W9-AND-652

Pronunciation Symbols

ə ...... banana, collect, abut

ˈə, ˌə ...... humdrum, abut

ᵊ ...... immediately preceding \l\, \n\, \m\, \ŋ\, as in battle, mitten, eaten, and sometimes cap and bells \-ᵊm-\, lock and key \-ᵊŋ-\; immediately following \l\, \m\, \r\, as often in French table, prisme, titre

ər ...... operation, further, urger

ˈər-, ˈə-r ...... as in two different pronunciations of hurry \ˈhər-ē, ˈhə-rē\

a ...... mat, map, mad, gag, snap, patch

ā ...... day, fade, date, aorta, drape, cape

ä ...... bother, cot, and, with most American speakers, father, cart

ȧ ...... father as pronounced by speakers who do not rhyme it with bother

au̇ ...... now, loud, out

b ...... baby, rib

ch ...... chin, nature \ˈnā-chər\ (actually, this sound is \t\ + \sh\)

d ...... did, adder

e ...... bet, bed, peck

ˈē, ˌē ...... beat, nosebleed, evenly, easy

ē ...... easy, mealy

f ...... fifty, cuff

g ...... go, big, gift

h ...... hat, ahead

hw ...... whale as pronounced by those who do not have the same pronunciation for both *whale* and *wail*

i ...... tip, banish, active

ī ...... site, side, buy, tripe (actually, this sound is \ä\ + \i\, or \ȧ\ + \i\)

j ...... job, gem, edge, join, judge (actually, this sound is \d\ + \zh\)

k ...... kin, cook, ache

k̲ ...... German ich, Buch

l ...... lily, pool

m ...... murmur, dim, nymph

n ...... no, own

ⁿ ...... indicates that a preceding vowel or diphthong is pronounced with the nasal passages open, as in French *un bon vin blanc* \œⁿ-bōⁿ-vaⁿ-bläⁿ\

ŋ ...... sing \ˈsiŋ\, singer \ˈsiŋ-ər\, finger \ˈfiŋ-gər\, ink \ˈiŋk\

ō ...... bone, know, beau

ȯ ...... saw, all, gnaw

œ ...... French boeuf, German Hölle

œ̄ ...... French feu, German Höhle

ȯi ...... coin, destroy, sawing

p ...... pepper, lip

r ...... red, car, rarity

s ...... source, less

sh ...... with nothing between, as in shy, mission, machine, special (actually, this is a single sound, not two); with a hyphen between, two sounds as in death's-head \ˈdeths-ˌhed\

t ...... tie, attack

th ...... with nothing between, as in thin, ether (actually, this is a single sound, not two); with a hyphen between, two sounds as in knighthood \ˈnīt-ˌhu̇d\

t͟h ...... then, either, this (actually, this is a single sound, not two)

ü ...... rule, youth, union \ˈyün-yən\, few \ˈfyü\

u̇ ...... pull, wood, book, curable \ˈkyu̇r-ə-bəl\

ue ...... German füllen, hübsch

ue̅ ...... French rue, German fühlen

v ...... vivid, give

w ...... we, away; in some words having final \(ˌ)ō\ a variant \ə-w\ occurs before vowels, as in \ˈfäl-ə-wiŋ\, covered by the variant \ə(-w)\ at the entry word

y ...... yard, young, cue \ˈkyü\, union \ˈyün-yən\

ʸ ...... indicates that during the articulation of the sound represented by the preceding character the front of the tongue has substantially the position it has for the articulation of the first sound of *yard*, as in French *digne* \dēnʸ\

yü ...... youth, union, cue, few, mute

yu̇ ...... curable, fury

z ...... zone, raise

zh ...... with nothing between, as in vision, azure \ˈazh-ər\ (actually, this is a single sound, not two); with a hyphen between, two sounds as in gazehound \ˈgāz-ˌhau̇nd\

\ ...... slant line used in pairs to mark the beginning and end of a transcription: \ˈpen\

ˈ ...... mark preceding a syllable with primary (strongest) stress: \ˈpen-mən-ˌship\

ˌ ...... mark preceding a syllable with secondary (next-strongest) stress: \ˈpen-mən-ˌship\

- ...... mark of syllable division

( ) ...... indicate that what is symbolized between is present in some utterances but not in others: *factory* \ˈfak-t(ə-)rē\

WEBSTER'S New Collegiate Dictionary

WEBSTER'S

New Collegiate Dictionary

A Merriam-Webster®

G. & C. MERRIAM COMPANY
Springfield, Massachusetts, U.S.A.

Copyright © 1974 by G. & C. Merriam Co.
Previous edition copyright © 1973 by G. & C. Merriam Co.

Philippines Copyright 1974 by G. & C. Merriam Co.
Previous edition Philippines Copyright 1973 by G. & C. Merriam Co.

Library of Congress Cataloging in Publication Data
Main entry under title:

Webster's new collegiate dictionary.

"Based on Webster's third new international dictionary."
"A Merriam-Webster."
Editions for 1898–1948 have title: Webster's collegiate dictionary; 1949–61 and 1973– editions have title: Webster's new collegiate dictionary; 1963–72 editions have title: Webster's seventh new collegiate dictionary.
1. English language—Dictionaries.
PE1628.W4M4 1974 423 72-19984
ISBN 0-87779-318-2 (plain)
0-87779-319-0 (indexed)
0-87779-320-4 (Buksyn)

COLLEGIATE is a registered trademark.

All rights reserved. No part of this work covered by the copyrights hereon may be reproduced or copied in any form or by any means—graphic, electronic, or mechanical, including photocopying, recording, taping, or information and retrieval systems—without written permission of the publisher.

Made in the United States of America

6

Contents

Preface 6a

Explanatory Chart 8a

Explanatory Notes 10a

The English Language and its History 20a

Abbreviations in this Work 31a

Pronunciation Symbols 32a

Dictionary of the English Language 1

Foreign Words and Phrases 1366

Biographical Names 1371

Geographical Names 1415

Colleges and Universities 1503

Signs and Symbols 1517

A Handbook of Style 1520

Index 1536

Preface

Webster's New Collegiate Dictionary is a completely new volume in the Merriam-Webster series of dictionaries. It is a general dictionary edited for use in school or college, in the office, and in the home—in short, wherever information about English words is likely to be sought. The average user should rarely have occasion to look for information about the vocabulary of present-day English that is not available within these pages.

The first Merriam-Webster Collegiate appeared in 1898 and quickly won the esteem of student and general reader. A second edition was published in 1910, and subsequent editions came out in 1916, 1931, 1936, 1949, and 1963. This eighth in the series incorporates the best of the time-tested features of its predecessors and introduces new features designed to add to its usefulness. Its more than 1500 pages make it the most comprehensive Merriam-Webster Collegiate ever published.

The heart of Webster's New Collegiate Dictionary is the more than 1300 pages given over to the A–Z vocabulary. The information there set down derives not only from the 10,000,000 citations which were available to the editors of Webster's Third New International Dictionary and the 1963 Collegiate but also from the considerably more than 1,000,000 citations collected since the publication of these books. Thus each entry is based on a constantly updated file of actual English usage.

Those entries known to be trademarks or service marks are so labeled and are treated in accordance with a formula approved by the United States Trademark Association. No entry in this dictionary, however, should be regarded as affecting the validity of any trademark or service mark.

A noteworthy feature of the vocabulary section is the nearly 900 pictorial illustrations, many of which were drawn especially for this book. These illustrations were selected not simply for their decorative function but particularly for their value in clarifying definitions.

The front matter—those pages preceding the A–Z vocabulary—contains two important sections. The Explanatory Notes should be read by every user of the dictionary since a thorough understanding of the information contained in them will contribute markedly to the value of this book. And all users of the dictionary are urged to read the lucid essay on the English language which was written for this Collegiate by Professor W. Nelson Francis of Brown University.

The back matter—those pages following the A–Z vocabulary—contains several sections that dictionary users have long found helpful. These include more than five hundred Foreign Words and Phrases that occur frequently in English texts but that have not become part of the English vocabulary; several thousand proper names that are entered under the separate headings Biographical Names and Geographical Names; and a list of the Colleges and Universities of the United States and Canada. There is also a Handbook of Style in which various stylistic conventions (as of punctuation and capitalization) are concisely summarized.

Webster's New Collegiate Dictionary has been edited by the trained staff of the G. & C. Merriam Co. It is the result of a collaborative effort, and it would be invidious to single out particular editors for special mention. At the same time, it would be ungracious to observe the anonymity which is often the lot of the present-day lexicographer, and so a list of those who contributed substantially to the completion of this book is printed below.

Webster's New Collegiate Dictionary is the product of a company that has been publishing dictionaries for more than 125 years. It is offered to the user with the conviction that it will serve him well.

Henry Bosley Woolf
Editor in Chief

Editorial Staff

Editor in Chief

Henry Bosley Woolf

Senior Editors

Edward Artin • F. Stuart Crawford • E. Ward Gilman • Mairé Weir Kay • Roger W. Pease, Jr.

Associate Editors

Robert D. Copeland • Grace A. Kellogg • Hubert P. Kelsey • James G. Lowe • George M. Sears

Assistant Editors

William Parr Black • Kathryn K. Flynn • Dolores R. Harris • Laverne W. King • Kerry W. Metz • Trudy A. Perkins • James E. Shea, Jr. • Anne H. Soukhanov • Raymond R. Wilson

Editorial Assistants

Dwight H. Day, Jr. • Philip B. Dickinson • Kathleen M. Doherty • L. Aimee Garn • Peter B. Kent

Editorial Consultants

Charlotte A. Bridgman • Philip W. Cummings • Philip B. Gove

Librarian

Marion D. Ware

Departmental Secretary

Hazel O. Lord

Head of Typing Room

Evelyn G. Summers

Clerks and Typists

Maude L. Barnes • Esther L. Gauthier • Mildred A. Lindsay • Maureen E. McCartney • Mildred M. McWha • Catherine T. Meaney • Frances W. Muldrew • Mildred C. Paquette • Genevieve M. Sherry • Francine A. Socha

- angle brackets PAGE 16a
- antonym PAGE 18a
- binomial PAGE 18a
- boldface colon PAGE 17a
- boldface type PAGE 10a
- capitalization label PAGE 14a
- centered periods PAGE 10a
- cognate cross-reference PAGE 18a
- cutback inflected forms PAGE 13a
- definition PAGE 17a
- directional cross-reference PAGE 18a
- equal variant PAGE 11a
- etymology PAGE 14a
- functional label PAGE 12a
- homographs PAGE 10a
- illustrative quotation PAGE 16a
- inflected forms PAGES 12a, 13a
- inflectional cross-reference PAGE 18a
- lightface type PAGE 10a
- lowercase PAGE 14a
- main entry PAGE 10a
- major stress PAGE 11a

pachy·der·ma·tous \ˌpak-i-ˈdər-mət-əs\ *adj* [deriv. of Gk *pachys* + *dermat-, derma* skin] **1 :** of or relating to the pachyderms **2 a :** THICK, THICKENED <~ skin> **b :** CALLOUS, INSENSITIVE — **pachy·der·ma·tous·ly** *adv*

pam·per \ˈpam-pər\ *vt* **pam·pered; pam·per·ing** \-p(ə-)riŋ\ [ME *pamperen,* prob. of D origin; akin to Flem *pamperen* to pamper] **1** *archaic* **:** to cram with rich food **:** GLUT **2 a :** to treat with extreme or excessive care and attention <~*ed* their guests> **b :** GRATIFY, HUMOR <enabled him to ~ his wanderlust —*New Yorker*> *syn* see INDULGE *ant* chasten — **pam·per·er** \-pər-ər\ *n*

pa·pa·ya \pə-ˈpī-ə\ *n* [Sp, of AmerInd origin; akin to Otomac *papai*] **:** a tropical American tree (*Carica papaya* of the family Caricaceae, the papaya family) with large oblong yellow edible fruit; *also* **:** its fruit

[2]**pa·per** *vb* **pa·pered; pa·per·ing** \ˈpā-p(ə-)riŋ\ *vt* **1** *archaic* **:** to put down or describe in writing **2 :** to fold or enclose in paper **3 :** to cover or line with paper; *esp* **:** to apply wallpaper to **4 :** to fill by giving out free passes <~ the theater for opening night> **5 :** to cover (an area) with advertising bills, circulars, or posters ~ *vi* **:** to hang wallpaper — **pa·per·er** \-pər-ər\ *n*

paper tiger *n* **:** one that is outwardly powerful or dangerous but inwardly weak or ineffectual <necessary to show that the . . . military presence was not a *paper tiger* —Kaye Whiteman>

[2]**Paphian** *n* **1 :** a native or inhabitant of Paphos **2** *often not cap* **:** PROSTITUTE

pap·il·lo·ma \ˌpap-ə-ˈlō-mə\ *n, pl* **-mas** *or* **-ma·ta** \-mət-ə\ **1 :** a benign tumor (as a wart) due to overgrowth of epithelial tissue on papillae of vascular connective tissue (as of the skin) **2 :** an epithelial tumor caused by a virus — **pap·il·lo·ma·tous** \-ˈlō-mət-əs\ *adj*

par·a·lyse *Brit var of* PARALYZE

pa·ram·e·ter·ize \pə-ˈram-ət-ə-ˌrīz\ *or* **pa·ram·e·trize** \-ˈram-ə-ˌtrīz\ *vt* **-ter·ized** *or* **-trized; -ter·iz·ing** *or* **-triz·ing :** to express in terms of parameters — **pa·ram·e·ter·iza·tion** \-ˌram-ət-ə-rə-ˈzā-shən, -ə-trə-ˈzā-\ *or* **pa·ram·e·tri·za·tion** \-ə-trə-ˈzā-\ *n*

pa·rang \ˈpär-ˌaŋ\ *n* [Malay] **:** a short sword, cleaver, or machete common in Malaysia and Indonesia

parasympathetic nervous system *n* **:** the part of the autonomic nervous system that contains chiefly cholinergic fibers, that tends to induce secretion, to increase the tone and contractility of smooth muscle, and to cause the dilatation of blood vessels, and that consists of a cranial and a sacral part — compare SYMPATHETIC NERVOUS SYSTEM

ped·dler *or* **ped·lar** \ˈped-lər\ *n* **:** one who peddles: as **a :** one who offers merchandise (as fresh produce) for sale along the street or from door to door **b :** one who deals in or promotes something intangible (as a personal asset or an idea) <influence ~*s*>

[1]**pe·des·tri·an** \pə-ˈdes-trē-ən\ *adj* [L *pedestr-, pedester,* lit., going on foot, fr. *pedes* one going on foot, fr. *ped-, pes* foot — more at FOOT] **1 :** COMMONPLACE, UNIMAGINATIVE **2 a :** going or performed on foot **b :** of, relating to, or designed for walking <a ~ mall>

peg leg *n* [[3]*peg*] **:** an artificial leg; *esp* **:** one fitted at the knee

[1]**pen·i·tent** \-tənt\ *adj* [ME, fr. MF, fr. L *paenitent-, paenitens,* fr. prp. of *paenitēre* to be sorry; akin to L *paene* almost — more at PATIENT] **:** feeling or expressing humble or regretful pain or sorrow for sins or offenses **:** REPENTANT — **pen·i·tent·ly** *adv*

[2]**penitent** *n* **1 :** a person who repents of sin **2 :** a person under church censure but admitted to penance esp. under the direction of a confessor

per·cent·age \pər-ˈsent-ij\ *n* **1 :** a part of a whole expressed in hundredths **2 a :** a share of winnings or profits **b :** ADVANTAGE, PROFIT <no ~ in going around looking like an old sack of laundry —Wallace Stegner> **3 :** an indeterminate part **:** PROPORTION **4 a :** PROBABILITY **b :** favorable odds

per·jure \ˈpər-jər\ *vt* **per·jured; per·jur·ing** \ˈpərj-(ə-)riŋ\ [MF *perjurer,* fr. L *perjurare,* fr. *per-* to destruction, to the bad + *jurare* to swear — more at PER-, JURY] **1** *obs* **:** to cause to commit perjury **2 :** to make a perjurer of (oneself)

pies *pl of* PI *or of* PIE

[4]**pile** *vb* **piled; pil·ing** *vt* **1 :** to lay or place in a pile **:** STACK **2 :** to heap in abundance **:** LOAD <*piled* potatoes on his plate> ~ *vi* **1 :** to form a pile **:** ACCUMULATE **2 :** to move or press forward in or as if in a mass **:** CROWD <*piled* into a car>

pile driver *n* **1 :** a machine for driving down piles with a pile hammer or a steam or air hammer **2 :** an operator of a pile driver

pil·grim \ˈpil-grəm\ *n* [ME, fr. OF *peligrin,* fr. LL *pelegrinus,* alter. of L *peregrinus* foreigner, fr. *peregrinus* foreign, fr. *pereger* being abroad, fr. *per* through + *agr-, ager* land — more at FOR, ACRE] **1 :** one who journeys in foreign lands **:** WAYFARER **2 :** one who travels to a shrine or holy place as a devotee **3** *cap* **:** one of the English colonists settling at Plymouth in 1620

pinch·beck \ˈpinch-ˌbek\ *n* [Christopher *Pinchbeck* †1732 E watchmaker] **1 :** an alloy of copper and zinc used esp. to imitate gold in jewelry **2 :** something counterfeit or spurious — **pinch·beck** *adj*

Explanatory Chart

pin·cush·ion \'pin-ˌkush-ən\ *n* **:** a small cushion in which pins may be stuck ready for use

[2]**pine** *n*, *often attrib* [ME, fr. OE *pīn*, fr. L *pinus*; akin to Gk *pitys* pine, L *opimus* fat — more at FAT] **1 :** any of a genus (*Pinus* of the family Pinaceae, the pine family) of coniferous evergreen trees which have slender elongated needles and some of which are valuable timber trees or ornamentals **2 :** the straight-grained white or yellow usu. durable and resinous wood of a pine varying from extreme softness in the white pine to hardness in the longleaf pine **3 :** any of various Australian coniferous trees (as of the genera *Callitris, Araucaria,* or *Cupressus*) **4 :** PINEAPPLE — **piny** *or* **pin·ey** \'pī-nē\ *adj*

post·card \'pōs(t)-ˌkärd\ *n* **1 :** a card on which a message may be written for mailing without an envelope and to which the sender must affix a stamp **2 :** POSTAL CARD 1

post–free \'pōs(t)-'frē\ *adj*, *chiefly Brit* **:** POSTPAID

post·mas·ter \-ˌmas-tər\ *n* **1 :** one who has charge of a post office **2 :** one who has charge of a station for the accommodation of travelers or who supplies post-horses — **post·mas·ter·ship** \-ˌship\ *n*

[2]**private** *n* **1** *archaic* **:** one not in public office **2** *obs* **:** PRIVACY **3 a :** a person of low rank in various organizations (as a police or fire department) **b :** an enlisted man of the lowest rank in the marine corps or of one of the two lowest ranks in the army — **in private :** not openly or in public

pro·gram·mer *also* **pro·gram·er** \'prō-ˌgram-ər, -grə-mər\ *n* **:** one that programs: as **a :** one that prepares and tests programs for mechanisms **b :** a person or device that programs a mechanism **c :** one that prepares educational programs

pro·jec·tor \prə-'jek-tər\ *n* **1 :** one that plans a project; *specif* **:** PROMOTER **2 :** one that projects: as **a :** a device for projecting a beam of light **b :** an optical instrument for projecting an image upon a surface **c :** a machine for projecting motion pictures on a screen **3 :** an imagined line from an object to a surface along which projection takes place

pro·jet \prō-'zhā, 'prō-ˌ\ *n, pl* **projets** \-'zhā(z), -ˌzhā(z)\ [F, fr. MF *pourjet*] **1 :** PLAN; *esp* **:** a draft of a proposed measure or treaty **2 :** a projected or proposed design

pro·mote \prə-'mōt\ *vt* **pro·mot·ed; pro·mot·ing** [L *promotus*, pp. of *promovēre*, lit., to move forward, fr. *pro-* forward + *movēre* to move] **1 a :** to advance in station, rank, or honor **:** RAISE **b :** to change (a pawn) into a piece in chess by moving to the eighth rank **c :** to advance (a student) from one grade to the next higher grade **2 a :** to contribute to the growth or prosperity of **:** FURTHER <~ international understanding> **b :** to help bring (as an enterprise) into being **:** LAUNCH **c :** to present (merchandise) for public acceptance through advertising and publicity **3** *slang* **:** to get possession of by doubtful means or by ingenuity ***syn*** see ADVANCE ***ant*** impede

proph·et \'präf-ət\ *n* [ME *prophete*, fr. OF, fr. L *propheta*, fr. Gk *prophētēs*, fr. *pro* for + *phanai* to speak — more at FOR, BAN] **1 :** one who utters divinely inspired revelations; *specif, often cap* **:** the writer of one of the prophetic books of the Old Testament **2 :** one gifted with more than ordinary spiritual and moral insight; *esp* **:** an inspired poet **3 :** one who foretells future events **:** PREDICTOR <a weather ~> **4 :** an effective or leading spokesman for a cause, doctrine, or group <he is first the student and then the ~ of power —Alfred Kazin> **5** *Christian Science* **a :** a spiritual seer **b :** disappearance of material sense before the conscious facts of spiritual Truth — **proph·et·ess** \-ət-əs\ *n*

pro·rate \(')prō-'rāt\ *vb* **pro·rat·ed; pro·rat·ing** [*pro rata*] *vt* **:** to divide, distribute, or assess proportionately ~ *vi* **:** to make a pro rata distribution

pro·spec·tive \prə-'spek-tiv *also* 'prä-ˌ, prō-', prä-'\ *adj* **1 :** likely to come about **:** EXPECTED <the ~ benefits of this law> **2 :** likely to be or become <a ~ mother> — **pro·spec·tive·ly** *adv*

pun·gent \-jənt\ *adj* [L *pungent-, pungens*, prp. of *pungere* to prick, sting; akin to L *pugnus* fist, *pugnare* to fight, Gk *pygmē* fist] **1 :** having a stiff and sharp point <~ leaves> **2 :** sharply painful; *also* **:** POIGNANT **3 a :** marked by a sharp incisive quality **:** CAUSTIC <a ~ denunciation> **b :** being to the point **:** highly expressive <~ prose> **4 :** causing a sharp or irritating sensation; *esp* **:** ACRID — **pun·gent·ly** *adv*

syn PUNGENT, PIQUANT, POIGNANT, RACY *shared meaning element* **:** sharp and stimulating to the mind or senses ***ant*** bland

pur·blind \'pər-ˌblīnd\ *adj* [ME *pur blind*, fr. *pur* purely, wholly, fr. *pur* pure] **1 a** *obs* **:** wholly blind **b :** partly blind **2 :** lacking in vision, insight, or understanding **:** OBTUSE — **pur·blind·ly** \-ˌblīn-(d)lē\ *adv* — **pur·blind·ness** \-ˌblīn(d)-nəs\ *n*

pur·dah \'pərd-ə\ *n* [Hindi *parda*, lit., screen, veil] **:** seclusion of women from public observation among Muslims and some Hindus esp. in India

Py·ram·i·don \pə-'ram-ə-ˌdän\ *trademark* — used for aminopyrine

pyre \'pī(ə)r\ *n* [L *pyra*, fr. Gk, fr. *pyr* fire — more at FIRE] **:** a combustible heap for burning a dead body as a funeral rite; *broadly* **:** a pile of material to be burned <a ~ of dead leaves>

minor stress
PAGE 11a

often attrib
PAGE 14a

pronunciation
PAGES 11a, 12a

regional label
PAGE 16a

run-on entry (undefined)
PAGE 11a

run-on entry (defined)
PAGE 11a

secondary variant
PAGE 11a

sense divider
PAGE 17a

sense letter
PAGE 17a

sense numeral
PAGE 17a

small capitals
PAGE 18a

stylistic label
PAGE 16a

subject label
PAGE 16a

swung dash (boldface)
PAGE 12a

swung dash (lightface)
PAGE 16a

synonymous cross-reference
PAGES 18a, 19a

synonym list
PAGE 19a

temporal label
PAGES 15a, 16a

uppercase
PAGE 14a

usage note
PAGES 16a, 17a

verbal illustration
PAGE 16a

Explanatory Notes

Entries

A boldface letter or a combination of such letters set flush with the left-hand margin of each column of type is a main entry. The main entry may consist of letters set solid, of letters joined by a hyphen, or of letters separated by one or more spaces:

teach ... *vb*

teach-in ... *n*

teaching fellow *n*

The material in lightface type that follows each main entry on the same line and on succeeding indented lines explains and justifies its inclusion in the dictionary.

The main entries follow one another in alphabetical order letter by letter: *book of account* follows *bookmobile*. Those containing an Arabic numeral are alphabetized as if the numeral were spelled out: *3-D* comes between *three-color* and *three-decker*. Those derived from proper names beginning with abbreviated forms of *Mac-* are alphabetized as if spelled *mac-*: *McCoy* comes after *macaroon* and before *mace*. Those that often begin with the abbreviation *St.* in common usage have the abbreviation spelled out: *Saint Martin's summer*.

A pair of guide words is printed at the top of each page. These indicate that the entries falling alphabetically between the words at the top of the outer column of each page are found on that page.

The guide words are the alphabetically first and usually the alphabetically last entries on the page:

aposelene ● appellation

Occasionally the last printed entry is not the alphabetically last entry. On page 124, for example, *bold-faced* is the last printed entry, but *boldness*, run on at *bold*, is the alphabetically last entry and is therefore the second guide word. The alphabetically last entry is not used, however, if it follows alphabetically the first guide word on the succeeding page. Thus on page 113 *bitterness* is not a guide word because it follows alphabetically the fourth homograph *bitter* which is the first guide word on page 114. Any boldface word—a main entry with definition, a variant, an inflected form, a defined or undefined run-on, or an entry in a list of self-explanatory words—may be used as a guide word.

When one main entry has exactly the same written form as another, the two are distinguished by superscript numerals preceding each word:

[1]**man** ... *n*	[1]**quail** ... *n*
[2]**man** *vt*	[2]**quail** *vb*

Sometimes such homographs are related: the two entries *man* are derived from the same root. Sometimes there is no relationship: the two entries *quail* are unrelated beyond the accident of spelling. The order of homographs is usually historical: the one first used in English is entered first.

Words precede word elements made up of the same letters; solid compounds precede hyphened compounds; hyphened compounds precede open compounds; and lowercase entries precede those with an initial capital:

mini ... *n*

mini- *comb form*

work·up ... *n*

work–up ... *n*

work up ... *vt*

ti·ta·nia ... *n*

Ti·ta·nia ... *n*

The centered periods within entry words indicate division points at which a hyphen may be put at the end of a line of print or writing. Thus the noun *re·frig·er·a·tor* may be ended on one line with:

re-
refrig-
refriger-
refrigera-

and continued on the next with:

-frigerator
-erator
-ator
-tor

Centered periods are not shown after a single initial letter or before a single terminal letter because printers seldom cut off a single letter:

aplomb ... *n*

hoary ... *adj*

idea ... *n*

Nor are they shown at the second and succeeding homographs of a word:

[1]**mas·ter** ... *n*

[2]**master** *vt*

[3]**master** *adj*

There are acceptable alternative end-of-line divisions just as there are acceptable variant spellings and pronunciations. It is, for example, all but impossible to produce a convincing argument that either of the divisions *aus·ter·i·ty*, *au·ster·i·ty* is better than the other. But space cannot be taken for entries like *aus·ter·i·ty or au·ster·i·ty*, and *au·s·ter·i·ty* would likely be confusing to many. No more than one division is, therefore, shown for any entry in this dictionary.

Many words have two or more common pronunciation variants, and the same end-of-line division is not always appropriate for each of them. The division *pi·an·ist*, for example, best fits the variant \pē-ˈan-əst\ whereas the division *pi·a·nist* best fits the variant \ˈpē-ə-nəst\. In instances like this, the division falling farthest to the left is used, regardless of the order of the pronunciations:

pi·a·nist \pē-ˈan-əst, ˈpē-ə-nəst\

When a main entry is followed by the word *or* and another spelling, the two spellings are equal variants. Both are standard, and either one may be used according to personal inclination:

the·ater *or* **the·atre**

If two variants joined by *or* are out of alphabetical order, they remain equal variants. The one printed first is, however, slightly more common than the second:

coun·sel·or *or* **coun·sel·lor**

When another spelling is joined to the main entry by the word *also*, the spelling after *also* is a secondary variant and occurs less frequently than the first:

lov·able *also* **love·able**

Secondary variants belong to standard usage and may be used according to personal inclination. If there are two secondary variants, the second is joined to the first by *or*. Once the word *also* is used to signal a secondary variant, all following variants are joined by *or*:

[1]**Shake·spear·ean** *or* **Shake·spear·ian** *also* **Shak·sper·ean** *or* **Shak·sper·ian**

Variants whose spelling places them alphabetically more than a column away from the main entry are entered at their own alphabetical places and usually not at the main entry:

Cha·nu·kah ... *var of* HANUKKAH

rime, rimer, rimester *var of* RHYME, RHYMER, RHYMESTER

Variants having a usage label appear only at their own alphabetical places:

fla·vour *chiefly Brit var of* FLAVOR

agin ... *dial var of* AGAINST

To show all the stylings that are found for English compounds would require space that can be better used for other information. So this dictionary limits itself to a single styling for a compound:

week·end

red–eye

high school

When a compound is widely used and one styling predominates, that styling is shown. When a compound is uncommon or when the evidence indicates that two or three stylings are approximately equal in frequency, the styling shown is based on the analogy of parallel compounds.

A main entry may be followed by one or more derivatives or by a homograph with a different functional label. These are run-on entries. Each is introduced by a lightface dash and each has a functional label. They are not defined, however, since their meanings are readily derivable from the meaning of the root word:

[2]**question** *vt* ... — **ques·tion·er** *n*

[1]**fun·ny** ... *adj* ... — **fun·ni·ly** ... *adv* — **fun·ni·ness** ... *n*

mu·tant ... *adj* ... — **mutant** *n*

A main entry may be followed by one or more phrases containing the entry word or an inflected form of it. These are also run-on entries. Each is introduced by a lightface dash but there is no functional label. They are, however, defined since their meanings are more than the sum of the meanings of their elements:

[1]**call** ... *vb* ... — **call one's bluff :** ...

[2]**mend** *n* ... — **on the mend :** ...

Defined phrases of this sort are run on at the entry constituting the first major element in the phrase. When there are variants, however, the run-on appears at the entry constituting the first major invariable element in the phrase:

[1]**clock** ... *n* ... — **kill the clock** *or* **run out the clock :** ...

[1]**seed** ... *n* ... — **go to seed** *or* **run to seed :** ...

Attention is called to the definition of *vocabulary entry* on page 1310. The term *dictionary entry* includes all vocabulary entries as well as all boldface entries in the separate sections of the back matter headed "Foreign Words and Phrases," "Biographical Names," "Geographical Names," and "Colleges and Universities."

Pronunciation

The matter between a pair of reversed virgules \ \ following the entry word indicates the pronunciation. The symbols used are explained in the chart printed inside the front and back covers of this dictionary and on page 32a. For a detailed discussion of these symbols and related matters, the serious student is referred to "A Guide to Pronunciation" in Webster's Third New International Dictionary.

A hyphen is used in the pronunciation to show syllabic division. These hyphens sometimes coincide with the centered periods in the entry word that indicate end-of-line division; sometimes they do not:

dis·cov·er \dis-ˈkəv-ər\

[1]**met·ric** \ˈme-trik\

A high-set mark ˈ indicates major (primary) stress or accent; a low-set mark ˌ indicates minor (secondary) stress or accent:

rough·neck \ˈrəf-ˌnek\

The stress mark stands at the beginning of the syllable that receives the stress.

The presence of variant pronunciations indicates that not all educated speakers pronounce words the same way. A second-place variant is not to be regarded as less acceptable than the pronunciation that is given first. It may, in fact, be used by as many educated speakers as the first variant, but the requirements of the printed page are such that one must precede the other:

apri·cot \ˈap-rə-ˌkät, ˈā-prə-\

for·eign \ˈfȯr-ən, ˈfär-\

A variant that is appreciably less common than the preceding variant is preceded by the word *also*:

col·league \ˈkäl-ˌēg *also* -ig\

Sometimes a regional label precedes a variant:

[1]**great** \ˈgrāt, *South also* ˈgre(ə)t\

Symbols enclosed by parentheses represent elements that are present in the pronunciation of some speakers but are absent from the pronunciation of other speakers, elements that are present in some but absent from other utterances of the same speaker, or elements whose presence or absence is uncertain:

hap·pen . . . *vi* . . . **hap·pen·ing** \'hap-(ə-)niŋ\

sat·is·fac·to·ry \ˌsat-əs-'fak-t(ə-)rē\

re·sponse \ri-'spän(t)s\

Thus, the parentheses at *happening* mean that there are some who pronounce the \ə\ between \p\ and \n\ and others who do not pronounce it.

When a main entry has less than a full pronunciation, the missing part is to be supplied from a pronunciation in a preceding entry or within the same pair of reversed virgules:

cham·pi·on·ship \-ˌship\

Ma·dei·ra \mə-'dir-ə, -'der-\

The pronunciation of the first three syllables of *championship* is found at the main entry *champion*:

[1]**cham·pi·on** \'cham-pē-ən\

The hyphens before and after \'der\ in the pronunciation of *Madeira* indicate that both the first and the last parts of the pronunciation are to be taken from the immediately preceding pronunciation.

In general, no pronunciation is indicated for open compounds consisting of two or more English words that have own-place entry:

kangaroo court *n*

Only the first entry in a sequence of numbered homographs is given a pronunciation if their pronunciations are the same:

[1]**re·ward** \ri-'wȯ(ə)rd\

[2]**reward**

Pronunciations are shown for obsolete words only if they occur in Shakespeare:

clois·tress \'klȯi-strəs\ *n, obs*

The pronunciation of unpronounced derivatives and compounds run on at a main entry is a combination of the pronunciation at the main entry and the pronunciation of the suffix or final element as given at its alphabetical place in the vocabulary:

— **oval·ness** *n*

— **over one's head**

Thus, the pronunciation of *ovalness* is the sum of the pronunciations given at *oval* and *-ness*; that of *over one's head*, the sum of the pronunciation of the three elements that make up the phrase.

Partial pronunciations are usually shown when two or more variants have a part in common. When a variation of stress is involved, a partial pronunciation may be terminated at the stress mark which stands at the beginning of a syllable not shown:

di·verse \dī-'vərs, də-', 'dī-ˌ\

an·cho·vy \'an-ˌchō-vē, an-'\

In some cases the pronunciation of a word or compound shows no major (primary) stress. One such class of words includes those that occur in main entries only as elements of an open compound. The stress shown for these words is the usual stress in the compound and may be less than major (primary):

clum·ber spaniel \ˌkləm-bər-\

In other contexts the word may have major (primary) stress, as in "Is that spaniel a clumber?"

Functional Labels

An italic label indicating a part of speech or some other functional classification follows the pronunciation or, if no pronunciation is given, the main entry. The eight traditional parts of speech are indicated as follows:

de·cep·tive . . . *adj*	**war·den** . . . *n*
hap·pi·ly . . . *adv*	**of** . . . *prep*
be·cause . . . *conj*	**they** . . . *pron*
hey . . . *interj*	**re·lax** . . . *vb*

If a verb is both transitive and intransitive, the labels *vt* and *vi* introduce the subdivisions:

pen·e·trate . . . *vb* . . . *vt* . . . ~ *vi*

A boldface swung dash **~** is used to stand for the main entry (as *penetrate*) and separate the subdivisions of the verb. If there is no subdivision, *vt* or *vi* takes the place of *vb*:

in·fect . . . *vt*

[2]**vacation** *vi*

Labeling a verb as transitive, however, does not preclude occasional intransitive use (as in absolute constructions).

Other italicized labels used to indicate functional classifications that are not traditional parts of speech are:

alt . . . *abbr*	**-ness** . . . *n suffix*
tele- *or* **tel-** *comb form*	**-ize** . . . *vb suffix*
-onym . . . *n comb form*	**Fe** *symbol*
-gen·ic . . . *adj comb form*	**Fris·bee** . . . *trademark*
[1]**pro-** *prefix*	**must** . . . *verbal auxiliary*
Air Express *service mark*	**gid·dap** . . . *vb imper*
[1]**-ic** . . . *adj suffix*	**me·seems** . . . *vb impersonal*
[2]**-ly** *adv suffix*	

Two functional labels are sometimes combined:

zilch . . . *adj or n*

[1]**le·ga·to** . . . *adv or adj*

Inflected Forms

NOUNS

The plurals of nouns are shown in this dictionary when suffixation brings about a change of final *-y* to *-i-*, when the noun ends in a consonant plus *-o* or in *-ey*, when the noun ends in *-oo*, when the noun has an irregular plural or a zero plural or a foreign plural, when the noun is a compound that pluralizes any element but the last, when the noun has variant plurals, and when it is believed that the dictionary user might have reasonable doubts about the spelling of the plural or when the plural is spelled in a way contrary to expectations:

[2]**fly** *n, pl* **flies**

to·ma·to . . . *n, pl* **-toes**

val·ley . . . *n, pl* **valleys**

[2]**boo** *n, pl* **boos**

[1]**mouse** . . . *n, pl* **mice**

sheep . . . *n, pl* **sheep**

alum·nus . . . *n, pl* **-ni**

moth·er–in–law . . . *n, pl* **mothers–in–law**

¹seed . . . *n, pl* **seed** *or* **seeds**

¹pi . . . *n, pl* **pis**

³dry *n, pl* **drys**

Cutback inflected forms are used when the noun has three or more syllables:

an·i·mos·i·ty . . . *n, pl* **-ties**

The plurals of nouns are usually not shown when the base word is unchanged by suffixation, when the noun is a compound whose second element is readily recognizable as a regular free form entered at its own place, or when the noun is unlikely to occur in the plural:

¹cat . . . *n*

¹church . . . *n*

gad·fly . . . *n*

al·che·my . . . *n*

Nouns that are plural in form and that regularly occur in plural construction are labeled *n pl*:

en·vi·rons . . . *n pl*

Nouns that are plural in form but that are not always construed as plurals are appropriately labeled:

ge·net·ics . . . *n pl but sing in constr*

forty winks *n pl but sing or pl in constr*

A noun that is singular in construction takes a singular verb when it is used as a subject; a noun that is plural in construction takes a plural verb when it is used as a subject.

VERBS

The principal parts of verbs are shown in this dictionary when suffixation brings about a doubling of a final consonant or an elision of a final *-e* or a change of final *-y* to *-i-*, when final *-c* changes to *-ck* in suffixation, when the verb ends in *-ey*, when the inflection is irregular, when there are variant inflected forms, and when it is believed that the dictionary user might have reasonable doubts about the spelling of an inflected form or when the inflected form is spelled in a way contrary to expectations:

³brag *vb* **bragged; brag·ging**

¹blame . . . *vt* **blamed; blam·ing**

¹spy . . . *vb* **spied; spy·ing**

²pic·nic . . . *vi* **pic·nicked; pic·nick·ing**

²volley *vb* **vol·leyed; vol·ley·ing**

³ring *vb* **rang** . . .; **rung** . . .; **ring·ing**

⁴bias *vt* **bi·ased** *or* **bi·assed; bi·as·ing** *or* **bi·as·sing**

²visa *vt* **vi·saed** . . .; **vi·sa·ing**

²chagrin *vt* **cha·grined** . . .; **cha·grin·ing**

The principal parts of a regularly inflected verb are shown when it is desirable to indicate the pronunciation of one of the inflected forms:

³spell *vb* **spelled** \ˈspeld, ˈspelt\; **spell·ing**

²but·ton . . . *vb* **but·toned; but·ton·ing** \ˈbət-niŋ, -ᵊn-iŋ\

Cutback inflected forms are often used when the verb has three or more syllables, when it is a disyllable that ends in *-l* and has variant spellings, and when it is a compound whose second element is readily recognized as an irregular verb:

de·i·fy . . . *vt* **-fied; -fy·ing**

²carol *vb* **-oled** *or* **-olled; -ol·ing** *or* **-ol·ling**

with·draw *vb* **-drew** . . .; **-drawn** . . .; **-draw·ing**

The principal parts of verbs are usually not shown when the base word is unchanged by suffixation or when the verb is a compound whose second element is readily recognizable as a regular free form entered at its own place:

⁴halt . . . *vi*

dis·sat·is·fy . . . *vb*

ADJECTIVES & ADVERBS

The comparative and superlative forms of adjectives and adverbs are shown in this dictionary when suffixation brings about a doubling of a final consonant or an elision of a final *-e* or a change of final *-y* to *-i-*, when the word ends in *-ey*, when the inflection is irregular, and when there are variant inflected forms:

¹red . . . *adj* **red·der; red·dest**

¹bare . . . *adj* **bar·er; bar·est**

¹heavy . . . *adj* **heavi·er; -est**

¹ear·ly . . . *adv* **ear·li·er; -est**

hom·ey *also* **homy** . . . *adj* **hom·i·er; -est**

¹good . . . *adj* **bet·ter** . . .; **best**

²ill . . . *adv* **worse; worst**

¹shy . . . *adj* **shi·er** *or* **shy·er** . . .; **shi·est** *or* **shy·est**

Adjectives and adverbs of two or more syllables are usually cut back:

come·ly . . . *adj* **come·li·er; -est**

²easy *adv* **eas·i·er; -est**

The comparative and superlative forms of regularly inflected adjectives and adverbs are shown when it is desirable to indicate the pronunciation of the inflected forms:

¹long \ˈlȯŋ\ *adj* **lon·ger** \ˈlȯŋ-gər\; **lon·gest** \ˈlȯŋ-gəst\

The inclusion of inflected forms in *-er* and *-est* at adjective and adverb entries means nothing more about the use of *more* and *most* with these adjectives and adverbs than that their comparative and superlative degrees may be expressed in either way: *lazier* or *more lazy*; *laziest* or *most lazy*.

At a few adjective entries only the superlative form is shown:

mere . . . *adj* **mer·est**

The absence of the comparative form indicates that there is no evidence of its use.

The comparative and superlative forms of adjectives and adverbs are not shown when the base word is unchanged by suffixation or when the word is a compound whose second element is readily recognizable as a regular free form entered at its own place:

¹full . . . *adj*

un·lucky . . . *adj*

The comparative and superlative forms of adverbs are not shown when they are identical with the inflected forms of a preceding adjective homograph:

¹hot . . . *adj* **hot·ter; hot·test**

²hot *adv*

Inflected forms are not shown at undefined run-ons or at some entries bearing a limiting label:

Jac·o·bin . . . *n* . . . — **jac·o·bin·ize** . . . *vt*

²lampoon *vt* . . . — **lam·poon·ery** . . . *n*

¹net . . . *n* . . . — **net·ty** . . . *adj*

²cote . . . *vt* . . . *obs* : to pass by

crouse . . . *adj* . . . *chiefly Scot* : BRISK, LIVELY

Capitalization

Most entries in this dictionary begin with a lowercase letter. A few of these have an italicized label *often cap*, which indicates that the word is as likely to be capitalized as not, that it is as acceptable with an uppercase initial as it is with one in lowercase. Some entries begin with an uppercase letter, which indicates that the word is usually capitalized. The absence of an initial capital or of an *often cap* label indicates that the word is not ordinarily capitalized:

mas·sive ... *adj*

an·gli·cize ... *vt* ... *often cap*

Swiss ... *n*

The capitalization of entries that are open or hyphened compounds is similarly indicated by the form of the entry or by an italicized label:

ice cream ... *n*

¹french fry *vt, often cap 1st F*

neo–im·pres·sion·ism ... *n, often cap N&I*

non–Com·mu·nist ... *adj*

Irish setter *n*

Memorial Day *n*

A word that is capitalized in some senses and lowercase in others shows variations from the form of the main entry by the use of italicized labels at the appropriate senses:

Gyp·sy ... *n* ... **3** *not cap*

Sal·va·tion·ist ... *n* ... **2** *often not cap*

¹mass ... *n* ... **1** *cap*

es·tab·lish·ment ... *n* ... **2** ... **b** *often cap*

Attributive Nouns

The italicized label *often attrib* placed after the functional label *n* indicates that the noun is often used as an adjective equivalent in attributive position before another noun:

ap·ple ... *n, often attrib*

¹dog ... *n, often attrib*

Examples of the attributive use of these nouns are *apple pie* and *dog license.*

While any noun may occasionally be used attributively, the label *often attrib* is limited to those having broad attributive use. This label is not used when an adjective homograph (as *iron* or *paper*) is entered. And it is not used at open compounds (as *X ray*) that may be used attributively with an inserted hyphen (as in *X-ray therapy*).

Etymology

The matter in boldface square brackets preceding the definition is the etymology. Meanings given in roman type within these brackets are not definitions of the entry, but are meanings of the Middle English, Old English, or non-English words within the brackets.

The etymology traces a vocabulary entry as far back as possible in English (as to Old English), tells from what language and in what form it came into English, and (except in the case of such words outside the general vocabulary of English as *dacha* and *talipot*) traces the pre-English source as far back as possible. These etyma are printed in italics.

The etymology usually gives the Middle English and the Old English forms of words in the following style:

¹reed ... *n* [ME *rede,* fr. OE *hrēod* ...]

¹hate ... *n* [ME, fr. OE *hete* ...]

An etymology in which a word is traced back to Middle English but not to Old English indicates that the word is found in Middle English but not in those texts that have survived from the Old English period:

¹clog ... *n* [ME *clogge* short thick piece of wood]

¹rub ... *vb* [ME *rubben;* akin to Icel *rubba* to scrape]

An etymology in which a word is traced back directly to Old English with no intervening mention of Middle English indicates that the word has not survived continuously from Old English times to the present. Rather, it died out after the Old English period and has been revived in modern times:

Geat ... *n* [OE *Gēat*]

thegn ... *n* [OE ...]

The etymology gives the language from which words borrowed into English have come. It also gives the form or a transliteration of the word in that language if the form differs from that in English:

¹fes·ti·val ... *adj* [ME, fr. MF, fr. L *festivus* festive]

linn ... *n* [ScGael *linne* pool]

¹school ... *n* [ME *scole,* fr. OE *scōl,* fr. L *schola* ...]

smor·gas·bord ... *n* [Sw *smörgåsbord* ...]

In a few cases the expression "deriv. of" replaces the more usual "fr." This expression indicates that one or more intermediate steps have been omitted in tracing the derivation of the form preceding the expression from the form following it:

¹gal·ley ... *n* [... OF *galie,* deriv. of MGk *galea*]

An etymology is not usually given for a word created in English by the combination of existing constituents or by functional shift. This indicates that the identity of the constituents is expected to be self-evident to the user:

like·ness ... *n* **1 :** the quality or state of being like

tone–deaf ... *adj* **:** relatively insensitive to differences in musical pitch

tooth·paste ... *n* **:** a paste for cleaning the teeth

profit system *n* **:** FREE ENTERPRISE

²wheel *vi* **1 :** to turn on or as if on an axis ...

In the case of a family of words obviously related to a common English word but differing from it by containing various easily recognizable suffixes, an etymology is usually given only at the base word, even though some of the derivatives may have been formed in a language other than English:

¹im·mor·tal ... *adj* [ME, fr. L *immortalis* ...] **1 :** exempt from death

im·mor·tal·i·ty ... *n* **:** the quality or state of being immortal

The word *immortality* was actually borrowed into Middle English (via Middle French) from Latin *immortalitas.*

Much of the technical vocabulary of the sciences and

other specialized studies consists of words or word elements that are current in two or more languages, with only such slight modifications as are necessary to adapt them to the structure of the individual language in each case. Many words and word elements of this kind have become sufficiently a part of the general vocabulary of English as to require entry in an abridged dictionary. Because of the vast extent of the relevant published material in many languages and in many scientific and other specialized fields, it is impracticable to ascertain the language of origin of every such term. Yet it would not be accurate to formulate a statement about the origin of any such term in a way that could be interpreted as implying that it was coined in English. Accordingly, whenever a term that is entered in this dictionary belongs recognizably to this class of internationally current terms and whenever no positive evidence is at hand to show that it was coined in English, the etymology recognizes its international status and the possibility that it originated elsewhere than in English by use of the label ISV (for International Scientific Vocabulary):

mega·watt ... *n* [ISV]

phy·lo·ge·net·ic ... *adj* [ISV, fr. NL *phylogenesis* ...]

[1]-ol ... *n suffix* [ISV, fr. *alcohol*]

An etymology beginning with the name of a language (including ME or OE) and not giving the foreign (or Middle English or Old English) form indicates that this form is the same as that of the entry word:

[1]tan·go ... *n* ... [AmerSp]

[1]po·grom ... *n* [Yiddish, fr. Russ ...]

[1]gang ... *n* [ME, fr. OE ...]

An etymology beginning with the name of a language (including ME or OE) and not giving the foreign (or Middle English or Old English) meaning indicates that this meaning is the same as that expressed in the first definition in the entry:

vig·or·ous ... *adj* [ME, fr. MF, fr. OF, fr. *vigor*] **1 :** possessing vigor

When an entry word is derived from an earlier Modern English word that is not entered in this dictionary, the meaning of such a word is given in parentheses:

[3]press *vb* [alter. of obs. *prest* (to enlist by giving pay in advance)]

Small superscript figures following words or syllables in an etymology refer to the tone of the word or syllable which they follow. They are, accordingly, used only with forms cited from tone languages:

chow mein ... *n* [Chin (Pek) *ch'ao*[3] *mien*[4], fr. *ch'ao*[3] to fry + *mien*[4] dough]

[1]voo·doo ... *n* ... [LaF *voudou*, of African origin; akin to Ewe *vo*[1]*du*[3] tutelary deity, demon]

When the source of a word appearing as a main entry is unknown, the expression "origin unknown" is usually used. Only in rare and exceptional circumstances (as with some ethnic names) does the absence of an etymology mean that it has not been possible to furnish any informative etymology. More often, it means that no etymology is believed to be necessary. This is the case, for instance, with most of the entries identified as variants and with many derivatives.

When a word has been traced back to the earliest language in which it is attested, and if this is an Indo-European language, selected cognates in other Indo-European languages (especially Old High German, Latin, and Greek) are usually given:

[1]one ... *adj* [ME *on*, fr. OE *ān*; akin to OHG *ein* one, L *unus* (OL *oinos*), Skt *eka*]

equine ... *adj* [L *equinus*, fr. *equus* horse; akin to OE *eoh* horse, Gk *hippos*]

Sometimes, however, to avoid space-consuming repetition, the expression "more at" directs the user to another entry where the cognates are given:

[2]thought *n* [ME, fr. OE *thōht*; akin to OE *thencan* to think — more at THINK]

Besides the use of "akin to" to denote an ordinary cognate relationship, some etymologies make special use of "akin to" as part of a longer formula "of— origin; akin to—," This formula indicates that a word was borrowed from some language belonging to a group of languages whose name is inserted in the blank before the word *origin*, that it is impossible to say that the word in question is a borrowing of a particular attested word in a particular language of the source group, and that the form cited in the blank after the expression *akin to* is a cognate of the word in question as attested within the source group:

[1]ca·noe ... *n* [F, fr. NL *canoa*, fr. Sp, fr. Arawakan, of Cariban origin; akin to Galibi *canaoua*]

[2]cant *n* [ME, prob. fr. MD or ONF; MD, edge, corner, fr. ONF, fr. L *canthus*, *cantus* iron tire, perh. of Celt origin; akin to W *cant* rim; akin to Gk *kanthos* corner of the eye]

This last example shows the two contrasting uses of "akin to." The word cited immediately after "of Celt origin; akin to" is a Celtic cognate of the presumed Celtic source word from which the Latin word was borrowed. The word cited after the second "akin to" is a further cognate from another Indo-European language.

When the origin of a word is traced to the name of a person or place not further identified, additional information may be found in the Biographical Names or Geographical Names section in the back matter:

new·ton ... *n* [Sir Isaac *Newton*]

cal·i·co ... *n* ... [*Calicut*, India]

Usage

Three types of status labels are used in this dictionary —temporal, regional, and stylistic—to signal that a word or a sense of a word is not part of the standard vocabulary of English.

The temporal label *obs* for "obsolete" means that there is no evidence of use since 1755:

egal ... *adj* ... *obs*

har·di·ment ... *n* ... **2** *obs*

The label *obs* is a comment on the word being defined. When a thing, as distinguished from the word used to designate it, is obsolete, appropriate orientation is usually given in the definition:

[1]cat·a·pult ... *n* ... **1 :** an ancient military device for hurling missiles

[2]ruff *n* ... **1 :** a wheel-shaped stiff collar worn by men and women of the late 16th and early 17th centuries

The temporal label *archaic* means that a word or sense once in common use is found today only sporadically or in special contexts:

eft·soons ... *adv* ... *archaic*

[2]tender ... *vt* ... **2** *archaic*

A word or sense limited in use to a specific region of the U.S. has a label that corresponds loosely to one of the areas defined in Hans Kurath's *Word Geography of the Eastern United States*. The adverb *chiefly* precedes a label when the word has some currency outside the specified region, and a double label is used to indicate considerable currency in each of two specific regions:

ban·nock ... *n* ... **2** *NewEng*

ban·quette ... *n* ... **1** ... **b** *South*

cal·cu·late ... *vt* ... **3** *chiefly North*

can·ti·na ... *n* ... **1** *Southwest*

em·bar·ca·de·ro ... *n* ... *West*

goo·ber ... *n* ... *South & Midland*

jolt–wag·on ... *n, Midland*

[1]pot·latch ... *n* ... **2** *Northwest*

Words current in all regions of the U.S. have no label.

A word or sense limited in use to one of the other countries of the English-speaking world has an appropriate regional label:

bairn ... *n* ... *chiefly Scot*

be·gor·ra ... *interj* ... *Irish*

bil·la·bong ... *n* ... **1** *Austral*

com·man·do ... *n* ... **1** *So Afr*

corn flour *n, Brit*

foot·ball ... *n* **1** ... **e** *Canad*

[3]gang *vi* ... *Scot*

gar·ron ... *n* ... *Scot & Irish*

The label *dial* for "dialect" indicates that the pattern of use of a word or sense is too complex for summary labeling: it usually includes several regional varieties of American English or of American and British English:

crit·ter ... *n* ... *dial*

The label *dial Brit* indicates currency in several dialects of the British Commonwealth; *dial Eng* indicates currency in one or more provincial dialects of England:

[1]lair ... *n* ... **1** *dial Brit*

few·trils ... *n* ... *dial Eng*

The stylistic label *slang* is used with words or senses that are especially appropriate in contexts of extreme informality, that usually have a currency not limited to a particular region or area of interest, and that are composed typically of shortened forms or extravagant or facetious figures of speech:

clip joint *n* **1** *slang* **:** a place of public entertainment (as a nightclub) that makes a practice of defrauding patrons (as by overcharging)

horn·swog·gle ... *vt* ... *slang* **:** BAMBOOZLE, HOAX

[1]prof ... *n, slang* **:** PROFESSOR

There is no satisfactory objective test for slang, especially with reference to a word out of context. No word, in fact, is invariably slang, and many standard words can be given slang applications.

The stylistic label *nonstand* for "nonstandard" is used for a few words or senses that are disapproved by many but that have some currency in reputable contexts:

ir·re·gard·less ... *adv* ... *nonstand*

[1]lay ... *vi* ... **2** *nonstand*

The stylistic label *substand* for "substandard" is used for those words or senses that conform to a widespread pattern of usage that differs in choice of word or form from that of the prestige group of the community:

ain't ... **2** *substand*

learn ... *vt* ... **2 a** *substand*

A subject label or guide phrase is sometimes used to indicate the specific application of a word or sense:

ape·ri·od·ic ... *adj* ... **3** *cryptology*

hemi·he·dral ... *adj* ... *of a crystal*

lose ... *vi* ... **3** *of a timepiece*

In general, however, subject orientation is given in the definition:

Gun·ther ... *n* ... **:** a Burgundian king and husband of Brunhild in Germanic legend

blitz ... *n* ... **2 b :** a rush of the passer by the defensive linebackers in football

Definitions are sometimes followed by verbal illustrations that show a typical use of the word in context. These illustrations are enclosed in angle brackets, and the word being illustrated is usually replaced by a lightface swung dash. The swung dash stands for the boldface entry word, and it may be followed by an italicized suffix:

large–print ... *adj* ... <~ books>

[3]low *adj* ... **11** ... <had a ~ opinion of him>

[2]mess ... *vi* ... **4 c** ... <~*ing* in other people's affairs>

proud ... *adj* ... **2 b** ... <the ~*est* moment in her life>

The swung dash is not used when the form of the boldface entry word is changed in suffixation, and it is not used for open compounds:

[1]dare ... *vt* ... **1 a** ... <*dared* him to jump>

upper hand *n* ... <was determined not to let his opponent get the *upper hand*>

Illustrative quotations are also used to show words in typical contexts:

[1]with·in ... *adv* **2** ... <search ~ for a creative impulse — Kingman Brewster, Jr.>

Omissions in quotations are indicated by suspension points:

[1]jog ... *vi* ... **1 :** ... < his ... holster *jogging* against his hip —Thomas Williams>

Definitions are sometimes followed by usage notes that give supplementary information about such matters as idiom, syntax, semantic relationship, and status. A usage note is introduced by a lightface dash:

[1]stead ... *n* ... **2 :** ... — used chiefly in the phrase *to stand one in good stead*

[3]zero *vt* ... **2 a :** ... — usu. used with *in*

ad·e·noid ... *n* ... **:** ... — usu. used in pl.

[1]guide ... *n* ... **3 :** ... — used esp. in commands

[1]pi·a·nis·si·mo ... *adv or adj* ... **:** ... — used as a direction in music

dick ... *n* ... **2 :** ... — usu. considered vulgar

Po·lack ... *n* ... **2 :** ... — usu. used disparagingly

Two or more usage notes are separated by a semicolon:

[2]cat ... *vi* ... — often used with *around;* often considered vulgar

Sometimes a usage note is used in place of a definition. Some function words (as conjunctions and prepositions) have little or no semantic content; most interjections express feelings but are otherwise untranslatable into meaning; and some other words (as oaths and honorific titles) are more amenable to comment than to definition:

[1]**if** ... *conj* ... **3** — used as a function word to introduce an exclamation expressing a wish

[1]**for** ... *prep* ... **9** — used as a function word to indicate duration of time or extent of space

[2]**ouch** *interj* ... — used esp. to express sudden pain

[3]**gad** *interj* ... — used as a mild oath

[1]**lord** ... *n* ... **4** — used as a British title

Sense Division

A boldface colon is used in this dictionary to introduce a definition:

deb·u·tante ... *n* ... **:** a young woman making her formal entrance into society

It is also used to separate two or more definitions of a single sense:

[2]**imitation** *adj* **:** resembling something else that is usu. genuine and of better quality **:** not real

Boldface Arabic numerals separate the senses of a word that has more than one sense:

[2]**quiz** *vt* ... **1 :** to make fun of **:** MOCK **2 :** to look at inquisitively **3 :** to question closely

Boldface lowercase letters separate the subsenses of a word:

[1]**pack** ... *n* ... **2 a :** the contents of a bundle **b :** a large amount or number **:** HEAP **c :** a full set of playing cards

Lightface numerals in parentheses indicate a further division of subsenses:

[1]**re·treat** ... *n* ... **1 a** (1) **:** an act or process of withdrawing ... (2) **:** the process of receding ... **b** (1) **:** the usu. forced withdrawal of troops ... (2) **:** a signal for retreating ...

A lightface colon following a definition and immediately preceding two or more subsenses indicates that the subsenses are subsumed by the preceding definition:

huge ... *adj* ... **:** very large or extensive: as **a :** of great size or area **b :** great in scale or degree ... **c :** great in scope or character

[1]**pe·cu·liar** ... *adj* ... **3 :** different from the usual or normal: **a :** SPECIAL, PARTICULAR **b :** CURIOUS **c :** ECCENTRIC, QUEER

The word *as* may or may not follow the lightface colon. Its presence (as at *huge*) indicates that the following subsenses are typical or significant examples. Its absence (as at *peculiar*) indicates that the subsenses which follow are exhaustive.

The system of separating the various senses of a word by numerals and letters is a lexical convenience. It reflects something of their semantic relationship, but it does not evaluate senses or set up a hierarchy of importance among them.

Sometimes a particular semantic relationship between senses is suggested by the use of one of four italic sense dividers: *esp*, *specif*, *also*, or *broadly*.

The sense divider *esp* (for *especially*) is used to introduce the most common meaning subsumed in the more general preceding definition:

chick ... *n* **1 a :** CHICKEN; *esp* **:** one newly hatched

The sense divider *specif* (for *specifically*) is used to introduce a common but highly restricted meaning subsumed in the more general preceding definition:

[2]**pitcher** *n* **:** one that pitches; *specif* **:** the player that pitches in a game of baseball

The sense divider *also* is used to introduce a meaning that is closely related to but may be considered less important than the preceding sense:

Mo·selle ... *n* ... a white table wine made in the valley of the Moselle; *also* **:** a similar wine made elsewhere

The sense divider *broadly* is used to introduce an extended or wider meaning of the preceding definition:

bull's–eye ... *n* ... **3 b :** a shot that hits the bull's-eye; *broadly* **:** something that precisely attains a desired end

The order of senses is historical: the sense known to have been first used in English is entered first. This is not to be taken to mean, however, that each sense of a multisense word developed from the immediately preceding sense. It is altogether possible that sense 1 of a word has given rise to sense 2 and sense 2 to sense 3, but frequently sense 2 and sense 3 may have arisen independently of one another from sense 1.

Information coming between the entry word and the first definition of a multisense word applies to all senses and subsenses. Information applicable only to some senses or subsenses is given between the appropriate boldface numeral or letter and the symbolic colon:

ole·in ... *n* ... **2** *also* **ole·ine** \-ən, -ˌēn\

cru·ci·fix·ion ... *n* ... **1 a** ... **b** *cap*

[1]**tile** ... *n* ... **1** *pl* **tiles** *or* **tile a :** ...

[2]**palm** *n* ... **3** [L *palmus*, fr. *palma*]

When an italicized label or guide phrase follows a boldface numeral, the label or phrase applies only to that specific numbered sense and its subsenses. It does not apply to any other boldface numbered senses:

ro·ta ... *n* ... **1** *chiefly Brit* **:** ... **2** *cap* ...

ro·man·ti·cism ... *n* **1 :** ... **2** *often cap* **a** (1) **:** ... (2) **:** ... **b :** ...

At *rota*, the *chiefly Brit* label applies to sense **1** but not to sense **2**. The *cap* label applies to sense **2** but not to sense **1**.

At *romanticism*, the *often cap* label applies to all the subsenses of sense **2** but not to sense **1**.

When an italicized label or guide phrase follows a boldface letter, the label or phrase applies only to that specific lettered sense and its subsenses. It does not apply to any other boldface lettered senses:

[1]**hearse** ... *n* ... **2 a** *archaic* **:** ... **b** *obs*

The *archaic* label applies to sense **2a** but not to sense **2b**. The *obs* label applies to sense **2b** but not to sense **2a**.

When an italicized label or guide phrase follows a parenthesized numeral, the label or phrase applies only to that specific numbered sense:

[1]**mat·ter** ... *n* ... **1** ... **h** (1) *obs* **:** REASON, CAUSE

The *obs* label applies to sense **1h** (1) and to no other subsenses of the word.

Names of Plants & Animals

An entry that defines the name of a plant or animal (as peach or lion) is a taxonomic entry. Such entries employ in part a formal codified vocabulary of New Latin names—taxa—that has been developed and used by biologists in accordance with international codes of botanical and of zoological nomenclature for the purpose of identifying and indicating the relationships of plants and animals. Names of taxa higher than the genus (as class, order, and family) are capitalized plural nouns which are often used with singular verbs and which are not abbreviated in normal use.

The genus is the fundamental taxon. It names a group of closely related kinds of plants (as *Prunus*, which includes the wild and cultivated cherries, apricots, peaches, and almonds) or animals (as *Felis*, which includes domestic and wild cats, lions, tigers, and cougars). It is a capitalized singular noun.

Each organism has one—and only one—correct name under these codes. The name for a species—the binomial or species name—consists of a singular capitalized genus name combined with an uncapitalized specific epithet. For a variety or subspecies—a trinomial, variety name, or subspecies name—the name adds a similar varietal or subspecific epithet. Thus the cultivated cabbage (*Brassica oleracea capitata*), the cauliflower (*Brassica oleracea botrytis*), and the brussels sprout (*Brassica oleracea gemmifera*) belong to the same species (*Brassica oleracea*) of cole.

Taxa in this dictionary are enclosed in parentheses and usually come immediately after the primary orienting noun. Genus names as well as binomials and trinomials are italicized, but names of taxa above the genus are not italicized:

ba·sid·io·my·cete ... *n* ... **:** any of a large class (Basidiomycetes) of higher fungi having septate hyphae, bearing spores on a basidium, and including rusts, smuts, mushrooms, and puffballs

rob·in ... *n* **1 a :** a small European thrush (*Erithacus rubecola*) resembling a warbler and having a brownish olive back and yellowish red throat and breast **b :** any of various Old World songbirds that are related to or resemble the European robin **2 :** a large No. American thrush (*Turdus migratorius*) with olivaceous gray upperparts, blackish head and tail, black and whitish streaked throat, and chiefly dull reddish breast and underparts

Taxa are used in this dictionary to provide precise technical identifications through which defined terms may be pursued in technical writing. Because of their specialized nature, however, taxa do not have separate entries.

Taxonomic entries are usually oriented indirectly to higher taxa by other vernaculars (as by *alga* at *seaweed* or *thrush* at *robin*) or by technical adjectives (as by *composite* at *daisy*, *leguminous* at *pea*, or *teleost* at *perch*). Among the higher plants, except the composites and legumes and a few obscure tropical groups, such orientation is by a vernacular family name that is linked at the corresponding taxonomic entry to its technical equivalent:

beech ... *n* ... **:** any of a genus (*Fagus* of the family Fagaceae, the beech family) of hardwood trees with smooth gray bark and small edible nuts; *also* **:** its wood

oak ... *n* ... **1 a :** a tree or shrub (genera *Quercus* or *Lithocarpus*) of the beech family that produces a rounded one-seeded thin-shelled nut surrounded at the base by an indurated cup

A genus name may be abbreviated to its initial letter when it is used more than once in senses not separated by a boldface number:

nas·tur·tium ... *n* ... **:** any of a genus (*Tropaeolum* of the family Tropaeolaceae, the nasturtium family) of herbs with showy spurred flowers and pungent seeds; *esp* **:** either of two widely cultivated ornamentals (*T. majus* and *T. minus*)

Cross-Reference

Four different kinds of cross-references are used in this dictionary: directional, synonymous, cognate, and inflectional. In each instance the cross-reference is readily recognized by the lightface small capitals in which it is printed.

A cross-reference following a lightface dash and beginning with *see* or *compare* is a directional cross-reference. It directs the dictionary user to look elsewhere for further information. A *compare* cross-reference is regularly appended to a definition; a *see* cross-reference may stand alone:

plea ... *n* ... **2** ... **a** ... — compare DEMURRER

[1]scru·ple ... *n* ... **1** —see WEIGHT table

A cross-reference immediately following a boldface colon is a synonymous cross-reference. It may stand alone as the only definitional matter for an entry or for a sense or subsense of an entry; it may follow an analytical definition; it may be one of two synonymous cross-references separated by a comma:

mul·ti·syl·lab·ic ... *adj* **:** POLYSYLLABIC

drain·age ... *n* ... **2 :** a device for draining **:** DRAIN

drip·py ... *adj* ... **1 :** RAINY, DRIZZLY

A synonymous cross-reference indicates that a definition at the entry cross-referred to can be substituted as a definition for the entry or the sense or subsense in which the cross-reference appears.

A cross-reference following an italic *var of* is a cognate cross-reference:

fiord *var of* FJORD

Sometimes a cognate cross-reference has a limiting label preceding *var of* as a specific indication that the variant is not standard English:

mair ... *chiefly Scot var of* MORE

quare ... *dial var of* [1]QUEER

sher·ris ... *archaic var of* SHERRY

A cross-reference following an italic label that identifies an entry as an inflected form of a noun, of an adjective or adverb, or of a verb is an inflectional cross-reference. Inflectional cross-references appear only when the inflected form falls at least a column away from the entry cross-referred to:

mice *pl of* MOUSE

sang *past of* SING

Synonyms & Antonyms

Synonymous words believed to be of interest to the dictionary user are listed in groups following the entry of one of the words in the group. (See, for example, *talkative* on page 1189.) They are signaled by an indented boldface italic ***syn***. They are followed by a brief statement of their common denotation which is called the "shared meaning element" and by a list of antonyms which is identified by a prefixed boldface italic ***ant*** and is specific to the first member of the group.

Synonymous words believed to present special problems to the dictionary user are similarly listed and are, further, clearly discriminated and illustrated in an accompanying paragraph. (See, for example, [1]*gaudy* on page 475.)

When a word is included in a synonym list, the main entry of that word is followed by a run-on ***syn*** see—which refers to the entry where the synonym list may be found. Where appropriate, the run-on is followed by ***ant*** and any antonyms specific to the word. (See, for example, *facetious* on page 410.)

Combining Forms, Prefixes & Suffixes

An entry that begins or ends with a hyphen is a word element that forms part of an English compound:

self- *comb form*

-l·o·gy . . . *n comb form* . . . <phraseo*logy*>

-lyze . . . *vb comb form* . . . <electro*lyze*>

pre- *prefix* . . . <*pre*historic>

¹-er . . . *adj suffix or adv suffix* . . . <hott*er*> <dri*er*>

-ism . . . *n suffix* . . . <barbarian*ism*>

-fy . . . *vb suffix* . . . <citi*fy*>

Combining forms, prefixes, and suffixes are entered in this dictionary for three reasons: to make easier the writing of etymologies of words in which these word elements occur over and over again; to make understandable the meaning of many undefined run-ons which for reasons of space would be omitted if they had to be given etymologies and definitions; and to make recognizable the meaningful elements of new words that are not well enough established in the language to warrant dictionary entry.

Lists of Undefined Words

Lists of undefined words occur after the entries of the prefixes **non-**, **re-**, and **un-**. These words are not defined because they are self-explanatory: their meanings are simply the sum of a meaning of the prefix combined with a meaning of the root word.

Abbreviations & Symbols

Abbreviations and symbols for chemical elements are included as main entries in the vocabulary:

acct *abbr*

Au *symbol*

Abbreviations have been normalized to one form. In practice, however, there is considerable variation in the use of periods and in capitalization (as *mph*, *m.p.h.*, *Mph*, and *MPH*), and stylings other than those given in this dictionary are often acceptable.

Abbreviations regularly used in this dictionary are listed separately on page 31a.

Symbols that are not capable of being alphabetized are included in a separate section of the back matter headed "Signs and Symbols."

The English Language and Its History

W. Nelson Francis
Professor of Linguistics and English
Brown University

English is undoubtedly the most important of the world's languages at the present time. In number of speakers it ranks second,[1] with approximately 275 million native speakers, compared with 585 million native speakers of Mandarin Chinese. Spanish comes next, with 185 million, followed by Russian with 140 million and Bengali and Hindu-Urdu with 125 million each. Importance is not measured only by numbers, however. The uses to which a language is put and the extent of its international exposure are at least as important as the sheer bulk of native speakers. The worldwide use of English in diplomacy, commerce, and science is evidence of its importance in this regard, and serves to explain why many millions around the world find it desirable and sometimes necessary to learn it as a second language.

It is not the intrinsic superiority of English over other languages that has made it the premier world language. If it is richer in vocabulary, more flexible in grammar, and more expressive than other languages (and some would question at least the last two of these claims), these qualities are the results, not the causes, of its importance in the world. Simply stated, what makes a language important is the importance of the people who use it and the uses to which they put it. Since the eighteenth century, speakers of English—at first from the British Isles and later from America and the dominions—have played a dominant role in colonial expansion, industrial and technological development, and world politics. The position of English in the world is the direct result of the history of those who speak it.

What is modern English, this great world language, like? Before we can answer that question at all meaningfully, we must deal with the broader questions What is a language like? and What qualities, if any, are shared by all languages, regardless of their relative prominence or obscurity? These are questions which are central to the study called linguistics. They cannot be completely answered by linguistics in its present state; probably they will never be completely answered. But linguistics has progressed sufficiently so that partial answers, dealing with the larger aspects of the questions, can be tentatively suggested. Like the answers put forward by most sciences, these are subject to revision in the future as new insights and new techniques are brought to bear and new minds take up the old problems from new angles. All we can say is that this is what we know, or think we know, now.

In the first place, language is a uniquely human possession, at least in that little corner of the universe that we know about. All races, tribes, and families of men have language; no animals do. Some people might question the second of these statements, since we know that animals communicate with one another by sounds. But when we identify the particular qualities of genuine language, we discover that animal communication systems are different in several fundamental ways. Why this is so, when we share so much of our anatomy, physiology, and psychology with the animals, especially the apes and monkeys, science cannot yet clearly explain. It seems to be largely due to the structure of our brains, though other physical differences, especially in the anatomy of the throat and mouth, may have something to do with it. Much research is going on now in the attempt to answer this question. Meanwhile it is certainly a deeply ingrained part of our human nature to consider language as belonging to man alone. There is something a bit eerie about those animals, mostly birds, which can be taught to mimic the sounds of language. All the stories, whether fables, fairy tales, or fantasies, that endow animals with speech also give them other human qualities as well, so that they cease to be animals and become humans in disguise. On the other hand, we find it hard to imagine a human society lacking language. None has ever been found. If there still are tribes unknown to us living in isolation in Amazonian jungles, we are confident that they have language.

It is paradoxical that in spite of this universality of language among humans it still must be learned afresh by each individual person. There is considerable debate among linguists and psychologists as to how much of our linguistic ability we inherit and how much we have to learn from others. A conservative position would be that we inherit a remarkable aptitude for learning language, or at least one language, together with a very strong motivation to learn it early in life. Some linguists go much farther, as far as to maintain that we inherit not only an aptitude and a desire to learn, but actually a good part of the underlying system that is much the same in all languages. In any case, three conditions meet together to allow us to learn a language rapidly and successfully while we are still very young children: aptitude, strong motivation, and exposure to older people actually using language as they go about their lives. All normal children seem to have the first two of these; the third supplies the input which decides what particular language, or sometimes languages, we learn. It is thus a factor of our heredity that we are able and eager to learn a language, and an accident of our environment that the language we learn is English or French or some other of the three thousand or so living languages. The normal circumstance is to learn the language surrounding us in early childhood and to speak it the rest of our lives; it is our NATIVE SPEECH or MOTHER TONGUE. Occasionally the environment is such that the child learns two mother tongues at the same time and is thus a native bilingual. Even more rarely, the child

[1] According to figures compiled by the Center for Applied Linguistics, Arlington, Va., in 1972.

may begin with one native speech but switch to another at such an early age that he forgets the first one completely. Whatever the situation, it is wholly a result of the environment. Most people are monolingual native speakers simply because most families and communities are homogeneously monolingual.

The fact that every normal human learns whatever language he happens to be surrounded by in childhood and that the amount of time and effort expended in this learning seems to be about the same for all languages suggests that languages must be essentially similar in their general form, however different they may be in details. Linguistics supports this supposition. It is possible to list a large number of qualities as being characteristic of language in general and hence of all known languages. Linguists call these LANGUAGE UNIVERSALS.

In the first place, languages are very versatile and adaptable. Their versatility is shown by the fact that all kinds of people, from scholars and mystics to laborers and mechanics, can make use of the same language to carry on their work, their social life, their thoughts, and their recreations. There are differences between the ways in which these different groups use their language, but it is at bottom the same means of communication. Another sign of the versatility of language is the fact that speakers are constantly saying new things that they never heard before, and others understand their utterances with equal ease, often without even realizing that they are new. This is one of the great differences between language proper and the pseudolanguages used by animals. So far as we know, all animal communications consist of a relatively short list of utterances which cannot be changed, expanded, or used in new and different ways. An animal "language", then, is rather like one of those little pocket phrase books for travelers. Even if he memorizes the book, the traveler is restricted to the immediate practical needs covered by the repertory of messages in the book. He can ask the way to his hotel or the price of a souvenir, but he can't comment very effectively on the sunset or describe the way things are in his hometown. And if something he says moves a speaker of the language to engage in real conversation, the traveler is lost. But two speakers of the same language, even though they may be very different in background, experience, education, and personality, can find a way to talk about anything they want to, using sentences that were never printed in any phrase book because nobody ever used them before.

The adaptability of language is related to its versatility. Like other human institutions, a language is adjusted by long use to the particular needs of the people and the society that use it. When these needs change, the language also changes, usually much more rapidly than most other institutions. This is why it is that in 1500 years—a relatively short space of time in human history—English has changed from the language of a rough, warlike, rather savage, agrarian, tribal society like that of the Anglo-Saxons to the typical language of the most complicated technological civilization yet developed on earth. It has always been easily adjusted to meet the new needs put upon it by a new religion, a new social system, an age of worldwide exploration, conquest, and colonization, and a series of political, agricultural, industrial, scientific, technological, and electronic revolutions. Other languages have done the same, and the process is going on today as the peoples of many different cultures around the world cope with the problem of adapting to Western society. Here again language shows itself fundamentally different from the communication systems of animals. A group of animals transplanted from their natural habitat to a new and different one do not devise new cries to deal with the new circumstances. They have only their little phrase book of specific and unalterable utterances, many of which are irrelevant to their new condition.

The versatility and adaptability that characterize all languages, as well as the fact that they all can be learned readily by any people, come from their organization or structure. Basically a language consists of four main parts or systems, each of which has its own organization while also being related to the others. First, and certainly most obvious in a dictionary like this one, is the VOCABULARY or LEXICON, a relatively large collection of words and word parts. Then there is the GRAMMAR, a set of rules governing the ways in which items from the lexicon can be combined into larger units. These words and sentences are related to the vast variety of things, events, and ideas that we talk about by a system of meanings, a SEMANTIC SYSTEM. Finally a tightly organized system of sound patterns, which linguists call the PHONOLOGY, controls the way in which the strings of words put in order according to the grammar are translated into sounds that can be spoken and heard. All languages have these four parts. Many languages, including English, have a fifth part, a WRITING SYSTEM, which supplies an alternative, visual way in which the ordered strings of words can be expressed. Unlike the other four systems, which seem to be as old as language itself, writing is a relatively new invention, probably not more than 6000 years old. Usually it is a kind of visual imitation of the phonology, using about the same number of units and following the same patterns of arrangement, though some writing systems—notably the Chinese—are based directly on the words themselves, rather than on the way they sound.

The vocabulary is the most loosely organized of the systems of language, and hence the one most open to change. It is relatively easy to add a new word to it. There are three requirements: first a need, second an inventive person, and third a group of speakers to pick up the new word and use it. The need may be of various kinds, the most obvious of which is some new element in the culture that must be named. Thus when lysergic acid diethylamide, which had been known to chemists under that ponderous name for some time, began to be used widely as a hallucinogenic drug, its name became shortened to LSD. There was also a need for a word to describe the people who use it. They could have been called *lysergic acid diethylamide users* or *LSD addicts*, but the inventiveness of some anonymous word coiner came up with *acidhead*, neatly combining a quality of the substance itself with the part of the body affected. Since the group that took up this term consisted chiefly of the drug users themselves and their associates on the fringes of society, the new word was at first considered slang, but it has now been used so widely that it has become an item in the regular vocabulary of English. Its future, like that of most slang words as well as many words in the more respectable part of the vocabulary, is in doubt, for social, not linguistic, reasons. If the use of LSD turns out to be a passing fad, the term will die out with the practice, and a future generation will find it as quaint as the present one finds outmoded expressions of the twenties, like *lounge lizard* and *flapper*.

The need may be of other kinds as well. Sometimes words acquire associations with unpleasant, antisocial, or otherwise undesirable ideas or experiences, so that people become reluctant to use them. There is then a need for a substitute that people find innocuous enough to use in ordinary conversation. Men who work on the land were once called *villains* in English (ultimately from the Latin word *villa* 'farm'); now they are called *farm labourers* or even *agricultural labourers* in England and *farmhands* in the United States. Sometimes the need is for more controllable precision, as in technical and scientific language. Thus linguists coined the word *phoneme* when the older *speech-sound* turned out to be too general and vague. Or the need may be for vocabulary items that identify the speaker with a particular social group. The special vocabularies of sailors, surfers, skiers, airplane pilots, and hundreds of other groups are full of terms which in a way serve the need for precision, but also serve to show that the speaker is "in" and to mystify and exclude those who are "out". Often these terms have perfectly good synonyms in the regular vocabulary. This is an old social use of language. Shakespeare makes amusing use of it when he shows that Prince Hal got along so well with the tavern *drawers* (waiters) that they taught him their "in" language. As the Prince puts it:

> They call drinking deep, dying scarlet; and when you breathe in your watering, they cry 'hem!' and bid you play it off. To conclude, I am so good a proficient in one quarter of an hour that I can drink with any tinker in his own language during my life. [1 Henry IV, II.iv]

The sources of new vocabulary items are many and varied and may change in popularity from one period to another or from one language to another. Very commonly the new words are not new at all in form, but are simply new uses of established words, such as the modern *acid* for *LSD* or Prince Hal's *dying scarlet* for drinking deep. Commonly also new combinations of old words or word parts are put together into what linguists call COMPOUNDS. The term *acidhead* is an example using whole words. The newly popular *astronaut* uses two word parts, originally from Greek, which are already familiar through their appearance in words like *astronomy* and *nautical*. Once a new word is established, a whole family of new words can be made out of it by the process of DERIVATION, the adding on of prefixes and suffixes primarily to change the grammatical function of the word. Thus as soon as English had *psychiatry* (ultimately from Greek elements meaning 'soul' and 'doctor'), the related *psychiatrist* and *psychiatric* were easily added. In English, as in many languages which at some time in their history have been in contact with one or more other languages, it is common to get new words by BORROWING. This is the process which accounts for the fact that a large majority of the words in the English lexicon are ultimately Latin or French. These four —transferred meaning, compounding, derivation, and borrowing—are the major ways in which a language gets new words. There are several minor ways as well, among which may be mentioned CLIPPING (as in *mini* from *miniskirt,* itself a compound), BLENDS (as in *brunch* from *breakfast* plus *lunch*), IMITATIONS (as in the verb *whiz*), ACRONYMS (as in *NASA* from *National Aeronautics and Space Administration*), ABBREVIATIONS (as in *emcee* and *deejay* for *master of ceremonies* and *disc jockey*), and COINAGES (*boondoggle, quark*). The last are the rarest of all, at least in English. We seem to resist the idea of making up a word completely afresh, without any reference to words already in existence.

Just as new words keep coming into the language, so old ones keep going out of use and eventually out of memory. The usual reason is that the things they refer to are no longer talked about; the generation born since World War II does not know words like *stuka* and *panzer,* which refer to modes of warfare that are no longer employed. Sometimes, however, an old word will be replaced by a new one for no apparent reason, as in the case of *eme,* the Old English word replaced by its French synonym *uncle*. These processes are natural ones, too, common to all languages. As the great lexicographer Samuel Johnson said, in answer to Swift's wish that words should be prevented from becoming obsolete, "But what makes a word obsolete, more than general agreement to forbear it? and how shall it be continued, when it conveys an offensive idea, or recalled again into the mouths of mankind, when it has once by disuse become unfamiliar, and by unfamiliarity unpleasing." [from Preface to *A Dictionary of the English Language,* 1755]

The other part of the central core of a language is its grammar. The largest and most complicated vocabulary would be of little value without a grammar to control the ways in which words can be put together to make larger constructions. Without a grammar the lexicon is only a list of separate items, like the entries in this dictionary. Many of these words can be used alone to make brief messages, but mostly they depend on being combined with other words to make utterances worth saying or listening to. Nor is it enough simply to put words alongside each other, in the fashion of the classic "Me Tarzan you Jane." Any sentence in this essay, any definition in this dictionary, will illustrate how complex and how delicate are the conventions governing combinations of words. They are not just strung along like beads in a necklace; they are fitted together into interlocking arrangements as intricate as the works of a watch. A change in the relationships of the parts usually changes the whole utterance: consider the difference between *Rats are our enemies* and *Our enemies are rats.* The words are the same but the messages are different.

There are various ways we can look at the grammar of a language. One analogy might be the rules of such a game as chess. The basic rules of chess are quite simple. There are only six kinds of pieces, each of which has the privilege of moving in a particular way. When certain combinations occur, certain moves are obligatory. Otherwise the player has many options each time it is his turn to move. As they move in turn, the two players construct a series of patterns on the board which is not like any series either of them has seen before. In the same way the words of a language are classified as belonging to certain classes, traditionally called PARTS OF SPEECH. The functions of these are different, just as the moves of the chess pieces are. Nouns can be subjects and objects, adjectives are modifiers, pronouns substitute for nouns, and so on. The rules are more complicated than those of chess, but not so complicated that they cannot be learned by a five-year-old child. Just as the chess players create a new game, unlike any other played in the past, so the speaker is constantly making up new sentences, many —perhaps most—of which are unlike any he ever heard or spoke in the past. The secret is in the fact that the grammar rules may be applied in many different combinations, some of them over and over, as sentences are created. Here is the major difference between animal communication and human language. Animal communication, again like the traveler's phrase book, has little or no grammar. Neither the animal nor the traveler has the power to use rules in new combinations to make original utterances. When we consider this fact, we realize that grammar is one of the greatest of all human inventions.

Another way of looking at grammar is to consider it as a set of patterns of behavior which the person using the language has somehow built into his mental structure. These patterns are sometimes called rules, but they are rules in a different sense from the rules of a game. These latter are imposed from the outside and consciously learned. But the rules of grammar, particularly those of the native language, are, as it were, invented by the child as he learns the language; they are largely unconscious, self-invented, and self-imposed. Only if he should happen to study formal grammar much later in life will the speaker encounter explicit formulations of these rules, and even then he may not recognize them. It seems rather paradoxical that many people find the study of grammar difficult, when all it is is an attempt to formulate what they themselves invented when they were children!

When grammar is looked at in this way, it is easy to see why it is much less subject to change than is vocabulary. The grammar rules are a closely integrated system, so that if a change is made in one part it may affect many other parts of the system. The vocabulary, on the other hand, is like the population of a city, where individuals may be born and die, or move in from outside, with only minor effects on the whole organization. As we shall see when we retrace the history of English, there have been a good many changes in the grammar of English, but they have occurred very slowly and gradually over a long period of time. In many of its aspects English grammar is still much like that of German, although the two languages, once the same, diverged and went their separate ways two thousand years ago.

The third major system of language is the sound system, or phonology. It is important because it controls the principal channel through which we send messages back and forth to each other. No matter how large a person's vocabulary and how carefully constructed his sentences, he would not be able to communicate normally if he did not know how to turn them into the modulated flow of sound we call speech. Underlying this continuous flow is a tightly organized system, which depends on our ability to make and to recognize sounds that contrast with one another. Thus for the middle part of *pit* we make a sound which is clearly different from the middle sounds of *pat* and *pot*. Similarly we contrast the first part of *pit* with the first part of *bit* or *nit*, and the last part with the last part of *pick*. There doesn't happen to be an English word *pid*, but if there were we would never confuse it with *pit* or *bid* or *pod*. There are normally only 25 to 50 of these contrasting sound units in a language (30 to 40 in English, depending on the dialect), but they are enough to permit us to give each word its characteristic shape. There are, of course, many cases of HOMOPHONES (words that sound alike) like *doe* and *dough*, but we are seldom confused by these because they usually appear in different contexts.

In addition to these contrasting units, which linguists call PHONEMES, each language has quite rigorous rules about how they may be combined in syllables and words. They cannot be strung along in any and all possible combinations. In a language like Hawaiian, for example, each syllable must be either just a vowel or a single consonant followed by a vowel. The few Hawaiian words and names we all know illustrate this rule: *hula, aloha, Honolulu, Waikiki*. In contrast, English syllables have only one vowel or diphthong but may have as many as three consonants before it and three after, as in *splints*. But the rules governing which consonants may be used are quite strict. For example, if there are three at the beginning of a word, the first must be *s*, the second *p, t*, or *k*, and the third *r, l, w*, or *y* (remember we are talking about sounds, not spellings). If you will look in the *s*-section of this dictionary, you will find how closely this rule is followed; the only words that break this rule are recent borrowings from other languages, and even these are usually changed to fit the English pattern.

A third part of the sound system concerns not the individual sounds but the features of rhythm, accent, and even musical pitch which are part of the flow of speech. Since most of these are related to whole clauses and sentences, rather than individual words, they are not given much attention in a dictionary, which deals primarily with single words. But an important exception is STRESS, which in English is a feature of individual words. The rules for assigning stress to the correct syllables of an English word are quite rigorous, and the native speaker of English knows them as he knows the rules of grammar. But there are some doubtful cases, such as *contemplative, hospitable*, and *altimeter*, for which we turn to the dictionary.

Because of its tight structure, the phonological system of a language does not usually change very much or very fast. Such changes as do occur usually affect the minor details of pronunciation, rather than the underlying system of contrasts. But this may change also, by the addition or disappearance of phonemes, by changes in the combining rules, or in the rules of stress. Thus Chaucer's English of six hundred years ago had a frictional sound made in the back of the mouth, as in modern German *Nacht*, and the ancestor of our word *courage* had three syllables with the stress on the second \kü-ˈrä-jə\.

As has been already noted, writing systems are comparatively recent innovations, as compared to the venerable antiquity of language itself with its basic systems of vocabulary, grammar, and phonology. The human race got along for several hundred thousand years with only the channel of speech through which to communicate verbal messages. But when societies became so complex that their essential records could no longer be kept in the memories of men and when they found it necessary to transmit at a distance messages that could not be entrusted safely to the memory of a messenger, various modes of writing were invented. The earliest of these seem to have been based on the word as a unit, and made use of a separate symbol or CHARACTER, originally a conventionalized picture, for each word. The Chinese system is still based on this principle, with some modifications. Systems of this sort have certain advantages, the chief of which is that they are largely independent of pronunciation. In fact, the Chinese system is used by a number of different languages, so that people who cannot understand one another's speech can communicate by writing. But the disadvantage of having to invent and learn to read and draw thousands of characters to represent the vocabulary of a language led people to devise new types of writing systems, based on the phonological structure, which, as we have seen, has many fewer units than the vocabulary and was already in full development as a channel of communication. At first the syllable was used as the unit to be represented. Symbols representing syllables could be strung along in the same order as the syllables of speech, usually with some additional indication as to where the boundaries between words fell. Finally the phoneme became the unit to be represented, and the ALPHABET was born. Most present-day writing systems are alphabetic, though because of accidents of history they have departed more or less from the principle of consistently representing each phoneme by a single character. Alphabets are rather readily adaptable to other languages besides those for which they were originally developed. Thus our Roman alphabet, originally devised for Latin, has been adopted by most of the languages of western Europe and the New World. Other familiar alphabets are the Cyrillic, used for Russian and other Slavic languages; the Arabic, used also for Persian and Urdu and formerly for Turkish; the Hebrew, also used for Yiddish; the Devanagari of India; and the Greek.

Alphabetic writing systems resemble phonological systems in that they have a relatively small number of units and a set of rules, sometimes quite elaborate, governing the ways in which the units may and may not be combined. Some of these rules are, as might be expected, simply reflections of the rules of the phonology. But others belong to the writing systems themselves. In English, for example, though we have many words ending in the sounds of *v* and *j*, there is a strong rule, with very few exceptions, against ending a word with either of these letters. Instead we write *-ge* or *-dge* for a final *j*-sound and *-ve* for a final *v*-sound. There is also a rule against doubling these letters, and *k* as well, even for the usual purpose of indicating that the preceding vowel is short. So we write *liver, flicker,* and *badger,* instead of the more consistent *livver, flikker, bajjer.*[2] It is these rules, which are known unconsciously by all literate users of English, that give English its characteristic look on the page. Combinations like *zdenek, lliiji,* and *mbau* simply don't look English, while *flace, crasp,* and *splick* could very well represent English words, though they don't happen to. In short, our system, for all its inconsistencies, is indeed a system and one which most people can learn to use easily and accurately. But it is also true that checking on spelling is one of the most common reasons for using the dictionary.

The semantic system has been left to the last partly because we know least about it in a formal way. It is probably not obvious to the ordinary observer that there is such a system. Everyone knows that meaning is an important part of language, but somehow they feel that words and sentences represent meaning directly, without the intervention of another formal system. But a little thought about how language works, and especially some comparisons of how different languages convey similar facts and ideas, leads us to the conclusion that there is a quite elaborate formally structured system between the infinite variety of the outside world and our ways of talking about it. Take the question of measurements. English, like the other languages in the western European tradition, has an elaborate system of ways of describing the size of things in terms of abstract standard units that can be counted, added, subtracted, multiplied, and divided. If asked how big a book or a desk is, we think of applying a ruler to it and giving the answer in inches or feet and fractions of these units. The whole repertory of miles, pounds, pints, cubic feet, acres, and all the rest is based on this underlying assumption that numerically manipulable standard units are the way to measure things. We are so committed to this way of measuring that we can hardly imagine any other. But many cultures, and the languages associated with them, measure distance in terms of time; two localities may be "two days' journey" apart. According to our system, one 20-mile stretch across country is equal to another, though the first may be across a level plain and the other across rough broken country or through a jungle. Another system might find these two not equal at all; the first might be "half a day's walk" and the second "two days' walk."[3]

Another illustration of the formal structuring of meanings, also taken from the general area of measurements, is the description of dimensions. In English we do this with pairs of words signifying opposite poles of measurement along a certain line, such as *tall : short* and *far : near.* Furthermore we have two sets of these, one set in which the line of measurement is related to a fixed point, often but not always that of the observer or speaker, and another set in which the line of measurement is related rather to the shape of the object being measured. Thus the first set has three main pairs: *far* and *near* (measured along a line extending from the observer in a specified direction), *high* and *low* (measured along a vertical line perpendicular to the observer's line of sight), *wide* and *narrow* (measured along a horizontal line perpendicular to the observer's line of sight). The second set has more dimensions—at least five—but they are still signified by pairs of opposed words: *large* (*big*) and *small* (*little*), *long* and *short, tall* and *short, deep* and *shallow, wide* (*broad*) and *narrow, thick* and *thin.* A further interesting point about English is that in each of these pairs one, which is somehow the larger one, is chosen for giving a neutral measurement or asking a neutral question about one of the dimensions. We say "The door is three feet *wide,*" "The water is three feet *deep,*" or "How *tall* is John?" rather than "The door is three feet *narrow,*" "The water is three feet *shallow,*" or "How *short* is John?" We would say the latter if someone else had already said "John is quite short," and even then the answer would be "He is only five feet *tall.*" Similarly we choose the larger dimension for the neutral nouns describing these dimensions: the *length* of the journey, the *height* of the building, the *depth* of the water. There are also nouns for the small dimensions, but they are all what linguists would call SEMANTICALLY MARKED. Note that "the *shortness* of the journey," "the *lowness* of the building," "the *shallowness* of the water" all convey special meanings beyond a mere neutral indication of dimension. It is clear that systems like these are not merely parts of the natural world; they impose a structural framework on the natural world which makes it easier to talk about it. This is what we mean by speaking of a semantic system that is part of language.

The relationships among these various systems are quite complex, but they may be suggested in a diagram such as this:

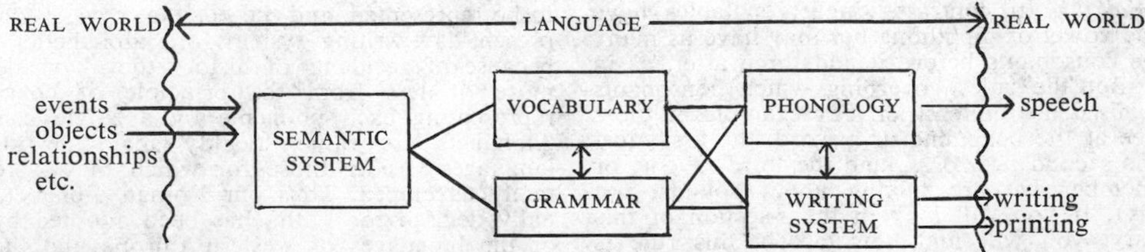

2 A few violations of this rule are beginning to appear, usually in slang, dialectal, and humorous words like *flivver* and *yakking.*

3 One unit of distance in terms of time that we do use is the *light-year.* But since the speed of light is constant, this is still an abstract standard: it is simply easier to say "one light-year" than "5,878,000,000,000 miles."

Here we see language, which is inside the minds of people, in contact with the outside world in two places, which scientists might call *interfaces.* At one end the semantic system sorts out, classifies, and arranges the jumble of events, objects, and relationships fed in by the outside world. At the other, the phonology and the writing system give instructions which control the actual performance of the speaker or writer. Within language itself, the internal structures of the various parts, as well as the relationships among them, are very complicated. It is the function of the dictionary to give information about many of these. Thus the main entries, in giving the correct spelling, indicate the relationship between the vocabulary and the writing system. Pronunciation cues indicate the relationship between vocabulary and phonology; definitions, that between vocabulary and the semantic system and sometimes between the semantic system and the real world. Each word is also classified under one or more parts of speech, which suggests the relationship between vocabulary and grammar. Thus the dictionary, centering on the vocabulary, also involves all the other parts of language.

The History of English

Language, like all other aspects of human culture, is constantly changing. This is implied in a good deal that is said above. Certainly the adaptability of language is one of the major sources of change; as the circumstances and needs of the speakers of a language change, they change the language to meet them. This is particularly apparent in vocabulary, where change is easiest to observe and most rapid. There are many words in this dictionary which were not included in Webster's Third New International Dictionary, published only twelve years ago. Less obviously, there are words now considered obsolete that were in current use not many decades ago. It is, of course, harder to decide that a word has left the vocabulary than that one has joined it, because the old words are enshrined in the older books even though people may not use them in speech. Hence the vocabulary, and the dictionary that reports it, has a category of ARCHAIC words—museum specimens, no longer completely alive, but still needed in special ways.

Change goes on in other parts of the language as well, though it is harder to observe. Anyone who has lived a moderately long life is not using exactly the same grammar and pronunciation that he learned as a child, though he himself is usually unaware of the changes that have taken place. These changes usually happen so slowly and gradually that they are imperceptible to the people in whose language they occur. It is only when we look back over a period of a century or more that language begins to look a little old-fashioned. Until recently it has not been possible to compare a person's pronunciation at various ages, as well as to observe what changes take place across the generations. Modern means of voice recording will make this possible in the future.

In order to see how the old-fashioned quality of language ultimately changes to complete unintelligibility if we go far enough back in time, let us take a retrospective trip into the older stages of English, making stops every two hundred years or so. The passages which will be used for illustration are all quite formal documents—in all cases but one they are public notices or proclamations—so that their kind of language is the kind that changes most slowly. Slang, informal conversation, personal letters, are all more unstable and changeable than the formal language of laws, legal documents, public announcements, and royal proclamations, which tends to retain archaic vocabulary and to some extent grammar as well. Yet we shall see that when we go back as far as five and a half centuries, even this conservative formal language becomes quite strange.

Our first example is from a document which is—or at least ought to be—familiar to all Americans: the Declaration of Independence, 1776.

Prudence, indeed, will dictate that Governments long established should not be changed for light and transient causes; and accordingly all experience hath shewn, that mankind are more disposed to suffer, while evils are sufferable, than to right themselves by abolishing the forms to which they are accustomed. But when a long train of abuses and usurpations, pursuing invariably the same Object, evinces a design to reduce them under absolute Despotism, it is their right, it is their duty, to throw off such Government, and to provide new Guards for their future security.—Such has been the patient sufferance of these Colonies; and such is now the necessity which constrains them to alter their former Systems of Government. The history of the present King of Great Britain is a history of repeated injuries and usurpations, all having in direct object the establishment of an absolute Tyranny over these States.

Probably what strikes the twentieth-century reader of this passage first is its extreme formality. It may even take a bit of study to realize that "the forms to which they are accustomed" means what we would more informally express as "the type of government they are used to," and we would feel easier with "the need that forces them to change the government" than we do with "the necessity which constrains them to alter their former Systems of Government." The more formal passages are still quite possible in modern English, however. It is rather a matter of style than age which makes them seem a bit out-of-date to us. The same may be said of the fact that the subjects of a good many of the sentences are abstract qualities: "Prudence . . . will dictate," "experience hath shewn," "necessity . . . constrains"—it is as though the actors in the drama were these abstractions, rather than people. But this is a characteristic feature of eighteenth-century style, which helps to emphasize that the only actual person mentioned is the villain, "the present King of Great Britain."

When we look a bit more closely, however, we find some features of vocabulary and grammar that are indeed old-fashioned to the point of being archaic. Words like *suffer, train, reduce,* and *object* are used in ways and with meanings that present-day writers would not use; we would be more likely to say *endure, series* or *succession, subject,* and *aim*. In grammar we note the form *hath,* which was already archaic in 1776, the treatment of *mankind* as a plural noun (*mankind are*), and the unusual word order of *Governments long established* and *pursuing invariably the same Object*. And *shew,* a variant spelling of *show,* long ago passed from common use.

What these various matters of style, vocabulary, and grammar add up to is a slight feeling of strangeness that can be a barrier to full understanding. The cautious reader might feel the need to go to the dictionary to check such words as *transient* and *suffer*. Nor would he expect the modern Congress, no matter how formal the situation, to produce a document quite like this. But he can still accept it as essentially his own language.

We go back another hundred and fifty years for the next example, a selection from a pamphlet written by John Winthrop and others of the Puritan pioneers from their ship, the *Arbella,* which was just about to set out across the ocean to establish Boston and the other settlements of the Massachusetts Bay Colony. The year is 1630, and the document bears a long and quaint title, *The Humble Request of His Maiesties loyall Subjects, the Governour and the Company late gone for New-England; To the rest of their Brethren, in and of the Church of England. For the obtaining of their Prayers and the removall of suspitions, and misconstructions of their Intentions*. Like many seventeenth-century titles, this one is really a summary of what the little pamphlet is about. The colonists are writing to those they are leaving behind, asking for understanding of their motives in leaving their country and their church to set up new settlements and a new church in the New World.

> If any there be, who through want of cleare intelligence of our course, or tendernesse of affection towards us, cannot conceive so well of our way as we could desire, we would intreat such not to despise us, nor to desert us in their prayers & affections, but to consider rather, that they are so much the more bound to expresse the bowels of their compassion towards us, remembring alwaies that both Nature and Grace, doth ever binde us to relieve and rescue with our utmost & speediest power, such as are deare unto us, when wee conceive them to be running uncomfortable hazards.
>
> What goodnes you shall extend to us in this or any other Christian kindnesse, wee your Brethren in CHRIST IESVS shall labour to repay in what dutie wee are or shall be able to performe, promising so farre as God shall enable us to give him no rest on your behalfes, wishing our heads and hearts may be as fountaines of teares for your everlasting welfare, when wee shall be in our poore Cottages in the wildernesse, . . .

Certainly one thing that strikes us here is the complexity of the sentences. The whole passage of 182 words comprises only two sentences; actually the second sentence has been broken off before its end, and runs on in the original for 23 more words. In spite of this, however, its tone is more personal and less abstract than that of the Declaration; the actors are people ("wee" and "you") rather than abstractions like "Prudence" and "necessity". Perhaps because of this more familiar tone, the vocabulary presents relatively few problems, though even in the first clause we realize that *want, intelligence,* and *affection* are being used in senses no longer current today—we would say *lack, understanding* or *knowledge,* and *feeling* (note that we now use just the word *affection* to mean what is here expressed by *tendernesse of affection*).

In other matters, however, the passage clearly declares itself as older than the Declaration. Even the spelling, which in our day is strictly standardized, is different, particularly in the matter of putting a final *-e* onto a good many words which we end with a consonant: *cleare, expresse, binde, deare, farre,* etc. Other spellings which are no longer current are *alwaies, wee,* and *dutie*. But it is probably the combination of grammatical complexity and archaic turns of phrase that gives the passage its antique flavor. A modern translation of the first sentence might go somewhat like this:

> If there are any people who, either because of lack of understanding of what we are doing or because of their fondness for us, do not approve our actions as highly as we would like them to, we ask them not to despise us or to give up praying for us and loving us. Instead, they should realize that they have a greater obligation to show us their affection and understanding. They should remember that it is both natural and moral to do our best to help save those we love when we think they are taking dangerous risks.

Here the original sentence of 105 words has been broken up into three sentences, much of the complicated sentence-structure has been simplified, and quaint turns of phrase like "the bowels of their compassion" have been put into ordinary modern English. Though the reader may miss the old-fashioned flavor of the original, it is safe to say he is clearer about what is being said.

In spite of the fact that the second of these passages is 340 years old, both of them fall into what linguists call the Modern English period. Our next example, however, goes back another two centuries into what we call Middle English. It is "A Crye Made for a Commune Passage Toward Hareflieu," actually a proclamation issued in the name of King Henry V for the assembling of supplies in support of his invasion of France in 1415.

> Be ther proclamacioun made, that alle manere of men, marchauntz, artificers, or other, of what estat, degre, or condicioun, that euere they be, that willen toward oure liege lorde the kyng, beyng atte harflewe in the costes of Normandye, that god him spede, with corne, brede, mele, or flour, wyne, ale, or biere, fyssh, flessh or any other viteille, clothe, lynnen, wollen or eny merchaundise, shertys, breches, doublettys, hosen, shone, or eny other manere ware of armure, artilrye, or of othere stuffe, lette hem apparaille and make redy betwen this and to-day seuenyght their bodyes, goodes, merchaundyses, ware, stoffure, viteille, what that euer it be; and in the mene while come to the Mair, and he shall dispose and assigne theym redy shippyng and passage vnto the forseide costes. [Text from Chambers & Daunt, *A Book of London English 1384–1425,* Oxford, 1931]

The first thing that the modern reader notices about this passage is undoubtedly the spelling. Just about half the running words are spelled differently from their modern forms. When we consider individual words, the difference is even more striking: only 29 of the 83 different words in the passage are spelled as in modern English. This certainly contributes to the superficial strangeness of the passage, but a closer look reveals that this in itself does not constitute a serious barrier to understanding, since most if not all of the words are easily identified in spite of their different spellings. In most cases the spellings conform to the general rules of modern English, the difference being in the alternatives chosen: thus *spede, mele,* and *mene* are perfectly possible modern spellings but they don't happen to be the accepted ways of spelling *speed, meal,* and *mean*. Some spellings, however, seem to indicate pronunciation differences. Thus *shertys* and *doublettys* for *shirts* and *doublets,* and perhaps *costes* for *coasts,* suggest that the plural ending in these words which end in *-t* was a full syllable, as it is to this day in some regional dialects where *posts* is pronounced as if spelled *postiz.*

Looking at the vocabulary of the proclamation, we find that once we get past the spelling so that we can identify the words, virtually all of them are still current in English. In fact, only *stoffure* ("material used for furnishing, supply, or outfit") is listed as completely obsolete by the Oxford English Dictionary. Nobody wears a *doublet* ("a quilted undergarment reinforced by rings of mail and worn under armor") nowadays, but the word turns up in enough historical fiction to be entered unlabeled in Webster's Third New International Dictionary. (The thing, not the word, is obsolete.) And *seuenyght,* which appears in the same dictionary under its later form *sennight,* is labeled archaic and illustrated by quotations from the seventeenth and eighteenth centuries. Some might wonder at *viteille,* but in its later form *victuals* it is still occasionally used.

It is another matter, however, when we consider the meanings of the words. A large number of them, including some of the most familiar ones, are used in senses that are either quite infrequent or impossible in modern English. Among these we might list *manere* ('kind'), *artificers* ('craftsmen'), *estat* ('rank'), *spede* ('help, prosper'), *artilrye* ('arms, munitions'), *apparaille* ('prepare'), *to-day seuenyght* ('a week from today'), *dispose* ('order'). Since these are some of the key words in the passage, to give them their usual modern meanings would distort its total meaning quite badly. Once again we are reminded that changes in the meanings of words that remain in the language are probably more important in their effect than the coming in of new words or the passing away of old ones.

Another fact about the vocabulary that we become aware of in studying this passage is that there are two major sources of English words: native English and borrowed Romance. We are reminded that for about two centuries before this proclamation was written it had been quite common for writers and speakers of English, many of whom also knew and used French, to slip French words into their English. Many of these words were taken up by others and eventually naturalized in English. In this passage 23 of the 83 different words, or about 30%, are from French. They include *proclamacioun, manere, marchauntz, artificers, estat, degre, condicioun,* and so on down to *passage* and *costes.* The native words make up 70% of the vocabulary but 77% of the running words, since many of them are the little grammatical words that are frequently repeated, like *that, and, or, the,* and *other.* Some, however, are important "content" words like *lorde, kyng, corne, ale, fyssh, wollen,* and *shertys.* Since the language of the proclamation is legalistic and hence rather repetitious, we sometimes find a native word and its French synonym coupled together, as in *apparaille and make redy* or *shippyng and passage.* But this is probably accidental, since other repetitive strings may be all French words (*dispose and assigne*) or mixed (*goodes, merchaundyses, ware*—native, French, native). It is of some interest to compare the percentages of native and French words in this passage with that in our most recent example, the selection from the Declaration of Independence, in which 48% are native, 42% French, and 9% direct from Latin. Obviously the habit of borrowing continued during the period of three and a half centuries between Henry V and our founding fathers.

The grammar, too, of this passage is more than a bit strange to the modern reader. The opening phrase is impossible in modern English, even of the most formal sort; we would have to say "Let there be made a proclamation" or more likely "Let it be proclaimed". Modern English has made a whole new set of indefinite pronouns by tacking *ever* onto *who, which,* and *what;* here, as in *of what estat . . . that euere they be,* the *ever* is still a separate adverb. Plural forms like *hosen* and *shone* have gone out; *hose* has become a sort of plural without a singular, like *trousers* and *scissors,* while *shone* has adopted the regular plural ending and become *shoes.* In sum, while the passage is clearly English, the modern reader inexperienced in the Middle English of Chaucer and his contemporaries has difficulties in reading it.

These difficulties increase considerably when we go back another century and a half to 1258. Here is part of a proclamation by another King Henry, the Third, in which he confirms his acceptance of the Provisions of Oxford, a document which a group of barons had forced him to sign in much the same way the Magna Carta had been extracted from King John forty-odd years earlier.

> Henri, þurȝ Godes fultume King on Englene-loande, Lhoauerd on Yrloande, Duk on Normandi, on Aquitaine, and Eorl on Aniow, send igretinge to alle hise holde, ilærde and ileawede, on Huntendoneschire. Þæt witen ȝe wel alle þæt we willen and vnnen þæt, þæt vre rædesmen alle, oþer þe moare dæl of heom, þæt beoþ ichosen þurȝ us and þurȝ þæt loandes folk on vre kuneriche, habbeþ idon and shullen don in þe worþnesse of Gode and on vre treowþe, for þe freme of þe loande þurȝ þe besiȝte of þan toforeniseide redesmen, beo stedefæst and ilestinde in alle þinge a buten ænde. And we hoaten alle vre treowe in þe treowþe þæt heo vs oȝen, þæt heo stedefæstliche healden and swerien to healden and to werien þo isetnesses þæt beon imakede and beon to makien, þurȝ þan toforeniseide rædesmen, oþer þurȝ þe moare dæl of heom, alswo alse hit is biforen iseid; and þæt æhc oþer helpe þæt for to done bi þan ilche oþe aȝenes alle men riȝt for to done and to foangen. [Text from Dickins & Wilson, *Early Middle English Texts,* Cambridge, 1951]

One surprising thing about this document is that it is in English at all, rather than in French, which was the official language of the government at this time. Actually it was promulgated in French as well; the parallel English version is probably the result of a contemporary nationalistic movement to restore English to official use. In any case, the modern reader probably finds the English version as difficult as he would the French. A modern translation might go somewhat as follows:

> Henry, by the grace of God King of England, Lord of Ireland, Duke of Normandy and Aquitaine, and Earl of Anjou, sends greetings to all his subjects, both clerical and lay, in Huntingdonshire. You are all to know well that we will and agree that whatever all our councillors, or the majority of them, who have been chosen by us and by the common people in our kingdom have done and shall do, to the honor of God and in fidelity to us, for the benefit of the country by the wisdom of the said councillors, is to be firm and lasting in all respects without end. And we command all our faithful followers by the loyalty that they owe to us to hold firmly and swear to hold and to defend the provisions that have been made and are to be made by the aforesaid councillors, or the majority of them, as is stated above; and [we further command] them to help one another to do so, by virtue of that same oath—to render justice to and receive it from all men.

Once again, spelling is the first obstacle to the

modern reader who attempts to interpret the original. For one thing, there are three strange letters in the alphabet: þ, called 'thorn', which stands for the sounds now spelled *th;* ȝ, called 'yogh', which represents consonantal *y* at the beginning of a word or medially before a stressed vowel, *gh* at the end of a word or before another consonant, and *w* between vowels; and æ, called 'ash', which spells the vowel of modern English *hat.* With these clues it is easier to see that þurȝ is our word *through* or *thorough,* ȝe is the pronoun *ye,* an archaic form of *you,* riȝt is *right,* oȝen is *owe* or *own,* and þæt is *that.* A few more hints help a bit more, such as that *u* and *v* are used interchangeably for both the vowel *u* and the consonant *v,* with *v* appearing at the beginnings of words and *u* in the middle, so that vre is *ure* (= *our*); and that *oa* is used to spell an *aw*-type of vowel, as it still is in one word, *broad.*

But even if the spelling were to be completely converted to modern forms, we would still have difficulties with words. A major reason for this is that, although the proclamation was written nearly two centuries after the Norman Conquest, it comes before the great influx of French words into the language. In fact, the same nationalistic motives mentioned above may have led the writer (quite possibly the translator, since it is likely that the French version was written first) to consciously avoid using any French words at all. In any case, except for the title *Duk,* the king's given name *Henri,* and the names of the three French provinces where he claimed feudal title—*Normandi, Aquitaine,* and *Aniow*—there are no French words at all in this selection. Instead, the proclamation frequently uses Old English words and phrases that have since been replaced by French synonyms and hence have become obsolete. Some of these, with their modern equivalents, are:

þurȝ Godes fultume	through God's help
holde	subjects, vassals
vnnen	agree
rædesmen	councillors, advisors
moare dæl	larger part, majority
þæt loandes folk	the common people
freme	benefit
hoaten	command
treowþe	loyalty, fidelity
werien	defend, protect
isetnesses	agreements, provisions
foangen	receive

With the exception of *protect* and *defend,* which were taken directly from Latin, and the native word *help,* all the words in the righthand column are of French origin. It is obvious that what amounted to a virtual revolution in the English vocabulary, especially its more formal layers, took place in the century and a half between Henry III and Henry V.

In grammar as well we find forms and constructions that are no longer current, though here the change has been more gradual. We may observe, for example, the contrast between the ending *-ing,* which marks verbal nouns, and *-ind,* which marks present participles, as in the words *igretinge* and *ilestinde.* At a somewhat later date, this distinction, which still prevails in modern German, was lost, and the *-ing* ending came to be used for both. This is in a way unfortunate since it can lead to ambiguity, as in *pursuing girls may be fun*—which can mean either 'the pursuit of girls' (verbal noun) or 'girls who pursue' (participle). Another grammatical marker that has since disappeared is the prefix *i-,* descended from an earlier *ge-,* which frequently appears with past participles, as in *idon, imakede,* and *iseid.* This prefix *ge-* has also survived in modern German. For the most part the word order is not far different from that of modern English, as comparison of the original with the translation will show. But word order such as *æhc oþer helpe þæt for to done* ('each the other help that for to do'), with two instances of the direct object coming before the verb, has to be changed to *each help the other to do that* to accord with modern grammar.

All these things—strange spelling, often reflecting a quite different pronunciation, obsolete words, and grammatical differences—add up to making the language of this passage seem like a foreign language, though paradoxically its freedom from French words makes it very pure English for its time. By the time we take another giant step backward, this time of nearly two and a half centuries, we are indeed dealing with an almost wholly unfamiliar language, in spite of the fact that we can trace an unbroken tradition of nearly a thousand years down to our own time. Linguists call this language OLD ENGLISH or ANGLO-SAXON. Here is part of another royal document, a writ, dated 1020, of King Cnut (or Canute, as he is more commonly known), a Danish Viking who was king of England for twenty years (1016–35) and of Denmark and Norway for shorter periods. He had just returned to England from a successful expedition to Denmark to make good his claim to the throne there, and put out this writ to reassure the English people of his intent to keep the peace. As a Dane, it is quite likely that he did not himself speak English, but had this document written by some clerk of his household. Also, in spite of his pagan background he had become a Christian, a fact which he emphasizes strongly in this document.

> Cnut cyning gret his arcebiscopas and his leodbiscopas and Þurcyl eorl and ealle his eorlas and ealne his þeodscype, twelfhynde and twyhynde, gehadode and læwede, on Englalande freondlice. And ic cyðe eow, þæt ic wylle beon hold hlaford and unswicende to godes gerihtum and to rihtre woroldlage.
>
> Ic nam me to gemynde þa gewritu and þa word, þe se arcebiscop Lyfing me fram þam papan brohte of Rome, þæt ic scolde æghwær godes lof upp aræran and unriht alecgan and full frið wyrcean be ðære mihte, þe me god syllan wolde.
>
> Nu ne wandode ic na minum sceattum, þa hwile þe eow unfrið on handa stod: nu ic mid godes fultume þæt totwæmde mid minum scattum. Þa cydde man me, þæt us mara hearm to fundode, þonne us wel licode: and þa for ic me sylf mid þam mannum þe me mid foron into Denmearcon, þe eow mæst hearm of com: and þæt hæbbe mid godes fultume forene forfangen, þæt eow næfre heonon forð þanon nan unfrið to ne cymð, þa hwile þe ge me rihtlice healdað and min lif byð. [Text from Kaiser, *Medieval English,* Berlin, 1958]

There is no doubt about this being virtually as strange as a foreign language. Only a few words—mostly pronouns and other function words—look like their modern descendants: *his, and, on, to, me, us, into.* There is another new character, ð, called 'edh', which is in variation with þ as a means of writing the sounds we spell with *th.* Even a full understanding of the spelling conventions would not help the modern reader very much. He cannot understand it without a translation, which might go as follows:

> Canute the king greets his archbishops and his provincial bishops and Earl Thurcyl and all his earls and all his people, rich and poor, ordained and lay, in England, in friendly fashion. And I assure you that I wish to be a gracious lord and devoted to the laws of God and to just human law.
>
> I have remembered the writs and the words that Archbishop Lyfing brought me from the Pope of Rome, [to the effect] that I should in all ways support the praise of God and put down injustice and promote perfect peace to the extent of the strength

that God would grant me.

I have never spared my wealth as long as discord was among you; now with God's help I have dispersed it [discord] with my wealth. When I was informed that more affliction had come upon us than we could put up with, then I went myself to Denmark with those men who caused you the most injury; and with God's help I have now seen to it that from this time on no breach of the peace will ever come to you from that source, so long as you obey me properly and my life endures.

With the exception of the ecclesiastical titles *arcebiscop* and *leodbiscop* and the Danish names Cnut and Thurcyl, the vocabulary here is totally English. Many of the words have survived into modern English, with changes in spelling that reflect changes in pronunciation: *cyning* (*king*), *hlaford* (*lord*), *brohte* (*brought*), *scolde* (*should*), *licode* (*liked*), *rihtlice* (*rightly*), etc. But many have become obsolete during the nine and a half centuries since this was written: *þeodscype* ('people'), *cyðe,* past *cydde* ('make known'), *unswicende* ('unyielding'), *lof* ('praise'), *frið* ('peace'), *wandode,* from *wandian* ('hesitate, omit'), etc. Of the 96 different words in the passage, 31 are now obsolete and 7 more have undergone rather drastic changes of meaning, so that even if the reader knew enough about Old English spelling to recognize the survivors, he would have to go to a dictionary of Old English for the meanings of 40% of the words.

In terms of grammar also, this English of 1020 shows more clearly its affiliation with the other Germanic languages. As in modern German, not only nouns but adjectives and even the definite article are INFLECTED; that is, they have special endings indicating the case, number, and sometimes gender. Some examples illustrating this:

se arcebiscop	'the archbishop'	masculine singular nominative
þam papan	'the pope'	masculine singular dative
ðære mihte	'the might'	feminine singular dative
þa gewritu	'the writs'	neuter plural accusative
þam mannum	'the men'	masculine plural dative
ealle his eorlas	'all his earls'	masculine plural accusative
ealne his þeodscype	'all his people'	masculine singular accusative
min lif	'my life'	neuter singular nominative
minum sceattum	'my treasures'	masculine plural dative

Verbs also have inflections, many of which have survived into modern English. We still have the distinction between STRONG verbs—those that form the past tense by changing the stem vowel—and WEAK verbs —those that add an ending containing a *d* or *t*.[4] The following are some forms from this passage illustrating these two types:

Strong past tense forms
- nam, from niman, 'take'
- stod, from standan, 'stand'
- for (sing.) and foron (plural) from faran, 'go, travel'
- com, from cuman, 'come'

Weak past tense forms
- brohte, from bringan, 'bring'
- wandode, from wandian, 'omit, neglect'
- totwæmde, from totwæman, 'break up, scatter'
- cydde, from cyðan, 'proclaim, make known'

In another important grammatical feature, the order of the elements in constructions, this passage shows many differences from modern English. In fact, only the subject-verb-object order of main clauses, as in *Cnut cyning gret his arcebiscopas,* is the same as ours. This is inverted if an adverb begins the sentence, as in *þa for ic* 'then went I.' This inversion survives today with only a few adverbs, such as *never* and *seldom*. The order in subordinate clauses, however, is quite different from ours. Here the rule is that the verb comes at the end of the clause, which makes the other elements come in an order that seems very unnatural to us, especially when it is combined with the practice of putting prepositions after their objects, often with other elements in between. All this is illustrated by *þe eow mæst hearm of com* ('whom to you most harm from came') and *þæt eow næfre heonon forð þanon nan unfrið to ne cymð* ('that you never hence forth thence no war to not comes'), where *eow* is the object of the preposition *to,* which doesn't come until seven words later. This last clause also illustrates the manner of emphasizing negation by multiple negative forms, which is still common in substandard speech ("I ain't never had no luck") but is generally considered unacceptable in standard English.

Many more points of difference could be found by further analysis of this passage, but this is enough to show that when we trace English back as much as two-thirds of its 1500-year history we discover that it has many of the features which we associate with a foreign language. In fact, we could only continue our backward journey by means of written texts about three centuries farther. After that we would come to a time when English was rarely or never written down, and we would have to depend on the various ingenious indirect methods which philologists use to reconstruct the unwritten early stages of the history of a language. By these methods we could push our horizon back to the time, about the beginning of the Christian era, when English was not a separate language at all but simply one of the dialects of the common Germanic language of northern Europe. By even more ingenious methods, involving comparison with other language families like Celtic, Slavic, Indic, Latin, and Greek, we can go back another two or three thousand years and draw hypothetical inferences about the common Indo-European tongue from which most of the languages of Europe ultimately derive. That is as far as we can go. Tens, perhaps hundreds, of thousands of years of the history of our language are irretrievably lost in the mists of time.

4 Some weak verbs such as *deal—dealt* and *creep—crept* also show vowel change in the past, but this is due to vowel shortening in Middle English, much later than the vowel shifts in strong verbs which go back to Proto-Germanic.

TABULAR HISTORY OF THE ENGLISH LANGUAGE

Date & Period	Historical Events	Linguistic Events
About 3000 B.C. Proto-Indo-European	Neolithic Age. Indo-Europeans living in north central Europe.	Indo-European undifferentiated, except dialectally.
3000–500 B.C. Indo-European Proto-Germanic	Extensive migrations of Indo-European speakers to India, Greece, and western Europe.	Differentiation of Indo-European language families, including Germanic. Earliest documents in Sanskrit, Greek, etc.
500–0 B.C. Germanic	Celts in Britain. Contact of Roman Empire with Germanic peoples.	Germanic undifferentiated except dialectally. First borrowings from Latin.
0–300 A.D. West Germanic	Expansion and power of Roman Empire. Romanization of Britain. Growth and migrations of Germanic tribes.	Differentiation of West, North, and East branches of Germanic. Continued Latin borrowings.
300–500 Proto Old English	Breakup of Roman Empire. Anglo-Saxon invasions of Britain.	Beginnings of differentiation of Vulgar Latin. Emergence of Old English. Contact with Celts. Oldest Germanic documents (Gothic Bible c. 350).
500–700 Early Old English	Conversion of Anglo-Saxons. Northumbrian culture. Earliest surviving literature.	Borrowings from Latin and occasionally Celtic. Increased diversity of dialects. Adoption of alphabet.
700–1000 Old English	Danish and Norse raids and invasions. Alfred and the political ascendancy of Wessex. Establishment of the Danelaw. Cynewulf, Aelfric, and other writers.	West Saxon dominant dialect. More Latin borrowings. Development of Old French and other Romance languages.
1000–1150 Late Old English	Viking raids; Danish kings of England. Norman Conquest. Replacement of native ruling class by French speakers.	Extensive borrowings from Norse, especially in the North. French the official language. English "submerged". Further differentiation of dialects.
1150–1300 Early Middle English	Gradual loss of continental possessions of English kings. Continued dominance of French speakers in politics, law, church. Beginnings of revival of literature in English.	Breakdown and loss of Old English inflections. Extensive phonological and syntactic changes. Borrowings from French (Anglo-Norman).
1300–1475 Middle English	Hundred Years' War. Growth of nationalism; decay of feudalism. Chaucer, Gower, Langland, "Gawain Poet", Wyclif. Mystery and Morality plays.	Emergence of English (dialect of London) as the standard literary and official language. Extensive borrowings from French.
1475–1650 Early Modern English	Caxton and printing. Renaissance humanism: revived study of Greek and Latin classics. Spenser, Shakespeare, Milton, biblical translations. Age of discovery and exploration.	Great vowel shift and loss of final -e. Beginning of standardized spelling. Extensive borrowings from Latin, some from Greek. Changes in grammar, especially verb system.
1650–1800 Later Modern English	Settlement of America and growth of British Empire. Opening of India and the Orient. Beginnings of industrial and scientific revolutions. Augustan age and Enlightenment.	Development of American and other colonial dialects. Spread of English around the world; borrowings from many languages. Johnson's Dictionary. Prescriptive grammarians (Lowth).
1800– Recent and Present-Day English	Independence and expansion of U.S. General education and literacy. Acceleration of scientific, industrial, and technological research and development. Journalism, telephone, radio, motion pictures, television.	Growth of scientific and technical vocabularies. English as dominant world language. Development of linguistics. Oxford, Century, and Merriam-Webster dictionaries. Extensive study and teaching of grammar.

Abbreviations in This Work

A.&M.	Agricultural and Mechanical
ab	about
abbr	abbreviation
abl	ablative
Acad	Academy
acc	accusative
act	active
A.D.	anno Domini
adj	adjective
adv	adverb
AF	Anglo-French
Afrik	Afrikaans
Agric	Agriculture
Alb	Albanian
alter	alteration
Am	America, American
Amer	American
AmerF	American French
AmerInd	American Indian
AmerSp	American Spanish
anc	ancient, anciently
anthropol	anthropology
aor	aorist
Ar	Arabic
Arab	Arabian
Aram	Aramaic
archaeol	archaeologist
Arm	Armenian
art	article
Assyr	Assyrian
astron	astronomer, astronomy
attrib	attributive
atty	attorney
aug	augmentative
Austral	Australian
Av	Avestan
AV	Authorized Version
b	born
Bab	Babylonian
bacteriol	bacteriologist
B.C.	before Christ, British Columbia
Belg	Belgian
Beng	Bengali
bib	biblical
biochem	biochemist
Braz	Brazilian
Bret	Breton
Brit	Britain, British
bro	brother
Bulg	Bulgarian
C	centigrade, College
Canad	Canadian
CanF	Canadian French
Cant	Cantonese
cap	capital, capitalized
Catal	Catalan
caus	causative
Celt	Celtic
cen	central
cent	century
chem	chemist
Chin	Chinese
comb	combining
Comm	Community
compar	comparative
Confed	Confederate
conj	conjugation, conjunction
constr	construction
contr	contraction
Copt	Coptic
Corn	Cornish
criminol	criminologist
d	died
D	Dutch
Dan	Danish
dat	dative
dau	daughter
def	definite
deriv	derivative
dial	dialect
dim	diminutive
disc	discovered
Dor	Doric
dram	dramatist
Du	Dutch
DV	Douay Version
e	eastern
E	east, eastern, English
econ	economist
Ed	Education
educ	educator
Egypt	Egyptian
emp	emperor
Eng	England, English
equiv	equivalent
Esk	Eskimo
esp	especially
est	estimated
Eth	Ethiopic
ethnol	ethnologist
F	Fahrenheit, French
fem	feminine
Finn	Finnish
fl	flourished
Flem	Flemish
fr	from
Fr	France, French
freq	frequentative
Fris	Frisian
ft	feet
fut	future
G	German
Gael	Gaelic
gen	general, genitive
Ger	German
Gk	Greek
Gmc	Germanic
Goth	Gothic
gov	governor
govt	government
Gr Brit	Great Britain
Heb	Hebrew
hist	historian
Hitt	Hittite
Hung	Hungarian
I	island
Icel	Icelandic
IE	Indo-European
imit	imitative
imper	imperative
incho	inchoative
indef	indefinite
indic	indicative
infin	infinitive
Inst	Institute
instr	instrumental
intens	intensive
interj	interjection
interrog	interrogative
Ion	Ionic
Ir	Irish
IrGael	Irish Gaelic
irreg	irregular
ISV	International Scientific Vocabulary
It, Ital	Italian
Jap	Japanese
Jav	Javanese
L	Latin
LaF	Louisiana French
lat	latitude
Lat	Latin
LG	Low German
LGk	Late Greek
LHeb	Late Hebrew
lit	literally, literary
Lith	Lithuanian
LL	Late Latin
long	longitude
m	miles
manuf	manufacturer
masc	masculine
math	mathematician
MBret	Middle Breton
MD	Middle Dutch
ME	Middle English
Mech	Mechanical
Med	Medical
Mex	Mexican, Mexico
MexSp	Mexican Spanish
MF	Middle French
MFlem	Middle Flemish
MGk	Middle Greek
MHG	Middle High German
mil	military
min	minister
MIr	Middle Irish
ML	Medieval Latin
MLG	Middle Low German
modif	modification
MPer	Middle Persian
MS	manuscript
mt	mountain
Mt	Mount
MW	Middle Welsh
n	northern, noun
N	north, northern
naut	nautical
NE	New England
neut	neuter
NewEng	New England
NGk	New Greek
NGmc	North Germanic
NHeb	New Hebrew
NL	New Latin
nom	nominative
nonstand	nonstandard
Norw	Norwegian
nov	novelist
n pl	noun plural
obs	obsolete
occas	occasionally
OE	Old English
OF	Old French
OFris	Old Frisian
OHG	Old High German
OIr	Old Irish
OIt	Old Italian
OL	Old Latin
ON	Old Norse
ONF	Old North French
OPer	Old Persian
OPg	Old Portuguese
OProv	Old Provençal
OPruss	Old Prussian
orig	originally
OS	Old Saxon
OSlav	Old Slavic
OSp	Old Spanish
OW	Old Welsh
PaG	Pennsylvania German
part	participle
pass	passive
Pek	Pekingese
Per, Pers	Persian
perf	perfect
perh	perhaps
pers	person
Pg	Portuguese
philos	philosopher
PhilSp	Philippine Spanish
physiol	physiologist
pl	plural
Pol	Polish
polit	political, politician
pop	population
Port	Portuguese
pp	past participle
prec	preceding
prep	preposition
pres	present, president
prob	probably
pron	pronoun, pronunciation
pronunc	pronunciation
Prov	Provençal
prp	present participle
Pruss	Prussian
pseud	pseudonym
psychol	psychologist
R.C.	Roman Catholic
redupl	reduplication
refl	reflexive
rel	relative
resp	respectively
rev	revolution
Rom	Roman
RSV	Revised Standard Version
Rum	Rumanian
Russ	Russian
S	south, southern
Sc	Scotch, Scots
Scand	Scandinavian
ScGael	Scottish Gaelic
Sch	School
Scot	Scotland, Scottish
secy	secretary
Sem	Seminary, Semitic
Serb	Serbian
Shak	Shakespeare
sing	singular
Skt	Sanskrit
Slav	Slavic
So Afr	South Africa
sociol	sociologist
Sp, Span	Spanish
specif	specifically
spp	species
St	Saint
Ste	Sainte
subj	subjunctive
substand	substandard
superl	superlative
Sw, Swed	Swedish
syn	synonym, synonymy
Syr	Syriac
Tag	Tagalog
Tech	Technology
theol	theologian
Theol	Theological
Toch	Tocharian
trans	translation
treas	treasury
Turk	Turkish
U	University
usu	usually
var	variant
vb	verb
vi	verb intransitive
VL	Vulgar Latin
voc	vocative
vt	verb transitive
W	Welsh, west, western
WGmc	West Germanic
zool	zoologist

syn ABASE, DEMEAN, DEBASE, DEGRADE, HUMBLE, HUMILIATE *shared meaning element* : to lessen in dignity or status ***ant*** exalt, extol

abash \ə-'bash\ *vt* [ME *abaishen,* fr. (assumed) MF *abaiss-, abair* to astonish, alter. of MF *esbair,* fr. *ex-* + *baer* to yawn — more at ABEYANCE] : to destroy the self-possession or self-confidence of : DISCONCERT ***syn*** see EMBARRASS ***ant*** embolden, reassure — **abash·ment** \-mənt\ *n*

abate \ə-'bāt\ *vb* **abat·ed; abat·ing** [ME *abaten,* fr. OF *abattre* to beat down — more at REBATE] *vt* **1 :** to put an end to : NULLIFY <~ a nuisance> **2 a :** to reduce in degree or intensity : MODERATE **b :** to reduce in value or amount : make less esp. by way of relief <~ a tax> **3 :** DEDUCT, OMIT <~ part of the price> **4 a :** to beat down or cut away so as to leave a figure in relief **b** *obs* : BLUNT **5 :** DEPRIVE ~ *vi* **1 :** to decrease in force or intensity **2 a :** to become defeated or become null or void **b :** to decrease in amount or value — **abat·er** *n*

syn* 1** see DECREASE ***ant augment, accelerate (*as speed*), intensify (*as hopes, a fever*)

2 ABATE, SUBSIDE, WANE, EBB *shared meaning element* : to die down in force or intensity ***ant*** rise, revive

abate·ment \ə-'bāt-mənt\ *n* **1 :** the act or process of abating : the state of being abated **2 :** an amount abated; *esp* : a deduction from the full amount of a tax

ab·a·tis \'ab-ə-ˌtē, 'ab-ət-əs\ *n, pl* **ab·a·tis** \'ab-ə-ˌtēz\ *or* **ab·a·tis·es** \-ət-ə-səz\ [F, fr. *abattre*] : a defensive obstacle formed by felled trees with sharpened branches facing the enemy

A battery *n* : a battery used to heat the filaments or cathode heaters of electron tubes

ab·at·toir \'ab-ə-ˌtwär\ *n* [F, fr. *abattre*] : SLAUGHTERHOUSE

ab·ax·i·al \(ˈ)a-'bak-sē-əl\ *adj* : situated out of or directed away from the axis

ab·ba·cy \'ab-ə-sē\ *n, pl* **-cies** [ME *abbatie,* fr. LL *abbatia*] : the office, dignity, jurisdiction, or tenure of an abbot

Ab·bas·id \ə-'bas-əd, 'ab-ə-səd\ *n* : a member of a dynasty of caliphs ruling the Muslim Empire (750–1258) and claiming descent from Abbas the uncle of Muhammad

ab·ba·tial \ə-'bā-shəl, a-\ *adj* : of or relating to an abbot, abbess, or abbey

ab·bé \a-'bā, 'ab-ˌā\ *n* [F, fr. LL *abbat-, abbas*] : a member of the French secular clergy in major or minor orders — used as a title

ab·bess \'ab-əs\ *n* [ME *abbesse,* fr. OF, fr. LL *abbatissa,* fem. of *abbat-, abbas*] : a woman who is the superior of a convent of nuns

Abbe·vil·li·an \ˌab-(ə-)ˈvil-ē-ən\ *adj* [*Abbeville,* France] : of or relating to an early lower Paleolithic culture characterized by bifacial stone hand axes

ab·bey \'ab-ē\ *n, pl* **abbeys** [ME, fr. OF *abaïe,* fr. LL *abbatia* abbey, fr. *abbat-, abbas*] **1 a :** a monastery ruled by an abbot **b :** a convent ruled by an abbess **2 :** an abbey church

ab·bot \'ab-ət\ *n* [ME *abbod,* fr. OE, fr. LL *abbat-, abbas,* fr. LGk *abbas,* fr. Aram *abbā* father] : the superior of a monastery for men

ab·bre·vi·ate \ə-'brē-vē-ˌāt\ *vt* **-at·ed; -at·ing** [ME *abbreviaten,* fr. LL *abbreviatus,* pp. of *abbreviare* — more at ABRIDGE] : to make briefer; *esp* : to reduce to a shorter form intended to stand for the whole ***syn*** see SHORTEN ***ant*** lengthen — **ab·bre·vi·a·tor** \-ˌāt-ər\ *n*

ab·bre·vi·a·tion \ə-ˌbrē-vē-'ā-shən\ *n* **1 :** the act or result of abbreviating : ABRIDGMENT **2 :** a shortened form of a written word or phrase used in place of the whole <*amt* is an ~ for *amount*>

[1]**ABC** \ˌā-(ˌ)bē-'sē\ *n, pl* **ABC's** *or* **ABCs** \-'sēz\ **1 :** ALPHABET — usu. used in pl. **2 a :** the rudiments of reading, writing, and spelling — usu. used in pl. **b :** the rudiments of a subject

[2]**ABC** *abbr* **1** American Bowling Congress **2** American Broadcasting Company **3** Australian Broadcasting Company

ABCD *abbr* accelerated business collection and delivery

ABC powers *n pl, often cap P* : Argentina, Brazil, and Chile

ABC soil *n* : a soil that has a well-differentiated profile with distinct A-, B-, and C-horizons

abd *or* **abdom** *abbr* abdomen; abdominal

ABD *abbr* all but dissertation

Ab·di·as \ab-'dī-əs\ *n* [LL, fr. Gk] : OBADIAH

ab·di·cate \'ab-di-ˌkāt\ *vb* **-cat·ed; -cat·ing** [L *abdicatus,* pp. of *abdicare,* fr. *ab-* + *dicare* to proclaim — more at DICTION] *vt* : to relinquish (as sovereign power) formally ~ *vi* : to renounce a throne, high office, dignity, or function — **ab·di·ca·ble** \-kə-bəl\ *adj* — **ab·di·ca·tion** \ˌab-di-'kā-shən\ *n* — **ab·di·ca·tor** \'ab-di-ˌkāt-ər\ *n*

syn ABDICATE, RENOUNCE, RESIGN *shared meaning element* : to give up formally or definitely ***ant*** assume (*as power, office*), usurp

ab·do·men \'ab-də-mən, ab-'dō-mən\ *n* [MF & L; MF, fr. L] **1 :** the part of the body between the thorax and the pelvis; *also* : the cavity of this part of the trunk containing the chief viscera **2 :** the posterior section of the body behind the thorax in an arthropod — see INSECT illustration — **ab·dom·i·nal** \ab-'däm-ən-ᵊl\ *adj* — **ab·dom·i·nal·ly** \-ē\ *adv*

ab·duce \ab-'d(y)üs\ *vt* **ab·duced; ab·duc·ing** [L *abducere*] : ABDUCT

ab·du·cens \ab-'d(y)ü-ˌsenz\ *n, pl* **ab·du·cen·tes** \ˌab-d(y)ù-'sent-(ˌ)ēz\ : ABDUCENS NERVE

abducens nerve *n* [NL *abducent; abducens,* fr. L, prp.] : either of the 6th pair of cranial nerves which are motor nerves that supply muscles of the eye — called also *abducent nerve*

ab·du·cent \ab-'d(y)üs-ᵊnt\ *adj* [L *abducent-, abducens,* prp. of *abducere*] : serving to abduct <an ~ muscle>

ab·duct \ab-'dəkt\ *vt* [L *abductus,* pp. of *abducere,* lit., to lead away, fr. *ab-* + *ducere* to lead — more at TOW] **1 :** to carry off (as a person) by force **2 :** to draw away (as a limb) from a position near or parallel to the median axis of the body; *also* : to move (similar parts) apart — **ab·duc·tor** \-'dək-tər\ *n*

ab·duc·tion \ab-'dək-shən\ *n* **1 :** the action of abducting : the condition of being abducted **2 :** the unlawful carrying away of a woman for marriage or intercourse

abeam \ə-'bēm\ *adv or adj* : on a line at right angles to a ship's keel

[1]**abe·ce·dar·i·an** \ˌā-bē-(ˌ)sē-'der-ē-ən\ *n* [ME *abecedary,* fr. ML *abecedarium* alphabet, fr. LL, neut. of *abecedarius* of the alphabet, fr. the letters *a* + *b* + *c* + *d*] : one learning the rudiments of something (as the alphabet)

[2]**abecedarian** *adj* **1 a :** of or relating to the alphabet **b :** alphabetically arranged **2 :** RUDIMENTARY

abed \ə-'bed\ *adv or adj* : in bed

Abel \'ā-bəl\ *n* [LL, fr. Gk, fr. Heb *Hebhel*] : a son of Adam and Eve killed by his brother Cain

Abe·li·an \ə-'bē-lē-ən\ *adj* [Niels *Abel* †1829 Norw. mathematician] : COMMUTATIVE 2 <~ group> <~ ring>

abel·mosk \'ā-bəl-ˌmäsk\ *n* [deriv. of Ar *abū -l- misk* father of the musk] : a bushy herb (*Hibiscus moschatus*) of the mallow family native to tropical Asia and the East Indies whose musky seeds are used in perfumery and in flavoring coffee

Ab·er·deen An·gus \ˌab-ər-ˌdē-'naŋ-gəs\ *n* [*Aberdeen & Angus,* counties in Scotland] : any of a breed of black hornless beef cattle originating in Scotland

[1]**ab·er·rant** \a-'ber-ənt\ *adj* [L *aberrant-, aberrans,* prp. of *aberrare* to go astray, fr. *ab-* + *errare* to wander, err] **1 :** straying from the right or normal way **2 :** deviating from the usual or natural type : ATYPICAL — **ab·er·rance** \-ən(t)s\ *n* — **ab·er·ran·cy** \-ən-sē\ *n* — **ab·er·rant·ly** *adv*

[2]**aberrant** *n* **1 :** an aberrant natural group, individual, or structure **2 :** a person whose behavior departs substantially from the standard

ab·er·rat·ed \'ab-ə-ˌrāt-əd\ *adj* [L *aberratus*] : ABERRANT

ab·er·ra·tion \ˌab-ə-'rā-shən\ *n* [L *aberratus,* pp. of *aberrare*] **1 :** the act of being aberrant esp. from a moral standard or normal state **2 :** failure of a mirror, refracting surface, or lens to produce exact point-to-point correspondence between an object and its image **3 :** unsoundness or disorder of the mind **4 :** a small periodic change of apparent position in celestial bodies due to the combined effect of the motion of light and the motion of the observer **5 :** an aberrant organ or individual : SPORT 5 — **ab·er·ra·tion·al** \-shnəl, -shən-ᵊl\ *adj*

abet \ə-'bet\ *vt* **abet·ted; abet·ting** [ME *abetten,* fr. MF *abeter,* fr. OF, fr. *a-* (fr. L *ad-*) + *beter* to bait, of Gmc origin; akin to OE *bǣtan* to bait] **1 :** to actively second and encourage (an activity or plan) : FORWARD **2 :** to assist or support in the achievement of a purpose <*abetted* the cause of justice> ***syn*** see INCITE ***ant*** deter — **abet·ment** \-mənt\ *n* — **abet·tor** *or* **abet·ter** \-'bet-ər\ *n*

abey·ance \ə-'bā-ən(t)s\ *n* [MF *abeance* expectation, fr. *abaer* to desire, fr. *a-* + *baer* to yawn, fr. ML *batare*] **1 :** a lapse in succession during which there is no person in whom a title is vested **2 :** temporary inactivity : SUSPENSION

abey·ant \-ənt\ *adj* [back-formation fr. *abeyance*] : being in abeyance ***syn*** see LATENT ***ant*** operative, active

ab·hor \əb-'hȯ(ə)r, ab-\ *vt* **ab·horred; ab·hor·ring** [ME *abhorren,* fr. L *abhorrēre,* fr. *ab-* + *horrēre* to shudder — more at HORROR] **1 :** to regard with extreme repugnance : LOATHE **2 :** to turn aside or keep away from esp. in scorn or shuddering fear : REJECT <the university should ~ mediocrity — Walter Moberly>

syn see HATE ***ant*** admire (*as people or deeds*), enjoy (*things which are a matter of taste*) — **ab·hor·rer** \-'hȯr-ər\ *n*

ab·hor·rence \əb-'hȯr-ən(t)s, -'här-\ *n* **1 a :** the act or state of abhorring **b :** the feeling of one who abhors **2 :** one that is abhorred

ab·hor·rent \-ənt\ *adj* [L *abhorrent-, abhorrens,* prp. of *abhorrēre*] **1 a** *archaic* : strongly opposed **b :** feeling or showing abhorrence **2 :** not agreeable : CONTRARY <a notion ~ to their philosophy> **3 :** being so repugnant as to stir up positive antagonism <acts ~ to every right-minded person> ***syn*** see REPUGNANT ***ant*** congenial — **ab·hor·rent·ly** *adv*

Abib \ä-'vēv\ *n* [Heb *Ābhībh,* lit., ear of grain] : the 1st month of the ancient Hebrew calendar corresponding to Nisan

abid·ance \ə-'bīd-ᵊn(t)s\ *n* **1 :** an act or state of abiding : CONTINUANCE **2 :** COMPLIANCE <~ by the rules>

abide \ə-'bīd\ *vb* **abode** \-'bōd\ *or* **abid·ed; abid·ing** [ME *abiden,* fr. OE *ābīdan,* fr. *ā-,* perfective prefix + *bīdan* to bide; akin to OHG *ir-,* perfective prefix] *vt* **1** *archaic* : to wait for : AWAIT **2 a :** to endure without yielding : WITHSTAND **b :** to bear patiently : TOLERATE <cannot ~ such bigots> **3 :** to accept without objection ~ *vi* **1 :** to remain stable or fixed in a state **2 :** to continue in a place : SOJOURN ***syn*** see STAY, CONTINUE, BEAR — **abid·er** *n* — **abide by 1 :** to conform to **2 :** to acquiesce in

abid·ing \ə-'bīd-iŋ\ *adj* : ENDURING, CONTINUING <an ~ interest in nature> — **abid·ing·ly** \-iŋ-lē\ *adv*

ab·i·gail \'ab-ə-ˌgāl\ *n* [*Abigail,* servant in *The Scornful Lady,* a play by Francis Beaumont & John Fletcher] : a lady's personal maid

abil·i·ty \ə-'bil-ət-ē\ *n, pl* **-ties** [ME *abilite,* fr. MF *habilité,* fr. L *habilitat-, habilitas,* fr. *habilis* apt, skillful — more at ABLE] **1 a :** the quality or state of being able; *esp* : physical, mental, or legal power to perform **b :** competence in doing : SKILL **2 :** natural talent or acquired proficiency : APTITUDE <children whose *abilities* warrant higher education>

-abil·i·ty *also* **-ibil·i·ty** \ə-'bil-ət-ē\ *n suffix* [ME *-abilite, -ibilite,* fr. MF *-abilité, -ibilité,* fr. L *-abilitas, -ibilitas,* fr. *-abilis, -ibilis,* -able + *-tas* -ty] : capacity, fitness, or tendency to act or be acted on in a (specified) way <ensil*ability*>

ab in·i·tio \ˌab-ə-'nish-ē-ˌō\ *adv* [L] : from the beginning

abio·gen·e·sis \ˌā-ˌbī-ō-'jen-ə-səs\ *n* [NL, fr. [2]*a-* + *bio-* + L *genesis*] : the origination of living from lifeless matter — **abio·ge·net·ic** \-ō-jə-'net-ik\ *or* **abio·ge·net·i·cal** \-i-kəl\ *adj* — **abio·ge·net·i·cal·ly** \-k(ə-)lē\ *adv* — **abi·og·e·nist** \ˌā-(ˌ)bī-'äj-ə-nəst\ *n*

abi·o·log·i·cal \ˌā-ˌbī-ə-'läj-i-kəl\ *adj* : not biological; *esp* : not involving or produced by organisms <~ synthesis of amino acids> — **abi·o·log·i·cal·ly** \-i-k(ə-)lē\ *adv*

abi·ot·ic \ˌā-(ˌ)bī-'ät-ik\ *adj* : not biotic : ABIOLOGICAL — **abi·ot·i·cal·ly** \-i-k(ə-)lē\ *adv*

ab·ject \'ab-ˌjekt, ab-'\ *adj* [ME, fr. L *abjectus,* fr. pp. of *abicere* to cast off, fr. *ab-* + *jacere* to throw — more at JET] **1 :** sunk to or existing in a low state or condition <to lowest pitch of ~ fortune

thou art fallen —John Milton> **2 a** : cast down in spirit : SERVILE, SPIRITLESS <a man made ~ by suffering> **b** : showing utter hopelessness or resignation <~ surrender> **3** : expressing or offered in a humble and often ingratiating spirit <~ flattery> <an ~ apology> ***syn*** see MEAN ***ant*** exalted (*as in rank or mood*), imperious (*as in manner*) — **ab·ject·ly** \ˈab-ˌjek-(t)lē, ab-ˈ\ *adv* — **ab·ject·ness** \-ˌjek(t)-nəs, -ˈjek(t)-\ *n*

ab·jec·tion \ab-ˈjek-shən\ *n* **1** : a low or downcast state : DEGRADATION **2** : the act of making abject : HUMBLING, REJECTION <I protest . . . this vile ~ of youth to age — G. B. Shaw>

ab·ju·ra·tion \ˌab-jə-ˈrā-shən\ *n* **1** : the act or process of abjuring **2** : an oath of abjuring

ab·jure \ab-ˈju̇(ə)r\ *vt* **ab·jured; ab·jur·ing** [ME *abjuren*, fr. MF or L; MF *abjurer*, fr. L *abjurare*, fr. *ab-* + *jurare* to swear — more at JURY] **1 a** : to renounce upon oath **b** : to reject solemnly **2** : to abstain from : AVOID <~ extravagance> — **ab·jur·er** *n*
syn ABJURE, RENOUNCE, FORSWEAR, RECANT, RETRACT *shared meaning element* : to withdraw a vow or a given word ***ant*** pledge (*as allegiance, a vow*), elect (*as a way of life, an end*)

abl *abbr* ablative

ab·late \a-ˈblāt\ *vb* **ab·lat·ed; ab·lat·ing** [L *ablatus* (suppletive pp. of *auferre* to remove, fr. *au-* away + *ferre* to carry), fr. *ab-* + *latus*, suppletive pp. of *ferre* — more at UKASE, BEAR, TOLERATE] *vt* : to remove by cutting, erosion, melting, evaporation, or vaporization ~ *vi* : to become ablated

ab·la·tion \a-ˈblā-shən\ *n* : the process of ablating: as **a** : surgical removal **b** : removal of a part (as the outside of a nose cone) by melting or vaporization

1ab·la·tive \ˈab-lət-iv\ *adj* : of, relating to, or constituting a grammatical case expressing typically the relations of separation and source and also frequently such relations as cause or instrument — **ablative** *n*

2ab·la·tive \a-ˈblāt-iv\ *adj* **1** : of or relating to ablation **2** : tending to ablate <~ material on a nose cone> — **ab·la·tive·ly** *adv*

ablative absolute \ˌab-lət-iv-\ *n* : a construction in Latin in which a noun or pronoun and its adjunct both in the ablative case form together an adverbial phrase expressing generally the time, cause, or an attendant circumstance of an action

ab·laut \ˈäp-ˌlau̇t, ˈab-\ *n* [G, fr. *ab* away from + *laut* sound] : a systematic variation of vowels in the same root or affix or in related roots or affixes esp. in the Indo-European languages that is usu. paralleled by differences in use or meaning (as in *sing, sang, sung, song*)

ablaze \ə-ˈblāz\ *adj or adv* **1** : being on fire **2** : having radiant light or bright color : GLOWING <his face all ~ with excitement — Bram Stoker>

able \ˈā-bəl\ *adj* **abler** \-b(ə-)lər\; **ablest** \-b(ə-)ləst\ [ME, fr. MF, fr. L *habilis* apt, fr. *habēre* to have — more at HABIT] **1 a** : having sufficient power, skill, or resources to accomplish an object **b** : susceptible to action or treatment **2** : marked by intelligence, knowledge, skill, or competence
syn ABLE, CAPABLE, COMPETENT, QUALIFIED *shared meaning element* : having power or fitness (as for work or a way of life) ***ant*** inept, unable

-able *also* **-ible** \ə-bəl\ *adj suffix* [ME, fr. OF, fr. L *-abilis, -ibilis*, fr. *-a-, -i-*, verb stem vowels + *-bilis* capable or worthy of] **1** : capable of, fit for, or worthy of (being so acted upon or toward) — chiefly in adjectives derived from verbs <break*able*> <collect*ible*> **2** : tending, given, or liable to <knowledge*able*> <perish*able*>

able-bod·ied \ˌā-bəl-ˈbäd-ēd\ *adj* : having a sound strong body

able-bodied seaman *n* : ABLE SEAMAN

able seaman *n* : an experienced deck-department seaman qualified to perform routine duties at sea

abloom \ə-ˈblüm\ *adj* : abounding with blooms : BLOOMING <parks ~ with roses>

ab·lut·ed \ə-ˈblüt-əd, a-\ *adj* [back-formation fr. *ablution*] : washed clean

ab·lu·tion \ə-ˈblü-shən, a-ˈblü-\ *n* [ME, fr. MF or L; MF, fr. L *ablution-, ablutio*, fr. *ablutus*, pp. of *abluere* to wash away, fr. *ab-* + *lavere* to wash — more at LYE] **1** : the washing of one's body or part of it (as in a religious rite) **2** *pl* : a building housing bathing and toilet facilities on a military base — **ab·lu·tion·ary** \-shə-ˌner-ē\ *adj*

ably \ˈā-blē\ *adv* : in an able manner

ABM \ˌā-(ˌ)bē-ˈem\ *n* : ANTIBALLISTIC MISSILE

abn *abbr* airborne

Ab·na·ki \ab-ˈnäk-ē\ *n, pl* **Abnaki** or **Abnakis** **1** : a member of an Amerindian people of Maine and southern Quebec **2** : an Algonquian language of the Abnaki and Penobscot peoples

ab·ne·gate \ˈab-ni-ˌgāt\ *vt* **-gat·ed; -gat·ing** [back-formation fr. *abnegation*] **1** : SURRENDER, RELINQUISH <*abnegated* his powers> **2** : DENY, RENOUNCE <*abnegated* his God> — **ab·ne·ga·tor** \-ˌgāt-ər\ *n*

ab·ne·ga·tion \ˌab-ni-ˈgā-shən\ *n* [LL *abnegation-, abnegatio*, fr. L *abnegatus*, pp. of *abnegare* to refute, fr. *ab-* + *negare* to deny — more at NEGATE] : DENIAL; *esp* : SELF-DENIAL

1ab·nor·mal \(ˈ)ab-ˈnȯr-məl\ *adj* [F *anormal*, fr. ML *anormalis*, fr. L *a-* + LL *normalis* normal] **1** : deviating from the normal or average; *esp* : markedly irregular <~ behavior> **2** : characterized by mental deficiency or disorder <~ children> — **ab·nor·mal·ly** \-mə-lē\ *adv*

2abnormal *n* : an abnormal person

ab·nor·mal·i·ty \ˌab-nər-ˈmal-ət-ē, -(ˌ)nȯr-\ *n, pl* **-ties** **1** : the quality or state of being abnormal **2** : something abnormal

abnormal psychology *n* : the psychology of mental and behavioral disorder : PSYCHOPATHOLOGY

abo \ˈab-(ˌ)ō\ *n, pl* **ab·os** *Austral* : ABORIGINE

1aboard \ə-ˈbō(ə)rd, -ˈbȯ(ə)rd\ *adv* **1** : on, onto, or within a car, ship, or airplane <climb ~> **2** : ALONGSIDE **3** *baseball* : on base

2aboard *prep* : ON, ONTO, WITHIN <go ~ ship> <~ a plane>

abode \ə-ˈbōd\ *n* [ME *abod*, fr. *abiden* to abide] **1** *obs* : WAIT, DELAY **2** : a temporary stay : SOJOURN **3** : the place where one abides : HOME

aboil \ə-ˈbȯi(ə)l\ *adj or adv* **1** : being at the boiling point : BOILING **2** : intensely excited or stirred up <the meeting was ~ with controversy>

abol·ish \ə-ˈbäl-ish\ *vt* [ME *abolisshen*, fr. MF *aboliss-*, stem of *abolir*, fr. L *abolēre*, prob. back-formation fr. *abolescere* to disappear, fr. *ab-* + *-olescere* (as in *adolescere* to grow up) — more at ADULT] **1** : to do away with wholly : ANNUL **2** : to destroy completely — **abol·ish·able** \-ə-bəl\ *adj* — **abol·ish·er** *n* — **abol·ish·ment** \-mənt\ *n*
syn ABOLISH, ANNIHILATE, EXTINGUISH *shared meaning element* : to make nonexistent or wholly ineffective or inactive ***ant*** establish

ab·o·li·tion \ˌab-ə-ˈlish-ən\ *n* [MF, fr. L *abolition-, abolitio*, fr. *abolitus*, pp. of *abolēre*] **1** : the act of abolishing : the state of being abolished **2** : the abolishing of slavery — **ab·o·li·tion·ary** \-ˈlish-ə-ˌner-ē\ *adj*

ab·o·li·tion·ism \-ˈlish-ə-ˌniz-əm\ *n* : principles or measures fostering abolition esp. of slavery — **ab·o·li·tion·ist** \-ˈlish-(ə-)nəst\ *n or adj*

ab·oma·sum \ˌab-ō-ˈmā-səm\ *n, pl* **-sa** \-sə\ [NL, fr. L *ab-* + *omasum* tripe of a bullock] : the fourth or true digestive stomach of a ruminant — **ab·oma·sal** \-səl\ *adj*

A-bomb \ˈā-ˌbäm\ *n* : ATOM BOMB — **A-bomb** *vb*

abom·i·na·ble \ə-ˈbäm-(ə-)nə-bəl\ *adj* **1** : worthy of or causing disgust or hatred : DETESTABLE <the ~ treatment of the poor> **2** : quite disagreeable or unpleasant <~ weather> — **abom·i·na·bly** \-blē\ *adv*

abominable snow·man \-ˈsnō-mən, -ˌman\ *n, often cap A&S* : a mysterious animal reported as existing in the high Himalayas and usu. thought to be a bear

abom·i·nate \ə-ˈbäm-ə-ˌnāt\ *vt* **-nat·ed; -nat·ing** [L *abominatus*, pp. of *abominari*, lit., to deprecate as an ill omen, fr. *ab-* + *omin-, omen* omen] : to hate or loathe intensely : ABHOR ***syn*** see HATE ***ant*** esteem, enjoy — **abom·i·na·tor** \-ˌnāt-ər\ *n*

abom·i·na·tion \ə-ˌbäm-ə-ˈnā-shən\ *n* **1** : something abominable **2** : extreme disgust and hatred : LOATHING

ab·oral \(ˈ)a-ˈbōr-əl, -ˈbȯr-\ *adj* : situated opposite to or away from the mouth — **ab·oral·ly** \-ə-lē\ *adv*

1ab·orig·i·nal \ˌab-ə-ˈrij-nəl, -ən-ᵊl\ *adj* **1** : being the first of its kind present in a region and often primitive in comparison with more advanced types **2** : of or relating to aborigines ***syn*** see NATIVE — **ab·orig·i·nal·ly** \-ē\ *adv*

2aboriginal *n* : ABORIGINE; *specif* : an Australian aborigine

ab·orig·i·ne \ˌab-ə-ˈrij-ə-(ˌ)nē\ *n* [L *aborigines*, pl., fr. *ab origine* from the beginning] **1** : an aboriginal inhabitant esp. as contrasted with an invading or colonizing people **2** *pl* : the original fauna and flora of a geographical area

aborn·ing \ə-ˈbȯ(ə)r-niŋ\ *adv* [¹*a-* + E dial. *borning* (birth)] : while being born or produced <a resolution that died ~>

1abort \ə-ˈbȯ(ə)rt\ *vb* [L *abortare*, fr. *abortus*, pp. of *aboriri* to miscarry, fr. *ab-* + *oriri* to rise, be born — more at RISE] *vi* **1** : to bring forth premature or stillborn offspring **2** : to become checked in development so as to remain rudimentary or to shrink away ~ *vt* **1 a** : to give birth to prematurely **b** : to terminate the pregnancy of before term **2 a** : to terminate prematurely : CANCEL <~ a project> <~ a spaceflight> **b** : to stop in the early stages <~ a disease> — **abort·er** *n*

2abort *n* : the premature termination of the flight of an aircraft on a combat or bombing mission; *also* : such termination of an action, procedure, or mission relating to a rocket or spacecraft <a launch ~>

abor·ti·fa·cient \ə-ˌbȯrt-ə-ˈfā-shənt\ *adj* : inducing abortion — **abortifacient** *n*

abor·tion \ə-ˈbȯr-shən\ *n* **1** : the expulsion of a nonviable fetus: as **a** : spontaneous expulsion of a human fetus during the first 12 weeks of gestation — compare MISCARRIAGE **b** : induced abortion **2** : MONSTROSITY **3 a** : arrest of development (as of a part or process) resulting in imperfection **b** : a result of such arrest

abor·tion·ist \-sh(ə-)nəst\ *n* : a producer of abortions

abor·tive \ə-ˈbȯrt-iv\ *adj* **1** *obs* : prematurely born **2** : FRUITLESS, UNSUCCESSFUL **3** : imperfectly formed or developed **4** : tending to cut short — **abor·tive·ly** *adv* — **abor·tive·ness** *n*

ABO system \ˌā-(ˌ)bē-ˈō-\ *n* : the basic system of antigens of human blood behaving in heredity as an allelic unit to produce any of the four blood groups A, B, AB, or O — called also *ABO group*

abound \ə-ˈbau̇nd\ *vi* [ME *abounden*, fr. MF *abonder*, fr. L *abundare*, fr. *ab-* + *unda* wave — more at WATER] **1** : to be present in large numbers or in great quantity : be prevalent **2** : to become copiously supplied <the old edition *~ed* in . . . coloured pictures — *Times Lit. Supp.*> <institutions ~ with evidence of his success — *Johns Hopkins Mag.*>

1about \ə-ˈbau̇t\ *adv* [ME, fr. OE *abūtan*, fr. ¹*a-* + *būtan* outside — more at BUT] **1** : on all sides : AROUND **2 a** : in rotation **b** : around the outside **3 a** : APPROXIMATELY **b** : ALMOST <~ starved> **4** : here and there **5** : in the vicinity : NEAR **6** : in succession : ALTERNATELY <turn ~ is fair play> **7** : in the opposite direction <face ~ > <the other way ~>

2about *prep* **1** : on every side of : AROUND **2 a** : in the immediate neighborhood of : NEAR **b** : on or near the person of **c** : in the makeup of <a mature wisdom ~ him> **d** : at the command of <has his wits ~ him> **3 a** : engaged in **b** : on the verge of <~ to join the army> **4** : with regard to : CONCERNING

5 : over or in different parts of **6** — used with the negative to express intention or determination <is not ~ to quit>
[3]about *adj* **1 :** moving from place to place; *specif* **:** out of bed **2 :** AROUND 2
about-face \ə-ˈbau̇t-ˈfās\ *n* [fr. the imper. phrase *about face*] **1 :** a 180° turn to the right from the position of attention **2 :** a reversal of direction **3 :** a reversal of attitude or point of view — **about-face** *vi*
[1]above \ə-ˈbəv\ *adv* [ME, fr. OE *abufan*, fr. *a-* + *bufan* above, fr. *be-* + *ufan* above; akin to OE *ofer* over] **1 a :** in the sky **:** OVERHEAD **b :** in or to heaven **2 a :** in or to a higher place **b :** higher on the same page or on a preceding page **c :** UPSTAIRS **3 :** in or to a higher rank or number <30 and ~> **4** *archaic* **:** in addition **:** BESIDES **5 :** UPSTAGE
[2]above *prep* **1 :** in or to a higher place than **:** OVER **2 a :** superior to (as in rank, quality, or degree) **b :** out of reach of **c :** in preference to **d :** too proud or honorable to stoop to **3 :** exceeding in number, quantity, or size **:** more than
[3]above *n* **1 a :** something that is above **b :** a person whose name is written above **2 a :** a higher authority **b :** HEAVEN
[4]above *adj* **:** written or discussed higher on the same page or on a preceding page
above all *adv* **:** before every other consideration **:** ESPECIALLY
[1]above·board \ə-ˈbəv-ˌbō(ə)rd, -ˌbȯ(ə)rd\ *adv* [fr. the difficulty of cheating at cards when the hands are above the table] **:** in a straightforward manner **:** OPENLY
[2]aboveboard *adj* **:** free from all traces of deceit or duplicity ***syn*** see STRAIGHTFORWARD ***ant*** underhand, underhanded
above·ground \ə-ˈbəv-ˌgrau̇nd\ *adj* **1 :** located on or above the surface of the ground **2 :** existing, produced, or published by or within the establishment <~ movies>
ab ovo \a-ˈbō-(ˌ)vō\ *adv* [L, lit., from the egg] **:** from the beginning
abp *abbr* archbishop
abr *abbr* abridged; abridgment
ab·ra·ca·dab·ra \ˌab-rə-kə-ˈdab-rə\ *n* [LL] **1 :** a magical charm or incantation used to ward off calamity **2 :** unintelligible language **:** GIBBERISH
abrad·ant \ə-ˈbrād-ᵊnt\ *n* **:** ABRASIVE
abrade \ə-ˈbrād\ *vb* **abrad·ed; abrad·ing** [L *abradere* to scrape off, fr. *ab-* + *radere* to scrape — more at RAT] *vt* **1 a :** to rub or wear away esp. by friction **:** ERODE **b :** to irritate or roughen by rubbing **2 :** to wear down in spirit **:** IRRITATE, WEARY ~ *vi* **:** to undergo abrasion — **abrad·able** \-ˈbrād-ə-bəl\ *adj* — **abrad·er** *n*
Abra·ham \ˈā-brə-ˌham\ *n* [LL, fr. Gk *Abraam*, fr. Heb *ʼAbhrāhām*] **:** an Old Testament patriarch and founder of the Hebrew people
abra·sion \ə-ˈbrā-zhən\ *n* [ML *abrasion-*, *abrasio*, fr. L *abrasus*, pp. of *abradere*] **1 a :** a wearing, grinding, or rubbing away by friction **b :** IRRITATION **2 :** an abraded area of the skin or mucous membrane
[1]abra·sive \ə-ˈbrā-siv, -ziv\ *adj* **:** tending to abrade **:** causing irritation <~ relationships> — **abra·sive·ly** *adv* — **abra·sive·ness** *n*
[2]abrasive *n* **:** a substance (as emery or pumice) used for abrading, smoothing, or polishing
ab·re·act \ˌab-rē-ˈakt\ *vt* [part trans. of G *abreagieren*, fr. *ab* away from + *reagieren* to react] **:** to release (a repressed or forgotten emotion) by or as if by verbalization esp. in psychoanalysis — **ab·re·ac·tion** \-ˈak-shən\ *n*
abreast \ə-ˈbrest\ *adv or adj* **1 :** beside one another with bodies in line <columns of men five ~> **2 :** up to a particular standard or level esp. of knowledge of recent developments <keeps ~ of the latest trends>
abridge \ə-ˈbrij\ *vt* **abridged; abridg·ing** [ME *abregen*, fr. MF *abregier*, fr. LL *abbreviare*, fr. L *ad-* + *brevis* short — more at BRIEF] **1 a** *archaic* **:** DEPRIVE **b :** to reduce in scope **:** DIMINISH <attempts to ~ the right of free speech> **2 :** to shorten in duration or extent <modern transportation that ~*s* distance> **3 :** to shorten by omission of words without sacrifice of sense **:** CONDENSE ***syn*** see SHORTEN ***ant*** expand, extend — **abridg·er** *n*
abridg·ment *or* **abridge·ment** \ə-ˈbrij-mənt\ *n* **1 :** the action of abridging **:** the state of being abridged **2 :** a shortened form of a work retaining the general sense and unity of the original
syn ABRIDGMENT, ABSTRACT, SYNOPSIS, CONSPECTUS, EPITOME *shared meaning element* **:** a shorter version of a larger work or treatment
ant expansion
abroach \ə-ˈbrōch\ *adv or adj* **1 :** in a condition for letting out a liquid (as wine) <a cask set ~> **2 :** in action or agitation **:** ASTIR <mischiefs that I set ~ —Shak.>
abroad \ə-ˈbrȯd\ *adv or adj* **1 :** over a wide area **:** WIDELY **2 :** away from one's home **3 :** beyond the boundaries of one's country **4 :** in wide circulation **:** ABOUT **5 :** wide of the mark **:** ASTRAY
ab·ro·gate \ˈab-rə-ˌgāt\ *vt* **-gat·ed; -gat·ing** [L *abrogatus*, pp. of *abrogare*, fr. *ab-* + *rogare* to ask, propose a law — more at RIGHT] **1 :** to abolish by authoritative action **:** ANNUL **2 :** to do away with ***syn*** see NULLIFY ***ant*** establish, fix (*as a right or custom*) — **ab·ro·ga·tion** \ˌab-rə-ˈgā-shən\ *n*
abrupt \ə-ˈbrəpt\ *adj* [L *abruptus*, fr. pp. of *abrumpere* to break off, fr. *ab-* + *rumpere* to break — more at REAVE] **1 a :** broken off **b :** suddenly terminating as if cut or broken off <~ plant filaments> **2 a :** occurring without warning **:** UNEXPECTED <~ weather changes> **b :** unceremoniously curt <an ~ manner> **c :** marked by sudden changes in subject matter **:** DISCONNECTED **3 :** rising or dropping sharply as if broken off <a high ~ bank bounded the stream> ***syn*** **1** see STEEP **2** see PRECIPITATE ***ant*** deliberate, leisurely — **abrupt·ly** \ə-ˈbrəp-(t)lē\ *adv* — **abrupt·ness** \ə-ˈbrəp(t)-nəs\ *n*
abrup·tion \ə-ˈbrəp-shən\ *n* **:** a sudden breaking off or away
abs *abbr* **1** absolute **2** abstract
ABS *abbr* American Bible Society
ab·scess \ˈab-ˌses\ *n* [L *abscessus*, lit., act of going away, fr. *abscessus*, pp. of *abscedere* to go away, fr. *abs-*, *ab-* + *cedere* to go — more at CEDE] **:** a localized collection of pus surrounded by inflamed tissue — **ab·scessed** \-ˌsest\ *adj*
ab·scise \ab-ˈsīz\ *vb* **ab·scised; ab·scis·ing** [L *abscisus*, pp. of *abscidere*, fr. *abs-* + *caedere* to cut — more at CONCISE] *vt* **:** to cut off by abscission ~ *vi* **:** to separate by abscission
ab·scis·ic acid \ˌab-ˌsiz-ik-, -ˌsis-\ *n* [*abscis*ion (var. of *abscission*) + *-ic*] **:** a plant hormone $C_{15}H_{20}O_4$ that is widespread in nature and is made synthetically and that typically promotes leaf abscission and dormancy and has an inhibitory effect on cell elongation — called also *abscisin II*, *dormin*
ab·sci·sin *also* **ab·scis·sin** \ˈab-sə-sən, ab-ˈsis-ᵊn\ *n* [*abscision*, *abscission* + *-in*] **:** any of a group of plant regulatory substances orig. found in young cotton bolls that tend to promote leaf abscission and inhibit various growth processes — compare ABSCISIC ACID
ab·scis·sa \ab-ˈsis-ə\ *n, pl* **abscissas** *also* **ab·scis·sae** \-ˈsis-(ˌ)ē\ [NL, fr. L, fem. of *abscissus*, pp. of *abscindere* to cut off, fr. *ab-* + *scindere* to cut — more at SHED] **:** the horizontal coordinate of a point in a plane Cartesian coordinate system obtained by measuring parallel to the x-axis — compare ORDINATE

AP abscissa of point *P*

ab·scis·sion \ab-ˈsizh-ən\ *n* [L *abscission-*, *abscissio*, fr. *abscissus*] **1 :** the act or process of cutting off **:** REMOVAL **2 :** the natural separation of flowers, fruit, or leaves from plants at a special separation layer
ab·scond \ab-ˈskänd\ *vi* [L *abscondere* to hide away, fr. *abs-* + *condere* to store up, conceal — more at CONDIMENT] **:** to depart secretly and hide oneself — **ab·scond·er** *n*
ab·sence \ˈab-sən(t)s\ *n* **1 :** the state of being absent **2 :** the period of time that one is absent **3 :** WANT, LACK <an ~ of detail> **4 :** inattention to present surroundings or occurrences <~ of mind>
[1]ab·sent \ˈab-sənt\ *adj* [ME, fr. MF, fr. L *absent-*, *absens*, prp. of *abesse* to be absent, fr. *ab-* + *esse* to be — more at IS] **1 :** not present or attending **:** MISSING **2 :** not existing **:** LACKING <danger in a situation where power is ~ —M. H. Trytten> **3 :** INATTENTIVE, PREOCCUPIED — **ab·sent·ly** *adv*
[2]ab·sent \ab-ˈsent\ *vt* **:** to keep (oneself) away
ab·sen·tee \ˌab-sən-ˈtē\ *n* **:** one that is absent or that absents himself; *specif* **:** a proprietor that lives away from his estate or business — **absentee** *adj*
absentee ballot *n* **:** a ballot submitted (as by mail) in advance of an election by a voter who is unable to be present at the polls
ab·sen·tee·ism \ˌab-sən-ˈtē-ˌiz-əm\ *n* **1 :** prolonged absence of an owner from his property **2 :** chronic absence from duty (as work)
absentee voter *n* **:** a registered voter who is permitted to vote by absentee ballot
ab·sent·mind·ed \ˌab-sənt-ˈmīn-dəd\ *adj* **:** lost in thought and unaware of one's surroundings or action **:** PREOCCUPIED; *also* **:** given to absence of mind — **ab·sent·mind·ed·ly** *adv* — **ab·sent·mind·ed·ness** *n*
absent without leave *adj* **:** absent without authority from one's place of duty in the armed forces
ab·sinthe *or* **ab·sinth** \ˈab-ˌsin(t)th\ *n* [F *absinthe*, fr. L *absinthium*, fr. Gk *apsinthion*] **1 :** WORMWOOD 1; *esp* **:** a common European wormwood (*Artemisia absinthium*) **2 :** a green liqueur flavored with wormwood or a substitute, anise, and other aromatics
ab·so·lute \ˈab-sə-ˌlüt, ˌab-sə-ˈ\ *adj* [ME *absolut*, fr. L *absolutus*, fr. pp. of *absolvere* to set free, absolve] **1 a :** free from imperfection **:** PERFECT **b :** free or relatively free from mixture **:** PURE <~ alcohol> **c :** OUTRIGHT, UNMITIGATED <an ~ lie> **2 :** being, governed by, or characteristic of a ruler or authority completely free from constitutional or other restraint **3 a :** standing apart from a normal or usual syntactical relation with other words or sentence elements <the ~ construction *this being the case* in the sentence "this being the case, let us go"> **b** *of an adjective or possessive pronoun* **:** standing alone without a modified substantive <*blind* in "help the blind" and *ours* in "your work and ours" are ~> **c** *of a verb* **:** having no object in the particular construction under consideration though normally transitive <*kill* in "if looks could kill" is an ~ verb> **4 :** having no restriction, exception, or qualification <an ~ requirement> <~ freedom> **5 :** POSITIVE, UNQUESTIONABLE <~ proof> **6 a :** independent of arbitrary standards of measurement **b :** relating to or derived in the simplest manner from the fundamental units of length, mass, and time <~ electric units> **c :** relating to the absolute-temperature scale <10° ~> **7 :** FUNDAMENTAL, ULTIMATE <~ knowledge> **8 :** perfectly embodying the nature of a thing <~ justice> **9 :** being self-sufficient and free of external references or relationships <an ~ term in logic> <~ music> **10 :** measuring or representing the distance from an aircraft to the ground or water beneath — **absolute** *n* — **ab·so·lute·ly** *adv* — **ab·so·lute·ness** *n*
absolute ceiling *n* **:** the maximum height above sea level at which a particular airplane can maintain horizontal flight under standard air conditions — called also *ceiling*
absolute humidity *n* **:** the amount of water vapor present in a unit volume of air
absolute magnitude *n* **:** the intrinsic luminosity of a celestial body (as a star) if viewed from a distance of 10 parsecs
absolute pitch *n* **1 :** the position of a tone in a standard scale independently determined by its rate of vibration **2 :** the ability to sing or name a note asked for or heard
absolute scale *n* **:** a temperature scale based on absolute zero
absolute space *n* **:** SPACE 4b
absolute temperature *n* **:** temperature measured on the absolute scale
absolute value *n* **1 :** the numerical value of a real number irrespective of sign **2 :** the positive square root of the sum of the squares of the real and imaginary parts of a complex number

absolute zero *n* : a hypothetical temperature characterized by complete absence of heat and equivalent to approximately −273.16°C or −459.69°F

ab·so·lu·tion \ˌab-sə-ˈlü-shən\ *n* : the act of absolving; *specif* : a remission of sins pronounced by a priest (as in the sacrament of penance)

ab·so·lut·ism \ˈab-sə-ˌlüt-ˌiz-əm\ *n* **1 a** : a political theory that absolute power should be vested in one or more rulers **b** : government by an absolute ruler or authority : DESPOTISM **2** : advocacy of a rule by absolute standards or principles **3** : an absolute standard or principle — **ab·so·lut·ist** \-ˌlüt-əst\ *n or adj* — **ab·so·lu·tis·tic** \ˌab-sə-(ˌ)lü-ˈtis-tik\ *adj*

ab·so·lut·ize \ˈab-sə-ˌlüt-ˌiz\ *vt* **-ized; -iz·ing** : to make absolute : convert into an absolute

ab·solve \əb-ˈzälv, -ˈsälv, -ˈzölv, -ˈsölv\ *vt* **ab·solved; ab·solv·ing** [ME *absolven*, fr. L *absolvere*, fr. *ab-* + *solvere* to loosen — more at SOLVE] **1** : to set free from an obligation or the consequences of guilt **2** : to remit (a sin) by absolution — **ab·solv·er** *n*

ab·sorb \əb-ˈsȯ(ə)rb, -ˈzȯ(ə)rb\ *vt* [MF *absorber*, fr. L *absorbēre*, fr. *ab-* + *sorbēre* to suck up; akin to Gk *rhophein* to suck up] **1** : to take in and make part of an existent whole <the capacity of China to ~ invaders> **2 a** : to suck up or take up <a sponge ~*s* water> <charcoal ~*s* gas> <plant roots ~ water> **b** : to take in <convictions ~*ed* in youth —M. R. Cohen> **3** : to engage or engross wholly <~*ed* in thought> **4 a** : to receive without recoil or echo <provided with a sound-*absorbing* surface> **b** : to transform (radiant energy) into a different form usu. with a resulting rise in temperature <the earth ~*s* the sun's rays> **5** : to take over (a cost) — **ab·sorb·abil·i·ty** \əb-ˌsȯr-bə-ˈbil-ət-ē, -ˌzȯr-\ *n* — **ab·sorb·able** \əb-ˈsȯr-bə-bəl, -ˈzȯr-\ *adj* — **ab·sorb·er** *n*

syn **1** ABSORB, IMBIBE, ASSIMILATE *shared meaning element* : to take in and incorporate something (as into the substance or mind) ***ant*** dissipate (*as time, energies*)
2 see MONOPOLIZE

ab·sor·bance \əb-ˈsȯr-bən(t)s, -ˈzȯr-\ *n* : ABSORBENCY 2

ab·sor·ben·cy \əb-ˈsȯr-bən-sē, -ˈzȯr-\ *n, pl* **-cies** **1** : the quality or state of being absorbent **2** *or* **ab·sor·ban·cy** : the ability of a layer of a substance to absorb radiation expressed mathematically as the negative common logarithm of transmittance

ab·sor·bent *also* **ab·sor·bant** \-bənt\ *adj* [L *absorbent-, absorbens*, prp. of *absorbēre*] : able to absorb <as ~ as a sponge> — **absorbent** *also* **absorbant** *n*

ab·sorb·ing *adj* : fully taking one's attention : ENGROSSING <an ~ novel> — **ab·sorb·ing·ly** \-biŋ-lē\ *adv*

ab·sorp·tance \əb-ˈsȯrp-tən(t)s, -ˈzȯrp-\ *n* [*absorpt*ion + *-ance*] : the ratio of the radiant energy absorbed by a body to that incident upon it

ab·sorp·tion \əb-ˈsȯrp-shən, -ˈzȯrp-\ *n* [F & L; F, fr. L *absorption-, absorptio*, fr. *absorptus*, pp. of *absorbēre*] **1 a** : the process of absorbing or of being absorbed — compare ADSORPTION **b** : interception of radiant energy or sound waves **2** : entire occupation of the mind <~ in his work> — **ab·sorp·tion·al** \-shnəl, -shən-ᵊl\ *adj* — **ab·sorp·tive** \-tiv\ *adj*

ab·stain \əb-ˈstān\ *vi* [ME *absteinen*, fr. MF *abstenir*, fr. L *abstinēre*, fr. *abs-, ab-* + *tenēre* to hold — more at THIN] : to refrain deliberately and often with an effort of self-denial from an action or practice ***syn*** see REFRAIN — **ab·stain·er** *n*

ab·ste·mi·ous \ab-ˈstē-mē-əs\ *adj* [L *abstemius*, fr. *abs-* + *temetum* mead; akin to L *tenebrae* darkness — more at TEMERITY] **1** : sparing esp. in eating or drinking **2** : sparingly used or indulged in <~ diet> — **ab·ste·mi·ous·ly** *adv*

ab·sten·tion \əb-ˈsten-chən\ *n* [LL *abstention-, abstentio*, fr. L *abstentus*, pp. of *abstinere*] : the act or practice of abstaining — **ab·sten·tious** \-chəs\ *adj*

ab·sti·nence \ˈab-stə-nən(t)s\ *n* [ME, fr. OF, fr. L *abstinentia*, fr. *abstinent-, abstinens*, prp. of *abstinēre*] **1** : voluntary forbearance esp. from indulgence of appetite or from eating some foods : ABSTENTION **2** : habitual abstaining from intoxicating beverages — **ab·sti·nent** \-nənt\ *adj* — **ab·sti·nent·ly** *adv*

abstr *abbr* abstract

[1]**ab·stract** \ab-ˈstrakt, ˈab-ˌ\ *adj* [ML *abstractus*, fr. L, pp. of *abstrahere* to draw away, fr. *abs-, ab-* + *trahere* to draw — more at DRAW] **1 a** : disassociated from any specific instance <~ entity> **b** : difficult to understand : ABSTRUSE <~ problems> **c** : IDEAL <~ justice> **d** : insufficiently factual : FORMAL <possessed only an ~ right> **2** : expressing a quality apart from an object <the word *poem* is concrete, *poetry* is ~> **3 a** : dealing with a subject in its abstract aspects : THEORETICAL <~ science> **b** : IMPERSONAL, DETACHED <the ~ compassion of a surgeon —*Time*> **4** : having only intrinsic form with little or no attempt at pictorial representation <~ painting> — **ab·stract·ly** \ab-ˈstrak-(t)lē, ˈab-ˌ\ *adv* — **ab·stract·ness** \ab-ˈstrak(t)-nəs, ˈab-ˌ\ *n*

[2]**ab·stract** \ˈab-ˌstrakt, *in sense 2 also* ab-ˈ\ *n* [ME, fr. L *abstractus*] **1** : a summary of points (as of a writing) usu. presented in skeletal form **2** : an abstract thing or state **3** : ABSTRACTION 4 ***syn*** see ABRIDGMENT ***ant*** amplification

[3]**ab·stract** \ab-ˈstrakt, ˈab-ˌ, *in sense 3 usu* ˈab-ˌ\ *vt* **1** : REMOVE, SEPARATE **2** : to consider apart from application to a particular instance **3** : to make an abstract of : SUMMARIZE **4** : to draw away the attention of **5** : STEAL, PURLOIN ~ *vi* : to make an abstraction — **ab·stract·able** \-ˈstrak-tə-bəl, -ˌstrak-\ *adj* — **ab·stac·tor** *or* **ab·stract·er** \-tər\ *n*

ab·stract·ed \ab-ˈstrak-təd, ˈab-ˌ\ *adj* : PREOCCUPIED, ABSENTMINDED <the ~ look of a professor> — **ab·stract·ed·ly** *adv* — **ab·stract·ed·ness** *n*

abstract expressionism *n* : art in which the artist attempts to convey his attitudes and emotions through nonrepresentational means — **abstract expressionist** *n*

ab·strac·tion \ab-ˈstrak-shən\ *n* **1 a** : the act or process of abstracting : the state of being abstracted **b** : an abstract idea or term **2** : absence of mind **3** : abstract quality or character **4** : an abstract composition or creation in art — **ab·strac·tion·al** \-shnəl, -shən-ᵊl\ *adj* — **ab·strac·tive** \ab-ˈstrak-tiv, ˈab-ˌ\ *adj*

ab·strac·tion·ism \ab-ˈstrak-shə-ˌniz-əm\ *n* : the principles or practice of creating abstract art — **ab·strac·tion·ist** \-sh(ə-)nəst\ *adj or n*

abstract of title : a summary statement of the successive conveyances and other facts on which a person's title to a piece of land rests

ab·strict \ab-ˈstrikt\ *vt* [*ab-* + L *strictus*, pp. of *stringere* to draw tight — more at STRAIN] : to cut off in or as if in abstriction

ab·stric·tion \-ˈstrik-shən\ *n* : the formation of spores by the cutting off of portions of the sporophore through the growth of septa

ab·struse \əb-ˈstrüs, ab-\ *adj* [L *abstrusus*, fr. pp. of *abstrudere* to conceal, fr. *abs-, ab-* + *trudere* to push — more at THREAT] : difficult to comprehend : RECONDITE <the ~ calculations of mathematicians> — **ab·struse·ly** *adv* — **ab·struse·ness** *n*

ab·stru·si·ty \-ˈstrü-sət-ē\ *n, pl* **-ties** **1** : the quality or state of being abstruse : ABSTRUSENESS **2** : something that is abstruse

[1]**ab·surd** \əb-ˈsərd, -ˈzərd\ *adj* [MF *absurde*, fr. L *absurdus*, fr. *ab-* + *surdus* deaf, stupid — more at SURD] **1** : ridiculously unreasonable, unsound, or incongruous **2** : having no rational or orderly relationship to man's life : MEANINGLESS; *also* : lacking order or value **3** : dealing with the absurd or with absurdism — **ab·surd·ly** *adv* — **ab·surd·ness** *n*

[2]**absurd** *n* : the state or condition in which man exists in an irrational and meaningless universe and in which man's life has no meaning outside his own existence

ab·surd·ism \-ˌiz-əm\ *n* : a philosophy based on the belief that man exists in an irrational and meaningless universe and that his search for order brings him into conflict with his universe — compare EXISTENTIALISM — **ab·surd·ist** \-əst\ *n or adj*

ab·sur·di·ty \əb-ˈsərd-ət-ē, -ˈzərd-\ *n, pl* **-ties** **1** : the quality or state of being absurd : ABSURDNESS **2** : something that is absurd

absurd theater *n* : THEATER OF THE ABSURD

abub·ble \ə-ˈbəb-əl\ *adj* **1** : being in the process of bubbling : EFFERVESCENT **2** : being in a state of agitated activity or motion : ASTIR

abuild·ing \ə-ˈbil-diŋ\ *adj* : being in the process of building or of being built

abun·dance \ə-ˈbən-dən(t)s\ *n* **1** : an ample quantity : PROFUSION **2** : AFFLUENCE, WEALTH **3** : relative degree of plentifulness <low ~*s* of uranium and thorium —H. C. Urey>

abun·dant \-dənt\ *adj* [ME, fr. MF, fr. L *abundant-, abundans*, prp. of *abundare* to abound] **1 a** : marked by great plenty (as of resources) <a fair and ~ land> **b** : amply supplied : ABOUNDING <~ with fly life and other natural trout food —Alexander MacDonald> **2** : occurring in abundance <~ rainfall> ***syn*** see PLENTIFUL ***ant*** scarce — **abun·dant·ly** *adv*

abundant year *n* : PERFECT YEAR

[1]**abuse** \ə-ˈbyüz\ *vt* **abused; abus·ing** [ME *abusen*, fr. MF *abuser*, fr. L *abusus*, pp. of *abuti*, fr. *ab-* + *uti* to use — more at USE] **1** : to attack in words : REVILE **2** *obs* : DECEIVE **3** : to put to a wrong or improper use <~ a privilege> **4** : to use so as to injure or damage : MALTREAT <~ a dog> — **abus·able** \-ˈbyü-zə-bəl\ *adj* — **abus·er** *n*

[2]**abuse** \ə-ˈbyüs\ *n* **1** : a corrupt practice or custom **2** : improper use or treatment : MISUSE <drug ~> **3** *obs* : a deceitful act : DECEPTION **4** : abusive language **5** : physical maltreatment

syn ABUSE, VITUPERATION, INVECTIVE, OBLOQUY, SCURRILITY, BILLINGSGATE *shared meaning element* : vehemently expressed condemnation or disapproval ***ant*** adulation

abu·sive \ə-ˈbyü-siv, -ziv\ *adj* **1** : characterized by wrong or improper use or action : CORRUPT <~ financial practices> **2 a** : characterized by or serving for verbal abuse **b** : physically injurious <received ~ treatment> — **abu·sive·ly** *adv* — **abu·sive·ness** *n*

abut \ə-ˈbət\ *vb* **abut·ted; abut·ting** [ME *abutten*, partly fr. OF *aboter* to border on, fr. *a-* (fr. L *ad-*) + *bout* blow, end, fr. *boter* to strike; partly fr. OF *abuter* to come to an end, fr. *a-* + *but* end, aim — more at [1]BUTT, [3]BUTT] *vi* **1** : to touch along a border or with a projecting part <land ~*s* on the road> **2 a** : to terminate at a point of contact **b** : to lean for support ~ *vt* **1** : to border on : TOUCH **2** : to cause to abut — **abut·ter** *n*

abu·ti·lon \ə-ˈbyüt-ᵊl-ˌän\ *n* [NL, genus name, fr. Ar *awbūtīlūn* abutilon] : any of a genus (*Abutilon*) of plants of the mallow family with usu. lobed leaves and showy solitary bell-shaped flowers

abut·ment \ə-ˈbət-mənt\ *n* **1** : the place at which abutting occurs **2 a** : the part of a structure that directly receives thrust or pressure (as of an arch) **b** : an anchorage for the cables of a suspension bridge or aerial railway

abut·tals \ə-ˈbət-ᵊlz\ *n pl* : the boundaries of lands with respect to adjacent lands

abut·ting *adj* : that abuts or serves as an abutment : ADJOINING, BORDERING ***syn*** see ADJACENT

abuzz \ə-ˈbəz\ *adj* : filled or resounding with or as if with a buzzing sound <a lake ~ with outboards> <a town ~ with excitement>

aby *or* **abye** \ə-ˈbī\ *vt* [ME *abien*, fr. OE *ābycgan*, fr. *ā-* + *bycgan* to buy — more at ABIDE, BUY] *archaic* : to suffer a penalty for

abysm \ə-ˈbiz-əm\ *n* [ME *abime*, fr. OF *abisme*, modif. of LL *abyssus*] : ABYSS <the dark backward and ~ of time —Shak.>

abys·mal \ə-ˈbiz-məl\ *adj* **1 a** : having immense or fathomless extension downward, backward, or inward <an ~ cliff> **b** : immeasurably great : PROFOUND <~ ignorance> <the ~ sufferings of the dispossessed> **2** : ABYSSAL ***syn*** see DEEP — **abys·mal·ly** \-mə-lē\ *adv*

abyss \ə-ˈbis\ *n* [ME *abissus*, fr. LL *abyssus*, fr. Gk *abyssos*, fr. *abyssos* bottomless, fr. *a-* + *byssos* depth; akin to Gk *bathys* deep

— more at BATHY-] **1 :** the bottomless gulf, pit, or chaos of the old cosmogonies **2 a :** an immeasurably deep gulf or great space **b :** intellectual or spiritual profundity

abys·sal \ə-ˈbis-əl\ *adj* **1 :** UNFATHOMABLE a **2 :** of or relating to the bottom waters of the ocean depths

Ab·ys·sin·i·an cat \ˌab-ə-ˌsin-ē-ən-, -ˌsin-yən-\ *n* [*Abyssinia,* kingdom in Africa] **:** any of a breed of small slender cats of African origin with short brownish hair ticked with darker color

ac *abbr* **1** account **2** money of account

[1]**Ac** *abbr* altocumulus

[2]**Ac** *symbol* actinium

AC *abbr* **1** alternating current **2** [L *ante Christum*] before Christ **3** [L *ante cibum*] before meals **4** area code **5** athletic club

ac- — see AD-

-ac \ˌak, *in a few words* ik *or* ək\ *n suffix* [NL *-acus* of or relating to, fr. Gk *-akos*] **:** one affected with <nostalgi*ac*>

aca·cia \ə-ˈkā-shə\ *n* [NL, genus name, fr. L, acacia tree, fr. Gk *akakia* shittah] **1 :** any of a genus (*Acacia*) of woody leguminous plants of warm regions with leaves pinnate or reduced to phyllodes and white or yellow flower clusters **2 :** GUM ARABIC

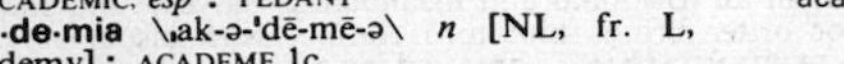

acacia 1

acad *abbr* academic; academy

ac·a·deme \ˈak-ə-ˌdēm\ *n* [irreg. fr. NL *academia*] **1 a :** a place of instruction **:** SCHOOL **b :** the academic environment **c** (1) **:** the academic community (2) **:** academic life **2 :** ACADEMIC; *esp* **:** PEDANT

ac·a·de·mia \ˌak-ə-ˈdē-mē-ə\ *n* [NL, fr. L, academy] **:** ACADEME 1c

[1]**ac·a·dem·ic** \ˌak-ə-ˈdem-ik\ *also* **ac·a·dem·i·cal** \-i-kəl\ *adj* **1 a :** of, relating to, or associated with an academy or school esp. of higher learning **b :** of or relating to performance in academic courses **c :** very learned but inexperienced in practical matters <~ thinkers> **d :** based on formal study esp. at an institution of higher learning **2 :** of or relating to literary or art rather than technical or professional studies **3 :** conforming to the traditions or rules of a school (as of literature or art) or an official academy **:** CONVENTIONAL **4 a :** theoretical without having an immediate or practical bearing **:** ABSTRACT <an ~ question> **b :** having no practical or useful significance ***syn*** see PEDANTIC, THEORETICAL — **ac·a·dem·i·cal·ly** \-ik (ə-) lē\ *adv*

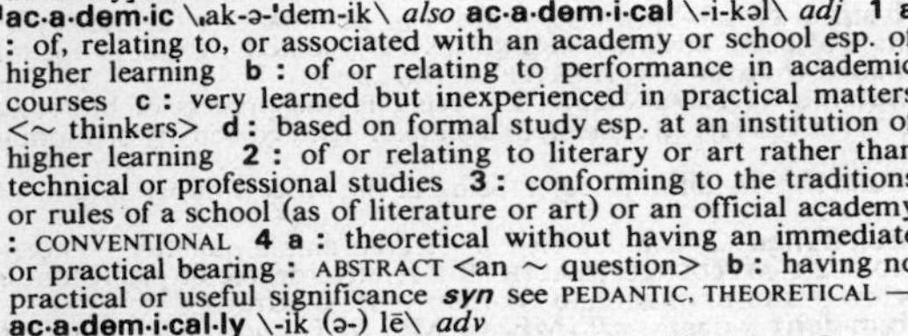

[2]**academic** *n* **1 :** a member of an institution of learning **2 :** one who is academic in background, outlook, or methods

academic freedom *n* **:** freedom to teach or to learn without interference (as by government officials)

ac·a·de·mi·cian \ˌak-əd-ə-ˈmish-ən, ə-ˌkad-ə-\ *n* **1 a :** a member of an academy for promoting science, art, or literature **b :** a follower of an artistic or philosophical tradition or a promoter of its ideas **2 :** ACADEMIC

ac·a·dem·i·cism \ˌak-ə-ˈdem-ə-ˌsiz-əm\ *also* **acad·e·mism** \ə-ˈkad-ə-ˌmiz-əm\ *n* **1 :** the doctrines of Plato's Academy; *specif* **:** the skeptical doctrines of the later Academy holding that nothing can be known — compare PYRRHONISM **2 :** purely speculative thoughts and attitudes

academic year *n* **:** the annual period of sessions of an educational institution usu. beginning in September and ending in June

acad·e·my \ə-ˈkad-ə-mē\ *n, pl* **-mies** [L *academia,* fr. Gk *Akadēmeia,* fr. *Akadēmeia,* gymnasium where Plato taught, fr. *Akadēmos* Attic mythological hero] **1** *cap* **a :** the school for advanced education founded by Plato **b :** the philosophical doctrines associated with Plato's Academy: (1) **:** PLATONISM (2) **:** ACADEMICISM **2 a :** a school usu. above the elementary level; *esp* **:** a private high school **b :** a high school or college in which special subjects or skills are taught **c :** higher education <the functions of the ~ in modern society> **3 :** a society of learned persons organized to advance art, science, or literature **4 :** a body of established opinion in a particular field widely accepted as authoritative

Aca·di·an \ə-ˈkād-ē-ən\ *n* **1 :** a native or inhabitant of Acadia **2 a :** a Louisianian descended from French-speaking immigrants from Acadia **b :** a dialect of French spoken by Acadians — **Acadian** *adj*

AC and U *abbr* Association of Colleges and Universities

acanth- *or* **acantho-** *comb form* [NL, fr. Gk *akanth-, akantho-,* fr. *akantha;* akin to ON *ögn* awn — more at AWN] **:** thorn **:** spine <*acanth*ous> <*acantho*cephalan>

acan·tho·ceph·a·lan \ə-ˌkan(t)-thə-ˈsef-ə-lən\ *n* [deriv. of *acanth-* + Gk *kephalē* head — more at CEPHALIC] **:** any of a group (Acanthocephala) of intestinal worms with a hooked proboscis that as adults lack a digestive tract and absorb food through the body wall — **acanthocephalan** *adj*

ac·an·thop·ter·yg·i·an \ˌak-ən-ˌthäp-tə-ˈrij-ē-ən\ *n* [deriv. of *acanth-* + Gk *pteryg-, pteryx* wing, fin — more at PTERYGOID] **:** any of a major division (Acanthopterygii) of teleost fishes including most spiny-finned fishes (as basses, perches, and mackerels) and some soft-finned fishes — **acanthopterygian** *adj*

acan·thus \ə-ˈkan(t)-thəs\ *n, pl* **acan·thus·es** *also* **acan·thi** \-ˈkan-ˌthī\ [NL, genus name, fr. Gk *akanthos,* a hellebore, fr. *akantha*] **1 :** any of a genus (*Acanthus* of the family Acanthaceae, the acanthus family) of prickly herbs of the Mediterranean region **2 :** an ornamentation (as in a Corinthian capital) representing or suggesting the leaves of the acanthus

acanthus 2

a cap·pel·la *also* **a ca·pel·la** \ˌäk-ə-ˈpel-ə\ *adv or adj* [It *a cappella* in chapel style] **:** without instrumental accompaniment

ac·a·ri·a·sis \ˌak-ə-ˈrī-ə-səs\ *n* **:** infestation with or disease caused by mites

ac·a·rid \ˈak-ə-rəd\ *n* **:** any of an order (Acarina) of arachnids including the mites and ticks; *esp* **:** a typical mite (family Acaridae) — **acarid** *adj*

ac·a·roid resin \ˈak-ə-ˌrȯid-\ *n* [NL *acaroides*] **:** an alcohol-soluble resin from Australian grass trees

acar·pel·ous *or* **acar·pel·lous** \(ˈ)ā-ˈkär-pə-ləs\ *adj* **:** having no carpels

ac·a·rus \ˈak-ə-rəs\ *n, pl* **-ri** \-ˌrī\ [NL, genus name, fr. Gk *akari,* a mite] **:** MITE; *esp* **:** one of a formerly extensive genus (*Acarus*)

acat·a·lec·tic \(ˌ)ā-ˌkat-ᵊl-ˈek-tik\ *adj* [LL *acatalecticus,* fr. *acatalectus,* fr. Gk *akatalēktos,* fr. *a-* + *katalēgein* to leave off — more at CATALECTIC] **:** not catalectic <~ verse> — **acatalectic** *n*

acau·les·cent \ˌā-kȯ-ˈles-ᵊnt\ *adj* [*a-* + L *caulis* stem — more at HOLE] **:** having no stem or appearing to have none — **acau·les·cence** \-ᵊn(t)s\ *n*

acc *abbr* accusative

ACC *abbr* Air Coordinating Committee

ac·cede \ak-ˈsēd\ *vi* **ac·ced·ed; ac·ced·ing** [ME *acceden,* fr. L *accedere* to go to, be added, fr. *ad-* + *cedere* to go — more at CEDE] **1** *archaic* **:** APPROACH **2 a :** to become a party (as to an agreement) **b :** to express approval or give consent often in response to urging **:** CONCEDE **3 :** to enter upon an office or position ***syn*** see ASSENT ***ant*** demur

ac·ce·le·ran·do \(ˌ)ä-ˌchel-ə-ˈrän-(ˌ)dō\ *adv or adj* [It, lit., accelerating, fr. L *accelerandum,* gerund of *accelerare*] **:** gradually faster — used as a direction in music

ac·cel·er·ate \ik-ˈsel-ə-ˌrāt, ak-\ *vb* **-at·ed; -at·ing** [L *acceleratus,* pp. of *accelerare,* fr. *ad-* + *celer* swift — more at CELERITY] *vt* **1 :** to bring about at an earlier time **2 :** to cause to move faster; *also* **:** to cause to undergo acceleration **3 a :** to hasten the progress or development of **b :** to cause to grow **:** INCREASE <~ food production> **4 a :** to enable (a student) to complete a course in less than usual time **b :** to speed up (a course of study) ~ *vi* **1 a :** to move faster **:** gain speed **b :** GROW, INCREASE <believed inflation was *accelerating*> **2 :** to follow a speeded-up educational program — **ac·cel·er·at·ing·ly** \-ˌrāt-iŋ-lē\ *adv*

ac·cel·er·a·tion \ik-ˌsel-ə-ˈrā-shən, (ˌ)ak-\ *n* **1 :** the act or process of accelerating **:** the state of being accelerated **2 :** change of velocity; *also* **:** the rate of this change

acceleration of gravity : the acceleration of a freely falling body under the influence of gravity expressed as the rate of increase of velocity per unit of time with the value at sea level in latitude 45 degrees being 980.1018 centimeters per second per second

acceleration principle *n* **:** a theory in economics: an increase or decrease in income induces a corresponding but magnified change in investment

ac·cel·er·a·tive \ik-ˈsel-ə-ˌrāt-iv, ak-\ *adj* **:** of, relating to, or tending to cause acceleration **:** ACCELERATING

ac·cel·er·a·tor \ik-ˈsel-ə-ˌrāt-ər, ak-\ *n* **:** one that accelerates: as **a :** a muscle or nerve that speeds the performance of an action **b :** a device for increasing the speed of a motor vehicle engine; *esp* **:** a foot-operated throttle that varies the supply of fuel-air mixture to the combustion chamber **c :** a substance that speeds a chemical reaction **d :** an apparatus for imparting high velocities to charged particles (as electrons)

ac·cel·er·om·e·ter \ik-ˌsel-ə-ˈräm-ət-ər, ak-\ *n* [ISV *acceler*ation + *-o-* + *-meter*] **:** an instrument for measuring acceleration or for detecting and measuring vibrations

[1]**ac·cent** \ˈak-ˌsent\ *n* [MF, fr. L *accentus,* fr. *ad-* + *cantus* song, fr. *cantus,* pp. of *canere* to sing — more at CHANT] **1 :** a distinctive manner of expression: as **a :** the inflection, tone, or choice of words taken to be unique in or highly characteristic of an individual — usu. used in pl. **b :** speech habits typical of the natives or residents of a region or of any other group **2 :** an articulative effort giving prominence to one syllable over adjacent syllables; *also* **:** the prominence thus given a syllable **3 :** rhythmically significant stress on the syllables of a verse usu. at regular intervals **4** *archaic* **:** UTTERANCE **5 a :** a mark (as ´, ˋ, ˆ) used in writing or printing to indicate a specific sound value, stress, or pitch, to distinguish words otherwise identically spelled, or to indicate that an ordinarily mute vowel should be pronounced **b :** an accented letter **6 a :** greater stress given to one musical tone than to its neighbors **b** (1) **:** the principle of regularly recurring stresses which serve to distribute a succession of pulses into measures (2) **:** special emphasis placed exceptionally upon tones not subject to such accent **c :** ACCENT MARK 2 **7 a :** emphasis laid on a part of an artistic design or composition **b :** an emphasized detail or area; *esp* **:** a small detail in sharp contrast with its surroundings **c :** a substance or object used for emphasis **8 :** a mark placed to the right of a letter or number and usu. slightly above it: **a** (1) **:** a double prime (2) **:** PRIME **b :** a mark used singly with numbers to denote minutes and doubly to denote seconds of time or to denote minutes and seconds of an angle or arc **c :** a mark used singly with numbers to denote feet and doubly to denote inches **9 :** special concern or attention **:** EMPHASIS <an ~ on youth> — **ac·cent·less** \-ləs\ *adj*

[2]**ac·cent** \ˈak-ˌsent, ak-ˈ\ *vt* **1 a :** to pronounce with accent **:** STRESS **b :** to mark with a written or printed accent **2 :** to give prominence to **:** make more prominent

accent mark *n* **1 :** ACCENT 5a, 8 **2 a :** a symbol used to indicate musical stress **b :** a mark placed after a letter designating a note of music to indicate in which octave the note occurs

accent mark 2a

ac·cen·tu·al \ak-ˈsench-(ə-)wəl\ *adj* [L *accentus*] **:** of, relating to, or characterized by accent; *specif* **:** based on accent rather than on quantity or syllabic recurrence — **ac·cen·tu·al·ly** \-ē\ *adv*

ac·cen·tu·ate \ak-ˈsen-chə-ˌwāt, ik-\ *vt* **-at·ed; -at·ing** [ML *accentuatus,* pp. of *accentuare,* fr. L *accentus*] **:** ACCENT, EMPHASIZE — **ac·cen·tu·a·tion** \(ˌ)ak-ˌsen-chə-ˈwā-shən, ik-\ *n*

ac·cept \ik-ˈsept, ak-\ *vb* [ME *accepten,* fr. MF *accepter,* fr. L *acceptare,* fr. *acceptus,* pp. of *accipere* to receive, fr. *ad-* + *capere* to take — more at HEAVE] *vt* **1 a :** to receive with consent <~ a gift> **b :** to be able or designed to take or hold (something applied) <a surface that will not ~ ink> **2 :** to give admittance or approval to <~ her as one of the group> **3 a :** to endure without protest <~ poor living conditions> **b :** to regard as proper, normal, or inevitable <the idea of universal education is widely ~*ed*> **c :** to receive as true <refused to ~ the hypothesis> **d :** to receive into the mind : UNDERSTAND <users of a language ~ words to mean certain things> **4 a :** to make a favorable response to <~ an offer> **b :** to undertake the responsibility of <~ a job> **5 :** to assume an obligation to pay **6 :** to receive (a legislative report) officially ~ *vi* **:** to receive favorably something offered — usu. used with *of* **syn** see RECEIVE — **ac·cept·ing·ly** \-ˈsep-tiŋ-lē\ *adv* — **ac·cept·ing·ness** \-iŋ-nəs\ *n*

ac·cept·able \ik-ˈsep-tə-bəl, ak-\ *adj* **1 :** capable or worthy of being accepted <no compromise would be ~> **2 a :** WELCOME, PLEASING <compliments are always ~> **b :** barely satisfactory or adequate <performances varied from excellent to ~> — **ac·cept·abil·i·ty** \ik-ˌsep-tə-ˈbil-ət-ē, (ˌ)ak-\ *n* — **ac·cept·able·ness** \ik-ˈsep-tə-bəl-nəs, ak-\ *n* — **ac·cept·ably** \-blē\ *adv*

ac·cep·tance \ik-ˈsep-tən(t)s, ak-\ *n* **1 :** the act of accepting **:** APPROVAL **2 :** the quality or state of being accepted or acceptable **3:** an agreeing either expressly or by conduct to the act or offer of another so that a contract is concluded and the parties become legally bound **4 a :** the act of accepting a time draft or bill of exchange for payment when due according to the specified terms **b :** an accepted draft or bill of exchange **5 :** ACCEPTATION 2

ac·cep·tant \-tənt\ *adj* **:** willing to accept **:** RECEPTIVE

ac·cep·ta·tion \ˌak-ˌsep-ˈtā-shən\ *n* **1 :** ACCEPTANCE; *esp* **:** favorable reception or approval **2:** a generally accepted meaning of a word or understanding of a concept **syn** see MEANING

ac·cept·ed *adj* **:** generally approved or used — **ac·cept·ed·ly** *adv*

ac·cept·er \ik-ˈsep-tər, ak-\ *n* **1:** one that accepts **2 :** ACCEPTOR 2

ac·cep·tive \ak-ˈsep-tiv\ *adj* **1 :** RECEPTIVE **2 :** ACCEPTABLE

ac·cep·tor \ik-ˈsep-tər, ak-\ *n* **1 :** ACCEPTER 1 **2 :** one that accepts an order or a bill of exchange **3 :** a compound, atom, or elementary particle capable of combining with another entity (as an atom, radical, or elementary particle) — compare DONOR 3a

[1]**ac·cess** \ˈak-ˌses\ *n* [ME, fr. MF & L; MF *acces* arrival, fr. L *accessus* approach, fr. *accessus*, pp. of *accedere* to approach — more at ACCEDE] **1 a :** ONSET 2 **b :** a fit of intense feeling **:** OUTBURST **2 a :** permission, liberty, or ability to enter, approach, communicate with, or pass to and from **b :** freedom or ability to obtain or make use of **c :** a way or means of access **d :** the action of going to or reaching **3 :** an increase by addition

[2]**access** *vt* **:** to get at **:** gain access to <accumulator and index registers can be ~*ed* by the programmer — *Datamation*>

ac·ces·si·ble \ik-ˈses-ə-bəl, ak-\ *adj* **1 :** usable for access **2 a :** capable of being reached <~ by rail> **b:** easy to get along with <~ people> **3:** capable of being influenced **:** OPEN **4:** capable of being used or seen — **ac·ces·si·bil·i·ty** \ik-ˌses-ə-ˈbil-ət-ē, ak-\ *n* — **ac·ces·si·ble·ness** \ik-ˈses-ə-bəl-nəs, ak-\ *n* — **ac·ces·si·bly** \-blē\ *adv*

[1]**ac·ces·sion** \ik-ˈsesh-ən, ak-\ *n* **1 :** something added **:** ACQUISITION **2 a :** the act of becoming joined **:** ADHERENCE **b :** the act by which one nation becomes party to an agreement already in force between other powers **3 a :** increase by something added **b :** acquisition of additional property by growth, increase, or other addition to existing property **4 :** the act of assenting or agreeing **5 a :** an act of coming near or to **:** APPROACH, ADMITTANCE **b :** the act of coming to high office or a position of honor or power **6 :** a sudden fit or outburst **:** ACCESS — **ac·ces·sion·al** \-ˈsesh-nəl, -ən-ᵊl\ *adj*

[2]**accession** *vt* **:** to record in order of acquisition

ac·ces·so·ri·al \ˌak-sə-ˈsōr-ē-əl, -ˈsȯr-\ *adj* **1 :** of or relating to an accessory <~ liability> **2 :** of, relating to, or constituting an accession **:** SUPPLEMENTARY <~ services>

ac·ces·so·rize \ik-ˈses-ə-ˌrīz, ak-\ *vb* **-rized; -riz·ing** *vt* **:** to furnish with accessories ~ *vi* **:** to wear clothing accessories

[1]**ac·ces·so·ry** *also* **ac·ces·sa·ry** \ik-ˈses-(ə-)rē, ak-\ *n, pl* **-ries** **1 a :** a thing of secondary or subordinate importance **:** ADJUNCT **b :** an object or device not essential in itself but adding to the beauty, convenience, or effectiveness of something else <auto *accessories*> <clothing *accessories*> **2 a :** a person not actually or constructively present but contributing as an assistant or instigator to the commission of an offense — called also *accessory before the fact* **b :** one who knowing that a crime has been committed aids or shelters the offender with intent to defeat justice — called also *accessory after the fact*

[2]**accessory** *adj* **1 :** aiding or contributing in a secondary way **:** SUPPLEMENTARY **2 :** assisting as a subordinate; *esp* **:** contributing to a crime but not as the chief agent **3 :** present in a minor amount and not essential as a constituent <an ~ mineral in a rock>

accessory fruit *n* **:** a fruit (as the apple) of which a conspicuous part consists of tissue other than that of the ripened ovary

accessory nerve *n* **:** either of a pair of motor nerves that are the 11th cranial nerves of higher vertebrates, arise from the medulla and the upper part of the spinal cord, and supply chiefly the pharynx and muscles of the upper chest, back, and shoulders

accessory shoe *n* **:** SHOE 5b

access road *n* **:** a road that provides access to a particular area

access time *n* **:** the time lag between the time stored information (as in a computer) is requested and the time it is delivered

ac·ciac·ca·tu·ra \(ˌ)ä-ˌchäk-ə-ˈtu̇r-ə\ *n* [It, lit., crushing] **:** a discordant note sounded with a principal note or chord and immediately released

ac·ci·dence \ˈak-səd-ən(t)s, -sə-ˌden(t)s\ *n* [L *accidentia* inflections of words, nonessential qualities, pl. of *accident-, accidens,* n.] **:** a part of grammar that deals with inflections

ac·ci·dent \ˈak-səd-ənt, -sə-ˌdent\ *n* [ME, fr. MF, fr. L *accident-, accidens* nonessential quality, chance, fr. prp. of *accidere* to happen, fr. *ad-* + *cadere* to fall — more at CHANCE] **1 a :** an event occurring by chance or arising from unknown causes **b :** lack of intention or necessity **:** CHANCE <met by ~ rather than by design> **2 a :** an unfortunate event resulting from carelessness, unawareness, ignorance, or a combination of causes **b :** an unexpected happening causing loss or injury which is not due to any fault or misconduct on the part of the person injured but from the consequences of which he may be entitled to some legal relief **3 :** a nonessential property of an entity or circumstance <the ~ of appearance> **4 :** an irregularity of a surface (as of the moon)

[1]**ac·ci·den·tal** \ˌak-sə-ˈdent-ᵊl\ *adj* **1 :** arising from extrinsic causes **:** NONESSENTIAL **2 a :** occurring unexpectedly or by chance **b :** happening without intent or through carelessness and often with unfortunate results — **ac·ci·den·tal·ly** \-ˈdent-lē, -ᵊl-ē\ *also* **ac·ci·dent·ly** \-ˈdent-lē\ *adv* — **ac·ci·den·tal·ness** \-ˈdent-ᵊl-nəs\ *n*

syn **1** ACCIDENTAL, FORTUITOUS, CONTINGENT, CASUAL *shared meaning element* **:** happening by chance **ant** planned

2 ACCIDENTAL, INCIDENTAL, ADVENTITIOUS *shared meaning element* **:** not part of the real or essential element of something **ant** essential

[2]**accidental** *n* **1 :** a nonessential property **2 a :** a chromatically altered note (as a sharp or flat) foreign to a key indicated by a signature **b :** a prefixed sign indicating an accidental

accident insurance *n* **:** insurance against loss through accidental bodily injury to the insured

accident-prone *adj* **1 :** having a greater than average number of accidents **2 :** having personality traits that predispose to accidents

ac·cip·i·ter \ak-ˈsip-ət-ər\ *n* [NL, genus name, fr. L, hawk] **:** any of a genus (*Accipiter*) of medium-sized short-winged long-legged hawks with low darting flight; *broadly* **:** a hawk (as of the family Accipitridae, the accipiter family) of similar appearance or habit of flight — **ac·cip·i·trine** \-ˈsip-ə-ˌtrīn\ *adj or n*

[1]**ac·claim** \ə-ˈklām\ *vb* [L *acclamare,* lit., to shout at, fr. *ad-* + *clamare* to shout — more at CLAIM] *vt* **1 :** APPLAUD, PRAISE **2 :** to declare by acclamation ~ *vi* **:** to shout praise or applause — **ac·claim·er** *n*

[2]**acclaim** *n* **1 :** the act of acclaiming **2 :** PRAISE, APPLAUSE

ac·cla·ma·tion \ˌak-lə-ˈmā-shən\ *n* [L *acclamation-, acclamatio,* fr. *acclamatus,* pp. of *acclamare*] **1 :** a loud eager expression of approval, praise, or assent **2 :** an overwhelming affirmative vote by cheers, shouts, or applause rather than by ballot

ac·cli·mate \ə-ˈklī-mət, ˈak-lə-ˌmāt\ *vb* **-mat·ed; -mat·ing** [F *acclimater,* fr. *a-* (fr. L *ad-*) + *climat* climate] **:** ACCLIMATIZE

ac·cli·ma·tion \ˌak-ˌlī-ˈmā-shən, -lə-\ *n* **:** acclimatization esp. under controlled (as laboratory) conditions

ac·cli·ma·ti·za·tion \ə-ˌklī-mət-ə-ˈzā-shən\ *n* **:** the process or result of acclimatizing

ac·cli·ma·tize \ə-ˈklī-mə-ˌtīz\ *vb* **-tized; -tiz·ing** *vt* **:** to adapt to a new temperature, altitude, climate, environment, or situation ~ *vi* **:** to become acclimatized — **ac·cli·ma·tiz·er** *n*

ac·cliv·i·ty \ə-ˈkliv-ət-ē, a-\ *n, pl* **-ties** [L *acclivitas,* fr. *acclivis* ascending, fr. *ad-* + *clivus* slope — more at DECLIVITY] **:** an ascending slope (as of a hill)

ac·co·lade \ˈak-ə-ˌlād\ *n* [F, fr. *accoler* to embrace, fr. (assumed) VL *accollare,* fr. L *ad-* + *collum* neck — more at COLLAR] **1 :** a ceremonial embrace **2 a :** a ceremony or salute to mark the conferring of knighthood **b :** a ceremony marking the recognition of special merit **3 a :** a mark of acknowledgment **:** AWARD **b :** an expression of praise **4 :** a brace or a line used in music to join two or more staffs carrying simultaneous parts

ac·com·mo·date \ə-ˈkäm-ə-ˌdāt\ *vb* **-dat·ed; -dat·ing** [L *accommodatus,* pp. of *accommodare,* fr. *ad-* + *commodare* to make fit, fr. *commodus* suitable — more at COMMODE] *vt* **1 :** to make fit, suitable, or congruous **2 :** to bring into agreement or concord **:** RECONCILE **3 :** to furnish with something desired, needed, or suited: **a :** to grant a loan to esp. without security **b :** to provide with lodgings **:** HOUSE **4 a :** to make room for **b :** to hold without crowding or inconvenience **5 :** to give consideration to **:** allow for <~ the special interests of various groups> ~ *vi* **:** to adapt oneself; *also* **:** to undergo visual accommodation **syn 1** see ADAPT **ant** constrain **2** see OBLIGE **ant** incommode — **ac·com·mo·da·tive** \-ˌdāt-iv\ *adj* — **ac·com·mo·da·tive·ness** *n*

ac·com·mo·dat·ing *adj* **:** HELPFUL, OBLIGING — **ac·com·mo·dat·ing·ly** \-ˌdāt-iŋ-lē\ *adv*

ac·com·mo·da·tion \ə-ˌkäm-ə-ˈdā-shən\ *n* **1 :** something supplied for convenience or to satisfy a need: as **a :** lodging, food, and services or seat, berth, or other space occupied together with services available — usu. used in pl. <tourist ~*s* on the boat> <overnight ~*s*> **b :** a public conveyance (as a train) that stops at all or nearly all points **c :** LOAN **2 :** the act of accommodating **:** the state of being accommodated: as **a :** the provision of what is needed or desired for convenience **b :** ADAPTATION, ADJUSTMENT **c :** an adjustment of differences **:** SETTLEMENT **d :** the automatic adjustment of the eye for seeing at different distances effected chiefly by changes in the convexity of the crystalline lens; *also* **:** the range over which such adjustment is possible — **ac·com·mo·da·tion·al** \-shnəl, -shən-ᵊl\ *adj*

accommodation ladder *n* **:** a light ladder or stairway hung over the side of a ship for ascending from or descending to small boats

accommodation paper *n* **:** a bill, draft, or note made, drawn, accepted, or endorsed by one person for another without consideration to enable that other to raise money or obtain credit

ac·com·mo·da·tor \ə-ˈkäm-ə-ˌdāt-ər\ *n* **:** one that accommodates; *esp* **:** a part-time or special-occasion domestic worker

ac·com·pa·ni·ment \ə-ˈkəmp-(ə-)nē-mənt\ *n* **1 :** a subordinate instrumental or vocal part designed to support or complement a principal voice or instrument **2 a :** an addition (as an ornament)

intended to give completeness or symmetry : COMPLEMENT **b** : an accompanying situation or occurence : CONCOMITANT
ac·com·pa·nist \ə-ˈkəmp-(ə-)nəst\ *n* : one (as a pianist) who plays an accompaniment
ac·com·pa·ny \ə-ˈkəmp-(ə-)nē\ *vb* **-nied; -ny·ing** [ME *accompanien,* fr. MF *acompaignier,* fr. *a-* (fr. L *ad-*) + *compaing* companion, fr. LL *companio*] *vt* **1 :** to go with or attend as an associate or companion **2 :** to perform an accompaniment to or for **3 a :** to cause to be in association : add or join to <*accompanied* his advice with a warning> **b :** to be in association with <the pictures that ~ the text> ~ *vi* : to perform an accompaniment
syn ACCOMPANY, ATTEND, ESCORT *shared meaning element* **:** to go along with
ac·com·plice \ə-ˈkäm-pləs, -ˈkəm-\ *n* [alter. (fr. incorrect division of *a complice*) of *complice*] **:** one associated with another esp. in wrongdoing
ac·com·plish \ə-ˈkäm-plish, -ˈkəm-\ *vt* [ME *accomplisshen,* fr. MF *acompliss-,* stem of *acomplir,* fr. (assumed) VL *accomplēre,* fr. L *ad-* + *complēre* to fill up — more at COMPLETE] **1 :** to bring to a successful conclusion : carry to completion <when they had ~*ed* their journey> <I hope to ~ much more today> **2 :** to attain to (a measure of time or distance) : COVER <at that rate will ~ only half the distance> **3** *archaic* **a :** to equip thoroughly **b :** PERFECT ***syn*** see PERFORM — **ac·com·plish·able** \-ə-bəl\ *adj* — **ac·com·plish·er** *n*
ac·com·plished *adj* **1 :** COMPLETED, EFFECTED <an ~ fact> **2 a :** complete in acquirements as the result of practice or training <an ~ dancer> **b :** having many social accomplishments
ac·com·plish·ment \ə-ˈkäm-plish-mənt, -ˈkəm-\ *n* **1 :** the act of accomplishing : COMPLETION **2 :** something accomplished : ACHIEVEMENT **3 a :** a quality or ability equipping one for society **b:** a special skill or ability acquired by training or practice
[1]**ac·cord** \ə-ˈkȯ(ə)rd\ *vb* [ME *accorden,* fr. OF *acorder,* fr. (assumed) VL *accordare,* fr. L *ad-* + *cord-, cor* heart — more at HEART] *vt* **1 :** to bring into agreement : RECONCILE **2 a :** to grant as suitable or proper **b :** to allow as a concession **c :** to confer something on as an award **d :** to assign as a portion ~ *vi* **1** *archaic* **:** to arrive at an agreement **2** *obs* **:** to give consent **3 :** to exhibit perfect fitness in a relationship or association : adjust or fit harmoniously ***syn*** **1** see AGREE ***ant*** conflict **2** see GRANT ***ant*** withhold
[2]**accord** *n* [ME, fr. OF *acort,* fr. *acorder*] **1 a :** AGREEMENT, CONFORMITY <acted in ~ with the company's policy> **b :** a formal act of agreement : TREATY **2 :** balanced interrelationship : HARMONY **3** *obs* **:** ASSENT **4 :** voluntary or spontaneous impulse to act <gave generously of their own ~>
ac·cor·dance \ə-ˈkȯrd-ᵊn(t)s\ *n* **1 :** AGREEMENT, CONFORMITY <in ~ with a rule> **2 :** the act of granting
ac·cor·dant \-ᵊnt\ *adj* **1 :** CONSONANT, AGREEING **2 :** HARMONIOUS, CORRESPONDENT — **ac·cor·dant·ly** *adv*
ac·cord·ing as *conj* **1 :** in accord with the way in which **2 a :** depending on how **b :** depending on whether : IF
ac·cord·ing·ly \ə-ˈkȯrd-iŋ-lē\ *adv* **1 :** in accordance : CORRESPONDINGLY **2 :** CONSEQUENTLY, SO
according to *prep* **1 :** in conformity with **2 :** as stated or attested by **3 :** depending on
[1]**ac·cor·di·on** \ə-ˈkȯrd-ē-ən\ *n* [G *akkordion,* fr. *akkord* chord, fr. F *accord,* fr. OF *acort*] **:** a portable keyboard wind instrument in which the wind is forced past free reeds by means of a hand-operated bellows — **ac·cor·di·on·ist** \-ē-ə-nəst\ *n*

accordion

[2]**accordion** *adj* **:** folding or creased or hinged to fold like an accordion <an ~ pleat> <an ~ door>
ac·cost \ə-ˈkȯst, -ˈkäst\ *vt* [MF *accoster,* deriv. of L *ad-* + *costa* rib, side — more at COAST] **:** to approach and speak to often in a challenging or aggressive way
ac·couche·ment \ˌa-ˌküsh-ˈmä^n, ə-ˈküsh-ˌ\ *n* [F] **:** LYING-IN; *esp* **:** PARTURITION
ac·cou·cheur \ˌa-ˌkü-ˈshər\ *n* [F] **:** one that assists at a birth <without President Truman as ~ there would have been no Israel —B. C. Crum>; *esp* **:** OBSTETRICIAN
[1]**ac·count** \ə-ˈkaůnt\ *n* **1** *archaic* **:** RECKONING, COMPUTATION **2 a :** a record of debit and credit entries chronologically posted to a ledger page to cover transactions involving a particular item or a particular person or concern **b :** a statement of transactions during a fiscal period **3 :** a collection of items to be balanced — usu. used in pl. **4 :** a statement explaining one's conduct **5 a :** a periodically rendered calculation listing charged purchases and credits <a grocery ~> **b :** the patronage involved in establishing or maintaining an account : BUSINESS<glad to get that customer's ~> **6 a :** VALUE, IMPORTANCE <a man of no ~> **b :** ESTEEM, JUDGMENT <he stands high in their ~> **7 :** PROFIT, ADVANTAGE <turned his wit to good ~> **8 a :** a statement or exposition of reasons, causes, grounds, or motives <no satisfactory ~ of these phenomena> **b :** a reason for an action : BASIS <on all ~*s* you must do it> **c :** careful thought : CONSIDERATION <left nothing out of ~> **9 :** a statement of facts or events : RELATION <a newspaper ~> **10 :** HEARSAY, REPORT — usu. used in pl. <by all ~*s* a rich man> **11 :** a sum of money or its equivalent deposited in the common cash of a bank and subject to withdrawal by the depositor — **on account of :** for the sake of : by reason of : because of — **on no account :** under no circumstances — **on one's own account 1 :** on one's own behalf **2 :** at one's own risk **3 :** by oneself : on one's own
[2]**account** *vb* [ME *accounten,* fr. MF *acompter,* fr. *a-* (fr. L *ad-*) + *compter* to count] *vt* **1 :** to probe into : ANALYZE **2 :** to think of as : CONSIDER <~*s* himself lucky> ~ *vi* **1 :** to furnish a justifying analysis or explanation — used with *for* **2 a :** to be the sole or primary factor — used with *for* **b :** to bring about the capture, death, or destruction of something <~*ed* for two rabbits>
ac·count·able \ə-ˈkaůnt-ə-bəl\ *adj* **1 :** subject to giving an account : ANSWERABLE **2 :** capable of being accounted for : EXPLAINABLE — **ac·count·abil·i·ty** \-ˌkaůnt-ə-ˈbil-ət-ē\ *n* — **ac·count·able·ness** \-ˈkaůnt-ə-bəl-nəs\ *n* — **ac·count·ably** \-blē\ *adv*
ac·coun·tan·cy \ə-ˈkaůnt-ᵊn-sē\ *n* **:** the profession or practice of accounting
ac·coun·tant \ə-ˈkaůnt-ᵊnt\ *n* **1 :** one that gives an account or is accountable **2 :** one who is skilled in the practice of accounting or who is in charge of public or private accounts — **ac·coun·tant·ship** \-ᵊn(t)-ˌship\ *n*
account book *n* **:** a book in which accounts are kept : LEDGER
account executive *n* **:** a business executive (as in an advertising agency) responsible for the management of a client's account
ac·count·ing \ə-ˈkaůnt-iŋ\ *n* **1 :** the system of recording and summarizing business and financial transactions in books and analyzing, verifying, and reporting the results; *also* **:** the principles and procedures of accounting **2 a :** practical application of accounting **b :** an instance of applying the principles and procedures of accounting
accounting machine *n* **:** a business machine that is key-operated or uses stored data (as punch cards) and that tabulates, adds, subtracts, or totals
account payable *n, pl* **accounts payable :** the balance due to a creditor on a current account
account receivable *n, pl* **accounts receivable :** a balance due from a debtor on a current account
ac·cou·tre *or* **ac·cou·ter** \ə-ˈküt-ər\ *vt* **-cou·tred** *or* **-cou·tered; -cou·tring** *or* **-cou·ter·ing** \-ˈküt-ə-riŋ, -ˈkü-triŋ\ [F *accoutrer,* fr. MF *acoustrer,* fr. *a-* + *costure* seam, fr. (assumed) VL *consutura,* fr. L *consutus,* pp. of *consuere* to sew together, fr. *com-* + *suere* to sew — more at SEW] **:** to provide with equipment or furnishings : OUTFIT ***syn*** see FURNISH
ac·cou·tre·ment *or* **ac·cou·ter·ment** \ə-ˈkü-trə-mənt, -ˈküt-ər-mənt\ *n* **1 :** the act of accoutering : the state of being accoutered **2 a :** an article of equipment or dress esp. when used as an accessory **b:** EQUIPMENT, TRAPPINGS; *specif* **:** a soldier's outfit usu. not including clothes and weapons — usu. used in pl. **3 :** an identifying and often superficial characteristic
ac·cred·it \ə-ˈkred-ət\ *vt* [F *accréditer,* fr. *ad-* + *crédit* credit] **1 :** to consider or recognize as outstanding **2 :** to give official authorization to or approval of: **a :** to provide with credentials; *esp* **:** to send (an envoy) with letters of authorization **b :** to recognize or vouch for as conforming with a standard **c :** to recognize (an educational institution) as maintaining standards that qualify the graduates for admission to higher or more specialized institutions or for professional practice **3 :** CREDIT ***syn*** see APPROVE — **ac·cred·i·table** \-ə-bəl\ *adj* — **ac·cred·i·ta·tion** \ə-ˌkred-ə-ˈtā-shən\ *n*
ac·crete \ə-ˈkrēt\ *vb* **ac·cret·ed; ac·cret·ing** [back-formation fr. *accretion*] *vi* **:** to grow or become attached by accretion ~ *vt* **:** to cause to adhere or become attached : ACCUMULATE
ac·cre·tion \ə-ˈkrē-shən\ *n* [L *accretion-, accretio,* fr. *accretus,* pp. of *accrescere* — more at ACCRUE] **1 :** the process of growth or enlargement: as **a :** increase by external addition or accumulation (as by adhesion of external parts or particles) **b :** the increase of land by the gradual or imperceptible action of natural forces **2 :** a product of accretion; *esp* **:** an extraneous addition <~*s* of grime> **3 :** coherence of separate particles : CONCRETION — **ac·cre·tion·ary** \-shə-ˌner-ē\ *adj* — **ac·cre·tive** \ə-ˈkrēt-iv\ *adj*
ac·cru·al \ə-ˈkrü-əl\ *n* **1 :** the action or process of accruing **2 :** something that accrues or has accrued
ac·crue \ə-ˈkrü\ *vb* **ac·crued; ac·cru·ing** [ME *acreuen,* prob. fr. MF *acreue* increase, fr. *acreistre* to increase, fr. L *accescere,* fr. *ad-* + *crescere* to grow — more at CRESCENT] *vi* **1 :** to come into existence as a legally enforceable claim **2 :** to come by way of increase or addition : arise as a growth or a result **3 :** to be periodically accumulated whether as an increase or a decrease ~ *vt* **:** COLLECT, ACCUMULATE — **ac·cru·able** \-ˈkrü-ə-bəl\ *adj* — **ac·crue·ment** \-ˈkrü-mənt\ *n*
acct *abbr* account; accountant
ac·cul·tur·ate \ə-ˈkəl-chə-ˌrāt\ *vt* **-at·ed; -at·ing** [back-formation fr. *acculturation*] **:** to change through acculturation
ac·cul·tur·a·tion \ə-ˌkəl-chə-ˈrā-shən\ *n* **1 :** a process of intercultural borrowing between diverse peoples resulting in new and blended patterns; *esp* **:** modifications in a primitive culture resulting from contact with an advanced society **2 :** the process beginning at infancy by which a human being acquires the culture of his society — **ac·cul·tur·a·tion·al** \-shnəl, -shən-ᵊl\ *adj* — **ac·cul·tur·a·tive** \ə-ˈkəl-chə-ˌrāt-iv\ *adj*
ac·cu·mu·late \ə-ˈkyü-myə-ˌlāt\ *vb* **-lat·ed; -lat·ing** [L *accumulatus,* pp. of *accumulare,* fr. *ad-* + *cumulare* to heap up — more at CUMULATE] *vt* **1 :** to heap or pile up : AMASS <~ a fortune> **2 :** COLLECT, GATHER <a composer *accumulating* one award after another> ~ *vi* **:** to increase in quantity or number
ac·cu·mu·la·tion \ə-ˌkyü-myə-ˈlā-shən\ *n* **1 :** the action or process of accumulating : the state of being or having accumulated **2 :** increase or growth by addition esp. when continuous or repeated <~ of interest> **3 :** something that has accumulated or has been accumulated
ac·cu·mu·la·tive \ə-ˈkyü-myə-ˌlāt-iv, -lət-\ *adj* **1 :** CUMULATIVE <an age of rapid and ~ change> **2 :** tending or given to accumulation — **ac·cu·mu·la·tive·ly** *adv* — **ac·cu·mu·la·tive·ness** *n*
ac·cu·mu·la·tor \ə-ˈkyü-myə-ˌlāt-ər\ *n* **:** one that accumulates: as **a :** SHOCK ABSORBER **b** *Brit* **:** STORAGE CELL **c :** a part (as in a computer) where numbers are totaled or stored

ac·cu·ra·cy \ˈak-yə-rə-sē\ *n, pl* **-cies** **1 :** freedom from mistake or error : CORRECTNESS **2 a :** conformity to truth or to a standard or model : EXACTNESS **b :** degree of conformity of a measure to a standard or a true value

ac·cu·rate \ˈak-yə-rət\ *adj* [L *accuratus,* fr. pp. of *accurare* to take care of, fr. *ad-* + *cura* care — more at CURE] **1 :** free from error esp. as the result of care <~ methods> **2 :** conforming exactly to truth or to a standard : EXACT <~ instruments> ***syn*** see CORRECT ***ant*** inaccurate — **ac·cu·rate·ly** \-yə-rət-lē, -yərt-\ *adv* — **ac·cu·rate·ness** \-yə-nət-nəs\ *n*

ac·cursed \ə-ˈkərst, -ˈkər-səd\ *or* **ac·curst** \ə-ˈkərst\ *adj* [ME *acursed,* fr. pp. of *acursen* to consign to destruction with a curse, fr. *a-* (fr. OE *ā,* perfective prefix) + *cursen* to curse — more at ABIDE] **1 :** being under a curse **2 :** DAMNABLE, DETESTABLE — **ac·curs·ed·ly** \-ˈkər-səd-lē\ *adv* — **ac·curs·ed·ness** \-ˈkər-səd-nəs\ *n*

accus *abbr* accusative

ac·cus·al \ə-ˈkyü-zəl\ *n* : ACCUSATION

ac·cu·sa·tion \ˌak-yə-ˈzā-shən\ *n* **1 :** the act of accusing : the state or fact of being accused **2 :** a charge of wrongdoing : ALLEGATION

[1]ac·cu·sa·tive \ə-ˈkyü-zət-iv\ *adj* [ME, fr. MF or L; MF *accusatif,* fr. L *accusativus,* fr. *accusatus,* pp. of *accusare*] **1 :** of, relating to, or being the grammatical case that marks the direct object of a verb or the object of any of several prepositions **2 :** ACCUSATORY

[2]accusative *n* **:** the accusative case of a language : a form in the accusative case

ac·cu·sa·to·ry \ə-ˈkyü-zə-ˌtōr-ē, -ˌtȯr-\ *adj* **:** containing or expressing accusation : ACCUSING

ac·cuse \ə-ˈkyüz\ *vb* **ac·cused; ac·cus·ing** [ME *accusen,* fr. OF *acuser,* fr. L *accusare* to call to account, fr. *ad-* + *causa* lawsuit, cause] *vt* **1 :** to charge with a fault or offense : BLAME **2 :** to charge with an offense judicially or by a public process ~ *vi* **:** to bring an accusation — **ac·cus·er** \ə-ˈkyü-zər\ *n* — **ac·cus·ing·ly** \-ˈkyü-ziŋ-lē\ *adv*

ac·cused *n, pl* **accused :** one charged with an offense; *esp* **:** the defendant in a criminal case

ac·cus·tom \ə-ˈkəs-təm\ *vt* [ME *accustomen,* fr. MF *acostumer,* fr. *a-* (fr. L *ad-*) + *costume* custom] **:** to make familiar through use or experience : HABITUATE — **ac·cus·tom·ation** \-ˌkəs-tə-ˈmā-shən\ *n*

ac·cus·tomed \ə-ˈkəs-təmd\ *adj* **1 :** familiar through use or experience : often used or practiced <her ~ cheerfulness> **2 :** being in the habit or custom <~ to making decisions> ***syn*** see USUAL ***ant*** unaccustomed — **ac·cus·tomed·ness** \-təm(d)-nəs\ *n*

[1]ace \ˈās\ *n* [ME *as,* fr. OF, fr. L, unit, a copper coin] **1 a :** a die face marked with one spot **b :** a playing card marked in its center with one large pip **c :** a domino end marked with one spot **2 :** a very small amount or degree : PARTICLE **3 :** a score made by a single stroke; *specif* **:** a point scored on a shot (as a service in tennis or handball) that an opponent fails to touch **4 :** a golf score of one stroke on a hole; *also* **:** a hole made in one stroke **5 :** a combat pilot who has brought down at least five enemy airplanes **6 :** one that excels at something — **ace in the hole 1 :** an ace dealt face down to a player (as in stud poker) and not exposed until the showdown **2 :** an effective and decisive argument or resource held in reserve — **within an ace of :** on the point of : very near to <came *within an ace of* winning>

[2]ace *vt* **aced; ac·ing 1 :** to score an ace against (an opponent) **2 :** to make (a hole in golf) in one stroke

[3]ace *adj* **:** of first or high rank or quality

ACE *abbr* American Council on Education

-a·ce·ae \ˈā-sē-ˌē\ *n pl suffix* [NL, fr. L, fem. pl. of *-aceus* -aceous] **:** plants of the nature of <Ros*aceae*> — in names of families of plants; formerly in names of orders of plants

ace·dia \ə-ˈsēd-ē-ə\ *n* [LL, fr. Gk *akēdeia,* fr. *a-* + *kēdos* care, grief — more at HATE] **:** APATHY, BOREDOM

acel·da·ma \ə-ˈsel-də-mə\ *n* [fr. *Aceldama,* field bought by Judas with the money received for betraying Christ (Acts 1:18–19), fr. Gk *Akeldama,* fr. Aram *ḥaqēl dĕmā,* lit., field of blood] **1 :** a place of bloodshed **2 :** a place associated with evil

acel·lu·lar \(ˈ)ā-ˈsel-yə-lər\ *adj* **:** containing no cells : not divided into cells

acen·tric \(ˈ)ā-ˈsen-trik\ *adj* **:** lacking a centromere <~ chromosomes>

-a·ceous \ˈā-shəs\ *adj suffix* [L *-aceus*] **1 a :** characterized by : full of <set*aceous*> **b :** consisting of <carbon*aceous*> : having the nature or form of <tuff*aceous*> **2 a :** of or relating to a group of animals typified by (such) a form <cet*aceous*> or characterized by (such) a feature <crust*aceous*> **b :** of or relating to a plant family typified by (such) a genus <ros*aceous*>

aceph·a·lous \(ˈ)ā-ˈsef-ə-ləs, ə-ˈsef-\ *adj* [Gk *akephalos,* fr. *a-* + *kephalē* head — more at CEPHALIC] **1 :** lacking a head or having the head reduced **2 :** lacking a governing head or chief

ace·quia \ə-ˈsä-kē-ə, ä-\ *n* [Sp, fr. Ar *as-sāqiyah* the irrigation stream] *Southwest* **:** an irrigation ditch or canal

acerb \ə-ˈsərb, a-\ *adj* [F or L; F *acerbe,* fr. L *acerbus,* fr. *acer*] **:** acid in temper, mood, or tone

ac·er·bate \ˈas-ər-ˌbāt\ *vt* **-bat·ed; -bat·ing :** IRRITATE, EXASPERATE

acer·bic \ə-ˈsər-bik\ *adj* **:** ACERB — **acer·bi·cal·ly** \-bi-k(ə-)lē\ *adv*

acer·bi·ty \ə-ˈsər-bət-ē\ *n, pl* **-ties :** acidity of manner or mood ***syn*** see ACRIMONY ***ant*** mellowness

ac·er·o·la \ˌas-ə-ˈrō-lə\ *n* [Amer Sp, fr. Sp, fruit of a shrub (*Crataegus azarolus*), fr. Ar *az-zuʿrūr*] **:** a West Indian shrub (genus *Malpighia*) with mildly acid cherrylike fruits very rich in vitamin C

ac·er·ose \ˈas-ə-ˌrōs\ *adj* [L *acer* sharp — more at EDGE] **:** shaped like a needle <~ leaves>

acer·vate \ə-ˈsər-vət, ˈas-ər-ˌvāt\ *adj* [L *acervatus,* pp. of *acervare* to heap up, fr. *acervus* heap] **:** growing in heaps or closely compacted clusters — **acer·vate·ly** *adv* — **ac·er·va·tion** \ˌas-ər-ˈvā-shən\ *n*

acet- *or* **aceto-** *comb form* [F & L; F *acét-,* fr. L *acet-,* fr. *acetum*] **:** acetic acid : acetic <*acet*yl>

ac·e·tab·u·lar·ia \ˌas-ə-ˌtab-yə-ˈlar-ē-ə, -ˈler-\ *n* [NL, genus name, fr. L *acetabulum* vinegar cup] **:** a large single-celled green alga (genus *Acetabularia*) of warm seas that resembles a small mushroom in form

ac·e·tab·u·lum \-ˈtab-yə-ləm\ *n, pl* **-lums** *or* **-la** \-lə\ [L, lit., vinegar cup, fr. *acetum* vinegar] **1 a :** the cup-shaped socket in the hipbone **b :** the cavity by which the leg of an insect articulates with the body **2 :** a sucker of an invertebrate (as a trematode or leech) — **ac·e·tab·u·lar** \-lər\ *adj*

ac·e·tal \ˈas-ə-ˌtal\ *n* [G *azetal,* fr. *azet-* acet- + *al*kohol alcohol] **:** any of various compounds characterized by the grouping $C(OR)_2$ and obtained esp. by heating aldehydes or ketones with alcohols

ac·et·al·de·hyde \ˌas-ə-ˈtal-də-ˌhīd\ *n* [ISV] **:** a colorless volatile water-soluble liquid aldehyde C_2H_4O used chiefly in organic synthesis

acet·amide \ə-ˈset-ə-ˌmīd, ˌas-ət-ˈam-ˌīd\ *n* [G *azetamid,* fr. *azet-* + *amid* amide] **:** a white crystalline amide C_2H_5NO of acetic acid used esp. as a solvent and in organic synthesis

ac·et·amin·o·phen \ˌas-ət-ə-ˈmin-ə-fən\ *n* [*acet-* + *amino-* + *phen*ol] **:** a crystalline compound $C_8H_9NO_2$ that is a hydroxy derivative of acetanilide and is used in chemical synthesis and in medicine to relieve pain and fever

ac·et·an·i·lide *or* **ac·et·an·i·lid** \ˌas-ə-ˈtan-ᵊl-ˌīd, -ᵊl-əd\ *n* [ISV] **:** a white crystalline compound C_8H_9NO that is derived from aniline and acetic acid and is used esp. to check pain or fever

ac·e·tate \ˈas-ə-ˌtāt\ *n* **1 :** a salt or ester of acetic acid **2 :** cellulose acetate or one of its products **3 :** a phonograph recording disk made of an acetate or coated with cellulose acetate

ace·tic \ə-ˈsēt-ik\ *adj* [prob. fr. F *acétique,* fr. L *acetum* vinegar, fr. *acēre* to be sour, fr. *acer* sharp — more at EDGE] **:** of, relating to, or producing acetic acid or vinegar

acetic acid *n* **:** a colorless pungent liquid acid $C_2H_4O_2$ that is the chief acid of vinegar and that is used esp. in synthesis (as of plastics)

ace·ti·fy \ə-ˈsēt-ə-ˌfī, -ˈset-\ *vt* **-fied; -fy·ing :** to turn into acetic acid or vinegar — **ace·ti·fi·ca·tion** \-ˌsēt-ə-fə-ˈkā-shən, -ˌset-\ *n* — **ace·ti·fi·er** \ˈsēt-ə-ˌfī(-ə)r, -ˈset-\ *n*

ace·to·ace·tic acid \ˌas-ə-tō-ə-ˌsēt-ik-, ə-ˌsēt-ō-\ *n* [part trans. of G *azetessigsäure,* fr. *azet-* acet- + *essigsäure* acetic acid] **:** an unstable acid $C_4H_6O_3$ found in abnormal urine

ac·e·tone \ˈas-ə-ˌtōn\ *n* [G *azeton,* fr. L *acetum*] **:** a volatile fragrant flammable liquid ketone C_3H_6O used chiefly as a solvent and in organic synthesis and found abnormally in urine — **ac·e·ton·ic** \ˌas-ə-ˈtän-ik\ *adj*

ac·e·to·phe·net·i·din \ˌas-ə-ˌtō-fə-ˈnet-əd-ən, ə-ˌsēt-ō-\ *n* [ISV] **:** a white crystalline compound $C_{10}H_{13}NO_2$ that is used to ease pain or fever

ace·tous \ə-ˈsēt-əs\ *adj* **:** relating to or producing vinegar; *also* **:** SOUR, VINEGARY

ace·tyl \ə-ˈsēt-ᵊl, ˈas-ət-\ *n* **:** the radical CH_3CO of acetic acid

acet·y·late \ə-ˈset-ᵊl-ˌāt\ *vt* **-lat·ed; -lat·ing :** to introduce the acetyl radical into (a compound) — **acet·y·la·tion** \-ˌset-ᵊl-ˈā-shən\ *n* — **acet·y·la·tive** \-ˈset-ᵊl-ˌāt-iv\ *adj*

ace·tyl·cho·line \ə-ˌsēt-ᵊl-ˈkō-ˌlēn\ *n* [ISV] **:** a compound $C_7H_{17}NO_3$ released at autonomic nerve endings, active in the transmission of the nerve impulse, and formed enzymatically in the tissues from choline — **ace·tyl·cho·lin·ic** \-kō-ˈlin-ik\ *adj*

ace·tyl·cho·lin·es·ter·ase \-ˌkō-lə-ˈnes-tə-ˌrās, -ˌrāz\ *n* [*acetylcholine* + *esterase*] **:** an enzyme that promotes the hydrolysis of acetylcholine

ace·tyl-coA \ə-ˌsēt-ᵊl-ˌkō-ˈā\ *n* **:** ACETYL COENZYME A

acetyl coenzyme A *n* **:** a compound $C_{25}H_{38}N_7O_{17}P_3S$ formed as an intermediate in metabolism and active as a coenzyme in biological acetylations

acet·y·lene \ə-ˈset-ᵊl-ən, -ᵊl-ˌēn\ *n* **:** a colorless gaseous hydrocarbon $HC{\equiv}CH$ made esp. by the action of water on calcium carbide and used chiefly in organic synthesis and as a fuel (as in welding and soldering) — **acet·y·le·nic** \ə-ˌset-ᵊl-ˈē-nik, -ˈen-ik\ *adj*

ace·tyl·sa·lic·y·late \ə-ˌsēt-ᵊl-sə-ˈlis-ə-ˌlāt\ *n* **:** a salt or ester of acetylsalicylic acid

ace·tyl·sal·i·cyl·ic acid \ə-ˈsēt-ᵊl-ˌsal-ə-ˌsil-ik-\ *n* [ISV] **:** ASPIRIN 1

Acha·tes \ə-ˈkāt-ēz\ *n* [L] **1 :** a faithful companion of Aeneas in Vergil's *Aeneid* **2 :** a faithful friend

[1]ache \ˈāk\ *vi* **ached; ach·ing** [ME *aken,* fr. OE *acan;* akin to LG *äken* to hurt] **1 a :** to suffer a usu. dull persistent pain **b :** to become distressed or disturbed (as with anxiety or regret) **c :** to feel compassion **2 :** to become filled with painful yearning — **ach·ing·ly** \ˈā-kiŋ-lē\ *adv*

[2]ache *n* **1 :** a usu. dull persistent pain **2 :** a condition marked by aching

achene \ə-ˈkēn\ *n* [NL *achaenium,* fr. *a-* + Gk *chainein* to yawn — more at YAWN] **:** a small dry indehiscent one-seeded fruit developing from a simple ovary and usu. having a thin pericarp attached to the seed at only one point — **ache·ni·al** \ə-ˈkē-nē-əl\ *adj*

Ach·er·on \ˈak-ə-ˌrän, -rən\ *n* [Gk *Acherōn*] **:** a river in Hades

Acheu·le·an *or* **Acheu·li·an** \ə-ˈshü-lē-ən\ *adj* [F *Acheuléen,* fr. St. *Acheul,* near Amiens, France] **:** of or relating to a lower Paleolithic culture characterized by bifacial tools with round cutting edges

à che·val \ˌäsh-ə-ˈväl\ *adv* [F, lit., on horseback] **1 :** with a leg on each side : ASTRIDE **2 :** in such a way as to straddle a line on the layout of a game of chance (as roulette) or be split between two numbers, cards, or events

achieve \ə-ˈchēv\ *vb* **achieved; achiev·ing** [ME *acheven,* fr. MF *achever* to finish, fr. *a-* (fr. L *ad-*) + *chief* end, head — more at CHIEF] *vt* **1** : to carry out successfully : ACCOMPLISH <~ a low unemployment rate> **2** : to get as the result of exertion : WIN <~ greatness> ~ *vi* : to attain a desired end or aim ***syn*** see PERFORM, REACH — **achiev·able** \-ˈchē-və-bəl\ *adj* — **achiev·er** *n*

achieve·ment \ə-ˈchēv-mənt\ *n* **1** : the act of achieving : successful completion : ACCOMPLISHMENT **2 a** : a result brought about by resolve, persistence, or endeavor **b** : a great or heroic deed **3** : the quality and quantity of a student's work ***syn*** see FEAT

Achil·les \ə-ˈkil-ēz\ *n* [L, fr. Gk *Achilleus*] : the greatest warrior among the Greeks at Troy and slayer of Hector

Achilles' heel *n* [fr. the story that Achilles was vulnerable only in the heel] : a vulnerable point

Achilles tendon *n* : the strong tendon joining the muscles in the calf of the leg to the bone of the heel

achla·myd·e·ous \ˌak-lə-ˈmid-ē-əs, ˌā-klə-\ *adj* [*a-* + Gk *chlamyd-, chlamys* mantle] : lacking both calyx and corolla

achlor·hyd·ria \ˌā-ˌklōr-ˈhid-rē-ə, -ˌklȯr-\ *n* [NL, fr. *a-* + *chlor*ine + *hydr*ogen] absence of hydrochloric acid from the gastric juice — **achlor·hy·dric** \-ˈhid-rik, -ˈhī-drik\ *adj*

achon·drite \(ˈ)ā-ˈkän-ˌdrīt\ *n* : a stony meteorite without rounded grains — **achon·drit·ic** \ˌā-ˌkän-ˈdrit-ik\ *adj*

achon·dro·pla·sia \ˌā-ˌkän-drə-ˈplā-zh(ē-)ə\ *n* [NL] : failure of normal development of cartilage resulting in dwarfism — **achon·dro·plas·tic** \-ˈplas-tik\ *adj*

ach·ro·mat \ˈak-rə-ˌmat\ *n* : ACHROMATIC LENS

achromat- *or* **achromato-** *comb form* [Gk *achrōmatos* colorless, fr. *a-* + *chrōmat-, chrōma* color — more at CHROMATIC] : achromatic <*achromatism*>

ach·ro·mat·ic \ˌak-rə-ˈmat-ik\ *adj* **1** : refracting light without dispersing into its constituent colors : giving images practically free from extraneous colors <an ~ telescope> **2** : not readily colored by the usual staining agents **3** : possessing no hue : being black, gray, or white : NEUTRAL **4** : being without accidentals or modulation : DIATONIC — **ach·ro·mat·i·cal·ly** \-i-k(ə-)lē\ *adv* — **ach·ro·ma·tic·i·ty** \ˌak-rō-mə-ˈtis-ət-ē\ *n* — **achro·ma·tize** \(ˈ)ā-ˈkrō-mə-ˌtīz, a-\ *vt*

achromatic lens *n* : a lens made by combining lenses of different glasses having different focal powers so that the light emerging from the lens forms an image practically free from unwanted colors

CROWN GLASS
FLINT GLASS
achromatic lens

achro·ma·tism \(ˈ)ā-ˈkrō-mə-ˌtiz-əm, a-\ *n* : the quality or state of being achromatic

achy \ˈā-kē\ *adj* **ach·i·er; ach·i·est** : afflicted with aches — **ach·i·ness** *n*

acic·u·la \ə-ˈsik-yə-lə\ *n, pl* **-lae** \-ˌlē\ *or* **-las** [NL, fr. LL, ornamental pin — more at AGLET] : a needlelike spine, bristle, or crystal — **acic·u·lar** \-lər\ *adj* — **acic·u·late** \-lət, -ˌlāt\ *adj*

¹ac·id \ˈas-əd\ *adj* [F or L; F *acide,* fr. L *acidus,* fr. *acēre* to be sour — more at ACETIC] **1 a** : sour, sharp, or biting to the taste **b** : sharp, biting, or sour in manner, disposition, or nature <an ~ individual> **c** : sharply clear, discerning, or pointed <an ~ wit> **d** : piercingly intense and often jarring <~ yellow> **2 a** : of, relating to, or being an acid; *also* : having the reactions or characteristics of an acid <~ soil> <an ~ solution> **b** *of salts and esters* : derived by partial exchange of replaceable hydrogen <~ sodium carbonate $NaHCO_3$> **c** : marked by or resulting from an abnormally high concentration of acid <~ indigestion> **3** : relating to or made by a process (as in making steel) in which the furnace is lined with acidic material and an acidic slag is used **4** : rich in silica <~ rocks> ***syn*** see SOUR ***ant*** sweet, alkaline — **ac·id·ly** *adv* — **ac·id·ness** *n*

²acid *n* **1** : a sour substance; *specif* : any of various typically water-soluble and sour compounds that are capable of reacting with a base to form a salt, that redden litmus, that are hydrogen-containing molecules or ions able to give up a proton to a base, or that are substances able to accept an unshared pair of electrons from a base **2** : something incisive, biting, or sarcastic <a social satire dripping with ~> **3** : LSD

ac·id–fast \ˈas-əd-ˌfast\ *adj* : not easily decolorized by acids

ac·id·head \-ˌhed\ *n* : an individual who uses LSD

acid·ic \ə-ˈsid-ik, a-\ *adj* **1** : acid-forming **2** : ACID

acid·i·fi·er \ə-ˈsid-ə-ˌfī(-ə)r\ *n* : one that acidifies; *esp* : a substance used to increase soil acidity

acid·i·fy \-ˌfī\ *vb* **-fied; -fy·ing** *vt* **1** : to make acid **2** : to convert into an acid ~ *vi* : to become acid — **acid·i·fi·cation** \-ˌsid-ə-fə-ˈkā-shən\ *n*

ac·i·dim·e·ter \ˌas-ə-ˈdim-ət-ər\ *n* : an apparatus for measuring the strength or the amount of acid present in a solution — **acid·i·met·ric** \ə-ˌsid-ə-ˈme-trik\ *adj* — **ac·i·dim·e·try** \ˌas-ə-ˈdim-ə-trē\ *n*

acid·i·ty \ə-ˈsid-ət-ē\ *n, pl* **-ties 1** : the quality, state, or degree of being acid : TARTNESS **2** : the quality or state of being excessively or abnormally acid

acid·o·phile \ə-ˈsid-ə-ˌfīl\ *or* **acid·o·phil** \-ˌfil\ *n* : an acidophilic substance, tissue, or organism

ac·i·do·phil·ic \ˌas-ə-dō-ˈfil-ik\ *adj* **1** : staining readily with acid stains **2** : preferring or thriving in a relatively acid environment

ac·i·doph·i·lus milk \ˌas-ə-ˌdäf-(ə-)ləs-\ *n* [NL *Lactobacillus acidophilus,* lit., acidophilic Lactobacillus] : milk fermented by any of several bacteria and used therapeutically to change the intestinal flora

ac·i·do·sis \ˌas-ə-ˈdō-səs\ *n* : an abnormal state of reduced alkalinity of the blood and of the body tissues — **ac·i·dot·ic** \-ˈdät-ik\ *adj*

acid phosphatase *n* : a phosphatase (as the phosphomonoesterase from the prostate gland) active in acid medium

acid rock *n* : rock music with lyrics having cryptic reference to a drug (as LSD)

acid test *n* : a severe or crucial test

acid·u·late \ə-ˈsij-ə-ˌlāt\ *vt* **-lat·ed; -lat·ing** [L *acidulus*] : to make acid or slightly acid — **acid·u·la·tion** \-ˌsij-ə-ˈlā-shən\ *n*

acid·u·lent \ə-ˈsij-ə-lənt\ *adj* [F *acidulant,* fr. prp. of *aciduler* to acidulate, fr L *acidulus*] : ACIDULOUS

acid·u·lous \ə-ˈsij-ə-ləs\ *adj* [L *acidulus* sourish, fr. *acidus*] : somewhat acid in taste or manner : HARSH ***syn*** see SOUR ***ant*** saccharine

ac·i·nar \ˈas-ə-nər, -ˌnär\ *adj* : of, relating to, or comprising an acinus <pancreatic ~ cells>

ac·i·nus \ˈas-ə-nəs\ *n, pl* **-ni** \-ˌnī\ [NL, fr. L, berry, berry seed] : one of the small sacs in a racemose gland lined with secreting cells — **ac·i·nous** \-nəs\ *adj*

ack *abbr* acknowledge; acknowledgment

ack–ack \ˈak-ˌak\ *n* [Brit. signalmen's telephone pron. of *AA,* abbr. of *antiaircraft*] : an antiaircraft gun; *also* : antiaircraft fire

ac·knowl·edge \ik-ˈnäl-ij, ak-\ *vt* **-edged; -edg·ing** [*ac-* (as in *accord*) + *knowledge*] **1** : to own or admit knowledge of or agreement with **2** : to recognize the rights, authority, or status of **3 a** : to express gratitude or obligation for **b** : to take notice of **c** : to make known the receipt of **4** : to recognize as genuine or valid <~ a debt> — **ac·knowl·edge·able** \-ə-bəl\ *adj*

syn ACKNOWLEDGE, ADMIT, OWN, AVOW, CONFESS *shared meaning element* : to disclose against one's will or inclination. ACKNOWLEDGE implies the disclosure of what has been or might have been withheld <*acknowledge* a fault> ADMIT often stresses reluctance in disclosing or conceding <at last the government . . . *admitted* its mistake — which governments seldom do — Willa Cather> OWN applies especially to acknowledgment of something in close relation to oneself <finally *owned* that he was responsible> AVOW implies open or bold declaration of what one might be expected to be silent about <had an *avowed* hostility to his family> CONFESS usually applies to something felt to be wrong; thus, one *admits* an error but *confesses* a crime. In less specific use it may imply no more than deference to the opinion of another <I *confess* that I don't follow your reasoning> ***ant*** deny

ac·knowl·edged \-ijd\ *adj* : generally recognized, accepted, or admitted — **ac·knowl·edged·ly** \-ij-(ə-)dlē\ *adv*

ac·knowl·edg·ment *also* **ac·knowl·edge·ment** \ik-ˈnäl-ij-mənt, ak-\ *n* **1 a** : the act of acknowledging **b** : recognition or favorable notice of an act or achievement **2** : a thing done or given in recognition of something received **3** : a declaration or avowal of one's act or of a fact to give it legal validity

aclin·ic line \(ˌ)ā-ˌklin-ik-\ *n* [²*a-* + *clinic*] : an imaginary line roughly parallel to the geographical equator and passing through those points where a magnetic needle has no dip

ACLS *abbr* American Council of Learned Societies

ACLU *abbr* American Civil Liberties Union

ACM *abbr* Association for Computing Machinery

ac·me \ˈak-mē\ *n* [Gk *akmē* point, highest point — more at EDGE] : the highest point or stage; *esp* : one that represents perfection of the thing expressed <she was the ~ of courtesy> ***syn*** see SUMMIT

ac·ne \ˈak-nē\ *n* [Gk *aknē* eruption of the face, MS var. of *akmē,* lit., point] : a disorder of the skin caused by inflammation of the skin glands and hair follicles; *specif* : one found chiefly in adolescents and marked by pimples esp. on the face — **ac·ned** \-nēd\ *adj*

acock \ə-ˈkäk\ *adj or adv* : being in a cocked position <a dog listening with ears ~>

acold \ə-ˈkōld\ *adj* [ME] *archaic* : COLD, CHILLED <the owl, for all his feathers, was ~ — John Keats>

ac·o·lyte \ˈak-ə-ˌlīt\ *n* [ME *acolite,* fr. OF & ML; OF, fr. ML *acoluthus,* fr. MGk *akolouthos,* fr. Gk, adj., following, fr. *a-, ha-* (akin to Gk *homos* same) + *keleuthos* path — more at SAME] **1** : one who assists the clergyman in a liturgical service by performing minor duties **2** : one who attends or assists : FOLLOWER <helped by his admiring ~*s*>

ac·o·nite \ˈak-ə-ˌnīt\ *n* **1** : ACONITUM 1; *esp* : a common monkshood (*Aconitum napellus*) **2** : the dried tuberous root of a monkshood (*Aconitum napellus*) formerly used as a sedative

ac·o·ni·tum \ˌak-ə-ˈnīt-əm\ *n* [NL, genus name, fr. L aconitum, fr. Gk *akoniton*] **1** : any of a genus (*Aconitum*) of usu. bluish flowered poisonous herbs of the buttercup family — compare MONKSHOOD, WOLFSBANE **2** : ACONITE 2

acorn \ˈā-ˌkȯ(ə)rn, -kərn\ *n* [ME *akern,* fr. OE *æcern;* akin to MHG *ackeran* acorns collectively, Russ *yagoda* berry] : the nut of the oak usu. seated in or surrounded by a hard woody cupule of indurated bracts

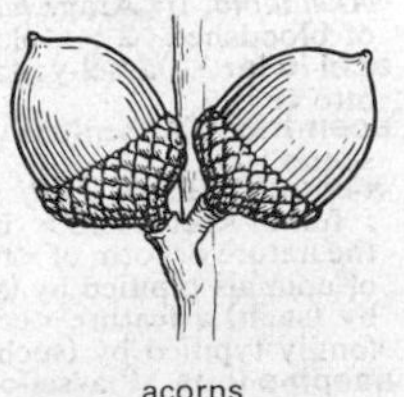
acorns

acorn squash *n* : an acorn-shaped dark green winter squash with a ridged surface and sweet yellow to orange flesh

acorn tube *n* : a very small vacuum tube that resembles an acorn in shape and is used at extremely high frequencies

acorn worm *n* : any of a group (Enteropneusta) of burrowing wormlike marine animals having an acorn-shaped proboscis and usu. classed with the chordates

acous·tic \ə-ˈkü-stik\ *adj* [Gk *akoustikos* of hearing, fr. *akouein* to hear — more at HEAR] **1** : of or relating to the sense or organs of hearing, to sound, or to the science of sounds <~ apparatus of the ear> <~ energy>; as **a** : deadening or absorbing sound <~ tile> **b** : operated by or utilizing sound waves **2** : of, relating to, or being a musical instrument whose sound is not electronically modified — **acous·ti·cal** \-sti-kəl\ *adj* — **acous·ti·cal·ly** \-k(ə-)lē\ *adv*

ac·ous·ti·cian \ˌak-ˌü-ˈstish-ən, ə-ˌkü-\ *n* : a specialist in acoustics

acous·tics \ə-ˈkü-stiks\ *n pl but sing or pl in constr* **1** : a science that deals with the production, control, transmission, reception, and effects of sound **2** *also* **acoustic** : the sum of the qualities that determine the value of an enclosure (as an auditorium) as to distinct hearing

ACP *abbr* American College of Physicians

acpt *abbr* acceptance

ac·quaint \ə-ˈkwānt\ *vt* [ME *aquainten,* fr. OF *acointier,* fr. ML *accognitare,* fr. LL *accognitus,* pp. of *accognoscere* to know perfectly, fr. L *ad-* + *cognoscere* to know — more at COGNITION]

1 : to cause to know personally <was ~*ed* with the mayor> **2 :** to make familiar : cause to know firsthand ***syn*** see INFORM

ac·quain·tance \ə-'kwānt-ᵊn(t)s\ *n* **1 a :** personal knowledge : FAMILIARITY **b :** the state of being acquainted **2 a :** the persons with whom one is acquainted <should auld ~ be forgot — Robert Burns> **b :** a person whom one knows but who is not a particularly close friend — **ac·quain·tance·ship** \-ˌship\ *n*

ac·qui·esce \ˌak-wē-'es\ *vi* **-esced; -esc·ing** [F *acquiescer,* fr. L *acquiescere,* fr. *ad-* + *quiescere* to be quiet — more at QUIET] : to accept or comply tacitly or passively ***syn*** see ASSENT ***ant*** object

ac·qui·es·cence \ˌak-wē-'es-ᵊn(t)s\ *n* **1 :** the act of acquiescing : the state of being acquiescent **2 :** an instance of acquiescing

ac·qui·es·cent \ˌak-wē-'es-ᵊnt\ *adj* [L *acquiescent-, acquiescens,* prp. of *acquiescere*] : inclined to acquiesce : ACQUIESCING — **ac·qui·es·cent·ly** *adv*

ac·quir·able \ə-'kwī-rə-bəl\ *adj* : capable of being acquired

ac·quire \ə-'kwī(ə)r\ *vt* **ac·quired; ac·quir·ing** [ME *aqueren,* fr. MF *aquerre,* fr. L *acquirere,* fr. *ad-* + *quaerere* to seek, obtain] **1 :** to get as one's own: **a :** to come into possession or control of often by unspecified means **b :** to come to have as a new or additional characteristic, trait, or ability (as by sustained effort or through environmental forces) <~ fluency in French> <bacteria that ~ tolerance to antibiotics> **2 :** to locate and hold (a desired object) in a detector < ~ a target by radar> ***syn*** see GET ***ant*** forfeit

ac·quire·ment \ə-'kwī(ə)r-mənt\ *n* **1 :** the act of acquiring **2 :** an attainment of mind or body usu. resulting from continued endeavor

ac·qui·si·tion \ˌak-wə-'zish-ən\ *n* [ME *acquisicioun,* fr. MF or L; MF *acquisition,* fr. L *acquisition-, acquisitio,* fr. *acquisitus,* pp. of *acquirere*] **1 :** the act of acquiring **2 :** something acquired or gained **3 :** the acquiring of library materials (as books and periodicals) by purchase, exchange, or gift — **ac·qui·si·tion·al** \-shnəl, -shən-ᵊl\ *adj* — **ac·quis·i·tor** \ə-'kwiz-ət-ər\ *n*

ac·quis·i·tive \ə-'kwiz-ət-iv\ *adj* : strongly desirous of acquiring and possessing ***syn*** see COVETOUS ***ant*** sacrificing, abnegating — **ac·quis·i·tive·ly** *adv* — **ac·quis·i·tive·ness** *n*

ac·quit \ə-'kwit\ *vt* **ac·quit·ted; ac·quit·ting** [ME *aquiten,* fr. OF *aquiter,* fr. *a-* (fr. L *ad-*) + *quite* free of — more at QUIT] **1 a** *archaic* : to pay off (as a claim or debt) **b** *obs* : REPAY, REQUITE **2 :** to discharge completely (as from an obligation or accusation) <the court *acquitted* the prisoner> **3 :** to conduct (oneself) satisfactorily esp. under stress <the recruits *acquitted* themselves like veterans> ***syn*** see BEHAVE — **ac·quit·ter** *n*

ac·quit·tal \ə-'kwit-ᵊl\ *n* : a setting free from the charge of an offense by verdict, sentence, or other legal process

ac·quit·tance \ə-'kwit-ᵊn(t)s\ *n* : a document evidencing a discharge from an obligation; *esp* : a receipt in full

acr- *or* **acro-** *comb form* [MF or Gk; MF *acro-,* fr. Gk *akr-, akro-,* fr. *akros* topmost, extreme; akin to Gk *akmē* point — more at EDGE] **1 :** beginning : end : tip <*acro*nym> **2 a :** top : peak : summit <*acro*dont> **b :** height <*acro*phobia> **c :** extremity of the body <*acro*cyanosis>

ac·ra·sin \'ak-rə-sən\ *n* [NL *Acrasia,* genus of fungi related to the slime molds + *-in*] : a substance and esp. cyclic AMP secreted by the individual cells of a slime mold and causing them to aggregate into a multicellular mass

acre \'ā-kər\ *n* [ME, fr. OE *æcer;* akin to OHG *ackar* field, L *ager,* Gk *agros,* L *agere* to drive — more at AGENT] **1 a** *archaic* : a field esp. of arable or pasture land **b** *pl* : LANDS, ESTATE **2 :** any of various units of area; *esp* : a unit in the U.S. and England equal to 160 square rods <a lake of 9 ~*s*> — see WEIGHT table **3 :** a broad expanse or great quantity <~*s* of time devoted to trivia>

acre·age \'ā-k(ə-)rij\ *n* : area in acres : ACRES

acre–foot \'ā-kər-'fu̇t\ *n* : the volume (as of irrigation water) that would cover one acre to a depth of one foot

acre–inch \'ā-kə-'rinch\ *n* : one twelfth of an acre-foot

ac·rid \'ak-rəd\ *adj* [modif. of L *acr-, acer* sharp — more at EDGE] **1 :** sharp and harsh or unpleasantly pungent in taste or odor : IRRITATING, CORROSIVE **2 :** deeply or violently bitter : ACRIMONIOUS <an ~ denunciation> — **acrid·i·ty** \a-'krid-ət-ē, ə-\ *n* — **ac·rid·ly** \'ak-rəd-lē\ *adv* — **ac·rid·ness** *n*

ac·ri·dine \'ak-rə-ˌdēn\ *n* : a colorless crystalline compound $C_{13}H_9N$ occurring in coal tar and important as the parent compound of dyes and pharmaceuticals

ac·ri·fla·vine \ˌak-rə-'flā-ˌvēn, -vən\ *n* [*acri*dine + *flavine*] : a yellow dye $C_{14}H_{14}N_3Cl$ used as an antiseptic esp. for wounds

Ac·ri·lan \'ak-rə-ˌlan, -lən\ *trademark* — used for an acrylic fiber

ac·ri·mo·ni·ous \ˌak-rə-'mō-nē-əs\ *adj* : caustic, biting, or rancorous esp. in feeling, language, or manner <an ~ dispute> — **ac·ri·mo·ni·ous·ly** *adv* — **ac·ri·mo·ni·ous·ness** *n*

ac·ri·mo·ny \'ak-rə-ˌmō-nē\ *n, pl* **-nies** [MF or L; MF *acrimonie,* fr. L *acrimonia,* fr. *acr-, acer*] : harsh or biting sharpness esp. of words, manner, or disposition

syn ACRIMONY, ACERBITY, ASPERITY *shared meaning element* : temper or language marked by angry irritation ***ant*** suavity

ac·ro·bat \'ak-rə-ˌbat\ *n* [F & Gk; F *acrobate,* fr. Gk *akrobatēs,* fr. *akrobatos* walking up high, fr. *akros* + *bainein* to go — more at COME] **1 :** one that performs gymnastic feats requiring skillful control of the body **2 :** one adept at swiftly changing his position or viewpoint <a political ~> — **ac·ro·bat·ic** \ˌak-rə-'bat-ik\ *adj* — **ac·ro·bat·i·cal·ly** \-i-k(ə-)lē\ *adv*

ac·ro·bat·ics \ˌak-rə-'bat-iks\ *n pl but sing or pl in constr* **1 :** the art, performance, or activity of an acrobat **2 :** a spectacular, showy, or startling performance involving great agility

ac·ro·car·pous \ˌak-rō-'kär-pəs\ *adj* [NL *acrocarpus,* fr. Gk *akrokarpos* bearing fruit at the top, fr. *akr-* acr- + *-karpos* -carpous] *of a moss* : having the archegonia and hence the capsules terminal on the stem

ac·ro·cen·tric \-'sen-trik\ *adj* [*acr-* + *-centric*] : having the centromere situated so that one chromosomal arm is much shorter than the other — **acrocentric** *n*

ac·ro·dont \'ak-rə-ˌdänt\ *adj* **1** *of teeth* : consolidated with the summit of the alveolar ridge without sockets **2 :** having acrodont teeth

acro·le·in \ə-'krō-lē-ən\ *n* [ISV *acr-* (fr. L *acr-, acer*) + L *olēre* to smell — more at ODOR] : a colorless irritant pungent liquid aldehyde C_3H_4O obtained by dehydration of glycerol or destructive distillation of fats

ac·ro·meg·a·ly \ˌak-rō-'meg-ə-lē\ *n* [F *acromégalie,* fr. *acr-* + Gk *megal-, megas* large — more at MUCH] : chronic hyperpituitarism marked by progressive enlargement of hands, feet, and face — **ac·ro·me·gal·ic** \-mə-'gal-ik\ *adj or n*

ac·ro·nym \'ak-rə-ˌnim\ *n* [*acr-* + *-onym* (as in *homonym*)] : a word (as *radar or snafu*) formed from the initial letter or letters of each of the successive parts or major parts of a compound term — **ac·ro·nym·ic** \ˌak-rə-'nim-ik\ *adj* — **ac·ro·nym·i·cal·ly** \-i-k(ə-)lē\ *adv*

acrop·e·tal \ə-'kräp-ət-ᵊl, a-\ *adj* [*acr-* + *-petal* (as in *centripetal*)] : proceeding from the base toward the apex or from below upward — **acrop·e·tal·ly** \-ᵊl-ē\ *adv*

ac·ro·pho·bia \ˌak-rə-'fō-bē-ə\ *n* [NL] : abnormal dread of being at a great height

acrop·o·lis \ə-'kräp-ə-ləs\ *n* [Gk *akropolis,* fr. *akr-* acr- + *polis* city — more at POLICE] : the upper fortified part of an ancient Greek city (as Athens)

[1]across \ə-'krȯs\ *adv* [ME *acros,* fr. AF *an crois,* fr. *an* in (fr. L *in*) + *crois* cross, fr. L *crux* — more at IN, CROSS] **1 :** in a position reaching from one side to the other : CROSSWISE **2 :** to or on the opposite side **3 :** so as to be understandable, acceptable, or successful : OVER <get an argument ~ >

[2]across *prep* **1 a :** from one side to the opposite side of : OVER, THROUGH <swam ~ the river> **b :** on the opposite side of <lives ~ the street from us> **2 :** so as to intersect or pass through at an angle <sawed ~ the grain of the wood> **3 :** into transitory contact with <ran ~ an old friend in the store>

[3]across *adj* : being in a crossed position

across–the–board *adj* **1 :** placed in combination to win, place, or show <an ~ racing bet> **2 :** embracing or affecting all classes or categories : BLANKET <an ~ pay raise>

acros·tic \ə-'krȯs-tik, -'kräs-\ *n* [MF & Gk; MF *acrostiche,* fr. Gk *akrostichis,* fr. *akr-* acr- + *stichos* line; akin to *steichein* to go — more at STAIR] **1 :** a composition usu. in verse in which sets of letters (as the initial or final letters of the lines) taken in order form a word or phrase or a regular sequence of letters of the alphabet **2 :** ACRONYM **3 :** a series of words of equal length arranged to read the same horizontally or vertically — **acrostic** *also* **acros·ti·cal** \-ti-kəl\ *adj* — **acros·ti·cal·ly** \-ti-k(ə-)lē\ *adv*

ACRR *abbr* American Council on Race Relations

ac·ry·late \'ak-rə-ˌlāt\ *n* **1 :** a salt or ester of acrylic acid **2 :** ACRYLIC RESIN

[1]acryl·ic \ə-'kril-ik\ *adj* [ISV *ac*rolein + *-yl* + *-ic*] : of or relating to acrylic acid or its derivatives <~ polymers>

[2]acrylic *n* **1 a :** ACRYLIC RESIN **b :** a paint in which the vehicle is an acrylic resin **c :** a painting done in an acrylic resin **2 :** ACRYLIC FIBER

acrylic acid *n* : an unsaturated liquid acid $C_3H_4O_2$ that is obtained by synthesis and that polymerizes readily to form useful products (as constituents for varnishes and lacquers)

acrylic fiber *n* : a quick-drying synthetic textile fiber made by polymerization of acrylonitrile usu. with other monomers

acrylic resin *n* : a glassy thermoplastic made by polymerizing acrylic or methacrylic acid or a derivative of either and used for cast and molded parts or as coatings and adhesives

ac·ry·lo·ni·trile \ˌak-rə-lō-'nī-trəl, -ˌtrēl\ *n* : a colorless volatile flammable liquid nitrile C_3H_3N used chiefly in organic synthesis and for polymerization

ACS *abbr* **1** American Chemical Society **2** American College of Surgeons

[1]act \'akt\ *n* [ME, partly fr. L *actus* doing, act, fr. *actus,* pp. of *agere* to drive, do; partly fr. L *actum* thing done, record, fr. neut. of *actus,* pp. — more at AGENT] **1 a :** a thing done : DEED **b :** something done voluntarily **2 :** a state of real existence rather than possibility **3 :** the formal product of a legislative body : STATUTE; *also* : a decision or determination of a sovereign, a legislative council, or a court of justice **4 :** the process of doing **5** *often cap* : a formal record of something done or transacted **6 a :** one of the principal divisions of a theatrical work (as a play or opera) **b :** one of the successive parts or performances in a variety show or circus **7 :** a display of affected behavior : PRETENSE ***syn*** see ACTION

[2]act *vt* **1** *obs* : ACTUATE, ANIMATE **2 a :** to represent or perform by action esp. on the stage **b :** FEIGN, SIMULATE **c :** IMPERSONATE **3 :** to play the part of as if in a play <~ the man of the world> **4 :** to behave in a manner suitable to <~ your age> ~ *vi* **1 a :** to perform on the stage **b :** to behave as if performing on the stage : PRETEND **2 :** to take action : MOVE <think before ~*ing*> <~*ed* favorably on the recommendation> **3 :** to conduct oneself : BEHAVE <~ like a fool> **4 :** to perform a specified function : SERVE <trees ~*ing* as a windbreak> **5 :** to produce an effect : WORK <wait for a medicine to ~ > **6** *of a play* : to be capable of being performed <the play ~*s* well> **7 :** to give a decision or award — **act·abil·i·ty** \ˌak-tə-'bil-ət-ē\ *n* — **act·able** \'ak-tə-bəl\ *adj*

[3]act *abbr* **1** active **2** actor **3** actual

ACT *abbr* **1** American College Test **2** Association of Classroom Teachers **3** Australian Capital Territory

Ac·tae·on \ak-'tē-ən\ *n* [L, fr. Gk *Aktaiōn*] **:** a hunter turned into a stag and killed by his own hounds for having seen Artemis bathing
actg *abbr* acting
ACTH \ˌā-ˌsē-(ˌ)tē-'āch\ *n* [*a*drenocorti*co*t*rophic *h*ormone] **:** ADRENOCORTICOTROPHIC HORMONE
ac·tin \'ak-tən\ *n* [ISV, fr. L *actus*] **:** a protein of muscle that is active in muscular contraction
actin- *or* **actini-** *or* **actino-** *comb form* [NL, ray, fr. Gk *aktin-, aktino-*, fr. *aktin-, aktis:* akin to OE *ūhte* morning twilight, L *noct-, nox* night — more at NIGHT] **1 a :** having a radiate form <*Actino*myces> **b :** actinian <*actini*form> **2 a :** actinic <*actini*um> **b :** actinic radiation (as X rays) <*actino*therapy>
[1]act·ing \'ak-tiŋ\ *adj* **1 :** holding a temporary rank or position **:** performing services temporarily <~ president> **2 a :** suitable for stage performance <an ~ play> **b :** prepared with directions for actors <an ~ text of a play>
[2]acting *n* **:** the art or practice of representing a character on a stage or before cameras
ac·tin·ia \ak-'tin-ē-ə\ *n, pl* **-i·ae** \-ē-ˌē\ *or* **-i·as** [NL, fr. Gk *aktin-, aktis*] **:** SEA ANEMONE; *also* **:** a related animal — **ac·tin·i·an** \-ē-ən\ *adj or n*
ac·tin·ic \ak-'tin-ik\ *adj* **:** of, relating to, or exhibiting actinism — **ac·tin·i·cal·ly** \-i-k(ə-)lē\ *adv*
actinic ray *n* **:** a radiation having marked photochemical action
ac·ti·nide \'ak-tə-ˌnīd\ *n* [ISV] **:** any element in a series of elements of increasing atomic numbers beginning with actinium (89) or thorium (90) and ending with element of atomic number 103 — see PERIODIC TABLE table
ac·ti·nism \'ak-tə-ˌniz-əm\ *n* **:** the property of radiant energy esp. in the visible and ultraviolet spectral regions by which chemical changes are produced
ac·tin·i·um \ak-'tin-ē-əm\ *n* [NL] **:** a radioactive trivalent metallic element that resembles lanthanum in chemical properties and that is found esp. in pitchblende — see ELEMENT table
ac·tin·o·lite \ak-'tin-ᵊl-ˌīt\ *n* **:** a bright or grayish green amphibole occurring in fibrous, radiated, or columnar forms
ac·ti·nom·e·ter \ˌak-tə-'näm-ət-ər\ *n* **1 :** an instrument for measuring the direct heating power of the sun's rays **2 :** an instrument for measuring the actinic power of radiant energy or for determining photographic exposure to be given — **ac·ti·no·me·tric** \-nō-'me-trik\ *adj* — **ac·ti·nom·e·try** \-'näm-ə-trē\ *n*
ac·ti·no·mor·phic \ˌak-tə-nō-'mȯr-fik\ *also* **ac·ti·no·mor·phous** \-fəs\ *adj* [ISV] **:** being radially symmetrical and capable of division into essentially symmetrical halves by any longitudinal plane passing through the axis — **ac·ti·no·mor·phy** \'ak-tə-nō-ˌmȯr-fē\ *n*
ac·ti·no·my·ces \ˌak-tə-nō-'mī-ˌsēz\ *n, pl* **actinomyces** [NL, genus name, fr. *actin-* + Gk *mykēt-, mykēs* fungus; akin to Gk *myxa* mucus — more at MUCUS] **:** any of a genus (*Actinomyces*) of filamentous bacteria including both soil-inhabiting saprophytes and disease-producing parasites — **ac·ti·no·my·ce·tal** \-mī-'sēt-ᵊl\ *adj*
ac·ti·no·my·cete \ˌak-tə-nō-'mī-ˌsēt, -mī-'sēt\ *n* [deriv. of Gk *aktin-, aktis* + *mykēt-, mykēs*] **:** any of an order (Actinomycetales) of filamentous or rod-shaped bacteria including the actinomyces and streptomyces — **ac·ti·no·my·ce·tous** \-mī-'sēt-əs\ *adj*
ac·ti·no·my·cin \ˌak-tə-nō-'mīs-ᵊn\ *n* **:** any of various red or yellow-red mostly toxic polypeptide antibiotics isolated from soil bacteria (esp. *Streptomyces antibioticus*)
ac·ti·no·my·co·sis \ˌak-tə-nō-mī-'kō-səs\ *n* **:** infection with or disease caused by actinomycetes; *esp.* **:** a chronic disease of cattle, swine, and man characterized by hard granulomatous masses usu. in mouth and jaw — **ac·ti·no·my·cot·ic** \-'kät-ik\ *adj*
ac·ti·non \'ak-tə-ˌnän\ *n* [NL, fr. *actinium*] **:** a gaseous radioactive isotope of radon that has a half-life of about 4 seconds
ac·ti·no·ura·ni·um \ˌak-tə-nō-yu̇-'rā-nē-əm\ *n* [NL, fr. *actinium* + *uranium*] **:** the uranium isotope of mass 235
ac·ti·no·zo·an \ˌ-nō-'zō-ən\ *n* [*actin-* + Gk *zōion* animal; akin to Gk *zōē* life — more at QUICK] **:** ANTHOZOAN — **actinozoan** *adj*
ac·tion \'ak-shən\ *n* **1 :** a proceeding in a court of justice by which one demands or enforces one's right **2 :** the bringing about of an alteration by force or through a natural agency **3 :** the manner or method of performing: **a :** the deportment of an actor or speaker or his expression by means of attitude, voice, and gesture **b :** the style of movement of the feet and legs (as of a horse) **c :** a function of the body or one of its parts **4 :** an act of will **5 a :** a thing accomplished usu. over a period of time, in stages, or with the possibility of repetition <an ~, the product and expression of exerted force —Thomas Carlyle> **b** *pl* **:** BEHAVIOR, CONDUCT <somber ~*s*> **c :** INITIATIVE, ENTERPRISE <a man of ~> **6 a** (1) **:** an engagement between troops or ships (2) **:** combat in war <gallantry in ~> **b** (1) **:** an event or series of events forming a literary composition (2) **:** the unfolding of the events of a drama or work of fiction **:** PLOT (3) **:** the movement of incidents in a plot **c :** the combination of circumstances that constitute the subject matter of a painting or sculpture **7 a :** an operating mechanism **b :** the manner in which a mechanism operates **8 a :** the price movement and trading volume of a commodity, security, or market **b :** the process of betting including the offering and acceptance of a bet and determination of a winner **9 :** the most vigorous, productive, or exciting activity in a particular field, area, or group <they itch to go where the ~ is —D. J. Henahan>
***syn* 1** ACTION, ACT, DEED *shared meaning element* **:** something done or effected
2 see BATTLE
ac·tion·able \'ak-sh(ə-)nə-bəl\ *adj* **:** subject to or affording ground for an action or suit at law — **ac·tion·ably** \-blē\ *adv*
ac·tion·less \'ak-shən-ləs\ *adj* **:** marked by inaction **:** IMMOBILE
action painting *n* **:** abstract expressionism marked esp. by the use of spontaneous techniques (as dribbling, splattering, or smearing)
action potential *n* **:** a recorded change in potential (as between the inside of a nerve cell and the extracellular medium) during activity of a cell or tissue
ac·ti·vate \'ak-tə-ˌvāt\ *vb* **-vat·ed; -vat·ing** *vt* **:** to make active or more active: as **a**(1) **:** to make (as molecules) reactive or more reactive (2) **:** to convert (as a provitamin) into a biologically active derivative **b :** to make (a substance) radioactive, luminescent, photosensitive, or photoconductive **c :** to treat (as carbon or alumina) esp. so as to improve adsorptive properties **d :** to aerate (sewage) so as to favor the growth of organisms that decompose organic matter **e** (1) **:** to set up or formally institute (as a military unit) with the necessary personnel and equipment (2) **:** to put (an individual or unit) on active duty ~ *vi* **:** to become active ***syn*** see VITALIZE ***ant*** arrest — **ac·ti·va·tion** \ˌak-tə-'vā-shən\ *n* — **ac·ti·va·tor** \'ak-tə-ˌvāt-ər\ *n*
activated carbon *n* **:** a highly adsorbent powdered or granular carbon made usu. by carbonization and chemical activation and used chiefly for purifying by adsorption — called also *activated charcoal*
activation analysis *n* **:** analysis to determine chemical elements in a material by bombarding it with neutrons to produce radioactive atoms whose radiations are characteristic of the elements present
ac·tive \'ak-tiv\ *adj* [ME, fr. MF or L; MF *actif*, fr. L *activus*, fr. *actus*, pp. of *agere* to drive, do — more at AGENT] **1 :** characterized by action rather than by contemplation or speculation **2 :** productive of action or movement **3 a** *of a verb form or voice* **:** asserting that the person or thing represented by the grammatical subject performs the action represented by the verb <*hits* in "he hits the ball" is ~> **b :** expressing action as distinct from mere existence or state **4 :** quick in physical movement **:** LIVELY **5 :** marked by vigorous activity **:** BUSY <the stock market was ~> **6 :** requiring vigorous action or exertion <~ sports> **7 :** having practical operation or results **:** EFFECTIVE <an ~ law> **8 a :** disposed to action **:** ENERGETIC <~ interest> **b :** engaged in an action or activity **:** PARTICIPATING <an ~ club member> **9 :** engaged in full-time service esp. in the armed forces <~ duty> **10 :** marked by present operation, transaction, movement, or use <~ account> **11 a :** capable of acting or reacting **:** ACTIVATED <~ nitrogen> <~ charcoal> **b :** tending to progress or to cause degeneration <~ tuberculosis> **c :** exhibiting optical activity **12 :** still eligible to win the pot in poker **13 :** moving down the line **:** visiting in the set — used of couples in contredanses or square dances — **active** *n* — **ac·tive·ly** *adv* — **ac·tive·ness** *n*
active immunity *n* **:** usu. long-lasting immunity that is acquired through production of antibodies within the organism in response to the presence of antigens — compare PASSIVE IMMUNITY
active transport *n* **:** movement of a chemical substance by the expenditure of energy through a gradient (as across a cell membrane) in concentration or electrical potential and opposite to the direction of normal diffusion
ac·tiv·ism \'ak-ti-ˌviz-əm\ *n* **:** a doctrine or practice that emphasizes direct vigorous action (as a mass demonstration) in support of or opposition to one side of a controversial issue — **ac·tiv·ist** \-vəst\ *n or adj* — **ac·tiv·is·tic** \ˌak-ti-'vis-tik\ *adj*
ac·tiv·i·ty \ak-'tiv-ət-ē\ *n, pl* **-ties 1 :** the quality or state of being active **2 :** vigorous or energetic action **:** LIVELINESS **3 :** natural or normal function: as **a :** a process (as digestion) that an organism carries on or participates in by virtue of being alive **b :** similar process actually or potentially involving mental function; *specif* **:** an educational procedure designed to stimulate learning by firsthand experience **4 :** an active force **5 a :** a pursuit in which a person is active **b :** a form of organized, supervised, often extracurricular recreation **6 :** an organizational unit for performing a specific function; *also* **:** its function or duties
act of God : an extraordinary interruption by a natural cause (as a flood or earthquake) of the usual course of events that experience, prescience, or care cannot reasonably foresee or prevent
ac·to·my·o·sin \ˌak-tə-'mī-ə-sən\ *n* [ISV *actin* + *-o-* + *myosin*] **:** a viscous contractile complex of actin and myosin concerned together with ATP in muscular contraction
ac·tor \'ak-tər\ *n* **1 :** one that acts **:** DOER **2 a :** one who represents a character in a dramatic production **b :** a theatrical performer **c :** one that behaves as if acting a part **3 :** one that takes part in any affair **:** PARTICIPANT — **ac·tor·ish** \-tə-rish\ *adj* — **ac·tress** \-trəs\ *n*
act out *vt* **1 a :** to represent in action <children *act out* what they read> **b :** to translate into action <unwilling to *act out* their beliefs> **2 :** to express (repressed or unconscious impulses) in overt behavior without awareness or insight esp. during psychoanalytic investigation
Acts \'akts\ *n pl but sing in constr* **:** a book in the New Testament narrating the beginnings of the Church — called also *Acts of the Apostles;* see BIBLE table
ac·tu·al \'ak-ch(ə-w)əl, 'aksh-wəl\ *adj* [ME *actuel*, fr. MF, fr. LL *actualis*, fr. L *actus* act] **1** *obs* **:** ACTIVE **2 a :** existing in act and not merely potentially **b :** existing in fact or reality <~ and imagined conditions> **c :** not false or apparent <~ costs> **3 :** existing or occurring at the time **:** CURRENT <caught in the ~ commission of a crime> ***syn*** see REAL ***ant*** ideal, imaginary
actual cash value *n* **:** the amount necessary to replace or restore lost, stolen, or damaged property (as an automobile)
ac·tu·al·i·ty \ˌak-chə-'wal-ət-ē\ *n, pl* **-ties 1 :** the quality or state of being actual **2 :** something that is actual **:** FACT, REALITY <possible risks which have been seized upon as *actualities* —T. S. Eliot>
ac·tu·al·ize \'ak-ch(ə-w)ə-ˌlīz, 'aksh-wə-\ *vb* **-ized; -iz·ing** *vt* **:** to make actual ~ *vi* **:** to become actual — **ac·tu·al·iza·tion** \ˌak-ch(ə-w)ə-lə-'zā-shən, ˌaksh-wə-\ *n*
ac·tu·al·ly \'ak-ch(ə-w)ə-lē, 'aksh-(wə-)lē\ *adv* **1 :** in act or in fact **:** REALLY <nominally but not ~ independent —Karl Loewenstein> **2 :** at the present moment <the party ~ in power> **3 :** in point of fact **:** in truth <she ~ spoke Latin>
ac·tu·ar·i·al \ˌak-chə-'wer-ē-əl\ *adj* **1 :** of or relating to actuaries **2 :** relating to statistical calculation esp. of life expectancy — **ac·tu·ar·i·al·ly** \-ē-ə-lē\ *adv*

ac·tu·ary \ˈak-chə-ˌwer-ē\ *n, pl* **-ar·ies** [L *actuarius* shorthand writer, fr. *actum* record — more at ACT] **1** *obs* **:** CLERK, REGISTRAR **2 :** one who calculates insurance and annuity premiums, reserves, and dividends

ac·tu·ate \ˈak-chə-ˌwāt\ *vt* **-at·ed; -at·ing** [ML *actuatus,* pp. of *actuare,* fr. L *actus* act] **1 :** to put into mechanical action or motion **2 :** to move to action **syn** see MOVE — **ac·tu·a·tion** \ˌak-chə-ˈwā-shən\ *n*

ac·tu·a·tor \ˈak-chə-ˌwāt-ər\ *n* **:** one that actuates; *specif* **:** a mechanism for moving or controlling something indirectly instead of by hand

act up *vi* **1 :** to act in a way different from that which is normal or expected: as **a :** to behave in an unruly, recalcitrant, or capricious manner **b :** to show off **c :** to function improperly <this typewriter is *acting up* again> **2 :** to become active or acute after being quiescent <her rheumatism started to *act up*>

acu·ity \ə-ˈkyü-ət-ē\ *n, pl* **-ities** [MF *acuité,* fr. OF *agüeté,* fr. *agu* sharp, fr. L *acutus*] **:** keenness of perception **:** SHARPNESS

acu·le·ate \ə-ˈkyü-lē-ət\ *adj* [L *aculeatus* having stings, fr. *aculeus,* dim. of *acus*] **:** having a sting <~ insects>

acu·men \ə-ˈkyü-mən\ *n* [L *acumin-, acumen,* lit., point, fr. *acuere*] **:** keenness and depth of perception, discernment, or discrimination esp. in practical matters **:** SHREWDNESS **syn** see DISCERNMENT

[1]**acu·mi·nate** \ə-ˈkyü-mə-nət\ *adj* **:** tapering to a slender point **:** POINTED

[2]**acu·mi·nate** \-ˌnāt\ *vb* **-nat·ed; -nat·ing** *vt* **:** to make sharp or acute ~ *vi* **:** to taper or come to a point — **acu·mi·na·tion** \ə-ˌkyü-mə-ˈnā-shən\ *n*

acu·punc·ture \ˈak-yu̇-ˌpəŋ(k)-chər\ *n* [L *acus* + E *puncture*] **:** an orig. Chinese practice of puncturing the body (as with needles) to cure disease or relieve pain

acute \ə-ˈkyüt\ *adj* **acut·er; acut·est** [L *acutus,* pp. of *acuere* to sharpen, fr. *acus* needle; akin to L *acer* sharp — more at EDGE] **1 :** ending in a sharp point: as **a :** being or forming an angle measuring less than 90 degrees <~ angle> **b :** composed of acute angles <~ triangle> **2 a :** marked by keen discernment or intellectual preception esp. of subtle distinctions **:** PENETRATING <an ~ thinker> **b :** responsive to slight impressions or stimuli <~ observer> **3 :** of a kind to act keenly on the senses; *esp* **:** characterized by sharpness or severity <~ pain> **4 a :** having a sudden onset, sharp rise, and short course <~ disease> **b :** lasting a short time <~ experiments> **5 :** seriously demanding urgent attention <an ~ housing shortage> **6 a** *of an accent mark* **:** having the form ˊ **b :** marked with an acute accent **c :** of the variety indicated by an acute accent — **acute·ly** *adv* — **acute·ness** *n*

syn 1 see SHARP **ant** obtuse

2 ACUTE, CRITICAL, CRUCIAL *shared meaning element* **:** full of uncertainty as to outcome **ant** chronic

ACV *abbr* **1** actual cash value **2** air-cushion vehicle

acy·clic \(ˈ)ā-ˈsī-klik, -ˈsik-lik\ *adj* **1 :** not cyclic; *esp* **:** not disposed in cycles or whorls **2 :** having an open-chain structure; *esp* **:** ALIPHATIC <an ~ compound>

ac·yl \ˈas-əl\ *n* [ISV, fr. *acid*] **:** a radical derived usu. from an organic acid by removal of the hydroxyl from all acid groups

[1]**ad** \ˈad\ *n* **:** ADVERTISEMENT 2

[2]**ad** *n* **:** ADVANTAGE 4

AD *abbr* **1** active duty **2** after date **3** air-dried **4** anno Domini — often printed in small capitals **5** assembly district

ad- *or* **ac-** *or* **af-** *or* **ag-** *or* **al-** *or* **ap-** *or* **as-** *or* **at-** *prefix* [ME, fr. MF, OF & L; MF, fr. OF, fr. L, fr. *ad* — more at AT] **1 :** to **:** toward — usu. *ac-* before *c, k,* or *q* <*ac*culturation> and *af-* before *f* and *ag-* before *g* <*ag*grade> and *al-* before *l* <*al*literation> and *ap-* before *p* <*ap*proximal> and *as-* before *s* <*as*suasive> and *at-* before *t* <*at*tune> and *ad-* before other sounds but sometimes *ad-* even before one of the listed consonants <*ad*sorb> **2 :** near **:** adjacent to — in this sense always in the form *ad-* <*ad*renal>

-ad \ˌad, əd\ *adv suffix* [L *ad*] **:** in the direction of **:** toward <cephal*ad*>

ADA *abbr* **1** Americans for Democratic Action **2** average daily attendance

ad·age \ˈad-ij\ *n* [MF, fr. L *adagium,* fr. *ad-* + *-agium* (akin to *aio* I say); akin to Gk *ē* he spoke] **:** a saying often in metaphorical form that embodies a common observation

[1]**ada·gio** \ə-ˈdäj-(ē-ˌ)ō, -ˈdäzh-\ *adv or adj* [It, fr. *ad* to + *agio* ease] **:** in an easy graceful manner **:** SLOWLY — used chiefly as a direction in music

[2]**adagio** *n, pl* **-gios 1 :** a musical composition or movement in adagio tempo **2 :** a ballet duet by a man and woman or a mixed trio displaying difficult feats of balance, lifting, or spinning

[1]**Ad·am** \ˈad-əm\ *n* [ME, fr. LL, fr. Gk, fr. Heb *Ādhām*] **1 :** the first man and father by Eve of Cain and Abel **2 :** the unregenerate nature of man — used esp. in the phrase *the old Adam* — **Adam·ic** \ə-ˈdam-ik\ *or* **Adam·i·cal** \-i-kəl\ *adj*

[2]**Adam** *adj* [Robert *Adam* †1792 & James *Adam* †1794 Sc designers] **:** of or relating to an 18th century style of furniture characterized by straight lines, surface decoration, and conventional designs (as festooned garlands and medallions)

ad·a·mance \ˈad-ə-mən(t)s\ *n* **:** ADAMANCY

ad·a·man·cy \-mən-sē\ *n* [[2]*adamant* + *-cy*] **:** unyielding quality **:** OBSTINACY

adam–and–eve \ˌad-ə-mən-ˈ(d)ēv\ *n* **:** PUTTYROOT

[1]**ad·a·mant** \ˈad-ə-mənt *also* -ˌmant\ *n* [ME, fr. OF, fr. L *adamant-, adamas* hardest metal, diamond, fr. Gk] **1 :** a stone (as a diamond) formerly believed to be of impenetrable hardness **2 :** an unbreakable or extremely hard substance

[2]**adamant** *adj* **:** unshakable or immovable esp. in opposition **:** UNYIELDING **syn** see INFLEXIBLE **ant** yielding — **ad·a·mant·ly** *adv*

ad·a·man·tine \ˌad-ə-ˈman-ˌtēn, -ˌtīn, -ˈmant-ᵊn\ *adj* [ME, fr. L *adamantinus,* fr. Gk *adamantinos,* fr. *adamant-, adamas*] **1 :** made of or having the quality of adamant **2 :** rigidly firm **:** UNYIELDING **3 :** resembling the diamond in hardness or luster

Adam's apple *n* **:** the projection in the front of the neck formed by the largest cartilage of the larynx — see LARYNX illustration

Adam's needle *n* **:** any of several yuccas

adapt \ə-ˈdapt\ *vb* [F or L; F *adapter,* fr. L *adaptare,* fr. *ad-* + *aptare* to fit, fr. *aptus* apt, fit] *vt* **:** to make fit (as for a specific or new use or situation) often by modification ~ *vi* **:** to become adapted — **adapt·ed·ness** *n*

syn ADAPT, ADJUST, ACCOMMODATE, CONFORM, RECONCILE *shared meaning element* **:** to bring one into correspondence with another **ant** unfit

adapt·able \ə-ˈdap-tə-bəl\ *adj* **:** capable of being adapted **:** SUITABLE **syn** see PLASTIC **ant** inadaptable, unadaptable — **adapt·abil·i·ty** \-ˌdap-tə-ˈbil-ət-ē\ *n*

ad·ap·ta·tion \ˌad-ˌap-ˈtā-shən, -əp-\ *n* **1 :** the act or process of adapting **:** the state of being adapted **2 :** adjustment to environmental conditions: as **a :** adjustment of a sense organ to the intensity or quality of stimulation **b :** modification of an organism or its parts that makes it more fit for existence under the conditions of its environment **3 :** something that is adapted; *specif* **:** a composition rewritten into a new form — **ad·ap·ta·tion·al** \-shnəl, -shən-ᵊl\ *adj* — **ad·ap·ta·tion·al·ly** \-ē\ *adv*

adapt·er *also* **adap·tor** \ə-ˈdap-tər\ *n* **1 :** one that adapts **2 a :** a device for connecting two parts (as of different diameters) of an apparatus **b :** an attachment for adapting apparatus for uses not orig. intended

adap·tion \ə-ˈdap-shən\ *n* **:** ADAPTATION

adap·tive \ə-ˈdap-tiv\ *adj* **:** showing or having a capacity for or tendency toward adaptation — **adap·tive·ly** *adv* — **adap·tive·ness** *n* — **ad·ap·tiv·i·ty** \ˌad-ˌap-ˈtiv-ət-ē\ *n*

Adar \ä-ˈdär\ *n* [ME, fr. Heb *Adhār*] **:** the 6th month of the civil year or the 12th month of the ecclesiastical year in the Jewish calendar — see MONTH table

Adar She·ni \ä-ˌdär-shā-ˈnē\ *n* [Heb *Ădhār Shēnī* second Adar] **:** VEADAR

ad·ax·i·al \(ˈ)a-ˈdak-sē-əl\ *adj* **:** situated on the same side as or facing the axis (as of an organ)

ADC *abbr* **1** aide-de-camp **2** Aid to Dependent Children **3** Air Defense Command **4** assistant division commander

add \ˈad\ *vb* [ME, *adden,* fr. L *addere,* fr. *ad-* + *-dere* to put — more at DO] *vt* **1 :** to join or unite so as to bring about an increase or improvement <~*s* 60 acres to his land> <wine ~*s* a creative touch to cooking> **2 :** to say further **:** APPEND **3 :** to combine (numbers) into an equivalent simple quantity or number **4 :** to include as a member of a group <don't forget to ~ me in> ~ *vi* **1 a :** to perform addition **b :** to come together or unite by addition **2 a :** to serve as an addition <the movie will ~ to his fame> **b :** to make an addition **:** ENLARGE — **add·able** *or* **add·ible** \ˈad-ə-bəl\ *adj*

ADD *abbr* American Dialect Dictionary

ad·dax \ˈad-ˌaks\ *n, pl* **ad·dax·es** [L] **:** a large light-colored antelope (*Addax nasomaculata*) of No. Africa, Arabia, and Syria

ad·dend \ˈad-ˌend, ə-ˈdend\ *n* [short for *addendum*] **:** a number to be added to another

ad·den·dum \ə-ˈden-dəm\ *n, pl* **-da** \-də\ [L, neut. of *addendus,* gerundive of *addere*] **1 :** a thing added **:** ADDITION **2 :** a supplement to a book — often used in pl. but sing. in constr.

[1]**ad·der** \ˈad-ər\ *n* [ME, alter. (by incorrect division of *a naddre*) of *naddre,* fr. OE *nǣdre;* akin to OHG *nātara* adder, L *natrix* water snake] **1 :** the common venomous viper (*Vipera berus*) of Europe; *broadly* **:** a terrestrial viper (family Viperidae) **2 :** any of several No. American snakes (as the hognose snakes) that are harmless but are popularly believed to be venomous

[2]**add·er** \ˈad-ər\ *n* **:** one that adds; *esp* **:** a device (as in a computer) that performs addition

ad·der's–tongue \ˈad-ərz-ˌtəŋ\ *n* **1 :** a fern (genus *Ophioglossum,* family Ophioglossaceae) whose fruiting spike resembles a serpent's tongue **2 :** DOGTOOTH VIOLET

[1]**ad·dict** \ə-ˈdikt\ *vt* [L *addictus,* pp. of *addicere* to favor, fr. *ad-* + *dicere* to say — more at DICTION] **1 :** to devote or surrender (oneself) to something habitually or obsessively <~*ed* to gambling> **2 :** to cause (a person) to become physiologically dependent upon a drug

[2]**ad·dict** \ˈad-(ˌ)ikt\ *n* **1 :** one who is addicted to a drug **2 :** DEVOTEE 2 <a detective novel ~>

ad·dic·tion \ə-ˈdik-shən\ *n* **1 :** the quality or state of being addicted <~ to reading> **2 :** compulsive physiological need for a habit-forming drug (as heroin) — compare HABITUATION

ad·dic·tive \ə-ˈdik-tiv\ *adj* **:** causing or characterized by addiction

Ad·di·son's disease \ˈad-ə-sənz-\ *n* [Thomas *Addison* †1860 E physician] **:** a destructive disease marked by deficient secretion of the adrenal cortical hormone and characterized by extreme weakness, loss of weight, low blood pressure, gastrointestinal disturbances, and brownish pigmentation of the skin and mucous membranes

ad·di·tion \ə-ˈdish-ən\ *n* [ME, fr. MF, fr. L *addition-, additio,* fr. *additus,* pp. of *addere*] **1 :** the result of adding **:** INCREASE **2 :** the act or process of adding; *esp* **:** the operation of combining numbers so as to obtain an equivalent simple quantity **3 :** a part added (as to a building or residential section) **4 :** direct chemical combination of substances into a single product — **in addition :** [1]BESIDES, ALSO — **in addition to :** over and above

ad·di·tion·al \ə-ˈdish-nəl, -ˈdish-ən-ᵊl\ *adj* **:** existing by way of addition **:** ADDED — **ad·di·tion·al·ly** \-ē\ *adv*

[1]**ad·di·tive** \ˈad-ət-iv\ *adj* **1 :** of, relating to, or characterized by addition **2 :** produced by addition — **ad·di·tive·ly** *adv* — **ad·di·tiv·i·ty** \ˌad-ə-ˈtiv-ət-ē\ *n*

[2]additive *n* **:** a substance added to another in relatively small amounts to impart or improve desirable properties or suppress undesirable properties <food ~*s*>
additive identity *n* **:** an identity element (as 0 in the group of whole numbers under the operation of addition) that in a given mathematical system leaves unchanged any element to which it is added
additive inverse *n* **:** a number of opposite sign with respect to a given number so that addition of the two numbers gives zero <the *additive inverse* of 4 is −4>
[1]ad·dle \'ad-ᵊl\ *adj* [ME *adel* filth, fr. OE *adela;* akin to MLG *adele* liquid manure] **1** *of an egg* **:** ROTTEN **2 :** CONFUSED, MUDDLED
[2]addle *vb* **ad·dled; ad·dling** \'ad-liŋ, -ᵊl-iŋ\ *vt* **:** to throw into confusion **:** CONFOUND ~ *vi* **1 :** to become rotten **:** SPOIL **2 :** to become confused
ad·dle·pat·ed \,ad-ᵊl-'pāt-əd\ *adj* **1 :** being mixed up **:** CONFUSED **2 :** ECCENTRIC
addn *abbr* addition
addnl *abbr* additional
[1]ad·dress \ə-'dres\ *vb* [ME *adressen,* fr. MF *adresser,* fr. *a-* (fr. L *ad-*) + *dresser* to arrange — more at DRESS] *vt* **1** *archaic* **a :** DIRECT, AIM **b :** to direct to go **:** SEND **2** *archaic* **:** to make ready; *esp* **:** DRESS **3 a :** to direct the efforts or attention of (oneself) <will ~ himself to the problem> **b :** to deal with **:** TREAT <intrigued by the chance to ~ important issues — I. L. Horowitz> **4 a :** to communicate directly <~*es* his thanks to his host> **b :** to speak or write directly to; *esp* **:** to deliver a formal speech to **5 a :** to mark directions for delivery on <~ a letter> **b :** to consign to the care of another (as an agent or factor) **6 :** to greet by a prescribed form **7 :** to adjust the club preparatory to hitting (a golf ball) ~ *vi, obs* **:** to direct one's speech or attentions — **ad·dress·er** *n*
[2]ad·dress \ə-'dres, *for 5 & 7 & less often 4 also* 'ad-,res\ *n* **1 :** dutiful and courteous attention esp. in courtship — usu. used in pl. **2 a :** readiness and capability for dealing (as with a person or problem) skillfully and smoothly **:** ADROITNESS **b** *obs* **:** a making ready; *also* **:** a state of preparedness **3 a :** manner of bearing onself <a man of rude ~> **b :** manner of speaking or singing **:** DELIVERY **4 :** a formal communication; *esp* **:** a prepared speech delivered to a special audience or on a special occasion **5 a :** a place where a person or organization may be communicated with **b :** directions for delivery on the outside of an object (as a letter or package) **c :** the designation of place of delivery placed between the heading and salutation on a business letter **6 :** a preparatory position of the player and club in golf **7 :** a location (as in the memory of a computer) where particular information is stored; *also* **:** the digits that identify such a location ***syn*** see TACT ***ant*** maladroitness
ad·dress·able \ə-'dres-ə-bəl\ *adj* **:** accessible through an address <~ registers in a computer>
ad·dress·ee \,ad-,res-'ē, ə-,dres-'ē\ *n* **:** one to whom something is addressed
ad·duce \ə-'d(y)üs\ *vt* **ad·duced; ad·duc·ing** [L *adducere,* lit., to lead to, fr. *ad-* + *ducere* to lead — more at TOW] **:** to offer as example, reason, or proof in discussion or analysis — **ad·duc·er** *n*
syn ADDUCE, CITE, ADVANCE, ALLEGE *shared meaning element* **:** to bring forward (as in explanation, proof, or demonstration)
[1]ad·duct \ə-'dəkt, a-\ *vt* [L *adductus,* pp. of *adducere*] **:** to draw (as a limb) toward or past the median axis of the body; *also* **:** to bring together (similar parts) <~ the fingers> — **ad·duc·tive** \-'dək-tiv\ *adj*
[2]ad·duct \'ad-,əkt\ *n* [G *addukt,* fr. L *adductus*] **:** a chemical addition product
ad·duc·tion \ə-'dək-shən, a-\ *n* **1 :** the action of adducting **:** the state of being adducted **2 :** the act or action of adducing or bringing forward
ad·duc·tor \-'dək-tər\ *n* [NL, fr. L, one that draws to, fr. *adductus*] **1 :** a muscle that draws a part toward the median line of the body or toward the axis of an extremity **2 :** a muscle that closes the valves of a bivalve mollusk
add up *vi* **1 :** AMOUNT — used with *to* <the play *adds up* to a lot of laughs> **2 :** to come to the expected total <the bill doesn't *add up*> ~ *vt* **:** to form an opinion of <*added* him *up* at a glance>
-ade \'ād\ *n suffix* [ME, fr. MF, fr. OProv *-ada,* fr. LL *-ata,* fr. L, fem. of *-atus* -ate] **1 :** act **:** action <block*ade*> **2 :** product; *esp* **:** sweet drink <lime*ade*>
Adé·lie penguin \ə-,dā-lē-\ *n* [*Adélie* Coast, Antarctica] **:** a small antarctic penguin (*Pygoscelis adeliae*) — called also *Adélie*
-adel·phous \ə-'del-fəs\ *adj comb form* [prob. fr. NL *-adelphus,* fr. Gk *adelphos* brother, fr. *ha-, a-* (akin to *homos* same) + *delphys* womb — more at SAME, DOLPHIN] **:** having (such or so many) stamen fascicles <mon*adelphous*>
aden- *or* **adeno-** *comb form* [NL, fr. Gk, fr. *aden-, adēn;* akin to L *inguen* groin, Gk *nephros* kidney — more at NEPHRITIS] **:** gland <*aden*itis>
ad·e·nine \'ad-ᵊn-,ēn\ *n* [ISV, fr. its presence in glandular tissue] **:** a purine base $C_5H_3N_4NH_2$ that codes hereditary information in the genetic code in DNA and RNA — compare CYTOSINE, GUANINE, THYMINE, URACIL
ad·e·ni·tis \,ad-ᵊn-'īt-əs\ *n* [NL] **:** inflammation of one or more lymph nodes
ad·e·no·car·ci·no·ma \,ad-ᵊn-(,ō)-,kärs-ᵊn-'ō-mə\ *n* [NL] **:** a malignant tumor originating in glandular epithelium — **ad·e·no·car·ci·no·ma·tous** \-mət-əs\ *adj*
ad·e·no·hy·poph·y·sis \-hī-'päf-ə-səs\ *n, pl* **-y·ses** \-ə-,sēz\ [NL] **:** the anterior glandular lobe of the pituitary gland — **ad·e·no·hy·poph·y·se·al** \-(,)hī-,päf-ə-'sē-əl\ *or* **ad·e·no·hy·po·phys·i·al** \-,hī-pə-'fiz-ē-əl\ *adj*
ad·e·noid \'ad-ᵊn-,òid, 'ad-,nòid\ *n* [Gk *adenoeidēs* glandular, fr. *adēn*] **:** an enlarged mass of lymphoid tissue at the back of the pharynx characteristically obstructing breathing — usu. used in pl. — **adenoid** *adj*
ad·e·noi·dal \,ad-ᵊn-'òid-ᵊl\ *adj* **1 :** of or relating to the adenoids **2 :** typical or suggestive of one affected with abnormally enlarged adenoids <an ~ tenor> <~ breathing>
ad·e·no·ma \,ad-ᵊn-'ō-mə\ *n, pl* **-nomas** *or* **-no·ma·ta** \-mət-ə\ [NL *adenomat-, adenoma*] **:** a benign tumor of a glandular structure or of glandular origin — **ad·e·no·ma·tous** \-mət-əs\ *adj*
aden·o·sine \ə-'den-ə-,sēn\ *n* [ISV, blend of *adenine* & *ribose*] **:** a nucleoside $C_{10}H_{13}N_5O_4$ that is a constituent of ribonucleic acid yielding adenine and ribose on hydrolysis
adenosine diphosphate *n* **:** ADP
adenosine mo·no·phos·phate \-,män-ə-'fäs-,fāt, -,mō-nə-\ *n* **1 :** AMP **2 :** CYCLIC AMP
adenosine tri·phos·pha·tase \-trī-'fäs-fə-,tās, -,tāz\ *n* **:** ATPASE
adenosine tri·phos·phate \-trī-'fäs-,fāt\ *n* **:** ATP
ad·e·no·vi·rus \,ad-ᵊn-ō-'vī-rəs\ *n* [*aden*oid + *-o-* + *virus*] **:** any of a group of DNA-containing viruses orig. identified in human adenoid tissue, causing respiratory diseases (as catarrh), and including some capable of inducing malignant tumors in experimental animals — **ad·e·no·vi·ral** \-rəl\ *adj*
ad·e·nyl \'ad-ᵊn-,il\ *n* **:** an univalent radical $C_5H_4N_5$ derived from adenine
adenyl cy·clase \-'sī-,klās, -,klāz\ *n* **:** an enzyme that catalyzes the formation of cyclic AMP from ATP
ad·e·nyl·ic acid \,ad-ᵊn-,il-ik-\ *n* **:** a nucleotide $C_{10}H_{14}N_5O_7P$ formed by partial hydrolysis of RNA or ATP
[1]ad·ept \'ad-,ept\ *n* [NL, *adeptus,* alchemist who has attained the knowledge of how to change base metals into gold, fr. L, pp. of *adipisci* to attain, fr. *ad-* + *apisci* to reach — more at APT] **:** a highly skilled or well-trained individual **:** EXPERT <an ~ at chess>
[2]adept \ə-'dept\ *adj* **:** thoroughly proficient **:** EXPERT ***syn*** see PROFICIENT ***ant*** inadept, inept, bungling — **adept·ly** \-'dep-(t)lē\ *adv* — **adept·ness** \-'dep(t)-nəs\ *n*
ad·e·qua·cy \'ad-i-kwə-sē\ *n, pl* **-cies :** the quality or state of being adequate
ad·e·quate \-kwət\ *adj* [L *adaequatus,* pp. of *adaequare* to make equal, fr. *ad-* + *aequare* to equal — more at EQUATE] **1 a :** sufficient for a specific requirement <~ taxation of goods>; *esp* **:** barely sufficient or satisfactory <her first performance was merely ~> **2 :** lawfully and reasonably sufficient ***syn*** see SUFFICIENT ***ant*** inadequate — **ad·e·quate·ly** *adv* — **ad·e·quate·ness** *n*
ad eun·dem \,ad-ē-'ən-dəm\ *or* **ad eundem gra·dum** \-'grād-əm\ *adv or adj* [NL *ad eundem gradum*] **:** to, in, or of the same rank — used esp. of the honorary granting of academic standing or a degree by a university to one whose actual work was done elsewhere
[1]à deux \ä-'də(r), à-dœ̄\ *adj* [F] **:** involving two people esp. in private <a cozy evening *à deux*>
[2]à deux *adv* **:** privately or intimately with only two present <dining *à deux*>
ADF *abbr* automatic direction finder
ADH *abbr* antidiuretic hormone
ad·here \ad-'hi(ə)r, əd-\ *vb* **ad·hered; ad·her·ing** [MF or L; MF *adhérer,* fr. L *adhaerēre,* fr. *ad-* + *haerēre* to stick — more at HESITATE] *vi* **1 :** to give support or maintain loyalty **2** *obs* **:** to be consistent **:** ACCORD **3 :** to hold fast or stick by or as if by gluing, suction, grasping, or fusing **4 :** to bind oneself to observance ~ *vt* **:** to cause to stick fast ***syn*** see STICK
ad·her·ence \-'hir-ən(t)s\ *n* **1 :** the act, action, or quality of adhering **2 :** steady or faithful attachment **:** FIDELITY
syn ADHERENCE, ADHESION *shared meaning element* **:** a sticking to or together ***ant*** nonadherence
ad·her·end \-'hi(ə)r-,end, ,ad-,hi(ə)r-'\ *n* [*adhere* + *-end* (as in *addend*)] **1 :** the surface to which an adhesive adheres **2 :** one of the bodies held to another by an adhesive
[1]ad·her·ent \ad-'hir-ənt, əd-\ *adj* [ME, fr. MF or L; MF *adhérent,* fr. L *adhaerent-, adhaerens,* prp. of *adhaerēre*] **1 :** able or tending to adhere **2 :** connected or associated with esp. by contract **3 :** ADNATE — **ad·her·ent·ly** *adv*
[2]adherent *n* **:** one that adheres: as **a :** a follower of a leader, party, or profession **b :** a believer in or advocate esp. of a particular idea or church ***syn*** see FOLLOWER ***ant*** renegade
ad·he·sion \ad-'hē-zhən, əd-\ *n* [F or L; F *adhésion,* fr. L *adhaesion-, adhaesio,* fr. *adhaesus,* pp. of *adhaerēre*] **1 :** steady or firm attachment **:** ADHERENCE **2 :** the action or state of adhering; *specif* **:** a union of bodily parts by growth **3 :** tissues abnormally united by fibrous tissue resulting from an inflammatory process **4 :** agreement to join **5 :** the molecular attraction exerted between the surfaces of bodies in contact ***syn*** see ADHERENCE ***ant*** nonadhesion — **ad·he·sion·al** \-'hēzh-nəl, -'hē-zhən-ᵊl\ *adj*
[1]ad·he·sive \-'hē-siv, -ziv\ *adj* **1 :** tending to remain in association or memory **2 :** tending to adhere or cause adherence **3 :** prepared for adhering **:** STICKY — **ad·he·sive·ly** *adv* — **ad·he·sive·ness** *n*
[2]adhesive *n* **1 :** an adhesive substance (as glue or cement) **2 :** a postage stamp with a gummed back
adhesive tape *n* **:** tape coated on one side with an adhesive mixture; *esp* **:** one used for covering wounds
[1]ad hoc \(')ad-'häk, -'hōk\ *adv* [L, for this] **:** for the particular end or case at hand without consideration of wider application
[2]ad hoc *adj* **:** concerned with a particular end or purpose <an *ad hoc* investigating committee>
[1]ad ho·mi·nem \(')ad-'häm-ə-,nem\ *adj* [NL, lit., to the man] **1 :** appealing to a person's feelings or prejudices rather than his intellect **2 :** marked by an attack on an opponent's character rather than by an answer to his contentions
[2]ad hominem *adv* **:** in an ad hominem manner <was arguing *ad hominem*>
adi·a·bat·ic \,ad-ē-ə-'bat-ik, ,ā-,dī-ə-\ *adj* [Gk *adiabatos* impassable, fr. *a-* + *diabatos* passable, fr. *diabainein* to go across, fr. *dia-* + *bainein* to go — more at COME] **:** occurring without loss or gain of heat <~ expansion of a body of air> — **adi·a·bat·i·cal·ly** \-i-k(ə-)lē\ *adv*
adieu \ə-'d(y)ü\ *n, pl* **adieus** *or* **adieux** \ə-'d(y)üz\ [ME, fr. MF, fr. *a* (fr. L *ad*) + *Dieu* God, fr. L *Deus* — more at AT, DEITY] **:** FAREWELL — often used interjectionally

ad in·fi·ni·tum \ˌad-ˌin-fə-ˈnīt-əm\ *adv or adj* [L] **:** without end or limit
ad int *abbr* ad interim
¹ad in·ter·im \(ˈ)ad-ˈin-tə-rəm, -ˌrim\ *adv* [L] **:** for the intervening time **:** TEMPORARILY
²ad interim *adj* **:** made or serving ad interim
adi·os \ˌad-ē-ˈōs, ˌäd-\ *interj* [Sp *adiós,* fr. *a* (fr. L *ad*) + *Dios* God, fr. L *Deus*] — used to express farewell
ad·i·pose \ˈad-ə-ˌpōs\ *adj* [NL *adiposus,* fr. L *adip-, adeps* fat, fr. Gk *aleipha;* akin to Gk *lipos* fat — more at LEAVE] **:** of or relating to animal fat **:** FATTY — **ad·i·pos·i·ty** \ˌad-ə-ˈpäs-ət-ē\ *n*
adipose tissue *n* **:** connective tissue in which fat is stored and which has the cells distended by droplets of fat
ad·it \ˈad-ət\ *n* [L *aditus* approach, fr. *aditus,* pp. of *adire* to go to, fr. *ad-* + *ire* to go — more at ISSUE] **:** a nearly horizontal passage from the surface in a mine
ADIZ *abbr* air defense identification zone
adj *abbr* **1** adjective **2** adjunct **3** adjustment **4** adjutant
ad·ja·cen·cy \ə-ˈjās-ᵊn-sē\ *n, pl* **-cies 1 :** something that is adjacent **2 :** the quality or state of being adjacent **:** CONTIGUITY
ad·ja·cent \ə-ˈjās-ᵊnt\ *adj* [ME, fr. MF or L; MF, fr. L *adjacent-, adjacens,* prp. of *adjacēre* to lie near, fr. *ad-* + *jacēre* to lie; akin to L *jacere* to throw — more at JET] **1 a :** not distant **:** NEARBY <the city and ~ suburbs> **b :** having a common border <~ lots> **c :** immediately preceding or following **2** *of two angles* **:** having the vertex and one side in common — **ad·ja·cent·ly** *adv*
syn ADJACENT, ADJOINING, CONTIGUOUS, ABUTTING, CONTERMINOUS *shared meaning element* **:** being in proximity ***ant*** nonadjacent
ad·jec·ti·val \ˌaj-ik-ˈtī-vəl\ *adj* **1 :** ADJECTIVE **2 :** characterized by the use of adjectives — **ad·jec·ti·val·ly** \-və-lē\ *adv*
¹ad·jec·tive \ˈaj-ik-tiv\ *adj* [ME, fr. MF or LL; MF *adjectif,* fr. LL *adjectivus,* fr. L *adjectus,* pp. of *adjicere* to throw to, fr. *ad-* + *jacere* to throw — more at JET] **1 :** of, relating to, or functioning as an adjective <an ~ clause> **2 :** not standing by itself **:** DEPENDENT **3 :** requiring or employing a mordant <~ dyes> **4 :** PROCEDURAL <~ law> — **ad·jec·tive·ly** *adv*
²adjective *n* **:** a word belonging to one of the major form classes in any of numerous languages and typically serving as a modifier of a noun to denote a quality of the thing named, to indicate its quantity or extent, or to specify a thing as distinct from something else
ad·join \ə-ˈjȯin\ *vb* [ME *adjoinen,* fr. MF *adjoindre,* fr. L *adjungere,* fr. *ad-* + *jungere* to join — more at YOKE] *vt* **1 :** to add or attach by joining **2 :** to lie next to or in contact with ~ *vi* **:** to be close to or in contact with one another
ad·join·ing *adj* **:** touching or bounding at a point or line ***syn*** see ADJACENT ***ant*** detached, disjoined
ad·joint \ˈaj-ˌȯint\ *n* [F, fr. pp. of *adjoindre* to adjoin] **:** the transpose of a matrix in which each element is replaced by its cofactor
ad·journ \ə-ˈjərn\ *vb* [ME *ajournen,* fr. MF *ajourner,* fr. *a-* (fr. L *ad-*) + *jour* day — more at JOURNEY] *vt* **:** to suspend indefinitely or until a later stated time ~ *vi* **1 :** to suspend a session to another time or place or indefinitely **2 :** to move to another place
syn ADJOURN, PROROGUE, DISSOLVE *shared meaning element* **:** to terminate the activities of (as a legislature)
ad·journ·ment \-mənt\ *n* **1 :** the act of adjourning **2 :** the state or interval of being adjourned
ad·judge \ə-ˈjəj\ *vt* **ad·judged; ad·judg·ing** [ME *ajugen,* fr. MF *ajugier,* fr. L *adjudicare,* fr. *ad-* + *judicare* to judge — more at JUDGE] **1 a :** to decide or rule upon as a judge **:** ADJUDICATE **b :** to pronounce judicially **:** RULE **2** *archaic* **:** SENTENCE, CONDEMN **3 :** to hold or pronounce to be **:** DEEM <~ the book a success> **4 :** to award or grant judicially in a case of controversy
ad·ju·di·cate \ə-ˈjüd-i-ˌkāt\ *vb* **-cat·ed; -cat·ing** [L *adjudicatus,* pp. of *adjudicare*] *vt* **:** to settle judicially ~ *vi* **:** to act as judge — **ad·ju·di·ca·tive** \-ˌkāt-iv, -kət-\ *adj* — **ad·ju·di·ca·tor** \-ˌkāt-ər\ *n*
ad·ju·di·ca·tion \ə-ˌjüd-i-ˈkā-shən\ *n* **1 :** the act or process of adjudicating **2 a :** a judicial decision or sentence **b :** a decree in bankruptcy — **ad·ju·di·ca·to·ry** \-ˈjüd-i-kə-ˌtōr-ē, -ˌtȯr-\ *adj*
¹ad·junct \ˈaj-ˌəŋ(k)t\ *n* [L *adjunctum,* fr. neut. of *adjunctus,* pp. of *adjungere*] **1 :** something joined or added to another thing but not essentially a part of it **2 :** a word or word group that qualifies or completes the meaning of another word or other words and is not itself one of the principal structural elements in its sentence **3 :** a person associated with or assisting another — **ad·junc·tive** \a-ˈjəŋ(k)-tiv\ *adj*
²adjunct *adj* **1 :** added or joined as an accompanying object or circumstance **2 :** attached in a subordinate or temporary capacity to a staff <an ~ psychiatrist> — **ad·junct·ly** \ˈaj-ˌəŋ(k)-tlē, -ˌəŋ-klē\ *adv*
ad·junc·tion \a-ˈjəŋ(k)-shən\ *n* **:** the act or process of adjoining
ad·ju·ra·tion \ˌaj-ə-ˈrā-shən\ *n* **1 :** a solemn oath **2 :** an earnest or solemn urging or advising — **ad·jur·a·to·ry** \ə-ˈju̇r-ə-ˌtōr-ē, -ˌtȯr-\ *adj*
ad·jure \ə-ˈju̇(ə)r\ *vt* **ad·jured; ad·jur·ing** [ME *adjuren,* fr. MF & L; MF *ajurer,* fr. L *adjurare,* fr. *ad-* + *jurare* to swear — more at JURY] **1 :** to charge or command solemnly under or as if under oath or penalty of a curse **2 :** to entreat or advise earnestly ***syn*** see BEG
ad·just \ə-ˈjəst\ *vb* [F *ajuster,* fr. *a-* + *juste* exact, just] *vt* **1 a :** to bring to a more satisfactory state: (1) **:** SETTLE, RESOLVE (2) **:** RECTIFY **b :** to make correspondent or conformable **:** ADAPT **c :** to bring the parts of to a true or more effective relative position <~ a carburetor> **2 :** to reduce to a system **:** REGULATE **3 :** to determine the amount to be paid under an insurance policy in settlement of (a loss) ~ *vi* **1 :** to adapt or conform oneself (as to climate, food, or new working hours) **2 :** to achieve mental and behavioral balance between one's own needs and the demands of others ***syn*** see ADAPT — **adjust·abil·i·ty** \-ˌjəs-tə-ˈbil-ət-ē\ *n* — **ad·just·able** \-ˈjəs-tə-bəl\ *adj* — **adjus·tive** \-ˈjəs-tiv\ *adj*
ad·just·ed *adj* **1 :** accommodated to suit a particular set of circumstances or requirements **2 :** having achieved a harmonious relationship with the environment or with other individuals <a well-*adjusted* schoolchild>
ad·just·er *also* **ad·jus·tor** \ə-ˈjəs-tər\ *n* **:** one that adjusts; *esp* **:** an insurance agent who investigates personal or property damage and makes estimates for effecting settlements
ad·just·ment \ə-ˈjəs(t)-mənt\ *n* **1 :** the act or process of adjusting **2 :** a settlement of a claim or debt in a case in which the amount involved is uncertain or in which full payment is not made **3 :** the state of being adjusted **4 :** a means (as a mechanism) by which things are adjusted one to another **5 :** a correction or modification to reflect actual conditions — **ad·just·men·tal** \ə-ˌjəs(t)-ˈment-ᵊl, ˌaj-ˌəs(t)-\ *adj*
ad·ju·tan·cy \ˈaj-ət-ən-sē\ *n* **:** the office or rank of an adjutant
ad·ju·tant \ˈaj-ət-ənt\ *n* [L *adjutant-, adjutans,* prp. of *adjutare* to help — more at AID] **1 :** a staff officer in the army, air force, or marine corps who assists the commanding officer and is responsible esp. for correspondence **2 :** one who helps **:** ASSISTANT
adjutant general *n, pl* **adjutants general 1 :** the chief administrative officer of an army who is responsible esp. for the administration and preservation of personnel records **2 :** the chief administrative officer of a major military unit (as a division or corps)
¹ad·ju·vant \ˈaj-ə-vənt\ *adj* [F or L; F, fr. L *adjuvant-, adjuvans,* prp. of *adjuvare* to aid — more at AID] **:** serving to aid or contribute **:** AUXILIARY
²adjuvant *n* **:** one that helps or facilitates; *esp* **:** something that enhances the effectiveness of medical treatment
Ad·le·ri·an \äd-ˈlir-ē-ən, ad-\ *adj* [Alfred *Adler* †1937 Austrian psychiatrist] **:** of, relating to, or being a theory and technique of psychotherapy emphasizing the importance of feelings of inferiority, a will to power, and overcompensation in neurotic processes
¹ad–lib \ˈad-ˈlib\ *adj* [*ad lib*] **:** spoken, composed, or performed without preparation
²ad–lib *vb* **ad–libbed; ad–lib·bing** *vt* **:** to deliver spontaneously ~ *vi* **:** to improvise esp. lines or a speech — **ad–lib** *n*
ad lib *adv* [NL *ad libitum*] **1 :** in accordance with one's wishes **2 :** without restraint or limit
¹ad li·bi·tum \(ˈ)ad-ˈlib-ət-əm\ *adv* [NL, in accordance with desire] **:** ad lib <rats fed *ad libitum*>
²ad libitum *adj* **:** omissible according to a performer's wishes — used as a direction in music; compare OBBLIGATO
ad loc *abbr* [L *ad locum*] to or at the place
adm *abbr* administration; administrative
ADM *abbr* admiral
ad·man \ˈad-ˌman\ *n* **:** one who writes, solicits, or places advertisements
ad·mass \ˈad-ˌmas\ *adj* [*ad*vertising + *mass*] *chiefly Brit* **:** of, relating to, or characteristic of a society that devotes itself chiefly to the production, promotion, and consumption of material goods
ad·mea·sure \ad-ˈmezh-ər, -ˈmā-zhər\ *vt* **-sured; -sur·ing** [ME *amesuren,* fr. MF *amesurer,* fr. *a-* (fr. L *ad-*) + *mesurer* to measure] **:** to determine the proper share of **:** APPORTION
ad·mea·sure·ment \-ˈmezh-ər-mənt, -ˈmā-zhər-\ *n* **1 :** determination and apportionment of shares **2 :** determination or comparison of dimensions **3 :** DIMENSIONS, SIZE
Ad·me·tus \ad-ˈmēt-əs\ *n* [L, fr. Gk *Admētos*] **:** a king of Pherae who was saved from his fated death by the substitution of his wife Alcestis
admin *abbr* administration
ad·min·is·ter \əd-ˈmin-ə-stər\ *vb* **ad·min·is·tered; ad·min·is·ter·ing** \-st(ə-)riŋ\ [ME *administren,* fr. MF *administrer,* fr. L *administrare,* fr. *ad-* + *ministrare* to serve, fr. *minister* servant — more at MINISTER] *vt* **1 :** to manage or supervise the execution, use, or conduct of <~ a trust fund> **2 a :** to mete out **:** DISPENSE <~ punishment> **b :** to give ritually <~ the last rites> **c :** to give remedially <~ a dose of medicine> ~ *vi* **1 :** to perform the office of administrator **2 :** to furnish a benefit **:** MINISTER <~ to his ailing friend> **3 :** to manage affairs ***syn*** see EXECUTE — **ad·min·is·tra·ble** \-strə-bəl\ *adj* — **ad·min·is·trant** \-strənt\ *n*
ad·min·is·trate \-ˌstrāt\ *vt* **-trat·ed; -trat·ing** [L *administratus,* pp. of *administrare*] **:** ADMINISTER
ad·min·is·tra·tion \əd-ˌmin-ə-ˈstrā-shən, (ˌ)ad-\ *n* **1 :** the act or process of administering **2 :** performance of executive duties **:** MANAGEMENT **3 :** the execution of public affairs as distinguished from policymaking **4 a :** a body of persons who administer **b** *cap* **:** a group constituting the political executive in a presidential government **c :** a governmental agency or board **5 :** the term of office of an administrative officer or body — **ad·min·is·tra·tion·al** \-shnəl, -shən-ᵊl\ *adj* — **ad·min·is·tra·tion·ist** \-sh(ə-)nəst\ *n*
ad·min·is·tra·tive \əd-ˌmin-ə-ˌstrāt-iv, -strət-\ *adj* **:** of or relating to administration or an administration **:** EXECUTIVE — **ad·min·is·tra·tive·ly** *adv*
administrative county *n* **:** a British local administrative unit often not coincident with an older county
administrative law *n* **:** law dealing with the establishment, duties, and powers of and available remedies against authorized agencies in the executive branch of the government
ad·min·is·tra·tor \əd-ˈmin-ə-ˌstrāt-ər\ *n* **1 :** a person legally vested with the right of administration of an estate **2 a :** one that administers esp. business, school, or governmental affairs **b :** a priest appointed to administer a diocese or parish temporarily
ad·min·is·tra·trix \-ˌmin-ə-ˈstrā-triks\ *n, pl* **-tra·tri·ces** \-ˈstrā-trə-ˌsēz\ [NL] **:** a female administrator esp. of an estate
ad·mi·ra·ble \ˈad-m(ə-)rə-bəl\ *adj* **1** *obs* **:** exciting wonder **:** SURPRISING **2 :** deserving the highest esteem **:** EXCELLENT — **ad-**

mi·ra·bil·i·ty \ˌad-m(ə-)rə-ˈbil-ət-ē\ *n* — **ad·mi·ra·ble·ness** \ˈad-m(ə-)rə-bəl-nəs\ *n* — **ad·mi·ra·bly** \-blē\ *adv*

ad·mi·ral \ˈad-m(ə-)rəl\ *n* [ME, fr. MF *amiral* admiral & ML *admiralis* emir, *admirallus* admiral, fr. Ar *amīr -al-* commander of the (as in *amīr-al-baḥr* commander of the sea)] **1** *archaic* : the commander in chief of a navy **2 a** : FLAG OFFICER **b** : a commissioned officer in the navy or coast guard who ranks above a vice admiral and whose insignia is four stars — compare GENERAL **3** *archaic* : FLAGSHIP **4** : any of several brightly colored butterflies (family Nymphalidae)

admiral of the fleet : the highest-ranking officer of the British navy

ad·mi·ral·ty \ˈad-m(ə-)rəl-tē\ *n* **1** *cap* : the executive department or officers formerly having general authority over British naval affairs **2** : the court having jurisdiction of maritime questions; *also* : the system of law administered by admiralty courts

Admiralty mile *n* : NAUTICAL MILE a

ad·mi·ra·tion \ˌad-mə-ˈrā-shən\ *n* **1** *archaic* : WONDER **2** : an object of admiring esteem **3 a** : a feeling of delighted or astonished approbation **b** : the act or process of regarding with admiration

ad·mire \əd-ˈmī(ə)r\ *vt* **ad·mired; ad·mir·ing** [MF *admirer*, fr. L *admirari*, fr. *ad-* + *mirari* to wonder — more at SMILE] **1** *archaic* : to marvel at **2** : to regard with admiration **3** : to think highly of often in a somewhat impersonal manner <~ a man's capacity for work> ***syn*** see REGARD ***ant*** abhor — **ad·mir·er** *n* — **ad·mir·ing·ly** \-ˈmī-riŋ-lē\ *adv*

ad·mis·si·ble \əd-ˈmis-ə-bəl\ *adj* [F, fr. ML *admissibilis*, fr. L *admissus*, pp. of *admittere*] **1** : capable of being allowed or conceded : PERMISSIBLE <behavior that was hardly ~> **2** : capable or worthy of being admitted <foreign products ~ to a domestic market> — **ad·mis·si·bil·i·ty** \-ˌmis-ə-ˈbil-ət-ē\ *n*

ad·mis·sion \əd-ˈmish-ən\ *n* **1 a** : the granting of an argument or position not fully proved **b** : acknowledgment that a fact or statement is true **2 a** : the act or process of admitting **b** : the state or privilege of being admitted **c** : a fee paid at or for admission ***syn*** see ADMITTANCE — **ad·mis·sive** \-ˈmis-iv\ *adj*

ad·mit \əd-ˈmit\ *vb* **ad·mit·ted; ad·mit·ting** [ME *admitten*, fr. L *admittere*, fr. *ad-* + *mittere* to send — more at SMITE] *vt* **1 a** : to allow scope for : PERMIT **b** : to concede as true or valid <compelled to ~ his failure> **2** : to allow entry (as to a place, fellowship, or privilege) <each ticket ~*s* two persons> <*admitted* to the university> ~ *vi* **1** : to give entrance or access **2 a** : ALLOW, PERMIT <this order ~*s* of two interpretations> **b** : to make acknowledgment — used with *to* ***syn*** **1** see RECEIVE ***ant*** eject, expel **2** see ACKNOWLEDGE ***ant*** gainsay, disdain — **ad·mit·ted·ly** \-ˈmit-əd-lē\ *adv*

ad·mit·tance \əd-ˈmit-ᵊn(t)s\ *n* **1** : permission to enter a place : ENTRANCE **2** : the reciprocal of the impedance of a circuit ***syn*** ADMITTANCE, ADMISSION *shared meaning element* : permitted entry

ad·mix \ad-ˈmiks\ *vt* [back-formation fr. obs. *admixt* mingled (with), fr. ME, fr. L *admixtus*] : MINGLE, BLEND

ad·mix·ture \ad-ˈmiks-chər\ *n* [L *admixtus*, pp. of *admiscēre* to mix with, fr. *ad-* + *miscēre* to mix — more at MIX] **1 a** : the act of mixing **b** : the fact of being mixed **2 a** : something added by mixing **b** : a product of mixing : MIXTURE

ad·mon·ish \ad-ˈmän-ish\ *vt* [ME *admonesten*, fr. MF *admonester*, fr. (assumed) VL *admonestare*, alter. of L *admonēre* to warn, fr. *ad-* + *monēre* to warn — more at MIND] **1 a** : to indicate duties or obligations to **b** : to express warning or disapproval to esp. in a gentle, earnest, or solicitous manner **2** : to give friendly earnest advice or encouragement to ***syn*** see REPROVE — **ad·mon·ish·er** *n* — **ad·mon·ish·ing·ly** \-ish-iŋ-lē\ *adv* — **ad·mon·ish·ment** \-mənt\ *n*

ad·mo·ni·tion \ˌad-mə-ˈnish-ən\ *n* [ME *amonicioun*, fr. MF *amonition*, fr. L *admonition-, admonitio*, fr. *admonitus*, pp. of *admonēre*] **1** : gentle or friendly reproof **2** : counsel or warning against fault or oversight

ad·mon·i·to·ry \əd-ˈmän-ə-ˌtōr-ē, -ˌtȯr-\ *adj* : expressing admonition : WARNING — **ad·mon·i·to·ri·ly** \-ˌmän-ə-ˈtōr-ə-lē, -ˈtȯr-\ *adv*

admrx *abbr* administratrix

ad·nate \ˈad-ˌnāt\ *adj* [L *adgnatus*, pp. of *adgnasci* to grow on, fr. *ad-* + *nasci* to be born — more at NATION] : grown to a usu. unlike part esp. along a margin <a calyx ~ to the ovary> — **ad·na·tion** \ad-ˈnā-shən\ *n*

ad nau·se·am \ad-ˈnȯ-zē-əm\ *adv* [L] : to a sickening degree

ad·nexa \ad-ˈnek-sə\ *n pl* [NL, fr. L *annexa*, neut. pl. of *annexus*, pp. of *annectere* to bind to — more at ANNEX] : conjoined, subordinate, or associated anatomic parts; *specif* : the embryonic membranes and other temporary structures of the embryo — **ad·nex·al** \-səl\ *adj*

ado \ə-ˈdü\ *n* [ME, fr. *at do*, fr. *at* + *don, do* to do] **1** : fussy bustling excitement : TO-DO **2** : time-wasting bother over trivial details <wrote the paper without further ~> **3** : TROUBLE, DIFFICULTY ***syn*** see STIR

ado·be \ə-ˈdō-bē\ *n* [Sp, fr. Ar *aṭ-ṭub* the brick, fr. Copt *tōbe* brick] **1** : a brick or building material of sun-dried earth and straw **2** : a heavy clay used in making adobe bricks; *broadly* : alluvial or playa clay in desert or arid regions **3** : a structure made of adobe bricks

ad·o·les·cence \ˌad-ᵊl-ˈes-ᵊn(t)s\ *n* **1** : the state or process of growing up **2** : the period of life from puberty to maturity terminating legally at the age of majority

[1]**ad·o·les·cent** \-ᵊnt\ *n* [F, fr. L *adolescent-, adolescens*, prp. of *adolescere* to grow up — more at ADULT] : one that is in the state of adolescence

[2]**adolescent** *adj* : of, relating to, or being in adolescence — **ad·o·les·cent·ly** *adv*

Ado·nai \ˌäd-ə-ˈnȯi, -ˈnī\ *n* [Heb *adhōnāy*] — used as a name of the God of the Hebrews

Ado·nis \ə-ˈdän-əs, -ˈdō-nəs\ *n* [L, fr. Gk *Adōnis*] : a youth loved by Aphrodite, killed at hunting by a wild boar, and restored to Aphrodite from Hades

adopt \ə-ˈdäpt\ *vt* [MF or L; MF *adopter*, fr. L *adoptare*, fr. *ad-* + *optare* to choose — more at OPTION] **1** : to take by choice into a relationship; *specif* : to take voluntarily (a child of other parents) as one's own child **2** : to take up and practice or use as one's own <~ another's mannerisms> **3** : to accept formally and put into effect <~ a constitutional amendment> **4** : to choose (a textbook) for required study in a course — **adopt·abil·i·ty** \-ˌdäp-tə-ˈbil-ət-ē\ *n* — **adopt·able** \-ˈdäp-tə-bəl\ *adj* — **adopt·er** *n*
syn ADOPT, EMBRACE, ESPOUSE *shared meaning element* : to take (as an opinion, policy, or practice) as one's own ***ant*** repudiate, discard

adopt·ee \ə-ˌdäp-ˈtē\ *n* : one that is adopted

adop·tion \ə-ˈdäp-shən\ *n* : the act of adopting : the state of being adopted

adop·tion·ism *or* **adop·tian·ism** \-shə-ˌniz-əm\ *n, often cap* : the doctrine that Jesus of Nazareth became the Son of God by adoption — **adop·tion·ist** \-sh(ə-)nəst\ *n, often cap*

adop·tive \ə-ˈdäp-tiv\ *adj* **1** : of or relating to adoption **2** : made or acquired by adoption <the ~ father> **3** : tending to adopt — **adop·tive·ly** *adv*

ador·able \ə-ˈdōr-ə-bəl, -ˈdȯr-\ *adj* **1** : worthy of being adored **2** : extremely charming <an ~ child> — **ador·abil·i·ty** \-ˌdōr-ə-ˈbil-ət-ē, -ˌdȯr-\ *n* — **ador·able·ness** \-ˈdōr-ə-bəl-nəs, -ˈdȯr-\ *n* — **ador·ably** \-blē\ *adv*

ad·o·ra·tion \ˌad-ə-ˈrā-shən\ *n* : the act of adoring : the state of being adored

adore \ə-ˈdō(ə)r, -ˈdȯ(ə)r\ *vt* **adored; ador·ing** [MF *adorer*, fr. L *adorare*, fr. *ad-* + *orare* to speak, pray — more at ORATION] **1** : to worship or honor as a deity or as divine **2** : to regard with reverent admiration and devotion <at 40 he still *adored* his father> **3** : to be extremely fond of <always ~*s* a good time> ***syn*** see REVERE ***ant*** blaspheme — **ador·er** *n*

adorn \ə-ˈdȯ(ə)rn\ *vt* [ME *adornen*, fr. MF *adorner*, fr. L *adornare*, fr. *ad-* + *ornare* to furnish — more at ORNATE] : to decorate esp. with ornaments
syn ADORN, DECORATE, ORNAMENT, EMBELLISH, BEAUTIFY, DECK, GARNISH *shared meaning element* : to add something to for the purpose of making more attractive ***ant*** disfigure

adorn·ment \-mənt\ *n* **1** : the action of adorning : the state of being adorned **2** : something that adorns

adoze \ə-ˈdōz\ *adv or adj* : in a state of dozing

[1]**ADP** \ˌā-ˌdē-ˈpē, ā-ˈdē-ˌpē\ *n* [*a*denosine *d*i*p*hosphate] : an ester of adenosine that is reversibly converted to ATP for the storing of energy by the addition of a high-energy phosphate group — called also *adenosine diphosphate*

[2]**ADP** *abbr* automatic data processing

[1]**ad rem** \(ˈ)ad-ˈrem\ *adv* [L, to the thing] : to the point : RELEVANTLY

[2]**ad rem** *adj* : relevant to the point or purpose

adren- *or* **adreno-** *comb form* [*adrenal*] **1** : adrenal glands <*adreno*cortical> **2** : adrenaline <*adren*ergic>

[1]**ad·re·nal** \ə-ˈdrēn-ᵊl\ *adj* **1** : adjacent to the kidneys **2** : of, relating to, or derived from adrenal glands or secretion — **ad·re·nal·ly** \-ᵊl-ē\ *adv*

[2]**adrenal** *n* : ADRENAL GLAND

ad·re·nal·ec·to·my \ə-ˌdrēn-ᵊl-ˈek-tə-mē\ *n* : surgical removal of one or both adrenal glands — **ad·re·nal·ec·to·mized** \-ˌmīzd\ *adj*

adrenal gland *n* : either of a pair of complex endocrine organs near the anterior medial border of the kidney consisting of a mesodermal cortex that produces steroids like sex hormones and hormones concerned esp. with metabolic functions and an ectodermal medulla that produces adrenaline — called also *adrenal*

Adren·a·lin \ə-ˈdren-ᵊl-ən\ *trademark* — used for a preparation of levorotatory epinephrine

adren·a·line \ə-ˈdren-ᵊl-ən\ *n* : EPINEPHRINE

ad·ren·er·gic \ˌad-rə-ˈnər-jik\ *adj* [*adren-* + Gk *ergon* work — more at WORK] **1** : liberating or activated by adrenaline or a substance like adrenaline <an ~ nerve> **2** : resembling adrenaline

ad·re·no·cor·ti·cal \ə-ˌdrē-nō-ˈkȯrt-i-kəl\ *adj* : of, relating to, or derived from the cortex of the adrenal glands

ad·re·no·cor·ti·co·ste·roid \ə-ˈdrē-nō-ˌkȯrt-i-kō-ˈsti(ə)r-ˌȯid *also* -ˈste(ə)r-\ *n* : a steroid obtained from or resembling or having physiological effects like those of the adrenal cortex

ad·re·no·cor·ti·co·tro·phic \ə-ˈdrē-nō-ˌkȯrt-i-kō-ˈtrō-fik\ *or* **adre·no·cor·ti·co·trop·ic** \-ˈträp-ik\ *adj* : acting on or stimulating the adrenal cortex

adrenocorticotrophic hormone *n* : a protein hormone of the anterior lobe of the pituitary gland that stimulates the adrenal cortex — called also *ACTH*

ad·re·no·cor·ti·co·tro·phin \-ˈtrō-fən\ *n* : ADRENOCORTICOTROPHIC HORMONE

adrift \ə-ˈdrift\ *adv or adj* **1** : without motive power and without anchor or mooring **2** : without guidance or purpose

adroit \ə-ˈdrȯit\ *adj* [F, fr. *à droit* properly] **1** : dexterous in the use of the hands **2** : marked by shrewdness, craft, or resourcefulness in coping with difficulty or danger ***syn*** **1** see DEXTEROUS ***ant*** maladroit **2** see CLEVER ***ant*** stolid — **adroit·ly** *adv* — **adroit·ness** *n*

ad·sci·ti·tious \ˌad-sə-ˈtish-əs\ *adj* [L *adscitus*, fr. pp. of *adsciscere* to receive, fr. *ad-* + *sciscere* to accept, fr. *scire* to know — more at SCIENCE] : derived or acquired from something extrinsic

ad·sorb \ad-ˈsȯ(ə)rb, -ˈzȯ(ə)rb\ *vb* [*ad-* + *-sorb* (as in *absorb*)] *vt* : to take up and hold by adsorption ~ *vi* : to become adsorbed — **ad·sorb·able** \-ˈsȯr-bə-bəl, -ˈzȯr-\ *adj*

ad·sorb·ate \ad-ˈsȯr-bət, -ˈzȯr-, -ˌbāt\ *n* : an adsorbed substance

ad·sor·bent \-bənt\ *adj* : having the capacity or tendency to adsorb — **adsorbent** *n*

ad·sorp·tion \ad-ˈsȯrp-shən, -ˈzȯrp-\ *n* [irreg. fr. *adsorb*] : the adhesion in an extremely thin layer of molecules (as of gases, solutes, or liquids) to the surfaces of solid bodies or liquids with which they are in contact — compare ABSORPTION — **ad·sorp·tive** \-ˈsȯrp-tiv, -ˈzȯrp-\ *adj*

ad·u·lar·ia \ˌaj-ə-ˈlar-ē-ə, -ˈler-\ *n* [It *adularia,* fr. F *adulaire,* fr. *Adula,* Swiss mountain group] **:** a transparent or translucent orthoclase

ad·u·late \ˈaj-ə-ˌlāt\ *vt* **-lat·ed; -lat·ing** [back-formation fr. *adulation,* fr. ME, fr. MF, fr. L *adulation-, adulatio,* fr. *adulatus,* pp. of *adulari* to flatter] **:** to flatter or admire excessively or slavishly — **ad·u·la·tion** \ˌaj-ə-ˈlā-shən\ *n* — **ad·u·la·tor** \ˈaj-ə-ˌlāt-ər\ *n* — **ad·u·la·to·ry** \-lə-ˌtōr-ē, -ˌtȯr-\ *adj*

¹adult \ə-ˈdəlt, ˈad-ˌəlt\ *adj* [L *adultus,* pp. of *adolescere* to grow up, fr. *ad-* + *-olescere* (fr. *alescere* to grow) — more at OLD] **1 :** fully developed and mature **:** GROWN-UP **2 a :** of, relating to, or befitting adults <an ~ approach to a problem> **b :** restricted to adults <~ movies> ***syn*** see MATURE ***ant*** juvenile, puerile — **adult·hood** \ə-ˈdəlt-ˌhu̇d\ *n* — **adult·like** \ə-ˈdəlt-ˌlīk\ *adj* — **adult·ly** \ə-ˈdəlt-lē, ˈad-ˌəlt-\ *adv* — **adult·ness** \ə-ˈdəlt-nəs, ˈad-ˌəlt-\ *n*

²adult *n* **:** one that is adult; *esp* **:** a human being after an age (as 21) specified by law

adult education *n* **:** lecture or correspondence courses for adults usu. not otherwise engaged in formal study

adul·ter·ant \ə-ˈdəl-t(ə-)rənt\ *n* **:** an adulterating substance or agent — **adulterant** *adj*

¹adul·ter·ate \ə-ˈdəl-tə-ˌrāt\ *vt* **-at·ed; -at·ing** [L *adulteratus,* pp. of *adulterare,* fr. *ad-* + *alter* other — more at ELSE] **:** to corrupt, debase, or make impure by the addition of a foreign or inferior substance; *esp* **:** to prepare for sale by replacing more valuable with less valuable or inert ingredients — **adul·ter·a·tor** \-ˌrāt-ər\ *n*

²adul·ter·ate \ə-ˈdəl-t(ə-)rət\ *adj* **1 :** tainted with adultery **:** ADULTEROUS **2 :** being adulterated **:** SPURIOUS

adul·ter·a·tion \ə-ˌdəl-tə-ˈrā-shən\ *n* **1 :** the process of adulterating **:** the condition of being adulterated **2 :** an adulterated product

adul·ter·er \ə-ˈdəl-tər-ər\ *n* **:** one that commits adultery; *esp* **:** a man who commits adultery

adul·ter·ess \ə-ˈdəl-t(ə-)rəs\ *n* **:** a woman who commits adultery

adul·ter·ine \ə-ˈdəl-tə-ˌrīn, -ˌrēn\ *adj* **1 a :** marked by adulteration **:** SPURIOUS **b :** ILLEGAL **2 :** born of adultery

adul·ter·ous \ə-ˈdəl-t(ə-)rəs\ *adj* **:** relating to, characterized by, or given to adultery — **adul·ter·ous·ly** *adv*

adul·tery \ə-ˈdəl-t(ə-)rē\ *n, pl* **-ter·ies** [ME, alter. of *avoutrie,* fr. MF, fr. L *adulterium,* fr. *adulter* adulterer, back-formation fr. *adulterare*] **:** voluntary sexual intercourse between a married man and someone other than his wife or between a married woman and someone other than her husband; *also* **:** an act of adultery

ad·um·brate \ˈad-əm-ˌbrāt, a-ˈdəm-\ *vt* **-brat·ed; -brat·ing** [L *adumbratus,* pp. of *adumbrare,* fr. *ad-* + *umbra* shadow — more at UMBRAGE] **1 :** to foreshadow vaguely **:** INTIMATE **2 a :** to give a sketchy representation or outline of **b :** to suggest or disclose partially **3 :** OVERSHADOW, OBSCURE — **ad·um·bra·tion** \ˌad-(ˌ)əm-ˈbrā-shən\ *n* — **ad·um·bra·tive** \a-ˈdəm-brət-iv\ *adj* — **ad·um·bra·tive·ly** *adv*

adust \ə-ˈdəst\ *adj* [ME, fr. L *adustus,* pp. of *adurere* to set fire to, fr. *ad-* + *urere* to burn — more at EMBER] **1 :** SCORCHED, BURNED **2** *archaic* **:** of a sunburned appearance **3** *archaic* **:** of a gloomy appearance or disposition

adv *abbr* **1** adverb **2** [L *adversus*] against **3** advertisement; advertising **4** advisory

ad val *abbr* ad valorem

ad va·lo·rem \ˌad-və-ˈlōr-əm, -ˈlȯr-\ *adj* [L, according to the value] **:** imposed at a rate percent of the value as stated in an invoice <*ad valorem* tax on goods>

¹ad·vance \əd-ˈvan(t)s\ *vb* **ad·vanced; ad·vanc·ing** [ME *advauncen,* fr. OF *avancier,* fr. (assumed) VL *abantiare,* fr. L *abante* before, fr. *ab-* + *ante* before — more at ANTE-] *vt* **1 :** to bring or move forward **2 :** to accelerate the growth or progress of **3 :** to raise to a higher rank **4 :** to supply or furnish in expectation of repayment **5** *archaic* **:** to lift up **:** RAISE **6 a :** to bring forward in time; *esp* **:** to make earlier <~ the date of the meeting> **b :** to place later in time **7 :** to bring forward for notice, consideration, or acceptance **:** PROPOSE **8 :** to raise in rate **:** INCREASE <~ the rent> ~ *vi* **1 :** to move forward **:** PROCEED **2 :** to make progress **:** INCREASE <~ in age> **3 :** to rise in rank, position, or importance **4 :** to rise in rate or price — **ad·vanc·er** *n*

syn* 1** ADVANCE, PROMOTE, FORWARD, FURTHER *shared meaning element* **:** to help to move ahead ***ant retard, check
2 see ADDUCE

²advance *n* **1 :** a moving forward **2 a :** progress in development **:** IMPROVEMENT <an ~ in medical technique> **b :** a progressive step <the job meant a personal ~ forward> **3 :** a rise in price, value, or amount **4 :** a first step or approach made **:** OFFER <her attitude discouraged all ~*s*> **5 :** a provision of something (as money or goods) before a return is received; *also* **:** the money or goods supplied — **in advance :** BEFOREHAND — **in advance of :** ahead of

³advance *adj* **1 :** made, sent, or furnished ahead of time <an ~ payment> **2 :** going or situated before <an ~ party of soldiers>

ad·vanced *adj* **1 :** far on in time or course <a man ~ in years> **2 a :** beyond the elementary or introductory <~ chemistry> **b :** being beyond others in progress or development <an ~ country>

advanced degree *n* **:** a university degree (as a master's or doctor's degree) higher than a bachelor's

advance man *n* **1 :** a business representative (as of a theatrical company) who makes necessary arrangements for the public appearance of the company — called also *advance agent* **2 :** an aide (as of a political candidate) who makes a security check or handles publicity in advance

ad·vance·ment \əd-ˈvan(t)-smənt\ *n* **1 :** the action of advancing **:** the state of being advanced: **a :** promotion or elevation to a higher rank or position **b :** progression to a higher stage of development **2 :** an advance of money or value

¹ad·van·tage \əd-ˈvant-ij\ *n* [ME *avantage,* fr. MF, fr. *avant* before, fr. L *abante*] **1 :** superiority of position or condition <higher ground gave the enemy the ~> **2 a :** BENEFIT, GAIN; *esp* **:** benefit resulting from some course of action <a mistake which turned out to his ~> **b** *obs* **:** INTEREST 3a **3 :** a factor or circumstance of benefit to its possessor <lacked the ~*s* of an education> **4 :** the first point won in tennis after deuce; *also* **:** the score for it — **to advantage :** so as to produce a favorable impression or effect

²advantage *vt* **-taged; -tag·ing :** to give an advantage to **:** BENEFIT

ad·van·ta·geous \ˌad-ˌvan-ˈtā-jəs, -vən-\ *adj* **:** giving an advantage **:** FAVORABLE ***syn*** see BENEFICIAL ***ant*** disadvantageous — **ad·van·ta·geous·ly** *adv* — **ad·van·ta·geous·ness** *n*

ad·vec·tion \ad-ˈvek-shən\ *n* [L *advection-, advectio* act of bringing, fr. *advectus,* pp. of *advehere* to carry to, fr. *ad-* + *vehere* to carry — more at WAY] **:** the horizontal movement of a mass of air that causes changes in temperature or in other physical properties of the air — **ad·vec·tive** \-ˈvek-tiv\ *adj*

Ad·vent \ˈad-ˌvent\ *n* [ME, fr. ML *adventus,* fr. L, arrival, fr. *adventus,* pp.] **1 :** the period beginning four Sundays before Christmas and observed by some Christians as a season of prayer and fasting **2 a :** the coming of Christ at the Incarnation **b :** SECOND COMING **3** *not cap* **:** ARRIVAL, COMING <the ~ of spring>

Ad·vent·ism \ˈad-ˌvent-ˌiz-əm\ *n* **1 :** the doctrine that the second coming of Christ and the end of the world are near at hand **2 :** the principles and practices of Seventh-Day Adventists — **Ad·vent·ist** \əd-ˈvent-əst, ad-ˈ, ˈad-ˌ\ *adj or n*

ad·ven·ti·tia \ˌad-vən-ˈtish-ə, -(ˌ)ven-\ *n* [NL, alter. of L *adventicia,* neut. pl. of *adventicius* coming from outside, fr. *adventus,* pp.] **:** an external chiefly connective tissue covering of an organ; *esp* **:** the external coat of a blood vessel — **ad·ven·ti·tial** \-əl\ *adj*

ad·ven·ti·tious \ˌad-vən-ˈtish-əs, -(ˌ)ven-\ *adj* [L *adventicius*] **1 :** added from another source and not inherent or innate **2 :** arising or occurring sporadically or in other than the usual location <~ buds> ***syn*** see ACCIDENTAL ***ant*** inherent — **ad·ven·ti·tious·ly** *adv* — **ad·ven·ti·tious·ness** *n*

ad·ven·tive \ad-ˈvent-iv\ *adj* **1 :** introduced but not fully naturalized **2 :** ADVENTITIOUS 2 — **adventive** *n* — **ad·ven·tive·ly** *adv*

Advent Sunday *n* **:** the first Sunday in Advent

¹ad·ven·ture \əd-ˈven-chər\ *n* [ME *aventure,* fr. OF, fr. (assumed) VL *adventura,* fr. L *adventus,* pp. of *advenire* to arrive, fr. *ad-* + *venire* to come — more at COME] **1 a :** an undertaking involving danger and unknown risks **b :** the encountering of risks <the spirit of ~> **2 :** an exciting or remarkable experience <an ~ in exotic dining> **3 :** an enterprise involving financial risk

²adventure *vb* **ad·ven·tured; ad·ven·tur·ing** \-ˈvench-(ə-)riŋ\ *vt* **1 :** to expose to danger or loss **:** VENTURE **2 :** to venture upon **:** TRY ~ *vi* **1 :** to proceed despite danger or risk **2 :** to take the risk

ad·ven·tur·er \əd-ˈvench-(ə-)rər\ *n* **1 :** one that adventures: as **a :** SOLDIER OF FORTUNE **b :** one that engages in risky commercial enterprises for profit **2 :** one who seeks unmerited wealth or position esp. by playing on the credulity or prejudice of others

ad·ven·ture·some \əd-ˈven-chər-səm\ *adj* **:** inclined to take risks **:** VENTURESOME — **ad·ven·ture·some·ness** *n*

ad·ven·tur·ess \əd-ˈvench-(ə-)rəs\ *n* **:** a female adventurer; *esp* **:** a woman who seeks position or livelihood by questionable means

ad·ven·tur·ism \əd-ˈven-chə-ˌriz-əm\ *n* **:** ill-considered or rash improvisation or experimentation esp. in politics or foreign affairs in the absence or in defiance of consistent plans or principles — **ad·ven·tur·ist** \-ˈvench-(ə-)rəst\ *n* — **ad·ven·tur·is·tic** \-ˌven-chə-ˈris-tik\ *adj*

ad·ven·tur·ous \əd-ˈvench-(ə-)rəs\ *adj* **1 :** disposed to seek adventure or to cope with the new and unknown <an ~ explorer> **2 :** characterized by unknown dangers and risks <an ~ journey> — **ad·ven·tur·ous·ly** *adv* — **ad·ven·tur·ous·ness** *n*

syn ADVENTUROUS, VENTURESOME, DARING, DAREDEVIL, RASH, RECKLESS, FOOLHARDY *shared meaning element* **:** exposing oneself to danger beyond what is called for by duty or courage ***ant*** cautious

¹ad·verb \ˈad-ˌvərb\ *n* [MF *adverbe,* fr. L *adverbium,* fr. *ad-* + *verbum* word — more at WORD] **:** a word belonging to one of the major form classes in any of numerous languages, typically serving as a modifier of a verb, an adjective, another adverb, a preposition, a phrase, a clause, or a sentence, and expressing some relation of manner or quality, place, time, degree, number, cause, opposition, affirmation, or denial

²adverb *adj* **:** ADVERBIAL

ad·ver·bi·al \ad-ˈvər-bē-əl\ *adj* **:** of, relating to, or having the function of an adverb — **adverbial** *n* — **ad·ver·bi·al·ly** \-ə-lē\ *adv*

ad ver·bum \(ˈ)ad-ˈvər-bəm\ *adv* [L] **:** to a word **:** VERBATIM

¹ad·ver·sary \ˈad-və(r)-ˌser-ē\ *n, pl* **-sar·ies :** one that contends with, opposes, or resists **:** ENEMY ***syn*** see OPPONENT — **ad·ver·sari·ness** *n*

²adversary *adj* **1 :** of, relating to, or involving an adversary **2 :** having or involving antagonistic parties or interests <divorce can be an ~ proceeding>

ad·ver·sa·tive \əd-ˈvər-sət-iv, ad-\ *adj* **:** expressing antithesis, opposition, or adverse circumstance <the ~ conjunction *but*> — **adversative** *n* — **ad·ver·sa·tive·ly** *adv*

ad·verse \ad-ˈvərs, ˈad-ˌ\ *adj* [ME, fr. MF *advers,* fr. L *adversus,* pp. of *advertere*] **1 :** acting against or in a contrary direction **:** HOSTILE <hindered by ~ winds> **2 :** opposed to one's interests **:** UNFAVORABLE <an ~ verdict> **3 :** opposite in position <on the ~ page> — **ad·verse·ly** *adv* — **ad·verse·ness** *n*

syn ADVERSE, INIMICAL, ANTAGONISTIC, COUNTER, COUNTERACTIVE *shared meaning element* **:** so opposed as to cause often harmful interference ***ant*** propitious

ad·ver·si·ty \əd-ˈvər-sət-ē\ *n, pl* **-ties** **1 :** a condition of suffering, destitution, or affliction **2 :** a calamitous or disastrous experience ***syn*** see MISFORTUNE ***ant*** prosperity

1ad·vert \əd-ˈvərt\ *vi* [ME *adverten,* fr. MF & L; MF *advertir,* fr. L *advertere,* fr. *ad-* + *vertere* to turn — more at WORTH] **1 :** to pay heed or attention **2 :** to make a usu. slight or glancing reference : refer casually (as by interpolation) ***syn*** see REFER

2ad·vert \ˈad-ˌvərt\ *n, chiefly Brit* : ADVERTISEMENT

ad·ver·tence \əd-ˈvərt-ᵊns\ *n* **1 :** the action or process of adverting : ATTENTION **2 :** ADVERTENCY 1

ad·ver·ten·cy \-ᵊn-sē\ *n, pl* **-cies** **1 :** the quality or state of being advertent : HEEDFULNESS **2 :** ADVERTENCE 1

ad·ver·tent \-ᵊnt\ *adj* [L *advertent-, advertens,* prp. of *advertere*] : giving attention : HEEDFUL — **ad·ver·tent·ly** *adv*

ad·ver·tise \ˈad-vər-ˌtīz\ *vb* **-tised; -tis·ing** [ME *advertisen,* fr. MF *advertiss-,* stem of *advertir*] *vt* **1 :** to make known to : NOTIFY **2 a :** to make publicly and generally known <*advertising* their readiness to make concessions> **b :** to announce publicly esp. by a printed notice or a broadcast **c :** to call public attention to esp. by emphasizing desirable qualities so as to arouse a desire to buy or patronize ~ *vi* **:** to issue or sponsor advertising <~ for a secretary> ***syn*** see DECLARE — **ad·ver·tis·er** *n*

ad·ver·tise·ment \ˌad-vər-ˈtīz-mənt; əd-ˈvərt-əz-mənt, -ə-smənt\ *n* **1 :** the act or process of advertising **2 :** a public notice; *esp* : one published in the press or broadcast over the air

ad·ver·tis·ing *n* **1 :** the action of calling something to the attention of the public esp. by paid announcements **2 :** ADVERTISEMENTS <the magazine contains much ~> **3 :** the business of preparing advertisements for publication or broadcast

ad·vice \əd-ˈvīs\ *n* [ME, fr. OF *avis* opinion, prob. fr. the phrase *ce m'est a vis* that appears to me, part. trans. of L *mihi visum est* it seemed so to me, I decided] **1 :** recommendation regarding a decision or course of conduct : COUNSEL <he shall have power, by and with the ~ and consent of the Senate, to make treaties — *U.S. Constitution*> **2 :** information or notice given : INTELLIGENCE — usu. used in pl. **3 :** an official notice concerning a business transaction <a remittance ~>

ad·vis·able \əd-ˈvī-zə-bəl\ *adj* **:** fit to be advised or done : PRUDENT ***syn*** see EXPEDIENT ***ant*** inadvisable — **ad·vis·abil·i·ty** \-ˌvī-zə-ˈbil-ət-ē\ *n* — **ad·vis·able·ness** \-ˈvī-zə-bəl-nəs\ *n* — **ad·vis·ably** \-blē\ *adv*

ad·vise \əd-ˈvīz\ *vb* **ad·vised; ad·vis·ing** [MF *advisen,* fr. OF *aviser,* fr. *avis*] *vt* **1 a :** to give advice to : COUNSEL <~ her to try a drier climate> **b :** CAUTION, WARN <~ him of the danger> **c :** RECOMMEND <~ prudence> **2 :** to give information or notice to : INFORM <~ his friends of his marriage> ~ *vi* **1 :** to give advice <~ on legal matters> **2 :** to take counsel : CONSULT <~ with one's parents> — **ad·vis·er** *or* **ad·vi·sor** \-ˈvī-zər\ *n*

ad·vised \əd-ˈvīzd\ *adj* **:** thought out : CONSIDERED — usu. used in combination <ill-*advised* plans> — **ad·vis·ed·ly** \-ˈvī-zəd-lē\ *adv*

ad·vis·ee \əd-ˌvī-ˈzē\ *n* **:** one that is advised

ad·vise·ment \əd-ˈvīz-mənt\ *n* **:** careful consideration : DELIBERATION

1ad·vi·so·ry \əd-ˈvīz-(ə-)rē\ *adj* **1 :** having or exercising power to advise **2 :** containing or giving advice

2advisory *n, pl* **-ries** **:** a report giving information (as on the weather)

ad·vo·ca·cy \ˈad-və-kə-sē\ *n* **:** the act or process of advocating : SUPPORT

1ad·vo·cate \ˈad-və-kət, -ˌkāt\ *n* [ME *advocat,* fr. MF, fr. L *advocatus,* fr. pp. of *advocare* to summon, fr. *ad-* + *vocare* to call — more at VOICE] **1 :** one that pleads the cause of another; *specif* : one that pleads the cause of another before a tribunal or judicial court <the ~ for the defense> **2 :** one that defends or maintains a cause or proposal

2ad·vo·cate \-ˌkāt\ *vt* **-cat·ed; -cat·ing: :** to plead in favor of ***syn*** see SUPPORT — **ad·vo·ca·tion** \ˌad-və-ˈkā-shən\ *n* — **ad·vo·ca·tive** \ˈad-və-ˌkāt-iv\ *adj* — **ad·vo·ca·tor** \-ˌkāt-ər\ *n*

ad·vow·son \əd-ˈvau̇-zᵊn\ *n* [ME, fr. OF *avoueson,* fr. ML *advocation-, advocatio,* fr. L, act of calling, fr. *advocatus,* pp.] **:** the right in English law of presenting a nominee to a vacant ecclesiastical benefice

advt *abbr* advertisement

ady·nam·ic \ˌā(ˌ)dī-ˈnam-ik, ˌad-ə-ˈnam-\ *adj* [Gk *adynamia* lack of strength, fr. *a-* + *dynamis* power, fr. *dynasthai* to be able] **:** characterized by or causing a loss of strength or function

ad·y·tum \ˈad-ə-təm\ *n, pl* **-ta** \-tə\ [L, fr. Gk *adyton,* neut. of *adytos* not to be entered, fr. *a-* + *dyein* to enter; akin to Skt *upā-du* to put on] **:** the innermost sanctuary in an ancient temple open only to priests : SANCTUM

adz *or* **adze** \ˈadz\ *n* [ME *adse,* fr. OE *adesa*] **:** a cutting tool that has a thin arched blade set at right angles to the handle and is used chiefly for shaping wood

adzes: *1* carpenter's with flat head, *2* shipwright's with spur, *3* cooper's

ae \ˈā\ *adj* [ME (northern dial.) *a,* alter. of *an*] *chiefly Scot* : ONE

Ae·a·cus \ˈē-ə-kəs\ *n* [L, fr. Gk *Aiakos*] **:** a son of Zeus who was given the Myrmidons as followers and became on his death a judge of the underworld

AEC *abbr* Atomic Energy Commission

ae·cio·spore \ˈē-s(h)ē-ə-ˌspō(ə)r, -ˌspȯ(ə)r\ *n* **:** one of the spores arranged within an aecium in a series like a chain

ae·ci·um \ˈē-s(h)ē-əm\ *n, pl* **-cia** \-s(h)ē-ə\ [NL, fr. Gk *aikia* assault, fr. *aeikēs* unseemly, fr. *a-* + *eikōs* seemly, fr. participle of *eikenai* to seem] **:** the fruiting body of a rust fungus in which the first binucleate spores are usu. produced — **ae·cial** \-sh(ē-)əl\ *adj*

aë·des \ā-ˈēd-(ˌ)ēz\ *n, pl* **aëdes** [NL, genus name, fr. Gk *aēdēs* unpleasant, fr. *a-* + *ēdos* pleasure; akin to Gk *hēdys* sweet — more at SWEET] **:** any of a genus (*Aëdes*) of mosquitoes including the vector of yellow fever, dengue, and other diseases — see MOSQUITO illustration — **ae·dine** \-ˈē-ˌdīn\ *adj*

ae·dile \ˈē-ˌdīl\ *n* [L *aedilis,* fr. *aedes* temple — more at EDIFY] **:** an official in ancient Rome in charge of public works and games, police, and the grain supply

AEF *abbr* American Expeditionary Force

Ae·ge·an \i-ˈjē-ən\ *adj* [L *Aegaeus,* fr. Gk *Aigaios*] **1 :** of or relating to the arm of the Mediterranean sea east of Greece **2 :** of or relating to the chiefly Bronze Age civilization of the islands of the Aegean sea and the countries adjacent to it

ae·gis \ˈē-jəs\ *n* [L, fr. Gk *aigis* goatskin, perh. fr. *aig-, aix* goat; akin to Arm *aic* goat] **1 :** a shield or breastplate emblematic of majesty that was orig. associated chiefly with Zeus but later mainly with Athena **2 :** PROTECTION <under the ~ of the law> **3 :** AUSPICES, SPONSORSHIP <under the ~ of the education department>

Ae·gis·thus \i-ˈjis-thəs\ *n* [L, fr. Gk *Aigisthos*] **:** a lover of the married Clytemnestra slain with her by her son Orestes

-aemia — see -EMIA

Ae·ne·as \i-ˈnē-əs\ *n* [L, fr. Gk *Aineias*] **:** a son of Anchises and Aphrodite, defender of Troy, and hero of Vergil's *Aeneid*

Aeneo·lith·ic \ā-ˌē-nē-ō-ˈlith-ik\ *adj* [L *aeneus* of copper or bronze, fr. *aes* copper, bronze — more at ORE] **:** of or relating to a transitional period between the Neolithic and Bronze ages in which some copper was used

1ae·o·lian \ē-ˈō-lē-ən, -ˈōl-yən\ *adj* **1** *often cap* **:** of or relating to Aeolus **2 :** giving forth or marked by a soughing sound or musical tone produced by or as if by the wind

2aeolian *var of* EOLIAN

1Ae·o·lian \ē-ˈō-lē-ən, -ˈōl-yən\ *adj* **:** of or relating to Aeolis or its inhabitants

2Aeolian *n* **1 :** a member of a group of Greek peoples of Thessaly and Boeotia that colonized Lesbos and the adjacent coast of Asia Minor **2 :** AEOLIC

aeolian harp *n* **:** a box-shaped musical instrument having stretched strings usu. tuned in unison on which the wind produces varying harmonics over the same fundamental tone

1Ae·ol·ic \ē-ˈäl-ik\ *adj* **:** AEOLIAN

2Aeolic *n* **:** a group of ancient Greek dialects used by the Aeolians

ae·o·lo·trop·ic \ˌē-ə-lō-ˈträp-ik\ *adj* [Gk *aiolos* variegated] **:** ANISOTROPIC 1 — **ae·o·lot·ro·py** \-ˈlä-trə-pē\ *n*

Ae·o·lus \ˈē-ə-ləs\ *n* [L, fr. Gk *Aiolos*] **:** the Greek god of the winds

ae·on \ˈē-ən, ˈē-ˌän\ *n* [L, fr. Gk *aiōn* — more at AYE] **1 :** an immeasurably or indefinitely long period of time : AGE **2 :** a unit of time equal to one billion years — used in geology

ae·o·ni·an \ē-ˈō-nē-ən\ *or* **ae·on·ic** \-ˈän-ik\ *adj* **:** lasting for an immeasurably or indefinitely long period of time

ae·py·or·nis \ˌē-pē-ˈȯr-nəs\ *n* [NL, genus name, fr. Gk *aipys* high + *ornis* bird — more at ERNE] **:** any of a group (genus *Aepyornis* or order Aepyornithiformes) of gigantic ratite birds known only from remains found in Madagascar

aeq *abbr* [L *aequales*] equal

aer- *or* **aero-** *comb form* [ME *aero-,* fr. MF, fr. L, fr. Gk *aer-, aero-,* fr. *aēr*] **1 a :** air : atmosphere <*aer*ate> <*aero*biology> **b :** aerial and <*aero*marine> **2 :** gas <*aero*sol> **3 :** aviation <*aero*drome>

aer·ate \ˈa(-ə)r-ˌāt, ˈe(-ə)r-\ *vt* **aer·at·ed; aer·at·ing** **1 :** to supply (the blood) with oxygen by respiration **2 :** to supply or impregnate (as the soil or a liquid) with air **3 a :** to combine or charge with a gas (as carbon dioxide) **b :** to make effervescent — **aer·a·tion** \ˌa(-ə)r-ˈā-shən, ˌe(-ə)r-\ *n*

aer·a·tor \ˈa(-ə)r-ˌāt-ər, ˈe(-ə)r-\ *n* **:** one that aerates; *esp* **:** an apparatus for aerating something (as sewage)

aer·en·chy·ma \ˌa(ə)r-ˈeŋ-kə-mə, ˌe(ə)r-\ *n* [NL] **:** the spongy modified cork tissue of many aquatic plants that facilitates gaseous exchange and maintains buoyancy

1ae·ri·al \ˈar-ē-əl, ˈer-, ā-ˈir-ē-əl\ *adj* [L *aerius,* fr. Gk *aerios,* fr. *aēr*] **1 a :** of, relating to, or occurring in the air or atmosphere **b :** consisting of air <~ particles> **c :** existing or growing in the air rather than in the ground or in water **d :** LOFTY <~ spires> **e :** operating or operated overhead on elevated cables or rails <an ~ railroad> **2 :** suggestive of air: as **a :** lacking substance : THIN <fine and ~ distinctions> **b :** IMAGINARY, ETHEREAL <visions of ~ joy — P. B. Shelley> **3 a :** of or relating to aircraft <~ navigation> **b :** designed for use in, taken from, or operating from or against aircraft <~ photo> **c :** effected by means of aircraft <~ transportation> **4 :** of, relating to, or gained by the forward pass in football — **ae·ri·al·ly** \-ə-lē\ *adv*

2aer·i·al \ˈar-ē-əl, ˈer-\ *n* **1 :** ANTENNA 2 **2 :** FORWARD PASS

ae·ri·al·ist \ˈar-ē-ə-ləst, ˈer-, ā-ˈir-\ *n* **:** one that performs feats in the air or above the ground esp. on the flying trapeze

aerial ladder *n* **:** a mechanically operated extensible ladder usu. mounted on a fire truck

aerial perspective *n* **:** the expression of space in painting by gradation of color and distinctness

ae·rie \ˈa(ə)r-ē, ˈe(ə)r-, ˈi(ə)r-, ˈā-(ə-)rē\ *n* [ML *aerea,* fr. OF *aire,* fr. L *area* area, feeding place for animals] **1 :** the nest of a bird on a cliff or a mountaintop **2** *obs* **:** a brood of birds of prey **3 :** a dwelling on a height

1aero \ˈa(-ə)r-(ˌ)ō, ˈe(-ə)r-\ *adj* [*aero-*] **1 :** of or relating to aircraft or aeronautics <an ~ engine> **2 :** designed for aerial use <an ~ lens>

2aero *abbr* aeronautical; aeronautics

aero- — see AER-

aero·bal·lis·tics \ˌar-ō-bə-ˈlis-tiks, ˌer-\ *n pl but sing or pl in constr* **:** the ballistics of the flight of missiles and projectiles in the atmosphere — **aero·bal·lis·tic** \-tik\ *adj*

aer·o·bat·ics \ˌar-ə-ˈbat-iks, ˌer-\ *n pl but sing or pl in constr* [blend of *aer-* and *acrobatics*] **:** performance of stunts in an airplane or glider — **aer·o·bat·ic** \-ik\ *adj*

aer·obe \ˈa(-ə)r-ˌōb, ˈe(-ə)r-\ *n* [F *aérobie,* fr. *aér-* aer- + *-bie* (fr. Gk *bios* life) — more at QUICK] **:** an organism (as a bacterium) that lives only in the presence of oxygen

aer·o·bic \ˌa(ə)r-ˈrō-bik, ˌe(ə)r-\ *adj* **1 :** living, active, or occurring only in the presence of oxygen <~ respiration> **2 :** of, relating to, or induced by aerobes — **aer·o·bi·cal·ly** \-bi-k(ə-)lē\ *adv*

aero·bi·ol·o·gy \ˌar-ō-bī-ˈäl-ə-jē\ *n* [*aer-* + *biology*] **:** the science dealing with the occurrence, transportation, and effects of airborne microorganisms or biological objects (as viruses, pollen, or plant spores) — **aero·bi·o·log·i·cal** \-ˌbī-ə-ˈläj-i-kəl\ *adj* — **aero·bi·o·log·i·cal·ly** \-k(ə-)lē\ *adv*

aero·bi·o·sis \ˌar-ō-bī-ˈō-səs, ˌer-, -bē-\ *n, pl* **-o·ses** \-ˌsēz\ **:** life in the presence of air or oxygen — **aero·bi·ot·ic** \-ˈät-ik\ *adj* — **aero·bi·ot·i·cal·ly** \-i-k(ə-)lē\ *adv*

aero·drome \ˈar-ə-ˌdrōm, ˈer-\ *n, chiefly Brit* **:** AIRFIELD, AIRPORT

aero·dy·nam·i·cist \-ˈnam-ə-səst\ *n* **:** one who specializes in aerodynamics

aero·dy·nam·ics \ˌar-ō-dī-ˈnam-iks, ˌer-\ *n pl but sing or pl in constr* **:** a branch of dynamics that deals with the motion of air and other gaseous fluids and with the forces acting on bodies in motion relative to such fluids — **aero·dy·nam·ic** \-ik\ *or* **aero·dy·nam·i·cal** \-i-kəl\ *adj* — **aero·dy·nam·i·cal·ly** \-i-k(ə-)lē\ *adv*

aero·dyne \ˈar-ə-ˌdīn, ˈer-\ *n* [*aerodynamic*] **:** a heavier-than-air aircraft that derives its lift in flight from forces resulting from its motion through the air

aero·em·bo·lism \ˌar-ō-ˈem-bə-ˌliz-əm, ˌer-\ *n* **1 :** a gaseous embolism **2 :** a condition equivalent to caisson disease caused by rapid ascent to high altitudes and resulting exposure to rapidly lowered air pressure — called also *air bends*

aero·gram *or* **aero·gramme** \ˈar-ə-ˌgram, ˈer-\ *n* **:** AIR LETTER 2

aer·og·ra·pher \ˌa(ə)r-ˈräg-rə-fər, ˌe(ə)r-\ *n* **:** a navy warrant officer who observes and forecasts weather and surf conditions

aer·og·ra·phy \-fē\ *n* **:** METEOROLOGY

aer·o·lite \ˈar-ə-ˌlīt, ˈer-\ *also* **aero·lith** \-ˌlith\ *n* **:** a stony meteorite — **aer·o·lit·ic** \ˌar-ə-ˈlit-ik, ˌer-\ *adj*

aer·ol·o·gy \ˌa(ə)r-ˈäl-ə-jē, ˌe(ə)r-\ *n* **1 :** METEOROLOGY **2 :** a branch of meteorology that deals esp. with the air — **aer·o·log·i·cal** \ˌar-ə-ˈläj-i-kəl, ˌer-\ *adj* — **aer·ol·o·gist** \ˌa(ə)r-ˈäl-ə-jəst, ˌe(ə)r-\ *n*

aero·mag·net·ic \ˌar-ō-mag-ˈnet-ik, ˌer-\ *adj* **:** of, relating to, or derived from a study of the earth's magnetic field esp. from the air <an ~ survey>

aero·me·chan·ics \-mə-ˈkan-iks\ *n pl but sing or pl in constr* **:** mechanics that deals with the equilibrium and motion of gases and of solid bodies immersed in them

aero·med·i·cine \-ˈmed-ə-sən\ *n* **:** a branch of medicine that deals with the diseases and disturbances arising from flying and the associated physiological and psychological problems — **aero·med·i·cal** \-ˈmed-i-kəl\ *adj*

aero·me·te·or·o·graph \ˌar-ō-ˌmēt-ē-ˈȯr-ə-ˌgraf, ˌer-\ *n* **:** METEOROGRAPH; *esp* **:** one adapted for use on an airplane

aer·om·e·ter \ˌa(ə)r-ˈäm-ət-ər, ˌe(ə)r-\ *n* [prob. fr. F *aéromètre*, fr. *aér-* + *mètre* -meter] **:** an instrument for ascertaining the weight or density of air or other gases

aero·naut \ˈar-ə-ˌnȯt, ˈer-, -ˌnät\ *n* [F *aéronaute*, fr. *aér-* aer- + Gk *nautēs* sailor — more at NAUTICAL] **:** one that operates or travels in an airship or balloon

aero·nau·tics \ˌar-ə-ˈnȯt-iks\ *n pl but sing in constr* **1 :** a science dealing with the operation of aircraft **2 :** the art or science of flight — **aero·nau·ti·cal** \-i-kəl\ *or* **aero·nau·tic** \-ik\ *adj* — **aero·nau·ti·cal·ly** \-i-k(ə-)lē\ *adv*

aero·neu·ro·sis \ˌar-ō-n(y)u̇-ˈrō-səs, ˌer-\ *n* **:** a functional nervous disorder of airmen caused by emotional stress and characterized by physical symptoms (as restlessness, abdominal pains, and diarrhea)

aer·on·o·my \ˌa(ə)r-ˈän-ə-mē, ˌe(ə)r-\ *n* **:** a science that deals with the physics and chemistry of the upper atmosphere — **aer·on·o·mer** \-mər\ *n* — **aer·o·nom·ic** \ˌar-ə-ˈnäm-ik\ *or* **aer·o·nom·i·cal** \-i-kəl\ *adj* — **aer·o·nom·ics** \-iks\ *n pl but sing in constr* — **aer·on·o·mist** \ˌa(ə)r-ˈän-ə-məst, ˌe(ə)r-\ *n*

aero·pause \ˈar-ō-ˌpȯz, ˈer-\ *n* **:** the level above the earth's surface where the atmosphere becomes ineffective for human and aircraft functions

aero·plane \ˈar-ə-ˌplān, ˈer-\ *chiefly Brit var of* AIRPLANE

aero·sol \ˈar-ə-ˌsäl, ˈer-, -ˌsȯl\ *n* **1 :** a suspension of fine solid or liquid particles in gas <smoke, fog, and mist are ~*s*> **2 :** a substance (as an insecticide or cosmetic) dispensed from a pressurized container as an aerosol; *also* **:** the container for this

aero·sol·ize \-ˌīz\ *vt* **-ized; -iz·ing :** to disperse as an aerosol — **aero·sol·iza·tion** \ˌar-ə-ˌsäl-ə-ˈzā-shən, -ˌsȯl-\ *n*

[1]**aero·space** \ˈar-ō-ˌspās, ˈer-\ *n* **1 :** space comprising the earth's atmosphere and the space beyond **2 :** a physical science that deals with aerospace **3 :** the aerospace industry

[2]**aerospace** *adj* **:** of or relating to aerospace, to vehicles used in aerospace or the manufacture of such vehicles, or to travel in aerospace <~ research> <~ profits> <~ medicine>

aero·sphere \ˈar-ō-ˌsfi(ə)r, ˈer-\ *n* [F *aérosphère*, fr. *aér-* aer- + *sphère* sphere, fr. L *sphaera*] **:** the body of air around the earth

aero·stat \-ˌstat\ *n* [F *aérostat*, fr. *aér-* + *-stat*] **:** an aircraft that embodies one or more containers filled with a gas lighter than air and that is supported chiefly by buoyancy derived from the surrounding air

aero·stat·ics \ˌar-ō-ˈstat-iks, ˌer-\ *n pl but sing or pl in constr* [modif. of NL *aerostatica*, fr. *aer-* + *statica* statics] **:** a branch of statics that deals with the equilibrium of gaseous fluids and of solid bodies immersed in them

aero·ther·mo·dy·nam·ics \-ˌthər-mə-(ˌ)dī-ˈnam-iks\ *n pl but sing or pl in constr* **:** the thermodynamics of gases and esp. of air

[1]**aery** \ˈa(ə)r-ē, ˈe(ə)r-ē, ˈā-ə-rē\ *adj* **aer·ier; -est** [L *aerius* — more at AERIAL] **:** having an aerial quality **:** ETHEREAL <~ visions> — **aer·i·ly** \ˈar-ə-lē, ˈer-\ *adv*

[2]**aery** *like* AERIE\ *var of* AERIE

Aes·cu·la·pi·an \ˌes-kyə-ˈlā-pē-ən\ *adj* [*Aesculapius*, Greco-Roman god of medicine, fr. L, fr. Gk *Asklēpios*] **:** of or relating to Aesculapius or the healing art **:** MEDICAL

Ae·sir \ˈā-ˌsi(ə)r\ *n pl* [ON *Æsir*, pl. of *āss* god] **:** the principal race of Norse gods

Ae·so·pi·an \ē-ˈsō-pē-ən\ *also* **Ae·sop·ic** \-ˈsäp-ik\ *adj* **1 :** of, relating to, or characteristic of Aesop or his fables **2 :** conveying an innocent meaning to an outsider but a concealed meaning to an informed member of a conspiracy or underground movement <~ language>

aesthesio- — see ESTHESIO-

aes·thete \ˈes-ˌthēt\ *n* [back-formation fr. *aesthetic*] **:** one having or affecting sensitivity to the beautiful esp. in art

aes·thet·ic \es-ˈthet-ik, is-\ *adj* [G *ästhetisch*, fr. NL *aestheticus*, fr. Gk *aisthētikos* of sense perception, fr. *aisthanesthai* to perceive — more at AUDIBLE] **1 a :** of, relating to, or dealing with aesthetics or the beautiful <~ theories> **b :** ARTISTIC <a work of ~ value> **2 :** appreciative of, responsive to, or zealous about the beautiful — **aes·thet·i·cal** \-i-kəl\ *adj* — **aes·thet·i·cal·ly** \-i-k(ə-)lē\ *adv*

aesthetic distance *n* **:** the frame of reference that an artist creates by the use of technical devices in and around the work of art to differentiate it psychologically from reality

aes·the·ti·cian \ˌes-thə-ˈtish-ən\ *n* **:** a specialist in aesthetics

aes·thet·i·cism \es-ˈthet-ə-ˌsiz-əm, is-\ *n* **1 a :** a doctrine that the principles of beauty are basic to other and esp. moral principles **b :** the advocacy of artistic and aesthetic autonomy **2 :** devotion to or emphasis on beauty or the cultivation of the arts

aes·thet·ics \-ˈthet-iks\ *n pl but sing or pl in constr, also* **aes·thet·ic** \-ik\ **1 :** a branch of philosophy dealing with the nature of the beautiful and with judgments concerning beauty **2 :** the description and explanation of artistic phenomena and aesthetic experience by means of other sciences (as psychology, sociology, ethnology, or history) **3 :** a particular philosophical theory or conception of art or beauty

aes·ti·val \ˈes-tə-vəl\ *adj* [ME *estival*, fr. MF or L; MF, fr. L *aestivalis*, fr. *aestivus* of summer, fr. *aestas* summer — more at EDIFY] **:** of or relating to the summer

aes·ti·vate \-ˌvāt\ *vi* **-vat·ed; -vat·ing 1 :** to spend the summer usu. at one place **2 :** to pass the summer in a state of torpor — compare HIBERNATE

aes·ti·va·tion \ˌes-tə-ˈvā-shən\ *n* **1 :** the state of one that aestivates **2 :** the disposition or method of arrangement of floral parts in a bud

aet *or* **aetat** *abbr* [L *aetatis*] of age; aged

ae·ti·ol·o·gy *var of* ETIOLOGY

af *abbr* affix

AF *abbr* **1** air force **2** audio frequency

af- — see AD-

AFAM *abbr* Ancient Free and Accepted Masons

[1]**afar** \ə-ˈfär\ *adv* [ME *afer*, fr. *on fer* at a distance and *of fer* from a distance] **:** from, to, or at a great distance <roamed ~>

[2]**afar** *n* **:** a great distance <saw him from ~ >

AFB *abbr* air force base

AFC *abbr* **1** American Football Conference **2** automatic frequency control

A1C *abbr* airman first class

AFDC *abbr* Aid to Families with Dependent Children

afeard *or* **afeared** \ə-ˈfi(ə)rd\ *adj* [ME *afered*, fr. OE *āfǣred*, pp. of *āfǣran* to frighten, fr. *ā-*, perfective prefix + *fǣran* to frighten — more at ABIDE, FEAR] *dial* **:** AFRAID

aff *abbr* affirmative

af·fa·ble \ˈaf-ə-bəl\ *adj* [MF, fr. L *affabilis*, fr. *affari* to speak to, fr. *ad-* + *fari* to speak — more at BAN] **1 :** being pleasant and at ease in talking to others **2 :** characterized by ease and friendliness *syn* see GRACIOUS *ant* reserved — **af·fa·bil·i·ty** \ˌaf-ə-ˈbil-ət-ē\ *n* — **af·fa·bly** \-blē\ *adv*

af·fair \ə-ˈfa(ə)r, -ˈfe(ə)r\ *n* [ME & MF; ME *affaire*, fr. MF, fr. *a faire* to do] **1 a** *pl* **:** commercial, professional, or public business **b :** MATTER, CONCERN **2 :** a procedure, action, or occasion only vaguely specified; *also* **:** an object or collection of objects only vaguely specified <his house was a 2-story ~> **3** *also* **af·faire a :** a romantic or passionate attachment typically of limited duration **:** LIAISON 1b **b :** a matter occasioning public anxiety, controversy, or scandal **:** CASE

[1]**af·fect** \ˈaf-ˌekt\ *n* [L *affectus*, fr. *affectus*, pp.] **1** *obs* **:** FEELING, AFFECTION **2 :** the conscious subjective aspect of an emotion considered apart from bodily changes

[2]**af·fect** \ə-ˈfekt, a-\ *vb* [MF & L; MF *affecter*, fr. L *affectare*, fr. *affectus*, pp. of *afficere* to influence, fr. *ad-* + *facere* to do — more at DO] *vt* **1** *archaic* **:** to aim at **2 a** *archaic* **:** to have affection for **b :** to be given to **:** FANCY <~ flashy clothes> **3 :** to make a display of liking or using **:** CULTIVATE <~ a worldly manner> **4 :** to put on a pretense of **:** FEIGN <~ indifference, though deeply hurt> **5 :** to tend toward <drops of water ~ roundness> **6 :** FREQUENT ~ *vi, obs* **:** INCLINE 2 *syn* see ASSUME

[3]**affect** *vt* **:** to produce an effect upon: as **a :** to produce a material influence upon or alteration in <paralysis ~*ed* his limbs> **b :** to act upon (as a person or his mind or his feelings) so as to effect a response **:** INFLUENCE — **af·fect·abil·i·ty** \-ˌfek-tə-ˈbil-ət-ē\ *n* — **af·fect·able** \-ˈfek-tə-bəl\ *adj*

syn AFFECT, INFLUENCE, TOUCH, IMPRESS, STRIKE, SWAY *shared meaning element* **:** to produce or have an effect upon. AFFECT implies the action of a stimulus that can produce a response or reaction <the sight *affected* her to tears> INFLUENCE implies a force that brings about a change (as in nature or behavior) <our beliefs are *influenced* by our upbringing> <a drug that *influences* growth rates> TOUCH may carry a vivid suggestion of close contact and may connote stirring, arousing, or harming <plants *touched* by frost> <his emotions were *touched* by her distress> IMPRESS stresses the depth and persistence of the effect <only one of the plans *impressed* him> STRIKE, similar to but weaker than *impress*, may convey the notion of sudden sharp perception or appreciation <*struck* by the solemnity of the occasion> SWAY implies the acting of influences that are not resisted or are irresistible, with resulting change in character or course of action <he is *swayed* by fashion, by suggestion, by transient moods —H. L. Mencken>

af·fec·ta·tion \ˌaf-ˌek-ˈtā-shən\ *n* **1** *obs* **:** a striving after **2 a :** the act of taking on or displaying an attitude or mode of behavior not natural to oneself or not genuinely felt **b :** speech or conduct not natural to oneself **:** ARTIFICIALITY ***syn*** see POSE

af·fect·ed \ə-ˈfek-təd, a-\ *adj* **1 :** INCLINED, DISPOSED <was well ~ toward her> **2 a :** given to affection **b :** assumed artificially or falsely **:** PRETENDED <an ~ interest in art> — **af·fect·ed·ly** *adv* — **af·fect·ed·ness** *n*

af·fect·ing \ə-ˈfek-tiŋ, a-\ *adj* **:** evoking a strong emotional response ***syn*** see MOVING — **af·fect·ing·ly** \-tiŋ-lē\ *adv*

¹af·fec·tion \ə-ˈfek-shən\ *n* [ME, fr. MF *affection,* fr. L *affection-, affectio,* fr. *affectus,* pp.] **1 :** a moderate feeling or emotion **2 :** tender attachment **:** FONDNESS <she had a deep ~ for her parents> **3** *obs* **:** PARTIALITY, PREJUDICE **4 :** the feeling aspect (as in pleasure or displeasure) of consciousness **5 a :** PROPENSITY, DISPOSITION **b** *archaic* **:** AFFECTATION 2 ***syn*** see FEELING — **af·fec·tion·less** \-ləs\ *adj*

²affection *n* **1 :** the action of affecting **:** the state of being affected **2 a** (1) **:** a bodily condition (2) **:** DISEASE, MALADY **b :** ATTRIBUTE <shape and weight are ~*s* of bodies>

af·fec·tion·al \ə-ˈfek-shnəl, -shən-ᵊl\ *adj* **:** of or relating to the affections — **af·fec·tion·al·ly** \-ē\ *adv*

af·fec·tion·ate \ə-ˈfek-sh(ə-)nət\ *adj* **1** *obs* **:** mentally or emotionally affected or inclined **2 :** having affection or warm regard **:** LOVING **3 :** proceeding from affection **:** TENDER <~ care> — **af·fec·tion·ate·ly** *adv*

af·fec·tioned \-shənd\ *adj, archaic* **:** having a tendency, disposition, or inclination **:** DISPOSED

af·fec·tive \a-ˈfek-tiv\ *adj* **1 :** relating to, arising from, or influencing feelings or emotions **:** EMOTIONAL <~ disorders> **2 :** expressing emotion <~ language> — **af·fec·tive·ly** *adv* — **af·fec·tiv·i·ty** \ˌaf-ˌek-ˈtiv-ət-ē\ *n*

af·fect·less \ˈaf-ˌek-tləs, a-ˈfek-\ *adj* **:** UNFEELING <a ruthless ~ society> — **af·fect·less·ness** *n*

af·fen·pin·scher \ˈaf-ən-ˌpin-chər\ *n* [G, fr. *affe* monkey + *pinscher,* a breed of hunting dog] **:** any of a breed of small dogs with a stiff red, gray, or black coat, pointed ears, and bushy eyebrows, chin tuft, and mustache

af·fer·ent \ˈaf-ə-rənt, -ˌer-ənt\ *adj* [L *afferent-, afferens,* prp. of *afferre* to bring to, fr. *ad-* + *ferre* to bear — more at BEAR] **:** bearing or conducting inward; *specif* **:** conveying impulses toward a nerve center — compare EFFERENT — **af·fer·ent·ly** *adv*

¹af·fi·ance \ə-ˈfī-ən(t)s\ *n* [ME, fr. MF, fr. *affier* to pledge, trust, fr. ML *affidare* to pledge, fr. L *ad-* + (assumed) VL *fidare* to trust — more at FIANCÉ] *archaic* **:** TRUST, CONFIDENCE

²affiance *vt* **-anced; -anc·ing :** to solemnly promise (oneself or another) in marriage **:** BETROTH

af·fi·ant \ə-ˈfī-ənt\ *n* [MF, fr. prp. of *affier*] **:** one that swears to an affidavit; *broadly* **:** DEPONENT

af·fi·cio·na·do *var of* AFICIONADO

af·fi·da·vit \ˌaf-ə-ˈdā-vət\ *n* [ML, he has made an oath, fr. *affidare*] **:** a sworn statement in writing made esp. under oath or on affirmation before an authorized magistrate or officer

¹af·fil·i·ate \ə-ˈfil-ē-ˌāt\ *vb* **-at·ed; -at·ing** [ML *affiliatus,* pp. of *affiliare* to adopt as a son, fr. L *ad-* + *filius* son — more at FEMININE] *vt* **1 a :** to bring or receive into close connection as a member or branch **b :** to associate as a member <~*s* himself with the local club> **2 :** to trace the origin of ~ *vi* **:** to connect or associate oneself **:** COMBINE — **af·fil·i·a·tion** \-ˌfil-ē-ˈā-shən\ *n*

²af·fil·i·ate \-ˈfil-ē-ət\ *n* **:** an affiliated person or organization; *specif* **:** a company effectively controlled by another or associated with others under common ownership or control

af·fil·i·at·ed \-ē-ˌāt-əd\ *adj* **:** closely associated with another typically in a dependent or subordinate position <the university and its ~ medical school> ***syn*** see RELATED

¹af·fine \a-ˈfīn, ə-\ *n* [MF *affin,* fr. L *affinis,* fr. *affinis* related] **:** a relative by marriage

²affine *adj* [L *affinis,* adj.] **:** of, relating to, or being a transformation (as a translation, a rotation, or a uniform stretching) that carries straight lines into straight lines and parallel lines into parallel lines but may alter distance between points and angles between lines <~ geometry> — **af·fine·ly** *adv*

af·fined \a-ˈfīnd, ə-\ *adj* **1 :** joined in a close relationship **:** CONNECTED **2 :** bound by obligation

af·fin·i·ty \ə-ˈfin-ət-ē\ *n, pl* **-ties** [ME *affinite,* fr. MF or L; MF *afinité,* fr. L *affinitas,* fr. *affinis* bordering on, related by marriage, fr. *ad-* + *finis* end, border] **1 :** relationship by marriage **2 a :** sympathy marked by community of interest **:** KINSHIP **b :** ATTRACTION; *esp* **:** an attractive force between substances or particles that causes them to enter into and remain in chemical combination **c :** a person esp. of the opposite sex having a particular attraction for one **3 a :** likeness based on relationship or causal connection **b :** a relation between biological groups involving resemblance in structural plan and indicating community of origin ***syn*** see ATTRACTION, LIKENESS

af·firm \ə-ˈfərm\ *vb* [ME *affermen,* fr. MF *afermer,* fr. L *affirmare,* fr. *ad-* + *firmare* to make firm, fr. *firmus* firm — more at FIRM] *vt* **1 a :** VALIDATE, CONFIRM **b :** to state positively **2 :** to assert (as a judgment or decree) as valid or confirmed **3 :** to express dedication to <~ life by refusing to kill> ~ *vi* **1 :** to testify or declare by affirmation **2 :** to uphold a judgment or decree of a lower court ***syn*** see ASSERT ***ant*** deny — **af·firm·able** \ə-ˈfər-mə-bəl\ *adj* — **af·fir·mance** \ə-ˈfər-mən(t)s\ *n*

af·fir·ma·tion \ˌaf-ər-ˈmā-shən\ *n* **1 a :** the act of affirming **b :** something affirmed **:** a positive assertion **2 :** a solemn declaration made under the penalties of perjury by a person who conscientiously declines taking an oath

¹af·fir·ma·tive \ə-ˈfər-mət-iv\ *adj* **1 :** asserting a predicate of a subject **2 :** asserting that the fact is so **3 :** POSITIVE <~ approach> **4 :** favoring or supporting a proposition or motion — **af·fir·ma·tive·ly** *adv*

²affirmative *n* **1 :** an expression (as the word *yes*) of affirmation or assent **2 :** an affirmative proposition **3 :** the side that upholds the proposition stated in a debate

¹af·fix \ə-ˈfiks, a-\ *vt* [ML *affixare,* fr. L *affixus,* pp. of *affigere* to fasten to, fr. *ad-* + *figere* to fasten — more at DIKE] **1 :** to attach physically <~ a stamp to a letter> **2 :** to attach in any way **:** ADD, APPEND <~ a signature to a document> **3 :** IMPRESS <~*ed* his seal> ***syn*** see FASTEN ***ant*** detach — **af·fix·able** \-ˈfik-sə-bəl\ *adj* — **af·fix·a·tion** \ˌaf-ˌik-ˈsā-shən\ *n* — **af·fix·ment** \ə-ˈfik-smənt, a-\ *n*

²af·fix \ˈaf-ˌiks\ *n* **1 :** a sound or sequence of sounds or a letter or sequence of letters occurring as a bound form attached to the beginning or end of a word, base, or phrase or inserted within a word or base and serving to produce a derivative word or an inflectional form **2 :** APPENDAGE — **af·fix·al** \-ˌik-səl\ *or* **af·fix·i·al** \a-ˈfik-sē-əl\ *adj*

af·fla·tus \ə-ˈflāt-əs, a-\ *n* [L, act of blowing or breathing on, fr. *afflatus,* pp. of *afflare* to blow on, fr. *ad-* + *flare* to blow — more at BLOW] **:** a divine imparting of knowledge or power **:** INSPIRATION

af·flict \ə-ˈflikt\ *vt* [ME *afflicten,* fr. L *afflictus,* pp. of *affligere* to cast down, fr. *ad-* + *fligere* to strike — more at PROFLIGATE] **1** *obs* **a :** HUMBLE **b :** OVERTHROW **2 a :** to distress so severely as to cause persistent suffering or anguish **b :** TROUBLE, INJURE ***syn*** AFFLICT, TRY, TORMENT, TORTURE, RACK *shared meaning element* **:** to inflict on one something (as suffering, disease, or embarrassment) that he finds hard to bear ***ant*** comfort

af·flic·tion \ə-ˈflik-shən\ *n* **1 :** the state of being afflicted **2 a :** the cause of persistent pain or distress **b :** great suffering

af·flic·tive \ə-ˈflik-tiv\ adj **:** causing affliction **:** DISTRESSING, TROUBLESOME — **af·flic·tive·ly** *adv*

af·flu·ence \ˈaf-ˌlü-ən(t)s *also* a-ˈflü- *or* ə-\ *n* **1 a :** an abundant flow or supply **:** PROFUSION **b :** abundance of property **:** WEALTH **2 :** a flowing to or toward a point **:** INFLUX

af·flu·en·cy \-ən-sē\ *n, pl* **-cies :** AFFLUENCE

¹af·flu·ent \-ənt\ *adj* [ME, fr. MF, fr. L *affluent-, affluens,* prp. of *affluere* to flow to, flow abundantly, fr. *ad-* + *fluere* to flow — more at FLUID] **1 a :** flowing in abundance **:** COPIOUS **b :** having a generously sufficient and typically increasing supply of material possessions <our ~ society> **2 :** flowing toward ***syn*** see RICH ***ant*** impecunious, straitened — **af·flu·ent·ly** *adv*

²affluent *n* **1 :** a tributary stream **2 :** an affluent person

af·flux \ˈaf-ˌləks\ *n* [F or L; F, fr. L *affluxus,* pp. of *affluere*] **:** AFFLUENCE 2

af·ford \ə-ˈfō(ə)rd, -ˈfȯ(ə)rd\ *vt* [ME *aforthen,* fr. OE *geforthian* to carry out, fr. *ge-,* perfective prefix + *forthian* to carry out, fr. *forth* — more at CO-, FORTH] **1 a :** to manage to bear without serious detriment <you can't ~ to neglect your health> **b :** to be able to bear the cost of <he can't ~ to be out of work long> <~ a new coat> **2 a :** to have the capacity for providing esp. to one who seeks <her letters ~ no clue to her intentions> **b :** to make available or give forth as a consequence of nature **:** provide naturally or inevitably <the sun ~*s* warmth to the earth> <the roof ~*ed* a fine view> ***syn*** see GIVE — **af·ford·able** \-ˈfōrd-ə-bəl, -ˈfȯrd-\ *adj*

af·for·est \a-ˈfȯr-əst, -ˈfär-\ *vt* [ML *afforestare,* fr. L *ad-* + ML *forestis* forest — more at FOREST] **:** to establish forest cover on — **af·for·es·ta·tion** \(ˌ)a-ˌfȯr-ə-ˈstā-shən, -ˌfär-\ *n*

¹af·fray \ə-ˈfrā\ *n* [ME, fr. MF, fr. *affreer* to startle] **:** FRAY, BRAWL

²affray *vt* [ME *affraien,* fr. MF *affreer*] *archaic* **:** STARTLE, FRIGHTEN

af·fri·cate \ˈaf-ri-kət\ *n* [prob. fr. G *affrikata,* fr. L *affricata,* fem. of *affricatus,* pp. of *affricare* to rub against, fr. *ad-* + *fricare* to rub — more at FRICTION] **:** a stop and its immediately following release through the articulatory position for a continuant nonsyllabic consonant (as the \t\ and \sh\ that are the constituents of the \ch\ in *why choose*) — **af·fric·a·tive** \a-ˈfrik-ət-iv, ə-\ *n or adj*

af·fri·ca·tion \ˌaf-rə-ˈkā-shən\ *n* **:** conversion (as of a simple stop sound) into an affricate

¹af·fright \ə-ˈfrīt\ *vt* [fr. ME *afyrht, afright* frightened, fr. OE *āfyrht, pp. of āfyrhtan* to frighten, fr. *ā-,* perfective prefix + *fyrhtan* to fear; akin to OE *fyrhto* fright — more at ABIDE, FRIGHT] **:** FRIGHTEN, ALARM

²affright *n* **:** sudden and great fear **:** TERROR

¹af·front \ə-ˈfrənt\ *vt* [ME *afronten,* fr. MF *afronter* to defy, fr. (assumed) VL *affrontare,* fr. L *ad-* + *front-, frons* forehead — more at FRONT] **1 :** to insult esp. to the face by behavior or language **2 a :** to face in defiance **:** CONFRONT <~ death> **b** *obs* **:** to encounter face to face **3 :** to appear directly before ***syn*** see OFFEND

²affront *n* **1 :** a deliberate offense **:** INSULT <an ~ to his dignity> **2** *obs* **:** a hostile encounter

afft *abbr* affidavit

af·fu·sion \a-ˈfyü-zhən\ *n* [LL *affusion-, affusio,* fr. L *affusus,* pp. of *affundere* to pour on, fr. *ad-* + *fundere* to pour — more at FOUND] **:** an act of pouring a liquid on (as in baptism)

Af·ghan \ˈaf-ˌgan *also* -gən\ *n* [Pashto *afghānī*] **1 :** a native or inhabitant of Afghanistan **2 :** PASHTO **3** *not cap* **:** a blanket or shawl of colored wool knitted or crocheted in strips or squares **4** *not cap* **:** a Turkoman carpet of large size and long pile woven in geometric designs **5 :** AFGHAN HOUND — **Afghan** *adj*

Afghan hound *n* **:** a tall slim swift hunting dog native to the Near East with a coat of silky thick hair and a long silky topknot

af·ghani \af-ˈgan-ē, -ˈgän-\ *n* [Pashto *afghānī,* lit., Afghan] — see MONEY table

afi·cio·na·da \ə-ˌfish(-ē)-ə-ˈnäd-ə, -ˌfis-ē-, -ˌfē-sē-, -ˈnäd-(ˌ)ä\ *n* [Sp, fem. of *aficionado*] **:** a female aficionado <card-playing ~*s*>

afi·cio·na·do \-ˈnäd-(ˌ)ō\ *n, pl* **-dos** [Sp, fr. pp. of *aficionar* to inspire affection, fr. *afición* affection, fr. L *affection-, affectio* — more at AFFECTION] **:** DEVOTEE, FAN <~*s* of the bullfight> <movie ~*s*>

afield \ə-ˈfē(ə)ld\ *adv or adj* **1 :** to, in, or on the field <was weak at bat but strong ~> **2 :** away from home : ABROAD **3 :** out of the way : ASTRAY <irrelevant remarks that carried us far ~>
AFIPS *abbr* American Federation of Information Processing Societies
afire \ə-ˈfī(ə)r\ *adj or adv* : being on fire : BLAZING <set the house ~>
AFL *abbr* American Football League
aflame \ə-ˈflām\ *adj or adv* : AFIRE
af·la·tox·in \ˌaf-lə-ˈtäk-sən\ *n* [NL *Aspergillus flavus*, species of mold + E *toxin*] : any of several mycotoxins that are produced esp. in corn or oilseed meals by molds (as *Aspergillus flavus*) and are suspected of being carcinogenic
AFL–CIO *abbr* American Federation of Labor and Congress of Industrial Organizations
afloat \ə-ˈflōt\ *adj or adv* [ME *aflot*, fr. OE *on flot*, fr. *on* + *flot*, fr. *flot* deep water, sea; akin to OE *flēotan* to float — more at FLEET] **1 a :** borne on or as if on the water : FLOATING **b :** at sea **2 :** free of difficulties : SELF-SUFFICIENT <the inheritance kept them ~ for years> **3 a :** circulating about : RUMORED <nasty stories were ~> **b :** ADRIFT
aflut·ter \ə-ˈflət-ər\ *adj* **1 :** being in a flutter : FLUTTERING **2 :** nervously excited **3 :** filled with or marked by the presence of fluttering things <roofs ~ with flags>
afoot \ə-ˈfu̇t\ *adv or adj* **1 :** on foot **2 :** in the process of development : under way <something out of the ordinary was ~ — Hamilton Basso>
afore \ə-ˈfō(ə)r, -ˈfȯ(ə)r\ *adv or conj or prep* [ME, fr. OE *onforan*, fr. *on* + *foran* before — more at BEFORE] *chiefly dial* : BEFORE
afore·men·tioned \-ˈmen-chənd\ *adj* : mentioned previously
afore·said \-ˌsed\ *adj* : said or named before or above
afore·thought \-ˌthȯt\ *adj* : previously in mind : PREMEDITATED, DELIBERATE <with malice ~>
a for·ti·o·ri \ˌä-ˌfȯrt-ē-ˈō(ə)r-ē; ˌā-ˌfȯrt-ē-ˈō(ə)r-ˌī, -ˈō(ə)r-ē; -ē-ˈȯ(ə)r-\ *adv* [NL, lit., from the stronger (argument)] : with greater reason or more convincing force — used in drawing a conclusion that is inferred to be even more certain than another <the man of prejudice is, *a fortiori*, a man of limited mental vision>
afoul of \ə-ˈfau̇l-əv\ *prep* **1 :** in or into collision or entanglement with **2 :** in or into conflict with
Afr *abbr* Africa; African
Afr- *or* **Afro-** *comb form* [L, *Afr-*, *Afer*] : African <*Afr*american> : African and <*Afro*-Asiatic>
afraid \ə-ˈfrād, *South also* ə-ˈfre(ə)d\ *adj* [ME *affraied*, fr. pp. of *affraien* to frighten — more at AFFRAY] **1 :** filled with fear or apprehension <~ of machines> <~ for his job> **2 :** filled with concern or regret over an unwanted situation <I'm ~ I won't be able to go> **3 :** having a dislike for something : DISINCLINED, RELUCTANT <~ of hard work> ***syn*** see FEARFUL ***ant*** unafraid, sanguine
A–frame \ˈā-ˌfrām\ *n* : a building typically having triangular front and rear walls and a roof reaching to the ground
afreet *or* **afrit** \ˈaf-ˌrēt, ə-ˈfrēt\ *n* [Ar *ʿifrīt*] : a powerful evil jinn, demon, or monstrous giant in Arabic mythology
afresh \ə-ˈfresh\ *adv* : from a fresh beginning : ANEW, AGAIN
Af·ri·can \ˈaf-ri-kən\ *n* **1 :** a native or inhabitant of Africa **2 :** an individual of immediate or remote African ancestry; *esp* : NEGRO — **African** *adj* — **Af·ri·can·ness** \-kən-nəs\ *n*
Af·ri·can·der *or* **Af·ri·kan·der** \ˌaf-ri-ˈkan-dər\ *n* [Afrik *Afrikaner*, *Afrikaander*, lit., Afrikaner] : any of a breed of tall red large-horned humped southern African cattle used chiefly for meat or draft
Af·ri·can·ism \ˈaf-ri-kə-ˌniz-əm\ *n* **1 :** a characteristic feature (as a custom or belief) of African culture **2 :** a characteristic feature of an African language occurring in a non-African language **3 :** allegiance to the traditions, interests, or ideals of Africa
Af·ri·can·ist \-nəst\ *n* : a specialist in African languages or cultures
Af·ri·can·ize \-ˌnīz\ *vt* **-ized; -iz·ing 1 :** to cause to acquire a distinctively African trait **2 :** to bring under the control or the cultural or civil supremacy of Africans and esp. Negroes **3 :** to replace (a non-African) with an African — **Af·ri·can·iza·tion** \ˌaf-ri-kə-nə-ˈzā-shən\ *n*
African mahogany *n* : MAHOGANY 1b
African violet *n* : any of several tropical African plants (esp. *Saintpaulia ionantha*) of the gloxinia family widely grown as a houseplant for their velvety fleshy leaves and showy purple, pink, or white flowers
[1]**Af·ri·kaans** \ˌaf-ri-ˈkän(t)s, -ˈkänz, ˈaf-ri-ˌ\ *n* [Afrik, fr. *afrikaans*, adj., African, fr. obs. Afrik *afrikanisch*, fr. L *africanus*] : a language developed from 17th century Dutch that is one of the official languages of the Republic of So. Africa
[2]**Afrikaans** *adj* : of or relating to Afrikaners or Afrikaans
Af·ri·ka·ner \ˌaf-ri-ˈkän-ər\ *n* [Afrik, lit., African, fr. L *africanus*] : a So. African native of European descent; *esp* : an Afrikaans-speaking descendant of the 17th century Dutch settlers
[1]**Af·ro** \ˈaf-(ˌ)rō\ *adj* [prob. fr. *Afro-American*] : having the hair shaped into a round bushy mass
[2]**Afro** *n, pl* **Afros** : an Afro hairstyle
Af·ro–Amer·i·can \ˌaf-rō-ə-ˈmer-ə-kən\ *n* : an American of African and esp. of Negroid descent — **Afro–American** *adj*
Af·ro–Asi·at·ic languages \ˌaf-rō-ˌā-z(h)ē-ˌat-ik- *also* -shē-\ *n pl* : a family of languages widely distributed over southwestern Asia and northern Africa comprising the Semitic, Egyptian, Berber, Cushitic, and Chad subfamilies
[1]**aft** \ˈaft\ *adv* [ME *afte* back, fr. OE *æftan* from behind, behind; akin to OE *æfter*] : near, toward, or in the stern of a ship or the tail of an aircraft : ABAFT <called all hands ~>
[2]**aft** *adj* : REARWARD, [4]AFTER 2 <the ~ decks>
[3]**aft** *Scot var of* OFT
[4]**aft** *abbr* afternoon
AFT *abbr* American Federation of Teachers
[1]**af·ter** \ˈaf-tər\ *adv* [ME, fr. OE *æfter*; akin to OHG *aftar* after] : following in time or place : AFTERWARD, BEHIND, LATER <we arrived shortly ~> <returned 20 years ~>
[2]**after** *prep* **1 a :** behind in place **b (1) :** subsequent to in time or order **(2) :** subsequent to and in view of <~ all our advice> **2** — used as a function word to indicate the object of a stated or implied action <go ~ gold> **3 :** so as to resemble: as **a :** in accordance with **b :** with the same or a derived name **c :** in the characteristic manner of **d :** in imitation of
[3]**after** *conj* : subsequently to the time when
[4]**after** *adj* **1 :** later in time : SUBSEQUENT <in ~ years> **2 :** located toward the rear and esp. toward the stern of a ship or tail of an aircraft
[5]**after** *n* : AFTERNOON
after all *adv* : in spite of considerations to the contrary : NEVERTHELESS <decided to take the train *after all*>

Afro

af·ter·birth \ˈaf-tər-ˌbərth\ *n* : the placenta and fetal membranes that are expelled after delivery
af·ter·burn·er \-ˌbər-nər\ *n* **1 :** an auxiliary burner attached to the tail pipe of a turbojet engine for injecting fuel into the hot exhaust gases and burning it to provide extra thrust **2 :** a device for burning or catalytically destroying unburned or partially burned carbon compounds in exhaust (as from an automobile)
af·ter·care \-ˌke(ə)r, -ˌka(ə)r\ *n* : the care, treatment, help, or supervision given to persons discharged from an institution (as a hospital or prison)
af·ter·clap \-ˌklap\ *n* : an unexpected damaging or unsettling event following a supposedly closed affair
af·ter·damp \-ˌdamp\ *n* : a toxic gas mixture remaining after an explosion of firedamp in mines
af·ter·deck \-ˌdek\ *n* : the part of a deck abaft midships
af·ter·ef·fect \ˈaf-tə-rə-ˌfekt\ *n* : an effect that follows its cause after an interval
af·ter·glow \ˈaf-tər-ˌglō\ *n* **1 :** a glow remaining where a light has disappeared **2 :** a reflection of past splendor, success, or emotion
af·ter–hours \ˌaf-tə-ˈrau̇(-ə)rz\ *adj* **1 :** engaged in after closing time <~ drinking> **2 :** operating after a legal or conventional closing time <an ~ nightclub>
af·ter·im·age \ˈaf-tə-ˌrim-ij\ *n* : a usu. visual sensation occurring after stimulation by its external cause has ceased
af·ter·life \ˈaf-tər-ˌlīf\ *n* **1 :** an existence after death **2 :** a later period in one's life
af·ter·math \-ˌmath\ *n* [[4]*after* + *math* (mowing, crop)] **1 :** a second-growth crop — called also *rowen* **2 :** CONSEQUENCE, RESULT <stricken with guilt as an ~ of the accident> **3 :** the period immediately following a usu. ruinous event <in the ~ of the war>
af·ter·most \-ˌmōst\ *adj* : nearest the stern of a ship : farthest aft
af·ter·noon \ˌaf-tər-ˈnün\ *n* **1 :** the part of day between noon and sunset **2 :** a relatively late period (as of time or life) <in the ~ of the 19th century> — **afternoon** *adj*
af·ter·noons \-ˈnünz\ *adv* : in the afternoon repeatedly : on any afternoon
af·ter·piece \ˈaf-tər-ˌpēs\ *n* : a short usu. comic entertainment performed after a play
af·ters \ˈaf-tərz\ *n pl, Brit* : DESSERT
af·ter–shave \ˈaf-tər-ˌshāv\ *n* : a usu. scented lotion for use on the face after shaving
af·ter·taste \-ˌtāst\ *n* : persistence of a sensation (as of flavor or an emotion) after the stimulating agent or experience has gone
af·ter·tax \ˈaf-tər-ˌtaks\ *adj* : remaining after payment of taxes and esp. of income tax <an ~ profit>
af·ter·thought \-ˌthȯt\ *n* **1 :** an idea occurring later **2 :** a part, feature, or device not thought of originally
af·ter·time \-ˌtīm\ *n* : FUTURE
af·ter·ward \ˈaf-tə(r)-wərd\ *or* **af·ter·wards** \-wərdz\ *adv* : at a later or succeeding time : SUBSEQUENTLY, THEREAFTER
af·ter·word \-ˌwərd\ *n* : EPILOGUE 1
af·ter·world \-ˌwərld\ *n* : a future world : a world after death
Ag *symbol* [L *argentum*] silver
AG *abbr* **1** adjutant general **2** attorney general
ag- — see AD-
Aga·da \ə-ˈgäd-ə, -ˈgōd-\ *var of* HAGGADAH
again \ə-ˈgen, -ˈgin\ *adv* [ME, opposite, again fr. OE *ongēan* opposite, back, fr. *on* + *gēn*, *gēan* still, again; akin to OE *gēan*-against, OHG *gegin* against, toward] **1 :** in return : BACK <swore he would pay him ~ when he was able —Shak.> **2 :** another time : once more : ANEW <I shall not look upon his like ~ —Shak.> **3 :** on the other hand <he might go, and ~ he might not> **4 :** in addition : BESIDES, FURTHER <~, there is another matter to consider>
again and again *adv* : OFTEN, REPEATEDLY
[1]**against** \ə-ˈgen(t)st, -ˈgin(t)st\ *prep* [ME, alter. of *againes*, fr. *again*] **1 a :** directly opposite : FACING **b** *obs* : exposed to **2 a :** in opposition or hostility to **b :** unfavorable to **c :** as a defense or protection from **3 :** compared or contrasted with **4 :** in preparation or provision for **5 a :** in the direction of and into contact with **b :** in contact with **6 :** in a direction opposite to the motion or course of : counter to **7 a :** as a counterbalance to **b :** in exchange for **c :** as a charge on **8 :** before the background of

2against *conj, archaic* : in preparation for the time when : BEFORE <throw on another log of wood ~ father comes home —Charles Dickens>

Ag·a·mem·non \ˌag-ə-ˈmem-ˌnän, -nən\ *n* [L, fr. Gk *Agamemnōn*] : a king of Mycenae who was the leader of the Greeks in the Trojan War

aga·mete \ˌā-gə-ˈmēt, (ˈ)ā-ˈgam-ˌēt\ *n* [ISV, fr. Gk *agametos* unmarried, fr. *a-* + *gamein* to marry — more at GAMETE] : an asexual reproductive cell

agam·ic \(ˈ)ā-ˈgam-ik\ *adj* [Gk *agamos* unmarried, fr. *a-* + *gamos* marriage — more at BIGAMY] : ASEXUAL, PARTHENOGENETIC — **agam·i·cal·ly** \-i-k(ə-)lē\ *adv*

agam·ma·glob·u·lin·emia \ˌā-ˌgam-ə-ˌgläb-yə-lə-ˈnē-mē-ə\ *n* [NL, fr. *a-* + ISV *gamma globulin* + NL *-emia*] : a condition in which the body forms few or no gamma globulins or antibodies — **agam·ma·glob·u·lin·emic** \-ˈnē-mik\ *adj*

aga·mo·sper·my \(ˈ)ā-ˈgam-ə-ˌspər-mē, ˈag-ə-mō-ˌspər-\ *n* [Gk *agamos* + E *-spermy*] : APOGAMY; *specif* : apogamy in which sexual union is not completed and the embryo is produced from the innermost layer of the integument

ag·a·pan·thus \ˌag-ə-ˈpan(t)-thəs\ *n* [NL, genus name, fr. Gk *agapē* + *anthos* flower — more at ANTHOLOGY] : any of several African plants (genus *Agapanthus*) of the lily family cultivated for their umbels of showy blue or purple flowers

1agape \ə-ˈgāp *also* -ˈgap\ *adj or adv* **1** : wide open : GAPING <young birds with mouths ~ in expectation of food> **2** : being in a state of wonder

2aga·pe \ä-ˈgä-(ˌ)pā, ˈäg-ə-ˌpā\ *n* [LL, fr. Gk *agapē*, lit., love] **1** : LOVE 4a **2** : LOVE FEAST — **aga·pe·ic** \ˌäg-ə-ˈpā-ik\ *adj* — **aga·pe·i·cal·ly** \-ˈpā-ə-k(ə-)lē\ *adv*

agar \ˈäg-ˌär\ *n* [Malay *agar-agar*] **1** : a gelatinous colloidal extractive of a red alga (as of the genera *Gelidium, Gracilaria*, and *Eucheuma*) used esp. in culture media or as a gelling and stabilizing agent in foods **2** : a culture medium containing agar

agar–agar \ˌäg-ˌär-ˈäg-ˌär\ *n* [Malay] : AGAR

aga·ric \ˈag-ə-rik, ə-ˈgar-ik\ *n* [L *agaricum*, a fungus, fr. Gk *agarikon*] **1 a** : any of several pore fungi (genus *Fomes*) used esp. in the preparation of punk **b** : the dried fruiting body of a fungus (*F. officinalis*) formerly used in medicine **2** : any of a family (Agaricaceae) of fungi with the sporophore usu. resembling an umbrella and with numerous lamellae on the underside of the cap

ag·ate \ˈag-ət\ *n, often attrib* [MF, fr. L *achates*, fr. Gk *achatēs*] **1** : a fine-grained variegated chalcedony having its colors arranged in stripes, blended in clouds, or showing mosslike forms **2** : something made of or fitted with agate: as **a** : a drawplate used by gold-wire drawers **b** : a bookbinder's burnisher **c** : a playing marble of agate **3** : a size of type approximately 5½ point

agate line *n* : a space one column wide and $\frac{1}{14}$ inch deep used as a unit of measurement in publication advertising

ag·ate·ware \ˈag-ət-ˌwa(ə)r, -ˌwe(ə)r\ *n* **1** : pottery veined and mottled to resemble agate **2** : an enameled iron or steel ware for household utensils

aga·ve \ə-ˈgäv-ē\ *n* [NL *Agave*, genus name, fr. L, a daughter of Cadmus, fr. Gk *Agauē*] : any of a genus (*Agave*) of plants of the amaryllis family having spiny-margined leaves and flowers in tall spreading panicles and including some cultivated for their fiber or for ornament

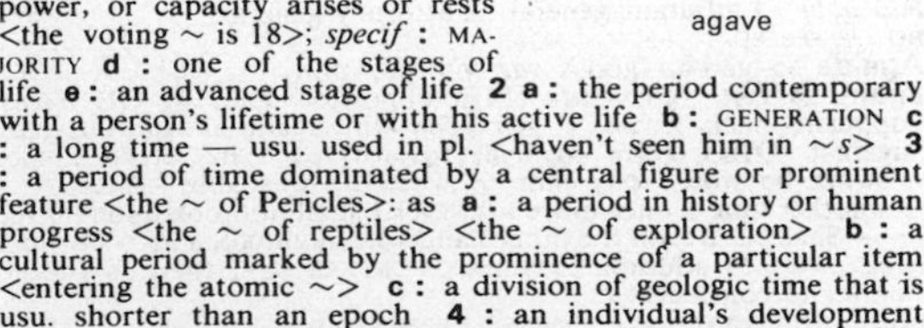

agave

agaze \ə-ˈgāz\ *adj* : engaged in the act of gazing

AGC *abbr* advanced graduate certificate

agcy *abbr* agency

1age \ˈāj\ *n* [ME, fr. OF *aage*, fr. (assumed) VL *aetaticum*, fr. L *aetat-, aetas*, fr. *aevum* lifetime — more at AYE] **1 a** : the part of an existence extending from the beginning to any given time <a boy 10 years of ~> **b** : LIFETIME **c** : the time of life at which some particular qualification, power, or capacity arises or rests <the voting ~ is 18>; *specif* : MAJORITY **d** : one of the stages of life **e** : an advanced stage of life **2 a** : the period contemporary with a person's lifetime or with his active life **b** : GENERATION **c** : a long time — usu. used in pl. <haven't seen him in ~*s*> **3** : a period of time dominated by a central figure or prominent feature <the ~ of Pericles>: as **a** : a period in history or human progress <the ~ of reptiles> <the ~ of exploration> **b** : a cultural period marked by the prominence of a particular item <entering the atomic ~> **c** : a division of geologic time that is usu. shorter than an epoch **4** : an individual's development measured in terms of the years requisite for like development of an average individual ***syn*** see PERIOD

2age *vb* **aged; ag·ing** *or* **age·ing** *vi* **1** : to become old : show the effects or the characteristics of increasing age **2 a** : to acquire a desirable quality by standing undisturbed for some time <after flour is milled it ~*s* —S. C. Prescott & B. E. Proctor> **b** : to become mellow or mature : RIPEN <this cheese has *aged* for nearly two years> ~ *vt* **1** : to cause to become old **2** : to bring to a state fit for use or to maturity

-age \ij\ *n suffix* [ME, fr. OF, fr. L *-aticum*] **1** : aggregate : collection <track*age*> **2 a** : action : process <haul*age*> **b** : cumulative result of <break*age*> **c** : rate of <dos*age*> **3** : house or place of <orphan*age*> **4** : state : rank <peon*age*> **5** : fee : charge <post*age*>

aged \ˈā-jəd, ˈājd; ˈājd *for 1b*\ *adj* **1** : grown old: as **a** : of an advanced age **b** : having attained a specified age <a man ~ 40 years> **c** : well advanced toward reduction to base level — used of topographic features **2** : typical of old age — **ag·ed·ness** \ˈā-jəd-nəs\ *n*

age–group \ˈāj-ˌgrüp\ *n* : a segment of a population that is of approximately the same age or is within a specified range of ages

age·less \ˈāj-ləs\ *adj* **1** : not growing old or showing the effects of age **2** : TIMELESS, ETERNAL <~ truths> — **age·less·ly** *adv* — **age·less·ness** *n*

age·long \ˈāj-ˌlȯŋ\ *adj* : lasting for an age : EVERLASTING

age–mate \-ˌmāt\ *n* : one who is of approximately the same age as another

agen·cy \ˈā-jən-sē\ *n, pl* **-cies** **1** : the capacity, condition, or state of acting or of exerting power : OPERATION **2** : a person or thing through which power is exerted or an end is achieved : INSTRUMENTALITY <communicated through the ~ of his ambassador> **3 a** : the office or function of an agent **b** : the relationship between a principal and his agent **4** : an establishment engaged in doing business for another <an advertising ~> **5** : an administrative division (as of a government) <the ~ for consumer protection>

agency shop *n* : a shop in which the union serves as the agent for and receives dues and assessments from all employees in the bargaining unit regardless of union membership

agen·da \ə-ˈjen-də\ *n* [L, neut. pl. of *agendum*, gerundive of *agere*] : a list, outline, or plan of things to be considered or done : PROGRAM <~*s* of faculty meetings> — **agen·da·less** \-də-ləs\ *adj*

agen·dum \-dəm\ *n, pl* **-da** \-də\ *or* **-dums** [L] **1** : AGENDA **2** : an item on an agenda

agene \ˈā-ˌjēn\ *n* [fr. *Agene*, a trademark] : the trichloride of nitrogen

agen·e·sis \(ˈ)ā-ˈjen-ə-səs\ *n* [NL] : lack or failure of development (as of a body part)

age·nize \ˈā-jə-ˌnīz\ *vt* **-nized; -niz·ing** : to treat (flour) with nitrogen trichloride

agent \ˈā-jənt\ *n* [ME, fr. ML *agent-, agens*, fr. L, prp. of *agere* to drive, lead, act, do; akin to ON *aka* to travel in a vehicle, Gk *agein* to drive, lead] **1 a** : something that produces or is capable of producing an effect : an active or efficient cause **b** : a chemically, physically, or biologically active principle **2** : one that acts or exerts power **3** : a person responsible for his acts **4** : a means or instrument by which a guiding intelligence achieves a result **5** : one who acts for or in the place of another by authority from him: as **a** : a representative, emissary, or official of a government <crown ~> <secret-service ~> **b** : one engaged in undercover activities (as espionage) : SPY <secret ~> ***syn*** see MEAN

agent–general *n, pl* **agents–general** : a chief agent; *specif* : the representative in England of a British dominion

agent pro·vo·ca·teur \ˈäzh-ˌäⁿ-prō-ˌväk-ə-ˈtər, ˈā-jənt-\ *n, pl* **agents provocateurs** \ˈäzh -ˌäⁿ-prō-ˌväk-ə-ˈtər, ˈā-jən(t)s-prō-\ [F, lit., provoking agent] : one employed to associate himself with members of a group or with suspected persons and by pretended sympathy with their aims or attitudes to incite them to some action that will make them liable to apprehension and punishment

agent·ry \ˈā-jən-trē\ *n, pl* **-ries** : the office, duties, or activities of an agent

age of consent : the age at which one is legally competent to give consent (as to marriage)

age of reason **1** : a period characterized by a prevailing belief in the use of reason; *esp* : the 18th century in England and France **2** : the time of life when one begins to be able to distinguish right from wrong

age–old \ˈā-ˈjōld\ *adj* : having existed for ages : ANCIENT

ag·er·a·tum \ˌaj-ə-ˈrāt-əm\ *n, pl* **-tums** [NL, genus name, fr. Gk *agēratos* ageless, fr. *a-* + *gēras* old age — more at CORN] : any of a large genus (*Ageratum*) of tropical American composite herbs often cultivated for their small showy heads of blue or white flowers; *also* : any of several related blue-flowered plants (genus *Eupatorium*)

Ag·ge·us \a-ˈgē-əs\ *n* [LL *Aggaeus*, fr. Gk *Aggaios*, fr. Heb *Ḥoggai*] : HAGGAI

1ag·gie \ˈag-ē\ *n* [*agate* + *-ie*] : a playing marble; *specif* : AGATE 2c

2aggie *n, often cap* [*agricultural* + *-ie*] : an agricultural school or college; *also* : a student at such an institution

ag·gior·na·men·to \ə-ˌjȯr-nə-ˈmen-(ˌ)tō\ *n, pl* **-tos** [It, fr. *aggiornare* to bring up to date, fr. *a* to (fr. L *ad-*) + *giorno* day, fr. LL *diurnum* day — more at JOURNEY] : a bringing up to date : MODERNIZATION <dedicated to the ~ of the church>

1ag·glom·er·ate \ə-ˈgläm-ə-ˌrāt\ *vt* **-at·ed; -at·ing** [L *agglomeratus*, pp. of *agglomerare* to heap up, join, fr. *ad-* + *glomer-, glomus* ball — more at CLAM] : to gather into a ball, mass, or cluster

2ag·glom·er·ate \-rət\ *adj* : gathered into a ball, mass, or cluster; *specif* : clustered or growing together but not coherent <an ~ flower head>

3ag·glom·er·ate \-rət\ *n* **1** : a jumbled mass or collection **2** : a rock composed of volcanic fragments of various sizes and degrees of angularity

ag·glom·er·a·tion \ə-ˌgläm-ə-ˈrā-shən\ *n* **1** : the action or process of collecting in a mass **2** : a heap or cluster of disparate elements <urban ~*s* knit together by the new railways —*Times Lit. Supp.*> — **ag·glom·er·a·tive** \-ˈgläm-ə-ˌrāt-iv\ *adj*

ag·glu·ti·na·bil·i·ty \ə-ˌglüt-ᵊn-ə-ˈbil-ət-ē\ *n* : capacity (as of red blood cells) to be agglutinated

1ag·glu·ti·nate \ə-ˈglüt-ᵊn-ət\ *adj* : AGGLUTINATIVE 2

2ag·glu·ti·nate \-ᵊn-ˌāt\ *vb* **-nat·ed; -nat·ing** [L *agglutinatus*, pp. of *agglutinare* to glue to, fr. *ad-* + *glutinare* to glue, fr. *glutin-, gluten* glue — more at GLUTEN] *vt* **1** : to cause to adhere : FASTEN **2** : to combine into a compound : attach to a base as an affix **3** : to cause to undergo agglutination ~ *vi* **1** : to unite or combine into a group or mass **2** : to form words by agglutination

ag·glu·ti·na·tion \ə-ˌglüt-ᵊn-ˈā-shən\ *n* **1** : the action or process of agglutinating **2** : a mass or group formed by the union of separate elements **3** : the formation of derivational or inflectional words by putting together constituents of which each expresses a single definite meaning **4** : a reaction in which particles (as red blood cells or bacteria) suspended in a liquid collect into clumps and which occurs esp. as a serologic response to a specific antibody

ag·glu·ti·na·tive \ə-ˈglüt-ᵊn-ˌāt-iv, -ət-\ *adj* **1** : ADHESIVE **2** : characterized by agglutination

ag·glu·ti·nin \ə-ˈglüt-ᵊn-ən\ *n* [ISV *agglutin*ation + *-in*] : a substance (as an antibody) producing agglutination

ag·glu·ti·no·gen \ə-ˈglüt-ᵊn-ə-jən\ *n* [*agglutinin* + *-o-* + *-gen*] : an antigen whose presence results in the formation of an agglutinin — **ag·glu·ti·no·gen·ic** \-ˌglüt-ᵊn-ə-ˈjen-ik\ *adj*

ag·gra·da·tion \ˌag-rə-ˈdā-shən\ *n* : a modification of the earth's surface in the direction of uniformity of grade by deposition

ag·grade \ə-ˈgrād\ *vt* [*ad-* + *grade*] : to fill with detrital material

ag·gran·dize \ə-ˈgran-ˌdīz, ˈag-rən-\ *vt* **-dized; -diz·ing** [F *agrandiss-*, stem of *agrandir*, fr. *a-* (fr. L *ad-*) + *grandir* to increase, fr. L *grandire*, fr. *grandis* great] **1** : to make great or greater : INCREASE, ENLARGE **2** : to make appear great or greater : praise highly <*aggrandized* the one and disparaged the other> **3** : to enhance the power, wealth, position, or reputation of <exploited the situation to ~ himself> — **ag·gran·dize·ment** \ə-ˈgran-dəz-mənt, -ˌdīz-; ˌag-rən-ˈdīz-\ *n* — **ag·gran·diz·er** \ə-ˈgran-ˌdī-zər, ˈag-rən-\ *n*

ag·gra·vate \ˈag-rə-ˌvāt\ *vt* **-vat·ed; -vat·ing** [L *aggravatus*, pp. of *aggravare* to make heavier, fr. *ad-* + *gravare* to burden, fr. *gravis* heavy — more at GRIEVE] **1** *obs* **a** : to make heavy : BURDEN **b** : INCREASE **2** : to make worse, more serious, or more severe : intensify unpleasantly <problems have been *aggravated* by neglect> **3 a** : to rouse to displeasure or anger by usu. persistent and often petty goading **b** : to produce inflammation in ***syn*** **1** see INTENSIFY ***ant*** alleviate **2** see IRRITATE

aggravated assault *n* : an assault that is more serious than a common assault: as **a** : an assault combined with an intent to commit a crime **b** : any of various assaults so defined by statute

ag·gra·va·tion \ˌag-rə-ˈvā-shən\ *n* **1** : the act, action, or result of aggravating; *esp* : an increasing in seriousness or severity **2** : an act or circumstance that intensifies or makes worse **3** : IRRITATION, PROVOCATION

[1]**ag·gre·gate** \ˈag-ri-gət\ *adj* [ME *aggregat*, fr. L *aggregatus*, pp. of *aggregare* to add to, fr. *ad-* + *greg-*, *grex* flock — more at GREGARIOUS] : formed by the collection of units or particles into a body, mass, or amount : COLLECTIVE: as **a** (1) : clustered in a dense mass or head <an ~ flower> (2) : formed from the several ovaries of a single flower **b** : composed of mineral crystals of one or more kinds or of mineral rock fragments **c** : taking all units as a whole : TOTAL <~ earnings> <~ sales> — **ag·gre·gate·ly** *adv* — **ag·gre·gate·ness** *n*

[2]**ag·gre·gate** \-ˌgāt\ *vt* **-gat·ed; -gat·ing** **1** : to collect or gather into a mass or whole **2** : to amount in the aggregate to : TOTAL

[3]**ag·gre·gate** \-gət\ *n* **1** : a mass or body of units or parts somewhat loosely associated with one another **2** : the whole sum or amount : SUM TOTAL **3 a** : an aggregate rock **b** : any of several hard inert materials (as sand, gravel, or slag) used for mixing with a cementing material to form concrete, mortar, or plaster **c** : a clustered mass of individual soil particles varied in shape, ranging in size from a microscopic granule to a small crumb, and considered the basic structural unit of soil **4** : SET 19 — **in the aggregate** : considered as a whole : COLLECTIVELY <knowledge of . . . man *in the aggregate* rather as an individual person —G. B. Dearing>

ag·gre·ga·tion \ˌag-ri-ˈgā-shən\ *n* **1 a** : the collecting of units or parts into a mass or whole **b** : the condition of being so collected **2** : a group, body, or mass composed of many distinct parts — **ag·gre·ga·tion·al** \-shnəl, -shən-ᵊl\ *adj*

ag·gre·ga·tive \ˈag-ri-ˌgāt-iv\ *adj* **1** : tending to aggregate **2** : of or relating to an aggregate — **ag·gre·ga·tive·ly** *adv*

ag·gress \ə-ˈgres\ *vi* : to commit aggression : act aggressively <westerners even ~*ed* against one another —A. E. Stevenson †1965>

ag·gres·sion \ə-ˈgresh-ən\ *n* [L *aggressus*, pp. of *aggredi* to attack, fr. *ad-* + *gradi* to step, go — more at GRADE] **1** : a forceful action or procedure (as an unprovoked attack) esp. when intended to dominate or master **2** : the practice of making attacks or encroachments; *esp* : unprovoked violation by one country of the territorial integrity of another **3** : hostile, injurious, or destructive behavior or outlook esp. when caused by frustration

ag·gres·sive \ə-ˈgres-iv\ *adj* **1 a** : tending toward or practicing aggression <~ behavior> **b** : marked by combative readiness <an ~ fighter> **2 a** : marked by driving forceful energy or initiative : ENTERPRISING <an ~ salesman> **b** : marked by obtrusive energy — **ag·gres·sive·ly** *adv* — **ag·gres·sive·ness** *n* — **ag·gres·siv·i·ty** \ˌag-ˌre-ˈsiv-ət-ē\ *n*

syn AGGRESSIVE, MILITANT, ASSERTIVE, SELF-ASSERTIVE, PUSHING *shared meaning element* : conspicuously or obtrusively active or energetic

ag·gres·sor \ə-ˈgres-ər\ *n* : one that commits or practices aggression

ag·grieve \ə-ˈgrēv\ *vt* **ag·grieved; ag·griev·ing** [ME *agreven*, fr. MF *agrever*, fr. L *aggravare* to make heavier] **1** : to give pain or trouble to : DISTRESS **2** : to inflict injury on

ag·grieved \ə-ˈgrēvd\ *adj* **1** : troubled or distressed in spirit **2 a** : showing or expressing grief, injury, or offense <an ~ plea> **b** : suffering from an infringement or denial of legal rights <~ minority groups> — **ag·griev·ed·ly** \-ˈgrē-vəd-lē\ *adv*

Aghan \ə-ˈgän\ *n* [Hindi, fr. Skt *Agrahāyana*] : a month of the Hindu year — see MONTH table

aghast \ə-ˈgast\ *adj* [ME *agast*, fr. pp. of *agasten* to frighten, fr. *a-* (perfective prefix) + *gasten* to frighten — more at ABIDE, GAST] : struck with terror, amazement, or horror : SHOCKED <were ~ when they heard of his defection>

ag·ile \ˈaj-əl\ *adj* [MF, fr. L *agilis*, fr. *agere* to drive, act — more at AGENT] **1** : marked by ready ability to move with quick easy grace **2** : mentally quick and resourceful — **ag·ile·ly** \-ə(l)-lē\ *adv*

syn AGILE, NIMBLE, BRISK, SPRY *shared meaning element* : acting or moving with easy alacrity ***ant*** torpid

agil·i·ty \ə-ˈjil-ət-ē\ *n, pl* **-ties** : the quality or state of being agile : NIMBLENESS, DEXTERITY <played with increasing ~>

agin \ə-ˈgin\ *dial var of* AGAINST

aging *pres part of* AGE

agin·ner \ə-ˈgin-ər\ *n* [*agin* + *-er*] *slang* : one who opposes change

agio \ˈaj-(ē-ˌ)ō\ *n, pl* **agios** [It, alter. of It dial. *lajjë*, fr. MGk *allagion* exchange, fr. Gk *allagē* exchange, fr. *allos* other — more at ELSE] : a premium or percentage paid for the exchange of one currency for another; *also* : the premium or discount on foreign bills of exchange

ag·i·tate \ˈaj-ə-ˌtāt\ *vb* **-tat·ed; -tat·ing** [L *agitatus*, pp. of *agitare*, freq. of *agere* to drive — more at AGENT] *vt* **1 a** *obs* : to give motion to **b** : to move with an irregular, rapid, or violent action <the storm *agitated* the sea> **2** : to excite and often trouble the mind or feelings of : DISTURB **3 a** : to discuss excitedly and earnestly **b** : to stir up public discussion of ~ *vi* : to attempt to arouse public feeling <*agitated* for better schools> ***syn*** **1** see SHAKE **2** see DISCOMPOSE ***ant*** calm, tranquilize — **ag·i·tat·ed·ly** *adv* — **ag·i·ta·tion** \ˌaj-ə-ˈtā-shən\ *n* — **ag·i·ta·tion·al** \-shnəl, -shən-ᵊl\ *adj*

ag·i·ta·tive \ˈaj-ə-ˌtāt-iv\ *adj* : causing or tending to cause agitation

ag·i·ta·to \ˌaj-ə-ˈtät-(ˌ)ō\ *adv or adj* [It, lit., agitated, fr. L *agitatus*] : in a restless and agitated manner — used as a direction in music

ag·i·ta·tor \ˈaj-ə-ˌtāt-ər\ *n* : one that agitates: as **a** : one who stirs up public feeling on controversial issues <political ~*s*> **b** : a device or an apparatus for stirring or shaking

ag·it·prop \ˈaj-ət-ˌpräp\ *n* [Russ, office of agitation and propaganda, fr. *agitatsiya* agitation + *propaganda*] : political and esp. pro-communist propaganda promulgated esp. in literature, drama, music, or art — **agitprop** *adj*

Aglaia \ə-ˈglī-ə, -ˈglā-(y)ə\ *n* [L, fr. Gk] : one of the three Graces

aglare \ə-ˈgla(ə)r, -ˈgle(ə)r\ *adj* : GLARING <his eyes ~ with fury> <buildings ~ in the sunlight>

agleam \ə-ˈglēm\ *adj* : reflecting light by gleaming

ag·let \ˈag-lət\ *n* [ME *aglet*, fr. MF *aguillette*, *aiguillette*, dim. of *aguille*, *aiguille* needle, fr. LL *acicula*, *acucula* ornamental pin, dim. of L *acus* needle, pin — more at ACUTE] **1** : the plain or ornamental tag covering the ends of a lace or point **2** : any of various ornamental studs, cords, or pins worn on clothing

agley \ə-ˈglā, -ˈglē, -ˈglī\ *adv* [Sc, lit., squintingly, fr. [1]*a-* + *gley* to squint] *chiefly Scot* : AWRY, WRONG <the best-laid schemes o' mice an' men gang aft ~ —Robert Burns>

aglit·ter \ə-ˈglit-ər\ *adj* : reflecting light by glittering

aglow \ə-ˈglō\ *adj* : radiant with warmth or excitement

agly·con \ag-ˈlī-ˌkän\ *or* **agly·cone** \-ˌkōn\ *n* [ISV *a-* (fr. Gk *ha-*, *a-* together) + *glyc-* + *-on*, *-one*] : an organic compound (as a phenol or alcohol) combined with the sugar portion of a glycoside

ag·nail \ˈag-ˌnāl\ *n* [ME, corn on the foot or toe, fr. OE *angnægl*, fr. *ang-* (akin to *enge* tight, painful) + *nægl* metal nail — more at ANGER, NAIL] : a sore or inflammation about a fingernail or toenail; *also* : HANGNAIL

[1]**ag·nate** \ˈag-ˌnāt\ *n* [L *agnatus*, fr. pp. of *agnasci* to be born in addition to, fr. *ad-* + *nasci* to be born — more at NATION] **1** : a relative whose kinship is traceable exclusively through males **2** : a paternal kinsman

[2]**agnate** *adj* **1** : related through male descent or on the father's side **2** : ALLIED, AKIN — **ag·nat·ic** \ag-ˈnat-ik\ *adj* — **ag·nat·i·cal·ly** \-i-k(ə-)lē\ *adv* — **ag·na·tion** \-ˈnā-shən\ *n*

Ag·ne·an \ˈäg-nē-ən\ *n* [*Agni*, ancient kingdom in Turkestan] : TOCHARIAN A

ag·nize \ag-ˈnīz\ *vt* **ag·nized; ag·niz·ing** [L *agn*oscere to acknowledge (fr. *ad-* + *noscere* to know) + E *-ize* (as in *recognize*) — more at KNOW] *archaic* : RECOGNIZE, ACKNOWLEDGE

ag·no·men \ag-ˈnō-mən\ *n, pl* **-nom·i·na** \-ˈnäm-ə-nə\ *or* **-no·mens** [L, irreg. fr. *ad-* + *nomen* name — more at NAME] : an additional cognomen given to a person by the ancient Romans (as in honor of some achievement)

[1]**ag·nos·tic** \ag-ˈnäs-tik, əg-\ *n* [Gk *agnōstos* unknown, unknowable, fr. *a-* + *gnōstos* known, fr. *gignōskein* to know — more at KNOW] : one who holds the view that any ultimate reality (as God) is unknown and prob. unknowable ***syn*** see ATHEIST — **ag·nos·ti·cism** \-tə-ˌsiz-əm\ *n*

[2]**agnostic** *adj* **1** : of, relating to, or being an agnostic or the beliefs of agnostics **2** : NONCOMMITTAL, UNDOGMATIC

Ag·nus Dei \ˌäg-ˌnüs-ˈdā(-ˌē), ˌän-ˌyüs-; ˌag-nəs-ˈdē-ˌī\ *n* [ME, fr. LL, lamb of God, fr. its opening words] **1** : a liturgical prayer addressed to Christ as Savior **2** : an image of a lamb often with a halo and a banner and cross as a symbol of Christ

Agnus Dei 2

ago \ə-ˈgō\ *adj or adv* [ME *agon*, *ago*, fr. pp. of *agon* to pass away, fr. OE *āgān*, fr. *ā-* (perfective prefix) + *gān* to go — more at ABIDE, GO] : earlier than the present time <10 years ~>

agog \ə-ˈgäg\ *adj* [MF *en gogues* in mirth] : full of intense interest or excitement : EAGER <the . . . court was ~ with gossip, scandal and intrigue —*Times Lit. Supp.*>

[1]**a-go-go** \ä-ˈgō-(ˌ)gō\ *n* [*Whisky à Gogo*, cafe and discotheque in Paris, France, from F *à gogo* galore, fr. MF] **1** : DISCOTHEQUE **2** : a usu. small intimate nightclub for dancing to live music and esp. rock'n'roll

[2]**a-go-go** *adj* : GO-GO

-a·gogue \ə-ˌgäg\ *n comb form* [F & NL; F, fr. LL *-agogus* promoting the expulsion of, fr. Gk *-agōgos,* fr. *agein* to lead; NL *-agogon,* fr. Gk, neut. of *-agōgos* — more at AGENT] **:** substance that promotes the secretion or expulsion of <emmen*agogue*>

agon \ˈäg-ˌän, ä-ˈgōn\ *n* [Gk *agōn*] **:** CONTEST, CONFLICT; *specif* **:** the dramatic conflict between the chief characters in a literary work

ag·o·nal \ˈag-ən-ᵊl\ *adj* **:** of, relating to, or associated with agony and esp. the death agony

agone \ə-ˈgȯn *also* -ˈgän\ *adj or adv, archaic* **:** AGO

agon·ic \(ˈ)ā-ˈgän-ik, ə-\ *adj* [Gk *agōnos* without angle, fr. *a-* + *gōnia* angle — more at -GON] **1 :** not forming an angle **2 :** being an imaginary line passing through points where there is no magnetic declination and where a freely suspended magnetic needle indicates true north

ag·o·nist \ˈag-ə-nəst\ *n* [LL *agonista* competitor, fr. Gk *agōnistēs,* fr. *agōnizesthai* to contend, fr. *agōn*] **1 :** one that is engaged in a struggle **2** [back-formation fr. *antagonist*] **:** a muscle that is checked and controlled by the opposing simultaneous contraction of another muscle

ag·o·nis·tic \ˌag-ə-ˈnis-tik\ *adj* **1 :** of or relating to the athletic contests of ancient Greece **2 :** ARGUMENTATIVE **3 :** striving for effect **:** STRAINED **4 :** of, relating to, or being aggressive or defensive social interaction (as fighting, fleeing, or submitting) between individuals usu. of the same species — **ag·o·nis·ti·cal** \-ti-kəl\ *adj* — **ag·o·nis·ti·cal·ly** \-k(ə-)lē\ *adv*

ag·o·nize \ˈag-ə-ˌnīz\ *vb* **-nized; -niz·ing** *vt* **:** to cause to suffer agony **:** TORTURE ~ *vi* **1 :** to suffer agony, torture, or anguish <~*s* over every decision> **2 :** STRUGGLE

ag·o·nized *adj* **:** characterized by, suffering, or expressing agony

ag·o·niz·ing *adj* **:** causing agony **:** PAINFUL <an ~ reappraisal of his policies> — **ag·o·niz·ing·ly** \-ˌnī-ziŋ-lē\ *adv*

ag·o·ny \ˈag-ə-nē\ *n, pl* **-nies** [ME *agonie,* fr. LL *agonia,* fr. Gk *agōnia* struggle, anguish, fr. *agōn* gathering, contest for a prize, fr. *agein* to lead, celebrate — more at AGENT] **1 a :** intense pain of mind or body **:** ANGUISH, TORTURE **b :** the struggle that precedes death **2 :** a violent struggle or contest **3 :** a strong sudden display (as of joy or delight) **:** OUTBURST ***syn*** see DISTRESS

agony column *n* **:** a newspaper column of personal advertisements relating esp. to missing relatives or friends

[1]**ag·o·ra** \ˈag-ə-rə\ *n, pl* **-ras** *or* **-rae** \-ˌrē, -ˌrī\ [Gk — more at GREGARIOUS] **:** a gathering place; *esp* **:** the marketplace in ancient Greece

[2]**ago·ra** \ˌäg-ə-ˈrä\ *n, pl* **ago·rot** \-ˈrōt\ [N Heb *agōrāh,* fr. Heb, a small coin] — see *pound* at MONEY table

ag·o·ra·pho·bia \ˌag-ə-rə-ˈfō-bē-ə\ *n* [NL, fr. Gk *agora* + NL *phobia*] **:** abnormal fear of crossing or of being in open spaces — **ag·o·ra·pho·bi·ac** \-ˈfō-bē-ˌak\ *n* — **ag·o·ra·pho·bic** \-ˈfō-bik, -ˈfäb-ik\ *adj*

agou·ti \ə-ˈgüt-ē\ *n* [F, fr. Sp. *agutí,* fr. Guarani] **1 :** a tropical American rodent (genus *Dasyprocta* or *Myoprocta*) about the size of a rabbit **2 :** a grizzled color of fur resulting from the barring of each hair in several alternate dark and light bands

agr *or* **agric** *abbr* agricultural; agriculture

agrafe *or* **agraffe** \ə-ˈgraf\ *n* [F *agrafe*] **:** a hook-and-loop fastening; *esp* **:** an ornamental clasp used on armor or costumes

agran·u·lo·cyte \(ˈ)ā-ˈgran-yə-lō-ˌsīt\ *n* **:** a leukocyte without cytoplasmic granules

agran·u·lo·cy·to·sis \ˌā-ˌgran-yə-lō-ˌsī-ˈtō-səs\ *n* **:** a destructive condition marked by severe decrease in blood granulocytes and often associated with the use of certain drugs

ag·ra·pha \ˈag-rə-fə\ *n pl* [Gk, neut. pl. of *agraphos* unwritten, fr. *a-* + *graphein* to write — more at CARVE] **:** sayings of Jesus not in the canonical gospels but found in other New Testament or early Christian writings

agraph·ia \(ˈ)ā-ˈgraf-ē-ə\ *n* [NL, fr. [2]*a-* + Gk *graphein* to write] **:** the pathologic loss of the ability to write

[1]**agrar·i·an** \ə-ˈgrer-ē-ən, -ˈgrar-\ *adj* [L *agrarius,* fr. *agr-, ager* field — more at ACRE] **1 :** of or relating to fields or lands or their tenure **2 a :** of, relating to, or characteristic of the farmer or his way of life **b :** organized or designed to promote agricultural interests <an ~ political party > <~ reforms>

[2]**agrarian** *n* **:** a member of an agrarian party or movement

agrar·i·an·ism \-ē-ə-ˌniz-əm\ *n* **:** a social or political movement designed to bring about land reforms or to improve the economic status of the farmer

agree \ə-ˈgrē\ *vb* **agreed; agree·ing** [ME *agreen,* fr. MF *agreer,* fr. *a-* (fr. L *ad-*) + *gre* will, pleasure, fr. L *gratum,* neut. of *gratus* pleasing, agreeable — more at GRACE] *vt* **1 :** ADMIT, CONCEDE **2 :** to settle on by common consent **:** ARRANGE ~ *vi* **1 :** to accept or concede something (as the views or wishes of another) typically after resolving points of disagreement **2 a :** to achieve or be in harmony (as of opinion, feeling, or purpose) **b :** to get along together **c :** to come to terms **3 a :** to be similar **:** CORRESPOND <both copies ~> **b :** to be consistent <the story ~*s* with the facts> **4 :** to be fitting, pleasing, or healthful **:** SUIT <this climate ~*s* with him> **5 :** to have an inflectional form denoting identity or a regular correspondence other than identity in a grammatical category (as gender, number, case, or person)

syn* 1** see ASSENT ***ant protest (*against*), differ (*with*)

2 AGREE, CONCUR, COINCIDE *shared meaning element* **:** to come into or be in harmony regarding a matter of opinion. AGREE implies complete accord usually attained by discussion and adjustment of differences <on some points we all can *agree*> CONCUR tends to suggest cooperative thinking or acting toward an end <for the creation of a masterwork of literature two powers must *concur,* the power of the man and the power of the moment —Matthew Arnold> but sometimes implies no more than approval (as of a decision reached by others). COINCIDE, used more often of opinions, judgments, wishes, or interests than of people, implies an agreement amounting to identity <their wishes *coincide* exactly with my desire> ***ant*** differ, disagree

3 AGREE, SQUARE, CONFORM, ACCORD, COMPORT, HARMONIZE, CORRESPOND *shared meaning element* **:** to go or exist together without conflict or incongruity ***ant*** differ (*from*)

agree·able \ə-ˈgrē-ə-bəl\ *adj* **1 :** pleasing to the mind or senses esp. as according well with one's tastes or needs <an ~ companion> <an ~ change> **2 :** ready or willing to agree or consent **3 :** being in harmony **:** CONSONANT ***syn*** see PLEASANT ***ant*** disagreeable — **agree·abil·i·ty** \-ˌgrē-ə-ˈbil-ət-ē\ *n* — **agree·able·ness** \-ˈgrē-ə-bəl-nəs\ *n* — **agree·ably** \-blē\ *adv*

agree·ment \ə-ˈgrē-mənt\ *n* **1 a :** the act or fact of agreeing **b :** harmony of opinion, action, or character **:** CONCORD **2 a :** an arrangement as to a course of action **b :** COMPACT, TREATY **3 a :** a contract duly executed and legally binding **b :** the language or instrument embodying such a contract

ag·ri·busi·ness \ˈag-rə-ˌbiz-nəs, -nəz\ *n* [*agri*culture + *business*] **:** a combination of the producing operations of a farm, the manufacture and distribution of farm equipment and supplies, and the processing, storage, and distribution of farm commodities

ag·ri·cul·tur·al \ˌag-ri-ˈkəlch-(ə-)rəl\ *adj* **:** of, relating to, used in, or concerned with agriculture — **ag·ri·cul·tur·al·ly** \-ē\ *adv*

ag·ri·cul·ture \ˈag-ri-ˌkəl-chər\ *n* [F, fr. L *agricultura,* fr. *ager* field + *cultura* cultivation — more at ACRE, CULTURE] **:** the science or art of cultivating the soil, producing crops, and raising livestock and in varying degrees the preparation of these products for man's use and their disposal (as by marketing) **:** FARMING — **ag·ri·cul·tur·ist** \ˌag-ri-ˈkəlch-(ə-)rəst\ *or* **ag·ri·cul·tur·al·ist** \-(ə-)rə-ləst\ *n*

ag·ri·mo·ny \ˈag-rə-ˌmō-nē\ *n, pl* **-nies** [ME, fr. MF & L; MF *aigremoine,* fr. L *agrimonia,* MS var. of *argemonia,* fr. Gk *argemōnē*] **:** a common yellow-flowered herb (genus *Agrimonia*) of the rose family having toothed leaves and fruits like burs; *also* **:** any of several similar or related plants

ag·ri·ol·o·gy \ˌag-rē-ˈäl-ə-jē\ *n* [Gk *agrios* wild, fr. *agros* field, country] **:** the comparative study of the customs of nonliterate peoples

agro- *comb form* [F, fr. Gk, fr. *agros* field — more at ACRE] **1 :** of or belonging to fields or soil **:** agricultural <*agro*logy> **2 :** agricultural and <*agro*-industrial>

ag·ro·bi·ol·o·gy \ˌag-rō-bī-ˈäl-ə-jē\ *n* **:** the study of plant nutrition and growth and crop production in relation to soil management — **ag·ro·bi·o·log·ic** \-ˌbī-ə-ˈläj-ik\ *or* **ag·ro·bi·o·log·i·cal** \-i-kəl\ *adj* — **ag·ro·bi·o·log·i·cal·ly** \-i-k(ə-)lē\ *adv*

ag·ro–in·dus·tri·al \ˌag-rō-in-ˈdəs-trē-əl\ *adj* **:** of or relating to production (as of power for industry and water for irrigation) for both industrial and agricultural purposes

agrol·o·gy \ə-ˈgräl-ə-jē\ *n* [ISV] **:** a branch of agriculture dealing with soils esp. in relation to crops — **ag·ro·log·ic** \ˌag-rə-ˈläj-ik\ *or* **ag·ro·log·i·cal** \-ˈläj-i-kəl\ *adj* — **ag·ro·log·i·cal·ly** \-i-k(ə-)lē\ *adv* — **agrol·o·gist** \ə-ˈgräl-ə-jəst\ *n*

agron·o·my \ə-ˈgrän-ə-mē\ *n* [prob. fr. F *agronomie,* fr. *agro-* + *-nomie* -nomy] **:** a branch of agriculture dealing with field-crop production and soil management — **ag·ro·nom·ic** \ˌag-rə-ˈnäm-ik\ *or* **ag·ro·nom·i·cal** \ˌag-rə-ˈnäm-i-kəl\ *adj* — **ag·ro·nom·i·cal·ly** \-i-k(ə-)lē\ *adv* — **agron·o·mist** \ə-ˈgrän-ə-məst\ *n*

aground \ə-ˈgrau̇nd\ *adv or adj* **1 :** on or onto the shore or the bottom of a body of water <a ship run ~> **2 :** on the ground <planes aloft and ~>

agt *abbr* agent

ague \ˈā-(ˌ)gyü\ *n* [ME, fr. MF *agüe,* fr. ML (*febris*) *acuta,* lit., sharp fever, fr. L, fem. of *acutus* sharp — more at ACUTE] **1 :** a fever (as malaria) marked by paroxysms of chills, fever, and sweating that recur at regular intervals **2 :** a fit of shivering **:** CHILL — **agu·ish** \ˈā-ˌgyü-ish\ *adj* — **agu·ish·ly** *adv*

ah \ˈä\ *interj* [ME] — used to express delight, relief, regret, or contempt

AH *abbr* **1** ampere-hour **2** anno hegirae **3** arts and humanities

aha \ä-ˈhä\ *interj* [ME] — used to express surprise, triumph, or derision

AHA *abbr* American Historical Association

ahead \ə-ˈhed\ *adv or adj* **1 a :** in a forward direction or position **:** FORWARD **b :** in front **2 :** in, into, or for the future <plan ~> <the years ~> **3 :** in or toward a more advantageous position <helped others to get ~> **4 :** at or to an earlier time **:** in advance <make payments ~>

ahead of *prep* **1 :** in front or advance of **2 :** in excess of **:** ABOVE

ahim·sa \ə-ˈhim-ˌsä\ *n* [Skt *ahiṁsā* noninjury] **:** the Hindu and Buddhist doctrine of refraining from harming any living being

ahis·tor·i·cal \ˌā-his-ˈtȯr-i-kəl, -ˈtär-\ *or* **ahis·tor·ic** \-ik\ *adj* **:** not concerned with or related to history, historical development, or tradition <the ~ attitudes of the radicals>

AHL *abbr* American Hockey League

ahold \ə-ˈhōld\ *n* [prob. fr. the phrase *a hold*] **:** HOLD <if you could get ~ of a representative who . . . would come along —Norman Mailer>

A–horizon *n* **:** the outer dark-colored layer of a soil profile consisting largely of partly disintegrated organic debris

ahoy \ə-ˈhȯi\ *interj* [*a-* (as in *aha*) + *hoy*] — used in hailing <ship ~>

Ah·ri·man \ˈär-i-mən, -ˌmän\ *n* [Per, modif. of Av *aṅrō mainyus* hostile spirit] **:** Ahura Mazda's antagonist who is a spirit of darkness and evil in Zoroastrianism

Ahu·ra Maz·da \ə-ˌhu̇r-ə-ˈmaz-də, ä-ˌhu̇r-\ *n* [Av *Ahuramazda,* lit., wise god] **:** the Supreme Being represented as a deity of goodness and light in Zoroastrianism

ai \ˈī, ä-ˈē\ *n* [Pg *ai* or Sp *aí,* fr. Tupi *ai*] **:** a sloth (genus *Bradypus*) with three claws on each front foot

AI *abbr* **1** ad interim **2** airborne intercept **3** air interception

AIA *abbr* American Institute of Architects

Ai·as \ˈī-əs\ *n* [Gk] **:** AJAX

ai·blins \ˈā-blənz\ *adv* [*able* + *-lings, -lins* -lings] *chiefly Scot* **:** PERHAPS

AIChE *abbr* American Institute of Chemical Engineers

[1]**aid** \ˈād\ *vb* [ME *eyden,* fr. MF *aider,* fr. L *adjutare,* fr. *adjutus,* pp. of *adjuvare,* fr. *ad-* + *juvare* to help] *vt* **:** to provide with what

is useful or necessary in achieving an end ~ *vi* : to give assistance *syn* see HELP *ant* injure — **aid·er** *n*

[2]aid *n* **1** : a subsidy granted to the king by the English parliament until the 18th century for an extraordinary purpose **2 a** : the act of helping **b** : help given : ASSISTANCE; *specif* : tangible means of assistance (as money or supplies) **3 a** : an assisting person or group — compare AIDE **b** : something by which assistance is given : an assisting device <an ~ to understanding> <a visual ~>; *specif* : HEARING AID **4** : a tribute paid by a vassal to his lord

AID *abbr* Agency for International Development

aide \'ād\ *n* [short for *aide-de-camp*] : a person who acts as an assistant; *specif* : a military officer acting as assistant to a superior

aide–de–camp \ˌād-di-'kamp, -'kän\ *n, pl* **aides–de–camp** \ˌād(z)-di-\ [F *aide de camp*, lit., camp assistant] : a military aide

aide–mé·moire \ˌād-mām-'wär\ *n, pl* **aide–mémoire** [F, fr. *aider* to aid + *mémoire* memory] **1** : an aid to the memory; *esp* : a mnemonic device **2** : a written summary or outline of important items of a proposed agreement or diplomatic communication : MEMORANDUM

aid·man \'ād-ˌman\ *n* : an army medical corpsman attached to a field unit

ai·grette \ā-'gret, 'ā-ˌ\ *n* [F] **1** : a spray of feathers (as of the egret) for the head **2** : a spray of gems worn on a hat or in the hair

ai·guille \ā-'gwē(ə)l, -'gwē\ *n* [F, lit., needle — more at AGLET] **1** : a sharp-pointed pinnacle of rock **2** : an instrument for boring holes in stone or other masonry materials

ai·guil·lette \ˌā-gwi-'let\ *n* [F — more at AGLET] : AGLET; *specif* : a shoulder cord worn by designated military aides — compare FOURRAGÈRE

ai·ki·do \ˌī-ki-'dō\ *n* [Jap *aikidō*, fr. *ai-* together, mutual + *ki* spirit + *dō* art] : a Japanese art of self-defense employing locks and holds and utilizing the principle of nonresistance to cause an opponent's own momentum to work against him

ail \'ā(ə)l\ *vb* [ME *eilen*, fr. OE *eglan*; akin to MLG *egelen* to annoy] *vt* : to give physical or emotional pain, discomfort, or trouble to ~ *vi* : to have something the matter; *esp* : to suffer ill health *syn* see TROUBLE

ai·lan·thus \ā-'lan(t)-thəs\ *n* [NL, genus name, fr. Amboinese *ai lanto*, lit., tree (of) heaven] : any of a small Asiatic genus (*Ailanthus* of the family Simaroubaceae, the ailanthus family) of chiefly tropical trees and shrubs with bitter bark, pinnate leaves, and terminal panicles of ill-scented greenish flowers

ai·le·ron \'ā-lə-ˌrän\ *n* [F, fr. dim. of *aile* wing] : a movable part of an airplane wing or a movable airfoil external to the wing at the trailing edge for imparting a rolling motion and thus providing lateral control —see AIRPLANE illustration

ail·ment \'ā(ə)l-mənt\ *n* **1** : a bodily disorder or chronic disease **2** : UNREST, UNEASINESS

ai·lu·ro·phile \ī-'lu̇r-ə-ˌfīl, ā-\ *n* [Gk *ailouros* cat] : a cat fancier : a lover of cats

ai·lu·ro·phobe \-ˌfōb\ *n* [Gk *ailouros* cat] : one who hates or fears cats

[1]aim \'ām\ *vb* [ME *aimen*, fr. MF *aesmer* & *esmer*; MF *aesmer*, fr. OF, fr. *a-* (fr. L *ad-*) + *esmer* to estimate, fr. L *aestimare* — more at ESTEEM] *vi* **1** : to direct a course; *specif* : to point a weapon at an object **2** : ASPIRE, INTEND <~*s* to reform the government> ~ *vt* **1** *obs* : GUESS, CONJECTURE **2 a** : POINT **b** : to direct to or toward a specified object or goal

[2]aim *n* **1** *obs* : MARK, TARGET **2 a** : the pointing of a weapon at a mark **b** : the ability to hit a target <his ~ was deadly> **c** : a weapon's accuracy or effectiveness **3** *obs* **a** : CONJECTURE, GUESS **b** : the directing of effort toward a goal **4** : a clearly directed intent or purpose *syn* see INTENTION — **aim·less** \-ləs\ *adj* — **aim·less·ly** *adv* — **aim·less·ness** *n*

ain \'ān\ *adj* [prob. fr. ON *eiginn*] *Scot* : OWN

ain't \'ānt\ [prob. contr. of *are not*] **1 a** : are not **b** : is not **c** : am not — though disapproved by many and more common in less educated speech, used orally in most parts of the U.S. by many educated speakers esp. in the phrase *ain't I* **2** *substand* **a** : have not **b** : has not

Ai·nu \'ī-(ˌ)nü\ *n, pl* **Ainu** *or* **Ainus** [Ainu, lit., man] **1** : a member of an indigenous Caucasoid people of Japan **2** : the language of the Ainu people

[1]air \'a(ə)r, 'e(ə)r\ *n, often attrib* [ME, fr. OF, fr. L *aer*, fr. Gk *aēr*] **1 a** : the mixture of invisible odorless tasteless gases (as nitrogen and oxygen) that surrounds the earth **b** : a light breeze **c** *archaic* : BREATH **2 a** : empty space **b** : NOTHINGNESS <vanished into thin ~> **c** : a sudden severance of relations <she gave him the ~> **3** : COMPRESSED AIR **4 a** (1) : AIRCRAFT <go by ~> (2) : AVIATION <~ safety> <~ rights> (3) : AIR FORCE <~ headquarters> **b** : the medium of transmission of radio waves; *also* : RADIO, TELEVISION <went on the ~> **5** : public utterance <he gave ~ to his opinion> **6 a** : the look, appearance, or bearing of a person esp. as expressive of some personal quality or emotion : DEMEANOR <an ~ of dignity> **b** : an artificial or affected manner : HAUGHTINESS <to put on ~*s*> **c** : outward appearance of a thing <an ~ of luxury> **d** : a surrounding or pervading influence : ATMOSPHERE <an ~ of mystery> **7** [prob. trans. of It *aria*] **a** *Elizabethan & Jacobean music* : an accompanied song or melody in usu. strophic form **b** : the chief voice part or melody in choral music **c** : TUNE, MELODY **8** : a football offense utilizing primarily the forward pass <behind by three touchdowns and forced to take to the ~> *syn* see POSE — **air·less** \-ləs\ *adj* — **air·less·ness** *n* — **up in the air** : not yet settled

[2]air *vt* **1** : to expose to the air for drying, purifying, or refreshing : VENTILATE — often used with *out* **2** : to expose to public view or bring to public notice **3** : to transmit by radio or television <~ a program> ~ *vi* : to become exposed to the open air *syn* see EXPRESS

air bag *n* : an automatically inflating bag in front of riders in an automobile to protect them from pitching forward into solid parts in case of an accident

air base *n* : a base of operations for military aircraft

air bends *n pl* : AEROEMBOLISM 2

air bladder *n* : a sac containing gas and esp. air; *esp* : a hydrostatic organ present in most fishes that serves as an accessory respiratory organ

air·borne \'a(ə)r-ˌbō(ə)rn, 'e(ə)r-, -ˌbȯ(ə)rn\ *adj* **1** : supported wholly by aerodynamic and aerostatic forces **2** : transported by air

air brake *n* **1** : a brake operated by a piston driven by compressed air **2** : a surface (as an aileron) that may be projected into the airstream for lowering the speed of an airplane

air·brush \-ˌbrəsh\ *n* : an atomizer for applying by compressed air a fine spray (as of paint or liquid color) — **airbrush** *vt*

air·burst \-ˌbərst\ *n* : the burst of a shell or bomb in the air

air·bus \-ˌbəs\ *n* : a short-range or medium-range subsonic jet passenger airplane

air cavalry *n* **1** : an army component that is transported in air vehicles and carries out the traditional cavalry missions of reconnaissance and security **2** : an army component organized for sustained ground combat and esp. equipped and adapted for transportation in air vehicles

air chief marshal *n* : a commissioned officer in the British air force who ranks with a general in the army

air coach *n* : a passenger airliner offering service at less than first-class rates usu. with curtailed accommodations

air commodore *n* : a commissioned officer in the British air force who ranks with a brigadier in the army

air–con·di·tion \ˌa(ə)r-kən-'dish-ən, ˌe(ə)r-\ *vt* [back-formation fr. *air conditioning*] : to equip (as a building) with an apparatus for washing air and controlling its humidity and temperature; *also* : to subject (air) to these processes — **air con·di·tion·er** \-'dish-(ə-)nər\ *n*

air–cool \'a(ə)r-'kül, 'e(ə)r-\ *vt* [back-formation fr. *air-cooled* & *air cooling*] : to cool the cylinders of (an internal-combustion engine) by air without the use of an intermediate medium

air·craft \'a(ə)r-ˌkraft, 'e(ə)r-\ *n, pl* **aircraft** *often attrib* : a weight-carrying structure for navigation of the air that is supported either by its own buoyancy or by the dynamic action of the air against its surfaces

aircraft carrier *n* : a warship with a flight deck on which airplanes can be launched and landed

air·crew \'a(ə)r-ˌkrü, 'e(ə)r-\ *n* : the crew manning an airplane

air–cushion vehicle *n* : GROUND-EFFECT MACHINE

air·drome \'a(ə)r-ˌdrōm, 'e(ə)r-\ *n* [alter. of *aerodrome*] : AIRPORT

air·drop \-ˌdräp\ *n* : delivery of cargo or personnel by parachute from an airplane in flight — **air–drop** *vt* — **air–drop·pa·ble** \-ˌdräp-ə-bəl\ *adj*

air–dry \-'drī\ *adj* : dry to such a degree that no further moisture is given up on exposure to air

Aire·dale terrier \ˌa(ə)r-ˌdāl-, ˌe(ə)r-\ *n* [*Airedale*, valley of the Aire river, England] : any of a breed of large terriers with a hard wiry coat that is dark on the back and sides and tan elsewhere — called also *Airedale*

Air Express *service mark* — used for package transport by air

air·field \'a(ə)r-ˌfēld, 'e(ə)r-\ *n* **1** : the landing field of an airport **2** : AIRPORT

air·flow \-ˌflō\ *n* : the motion of air (as around parts of an airplane in flight) relative to the surface of a body immersed in it

air·foil \-ˌfȯil\ *n* : a body (as an airplane wing or propeller blade) designed to provide a desired reaction force when in motion relative to the surrounding air

air force *n* **1** : the military organization of a nation for air warfare **2** : a unit of the U.S. Air Force higher than a division and lower than a command

air·frame \-ˌfrām\ *n* [*aircraft* + *frame*] : the structure of an airplane or rocket without the power plant

air·freight \-'frāt\ *n* : freight transport by air in volume; *also* : the charge for this service — **airfreight** *vt*

air·glow \-ˌglō\ *n* : light that is observed esp. during the night, that originates in the high atmosphere, and that is associated with photochemical reactions of gases caused by solar radiation

air gun *n* **1** : a rifle from which a projectile is propelled by compressed air **2** : any of various hand tools that work by compressed air; *esp* : AIRBRUSH

air·head \-ˌhed\ *n* ['*air* + *-head* (as in *beachhead*)] : an area in hostile territory secured usu. by airborne troops for further use in bringing in troops and materiel by air

air hole *n* **1 a** : a hole to admit or discharge air **b** : a spot not frozen over in ice **2** : AIR POCKET

air·ing \'a(ə)r-iŋ, 'e(ə)r-\ *n* **1** : exposure to air or heat for drying or freshening **2** : exposure to or exercise in the open air esp. to promote health or fitness **3** : exposure to public view or notice **4** : a radio or television broadcast

air lane *n* : a path customarily followed by airplanes

air letter *n* **1** : an airmail letter **2** : a sheet of airmail stationery that can be folded and sealed with the message inside and the address outside

air·lift \'a(ə)r-ˌlift, 'e(ə)r-\ *n* : a system of transporting cargo or passengers by aircraft usu. to an otherwise inaccessible area — **airlift** *vt*

air·line \-ˌlīn\ *n* : an air transportation system including its equipment, routes, operating personnel, and management

air line *n* : a straight line through the air between two points : BEELINE

air·lin·er \-ˌlī-nər\ *n* : an airplane operated by an airline

air lock *n* **1** : an intermediate chamber between the outer air and the working chamber of a pneumatic caisson; *also* : a similar intermediate chamber **2 :** a stoppage of flow caused by air being in a part where liquid ought to circulate

air·mail \'a(ə)r-ˈmā(ə)l, 'e(ə)r-, -ˌmāl\ *n* **:** the system of transporting mail by aircraft; *also* **:** the mail thus transported — **airmail** *vt*

air·man \-mən\ *n* **1 :** an enlisted man in the air force: as **a :** an enlisted man of one of the three ranks below sergeant **b :** an enlisted man ranking above an airman basic and below an airman first class **2 :** a civilian or military pilot, aviator, or aviation technician

airman basic *n* **:** an enlisted man of the lowest rank in the air force

airman first class *n* **:** an enlisted man in the air force ranking above an airman and below a sergeant

air·man·ship \'a(ə)r-mən-ˌship, 'e(ə)r-\ *n* **:** skill in piloting or navigating airplanes

air marshal *n* **:** a commissioned officer in the British air force who ranks with a lieutenant general in the army

air mass *n* **:** a body of air extending hundreds or thousands of miles horizontally and sometimes as high as the stratosphere and maintaining as it travels nearly uniform conditions of temperature and humidity at any given level

air mattress *n* **:** MATTRESS 1b

Air Medal *n* **:** a U.S. military decoration awarded for meritorious achievement while participating in an aerial flight

air mile *n* **:** a mile in air navigation; *specif* **:** a unit equal to 6076.1154 feet

air–mind·ed \'a(ə)r-ˈmīn-dəd, 'e(ə)r-\ *adj* **:** interested in aviation or in air travel — **air–mind·ed·ness** *n*

air·mo·bile \-ˌmō-bəl, -ˌbēl, -ˌbīl\ *adj* [*air* + [1]*mobile*] **:** of, relating to, or being a military unit whose members are transported to combat areas usu. by helicopter

air·park \-ˌpärk\ *n* **:** a small airport usu. near an industrial area

air piracy *n* **:** the hijacking of a flying airplane **:** SKYJACKING

air·plane \'a(ə)r-ˌplān, 'e(ə)r-\ *n* [alter. of *aeroplane*, prob. fr. LGk *aeroplanos* wandering in air, fr. Gk *aer-* + *planos* wandering, fr. *planasthai* to wander — more at PLANET] **:** a fixed-wing aircraft heavier than air that is driven by a screw propeller or by a high-velocity jet and supported by the dynamic reaction of the air against its wings

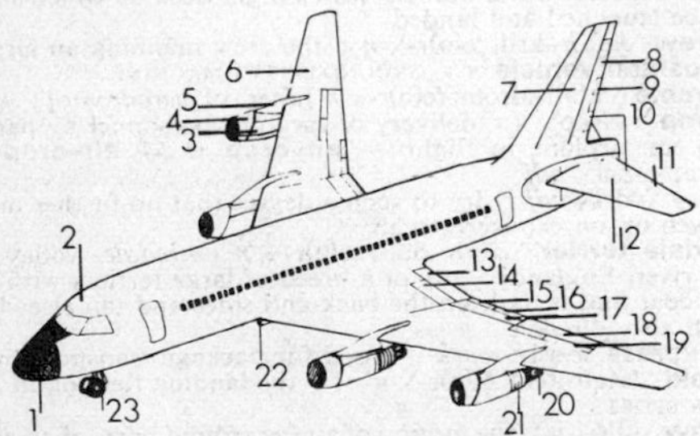

airplane: *1* weather radar, *2* cockpit, *3* jet engine, *4* engine pod, *5* pylon, *6* swept-back wing, *7* vertical stabilizer, *8* rudder, *9, 10* tabs, *11* elevator, *12* horizontal stabilizer, *13* inboard flap, *14* inboard spoiler, *15, 16* tabs, *17* aileron, *18* outboard flap, *19* outboard spoiler, *20* sound suppressor, *21* thrust reverser, *22* cabin air intake, *23* nose landing gear

air plant *n* **1 :** EPIPHYTE **2 :** a plant (genus *Kalanchoe*) that propagates new plants from the leaves

air pocket *n* **:** a condition of the atmosphere (as a local down current) that causes an airplane to drop suddenly

air police *n* **:** the military police of an air force

air·port \'a(ə)r-ˌpō(ə)rt, 'e(ə)r-, -ˌpȯ(ə)rt\ *n* **:** a tract of land or water that is maintained for the landing and takeoff of aircraft and for receiving and discharging passengers and cargo and that usu. has facilities for the shelter, supply, and repair of planes

air·post \-ˈpōst\ *n* **:** AIRMAIL

air power *n* **:** the military strength of a nation's air force

air pump *n* **:** a pump for exhausting air from a closed space or for compressing air or forcing it through other apparatus

air raid *n* **:** an attack by armed airplanes on a surface target

air right *n* **:** a property right to the space above a surface area or object

air sac *n* **1 :** one of the air-filled spaces in the body of a bird connected with the air passages of the lungs **2 :** ALVEOLUS 1b **3 :** a thin-walled dilation of a trachea occurring in many insects

air·screw \'a(ə)r-ˌskrü, 'e(ə)r-\ *n* **1 :** a screw propeller designed to operate in air **2** *Brit* **:** an airplane propeller

air·ship \-ˌship\ *n* **:** a lighter-than-air aircraft having propulsion and steering systems

air·sick \-ˌsik\ *adj* **:** affected with motion sickness associated with flying — **air·sick·ness** *n*

air·space \-ˌspās\ *n* **:** the space lying above the earth or above a certain area of land or water; *esp* **:** the space lying above a nation and coming under its jurisdiction

air·speed \-ˌspēd\ *n* **:** the speed (as of an airplane) with relation to the air — compare GROUND SPEED

air·stream \-ˌstrēm\ *n* **:** a current of air; *specif* **:** AIRFLOW

air strike *n* **:** an air attack

air·strip \-ˌstrip\ *n* **:** a runway without normal air base or airport facilities

[1]**airt** \'ärt, 'ert\ *n* [ME *art*, fr. ScGael *āird*] *chiefly Scot* **:** compass point **:** DIRECTION

[2]**airt** *vt*, *chiefly Scot* **:** DIRECT, GUIDE

air·tight \'a(ə)r-ˈtīt, 'e(ə)r-\ *adj* **1 :** impermeable to air or nearly so **2 a :** having no noticeable weakness, flaw, or loophole <an ~ argument> **b :** permitting no opportunity for an opponent to score <an ~ defense> — **air·tight·ness** *n*

air–to–air \ˌa(ə)rt-ə-ˈ(w)a(ə)r, ˌe(ə)rt-ə-ˈ(w)e(ə)r\ *adj* **:** launched from one airplane in flight at another **:** involving aircraft in flight <~ rockets> <~ combat>

air vice–marshal *n* **:** a commissioned officer in the British air force who ranks with a major general in the army

air·wave \'a(ə)r-ˌwāv, 'e(ə)r-\ *n* **1 :** the medium of radio and television transmission — usu. used in pl. **2 :** AIRWAY 4

air·way \-ˌwā\ *n* **1 :** a passage for a current of air (as in a mine or to the lungs) **2 :** a designated route along which airplanes fly from airport to airport; *esp* **:** such a route equipped with navigational aids **3 :** AIR LINE 2 **4 :** a channel of a designated radio frequency for broadcasting or other radio communication

air·wor·thy \-ˌwər-thē\ *adj* **:** fit for operation in the air <an ~ airplane> — **air·wor·thi·ness** *n*

airy \'a(ə)r-ē, 'e(ə)r-\ *adj* **air·i·er; -est 1 a :** of or relating to air **:** ATMOSPHERIC **b :** high in the air **:** LOFTY <~ perches> **c :** performed in air **:** AERIAL <~ leaps> **2 :** UNREAL, ILLUSORY <~ romances> **3 a :** being light and graceful in movement or manner **:** SPRIGHTLY, VIVACIOUS **b :** ETHEREAL **4 :** open to the free circulation of air **:** BREEZY **5 :** AFFECTED, PROUD <~ condescension>

aisle \'ī(ə)l\ *n* [ME *ile*, fr. MF *aile* wing, fr. L *ala*; akin to OE *eaxl* shoulder, L *axilla* armpit — more at AXIS] **1 :** the side of a church nave separated by piers from the nave proper — see BASILICA illustration **2 a :** a passage (as in a theater) separating sections of seats **b :** a passage (as in a store or warehouse) for inside traffic

ait \'āt\ *n* [ME, alter. of OE *īgeoth*, fr. *īg* island — more at ISLAND] *Brit* **:** a little island

aitch \'āch\ *n* [F *hache*, fr. (assumed) VL *hacca*] **:** the letter *h*

aitch·bone \'āch-ˌbōn\ *n* [ME *hachbon*, alter. (resulting from incorrect division of *a nachebon*) of (assumed) ME *nachebon*, fr. ME *nache* buttock (fr. MF, fr. LL *natica*, fr. L *natis*) + *bon* bone — more at NATES] **1 :** the hipbone esp. of cattle **2 :** the cut of beef containing the aitchbone

ajar \ə-ˈjär\ *adj or adv* [earlier *on char*, fr. *on* + *char* turn — more at CHARE] **:** being slightly open <a door ~>

Ajax \'ā-ˌjaks\ *n* [L, fr. Gk *Aias*] **1 :** a Greek hero in the Trojan War who kills himself because the armor of Achilles is awarded to Odysseus **2 :** a fleet-footed Greek hero in the Trojan war — called also *Ajax the Less*

AK *abbr* Alaska

AKA *abbr* also known as

Akan \'äk-ˌän\ *n, pl* **Akan** *or* **Akans 1 :** a language spoken over a wide area in Ghana and extending into the Ivory Coast **2 :** the Akan-speaking peoples

AKC *abbr* American Kennel Club

akim·bo \ə-ˈkim-(ˌ)bō\ *adj or adv* [ME *in kenebowe*] **1 :** having the hand on the hip and the elbow turned outward **2 :** set in a bent position <a tailor sitting with legs ~>

akin \ə-ˈkin\ *adj* **1 :** related by blood **:** descended from a common ancestor or prototype **2 :** essentially similar, related, or compatible ***syn*** see SIMILAR ***ant*** alien

Ak·ka·di·an \ə-ˈkād-ē-ən\ *n* **1 :** a Semitic inhabitant of central Mesopotamia before 2000 B.C. **2 :** an ancient Semitic language of Mesopotamia used from about the 28th to the 1st century B.C. — **Akkadian** *adj*

ak·va·vit \'äk-wə-ˌvēt, 'äk-vä-\ *var of* AQUAVIT

Al *symbol* aluminum

AL *abbr* **1** Alabama **2** American League **3** American Legion

al- — see AD-

[1]**-al** \əl, ᵊl\ *adj suffix* [ME, fr. OF & L; OF, fr. L *-alis*] **:** of, relating to, or characterized by <direction*al*> <fiction*al*>

[2]**-al** *n suffix* [ME *-aille*, fr. OF, fr. L *-alia*, neut. pl. of *-alis*] **:** action **:** process <rehears*al*>

[3]**-al** \ˌal, ˌȯl, əl, ᵊl\ *n suffix* [F, fr. *alcool* alcohol, fr. ML *alcohol*] **1 :** aldehyde <butan*al*> **2 :** acetal <butyr*al*>

ala \'ā-lə\ *n, pl* **alae** \-ˌlē\ [L — more at AISLE] **:** a wing or a winglike anatomic process or part — **alar** \'ā-lər\ *adj* — **ala·ry** \-lə-rē\ *adj*

a la *or* **à la** \ˌal-ə, ˌäl-ə, ˌäl-(ˌ)ä\ *prep* [F *à la*] **:** in the manner of

Ala *abbr* Alabama

ALA *abbr* **1** American Library Association **2** Automobile Legal Association

al·a·bas·ter \'al-ə-ˌbas-tər\ *n* [ME *alabastre*, fr. MF, fr. L *alabaster* vase of alabaster, fr. Gk *alabastros*] **1 :** a compact fine-textured usu. white and translucent gypsum often carved into vases and ornaments **2 :** a hard compact calcite or aragonite that is translucent and sometimes banded — **alabaster** *or* **al·a·bas·trine** \ˌal-ə-ˈbas-trən\ *adj*

a la carte \ˌal-ə-ˈkärt, ˌäl-\ *adv or adj* [F *à la carte* by the bill of fare] **:** according to a menu that prices each item separately

alack \ə-ˈlak\ *interj* [ME] *archaic* — used to express sorrow or regret

alac·ri·ty \ə-ˈlak-rət-ē\ *n* [L *alacritas*, fr. *alacr-*, *alacer* lively, eager; akin to OE & OHG *ellen* zeal] **:** promptness in response **:** cheerful readiness <accepted the invitation with ~> ***syn*** see CELERITY ***ant*** languor — **alac·ri·tous** \-rət-əs\ *adj*

Alad·din \ə-ˈlad-ᵊn\ *n* **:** a youth in the *Arabian Nights' Entertainments* who comes into possession of a magic lamp

al·a·me·da \ˌal-ə-ˈmēd-ə, -ˈmād-\ *n* [Sp, fr. *álamo* poplar] **:** a public promenade bordered with trees

a la mode \ˌal-ə-ˈmōd, ˌäl-\ *adj* [F *à la mode* according to the fashion] **1 :** FASHIONABLE, STYLISH **2 :** topped with ice cream

al·a·nine \'al-ə-ˌnēn\ *n* [G *alanin*, irreg. fr. *aldehyd* aldehyde] **:** a white crystalline amino acid $C_3H_7NO_2$ formed esp. by the hydrolysis of proteins

al·a·nyl \'al-ə-ˌnil\ *n* [ISV *alan*ine + *-yl*] **:** an acyl radical of alanine

[1]**alarm** \ə-ˈlärm\ *also* **ala·rum** \ə-ˈlär-əm, -ˈlar-\ *n* [ME *alarme*, *alarom*, fr. MF *alarme*, fr. OIt *all'arme*, lit., to the weapon] **1** *usu alarum*, *obs* **:** a call to arms <the angry trumpet sounds ~ —Shak.> **2 :** a signal (as a loud noise or flashing light) that warns or alerts; *also* **:** a device that signals <set the ~ to wake me at seven> **3 :** sudden sharp apprehension and fear resulting from the

perception of imminent danger **4 :** a warning notice ***syn*** see FEAR ***ant*** assurance, composure

²alarm *also* **alarum** *vt* **1 :** to give warning to : put on the alert **2 :** to strike with fear : TERRIFY **3 :** DISTURB, EXCITE — **alarm·ing·ly** \-ˈlär-miŋ-lē\ *adv*

alarm clock *n* **:** a clock that can be set to sound an alarm at a desired time

alarm·ism \ə-ˈlär-ˌmiz-əm\ *n* **:** the often unwarranted exciting of fears or warning of danger — **alarm·ist** \-məst\ *n or adj*

alarm reaction *n* **:** the complex of reactions of an organism to stress (as by increased hormonal activity)

alarums and excursions *n pl* **1 :** martial sounds and the movement of soldiers across the stage — used as a stage direction in Elizabethan drama **2 :** clamor, excitement, and feverish or disordered activity

alas \ə-ˈlas\ *interj* [ME, fr. OF, fr. *a* ah + *las* weary, fr. L *lassus* — more at LET] — used to express unhappiness, pity, or concern

Alas·kan malamute \ə-ˌlas-kən-\ *n* **:** any of a breed of powerful heavy-coated deep-chested dogs of Alaskan origin with erect ears, heavily cushioned feet, and plumy tail

Alas·ka time \ə-ˈlas-kə-\ *n* **:** the time of the 10th time zone west of Greenwich that includes central Alaska

alate \ˈā-ˌlāt\ *also* **alat·ed** \-ˌlāt-əd\ *adj* [L *alatus*, fr. *ala*] **:** having wings or a winglike part — **ala·tion** \ā-ˈlā-shən\ *n*

alb \ˈalb\ *n* [ME *albe*, fr. OE, fr. ML *alba*, fr. L, fem. of *albus* white] **:** a full-length white linen vestment with long sleeves that is gathered at the waist with a cincture and worn by a priest at Mass — see VESTMENT illustration

Alb *abbr* Albania; Albanian

al·ba·core \ˈal-bə-ˌkō(ə)r, -ˌkȯ(ə)r\ *n, pl* **-core** *or* **-cores** [Pg *albacor*, fr. Ar *al-bakūrah* the albacore] **1 :** a large pelagic tuna (*Thunnus alalunga*) with long pectoral fins that is a source of canned tuna; *broadly* **:** any of various tunas (as a bonito) **2 :** any of several carangid fishes

Al·ba·nian \al-ˈbā-nē-ən, -nyən *also* ȯl-\ *n* **1 :** a native or inhabitant of Albania **2 :** the Indo-European language of the Albanian people — see INDO-EUROPEAN LANGUAGES table — **Albanian** *adj*

al·ba·tross \ˈal-bə-ˌtrȯs, -ˌträs\ *n, pl* **-tross** *or* **-tross·es** [prob. alter. of *alcatras* (water bird), fr. Pg or Sp *alcatraz* pelican] **:** any of various large web-footed seabirds (family Diomedeidae) that are related to the petrels and include the largest seabirds

albatross

al·be·do \al-ˈbēd-(ˌ)ō\ *n, pl* **-dos** [LL, whiteness, fr. L *albus*] **:** reflective power; *specif* **:** the fraction of incident light or electromagnetic radiation that is reflected by a surface or body (as the moon or a cloud)

al·be·it \ȯl-ˈbē-ət, al-\ *conj* [ME, lit., all though it be] **:** conceding the fact that **:** even though ***syn*** see THOUGH

Al·bi·gen·ses \ˌal-bə-ˈjen-ˌsēz\ *n pl* [ML, pl. of *Albigensis*, lit., inhabitant of Albi, fr. *Albiga* (Albi), France] **:** members of a Catharistic sect of southern France between the 11th and 13th centuries — **Al·bi·gen·sian** \-ˈjen-chən, -ˈjen(t)-sē-ən\ *adj or n* — **Al·bi·gen·sian·ism** \-ˌiz-əm\ *n*

al·bi·nism \ˈal-bə-ˌniz-əm, al-ˈbī-\ *n* **:** the condition of an albino

al·bi·no \al-ˈbī-(ˌ)nō\ *n, pl* **-nos** *often attrib* [Pg, fr. Sp, fr. *albo* white, fr. L *albus*] **:** an organism exhibiting deficient pigmentation; *esp* **:** a human being or lower animal that is congenitally deficient in pigment and usu. has a milky or translucent skin, white or colorless hair, and eyes with pink or blue iris and deep-red pupil — **al·bin·ic** \-ˈbin-ik\ *adj*

al·bi·not·ic \ˌal-bə-ˈnät-ik\ *adj* [*albino* + *-tic* (as in *melanotic*)] **1 :** of, relating to, or affected with albinism **2 :** tending toward albinism

Al·bi·on \ˈal-bē-ən\ *n* [L] **1 :** Great Britain **2 :** England

al·bite \ˈal-ˌbīt\ *n* [Sw *albit*, fr. L *albus*] **:** a triclinic usu. white feldspar consisting of a sodium aluminum silicate $NaAlSi_3O_8$ — **al·bit·ic** \al-ˈbit-ik\ *adj*

al·bum \ˈal-bəm\ *n* [L, a white tablet, fr. neut. of *albus*] **1 a :** a book with blank pages for autographs, stamps, or photographs **b :** a paperboard container for a phonograph record **:** JACKET **c :** one or more long-playing phonograph records or tape recordings produced as a single unit <a 2-record ~> **2 :** a collection usu. in book form of literary selections, musical compositions, or pictures **:** ANTHOLOGY

al·bu·men \al-ˈbyü-mən\ *n* [L, fr. *albus*] **1 :** the white of an egg — see EGG illustration **2 :** ALBUMIN

al·bu·min \al-ˈbyü-mən\ *n* [ISV *albumen* + *-in*] **:** any of numerous simple heat-coagulable water-soluble proteins that occur in blood plasma or serum, muscle, the whites of eggs, milk, and other animal substances and in many plant tissues and fluids

¹al·bu·min·oid \-mə-ˌnȯid\ *adj* **:** resembling albumin **:** PROTEIN

²albuminoid *n* **1 :** PROTEIN **2 :** SCLEROPROTEIN

al·bu·min·ous \al-ˈbyü-mə-nəs\ *adj* **:** relating to, containing, or having the properties of albumen or albumin

al·bu·min·uria \(ˌ)al-ˌbyü-mə-ˈn(y)u̇r-ē-ə\ *n* [NL] **:** the presence of albumin in the urine often symptomatic of kidney disease — **al·bu·min·uric** \-ˈn(y)u̇(ə)r-ik\ *adj*

al·bu·mose \ˈal-byə-ˌmōs, -ˌmōz\ *n* [F, fr. *albumine* albumen + *-ose*] **:** any of various products of enzymatic protein hydrolysis

al·bur·num \al-ˈbər-nəm\ *n* [L, fr. *albus* white] **:** SAPWOOD

alc *abbr* alcohol

al·ca·ic \al-ˈkā-ik\ *adj, often cap* [LL *Alcaicus* of Alcaeus, fr. Gk *Alkaïkos*, fr. *Alkaios* Alcaeus, *fl ab* 600 B.C. Gk poet] **:** relating to or written in a verse or strophe marked by complicated variation of a dominant iambic pattern — **alcaic** *n*

al·cai·de *or* **al·cay·de** \al-ˈkīd-ē\ *n* [Sp *alcaide*, fr. Ar *al-qā'id* the captain] **:** a commander of a castle or fortress (as among Spaniards, Portuguese, or Moors)

al·cal·de \al-ˈkäl-dē\ *n* [Sp, fr. Ar *al-qadi* the judge] **:** the chief administrative and judicial officer of a Spanish town

al·ca·zar \al-ˈkäz-ər, -ˈkaz-\ *n* [Sp *alcázar*, fr. Ar *al-qaṣr* the castle] **:** a Spanish fortress or palace

Al·ces·tis \al-ˈses-təs\ *n* [L, fr. Gk *Alkēstis*] **:** the wife of Admetus who dies for her husband and is restored to him by Hercules

al·che·mist \ˈal-kə-məst\ *n* **:** one who studies or practices alchemy — **al·che·mis·tic** \ˌal-kə-ˈmis-tik\ *or* **al·che·mis·ti·cal** \-ti-kəl\ *adj*

al·che·mize \ˈal-kə-ˌmīz\ *vt* **-mized; -miz·ing :** to change by alchemy **:** TRANSMUTE

al·che·my \ˈal-kə-mē\ *n* [ME *alkamie, alquemie*, fr. MF or ML; MF *alquemie*, fr. ML *alchymia*, fr. Ar *al-kīmiyā'*, fr. *al* the + *kīmiyā* alchemy, fr. LGk *chēmeia*] **1 :** a medieval chemical science and speculative philosophy aiming to achieve the transmutation of the base metals into gold, the discovery of a universal cure for disease, and the discovery of a means of indefinitely prolonging life **2 :** a power or process of transforming something common into something precious — **al·chem·ic** \al-ˈkem-ik\ *or* **al·chem·i·cal** \-i-kəl\ *adj* — **al·chem·i·cal·ly** \-i-k(ə-)lē\ *adv*

Alc·me·ne \alk-ˈmē-nē\ *n* [Gk *Alkmēnē*] **:** the mother of Hercules by Zeus in the form of her husband Amphitryon

al·co·hol \ˈal-kə-ˌhȯl\ *n* [NL, fr. ML, powdered antimony, fr. OSp, fr. Ar *al-kuḥul* the powdered antimony] **1 :** a colorless volatile flammable liquid C_2H_6O that is the intoxicating agent in fermented and distilled liquors and is used also as a solvent — called also *ethyl alcohol* **2 :** any of various compounds that are analogous to ethyl alcohol in constitution and that are hydroxyl derivatives of hydrocarbons **3 :** liquor (as beer, wine, or whiskey) containing alcohol

¹al·co·hol·ic \ˌal-kə-ˈhȯl-ik, -ˈhäl-\ *adj* **1 a :** of, relating to, or caused by alcohol **b :** containing alcohol **2 :** affected with alcoholism — **al·co·hol·i·cal·ly** \-i-k(ə-)lē\ *adv*

²alcoholic *n* **:** one affected with alcoholism

al·co·hol·ism \ˈal-kə-ˌhȯ-ˌliz-əm\ *n* **1 :** continued excessive or compulsive use of alcoholic drinks **2 :** poisoning by alcohol; *esp* **:** a complex chronic psychological and nutritional disorder associated with excessive and usu. compulsive drinking

al·co·hol·ize \-ˌlīz\ *vt* **-ized; -iz·ing :** to treat or saturate with alcohol

al·co·hol·om·e·ter \ˌal-kə-ˌhȯ-ˈläm-ət-ər\ *n* [F *alcoolomètre*, fr. *alcool* alcohol + *-o-* + *-mètre* -meter] **:** a device for determining the alcoholic strength of liquids — **al·co·hol·om·e·try** \-ˈläm-ə-trē\ *n*

Al·co·ran \ˌal-kə-ˈran\ *n* [ME, fr. MF or ML; MF & ML, fr. Ar *al-qur'ān*, lit., the reading] *archaic* **:** KORAN

al·cove \ˈal-ˌkōv\ *n* [F *alcôve*, fr. Sp *alcoba*, fr. Ar *al-qubbah* the arch] **1 a :** a small recessed section of a room **:** NOOK **b :** an arched opening (as in a wall) **:** NICHE **2 :** SUMMERHOUSE — **al·coved** \-ˌkōvd\ *adj*

Al·cy·o·ne \al-ˈsī-ə-(ˌ)nē\ *n* [L, fr. Gk *Alkyonē*] **:** the brightest star in the Pleiades

ald *abbr* alderman

Al·deb·a·ran \al-ˈdeb-ə-rən\ *n* [Ar *al-dabarān*, lit., the follower] **:** a red star of the first magnitude that is seen in the eye of Taurus and is the brightest star in the Hyades

al·de·hyde \ˈal-də-ˌhīd\ *n* [G *aldehyd*, fr. NL *al. dehyd.*, abbr. of *alcohol dehydrogenatum* dehydrogenated alcohol] **:** ACETALDEHYDE; *broadly* **:** any of various highly reactive compounds typified by acetaldehyde and characterized by the group CHO — **al·de·hy·dic** \ˌal-də-ˈhīd-ik\ *adj*

al·der \ˈȯl-dər\ *n* [ME, fr. OE *alor*; akin to OHG *elira* alder, L *alnus*] **:** any of a genus (*Alnus*) of toothed-leaved trees or shrubs of the birch family growing in moist ground and having wood used by turners and bark used in dyeing and tanning

al·der·man \ˈȯl-dər-mən\ *n* [ME, fr. OE *ealdorman*, fr. *ealdor* parent (fr. *eald* old) + *man* — more at OLD] **1 :** a person governing a kingdom, district, or shire as viceroy for an Anglo-Saxon king **2 :** a magistrate ranking next below the mayor in an English or Irish city or borough **3 :** a member of a city legislative body — **al·der·man·ic** \ˌȯl-dər-ˈman-ik\ *adj*

al·dol \ˈal-ˌdȯl, -ˌdōl\ *n* [ISV *ald*ehyde + *-ol*] **:** a colorless beta-hydroxy aldehyde $C_4H_8O_2$ used esp. in organic synthesis; *broadly* **:** any of various similar aldehydes — **al·dol·iza·tion** \ˌal-ˌdȯ-lə-ˈzā-shən, -ˌdō-\ *n*

al·dol·ase \ˈal-də-ˌlās, -ˌlāz\ *n* [*aldol* + *-ase*] **:** a crystalline enzyme that occurs widely in living systems and catalyzes reversibly the cleavage of a fructose ester into triose sugars

al·dose \ˈal-ˌdōs, -ˌdōz\ *n* [ISV *ald*ehyde + *-ose*] **:** a sugar containing one aldehyde group per molecule

al·do·ste·rone \al-ˈdäs-tə-ˌrōn, ˌal-dō-stə-ˈrōn\ *n* [*ald*ehyde + *-o-* + *sterol* + *-one*] **:** a steroid hormone $C_{13}H_{16}N_2O$ of the adrenal cortex that functions in the regulation of the salt and water balance of the body

al·do·ste·ron·ism \-ˌrō-ˌniz-əm, -ˈrō-\ *n* **:** a condition that is characterized by excessive production and excretion of aldosterone and typically by loss of body potassium, muscular weakness, and elevated blood pressure

al·drin \ˈȯl-drən, ˈal-\ *n* [Kurt *Alder* †1958 G chemist + E *-in*] **:** an exceedingly poisonous cyclodiene insecticide $C_{12}H_6Cl_6$

ale \ˈā(ə)l\ *n* [ME, fr. OE *ealu*; akin to ON *öl* ale, L *alumen* alum] **1 :** a fermented liquor brewed esp. by rapid fermentation from an

infusion of malt with the addition of hops **2 :** an English country festival at which ale is the principal beverage
ale·a·tor·ic \ˌā-lē-ə-ˈtȯr-ik, -ˈtär-\ *adj* [L *aleatorius* of a gambler] **:** improvisatory or random in character <~ music>
ale·a·to·ry \ˈā-lē-ə-ˌtȯr-ē, -ˌtȯr-\ *adj* [L *aleatorius* of a gambler, fr. *aleator* gambler, fr. *alea* a dice game] **1 :** depending on an uncertain event or contingency as to both profit and loss <an ~ contract> **2 :** relating to luck and esp. to bad luck **3 :** ALEATORIC
alee \ə-ˈlē\ *adv* **:** on or toward the lee — compare AWEATHER
ale·house \ˈā(ə)l-ˌhau̇s\ *n* **:** a place where ale is sold to be drunk on the premises
Al·e·man·nic \ˌal-ə-ˈman-ik\ *n* [LL *alemanni*, of Gmc origin; akin to Goth *alamans* totality of people] **:** the group of dialects of German spoken in Alsace, Switzerland, and southwestern Germany
alem·bic \ə-ˈlem-bik\ *n* [ME, fr. MF & ML; MF *alambic* & ML *alembicum*, fr. Ar *al-anbīq*, fr. *al* the + *anbīq* still, fr. LGk *ambik-*, *ambix* alembic, fr. Gk, cap of a still] **1 :** an apparatus formerly used in distillation **2 :** something that refines or transmutes as if by distillation <philosophy . . . filtered through the ~ of Plato's mind — B. T. Shropshire>

alembic 1: *1* head, *2* cucurbit, *3* receiver, *4* lamp

aleph \ˈäl-ˌef, -əf\ *n* [Heb *āleph*, prob. fr. *eleph* ox] **:** the 1st letter of the Hebrew alphabet — see ALPHABET table
aleph–null \-ˈnəl\ *n* **:** the cardinal number of the set of all integers which is the smallest transfinite cardinal number
1alert \ə-ˈlərt\ *adj* [It *all' erta*, lit., on the ascent] **1 a :** watchful and prompt to meet danger or emergency **b :** quick to perceive and act **2 :** ACTIVE, BRISK ***syn* 1** see WATCHFUL ***ant*** supine **2** see INTELLIGENT — **alert·ly** *adv* — **alert·ness** *n*
2alert *n* **1 :** an alarm or other signal of danger **2 :** the state of readiness of those warned by an alert **3 :** the period during which an alert is in effect — **on the alert :** on the lookout esp. for danger or opportunity
3alert *vt* **:** to call to a state of readiness **:** WARN
-a·les \ˈā-(ˌ)lēz\ *n pl suffix* [NL, fr. L, pl. of *-alis* -al] **:** plants consisting of or related to — in the names of taxonomic orders
al·eu·rone \ˈal-yə-ˌrōn\ *n* [G *aleuron*, fr. Gk, flour; akin to Arm *alam* I grind] **:** protein matter in the form of minute granules or grains occurring in seeds in endosperm or in a special peripheral layer — **al·eu·ron·ic** \ˌal-yə-ˈrän-ik\ *adj*
Aleut \ə-ˈlüt\ *n* [Russ] **1 :** a member of a people of the Aleutian and Shumagin islands and the western part of Alaska peninsula **2 :** the language of the Aleuts
al·e·vin \ˈal-ə-vən\ *n* [F, fr. OF, fr. *alever* to lift up, rear (offspring), fr. L *allevare*, fr. *ad-* + *levare* to raise — more at LEVER] **:** a young fish; *esp* **:** the newly hatched salmon when still attached to the yolk sac
1ale·wife \ˈā(ə)l-ˌwīf\ *n* **:** a woman who keeps an alehouse
2alewife *n* **:** a food fish (*Alosa pseudoharengus*) of the herring family (Clupeidae) very abundant on the Atlantic coast; *also* **:** any of several related fishes (as the menhaden)
al·ex·an·der \ˌal-ig-ˈzan-dər, ˌel-\ *n, often cap* **:** an iced cocktail made from crème de cacao, sweet cream, and gin or brandy
Al·ex·an·dri·an \ˌal-ig-ˈzan-drē-ən, ˌel-\ *adj* **1 :** of or relating to Alexander the Great **2 :** HELLENISTIC
al·ex·an·drine \-ˈzan-drən\ *n, often cap* [MF *alexandrin*, adj., fr. *Alexandre* Alexander the Great †323 B.C. king of Macedonia; fr. its use in a poem on Alexander] **:** a line of verse of 12 syllables consisting regularly of 6 iambics with a caesura after the 3d iambic — **alexandrine** *adj*
al·ex·an·drite \-ˈzan-ˌdrīt\ *n* [G *alexandrit*, fr. *Alexander I* †1825 Russ emperor] **:** a grass-green chrysoberyl that shows a red color by transmitted or artificial light
alex·ia \ə-ˈlek-sē-ə\ *n* [NL, fr. *a-* + Gk *lexis* speech, fr. *legein* to speak — more at LEGEND] **:** aphasia characterized by loss of ability to read
Al·fa \ˈal-fə\ — a communications code word for the letter *a*
al·fal·fa \al-ˈfal-fə\ *n* [Sp, modif. of Ar dial. *al-fasfaṣah* the alfalfa] **:** a deep-rooted European leguminous plant (*Medicago sativa*) widely grown for hay and forage
al·fil·a·ria \(ˌ)al-ˌfil-ə-ˈrē-ə\ *n* [AmerSp *alfilerillo*, fr. Sp, dim. of *alfiler* pin, modif. of Ar *al-khilāl* the thorn] **:** a European weed (*Erodium cicutarium*) of the geranium family grown for forage in western America
al·for·ja \al-ˈfȯr-(ˌ)hä\ *n* [Sp, fr. Ar *al-khurj*] *West* **:** SADDLEBAG
al·fres·co \al-ˈfres-(ˌ)kō\ *adj or adv* [It] **:** taking place in the open air <an ~ lunch>
alg *abbr* algebra
alg- *or* **algo-** *comb form* [NL, fr. Gk *alg-*, fr. *algos*] **:** pain <*algo*phobia>
al·ga \ˈal-gə\ *n, pl* **al·gae** \ˈal-(ˌ)jē\ *also* **algas** [L, seaweed] **:** any of a group (Algae) of chiefly aquatic nonvascular plants (as seaweeds, pond scums, and stoneworts) with chlorophyll often masked by a brown or red pigment — **al·gal** \-gəl\ *adj* — **al·goid** \-ˌgȯid\ *adj*
al·gar·ro·ba \ˌal-gə-ˈrō-bə\ *n* [Sp, fr. Ar *al-kharrūbah* the carob] **1 :** CAROB **2** [MexSp, fr. Sp] **:** MESQUITE; *also* **:** its pods
al·ge·bra \ˈal-jə-brə\ *n* [ML, fr. Ar *al-jabr*, lit., the reduction] **1 a :** a generalization of arithmetic in which letters representing numbers are combined according to the rules of arithmetic **b :** a treatise on algebra **2 :** LINEAR ALGEBRA 2 **3 :** a logical or set calculus — **al·ge·bra·ist** \-ˌbrā-əst\ *n*
al·ge·bra·ic \ˌal-jə-ˈbrā-ik\ *adj* **1 :** relating to, involving, or according to the laws of algebra **2 :** involving only a finite number of repetitions of addition, subtraction, multiplication, division, extraction of roots, and raising to powers <~ equation> — compare TRANSCENDENTAL — **al·ge·bra·ical·ly** \-ˈbrā-ə-k(ə-)lē\ *adv*
algebraic number *n* **:** a root of an algebraic equation with rational coefficients
Al·ger·ish \ˈal-jə-rish\ *adj* **:** of, relating to, or characteristic of the works of Horatio Alger in which success is achieved through self-reliance and hard work
-al·gia \ˈal-j(ē-)ə\ *n comb form* [Gk, fr. *algos*] **:** pain <neur*algia*>
al·gi·cide \ˈal-jə-ˌsīd\ *n* [*alga* + *-i-* + *-cide*] **:** an agent used to kill algae — **al·gi·cid·al** \ˌal-jə-ˈsīd-ᵊl\ *adj*
al·gid \ˈal-jəd\ *adj* [L *algidus*, fr. *algēre* to feel cold; akin to Icel *elgur* slush] **:** CHILL, COLD — **al·gid·i·ty** \al-ˈjid-ət-ē\ *n*
al·gin \ˈal-jən\ *n* **:** any of various colloidal substances from marine brown algae: as **a :** ALGINIC ACID **b :** a soluble salt of alginic acid used esp. as a stabilizer or emulsifier
al·gi·nate \ˈal-jə-ˌnāt\ *n* **:** a salt of alginic acid
al·gin·ic acid \(ˌ)al-ˌjin-ik-\ *n* [ISV *algin* + *-ic*] **:** an insoluble colloidal acid $(C_6H_8O_6)_n$ that in the form of its salts is a constituent of the cell walls of brown algae
Al·gol \ˈal-ˌgäl, -ˌgȯl\ *n* [Ar *al-ghūl*, lit., the ghoul] **:** a binary star in the constellation Perseus whose larger component revolves about and eclipses the smaller brighter star causing periodic variation in brightness
AL·GOL *or* **Al·gol** \ˈal-ˌgäl, -ˌgȯl\ *n* [*algo*rithmic *l*anguage] **:** an algebraic and logical language for programming a computer
al·go·lag·nia \ˌal-gō-ˈlag-nē-ə\ *n* [NL, fr. *alg-* + Gk *lagneia* lust] **:** pleasure in inflicting or suffering pain — **al·go·lag·nic** \-nik\ *adj* — **al·go·lag·nist** \-nəst\ *n*
al·gol·o·gy \al-ˈgäl-ə-jē\ *n* **:** the study or science of algae — **al·go·log·i·cal** \ˌal-gə-ˈläj-i-kəl\ *adj* — **al·go·log·i·cal·ly** \-k(ə-)lē\ *adv* — **al·gol·o·gist** \al-ˈgäl-ə-jəst\ *n*
al·gom·e·ter \al-ˈgäm-ət-ər\ *n* **:** an instrument for measuring the smallest pressure that induces pain — **al·go·met·ric** \ˌal-gə-ˈme-trik\ *or* **al·go·met·ri·cal** \-tri-kəl\ *adj* — **al·gom·e·try** \al-ˈgäm-ə-trē\ *n*
Al·gon·ki·an \al-ˈgäŋ-kē-ən\ *adj* **:** PROTEROZOIC
Al·gon·qui·an \al-ˈgän-kwē-ən, -ˈgäŋ-\ *or* **Al·gon·quin** \-kwən\ *or* **Al·gon·ki·an** \-ˈgäŋ-kē-ən\ *or* **Al·gon·kin** \-ˈgäŋ-kən\ *n* [CanF *Algonquin*] **1 :** an Amerindian people of the Ottawa river valley **2** *usu Algonquin* **:** a dialect of Ojibwa **3** *usu Algonquian* **:** a stock of Indian languages spoken from Labrador to Carolina and westward to the Great Plains **4** *usu Algonquian* **:** a member of the Amerindian peoples speaking Algonquian languages **5** *Algonkian* **:** the Algonkian era or system or group of systems
al·go·pho·bia \ˌal-gə-ˈfō-bē-ə\ *n* [NL] **:** morbid fear of pain
al·go·rithm \ˈal-gə-ˌrith-əm\ *n* [alter. of ME *algorisme*, fr. OF & ML; OF, fr. ML *algorismus*, fr. Ar *al-khuwārizmi*, *fr. al-Khuwārizmi fl* 825 A.D. Arab mathematician] **:** a procedure for solving a mathematical problem (as of finding the greatest common divisor) in a finite number of steps that frequently involves repetition of an operation; *broadly* **:** a step-by-step procedure for solving a problem or accomplishing some end — **al·go·rith·mic** \ˌal-gə-ˈrith-mik\ *adj*
Al·ham·bra \al-ˈham-brə\ *n* [Sp, fr. Ar *al-ḥamrā'* the red house] **:** the palace of the Moorish kings at Granada, Spain
Al·ham·bra·ic \ˌal-ˌham-ˈbrā-ik\ *adj* **:** ALHAMBRESQUE
Al·ham·bresque \ˌal-ˌham-ˈbresk\ *adj* **:** made or decorated after the fanciful style of the ornamentation in the Alhambra
ali- *comb form* [L, fr. *ala* — more at AISLE] **:** wing <*ali*form>
1alias \ˈā-lē-əs, ˈāl-yəs\ *adv* [L, otherwise, fr. *alius* other — more at ELSE] **:** otherwise called **:** otherwise known as
2alias *n* **:** an assumed name
Ali Ba·ba \ˌal-ē-ˈbäb-ə\ *n* **:** a woodcutter in the *Arabian Nights' Entertainments* who enters the cave of the Forty Thieves by using the password *Sesame*
1al·i·bi \ˈal-ə-ˌbī\ *n* [L, elsewhere, fr. *alius*] **1 :** the plea of having been at the time of the commission of an act elsewhere than at the place of commission; *also* **:** the fact or state of having been elsewhere at the time **2 :** a plausible excuse usu. intended to avert blame or punishment (as for failure or negligence) ***syn*** see APOLOGY
2alibi *vb* **-bied; -bi·ing** *vi* **:** to offer an excuse ~ *vt* **:** to exonerate by an alibi
ali·cy·clic \ˌal-ə-ˈsī-klik, -ˈsik-lik\ *adj* [ISV *ali*phatic + *cyclic*] **:** combining the properties of aliphatic and cyclic compounds
al·i·dade \ˈal-ə-ˌdād\ *n* [ME *allidatha*, fr. ML *alhidada*, fr. Ar *al-ʻidādah* the revolving radius of a circle] **:** a rule equipped with simple or telescopic sights and used for determination of direction: as **a :** a part of an astrolabe **b :** a part of a surveying instrument consisting of the telescope and its attachments
1alien \ˈā-lē-ən, ˈāl-yən\ *adj* [ME, fr. OF, fr. L *alienus*, fr. *alius*] **1 a :** belonging or relating to another person, place, or thing **:** STRANGE **b :** relating, belonging, or owing allegiance to another country or government **:** FOREIGN **2 :** differing in nature or character typically to the point of incompatibility ***syn*** see EXTRINSIC ***ant*** akin, assimilable — **alienly** *adv* — **alien·ness** \-lē-ən-nəs, -yən-nəs\ *n*
2alien *n* **1 :** a person of another family, race, or nation **2 :** a foreign-born resident who has not been naturalized and is still a subject or citizen of a foreign country; *broadly* **:** a foreign-born citizen
3alien *vt* **1 :** ALIENATE, ESTRANGE **2 :** to make over (as property)
alien·able \ˈāl-yə-nə-bəl, ˈā-lē-ə-nə-\ *adj* **:** transferable to the ownership of another — **alien·abil·i·ty** \ˌāl-yə-nə-ˈbil-ət-ē, ˌā-lē-ə-nə-\ *n*
alien·age \ˈāl-yə-nij, ˈā-lē-ə-nij\ *n* **:** the status of an alien
alien·ate \ˈā-lē-ə-ˌnāt, ˈāl-yə-\ *vt* **-at·ed; -at·ing 1 :** to convey or transfer (as property or a right) usu. by a specific act rather than the due course of law **2 :** to make unfriendly, hostile, or indifferent where attachment formerly existed **3 :** to cause to be withdrawn or diverted ***syn* 1** see TRANSFER **2** see ESTRANGE ***ant*** unite, reunite — **alien·ator** \-ˌnāt-ər\ *n*
alien·ation \ˌā-lē-ə-ˈnā-shən, ˌāl-yə-\ *n* **1 :** a conveyance of property to another **2 :** a withdrawing or separation of a person or his affections from an object or position of former attachment **:** ISOLATION, EXILE <~ . . . from the values of one's society and family — S. L. Halleck>
alien·ee \-ˈnē\ *n* **:** one to whom property is transferred
alien·ism \ˈā-lē-ə-ˌniz-əm, ˈāl-yə-\ *n* **:** ALIENAGE

alien·ist \-nəst\ *n* [F *aliéniste,* fr. *aliéné* insane, fr. L *alienatus,* pp. of *alienare* to estrange, fr. *alienus*] **:** one that treats diseases of the mind; *esp* **:** a specialist in legal aspects of psychiatry

alien·or \ˌā-lē-ə-ˈnȯ(ə)r, ˌāl-yə-\ *n* **:** one who transfers property to another

ali·form \ˈā-lə-ˌfȯrm, ˈal-ə-\ *adj* **:** having winglike extensions **:** wing-shaped

1alight \ə-ˈlīt\ *vi* **alight·ed** *also* **alit** \ə-ˈlit\; **alight·ing** [ME *alighten,* fr. OE *ālīhtan,* fr. *ā-* (perfective prefix) + *līhtan* to alight — more at ABIDE, LIGHT] **1 :** to come down from something: as **a :** DISMOUNT **b :** DEPLANE **2 :** to descend from the air and settle **:** LAND **3** *archaic* **:** to come by chance — **alight·ment** *n*

2alight *adj* **1** *chiefly Brit* **:** being on fire **2 :** lighted up **:** ILLUMINATED

align *also* **aline** \ə-ˈlīn\ *vb* [F *aligner,* fr. OF, fr. *a-* (fr. L *ad-*) + *ligne* line, fr. L *linea*] *vt* **1 :** to bring into line or alignment **2 :** to array on the side of or against a party or cause ~ *vi* **1 :** to get or fall into line **2 :** to be in or come into precise adjustment or correct relative position ***syn*** see LINE — **align·er** *n*

align·ment *also* **aline·ment** \ə-ˈlīn-mənt\ *n* **1 :** the act of aligning or state of being aligned; *esp* **:** the proper positioning or state of adjustment of parts (as of a mechanical or electronic device) in relation to each other **2 a :** a forming in line **b :** the line thus formed **3 :** the ground plan (as of a railroad or fieldwork) in distinction from the profile **4 :** an arrangement of groups or forces in relation to one another <sectional ~*s* within the political party>

1alike \ə-ˈlīk\ *adj* [ME *ilik* (alter. of *ilich*) & *alik,* alter. of OE *onlīc,* fr. *on* + *līc* body — more at LIKE] **:** exhibiting close resemblance without being identical <~ in their beliefs> ***syn*** see SIMILAR ***ant*** different — **alike·ness** *n*

2alike *adv* **:** in the same manner, form, or degree **:** EQUALLY <was denounced by teachers and students ~>

1al·i·ment \ˈal-ə-mənt\ *n* [ME, fr. L *alimentum,* fr. *alere* to nourish — more at OLD] **:** FOOD, NUTRIMENT; *also* **:** SUSTENANCE

2al·i·ment \-ˌment\ *vt* **:** to give aliment to **:** NOURISH, SUSTAIN

al·i·men·ta·ry \ˌal-ə-ˈment-ə-rē, -ˈmen-trē\ *adj* **1 :** of or relating to nourishment or nutrition **2 :** furnishing sustenance or maintenance

alimentary canal *n* **:** the tubular passage that extends from mouth to anus and functions in digestion and absorption of food and elimination of residual waste

al·i·men·ta·tion \ˌal-ə-mən-ˈtā-shən, -ˌmen-\ *n* **:** the act or process of affording nutriment; *also* **:** the state or mode of being nourished — **al·i·men·ta·tive** \ˌal-ə-ˈment-ət-iv\ *adj*

al·i·mo·ny \ˈal-ə-ˌmō-nē\ *n, pl* **-nies** [L *alimonia* sustenance, fr. *alere*] **1 :** the means of living **:** MAINTENANCE **2 :** an allowance made to a woman for her support by a man pending or after her legal separation or divorce from him

A-line \ˈā-ˌlīn\ *adj* **:** having a flared bottom and a close-fitting top — used of a garment <an ~ skirt>

Al·i·oth \ˈal-ē-ˌäth, -ˌōth\ *n* [Ar *alyat* fat tail of a sheep] **:** a star of the second magnitude in the handle of the Big Dipper

al·i·phat·ic \ˌal-ə-ˈfat-ik\ *adj* [ISV, fr. Gk *aleiphat-, aleiphar* oil, fr. *aleiphein* to smear; akin to Gk *lipos* fat — more at LEAVE] **:** of, relating to, or derived from fat; *specif* **:** belonging to a group of organic compounds having an open-chain structure and consisting of the paraffin, olefin, and acetylene hydrocarbons and their derivatives

al·i·quot \ˈal-ə-ˌkwät, -kwət\ *adj* [ML *aliquotus,* fr. L *aliquot* some, several, fr. *alius* other + *quot* how many — more at ELSE, QUOTA] **1 :** contained an exact number of times in something else — used of a divisor or part <5 is an ~ part of 15> <an ~ portion of a solution> **2 :** FRACTIONAL <an ~ part of invested capital> — **aliquot** *n*

alive \ə-ˈlīv\ *adj* [ME, fr. OE *on life,* fr. *on* + *līf* life] **1 :** having life **:** not dead or inanimate **2 :** still in existence, force, or operation **:** ACTIVE <kept hope ~> **3 :** knowing or realizing the existence of **:** SENSITIVE <~ to the danger> **4 :** marked by alertness, acitivity, or briskness **5 :** marked by much life, animation, or activity **:** SWARMING **6** — used as an intensive following the noun <the proudest boy ~> ***syn*** **1** see LIVING ***ant*** dead, defunct **2** see AWARE ***ant*** blind (*to*) — **alive·ness** *n*

ali·yah \ä-ˈlē-(ˌ)yä\ *n* [NHeb *ʿalīyāh,* fr. Heb, ascent] **1 :** the action of going up or of being called to the reading desk of the synagogue to read from the Scriptures **2 :** the immigration of Jews to Israel

aliz·a·rin \ə-ˈliz-ə-rən\ *n* [prob. fr. F *alizarine*] **1 :** an orange or red crystalline compound $C_{14}H_8O_4$ formerly prepared from madder and now made synthetically and used esp. to dye Turkey reds and in making red pigments **2 :** any of various acid, mordant, and solvent dyes derived like alizarin proper from anthraquinone

alk *abbr* alkaline

al·ka·hest \ˈal-kə-ˌhest\ *n* [NL *alchahest*] **:** the universal solvent believed by the alchemists to exist — **al·ka·hes·tic** \ˌal-kə-ˈhes-tik\ *adj*

al·ka·les·cence \ˌal-kə-ˈles-ᵊn(t)s\ *n* **:** the property or degree of being alkaline — **al·ka·les·cent** \-ᵊnt\ *adj*

al·ka·li \ˈal-kə-ˌlī\ *n, pl* **-lies** *or* **-lis** [ME, fr. ML, fr. Ar *al-qili* the ashes of the plant saltwort] **1 :** a soluble salt obtained from the ashes of plants and consisting largely of potassium or sodium carbonate; *broadly* **:** a substance (as a hydroxide or carbonate of an alkali metal) having marked basic properties — compare BASE 7 **2 :** ALKALI METAL **3 :** a soluble salt or a mixture of soluble salts present in some soils of arid regions in quantity detrimental to agriculture

al·ka·li·fy \al-ˈkal-ə-ˌfī, ˈal-kə-lə-\ *vb* **-fied; -fy·ing** *vt* **:** to convert or change into an alkali **:** make alkaline ~ *vi* **:** to become alkaline

alkali metal *n* **:** any of the univalent mostly basic metals of group I of the periodic table comprising lithium, sodium, potassium, rubidium, cesium, and francium

al·ka·lim·e·ter \ˌal-kə-ˈlim-ət-ər\ *n* [F *alcalimètre,* fr. *alcali* alkali + *-mètre* -meter] **:** an apparatus for measuring the strength or the amount of alkali in a mixture or solution — **al·ka·lim·e·try** \-ˈlim-ə-trē\ *n*

al·ka·line \ˈal-kə-lən, -ˌlīn\ *adj* **:** of, relating to, or having the properties of an alkali; *esp* **:** having a pH of more than 7 — **al·ka·lin·i·ty** \ˌal-kə-ˈlin-ət-ē\ *n*

alkaline earth *n* **1 :** an oxide of any of several bivalent strongly basic metals comprising calcium, strontium, and barium and sometimes also magnesium, radium, or less often beryllium **2 :** ALKALINE-EARTH METAL

alkaline-earth metal *n* **:** any of the metals whose oxides are the alkaline earths

alkaline phosphatase *n* **:** a phosphatase (as the phosphomonoesterase from blood plasma or milk) active in alkaline medium

al·ka·lin·ize \ˈal-kə-lə-ˌnīz\ *vt* **-ized; -iz·ing :** to make alkaline — **al·ka·lin·iza·tion** \ˌal-kə-ˌlin-ə-ˈzā-shən, -lə-nə-\ *n*

al·ka·loid \ˈal-kə-ˌlȯid\ *n* **:** any of numerous usu. colorless, complex, and bitter organic bases (as morphine or codeine) containing nitrogen and usu. oxygen that occur esp. in seed plants — **al·ka·loi·dal** \ˌal-kə-ˈlȯid-ᵊl\ *adj*

al·ka·lo·sis \ˌal-kə-ˈlō-səs\ *n* **:** a condition of increased alkalinity of the blood and tissues

al·ka·net \ˈal-kə-ˌnet\ *n* [ME, fr. OSp *alcaneta,* dim. of *alcana* henna shrub, fr. ML *alchanna,* fr. Ar *al-ḥinnāʾ* the henna] **1 a :** a European plant (*Alkanna tinctoria*) of the borage family; *also* **:** its root **b :** a red dyestuff prepared from the root **2 :** BUGLOSS

alk·oxy \ˈal-ˌkäk-sē\ *adj* [ISV *alkyl* + *oxygen*] **:** of, relating to, or containing a univalent radical composed of an alkyl group united with oxygen

alky *abbr* alkalinity

al·kyd \ˈal-kəd\ *n* [blend of *alkyl* and *acid*] **:** any of numerous thermoplastic or thermosetting synthetic resins made by heating polyhydroxy alcohols with polybasic acids or their anhydrides and used esp. for protective coatings

al·kyl \ˈal-kəl\ *n* [prob. fr. G, fr. *alkohol* alcohol, fr. ML *alcohol*] **1 a :** a univalent aliphatic radical C_nH_{2n+1} (as methyl) **b :** any univalent aliphatic, aromatic-aliphatic, or alicyclic hydrocarbon radical **2 :** a compound of alkyl radicals with a metal — **al·kyl·ic** \al-ˈkil-ik\ *adj*

al·kyl·ate \ˈal-kə-ˌlāt\ *vt* **-at·ed; -at·ing :** to introduce one or more alkyl groups into (a compound)

al·kyl·ation \ˌal-kə-ˈlā-shən\ *n* **:** the act or process of alkylating esp. for producing high-octane fuel

1all \ˈȯl\ *adj* [ME *all, al,* fr. OE *eall;* akin to OHG *al* all] **1 a :** the whole amount or quantity of <sat up ~ night> **b :** as much as possible <spoke in ~ seriousness> **2 a :** every member or individual component of <~ men will go> <~ five children were present> **b** — used in logic as a verbalized equivalent of the universal quantifier **3 :** the whole number or sum of <~ the angles of a triangle are equal to two right angles> **4 :** EVERY <~ manner of hardship> **5 :** any whatever <beyond ~ doubt> **6 :** nothing but **:** ONLY: **a :** completely taken up with, given to, or absorbed by <became ~ attention> **b :** having or seeming to have (some physical feature) in conspicuous excess or prominence <~ thumbs> **c :** paying full attention with <~ ears> **7** *dial* **:** used up **:** entirely consumed — used esp. of food and drink **8 :** being more than one person or thing — **all the :** as much of . . . as **:** as much of a . . . as <*all the* home I ever had>

2all *adv* **1 :** WHOLLY, ALTOGETHER <sat ~ alone> — often used as an intensive <~ out of proportion> **2** *obs* **:** EXCLUSIVELY, ONLY **3** *archaic* **:** JUST **4 :** so much <~ the better for it> **5 :** for each side **:** APIECE <the score is two ~>

3all *pron* **1 :** the whole number, quantity, or amount **:** TOTALITY <~ that I have> <~ of us> <~ of the books> **2 :** EVERYBODY, EVERYTHING <sacrificed ~ for love> — **all in all :** on the whole **:** generally <*all in all,* things might have been worse> — **at all :** in any way — usu. used with a negative <no good *at all*>

4all *n* **:** the whole of one's possessions or of what one prizes <gave his ~ for the cause>

all- *or* **allo-** *comb form* [Gk, fr. *allos* other — more at ELSE] **1 :** other **:** different **:** atypical <*allo*gamous> <*allo*merism> **2** *allo-* **:** isomeric form or variety of (a specified chemical compound) **3** *allo-* **:** being one of a group whose members together constitute a structural unit esp. of a language <*allo*phone>

1al·la bre·ve \ˌal-ə-ˈbrev, ˌäl-ə-ˈbrev-(ˌ)ā\ *adv or adj* [It, lit., according to the breve] **:** in duple or quadruple time with the beat represented by the half note

2alla breve *n* **:** the sign marking a piece or passage to be played alla breve; *also* **:** a passage so marked

alla breve

Al·lah \ˈal-ə, ä-ˈlä\ *n* [Ar *allāh*] **:** the Supreme Being of the Muslims

1all-Amer·i·can \ˌȯ-lə-ˈmer-ə-kən\ *adj* **1 :** composed wholly of American elements **2 :** representative of the ideals of the U.S. <an ~ boy> **3 a :** selected (as by a poll of journalists) as one of the best in the U.S. in a particular category at a particular time <an ~ quarterback> **b :** made up of all-American participants <an ~ basketball team> **4 :** of or relating to the American nations as a group

2all-American *n* **:** one (as an athlete) that is voted all-American

al·lan·to·is \ə-ˈlant-ə-wəs\ *n, pl* **al·lan·to·ides** \ˌal-ən-ˈtō-ə-ˌdēz, ˌal-ˌan-\ [NL, deriv. of Gk *allant-, allas* sausage] **:** a vascular fetal membrane of reptiles, birds, or mammals that is formed as a pouch from the hindgut and that in placental mammals is intimately associated with the chorion in formation of the placenta — **al·lan·to·ic** \ˌal-ən-ˈtō-ik, ˌal-ˌan-\ *adj*

al·lar·gan·do \ˌäl-ˌär-ˈgän-(ˌ)dō\ *adj or adv* [It, widening, verbal of *allargare* to widen, fr. *al-* (fr. L *ad-*) + *largare* to widen] : becoming gradually broader with the same or greater volume — used as a direction in music

all–around \ˌȯ-lə-ˈrau̇nd\ adj **1 :** competent in many fields <an ~ man of letters> **2 :** having general utility **3 :** considered in or encompassing all aspects : INCLUSIVE <the best ~ recording of the work to date> <good nature and ~ competence —G. H. Soule> ***syn*** see VERSATILE

al·lay \ə-ˈlā\ *vb* [ME *alayen,* fr. OE *ālecgan,* fr. *ā-* (perfective prefix) + *lecgan* to lay — more at ABIDE, LAY] *vt* **1 :** to subdue or reduce in intensity or severity : ALLEVIATE <wishing for a breeze to ~ the summer heat> **2 :** to make quiet : CALM ~ *vi, obs* : to diminish in strength : SUBSIDE ***syn*** see RELIEVE ***ant*** intensify

all but *adv* : very nearly : ALMOST <he *all but* disappeared from public notice>

all clear *n* : a signal that a danger has passed

all–day \ˌȯl-ˌdā\ *adj* **:** lasting for, occupying, or appearing throughout an entire day <an ~ trip>

al·le·ga·tion \ˌal-i-ˈgā-shən\ *n* **1 :** the act of alleging **2 :** a positive assertion; *specif* **:** a statement by a party to a legal action of what he undertakes to prove **3 :** an assertion unsupported and by implication regarded as unsupportable <vague ~*s* of misconduct>

al·lege \ə-ˈlej\ *vt* **al·leged; al·leg·ing** [ME *alleggen,* fr. OF *alleguer,* fr. L *allegare* to dispatch, cite, fr. *ad-* + *legare* to depute — more at LEGATE] **1 :** to assert without proof or before proving <the newspaper ~*s* the mayor's guilt> **2** *archaic* **:** to adduce or bring forward as a source or authority **3 :** to bring forward as a reason or excuse ***syn*** see ADDUCE ***ant*** contravene, traverse

al·leged \ə-ˈlejd, -ˈlej-əd\ *adj* **1 :** asserted to be true or to exist : AVOWED <an ~ miracle> **2 :** questionably true or of a specified kind : SO-CALLED <bought an ~ antique vase> — **al·leg·ed·ly** \-ˈlej-əd-lē\ *adv*

Al·le·ghe·ny spurge \ˌal-ə-ˌgā-nē- *also* ˌgen-ē\ *n* [*Allegheny* mts., U.S.A.] **:** a low herb or subshrub (*Pachysandra procumbens*) of the box family widely grown as a ground cover

al·le·giance \ə-ˈlē-jən(t)s\ *n* [ME *allegeaunce,* modif. of MF *ligeance,* fr. OF, fr. *lige* liege] **1 a :** the obligation of a feudal vassal to his liege lord **b** (1) **:** the fidelity owed by a subject or citizen to his sovereign or government (2) **:** the obligation of an alien to the government under which he resides **2 :** devotion or loyalty to a person, group, or cause ***syn*** see FIDELITY ***ant*** treachery, treason

al·le·giant \-jənt\ *adj* : giving allegiance : LOYAL

al·le·gor·i·cal \ˌal-ə-ˈgȯr-i-kəl, -ˈgär-\ *adj* **1 :** of, relating to, or having the characteristics of allegory **2 :** having hidden spiritual meaning that transcends the literal sense of a sacred text — **al·le·gor·i·cal·ly** \-k(ə-)lē\ *adv* — **al·le·gor·i·cal·ness** \-kəl-nəs\ *n*

al·le·go·rist \ˈal-ə-ˌgōr-əst, -ˌgȯr-\ *n* **:** a writer of allegory

al·le·go·ri·za·tion \ˌal-ə-ˌgōr-ə-ˈzā-shən, -ˌgȯr-, -gər-\ *n* **:** allegorical representation or interpretation

al·le·go·rize \ˈal-ə-ˌgōr-ˌīz, -ˌgȯr-, -gər-\ *vb* **-rized; -riz·ing** *vt* **1 :** to make into allegory **2 :** to treat or explain as allegory ~ *vi* **1 :** to give allegorical explanations **2 :** to compose or use allegory — **al·le·go·riz·er** *n*

al·le·go·ry \ˈal-ə-ˌgōr-ē, -ˌgȯr-\ *n, pl* **-ries** [ME *allegorie,* fr. L *allegoria,* fr. Gk *allēgoria,* fr. *allēgorein* to speak figuratively, fr. *allos* other + *-agorein* to speak publicly, fr. *agora* assembly — more at ELSE, GREGARIOUS] **1 a :** the expression by means of symbolic fictional figures and actions of truths or generalizations about human existence **b :** an instance (as in a story or painting) of such expression **2 :** a symbolic representation : EMBLEM

1al·le·gret·to \ˌal-ə-ˈgret-(ˌ)ō, ˌäl-\ *adv or adj* [It, fr. *allegro*] **:** faster than andante but not so fast as allegro — used as a direction in music

2allegretto *n, pl* **-tos :** a musical composition or movement in allegretto tempo

1al·le·gro \ə-ˈleg-(ˌ)rō, -ˈlā-(ˌ)grō\ *adv or adj* [It, merry, fr. (assumed) VL *alecrus* lively, alter. of L *alacr-, alacer* — more at ALACRITY] : in a brisk lively manner — used as a direction in music

2allegro *n, pl* **-gros :** a musical composition or movement in allegro tempo

al·lele \ə-ˈlē(ə)l\ *n* [G *allel,* short for *allelomorph*] **1 :** either of a pair of alternative Mendelian characters (as smooth and wrinkled seed in the pea) **2 :** one of a group of genes that occur alternatively at a given locus — **al·le·lic** \-ˈlē-lik, -ˈlel-ik\ *adj* — **al·lel·ism** \-ˈlē(ə)l-ˌiz-əm, -ˈlel-ˌiz-\ *n*

al·le·lo·morph \ə-ˈlel-ə-ˌmȯrf, -ˈlē-lə-\ *n* [Gk *allēlōn* of each other (fr. *allos* one . . . the other, fr. *allos* other) + *morphē* form — more at ELSE] : ALLELE — **al·le·lo·mor·phic** \ə-ˌlel-ə-ˈmȯr-fik, -ˌlē-lə-\ *adj* — **al·le·lo·mor·phism** \ə-ˈlel-ə-ˌmȯr-ˌfiz-əm, -ˈlē-lə-\ *n*

al·le·lu·ia \ˌal-ə-ˈlü-yə\ *interj* [ME, fr. LL, fr. Gk *allēlouia,* fr. Heb *halalūyāh* praise ye Jehovah] : HALLELUJAH

al·le·mande \ˈal-ə-ˌman(d), -mən, -ˌmänd\ *n, often cap* [F, fr. fem. of *allemand* German] **1 a :** a 17th and 18th century court dance developed in France from a German folk dance **b :** a dance step with arms interlaced **2 :** a musical composition or movement in moderate tempo and duple or quadruple time

all–em·brac·ing \ˌȯ-lim-ˈbrā-siŋ\ *adj* : COMPLETE, SWEEPING <an ~ charity toward his fellowmen>

al·ler·gen \ˈal-ər-jən\ *n* **:** a substance that induces allergy — **al·ler·gen·ic** \ˌal-ər-ˈjen-ik\ *adj*

al·ler·gic \ə-ˈlər-jik\ *adj* **1 :** of, relating to, or inducing allergy **2 :** disagreeably sensitive : ANTIPATHETIC <~ to marriage>

al·ler·gist \ˈal-ər-jəst\ *n* **:** a specialist in allergy

al·ler·gy \ˈal-ər-jē\ *n, pl* **-gies** [G *allergie,* fr. *all-* + Gk *ergon* work — more at WORK] **1 :** altered bodily reactivity (as anaphylaxis) to an antigen in response to a first exposure <his bee-venom ~ may render a second sting fatal> **2 :** exaggerated or pathological reaction (as by sneezing, respiratory embarrassment, itching, or skin rashes) to substances, situations, or physical states that are without comparable effect on the average individual **3 :** medical practice concerned with allergies **4 :** a feeling of antipathy or repugnance

al·le·thrin \ˈal-ə-thrən\ *n* [*all*yl + pyr*ethrin*] : a light yellow viscous oily synthetic insecticide $C_{19}H_{26}O_3$ used esp. in household aerosols

al·le·vi·ate \ə-ˈlē-vē-ˌāt\ *vt* **-at·ed; -at·ing** [LL *alleviatus,* pp. of *alleviare,* fr. L *ad-* + *levis* light — more at LIGHT] : RELIEVE, LESSEN: as **a :** to make (as suffering) more bearable <her sympathy *alleviated* his distress> **b :** to partially remove or correct ***syn*** see RELIEVE ***ant*** aggravate — **al·le·vi·a·tion** \-ˌlē-vē-ˈā-shən\ *n* — **al·le·vi·a·tor** \-ˈlē-vē-ˌāt-ər\ *n*

al·le·vi·a·tive \ə-ˈlē-vē-ˌāt-iv\ *or* **al·le·vi·a·to·ry** \-vē-ə-ˌtōr-ē, -ˌtȯr-\ *adj* **:** tending to alleviate : PALLIATIVE

1al·ley \ˈal-ē\ *n, pl* **alleys** [ME, fr. MF *alee,* fr. OF, fr. *aler* to go, modif. of L *ambulare* to walk] **1 :** a garden or park walk bordered by trees or bushes **2 a** (1) **:** a grassed enclosure for bowling or skittles (2) **:** a hardwood lane for bowling; *also* **:** a room or building housing a group of such lanes **b :** the space on each side of a tennis doubles court between the sideline and the service sideline **3 :** a narrow street; *esp* **:** a thoroughfare through the middle of a block giving access to the rear of lots or buildings — **up one's alley** *also* **down one's alley :** suited to one's own tastes or abilities

2alley *n, pl* **alleys** [by shortening and alter. fr. *alabaster*] : a playing marble; *esp* **:** one of superior quality

al·ley·way \ˈal-ē-ˌwā\ *n* **1 :** a narrow passageway **2 :** ALLEY 3

All Fools' Day *n* : APRIL FOOLS' DAY

all fours *n pl* **1 a :** all four legs of a quadruped **b :** the two legs and two arms of a person when used to support the body **2** *sing in constr* **:** any of various card games in which points are scored for the high trump, low trump, jack of trumps, and game

all get–out \ˌȯl-get-ˈau̇t, -git-\ *n* **:** the utmost conceivable degree — used in comparisons to suggest something superlative <is handsome as *all get-out* and has a deft way with the ladies — John McCarten>

all hail *interj* — used to express greeting, welcome, or acclamation

All·hal·lows \ȯl-ˈhal-(ˌ)ōz, -əz\ *n, pl* **Allhallows** [short for *All Hallows' Day*] : ALL SAINTS' DAY

all·heal \ˈȯl-ˌhēl\ *n* **:** any of several plants (as valerian or self-heal) used esp. in folk medicine

al·li·a·ceous \ˌal-ē-ˈā-shəs\ *adj* [L *allium*] **:** resembling garlic or onion esp. in smell or taste

al·li·ance \ə-ˈlī-ən(t)s\ *n* **1 a :** the state of being allied **:** the action of allying **b :** a bond or connection between families, states, parties, or individuals <a closer ~ between government and industry> **2 :** an association to further the common interests of the members; *specif* **:** a confederation of nations by formal treaty **3 :** union by relationship in qualities : AFFINITY **4 :** a treaty of alliance

al·lied \ə-ˈlīd, ˈal-ˌīd\ *adj* **1 :** having or being in close association : CONNECTED <a strong personal pride ~ with the utmost probity> <two families ~ by marriage> **2 :** joined in alliance by compact or treaty; *specif, cap* **:** of or relating to the nations united against the Central European powers in World War I or those united against the Axis powers in World War II **3 a :** related esp. by common properties or qualities <heraldry and ~ subjects> **b :** related genetically ***syn*** see RELATED

al·li·ga·tor \ˈal-ə-ˌgāt-ər\ *n* [Sp *el lagarto* the lizard, fr. *el* the (fr. L *ille* that) + *lagarto* lizard, fr. (assumed) VL *lacartus,* fr. L *lacertus, lacerta* — more at LARIAT, LIZARD] **1 a :** either of two crocodilians (genus *Alligator*) having broad heads not tapering to the snout and a special pocket in the upper jaw for reception of the enlarged lower fourth tooth **b :** CROCODILIAN **2 :** leather made from alligator hide

alligator 1a

alligator pear *n* : AVOCADO

alligator snapper *n* **:** a snapping turtle (*Macrochelys temminckii*) of the rivers of the Gulf states that may reach nearly 150 pounds in weight and 5 feet in length

all–im·por·tant \ˌȯ-lim-ˈpȯrt-ᵊnt, -ənt\ *adj* **:** of very great or greatest importance <an ~ question>

all–in·clu·sive \ˌȯ-lin-ˈklü-siv, -ziv\ *adj* **:** including everything <a broader and more nearly ~ view> — **all–in·clu·sive·ness** *n*

al·lit·er·ate \ə-ˈlit-ə-ˌrāt\ *vb* **-at·ed; -at·ing** [back-formation fr. *alliteration*] *vi* **1 :** to form an alliteration **2 :** to write or speak alliteratively ~ *vt* **:** to arrange or place so as to make alliteration <~ syllables in a sentence>

al·lit·er·a·tion \ə-ˌlit-ə-ˈrā-shən\ *n* [*ad-* + L *littera* letter] **:** the repetition of usu. initial consonant sounds in two or more neighboring words or syllables (as *w*ild and *w*oolly, *thr*eatening *thr*ongs) — called also *head rhyme, initial rhyme*

al·lit·er·a·tive \ə-ˈlit-ə-ˌrāt-iv, -rət-\ *adj* **:** of, relating to, or marked by alliteration — **al·lit·er·a·tive·ly** *adv*

al·li·um \ˈal-ē-əm\ *n* [NL, genus name, fr. L, garlic] **:** any of a large genus (*Allium*) of bulbous herbs of the lily family including the onion, garlic, chive, leek, and shallot

all–night \ˌȯl-ˌnīt\ *adj* **1 :** lasting throughout the night <an ~ poker game> **2 :** open throughout the night <an ~ diner>

allo *abbr* allegro

allo- — see ALL-

al·lo·ca·ble \ˈal-ə-kə-bəl\ *adj* **1 :** capable of being allocated **2 :** assignable in accounting to a particular account or to a particular period of time

al·lo·cate \ˈal-ə-ˌkāt\ *vt* **-cat·ed; -cat·ing** [ML *allocatus,* pp. of *allocare,* fr. L *ad-* + *locare* to place, fr. *locus* place — more at STALL] **1 :** to apportion for a specific purpose or to particular persons or things : DISTRIBUTE <~ tasks among human and automated components> **2 :** to set apart or earmark : DESIGNATE <~

a section of the building for special research purposes> ***syn*** see ALLOT — **al·lo·cat·able** \-ˌkāt-ə-bəl\ *adj* — **al·lo·ca·tion** \ˌal-ə-ˈkā-shən\ *n* — **al·lo·ca·tor** \ˈal-ə-ˌkāt-ər\ *n*

al·lo·cu·tion \ˌal-ə-ˈkyü-shən\ *n* [L *allocution-, allocutio,* fr. *allocutus,* pp. of *alloqui* to speak to, fr. *ad-* + *loqui* to speak] : a formal speech; *esp* : an authoritative or hortatory address

al·log·a·mous \ə-ˈläg-ə-məs\ *adj* : reproducing by cross-fertilization — **al·log·a·my** \-mē\ *n*

al·lo·ge·ne·ic \ˌal-ō-jə-ˈnē-ik\ *adj* [*all-* + *-geneic* (as in *syngeneic*)] : sufficiently unlike genetically to interact antigenically

al·lo·graft \ˈal-ə-ˌgraft\ *n* : a homograft between allogeneic individuals

al·lo·graph \ˈal-ə-ˌgraf\ *n* **1** : a letter of an alphabet in a particular shape (as A or a) **2** : a letter or combination of letters that is one of several ways of representing one phoneme (as *pp* in *hopping* representing the phoneme *p*) — **al·lo·graph·ic** \ˌal-ə-ˈgraf-ik\ *adj*

al·lom·er·ism \ə-ˈläm-ə-ˌriz-əm\ *n* : variability in chemical constitution without variation in crystalline form — **al·lom·er·ous** \-rəs\ *adj*

al·lom·e·try \ə-ˈläm-ə-trē\ *n* : relative growth of a part in relation to an entire organism; *also* : the measure and study of such growth — **al·lo·me·tric** \ˌal-ə-ˈme-trik\ *adj*

¹al·lo·morph \ˈal-ə-ˌmȯrf\ *n* [ISV] **1** : any of two or more distinct crystalline forms of the same substance **2** : a pseudomorph that has undergone change or substitution of material — **al·lo·mor·phic** \ˌal-ə-ˈmȯr-fik\ *adj* — **al·lo·mor·phism** \ˈal-ə-ˌmȯr-ˌfiz-əm\ *n*

²allomorph *n* [*allo-* + *morpheme*] : one of two or more forms that a morpheme has at different points in the language <the *-es* \əz\ of *dishes,* the *-s* \z\ of *dreams,* the *-s* \s\ of *traps,* the *-en* \ən\ of *oxen,* the vowel modification distinguishing *teeth* from *tooth,* and the zero suffix of *sheep* in *those sheep* are ~*s* of the same morpheme> — **al·lo·mor·phic** \ˌal-ə-ˈmȯr-fik\ *adj* — **al·lo·mor·phism** \ˈal-ə-ˌmȯr-ˌfiz-əm\ *n*

al·longe \a-ˈlō^{n}zh\ *n* [F, lit., lengthening] : RIDER 2a

al·lo·path \ˈal-ə-ˌpath\ *n* : one who practices allopathy

al·lop·a·thy \ə-ˈläp-ə-thē\ *n* [G *allopathie,* fr. *all-* + *-pathie* -pathy] **1** : a system of medical practice that combats disease (as gonorrhea) by treatments (as by exciting nonspecific inflammation through the injection of silver nitrate) that produce effects different from those produced by the disease treated **2** : a system of medical practice making use of all measures proved of value in treatment of disease : conventional medicine exclusive of homeopathy — **al·lo·path·ic** \ˌal-ə-ˈpath-ik\ *adj* — **al·lo·path·i·cal·ly** \-i-k(ə-)lē\ *adv*

al·lo·pat·ric \ˌal-ə-ˈpa-trik\ *adj* [*all-* + Gk *patra* fatherland, fr. *patēr* father — more at FATHER] : occurring in different areas or in isolation <~ speciation> — **al·lo·pat·ri·cal·ly** \-tri-k(ə-)lē\ *adv* — **al·lop·a·try** \ə-ˈläp-ə-trē\ *n*

al·lo·phane \ˈal-ə-ˌfān\ *n* [Gk *allophanēs* appearing otherwise, fr. *all-* + *phainesthai* to appear, pass. of *phainein* to show — more at FANCY] : an amorphous translucent mineral of various colors often occurring in incrustations or stalactite forms and consisting of a hydrous aluminum silicate

al·lo·phone \ˈal-ə-ˌfōn\ *n* [*allo-* + *phone*] : one of two or more variants of the same phoneme <the aspirated *p* of *pin* and the nonaspirated *p* of *spin* are ~*s* of the phoneme *p*> — **al·lo·phon·ic** \ˌal-ə-ˈfän-ik\ *adj*

al·lo·pu·ri·nol \ˌal-ō-ˈpyu̇r-ə-ˌnȯl, -ˌnōl\ *n* [*all-* + *purine* + *-ol*] : a drug $C_5H_4N_4O$ used to promote excretion of uric acid

all–or–none \ˌȯ-lər-ˈnən\ *adj* : marked either by entire or complete operation or effect or by none at all <~ response of a nerve cell>

all–or–noth·ing \-ˈnəth-iŋ\ *adj* **1** : ALL-OR-NONE **2 a** : accepting no less than everything <he's an ~ perfectionist> **b** : risking everything <playing an ~ game>

al·lo·ste·ric \ˌal-ə-ˈster-ik, -ˈsti(ə)r-\ *adj* [*all-* + *steric*] : of, relating to, or being change (as inhibition) in enzyme activity caused by alteration of an enzyme at a point other than its enzymatically active site — **al·lo·ste·ri·cal·ly** \-i-k(ə-)lē\ *adv*

al·lot \ə-ˈlät\ *vt* **al·lot·ted; al·lot·ting** [ME *alotten,* fr. MF *aloter,* fr. *a-* (fr. L *ad-*) + *lot,* of Gmc origin; akin to OE *hlot* lot] **1** : to assign as a share or portion <~ 10 minutes for the speech> **2** : to distribute by or as if by lot <~ hotel rooms to members of the delegation> — **al·lot·ter** *n*

syn ALLOT, ASSIGN, APPORTION, ALLOCATE *shared meaning element* : to give as a share, portion, role, or lot

al·lot·ment \ə-ˈlät-mənt\ *n* **1** : the act of allotting : APPORTIONMENT **2** : something that is allotted

al·lo·trans·plant \ˌal-ō-tran(t)s-ˈplant\ *vt* : to transplant as a homograft — **al·lo·trans·plant** \-ˈtran(t)s-ˌ\ *n* — **al·lo·trans·plan·ta·tion** \-ˌtran(t)s-ˌplan-ˈtā-shən\ *n*

al·lo·trope \ˈal-ə-ˌtrōp\ *n* [ISV, back-formation fr. *allotropy*] : a form showing allotropy — **al·lo·trop·ic** \ˌal-ə-ˈträp-ik\ *adj* — **al·lo·trop·i·cal·ly** \-i-k(ə-)lē\ *adv*

al·lot·ro·py \ə-ˈlä-trə-pē\ *n, pl* **-pies** : the existence of a substance and esp. an element in two or more different forms (as of crystals) usu. in the same phase

all' ot·ta·va \ˌal-ə-ˈtäv-ə, ˌäl-ō-\ *adv or adj* [It, at the octave] : OTTAVA

al·lot·tee \ə-ˌlät-ˈē\ *n* : one to whom an allotment is made

al·lo·type \ˈal-ə-ˌtīp\ *n* : an isoantigenic immunoglobulin — **al·lo·typ·ic** \ˌal-ə-ˈtip-ik\ *adj* — **al·lo·typ·i·cal·ly** \-i-k(ə-)lē\ *adv* — **al·lo·typy** \ˈal-ə-ˌtī-pē\ *n*

all–out \ˈȯ-ˈlau̇t\ *adj* : made with maximum effort : THOROUGHGOING <an ~ effort to win the contest>

all out *adv* : with full determination or enthusiasm : with maximum effort — used chiefly in the phrase *go all out*

¹all·over \ˈȯ-ˌlō-vər\ *adj* : covering the whole extent or surface <a sweater with an ~ pattern>

²allover *n* **1** : an embroidered, printed, or lace fabric with a design covering most of the surface **2** : a pattern or design in which a single unit is repeated so as to cover an entire surface

all over *adv* **1** : over the whole extent <decorated *all over* with a flower pattern> **2** : EVERYWHERE <looked *all over* for the missing book> **3** : in every respect : THOROUGHLY <she is her mother *all over*>

all–overs \ˈȯ-ˌlō-vərz\ *n pl, chiefly South & Midland* : a feeling of nervousness : FIDGETS <I don't like such stories . . . they give me the ~ — J. C. Harris>

al·low \ə-ˈlau̇\ *vb* [ME *allowen,* fr. MF *alouer* to place, (fr. ML *allocare*) & *allouer* to approve, fr. L *adlaudare* to extol, fr. *ad-* + *laudare* to praise — more at ALLOCATE, LAUD] *vt* **1 a** : to assign as a share or suitable amount (as of time or money) <~ an hour for lunch> **b** : to reckon as a deduction or an addition <~ a gallon for leakage> **2** : ADMIT, CONCEDE <must ~ that money causes problems in marriage> **3 a** : PERMIT <doesn't ~ people to smoke in his home> **b** : to forbear or neglect to restrain or prevent <~ the dog to roam> **4** *dial* **a** : to be of the opinion : THINK **b** : INTEND, PLAN ~ *vi* **1** : to make a possibility : ADMIT — used with *of* <evidence that ~*s* of only one conclusion> **2** : to make allowance — used with *for* <~ for expansion> **3** *dial* : SUPPOSE, CONSIDER ***syn*** see LET ***ant*** inhibit

al·low·able \ə-ˈlau̇-ə-bəl\ *adj* : PERMISSIBLE — **al·low·able·ness** *n* — **al·low·ably** \-blē\ *adv*

¹al·low·ance \ə-ˈlau̇-ən(t)s\ *n* **1 a** : a share or portion allotted or granted **b** : a sum granted as a reimbursement or bounty or for expenses <salary includes cost-of-living ~>; *esp* : a sum regularly provided for personal or household expenses <each child has an ~> **c** : a fixed or available amount <provide an ~ of time for recreation> **d** : a reduction from a list price or stated price <a trade-in ~> **2** : an imposed handicap (as in a race) **3** : an allowed dimensional difference between mating parts of a machine **4** : the act of allowing : PERMISSION **5** : the taking into account of mitigating circumstances or contingencies ***syn*** see RATION

²allowance *vt* **-anced; -anc·ing** **1** : to put on a fixed allowance (as of food and drink) **2** : to supply in a fixed or regular quantity

al·low·ed·ly \ə-ˈlau̇-əd-lē\ *adv* : by allowance : ADMITTEDLY

al·lox·an \ə-ˈläk-sən\ *n* [G, fr. *all*antoin, a chemical found in the allantoic membrane of cows + *ox*alsäure oxalic acid + *-an*] : a crystalline compound $C_4H_2N_2O_4$ causing diabetes mellitus when injected into experimental animals; *also* : one of its similarly acting derivatives

¹al·loy \ˈal-ˌȯi, ə-ˈlȯi\ *n* [MF *aloi,* fr. *aloier* to combine, fr. L *alligare* to bind — more at ALLY] **1** : the degree of mixture with base metals : FINENESS **2** : a substance composed of two or more metals or of a metal and a nonmetal intimately united usu. by being fused together and dissolving in each other when molten; *also* : the state of union of the components **3** *archaic* : a metal mixed with a more valuable metal to give durability or some other desired quality **4 a** : an admixture that lessens value **b** : an impairing alien element **5** : a compound, mixture, or union of different things : AMALGAM <an ethnic ~ of many peoples>

²al·loy \ə-ˈlȯi, ˈal-ˌȯi\ *vt* **1** : to reduce the purity of by mixing with a less valuable metal **2** : to mix so as to form an alloy **3 a** : to impair or debase by admixture **b** : TEMPER, MODERATE ~ *vi* : to lend itself to being alloyed <iron ~*s* well>

all–pow·er·ful \ˈȯl-ˈpau̇(-ə)r-fəl\ *adj* : having complete or sole power

all–pur·pose \-ˈpər-pəs\ *adj* : suited for many purposes or uses

¹all right \(ˈ)ȯl-ˈrīt, *esp for 2* ˈȯl-ˌ\ *adv* **1** : well enough <does *all right* in school> **2** : very well : YES <*all right,* let's go> **3** : beyond doubt : CERTAINLY <he has pneumonia *all right*>

²all right \(ˈ)ȯl-ˈ\ *adj* **1** : SATISFACTORY <the film is *all right* for children> **2** : SAFE, WELL <he was ill but he's *all right* now> **3** : AGREEABLE, PLEASING — usu. used as a generalized term of approval

all–round \ˈȯl-ˈrau̇nd\ *var of* ALL-AROUND

All Saints' Day *n* : November 1 observed in Western liturgical churches as a Christian feast in honor of all the saints

all·seed \ˈȯl-ˌsēd\ *n* : any of several many-seeded plants (as knotgrass)

All Souls' Day *n* : November 2 observed as a day of prayer for the souls of the faithful departed

all·spice \ˈȯl-ˌspīs\ *n* **1** : the berry of a West Indian tree (*Pimenta dioica*) of the myrtle family; *also* : the allspice tree **2** : a mildly pungent and aromatic spice prepared from allspice berries

¹all–star \ˌȯl-ˌstär\ *adj* : composed wholly or chiefly of stars or of outstanding performers or participants <an ~ cast>

²all–star \ˈȯl-ˌstär\ *n* : a member of an all-star team <major league ~*s*>

all that \(ˈ)ȯl-ˈt͟hat\ *adv* : to an indicated or suggested extent or degree : SO <didn't take his threats *all that* seriously>

all the same *adv* : NEVERTHELESS <she was very tired but enjoyed the play *all the same*>

all–time \ˌȯl-ˌtīm\ *adj* **1** : FULL-TIME **2** : exceeding all others of all time <an ~ best seller>

all told *adv* : with everything taken into account : in all

al·lude \ə-ˈlüd\ *vi* **al·lud·ed; al·lud·ing** [L *alludere,* lit., to play with, fr. *ad-* + *ludere* to play — more at LUDICROUS] : to make indirect reference ***syn*** see REFER

¹al·lure \ə-ˈlu̇(ə)r\ *vt* **al·lured; al·lur·ing** [ME *aluren,* fr. MF *alurer,* fr. OF, fr. *a-* (fr. L *ad-*) + *loire* lure — more at LURE] : to entice by charm or attraction ***syn*** see ATTRACT ***ant*** repel — **al·lure·ment** \-ˈlu̇(ə)r-mənt\ *n*

²allure *n* : power of attraction or fascination : CHARM

al·lu·sion \ə-ˈlü-zhən\ *n* [LL *allusion-, allusio,* fr. L *allusus,* pp. of *alludere*] **1** : the act of alluding or hinting at **2** : an implied or indirect reference esp. when used in literature; *also* : the use of such references — **al·lu·sive** \-ˈlü-siv, -ziv\ *adj* — **al·lu·sive·ly** *adv* — **al·lu·sive·ness** *n*

1al·lu·vi·al \ə-'lü-vē-əl\ *adj* **:** relating to, composed of, or found in alluvium <~ soil> <~ diamonds>
2alluvial *n* **:** an alluvial deposit
alluvial fan *n* **:** the alluvial deposit of a stream where it issues from a gorge upon a plain or of a tributary stream at its junction with the main stream
al·lu·vi·on \ə-'lü-vē-ən\ *n* [L *alluvion-, alluvio,* fr. *alluere* to wash against, fr. *ad-* + *lavere* to wash — more at LYE] **1 :** the wash or flow of water against a shore **2 :** FLOOD, INUNDATION **3 :** ALLUVIUM **4 :** an accession to land by the gradual addition of matter (as by deposit of alluvium) that then belongs to the owner of the land to which it is added; *also* **:** the land so added
al·lu·vi·um \-vē-əm\ *n, pl* **-vi·ums** *or* **-via** \-vē-ə\ [LL, neut. of *alluvius* alluvial, fr. L *alluere*] **:** clay, silt, sand, gravel, or similar detrital material deposited by running water
1al·ly \ə-'lī, 'al-,ī\ *vb* **al·lied; al·ly·ing** [ME *allien,* fr OF *alier,* fr. L *alligare* to bind to, fr. *ad-* + *ligare* to bind — more at LIGATURE] *vt* **1 :** to unite or form a connection between **:** ASSOCIATE <*allied* himself with a wealthy family by marriage> **2 :** to connect or form a relation between (as by likeness or compatibility) **:** RELATE ~ *vi* **:** to form or enter into an alliance
2al·ly \'al-,ī, ə-'lī\ n, *pl* **allies 1 :** a plant or animal linked to another by genetic or evolutionary relationship **2 :** a sovereign or state associated with another by treaty or league **3 :** one that is associated with another as a helper **:** AUXILIARY
-al·ly \(ə-)lē\ *adv suffix* [1*-al* + *-ly*] **:** 2-LY <terrific*ally*> — in adverbs formed from adjectives in *-ic* with no alternative form in *-ical*
al·lyl \'al-əl\ *n* [ISV, fr. L *allium* garlic]**:** an unsaturated univalent radical C_3H_5 compounds of which are found in the oils of garlic and mustard — **al·lyl·ic** \ə-'lil-ik, a-\ *adj*
al·ma·gest \'al-mə-,jest\ *n* [ME *almageste,* fr. MF & ML, fr. Ar *al-majusti* the almagest, fr. *al* the + Gk *megistē,* fem. of *megistos,* superl. of *megas* great — more at MUCH] **:** any of several early medieval treatises on a branch of knowledge
al·ma ma·ter \,al-mə-'mät-ər\ *n* [L, fostering mother] **1 :** a school, college, or university which one has attended or from which one has graduated **2 :** the song or hymn of a school, college, or university
al·ma·nac \'ȯl-mə-,nak, 'al-\ *n* [ME *almenak,* fr. ML *almanach,* prob. fr. Ar *al-manākh* the almanac] **1 :** a publication containing astronomical and meteorological data arranged according to the days, weeks, and months of a given year and often including a miscellany of other information **2 :** a usu. annual publication containing statistical, tabular, and general information
al·man·dine \'al-mən-,dēn\ *n* [ME *alabandine,* fr. ML *alabandina,* fr. *Alabanda* ancient city in Asia Minor] **1 :** ALMANDITE **2 :** a violet variety of the ruby spinel or sapphire **3 :** the purple Indian garnet
al·man·dite \'al-mən-,dīt\ *n* [alter. of *almandine*] **:** a deep red garnet consisting of an iron aluminum silicate $Fe_3Al_2(SiO_4)_3$
1al·mighty \ȯl-'mīt-ē\ *adj* [ME, fr. OE *ealmihtig,* fr. *eall* all + *mihtig* mighty] **1** *often cap* **:** having absolute power over all <*Almighty* God> **2 :** relatively unlimited in power **3 :** great in magnitude or seriousness — **al·mighti·ness** *n, often cap*
2almighty *adv* **:** to a great degree **:** EXTREMELY <although he did not precisely starve, he was ~ hungry — W. A. Swanberg>
Almighty *n* **:** GOD 1 — used with *the*
al·mond \'äm-ənd, 'am-; 'al-mənd\ *n* [ME *almande,* fr. OF, fr. LL *amandula,* alter. of L *amygdala,* fr. Gk *amygdalē*] **1 a :** a small tree (*Prunus amygdalus*) of the rose family with flowers and young fruit resembling those of the peach **b :** the drupaceous fruit of the almond; *esp* **:** its ellipsoidal edible kernel used as a nut **2 :** any of several fruits similar to the almond; *also* **:** the trees producing them

almonds 1b

al·mond-eyed \,äm-ən-'dīd, ,am-; ,al-mən-\ *adj* **:** having narrow slant almond-shaped eyes
almond green *n* **:** a variable color averaging a moderate yellowish green
al·mo·ner \'al-mə-nər, 'äm-ə-\ *n* [ME *almoiner,* fr. OF *almosnier,* fr. *almosne* alms, fr. LL *eleemosyna*] **1 :** one who distributes alms **2** *Brit* **:** a social-service worker in a hospital
al·most \'ȯl-,mōst, ȯl-'\ *adv* [ME, fr. OE *ealmǣst,* fr. *eall* + *mǣst* most] **:** very nearly but not exactly or entirely
alms \'ämz, 'älmz\ *n, pl* **alms** [ME *almesse, almes,* fr. OE *ælmesse, ælms;* akin to OHG *alamuosan* alms; both fr. a prehistoric WGmc word borrowed fr. LL *eleemosyna* alms, fr. Gk *eleēmosynē* pity, alms, fr. *eleēmōn* merciful, fr. *eleos* pity] **1** *archaic* **:** CHARITY **2 :** something (as money or food) given freely to relieve the poor — **alms·giv·er** \-,giv-ər\ *n* — **alms·giv·ing** \-,giv-iŋ\ *n*
alms·house \-,hau̇s\ *n* **1** *Brit* **:** a privately financed home for the poor **2** *archaic* **:** POORHOUSE
alms·man \-mən\ *n* **:** a recipient of alms
al·ni·co \'al-ni-,kō\ *n* [*al*uminum + *ni*ckel + *co*balt]**:** a powerful permanent-magnet alloy containing iron, nickel, aluminum, and one or more of the elements cobalt, copper, and titanium
al·oe \'al-(,)ō\ *n* [ME, fr. LL, fr. L, dried juice of aloe leaves, fr. Gk *aloē* dried juice of aloe leaves] **1** *pl* **:** the fragrant wood of an East Indian tree (*Aquilaria agallocha*) of the mezereon family **2 a :** any of a large genus (*Aloe*) of succulent chiefly southern African plants of the lily family with basal leaves and spicate flowers **b :** the dried juice of the leaves of various aloes used as a purgative and tonic — usu. used in pl. but sing. in constr. **3 :** any of a genus (*Furcraea*) of American plants of the amaryllis family somewhat like the African aloes
1aloft \ə-'lȯft\ *adv* [ME, fr. ON *ā lopt,* fr. *ā* on, in + *lopt* air — more at ON, LOFT] **1 :** at or to a great height **2 :** in the air; *esp* **:** in flight (as in an airplane) <meals served ~> **3 :** at, on, or to the masthead or the higher rigging
2aloft *prep* **:** on top of **:** ABOVE <bright signs ~ hotels>
alog·i·cal \(')ā-'läj-i-kəl\ *adj* **:** being outside the bounds of that to which logic can apply — **alog·i·cal·ly** \-k(ə-)lē\ *adv*
alo·ha \ə-'lō-(h)ə, ä-, -,(h)ä\ *interj* [Hawaiian, fr. *aloha* love] — used as a greeting or farewell
aloha shirt *n* **:** a loose brightly colored Hawaiian sport shirt
al·o·in \'al-ə-wən\ *n* **:** a bitter yellow crystalline cathartic obtained from the aloe
1alone \ə-'lōn\ *adj* [ME, fr. *al* all + *one* one] **1 :** separated from others **:** ISOLATED **2 :** exclusive of anyone or anything else **:** ONLY **3 a :** considered without reference to any other <the children ~ would eat that much> **b :** INCOMPARABLE, UNIQUE <~ in his ability to solve fiscal problems> — **alone·ness** \-'lōn-nəs\ *n*
syn ALONE, SOLITARY, LONELY, LONESOME, LONE, LORN, FORLORN, DESOLATE *shared meaning element* **:** isolated from others. ALONE stresses the objective fact of being by oneself with slighter notion of emotional involvement than most of the remaining terms <everyone needs to be *alone* sometimes> SOLITARY may indicate isolation as a chosen course <glorying in the calm of her *solitary* life> but more often it suggests sadness and a sense of loss <left *solitary* by the death of his wife> LONELY adds to *solitary* a suggestion of longing for companionship <felt *lonely* and forsaken> LONESOME heightens the implication of dreariness and longing <an only child often leads a *lonesome* life> LONE may replace *lonely* or *lonesome* but typically is as objective as *alone* <a *lone* robin pecking at the lawn> LORN suggests recent separation or bereavement <when *lorn* lovers sit and droop — W. M. Praed> FORLORN stresses dejection, woe, and listlessness at separation from one held dear <a *forlorn* lost child> DESOLATE implies a sharp and poignant sense of loneliness ***ant*** accompanied
2alone *adv* **1 :** SOLELY, EXCLUSIVELY **2 :** without aid or support
1along \ə-'lȯŋ\ *prep* [ME, fr. OE *andlang,* fr. *and-* against + *lang* long — more at ANTE-] **1 :** in a line parallel with the length or direction of **2 :** in the course of **3 :** in accordance with **:** IN
2along *adv* **1 :** FORWARD, ON <move ~> **2 :** from one to another <word was passed ~> **3 a :** as a companion <brought his wife ~> **b :** in association — used with *with* <work ~ with colleagues> **4 :** at or to an advanced point <plans are far ~> **5 :** in addition **:** ALSO — often used with *with* <a bill came ~ with the package> **6 :** at hand **:** as a necessary or useful item <had his gun ~> **7 :** on hand **:** THERE <tell him I'll be ~ to see him> — **all along :** all the time <knew the truth *all along*>
along of *prep* [ME *ilong on,* fr. OE *gelang on,* fr. *ge-,* associative prefix + *lang* — more at CO-] *dial* **:** because of
along·shore \ə-'lȯŋ-'shō(ə)r, -'shȯ(ə)r\ *adv or adj* **:** along the shore or coast <walked ~> <~ currents>
1along·side \-,sīd\ *adv* **1 :** along the side **:** in parallel position **2 :** at the side **:** close by <a guard with a prisoner ~>
2alongside *prep* **:** side by side with; *specif* **:** parallel to
alongside of *prep* **:** ALONGSIDE
1aloof \ə-'lüf\ *adv* [obs. *aloof* (to windward)] **:** at a distance **:** out of involvement
2aloof *adj* **:** removed or distant in interest or feeling **:** RESERVED syn see INDIFFERENT ***ant*** familiar, close — **aloof·ly** *adv* — **aloof·ness** *n*
al·o·pe·cia \,al-ə-'pē-sh(ē-)ə\ *n* [ME *allopicia,* fr. L *alopecia,* fr. Gk *alōpekia,* fr. *alōpek-, alōpēx* fox — more at VULPINE]**:** loss of hair, wool, or feathers **:** BALDNESS — **al·o·pe·cic** \-'pē-sik\ *adj*
aloud \ə-'lau̇d\ *adv* [ME, fr. 1*a-* + *loud*] **1** *archaic* **:** in a loud manner **:** LOUDLY **2 :** with the speaking voice
alow \ə-'lō\ *adv* [ME, fr. 1*a-* + *low*] **:** BELOW <~ in the ship's hold>
alp \'alp\ *n* [back-formation fr. *Alps,* mountain system of Europe] **1 :** a high rugged mountain **2 :** something suggesting an alp in height, size, or ruggedness
al·paca \al-'pak-ə\ *n* [Sp, fr. Aymara *allpaca*] **1 :** a mammal with fine long woolly hair that is domesticated in Peru and is prob. a variety of the guanaco **2 a :** wool of the alpaca **b (1) :** a thin cloth made of or containing this wool **(2) :** a rayon or cotton imitation of this cloth

alpaca 1

al·pen·glow \'al-pən-,glō\ *n* [prob. part trans. of G *Alpenglühen,* fr. *Alpen* Alps + *glühen* glow] **:** a reddish glow seen near sunset or sunrise on the summits of mountains
al·pen·stock \'al-pən-,stäk\ *n* [G, fr. *Alpen* + *stock* staff] **:** a long iron-pointed staff used in mountain climbing
al·pes·trine \al-'pes-trən\ *adj* [ML *alpestris* mountainous, fr. L *Alpes* Alps] **:** growing at high elevations but not above the timberline **:** SUBALPINE
1al·pha \'al-fə\ *n* [ME, fr. L, fr. Gk, of Sem origin; akin to Heb *āleph* aleph] **1 :** the 1st letter of the Greek alphabet — see ALPHABET table **2 :** something that is first **:** BEGINNING **3 :** the chief or brightest star of a constellation
2alpha *or* α **-** *adj* **:** closest in the structure of an organic molecule to a particular group or atom <α-substitution> <α-naphthol>
3alpha *adj* **:** ALPHABETIC
al·pha–ad·ren·er·gic \'al-fə-,ad-rə-'nər-jik\ *adj* **:** of, relating to, or being an alpha-receptor <~ blocking action>
alpha and omega *n* [fr. the fact that alpha and omega are respectively the first and last letters of the Greek alphabet] **1 :** the beginning and ending **2 :** the principal element
al·pha·bet \'al-fə-,bet, -bət\ *n* [ME *alphabete,* fr. LL *alphabetum,* fr. Gk *alphabētos,* fr. *alpha* + *bēta* beta] **1 a :** a set of letters or other characters with which one or more languages are written esp. if arranged in a customary order **b :** a system of signs or signals that serve as equivalents for letters **2 :** RUDIMENTS, ELEMENTS
al·pha·bet·ic \,al-fə-'bet-ik\ *or* **al·pha·bet·i·cal** \-i-kəl\ *adj* **1 :** of, relating to, or employing an alphabet **2 :** arranged in the order of the letters of the alphabet — **al·pha·bet·i·cal·ly** \-i-k(ə-)lē\ *adv*

ALPHABET TABLE

Showing the letters of five non-Roman alphabets and the transliterations used in the etymologies

HEBREW[1,4]

Letter	Name	Transliteration
א	aleph	ʼ [2]
ב	beth	b, bh
ג	gimel	g, gh
ד	daleth	d, dh
ה	he	h
ו	waw	w
ז	zayin	z
ח	heth	ḥ
ט	teth	ṭ
י	yod	y
כ ך	kaph	k, kh
ל	lamed	l
מ ם	mem	m
נ ן	nun	n
ס	samekh	s
ע	ayin	ʽ
פ ף	pe	p, ph
צ ץ	sadhe	ṣ
ק	qoph	q
ר	resh	r
שׂ	sin	ś
שׁ	shin	sh
ת	taw	t, th

ARABIC[3,4]

Alone	Joined to preceding	Joined to both	Joined to following	Name	Transliteration
ا	ـا			alif	ʼ [5]
ب	ـب	ـبـ	بـ	bā	b
ت	ـت	ـتـ	تـ	tā	t
ث	ـث	ـثـ	ثـ	thā	th
ج	ـج	ـجـ	جـ	jīm	j
ح	ـح	ـحـ	حـ	ḥā	ḥ
خ	ـخ	ـخـ	خـ	khā	kh
د	ـد			dāl	d
ذ	ـذ			dhāl	dh
ر	ـر			rā	r
ز	ـز			zāy	z
س	ـس	ـسـ	سـ	sīn	s
ش	ـش	ـشـ	شـ	shīn	sh
ص	ـص	ـصـ	صـ	ṣād	ṣ
ض	ـض	ـضـ	ضـ	ḍād	ḍ
ط	ـط	ـطـ	طـ	ṭā	ṭ
ظ	ـظ	ـظـ	ظـ	ẓā	ẓ
ع	ـع	ـعـ	عـ	ʽayn	ʽ
غ	ـغ	ـغـ	غـ	ghayn	gh
ف	ـف	ـفـ	فـ	fā	f
ق	ـق	ـقـ	قـ	qāf	q
ك	ـك	ـكـ	كـ	kāf	k
ل	ـل	ـلـ	لـ	lām	l
م	ـم	ـمـ	مـ	mīm	m
ن	ـن	ـنـ	نـ	nūn	n
ه	ـه	ـهـ	هـ	hā	h[6]
و	ـو			wāw	w
ى	ـى	ـيـ	يـ	yā	y

GREEK[7]

Letter	Name	Transliteration
Α α	alpha	a
Β β	beta	b
Γ γ	gamma	g, n
Δ δ	delta	d
Ε ε	epsilon	e
Ζ ζ	zeta	z
Η η	eta	ē
Θ θ	theta	th
Ι ι	iota	i
Κ κ	kappa	k
Λ λ	lambda	l
Μ μ	mu	m
Ν ν	nu	n
Ξ ξ	xi	x
Ο ο	omicron	o
Π π	pi	p
Ρ ρ	rho	r, rh
Σ σ ς	sigma	s
Τ τ	tau	t
Υ υ	upsilon	y, u
Φ φ	phi	ph
Χ χ	chi	ch
Ψ ψ	psi	ps
Ω ω	omega	ō

RUSSIAN[8]

А а	a
Б б	b
В в	v
Г г	g
Д д	d
Е е	e
Ж ж	zh
З з	z
И и Й й	i, ĭ
К к	k
Л л	l
М м	m
Н н	n
О о	o
П п	p
Р р	r
С с	s
Т т	t
У у	u
Ф ф	f
Х х	kh
Ц ц	ts
Ч ч	ch
Ш ш	sh
Щ щ	shch
Ъ ъ[9]	”
Ы ы	y
Ь ь[10]	’
Э э	e
Ю ю	yu
Я я	ya

SANSKRIT[11]

अ	a	ञ	ñ
आ	ā	ट	ṭ
इ	i	ठ	ṭh
ई	ī	ड	ḍ
उ	u	ढ	ḍh
ऊ	ū	ण	ṇ
ऋ	ṛ	त	t
ॠ	ṝ	थ	th
ऌ	ḷ	द	d
ॡ	ḹ	ध	dh
ए	e	न	n
ऐ	ai	प	p
ओ	o	फ	ph
औ	au	ब	b
ं	ṃ	भ	bh
ः	ḥ	म	m
क	k	य	y
ख	kh	र	r
ग	g	ल	l
घ	gh	व	v
ङ	ṅ	श	ś
च	c	ष	ṣ
छ	ch	स	s
ज	j	ह	h
झ	jh		

1 See ALEPH, BETH, etc., in the vocabulary. Where two forms of a letter are given, the one at the right is the form used at the end of a word. 2 Not represented in transliteration when initial. 3 The left column shows the form of each Arabic letter that is used when it stands alone, the second column its form when it is joined to the preceding letter, the third column its form when it is joined to both the preceding and the following letter, and the right column its form when it is joined to the following letter only. In the names of the Arabic letters, *ā*, *ī*, and *ū* respectively are pronounced like *a* in *father*, *i* in *machine*, *u* in *rude*. 4 Hebrew and Arabic are written from right to left. The Hebrew and Arabic letters are all primarily consonants; a few of them are also used secondarily to represent certain vowels, but full indication of vowels, when provided at all, is by means of a system of dots or strokes adjacent to the consonantal characters. 5 Alif represents no sound in itself, but is used principally as an indicator of the presence of a glottal stop (transliterated ’ medially and finally; not represented in transliteration when initial) and as the sign of a long *a*. 6 When ه has two dots above it (ة), it is called *tā marbūta* and, if it immediately precedes a vowel, is transliterated *t* instead of *h*. 7 See ALPHA, BETA, GAMMA, etc., in the vocabulary. The letter gamma is transliterated *n* only before velars; the letter upsilon is transliterated *u* only as the final element in diphthongs. 8 See CYRILLIC in the vocabulary. 9 This sign indicates that the immediately preceding consonant is not palatalized even though immediately followed by a palatal vowel. 10 This sign indicates that the immediately preceding consonant is palatalized even though not immediately followed by a palatal vowel. 11 The alphabet shown here is the Devanagari. When vowels are combined with preceding consonants they are indicated by various strokes or hooks instead of by the signs here given, or, in the case of short *a*, not written at all. Thus the character क represents *ka;* the character का, *kā;* the character कि, *ki;* the character की, *kī;* the character कु, *ku;* the character कू, *kū;* the character कृ, *kṛ;* the character कॄ, *kṝ;* the character के, *ke;* the character कै, *kai;* the character को, *ko;* the character कौ, *kau;* and the character क्, *k* without any following vowel. There are also many compound characters representing combinations of two or more consonants.

al·pha·bet·iza·tion \ˌal-fə-ˌbet-ə-ˈzā-shən\ *n* **1 :** the act or process of alphabetizing **2 :** an alphabetically arranged series, list, or file

al·pha·bet·ize \ˈal-fə-bə-ˌtīz\ *vt* **-ized; -iz·ing** **1 :** to furnish with an alphabet **2 :** to arrange alphabetically — **al·pha·bet·iz·er** *n*

alpha globulin *n* [ISV] **:** any of several globulins of plasma or serum that have at alkaline pH the greatest electrophoretic mobility next to albumin — compare BETA GLOBULIN, GAMMA GLOBULIN

al·pha–he·lix \ˌal-fə-ˈhē-liks\ *n* **:** the coiled structural arrangement of many proteins consisting of a single spiral amino-acid chain that is stabilized by hydrogen bonds

alpha iron *n* **:** the form of iron stable below 910°C

al·pha·mer·ic \ˌal-fə-ˈmer-ik\ *or* **al·pha·mer·i·cal** \-i-kəl\ *adj* [*alpha*bet + nu*meric*, nu*merical*] **:** ALPHANUMERIC

al·pha·nu·mer·ic \-n(y)ü-ˈmer-ik\ *also* **al·pha·nu·mer·i·cal** *adj* [*alpha*bet + *numeric, numerical*] **1 :** consisting of both letters and numbers and often other symbols (as punctuation marks and mathematical symbols) as well <an ~ code>; *also* **:** being a character in an alphanumeric system **2 :** capable of using alphanumeric characters <an ~ computer> — **al·pha·nu·mer·i·cal·ly** \-i-k(ə-)lē\ *adv*

alpha particle *n* **:** a positively charged nuclear particle identical with the nucleus of a helium atom that consists of two protons and two neutrons and is ejected at high speed in certain radioactive transformations

alpha privative *n* **:** the prefix *a-* or *an-* expressing negation in Greek and in English

alpha ray *n* **1 :** an alpha particle moving at high speed (as in radioactive emission) **2 :** a stream of alpha particles — called also *alpha radiation*

al·pha–re·cep·tor \ˈal-fə-ri-ˌsep-tər\ *n* **:** a receptor that is associated with vasoconstriction, relaxation of intestinal muscle, and contraction of the nictitating membrane, iris dilator muscle, splenic smooth muscle, and muscular layer of the wall of the uterus — called also *alpha-adrenergic receptor*

Al·phe·us \al-ˈfē-əs\ *n* [L, fr. Gk *Alpheios*] **:** a Greek river-god who pursues the nymph Arethusa and is finally united with her

al·pine \ˈal-ˌpīn\ *n* **1 :** a plant native to alpine or boreal regions that is often grown for ornament **2** *cap* **:** a person possessing Alpine physical characteristics

Alpine *adj* **1** *often not cap* **:** of, relating to, or resembling the Alps or any mountains **2** *often not cap* **:** of, relating to, or growing in the biogeographic zone including the elevated slopes above timberline **3 :** of or relating to a type of stocky broad-headed white men of medium height with brown hair or eyes often regarded as constituting a branch of the Caucasian race **4 :** of or relating to competitive ski events consisting of slalom and downhill racing — compare NORDIC

al·pin·ism \ˈal-pə-ˌniz-əm\ *n, often cap* **:** mountain climbing in the Alps or other high mountains — **al·pin·ist** \-nəst\ *n*

al·ready \ȯl-ˈred-ē\ *adv* [ME *al redy*, fr. *al redy*, adj., wholly ready, fr. *al* all + *redy* ready] **:** prior to a specified or implied past, present, or future time **:** by this time **:** PREVIOUSLY <he had ~ left when I called>

al·right \(ˈ)ȯl-ˈrīt, ˈȯl-ˌ\ *adv or adj* [ME, fr. *al* + *right*] **:** ALL RIGHT <the first two years of the medical school were ~ — Gertrude Stein>

Al·sa·tian \al-ˈsā-shən\ *n* [ML *Alsatia* Alsace] **:** GERMAN SHEPHERD

al·sike clover \ˌal-ˌsak-, -ˌsīk-\ *n* [*Alsike*, Sweden] **:** a European perennial clover (*Trifolium hybridum*) much used as a forage plant

al·so \ˈȯl-(ˌ)sō\ *adv* [ME, fr. OE *eallswā*, fr. *eall* all + *swā* so — more at SO] **1 :** LIKEWISE 1 **2 :** in addition **:** TOO

al·so–ran \-ˌran\ *n* **1 :** a horse or dog that finishes out of the money in a race **2 :** a contestant that does not win **3 :** one that is competitively of little importance <was just an ~ in the scramble for . . . privileges — C. A. Buss>

alt *abbr* **1** alternate **2** altitude **3** alto

Alta *abbr* Alberta

Al·ta·ic \al-ˈtā-ik\ *adj* **1 :** of or relating to the Altai mountains **2 :** of, relating to, or constituting a language family comprising the Turkic, Tungusic, and Mongolic subfamilies

Al·tair \al-ˈtī(ə)r, -ˈta(ə)r, -ˈte(ə)r, ˈal-ˌ\ *n* [Ar *al-ṭā'ir*, lit., the flier] **:** the first magnitude star Alpha (α) Aquilae

al·tar \ˈȯl-tər\ *n, often attrib* [ME *alter*, fr. OE *altar*, fr. L *altare*; akin to L *adolēre* to burn up] **1 :** a usu. raised structure or place on which sacrifices are offered or incense is burned in worship **2 :** a table on which the eucharistic elements are consecrated or which serves as a center of worship or ritual — see BASILICA illustration

altar boy *n* **:** a boy who assists the celebrant in a liturgical service

altar call *n* **:** an appeal by an evangelist to worshipers to come forward to signify their decision to commit their lives to Christ

altar of repose *often cap A&R* **:** REPOSITORY 2

al·tar·piece \ˈȯl-tər-ˌpēs\ *n* **:** a work of art that decorates the space above and behind an altar

altar rail *n* **:** a railing in front of an altar separating the chancel from the body of the church

altar stone *n* **:** a stone slab with a compartment containing the relics of martyrs that forms an essential part of a Roman Catholic altar

alt·az·i·muth \(ˈ)al-ˈtaz-(ə-)məth\ *n* [ISV *alt*itude + *azimuth*] **:** a telescope mounted so that it can swing horizontally and vertically; *also* **:** any of several other similarly mounted instruments

al·ter \ˈȯl-tər\ *vb* **al·tered; al·ter·ing** \-t(ə-)riŋ\ [ME *alteren*, fr. MF *alterer*, fr. ML *alterare*, fr. L *alter* other (of two); akin to L *alius* other — more at ELSE] *vt* **1 :** to make different without changing into something else **2 :** CASTRATE, SPAY ~ *vi* **:** to become different *syn* see CHANGE *ant* fix — **al·ter·abil·i·ty** \ˌȯl-t(ə-)rə-ˈbil-ət-ē\ *n* — **al·ter·able** \ˈȯl-t(ə-)rə-bəl\ *adj* — **al·ter·ably** \-blē\ *adv* — **al·ter·er** \-tər-ər\ *n*

al·ter·ation \ˌȯl-tə-ˈrā-shən\ *n* **1 :** the act or process of altering **:** the state of being altered **2 :** the result of altering **:** MODIFICATION

al·ter·ative \ˈȯl-tə-ˌrāt-iv, -rət-\ *n* **:** a drug used empirically to alter favorably the course of an ailment

al·ter·cate \ˈȯl-tər-ˌkāt\ *vi* **-cat·ed; -cat·ing** [L *altercatus*, pp. of *altercari*, fr. *alter*] **:** to dispute angrily or noisily **:** WRANGLE

al·ter·ca·tion \ˌȯl-tər-ˈkā-shən\ *n* **:** a noisy heated angry dispute; *also* **:** noisy controversy *syn* see QUARREL

al·ter ego \ˌȯl-tə-ˈrē-(ˌ)gō *also* -ˈreg-(ˌ)ō\ *n* [L, lit., second I] **:** a second self; *esp* **:** a trusted friend

¹al·ter·nate \ˈȯl-tər-nət *also* ˈal-\ *adj* [L *alternatus*, pp. of *alternare*, fr. *alternus* alternate, fr. *alter*] **1 :** occurring or succeeding by turns <a day of ~ sunshine and rain> **2 a :** arranged first on one side and then on the other at different levels or points along an axial line <~ leaves> — compare OPPOSITE **b :** arranged one above or alongside the other **3 :** every other **:** every second <he works on ~ days> **4 :** constituting an alternative <took the ~ route home> *syn* see INTERMITTENT *ant* consecutive — **al·ter·nate·ly** *adv*

²al·ter·nate \-ˌnāt\ *vb* **-nat·ed; -nat·ing** *vt* **1 :** to perform by turns or in succession **2 :** to cause to alternate ~ *vi* **:** to change from one to another repeatedly <storms *alternated* with sunshine>

³al·ter·nate \-nət\ *n* **1 :** ALTERNATIVE **2 :** one that substitutes for or alternates with another

alternate angle *n* **:** one of a pair of angles on opposite sides of a transversal at its intersection with two other lines: **a :** one of a pair of angles inside the two intersected lines — called also *alternate interior angle* **b :** one of a pair of angles outside the two intersected lines — called also *alternate exterior angle*

alternating current *n* **:** an electric current that reverses its direction at regularly recurring intervals — abbr. *AC*

alternating group *n* **:** a permutation group whose elements comprise those permutations of *n* objects which can be formed from the original order by making consecutively an even number of interchanges of pairs of objects

al·ter·na·tion \ˌȯl-tər-ˈnā-shən *also* ˌal-\ *n* **1 a :** the act or process of alternating or causing to alternate **b :** alternating occurrence **:** SUCCESSION **2 :** DISJUNCTION 2a **3 :** the occurrence of different allomorphs or allophones

alternation of generations : the occurrence of two or more forms differently produced in the life cycle of a plant or animal usu. involving the regular alternation of a sexual with an asexual generation but not infrequently consisting of alternation of a dioecious generation with one or more parthenogenetic generations

¹al·ter·na·tive \ȯl-ˈtər-nət-iv, al-\ *adj* **1 :** offering or expressing a choice <several ~ plans> **2 :** ALTERNATE — **al·ter·na·tive·ly** *adv* — **al·ter·na·tive·ness** *n*

²alternative *n* **1 a :** a proposition or situation offering a choice between two or more things only one of which may be chosen **b :** an opportunity for deciding between two or more courses or propositions **2 :** one of two or more things, courses, or propositions to be chosen *syn* see CHOICE

al·ter·na·tor \ˈȯl-tər-ˌnāt-ər *also* ˈal-\ *n* **:** an electric generator for producing alternating current

al·thaea *or* **al·thea** \al-ˈthē-ə\ *n* [L *althaea* marsh mallow, fr. Gk *althaia*] **1 :** ROSE OF SHARON 2 **2 :** a hollyhock or related plant (genus *Althaea*)

alt·horn \ˈalt-ˌhȯ(ə)rn\ *n* [G, fr. *alt* alto + *horn* horn] **:** an alto saxhorn

al·though *also* **al·tho** \ȯl-ˈt͟hō\ *conj* [ME *although*, fr. *al* all + *though*] **:** in spite of the fact that **:** even though *syn* see THOUGH

al·tim·e·ter \al-ˈtim-ət-ər, ˈal-tə-ˌmēt-ər\ *n* [L *altus* + E *-meter*] **:** an instrument for measuring altitude; *specif* **:** an aneroid barometer designed to register changes in atmospheric pressure accompanying changes in altitude — **al·tim·e·try** \al-ˈtim-ə-trē\ *n*

al·ti·pla·no \ˌal-ti-ˈplän-(ˌ)ō\ *n, pl* **-nos** [AmerSp, fr. L *altus* + *planum* plain] **:** a high plateau or plain **:** TABLELAND

al·ti·tude \ˈal-tə-ˌt(y)üd\ *n* [ME, fr. L *altitudo* height, depth, fr. *altus* high, deep — more at OLD] **1 a :** the angular elevation of a celestial object above the horizon **b :** the vertical elevation of an object above sea level **c :** the perpendicular distance from a vertex of a geometric figure to the opposite side or from a side or face to a parallel side or face; *esp* **:** the altitude on a base **2 :** the highest level of a quality or feeling <the ~ of passion> **3 a :** vertical distance or extent **b :** position at a height **c :** an elevated region **:** EMINENCE — usu. used in pl. *syn* see HEIGHT — **al·ti·tu·di·nal** \ˌal-tə-ˈt(y)üd-nəl, -ᵊn-əl\ *adj* — **al·ti·tu·di·nous** \-ˈt(y)üd-nəs, -ᵊn-əs\ *adj*

altitude sickness *n* **:** the effects (as nosebleed or nausea) of oxygen deficiency in the blood and tissues developed in rarefied air at high altitudes

¹al·to \ˈal-(ˌ)tō\ *n, pl* **altos** [It, lit., high, fr. L *altus*] **1 a :** COUNTERTENOR **b :** CONTRALTO **2 :** the second highest part in 4-part harmony **3 :** a member of a family of instruments having a range lower than that of the treble or soprano

²alto *adj* **:** relating to or having the range or part of an alto

al·to·cu·mu·lus \ˌal-tō-ˈkyü-myə-ləs\ *n, pl* **-li** \-ˌlī, -ˌlē\ [NL, fr. L *altus* + NL *-o-* + *cumulus*] **:** a fleecy cloud formation consisting of large whitish globular cloudlets with shaded portions — see CLOUD illustration

¹al·to·geth·er \ˌȯl-tə-ˈget͟h-ər\ *adv* [ME *altogedere*, fr. *al* all + *togedere* together] **1 :** WHOLLY, THOROUGHLY <an ~ different problem> **2 :** in all **:** all told **3 :** on the whole **:** in the main

²altogether *n* **:** NUDE — used with *the* <posed in the ~>

al·to–re·lie·vo *or* **al·to–ri·lie·vo** \ˌal-(ˌ)tō-ri-ˈlē-(ˌ)vō, ˌäl-(ˌ)tō-rēl-ˈyā-(ˌ)vō\ *n, pl* **alto–relievos** *or* **al·to–ri·lie·vi** \ˌäl-(ˌ)tō-rēl-ˈyā-(ˌ)vē\ [It *alto rilievo*] **1 :** HIGH RELIEF **2 :** a sculpture in high relief

al·to·stra·tus \ˌal-tō-ˈstrāt-əs, -ˈstrat-\ *n, pl* **-ti** \-ˌī\ [NL, fr. L *altus* + NL *-o-* + *stratus*] **:** a cloud formation similar to cirrostratus but darker and at a lower level — see CLOUD illustration

al·tri·cial \al-ˈtrish-əl\ *adj* [L *altric-, altrix* fem. of *altor* one who nourishes, fr. *altus* pp. of *alere* to nourish — more at OLD] **:** having the young hatched in a very immature and helpless condition so as to require care for some time — compare PRECOCIAL

al·tru·ism \ˈal-trü-ˌiz-əm\ *n* [F *altruisme*, fr. *autrui* other people, fr. OF, oblique case form of *autre* other, fr. L *alter*] **:** unselfish regard for or devotion to the welfare of others — **al·tru·ist** \-trü-əst\ *n* — **al·tru·is·tic** \ˌal-trü-ˈis-tik\ *adj* — **al·tru·is·ti·cal·ly** \-ti-k(ə-)lē\ *adv*

al·u·la \ˈal-yə-lə\ *n, pl* **-lae** \-ˌlē, -ˌlī\ [NL, fr. L, dim. of *ala* wing — more at AISLE] : BASTARD WING — **al·u·lar** \-lər\ *adj*

al·um \ˈal-əm\ *n* [ME, fr. MF *alum, alun,* fr. L *alumen* — more at ALE] **1** : a potassium aluminum sulfate $KAl(SO_4)_2.12H_2O$ or an ammonium aluminum sulfate $NH_4Al(SO_4)_2.12H_2O$ used esp. as an emetic and as an astringent and styptic **2** : any of various double salts isomorphous with potash alum **3** : ALUMINUM SULFATE

alu·mi·na \ə-ˈlü-mə-nə\ *n* [NL, fr. L *alumin-, alumen* alum] : aluminum oxide Al_2O_3 occurring native as corundum and in hydrated forms (as in bauxite)

alu·mi·nate \-nət\ *n* : a compound of alumina with a metallic oxide

alu·mi·nif·er·ous \ə-ˌlü-mə-ˈnif-(ə-)rəs\ *adj* : containing alum or aluminum

al·u·min·i·um \ˌal-yə-ˈmin-ē-əm\ *n* [NL, fr. *alumina*] *chiefly Brit* : ALUMINUM

alu·mi·nize \ə-ˈlü-mə-ˌnīz\ *vt* **-nized; -niz·ing** : to treat or coat with aluminum

alu·mi·no·sil·i·cate \ə-ˌlü-mə-nō-ˈsil-ə-ˌkāt, -ˈsil-i-kət\ *n* [L *alumin-, alumen* + *-o-* + ISV *silicate*] : a combined silicate and aluminate

alu·mi·nous \ə-ˈlü-mə-nəs\ *adj* : of, relating to, or containing alum or aluminum

alu·mi·num \ə-ˈlü-mə-nəm\ *n, often attrib* [NL, fr. *alumina*] : a bluish silver-white malleable ductile light trivalent metallic element with good electrical and thermal conductivity, high reflectivity, and resistance to oxidation that is the most abundant metal in the earth's crust occurring always in combination — see ELEMENT table

aluminum sulfate *n* : a colorless salt $Al_2(SO_4)_3$ usu. made by treating bauxite with sulfuric acid and used in making paper, in water purification, and in tanning

alum·na \ə-ˈləm-nə\ *n, pl* **-nae** \-(ˌ)nē\ [L, fem. of *alumnus*] : a girl or woman who has attended or has graduated from a particular school, college, or university

alum·nus \ə-ˈləm-nəs\ *n, pl* **-ni** \-ˌnī\ [L, foster son, pupil, fr. *alere* to nourish — more at OLD] **1** : one who has attended or has graduated from a particular school, college, or university **2** : one who is a former member, employee, contributor, or inmate <former juvenile delinquent, hoodlum, ~ of reform schools — *Newsweek*>

al·um·root \ˈal-əm-ˌrüt, -ˌrůt\ *n* **1** : any of several No. American herbs (genus *Heuchera*) of the saxifrage family; *esp* : one (*H. americana*) with an astringent root **2** : WILD GERANIUM 1

al·u·nite \ˈal-(y)ə-ˌnīt\ *n* [F, fr. *alun* alum] : a mineral $K(AlO)_3(SO_4)_2.3H_2O$ consisting of a hydrous potassium aluminum sulfate and occurring massive or in rhombohedral crystals

al·ve·o·lar \al-ˈvē-ə-lər\ *adj* **1** : of, relating to, resembling, or having alveoli **2** : of, relating to, or constituting the part of the jaws where the teeth arise, the air cells of the lungs, or glands with secretory cells about a central space **3** : articulated with the tip of the tongue touching or near the teethridge — **al·ve·o·lar·ly** *adv*

al·ve·o·late \-lət\ *adj* : pitted like a honeycomb — **al·ve·o·la·tion** \(ˌ)al-ˌvē-ə-ˈlā-shən\ *n*

al·ve·o·lus \al-ˈvē-ə-ləs\ *n, pl* **-li** \-ˌlī, -(ˌ)lē\ [NL, fr. L, dim. of *alveus* cavity, hollow, fr. *alvus* belly; akin to ON *hvannjōli* stalk of angelica, Gk *aulos,* a reed instrument] **1** : a small cavity or pit: as **a** : a socket for a tooth **b** : an air cell of the lungs **c** : an acinus of a compound gland **d** : a cell or compartment of a honeycomb **2** : TEETHRIDGE

alw *abbr* allowance

al·way \ˈȯl-(ˌ)wā\ *adv* [ME] *archaic* : ALWAYS

al·ways \ˈȯl-wēz, -wəz, -(ˌ)wāz\ *adv* [ME *alway, alwayes,* fr. OE *ealne weg,* lit., all the way, fr. *ealne* (acc. of *eall* all) + *weg* (acc.) way — more at WAY] **1** : at all times : INVARIABLY **2** : FOREVER, PERPETUALLY **3** : at any rate : in any event <as a last resort one can ~ work>

Al·yce clover \ˌal-əs-\ *n* [prob. by folk etymology fr. NL *Alysicarpus,* genus name, fr. Gk *halysis* chain + *karpos* fruit] : a low spreading annual Old World legume (*Alysicarpus vaginalis*) used in the southern U.S. as a cover crop and for hay and pasturage

alys·sum \ə-ˈlis-əm\ *n* [NL, fr. Gk *alysson,* plant believed to cure rabies, fr. neut. of *alyssos* curing rabies, fr. *a-* + *lyssa* rabies] **1** : any of a genus (*Alyssum*) of Old World herbs of the mustard family with small yellow racemose flowers **2** : SWEET ALYSSUM

am [ME, fr. OE *eom;* akin to ON *em* am, L *sum,* Gk *eimi,* OE *is* is] *pres 1st sing of* BE

[1]**Am** *abbr* America; American

[2]**Am** *symbol* americium

AM *abbr* **1** airmail **2** Air Medal **3** amplitude modulation **4** [L *anno mundi*] in the year of the world — often printed in small capitals **5** ante meridiem **6** [NL *artium magister*] master of arts

ama \ˈäm-(ˌ)ä\ *n, pl* **amas or ama** [Jap] : a Japanese diver esp. for pearls

AMA *abbr* American Medical Association

amah \ˈäm-(ˌ)ä\ *n* [Pg *ama* wet nurse, fr. ML *amma*] : an Oriental female servant; *esp* : a Chinese nurse

amain \ə-ˈmān\ *adv* **1** : with all one's might <down came the storm, and smote ~ the vessel — H. W. Longfellow> **2 a** : at full speed **b** : in great haste **3** : to a high degree : EXCEEDINGLY <they whom I favour thrive in wealth ~ — John Milton>

Ama·le·kite \ˈam-ə-ˌlek-ˌīt, ə-ˈmal-ə-ˌkīt\ *n* [Heb *ʽAmālēqī,* pl. fr. *ʽAmālēq* Amalek, grandson of Esau] : a member of an ancient nomadic people living south of Canaan

amal·gam \ə-ˈmal-gəm\ *n* [ME *amalgame,* fr. MF, fr. ML *amalgama*] **1** : an alloy of mercury with another metal that is solid or liquid at room temperature according to the proportion of mercury present and is used esp. in making tooth cements **2** : a mixture of different elements

amal·gam·ate \-gə-ˌmāt\ *vt* **-at·ed; -at·ing** : to unite in or as if in an amalgam; *esp* : to merge into a single body ***syn*** see MIX — **amal·gam·ator** \-ˌmāt-ər\ *n*

amal·gam·ation \ə-ˌmal-gə-ˈmā-shən\ *n* **1 a** : the action or process of amalgamating : UNITING **b** : the state of being amalgamated **2** : the result of amalgamating : AMALGAM **3** : CONSOLIDATION, MERGER <~ of two corporations> — **amal·gam·ative** \-ˈmal-gə-ˌmāt-iv\ *adj*

am·a·ni·ta \ˌam-ə-ˈnīt-ə, -ˈnēt-\ *n* [NL, genus name, fr. Gk *amanitai,* pl., a kind of fungus] : any of various mostly poisonous white-spored fungi (genus *Amanita*) with the volva separate from the cap

aman·ta·dine \ə-ˈmant-ə-ˌdēn\ *n* [ISV *adamant*ane ($C_{10}H_{16}$) + am*ine*] : an antiviral drug used esp. to prevent infection (as by an influenza virus) by interfering with virus penetration into host cells

aman·u·en·sis \ə-ˌman-yə-ˈwen(t)-səs\ *n, pl* **-en·ses** \-(ˌ)sēz\ [L, fr. (*servus*) *a manu* slave with secretarial duties] : one employed to write from dictation or to copy manuscript

am·a·ranth \ˈam-ə-ˌran(t)th\ *n* [L *amarantus,* a flower, fr. Gk *amaranton,* fr. neut. of *amarantos* unfading, fr. *a-* + *marainein* to waste away — more at SMART] **1** : a flower that never fades **2** : any of a large genus (*Amaranthus* of the family Amaranthaceae, the amaranth family) of coarse herbs including pigweeds and various forms cultivated for their showy flowers **3** : a dark reddish purple

am·a·ran·thine \ˌam-ə-ˈran(t)-thən, -ˈran-ˌthīn\ *adj* **1 a** : of or relating to an amaranth **b** : that does not fade : UNDYING **2** : of the color amaranth

am·a·ryl·lis \ˌam-ə-ˈril-əs\ *n* [NL, genus name, prob. fr. L, name of a shepherdess in Vergil's *Eclogues*] : any of a genus (*Amaryllis* of the family Amaryllidaceae, the amaryllis family) of bulbous African herbs with showy umbellate flowers; *also* : a plant of any of several related genera (as *Hippeastrum* or *Sprekelia*)

amass \ə-ˈmas\ *vb* [MF *amasser,* fr. OF, fr. *a-* (fr. L *ad-*) + *masser* to gather into a mass, fr. *masse* mass] *vt* **1** : to collect for oneself : ACCUMULATE <~ a great fortune> **2** : to collect into a mass : GATHER <~ the wool into a large ball> ~ *vi* : to come together : ASSEMBLE — **amass·er** *n* — **amass·ment** \-mənt\ *n*

am·a·teur \ˈam-ə-ˌtər, -ət-ər, -ə-ˌt(y)u̇(ə)r, -ə-ˌchu̇(ə)r, -ə-chər\ *n* [F, fr. L *amator* lover, fr. *amatus,* pp. of *amare* to love] **1** : DEVOTEE, ADMIRER **2** : one who engages in a pursuit, study, science, or sport as a pastime rather than as a profession **3** : one lacking in experience and competence in an art or science — **amateur** *adj* — **am·a·teur·ish** \ˌam-ə-ˈtər-ish, -ˈt(y)u̇(ə)r-\ *adj* — **am·a·teur·ish·ly** *adv* — **am·a·teur·ish·ness** *n* — **am·a·teur·ism** \ˈam-ə-ˌtər-ˌiz-əm, -ət-ə-ˌriz-, -ə-ˌt(y)u̇(ə)r-ˌiz-, -ˌchu̇(ə)r-ˌiz-, -chə-ˌriz-\ *n*

syn AMATEUR, DILETTANTE, DABBLER, TYRO *shared meaning element* : one who follows a pursuit without attaining proficiency or professional status ***ant*** professional, expert

Ama·ti \ä-ˈmät-ē,ə-\ *n, pl* **Amatis** : a violin made by a member of the Amati family of Cremona

am·a·tive \ˈam-ət-iv\ *adj* [ML *amativus,* fr. L *amatus*] : disposed or disposing to love : AMOROUS — **am·a·tive·ly** *adv* — **am·a·tive·ness** *n*

am·a·tol \ˈam-ə-ˌtȯl, -ˌtäl, -ˌtōl\ *n* [ISV *am*monium + connective *-a-* + trinitro*tol*uene] : an explosive consisting of ammonium nitrate and trinitrotoluene

am·a·to·ry \ˈam-ə-ˌtōr-ē, -ˌtȯr-\ *adj* : of, relating to, or expressing sexual love

am·au·ro·sis \ˌam-ȯ-ˈrō-səs\ *n, pl* **-ro·ses** \-ˌsēz\ [NL, fr. Gk *amaurōsis,* lit., dimming, fr. *amauroun* to dim, fr. *amauros* dim] : decay of sight occurring without perceptible external change — **am·au·rot·ic** \-ˈrät-ik\ *adj*

[1]**amaze** \ə-ˈmāz\ *vb* **amazed; amaz·ing** [ME *amasen,* fr. OE *āmasian,* fr. *ā-* (perfective prefix) + (assumed) *masian* to confuse — more at ABIDE] *vt* **1** *obs* : BEWILDER, PERPLEX **2** : to fill with wonder : ASTOUND ~ *vi* : to show or cause astonishment <his calmness continues to ~> ***syn*** see SURPRISE — **amaz·ing·ly** \-ˈmā-ziŋ-lē\ *adv*

[2]**amaze** *n* : AMAZEMENT

amaze·ment \ə-ˈmāz-mənt\ *n* **1** *obs* : CONSTERNATION, BEWILDERMENT **2** : the quality or state of being amazed

am·a·zon \ˈam-ə-ˌzän, -ə-zən\ *n* [ME, fr. L, fr. Gk *Amazōn*] **1** *cap* : a member of a race of female warriors repeatedly warring with the Greeks of classical mythology **2** : a tall strong masculine woman : VIRAGO

Am·a·zo·nian \ˌam-ə-ˈzō-nē-ən, -nyən\ *adj* **1 a** : relating to, resembling, or befitting an Amazon **b** *not cap* : MASCULINE, WARLIKE <an *amazonian* woman> **2** : of or relating to the Amazon river or its valley

am·a·zon·ite \ˈam-ə-zə-ˌnīt\ *or* **am·a·zon·stone** \-zən-ˌstōn\ *n* [*Amazon* river] : an apple-green or bluish-green microcline

amb *abbr* ambassador

am·bage \ˈam-bij\ *n, pl* **am·ba·ges** \am-ˈbā-(ˌ)jēz, ˈam-bij-əz\ [back-formation fr. ME *ambages,* fr. MF or L; MF, fr. L, fr. *ambi-* + *agere* to drive — more at AGENT] **1** *archaic* : AMBIGUITY, CIRCUMLOCUTION — usu. used in pl. **2** *pl, archaic* : indirect ways or proceedings — **am·ba·gious** \am-ˈbā-jəs\ *adj*

am·bas·sa·dor \am-ˈbas-əd-ər, əm-, im-\ *n* [ME *ambassadour,* fr. MF *ambassadeur,* of Gmc origin; akin to OHG *ambaht* service] **1** : an official envoy; *esp* : a diplomatic agent of the highest rank accredited to a foreign government or sovereign as the resident representative of his own government or sovereign or appointed for a special and often temporary diplomatic assignment **2 a** : an authorized representative or messenger **b** : an unofficial representative <travelers abroad should be ~*s* of goodwill> — **am·bas·sa·do·ri·al** \-ˌbas-ə-ˈdōr-ē-əl, -ˈdȯr-\ *adj* — **am·bas·sa·dor·ship** \-ˈbas-əd-ər-ˌship\ *n*

ambassador–at–large *n, pl* **ambassadors–at–large** : a minister of the highest rank not accredited to a particular foreign government or sovereign

ə abut	ᵊ kitten	ər further	a back	ā bake	ä cot, cart
au̇ out	ch chin	e less	ē easy	g gift	i trip	ī life
j joke	ŋ sing	ō flow	ȯ flaw	ȯi coin	th thin	th this
ü loot	u̇ foot	y yet	yü few	yu̇ furious	zh vision

am·bas·sa·dress \am-ˈbas-ə-drəs, əm-, im-\ *n* **1 :** a female ambassador **2 :** the wife of an ambassador

am·beer \ˈam-ˌbi(ə)r\ *n* [prob. alter. of *amber;* fr. its color] *chiefly South & Midland* **:** TOBACCO JUICE

1**am·ber** \ˈam-bər\ *n* [ME *ambre,* fr. MF, fr. ML *ambra,* fr. Ar *ʿanbar* ambergris] **1 :** a hard yellowish to brownish translucent fossil resin that takes a fine polish and is used chiefly in making ornamental objects (as beads) **2 :** a variable color averaging a dark orange yellow

2**amber** *adj* **1 :** consisting of amber **2 :** resembling amber; *esp* **:** having the color amber

am·ber·gris \ˈam-bər-ˌgris, -ˌgrēs\ *n* [ME *ambregris,* fr. MF *ambre gris,* fr. *ambre* + *gris* gray — more at GRIZZLE] **:** a waxy substance found floating in or on the shores of tropical waters, believed to originate in the intestines of the sperm whale, and used in perfumery as a fixative

am·ber·jack \-ˌjak\ *n* [fr. its color] **:** any of several carangid fishes (genus *Seriola*); *esp* **:** a large vigorous sport fish (*S. dumerili*) of the western Atlantic

ambi- *prefix* [L *ambi-, amb-* both, around; akin to L *ambo* both, Gk *amphō* both, *amphi* around — more at BY] **:** both <*ambi*valent>

am·bi·dex·ter·i·ty \ˌam-bi-(ˌ)dek-ˈster-ət-ē\ *n* **:** the quality or state of being ambidextrous

am·bi·dex·trous \ˌam-bi-ˈdek-strəs\ *adj* [LL *ambidexter,* fr. L *ambi-* + *dexter*] **1 :** using both hands with equal ease **2 :** unusually skillful **:** VERSATILE **3 :** characterized by duplicity **:** DOUBLE-DEALING — **am·bi·dex·trous·ly** *adv*

am·bi·ence *or* **am·bi·ance** \ˈam-bē-ən(t)s, äⁿ-byäⁿs\ *n* [F *ambiance,* fr. *ambiant* ambient] **:** a surrounding or pervading atmosphere **:** ENVIRONMENT

1**am·bi·ent** \ˈam-bē-ənt\ *adj* [L *ambient-, ambiens,* prp. of *ambire* to go around, fr. *ambi-* + *ire* to go — more at ISSUE] **:** surrounding on all sides **:** ENCOMPASSING

2**ambient** *n* **:** an encompassing atmosphere **:** ENVIRONMENT

am·bi·gu·i·ty \ˌam-bə-ˈgyü-ət-ē\ *n, pl* **-ities 1 a :** the quality or state of being ambiguous in meaning <~ is often a feature of poetry> **b :** an ambiguous word or expression **2 :** UNCERTAINTY <the basic ~ of her self-image>

am·big·u·ous \am-ˈbig-yə-wəs\ *adj* [L *ambiguus,* fr. *ambigere* to wander about, fr. *ambi-* + *agere* to drive — more at AGENT] **1 a :** doubtful or uncertain esp. from obscurity or indistinctness <eyes of an ~ color> **b :** INEXPLICABLE **2 :** capable of being understood in two or more possible senses *syn* see OBSCURE *ant* explicit — **am·big·u·ous·ly** *adv* — **am·big·u·ous·ness** *n*

am·bi·sex·trous \ˌam-bi-ˈsek-strəs\ *adj* [alter. (influenced by *ambidextrous*) of *ambisexual* (common to both sexes)] **1 :** not distinguishable as male or female <~ clothing> **2 :** including males and females <an ~ party>

am·bit \ˈam-bət\ *n* [ME, fr. L *ambitus,* fr. *ambitus,* pp. of *ambire*] **1 :** CIRCUIT, COMPASS **2 :** the bounds or limits of a place or district **3 :** a sphere of action, expression, or influence **:** SCOPE

1**am·bi·tion** \am-ˈbish-ən\ *n* [ME, fr. MF or L; MF, fr. L *ambition-ambitio,* lit., going around, fr. *ambitus,* pp.] **1 a :** an ardent desire for rank, fame, or power **b :** desire to achieve a particular end **2 :** the object of ambition **3 :** a desire for activity or exertion <felt sick and had no ~> — **am·bi·tion·less** \-ləs\ *adj*

syn AMBITION, ASPIRATION, PRETENSION *shared meaning element* **:** strong desire for advancement or success

2**ambition** *vt* **:** to have as one's ambition **:** DESIRE

am·bi·tious \am-ˈbish-əs\ *adj* **1 a :** having or controlled by ambition **b :** having a desire to achieve a particular goal **:** ASPIRING **2 :** resulting from, characterized by, or showing ambition — **am·bi·tious·ly** *adv* — **am·bi·tious·ness** *n*

am·biv·a·lence \am-ˈbiv-ə-lən(t)s\ *n* [ISV] **1 :** simultaneous attraction toward and repulsion from an object, person, or action **2 a :** continual fluctuation (as between one thing and its opposite) **b :** uncertainty as to which approach to follow — **am·biv·a·lent** \-lənt\ *adj* — **am·biv·a·lent·ly** *adv*

am·bi·ver·sion \ˌam-bi-ˈvər-zhən, -shən\ *n* [*ambi-* + *-version* (as in *introversion*)] **:** the personality configuration of an ambivert — **am·bi·ver·sive** \-ˈvər-siv, -ziv\ *adj*

am·bi·vert \ˈam-bi-ˌvərt\ *n* [*ambi-* + *-vert* (as in *introvert*)] **:** a person having characteristics of both extrovert and introvert

1**am·ble** \ˈam-bəl\ *vi* **am·bled; am·bling** \-b(ə-)liŋ\ [ME *amblen,* fr. MF *ambler,* fr. L *ambulare* to walk] **:** to go at or as if at an amble **:** SAUNTER — **am·bler** \-b(ə-)lər\ *n*

2**amble** *n* **1 a :** an easy gait of a horse in which the legs on the same side of the body move together **b :** 7RACK b **2 :** an easy gait **3 :** a leisurely walk

am·blyg·o·nite \am-ˈblig-ə-ˌnīt\ *n* [G *amblygonit,* fr. Gk *amblygōnios* obtuse-angled, fr. *amblys* blunt, dull + *gōnia* angle; akin to L *molere* to grind — more at MEAL, -GON] **:** a mineral (Li,Na)-$AlPO_4$(F,OH) consisting of basic lithium aluminum phosphate commonly containing sodium and fluorine and occurring in white cleavable masses

am·bly·opia \ˌam-blē-ˈō-pē-ə\ *n* [NL, fr. Gk *amblyōpia,* fr. *amblys* + *-ōpia* -opia] **:** dimness of sight without apparent change in the eye structures associated esp. with toxic effects or dietary deficiencies — **am·bly·opic** \-ˈōpik, -ˈäp-ik\ *adj*

am·bo·cep·tor \ˈam-bō-ˌsep-tər\ *n* [ISV *ambi-* + *receptor*] **:** the lytic antibody used in complement-fixation tests

Am·boi·nese \ˌam-ˌbȯi-ˈnēz, -ˈnēs, am-ˈbȯi-ˌ\ *or* **Am·bo·nese** \ˌam-bə-ˈnēz, -ˈnēs\ *n, pl* **Amboinese** *or* **Ambonese** [*Amboina* (*Ambon*) + *-ese*] **1 :** a native or inhabitant of Ambon **2 :** the language of the people of Ambon

am·boy·na *or* **am·boi·na** \am-ˈbȯi-nə\ *n* [*Amboina,* Moluccas, Indonesia] **:** a mottled curly-grained wood of a leguminous tree (*Pterocarpus indicus*) of southeastern Asia

am·bro·sia \am-ˈbrō-zh(ē-)ə\ *n* [L, fr. Gk, lit., immortality, fr. *ambrotos* immortal, fr. *a-* + *-mbrotos* (akin to *brotos* mortal) — more at MURDER] **1 a :** the food of the Greek and Roman gods **b :** the ointment or perfume of the gods **2 :** something extremely pleasing to taste or smell **3 :** a dessert made of oranges and shredded coconut — **am·bro·sial** \-zh(ē-)əl\ *adj* — **am·bro·sial·ly** \-ē\ *adv*

am·bro·type \ˈam-brə-ˌtīp\ *n* [Gk *ambro*tos + E *type*] **:** a positive picture made of a photographic negative on glass backed by a dark surface

am·bry \ˈam-brē; ˈäm-rē, ˈȯm-\ *n, pl* **ambries** [ME *armarie,* fr. OF, fr. L *armarium,* fr. *arma* weapons — more at ARM] **1 :** a recess in a church wall (as for holding sacramental vessels) **2** *dial chiefly Brit* **:** PANTRY

ambs·ace \ˈām-ˌzās\ *n* [ME *ambes as,* fr. OF, fr. *ambes* both + *as* aces] *archaic* **:** the lowest throw at dice; *also* **:** something worthless or unlucky

am·bu·la·crum \ˌam-byə-ˈlak-rəm, -ˈlāk-\ *n, pl* **-cra** \-rə\ [NL, fr. L, alley, fr. *ambulare* to walk] **:** one of the radial areas of echinoderms along which run the principal nerves, blood vessels, and elements of the water-vascular system — **am·bu·la·cral** \-rəl\ *adj*

am·bu·lance \ˈam-byə-lən(t)s\ *n* [F, field hospital, fr. *ambulant* itinerant, fr. L *ambulant-, ambulans,* prp. of *ambulare*] **:** a vehicle equipped for transporting the injured or sick

ambulance chaser *n* **:** a lawyer or lawyer's agent who incites accident victims to sue for damages — **ambulance chasing** *n*

am·bu·lant \ˈam-byə-lənt\ *adj* **:** moving about **:** AMBULATORY

am·bu·late \-ˌlāt\ *vi* **-lat·ed; -lat·ing** [L *ambulatus,* pp. of *ambulare*] **:** to move from place to place **:** WALK — **am·bu·la·tion** \ˌam-byə-ˈlā-shən\ *n*

1**am·bu·la·to·ry** \ˈam-byə-lə-ˌtōr-ē, -ˌtȯr-\ *adj* **1 :** of, relating to, or adapted to walking; *also* **:** occurring while walking **2 :** moving from place to place **:** ITINERANT **3 :** capable of being altered <a will is ~ until the testator's death> **4 a :** able to walk about and not bedridden **b :** involving an individual who is able to walk about <~ medical care> — **am·bu·la·to·ri·ly** \ˌam-byə-lə-ˈtōr-ə-lē, -ˈtȯr-\ *adv*

2**ambulatory** *n, pl* **-ries :** a sheltered place (as in a cloister or church) for walking

am·bus·cade \ˈam-bə-ˌskād, ˌam-bə-ˈ\ *n* [MF *embuscade,* modif. of OIt *imboscata,* fr. *imboscare* to place in ambush, fr. *in* (fr. L) + *bosco* forest, perh. of Gmc origin; akin to OHG *busc* forest — more at IN, BUSH] **:** AMBUSH — **ambuscade** *vb* — **am·bus·cad·er** *n*

1**am·bush** \ˈam-ˌbu̇sh\ *vb* [ME *embushen,* fr. OF *embuschier,* fr. *en* in (fr. L *in*) + *busche* stick of firewood] *vt* **1 :** to station in ambush **2 :** to attack from an ambush **:** WAYLAY ~ *vi* **:** to lie in wait **:** LURK *syn* see SURPRISE — **am·bush·er** *n* — **am·bush·ment** \-mənt\ *n*

2**ambush** *n* **1 :** a trap in which concealed persons lie in wait to attack by surprise **2 :** the persons stationed in ambush; *also* **:** their concealed position

amdt *abbr* amendment

ameba, ameban, amebic, ameboid *var of* AMOEBA, AMOEBAN, AMOEBIC, AMOEBOID

am·e·bi·a·sis \ˌam-i-ˈbī-ə-səs\ *n* **:** infection with or disease caused by amoebas

ame·bic dysentery \ə-ˌmē-bik-\ *n* **:** acute intestinal amebiasis of man caused by an amoeba (*Endamoeba histolytica*) and marked by dysentery, griping pain, and erosion of the intestinal wall

amebocyte *var of* AMOEBOCYTE

âme dam·née \äm-dä-nā\ *n, pl* **âmes damnées** \äm-dä-nā(z)\ [F, lit., damned soul] **:** a willing tool of another person

ameer *var of* EMIR

ame·lio·rate \ə-ˈmēl-yə-ˌrāt, -ˈmē-lē-ə-\ *vb* **-rat·ed; -rat·ing** [alter. of *meliorate*] *vt* **:** to make better or more tolerable ~ *vi* **:** to grow better *syn* see IMPROVE *ant* worsen, deteriorate — **ame·lio·ra·tion** \-ˌmēl-yə-ˈrā-shən, -ˌmē-lē-ə-\ *n* — **ame·lio·ra·tive** \-ˈmēl-yə-ˌrāt-iv, -ˈmē-lē-ə-\ *adj* — **ame·lio·ra·tor** \-ˌrāt-ər\ *n* — **ame·lio·ra·to·ry** \-rə-ˌtōr-ē, -ˌtȯr-\ *adj*

amen \(ˈ)ā-ˈmen, (ˈ)ä-; ˈä- *when sung*\ *interj* [ME, fr. OE, fr. LL, fr. Gk *amēn,* fr. Heb *āmēn*] — used to express solemn ratification (as of an expression of faith) or hearty approval (as of an assertion)

ame·na·ble \ə-ˈmē-nə-bəl, -ˈmen-ə-\ *adj* [prob. fr. (assumed) AF, fr. MF *amener* to lead up, fr. OF, fr. *a-* (fr. L *ad-*) + *mener* to lead, fr. L *minare* to drive, fr. *minari* to threaten — more at MOUNT] **1 :** liable to be brought to account **:** ANSWERABLE <citizens ~ to the law> **2 a :** capable of submission (as to judgment or test) <the data is ~ to analysis> **b :** readily brought to yield or submit **:** TRACTABLE <a child ~ to discipline> *syn* **1** see RESPONSIBLE **2** see OBEDIENT *ant* recalcitrant, refractory — **ame·na·bil·i·ty** \-ˌmē-nə-ˈbil-ət-ē, -ˌmen-ə-\ *n* — **ame·na·bly** \-ˈmē-nə-blē, -ˈmen-ə-\ *adv*

amen corner \ˌā-ˌmen-\ *n* **:** a conspicuous corner in a church occupied by fervent worshipers

amend \ə-ˈmend\ *vb* [ME *amenden,* fr. OF *amender,* modif. of L *emendare,* fr. *e, ex* out + *menda* fault; akin to L *mendax* lying, *mendicus* beggar, Skt *mindā* physical defect] *vt* **1 :** to put right; *specif* **:** to make emendations in (as a text) **2 a :** to change or modify for the better **:** IMPROVE <~ the situation> **b :** to alter esp. in phraseology; *specif* **:** to alter formally by modification, deletion, or addition <~ the constitution> ~ *vi* **:** to reform oneself *syn* see CORRECT *ant* debase, impair — **amend·able** \-ˈmen-də-bəl\ *adj* — **amend·er** *n*

amen·da·to·ry \ə-ˈmen-də-ˌtōr-ē, -ˌtȯr-\ *adj* [*amend* + *-atory* (as in *emendatory*)] **:** CORRECTIVE

amend·ment \ə-ˈmen(d)-mənt\ *n* **1 :** the act of amending esp. for the better **:** CORRECTION **2 :** a substance that aids plant growth indirectly by improving the condition of the soil **3 a :** the process of amending by parliamentary or constitutional procedure **b :** an alteration proposed or effected by this process <the 18th ~>

amends \ə-ˈmen(d)z\ *n pl but sing or pl in constr* [ME *amendes,* fr. OF, pl. of *amende* reparation, fr. *amender*] **:** compensation for a loss or injury **:** RECOMPENSE

ame·ni·ty \ə-ˈmen-ət-ē, -ˈmē-nət-\ *n, pl* **-ties** [ME *amenite,* fr. L *amoenitat-, amoenitas,* fr. *amoenus* pleasant] **1 a :** the quality of being pleasant or agreeable **b** (1) **:** the attractiveness and value of real estate or of a residential structure (2) **:** a feature conducive to such attractiveness and value **2 :** something that conduces to material comfort or convenience **3 :** something (as a conventional social gesture) that conduces to smoothness or pleasantness of social intercourse

amen·or·rhea \ā-ˌmen-ə-ˈrē-ə, ˌäm-ˌen-\ *n* [NL, fr. *a-* + Gk *mēn* month + NL *-o-* + *-rrhea* — more at MOON] **:** abnormal absence or suppression of the menstrual discharge — **amen·or·rhe·ic** \-ˈrē-ik\ *adj*

ament \ˈam-ənt, ˈā-mənt\ *n* [NL *amentum,* fr. L, thong, strap] **:** an indeterminate spicate inflorescence (as in the willow) bearing scaly bracts and apetalous unisexual flowers — **amen·ta·ceous** \ˌam-ən-ˈtā-shəs, ˌā-mən-\ *adj* — **amen·tif·er·ous** \-ˈtif-(ə-)rəs\ *adj*

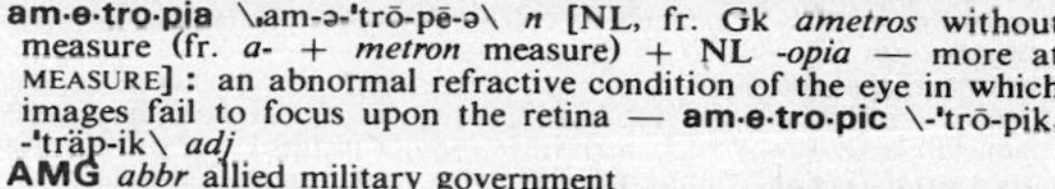

staminate ament

amen·tia \(ˈ)ā-ˈmen-ch(ē-)ə, (ˈ)ä-\ *n* [NL, fr. L, madness, fr. *ament-, amens* mad, fr. *a-* (fr. *ab-*) + *ment-, mens* mind — more at MIND] **:** mental deficiency; *specif* **:** a condition of lack of development of intellectual capacity

Amer *abbr* America; American

Am·er·asian \ˌam-ə-ˈrā-zhən, -shən\ *n* [*American* + *Asian*] **:** a person of mixed American and Asian descent; *esp* **:** one whose mother is Asian and whose father is American

amerce \ə-ˈmərs\ *vt* **amerced; amerc·ing** [ME *amercien,* fr. AF *amercier,* fr. OF *a merci* at (one's) mercy] **:** to punish by a fine whose amount is fixed by the court; *broadly* **:** PUNISH — **amerce·ment** \-ˈmər-smənt\ *n* — **amer·cia·ble** \-ˈmər-sē-ə-bəl, -ˈmər-shə-bəl\ *adj*

[1]**Amer·i·can** \ə-ˈmer-ə-kən\ *n* **1 :** an Indian of No. America or So. America **2 :** a native or inhabitant of No. America or So. America **3 :** a citizen of the U.S.

[2]**American** *adj* **1 :** of or relating to America **2 :** of or relating to the U.S. or its possessions or original territory **3 :** of or relating to the division of mankind that comprises the Indians of No. America and So. America — **Amer·i·can·ness** \-kən-nəs\ *n*

Amer·i·ca·na \ə-ˌmer-ə-ˈkan-ə, -ˈkän-, -ˈkā-nə\ *n pl* **:** materials concerning or characteristic of America, its civilization, or its culture; *also* **:** a collection of such materials

American chameleon *n* **:** a lizard (*Anolis carolinensis*) of the southeastern U.S.

American cheese *n* **:** a process cheese made from American cheddar cheese

American dream *n* **:** an American social ideal that stresses egalitarianism and esp. material prosperity

American elm *n* **:** a large elm (*Ulmus americana*) with gradually spreading branches and pendulous branchlets that is common in eastern No. America

American English *n* **:** the native language of most inhabitants of the U.S. — used esp. with the implication that it is clearly distinguishable from British English yet not so divergent as to be a separate language

American foxhound *n* **:** any of an American breed of foxhounds that are smaller than the English foxhound but with longer ears and that have a dense hard glossy coat usu. of black, tan, and white, straight forelegs, and powerful hindquarters

American Indian *n* **:** a member of any of the aboriginal peoples of the western hemisphere except usu. the Eskimos constituting one of the divisions of the Mongoloid stock

American Indian Day *n* **:** the fourth Friday in September observed in honor of the American Indian

Amer·i·can·ism \ə-ˈmer-ə-kə-ˌniz-əm\ *n* **1 :** a characteristic feature of American English esp. as contrasted with British English **2 :** attachment or allegiance to the traditions, interests, or ideals of the U.S. **3 a :** a custom or trait peculiar to America **b :** the political principles and practices essential to American national culture

Amer·i·can·ist \-kə-nəst\ *n* **1 :** a specialist in the languages or cultures of the aboriginal inhabitants of America **2 :** a specialist in American culture or history

American ivy *n* **:** VIRGINIA CREEPER

Amer·i·can·iza·tion \ə-ˌmer-ə-kə-nə-ˈzā-shən\ *n* **1 :** the act or process of Americanizing **2 :** instruction of foreigners (as immigrants) in English and in U.S. history, government, and culture

Amer·i·can·ize \ə-ˈmer-ə-kə-ˌnīz\ *vb* **-ized; iz·ing** *vt* **:** to cause to acquire or conform to American characteristics ~ *vi* **:** to acquire or conform to American traits

American plan *n* **:** a hotel plan whereby the daily rates cover the costs of the room and meals — compare EUROPEAN PLAN

American saddle horse *n* **:** a 3-gaited or 5-gaited saddle horse of a breed developed chiefly in Kentucky from Thoroughbreds and native stock

American Standard Version *n* **:** an American version of the Bible based on the Revised Version and published in 1901 — called also *American Revised Version*

American trotter *n* **:** STANDARDBRED

American water spaniel *n* **:** a medium-sized spaniel of American origin with a thick curly chocolate or liver-colored coat

am·er·i·ci·um \ˌam-ə-ˈris(h)-ē-əm\ *n* [NL, fr. *America* + NL *-ium*] **:** a radioactive metallic element produced by bombardment of uranium with high-energy helium nuclei — see ELEMENT table

Amerind *abbr* American Indian

Am·er·in·di·an \ˌam-ə-ˈrin-dē-ən\ *n* [*American* + *Indian*] **:** AMERICAN INDIAN — **Am·er·ind** \ˈam-ə-ˌrind\ *n* — **Amerindian** *adj* — **Am·er·in·dic** \ˌam-ə-ˈrin-dik\ *adj*

âmes damnées *pl of* ÂME DAMNÉE

am·e·thop·ter·in \ˌam-ə-ˈthäp-tə-rən\ *n* [*amin-* + *meth-* + *pteroic* acid + *-in*] **:** METHOTREXATE

am·e·thyst \ˈam-ə-thəst, -(ˌ)thist\ *n* [ME *amatiste,* fr. OF & L; OF, fr. L *amethystus,* fr. Gk *amethystos,* lit., remedy against drunkenness, fr. *a-* + *methyein* to be drunk, fr. *methy* wine — more at MEAD] **1 a :** a clear purple or bluish violet variety of crystallized quartz that is much used as a jeweler's stone **b :** a deep purple variety of corundum **2 :** a variable color averaging a moderate purple — **am·e·thys·tine** \ˌam-ə-ˈthis-tən\ *adj*

am·e·tro·pia \ˌam-ə-ˈtrō-pē-ə\ *n* [NL, fr. Gk *ametros* without measure (fr. *a-* + *metron* measure) + NL *-opia* — more at MEASURE] **:** an abnormal refractive condition of the eye in which images fail to focus upon the retina — **am·e·tro·pic** \-ˈtrō-pik, -ˈträp-ik\ *adj*

AMG *abbr* allied military government

Am·har·ic \am-ˈhar-ik\ *n* **:** the Semitic language that is the official language of Ethiopia — **Amharic** *adj*

ami·a·ble \ˈā-mē-ə-bəl\ *adj* [ME, fr. MF, fr. LL *amicabilis* friendly, fr. L *amicus* friend; akin to L *amare* to love] **1** *archaic* **:** PLEASING, ADMIRABLE **2 a :** generally agreeable <an ~ musical comedy> **b :** having a friendly, sociable, and congenial disposition — **ami·a·bil·i·ty** \ˌā-mē-ə-ˈbil-ət-ē\ *n* — **ami·a·ble·ness** \ˈā-mē-ə-bəl-nəs\ *n* — **ami·a·bly** \-blē\ *adv*

syn AMIABLE, GOOD-NATURED, OBLIGING, COMPLAISANT *shared meaning element* **:** having or showing a will to please ***ant*** unamiable

am·i·an·thus \ˌam-ē-ˈan(t)-thəs\ *or* **am·i·an·tus** \-ˈant-əs\ *n* [L *amiantus,* fr. Gk *amiantos,* fr. *amiantos* unpolluted, fr. *a-* + *miainein* to pollute] **:** fine silky asbestos

am·i·ca·ble \ˈam-i-kə-bəl\ *adj* [ME, fr. LL *amicabilis*] **:** characterized by friendly goodwill **:** PEACEABLE — **am·i·ca·bil·i·ty** \ˌam-i-kə-ˈbil-ət-ē\ *n* — **am·i·ca·ble·ness** \ˈam-i-kə-bəl-nəs\ *n* — **am·i·ca·bly** \-blē\ *adv*

syn AMICABLE, NEIGHBORLY, FRIENDLY *shared meaning element* **:** exhibiting goodwill and an absence of antagonism ***ant*** antagonistic

am·ice \ˈam-əs\ *n* [ME *amis,* prob. fr. MF, pl. of *amit,* fr. ML *amictus,* fr. L, cloak, fr. *amictus,* pp. of *amicire* to wrap around, fr. *am-, amb-* around + *jacere* to throw — more at AMBI-, JET] **:** a liturgical vestment made of an oblong piece of cloth usu. of white linen and worn about the neck and shoulders and partly under the alb — see VESTMENT illustration

ami·cus cu·ri·ae \ə-ˌmē-kə-ˈsk(y)u̇r-ē-ˌī\ *n, pl* **ami·ci curiae** \-ˌmē-(ˌ)kē-ˈk(y)u̇r-\ [NL, lit., friend of the court] **:** one (as a professional person or organization) that is not a party to a particular litigation but that is permitted by the court to advise it in respect to some matter of law that directly affects the case in question

amid \ə-ˈmid\ *or* **amidst** \-ˈmidst, -ˈmitst\ *prep* [*amid* fr. ME *amidde,* fr. OE *onmiddan,* fr. *on* + *middan,* dat. of *midde* mid; *amidst* fr. ME *amiddes,* fr. *amidde* + *-es* -s] **1 :** in or into the middle of **:** AMONG **2 :** DURING

amid- *or* **amido-** *comb form* [ISV, fr. *amide*] **1 :** containing the group NH_2 characteristic of amides united to a radical of acid character <*amido*sulfuric> **2 :** AMIN- <*amido*phenol>

am·i·dase \ˈam-ə-ˌdās, -ˌdāz\ *n* [ISV *amide* + *-ase*] **:** an enzyme that hydrolyzes acid amides usu. with the liberation of ammonia

am·ide \ˈam-ˌīd, -əd\ *n* [ISV, fr. NL *ammonia*] **:** a compound resulting from replacement of an atom of hydrogen in ammonia by an element or radical or of one or more atoms of hydrogen in ammonia by univalent acid radicals — compare IMIDE — **amid·ic** \ə-ˈmid-ik, a-\ *adj*

ami·do \ə-ˈmēd-(ˌ)ō, ˈam-ə-ˌdō\ *adj* [*amid-*] **1 :** relating to or containing the group NH_2 or a substituted group NHR or NR_2 united to a radical of acid character — compare AMINO **2 :** AMINO

am·i·dol \ˈam-ə-ˌdȯl, -ˌdōl\ *n* [G, fr. *Amidol,* a trademark] **:** a colorless crystalline salt $C_6H_8N_2O.2HCl$ used chiefly as a photographic developer

amid·ships \ə-ˈmid-ˌships\ *adv* **1 :** in or toward the part of a ship midway between the bow and the stern **2 :** in or toward the middle

ami·go \ə-ˈmē-(ˌ)gō, ä-\ *n, pl* **-gos** [Sp, fr. L *amicus* — more at AMIABLE] **:** FRIEND

amin- *or* **amino-** *comb form* [ISV, fr. *amine*] **:** containing the group NH_2 united to a radical other than an acid radical <*amino*benzoic acid>

amine \ə-ˈmēn, ˈam-ˌēn\ *n* [ISV, fr. NL *ammonia*] **1 :** any of various basic compounds derived from ammonia by replacement of hydrogen by one or more univalent hydrocarbon radicals **2 :** a compound containing one or more halogen atoms attached to nitrogen — **ami·nic** \ə-ˈmē-nik, a-, -ˈmin-ik\ *adj*

ami·no \ə-ˈmē-(ˌ)nō\ *adj* [*amin-*] **:** relating to or containing the group NH_2 or a substituted group NHR or NR_2 united to a radical other than an acid radical — compare AMIDO

amino acid *n* **:** an amphoteric organic acid containing the amino group NH_2; *esp* **:** any of the alpha-amino acids that are the chief components of proteins and are synthesized by living cells or are obtained as essential components of the diet

ami·no·ac·id·uria \ə-ˌmē-nō-ˌas-ə-ˈd(y)u̇r-ē-ə\ *n* [NL] **:** a condition in which one or more amino acids are excreted in excessive amounts

ami·no·ben·zo·ic acid \ə-ˌmē-nō-ben-ˌzō-ik-\ *n* [ISV] **:** any of three crystalline derivatives $C_7H_7NO_2$ of benzoic acid of which the yellowish para-substituted acid is a growth factor of the vitamin B complex and of folic acids

amino nitrogen *n* **:** nitrogen occurring as a constituent of the amino group

am·i·noph·yl·line \ˌam-ə-ˈnäf-ə-lən\ *n* [*amin-* + theo*phylline*] **:** a compound of theophylline and the diamine of ethylene that has various medical and veterinary uses

ami·no·py·rine \ə-ˌmē-nō-ˈpī(ə)r-ˌēn\ *n* [ISV, fr. *amin-* + anti*pyrine*] **:** a white crystalline compound $C_{13}H_{17}N_3O$ that is used to relieve fever and pain and that can cause a dangerous blood disorder in some users

ami·no·sal·i·cyl·ic acid \ə-ˈmē-nō-ˌsal-ə-ˌsil-ik-\ *n* **:** any of four isomeric derivatives $C_7H_7O_3N$ of salicylic acid that have a single amino group; *esp* **:** PARA-AMINOSALICYLIC ACID

ami·no·trans·fer·ase \-ˈtran(t)s-fə-ˌrās, -ˌrāz\ *n* **:** TRANSAMINASE

ə abut	ᵊ kitten	ər further	a back	ā bake	ä cot, cart
au̇ out	ch chin	e less	ē easy	g gift	i trip	ī life
j joke	ŋ sing	ō flow	ȯ flaw	ȯi coin	th thin	t͟h this
ü loot	u̇ foot	y yet	yü few	yu̇ furious	zh vision

ami·no·tri·azole \ə-ˌmē-nō-ˈtrī-ə-ˌzōl\ *n* [*amin-* + *triazole*] : AMITROLE

amir *var of* EMIR

Amish \ˈäm-ish, ˈam-, ˈām-\ *adj* [prob. fr. G *amisch,* fr. Jacob *Amman* or *Amen fl* 1693 Swiss Mennonite bishop] : of or relating to a strict sect of Mennonite followers of Amman that settled in America chiefly in the 18th century — **Amish** *n*

¹amiss \ə-ˈmis\ *adv* **1 a** : in a mistaken way : WRONGLY <if you think he is guilty, you judge ~> **b** : ASTRAY <something had gone ~> **2** : in a faulty way : IMPERFECTLY

²amiss *adj* **1** : not being in accordance with right order **2** : FAULTY, IMPERFECT **3** : out of place in given circumstances — usu. used with a negative <a few pertinent remarks may not be ~ here>

ami·to·sis \ˌā-mī-ˈtō-səs\ *n* [NL, fr. ²*a-* + *mitosis*] : cell division by simple cleavage of the nucleus and division of the cytoplasm without spindle formation or appearance of chromosomes — **ami·tot·ic** \-ˈtät-ik\ *adj* — **ami·tot·i·cal·ly** \-i-k(ə-)lē\ *adv*

am·i·trip·ty·line \ˌam-ə-ˈtrip-tə-ˌlēn\ *n* [origin unknown] : an antidepressant drug $C_{20}H_{23}N$

am·i·trole \ˈam-ə-ˌtrōl\ *n* [*amin-* + *triazole*] : a systemic herbicide $C_2H_4N_4$ used in areas other than food croplands

am·i·ty \ˈam-ət-ē\ *n, pl* **-ties** [ME *amite,* fr. MF *amité,* fr. ML *amicitas,* fr. L *amicus* friend — more at AMIABLE] : FRIENDSHIP; *esp* : friendly relations between nations

am·me·ter \ˈam-ˌēt-ər\ *n* [*ampere* + *-meter*] : an instrument for measuring electric current in amperes

am·mine \ˈam-ˌēn, a-ˈmēn\ *n* [ISV *ammonia* + *-ine*] **1** : a molecule of ammonia as it exists in a coordination complex <hex-*ammine*-cobalt chloride $CoN_6H_{18}Cl_3$> **2** : an ammino compound

am·mi·no \ˈam-ə-ˌnō, a-ˈmē-(ˌ)nō\ *adj* [ISV *ammino-,* fr. *ammine*] : of, relating to, or being an ammine

am·mo \ˈam-(ˌ)ō\ *n* [by shortening & alter.] : AMMUNITION

am·mo·nia \ə-ˈmō-nyə\ *n* [NL, fr. L *sal ammoniacus* sal ammoniac, lit., salt of Ammon, fr. Gk *ammōniakos* of Ammon, fr. *Ammōn* Ammon, Amen, an Egyptian god near one of whose temples it was prepared] **1** : a pungent colorless gaseous alkaline compound of nitrogen and hydrogen NH_3 that is very soluble in water and can easily be condensed to a liquid by cold and pressure **2** : AMMONIA WATER

am·mo·ni·ac \ə-ˈmō-nē-ˌak\ *n* [ME & L; ME, fr. L *ammoniacum,* fr. Gk *ammōniakon,* fr. neut. of *ammōniakos* of Ammon] : the aromatic gum resin of a Persian herb (*Dorema ammoniacum*) of the carrot family used as an expectorant and stimulant and in plasters

am·mo·ni·a·cal \ˌam-ə-ˈnī-ə-kəl\ *or* **am·mo·ni·ac** \ə-ˈmō-nē-ˌak\ *adj* : of, relating to, containing, or having the properties of ammonia

am·mo·ni·ate \ə-ˈmō-nē-ˌāt\ *vt* **-at·ed; -at·ing** **1** : to combine or impregnate with ammonia or an ammonium compound **2** : to subject to ammonification — **am·mo·ni·a·tion** \-ˌmō-nē-ˈā-shən\ *n*

ammonia water *n* : a water solution of ammonia

am·mo·ni·fi·ca·tion \ə-ˌmän-ə-fə-ˈkā-shən, -ˌmō-nə-\ *n* **1** : the act or process of ammoniating **2** : decomposition with production of ammonia or ammonium compounds esp. by the action of bacteria on nitrogenous organic matter — **am·mo·ni·fi·er** \-ˈmän-ə-ˌfī(-ə)r, -ˈmō-nə-\ *n* — **am·mo·ni·fy** \-ˌfī\ *vb*

am·mo·nite \ˈam-ə-ˌnīt\ *n* [NL *ammonites,* fr. L *cornu Ammonis,* lit., horn of Ammon] : any of numerous flat spiral fossil shells of cephalopods (order Ammonoidea) esp. abundant in the Mesozoic age — **am·mo·nit·ic** \ˌam-ə-ˈnit-ik\ *adj*

Am·mon·ite \ˈam-ə-ˌnīt\ *n* [LL *Ammonites,* fr. Heb *ʽAmmōn,* Ammon (son of Lot), descendant of Ammon] : a member of a Semitic people who in Old Testament times lived east of the Jordan between the Jabbok and the Arnon — **Ammonite** *adj*

am·mo·ni·um \ə-ˈmō-nē-əm\ *n* [NL, fr. *ammonia*] : an ion NH_4^+ or radical NH_4 derived from ammonia by combination with a hydrogen ion or atom and known in compounds (as salts) that resemble in properties the compounds of the alkali metals and in organic compounds (as quaternary ammonium compounds)

ammonium carbonate *n* : a carbonate of ammonium; *specif* : the commercial mixture of the bicarbonate and carbamate used esp. in smelling salts

ammonium chloride *n* : a white crystalline volatile salt NH_4Cl that is used in dry cells and as an expectorant — called also *sal ammoniac*

ammonium cyanate *n* : an inorganic white crystalline salt N_2H_4OC that can be converted into organic urea

ammonium hydroxide *n* : a weakly basic compound NH_5O that is formed when ammonia dissolves in water and that exists only in solution

ammonium nitrate *n* : a colorless crystalline salt $N_2H_4O_3$ used in explosives and fertilizers

ammonium phosphate *n* : a phosphate of ammonium; *esp* : a white crystalline compound $N_2H_9PO_4$ used esp. as a fertilizer and as a fire retardant

ammonium sulfate *n* : a colorless crystalline salt $N_2H_8SO_4$ used chiefly as a fertilizer

am·mo·noid \ˈam-ə-ˌnȯid\ *n* : AMMONITE

am·mu·ni·tion \ˌam-yə-ˈnish-ən\ *n* [obs. F *amunition,* fr. MF, alter. of *munition*] **1 a** : the projectiles with their fuzes, propelling charges, and primers fired from guns **b** : explosive military items (as grenades or bombs) **2** : material for use in attacking or defending a position <derived their critical ~ from . . . Aristotelian doctrines — R. A. Hall *b*1911>

Amn *abbr* airman

am·ne·sia \am-ˈnē-zhə\ *n* [NL, fr. Gk *amnēsia* forgetfulness, prob. alter. of *amnēstia*] **1** : loss of memory due usu. to brain injury, shock, fatigue, repression, or illness **2** : a gap in one's memory — **am·ne·si·ac** \-z(h)ē-ˌak\ *or* **am·ne·sic** \-zik, -sik\ *adj or n* — **am·nes·tic** \-ˈnes-tik\ *adj*

am·nes·ty \ˈam-nə-stē\ *n, pl* **-ties** [Gk *amnēstia* forgetfulness, fr. *amnēstos* forgotten, fr. *a-* + *mnasthai* to remember — more at MIND] : the act of an authority (as a government) by which pardon is granted to a large group of individuals — **amnesty** *vt*

am·nio·cen·te·sis \ˌam-nē-ō-(ˌ)sen-ˈtē-səs\ *n* [NL, fr. *amnion* + *centesis* puncture, fr. Gk *kentesis,* fr. *kentein* to prick — more at CENTER] : the surgical insertion of a hollow needle through the abdominal wall and uterus of a pregnant female esp. to obtain amniotic fluid for the determination of sex or chromosomal abnormality

am·ni·on \ˈam-nē-ˌän, -ən\ *n, pl* **amnions** *or* **am·nia** \-nē-ə\ [NL, fr. Gk, caul, prob. fr. dim. of *amnos* lamb — more at YEAN] **1** : a thin membrane forming a closed sac about the embryos of reptiles, birds, and mammals and containing a serous fluid in which the embryo is immersed **2** : a membrane analogous to the amnion and occurring in various invertebrates — **am·ni·ote** \-nē-ˌōt\ *adj or n* — **am·ni·ot·ic** \ˌam-nē-ˈät-ik\ *adj*

amo·bar·bi·tal \ˌam-ō-ˈbär-bə-ˌtȯl\ *n* [*amyl* + *-o-* + *barbital*] : a barbiturate $C_{11}H_{18}N_2O_3$ used as a hypnotic and sedative; *also* : its sodium salt

amoe·ba \ə-ˈmē-bə\ *n, pl* **-bas** *or* **-bae** \-(ˌ)bē\ [NL, genus name, fr. Gk *amoibē* change, fr. *ameibein* to change — more at MIGRATE] : any of a large genus (*Amoeba*) of naked rhizopod protozoans with lobed and never anastomosing pseudopodia and without permanent organelles or supporting structures that are widely distributed in fresh and salt water and moist terrestrial situations; *broadly* : a naked rhizopod or other amoeboid protozoan — **amoe·bic** \-bik\ *also* **amoe·ban** \-bən\ *adj*

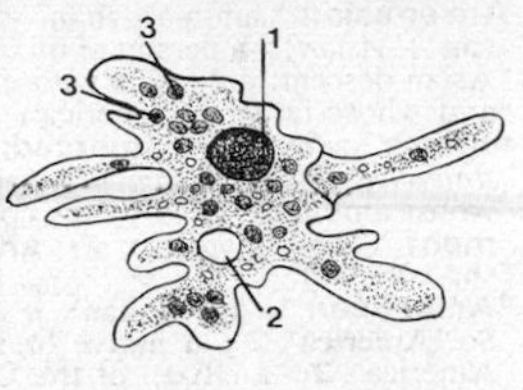

amoeba: *1* nucleus, *2* contractile vacuole, *3* food vacuoles

am·oe·bi·a·sis *var of* AMEBIASIS

amoe·bo·cyte \ə-ˈmē-bə-ˌsīt\ *n* : a cell (as a phagocyte) having amoeboid form or movements

amoe·boid \-ˌbȯid\ *adj* : resembling an amoeba specif. in moving or changing in shape by means of protoplasmic flow

¹amok \ə-ˈmək, -ˈmäk\ *adv* [Malay *amok*] **1** : in a murderously frenzied state **2 a** : in a violently raging manner <a virus that had run ~> **b** : in an undisciplined or faulty manner

²amok *adj* : possessed with a murderous or violently uncontrollable frenzy

³amok *n* : a murderous frenzy that occurs chiefly among Malays

amo·le \ə-ˈmō-lē\ *n* [Sp. fr. Nahuatl *amolli* soap] : a plant part (as a root) possessing detergent properties and serving as a substitute for soap; *also* : a plant so used

among \ə-ˈməŋ\ *also* **amongst** \-ˈməŋ(k)st\ *prep* [*among* fr. ME, fr. OE *on gemonge,* fr. *on* + *gemonge,* dat. of *gemong* crowd, fr. *ge-* (associative prefix) + *-mong* (akin to OE *mengan* to mix); *amongst* fr. ME *amonges,* fr. *among* + *-es* -s — more at CO-, MINGLE] **1** : in or through the midst of : surrounded by **2** : in company or association with <living ~ artists> **3** : by or through the aggregate of <discontent ~ the poor> **4** : in the number or class of <wittiest ~ poets> <~ other things he was president of his college class> **5** : in shares to each of <divided ~ the heirs> **6 a** : through the reciprocal acts of <quarrel ~ themselves> **b** : through the joint action of <made a fortune ~ themselves>

amon·til·la·do \ə-ˌmän-tə-ˈläd-(ˌ)ō, -ti(l)-ˈyäth-(ˌ)ō\ *n, pl* **-dos** [Sp, fr. *a* to + *montilla* a wine from Montilla, Spain] : a pale dry sherry

amor·al \(ˈ)ā-ˈmȯr-əl, (ˈ)a-, -ˈmär-\ *adj* **1 a** : being neither moral nor immoral; *specif* : lying outside the sphere to which moral judgments apply **b** : lacking moral sensibility <infants are ~> **2** : being outside or beyond the moral order or a particular code of morals <~ customs> *syn* see IMMORAL — **amor·al·ism** \-ə-ˌliz-əm\ *n* — **amo·ral·i·ty** \ˌā-mə-ˈral-ət-ē, ˌa-, -(ˌ)mō-\ *n* — **amor·al·ly** \(ˈ)ā-ˈmȯr-ə-lē, (ˈ)a-, -ˈmär-\ *adv*

amo·ret·to \ˌam-ə-ˈret-(ˌ)ō, ˌäm-\ *n, pl* **-ti** \-(ˌ)ē\ *or* **amorettos** [It, dim. of *amore* love, cupid, fr. L *amor*] : CUPID, CHERUB 2

am·or·ist \ˈam-ə-rəst\ *n* **1** : a devotee of love and esp. sexual love : GALLANT **2** : one that writes about romantic love — **am·or·is·tic** \ˌam-ə-ˈris-tik\ *adj*

Am·o·rite \ˈam-ə-ˌrīt\ *n* [Heb *Ĕmōrī*] : a member of one of various Semitic peoples living in Mesopotamia, Syria, and Palestine during the 3d and 2d millenia B.C. — **Amorite** *adj*

am·o·rous \ˈam-(ə-)rəs\ *adj* [ME, fr. MF, fr. ML *amorosus,* fr. L *amor* love, fr. *amare* to love] **1** : strongly moved by love and esp. sexual love <~ women> **2** : being in love : ENAMORED — usu. used with *of* <~ of the girl> **3 a** : indicative of love <received ~ glances from her partner> **b** : of or relating to love <an ~ novel> — **am·o·rous·ly** *adv* — **am·o·rous·ness** *n*

amor·phism \ə-ˈmȯr-ˌfiz-əm\ *n* : amorphous quality

amor·phous \-fəs\ *adj* [Gk *amorphos,* fr. *a-* + *morphē* form] **1 a** : having no definite form : SHAPELESS <an ~ cloud mass> **b** : being without definite character or nature : UNCLASSIFIABLE **c** : lacking organization or unity **2** : having no real or apparent crystalline form : UNCRYSTALLIZED <an ~ mineral> — **amor·phous·ly** *adv* — **amor·phous·ness** *n*

amort \ə-ˈmȯ(ə)rt\ *adj* [short for *all-a-mort,* by folk etymology fr. MF *a la mort* to the death] *archaic* : being at the point of death

am·or·ti·za·tion \ˌam-ərt-ə-ˈzā-shən *also* ə-ˌmȯrt-\ *n* **1** : the act or process of amortizing **2** : the result of amortizing

am·or·tize \ˈam-ər-ˌtīz *also* ə-ˈmȯr-\ *vt* **-tized; -tiz·ing** [ME *amortisen* to deaden, alienate in mortmain, modif. of MF *amortiss-,* stem of *amortir,* fr. (assumed) VL *admortire* to deaden, fr. L *ad-* + *mort-, mors* death — more at MURDER] : to provide for the gradual extinguishment of (as a mortgage) usu. by contribution to a sinking fund at the time of each periodic interest payment — **am·or·tiz·able** \-ˌtī-zə-bəl\ *adj*

Amos \ˈā-məs\ *n* [Heb *ʽĀmōs*] **1** : a Hebrew prophet of the 8th century B.C. **2** : a prophetic book of canonical Jewish and Christian Scripture — see BIBLE table

[1]amount \ə-'mau̇nt\ *vi* [ME *amounten,* fr. OF *amonter,* fr. *amont* upward, fr. *a-* (fr. L *ad-*) + *mont* mountain — more at MOUNT] **1 :** to add up <the bill ~*s* to $10> **2 :** to be equivalent <acts that ~ to treason>
[2]amount *n* **1 :** the total number or quantity : AGGREGATE **2 a :** the whole effect, significance, or import **b :** the quantity at hand or under consideration <has an enormous ~ of energy> **3 :** a principal sum and the interest on it
amour \ə-'mu̇(ə)r, ä-, a-\ *n* [ME, love, affection, fr. OF, fr. OProv *amor,* fr. L, fr. *amare* to love] **:** a usu. illicit love affair
amour pro·pre \ˌam-ˌu̇r-'prōprᵊ, ˌäm-, -'prȯprᵊ\ *n* [F *amour-propre,* lit., love of oneself] **:** SELF-ESTEEM
Amoy \ä-'mȯi, a-, ə-\ *n* **:** the dialect of Chinese spoken in and near Amoy in southeastern China
amp *abbr* ampere
AMP \ˌā-ˌem-'pē\ *n* [*a*denosine *m*ono*p*hosphate] **:** a mononucleotide of adenine $C_{10}H_{12}N_5O_3H_2PO_4$ that was orig. isolated from mammalian muscle and is reversibly convertible to ADP and ATP in metabolic reactions — called also *adenosine monophosphate;* compare CYCLIC AMP
am·per·age \'am-p(ə-)rij, -ˌpi(ə)r-ij\ *n* **:** the strength of a current of electricity expressed in amperes
am·pere \'am-ˌpi(ə)r *also* -ˌpe(ə)r\ *n* [Andre M. *Ampère* †1836 F physicist] **1 :** the practical mks unit of electric current that is equivalent to a flow of one coulomb per second or to the steady current produced by one volt applied across a resistance of one ohm **2 :** a unit of electric current equal to a constant current that when maintained in two straight parallel conductors of infinite length and negligible circular sections one meter apart in a vacuum produces between the conductors a force equal to 2×10^{-7} newton per meter of length
ampere-hour *n* **:** a unit quantity of electricity equal to the quantity carried past any point of a circuit in one hour by a steady current of one ampere
ampere-turn *n* **:** the mks unit of magnetomotive force equal to the magnetomotive force around a path that links with one turn of wire carrying an electric current of one ampere
am·per·sand \'am-pər-ˌsand\ *n* [alter. of *and* (&)*per se and,* lit., (the character) & by itself (is the word) *and*] **:** a character typically & standing for the word *and*
am·phet·amine \am-'fet-ə-ˌmēn, -mən\ *n* [ISV *a*lpha + *m*ethyl + *phen-* + *et*hyl + *amine*] **1 :** a compound $C_9H_{13}N$ used esp. as an inhalant and in solution as a spray in head colds and hay fever **2 :** any of various derivatives of amphetamine used as stimulants for the central nervous system: as **a :** a white crystalline compound $C_{18}H_{28}N_2O_4S$ — called also *amphetamine sulfate* **b :** a compound consisting of the dextrorotatory form of amphetamine sulfate — called also *dextroamphetamine*
amphi- *or* **amph-** *prefix* [L *amphi-* around, on both sides, fr. Gk *amphi-, amph-,* fr. *amphi* — more at AMBI-] **:** on both sides **:** of both kinds **:** both <*amphi*biotic> <*amphi*stylar>
am·phib·ia \am-'fib-ē-ə\ *n pl* **:** AMPHIBIANS
am·phib·i·an \-ē-ən\ *n* [deriv. of Gk *amphibion* amphibious being, fr. neut. of *amphibios*] **1 :** an amphibious organism; *esp* **:** any of a class (Amphibia) of cold-blooded vertebrates (as frogs, toads, or newts) intermediate in many characters between fishes and reptiles and having gilled aquatic larvae and air-breathing adults **2 :** an airplane designed to take off from and land on either land or water **3 :** a flat-bottomed vehicle that moves on tracks having finlike extensions by means of which it is propelled on land or water — **amphibian** *adj*
am·phib·i·ous \am-'fib-ē-əs\ *adj* [Gk *amphibios,* lit., living a double life, fr. *amphi-* + *bios* mode of life — more at QUICK] **1 :** able to live both on land and in water <~ plants> **2 a :** relating to or adapted for both land and water <~ vehicles> **b :** executed by coordinated action of land, sea, and air forces organized for invasion; *also* **:** trained or organized for such action <~ forces> **3 :** combining two characteristics — **am·phib·i·ous·ly** *adv* — **am·phib·i·ous·ness** *n*
am·phi·bole \'am(p)-fə-ˌbōl\ *n* [F, fr. LL *amphibolus,* fr. Gk *amphibolos* ambiguous fr. *amphiballein* to throw round, doubt, fr. *amphi-* + *ballein* to throw — more at DEVIL] **1 :** HORNBLENDE **2 :** any of a group of minerals $A_2B_5(Si, Al)_8O_{22}(OH)_2$ with like crystal structures usu. containing three groups of metal ions
am·phib·o·lite \am-'fib-ə-ˌlīt\ *n* **:** a usu. metamorphic rock consisting essentially of amphibole — **am·phib·o·lit·ic** \(ˌ)am-ˌfib-ə-'lit-ik\ *adj*
am·phi·brach \'am(p)-fə-ˌbrak\ *n* [L *amphibrachys,* fr. Gk, lit., short at both ends, fr. *amphi-* + *brachys* short — more at BRIEF] **:** a metrical foot consisting of a long syllable between two short syllables in quantitative verse or of a stressed syllable between two unstressed syllables in accentual verse <*romantic* is an accentual ~> — **am·phi·brach·ic** \ˌam(p)-fə-'brak-ik\ *adj*
am·phic·ty·o·ny \am-'fik-tē-ə-nē\ *n, pl* **-nies** [Gk *amphiktyonia*] **:** an association of neighboring states in ancient Greece to defend a common religious center; *broadly* **:** an association of neighboring states for their common interest — **am·phic·ty·on·ic** \(ˌ)am-ˌfik-tē-'än-ik\ *adj*
am·phi·dip·loid \ˌam(p)-fi-'dip-ˌlȯid\ *adj, of an interspecific hybrid* **:** having a complete diploid chromosome set from each parent strain — **amphidiploid** *n* — **am·phi·dip·loi·dy** \-ˌlȯid-ē\ *n*
am·phim·a·cer \am-'fim-ə-sər\ *n* [L *amphimacrus,* fr. Gk *amphimakros,* lit., long at both ends, fr. *amphi-* + *makros* long — more at MEAGER] **:** a metrical foot consisting of a short syllable between two long syllables in quantitative verse or of an unstressed syllable between two stressed syllables in accentual verse <*twenty-two* is an accentual ~>
am·phi·mic·tic \ˌam(p)-fi-'mik-tik\ *adj* [ISV *amphi-* + Gk *miktos* blended, fr. *mignynai*] **:** capable of interbreeding freely and of producing fertile offspring — **am·phi·mic·ti·cal·ly** \-ti-k(ə-)lē\ *adv*
am·phi·mix·is \-'mik-səs\ *n, pl* **-mix·es** \-ˌsēz\ [NL, fr. *amphi-* + Gk *mixis* mingling, fr. *mignynai* to mix — more at MIX] **:** the union of germ cells in sexual reproduction
Am·phi·on \am-'fī-ən\ *n* [L, fr. Gk *Amphiōn*] **:** a musician who built the walls of Thebes by charming the stones into place with his lyre
am·phi·ox·us \ˌam(p)-fē-'äk-səs\ *n, pl* **-oxi** \-ˌsī\ *or* **-ox·us·es** [NL, fr. *amphi-* + Gk *oxys* sharp] **:** any of a genus (*Branchiostoma*) of lancelets; *broadly* **:** LANCELET
am·phi·ploid \'am(p)-fi-ˌplȯid\ *adj, of an interspecific hybrid* **:** having at least one complete diploid set of chromosomes derived from each ancestral species — **amphiploid** *n* — **am·phi·ploi·dy** \-ˌplȯid-ē\ *n*
am·phi·pod \-ˌpäd\ *n* [deriv. of Gk *amphi-* + *pod-, pous* foot — more at FOOT] **:** any of a large group (Amphipoda) of small crustaceans (as the sand flea) with a laterally compressed body — **amphipod** *adj*
am·phi·pro·style \ˌam(p)-fi-'prō-ˌstīl\ *adj* [L *amphiprostylos,* fr. Gk, fr. *amphi-* + *prostylos* having pillars in front, fr. *pro-* + *stylos* pillar — more at STEER] **:** having columns at each end only <an ~ building> — **amphiprostyle** *n*
am·phis·bae·na \ˌam(p)-fəs-'bē-nə\ *n* [L, fr. Gk *amphisbaina,* fr. *amphis* on both sides (fr. *amphi* around) + *bainein* to walk, go — more at BY, COME] **:** a serpent in classical mythology having a head at each end and capable of moving in either direction — **am·phis·bae·nic** \-nik\ *adj*
am·phi·sty·lar \ˌam(p)-fi-'stī-lər\ *adj* **:** having columns at both ends or on both sides <an ~ building>
am·phi·the·ater \'am(p)-fə-ˌthē-ət-ər\ *n* [L *amphitheatrum,* fr. Gk *amphitheatron,* fr. *amphi-* + *theatron* theater] **1 :** an oval or circular building with rising tiers of seats ranged about an open space and used in ancient Rome esp. for contests and spectacles **2 a :** a very large auditorium **b :** a room with a gallery from which doctors and students may observe surgical operations **c :** a rising gallery in a modern theater **d :** a flat or gently sloping area surrounded by abrupt slopes **3 :** a place of public games or contests — **am·phi·the·at·ric** \ˌam(p)-fə-thē-'a-trik\ *or* **am·phi·the·at·ri·cal** \-tri-kəl\ *adj* — **am·phi·the·at·ri·cal·ly** \-tri-k(ə-)lē\ *adv*
am·phit·ro·pous \am-'fi-trə-pəs\ *adj* **:** having the ovule inverted but with the attachment near the middle of one side
Am·phit·ry·on \am-'fi-trē-ən\ *n* [Gk *Amphitryōn*] **:** the husband of Alcmene
am·pho·ra \'am(p)-fə-rə\ *n, pl* **-rae** \-ˌrē, -ˌrī\ *or* **-ras** [L, modif. of Gk *amphoreus, amphiphoreus,* fr. *amphi-* + *phoreus* bearer, fr. *pherein* to bear — more at BEAR] **1 :** an ancient Greek jar or vase with a large oval body, narrow cylindrical neck, and two handles that rise almost to the level of the mouth **2 :** a 2-handled vessel shaped like an amphora
am·pho·ter·ic \ˌam(p)-fə-'ter-ik\ *adj* [ISV, fr. Gk *amphoteros* each of two, fr. *amphō* both — more at AMBI-] **:** partly one and partly the other; *specif* **:** capable of reacting chemically either as an acid or as a base
am·pho·ter·i·cin \-'ter-ə-sən\ *n* [*amphoteric* + *-in*] **:** either of two antibiotic drugs obtained from a soil actinomycete (*Streptomyces nodosus*); *esp* **:** the one useful against deep-seated and systemic fungal infections — called also *amphotericin B*
amp hr *abbr* ampere-hour
am·pi·cil·lin \ˌam-pə-'sil-ən\ *n* [*am*in- + *pen*i*cillin*] **:** an antibiotic of the penicillin group that is effective against gram-negative bacteria
am·ple \'am-pəl\ *adj* **am·pler** \-p(ə-)lər\; **am·plest** \-p(ə-)ləst\ [MF, fr. L *amplus*] **1 :** generous or more than adequate in size, scope, or capacity <there was room for an ~ garden> **2 :** generously sufficient to satisfy a requirement or need <they had ~ money for the trip> **3 :** BUXOM, PORTLY <an ~ figure> ***syn* 1** see SPACIOUS **2** see PLENTIFUL ***ant*** meager, scant — **am·ple·ness** \-pəl-nəs\ *n* — **am·ply** \-plē\ *adv*
am·plex·i·caul \am-'plek-sə-ˌkȯl\ *adj* [NL *amplexicaulis,* fr. L *amplexus* (pp. of *amplecti* to entwine, fr. *ambi-* + *plectere* to braid) + *-i-* + *caulis* stem — more at HOLE] *of a leaf* **:** sessile with the base or stipules surrounding the stem
am·plex·us \am-'plek-səs\ *n* [NL, fr. L, embrace, fr. *amplexus,* pp.] **:** the mating embrace of a frog or toad during which eggs are shed into the water and there fertilized
am·pli·dyne \'am-plə-ˌdīn\ *n* [*ampli*fier + Gk *dyn*amis power — more at DYNAMIC] **:** a direct-current generator that by the use of compensating coils and a short circuit across two of its brushes precisely controls a large power output whenever a small power input is varied in the field winding of the generator
am·pli·fi·ca·tion \ˌam-plə-fə-'kā-shən\ *n* **1 :** an act, example, or product of amplifying **2 a :** the particulars by which a statement is expanded **b :** an expanded statement
am·pli·fi·er \'am-plə-ˌfī(-ə)r\ *n* **:** one that amplifies; *specif* **:** a device usu. employing electron tubes or transistors to obtain amplification of voltage, current, or power
am·pli·fy \-ˌfī\ *vb* **-fied; -fy·ing** [ME *amplifien,* fr. MF *amplifier,* fr. L *amplificare,* fr. *amplus*] *vt* **1 :** to expand (as a statement) by the use of detail or illustration or by closer analysis **2 :** to make larger or greater (as in amount, importance, or intensity) **:** INCREASE **3 :** to utilize (an input of power) so as to obtain an output of greater magnitude through the relay action of a transducer ~ *vi* **:** to expand one's remarks or ideas ***syn*** see EXPAND ***ant*** abridge, condense
am·pli·tude \-ˌt(y)üd\ *n* **1 :** the quality or state of being ample **:** FULLNESS **2 :** the extent or range of a quality, property, process, or phenomenon: as **a :** the extent of a vibratory movement (as of a pendulum) measured from the mean position to an extreme **b :** the maximum departure of the value of an alternating current or

wave from the average value **3 :** the arc of the horizon between the true east or west point and the foot of the vertical circle passing through any star or object
amplitude modulation *n* **1 :** modulation of the amplitude of a radio carrier wave in accordance with the strength of the audio or other signal **2 :** a broadcasting system using amplitude modulation — abbr. *AM;* compare FREQUENCY MODULATION
am·pul *or* **am·pule** *or* **am·poule** \'am-ˌpyü(ə)l, -pül\ *n* [ME *ampulle* flask, fr. OE & OF; OE *ampulle* & OF *ampoule,* fr. L *ampulla*] **1 :** a hermetically sealed small bulbous glass vessel that is used to hold a solution for hypodermic injection **2 :** a vial resembling an ampul
am·pul·la \am-'pu̇l-ə, -'pəl-\ *n, pl* **-lae** \-(ˌ)ē, -ˌī\ [ME, fr. OE, fr. L, dim. of *amphora*] **1 :** a glass or earthenware flask with a globular body and two handles used esp. by the ancient Romans to hold ointment, perfume, or wine **2 :** a saccular anatomic swelling or pouch — **am·pul·lar** \-ər\ *adj*
am·pu·tate \'am-pyə-ˌtāt\ *vt* **-tat·ed; -tat·ing** [L *amputatus,* pp. of *amputare,* fr. *am-, amb-* around + *putare* to cut, prune — more at AMBI-, PAVE] **:** to cut or lop off; *esp* **:** to cut (as a limb) from the body — **am·pu·ta·tion** \ˌam-pyə-'tā-shən\ *n* — **am·pu·ta·tor** \'am-pyə-ˌtāt-ər\ *n*
am·pu·tee \ˌam-pyə-'tē\ *n* **:** one that has had a limb amputated
AMS *abbr* Agricultural Marketing Service
amt *abbr* amount
am·trac *or* **am·track** \'am-ˌtrak\ *n* [*am*phibious + *trac*tor] **:** AMPHIBIAN 3
AMU *abbr* atomic mass unit
amuck \ə-'mək\ *var of* AMOK
am·u·let \'am-yə-lət\ *n* [L *amuletum*] **:** a charm (as an ornament) often inscribed with a magic incantation or symbol to protect the wearer against evil (as disease or witchcraft) or to aid him ***syn*** see FETISH
amuse \ə-'myüz\ *vb* **amused; amus·ing** [MF *amuser,* fr. OF, fr. *a-* (fr. L *ad-*) + *muser* to muse] *vt* **1 a** *archaic* **:** to divert the attention so as to deceive **:** BEMUSE **b** *obs* **:** to occupy the attention of **:** ABSORB **c** *obs* **:** DISTRACT, BEWILDER **2 a :** to entertain or occupy in a light, playful, or pleasant manner <~ the child with a story> **b :** to appeal to the sense of humor of <the joke doesn't ~ me> ~ *vi, obs* **:** MUSE — **amus·ed·ly** \-'myü-zəd-lē\ *adv* — **amus·er** *n*
syn AMUSE, DIVERT, ENTERTAIN *shared meaning element* **:** to pass or cause to pass one's time pleasantly ***ant*** bore
amuse·ment \ə-'myüz-mənt\ *n* **1 :** a means of amusing or entertaining <what are her favorite ~*s*> **2 :** the condition of being amused <his ~ knew no bounds> **3 :** pleasurable diversion **:** ENTERTAINMENT <plays the piano for ~>
amusement park *n* **:** a commercially operated park with various devices for entertainment and booths for the sale of food and drink
amus·ing \ə-'myü-ziŋ\ *adj* **:** giving amusement **:** DIVERTING — **amus·ing·ly** \-ziŋ-lē\ *adv* — **amus·ing·ness** *n*
amu·sive \ə-'myü-ziv, -siv\ *adj* **:** tending to amuse or arouse mirth **:** AMUSING
AMVETS \'am-ˌvets\ *abbr* American Veterans (of World War II)
amyg·da·la \ə-'mig-də-lə\ *n, pl* **-lae** \-ˌlē, -ˌlī\ [NL, fr. L, almond, fr. Gk *amygdalē*] **:** an almond-shaped mass of gray matter in the roof of a lateral ventricle of the brain
amyg·da·lin \-lən\ *n* [NL *Amygdalus,* genus name, fr. LL, almond tree, fr. Gk *amygdalos;* akin to Gk *amygdalē*] **:** a white crystalline cyanogenetic glucoside $C_{20}H_{27}NO_{11}$ found esp. in the bitter almond (*Amygdalus communis amara*)
¹amyg·da·loid \-ˌlȯid\ *n* [Gk *amygdaloeidēs,* adj.] **:** an igneous and usu. volcanic rock orig. containing small cavities filled with deposits of different minerals (as chalcedony or calcite) — **amyg·da·loi·dal** \-ˌmig-də-'lȯid-ᵊl\ *adj*
²amygdaloid *adj* [Gk *amygdaloeidēs,* fr. *amygdalē* almond] **1 :** almond-shaped **2 :** of or relating to an amygdala
am·yl \'am-əl\ *n* [blend of *amyl-* and *-yl*] **:** a univalent hydrocarbon radical C_5H_{11} that occurs in various isomeric forms and is derived from pentane — called also *pentyl*
amyl- *or* **amylo-** *comb form* [LL *amyl-,* fr. L *amylum,* fr. Gk *amylon,* fr. neut. of *amylos* not ground at the mill, fr. *a-* + *mylē* mill — more at MEAL] **:** starch <*amyl*ase>
am·y·la·ceous \ˌam-ə-'lā-shəs\ *adj* **:** of, relating to, or having the characteristics of starch **:** STARCHY
amyl acetate *n* **:** BANANA OIL 1
amyl alcohol *n* **:** any of eight isomeric alcohols $C_5H_{12}O$ used esp. as solvents and in making esters; *also* **:** either of two commercially produced mixtures of amyl alcohols obtained from fusel oil or derived from pentanes and used esp. as solvents
am·y·lase \'am-ə-ˌlās, -ˌlāz\ *n* **:** any of the enzymes (as amylopsin) that accelerate the hydrolysis of starch and glycogen or their intermediate hydrolysis products
¹am·y·loid \-ˌlȯid\ *or* **am·y·loi·dal** \ˌam-ə-'lȯid-ᵊl\ *adj* **:** resembling or containing amylum
²amyloid *n* **1 :** a nonnitrogenous starchy food **2 :** a waxy translucent substance consisting of protein in combination with polysaccharides that is deposited in some animal organs under abnormal conditions
am·y·loid·osis \ˌam-ə-ˌlȯi-'dō-səs\ *n* [NL] **:** a condition characterized by the deposition of amyloid in organs or tissues of the animal body
am·y·lol·y·sis \ˌam-ə-'läl-ə-səs\ *n* [NL] **:** the conversion of starch into soluble products (as dextrins and sugars) esp. by enzymes — **am·y·lo·lyt·ic** \-lō-'lit-ik\ *adj*
am·y·lo·pec·tin \ˌam-ə-lō-'pek-tən\ *n* **:** a component of starch that has a high molecular weight and branched structure and does not tend to gel in aqueous solutions
am·y·lop·sin \ˌam-ə-'läp-sən\ *n* [*amyl-* + *-psin* (as in *trypsin*)] **:** the amylase of the pancreatic juice
am·y·lose \'am-ə-ˌlōs, -ˌlōz\ *n* **1 :** any of various polysaccharides (as starch or cellulose) **2 :** a component of starch characterized by its straight chains of glucose units and by the tendency of its aqueous solutions to set to a stiff gel **3 :** any of various compounds $(C_6H_{10}O_5)_x$ obtained by the hydrolysis of starch
am·y·lum \-ləm\ *n* [L — more at AMYL-] **:** STARCH
amyo·to·nia \ˌā-ˌmī-ə-'tō-nē-ə\ *n* [NL] **:** deficiency of muscle tone
¹an \ən, (ˈ)an\ *indefinite article* [ME, fr. OE *ān* one — more at ONE] **:** ²A — in standard speech and writing used (1) invariably before words beginning with a vowel letter and sound <*an* oak>; (2) invariably before *h*-initial words in which the *h* is silent <*an* honor>; (3) frequently before *h*-initial words which have in an initial unstressed syllable an \h\ sound often lost after the *an* <*an* historian>; (4) sometimes esp. in England before words like *union* and *European* whose initial letter is a vowel and whose initial sounds are \yü\ or \yu̇\
²an *or* **an'** *conj* **1** *see* AND \ **:** AND **2** \(ˈ)an\ *archaic* **:** IF
³an *abbr* annum
an- — see A-
¹-an *or* **-ian** *also* **-ean** *n suffix* [*-an* & *-ian* fr. ME *-an, -ian,* fr. OF & L; OF *-ien,* fr. L *-ianus,* fr. *-i-* + *-anus,* adj. suffix; *-ean* fr. such words as *Mediterranean, European*] **1 :** one that is of or relating to <Americ*an*> <Boston*ian*> **2 :** one skilled in or specializing in <phonetic*ian*>
²-an *or* **-ian** *also* **-ean** *adj suffix* **1 :** of or belonging to <Americ*an*> <Florid*ian*> **2 :** characteristic of **:** resembling <Mozart*ean*>
³-an *n suffix* [ISV *-an, -ane,* alter. of *-ene, -ine,* & *-one*] **1 :** unsaturated carbon compound <tol*an*> **2 :** anhydride of a carbohydrate <dextr*an*>
¹ana \'an-ə\ *adv* [ME, fr. ML, fr. Gk, at the rate of, lit., up] **:** of each an equal quantity — used in prescriptions
²ana \'an-ə, 'än-ə, 'ā-nə\ *n, pl* **ana** *or* **anas** [*-ana*] **1 :** a collection of the memorable sayings of a person **2 :** a collection of anecdotes or interesting or curious information about a person or a place
ANA *abbr* **1** American Newspaper Association **2** American Nurses Association **3** Association of National Advertisers
ana- *or* **an-** *prefix* [L, fr. Gk, up, back, again, fr. *ana* up — more at ON] **1 :** up **:** upward <*ana*bolism> **2 :** back **:** backward <*ana*tropous>
-ana \'an-ə, 'än-ə, 'ā-nə\ *or* **-i·ana** \ē-'\ *n pl suffix* [NL, fr. L, neut. pl. of *-anus* -an & *-ianus* -ian] **:** collected items of information esp. anecdotal or bibliographical concerning <American*a*> <Johnson*iana*>
ana·bap·tism \ˌan-ə-'bap-ˌtiz-əm\ *n* [NL *anabaptismus,* fr. LGk *anabaptismos* rebaptism, fr. *anabaptizein* to rebaptize, fr. *ana-* again + *baptizein* to baptize] **1** *cap* **a :** the doctrine or practices of the Anabaptists **b :** the Anabaptist movement **2 :** the baptism of one previously baptized
Ana·bap·tist \-'bap-təst\ *n* **:** a Protestant sectarian of a radical movement arising in Zurich in 1524 and advocating the baptism and church membership of adult believers only, nonresistance, and the separation of church and state — **Anabaptist** *adj*
anab·a·sis \ə-'nab-ə-səs\ *n, pl* **-a·ses** \-ˌsēz\ [Gk, inland march, fr. *anabainein* to go up or inland, fr. *ana-* + *bainein* to go — more at COME] **1 :** a going or marching up **:** ADVANCE; *esp* **:** a military advance **2** [fr. the retreat of Gk mercenaries in Asia Minor described in the *Anabasis* of Xenophon] **:** a difficult and dangerous military retreat
an·a·bat·ic \ˌan-ə-'bat-ik\ *adj* [Gk *anabatos,* verbal of *anabainein*] **:** moving upward **:** RISING <an ~ wind>
ana·bi·o·sis \ˌan-ə-bī-'ō-səs, -bē-\ *n, pl* **-o·ses** \-'ō-ˌsēz\ [NL, fr. Gk *anabiōsis* return to life, fr. *anabioun* to return to life, fr. *ana-* + *bios* life — more at QUICK] **:** a state of suspended animation induced in some organisms by desiccation — **ana·bi·ot·ic** \-'ät-ik\ *adj*
anab·o·lism \ə-'nab-ə-ˌliz-əm\ *n* [ISV *ana-* + *-bolism* (as in *metabolism*)] **:** the constructive part of metabolism concerned esp. with macromolecular synthesis — **an·a·bo·lic** \ˌan-ə-'bäl-ik\ *adj*
anach·ro·nism \ə-'nak-rə-ˌniz-əm\ *n* [prob. fr. MGk *anachronismos,* fr. *anachronizesthai* to be an anachronism, fr. LGk *anachronizein* to be late, fr. Gk *ana-* + *chronos* time] **1 :** an error in chronology; *esp* **:** a chronological misplacing of persons, events, objects, or customs in regard to each other **2 :** a person or a thing that is chronologically out of place; *esp* **:** one from a former age that is incongruous in the present — **anach·ro·nis·tic** \ə-ˌnak-rə-'nis-tik\ *also* **ana·chron·ic** \ˌan-ə-'krän-ik\ *or* **anach·ro·nous** \ə-'nak-rə-nəs\ *adj* — **anach·ro·nis·ti·cal·ly** \ə-ˌnak-rə-'nis-ti-k(ə-)lē\ *also* **anach·ro·nous·ly** *adv*
an·a·clit·ic \ˌan-ə-'klit-ik\ *adj* [Gk *anaklitos,* verbal of *anaklinein* to lean upon, fr. *ana-* + *klinein* to lean — more at LEAN] **:** characterized by dependence of libido on a nonsexual instinct
an·a·co·lu·thon \ˌan-ə-kə-'lü-ˌthän\ *n, pl* **-tha** \-thə\ *or* **-thons** [LL, fr. LGk *anakolouthon* inconsistency in logic, fr. Gk, neut. of *anakolouthos,* inconsistent, fr. *an-* + *akolouthos* following, fr. *ha-, a-* together + *keleuthos* path; akin to Gk *hama* together — more at SAME] **:** syntactical inconsistency or incoherence within a sentence; *esp* **:** the shift from one construction to another (as in "you really ought — well, do it your own way") — **an·a·co·lu·thic** \-thik\ *adj* — **an·a·co·lu·thi·cal·ly** \-thi-k(ə-)lē\ *adv*
an·a·con·da \ˌan-ə-'kän-də\ *n* [prob. modif. of Sinhalese *henakandayā* a slender green snake] **:** a large semiaquatic snake (*Eunectes murinus*) of the boa family of tropical So. America that crushes its prey in its coils; *broadly* **:** a large constricting snake
anac·re·on·tic \ə-ˌnak-rē-'änt-ik\ *n* **:** a poem in the manner of Anacreon; *esp* **:** a drinking song or light lyric
Anacreontic *adj* [L *anacreonticus,* fr. *Anacreont-, Anacreon* Anacreon, fr. Gk *Anakreont-, Anakreōn*] **1 :** of, relating to, or resembling the poetry of Anacreon **2 :** convivial or amatory in tone or theme
an·a·cru·sis \ˌan-ə-'krü-səs\ *n, pl* **-cru·ses** \-ˌsēz\ [NL, fr. Gk *anakrousis* beginning of a song, fr. *anakrouein* to begin a song, fr. *ana-* + *krouein* to strike, beat; akin to Lith *krušti* to stamp] **1 :** one or more syllables at the beginning of a line of poetry that are regarded as preliminary to and not a part of the metrical pattern **2 :** UPBEAT; *specif* **:** one or more notes or tones preceding the first downbeat of a musical phrase

ana·cul·ture \'an-ə-ˌkəl-chər\ *n* [ISV] : a mixed bacterial culture; *esp* : one used in the preparation of autogenous vaccines

an·a·dem \'an-ə-ˌdem\ *n* [L *anadema*, fr. Gk *anadēma*, fr. *anadein* to wreathe, fr. *ana-* + *dein* to bind — more at DIADEM] *archaic* : a wreath for the head : GARLAND

ana·di·plo·sis \ˌan-əd-ə-'plō-səs, ˌan-ə-(ˌ)dī-'plō-\ *n, pl* **-plo·ses** \-ˌsēz\ [LL, fr. Gk *anadiplōsis*, lit., repetition, fr. *anadiploun* to double, fr. *ana-* + *diploun* to double — more at DIPLOMA] : repetition of a prominent and usu. the last word in one phrase or clause at the beginning of the next (as in "rely on his honor — honor such as his?")

anad·ro·mous \ə-'nad-rə-məs\ *adj* [Gk *anadromos* running upward, fr. *anadramein* to run upward, fr. *ana-* + *dramein* to run — more at DROMEDARY] : ascending rivers from the sea for breeding <shad are ~>

anae·mia, anae·mic *var of* ANEMIA, ANEMIC

an·aer·obe \'an-ə-ˌrōb; (ˈ)an-'a(-ə)r-ˌōb, -'e(-ə)r-\ *n* [ISV] : an anaerobic organism

an·aer·o·bic \ˌan-ə-'rō-bik; ˌan-ˌa(-ə)r-'ō-, -ˌe(-ə)r-\ *adj* **1** : living, active, or occurring in the absence of free oxygen <~ respiration> **2** : relating to or induced by anaerobes — **an·aer·o·bi·cal·ly** \-bi-k(ə-)lē\ *adv*

an·aero·bi·o·sis \ˌan-ə-rō-(ˌ)bī-'ō-səs, -bē-; ˌan-ˌa(-ə)r-ō-, -ˌe(-ə)r-\ *n pl* **-o·ses** \-'ō-ˌsēz\ : life in the absence of air or free oxygen

an·aes·the·sia, an·aes·thet·ic *var of* ANESTHESIA, ANESTHETIC

ana·glyph \'an-ə-ˌglif\ *n* [LL *anaglyphus* embossed, fr. Gk *anaglyphos*, fr. *anaglyphein* to emboss, fr. *ana-* + *glyphein* to carve — more at CLEAVE] **1** : a sculptured, chased, or embossed ornament worked in low relief **2** : a stereoscopic motion or still picture in which the right component of a composite image usu. red in color is superposed on the left component in a contrasting color to produce a three-dimensional effect when viewed through correspondingly colored filters in the form of spectacles — **ana·glyph·ic** \ˌan-ə-'glif-ik\ *adj*

an·a·go·ge *or* **an·a·go·gy** \'an-ə-ˌgō-jē\ *n, pl* **-ges** *or* **-gies** [LL *anagoge*, fr. LGk *anagōgē*, fr. Gk, reference, fr. *anagein* to refer, fr. *ana-* + *agein* to lead — more at AGENT] : interpretation of a word, passage, or text (as of Scripture or poetry) that finds beyond the literal, allegorical, and moral senses a fourth and ultimate spiritual or mystical sense — **an·a·gog·ic** \ˌan-ə-'gäj-ik\ *or* **an·a·gog·i·cal** \-i-kəl\ *adj* — **an·a·gog·i·cal·ly** \-i-k(ə-)lē\ *adv*

¹ana·gram \'an-ə-ˌgram\ *n* [prob. fr. MF *anagramme*, fr. NL *anagrammat-, anagramma*, modif. of Gk *anagrammatismos*, fr. *anagrammatizein* to transpose letters, fr. *ana-* + *grammat-, gramma* letter — more at GRAM] **1** : a word or phrase made by transposing the letters of another word or phrase **2** *pl but sing in constr* : a game in which words are formed by rearranging the letters of other words or by arranging letters taken (as from a stock of cards or blocks) at random — **ana·gram·mat·ic** \ˌan-ə-grə-'mat-ik\ *or* **ana·gram·mat·i·cal** \-i-kəl\ *adj* — **ana·gram·mat·i·cal·ly** \-i-k(ə-)lē\ *adv*

²anagram *vt* **-grammed; -gram·ming** **1** : ANAGRAMMATIZE **2** : to rearrange (the letters of a text) in order to discover a hidden message

ana·gram·ma·tize \ˌan-ə-'gram-ə-ˌtīz\ *vt* **-tized; -tiz·ing** : to transpose (as letters in a word) so as to form an anagram — **ana·gram·ma·ti·za·tion** \-ˌgram-ət-ə-'zā-shən\ *n*

¹anal \'ān-ᵊl\ *adj* **1** : of, relating to, or situated near the anus **2 a** : of, relating to, or characterized by the stage of psychosexual development in psychoanalytic theory during which the child is concerned esp. with its feces **b** : of, relating to, or characterized by personality traits (as parsimony, meticulousness, and ill humor) considered typical of fixation at the anal stage of development — **anal·ly** \-ᵊl-ē\ *adv*

²anal *abbr* **1** analogy **2** analysis; analytic

anal·cime \ə-'nal-ˌsēm\ *n* [F, fr. Gk *analkimos* weak, fr. *an-* + *alkimos* strong, fr. *alkē* strength] : a white or slightly colored mineral $NaAlSi_2O_6.H_2O$ occurring in various igneous rocks massive or in crystals — **anal·ci·mic** \-ˌnal-'sē-mik, -'sim-ik\ *adj*

anal·cite \ə-'nal-ˌsīt\ *n* : ANALCIME

an·a·lects \'an-ᵊl-ˌek(t)s\ *also* **an·a·lec·ta** \ˌan-ᵊl-'ek-tə\ *n pl* [NL *analecta*, fr. Gk *analekta*, neut. pl. of *analektos*, verbal of *analegein* to collect, fr. *ana-* + *legein* to gather — more at LEGEND] : selected miscellaneous written passages

an·a·lem·ma \ˌan-ə-'lem-ə\ *n* [L, sundial on a pedestal, fr. Gk *analēmma*, lofty structure, sundial, fr. *analambanein* to take up, fr. *ana-* + *lambanein* to take — more at LATCH] : a graduated scale having the shape of a figure 8 and showing the sun's declination and the equation of time for each day of the year — **an·a·lem·mat·ic** \-le-'mat-ik, -lə-\ *adj*

an·a·lep·tic \ˌan-ᵊl-'ep-tik\ *adj* [Gk *analēptikos*, fr. *analambanein* to take up, restore] : RESTORATIVE; *esp* : stimulant to the central nervous system — **analeptic** *n*

an·al·ge·sia \ˌan-ᵊl-'jē-zhə, -z(h)ē-ə\ *n* [NL, fr. Gk *analgēsia*, fr. *an-* + *algēsis* sense of pain, fr. *algein* to suffer pain, fr. *algos* pain] : insensibility to pain without loss of consciousness — **an·al·ge·sic** \-'jē-zik, -sik\ *adj or n* — **an·al·get·ic** \-'jet-ik\ *adj or n*

anal·i·ty \ā-'nal-ət-ē\ *n, pl* **-ties** : the psychological state or quality of being anal

an·a·log *also* **an·a·logue** \'an-ᵊl-ˌȯg, -ˌäg\ *adj* : of or relating to an analog computer

analog computer *n* : a computer that operates with numbers represented by directly measurable quantities (as voltages or rotations) — compare DIGITAL COMPUTER, HYBRID COMPUTER

an·a·log·i·cal \ˌan-ᵊl-'äj-i-kəl\ *also* **an·a·log·ic** \-ik\ *adj* **1** : of, relating to, or based on analogy **2** : expressing or implying analogy — **an·a·log·i·cal·ly** \-i-k(ə-)lē\ *adv*

anal·o·gist \ə-'nal-ə-jəst\ *n* : one who searches for or reasons from analogies

anal·o·gize \-ˌjīz\ *vb* **-gized; -giz·ing** *vi* : to use or exhibit analogy ~ *vt* : to compare by analogy

anal·o·gous \ə-'nal-ə-gəs\ *adj* [L *analogus*, fr. Gk *analogos*, lit., proportionate, fr. *ana-* + *logos* reason, ratio, fr. *legein* to gather, speak — more at LEGEND] **1** : showing an analogy or a likeness that permits one to draw an analogy : COMPARABLE **2** : being or related to as an analogue ***syn*** see SIMILAR — **anal·o·gous·ly** *adv* — **anal·o·gous·ness** *n*

analogue *or* **an·a·log** \'an-ᵊl-ˌȯg, -ˌäg\ *n* [F *analogue*, fr. *analogue* analogous, fr. Gk *analogos*] **1** : something that is analogous or similar to something else **2** : an organ similar in function to an organ of another animal or plant but different in structure and origin **3** : a chemical compound structurally similar to another but differing often by a single element of the same valence and group of the periodic table as the element it replaces ***syn*** see PARALLEL

anal·o·gy \ə-'nal-ə-jē\ *n, pl* **-gies** **1** : inference that if two or more things agree with one another in some respects they will prob. agree in others **2** : resemblance in some particulars between things otherwise unlike : SIMILARITY **3** : correspondence between the members of pairs or sets of linguistic forms that serves as a basis for the creation of another form **4** : correspondence in function between anatomical parts of different structure and origin — compare HOMOLOGY ***syn*** see LIKENESS

analogy test *n* : a reasoning test that requires the person tested to supply the missing term in a proportion (as *darkness* in the proportion *day:light::night:* . . .)

an·al·pha·bet \(ˈ)an-'al-fə-ˌbet, -bət\ *n* [Gk *analphabētos* not knowing the alphabet, fr. *an-* + *alphabētos* alphabet] : one who cannot read : ILLITERATE — **an·al·pha·bet·ic** \ˌan-ˌal-fə-'bet-ik\ *adj or n* — **an·al·pha·bet·ism** \(ˈ)an-'al-fə-bə-ˌtiz-əm\ *n*

anal·y·sand \ə-'nal-ə-ˌsand\ *n* [*analyse* + *-and* (as in *multiplicand*)] : one who is undergoing psychoanalysis

an·a·lyse *chiefly Brit var of* ANALYZE

anal·y·sis \ə-'nal-ə-səs\ *n, pl* **-y·ses** \-ˌsēz\ [NL, fr. Gk, fr. *analyein* to break up, fr. *ana-* + *lyein* to loosen — more at LOSE] **1** : separation of a whole into its component parts **2 a** : an examination of a complex, its elements, and their relations **b** : a statement of such an analysis **3** : the use of function words instead of inflectional forms as a characteristic device of a language **4 a** : the identification or separation of ingredients of a substance **b** : a statement of the constituents of a mixture **5 a** : proof of a mathematical proposition by assuming the result and deducing a valid statement by a series of reversible steps **b** (1) : a branch of mathematics concerned mainly with functions and limits (2) : CALCULUS 3b **6 a** : a method in philosophy of resolving complex expressions into simpler or more basic ones **b** : clarification of an expression by an elucidation of its use in discourse **7** : PSYCHOANALYSIS

analysis of variance : analysis of variation in an experimental outcome and esp. of a statistical variance in order to determine the contributions of given factors or variables to the variance

analysis si·tus \-'sīt-əs, -'sēt-; -'sī-ˌtüs, -'sē-\ *n* [NL, lit., analysis of situation] : TOPOLOGY 2a

an·a·lyst \'an-ᵊl-əst\ *n* [prob. fr. *analyze*] **1** : a person who analyzes or who is skilled in analysis **2** : PSYCHOANALYST **3** : SYSTEMS ANALYST

an·a·lyt·ic \ˌan-ᵊl-'it-ik\ *adj* [LL *analyticus*, fr. Gk *analytikos*, fr. *analyein*] **1** : of or relating to analysis or analytics; *esp* : separating something into component parts or constituent elements **2** : skilled in or using analysis esp. in thinking or reasoning <a keenly ~ man> **3** : not synthetic; *esp* : logically necessary : TAUTOLOGOUS <an ~ truth> **4** : characterized by analysis rather than inflection <~ languages> **5** : PSYCHOANALYTIC **6** : treated or treatable by or using the methods of algebra and calculus **7 a** *of a function of a real variable* : capable of being expanded in a Taylor's series in powers of $x - h$ in some neighborhood of the point h **b** *of a function of a complex variable* : differentiable at every point in some neighborhood of a given point or points ***syn*** see LOGICAL — **an·a·lyt·i·cal** \-i-kəl\ *adj* — **an·a·lyt·i·cal·ly** \-i-k(ə-)lē\ *adv* — **an·a·ly·tic·i·ty** \ˌan-ᵊl-ə-'tis-ət-ē\ *n*

analytic geometry *n* : the study of geometric properties by means of algebraic operations upon symbols defined in terms of a coordinate system — called also *coordinate geometry*

analytic philosophy *n* : PHILOSOPHICAL ANALYSIS

an·a·lyt·ics \ˌan-ᵊl-'it-iks\ *n pl but sing or pl in constr* : the method of logical analysis

an·a·ly·za·tion \ˌan-ᵊl-ə-'zā-shən\ *n* : ANALYSIS

an·a·lyze \'an-ᵊl-ˌīz\ *vt* **-lyzed; -lyz·ing** [prob. irreg. fr. *analysis*] **1** : to study or determine the nature and relationship of the parts of by analysis <~ a traffic pattern> **2** : to subject to scientific or grammatical analysis **3** : PSYCHOANALYZE — **an·a·lyz·abil·i·ty** \ˌan-ᵊl-ˌī-zə-'bil-ət-ē\ *n* — **an·a·lyz·able** \'an-ᵊl-ˌī-zə-bəl\ *adj*

syn ANALYZE, RESOLVE, DISSECT, BREAK DOWN *shared meaning element* : to divide a complex whole into its component parts or constituent elements ***ant*** compose, compound, construct

an·am·ne·sis \ˌan-ˌam-'nē-səs\ *n, pl* **-ne·ses** \-ˌsēz\ [NL, fr. Gk *anamnēsis*, fr. *anamimnēskesthai* to remember, fr. *ana-* + *mimnēskesthai* to remember — more at MIND] **1** : a recalling to mind : REMINISCENCE **2** : a preliminary case history of a medical or psychiatric patient

an·am·nes·tic \-'nes-tik\ *adj* [Gk *anamnēstikos* easily recalled, fr. *anamimnēskesthai*] **1** : of or relating to an anamnesis **2** : of or relating to a secondary response to an immunogenic substance after serum antibodies can no longer be detected in the blood — **an·am·nes·ti·cal·ly** \-ti-k(ə-)lē\ *adv*

ana·mor·phic \ˌan-ə-'mȯr-fik\ *adj* [NL *anamorphosis* distorted optical image] : producing or having different magnification of the image in each of two perpendicular directions — used of an optical device or its image

ə abut ᵊ kitten ər further a back ā bake ä cot, cart
aů out ch chin e less ē easy g gift i trip ī life
j joke ŋ sing ō flow ȯ flaw ȯi coin th thin t͟h this
ü loot ů foot y yet yü few yů furious zh vision

An·a·ni·as \ˌan-ə-ˈnī-əs\ *n* [Gk, prob. fr. Heb *Ḥănanyāh*] **1 :** an early Christian struck dead for lying about his donation to the church **2 :** a Christian of Damascus who baptized Paul **3 :** LIAR

an·a·pest \ˈan-ə-ˌpest\ *n* [L *anapaestus,* fr. Gk *anapaistos,* lit., struck back (a dactyl reversed), fr. (assumed) Gk *anapaiein* to strike back, fr. Gk *ana-* + *paiein* to strike] **1 :** a metrical foot consisting of two short syllables followed by one long syllable or of two unstressed syllables followed by one stressed syllable (as *un-abridged*) — compare DACTYL **2 :** a verse written in anapests — **an·a·pes·tic** \ˌan-ə-ˈpes-tik\ *adj or n*

ana·phase \ˈan-ə-ˌfāz\ *n* [ISV] **:** the stage of mitosis and meiosis in which the chromosomes move toward the poles of the spindle — **ana·pha·sic** \ˌan-ə-ˈfā-zik\ *adj*

anaph·o·ra \ə-ˈnaf-ə-rə\ *n* [LL, fr. LGk, fr. Gk, act of carrying back, reference fr. *anapherein* to carry back, refer, fr. *ana-* + *pherein* to carry — more at BEAR] **1 :** repetition of a word or phrase at the beginning of two or more successive clauses or verses esp. for rhetorical or poetic effect — compare EPISTROPHE **2 :** use of a grammatical substitute (as a pronoun or a pro-verb) to refer to a preceding word or group of words

an·a·phor·ic \ˌan-ə-ˈfȯr-ik, -ˈfär-\ *adj* **:** referring to a preceding word or group of words <the ~ *does* in "she dances better than he does">

an·aph·ro·di·sia \ˌan-ˌaf-rə-ˈdizh-(ē)ə\ *n* [NL, fr. *a-* + Gk *aphrodisios* sexual — more at APHRODISIAC] **:** absence or impairment of sexual desire — **an·aph·ro·dis·i·ac** \-ˈdiz-ē-ˌak\ *adj or n*

ana·phy·lac·tic \ˌan-ə-fə-ˈlak-tik\ *adj* **:** of, relating to, affected by, or causing anaphylaxis <~ shock> — **ana·phy·lac·ti·cal·ly** \-ti-k(ə-)lē\ *adv*

ana·phy·lac·toid \-ˈlak-ˌtȯid\ *adj* **:** resembling anaphylaxis

ana·phy·lax·is \-ˈlak-səs\ *n, pl* **-lax·es** \-ˌsēz\ [NL, fr. *ana-* + *-phylaxis* (as in *prophylaxis*)] **:** hypersensitivity (as to foreign proteins or drugs) resulting from sensitization following prior contact with the causative agent

an·a·pla·sia \ˌan-ə-ˈplā-zh(ē-)ə\ *n* [NL] **:** reversion of cells to a more primitive or undifferentiated form — **an·a·plas·tic** \-ˈplas-tik\ *adj*

an·arch \ˈan-ˌärk\ *n* [back-formation fr. *anarchy*] **:** a leader or advocate of revolt or anarchy

an·ar·chic \a-ˈnär-kik, ə-\ *adj* **1 a :** of, relating to, or advocating anarchy **b :** likely to bring about anarchy <~ violence> **2 :** lacking order, regularity, or definiteness <~ art forms>

an·ar·chism \ˈan-ər-ˌkiz-əm, -ˌär-\ *n* **1 :** a political theory holding all forms of governmental authority to be unnecessary and undesirable and advocating a society based on voluntary cooperation and free association of individuals and groups **2 :** the advocacy or practice of anarchistic principles

an·ar·chist \ˈan-ər-kəst, -ˌär-\ *n* **1 :** one who rebels against any authority, established order, or ruling power **2 :** one who believes in, advocates, or promotes anarchism or anarchy; *esp* **:** one who uses violent means to overthrow the established order — **anarchist** *or* **an·ar·chis·tic** \ˌan-ər-ˈkis-tik, -(ˌ)är-\ *adj*

an·ar·cho–syn·di·cal·ism \a-ˌnär-kō-ˈsin-di-kə-ˌliz-əm, ˌan-ər-kō-\ *n* **:** SYNDICALISM — **an·ar·cho–syn·di·cal·ist** \-kə-ləst\ *n or adj*

an·ar·chy \ˈan-ər-kē, -ˌär-\ *n* [ML *anarchia,* fr. Gk, fr. *anarchos* having no ruler, fr. *an-* + *archos* ruler — more at ARCH-] **1 a :** absence of government **b :** a state of lawlessness or political disorder due to the absence of governmental authority **c :** a utopian society made up of individuals who have no government and who enjoy complete freedom **2 :** absence of order **:** DISORDER **3 :** ANARCHISM

an·ar·thria \a-ˈnär-thrē-ə\ *n* [NL, fr. Gk *anarthros* inarticulate, fr. *an-* + *arthron* joint — more at ARTHR-] **:** inability to articulate words as a result of brain lesion

an·a·sar·ca \ˌan-ə-ˈsär-kə\ *n* [NL, fr. *ana-* + Gk *sark-, sarx* flesh — more at SARCASM] **:** edema with accumulation of serum in the connective tissue — **ana·sar·cous** \-kəs\ *adj*

an·astig·mat \a-ˈnas-tig-ˌmat, ˌan-ə-ˈstig-\ *n* [G, back-formation fr. *anastigmatisch* anastigmatic] **:** an anastigmatic lens

an·astig·mat·ic \ˌan-ə-(ˌ)stig-ˈmat-ik, ˌan-ˌas-tig-\ *adj* [ISV] **:** not astigmatic — used esp. of lenses that are able to form approximately point images of object points

anas·to·mose \ə-ˈnas-tə-ˌmōz, -ˌmōs\ *vb* **-mosed; -mos·ing** [prob. back-formation fr. *anastomosis*] *vt* **:** to connect or join by anastomosis ~ *vi* **:** to communicate by anastomosis

anas·to·mo·sis \ə-ˌnas-tə-ˈmō-səs\ *n, pl* **-mo·ses** \-ˌsēz\ [LL, fr. Gk *anastomōsis,* fr. *anastomoun* to provide with an outlet, fr. *ana-* + *stoma* mouth, opening — more at STOMACH] **1 :** the union of parts or branches (as of streams, blood vessels, or leaf veins) so as to intercommunicate **:** INOSCULATION **2 :** a product of anastomosis **:** NETWORK — **anas·to·mot·ic** \-ˈmät-ik\ *adj*

anas·tro·phe \ə-ˈnas-trə-(ˌ)fē\ *n* [ML, fr. Gk *anastrophē,* lit., turning back, fr. *anastrephein* to turn back, fr. *ana-* + *strephein* to turn — more at STROPHE] **:** inversion of the usual syntactical order of words for rhetorical effect — compare HYSTERON PROTERON

anat *abbr* anatomical; anatomy

an·a·tase \ˈan-ə-ˌtās, -ˌtāz\ *n* [F, fr. Gk *anatasis* extension, fr. *anateinein* to extend, fr. *ana-* + *teinein* to stretch — more at THIN] **:** a tetragonal titanium dioxide used esp. as a white pigment

anath·e·ma \ə-ˈnath-ə-mə\ *n* [LL *anathemat-, anathema,* fr. Gk, thing devoted to evil, curse, fr. *anatithenai* to set up, dedicate, fr. *ana-* + *tithenai* to place, set — more at DO] **1 a :** a ban or curse solemnly pronounced by ecclesiastical authority and accompanied by excommunication **b :** the denunciation of something as accursed **c :** a vigorous denunciation **:** CURSE **2 a :** one that is cursed by ecclesiastical authority **b :** one that is intensely disliked or loathed <men whose names were ~ —Thomas Wolfe>

anath·e·ma·tize \-ˌtīz\ *vt* **-tized; -tiz·ing :** to pronounce an anathema upon *syn* see EXECRATE

An·a·to·lian \ˌan-ə-ˈtō-lē-ən, -ˈtōl-yən\ *n* **1 :** a native or inhabitant of Anatolia and specif. of the western plateau lands of Turkey in Asia **2 :** a branch of the Indo-European language family that includes a group of extinct languages of ancient Anatolia — see INDO-EUROPEAN LANGUAGES table — **Anatolian** *adj*

an·a·tom·i·co- \ˌan-ə-ˈtäm-i-(ˌ)kō\ *or* **anat·o·mo-** \ə-ˈnat-ə-(ˌ)mō\ *comb form* **:** anatomical and **:** anatomical <*anatomico*pathological> <*anatomo*clinical>

anat·o·mist \ə-ˈnat-ə-məst\ *n* **1 :** a student of anatomy; *esp* **:** one skilled in dissection **2 :** one who analyzes minutely and critically <an ~ of urban society>

anat·o·mize \-ˌmīz\ *vt* **-mized; -miz·ing 1 :** to cut in pieces in order to display or examine the structure and use of the parts **:** DISSECT **2 :** ANALYZE

anat·o·my \ə-ˈnat-ə-mē\ *n, pl* **-mies** [LL *anatomia* dissection, fr. Gk *anatomē,* fr. *anatemnein* to dissect, fr. *ana-* + *temnein* to cut — more at TOME] **1 :** a branch of morphology that deals with the structure of organisms **2 :** a treatise on anatomic science or art **3 :** the art of separating the parts of an animal or plant in order to ascertain their position, relations, structure, and function **:** DISSECTION **4** *obs* **:** a body dissected or to be dissected **5 :** structural makeup esp. of an organism or any of its parts **6 :** a separating or dividing into parts for detailed examination **:** ANALYSIS **7 a** (1) **:** SKELETON (2) **:** MUMMY **b :** the human body — **an·a·tom·ic** \ˌan-ə-ˈtäm-ik\ *or* **an·a·tom·i·cal** \-i-kəl\ *adj* — **an·a·tom·i·cal·ly** \-i-k(ə-)lē\ *adv*

ana·tox·in \ˌan-ə-ˈtäk-sən\ *n* [ISV *ana-* + *toxin*] **:** TOXOID

anat·ro·pous \ə-ˈna-trə-pəs\ *adj* **:** having the ovule inverted so that the micropyle is bent down to the funiculus to which the body of the ovule is united

anc *abbr* ancient

-ance \ən(t)s, ᵊn(t)s\ *n suffix* [ME, fr. OF, fr. L *-antia,* fr. *-ant-, -ans* -ant + *-ia* -y] **1 :** action or process <further*ance*> **:** instance of an action or process <perform*ance*> **2 :** quality or state **:** instance of a quality or state <protuber*ance*> **3 :** amount or degree <conduct*ance*>

an·ces·tor \ˈan-ˌses-tər\ *n* [ME *ancestre,* fr. OF, fr. L *antecessor* one that goes before, fr. *antecessus,* pp. of *antecedere* to go before, fr. *ante-* + *cedere* to go — more at CEDE] **1 a :** one from whom a person is descended and who is usu. more remote in the line of descent than a grandparent **b :** FOREFATHER 2 **2 :** FORERUNNER, PROTOTYPE **3 :** a progenitor of a more recent or existing species or group — **an·ces·tress** \-trəs\ *n*

ancestor worship *n* **:** the custom of venerating deceased ancestors who are considered still a part of the family and whose spirits are believed to have the power of intervention in the affairs of the living

an·ces·tral \an-ˈses-trəl\ *adj* **:** of, relating to, or inherited from an ancestor <~ estates> — **an·ces·tral·ly** \-trə-lē\ *adv*

an·ces·try \ˈan-ˌses-trē\ *n* **1 :** line of descent **:** LINEAGE; *specif* **:** honorable, noble, or aristocratic descent **2 :** persons initiating or comprising a line of descent **:** ANCESTORS

An·chi·ses \an-ˈkī-(ˌ)sēz, aŋ-\ *n* [L, fr. Gk *Anchisēs*] **:** the father of Aeneas rescued by his son from the burning city of Troy

[1]**an·chor** \ˈaŋ-kər\ *n, often attrib* [ME *ancre,* fr. OE *ancor,* fr. L *anchora,* fr. Gk *ankyra;* akin to L *uncus* hook — more at ANGLE] **1 :** a device usu. of metal attached to a ship or boat by a cable and cast overboard to hold it in a particular place by means of a fluke that digs into the bottom **2 :** a reliable support **:** MAINSTAY **3 :** something that serves to hold an object firmly **4 :** an object shaped like a ship's anchor **5 :** ANCHORMAN **6** *pl, slang* **:** the brakes of a motor vehicle — **an·chor·less** \-ləs\ *adj*

anchor 1: *1* ring, *2* stock, *3* shank, *4* bill, *5* fluke, *6* arm, *7* throat, *8* crown

[2]**anchor** *vb* **an·chored; an·chor·ing** \-k(ə-)riŋ\ *vt* **1 :** to hold in place in the water by an anchor **2 :** to secure firmly **:** FIX **3 :** to serve as an anchorman on <~*ing* a television interview program —Charles Mandel> ~ *vi* **1 :** to cast anchor **2 :** to become fixed

an·chor·age \ˈaŋ-k(ə-)rij\ *n* **1 a :** the act of anchoring **:** the condition of lying at anchor **b :** a place where vessels anchor **:** a place suitable for anchoring **2 :** a means of securing **:** a source of reassurance <this ~ of Christian hope —T. O. Wedel> **3 :** something that provides a secure hold

an·cho·ress \ˈaŋ-k(ə-)rəs\ *or* **an·cress** \-krəs\ *n* [ME *ankeresse,* fr. *anker* hermit, fr. OE *ancor,* fr. OIr *anchara,* fr. LL *anachoreta*] **:** a female anchorite

an·cho·rite \ˈaŋ-kə-ˌrīt\ *also* **an·cho·ret** \-ˌret\ *n* [ME, fr. ML *anchorita,* alter. of LL *anachoreta,* fr. LGk *anachōrētēs,* fr. Gk *anachōrein* to withdraw, fr. *ana-* + *chōrein* to make room, fr. *chōros* place; akin to Gk *chēros* left, bereaved — more at HEIR] **:** one who lives in seclusion usu. for religious reasons — **an·cho·rit·ic** \ˌaŋ-kə-ˈrit-ik\ *adj* — **an·cho·rit·i·cal·ly** \-i-k(ə-)lē\ *adv*

an·chor·man \ˈaŋ-kər-ˌman\ *n* **1 :** one who is last: as **a :** the member of a team who competes last <the ~ on a relay team> **b :** one who has the lowest scholastic standing in his graduating class **2 :** a broadcaster who coordinates the related activities of other usu. remotely located broadcasters so as to produce a coherent program **3 :** MODERATOR 2c

an·cho·vy \ˈan-ˌchō-vē, an-ˈ\ *n, pl* **-vies** *or* **-vy** [Sp *anchova*] **:** any of numerous small fishes (family Engraulidae) resembling herrings; *esp* **:** a common Mediterranean fish (*Engraulis encrasicholus*) used esp. for making sauces and relishes

an·cien ré·gime \äⁿs-yaⁿ-rā-zhēm\ *n* [F, lit., old regime] **1 :** the political and social system of France before the Revolution of 1789 **2 :** a system or mode no longer prevailing

[1]**an·cient** \ˈān-shənt, -chənt, ˈāŋ(k)-shənt\ *adj* [ME *ancien,* fr. MF, fr. (assumed) VL *anteanus,* fr. L *ante* before — more at ANTE-] **1 :** having had an existence of many years **2 :** of or relating to a remote period, to a time early in history, or to those living in such a period or time; *specif* **:** of or relating to the historical period beginning with the earliest known civilizations and extending to the fall of the western Roman Empire in 476 **3 :** having the qualities of age or long existence: **a :** VENERABLE **b :** OLD-FASHIONED, ANTIQUE *syn* see OLD *ant* modern — **an·cient·ness** *n*

[2]**ancient** *n* **1 :** an aged living being <a penniless ~ > **2 :** one who lived in ancient times: **a** *pl* **:** the civilized people of antiquity;

esp : those of the classical nations **b** : one of the classical authors <Plutarch and other ~*s*> **3** : an ancient coin

[3]**ancient** *n* [alter. of *ensign*] **1** *archaic* : ENSIGN, STANDARD, FLAG **2** *obs* : the bearer of an ensign

ancient history *n* **1** : the history of ancient times **2** : knowledge or information (as of something in the recent past) that is widespread and has lost its initial freshness or importance : common knowledge

an·cient·ly *adv* : in ancient times : long ago

an·cient·ry \-rē\ *n* : ANTIQUITY, ANCIENTNESS

an·cil·la \an-'sil-ə\ *n, pl* **-lae** \-(ˌ)ē\ [L, female servant] : AID, HELPER

an·cil·lary \'an(t)-sə-ˌler-ē, *esp Brit* an-'sil-ə-rē\ *adj* **1** : SUBORDINATE, SUBSIDIARY <the main factory and its ~ plants> **2** : AUXILIARY, SUPPLEMENTARY <the need for ~ evidence> — **ancillary** *n*

an·con \'aŋ-ˌkän\ *n, pl* **an·co·nes** \aŋ-'kō-nēz\ [L, fr. Gk *ankōn* elbow; akin to L *uncus* hook] : a bracket, elbow, or console used as an architectural support

-an·cy \ən-sē, ᵊn-\ *n suffix* [L *-antia* — more at -ANCE] : quality or state <piqu*ancy*>

an·cy·lo·sto·mi·a·sis \ˌaŋ-ki-lō-stə-'mī-ə-səs, ˌan(t)-sə-\ *n, pl* **-a·ses** \-ˌsēz\ [NL, fr. *Ancylostoma*, genus of hookworms, fr. Gk *ankylos* hooked + *stoma* mouth; akin to L *incus* hook — more at ANGLE, STOMACH] : infestation with or disease caused by hookworms; *esp* : a lethargic anemic state in man due to blood loss through the feeding of hookworms in the small intestine

and \ən(d), (ˈ)an(d), *usu* ᵊn(d) *after* t, d, s *or* z, *often* ᵊm *after* p *or* b, *sometimes* ᵊŋ *after* k *or* g\ *conj* [ME, fr. OE; akin to OHG *unti* and] **1** — used as a function word to indicate connection or addition esp. of items within the same class or type; used to join sentence elements of the same grammatical rank or function **2** — used as a function word to express logical modification, consequence, antithesis, or supplementary explanation **3** *obs* : IF **4** — used in logic as a sentential connective that forms a complex sentence which is true only if both constituent sentences are true — compare CONJUNCTION — **and how** \'and-'hau̇\ — used to emphasize the preceding idea — **and so forth** \ən-'sō-ˌfȯrth, -ˌfōrth\ **1** : and others or more of the same or similar kind **2** : further in the same or similar manner **3** : and the rest **4** : and other things — **and so on** \ən-'sō-ˌȯn, -ˌän\ : and so forth

AND \'and\ *n* : a logical operator equivalent to the sentential connective *and* <~ gate in a computer>

an·da·lu·site \ˌan-də-'lü-ˌsīt\ *n* [F *andalousite*, fr. *Andalousie* Andalusia, region in Spain] : a mineral Al_2SiO_5 consisting of a silicate of aluminum usu. in thick nearly square orthorhombic prisms of various colors

[1]**an·dan·te** \än-'dän-(ˌ)tā, -'dänt-ē; an-'dant-ē\ *adv or adj* [It, lit., going, prp. of *andare* to go] : moderately slow — used as a direction in music

[2]**andante** *n* : a musical composition or movement in andante tempo

[1]**an·dan·ti·no** \ˌän-ˌdän-'tē-(ˌ)nō\ *adv or adj* [It, dim of *andante*] : slightly faster than andante — used as a direction in music

[2]**andantino** *n, pl* **-nos** : a musical composition or movement in andantino tempo

an·des·ite \'an-di-ˌzīt\ *n* [G *andesit*, fr. *Andes*] : an extrusive usu. dark grayish rock consisting essentially of oligoclase or feldspar — **an·des·it·ic** \ˌan-di-'zit-ik\ *adj*

and·iron \'an-ˌdī(-ə)rn\ *n* [ME *aundiren*, modif. of OF *andier*] : one of a pair of metal supports for firewood used on a hearth and made of a horizontal bar mounted on short legs with usu. a vertical shaft surmounting the front end

and/or \'an-'dȯ(ə)r\ *conj* — used as a function word to indicate that two words or expressions are to be taken together or individually

andr- *or* **andro-** *comb form* [MF, fr. L, fr. Gk, fr. *andr-*, *anēr* man (male); akin to Oscan *ner* man, Skt *nr*, OIr *nert* strength] **1** : man <*andro*phobia> **2** : male <*andr*oecium>

an·dra·dite \an-'dräd-ˌīt, 'an-drə-ˌdīt\ *n* [José B. de *Andrada* e Silva †1838 Brazilian geologist] : a garnet $Ca_3Fe_2(SiO_4)_3$ of any of various colors ranging from yellow and green to brown and black

An·dro·cles \'an-drə-ˌklēz\ *n* [L, fr. Gk *Androklēs*] : a fabled Roman slave spared in the arena by a lion from whose foot he had years before extracted a thorn

an·droe·ci·um \an-'drē-s(h)ē-əm\ *n, pl* **-cia** \-s(h)ē-ə\ [NL, fr. *andr-* + Gk *oikion*, dim of *oikos* house — more at VICINITY] : the aggregate of microsporophylls in the flower of a seed plant

an·dro·gen \'an-drə-jən\ *n* [ISV] : a male sex hormone (as testosterone) — **an·dro·gen·ic** \ˌan-drə-'jen-ik\ *adj*

an·drog·y·nous \an-'dräj-ə-nəs\ *adj* [L *androgynus* hermaphrodite, fr. Gk *androgynos*, fr. *andr-* + *gynē* woman — more at QUEEN] **1** : having the characteristics or nature of both male and female **2** : bearing both staminate and pistillate flowers in the same cluster with the male flowers uppermost — **an·drog·y·ny** \-nē\ *n*

an·droid \'an-ˌdrȯid\ *n* [LGk *androeidēs* manlike, fr. Gk *andr-* + *-oeides* -oid] : an automaton with a human form

An·drom·a·che \an-'dräm-ə-(ˌ)kē\ *n* [L, fr. Gk *Andromachē*] : the wife of Hector

An·drom·e·da \an-'dräm-əd-ə\ *n* [L, fr. Gk *Andromedē*] **1** : an Ethiopian princess of classical mythology rescued from a monster by her future husband Perseus **2** [L (gen. *Andromedae*)] : a northern constellation directly south of Cassiopeia between Pegasus and Perseus

an·dros·ter·one \an-'dräs-tə-ˌrōn\ *n* [ISV *andr-* + *sterol* + *-one*] : an androgenic hormone that is a hydroxy ketone $C_{19}H_{30}O_2$ and is found in human male and female urine

-an·drous \'an-drəs\ *adj comb form* [NL *-andrus*, fr. Gk *-andros* having (such or so many) men, fr. *andr-*, *anēr*] : having (such or so many) stamens <mon*androus*>

ane \'ān\ *adj or n or pron, chiefly Scot* : ONE

-ane \ˌān\ *n suffix* [ISV *-an*, *-ane*, alter. of *-ene*, *-ine*, & *-one*] **1** : [3]AN 1 <tol*ane*> **2** : saturated or completely hydrogenated carbon compound (as a hydrocarbon) <meth*ane*>

an·ec·dot·age \'an-ik-ˌdōt-ij\ *n* : the telling of anecdotes; *also* : ANECDOTES

an·ec·dot·al \ˌan-ik-'dōt-ᵊl\ *adj* **1** : relating to, characteristic of, or containing anecdotes **2** : having the form or style of anecdotes **3** : depicting an anecdote <~ art> — **an·ec·dot·al·ly** \-ᵊl-ē\ *adv*

an·ec·dote \'an-ik-ˌdōt\ *n* [F, fr. Gk *anekdota* unpublished items, fr. neut. pl. of *anekdotos* unpublished, fr. *a-* + *ekdidonai* to publish, fr. *ex* out + *didonai* to give — more at EX-, DATE] : a usu. short narrative of an interesting, amusing, or biographical incident

an·ec·dot·ic \ˌan-ik-'dät-ik\ *or* **an·ec·dot·i·cal** \-'dät-i-kəl\ *adj* **1** : ANECDOTAL **2** : given to or skilled in telling anecdotes — **an·ec·dot·i·cal·ly** \-'dät-i-k(ə-)lē\ *adv*

an·ec·dot·ist \'an-ik-ˌdōt-əst\ *or* **an·ec·dot·al·ist** \ˌan-ik-'dōt-ᵊl-əst\ *n* : one who is given to or is skilled in telling anecdotes

an·echo·ic \ˌan-i-'kō-ik\ *adj* : free from echoes and reverberations <an ~ chamber>

anem- *or* **anemo-** *comb form* [prob. fr. F *anémo-*, fr. GK *anem-*, *anemo-*, fr. *anemos* — more at ANIMATE] : wind <*anemo*meter>

ane·mia \ə-'nē-mē-ə\ *n* [NL, fr. Gk *anaimia* bloodlessness, fr. *a-* + *-aimia* -emia] **1 a** : a condition in which the blood is deficient in red blood cells, in hemoglobin, or in total volume **b** : ISCHEMIA **2** : lack of vitality — **ane·mic** \ə-'nē-mik\ *adj* — **ane·mi·cal·ly** \-mi-k(ə-)lē\ *adv*

anemo·graph \ə-'nem-ə-ˌgraf\ *n* : a recording anemometer — **anemo·graph·ic** \-ˌnem-ə-'graf-ik\ *adj*

an·e·mom·e·ter \ˌan-ə-'mäm-ət-ər\ *n* : an instrument for measuring and indicating the force or speed of the wind — **an·e·mo·met·ric** \ˌan-ə-mō-'me-trik\ *also* **an·e·mo·met·ri·cal** \-tri-kəl\ *adj*

anemometer

an·e·mom·e·try \ˌan-ə-'mäm-ə-trē\ *n* : the act or process of ascertaining the force, speed, and direction of wind

anem·o·ne \ə-'nem-ə-nē\ *n* [L, fr. Gk *anemōnē*] **1** : any of a large genus (*Anemone*) of the buttercup family having lobed or divided leaves and showy flowers without petals but with conspicuous often colored sepals **2** : SEA ANEMONE

an·e·moph·i·lous \ˌan-ə-'mäf-ə-ləs\ *adj* : normally wind-pollinated — **an·e·moph·i·ly** \-lē\ *n*

anent \ə-'nent\ *prep* [ME *onevent*, *anent*, fr. OE *on efen* alongside, fr. *on* + *efen* even] : ABOUT, CONCERNING

an·er·oid \'an-ə-ˌrȯid\ *adj* [F *anéroïde*, fr. Gk *a-* + LGk *nēron* water, fr. Gk, neut. of *nearos*, *nēros* fresh; akin to Gk *neos* new — more at NEW] : containing no liquid or actuated without the use of liquid <an ~ manometer>

aneroid barometer *n* : a barometer in which the action of atmospheric pressure in bending a metallic surface is made to move a pointer

an·es·the·sia \ˌan-əs-'thē-zhə\ *n* [NL, fr. Gk *anaisthēsia* insensibility, fr. *a-* + *aisthēsis* perception, fr. *aisthanesthai* to perceive — more at AUDIBLE] : loss of sensation with or without loss of consciousness

an·es·the·si·ol·o·gist \-ˌthē-zē-'äl-ə-jəst\ *n* : ANESTHETIST; *specif* : a physician specializing in anesthesiology

an·es·the·si·ol·o·gy \-jē\ *n* : a branch of medical science dealing with anesthesia and anesthetics

[1]**an·es·thet·ic** \ˌan-əs-'thet-ik\ *adj* **1** : of, relating to, or capable of producing anesthesia **2** : lacking awareness or sensitivity <unmoved and quite ~ to his presence —S. J. Perelman> — **an·es·thet·i·cal·ly** \-i-k(ə-)lē\ *adv*

[2]**anesthetic** *n* **1** : a substance that produces anesthesia **2** : something that brings relief : PALLIATIVE

anes·the·tist \ə-'nes-thət-əst\ *n* : one who administers anesthetics

anes·the·tize \-thə-ˌtīz\ *vt* **-tized; -tiz·ing** : to subject to anesthesia

an·es·trous \(ˈ)an-'es-trəs\ *adj* **1** : not exhibiting estrus **2** : of or relating to anestrus

an·es·trus \-trəs\ *n* [NL, fr. *a-* + *estrus*] : the period of sexual quiescence between two periods of sexual activity in cyclically breeding mammals

an·eu·ploid \'an-yü-ˌplȯid\ *adj* [*an-* + *euploid*] : having or being a chromosome number that is not an exact multiple of the usu. haploid number — **aneuploid** *n* — **an·eu·ploi·dy** \-ˌplȯid-ē\ *n*

an·eu·rysm *also* **an·eu·rism** \'an-yə-ˌriz-əm\ *n* [Gk *aneurysma* fr. *aneurynein* to dilate, fr. *ana-* + *eurynein* to stretch, fr. *eurys* wide — more at EURY-] : a permanent abnormal blood-filled dilatation of a blood vessel resulting from disease of the vessel wall — **an·eu·rys·mal** \ˌan-yə-'riz-məl\ *adj*

anew \ə-'n(y)ü\ *adv* [ME *of newe*, fr. OE *of nīwe*, fr. *of* + *nīwe* new] **1** : for an additional time : AFRESH **2** : in a new or different form

an·frac·tu·os·i·ty \(ˌ)an-ˌfrak-chə-'wäs-ət-ē\ *n, pl* **-ties** **1** : the quality or state of being anfractuous **2** : a winding channel or course; *esp* : an intricate path or process (as of the mind)

an·frac·tu·ous \an-'frak-chə-wəs\ *adj* [F *anfractueux*, fr. LL *anfractuosus*, fr. L *anfractus* coil, bend, fr. *anfractus* crooked, fr. *an-* (fr. *ambi-* around) + *fractus*, pp. of *frangere* to break — more at AMBI-, BREAK] : full of windings and intricate turnings : TORTUOUS

Ang *abbr* Anglesey

an·ga·ry \'aŋ-gə-rē\ *n* [LL *angaria* service to a lord, fr. Gk *angareia* compulsory public service, fr. *angaros* Persian courier] : the right in international law of a belligerent to seize, use, or destroy property of neutrals

an·gel \'ān-jəl\ *n* [ME, fr. OF *angele*, fr. LL *angelus*, fr. Gk *angelos*, lit., messenger] **1 a :** a spiritual being superior to man in power and intelligence **b** *pl* **:** an order of angels — see CELESTIAL HIERARCHY **2 :** an attendant spirit or guardian **3 :** a white-robed winged figure of human form in fine art **4 :** MESSENGER, HARBINGER <~ of death> **5 :** a person believed to resemble an angel **6** *Christian Science* **:** a message originating from God in his aspects of Truth and Love **7 :** one (as a backer of a theatrical venture) who aids or supports with money or influence — **an·gel·ic** \an-'jel-ik\ *or* **an·gel·i·cal** \-i-kəl\ *adj* — **an·gel·i·cal·ly** \-i-k(ə-)lē\ *adv*

an·gel·fish \'ān-jel-,fish\ *n* **1 :** any of several compressed bright-colored teleost fishes (family Chaetodontidae) of warm seas **2 :** SCALARE

angel food cake *n* **:** a usu. white sponge cake made of flour, sugar, and whites of eggs

an·gel·i·ca \an-'jel-i-kə\ *n* [NL, genus name, fr. ML, fr. LL, fem. of *angelicus* angelic, fr. LGk *angelikos*, fr. Gk, of a messenger, fr. *angelos*] **1 :** any of a genus (*Angelica*) of herbs of the carrot family; *esp* **:** a biennial (*A. archangelica*) whose roots and fruit furnish a flavoring oil **2** *cap* **:** a sweet dessert wine produced in California

angelica tree *n* **:** HERCULES'-CLUB 1

An·ge·lus \'an-jə-ləs\ *n* [ML, fr. LL, angel; fr. the first word of the opening versicle] **1 :** a devotion of the Western church that commemorates the Incarnation and is said morning, noon, and evenings **2 :** a bell announcing the time for the Angelus

¹an·ger \'aŋ-gər\ *n* [ME, affliction, anger, fr. ON *angr* grief; akin to OE *enge* narrow, L *angere* to strangle, Gk *anchein*] **1 :** a strong feeling of displeasure and usu. of antagonism **2 :** RAGE 2 — **an·ger·less** \-ləs\ *adj*

syn ANGER, IRE, RAGE, FURY, INDIGNATION, WRATH *shared meaning element* **:** emotional excitement induced by intense displeasure. ANGER, the most general term, names the reaction but in itself conveys nothing about intensity or justification or manifestation of the emotional state <tried to hide his *anger*> <Moses' *anger* waxed hot —Exod 32:19 (AV)> IRE, more frequent in literary contexts, may suggest greater intensity than *anger*, often with an evident display of feeling <cheeks flushed dark with *ire*> RAGE suggests loss of self-control from violence of emotion <screaming with *rage*> FURY is overmastering destructive rage merging on madness <in his *fury* made sudden decisions which would prove utterly disastrous —W. L. Shirer> INDIGNATION stresses righteous anger at what one considers unfair, mean, or shameful <behavior that caused general *indignation*> WRATH may imply either rage or indignation but is likely to suggest a desire or intent to revenge or punish <rose in his *wrath* and struck his tormentor to the floor> *ant* pleasure, gratification, forbearance

²anger *vb* **an·gered; an·ger·ing** \-g(ə-)riŋ\ *vt* **:** to make angry ~ *vi* **:** to become angry

An·ge·vin \'an-jə-vən\ *adj* [F, fr. OF, fr. ML *andegavinus*, fr. *Andegavia* Anjou] **:** of, relating to, or characteristic of Anjou or the Plantagenets — **Angevin** *n*

angi- *or* **angio-** *comb form* [NL, fr. Gk *angei-*, *angeio-*, fr. *angeion* vessel, blood vessel, dim. of *angos* vessel] **1 :** blood or lymph vessel **:** blood vessels and <*angi*oma> <*angio*cardiography> **2 :** seed vessel <*angio*carpous>

an·gi·na \an-'jī-nə, 'an-jə-\ *n* [L, quinsy, fr. *angere*] **:** a disease marked by spasmodic attacks of intense suffocative pain: as **a :** a severe inflammatory or ulcerated condition of the mouth or throat **b :** ANGINA PECTORIS — **an·gi·nal** \an-'jīn-ᵊl, 'an-jən-\ *adj* — **an·gi·nose** \'an-jə-,nōs\ *adj*

angina pec·to·ris \-'pek-t(ə-)rəs\ *n* [NL, lit., angina of the chest] **:** a disease marked by brief paroxysmal attacks of chest pain precipitated by deficient oxygenation of the heart muscles

an·gio·car·di·og·ra·phy \'an-jē-ō-,kärd-ē-'äg-rə-fē\ *n* **:** the roentgenographic visualization of the heart and its blood vessels after injection of a radiopaque substance — **an·gio·car·dio·graph·ic** \-ē-ə-'graf-ik\ *adj*

an·gio·car·pous \,an-jē-ō-'kär-pəs\ *or* **an·gio·car·pic** \-pik\ *adj* **:** having or being fruit enclosed within an external covering — **an·gio·car·py** \'an-jē-ō-,kär-pē\ *n*

an·gi·og·ra·phy \,an-jē-'äg-rə-fē\ *n*: the roentgenographic visualization of the blood vessels after injection of a radiopaque substance — **an·gio·graph·ic** \,an-jē-ə-'graf-ik\ *adj*

an·gi·ol·o·gy \,an-jē-'äl-ə-jē\ *n* **:** the study of blood vessels and lymphatics

an·gi·o·ma \,an-jē-'ō-mə\ *n* **:** a tumor composed chiefly of blood vessels or lymph vessels — **an·gi·o·ma·tous** \-mət-əs\ *adj*

an·gio·sperm \'an-jē-ə-,spərm\ *n* [deriv. of NL *angi-* + Gk *sperma* seed — more at SPERM] **:** any of a class (Angiospermae) of vascular plants (as orchids or roses) having the seeds in a closed ovary — **an·gio·sper·mous** \,an-jē-ə-'spər-məs\ *adj*

an·gio·ten·sin \,an-jē-ō-'ten(t)-sən\ *n* [*angi-* + hyper*tension* + *-in*] **:** either of two forms of a kinin with marked vasoconstrictive action; *esp* **:** the one used in treatment of shock — called also *angiotensin II*

an·gio·ten·sin·ase \-sə-,nās, -,nāz\ *n* **:** any of several enzymes in the blood that hydrolyze angiotensin

Angl *abbr* Anglican

¹an·gle \'aŋ-gəl\ *n* [ME, fr. MF, fr. L *angulus*; akin to OE *anclēow* ankle] **1 :** a corner whether constituting a projecting part or a partially enclosed space <they sheltered in an ~ of the building> **2 a :** the figure formed by two lines extending from the same point or by two surfaces diverging from the same line **b :** a measure of the amount of turning necessary to bring one line or plane into coincidence with or parallel to another **3 a :** the precise viewpoint from which something is observed or considered; *also* **:** the aspect seen from such an angle **b (1) :** a special approach, point of attack, or technique for accomplishing an objective **(2) :** an often improper or illicit method of obtaining advantage <he always had an ~ to beat the other fellow> **4 :** a sharply divergent course <the road went off at an ~> **5 :** a position to the side of an opponent in football from which a player may block his opponent more effectively or without penalty — usu. used in the phrases *get an angle* or *have an angle* **syn** see PHASE — **an·gled** \-gəld\ *adj*

angles 2a: *1* obtuse, *2* right, *3* acute

²angle *vb* **an·gled; an·gling** \-g(ə-)liŋ\ *vt* **1 :** to turn, move, or direct at an angle **2 :** to present (as a news story) from a particular or prejudiced point of view **:** SLANT ~ *vi* **:** to turn or proceed at an angle

³angle *vi* **an·gled; an·gling** \-g(ə-)liŋ\ [ME *angelen*, fr. *angel* fishhook, fr. OE, fr. *anga* hook; akin to OHG *ango* hook, L *uncus*, Gk *onkos* barbed hook, *ankos* glen] **1 :** to fish with a hook **2 :** to use artful means to attain an objective <*angled* for an invitation>

angle bracket *n* **:** BRACKET 3b

An·gle·doz·er \'aŋ-gəl-,dō-zər\ *trademark* — used for a tractor-driven pusher and scraper with the blade at an angle for pushing material to one side

angle iron *n* **1 :** an iron cleat for joining parts of a structure at an angle **2 :** a piece of structural steel rolled with an L-shaped section

angle of attack : the acute angle between the direction of the relative wind and the chord of an airfoil

angle of depression : the angle formed by the line of sight and the horizontal plane for an object below the horizontal

angle of elevation : the angle formed by the line of sight and the horizontal plane for an object above the horizontal

angle of incidence : the angle that a line (as a ray of light) falling on a surface makes with a perpendicular to the surface at the point of incidence

angle of reflection : the angle between a reflected ray and the normal drawn at the point of incidence to a reflecting surface

angle of refraction : the angle between a refracted ray and the normal drawn at the point of incidence to the interface at which refraction occurs

an·gler \'aŋ-glər\ *n* **1 :** one that angles **2 :** any of several pediculate fishes; *esp* **:** one (*Lophius piscatorius*) having a large flattened head and wide mouth with a lure on the head and fleshy mouth appendages used to attract smaller fishes as prey

An·gles \'aŋ-gəlz\ *n pl* [L *Angli*, of Gmc origin; akin to OE *Engle* Angles] **:** a Germanic people that invaded England along with the Saxons and Jutes in the 5th century A.D. and merged with them to form the Anglo-Saxon peoples

angle shot *n* **:** a picture taken with the camera pointed at an angle from the horizontal

an·gle·site \'aŋ-gəl-,sīt, -glə-\ *n* [F *anglésite*, fr. *Anglesey* island, Wales] **:** a mineral $PbSO_4$ consisting of lead sulfate formed by the oxidation of galena

an·gle·worm \'aŋ-gəl-,wərm\ *n* **:** EARTHWORM

An·gli·an \'aŋ-glē-ən\ *n* **1 :** a member of the Angles **2 :** the Old English dialects of Mercia and Northumbria — **Anglian** *adj*

An·gli·can \'aŋ-gli-kən\ *adj* [ML *anglicanus*, fr. *anglicus* English, fr. LL *Angli* English people, fr. L, Angles] **1 :** of or relating to the established episcopal Church of England and churches of similar faith and order in communion with it **2 :** of or relating to England or the English nation — **Anglican** *n* — **An·gli·can·ism** \-kə-,niz-əm\ *n*

an·gli·ce \'aŋ-glə-(,)sē\ *adv, often cap* [ML, adv. of *anglicus*] **:** in English; *esp* **:** in readily understood English <the city of Napoli, ~ Naples>

an·gli·cism \'aŋ-glə-,siz-əm\ *n, often cap* [ML *anglicus* English] **1 :** a characteristic feature of English occurring in another language **2 :** adherence or attachment to English customs or ideas

An·gli·cist \'aŋ-glə-səst\ *n* **:** a specialist in English linguistics

an·gli·cize \'aŋ-glə-,sīz\ *vt* **-cized; -ciz·ing** *often cap* **1 :** to make English in quality or characteristics **2 :** to adapt (a foreign word or phrase) to English usage; *esp* **:** to borrow into English without alteration of form or spelling and with or without change in pronunciation — **an·gli·ci·za·tion** \,aŋ-glə-sə-'zā-shən\ *n, often cap*

an·gling \'aŋ-gliŋ\ *n* **:** the act of one who angles; *esp* **:** the act or sport of fishing with hook and line

An·glist \'aŋ-gləst\ *n* **:** ANGLICIST

An·glo \'aŋ-(,)glō\ *n, pl* **Anglos** [in sense 2, fr. MexSp, fr. Sp *anglo-americano* Anglo-American] **1 :** ANGLO-AMERICAN **2 :** a Caucasian inhabitant of the U.S. of non-Latin extraction — **Anglo** *adj*

Anglo- *comb form* [NL, fr. LL *Angli*] **1 :** English <*Anglo*-Norman> **2 :** English and <*Anglo*-Japanese>

An·glo–Amer·i·can \,aŋ-glō-ə-'mer-ə-kən\ *n* **1 :** an inhabitant of the U.S. of English origin or descent **2 :** a North American whose native language is English and whose culture is of English origin — **Anglo–American** *adj*

An·glo–Cath·o·lic \-'kath-(ə-)lik\ *adj* **:** of or relating to a High Church movement in Anglicanism emphasizing its continuity with historic Catholicism and fostering Catholic dogmatic and liturgical traditions — **Anglo–Catholic** *n* — **An·glo–Cathol·i·cism** \-kə-'thäl-ə-,siz-əm\ *n*

An·glo–French \-'french\ *n* **:** the French language used in medieval England

An·glo–Nor·man \-'nȯr-mən\ *n* **1 :** one of the Normans living in England after the Conquest **2 :** the form of Anglo-French used by Anglo-Normans

an·glo·phile \'aŋ-glə-,fīl\ *also* **an·glo·phil** \-,fil\ *n, often cap* [F, fr. *anglo-* + *-phile*] **:** one who greatly admires or favors England and things English — **an·glo·phil·ic** \,aŋ-glə-'fil-ik\ *adj, often cap* — **an·gloph·i·lism** \aŋ-'gläf-ə-,liz-əm\ *n, often cap* — **an·gloph·i·ly** \aŋ-'gläf-ə-lē\ *n*

an·glo·phil·ia \,aŋ-glə-'fil-ē-ə\ *n, often cap* **:** excessive admiration of or partiality for England or English ways — **an·glo·phil·i·ac** \-ē-,ak\ *adj, often cap*

an·glo·phobe \'aŋ-glə-,fōb\ *n, often cap* [prob. fr. F, fr. *anglo-* + *-phobe*]**:** one who is averse to England and things English —

an·glo·pho·bia \ˌaŋ-glə-ˈfō-bē-ə\ *n, often cap* — **an·glo·pho·bic** \-bik\ *adj, often cap*

an·glo·phone \ˈaŋ-glə-ˌfōn\ *adj, often cap* : consisting of or belonging to an English-speaking population — **Anglophone** *n*

An·glo–Sax·on \ˌaŋ-glō-ˈsak-sən\ *n* [NL *Anglo-Saxones*, pl., alter. of ML *Angli Saxones*, fr. L *Angli* Angles + LL *Saxones* Saxons] **1 :** a member of the Germanic peoples conquering England in the 5th century A.D. and forming the ruling class until the Norman conquest — compare ANGLES, JUTE, SAXON **2 :** ENGLISHMAN; *specif* : a person descended from the Anglo-Saxons **3 :** OLD ENGLISH 1 **4 :** direct plain English — **Anglo–Saxon** *adj*

an·go·ra \aŋ-ˈgōr-ə, an-, -ˈgȯr-\ *n* **1 :** the hair of the Angora rabbit or Angora goat — called also *angora wool* **2 :** a yarn of Angora rabbit hair used esp. for knitting **3** *cap* **a :** ANGORA CAT **b :** ANGORA GOAT **c :** ANGORA RABBIT

Angora cat *n* [*Angora* (Ankara), Turkey] : a long-haired domestic cat

Angora goat *n* : any of a breed or variety of the domestic goat raised for its long silky hair which is the true mohair

Angora rabbit *n* : a long-haired usu. white rabbit with red eyes that is raised for fine wool

an·gos·tu·ra bark \ˌaŋ-gə-ˈst(y)u̇r-ə-\ *n* [*Angostura* (now Ciudad Bolívar), Venezuela] : the aromatic bitter bark of either of two So. American trees (*Galipea officinalis* and *Cusparia trifoliata*) of the rue family that is used as a tonic and antipyretic

an·gry \ˈaŋ-grē\ *adj* **an·gri·er; -est 1 :** feeling or showing anger : WRATHFUL **2 a :** indicative of or proceeding from anger <~ words> **b :** seeming to show anger or to threaten in an angry manner <an ~ sky> **3 :** painfully inflamed <an ~ rash> — **an·gri·ly** \-grə-lē\ *adv* — **an·gri·ness** \-grē-nəs\ *n*

angry young man *n* : one of a group of mid-20th century British authors whose works express the bitterness of the lower classes toward the established sociopolitical system and toward the mediocrity and hypocrisy of the middle and upper classes

angst \ˈäŋ(k)st\ *n* [Dan & G; Dan, fr. G; akin to L *angustus*] : a feeling of anxiety : DREAD

ang·strom \ˈaŋ-strəm *also* ˈȯŋ-\ *n* [Anders J. *Ångström* †1874 Sw physicist] : a unit of wavelength of light equal to one ten-billionth of a meter

[1]**an·guish** \ˈaŋ-gwish\ *n* [ME *angwisshe*, fr. OF *angoisse*, fr. L *angustiae*, pl., straits, distress fr. *angustus* narrow; akin to OE *enge* narrow — more at ANGER] : extreme pain or distress of body or mind ***syn*** see SORROW ***ant*** relief

[2]**anguish** *vi* : to suffer intense pain or sorrow ~ *vt* : to cause to suffer anguish or distress

an·guished *adj* **1 :** suffering anguish : TORMENTED <the ~ martyrs> **2 :** expressing anguish : AGONIZED <~ cries>

an·gu·lar \ˈaŋ-gyə-lər\ *adj* [MF or L; MF *angulaire*, fr. L *angularis*, fr. *angulus* angle] **1 a :** having one or more angles **b :** forming an angle : sharp-cornered **2 :** measured by an angle <~ distance> **3 a :** stiff in character or manner **b :** having the bones prominent from lack of plumpness — **an·gu·lar·ly** *adv*

an·gu·lar·i·ty \ˌaŋ-gyə-ˈlar-ət-ē\ *n, pl* **-ties 1 :** the quality of being angular **2** *pl* : angular outlines or characteristics

angular momentum *n* : a vector quantity that is the measure of the intensity of rotational motion, that is equal in classical physics to the product of the angular velocity of a rotating body or system and its moment of inertia with respect to the rotation axis, and that is directed along the rotation axis

angular velocity *n* : the time rate of change of angular position that has direction and sense such that the motion appears clockwise to one looking in the direction of the vector

an·gu·la·tion \ˌaŋ-gyə-ˈlā-shən\ *n* **1 :** the action of making angular **2 :** an angular position, formation, or shape

An·gus \ˈaŋ-gəs\ *n* [*Angus*, county in Scotland] : ABERDEEN ANGUS

an·hin·ga \an-ˈhiŋ-gə\ *n* [Pg, fr. Tupi] : SNAKEBIRD; *esp* : WATER TURKEY

anhyd *abbr* anhydrous

an·hy·dride \(ˈ)an-ˈhī-ˌdrīd\ *n* : a compound derived from another (as an acid) by removal of the elements of water

an·hy·drite \-ˌdrīt\ *n* [G *anhydrit*, fr. Gk *anydros*] : a mineral $CaSO_4$ consisting of an anhydrous calcium sulfate that is usu. massive and white or slightly colored

an·hy·drous \-drəs\ *adj* [Gk *anydros*, fr. *a-* + *hydōr* water — more at WATER] : free from water and esp. water of crystallization

ani \ä-ˈnē\ *n* [Sp *aní*, or Pg *ani*, fr. Tupi *ani*] : any of several black cuckoos (genus *Crotaphagus*) of the warmer parts of America

anile \ˈan-ˌīl, ˈā-ˌnīl\ *adj* [L *anilis*, fr. *anus* old woman; akin to OHG *ano* grandfather] : of or resembling a doddering old woman; *esp* : FLIGHTY — **anil·i·ty** \a-ˈnil-ət-ē, ā-, ə-\ *n*

an·i·line \ˈan-ᵊl-ən\ *n* [G *anilin*, fr. *anil* indigo, fr. F, fr. Pg, fr. Ar *an-nīl* the indigo plant, fr. Skt *nīlī* indigo, fr. fem. of *nīla* dark blue] : an oily liquid poisonous amine $C_6H_5NH_2$ obtained esp. by the reduction of nitrobenzene and used chiefly in organic synthesis (as of dyes)

aniline dye *n* : a dye made by the use of aniline or one chemically related to such a dye; *broadly* : a synthetic organic dye

ani·lin·gus \ˌā-ni-ˈliŋ-gəs\ *or* **ani·linc·tus** \-ˈliŋ(k)-təs\ *n* [NL, fr. *anus* + *-i-* + *-lingus*, *-linctus* (as in *cunnilingus*, *cunnilinctus*)] : erotic stimulation achieved by contact between mouth and anus

an·i·ma \ˈan-ə-mə\ n [NL, fr. L, soul] : an individual's true inner self that in the analytic psychology of C. G. Jung reflects archetypal ideals of conduct; *esp* : an inner feminine part of the male personality — compare PERSONA 2

an·i·mad·ver·sion \ˌan-ə-ˌmad-ˈvər-zhən, -məd-, -ˈvər-shən\ *n* [L *animadversion-*, *animadversio*, fr. *animadversus*, pp. of *animadvertere*] **1 :** a critical and usu. censorious remark **2 :** adverse and typically ill-natured or unfair criticism
syn ANIMADVERSION, STRICTURE, ASPERSION, REFLECTION *shared meaning element* : adverse criticism ***ant*** commendation

an·i·mad·vert \-ˈvərt\ *vb* [L *animadvertere* to pay attention to, censure, fr. *animum advertere*, lit., to turn the mind to] *vt, archaic* : NOTICE, OBSERVE ~ *vi* : to make an animadversion ***syn*** see REMARK

[1]**an·i·mal** \ˈan-ə-məl\ *n* [L, fr. *animale*, neut. of *animalis* animate, fr. *anima* soul] **1 :** any of a kingdom (Animalia) of living beings typically differing from plants in capacity for spontaneous movement and rapid motor response to stimulation **2 a :** one of the lower animals as distinguished from man **b :** MAMMAL **3 :** a human being considered chiefly with regard to his physical nature **4 :** ANIMALITY 2 — **an·i·mal·like** \-məl-ˌ(l)īk\ *adj* — **an·i·mal·ness** \-məl-nəs\ *n*

[2]**animal** *adj* **1 :** of, relating to, or derived from animals **2 a** : of or relating to the physical or sentient as contrasted with the intellectual or rational **b :** SENSUAL, FLESHLY **3 :** of or relating to the animal pole of an egg or to the part from which ectoderm normally develops ***syn*** see CARNAL ***ant*** rational — **an·i·mal·ly** \-mə-lē\ *adv*

animal cracker *n* : a small animal-shaped cracker

an·i·mal·cule \ˌan-ə-ˈmal-(ˌ)kyü(ə)l\ *or* **an·i·mal·cu·lum** \-ˈmal-kyə-ləm\ *n, pl* **-cules** *or* **-cu·la** \-kyə-lə\ [NL *animalculum*, dim. of L *animal*] : a minute usu. microscopic organism — **an·i·mal·cu·lar** \-kyə-lər\ *adj*

animal heat *n* : heat produced in the body of a living animal by functional chemical and physical activities

animal husbandry *n* : a branch of agriculture concerned with the production and care of domestic animals

an·i·mal·ism \ˈan-ə-mə-ˌliz-əm\ *n* **1 a** (1) **:** the qualities typical of animals; *esp* : buoyant health and uninhibited vitality (2) : the exercise of these qualities **b :** preoccupation with the satisfaction of physical drives or wants **2 :** a theory that human beings are nothing more than animals — **an·i·mal·ist** \-mə-ləst\ *n* — **an·i·mal·is·tic** \ˌan-ə-mə-ˈlis-tik\ *adj*

an·i·mal·i·ty \ˌan-ə-ˈmal-ət-ē\ *n* **1 :** ANIMALISM 1a (1) **2 a :** the state of being an animal **b :** animal nature **3 :** the animal world

an·i·mal·ize \ˈan-ə-mə-ˌlīz\ *vt* **-ized; -iz·ing 1 :** to represent in animal form **2 a :** BRUTALIZE <men *animalized* by the war> **b** : SENSUALIZE <*animalized* by passion> — **an·i·mal·iza·tion** \ˌan-ə-mə-lə-ˈzā-shən\ *n*

animal kingdom *n* : the one of the three basic groups of natural objects that includes all living and extinct animals — compare MINERAL KINGDOM, PLANT KINGDOM

animal magnetism *n* : a force held to reside in some individuals by which a strong quasi-hypnotic influence can be exerted

animal pole *n* : the point on the surface of an egg that is diametrically opposite to the vegetal pole and usu. marks the most active part of the protoplasm or the part containing least yolk

animal spirits *n pl* : vivacity arising from physical health and energy

animal starch *n* : GLYCOGEN

[1]**an·i·mate** \ˈan-ə-mət\ *adj* [ME, fr. L *animatus*, pp. of *animare* to give life to, fr. *anima* breath, soul; akin to OE *ōthian* to breathe, L *animus* spirit, mind, courage, Gk *anemos* wind] **1 a :** possessing life : ALIVE **b :** of the kind or class of which life is a characteristic <all ~ creation> **2 :** of or relating to animal life as opposed to plant life **3 :** full of life : ANIMATED ***syn*** see LIVING ***ant*** inanimate — **an·i·mate·ly** *adv* — **an·i·mate·ness** *n*

[2]**an·i·mate** \-ˌmāt\ *vt* **-mat·ed; -mat·ing 1 :** to give spirit and support to : ENCOURAGE **2 a :** to give life to **b :** to give vigor and zest to **3 :** to move to action **4 a :** to make or design in such a way that apparently spontaneous lifelike movement is effected **b** : to produce in the form of an animated cartoon ***syn*** see QUICKEN

an·i·mat·ed \-ˌmāt-əd\ *adj* **1 a :** endowed with life or the qualities of life : ALIVE <viruses that can behave as ~ bodies or inert crystals> **b :** full of movement and activity **c :** full of vigor and spirit : VIVACIOUS <an ~ discussion> **2 :** having the appearance of something alive **3 :** made in the form of an animated cartoon ***syn* 1** see LIVING ***ant*** inert **2** see LIVELY — **an·i·mat·ed·ly** *adv*

animated cartoon *n* **1 :** a motion picture made from a series of drawings simulating motion by means of slight progressive changes **2 :** ANIMATION 2a

an·i·ma·tion \ˌan-ə-ˈmā-shən\ *n* **1 :** the act of animating : the state of being animate or animated **2 a :** a motion picture made by photographing successive positions of inanimate objects (as puppets or mechanical parts) **b :** ANIMATED CARTOON 1 **3 :** the preparation of animated cartoons

an·i·ma·to \ˌan-ə-ˈmät-(ˌ)ō\ *adv or adj* [It, fr. L *animatus*] : with animation — used as a direction in music

an·i·ma·tor \ˈan-ə-ˌmāt-ər\ *n* : one that contributes to the production of an animated cartoon

an·i·mism \ˈan-ə-ˌmiz-əm\ *n* [G *animismus*, fr. L *anima* soul] **1** : a doctrine that the soul is the vital principle of organic development **2 :** attribution of conscious life to nature or natural objects **3 :** belief in the existence of spirits separable from bodies — **an·i·mist** \-məst\ *n* — **an·i·mis·tic** \ˌan-ə-ˈmis-tik\ *adj*

an·i·mos·i·ty \ˌan-ə-ˈmäs-ət-ē\ *n, pl* **-ties** [ME *animosite*, fr. MF or LL; MF *animosité*, fr. LL *animositat-*, *animositas*, fr. L *animosus* spirited, fr. *animus*] : ill will or resentment tending toward active hostility ***syn*** see ENMITY

an·i·mus \ˈan-ə-məs\ *n* [L, spirit, mind, courage, anger] **1 :** basic attitude or governing spirit : DISPOSITION, INTENTION **2 :** a usu. prejudiced and often spiteful or malevolent ill will **3 :** an inner masculine part of the female personality in the analytic psychology of C. G. Jung ***syn*** see ENMITY ***ant*** favor

an·ion \ˈan-ˌī-ən\ *n* [Gk, neut. of *aniōn*, prp. of *anienai* to go up, fr. *ana-* + *ienai* to go — more at ISSUE] : the ion in an electrolyzed solution that migrates to the anode; *broadly* : a negatively charged ion

an·ion·ic \ˌan-(ˌ)ī-ˈän-ik\ *adj* **1 :** of or relating to anions **2 :** characterized by an active and esp. surface-active anion — **an·ion·i·cal·ly** \-i-k(ə-)lē\ *adv*

anis- *or* **aniso-** *comb form* [NL, fr. Gk, fr. *anisos*, fr. *a-* + *isos* equal] **:** unequal <*aniseikonia*> <*anisodactylous*>

an·ise \ˈan-əs\ *n* [ME *anis*, fr. OF, fr. L *anisum*, fr. Gk *annēson*, *anison*] **:** an herb (*Pimpinella anisum*) of the carrot family having carminative and aromatic seeds; *also* **:** ANISEED

ani·seed \ˈan-ə(s)-ˌsēd\ *n* [ME *anis seed*, fr. *anis* + *seed*] **:** the seed of anise often used as a flavoring in cordials and in cooking

an·is·ei·ko·nia \ˌan-ˌī-ˌsī-ˈkō-nē-ə\ *n* [NL, fr. *anis-* + Gk *eikōn* image — more at ICON] **:** a defect of binocular vision in which the two retinal images of an object differ in size — **an·is·ei·kon·ic** \-ˈkän-ik\ *adj*

an·is·ette \ˌan-ə-ˈset, -ˈzet\ *n* [F, fr. *anis*] **:** a usu. colorless sweet liqueur flavored with aniseed

an·isog·a·mous \ˌan-(ˌ)ī-ˈsäg-ə-məs\ *also* **an·iso·gam·ic** \-ˌī-sə-ˈgam-ik\ *adj* **:** characterized by fusion of heterogamous gametes or of individuals that usu. differ chiefly in size <~ reproduction> — **an·isog·a·my** \-(ˌ)ī-ˈsäg-ə-mē\ *n*

an·iso·me·tro·pia \ˌan-ˌī-sə-mə-ˈtrō-pē-ə\ *n* [NL, fr. Gk *anisometros* of unequal measure (fr. *anis-* + *metron* measure) + NL *-opia* — more at MEASURE] **:** unequal refractive power in the two eyes — **an·iso·me·tro·pic** \-ˈträp-ik, -ˈtrō-pik\ *adj*

an·iso·trop·ic \ˌan-ˌī-sə-ˈträp-ik\ *adj* **1 :** exhibiting properties with different values when measured along axes in different directions <an ~ crystal> **2 :** assuming different positions in response to external stimuli — **an·iso·trop·i·cal·ly** \-i-k(ə-)lē\ *adv* — **an·isot·ro·py** \-(ˌ)ī-ˈsä-trə-pē\ *or* **an·isot·ro·pism** \-ˌpiz-əm\ *n*

an·ker·ite \ˈaŋ-kə-ˌrīt\ *n* [G *ankerit*, fr. M. J. *Anker* †1843 Austrian mineralogist] **:** a dolomitic iron-containing mineral $Ca(Fe,Mg,Mn)(CO_3)_2$

ankh \ˈaŋk\ *n* [Egypt *ʿnḫ*] **:** a cross having a loop for its upper vertical arm and serving esp. in ancient Egypt as an emblem of life

ankh

an·kle \ˈaŋ-kəl\ *n* [ME *ankel*, fr. OE *ancleōw*; akin to OHG *anchlāo* ankle, L *angulus* angle] **1 :** the joint between the foot and the leg; *also* **:** the region of this joint **2 :** the joint between the cannon bone and pastern (as in the horse)

an·kle·bone \ˌan-kəl-ˈbōn, ˈaŋ-kəl-ˌ\ *n* **:** TALUS 1

an·klet \ˈaŋ-klət\ *n* **1 :** something (as an ornament) worn around the ankle **2 :** a short sock reaching slightly above the ankle **3 :** a woman's or child's low shoe having one or more ankle straps

an·ky·lose \ˈaŋ-ki-ˌlōs, -ˌlōz\ *vb* **-losed; -los·ing** [back-formation fr. *ankylosis*] *vt* **:** to unite or stiffen by ankylosis ~ *vi* **:** to undergo ankylosis

an·ky·lo·sis \ˌaŋ-ki-ˈlō-səs\ *n, pl* **-lo·ses** \-ˌsēz\ [NL, fr. Gk *ankylōsis*, fr. *ankyloun* to make crooked, fr. *ankylos* crooked; akin to L *uncus* hooked — more at ANGLE] **1 :** stiffness or fixation of a joint by disease or surgery **2 :** union of separate bones or hard parts to form a single bone or part — **an·ky·lot·ic** \-ˈlät-ik\ *adj*

an·la·ge \ˈän-ˌläg-ə\ *n, pl* **-gen** \-ən\ *also* **-ges** \-əz\ [G, lit., act of laying on] **:** the foundation of a subsequent development; *specif* **:** the first recognizable commencement of a developing part or organ in an embryo

ann *abbr* **1** annals **2** annual

an·na \ˈän-ə\ *n* [Hindi *ānā*] **1 :** a former monetary unit of Burma, India, and Pakistan equal to 1/16 rupee **2 :** a coin representing one anna

an·nal·ist \ˈan-ᵊl-əst\ *n* **:** a writer of annals **:** HISTORIAN — **an·nal·is·tic** \ˌan-ᵊl-ˈis-tik\ *adj*

an·nals \ˈan-ᵊlz\ *n pl* [L *annales*, fr. pl. of *annalis* yearly — more at ANNUAL] **1 :** a record of events arranged in yearly sequence **2 :** historical records **:** CHRONICLES **3 :** records of the activities of an organization *syn* see HISTORY

An·nam·ese \ˌan-ə-ˈmēz, -ˈmēs\ *n, pl* **Annamese** [*Annam*, region of Vietnam] **1 a :** a Mongolian people inhabiting Vietnam **b** *or* **An·nam·ite** \ˈan-ə-ˌmīt\ **:** a member of this people **2 :** the language of the Annamese people **:** VIETNAMESE — **Annamese** *adj* — **Annamite** *adj*

an·nat·to \ə-ˈnät-(ˌ)ō\ *n* [of Cariban origin; akin to Galibi *annoto* tree producing annatto] **:** a yellowish red dyestuff made from the pulp around the seeds of a tropical tree (*Bixa orellana*, family Bixaceae)

an·neal \ə-ˈnē(ə)l\ *vt* [ME *anelen*, fr. OE *onǣlan*, fr. *on* + *ǣlan* to set on fire, burn, fr. *āl* fire; akin to OE *ād* funeral pyre — more at EDIFY] **1 :** to heat (as glass) in order to fix laid-on colors **2 :** to heat and then cool (as steel or glass) usu. for softening and making less brittle **3 :** STRENGTHEN, TOUGHEN

an·ne·lid \ˈan-ᵊl-əd\ *n* [deriv. of L *anellus* little ring — more at ANNULET] **:** any of a phylum (Annelida) of coelomate and usu. elongated segmented invertebrates (as earthworms, various marine worms, and leeches) — **annelid** *adj* — **an·nel·i·dan** \ə-ˈnel-əd-ᵊn, a-\ *adj or n*

annelid: *1* nereis, *2* leech, *3* earthworm

[1]an·nex \ə-ˈneks, ˈan-ˌeks\ *vt* [ME *annexen*, fr. MF *annexer*, fr. OF, fr. *annexe* joined, fr. L *annexus*, pp. of *annectere* to bind to, fr. *ad-* + *nectere* to bind] **1 :** to attach as a quality, consequence, or condition **2** *archaic* **:** to join together materially **:** UNITE **3 :** SUBJOIN, APPEND **4 :** to incorporate (a country or other territory) within the domain of a state **5 :** to obtain or take for oneself — **an·nex·ation** \ˌan-ˌek-ˈsā-shən\ *n* — **an·nex·ation·al** \-shnəl, -shən-ᵊl\ *adj* — **an·nex·ation·ist** \-sh(ə-)nəst\ *n*

[2]an·nex \ˈan-ˌeks, -iks\ *n* **:** something annexed or appended: as **a :** an added stipulation or statement **:** APPENDIX **b :** a subsidiary or supplementary structure **:** WING

an·nexe \ˈan-ˌeks, -iks\ *chiefly Brit var of* [2]ANNEX

An·nie Oak·ley \ˌan-ē-ˈō-klē\ *n, pl* **Annie Oakleys** [*Annie Oakley* †1926 Am markswoman; fr. the resemblance of a punched pass to a playing card with bullet holes through the spots] **:** a free ticket (as to a theater)

an·ni·hi·late \ə-ˈnī-ə-ˌlāt\ *vb* **-lat·ed; -lat·ing** [LL *annihilatus*, pp. of *annihilare* to reduce to nothing, fr. L *ad-* + *nihil* nothing — more at NIL] *vt* **1 a :** to cause to be of no effect **:** NULLIFY **b :** to destroy the substance or force of **2 :** to regard as of no consequence **3 :** to cause to cease to exist **4 a :** to destroy a considerable part of <the army was *annihilated*> **b :** to vanquish completely **:** ROUT ~ *vi* **:** to cease to exist **:** VANISH — used of a particle and its antiparticle upon coming together *syn* see ABOLISH — **an·ni·hi·la·tion** \-ˌnī-ə-ˈlā-shən\ *n* — **an·ni·hi·la·tive** \ə-ˈnī-ə-ˌlāt-iv\ *adj* — **an·ni·hi·la·tor** \-ˌlāt-ər\ *n* — **an·ni·hi·la·to·ry** \-ˈnī-ə-lə-ˌtōr-ē, -ˌtȯr\ *adj*

an·ni·ver·sa·ry \ˌan-ə-ˈvərs-(ə-)rē\ *n, pl* **-ries** *often attrib* [ME *anniversarie*, fr. ML, *anniversarium*, fr. L, neut. of *anniversarius* returning annually, fr. *annus* year + *versus*, pp. of *vertere* to turn — more at ANNUAL, WORTH] **1 :** the annual recurrence of a date marking a notable event **2 :** the celebration of an anniversary

an·no Do·mi·ni \ˌan-(ˌ)ō-ˈdäm-ə-nē, -ˈdō-mə-, -ˌnī\ *adv, often cap A* [ML, in the year of the Lord] — used to indicate that a time division falls within the Christian era

an·no he·gi·rae \-hi-ˈjī(ə)r-(ˌ)ē, -ˈhej-ə-ˌrē\ *adv, often cap A&H* [NL, in the year of the Hegira] — used to indicate that a time division falls within the Muslim era

an·no·tate \ˈan-ə-ˌtāt\ *vb* **-tat·ed; -tat·ing** [L *annotatus*, pp. of *annotare*, fr. *ad-* + *notare* to mark — more at NOTE] *vi* **:** to make or furnish critical or explanatory notes or comment ~ *vt* **:** to make or furnish annotations for (a literary work or subject) — **an·no·ta·tive** \-ˌtāt-iv\ *adj* — **an·no·ta·tor** \-ˌtāt-ər\ *n*

an·no·ta·tion \ˌan-ə-ˈtā-shən\ *n* **1 :** the act of annotating **2 :** a note added by way of comment or explanation

an·nounce \ə-ˈnaun(t)s\ *vb* **-nounced; -nounc·ing** [ME *announcen*, fr. MF *annoncer*, fr. L *annuntiare*, fr. *ad-* + *nuntiare* to report, fr. *nuntius* messenger] *vt* **1 :** to make known publicly **:** PROCLAIM <*announced* their engagement> **2 a :** to give notice of the arrival, presence, or readiness of <~ dinner> **b :** to indicate beforehand **:** FORETELL **3 :** to serve as an announcer of ~ *vi* **1 :** to serve as an announcer **2 :** to declare one's candidacy **:** give one's political support *syn* see DECLARE

an·nounce·ment \ə-ˈnaun(t)-smənt\ *n* **1 :** the act of announcing or of being announced **2 :** a public notification or declaration **3 :** a piece of formal stationery designed for a social or business announcement

an·nounc·er \ə-ˈnaun(t)-sər\ *n* **:** one that announces; *esp* **:** one that introduces television or radio programs, makes commercial announcements, reads news summaries, and gives station identification

an·noy \ə-ˈnȯi\ *vb* [ME *anoien*, fr. OF *enuier*, fr. LL *inodiare* to make loathsome, fr. L *in* + *odium* hatred — more at ODIUM] *vt* **1 :** to disturb or irritate esp. by repeated acts **:** VEX **2 :** to harass esp. by quick and brief attacks ~ *vi* **:** to be a source of annoyance — **an·noy·er** *n*

syn **1** ANNOY, VEX, IRK, BOTHER *shared meaning element* **:** to disturb and nervously upset a person ***ant*** soothe
2 see WORRY

an·noy·ance \ə-ˈnȯi-ən(t)s\ *n* **1 :** the act of annoying or of being annoyed **2 :** the state or feeling of being annoyed **:** VEXATION **3 :** a source of vexation or irritation **:** NUISANCE

an·noy·ing *adj* **:** causing vexation **:** IRRITATING — **an·noy·ing·ly** \-iŋ-lē\ *adv*

[1]an·nu·al \ˈan-yə(-wə)l\ *adj* [ME, fr. MF & LL; MF *annuel*, fr. LL *annualis*, blend of L *annuus* yearly (fr. *annus* year) and L *annalis* yearly (fr. *annus* year); akin to Goth *athnam* (dat. pl.) years, Skt *atati* he walks, goes] **1 :** covering the period of a year <~ rainfall> **2 :** occurring or performed once a year **:** YEARLY <an ~ reunion> **3 :** completing the life cycle in one growing season — **an·nu·al·ly** \-ē\ *adv*

[2]annual *n* **1 :** a publication appearing yearly **2 :** an event that occurs yearly **3 :** something that lasts one year or season; *specif* **:** an annual plant

annual ring *n* **:** the layer of wood produced by a single year's growth of a woody plant

an·nu·itant \ə-ˈn(y)ü-ət-ənt\ *n* **:** a beneficiary of an annuity

an·nu·ity \ə-ˈn(y)ü-ət-ē\ *n, pl* **-ities** [ME *annuite*, fr. MF *annuité*, fr. ML *annuitat-*, *annuitas*, fr. L *annuus* yearly] **1 :** an amount payable yearly or at other regular intervals **2 :** the right to receive or the obligation to pay an annuity **3 :** a contract or agreement providing for the payment of an annuity

an·nul \ə-ˈnəl\ *vt* **an·nulled; an·nul·ling** [ME *annullen*, fr. MF *annuller*, fr. LL *annullare*, fr. L *ad-* + *nullus* not any — more at NULL] **1 :** to reduce to nothing **:** OBLITERATE **2 :** to make ineffective or inoperative **:** NEUTRALIZE <~ the drug's effect> **3 :** to declare or make legally invalid or void <wants his marriage *annulled*> *syn* see NULLIFY

an·nu·lar \ˈan-yə-lər\ *adj* [MF or L; MF *annulaire*, fr. L *annularis*, fr. *annulus*] **:** of, relating to, or forming a ring — **an·nu·lar·i·ty** \ˌan-yə-ˈlar-ət-ē\ *n* — **an·nu·lar·ly** \ˈan-yə-lər-lē\ *adv*

annular eclipse *n* **:** an eclipse in which a thin outer ring of the sun's disk is not covered by the apparently smaller dark disk of the moon

an·nu·late \ˈan-yə-lət, -ˌlāt\ *or* **an·nu·lat·ed** \-ˌlāt-əd\ *adj* **:** furnished with or composed of rings **:** RINGED — **an·nu·late·ly** *adv*

an·nu·la·tion \ˌan-yə-ˈlā-shən\ *n* **:** formation of rings; *also* **:** RING

an·nu·let \ˈan-yə-lət\ *n* [modif. of MF *annelet*, dim. of *anel*, fr. L *anellus*, dim. of *annulus*] **1 :** a little ring **2 :** a small architectural molding or ridge forming a ring

an·nul·ment \ə-ˈnəl-mənt\ *n* **1 :** the act of annulling or of being annulled **2 :** a judicial pronouncement declaring a marriage invalid

an·nu·lus \ˈan-yə-ləs\ *n, pl* **-li** \-ˌlī, -lē\ *also* **-lus·es** [L, dim. of *anus* ring, anus — more at ANUS] **1 :** RING **2 :** a part, structure, or marking resembling a ring; as **a :** a line of cells around a fern sporangium that ruptures the sporangium by contracting **b :** a growth ring (as on the scale of a fish) that is used in estimating age

an·nun·ci·ate \ə-'nən(t)-sē-,āt\ *vt* **-at·ed; -at·ing :** ANNOUNCE

an·nun·ci·a·tion \ə-,nən(t)-sē-'ā-shən\ *n* [ME *annunciacioun,* fr. MF *anunciation,* fr. LL *annuntiation-, annuntiatio,* fr. L *annuntiatus,* pp. of *annuntiare* — more at ANNOUNCE] **1 :** the act of announcing or of being announced **:** ANNOUNCEMENT **2** *cap* **:** March 25 observed as a church festival in commemoration of the announcement of the Incarnation to the Virgin Mary

an·nun·ci·a·tor \ə-'nən(t)-sē-,āt-ər\ *n* **:** one that annunciates; *specif* **:** a usu. electrically controlled signal board or indicator — **an·nun·ci·a·to·ry** \-sē-ə-,tōr-ē, -,tȯr-\ *adj*

an·nus mi·ra·bi·lis \,an-ə-smə-'räb-ə-ləs, ,än-\ *n, pl* **an·ni mi·ra·bi·les** \'an-,ī-mə-'räb-ə-,lēz, 'än-(,)ē-mə-'räb-ə-,lās\ [NL] **:** wonderful year — used of an esp. notable year

an·ode \'an-,ōd\ *n* [Gk *anodos* way up, fr. *ana-* + *hodos* way — more at CEDE] **1 :** the positive terminal of an electrolytic cell — compare CATHODE **2 :** the negative terminal of a primary cell or of a storage battery that is delivering current **3 :** the electron-collecting electrode of an electron tube — **an·od·ic** \a-'näd-ik\ or **an·od·al** \-'nōd-ᵊl\ *adj* — **an·od·i·cal·ly** \-i-k(ə-)lē\ *or* **an·od·al·ly** \-ᵊl-ē\ *adv*

an·od·ize \'an-ə-,dīz\ *vt* **-ized; -iz·ing :** to subject (a metal) to electrolytic action as the anode of a cell in order to coat with a protective or decorative film — **an·od·iza·tion** \,an-,ōd-ə-'zā-shən, -əd-\ *n*

¹an·o·dyne \'an-ə-,dīn\ *adj* [L *anodynos,* fr. Gk *anōdynos,* fr. *a-* + *odynē* pain; akin to OE *etan* to eat] **:** serving to assuage pain

²anodyne *n* **1 :** a drug that allays pain **2 :** something that soothes, calms, or comforts <the ~ of bridge, a comfortable book, or sport — Harrison Smith> — **an·o·dyn·ic** \,an-ə-'din-ik\ *adj*

anoint \ə-'nȯint\ *vt* [ME *anointen,* fr. MF *enoint,* pp. of *enoindre,* fr. L *inunguere,* fr. *in-* + *unguere* to smear — more at OINTMENT] **1 :** to smear or rub with oil or an oily substance **2 a :** to apply oil to as a sacred rite esp. for consecration **b :** to designate as if through the rite of anointment **:** CONSECRATE — **anoint·er** *n* — **anoint·ment** \-mənt\ *n*

anom·a·lis·tic \ə-,näm-ə-'lis-tik\ *adj* **:** of or relating to the astronomical anomaly — **anom·a·lis·ti·cal** \-ti-kəl\ *adj*

anom·a·lous \ə-'näm-ə-ləs\ *adj* [LL *anomalus,* fr. Gk *anōmalos,* lit., uneven, fr. *a-* + *homalos* even, fr. *homos* same — more at SAME] **1 :** deviating from a general rule, method, or analogy **:** ABNORMAL **2 :** being out of keeping with accepted notions of fitness or order; *also* **:** inconsistent with what would naturally be expected ***syn*** see IRREGULAR — **anom·a·lous·ly** *adv* — **anom·a·lous·ness** *n*

anom·a·ly \ə-'näm-ə-lē\ *n, pl* **-lies 1 :** the angular distance of a planet from its perihelion as seen from the sun **2 :** deviation from the common rule **:** IRREGULARITY **3 :** something anomalous; *esp* **:** something that deviates in excess of normal variation ***syn*** see PARADOX

an·o·mie *or* **an·o·my** \'an-ə-mē\ *n* [F *anomie,* fr. Gk *anomia* lawlessness, fr. *anomos* lawless, fr. *a-* + *nomos* law, fr. *nemein* to distribute — more at NIMBLE] **:** a state of society in which normative standards of conduct and belief are weak or lacking; *also* **:** a similar condition in an individual commonly characterized by disorientation, anxiety, and isolation — **ano·mic** \ə-'näm-ik, -'nō-mik\ *adj*

¹anon \ə-'nän\ *adv* [ME, fr. OE *on ān,* fr. *on* in + *ān* one — more at ON, ONE] **1** *obs* **:** at once **:** IMMEDIATELY **2** *archaic* **:** SOON, PRESENTLY **3 :** at another time

²anon *abbr* anonymous; anonymously

an·o·nym \'an-ə-,nim\ *n* **1 :** one who is anonymous **2 :** PSEUDONYM

an·o·nym·i·ty \,an-ə-'nim-ət-ē\ *n, pl* **-ties 1 :** the quality or state of being anonymous **2 :** one that is anonymous

anon·y·mous \ə-'nän-ə-məs\ *adj* [LL *anonymus,* fr. Gk *anōnymos,* fr. *a-* + *onyma* name — more at NAME] **1 :** having or giving no name <an ~ author> **2 :** of unknown or unnamed origin <~ gifts> **3 :** marked by lack of individuality or personality <the gray ~ streets — William Styron> — **anon·y·mous·ly** *adv* — **anon·y·mous·ness** *n*

anoph·e·les \ə-'näf-ə-,lēz\ *n* [NL, genus name, fr. Gk *anōphelēs* useless, fr. *a-* + *ophelos* advantage, help; akin to OE *ō-* behind, OHG *ā-,* Skt *ā-* toward and to Skt *phalam* fruit, profit] **:** any of a genus (*Anopheles*) of mosquitoes that includes all mosquitoes which transmit malaria to man — see MOSQUITO illustration — **anoph·e·line** \-,līn\ *adj or n*

an·o·rak \'an-ə-,rak\ *n* [Greenland Esk *ánorâq*] **:** PARKA

an·o·rec·tic \,an-ə-'rek-tik\ *or* **an·o·ret·ic** \-'ret-ik\ *adj* [Gk *anorektos,* fr. *an-* ²a- + *oregein* to reach after] **1 :** lacking appetite **2 :** causing loss of appetite

an·orex·ia \,an-ə-'rek-sē-ə\ *n* [NL, fr. Gk, fr. *a-* + *orexis* appetite, fr. *oregein* to stretch out, reach after — more at RIGHT] **:** loss of appetite esp. when prolonged — **an·orexi·gen·ic** \,an-ə-,rek-sə-'jen-ik\ *adj*

an·or·thite \ə-'nȯr-,thīt\ *n* [F, fr. *a-* + Gk *orthos* straight — more at ARDUOUS] **:** a white, grayish, or reddish feldspar $CaAl_2Si_2O_8$ occurring in many igneous rocks — **an·or·thit·ic** \,an-,ȯr-'thit-ik\ *adj*

an·or·tho·site \ə-'nȯr-thə-,sīt\ *n* [F *anorthose,* a feldspar, fr. *a-* + Gk *orthos*] **:** a granular plutonic igneous rock composed almost exclusively of a soda-lime feldspar (as labradorite)

an·os·mia \a-'näz-mē-ə\ *n* [NL, fr. *a-* + Gk *osmē* smell — more at ODOR] **:** loss or impairment of the sense of smell — **an·os·mic** \-mik\ *adj*

¹an·oth·er \ə-'nəth-ər\ *adj* **1 :** different or distinct from the one first considered <the same scene viewed from ~ angle> **2 :** some other **:** LATER <do it ~ time> **3 :** being one more in addition to one or more of the same kind **:** NEW <have ~ piece of pie>

²another *pron* **1 :** an additional one **:** one more **2 :** one that is different from the first or present one **3 :** one of a group of unspecified or indefinite things

anoth·er–guess \ə-'nəth-ər-,ges\ *adj* [alter. of *anothergates,* fr. *¹another* + *gate*] *archaic* **:** of another sort

an·ovu·lant \a-'näv-yə-lənt, -'nōv-\ *n* [²*a-* + *ovulate* + *-ant*] **:** a drug that suppresses ovulation — **anovulant** *adj*

an·ovu·la·to·ry \(')an-'äv-yə-lə-,tōr-ē, -'ōv-, -,tȯr-\ *adj* [²*a-* + *ovulate* + *-ory*] **1 :** not involving or associated with ovulation <~ bleeding> **2 :** suppressing ovulation

an·ox·emia \,an-,äk-'sē-mē-ə\ *n* [NL] **:** a condition of subnormal oxygenation of the arterial blood — **an·ox·emic** \-mik\ *adj*

an·ox·ia \a-'näk-sē-ə\ *n* [NL] **:** hypoxia esp. of such severity as to result in permanent damage — **an·ox·ic** \-sik\ *adj*

ans *abbr* answer

an·ser·ine \'an(t)-sə-,rīn\ *adj* [L *anserinus,* fr. *anser* goose — more at GOOSE] **:** of, relating to, or resembling a goose

¹an·swer \'an(t)-sər\ *n* [ME, fr. OE *andswaru;* akin to ON *andsvar* answer; both fr. a prehistoric WGmc-NGmc compound whose first constituent is represented by OE *and-* against, and whose second constituent is akin to OE *swerian* to swear — more at ANTE-] **1 a :** something spoken or written in reply to a question **b :** a correct response **2 a :** a reply to a charge **:** DEFENSE **b :** a rejoinder made by the defendant in an equity case in reply to the charges made by the complainant in his bill **3 :** something done in response <his only ~ was to walk out> **4 :** a solution of a problem <the ~ to a chess problem>

²answer *vb* **an·swered; an·swer·ing** \'an(t)s-(ə-)riŋ\ *vi* **1 :** to speak or write in reply **2 a :** to be or make oneself responsible or accountable **b :** to make amends **:** ATONE **3 :** to be in conformity or correspondence <~*ed* to the description> **4 :** to act in response to an action performed elsewhere or by another **5 :** to be adequate **:** SERVE ~ *vt* **1 a :** to speak or write in reply to **b :** to say or write by way of reply **2 :** to reply in rebuttal, justification, or explanation **3 a :** to correspond to **b :** to be adequate or usable for **:** serve the purpose of often in a temporary or expedient manner **4** *obs* **:** to atone for **5 :** to act in response to **6 :** to offer a solution for; *esp* **:** SOLVE — **an·swer·er** \'an(t)-sər-ər\ *n*

syn **1** ANSWER, RESPOND, REPLY, REJOIN, RETORT *shared meaning element* **:** to say or write or do something in return
2 see SATISFY

an·swer·able \'an(t)s-(ə-)rə-bəl\ *adj* **1 :** liable to be called to account **:** RESPONSIBLE **2** *archaic* **:** SUITABLE, ADEQUATE **3** *archaic* **:** ACCORDANT, CORRESPONDING **4 :** capable of being refuted

answering service *n* **:** a commercial service that answers telephone calls for its clients

¹ant \'ant\ *n* [ME *ante, emete,* fr. OE *æmette;* akin to OHG *āmeiza* ant] **:** any of a family (Formicidae) of colonial hymenopterous insects with a complex social organization and various castes performing special duties

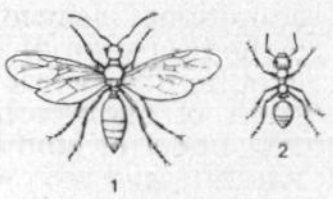

1 2

ants: *1* winged male, *2* worker

²ant *abbr* **1** antenna **2** antonym

Ant *abbr* **1** Antarctica **2** Antrim

ant- — see ANTI-

¹-ant \ənt, ᵊnt\ *n suffix* [ME, fr. OF, fr. *-ant,* prp. suffix, fr. L *-ant, -ans,* prp. suffix of first conjugation, fr. *-a-* (stem vowel of first conjugation) + *-nt-, -ns,* prp. suffix; akin to OE *-nde,* prp. suffix, Gk *-nt-, -n,* part. suffix] **1 a :** one that performs (a specified action) **:** personal or impersonal agent <claim*ant*> <cool*ant*> **b :** thing that promotes (a specified action or process) <expector*ant*> **2 :** one connected with <annuit*ant*> **3 :** thing that is acted upon (in a specified manner) <inhal*ant*>

²-ant *adj suffix* **1 :** performing (a specified action) or being (in a specified condition) <somnambul*ant*> **2 :** promoting (a specified action or process) <expector*ant*>

an·ta \'ant-ə\ *n, pl* **antas** *or* **an·tae** \'an-,tē, -,tī\ [L; akin to ON *önd* anteroom] **:** a pier produced by thickening a wall at its termination

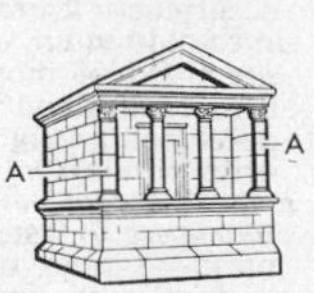

A A

A, A antas

ANTA *abbr* American National Theater and Academy

ant·ac·id \(')ant-'as-əd\ *adj* **:** counteractive of acidity — **antacid** *n*

An·tae·an \an-'tē-ən\ *adj* [*Antaeus,* a giant overcome by Hercules] **1 :** having superhuman strength **2 :** MAMMOTH

an·tag·o·nism \an-'tag-ə-,niz-əm\ *n* **1 a :** actively expressed opposition, hostility, or antipathy <~ between factions> **b :** opposition of a conflicting force, tendency, or principle <the ~ of democracy to dictatorship> **2 :** opposition in physiological action; *esp* **:** interaction of two or more substances such that the action of any one of them on living cells or tissues is lessened ***syn*** see ENMITY ***ant*** accord, comity

an·tag·o·nist \-nəst\ *n* **1 :** one that opposes another esp. in combat **:** ADVERSARY **2 :** an agent of physiological antagonism: as **a :** a muscle that contracts with and limits the action of an agonist with which it is paired — called also *antagonistic muscle* **b :** a drug that opposes the action of another ***syn*** see OPPONENT

an·tag·o·nis·tic \(,)an-,tag-ə-'nis-tik\ *adj* **:** characterized by or resulting from antagonism **:** OPPOSING ***syn*** see ADVERSE ***ant*** favoring, favorable — **an·tag·o·nis·ti·cal·ly** \-ti-k(ə-)lē\ *adv*

an·tag·o·nize \an-'tag-ə-,nīz\ *vt* **-nized; -niz·ing** [Gk *antagōnizesthai,* fr. *anti-* + *agōnizesthai* to struggle, fr. *agōn* contest — more at AGONY] **1 :** to act in opposition to **:** COUNTERACT **2 :** to incur or provoke the hostility of ***syn*** see OPPOSE

ə abut   ᵊ kitten   ər further   a back   ā bake   ä cot, cart
aů out   ch chin   e less   ē easy   g gift   i trip   ī life
j joke   ŋ sing   ō flow   ȯ flaw   ȯi coin   th thin   th this
ü loot   ů foot   y yet   yü few   yů furious   zh vision

ant·arc·tic \(ˈ)ant-ˈärk-tik, -ˈärt-ik\ *adj, often cap* [ME *antartik,* fr. L *antarcticus,* fr. Gk *antarktikos,* fr. *anti-* + *arktikos* arctic] : of or relating to the south pole or to the region near it

antarctic circle *n, often cap A&C* : a small circle of the earth that is parallel to its equator and that is approximately 23°27′ from the south pole

An·tar·es \an-ˈta(ə)r-(ˌ)ēz, -ˈte(ə)r-\ *n* [Gk *Antarēs*] : a giant red star of very low density that is the brightest star in Scorpio

ant bear *n* : a large anteater (*Myrmecophaga jubata*) of So. America with a shaggy gray fur, a black band across the breast, and a white stripe on the shoulder

ant bear

ant cow *n* : an aphid from which ants obtain honeydew

1an·te \ˈant-ē\ *n* [*ante-*] **1** : a poker stake usu. put up before the deal to build the pot <the dealer called for a dollar ~> **2** : an amount paid : PRICE <these improvements would raise the ~>

2ante *vt* **an·ted; an·te·ing** : to put up (an ante); *also* : PAY, PRODUCE — often used with *up*

ante- *prefix* [ME, fr. L, fr. *ante* before, in front of; akin to OE *and-* against, Gk *anti* before, against — more at END] **1 a** : prior : earlier <*ante*type> **b** : anterior : forward <*ante*room> **2 a** : prior to : earlier than <*ante*diluvian> **b** : in front of <*ante*choir>

ant·eat·er \ˈant-ˌēt-ər\ *n* : any of several mammals that feed largely or entirely on ants: as **a** : an edentate with a long narrow snout, a long tongue, and enormous salivary glands **b** : ECHIDNA **c** : AARDVARK

an·te·bel·lum \ˌant-i-ˈbel-əm\ *adj* [L *ante bellum* before the war] : existing before a war; *esp* : existing before the Civil War <an ~ brick mansion>

an·te·cede \ˌant-ə-ˈsēd\ *vt* **-ced·ed; -ced·ing** [L *antecedere,* fr. *ante-* + *cedere* to go — more at CEDE] : PRECEDE

an·te·ced·ence \-ˈsēd-ᵊn(t)s\ *n* : PRIORITY, PRECEDENCE

1an·te·ced·ent \ˌant-ə-ˈsēd-ᵊnt\ *n* [ME, fr. ML & L; ML *antecedent-, antecedens,* fr. L, logical antecedent, lit., one that goes before, fr. neut. of *antecedent-, antecedens,* prp. of *antecedere*] **1** : a substantive word, phrase, or clause referred to by a pronoun (as *John* in "I saw John and spoke to him"); *broadly* : a word or group of words replaced and referred to by a substitute **2** : the conditional element in a proposition (as *if A* in "if A, then B") **3** : the first term of a mathematical ratio **4 a** : a preceding event, condition, or cause **b** *pl* : the significant events, conditions, and traits of one's earlier life **5 a** : a predecessor in a series; *esp* : a model or stimulus for later developments **b** *pl* : ANCESTORS, PARENTS ***syn*** see CAUSE

2antecedent *adj* **1** : prior in time or order **2** : causally or logically prior ***syn*** see PRECEDING ***ant*** subsequent, consequent — **an·te·ced·ent·ly** *adv*

an·te·ces·sor \ˌant-i-ˈses-ər\ *n* [ME *antecessour,* fr. L *antecessor* — more at ANCESTOR] : one that goes before : PREDECESSOR

an·te·cham·ber \ˈant-i-ˌchām-bər\ *n* [F *antichambre,* fr. MF, fr. It *anti-* (fr. L *ante-*) + MF *chambre* room — more at CHAMBER] : ANTEROOM

an·te·choir \ˈant-i-ˌkwī(ə)r\ *n* : a space enclosed or reserved for the clergy and choristers at the entrance to a choir

1an·te·date \ˈant-i-ˌdāt\ *n* : a date assigned to an event or document earlier than the actual date of the event or document

2an·te·date \ˈant-i-ˌdāt, ˌant-i-ˈ\ *vt* **1 a** : to date as of a time prior to that of execution **b** : to assign to a date prior to that of actual occurrence **2** *archaic* : ANTICIPATE **3** : to precede in time

an·te·di·lu·vi·an \ˌant-i-də-ˈlü-vē-ən, -(ˌ)dī-\ *adj* [*ante-* + L *diluvium* flood — more at DELUGE] **1** : of or relating to the period before the flood described in the Bible **2** : made, evolved, or developed a long time ago : ANTIQUATED <an ~ automobile> — **antediluvian** *n*

an·te·fix \ˈant-i-ˌfiks\ *n* [L *antefixum,* fr. neut. of *antefixus,* pp. of *antefigere* to fasten before, fr. *ante-* + *figere* to fasten — more at DIKE] **1** : an ornament at the eaves of a classical building concealing the ends of the joint tiles of the roof **2** : an ornament of the molding of a classic cornice — **an·te·fix·al** \ˌant-i-ˈfik-səl\ *adj*

an·te·lope \ˈant-ᵊl-ˌōp\ *n, pl* **-lope** *or* **-lopes** [ME, fabulous heraldic beast, prob. fr. MF *antelop* savage animal with sawlike horns, fr. ML *anthalopus,* fr. LGk *antholop-, antholops*] **1 a** : any of various Old World ruminant mammals (family Bovidae) that differ from the true oxen esp. in lighter racier build and horns directed upward and backward **b** : PRONGHORN **2** : leather from antelope hide

an·te me·ri·di·em \ˈant-i-mə-ˈrid-ē-əm, -ē-ˌem\ *adj* [L] : being before noon — abbr. *a.m.*

an·te·mor·tem \-ˈmȯrt-əm\ *adj* [L *ante mortem*] : preceding death

an·te·na·tal \-ˈnāt-ᵊl\ *adj* : of or relating to an unborn child : PRENATAL; *also* : occurring during pregnancy

an·ten·na \an-ˈten-ə\ *n, pl* **-nae** \-(ˌ)ē\ *or* **-nas** [ML, fr. L, sail yard] **1** : a movable segmented organ of sensation on the head of insects, myriopods, and crustaceans — see INSECT illustration **2** *pl antennas* : a usu. metallic device (as a rod or wire) for radiating or receiving radio waves — **an·ten·nal** \-ˈten-ᵊl\ *adj*

an·ten·nule \an-ˈten-(ˌ)yü(ə)l\ *n* : a small antenna or similar appendage

an·te·pen·di·um \ˌant-i-ˈpen-dē-əm\ *n, pl* **-di·ums; -dia** \-dē-ə\ [ML, fr. L *ante-* + *pendēre* to hang — more at PENDANT] : a hanging for the front of an altar, pulpit, or lectern

an·te·pe·nult \ˌant-i-ˈpē-ˌnəlt, -pi-ˈ\ *also* **an·te·pen·ul·ti·ma** \-pi-ˈnəl-tə-mə\ *n* [LL *antepaenultima,* fem. of *antepaenultimus* preceding the next to last, fr. L *ante-* + *paenultimus* penultimate] : the 3d syllable of a word counting from the end (as *cu* in *accumulate*) — **an·te·pen·ul·ti·mate** \-pi-ˈnəl-tə-mət\ *adj or n*

an·te·ri·or \an-ˈtir-ē-ər\ *adj* [L, compar. of *ante* before — more at ANTE-] **1 a** : situated before or toward the front **b** : ABAXIAL **2 a** : coming before in time : ANTECEDENT **b** : logically prior ***syn*** see PRECEDING ***ant*** posterior — **an·te·ri·or·ly** *adv*

an·tero- \ˌant-ə-(ˌ)rō\ *comb form* [NL, fr. L *anterior*] : anterior <*antero*parietal> : anterior and <*antero*lateral> : from front to <*antero*posterior>

an·te·room \ˈant-i-ˌrüm, -ˌrům\ *n* : an outer room that leads to another usu. more important room and that is often used as a waiting room

anth- — see ANTI-

an·the·lion \ant-ˈhēl-yən, an-ˈthēl-\ *n, pl* **-lia** \-yə\ *or* **-lions** [Gk *anthēlion,* fr. neut. of *anthēlios* opposite the sun, fr. *anti-* + *hēlios* sun — more at SOLAR] : a somewhat bright white spot appearing on the parhelic circle opposite the sun

an·thel·min·tic \ˌant-ˌhel-ˈmint-ik, ˌan-ˌthel-\ *adj* [*anti-* + Gk *helminth-, helmis* worm — more at HELMINTH] : expelling or destroying parasitic worms esp. of the intestine — **anthelmintic** *n*

an·them \ˈan(t)-thəm\ *n* [ME *antem,* fr. OE *antefn,* fr. LL *antiphona,* fr. LGk *antiphōna,* pl. of *antiphōnon,* fr. Gk, neut. of *antiphōnos* responsive, fr. *anti-* + *phōnē* sound — more at BAN] **1 a** : a psalm or hymn sung antiphonally or responsively **b** : a sacred vocal composition with words usu. from the Scriptures **2** : a song or hymn of praise or gladness

an·the·mi·on \an-ˈthē-mē-ən\ *n, pl* **-mia** \-mē-ə\ [Gk, fr. dim. of *anthemon* flower, fr. *anthos* — more at ANTHOLOGY] : an ornament of floral or foliated forms arranged in a radiating cluster but always flat (as in relief sculpture or in painting)

an·ther \ˈan(t)-thər\ *n* [NL *anthera,* fr. L, medicine made fr. flowers, fr. Gk *anthēra,* fr. fem. of *antheros* flowery, fr. *anthos*] : the part of a stamen that develops and contains pollen and is usu. borne on a stalk — see FLOWER illustration — **an·ther·al** \-thə-rəl\ *adj*

an·ther·id·i·um \ˌan(t)-thə-ˈrid-ē-əm\ *n, pl* **-id·ia** \-ē-ə\ [NL, fr. *anthera*] : the male reproductive organ of a cryptogamous plant — **an·ther·id·i·al** \-ē-əl\ *adj*

an·the·sis \an-ˈthē-səs\ *n* [NL, fr. Gk *anthēsis* bloom, fr. *anthein* to flower, fr. *anthos*] : the action or period of opening of a flower

ant·hill \ˈant-ˌhil\ *n* : a mound thrown up by ants or termites in digging their nest

an·tho·cy·a·nin \ˌan(t)-thə-ˈsī-ə-nən\ *also* **an·tho·cy·an** \-ˈsī-ən, -ˌan\ *n* [Gk *anthos* + *kyanos* dark blue] : any of various soluble glycoside pigments producing blue to red coloring in flowers and plants

an·thol·o·gist \an-ˈthäl-ə-jəst\ *n* : a compiler of an anthology

an·thol·o·gize \-ˌjīz\ *vt* **-gized; -giz·ing** : to compile or publish in an anthology — **an·thol·o·giz·er** \-ˌjī-zər\ *n*

an·thol·o·gy \an-ˈthäl-ə-jē\ *n, pl* **-gies** [NL *anthologia* collection of epigrams, fr. MGk, fr. Gk, flower gathering, fr. *anthos* flower + *logia* collecting, fr. *legein* to gather; akin to Skt *andha* herb — more at LEGEND] : a collection of selected literary pieces or passages

an·thoph·a·gous \an-ˈthäf-ə-gəs\ *adj* [Gk *anthos* + E *-phagous*] : feeding on flowers — **an·thoph·a·gy** \-ə-jē\ *n*

an·tho·zo·an \ˌan(t)-thə-ˈzō-ən\ *n* [deriv. of Gk *anthos* + *zōion* animal; akin to Gk *zōē* life — more at QUICK] : any of a class (Anthozoa) of marine coelenterates (as the corals and sea anemones) having polyps with radial partitions — **anthozoan** *adj*

an·thra·cene \ˈan(t)-thrə-ˌsēn\ *n* : a crystalline cyclic hydrocarbon $C_{14}H_{10}$ obtained from coal-tar distillation

an·thra·cite \ˈan(t)-thrə-ˌsīt\ *n* [Gk *anthrakitis,* fr. *anthrak-, anthrax* coal] : a hard natural coal of high luster differing from bituminous coal in containing little volatile matter — **an·thra·cit·ic** \ˌan(t)-thrə-ˈsit-ik\ *adj*

an·thrac·nose \an-ˈthrak-ˌnōs\ *n* [F, fr. Gk *anthrak-, anthrax* + *nosos* disease] : any of numerous destructive plant diseases caused by imperfect fungi and characterized by often dark sunken lesions or blisters

an·thra·ni·late \an-ˈthran-ᵊl-ˌāt, ˌan-thrə-ˈnil-ˌāt\ *n* : a salt or ester of anthranilic acid

an·thra·nil·ic acid \ˌan(t)-thrə-ˌnil-ik-\ *n* [ISV *anthra*cene + *anil*ine] : a crystalline acid $NH_2C_6H_4COOH$ used as an intermediate in the manufacture of dyes (as indigo), pharmaceuticals, and perfumes

an·thra·qui·none \ˌan(t)-thrə-kwin-ˈōn, -ˈkwin-ˌōn\ *n* [prob. fr. F, fr. *anthracene* + *quinone*] : a yellow crystalline ketone $C_{14}H_8O_2$ derived from anthracene and used esp. in the manufacture of dyes

an·thrax \ˈan-ˌthraks\ *n* [ME *antrax* carbuncle, fr. L *anthrax,* fr. Gk, coal, carbuncle] : an infectious disease of warm-blooded animals (as cattle and sheep) caused by a spore-forming bacterium (*Bacillus anthracis*), transmissible to man esp. by the handling of infected products (as hair), and characterized by external ulcerating nodules or by lesions in the lungs

anthrop *abbr* anthropological; anthropology

anthrop- *or* **anthropo-** *comb form* [L *anthropo-,* fr. Gk *anthrōp-, anthrōpo-,* fr. *anthrōpos*] : human being <*anthropo*genesis>

an·throp·ic \an-ˈthräp-ik\ *or* **an·throp·i·cal** \-i-kəl\ *adj* [Gk *anthrōpikos,* fr. *anthrōpos*] : of or relating to mankind or the period of man's existence on earth

an·thro·po·cen·tric \ˌan(t)-thrə-pə-ˈsen-trik\ *adj* **1** : considering man to be the most significant entity of the universe **2** : interpreting or regarding the world in terms of human values and experiences — **an·thro·po·cen·tri·cal·ly** \-tri-k(ə-)lē\ *adv* — **an·thro·po·cen·tric·i·ty** \-pō-(ˌ)sen-ˈtris-ət-ē\ *n*

an·thro·po·gen·e·sis \ˌan(t)-thrə-pə-ˈjen-ə-səs\ *n* [NL, fr. *anthrop-* + L *genesis*] : the study of the origin and development of man — **an·thro·po·ge·net·ic** \-(ˌ)pō-jə-ˈnet-ik\ *adj*

an·thro·po·gen·ic \-pə-ˈjen-ik\ *adj* : of, relating to, or influenced by the impact of man on nature <~ ecosystems>

an·thro·pog·ra·phy \ˌan(t)-thrə-ˈpäg-rə-fē\ *n* : a branch of anthropology dealing with the distribution of man as distinguished by physical character, language, institutions, and customs

1an·thro·poid \ˈan(t)-thrə-ˌpȯid\ *adj* [Gk *anthrōpoeidēs,* fr. *anthrōpos*] **1** : resembling man **2** : resembling an ape <~ gangsters>

[2]**anthropoid** *n* **:** any of several large tailless semierect apes (family Pongidae)
anthropoid ape *n* **:** APE 1b
an·thro·pol·o·gy \ˌan(t)-thrə-ˈpäl-ə-jē\ *n* [NL *anthropologia,* fr. *anthrop-* + *-logia* -logy] **1 :** the science of man; *esp* **:** the study of man in relation to distribution, origin, classification, and relationship of races, physical character, environmental and social relations, and culture **2 :** teaching about the origin, nature, and destiny of man esp. from the perspective of his relation to God — **an·thro·po·log·i·cal** \-pə-ˈläj-i-kəl\ *adj* — **an·thro·po·log·i·cal·ly** \-i-k(ə-)lē\ *adv* — **an·thro·pol·o·gist** \ˌan(t)-thrə-ˈpäl-ə-jəst\ *n*
an·thro·pom·e·try \ˌan(t)-thrə-ˈpäm-ə-trē\ *n* [F *anthropométrie,* fr. *anthrop-* + *-métrie* -metry] **:** the study of human body measurements esp. on a comparative basis — **an·thro·po·met·ric** \-pə-ˈme-trik\ *or* **an·thro·po·met·ri·cal** \-tri-kəl\ *adj* — **an·thro·po·met·ri·cal·ly** \-tri-k(ə-)lē\ *adv*
an·thro·po·mor·phic \ˌan(t)-thrə-pə-ˈmȯr-fik\ *adj* [LL, *anthropomorphus* of human form, fr. Gk *anthrōpomorphos,* fr. *anthrōp-* + *-morphos* -morphous] **1 :** described or thought of as having a human form or human attributes <~ deities> **2 :** ascribing human characteristics to nonhuman things <~ supernaturalism> — **an·thro·po·mor·phi·cal·ly** \-fi-k(ə-)lē\ *adv*
an·thro·po·mor·phism \-ˌfiz-əm\ *n* **:** an interpretation of what is not human or personal in terms of human or personal characteristics **:** HUMANIZATION — **an·thro·po·mor·phist** \-fəst\ *n*
an·thro·po·mor·phize \-ˌfīz\ *vt* **-phized; -phiz·ing :** to attribute human form or personality to
an·thro·po·pa·thism \ˌan(t)-thrə-ˈpäp-ə-ˌthiz-əm, -pō-ˈpath-ˌiz-\ *n* [LGk *anthrōpopatheia* humanity, fr. Gk *anthrōpopathēs* having human feelings, fr. *anthrōp-* + *pathos* experience — more at PATHOS] **:** the ascription of human feelings to something not human
an·thro·poph·a·gous \ˌan(t)-thrə-ˈpäf-ə-gəs\ *adj* **:** feeding on human flesh — **an·thro·poph·a·gy** \-ə-jē\ *n*
an·thro·poph·a·gus \-ə-gəs\ *n, pl* **-a·gi** \-ə-ˌgī, -ˌjī, -ˌgē\ [L, fr. Gk *anthrōpophagos,* fr. *anthrōp-* + *-phagos* -phagous] **:** MAN-EATER, CANNIBAL
an·thro·pos·o·phy \ˌan(t)-thrə-ˈpäs-ə-fē\ *n* **:** a 20th century religious system growing out of theosophy and centering on man rather than God
[1]**an·ti** \ˈan-ˌtī, ˈant-ē\ *n, pl* **antis** [*anti-*] **:** one that is opposed
[2]**anti** *prep* **:** opposed to **:** AGAINST
anti- *or* **ant-** *or* **anth-** *prefix* [*anti-* fr. ME, fr. OF & L; OF, fr. L, against, fr. Gk, fr. *anti-; ant-* fr. ME, fr. L, against, fr. Gk, fr. *anti; anth-* fr. L, against, fr. Gk, fr. *anti* — more at ANTE-] **1 a :** of the same kind but situated opposite, exerting energy in the opposite direction, or pursuing an opposite policy <*anti*clinal> **b :** one that is opposite in kind to <*anti*climax> **2 a :** opposing or hostile to in opinion, sympathy, or practice <*anti*-Semite> **b :** opposing in effect or activity <*ant*acid> <*anti*catalyst> **3 :** combating or defending against <*anti*aircraft> <*anti*missile>
[1]**an·ti·air·craft** \ˌant-ē-ˈa(ə)r-ˌkraft, -ˈe(ə)r-\ *adj* **:** designed for or concerned with defense against air attack
[2]**antiaircraft** *n* **:** an antiaircraft weapon
an·ti·anx·i·ety \ˌant-ē-(ˌ)aŋ-ˈzī-ət-ē\ *adj* **:** tending to prevent or relieve anxiety <~ drugs>
an·ti·ar·rhyth·mic \ˌant-ē-(ˌ)ā-ˈrith-mik, ˌan-ˌtī-\ *adj* **:** tending to prevent or relieve arrhythmia <an ~ agent>
an·ti–art \-ˈärt\ *n* **:** art based on premises antithetical to traditional or popular art forms; *specif* **:** DADA
an·ti·au·thor·i·tar·i·an \-ȯ-ˌthär-ə-ˈter-ē-ən, -ə-ˌthär-, -ˌthȯr-\ *adj* **:** opposing or hostile to authoritarians or authoritarianism — **an·ti·au·thor·i·tar·i·an·ism** \-ˌiz-əm\ *n*
an·ti·aux·in \-ˈȯk-sən\ *n* **:** a plant substance that opposes or suppresses the natural effect of an auxin
an·ti·bac·te·ri·al \ˌant-i-bak-ˈtir-ē-əl, ˌan-ˌtī-\ *adj* **:** directed or effective against bacteria
an·ti·bal·lis·tic missile \ˌant-i-bə-ˌlis-tik-, ˌan-ˌtī-\ *n* **:** a missile for intercepting and destroying ballistic missiles
an·ti·bi·o·sis \-bī-ˈō-səs, -bē-\ *n* [NL] **:** antagonistic association between organisms to the detriment of one of them or between one organism and a metabolic product of another
[1]**an·ti·bi·ot·ic** \-bī-ˈät-ik, -bē-\ *adj* **1 :** tending to prevent, inhibit, or destroy life **2 :** of or relating to antibiosis or antibiotics — **an·ti·bi·ot·i·cal·ly** \-i-k(ə-)lē\ *adv*
[2]**antibiotic** *n* **:** a substance produced by a microorganism and able in dilute solution to inhibit or kill another microorganism
an·ti·black \-ˈblak\ *adj* **:** opposed or hostile to people belonging to the Negro race <his ~ attitude> — **an·ti·black·ism** \-ˌiz-əm\ *n*
an·ti·body \ˈant-i-ˌbäd-ē\ *n* **:** any of the body globulins that combine specifically with antigens and neutralize toxins, agglutinate bacteria or cells, and precipitate soluble antigens
[1]**an·tic** \ˈant-ik\ *n* **1 :** a ludicrous act or action **:** CAPER <childish ~s> **2** *archaic* **:** a performer of a grotesque or ludicrous part **:** BUFFOON
[2]**antic** *adj* [It *antico* ancient, fr. L *antiquus* — more at ANTIQUE] **1** *archaic* **:** GROTESQUE, BIZARRE **2 a :** characterized by clownish extravagance or absurdity **b :** whimsically gay **:** FROLICSOME — **an·ti·cal·ly** \-i-k(ə-)lē\ *adv*
an·ti·can·cer \ˌant-i-ˈkan(t)-sər, ˌan-ˌtī-\ *also* **an·ti·can·cer·ous** \-ˈkan(t)s-(ə-)rəs\ *adj* **:** used or effective against cancer <~ drugs>
an·ti·cat·a·lyst \-ˈkat-ᵊl-əst\ *n* **1 :** an agent that retards a chemical reaction **2 :** a catalytic poison
an·ti·cho·lin·er·gic \-ˌkō-lə-ˈnər-jik\ *adj* **:** opposing or annulling the physiologic action of acetylcholine — **anticholinergic** *n*
an·ti·cho·lin·es·ter·ase \-ˈnes-tə-ˌrās, -ˌrāz\ *n* **:** a substance that inhibits a cholinesterase by combination with it
An·ti·christ \ˈant-i-ˌkrīst\ *n* [ME *anticrist,* fr. OF & LL; OF, fr. LL *Antichristus,* fr. Gk *Antichristos,* fr. *anti-* + *Christos* Christ] **1 :** one who denies or opposes Christ; *specif* **:** a great antagonist expected to fill the world with wickedness but to be conquered forever by Christ at his second coming **2 :** a false Christ
an·tic·i·pant \an-ˈtis-ə-pənt\ *adj* **:** EXPECTANT, ANTICIPATING — usu. used with *of* — **anticipant** *n*
an·tic·i·pate \an-ˈtis-ə-ˌpāt\ *vb* **-pat·ed; -pat·ing** [L *anticipatus,* pp. of *anticipare,* fr. *ante-* + *-cipare* (fr. *capere* to take) — more at HEAVE] *vt* **1 :** to give advance thought, discussion, or treatment to **2 :** to meet (an obligation) before a due date **3 :** to foresee and deal with in advance **:** FORESTALL **4 :** to use or expend in advance of actual possession **5 :** to act before (another) often so as to check or counter **6 :** to look forward to as certain **:** EXPECT ~ *vi* **:** to speak or write in knowledge or expectation of later matter ***syn*** see FORESEE — **an·tic·i·pat·able** \-ˌpāt-ə-bəl\ *adj* — **an·tic·i·pa·tor** \-ˌpāt-ər\ *n*
an·tic·i·pa·tion \(ˌ)an-ˌtis-ə-ˈpā-shən\ *n* **1 :** the use of money before it is available; *esp* **:** the taking or alienation of the income of a trust estate before it is due **2 a :** a prior action that takes into account or forestalls a later action **b :** the act of looking forward; *specif* **:** pleasurable expectation **3 a :** visualization of a future event or state **b :** an object or form that anticipates a later type **4 :** the early sounding of one or more tones of a succeeding chord to form a temporary dissonance — compare SUSPENSION ***syn*** see PROSPECT
an·tic·i·pa·tive \an-ˈtis-ə-ˌpāt-iv, -pət-\ *adj* **:** given to or engaged in anticipation — **an·tic·i·pa·tive·ly** *adv*
an·tic·i·pa·to·ry \an-ˈtis-ə-pə-ˌtōr-ē, -ˌtȯr-\ *adj* **:** characterized by anticipation **:** ANTICIPATING
an·ti·cler·i·cal \ˌant-i-ˈkler-i-kəl, ˌan-ˌtī-\ *adj* **:** opposed to clericalism or to the interference or influence of the clergy in secular affairs — **anticlerical** *n* — **an·ti·cler·i·cal·ism** \-kə-ˌliz-əm\ *n* — **an·ti·cler·i·cal·ist** \-ləst\ *n*
an·ti·cli·mac·tic \ˌant-i-klī-ˈmak-tik\ *also* **an·ti·cli·mac·ti·cal** \-ti-kəl\ *adj* **:** of, relating to, or marked by anticlimax — **an·ti·cli·mac·ti·cal·ly** \-ti-k(ə-)lē\ *adv*
an·ti·cli·max \-ˈklī-ˌmaks\ *n* **1 :** the usu. sudden transition in writing or speaking from a significant idea to a trivial or ludicrous idea; *also* **:** an instance of this transition **2 :** an event (as at the end of a series) that is strikingly less important than what has preceded it
an·ti·cli·nal \-ˈklīn-ᵊl\ *adj* [*anti-* + Gk *klinein* to lean — more at LEAN] **:** inclining in opposite directions; *specif* **:** of or relating to a geological anticline
an·ti·cline \ˈant-i-ˌklīn\ *n* [back-formation fr. *anticlinal*] **:** an arch of stratified rock in which the layers bend downward in opposite directions from the crest — compare SYNCLINE

cross section of strata showing anticline

an·ti·clock·wise \ˌant-i-ˈkläk-ˌwīz, ˌan-ˌtī-\ *adj or adv* **:** COUNTERCLOCKWISE
an·ti·co·ag·u·lant \-kō-ˈag-yə-lənt\ *n* **:** a substance that hinders the clotting of blood
an·ti·co·ag·u·late \-ˌlāt\ *vt* [back-formation fr. *anticoagulant*] **:** to hinder the clotting of the blood of esp. by treatment with an anticoagulant — **an·ti·co·ag·u·la·tion** \-ˌag-yə-ˈlā-shən\ *n*
an·ti·co·don \-ˈkō-ˌdän\ *n* [*anti-* + *codon*] **:** a triplet of nucleotide bases in transfer RNA that is believed to identify the amino acid carried and to bind to a complementary codon in messenger RNA during protein synthesis at a ribosome
an·ti·con·vul·sant \-kən-ˈvəl-sənt\ *or* **an·ti·con·vul·sive** \-siv\ *adj* **:** used in tending to control or ward off convulsions (as in epilepsy) — **anticonvulsant** *n*
an·ti·cy·clone \ˌant-i-ˈsī-ˌklōn\ *n* **1 :** a system of winds that rotates about a center of high atmospheric pressure clockwise in the northern hemisphere and counterclockwise in the southern, that usu. advances at 20 to 30 miles per hour, and that usu. has a diameter of 1500 to 2500 miles **2 :** HIGH 2 — **an·ti·cy·clon·ic** \-sī-ˈklän-ik\ *adj*
an·ti·de·pres·sant \ˌant-i-di-ˈpres-ᵊnt, ˌan-ˌtī-\ *or* **an·ti·de·pres·sive** \-ˈpres-iv\ *adj* **:** used or tending to relieve or prevent psychic depression — **antidepressant** *n*
an·ti·de·riv·a·tive \-di-ˈriv-ət-iv\ *n* **:** INDEFINITE INTEGRAL
an·ti·di·uret·ic \ˌant-i-ˌdī-yü-ˈret-ik\ *n* **:** a substance that tends to check or oppose excretion of urine — **antidiuretic** *adj*
antidiuretic hormone *n* **:** VASOPRESSIN
an·ti·dot·al \ˌant-i-ˈdōt-ᵊl\ *adj* **:** of, relating to, or acting as an antidote — **an·ti·dot·al·ly** \-ᵊl-ē\ *adv*
an·ti·dote \ˈant-i-ˌdōt\ *n* [ME *antidot,* fr. L *antidotum,* fr. Gk *antidotos,* fr. fem. of *antidotos* given as an antidote, fr. *antididonai* to give as an antidote, fr. *anti-* + *didonai* to give — more at DATE] **1 :** a remedy to counteract the effects of poison **2 :** something that relieves, prevents, or counteracts <an ~ to the mechanization of our society>
an·ti·elec·tron \ˌant-ē-ə-ˈlek-ˌträn, ˌan-ˌtī-\ *n* **:** POSITRON
an·ti·en·zyme \-ˈen-ˌzīm\ *n* **:** an inhibitor of enzyme action; *esp* **:** one produced by living cells
an·ti·es·tab·lish·ment \-is-ˈtab-lish-mənt\ *adj* **:** opposed or hostile to the social, political, economic, or moral principles of a ruling class (as of a nation)
an·ti–fed·er·al·ist \ˌant-i-ˈfed-(ə-)rə-ləst, ˌan-ˌtī-\ *n, often cap A & F* **:** a member of the group that opposed the adoption of the U.S. Constitution
an·ti·fer·til·i·ty \-fər-ˈtil-ət-ē\ *adj* **:** intended to control excess or unwanted fertility **:** CONTRACEPTIVE <~ agents>
an·ti·foul·ing \-ˈfau̇-liŋ\ *adj* **:** intended to prevent fouling of underwater structures (as the bottoms of ships) <~ paint>
an·ti·freeze \ˈant-i-ˌfrēz\ *n* **:** a substance added to a liquid (as the water in an automobile engine) to lower its freezing point

an·ti·fun·gal \ˌant-i-ˈfəŋ-gəl, ˌan-ˌtī-\ *adj* **:** used or effective against fungi **:** FUNGICIDAL <~ drugs>

an·ti·gen \ˈant-i-jən\ *n* [ISV] **:** a usu. protein or carbohydrate substance (as a toxin or enzyme) that when introduced into the body stimulates the production of an antibody — **an·ti·gen·ic** \ˌant-i-ˈjen-ik\ *adj* — **an·ti·gen·i·cal·ly** \-i-k(ə-)lē\ *adv* — **an·ti·ge·nic·i·ty** \-jə-ˈnis-ət-ē\ *n*

an·ti·glob·u·lin \ˌant-i-ˈgläb-yə-lən, ˌan-ˌtī-\ *n* **:** an antibody that combines with and precipitates globulin

An·tig·o·ne \an-ˈtig-ə-(ˌ)nē\ *n* [Gk *Antigonē*] **:** a daughter of Oedipus and Jocasta who buries her brother Polynices' body against the order of her uncle Creon

[1]an·ti·grav·i·ty \ˌant-i-ˈgrav-ət-ē, ˌan-ˌtī-\ *adj* **:** reducing or canceling the effect of gravity or protecting against it

[2]antigravity *n* **:** a hypothetical effect resulting from cancellation or reduction of a gravitational field

an·ti·he·mo·phil·ic \ˌant-i-ˌhē-mə-ˈfil-ik, ˌan-ˌtī-\ *adj* **:** counteracting the bleeding tendency in hemophilia

an·ti–he·ro \ˈant-i-ˌhē-(ˌ)rō, ˈan-ˌtī-, -ˌhi(ə)r-(ˌ)ō\ *n* **:** a protagonist who is notably lacking in heroic qualities (as courage or unselfishness) — **an·ti–he·ro·ic** \ˌant-i-hi-ˈrō-ik, ˌan-ˌtī-\ *adj*

an·ti·his·ta·mine \ˌant-i-ˈhis-tə-ˌmēn, ˌan-ˌtī-, -mən\ *n* **:** any of various compounds used for treating allergic reactions and cold symptoms presumably by inactivating histamine — **an·ti·his·ta·min·ic** \-ˌhis-tə-ˈmin-ik\ *adj or n*

an·ti·hu·man \ˌant-i-ˈhyü-mən, ˌan-ˌtī-, -ˈyü-\ *adj* **:** acting or being against man; *esp* **:** reacting strongly with human antigens

an·ti·hy·per·ten·sive \-ˌhī-pər-ˈten(t)-siv\ *n* **:** a substance that is effective against high blood pressure — **antihypertensive** *adj*

an·ti–in·flam·ma·to·ry \ˌant-ē-in-ˈflam-ə-ˌtōr-ē, ˌan-ˌtī-, -ˌtȯr-\ *adj* **:** counteracting inflammation

an·ti·knock \ˌant-i-ˈnäk\ *n* **:** a substance used as a fuel or fuel additive to prevent knocking in an internal-combustion engine

an·ti·leu·ke·mic \ˌant-i-lü-ˈkē-mik, ˌan-ˌtī-\ *adj* **:** counteracting the effects of leukemia

an·ti·lit·ter \-ˈlit-ər\ *adj* **:** serving to prevent or discourage the littering of public areas <~ laws>

antilog *abbr* antilogarithm

an·ti·log·a·rithm \ˌant-i-ˈlȯg-ə-ˌrith-əm, ˌan-ˌtī-, -ˈläg-\ *n* **:** the number corresponding to a given logarithm

an·ti·lym·pho·cyte serum \-ˈlim(p)-fə-ˌsīt-\ *n* **:** a serum used for suppressing graft rejection caused by lymphocyte-controlled immune responses in organ or tissue transplant recipients

an·ti·lym·pho·cyt·ic serum \ˌant-i-ˌlim-fə-ˌsit-ik-, ˌan-ˌtī-\ *n* **:** ANTILYMPHOCYTE SERUM

an·ti·ma·cas·sar \ˌant-i-mə-ˈkas-ər\ *n* [*anti-* + *Macassar* (*oil*) (a hairdressing)] **:** a cover to protect the back or arms of furniture

an·ti·mag·net·ic \ˌant-i-mag-ˈnet-ik, ˌan-ˌtī-\ *adj, of a watch* **:** having a balance unit composed of alloys that will not remain magnetized

an·ti·ma·lar·i·al \-mə-ˈler-ē-əl\ *adj* **:** serving to prevent, check, or cure malaria — **antimalarial** *n*

an·ti·mat·ter \ˈant-i-ˌmat-ər\ *n* **:** matter composed of the counterparts of ordinary matter, antiprotons instead of protons, positrons instead of electrons, and antineutrons instead of neutrons

an·ti·me·tab·o·lite \ˌant-i-mə-ˈtab-ə-ˌlīt, ˌan-ˌtī-\ *n* **:** a substance that replaces or inhibits the utilization of a metabolite

an·ti·mi·cro·bi·al \ˌant-i-mī-ˈkrō-bē-əl\ *adj* **:** destroying or inhibiting the growth of microorganisms — **antimicrobial** *n*

an·ti·mis·sile missile \ˌant-i-ˈmis-əl-, ˌan-ˌtī-; *chiefly Brit* ˌant-i-ˈmis-ˌīl-\ *n* **:** ANTIBALLISTIC MISSILE

an·ti·mi·tot·ic \ˌant-i-mī-ˈtät-ik\ *adj* **:** inhibiting division of the cell nucleus — **antimitotic** *n*

an·ti·mo·ni·al \ˌant-ə-ˈmō-nē-əl\ *adj* **:** of, relating to, or containing antimony — **antimonial** *n*

an·ti·mon·ic \-ˈmän-ik\ *adj* **:** of, relating to, or derived from antimony with a valence of five

an·ti·mo·ni·ous \-ˈmō-nē-əs\ *adj* **:** of, relating to, or derived from antimony with a valence of three

an·ti·mo·ny \ˈant-ə-ˌmō-nē\ *n* [ME *antimonie*, fr. ML *antimonium*] **1 :** STIBNITE **2 :** a trivalent and pentavalent metalloid commonly metallic silvery white, crystalline, and brittle element that is used esp. as a constituent of alloys and in medicine — see ELEMENT table

an·ti·my·cin A \ˌant-i-ˌmīs-ᵊn-ˈā\ *n* [*anti-* + *myc-* + *-in*] **:** a crystalline antibiotic $C_{28}H_{40}N_2O_9$ used esp. as a fungicide, insecticide, and miticide — called also *antimycin*

an·ti·neo·plas·tic \ˌant-i-ˌnē-ə-ˈplas-tik, ˌan-ˌtī-\ *adj* **:** inhibiting or preventing the growth and spread of neoplasms or malignant cells

an·ti·neu·tri·no \-n(y)ü-ˈtrē-(ˌ)nō\ *n* **:** the antiparticle of the neutrino

an·ti·neu·tron \-ˈn(y)ü-ˌträn\ *n* **:** an uncharged particle of mass equal to that of the neutron but having a magnetic moment in the opposite direction

ant·ing \ˈant-iŋ\ *n* **:** the deliberate placing by some passerine birds of living ants among the feathers

an·ti·node \ˈant-i-ˌnōd, ˈan-ˌtī-\ *n* [ISV] **:** a region of maximum amplitude situated between adjacent nodes in a vibrating body — **an·ti·nod·al** \ˌant-i-ˈnōd-ᵊl, ˌan-ˌtī-\ *adj*

an·ti·no·mi·an \ˌant-i-ˈnō-mē-ən\ *n* [ML *antinomus*, fr. L *anti-* + Gk *nomos* law] **1 :** one who holds that under the gospel dispensation of grace the moral law is of no use or obligation because faith alone is necessary to salvation **2 :** one who rejects a socially established morality — **antinomian** *adj* — **an·ti·no·mi·an·ism** \-mē-ə-ˌniz-əm\ *n*

an·tin·o·my \an-ˈtin-ə-mē\ *n, pl* **-mies** [G *antinomie*, fr. L *antinomia* conflict of laws, fr. Gk, fr. *anti-* + *nomos* law — more at NIMBLE] **1 :** a contradiction between two apparently equally valid principles or between inferences correctly drawn from such principles **2 :** conflict (as of principles, ideas, or aspirations) insoluble in the light of available knowledge ***syn*** see PARADOX

an·ti·nov·el \ˈant-i-ˌnäv-əl, ˈan-ˌtī-\ *n* **:** a work of fiction that lacks most or all of the traditional features of the novel — **an·ti·nov·el·ist** \-ˌnäv-(ə-)ləst\ *n*

an·ti·nu·cle·on \ˌant-i-ˈn(y)ü-klē-ˌän, ˌan-ˌtī-\ *n* **:** the antiparticle of the nucleon

an·ti·ox·i·dant \ˌant-ē-ˈäk-səd-ənt, ˌan-ˌtī-\ *n* **:** a substance that opposes oxidation or inhibits reactions promoted by oxygen or peroxides — **antioxidant** *adj*

an·ti·par·a·sit·ic \ˌant-i-ˌpar-ə-ˈsit-ik, ˌan-ˌtī-\ *adj* **:** acting against parasites

an·ti·par·ti·cle \ˈant-i-ˌpärt-i-kəl, ˈan-ˌtī-\ *n* **:** an elementary particle identical to another elementary particle in mass but opposite to it in electric and magnetic properties — used of either of a pair of particles whose encounter results in mutual annihilation

an·ti·pas·to \ˌant-i-ˈpas-(ˌ)tō, ˌänt-i-ˈpäs-\ *n, pl* **-tos** [It, fr. *anti-* (fr. L *ante-*) + *pasto* food, fr. L *pastus*, fr. *pastus*, pp. of *pascere* to feed — more at FOOD] **:** HORS D'OEUVRE

an·ti·pa·thet·ic \ˌant-i-pə-ˈthet-ik\ *adj* **1 :** having a natural aversion <a person ~ to violence> **2 :** arousing or showing antipathy — **an·ti·pa·thet·i·cal·ly** \-i-k(ə-)lē\ *adv*

an·tip·a·thy \an-ˈtip-ə-thē\ *n, pl* **-thies** [L *antipathia*, fr. Gk *antipatheia*, fr. *antipathēs* of opposite feelings, fr. *anti-* + *pathos* experience — more at PATHOS] **1** *obs* **:** opposition in feeling **2 :** settled aversion or dislike **:** DISTASTE **3 :** an object of aversion ***syn*** see ENMITY ***ant*** taste (*for*), affection (*for*)

an·ti·pe·ri·od·ic \-ˌpir-ē-ˈäd-ik\ *adj* [ISV] **:** preventing periodic returns of disease — **antiperiodic** *n*

an·ti·per·son·nel \ˌant-i-ˌpərs-ᵊn-ˈel, ˌan-ˌtī-\ *adj* **:** designed for use against military personnel <an ~ mine>

an·ti·per·spi·rant \-ˈpər-sp(ə-)rənt\ *n* **:** a cosmetic preparation used to check excessive perspiration

an·ti·phlo·gis·tic \-flə-ˈjis-tik\ *adj* **:** counteracting inflammation — **antiphlogistic** *n*

an·ti·phon \ˈant-ə-fən, -ˌfän\ *n* [LL *antiphona* — more at ANTHEM] **1 :** a psalm, anthem, or verse sung responsively **2 :** a verse usu. from Scripture said or sung before and after a canticle, psalm, or psalm verse as part of the liturgy

[1]an·tiph·o·nal \an-ˈtif-ən-ᵊl\ *n* **:** ANTIPHONARY

[2]antiphonal *adj* **:** of or relating to an antiphon or antiphony — **an·tiph·o·nal·ly** \-ᵊl-ē\ *adv*

an·tiph·o·nary \an-ˈtif-ə-ˌner-ē\ *n, pl* **-nar·ies 1 :** a book containing a collection of antiphons **2 :** a book containing the choral parts of the Divine Office

an·tiph·o·ny \an-ˈtif-ə-nē\ *n, pl* **-nies :** responsive alternation between two groups esp. of singers

an·tiph·ra·sis \an-ˈtif-rə-səs\ *n, pl* **-ra·ses** \-ˌsēz\ [LL, fr. Gk, fr. *anti-* + *phrasis* diction — more at PHRASE] **:** the usu. ironic or humorous use of words in senses opposite to the generally accepted meanings <"the child is a giant of 3 feet 4 inches" is an example of ~>

[1]an·tip·o·dal \an-ˈtip-əd-ᵊl\ *adj* **1 :** of or relating to the antipodes; *specif* **:** situated at the opposite side of the earth or moon <an ~ meridian> <an ~ continent> **2 :** diametrically opposite <an ~ point on a sphere> **3 :** OPPOSED

[2]antipodal *n* **:** any of three cells in the female gametophyte of most angiosperms that are grouped at the end of the embryo sac farthest from the micropyle

an·ti·pode \ˈant-ə-ˌpōd\ *n, pl* **an·tip·o·des** \an-ˈtip-ə-ˌdēz\ [ME *antipodes*, pl., persons dwelling at opposite points on the globe, fr. L, fr. Gk, fr. pl. of *antipod-*, *antipous* with feet opposite, fr. *anti-* + *pod-*, *pous* foot — more at FOOT] **1 :** the parts of the earth diametrically opposite — usu. used in pl. **2 :** the exact opposite or contrary — **an·tip·o·de·an** \(ˌ)an-ˌtip-ə-ˈdē-ən\ *adj*

an·ti·po·et·ic \ˌant-i-pō-ˈet-ik, ˌan-ˌtī-\ *adj* **:** of, relating to, or characterized by opposition to traditional poetic technique or style

an·ti·pol·lu·tion \-pə-ˈlü-shən\ *adj* **:** designed to prevent, reduce, or eliminate pollution <~ laws> — **antipollution** *n*

an·ti·pope \ˈant-i-ˌpōp\ *n* [MF *antipape*, fr. ML *antipapa*, fr. *anti-* + *papa* pope] **:** one elected or claiming to be pope in opposition to the pope canonically chosen

an·ti·pov·er·ty \ˌant-i-ˈpäv-ərt-ē, ˌan-ˌtī-\ *adj* **:** of or relating to action designed to relieve poverty <~ programs>

an·ti·pro·ton \-ˈprō-ˌtän\ *n* **:** the antiparticle of the proton

an·ti·psy·chot·ic \ˌant-i-sī-ˈkät-ik\ *adj* **:** tending to alleviate psychosis or psychotic states <an ~ drug> — **antipsychotic** *n*

an·ti·py·ret·ic \-pī-ˈret-ik\ *n* **:** an agent that reduces fever — **antipyretic** *adj*

an·ti·py·rine \-ˈpī(ə)r-ˌēn\ *n* [fr. *Antipyrine*, a trademark] **:** a white crystalline compound $C_{11}H_{12}N_2O$ used to relieve fever, pain, or rheumatism

antiq *abbr* antiquarian; antiquary

[1]an·ti·quar·i·an \ˌant-ə-ˈkwer-ē-ən\ *n* **:** one who collects or studies antiquities

[2]antiquarian *adj* **1 :** of or relating to antiquarians or antiquities **2 :** dealing in old or rare books — **an·ti·quar·i·an·ism** \-ē-ə-ˌniz-əm\ *n*

an·ti·quary \ˈant-ə-ˌkwer-ē\ *n, pl* **-quar·ies :** ANTIQUARIAN

an·ti·quate \ˈant-ə-ˌkwāt\ *vt* **-quat·ed; -quat·ing** [LL *antiquatus*, pp. of *antiquare*, fr. L *antiquus*] **:** to make old or obsolete — **an·ti·qua·tion** \ˌant-ə-ˈkwā-shən\ *n*

an·ti·quat·ed *adj* **1 :** OBSOLETE <a calendar becomes ~ —A. L. Kroeber> **2 :** outmoded or discredited by reason of age **:** being out of style or fashion <~ methods of farming> **3 :** advanced in age ***syn*** see OLD ***ant*** modish

[1]an·tique \an-ˈtēk\ *adj* [MF, fr. L *antiquus*, fr. *ante* before — more at ANTE-] **1 :** existing since ancient or former times **:** belonging to antiquity <a few of the ~ virtues still persist> **2 :** belonging to earlier times **:** ANCIENT <ruins of an ~ city> **3 a :** being in the style or fashion of former times <~ manners and graces> **b :** made in or representative of the work of an earlier period <~ mirrors>; *also* **:** being an antique **4 :** selling or exhibiting antiques <an ~ show> ***syn*** see OLD ***ant*** modern, current

[2]antique *n* **1 :** a relic or object of ancient times or of an earlier period than the present **2 :** a work of art, piece of furniture, or decorative object made at an earlier period and according to various customs laws at least 100 years ago

[3]**antique** *vt* **-tiqued; -tiquing :** to finish or refinish in antique style : give an appearance of age to

an·tiq·ui·ty \an-ˈtik-wət-ē\ *n, pl* **-ties** **1 :** ancient times; *esp* : those before the Middle Ages **2 :** the quality of being ancient **3** *pl* **a :** relics or monuments (as coins, statues, or buildings) of ancient times **b :** matters relating to the life or culture of ancient times **4 :** the people of ancient times

an·ti·rac·ism \ˌant-i-ˈrā-ˌsiz-əm, ˌan-ˌtī- *also* -ˌshiz-\ *n* **:** adherence to the view that racism is a social evil

an·ti·rheu·mat·ic \-rü-ˈmat-ik\ *adj* **:** alleviating or preventing rheumatism — **antirheumatic** *n*

an·tir·rhi·num \ˌant-ə-ˈrī-nəm\ *n* [NL, genus name, fr. L, snapdragon, fr. Gk *antirrhinon*, fr. *anti-* like (fr. *anti* against, equivalent to) + *rhin-, rhis* nose — more at ANTI-] **:** any of a large genus (*Antirrhinum*) of herbs (as the snapdragon) of the figwort family with bright-colored irregular flowers

antis *pl of* ANTI

an·ti–Sem·i·tism \ˌant-i-ˈsem-ə-ˌtiz-əm, ˌan-ˌtī-\ *n* **:** hostility toward or discrimination against Jews as a religious or racial group — **an·ti–Se·mit·ic** \-sə-ˈmit-ik\ *adj* — **an·ti–Sem·ite** \-ˈsem-ˌīt\ *n*

an·ti·sep·sis \ˌant-ə-ˈsep-səs\ *n* **:** the inhibiting of the growth and multiplication of microorganisms by antiseptic means

[1]**an·ti·sep·tic** \ˌant-ə-ˈsep-tik\ *adj* [*anti-* + Gk *sēptikos* putrefying, septic] **1 a :** opposing sepsis, putrefaction, or decay; *esp*: preventing or arresting the growth of microorganisms (as on living tissue) **b :** acting or protecting like an antiseptic **2 :** relating to or characterized by the use of antiseptics **3 a :** scrupulously clean : ASEPTIC **b :** extremely neat or orderly; *esp* **:** neat to the point of being bare or uninteresting **c :** free from what is held to be contaminating **4 :** IMPERSONAL, DETACHED; *esp* **:** coldly impersonal <"acceptable losses on the battlefield" is another ~ phrase> — **an·ti·sep·ti·cal·ly** \-ti-k(ə-)lē\ *adv*

[2]**antiseptic** *n* **:** a substance that checks the growth or action of microorganisms esp. in or on living tissue; *also* **:** GERMICIDE

an·ti·se·rum \ˈant-i-ˌsir-əm, ˈan-ˌtī-, -ˌser-\ *n* [ISV] **:** a serum containing antibodies

an·ti·slav·ery \ˌant-i-ˈslāv-(ə-)rē, ˌan-ˌti-\ *n* **:** opposition to slavery

an·ti·smog \-ˈsmäg *also* -ˈsmȯg\ *adj* **:** designed to reduce pollutants contributing to the formation of smog <~ devices for automobiles>

an·ti·so·cial \-ˈsō-shəl\ *adj* **1 :** hostile or harmful to organized society; *esp* **:** being or marked by behavior deviating sharply from the social norm **2 :** averse to the society of others **:** UNSOCIABLE ***syn*** see UNSOCIAL ***ant*** social

an·ti·spas·mod·ic \-spaz-ˈmäd-ik\ *adj* **:** capable of preventing or relieving spasms or convulsions — **antispasmodic** *n*

an·ti·spec·u·la·tion \-ˌspek-yə-ˈlā-shən\ *adj* **:** directed against or designed to control speculation

an·tis·tro·phe \an-ˈtis-trə-(ˌ)fē\ *n* [LL, fr. Gk *antistrophē*, fr. *anti-* + *strophē* strophe] **1 :** a returning movement in Greek choral dance exactly answering to a previous strophe; *specif* **:** the part of a choral song delivered during this movement **2 a :** the repetition of words in reversed order **b :** the repetition of a word or phrase at the end of successive clauses — **an·ti·stroph·ic** \ˌant-ə-ˈsträf-ik\ *adj* — **an·ti·stroph·i·cal·ly** \-i-k(ə-)lē\ *adv*

an·ti·sub·ma·rine \ˌant-i-ˈsəb-mə-ˌrēn, ˌan-ˌtī-, -ˌsəb-mə-ˈ\ *adj* **:** designed or waged to destroy submarines <an ~ gun> <~ warfare>

an·ti·sym·met·ric \-sə-ˈme-trik\ *adj* **:** relating to or being a relation (as "is a subset of") that implies equality of any two quantities for which it holds in both directions <the relation *R* is ~ if *aRb* and *bRa* implies *a*=*b*>

an·ti·tank \-ˈtaŋk\ *adj* **:** designed to destroy or check tanks <an ~ gun>

an·tith·e·sis \an-ˈtith-ə-səs\ *n, pl* **-e·ses** \-ˌsēz\ [LL, fr. Gk, lit., opposition, fr. *antitithenai* to oppose, fr. *anti-* + *tithenai* to set — more at DO] **1 a** (1)**:** the rhetorical contrast of ideas by means of parallel arrangements of words, clauses, or sentences (as in "action, not words" or "they promised freedom and provided slavery") (2) **:** OPPOSITION, CONTRAST <the ~ of prose and verse> **b** (1)**:** the second of two opposing constituents of an antithesis (2)**:** the direct opposite **2 :** the second stage of a dialectic process

an·ti·thet·i·cal \ˌant-ə-ˈthet-i-kəl\ *or* **an·ti·thet·ic** \-ˈthet-ik\ *adj* **1 :** constituting or marked by antithesis **2 :** being in direct and unequivocal opposition ***syn*** see OPPOSITE — **an·ti·thet·i·cal·ly** \-i-k(ə-)lē\ *adv*

an·ti·thy·roid \ˌant-i-ˈthī-ˌrȯid\ *adj* **:** able to counteract excessive thyroid activity

an·ti·tox·ic \-ˈtäk-sik\ *adj* **1 :** counteracting poison **2 :** of, relating to, or being an antitoxin

an·ti·tox·in \ˌant-i-ˈtäk-sən\ *n* [ISV] **:** an antibody formed in the body as a result of the introduction of a toxin and capable of neutralizing the specific toxin that stimulated its production and produced commercially in animals by injection of a toxin or toxoid (as of human disease) with the resulting serum being used to counteract the toxin in other individuals; *also***:** a serum containing antitoxins

an·ti·trades \ˈant-i-ˌtrādz, ˈan-ˌtī-\ *n pl* **1 :** the prevailing westerly winds of middle latitudes **2 :** the westerly winds above the trade winds

an·ti·trust \ˌant-i-ˈtrəst, ˌan-ˌtī-\ *adj* **:** of or relating to legislation or opposition to trusts or combinations; *specif* **:** consisting of laws to protect trade and commerce from unlawful restraints and monopolies or unfair business practices

an·ti·trust·er \-ˈtrəs-tər\ *n* **:** one who advocates or enforces antitrust provisions of the law

an·ti·tu·ber·cu·lous \-t(y)ù-ˈbər-kyə-ləs\ *also* **an·ti·tu·ber·cu·lar** \-ˈbər-kyə-lər\ *adj* **:** used or effective against tuberculosis

an·ti·tu·mor \-ˈt(y)ü-mər\ *also* **an·ti·tu·mor·al** \-mə-rəl\ *adj* **:** ANTICANCER

an·ti·tus·sive \-ˈtəs-iv\ *adj* **:** tending or having the power to control or prevent cough — **antitussive** *n*

an·ti–uto·pia \ˌant-i-yù-ˈtō-pē-ə, ˌan-ˌtī-\ *n* **:** a place, state, or condition of social, political, and economic discord

[1]**an·ti–uto·pi·an** \-pē-ən\ *adj* **:** of, relating to, or having the characteristics of an anti-utopia

[2]**anti–utopian** *n* **:** one that believes in or predicts an anti-utopia

an·ti·ven·in \ˌant-i-ˈven-ən, ˌan-ˌtī-\ *n* [ISV] **:** an antitoxin to a venom **:** an antiserum containing such antitoxin

an·ti·vi·ral \ˌan-ti-ˈvī-rəl\ *adj* **:** acting to make a virus ineffective

an·ti·vi·ta·min \ˈant-i-ˌvīt-ə-mən\ *n* **:** a substance that makes a vitamin ineffective

an·ti·white \ˌant-i-ˈhwīt, ˌan-ˌtī-, -ˈwīt\ *adj* **:** opposed or hostile to people belonging to a light-skinned race <~ propaganda> — **an·ti·whit·ism** \-ˈhwīt-ˌiz-əm, -ˈwīt-\ *n*

ant·ler \ˈant-lər\ *n* [ME *aunteler*, fr. MF *antoillier*, fr. (assumed) VL *anteoculare*, fr. neut. of *anteocularis* located before the eye, fr. L *ante-* + *oculus* eye — more at EYE] **:** the solid deciduous horn of an animal of the deer family; *also* **:** a branch of this horn — **ant·lered** \-lərd\ *adj*

4
3
2
1

antlers: *1* brow antler, *2* bay antler, *3* royal antler, *4* surroyal

ant lion *n* **:** any of various neuropterous insects (as of the genus *Myrmeleon*) having a long-jawed larva that digs a conical pit in which it lies in wait to catch insects (as ants) on which it feeds

An·to·ni·an \an-ˈtō-nē-ən\ *n* [L *Antonius* Anthony] **:** a member of one of several monastic communities (as the Armenian Antonians) that follow a rule derived from St. Anthony

ant·onym \ˈant-ə-ˌnim\ *n* **:** a word of opposite meaning <the usual ~ of *good* is *bad*, of *hot* is *cold*> — **ant·onym·ic** \ˌant-ə-ˈnim-ik\ *adj* — **an·ton·y·mous** \an-ˈtän-ə-məs\ *adj* — **an·ton·y·my** \-mē\ *n*

an·tre \ˈant-ər\ *n* [F, fr. L *antrum*] **:** CAVE 1

an·trorse \ˈan-ˌtrȯ(ə)rs\ *adj* [NL *antrorsus*, irreg. fr. L *anterior* + *-orsus* (as in *dextrorsus* toward the right) — more at DEXTRORSE] **:** directed forward or upward — **an·trorse·ly** *adv*

an·trum \ˈan-trəm\ *n, pl* **an·tra** \-trə\ [LL, fr. L, cave, fr. Gk *antron*]**:** the cavity of a hollow organ or a sinus — **an·tral** \-trəl\ *adj*

an·uran \ə-ˈn(y)ùr-ən, a-\ *adj or n* [deriv. of *a-* + Gk *oura* tail — more at SQUIRREL] **:** SALIENTIAN

an·uria \ə-ˈn(y)ùr-ē-ə, a-\ *n* [NL] **:** absence or defective excretion of urine — **an·uric** \-ˈn(y)ùr-ik\ *adj*

an·urous \ə-ˈn(y)ùr-əs, a-\ *adj* **:** having no tail

anus \ˈā-nəs\ *n* [L; akin to OIr *āinne* anus]**:** the posterior opening of the alimentary canal

an·vil \ˈan-vəl\ *n* [ME *anfilt*, fr. OE; akin to OHG *anafalz* anvil; both fr. a prehistoric WGmc compound whose first constituent is represented by OE *an* on, and whose second constituent is akin to Sw dial. *filta* to beat; akin to L *pellere* to beat — more at ON, FELT] **1 :** a heavy usu. steel-faced iron block on which metal is shaped (as by hand hammering) **2 :** INCUS

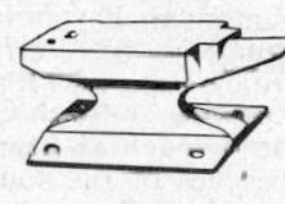

anvil 1

anx·i·ety \aŋ-ˈzī-ət-ē\ *n, pl* **-eties** [L *anxietas*, fr. *anxius*] **1 a :** painful or apprehensive uneasiness of mind usu. over an impending or anticipated ill **b :** fearful concern or interest **c :** a cause of anxiety **2 :** an abnormal and overwhelming sense of apprehension and fear often marked by physiological signs (as sweating, tension, and increased pulse), by doubt concerning the reality and nature of the threat, and by self-doubt about one's capacity to cope with it ***syn*** see CARE ***ant*** security

anx·ious \ˈaŋ(k)-shəs\ *adj* [L *anxius*; akin to L *angere* to strangle, distress — more at ANGER] **1 :** characterized by extreme uneasiness of mind or brooding fear about some contingency **:** WORRIED **2 :** characterized by, resulting from, or causing anxiety **:** WORRYING **3 :** ardently or earnestly wishing ***syn*** see EAGER ***ant*** loath — **anx·ious·ly** *adv* — **anx·ious·ness** *n*

[1]**any** \ˈen-ē\ *adj* [ME, fr. OE *ǣnig*; akin to OHG *einag* any, OE *ān* one — more at ONE] **1 :** one or some indiscriminately of whatever kind: **a :** one or another taken at random <ask ~ man you meet> **b :** EVERY — used to indicate one selected without restriction <~ child would know that> **2 :** one, some, or all indiscriminately of whatever quantity: **a :** one or more — used to indicate an undetermined number or amount <have you ~ money> **b :** ALL — used to indicate a maximum or whole <needs ~ help he can get> **c :** a or some without reference to quantity or extent **3 a :** unmeasured or unlimited in amount, number, or extent <~ quantity you desire> **b :** appreciably large or extended <could not endure it ~ length of time>

[2]**any** *pron, sing or pl in constr* **1 :** any person or persons **:** ANYBODY **2 a :** any thing or things **b :** any part, quantity, or number

[3]**any** *adv* **:** to any extent or degree **:** at all <was never ~ good>

any·body \-ˌbäd-ē, -bəd-\ *pron* **:** any person **:** ANYONE

any·how \-ˌhaù\ *adv* **1 a :** in any manner whatever **b :** in a haphazard manner **2 a :** at any rate **b :** in any event

any·more \ˌen-ē-ˈmō(ə)r, -ˈmȯ(ə)r\ *adv* **:** at the present time **:** NOW — usu. used in a negative context

any·one \-(ˌ)wən\ *pron* **:** any person at all **:** ANYBODY

any·place \-ˌplās\ *adv* **:** in any place **:** ANYWHERE

[1]**any·thing** \-ˌthiŋ\ *pron* **:** any thing whatever

[2]**anything** *adv* **:** at all

any·time \ˈen-ē-ˌtīm\ *adv* **:** at any time whatever

any·way \-ˌwā\ *adv* **1 :** ANYWISE **2 :** in any case **:** ANYHOW

any·ways \-ˌwāz\ *adv* **1** *archaic* **:** ANYWISE **2** *chiefly dial* **:** in any case

[1]**any·where** \-ˌ(h)we(ə)r, -ˌ(h)wa(ə)r, -(h)wər\ *adv* **1 :** at, in, or to any place or point **2 :** at all **:** to any extent **3** — used as a function word to indicate limits of variation <~ from 40 to 60 students>
[2]**anywhere** *n* **:** any place
any·wise \ˈen-ē-ˌwīz\ *adv* **:** in any way whatever **:** at all
An·zac \ˈan-ˌzak\ *n* [*A*ustralian and *N*ew *Z*ealand *A*rmy *C*orps] **:** a soldier from Australia or New Zealand
AO *abbr* **1** account of **2** and others
AOH *abbr* Ancient Order of Hibernians
A–OK \ˌā-(ˌ)ō-ˈkā\ *adv or adj* **:** very definitely OK
A1 \ˈā-ˈwən\ *adj* **1 :** having the highest possible classification — used of a ship **2 :** of the finest quality **:** FIRST-RATE
aor *abbr* aorist
ao·rist \ˈā-ə-rəst, ˈe-ə-\ *n* [LL & Gk; LL *aoristos,* fr. Gk, fr. *aoristos* undefined, fr. *a-* + *horistos* definable, fr. *horizein* to define — more at HORIZON] **:** an inflectional form of a verb typically denoting simple occurrence of an action without reference to its completeness, duration, or repetition — **aorist** *or* **ao·ris·tic** \ˌā-ə-ˈris-tik, ˌe-ə-\ *adj* — **ao·ris·ti·cal·ly** \-ti-k(ə-)lē\ *adv*
aort- *or* **aorto-** *comb form* **:** aorta **:** aortic and <*aorto*esophageal>
aor·ta \ā-ˈȯrt-ə\ *n, pl* **-tas** *or* **-tae** \-ē\ [NL, fr. Gk *aortē,* fr. *aeirein* to lift] **:** the great trunk artery that carries blood from the heart to be distributed by branch arteries through the body — see HEART illustration — **aor·tal** \-ˈȯrt-ᵊl\ *adj* — **aor·tic** \-ˈȯrt-ik\ *adj*
aortic arch *n* **:** one of the arterial branches in vertebrate embryos that exist in a series of pairs with one on each side of the embryo, connect the ventral arterial system lying anterior to the heart to the dorsal arterial system above the alimentary tract, and persist in adult fishes but are reduced or much modified in the adult of higher forms
aor·tog·ra·phy \ˌā-ˌȯr-ˈtäg-rə-fē\ *n* **:** arteriography of the aorta — **aor·to·graph·ic** \(ˌ)ā-ˌȯrt-ə-ˈgraf-ik\ *adj*
aou·dad \ˈaů-ˌdad, ˈä-ů-\ *n* [F, fr. Berber *audad*] **:** a wild sheep (*Ammotragus lervia*) of No. Africa
à ou·trance \ˌä-ˌü-ˈträ^ns\ *adv* [F] **:** to the limit **:** UNSPARINGLY
ap *abbr* **1** apostle **2** apothecaries'
AP *abbr* **1** additional premium **2** airplane **3** American plan **4** antipersonnel **5** arithmetic progression **6** armor-piercing **7** Associated Press **8** author's proof
[1]**ap-** — see AD-
[2]**ap-** — see APO-
APA *abbr* **1** American Philological Association **2** American Philosophical Association **3** American Psychiatric Association **4** American Psychological Association
apace \ə-ˈpās\ *adv* [ME, prob. fr. MF *à pas* on step] **1 :** at a quick pace **:** SWIFTLY **2 :** ABREAST — used with *of* or *with*
Apache \ə-ˈpach-ē, *in sense 3* ə-ˈpash\ *n, pl* **Apache** *or* **Apach·es** \-ˈpach-ēz, -ˈpash(-əz)\ [Sp] **1 a :** a group of Amerindian peoples of the southwestern U.S. **b :** a member of any of these peoples **2 :** any of the Athapaskan languages of the Apache people **3** *not cap* [F, fr. *Apache* Apache Indian] **a :** a member of a gang of criminals esp. in Paris **b :** RUFFIAN
ap·a·nage *var of* APPANAGE
ap·a·re·jo \ˌap-ə-ˈrā-(ˌ)(h)ō\ *n, pl* **-jos** [AmerSp] **:** a packsaddle of stuffed leather or canvas
[1]**apart** \ə-ˈpärt\ *adv* [ME, fr. MF *a part,* lit., to the side] **1 a :** at a little distance <tried to keep ~ from the family squabbles> **b :** away from one another in space or time <towns 20 miles ~> **2 a :** as a separate unit **:** INDEPENDENTLY <viewed ~, his arguments were unsound> **b :** so as to separate one from another <found it hard to tell the twins ~> **3 :** excluded from consideration **:** ASIDE <a few blemishes ~, the novel is excellent> **4 :** in or into two or more parts **:** to pieces <had to take the engine ~>
[2]**apart** *adj* **1 :** SEPARATE, ISOLATED **2 :** holding different opinions **:** DIVIDED — **apart·ness** *n*
apart from *prep* **:** other than **:** BESIDES
apart·heid \ə-ˈpär-ˌtāt, -ˌtīt\ *n* [Afrik, lit., separateness] **:** racial segregation; *specif* **:** a policy of segregation and political and economic discrimination against non-European groups in the Republic of So. Africa
apart·ment \ə-ˈpärt-mənt\ *n* [F *appartement,* fr. It *appartamento*] **1 :** a room or set of rooms fitted esp. with housekeeping facilities and used as a dwelling **2 :** a building made up of individual dwelling units — **apart·men·tal** \ə-ˌpärt-ˈment-ᵊl\ *adj*
apartment hotel *n* **:** an apartment house containing suites equipped for housekeeping purposes and in addition furnished rooms and dining service for transient and permanent guests
apartment house *n* **:** a building containing separate residential apartments — called also *apartment building*
ap·a·thet·ic \ˌap-ə-ˈthet-ik\ *adj* **1 :** having or showing little or no feeling or emotion **:** SPIRITLESS **2 :** having little or no interest or concern **:** INDIFFERENT ***syn*** see IMPASSIVE ***ant*** alert — **ap·a·thet·i·cal·ly** \-i-k(ə-)lē\ *adv*
ap·a·thy \ˈap-ə-thē\ *n* [Gk *apatheia,* fr. *apathēs* without feeling, fr. *a-* + *pathos* emotion — more at PATHOS] **1 :** lack of feeling or emotion **:** IMPASSIVENESS **2 :** lack of interest or concern **:** INDIFFERENCE
ap·a·tite \ˈap-ə-ˌtīt\ *n* [G *apatit,* fr. Gk *apatē* deceit] **:** any of a group of calcium phosphate minerals of the approximate general formula $Ca_5(F,Cl,OH,\frac{1}{2}CO_3)(PO_4)_3$ occurring variously as hexagonal crystals, as granular masses, or in fine-grained masses as the chief constituent of phosphate rock and of bones and teeth; *specif* **:** calcium phosphate fluoride $Ca_5F(PO_4)_3$
APB *abbr* all points bulletin
[1]**ape** \ˈāp\ *n* [ME, fr. OE *apa;* akin to OHG *affo* ape] **1 a :** MONKEY; *esp* **:** one of the larger tailless or short-tailed Old World forms **b :** any of a family (Pongidae) of large semierect primates (as the chimpanzee or gorilla) — called also *anthropoid ape* **2 a :** MIMIC **b :** a large uncouth person — **ape·like** \ˈā-ˌplīk\ *adj*
[2]**ape** *vt* **aped; ap·ing :** to copy closely but often clumsily and ineptly <servants *aping* the ways of their betters> ***syn*** see COPY — **ap·er** *n*
apeak \ə-ˈpēk\ *adj or adv* [alter. of earlier *apike,* prob. fr. *a-* + *pike*] **:** being in a vertical position <with oars ~>
ape–man \ˈāp-ˈman, -ˌman\ *n* **:** a primate (as pithecanthropus) intermediate in character between Homo sapiens and the higher apes
aper·çu \ȧ-per-sūē, ˌap-ər-ˈsü\ *n, pl* **aperçus** \-sūē(z), -ˈsüz\ [F] **1 :** an immediate impression; *esp* **:** INSIGHT 2 **2 :** a brief survey or sketch **:** OUTLINE
ape·ri·ent \ə-ˈpir-ē-ənt\ *adj* [L *aperient-, aperiens,* prp. of *aperire*] **:** gently moving the bowels **:** LAXATIVE — **aperient** *n*
ape·ri·od·ic \ˌā-ˌpir-ē-ˈäd-ik\ *adj* **1 :** of irregular occurrence <~ floods> **2 :** not having periodic vibrations **:** not oscillatory **3** *cryptology* **:** not repeating or not repeating with a short or easily discoverable period <an ~ key> — **ape·ri·od·i·cal·ly** \-i-k(ə-)lē\ *adv* — **ape·ri·o·dic·i·ty** \-ē-ə-ˈdis-ət-ē\ *n*
aper·i·tif \ˌäp-ˌer-ə-ˈtēf, ə-ˈper-ə-ˌ\ *n* [F *apéritif* aperient, aperitif, fr. MF *aperitif,* adj., aperient, fr. ML *aperitivus,* irreg. fr. L *aperire*] **:** an alcoholic drink taken before a meal as an appetizer
ap·er·ture \ˈap-ə(r)-ˌchů(ə)r, -chər, -ˌt(y)ů(ə)r\ *n* [ME, fr. L *apertura,* fr. *apertus,* pp. of *aperire* to open — more at WEIR] **1 :** an opening or open space **:** HOLE **2 a :** the opening in a photographic lens that admits the light **b :** the diameter of the stop in an optical system that determines the diameter of the bundle of rays traversing the instrument **c :** the diameter of the objective lens or mirror of a telescope
syn APERTURE, INTERSTICE, ORIFICE *shared meaning element* **:** an opening allowing passage through or in and out
apet·al·ous \(ˈ)ā-ˈpet-ᵊl-əs\ *adj* **:** having no petals — **apet·aly** \-ᵊl-ē\ *n*
apex \ˈā-ˌpeks\ *n, pl* **apex·es** *or* **api·ces** \ˈā-pə-ˌsēz, ˈap-ə-\ [L] **1 a :** the uppermost point **:** VERTEX <the ~ of a mountain> **b :** the narrowed or pointed end **:** TIP <the ~ of the tongue> **2 :** the highest or culminating point <the ~ of his career> ***syn*** see SUMMIT
aphaer·e·sis *or* **apher·e·sis** \ə-ˈfer-ə-səs\ *n, pl* **-e·ses** \-ˌsēz\ [LL, fr. Gk *aphairesis,* lit., taking off, fr. *aphairein* to take away, fr. *apo-* + *hairein* to take] **:** the loss of one or more sounds or letters at the beginning of a word (as in *round* for *around* and *coon* for *raccoon*) — **aph·ae·ret·ic** \ˌaf-ə-ˈret-ik\ *adj*
aph·a·nite \ˈaf-ə-ˌnīt\ *n* [F, fr. Gk *aphanēs* invisible, fr. *a-* + *phainesthai* to appear — more at PHENOMENON] **:** a dark rock of such close texture that its separate grains are invisible to the naked eye — **aph·a·nit·ic** \ˌaf-ə-ˈnit-ik\ *adj*
apha·sia \ə-ˈfā-zh(ē-)ə\ *n* [NL, fr. Gk, fr. *a-* + *-phasia*] **:** loss or impairment of the power to use words usu. resulting from a brain lesion — **apha·si·ac** \-zē-ˌak\ *adj* — **apha·sic** \-zik\ *n or adj*
aph·elion \a-ˈfēl-yən\ *n, pl* **-elia** \-yə\ [NL, fr. *apo-* + Gk *hēlios* sun — more at SOLAR] **:** the point of a planet's or comet's orbit most distant from the sun — compare PERIHELION
aph·e·sis \ˈaf-ə-səs\ *n, pl* **-e·ses** \-ˌsēz\ [NL, fr. Gk, release, fr. *aphienai* to let go, fr. *apo-* + *hienai* to send — more at JET] **:** aphaeresis consisting of the loss of a short unaccented vowel (as in *lone* for *alone*) — **aphet·ic** \ə-ˈfet-ik\ *adj* — **aphet·i·cal·ly** \-i-k(ə-)lē\ *adv*
aphid \ˈā-fəd, ˈaf-əd\ *n* **:** any of numerous small sluggish homopterous insects (superfamily Aphidoidea) that suck the juices of plants
aphis \ˈā-fəs, ˈaf-əs\ *n, pl* **aphi·des** \ˈā-fə-ˌdēz, ˈaf-ə-\ [NL *Aphid-, Aphis,* genus name] **:** an aphid of a common genus (*Aphis*); *broadly* **:** APHID
aphis lion *n* **:** any of several insect larvae (as a lacewing or ladybug larva) that feed on aphids
aph·o·late \ˈaf-ə-ˌlāt\ *n* [prob. fr. *az-* + *pho*sphine + *-late* (of unknown origin)] **:** a chemosterilant esp. effective in controlling houseflies
apho·nia \(ˈ)ā-ˈfō-nē-ə\ *n* [NL, fr. Gk *aphōnia,* fr. *aphōnos* voiceless, fr. *a-* + *phōnē* sound — more at BAN] **:** loss of voice and of all but whispered speech — **apho·nic** \-ˈfän-ik, -ˈfō-nik\ *adj*
aph·o·rism \ˈaf-ə-ˌriz-əm\ *n* [MF *aphorisme,* fr. LL *aphorismus,* fr. Gk *aphorismos* definition, aphorism, fr. *aphorizein* to define, fr. *apo-* + *horizein* to bound — more at HORIZON] **1 :** a concise statement of a principle **2 :** a terse formulation of a truth or sentiment **:** ADAGE — **aph·o·rist** \-rəst\ *n* — **aph·o·ris·tic** \ˌaf-ə-ˈris-tik\ *adj* — **aph·o·ris·ti·cal·ly** \-ti-k(ə-)lē\ *adv*
aph·o·rize \ˈaf-ə-ˌrīz\ *vi* **-rized; -riz·ing :** to write or speak in or as if in aphorisms
apho·tic \(ˈ)ā-ˈfōt-ik\ *adj* **:** lacking light <the ~ zone in the ocean>
aph·ro·dis·i·ac \ˌaf-rə-ˈdiz-ē-ˌak\ *adj* [Gk *aphrodisiakos* sexual, fr. *aphrodisia* sexual pleasures, fr. neut. pl. of *aphrodisios* of Aphrodite, fr. *Aphroditē*] **:** exciting sexual desire — **aphrodisiac** *n* — **aph·ro·di·si·a·cal** \ˌaf-rəd-ə-ˈzī-ə-kəl, -ˈsī-\ *adj*
Aph·ro·di·te \ˌaf-rə-ˈdīt-ē\ *n* [Gk *Aphroditē*] **:** the Greek goddess of love and beauty — compare VENUS
aphyl·lous \(ˈ)ā-ˈfil-əs\ *adj* [Gk *aphyllos,* fr. *a-* + *phyllon* leaf — more at BLADE] **:** not having foliage leaves — **aphyl·ly** \ˈā-ˌfil-ē\ *n*
API *abbr* **1** air position indicator **2** American Petroleum Institute
api·an \ˈā-pē-ən\ *adj* [L *apianus,* fr. *apis*] **:** of or relating to bees
api·ar·i·an \ˌā-pē-ˈer-ē-ən\ *adj* **:** of or relating to beekeeping or bees
api·a·rist \ˈā-pē-ə-rəst, -pē-ˌer-əst\ *n* **:** BEEKEEPER
api·ary \ˈā-pē-ˌer-ē\ *n, pl* **-ar·ies** [L *apiarium,* fr. *apis* bee] **:** a place where bees are kept; *esp* **:** a collection of hives or colonies of bees kept for their honey
api·cal \ˈā-pi-kəl *also* ˈap-i-\ *adj* [prob. fr. NL *apicalis,* fr. L *apic-, apex*] **1 :** of, relating to, or situated at an apex **2 :** of, relating to, or formed with the tip of the tongue <*n, l,* and *r* are ~ consonants> — **api·cal·ly** \-k(ə-)lē\ *adv*
apical dominance *n* **:** inhibition of the growth of lateral buds by the terminal bud of a shoot
apic·u·late \ə-ˈpik-yə-lət, ā-\ *adj* [NL *apiculus,* dim. of L *apic-, apex*] **:** ending abruptly in a small distinct point <an ~ leaf>
api·cul·ture \ˈā-pə-ˌkəl-chər\ *n* [prob. fr. F, fr. L *apis* bee + F *culture*] **:** the keeping of bees esp. on a large scale — **api·cul·tur·al** \ˌā-pə-ˈkəlch(-ə)-rəl\ *adj* — **api·cul·tur·ist** \-rəst\ *n*
apiece \ə-ˈpēs\ *adv* **:** for each one **:** INDIVIDUALLY

Apis \ˈā-pəs\ *n* [L, fr. Gk, fr. Egypt *ḥp*] **:** a sacred bull worshiped by the ancient Egyptians

ap·ish \ˈā-pish\ *adj* **:** resembling an ape: as **a :** given to slavish imitation **b :** extremely silly or affected — **ap·ish·ly** *adv* — **ap·ish·ness** *n*

apla·cen·tal \ˌā-plə-ˈsent-ᵊl\ *adj* **:** having or developing no placenta

ap·la·nat·ic \ˌap-lə-ˈnat-ik\ *adj* [*a-* + Gk *planasthai* to wander — more at PLANET] **:** free from or corrected for spherical aberration <an ~ lens>

apla·sia \(ˌ)ā-ˈplā-zh(ē-)ə, ə-\ *n* [NL, fr. [2]*a-* + *-plasia*] **:** incomplete or faulty development of an organ or part — **aplas·tic** \(ˌ)ā-ˈplas-tik\ *adj*

[1]**aplen·ty** \ə-ˈplent-ē\ *adj* **:** being in plenty or abundance <money ~ for all his needs>

[2]**aplenty** *adv* **1 :** in abundance **:** PLENTIFULLY **2 :** very much **:** EXTREMELY <scared ~>

ap·lite \ˈap-ˌlīt\ *n* [prob. fr. G *aplit,* fr. Gk *haploos* simple — more at HAPL-] **:** a fine-grained light-colored granite consisting almost entirely of quartz and feldspar — **ap·lit·ic** \a-ˈplit-ik\ *adj*

aplomb \ə-ˈpläm, -ˈpləm\ *n* [F, lit., perpendicularity, fr. MF, fr. *a plomb,* lit., according to the plummet] **:** complete and confident composure or self-assurance **:** POISE ***syn*** see CONFIDENCE ***ant*** shyness

ap·nea *or* **ap·noea** \ˈap-nē-ə\ *n* [NL] **1 :** transient cessation of respiration **2 :** ASPHYXIA — **ap·ne·ic** \-nē-ik\ *adj*

APO *abbr* army post office

apo- *or* **ap-** *prefix* [ME, fr. MF & L; MF, fr. L, fr. Gk, fr. *apo* — more at OF] **1 :** away from **:** off <*ap*helion> **2 :** detached **:** separate <*apo*carpous> **3:** formed from **:** related to <*apo*morphine>

Apoc *abbr* **1** Apocalypse **2** Apocrypha; apocryphal

apoc·a·lypse \ə-ˈpäk-ə-ˌlips\ *n* [ME, revelation, Revelation, fr. LL *apocalypsis,* fr. Gk *apokalypsis,* fr. *apokalyptein* to uncover, fr. *apo-* + *kalyptein* to cover — more at HELL] **1 a :** one of the Jewish and Christian writings of 200 B.C. to A.D. 150 marked by pseudonymity, symbolic imagery, and the expectation of an imminent cosmic cataclysm in which God destroys the ruling powers of evil and raises the righteous to life in a messianic kingdom **b** *cap* **:** REVELATION 2 **2 :** something viewed as a prophetic revelation

apoc·a·lyp·tic \ə-ˌpäk-ə-ˈlip-tik\ *also* **apoc·a·lyp·ti·cal** \-ti-kəl\ *adj* **1 :** of, relating to, or resembling an apocalypse **2 :** forecasting the ultimate destiny of the world **:** PROPHETIC **3 :** foreboding imminent disaster or final doom **:** TERRIBLE **4 :** wildly unrestrained in making predictions **:** GRANDIOSE **5:** ultimately decisive **:** CLIMACTIC — **apoc·a·lyp·ti·cal·ly** \-ti-k(ə-)lē\ *adv*

apoc·a·lyp·ti·cism \-tə-ˌsiz-əm\ *or* **apoc·a·lyp·tism** \ə-ˈpäk-ə-ˌlip-ˌtiz-əm\ *n* **:** apocalyptic expectation; *esp* **:** a doctrine concerning an imminent end of the world and an ensuing general resurrection and final judgment

apoc·a·lyp·tist \ə-ˈpäk-ə-ˌlip-təst\ *n* **:** the writer of an apocalypse

apo·car·pous \ˌap-ə-ˈkär-pəs\ *adj* **:** having the carpels of the gynoecium separate — **apo·car·py** \ˈap-ə-ˌkär-pē\ *n*

apo·chro·mat·ic \ˌap-ə-krō-ˈmat-ik\ *adj* [ISV] **:** free from chromatic and spherical aberration <an ~ lens>

apoc·o·pe \ə-ˈpäk-ə-(ˌ)pē\ *n* [LL, fr. Gk *apokopē,* lit., cutting off, fr. *apokoptein* to cut off, fr. *apo-* + *koptein* to cut — more at CAPON] **:** the loss of one or more sounds or letters at the end of a word (as in *sing* from Old English *singan*)

apo·crine \ˈap-ə-krən, -ˌkrīn, -ˌkrēn\ *adj* [ISV *apo-* + Gk *krinein* to separate — more at CERTAIN] **:** producing a secretion by separation of part of the cytoplasm of the secreting cells

apoc·ry·pha \ə-ˈpäk-rə-fə\ *n pl but sing or pl in constr* [ML, fr. LL, neut. pl. of *apocryphus* secret, not canonical, fr. Gk *apokryphos* obscure, fr. *apokryptein* to hide away, fr. *apo-* + *kryptein* to hide — more at CRYPT] **1 :** writings or statements of dubious authenticity **2** *cap* **a :** books included in the Septuagint and Vulgate but excluded from the Jewish and Protestant canons of the Old Testament — see BIBLE table **b :** early Christian writings not included in the New Testament

apoc·ry·phal \-fəl\ *adj* **1** *often cap* **:** of or resembling the Apocrypha **2 :** of doubtful authenticity **:** SPURIOUS ***syn*** see FICTITIOUS — **apoc·ry·phal·ly** \-fə-lē\ *adv* — **apoc·ry·phal·ness** *n*

apo·cyn·thi·on \ˌap-ə-ˈsin(t)-thē-ən\ *n* [NL, fr. *apo-* + *Cynthia*] **:** APOLUNE

ap·o·dal \ˈap-əd-ᵊl\ *or* **ap·o·dous** \-əd-əs\ *adj* [Gk *apod-, apous,* fr. *a-* + *pod-, pous* foot — more at FOOT] **:** having no feet or analogous appendages <eels are ~>

apo·dic·tic \ˌap-ə-ˈdik-tik\ *also* **apo·deic·tic** \-ˈdīk-tik\ *adj* [L *apodicticus,* fr. Gk *apodeiktikos,* fr. *apodeiknynai* to demonstrate, fr. *apo-* + *deiknynai* to show — more at DICTION] **:** expressing or of the nature of necessary truth or absolute certainty — **apo·dic·ti·cal·ly** \-ti-k(ə-)lē\ *adv*

apod·o·sis \ə-ˈpäd-ə-səs\ *n, pl* **-o·ses** \-ˌsēz\ [NL, fr. Gk, fr. *apodidonai* to give back, deliver, fr. *apo-* + *didonai* to give — more at DATE] **:** the main clause of a conditional sentence — compare PROTASIS

apo·en·zyme \ˌap-ō-ˈen-ˌzīm\ *n* [ISV] **:** a protein that forms an active enzyme system by combination with a coenzyme and determines the specificity of this system for a substrate

apog·a·my \ə-ˈpäg-ə-mē\ *n* [ISV] **:** development of a sporophyte from a gametophyte without fertilization — **apo·gam·ic** \ˌap-ə-ˈgam-ik\ *or* **apog·a·mous** \əˈpäg-ə-məs\ *adj*

apo·gee \ˈap-ə-(ˌ)jē\ *n* [F *apogée,* fr. NL *apogaeum,* fr. Gk *apogaion,* fr. neut. of *apogeios, apogaios* far from the earth, fr. *apo-* + *gē* earth] **1 :** the point in the orbit of a satellite of the earth or of a vehicle orbiting the earth that is at the greatest distance from the center of the earth; *also* **:** the point farthest from a planet or a satellite (as the moon) reached by an object orbiting it — compare PERIGEE **2 :** the farthest or highest point **:** CULMINATION <Aegean civilization reached its ~ in Crete> — **apo·ge·an** \ˌap-ə-ˈjē-ən\ *adj*

apolit·i·cal \ˌā-pə-ˈlit-i-kəl\ *adj* **1 :** having an aversion for or no interest or involvement in political affairs **2 :** having no political significance — **apolit·i·cal·ly** \-k(ə-)lē\ *adv*

Ap·ol·lin·i·an \ˌap-ə-ˈlin-ē-ən\ *adj* **:** APOLLONIAN

Apol·lo \ə-ˈpäl-(ˌ)ō\ *n* [L *Apollin-, Apollo,* fr. Gk *Apollōn*] **:** the Greek god and in later times the Roman god of sunlight, prophecy, music, and poetry

Ap·ol·lo·ni·an \ˌap-ə-ˈlō-nē-ən\ *adj* **1 :** of, relating to, or resembling the god Apollo **2 :** harmonious, measured, ordered, or balanced in character

Apol·lyon \ə-ˈpäl-yən, -ˈpäl-ē-ən\ *n* [Gk *Apollyōn*] **:** the angel of the bottomless pit in the Book of Revelation

[1]**apol·o·get·ic** \ə-ˌpäl-ə-ˈjet-ik\ *adj* [Gk *apologētikos,* fr. *apologeisthai* to defend, fr. *apo-* + *logos* speech] **1 a :** offered in defense or vindication <the ~ writings of the early Christians> **b :** offered by way of excuse or apology <an ~ smile> **2 :** regretfully acknowledging fault or failure **:** CONTRITE <was most ~ about his mistake> — **apol·o·get·i·cal·ly** \-i-k(ə-)lē\ *adv*

[2]**apologetic** *n* **:** APOLOGETICS

apol·o·get·ics \-iks\ *n pl but sing or pl in constr* **1 :** systematic argumentative discourse in defense (as of a doctrine) **2 :** a branch of theology devoted to the defense of the divine origin and authority of Christianity

ap·o·lo·gia \ˌap-ə-ˈlō-j(ē-)ə\ *n* [LL] **:** a defense esp. of one's opinions, position, or actions <the finest ~ or explanation of what drives a man to devote his life to pure mathematics —*Brit. Book News*> ***syn*** see APOLOGY

apol·o·gist \ə-ˈpäl-ə-jəst\ *n* **:** one who speaks or writes in defense of a faith, a cause, or an institution

apol·o·gize \-ˌjīz\ *vi* **-gized; -giz·ing :** to make an apology — **apol·o·giz·er** *n*

ap·o·logue \ˈap-ə-ˌlȯg, -ˌläg\ *n* [F, fr. L *apologus,* fr. Gk *apologos,* fr. *apo-* + *logos* speech, narrative] **:** an allegorical narrative usu. intended to convey a moral

apol·o·gy \ə-ˈpäl-ə-jē\ *n, pl* **-gies** [MF or LL; MF *apologie,* fr. LL *apologia,* fr. Gk, fr. *apo-* + *logos* speech — more at LEGEND] **1 a :** a formal justification **:** DEFENSE **b :** EXCUSE 2a **2 :** an admission of error or discourtesy accompanied by an expression of regret **3 :** a poor substitute **:** MAKESHIFT

syn APOLOGY, APOLOGIA, EXCUSE, PLEA, PRETEXT, ALIBI *shared meaning element* **:** matter offered in explanation or defense (as of an act, a policy, or a view). APOLOGY usually applies to an expression of regret for a mistake or wrong with implied admission of guilt or fault and with or without reference to palliating circumstances <said by way of *apology* that he would have met them if he could> Sometimes *apology,* like APOLOGIA, implies not admission of guilt or regret but a desire to clear the grounds for some course, belief, or position <the speech was an effective *apology* for his foreign policy> EXCUSE implies an intent to avoid or remove blame or censure <used his illness as an *excuse* for missing the meeting> PLEA stresses argument or appeal for understanding or sympathy or mercy <their *pleas* for help were ignored> PRETEXT suggests subterfuge and the offering of false reasons or motives in excuse or explanation <used any *pretext* to get out of work> ALIBI implies a desire to shift blame or evade punishment and imputes plausibility rather than truth to the explanation offered <his *alibi* failed to stand scrutiny>

apo·lune \ˈap-ə-ˌlün\ *n* [*apo-* + L *luna* moon — more at LUNAR] **:** the point in the path of a body orbiting the moon that is farthest from the center of the moon — compare PERILUNE

apo·mict \ˈap-ə-ˌmikt\ *n* [prob. back-formation fr. ISV *apomictic,* fr. *apo-* + Gk *mignynai* to mix — more at MIX] **:** one produced or reproducing by apomixis — **apo·mic·tic** \ˌap-ə-ˈmik-tik\ *adj* — **apo·mic·ti·cal·ly** \-ti-k(ə-)lē\ *adv*

apo·mix·is \ˌap-ə-ˈmik-səs\ *n, pl* **-mix·es** \-ˌsēz\ [NL, fr. *apo-* + Gk *mixis* act of mixing, fr. *mignynai*] **:** reproduction (as apogamy or parthenogenesis) involving specialized generative tissues but not dependent on fertilization

apo·mor·phine \ˌap-ə-ˈmȯr-ˌfēn\ *n* [ISV] **:** an artificial crystalline alkaloid $C_{17}H_{17}NO_2$ from morphine with a powerful emetic action

apo·neu·ro·sis \ˌap-ə-n(y)u̇-ˈrō-səs\ *n* [NL, fr. Gk *aponeurōsis,* fr. *aponeurousthai* to pass into a tendon, fr. *apo-* + *neuron* sinew — more at NERVE] **:** any of the thicker and denser of the deep fasciae that cover, invest, and form the terminations and attachments of various muscles and differ from tendons in being flat and thin — **apo·neu·rot·ic** \-ˈrät-ik\ *adj*

apo·phyl·lite \ˌap-ə-ˈfil-ˌīt, ə-ˈpäf-ə-ˌlīt\ *n* [F, fr. *apo-* + Gk *phyllon* leaf] **:** a mineral $KCa_4Si_8O_{20}(F,OH).8H_2O$ composed of a hydrous potassium calcium silicate related to the zeolites and usu. found in transparent square prisms or white or grayish masses

apoph·y·sis \ə-ˈpäf-ə-səs\ *n, pl* **-y·ses** \-ˌsēz\ [NL, fr. Gk, fr. *apo-* + *phyein* to bring forth — more at BE] **:** an expanded or projecting part esp. of an organism — **apoph·y·se·al** \ə-ˌpäf-ə-ˈsē-əl\ *adj*

ap·o·plec·tic \ˌap-ə-ˈplek-tik\ *adj* [F or LL; F *apoplectique,* fr. LL *apoplecticus,* fr. Gk *apoplēktikos,* fr. *apoplēssein*] **1 :** of, relating to, or causing apoplexy **2 :** affected with, inclined to, or showing symptoms of apoplexy **3 :** of a kind to cause apoplexy; *esp* **:** highly excited <flew into an ~ rage> — **ap·o·plec·ti·cal·ly** \-ti-k(ə-)lē\ *adv*

ap·o·plexy \ˈap-ə-ˌplek-sē\ *n* [ME *apoplexie,* fr. MF & LL; MF, fr. LL *apoplexia,* fr. Gk *apoplēxia,* fr. *apoplēssein* to cripple by a stroke, fr. *apo-* + *plēssein* to strike — more at PLAINT] **:** sudden diminution or loss of consciousness, sensation, and voluntary motion caused by rupture or obstruction (as by a clot) of an artery of the brain

aport \ə-ˈpō(ə)rt, -ˈpȯ(ə)rt\ *adv* **:** on or toward the left side of a ship <put the helm hard ~>

apo·se·le·ne \ˌap-ō-sə-ˈlē-nē\ *n* [ISV *apo-* + Gk *selēnē* moon — more at SELENIUM] : APOLUNE
apo·se·mat·ic \ˌap-ə-si-ˈmat-ik\ *adj* : being conspicuous and serving to warn <~ coloration> — **apo·se·mat·i·cal·ly** \-i-k(ə-)lē\ *adv*
ap·o·si·o·pe·sis \ˌap-ə-ˌsī-ə-ˈpē-səs\ *n, pl* **-pe·ses** \-ˌsēz\ [LL, fr. Gk *aposiōpēsis*, fr. *aposiōpan* to be quite silent, fr. *apo-* + *siōpan* to be silent, fr. *siōpē* silence] : the leaving of a thought incomplete usu. by a sudden breaking off (as in "his behavior was — but I blush to mention that") — **ap·o·si·o·pet·ic** \-ˈpet-ik\ *adj*
apos·ta·sy \ə-ˈpäs-tə-sē\ *n, pl* **-sies** [ME *apostasie*, fr. LL *apostasia*, fr. Gk, lit., revolt, fr. *aphistasthai* to revolt, fr. *apo-* + *histasthai* to stand — more at STAND] **1** : renunciation of a religious faith **2** : abandonment of a previous loyalty : DEFECTION
apos·tate \ə-ˈpäs-ˌtāt, -tət\ *n* : one who commits apostasy — **apos·tate** *adj*
apos·ta·tize \ə-ˈpäs-tə-ˌtīz\ *vi* **-tized; -tiz·ing** : to commit apostasy
a pos·te·ri·o·ri \ˌä-(ˌ)pō-ˌstir-ē-ˈō(ə)r-ē, -ˌster-; ˌā-(ˌ)pä-ˌstir-ē-ˈō(ə)r-ˌī, -(ˌ)pō-, -ˈō(ə)r-ē; -ˈō(ə)r-\ *adj* [L, lit., from the latter] **1** : INDUCTIVE **2** : relating to or derived by reasoning from observed facts — compare A PRIORI — **a posteriori** *adv*
apos·tle \ə-ˈpäs-əl\ *n* [ME, fr. OF & OE; OF *apostle* & OE *apostol*, fr. LL *apostolus*, fr. Gk *apostolos*, fr. *apostellein* to send away, fr. *apo-* + *stellein* to send — more at STALL] **1** : one sent on a mission: as **a** : one of an authoritative New Testament group sent out to preach the gospel and made up esp. of Christ's 12 original disciples and Paul **b** : the first prominent Christian missionary to a region or group **2 a** : one who initiates a great moral reform or who first advocates an important belief or system **b** : an ardent supporter : ADHERENT <an ~ of liberal tolerance> **3** : the highest ecclesiastical official in some church organizations **4** : one of a Mormon administrative council of 12 men — **apos·tle·ship** \-ˌship\ *n*
Apostles' Creed *n* : a Christian statement of belief ascribed to the Twelve Apostles and used esp. in public worship
apos·to·late \ə-ˈpäs-tə-ˌlāt, -lət\ *n* [LL *apostolatus*, fr. *apostolus*] **1** : the office or mission of an apostle **2** : an association of persons dedicated to the propagation of a religion or a doctrine
ap·os·tol·ic \ˌap-ə-ˈstäl-ik\ *adj* **1 a** : of or relating to an apostle **b** : of, relating to, or conforming to the teachings of the New Testament apostles **2 a** : of or relating to a succession of spiritual authority from the apostles held (as by Roman Catholics, Anglicans, and Eastern Orthodox) to be perpetuated by successive ordinations of bishops and to be necessary for the validity of sacraments and orders **b** : PAPAL — **apos·to·lic·i·ty** \ə-ˌpäs-tə-ˈlis-ət-ē\ *n*
apostolic delegate *n* : an ecclesiastical representative of the Holy See in a country that has no formal diplomatic relations with it
Apostolic Father *n* : a church father of the first or second century A.D.
1apos·tro·phe \ə-ˈpäs-trə-(ˌ)fē\ *n* [L, fr. Gk *apostrophē*, lit., act of turning away, fr. *apostrephein* to turn away, fr. *apo-* + *strephein* to turn — more at STROPHE] : the addressing of a usu. absent person or a usu. personified thing rhetorically <Carlyle's "O Liberty, what things are done in thy name!" is an example of ~> — **ap·os·troph·ic** \ˌap-ə-ˈsträf-ik\ *adj*
2apostrophe *n* [MF & LL; MF, fr. LL *apostrophus*, fr. Gk *apostrophos*, fr. *apostrophos* turned away, fr. *apostrephein*] : a mark ' used to indicate the omission of letters or figures, the possessive case, or the plural of letters or figures — **apostrophic** *adj*
apos·tro·phize \ə-ˈpäs-trə-ˌfīz\ *vb* **-phized; -phiz·ing** *vt* : to address by or in apostrophe ~ *vi* : to make use of apostrophe
apothecaries' measure *n* : a measure of capacity used chiefly by pharmacists — see WEIGHT table
apothecaries' weight *n* : a system of weights used chiefly by pharmacists — see WEIGHT table
apoth·e·cary \ə-ˈpäth-ə-ˌker-ē\ *n, pl* **-car·ies** [ME *apothecarie*, fr. ML *apothecarius*, fr. LL, shopkeeper, fr. L *apotheca* storehouse, fr. Gk *apothēkē*, fr. *apotithenai* to put away, fr. *apo-* + *tithenai* to put — more at DO] **1** : one who prepares and sells drugs or compounds for medicinal purposes **2** : PHARMACY
apo·the·ci·um \-ˈthē-s(h)ē-əm\ *n, pl* **-cia** \-s(h)ē-ə\ [NL, fr. L *apotheca*] : a spore-bearing structure in many lichens and fungi consisting of a discoid or cupped body bearing asci on the exposed flat or concave surface — **apo·the·cial** \-sh(ē-)əl, -sē-əl\ *adj*
ap·o·thegm \ˈap-ə-ˌthem\ *n* [Gk *apophthegmat-*, *apophthegma*, fr. *apophthengesthai* to speak out, fr. *apo-* + *phthengesthai* to utter] : a short, pithy, and instructive saying or formulation : APHORISM — **ap·o·theg·mat·ic** \ˌap-ə-theg-ˈmat-ik\ *or* **ap·o·theg·mat·i·cal** \-i-kəl\ *adj* — **ap·o·theg·mat·i·cal·ly** \-i-k(ə-)lē\ *adv*
ap·o·them \ˈap-ə-ˌthem\ *n* [ISV *apo-* + *-them* (fr. Gk *thema* something laid down, theme)] : the perpendicular from the center of a regular polygon to one of the sides
apo·the·o·sis \ə-ˌpäth-ē-ˈō-səs, ˌap-ə-ˈthē-ə-səs\ *n, pl* **-o·ses** \-ˌsēz\ [LL, fr. Gk *apotheōsis*, fr. *apotheoun* to deify, fr. *apo-* + *theos* god] **1** : elevation to divine status : DEIFICATION **2** : the perfect example : QUINTESSENCE <she is the ~ of womanhood> — **apo·the·o·size** \ˌap-ə-ˈthē-ə-ˌsīz, ə-ˈpäth-ē-ə-\ *vt*
apo·tro·pa·ic \ˌap-ə-trō-ˈpā-ik\ *adj* [Gk *apotropaios*, fr. *apotrepein* to avert, fr. *apo-* + *trepein* to turn — more at TROPE] : designed to avert evil <an ~ ritual> — **apo·tro·pa·i·cal·ly** \-ˈpā-ə-k(ə-)lē\ *adv*
app *abbr* **1** apparatus **2** appendix
ap·pall *also* **ap·pal** \ə-ˈpȯl\ *vb* **ap·palled; ap·pall·ing** [ME *appallen*, fr. MF *apalir*, fr. OF, fr. *a-* (fr. L *ad-*) + *palir* to grow pale, fr. L *pallescere*, incho. of *pallēre* to be pale — more at FALLOW] *vi, obs* : WEAKEN, FAIL ~ *vt* : to overcome with consternation, shock, or dismay ***syn*** see DISMAY ***ant*** nerve, embolden
ap·pall·ing *adj* : inspiring horror, dismay, or disgust <living under ~ conditions> ***syn*** see FEARFUL ***ant*** reassuring — **ap·pall·ing·ly** \-ˈpȯ-liŋ-lē\ *adv*
Ap·pa·loo·sa \ˌap-ə-ˈlü-sə\ *n* [prob. fr. *Palouse*, an Indian people of Wash. and Idaho] : a rugged saddle horse of a breed developed in western No. America that has a mottled skin, vertically striped hooves, and a blotched or dotted patch of white hair over the rump and loins
ap·pa·nage \ˈap-ə-nij\ *n* [F *apanage*, fr. OF, fr. *apaner* to provide for a younger offspring, fr. OProv *apanar* to support, fr. *a-* (fr. L *ad-*) + *pan* bread, fr. L *panis* — more at FOOD] **1 a** : a grant (as of land or revenue) made by a sovereign or a legislative body to a dependent member of the royal family or a principal liege man **b** : a property or privilege appropriated to or by a person as his share **2** : a rightful endowment or adjunct
ap·pa·rat \ˈap-ə-ˌrat, ˌäp-ə-ˈrät\ *n* [Russ] : APPARATUS 2
ap·pa·ra·tchik \ˌäp-ə-ˈräch-ik\ *n, pl* **-ratchiks** *or* **-ra·tchi·ki** \-ˈräch-ə-(ˌ)kē\ [Russ, fr. *apparat*] : a member of a Communist apparat
ap·pa·ra·tus \ˌap-ə-ˈrat-əs, -ˈrāt-\ *n, pl* **-tus·es** *or* **-tus** [L, fr. *apparatus*, pp. of *apparare* to prepare, fr. *ad-* + *parare* to prepare — more at PARE] **1 a** : a set of materials or equipment designed for a particular use **b** : an instrument or appliance designed for a specific operation **c** : a group of organs having a common function **2** : the functional machinery by means of which a systematized activity is carried out; *esp* : the organization of a political party or an underground movement
1ap·par·el \ə-ˈpar-əl\ *vt* **-eled** *or* **-elled; -el·ing** *or* **-el·ling** [ME *appareillen*, fr. OF *apareillier* to prepare, fr. (assumed) VL *appariculare*, irreg. fr. L *apparare*] **1** : to put clothes on : DRESS **2** : ADORN, EMBELLISH
2apparel *n* **1** : the equipment (as sails and rigging) of a ship **2** : personal attire : CLOTHING **3** : something that clothes or adorns <the bright ~ of spring>
ap·par·ent \ə-ˈpar-ənt, -ˈper-\ *adj* [ME, fr. OF *aparent*, fr. L *apparent-*, *apparens*, prp. of *apparēre* to appear] **1** : open to view : VISIBLE **2** : clear or manifest to the understanding **3** : appearing as actual to the eye or mind **4** : having an indefeasible right to succeed to a title or estate **5** : manifest to the senses or mind as real or true on the basis of evidence that may or may not be factually valid <his ~ absorption was belied by his rigid pose> — **ap·par·ent·ly** \-ˈpar(-ə)nt-lē, -ˈper(-ə)nt-\ *adv* — **ap·par·ent·ness** \-ˈpar-ənt-nəs, -ˈper-\ *n*
syn **1** APPARENT, ILLUSORY, ILLUSIONARY, SEEMING, OSTENSIBLE *shared meaning element* : not actually being what it appears to be ***ant*** real
2 see EVIDENT ***ant*** unintelligible
apparent time *n* : the time of day indicated by the hour angle of the sun or by a sundial
ap·pa·ri·tion \ˌap-ə-ˈrish-ən\ *n* [ME *apparicioun*, fr. LL *apparition-*, *apparitio* appearance, fr. L *apparitus*, pp. of *apparēre*] **1 a** : an unusual or unexpected sight : PHENOMENON **b** : a ghostly figure **2** : the act of becoming visible : APPEARANCE — **ap·pa·ri·tion·al** \-ˈrish-nəl, -ən-ᵊl\ *adj*
ap·par·i·tor \ə-ˈpar-ət-ər\ *n* [L, fr. *apparitus*] : an official formerly sent to carry out the orders of a magistrate, judge, or court
1ap·peal \ə-ˈpē(ə)l\ *n* **1** : a legal proceeding by which a case is brought from a lower to a higher court for rehearing **2** : a criminal accusation **3 a** : an application (as to a recognized authority) for corroboration, vindication, or decision **b** : an earnest plea : ENTREATY **4** : the power of arousing a sympathetic response : ATTRACTION <movies had a great ~ for him>
2appeal *vb* [ME *appelen* to accuse, appeal, fr. MF *apeler*, fr. L *appellare*, fr. *appellere* to drive to, fr. *ad-* + *pellere* to drive — more at FELT] *vt* **1** : to charge with a crime : ACCUSE **2** : to take proceedings to have (a case) reheard in a higher court ~ *vi* **1** : to take a case to a higher court for rehearing **2** : to call upon another for corroboration, vindication, or decision **3** : to make an earnest request **4** : to arouse a sympathetic response — **ap·peal·abil·i·ty** \-ˌpē-lə-ˈbil-ət-ē\ *n* — **ap·peal·able** \-ˈpē-lə-bəl\ *adj* — **ap·peal·er** *n*
ap·peal·ing \ə-ˈpē-liŋ\ *adj* **1** : having appeal : PLEASING **2** : marked by earnest entreaty : IMPLORING — **ap·peal·ing·ly** \-liŋ-lē\ *adv*
ap·pear \ə-ˈpi(ə)r\ *vi* [ME *apperen*, fr. OF *aparoir*, fr. L *apparēre*, fr. *ad-* + *parēre* to show oneself; akin to Gk *peparein* to display] **1 a** : to be or come in sight <the sun ~*s* on the horizon> **b** : to show up <~*s* promptly at eight each day> **2** : to come formally before an authoritative body <must ~ in court today> **3** : to have an outward aspect <~*s* happy enough> **4** : to become evident or manifest <there ~*s* growing evidence to the contrary> **5** : to come into public view <first ~*ed* on a television variety show> **6** : to come into existence <man ~*s* late in the evolutionary chain> ***syn*** see SEEM
ap·pear·ance \ə-ˈpir-ən(t)s\ *n* **1 a** : the act, action, or process of appearing **b** : the coming into court of a party in an action or his attorney **2 a** : outward aspect : LOOK <had a fierce ~> **b** : external show : SEMBLANCE <although hostile, he tried to preserve an ~ of neutrality> **c** *pl* : outward indication <would do anything to keep up ~*s*> **3 a** : a sense impression or aspect of a thing <the blue of distant hills is only an ~> **b** : the world of sensible phenomena **4 a** : something that appears : PHENOMENON **b** : an instance of appearing : OCCURRENCE
ap·pease \ə-ˈpēz\ *vt* **ap·peased; ap·peas·ing** [ME *appesen*, fr. OF *apaisier*, fr. *a-* (fr. L *ad-*) + *pais* peace — more at PEACE] **1** : to bring to a state of peace or quiet : CALM **2** : to cause to subside : ALLAY <~ his hunger> **3** : PACIFY, CONCILIATE; *esp* : to buy off (an aggressor) by concessions usu. at the sacrifice of principles — **ap·peas·able** \-ˈpē-zə-bəl\ *adj* — **ap·pease·ment** \ə-ˈpēz-mənt\ *n* — **ap·peas·er** *n*
1ap·pel·lant \ə-ˈpel-ənt\ *adj* : of or relating to an appeal : APPELLATE
2appellant *n* : one that appeals; *specif* : one that appeals from a judicial decision or decree
ap·pel·late \ə-ˈpel-ət\ *adj* [L *appellatus*, pp. of *appellare*] : of, relating to, or recognizing appeals; *specif* : having the power to review the judgment of another tribunal <an ~ court>
ap·pel·la·tion \ˌap-ə-ˈlā-shən\ *n* **1** *archaic* : the act of calling by a name **2** : an identifying name or title : DESIGNATION

ap·pel·la·tive \ə-ˈpel-ət-iv\ *adj* **1 :** of or relating to a common noun **2 :** of, relating to, or inclined to the giving of names — **ap·pel·la·tive** *n* — **ap·pel·la·tive·ly** *adv*

ap·pel·lee \ˌap-ə-ˈlē\ *n* **:** one against whom an appeal is taken

ap·pend \ə-ˈpend\ *vt* [F *appendre,* fr. LL *appendere,* fr. L, to weigh, fr. *ad-* + *pendere* to weigh — more at PENDANT] **1 :** ATTACH, AFFIX **2 :** to add as a supplement or appendix (as in a book)

ap·pend·age \ə-ˈpen-dij\ *n* **1 :** an adjunct to something larger or more important **:** APPURTENANCE **2 :** a dependent or subordinate person **3 :** a subordinate or derivative body part; *esp* **:** a limb or analogous part (as a seta)

ap·pen·dant \ə-ˈpen-dənt\ *adj* **1 :** associated as an attendant circumstance **2 :** belonging as a right — used of annexed land in English law **3 :** attached as an appendage <a seal ~ to a document> — **appendant** *n*

ap·pen·dec·to·my \ˌap-ən-ˈdek-tə-mē\ *n, pl* **-mies** [L *appendic-, appendix* + E *-ectomy*] **:** surgical removal of the vermiform appendix

ap·pen·di·ci·tis \ə-ˌpen-də-ˈsīt-əs\ *n* **:** inflammation of the vermiform appendix

ap·pen·dic·u·lar \ˌap-ən-ˈdik-yə-lər\ *adj* **:** of or relating to an appendage and esp. a limb <the ~ skeleton>

ap·pen·dix \ə-ˈpen-diks\ *n, pl* **-dix·es** *or* **-di·ces** \-də-ˌsēz\ [L *appendic-, appendix,* fr. *appendere*] **1 a :** APPENDAGE **b :** supplementary material usu. attached at the end of a piece of writing **2 :** a bodily outgrowth or process; *specif* **:** VERMIFORM APPENDIX

ap·per·ceive \ˌap-ər-ˈsēv\ *vt* **-ceived; -ceiv·ing** [ME *apperceiven,* fr. OF *aperceivre,* fr. *a-* (fr. L *ad-*) + *perceivre* to perceive] **:** to have apperception of

ap·per·cep·tion \-ˈsep-shən\ *n* [F *aperception,* fr. *apercevoir*] **1 :** introspective self-consciousness **2 :** mental perception; *esp* **:** the process of understanding something perceived in terms of previous experience ***syn*** see RECOGNITION — **ap·per·cep·tive** \-ˈsep-tiv\ *adj*

ap·per·tain \ˌap-ər-ˈtān\ *vi* [ME *apperteinen,* fr. MF *apartenir,* fr. LL *appertinēre,* fr. L *ad-* + *pertinēre* to belong — more at PERTAIN] **:** to belong or be connected as a rightful part or attribute **:** PERTAIN

ap·pe·tence \ˈap-ət-ən(t)s\ *n* **:** APPETENCY

ap·pe·ten·cy \ˈap-ət-ən-sē\ *n, pl* **-cies** [L *appetentia,* fr. *appetent-, appetens,* prp. of *appetere*] **1 :** a fixed and strong desire **:** APPETITE **2 :** a natural affinity (as between chemicals) — **ap·pe·tent** \-ənt\ *adj*

ap·pe·tite \ˈap-ə-ˌtīt\ *n* [ME *apetit,* fr. MF, fr. L *appetitus,* fr. *appetitus,* pp. of *appetere* to strive after, fr. *ad-* + *petere* to go to — more at FEATHER] **1 :** one of the instinctive desires necessary to keep up organic life; *esp* **:** the desire to eat **2 a :** an inherent craving <an insatiable ~ for work> **b :** TASTE, PREFERENCE <the cultural ~*s* of the time —J. D. Hart> — **ap·pe·ti·tive** \-ˌtīt-iv\ *adj*

ap·pe·tiz·er \ˈap-ə-ˌtī-zər\ *n* **:** a food or drink that stimulates the appetite and is usu. served before a meal

ap·pe·tiz·ing \-ˌtī-ziŋ\ *adj* **:** appealing to the appetite esp. in appearance or aroma ***syn*** see PALATABLE ***ant*** unappetizing — **ap·pe·tiz·ing·ly** \-ziŋ-lē\ *adv*

Ap·pi·an Way \ˌap-ē-ən-\ *n* [*Appius* Claudius Caecus *fl* 300 B.C. Roman statesman] **:** an ancient paved highway extending from Rome to Brundisium

appl *abbr* applied

ap·plaud \ə-ˈplȯd\ *vb* [MF or L; MF *applaudir,* fr. L *applaudere,* fr. *ad-* + *plaudere* to applaud] *vi* **:** to express approval esp. by clapping the hands ~ *vt* **1 :** to express approval of **:** PRAISE <~ her efforts to lose weight> **2 :** to show approval of esp. by clapping the hands — **ap·plaud·able** \-ə-bəl\ *adj* — **ap·plaud·ably** \-blē\ *adv* — **ap·plaud·er** *n*

ap·plause \ə-ˈplȯz\ *n* [ML *applausus,* fr. L, clashing noise, fr. *applausus,* pp. of *applaudere*] **1 :** approval publicly expressed (as by clapping the hands) **2 :** marked commendation **:** ACCLAIM <the kind of ~ every really creative writer wants—Robert Tallant>

ap·ple \ˈap-əl\ *n, often attrib* [ME *appel,* fr. OE *æppel;* akin to OHG *apful* apple, OSlav *ablŭko*] **1 :** the fleshy usu. rounded and red or yellow edible pome fruit of a tree (genus *Malus*) of the rose family; *also* **:** an apple tree **2 :** a fruit or other vegetable production suggestive of an apple — **apple of one's eye :** one that is highly cherished <his daughter is the *apple of his eye*>

ap·ple·jack \-ˌjak\ *n* **:** brandy distilled from cider; *also* **:** an alcoholic beverage traditionally made by freezing hard cider

apple maggot *n* **:** a two-winged fly (*Rhagoletis pomonella*) whose larva burrows in and feeds esp. on apples

ap·ple–pie \ˌap-əl-ˌpī\ *adj* **1 :** EXCELLENT, PERFECT <~ order> **2 :** of, relating to, or characterized by traditionally American values (as honesty or simplicity) <is the epitome of ~ wholesomeness>

ap·ple–pol·ish \ˈap-əl-ˌpäl-ish\ *vb* [fr. the traditional practice of schoolchildren bringing a shiny apple as a gift to their teacher] *vi* **:** to attempt to ingratiate oneself **:** TOADY ~ *vt* **:** to curry favor with (as by flattery) — **ap·ple–pol·ish·er** *n*

Ap·ple·ton layer \ˌap-əl-tən-, -əlt-ən-\ *n* [Sir Edward *Appleton* †1965 E physicist] **:** F LAYER

ap·pli·ance \ə-ˈplī-ən(t)s\ *n* **1 :** an act of applying **2 a :** a piece of equipment for adapting a tool or machine to a special purpose **:** ATTACHMENT **b :** an instrument or device designed for a particular use; *specif* **:** a household or office device (as a stove, fan, or refrigerator) operated by gas or electric current **3** *obs* **:** COMPLIANCE

ap·pli·ca·ble \ˈap-li-kə-bəl *also* ə-ˈplik-ə-\ *adj* **:** capable of or suitable for being applied **:** APPROPRIATE <there are several statutes ~ to the case> ***syn*** see RELEVANT ***ant*** inapplicable — **ap·pli·ca·bil·i·ty** \ˌap-li-kə-ˈbil-ət-ē *also* ə-ˌplik-ə-\ *n*

ap·pli·cant \ˈap-li-kənt\ *n* **:** one who applies <a job ~>

ap·pli·ca·tion \ˌap-lə-ˈkā-shən\ *n* [ME *applicacioun,* fr. L *application-, applicatio* inclination, fr. *applicatus,* pp. of *applicare*] **1 :** an act of applying: **a** (1) **:** an act of putting to use <~ of new techniques> (2) **:** a use to which something is put <new ~*s* for old remedies> **b :** an act of administering or superposing <~ of paint to a house> **c :** assiduous attention <succeeds by ~ to his studies> **2 a :** REQUEST, PETITION <an ~ for financial aid> **b :** a form used in making a request **3 :** the practical inference to be derived from a discourse (as a moral tale) **4 :** a medicated or protective layer or material <an oily ~ for dry skin> **5 :** capacity for practical use <words of varied ~>

ap·pli·ca·tive \ˈap-lə-ˌkāt-iv, ə-ˈplik-ət-\ *adj* **1 :** APPLICABLE, PRACTICAL **2 :** put to use **:** APPLIED — **ap·pli·ca·tive·ly** *adv*

ap·pli·ca·tor \ˈap-lə-ˌkāt-ər\ *n* **:** one that applies; *specif* **:** a device for applying a substance (as medicine or polish)

ap·pli·ca·to·ry \ˈap-li-kə-ˌtōr-ē, -ˌtȯr-, ə-ˈplik-ə-\ *adj* **:** capable of being applied

ap·plied \ə-ˈplīd\ *adj* **:** put to practical use; *esp* **:** applying general principles to solve definite problems <~ sciences>

[1]ap·pli·qué \ˌap-lə-ˈkā\ *n* [F, pp. of *appliquer* to put on, fr. L *applicare*] **:** a cutout decoration fastened to a larger piece of material

[2]appliqué *vt* **-quéd; -qué·ing :** to apply (as a decoration or ornament) to a larger surface **:** OVERLAY

ap·ply \ə-ˈplī\ *vb* **ap·plied; ap·ply·ing** [ME *applien,* fr. MF *aplier,* fr. L *applicare,* fr. *ad-* + *plicare* to fold — more at PLY] *vt* **1 a :** to put to use esp. for some practical purpose <*applies* pressure to get what he wants> **b :** to bring into action <~ the brakes> **c :** to lay or spread on <~ varnish to a table> **d :** to put into operation or effect <~ a law> **2 :** to employ diligently or with close attention <should ~ himself to his work> ~ *vi* **1 :** to have relevance or a valid connection <this rule *applies* to freshmen only> **2 :** to make an appeal or request esp. in the form of a written application <~ for a job> — **ap·pli·er** \-ˈplī(-ə)r\ *n*

ap·pog·gia·tu·ra \ə-ˌpäj-ə-ˈtu̇r-ə\ *n* [It, lit., support] **:** an embellishing note or tone preceding an essential melodic note or tone and usu. written as a note of smaller size

long written played
short written played
double written played

appoggiatura

ap·point \ə-ˈpȯint\ *vb* [ME *appointen,* fr. MF *apointier* to arrange, fr. *a-* (fr. L *ad-*) + *point*] *vt* **1 a :** to fix or set offically <~ a trial date> **b :** to name officially <will ~ him director of the program> **c** *archaic* **:** ARRANGE **d :** to determine the disposition of (an estate) to someone by virtue of a power of appointment **2 :** to provide with complete and usu. appropriate or elegant furnishings or equipment ~ *vi* **:** to exercise a power of appointment ***syn*** see FURNISH

ap·poin·tee \ə-ˌpȯin-ˈtē, ˌa-\ *n* **1 :** one who is appointed **2 :** one to whom an estate is appointed

ap·point·ive \ə-ˈpȯint-iv\ *adj* **:** of, relating to, or filled by appointment <an ~ office>

ap·point·ment \ə-ˈpȯint-mənt\ *n* **1 a :** an act of appointing **:** DESIGNATION **b :** the designation by virtue of a vested power of a person to enjoy an estate **2 :** a nonelective office or position <holds an academic ~> **3 :** an arrangement for a meeting **:** ENGAGEMENT **4 :** EQUIPMENT, FURNISHINGS — usu. used in pl.

ap·por·tion \ə-ˈpōr-shən, -ˈpȯr-\ *vt* **ap·por·tioned; ap·por·tion·ing** \-sh(ə-)niŋ\ [MF *apportionner,* fr. *a-* (fr. L *ad-*) + *portionner* to portion] **:** to divide and share out according to a plan; *esp* **:** to make a proportionate division or distribution of ***syn*** see ALLOT

ap·por·tion·ment \-shən-mənt\ *n* **:** an act or result of apportioning; *esp* **:** the apportioning of representatives or taxes among the states according to U.S. law

ap·pose \a-ˈpōz\ *vt* **ap·posed; ap·pos·ing** [MF *aposer,* fr. OF, fr. *a-* + *poser* to put — more at POSE] **1** *archaic* **:** to put before **:** apply (one thing) to another **2 :** to place in juxtaposition or proximity

ap·po·site \ˈap-ə-zət\ *adj* [L *appositus,* fr. pp. of *apponere* to place near, fr. *ad-* + *ponere* to put — more at POSITION] **:** highly pertinent or appropriate **:** APT ***syn*** see RELEVANT ***ant*** inapposite, inapt — **ap·po·site·ly** *adv* — **ap·po·site·ness** *n*

ap·po·si·tion \ˌap-ə-ˈzish-ən\ *n* **1 a :** a grammatical construction in which two usu. adjacent nouns having the same referent stand in the same syntactical relation to the rest of a sentence (as *the poet* and *Burns* in "a biography of the poet Burns") **b :** the relation of one of such a pair of nouns or noun equivalents to the other **2 a :** an act or instance of apposing; *specif* **:** the deposition of successive layers upon those already present (as in cell walls) **b :** the state of being apposed — **ap·po·si·tion·al** \-ˈzish-nəl, -ən-ᵊl\ *adj* — **ap·po·si·tion·al·ly** \-ē\ *adv*

ap·pos·i·tive \ə-ˈpäz-ət-iv, a-\ *adj* **:** of, relating to, or standing in grammatical apposition — **appositive** *n* — **ap·pos·i·tive·ly** *adv*

ap·prais·al \ə-ˈprā-zəl\ *n* **:** an act or instance of appraising; *esp* **:** a valuation of property by the estimate of an authorized person

ap·praise \ə-ˈprāz\ *vt* **ap·praised; ap·prais·ing** [ME *appreisen,* fr. MF *aprisier* to apprize] **1 :** to set a value on **:** estimate the amount of **2 :** to evaluate the worth, significance, or status of; *esp* **:** to give an expert judgment of the value or merit of ***syn*** see ESTIMATE — **ap·praise·ment** \-ˈprāz-mənt\ *n* — **ap·prais·er** *n* — **ap·prais·ing** *adj* — **ap·prais·ing·ly** \-ˈprā-ziŋ-lē\ *adv*

ap·pre·cia·ble \ə-ˈprē-shə-bəl\ *adj* **:** capable of being perceived or measured ***syn*** see PERCEPTIBLE ***ant*** inappreciable — **ap·pre·cia·bly** \-blē\ *adv*

ap·pre·ci·ate \ə-ˈprē-shē-ˌāt\ *vb* **-at·ed; -at·ing** [LL *appretiatus,* pp. of *appretiare,* fr. L *ad-* + *pretium* price — more at PRICE] *vt* **1 a :** to grasp the nature, worth, quality, or significance of <can't ~ the difference between right and wrong> **b :** to value or admire highly <think no one ~*s* his endeavors> **c :** to judge with heightened perception or understanding **:** be fully aware of <must experience it to ~ it> **d :** to recognize with gratitude <certainly ~*s* your kindness> **2 :** to increase the value of ~ *vi* **:** to increase

in number or value — **ap·pre·ci·a·tor** \-ˌāt-ər\ *n* — **ap·pre·cia·to·ry** \-shə-ˌtōr-ē, -ˌtȯr-\ *adj*
syn **1** see UNDERSTAND ***ant*** depreciate
2 APPRECIATE, VALUE, PRIZE, TREASURE, CHERISH *shared meaning element* **:** to hold in high esteem ***ant*** despise

ap·pre·ci·a·tion \ə-ˌprē-shē-ˈā-shən\ *n* **1 a :** sensitive awareness; *esp* **:** recognition of aesthetic values **b :** JUDGMENT, EVALUATION; *esp* **:** a favorable critical estimate **c :** an expression of admiration, approval, or gratitude **2 :** increase in value

ap·pre·cia·tive \ə-ˈprē-shət-iv *also* -shē-ˌāt-\ *adj* **:** having or showing appreciation — **ap·pre·cia·tive·ly** *adv* — **ap·pre·cia·tive·ness** *n*

ap·pre·hend \ˌap-ri-ˈhend\ *vb* [ME *apprehenden,* fr. L *apprehendere,* lit., to seize, fr. *ad-* + *prehendere* to seize — more at PREHENSILE] *vt* **1 :** ARREST, SEIZE <~ a thief> **2 a :** to become aware of **:** PERCEIVE **b :** to anticipate esp. with anxiety, dread, or fear **3 :** to grasp with the understanding **:** recognize the meaning of ~ *vi* **:** UNDERSTAND, GRASP ***syn*** see FORESEE

ap·pre·hen·si·ble \ˌap-ri-ˈhen(t)-sə-bəl\ *adj* **:** capable of being apprehended — **ap·pre·hen·si·bly** \-blē\ *adv*

ap·pre·hen·sion \ˌap-ri-ˈhen-chən\ *n* [ME, fr. LL *apprehension-, apprehensio,* fr. L *apprehensus,* pp. of *apprehendere*] **1 a :** the act or power of perceiving or comprehending <a man of dull ~> **b :** the result of apprehending mentally **:** CONCEPTION <according to popular ~> **2 :** seizure by legal process **:** ARREST **3 :** suspicion or fear esp. of future evil **:** FOREBODING

ap·pre·hen·sive \-ˈhen(t)-siv\ *adj* **1 :** capable of apprehending or quick to do so **:** DISCERNING **2 :** having apprehension **:** COGNIZANT **3 :** viewing the future with anxiety or alarm ***syn*** see FEARFUL ***ant*** confident — **ap·pre·hen·sive·ly** *adv* — **ap·pre·hen·sive·ness** *n*

¹ap·pren·tice \ə-ˈprent-əs\ *n* [ME *aprentis,* fr. MF, fr. OF, fr. *aprendre* to learn, fr. L *apprendere, apprehendere*] **1 a :** one bound by indenture to serve another for a prescribed period with a view to learning an art or trade **b :** one who is learning by practical experience under skilled workers a trade, art, or calling **2 :** an inexperienced person **:** NOVICE <an ~ in cooking> — **ap·pren·tice·ship** \-ə(sh)-ˌship, -əs-ˌship\ *n*

²apprentice *vt* **-ticed; -tic·ing :** to set at work as an apprentice; *esp* **:** to bind to an apprenticeship by contract or indenture

ap·pressed \a-ˈprest\ *adj* [L *appressus,* pp. of *apprimere* to press to, fr. *ad-* + *premere* to press — more at PRESS] **:** pressed close to or lying flat against something <leaves ~ against the stem>

ap·prise \ə-ˈprīz\ *vt* **ap·prised; ap·pris·ing** [F *appris,* pp. of *apprendre* to learn, teach, fr. OF *aprendre*] **:** to give notice to **:** TELL ***syn*** see INFORM

ap·prize \ə-ˈprīz\ *vt* **ap·prized; ap·priz·ing** [ME *apprisen,* fr. MF *aprisier,* fr. OF, fr. *a-* (fr. L *ad-*) + *prisier* to appraise — more at PRIZE] **:** VALUE, APPRECIATE

¹ap·proach \ə-ˈprōch\ *vb* [ME *approchen,* fr. OF *aprochier,* fr. LL *appropiare,* fr. L *ad-* + *prope* near; akin to L *pro* before — more at FOR] *vt* **1 a :** to draw closer to **:** NEAR <~ the podium> **b :** to come very near to **:** be almost the same as <its mathematics ~*es* mysticism —Theodore Sturgeon> **2 a :** to make advances to esp. in order to create a desired result <was ~*ed* by several Broadway producers> **b :** to take preliminary steps toward accomplishment or full knowledge or experience of <~ the subject with an open mind> ~ *vi* **1 :** to draw nearer <dawn ~*es*> **2 :** to make an approach in golf ***syn*** see MATCH

²approach *n* **1 a :** an act or instance of approaching <the ~ of summer> **b :** APPROXIMATION <in this book he makes his closest ~ to greatness> **2 a :** the taking of preliminary steps toward a particular purpose <experimenting with new lines of ~> **b :** a particular manner of taking such steps <a highly individual ~ to language> **3 :** a means of access **:** AVENUE **4 a :** a golf shot from the fairway toward the green **b :** the steps taken by a bowler before he delivers the ball; *also* **:** the part of the alley behind the foul line from which the bowler delivers the ball

ap·proach·able \ə-ˈprō-chə-bəl\ *adj* **:** capable of being approached **:** ACCESSIBLE; *specif* **:** easy to meet or deal with — **ap·proach·abil·i·ty** \-ˌprō-chə-ˈbil-ət-ē\ *n*

ap·pro·bate \ˈap-rə-ˌbāt\ *vt* **-bat·ed; -bat·ing** [ME *approbaten,* fr. L *approbatus,* pp. of *approbare*] **:** APPROVE, SANCTION — **ap·pro·ba·to·ry** \ˈap-rə-bə-ˌtōr-ē, ə-ˈprō-bə-, -ˌtȯr-\ *adj*

ap·pro·ba·tion \ˌap-rə-ˈbā-shən\ *n* **1** *obs* **:** PROOF **2 a :** an act of approving formally or officially **b :** COMMENDATION, PRAISE

¹ap·pro·pri·ate \ə-ˈprō-prē-ˌāt\ *vt* **-at·ed; -at·ing** [ME *appropriaten,* fr. LL *appropriatus,* pp. of *appropriare,* fr. L *ad-* + *proprius* own] **1 :** to take exclusive possession of **:** ANNEX <no one should ~ a common benefit> **2 :** to set apart for or assign to a particular purpose or use <~ money for the research program> **3 :** to take or make use of without authority or right — **ap·pro·pri·a·ble** \-prē-ə-bəl\ *adj* — **ap·pro·pri·a·tor** \-prē-ˌāt-ər\ *n*
syn APPROPRIATE, PREEMPT, ARROGATE, CONFISCATE *shared meaning element* **:** to seize high-handedly

²ap·pro·pri·ate \ə-ˈprō-prē-ət\ *adj* **:** especially suitable or compatible **:** FITTING ***syn*** see FIT ***ant*** inappropriate — **ap·pro·pri·ate·ly** *adv* — **ap·pro·pri·ate·ness** *n*

ap·pro·pri·a·tion \ə-ˌprō-prē-ˈā-shən\ *n* **1 :** an act or instance of appropriating **2 :** something that has been appropriated; *specif* **:** money set aside by formal action for a specific use — **ap·pro·pri·a·tive** \-ˈprō-prē-ˌāt-iv\ *adj*

ap·prov·able \ə-ˈprü-və-bəl\ *adj* **:** capable of being approved — **ap·prov·ably** \-blē\ *adv*

ap·prov·al \ə-ˈprü-vəl\ *n* **:** an act or instance of approving **:** APPROBATION — **on approval :** subject to a prospective buyer's acceptance or refusal <took the suit home *on approval*>

ap·prove \ə-ˈprüv\ *vb* **ap·proved; ap·prov·ing** [ME *approven,* fr. OF *aprover,* fr. L *approbare,* fr. *ad-* + *probare* to prove — more at PROVE] *vt* **1** *obs* **:** PROVE, ATTEST **2 :** to have or express a favorable opinion of <couldn't ~ his conduct> **3 a :** to accept as satisfactory <hopes he will ~ the date of the meeting> **b :** to give formal or official sanction to **:** RATIFY <Congress *approved* the proposed budget> ~ *vi* **:** to take a favorable view <doesn't ~ of fighting> — **ap·prov·ing·ly** \-ˈprü-viŋ-lē\ *adv*
syn APPROVE, ENDORSE, SANCTION, ACCREDIT, CERTIFY *shared meaning element* **:** to hold or express a favorable opinion ***ant*** disapprove

approved school *n, Brit* **:** a school for juvenile delinquents

approx *abbr* approximate; approximately

¹ap·prox·i·mate \ə-ˈpräk-sə-mət\ *adj* [LL *approximatus,* pp. of *approximare* to come near, fr. L *ad-* + *proximare* to come near — more at PROXIMATE] **1 :** nearly correct or exact **2 :** located close together <~ leaves> — **ap·prox·i·mate·ly** *adv*

²ap·prox·i·mate \-ˌmāt\ *vb* **-mat·ed; -mat·ing** *vt* **1 a :** to bring near or close **b :** to bring (cut edges of tissue) together **2 :** to come near to **:** APPROACH <a child tries to ~ his parents' speech> ~ *vi* **:** to come close

ap·prox·i·ma·tion \ə-ˌpräk-sə-ˈmā-shən\ *n* **1 :** the act or process of drawing together **2 :** the quality or state of being close or near <an ~ to the truth> **3 :** something that is approximate; *esp* **:** a mathematical quantity that is close in value to but not the same as a desired quantity — **ap·prox·i·ma·tive** \-ˈpräk-sə-ˌmāt-iv\ *adj* — **ap·prox·i·ma·tive·ly** *adv*

appt *abbr* appoint; appointed; appointment

apptd *abbr* appointed

ap·pur·te·nance \ə-ˈpərt-nən(t)s, -ᵊn-ən(t)s\ *n* **1 :** an incidental right (as a right-of-way) attached to a principal property right and passing in possession with it **2 :** a subordinate part or adjunct <the ~ of welcome is fashion and ceremony—Shak.> **3** *pl* **:** accessory objects **:** APPARATUS

ap·pur·te·nant \ə-ˈpərt-nənt, -ᵊn-ənt\ *adj* [ME *apertenant,* fr. MF, fr. OF, prp. of *apartenir* to belong — more at APPERTAIN] **1 :** constituting a legal accompaniment **2 :** AUXILIARY, ACCESSORY — **appurtenant** *n*

Apr *abbr* April

aprax·ia \(ˈ)ā-ˈprak-sē-ə\ *n* [NL, fr. Gk, inaction, fr. *a-* + *praxis* action, fr. *prassein* to do — more at PRACTICAL] **:** loss or impairment of the ability to execute complex coordinated movements — **aprac·tic** \-ˈprak-tik\ *or* **aprax·ic** \-ˈprak-sik\ *adj*

après–ski \ˌäp-ˌrā-ˈskē, ˌap-\ *n* [F *après* after + *ski* ski, skiing] **:** social activity (as at a ski lodge) after a day's skiing — **après–ski** *adj*

apri·cot \ˈap-rə-ˌkät, ˈā-prə-\ *n, often attrib* [alter. of earlier *abrecock,* deriv. of Ar *al-birqūq* the apricot] **1 a :** the oval orange-colored fruit of a temperate-zone tree (*Prunus armeniaca*) resembling the related peach and plum in flavor **b :** a tree that bears apricots **2 :** a variable color averaging a moderate orange

April \ˈā-prəl\ *n* [ME, fr. OF & L; OF *avrill,* fr. L *Aprilis*] **:** the 4th month of the Gregorian calendar

April fool *n* **:** the butt of a joke or trick played on April Fools' Day; *also* **:** such a joke or trick

April Fools' Day *n* **:** April 1 characteristically marked by the playing of practical jokes

a pri·o·ri \ˌä-prē-ˈō(ə)r-ē, ap-rē-; ˌā-(ˌ)prī-ˈō(ə)r-ˌī, ˌā-prē-ˈō(ə)r-ē; -ˈȯ(ə)r-\ *adj* [L, from the former] **1 a :** DEDUCTIVE **b :** relating to or derived by reasoning from self-evident propositions — compare A POSTERIORI **c :** presupposed by experience **2 :** being without examination or analysis **:** PRESUMPTIVE — **a priori** *adv* — **apri·or·i·ty** \-ˈȯr-ət-ē\ *n*

apron \ˈā-prən, -pərn\ *n, often attrib* [ME, alter. (resulting fr. incorrect division of *a napron*) of *napron,* fr. MF *naperon,* dim. of *nape* cloth, modif. of L *mappa* napkin — more at MAP] **1 :** a garment usu. of cloth, plastic, or leather usu. tied around the waist and used to protect clothing or adorn a costume **2 :** something that suggests or resembles an apron in shape, position, or use: as **a :** the lower member under the sill of the interior casing of a window **b :** an upward or downward vertical extension of a sink or lavatory **c :** a piece of waterproof cloth spread out (as before the seat of a vehicle) as a protection from rain or mud **d :** a covering (as of sheet metal) for protecting parts of machinery **e :** an endless belt for carrying material **f :** an extensive fan-shaped deposit of detritus **g :** the part of the stage in front of the proscenium arch **h :** the area along the waterfront edge of a pier or wharf **i :** a shield (as of concrete, planking, or brushwood) along the bank of a river, along a seawall, or below a dam **j :** the extensive paved part of an airport immediately adjacent to the terminal area or hangars

apron string *n* **:** the string of an apron — usu. used in pl. as a symbol of dominance or complete control <though 40 years old he was still tied to his mother's *apron strings*>

¹ap·ro·pos \ˌap-rə-ˈpō, ˈap-rə-ˌ\ *adv* [F *à propos,* lit., to the purpose] **1 :** at an opportune time **:** SEASONABLY **2 :** by the way

²apropos *adj* **:** being both relevant and opportune ***syn*** see RELEVANT

³apropos *prep* **:** apropos of

apropos of *prep* **:** with regard to **:** CONCERNING

apse \ˈaps\ *n* [ML & L; ML *apsis,* fr. L] **1 :** a projecting part of a building (as a church) that is usu. semicircular in plan and vaulted — see BASILICA illustration **2 :** APSIS 1

ap·si·dal \ˈap-səd-ᵊl\ *adj* **:** of or relating to an apse

ap·sis \ˈap-səs\ *n, pl* **ap·si·des** \-sə-ˌdēz\ [NL *apsid-, apsis,* fr. L, arch, orbit, fr. Gk *hapsid-, hapsis,* fr. *haptein* to fasten] **1 :** the point in an astronomical orbit at which the distance of the body from the center of attraction is either greatest or least **2 :** APSE 1

¹apt \ˈapt\ *adj* [ME, fr. L *aptus,* lit., fastened, fr. pp. of *apere* to fasten; akin to L *apisci* to reach, *apud* near, Skt *āpta* fit] **1 :** unusually fitted or qualified **:** READY <proved an ~ tool in the hands of the conspirators> **2 a :** having a tendency **:** LIKELY <plants ~ to suffer from drought> **b :** ordinarily disposed **:** INCLINED <~ to accept what is plausible as true> **3 :** suited to a purpose; *esp* **:** being to the point <an ~ quotation> **4 :** keenly intelligent and responsive ***syn*** **1** see FIT ***ant*** inapt, inept **2** see QUICK — **apt·ly** \ˈap-(t)lē\ *adv* — **apt·ness** \ˈap(t)-nəs\ *n*

²apt *abbr* **1** apartment **2** aptitude

ap·ter·ous \ˈap-tə-rəs\ *adj* [Gk *apteros,* fr. *a-* + *pteron* wing — more at FEATHER] **:** lacking wings <~ insects>

ap·ter·yx \'ap-tə-riks\ *n* [NL, fr. *a-* + Gk *pteryx* wing; akin to Gk *pteron*] : KIWI
ap·ti·tude \'ap-tə-,t(y)üd\ *n* **1** : capacity for learning : APTNESS **2 a** : INCLINATION, TENDENCY **b** : a natural ability : TALENT **3** : general suitability *syn* see GIFT — **ap·ti·tu·di·nal** \,ap-tə-'t(y)üd-nəl, -ᵊn-əl\ *adj* — **ap·ti·tu·di·nal·ly** \-ē\ *adv*
ap·y·rase \'ap-ə-,rās, -,rāz\ *n* [*a*denosine + *py*rophosphate + *-ase*] : any of several enzymes that hydrolyze ATP with the liberation of phosphate
aq *abbr* aqua; aqueous
aqua \'ak-wə, 'äk-\ *n, pl* **aquae** \'ak-(,)wē, 'äk-,wī\ *or* **aquas** [L— more at ISLAND] **1** : WATER; *esp* : an aqueous solution (as of a volatile substance) **2** : a light greenish blue color
aqua·cade \'ak-wə-,kād, 'äk-\ *n* [*Aquacade*, a water entertainment spectacle orig. at Cleveland, Ohio (1937)] : a water spectacle that consists usu. of exhibitions of swimming and diving with musical accompaniment
Aqua·dag \-,dag\ *trademark* — used for a colloidal suspension of fine particles of graphite in water for use as a lubricant
aqua·for·tis \,ak-wə-'fört-əs, ,äk-\ *n* [NL *aqua fortis*, lit., strong water] : NITRIC ACID
aqua·lung·er \'ak-wə-,ləŋ-ər, 'äk-\ *n* [fr. *Aqua-lung*, a trademark] : SCUBA DIVER
aqua·ma·rine \,ak-wə-mə-'rēn, ,äk-\ *n* [NL *aqua marina*, fr. L, sea water] **1** : a transparent beryl that is blue, blue-green, or green in color **2** : a pale blue to light greenish blue
aqua·naut \'ak-wə-,nȯt, 'äk-\ *n* [L *aqua* + E *-naut* (as in *aeronaut*)] : a scuba diver who lives and operates both inside and outside an underwater shelter for an extended period
aqua·plane \'ak-wə-,plān, 'äk-\ *n* : a board towed behind a speeding motorboat and ridden by a person standing on it — **aquaplane** *vi* — **aqua·plan·er** *n*
aqua pu·ra \,ak-wə-'pyu̇r-ə, ,äk-\ *n* [L] : pure water
aqua re·gia \-'rē-j(ē-)ə\ *n* [NL, lit., royal water] : a mixture of nitric and hydrochloric acids that dissolves gold or platinum
aqua·relle \,ak-wə-'rel, ,äk-\ *n* [F, fr. obs. It *acquarella* (now *acquerello*), fr. *acqua* water, fr. L *aqua*] : a drawing usu. in transparent watercolor — **aqua·rell·ist** \-'rel-əst\ *n*
aquar·ist \ə-'kwar-əst, -'kwer-\ *n* : one who keeps an aquarium
aquar·i·um \ə-'kwar-ē-əm, -'kwer-\ *n, pl* **-i·ums** *or* **-ia** \-ē-ə\ [L, watering place for cattle, fr. neut. of *aquarius* of water, fr. *aqua*] **1** : a container (as a glass tank) or an artificial pond in which living aquatic animals or plants are kept **2** : an establishment where aquatic collections of living organisms are kept and exhibited
Aquar·i·us \-ē-əs\ *n* [L (gen. *Aquarii*), lit., water carrier] **1** : a constellation south of Pegasus pictured as a man pouring water **2 a** : the 11th sign of the zodiac in astrology — see ZODIAC table **b** : one born under this sign
¹aquat·ic \ə-'kwät-ik, -'kwat-\ *adj* **1** : growing or living in or frequenting water **2** : taking place in or on water <~ sports> — **aquat·i·cal·ly** \-i-k(ə-)lē\ *adv*
²aquatic *n* **1** : an aquatic animal or plant **2** *pl but sing or pl in constr* : water sports
aqua·tint \'ak-wə-,tint, 'äk-\ *n* [It *acqua tinta* dyed water] : a method of etching a printing plate so that tones similar to watercolor washes can be reproduced; *also* : a print made from a plate so etched — **aquatint** *vt* — **aqua·tint·er** *n* — **aqua·tint·ist** \-əst\ *n*
aqua·vit \'äk-wə-,vēt\ *n* [Sw, Dan & Norw *akvavit*, fr. ML *aqua vitae*] : a clear Scandinavian liquor flavored with caraway seeds
aqua vi·tae \,ak-wə-'vīt-ē, ,äk-\ *n* [ME, fr. ML, lit., water of life] **1** : ALCOHOL **2** : a strong alcoholic liquor
aq·ue·duct \'ak-wə-,dəkt\ *n* [L *aquaeductus*, fr. *aquae* (gen. of *aqua*) + *ductus* act of leading — more at DUCT] **1 a** : a conduit for water; *esp* : one for carrying a large quantity of flowing water **b** : a structure for conveying a canal over a river or hollow **2** : a canal or passage in a part or organ
aque·ous \'ā-kwē-əs, 'ak-wē-\ *adj* [ML *aqueus*, fr. L *aqua*] **1 a** : of, relating to, or resembling water **b** : made from, with, or by water **2** : of or relating to the aqueous humor — **aque·ous·ly** *adv*
aqueous humor *n* : a limpid fluid occupying the space between the crystalline lens and the cornea of the eye
aqui·cul·ture *or* **aqua·cul·ture** \'ak-wə-,kəl-chər, 'äk-\ *n* [L *aqua* + E *-culture* (as in *agriculture*)] **1** : the cultivation of the natural produce of water **2** : HYDROPONICS — **aqui·cul·tur·al** \,ak-wə-'kəlch-(ə-)rəl, ,äk-\ *adj*
aqui·fer \'ak-wə-fər, 'äk-\ *n* [NL, fr. L *aqua* + *-fer*] : a water-bearing stratum of permeable rock, sand, or gravel — **aquif·er·ous** \a-'kwif-ə-rəs, ä-\ *adj*
Aq·ui·la \'ak-wə-lə\ *n* [L (gen. *Aquilae*), lit., eagle] : a northern constellation in the Milky Way southerly from Lyra and Cygnus
aq·ui·le·gia \,ak-wə-'lē-j(ē-)ə\ *n* [NL] : COLUMBINE
aq·ui·line \'ak-wə-,līn, -lən\ *adj* [L *aquilinus*, fr. *aquila* eagle] **1** : of, relating to, or resembling an eagle **2** : curving like an eagle's beak <an ~ nose> — **aq·ui·lin·i·ty** \,ak-wə-'lin-ət-ē\ *n*
aquiv·er \ə-'kwiv-ər\ *adj* : marked by trembling or quivering <all ~ with excitement>
¹ar \'är\ *n* [ME] : the letter *r*
²ar *abbr* arrival; arrive
Ar *symbol* argon
AR *abbr* **1** acknowledgment of receipt **2** all rail **3** all risks **4** annual return **5** Arkansas **6** army regulation **7** autonomous republic
-ar \ər *also* ,är\ *adj suffix* [ME, fr. L *-aris*, alter. of *-alis* -al] : of or relating to <molecul*ar*> : being <spectacul*ar*> : resembling <oracul*ar*>
¹Ar·ab \'ar-əb, *in sense 2 often* 'ā-,rab\ *n* [ME, fr. L *Arabus, Arabs*, fr. Gk *Arab-, Araps*, fr. Ar *'Arab*] **1 a** : a member of the Semitic people of the Arabian peninsula **b** : a member of an Arabic-speaking people **2** *not cap* : STREET ARAB **3** : a horse of the stock used by the natives of Arabia and adjacent regions; *specif* : a horse of a breed noted for its graceful build, speed, intelligence, and spirit — **Arab** *adj*
²Arab *abbr* Arabian; Arabic

¹ar·a·besque \,ar-ə-'besk\ *adj* [F, fr. It *arabesco* Arabian in fashion, fr. *Arabo* Arab, fr. L *Arabus*] : of, relating to, or being in the style of arabesque
²arabesque *n* **1** : an ornament or style that employs flower, foliage, or fruit and sometimes animal and figural outlines to produce an intricate pattern of interlaced lines **2** : a posture in ballet in which the body is bent forward from the hip on one leg with the corresponding arm extended forward and the other arm and leg backward **3** : a contrived intricate pattern of verbal expression <~*s* of alliteration —C. E. Montague>

arabesque 1

Ara·bi·an coffee \ə-,rā-bē-ən-\ *n* : COFFEE TREE 1a
Arabian horse *n* : ARAB 3
¹Ar·a·bic \'ar-ə-bik\ *adj* **1** : of, relating to, or characteristic of Arabia or the Arabs **2** : of, relating to, or constituting Arabic **3** : of or relating to Arabic numerals
²Arabic *n* : a Semitic language orig. of the Arabs of the Hejaz and Nejd that is now the prevailing speech of Arabia, Jordan, Lebanon, Syria, Iraq, Egypt, and parts of northern Africa
Arabic alphabet *n* : the alphabet of 28 letters derived from the Aramaic which is used for writing Arabic and also with adaptations for numerous other languages of Asia, Africa, and Europe of peoples professing the Muslim religion
arab·i·cize \ə-'rab-ə-,sīz\ *vt* **-cized; -ciz·ing** *often cap* **1** : to adapt (a language or elements of a language) to the phonetic or structural pattern of Arabic **2** : ARABIZE 1
Arabic numeral *n*, : one of the number symbols 0, 1, 2, 3, 4, 5, 6, 7, 8, 9 — see NUMBER table
arab·i·nose \ə-'rab-ə-,nōs, -,nōz\ *n* [ISV *arabin* (the solid principle in gum arabic, fr. *gum arabic* + *-in*) + *-ose*] : a crystalline aldose sugar $C_5H_{10}O_5$ of the pentose class
ara·bi·no·side \,ar-ə-'bin-ə-,sīd, ə-'rab-ə-nō-,sīd\ *n* : a glycoside that yields arabinose on hydrolysis
Ar·ab·ist \'ar-ə-bəst\ *n* : a specialist in the Arabic language or in Arabic culture
ar·ab·ize \'ar-ə-,bīz\ *vt* **-ized; -iz·ing** *often cap* **1 a** : to cause to acquire Arabic customs, manners, speech, or outlook **b** : to modify (a racial or national stock) by an admixture of Arab blood **2** : ARABICIZE 1
¹ar·a·ble \'ar-ə-bəl\ *adj* [MF or L; MF, fr. L *arabilis*, fr. *arare* to plow; akin to OE *erian* to plow, Gk *aroun*] : fit for or cultivated by plowing or tillage — **ar·a·bil·i·ty** \,ar-ə-'bil-ət-ē\ *n*
²arable *n* : land that is tilled or tillable
arach·nid \ə-'rak-nəd\ *n* [deriv. of Gk *arachnē* spider] : any of a class (Arachnida) of arthropods comprising mostly air-breathing invertebrates, including the spiders and scorpions, mites, and ticks, and having a segmented body divided into two regions of which the anterior bears four pairs of legs but no antennae — **arachnid** *adj*
¹arach·noid \ə-'rak-,nȯid\ *n* [NL *arachnoides*, fr. Gk *arachnoeidēs*, like a cobweb, fr. *arachnē* spider, spider's web] : a thin membrane of the brain and spinal cord that lies between the dura mater and the pia mater
²arachnoid *adj* **1** : of or relating to the arachnoid membrane **2** : covered with or composed of soft loose hairs or fibers
³arachnoid *adj* [deriv. of Gk *arachnē*] : resembling or related to the arachnids
ara·go·nite \ə-'rag-ə-,nīt, 'ar-ə-gə-\ *n* [G *aragonit*, fr. *Aragon*, Spain] : a mineral $CaCO_3$ consisting like calcite of calcium carbonate but differing from calcite in its orthorhombic crystallization, greater density, and less distinct cleavage — **ara·go·nit·ic** \ə-,rag-ə-'nit-ik, ,ar-ə-gə-\ *adj*
Ar·a·mae·an \,ar-ə-'mē-ən\ *n* [L *Aramaeus*, fr. Gk *Aramaios*, fr. Heb *'Arām* Aram, ancient name for Syria] **1** : a member of a Semitic people of the second millennium B.C. in Syria and Upper Mesopotamia **2** : ARAMAIC — **Aramaean** *adj*
Ar·a·ma·ic \,ar-ə-'mā-ik\ *n* : a Semitic language known since the ninth century B.C. as the speech of the Aramaeans and later used extensively in southwest Asia as a commercial and governmental language and adopted as their customary speech by various non-Aramaean peoples including the Jews after the Babylonian exile
Aramaic alphabet *n* **1** : an extinct North Semitic alphabet dating from the ninth century B.C. which was for several centuries the commercial alphabet of southwest Asia and the parent of other alphabets (as Syriac and Arabic) **2** : the square Hebrew alphabet as distinguished from the early Hebrew alphabet
ara·ne·id \ə-'rā-nē-əd, ,ar-ə-'\ *n* [deriv. of L *aranea* spider] : SPIDER 1 — **ar·a·ne·idal** \,ar-ə-'nē-əd-ᵊl\ *adj* — **ar·a·ne·idan** \-əd-ᵊn\ *adj or n*
Arap·a·ho *or* **Arap·a·hoe** \ə-'rap-ə-,hō\ *n, pl* **Arapaho** *or* **Arapahos** *or* **Arapahoe** *or* **Arapahoes** : a member of an Amerindian people of the plains region ranging from Saskatchewan and Manitoba to New Mexico and Texas
ar·a·pai·ma \,ar-ə-'pī-mə\ *n* [Pg & Sp, of Tupian origin; akin to Mura *uarapâinu* pirarucu] : PIRARUCU
ar·a·ro·ba \,ar-ə-'rō-bə\ *n* [Pg, of Tupian origin; akin to Tupi *araribá*, a Brazilian tree] : GOA POWDER
Arau·ca·ni·an \ə-,rau̇-'kän-ē-ən, ,ar-,ȯ-'kān-\ *also* **Arau·can** \ə-'rau̇-kən\ *n* [Sp *araucano*, fr. *Arauco*, province in Chile] **1** : a member of a group of Indian peoples of south central Chile and adjacent regions of Argentina **2** : the language of the Araucanian people that constitutes an independent language family — **Araucanian** *adj*

ar·au·car·ia \ˌar-ˌȯ-ˈkar-ē-ə\ *n* [NL, genus name, fr. *Arauco*] **:** any of a genus (*Araucaria*) of So. American or Australian trees of the pine family — **ar·au·car·i·an** \-ē-ən\ *adj*

Ar·a·wak \ˈar-ə-ˌwäk\ *n, pl* **Arawak** *or* **Arawaks 1 :** a member of an American Indian people of the Arawakan group now living chiefly along the coast of Guyana **2 :** the language of the Arawak people

Ar·a·wak·an \ˌar-ə-ˈwäk-ən\ *n, pl* **Arawakan** *or* **Arawakans 1 :** a member of a group of Indian peoples of South America and the West Indies **2 :** the language family of the Arawakan peoples

ar·ba·lest *or* **ar·ba·list** \ˈär-bə-ləst\ *n* [ME *arblast*, fr. OE, fr. OF *arbaleste*, fr. LL *arcuballista*, fr. L *arcus* bow + *ballista* — more at ARROW] **:** CROSSBOW; *esp* **:** a medieval military weapon with a steel bow used to throw balls, stones, and quarrels — **ar·ba·lest·er** \-ˌles-tər\ *n*

ar·bi·ter \ˈär-bət-ər\ *n* [ME *arbitre*, fr. MF, fr. L *arbitr-, arbiter*] **1 :** a person with power to decide a dispute **:** JUDGE **2 :** a person or agency having absolute power of judging and determining

arbiter el·e·gan·ti·a·rum \-ˌel-ə-ˌgan-shē-ˈar-əm, -ˈer-\ *n* [L, arbiter of refinements] **:** one who prescribes, rules on, or is a recognized authority on matters of social behavior and taste

ar·bi·tra·ble \ˈär-bə-trə-bəl, är-ˈbi-\ *adj* **:** subject to decision by arbitration

[1]**ar·bi·trage** \ˈär-bə-ˌträzh\ *n* [F, fr. MF, arbitration, fr. OF, fr. *arbitrer* to render judgment, fr. L *arbitrari*, fr. *arbitr-, arbiter*] **:** simultaneous purchase and sale of the same or equivalent security in order to profit from price discrepancies

[2]**arbitrage** *vi* **-traged; -trag·ing :** to engage in arbitrage

ar·bi·tra·geur \ˌär-bə-(ˌ)trä-ˈzhər\ *or* **ar·bi·trag·er** \ˈär-bə-ˌträzh-ər\ *n* [F *arbitrageur*, fr. *arbitrage* + *eur* -or] **:** one that practices arbitrage

ar·bi·tral \ˈär-bə-trəl\ *adj* **:** of or relating to arbiters or arbitration

ar·bit·ra·ment \är-ˈbi-trə-mənt\ *n* [ME, fr. MF *arbitrement*, fr. *arbitrer*] **1** *archaic* **:** the right or power of deciding **2 :** the settling of a dispute by an arbiter **:** ARBITRATION **3 :** the judgment given by an arbitrator

ar·bi·trary \ˈär-bə-ˌtrer-ē\ *adj* **1 :** depending on choice or discretion; *specif* **:** determinable by decision of a judge or tribunal **2 a :** arising from will or caprice **b :** selected at random and without reason **3 :** DESPOTIC, TYRANNICAL <~ rule> — **ar·bi·trari·ly** \ˌär-bə-ˈtrer-ə-lē\ *adv* — **ar·bi·trari·ness** \ˈär-bə-ˌtrer-ē-nəs\ *n*

ar·bi·trate \ˈär-bə-ˌtrāt\ *vb* **-trat·ed; -trat·ing** *vi* **:** to act as arbitrator <a committee appointed to ~ between the company and the union> ~ *vt* **1 :** to act as arbiter upon **2 :** to submit or refer for decision to an arbiter <agreed to ~ their differences> **3** *archaic* **:** DECIDE, DETERMINE — **ar·bi·tra·tive** \-ˌtrāt-iv\ *adj*

ar·bi·tra·tion \ˌär-bə-ˈtrā-shən\ *n* **:** the act of arbitrating; *esp* **:** the hearing and determination of a case in controversy by a person chosen by the parties or appointed under statutory authority — **ar·bi·tra·tion·al** \-shnəl, -shən-ᵊl\ *adj*

ar·bi·tra·tor \ˈär-bə-ˌtrāt-ər\ *n* **1 :** a person chosen to settle differences between two parties in controversy **2 :** ARBITER

[1]**ar·bor** \ˈär-bər\ *n* [ME *erber* plot of grass, arbor, fr. OF *herbier* plot of grass, fr. *herbe* herb, grass] **:** a bower of vines or branches or of latticework covered with climbing shrubs or vines

[2]**arbor** *n* [L, tree, shaft] **1 a :** a main shaft or beam **b :** a spindle or axle of a wheel **c :** a shaft on which a revolving cutting tool is mounted **d :** a spindle on a cutting machine that holds the work to be cut **2** *pl* **ar·bo·res** \ˈär-bə-ˌrēz\ **:** a tree as distinguished from a shrub

Arbor Day *n* [L *arbor* tree] **:** a day designated for planting trees

ar·bo·re·al \är-ˈbōr-ē-əl, -ˈbȯr-\ *adj* [L *arboreus* of a tree, fr. *arbor*] **1 :** of, relating to, or resembling a tree **2 :** inhabiting or frequenting trees <~ monkeys> — **ar·bo·re·al·ly** \-ə-lē\ *adv*

ar·bo·re·ous \-ē-əs\ *adj* **1 :** WOODED **2 :** ARBOREAL <an ~ palm> <an ~ bird>

ar·bo·res·cence \ˌär-bə-ˈres-ᵊn(t)s\ *n* **:** the condition of being arborescent

ar·bo·res·cent \-ᵊnt\ *adj* **:** resembling a tree in properties, growth, structure, or appearance — **ar·bo·res·cent·ly** *adv*

ar·bo·re·tum \ˌär-bə-ˈrēt-əm\ *n, pl* **-retums** *or* **-re·ta** \-ˈrēt-ə\ [NL, fr. L, place grown with trees, fr. *arbor*] **:** a place where trees, shrubs, and herbaceous plants are cultivated for scientific and educational purposes

ar·bo·ri·cul·ture \ˈär-bə-rə-ˌkəl-chər; är-ˈbōr-ə-, -ˈbȯr-\ *n* [[2]*arbor* + *-i-* + *culture*] **:** the cultivation of trees and shrubs esp. for ornament — **ar·bo·ri·cul·tur·ist** \ˌär-bə-rə-ˈkəlch-(ə-)rəst; är-ˌbōr-ə-, -ˌbȯr-\ *n*

ar·bor·ist \ˈär-bə-rəst\ *n* **:** a specialist in the care and maintenance of trees

ar·bo·ri·za·tion \ˌär-bə-rə-ˈzā-shən\ *n* **:** formation of or into an arborescent figure or arrangement; *also* **:** such a figure or arrangement

ar·bo·rize \ˈär-bə-ˌrīz\ *vi* **-rized; -riz·ing :** to branch freely and repeatedly

ar·bor·vi·tae \ˌär-bər-ˈvīt-ē\ *n* [NL *arbor vitae*, lit., tree of life] **:** any of various evergreen trees (esp. genus *Thuja*) of the pine family that usu. have closely overlapping or compressed scale leaves and are often grown for ornament and in hedges

ar·bour *chiefly Brit var of* ARBOR

ar·bo·vi·rus \ˌär-bə-ˈvī-rəs\ *n* [*ar*thropod-*bo*rne *virus*] **:** any of various viruses transmitted by arthropods and including the causative agents of encephalitis, yellow fever, and dengue

ar·bu·tus \är-ˈbyüt-əs\ *n* [NL, genus name, fr. L, strawberry tree] **1 :** any of a genus (*Arbutus*) of shrubs and trees of the heath family with white or pink flowers and scarlet berries **2 :** a trailing plant (*Epigaea repens*) of the heath family that occurs in eastern No. America and bears fragrant pinkish flowers in early spring

[1]**arc** \ˈärk\ *n* [ME *ark*, fr. MF *arc* bow, fr. L *arcus* bow, arch, arc — more at ARROW] **1 :** the apparent path described above and below the horizon by a celestial body (as the sun) **2 :** something arched or curved **3 :** a sustained luminous discharge of electricity across a gap in a circuit or between electrodes; *also* **:** ARC LAMP **4 :** a continuous portion (as of a circle or ellipse) of a curved line

[2]**arc** *vi* **1 :** to form an electric arc **2 :** to follow an arc-shaped course

[3]**arc** *adj* [*arc sine* arc or angle (corresponding to the) sine (of so many degrees)] **:** INVERSE 2 — used with the trigonometric functions and hyperbolic functions <~ sine>

ARC *abbr* American Red Cross

ar·cade \är-ˈkād\ *n* [F, fr. It *arcata*, fr. *arco* arch, fr. L *arcus*] **1 :** a long arched building or gallery **2 :** an arched covered passageway or avenue (as between shops) **3 :** a series of arches with their columns or piers

ar·cad·ed \-ˈkād-əd\ *adj* **:** formed in or furnished or decorated with arches or arcades

ar·ca·dia \är-ˈkād-ē-ə\ *n, often cap* [*Arcadia*, region of ancient Greece frequently chosen as background for pastoral poetry] **:** a region or scene of simple pleasure and quiet

Ar·ca·di·an \är-ˈkād-ē-ən\ *n* **1** *often not cap* **:** a person who lives a simple quiet life **2 :** a native or inhabitant of Arcadia **3 :** the dialect of ancient Greek used in Arcadia — **arcadian** *adj, often cap*

ar·cad·ing \är-ˈkād-iŋ\ *n* **:** a series of arches or arcades used in the construction or decoration esp. of a building

Ar·ca·dy \ˈär-kəd-ē\ *n* **:** ARCADIA

ar·cane \är-ˈkān\ *adj* [L *arcanus*] **:** known or knowable only to one having the key **:** SECRET <~ rites> ***syn*** see MYSTERIOUS

ar·ca·num \är-ˈkā-nəm\ *n, pl* **-na** \-nə\ [L, fr. neut. of *arcanus* secret, fr. *arca* chest — more at ARK] **1 :** mysterious knowledge known only to the initiate **2 :** ELIXIR 1

arc cosecant *n* **:** the inverse function to the cosecant <if y is the cosecant of θ, then θ is the *arc cosecant* of y> — symbol *arc csc* or csc^{-1}

arc cosine *n* **:** the inverse function to the cosine <if y is the cosine of θ, then θ is the *arc cosine* of y> — symbol *arc cos* or cos^{-1}

arc cotangent *n* **:** the inverse function to the cotangent <if y is the cotangent of θ, then θ is the *arc cotangent* of y> — symbol *arc cot* or cot^{-1}

[1]**arch** \ˈärch\ *n* [ME *arche*, fr. OF, fr. (assumed) VL *arca*, fr. L *arcus* — more at ARROW] **1 :** a typically curved structural member spanning an opening and serving as a support (as for the wall or other weight above the opening) **2 a :** something resembling an arch in form or function; *esp* **:** either of two vaulted portions of the bony structure of the foot that impart elasticity to it **b :** a curvature having the form of an arch **3 :** ARCHWAY

arches 1: *1* round: *imp* impost, *sp* springer, *v* voussoir, *k* keystone, *ext* extrados, *int* intrados, *2* horseshoe, *3* lancet, *4* ogee, *5* trefoil, *6* basket-handle, *7* Tudor

[2]**arch** *vt* **1 :** to cover or provide with an arch **2 :** to form or bend into an arch ~ *vi* **1 :** to form an arch **2 :** to take an arch-shaped course

[3]**arch** *adj* [*arch-*] **1 :** PRINCIPAL, CHIEF <an *arch*-villain> **2** [*arch-* (as in *archrogue*)] **a :** cleverly sly and alert **b :** playfully saucy ***syn*** see SAUCY — **arch·ly** *adv* — **arch·ness** *n*

[4]**arch** *abbr* **1** archaic **2** archery **3** architect; architectural; architecture

[1]**arch-** *prefix* [ME *arche-, arch-*, fr. OE & OF; OE *arce-*, fr. LL *arch-* & L *archi-*; OF *arch-*, fr. LL *arch-* & L *archi-*, fr. Gk *arch-, archi-*, fr. *archein* to begin, rule; akin to Gk *archē* beginning, rule, *archos* ruler] **1 :** chief **:** principal <*arch*enemy> **2 :** extreme **:** most fully embodying the qualities of his or its kind <*arch*rogue>

[2]**arch-** — see ARCHI-

[1]**-arch** \ˌärk, *in a few words also* ərk\ *n comb form* [ME *-arche*, fr. OF & LL & L; OF *-arche*, fr. LL *-archa*, fr. L *-arches, -archus*, fr. Gk *-archēs, -archos*, fr. *archein*] **:** ruler **:** leader <matri*arch*>

[2]**-arch** \ˌärk\ *adj comb form* [prob. fr. G, fr. Gk *archē* beginning] **:** having (such) a point or (so many) points of origin <end*arch*>

archae- *or* **archaeo-** *also* **archeo-** *comb form* [Gk *archaio-*, fr. *archaios* ancient, fr. *archē* beginning] **:** ancient **:** primitive <*Archaeo*pteryx> <*Archeo*zoic>

ar·chae·ol·o·gist *or* **ar·che·ol·o·gist** \ˌär-kē-ˈäl-ə-jəst\ *n* **:** a specialist in archaeology

ar·chae·ol·o·gy *or* **ar·che·ol·o·gy** \-jē\ *n* [F *archéologie*, fr. LL *archaeologia* antiquarian lore, fr. Gk *archaiologia*, fr. *archaio-* + *-logia* -logy] **1 :** the scientific study of material remains (as fossil relics, artifacts, and monuments) of past human life and activities **2 :** remains of the culture of a people **:** ANTIQUITIES — **ar·chae·o·log·i·cal** \ˌär-kē-ə-ˈläj-i-kəl\ *adj* — **ar·chae·o·log·i·cal·ly** \-k(ə-)lē\ *adv*

ar·chae·op·ter·yx \ˌär-kē-ˈäp-tə-riks\ *n* [NL, genus name, fr. *archae-* + Gk *pteryx* wing; akin to Gk *pteron* wing — more at FEATHER] **:** a primitive bird (genus *Archaeopteryx*) of the Upper Jurassic period of Europe with reptilian characteristics

ar·chae·or·nis \ˌär-kē-ˈȯr-nəs\ *n* [NL, genus name, fr. *archae-* + Gk *ornis* bird — more at ERNE] **:** any of a genus (*Archaeornis*) of Upper Jurassic toothed birds

ar·cha·ic \är-ˈkā-ik\ *adj* [F or Gk; F *archaïque*, fr. Gk *archaïkos*, fr. *archaios*] **1 :** of, relating to, or characteristic of an earlier or more primitive time **:** ANTIQUATED <~ legal traditions> **2 :** having the characteristics of the language of the past and surviving chiefly in specialized uses **3 :** surviving from an earlier period; *specif* **:** typical of a previously dominant evolutionary stage ***syn*** see OLD ***ant*** up-to-date — **ar·cha·i·cal·ly** \-i-k(ə-)lē\ *adv*

archaic smile *n* : an expression that resembles a smile and is characteristic of early Greek sculpture

ar·cha·ism \'är-kē-ˌiz-əm, -(ˌ)kā-ˌiz-\ *n* [NL *archaïsmus,* fr. Gk *archaïsmos,* fr. *archaios*] **1** : the use of archaic diction or style **2** : an instance of archaic usage **3** : something that is outmoded or old-fashioned <judicial ~> — **ar·cha·ist** \-əst\ *n* — **ar·cha·is·tic** \ˌär-kē-'is-tik, -(ˌ)kā-\ *adj* — **ar·cha·ize** \'är-kē-ˌīz, -(ˌ)kā-\ *vb*

arch·an·gel \'är-ˌkān-jəl\ *n* [ME, fr. OF or LL; OF *archangele,* fr. LL *archangelus,* fr. Gk *archangelos,* fr. *arch-* + *angelos* angel] **1** : a chief angel **2** *pl* : an order of angels — see CELESTIAL HIERARCHY — **arch·an·gel·ic** \ˌär-(ˌ)kan-'jel-ik\ *adj*

arch·bish·op \(')ärch-'bish-əp\ *n* [ME, fr. OE *arcebiscop,* fr. LL *archiepiscopus,* fr. LGk *archiepiskopos,* fr. *archi-* + *episkopos* bishop — more at BISHOP] : a bishop at the head of an ecclesiastical province or one of equivalent honorary rank — **arch·bish·op·ric** \-ə-(ˌ)prik\ *n*

arch·dea·con \(')ärch-'dē-kən\ *n* [ME *archedeken,* fr. OE *arcediacon,* fr. LL *archidiaconus,* fr. LGk *archidiakonos,* fr. Gk *archi-* + *diakonos* deacon] : a clergyman having the duty of assisting a diocesan bishop in ceremonial functions or administrative work — **arch·dea·con·ate** \-kə-nət\ *n*

arch·dea·con·ry \-kən-rē\ *n, pl* **-ries** : the district or residence of an archdeacon

arch·di·o·cese \(')ärch-'dī-ə-səs, -ˌsēz, -ˌsēs\ *n* : the diocese of an archbishop — **arch·di·oc·e·san** \ˌärch-dī-'äs-ə-sən\ *adj*

arch·du·cal \(')ärch-'d(y)ü-kəl\ *adj* [F *archiducal,* fr. *archiduc*] : of or relating to an archduke or archduchy

arch·duch·ess \-'dəch-əs\ *n* [F *archiduchesse,* fem. of *archiduc* archduke, fr. MF *archeduc*] **1** : the wife or widow of an archduke **2** : a woman having in her own right a rank equal to that of an archduke

arch·duchy \-'dəch-ē\ *n* [F *archiduché,* fr. MF *archeduché,* fr. *arche-* arch- + *duché* duchy] : the territory of an archduke or archduchess

arch·duke \-'d(y)ük\ *n* [MF *archeduc,* fr. *arche-* arch- + *duc* duke] : a sovereign prince; *specif* : a prince of the imperial family of Austria — **arch·duke·dom** \-dəm\ *n*

Ar·che·an *or* **Ar·chae·an** \är-'kē-ən\ *adj* [Gk *archaios*] : of, relating to, or being the earlier part of the Precambrian era or the oldest known group of rocks; *also* : PRECAMBRIAN — **Archean** *n*

arched \'ärcht\ *adj* : made with, formed in, or covered with an arch <an ~ beam> <an ~ door>

ar·che·go·ni·al \ˌär-ki-'gō-nē-əl\ *adj* : of or relating to an archegonium; *also* : ARCHEGONIATE

¹ar·che·go·ni·ate \-nē-ət\ *adj* : bearing archegonia

²archegoniate *n* : a plant (as a moss, fern, horsetail, or club moss) that bears archegonia

ar·che·go·ni·um \-nē-əm\ *n, pl* **-nia** \-nē-ə\ [NL, fr. Gk *archegonos* originator, fr. *archein* to begin + *gonos* procreation; akin to Gk *gignesthai* to be born — more at ARCH-, KIN] : the flask-shaped female sex organ of mosses, ferns, and some gymnosperms

arch·en·e·my \(')är-'chen-ə-mē\ *n, pl* **-mies** : a principal enemy

arch·en·ter·on \är-'kent-ə-ˌrän, -rən\ *n* [NL] : the cavity of the gastrula of an embryo

archeol *abbr* archeology

Ar·cheo·zo·ic *also* **Ar·chaeo·zo·ic** \ˌär-kē-ə-'zō-ik\ *adj* : of, relating to, or being the earliest era of geological history; *also* : relating to the system of rocks formed in this era — see GEOLOGIC TIME table — **Archeozoic** *n*

ar·cher \'är-chər\ *n* [ME, fr. OF, fr. LL *arcarius,* alter. of *arcuarius,* fr. *arcuarius* of a bow, fr. L *arcus* bow — more at ARROW] **1** : one who uses a bow and arrow — called also *bowman* **2** *cap* : SAGITTARIUS

ar·chery \'ärch-(ə-)rē\ *n* **1** : the art, practice, or skill of shooting with bow and arrow **2** : an archer's weapons **3** : a body of archers

ar·che·spore \'är-ki-ˌspō(ə)r, -ˌspȯ(ə)r\ *or* **ar·che·spo·ri·um** \ˌär-ki-'spōr-ē-əm, -'spȯr-\ *n, pl* **-spores** *or* **-spo·ria** \-ē-ə\ [NL *archesporium,* fr. *arche-* (as in *archegonium*) + *-sporium* (fr. *spora* spore)] : the cell or group of cells from which spore mother cells develop — **ar·che·spo·ri·al** \ˌär-ki-'spōr-ē-əl, -'spȯr-\ *adj*

ar·che·type \'är-ki-ˌtīp\ *n* [L *archetypum,* fr. Gk *archetypon,* fr. neut. of *archetypos* archetypal, fr. *archein* + *typos* type] **1** : the original pattern or model of which all things of the same type are representations or copies : PROTOTYPE **2** : IDEA 1a **3** : an inherited idea or mode of thought in the psychology of C. G. Jung that is derived from the experience of the race and is present in the unconscious of the individual — **ar·che·typ·al** \ˌär-ki-'tī-pəl\ *or* **ar·che·typ·i·cal** \-'tip-i-kəl\ *adj* — **ar·che·typ·al·ly** \-pə-lē\ *or* **ar·che·typ·i·cal·ly** \-i-k(ə-)lē\ *adv*

arch·fiend \(')ärch-'fēnd\ *n* : a chief fiend; *esp* : SATAN

archi- *or* **arch-** *prefix* [F or L; F, fr. L, fr. Gk — more at ARCH-] **1** : chief : principal <*archi*blast> **2** : primitive : original : primary <*arch*enteron> <*archi*carp>

ar·chi·carp \'är-ki-ˌkärp\ *n* : the female sex organ in ascomycetous fungi consisting usu. of a filamentous trichogyne and a basal fertile ascogonium

ar·chi·di·ac·o·nal \ˌär-ki-dī-'ak-ən-ᵊl\ *adj* [LL *archidiaconus* archdeacon] : of or relating to an archdeacon

ar·chi·epis·co·pal \ˌär-kē-ə-'pis-kə-pəl\ *adj* [ML *archiepiscopalis,* fr. LL *archiepiscopus* archbishop — more at ARCHBISHOP] : of or relating to an archbishop — **ar·chi·epis·co·pal·ly** \-pə-lē\ *adv* — **ar·chi·epis·co·pate** \-pət, -ˌpāt\ *n*

ar·chil \'är-chəl\ *n* [ME *orchell*] **1** : a violet dye obtained from lichens (genera *Roccella* and *Lecanora*) **2** : a plant that yields archil

ar·chi·man·drite \ˌär-kə-'man-ˌdrīt\ *n* [LL *archimandrites,* fr. LGk *archimandritēs,* fr. Gk *archi-* + LGk *mandra* monastery, fr. Gk, fold, pen] : a dignitary in an Eastern church ranking below a bishop; *specif* : the superior of a large monastery or group of monasteries

Ar·chi·me·des' screw \ˌär-kə-ˌmēd-ēz-\ *n* : a device made of a tube bent spirally around an axis or of a broad-threaded screw encased by a cylinder and used to raise water

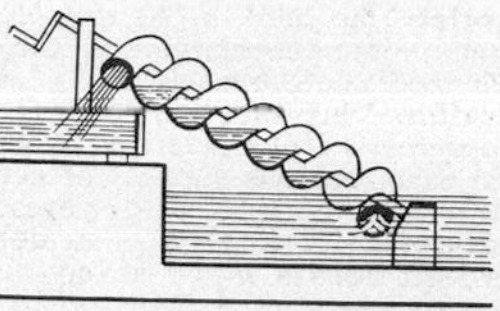

Archimedes' screw

ar·chi·pe·lag·ic \ˌär-kə-pə-'laj-ik, ˌär-chə-\ *adj* : of, relating to, or located in an archipelago

ar·chi·pel·a·go \ˌär-kə-'pel-ə-ˌgō, ˌär-chə-\ *n, pl* **-goes** *or* **-gos** [*Archipelago* Aegean sea, fr. It *Arcipelago,* lit., chief sea, fr. *arci-* (fr. L *archi-*) + Gk *pelagos* sea — more at FLAKE] **1** : an expanse of water with many scattered islands **2** : a group of islands

ar·chi·tect \'är-kə-ˌtekt\ *n* [MF *architecte,* fr. L *architectus,* fr. Gk *architektōn* master builder, fr. *archi-* + *tektōn* builder, carpenter — more at TECHNICAL] **1** : one who designs buildings and superintends their construction **2** : one who plans and achieves a difficult objective <the great ~ of the military victory —*Time*>

ar·chi·tec·ton·ic \ˌär-kə-ˌtek-'tän-ik\ *adj* [L *architectonicus,* fr. Gk *architektonikos,* fr. *architektōn*] **1** : of, relating to, or according with the principles of architecture : ARCHITECTURAL **2** : resembling architecture in structure or organization — **ar·chi·tec·ton·i·cal·ly** \-i-k(ə-)lē\ *adv*

ar·chi·tec·ton·ics \-'tän-iks\ *n pl but sing or pl in constr, also* **ar·chi·tec·ton·ic** \-ik\ **1** : the science of architecture **2 a** : the structural design of an entity **b** : the system of structure

ar·chi·tec·tur·al \ˌär-kə-'tek-chə-rəl, -'tek-shrəl\ *adj* : of, relating to, or conforming to the rules of architecture — **ar·chi·tec·tur·al·ly** \-ē\ *adv*

ar·chi·tec·ture \'är-kə-ˌtek-chər\ *n* **1** : the art or science of building; *specif* : the art or practice of designing and building structures and esp. habitable ones **2** : formation or construction as or as if as the result of conscious act **3** : architectural product or work **4** : a method or style of building

ar·chi·trave \'är-kə-ˌtrāv\ *n* [MF, fr. OIt, fr. *archi-* + *trave* beam, fr. L *trabs* — more at THORP] **1** : the lowest division of an entablature resting in classical architecture immediately on the capital of the column — see ENTABLATURE illustration **2** : the molding around a rectangular opening (as a door)

ar·chi·val \är-'kī-vəl\ *adj* : relating to, contained in, or constituting archives

¹ar·chive \'är-ˌkīv\ *n* [F & L; F, fr. L *archivum,* fr. Gk *archeion* government house (in pl., official documents), fr. *archē* rule, government — more at ARCH-] : a place in which public records or historical documents are preserved; *also* : the material preserved — often used in pl.

²archive *vt* **ar·chived; ar·chiv·ing** : to file or collect (as records or documents) in an archive or other repository

ar·chi·vist \'är-kə-vəst, -ˌkī-\ *n* : a person in charge of archives

ar·chi·volt \'är-kə-ˌvōlt\ *n* [It *archivolto,* fr. ML *archivoltum*] : an ornamental molding around an arch corresponding to an architrave

ar·chon \'är-ˌkän, -kən\ *n* [L, fr. Gk *archōn,* fr. prp. of *archein*] **1** : a chief magistrate in ancient Athens **2** : a presiding officer

arch·priest \(')ärch-'prēst\ *n* : a priest who occupies a preeminent position

arch·way \'ärch-ˌwā\ *n* : a way or passage under an arch; *also* : an arch over a passage

-ar·chy \ˌär-kē, *in a few words also* ər-kē\ *n comb form* [ME *-archie,* fr. MF, fr. L *-archia,* fr. Gk, fr. *archein* to rule — more at ARCH-] : rule : government <squire*archy*>

arc lamp *n* : an electric lamp that produces light by an arc made when a current passes between two incandescent electrodes surrounded by gas — called also *arc light*

ar·co \'är-(ˌ)kō\ *adv or adj* [It, fr. *arco* bow, fr. L *arcus*] : with the bow — usu. used as a direction in music for players of stringed instruments; compare PIZZICATO

arc secant *n* : the inverse function to the secant <if y is the secant of θ, then θ is the *arc secant* of y> — symbol *arc sec* or sec^{-1}

arc sine *n* : the inverse function to the sine <if y is the sine of θ, then θ is the *arc sine* of y> — symbol *arc sin* or sin^{-1}

arc tangent *n* : the inverse function to the tangent <if y is the tangent of θ, then θ is the *arc tangent* of y> — symbol *arc tan* or tan^{-1}

¹arc·tic \'ärk-tik, 'ärt-ik\ *adj* [ME *artik,* fr. L *arcticus,* fr. Gk *arktikos,* fr. *arktos* bear, Ursa Major, north; akin to L *ursus* bear] **1** *often cap* : of or relating to the region around the north pole to approximately 65° N **2 a** : bitter cold : FRIGID **b** : cold in temper or mood <an ~ smile> — **arc·ti·cal·ly** \-(t)i-k(ə-)lē\ *adv*

²arc·tic \'ärt-ik, 'ärk-tik\ *n* : a rubber overshoe reaching to the ankle or above

arctic circle *n, often cap A&C* : a small circle of the earth that is parallel to its equator and that is approximately 23° 27′ from the north pole and circumscribes the frigid zone

Arc·tu·rus \ärk-'t(y)u̇r-əs\ *n* [L, fr. Gk *Arktouros,* lit., bear watcher] : a giant fixed star of the first magnitude in Boötes

ar·cu·ate \'är-kyə-wət, -ˌwāt\ *adj* [L *arcuatus,* pp. of *arcuare* to bend like a bow, fr. *arcus* bow] : curved like a bow <an ~ cloud> <an ~ vein of a leaf> — **ar·cu·ate·ly** *adv*

-ard \ərd\ *also* **-art** \ərt\ *n suffix* [ME, fr. OF, of Gmc origin; akin to OHG *-hart* (in personal names such as *Gērhart* Gerard), OE *heard* hard] : one that is characterized by performing some action, possessing some quality, or being associated with some thing esp. conspicuously or excessively <bragg*art*> <dull*ard*> <poll*ard*>

ar·deb \ˈär-ˌdeb\ *n* [Ar *ardabb, irdabb*] **:** any of numerous Egyptian units of capacity; *esp* **:** the customs unit equal to 5.44 imperial or 5.619 U.S. bushels

ar·dent \ˈärd-ᵊnt\ *adj* [ME, fr. MF, fr. L *ardent-, ardens* prp. of *ardēre*] **1 :** characterized by warmth of feeling typically expressed in eager zealous support or activity **2 :** FIERY, HOT <an ~ sun> **3 :** SHINING, GLOWING <~ eyes> ***syn*** see IMPASSIONED ***ant*** cool — **ar·den·cy** \-ᵊn-sē\ *n* — **ar·dent·ly** *adv*

ardent spirits *n pl* **:** strong distilled liquors

ar·dor \ˈärd-ər\ *n* [ME *ardour*, fr. MF & L; MF, fr. L *ardor*, fr. *ardēre* to burn; akin to OHG *essa* forge, L *aridus* dry] **1 a :** an often restless or transitory warmth of feeling <the sudden ~ *s* of youth> **b :** extreme vigor or energy **:** INTENSITY **c :** ZEAL, LOYALTY **2 :** strong or burning heat ***syn*** see PASSION

ar·dour *chiefly Brit var of* ARDOR

ar·du·ous \ˈärj-(ə-)wəs\ *adj* [L *arduus* high, steep, difficult; akin to ON *örthigr* high, steep, Gk *orthos* straight] **1 a :** hard to accomplish or achieve **:** DIFFICULT <years of ~ training> **b :** marked by great labor or effort **:** STRENUOUS <a life of ~ toil —A. C. Cole> **2 :** hard to climb **:** STEEP ***syn*** see HARD ***ant*** light, facile — **ar·du·ous·ly** *adv* — **ar·du·ous·ness** *n*

¹are [ME, fr. OE *earun;* akin to ON *eru, erum* are, OE *is* is] *pres 2d sing or pres pl of* BE

²are \ˈa(ə)r, ˈe(ə)r, ˈär\ *n* [F, fr. L *area*] — see METRIC SYSTEM table

ar·ea \ˈar-ē-ə, ˈer-\ *n* [L, piece of level ground, threshing floor, fr. *arēre* to be dry; akin to L *ardor*] **1 :** a level piece of ground **2 :** the surface included within a set of lines; *specif* **:** the number of unit squares equal in measure to the surface — see METRIC SYSTEM table, WEIGHT table **3 :** AREAWAY <went down the steps into the ~ of a house —James Joyce> **4 :** a particular extent of space or surface or one serving a special function **5 :** the scope of a concept, operation, or activity **:** FIELD <the whole ~ of foreign policy> **6 :** a part of the cerebral cortex having a particular function — **ar·e·al** \-ē-əl\ *adj* — **ar·e·al·ly** \-ə-lē\ *adv*

area code *n* **:** a 3-digit number that identifies each telephone service area in a country (as the U.S. or Canada)

area·way \ˈar-ē-ə-ˌwā, ˈer-\ *n* **:** a sunken space affording access, air, and light to a basement

are·ca \ə-ˈrē-kə, ˈar-i-kə\ *n* [NL, genus name, fr. Pg, fr. Malayalam *atekka*] **:** any of several tropical Asian palms (*Areca* or related genera); *esp* **:** BETEL PALM

arec·o·line \ə-ˈrek-ə-ˌlēn\ *n* [ISV *areca* + *-ol* + *-ine*] **:** a toxic alkaloid $C_8H_{13}NO_2$ that has parasympathomimetic effects, is used as a veterinary anthelmintic, and occurs naturally in betel nuts

are·na \ə-ˈrē-nə\ *n* [L *harena, arena* sand, sandy place] **1 :** an area in a Roman amphitheater for gladiatorial combats **2 a :** an enclosed area used for public entertainment **b :** a building containing an arena **3 :** a sphere of interest or activity **:** SCENE <the political ~>

ar·e·na·ceous \ˌar-ə-ˈnā-shəs\ *adj* [L *arenaceus*, fr. *arena*] **1 :** resembling, made of, or containing sand or sandy particles **2 :** growing in sandy places

arena theater *n* **:** a theater in which the stage is located in the center of the auditorium — called also *theater-in-the-round*

ar·e·nic·o·lous \ˌar-ə-ˈnik-ə-ləs\ *adj* [L *arena* + E *-i-* + *-colous*] **:** living, burrowing, or growing in sand

aren't \(ˈ)ärnt, ˈär-ənt\ **1 :** are not **2 :** am not — used in questions

ar·eo·cen·tric \ˌar-ē-ō-ˈsen-trik\ *adj* [Gk *Areios* of Ares, fr. *Arēs*] **:** having or relating to the planet Mars as a center

are·o·la \ə-ˈrē-ə-lə\ *n, pl* **-lae** \-ˌlē\ *or* **-las** [NL, fr. L, small open space, dim. of *area*] **:** a small area between things or about something; *esp* **:** a colored ring (as about the nipple, a vesicle, or a pustule) — **are·o·lar** \-lər\ *adj* — **are·o·late** \-lət\ *adj* — **are·o·la·tion** \ə-ˌrē-ə-ˈlā-shən, ˌar-ē-ə-\ *n*

ar·e·ole \ˈar-ē-ˌōl\ *n* **:** a small pit or cavity

Ar·e·op·a·gite \ˌar-ē-ˈäp-ə-ˌjīt, -ˌgīt\ *n* **:** a member of the Areopagus — **Ar·e·op·a·git·ic** \-ˌäp-ə-ˈjit-ik\ *adj*

Ar·e·op·a·gus \-ˈäp-ə-gəs\ *n* [L, fr. Gk *Areios pagos*, fr. *Areios pagos* (lit., hill of Ares), a hill in Athens where the tribunal met] **:** the supreme tribunal of Athens

Ar·es \ˈa(ə)r-(ˌ)ēz, ˈe(ə)r-\ *n* [Gk *Arēs*] **:** the Greek god of war — compare MARS

arête \ə-ˈrāt\ *n* [F, lit., fish bone, fr. LL *arista*, fr. L, beard of grain] **:** a sharp-crested ridge in rugged mountains

ar·e·thu·sa \ˌar-ə-ˈth(y)ü-zə\ *n* [L, fr. Gk *Arethousa*] **1** *cap* **:** a wood nymph who fleeing the advances of the river god Alpheus was changed into a fountain **2 :** any of a genus (*Arethusa*) of bog orchids with a single linear leaf and solitary purple flower

arg *abbr* **1** argent **2** argument

Arg *abbr* Argyll

ar·ga·li \ˈär-gə-lē\ *n* [Mongolian] **:** a large Asiatic wild sheep (*Ovis ammon*) noted for its large horns; *also* **:** any of several other large wild sheep (as the bighorn)

Ar·gand diagram \ˌär-ˌgän-, -ˌgan-\ *n* [John Robert *Argand* †1825 F mathematician] **:** a conventional diagram in which the complex number $x + iy$ is represented by the point whose rectangular coordinates are x and y

ar·gent \ˈär-jənt\ *n* [ME, fr. MF & L; MF, fr. L *argentum;* akin to L *arguere* to make clear, Gk *argyros* silver, *argos* white] **1** *archaic* **:** the metal silver; *also* **:** WHITENESS **2 :** the heraldic color silver or white — **argent** *adj*

ar·gen·tic \är-ˈjent-ik\ *adj* **:** of, relating to, or containing silver esp. when bivalent

ar·gen·tif·er·ous \ˌär-jən-ˈtif-(ə-)rəs\ *adj* **:** producing or containing silver

¹ar·gen·tine \ˈär-jən-ˌtīn, -ˌtēn\ *adj* **:** SILVER, SILVERY

²argentine *n* **:** SILVER; *also* **:** any of various materials resembling it

ar·gen·tite \ˈär-jən-ˌtīt\ *n* **:** native silver sulfide Ag_2S having a metallic luster and dark lead-gray color and constituting a valuable ore of silver

ar·gen·tous \är-ˈjent-əs\ *adj* **:** of, relating to, or containing silver esp. when univalent

ar·gil \ˈär-jəl\ *n* [ME, fr. L *argilla*, fr. Gk *argillos;* akin to Gk *argos* white] **:** CLAY; *esp* **:** potter's clay

ar·gil·la·ceous \ˌär-jə-ˈlā-shəs\ *adj* **:** of, relating to, or containing clay or clay minerals **:** CLAYEY

ar·gil·lite \ˈär-jə-ˌlīt\ *n* **:** a compact argillaceous rock differing from shale in being cemented by silica and from slate in having no slaty cleavage

ar·gi·nase \ˈär-jə-ˌnās, -ˌnāz\ *n* [ISV] **:** a crystalline enzyme that converts naturally occurring arginine into ornithine and urea

ar·gi·nine \ˈär-jə-ˌnēn\ *n* [G *arginin*] **:** a crystalline basic amino acid $C_6H_{14}N_4O_2$ derived from guanidine

Ar·give \ˈär-ˌjīv, -ˌgīv\ *adj* [L *Argivus*, fr. Gk *Argeios*, lit., of Argos, fr. *Argos* city-state of ancient Greece] **:** of or relating to the Greeks or Greece and esp. the Achaean city of Argos or the surrounding territory of Argolis — **Argive** *n*

Ar·go \ˈär-(ˌ)gō\ *n* [L (gen. *Argus*), fr. Gk *Argō*] **:** a large constellation in the southern hemisphere lying principally between Canis Major and the Southern Cross

ar·gol \ˈär-ˌgōl\ *n* [ME *argoile*] **:** crude tartar deposited in wine casks during aging

ar·gon \ˈär-ˌgän\ *n* [Gk, neut. of *argos* idle, lazy, fr. *a-* + *ergon* work; fr. its relative inertness — more at WORK] **:** a colorless odorless gaseous element found in the air and in volcanic gases and used esp. as a filler for electric bulbs and electron tubes — see ELEMENT table

ar·go·naut \ˈär-gə-ˌnȯt, -ˌnät\ *n* [L *Argonautes*, fr. Gk *Argonautēs*, fr. *Argō*, ship in which the Argonauts sailed + *nautēs* sailor — more at NAUTICAL] **1 a** *cap* **:** one of a band of heroes sailing with Jason in quest of the Golden Fleece **b :** an adventurer engaged in a quest **2 :** PAPER NAUTILUS

ar·go·sy \ˈär-gə-sē\ *n, pl* **-sies** [modif. of It *ragusea* Ragusan vessel, fr. *Ragusa*, Dalmatia (now Dubrovnik, Yugoslavia)] **1 :** a large ship; *esp* **:** a large merchant ship <three of your *argosies* are . . . come to harbor—Shak.> **2 :** a fleet of ships **3 :** a rich supply <an ~ of railway folklore —F.P. Donovan>

ar·got \ˈär-gət, -(ˌ)gō\ *n* [F] **:** an often more or less secret vocabulary and idiom peculiar to a particular group <the American Negro has . . . developed his own ~, partly to put the white man off, partly to put him down —Daniel Stern> ***syn*** see DIALECT

ar·gu·able \ˈär-gyə-wə-bəl\ *adj* **:** open to argument, dispute, or question — **ar·gu·ably** \-blē\ *adv*

ar·gue \ˈär-(ˌ)gyü, -gyə(-w)\ *vb* **ar·gued; ar·gu·ing** [ME *arguen*, fr. MF *arguer* to accuse, reason & L *arguere* to make clear; MF *arguer*, fr. L *argutare* to prate, fr. *argutus* clear, noisy, fr. pp. of *arguere*] *vi* **1 :** to give reasons for or against something **:** REASON **2 :** to contend or disagree in words **:** DISPUTE ~ *vt* **1 :** to give evidence of **:** INDICATE **2 :** to consider the pros and cons of **:** DISCUSS **3 :** to prove or try to prove by giving reasons **:** MAINTAIN **4 :** to persuade by giving reasons **:** INDUCE ***syn*** see DISCUSS — **ar·gu·er** \-gyə-wər\ *n*

ar·gu·fy \ˈär-gyə-ˌfī\ *vb* **-fied; -fy·ing** *vt* **:** DISPUTE, DEBATE ~ *vi* **:** WRANGLE — **ar·gu·fi·er** \-ˌfī(-ə)r\ *n*

ar·gu·ment \ˈär-gyə-mənt\ *n* [ME, fr. MF, fr. L *argumentum*, fr. *arguere*] **1** *obs* **:** an outward sign **:** INDICATION **2 :** a reason given in proof or rebuttal **3 a :** the act or process of arguing **:** ARGUMENTATION **b :** a coherent series of reasons offered **c :** QUARREL, DISAGREEMENT **4 :** an abstract or summary esp. of a literary work <a later editor added an ~ to the poem> **5 :** the subject matter esp. of a literary work **6 a :** one of the independent variables upon whose value that of a function depends **b :** the angle that fixes the direction of a complex number <if $a + bi$ is written as $re^{i\theta} = r(\cos\theta + i\sin\theta)$ then θ is the ~>

ar·gu·men·ta·tion \ˌär-gyə-mən-ˈtā-shən, -ˌmen-\ *n* **1 :** the act or process of forming reasons and of drawing conclusions and applying them to a case in discussion **2 :** DEBATE, DISCUSSION

ar·gu·men·ta·tive \ˌär-gyə-ˈment-ət-iv\ *also* **ar·gu·men·tive** \-ˈment-iv\ *adj* **1 :** characterized by argument **:** CONTROVERSIAL **2 :** given to argument **:** DISPUTATIOUS <~ to the point of being cantankerous —J. S. Clarke> — **ar·gu·men·ta·tive·ly** *adv*

ar·gu·men·tum \ˌär-gyə-ˈment-əm\ *n, pl* **-men·ta** \-ˈment-ə\ [L] **:** ARGUMENT 3b

Ar·gus \ˈär-gəs\ *n* [L, fr. Gk *Argos*] **1 :** a hundred-eyed monster of Greek legend **2 :** a watchful guardian

Ar·gus–eyed \ˌär-gə-ˈsīd\ *adj* **:** vigilantly observant

ar·gy–bar·gy \ˌär-gē-ˈbär-gē\ *n* [redupl. of Sc & E dial. *argy*, alter. of *argue*] *chiefly Brit* **:** a lively discussion **:** ARGUMENT, DISPUTE

ar·gyle *also* **ar·gyll** \ˈär-ˌgīl, är-ˈ\ *n, often cap* [*Argyle, Argyll*, branch of the Scottish clan of Campbell, fr. whose tartan the design was adapted] **:** a geometric knitting pattern of varicolored diamonds in solid and outline shapes on a single background color; *also* **:** a sock knit in this pattern

Ar·gy·rol \ˈär-jə-ˌrȯl, -ˌrōl\ *trademark* — used for a silver-protein compound whose aqueous solution is used as a local antiseptic esp. for mucous membranes

ar·hat \ˈär-(ˌ)hət\ *n* [Skt, fr. prp. of *arhati* he deserves; akin to Gk *alphein* to gain] **:** a Buddhist who has reached the stage of enlightenment — **ar·hat·ship** \-ˌship\ *n*

aria \ˈär-ē-ə\ *n* [It, lit., atmospheric air, modif. of L *aer*] **:** AIR, MELODY, TUNE; *specif* **:** an accompanied elaborate melody sung (as in an opera) by a single voice

Ar·i·ad·ne \ˌar-ē-ˈad-nē\ *n* [L, fr. Gk *Ariadnē*] **:** a daughter of Minos who gives Theseus the thread whereby he escapes from the labyrinth

Ar·i·an \ˈar-ē-ən, ˈer-\ *adj* **:** of or relating to Arius or his doctrines esp. that the Son is not of the same substance as the Father but was created as an agent for creating the world — **Arian** *n* — **Ar·i·an·ism** \-ə-ˌniz-əm\ *n*

-ar·i·an \ˈer-ē-ən, ˈar-\ *n suffix* [L *-arius* -ary] **1 :** believer <necessit*arian*> **:** advocate <latitudin*arian*> **2 :** producer <discipl in*arian*>

ARIBA *abbr* Associate of the Royal Institute of British Architects

ari·bo·fla·vin·osis \ˌā-ˌrī-bə-ˌflā-və-ˈnō-səs\ *n* [NL] **:** a deficiency disease due to inadequate intake of riboflavin

ar·id \'ar-əd\ *adj* [F or L; F *aride*, fr. L *aridus* — more at ARDOR] **1 :** excessively dry; *specif* **:** having insufficient rainfall to support agriculture **2 :** lacking in interest and life **:** JEJUNE ***syn*** see DRY ***ant*** moist, verdant — **arid·i·ty** \ə-'rid-ət-ē, a-\ *n* — **ar·id·ness** \'ar-əd-nəs\ *n*

Ar·i·el \'ar-ē-əl, 'er-\ *n* **1 :** a supernatural prankster in Shakespeare's *The Tempest* **2 :** the inner satellite of Uranus

Ar·i·es \'ar-ē-ˌēz, 'er-\ *n* [L (gen. *Arietis*), lit., ram; akin to Gk *eriphos* kid, OIr *heirp* doe] **1 :** a constellation between Pisces and Taurus pictured as a ram **2 a :** the 1st sign of the zodiac in astrology — see ZODIAC table **b :** one born under this sign

ari·et·ta \ˌär-ē-'et-ə, ˌar-\ *n* [It, dim. of *aria*] **:** a short aria

aright \ə-'rīt\ *adv* [ME, fr. OE *ariht*, fr. [1]*a-* + *riht* right] **:** RIGHTLY, CORRECTLY <if I remember ~>

ar·il \'ar-əl\ *n* [prob. fr. NL *arillus*, fr. ML, raisin, grape seed] **:** an exterior covering or appendage of some seeds that develops after fertilization as an outgrowth from the ovule stalk — **ar·iled** \'ar-əld\ *adj* — **ar·il·late** \'ar-ə-ˌlāt\ *adj*

ari·o·so \ˌär-ē-'ō-(ˌ)sō, -(ˌ)zō\ *n, pl* **-sos** *also* **-si** \-(ˌ)sē, -(ˌ)zē\ [It, fr. *aria*] **:** a musical passage or composition having a mixture of free recitative and metrical song

arise \ə-'rīz\ *vi* **arose** \-'rōz\; **aris·en** \-'riz-ᵊn\; **aris·ing** \-'rī-ziŋ\ [ME *arisen*, fr. OE *ārīsan*, fr. *ā-*, perfective prefix + *risan* to rise — more at ABIDE] **1 :** to get up **:** RISE **2 a :** to originate from a source **b :** to come into being or to attention **3 :** ASCEND ***syn*** see SPRING

aris·ta \ə-'ris-tə\ *n, pl* **-tae** \-(ˌ)tē, -ˌtī\ *or* **-tas** [NL, fr. L, beard of grain] **:** a bristlelike structure or appendage — **aris·tate** \-ˌtāt\ *adj*

ar·is·toc·ra·cy \ˌar-ə-'stäk-rə-sē\ *n, pl* **-cies** [MF & LL; MF *aristocratie*, fr. LL *aristocratia*, fr. Gk *aristokratia*, fr. *aristos* best + *-kratia* -cracy] **1 :** government by the best individuals or by a small privileged class **2 a :** a government in which power is vested in a minority consisting of those believed to be best qualified **b :** a state with such a government **3 :** a governing body or upper class usu. made up of an hereditary nobility **4 :** the aggregate of those believed to be superior

aris·to·crat \ə-'ris-tə-ˌkrat, a-; 'ar-ə-stə-\ *n* **1 :** a member of an aristocracy; *esp* **:** NOBLE **2 a :** one who has the bearing and viewpoint typical of the aristocracy **b :** one who favors aristocracy

aris·to·crat·ic \ə-ˌris-tə-'krat-ik, (ˌ)a-ˌris-tə-, ˌar-ə-stə-\ *adj* [MF *aristocratique*, fr. ML *aristocraticus*, fr. Gk *aristokratikos*, fr. *aristos* + *-kratikos* -cratic] **1 :** belonging to, having the qualities of, or favoring aristocracy **2 a :** socially exclusive <an ~ neighborhood> **b :** SNOBBISH — **aris·to·crat·i·cal·ly** \-i-k(ə-)lē\ *adv*

Ar·is·to·te·lian *or* **Ar·is·to·te·lean** \ˌar-ə-stə-'tēl-yən\ *adj* [L *Aristoteles* Aristotle, fr. Gk *Aristotelēs*] **:** of or relating to the Greek philosopher Aristotle or his philosophy — **Aristotelian** *n* — **Ar·is·to·te·lian·ism** \-yə-ˌniz-əm\ *n*

arith *abbr* arithmetic; arithmetical

arith·me·tic \ə-'rith-mə-ˌtik\ *n* [ME *arsmetrik*, fr. OF *arismetique*, fr. L *arithmetica*, fr. Gk *arithmētikē*, fr. fem. of *arithmētikos* arithmetical, fr. *arithmein* to count, fr. *arithmos* number; akin to Gk *arariskein* to fit] **1 a :** a branch of mathematics that deals with real numbers including sometimes the transfinite cardinals and computations with them **b :** a treatise on arithmetic **2 :** COMPUTATION, CALCULATION — **ar·ith·met·ic** \ˌar-ith-'met-ik\ *or* **ar·ith·met·i·cal** \-i-kəl\ *adj* — **ar·ith·met·i·cal·ly** \-i-k(ə-)lē\ *adv* — **arith·me·ti·cian** \ə-ˌrith-mə-'tish-ən\ *n*

arithmetic mean *n* **:** a value that is computed by dividing the sum of a set of terms by the number of terms

arithmetic progression *n* **:** a progression (as 3, 5, 7, 9) in which the difference between any term and its predecessor is constant

-ar·i·um \'ar-ē-əm, 'er-\ *n suffix, pl* **-ariums** *or* **-ar·ia** \-ē-ə\ [L, fr. neut. of *-arius* -ary] **:** thing or place relating to or connected with <planet*arium*>

Ariz *abbr* Arizona

ark \'ärk\ *n* [ME, fr. OE *arc*; akin to OHG *arahha* ark; both fr. a prehistoric Gmc word borrowed fr. L *arca* chest; akin to L *arcēre* to hold off, defend, Gk *arkein*] **1 a :** a boat or ship held to resemble that in which Noah and his family were preserved from the Deluge **b :** something that affords protection and safety **2 a :** the sacred chest representing to the Hebrews the presence of God among them **b :** a repository traditionally in or against the wall of a synagogue for the scrolls of the Torah

Ark *abbr* Arkansas

[1]**arm** \'ärm\ *n* [ME, fr. OE *earm*; akin to L *armus* shoulder, Gk *harmos* joint, L *arma* weapons, *ars* skill, Gk *arariskein* to fit] **1 :** a human upper limb; *esp* **:** the part between the shoulder and the wrist **2 :** something like or corresponding to an arm: as **a :** the forelimb of a vertebrate **b :** a limb of an invertebrate animal **c :** a branch or lateral shoot of a plant **d :** a slender part of a structure, machine, or an instrument projecting from a main part, axis, or fulcrum **e :** the end of a ship's yard; *also* **:** the part of an anchor from the crown to the fluke **3 :** an inlet of water (as from the sea) **4 :** POWER, MIGHT <the long ~ of the law> **5 :** a support (as on a chair) for the elbow and forearm **6 :** SLEEVE **7 :** a functional division of a group or activity <the logistical ~ of the air force> — **armed** \'ärmd\ *adj* — **arm·less** \'ärm-ləs\ *adj* — **arm·like** \-ˌlīk\ *adj*

[2]**arm** *vb* [ME *armen*, fr. OF *armer*, fr. L *armare*, fr. *arma* weapons, tools] *vt* **1 :** to furnish or equip with weapons **2 :** to furnish with something that strengthens or protects **3 :** to fortify morally **4 :** to equip or ready for action or operation <~ a bomb> ~ *vi* **:** to prepare oneself for struggle or resistance ***syn*** see FURNISH

[3]**arm** *n* [ME *armes* (pl.) weapons, fr. OF, fr. L *arma*] **1 a :** a means of offense or defense; *esp* **:** FIREARM **b :** a combat branch (as of an army) **c :** an organized branch of national defense (as the navy) **2** *pl* **a :** the hereditary heraldic devices of a family **b :** heraldic devices adopted by a government **3** *pl* **a :** active hostilities **:** WARFARE **b :** military service

Arm *abbr* **1** Armagh **2** Armenian

ar·ma·da \är-'mäd-ə, -'mad-, -'mād-\ *n* [Sp, fr. ML *armata* army, fleet, fr. L, fem. of *armatus*, pp. of *armare*] **1 :** a fleet of warships **2 :** a large force of moving things <an ~ of fishing boats>

ar·ma·dil·lo \ˌär-mə-'dil-(ˌ)ō\ *n, pl* **-los** [Sp, fr. dim. of *armado* armed one, fr. L *armatus*] **:** any of several burrowing chiefly nocturnal edentate mammals (family Dasypodidae) of warm parts of the Americas having body and head encased in an armor of small bony plates in which many of them can curl up into a ball when attacked

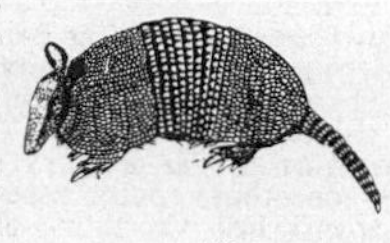

armadillo

Ar·ma·ged·don \ˌär-mə-'ged-ᵊn\ *n* [Gk *Armageddōn, Harmagedōn*, scene of the battle foretold in Rev 16:14–16] **1 a :** a final and conclusive battle between the forces of good and evil **b :** the site or time of Armageddon **2 :** a vast decisive conflict

Ar·ma·gnac \'är-mən-ˌyak\ *n* [F, fr. *Armagnac*, region in southwest France] **:** a brown dry brandy produced in the Gers district of France

ar·ma·ment \'är-mə-mənt\ *n* [F *armement*, fr. L *armamenta* (pl.) utensils, military or naval equipment, fr. *armare* to arm, equip] **1 :** a military or naval force **2 a :** the aggregate of a nation's military strength **b :** arms and equipment (as of a combat unit) **c :** means of protection or defense **:** ARMOR **3 :** the process of preparing for war

ar·ma·men·tar·i·um \ˌär-mə-ˌmen-'ter-ē-əm, -mən-\ *n, pl* **-tar·ia** \-ē-ə\ [L, armory, fr. *armamenta*] **1 :** the equipment and methods used esp. in medicine **2 :** matter available or utilized for an undertaking or field of activity <a whole ~ of devices to create an illusion of real life —Kenneth Rexroth>

ar·ma·ture \'är-mə-ˌchu̇(ə)r, -chər, -ˌt(y)u̇(ə)r\ *n* [L *armatura* armor, equipment, fr. *armatus*] **1 :** an organ or structure (as teeth or thorns) for offense or defense **2 a :** a piece of soft iron or steel that connects the poles of a magnet or of adjacent magnets **b :** a part which consists essentially of coils of wire around a metal core and in which electric current is induced in a generator or in which the input current interacts with a magnetic field to produce torque in a motor **c :** the movable part of an electromagnetic device (as a loudspeaker) **d :** a framework used by a sculptor to support a figure being modeled in a plastic material

[1]**arm·chair** \'ärm-ˌche(ə)r, -ˌcha(ə)r, 'ärm-'\ *n* **:** a chair with armrests

[2]**armchair** *adj* **1 :** remote from direct dealing with problems <~ strategists> **2 :** sharing vicariously in another's experiences <an ~ traveler>

armed forces *n pl* **:** the combined military, naval, and air forces of a nation

Ar·me·nian \är-'mē-nē-ən, -nyən\ *n* **1 :** a member of a people dwelling chiefly in Armenia **2 :** the Indo-European language of the Armenians — see INDO-EUROPEAN LANGUAGES table — **Armenian** *adj*

arm·ful \'ärm-ˌfu̇l\ *n, pl* **armfuls** \-ˌfu̇lz\ *or* **arms·ful** \'ärmz-ˌfu̇l\ **:** as much as the arm can hold

arm·hole \'ärm-ˌhōl\ *n* **:** an opening for the arm in a garment

ar·mi·ger \'är-mi-jər\ *n* [ML, fr. L, armor-bearer, fr. *armiger* bearing arms, fr. *arma* arms + *-ger* -gerous] **1 :** SQUIRE **2 :** one entitled to bear heraldic arms — **ar·mig·er·al** \är-'mij-ə-rəl\ *adj*

ar·mig·er·ous \är-'mij-ə-rəs\ *adj* **:** bearing heraldic arms

ar·mil·la·ry sphere \ˌär-mə-ˌler-ē-, är-ˌmil-ə-rē-\ *n* [F *sphère armillaire*, fr. ML *armilla*, fr. L, bracelet, iron ring, fr. *armus* arm, shoulder; akin to OE *earm* arm] **:** an old astronomical instrument composed of rings representing the positions of important circles of the celestial sphere

Ar·min·i·an \är-'min-ē-ən\ *adj* **:** of or relating to Arminius or his doctrines opposing the absolute predestination of strict Calvinism and maintaining the possibility of salvation for all — **Armin·ian** *n* — **Ar·min·i·an·ism** \-ē-ə-ˌniz-əm\ *n*

armor 1: *1* helmet, *2* gorget, *3* shoulder piece, *4* pallette, *5* breastplate, *6* brassard, *7* elbow piece, *8* skirt of tasses, *9* tuille, *10* gauntlet, *11* cuisse, *12* knee piece, *13* jambeau, *14* solleret

ar·mi·stice \'är-mə-stəs\ *n* [F or NL; F, fr. NL *armistitium*, fr. L *arma* + *-stitium* (as in *solstitium* solstice)] **:** temporary suspension of hostilities by agreement between the opponents **:** TRUCE

Armistice Day *n* [fr. the armistice terminating World War I on November 11, 1918] **:** VETERANS DAY — used before the official adoption of *Veterans Day* in 1954

arm·let \'ärm-lət\ *n* **1 :** a band (as of cloth or metal) worn around the upper arm **2 :** a small arm (as of the sea)

ar·moire \ärm-'wär, 'är-mər\ *n* [MF, fr. OF *armaire*, fr. L *armarium*, fr. *arma*] **:** a usu. large cupboard, wardrobe, or clothespress

ar·mor \'är-mər\ *n* [ME *armure*, fr. OF, fr. L *armatura* — more at ARMATURE] **1 :** defensive covering for the body; *esp* **:** covering (as of metal) used in combat **2 :** a quality or circumstance that affords protection <the ~ of prosperity> **3 a :** a usu. metallic protective covering (as for a ship, fort, airplane, or automobile) **b :** a protective covering (as a diver's suit, the covering of a plant or animal, or a sheathing for wire, cordage, or hose) **4 :** armored forces and vehicles (as tanks) — **armor** *vt* — **ar·mored** \-mərd\ *adj* — **ar·mor·less** \-mər-ləs\ *adj*

1ar·mor–clad \ˈär-mər-ˌklad\ *adj* **:** sheathed in or protected by armor

2armor–clad *n* **:** an armor-clad warship

armored scale *n* **:** any of numerous scales constituting a family (Diaspididae) and having a firm covering of wax best developed in the female

ar·mor·er \ˈär-mər-ər\ *n* **1 :** one that makes armor or arms **2 :** one that repairs, assembles, and tests firearms

ar·mo·ri·al \är-ˈmōr-ē-əl, -ˈmȯr-\ *adj* [*armory* (heraldry)] **:** of, relating to, or bearing heraldic arms — **ar·mo·ri·al·ly** \-ē-ə-lē\ *adv*

Ar·mor·i·can \är-ˈmȯr-i-kən, -ˈmär-\ *or* **Ar·mor·ic** \-ik\ *n* **:** a native or inhabitant of Armorica; *esp* **:** BRETON — **Armorican** *or* **Armoric** *adj*

ar·mory \ˈärm-(ə-)rē\ *n, pl* **ar·mor·ies** **1 a :** a supply of arms for defense or attack **b :** a collection of available resources **2 :** a place where arms and military equipment are stored; *esp* **:** one used for training military reserve personnel **3 :** a place where arms are manufactured

ar·mour \ˈär-mər\ *chiefly Brit var of* ARMOR

arm·pit \ˈärm-ˌpit\ *n* **:** the hollow beneath the junction of the arm and shoulder

arm·rest \-ˌrest\ *n* **:** a support for the arm

arm–twist·ing \-ˌtwis-tiŋ\ *n* **:** the use of direct personal pressure in order to achieve a desired end <for all the ~, the . . . vote on the measure was unexpectedly tight —*Newsweek*>

arm wrestling *n* **:** a form of wrestling in which two opponents sit face to face gripping usu. their right hands and setting corresponding elbows firmly on a surface (as a tabletop) in an attempt to force each other's arm down — called also *Indian wrestling*

ar·my \ˈär-mē\ *n, pl* **armies** [ME *armee*, fr. MF, fr. ML *armata* — more at ARMADA] **1 a :** a large organized body of men armed and trained for war esp. on land **b :** a unit capable of independent action and consisting usu. of a headquarters, two or more corps, and auxiliary troops **c** *often cap* **:** the complete military organization of a nation for land warfare **2 :** a great multitude <an ~ of bicycles —Norm Fruchter> **3 :** a body of persons organized to advance a cause

army ant *n* **:** any of various nomadic social ants (subfamily Dorylinae)

ar·my·worm \ˈär-mē-ˌwərm\ *n* **:** any of numerous moths whose larvae travel in multitudes from field to field destroying grass, grain, and other crops; *esp* **:** the common armyworm (*Pseudaletia unipuncta*) of the northern U.S.

ar·ni·ca \ˈär-ni-kə\ *n* [NL, genus name] **1 :** any of many composite herbs (genus *Arnica*) including some with bright yellow ray flowers **2 :** the dried flower heads of an arnica (esp. *Arnica montana*) used esp. in the form of a tincture as a liniment (as for sprains or bruises); *also* **:** this tincture

ar·oid \ˈa(ə)r-ˌȯid, ˈe(ə)r-\ *adj* [NL *Arum*] **:** of or relating to the arum family — **aroid** *n*

aroint \ə-ˈrȯint\ *vb imper* [origin unknown] *archaic* **:** BEGONE <~ thee, witch —Shak.>

aro·ma \ə-ˈrō-mə\ *n* [ME *aromat* spice, fr. OF, fr. L *aromat-, aroma*, fr. Gk *arōmat-, arōma*] **1 a :** a distinctive pervasive and usu. pleasant or savory smell; *broadly* **:** ODOR **b :** the bouquet of a wine **2 :** a distinctive quality or atmosphere **:** FLAVOR <the ~ of enjoyment —Stella D. Gibbons> ***syn*** see SMELL

1ar·o·mat·ic \ˌar-ə-ˈmat-ik\ *adj* **1 :** of, relating to, or having aroma: **a :** FRAGRANT **b :** having a strong smell **c :** having a distinctive quality **2 :** of, relating to, or characterized by the presence of at least one benzene ring — used of cyclic hydrocarbons and their derivatives — **ar·o·mat·i·cal·ly** \-i-k(ə-)lē\ *adv* — **aro·ma·tic·i·ty** \ˌar-ə-mə-ˈtis-ət-ē, ə-ˌrō-mə-\ *n* — **ar·o·mat·ic·ness** \ˌar-ə-ˈmat-ik-nəs\ *n*

2aromatic *n* **1 :** an aromatic plant, drug, or medicine **2 :** an aromatic organic compound

aro·ma·tize \ə-ˈrō-mə-ˌtīz\ *vt* **-tized; -tiz·ing** **1 :** to make aromatic **:** FLAVOR **2 :** to convert into one or more aromatic compounds — **aro·ma·ti·za·tion** \-ˌrō-mət-ə-ˈzā-shən\ *n*

arose *past of* ARISE

1around \ə-ˈrau̇nd\ *adv* [ME, fr. 1*a-* + *round*] **1 a :** in circumference <a tree five feet ~> **b :** in, along, or through a circuit <the road goes ~ by the lake> **2 a :** on all or various sides <papers lying ~> **b :** in close from all sides so as to surround **c :** NEARBY **3 a :** here and there in various places **b :** to a particular place **4 a :** in rotation or succession **b :** from beginning to end **:** THROUGH <mild the year ~> **5 :** in or to an opposite direction or position **6 :** in the neighborhood of **:** APPROXIMATELY

2around *prep* **1 a :** on all sides of **b :** so as to encircle or enclose <seated ~ the table> **c :** so as to avoid or get past **:** on or to another side of <went ~ the lake> <got ~ his objections> **d :** NEAR **2 :** in all directions outward from **3 :** here and there in or throughout <barnstorming ~ the country> **4 :** so as to have a center or basis in <a society organized ~ kinship ties>

3around *adj* **1 :** ABOUT 1 <has been up and ~ for two days> **2 :** being in existence, evidence, or circulation <the most intelligent of the artists ~ today —R. M. Coates>

around–the–clock *adj* **:** being in effect, continuing, or lasting 24 hours a day **:** CONSTANT

arouse \ə-ˈrau̇z\ *vb* **aroused; arous·ing** [*a-* (as in *arise*) + *rouse*] *vt* **1 :** to awaken from sleep **2 :** to rouse to action **:** EXCITE <the book *aroused* debate> ~ *vi* **:** to awake from sleep **:** STIR — **arous·al** \-ˈrau̇-zəl\ *n*

ARP *abbr* air-raid precautions

ar·peg·gio \är-ˈpej-(ē-ˌ)ō\ *n, pl* **-gios** [It, fr. *arpeggiare* to play on the harp, fr. *arpa* harp, of Gmc origin; akin to OHG *harpha* harp] **1 :** production of the tones of a chord in succession and not simultaneously **2 :** a chord played in arpeggio

ar·pent \är-ˈpä^{n}\ *n, pl* **arpents** \-ˈpä^{n}(z)\ [MF] **1 :** any of various old French units of land area; *esp* **:** one used in French sections of Canada and the U.S. equal to about 0.85 acre **2 :** a unit of length equal to one side of a square arpent

arquebus \ˈär-\ *var of* HARQUEBUS

arr *abbr* **1** arranged **2** arrival; arrive

Written Played

arpeggio 2

ar·rack \ˈar-ək, ə-ˈrak\ *n* [Ar ʿ*araq* sweet juice, liquor] **:** an alcoholic beverage of the Far East or Near East; *esp* **:** one distilled from the juice of the coconut palm or from a mash of rice and molasses

ar·raign \ə-ˈrān\ *vt* [ME *arreinen*, fr. MF *araisner*, fr. OF, fr. *a-* (fr. L *ad-*) + *raisnier* to speak, fr. (assumed) VL *rationare*, fr. L *ration-, ratio* reason — more at REASON] **1 :** to call (a prisoner) before a court to answer to an indictment **:** CHARGE **2 :** to accuse of wrong, inadequacy, or imperfection — **ar·raign·ment** \-mənt\ *n*

ar·range \ə-ˈrānj\ *vb* **-ranged; -rang·ing** [ME *arangen*, fr. MF *arangier*, fr. OF, fr. *a-* + *rengier* to set in a row, fr. *reng* row — more at RANK] *vt* **1 :** to put into a proper order or into a correct or suitable sequence, relationship, or adjustment <~ flowers in a vase> <~ cards alphabetically> **2 :** to make preparations for **:** PLAN <*arranged* a reception for the visitor> **3 :** to bring about an agreement or understanding concerning **:** SETTLE <~ an exchange of war prisoners> **4 a :** to adapt (a musical composition) by scoring for voices or instruments other than those for which orig. written **b :** ORCHESTRATE ~ *vi* **1 :** to bring about an agreement or understanding <*arranged* to have a table at the restaurant> **2 :** to make preparations **:** PLAN <*arranged* for a vacation with his family> ***syn*** **1** see ORDER **2** see NEGOTIATE ***ant*** disarrange, derange — **ar·rang·er** *n*

ar·range·ment \ə-ˈrānj-mənt\ *n* **1 a :** the act of arranging <the ~ of the details was quickly accomplished> **b :** the state of being arranged **:** ORDER <everything in neat ~> **2 :** something arranged: as **a :** a preliminary measure **:** PREPARATION <travel ~*s*> **b :** an adaptation of a musical composition by rescoring **c :** an informal agreement or settlement esp. on personal, social, or political matters <~*s* under the new regime> **3 :** something made by arranging parts or things together <a floral ~>

ar·rant \ˈar-ənt\ *adj* [alter. of *errant*] **:** being notoriously without moderation **:** EXTREME <we are ~ knaves, all; believe none of us —Shak.> ***syn*** see OUTRIGHT — **ar·rant·ly** *adv*

ar·ras \ˈar-əs\ *n, pl* **arras** [ME, fr. *Arras*, France] **1 :** a tapestry of Flemish origin used esp. for wall hangings and curtains **2 :** a wall hanging or screen of tapestry

1ar·ray \ə-ˈrā\ *vt* [ME *arrayen*, fr. OF *arayer*, fr. (assumed) VL *arredare*, fr. L *ad-* + a base of Gmc origin; akin to Goth *garaiths* arranged — more at READY] **1 a :** to set or place in order **:** draw up **:** MARSHAL **b :** to set or set forth in order (as a jury) for the trial of a cause **2 :** to dress or decorate esp. in splendid or impressive attire **:** ADORN ***syn*** see LINE — **ar·ray·er** *n*

2array *n* **1 a :** a regular and imposing grouping or arrangement **:** ORDER **b :** military order <forces in ~> **c :** an orderly listing of jurors impaneled **d :** a group of individuals or kinds that has a definite modal point forming a center of variations **2 a :** CLOTHING, ATTIRE **b :** rich or beautiful apparel **:** FINERY **3 :** a body of soldiers **:** MILITIA <the baron and his feudal ~> **4 :** an imposing group **:** large number <faced a whole ~ of problems> **5 a :** a number of mathematical elements arranged in rows and columns **b :** a series of statistical data arranged in classes in order of magnitude **6 :** an arrangement of computer memory elements (as magnetic cores) in a single plane

ar·rear \ə-ˈri(ə)r\ *n* [ME *arrere* behind, backward, fr. MF, fr. (assumed) VL *ad retro* backward, fr. L *ad* to + *retro* backward, behind — more at AT, RETRO-] **1 :** the state of being behind in the discharge of obligations — usu. used in pl. <in ~*s* with his payments> **2 a :** an unfinished duty — usu. used in pl. <~*s* of work that have piled up> **b :** an unpaid and overdue debt — usu. used in pl. <paying off the ~*s* of the past several months>

ar·rear·age \-ij\ *n* **1 :** the condition of being in arrears **2 :** something that is in arrears; *esp* **:** something unpaid and overdue

1ar·rest \ə-ˈrest\ *vt* [ME *aresten*, fr. MF *arester* to rest, arrest, fr. (assumed) VL *arrestare*, fr. L *ad-* + *restare* to remain, rest] **1 a :** to bring to a stop <sickness ~*ed* his activities> **b :** CHECK, SLOW **c :** to make inactive <an ~*ed* tumor> **2 :** SEIZE, CAPTURE; *specif* **:** to take or keep in custody by authority of law **3 :** to catch suddenly and engagingly — **ar·rest·er** *or* **ar·res·tor** \-ˈres-tər\ *n* — **ar·rest·ment** \-ˈres(t)-mənt\ *n*

2arrest *n* **1 a :** the act of stopping **b :** the condition of being stopped **2 :** the taking or detaining in custody by authority of law **3 :** a device for arresting motion — **under arrest** **:** in legal custody

ar·res·tant \ə-ˈres-tənt\ *n* **:** a substance that causes an insect to stop locomotion and begin to feed

arrest·ee \ə-ˌres-ˈtē\ *n* **:** one that is under arrest

ar·rest·ing \ə-ˈres-tiŋ\ *adj* **:** catching the attention **:** STRIKING, IMPRESSIVE — **ar·rest·ing·ly** \-tiŋ-lē\ *adv*

ar·rhyth·mia \ā-ˈrith-mē-ə\ *n* [NL, fr. Gk, lack of rhythm, fr. *arrhythmos* unrhythmical, fr. *a-* + *rhythmos* rhythm] **:** an alteration in rhythm of the heartbeat either in time or force

ar·rhyth·mic \-mik\ *adj* [Gk *arrhythmos*] **:** lacking rhythm or regularity <~ locomotor activity> — **ar·rhyth·mi·cal** \-mi-kəl\ *adj* — **ar·rhyth·mi·cal·ly** \-mi-k(ə-)lē\ *adv*

ar·ri·ère–ban \ˌar-ē-ˌe(ə)r-ˈbän, -ˈban\ *n* [F] **:** a proclamation of a king (as of France) calling his vassals to arms; *also* **:** the body of vassals summoned

ar·ri·ère–pen·sée \-pä^{n}-ˈsā\ *n* [F, fr. *arrière* in back + *pensée* thought] **:** mental reservation

ar·ris \ˈar-əs\ *n, pl* **arris** *or* **ar·ris·es** [prob. modif. of MF *areste*, lit., fishbone, fr. LL *arista* — more at ARÊTE] **:** the sharp edge or salient angle formed by the meeting of two surfaces esp. in moldings

ar·riv·al \ə-ˈrī-vəl\ *n* **1 :** the act of arriving **2 :** the attainment of an end or state **3 :** one that has recently reached a destination

ar·rive \ə-ˈrīv\ *vi* **ar·rived; ar·riv·ing** [ME *ariven*, fr. OF *ariver*, fr. (assumed) VL *arripare* to come to shore, fr. L *ad-* + *ripa* shore — more at RIVE] **1 a :** to reach a destination **b :** to make an appearance <all the guests have *arrived*> **2 a** *archaic* **:** HAPPEN **b :** to be near in time **:** COME <the moment has *arrived*> **3 :** to achieve success — **ar·riv·er** *n* — **arrive at** : to reach by effort or thought <have *arrived at* a decision>

ar·ri·vé \ˌar-i-ˈvā\ *n* [F, fr. pp. of *arriver* to arrive, fr. OF *ariver*] : one who has risen rapidly to success, power, or fame

ar·ri·viste \-ˈvēst\ *n* [F, fr. *arriver*] : one that is a new and uncertain arrival (as in social position or artistic endeavor)

ar·ro·ba \ə-ˈrō-bə\ *n* [Sp & Pg, fr. Ar *ar-rub'*, lit., the quarter] **1** : an old Spanish unit of weight equal to about 25 pounds used in some Spanish-American countries **2** : an old Portuguese unit of weight equal to about 32 pounds used in Brazil

ar·ro·gance \ˈar-ə-gən(t)s\ *n* : a feeling of superiority manifested in an overbearing manner or presumptuous claims

ar·ro·gant \-gənt\ *adj* [ME, fr. L *arrogant-, arrogans*, prp. of *arrogare*] **1** : exaggerating or disposed to exaggerate one's own worth or importance in an overbearing manner <an ~ official> **2** : proceeding from or characterized by arrogance <~ manners> ***syn*** see PROUD ***ant*** meek, unassuming — **ar·ro·gant·ly** *adv*

ar·ro·gate \-ˌgāt\ *vt* **-gat·ed; -gat·ing** [L *arrogatus*, pp. of *arrogare*, fr. *ad-* + *rogare* to ask — more at RIGHT] **1 a** : to claim or seize without justification **b** : to make undue claims to having : ASSUME **2** : to claim on behalf of another : ASCRIBE ***syn*** see APPROPRIATE — **ar·ro·ga·tion** \ˌar-ə-ˈgā-shən\ *n*

ar·ron·disse·ment \ə-ˈrän-də-smənt, ˈar-ˌōⁿ-(ˌ)dē-ˈsmäⁿ\ *n* [F] **1** : the largest division of a French department **2** : an administrative district of some large French cities

ar·row \ˈar-(ˌ)ō, -ə(-w)\ *n* [ME *arwe*, fr. OE; akin to Goth *arhwazna* arrow, L *arcus* bow, arch, arc] **1** : a missile weapon shot from a bow and usu. having a slender shaft, a pointed head, and feathers at the butt **2** : something shaped like an arrow; *esp* : a mark (as on a map or signboard) to indicate direction

ar·row·head \ˈar-ō-ˌhed, ˈar-ə-\ *n* **1** : the usu. separate wedge-shaped striking end of an arrow **2** : something resembling an arrowhead **3** : any of a genus (*Sagittaria*) of plants of the water-plantain family with leaves shaped like arrowheads

ar·row·root \-ˌrüt, -ˌru̇t\ *n* **1 a** : any of a genus (*Maranta* of the family Marantaceae, the arrowroot family) of tropical American plants with tuberous roots; *esp* : one (*M. arundinacea*) whose roots yield a nutritive starch **b** : any of several plants (as coontie) that yield starch **2** : starch yielded by an arrowroot

ar·row·wood \-ˌwu̇d\ *n* : any of several shrubs (as several viburnums) having tough pliant shoots formerly used to make arrows

ar·row·worm \-ˌwərm\ *n* : CHAETOGNATH

ar·rowy \ˈar-ə-wē\ *adj* **1** : consisting of arrows **2** : resembling or suggesting an arrow; *esp* : swiftly moving

ar·royo \ə-ˈrȯi-ə, -(ˌ)ō\ *n, pl* **-royos** [Sp] **1** : a watercourse (as a creek or stream) in an arid region **2** : a water-carved gully or channel

ARS *abbr* Agricultural Research Service

arse *var of* ASS

ar·se·nal \ˈärs-nəl, -ᵊn-əl\ *n* [It *arsenale*, modif. of Ar *dār ṣinā'ah* house of manufacture] **1 a** : an establishment for the manufacture or storage of arms and military equipment **b** : a collection of weapons **2** : STORE, REPERTORY <the team's ~ of experienced players>

ar·se·nate \ˈärs-nət, -ᵊn-ət, -ᵊn-ˌāt\ *n* : a salt or ester of an arsenic acid

¹ar·se·nic \ˈärs-nik, -ᵊn-ik\ *n* [ME, fr. MF & L; MF, fr. L *arsenicum*, fr. Gk *arsenikon, arrhenikon* yellow orpiment, fr. Syr *zarnīg*, of Iranian origin; akin to Av *zaranya* gold, Skt *hari* yellowish — more at YELLOW] **1** : a trivalent and pentavalent solid poisonous element that is commonly metallic steel-gray, crystalline, and brittle — see ELEMENT table **2** : a poisonous trioxide As_2O_3 or As_4O_6 of arsenic used esp. as an insecticide or weed killer — called also *arsenic trioxide*

²ar·sen·ic \är-ˈsen-ik\ *adj* : of, relating to, or containing arsenic esp. with a valence of five

ar·sen·i·cal \är-ˈsen-i-kəl\ *adj* : of, relating to, or containing arsenic <an ~ drug> — **arsenical** *n*

ar·se·nic trisulfide \ˌärs-nik-, -ᵊn-ik-\ *n* : a yellow compound As_2S_3 occurring native as orpiment or prepared artificially and used in fireworks and as a pigment

ar·se·nide \ˈärs-ᵊn-ˌīd\ *n* : a binary compound of arsenic with a more positive element

ar·se·ni·ous \är-ˈsē-nē-əs\ *adj* : of, relating to, or containing arsenic esp. when trivalent

ar·se·nite \ˈärs-ᵊn-ˌīt\ *n* : a salt or ester of an arsenious acid

ar·se·no·py·rite \ˌärs-ᵊn-ō-ˈpī(ə)r-ˌīt\ *n* : a mineral FeAsS consisting of a combined sulfide and arsenide of iron occurring in prismatic orthorhombic crystals or in masses or grains

ar·sine \är-ˈsēn, ˈär-ˌ\ *n* [ISV, fr. *arsenic*] : a colorless flammable extremely poisonous gas AsH_3 with an odor like garlic; *also* : a derivative of arsine

ar·sis \ˈär-səs\ *n, pl* **ar·ses** \-ˌsēz\ [LL & Gk; LL, raising of the voice, accented part of foot, fr. Gk, upbeat, less important part of foot, lit., act of lifting, fr. *aeirein, airein* to lift] **1 a** : the lighter or shorter part of a poetic foot esp. in quantitative verse **b** : the accented or longer part of a poetic foot esp. in accentual verse **2** : the unaccented part of a musical measure — compare THESIS

ar·son \ˈärs-ᵊn\ *n* [obs. F, fr. OF, fr. *ars*, pp. of *ardre* to burn, fr. L *ardēre* — *more at* ARDOR]: the malicious or fraudulent burning of property (as a building) — **ar·son·ist** \-əst\ *n* — **ar·son·ous** \-əs\ *adj*

ars·phen·a·mine \ärs-ˈfen-ə-ˌmēn, -mən\ *n* [ISV *arsenic* + *phenamine*] : a light-yellow toxic hygroscopic powder $C_{12}Cl_2H_{14}As_2N_2O_2.2H_2O$ formerly used in the treatment of spirochetal diseases

¹art \(ˈ)ärt, ərt\ [ME, fr. OE *eart*; akin to ON *est, ert* (thou) art, OE *is* is] *archaic pres 2d sing of* BE

²art \ˈärt\ *n* [ME, fr. OF, fr. L *art-, ars* — more at ARM] **1** : skill acquired by experience, study, or observation <the ~ of making friends> **2 a** : a branch of learning: (1) : one of the humanities (2) *pl* : LIBERAL ARTS **b** *archaic* : LEARNING, SCHOLARSHIP **3** : an occupation requiring knowledge or skill <the ~ of organ building> **4 a** : the conscious use of skill and creative imagination esp. in the production of aesthetic objects; *also* : works so produced **b** (1) : FINE ARTS (2) : one of the fine arts (3) : a graphic art **5 a** *archaic* : a skillful plan **b** : the quality or state of being artful **6** : decorative or illustrative elements in printed matter ***syn*** ART, SKILL, CUNNING, ARTIFICE, CRAFT *shared meaning element* : the faculty of carrying out expertly what is planned or devised

³art *abbr* **1** article **2** artificial **3** artillery

-art — see -ARD

art de·co \ˌär(t)-dā-ˈkō, (ˈ)är(t)-ˈdā-(ˌ)-\ *n, often cap A&D* [F *Art Déco*, fr. *Exposition Internationale des Arts Decoratifs*, an exposition of decorative arts held in Paris, France, in 1925] : a pervasive decorative style of the 1920s and 1930s characterized esp. by bold outlines, streamlined and rectilinear forms, and the use of new materials (as plastic)

artefact *var of* ARTIFACT

ar·tel \är-ˈtel(-yə)\ *n* [Russ *artel'*, fr. It *artieri*, pl. of *artiere* artisan, fr. *arte* art] : COLLECTIVE FARM

Ar·te·mis \ˈärt-ə-məs\ *n* [Gk] : a Greek goddess often portrayed as a virgin huntress and identified as a moon goddess — compare DIANA

ar·te·mi·sia \ˌärt-ə-ˈmizh-(ē-)ə, -ˈmiz-ē-ə\ *n* [NL, genus name, fr. L, artemisia, fr. Gk] : any of a genus (*Artemisia*) of composite herbs and shrubs with strong-smelling foliage

arteri- *or* **arterio-** *comb form* [MF, fr. LL, fr. Gk *artēri-, artērio-*, fr. *artēria* artery] **1** : artery <*arterio*logy> **2** : arterial and <*arterio*venous>

¹ar·te·ri·al \är-ˈtir-ē-əl\ *adj* **1 a** : of or relating to an artery **b** : relating to or being the bright red blood present in most arteries that has been oxygenated in lungs or gills **2** : of, relating to, or constituting through-traffic facilities — **ar·te·ri·al·ly** \-ē-ə-lē\ *adv*

²arterial *n* : a through street or arterial highway

ar·te·ri·al·ize \är-ˈtir-ē-ə-ˌlīz\ *vt* **-ized; -iz·ing** : to transform (venous blood) into arterial blood by oxygenation — **ar·te·ri·al·iza·tion** \-ˌtir-ē-ə-lə-ˈzā-shən\ *n*

ar·te·rio·gram \är-ˈtir-ē-ə-ˌgram\ *n* [ISV] : a roentgenogram of an artery made by arteriography

ar·te·ri·og·ra·phy \är-ˌtir-ē-ˈäg-rə-fē\ *n, pl* **-phies** [ISV] : the roentgenographic visualization of an artery after injection of a special substance — **ar·te·rio·graph·ic** \-ē-ə-ˈgraf-ik\ *adj*

ar·te·ri·ole \är-ˈtir-ē-ˌōl\ *n* [F or NL; F *artériole*, prob. fr. NL *arteriola*, dim. of L *arteria*] : one of the small terminal twigs of an artery that ends in capillaries — **ar·te·ri·o·lar** \-ˌtir-ē-ˈō-lär, -lər\ *adj*

ar·te·rio·scle·ro·sis \är-ˌtir-ē-ō-sklə-ˈrō-səs\ *n* [NL] : a chronic disease characterized by abnormal thickening and hardening of the arterial walls — **ar·te·rio·scle·rot·ic** \-ˈrät-ik\ *adj or n*

ar·te·rio·ve·nous \-ˈvē-nəs\ *adj* [ISV] : of, relating to, or connecting the arteries and veins

ar·ter·i·tis \ˌärt-ə-ˈrīt-əs\ *n* [NL] : arterial inflammation

ar·tery \ˈärt-ə-rē\ *n, pl* **-ter·ies** [ME *arterie*, fr. L *arteria*, fr. Gk *artēria*; akin to Gk *aortē* aorta] **1** : one of the tubular branching muscular- and elastic-walled vessels that carry blood from the heart through the body **2** : a channel (as a river or highway) of transportation or communication; *esp* : the principal channel in a branching system

ar·te·sian well \är-ˌtē-zhən-\ *n* [F *artésien*, lit., of Artois, fr. OF, fr. *Arteis* Artois, France] **1** : a well made by boring into the earth until water is reached which from internal pressure flows up like a fountain **2** : a deep-bored well

art film *n* : a motion picture produced as an artistic effort

art form *n* : a recognized form (as a symphony) or medium (as sculpture) of artistic expression

art·ful \ˈärt-fəl\ *adj* **1** : performed with or showing art or skill <an ~ performance on the violin> **2** : ARTIFICIAL <trim walks and ~ bowers —William Wordsworth> **3 a** : using or characterized by art and skill : DEXTEROUS <an ~ prose stylist> **b** : adroit in attaining an end often by insinuating or indirect means : WILY <an ~ cross-examiner> ***syn*** see SLY ***ant*** artless — **art·ful·ly** \-fə-lē\ *adv* — **art·ful·ness** *n*

art glass *n* : articles of glass designed primarily for decorative purposes; *esp* : novelty glassware

art-historical *adj* : of or relating to the history of art <~ method>

art house *n* : ART THEATER

arthr- *or* **arthro-** *comb form* [L, fr. Gk, fr. *arthron*; akin to Gk *arariskein* to fit — more at ARM] : joint <*arthr*algia> <*arthro*pathy>

ar·thral·gia \är-ˈthral-j(ē-)ə\ *n* [NL] : neuralgic pain in one or more joints — **ar·thral·gic** \-jik\ *adj*

ar·thrit·ic \är-ˈthrit-ik\ *adj* **1** : of, relating to, or affected with arthritis **2** : being or showing effects associated with aging <~ anxiety> — **arthritic** *n* — **ar·thrit·i·cal·ly** \-i-k(ə-)lē\ *adv*

ar·thri·tis \är-ˈthrīt-əs\ *n, pl* **-thrit·i·des** \-ˈthrit-ə-ˌdēz\ [L, fr. Gk, fr. *arthron*]: inflammation of joints due to infectious, metabolic, or constitutional causes

ar·throd·e·sis \är-ˈthräd-ə-səs\ *n, pl* **-e·ses** \-ˌsēz\ [NL, fr. *arthr-* + Gk *desis* binding, fr. *dein* to bind]: the surgical immobilization of a joint so that the bones grow solidly together : artificial ankylosis

ar·throp·a·thy \är-ˈthräp-ə-thē\ *n, pl* **-thies** : a disease of a joint

ar·thro·pod \ˈär-thrə-ˌpäd\ *n* [NL *Arthropoda*, group name, fr. *arthr-* + Gk *pod-, pous* foot — more at FOOT] : any of a phylum (Arthropoda) of invertebrate animals (as insects, arachnids, and crustaceans) that have a jointed body and limbs, usu. a chitinous shell molted at intervals, and the brain dorsal to the alimentary canal and connected with a ventral chain of ganglia

Ashan·ti \ə-'shant-ē, -'shänt-\ *n, pl* **Ashanti** *or* **Ashantis** [Ashanti *A*[1]*san*[3]*te*[1]] **1 :** a West African people of Ghana **2 :** the dialect of Akan spoken by the Ashanti people

ash·can \'ash-ˌkan\ *adj, often cap* **:** of or relating to a group of 20th century American painters who depicted city life realistically <~ school>

ash can *n* **1 :** a metal receptacle for refuse **2** *slang* **:** DEPTH CHARGE

1**ash·en** \'ash-ən\ *adj* **:** of, relating to, or made from the wood of the ash tree

2**ashen** *adj* **1 :** consisting of or resembling ashes **2 :** of the color of ashes **3 :** deadly pale **:** BLANCHED <his face was ~ with fear>

Ash·er \'ash-ər\ *n* [Heb *Āshēr*] **:** a son of Jacob and the traditional eponymous ancestor of one of the tribes of Israel

Ash·ke·nazi \ˌash-kə-'naz-ē\ *n, pl* **-naz·im** \-'naz-əm\ [Heb *Ashkĕnāzī*] **:** a member of one of the two great divisions of Jews comprising the eastern European Yiddish-speaking Jews — **Ash·ke·naz·ic** \-'naz-ik\ *adj*

ash·lar \'ash-lər\ *n* [ME *asheler,* fr. MF *aisselier* a traverse beam, fr. OF, fr. *ais* board, fr. L *axis,* alter. of *assis*] **1 :** hewn or squared stone; *also* **:** masonry of such stone **2 :** a thin squared and dressed stone for facing a wall of rubble or brick

ashore \ə-'shō(ə)r, -'shȯ(ə)r\ *adv* **:** on or to the shore

ash·ram \'äsh-rəm\ *n* [Skt *āśrama,* fr. *ā* toward + *śrama* religious exercise] **1 a :** a secluded dwelling of a Hindu sage **b :** the group of disciples instructed there **2 :** a religious retreat

Ash·to·reth \'ash-tə-ˌreth\ *n* [Heb *'Ashtōreth*] **:** ASTARTE

ash·tray \'ash-ˌtrā\ *n* **:** a receptacle for tobacco ashes and for cigar and cigarette butts

Ashur \'ä-ˌshu̇(ə)r\ *n* [Assyrian *Ashūr*] **:** the chief deity of the Assyrian pantheon

Ash Wednesday *n* **:** the first day of Lent

ashy \'ash-ē\ *adj* **ash·i·er; -est 1 :** of or relating to ashes **2 :** deadly pale

ASI *abbr* airspeed indicator

Asian \'ā-zhən, -shən\ *adj* **:** of, relating to, or characteristic of the continent of Asia or its people — **Asian** *n*

Asian influenza *n* **:** influenza caused by a mutant strain of the influenza virus

Asi·at·ic \ˌā-z(h)ē-'at-ik\ *adj* **:** ASIAN — sometimes taken to be offensive — **Asiatic** *n*

Asiatic cholera *n* **:** an acute infectious epidemic cholera of Asiatic origin caused by a bacterium (*Vibrio comma*)

1**aside** \ə-'sīd\ *adv* **1 :** to or toward the side <stepped ~> **2 :** out of the way **:** AWAY **3 :** set to one side <jesting ~>

2**aside** *prep, obs* **:** BEYOND, PAST

3**aside** *n* **1 :** an utterance meant to be inaudible to someone; *esp* **:** an actor's speech heard by the audience but supposedly not by other characters on stage **2 :** a straying from the theme **:** DIGRESSION

aside from *prep* **1 :** in addition to **:** BESIDES **2 :** except for

as if *conj* **1 :** as it would be if <it was *as if* he had lost his last friend> **2 :** as one would do if <he ran *as if* ghosts were chasing him> **3 :** THAT <it seemed *as if* the day would never end>

Asin \'äs-(ˌ)in\ *n* [Hindi *Asin,* fr. Skt *Aśvina*] **:** a month of the Hindu year — see MONTH table

as·i·nine \'as-ᵊn-ˌīn\ *adj* [L *asininus,* fr. *asinus* ass] **1 :** of, relating to, or resembling an ass **2 :** marked by inexcusable failure to exercise intelligence or sound judgment <an ~ excuse> ***syn*** see SIMPLE ***ant*** sensible, judicious — **as·i·nine·ly** *adv* — **as·i·nin·i·ty** \ˌas-ᵊn-'in-ət-ē\ *n*

ask \'ask\ *vb* **asked** \'as(k)t\; **ask·ing** [ME *asken,* fr. OE *āscian;* akin to OHG *eiscōn* to ask, L *aeruscare* to beg] *vt* **1 a :** to call on for an answer **b :** to put a question about **c :** SPEAK, UTTER <~ a question> **2 a :** to make a request of <she *~ed* her teacher for help> **b :** to make a request for <she *~ed* help from her teacher> **3 :** to call for **:** REQUIRE **4 :** to set as a price <*~ed* $3000 for the car> **5 :** INVITE ~ *vi* **1 :** to seek information **2 :** to make a request <*~ed* for food> **3 :** LOOK — often used in the phrase *ask for trouble* — **ask·er** *n*

syn **1** ASK, QUESTION, INTERROGATE, QUERY, INQUIRE *shared meaning element* **:** to address a person in an attempt to elicit information

2 ASK, REQUEST, SOLICIT *shared meaning element* **:** to seek to obtain by making one's wants known

askance \ə-'skan(t)s\ *also* **askant** \-'skant\ *adv* [origin unknown] **1 :** with a side glance **:** OBLIQUELY **2 :** with disapproval or distrust **:** SCORNFULLY

as·ke·sis \ə-'skē-səs\ *var of* ASCESIS

askew \ə-'skyü\ *adv or adj* [prob. fr. *a-* + *skew*] **:** out of line **:** AWRY <the picture hung ~> — **askew·ness** *n*

ASLA *abbr* American Society of Landscape Architects

1**aslant** \ə-'slant\ *adv or adj* **:** in a slanting direction **:** OBLIQUELY

2**aslant** *prep* **:** over or across in a slanting direction

1**asleep** \ə-'slēp\ *adj* **1 :** being in a state of sleep **2 :** DEAD **3 :** lacking sensation **:** NUMB **4 a :** INACTIVE, SLUGGISH **b :** not alert **:** INDIFFERENT

2**asleep** *adv* **1 :** into a state of sleep **2 :** into the sleep of death **3 :** into a state of inactivity, sluggishness, or indifference

as long as *conj* **1 :** provided that <can do as they like *as long as* they have a B average> **2 :** inasmuch as **:** SINCE <*as long as* you're going, I'll go too>

aslope \ə-'slōp\ *adj or adv* **:** being in a sloping or slanting position or direction

ASME *abbr* American Society of Mechanical Engineers

aso·cial \(ˈ)ā-'sō-shəl\ *adj* **:** not social: as **a :** rejecting or lacking the capacity for social interaction <an ~ or reclusive attitude — A. T. Weaver> **b :** ANTISOCIAL ***syn*** see UNSOCIAL ***ant*** social

as of *prep* **:** ON, AT, FROM <takes effect *as of* July 1>

1**asp** \'asp\ *n* [ME] **:** ASPEN

2**asp** *n* [ME *aspis,* fr. L, fr. Gk] **:** a small venomous snake of Egypt variously identified as the cerastes or a small African cobra (*Naja haje*)

as·par·a·gine \ə-'spar-ə-ˌjēn\ *n* [F, fr. L *asparagus*] **:** a white crystalline amino acid $C_4H_8N_2O_3$ that is an amide of aspartic acid and serves as a storage depot for amino groups in many plants

as·par·a·gus \ə-'spar-ə-gəs\ *n* [NL, genus name, fr. L, asparagus plant, fr. Gk *asparagos;* akin to Gk *spargan* to swell — more at SPARK] **:** any of a genus (*Asparagus*) of Old World perennial plants of the lily family having much-branched stems, minute scalelike leaves, and linear cladophylls; *esp* **:** one (*A. officinalis*) widely cultivated for its edible young shoots

as·par·tate \ə-'spär-ˌtāt\ *n* **:** a salt or ester of aspartic acid

as·par·tic acid \ə-ˌspärt-ik-\ *n* [ISV, irreg. fr. L *asparagus*] **:** a crystalline amino acid $C_4H_7NO_4$ found esp. in plants

as·par·to·ki·nase \ə-ˌspärt-ō-'kī-ˌnās, -ˌnāz\ *n* [*aspartic* acid + *-o-* + *kinase*] **:** an enzyme that catalyzes the phosphorylation of aspartic acid by ATP

as·pect \'as-ˌpekt\ *n* [ME, fr. L *aspectus,* fr. *aspectus,* pp. of *aspicere* to look at, fr. *ad-* + *specere* to look — more at SPY] **1 a :** the position of planets or stars with respect to one another held by astrologers to influence human affairs; *also* **:** the apparent position (as conjunction) of a body in the solar system with respect to the sun **b :** a position facing a particular direction **:** EXPOSURE **c :** the manner of presentation of a plane to a fluid through which it is moving or to a current **2 a** (1) **:** appearance to the eye or mind (2) **:** a particular appearance of countenance: MIEN <a man surly in ~> **b :** a particular status or phase in which something appears or may be regarded <studied every ~ of the question> **3** *archaic* **:** an act of looking **:** GAZE **4 a :** the nature of the action of a verb as to its beginning, duration, completion, or repetition and without reference to its position in time **b :** a set of inflected verb forms that indicate aspect ***syn*** see PHASE — **as·pec·tu·al** \a-'spek-chə(-wə)l\ *adj*

aspect ratio *n* **:** a ratio of one dimension to another: as **a :** the ratio or span to mean chord of an airfoil **b :** the ratio of the width of a television or motion-picture image to its height

as·pen \'as-pən\ *n* [alter of ME *asp,* fr. OE *æspe;* akin to OHG *aspa* aspen, Latvian *apsa*] **:** any of several poplars (esp. *Populus tremula* of Europe and *P. tremuloides* and *P. grandidentata* of No. America) with leaves that flutter in the lightest wind because of their flattened petioles — **aspen** *adj*

as·per·ges \ə-'spər-(ˌ)jēz\ *n* [L, thou wilt sprinkle, fr. *aspergere*] **:** a ceremony of sprinkling altar, clergy, and people with holy water

as·per·gil·lo·sis \ˌas-pər-(ˌ)jil-'ō-səs\ *n, pl* **-lo·ses** \-ˌsēz\ **:** infection with or disease caused (as in poultry) by molds (genus *Aspergillus*)

as·per·gil·lum \ˌas-pər-'jil-əm\ *n, pl* **-la** \-ə\ *or* **-lums** [NL, fr. L *aspergere*] **:** a brush or small perforated container with a handle that is used for sprinkling holy water in a liturgical service

as·per·gil·lus \-'jil-əs\ *n, pl* **-gil·li** \-'jil-ˌī\ [NL, genus name, fr. *aspergillum*] **:** any of a genus (*Aspergillus*) of ascomycetous fungi with branched radiate sporophores including many common molds

as·per·i·ty \a-'sper-ət-ē, ə-\ *n, pl* **-ties** [ME *asprete,* fr. OF *aspreté,* fr. *aspre* rough, fr. L *asper*] **1 :** RIGOR, SEVERITY **2 a :** roughness of surface **:** UNEVENNESS **b :** roughness of sound **3 :** roughness of manner or of temper **:** HARSHNESS ***syn*** see ACRIMONY ***ant*** amenity

as·perse \ə-'spərs, a-\ *vt* **as·persed; as·pers·ing** [L *aspersus,* pp. of *aspergere,* fr. *ad-* + *spargere* to scatter — more at SPARK] **1 :** SPRINKLE; *esp* **:** to sprinkle with holy water **2 :** to attack with evil reports or false or injurious charges ***syn*** see MALIGN

as·per·sion \ə-'spər-zhən, -shən\ *n* **1 :** a sprinkling with water esp. in religious ceremonies **2 a :** the act of calumniating **:** DEFAMATION **b :** a calumnious expression <he cast *~s* on her integrity> ***syn*** see ANIMADVERSION

as·phalt \'as-ˌfȯlt\ *or* **as·phal·tum** \as-'fȯl-təm\ *n* [ME *aspalt,* fr. LL *aspaltus,* fr. Gk *asphaltos*] **1 :** a brown to black bituminous substance that is found in natural beds and is also obtained as a residue in petroleum or coal-tar refining and that consists chiefly of hydrocarbons **2 :** an asphaltic composition used for pavements and as a waterproof cement — **as·phal·tic** \as-'fȯl-tik\ *adj*

as·phalt·ite \'as-ˌfȯl-ˌtīt\ *n* **:** a native asphalt occurring in vein deposits below the surface of the ground

asphalt jungle *n* **:** a big city or a specified part of a big city

aspher·ic \(ˈ)ā-'sfi(ə)r-ik, -'sfer-\ *or* **aspher·i·cal** \-i-kəl\ *adj* **1 :** departing slightly from the spherical form <~ optical surface> **2 :** free from spherical aberration <an ~ lens>

as·pho·del \'as-fə-ˌdel\ *n* [L *asphodelus,* fr. Gk *asphodelos*] **:** any of various Old World usu. perennial herbs (esp. genera *Asphodelus* and *Asphodeline*) of the lily family with flowers in long erect racemes

as·phyx·ia \as-'fik-sē-ə, əs-\ *n* [NL, fr. Gk, stopping of the pulse, fr. *a-* + *sphyzein* to throb] **:** a lack of oxygen or excess of carbon dioxide in the body that is usu. caused by interruption of breathing and that causes unconsciousness

as·phyx·i·ate \-sē-ˌāt\ *vb* **-at·ed; -at·ing** *vt* **:** to cause asphyxia in; *also* **:** to kill or make unconscious through want of adequate oxygen, presence of noxious agents, or other obstruction to normal breathing ~ *vi* **:** to become asphyxiated — **as·phyx·i·a·tion** \-ˌfik-sē-'ā-shən\ *n* — **as·phyx·i·a·tor** \-'fik-sē-ˌāt-ər\ *n*

1**as·pic** \'as-pik\ *n* [MF, alter. of *aspe,* fr. L *aspis*] *obs* **:** 2ASP

2**aspic** *n* [F, lit., asp] **:** a savory jelly (as of fish or meat stock) used cold to garnish meat or fish or to make a mold of meat, fish, or vegetables

as·pi·dis·tra \ˌas-pə-'dis-trə\ *n* [NL, irreg. fr. Gk *aspid-, aspis* shield] **:** an Asiatic plant (*Aspidistra lurida*) of the lily family that has large basal leaves and is often grown as a foliage plant

1**as·pi·rant** \'as-p(ə-)rənt, ə-'spī-rənt\ *n* **:** one who aspires <presidential *~s*>

2**aspirant** *adj* **:** seeking to attain a desired position or status

1**as·pi·rate** \'as-pə-ˌrāt\ *vt* **-rat·ed; -rat·ing** [L *aspiratus,* pp. of *aspirare*] **1 :** to pronounce (a vowel, a consonant, or a word) with an accompanying *h*-sound **2 a :** to draw by suction **b :** to remove (as blood) by aspiration

2**as·pi·rate** \'as-p(ə-)rət\ *n* **1 :** an independent sound \h\ or a character (as the letter *h*) representing it **2 :** a consonant having

aspiration as its final component <in English the *p* of *pit* represents an ~> **3 :** material removed by aspiration
as·pi·ra·tion \ˌas-pə-ˈrā-shən\ *n* **1 :** the pronunciation or addition of an aspirate; *also* **:** the aspirate or its symbol **2 :** a drawing of something in, out, up, or through by or as if by suction: as **a :** the act of breathing and esp. of breathing in **b :** the withdrawal of fluid from the body **c :** the taking of foreign matter into the lungs with the respiratory current **3 a :** a strong desire to achieve something high or great **b :** an object of such desire ***syn*** see AMBITION
as·pi·ra·tor \ˈas-pə-ˌrāt-ər\ *n* **:** an apparatus for producing suction or moving or collecting materials by suction; *esp* **:** a hollow tubular instrument connected with a partial vacuum and used to remove fluid or tissue or foreign bodies from the body
as·pire \ə-ˈspī(ə)r\ *vi* **as·pired; as·pir·ing** [ME *aspiren,* fr. MF or L; MF *aspirer,* fr. L *aspirare,* lit., to breathe upon, fr. *ad-* + *spirare* to breathe — more at SPIRIT] **1 :** to seek to attain or accomplish a particular goal <*aspired* to a career in medicine> **2 :** ASCEND, SOAR — **as·pir·er** *n*
as·pi·rin \ˈas-p(ə-)rən\ *n, pl* **aspirin** *or* **aspirins** [ISV, fr. *a*cetyl + *spir*aeic acid (former name of salicylic acid), fr. NL *Spiraea,* genus of shrubs — more at SPIREA] **1 :** a white crystalline derivative $C_9H_8O_4$ of salicylic acid used for relief of pain and fever **2 :** a tablet of aspirin
ASR *abbr* **1** airport surveillance radar **2** air-sea rescue
as regards *or* **as respects** *prep* **:** in regard to **:** with respect to
¹ass \ˈas\ *n* [ME, fr. OE *assa,* perh. fr. OIr *asan,* fr. L *asinus*] **1 :** any of several hardy gregarious mammals (genus *Equus*) that are smaller than the horse, have long ears, and include the donkey **2 :** a stupid, obstinate, or perverse person

asses 1

²ass \ˈas\ *or* **arse** \ˈas, ˈärs\ *n* [ME *ars, ers,* fr. OE *ærs, ears;* akin to OHG & ON *ars* buttocks, Gk *orrhos,* Arm *or,* Hitt *arraš,* OIr *err* tail] **1 a :** BUTTOCKS — often considered vulgar **b :** ANUS — often considered vulgar **2 :** sexual intercourse — usu. considered vulgar
as·sa·fet·i·da *or* **as·sa·foe·ti·da** *var of* ASAFETIDA
as·sai \ä-ˈsī\ *adv* [It, fr. (assumed) VL *ad satis* enough — more at ASSET] **:** VERY — used with tempo direction in music <allegro ~>
as·sail \ə-ˈsā(ə)l\ *vt* [ME *assailen,* fr. OF *asaillir,* fr. (assumed) VL *assalire,* alter. of L *assilire* to leap upon, fr. *ad-* + *salire* to leap — more at SALLY] **:** to attack violently with blows or words ***syn*** see ATTACK — **as·sail·able** \-ˈsā-lə-bəl\ *adj* — **as·sail·ant** \-ˈsā-lənt\ *n*
As·sam·ese \ˌas-ə-ˈmēz, -ˈmēs\ *n, pl* **Assamese 1 :** a native or inhabitant of Assam, India **2 :** the Indic language of Assam
as·sas·sin \ə-ˈsas-ᵊn\ *n* [ML *assassinus,* fr. Ar *ḥashshāshīn,* pl. of *ḥashshāsh* one addicted to hashish] **1** *cap* **:** one of a secret order of Muslims that at the time of the Crusades terrorized Christians and other enemies by secret murder committed under the influence of hashish **2 :** MURDERER; *esp* **:** one that murders a politically important person either for hire or from fanatical motives
as·sas·si·nate \ə-ˈsas-ᵊn-ˌāt\ *vt* **-nat·ed; -nat·ing 1 :** to murder by sudden or secret attack usu. for impersonal reasons <~ a senator> <arranged to have his estranged wife *assassinated*> **2 :** to injure or destroy unexpectedly and treacherously ***syn*** see KILL — **as·sas·si·na·tion** \-ˌsas-ᵊn-ˈā-shən\ *n* — **as·sas·si·na·tor** \-ˈsas-ᵊn-ˌāt-ər\ *n*
assassin bug *n* **:** any of a family (Reduviidae) of bugs that are usu. predatory on insects though some suck the blood of mammals **:** CONENOSE
¹as·sault \ə-ˈsȯlt\ *n* [ME *assaut,* fr. OF, fr. (assumed) VL *assaltus,* fr. *assaltus,* pp. of *assalire*] **1 :** a violent physical or verbal attack **2 a :** an apparently violent attempt or a willful offer with force or violence to do hurt to another without the actual doing of the hurt threatened (as by lifting the fist in a threatening manner) — compare BATTERY 1b **b :** RAPE
²assault *vt* **1 :** to make an assault on **2 :** RAPE ~ *vi* **:** to make an assault ***syn*** see ATTACK — **as·sault·er** *n* — **as·saul·tive** \-ˈsȯl-tiv\ *adj* — **as·saul·tive·ly** *adv* — **as·saul·tive·ness** *n*
assault boat *n* **:** a small portable boat used in an amphibious military attack or in land warfare for crossing rivers or lakes
¹as·say \ˈas-ˌā, a-ˈsā\ *n* [ME, fr. OF *essai, assai* test, effort — more at ESSAY] **1** *archaic* **:** TRIAL, ATTEMPT **2 :** examination and determination as to characteristics (as weight, measure, or quality) **3 :** analysis (as of an ore or drug) to determine the presence, absence, or quantity of one or more components **4 :** a substance to be assayed; *also* **:** the tabulated result of assaying
²as·say \a-ˈsā, ˈas-ˌā\ *vt* **1 :** TRY, ATTEMPT **2 a :** to analyze (as an ore) for one or more valuable components **b :** to judge the worth of **:** ESTIMATE ~ *vi* **:** to prove up in an assay — **as·say·er** *n*
as·se·gai *or* **as·sa·gai** \ˈas-i-ˌgī\ *n* [deriv. of Ar *az-zaghāya* the assegai, fr. *al-* the + *zaghāya* assegai] **:** a slender hardwood spear or light javelin usu. tipped with iron and used in southern Africa
as·sem·blage \ə-ˈsem-blij, *for 3 also* ˌas-ˌäm-ˈbläzh\ *n* **1 :** a collection of persons or things **:** GATHERING **2 :** the act of assembling **:** the state of being assembled **3 a :** an artistic composition made from scraps, junk, and odds and ends (as of paper, cloth, wood, stone, or metal) **b :** the art of making assemblages
as·sem·blag·ist \-blij-əst, -ˈbläzh-əst\ *n* **:** an artist who specializes in assemblages
as·sem·ble \ə-ˈsem-bəl\ *vb* **as·sem·bled; as·sem·bling** \-b(ə-)liŋ\ [ME *assemblen,* fr. OF *assembler,* fr. (assumed) VL *assimulare,* fr. L *ad-* + *simul* together — more at SAME] *vt* **1 :** to bring together (as in a particular place or for a particular purpose) **2 :** to fit together the parts of ~ *vi* **:** to meet together **:** CONVENE ***syn*** see GATHER
as·sem·bler \-b(ə-)lər\ *n* **1 :** one that assembles **2 :** a computer program that automatically converts instructions written in a symbolic code into the equivalent machine code
as·sem·bly \ə-ˈsem-blē\ *n, pl* **-blies** [ME *assemblee,* fr. MF, fr. OF, fr. *assembler*] **1 :** a company of persons gathered for deliberation and legislation, worship, or entertainment **2** *cap* **:** a legislative body; *specif* **:** the lower house of a legislature **3 :** ASSEMBLAGE 1, 2 **4 :** a signal given by drum, bugle, trumpet, or all field music for troops to assemble or fall in **5 a :** the fitting together of manufactured parts into a complete machine, structure, or unit of a machine **b :** a collection of parts so assembled **6 :** the translation of symbolic code to machine code by an assembler
assembly language *n* **:** a symbolic language for programming a computer that is a close approximation of machine language
assembly line *n* **1 :** an arrangement of machines, equipment, and workers in which work passes from operation to operation in direct line until the product is assembled **2 :** a process for turning out a finished product in a mechanically efficient manner <academic *assembly lines*>
as·sem·bly·man \ə-ˈsem-blē-mən\ *n* **:** a member of an assembly
Assembly of God : a congregation belonging to a Pentecostal body founded in the U.S. in 1914
as·sem·bly·wom·an \-ˌwu̇m-ən\ *n* **:** a female member of an assembly
¹as·sent \ə-ˈsent\ *vi* [ME *assenten,* fr. OF *assenter,* fr. L *assentari,* fr. *assentire,* fr. *ad-* + *sentire* to feel — more at SENSE] **:** to agree to something esp. after thoughtful consideration **:** CONCUR — **as·sen·tor** *or* **as·sent·er** \-ˈsent-ər\ *n*
syn ASSENT, CONSENT, ACCEDE, ACQUIESCE, AGREE, SUBSCRIBE *shared meaning element* **:** to concur with what has been proposed ***ant*** dissent
²assent *n* **:** an act of assenting **:** ACQUIESCENCE, AGREEMENT
as·sen·ta·tion \ˌas-ᵊn-ˈtā-shən, ˌas-ˌen-\ *n* **:** ready assent esp. when insincere or obsequious
as·sert \ə-ˈsərt\ *vt* [L *assertus,* pp. of *asserere,* fr. *ad-* + *serere* to join — more at SERIES] **1 :** to state or declare positively and often forcefully or aggressively **2 a :** to demonstrate the existence of <~ his manhood —James Joyce> **b :** POSIT, POSTULATE
syn* 1** ASSERT, DECLARE, AFFIRM, PROTEST, AVOW *shared meaning element* **:** to state or put forward positively usu. in anticipation of or in the face of denial or objection ***ant deny, controvert
2 see MAINTAIN
— **assert oneself :** to compel recognition esp. of one's rights
as·ser·tion \ə-ˈsər-shən\ *n* **:** the act of asserting; *also* **:** DECLARATION, AFFIRMATION
as·ser·tive \ə-ˈsərt-iv\ *adj* **:** disposed to or characterized by bold or confident assertion ***syn*** see AGGRESSIVE ***ant*** retiring, acquiescent — **as·ser·tive·ly** *adv* — **as·ser·tive·ness** *n*
asses *pl of* AS *or of* ASS
as·sess \ə-ˈses\ *vt* [ME *assessen,* prob. fr. ML *assessus,* pp. of *assidēre,* fr. L, to sit beside, assist in the office of a judge — more at ASSIZE] **1 :** to determine the rate or amount of (as a tax) **2 a :** to impose (as a tax) according to an established rate **b :** to subject to a tax, charge, or levy **3 :** to make an official valuation of (property) for the purposes of taxation **4 :** to determine the importance, size, or value of ***syn*** see ESTIMATE — **as·sess·able** \-ˈses-ə-bəl\ *adj*
as·sess·ment \ə-ˈses-mənt\ *n* **1 :** the act or an instance of assessing **:** APPRAISAL **2 :** the amount assessed
as·ses·sor \ə-ˈses-ər\ *n* **1 :** an official who assists a judge or magistrate **2 :** an official who assesses property for taxation
as·set \ˈas-ˌet\ *n* [back-formation fr. *assets,* sing., sufficient property to pay debts and legacies, fr. AF *asetz,* fr. OF *assez* enough, fr. (assumed) VL *ad satis,* fr. L *ad* to + *satis* enough — more at AT, SAD] **1** *pl* **a :** the property of a deceased person subject by law to the payment of his debts and legacies **b :** the entire property of all sorts of a person, association, corporation, or estate applicable or subject to the payment of his or its debts **2 :** ADVANTAGE, RESOURCE <his wit is his chief ~> **3** *pl* **:** the items on a balance sheet showing the book value of property owned
as·sev·er·ate \ə-ˈsev-ə-ˌrāt\ *vt* **-at·ed; -at·ing** [L *asseveratus,* pp. of *asseverare,* fr. *ad-* + *severus* severe] **:** to affirm or aver positively or earnestly — **as·sev·er·a·tion** \-ˌsev-ə-ˈrā-shən\ *n* — **as·sev·er·a·tive** \-ˈsev-ə-ˌrāt-iv\ *adj*
as·si·du·ity \ˌas-ə-ˈd(y)ü-ət-ē\ *n, pl* **-ities 1 :** the quality or state of being assiduous **:** DILIGENCE **2 :** solicitous or obsequious attention to a person
as·sid·u·ous \ə-ˈsij-(ə-)wəs\ *adj* [L *assiduus,* fr. *assidēre*] **:** marked by careful unremitting attention or persistent application <~ patrons of the opera> ***syn*** see BUSY ***ant*** desultory — **as·sid·u·ous·ly** *adv* — **as·sid·u·ous·ness** *n*
¹as·sign \ə-ˈsīn\ *vt* [ME *assignen,* fr. OF *assigner,* fr. L *assignare,* fr. *ad-* + *signare* to mark, fr. *signum* mark, sign] **1 :** to transfer (property) to another esp. in trust or for the benefit of creditors **2 a :** to appoint to a post or duty **b :** PRESCRIBE <~ the lesson> **3 :** to fix authoritatively **:** SPECIFY <~ a limit> **4 :** to ascribe with assurance esp. as motive or reason ***syn*** see ALLOT, ASCRIBE — **as·sign·abil·i·ty** \-ˌsī-nə-ˈbil-ət-ē\ *n* — **as·sign·able** \-ˈsī-nə-bəl\ *adj* — **as·sign·er** \ə-ˈsī-nər\ *or* **as·sign·or** \ˌas-ə-ˈnȯ(ə)r, ˌas-ˌī-, ə-ˌsī-\ *n*
²assign *n* **:** ASSIGNEE
as·si·gnat \ˌas-(ˌ)ēn-ˈyä, ˈas-ig-ˌnat\ *n* [F, fr. L *assignatus,* pp. of *assignare*] **:** a bill issued as currency by the French Revolutionary government (1790–95) on the security of expropriated lands
as·sig·na·tion \ˌas-ig-ˈnā-shən\ *n* **1 :** the act of assigning or the assignment made; *esp* **:** ALLOTMENT **2 :** TRYST <returned from an

ə abut ᵊ kitten ər further a back ā bake ä cot, cart
au̇ out ch chin e less ē easy g gift i trip ī life
j joke ŋ sing ō flow ȯ flaw ȯi coin th thin th this
ü loot u̇ foot y yet yü few yu̇ furious zh vision

~ with his mistress —W. B. Yeats> — **as·sig·na·tion·al** \-shnəl, -shən-ᵊl\ *adj*

assigned risk *n* **:** a poor risk (as an accident-prone motorist) that insurance companies would normally reject but are forced to insure by state law

as·sign·ee \ˌas-ə-ˈnē, ˌas-ˌī-, ə-ˌsī-\ *n* **1 :** a person to whom an assignment is made **2 :** a person appointed to act for another **3 :** a person to whom a right or property is legally transferred

as·sign·ment \ə-ˈsīn-mənt\ *n* **1 :** the act of assigning **2 a :** a position, post, or office to which one is assigned **b :** a specified task or amount of work assigned or undertaken as if assigned by authority **3 :** the transfer of property; *esp* **:** the transfer of property to be held in trust or to be used for the benefit of creditors ***syn*** see TASK

as·sim·i·la·ble \ə-ˈsim-ə-lə-bəl\ *adj* **:** capable of being assimilated — **as·sim·i·la·bil·i·ty** \-ˌsim-ə-lə-ˈbil-ət-ē\ *n*

[1]as·sim·i·late \ə-ˈsim-ə-ˌlāt\ *vb* **-lat·ed; -lat·ing** [ML *assimilatus,* pp. of *assimilare,* fr. L *assimulare* to make similar, fr. *ad-* + *simulare* to make similar, simulate] *vt* **1 a :** to take in and appropriate as nourishment **:** absorb into the system **b :** to take into the mind and thoroughly comprehend **2 a :** to make similar **b :** to alter by assimilation **c :** to absorb into the cultural tradition of a population or group <the community *assimilated* many immigrants> **3 :** COMPARE, LIKEN ~ *vi* **:** to become assimilated ***syn*** see ABSORB — **as·sim·i·la·tor** \-ˌlāt-ər\ *n*

[2]as·sim·i·late \-lət, -ˌlāt\ *n* **:** something that is assimilated

as·sim·i·la·tion \ə-ˌsim-ə-ˈlā-shən\ *n* **1 a :** an act, process, or instance of assimilating **b :** the state of being assimilated **2 :** the incorporation or conversion of nutrients into protoplasm that in animals follows digestion and absorption and in higher plants involves both photosynthesis and root absorption **3 :** adaptation of a sound to an adjacent sound <in the word *cupboard* the \p\ sound of the word *cup* has undergone complete ~> ***syn*** see RECOGNITION

as·sim·i·la·tion·ism \-shə-ˌniz-əm\ *n* **:** a policy of assimilating differing racial or cultural groups — **as·sim·i·la·tion·ist** \-sh(ə-)nəst\ *n or adj*

as·sim·i·la·tive \ə-ˈsim-ə-ˌlāt-iv, -lət-\ *adj* **:** of, relating to, or causing assimilation

as·sim·i·la·to·ry \ə-ˈsim-ə-lə-ˌtōr-ē, -ˌtȯr-\ *adj* **:** ASSIMILATIVE

[1]as·sist \ə-ˈsist\ *vb* [MF or L; MF *assister* to help, stand by, fr. L *assistere,* fr. *ad-* + *sistere* to cause to stand; akin to L *stare* to stand — more at STAND] *vi* **1 :** to give support or aid **2 :** to be present as a spectator ~ *vt* **:** to give usu. supplementary support or aid to <~ a lame man up the stairs> ***syn*** see HELP ***ant*** hamper, impede

[2]assist *n* **1 :** an act of assistance **:** AID **2 :** the action of a player who by passing a ball or puck enables a teammate to make a putout or score a goal **3 :** a mechanical device that provides assistance

as·sis·tance \ə-ˈsis-tən(t)s\ *n* **:** the act of assisting or the help supplied **:** AID <financial and technical ~>

as·sis·tant \-tənt\ *n* **:** one who assists **:** HELPER; *also* **:** an auxiliary device or substance — **assistant** *adj*

assistant professor *n* **:** a member of a college or university faculty who ranks above an instructor and below an associate professor — **assistant professorship** *n*

as·sis·tant·ship \ə-ˈsis-tən(t)-ˌship\ *n* **:** an appointment awarded on an annual basis to a qualified graduate student that requires part-time teaching, research, or residence hall duties and carries a stipend

as·size \ə-ˈsīz\ *n* [ME *assise,* fr. OF, session, settlement, fr. *asseoir* to seat, fr. (assumed) VL *assedēre,* fr. L *assidēre* to sit beside, assist in the office of a judge, fr. *ad-* + *sedēre* to sit — more at SIT] **1 :** an enactment made by a legislative assembly **:** ORDINANCE **2 a :** a statute regulating weights and measures of articles sold in the market **b :** the regulation of the price of bread or ale by the price of grain **3 :** a fixed or customary standard **4 a :** a judicial inquest **b :** an action to be decided by such an inquest, the writ for instituting it, or the verdict or finding rendered by the jury **5 a :** the periodical sessions of the superior courts in English counties for trial of civil and criminal cases — usu. used in pl. **b :** the time or place of holding such a court, the court itself, or a session of it — usu. used in pl.

assn *abbr* association

assoc *also* **asso** *abbr* **1** associate **2** association

as·so·cia·ble \ə-ˈsō-sh(ē-)ə-bəl, -sē-ə-\ *adj* **:** capable of being associated, joined, or connected in thought

[1]as·so·ci·ate \ə-ˈsō-s(h)ē-ˌāt\ *vb* **-at·ed; -at·ing** [ME *associat* associated, fr. L *associatus,* pp. of *associare* to unite, fr. *ad-* + *sociare* to join, fr. *socius* companion — more at SOCIAL] *vt* **1 :** to join as a partner, friend, or companion **2** *obs* **:** to keep company with **:** ATTEND **3 :** to join or connect together **:** COMBINE; *specif* **:** to subject to chemical association **4 :** to bring together in any of various ways (as in memory or imagination) ~ *vi* **1 :** to come together as partners, friends, or companions **2 :** to combine or join with other parts **:** UNITE ***syn*** see JOIN

[2]as·so·ci·ate \ə-ˈsō-s(h)ē-ət, -shət-, -s(h)ē-ˌāt\ *adj* **1 :** closely connected (as in function or office) with another **2 :** closely related esp. in the mind **3 :** having secondary or subordinate status <~ membership in a society>

[3]as·so·ciate *like* [2]\ *n* **1 :** a fellow worker **:** PARTNER, COLLEAGUE **2 :** COMPANION, COMRADE **3** *often cap* **:** a degree conferred esp. by a junior college <~ in arts> — **as·so·ciate·ship** \-ˌship\ *n*

associate professor *n* **:** a member of a college or university faculty who ranks above an assistant professor and below a professor — **associate professorship** *n*

as·so·ci·a·tion \ə-ˌsō-sē-ˈā-shən, -shē-\ *n* **1 a :** the act of associating **b :** the state of being associated **:** PARTNERSHIP, COMBINATION **2 :** an organization of persons having a common interest **:** SOCIETY **3 :** something linked in memory or imagination with a thing or person **4 :** the process of forming mental connections or bonds between sensations, ideas, or memories **5 :** the formation of polymers by linkage through hydrogen bonds or of loosely bound chemical complexes **6 :** a major unit in ecological community organization characterized by essential uniformity and usu. by two or more dominant species — **as·so·ci·a·tion·al** \-shnəl, -shən-ᵊl\ *adj*

association football *n* **:** SOCCER

as·so·cia·tive \ə-ˈsō-s(h)ē-ˌāt-iv, -shət-iv\ *adj* **1 :** of or relating to association esp. of ideas or images **2 :** dependent on or acquired by association or learning **3 :** combining elements such that when the order of the elements is preserved the result is independent of the grouping <addition is ~ since (a + b) + c = a + (b + c)> — **as·so·cia·tive·ly** *adv* — **as·so·cia·tiv·i·ty** \-ˌsō-s(h)ē-ə-ˈtiv-ət-ē, -shə-ˈtiv-\ *n*

as·soil \ə-ˈsȯi(ə)l\ *vt* [ME *assoilen,* fr. OF *assoldre,* fr. L *absolvere* to absolve] **1** *archaic* **:** ABSOLVE, PARDON **2** *archaic* **:** ACQUIT, CLEAR **3** *archaic* **:** EXPIATE — **as·soil·ment** \-mənt\ *n, archaic*

as·so·nance \ˈas-ə-nən(t)s\ *n* [F, fr. L *assonare* to answer with the same sound, fr. *ad-* + *sonare* to sound — more at SOUND] **1 :** resemblance of sound in words or syllables **2 a :** relatively close juxtaposition of similar sounds esp. of vowels **b :** repetition of vowels without repetition of consonants (as in *stony* and *holy*) used as an alternative to rhyme in verse — **as·so·nant** \-nənt\ *adj or n*

as soon as *conj* **:** immediately at or just after the time that

as·sort \ə-ˈsȯ(ə)rt\ *vb* [MF *assortir,* fr. *a-* (fr. L *ad-*) + *sorte* sort] *vt* **1 :** to distribute into groups of a like kind **:** CLASSIFY **2 :** to supply with an assortment or variety (as of goods) ~ *vi* **1 :** to agree in kind **:** HARMONIZE **2 :** to keep company **:** ASSOCIATE — **as·sor·ta·tive** \-ˈsȯrt-ət-iv\ *adj* — **as·sort·er** *n*

as·sort·ed \-ˈsȯrt-əd\ *adj* **1 :** consisting of various kinds **2 :** suited by nature, character, or design **:** MATCHED <an ill-*assorted* pair>

as·sort·ment \-ˈsȯ(ə)rt-mənt\ *n* **1 a :** the act of assorting **b :** the state of being assorted **2 :** a collection of assorted things or persons

ASSR *abbr* Autonomous Soviet Socialist Republic

asst *abbr* assistant

asstd *abbr* **1** assented **2** assorted

as·suage \ə-ˈswāj\ *vt* **as·suaged; as·suag·ing** [ME *aswagen,* fr. OF *assouagier,* fr. (assumed) VL *assuaviare,* fr. L *ad-* + *suavis* sweet — more at SWEET] **1 :** to lessen the intensity of (something that pains or distresses) **:** EASE **2 :** PACIFY, QUIET **3 :** to put an end to by satisfying **:** APPEASE, QUENCH <he *assuaged* his hunger with a sandwich> ***syn*** see RELIEVE ***ant*** exacerbate, intensify — **as·suage·ment** \-ˈswāj-mənt\ *n*

as·sua·sive \ə-ˈswā-siv, -ziv\ *adj* **:** having a pleasantly soothing quality or effect **:** CALMING

as·sume \ə-ˈsüm\ *vt* **as·sumed; as·sum·ing** [ME *assumen,* fr. L *assumere,* fr. *ad-* + *sumere* to take — more at CONSUME] **1 a :** to take up or in **:** RECEIVE **b :** to take into partnership, employment, or use **2 a :** to take to or upon oneself **:** UNDERTAKE **b :** to put on (clothing) **:** DON **3 :** SEIZE, USURP **4 :** to pretend to have or be **:** FEIGN <*assumed* an air of confidence in spite of her dismay> **5 :** to take as granted or true **:** SUPPOSE **6 :** to take over (the debts of another) as one's own — **as·sum·abil·i·ty** \-ˌsü-mə-ˈbil-ət-ē\ *n* — **as·sum·able** \-ˈsü-mə-bəl\ *adj* — **as·sum·ably** \-blē\ *adv*

syn ASSUME, AFFECT, PRETEND, SIMULATE, FEIGN, COUNTERFEIT, SHAM *shared meaning element* **:** to put on a false or deceptive appearance

as·sum·ing *adj* **:** PRETENTIOUS, PRESUMPTUOUS

as·sump·sit \ə-ˈsəm(p)-sət\ *n* [NL, he undertook, fr. *assumere* to undertake, fr. L] **1 a :** a common-law action alleging damage from a breach of agreement **b :** an action to recover damages for breach of contract or promise **2 :** a promise or contract not under seal on which an action of assumpsit may be brought

as·sump·tion \ə-ˈsəm(p)-shən\ *n* [ME, fr. LL *assumption-, assumptio,* fr. L, taking up, fr. *assumptus,* pp. of *assumere*] **1 a :** the taking up of a person into heaven **b** *cap* **:** August 15 observed in commemoration of the Assumption of the Virgin Mary **2 :** a taking to or upon oneself <a delay in the ~ of his new position> **3 :** the act of laying claim to or taking possession of <the ~ of power> **4 :** ARROGANCE, PRETENSION **5 a :** the supposition that something is true **b :** a fact or statement (as a proposition, axiom, postulate, or notion) taken for granted **6 :** the taking over of another's debts

as·sump·tive \ə-ˈsəm(p)-tiv\ *adj* **1 :** taken as one's own **2 :** taken for granted <~ beliefs> **3 :** making undue claims **:** ASSUMING <an ~ person>

as·sur·ance \ə-ˈshu̇r-ən(t)s\ *n* **1 :** the act or action of assuring: as **a :** PLEDGE, GUARANTEE **b :** the act of conveying real property; *also* **:** the instrument by which it is conveyed **c** *chiefly Brit* **:** INSURANCE **2 :** the state of being assured: as **a :** a being sure and safe **:** SECURITY **b :** a being certain in the mind **:** freedom from doubt <the puritan's ~ of salvation> **c :** confidence of mind or manner **:** easy freedom from self-doubt or uncertainty; *also* **:** excessive self-confidence **:** BRASHNESS, PRESUMPTION **3 :** something that inspires or tends to inspire confidence <gave repeated ~*s* of his goodwill> ***syn*** **1** see CERTAINTY ***ant*** mistrust, dubiousness **2** see CONFIDENCE ***ant*** diffidence

as·sure \ə-ˈshu̇(ə)r\ *vt* **as·sured; as·sur·ing** [ME *assuren,* fr. MF *assurer,* fr. ML *assecurare,* fr. L *ad-* + *securus* secure] **1 :** to make safe (as from risks or against overthrow) **:** INSURE **2 :** to give confidence to **:** REASSURE **3 :** to make sure or certain **:** CONVINCE **4 :** to inform positively <*assured* her of his fidelity> **5 :** to make certain the coming or attainment of **:** GUARANTEE <worked hard to ~ accuracy> ***syn*** see ENSURE

[1]as·sured \ə-ˈshu̇(ə)rd\ *adj* **1 :** characterized by certainty or security **:** GUARANTEED <an ~ market> **2 a :** characterized by self-confidence <an ~ dancer> **b :** characterized by smug self-satisfaction **:** COMPLACENT **3 :** satisfied as to the certainty or truth of a matter **:** CONVINCED — **as·sured·ly** \-ˈshu̇r-əd-lē, -ˈshu̇(ə)rd-\ *adv* — **as·sured·ness** \-ˈshu̇r-əd-nəs, -ˈshu̇(ə)rd-\ *n*

[2]assured *n, pl* **assured** *or* **assureds :** INSURED

as·sur·er \ə-ˈshu̇r-ər\ *or* **as·sur·or** \ə-ˈshu̇r-ər, ə-ˌshu̇r-ˈȯ(ə)r\ *n* **:** one that assures **:** INSURER

as·sur·gent \ə-'sər-jənt\ *adj* [L *assurgent-, assurgens,* prp. of *assurgere* to rise, fr. *ad-* + *surgere* to rise — more at SURGE] : moving upward : RISING; *esp* : ASCENDANT 1b
assy *abbr* assembly
Assyr *abbr* Assyrian
As·syr·i·an \ə-'sir-ē-ən\ *n* **1 :** a member of an ancient Semitic race forming the Assyrian nation **2 :** the Semitic language of the Assyrians — **Assyrian** *adj*
As·syr·i·ol·o·gist \ə-ˌsir-ē-'äl-ə-jəst\ *n* : a specialist in Assyriology
As·syr·i·ol·o·gy \-jē\ *n* : the science or study of the history, language, and antiquities of ancient Assyria and Babylonia — **As·syr·i·o·log·i·cal** \-ˌsir-ē-ə-'läj-i-kəl\ *adj*
-ast \ˌast, əst\ *n suffix* [ME, fr. L *-astes,* fr. Gk *-astēs,* fr. verbs in *-azein*] : one connected with <ecdysi*ast*>
astar·board \ə-'stär-bərd\ *adv* : toward or on the starboard side of a ship <put the helm hard ~>
As·tar·te \ə-'stärt-ē\ *n* [L, fr. Gk *Astartē*] : the Phoenician goddess of fertility and of sexual love
astat·ic \(ˈ)ā-'stat-ik\ *adj* **1 :** not static : not stable or steady **2 :** having little or no tendency to take a fixed or definite position or direction — **astat·i·cal·ly** \-i-k(ə-)lē\ *adv* — **astat·i·cism** \-'stat-ə-ˌsiz-əm\ *n*
as·ta·tine \'as-tə-ˌtēn\ *n* [Gk *astatos* unsteady, fr. *a-* + *statos* standing, fr. *histanai* to cause to stand — more at STAND] : a radioactive halogen element discovered by bombarding bismuth with helium nuclei and also formed by radioactive decay — see ELEMENT table
as·ter \'as-tər\ *n* **1** [NL, genus name, fr. L, aster, fr. Gk *aster-, astēr* star, aster — more at STAR] : any of various chiefly fall-blooming leafy-stemmed composite herbs (*Aster* and closely related genera) with often showy heads containing tubular flowers or both tubular and ray flowers — compare CHINA ASTER **2** [NL, fr. Gk *aster-, astēr*] : a system of gelated cytoplasmic rays typically arranged radially about a centrosome at either end of the mitotic spindle and sometimes persisting between mitoses
-as·ter \ˌas-tər, 'as-\ *n suffix* [ME, fr. L, suffix denoting partial resemblance] : one that is inferior, worthless, or not genuine <critic*aster*>
as·te·ria \a-'stir-ē-ə\ *n* [L, a precious stone, fr. Gk, fem. of *asterios* starry, fr. *aster-, astēr*] : a gem stone cut to show asterism
as·te·ri·at·ed \-ē-ˌāt-əd\ *adj* [Gk *asterios*] : exhibiting asterism <~ sapphire>
1as·ter·isk \'as-tə-ˌrisk\ *n* [LL *asteriscus,* fr. Gk *asteriskos,* lit., little star, dim. of *aster-, astēr*] : the character * used in printing or writing as a reference mark, as an indication of the omission of letters or words, or to denote a hypothetical or nonoccurring linguistic form — **as·ter·isk·less** \-ləs\ *adj*
2asterisk *vt* : to mark with an asterisk : STAR
as·ter·ism \'as-tə-ˌriz-əm\ *n* [Gk *asterismos,* fr. *asterizein* to arrange in constellations, fr. *aster-, astēr*] **1 a :** CONSTELLATION **b :** a small group of stars **2 :** a star-shaped figure exhibited by some crystals by reflected light (as in a star sapphire) or by transmitted light (as in some mica) **3 :** three asterisks arranged in the form of a pyramid (as ⁎⁎⁎ or ⁂) esp. in order to direct attention to a following passage
astern \ə-'stərn\ *adv or adj* **1 :** behind a ship **2 :** at or toward the stern of a ship **3 :** STERNFOREMOST, BACKWARD
1as·ter·oid \'as-tə-ˌrȯid\ *n* [Gk *asteroeidēs* starlike, fr. *aster-, astēr*] **1 :** one of thousands of small planets between Mars and Jupiter with diameters from a fraction of a mile to nearly 500 miles **2 :** STARFISH — **aster·oi·dal** \ˌas-tə-'rȯid-ᵊl\ *adj*
2asteroid *adj* **1 :** resembling a star **2 :** of or resembling a starfish
as·the·nia \as-'thē-nē-ə\ *n* [NL, fr. Gk *astheneia,* fr. *asthenēs* weak, fr. *a-* + *sthenos* strength] : lack or loss of strength : DEBILITY
as·then·ic \as-'then-ik\ *adj* **1 :** of, relating to, or exhibiting asthenia : WEAK **2 :** characterized by slender build and slight muscular development : ECTOMORPHIC
as·theno·sphere \as-'then-ə-ˌsfi(ə)r\ *n* [Gk *asthenēs* weak + E *-o-* + *sphere*] : a hypothetical zone of the earth which lies beneath the lithosphere and within which the material is believed to yield readily to persistent stresses
asth·ma \'az-mə\ *n* [ME *asma,* fr. ML, modif. of Gk *asthma*] : a condition often of allergic origin that is marked by continuous or paroxysmal labored breathing accompanied by wheezing, by a sense of constriction in the chest, and often by attacks of coughing or gasping — **asth·mat·ic** \az-'mat-ik\ *adj or n* — **asth·mat·i·cal·ly** \-i-k(ə-)lē\ *adv*
as though *conj* : as if
as·tig·mat·ic \ˌas-tig-'mat-ik\ *adj* [*a-* + Gk *stigmat-, stigma* mark — more at STIGMA] **1 :** affected with, relating to, or correcting astigmatism **2 :** showing incapacity for observation or discrimination <an ~ fanaticism, a disregard for the facts—*N. Y. Herald Tribune*> — **as·tig·mat·i·cal·ly** \-i-k(ə-)lē\ *adv*
astig·ma·tism \ə-'stig-mə-ˌtiz-əm\ *n* **1 :** a defect of an optical system (as a lens) in consequence of which rays from a point fail to meet in a focal point resulting in a blurred and imperfect image **2 :** a defect of vision due to astigmatism of the refractive system of the eye and esp. to corneal irregularity **3 :** distorted understanding suggestive of the blurred vision of an astigmatic person
astir \ə-'stər\ *adj* **1 :** exhibiting activity **2 :** being out of bed : UP
ASTM *abbr* American Society for Testing and Materials
as to *prep* **1 :** with regard or reference to : as for : ABOUT <at a loss *as to* how to explain the mistake> **2 :** according to : BY <graded *as to* size and color>
as·ton·ied \ə-'stän-ēd\ *adj* [ME, fr. pp. of *astonien*] **1** *archaic* : deprived briefly of the power to act : DAZED **2** *archaic* : filled with consternation or dismay
as·ton·ish \ə-'stän-ish\ *vt* [prob. fr. earlier *astony* (fr. ME *astonen, astonien,* fr. OF *estoner,* fr. — assumed — VL *extonare,* fr. L *ex-* + *tonare* to thunder) + *-ish* (as in *abolish*) — more at THUNDER] **1** *obs* : to strike with sudden fear **2 :** to strike with sudden wonder or surprise ***syn*** see SURPRISE
as·ton·ish·ing \-iŋ\ *adj* : causing astonishment : SURPRISING — **as·ton·ish·ing·ly** \-iŋ-lē\ *adv*
as·ton·ish·ment \ə-'stän-ish-mənt\ *n* **1 a :** the state of being astonished **b :** CONSTERNATION **c :** AMAZEMENT **2 :** a cause of amazement or wonder
1as·tound \ə-'stau̇nd\ *adj* [ME *astoned,* fr. pp. of *astonen*] *archaic* : overwhelmed with astonishment or amazement : ASTOUNDED
2astound *vt* : to fill with bewilderment and wonder ***syn*** see SURPRISE
as·tound·ing \ə-'stau̇n-diŋ\ *adj* : causing astonishment or amazement — **as·tound·ing·ly** \-diŋ-lē\ *adv*
ASTP *abbr* army specialized training program
astr- *or* **astro-** *comb form* [ME *astro-,* fr. OF, fr. L *astr-, astro-,* fr. Gk, fr. *astron* — more at STAR] **1 :** star : heavens : outer space : astronomical <*astro*physics> **2 :** aster of a cell <*astro*sphere>
1astrad·dle \ə-'strad-ᵊl\ *adv* : on or above and extending onto both sides : ASTRIDE
2astraddle *prep* : with one leg on each side of : ASTRIDE
as·tra·gal \'as-tri-gəl\ *n* [L *astragalus,* fr. Gk *astragalos* anklebone, molding] **1 :** a narrow half-round molding **2 :** a projecting strip on the edge of a folding door
as·trag·a·lus \ə-'strag-ə-ləs\ *n, pl* **-li** \-ˌlī, -ˌlē\ [NL, fr. Gk *astragalos*] **1 :** one of the proximal bones of the tarsus of the higher vertebrates — compare TALUS 1 **2 :** ASTRAGAL
as·tra·khan *or* **as·tra·chan** \'as-trə-kən, -ˌkan\ *n, often cap* [*Astrakhan,* U.S.S.R.] **1 :** karakul of Russian origin **2 :** a cloth with a usu. wool, curled, and looped pile resembling karakul
as·tral \'as-trəl\ *adj* [LL *astralis,* fr. L *astrum* star, fr. Gk *astron* — more at STAR] **1 a :** of or relating to the stars **b :** consisting of stars : STARRY **2 :** of or relating to a mitotic aster **3 :** of or consisting of a supersensible substance held in theosophy to be next above the tangible world in refinement **4 a :** VISIONARY **b :** elevated in station or position : EXALTED — **as·tral·ly** \-trə-lē\ *adv*
astray \ə-'strā\ *adv or adj* [ME, fr. MF *estraié* wandering, fr. *estraier* to stray — more at STRAY] **1 :** off the right path or route : STRAYING **2 :** in error : away from a proper or desirable course or development
1astride \ə-'strīd\ *adv* **1 :** with one leg on each side <rode her horse ~> **2 :** with the legs stretched wide apart <standing ~ with arms folded>
2astride *prep* **1 :** on or above and with one leg on each side of **2 :** placed or lying on both sides of **3 :** extending over or across : SPANNING, BRIDGING
1as·trin·gent \ə-'strin-jənt\ *adj* [prob. fr. MF, fr. L *astringent-, astringens,* prp. of *astringere* to bind fast, fr. *ad-* + *stringere* to bind tight — more at STRAIN] **1 :** able to draw together the soft organic tissues : STYPTIC, PUCKERY <~ lotions> <an ~ fruit> **2 :** suggestive of an astringent effect upon tissue : rigidly severe : AUSTERE <dry ~ comments>; *also* : TONIC — **as·trin·gen·cy** \-jən-sē\ *n* — **as·trin·gent·ly** *adv*
2astringent *n* : an astringent agent or substance
as·tro·bi·ol·o·gy \ˌas-trō-(ˌ)bī-'äl-ə-jē\ *n* : EXOBIOLOGY — **as·tro·bi·o·log·i·cal** \-ˌbī-ə-'läj-i-kəl\ *adj* — **as·tro·bi·ol·o·gist** \-(ˌ)bī-'äl-ə-jəst\ *n*
as·tro·cyte \'as-trə-ˌsīt\ *n* [ISV] : a star-shaped cell (as of the neuroglia) — **as·tro·cyt·ic** \ˌas-trə-'sit-ik\ *adj*
as·tro·cy·to·ma \ˌas-trə-sī-'tō-mə\ *n, pl* **-mas** *or* **-ma·ta** \-mət-ə\ [NL] : a nerve-tissue tumor composed of astrocytes
as·tro·dome \'as-trə-ˌdōm\ *n* [ISV] : a transparent dome in the upper surface of an airplane from within which the navigator makes celestial observations
astrol *abbr* astrology
as·tro·labe \'as-trə-ˌlāb\ *n* [ME, fr. MF & ML; MF, fr. ML *astrolabium,* fr. LGk *astrolabion,* dim. of Gk *astrolabos,* fr. *astr-* + *lambanein* to take — more at LATCH] : a compact instrument used to observe the position of celestial bodies before the invention of the sextant

astrolabe

as·trol·o·ger \ə-'sträl-ə-jər\ *n* : one who practices astrology
as·trol·o·gy \ə-'sträl-ə-jē\ *n* [ME *astrologie,* fr. MF, fr. L *astrologia,* fr. Gk, fr. *astr-* + *-logia* -logy] **1** *obs* : ASTRONOMY **2 :** the divination of the supposed influences of the stars and planets on human affairs and terrestrial events by their positions and aspects — **as·tro·log·i·cal** \ˌas-trə-'läj-i-kəl\ *adj* — **as·tro·log·i·cal·ly** \-k(ə-)lē\ *adv*
astron *abbr* astronomer; astronomy
as·tro·naut \'as-trə-ˌnȯt, -ˌnät\ *n* [*astr-* + *-naut* (as in *aeronaut*)] : a person who travels beyond the earth's atmosphere; *also* : a trainee for spaceflight
as·tro·nau·tics \ˌas-trə-'nȯt-iks\ *n pl but sing or pl in constr* **1 :** the science of the construction and operation of vehicles for travel in space beyond the earth's atmosphere **2 :** navigation in space beyond the earth's atmosphere — **as·tro·nau·tic** \-ik\ *or* **as·tro·nau·ti·cal** \-i-kəl\ *adj* — **as·tro·nau·ti·cal·ly** \-i-k(ə-)lē\ *adv*
as·tro·nav·i·ga·tion \ˌas-trō-ˌnav-ə-'gā-shən\ *n* : CELESTIAL NAVIGATION
as·tron·o·mer \ə-'strän-ə-mər\ *n* : one who is skilled in astronomy or who makes observations of celestial phenomena
as·tro·nom·i·cal \ˌas-trə-'näm-i-kəl\ *or* **as·tro·nom·ic** \-ik\ *adj* **1 :** of or relating to astronomy **2 :** enormously or inconceivably large <~ numbers> — **as·tro·nom·i·cal·ly** \-i-k(ə-)lē\ *adv*

astronomical unit *n* : a unit of length used in astronomy equal to the mean distance of the earth from the sun or about 93 million miles
as·tron·o·my \ə-ˈsträn-ə-mē\ *n, pl* **-mies** [ME *astronomie,* fr. OF, fr. L *astronomia,* fr. Gk, fr. *astr-* + *-nomia* -nomy] **1 :** the science of the celestial bodies and of their magnitudes, motions, and constitution **2 :** a treatise on astronomy
as·tro·pho·tog·ra·phy \ˌas-(ˌ)trō-fə-ˈtäg-rə-fē\ *n* [ISV] : photography as used in astronomical investigations
as·tro·phys·ics \ˌas-trə-ˈfiz-iks\ *n pl but sing or pl in constr* [ISV] : a branch of astronomy dealing with the physical and chemical constitution of the celestial bodies — **as·tro·phys·i·cal** \-i-kəl\ *adj* — **as·tro·phys·i·cist** \-ˈfiz-(ə-)səst\ *n*
as·tro·sphere \ˈas-trə-ˌsfi(ə)r\ *n* [ISV] : an aster exclusive of the centrosome
as·tute \ə-ˈst(y)üt, a-\ *adj* [L *astutus,* fr. *astus* craft] : exhibiting combined shrewdness and perspicacity often to the point of being artful or crafty <an ~ observer> <an ~ appeal to the weakness of his victim> ***syn*** see SHREWD ***ant*** gullible — **as·tute·ly** *adv* — **as·tute·ness** *n*
As·ty·a·nax \ə-ˈstī-ə-ˌnaks\ *n* [Gk] : a son of Hector and Andromache hurled by the Greeks from the walls of Troy
asun·der \ə-ˈsən-dər\ *adv or adj* **1 :** into parts <torn ~> **2 :** apart from each other in position <wide ~>
ASV *abbr* American Standard Version
aswarm \ə-ˈswȯ(ə)rm\ *adj* : filled to overflowing : SWARMING <streets ~ with people>
aswirl \ə-ˈswər(-ə)l\ *adj* : moving with a whirling motion
aswoon \ə-ˈswün\ *adj* : being in a swoon : DAZED
asy·lum \ə-ˈsī-ləm\ *n* [ME, fr. L, fr. Gk *asylon,* neut. of *asylos* inviolable, fr. *a-* + *sylon* right of seizure] **1 :** an inviolable place of refuge and protection giving shelter to criminals and debtors : SANCTUARY **2 :** a place of retreat and security : SHELTER **3 a :** the protection or inviolability afforded by an asylum : REFUGE **b :** protection from arrest and extradition given esp. to political refugees by a nation or by an embassy or other agency enjoying diplomatic immunity **4 :** an institution for the relief or care of the destitute or afflicted and esp. the insane
asym·met·ric \ˌā-sə-ˈme-trik\ *or* **asym·met·ri·cal** \-tri-kəl\ *adj* [Gk *asymmetria* lack of proportion, fr. *asymmetros* ill-proportioned, fr. *a-* + *symmetros* symmetrical — more at SYMMETRY] **1 :** not symmetrical **2 :** characterized by being bonded to different atoms or groups — **asym·met·ri·cal·ly** \-k(ə-)lē\ *adv* — **asym·me·try** \(ˈ)ā-ˈsim-ə-trē\ *n*
asymp·tom·at·ic \ˌā-ˌsim(p)-tə-ˈmat-ik\ *adj* : presenting no subjective evidence of disease — **asymp·tom·at·i·cal·ly** \-i-k(ə-)lē\ *adv*
as·ymp·tote \ˈas-əm(p)-ˌtōt\ *n* [prob. fr. (assumed) NL *asymptotus,* fr. Gk *asymptōtos,* fr. *asymptōtos* not meeting, fr. *a-* + *sympiptein* to meet — more at SYMPTOM] : a straight line associated with a curve such that as a point moves along an infinite branch of the curve the distance from the point to the line approaches zero and the slope of the curve at the point approaches the slope of the line — **as·ymp·tot·ic** \ˌas-əm(p)-ˈtät-ik\ *adj* — **as·ymp·tot·i·cal·ly** \-i-k(ə-)lē\ *adv*

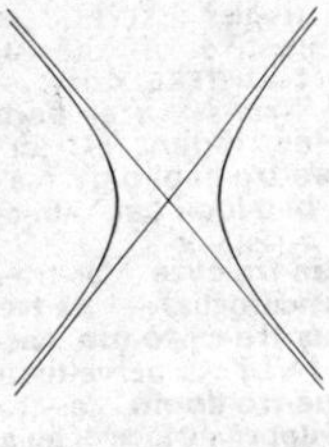

asymptotes to the hyperbola

asyn·ap·sis \ˌā-sə-ˈnap-səs\ *n, pl* **-ap·ses** \-ˌsēz\ [NL [2]*a-* + *synapsis*] : failure of pairing of homologous chromosomes in meiosis
asyn·chro·nous \-krə-nəs\ *adj* : not synchronous — **asyn·chro·nous·ly** *adv*
asyn·chro·ny \-krə-nē\ *or* **asyn·chro·nism** \(ˈ)ā-ˈsiŋ-krə-ˌniz-əm, -ˈsin-\ *n* : the quality or state of being asynchronous : absence or lack of concurrence in time
as·yn·det·ic \ˌas-ᵊn-ˈdet-ik\ *adj* : marked by asyndeton — **as·yn·det·i·cal·ly** \-i-k(ə-)lē\ *adv*
asyn·de·ton \ə-ˈsin-də-ˌtän, (ˈ)ā-ˈsin-\ *n, pl* **-tons** *or* **-ta** \-dət-ə\ [LL, fr. Gk, fr. neut. of *asyndetos* unconnected, fr. *a-* + *syndetos* bound together, fr. *syndein* to bind together, fr. *syn-* + *dein* to bind — more at DIADEM] : omission of the conjunctions that ordinarily join coordinate words or clauses (as in "I came, I saw, I conquered")
[1]**at** \ət, (ˈ)at\ *prep* [ME, fr. OE *æt;* akin to OHG *az* at, L *ad*] **1** — used as a function word to indicate presence or occurrence in, on, or near <staying ~ a hotel> <~ a party> <sick ~ heart> **2** — used as a function word to indicate the goal of an indicated or implied action or motion <aim ~ the target> <laugh ~ him> <creditors are ~ him again> **3** — used as a function word to indicate that with which one is occupied or employed <~ work> <~ the controls> <an expert ~ chess> **4** — used as a function word to indicate situation in an active or passive state or condition <a criminal ~ liberty> <~ rest> **5** — used as a function word to indicate the means, cause, or manner <sold ~ auction> <laughed ~ his joke> <act ~ your own discretion> **6 a** — used as a function word to indicate the rate, degree, or position in a scale or series <the temperature ~ 90> <~ first> **b** — used as a function word to indicate age or position in time <will retire ~ 65> <awoke ~ midnight>
[2]**at** \ˈät\ *n, pl* **at** [Siamese] — see *kip* at MONEY table
[3]**at** *abbr* **1** airtight **2** atomic
At *symbol* astatine
AT *abbr* **1** air temperature **2** ampere-turn
at- — see AD-
At·a·brine \ˈat-ə-brən, -ˌbrēn\ *trademark* — used for quinacrine
At·a·lan·ta \ˌat-ᵊl-ˈant-ə\ *n* [L, fr. Gk *Atalantē*] : a Greek maiden of mythology who challenged each of her suitors to a footrace and was eventually defeated by and married to Hippomenes
at all \ət-ˈȯl, ə-ˈtȯl, at-ˈȯl\ *adv* : in any way or respect : to the least extent or degree : under any circumstances <doesn't smoke *at all*>
at·a·man \ˌat-ə-ˈman\ *n* [Russ] : HETMAN
at·a·mas·co lily \ˌat-ə-ˈmas-(ˌ)kō-\ *n* [*attamusco,* lit., it is red (in some Algonquian language of Virginia)] : any of a genus (*Zephyranthes*) of American bulbous herbs of the amaryllis family with pink, white, or yellowish flowers
at·a·rac·tic \ˌat-ə-ˈrak-tik\ *or* **at·a·rax·ic** \-ˈrak-sik\ *n* [*ataractic* fr. Gk *ataraktos* calm, fr. *a-* + *tarassein* to disturb; *ataraxic* fr. Gk *ataraxia* calmness, fr. *a-* + *tarassein* — more at DREG] : a tranquilizer drug — **ataractic** *adj*
at·a·vism \ˈat-ə-ˌviz-əm\ *n* [F *atavisme,* fr. L *atavus* ancestor] **1 :** recurrence in an organism or in any of its parts of a form typical of ancestors more remote than the parents usu. due to genetic recombination **2 :** an individual or character manifesting atavism : THROWBACK — **at·a·vist** \-vəst\ *n* — **at·a·vis·tic** \ˌat-ə-ˈvis-tik\ *adj* — **at·a·vis·ti·cal·ly** \-ti-k(ə-)lē\ *adv*
atax·ia \ə-ˈtak-sē-ə, (ˈ)ā-\ *n* [Gk, fr. *a-* + *tassein* to put in order — more at TACTICS] **1 :** lack of order : CONFUSION **2 :** an inability to coordinate voluntary muscular movements that is symptomatic of some nervous disorders — **atax·ic** \-sik\ *adj*
at bat \ət-ˈbat\ *n* : an official time at bat charged to a baseball batter except when he gets a base on balls or a sacrifice hit, is hit by a pitched ball, or is interfered with by the catcher <three hits in five *at bats*>
[1]**ate** *past of* EAT
[2]**ate** \ˈät-ē, ˈāt-; ˈä-ˌtā, ˈā-ˌtē\ *n* [Gk *atē*] : blind impulse, reckless ambition, or excessive folly that drives men to ruin
[1]**-ate** \ət, ˌāt\ *n suffix* [ME *-at,* fr. OF, fr. L *-atus, -atum,* masc. & neut. of *-atus,* pp. ending] **1 :** one acted upon (in a specified way) <distill*ate*> **2** [NL *-atum,* fr. L] : chemical compound or complex anion derived from a (specified) compound or element <phenol*ate*> <ferr*ate*>; *esp* : salt or ester of an acid with a name ending in *-ic* and not beginning with *hydro-* <bor*ate*>
[2]**-ate** *n suffix* [ME *-at,* fr. OF, fr. L *-atus,* fr. *-atus,* pp. ending] : office : function : rank : group of persons holding a (specified) office or rank or having a (specified) function <vicar*ate*>
[3]**-ate** *adj suffix* [ME *-at,* fr. L *-atus,* fr. pp. ending of 1st conj. verbs, fr. *-a-,* stem vowel of 1st conj. + *-tus,* pp. suffix — more at -ED] : marked by having <crani*ate*>
[4]**-ate** \ˌāt\ *vb suffix* [ME *-aten,* fr. L *-atus,* pp. ending] : act on (in a specified way) <insul*ate*> : cause to be modified or affected by <camphor*ate*> : cause to become <activ*ate*> : furnish with <capacit*ate*>
At·e·brin \ˈat-ə-brən\ *trademark* — used for quinacrine
-at·ed \ˌāt-əd\ *adj suffix* : [3]-ATE <locul*ated*>
at·el·ec·ta·sis \ˌat-ᵊl-ˈek-tə-səs\ *n, pl* **-ta·ses** \-ˌsēz\ [NL, fr. Gk *atelēs* incomplete, defective (fr. *a-* [2]*a-* + *telos* end) + *ektasis* extension, fr. *ekteinein* to stretch out, fr. *ex-* + *teinein* to stretch — more at WHEEL, THIN] : collapse of the expanded lung; *also* : defective expansion of the pulmonary alveoli at birth
ate·lier \ˌat-ᵊl-ˈyā\ *n* [F] **1 :** an artist's or designer's studio or workroom **2 :** WORKSHOP
a tem·po \ä-ˈtem-(ˌ)pō\ *adv or adj* [It] : in time — used as a direction in music to return to the original rate of speed
a ter·go \ä-ˈte(ə)r-(ˌ)gō\ *adv* [L] : from behind
Ate·ri·an \ə-ˈtir-ē-ən\ *adj* [F *atérien,* fr. Bir el-*Ater* (Constantine), Algeria] : of or relating to a Paleolithic culture of northern Africa characterized by Mousterian features, tanged arrow points, and leaf-shaped spearheads
Ath·a·na·sian \ˌath-ə-ˈnā-zhən, -ˈnā-shən\ *adj* : of or relating to Athanasius or his advocacy of the homoousian doctrine against Arianism
Athanasian Creed *n* : a Christian creed originating in Europe about A.D. 400 and relating esp. to the Trinity and Incarnation
Ath·a·pas·kan *or* **Ath·a·pas·can** \ˌath-ə-ˈpas-kən\ *or* **Ath·a·bas·can** *or* **Ath·a·bas·kan** \-ˈbas-\ *n* [Cree *Athap-askaw,* an Athapaskan people, lit., grass or reeds here and there] **1 :** a language stock of the Na-dene group in No. America **2 :** a member of a people speaking an Athapaskan language
athe·ism \ˈā-thē-ˌiz-əm\ *n* [MF *athéisme,* fr. *athée* atheist, fr. Gk *atheos* godless, fr. *a-* + *theos* god] **1 a :** a disbelief in the existence of deity **b :** the doctrine that there is no deity **2 :** UNGODLINESS, WICKEDNESS
athe·ist \ˈā-thē-əst\ *n* : one who denies the existence of God — **athe·is·tic** \ˌā-thē-ˈis-tik\ *or* **athe·is·ti·cal** \ˌā-thē-ˈis-ti-kəl\ *adj* — **athe·is·ti·cal·ly** \-ti-k(ə-)lē\ *adv*
syn ATHEIST, AGNOSTIC, DEIST, FREETHINKER, UNBELIEVER, INFIDEL *shared meaning element* : one who does not take an orthodox religious position ***ant*** theist
ath·e·ling \ˈath-ə-liŋ, ˈat͟h-\ *n* [ME, fr. OE *ætheling,* fr. *æthelu* nobility, akin to OHG *adal* nobility] : an Anglo-Saxon prince or nobleman; *esp* : the heir apparent or a prince of the royal family
ath·e·nae·um *or* **ath·e·ne·um** \ˌath-ə-ˈnē-əm\ *n* [L *Athenaeum,* a school in ancient Rome for the study of arts, fr. Gk *Athēnaion,* a temple of Athena, fr. *Athēnē*] **1 :** a literary or scientific association **2 :** a building or room in which books, periodicals, and newspapers are kept for use
Athe·ne \ə-ˈthē-nē\ *or* **Athe·na** \-nə\ *n* [Gk *Athēnē* & L *Athena,* fr. Gk *Athēnē*] : the Greek goddess of wisdom — compare MINERVA
ath·ero·gen·e·sis \ˌath-ə-rō-ˈjen-ə-səs\ *n* : the production of atheroma
ath·ero·gen·ic \-ˈjen-ik\ *adj* [*atheroma* + *-genic*] : relating to or producing degenerative changes in arterial walls <~ diet>
ath·er·o·ma \ˌath-ə-ˈrō-mə\ *n* [NL *atheromat-, atheroma,* fr. L, a tumor containing matter resembling gruel, fr. Gk *athērōma,* fr. *athēra* gruel] : fatty degeneration of the inner coat of the arteries — **ath·er·o·ma·to·sis** \-ˌrō-mə-ˈtō-səs\ *n* — **ath·er·o·ma·tous** \-ˈrō-mət-əs\ *adj*
ath·ero·scle·ro·sis \ˌath-ə-rō-sklə-ˈrō-səs\ *n* [NL, fr. *atheroma* + *sclerosis*] : an arteriosclerosis characterized by the deposition of fatty substances in and fibrosis of the inner layer of the arteries — **ath·ero·scle·rot·ic** \-sklə-ˈrät-ik\ *adj* — **ath·ero·scle·rot·i·cal·ly** \-i-k(ə-)lē\ *adv*
athirst \ə-ˈthərst\ *adj* [ME, fr. OE *ofthyrst,* pp. of *ofthyrstan* to suffer from thirst, fr. *of* off, from + *thyrstan* to thirst — more at

OF] **1** *archaic* : THIRSTY **2** : having a strong eager desire <I that for ever feel ~ for glory —John Keats> ***syn*** see EAGER

ath·lete \'ath-,lēt\ *n* [ME, fr. L *athleta,* fr. Gk *athlētēs,* fr. *athlein* to contend for a prize, fr. *athlon* prize, contest] : one who is trained or skilled in exercises, sports, or games requiring physical strength, agility, or stamina

athlete's foot *n* : ringworm of the feet

ath·let·ic \ath-'let-ik\ *adj* **1** : of or relating to athletes or athletics **2** : characteristic of an athlete; *esp* : VIGOROUS, ACTIVE **3** : characterized by heavy frame, large chest, and powerful muscular development : MESOMORPHIC **4** : used by athletes — **ath·let·i·cal·ly** \-i-k(ə-)lē\ *adv* — **ath·let·i·cism** \-'let-ə-,siz-əm\ *n*

ath·let·ics \ath-'let-iks\ *n pl but sing or pl in constr* **1 a** : exercises, sports, or games engaged in by athletes **b** *Brit* : track-and-field sports **2** : the practice or principles of athletic activities

athletic supporter *n* : a supporter for the genitals worn by men participating in sports or strenuous activities

ath·o·dyd \'ath-ə-,did\ *n* [*aero-thermodynamic duct*] : a jet engine (as a ramjet engine) consisting essentially of a continuous duct of varying diameter which admits air at the forward end, adds heat to it by the combustion of fuel, and discharges it from the after end

at home \ət-'hōm\ *n* : a reception given at one's home

-athon \ə-,thän\ *n comb form* [*marathon*] : contest of endurance <talk*athon*>

ath·ro·cyte \'ath-rə-,sīt\ *n* [Gk *athroos* together, collected + ISV *-cyte*] : a cell capable of picking up foreign material and storing it in granular form in its cytoplasm — **ath·ro·cy·to·sis** \,ath-rə-sī-'tō-səs\ *n*

¹athwart \ə-'thwȯ(ə)rt, *naut often* -'thȯ(ə)rt\ *adv* **1** : across esp. in an oblique direction **2** : in opposition to the right or expected course <and quite ~ goes all decorum —Shak.>

²athwart *prep* **1** : ACROSS <a row of stepping-stones set ~ the creek —Eden Phillpotts> **2** : in opposition to <a procedure directly ~ the New England prejudices —R. G. Cole>

athwart·ship \-,ship\ *adj* : being across the ship from side to side <~ and longitudinal framing>

athwart·ships \-,ships\ *adv* : across the ship from side to side

atilt \ə-'tilt\ *adv or adj* **1** : in a tilted position **2** : with lance in hand <run ~ at death—Shak.>

atin·gle \ə-'tiŋ-gəl\ *adj* : tingling esp. with excitement or exhilaration

-a·tion \'ā-shən\ *n suffix* [ME *-acioun,* fr. OF *-ation,* fr. L *-ation-, -atio,* fr. *-atus* -ate + *-ion-, -io* -ion] : action or process <flirt*ation*> : something connected with an action or process <discolor*ation*>

-a·tive \,āt-iv, ət-\ *adj suffix* [ME, fr. MF *-atif,* fr. L *-ativus,* fr. *-atus* + *-ivus* -ive] : of, relating to, or connected with <authorit*ative*> : tending to <talk*ative*>

At·ka mackerel \,at-kə-, ,ät-\ *n* [*Atka* Island, Alaska] : a greenling (*Pleurogrammus monopterygius*) of Alaska and adjacent regions valued as a food fish

Atl *abbr* Atlantic

¹At·lan·te·an \,at-,lan-'tē-ən, ət-'lant-ē-\ *adj* : of, relating to, or resembling Atlas : STRONG

²Atlantean *adj* : of or relating to Atlantis

At·lan·tic \ət-'lant-ik, at-\ *adj* **1 a** : of, relating to, or found in, on, or near the Atlantic ocean **b** : of, relating to, or found on or near the east coast of the U.S. **2** : of or relating to the nations that border the Atlantic ocean <the ~ community>

Atlantic croaker *n* : a small but important food fish (*Micropogan undulatus*) of the Gulf coast and the Atlantic coast south of Cape Cod — called also *hardhead*

At·lan·ti·cism \-'lant-ə-,siz-əm\ *n* [*Atlantic* (*ocean*)] : a policy of military cooperation between European and No. American powers — **At·lan·ti·cist** \-səst\ *n*

Atlantic time *n* [*Atlantic* (*ocean*)] : the time of the 4th time zone west of Greenwich that includes the Canadian Maritime Provinces, Puerto Rico, and the Virgin Islands — called also *Atlantic standard time*

At·lan·tis \ət-'lant-əs, at-\ *n* : a fabled island that was traditionally placed west of the Strait of Gibraltar and that was swallowed up by the sea

at·las \'at-ləs\ *n* [L *Atlant-, Atlas,* fr. Gk] **1** *cap* : a Titan who for his part in the Titans' revolt against the gods was obliged to support the heavens with his head and hands **2** *cap* : one who bears a heavy burden **3 a** : a bound collection of maps **b** : a bound collection of tables, charts, or plates **4** : the first vertebra of the neck **5** *pl usu* **at·lan·tes** \ət-'lant-(,)ēz, at-\ : a figure or half figure of a man used as a column to support an entablature

at·latl \'ät-,lät-ᵊl\ *n* [of Uto-Aztecan origin; akin to Nahuatl *atlatl* atlatl] : a device for throwing a spear or dart that consists of a rod or board with a projection (as a hook or thong) at the rear end to hold the weapon in place until released

At·li \'ät-lē\ *n* [ON] : a king of the Huns figuring in Germanic legend and corresponding to the historical Attila

atm *abbr* atmosphere; atmospheric

at·man \'ät-mən\ *n, often cap* [Skt *ātman,* lit., breath, soul; akin to OHG *ātum* breath] **1** *Hinduism* : the innermost essence of each individual **2** *Hinduism* : the supreme universal self : BRAHMA 1

at·mom·e·ter \at-'mäm-ət-ər\ *n* [Gk *atmos* + E *-meter*] : an instrument for measuring the evaporating capacity of the air

at·mo·sphere \'at-mə-,sfi(ə)r\ *n* [NL *atmosphaera,* fr. Gk *atmos* vapor + L *sphaera* sphere; akin to Gk *aēnai* to blow — more at WIND] **1 a** : a gaseous mass enveloping a celestial body (as a planet) **b** : the whole mass of air surrounding the earth **2** : the air of a locality **3** : a surrounding influence or environment <an ~ of mutual trust> **4** : a unit of pressure equal to the pressure of the air at sea level or approximately 14.7 pounds to the square inch **5 a** : the overall aesthetic effect of a work of art **b** : a dominant aesthetic or emotional effect or appeal — **at·mo·sphered** \-,sfi(ə)rd\ *adj*

at·mo·spher·ic \,at-mə-'sfi(ə)r-ik, -'sfer-\ *adj* **1 a** : of or relating to the atmosphere **b** : resembling the atmosphere : AIRY **c** : occurring in or actuated by the atmosphere **2** : having, marked by, or contributing aesthetic or emotional atmosphere — **at·mo·spher·i·cal·ly** \-i-k(ə-)lē\ *adv*

at·mo·spher·ics \-iks\ *n pl* : audible disturbances produced in radio receiving apparatus by atmospheric electrical phenomena (as lightning); *also* : the electrical phenomena causing these disturbances

atmospheric tide *n* : TIDE 2a(5)

at·mo·sphe·ri·um \,at-mə-'sfir-ē-əm\ *n* [*atmosphere* + *-ium* (as in *planetarium*)] : an optical device for projecting images of meteorological phenomena (as clouds) on the inside of a dome; *also* : a room housing this device

at no *abbr* atomic number

atoll \'a-,tȯl, -,täl, -,tōl, 'ā-\ *n* [*atolu,* native name in the Maldive Islands] : a coral island consisting of a reef surrounding a lagoon

atoll

at·om \'at-əm\ *n* [ME, fr. L *atomus,* fr. Gk *atomos,* fr. *atomos* indivisible, fr. *a-* + *temnein* to cut — more at TOME] **1** : one of the minute indivisible particles of which according to ancient materialism the universe is composed **2** : a tiny particle : BIT **3 a** : the smallest particle of an element that can exist either alone or in combination **b** : a group of such particles constituting the smallest quantity of a radical **4** : the atom considered as a source of vast potential energy

atom bomb *n* **1** : a bomb whose violent explosive power is due to the sudden release of atomic energy resulting from the splitting of nuclei of a heavy chemical element (as plutonium or uranium) by neutrons in a very rapid chain reaction — called also *atomic bomb, fission bomb* **2** : a bomb whose explosive power is due to the release of atomic energy — **atom–bomb** *vt*

atom·ic \ə-'täm-ik\ *adj* **1** : of, relating to, or concerned with atoms, atomic energy, or atomic bombs **2** : MINUTE **3** *of a chemical element* : existing in the state of separate atoms — **atom·i·cal·ly** \-i-k(ə-)lē\ *adv*

atomic clock *n* : a precision clock that depends for its operation on an electrical oscillator regulated by the natural vibration frequencies of an atomic system (as a beam of cesium atoms)

atomic cocktail *n* : a radioactive substance (as iodide of sodium) dissolved in water and administered orally to patients with cancer

atomic energy *n* : energy that can be liberated by changes in the nucleus of an atom (as by fission of a heavy nucleus or fusion of light nuclei into heavier ones with accompanying loss of mass)

at·o·mic·i·ty \,at-ə-'mis-ət-ē\ *n* **1 a** : VALENCE **b** : the number of atoms in the molecule of an element **c** : the number of replaceable atoms or groups in the molecule of a compound **2** : the state of consisting of atoms

atomic mass *n* : the mass of any species of atom usu. expressed in atomic mass units

atomic mass unit *n* : a unit of mass for expressing masses of atoms, molecules, or nuclear particles equal to $\frac{1}{12}$ of the atomic mass of the most abundant carbon isotope $_6C^{12}$

atomic number *n* : an experimentally determined number characteristic of a chemical element that represents the number of protons in the nucleus which in a neutral atom equals the number of electrons outside the nucleus and that determines the place of the element in the periodic table — see ELEMENT table

atomic pile *n* : REACTOR 3b — called also *atomic reactor*

atom·ics \ə-'täm-iks\ *n pl but sing in constr* : the science of atoms esp. when involving atomic energy

atomic theory *n* **1** : a theory of the nature of matter: all material substances are composed of minute particles or atoms of a comparatively small number of kinds and all the atoms of the same kind are uniform in size, weight, and other properties — called also *atomic hypothesis* **2** : any of several theories of the structure of the atom; *esp* : one based on experimentation and theoretical considerations holding that the atom is composed essentially of a small positively charged comparatively heavy nucleus surrounded by a comparatively large arrangement of electrons

atomic weight *n* : the average relative weight of an element referred to some element taken as a standard with oxygen of atomic weight 16 or usu. with carbon of atomic weight 12 being taken as a basis — see ELEMENT table

at·om·ism \'at-ə-,miz-əm\ *n* : a doctrine that the universe is composed of simple indivisible minute particles — **at·om·ist** \-məst\ *n*

at·om·is·tic \,at-ə-'mis-tik\ *adj* **1** : of or relating to atoms or atomism **2** : composed of many simple elements; *also* : divided into unconnected or antagonistic fragments <an ~ society> — **at·om·is·ti·cal·ly** \-ti-k(ə-)lē\ *adv*

at·om·is·tics \-tiks\ *n pl but sing in constr* : a science dealing with the atom or with the use of atomic energy

at·om·ize \'at-ə-,mīz\ *vt* **-ized; -iz·ing** **1** : to reduce to minute particles or to a fine spray **2** : to treat as made up of many discrete units **3** : to subject to atomic bombing — **at·om·iza·tion** \,at-ə-mə-'zā-shən\ *n*

at·om·iz·er \'at-ə-ˌmī-zər\ *n* **:** an instrument for atomizing usu. a perfume or disinfectant

atom smasher *n* **:** ACCELERATOR d

at·o·my \'at-ə-mē\ *n, pl* **-mies** [irreg. fr. L *atomi,* pl. of *atomus* atom] **:** a tiny particle **:** ATOM, MITE

aton·al \(ˈ)ā-'tōn-ᵊl, (ˈ)a-\ *adj* **:** marked by avoidance of traditional musical tonality; *esp* **:** organized without reference to key or tonal center and using the tones of the chromatic scale impartially — **aton·al·ism** \-ᵊl-ˌiz-əm\ *n* — **aton·al·ist** \-ᵊl-əst\ *n* — **aton·al·is·tic** \ˌā-ˌtōn-ᵊl-'is-tik, ˌa-\ *adj* — **ato·nal·i·ty** \ˌā-tō-ˌnal-ət-ē, ˌa-\ *n* — **aton·al·ly** \(ˈ)ā-'tōn-ᵊl-ē, (ˈ)a-\ *adv*

atone \ə-'tōn\ *vb* **atoned; aton·ing** [ME *atonen* to become reconciled, fr. *at on* in harmony, fr. *at* + *on* one] *vt* **1** *obs* **:** RECONCILE **2 :** to supply satisfaction for **:** EXPIATE ~ *vi* **:** to make amends

atone·ment \ə-'tōn-mənt\ *n* **1** *obs* **:** RECONCILIATION **2 :** the reconciliation of God and man through the sacrificial death of Jesus Christ **3 :** reparation for an offense or injury **:** SATISFACTION <made ~ for his cruelty> **4** *Christian Science* **:** the exemplifying of man's oneness with God

aton·ic \(ˈ)ā-'tän-ik, (ˈ)a-\ *adj* **1 :** characterized by atony **2 :** uttered without accent or stress — **ato·nic·i·ty** \ˌā-tō-'nis-ət-ē, ˌat-ə-'nis-\ *n*

at·o·ny \'at-ᵊn-ē\ *n* [LL *atonia,* fr. Gk, fr. *atonos* without tone, fr. *a-* + *tonos* tone] **:** lack of physiological tone esp. of a contractile organ

[1]**atop** \ə-'täp\ *prep* **:** on top of

[2]**atop** *adj* **:** being on, to, or at the top

at·o·py \'at-ə-pē\ *n* [Gk *atopia* uncommonness, fr. *atopos* out of the way, uncommon, fr. *a-* + *topos* place — more at TOPIC] **:** a probably hereditary allergy characterized by symptoms (as asthma, hay fever, or hives) produced upon exposure to the exciting antigen without inoculation — **atop·ic** \(ˈ)ā-'täp-ik, -'tō-pik\ *adj*

-a·tor *n suffix* [ME *-atour,* fr. OF & L; OF, fr. L *-ator,* fr. *-atus* -ate + *-or*] **:** one that does <totaliz*ator*>

ATP \ˌā-ˌtē-'pē, ā-'tē-ˌpē\ *n* [*a*denosine *t*ri*p*hosphate] **:** an adenosine ester derivative $C_{10}H_{16}N_5O_{13}P_3$ that supplies energy for many biochemical cellular processes by undergoing enzymatic hydrolysis esp. to ADP — called also *adenosine triphosphate*

ATPase \ˌā-ˌtē-'pē-ˌās, -ˌāz\ *n* **:** an enzyme that hydrolyzes ATP; *esp* **:** one that hydrolyzes ATP to ADP and inorganic phosphate

at·ra·bil·ious \ˌa-trə-'bil-yəs\ *adj* [L *atra bilis* black bile] **1 :** given to or marked by melancholy **:** GLOOMY **2 :** ILL-NATURED, PEEVISH — **at·ra·bil·ious·ness** *n*

at·ra·zine \'a-trə-ˌzēn\ *n* [ISV *atr-* (prob. fr. L *atr-, ater* black, dark) + tri*azine*] **:** a photosynthesis-inhibiting persistent herbicide $C_8H_{14}ClN_5$ used esp. to kill annual weeds and quack grass

atrem·ble \ə-'trem-bəl\ *adj* **:** shaking involuntarily **:** TREMBLING <he was white as death and all ~ —Robert Coover>

atre·sia \ə-'trē-zhə\ *n* [NL, fr. [2]*a-* + Gk *trēsis* perforation, fr. *tetrainein* to pierce — more at THROW] **1 :** absence or closure of a natural passage of the body **2 :** involution of a part (as an ovarian follicle)

Atreus \'ā-ˌtrüs, -trē-əs\ *n* [Gk] **:** a king of Mycenae who was the father of Agamemnon and Menelaus

atrio·ven·tric·u·lar \ˌā-trē-ō-ven-'trik-yə-lər, -vən-\ *adj* [NL *atrium* + E *ventricular*] **:** of, relating to, or located between an atrium and ventricle of the heart

atrip \ə-'trip\ *adj, of an anchor* **:** AWEIGH

atri·um \'ā-trē-əm\ *n, pl* **atria** \-trē-ə\ *also* **atri·ums** [L] **1 :** the central hall of a Roman house **2** [NL, fr. L] **:** an anatomical cavity or passage; *esp* **:** the main chamber of an auricle of the heart or the entire auricle **3 :** a rectangularly shaped open patio around which a house is built — **atri·al** \-trē-əl\ *adj*

atro·cious \ə-'trō-shəs\ *adj* [L *atroc-, atrox* gloomy, atrocious, fr. *atr-, ater* black + *-oc-, -ox* (akin to Gk *ōps* eye) — more at EYE] **1 :** extremely wicked, brutal, or cruel **:** BARBARIC **2 :** APPALLING, HORRIFYING <the ~ weapons of modern war> **3 a :** utterly revolting **:** ABOMINABLE <~ working conditions> **b :** of very poor quality <~ handwriting> ***syn*** see OUTRAGEOUS — **atro·cious·ly** *adv* — **atro·cious·ness** *n*

atroc·i·ty \ə-'träs-ət-ē\ *n, pl* **-ties 1 :** the quality or state of being atrocious **2 :** an atrocious act, object, or situation

[1]**at·ro·phy** \'a-trə-fē\ *n, pl* **-phies** [LL *atrophia,* fr. Gk, fr. *atrophos* ill fed, fr. *a-* + *trephein* to nourish; akin to Gk *thrombos* clot, curd] **1 :** decrease in size or wasting away of a body part or tissue; *also* **:** arrested development or loss of a part or organ incidental to the normal development or life of an animal or plant **2 :** a wasting away or progressive decline **:** DEGENERATION <the ~ of freedom> — **atro·phic** \(ˈ)ā-'trō-fik\ *adj*

[2]**atrophy** *vb* **-phied; -phy·ing** *vi* **:** to undergo atrophy ~ *vt* **:** to cause to undergo atrophy

at·ro·pine \'a-trə-ˌpēn\ *n* [G *atropin,* fr. NL *Atropa,* genus name of belladonna, fr. Gk *Atropos*] **:** a poisonous white crystalline alkaloid $C_{17}H_{23}NO_3$ from belladonna and related plants used esp. to relieve spasms and to dilate the pupil of the eye

att *abbr* **1** attached **2** attention **3** attorney

at·tach \ə-'tach\ *vb* [ME *attachen,* fr. MF *attacher,* fr. OF *estachier,* fr. *estache* stake, of Gmc origin; akin to OE *staca* stake] *vt* **1 :** to take by legal authority esp. under a writ <the court's sheriffs ~*ed* his property> **2 :** to bring (oneself) into an association **3 :** to bind by personal ties (as of affection or sympathy) <was strongly ~*ed* to his family> **4 :** to make fast to (as by tying or gluing) <~ a label to a package> **5 :** ASCRIBE, ATTRIBUTE <~*ed* great importance to public opinion polls> ~ *vi* **:** to become attached **:** ADHERE ***syn*** see FASTEN ***ant*** detach — **at·tach·able** \-'tach-ə-bəl\ *adj*

at·ta·ché \ˌat-ə-'shā, ˌa-ˌta-, ə-ˌta-\ *n* [F, pp. of *attacher*] **1 :** a technical expert on the diplomatic staff of his country at a foreign capital <a military ~> **2 :** ATTACHÉ CASE

at·ta·ché case \ə-'tash-(ˌ)ā-, ; ˌat-ə-'shā-, ˌa-ˌta-\ *n* **:** a small thin suitcase used esp. for carrying business papers

at·tached \ə-'tacht\ *adj* **:** permanently fixed when adult <~ barnacles>

at·tach·ment \ə-'tach-mənt\ *n* **1 :** a seizure by legal process; *also* **:** the writ or precept commanding such seizure **2 a :** the state of being personally attached **:** FIDELITY <~ to a cause> **b :** affectionate regard <a deep ~ to natural beauty> **3 :** a device attached to a machine or implement **4 :** the physical connection by which one thing is attached to another **5 :** the process of physically attaching

[1]**at·tack** \ə-'tak\ *vb* [MF *attaquer,* fr. (assumed) OIt *estaccare* to attach, fr. *stacca* stake, of Gmc origin; akin to OE *staca*] *vt* **1 :** to set upon forcefully **2 :** to threaten (a piece in chess) with immediate capture **3 :** to assail with unfriendly or bitter words **4 :** to begin to affect or to act on injuriously **5 :** to set to work on ~ *vi* **:** to make an attack
syn ATTACK, ASSAIL, ASSAULT, BOMBARD, STORM *shared meaning element* **:** to make an onslaught on

[2]**attack** *n* **1 :** the act of attacking **:** ASSAULT **2 :** a belligerent or antagonistic action **3 :** the beginning of destructive action (as by a chemical agent) **4 :** the setting to work on some undertaking <made a new ~ on the problem> **5 :** the act or manner of beginning a musical tone or phrase **6 :** a fit of sickness; *esp* **:** an active episode of a chronic or recurrent disease **7 a :** an offensive or scoring action <won the game with an eight-hit ~> **b :** offensive players or the positions taken up by them

at·tack·man \-ˌman\ *n* **:** a player (as in lacrosse) assigned to an offensive zone or position

at·tain \ə-'tān\ *vb* [ME *atteynen,* fr. OF *ataindre,* fr. (assumed) VL *attangere,* fr. L *attingere,* fr. *ad-* + *tangere* to touch — more at TANGENT] *vt* **1 :** to reach as an end **:** GAIN, ACHIEVE <~ a goal> <struggled to ~ a natural effect> **2 :** to come into possession of **:** OBTAIN <he ~*ed* preferment over his fellows> **3 :** to come to as the end of a progression or course of movement <they ~*ed* the top of the hill> <~ a ripe old age> ~ *vi* **:** to come or arrive by motion, growth, or effort ***syn*** see REACH — **at·tain·abil·i·ty** \-ˌtā-nə-'bil-ət-ē\ *n* — **at·tain·able** \-'tā-nə-bəl\ *adj* — **at·tain·able·ness** *n*

at·tain·der \ə-'tān-dər\ *n* [ME *attaynder,* fr. MF *ataindre* to accuse, attain] **1 :** extinction of the civil rights and capacities of a person upon sentence of death or outlawry usu. after a conviction of treason **2** *obs* **:** DISHONOR

at·tain·ment \ə-'tān-mənt\ *n* **1 :** the act of attaining **:** the condition of being attained **2 :** something attained **:** ACCOMPLISHMENT <scientific ~*s*>

[1]**at·taint** \ə-'tānt\ *vt* [ME *attaynten,* fr. MF *ataint,* pp. of *ataindre*] **1 :** to affect by attainder **2 a** *obs* **:** INFECT, CORRUPT **b** *archaic* **:** TAINT, SULLY **3** *archaic* **:** ACCUSE

[2]**attaint** *n, obs* **:** a stain upon honor or purity **:** DISGRACE

at·tar \'at-ər, 'a-ˌtär\ *n* [Per *'atir* perfumed, fr. Ar, fr. *'itr* perfume] **:** a fragrant essential oil (as from rose petals); *also* **:** FRAGRANCE

[1]**at·tempt** \ə-'tem(p)t\ *vt* [L *attemptare,* fr. *ad-* + *temptare* to touch, try — more at TEMPT] **1 :** to make an effort to do, accomplish, solve, or effect <~*ed* to swim the swollen river> **2** *archaic* **:** TEMPT **3** *archaic* **:** to try to subdue **:** ATTACK — **at·tempt·able** \-'tem(p)-tə-bəl\ *adj*
syn ATTEMPT, TRY, ENDEAVOR, ESSAY, STRIVE, STRUGGLE *shared meaning element* **:** to make an effort to do or accomplish ***ant*** succeed

[2]**attempt** *n* **1 :** the act or an instance of attempting; *esp* **:** an unsuccessful effort **2** *archaic* **:** ATTACK, ASSAULT

at·tend \ə-'tend\ *vb* [ME *attenden,* fr. OF *atendre,* fr. L *attendere,* lit., to stretch to, fr. *ad-* + *tendere* to stretch — more at THIN] *vt* **1** *archaic* **:** to give heed to **2 :** to look after **:** take charge of **3** *archaic* **a :** to wait for **b :** to be in store for **4 a :** to go or stay with as a companion, nurse, or servant **b :** to visit professionally as a physician **5 :** to be present with **:** ACCOMPANY **6 :** to be present at ~ *vi* **1 :** to apply oneself <~ to your work> **2 :** to apply the mind or pay attention **:** HEED **3 :** to be ready for service <ministers who ~ upon the king> **4** *obs* **:** WAIT, STAY **5 :** to take charge **:** SEE <I'll ~ to that> ***syn*** see TEND, ACCOMPANY — **at·tend·er** *n*

at·ten·dance \ə-'ten-dən(t)s\ *n* **1 :** the act or fact of attending <a physician in ~> **2 a :** the persons or number of persons attending <daily ~ at the fair dwindled> **b :** the number of times a person attends

[1]**at·ten·dant** \ə-'ten-dənt\ *adj* **:** accompanying or following as a consequence <problems ~ upon pollution>

[2]**attendant** *n* **1 :** one who attends another to perform a service; *esp* **:** an employee who waits on customers <a parking-lot ~> **2 :** something that accompanies **:** CONCOMITANT **3 :** ATTENDEE

at·tend·ee \ə-ˌten-'dē, ˌa-\ *n* **:** one who is present on a given occasion or at a given place **:** ATTENDER <~*s* at a convention>

at·tend·ing \ə-'ten-diŋ\ *adj* **:** serving as a physician on the staff of a teaching hospital <~ surgeon>

at·ten·tion \ə-'ten-chən\ *n* [ME *attencioun,* fr. L *attention-, attentio,* fr. *attentus,* pp. of *attendere*] **1 a :** the act or state of attending esp. through applying the mind to an object of sense or thought **b :** a condition of readiness for such attention involving esp. a selective narrowing or focusing of consciousness and receptivity **2 :** OBSERVATION, NOTICE; *esp* **:** consideration with a view to action <a problem requiring prompt ~> **3 a :** an act of civility or courtesy esp. in courtship **b :** sympathetic consideration of the needs and wants of others **:** ATTENTIVENESS **4 :** a position assumed by a soldier with heels together, body erect, arms at the sides, and eyes to the front — often used as a command — **at·ten·tion·al** \-'tench-nəl, -'ten-chən-ᵊl\ *adj*

attention line *n* **:** a line usu. placed above the salutation in a business letter directing the letter to one specified

attention span *n* **:** the length of time during which an individual is able to concentrate

at·ten·tive \ə-'tent-iv\ *adj* **1 :** MINDFUL, OBSERVANT <~ to what he is doing> **2 :** heedful of the comfort of others **:** SOLICITOUS **3 :** offering attentions in or as if in the role of a suitor ***syn*** see THOUGHTFUL ***ant*** inattentive, neglectful — **at·ten·tive·ly** *adv* — **at·ten·tive·ness** *n*

[1]**at·ten·u·ate** \ə-'ten-yə-ˌwāt\ *vb* **-at·ed; -at·ing** [L *attenuatus,* pp. of *attenuare* to make thin, fr. *ad-* + *tenuis* thin — more at THIN]

vt **1 :** to make thin or slender **2 :** to lessen the amount, force, or value of : WEAKEN **3 :** to reduce the severity, virulence, or vitality of **4 :** to make thin in consistency : RAREFY ~ *vi* **:** to become thin, fine, or less — **at·ten·u·a·tion** \-ˌten-yə-ˈwā-shən\ *n*

2at·ten·u·ate \ə-ˈten-yə-wət\ *adj* **1 :** attenuated esp. in thickness, density, or force **2 :** tapering gradually usu. to a long slender point <~ leaves>

at·ten·u·a·tor \-yə-ˌwāt-ər\ *n* **:** a device for attenuating; *esp* **:** one for reducing the amplitude of an electrical signal without appreciable distortion

at·test \ə-ˈtest\ *vb* [MF *attester,* fr. L *attestari,* fr. *ad-* + *testis* witness — more at TESTAMENT] *vt* **1 a :** to affirm to be true or genuine; *specif* **:** to authenticate by signing as a witness **b :** to authenticate officially **2 :** to establish or verify the usage of **3 :** to be proof of **:** MANIFEST <the ruins of the city ~ to its ancient magnificence> **4 :** to put on oath ~ *vi* **:** to bear witness **:** TESTIFY <~ to the truth of the statement> — **at·tes·ta·tion** \ˌa-ˌtes-ˈtā-shən, ˌat-ə-ˈstā-\ *n* — **at·test·er** \ə-ˈtes-tər\ *n*

at·tic \ˈat-ik\ *n* [F *attique,* fr. *attique* of Attica, fr. L *Atticus*] **1 :** a low story or wall above the main order of a facade in the classical styles **2 :** a room behind an attic **3 :** a room or a space immediately below the roof of a building **:** GARRET

1At·tic \ˈat-ik\ *adj* [L *Atticus,* fr. Gk *Attikos,* fr. *Attikē* Attica, Greece] **1 :** Athenian **2 :** marked by simplicity, purity, and refinement <an ~ prose style>

2Attic *n* **:** a dialect of ancient Greek orig. used in Attica and later the literary language of the Greek-speaking world

at·ti·cism \ˈat-ə-ˌsiz-əm\ *n, often cap* **1 :** a characteristic feature of Attic Greek occurring in another language or dialect **2 :** a witty or well-turned phrase

1at·tire \ə-ˈtī(ə)r\ *vt* **-tired; -tir·ing** [ME *attiren,* fr. OF *atirier,* fr. *a-* (fr. L *ad-*) + *tire* order, rank, of Gmc origin; akin to OE *tīr* glory; akin to L *deus* god — more at DEITY] **:** to put garments on **:** DRESS, ARRAY; *esp* **:** to clothe in fancy or rich garments

2attire *n* **1 :** DRESS, CLOTHES; *esp* **:** splendid or decorative clothing **2 :** the antlers or antlers and scalp of a stag or buck

at·ti·tude \ˈat-ə-ˌt(y)üd\ *n* [F, fr. It *attitudine,* fr. *attitudine* aptitude, fr. LL *aptitudin-, aptitudo* fitness — more at APTITUDE] **1 :** the arrangement of the parts of a body or figure **:** POSTURE **2 a :** a mental position with regard to a fact or state **b :** a feeling or emotion toward a fact or state **3 :** a position assumed for a specific purpose <a threatening ~> **4 :** a ballet position similar to the arabesque in which the raised leg is bent at the knee **5 :** the position of an aircraft or spacecraft determined by the relationship between its axes and a reference datum (as the horizon or a particular star) **6 :** an organismic state of readiness to respond in a characteristic way to a stimulus (as an object, concept, or situation) ***syn*** see POSITION

at·ti·tu·di·nal \ˌat-ə-ˈt(y)üd-nəl, -ᵊn-əl\ *adj* [*attitude* + *-inal* (as in *aptitudinal,* fr. L *aptitudin-, aptitudo*)] **:** relating to, based on, or expressive of personal attitudes or feelings <~ judgment>

at·ti·tu·di·nize \ˌat-ə-ˈt(y)üd-ᵊn-ˌīz\ *vi* **-nized; -niz·ing :** to assume an affected mental attitude **:** POSE

attn *abbr* attention

at·to- \ˈat-(ˌ)ō\ *comb form* [ISV, fr. Dan or Norw *atten* eighteen, fr. ON *āttjān;* akin to OE *eahtatīene* eighteen] **:** one quintillionth (10^{-18}) part of <*atto*gram>

at·torn \ə-ˈtərn\ *vi* [ME *attournen,* fr. MF *atorner,* fr. OF, fr. *a-* (fr. L *ad-*) + *torner* to turn] **:** to agree to become tenant to a new owner or landlord of the same property — **at·torn·ment** \-mənt\ *n*

at·tor·ney \ə-ˈtər-nē\ *n, pl* **-neys** [ME *attourney,* fr. MF *atorné,* pp. of *atorner*] **:** one who is legally appointed by another to transact business for him; *specif* **:** a legal agent qualified to act for suitors and defendants in legal proceedings — **at·tor·ney·ship** \-ˌship\ *n*

attorney-at-law *n, pl* **attorneys-at-law :** a practitioner in a court of law who is legally qualified to prosecute and defend actions in such court on the retainer of clients

attorney general *n, pl* **attorneys general** *or* **attorney generals :** the chief law officer of a nation or state who represents the government in litigation and serves as its principal legal advisor

at·tract \ə-ˈtrakt\ *vb* [ME *attracten,* fr. L *attractus,* pp. of *attrahere,* fr. *ad-* + *trahere* to draw — more at DRAW] *vt* **:** to cause to approach or adhere: as **a :** to pull to or toward oneself or itself <a magnet ~s iron> **b :** to draw by appeal to natural or excited interest, emotion, or aesthetic sense **:** ENTICE <~ attention> ~ *vi* **:** to exercise attraction — **at·tract·able** \-ˈtrak-tə-bəl\ *adj* — **at·trac·tor** \-ˈtrak-tər\ *n*

syn ATTRACT, ALLURE, CHARM, CAPTIVATE, FASCINATE, BEWITCH, ENCHANT *shared meaning element* **:** to draw another by exerting a compelling influence ***ant*** repel

at·trac·tant \ə-ˈtrak-tənt\ *n* **:** something that attracts; *esp* **:** a substance (as a pheromone) that attracts insects or other animals

at·trac·tion \ə-ˈtrak-shən\ *n* **1 a :** the act, process, or power of attracting **b :** personal charm **2 :** the action or power of drawing forth a response **:** an attractive quality **3 :** a force acting mutually between particles of matter, tending to draw them together, and resisting their separation **4 :** something that attracts or is intended to attract people by appealing to their desires and tastes <~s at the local theater>

syn ATTRACTION, AFFINITY, SYMPATHY *shared meaning element* **:** the relationship existing between persons or things that are naturally or involuntarily drawn together

at·trac·tive \ə-ˈtrak-tiv\ *adj* **1 :** having or relating to the power to attract <~ forces between molecules> <an ~ offer> **2 :** arousing interest or pleasure **:** CHARMING <an ~ smile> — **at·trac·tive·ly** *adv* — **at·trac·tive·ness** *n* — **at·trac·tiv·i·ty** \ə-ˌtrak-ˈtiv-ət-ē, ˌa-ˌtrak-\ *n*

attrib *abbr* attributive; attributively

1at·tri·bute \ˈa-trə-ˌbyüt\ *n* [ME, fr. L *attributus,* pp. of *attribuere* to attribute, fr. *ad-* + *tribuere* to bestow — more at TRIBUTE] **1 :** an inherent characteristic; *also* **:** an accidental quality **2 :** an object closely associated with or belonging to a specific person, thing, or office <a scepter is the ~ of power>; *esp* **:** such an object used for identification in painting or sculpture **3 :** a word ascribing a quality; *esp* **:** ADJECTIVE

2at·trib·ute \ə-ˈtrib-yət\ *vt* **-ut·ed; -ut·ing 1 :** to explain by indicating a cause <*attributed* his success to his coach> **2 a :** to regard as a characteristic of a person or thing **b :** to reckon as made or originated in an indicated fashion <*attributed* the invention to a Russian> **c :** CLASSIFY, DESIGNATE ***syn*** see ASCRIBE — **at·trib·ut·able** \-yət-ə-bəl\ *adj* — **at·trib·ut·er** *n*

at·tri·bu·tion \ˌa-trə-ˈbyü-shən\ *n* **1 :** the act of attributing; *esp* **:** the ascribing of a work (as of literature or art) to a particular author or artist **2 :** an ascribed quality, character, or right — **at·tri·bu·tion·al** \-shnəl, -shən-ᵊl\ *adj*

at·trib·u·tive \ə-ˈtrib-yət-iv\ *adj* **1 :** relating to or of the nature of an attribute **:** ATTRIBUTING **2 :** joined directly to a modified noun without a linking verb <*city* in *city streets* is an ~ noun> — **attributive** *n* — **at·trib·u·tive·ly** *adv*

at·trit·ed \ə-ˈtrīt-əd\ *adj* **:** worn by attrition

at·tri·tion \ə-ˈtrish-ən\ *n* [L *attrition-, attritio,* fr. *attritus,* pp. of *atterere* to rub against, fr. *ad-* + *terere* to rub — more at THROW] **1** [ME *attricioun,* fr. (assumed) ML *attrition-, attritio,* fr. L] **:** sorrow for one's sins that arises from a motive other than that of the love of God **2 :** the act of rubbing together **:** FRICTION; *also* **:** the act of wearing or grinding down by friction **3 :** the act of weakening or exhausting by constant harassment or abuse **4 :** a reduction (as in personnel) chiefly as a result of resignation, retirement, or death — **at·tri·tion·al** \-ˈtrish-nəl, -ˈtrish-ən-ᵊl\ *adj*

at·tune \ə-ˈt(y)ün\ *vt* **:** to bring into harmony **:** TUNE — **at·tune·ment** \-mənt\ *n*

atty *abbr* attorney

atty gen *abbr* attorney general

atwit·ter \ə-ˈtwit-ər\ *adj* **:** nervously concerned **:** EXCITED <gossips ~ with speculation —*Time*>

at wt *abbr* atomic weight

atyp·i·cal \(ˈ)ā-ˈtip-i-kəl\ *adj* **:** not typical **:** IRREGULAR, UNUSUAL — **atyp·i·cal·i·ty** \ˌā-ˌtip-ə-ˈkal-ət-ē\ *n* — **atyp·i·cal·ly** \(ˈ)ā-ˈtip-i-k(ə-)lē\ *adv*

Au *symbol* [L *aurum*] gold

AU *abbr* angstrom unit

au·bade \ō-ˈbäd\ *n* [F, fr. (assumed) OProv *aubada,* fr. OProv *alba, auba* dawn, fr. (assumed) VL *alba,* fr. L, fem. of *albus* white] **1 :** a song or poem greeting the dawn **2 a :** a morning love song **b :** a song or poem of lovers parting at dawn **3 :** morning music — compare NOCTURNE

1au·burn \ˈȯ-bərn\ *adj* [ME *auborne* blond, fr. MF, fr. ML *alburnus* whitish, fr. L *albus*] **1 :** of the color auburn **2 :** of a reddish brown color

2auburn *n* **:** a moderate brown

Au·bus·son \ˌō-bə-ˈsōⁿ\ *n* [*Aubusson,* France] **1 :** a figured scenic tapestry used for wall hangings and upholstery **2 :** a rug woven to resemble Aubusson tapestry

AUC \ˌā-(ˌ)yü-ˈsē\ *abbr* [L *ab urbe condita*] from the year of the founding of the city (of Rome)

au cou·rant \ˌō-kü-ˈräⁿ\ *adj* [F, lit., in the current] **1 :** fully informed **:** UP-TO-DATE **2 :** fully familiar **:** CONVERSANT

1auc·tion \ˈȯk-shən\ *n* [L *auction-, auctio,* lit., increase, fr. *auctus,* pp. of *augēre* to increase — more at EKE] **1 :** a public sale of property to the highest bidder **2 :** the act or process of bidding in some card games

2auction *vt* **auc·tioned; auc·tion·ing** \-sh(ə-)niŋ\ **:** to sell at auction <~*ed* off his library>

auction bridge *n* **:** a bridge game differing from contract bridge in that tricks made in excess of the contract are scored toward game

auc·tion·eer \ˌȯk-shə-ˈni(ə)r\ *n* **:** an agent who sells goods at auction — **auctioneer** *vt*

auc·to·ri·al \ȯk-ˈtōr-ē-əl, -ˈtȯr-\ *adj* [L *auctor* author — more at AUTHOR] **:** of or relating to an author

aud *abbr* audit; auditor

au·da·cious \ȯ-ˈdā-shəs\ *adj* [MF *audacieux,* fr. *audace* boldness, fr. L *audacia,* fr. *audac-, audax* bold, fr. *audēre* to dare, fr. *avidus* eager — more at AVID] **1 a :** intrepidly daring **:** ADVENTUROUS <an ~ mountain climber> **b :** recklessly bold **:** RASH **2 :** contemptuous of law, religion, or decorum **:** INSOLENT **3 :** marked by originality and verve <a bright ~ comedy about love> — **au·da·cious·ly** *adv* — **au·da·cious·ness** *n*

au·dac·i·ty \ȯ-ˈdas-ət-ē\ *n, pl* **-ties** [ME *audacite,* fr. L *audac-, audax*] **1 :** the quality or state of being audacious: **a :** intrepid boldness **b :** bold or arrogant disregard of normal restraints **2 :** an audacious act — usu. used in pl. ***syn*** see TEMERITY ***ant*** circumspection

1au·di·ble \ˈȯd-ə-bəl\ *adj* [LL *audibilis,* fr. L *audire* to hear; akin to Gk *aisthanesthai* to perceive, Skt *āvis* evidently] **:** heard or capable of being heard — **au·di·bil·i·ty** \ˌȯd-ə-ˈbil-ət-ē\ *n* — **au·di·bly** \ˈȯd-ə-blē\ *adv*

2audible *n* **:** AUTOMATIC 2

au·di·ence \ˈȯd-ē-ən(t)s, ˈäd-\ *n* [ME, fr. MF, fr. L *audientia,* fr. *audient-, audiens,* prp. of *audire*] **1 :** the act or state of hearing **2 a :** a formal hearing or interview <an ~ with the pope> **b :** an opportunity of being heard <he would succeed if he were once given ~> **3 a :** a group of listeners or spectators **b :** the reading public **4 :** FOLLOWING

au·di·ent \-ənt\ *n* [L *audient-, audiens,* prp.] **:** one that hears

au·dile \ˈȯ-ˌdīl\ *n* [L *audire* to hear] **:** a person whose mental imagery is auditory rather than visual or motor — **audile** *adj*

aud·ing \ˈȯd-iŋ\ *n* [L *audire* + E *-ing*] **:** the process of hearing, recognizing, and interpreting a spoken language

ə abut	ᵊ kitten	ər further	a back	ā bake	ä cot, cart
aù out	ch chin	e less	ē easy	g gift	i trip	ī life
j joke	ŋ sing	ō flow	ȯ flaw	ȯi coin	th thin	t͟h this
ü loot	ù foot	y yet	yü few	yù furious	zh vision

1au·dio \'ȯd-ē-,ō\ *adj* [*audio-*] **1 :** of or relating to acoustic, mechanical, or electrical frequencies corresponding to normally audible sound waves which are of frequencies approximately from 15 to 20,000 cycles per second **2 a :** of or relating to sound or its reproduction and esp. high-fidelity reproduction **b :** relating to or used in the transmission or reception of sound — compare VIDEO
2audio *n* **1 :** the transmission, reception, or reproduction of sound **2 :** the section of television or motion picture equipment that deals with sound **3 :** an audio signal; *broadly* **:** SOUND
audio- *comb form* [L *audire* to hear] **1 :** hearing <*audio*meter> **2 :** sound <*audio*phile> **3 :** auditory and <*audio*visual>
au·dio·gen·ic \,ȯd-ē-ō-'jen-ik\ *adj* **:** produced by frequencies corresponding to sound waves — used esp. of epileptoid responses <~ seizures>
au·dio–lin·gual \,ȯd-ē-ō-'liŋ-g(yə-)wəl\ *adj* **:** involving a drill routine of listening and speaking in language learning
au·di·ol·o·gy \,ȯd-ē-'äl-ə-jē\ *n* **:** a branch of science dealing with hearing; *specif* **:** therapy of individuals having impaired hearing — **au·di·o·log·i·cal** \-ē-ə-'läj-i-kəl\ *adj* — **au·di·ol·o·gist** \-ē-'äl-ə-jəst\ *n*
au·di·om·e·ter \,ȯd-ē-'äm-ət-ər\ *n* **:** an instrument used in measuring the acuity of hearing — **au·dio·met·ric** \-ē-ō-'me-trik\ *adj* — **au·di·om·e·try** \-ē-'äm-ə-trē\ *n*
au·dio·phile \'ȯd-ē-ō-,fīl\ *n* **:** one who is enthusiastic about sound reproduction and esp. music from high-fidelity broadcasts or recordings
au·dio·tape \,ȯd-ē-ō-'tāp\ *n* **:** a tape recording of sound
au·dio·vi·su·al \,ȯd-ē-(,)ō-'vizh-(ə-)wəl, -'vizh-əl\ *adj* **1 :** of or relating to both hearing and sight **2 :** designed to aid in learning or teaching by making use of both hearing and sight <an extensive ~ department of films and recordings>
au·dio·vi·su·als \-wəlz, -əlz\ *n pl* **:** instructional materials (as filmstrips accompanied by recordings) that make use of both sight and sound
1au·dit \'ȯd-ət\ *n* [ME, fr. L *auditus* act of hearing, fr. *auditus*, pp.] **1 a :** a formal or official examination and verification of an account book **b :** a methodical examination and review **2 :** the final report of an examination of books of account by auditors — **au·dit·able** \-ə-bəl\ *adj*
2audit *vt* **1 :** to examine with intent to verify <~ the account books> **2 :** to attend (a course) without working for or expecting to receive formal credit
1au·di·tion \ȯ-'dish-ən\ *n* [MF or L; MF, fr. L *audition-, auditio*, fr. *auditus*, pp. of *audire*] **1 :** the power or sense of hearing **2 :** the act of hearing; *esp* **:** a critical hearing <an ~ of new recordings> **3 :** a trial performance to appraise an entertainer's merits
2audition *vb* **au·di·tioned; au·di·tion·ing** \-'dish-(ə-)niŋ\ *vt* **:** to test in an audition ~ *vi* **:** to give a trial performance
au·di·tive \'ȯd-ət-iv\ *adj* **:** AUDITORY
au·di·tor \'ȯd-ət-ər\ *n* **1 :** one that hears or listens; *esp* **:** one that is a member of an audience **2 :** one authorized to examine and verify accounts **3 :** one that audits a course of study **4 :** one that hears (as a court case) in the capacity of judge
au·di·to·ri·um \,ȯd-ə-'tōr-ē-əm, -'tȯr-\ *n* **1 :** the part of a public building where an audience sits **2 :** a room, hall, or building used for public gatherings
1au·di·to·ry \'ȯd-ə-,tōr-ē, -,tȯr-\ *n* [ME *auditorie*, fr. L *auditorium* auditorium] **1** *archaic* **:** AUDIENCE **2** *archaic* **:** AUDITORIUM
2au·di·to·ry *adj* [LL *auditorius*] **:** of, relating to, or experienced through hearing
auditory nerve *n* **:** either of the 8th pair of cranial nerves connecting the inner ear with the brain and transmitting impulses concerned with hearing and balance — see EAR illustration
au fait \ō-'fā\ *adj* [F, lit., to the point] **1 :** fully competent **:** CAPABLE **2 :** fully informed **:** FAMILIAR **3 :** socially correct
Auf·klä·rung \'au̇f-,klā-rəŋ, -,kler-əŋ\ *n* [G] **:** ENLIGHTENMENT 2
au fond \ō-fōⁿ\ *adv* [F] **:** at bottom **:** FUNDAMENTALLY
auf Wie·der·seh·en \au̇f-'vēd-ər-,zā(-ə)n\ *interj* [G, lit., till seeing again] — used to express farewell
aug *abbr* augmentative
Aug *abbr* August
Au·ge·an \ȯ-'jē-ən\ *adj* [L *Augeas*, king of Elis, fr. Gk *Augeias;* fr. the legend that his stable, left neglected for 30 years, was finally cleaned by Hercules] **:** extremely formidable or difficult and occas. distasteful <an ~ task>
Augean stable *n* **:** a condition or place marked by great accumulation of filth or corruption — usu. used in pl. <every government should attend to cleaning its own *Augean stables*>
au·gend \'ȯ-,jend\ *n* [L *augendus*, gerundive of *augēre* to increase — more at EKE] **:** a quantity to which an addend is added
au·ger \'ȯ-gər\ *n* [ME, alter. (resulting from incorrect division of *a nauger*) of *nauger*, fr. OE *nafogār;* akin to OHG *nabugēr* auger; both fr. a prehistoric WGmc-NGmc compound whose constituents are represented by OE *nafu*, nave and *gār* spear — more at GORE] **1 :** a tool for boring holes in wood consisting of a shank with a crosswise handle for turning, a central tapered screw, and a pair of cutting lips **2 :** any of various instruments or devices made like an auger and used for boring (as in soil), forcing (as through a meat grinder), or for moving material (as in a snow thrower)

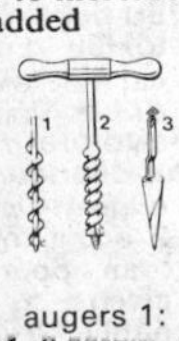

augers 1: *1, 2* screw, *3* tapering pod

1aught \'ȯt, 'ät\ *pron* [ME, fr. OE *āwiht*, fr. *ā* ever + *wiht* creature, thing — more at AYE, WIGHT] **1** *archaic* **:** ANYTHING **2 :** ALL <for ~ I care>
2aught *adv, archaic* **:** at all
3aught *n* [alter. (resulting from incorrect division of *a naught*) of *naught*] **1 :** ZERO, CIPHER **2** *archaic* **:** NONENTITY, NOTHING
au·gite \'ȯ-,jīt\ *n* [L *augites*, a precious stone, fr. Gk *augitēs*] **1 :** a mineral consisting of an aluminous usu. black or dark green pyroxene that is found in igneous rocks **2 :** PYROXENE — **au·git·ic** \ȯ-'jit-ik\ *adj*
1aug·ment \ȯg-'ment\ *vb* [ME *augmenten*, fr. MF *augmenter*, fr. LL *augmentare*, fr. *augmentum* increase, fr. *augēre* to increase — more at EKE] *vi* **:** to become augmented ~ *vt* **1 :** to make (something well or adequately developed) greater, more numerous, larger, or more intense **2 :** to add an augment to ***syn*** see INCREASE ***ant*** abate — **aug·ment·able** \-ə-bəl\ *adj* — **aug·ment·er** *or* **aug·men·tor** \-'ment-ər\ *n*
2aug·ment \'ȯg-,ment\ *n* **:** a vowel prefixed or a lengthening of the initial vowel to mark past time esp. in Greek and Sanskrit verbs
aug·men·ta·tion \,ȯg-mən-'tā-shən, -,men-\ *n* **1 a :** the act or process of augmenting **b :** the state of being augmented **2 :** something that augments **:** ADDITION
1aug·men·ta·tive \ȯg-'ment-ət-iv\ *adj* **1 :** able to augment **2 :** indicating large size and sometimes awkwardness or unattractiveness — used of words and affixes; compare DIMINUTIVE
2augmentative *n* **:** an augmentative word or affix
aug·ment·ed \ȯg-'ment-əd\ *adj, of a musical interval* **:** made one half step greater than major or perfect <an ~ fifth>
augmented matrix *n* **:** a matrix whose elements are the coefficients of a set of simultaneous linear equations with the constant terms of the equations entered in an added column
au gra·tin \ō-'grat-ᵊn, ȯ-, -'grät-\ *adj* [F, lit., with the burnt scrapings from the pan] **:** covered with bread crumbs, butter, and cheese and then browned
1au·gur \'ȯ-gər\ *n* [L; prob. akin to L *augēre*] **1 :** an official diviner of ancient Rome **2 :** one held to foretell events by omens
2augur *vt* **1 :** to foretell esp. from omens **2 :** to give promise of **:** PRESAGE <higher pay ~*s* a better future> ~ *vi* **:** to predict the future esp. from omens
au·gu·ry \'ȯ-gyə-rē, -gə-\ *n, pl* **-ries 1 :** divination from omens or portents or from chance events (as the fall of lots) **2 :** OMEN, PORTENT
au·gust \ȯ-'gəst\ *adj* [L *augustus;* akin to L *augēre* to increase] **:** marked by majestic dignity or grandeur — **au·gust·ly** *adv* — **au·gust·ness** \-'gəs(t)-nəs\ *n*
Au·gust \'ȯ-gəst\ *n* [ME, fr. OE, fr. L *Augustus*, fr. *Augustus* Caesar] **:** the 8th month of the Gregorian calendar
Au·gus·tan \ȯ-'gəs-tən, ə-\ *adj* **1 :** of, relating to, or characteristic of Augustus Caesar or his age **2 :** of, relating to, or characteristic of the neoclassical period in England — **Augustan** *n*
1Au·gus·tin·i·an \,ȯ-gə-'stin-ē-ən\ *adj* **1 :** of or relating to St. Augustine or his doctrines **2 :** of or relating to any of several orders under a rule ascribed to St. Augustine — **Au·gus·tin·i·an·ism** \-ē-ə-,niz-əm\ *n*
2Augustinian *n* **1 :** a follower of St. Augustine **2 :** a member of an Augustinian order; *specif* **:** a friar of the Hermits of St. Augustine founded in 1256 and devoted to educational, missionary, and parish work
au jus \ō-'zhü(s), -'jüs; ō-zhuē\ *adj* [F, lit., with juice] **:** served in the juice obtained from roasting
auk \'ȯk\ *n* [Norw or Icel *alk, alka*, fr. ON *ālka;* akin to L *olor* swan] **:** any of several black and white short-necked diving seabirds (family Alcidae) that breed in colder parts of the northern hemisphere
auk·let \'ȯ-klət\ *n* **:** any of several small auks of the No. Pacific coasts
auld \'ȯl(d), 'äl(d)\ *adj, chiefly Scot* **:** OLD
auld lang syne \,ōl-,(d)aŋ-'zīn, ,ōl-,(d)laŋ-, ,ōl-\ *n* [Sc, lit., old long ago] **:** the good old times

great auk

au na·tu·rel \,ō-,nat-ə-'rel\ *adj* [F] **1 a :** being in natural style or condition **b :** NUDE **2 :** cooked plainly
aunt \'ant, 'ånt\ *n* [ME, fr. OF *ante*, fr. L *amita;* akin to OHG *amma* mother, nurse, Gk *amma* nurse] **1 :** the sister of one's father or mother **2 :** the wife of one's uncle — **aunt·hood** \-,hu̇d\ *n* — **aunt·like** \-,līk\ *adj* — **aunt·ly** *adj*
Aunt Sal·ly \-'sal-ē\ *n, pl* **Aunt Sallies** [*Aunt Sally*, name given to an effigy of a woman smoking a pipe set up as an amusement attraction at English fairs for patrons to throw missiles at] **1** *Brit* **:** STRAW MAN 1 **2** *Brit* **:** one that is set up to invite attack or criticism **:** TARGET
au pair girl \'ō-'pa(ə)r-, -'pe(ə)r-\ *n* [F *au pair*, on even terms] **:** a foreign girl living in England who does domestic work for a family in return for room and board and the opportunity to learn the English language — called also *au pair*
aur- *or* **auri-** *comb form* [L, fr. *auris* — more at EAR] **1 :** ear <*aural*> <*auri*scope> **2 :** aural and <*auri*nasal>
au·ra \'ȯr-ə\ *n* [ME, fr. L, air, breeze, fr. Gk; akin to Gk *aēr* air] **1 a :** a subtle sensory stimulus (as an aroma) **b :** a distinctive atmosphere surrounding a given source <the place had an ~ of mystery> **2 :** a luminous radiation **:** NIMBUS **3 :** a subjective sensation (as of lights) experienced before an attack of some nervous disorders
au·ral \'ȯr-əl\ *adj* **:** of or relating to the ear or to the sense of hearing — **au·ral·ly** \-ə-lē\ *adv*
aurar *pl of* EYRIR
au·re·ate \'ȯr-ē-ət\ *adj* [ME *aureat*, fr. ML *aureatus* decorated with gold, fr. L *aureus* golden — more at ORIOLE] **1 :** of a golden color or brilliance **2 :** marked by grandiloquent and rhetorical style
au·re·ole \'ȯr-ē-,ōl\ *or* **au·re·o·la** \ȯ-'rē-ə-lə\ *n* [ME *aureole* heavenly crown worn by saints, fr. ML *aureola*, fr. L, fem. of *aureolus* golden — more at ORIOLE] **1 :** a radiant light around the head or body of a representation of a sacred personage **2 :** RADIANCE, AURA <had about him an ~ of youth and health> **3 :** the luminous area surrounding the sun or other bright light when seen through thin cloud or mist **:** CORONA **4 :** a ring-shaped zone around an igneous intrusion — **aureole** *vt*
Au·reo·my·cin \,ȯr-ē-ō-'mīs-ᵊn\ *trademark* — used for chlortetracycline
au re·voir \,ōr-əv-'wär, ,ȯr-\ *n* [F, lit., till seeing again] **:** GOOD-BYE — often used interjectionally
au·ric \'ȯr-ik\ *adj* [L *aurum* gold — more at ORIOLE] **:** of, relating to, or derived from gold esp. when trivalent

au·ri·cle \'ȯr-i-kəl\ *n* [L *auricula,* fr. dim. of *auris* ear] **1 a** : PINNA 2b **b** : the chamber or either of the chambers of the heart that receives blood from the veins and forces it into the ventricle or ventricles — see HEART illustration **2** : an angular or ear-shaped anatomic lobe or process

au·ric·u·la \ȯ-'rik-yə-lə\ *n* [NL, fr. L, external ear] **1** : a yellow-flowered Alpine primrose (*Primula auricula*) **2** : AURICLE

au·ric·u·lar \ȯ-'rik-yə-lər\ *adj* **1** : of, relating to, or using the ear or the sense of hearing **2** : told privately <an ~ confession> **3** : understood or recognized by the sense of hearing **4** : of or relating to an auricle or auricula

au·ric·u·late \ȯ-'rik-yə-lət\ *adj* : having ears or auricles

au·ric·u·lo·ven·tric·u·lar \ȯ-ˌrik-yə-(ˌ)lō-ven-'trik-yə-lər, -vən-\ *adj* : ATRIOVENTRICULAR

au·rif·er·ous \ȯ-'rif-(ə-)rəs\ *adj* [L *aurifer,* fr. *aurum* + *-fer* -ferous] : gold-bearing

Au·ri·ga \ȯ-'rī-gə\ *n* [L (gen. *Aurigae*), lit., charioteer] : a constellation between Perseus and Gemini

Au·ri·gna·cian \ˌȯr-ēn-'yā-shən\ *adj* [F *aurignacien,* fr. *Aurignac,* France] : of or relating to an Upper Paleolithic culture marked by finely made artifacts of stone and bone, paintings, and engravings

au·rochs \'au̇(ə)r-ˌäks, 'ȯ(ə)r-\ *n, pl* **aurochs** [G, fr. OHG *ūrohso,* fr. *ūro* aurochs + *ohso* ox; akin to OE *ūr* aurochs — more at OX] **1** : URUS **2** : WISENT

au·ro·ra \ə-'rōr-ə, ȯ-, -'rȯr-\ *n, pl* **auroras** *or* **au·ro·rae** \-(ˌ)ē\ [L — more at EAST] **1** *cap* : the Roman goddess of dawn — compare EOS **2** : DAWN **3 a** : AURORA BOREALIS **b** : AURORA AUSTRALIS — **au·ro·ral** \-əl\ *adj* — **au·ro·re·an** \-ē-ən\ *adj*

aurora aus·tra·lis \-ȯ-'strā-ləs, -ä-'strā-\ *n* [NL, lit., southern aurora] : a phenomenon in the southern hemisphere corresponding to the aurora borealis in the northern hemisphere

aurora bo·re·al·is \-ˌbōr-ē-'al-əs, -ˌbȯr-\ *n* [NL, lit., northern dawn] : a luminous phenomenon that consists of streamers or arches of light in the sky at night, is held to be of electrical origin, and appears to best advantage in the arctic regions

au·rous \'ȯr-əs\ *adj* [ISV, fr. L *aurum* gold — more at ORIOLE] : of, relating to, or containing gold esp. when univalent

AUS *abbr* Army of the United States

aus·cul·tate \'ȯ-skəl-ˌtāt\ *vt* **-tat·ed; -tat·ing** [back-formation fr. *auscultation*] : to examine by auscultation — **aus·cul·ta·to·ry** \ȯ-'skəl-tə-ˌtōr-ē, -ˌtȯr-\ *adj*

aus·cul·ta·tion \ˌȯ-skəl-'tā-shən\ *n* [L *auscultation-, auscultatio* act of listening, fr. *auscultatus,* pp. of *auscultare* to listen; akin to L *auris* ear — more at EAR] : the act of listening to sounds arising within organs (as the lungs) as an aid to diagnosis and treatment

aus·land·er \'au̇-ˌslen-dər, -ˌslan-\ *n* [G *ausländer,* lit., outlander] : OUTSIDER, FOREIGNER

aus·pi·cate \'ȯ-spə-ˌkāt\ *vt* **-cat·ed; -cat·ing** [L *auspicatus,* pp. of *auspicari* to take auspices, fr. *auspic-, auspex*] : to initiate or enter upon esp. under circumstances or with a procedure (as drinking a toast) calculated to ensure good luck

aus·pice \'ȯ-spəs\ *n, pl* **aus·pic·es** \-spə-səz, -ˌsēz\ [L *auspicium,* fr. *auspic-, auspex* diviner by birds, fr. *avis* bird + *specere* to look, look at — more at AVIARY, SPY] **1** : observation by an augur esp. of the flight and feeding of birds to discover omens **2** : a prophetic sign; *esp* : a favorable sign **3** *pl* : kindly patronage and guidance : PROTECTION <under the ~*s* of the cultural exchange program>

aus·pi·cious \ȯ-'spish-əs\ *adj* **1** : affording a favorable auspice : PROPITIOUS <made an ~ beginning by getting an A> **2** : attended by good auspices : PROSPEROUS <an ~ year> ***syn*** see FAVORABLE ***ant*** inauspicious, ill-omened — **aus·pi·cious·ly** *adv* — **aus·pi·cious·ness** *n*

Aus·sie \'ȯ-sē, 'äs-ē\ *n* [*Aus*tralian + *-ie*] : a native or inhabitant of Australia

aus·ten·ite \'ȯs-tə-ˌnīt, 'äs-\ *n* [F, fr. Sir W. C. Roberts-*Austen* †1902 E metallurgist] : a solid solution in iron of carbon and sometimes other solutes that occurs as a constituent of steel under certain conditions — **aus·ten·it·ic** \ˌȯs-tə-'nit-ik, ˌäs-\ *adj*

aus·tere \ȯ-'sti(ə)r\ *adj* [ME, fr. MF, fr. L *austerus,* fr. Gk *austēros* harsh, severe; akin to Gk *hauos* dry — more at SERE] **1 a** : stern and forbidding in appearance and manner <~ Puritan colonists> **b** : SOMBER, GRAVE <dressed all in ~ black for the funeral> **2** : rigidly abstemious : ASCETIC <an ~ old hermit living on berries and roots> **3** : UNADORNED, SIMPLE <an ~ chair with a straight back> ***syn*** see SEVERE ***ant*** ardent (*as of persons*), exuberant (*as of style*) — **aus·tere·ly** *adv* — **aus·tere·ness** *n*

aus·ter·i·ty \ȯ-'ster-ət-ē\ *n, pl* **-ties** **1** : the quality or state of being austere **2 a** : an austere act, manner, or attitude **b** : an ascetic practice **3** : enforced or extreme economy

¹Austr- *or* **Austro-** *comb form* [ME *austr-,* fr. L, fr. *Austr-, Auster* south wind; akin to L *aurora* dawn — more at EAST] **1** : south : southern <*Austro*asiatic> **2** : Australian and <*Austro*-Malayan>

²Austr- *or* **Austro-** *comb form* [prob. fr. NL, fr. *Austria*] : Austrian and <*Austro*-Hungarian>

aus·tral \'ȯs-trəl, 'äs-\ *adj* **1** : SOUTHERN **2** *cap* : AUSTRALIAN

Aus·tra·lia Day \ȯ-'strāl-yə-, ä-\ *n* : a national holiday in Australia observed in commemoration of the landing of the British at Sydney Cove in 1788 and observed on Jan. 26 if a Monday and otherwise on the next Monday

¹Aus·tra·lian \ȯ-'strāl-yən, ä-\ *n* : a native or inhabitant of the Australian commonwealth

²Australian *adj* **1** : of, relating to, or characteristic of the continent or commonwealth of Australia, its inhabitants, or the languages spoken there **2** : of, relating to, or being a biogeographic region that comprises Australia and the islands north of it from the Celebes eastward, Tasmania, New Zealand, and Polynesia

Australian ballot *n* : an official ballot printed at public expense on which the names of all the nominated candidates and proposals appear and which is distributed only at the polling place and marked in secret

Australian pine *n* : any of several casuarinas (esp. *Casuarina equisetifolia*) now widely grown as ornamentals in warm regions (as Florida)

Australian Rules football *n* : a game resembling rugby that is played between two teams of 18 players on a field 180–190 yards long that has four goalposts at each end

Australian terrier *n* : a small rather short-legged usu. grayish wirehaired terrier of Australian origin

Aus·tra·loid \'ȯs-trə-ˌlȯid, 'äs-\ *adj* [*Austral*ia + E *-oid*] : of or relating to an ethnic group including the Australian aborigines and other peoples of southern Asia and Pacific islands sometimes including the Ainu — **Australoid** *n*

aus·tra·lo·pith·e·cine \ȯ-ˌstrā-lō-'pith-ə-ˌsīn, ä-; ˌȯs-trə-, ˌäs-\ *adj* [deriv. of L *australis* southern (fr. *Austr-, Auster*) + Gk *pithēkos* ape — more at PITHECANTHROPUS] : of or relating to extinct southern African hominids (esp. genus *Australopithecus*) with near-human dentition and a relatively small brain — **australopithecine** *n*

Aus·tral·orp \'ȯs-trə-ˌlȯ(ə)rp, 'äs-\ *n* [*Austral*ian + *Orp*ington] : a usu. black domestic fowl developed in Australia and valued for egg production

Aus·tro·asi·at·ic \'ȯs-(ˌ)trō-ˌā-z(h)ē-'at-ik, 'äs- *also* -ˌā-shē-\ *adj* : of, relating to, or constituting a family of languages once widespread over northeastern India and Indochina

Aus·tro·ne·sian \ˌȯs-trə-'nē-zhən, ˌäs-, -shən\ *adj* [*Austronesia,* islands of the southern Pacific] : of, relating to, or constituting a family of agglutinative languages spoken in the area extending from Madagascar eastward through the Malay peninsula and archipelago to Hawaii and Easter Island and including practically all the native languages of the Pacific Islands with the exception of the Australian, Papuan, and Negrito languages

aut- *or* **auto-** *comb form* [Gk, fr. *autos* same, -self, self] **1** : self : same one <*aut*ism> <*auto*biography> **2** : automatic : self-acting : self-regulating <*auto*dyne>

au·ta·coid \'ȯt-ə-ˌkȯid\ *n* [*aut-* + Gk *akos* remedy; akin to OIr *hicc* healing] : a specific organic substance (as a hormone) forming in one part of the body, moving in the body fluid or the sap, and modifying the activity of the cells of another part — **au·ta·coi·dal** \ˌȯt-ə-'kȯid-ᵊl\ *adj*

au·tar·chic \ȯ-'tär-kik\ *adj* : AUTARKIC — **au·tar·chi·cal** \-ki-kəl\ *adj*

¹au·tar·chy \'ȯ-ˌtär-kē\ *n, pl* **-chies** [Gk *autarchia,* fr. *aut-* + *-archia* -archy] **1** : absolute sovereignty **2** : absolute or autocratic rule

²autarchy *n* [by alter.] : AUTARKY

au·tar·kic \ȯ-'tär-kik\ *adj* : of, relating to, or marked by autarky — **au·tar·ki·cal** \-ki-kəl\ *adj*

au·tar·ky \'ȯ-ˌtär-kē\ *n* [G *autarkie,* fr. Gk *autarkeia,* fr. *autarkēs* self-sufficient, fr. *aut-* + *arkein* to defend, suffice — more at ARK] **1** : SELF-SUFFICIENCY, INDEPENDENCE; *specif* : national economic self-sufficiency and independence **2** : a policy of establishing a self-sufficient and independent national economy

aut·ecol·o·gy \ˌȯt-i-'käl-ə-jē, ˌȯt-ē-\ *n* [ISV] : ecology dealing with individual organisms or individual kinds of organisms — **aut·eco·log·i·cal** \ˌȯt-ˌē-kə-'läj-i-kəl, -ˌek-ə-\ *adj*

au·teur theory \ō-'tər-\ *n* [part trans. of F *politique des auteurs,* fr. *auteur* author; fr. the view that directors are the true authors of a film] : a theory in motion-picture criticism that views the director as the primary creative force in a motion picture

auth *abbr* **1** authentic **2** author **3** authorized

au·then·tic \ə-'thent-ik, ȯ-\ *adj* [ME *autentik,* fr. MF *autentique,* fr. LL *authenticus,* fr. Gk *authentikos,* fr. *authentēs* perpetrator, master, fr. *aut-* + *-hentēs* (akin to Gk *anyein* to accomplish, Skt *sanoti* he gains)] **1** *obs* : AUTHORITATIVE **2** : worthy of acceptance or belief as conforming to fact or reality : TRUSTWORTHY **3 a** : not imaginery, false, or imitation <one of the few remaining ~ colonial buildings> **b** : conforming to an original so as to reproduce essential features <an ~ reproduction of a colonial farmhouse> **4 a** *of a church mode* : ranging upward from the keynote — compare PLAGAL 1 **b** *of a cadence* : progressing from the dominant chord to the tonic — compare PLAGAL 2 — **au·then·ti·cal·ly** \-i-k(ə-)lē\ *adv* — **au·then·tic·i·ty** \ˌȯ-ˌthen-'tis-ət-ē, -thən-\ *n*

syn AUTHENTIC, GENUINE, VERITABLE, BONA FIDE *shared meaning element* : being actually and precisely what is claimed. AUTHENTIC stresses fidelity to actuality and fact and may imply authority or trustworthiness in determining this relationship <confirmed both by legend and *authentic* record —J. A. Froude> GENUINE implies accordance with an original or type without counterfeiting, admixture, or adulteration <*genuine* maple syrup> or it may stress sincerity or the absence of factitiousness <*genuine* piety> VERITABLE implies a correspondence with truth and typically conveys a suggestion of affirmation <though Christ be the *veritable* Son of God — A. T. Quiller-Couch> or in figurative or hyperbolic contexts asserts the justice of the designation <he is a *veritable* fool> BONA FIDE, often interchangeable with *authentic* or *genuine,* can distinctively apply when good faith or sincerity is in question <a *bona fide* sale of securities> ***ant*** spurious

au·then·ti·cate \ə-'thent-i-ˌkāt, ȯ-\ *vt* **-cat·ed; -cat·ing** : to prove or serve to prove the authenticity of ***syn*** see CONFIRM ***ant*** impugn — **au·then·ti·ca·tion** \-ˌthent-i-'kā-shən\ *n* — **au·then·ti·ca·tor** \-'thent-i-ˌkāt-ər\ *n*

au·thor \'ȯ-thər\ *n* [ME *auctour,* fr. ONF, fr. L *auctor* promoter, originator, author, fr. *auctus,* pp. of *augēre* to increase — more at EKE] **1** : the writer of a literary work (as a book) **2 a** : one that originates or gives existence : SOURCE <trying to track down the ~ of the rumor> <the ~ of a theory> **b** *cap* : GOD 1 ***syn*** see MAKER — **au·thor·ess** \'ȯ-th(ə-)rəs\ *n* — **au·tho·ri·al** \ȯ-'thōr-ē-əl, -'thȯr-\ *adj*

au·thor·i·tar·i·an \ȯ-ˌthär-ə-ˈter-ē-ən, ə-, -ˌthȯr-\ *adj* **1 :** of, relating to, or favoring blind submission to authority <had ~ parents> **2 :** of, relating to, or favoring a concentration of power in a leader or an elite not constitutionally responsible to the people — **authoritarian** *n* — **au·thor·i·tar·i·an·ism** \-ē-ə-ˌniz-əm\ *n*

au·thor·i·ta·tive \ə-ˈthär-ə-ˌtāt-iv, ȯ-, -ˈthȯr-\ *adj* **1 a :** having or proceeding from authority : OFFICIAL <~ church doctrine> **b :** entitled to credit or acceptance : CONCLUSIVE <a most ~ literary critique> **2 :** DICTATORIAL, PEREMPTORY — **au·thor·i·ta·tive·ly** *adv* — **au·thor·i·ta·tive·ness** *n*

au·thor·i·ty \ə-ˈthär-ət-ē, ȯ-, -ˈthȯr-\ *n, pl* **-ties** [ME *auctorite,* fr. OF *auctorité,* fr. L *auctoritat-, auctoritas* opinion, decision, power, fr. *auctor*] **1 a** (1) **:** a citation (as from a book or file) used in defense or support (2) **:** the source from which the citation is drawn **b** (1) **:** a conclusive statement or set of statements (as an official decision of a court) (2) **:** a decision taken as a precedent (3) **:** TESTIMONY **c :** an individual cited or appealed to as an expert **2 a :** power to influence or command thought, opinion, or behavior **b :** freedom granted by one in authority : RIGHT **3 a :** persons in command; *specif* **:** GOVERNMENT **b :** a governmental agency or corporation to administer a revenue-producing public enterprise <the transit ~> **4 a :** GROUNDS, WARRANT <had excellent ~ for his strange actions> **b :** convincing force : WEIGHT <his strong tenor lent ~ to the performance> ***syn*** see INFLUENCE

au·tho·ri·za·tion \ˌȯ-th(ə-)rə-ˈzā-shən\ *n* **1 :** the act of authorizing **2 :** an instrument that authorizes : SANCTION

au·tho·rize \ˈȯ-thə-ˌrīz\ *vt* **-rized; -riz·ing 1 :** to invest esp. with legal authority : EMPOWER <*authorized* to act for her husband> **2 :** to establish by or as if by authority : SANCTION <a custom *authorized* by time> **3** *archaic* **:** to furnish a ground for : JUSTIFY — **au·tho·riz·er** *n*

Authorized Version *n* **:** a revision of the English Bishops' Bible carried out under James I, published in 1611, and widely used by Protestants

au·thor·ship \ˈȯ-thər-ˌship\ *n* **1 :** the profession of writing **2 a :** the origin of a literary production **b :** the state or act of creating or causing

au·tism \ˈȯ-ˌtiz-əm\ *n* **:** absorption in self-centered subjective mental activity (as daydreams, fantasies, delusions, and hallucinations) esp. when accompanied by marked withdrawal from reality — **au·tis·tic** \ȯ-ˈtis-tik\ *adj*

[1]**au·to** \ˈȯt-(ˌ)ō, ˈät-\ *n, pl* **autos :** AUTOMOBILE

[2]**auto** *abbr* automatic

[1]**auto-** — see AUT-

[2]**auto-** *comb form* [[1]*automobile*] **:** self-propelling : automotive <*auto*truck>

au·to·an·ti·body \ˌȯt-(ˌ)ō-ˈant-i-ˌbäd-ē\ *n* **:** an antibody against one of the constituents of the tissues of the individual that produces it

au·to·bahn \ˈȯt-ō-ˌbän, ˈau̇t-\ *n* [G, fr. *auto* + *bahn* road] **:** a German expressway

au·to·bio·graph·i·cal \ˌȯt-ə-ˌbī-ə-ˈgraf-i-kəl\ *also* **au·to·bio·graph·ic** \-ik\ *adj* **:** of, relating to, or of the nature of an autobiography — **au·to·bio·graph·i·cal·ly** \-i-k(ə-)lē\ *adv*

au·to·bi·og·ra·phy \ˌȯt-ə-bī-ˈäg-rə-fē, -bē-\ *n* **:** the biography of a person narrated by himself — **au·to·bi·og·ra·pher** \-fər\ *n*

au·to·bus \ˈȯt-ō-ˌbəs\ *n* [*auto* + *bus*] **:** OMNIBUS 1

au·to·cade \ˈȯt-ō-ˌkād\ *n* **:** MOTORCADE

au·to·ca·tal·y·sis \ˌȯt-ō-kə-ˈtal-ə-səs\ *n, pl* **-y·ses** \-ˌsēz\ [NL] **:** catalysis of a reaction by one of its products — **au·to·cat·a·lyt·ic** \-ˌkat-ᵊl-ˈit-ik\ *adj*

au·to·ceph·a·lous \ˌȯt-ō-ˈsef-ə-ləs\ *adj* [LGk *autokephalos,* fr. Gk *aut-* + *kephalē* head — more at CEPHALIC] **:** being independent of external and esp. patriarchal authority — used esp. of Eastern national churches

au·toch·thon \ȯ-ˈtäk-thən\ *n, pl* **-thons** *or* **-tho·nes** \-thə-ˌnēz\ [Gk *autochthōn,* fr. *aut-* + *chthōn* earth — more at HUMBLE] **1 a :** one held to have sprung from the ground he inhabits **b :** ABORIGINE, NATIVE **2 :** something that is autochthonous; *esp* **:** an indigenous plant or animal — **au·toch·tho·nism** \-thə-ˌniz-əm\ *n*

au·toch·tho·nous \ȯ-ˈtäk-thə-nəs\ *adj* **:** INDIGENOUS, NATIVE — **au·toch·tho·nous·ly** *adv* — **au·toch·tho·ny** \-nē\ *n*

[1]**au·to·clave** \ˈȯt-ō-ˌklāv\ *n* [F, fr. *aut-* + L *clavis* key — more at CLAVICLE] **:** an apparatus (as for sterilizing) using superheated steam under pressure

[2]**autoclave** *vt* **-claved; -clav·ing :** to subject to the action of an autoclave

au·toc·ra·cy \ȯ-ˈtäk-rə-sē\ *n, pl* **-cies 1 :** government in which one person possesses unlimited power **2 :** the authority or rule of an autocrat **3 :** a community or state governed by autocracy

au·to·crat \ˈȯt-ə-ˌkrat\ *n* [F *autocrate,* fr. Gk *autokratēs* ruling by oneself, absolute, fr. *aut-* + *-kratēs* ruling — more at -CRAT] **1 :** a person (as a monarch) ruling with unlimited authority **2 :** one who has undisputed influence or power

au·to·crat·ic \ˌȯt-ə-ˈkrat-ik\ *adj* **1 :** of, relating to, or being an autocracy : ABSOLUTE <an ~ government> **2 :** characteristic of or resembling an autocrat : DESPOTIC <an ~ ruler> — **au·to·crat·i·cal** \-i-kəl\ *adj* — **au·to·crat·i·cal·ly** \-i-k(ə-)lē\ *adv*

au·to·cross \ˈȯt-ō-ˌkrȯs, ˈät-\ *n* [*auto*] **:** an automobile gymkhana

au·to–da–fé \ˌau̇t-ō-də-ˈfā, ˌȯt-\ *n, pl* **au·tos–da–fé** \-ōz-də-\ [Pg *auto da fé,* lit., act of the faith] **:** the ceremony accompanying the pronouncement of judgment by the Inquisition and followed by the execution of sentence by the secular authorities; *broadly* **:** the burning of a heretic

au·to·di·dact \ˌȯt-ō-ˈdī-ˌdakt, -dī-ˈ, -də-ˈ\ *n* [Gk *autodidaktos* self-taught, fr. *aut-* + *didaktos* taught, fr. *didaskein* to teach — more at DOCILE] **:** a self-taught person — **au·to·di·dac·tic** \-dī-ˈdak-tik, -də-\ *adj*

au·to·dyne \ˈȯt-ə-ˌdīn\ *n* [ISV *aut-* + hetero*dyne*] **:** a heterodyne in which the auxiliary current is generated in the device used for rectification

au·toe·cious \ȯ-ˈtē-shəs\ *adj* [*aut-* + Gk *oikia* house — more at VICINITY] **:** passing through all life stages on the same host <~ rusts> — **au·toe·cious·ly** *adv* — **au·toe·cism** \-ˈtē-ˌsiz-əm\ *n*

au·to·er·o·tism \ˌȯt-ō-ˈer-ə-ˌtiz-əm\ *or* **au·to·erot·i·cism** \-i-ˈrät-ə-ˌsiz-əm\ *n* **1 :** sexual gratification obtained solely through one's own organism **2 :** sexual feeling arising without known external stimulation — **au·to·erot·ic** \-i-ˈrät-ik\ *adj* — **au·to·erot·i·cal·ly** \-i-k(ə-)lē\ *adv*

au·tog·a·my \ȯ-ˈtäg-ə-mē\ *n* [ISV] **:** SELF-FERTILIZATION: as **a :** pollination of a flower by its own pollen **b :** conjugation of two sister cells or sister nuclei of protozoans or fungi — **au·tog·a·mous** \-məs\ *adj*

au·to·gen·e·sis \ˌȯt-ō-ˈjen-ə-səs\ *n* [NL] **:** ABIOGENESIS — **au·to·ge·net·ic** \-jə-ˈnet-ik\ *adj* — **au·to·ge·net·i·cal·ly** \-i-k(ə-)lē\ *adv*

au·tog·e·nous \ȯ-ˈtäj-ə-nəs\ *or* **au·to·gen·ic** \ˌȯt-ə-ˈjen-ik\ *adj* [Gk *autogenēs,* fr. *aut-* + *-genēs* born, produced — more at -GEN] **1 :** produced independently of external influence or aid : ENDOGENOUS **2 :** originating or derived from sources within the same individual <an ~ graft> <~ vaccine> **3 :** requiring a meal of blood to produce viable eggs <~ mosquitoes> — **au·tog·e·nous·ly** *adv*

au·to·gi·ro *also* **au·to·gy·ro** \ˌȯt-ō-ˈjī(ə)r-(ˌ)ō\ *n, pl* **-ros** [fr. *Autogiro,* a trademark] **:** a rotary-wing aircraft that employs a propeller for forward motion and a freely rotating rotor for lift

au·to·graft \ˈȯt-ō-ˌgraft\ *n* **:** a tissue or organ that is transplanted from one part to another part of the same body — **autograft** *vt*

[1]**au·to·graph** \ˈȯt-ə-ˌgraf\ *n* [LL *autographum,* fr. L, neut. of *autographus* written with one's own hand, fr. Gk *autographos,* fr. *aut-* + *-graphos* written — more at -GRAPH] **1 :** something written or made with one's own hand: **a :** an original manuscript or work of art **b :** a person's handwritten signature **2 :** a representation or trace of an object produced in a photographic emulsion by the mechanical, electrical, chemical, or radiation effects of the object itself — **au·tog·ra·phy** \ȯ-ˈtäg-rə-fē\ *n*

[2]**autograph** *vt* **1 :** to write with one's own hand **2 :** to write one's signature in or on

au·to·graph·ic \ˌȯt-ə-ˈgraf-ik\ *adj* **1 :** of, relating to, or constituting an autograph **2 a** *of an instrument* **:** SELF-RECORDING **b** *of a record* **:** recorded by a self-recording instrument — **au·to·graph·i·cal·ly** \-i-k(ə-)lē\ *adv*

Au·to·harp \ˈȯt-ō-ˌhärp\ *trademark* — used for a zither with button-controlled dampers for selected strings

au·to·hyp·no·sis \ˌȯt-ō-hip-ˈnō-səs\ *n* [NL] **:** self-induced and usu. automatic hypnosis — **au·to·hyp·not·ic** \-ˈnät-ik\ *adj*

au·to·im·mune \-im-ˈyün\ *adj* **:** of, relating to, or caused by autoantibodies <~ diseases> — **au·to·im·mu·ni·ty** \-ˈyü-nət-ē\ *n* — **au·to·im·mu·ni·za·tion** \-ˌim-yə-nə-ˈzā-shən *also* -im-ˌyü-\ *n*

au·to·in·fec·tion \-in-ˈfek-shən\ *n* [ISV] **:** reinfection with larvae produced by parasitic worms already in the body

au·to·in·oc·u·la·tion \ˌȯt-ō-in-ˌäk-yə-ˈlā-shən\ *n* [ISV] **1 :** inoculation with vaccine prepared from material from one's own body **2 :** spread of infection from one part to other parts of the same body

au·to·in·tox·i·ca·tion \-in-ˌtäk-sə-ˈkā-shən\ *n* [ISV] **:** a state of being poisoned by toxic substances produced within the body

au·to·load·ing \ˌȯt-ō-ˈlōd-iŋ\ *adj* **:** SEMIAUTOMATIC b

au·tol·o·gous \ȯ-ˈtäl-ə-gəs\ *adj* [*aut-* + *-ologous* (as in *homologous*)] **:** derived from the same individual

au·tol·y·sate \ȯ-ˈtäl-ə-ˌsāt, -ˌzāt\ *n* **:** a product of autolysis

au·tol·y·sin \-ə-sən\ *n* **:** a substance that produces autolysis

au·tol·y·sis \-ə-səs\ *n* [NL] **:** breakdown of all or part of a cell or tissue by self-produced enzymes — **au·to·lyt·ic** \ˌȯt-ᵊl-ˈit-ik\ *adj*

au·to·mak·er \ˈȯt-ō-ˌmā-kər, ˈät-\ *n* **:** a manufacturer of automobiles

au·to·ma·nip·u·la·tion \ˌȯt-ō-mə-ˌnip-yə-ˈlā-shən\ *n* **:** physical stimulation of the genital organs by oneself — **au·to·ma·nip·u·la·tive** \-ˈnip-yə-ˌlāt-iv\ *adj*

Au·to·mat \ˈȯt-ə-ˌmat\ *service mark* — used for a cafeteria in which food is obtained esp. from coin-operated compartments

au·to·mate \ˈȯt-ə-ˌmāt\ *vb* **-mat·ed; -mat·ing** [back-formation fr. *automation*] *vt* **1 :** to operate by automation **2 :** to convert to largely automatic operation : AUTOMATIZE ~ *vi* **:** to undergo automation — **au·to·mat·able** \-ˌmāt-ə-bəl\ *adj*

[1]**au·to·mat·ic** \ˌȯt-ə-ˈmat-ik\ *adj* [Gk *automatos* self-acting, fr. *aut-* + *-matos* (akin to L *ment-, mens* mind) — more at MIND] **1 a :** largely or wholly involuntary; *esp* **:** REFLEX 5 <~ blinking of the eyelids> **b :** acting or done spontaneously or unconsciously **c :** resembling an automaton : MECHANICAL <knew the lesson so well that her answers were ~> **2 :** having a self-acting or self-regulating mechanism **3** *of a firearm* **:** using either gas pressure or force of recoil and mechanical spring action for repeatedly ejecting the empty cartridge shell, introducing a new cartridge, and firing it ***syn*** see SPONTANEOUS — **au·to·mat·i·cal·ly** \-i-k(ə-)lē\ *adv* — **au·to·ma·tic·i·ty** \-mə-ˈtis-ət-ē, -ma-\ *n*

[2]**automatic** *n* **1 :** a machine or apparatus that operates automatically: as **a :** an automatic firearm **b :** an automatic gear-shifting mechanism **2 :** a substitute offensive or defensive play called at the line of scrimmage in football — called also *audible*

automatic pilot *n* **:** a device for automatically steering ships, aircraft, and spacecraft — called also *autopilot*

automatic writing *n* **:** writing performed without conscious intention and sometimes without awareness as if of telepathic or spiritualistic origin

au·to·ma·tion \ˌȯt-ə-ˈmā-shən\ *n* [[1]*automatic*] **1 :** the technique of making an apparatus, a process, or a system operate automatically **2 :** the state of being operated automatically **3 :** automatically controlled operation of an apparatus, process, or system by mechanical or electronic devices that take the place of human organs of observation, effort, and decision

au·tom·a·tism \ȯ-ˈtäm-ə-ˌtiz-əm\ *n* [F *automatisme,* fr. *automate* automaton, fr. L *automaton*] **1 a :** the quality or state of being automatic **b :** an automatic action **2 :** a theory that views the body as a machine and consciousness as a noncontrolling adjunct of the body **3 :** the power or fact of moving independently of external stimuli or under the influence of external stimuli but independent of conscious control **4 :** suspension of the conscious mind to release subconscious images — **au·tom·a·tist** \-ˈtäm-ət-əst\ *n*

au·tom·a·ti·za·tion \ȯ-ˌtäm-ət-ə-ˈzā-shən\ *n* : AUTOMATION

au·tom·a·tize \ȯ-ˈtäm-ə-ˌtīz\ *vt* **-tized; -tiz·ing** [[1]*automatic*] : to make automatic

au·tom·a·ton \ȯ-ˈtäm-ət-ən, -ə-ˌtän\ *n, pl* **-atons** *or* **-a·ta** \-ət-ə, -ə-ˌtä\ [L, fr. Gk, neut. of *automatos*] **1** : a mechanism that is relatively self-operating; *esp* : ROBOT **2** : a machine or control mechanism designed to follow automatically a predetermined sequence of operations or respond to encoded instructions **3** : an individual who acts in a mechanical fashion

[1]**au·to·mo·bile** \ˌȯt-ə-mō-ˈbē(ə)l, ˈȯt-ə-mō-ˌbēl, ˌȯt-ə-ˈmō-ˌbēl\ *adj* [F, fr. *aut-* + *mobile*] : AUTOMOTIVE

[2]**automobile** *n* : a usu. four-wheeled automotive vehicle designed for passenger transportation and commonly propelled by an internal-combustion engine using a volatile fuel — **automobile** *vi* — **au·to·mo·bil·ist** \-ˈbē-ləst, -ˌbē-\ *n*

au·to·mor·phism \ˌȯt-ə-ˈmȯr-ˌfiz-əm\ *n* [*aut-* + iso*morphism*] : an isomorphism of a set (as a group) with itself

au·to·mo·tive \ˌȯt-ə-ˈmōt-iv\ *adj* **1** : SELF-PROPELLED **2** : of, relating to, or concerned with automotive vehicles or machines

au·to·nom·ic \ˌȯt-ə-ˈnäm-ik\ *adj* **1 a** : acting independently of volition <~ reflexes> **b** : relating to, affecting, or controlled by the autonomic nervous system **2** : due to internal causes or influences : SPONTANEOUS — **au·to·nom·i·cal·ly** \-i-k(ə-)lē\ *adv*

autonomic nervous system *n* : a part of the vertebrate nervous system that innervates smooth and cardiac muscle and glandular tissues and governs involuntary actions and that consists of the sympathetic nervous system and the parasympathetic nervous system

au·ton·o·mist \ȯ-ˈtän-ə-məst\ *n* : one who advocates autonomy

au·ton·o·mous \ȯ-ˈtän-ə-məs\ *adj* [Gk *autonomos* independent, fr. *aut-* + *nomos* law — more at NIMBLE] **1** : of, relating to, or marked by autonomy **2 a** : having the right or power of self-government **b** : undertaken or carried on without outside control : SELF-CONTAINED <an ~ school system> **3 a** : existing or capable of existing independently <an ~ zooid> **b** : responding, reacting, or developing independently of the whole <an ~ growth> **4** : controlled by the autonomic nervous system *syn* see FREE — **au·ton·o·mous·ly** *adv*

au·ton·o·my \-mē\ *n, pl* **-mies** **1** : the quality or state of being self-governing; *esp* : the right of self-government **2** : a self-governing state **3** : self-directing freedom and esp. moral independence

au·to·phyte \ˈȯt-ə-ˌfīt\ *n* : a plant capable of synthesizing its own food from simple inorganic substances — **au·to·phyt·ic** \ˌȯt-ə-ˈfit-ik\ *adj* — **au·to·phyt·i·cal·ly** \-i-k(ə-)lē\ *adv*

au·to·pi·lot \ˈȯt-ō-ˌpī-lət\ *n* : AUTOMATIC PILOT

au·to·plas·tic \ˌȯt-ō-ˈplas-tik\ *adj* : of, relating to, or involving repair of lesions with tissue from the same body — **au·to·plas·ti·cal·ly** \-ti-k(ə-)lē\ *adv* — **au·to·plas·ty** \ˈȯt-ō-ˌplas-tē\ *n*

au·top·sy \ˈȯ-ˌtäp-sē, ˈȯt-əp-\ *n, pl* **-sies** [Gk *autopsia* act of seeing with one's own eyes, fr. *aut-* + *opsis* sight, fr. *opsesthai* to be going to see — more at OPTIC] : POSTMORTEM EXAMINATION — **autopsy** *vt*

au·to·ra·dio·graph \ˌȯt-ō-ˈrād-ē-ə-ˌgraf\ *or* **au·to·ra·dio·gram** \-ˌgram\ *n* [ISV] : an image produced on a photographic film or plate by the radiations from a radioactive substance in an object which is in close contact with the emulsion — **au·to·ra·dio·graph·ic** \-ˌrād-ē-ə-ˈgraf-ik\ *adj* — **au·to·ra·di·og·ra·phy** \-ˌrād-ē-ˈäg-rə-fē\ *n*

au·to·ro·ta·tion \-rō-ˈtā-shən\ *n* : the turning of the rotor of an autogiro or a helicopter with the resulting lift caused solely by the aerodynamic forces induced by motion of the rotor along its flight path — **au·to·ro·tate** \-ˈrō-ˌtāt\ *vi* — **au·to·ro·ta·tion·al** \-rō-ˈtā-shnəl, -shən-ᵊl\ *adj*

autos–da–fé *pl of* AUTO-DA-FE

au·to·sex·ing \ˈȯt-ō-ˌsek-siŋ\ *adj* : showing different characters in the two sexes at birth or hatching

au·to·some \ˈȯt-ə-ˌsōm\ *n* : a chromosome other than a sex chromosome — **au·to·so·mal** \ˌȯt-ə-ˈsō-məl\ *adj* — **au·to·so·mal·ly** \-mə-lē\ *adv*

au·to·stra·da \ˌau̇t-ō-ˈsträd-ə, ˌȯt-ō-\ *n, pl* **-stradas** *or* **-stra·de** \-ˈsträd-(ˌ)ā\ [It, fr. *auto*mobile + *strada* street, fr. LL *strata* paved road — more at STREET] : a high-speed multilane highway first developed in Italy

au·to·sug·ges·tion \ˌȯt-ō-sə(g)-ˈjes(h)-chən\ *n* [ISV] : an influencing of one's own attitudes, behavior, or physical condition by mental processes other than conscious thought : SELF-HYPNOSIS — **au·to·sug·gest** \-sə(g)-ˈjest\ *vt*

au·to·te·lic \ˌȯt-ō-ˈtel-ik, -ˈtē-lik\ *adj* [Gk *autotelēs*, fr. *aut-* + *telos* end — more at WHEEL] : having a purpose in itself

au·to·tet·ra·ploi·dy \ˌȯt-ō-ˈte-trə-ˌplȯid-ē\ *n* : the state of having four genomes due to doubling of the ancestral chromosome complement — **au·to·tet·ra·ploid** \-ˌplȯid\ *adj or n*

au·tot·o·mize \ȯ-ˈtät-ə-ˌmīz\ *vb* **-mized; -miz·ing** *vt* : to effect autotomy of ~ *vi* : to undergo autotomy

au·tot·o·my \-mē\ *n* [ISV] : reflex separation of a part from the body : division of the body into two or more pieces — **au·to·tom·ic** \ˌȯt-ə-ˈtäm-ik\ *or* **au·to·to·mous** \ȯ-ˈtät-ə-məs\ *adj*

au·to·trans·form·er \-tran(t)s-ˈfȯr-mər\ *n* : a transformer in which the primary and secondary coils have part or all of their turns in common

au·to·trans·plant \-ˈtran(t)s-ˌplant\ *n* : AUTOGRAFT — **au·to·trans·plant** \-tran(t)s-ˈ\ *vt*

au·to·trans·plan·ta·tion \-ˌtran(t)s-ˌplan-ˈtā-shən\ *n* : the action of autotransplanting : the condition of being autotransplanted

au·to·troph \ˈȯt-ə-ˌtrōf, -ˌträf\ *n* [G, fr. *autotroph*, adj.] : an autotrophic organism — **au·tot·ro·phy** \ȯ-ˈtä-trə-fē\ *n*

au·to·tro·phic \ˌȯt-ə-ˈtrō-fik\ *adj* [prob. fr. G *autotroph*, fr. Gk *autotrophos* supplying one's own food, fr. *aut-* + *trephein* to nourish — more at ATROPHY] **1** : needing only carbon dioxide or carbonates as a source of carbon and a simple inorganic nitrogen compound for metabolic synthesis **2** : not requiring a specified exogenous factor for normal metabolism — **au·to·tro·phi·cal·ly** \-fi-k(ə-)lē\ *adv*

au·tumn \ˈȯt-əm\ *n* [ME *autumpne*, fr. L *autumnus*] **1** : the season between summer and winter comprising in the northern hemisphere usu. the months of September, October, and November or as reckoned astronomically extending from the September equinox to the December solstice — called also *fall* **2** : a period of maturity or incipient decline <in the ~ of her life> — **au·tum·nal** \ȯ-ˈtəm-nəl\ *adj* — **au·tum·nal·ly** \-nə-lē\ *adv*

autumn crocus *n* : an autumn-blooming colchicum

au·tun·ite \ō-ˈtən-ˌīt, ˈȯt-ᵊn-\ *n* [*Autun*, France] : a radioactive lemon-yellow mineral $Ca(UO_2)(PO_4)_2.10–12H_2O$ occurring in tabular crystals with basal cleavage and in scales resembling those of mica

aux *or* **auxil** *abbr* auxiliary

aux·e·sis \ȯg-ˈzē-səs, ȯk-ˈsē-\ *n* [NL, fr. Gk *auxēsis* increase, growth, fr. *auxein* to increase — more at EKE] : GROWTH; *specif* : increase of cell size without cell division — **aux·et·ic** \-ˈzet-ik, -ˈset-\ *adj* — **aux·et·i·cal·ly** \-i-k(ə-)lē\ *adv*

[1]**aux·il·ia·ry** \ȯg-ˈzil-yə-rē, -ˈzil-(ə-)rē\ *adj* [L *auxiliaris*, fr. *auxilium* help; akin to Gk *auxein* to increase] **1 a** : offering or providing help **b** : functioning in a subsidiary capacity <an ~ branch of the state university> **2** *of a verb* : accompanying another verb and typically expressing person, number, mood, or tense **3 a** : SUPPLEMENTARY **b** : RESERVE <an ~ power plant> **4** : equipped with sails and a supplementary inboard engine

[2]**auxiliary** *n, pl* **-ries** **1 a** : an auxiliary person, group, or device; *specif* : a member of a foreign force serving a nation at war **b** : a Roman Catholic titular bishop assisting a diocesan bishop and not having the right of succession **2** : an auxiliary boat or ship **3** : an auxiliary verb

aux·in \ˈȯk-sən\ *n* [ISV, fr. Gk *auxein*] : an organic substance that is able in low concentrations to promote elongation of plant shoots and usu. to control other specific growth effects; *broadly* : PLANT HORMONE — **aux·in·ic** \ȯk-ˈsin-ik\ *adj* — **aux·in·i·cal·ly** \-i-k(ə-)lē\ *adv*

auxo·troph \ˈȯk-sə-ˌtrōf, -ˌträf\ *n* : an auxotrophic strain or individual — **aux·ot·ro·phy** \ȯk-ˈsät-rə-fē\ *n*

auxo·tro·phic \ˌȯk-sə-ˈtrō-fik\ *adj* [Gk *auxein* to increase + *-o-* + E *-trophic*] : requiring a specific growth substance beyond the minimum required for normal metabolism and reproduction <~ mutants of bacteria>

av *abbr* **1** avenue **2** average **3** avoirdupois

AV *abbr* **1** ad valorem **2** audiovisual **3** Authorized Version

[1]**avail** \ə-ˈvā(ə)l\ *vb* [ME *availen*, prob. fr. *a-* (as in *abaten* to abate) + *vailen* to avail — more at VAIL] *vi* : to be of use or advantage : SERVE <our best efforts did not ~> ~ *vt* **1** : to be of use or advantage to : PROFIT **2** : to result in : bring about <his efforts ~*ed* him nothing> — **avail oneself of** *also* **avail of** : to make use of : take advantage of

[2]**avail** *n* **1** : advantage toward attainment of a goal or purpose : USE <effort was of little ~> **2** *pl, archaic* : profits or proceeds esp. from a business or from the sale of property

avail·abil·i·ty \ə-ˌvā-lə-ˈbil-ət-ē\ *n, pl* **-ties** **1** : the quality or state of being available **2** : an available person or thing

avail·able \ə-ˈvā-lə-bəl\ *adj* **1** *archaic* : having a beneficial effect **2** : VALID — used of a legal plea or charge **3** : present or ready for immediate use **4** : ACCESSIBLE, OBTAINABLE <articles ~ in any drugstore> **5** : qualified or willing to do something or to assume a responsibility <~ candidates> **6** : present in such chemical or physical form as to be usable (as by a plant) <~ nitrogen> <~ water> — **avail·able·ness** *n* — **avail·ably** \-blē\ *adv*

[1]**av·a·lanche** \ˈav-ə-ˌlanch\ *n* [F, fr. F dial. *lavantse, avalantse*] **1** : a large mass of snow, ice, earth, rock, or other material in swift motion down a mountainside or over a precipice **2** : a sudden great or overwhelming rush or accumulation of something <office workers tied down with an ~ of paper work> **3** : a cumulative process in which electrons or charge carriers accelerated by an electric field produce additional electrons or charge carriers through collisions (as with gas molecules)

[2]**avalanche** *vb* **-lanched; -lanch·ing** *vi* : to descend in an avalanche ~ *vt* : OVERWHELM, FLOOD

Av·a·lon \ˈav-ə-ˌlän\ *n* : a paradise in Arthurian legend to which Arthur is carried after his death

[1]**avant–garde** \ˌäv-ˌän(t)-ˈgärd, ˌav-, ˌäv-; ə-ˈvänt-, ; ˌav-ˌōⁿ-, ˌav-ˌȯn(t)-ˈ\ *n* [F, vanguard] : an intelligentsia that develops new or experimental concepts esp. in the arts — **avant–gard·ism** \-ˈgärd-ˌiz-əm\ *n* — **avant–gard·ist** \-ˈgärd-əst\ *n*

[2]**avant–garde** *adj* : of or relating to an avant-garde <~ writers>

av·a·rice \ˈav-(ə-)rəs\ *n* [ME, fr. OF, fr. L *avaritia*, fr. *avarus* avaricious, fr. *avēre* to covet — more at AVID] : excessive or insatiable desire for wealth or gain : GREEDINESS, CUPIDITY

av·a·ri·cious \ˌav-ə-ˈrish-əs\ *adj* : greedy of gain : excessively acquisitive esp. in seeking to hoard riches *syn* see COVETOUS *ant* generous — **av·a·ri·cious·ly** *adv* — **av·a·ri·cious·ness** *n*

avast \ə-ˈvast\ *vb imper* [perh. fr. D *houd vast* hold fast] — a nautical command to stop or cease

av·a·tar \ˈav-ə-ˌtär\ *n* [Skt *avatāra* descent, fr. *avatarati* he descends, fr. *ava-* away + *tarati* he crosses over — more at UKASE, THROUGH] **1** : the incarnation of a Hindu deity (as Vishnu) **2 a** : an incarnation in human form **b** : an embodiment (as of a concept or philosophy) usu. in a person **3** : a variant phase or version of a continuing basic entity

avaunt \ə-ˈvȯnt, -ˈvänt\ *adv* [ME, fr. MF *avant*, fr. L *abante* forward, before, fr. *ab* from + *ante* before — more at OF, ANTE-] : AWAY, HENCE

AVC *abbr* **1** American Veterans Committee **2** automatic volume control

avdp *abbr* avoirdupois

[1]**ave** \ˈäv-(ˌ)ā\ *n* [ME, fr. L, hail] **1 :** an expression of greeting or of leave-taking **:** FAREWELL **2** *often cap* **:** AVE MARIA

[2]**ave** *abbr* avenue

avel·lan \ə-ˈvel-ən\ *or* **avel·lane** \ə-ˈvel-ˌān, ˈav-ə-ˌlān\ *adj* [L *abellana, avellana* filbert, fr. fem. of *Abellanus* of Abella, fr. *Abella,* ancient town in Italy] *of a heraldic cross* **:** having the four arms shaped like conventionalized filberts — see CROSS illustration

Ave Ma·ria \ˌäv-(ˌ)ā-mə-ˈrē-ə\ *n* [ME, fr. ML, hail, Mary] **:** HAIL MARY

avenge \ə-ˈvenj\ *vt* **avenged; aveng·ing** [ME *avengen,* prob. fr. *a-* (as in *abaten* to abate) + *vengen* to avenge, fr. OF *vengier* — more at VENGEANCE] **1 :** to take vengeance for or on behalf of **2 :** to exact satisfaction for (a wrong) by punishing the wrongdoer — **aveng·er** *n*

syn AVENGE, REVENGE *shared meaning element* **:** to punish one who has wronged oneself or another

av·ens \ˈav-ənz\ *n, pl* **avens** [ME *avence,* fr. OF] **:** any of a genus (*Geum*) of perennial herbs of the rose family with white, purple, or yellow flowers

av·en·tail \ˈav-ən-ˌtāl\ *n* [ME, modif. of OF *ventaille*] **:** VENTAIL

aven·tu·rine \ə-ˈven-chə-ˌrēn, -rən\ *n* [F, fr. *aventure* chance — more at ADVENTURE] **1 :** glass containing opaque sparkling particles of foreign material usu. copper or chromic oxide **2 :** a translucent quartz spangled throughout with scales of mica or other mineral

av·e·nue \ˈav-ə-ˌn(y)ü\ *n* [MF, fr. fem. of *avenu,* pp. of *avenir* to come to, fr. L *advenire* — more at ADVENTURE] **1 :** a way of access **:** ROUTE **2 :** a channel for pursuing a desired object <~*s* of communication> **3 a** *chiefly Brit* **:** the principal walk or driveway to a house situated off a main road **b :** a broad passageway bordered by trees **4 :** an often broad street or road

aver \ə-ˈvər\ *vt* **averred; aver·ring** [ME *averren,* fr. MF *averer,* fr. ML *adverare* to confirm as authentic, fr. L *ad-* + *verus* true — more at VERY] **1 a :** to verify or prove to be true in pleading a cause **b :** to allege or assert in pleading **2 :** to declare positively

[1]**av·er·age** \ˈav-(ə-)rij\ *n* [modif. of MF *avarie* damage to ship or cargo, fr. OIt *avaria,* fr. Ar *ʽawārīyah* damaged merchandise] **1 :** sundry petty charges regularly defrayed by the master of a ship and usu. included in the freight **2 a :** a less than total loss sustained by a ship or cargo **b :** a charge arising from damage caused by sea perils customarily distributed equitably and proportionately among all chargeable with it **3 a :** a single value (as a mean, mode, or median) that summarizes or represents the general significance of a set of unequal values **b :** MEAN 1b **4 a :** an estimation of or approximation to an arithmetic mean **b :** a level (as of intelligence) typical of a group, class, or series <above the ~> **5 :** a ratio expressing the average performance esp. of an athletic team or an athlete computed according to the number of opportunities for successful performance

syn AVERAGE, MEAN, MEDIAN, NORM *shared meaning element* **:** something (as a quantity) that represents a middle point between extremes ***ant*** maximum, minimum

[2]**average** *adj* **1 :** equaling an arithmetic mean **2 a :** being about midway between extremes <a man of ~ height> **b :** not out of the ordinary **:** COMMON <the ~ person> — **av·er·age·ly** *adv* — **av·er·age·ness** *n*

[3]**average** *vb* **av·er·aged; av·er·ag·ing** *vi* **1 a :** to be or come to an average <the gain *averaged* out to 20 percent> **b :** to have a medial value of <a color *averaging* a pale purple> **2 :** to buy on a falling market or sell on a rising market additional shares or commodities so as to obtain a more favorable average price — usu. used with *down* or *up* ~ *vt* **1 :** to do, get, or have on the average or as an average sum or quantity <~*s* 12 hours of work a day> **2 :** to find the arithmetic mean of (a series of unequal quantities) **3 a :** to bring toward the average **b :** to divide among a number proportionately

aver·ment \ə-ˈvər-mənt\ *n* **1 :** the act of averring **2 :** something that is averred **:** AFFIRMATION

averse \ə-ˈvərs\ *adj* [L *aversus,* pp. of *avertere*] **:** having an active feeling of repugnance or distaste <~ to strenuous exercise> ***syn*** see DISINCLINED ***ant*** avid (*of* or *for*), athirst (*for*) — **averse·ly** *adv* — **averse·ness** *n*

aver·sion \ə-ˈvər-zhən, -shən\ *n* **1** *obs* **:** the act of turning away **2 a :** a feeling of repugnance toward something with a desire to avoid or turn from it <regards drunkenness with ~> **b :** a settled dislike **:** ANTIPATHY <expressed an ~ to parties> **3** *archaic* **:** one that is the object of aversion

aver·sive \ə-ˈvər-siv, -ziv\ *adj* **:** tending to avoid or causing avoidance of a noxious or punishing stimulus <behavior modification by ~ stimulation>

avert \ə-ˈvərt\ *vt* [ME *averten,* fr. MF *avertir,* fr. L *avertere,* fr. *ab-* + *vertere* to turn — more at WORTH] **1 :** to turn away or aside (as the eyes) in avoidance **2 :** to see coming and ward off **:** AVOID ***syn*** see PREVENT

Aves·ta \ə-ˈves-tə\ *n* [MPer *Avastāk,* lit., original text] **:** the book of the sacred writings of Zoroastrianism

Aves·tan \-tən\ *n* **:** one of the two ancient languages of Old Iranian and of the sacred books of Zoroastrianism — see INDO-EUROPEAN LANGUAGES table — **Avestan** *adj*

avg *abbr* average

av·gas \ˈav-ˌgas\ *n* [*aviation gasoline*] **:** gasoline for airplanes

avi·an \ˈā-vē-ən\ *adj* [L *avis*] **:** of, relating to, or derived from birds

avi·an·ize \-vē-ə-ˌnīz\ *vt* **-ized; -iz·ing :** to modify or attenuate (as a virus) by repeated culture in the developing chick embryo

avi·a·rist \ˈā-vē-ə-rəst, -vē-ˌer-əst\ *n* **:** one who keeps an aviary

avi·ary \ˈā-vē-ˌer-ē\ *n, pl* **-ar·ies** [L *aviarium,* fr. *avis* bird; akin to Gk *aetos* eagle] **:** a place for keeping birds confined

avi·ate \ˈā-vē-ˌāt, ˈav-ē-\ *vi* **-at·ed; -at·ing** [back-formation fr. *aviation*] **:** to navigate the air (as in an airplane)

avi·a·tion \ˌā-vē-ˈā-shən, ˌav-ē-\ *n, often attrib* [F, fr. L *avis*] **1 :** the operation of heavier-than-air aircraft **2 :** military airplanes **3 :** airplane manufacture, development, and design

aviation cadet *n* **:** one in training for a military or naval commission with an aeronautical rating

avi·a·tor \ˈā-vē-ˌāt-ər, ˈav-ē-\ *n* **:** the operator or pilot of an airplane

avi·a·tress \-ˌā-trəs\ *n* **:** AVIATRIX

avi·a·trix \ˌā-vē-ˈā-triks, ˌav-ē-\ *n, pl* **-trix·es** \-trik-səz\ *or* **-tri·ces** \-trə-ˌsēz\ **:** a woman aviator

avi·cul·ture \ˈā-və-ˌkəl-chər, ˈav-ə-\ *n* [L *avis* + E *culture*] **:** the raising and care of birds and esp. of wild birds in captivity — **avi·cul·tur·ist** \ˌā-və-ˈkəlch-(ə-)rəst, ˌav-ə-\ *n*

av·id \ˈav-əd\ *adj* [F or L; F *avide,* fr. L *avidus,* fr. *avēre* to covet; akin to Goth *awi*liuth thanks, Gk en*ēēs* gentle] **1 :** desirous to the point of greed **:** urgently eager **:** GREEDY <~ fondness for publicity> **2 :** characterized by enthusiasm and vigorous pursuit <~ readers> ***syn*** see EAGER ***ant*** indifferent, averse — **av·id·ly** *adv* — **av·id·ness** *n*

av·i·din \ˈav-əd-ən\ *n* [fr. its avidity for biotin] **:** a protein found in white of egg that combines with biotin and makes it inactive

avid·ity \ə-ˈvid-ət-ē, a-\ *n, pl* **-ities 1 :** the quality or state of being avid: **a :** keen eagerness **b :** consuming greed **2 a :** the strength of an acid or base dependent on its degree of dissociation **b :** AFFINITY 2b

avi·fau·na \ˌā-və-ˈfȯn-ə, ˌav-ə-, -ˈfän-ə\ *n* [NL, fr. L *avis* + NL *fauna*] **:** the birds or the kinds of birds of a region, period, or environment — **avi·fau·nal** \-ᵊl\ *adj* — **avi·fau·nal·ly** \-ᵊl-ē\ *adv* — **avi·fau·nis·tic** \-fȯ-ˈnis-tik, -fä-\ *adj*

av·i·ga·tion \ˌav-ə-ˈgā-shən\ *n* [L *avis* + E *-gation* (as in *navigation*)] **:** the navigation of airplanes

avi·on·ics \ˌā-vē-ˈän-iks, ˌav-ē-\ *n pl* [*avi*ation electr*onics*] **:** the development and production of electrical and electronic devices for use in aviation, missilery, and astronautics; *also* **:** the devices and systems so developed — **avi·on·ic** \-ik\ *adj*

avir·u·lent \(ˈ)ā-ˈvir-(y)ə-lənt\ *adj* [ISV] **:** not virulent — compare NONPATHOGENIC

avi·ta·min·osis \ˌā-ˌvīt-ə-mə-ˈnō-səs\ *n, pl* **-o·ses** \-ˌsēz\ **:** disease (as pellagra) resulting from a deficiency of one or more vitamins — **avi·ta·min·ot·ic** \-mə-ˈnät-ik\ *adj*

avn *abbr* aviation

avo \ˈav-(ˌ)ü\ *n, pl* **avos** [Pg, fr. *avo* fractional part, fr. *-avo* ordinal suffix (as in *oitavo* eighth, fr. L *octavus*) — more at OCTAVE] — see *pataca* at MONEY table

av·o·ca·do \ˌav-ə-ˈkäd-(ˌ)ō, ˌäv-\ *n, pl* **-dos** *also* **-does** [modif. of Sp *aguacate,* fr. Nahuatl *ahuscatl*] **:** the pulpy green or purple edible fruit of various tropical American trees (genus *Persea*) of the laurel family; *also* **:** a tree bearing avocados — called also *alligator pear, avocado pear*

av·o·ca·tion \ˌav-ə-ˈkā-shən\ *n* [L *avocation-, avocatio,* fr. *avocatus,* pp. of *avocare* to call away, fr. *ab-* + *vocare* to call, fr. *voc-, vox* voice — more at VOICE] **1** *archaic* **:** DIVERSION, DISTRACTION **2 :** a subordinate occupation pursued in addition to one's vocation esp. for enjoyment **:** HOBBY **3 :** customary employment **:** VOCATION — **av·o·ca·tion·al** \-shnəl, -shən-ᵊl\ *adj* — **av·o·ca·tion·al·ly** \-ē\ *adv*

av·o·cet \ˈav-ə-ˌset\ *n* [F & It; F *avocette,* fr. It *avocetta*] **:** any of several rather large long-legged shorebirds (genus *Recurvirostra*) with webbed feet and slender upward-curving bill

avoid \ə-ˈvȯid\ *vt* [ME *avoiden,* fr. OF *esvuidier,* fr. *es-* (fr. L *ex-*) + *vuidier* to empty — more at VOID] **1** *obs* **:** VOID, EXPEL **2** *archaic* **:** to depart or withdraw from **:** LEAVE **3 :** to make legally void **:** ANNUL <~ a plea> **4 a :** to keep away from **:** SHUN **b :** to prevent the occurrence or effectiveness of **c :** to refrain from ***syn*** see ESCAPE — **avoid·able** \-ə-bəl\ *adj* — **avoid·ably** \-blē\ *adv* — **avoid·er** *n*

avoid·ance \ə-ˈvȯid-ᵊn(t)s\ *n* **1** *obs* **a :** an action of emptying, vacating, or clearing away **b :** OUTLET **2 :** ANNULMENT **3 :** an act or practice of avoiding

av·oir·du·pois \ˌav-ərd-ə-ˈpȯiz, ˈav-ərd-ə-ˌ\ *n* [ME *avoir de pois* goods sold by weight, fr. OF, lit., goods of weight] **1 :** AVOIRDUPOIS WEIGHT **2 :** WEIGHT, HEAVINESS; *esp* **:** personal weight

avoirdupois weight *n* **:** the series of units of weight based on the pound of 16 ounces and the ounce of 16 drams — see WEIGHT table

avouch \ə-ˈvau̇ch\ *vt* [ME *avouchen* to cite as authority, fr. MF *avochier* to summon, fr. L *advocare* — more at ADVOCATE] **1 :** to declare as a matter of fact or as a thing that can be proved **:** AFFIRM **2 :** to vouch for **:** CORROBORATE **3 a :** to acknowledge (as an act) as one's own **b :** CONFESS, AVOW

avouch·ment \-mənt\ *n* **:** an act of avouching **:** AVOWAL

avow \ə-ˈvau̇\ *vt* [ME *avowen,* fr. OF *avouer,* fr. L *advocare*] **1 :** to declare assuredly **2 :** to declare openly, bluntly, and without shame <ever ready to ~ his reactionary outlook> ***syn* 1** see ASSERT **2** see ACKNOWLEDGE ***ant*** disavow — **avow·ed·ly** \-ˈvau̇-əd-lē\ *adv* — **avow·er** \-ˈvau̇(-ə)r\ *n*

avow·al \-ˈvau̇(-ə)l\ *n* **:** an open declaration or acknowledgment

avulse \ə-ˈvəls\ *vt* **avulsed; avuls·ing** [L *avulsus,* pp. of *avellere* to tear off, fr. *ab-* + *vellere* to pluck — more at VULNERABLE] **:** to separate by avulsion

avul·sion \ə-ˈvəl-shən\ *n* **:** a forcible separation or detachment: as **a :** a tearing away of a body part accidentally or surgically **b :** a sudden cutting off of land by flood, currents, or change in course of a body of water; *esp* **:** one separating land from one person's property and joining it to another's

avun·cu·lar \ə-ˈvəŋ-kyə-lər\ *adj* [L *avunculus* maternal uncle — more at UNCLE] **1 :** of or relating to an uncle **2 :** suggestive of an uncle esp. in kindliness or geniality <~ indulgence>

aw \ˈȯ\ *interj* — used to express mild sympathy, remonstrance, incredulity, or disgust

AW *abbr* **1** actual weight **2** aircraft warning **3** all water **4** articles of war **5** automatic weapon

await \ə-ˈwāt\ *vb* [ME *awaiten,* fr. ONF *awaitier,* fr. *a-* (fr. L *ad-*) + *waitier* to watch — more at WAIT] *vt* **1** *obs* **:** to lie in wait for **2 a :** to wait for **b :** to remain in abeyance until <a treaty ~*ing* ratification> **3 :** to be ready or waiting for <wondered what ~*ed*

him at the end of his journey> ~ *vi* **1** *obs* : ATTEND **2** : to stay or be in waiting : WAIT **3** : to be in store ***syn*** see EXPECT ***ant*** despair

[1]**awake** \ə-ˈwāk\ *vb* **awoke** \-ˈwōk\ *also* **awaked** \-ˈwākt\; **awaked** *also* **awoke** *or* **awo·ken** \-ˈwō-kən\; **awak·ing** *vi* **1** : to cease sleeping **2** : to become aroused or active again **3** : to become conscious or aware of something <*awoke* to their danger> ~ *vt* **1** : to arouse from sleep or a sleeplike state **2** : to make active : stir up <*awake* old memories>

[2]**awake** *adj* : roused from or as if from sleep ***syn*** see AWARE

awak·en \ə-ˈwā-kən\ *vb* **awak·ened; awak·en·ing** \-ˈwāk-(ə-)niŋ\ [ME *awakenen*, fr. OE *awæcnian*, fr. *a-* + *wæcnian* to waken] : AWAKE — **awak·en·er** \-ˈwāk-(ə-)nər\ *n*

[1]**award** \ə-ˈwȯ(ə)rd\ *vt* [ME *awarden* to decide, fr. ONF *eswarder*, fr. *es-* (fr. L *ex-*) + *warder* to guard, of Gmc origin; akin to OHG *wartēn* to watch — more at WARD] **1** : to give by judicial decree or after careful weighing of evidence **2** : to confer or bestow as being deserved or merited or needed <~ scholarships to ghetto students> ***syn*** see GRANT — **award·able** \-ˈwȯrd-ə-bəl\ *adj* — **award·er** \-ˈwȯrd-ər\ *n*

[2]**award** *n* **1 a** : a judgment or final decision; *esp* : the decision of arbitrators in a case submitted to them **b** : the document containing the decision of arbitrators **2** : something that is conferred or bestowed esp. on the basis of merit or need

award·ee \ə-ˌwȯr-ˈdē, -ˈwȯr-ˌ\ *n* : one that receives an award

aware \ə-ˈwa(ə)r, -ˈwe(ə)r\ *adj* [ME *iwar*, fr. OE *gewær*, fr. *ge-* (associative prefix) + *wær* wary — more at CO-, WARY] **1** *archaic* : WATCHFUL, WARY **2** : having or showing realization, perception, or knowledge — **aware·ness** *n*

syn AWARE, COGNIZANT, CONSCIOUS, SENSIBLE, ALIVE, AWAKE *shared meaning element* : having knowledge of something and esp. of something not generally known or apparent ***ant*** unaware

awash \ə-ˈwȯsh, -ˈwäsh\ *adj* **1 a** : alternately covered and exposed by waves or tide **b** : washing about : AFLOAT **c** : covered with water : FLOODED **2** : marked by an abundance <a post office ~ with holiday mail>

[1]**away** \ə-ˈwā\ *adv* **1** : on the way : ALONG <get ~ early> **2** : from this or that place : HENCE, THENCE <go ~> **3 a** : in a secure place or manner <locked ~> <tucked ~> **b** : in another direction **4** : out of existence : to an end <echoes dying ~> **5** : from one's possession <gave ~ a fortune> **6 a** : ON, UNINTERRUPTEDLY <clocks ticking ~> **b** : without hesitation or delay **7** : by a long distance or interval : FAR <~ back in 1910>

[2]**away** *adj* **1** : absent from a place : GONE <~ for the weekend> **2** : DISTANT <a lake 10 miles ~> **3** : played on an opponent's grounds <home and ~ games> **4** *baseball* : OUT <two ~ in the 9th> — **away·ness** *n*

[1]**awe** \ˈȯ\ *n* [ME, fr. ON *agi*; akin to OE *ege* awe, Gk *achos* pain] **1** *archaic* **a** : DREAD, TERROR **b** : the power to inspire dread **2** : emotion in which dread, veneration, and wonder are variously mingled: as **a** : profound and humbly fearful reverence inspired by deity or by something sacred or mysterious **b** : submissive and admiring fear inspired by authority or power <they stood in ~ of the king> **c** : wondering reverence tinged with fear inspired by the sublime ***syn*** see REVERENCE

[2]**awe** *vt* **awed; aw·ing** : to inspire with awe

awea·ry \ə-ˈwi(ə)r-ē\ *adj, archaic* : being weary

aweath·er \ə-ˈwe*th*-ər\ *adv* : on or toward the weather or windward side — compare ALEE

awed \ˈȯd\ *adj* : showing awe <~ respect>

aweigh \ə-ˈwā\ *adj* : raised just clear of the ground — used of an anchor

awe·less *or* **aw·less** \ˈȯ-ləs\ *adj* **1** : feeling no awe **2** *obs* : inspiring no awe

awe·some \ˈȯ-səm\ *adj* **1** : expressive of awe <~ tribute> **2** : inspiring awe <an ~ sight> — **awe·some·ly** *adv* — **awe·some·ness** *n*

awe·struck \-ˌstrək\ *also* **awe·strick·en** \-ˌstrik-ən\ *adj* : filled with awe

[1]**aw·ful** \ˈȯ-fəl\ *adj* **1** : inspiring awe **2** : filled with awe: as **a** *obs* : AFRAID, TERRIFIED **b** : deeply respectful or reverential **3** : extremely disagreeable or objectionable **4** : exceedingly great — used as an intensive <they took an ~ chance> ***syn*** see FEARFUL — **aw·ful·ly** \ˈȯ-fə-lē, *esp as adv of adj senses 3 & 4* -flē\ *adv* — **aw·ful·ness** \-fəl-nəs\ *n*

[2]**awful** *adv* : VERY, EXTREMELY <~ tired>

awhile \ə-ˈhwī(ə)l, ə-ˈwī(ə)l\ *adv* : for a while

awhirl \ə-ˈhwər(-ə)l, -ˈwər(-ə)l\ *adj* : characterized by whirling

awk·ward \ˈȯ-kwərd\ *adj* [ME *awkeward* in the wrong direction, fr. *awke* turned the wrong way, fr. ON *öfugr*; akin to OHG *abuh* turned the wrong way, L *opacus* obscure] **1** *obs* : PERVERSE **2** *archaic* : UNFAVORABLE, ADVERSE **3** : lacking dexterity or skill (as in the use of hands) <~ with a needle and thread> **b** : showing lack of expertness <~ pictures> **4 a** : lacking ease or grace (as of movement or expression) **b** : lacking the right proportions, size, or harmony of parts : UNGAINLY **5 a** : lacking social grace and assurance **b** : causing embarrassment <an ~ moment> **6** : poorly adapted for use or handling <an ~ load> **7** : requiring caution <an ~ diplomatic situation> — **awk·ward·ly** *adv* — **awk·ward·ness** *n*

syn AWKWARD, CLUMSY, MALADROIT, INEPT, GAUCHE *shared meaning element* : not marked by ease and smoothness (as in acting or functioning) ***ant*** handy, deft, graceful

awl \ˈȯl\ *n* [ME *al*, fr. ON *alr*; akin to OHG *āla* awl, Skt *ārā*] : a pointed instrument for marking surfaces or piercing small holes (as in leather or wood)

awl–shaped \-ˌshāpt\ *adj* : shaped like an awl; *specif* : being linear and tapering to a fine point

aw·mous \ˈä-məs, ˈȯ-\ *n* [ME (northern dial.) *almouse*, fr. ON *almusa*, fr. OS *almōsa* or OHG *alamuosan*] *Scot* : ALMS

awn \ˈȯn\ *n* [ME, fr. OE *agen*, fr. ON *ögn*; akin to OHG *agana* awn, OE *ecg* edge — more at EDGE] : one of the slender bristles that terminate the glumes of the spikelet in some cereal and other grasses; *broadly* : a small pointed process — **awned** \ˈȯnd\ *adj* — **awn·less** \ˈȯn-ləs\ *adj*

awls: *1* ordinary, *2* sewing

aw·ning \ˈȯn-iŋ, ˈän-\ *n* [origin unknown] **1** : a rooflike cover extending over or before a place (as over the deck of a ship or before a window) as a shelter **2** : a shelter resembling an awning — **aw·ninged** \-iŋd\ *adj*

awoke *past of* AWAKE

awoken *past part of* AWAKE

[1]**AWOL** \ˈā-ˌwȯl, ˌā-ˌdəb-əl-yü-ˌō-ˈel\ *adj, often not cap* [*a*bsent *w*ith*o*ut *l*eave] : absent without leave

[2]**AWOL** *n, often not cap* : one who is AWOL

awry \ə-ˈrī\ *adv or adj* **1** : in a turned or twisted position or direction : ASKEW **2** : out of the right or hoped-for course : AMISS

[1]**ax** *or* **axe** \ˈaks\ *n* [ME, fr. OE *æcx*; akin to OHG *ackus* ax, L *ascia*, Gk *axinē*] **1** : a cutting tool that consists of a heavy edged head fixed to a handle with the edge parallel to the handle and that is used esp. for felling trees and chopping and splitting wood **2** : a hammer with a sharp edge for dressing or spalling stone **3** : abrupt removal (as from employment or from a budget) — **ax to grind** : an ulterior often selfish purpose to further

ax 1: *a* fireman's ax; *b-g* single-bit patterns: *b* Michigan, *c* Yankee, *d* Connecticut, *e* wedge, *f* rockaway, *g* Hudson Bay; *h-m* double-bit patterns: *h* crown, *i* Western, *j* peeling, *k* wedge, *l* Puget Sound falling, *m* forester's

[2]**ax** *or* **axe** *vt* **axed; ax·ing** **1 a** : to shape, dress, or trim with an ax **b** : to chop, split, or sever with an ax **2** : to remove abruptly (as from employment or from a budget)

[3]**ax** *abbr* **1** axiom **2** axis

ax·el \ˈak-səl, ˈäk-\ *n* [*Axel* Paulsen *fl* 1890 Norw figure skater] : a jump in figure skating from the outer forward edge of one skate with 1½ turns taken in the air and a return to the outer backward edge of the other skate

axe·nic \(ˈ)ā-ˈzen-ik, -ˈzēn-\ *adj* [*a-* + Gk *xenos* strange] : free from other living organisms — **axe·ni·cal·ly** \-i-k(ə-)lē\ *adv*

ax·i·al \ˈak-sē-əl\ *or* **ax·al** \-səl\ *adj* **1** : of, relating to, or having the characteristics of an axis **2 a** : situated around, in the direction of, on, or along an axis **b** : extending in a direction essentially perpendicular to the plane of a cyclic structure (as of cyclohexane) <~ hydrogens> — compare EQUATORIAL — **ax·i·al·i·ty** \ˌak-sē-ˈal-ət-ē\ *n* — **ax·i·al·ly** \ˈak-sē-ə-lē\ *adv*

axial skeleton *n* : the skeleton of the trunk and head

ax·il \ˈak-səl, -ˌsil\ *n* [NL *axilla*, fr. L] : the angle between a branch or leaf and the axis from which it arises

ax·ile \-ˌsīl\ *adj* : relating to or situated in an axis

ax·il·la \ag-ˈzil-ə, ak-ˈsil-\ *n, pl* **-lae** \-(ˌ)ē, -ˌī\ *or* **-las** [L] : ARMPIT

ax·il·lar \ag-ˈzil-ər, ak-ˈsil-, ˈag-zəl-, ˈak-səl-, -ˌär\ *n* : an axillary part (as a vein, nerve, or feather)

[1]**ax·il·lary** \ˈak-sə-ˌler-ē\ *adj* **1** : of, relating to, or located near the axilla **2** : situated in or growing from an axil <~ buds>

[2]**axillary** *n, pl* **-lar·ies** : AXILLAR; *esp* : one of the feathers arising from the axilla and closing the space between the flight feathers and body of a flying bird

axillary bud *n* : LATERAL BUD

ax·i·o·log·i·cal \ˌak-sē-ə-ˈläj-i-kəl\ *adj* : of or relating to axiology — **ax·i·o·log·i·cal·ly** \-i-k(ə-)lē\ *adv*

ax·i·ol·o·gy \ˌak-sē-ˈäl-ə-jē\ *n* [Gk *axios* + ISV *-logy*] : the study of the nature, types, and criteria of values and of value judgments esp. in ethics

ax·i·om \ˈak-sē-əm\ *n* [L *axioma*, fr. Gk *axiōma*, lit., honor, fr. *axioun* to think worthy, fr. *axios* worth, worthy; akin to Gk *agein* to drive — more at AGENT] **1** : a maxim widely accepted on its intrinsic merit **2 a** : a proposition regarded as a self-evident truth **b** : POSTULATE 1

ax·i·om·at·ic \ˌak-sē-ə-ˈmat-ik\ *adj* [MGk *axiōmatikos*, fr. Gk, honorable, fr. *axiōmat-*, *axiōma*] : of, relating to, or having the nature of an axiom : widely accepted as self-evident — **ax·i·om·at·i·cal·ly** \-i-k(ə-)lē\ *adv*

ax·is \ˈak-səs\ *n, pl* **ax·es** \-ˌsēz\ [L, axis, axle; akin to OE *eax* axis, axle, Gk *axōn*, L *axilla* armpit, *agere* to drive — more at AGENT] **1 a** : a straight line about which a body or a geometric figure rotates or may be supposed to rotate **b** : a straight line with respect to which a body or figure is symmetrical **c** : a straight line that bisects at right angles a system of parallel chords of a curve and divides the curve into two symmetrical parts **d** : a straight line about which a line, curve, or plane figure is conceived to revolve in generating a solid of revolution **e** : one of the reference lines of a coordinate system **2 a** : the second vertebra of the neck that serves as a pivot for the head to turn on **b** : any of various central, fundamental, or axial parts **3** : a plant stem **4** : one of several imaginary lines assumed in describing the positions of the planes by which a crystal is bounded and the positions of atoms in the structure of the crystal **5** : a main line of direction, motion, growth, or extension **6 a** : an implied line in painting or sculpture through a composition to which elements in the composition are referred **b** : a line actually drawn and used as the basis of measurements in an architectural or other working drawing **7** : any of three fixed lines of reference in an airplane which are usu.

centroidal and mutually perpendicular and of which the first is the principal longitudinal line in the plane of symmetry, the second is perpendicular to the first in the plane of symmetry, and the third is perpendicular to the other two — called also respectively *longitudinal axis, normal axis, lateral axis* **8** : PARTNERSHIP, ALLIANCE

axi·sym·met·ric \ˌak-si-sə-ˈme-trik\ *also* **axi·sym·met·ri·cal** \-tri-kəl\ *adj* [*axis* + *symmetric*] : symmetric in respect to an axis — **axi·sym·met·ri·cal·ly** \-tri-k(ə-)lē\ *adv* — **axi·sym·me·try** \-ˈsim-ə-trē\ *n*

ax·le \ˈak-səl\ *n* [ME *axel-* (as in *axeltre*)] **1** *archaic* : AXIS **2 a** : a pin or shaft on or with which a wheel or pair of wheels revolves **b** (1) : the spindle of an axletree (2) : AXLETREE

axle·tree \-(ˌ)trē\ *n* [ME *axeltre,* fr. ON *öxultrē,* fr. *öxull* axle + *trē* tree] : a fixed bar or beam with bearings at its ends on which wheels (as of a cart) revolve

ax·man \ˈak-smən\ *n* : one who wields an ax

Ax·min·ster \ˈak-ˌsmin(t)-stər\ *n* [*Axminster,* England] : a machine-woven carpet with pile tufts inserted mechanically in a variety of textures and patterns

ax·o·lotl \ˈak-sə-ˌlät-ᵊl\ *n* [Nahuatl, lit., water doll] : any of several salamanders (genus *Ambystoma*) of mountain lakes of Mexico and the western U.S. that ordinarily live and breed without metamorphosing

ax·on \ˈak-ˌsän\ *also* **ax·one** \-ˌsōn\ *n* [NL *axon,* fr. Gk *axōn*] : a usu. long and single nerve-cell process that usu. conducts impulses away from the cell body — see NEURON illustration — **ax·o·nal** \ˈak-sən-ᵊl; ak-ˈsän-, -ˈsōn-\ *or* **ax·on·ic** \ak-ˈsän-ik, -ˈsōn-\ *adj*

ax·o·no·met·ric projection \ˌak-sə-nō-ˌme-trik-\ *n* [Gk *axōn* axis + E *-metric*] : a drawing projection in which an object is represented by means of its perpendicular projection on a surface in such a way that a rectangular solid appears as inclined and shows three faces

axo·plasm \ˈak-sə-ˌplaz-əm\ *n* [*axon* + *-plasm*] : the protoplasm of an axon — **axo·plas·mic** \ˌak-sə-ˈplaz-mik\ *adj*

ay \(ˈ)ī\ *interj* [MF *aymi* ay me] — usu. used with following *me* to express sorrow or regret

ayah \ˈī-ə; ˈä-yə, -(ˌ)yä\ *n* [Hindi *āyā,* fr. Pg *aia,* fr. L *avia* grandmother] : a nurse or maid native to India

AYC *abbr* American Youth Congress

AYD *abbr* American Youth for Democracy

[1]**aye** *also* **ay** \ˈā\ *adv* [ME, fr. ON *ei;* akin to OE *ā* always, L *aevum* age, lifetime, Gk *aiōn* age] : EVER, ALWAYS, CONTINUALLY <love that will ~ endure —W. S. Gilbert>

[2]**aye** *also* **ay** \ˈī\ *adv* [perh. fr. ME *ye, yie* — more at YEA] : YES <~, ~, sir>

[3]**aye** *also* **ay** \ˈī\ *n, pl* **ayes** : an affirmative vote or voter <the ~*s* have it>

aye–aye \ˈī-ˌī\ *n* [F, fr. Malagasy *aiay*] : a nocturnal lemur (*Daubentonia madagascariensis*) of Madagascar

AYH *abbr* American Youth Hostels

ayin \ˈī-ən\ *n* [Heb *ʿayin,* lit., eye] : the 16th letter of the Hebrew alphabet — see ALPHABET table

Ay·ma·ra \ˌī-mə-ˈrä\ *n, pl* **Aymara** *or* **Aymaras** [Sp *aymará*] **1** : a member of an Indian people of Bolivia and Peru **2 a** : the language of the Aymara people **b** : a language family of the Kechumaran stock comprising Aymara

Ayr *abbr* Ayrshire

Ayr·shire \ˈa(ə)r-ˌshi(ə)r, ˈe(ə)r-, -shər; ˈash-ˌi(ə)r\ *n* [*Ayrshire,* Scotland] : any of a breed of hardy dairy cattle originated in Ayr that vary in color from white to red or brown

az *abbr* **1** azimuth **2** azure

AZ *abbr* Arizona

az- *or* **azo-** *comb form* [ISV, fr. *azote*] : containing nitrogen esp. as the bivalent group N=N <*azine*>

aza- *or* **az-** *comb form* [ISV *az-* + *-a-*] : containing nitrogen in place of carbon and usu. the bivalent group NH for the group CH_2 or a single trivalent nitrogen atom for the group CH <*aza*guanine>

aza·lea \ə-ˈzāl-yə\ *n* [NL, genus name, fr. Gk, fem. of *azaleos* dry; akin to L *aridus* dry — more at ARDOR] : any of a genus or subgenus (*Azalea*) of rhododendrons with funnel-shaped corollas and usu. deciduous leaves including many species and hybrid forms cultivated as ornamentals

aza·thi·o·prine \ˌaz-ə-ˈthī-ə-ˌprēn\ *n* [*aza-* + *thio-* + *purine*] : a purine antimetabolite $C_9H_7N_7O_2S$ that is used esp. to suppress antibody production

Aza·zel \ə-ˈzā-zəl, ˈaz-ə-ˌzel\ *n* [Heb *ʿazāzēl*] : an evil spirit of the wilderness to which a scapegoat was sent by the ancient Hebrews in a ritual of atonement

AZC *abbr* American Zionist Council

azide \ˈā-ˌzīd, ˈaz-ˌīd\ *n* : a compound containing the group N_3 combined with an element or radical — **az·i·do** \ˈaz-ə-ˌdō\ *adj*

az·i·muth \ˈaz-(ə-)məth\ *n* [ME, fr. (assumed) ML, fr. Ar *as-sumūt* the azimuth, pl. of *as-samt* the way] **1** : an arc of the horizon measured between a fixed point (as true north) and the vertical circle passing through the center of an object usu. in astronomy and navigation clockwise from the north point through 360 degrees **2** : horizontal direction expressed as the angular distance between the direction of a fixed point (as the observer's heading) and the direction of the object — **az·i·muth·al** \ˌaz-ə-ˈməth-əl\ *adj* — **az·i·muth·al·ly** \-ˈməth-ə-lē\ *adv*

azimuthal equidistant projection *n* : a map projection of the surface of the earth so centered at any given point that a straight line radiating from the center to any other point represents the shortest distance and can be measured to scale

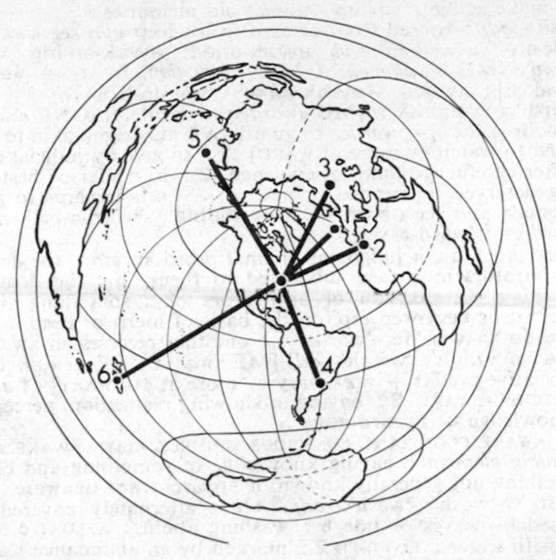

azimuthal equidistant projection, centered on Washington, D.C.: *1* London, *2* Algiers, *3* Moscow, *4* Buenos Aires, *5* Tokyo, *6* Auckland

azine \ˈā-ˌzēn, ˈaz-ˌēn\ *n* **1** : any of numerous organic compounds with a nitrogenous 6-membered ring **2** : a compound of the general formula RCH=NN=CHR or $R_2C{=}NN{=}CR_2$ formed by the action of hydrazine on aldehydes or ketones

azin·phos·meth·yl \ˌāz-ᵊn-(ˌ)fäs-ˈmeth-əl, ˌaz-\ *n* [*azine* + *phosphorus* + *methyl*] : an organophosphorus pesticide used against insects and mites

azo \ˈā-(ˌ)zō, ˈaz-(ˌ)ō\ *adj* [*az-*] : relating to or containing the bivalent group N=N united at both ends to carbon

azo dye *n* : any of numerous versatile dyes containing azo groups

azo·ic \(ˈ)ā-ˈzō-ik\ *adj* [*a-* + Gk *zōē* life — more at QUICK] : having no life; *specif* : of or relating to the part of geologic time that antedates life — compare ARCHEAN

azole \ˈā-ˌzōl, ˈaz-ˌōl\ *n* : any of numerous compounds characterized by a 5-membered ring containing at least one atom of nitrogen

azon·al \(ˈ)ā-ˈzōn-ᵊl\ *adj* : of, relating to, or being a soil or a major soil group marked by soils lacking well-developed horizons often because of immaturity — compare INTRAZONAL, ZONAL

azote \ˈā-ˌzōt, ˈaz-ˌōt\ *n* [F, irreg. fr. *a-* + Gk *zōē* life] : NITROGEN

azo·te·mia \ˌā-zō-ˈtē-mē-ə, ˌaz-ō-\ *n* [ISV *azote* + NL *-emia*] : an excess of nitrogenous bodies in the blood as a result of kidney insufficiency — **azo·te·mic** \-mik\ *adj*

az·oth \ˈaz-ˌȯth\ *n* [Ar *az-zāʾūq* the mercury] **1** : mercury regarded by alchemists as the first principle of metals **2** : the universal remedy of Paracelsus

azo·to·bac·ter \ā-ˈzōt-ə-ˌbak-tər\ *n* [NL, genus name, fr. ISV *azote* + NL *bacterium*] : any of a genus (*Azotobacter*) of large rod-shaped or spherical bacteria occurring in soil and sewage and fixing atmospheric nitrogen

azo·tu·ria \ˌā-zō-ˈt(y)u̇r-ē-ə\ *n* [ISV *azote* + NL *-uria*] : an excess of urea or other nitrogenous substances in the urine

Az·tec \ˈaz-ˌtek\ *n* [Sp *azteca,* fr. Nahuatl, pl. of *aztecatl*] **1 a** : a member of a Nahuatlan people that founded the Mexican empire conquered by Cortes in 1519 **b** : a member of any people under Aztec influence **2 a** : the language of the Aztec people **b** : NAHUATL — **Az·tec·an** \-ən\ *adj*

azure \ˈazh-ər\ *n* [ME *asur,* fr. OF *azur,* prob. fr. OSp, modif. of Ar *lāzaward,* fr. Per *lāzhuward*] **1** *archaic* : LAPIS LAZULI **2 a** : the blue color of the clear sky **b** : the heraldic color blue **3** : the unclouded sky — **azure** *adj*

azur·ite \ˈazh-ə-ˌrīt\ *n* [F, fr. *azur* azure] **1** : a mineral $Cu_3(OH)_2(CO_3)_2$ consisting of blue basic carbonate of copper, occurring in monoclinic crystals, in mass, and in earthy form, and constituting an ore of copper **2** : a semiprecious stone derived from azurite

azygo- *comb form* [ISV, fr. Gk *azygos*] : azygous

azygos *n* [NL, fr. Gk, unyoked, fr. *a-* + *zygon* yoke — more at YOKE] : an azygous anatomical part

azy·gous *or* **azy·gos** \(ˈ)ā-ˈzī-gəs\ *adj* [NL *azygos*] : not being one of a pair : SINGLE <an ~ vein>

1b \'bē\ *n, pl* **b's** *or* **bs** \'bēz\ *often cap, often attrib* **1 a :** the 2d letter of the English alphabet **b :** a graphic representation of this letter **c :** a speech counterpart of orthographic *b* **2 :** the 7th tone of a C-major scale **3 :** a graphic device for reproducing the letter *b* **4 :** one designated *b* esp. as the 2d in order or class **5 a :** a grade rating a student's work as good but short of excellent **b :** one graded or rated with a B **6 :** something shaped like the letter B

2b *abbr, often cap* **1** bachelor **2** bacillus **3** back **4** bag **5** bale **6** bass **7** basso **8** bat **9** Baumé **10** before **11** Bible **12** billion **13** bishop **14** black **15** blue **16** bolivar **17** book **18** born **19** brick **20** brightness **21** British **22** bulb **23** butut

B *symbol* **1** boron **2** magnetic induction

Ba *symbol* barium

BA *abbr* **1** bachelor of arts **2** batting average **3** Buenos Aires

baa *or* **ba** \'ba, 'bä\ *n* [imit.] **:** the bleat of a sheep — **baa** *vi*

BAA *abbr* bachelor of applied arts

BAAE *abbr* bachelor of aeronautical and astronautical engineering

baal \'bā(-ə)l\ *n, pl* **baals** *or* **baa·lim** \'bā-(ə-)ləm, 'bā-ə-ˌlim\ *often cap* [Heb *ba'al* lord] **:** any of numerous Canaanite and Phoenician local deities — **baal·ism** \'bā-(ə-)ˌliz-əm\ *n, often cap*

ba·ba \'bäb-(ˌ)ä, -ə\ *n* [F, fr. Pol, lit., old woman] **:** a rich cake soaked in a rum and sugar syrup

ba·bas·su \ˌbäb-ə-'sü\ *n* [Pg *babaçú*] **:** a tall pinnate-leaved palm (*Orbignya speciosa* or *O. martiana*) of northeastern Brazil with hard-shelled nuts yielding a valuable oil

1bab·bitt \'bab-ət\ *n* **:** a babbitt-metal lining for a bearing

2babbitt *vt* **:** to line or furnish with babbitt metal

Bab·bitt \'bab-ət\ *n* [George F. *Babbitt,* character in the novel *Babbitt* (1922) by Sinclair Lewis] **:** a business or professional man who conforms unthinkingly to prevailing middle-class standards — **Bab·bitt·ry** \-ə-trē\ *n*

babbitt metal *n* [Isaac *Babbitt* †1862 Am inventor] **:** an alloy used for lining bearings; *esp* **:** one containing tin, copper, and antimony

bab·ble \'bab-əl\ *vb* **bab·bled; bab·bling** \-(ə-)liŋ\ [ME *babelen,* prob. of imit. origin] *vi* **1 a :** to utter meaningless or unintelligible sounds **b :** to talk foolishly **:** PRATTLE **c :** to talk excessively **:** CHATTER **2 :** to make sounds as though babbling ~ *vt* **1 :** to utter in an incoherently or meaninglessly repetitious manner **2 :** to reveal by talk that is too free — **babble** *n* — **bab·ble·ment** \-əl-mənt\ *n* — **bab·bler** \-(ə-)lər\ *n*

Bab·cock test \ˌbab-ˌkäk-\ *n* [Stephen M. *Babcock* †1931 Am agricultural chemist] **:** a test for determining the fat content of milk and milk products

babe \'bāb\ *n* [ME, prob. of imit. origin] **1 a :** INFANT, BABY **b** *slang* **:** GIRL, WOMAN **2 :** a naive inexperienced person

Ba·bel \'bā-bəl, 'bab-əl\ *n* [Heb *Bābhel,* fr. Assyr-Bab *bāb-ilu* gate of god] **1 :** a city in Shinar where the building of a tower is held in the Book of Genesis to have been interrupted by the confusion of tongues **2** *often not cap* **a :** a confusion of sounds or voices **b :** a scene of noise or confusion

ba·be·sia \bə-'bē-zh(ē-)ə\ *n* [NL, genus name, fr. Victor *Babeș* †1926 Rumanian bacteriologist] **:** any of a family (Babesiidae and esp. genus *Babesia*) of sporozoans parasitic in mammalian red blood cells (as in Texas fever) and transmitted by the bite of a tick — called also *piroplasm*

bab·e·si·a·sis \ˌbab-ə-'zī-ə-səs\ *n* [NL] **:** an infection with or disease caused by babesias

ba·boon \ba-'bün, *chiefly Brit* bə-\ *n* [ME *babewin,* fr. MF *babouin,* fr. *baboue* grimace] **:** any of several large African and Asiatic primates (*Papio* and related genera of the family Cercopithecidae) having doglike muzzles and usu. short tails — **ba·boon·ish** \-'bü-nish\ *adj*

ba·bu \'bäb-(ˌ)ü\ *n* [Hindi *bābū,* lit., father] **1 :** a Hindu gentleman — a form of address corresponding to *Mr.* **2 a :** an Indian clerk who writes English **b :** an Indian having some education in English — often used disparagingly

ba·bul \bə-'bül\ *n* [Per *babūl*] **:** an acacia tree (*Acacia arabica*) widespread in northern Africa and across Asia that yields gum arabic and tannins as well as fodder and timber

ba·bush·ka \bə-'büsh-kə, -'bu̇sh-\ *n* [Russ, grandmother, dim. of *baba* old woman] **1 :** a usu. triangularly folded kerchief for the head **2 :** a head covering resembling a babushka

1ba·by \'bā-bē\ *n, pl* **babies** [ME, fr. *babe*] **1 a (1) :** an extremely young child; *esp* **:** INFANT **(2) :** an extremely young animal **b :** the youngest of a group **2 :** an infantile person **3 a** *slang* **:** GIRL, WOMAN — often used in address **b :** PERSON, THING **c** *slang* **:** BOY, MAN — often used in address — **baby** *adj* — **baby·hood** \-bē-ˌhu̇d\ *n* — **ba·by·ish** \-ish\ *adj*

2baby *vt* **ba·bied; ba·by·ing 1 :** to tend or indulge with often excessive or inappropriate care and solicitude <parents must resist the urge to ~ an only child> **2 :** to operate or treat with care <~ a new motor> *syn* see INDULGE

baby blue–eyes \-'blü-ˌīz\ *n pl but sing or pl in constr* **:** NEMOPHILA

baby carriage *n* **:** a four-wheeled push carriage usu. with a folding top — called also *baby buggy*

baby farm *n* **:** a place where care of babies is provided for a fee — **baby farming** *n*

baby grand *n* **:** a small grand piano five to six feet long

Bab·y·lon \'bab-ə-lən, -ˌlän\ *n* [*Babylon,* ancient city of Babylonia] **:** a city devoted to materialism and the pursuit of sensual pleasure

1Bab·y·lo·nian \ˌbab-ə-'lō-nyən, -nē-ən\ *n* **1 :** a native or inhabitant of ancient Babylonia or Babylon **2 :** the form of the Akkadian language used in ancient Babylonia

2Babylonian *adj* **1 :** of, relating to, or characteristic of Babylonia or Babylon, the Babylonians, or Babylonian **2 :** LUXURIOUS

baby's breath *n* **1 :** GYPSOPHILA **2 :** a bedstraw (*Galium sylvaticum*) with thin lanceolate leaves and white flowers

ba·by–sit \'bā-bē-ˌsit\ *vb* **-sat** \-ˌsat\; **-sit·ting** [back-formation fr. *baby-sitter*] *vi* **:** to care for children usu. during a short absence of the parents ~ *vt* **:** to baby-sit for — **ba·by–sit·ter** *n*

baby talk *n* **1 :** the syntactically imperfect speech or phonetically modified forms used by small children learning to talk **2 :** the consciously imperfect or mutilated speech or prattle often used by adults in speaking to small children

bac *abbr* [ML *baccalaureus*] bachelor

bac·ca \'bak-ə\ *n, pl* **bac·cae** \'bak-ˌsē, 'bak-ˌī\ [NL, fr. L *baca, bacca* berry] **:** BERRY 1c — **bac·cif·er·ous** \bak-'sif-(ə-)rəs\ *adj*

bac·ca·lau·re·ate \ˌbak-ə-'lȯr-ē-ət, -'lär-\ *n* [ML *baccalaureatus,* fr. *baccalaureus* bachelor, alter. of *baccalarius*] **1 :** the degree of bachelor conferred by universities and colleges **2 a :** a sermon to a graduating class **b :** the service at which this sermon is delivered

bac·ca·rat \ˌbäk-ə-'rä, ˌbak-\ *n* [F *baccara*] **:** a card game resembling chemin de fer in which three hands are dealt and players may bet either or both hands against the dealer's

bac·cate \'bak-ˌāt\ *adj* [L *bacca* berry] **1 :** pulpy throughout like a berry **2 :** bearing berries

Bac·chae \'bak-ˌē, -ˌī\ *n pl* [L, fr. Gk *Bakchai,* fr. *Bakchos* Bacchus] **1 :** the female attendants or priestesses of Bacchus **2 :** the women participating in the Bacchanalia

1bac·cha·nal \'bak-ən-ᵊl\ *adj* [L *bacchanalis* of Bacchus] **:** of, relating to, or suggestive of the Bacchanalia **:** BACCHANALIAN

2bac·cha·nal \'bak-ən-ᵊl, ˌbak-ə-'nal, ˌbäk-ə-'näl\ *n* **1 a :** a devotee of Bacchus; *esp* **:** one who celebrates the Bacchanalia **b :** REVELER **2 :** drunken revelry or carousal **:** BACCHANALIA

bac·cha·na·lia \ˌbak-ə-'nāl-yə\ *n, pl* **bacchanalia** [L, pl., fr. neut. pl. of *bacchanalis*] **1** *pl, cap* **:** a Roman festival of Bacchus celebrated with dancing, song, and revelry **2 :** a drunken feast **:** ORGY — **bac·cha·na·lian** \-'nāl-yən\ *adj or n*

bac·chant \bə-'kant, -'känt; 'bak-ənt\ *n, pl* **bacchants** *or* **bac·chantes** \bə-'kants, -'känts, -'kant-ēz, -'känt-ēz\ [L *bacchant-, bacchans,* fr. prp. of *bacchari* to take part in the orgies of Bacchus] **:** BACCHANAL — **bacchant** *adj* — **bac·chan·tic** \bə-'kant-ik, -'känt-\ *adj*

bac·chante \bə-'kant(-ē), -'känt(-ē)\ *n* [F, fr. L *bacchant-, bacchans*] **:** a priestess or female follower of Bacchus **:** MAENAD

bac·chic \'bak-ik\ *adj, often cap* **1 :** of or relating to Bacchus **2 :** of or relating to the Bacchanalia **:** BACCHANALIAN

Bac·chus \'bak-əs\ *n* [L, fr. Gk *Bakchos*] **:** the Greek god of wine — called also *Dionysus*

bach \'bach\ *vi* **:** to live as a bachelor — **bach** *n*

bach·e·lor \'bach-(ə-)lər\ *n* [ME *bacheler,* fr. OF, fr. ML *baccalarius* tenant farmer, squire, advanced student, of Celtic origin; akin to IrGael *bachlach* shepherd, peasant, fr. OIr *bachall* staff, fr. L *baculum* — more at BACTERIUM] **1 :** a young knight who follows the banner of another **:** KNIGHT BACHELOR **2 :** a person who has received what is usu. the lowest degree conferred by a four-year college, university, or professional school <~ of arts> **3 a :** an unmarried man **b :** a male animal (as a fur seal) without a mate during breeding time — **bach·e·lor·hood** \-ˌhu̇d\ *n*

bachelor's button *n* **:** a European composite (*Centaurea cyanus*) having flower heads with blue, pink, or white rays that is often cultivated in No. America — called also *cornflower*

ba·cil·la·ry \'bas-ə-ˌler-ē, bə-'sil-ə-rē\ *or* **ba·cil·lar** \bə-'sil-ər, 'bas-ə-lər\ *adj* [ML & NL *bacillus*] **1 :** shaped like a rod; *also* **:** consisting of small rods **2 :** of, relating to, or produced by bacilli

ba·cil·lus \bə-'sil-əs\ *n, pl* **-li** \-ˌī *also* -ē\ [NL, fr. ML, small staff, rod, dim. of L *baculus* staff, alter. of *baculum* — more at BACTERIUM] **1 :** any of a genus (*Bacillus*) of aerobic rod-shaped bacteria producing endospores that do not thicken the rod and including many saprophytes and some parasites (as *B. anthracis* of anthrax); *broadly* **:** a straight rod-shaped bacterium **2 :** BACTERIUM; *esp* **:** a disease-producing bacterium

bac·i·tra·cin \ˌbas-ə-'trās-ᵊn\ *n* [NL *Bacillus subtilis* (species of bacillus producing the toxin) + Margaret *Tracy b ab* 1936 Am child in whose tissues it was found] **:** a toxic antibiotic isolated from a bacillus (*Bacillus subtilis*) and usu. used topically against cocci

1back \'bak\ *n* [ME, fr. OE *bæc;* akin to OHG *bah* back] **1 a :** the rear part of the human body esp. from the neck to the end of the spine **b :** the corresponding part of a lower animal (as a quadruped) **c :** SPINAL COLUMN **d :** BACKBONE 4 **2 a :** the side or surface opposite the front or face **:** the rear part; *also* **:** the farther or reverse side **b :** something at or on the back for support <~ of a chair> **3 :** a position in some games (as football or soccer) behind the front line of players; *also* **:** a player in this position — **back·less** \'bak-ləs\ *adj*

2back *adv* **1 a :** to, toward, or at the rear **b :** in or into the past **:** AGO **c :** in or into a reclining position **d (1) :** under restraint **(2) :** in a delayed or retarded condition **2 a :** to, toward, or in a place from which a person or thing came **b :** to or toward a former state **c :** in return or reply — **back and forth :** backward and forward **:** from one place to another

3back *adj* **1 a :** being at or in the back <~ door> **b :** distant from a central or main area **:** REMOTE **c :** articulated at or toward the back of the oral passage **2 :** being in arrears **:** OVERDUE **3 :** moving or operating backward **4 :** not current <~ number of a magazine> **5 :** constituting the final nine holes of an 18-hole golf course

4back *vt* **1 a :** to support by material or moral assistance — often used with *up* **b :** SUBSTANTIATE **c (1) :** COUNTERSIGN, ENDORSE **(2) :** to assume financial responsibility for **2 :** to cause to go back or in reverse **3 a :** to furnish with a back **b :** to be at the back of ~ *vi* **1 :** to move backward **2** *of the wind* **:** to shift counterclockwise — compare VEER **3 :** to have the back in the direction of something ***syn*** see SUPPORT, RECEDE — **back and fill 1 :** to manage the sails of a ship so as to keep it clear of obstructions as it floats down with the current of a river or channel **2 :** to take opposite positions alternately **:** SHILLY-SHALLY

[5]**back** *n* [D *bak*] **:** a shallow vat or tub used esp. by brewers or dyers

back·ache \'bak-ˌāk\ *n* **:** a pain in the lower back

back away *vi* **:** to move back (as from a theoretical position) **:** WITHDRAW

back–bench·er \'bak-'ben-chər\ *n* **:** a rank-and-file member of a British legislature

back·bite \-ˌbīt\ *vb* **-bit; -bitten; -biting** *vt* **:** to say mean or spiteful things about **:** SLANDER ~ *vi* **:** to backbite a person — **back·bit·er** *n*

back·board \-ˌbō(ə)rd, -ˌbȯ(ə)rd\ *n* **:** a board placed at or serving as the back of something; *specif* **:** a rounded or rectangular board that is behind the basket on a basketball court and that serves to keep missed shots from going out-of-bounds and as a surface from which the ball can be made to rebound into the basket

back·bone \-'bōn, -ˌbōn\ *n* **1 :** SPINAL COLUMN, SPINE **2 a :** a chief mountain ridge, range, or system **b :** the foundation or most substantial or sturdiest part of something **3 :** firm and resolute character **4 :** the back of a book usu. lettered with the title and the author's and publisher's names ***syn*** see FORTITUDE ***ant*** spinelessness

back–check \-ˌchek\ *vi* **:** to skate back toward one's own goal while closely defending against the offensive rushes of an opposing player in ice hockey

back·coun·try \-ˌkən-trē\ *n* **:** a thinly settled rural area

back·court \-'kō(ə)rt, -'kȯ(ə)rt\ *n* **1 :** the area near or nearest the back boundary lines or back wall of the playing area in a net or court game **2 :** a basketball team's defensive half of the court; *also* **:** the part of the offensive half of the court farthest from the goal

back·court·man \-mən\ *n* **:** a guard on a basketball team

back·cross \'bak-ˌkrȯs\ *vt* [[2]*back*] **:** to cross (a first-generation hybrid) with or as if with one parent — **backcross** *n*

back dive *n* **:** a dive from a position facing the diving board

back down *vi* **:** to withdraw from a commitment or position

back·drop \'bak-ˌdräp\ *n* **1 :** a painted cloth hung across the rear of a stage **2 :** BACKGROUND

back·er \'bak-ər\ *n* **1 :** one that supports **2 :** one who works with backs or backing

back·field \-ˌfēld\ *n* **:** the football players whose positions are behind the line of scrimmage; *also* **:** the positions themselves

[1]**back·fire** \-ˌfī(ə)r\ *n* **1 :** a fire started to check an advancing forest or prairie fire by clearing an area **2 :** an improperly timed explosion of fuel mixture in the cylinder of an internal-combustion engine

[2]**backfire** *vi* **1 :** to make or undergo a backfire **2 :** to have the reverse of the desired or expected effect

back–formation *n* **1 :** a word formed by subtraction of a real or supposed affix from an already existing longer word (as *burgle* from *burglar*) **2 :** the formation of a back-formation

back·gam·mon \'bak-ˌgam-ən, bak-'\ *n* [perh. fr. [3]*back* + ME *gamen, game* game] **:** a board game played with dice and counters in which each player tries to move his counters along the board and at the same time to block or capture his opponent's counters

INNER TABLE OUTER TABLE

backgammon board with men arranged as at the beginning of a game

[1]**back·ground** \'bak-ˌgrau̇nd\ *n* **1 a :** the scenery or ground behind something **b :** the part of a painting representing what lies behind objects in the foreground **2 :** an inconspicuous position **3 a :** the conditions that form the setting within which something is experienced **b (1) :** the circumstances or events antecedent to a phenomenon or development **(2) :** information essential to understanding of a problem or situation **c :** the total of a person's experience, knowledge, and education **4 :** intrusive sound that interferes with received or recorded electronic signals

[2]**background** *vt* **:** to provide with background <~ a new employee>

background music *n* **:** music to accompany the dialogue or action of a motion picture or radio or television drama

[1]**back·hand** \'bak-ˌhand\ *n* **1 a :** a stroke (as in tennis) made with the back of the hand turned in the direction of movement **b :** a catch (as in baseball) made to the side of the body opposite the hand being used **2 :** handwriting whose strokes slant downward from left to right

backhand 1

[2]**backhand** *or* **back·hand·ed** \-'han-dəd\ *adv* **:** with a backhand

[3]**backhand** *vt* **:** to do, hit, or catch backhand

back·hand·ed \'bak-'han-dəd\ *adj* **1 :** using or made with a backhand **2 :** INDIRECT, DEVIOUS; *esp* **:** SARCASTIC — **back·hand·ed·ly** *adv*

back·hoe \-ˌhō\ *n* **:** an excavating machine whose bucket is rigidly attached to a hinged stick on the boom and is drawn toward the machine in operation

back·house \-ˌhau̇s\ *n* **:** an outdoor toilet

back·ing \'bak-iŋ\ *n* **1 :** something forming a back **2 a :** SUPPORT, AID **b :** endorsement esp. of a warrant by a magistrate

back judge *n* **:** a football official whose duties include keeping the game's official time and identifying eligible pass receivers

back·lash \'bak-ˌlash\ *n* **1 :** a sudden violent backward movement or reaction **2 :** a snarl in that part of a fishing line wound on the reel **3 :** a strong adverse reaction (as to a recent political or social development) — **back·lash·er** *n*

[1]**back·log** \-ˌlȯg, -ˌläg\ *n* **1 :** a large log at the back of a hearth fire **2 :** a reserve that promises continuing work and profit **3 :** an accumulation of tasks unperformed or materials not processed

[2]**backlog** *vb* **:** ACCUMULATE

back matter *n* **:** matter following the main text of a book

back mutation *n* **:** mutation of a previously mutated gene to its former condition

back of *prep* **:** BEHIND

back off *vi* **:** to back down

back out *vi* **:** to withdraw esp. from a commitment or contest

[1]**back·pack** \'bak-ˌpak\ *n* **1 a :** a load carried on the back **b :** a camping pack (as of canvas or nylon) supported by a usu. aluminum frame and carried on the back **2 :** a piece of equipment designed for use while being carried on the back

[2]**backpack** *vt* **:** to carry (food or equipment) on the back esp. in hiking ~ *vi* **:** to hike with a backpack — **back·pack·er** *n*

back·ped·al \'bak-ˌped-ᵊl\ *vi* **:** to retreat or move backward (as in boxing)

back·rest \-ˌrest\ *n* **:** a rest for the back

back room *n* **1 :** a room situated in the rear **2 :** the meeting place of a directing group that exercises its authority in an inconspicuous and indirect way

back·saw \'bak-ˌsȯ\ *n* **:** a saw with a metal rib along its back

back·scat·ter \-ˌskat-ər\ *or* **back·scat·ter·ing** \-ə-riŋ\ *n* **:** the scattering of radiation (as X rays) in a direction opposite to that of the incident radiation due to reflection from particles of the medium traversed; *also* **:** the radiation so reversed in direction

back·seat \-'sēt\ *n* **1 :** a seat in the back (as of an automobile) **2 :** an inferior position <won't take a ~ to anyone>

back·set \'bak-ˌset\ *n* **:** SETBACK

back·side \-'sīd\ *n* **:** BUTTOCKS — often used in pl.

back·slap \-ˌslap\ *vt* **:** to display excessive or effusive goodwill for ~ *vi* **:** to display excessive cordiality or good-fellowship — **back·slap·per** *n*

back·slide \-ˌslīd\ *vi* **-slid** \-ˌslid\; **-slid** *or* **-slid·den** \-ˌslid-ᵊn\; **-slid·ing** \-ˌslīd-iŋ\ **:** to lapse morally or in the practice of religion ***syn*** see LAPSE — **back·slid·er** \-ˌslīd-ər\ *n*

back·spin \-ˌspin\ *n* **:** a backward rotary motion of a ball

[1]**back·stage** \'bak-'stāj\ *adv* **1 :** in or to a backstage area **2 :** in private **:** SECRETLY

[2]**back·stage** \'bak-ˌstāj\ *adj* **1 :** of, relating to, or occurring in the area behind the proscenium and esp. in the dressing rooms **2 :** of or relating to the private lives of theater people **3 :** of or relating to the inner working or operation (as of an organization)

back·stairs \-ˌsta(ə)rz, -ˌste(ə)rz\ *adj* **1 :** SECRET, FURTIVE <~ political deals> **2 :** SORDID, SCANDALOUS <~ gossip>

back·stay \-ˌstā\ *n* **1 :** a stay extending from the mastheads to the side of a ship and slanting aft **2 :** a strengthening or supporting device at the back (as of a carriage or a shoe)

back·stitch \-ˌstich\ *n* **:** a hand stitch made by inserting the needle a stitch length to the right and bringing it up an equal distance to the left — **backstitch** *vb*

[1]**back·stop** \-ˌstäp\ *n* **1 :** something at the back serving as a stop: as **a :** a screen or fence for keeping a ball from leaving the field of play **b :** a stop (as a pawl) that prevents a backward movement (as of a wheel) **2 :** a player (as the catcher) whose position is behind the batter

[2]**backstop** *vt* **1 :** to serve as a backstop to **2 :** SUPPORT, BOLSTER

back·stretch \'bak-'strech\ *n* **:** the side opposite the homestretch on a racecourse

back·stroke \-ˌstrōk\ *n* **:** a swimming stroke executed on the back

back·swept \-ˌswept\ *adj* **:** swept or slanting backward

back swimmer *n* **:** a water bug (family Notonectidae) that swims on its back

back·swing \'bak-ˌswiŋ\ *n* **:** the movement of a club, racket, bat, or arm backward to a position from which the forward or downward swing is made

back·sword \-ˌsō(ə)rd, -ˌsȯ(ə)rd\ *n* **1 :** a single-edged sword **2 :** SINGLESTICK

back talk *n* **:** an impudent, insolent, or argumentative reply

back·track \'bak-ˌtrak\ *vi* **1 :** to retrace one's course **2 :** to reverse a position or stand

back·up \-ˌəp\ *n* **:** one that serves as a substitute or alternative <a ~ for a rocket>

back up \-'əp\ *vi* **:** to accumulate in a congested state <traffic *backed up* for miles> ~ *vt* **1 :** to hold back <a dam *backing up* a huge lake> **2 :** to move into a position behind (a teammate) in order to assist on a play (as in stopping a missed ball)

[1]**back·ward** \'bak-wərd\ *or* **back·wards** \-wərdz\ *adv* **1 a :** toward the back **b :** with the back foremost **2 a :** in a reverse or contrary direction or way **b :** toward the past **c :** toward a worse state

[2]**backward** *adj* **1 a :** directed or turned backward **b :** done or executed backward **2 :** DIFFIDENT, SHY **3 :** retarded in development — **back·ward·ly** *adv* — **back·ward·ness** *n*

[3]**backward** *n* **:** the part behind or past

back·wash \'bak-ˌwȯsh, -ˌwäsh\ *n* **1 :** backward movement (as of water or air) produced by a propelling force (as the motion of oars) **2 :** a consequence or by-product of an event **:** AFTERMATH

back·wa·ter \-ˌwȯt-ər, -ˌwät-\ *n* **1 a :** water turned back in its course by an obstruction, an opposing current, or the tide **b :** a body of water turned back **2 :** an isolated or backward place or condition

back·woods \-'wu̇dz\ *n pl but sing or pl in constr* **1 :** wooded or partly cleared areas on the frontier **2 :** a remote or culturally backward area — **back·woods·man** \-mən\ *n*

back·yard \-'yärd\ *n* **1 :** an area at the rear of a house **2 :** an area that is one's special domain

ba·con \ˈbā-kən\ *n* [ME, fr. MF, of Gmc origin; akin to OHG *bahho* side of bacon, *bah* back] **:** a side of a pig cured and smoked

Ba·co·ni·an \bā-ˈkō-nē-ən\ *adj* **1 :** of, relating to, or characteristic of Francis Bacon or his doctrines **2 :** of or relating to those who believe that Francis Bacon wrote the works usu. attributed to Shakespeare — **Baconian** *n*

bact *abbr* **1** bacterial **2** bacteriology **3** bacterium

bac·ter·emia \ˌbak-tə-ˈrē-mē-ə\ *n* [NL, alter. of *bacteriemia,* fr. *bacteri-* + *-emia*] **:** the usu. transient presence of bacteria or other microorganisms in the blood — **bac·ter·emic** \-mik\ *adj*

bacteri- *or* **bacterio-** *comb form* [NL *bacterium*] **:** bacteria <*bacteri*al> <*bacterio*lysis>

bacteria *pl of* BACTERIUM

bac·te·ri·al \bak-ˈtir-ē-əl\ *adj* **:** of, relating to, or caused by bacteria <a ~ chromosome> <~ infection> — **bac·te·ri·al·ly** \-ə-lē\ *adv*

bac·te·ri·cid·al \bak-ˌtir-ə-ˈsīd-ᵊl\ *adj* **:** destroying bacteria — **bac·te·ri·cid·al·ly** \-ᵊl-ē\ *adv* — **bac·te·ri·cide** \-ˈtir-ə-ˌsīd\ *n*

bac·ter·in \ˈbak-tə-rən\ *n* **:** a suspension of killed or attenuated bacteria for use as an antigen

bac·te·rio·chlo·ro·phyll \bak-ˌtir-ē-ō-ˈklōr-ə-ˌfil, -ˈklȯr-, -fəl\ *n* **:** a pyrrole derivative in photosynthetic bacteria related to the chlorophyll of higher plants

bac·te·rio·cin \bak-ˈtir-ē-ə-sən\ *n* [ISV *bacteri-* + *-cin* (as in *colicin*)] **:** an antibiotic (as colicin) produced by bacteria

bac·te·ri·ol·o·gy \(ˌ)bak-ˌtir-ē-ˈäl-ə-jē\ *n* [ISV] **1 :** a science that deals with bacteria and their relations to medicine, industry, and agriculture **2 :** bacterial life and phenomena — **bac·te·ri·o·log·ic** \bak-ˌtir-ē-ə-ˈläj-ik\ *or* **bac·te·ri·o·log·i·cal** \-ˈläj-i-kəl\ *adj* — **bac·te·ri·o·log·i·cal·ly** \-i-k(ə-)lē\ *adv* — **bac·te·ri·ol·o·gist** \(ˌ)bak-ˌtir-ē-ˈäl-ə-jəst\ *n*

bac·te·ri·ol·y·sis \(ˌ)bak-ˌtir-ē-ˈäl-ə-səs\ *n* [NL] **:** destruction or dissolution of bacterial cells — **bac·te·ri·o·lyt·ic** \bak-ˌtir-ē-ə-ˈlit-ik\ *adj*

bac·te·rio·phage \bak-ˈtir-ē-ə-ˌfāj, -ˌfäzh\ *n* [ISV] **:** any of various specific bacteriolytic viruses normally present in sewage and in body products — **bac·te·rio·phag·ic** \-ˌtir-ē-ə-ˈfaj-ik\ *or* **bac·te·ri·oph·a·gous** \(ˌ)bak-ˌtir-ē-ˈäf-ə-gəs\ *adj* — **bac·te·ri·oph·a·gy** \(ˌ)bak-ˌtir-ē-ˈäf-ə-jē\ *n*

bac·te·rio·sta·sis \bak-ˌtir-ē-ō-ˈstā-səs\ *n* [NL] **:** inhibition of the growth of bacteria without destruction

bac·te·rio·stat \-ˈtir-ē-ō-ˌstat\ *n* **:** an agent that causes bacteriostasis — **bac·te·rio·stat·ic** \-ˌtir-ē-ō-ˈstat-ik\ *adj* — **bac·te·rio·stat·i·cal·ly** \-i-k(ə-)lē\ *adv*

bac·te·ri·um \bak-ˈtir-ē-əm\ *n, pl* **-ria** \-ē-ə\ [NL, fr. Gk *baktērion* staff; akin to L *baculum* staff] **:** any of a class (Schizomycetes) of microscopic plants having round, rodlike, spiral, or filamentous single-celled or noncellular bodies often aggregated into colonies or motile by means of flagella, living in soil, water, organic matter, or the bodies of plants and animals, and being autotrophic, saprophytic, or parasitic in nutrition and important to man because of their chemical effects and as pathogens

bac·te·ri·uria \bak-ˌtir-ē-ˈ(y)u̇r-ē-ə\ *n* [NL] **:** the passage of bacteria in the urine

bac·te·rize \ˈbak-tə-ˌrīz\ *vt* **-rized; -riz·ing :** to subject to bacterial action — **bac·te·ri·za·tion** \ˌbak-tə-rə-ˈzā-shən\ *n*

bac·te·roid \ˈbak-tə-ˌrȯid\ *n* **1 :** an irregularly shaped bacterium (as a rhizobium) found esp. in root nodules of legumes **2 :** a microorganism like a bacterium found in cells of the fat body esp. of roaches

Bac·tri·an camel \ˌbak-trē-ən-\ *n* [fr. its habitat in ancient Bactria] **:** CAMEL 1b

[1]**bad** \ˈbad\ *adj* **worse** \ˈwərs\; **worst** \ˈwərst\ [ME] **1 a :** failing to reach an acceptable standard **:** POOR **b :** UNFAVORABLE <make a ~ impression> **c :** not fresh or sound **:** SPOILED, DILAPIDATED <~ fish> <the house was in ~ condition> **2 a :** morally objectionable **b :** MISCHIEVOUS, DISOBEDIENT **3 :** inadequate or unsuited to a purpose <a ~ plan> <~ lighting> **4 :** DISAGREEABLE, UNPLEASANT <~ news> **5 a :** INJURIOUS, HARMFUL **b :** SEVERE <a ~ cold> **6 :** INCORRECT, FAULTY <~ grammar> **7 a :** suffering pain or distress <felt generally ~> **b :** UNHEALTHY, DISEASED <~ teeth> **8 :** SORROWFUL, SORRY **9 :** INVALID, VOID <a ~ check> — **bad** *adv* — **bad·ly** *adv* — **bad·ness** *n*

syn BAD, EVIL, ILL, WICKED, NAUGHTY *shared meaning element* **:** not ethically or morally acceptable. BAD, a very general term, is applicable to anyone or anything reprehensible for whatever reason and to whatever degree <such a *bad* boy, he won't stay in the yard> <almost as *bad* . . . as kill a king, and marry with his brother —Shak.> EVIL may add to *bad* a strong suggestion of the sinister or baleful <watched silently with an *evil* glow in his eyes> <an *evil* deed> ILL may suggest an active malevolence or vicious intent <misled by *ill* counsel> or it may merely attribute objectionableness or inferiority to someone or something <a man held in *ill* repute> WICKED usually implies serious moral reprehensibility <the *wicked* sorcerers who have done people to death by their charms —J. G. Frazer> or it may suggest malevolence and malice <a brooding *wicked* spirit> NAUGHTY, once a close synonym of *wicked,* is now usually restricted to trivial misdeeds (as of children) or used to suggest reprehensibility in a light or playful way <a very *naughty* story> ***ant*** good

[2]**bad** *n* **1 :** something that is bad **2 :** an evil or unhappy state

bad blood *n* **:** ill feeling **:** BITTERNESS

bad·der·locks \ˈbad-ər-ˌläks\ *n pl but sing in constr* [origin unknown] **:** a large blackish seaweed (*Alaria esculenta*) often eaten as a vegetable in Europe

bad·die *or* **bad·dy** \ˈbad-ē\ *n, pl* **baddies :** one that is bad; *esp* **:** an opponent of the hero (as in fiction or motion pictures)

bade *past of* BID

badge \ˈbaj\ *n* [ME *bage, bagge*] **1 :** a device or token esp. of membership in a society or group **2 :** a characteristic mark **3 :** an emblem awarded for a particular accomplishment — **badge** *vt*

[1]**bad·ger** \ˈbaj-ər\ *n* [prob. fr. *badge;* fr. the white mark on its forehead] **1 a :** any of several sturdy burrowing mammals (genera *Meles* and *Taxidea* of the family Mustelidae) widely distributed in the northern hemisphere **b :** the pelt or fur of a badger **2** *cap* **:** a native or resident of Wisconsin — used as a nickname

[2]**badger** *vt* **bad·gered; bad·ger·ing** \ˈbaj-(ə-)riŋ\ [fr. the sport of baiting badgers] **:** to harass or annoy persistently ***syn*** see BAIT

ba·di·nage \ˌbad-ᵊn-ˈäzh\ *n* [F] **:** playful repartee **:** BANTER

bad·land \ˈbad-ˌland\ *n* **:** a region marked by intricate erosional sculpturing, scanty vegetation, and fantastically formed hills — usu. used in pl.

bad·min·ton \ˈbad-ˌmint-ᵊn\ *n* [*Badminton,* residence of the Duke of Beaufort, England] **:** a court game played with light long-handled rackets and a shuttlecock volleyed over a net

bad–mouth \ˈbad-ˌmau̇th, -ˌmau̇t͟h\ *vt* **:** to criticize severely and persistently

BAE *abbr* **1** bachelor of aeronautical engineering **2** bachelor of agricultural engineering **3** bachelor of architectural engineering **4** bachelor of art education **5** bachelor of arts in education

BAEd *abbr* bachelor of arts in education

Bae·de·ker \ˈbād-i-kər\ *n* [Karl *Baedeker* †1859 G publisher of guidebooks] **:** GUIDEBOOK

BAeE *abbr* bachelor of aeronautical engineering

BAEE *abbr* bachelor of arts in elementary education

[1]**baf·fle** \ˈbaf-əl\ *vt* **baf·fled; baf·fling** \-(ə-)liŋ\ [prob. alter. of ME (Sc) *bawchillen* to denounce, discredit publicly] **1 :** to defeat or check (as a person or his plans) by confusing or puzzling **:** DISCONCERT **2 a :** to check or break the force or flow of by or as if by a baffle **b :** to prevent (sound waves) from interfering with each other (as by a baffle) ***syn*** see FRUSTRATE — **baf·fle·ment** \-əl-mənt\ *n* — **baf·fler** \-(ə-)lər\ *n* — **baf·fling·ly** \ˈbaf-liŋ-lē\ *adv*

[2]**baffle** *n* **1 :** a device (as a plate, wall, or screen) to deflect, check, or regulate flow (as of a fluid or light) **2 :** a partition or cabinet to impede the exchange of sound waves between the front and back of a loudspeaker

baffling wind *n* **:** a light wind that frequently shifts from one point to another

[1]**bag** \ˈbag\ *n* [ME *bagge,* fr. ON *baggi*] **1 :** a usu. flexible container that may be closed for holding, storing, or carrying something: as **a :** PURSE; *esp* **:** HANDBAG **b :** a bag for game **c :** TRAVELING BAG **2 :** something resembling a bag: as **a :** a pouched or pendulous bodily part or organ; *esp* **:** UDDER **b :** a puffed-out sag or bulge in cloth **c :** a square white canvas container to mark a base in baseball **3 :** the amount contained in a bag **4 a** (1) **:** a quantity of game taken (2) **:** the maximum quantity of game permitted by law **b :** SPOILS **c :** a group of persons or things **5 :** a slovenly unattractive woman **6 :** something one likes or does well **7 a :** a way of life **b :** a characteristic manner of expression — **in the bag :** SURE, CERTAIN

[2]**bag** *vb* **bagged; bag·ging** *vi* **1 :** to swell out **:** BULGE **2 :** to hang loosely ~ *vt* **1 :** to cause to swell **2 :** to put into a bag **3 a :** to take (animals) as game **b :** to get possession of esp. by strategy or stealth **c :** CAPTURE, SEIZE **d :** to shoot down **:** DESTROY ***syn*** see CATCH

BAg *abbr* bachelor of agriculture

ba·gasse \bə-ˈgas\ *n* [F] **:** plant residue (as of sugarcane or grapes) left after a product (as juice) has been extracted

bag·a·telle \ˌbag-ə-ˈtel\ *n* [F, fr. It *bagattella*] **1 :** TRIFLE 1 **2 :** a game played with a cue and balls on an oblong table having cups or cups and arches at one end

ba·gel \ˈbā-gəl\ *n* [Yiddish *beygel,* deriv. of OHG *boug* ring; akin to OE *bēag* ring — more at BEE] **:** a hard glazed doughnut-shaped roll

bag·ful \ˈbag-ˌfu̇l\ *n* **1 :** as much or as many as a bag will hold **2 :** a large number or amount <had a ~ of tricks>

bag·gage \ˈbag-ij\ *n* [ME *bagage,* fr. MF, fr. *bague* bundle] **1 :** traveling bags and personal belongings of travelers **:** LUGGAGE **2 :** transportable equipment esp. of a military force **3 a :** superfluous or intrusive things or circumstances **b :** outmoded theories or practices **4** [prob. modif. of MF *bagasse,* fr. OProv *bagassa*] **a :** a worthless or contemptible woman; *esp* **:** PROSTITUTE **b :** a young woman or girl

bagpipe

bag·ging \ˈbag-iŋ\ *n* **:** material (as cloth) for bags

bag·gy \ˈbag-ē\ *adj* **bag·gi·er; -est :** loose, puffed out, or hanging like a bag <~ trousers> — **bag·gi·ly** \ˈbag-ə-lē\ *adv* — **bag·gi·ness** \ˈbag-ē-nəs\ *n*

bag·man \ˈbag-mən\ *n* **1** *chiefly Brit* **:** TRAVELING SALESMAN **2 :** a person who on behalf of another collects or distributes illicitly gained money

ba·gnio \ˈban-(ˌ)yō\ *n, pl* **bagnios** [It *bagno,* lit., public baths (fr. the use of Roman baths at Constantinople for imprisonment of Christian prisoners by the Turks), fr. L *balneum,* fr. Gk *balaneion;* akin to OHG *quellan* to gush — more at DEVIL] **1** *obs* **:** PRISON **2 :** BROTHEL

bag of waters : the double-walled fluid-filled sac that encloses and protects the fetus in the womb and that breaks releasing its fluid during the birth process

bag·pipe \ˈbag-ˌpīp\ *n* **:** a wind instrument consisting of a leather bag, a valve-stopped mouth tube, a reed melody pipe, and three or

four drone pipes — often used in pl. — **bag·pip·er** \-ˌpī-pər\ *n*
ba·guette \ba-ˈget\ *n* [F, lit., rod] **1 :** a small molding like but smaller than the astragal **2 :** a gem having the shape of a long narrow rectangle; *also* **:** the shape itself
bag·wig \ˈbag-ˌwig\ *n* **:** an 18th century wig with the back hair enclosed in a small silk bag
bag·worm \-ˌwərm\ *n* **:** any of a family (Psychidae) of moths with wingless females and plant-feeding larvae that live in a silk case covered with plant debris; *esp* **:** one (*Thyridopteryx ephemeraeformis*) often destructive to deciduous and evergreen trees of the eastern U.S.
bah \ˈbä, ˈba\ *interj* — used to express disdain or contempt
Ba·ha'i \bä-ˈhä-ˌē, -ˈhī\ *n, pl* **Baha'is** [Per *bahā'ī,* lit., of glory, fr. *bahā* glory] **:** an adherent of a religious movement originating among Shia Muslims in Iran in the 19th century and emphasizing the spiritual unity of mankind — **Baha'i** *adj* — **Ba·ha·ism** \-ˈhä-ˌiz-əm, -ˈhī-ˌiz-\ *n* — **Ba·ha·ist** \-ˈhä-(ˌ)ist\ *n*
Ba·ha·sa In·do·ne·sia \bə-ˌhäs-ə-ˌin-də-ˈnē-zhə, -shə\ *n* [Indonesian *bahasa indonésia,* lit., Indonesian language] **:** INDONESIAN 2b
Ba·hia grass \bə-ˈhē-ə-\ *n* [*Bahia,* state in Brazil] **:** a perennial tropical American grass (*Paspalpum notatum*) used in the southern U.S. as a pasture grass
baht \ˈbät\ *n, pl* **bahts** *or* **baht** [Thai *bāt*] — see MONEY table
1**bail** \ˈbā(ə)l\ *n* [ME, custody, security for appearance, fr. MF, custody, fr. *baillier* to have in charge, deliver, fr. ML *bajulare* to control, fr. L, to carry a load, fr. *bajulus* porter] **1 :** security given for the due appearance of a prisoner in order to obtain his release from imprisonment **2 :** the temporary release of a prisoner on bail **3 :** one who provides bail
2**bail** *vt* [In sense 1, fr. AF *baillier,* fr. F, to deliver; in other senses, fr. 1 *bail*] **1 :** to deliver (property) in trust to another for a special purpose and for a limited period **2 :** to release under bail **3 :** to procure the release of by giving bail — often used with *out* **4 :** to help from a predicament — used with *out* <~ *ing* out impoverished countries>
3**bail** *n* [ME *baille* bailey, fr. OF] *chiefly Brit* **:** a device for confining or separating animals
4**bail** *n* [ME *baille,* fr. MF, bucket, fr. ML *bajula* water vessel, fr. fem. of L *bajulus*] **:** a container used to remove water from a boat
5**bail** *vt* **1 :** to clear (water) from a boat by dipping and throwing over the side — usu. used with *out* **2 :** to clear water from by dipping and throwing — usu. used with *out* ~ *vi* **:** to parachute from an airplane — usu. used with *out* — **bail·er** *n*
6**bail** *n* [ME *beil, baile,* prob. of Scand origin; akin to Sw *bygel* bow, hoop; akin to OE *būgan* to bend — more at BOW] **1 a :** a supporting half hoop **b :** a hinged bar for holding paper against the platen of a typewriter **2 :** the usu. arched handle of a kettle or pail
bail·able \ˈbā-lə-bəl\ *adj* **1 :** entitled to bail **2 :** allowing bail <a ~ offense>
bail·ee \bā-ˈlē\ *n* **:** the person to whom property is bailed
bai·ley \ˈbā-lē\ *n, pl* **baileys** [ME *baili,* fr. OF *baille, balie* palisade, bailey] **1 :** the outer wall of a castle or any of several walls surrounding the keep **2 :** the space immediately within the external wall or between two outer walls of a castle
Bai·ley bridge \ˌbā-lē-\ *n* [Sir Donald *Bailey b*1901 E engineer] **:** a bridge designed for rapid construction from interchangeable latticed steel panels that are coupled with steel pins
bai·lie \ˈbā-lē\ *n* [ME] **1** *chiefly dial* **:** BAILIFF **2 :** a Scottish municipal magistrate corresponding to an English alderman
bai·liff \ˈbā-ləf\ *n* [ME *baillif, bailie,* fr. OF *baillif,* fr. *bail* custody, jurisdiction — more at BAIL] **1 a :** an official employed by a British sheriff to serve writs and make arrests and executions **b :** a minor officer of some U.S. courts usu. serving as a messenger or usher **2** *chiefly Brit* **:** one who manages an estate or farm — **bai·liff·ship** \-ˌship\ *n*
bai·li·wick \ˈbā-li-ˌwik\ *n* [ME *baillifwik,* fr. *baillif* + *wik* dwelling place, village, fr. OE *wīc;* akin to OHG *wīch* dwelling place, town; both fr. a prehistoric WGmc word borrowed fr. L *vicus* village — more at VICINITY] **1 :** the office or jurisdiction of a bailiff **2 :** a special domain
bail·ment \ˈbā(ə)l-mənt\ *n* **:** the act of bailing a person or property
bail·or \bā-ˈlȯ(ə)r, ˈbā-lər\ *or* **bail·er** \ˈbā-lər\ *n* **:** one who delivers goods or money to another in trust
bails·man \ˈbā(ə)lz-mən\ *n* **:** one who gives bail for another
bairn \ˈba(ə)rn, ˈbe(ə)rn\ *n* [ME *bern, barn,* fr. OE *bearn* & ON *barn;* akin to OHG *barn* child] *chiefly Scot* **:** CHILD
Bai·sakh \ˈbī-ˌsäk\ *n* [Hindi, fr. Skt *Vaiśākha*] **:** a month of the Hindu year — see MONTH table
1**bait** \ˈbāt\ *vb* [ME *baiten,* fr. ON *beita;* akin to OE *bǣtan* to bait, *bītan* to bite] *vt* **1 a :** to persecute or exasperate with unjust, malicious, or persistent attacks **b :** to nag at **c :** TEASE **2 a :** to harass (as a chained animal) with dogs usu. for sport **b :** to attack by biting and tearing **3 a :** to furnish with bait **b :** ENTICE, LURE **4 :** to give food and drink to (an animal) esp. on the road ~ *vi, archaic* **:** to stop for food and rest when traveling — **bait·er** *n*
syn BAIT, BADGER, HECKLE, HECTOR, CHIVY, HOUND *shared meaning element* **:** to harass persistently or annoyingly
2**bait** *n* [ON *beit* pasturage & *beita* food; akin to OE *bītan* to bite] **1 a :** something used in luring esp. to a hook or trap **b :** a poisonous material placed where it will be eaten by pests **2 :** LURE, TEMPTATION
bai·za \ˈbī-(ˌ)zä\ *n* [colloq. Ar, fr. Hindi *paisā*] — see *rial* at MONEY table
baize \ˈbāz\ *n* [MF *baies,* pl. of *baie* baize, fr. fem. of *bai* bay-colored] **:** a coarse woolen or cotton fabric napped to imitate felt
1**bake** \ˈbāk\ *vb* **baked; bak·ing** [ME *baken,* fr. OE *bacan;* akin to OHG *bahhan* to bake, Gk *phōgein* to roast] *vt* **1 :** to prepare (as food) by dry heat esp. in an oven **2 :** to dry or harden by subjecting to heat ~ *vi* **1 :** to prepare food by baking it **2 :** to become baked — **bak·er** *n*
2**bake** *n* **1 :** the act or process of baking **2 :** a social gathering at which a baked food is served
Ba·ke·lite \ˈbā-kə-ˌlīt, -ˌklīt\ *trademark* — used for any of various synthetic resins and plastics
baker's dozen *n* **:** THIRTEEN
bakers' yeast *n* **:** a yeast (as *Saccharomyces cerevisiae*) used or suitable for use as leaven
bak·ery \ˈbā-k(ə-)rē\ *n, pl* **-er·ies :** a place for baking or selling baked goods
bake·shop \ˈbāk-ˌshäp\ *n* **:** BAKERY
baking powder *n* **:** a powder used as a leavening agent in making baked goods (as quick breads) that consists of a carbonate, an acid substance, and starch or flour
baking soda *n* **:** SODIUM BICARBONATE
bak·sheesh \ˈbak-ˌshēsh, bak-ˈ\ *n, pl* **baksheesh** [Per *bakhshīsh,* fr. *bakhshīdan* to give; akin to Gk *phagein* to eat, Skt *bhajati* he allots] **:** TIP, GRATUITY
bal *abbr* balance
1**BAL** \ˌbē-ˌā-ˈel\ *n* [*B*ritish *A*nti-*L*ewisite] **:** a compound $C_3H_8OS_2$ developed as an antidote against lewisite and used against other arsenicals and against mercurials
2**BAL** *n* [*b*asic *a*ssembly *l*anguage] **:** a generalized assembly language for programming a computer with a small memory
Ba·laam \ˈbā-ləm\ *n* [Gk, fr. Heb *Bil'ām*] **:** an Old Testament prophet who is reproached by the ass he is riding and rebuked by God's angel while on the way to meet with an enemy of Israel
bal·a·lai·ka \ˌbal-ə-ˈlī-kə\ *n* [Russ] **:** a stringed instrument with a triangular body used esp. in the U.S.S.R.
1**bal·ance** \ˈbal-ən(t)s\ *n* [ME, fr. OF, fr. (assumed) VL *bilancia,* fr. LL *bilanc-, bilanx* having two scalepans, fr. L *bi-* + *lanc-, lanx* plate; akin to OE *eln* ell — more at ELL] **1 :** an instrument for weighing: as **a :** a beam that is supported freely in the center and has two pans of equal weight suspended from its ends **b :** a device that uses the elasticity of a spiral spring for measuring weight or force **c** *cap* **:** LIBRA **2 :** a means of judging or deciding **3 :** a counterbalancing weight, force, or influence **4 :** a vibrating wheel operating with a hairspring to regulate the movement of a timepiece **5 a :** stability produced by even distribution of weight on each side of the vertical axis **b :** equipoise between contrasting, opposing, or interacting elements **c :** equality between the totals of the two sides of an account **6 a :** an aesthetically pleasing integration of elements **b :** the juxtaposition in writing of syntactically parallel constructions containing similar or contrasting ideas **7 a :** physical equilibrium **b :** the ability to retain one's balance **8 a :** weight or force of one side in excess of another **b :** something left over **:** REMAINDER **c :** an amount in excess esp. on the credit side of an account **9 :** mental and emotional steadiness **10 :** the point on the trigger side of a rifle at which if the rifle is held the weight of the ends balance each other — **bal·anced** \-ən(t)st\ *adj* — **in the balance** *or* **in balance :** in an uncertain critical position **:** with the fate or outcome about to be determined — **on balance :** all things considered
2**balance** *vb* **bal·anced; bal·anc·ing** *vt* **1 a (1) :** to compute the difference between the debits and credits of (an account) **(2) :** to pay the amount due on **:** SETTLE **b (1) :** to arrange so that one set of elements exactly equals another <~ a mathematical equation> **(2) :** to complete (a chemical equation) so that the same number of atoms of each kind appears on each side **2 a :** COUNTERBALANCE, OFFSET **b :** to equal or equalize in weight, number, or proportion **3 a :** to compare the weight of in or as if in a balance **b :** to deliberate upon esp. by weighing opposing issues **:** PONDER **4 a :** to bring to a state or position of equipoise **b :** to poise in or as if in balance **c :** to bring into harmony or proportion ~ *vi* **1 :** to become balanced or established in balance **2 :** to be an equal counterpoise **3 :** FLUCTUATE, WAVER <contempt for the mind that ~*s* and waits —P. E. More> **4 :** to move with a swaying or swinging motion ***syn*** see COMPENSATE
balance beam *n* **1 :** a narrow wooden beam supported in a horizontal position approximately four feet above the floor and used for balancing feats in gymnastics **2 :** an event in gymnastics competition in which the balance beam is used
balance of payments : a summary of the international transactions of a country or region over a period of time including commodity and service transactions, capital transactions, and gold movements
balance of power : an equilibrium of power sufficient to discourage or prevent one nation or political party from imposing its will upon or interfering with the interests of another
balance of terror : an equilibrium of military power (as nuclear capability) between potentially opposing nations sufficient to deter one nation from waging war upon another
balance of trade : the difference in value over a period of time between a country's imports and exports
bal·anc·er \ˈbal-ən-sər\ *n* **:** one that balances; *specif* **:** HALTERE
balance sheet *n* **:** a statement of financial condition at a given date
balance wheel *n* **1 :** a wheel that regulates or stabilizes the motion of a mechanism **2 :** a balancing or stabilizing force <serve as a vital *balance wheel* in this country's overall educational and cultural relations — F. A. Young>
Ba·lante \bə-ˈlänt\ *n, pl* **Balante** *or* **Balantes** [F, fr. Balante *Bulanda*] **1 :** a member of a Negro people of Senegal and Angola **2 :** the language of the Balante people
bal·as \ˈbal-əs\ *n* [ME, fr. MF *balais,* fr. Ar *balakhsh,* fr. *Balakhshān,* ancient region of Afghanistan] **:** a ruby spinel of a pale rose-red or orange
ba·la·ta \bə-ˈlät-ə\ *n* [Sp, of Cariban origin; akin to Galibi *balata*] **:** a substance like gutta-percha that is the dried juice of tropical American trees (esp. *Manilkara bidentata*) of the sapodilla family and is used esp. in belting and golf balls; *also* **:** a tree yielding balata
bal·boa \bal-ˈbō-ə\ *n* [Sp, fr. Vasco Núñez de *Balboa* †1517 Sp explorer] — see MONEY table

bal·brig·gan \bal-ˈbrig-ən\ *n* [*Balbriggan*, Ireland] **:** a knitted cotton fabric used esp. for underwear or hosiery

bal·co·ny \ˈbal-kə-nē\ *n, pl* **-nies** [It *balcone*, fr. OIt, scaffold, of Gmc origin; akin to OHG *balko* beam — more at BALK] **1 :** a platform that projects from the wall of a building and is enclosed by a parapet or railing **2 :** an interior projecting gallery in a public building (as a theater) — **bal·co·nied** \-nēd\ *adj*

1bald \ˈbȯld\ *adj* [ME *balled;* akin to OE *bǣl* fire, pyre, Dan *baeldet* bald, L *fulica* coot, Gk *phalios* having a white spot] **1 a :** lacking a natural or usual covering (as of hair, vegetation, or nap) **b :** having little or no tread <~ tires> **2 :** UNADORNED **3 :** UNDISGUISED, PALPABLE **4 :** marked with white ***syn*** see BARE — **bald·ish** \ˈbȯl-dish\ *adj* — **bald·ly** \ˈbȯl-(d)lē\ *adv* — **bald·ness** \ˈbȯl(d)nəs\ *n*

2bald *vi* **:** to become bald

bal·da·chin \ˈbȯl-də-kən, ˈbal-\ *or* **bal·da·chi·no** \ˌbal-də-ˈkē-(ˌ)nō, ˌbäl-\ *n, pl* **baldachins** *or* **baldachinos** [It *baldacchino*, fr. *Baldacco* Baghdad, Iraq] **1 :** a rich embroidered fabric of silk and gold **2 :** a cloth canopy fixed or carried over an important person or a sacred object **3 :** an ornamental structure resembling a canopy used esp. over an altar

bald cypress *n* **:** either of two large swamp trees (*Taxodium distichum* and *T. ascendens*) of the southern U.S.; *also* **:** the hard red wood of bald cypress that is much used for shingles

bald eagle *n* **:** the common eagle (*Haliaeetus leucocephalus*) of No. America that is wholly dark when young but has a white head and neck feathers when mature and also a white tail when old

bald eagle

Bal·der \ˈbȯl-dər\ *n* [ON *Baldr*] **:** the son of Odin and Frigga and Norse god of light and peace slain through the trickery of Loki by a mistletoe sprig

bal·der·dash \ˈbȯl-dər-ˌdash\ *n* [origin unknown] **:** NONSENSE

bald–faced \ˈbȯl(d)-ˈfāst\ *adj* **:** BAREFACED

bald·head \ˈbȯld-ˌhed\ *n* **:** a bald-headed person

bald·pate \ˈbȯl(d)-ˌpāt\ *n* **1 :** BALDHEAD **2 :** a No. American widgeon (*Mareca americana*) with a white crown

bal·dric \ˈbȯl-drik\ *n* [ME *baudry, baudrik*] **:** an often ornamented belt worn over one shoulder to support a sword or bugle

1bale \ˈbā(ə)l\ *n* [ME, fr. OE *bealu;* akin to OHG *balo* evil, OSlav *bolŭ* sick man] **1 :** great evil **2 :** WOE, SORROW

2bale *n* [ME, fr. OF, of Gmc origin; akin to OHG *balla* ball] **:** a large bundle of goods; *specif* **:** a large closely pressed package of merchandise bound and usu. wrapped <a ~ of paper> <a ~ of hay>

3bale *vt* **baled; bal·ing :** to make up into a bale — **bal·er** *n*

ba·leen \bə-ˈlēn\ *n* [ME *baleine* whale, baleen, fr. L *balaena* whale, fr. Gk *phallaina;* akin to Gk *phallos* penis — more at BLOW] **:** WHALEBONE

bale·fire \ˈbā(ə)l-ˌfī(ə)r\ *n* [ME, fr. OE *bǣlfȳr* funeral fire, fr. *bǣl* pyre + *fȳr* fire — more at BALD] **:** an outdoor fire often used as a signal fire

bale·ful \-fəl\ *adj* **1 :** deadly or pernicious in influence **2 :** foreboding evil **:** OMINOUS ***syn*** see SINISTER — **bale·ful·ly** \-fə-lē\ *adv* — **bale·ful·ness** \-fəl-nəs\ *n*

1balk \ˈbȯk\ *n* [ME *balke*, fr. OE *balca;* akin to OHG *balko* beam, L *fulcire* to prop, Gk *phalanx* log, phalanx] **1 :** a ridge of land left unplowed as a dividing line or through carelessness **2 :** BEAM, RAFTER **3 :** HINDRANCE, CHECK **4 a :** the space behind the balkline on a billiard table **b:** any of the outside divisions made by the balklines **5 :** failure of a player to complete a motion; *esp* **:** an illegal motion of the pitcher in baseball while in position

2balk *vt* **1** *archaic* **:** to pass over or by **2 :** to check or stop by or as if by an obstacle **:** BLOCK ~ *vi* **1 :** to stop short and refuse to proceed **2 :** to refuse abruptly — used with *at* **3 :** to commit a balk in sports ***syn*** see FRUSTRATE ***ant*** forward — **balk·er** *n*

bal·kan·ize \ˈbȯl-kə-ˌnīz\ *vt* **-ized; -iz·ing** *often cap* [*Balkan* peninsula] **:** to break up (as a region) into smaller and often hostile units — **bal·kan·iza·tion** \ˌbȯl-kə-nə-ˈzā-shən\ *n, often cap*

balk·line \ˈbȯ-ˌklīn\ *n* **1 :** a line across a billiard table near one end behind which the cue balls are placed in making opening shots **2 a :** one of four lines parallel to the cushions of a billiard table dividing it into nine compartments **b :** a carom billiards game that sets restrictions (as in scoring) determined by these lines

balky \ˈbȯ-kē\ *adj* **balk·i·er; -est :** refusing or likely to refuse to proceed or act as directed or expected <a ~ mule> ***syn*** see CONTRARY — **balk·i·ness** *n*

1ball \ˈbȯl\ *n* [ME *bal*, fr. ON *böllr;* akin to OE *bealluc* testis, OHG *balla* ball, OE *bula* bull] **1 :** a round or roundish body or mass: as **a :** a spherical or ovoid body used in a game or sport **b :** EARTH, GLOBE **c :** a spherical or conical projectile; *also* **:** projectiles used in firearms **d :** a roundish protuberant anatomic structure; *esp* **:** the rounded eminence at the base of the thumb or great toe **2 a :** TESTIS — often considered vulgar **b** *pl* (1) **:** NONSENSE — often considered vulgar (2) **:** COURAGE — often considered vulgar **3 :** a game in which a ball is thrown, kicked, or struck; *esp* **:** BASEBALL **4 a :** the delivery of the ball <a pitcher whose ~ curves> **b :** a pitched baseball not struck at by the batter that fails to pass through the strike zone **c :** a hit or thrown ball in various games <foul ~> — **on the ball 1 :** marked by knowledgeableness and competence **:** ALERT <the other introductory essay . . . is much more *on the ball* —*Times Lit. Supp.*> <keep *on the ball*> **2 :** of ability or competence <if the teacher has something *on the ball*, the pupils won't squirm much — *New Yorker*>

2ball *vi* **:** to form or gather into a ball ~ *vt* **1 :** to form or gather into a ball <~*ed* the paper into a wad> **2 :** to have sexual intercourse with — usu. considered vulgar

3ball *n* [F *bal*, fr. OF, fr. *baller* to dance, fr. LL *ballare*, fr. Gk *ballizein;* akin to Skt *balbalīti* he whirls] **1 :** a large formal gathering for social dancing **2 :** a very pleasant experience **:** a good time

bal·lad \ˈbal-əd\ *n* [ME *balade* song sung while dancing, song, fr. MF, fr. OProv *balada* dance, song sung while dancing, fr. *balar* to dance, fr. LL *ballare*] **1 :** a simple song **:** AIR **2 a :** a narrative composition in rhythmic verse suitable for singing **b :** an art song accompanying a traditional ballad **3 :** a popular song; *esp* **:** a slow romantic or sentimental song — **bal·lad·ic** \bə-ˈlad-ik, ba-\ *adj*

bal·lade \bə-ˈläd, ba-\ *n* [ME *balade*, fr. MF, ballad, ballade] **1 :** a fixed verse form consisting usu. of three stanzas with recurrent rhymes, an envoi, and an identical refrain for each part **2 a :** an elaborate musical setting of a ballad **b :** a musical composition usu. for piano suggesting the epic ballad

bal·lad·eer \ˌbal-ə-ˈdi(ə)r\ *n* **:** a singer of ballads

bal·lad·ist \ˈbal-əd-əst\ *n* **:** one who writes or sings ballads

bal·lad·ry \ˈbal-ə-drē\ *n* **:** BALLADS

ballad stanza *n* **:** a stanza consisting of four lines with the first and third lines unrhymed iambic tetrameters and the second and fourth lines rhymed iambic trimeters

ball-and-socket joint *n* **1 :** a joint in which a ball moves within a socket so as to allow rotary motion in every direction within certain limits **2 :** an articulation (as the hip joint) in which the rounded head of one bone fits into a cuplike cavity of the other and admits movement in any direction — called also *enarthrosis*

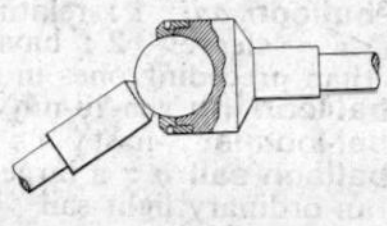
ball-and-socket joint 1

1bal·last \ˈbal-əst\ *n* [prob. fr. LG, of Scand origin; akin to Dan & Sw *barlast* ballast; akin to OE *baer* bare & to OE *blǣst* load — more at LAST] **1 :** a heavy substance used to improve the stability and control the draft of a ship or the ascent of a balloon **2 :** something that gives stability esp. in character or conduct <stated that his training had given him ~ and a sense of responsibility — *Current Biog.*> **3 :** gravel or broken stone laid in a railroad bed or used in making concrete **4 :** a resistance used to stabilize the current in a circuit (as of a fluorescent lamp) — **in ballast** *of a ship* **:** having only ballast for a load

2ballast *vt* **1 :** to steady or equip with or as if with ballast **2 :** to fill in (as a railroad bed) with ballast

ball bearing *n* **:** a bearing in which the journal turns upon loose hardened steel balls that roll easily in a race; *also* **:** one of the balls in such a bearing

ball boy *n* **:** a tennis court attendant who retrieves balls for the players

ball·car·ri·er \ˈbȯl-ˌkar-ē-ər\ *n* **:** the football player carrying the ball on an offensive play

ball cock *n* **:** an automatic valve whose opening and closing are controlled by a spherical float at the end of a lever

ball control *n* **:** an offensive strategy (as in football or basketball) in which a team tries to maintain possession of the ball for extended periods of time

bal·le·ri·na \ˌbal-ə-ˈrē-nə\ *n* [It, fr. *ballare* to dance, fr. LL] **:** a female ballet dancer **:** DANSEUSE

bal·let \ˈba-ˌlā, ba-ˈ\ *n* [F, fr. It *balletto*, dim. of *ballo* dance, fr. *ballare*] **1 a :** dancing in which conventional poses and steps are combined with light flowing figures (as leaps and turns) **b :** a theatrical art form using ballet dancing, music, and scenery to convey a story, theme, or atmosphere **2 :** music for a ballet **3 :** a group that performs ballets — **bal·let·ic** \ba-ˈlet-ik\ *adj*

ballet d'ac·tion \ˈba-ˌlā-daks-ˈyōⁿ, ba-ˈlā-\ *n, pl* **ballets d'action** \-ˌlā(z)-, -ˈlā(z)-\ [F, ballet of action] **:** a ballet with a plot

bal·let·o·mane \ba-ˈlet-ə-ˌmān\ *n* [*ballet* + *-o-* + *-mane* (fr. *mania*)] **:** a devotee of ballet — **bal·let·o·ma·nia** \-ˌlet-ə-ˈmā-nē-ə, -nyə\ *n*

ball–flow·er \ˈbȯl-ˌflau̇(-ə)r\ *n* **:** an architectural ornament consisting of a ball placed in the hollow of a circular flower

ball-flowers

ball hawk *n* **1 :** one skillful in taking the ball away from opponents (as in football or basketball) **2 :** a baseball outfielder skilled in catching fly balls

bal·lis·ta \bə-ˈlis-tə\ *n, pl* **-tae** \-ˌtē\ [L, fr. (assumed) Gk *ballistēs*, fr. *ballein* to throw — more at DEVIL] **:** an ancient military engine often in the form of a crossbow for hurling large missiles

bal·lis·tic \bə-ˈlis-tik\ *adj* [L *ballista*] **:** of or relating to ballistics or to a body in motion according to the laws of ballistics — **bal·lis·ti·cal·ly** \-ti-k(ə-)lē\ *adv*

ballistic missile *n* **:** a self-propelled missile guided in the ascent of a high-arch trajectory and freely falling in the descent

bal·lis·tics \bə-ˈlis-tiks\ *n pl but sing or pl in constr* **1 a :** the science of the motion of projectiles in flight **b :** the flight characteristics of a projectile **2 a :** the study of the processes within a firearm as it is fired **b :** the firing characteristics of a firearm or cartridge

bal·lis·to·car·dio·gram \bə-ˈlis-tō-ˈkärd-ē-ə-ˌgram\ *n* **:** the record made by a ballistocardiograph

bal·lis·to·car·dio·graph \-ˌgraf\ *n* [*ballistic* + *-o-* + *cardiograph*] **:** a device for measuring the amount of blood passing through the heart in a specified time by recording the recoil movements of the body that result from contraction of the heart muscle in ejecting

blood from the ventricles — **bal·lis·to·car·dio·graph·ic** \-ˌkärd-ē-ə-ˈgraf-ik\ *adj* — **bal·lis·to·car·di·og·ra·phy** \-ē-ˈäg-rə-fē\ *n*
ball lightning *n* **:** a rare form of lightning consisting of luminous balls that may move along solid objects or float in the air
ball of fire : a person of unusual energy, vitality, or drive
bal·lon \ba-ˈlō^{n}\ *n* [F, lit., balloon] **:** lightness of movement that exaggerates the duration of a ballet dancer's jump
bal·lo·net \ˌbal-ə-ˈnā\ *n* [F *ballonnet,* dim. of *ballon*] **:** a compartment of variable volume within the interior of a balloon or airship used to control ascent and descent
bal·lon·né \ˌbal-ə-ˈnā\ *n* [F, fr. *ballon*] **:** a wide circular jump in ballet usu. with a battement
1**bal·loon** \bə-ˈlün\ *n* [F *ballon* large football, balloon, fr. It dial. *ballone* large football, aug. of *balla* ball, of Gmc origin] **1 :** a nonporous bag of tough light material filled with heated air or a gas lighter than air so as to rise and float in the atmosphere **2 :** a toy consisting of an inflatable rubber bag **3 :** the outline enclosing words spoken or thought by a figure esp. in a cartoon
2**balloon** *vt* **:** INFLATE, DISTEND ~ *vi* **1 :** to ascend or travel in a balloon **2 :** to swell or puff out **:** EXPAND **3 :** to increase rapidly
3**balloon** *adj* **1 :** relating to, resembling, or suggesting a balloon <a ~ sleeve> **2 :** having a final installment that is much larger than preceding ones in a term or installment note
bal·loon·ing \bə-ˈlü-niŋ\ *n* **:** the act or sport of riding in a balloon
bal·loon·ist \-nəst\ *n* **:** one who ascends in a balloon
balloon sail *n* **:** a large light sail set in addition to or in place of an ordinary light sail
balloon tire *n* **:** a pneumatic tire with a flexible carcass and large cross section designed to provide cushioning through low pressure
balloon vine *n* **:** a tropical American vine (*Cardiospermum halicacabum*) of the soapberry family bearing large ornamental pods
1**bal·lot** \ˈbal-ət\ *n* [It *ballotta,* fr. It dial., dim. of *balla* ball] **1 a :** a small ball used in secret voting **b :** a sheet of paper used to cast a secret vote **2 a :** the action or system of secret voting **b :** the right to vote **c :** 1VOTE 1a **3 :** the number of votes cast
2**ballot** *vi* **:** to vote or decide by ballot — **bal·lot·er** *n*
bal·lotte·ment \bə-ˈlät-mənt\ *n* [F, lit., act of tossing, shaking, fr. *ballotter* to toss, fr. MF *baloter,* fr. *balotte* little ball, fr. It dial. *ballotta*] **:** a sharp upward pushing against the uterine wall with a finger for diagnosing pregnancy by feeling the return impact of the displaced fetus; *also* **:** a similar procedure for detecting a floating kidney
ball park *n* **:** a park in which ball games are played — **in the ball park** *slang* **:** approximately correct <concede that the industry estimate . . . is "*in the ball park*" —Ronald Kessler>
ball–point pen *n* **:** a pen having as the writing point a small rotating metal ball that inks itself by contact with an inner magazine
ball·room \ˈbȯl-ˌrüm, -ˌru̇m\ *n* **:** a large room for dances
ball up *vt* **:** to make a mess of **:** CONFUSE, MUDDLE <incompetents who *balled up* the whole program> ~ *vi* **:** to become badly muddled or confused
ball valve *n* **:** a valve in which a ball regulates the aperture by its rise and fall due to fluid pressure, a spring, or its own weight
bal·ly·hoo \ˈbal-ē-ˌhü\ *n, pl* **-hoos** [origin unknown] **1 :** a noisy attention-getting demonstration or talk **2 :** flamboyant, exaggerated, or sensational advertising or propaganda — **ballyhoo** *vt*
bal·ly·rag \-ˌrag\ *var of* BULLYRAG
balm \ˈbäm, ˈbälm\ *n* [ME *basme, baume,* fr. OF, fr. L *balsamum* balsam, fr. Gk *balsamon*] **1 :** a balsamic resin; *esp* **:** one from small tropical evergreen trees (genus *Commiphora* of the family Burseraceae) **2 :** an aromatic preparation (as a healing ointment) **3 :** any of various aromatic plants (as of the genera *Melissa* or *Monarda*) **4 :** a spicy aromatic odor **5 :** a soothing restorative agency
bal·ma·caan \ˌbal-mə-ˈkan, -ˈkän\ *n* [*Balmacaan,* estate near Inverness, Scotland] **:** a loose single-breasted overcoat usu. made of rough woolens and having raglan sleeves, a short turnover collar, and a closing that may be buttoned up to the throat
balm of Gil·e·ad \-ˈgil-ē-əd\ [*Giliad,* region of ancient Palestine known for its balm (Jer 8:22)] **1 :** a small evergreen African and Asian tree (*Commiphora meccanensis* of the family Burseraceae) with aromatic leaves; *also* **:** a fragant oleoresin from this tree **2 :** an agency that soothes, relieves, or heals **3 a :** BALSAM FIR **b :** either of two poplars: (1) **:** a hybrid northern tree (*Populus gileadensis*) with broadly cordate leaves that are pubescent esp. on the underside (2) **:** BALSAM POPLAR
bal·mor·al \bal-ˈmȯr-əl, -ˈmär-\ *n* [*Balmoral* Castle, Scotland] **1 :** a laced boot or shoe; *esp* **:** an oxford shoe with quarters meeting over a separate tongue **2** *often cap* **:** a round flat cap with a top projecting all around
balmy \ˈbäm-ē, ˈbäl-mē\ *adj* **balm·i·er; -est 1 a :** having the qualities of balm **:** SOOTHING **b :** MILD **2 :** FOOLISH, INSANE — **balm·i·ly** \-ə-lē\ *adv* — **balm·i·ness** \-ē-nəs\ *n*
bal·ne·ol·o·gy \ˌbal-nē-ˈäl-ə-jē\ *n* [ISV, fr. L *balneum* bath — more at BAGNIO] **:** the science of the therapeutic use of baths
1**ba·lo·ney** \bə-ˈlō-nē\ *var of* BOLOGNA
2**baloney** *n* [*bologna*] **:** pretentious nonsense **:** BUNKUM — often used as a generalized expression of disagreement <it is a wish-gratifying intellectual toy. And a lot of ~ —H. D. Scott>
bal·sa \ˈbȯl-sə\ *n* [Sp] **1 :** a tropical American tree (*Ochroma lagopus*) of the silk-cotton family with extremely light strong wood used esp. for floats; *also* **:** its wood **2 :** RAFT; *specif* **:** one made of two cylinders of metal or wood joined by a framework and used for landing through surf
bal·sam \ˈbȯl-səm\ *n* [L *balsamum*] **1 a :** an aromatic and usu. oily and resinous substance flowing from various plants; *esp* **:** any of several resinous substances containing benzoic or cinnamic acid and used esp. in medicine **b :** a preparation containing resinous substances and having a balsamic odor **2 a :** a balsam-yielding tree; *esp* **:** BALSAM FIR **b :** IMPATIENS; *esp* **:** a common garden ornamental (*Impatiens balsamina*) **3 :** BALM 5 — **bal·sam·ic** \bȯl-ˈsam-ik\ *adj*
balsam fir *n* **:** a resinous American evergreen tree (*Abies balsamea*) that is widely used for pulpwood and as a Christmas tree
balsam of Pe·ru \-pə-ˈrü\ **:** a leguminous balsam from a tropical American tree (*Myroxylon pereirae*) used in perfumery and medicine
balsam of To·lu \-tə-ˈlü\ [Santiago de *Tolú,* Colombia] **:** a balsam from a tropical American leguminous tree (*Myroxylon balsamum*) used esp. in cough syrups and perfumes
balsam poplar *n* **:** a No. American poplar (*Populus balsamifera*) that is often cultivated as a shade tree and has buds thickly coated with an aromatic resin — called also *balm of Gilead, hackmatack, tacamahac*
Bal·ti \ˈbəl-tē, ˈbȯl-\ *n* **:** a Tibeto-Burman language of northern Kashmir
Bal·tic \ˈbȯl-tik\ *adj* [ML (*mare*) *balticum* Baltic sea] **1 :** of or relating to the Baltic sea or to the states of Lithuania, Latvia, and Estonia **2 :** of or relating to a branch of the Indo-European languages containing Latvian, Lithuanian, and Old Prussian — see INDO-EUROPEAN LANGUAGES table
Bal·ti·more chop \ˌbȯl-tə-ˌmō(ə)r-, -ˌmȯ(ə)r-, -mər-\ *n* [fr. its strategic use by the Baltimore team] **:** a batted baseball that usu. bounces too high for an infielder to have time to catch it and make a putout at first base
Baltimore oriole *n* [George Calvert, Lord *Baltimore*] **:** a common American oriole (*Icterus galbula*) in which the male is brightly colored with orange, black, and white and the female is primarily brown and greenish yellow
Bal·to–Slav·ic \ˌbȯl-(ˌ)tō-ˈslav-ik, -ˈsläv-\ *n* **:** a subfamily of Indo-European languages consisting of the Baltic and the Slavic branches — see INDO-EUROPEAN LANGUAGES table
Ba·lu·chi \bə-ˈlü-chē\ *n, pl* **Baluchi** *or* **Baluchis** [Per *Balūchī*] **1 a :** an Indo-Iranian people of Baluchistan **b :** a member of this people **2 :** the Iranian language of the Baluchi people
bal·us·ter \ˈbal-ə-stər\ *n* [F *balustre,* fr. It *balaustro,* fr. *balaustra* wild pomegranate flower, fr. L *balaustium,* fr. Gk *balaustion;* fr. its shape] **1 :** an upright often vase-shaped support for a rail **2 :** an object or vertical member (as the leg of a table, a round in the back of a chair, or the stem of a glass) having a vaselike or turned outline
bal·us·trade \-ə-ˌstrād\ *n* [F, fr. It *balaustrata,* fr. *balaustro*] **:** a row of balusters topped by a rail; *also* **:** a low parapet or barrier
BAM *abbr* **1** bachelor of applied mathematics **2** bachelor of arts in music
Bam·ba·ra \bam-ˈbär-ə\ *n, pl* **Bambara** *or* **Bambaras 1 :** a member of a Negroid people of the upper Niger **2 :** a Mande language of the Bambara people
bam·bi·no \bam-ˈbē-(ˌ)nō, bäm-\ *n, pl* **-nos** *or* **-ni** \-(ˌ)nē\ [It, dim. of *bambo* child] **1 :** CHILD, BABY **2** *pl usu bambini* **:** a representation of the infant Christ
bam·boo \(ˈ)bam-ˈbü\ *n, pl* **bamboos** [Malay *bambu*] **:** any of various chiefly tropical woody or arborescent grasses (as of the genera *Bambusa, Arundinaria,* and *Dendrocalamus*) including some with hollow stems used for building, furniture, or utensils and young shoots used for food — **bamboo** *adj*

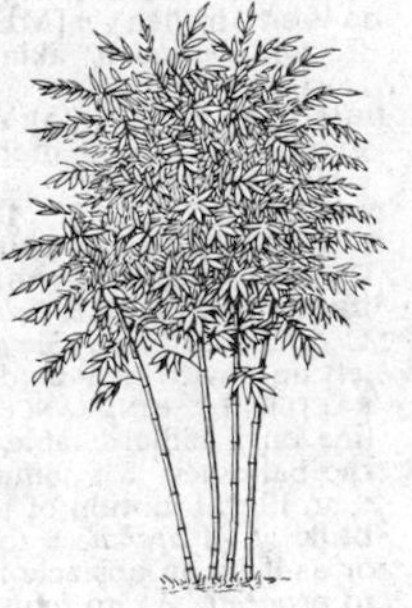
bamboo

bamboo curtain *n, often cap B&C* **:** a political, military, and ideological barrier in the Orient
bam·boo·zle \bam-ˈbü-zəl\ *vt* **bam·boo·zled; bam·boo·zling** \-ˈbüz-(ə-)liŋ\ [origin unknown] **:** to conceal one's true motives from esp. by elaborately feigning good intentions **:** HOODWINK — **bam·boo·zle·ment** \-ˈbü-zəl-mənt\ *n*
1**ban** \ˈban\ *vb* **banned; ban·ning** [ME *bannen* to summon, curse, fr. OE *bannan* to summon; akin to OHG *bannan* to command, L *fari* to speak, Gk *phanai* to say, *phōnē* sound, voice] *vt* **1** *archaic* **:** CURSE **2 :** to prohibit esp. by legal means or social pressure ~ *vi* **:** to utter curses or maledictions *syn* see FORBID
2**ban** *n* [ME, partly fr. *bannen* & partly fr. OF *ban,* of Gmc origin; akin to OHG *bannan* to command] **1 :** the summoning in feudal times of the king's vassals for military service **2 :** ANATHEMA, EXCOMMUNICATION **3 :** MALEDICTION, CURSE **4 :** legal prohibition **5 :** censure or condemnation esp. through public opinion
3**ban** \ˈbän\ *n, pl* **ba·ni** \ˈbän-(ˌ)ē\ [Rum] — see *leu* at MONEY table
ba·nal \bə-ˈnäl, -ˈnal; bə-ˈnal, ba-ˈ, bā-ˈ; ˈbān-ᵊl\ *adj* [F, fr. MF, of compulsory feudal service, possessed in common, commonplace, fr. *ban*] **1 :** lacking originality, freshness, or novelty **:** TRITE **2 :** COMMON, ORDINARY <a ~ inflammation> *syn* see INSIPID *ant* original — **ba·nal·i·ty** \bə-ˈnal-ət-ē *also* bā *or* ba\ *n* — **ba·nal·ly** \bə-ˈnäl-lē, -ˈnal; bə-ˈnal-lē, ba-, bā-; ˈbān-ᵊl-(l)ē\ *adv*
ba·nana \bə-ˈnan-ə, *esp Brit* -ˈnän-\ *n, often attrib* [Sp or Pg; Sp, fr. Pg, of African origin; akin to Wolof *banäna* banana] **1 :** an elongated usu. tapering tropical fruit with soft pulpy flesh enclosed in a soft usu. yellow rind **2 :** a widely cultivated perennial herb (genus *Musa* of the family Musaceae, the banana family) bearing bananas in compact pendent bunches
banana oil *n* **1 :** a colorless liquid acetate $C_7H_{14}O_2$ of amyl alcohol that has a pleasant fruity odor and is used as a solvent and in the manufacture of artificial fruit essences **2 :** a lacquer containing banana oil
banana seat *n* **:** an elongated bicycle saddle that often has an upward-curved back and a tapered front
banana split *n* **:** one or more scoops of ice cream served on a banana sliced in half lengthwise and usu. garnished with flavored syrups, fruits, nuts, and whipped cream
ba·nau·sic \bə-ˈnȯ-sik, -zik\ *adj* [Gk *banausikos* of an artisan, nonintellectual, vulgar, fr. *banausos* artisan] **1 a :** PRACTICAL, UTILITARIAN <a ~ approach to literature> **b :** DULL, PEDESTRIAN

<a ~ performance> **2 a :** VOCATIONAL <~ pursuits> **b :** concerned with or tending to seek material things : MATERIALISTIC <a ~ civilization>

1**band** \'band\ *n* [in senses 1 & 2, fr. ME *band, bond* something that constricts, fr. ON *band;* akin to OE *bindan* to bind; in other senses, fr. ME *bande* strip, fr. MF, fr. (assumed) VL *binda,* of Gmc origin; akin to OHG *binta* fillet; akin to OE *bindan*] **1 :** something that confines or constricts while allowing a degree of movement **2 :** something that binds or restrains legally, morally, or spiritually: as **a :** a restraining obligation or tie affecting one's relations to others or to a tradition **b** *archaic* **:** a formal promise or guarantee **c** *archaic* **:** a pledge given : SECURITY **3 :** a strip serving to join or hold things together: as **a :** BELT 2 **b :** a cord or strip across the backbone of a book to which the sections are sewn **4 :** a thin flat encircling strip esp. for binding: as **a :** a close-fitting strip that confines material at the waist, neck, or cuff of clothing **b :** a strip of cloth used to protect a newborn baby's navel — called also *bellyband* **c :** a ring of elastic **5 :** an elongated surface or section with parallel or roughly parallel sides; *specif* **:** a more or less well-defined range of wavelengths, frequencies, or energies of optical, electric, or acoustic radiation **6 :** a narrow strip serving chiefly as decoration: as **a :** a narrow strip of material applied as trimming to an article of dress **b** *pl* **:** a pair of strips hanging at the front of the neck as part of a clerical, legal, or academic dress **c :** a ring without raised portions **7 :** a group of grooves on a phonograph record containing recorded sound

2**band** *vt* **1 :** to affix a band to or tie up with a band **2 :** to finish with a band **3 a :** to attach (oneself) to a group **b :** to gather together or summon for a purpose <he ~*ed* all his resources together against the coming struggle> **c :** to unite in a company or confederacy <the farmers were ~*ed* against certain government controls> ~ *vi* **:** to unite for a common purpose — often used with *together* <fourteen of the largest cities have ~*ed* together in hopes of attacking the blight that is common to them all —J. B. Conant> — **band·er** *n*

3**band** *n* [MF *bande* troop] **:** a group of persons, animals, or things; *esp* **:** a group of musicians organized for ensemble playing and using chiefly woodwinds, brass, and percussion instruments — compare ORCHESTRA

1**ban·dage** \'ban-dij\ *n* [MF, fr. *bande*] **1 :** a strip of fabric used esp. to dress and bind up wounds **2 :** a flexible strip or band used to cover, strengthen, or compress something

2**bandage** *vt* **ban·daged; ban·dag·ing :** to bind, dress, or cover with a bandage — **ban·dag·er** *n*

Band-Aid \'ban-'dād\ *trademark* — used for a small adhesive strip with a gauze pad for covering minor wounds

ban·dan·na *or* **ban·dana** \ban-'dan-ə\ *n* [Hindi *bādhnū* a dyeing process involving the tying of cloth in knots, cloth so dyed, fr. *bādhnā* to tie, fr. Skt *badhnāti* he ties; akin to OE *bindan*] **:** a large figured handkerchief

band·box \'ban(d)-ˌbäks\ *n* **1 :** a usu. cylindrical box of paperboard or thin wood for holding light articles of attire **2 :** a structure (as a theater or baseball park) having relatively small interior dimensions

ban·deau \ban-'dō\ *n, pl* **ban·deaux** \-'dōz\ [F, dim. of *bande*] **1 :** a fillet or band esp. for the hair **2 :** BRASSIERE

band·ed \'ban-dəd\ *adj* **:** having or marked with bands <a ~ pattern of clouds>

ban·de·ri·lla \ˌban-də-'rē(l)-yə\ *n* [Sp, dim. of *bandera* banner] **:** a decorated barbed dart that the banderillero thrusts into the neck or shoulders of the bull in a bullfight

ban·de·ri·lle·ro \ˌban-də-(ˌ)rē(l)-'ye(ə)r-(ˌ)ō\ *n, pl* **-ros** [Sp, fr. *banderilla*] **:** one who thrusts in the banderillas in a bullfight

ban·de·role *or* **ban·de·rol** \'ban-də-ˌrōl\ *n* [F *banderole,* fr. It *banderuola,* dim. of *bandiera* banner, of Gmc origin; akin to Goth *bandwo* sign — more at BANNER] **1 :** a long narrow forked flag or streamer **2 :** a long scroll bearing an inscription or a device

ban·di·coot \'ban-di-ˌküt\ *n* [Telugu *pandikokku*] **1 :** any of several very large rats (*Nesokia* and related genera) of India and Ceylon destructive to rice fields and gardens **2 :** any of various small insectivorous and herbivorous marsupial mammals (family Peramelidae) of Australia, Tasmania, and New Guinea

ban·dit \'ban-dət\ *n* [It *bandito,* fr. pp. of *bandire* to banish, of Gmc origin; akin to OHG *bannan* to command — more at BAN] **1** *pl also* **ban·dit·ti** \ban-'dit-ē\ **a :** an outlaw who lives by plunder; *esp* **:** a member of a band of marauders **b :** a political terrorist : GUERRILLA **2 :** ROBBER **3 :** one who takes unfair advantage of others <the taxi ~*s* who tie up traffic —Bennett Cerf> **4 :** an enemy plane — **ban·dit·ry** \'ban-də-trē\ *n*

band·lead·er \'ban-ˌdlēd-ər\ *n* **:** the director of a band

band·mas·ter \'ban(d)-ˌmas-tər\ *n* **:** a conductor of a musical band

ban·dog \'ban-ˌdȯg\ *n* [ME *bandogge,* fr. *band* + *dogge* dog] **:** a dog kept tied to serve as a watchdog or because of its ferocity

ban·do·lier *or* **ban·do·leer** \ˌban-də-'li(ə)r\ *n* [MF *bandouliere,* deriv. of OSp *bando* band, of Gmc origin; akin to Goth *bandwo*] **:** a belt worn over the shoulder and across the breast often for the suspending or supporting of some article (as cartridges) or as a part of an official or ceremonial dress

ban·dore \'ban-ˌdō(ə)r, -ˌdȯ(ə)r\ *or* **ban·do·ra** \ban-'dōr-ə, -'dȯr-\ *n* [Sp *bandurria* or Pg *bandurra,* fr. LL *pandura* 3-stringed lute, fr. Gk *pandoura*] **:** a bass stringed instrument resembling a guitar

band razor *n* **:** a safety razor utilizing a cartridge that contains a narrow single-edged band of steel which may be advanced just enough to expose a new surface

band saw *n* **:** a saw in the form of an endless steel belt running over pulleys; *also* **:** a power sawing machine using this device

band shell *n* **:** a bandstand having at the rear a sounding board shaped like a huge concave seashell

bands·man \'ban(d)z-mən\ *n* **:** a member of a musical band

band·stand \'ban(d)-ˌstand\ *n* **:** a usu. roofed stand or raised platform on which a band or orchestra performs

b and w *abbr* black and white

band·wag·on \'ban-ˌdwag-ən\ *n* **1 :** a usu. ornate and high wagon for a band of musicians esp. in a circus parade **2 :** a party, faction, or cause that attracts adherents or amasses power by its timeliness, showmanship, or momentum

band·width \'ban-ˌdwidth\ *n* **:** the range within a band of wavelengths, frequencies, or energies

1**ban·dy** \'ban-dē\ *vb* **ban·died; ban·dy·ing** [prob. fr. MF *bander* to be tight, to bandy, fr. *bande* strip — more at BAND] *vt* **1 :** to bat (as a tennis ball) to and fro **2 a :** to toss from side to side or pass about from one to another often in a careless or inappropriate manner **b :** EXCHANGE; *esp* **:** to exchange (words) argumentatively **c :** to discuss lightly or banteringly **d :** to use in a glib or offhand manner — often used with *about* <~ these statistics about with considerable bravado —Richard Pollak> **3** *archaic* **:** to band together ~ *vi* **1** *obs* **:** CONTEND **2** *archaic* **:** UNITE

2**bandy** *n* [perh. fr. MF *bandé,* pp. of *bander*] **:** a game similar to hockey and believed to be its prototype

3**bandy** *adj* [prob. fr. *bandy* (hockey stick)] **1** *of legs* **:** BOWED **2 :** BOWLEGGED — **ban·dy-legged** \ˌban-dē-'leg(-ə)d, -'lāg(-ə)d\ *adj*

1**bane** \'bān\ *n* [ME, fr. OE *bana;* akin to OHG *bano* death, Av *banta* ill] **1 a** *obs* **:** MURDERER, SLAYER **b :** POISON **c :** DEATH, DESTRUCTION <money, thou ~ of bliss, and source of woe —George Herbert> **d :** WOE **2 :** a source of harm or ruin : CURSE <national frontiers have been more of a ~ than a boon for mankind —D. C. Thomson>

2**bane** *vt* **baned; ban·ing** *obs* **:** to kill esp. with poison

3**bane** *n* [ME (northern dial.) *ban,* fr. OE *bān*] *chiefly Scot* **:** BONE

bane·ber·ry \'bān-ˌber-ē\ *n* **:** the acrid poisonous berry of a plant (genus *Actaea*) of the buttercup family; *also* **:** the plant itself

bane·ful \'bān-fəl\ *adj* **1** *archaic* **:** POISONOUS **2 :** productive of destruction or woe **:** seriously harmful <a ~ influence> ***syn*** see PERNICIOUS ***ant*** beneficial — **bane·ful·ly** \-fə-lē\ *adv*

1**bang** \'baŋ\ *vb* [prob. of Scand origin; akin to Icel *banga* to hammer] *vt* **1 :** to strike sharply : BUMP <fell and ~*ed* his knee> **2 :** to knock, beat, or thrust vigorously often with a sharp noise **3 :** to have sexual intercourse with — often considered vulgar ~ *vi* **1 :** to strike with a sharp noise or thump <the falling chair ~*ed* against the wall> **2 :** to produce a sharp often metallic explosive or percussive noise or series of such noises

2**bang** *n* **1 :** a resounding blow **2 :** a sudden loud noise — often used interjectionally **3 a :** a sudden striking effect **b :** a quick burst of energy <start off with a ~> **c :** THRILL <I get a ~ out of all this —W. H. Whyte>

3**bang** *adv* **:** RIGHT, DIRECTLY <ran ~ up against more trouble>

4**bang** *n* [prob. short for *bangtail* (short tail)] **:** a fringe of banged hair — usu. used in pl.

5**bang** *vt* **:** to cut (as front hair) short and squarely across

ban·ga·lore torpedo \ˌbaŋ-gə-ˌlō(ə)r-, -ˌlȯ(ə)r-\ *n* [*Bangalore,* India] **:** a metal tube that contains explosives and a firing mechanism and is used to cut barbed wire and detonate buried mines

bang away *vi* **1 :** to work with determined effort <students *banging away* at their homework> **2 :** to attack persistently <police are going to keep *banging away* at you —E. S. Gardner>

bang·er \'baŋ-ər\ *n, Brit* **:** SAUSAGE

bang·kok \'baŋ-ˌkäk, baŋ-'\ *n* [earlier *bangkok,* a fine straw, fr. *Bangkok,* Thailand] **:** a hat woven of fine palm fiber in the Philippines

ban·gle \'baŋ-gəl\ *n* [Hindi *baṅglī*] **1 :** a stiff usu. ornamental bracelet or anklet slipped or clasped on **2 :** an ornamental disk that hangs loosely (as on a bracelet or tambourine)

Bang's disease \'baŋz-\ *n* [Bernhard L. F. *Bang* †1932 Dan veterinarian] **:** BRUCELLOSIS; *specif* **:** contagious abortion of cattle

bang·tail \'baŋ-ˌtāl\ *n* [*bangtail* (short tail)] **1 :** RACEHORSE **2 :** a wild horse

bang-up \'baŋ-ˌəp\ *adj* [1*bang*] **:** FIRST-RATE, EXCELLENT <a ~ job>

bang up \-'əp\ *vt* [1*bang*] **:** to cause extensive damage to

bani *pl of* BAN

ban·ish \'ban-ish\ *vt* [ME *banishen,* fr. MF *baniss-,* stem of *banir,* of Gmc origin; akin to OHG *bannan* to command — more at BAN] **1 :** to require by authority to leave a country **2 :** to drive out or remove from a home or place of usual resort or continuance **3 :** to clear away : DISPEL <his discovery ~*es* anxiety —Stringfellow Barr> — **ban·ish·er** *n* — **ban·ish·ment** \-ish-mənt\ *n*

syn BANISH, EXILE, DEPORT, TRANSPORT *shared meaning element* **:** to remove by authority or force from a country, state, or sovereignty

banjo

ban·is·ter *also* **ban·nis·ter** \'ban-ə-stər\ *n* [alter. of *baluster*] **1 :** one of the upright supports of a handrail alongside a staircase **2 a :** a handrail with its supporting posts **b :** HANDRAIL

ban·jo \'ban-(ˌ)jō\ *n, pl* **banjos** *also* **banjoes** [prob. of African origin; akin to Kimbundu *mbanza,* a similar instrument] **:** a musical instrument consisting of a drumlike body, a long fretted neck, and four or more strings that are strummed with the fingers — **ban·jo·ist** \-ˌjō-əst\ *n*

1**bank** \'baŋk\ *n* [ME, prob. of Scand origin; akin to ON *bakki* bank; akin to OE *benc* bench — more at BENCH] **1 :** a mound, pile, or ridge raised above the surrounding level: as **a :** a piled up mass of cloud or fog **b :** an undersea elevation rising esp. from the continental shelf **2 :** the rising ground bordering a lake, river, or sea or forming the edge of a cut or hollow **3 a :** a steep slope (as of a hill) **b :** the lateral inward tilt of a surface along a curve or of a vehicle (as an airplane) when taking a curve **4 :** a protective or cushioning rim or piece

[2]**bank** *vt* **1 a :** to raise a bank about **b :** to cover (as a fire) with fresh fuel and adjust the draft of air so as to keep in an inactive state **c :** to build (a curve) with the roadbed or track inclined laterally upward from the inside edge **2 :** to heap or pile in a bank **3 :** to drive (a ball in billiards) into a cushion **4 :** to form or group in a tier ~ *vi* **1 :** to rise in or form a bank — often used with *up* <clouds would ~ up about midday, and showers fall —William Beebe> **2 a :** to incline an airplane laterally **b** (1) **:** to incline laterally (2) **:** to follow a curve or incline <skiers ~*ing* around the turn>

[3]**bank** *n* [ME, fr. OF *banc* bench, of Gmc origin; akin to OE *benc*] **1 :** a bench for the rowers of a galley **2 :** a group or series of objects arranged near together in a row or a tier: as **a :** a row of keys on a typewriter **b :** a set of two or more elevators **3 :** one of the horizontal and usu. secondary or lower divisions of a headline

[4]**bank** *n* [ME, fr. MF or OIt; MF *banque,* fr. OIt *banca,* lit., bench, of Gmc origin; akin to OE *benc*] **1 a** *obs* **:** the table, counter, or place of business of a money changer **b :** an establishment for the custody, loan, exchange, or issue of money, for the extension of credit, and for facilitating the transmission of funds **2 :** a person conducting a gambling house or game; *specif* **:** DEALER **3 :** a supply of something held in reserve: as **a :** the fund of supplies (as money, chips, or pieces) held by the banker or dealer for use in a game **b :** a fund of pieces belonging to a game (as dominoes) from which the players draw **4 :** a place where something is held available <data ~>; *esp* **:** a depot for the collection and storage of a biological product of human origin for medical use

[5]**bank** *vi* **1 :** to keep a bank **2 :** to deposit money or have an account in a bank ~ *vt* **:** to deposit in a bank — **bank on :** to depend or rely on

bank·able \ˈbaŋ-kə-bəl\ *adj* **:** acceptable to or at a bank

bank acceptance *n* **:** a draft drawn on and accepted by a bank

bank annuities *n pl* **:** CONSOLS

bank·book \ˈbaŋk-ˌbu̇k\ *n* **:** the depositor's book in which a bank records his deposits and withdrawals — called also *passbook*

bank discount *n* **:** the interest discounted in advance on a note and computed on the face value of the note

[1]**bank·er** \ˈbaŋ-kər\ *n* **1 :** one that engages in the business of banking **2 :** the player who keeps the bank in various games

[2]**banker** *n* **:** a man or boat employed in the cod fishery on the Newfoundland banks

[3]**banker** *n* **:** a sculptor's or mason's workbench

banker's bill *n* **:** a bill of exchange drawn by a bank on a foreign bank

bank holiday *n* **1** *Brit* **:** LEGAL HOLIDAY **2 :** a period when banks in general are closed often by government fiat

bank·ing *n* **:** the business of a bank or a banker

bank line *n* [[1]*bank*] **:** a fishing line attached to the shore and not constantly tended by a fisherman

bank money *n* **:** a medium of exchange consisting chiefly of checks and drafts

bank note *n* **:** a promissory note issued by a bank payable to bearer on demand without interest and acceptable as money

bank paper *n* **1 :** circulating bank notes **2 :** bankable commercial paper (as drafts or bills)

bank rate *n* **:** the discount rate fixed by a central bank

[1]**bank·roll** \ˈbaŋ-ˌkrōl\ *n* **:** supply of money **:** FUNDS

[2]**bankroll** *vt* **:** to supply the capital for or pay the cost of (a business or project) — **bank·roll·er** *n*

[1]**bank·rupt** \ˈbaŋ-(ˌ)krəpt\ *n* [modif. of MF & OIt; MF *banqueroute* bankruptcy, fr. OIt *bancarotta,* fr. *banca* bank + *rotta* broken, fr. L *rupta,* fem. of *ruptus,* pp. of *rumpere* to break — more at BEREAVE] **1 a :** a person who has done any of the acts that by law entitle his creditors to have his estate administered for their benefit **b :** a person judicially declared subject to having his estate administered under the bankrupt laws for the benefit of his creditors **c :** a person who becomes insolvent **2 :** one who is destitute of a particular thing <a moral ~>

[2]**bankrupt** *vt* **1 :** to reduce to bankruptcy **2 :** IMPOVERISH <war had ~*ed* the nation's natural resources> ***syn*** see DEPLETE

[3]**bankrupt** *adj* **1 a :** reduced to a state of financial ruin **:** IMPOVERISHED; *specif***:** legally declared a bankrupt <the company went ~> **b :** of or relating to bankrupts or bankruptcy <~ laws> **2 a :** BROKEN, RUINED <a ~ professional career> **b :** DEPLETED, STERILE <a ~ old culture> **c :** DESTITUTE — used with *of* or *in* <~ of all merciful feelings>

bank·rupt·cy \ˈbaŋ-(ˌ)krəp-(t)sē\ *n, pl* **-cies** **1 :** the quality or state of being bankrupt **2 :** utter failure or impoverishment

bank shot *n* **1 :** a shot in billiards and pool in which a player banks the cue ball or the object ball **2 :** a shot in basketball played to rebound from the backboard into the basket

bank·sia \ˈbaŋ(k)-sē-ə\ *n* [NL, genus name, fr. Sir Joseph *Banks* †1820 E naturalist] **:** an Australian evergreen tree or shrub (genus *Banksia*) of the protea family with alternate leathery leaves and yellowish flowers in dense cylindrical heads

bank·side \ˈbaŋk-ˌsīd\ *n* **1 :** the slope of a bank esp. of a stream **2** *cap* **:** the bank of the Thames at Southwark

[1]**ban·ner** \ˈban-ər\ *n* [ME *banere,* fr. OF, of Gmc origin; akin to Goth *bandwo* sign; akin to ON *benda* to give a sign] **1 a :** a piece of cloth attached by one edge to a staff and used by a monarch, feudal lord, or commander as his standard and as a rallying point in battle **b :** FLAG 1 **c :** an ensign displaying a distinctive or symbolic device or legend; *esp* **:** one presented as an award of honor or distinction **2 :** a headline in large type running across a newspaper page **3 :** a strip of cloth on which a sign is painted <welcome ~*s* stretched across the street> **4 :** a name, slogan, or goal associated with a particular group or ideology <the new ~ is "community control" —F. M. Hechinger> — often used with *under* <69th production under its own ~ —T. J. Smith> <every new administration arrives . . . under the ~ of change —John Cogley>

[2]**banner** *adj* **1 :** distinguished from all others esp. in excellence <a ~ year for business> **2 :** prominent in support of a political party <a ~ Democratic county>

[1]**ban·ner·et** \ˈban-ə-rət, ˌban-ə-ˈret\ *n, often cap* [ME *baneret,* fr. OF, fr. *banere*] **:** a knight leading his vassals into the field under his own banner and therefore ranking above a knight bachelor

[2]**banneret** *also* **ban·ner·ette** *n* **:** a small banner

ban·ne·rol *also* **ban·ner roll** \ˈban-ə-ˌrōl\ *n* **:** BANDEROLE

ban·nock \ˈban-ək\ *n* [ME *bannok*] **1 :** an often unleavened bread of oat or barley flour baked in flat loaves **2** *NewEng* **:** CORN BREAD: *esp* **:** a thin cake baked on a griddle

banns \ˈbanz\ *n pl* [pl. of *bann,* fr. ME *bane, ban* proclamation, ban] **:** public announcement esp. in church of a proposed marriage

[1]**ban·quet** \ˈbaŋ-kwət, ˈban- *also* -ˌkwet\ *n* [MF, fr. OIt *banchetto,* fr. dim. of *banca* bench, bank] **:** an elaborate and often ceremonious meal for numerous people often in honor of a person

[2]**banquet** *vt* **:** to treat with a banquet **:** FEAST ~ *vi* **:** to partake of a banquet — **ban·quet·er** *n*

banquet room *n* **:** a large room (as in a restaurant or hotel) suitable for banquets

ban·quette \baŋ-ˈket, ban-\ *n* [F, fr. Prov *banqueta,* dim. of *banc* bench, of Gmc origin; akin to OE *benc* bench] **1 a :** a raised way along the inside of a parapet or trench for gunners or guns **b** *South* **:** SIDEWALK **2 a :** a long upholstered seat **b :** a sofa having one roll-over arm **c :** a built-in upholstered bench along a wall

Ban·quo \ˈbaŋ-(ˌ)kwō, ˈban-\ *n* **:** a murdered Scottish thane in Shakespeare's *Macbeth* whose ghost appears to Macbeth

ban·shee \ˈban-(ˌ)shē, ban-ˈ\ *n* [ScGael *bean-sìth,* fr. or akin to OIr *ben side* woman of fairyland] **:** a female spirit in Gaelic folklore whose appearance or wailing warns a family of the approaching death of a member

[1]**ban·tam** \ˈbant-əm\ *n* [*Bantam,* former residency in Java] **1 :** any of numerous small domestic fowls that are often miniatures of members of the standard breeds **2 :** a person of diminutive stature and often combative disposition

[2]**bantam** *adj* **1 :** SMALL, DIMINUTIVE **2 :** pertly combative **:** SAUCY

ban·tam·weight \-ˌwāt\ *n* **:** a boxer who weighs more than 112 but not more than 118 pounds

[1]**ban·ter** \ˈbant-ər\ *vb* [origin unknown] *vt* **1 :** to speak to or address in a witty and teasing manner **2** *archaic* **:** DELUDE **3** *chiefly South & Midland* **:** CHALLENGE ~ *vi* **:** to speak or act playfully or wittily — **ban·ter·er** \-ər-ər\ *n* — **ban·ter·ing·ly** \ˈbant-ə-riŋ-lē\ *adv*

[2]**banter** *n* **:** good-natured and usu. witty and animated joking <exchanged ~ with newsmen>

bant·ling \ˈbant-liŋ\ *n* [perh. modif. of G *bänkling* bastard, fr. *bank* bench, fr. OHG — more at BENCH] **:** a very young child

Ban·tu \ˈban-(ˌ)tü, ˈbän-\ *n, pl* **Bantu** *or* **Bantus** **1 a :** a family of Negroid peoples who occupy equatorial and southern Africa **b :** a member of any of these peoples **2 :** a group of African languages spoken generally south of a line from Cameroons to Kenya

Ban·tu·stan \ˌban-tü-ˈstan, ˌbän-tü-ˈstän\ *n* [*Bantu* + *-stan* land (as in *Hindustan*)] **:** an all-black enclave in the Republic of So. Africa with a limited degree of self-government

ban·yan \ˈban-yən\ *n* [earlier *banyan* Hindu merchant, fr. Hindi *baniyā;* fr. a banyan pagoda erected under a tree of the species in Iran] **:** an East Indian tree (*Ficus bengalensis*) of the mulberry family with branches that send out shoots which grow down to the soil and root to form secondary trunks

ban·zai \(ˈ)bän-ˈzī\ *n* [Jap] **:** a Japanese cheer or battle cry — usu. used interjectionally

banzai attack *n* **:** a mass attack by Japanese soldiers

bao·bab \ˈbau̇-ˌbab, ˈbā-ə-\ *n* [prob. native name in Africa] **:** a broad-trunked Old World tropical tree (*Adansonia digitata*) of the silk-cotton family with an edible acid fruit resembling a gourd and bark used in making paper, cloth, and rope

Bap *or* **Bapt** *abbr* Baptist

bap·ti·sia \bap-ˈtizh-(ē-)ə\ *n* [NL, genus name, fr. Gk *baptisis* a dipping, fr. *baptein*] **:** any of a genus (*Baptisia*) of No. American leguminous plants with showy papilionaceous flowers

bap·tism \ˈbap-ˌtiz-əm\ *n* **1 a :** a Christian sacrament marked by ritual use of water and admitting the recipient to the Christian community **b :** a non-Christian rite using water for ritual purification **c** *Christian Science* **:** purification by or submergence in Spirit **2 :** an act, experience, or ordeal by which one is purified, sanctified, initiated, or named — **bap·tis·mal** \bap-ˈtiz-məl\ *adj* — **bap·tis·mal·ly** \-mə-lē\ *adv*

baptismal name *n* **:** CHRISTIAN NAME 1

baptism of fire **1 :** a spiritual baptism by a gift of the Holy Spirit — often used in allusion to Acts 2:3-4; Mt. 3:11 (RSV) **2 :** an introductory or initial experience that is a severe ordeal; *specif* **:** a soldier's first exposure to enemy fire

bap·tist \ˈbap-təst\ *n* **1 :** one that baptizes **2** *cap* **:** a member or adherent of an evangelical Protestant denomination marked by congregational polity and baptism by immersion of believers only — **Baptist** *adj*

bap·tis·tery *or* **bap·tis·try** \ˈbap-tə-strē\ *n, pl* **-ter·ies** *or* **-tries** **:** a part of a church or formerly a separate building used for baptism

bap·tize \bap-ˈtīz, ˈbap-ˌ\ *vb* **bap·tized; bap·tiz·ing** [ME *baptizen,* fr. OF *baptiser,* fr. LL *baptizare,* fr. Gk *baptizein* to dip, baptize, fr. *baptos* dipped, fr. *baptein* to dip; akin to ON *kafa* to dive] *vt* **1 :** to administer baptism to **2 a :** to purify or cleanse spiritually esp. by a purging experience or ordeal **b :** INITIATE **3 :** to give a name to (as at baptism) **:** CHRISTEN ~ *vi* **:** to administer baptism — **bap·tiz·er** *n*

[1]**bar** \ˈbär\ *n, often attrib* [ME *barre,* fr. OF] **1 a :** a straight piece (as of wood or metal) that is longer than it is wide and has any of various uses (as for a lever, support, barrier, or fastening) **b :** a solid piece or block of material that is usu. rectangular and

considerably longer than it is wide **c :** a usu. rigid piece (as of wood or metal) longer than it is wide that is used as a handle or support; *esp* **:** a handrail used by ballet dancers to maintain balance while exercising **2 :** something that obstructs or prevents passage, progress, or action: as **a :** the complete and permanent destruction of an action or claim in law; *also* **:** a plea or objection that effects such destruction **b :** an intangible or nonphysical impediment **c :** a submerged or partly submerged bank (as of sand) along a shore or in a river often obstructing navigation **3 a** (1) **:** the railing in a courtroom that encloses the place about the judge where prisoners are stationed or where the business of the court is transacted in civil cases (2) **:** COURT, TRIBUNAL (3) **:** a particular system of courts (4) **:** an authority or tribunal that hands down judgment **b** (1) **:** the barrier in the English Inns of Court that formerly separated the seats of the benchers or readers from the body of the hall occupied by the students (2) **:** the whole body of barristers or lawyers qualified to practice in any jurisdiction (3) **:** the profession of barrister or lawyer **4 :** a straight stripe, band, or line much longer than it is wide: as **a :** one of two or more horizontal stripes on a heraldic shield **b :** a metal or embroidered strip worn on a military uniform esp. to indicate rank or service **5 a :** a counter at which food or esp. alcoholic beverages are served **b :** BARROOM **6 a :** a vertical line across the musical staff before the initial measure accent **b :** MEASURE **7 :** a lace and embroidery joining covered with buttonhole stitch for connecting various parts of the pattern in needlepoint lace and cutwork

bar 6a

[2]**bar** *vt* **barred; bar·ring 1 a :** to fasten with a bar **b :** to place bars across to prevent ingress or egress **2 :** to mark with bars **:** STRIPE **3 a :** to confine or shut in by or as if by bars **b :** to set aside **:** rule out **c :** to keep out **:** EXCLUDE **4 a :** to interpose legal objection to or to the claim of **b :** PREVENT, FORBID

[3]**bar** *prep* **:** EXCEPT

[4]**bar** *n* [G, fr. Gk *baros*] **1 :** a unit of pressure equal to one million dynes per square centimeter **2 :** the absolute cgs unit of pressure equal to one dyne per square centimeter

[5]**bar** *abbr* **1** barometer; barometric **2** barrel

Bar *abbr* Baruch

BAr *abbr* bachelor of architecture

BAR *abbr* Browning automatic rifle

bar- *or* **baro-** *comb form* [Gk *baros*; akin to Gk *barys* heavy — more at GRIEVE] **:** weight **:** pressure <*baro*meter>

Ba·rab·bas \bə-ˈrab-əs\ *n* [Gk, fr. Aram *Bar-abba*] **:** a Jewish prisoner according to Matthew, Mark, and John released in preference to Christ at the demand of the multitude

bar·a·thea \ˌbar-ə-ˈthē-ə\ *n* [fr. *Barathea*, a trademark] **:** a fabric that has a broken rib weave and a pebbly texture and that is made of silk, worsted, or synthetic fiber or a combination of these

[1]**barb** \ˈbärb\ *n* [ME *barbe* barb, beard, fr. MF, fr. L *barba* — more at BEARD] **1 a :** a sharp projection extending backward (as from the point of an arrow or fishhook) and preventing easy extraction; *also* **:** a sharp projection with its point similarly oblique to something else **b :** a biting or pointedly critical remark or comment **2 :** a medieval cloth headdress passing over or under the chin and covering the neck **3 :** [2]BARBEL **4 :** one of the side branches of the shaft of a feather **5 :** a plant hair or bristle ending in a hook

[2]**barb** *vt* **:** to furnish with a barb

[3]**barb** *n* [F *barbe*, fr. It *barbero*, fr. *barbero* of Barbary, fr. *Barberia* Barbary, coastal region in Africa] **1 :** any of a northern African breed of horses that are noted for speed and endurance and are related to Arabs **2 :** a pigeon of a domestic breed related to the carrier pigeons

bar·bar·ian \bär-ˈber-ē-ən, -ˈbar-\ *adj* [L *barbarus*] **1 :** of or relating to a land, culture, or people alien and usu. believed to be inferior to one's own **2 :** lacking refinement, learning, or artistic or literary culture — **barbarian** *n* — **bar·bar·i·an·ism** \-ē-ə-ˌniz-əm\ *n*

syn BARBARIAN, BARBARIC, BARBAROUS, SAVAGE *shared meaning element* **:** characteristic of uncivilized man ***ant*** civilized

bar·bar·ic \bär-ˈbar-ik\ *adj* **1 a :** of, relating to, or characteristic of barbarians **b :** possessing or characteristic of a cultural level more complex than primitive savagery but less sophisticated than advanced civilization **2 a :** marked by a lack of restraint **:** WILD **b :** having a bizarre, primitive, or unsophisticated quality ***syn*** see BARBARIAN ***ant*** restrained, refined, subdued — **bar·bar·i·cal·ly** \-i-k(ə-)lē\ *adv*

bar·ba·rism \ˈbär-bə-ˌriz-əm\ *n* **1 :** an idea, act, or expression that in form or use offends against contemporary standards of good taste or acceptability **2 a :** a barbarian or barbarous social or intellectual condition **:** BACKWARDNESS **b :** the practice or display of barbarian acts, attitudes, or ideas

bar·bar·i·ty \bär-ˈbar-ət-ē\ *n, pl* **-ties 1 :** BARBARISM **2 a :** barbarous cruelty **:** INHUMANITY **b :** an act or instance of barbarous cruelty

bar·ba·ri·za·tion \ˌbär-bə-rə-ˈzā-shən\ *n* **:** the act or process of barbarizing **:** the state of being barbarized

bar·ba·rize \ˈbär-bə-ˌrīz\ *vi* **-rized; -riz·ing :** to become barbarous ~ *vt* **:** to make barbarian or barbarous

bar·ba·rous \ˈbär-b(ə-)rəs\ *adj* [L *barbarus*, fr. Gk *barbaros* foreign, ignorant] **1 :** characterized by the occurrence of barbarisms **2 a :** UNCIVILIZED **b :** lacking culture or refinement **:** PHILISTINE **3 :** mercilessly harsh or cruel ***syn* 1** see BARBARIAN **2** see FIERCE ***ant*** clement — **bar·ba·rous·ly** *adv* — **bar·ba·rous·ness** *n*

Bar·ba·ry ape \ˌbär-b(ə-)rē-\ *n* [*Barbary*, Africa] **:** a tailless monkey (*Macaca sylvana*) of No. Africa and Gibraltar

Barbary Coast *n* **:** a district or section of a city noted as a center of gambling, prostitution, and riotous nightlife

bar·bate \ˈbär-ˌbāt\ *adj* [L *barbatus*, fr. *barba*] **:** bearded esp. with long stiff hairs

barbe \ˈbärb\ *n* [ME, fr. MF, lit., beard] **:** [1]BARB 2

[1]**bar·be·cue** \ˈbär-bi-ˌkyü\ *n* [AmerSp *barbacoa*, prob. fr. Taino] **1 :** an often portable fireplace over which meat and fish are roasted **2 :** a large animal (as a hog or steer) roasted or broiled whole or split over an open fire or barbecue pit **3 :** a social gathering esp. in the open air at which barbecued food is eaten

[2]**barbecue** *vt* **-cued; -cu·ing 1 :** to roast or broil on a rack over hot coals or on a revolving spit before or over a source of cooking heat **2 :** to cook in a highly seasoned vinegar sauce — **bar·be·cu·er** *n*

barbed \ˈbärbd\ *adj* **1 :** having barbs **2 :** characterized by pointed and biting criticism <~ witticisms> — **barbed·ness** \ˈbär-bəd-nəs, ˈbarb(d)-nəs\ *n*

barbed wire \ˈbä(r)b-ˈ(d)wī(ə)r\ *n* **:** twisted wires armed with barbs or sharp points — called also *barbwire*

[1]**bar·bel** \ˈbär-bəl\ *n* [ME, fr. MF, fr. (assumed) VL *barbellus*, dim. of L *barbus* barbel, fr. *barba* beard — more at BEARD] **:** a European freshwater cyprinid fish (*Barbus fluviatilis*) with four barbels on its upper jaw; *also* **:** any of various other fishes of this genus

[2]**bar·bel** *n* [obs. F, fr. MF, dim. of *barbe* barb, beard] **:** a slender tactile process on the lips of certain fishes (as catfishes)

bar·bell \ˈbär-ˌbel\ *n* **:** a bar with adjustable weighted disks attached to each end that is used for exercise and in weight lifting

bar·bel·late \ˈbär-bə-ˌlāt, bär-ˈbel-ət\ *adj* [NL *barbella* short stiff hair, dim. of L *barbula*, dim. of *barba*] **:** having short stiff hooked bristles or hairs <a ~ fruit>

[1]**bar·ber** \ˈbär-bər\ *n* [ME, fr. MF *barbeor*, fr. *barbe* beard — more at BARB] **:** one whose business is cutting and dressing hair, shaving and trimming beards, and performing related services

[2]**barber** *vb* **bar·bered; bar·ber·ing** \-b(ə-)riŋ\ *vt* **:** to perform the services of a barber for ~ *vi* **:** to perform the services of a barber

bar·ber·ry \ˈbär-ˌber-ē\ *n* [ME *barbere*, fr. MF *barbarin*, fr. Ar *barbārīs*] **:** any of a genus (*Berberis* of the family Berberidaceae, the barberry family) of shrubs having spines, yellow flowers, and oblong red berries

[1]**bar·ber·shop** \ˈbär-bər-ˌshäp\ *n* **:** a barber's place of business

[2]**barbershop** *adj* [fr. the old custom of men in barbershops forming quartets for impromptu singing of sentimental songs] **:** having a style of impromptu unaccompanied vocal harmonizing of popular songs esp. by a male quartet and marked by chromatically altered tones

barber's itch *n* **:** ringworm of the face and neck

bar·bet \ˈbär-bət\ *n* [prob. fr. [1]*barb*] **:** any of numerous nonpasserine tropical birds (family Capitonidae) with a stout bill bearing bristles and usu. swollen at the base

bar·bette \bär-ˈbet\ *n* [F, dim. of *barbe* headdress] **1 :** a mound of earth or a protected platform from which guns fire over a parapet **2 :** a cylinder of armor protecting a gun turret on a warship

bar·bi·can \ˈbär-bi-kən\ *n* [ME, fr. OF *barbacane*, fr. ML *barbacana*] **:** an outer defensive work; *esp* **:** a tower at a gate or bridge

bar·bi·cel \ˈbär-bə-ˌsel\ *n* [NL *barbicella*, dim. of L *barba*] **:** one of the small hook-bearing processes on a barbule of a feather

bar·bi·tal \ˈbär-bə-ˌtȯl\ *n* [*barbit*uric + *-al* (as in *Veronal*)] **:** a white crystalline addictive hypnotic $C_8H_{12}N_2O_3$ often administered in the form of its soluble sodium salt

bar·bi·tone \ˈbär-bə-ˌtōn\ *n* [*barbit*uric + *-one*] *Brit* **:** BARBITAL

bar·bi·tu·rate \bär-ˈbich-ə-rət, -ˌrāt; ˌbär-bə-ˈt(y)u̇r-ət, -ˈt(y)u̇(ə)r-ˌāt\ *n* **1 :** a salt or ester of barbituric acid **2 :** any of various derivatives of barbituric acid used esp. as sedatives, hypnotics, and antispasmodics

bar·bi·tu·ric acid \ˌbär-bə-ˌt(y)u̇r-ik-\ *n* [part trans. of G *barbitursäure*, irreg. fr. the name *Barbara* + ISV *uric* + G *säure* acid] **:** a synthetic crystalline acid $C_4H_4N_2O_3$ that is a derivative of pyrimidine

bar·bule \ˈbär-(ˌ)byü(ə)l\ *n* **:** a minute barb; *esp* **:** one of the processes that fringe the barbs of a feather

barb·wire *n* **:** BARBED WIRE

bar car *n* **:** a railroad car with facilities for preparing and serving refreshments and esp. drinks

bar·ca·role *or* **bar·ca·rolle** \ˈbär-kə-ˌrōl\ *n* [F *barcarolle*, fr. It *barcarola*, fr. *barcarolo* gondolier, fr. *barca* bark, fr. LL] **1 :** a Venetian boat song usu. in 6/8 or 12/8 time characterized by the alternation of a strong and weak beat that suggests a rowing rhythm **2 :** music imitating a barcarole

bar chart *n* **:** a graphic means of comparing quantities by rectangles with lengths proportional to the size of the quantities represented — called also *bar graph*

[1]**bard** \ˈbärd\ *n* [ME, fr. ScGael & MIr] **1 a :** a tribal poet-singer gifted in composing and reciting verses on heroes and their deeds **b :** a composer, singer, or declaimer of epic or heroic verse **2 :** POET — **bard·ic** \-ik\ *adj*

[2]**bard** *or* **barde** \ˈbärd\ *n* [MF *barde*, fr. OSp *barda*, fr. Ar *barda'ah*] **:** a piece of armor or ornament for a horse's neck, breast, or flank

[3]**bard** *vt* **:** to furnish with bards

bard·ol·a·ter \bär-ˈdäl-ət-ər\ *n* [*Bard (of Avon)*, epithet of Shakespeare + id*olater*] **:** one who idolizes Shakespeare — **bard·ol·a·try** \-ə-trē\ *n*

[1]**bare** \ˈba(ə)r, ˈbe(ə)r\ *adj* **bar·er; bar·est** [ME, fr. OE *bær*; akin to OHG *bar* naked, Lith *basas* barefoot] **1 a :** lacking a natural, usual, or appropriate covering **b** (1) **:** lacking clothing (2) *obs* **:** BAREHEADED **c :** UNARMED **2 :** open to view **:** EXPOSED **3 a :** unfurnished or scantily supplied **b :** DESTITUTE <~ of all safeguards> **4 a :** having nothing left over or added **:** MERE **b :** devoid of amplification or adornment **5** *obs* **:** WORTHLESS — **bare·ness** *n*

syn BARE, NAKED, NUDE, BALD, BARREN *shared meaning element* : deprived of naturally or conventionally appropriate covering ***ant*** covered

[2]**bare** *vt* **bared; bar·ing** : to make or lay bare : UNCOVER, REVEAL

[3]**bare** *archaic past of* BEAR

bare·back \-ˌbak\ *or* **bare·backed** \-ˈbakt\ *adv or adj* : on the bare back of a horse : without a saddle <a young boy riding ~> <learned ~ riding among the Indians>

bare bones *n pl* : the barest essentials, facts, or elements <stripped his proposition to its *bare bones* —A. H. Vandenberg †1951>

bare·faced \ˈba(ə)r-ˈfāst, ˈbe(ə)r-\ *adj* **1** : having the face uncovered: **a** : BEARDLESS **b** : wearing no mask **2 a** : OPEN, UNCONCEALED **b** : lacking scruples — **bare·faced·ly** \-ˈfā-səd-lē, -ˈfāst-lē\ *adv* — **bare·faced·ness** \-ˈfā-səd-nəs, -ˈfās(t)-nəs\ *n*

bare·foot \-ˌfu̇t\ *or* **bare·foot·ed** \-ˈfu̇t-əd\ *adv or adj* : with the feet bare : UNSHOD <went ~ most of the summer> <~ boy, with cheek of tan —J. G. Whittier>

ba·rege \bə-ˈrezh\ *n* [F *barège,* fr. *Barèges,* town in the Pyrenees, France] : a sheer fabric of open weave for women's clothing usu. made of wool in combination with silk or cotton

bare–hand·ed \ˈba(ə)r-ˈhan-dəd, ˈbe(ə)r-\ *adv or adj* **1** : without gloves **2** : without tools or weapons <fight an animal ~>

bare·head·ed \-ˈhed-əd\ *adv or adj* : without a hat or other covering for the head <go ~ in the hot sun> <a ~ boy who had lost his cap> — **bare·head·ed·ness** *n*

bare·knuck·le \-ˈnək-əl\ *or* **bare·knuck·led** \-əld\ *adj or adv* **1** : not using boxing gloves <champion ~ prizefighter of England —Dennis Craig> <the days in which men fought ~> **2** : having a fierce unrelenting character <a . . . ~ polemic —*Nat'l Review*> <fighting ~ in congress for his beliefs>

bare·ly *adv* **1** : SCARCELY, HARDLY <~ enough money to cover expenses> **2** : in a meager manner : PLAINLY <a ~ furnished room>

barf \ˈbärf\ *vi* [origin unknown] : VOMIT

bar·fly \ˈbär-ˌflī\ *n* : a drinker who frequents bars

[1]**bar·gain** \ˈbär-gən\ *n, often attrib* **1** : an agreement between parties settling what each gives or receives in a transaction between them or what course of action or policy each pursues in respect to the other **2** : something acquired by or as if by bargaining; *esp* : an advantageous purchase **3** : a transaction, situation, or event regarded in the light of its results — **in the bargain** *or* **into the bargain** : BESIDES

[2]**bargain** *vb* [ME *bargainen,* fr. MF *bargaignier,* of Gmc origin; akin to OE *borgian* to borrow — more at BURY] *vi* **1** : to negotiate over the terms of a purchase, agreement, or contract : HAGGLE **2** : to come to terms : AGREE ~ *vt* : to sell or dispose of by bargaining : BARTER — **bar·gain·er** *n* — **bargain for** : EXPECT

bargain basement *n* : a section of a store (as the basement) where merchandise is sold at reduced prices

bargain counter *n* : a counter where merchandise is sold at bargain prices

[1]**barge** \ˈbärj\ *n* [ME, fr. OF, fr. LL *barca*] : any of various boats: as **a** : a roomy usu. flat-bottomed boat used chiefly for the transport of goods on inland waterways and usu. propelled by towing **b** : a large motorboat supplied to the flag officer of a flagship **c** : a roomy pleasure boat; *esp* : a boat of state elegantly furnished and decorated

[2]**barge** *vb* **barged; barg·ing** *vt* : to carry by barge ~ *vi* **1** : to move ponderously or clumsily **2** : to thrust oneself heedlessly or unceremoniously

barge·board \ˈbärj-ˌbō(ə)rd, -ˌbȯ(ə)rd\ *n* [origin unknown] : an often ornamented board that conceals roof timbers projecting over gables

barg·ee \bär-ˈjē\ *n, Brit* : BARGEMAN

barge·man \ˈbärj-mən\ *n* : the master or a deckhand of a barge

bar graph *n* : BAR CHART

bar·hop \ˈbär-ˌhäp\ *vi* : to visit and drink at a series of bars in the course of an evening

bar·iat·rics \ˌbar-ē-ˈa-triks\ *n pl but sing in constr* [*bar-* + *-iatrics*] : a branch of medicine that deals with the treatment of obesity — **bar·ia·tri·cian** \ˌbar-ē-ə-ˈtrish-ən\ *n*

bar·ic \ˈbar-ik\ *adj* : of or relating to barium

ba·ri·lla \bə-ˈrē(l)-yə\ *n* [Sp *barrilla*] **1** : either of two European saltworts (*Salsola kali* and *S. soda*) or a related Algerian plant (*Halogeton souda*) **2** : an impure sodium carbonate made from barilla ashes and formerly used esp. in making soap and glass

bar·ite \ˈba(ə)r-ˌīt, ˈbe(ə)r-\ *n* [Gk *barytēs* weight, fr. *barys*] : barium sulfate $BaSO_4$ occurring as a mineral

[1]**bari·tone** \ˈbar-ə-ˌtōn\ *n* [F *baryton* or It *baritono,* fr. Gk *barytonos* deep sounding, fr. *barys* heavy + *tonos* tone — more at GRIEVE] **1 a** : a male singing voice of medium compass between bass and tenor **b** : one having such a voice **2** : a saxhorn similar in range and tone to the euphonium — called also *baritone horn* — **bari·tonal** \ˌbar-ə-ˈtōn-ᵊl\ *adj*

[2]**baritone** *adj* : relating to or having the range or part of a baritone

bar·i·um \ˈbar-ē-əm, ˈber-\ *n* [NL, fr. *bar-*] : a silver-white malleable toxic bivalent metallic element of the alkaline-earth group that occurs only in combination — see ELEMENT table

barium sulfate *n* : a colorless crystalline insoluble compound $BaSO_4$ that occurs in nature as barite, is obtained artificially by precipitation, and is used as a pigment and extender, as a filler, and as a substance opaque to X rays in medical photography of the alimentary canal

[1]**bark** \ˈbärk\ *vb* [ME *berken,* fr. OE *beorcan;* akin to ON *berkja* to bark, Lith *burgeti* to growl] *vi* **1 a** : to make the characteristic short loud cry of a dog **b** : to make a noise resembling a bark **2** : to speak in a curt loud and usu. angry tone : SNAP ~ *vt* **1** : to utter in a curt loud usu. angry tone **2** : to advertise by persistent outcry <newsboys ~*ed* their wares persistently> — **bark up the wrong tree** : to proceed under a misapprehension

[2]**bark** *n* **1 a** : the sound made by a barking dog **b** : a similar sound **2** : a short sharp peremptory tone of speech or utterance — **bark·less** \ˈbär-kləs\ *adj*

[3]**bark** *n* [ME, fr. ON *bark-, bǫrkr;* akin to MD & MLG *borke* bark] **1** : the tough exterior covering of a woody root or stem **2 a** : TANBARK **b** : CINCHONA 2 — **bark·less** \ˈbär-kləs\ *adj*

[4]**bark** *vt* **1** : to treat with an infusion of tanbark **2 a** : to strip the bark from; *specif* : GIRDLE 3 **b** : to rub off or abrade the skin of

[5]**bark** *n* [ME, fr. MF *barque,* fr. OProv *barca,* fr. LL] **1 a** : a small sailing ship **b** : a 3-masted ship with foremast and mainmast square-rigged and mizzenmast fore-and-aft rigged **2** : a craft propelled by sails or oars

bark 1b

bark beetle *n* : a beetle (family Scolytidae) that bores under the bark of trees both as larva and adult

bar·keep·er \ˈbär-ˌkē-pər\ *or* **bar·keep** \-ˌkēp\ *n* : BARTENDER

bar·ken·tine \ˈbär-kən-ˌtēn\ *n* [[5]*bark* + *-entine,* alter. of *-antine* (as in *brigantine*)] : a 3-masted ship having the foremast square-rigged and the mainmast and mizzenmast fore-and-aft rigged

[1]**bark·er** \ˈbär-kər\ *n* : one that barks; *esp* : a person who advertises by hawking at an entrance to a show

[2]**barker** *n* : one that removes or prepares bark

barky \ˈbär-kē\ *adj* **bark·i·er; -est** : covered with or resembling bark

bar·ley \ˈbär-lē\ *n* [ME *barly,* fr. OE *bærlic* of barley; akin to OE *bere* barley, L *far* spelt] : a cereal grass (genus *Hordeum,* esp. *H. vulgare*) having the flowers in dense spikes with long awns and three spikelets at each joint of the rachis; *also* : its seed used in malt beverages and in breakfast foods and stock feeds

bar·ley–bree \-ˌbrē\ *also* **bar·ley–broo** \-ˌbrü\ *n* [*barley* + Sc *bree* or *broo* (bree)] **1** *chiefly Scot* : WHISKEY **2** *chiefly Scot* : BEER, ALE

bar·ley·corn \-ˌkȯ(ə)rn\ *n* **1** : a grain of barley **2** : an old unit of length equal to the third part of an inch

bar·low \ˈbär-ˌlō\ *n* [Russell *Barlow* 18th cent. E knife maker] : a sturdy inexpensive jackknife

barm \ˈbärm\ *n* [ME *berme,* fr. OE *beorma;* akin to L *fermentum* yeast, *fervēre* to boil — more at BURN] : yeast formed on fermenting malt liquors

bar·maid \ˈbär-ˌmād\ *n* : a female bartender

bar·man \-mən\ *n* : BARTENDER

Bar·me·cid·al \ˌbär-mə-ˈsīd-ᵊl\ *or* **Bar·me·cide** \ˈbär-mə-ˌsīd\ *adj* [*Barmecide,* a wealthy Persian, who, in a tale of *The Arabian Nights,* invited a beggar to a feast of imaginary food] : providing only the illusion of plenty or abundance <a ~ feast>

[1]**bar mitz·vah** \bär-ˈmits-və\ *n, often cap B&M* [Heb *bar miṣwāh,* lit., son of the (divine) law] **1** : a Jewish boy who reaches his 13th birthday and attains the age of religious duty and responsibility **2** : the initiatory ceremony recognizing a boy as a bar mitzvah

[2]**bar mitzvah** *vt* **bar mitz·vahed; bar mitz·vah·ing** : to administer the ceremony of bar mitzvah to

barmy \ˈbär-mē\ *adj* **barm·i·er; -est** **1** : full of froth or ferment **2** : BALMY 2

barn \ˈbärn\ *n* [ME *bern,* fr. OE *bereærn,* fr. *bere* barley + *ærn* place] **1 a** : a usu. large building for the storage of farm products, for feed, and usu. for the housing of farm animals or farm equipment **b** : an unusually large and usu. bare building <a great ~ of a hotel —W. A. White> **2** : a large building for the housing of a fleet of vehicles (as trolley cars or trucks) — **barny** \ˈbär-nē\ *adj*

Bar·na·bas \ˈbär-nə-bəs\ *n* [Gk, fr. Aram *Barnebhūāh*] : a companion of the apostle Paul on his first missionary journey

bar·na·cle \ˈbär-ni-kəl\ *n* [ME *barnakille,* alter. of *bernake,* of Celt origin; akin to Corn *brennyk* limpet] **1** : a European goose (*Branta leucopsis*) that breeds in the arctic and is larger than the related brant — called also *barnacle goose* **2** : any of numerous marine crustaceans (order Cirripedia) with feathery appendages for gathering food that are free-swimming as larvae but fixed to rocks or floating logs as adults — **bar·na·cled** \-kəld\ *adj*

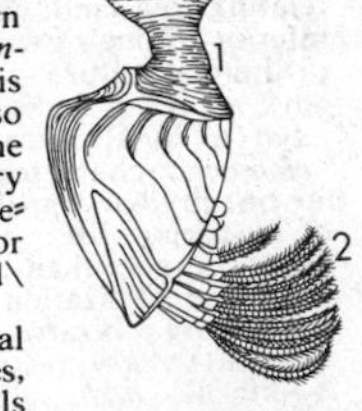

barnacle 2: *1* peduncle, *2* cirri

barn dance *n* : a rollicking American social dance orig. held in a barn with square dances, round dances, and traditional music and calls

barn lot *n, chiefly South & Midland* : BARNYARD

barn owl *n* : a widely distributed owl (*Tyto alba*) that has plumage mottled buff brown and gray above and chiefly white below, frequents barns and other buildings, and preys esp. on rodents

barn raising *n* : a gathering for the purpose of erecting a barn — compare [1]BEE 3

barn·storm \ˈbärn-ˌstȯrm\ *vi* **1** : to tour through rural districts staging theatrical performances usu. in one-night stands **2** : to travel from place to place making brief stops (as in a political campaign) **3** : to pilot one's airplane in sightseeing flights with passengers or in exhibition stunts in an unscheduled itinerant course esp. in rural districts ~ *vt* : to travel across while barnstorming — **barn·storm·er** *n*

[1]**barn·yard** \-ˌyärd\ *n* : a usu. fenced area adjoining a barn

[2]**barnyard** *adj* : EARTHY, SMUTTY, SCATOLOGICAL <~ humor>

baro- — see BAR-

baro·gram \ˈbar-ə-ˌgram\ *n* [ISV] : a barographic tracing

baro·graph \-ˌgraf\ *n* [ISV] : a self-registering barometer — **baro·graph·ic** \ˌbar-ə-ˈgraf-ik\ *adj*

ba·rom·e·ter \bə-ˈräm-ət-ər\ *n* **1** : an instrument for determining the pressure of the atmosphere and hence for assisting in judgment as to probable weather changes and for determining the height of an ascent **2** : something that serves to register fluctuations (as in public opinion) — **baro·met·ric** \ˌbar-ə-ˈme-trik\ *or* **baro·met·ri·cal** \-tri-kəl\ *adj* — **baro·met·ri·cal·ly** \-tri-k(ə-)lē\ *adv* — **ba·rom·e·try** \bə-ˈräm-ə-trē\ *n*

barometric pressure *n* **:** the pressure of the atmosphere usu. expressed in terms of the height of a column of mercury

bar·on \ˈbar-ən\ *n* [ME, fr. OF, of Gmc origin; akin to OHG *baro* freeman] **1 a :** one of a class of tenants holding his rights and title by military or other honorable service directly from a feudal superior (as a king) **b :** a lord of the realm **:** NOBLE, PEER **2 a :** a member of the lowest grade of the peerage in Great Britain **b :** a nobleman on the continent of Europe of varying rank **c :** a member of the lowest order of nobility in Japan **3 :** a man of great power or influence in some field of activity <cattle ~>

bar·on·age \-ə-nij\ *n* **:** the whole body of barons or peers **:** NOBILITY 2

bar·on·ess \-ə-nəs\ *n* **1 :** the wife or widow of a baron **2 :** a woman who holds a baronial title in her own right

bar·on·et \ˈbar-ə-nət, *US also* ˌbar-ə-ˈnet\ *n* **:** the holder of a rank of honor below a baron and above a knight

bar·on·et·age \-ij\ *n* **1 :** BARONETCY **2 :** the whole body of baronets

bar·on·et·cy \-sē\ *n* **:** the rank of a baronet

ba·rong \bə-ˈrȯŋ, -ˈräŋ\ *n* [native name in the Philippines] **:** a thick-backed thin-edged knife or sword used by the Moro

ba·ro·ni·al \bə-ˈrō-nē-əl\ *adj* **1 :** of or relating to a baron or the baronage **2 :** STATELY, AMPLE <a ~ room>

bar·ony \ˈbar-ə-nē\ *n, pl* **-on·ies** **1 :** the domain, rank, or dignity of a baron **2 :** a vast private landholding **3 :** a field of activity under the sway of an individual or a special group

[1]**ba·roque** \bə-ˈrōk, ba-, -ˈräk\ *n* [F, fr. Pg *barrôco*] **:** an irregularly shaped pearl

[2]**ba·roque** \bə-rōk, ba-, -ˈräk\ *adj* [F, fr. It *barocco*] **:** of, relating to, or having the characteristics of a style of artistic expression prevalent esp. in the 17th century that is marked generally by extravagant forms and elaborate and sometimes grotesque ornamentation and specifically also in architecture by dynamic opposition and the use of curved and plastic figures, in music by improvisation, contrasting effects, and powerful tensions, and in literature by complexity of form and bizarre, ingenious, and often ambiguous imagery — **ba·roque·ly** *adv*

baro·re·cep·tor \ˌbar-ō-ri-ˈsep-tər\ *n* [*bar-* + *receptor*] **:** a neural receptor (as of the arterial walls) sensitive to changes in environmental pressure

ba·rouche \bə-ˈrüsh\ *n* [G *barutsche*, fr. It *biroccio*, deriv. of LL *birotus* two-wheeled, fr. L *bi-* + *rota* wheel — more at ROLL] **:** a four-wheeled carriage with a driver's seat high in front, two double seats inside facing each other, and a folding top over the back seat

bar pilot *n* **:** a pilot who navigates a ship from a pilot station over a bar and often into a harbor or to the harbor docks

barque \ˈbärk\, **bar·quen·tine** \ˈbär-kən-ˌtēn\ *var of* BARK, BARKENTINE

[1]**bar·rack** \ˈbar-ək, -ik\ *n* [F *baraque* hut, fr. Catal *barraca*] **1 :** a building or set of buildings used esp. for lodging soldiers in garrison **2 a :** a structure resembling a shed or barn that provides temporary housing **b :** housing characterized by extreme plainness or dreary uniformity — usu. used in pl. in all senses

[2]**barrack** *vt* **:** to lodge in barracks

[3]**barrack** *vb* [origin unknown] *vi* **1** *chiefly Austral* **:** JEER, SCOFF **2** *chiefly Austral* **:** ROOT, CHEER — usu. used with *for* ~ *vt, chiefly Austral* **:** to shout at derisively or sarcastically — **bar·rack·er** *n*

barracks bag *n* **:** a fabric bag for carrying personal equipment

bar·ra·coon \ˌbar-ə-ˈkün\ *n* [Sp *barracón*, aug. of *barraca* hut, fr. Catal] **:** an enclosure or barracks formerly used for temporary confinement of slaves or convicts

bar·ra·cou·ta \ˌbar-ə-ˈküt-ə\ *n* [modif. of AmerSp *barracuda*] **1 :** a large marine food fish (*Thyrsites atun*) **2 :** BARRACUDA

bar·ra·cu·da \ˌbar-ə-ˈküd-ə\ *n, pl* **-da** *or* **-das** [AmerSp] **:** any of several predaceous marine fishes (genus *Sphyraena* of the family Sphyraenidae) of warm seas that include excellent food fishes as well as forms regarded as toxic

[1]**bar·rage** \ˈbär-ij\ *n* [F, fr. *barrer* to bar, fr. *barre* bar] **:** an artificial dam placed in a watercourse to increase the depth of water or to divert it into a channel for navigation or irrigation

[2]**bar·rage** \bə-ˈräzh, -ˈräj\ *n* [F (*tir de*) *barrage* barrier fire] **1 :** a barrier of fire esp. of artillery laid on a line close to friendly troops to screen and protect them **2 :** a rapid-fire massive or concentrated delivery or outpouring (as of speech or writing)

[3]**bar·rage** \bə-ˈräzh, -ˈräj\ *vt* **bar·raged; bar·rag·ing :** to deliver a barrage against

barrage balloon *n* **:** a small captive balloon used to support wires or nets as protection against air attacks

bar·ra·mun·da \ˌbar-ə-ˈmən-də\ *or* **bar·ra·mun·di** \-dē\ *n* [native name in Australia] **:** any of several Australian fishes: as **a :** a large red-fleshed lungfish (*Neoceratodus forsteri*) of Australian rivers used for food **b :** a river fish (*Scleropages leichhardtii*) that is used for food

bar·ran·ca \bə-ˈraŋ-kə\ *or* **bar·ran·co** \-(ˌ)kō\ *n, pl* **-cas** *or* **-cos** [Sp] **1 :** a deep gulley or arroyo with steep sides **2 :** a steep bank or bluff

bar·ra·tor *also* **bar·ra·ter** \ˈbar-ət-ər\ *n* **:** one who engages in barratry

bar·ra·try \ˈbar-ə-trē\ *n, pl* **-tries** [ME *barratrie*, fr. MF *baraterie* deception, fr. *barater* to deceive, exchange] **1 :** the purchase or sale of office or preferment in church or state **2 :** a fraudulent breach of duty on the part of a master of a ship or of the mariners to the injury of the owner of the ship or cargo **3 :** the persistent incitement of litigation

barred \ˈbärd\ *adj* **:** marked by or divided off by bars; *specif* **:** having alternate bands of different color <~ feather>

[1]**bar·rel** \ˈbar-əl\ *n* [ME *barel*, fr. MF *baril*] **1 :** a round bulging vessel of greater length than breadth that is usu. made of staves bound with hoops and has flat ends of equal diameter **2 a :** the amount contained in a barrel; *esp* **:** the amount (as 31 gal. of fermented beverage or 42 gal. of petroleum) fixed for a certain commodity used as a unit of measure **b :** a great quantity **3 :** a drum or cylindrical part: as **a :** the discharging tube of a gun **b :** the cylindrical metal box enclosing the mainspring of a timepiece **c :** the part of a fountain pen or of a pencil containing the ink or lead **d :** a cylindrical or tapering housing containing the optical components of a photographic-lens system and the iris diaphragm **e :** TUMBLING BARREL **f :** the fuel outlet from the carburetor on a gasoline engine **4 :** the trunk of a quadruped — see COW illustration — **bar·reled** \-əld\ *adj* — **on the barrel :** asking for or granting no credit **:** in cash — **over a barrel :** at a disadvantage **:** in an awkward position

[2]**barrel** *vb* **-reled** *or* **-relled; -rel·ing** *or* **-rel·ling** *vt* **:** to put or pack in a barrel ~ *vi* **:** to move at a high speed

barrel chair *n* **:** an upholstered chair with a high solid rounded back

bar·rel·ful \ˈbar-əl-ˌfu̇l\ *n, pl* **barrelfuls** \-ˌfu̇lz\ *or* **bar·rels·ful** \-əlz-ˌfu̇l\ **1 :** as much or as many as a barrel will hold **2 :** a large number or amount

bar·rel·house \ˈbar-əl-ˌhau̇s\ *n* **1 :** a cheap drinking and usu. dancing establishment **2 :** a style of jazz characterized by a very heavy beat and simultaneous improvisation by each player

barrel organ *n* **:** an instrument for producing music by the action of a revolving cylinder studded with pegs on a series of valves that admit air from a bellows to a set of pipes

barrel roll *n* **:** an airplane maneuver in which a complete revolution about the longitudinal axis is made

[1]**bar·ren** \ˈbar-ən\ *adj* [ME *bareine*, fr. OF *baraine*] **1 :** not reproducing: as **a :** incapable of producing offspring — used esp. of females or matings **b :** not yet or not recently pregnant **c :** habitually failing to fruit **2 :** not productive: as **a :** lacking a normal or adequate cover of vegetation or crops **:** DESOLATE <arid ~ soil> **b :** unproductive of results or gain **:** FRUITLESS <a ~ scheme> **3 :** DEVOID, LACKING — used with *of* <~ of excitement> **4 :** lacking interest, information, or charm **5 :** DULL, UNRESPONSIVE ***syn* 1** see STERILE ***ant*** fecund **2** see BARE — **bar·ren·ly** *adv* — **bar·ren·ness** \-ən-nəs\ *n*

[2]**barren** *n* **1 :** a tract of barren land **2** *pl* **:** an extent of usu. level land having an inferior growth of trees or little vegetation

bar·rette \bä-ˈret, bə-\ *n* [F, dim. of *barre* bar] **:** a clip or bar for holding a woman's hair in place

[1]**bar·ri·cade** \ˈbar-ə-ˌkād, ˌbar-ə-ˈ\ *vt* **-cad·ed; -cad·ing** **1 :** to block off or stop up with a barricade **2 :** to prevent access to by means of a barricade

[2]**barricade** *n* [F, fr. MF, fr. *barriquer* to barricade, fr. *barrique* barrel] **1 :** an obstruction or rampart thrown up across a way or passage to check the advance of the enemy **2 :** BARRIER, OBSTACLE **3** *pl* **:** a field of combat or dispute

bar·ri·ca·do \ˌbar-ə-ˈkād-(ˌ)ō\ *n, pl* **-does** [modif. of F *barricade*] *archaic* **:** BARRICADE — **barricado** *vt, archaic*

bar·ri·er \ˈbar-ē-ər\ *n* [ME *barrere*, fr. MF *barriere*, fr. *barre*] **1 a :** a material object or set of objects that separates, demarcates, or serves as a barricade **b :** an extension of the antarctic continental ice cap into the sea resting partly on the bottom **2** *pl, often cap* **:** a medieval war game in which combatants fight on foot with a fence or railing between them **3 :** the movable gate or device at the starting line in a racetrack **4 :** something immaterial that impedes or separates <~*s* of reserve> **5 :** a factor that tends to restrict the free movement, mingling, or interbreeding of individuals or populations <behavioral and geographic ~*s* to hybridization>

barrier reef *n* **:** a coral reef roughly parallel to a shore and separated from it by a lagoon

bar·ring \ˈbär-iŋ\ *prep* **:** excluding by exception **:** EXCEPTING

bar·rio \ˈbär-ē-ˌō, ˈbar-\ *n, pl* **-ri·os** [Sp, fr. Ar *barrī* of the open country, fr. *barr* outside, open country] **1 :** a ward, quarter, or district of a city or town in Spanish-speaking countries **2 :** a Spanish-speaking quarter or neighborhood in a city or town in the U.S. esp. in the Southwest

bar·ris·ter \ˈbar-ə-stər\ *n* [[1]*bar* + *-i-* + *-ster*] **:** a counsel admitted to plead at the bar and undertake the public trial of causes in an English superior court — compare SOLICITOR

bar·room \ˈbär-ˌrüm, -ˌru̇m\ *n* **:** a room or establishment whose main feature is a bar for the sale of liquor

[1]**bar·row** \ˈbar-(ˌ)ō, -ə(-w)\ *n* [ME *bergh*, fr. OE *beorg*; akin to OHG *berg* mountain, Skt *brhant* high] **1 :** MOUNTAIN, MOUND — used only in the names of hills in England **2 :** a large mound of earth or stones over the remains of the dead **:** TUMULUS

[2]**barrow** *n* [ME *barow*, fr. OE *bearg*; akin to OHG *barug* barrow, OE *borian* to bore] **:** a male hog castrated before sexual maturity

[3]**barrow** *n* [ME *barew*, fr. OE *bearwe*; akin to OE *beran* to carry — more at BEAR] **1 a :** HANDBARROW **b :** WHEELBARROW **2 :** a cart with a shallow box body, two wheels, and shafts for pushing it **:** PUSHCART

barrow boy *n* **:** a boy who sells goods (as fruit or vegetables) from a barrow

bar sinister *n* **1 :** a heraldic charge held to be a mark of bastardy **2 :** the fact or condition of being of illegitimate birth

Bart *abbr* baronet

bar·tend·er \ˈbär-ˌten-dər\ *n* **:** one that serves liquor at a bar

[1]**bar·ter** \ˈbärt-ər\ *vb* [ME *bartren*, fr. MF *barater*] *vi* **:** to trade by exchanging one commodity for another ~ *vt* **:** to trade or exchange by or as if by bartering — **bar·ter·er** \-ər-ər\ *n*

[2]**barter** *n* **1 :** the act or practice of carrying on trade by bartering **2 :** the thing given in exchange in bartering

Bar·tho·lin's gland \ˌbärt-ᵊl-ənz-, ˌbär-thə-lənz-\ *n* [Kaspar *Bartholin* †1738 Dan physician] **:** either of two oval racemose glands

---

ə abut   ᵊ kitten   ər further   a back   ā bake   ä cot, cart
au̇ out   ch chin   e less   ē easy   g gift   i trip   ī life
j joke   ŋ sing   ō flow   ȯ flaw   ȯi coin   th thin   t͟h this
ü loot   u̇ foot   y yet   yü few   yu̇ furious   zh vision

lying one to each side of the lower part of the vagina and secreting a lubricating mucus — compare COWPER'S GLAND

bar·ti·zan \'bärt-ə-zən, ˌbärt-ə-'zan\ *n* [ME *bretasinge,* fr. *bretasce* parapet — more at BRATTICE] : a small structure (as a turret) projecting from a building and serving esp. for lookout or defense

Ba·ruch \bə-'rük, 'bär-ˌük\ *n* [LL, fr. Gk *Barouch,* fr. Heb *Bārūkh*] : a homiletic book included in the Roman Catholic canon of the Old Testament and in the Protestant Apocrypha — see BIBLE table

bar·ware \'bär-ˌwa(ə)r, -ˌwe(ə)r\ *n* : equipment for outfitting a bar

bary·on \'bar-ē-ˌän\ *n* [ISV *bary-* (fr. Gk *barys* heavy) + [2]*-on* — more at GRIEVE] : any of a group of elementary particles with the same spin that have a mass equal to or greater than the proton — **bary·on·ic** \ˌbar-ē-'än-ik\ *adj*

ba·ry·ta \bə-'rīt-ə\ *n* [NL, modif. of Gk *barytēs* weight — more at BARITE] : any of several compounds of barium: as **a** : barium monoxide **b** : barium hydroxide **c** : BARIUM SULFATE — **ba·ryt·ic** \-'rit-ik\ *adj*

bar·yte \'ba(ə)r-ˌīt, 'be(ə)r-\ *or* **ba·ry·tes** \bə-'rīt-ēz\ *var of* BARITE

bary·tone \'bar-ə-ˌtōn\ *var of* BARITONE

BAS *abbr* **1** bachelor of applied science **2** bachelor of arts and sciences

bas·al \'bā-səl, -zəl\ *adj* **1 a** : relating to, situated at, or forming the base **b** : arising from the base of a stem <~ leaves> **2 a** : of or relating to the foundation, base, or essence : FUNDAMENTAL **b** : of, relating to, or being essential for maintaining the fundamental vital activities of an organism : MINIMAL **c** : used for teaching beginners <~ readers> — **ba·sal·ly** \-ē\ *adv*

basal body *n* : a minute distinctively staining cell organelle found at the base of a flagellum or cilium and resembling a centriole in structure — called also *basal granule, kinetosome*

basal cell *n* : one of the innermost cells of the deeper epidermis of the skin

basal metabolic rate *n* : the rate at which heat is given off by an organism at complete rest

basal metabolism *n* : the turnover of energy in a fasting and resting organism using energy solely to maintain vital cellular activity, respiration, and circulation as measured by the basal metabolic rate

ba·salt \bə-'sȯlt, 'bā-ˌ\ *n* [L *basaltes,* MS var. of *basanites* touchstone, fr. Gk *basanitēs* (*lithos*), fr. *basanos* touchstone, fr. Egypt *bḫnw*] : a dark gray to black dense to fine-grained igneous rock that consists of basic plagioclase, augite, and usu. magnetite — **ba·sal·tic** \bə-'sȯl-tik\ *adj*

bas·cule \'bas-(ˌ)kyü(ə)l\ *n* [F, seesaw] : an apparatus or structure (as a bridge) in which one end is counterbalanced by the other on the principle of the seesaw or by weights

[1]base \'bās\ *n, pl* **bas·es** \'bā-səz\ [ME, fr. MF, fr. L *basis,* fr. Gk, step, base, fr. *bainein* to go — more at COME] **1 a** : the bottom of something considered as its support : FOUNDATION **b** (1) : the lower part of a wall, pier, or column considered as a separate architectural feature (2) : the lower part of a complete architectural design **c** : a side or face of a geometrical figure from which an altitude can be constructed; *esp* : one on which the figure stands **d** : that part of a bodily organ by which it is attached to another more central structure of the organism **2 a** : a main ingredient <paint having a latex ~> **b** : a supporting or carrying ingredient (as of a medicine) **3** : the fundamental part of something : GROUNDWORK **4** : the lower part of a heraldic field **5 a** : the point or line from which a start is made in an action or undertaking **b** : a line in a survey which serves as the origin for computations **c** : the locality or the installations on which a military force relies for supplies or from which it initiates operations **d** : the number with reference to which a number system or a mathematical table is constructed; *esp* : the number of units in a given digit's place that is required to give one in the next higher place **e** : ROOT 6 **6 a** : the starting place or goal in various games **b** : any one of the four stations at the corners of a baseball infield **7** : any of various typically water-soluble and acrid or brackish tasting compounds capable of reacting with an acid to form a salt that are molecules or ions able to take up a proton from an acid or substances able to give up an unshared pair of electrons to an acid **8** : a price level at which a security previously actively declining in price resists further price decline **9** : a sum of money in business which is multiplied by a rate (as of interest) or of which a percent is taken **10** : the part of a transformational grammar consisting of rules and a lexicon that generates the deep structures of a language — **based** \'bāst\ *adj* — **base·less** \'bā-sləs\ *adj*

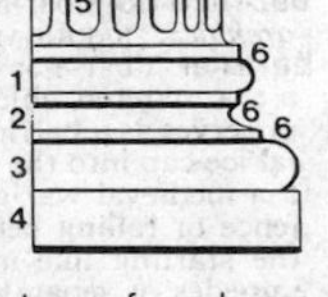

base of a column: *1* upper torus, *2* scotia, *3* lower torus, *4* plinth, *5* shaft, *6* fillets

syn BASE, BASIS, FOUNDATION, GROUND *shared meaning element* : something on which another thing is built up and by which it is supported *ant* top

— **off base** **1** : completely or absurdly mistaken **2** : UNAWARES

[2]base *vt* **based; bas·ing** **1** : to make, form, or serve as a base for **2** : to find a base or basis for — usu. used with *on* or *upon*

[3]base *adj* : constituting or serving as a base

[4]base *adj* [ME *bas,* fr. MF, fr. ML *bassus* short, low] **1** *archaic* : of little height **2** *obs* : low in place or position **3** *obs* : BASS **4** *archaic* : BASEBORN **5 a** : resembling a villein : SERVILE <a ~ tenant> **b** : held by villenage <~ tenure> **6 a** : being of comparatively low value and having relatively inferior properties (as resistance to corrosion) <a ~ metal such as iron> — compare NOBLE **b** : containing a larger than usual proportion of base metals <~ silver denarii> **7 a** : lacking or indicating the lack of higher qualities of mind or spirit : IGNOBLE <a ~ betrayal> **b** : lacking higher values : DEGRADING <a drab ~ way of life> **8** : of relatively little value — **base·ly** *adv* — **base·ness** *n*

syn BASE, LOW, VILE *shared meaning element* : contemptible because beneath what is expected of the average man. BASE stresses the ignoble and may suggest cruelty, treachery, greed, or grossness <*base* self-centered indulgence and selfish ambition —W. R. Inge> LOW may connote crafty cunning, vulgarity, or immorality and regularly implies an outraging of one's sense of decency or propriety <refused to listen to such *low* talk> VILE, the strongest of these words, tends to suggest disgusting depravity or filth <a *vile* remark> <matricide, the *vilest* of crimes> *ant* noble

base·ball \'bās-ˌbȯl\ *n, often attrib* : a game played with a bat and ball between two teams of nine players each on a large field centering on four bases that mark the course a runner must take to score; *also* : the ball used in this game

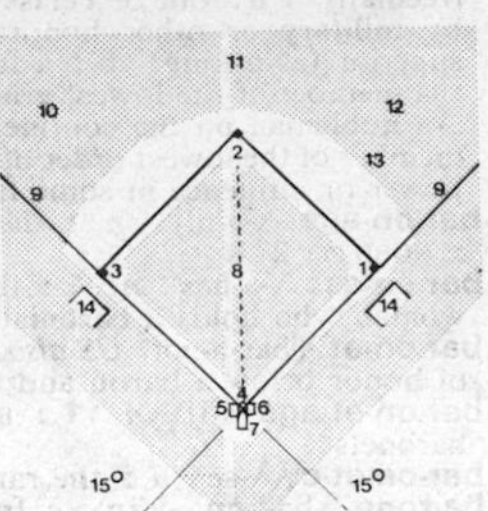

baseball field: *1* first base, *2* second base, *3* third base, *4* home base, *5* right-handed batter's box, *6* left-handed batter's box, *7* catcher's box, *8* pitcher's plate, *9* foul lines, *10* left field, *11* center field, *12* right field, *13* grass line, *14* coaches' boxes, *15* next batter's boxes

base·board \-ˌbō(ə)rd, -ˌbȯ(ə)rd\ *n* : a board situated at or forming the base of something; *specif* : a molding covering the joint of a wall and the adjoining floor

base·born \-'bȯ(ə)rn\ *adj* **1 a** : of humble birth : LOWLY **b** : of illegitimate birth : BASTARD **2** : MEAN, IGNOBLE

base burner *n* : a stove in which the fuel is fed from a hopper as the lower layer is consumed

base component *n* : BASE 10

base exchange *n* : a post exchange at a naval or air force base

base hit *n* : a hit in baseball that enables the batter to reach base safely without benefit of an error or fielder's choice

base·lev·el \'bā-ˌslev-əl\ *n* : the level below which a land surface cannot be reduced by running water

base·line \'bā-ˌslīn\ *n* **1** : a line serving as a base **2** : the area within which a baseball player must keep when running between bases **3** : the back line at each end of a court in various games (as tennis) **4** : FOUNDATION, BASIS 3

base·ment \'bā-smənt\ *n* [prob. fr. [1]*base*] **1** : the ground floor facade or interior in Renaissance architecture **2** : the part of a building that is wholly or partly below ground level **3** : the lowest or fundamental part of something **4** *chiefly New Eng* : TOILET, WASHROOM — **base·ment·less** \-ləs\ *adj*

basement membrane *n* : a usu. single-layered membrane of flat cells of connective tissue underlying the epithelial cells of many organs

ba·sen·ji \bə-'sen-jē, -'zen-\ *n* [of Bantu origin; akin to Lingala *basenji,* pl. of *mosenji* native] : any of an African breed of small compact curly-tailed chestnut-brown dogs that rarely bark

base on balls : an advance to first base given to a baseball player who during his turn at bat receives four pitches outside the strike zone that are not swung at

base path *n* : the area between the bases of a baseball field used by a base runner

base pay *n* : a rate or amount of pay for a standard work period, job, or position exclusive of additional payments or allowances

base runner *n* : a baseball player of the team at bat who is on base or is attempting to reach a base — **base·run·ning** *n*

[1]bash \'bash\ *vb* [origin unknown] *vt* : to strike violently : HIT; *also* : to injure or damage by striking : SMASH — usu. used with *in* ~ *vi* : CRASH — **bash·er** *n*

[2]bash *n* **1** : a forceful blow **2** : a festive social gathering : PARTY **3** : an important sports contest **4** : TRY, ATTEMPT

ba·shaw \bə-'shȯ\ *var of* PASHA

bash·ful \'bash-fəl\ *adj* [obs. *bash* (to be abashed)] **1** : socially shy or timid; *esp* : exhibiting an immature lack of savoir faire **2** : characterized by, showing, or resulting from extreme sensitiveness, self-consciousness or shyness <a ~ smile> *syn* see SHY *ant* forward, brazen — **bash·ful·ly** \-fə-lē\ *adv* — **bash·ful·ness** \-fəl-nəs\ *n*

[1]ba·sic \'bā-sik, -zik\ *adj* **1** : of, relating to, or forming the base or essence : FUNDAMENTAL **2** : constituting or serving as the basis or starting point **3 a** : of, relating to, containing, or having the character of a base **b** : having an alkaline reaction **4** *of rocks* : containing relatively little silica **5** : of, relating to, or made by a basic process — **ba·si·cal·ly** \-si-k(ə-)lē, -zi-\ *adv* — **ba·sic·i·ty** \bā-'sis-ət-ē\ *n*

[2]basic *n* **1** : something that is basic : FUNDAMENTAL <the ~*s* of biology> **2** : BASIC TRAINING

BA·SIC \'bā-sik, -zik\ *n* [*B*eginner's *A*ll-purpose *S*ymbolic *I*nstruction *C*ode] : a standardized language for programming and interacting with a computer

basic process *n* : a process of making steel carried on in a furnace lined with basic material and under a slag that is dominantly basic

basic slag *n* : a slag low in silica and high in base-forming oxides that is used in the basic process of steelmaking and that is then useful as a fertilizer

basic training *n* : the initial period of training of a military recruit

ba·sid·io·my·cete \bə-ˌsid-ē-ō-'mī-ˌsēt, -ˌmī-'sēt\ *n* [deriv. of NL *basidium* + Gk *mykēt-, mykēs* fungus — more at MYC-] : any of a large class (Basidiomycetes) of higher fungi having septate hyphae, bearing spores on a basidium, and including rusts, smuts, mushrooms, and puffballs — **ba·sid·io·my·ce·tous** \-ē-ō-ˌmī-'sēt-əs\ *adj*

ba·sid·io·spore \bə-'sid-ē-ə-ˌspō(ə)r, -ˌspȯ(ə)r\ *n* [NL *basidium* + E *-o-* + *spore*] : a spore produced by a basidium — **ba·sid·io·spo·rous** \-ˌsid-ē-ə-'spōr-əs, -'spȯr-; -ē-'äs-pə-rəs\ *adj*

ba·sid·i·um \bə-'sid-ē-əm\ *n, pl* **-ia** \-ē-ə\ [NL, fr. L *basis*] : a structure on a basidiomycete in which nuclear fusion occurs followed by meiosis and on which usu. four basidiospores are borne — **ba·sid·i·al** \-ē-əl\ *adj*

ba·si·fy \'bā-sə-ˌfī\ *vt* **-fied; -fy·ing** : to convert into a base or make alkaline — **ba·si·fi·ca·tion** \-ˌbā-sə-fə-'kā-shən\ *n*

ba·sil \'baz-əl, 'bās-, 'bas-, 'bāz-\ *n* [MF *basile,* fr. LL *basilicum,* fr. Gk *basilikon,* fr. neut. of *basilikos*] **:** any of several plants of the mint family: as **a :** SWEET BASIL **b :** BUSH BASIL

bas·i·lar \'baz-ə-lər, 'bas- *also* 'bāz- *or* 'bās-\ *also* **bas·i·lary** \-ˌler-ē\ *adj* [irreg. fr. *basis*] **:** of, relating to, or situated at the base

basilar membrane *n* **:** a membrane extending from the bony shelf of the cochlea to the outer wall and supporting the organ of Corti

Ba·sil·i·an \bə-'zil-ē-ən, -'sil-\ *n* **:** a member of the monastic order founded by St. Basil in the 4th century in Cappadocia — **Basilian** *adj*

ba·sil·i·ca \bə-'sil-i-kə, -'zil-\ *n* [L, fr. Gk *basilikē,* fr. fem. of *basilikos* royal, fr. *basileus* king] **1 :** an oblong building ending in a semicircular apse used in ancient Rome esp. for a court of justice and place of public assembly **2 :** an early Christian church building consisting of nave and aisles with clerestory and a large high transept from which an apse projects **3 :** a Roman Catholic church given ceremonial privileges — **ba·sil·i·can** \-kən\ *adj*

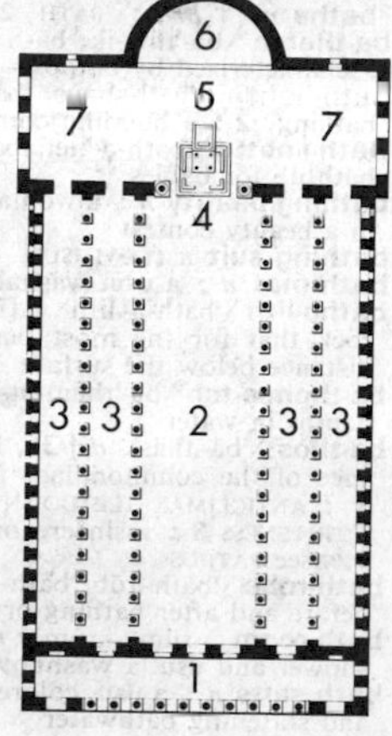

basilica 2: *1* narthex, *2* nave, *3* aisles, *4* altar, *5* bema, *6* apse, *7* transept

bas·i·lisk \'bas-ə-ˌlisk, 'baz-\ *n* [ME, fr. L *basiliscus,* fr. Gk *basiliskos,* fr. dim. of *basileus*] **1 :** a legendary reptile with fatal breath and glance **2 :** any of several crested tropical American lizards (genus *Basiliscus*) related to the iguanas and noted for their ability to run on their hind legs — **basilisk** *adj*

basil thyme *n* **:** CALAMINT

ba·sin \'bās-ᵊn\ *n* [ME, fr. OF *bacin,* fr. LL *bacchinon*] **1 a :** an open usu. circular vessel with sloping or curving sides used typically for holding water for washing **b :** the quantity contained in a basin **2 a :** a dock built in a tidal river or harbor **b :** an enclosed or partly enclosed water area **3 a :** a large or small depression in the surface of the land or in the ocean floor **b :** the entire tract of country drained by a river and its tributaries **c :** a great depression in the surface of the lithosphere occupied by an ocean **4 :** a broad area of the earth beneath which the strata dip usu. from the sides toward the center — **ba·sin·al** \-ᵊn-əl\ *adj* — **ba·sined** \-ᵊnd\ *adj*

bas·i·net \ˌbas-ə-'net\ *n* [ME *bacinet,* fr. OF, dim. of *bacin*] **:** a light often pointed steel helmet

ba·sip·e·tal \bā-'sip-ət-ᵊl, -'zip-\ *adj* [L *basis* + *petere* to go toward — more at FEATHER] **:** proceeding from the apex toward the base or from above downward — **ba·sip·e·tal·ly** \-ᵊl-ē\ *adv*

ba·sis \'bā-səs\ *n, pl* **ba·ses** \-ˌsēz\ [L — more at BASE] **1 :** FOUNDATION **2 :** the principal component of something **3 :** something on which something else is constructed or established **4 :** the basic principle **5 :** a set of linearly independent vectors in a vector space such that any vector in the vector space can be expressed as a linear combination of them with appropriately chosen coefficients ***syn*** see BASE

bask \'bask\ *vb* [ME *basken,* fr. ON *bathask,* refl. of *batha* to bathe; akin to OE *bæth* bath] *vi* **1 :** to lie in or expose oneself to a pleasant warmth or atmosphere **2 :** to take pleasure or derive enjoyment ~ *vt, obs* **:** to warm by continued exposure to heat

bas·ket \'bas-kət\ *n* [ME, prob. fr. (assumed) ONF *baskot;* akin to OF *baschoue* wooden vessel; both fr. L *bascauda* dishpan, of Celt origin; akin to MIr *basc* necklace — more at FASCIA] **1 a :** a receptacle made of interwoven material (as osiers) **b :** any of various lightweight usu. wood containers **c :** the quantity contained in a basket **2 :** something that resembles a basket esp. in shape or use **3 a :** a net open at the bottom and suspended from a metal ring that constitutes the goal in basketball **b :** a field goal in basketball — **bas·ket·ful** \-ˌfu̇l\ *n* — **bas·ket·like** \-ˌlīk\ *adj* — **bas·ket·work** \-ˌwərk\ *n*

bas·ket·ball \-ˌbȯl\ *n, often attrib* **:** a usu. indoor court game between two teams of usu. five players each who score by tossing an inflated ball through a raised goal; *also* **:** the ball used in this game

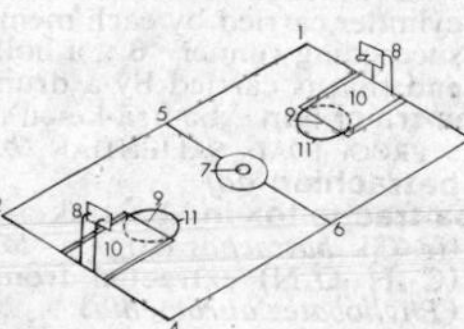

basketball court: *1-2, 3-4* sidelines, *1-3, 2-4* end lines, *5-6* division line, *7* center circle, *8* backboards and baskets, *9* free throw line, *10* lane, *11* free throw circle

basket case *n* **1 :** one who has all four limbs amputated **2 :** one that is totally incapacitated or inoperative

basket fern *n* **1 :** MALE FERN **2 :** a tropical American sword fern (*Nephrolepis pectinata*)

basket–handle arch *n* **:** a low-crowned elliptical arch drawn from three or more centers — see ARCH illustration

basket hilt *n* **:** a hilt with a basket-shaped guard to protect the hand — **bas·ket–hilt·ed** \ˌbas-kət-'hil-təd\ *adj*

Basket Maker *n* **1 :** any of three stages of an ancient culture of the plateau area of southwestern U.S. that preceded and formed one cultural development with the Pueblo **2 :** a member of the people who produced the Basket Maker culture

basket–of–gold *n* **:** a European perennial herb (*Alyssum saxatile*) widely cultivated for its grayish foliage and yellow flowers

bas·ket·ry \'bas-kə-trē\ *n, pl* **-ries 1 :** the art or craft of making baskets or objects woven like baskets **2 :** objects produced by basketry

basket star *n* **:** an echinoderm (order Euryalida) resembling a starfish with slender complexly branched interlacing arms

basket weave *n* **:** a textile weave resembling the checkered pattern of a plaited basket

bas·ket·work \'bas-kət-ˌwərk\ *n* **:** BASKETRY 2

bas mitz·vah \bä-'smits-və\ *n, often cap B&M* [Heb *bath miṣwāh,* lit., daughter of the (divine) law] **1 :** a Jewish girl who at about 13 years of age assumes religious responsibilities **2 :** the initiatory ceremony recognizing a girl as a bas mitzvah

ba·so·phil \'bā-sə-ˌfil, -zə-\ *or* **ba·so·phile** \-ˌfīl\ *n* **:** a basophilic substance or structure; *esp* **:** a white blood cell with basophilic granules

ba·so·phil·ia \ˌbā-sə-'fil-ē-ə, -zə-\ *n* [NL] **1 :** tendency to stain with basic dyes **2 :** an abnormality in which some tissue element has increased basophilia

ba·so·phil·ic \-'fil-ik\ *adj* [ISV *base* + *-o-* + *-philic*] **:** staining readily with basic stains

Basque \'bask\ *n* [F, fr. L *Vasco*] **1 :** one of a people of obscure origin inhabiting the western Pyrenees on the Bay of Biscay **2 :** the language of the Basques of unknown relationship **3** *not cap* **:** a tight-fitting bodice for women — **Basque** *adj*

bas–re·lief \ˌbä-ri-'lēf\ *n* [F, fr. *bas* low + *relief* raised work] **1 :** sculptural relief in which the projection from the surrounding surface is slight and no part of the modeled form is undercut **2 :** sculpture executed in bas-relief

[1]bass \'bas\ *n, pl* **bass** *or* **bass·es** [ME *base,* alter. of OE *bærs;* akin to OE *byrst* bristle — more at BRISTLE] **:** any of numerous edible spiny-finned fishes (esp. families Centrarchidae and Serranidae)

[2]bass \'bās\ *adj* [ME *bas* base] **1 :** deep or grave in tone **2 a :** of low pitch **b :** relating to or having the range or part of a bass

[3]bass \'bās\ *n* **1 :** a deep or grave tone **:** a low-pitched sound **2 a :** the lowest part in 4-part harmony **b :** the lower half of the whole vocal or instrumental tonal range — compare TREBLE **c :** the lowest adult male singing voice; *also* **:** a person having this voice **d :** a member of a family of instruments having the lowest range; *esp* **:** DOUBLE BASS

[4]bass \'bas\ *n* [alter. of *bast*] **1 :** a coarse tough fiber from palms **2 :** BASSWOOD 1

bass clef *n* **1 :** a clef placing the F below middle C on the fourth line of the staff **2 :** the bass staff

bass clef 1

bass drum *n* **:** a large drum having two heads and giving a booming sound of low indefinite pitch — see DRUM illustration

bas·set hound \'bas-ət-\ *n* [F, *basset,* fr. MF, fr. *basset* short, fr. *bas* low — more at BASE] **:** any of an old French breed of short-legged slow-moving hunting dogs with very long ears and crooked front legs — called also *basset*

bass fiddle *n* **:** the double bass esp. as used in jazz orchestras

bass horn *n* **:** TUBA

bas·si·net \ˌbas-ə-'net\ *n* [prob. modif. of F *barcelonnette,* dim. of *berceau* cradle] **1 :** a baby's basketlike bed (as of wickerwork or plastic) often with a hood over one end **2 :** a perambulator that resembles a bassinet

bass·ist \'bā-səst\ *n* **:** a double bass player

bas·so \'bas-(ˌ)ō, 'bäs-\ *n, pl* **bassos** *or* **bas·si** \'bäs-ˌē\ [It, fr. ML *bassus,* fr. *bassus* short, low] **:** a bass singer; *esp* **:** an operatic bass

bas·soon \bə-'sün, ba-\ *n* [F *basson,* fr. It *bassone,* fr. *basso*] **:** a tenor or bass double-reed woodwind instrument having a long U-shaped conical tube connected to the mouthpiece by a thin metal tube and a usual range two octaves lower than that of the oboe — **bas·soon·ist** \-'sü-nəst\ *n*

bassoon

bas·so pro·fun·do \ˌbas(ˌ)ō-prə-'fən-(ˌ)dō, ˌbäs-, -'fün-\ *n, pl* **basso profun·dos** [It, lit., deep bass] **1 :** a deep heavy bass voice with an exceptionally low range **2 :** a person having a basso profundo voice

bas·so–re·lie·vo *also* **bas·so–ri·lie·vo** \ˌbas-(ˌ)ō-ri-'lē-(ˌ)vō, ˌbäs-(ˌ)ō-rēl-'yā-(ˌ)vō\ *n* [It *bassorilievo,* fr. *basso* low + *rilievo* relief] **:** BAS-RELIEF

bass viol *n* **1 :** the largest member of the viol family **:** VIOLA DA GAMBA **2 :** DOUBLE BASS

bass·wood \'bas-ˌwu̇d\ *n* **1 :** any of several New World lindens; *esp* **:** LINDEN 1b **2 :** the straight-grained white wood of a basswood

bast \'bast\ *n* [ME, fr. OE *bæst;* akin to OHG & ON *bast*] **1 :** PHLOEM **2 :** a strong woody fiber obtained chiefly from the phloem of plants and used esp. in cordage, matting, and fabrics

[1]bas·tard \'bas-tərd\ *n* [ME, fr. OF] **1 :** an illegitimate child **2 :** something that is spurious, irregular, inferior, or of questionable origin **3 a :** an offensive or disagreeable person — used as a generalized term of abuse **b :** MAN, FELLOW — **bas·tard·ly** *adj*

[2]bastard *adj* **1 :** ILLEGITIMATE **2 :** of inferior breed or stock **:** MONGREL **3 :** of abnormal shape or irregular size **4 :** of a kind similar to but inferior to or less typical than some standard <~ measles> **5 :** lacking genuineness or authority **:** FALSE

bas·tard·ize \'bas-tər-ˌdīz\ *vt* **-ized; -iz·ing 1 :** to declare or prove to be a bastard **2 :** to reduce from a higher to a lower state or condition **:** DEBASE — **bas·tard·iza·tion** \ˌbas-tərd-ə-'zā-shən\ *n*

ə abut ᵊ kitten ər further a back ā bake ä cot, cart
au̇ out ch chin e less ē easy g gift i trip ī life
j joke ŋ sing ō flow ȯ flaw ȯi coin th thin t͟h this
ü loot u̇ foot y yet yü few yu̇ furious zh vision

bastard wing *n* **:** the process of a bird's wing corresponding to the thumb and bearing a few short quills — called also *alula*
bas·tardy \'bas-tərd-ē\ *n, pl* **-tard·ies** **1 :** the quality or state of being a bastard **:** ILLEGITIMACY **2 :** the begetting of an illegitimate child
1**baste** \'bāst\ *vt* **bast·ed; bast·ing** [ME *basten,* fr. MF *bastir,* of Gmc origin; akin to OHG *besten* to patch; akin to OE *bæst* bast] **:** to sew with long loose stitches in order to hold something in place temporarily — **bas·ter** *n*
2**baste** *vt* **bast·ed; bast·ing** [origin unknown] **:** to moisten (as meat) at intervals with a liquid (as melted butter, fat, or pan drippings) esp. during cooking — **bast·er** *n*
3**baste** *vt* **bast·ed; bast·ing** [prob. fr. ON *beysta;* akin to OE *bēatan* to beat] **1 :** to beat severely or soundly **:** THRASH **2 :** to scold vigorously **:** BERATE
bas·tille *or* **bas·tile** \ba-'stē(ə)l\ *n* [F *bastille,* fr. the *Bastille,* tower in Paris used as a prison] **:** PRISON, JAIL
Bastille Day *n* **:** July 14 observed in France as a national holiday in commemoration of the fall of the Bastille in 1789
1**bas·ti·na·do** \,bas-tə-'näd-(,)ō, -'näd-\ *or* **bas·ti·nade** \,bas-tə-'näd, -'näd\ *n, pl* **-na·does** *or* **-nades** [Sp *bastonada,* fr. *bastón* stick, fr. LL *bastum*] **1 :** a blow with a stick or cudgel **2 a :** a beating esp. with a stick **b :** a punishment consisting of beating the soles of the feet with a stick **3 :** STICK, CUDGEL
2**bastinado** *vt* **-doed; -do·ing :** to subject to repeated blows
1**bast·ing** \'bā-stiŋ\ *n* **1 :** the action of a sewer who bastes **2 a :** the thread used by a baster **b :** the stitching made by a baster
2**basting** *n* **1 :** the action of one that bastes food **2 :** the liquid used by a baster
3**basting** *n* **:** a severe beating
bas·tion \'bas-chən\ *n* [MF, fr. *bastille* fortress, modif. of OProv *bastida,* fr. *bastir* to build, of Gmc origin; akin to OHG *besten* to patch] **1 :** a projecting part of a fortification **2 :** a fortified area or position **3 :** something that is considered a stronghold **:** BULWARK — **bas·tioned** \-chənd\ *adj*
bast ray *n* **:** PHLOEM RAY
Ba·su·to \bə-'süt-(,)ō\ *n, pl* **Basuto** *or* **Basutos :** one of the Bantu-speaking people of Basutoland
1**bat** \'bat\ *n* [ME, fr. OE *batt,* prob. of Celt origin; akin to Gaulish anda*bata,* a gladiator — more at BATTLE] **1 :** a stout solid stick **:** CLUB **2 :** a sharp blow **:** STROKE **3 a :** a wooden implement used for hitting the ball in various games **b :** a racket used in various games (as squash) **c :** the short whip used by a jockey **4 a :** BATSMAN **b :** a turn at batting — usu. used in the phrase *at bat* **5 :** BATTING 2 — usu. used in pl. **6** *Brit* **:** GAIT **7 :** BINGE — **off one's own bat :** through one's own efforts <won the game *off his own bat*> — **off the bat :** without delay **:** IMMEDIATELY
2**bat** *vb* **bat·ted; bat·ting** *vt* **1 :** to strike or hit with or as if with a bat **2 a :** to advance (a base runner) by batting **b :** to have a batting average of **3 :** to compose esp. in a casual, careless, or hurried manner — usu. used with *out* **4 :** to discuss at length **:** consider in detail ~ *vi* **1 a :** to strike or hit a ball with a bat **b :** to take one's turn at bat **2 :** to wander aimlessly — **bat the breeze :** CHAT 2
3**bat** *n* [alter. of ME *bakke,* prob. of Scand origin, akin to OSw natt*bakka* bat] **:** any of an order (Chiroptera) of nocturnal placental flying mammals with forelimbs modified to form wings
4**bat** *vt* **bat·ted; bat·ting** [prob. alter of 2*bate*] **:** to wink esp. in surprise or emotion <never *batted* an eye>
BAT *abbr* bachelor of arts in teaching
bat·boy \'bat-,bȯi\ *n* **:** a boy employed to look after the equipment (as bats) of a baseball team
1**batch** \'bach\ *n* [ME *bache;* akin to OE *bacan* to bake] **1 :** the quantity baked at one time **:** BAKING **2 a :** the quantity of material prepared or required for one operation; *specif* **:** a mixture of raw materials ready for fusion into glass **b :** the quantity produced at one operation **c :** a group of jobs to be run on a computer at one time with the same program <~ processing> **3 :** a group of persons or things **:** LOT
2**batch** *vt* **:** to bring together or process as a batch — **batch·er** *n*
3**batch** *var of* BACH
1**bate** \'bāt\ *vb* **bat·ed; bat·ing** [ME *baten,* short for *abaten* to abate] *vt* **1 :** to reduce the force or intensity of **:** RESTRAIN <with *bated* breath> **2 :** to take away **:** DEDUCT **3** *archaic* **:** to lower esp. in amount or estimation **4** *archaic* **:** BLUNT ~ *vi, obs* **:** DIMINISH, DECREASE
2**bate** *vi* **bat·ed; bat·ing** [ME *baten,* fr. MF *batre* to beat — more at DEBATE] *of a falcon* **:** to beat the wings impatiently
ba·teau \ba-'tō\ *n, pl* **ba·teaux** \-'tō(z)\ [CanF, fr. F, fr. OF *batel,* fr. OE *bāt* boat — more at BOAT] **:** any of various small craft; *esp* **:** a flat-bottomed boat with raked bow and stern and flaring sides
Bates·ian mimicry \,bāt-sē-ən-\ *n* [Henry Walter *Bates* †1892 E naturalist] **:** resemblance of an innocuous species to another that is protected from predators by repellent qualities (as unpalatability)
bat·fish \'bat-,fish\ *n* **:** any of several fishes with winglike processes: as **a :** any of several flattened pediculate fishes (as a common West Indian form *Ogcocephalus vespertilio*) **b :** a flying gurnard (*Dactylopterus volitans*) of the Atlantic **c :** a California stingray (*Aetobatus californicus*)
bat·fowl \-,faul\ *vi* **:** to catch birds at night by blinding them with a light and knocking them down with a stick or netting them
1**bath** \'bath, 'bȧth\ *n, pl* **baths** \'bat͟hz, 'baths, 'bȧt͟hz, 'bȧths\ [ME, fr. OE *bæth;* akin to OHG *bad* bath, OE *bacan* to bake] **1 :** a washing or soaking (as in water or steam) of all or part of the body **2 a :** water used for bathing **b** (1) **:** a contained liquid for a special purpose (2) **:** a receptacle holding the liquid **c** (1) **:** a medium for regulating the temperature of something placed in or on it (2) **:** a vessel containing this medium **3 a :** BATHROOM **b :** a building containing an apartment or a series of rooms designed for bathing **c :** SPA — usu. used in pl. **4 :** the quality or state of being covered with a liquid **5 :** BATHTUB
2**bath** *vt, Brit* **:** to give a bath to ~ *vi, Brit* **:** to take a bath
3**bath** *n* [Heb] **:** an ancient Hebrew liquid measure corresponding to the ephah of dry measure

bath- *or* **batho-** *comb form* [ISV, fr. Gk *bathos,* fr. *bathys* deep — more at BATHY-] **:** depth <*bath*ometer>
bath chair \'bath-, 'bȧth-\ *n, often cap B* [*Bath,* England] **:** a hooded and sometimes glassed wheeled chair used esp. by invalids; *broadly* **:** WHEELCHAIR
1**bathe** \'bāt͟h\ *vb* **bathed; bath·ing** [ME *bathen,* fr. OE *bathian;* akin to OE *bæth* bath] *vt* **1 :** to wash in a liquid (as water) **2 :** MOISTEN, WET **3 :** to apply water or a liquid medicament to **4 :** to flow along the edge of **:** LAVE **5 :** to suffuse with or as if with light ~ *vi* **1 :** to take a bath **2 :** to go swimming **3 :** to become immersed or absorbed — **bath·er** \'bā-t͟hər\ *n*
2**bathe** *n* **1** *Brit* **:** 1BATH **2** *Brit* **:** SWIM, DIP
ba·thet·ic \bə-'thet-ik, bā-\ *adj* [*bathos* + *-etic* (as in *pathetic*)] **:** characterized by bathos — **ba·thet·i·cal·ly** \-i-k(ə-)lē\ *adv*
bath·house \'bath-,haus, 'bȧth-\ *n* **1 :** a building equipped for bathing **2 :** a building containing dressing rooms for bathers
Bath·i·nette \,bath-ə-'net, ,bȧth-\ *trademark* — used for a portable bathtub for babies
bathing beauty *n* **:** a woman in a bathing suit who is a contestant in a beauty contest
bathing suit *n* **:** SWIMSUIT
bath mat *n* **:** a usu. washable mat used in a bathroom
batho·lith \'bath-ə-,lith\ *n* [ISV] **:** a great mass of intruded igneous rock that for the most part stopped in its rise a considerable distance below the surface — **batho·lith·ic** \,bath-ə-'lith-ik\ *adj*
ba·thom·e·ter \bə-'thäm-ət-ər\ *n* **:** an instrument for measuring depths in water
ba·thos \'bā-,thäs\ *n* [Gk, lit., depth] **1 a :** the sudden appearance of the commonplace in otherwise elevated matter or style **b :** ANTICLIMAX, LETDOWN **2 :** exceptional commonplaceness **:** TRITENESS **3 :** insincere or overdone pathos **:** SENTIMENTALISM *syn* see PATHOS
bath·robe \'bath-,rōb, 'bȧth-\ *n* **:** a loose usu. absorbent robe worn before and after bathing or as a dressing gown
bath·room \,rüm, -,ru̇m\ *n* **:** a room containing a bathtub or shower and usu. a washbowl and toilet
bath salts *n* **:** a usu. colored crystalline compound for perfuming and softening bathwater
bath·tub \-,təb\ *n* **:** a usu. fixed tub for bathing — **bath·tub·ful** \-,fu̇l\ *n*
bathtub gin *n* **:** a usu. strong liquor often made illicitly under makeshift conditions from spirits flavored with essential oils
bath·wa·ter \'bath-,wȯt-ər, 'bȧth-, -,wät-ər\ *n* **:** water for a bath
bathy- *comb form* [ISV, fr. Gk, fr. *bathys* deep; akin to Skt *gāhate* he dives into] **1 :** deep **:** depth <*bathy*al> **2 :** deep-sea <*bathy*sphere>
bathy·al \'bath-ē-əl\ *adj* **:** DEEP-SEA
bathy·met·ric \,bath-i-'me-trik\ *adj* **:** of or relating to bathymetry — **bathy·met·ri·cal** \-tri-kəl\ *adj* — **bathy·met·ri·cal·ly** \-tri-k(ə-)lē\ *adv*
ba·thym·e·try \bə-'thim-ə-trē\ *n, pl* **-tries** [ISV] **:** the measurement of depths of water in oceans, seas, and lakes
bathy·pe·lag·ic \,bath-i-pə-'laj-ik\ *adj* [*bathy-* + *pelagic*] **:** of, relating to, or living in the ocean depths esp. between 2000 and 12,000 feet
bathy·scaphe \'bath-i-,skaf, -,skāf\ *also* **bathy·scaph** \-,skaf\ *n* [ISV *bathy-* + Gk *skaphē* light boat] **:** a navigable submersible ship for deep-sea exploration having a spherical watertight cabin attached to its underside
bathy·sphere \-,sfi(ə)r\ *n* **:** a strongly built steel diving sphere for deep-sea observation
ba·tik \bə-'tēk, 'bat-ik\ *n* [Malay] **1 a :** an Indonesian method of hand-printing textiles by coating with wax the parts not to be dyed **b :** a design so executed **2 :** a fabric printed by batik
bat·ing \'bāt-iŋ\ *prep* **:** with the exception of **:** EXCEPTING
ba·tiste \bə-'tēst, ba-\ *n* [F] **:** a fine soft sheer fabric of plain weave made of various fibers
bat·man \'bat-mən\ *n* [deriv. of Gk *bastizein* to carry] **:** an orderly of a British military officer
bat mitz·vah \bät-'mits-və\ *often cap B&M, var of* BAS MITZVAH
ba·ton \bə-'tän, ba-, -'tōn *also* 'bat-ən\ *n* [F *bâton,* fr. OF *baston,* fr. LL *bastum* stick] **1 :** CUDGEL, TRUNCHEON **2 :** a staff borne as a symbol of office **3 :** a narrow heraldic bend **4 :** a stick or wand with which a leader directs a band or orchestra **5 :** a hollow cylinder carried by each member of a relay team and passed to the succeeding runner **6 :** a hollow metal rod with a ball usu. at one end that is carried by a drum major or drum majorette
ba·tra·chi·an \bə-'trā-kē-ən\ *n* [deriv. of Gk *batrachos* frog] **:** FROG, TOAD, SALIENTIAN; *broadly* **:** a vertebrate amphibian — **batrachian** *adj*
ba·tracho·tox·in \bə-,trak-ə-'täk-sən, ,ba-trə-kō-\ *n* [ISV *batracho-* (fr. Gk *batrachos* frog) + *toxin*] **:** a very powerful steroid venom ($C_{24}H_{33}O_4N$) extracted from the skin of a So. American frog (*Phyllobates aurotaenia*)
bats·man \'bat-smən\ *n* **:** a batter esp. in cricket
batt *var of* BAT
bat·tai·lous \'bat-əl-əs\ *adj* [ME *bataillous,* fr. MF *bataillos,* fr. *bataille* battle] *archaic* **:** ready for battle **:** WARLIKE
bat·ta·lia \bə-'tāl-yə, -'tal-\ *n* [It *battaglia*] **1** *obs* **:** a large body of men in battle array **2** *archaic* **:** order of battle
bat·tal·ion \bə-'tal-yən\ *n* [MF *bataillon,* fr. OIt *battaglione,* aug. of *battaglia* company of soldiers, battle, fr. LL *battalia* combat — more at BATTLE] **1 :** a considerable body of troops organized to act together **:** ARMY **2 :** a military unit composed of a headquarters and two or more companies, batteries, or similar units **3 :** a large group <a ~ of instructors teaching elementary composition —Douglas Bush>
batteau *var of* BATEAU
bat·te·ment \,bat-(ə-)'män\ *n* [F, fr. *battre* to beat (fr. L *battuere*) + *-ment*— more at BATTLE] **:** a ballet movement in which the foot is extended in any direction usu. followed by a beat against the supporting foot
1**bat·ten** \'bat-ən\ *vb* **bat·tened; bat·ten·ing** \'bat-niŋ, -ən-iŋ\ [prob. fr. ON *batna* to improve] *vi* **1 a :** to grow fat **b :** to feed

gluttonously **2 :** to grow prosperous esp. at the expense of another ~ *vt* **:** FATTEN

2**batten** *n* [F *bâton*] **1 a** *Brit* **:** a piece of lumber used esp. for flooring **b :** a thin narrow strip of lumber used esp. to seal or reinforce a joint **2 :** a strip, bar, or support resembling or used similarly to a batten

3**batten** *vt* **bat·tened; bat·ten·ing** \'bat-niŋ, -ᵊn-iŋ\ **:** to furnish or fasten with battens — often used with *down*

1**bat·ter** \'bat-ər\ *vb* [ME *bateren*, prob. freq. of *batten* to bat, fr. *bat*] *vt* **1 a :** to beat with successive blows so as to bruise, shatter, or demolish **b :** BOMBARD **2 :** to subject to strong, overwhelming, or repeated attack **3 :** to wear or damage by hard usage or blows <a ~*ed* old hat> ~ *vi* **:** to strike heavily and repeatedly **:** BEAT ***syn*** see MAIM

2**batter** *n* [ME *bater*, prob. fr. *bateren*] **1 :** a mixture that consists of flour, liquid, and other ingredients and is thin enough to pour or drop from a spoon **2 :** an instance of battering **3 :** a damaged area on a printing surface

3**batter** *vt* [origin unknown] **:** to give a receding upward slope to (as a wall)

4**batter** *n* **:** a receding upward slope of the outer face of a structure

5**batter** *n* **:** one that bats; *esp* **:** the player whose turn it is to bat

bat·te·rie \ˌbat-ə-'rē\ *n* [F, lit., beating — more at BATTERY] **:** a ballet movement consisting of beating together the feet or calves of the legs during a leap

battering ram *n* **1 :** a military siege engine consisting of a large wooden beam with a head of iron used in ancient times to beat down the walls of a besieged place **2 :** a heavy metal bar with handles used (as by firemen) to batter down doors and walls

bat·tery \'bat-ə-rē, 'ba-trē\ *n, pl* **-ter·ies** [MF *batterie*, fr. OF, fr. *battre* to beat, fr. L *battuere* — more at BATTLE] **1 a :** the act of battering or beating **b :** the unlawful beating or use of force on a person without his consent — compare ASSAULT 2a **2 a :** a grouping of artillery pieces for tactical purposes **b :** the guns of a warship **3 :** an artillery unit in the army equivalent to a company **4 a :** a combination of apparatus for producing a single electrical effect **b :** a group of two or more cells connected together to furnish electric current; *also* **:** a single cell that furnishes electric current <a flashlight ~> **5 a :** a number of similar articles, items, or devices arranged, connected, or used together **:** SET, SERIES **b :** an impressive or imposing group **:** ARRAY **6 :** the position of readiness of a gun for firing **7 :** the pitcher and catcher of a baseball team

bat·ting \'bat-iŋ\ *n* **1 a :** the act of one who bats **b :** the use of or ability with a bat **2 :** layers or sheets of raw cotton or wool used for lining quilts or for stuffing or packaging

batting average *n* **1 :** a ratio (as a rate per thousand) of base hits to official times at bat for a baseball player **2 :** a record of achievement or accomplishment <an almost unbelievably high *batting average* in gaining and holding the friendship of the home folk —G. S. Perry>

1**bat·tle** \'bat-ᵊl\ *n, often attrib* [ME *batel*, fr. OF *bataille* battle, fortifying tower, battalion, fr. LL *battalia* combat, alter. of *battualia* fencing exercises, fr. L *battuere* to beat, of Celt origin; akin to Gaulish anda*bata*, a gladiator; akin to L *fatuus* foolish, Russ *bat* cudgel] **1 :** a general encounter between armies, ships of war, or airplanes **2 :** a combat between two persons **3** *archaic* **:** BATTALION **4 :** an extended contest, struggle, or controversy ***syn*** BATTLE, ENGAGEMENT, ACTION *shared meaning element* **:** a meeting between opposing forces

2**battle** *vb* **bat·tled; bat·tling** \'bat-liŋ, -ᵊl-iŋ\ *vi* **1 :** to engage in battle **:** FIGHT **2 :** to contend with full strength, vigor, craft, or resources **:** STRUGGLE ~ *vt* **1 :** to fight against **2 :** to force (as one's way) by battling — **bat·tler** \-lər, -ᵊl-ər\ *n*

3**battle** *vt* **bat·tled; bat·tling** [ME *batailen*, fr. MF *bataillier* to fortify, fr. OF, fr. *bataille*] *archaic* **:** to fortify with battlements

bat·tle–ax \'bat-ᵊl-ˌaks\ *n* **1 :** a broadax formerly used as a weapon of war **2 :** a quarrelsome domineering woman

battle cruiser *n* **:** a large heavily armed warship that is lighter, faster, and more maneuverable than a battleship

battle cry *n* **:** WAR CRY

battle fatigue *n* **:** COMBAT FATIGUE — **bat·tle–fa·tigued** *adj*

bat·tle·field \'bat-ᵊl-ˌfēld\ *n* **1 :** a place where a battle is fought **2 :** an area of conflict

bat·tle·front \-ˌfrənt\ *n* **:** the military sector in which actual combat takes place

bat·tle·ground \-ˌgraund\ *n* **:** BATTLEFIELD

battle group *n* **:** a military unit normally made up of five companies

bat·tle·ment \'bat-ᵊl-mənt\ *n* [ME *batelment*, fr. MF *bataille*] **:** a parapet with open spaces that surmounts a wall and is used for defense or decoration — **bat·tle·ment·ed** \-ˌment-əd\ *adj*

1 2 3 1 2

battlements: *1* crenels, *2* merlons, *3* machicolations

battle royal *n, pl* **battles royal** *or* **battle royals 1 a :** a fight participated in by more than two combatants; *esp* **:** one in which the last man in the ring or on his feet is declared the winner **b :** a violent struggle **2 :** a heated dispute

bat·tle·ship \'bat-ᵊl-ˌship\ *n* [short for *line-of-battle ship*] **:** a warship of the largest and most heavily armed and armored class

bat·tle·wag·on \-ˌwag-ən\ *n* **:** BATTLESHIP

bat·tu \ba-'t(y)ü\ *adj* [F, fr. pp. of *battre* to beat] *of a ballet movement* **:** performed with a striking together of the legs

bat·tue \ba-'t(y)ü\ *n* [F, fr. *battre* to beat] **:** the beating of woods and bushes to flush game; *also* **:** a hunt in which this procedure is used

bat·ty \'bat-ē\ *adj* **bat·ti·er; -est 1 :** of, relating to, or resembling a bat **2 :** mentally unstable **:** CRAZY — **bat·ti·ness** *n*

bau·ble \'bò-bəl, 'bäb-əl\ *n* [ME *babel*, fr. MF] **1 :** TRINKET **2 :** a fool's scepter **3 :** TRIFLE

Bau·cis \'bò-səs\ *n* [L, fr. Gk *Baukis*] **:** the wife of Philemon who with him presided over a temple of Zeus

baud \'bòd, 'bōd\ *n, pl* **baud** *also* **bauds** [*baud* (telegraphic transmission speed unit), fr. J. M. E. *Baudot* †1903 F inventor] **:** a variable unit of data transmission speed usu. equal to one bit per second

bau·drons \'bòd-rənz, 'bòth-\ *n* [ME] *Scot* **:** CAT

Bau·haus \'baù-ˌhaùs\ *adj* [G *Bauhaus*, lit., architecture house, school founded by Gropius] **:** of, relating to, or influenced by a school of design noted esp. for a program that synthesized technology, craftsmanship, and design aesthetics

baulk *chiefly Brit var of* BALK

Bau·mé \bō-'mā\ *adj* [Antoine *Baumé*] **:** being, calibrated in accordance with, or according to either of two arbitrary hydrometer scales for liquids lighter than water or for liquids heavier than water that indicate specific gravity in degrees

baux·ite \'bòk-ˌsīt, 'bäk-\ *n* [F *bauxite*, fr. Les *Baux*, near Arles, France] **:** an impure mixture of earthy hydrous aluminum oxides and hydroxides that commonly contains similar compounds of iron and occas. of manganese, usu. has a concretionary or oolitic structure, and is the principal source of aluminum — **baux·it·ic** \bòk-'sit-ik, bäk-\ *adj*

Bav *abbr* Bavaria; Bavarian

Ba·var·i·an \bə-'ver-ē-ən, -'var-\ *n* **1 :** a native or inhabitant of Bavaria **2 :** the High German dialect of Bavaria and Austria — **Bavarian** *adj*

baw·bee *or* **bau·bee** \'bò-(ˌ)bē, bò-'\ *n* [prob. fr. Alexander Orrok, laird of Sille*bawbe fl* 1538 Sc master of the mint] **1 a :** any of various Scottish coins of small value **b :** an English halfpenny **2 :** TRIFLE

baw·cock \'bò-ˌkäk\ *n* [F *beau coq*, fr. *beau* fine + *coq* fellow, cock] *archaic* **:** a fine fellow

bawd \'bòd\ *n* [ME *bawde*] **1** *obs* **:** PANDER **2 a :** one who keeps a house of prostitution **:** MADAM **b :** PROSTITUTE

bawd·ry \'bò-drē\ *n* [ME *bawderie*, fr. *bawde*] **1** *obs* **:** UNCHASTITY **2 :** suggestive, coarse, or obscene language

1**bawdy** \'bòd-ē\ *adj* **bawd·i·er; -est** [*bawd*] **1 :** OBSCENE, LEWD **2 :** boisterously or humorously indecent — **bawd·i·ly** \'bòd-ᵊl-ē\ *adv* — **bawd·i·ness** \'bòd-ē-nəs\ *n*

2**bawdy** *n* [prob. fr. 1*bawdy*] **:** BAWDRY 2

1**bawl** \'bòl\ *vb* [ME *baulen*, prob. of Scand origin; akin to Icel *baula* to low] *vi* **1 :** to cry out loudly and unrestrainedly **:** YELL, BELLOW **2 :** to cry loudly **:** WAIL ~ *vt* **:** to cry out at the top of one's voice — **bawl·er** *n*

2**bawl** *n* **:** a loud prolonged cry **:** OUTCRY

bawl out *vt* **:** to reprimand loudly or severely

1**bay** \'bā\ *adj* [ME, fr. MF *bai*, fr. L *badius*; akin to OIr *buide* yellow] **:** reddish brown <a ~ mare>

2**bay** *n* **1 :** a bay-colored animal; *specif* **:** a horse with a bay-colored body and black mane, tail, and points — compare 1CHESTNUT 4, 1SORREL 1a **2 :** a reddish brown

3**bay** *n* [ME, berry, fr. MF *baie*, fr. L *baca*] **1 a :** LAUREL 1 **b :** any of several shrubs or trees (as of the genera *Magnolia, Myrica,* and *Gordonia*) resembling the laurel **2 a :** a garland or crown esp. of laurel given as a prize for victory or excellence **b :** HONOR, FAME — usu. used in pl.

4**bay** *n* [ME, fr. MF *baee* opening, fr. OF, fr. fem. of *baé*, pp. of *baer* to gape, yawn — more at ABEYANCE] **1 :** a principal compartment of the walls, roof, or other part of a building or of the whole building **2 :** a main division of a structure: as **a :** a compartment in a barn **b :** BAY WINDOW **c :** the forward part of a ship on each side between decks often used as a ship's hospital **d (1) :** a longitudinal part of an elongated aircraft structure lying between two adjacent transverse members or walls **(2) :** any of several compartments in the fuselage of an airplane **e :** a compartment (as in a service station) for a car **3 :** a vertical support on which various pieces of electronic apparatus are mounted

5**bay** *vb* [ME *baien, abaien*, fr. OF *abaiier*, of imit. origin] *vi* **1 :** to bark with prolonged tones **2 :** to cry out **:** SHOUT ~ *vt* **1 :** to bark at **2 :** to bring to bay **3 :** to pursue with barking **4 :** to utter in deep prolonged tones

6**bay** *n* **1 :** the position of one unable to retreat and forced to face danger <brought his quarry to ~> **2 :** the position of one checked <police kept the rioters at ~> **3 :** a baying of dogs

7**bay** *n, often attrib* [ME *baye*, fr. MF *baie*] **1 :** an inlet of the sea or other body of water usu. smaller than a gulf **2 :** a small body of water set off from the main body **3 :** any of various terrestrial formations resembling a bay of the sea

ba·ya·dere \'bī-ə-ˌdi(ə)r, -ˌde(ə)r\ *n* [F *bayadère* Hindu dancing girl] **:** a fabric with horizontal stripes in strongly contrasted colors

bay antler \'bā-\ *n* [earlier *bes antler*, fr. ME *bes-* secondary (fr. MF, fr. L *bis-* twice) + E *antler*] **:** the second tine from the base of a stag's antler — see ANTLER illustration

bay·ber·ry \'bā-ˌber-ē\ *n* **1 :** a West Indian tree (*Pimenta racemosa*) of the myrtle family yielding a yellow aromatic oil **2 a :** a hardy shrub (*Myrica pensylvanica*) of coastal eastern No. America bearing dense clusters of small globular nuts covered with grayish white wax; *also* **:** WAX MYRTLE **b :** the fruit of a bayberry

Bayes·ian \'bā-zē-ən, -zhən\ *adj* [Thomas *Bayes* †1761 E mathematician] **:** being or relating to a theory (as of decision or of statistical inference) in which probabilities are associated with individual events or statements and not merely with sequences of events (as in frequency theories)

bay leaf *n* **:** the dried leaf of the European laurel used in cooking

ə abut	ᵊ kitten	ər further	a back	ā bake	ä cot, cart
aù out	ch chin	e less	ē easy	g gift	i trip	ī life
j joke	ŋ sing	ō flow	ò flaw	òi coin	th thin	th this
ü loot	ù foot	y yet	yü few	yù furious	zh vision

[1]**bay·o·net** \'bā-ə-nət, -ˌnet, ˌbā-ə-'net\ *n* [F *baïonnette,* fr. *Bayonne,* France] **:** a steel blade attached at the muzzle end of a shoulder arm and used in hand-to-hand combat

[2]**bayonet** *vb* **-net·ed** *also* **-net·ted; -net·ing** *also* **net·ting** *vt* **1 :** to stab with a bayonet **2 :** to compel or drive by or as if by the bayonet ~ *vi* **:** to use a bayonet

bay·ou \'bī-(ˌ)(y)ō, -(ˌ)(y)ü, -(y)ə\ *n* [LaF, fr. Choctaw *bayuk*] **1 :** a creek, secondary watercourse, or minor river that is tributary to another body of water **2 :** any of various usu. marshy or sluggish bodies of water

bay rum *n* **:** a fragrant cosmetic and medicinal liquid distilled from the leaves of the West Indian bayberry or usu. prepared from essential oils, alcohol, and water

Bay Stat·er \'bā-ˌstāt-ər\ *n* **:** a native or resident of Massachusetts — used as a nickname

bay window *n* **1 :** a window or series of windows forming a bay or recess in a room and projecting outward from the wall **2 :** POTBELLY

ba·zaar \bə-'zär\ *n* [Per *bāzār*] **1 :** an Oriental market consisting of rows of shops or stalls selling miscellaneous goods **2 a :** a place for the sale of goods **b :** DEPARTMENT STORE **3 :** a fair for the sale of articles esp. for charitable purposes

ba·zoo·ka \bə-'zü-kə\ *n* [*bazooka* (a crude musical instrument made of pipes and a funnel)] **:** a light portable shoulder weapon consisting of an open-breech smoothbore firing tube that launches armor-piercing rockets

[1]**BB** \'bē-(ˌ)bē\ *n* **1 :** a shot pellet 0.18 inch in diameter for use in a shotgun cartridge **2 :** a shot pellet 0.175 inch in diameter for use in a gun that propels shot by compressed air produced by a plunger operated by a spring

[2]**BB** *abbr* **1** bachelor of business **2** ball bearing **3** base on balls **4** blue book **5** B'nai B'rith

BBA *abbr* bachelor of business administration

B battery *n* **:** an electric battery connected in the plate circuit of an electron tube to cause flow of electron current in the tube

BBB *abbr* Better Business Bureau

BBC *abbr* British Broadcasting Corporation

BBE *abbr* bachelor of business education

bbl *abbr* barrel; barrels

BC *abbr* **1** bachelor of commerce **2** before Christ — often printed in small capitals **3** British Columbia

BCD *abbr* binary-coded decimal

BCE *abbr* **1** bachelor of chemical engineering **2** bachelor of civil engineering

BCG vaccine \ˌbē-(ˌ)sē-'jē-\ *n* [*b*acillus, *C*almette-*G*uérin (an attenuated strain of tubercle bacilli), fr. Albert *Calmette* †1933 and Camille *Guérin* †1961 F bacteriologists] **:** a vaccine prepared from a living attenuated strain of tubercle bacilli and used to vaccinate human beings against tuberculosis

BCh *abbr* bachelor of chemistry

BChE *abbr* bachelor of chemical engineering

BCL *abbr* **1** bachelor of canon law **2** bachelor of civil law

bcn *abbr* beacon

B complex *n* **:** VITAMIN B COMPLEX

BCS *abbr* **1** bachelor of chemical science **2** bachelor of commercial science

BCSE *abbr* Board of Civil Service Examiners

BC soil \'bē-'sē-\ *n* **:** a soil whose profile has only B-horizons and C-horizons

bd *abbr* **1** board **2** bound **3** boundary **4** bundle

BD *abbr* **1** bachelor of divinity **2** bank draft **3** barrels per day **4** bills discounted **5** bomb disposal **6** brought down

BDA *abbr* **1** bachelor of domestic arts **2** bachelor of dramatic art

bdel·li·um \'del-ē-əm\ *n* [ME, fr. L, fr. Gk *bdellion*] **:** a gum resin similar to myrrh obtained from various trees (genus *Commiphora*) of the East Indies and Africa

bdel·lo·vi·brio \ˌdel-ō-'vib-rē-ˌō\ *n* [NL, genus name, fr. Gk *bdella* leech + NL *vibrio*] **:** a bacterium (genus *Bdellovibrio*) that is parasitic on other bacteria

bd ft *abbr* board foot

bdl *or* **bdle** *abbr* bundle

bdrm *abbr* bedroom

be \(')bē\ *vb, past 1st & 3d sing* **was** \(')wəz, 'wäz\; *2d sing* **were** \(')wər\; *pl* **were;** *past subjunctive* **were;** *past part* **been** \(')bin, *chiefly Brit* (')bēn\; *pres part* **be·ing** \'bē-iŋ\; *pres 1st sing* **am** \əm, (')am\; *2d sing* **are** \ər, (')är\; *3d sing* **is** \(')iz, əz\; *pl* **are;** *pres subjunctive* **be** [ME *been,* fr. OE *bēon;* akin to OHG *bim* am, L *fui* I have been, *futurus* about to be, *fieri* to become, be done, Gk *phynai* to be born, be by nature, *phyein* to bring forth] *vi* **1 a :** to equal in meaning **:** have the same connotation as **:** SYMBOLIZE <God *is* love> <January *is* the first month> <let *x* ~ 10> **b :** to have identity with <the first person I met *was* my brother> **c :** to constitute the same class as **d :** to have a specified qualification or characterization <the leaves *are* green> **e :** to belong to the class of <the fish *is* a trout> — used regularly in senses 1a through 1e as the copula of simple predication **2 a :** to have an objective existence **:** have reality or actuality **:** LIVE <I think, therefore I *am*> <once upon a time there *was* a knight> **b :** to have, maintain, or occupy a place, situation, or position <the book *is* on the table> **c :** to remain unmolested, undisturbed, or uninterrupted — used only in infinitive form <let him ~> **d :** to take place **:** OCCUR <the concert *was* last night> **e** *archaic* **:** BELONG, BEFALL ~ *verbal auxiliary* **1** — used with the past participle of transitive verbs as a passive-voice auxiliary <the money *was* found> <the house is *being* built> **2** — used as the auxiliary of the present participle in progressive tenses expressing continuous action <he *is* reading> <I have *been* sleeping> **3** — used with the past participle of some intransitive verbs as an auxiliary forming archaic perfect tenses <Christ *is* risen from the dead — 1 Cor 15:20 (DV)> **4** — used with the infinitive with *to* to express futurity, arrangement in advance, or obligation <I *am* to interview him today> <he *was* to become famous>

Be *symbol* beryllium

BE *abbr* **1** bachelor of education **2** bachelor of engineering **3** bill of exchange

be- *prefix* [ME, fr. OE *bi-, be-;* akin to OE *bī* by, near — more at BY] **1 :** on **:** around **:** over <*be*daub> <*be*smear> **2 :** to a great or greater degree **:** thoroughly <*be*fuddle> <*be*rate> **3 :** excessively **:** ostentatiously — in intensive verbs formed from simple verbs <*be*deck> and in adjectives based on adjectives ending in *-ed* <*be*ribboned> **4 :** about **:** to **:** at **:** upon **:** against **:** across <*be*stride> <*be*speak> **5 :** make **:** cause to be **:** treat as <*be*little> <*be*fool> <*be*friend> **6 :** call or dub esp. excessively <*be*doctor> **7 :** affect, afflict, treat, provide, or cover with esp. excessively <*be*devil> <*be*fog>

Bé *abbr* Baumé

[1]**beach** \'bēch\ *n* [origin unknown] **1 :** shore pebbles **:** SHINGLE **2 a :** a shore of an ocean, sea, or lake or the bank of a river covered by sand, gravel, or larger rock fragments **b :** a seashore area

[2]**beach** *vt* **1 :** to run or drive ashore **2 :** to make (a person) incapable or ineffective **:** DISABLE

beach ball *n* **:** a large inflated ball for use at the beach

beachboy *n* **:** a male beach attendant (as at a club or hotel)

beach break *n* **:** a wave that breaks close to the shore

beach buggy *n* **:** a motor vehicle with oversize tires for use on sand beaches

beach·comber \'bēch-ˌkō-mər\ *n* **1 :** a white man living as a drifter or loafer esp. on the islands of the So. Pacific **2 :** one who searches along a shore for useful or salable flotsam and refuse — **beach·comb** \-ˌkōm\ *vb*

beach flea *n* **:** any of numerous amphipod crustaceans (family Orchestiidae) living on ocean beaches and leaping like fleas

beach·front \'bēch-ˌfrənt\ *n* **:** a strip of land that fronts a beach — called also *shorefront*

beach grass *n* **:** any of several tough strongly rooted grasses that grow on exposed sandy shores; *esp* **:** a rhizomatous perennial (genus *Ammophila*) widely planted to bind sandy slopes

beach·head \'bēch-ˌhed\ *n* **1 :** an area on a hostile shore occupied to secure further landing of troops and supplies **2 :** FOOTHOLD

beach pea *n* **:** a wild pea (*Lathyrus maritimus*) with tough roots and purple flowers found along sandy seashores

beach plum *n* **:** a shrubby plum (*Prunus maritima*) having showy white flowers and growing along the northeastern coast of North America; *also* **:** its dark purple edible fruit that is often used in jams and jellies

beach·side \'bēch-ˌsīd\ *adj* **:** located on a beach

beach wagon *n* **:** STATION WAGON

beach·wear \'bēch-ˌwa(ə)r, -ˌwe(ə)r\ *n* **:** clothing for wear at a beach

beachy \'bē-chē\ *adj* **:** covered with pebbles or shingle

[1]**bea·con** \'bē-kən\ *n* [ME *beken,* fr. OE *bēacen* sign; akin to OHG *bouhhan* sign] **1 :** a signal fire commonly on a hill, tower, or pole **2 a :** a lighthouse or other signal for guidance **b :** a radio transmitter emitting signals for guidance of aircraft **3 :** a source of light or inspiration

[2]**beacon** *vt* **:** to furnish with a beacon ~ *vi* **:** to shine as a beacon

[1]**bead** \'bēd\ *n* [ME *bede* prayer, prayer bead, fr. OE *bed, gebed* prayer; akin to OE *biddan* to entreat, pray — more at BID] **1 a** *obs* **:** PRAYER — usu. used in pl. **b** *pl* **:** a series of prayers and meditations made with a rosary **2 :** a small piece of material pierced for threading on a string or wire (as in a rosary) **3** *pl* **a :** ROSARY **b :** a necklace of beads or pearls **4 :** a small ball-shaped body: as **a :** a drop of sweat or blood **b :** a bubble formed in or on a beverage **c :** a small metal knob on a firearm used as a front sight **d :** a blob or a line of weld metal **e :** a glassy drop of flux (as borax) used as a solvent and color test for several metallic oxides and salts **5 :** a projecting rim, band, or molding

[2]**bead** *vt* **1 :** to furnish, adorn or cover with beads or beading **2 :** to string together like beads ~ *vi* **:** to form into a bead

bead·ing *n* **1 :** material or a part or a piece consisting of a bead **2 :** a beaded molding **3 :** an openwork trimming **4 :** BEADWORK

bea·dle \'bēd-ᵊl\ *n* [ME *bedel,* fr. OE *bydel;* akin to OHG *butil* bailiff, OE *bēodan* to command — more at BID] **:** a minor parish official whose duties include ushering and preserving order at services and sometimes civil functions

bead·roll \'bē-ˌdrōl\ *n* [fr. the reading in church of a list of names of persons for whom prayers are to be said] **1 :** a list of names **:** CATALOG **2 :** ROSARY

beads·man \'bēdz-mən\ *n, archaic* **:** one who prays for another

bead·work \'bē-ˌdwərk\ *n* **1 :** ornamental work in beads **2 :** joinery beading

beady \'bēd-ē\ *adj* **1 a :** resembling beads **b :** small, round, and shiny with interest or greed <~ eyes> **2 :** marked by bubbles or beads <a ~ liquor>

bea·gle \'bē-gəl\ *n* [ME *begle*] **:** a small short-legged smooth-coated hound

beak \'bēk\ *n* [ME *bec,* fr. OF, fr. L *beccus,* of Gaulish origin] **1 a :** the bill of a bird; *esp* **:** the bill of a bird of prey adapted for striking and tearing **b** (1) **:** any of various rigid projecting mouth structures (as of a turtle) (2) **:** the elongated sucking mouth of some insects (as the typical bugs) **c :** the human nose **2 :** a pointed structure or formation: **a :** a metal-pointed beam projecting from the bow of an ancient galley for piercing an enemy ship **b :** the spout of a vessel **c :** a continuous slight architectural projection ending in an arris — see MOLDING illustration **d :** a process suggesting the beak of a bird **3** *chiefly Brit* **a :** MAGISTRATE **b :** HEADMASTER — **beaked** \'bēkt\ *adj*

bea·ker \'bē-kər\ *n* [ME *biker,* fr. ON *bikarr,* prob. fr. OS *bikeri;* akin to OHG *behhari* beaker; both fr. a prehistoric WGmc word borrowed fr. ML *bicarius* beaker, fr. Gk *bikos* earthen jug] **1 :** a large drinking cup that has a wide mouth and is sometimes supported on a standard **2 :** a deep widemouthed and often projecting-lipped thin vessel used esp. by chemists and pharmacists

be–all and end–all \'bē-ˌó-lən-'(d)en-ˌdól\ *n* **:** prime cause **:** essential element

1**beam** \'bēm\ *n* [ME *beem,* fr. OE *bēam* tree, beam; akin to OHG *boum* tree] **1 a** **:** a long piece of heavy often squared timber suitable for use in construction **b :** a wood or metal cylinder in a loom on which the warp is wound **c :** the part of a plow to which handles, standard, and colter are attached **d :** the bar of a balance from which scales hang **e :** one of the principal horizontal supporting members of a building or ship <a steel ~ supporting a floor>; *also* **:** BOOM, SPAR <the ~ of a crane> **f :** the extreme width of a ship at the widest part **g :** an oscillating lever on a central axis receiving motion at one end from an engine piston rod and transmitting it at the other **2 a :** a ray or shaft of light **b :** a collection of nearly parallel rays (as X rays) or particles (as electrons) **c :** a constant directional radio signal transmitted for the guidance of pilots; *also* **:** the course indicated by a radio beam **3 :** the main stem of a deer's antler **4 :** the width of the buttocks — **on the beam** **1 :** following a guiding beam **2 :** proceeding or operating correctly

2**beam** *vt* **1 :** to emit in beams or as a beam **2 :** to support with beams **3 a :** to aim (a broadcast) by directional antennas **b :** to direct to a particular audience ~ *vi* **1 :** to send out beams of light **2 :** to smile with joy

beam–ends \'bē-'men(d)z\ *n pl* **:** the ends of a ship's beams — **on her beam–ends :** inclined so much on one side that the beams approach a vertical position

beam·ish \'bē-mish\ *adj* **:** beaming and bright with optimism, promise, or achievement — **beam·ish·ly** *adv*

beamy \'bē-mē\ *adj* **1 :** emitting beams of light **:** RADIANT **2 :** broad in the beam <a ~ cargo ship>

1**bean** \'bēn\ *n* [ME *bene,* fr. OE *bēan;* akin to OHG *bōna* bean] **1 a :** BROAD BEAN **b :** the seed of any of various erect or climbing leguminous plants (esp. genera *Phaseolus, Dolichos,* and *Vigna*) other than the broad bean **c :** a plant bearing beans **d :** a bean pod used when immature as a vegetable **2 a :** a valueless item **b** *pl* **:** a small amount <didn't know ~*s* about it> **3 :** any of various seeds or fruits that resemble beans or bean pods <catalpa ~>; *also* **:** a plant producing these **4 :** a protuberance on the upper mandible of waterfowl **5 :** HEAD, BRAIN **6** *pl* **:** EXUBERANCE — used in the phrase *full of beans*

2**bean** *vt* **:** to strike (a person) on the head with an object

bean·ball \'bēn-,bȯl\ *n* **:** a pitched baseball thrown at a batter's head

bean curd *n* **:** a soft vegetable cheese that is extensively eaten in the Orient and is prepared by treating soybean milk with coagulants (as magnesium chloride or dilute acids)

bean·ie \'bē-nē\ *n* **:** a small round tight-fitting skullcap worn esp. by schoolboys and college freshmen

beano \'bē-(,)nō\ *n, pl* **beanos** [by alter.] **:** BINGO

bean sprouts *n pl* **:** the sprouts of bean seeds esp. of the mung bean

bean tree *n* **:** any of several trees having fruits resembling a bean pod**:** as **a :** a yellow-flowered Australian leguminous tree (*Castanospermum australe*) with large pods containing seeds like chestnuts **b :** CATALPA

1**bear** \'ba(ə)r, 'be(ə)r\ *n, pl* **bears** *often attrib* [ME *bere,* fr. OE *bera;* akin to OE *brūn* brown] **1** *or pl* **bear :** any of a family (Ursidae of the order Carnivora) of large heavy mammals having long shaggy hair, rudimentary tail, and plantigrade feet and feeding largely on fruit and insects as well as on flesh **2 :** a surly, uncouth, or shambling person **3** [prob. fr. the proverb about *selling the bearskin before catching the bear*] **:** one that sells securities or commodities in expectation of a price decline — compare BULL

2**bear** *vb* **bore** \'bō(ə)r, 'bȯ(ə)r\; **borne** \'bō(ə)rn, 'bȯ(ə)rn\ *also* **born** \'bȯ(ə)rn\; **bear·ing** [ME *beren,* fr. OE *beran;* akin to OHG *beran* to carry, L *ferre,* Gk *pherein*] *vt* **1 a :** to move while holding up and supporting **b :** to be equipped or furnished with **c :** to hold in the mind **d :** DISSEMINATE **e :** BEHAVE, CONDUCT <~*ing* himself well> **f :** to have as a feature or characteristic **g :** to give as testimony <~ false witness> **h :** to have as an identification <*bore* the name of John> **i :** LEAD, ESCORT **j :** RENDER, GIVE **2 a :** to give birth to **b :** to produce as yield **c** (1) **:** to permit growth of (2) **:** CONTAIN <oil-*bearing* shale> **3 a :** to support the weight of **:** SUSTAIN **b :** to put up with esp. without giving way <couldn't ~ his wife's family> **c :** ASSUME, ACCEPT **d :** to hold above, on top, or aloft **e :** to admit of **:** ALLOW **f :** to call for as suitable or essential <his odd behavior ~*s* watching> **4 :** THRUST, PRESS ~ *vi* **1 a :** to force one's way **b :** to be situated **:** LIE **c :** to extend in a direction indicated or implied **d :** to become directed **e :** to go or incline in an indicated direction <road ~*s* to the right> **2 a :** APPLY, PERTAIN **b :** to exert influence or force **3 :** to support a weight or strain — often used with *up* **4 :** to produce fruit **:** YIELD
syn **1** see CARRY
2 BEAR, SUFFER, ENDURE, ABIDE, TOLERATE, STAND, BROOK *shared meaning element* **:** to put up with something trying or painful — **bear a hand :** to join in and help out — **bear fruit :** to come to satisfying fruition, production, or development — **bear in mind :** to think of esp. as a warning **:** REMEMBER

bear·able \'bar-ə-bəl, 'ber-\ *adj* **:** capable of being borne — **bear·abil·i·ty** \,bar-ə-'bil-ət-ē, ,ber-\ *n* — **bear·ably** \-blē\ *adv*

bear·bait·ing \'ba(ə)r-,bāt-iŋ, 'be(ə)r-\ *n* **:** the practice of setting dogs on a chained bear

bear·ber·ry \-,ber-ē\ *n* **1 :** a trailing evergreen plant (*Arctostaphylos uva-ursi*) of the heath family with astringent foliage and red berries **2 :** the large cranberry (*Vaccinium macrocarpon*) **3 :** CASCARA BUCKTHORN

1**beard** \'bi(ə)rd\ *n* [ME *berd,* fr. OE *beard;* akin to OHG *bart* beard, L *barba*] **1 :** the hair that grows on a man's face often excluding the mustache **2 :** a hairy or bristly appendage or tuft **3 :** BEVEL 3; *also* **:** the bevel plus the shoulder — **beard·ed** \-əd\ *adj* — **beard·ed·ness** *n* — **beard·less** \-ləs\ *adj*

2**beard** *vt* **1 :** to furnish with a beard **2 :** to confront and oppose with boldness, resolution, and often effrontery **:** DEFY

bear down *vt* **:** OVERCOME, OVERWHELM ~ *vi* **:** to exert full strength and concentrated attention — **bear down on 1 :** EMPHASIZE **2 :** to weigh heavily on **:** BURDEN

beard·tongue \'bi(ə)rd-,təŋ\ *n* **:** PENTSTEMON

bear·er \'bar-ər, 'ber-\ *n* **:** one that bears: as **a :** PORTER **b :** a plant yielding fruit **c :** PALLBEARER **d :** one holding a check, draft, or other order for payment esp. if marked payable to bearer

bear grass *n* **:** any of several plants (genera *Yucca, Nolina,* or *Xerophyllum*) of the lily family chiefly of the southern and western U.S. with foliage resembling coarse blades of grass

bear hug *n* **:** a rough tight embrace

bear·ing *n* **1 :** the manner in which one bears or comports oneself <a man of erect and soldierly ~> **2 a :** the act, power, or time of bringing forth offspring or fruit **b :** a product of bearing **:** CROP **3 :** PRESSURE, THRUST **4 a :** an object, surface, or point that supports **b :** a machine part in which another part (as a journal or pin) turns or slides **5 :** a figure borne on a heraldic field **6 a :** the situation or horizontal direction of one point with respect to another or to the compass **b :** a determination of position **c** *pl* **:** comprehension of one's position, environment, or situation **d :** RELATION, CONNECTION; *also* **:** PURPORT **7 :** the part of a structural member that rests upon its supports
syn BEARING, DEPORTMENT, DEMEANOR, MIEN, MANNER, CARRIAGE *shared meaning element* **:** the way in which a person outwardly manifests his personality or attitude

bearing rein *n* **:** CHECKREIN 1

bear·ish \'ba(ə)r-ish, 'be(ə)r-\ *adj* **1 :** resembling a bear in roughness, gruffness, or surliness **2 a :** marked by, tending to cause, or fearful of falling prices (as in a stock market) **b :** PESSIMISTIC — **bear·ish·ly** *adv* — **bear·ish·ness** *n*

bé·ar·naise sauce \,bā-är-,nāz-, -ər-\ *n* [F *béarnaise,* fem. of *béarnais* of Béarn, France] **:** hollandaise sauce flavored with wine, shallots, and herbs

bear out *vt* **:** CONFIRM, SUBSTANTIATE <research *bore out* his theory>

bear·skin \'ba(ə)r-,skin, 'be(ə)r-\ *n* **:** an article made of the skin of a bear; *esp* **:** a military hat made of the skin of a bear

bear up *vt* **:** SUPPORT, ENCOURAGE ~ *vi* **:** to summon up courage, resolution, or strength <*bearing up* under the strain>

beast \'bēst\ *n* [ME *beste,* fr. OF, fr. L *bestia*] **1 a :** an animal as distinguished from a plant **b :** a lower animal as distinguished from man **c :** a four-footed mammal as distinguished from man, lower vertebrates, and invertebrates **d :** an animal under human control **2 :** a contemptible person

beast epic *n* **:** a poem with epic conventions in which animals speak and act like human beings

beast fable *n* **:** a usu. didactic prose or verse fable in which animals speak and act like human beings

beas·tings \'bē-stiŋz\ *n pl but sing or pl in constr* [ME *bestynge,* fr. OE *bȳsting,* fr. *bēost* beastings] **:** the colostrum esp. of a cow

1**beast·ly** \'bēst-lē\ *adj* **beast·li·er; -est** **1 :** of, relating to, or resembling a beast **:** BESTIAL **2 :** ABOMINABLE, DISAGREEABLE <~ weather> — **beast·li·ness** *n*

2**beastly** *adv* **:** VERY <a ~ cold day>

beast of burden : an animal employed to carry heavy material or to perform other heavy work (as pulling a plow)

1**beat** \'bēt\ *vb* **beat; beat·en** \'bēt-ᵊn\ *or* **beat; beat·ing** [ME *beten,* fr. OE *bēatan;* akin to OHG *bōzan* to beat, L *-futare* to beat, *fustis* club] *vt* **1 :** to strike repeatedly: **a :** to hit repeatedly so as to inflict pain — often used with *up* **b :** to walk on **:** TREAD **c :** to strike directly against forcefully and repeatedly **:** dash against **d :** to flap or thrash at vigorously **e :** to strike at in order to rouse game; *also* **:** to range over in or as if in quest of game **f :** to mix by stirring **:** WHIP — often used with *up* **g :** to strike repeatedly in order to produce music or a signal <~ a drum> **2 a :** to drive or force by blows **b :** to pound into a powder, paste, or pulp **c :** to make by repeated treading or driving over **d** (1) **:** to dislodge by repeated hitting (2) **:** to lodge securely by repeated striking **e :** to shape by beating <~ swords into plowshares>; *esp* **:** to flatten thin by blows **f :** to sound or express esp. by drumbeat **3 :** to cause to strike or flap repeatedly **4 a :** OVERCOME, DEFEAT; *also* **:** SURPASS — often used with *out* **b :** to prevail despite <~ the odds> **c :** BEWILDER, BAFFLE **d** (1) **:** FATIGUE, EXHAUST (2) **:** to leave dispirited, irresolute, or hopeless **e :** CHEAT, SWINDLE **5 a** (1) **:** to act ahead of usu. so as to forestall (2) **:** to report a news item in advance of **b :** to come or arrive before **c :** CIRCUMVENT <~ the system> **6 :** to indicate by beating <~ the tempo> ~ *vi* **1 a :** to become forcefully impelled **:** DASH **b :** to glare or strike with oppressive intensity **c :** to sustain distracting activity **d :** to beat a drum **2 a** (1) **:** PULSATE, THROB (2) **:** TICK **b :** to sound upon being struck **3 a :** to strike repeated blows **b :** to strike the air **:** FLAP **c :** to strike cover in order to rouse game; *also* **:** to range or scour for or as if for game **4 :** to progress with much difficulty — **beat about the bush** *or* **beat around the bush :** to fail or refuse to come to the point in discourse — **beat it 1 :** to hurry away **:** SCRAM **2 :** HURRY, RUSH — **beat one's brains out :** to try intently to resolve something difficult by thinking — **beat the bushes :** to search thoroughly through all possible areas — **beat the rap :** to escape or evade the penalties connected with an accusation or charge

2**beat** *n* **1 a :** a single stroke or blow esp. in a series; *also* **:** PULSATION, TICK **b :** a sound produced by or as if by beating **c :** a driving impact or force **2 :** one swing of the pendulum or balance of a timepiece **3 :** each of the pulsations of amplitude produced by the union of sound or radio waves or electric currents having different frequencies **4 :** an accented stroke (as of one leg or foot against the other) in dancing **5 a :** a metrical or rhythmic stress in poetry or music or the rhythmic effect of these stresses **b :** the tempo indicated (as by a conductor) to a musical performer **c :** the pronounced rhythm that is the characteristic driving force in jazz or rock music; *also* : [2]ROCK 2 **6 :** a regularly traversed round <the cop on the ~> **7 a :** something that excels <I've never seen the ~ of it> **b :** the reporting of a news story ahead of competitors **8 :** DEADBEAT **9 a :** an act of beating to windward **b :** one of the reaches so traversed : TACK — **beat·less** \-ləs\ *adj*

[3]**beat** *adj* [ME *beten, bete,* fr. pp. of *beten*] **1 a :** being in a state of exhaustion : EXHAUSTED **b :** sapped of resolution or morale **2 :** of, relating to, or being beatniks <~ poets>

[4]**beat** *n* : BEATNIK

beat·en \'bēt-ᵊn\ *adj* **1 :** hammered into a desired shape <~ gold> **2 :** much trodden and worn smooth; *also* : FAMILIAR <a ~ path> **3 :** being in a state of exhaustion : EXHAUSTED

beat·er \'bēt-ər\ *n* **1 :** one that beats: as **a :** EGGBEATER **b :** a rotary blade attached to an electric mixer **c :** DRUMSTICK 1 **2 :** one that strikes bushes or other cover to rouse game **3 :** an advance publicity agent

be·atif·ic \ˌbē-ə-'tif-ik\ *adj* [L *beatificus* making happy, fr. *beatus* happy, fr. pp. of *beare* to bless; akin to L *bonus* good — more at BOUNTY] **1 :** of, possessing, or imparting beatitude **2 :** having a blissful or benign appearance : SAINTLY, ANGELIC <a ~ smile> — **be·atif·i·cal·ly** \-i-k(ə-)lē\ *adv*

beatific vision *n* : the direct knowledge of God enjoyed by the blessed in heaven

be·at·i·fy \bē-'at-ə-ˌfī\ *vt* **-fied; -fy·ing** [MF *beatifier,* fr. LL *beatificare,* fr. L *beatus*] **1 :** to make supremely happy **2 :** to declare to have attained the blessedness of heaven and authorize the title "Blessed" and limited public religious honor — **be·at·i·fi·ca·tion** \-ˌat-ə-fə-'kā-shən\ *n*

beat·ing \'bēt-iŋ\ *n* **1 :** an act of striking with repeated blows so as to injure or damage; *also* : the injury or damage thus inflicted **2 :** PULSATION **3 :** SETBACK, DEFEAT

beating reed *n* : a reed in a musical instrument that vibrates against the edges of an air opening (as in a clarinet or organ pipe) to which it is attached — compare FREE REED

be·at·i·tude \bē-'at-ə-ˌt(y)üd\ *n* [L *beatitudo,* fr. *beatus*] **1 a :** a state of utmost bliss **b** — used as a title for a primate esp. of an Eastern church **2 :** any of the declarations made in the Sermon on the Mount (Mt 5:3–12) beginning in the AV "Blessed are"

beat·nik \'bēt-nik\ *n* [[3]*beat* + Yiddish *-nik,* suffix denoting a person, fr. Russ & Pol] : a person who rejects the mores of established society (as by dressing and behaving unconventionally) and indulges in exotic philosophizing and self-expression

beat out *vt* **1 :** to make or perform by or as if by beating **2 :** to mark or accompany by beating **3 :** to turn (a routine ground ball) into a hit in baseball by fast running to first base

Be·atrice *n* [It] \ˌbā-ä-'trē-(ˌ)chā, 'bē-ə-trəs\: a Florentine woman immortalized in Dante's *Vita Nuova* and *Divina Commedia*

beau \'bō\ *n, pl* **beaux** \'bōz\ *or* **beaus** [F, fr. *beau* beautiful, fr. L *bellus* pretty] **1 :** DANDY **2 :** a man who is a frequent or steady escort of a woman : BOYFRIEND

Beau Brum·mell \bō-'brəm-əl\ *n* [nickname of G. B. *Brummell*] : DANDY

BEAUFORT SCALE

BEAUFORT NUMBER	NAME	MILES PER HOUR	DESCRIPTION
0	calm	less than 1	calm; smoke rises vertically
1	light air	1–3	direction of wind shown by smoke but not by wind vanes
2	light breeze	4–7	wind felt on face; leaves rustle; ordinary vane moved by wind
3	gentle breeze	8–12	leaves and small twigs in constant motion; wind extends light flag
4	moderate breeze	13–18	raises dust and loose paper; small branches are moved
5	fresh breeze	19–24	small trees in leaf begin to sway; crested wavelets form on inland waters
6	strong breeze	25–31	large branches in motion; telegraph wires whistle; umbrellas used with difficulty
7	moderate gale (*or* near gale)	32–38	whole trees in motion; inconvenience in walking against wind
8	fresh gale (*or* gale)	39–46	breaks twigs off trees; generally impedes progress
9	strong gale	47–54	slight structural damage occurs; chimney pots and slates removed
10	whole gale (*or* storm)	55–63	trees uprooted; considerable structural damage occurs
11	storm (*or* violent storm)	64–72	very rarely experienced; accompanied by widespread damage
12	hurricane*	73–136	devastation occurs

*The U.S. uses 74 statute mph as the speed criterion for hurricane.

Beau·fort scale \ˌbō-fərt-\ *n* [Sir Francis *Beaufort*] : a scale in which the force of the wind is indicated by numbers from 0 to 12

beau geste \bō-'zhest\ *n, pl* **beaux gestes** *or* **beau gestes** \bō-'zhest\ [F, lit., beautiful gesture] **1 :** a graceful or magnanimous gesture **2 :** an ingratiating conciliatory gesture

beau ide·al \ˌbō-ī-'dē(-ə)l\ *n, pl* **beau ideals** [F *beau idéal* ideal beauty] : the perfect type or model

Beau·jo·lais \ˌbō-zhō-'lā\ *n* [F, fr. *Beaujolais,* region of central France] : a French red table wine

Beau·mé *var of* BAUMÉ

beau monde \bō-'mänd, -mōⁿd\ *n, pl* **beau mondes** \-'män(d)z\ *or* **beaux mondes** \bō-mōⁿd\ [F, lit., fine world] : the world of high society and fashion

beau·te·ous \'byüt-ē-əs\ *adj* [ME, fr. *beaute*] : BEAUTIFUL — **beau·te·ous·ly** *adv* — **beau·te·ous·ness** *n*

beau·ti·cian \byü-'tish-ən\ *n* [*beauty* + *-ician*] : COSMETOLOGIST

beau·ti·ful \'byüt-i-fəl\ *adj* **1 :** having qualities of beauty : exciting aesthetic pleasure **2 :** generally pleasing : EXCELLENT — **beau·ti·ful·ly** \-f(ə-)lē\ *adv* — **beau·ti·ful·ness** \-fəl-nəs\ *n*

syn BEAUTIFUL, LOVELY, HANDSOME, PRETTY, COMELY, FAIR *shared meaning element* : pleasing to the mind, spirit, or senses ***ant*** ugly

beautiful people *n pl, often cap B & P* : people who are identified with international society

beau·ti·fy \'byüt-ə-ˌfī\ *vb* **-fied; -fy·ing** *vt* : to make beautiful or add beauty to : EMBELLISH ~ *vi* : to grow beautiful ***syn*** see ADORN — **beau·ti·fi·ca·tion** \ˌbyüt-ə-fə-'kā-shən\ *n* — **beau·ti·fi·er** \'byüt-ə-ˌfī(-ə)r\ *n*

beau·ty \'byüt-ē\ *n, pl* **beauties** [ME *beaute,* fr. OF *biauté,* fr. *bel, biau* beautiful, fr. L *bellus* pretty; akin to L *bonus* good — more at BOUNTY] **1 :** the quality or aggregate of qualities in a person or thing that gives pleasure to the senses or pleasurably exalts the mind or spirit : LOVELINESS **2 :** a beautiful person or thing; *esp* : a beautiful woman **3 :** a brilliant, extreme, or egregious example or instance <that mistake was a ~> **4 :** a particularly graceful, ornamental, or excellent quality

beauty bush *n* : a Chinese shrub (*Kolkwitzia amabilis*) of the honeysuckle family with pinkish flowers and bristly fruit

beauty shop *n* : an establishment or department where hairdressing, facials, and manicures are done — called also *beauty parlor, beauty salon*

beauty spot *n* **1 :** [1]PATCH 2 **2 a :** NEVUS **b :** a minor blemish

beaux arts \bō-'zär\ *n pl* [F] : FINE ARTS

beaux espirits *pl of* BEL ESPRIT

[1]**bea·ver** \'bē-vər\ *n, pl* **beavers** [ME *bever,* fr. OE *beofor;* akin to OHG *bibar* beaver, OE *brūn* brown] **1** *or pl* **beaver a :** either of two large semiaquatic rodents (genus *Castor*) having webbed hind feet and a broad flat tail, constructing dams and underwater lodges, and yielding valuable fur and castor **b :** the fur or pelt of the beaver **2 a :** a hat made of beaver fur or a fabric imitation **b :** SILK HAT **3 :** a heavy fabric of felted wool or of cotton napped on both sides

[2]**beaver** *n* [ME *baviere,* fr. MF] **1 :** a piece of armor protecting the lower part of the face **2 :** a helmet visor

[3]**beaver** *vi* : to work energetically <~*ing* away at the problem>

bea·ver·board \'bē-vər-ˌbō(ə)rd, -ˌbò(ə)rd\ *n* [fr. *Beaver Board,* a trademark] : a fiberboard used for partitions and ceilings

be·bop \'bē-ˌbäp\ *n* [imit.] : BOP — **be·bop·per** *n*

BEC *abbr* Bureau of Employees' Compensation

be·calm \bi-'käm, -'kälm\ *vt* **1 :** to keep motionless by lack of wind **2 :** to make calm : SOOTHE

be·cause \bi-'kòz, -(ˈ)kəz\ *conj* [ME *because that, because,* fr. *by cause that*] **1 :** for the reason that : SINCE <rested ~ he was tired> **2 :** the fact that : THAT <the latter fact, we suggest, was because the world was . . . particularly attentive at that moment to the subject of violence —*Times Lit. Supp.*>

because of *prep* : by reason of : on account of

bec·ca·fi·co \ˌbek-ə-'fē-(ˌ)kō\ *n, pl* **-cos** *or* **-coes** [It, fr. *beccare* to peck + *fico* fig, fr. L *ficus*] : any of various European songbirds that are sometimes served as a table delicacy

bé·cha·mel \ˌbā-shə-'mel\ *n* [F *sauce béchamelle,* fr. Louis de *Béchamel* †1703 F courtier] : a white sauce sometimes enriched with cream

be·chance \bi-'chan(t)s\ *vb, archaic* : BEFALL

bêche–de–mer \ˌbesh-də-'me(ə)r, ˌbāsh-\ *n* [F, lit., sea grub] **1** *pl* **bêche–de–mer** *or* **bêches–de–mer** \ˌbesh-(əz-)də-, ˌbāsh-\: TREPANG **2** *cap B&M* : a lingua franca based on English and used esp. in New Guinea, the Bismarck archipelago, and the Solomon islands

[1]**beck** \'bek\ *n* [ME *bek,* fr. ON *bekkr;* akin to OE *bæc* brook, OHG *bah,* MIr *būal* flowing water] *Brit* : CREEK 2

[2]**beck** *vt* [ME *becken,* alter. of *beknen*] *archaic* : BECKON

[3]**beck** *n* **1** *chiefly Scot* : BOW, CURTSY **2 a :** a beckoning gesture **b :** SUMMONS, BIDDING — **at one's beck and call :** in obedient readiness to obey any command

beck·et \'bek-ət\ *n* [origin unknown] : a device for holding something in place: as **a :** a grommet or a loop of rope with a knot at one end to catch in an eye at the other **b :** a ring of rope or metal **c :** a loop of rope (as for a handle)

becket bend *n* : SHEET BEND

beck·on \'bek-ən\ *vb* **beck·oned; beck·on·ing** \'bek-(ə-)niŋ\ [ME *beknen,* fr. OE *biecnan,* fr. *bēacen* sign — more at BEACON] *vi* **1 :** to summon or signal typically with a wave or nod **2 :** to appear inviting : ATTRACT ~ *vt* : to beckon to — **beckon** *n*

be·cloud \bi-'klau̇d\ *vt* **1 :** to obscure with or as if with a cloud **2 :** to prevent clear perception or realization of : MUDDLE <prejudices that ~ his judgment>

be·come \bi-'kəm\ *vb* **-came** \-'kām\; **-come; -com·ing** [ME *becomen* to come to, become, fr. OE *becuman,* fr. *be-* + *cuman* to come] *vi* **1 a :** to come into existence **b :** to come to be <~ sick> **2 :** to undergo change or development ~ *vt* : to suit or be suitable to <her clothes ~ her> — **become of :** to happen to

be·com·ing \-'kəm-iŋ\ *adj* : SUITABLE, FITTING; *esp* : attractively suitable — **be·com·ing·ly** \-iŋ-lē\ *adv*

[1]**bed** \ˈbed\ *n* [ME, fr. OE *bedd;* akin to OHG *betti* bed, L *fodere* to dig] **1 a :** a piece of furniture on or in which one may lie and sleep **b (1) :** a place of marital sex relations **(2) :** marital relationship **c :** a place for sleeping **d :** SLEEP; *also* **:** a time for sleeping <took a walk before ~> **e (1) :** a mattress filled with soft material **(2) :** BEDSTEAD **f :** the equipment and services needed to care for one hospitalized patient or hotel guest **2 :** a flat or level surface: as **a :** a plot of ground prepared for plants; *also* **:** the plants grown in such a plot **b :** the bottom of a body of water; *esp* **:** an area of sea bottom supporting a heavy growth of a particular organism <an oyster ~> **3 :** a supporting surface or structure **:** FOUNDATION; *esp* **:** the earthwork that supports the ballast and track of a railroad **4 :** LAYER, STRATUM **5 a :** the place or material in which a block or brick is laid **b :** the lower surface of a brick, slate, or tile **6 :** a mass or heap resembling a bed <a ~ of ashes> — **in bed :** in the act of sexual intercourse

[2]**bed** *vb* **bed·ded; bed·ding** *vt* **1 a :** to furnish with a bed or bedding **:** settle in sleeping quarters — often used with *down* **b :** to put, take, or send to bed **2 a :** EMBED **b :** to plant or arrange in beds **c :** BASE, ESTABLISH **3 a :** to lay flat or in a layer **b :** to make a bed in or of ~ *vi* **1 a :** to find or make sleeping accommodations **b :** to go to bed **2 :** to form a layer **3 :** to lie flat or flush

BEd *abbr* bachelor of education

be·dab·ble \bi-ˈdab-əl\ *vt* **:** to wet or soil by dabbling

be·daub \bi-ˈdȯb, -ˈdäb\ *vt* **1 :** to daub over **:** BESMEAR **2 :** to ornament with vulgar excess

be·daz·zle \bi-ˈdaz-əl\ *vt* **1 :** to confuse by a strong light **:** DAZZLE **2 :** to impress forcefully **:** ENCHANT — **be·daz·zle·ment** \-mənt\ *n*

bed board *n* **:** a stiff thin wide board inserted usu. between bedspring and mattress esp. to give support to one's back or to protect a mattress from sagging springs

bed·bug \ˈbed-ˌbəg\ *n* **:** a wingless bloodsucking bug (*Cimex lectularius*) sometimes infesting houses and esp. beds and feeding on human blood

bed·cham·ber \-ˌchām-bər\ *n* **:** BEDROOM

bed check *n* **:** a night inspection to check the presence of persons (as soldiers) required by regulations to be in bed or in quarters

bed·clothes \ˈbed-ˌklō(t͟h)z\ *n pl* **:** the covering (as sheets and blankets) used on a bed

bed·der \ˈbed-ər\ *n* **1 :** one that makes up beds **2 :** a bedding plant

[1]**bed·ding** \ˈbed-iŋ\ *n* [ME, fr. OE, fr. *bedd*] **1 :** BEDCLOTHES **2 :** a bottom layer **:** FOUNDATION **3 :** material to provide a bed for livestock **4 :** STRATIFICATION

[2]**bedding** *adj* [fr. gerund of [2]*bed*] **:** appropriate or adapted for culture in open-air beds

be·deck \bi-ˈdek\ *vt* **:** to clothe with finery **:** deck out

be·dev·il \bi-ˈdev-əl\ *vt* **1 :** to possess with or as if with a devil **2 :** to change for the worse **:** SPOIL **3 :** to drive frantic **:** HARASS **4 :** to confuse utterly **:** BEWILDER — **be·dev·il·ment** \-mənt\ *n*

be·dew \bi-ˈd(y)ü\ *vt* **:** to wet with or as if with dew

bed·fast \ˈbed-ˌfast\ *adj* **:** BEDRIDDEN

bed·fel·low \-ˌfel-(ˌ)ō, -ə(-w)\ *n* **1 :** one who shares a bed with another **2 :** a close associate **:** ALLY <political ~*s*>

Bed·ford cord \ˌbed-fərd-\ *n* [perh. fr. New *Bedford,* Massachusetts] **:** a clothing fabric with lengthwise ribs that resembles corduroy; *also* **:** the weave used in making this fabric

be·dight \bi-ˈdīt\ *vt* **be·dight·ed** *or* **bedight; be·dight·ing** *archaic* **:** EQUIP, ARRAY

be·dim \bi-ˈdim\ *vt* **1 :** to make less bright **2 :** to make indistinct **:** OBSCURE

Bed·i·vere \ˈbed-ə-ˌvi(ə)r\ *n* **:** a knight of the Round Table

be·di·zen \bi-ˈdīz-ᵊn, -ˈdiz-\ *vt* **:** to dress or adorn with gaudy finery — **be·di·zen·ment** \-mənt\ *n*

bed·lam \ˈbed-ləm\ *n* [*Bedlam,* popular name for the Hospital of St. Mary of Bethlehem, London, an insane asylum, fr. ME *Bedlem* Bethlehem] **1** *obs* **:** MADMAN, LUNATIC **2** *archaic* **:** a lunatic asylum **3 :** a place, scene, or state of uproar and confusion — **bedlam** *adj*

bed·lam·ite \-lə-ˌmīt\ *n* **:** MADMAN, LUNATIC — **bedlamite** *adj*

Bed·ling·ton terrier \ˌbed-liŋ-tən-\ *n* [*Bedlington,* England] **:** a swift rough-coated terrier of light build usu. groomed to resemble a lamb

bed·mate \ˈbed-ˌmāt\ *n* **:** one who shares one's bed; *esp* **:** a sexual partner

bed molding *n* **:** the molding of a cornice below the corona and above the frieze; *also* **:** a molding below a deep projection

bed of roses : a place or situation of agreeable ease

bed·ou·in *or* **bed·u·in** \ˈbed(-ə)-wən\ *n, pl* **bedouin** *or* **bedouins** *or* **beduin** *or* **beduins** *often cap* [F *bédouin,* fr. Ar *badāwī, bidwān,* pl. of *badawi* desert dweller] **:** a nomadic Arab of the Arabian, Syrian, or No. African deserts

bed·pan \ˈbed-ˌpan\ *n* **:** a shallow vessel used by a person in bed for urination or defecation

bed·plate \-ˌplāt\ *n* **:** a plate or framing used as a support

bed·post \-ˌpōst\ *n* **:** the usu. turned or carved post of a bed

be·drag·gle \bi-ˈdrag-əl\ *vt* **:** to wet thoroughly

be·drag·gled \bi-ˈdrag-əld\ *adj* **1 :** left wet and limp by or as if by rain **2 :** soiled and stained by or as if by trailing in mud **3 :** DILAPIDATED <~ buildings>

bed·rid·den \ˈbed-ˌrid-ᵊn\ *or* **bed·rid** \-ˌrid\ *adj* [alter. of ME *bedrede, bedreden,* fr. OE *bedreda,* fr. *bedreda* one confined to bed, fr. *bedd* bed + *-rida, -reda* rider, fr. *rīdan* to ride] **:** confined (as by illness) to bed

bed·rock \-ˈräk, -ˌräk\ *n* **1 :** the solid rock underlying unconsolidated surface materials (as soil) **2 a :** lowest point **:** NADIR **b :** BASIS — **bedrock** *adj*

bed·roll \-ˌrōl\ *n* **:** bedding rolled up for carrying

[1]**bed·room** \-ˌrüm, -ˌrům\ *n* **:** a room furnished with a bed and intended primarily for sleeping

[2]**bed·room** *adj* **1 :** dealing with, suggestive of, or inviting to sexual relations <a ~ farce> <~ eyes> **2 :** inhabited or used by commuters <~ suburbs>

Beds *abbr* Bedfordshire

[1]**bed·side** \ˈbed-ˌsīd\ *n* **:** the side of a bed **:** a place beside a bed

[2]**bedside** *adj* **1 :** of, relating to, or conducted at the bedside <a ~ diagnosis> **2 :** suitable for a bedridden person <~ reading>

bedside manner *n* **:** the manner that a physician assumes toward his patients

bed–sit·ter \ˈbed-ˌsit-ər\ *n* [*bed*room + *sit*ting room + *-er*] *Brit* **:** a one-room apartment serving as both bedroom and sitting room — called also *bed-sit, bed-sitting-room*

bed·so·nia \bed-ˈsō-nē-ə\ *n* [NL, fr. Sir Samuel P. *Bedson* †1969 E bacteriologist] **:** any of a group of viruses associated with some forms of arthritis in man and causing various infections in animals

bed·sore \ˈbed-ˌsō(ə)r, -ˌsȯ(ə)r\ *n* **:** an ulceration of tissue deprived of nutrition by prolonged pressure

bed·spread \-ˌspred\ *n* **:** a usu. ornamental cloth cover for a bed

bed·spring \-ˌspriŋ\ *n* **:** a spring supporting a mattress

bed·stead \-ˌsted, -ˌstid\ *n* **:** the framework of a bed

bed·straw \-ˌstrȯ\ *n* [fr. its use for mattresses] **:** any of a genus (*Galium*) of herbs of the madder family having angled stems, opposite or whorled leaves, and small flowers

bed table *n* **1 :** a small table used beside a bed **2 :** an adjustable table used (as for eating or writing) by a person in bed

bed·time \-ˌtīm\ *n* **:** a time for going to bed

bedtime story *n* **:** a simple story for young children that often deals with animals

bed warmer *n* **:** a covered pan containing hot coals used to warm a bed

bed–wet·ting \-ˌwet-iŋ\ *n* **:** enuresis esp. when occurring in bed during sleep —**bed wetter** *n*

[1]**bee** \ˈbē\ *n* [ME, fr. OE *bēo;* akin to OHG *bīa* bee, Lith *bitis*] **1 :** a social colonial hymenopterous insect (*Apis mellifera*) often kept in hives for the honey that it produces; *broadly* **:** any of numerous insects (superfamily Apoidea) that differ from the related wasps esp. in the heavier hairier body and in having sucking as well as chewing mouthparts, that feed on pollen and nectar, and that store both and often also honey **2 :** an eccentric notion **:** FANCY **3** [perh. fr. E dial. *been* help given by neighbors, fr. ME *bene* prayer, boon, fr. OE *bēn* prayer — more at BOON] **:** a gathering of people for a specific purpose <spelling ~> — **bee·like** \-ˌlīk\ *adj* — **bee in one's bonnet :** [1]BEE 2

[2]**bee** *n* [ME *beghe* metal ring, fr. OE *bēag;* akin to OE *būgan* to bend — more at BOW] **:** a piece of hard wood at the side of a bowsprit to reeve fore-topmast stays through

[3]**bee** *n* **:** the letter *b*

BEE *abbr* bachelor of electrical engineering

bee balm *n* **:** any of several mints (as monarda) attractive to bees; *esp* **:** OSWEGO TEA

bee·bee *var of* BB

bee·bread \ˈbē-ˌbred\ *n* **:** bitter yellowish brown pollen stored up in honeycomb cells and used mixed with honey by bees as food

beech \ˈbēch\ *n, pl* **beech·es** *or* **beech** [ME *beche,* fr. OE *bēce;* akin to OE *bōc* beech, OHG *buohha,* L *fagus,* Gk *phēgos* oak] **:** any of a genus (*Fagus* of the family Fagaceae, the beech family) of hardwood trees with smooth gray bark and small edible nuts; *also* **:** its wood — **beech·en** \ˈbē-chən\ *adj*

beech·drops \ˈbēch-ˌdräps\ *n pl but sing or pl in constr* **:** a low wiry plant (*Epifagus virginiana*) of the broomrape family parasitic on the roots of beeches

beech·nut \-ˌnət\ *n* **:** the nut of the beech

beef 1: *A* wholesale cuts: *1* shank, *2* round with rump and shank cut off, *3* rump, *4* sirloin, *5* short loin, *6* flank, *7* rib, *8* chuck, *9* plate, *10* brisket, *11* shank; *B* retail cuts: *a* heel pot roast, *b* round steak, *c* rump roast, *d* sirloin steak, *e* pinbone steak, *f* short ribs, *g* porterhouse steak, *h* T-bone steak, *i* club steak, *j* flank steak, *k* rib roast, *m* blade rib roast, *n* plate, *o* brisket, *p* crosscut shank, *q* arm pot roast, *r* boneless neck, *s* blade roast

bee eater *n* **:** any of a family (Meropidae) of brightly colored slender-billed insectivorous chiefly tropical Old World birds

[1]**beef** \ˈbēf\ *n, pl* **beefs** \ˈbēfs\ *or* **beeves** \ˈbēvz\ [ME, fr. OF *buef* ox, beef, fr. L *bov-, bos* head of cattle — more at COW] **1 :** the flesh of an adult domestic bovine (as a steer or cow) when killed for food **2 a :** an ox, cow, or bull in a full-grown or nearly full-grown state; *esp* **:** a steer or cow fattened for food <quality Texas *beeves*> <a herd of good ~> **b :** a dressed carcass of a beef animal **3 :** muscular flesh **:** BRAWN **4** *pl* **beefs :** COMPLAINT

[2]**beef** *vt* **:** to add weight, strength, or power to — usu. used with *up* ~ *vi* **:** COMPLAIN

beef·cake \ˈbēf-ˌkāk\ *n* **:** a photographic display of muscular male physiques — compare CHEESECAKE

beef cattle *n pl* **:** cattle developed primarily for the efficient production of meat and marked by capacity for rapid growth, heavy well-fleshed body, and stocky build

beef·eat·er \ˈbē-ˌfēt-ər\ *n* **:** a yeoman of the guard of an English monarch

bee fly *n* **:** any of numerous two-winged flies (family Bombyliidae) many of which resemble bees

beef·steak \'bēf-ˌstāk\ *n* : a steak of beef usu. from the hindquarter

beefsteak fungus *n* : a bright red edible pore fungus (*Fistulina hepatica*) that grows on dead trees

beef Stro·ga·noff \-'strȯ-gə-ˌnȯf, -'strō-\ *n* [Count Paul *Stroganoff*, 19th cent. Russ diplomat] : beef sliced thin and cooked in a sour-cream sauce

beef·wood \'bēf-ˌwu̇d\ *n* : any of several hard heavy reddish chiefly tropical woods used esp. for cabinetwork; *also* : a tree (as a casuarina) yielding beefwood

beefy \'bē-fē\ *adj* **beef·i·er; -est** **1** : full of beef **2** : BRAWNY, POWERFUL

bee·hive \'bē-ˌhīv\ *n* **1** : HIVE 1 **2** : something resembling a hive for bees: as **a** : a scene of crowded activity **b** : a conically shaped woman's hairdo — **beehive** *adj*

bee·keep·er \-ˌkē-pər\ *n* : one who raises bees — **bee·keep·ing** *n*

bee·line \-ˌlīn\ *n* [fr. the belief that nectar-laden bees return to their hives in a direct line] : a straight direct course

Beel·ze·bub \bē-'el-zi-ˌbəb, 'bel-zi-, 'bel-\ *n* [*Beelzebub*, prince of devils, fr. L, fr. Gk *Beelzeboub*, fr. Heb *Ba'al zĕbhūbh*, a Philistine god, lit., lord of flies] **1** : DEVIL **2** : a fallen angel in Milton's *Paradise Lost* ranking next to Satan

been *past part of* BE

1beep \'bēp\ *n* [imit.] : a sound (as from a horn or an electronic device) that serves as a signal or warning

2beep *vi* **1** : to sound a horn **2** : to make a beep ~ *vt* : to cause (as a horn) to sound — **beep·er** *n*

beer \'bi(ə)r\ *n* [ME *ber*, fr. OE *bēor*; akin to OHG *bior* beer] **1** : a malted and hopped somewhat bitter alcoholic beverage; *specif* : such a beverage brewed by slow fermentation **2** : a carbonated nonalcoholic or a fermented slightly alcoholic beverage with flavoring from roots or other plant parts <birch ~>

beery \'bi(ə)r-ē\ *adj* **beer·i·er; -est** **1** : affected or caused by beer <~ voices> **2** : smelling or tasting of beer <~ tavern>

bees·tings *var of* BEASTINGS

bees·wax \'bēz-ˌwaks\ *n* : WAX 1

beet \'bēt\ *n* [ME *bete*, fr. OE *bēte*, fr. L *beta*] : a biennial garden plant (genus *Beta*) of the goosefoot family with thick long-stalked edible leaves and swollen root used as a vegetable, as a source of sugar, or for forage; *also* : its root

beet armyworm *n* : an armyworm (*Spodoptera exigua*) that eats the foliage of beets, alfalfa, and vegetables

1bee·tle \'bēt-ᵊl\ *n* [ME *betylle*, fr. OE *bitula*, fr. *bitan* to bite] **1** : any of an order (Coleoptera) of insects having four wings of which the outer pair are modified into stiff elytra that protect the inner pair when at rest **2** : any of various insects resembling a beetle

2beetle *n* [ME *betel*, fr. OE *bietel*; akin to OE *bēatan* to beat] **1** : a heavy wooden hammering or ramming instrument **2** : a wooden pestle or bat for domestic tasks **3** : a machine for giving fabrics a lustrous finish

3beetle *adj* [ME *bitel-browed* having overhanging brows, prob. fr. *betylle*, *bitel* beetle] : being prominent and overhanging <~ brows>

4beetle *vi* **bee·tled; bee·tling** \'bēt-liŋ, -ᵊl-iŋ\ : PROJECT, JUT <to scale the *beetling* crags —R. L. Stevenson>

beet leafhopper *n* : a leafhopper (*Eutettix tenellus*) that transmits a virus disease to sugar beets and other plants in the western U.S.

bee tree *n* : a hollow tree in which honeybees nest

beet·root \'bē-ˌtrüt\ *n*, *chiefly Brit* : the root of the beet

bef *abbr* before

BEF *abbr* British Expeditionary Force

be·fall \bi-'fȯl\ *vb* **-fell** \-'fel\; **-fall·en** \-'fȯ-lən\ *vi* : to happen esp. as if by fate ~ *vt* : to happen to

be·fit \bi-'fit\ *vt* : to be proper or becoming to

be·fit·ting \-'fit-iŋ\ *adj* **1** : SUITABLE, APPROPRIATE **2** : PROPER, DECENT — **be·fit·ting·ly** \-iŋ-lē\ *adv*

be·fog \bi-'fȯg, -'fäg\ *vt* **1** : to make foggy : OBSCURE **2** : CONFUSE

be·fool \bi-'fül\ *vt* **1** : to make a fool of **2** : DELUDE, DECEIVE

1be·fore \bi-'fō(ə)r, -'fȯ(ə)r\ *adv* [ME, adv. & prep., fr. OE *beforan*, fr. *be-* + *foran* before, fr. *fore*] **1** : in advance : AHEAD **2** : at an earlier time : PREVIOUSLY

2before *prep* **1 a** (1) : in front of (2) : in the presence of <stood ~ the judge> **b** : under the jurisdiction or consideration of <the case ~ the court> **c** (1) : at the disposal of (2) : in store for **2** : preceding in time : earlier than **3** : in a higher or more important position than <put quantity ~ quality>

3before *conj* **1** : earlier than the time when **2** : sooner than

be·fore·hand \bi-'fō(ə)r-ˌhand, -'fȯ(ə)r-\ *adv or adj* **1 a** : in anticipation **b** : in advance **2** : ahead of time : EARLY — **be·fore·hand·ed·ness** \-ˌhan-dəd-nəs, -'han-\ *n*

be·fore·time \-ˌtīm\ *adv*, *archaic* : FORMERLY

be·foul \bi-'fau̇(ə)l\ *vt* : to make foul with or as if with dirt or filth

be·friend \bi-'frend\ *vt* : to act as a friend to

be·fud·dle \bi-'fəd-ᵊl\ *vt* **1** : to muddle or stupefy with or as if with drink **2** : CONFUSE, PERPLEX — **be·fud·dle·ment** \-mənt\ *n*

1beg \'beg\ *vb* **begged; beg·ging** [ME *beggen*] *vt* **1** : to ask for as a charity **2** : to ask earnestly for : ENTREAT **3 a** : EVADE, SIDESTEP <*begged* the real problems> **b** : to assume as established or proved <~ the question> ~ *vi* **1** : to ask for alms **2** : to ask earnestly <*begged* for mercy>
syn BEG, ENTREAT, BESEECH, IMPLORE, SUPPLICATE, ADJURE, IMPORTUNE *shared meaning element* : to ask or request urgently — **beg off** : to ask to be released from something

2beg *abbr* begin; beginning

be·gat \bi-'gat\ *archaic past of* BEGET

be·get \bi-'get\ *vt* **-got** \-'gät\; **-gotten** \-'gät-ᵊn\ *or* **-got; -get·ting** [ME *begeten*, alter. of *beyeten*, fr. OE *bigietan* — more at GET] **1** : to procreate as the father : SIRE **2** : to produce as an effect : CAUSE — **be·get·ter** *n*

1beg·gar \'beg-ər\ *n* [ME *beggere*, *beggare*, fr. *beggen* to beg + *-ere*, *-are* -er] **1** : one that begs; *esp* : one that lives by asking for gifts **2** : PAUPER **3** : FELLOW

2beggar *vt* **beg·gared; beg·gar·ing** \'beg-(ə-)riŋ\ **1** : to reduce to beggary **2** : to exceed the resources or abilities of <~*s* description>

beg·gar·ly \'beg-ər-lē\ *adj* **1** : befitting or resembling a beggar; *esp* : marked by extreme poverty **2** : contemptibly mean, scant, petty, or paltry *syn* see CONTEMPTIBLE — **beg·gar·li·ness** *n*

beg·gar's-lice \'beg-ərz-ˌlīs\ *or* **beg·gar-lice** \-ər-ˌlīs\ *n pl but sing or pl in constr* : any of several plants (as of the genera *Lappula*, *Hackelia*, and *Desmodium*) with prickly or adhesive fruits; *also* : one of these fruits

beg·gar-ticks *or* **beg·gar's-ticks** \-ˌtiks\ *n pl but sing or pl in constr* **1** : BUR MARIGOLD; *also* : its prickly achenes **2** : BEGGAR'S-LICE

beg·gar·weed \'beg-ər-ˌwēd\ *n* **1** : any of various plants (as a knotgrass, spurry, or dodder) that grow in waste ground **2** : any of several tick trefoils (genus *Desmodium*); *esp* : a West Indian forage plant (*D. tortuosum*) cultivated in the southern U.S.

beg·gary \'beg-ə-rē\ *n*, *pl* **-gar·ies** **1** : POVERTY, PENURY **2** : the class or occupation of beggars **3** : the act of begging : MENDICANCY

be·gin \bi-'gin\ *vb* **be·gan** \-'gan\; **be·gun** \-'gən\; **be·gin·ning** [ME *beginnen*, fr. OE *beginnan*; akin to OHG *biginnan* to begin, OE *onginnan*] *vi* **1 a** : to do the first part of an action : START **b** : to undergo initial steps **2 a** : to come into existence : ARISE **b** : to have a starting point **3** : to do or succeed in the least degree ~ *vt* **1** : to set about the activity of **2 a** : to call into being : FOUND **b** : ORIGINATE, INVENT **3** : to come first in
syn BEGIN, COMMENCE, START, INITIATE, INAUGURATE *shared meaning element* : to take the first step (as in a course, process, or operation) *ant* end

be·gin·ner \bi-'gin-ər\ *n* : one that begins something; *specif* : an inexperienced person

1be·gin·ning \bi-'gin-iŋ\ *n* **1** : the point at which something begins : START **2** : the first part **3** : ORIGIN, SOURCE **4 a** : a rudimentary stage or early period — usu. used in pl. **b** : something undeveloped or incomplete

2beginning *adj* **1** : just created or formed : INCIPIENT **2** : INTRODUCTORY, EARLY **3** : BASIC <~ chemistry> **4** : just becoming familiar with the rudiments or practice <a ~ machinist>

beginning rhyme *n* **1** : rhyme at the beginning of successive lines of verse **2** : ALLITERATION

be·gird \bi-'gərd\ *vt* **1** : GIRD 1a **2** : SURROUND, ENCOMPASS

be·gone \bi-'gȯn *also* -'gän\ *vi* [ME, fr. *be gone* (imper.)] : to go away : DEPART — used esp. in the imperative

be·go·nia \bi-'gōn-yə\ *n* [NL, genus name, fr. Michel *Bégon* †1710 F governor of Santo Domingo] : any of a large genus (*Begonia* of the family Begoniaceae, the begonia family) of tropical herbs having asymmetrical leaves and being widely cultivated as ornamentals

be·gor·ra \bi-'gȯr-ə, -'gär-\ *interj* [euphemism for *by God*] *Irish* — used as a mild oath

be·grime \bi-'grīm\ *vt* **be·grimed; be·grim·ing** **1** : to make dirty with grime **2** : SULLY, CORRUPT

be·grudge \bi-'grəj\ *vt* **1** : to give or concede reluctantly **2 a** : to look upon with reluctance or disapproval **b** : to take little pleasure in : be annoyed by **3** : to envy the pleasure or enjoyment of — **be·grudg·er** *n* — **be·grudg·ing·ly** \-'grəj-iŋ-lē\ *adv*

be·guile \bi-'gī(ə)l\ *vb* **be·guiled; be·guil·ing** *vt* **1** : to lead by deception **2 a** : HOODWINK **b** : to deprive by guile : CHEAT **3** : to while away esp. by some agreeable occupation **4** : to please or persuade by the use of wiles : CHARM ~ *vi* : to deceive by wiles *syn* see DECEIVE, WHILE — **be·guile·ment** \-'gī(ə)l-mənt\ *n* — **be·guil·er** \-'gī-lər\ *n* — **be·guil·ing·ly** \-'gī-liŋ-lē\ *adv*

be·guine \bi-'gēn\ *n* [AmerF *béguine*, fr. F *béguin* flirtation] : a vigorous popular dance of the islands of Saint Lucia and Martinique that somewhat resembles the rumba

Be·guine \'bā-ˌgēn, ˌbā-'\ *n* [MF] : a member of one of various ascetic and philanthropic communities of women not under vows founded chiefly in the Netherlands in the 13th century

be·gum \'bā-gəm, 'bē-\ *n* [Hindi *begam*] : a Muslim woman of high rank

be·half \bi-'haf, -'häf\ *n* [ME, fr. *by* + *half* half, side] : INTEREST, BENEFIT; *also* : SUPPORT, DEFENSE <argued in his ~> — **in behalf of** *or* **on behalf of** : in the interest of : as a representative of

be·have \bi-'hāv\ *vb* **be·haved; be·hav·ing** [ME *behaven*, fr. *be-* + *haven* to have, hold] *vt* **1** : to bear or comport (oneself) in a particular way **2** : to conduct (oneself) in a proper manner ~ *vi* **1** : to act, function, or react in a particular way **2** : to conduct oneself properly — **be·hav·er** *n*
syn BEHAVE, CONDUCT, COMPORT, DEPORT, ACQUIT *shared meaning element* : to act or to cause or allow (oneself) to act in a particular way *ant* misbehave

be·hav·ior \bi-'hā-vyər\ *n* [alter. of ME *behavour*, fr. *behaven*] **1** : the manner of conducting oneself **2 a** : anything that an organism does involving action and response to stimulation **b** : the response of an individual, group, or species to its environment **3** : the way in which something (as a machine) behaves — **be·hav·ior·al** \-vyə-rəl\ *adj* — **be·hav·ior·al·ly** \-rə-lē\ *adv*

behavioral science *n* : a science (as psychology, sociology, or anthropology) dealing with human action and seeking generalizations of man's behavior in society — **behavioral scientist** *n*

be·hav·ior·ism \bi-'hā-vyə-ˌriz-əm\ *n* : a doctrine holding that the proper concern of psychology is the objective evidence of behavior and that consciousness and mind cannot be meaningfully defined or studied — **be·hav·ior·ist** \-vyə-rəst\ *adj or n* — **be·hav·ior·is·tic** \-ˌhā-vyə-'ris-tik\ *adj*

be·hav·iour *chiefly Brit var of* BEHAVIOR

be·head \bi-'hed\ *vt* : to cut off the head of : DECAPITATE

be·he·moth \bi-'hē-məth, 'bē-ə-ˌmäth\ *n* [ME, fr. L, fr. Heb *běhēmōth*] **1** *often cap* : an animal described in Job 40:15–24 that is prob. the hippopotamus **2** : something of oppressive or monstrous size or power — **be·he·moth·ic** \ˌbē-ə-'mäth-ik\ *adj*

be·hest \bi-ˈhest\ *n* [ME, promise, command, fr. OE *behǣs* promise, fr. *behātan* to promise, fr. *be-* + *hātan* to command, promise — more at HIGHT] **1 :** an authoritative order **:** COMMAND **2 :** an urgent prompting <returned home at the ~ of his friends>

[1]**be·hind** \bi-ˈhīnd\ *adv* [ME *behinde*, fr. OE *behindan*, fr. *be-* + *hindan* from behind; akin to OE *hinder* behind — more at HIND] **1 a :** in the place, situation, or time that is being or has been departed from <stay ~> **b :** in, to, or toward the back <look ~> **2 a :** in a secondary or inferior position **b :** in arrears <~ in his payments> **c :** SLOW **3** *archaic* **:** still to come

[2]**behind** *prep* **1 a (1) :** in or to a place or situation in back of or to the rear of <look ~ you> <stayed ~ the troops> **(2) :** beyond in past time <left a great name ~ him> **b** — used as a function word to indicate something that lies between one thing (as an observer) and another <malice ~ the mask of friendship> **2** — used as a function word to indicate backwardness <~ his classmates in performance>, delay <~ schedule>, or deficiency <lagged ~ last year's sales> **3 a :** in the background of <the conditions ~ the strike> **b :** in a supporting position at the back of <solidly ~ their candidate> — **behind the times :** OLD-FASHIONED, OUT-OF-DATE

[3]**behind** *n* [[1]*behind*] **:** BUTTOCKS — sometimes considered vulgar

be·hind·hand \bi-ˈhīnd-ˌhand\ *adj* **1 :** being in arrears **2 a :** lagging behind the times **:** BACKWARD **b :** being in an inferior position **c :** being behind schedule ***syn*** see TARDY ***ant*** beforehand

behind-the-scenes *adj* **:** kept, made, or held in secret

be·hold \bi-ˈhōld\ *vb* **-held** \-ˈheld\; **-hold·ing** [ME *beholden* to keep, behold, fr. OE *behealdan*, fr. *be-* + *healdan* to hold] *vt* **1 :** to perceive through sight or apprehension **:** SEE **2 :** to gaze upon **:** OBSERVE ~ *vi* — used in the imperative esp. to call attention — **be·hold·er** *n*

be·hold·en \bi-ˈhōl-dən\ *adj* [ME, fr. pp. of *beholden*] **:** being under obligation for a favor or gift **:** INDEBTED

be·hoof \bi-ˈhüf\ *n* [ME *behof*, fr. OE *behōf*; akin to OE *hebban* to raise — more at HEAVE] **:** ADVANTAGE, PROFIT

be·hoove \bi-ˈhüv\ *or* **be·hove** \-ˈhōv\ *vb* **be·hooved** *or* **be·hoved; be·hoov·ing** *or* **be·hov·ing** [ME *behoven*, fr. OE *behōfian*, fr. *behōf*] *vt* **:** to be necessary, proper, or advantageous for <it ~*s* us to fight> ~ *vi* **:** to be necessary, fit, or proper

beige \ˈbāzh\ *n* [F] **1 :** cloth made of natural undyed wool **2 a :** a variable color averaging light grayish yellowish brown **b :** a pale to grayish yellow — **beige** *adj* — **beigy** \ˈbā-zhē\ *adj*

[1]**be·ing** \ˈbē-iŋ\ *n* **1 a :** the quality or state of having existence **b (1) :** something conceivable as existing **(2) :** something that actually exists **(3) :** the totality of existing things **c :** conscious existence **:** LIFE **2 :** the qualities that constitute an existent thing **:** ESSENCE; *esp* **:** PERSONALITY **3 :** a living thing; *esp* **:** PERSON

[2]**being** *adj* [prp. of *be*] **:** PRESENT — used in the phrase *for the time being*

Be·ja \ˈbā-jə\ *n, pl* **Beja 1 a :** a nomadic pastoral people living between the Nile and the Red sea **b :** a member of this people **2 :** the Cushitic language of the Beja people

bel \ˈbel\ *n* [Alexander Graham *Bell*] **:** ten decibels

be·la·bor \bi-ˈlā-bər\ *vt* **1 :** to work on or at to absurd lengths <~ the obvious> **2 a :** to beat soundly **b :** ASSAIL, ATTACK

be·la·bour *chiefly Brit var of* BELABOR

be·lat·ed \bi-ˈlāt-əd\ *adj* [pp. of *belate* (to make late)] **1 :** delayed beyond the usual time **2 :** existing or appearing past the normal or proper time — **be·lat·ed·ly** *adv* — **be·lat·ed·ness** *n*

be·laud \bi-ˈlȯd\ *vt* **:** to praise usu. to excess

[1]**be·lay** \bi-ˈlā\ *vb* [ME *beleggen* to beset, fr. OE *belecgan*, fr. *be-* + *lecgan* to lay] *vt* **1 a :** to secure (as a rope) by turns around a cleat, pin, or bitt **b :** to make fast **2 :** STOP **3 a :** to secure (a person) at the end of a rope **b :** to secure (a rope) to a person or object ~ *vi* **1 :** to be made fast **2 :** STOP, QUIT — used in the imperative <~ there> **3 :** to make a line fast by turns around a cleat, pin, or bitt

[2]**belay** *n* **1 :** the obtaining of a hold (as for a rope) during mountain climbing; *also* **:** a method of obtaining such a hold **2 :** something (as a projection of rock) to which a mountain climber's rope is anchored

bel can·to \ˌbel-ˈkän-(ˌ)tō\ *n* [It, lit., beautiful singing] **:** operatic singing originating in 17th century and 18th century Italy and stressing ease, purity, and evenness of tone production and an agile and precise vocal technique

belch \ˈbelch\ *vb* [ME *belchen*, fr. OE *bealcian*] *vi* **1 :** to expel gas suddenly from the stomach through the mouth **2 :** to erupt, explode, or detonate violently **3 :** to issue forth spasmodically **:** GUSH ~ *vt* **1 :** to eject or emit violently **2 :** to expel (gas) from the stomach suddenly **:** ERUCT — **belch** *n*

bel·dam *or* **bel·dame** \ˈbel-dəm\ *n* [ME *beldam* grandmother, fr. MF *bel* beautiful + ME *dam*] **:** an old woman; *esp* **:** HAG

be·lea·guer \bi-ˈlē-gər\ *vt* **-guered; -guer·ing** \-g(ə-)riŋ\ [D *belegeren*, fr. *be-* (akin to OE *be-*) + *leger* camp; akin to OHG *legar* bed — more at LAIR] **1 :** to surround with an army so as to prevent escape **:** BESIEGE **2 :** BESET, HARASS <~*ed* parents>

bel·em·nite \ˈbel-əm-ˌnīt\ *n* [F *bélemnite*, fr. Gk *belemnon* dart; akin to Gk *ballein* to throw — more at DEVIL] **:** a conical fossil shell of an extinct cephalopod (family Belemnitidae) — **bel·em·nit·ic** \ˌbel-əm-ˈnit-ik\ *adj*

bel es·prit \ˌbel-ə-ˈsprē, -e-\ *n, pl* **beaux es·prits** \ˌbō-ˌzes-ˈprē\ [F, lit., fine mind] **:** a person with a fine and gifted mind

bel·fry \ˈbel-frē\ *n, pl* **belfries** [ME *belfrey*, alter. of *berfrey*, fr. MF *berfrei*, deriv. of Gk *pyrgos phorētos* movable war tower] **1 :** a bell tower; *esp* **:** one surmounting or attached to another structure **2 :** a room in which a bell is hung in a tower **3 :** a cupola, turret, or framework for enclosing a bell

Belg *abbr* Belgian; Belgium

bel·ga \ˈbel-gə\ *n* [F, fr. L *Belga* Belgian] **:** a former Belgian monetary unit for use in foreign exchange equal to five francs

Bel·gae \ˈbel-ˌgī, -ˌjē\ *n pl* [L, pl. of *Belga*] **:** a people occupying northern France, Belgium, and England in Caesar's time — **Bel·gic** \-jik\ *adj*

Bel·gian \ˈbel-jən\ *n* **1 :** a native or inhabitant of Belgium **2 :** any of a Belgian breed of heavy usu. roan or chestnut draft horses — **Belgian** *adj*

Belgian hare *n* **:** any of a breed of slender dark-red domestic rabbits

Belgian Ma·li·nois \-ˌmal-ən-ˈwä\ *n* **:** any of a breed of squarely built working dogs closely related to the Belgian sheepdog and having relatively short straight hair with a dense undercoat — called also *Malinois*

Belgian sheepdog *n* **:** any of a breed of hardy black or gray dogs developed in Belgium esp. for herding sheep

Belgian Ter·vu·ren \-(ˌ)tər-ˈvyůr-ən, -ter-\ *n* [*Tervuren*, commune in Brabant, Belgium] **:** any of a breed of working dogs closely related to the Belgian sheepdog but having abundant long straight fawn-colored hair with black tips

Bel·go- \ˈbel-(ˌ)gō\ *comb form* [*Belgian*] **:** Belgian and <*Belgo-English*>

Be·lial \ˈbē-lē-əl, ˈbēl-yəl\ *n* [Gk, fr. Heb *bĕlīya'al* worthlessness] **1** — a biblical name of the devil or one of the fiends **2 :** one of the fallen angels in Milton's *Paradise Lost*

be·lie \bi-ˈlī\ *vt* **-lied; -ly·ing 1 a :** to give a false impression of **b :** to contrast with **2 a :** to prove (something) false **b :** to run counter to **:** CONTRADICT ***syn*** see MISREPRESENT — **be·li·er** \-ˈlī(-ə)r\ *n*

be·lief \bə-ˈlēf\ *n* [ME *beleave*, prob. alter. of OE *gelēafa*, fr. *ge-*, associative prefix + *lēafa*; akin to OE *lȳfan*] **1 :** a state or habit of mind in which trust or confidence is placed in some person or thing **2 :** something believed; *specif* **:** a tenet or body of tenets held by a group **3 :** conviction of the truth of some statement or the reality of some being or phenomenon esp. when based on examination of evidence

syn **1** BELIEF, FAITH, CREDENCE, CREDIT *shared meaning element* **:** an assent or act of assenting to something offered for acceptance. BELIEF may suggest mental acceptance without directly implying certitude or certainty on the part of the believer <had the strongest *belief* in his own capacity for success> FAITH implies certitude and full trust and confidence in the source whether there be objective evidence or not <*faith* is the substance of things hoped for, the evidence of things not seen —Heb. 11:1 (AV)> CREDENCE implies intellectual acceptance but conveys nothing about the validity of the grounds for acceptance <give *credence* to rumors> CREDIT implies acceptance on grounds short of proof and especially on the past reputation of the source <what *credit* can be attached to an anonymous report?> ***ant*** unbelief, disbelief
2 see OPINION

be·liev·able \-ˈlē-və-bəl\ *adj* **:** capable of being believed esp. as within the range of known possibility or probability ***syn*** see PLAUSIBLE ***ant*** unbelievable — **be·liev·abil·i·ty** \-ˌlē-və-ˈbil-ət-ē\ *n* — **be·liev·ably** \-ˈlē-və-blē\ *adv*

be·lieve \bə-ˈlēv\ *vb* **be·lieved; be·liev·ing** [ME *beleven*, fr. OE *belēfan*, fr. *be-* + *lȳfan*, *lēfan* to allow, believe; akin to OHG *gilouben* to believe, OE *lēof* dear — more at LOVE] *vi* **1 a :** to have a firm religious faith **b :** to accept trustfully and on faith <people who ~ in the natural goodness of man> **2 :** to have a firm conviction as to the reality or goodness of something <~ in exercise> **3 :** to hold an opinion **:** THINK ~ *vt* **1 :** to consider to be true or honest <~ the reports> **2 :** to hold as an opinion **:** SUPPOSE <I ~ it will rain soon> ***syn*** see KNOW — **be·liev·er** *n*

be·like \bi-ˈlīk\ *adv, archaic* **:** most likely **:** PROBABLY

be·lit·tle \bi-ˈlit-ᵊl\ *vt* **-lit·tled; -lit·tling** \-ˈlit-ᵊl-iŋ, -ˈlit-liŋ\ **1 :** to cause (a person or thing) to seem little or less **2 :** DISPARAGE **2** <~*s* her efforts> ***syn*** see DECRY ***ant*** aggrandize, magnify — **be·lit·tle·ment** \-ˈlit-ᵊl-mənt\ *n* — **be·lit·tler** \-ˈlit-ᵊl-ər, -ˈlit-lər\ *n*

be·live \bi-ˈlīv\ *adv* [ME *bilive*, fr. *by* + *live*, dat. of *lif* life] *Scot* **:** in due time **:** by and by

[1]**bell** \ˈbel\ *n* [ME *belle*, fr. OE; akin to OE *bellan* to roar — more at BELLOW] **1 :** a hollow metallic device that vibrates and gives forth a ringing sound when struck **2 :** the sounding of a bell as a signal **3 a :** a bell rung to tell the hour **b :** a stroke of such a bell esp. on shipboard **c :** the time so indicated **d :** a half hour period of a watch on shipboard indicated by the strokes of a bell — see SHIP'S BELLS table below **4 :** something having the form of a bell: as **a :** the corolla of a flower **b :** the flared end of a wind instrument **5 a :** a percussion instrument consisting of metal bars or tubes that when struck give out tones resembling bells — usu. used in pl. **b :** GLOCKENSPIEL

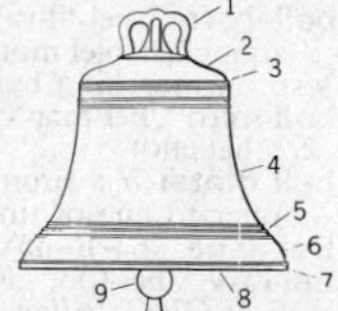

bell 1: *1* crown, *2* head, *3* shoulder, *4* waist, *5* bead lines, *6* sound bow, *7* lip, *8* mouth, *9* clapper

[2]**bell** *vt* **1 :** to provide with a bell **2 :** to make bell-mouthed ~ *vi* **:** to take the form of a bell **:** FLARE — **bell the cat :** to do a daring or risky deed

SHIP'S BELLS

NO. OF BELLS	HOUR (A.M. OR P.M.)		
1	12:30	4:30	8:30
2	1:00	5:00	9:00
3	1:30	5:30	9:30
4	2:00	6:00	10:00
5	2:30	6:30	10:30
6	3:00	7:00	11:00
7	3:30	7:30	11:30
8	4:00	8:00	12:00

[3]bell *vi* [ME *bellen,* fr. OE *bellan*] **:** to make a resonant bellowing or baying sound <the wild buck ~*s* from ferny brake —Sir Walter Scott>

[4]bell *n* **:** BELLOW, ROAR

bel·la·don·na \ˌbel-ə-ˈdän-ə\ *n* [It, lit., beautiful lady] **1 :** a European poisonous plant (*Atropa belladonna*) of the nightshade family having reddish bell-shaped flowers, shining black berries, and root and leaves that yield atropine — called also *deadly nightshade* **2 :** a medicinal extract (as atropine) from the belladonna plant

belladonna lily *n* **:** an amaryllis (*Amaryllis belladonna*) often cultivated for its fragrant usu. white or rose flowers

bell·bird \ˈbel-ˌbərd\ *n* **:** any of several birds whose notes suggest the sound of a bell

bell–bot·toms \ˈbel-ˈbät-əmz\ *n pl* **:** pants with wide flaring bottoms — **bell–bottom** *adj*

bell·boy \ˈbel-ˌbȯi\ *n* **:** BELLHOP

bell buoy *n* **:** a buoy with a bell that rings by the action of the waves

bell captain *n* **:** CAPTAIN 1h(2)

belle \ˈbel\ *n* [F, fr. fem. of *beau* beautiful — more at BEAU] **:** a popular and attractive girl or woman; *esp* **:** a girl or woman whose charm and beauty make her a favorite <the ~ of the ball>

Bel·leek \bə-ˈlēk\ *n* [*Belleek,* town in Northern Ireland] **:** a very thin translucent porcelain with a lustrous pearly glaze first produced in Ireland in the mid-nineteenth century — called also *Belleek china, Belleek ware*

Bel·ler·o·phon \bə-ˈler-ə-fən, -ˌfän\ *n* [L, fr. Gk *Bellerophōn*] **:** a legendary Greek hero noted for killing the Chimera

belles let·tres \bel-letrᵊ\ *n pl but sing in constr* [F, lit., fine letters] **:** literature that is an end in itself and not practical or purely informative; *specif* **:** light, entertaining, and often sophisticated literature

bel·le·trist \bel-ˈle-trəst\ *n* [*belles lettres*] **:** a writer of belles lettres — **bel·le·tris·tic** \ˌbel-ə-ˈtris-tik\ *adj*

bell·flow·er \ˈbel-ˌflau̇(-ə)r\ *n* **:** any of a genus (*Campanula* of the family Campanulaceae, the bellflower family) having an acrid juice, alternate leaves, and usu. showy bell-shaped flowers

bell·hop \-ˌhäp\ *n* [short for *bell-hopper*] **:** a hotel or club employee who escorts guests to rooms, assists them with luggage, and runs errands

bel·li·cose \ˈbel-i-ˌkōs\ *adj* [ME, fr. L *bellicosus,* fr. *bellicus* of war, fr. *bellum* war] **:** favoring or inclined to start quarrels or wars ***syn*** see BELLIGERENT ***ant*** pacific, amicable — **bel·li·cose·ly** *adv* — **bel·li·cose·ness** *n* — **bel·li·cos·i·ty** \ˌbel-i-ˈkäs-ət-ē\ *n*

-bel·lied \ˈbel-ēd\ *adj comb form* **:** having (such) a belly <a big-*bellied* man>

bel·lig·er·ence \bə-ˈlij(-ə)-rən(t)s\ *n* **:** an aggressive or truculent attitude, atmosphere, or disposition

bel·lig·er·en·cy \-rən-sē\ *n* **1 :** the state of being at war or in conflict; *specif* **:** the status of a legally recognized belligerent **2 :** BELLIGERENCE

bel·lig·er·ent \-rənt\ *adj* [modif. of L *belligerant-, belligerans,* prp. of *belligerare* to wage war, fr. *belliger* waging war, fr. *bellum* + *gerere* to wage — more at CAST] **1 :** waging war; *specif* **:** belonging to or recognized as a state at war and protected by and subject to the laws of war **2 :** inclined to or exhibiting assertiveness, hostility, or combativeness — **belligerent** *n* — **bel·lig·er·ent·ly** *adv*

syn BELLIGERENT, BELLICOSE, PUGNACIOUS, COMBATIVE, QUARRELSOME, CONTENTIOUS *shared meaning element* **:** having or taking an aggressive or truculent attitude ***ant*** friendly

bell jar *n* **:** a bell-shaped usu. glass vessel designed to cover objects or to contain gases or a vacuum

bell–ly·ra \ˈbel-ˈlī-rə\ *or* **bell lyre** \-ˌlī(ə)r\ *n* [*lyra* fr. L, lyre] **:** a glockenspiel mounted in a portable lyre-shaped frame and used esp. in marching bands

bell·man \ˈbel-mən\ *n* **1 :** a man (as a town crier) who rings a bell **2 :** BELLHOP

bell metal *n* **:** bronze that consists usu. of three to four parts of copper to one of tin and that is used for making bells

Bel·lo·na \bə-ˈlō-nə\ *n* [L] **:** the Roman goddess of war

bel·low \ˈbel-(ˌ)ō, -ə(-w)\ *vb* [ME *belwen,* fr. OE *bylgian;* akin to OE & OHG *bellan* to roar, Skt *bhāsate* he talks] *vi* **1 :** to make the loud deep hollow sound characteristic of a bull **2 :** to shout in a deep voice ~ *vt* **:** BAWL <~*s* the orders> — **bellow** *n*

bel·lows \ˈbel-(ˌ)ōz, -əz\ *n pl but sing or pl in constr* [ME *bely, below, belwes* — more at BELLY] **1 :** an instrument or machine that by alternate expansion and contraction draws in air through a valve or orifice and expels it through a tube; *also* **:** any of various other blowers **2 :** LUNGS **3 :** the pleated expansible part in a camera

bell·pull \ˈbel-ˌpu̇l\ *n* **:** a handle or knob attached to a cord by which one rings a bell; *also* **:** the cord itself

bell push *n* **:** a button that is pushed to ring a bell

bells \ˈbelz\ *n pl* **:** BELL-BOTTOMS

bell tower *n* **:** a tower that supports or shelters a bell

bell·weth·er \ˈbel-ˈweth-ər, -ˌweth-\ *n* [ME, leading sheep of a flock, leader, fr. *belle* bell + *wether;* fr. the practice of belling the leader of a flock] **:** one that takes the lead or initiative **:** LEADER

bell·wort \ˈbel-ˌwərt, -ˌwȯ(ə)rt\ *n* **:** any of a small genus (*Uvularia*) of herbs of the lily family with yellow drooping bell-shaped flowers

[1]bel·ly \ˈbel-ē\ *n, pl* **bellies** [ME *bely* bellows, belly, fr. OE *belg* bag, skin; akin to OHG *balg* bag, skin, OE *blāwan* to blow] **1 a :** ABDOMEN 1 **b :** the undersurface of an animal's body; *also* **:** hide from this part **c :** WOMB, UTERUS **d :** the stomach and its adjuncts **2 :** an internal cavity **:** INTERIOR **3 :** appetite for food **4 :** a surface or object curved or rounded like a human belly **5 a :** the part of a sail that swells out when filled with wind **b :** the enlarged fleshy body of a muscle **c :** the side of a piece of printer's type having the nick

[2]belly *vb* **bel·lied; bel·ly·ing :** SWELL, FILL

[1]bel·ly·ache \ˈbel-ē-ˌāk\ *n* **:** pain in the abdomen and esp. in the bowels **:** COLIC

[2]bellyache *vi* **:** to complain whiningly or peevishly **:** find fault — **bel·ly·ach·er** *n*

bel·ly·band \ˈbel-ē-ˌband\ *n* **:** a band around or across the belly **:** as **a :** GIRTH 1 **b :** BAND 4b

belly button *n* **:** NAVEL 1

belly dance *n* **:** a usu. solo dance emphasizing movements of the belly — **belly dance** *vi* — **belly dancer** *n*

belly flop *n* **:** a dive (as into water or in coasting prone on a sled) in which the front of the body strikes flat against another surface — called also *belly flopper* — **belly flop** *vi*

bel·ly·ful \ˈbel-ē-ˌfu̇l\ *n* **:** an excessive amount <a ~ of advice>

bel·ly–land \-ˌland\ *vi* **:** to land an airplane on its undersurface without use of landing gear — **belly landing** *n*

belly laugh *n* **:** a deep hearty laugh

be·long \bi-ˈlȯŋ\ *vi* [ME *belongen,* fr. *be-* + *longen* to be suitable — more at LONG] **1 a :** to be suitable, appropriate, or advantageous <a telephone ~*s* in every home> **b :** to be in a proper situation <a man of his ability ~*s* in teaching> **2 a :** to be the property of a person or thing — used with *to* **b :** to be attached or bound by birth, allegiance, or dependency **c :** to be a member of a club or organization **3 :** to be an attribute, part, adjunct, or function of a person or thing <nuts and bolts ~ to a car> **4 :** to be properly classified

be·long·ing \-ˈlȯŋ-iŋ\ *n* **1 :** POSSESSION — usu. used in pl. **2 :** close or intimate relationship <a sense of ~>

Belo·rus·sian \ˌbel-ō-ˈrəsh-ən\ *n* **1 :** a native or inhabitant of Belorussia, U.S.S.R. **2 :** the Slavic language of the Belorussians — **Belorussian** *adj*

be·loved \bi-ˈləv(-ə)d\ *adj* [ME, fr. pp. of *beloven* to love, fr. *be-* + *loven* to love] **:** dearly loved — **beloved** *n*

[1]be·low \bi-ˈlō\ *adv* [*be-* + *low,* adj.] **1 :** in or to a lower place **2 a :** on earth **b :** in or to Hades or hell **3 :** on or to a lower floor or deck **4 :** in, to, or at a lower rank or number **5 :** lower on the same page or on a following page **6 :** under the surface of the water

[2]below *prep* **1 :** in or to a lower place than **:** UNDER **2 :** inferior to (as in rank) **3 :** not suitable to the rank of **:** BENEATH

[3]below *n* **:** something that is below

[4]below *adj* **:** written or discussed lower on the same page or on a following page

Bel Pa·ese \ˌbel-pä-ˈā-zə, -zē\ *trademark* — used for a mild soft creamy cheese in a firm rind

Bel·shaz·zar \bel-ˈshaz-ər\ *n* [Heb *Bēlshaṣṣar*] **:** a son of Nebuchadnezzar and king of Babylon

[1]belt \ˈbelt\ *n* [ME, fr. OE; akin to OHG *balz* belt; both fr. a prehistoric WGmc-NGmc word borrowed fr. L *balteus* belt] **1 a :** a strip of flexible material worn esp. around the waist **b :** a similar article worn as a corset or for protection or safety **2 :** a continuous band of tough flexible material for transmitting motion and power or conveying materials **3 :** an area characterized by some distinctive feature (as of culture, habitation, geology, or life forms); *esp* **:** one suited to a particular crop <the corn ~> — **belt·ed** \ˈbel-təd\ *adj* — **belt·less** \ˈbelt-ləs\ *adj* — **below the belt :** UNFAIRLY — **under one's belt :** in one's possession **:** as part of one's experience

[2]belt *vt* **1 a :** to encircle or fasten with a belt **b :** to strap on **2 a :** to beat with or as if with a belt **:** THRASH **b :** STRIKE, HIT **3 :** to mark with a band **4 :** to sing in a forceful manner or style <~*ing* out popular songs> ~ *vi* **:** to move or act in a vigorous or violent manner

[3]belt *n* **1 :** a jarring blow **:** WHACK **2 :** DRINK <a ~ of brandy>

Bel·tane \ˈbel-tən\ *n* [ME, fr. ScGael *bealltain*] **1 :** the first day of May in the old Scottish calendar **2 :** the Celtic May Day festival

belt highway *n* **:** BELTWAY

belt·ing \ˈbel-tiŋ\ *n* **1 :** BELTS **2 :** material for belts

Belts·ville Small White \ˈbelts-ˌvil-, -vəl-\ *n* [*Beltsville,* Md.] **:** a small white domestic turkey of a variety developed by the U.S. Department of Agriculture

belt tightening *n* **:** a reduction in spending

belt up *vi, Brit* **:** to shut up

belt·way \ˈbelt-ˌwā\ *n* **:** a highway skirting an urban area

be·lu·ga \bə-ˈlü-gə\ *n* [Russ, fr. *belyĭ* white; akin to Gk *phainein* to show — more at FANCY] **1 :** a white sturgeon (*Acipenser huso*) of the Black sea, Caspian sea, and their tributaries **2** [Russ *belukha,* fr. *belyĭ*] **:** a cetacean (*Delphinapterus leucas*) that is about 10 feet long and white when adult

bel·ve·dere \ˈbel-və-ˌdi(ə)r\ *n* [It, lit., beautiful view] **:** a structure (as a cupola or a summerhouse) designed to command a view

BEM *abbr* **1** bachelor of engineering of mines **2** British Empire Medal

be·ma \ˈbē-mə\ *n* [LL & LGk; LL, fr. LGk *bēma,* fr. Gk, step, tribunal, fr. *bainein* to go — more at COME] **:** the part of an Eastern church containing the altar — see BASILICA illustration

Bem·ba \ˈbem-bə\ *n, pl* **Bemba** *or* **Bembas 1 :** a member of a primarily agricultural Bantu-speaking people of northern Rhodesia **2 :** a Bantu language of the Bemba people

be·med·aled *or* **be·med·alled** \bi-ˈmed-ᵊld\ *adj* **:** wearing or decorated with medals

be·mire \bi-ˈmī(ə)r\ *vt* **1 :** to soil with mud or dirt **2 :** to drag through or sink in mire

be·moan \bi-ˈmōn\ *vt* **1 :** to express deep grief or distress over <implores their pity, and his pain ~*s* —John Dryden> **2 :** to regard with displeasure, disapproval, or regret ***syn*** see DEPLORE

be·mock \bi-ˈmäk, -ˈmȯk\ *vt, archaic* **:** MOCK

be·muse \bi-ˈmyüz\ *vt* **1 :** to make confused **:** BEWILDER **2 :** to cause to become lost in thought — **be·mus·ed·ly** \-ˈmyü-zəd-lē\ *adv* — **be·muse·ment** \-ˈmyüz-mənt\ *n*

[1]ben \ˈben\ *adv* [ME, fr. OE *binnan,* fr. *be-* + *innan* within, from within, fr. *in*] *Scot* **:** WITHIN

[2]ben \(ˈ)ben\ *prep, Scot* **:** WITHIN

[3]ben \ˈben\ *n, Scot* **:** the inner room or parlor of a 2-room cottage

Bence–Jones protein \ˌben(t)s-ˌjōnz-\ *n* [Henry *Bence-Jones* †1873 E physician and chemist] **:** a globulin or a group of globulins found in the blood serum and urine in multiple myeloma and occas. in other bone diseases

[1]**bench** \ˈbench\ *n* [ME, fr. OE *benc;* akin to OHG *bank* bench] **1 a :** a long seat for two or more persons **b :** a thwart in a boat **c (1) :** a seat on which the members of an athletic team await a turn or opportunity to play **(2) :** the reserve players on a team **2 a :** the seat where a judge sits in court **b :** the office or dignity of a judge **c :** the place where justice is administered : COURT **d :** the persons who sit as judges **3 a :** a seat for an official **b :** the office or dignity of such an official **c :** the officials occupying such a bench **4 a :** a long worktable **b :** a table forming part of a machine **5 :** TERRACE, SHELF; *esp* : a former wave-cut shore of a sea or lake or floodplain of a river **6 a :** a platform on which a dog is placed at a dog show **b :** a dog show

[2]**bench** *vt* **1 :** to furnish with benches **2 a :** to seat on a bench **b (1) :** to remove from or keep out of a game **(2) :** to remove from the starting lineup **3 :** to exhibit (dogs) on a bench ~ *vi* : to form a bench by natural processes

bench·er \ˈben-chər\ *n* : one who sits on or presides at a bench

bench mark *n* **1 :** a mark on a permanent object indicating elevation and serving as a reference in topographical surveys and tidal observations **2** *usu* **benchmark a :** a point of reference from which measurements may be made **b :** something that serves as a standard by which others may be measured

bench show *n* : an exhibition of small animals in competition for prizes on the basis of points of physical conformation and condition

bench warrant *n* : a warrant issued by a presiding judge or by a court against a person guilty of contempt or indicted for a crime

[1]**bend** \ˈbend\ *n* [ME, fr. MF *bende,* of Gmc origin; akin to OHG *binta, bant* band — more at BAND] **1 :** a diagonal band that runs from the dexter chief to the sinister base on a heraldic shield **2 :** the half of a butt or a hide trimmed of the thinner parts **3** [ME, band, fr. OE *bend* fetter — more at BAND] **:** a knot by which one rope is fastened to another or to some object

[2]**bend** *vb* **bent** \ˈbent\; **bend·ing** [ME *bendan,* fr. OE *bendan;* akin to OE *bend* fetter] *vt* **1 :** to constrain or strain to tension <~ a bow> **2 a :** to turn or force from straight or even to curved or angular **b :** to force back to an original straight or even condition **c :** to force from a proper shape **3 :** FASTEN <~ a sail to its yard> **4 :** to make submissive : SUBDUE **5 a :** to cause to turn from a straight course : DEFLECT **b :** to guide or turn toward : DIRECT **c :** INCLINE, DISPOSE **6 :** to direct strenuously or with interest : APPLY ~ *vi* **1 :** to curve out of a straight line or position; *specif* : to incline the body in token of submission **2 :** INCLINE, TEND **3 :** to apply oneself vigorously <~*ing* to their work> **4 :** to make concessions : COMPROMISE ***syn*** see CURVE — **bend over backwards :** to make extreme efforts at concession

[3]**bend** *n* **1 :** the act or process of bending **:** the state of being bent **2 :** something that is bent: as **a :** a curved part of a stream **b :** [1]WALE 2 — usu. used in pl. **3** *pl but sing or pl in constr* : CAISSON DISEASE <a case of the ~*s*> — **around the bend :** MAD, CRAZY <afraid his friend was going *around the bend*>

ben·day \ˈben-ˈdā\ *adj, often cap* [*Ben*jamin *Day* †1916 Am printer] : involving a process for adding shaded or tinted areas made up of dots for reproduction by line engraving — **benday** *vt*

bend·er \ˈben-dər\ *n* **1 :** one that bends **2 :** SPREE

bend sinister *n* : a diagonal bend that runs from the sinister chief to the dexter base on a heraldic shield

[1]**be·neath** \bi-ˈnēth\ *adv* [ME *benethe,* fr. OE *beneothan,* fr. *be-* + *neothan* below; akin to OE *nithera* nether] **1 :** in or to a lower position : BELOW **2 :** directly under : UNDERNEATH

[2]**beneath** *prep* **1 a :** in or to a lower position than : BELOW **b :** directly under **c :** at the foot of **2 :** not suitable to the rank of **:** unworthy of **3 :** under the control, pressure, or influence of

ben·e·dict \ˈben-ə-ˌdikt\ *n* [alter. of *Benedick,* character in Shakespeare's *Much Ado about Nothing*] : a newly married man who has long been a bachelor

Ben·e·dic·tine \ˌben-ə-ˈdik-tən, -ˌtēn\ *n* : a monk or a nun of one of the congregations following the rule of St. Benedict and devoted esp. to scholarship and liturgical worship — **Benedictine** *adj*

bene·dic·tion \ˌben-ə-ˈdik-shən\ *n* [ME *benediccioun,* fr. LL *benediction-, benedictio,* fr. *benedictus,* pp. of *benedicere* to bless, fr. L, to speak well of, fr. *bene* well + *dicere* to say — more at BOUNTY, DICTION] **1 :** an expression of good wishes **2 :** the invocation of a blessing; *esp* : the short blessing with which public worship is concluded **3** *often cap* : a Roman Catholic or Anglo-Catholic devotion including the exposition of the eucharistic Host in the monstrance and the blessing of the people with it **4 :** something that promotes goodness or well-being

bene·dic·to·ry \-ˈdik-t(ə-)rē\ *adj* : of or expressing benediction

Bene·dic·tus \-ˈdik-təs\ *n* [LL, blessed, fr. pp. of *benedicere;* fr. its first word] **1 :** a canticle from Mt 21:9 beginning "Blessed is he that cometh in the name of the Lord" **2 :** a canticle from Lk 1:68 beginning "Blessed be the Lord God of Israel"

bene·fac·tion \ˌben-ə-ˈfak-shən\ *n* [LL *benefaction-, benefactio,* fr. L *bene factus,* pp. of *bene facere* to do good to, fr. *bene* + *facere* to do — more at DO] **1 :** the act of benefiting **2 :** a benefit conferred; *esp* : a charitable donation

bene·fac·tor \ˈben-ə-ˌfak-tər\ *n* : one that confers a benefit; *esp* : one that makes a gift or bequest — **bene·fac·tress** \-trəs\ *n*

be·nef·ic \bə-ˈnef-ik\ *adj* [L *beneficus,* fr. *bene* + *facere*] : BENEFICENT

ben·e·fice \ˈben-ə-fəs\ *n* [ME, fr. MF, fr. ML *beneficium,* fr. L, favor, promotion, fr. *beneficus*] **1 :** an ecclesiastical office to which the revenue from an endowment is attached **2 :** a feudal estate in lands : FIEF — **benefice** *vt*

be·nef·i·cence \bə-ˈnef-ə-sən(t)s\ *n* [L *beneficentia,* fr. *beneficus*] **1 :** the quality or state of being beneficent **2 :** BENEFACTION

be·nef·i·cent \-sənt\ *adj* [back-formation fr. *beneficence*] **1 :** doing or producing good; *esp* : performing acts of kindness and charity **2 :** BENEFICIAL — **be·nef·i·cent·ly** *adv*

ben·e·fi·cial \ˌben-ə-ˈfish-əl\ *adj* [L *beneficium* favor, benefit] **1 :** conferring benefits : conducive to personal or social well-being **2 :** receiving or entitling one to receive advantage, use, or benefit <the ~ owner of an estate> <a ~ legacy> — **ben·e·fi·cial·ly** \-ˈfish-ə-lē\ *adv* — **ben·e·fi·cial·ness** *n*

syn BENEFICIAL, ADVANTAGEOUS, PROFITABLE *shared meaning element* : bringing good or gain ***ant*** harmful, detrimental

ben·e·fi·cia·ry \ˌben-ə-ˈfish-ē-ˌer-ē, -ˈfish-(ə-)rē\ *n, pl* **-ries 1 :** one that benefits from something <*beneficiaries* of government programs> **2 a :** the person designated to receive the income of a trust estate **b :** the person named (as in an insurance policy) to receive proceeds or benefits — **beneficiary** *adj*

ben·e·fi·ci·ate \-ˈfish-ē-ˌāt\ *vt* **-at·ed; -at·ing :** to treat (a raw material) so as to improve properties; *esp* : to prepare (iron ore) for smelting — **ben·e·fi·ci·a·tion** \-ˌfish-ē-ˈā-shən\ *n*

[1]**ben·e·fit** \ˈben-ə-ˌfit\ *n* [ME, fr. AF *benfet,* fr. L *bene factum,* fr. neut. of *bene factus*] **1** *archaic* : an act of kindness : BENEFACTION **2 a :** something that promotes well-being : ADVANTAGE **b :** useful aid : HELP **3 a :** financial help in time of sickness, old age or unemployment **b :** a payment or service provided for under an annuity, pension plan, or insurance policy **4 :** an entertainment or social event to raise funds for a person or cause

[2]**benefit** *vb* **-fit·ed** \-ˌfit-əd\ *or* **-fit·ted; -fit·ing** *or* **-fit·ting** *vt* : to be useful or profitable to <medicines that ~ mankind> ~ *vi* : to receive benefit — **ben·e·fit·er** \-ˌfit-ər\ *n*

benefit of clergy 1 : clerical exemption from trial in a civil court **2 :** the ministration or sanction of the church <a couple living together without *benefit of clergy*>

be·nev·o·lence \bə-ˈnev(-ə)-lən(t)s\ *n* **1 :** disposition to do good **2 a :** an act of kindness **b :** a generous gift **3 :** a compulsory levy by certain English kings with no other authority than the claim of prerogative

be·nev·o·lent \-lənt\ *adj* [ME, fr. L *benevolent-, benevolens,* fr. *bene* + *volent-, volens,* prp. of *velle* to wish — more at WILL] **1 a :** marked by or disposed to doing good <a ~ donor> **b :** organized for the purpose of doing good <a ~ society> **2 :** marked by or suggestive of goodwill <~ smiles> — **be·nev·o·lent·ly** *adv* — **be·nev·o·lent·ness** *n*

Ben·gal·ee \ben-ˈgȯl-ē, beŋ-\ *n* [Hindi *Baṅgālī* Bengali] : a native or resident of Bangladesh — **Bengalee** *adj*

Ben·gali \ben-ˈgȯ-lē, beŋ-\ *n* [Hindi *Baṅgālī,* fr. *Baṅgāl* Bengal] **1 :** a native or resident of Bengal **2 :** a native or inhabitant of Bangladesh **3 :** the modern Indic language of Bengal — **Bengali** *adj*

ben·ga·line \ˈbeŋ-gə-ˌlēn\ *n* [F, fr. *Bengal*] : a fabric with a crosswise rib made from textile fibers (as rayon, nylon, cotton, or wool) often in combination

Ben·gal light \ˌben-ˌgȯl-, ˌbeŋ-\ *n* **1 :** a blue light used formerly for signaling and illumination **2 :** any of various colored lights or flares

BEngr *abbr* bachelor of engineering

BEngS *abbr* bachelor of engineering science

be·night·ed \bi-ˈnīt-əd\ *adj* **1 :** overtaken by darkness or night **2 :** existing in a state of intellectual, moral, or social darkness : UNENLIGHTENED — **be·night·ed·ly** *adv* — **be·night·ed·ness** *n*

be·nign \bi-ˈnīn\ *adj* [ME *benigne,* fr. MF, fr. L *benignus,* fr. *bene* well + *gigni* to be born, pass. of *gignere* to beget — more at BOUNTY, KIN] **1 :** of a gentle disposition : GRACIOUS <a ~ teacher> **2 a :** showing kindness and gentleness <~ faces> **b :** FAVORABLE <a ~ climate> **3 :** of a mild character <~ tumor> ***syn*** see KIND ***ant*** malign — **be·nig·ni·ty** \-ˈnig-nət-ē\ *n* — **be·nign·ly** \-ˈnīn-lē\ *adv*

be·nig·nan·cy \bi-ˈnig-nən-sē\ *n* : benignant quality

be·nig·nant \-nənt\ *adj* [*benign* + *-ant* (as in *malignant*)] **1 :** serenely mild and kindly : BENIGN **2 :** FAVORABLE, BENEFICIAL <a ~ power> ***syn*** see KIND ***ant*** malignant — **be·nig·nant·ly** *adv*

ben·i·son \ˈben-ə-sən, -zən\ *n* [ME *beneson,* fr. OF *beneiçon,* fr. LL *benediction-, benedictio*] : BLESSING, BENEDICTION

Ben·ja·min \ˈbenj-(ə-)mən\ *n* [Heb *Binyāmīn*] : a son of Jacob and the traditional eponymous ancestor of one of the tribes of Israel

ben·ne *or* **ben·ni** \ˈben-ē\ *n* [of African origin; akin to Mandingo *bĕne* sesame] : SESAME 1

ben·ny \ˈben-ē\ *n, pl* **bennies** [*Ben*zedrine + *-ie*] *slang* : a tablet of amphetamine taken as a stimulant

[1]**bent** \ˈbent\ *n* [ME, grassy place, bent grass, fr. OE *beonot-;* akin to OHG *binuz* rush] **1 :** unenclosed grassland **2 a (1) :** a reedy grass **(2) :** a stalk of stiff coarse grass **b :** any of a genus (*Agrostis*) including important chiefly perennial and rhizomatous pasture and lawn grasses with fine velvety or wiry herbage

[2]**bent** *adj* [ME, fr. pp. of *benden* to bend] **1 :** changed by bending out of an original straight or even condition <~ twigs> **2 :** strongly inclined : DETERMINED <was ~ on winning>

[3]**bent** *n* [irreg. fr. [2]*bend*] **1 a :** a strong inclination or interest : BIAS **b :** a special inclination or capacity : TALENT **2 :** capacity of endurance **3 :** a transverse framework (as in a bridge) to carry lateral as well as vertical loads ***syn*** see GIFT

Ben·tham·ism \ˈben(t)-thə-ˌmiz-əm\ *n* : the utilitarian philosophy of Jeremy Bentham and his followers — **Ben·tham·ite** \-ˌmīt\ *n*

ben·thic \ˈben(t)-thik\ *or* **ben·thal** \-thəl\ *adj* [*benthos*] **1 :** of, relating to, or occurring at the bottom of a body of water **2 :** of, relating to, or occurring in the depths of the ocean

ben·thon·ic \ben-ˈthän-ik\ *adj* [irreg. fr. *benthos*] : BENTHIC

ben·thos \ˈben-ˌthäs\ *n* [NL, fr. Gk, depth, deep sea; akin to Gk *bathys* deep — more at BATHY-] : organisms that live on or in the bottom of bodies of water

ben·ton·ite \ˈbent-ᵊn-ˌīt\ *n* [Fort *Benton,* Montana] : an absorptive and colloidal clay used esp. as a filler (as in paper) or carrier (as of drugs) — **ben·ton·it·ic** \ˌbent-ᵊn-ˈit-ik\ *adj*

ə abut ᵊ kitten ər further a back ā bake ä cot, cart
au̇ out ch chin e less ē easy g gift i trip ī life
j joke ŋ sing ō flow ȯ flaw ȯi coin th thin t͟h this
ü loot u̇ foot y yet yü few yu̇ furious zh vision

ben tro·va·to \ˌben-trō-ˈvät-(ˌ)ō\ *adj* [It, lit., well found] : characteristic or appropriate but not true

bent·wood \ˈbent-ˌwu̇d\ *adj* : made of wood that is bent and not cut into shape <~ furniture>

be·numb \bi-ˈnəm\ *vt* [ME *benomen,* fr. *benomen, benome,* pp. of *benimen* to deprive, fr. OE *beniman,* fr. *be-* + *niman* to take — more at NIMBLE] **1** : to make inactive : DEADEN **2** : to make numb esp. by cold

benz- *or* **benzo-** *comb form* [ISV, fr. *benzoin*] : related to benzene or benzoic acid <*benzo*phenone> <*benz*yl>

benz·al·de·hyde \ben-ˈzal-də-ˌhīd\ *n* [G *benzaldehyd,* fr. *benz-* + *aldehyd* aldehyde] : a colorless nontoxic aromatic liquid C_6H_5CHO found in essential oils (as in peach kernels) and used in flavoring and perfumery, in pharmaceuticals, and in synthesis of dyes

benz·an·thra·cene \ben-ˈzan(t)-thrə-ˌsēn\ *n* [ISV] : a crystalline feebly carcinogenic cyclic hydrocarbon $C_{18}H_{12}$ that is found in small amounts in coal tar

Ben·ze·drine \ˈben-zə-ˌdrēn\ *trademark* — used for amphetamine

ben·zene \ˈben-ˌzēn, ben-ˈ\ *n* [ISV *benz-* + *-ene*] : a colorless volatile flammable toxic liquid aromatic hydrocarbon C_6H_6 used in organic synthesis, as a solvent, and as a motor fuel — called also *benzol* — **ben·ze·noid** \ˈben-zə-ˌnȯid\ *adj*

benzene ring *n* : a structural arrangement of atoms held to exist in benzene and other aromatic compounds and marked by six carbon atoms linked by alternate single and double bonds in a planar symmetrical hexagon with each carbon attached to hydrogen in benzene itself or to other atoms or groups in substituted benzenes — called also *benzene nucleus;* compare META- 4b, ORTH- 4b, PARA- 2b

formula for benzene ring

ben·zi·dine \ˈben-zə-ˌdēn\ *n* [prob. fr. G *benzidin,* fr. *benzin* + *-idin* -idine] : a crystalline base $C_{12}H_{12}N_2$ prepared from nitrobenzene and used esp. in making dyes

benz·imid·azole \ˌben-ˌzim-ə-ˈdaz-ˌōl, ˌben-zə-ˈmid-ə-ˌzōl\ *n* [ISV *benz-* + *imidazole*] : a crystalline base $C_7H_6N_2$ that inhibits the growth of various organisms (as some viruses); *also* : one of its derivatives

ben·zine \ˈben-ˌzēn, ben-ˈ\ *n* [G *benzin,* fr. *benz-*] **1** : BENZENE **2** : any of various volatile flammable petroleum distillates used esp. as solvents or as motor fuels

ben·zo·ate \ˈben-zə-ˌwāt\ *n* : a salt or ester of benzoic acid

benzoate of soda : SODIUM BENZOATE

ben·zo·caine \ˈben-zə-ˌkān\ *n* [ISV] : a white crystalline ester $C_9H_{11}NO_2$ used as a local anesthetic

ben·zo·fu·ran \ˌben-zō-ˈfyu̇(ə)r-ˌan, -fyu̇-ˈran\ *n* [*benz-* + *furan*] : COUMARONE

ben·zo·ic acid \ben-ˌzō-ik-\ *n* [ISV, fr. *benzoin*] : a white crystalline acid $C_7H_6O_2$ found naturally (as in benzoin or in cranberries) or made synthetically and used esp. as a preservative of foods, in medicine, and in organic synthesis

ben·zo·in \ˈben-zə-wən, -ˌwēn; -ˌzōin\ *n* [MF *benjoin,* fr. OCatal *benjuí,* fr. Ar *lubān jāwī,* lit., frankincense of Java] **1** : a hard fragrant yellowish balsamic resin from trees (genus *Styrax*) of southeastern Asia used esp. in medication, as a fixative in perfumes, and as incense **2** : a white crystalline hydroxy ketone $C_{14}H_{12}O_2$ made from benzaldehyde **3 a** : a tree yielding benzoin **b** : SPICEBUSH 1

ben·zol \ˈben-ˌzȯl, -ˌzōl\ *n* [G, fr. *benz-* + *ol*] : BENZENE; *also* : a mixture of benzene and other aromatic hydrocarbons

ben·zo·phe·none \ˌben-zō-fi-ˈnōn, -ˈfē-ˌnōn\ *n* [ISV] : a colorless crystalline ketone $C_{13}H_{10}O$ used chiefly in perfumery

ben·zo·py·rene \ˌben-zō-ˈpī(ə)r-ˌēn, -pī-ˈrēn\ *or* **benz·py·rene** \benz-ˈpī(ə)r-ˌēn, ˌbenz-pī-ˈrēn\ *n* [ISV] : a yellow crystalline cancer-producing hydrocarbon $C_{20}H_{12}$ found in coal tar

ben·zo·yl \ˈben-zə-ˌwil\ *n* [G, fr. *benzoësäure* benzoic acid + Gk *hylē* matter, lit., wood] : the radical C_6H_5CO of benzoic acid

ben·zyl \ˈben-ˌzēl, -zəl\ *n* [ISV *benz-* + *-yl*] : a univalent radical $C_6H_5CH_2$ derived from toluene — **ben·zyl·ic** \ben-ˈzil-ik\ *adj*

Be·o·wulf \ˈbā-ə-ˌwu̇lf\ *n* : a legendary Geatish warrior and hero of the Old English poem *Beowulf*

be·paint \bi-ˈpānt\ *vt, archaic* : TINGE

be·queath \bi-ˈkwēth, -ˈkwēth\ *vt* [ME *bequethen,* fr. OE *becwethan,* fr. *be-* + *cwethan* to say — more at QUOTH] **1** : to give or leave by will — used esp. of personal property **2** : to hand down : TRANSMIT <ideas *~ed* to us by the 19th century> — **be·queath·al** \-əl\ *n*

be·quest \bi-ˈkwest\ *n* [ME, irreg. fr. *bequethen*] **1** : the act of bequeathing **2** : something bequeathed : LEGACY

be·rate \bi-ˈrāt\ *vt* : to scold or condemn vehemently and at length ***syn*** see SCOLD

Ber·ber \ˈbər-bər\ *n* [Ar *Barbar*] **1** : a member of a Caucasoid people of northern Africa west of Tripoli **2 a** : a branch of the Afro-Asiatic language family comprising languages spoken by various tribal groups (as the Tuareg or the Kabyle) in northern Africa **b** : any one of these languages

ber·ber·ine \ˈbər-bə-ˌrēn\ *n* [G *berberin,* fr. NL *berberis* barberry root, fr. ML *barberis,* fr. Ar *barbāris*] : a bitter crystalline yellow alkaloid $C_{20}H_{19}NO_5$ obtained from the roots of various plants (as barberry) and used as a tonic and antiperiodic

ber·ceuse \be(ə)r-ˈsə(r)z\ *n, pl* **ber·ceuses** \-ˈsə(r)z(-əz)\ [F] **1** : LULLABY **2** : a musical composition of a tranquil nature

be·reave \bi-ˈrēv\ *vt* **-reaved** *or* **-reft** \-ˈreft\; **-reav·ing** [ME *bereven,* fr. OE *berēafian,* fr. *be-* + *rēafian* to rob — more at REAVE] **1** *archaic* : to deprive of something — usu. used with *of* <madam, you have *bereft* me of all words —Shak.> **2** *archaic* : to take away (a valued or necessary possession) esp. by force

¹be·reaved *adj* : suffering the death of a loved one <~ parents>

²bereaved *n, pl* **bereaved** : one who is bereaved

be·reave·ment \bi-ˈrēv-mənt\ *n* : the state or fact of being bereaved; *esp* : the loss of a loved one by death

be·reft \-ˈreft\ *adj* **1 a** : deprived or robbed of the possession or use of something — used with *of* <both players are instantly ~ of their poise —A. E. Wier> **b** : lacking something needed, wanted, or expected — used with *of* <the book is . . . completely ~ of an index —*Times Lit. Supp.*> **2** : BEREAVED <a ~ daughter mourning here on the heights —B. A. Williams>

Ber·e·ni·ce's Hair \ˌber-ə-ˌnī-sēz-\ *n* : COMA BERENICES

be·ret \bə-ˈrā\ *n* [F *berret,* fr. Prov — more at BIRETTA] : a visorless usu. woolen cap with a tight headband and a soft full flat top

berg \ˈbərg\ *n* : ICEBERG

ber·ga·mot \ˈbər-gə-ˌmät\ *n* [F *bergamote,* fr. It *bergamotta,* of Turkic origin; akin to Turk *bey-armudu* prince's pear] **1** : a pear-shaped orange (*Citrus bergamia*) whose rind yields an essential oil used in perfumery **2** : any of several mints (genus *Monarda*)

be·rib·boned \bi-ˈrib-ənd\ *adj* : adorned with ribbons

beri·beri \ˌber-ē-ˈber-ē\ *n* [Sinhalese *bæribæri*] : a deficiency disease marked by inflammatory or degenerative changes of the nerves, digestive system, and heart and caused by a lack of or inability to assimilate thiamine

Be·ring time \ˈbi(ə)r-iŋ-, ˈbe(ə)r-\ *n* [*Bering* sea] : the time of the 11th time zone west of Greenwich that includes western Alaska and the Aleutian islands

Berke·le·ian *or* **Berke·ley·an** \ˈbär-klē-ən, ˈbər-; bär-ˈ, ˌbər-ˈ\ *adj* : of, relating to, or suggestive of Bishop Berkeley or his system of philosophical idealism — **Berkeleian** *n* — **Berke·le·ian·ism** \-ə-ˌniz-əm\ *n*

berke·li·um \ˈbər-klē-əm\ *n* [NL, fr. *Berkeley,* Calif.] : a radioactive metallic element produced by bombarding americium 241 with helium ions — see ELEMENT table

Berks *abbr* Berkshire

Berk·shire \ˈbərk-ˌshi(ə)r, -shər\ *n* [*Berkshire,* England] : any of a breed of medium-sized black swine with white markings

ber·lin \(ˌ)bər-ˈlin\ *n* [F *berline,* fr. *Berlin,* Germany] : a four-wheeled two-seated covered carriage with a hooded rear seat

berm *or* **berme** \ˈbərm\ *n* [F *berme,* fr. D *berm* strip of ground along a dike; akin to ME *brimme* brim] : a narrow shelf, path, or ledge typically at the top or bottom of a slope

Ber·mu·da grass \(ˌ)bər-ˈmyüd-ə-, *esp South* -ˈmüd-\ *n* [*Bermuda* islands, No. Atlantic] : a trailing stoloniferous southern European grass (*Cynodon dactylon*)

Bermuda rig *n* : a fore-and-aft rig marked by a triangular sail and a mast with an extreme rake

Ber·mu·das \(ˌ)bər-ˈmyüd-əz, *esp South* -ˈmüd-\ *n pl* : BERMUDA SHORTS

Bermuda shorts *n pl* : knee-length walking shorts

Ber·nese mountain dog \ˌbər-ˌnēz-, -ˌnēs-\ *n* [*Bern,* Switzerland] : any of a Swiss breed of large powerful long-coated black dogs with brown and white markings formerly used for draft

Ber·noul·li trial \ber-ˌnü-ē-, ˌbər-ˌnü-ˌ(y)ē-\ *n* [Jacques *Bernoulli* †1705 Swiss mathematician] : a statistical experiment that has two mutually exclusive outcomes each of which has a constant probability of occurrence

ber·ried \ˈber-ēd\ *adj* **1** : furnished with berries : BACCATE **2** : bearing eggs <a ~ lobster>

¹ber·ry \ˈber-ē, *esp in compounds in which a stressed syllable immediately precedes Brit often & US sometimes* b(ə-)rē\ *n, pl* **berries** [ME *berye,* fr. OE *berie;* akin to OHG *beri* berry] **1 a** : a pulpy and usu. edible fruit (as a strawberry, raspberry, or checkerberry) of small size irrespective of its structure **b** : a simple fruit (as a currant, grape, tomato, or banana) with a pulpy or fleshy pericarp **c** : the dry seed of some plants (as coffee) **2** : an egg of a fish or lobster

²ber·ry \ˈber-ē\ *vi* **ber·ried; ber·ry·ing** **1** : to bear or produce berries <a *~ing* shrub> **2** : to gather or seek berries

ber·ry·like \ˈber-ē-ˌlīk\ *adj* **1** : resembling a berry esp. in size or structure **2** : being small and rounded : COCCOID

ber·seem \(ˌ)bər-ˈsēm\ *n* [Ar *barsīm,* fr. Copt *bersīm*] : a succulent clover (*Trifolium alexandrinum*) cultivated as a forage plant and green-manure crop esp. in the alkaline soils of the Nile valley and in the southwestern U.S. — called also *Egyptian clover*

¹ber·serk \bə(r)-ˈsərk, ˌbər-, -ˈzərk, ˈbər-ˌ\ *or* **ber·serk·er** \-ər\ *n* [ON *berserkr,* fr. *björn* bear + *serkr* shirt] **1** : an ancient Scandinavian warrior frenzied in battle and held to be invulnerable **2** : one whose actions are marked by reckless defiance

²berserk *adj* : FRENZIED, CRAZED — usu. used in the phrase *go berserk* — **berserk** *adv*

¹berth \ˈbərth\ *n* [prob. fr. ²*bear* + *-th*] **1 a** : sufficient distance for maneuvering a ship **b** : safe distance — used esp. with *wide* **2 a** : the place where a ship lies when at anchor or at a wharf **b** : a space for an automotive vehicle at rest <a truck-loading ~> **3** : a place to sit or sleep esp. on a ship or vehicle : ACCOMMODATION **4 a** : a billet on a ship **b** : JOB, POSITION

²berth *vt* **1** : to bring into a berth **2** : to allot a berth to ~ *vi* : to come into a berth

ber·tha \ˈbər-thə\ *n* [F *berthe,* fr. *Berthe* (Bertha) †783 queen of the Franks] : a wide round collar covering the shoulders

Ber·til·lon system \ˈbərt-ᵊl-ˌän-, ˈbert-ē-ˌ(y)ōⁿ-\ *n* [Alphonse *Bertillon* †1914 F criminologist] : a system of identification of persons by a description based on anthropometric measurements, standardized photographs, notation of markings, color, thumb line impressions, and other data

Berw *abbr* Berwick

ber·yl \ˈber-əl\ *n* [ME, fr. OF *beril,* fr. L *beryllus,* fr. Gk *bēryllos,* of Indic origin; akin to Skt *vaidurya* cat's-eye] : a mineral $Be_3Al_2Si_6O_{18}$ consisting of a silicate of beryllium and aluminum of great hardness and occurring in green, bluish green, yellow, pink, or white hexagonal prisms

be·ryl·li·um \bə-ˈril-ē-əm\ *n* [NL, fr. Gk *bēryllion,* dim. of *bēryllos*] : a steel-gray light strong brittle toxic bivalent metallic element used chiefly as a hardening agent in alloys — see ELEMENT table

be·seech \bi-'sēch\ *vb* **-sought** \-'sȯt\ *or* **-seeched; -seech·ing** [ME *besechen,* fr. *be-* + *sechen* to seek] *vt* **1 :** to beg for urgently or anxiously **2 :** to request earnestly : IMPLORE ~ *vi* **:** to make supplication *syn* see BEG — **be·seech·ing·ly** \-'sē-chiŋ-lē\ *adv*
be·seem \bi-'sēm\ *vi, archaic* **:** to be fitting or becoming ~ *vt, archaic* **:** to be suitable to : BEFIT
be·set \bi-'set\ *vt* **1 :** to set or stud with or as if with ornaments **2 :** TROUBLE, HARASS <inflation ~*s* the economy> **3 a :** to set upon : ASSAIL <the settlers were ~ by savages> **b :** to hem in : SURROUND — **be·set·ment** \-mənt\ *n*
be·set·ting *adj* **:** constantly present or attacking : OBSESSIVE
be·shrew \bi-'shrü, *esp South* -'srü\ *vt, archaic* **:** CURSE
¹be·side \bi-'sīd\ *adv* [ME, adv. & prep., fr. OE *be sīdan* at or to the side, fr. *be* at (fr. *bī*) + *sīdan,* dat. & acc. of *sīde* side — more at BY] **1** *archaic* **:** NEARBY **2** *archaic* **:** BESIDES
²beside *prep* **1 a :** by the side of <walk ~ me> **b :** in comparison with **c :** on a par with **2 :** BESIDES — **beside oneself :** in a state of extreme excitement
¹be·sides \bi-'sīdz\ *adv* **1 :** over and above : ALSO **2 :** MOREOVER, FURTHERMORE
²besides *prep* **1 :** other than : EXCEPT **2 :** in addition to
³besides *adj* **:** ELSE
be·siege \bi-'sēj\ *vt* **1 :** to surround with armed forces **2 a :** to press with requests : IMPORTUNE **b :** to cause worry or distress to : BESET <doubts that *besieged* him> — **be·sieg·er** *n*
be·smear \bi-'smi(ə)r\ *vt* **:** SMEAR
be·smirch \bi-'smərch\ *vt* **:** SULLY, SOIL
be·som \'bē-zəm\ *n* [ME *beseme,* fr. OE *besma;* akin to OHG *besmo* broom] **1 :** BROOM 2; *esp* **:** one made of twigs **2 :** BROOM 1
be·sot \bi-'sät\ *vt* **be·sot·ted; be·sot·ting** [*be-* + *sot* (to stultify)] **:** to make dull or stupid; *esp* **:** to muddle with drunkenness or infatuation
be·spat·ter \bi-'spat-ər\ *vt* **:** SPATTER
be·speak \bi-'spēk\ *vt* **-spoke** \-'spōk\; **-spo·ken** \-'spō-kən\; **-speak·ing 1 :** to hire, engage, or claim beforehand **2 :** to speak to esp. with formality : ADDRESS **3 :** REQUEST <~ a favor> **4 a :** INDICATE, SIGNIFY <her performance ~*s* considerable practice> **b :** to show beforehand : FORETELL
be·spec·ta·cled \bi-'spek-ti-kəld, -ˌtik-əld\ *adj* **:** wearing spectacles
be·spoke \bi-'spōk\ *or* **be·spo·ken** \-'spō-kən\ *adj* [pp. of *bespeak*] **1** *Brit* **a :** CUSTOM-MADE **b :** dealing in or producing custom-made articles **2** *dial* **:** ENGAGED
be·sprent \bi-'sprent\ *adj* [ME *bespreynt,* fr. pp. of *besprengen* to besprinkle, fr. OE *besprengan*] *archaic* **:** sprinkled over
be·sprin·kle \bi-'spriŋ-kəl\ *vt* [ME *besprenkeln,* freq. of *besprengen*] **:** SPRINKLE
Bes·se·mer converter \ˌbes-ə-mər-\ *n* **:** the furnace used in the Bessemer process
Bessemer process *n* [Sir Henry *Bessemer*] **:** a process of making steel from pig iron by burning out carbon and other impurities by means of a blast of air forced through the molten metal
¹best \'best\ *adj, superlative of* GOOD [ME, fr. OE *betst;* akin to OE *bōt* remedy — more at BETTER] **1 :** excelling all others <the ~ student> **2 :** most productive of good or of advantage, utility, or satisfaction <what is the ~ thing to do> **3 :** MOST, LARGEST <it rained for the ~ part of their vacation>
²best *adv, superlative of* WELL **1 :** in the best way **2 :** MOST
³best *n* **1 :** the best state or part **2 :** one that is best <the ~ falls short> **3 :** the greatest degree of good or excellence **4 :** one's maximum effort <do your ~> **5 :** best clothes <Sunday ~> — **at best :** under the most favorable circumstances
⁴best *vt* **:** to get the better of : OUTDO
best–ball \'bes(t)-'bȯl\ *adj* **:** relating to or being a golf match in which one player competes against the best individual score of two or more players for each hole — compare FOUR-BALL
¹be·stead *also* **be·sted** \bi-'sted\ *adj* [ME *bested,* fr. *be-* + *sted,* pp. of *steden* to place] **1** *archaic* **:** SITUATED **2** *archaic* **:** BESET
²bestead *vt* **be·stead·ed; be·stead; be·stead·ing** [*be-* + *stead*] **1** *archaic* **:** HELP **2** *archaic* **:** to be useful to : AVAIL
bes·tial \'bes(h)-chəl, 'bēs(h)-\ *adj* [ME, fr. MF, fr. L *bestialis,* fr. *bestia* beast] **1 a :** of or relating to beasts **b :** resembling a beast **2 a :** lacking intelligence or reason **b :** marked by base or inhuman instincts or desires : BRUTAL — **bes·tial·ize** \-chə-ˌlīz\ *vt* — **bes·tial·ly** \-chə-lē\ *adv*
bes·ti·al·i·ty \ˌbes(h)-chē-'al-ət-ē, ˌbēs(h)-\ *n, pl* **-ties 1 :** the condition or status of a lower animal **2 :** display or gratification of bestial traits or impulses **3 :** sexual relations between a human being and a lower animal
bes·ti·ary \'bes(h)-chē-ˌer-ē, 'bēs(h)-\ *n, pl* **-ar·ies** [ML *bestiarium,* fr. L, neut. of *bestiarius* of beasts, fr. *bestia*] **:** a medieval allegorical or moralizing work on the appearance and habits of real or imaginary animals
be·stir \bi-'stər\ *vt* **:** to stir up : rouse to action
best man *n* **:** the principal groomsman at a wedding
be·stow \bi-'stō\ *vt* [ME *bestowen,* fr. *be-* + *stowe* place — more at STOW] **1 :** to put to use : APPLY <~*ed* his spare time on study> **2 :** to put in a particular or appropriate place : STOW **3 :** to provide with quarters : put up **4 :** to convey as a gift — usu. used with *on* or *upon syn* see GIVE — **be·stow·al** \-'stō-əl\ *n*
be·strew \bi-'strü\ *vt* **-strewed; -strewed** *or* **-strewn** \-'strün\; **-strew·ing 1 :** STREW **2 :** to lie scattered over
be·stride \bi-'strīd\ *vt* **-strode** \-'strōd\; **-strid·den** \-'strid-ᵊn\; **-strid·ing** \-'strīd-iŋ\ **1 :** to ride, sit, or stand astride : STRADDLE **2 :** to tower over : DOMINATE **3** *archaic* **:** to stride across
best–sell·er \'bes(t)-'sel-ər\ *n* **:** an article (as a book) whose sales are among the highest of its class — **best·sell·er·dom** \-dəm\ *n* — **best–sell·ing** \-'sel-iŋ\ *adj*
¹bet \'bet\ *n* [origin unknown] **1 a :** something that is laid, staked, or pledged typically between two parties on the outcome of a contest or a contingent issue : WAGER **b :** the act of giving such a pledge **2 :** something to wager on
²bet *vb* **bet** *also* **bet·ted; bet·ting** *vt* **1 a :** to stake on the outcome of an issue **b :** to be able to be sure that — usu. used in the expression *you bet* <you ~ I'll be there> **2 a :** to maintain with or as if with a bet **b :** to make a bet with ~ *vi* **:** to lay a bet
³bet *abbr* between
¹be·ta \'bāt-ə\ *n* [Gk *bēta,* of Sem origin; akin to Heb *bēth* beth] **1 :** the 2d letter of the Greek alphabet — see ALPHABET table **2 :** the second brightest star of a constellation **3 a :** BETA PARTICLE **b :** BETA RAY
²beta *or* β- *adj* **:** second in position in the structure of an organic molecule from a particular group or atom <~ substitution>
be·ta–ad·ren·er·gic \-ˌad-rə-'nər-jik\ *adj* **:** of, relating to, or being a beta-receptor <~ blocking action>
beta globulin *n* [ISV] **:** any of several globulins of plasma or serum that have electrophoretic mobilities intermediate between those of the alpha globulins and gamma globulins
be·ta·ine \'bēt-ə-ˌēn\ *n* [ISV, fr. L *beta* beet] **:** a sweet crystalline quaternary ammonium salt $C_5H_{11}NO_2$ occurring esp. in beet juice; *also* **:** its hydrate $C_5H_{13}NO_3$ or the chloride of this
be·take \bi-'tāk\ *vt* **-took** \-'tu̇k\; **-tak·en** \-'tā-kən\; **-tak·ing 1** *archaic* **:** COMMIT **2 :** to cause (oneself) to go
be·ta–ox·i·da·tion \'bāt-ə-ˌäk-sə-'dā-shən\ *n* **:** stepwise catabolism of fatty acids in which two-carbon fragments are successively removed from the carboxyl end of the chain
beta particle *n* **:** an electron or positron ejected from the nucleus of an atom during radioactive decay; *also* **:** a high-speed electron or positron
beta ray *n* **1 :** BETA PARTICLE **2 :** a stream of beta particles
be·ta–re·cep·tor \ˌbāt-ə-ri-'sep-tər\ *n* **:** a receptor that is associated with positive effects on heartthrob and muscular contractility, with vasodilation, and with inhibition of smooth muscle in the bronchi, intestine, and muscular layer of the wall of the uterus — called also *beta-adrenergic receptor*
be·ta·tron \'bāt-ə-ˌträn\ *n* [ISV] **:** an accelerator in which electrons are propelled by the inductive action of a rapidly varying magnetic field
be·tel \'bēt-ᵊl\ *n* [Pg, fr. Tamil *verrilai*] **:** a climbing pepper (*Piper betle*) whose dried leaves are chewed together with betel nut and lime as a stimulant masticatory esp. by southeastern Asians
Be·tel·geuse \'bēt-ᵊl-ˌjüs, 'bet-, -ˌjüz-, -ˌjə(r)z\ *n* [F *Bételgeuse,* fr. Ar *bayt al-jawzā'* Gemini, lit., the house of the twins (confused with Orion & Betelgeuse)] **:** a variable red giant star of the first magnitude near one shoulder of Orion
betel nut *n* **:** the astringent seed of the betel palm
betel palm *n* **:** an Asiatic pinnate-leaved palm (*Areca cathecu*) that has an orange-colored drupe with an outer fibrous husk
bête noire \ˌbet-nə-'wär, ˌbāt-\ *n, pl* **bêtes noires** \ˌbet-nə-'wär(z), ˌbāt-\ [F, lit., black beast] **:** a person or thing strongly detested or avoided : BUGBEAR
beth \'bāt(h), 'bās\ *n* [Heb *bēth,* fr. *bayith* house] **:** the 2d letter of the Hebrew alphabet — see ALPHABET table
beth·el \'beth-əl\ *n* [Heb *bēth'ēl* house of God] **1 :** a hallowed spot **2 a :** a chapel for Nonconformists **b :** a place of worship for seamen
be·think \bi-'thiŋk\ *vt* **-thought** \-'thȯt\; **-think·ing 1 a :** REMEMBER, RECALL **b :** to cause (oneself) to be reminded **2 :** to cause (oneself) to consider
be·tide \bi-'tīd\ *vt* **:** to happen to : BEFALL ~ *vi* **:** to happen esp. as if by fate
be·times \bi-'tīmz\ *adv* **1 :** in good time : EARLY **2** *archaic* **:** in a short time : SPEEDILY **3 :** at times : OCCASIONALLY
bê·tise \bā-'tēz\ *n, pl* **bê·tises** \-'tēz\ [F] **1 :** lack of good sense : STUPIDITY **2 :** an act of foolishness or stupidity
be·to·ken \bi-'tō-kən\ *vt* **be·to·kened; be·to·ken·ing** \-'tōk-(ə-)niŋ\ **1 :** to give evidence of : SHOW **2 :** to typify beforehand : PRESAGE
bet·o·ny \'bet-ᵊn-ē\ *n, pl* **-nies** [ME *betone,* fr. OF *betoine,* fr. L *vettonica, betonica,* fr. *Vettones,* an ancient people inhabiting the Iberian peninsula] **:** any of several woundworts (genus *Stachys*); *esp* **:** WOOD BETONY 1
be·tray \bi-'trā\ *vb* [ME *betrayen,* fr. *be-* + *trayen* to betray, fr. OF *trair,* fr. L *tradere* — more at TRAITOR] *vt* **1 :** to lead astray; *esp* **:** SEDUCE **2 :** to deliver to an enemy by treachery **3 :** to fail or desert esp. in time of need **4 a :** to reveal unintentionally **b :** SHOW, INDICATE **c :** to disclose in violation of confidence ~ *vi* **:** to prove false *syn* see REVEAL — **be·tray·al** \-'trā(-ə)l\ *n* — **be·tray·er** \-'trā-ər\ *n*
be·troth \bi-'träth, -'trȯth, -'trōth, *or with* th\ *vt* [ME *betrouthen,* fr. *be-* + *trouthe* truth, troth] **:** to promise to marry or give in marriage
be·troth·al \-'trōth-əl, -'trȯth-, -'trōth-\ *n* **1 :** the act of betrothing or fact of being betrothed **2 :** a mutual promise or contract for a future marriage
be·trothed *n* **:** the person to whom one is betrothed
bet·ta \'bet-ə\ *n* [NL] **:** any of a genus (*Betta*) of small brilliantly colored long-finned freshwater fishes (as the Siamese fighting fish) of southeastern Asia
¹bet·ter \'bet-ər\ *adj, comparative of* GOOD [ME *bettre,* fr. OE *betera;* akin to OE *bōt* remedy, Skt *bhadra* fortunate] **1 :** more than half **2 :** improved in health **3 :** of higher quality <ladies' ~ dresses>
²better *adv, comparative of* WELL **1 :** in a more excellent manner **2 a :** to a higher or greater degree <he knows the story ~ than you do> **b :** MORE <it is ~ than nine miles to the nearest gas station>
³better *n* **1 a :** something better **b :** a superior esp. in merit or rank **2 :** ADVANTAGE, VICTORY <get the ~ of him>

[4]**better** *vt* **1 :** to make better: as **a :** to make more tolerable or acceptable <trying to ~ the lot of slum dwellers> **b :** to make more complete or perfect <looked forward to ~*ing* her acquaintance with the new neighbors> **2 :** to surpass in excellence : EXCEL ~ *vi* **:** to become better ***syn*** see IMPROVE ***ant*** worsen

bet·ter·ment \'bet-ər-mənt\ *n* **1 :** a making or becoming better **2 :** an improvement that adds to the value of a property or facility

better–off \ˌbet-ə-'rȯf\ *adj* **:** being in comfortable economic circumstances <the ~ people live in the older section of town>

betting shop *n, Brit* **:** a shop where bets are taken

bet·tor *or* **bet·ter** \'bet-ər\ *n* **:** one that bets

[1]**be·tween** \bi-'twēn\ *prep* [ME *betwene,* prep. & adv., fr. OE *betwēonum,* fr. *be-* + *-twēonum* (dat. pl.) (akin to Goth *tweihnai* two each); akin to OE *twā* two] **1 a :** by the common action of **:** jointly engaging <shared the work ~ the two of them> <talks ~ the three —*Time*> **b :** in common to **:** shared by <divided ~ his four grandchildren> **2 a :** in the time, space, or interval that separates **b :** in intermediate relation to **3 a :** from one to the other of **b :** serving to join **:** CONNECTING <air service ~ the two cities> **c :** separating from <the line ~ fact and fancy> **4 :** in point of comparison of <not much to choose ~ the two coats> — **between you and me :** in confidence

[2]**between** *adv* **:** in an intermediate space or interval

be·tween·brain \-ˌbrān\ *n* **:** DIENCEPHALON

be·tween·ness \bi-'twēn-nəs\ *n* **:** the quality or state of being between two others in an ordered set

be·tween·times \bi-'twēn-ˌtīmz\ *adv* **:** at or during intervals

be·tween·whiles \-ˌhwīlz, -ˌwīlz\ *adv* **:** BETWEENTIMES

be·twixt \bi-'twikst\ *adv or prep* [ME, fr. OE *betwux,* fr. *be-* + *-twux* (akin to Goth *tweihnai*)] *archaic* **:** BETWEEN

betwixt and between *adv or adj* **:** in a midway position **:** neither one thing nor the other

Beu·lah \'byü-lə\ *n* **:** an idyllic land near the end of life's journey in Bunyan's *Pilgrim's Progress*

BeV *abbr* billion electron volts

[1]**bev·el** \'bev-əl\ *adj* **:** OBLIQUE, BEVELED

[2]**bevel** *n* [(assumed) MF, fr. OF *baif* with open mouth, fr. *baer* to yawn — more at ABEYANCE] **1 a :** the angle that one surface or line makes with another when they are not at right angles **b :** the slant or inclination of such a surface or line **2 :** an instrument consisting of two rules or arms jointed together and opening to any angle for drawing angles or adjusting surfaces to be given a bevel **3 :** the part of printing type extending from face to shoulder — see TYPE illustration

[3]**bevel** *vb* **-eled** *or* **-elled; -el·ing** *or* **-el·ling** \'bev-(ə-)liŋ\ *vt* **:** to cut or shape to a bevel ~ *vi* **:** INCLINE, SLANT

bevel gear *n* **:** one of a pair of toothed wheels whose working surfaces are inclined to nonparallel axes

bevel gears

bev·er·age \'bev-(ə-)rij\ *n* [ME, fr. MF *bevrage,* fr. *beivre* to drink, fr. L *bibere* — more at POTABLE] **:** a liquid for drinking; *esp* **:** one that is not water

bevy \'bev-ē\ *n, pl* **bev·ies** [ME *bevey*] **1 :** a large group or collection <a ~ of girls> **2 :** a group of animals and esp. quail together

be·wail \bi-'wā(ə)l\ *vt* **1 :** to wail over **2 :** to express deep sorrow for usu. by wailing and lamentation <wringing her hands and ~*ing* her fate> ***syn*** see DEPLORE

be·ware \bi-'wa(ə)r, -'we(ə)r\ *vb* [ME *been war,* fr. *been* to be + *war* careful — more at BE, WARE] *vi* **:** to be on one's guard <~ of the dog> ~ *vt* **1 :** to take care of **2 :** to be wary of

be·whis·kered \-'hwis-kərd, -'wis-\ *adj* **:** wearing whiskers

be·wigged \bi-'wigd\ *adj* **:** wearing a wig

be·wil·der \bi-'wil-dər\ *vt* **be·wil·dered; be·wil·der·ing** \-d(ə-)riŋ\ **1 :** to cause to lose one's bearings **2 :** to perplex or confuse esp. by a complexity, variety, or multitude of objects or considerations ***syn*** see PUZZLE — **be·wil·dered·ly** *adv* — **be·wil·dered·ness** *n* — **be·wil·der·ing·ly** \-d(ə-)riŋ-lē\ *adv*

be·wil·der·ment \-dər-mənt\ *n* **1 :** the quality or state of being bewildered **2 :** a bewildering tangle or confusion

be·witch \bi-'wich\ *vt* **1 a :** to influence or affect esp. injuriously by witchcraft **b :** to cast a spell over **2 :** to attract as if by the power of witchcraft <~*ed* by her beauty> ~ *vi* **:** to bewitch someone or something ***syn*** see ATTRACT — **be·witch·ery** \-(ə-)rē\ *n* — **be·witch·ing·ly** \-iŋ-lē\ *adv*

be·witch·ment \-'wich-mənt\ *n* **1 a :** the act or power of bewitching **b :** a spell that bewitches **2 :** the state of being bewitched

be·wray \bi-'rā\ *vt* [ME *bewreyen,* fr. *be-* + *wreyen* to accuse, fr. OE *wrēgan*] *archaic* **:** DIVULGE, BETRAY

bey \'bā\ *n* [Turk, gentleman, chief] **1 a :** a provincial governor in the Ottoman Empire **b :** the former native ruler of Tunis or Tunisia **2** — formerly used as a courtesy title in Turkey and Egypt

[1]**be·yond** \bē-'änd\ *adv* [ME, prep. & adv., fr. OE *begeondan,* fr. *be-* + *geondan* beyond, fr. *geond* yond — more at YOND] **1 :** on or to the farther side **:** FARTHER **2 :** in addition **:** BESIDES

[2]**beyond** *prep* **1 :** on or to the farther side of **:** at a greater distance than **2 a :** out of the reach or sphere of **b :** in a degree or amount surpassing **c :** out of the comprehension of **3 :** in addition to **:** over and above **:** BESIDES

[3]**beyond** *n* **1 :** something that lies beyond **2 :** something that lies outside the scope of ordinary experience; *specif* **:** [2]HEREAFTER

be·zant \'bez-ᵊnt, bə-'zant\ *n* [ME *besant,* fr. MF, fr. ML *Byzantius* Byzantine, fr. *Byzantium,* ancient name of Istanbul] **1 :** SOLIDUS 1 **2 :** a flat disk used in architectural ornament

be·zel \'bē-zəl, 'bez-əl\ *n* [prob. F dial., alter. of F *biseau*] **1 :** a sloping edge or face esp. on a cutting tool **2 :** the oblique side or face of a cut gem; *specif* **:** the upper faceted portion of a brilliant projecting from the setting — see BRILLIANT illustration **3 :** a rim that holds a transparent covering (as on a watch, clock, or headlight) or that is rotatable and has special markings (as on a watch)

be·zique \bə-'zēk\ *n* [F *bésique*] **:** a card game similar to pinochle that is played with a pack of 64 cards

be·zoar \'bē-ˌzō(ə)r, -ˌzȯ(ə)r\ *n* [F *bézoard,* fr. Sp *bezoar,* fr. Ar *bāzahr,* fr. Per *pād-zahr,* fr. *pād* protecting (against) + *zahr* poison] **:** any of various concretions found chiefly in the alimentary organs of ruminants and formerly believed to possess magical properties

bf *abbr* boldface

BF *abbr* **1** bachelor of forestry **2** board foot **3** brought forward

BFA *abbr* bachelor of fine arts

bg *abbr* **1** background **2** bag **3** beige **4** being

BG *abbr* brigadier general

B Gen *abbr* brigadier general

B–girl *n* [prob. fr. *bar* + *girl*] **:** a woman who entertains bar patrons and encourages them to spend freely

BH *abbr* **1** bill of health **2** Brinell hardness

Bha·don \'bäd-ˌōn\ *n* [Hindi *bhādō,* fr. Skt *bhādrapada,* fr. *Bhādrapada,* a constellation] **:** a month of the Hindu year — see MONTH table

Bha·ga·vad Gi·ta \ˌbäg-ə-ˌväd-'gēt-ə\ *n* [Skt *Bhagavadgītā,* lit., song of the blessed one (Krishna)] **:** a Hindu devotional work in poetic form

bhak·ti \'bək-tē\ *n* [Skt, lit., portion] **:** devotion to a deity constituting a way to salvation in Hinduism

bhang \'baŋ\ *n* [Hindi *bhāg*] **1 a :** HEMP 1 **b :** the leaves and flowering tops of uncultivated hemp **:** CANNABIS — compare MARIJUANA **2 :** an intoxicant product obtained from bhang — compare HASHISH

BHC \ˌbē-ˌāch-'sē\ *n* [*b*enzene *h*exa*c*hloride] **:** a compound $C_6H_6Cl_6$ that occurs in several stereoisomeric forms and is used as an insecticide — compare LINDANE

bhd *abbr* bulkhead

BHE *abbr* Bureau of Higher Education

BHL *abbr* **1** bachelor of Hebrew letters **2** bachelor of Hebrew literature

BHN *abbr* Brinell hardness number

Bhoj·puri \'bōj-ˌpu̇r-ē, 'bäj-, pə-rē\ *n* [Hindi *Bhojpurī,* fr. *Bhojpur,* village in Bihar] **:** the dialect of Bihari spoken in Western Bihar and the eastern United Provinces, India

B–horizon *n* **:** a soil layer immediately beneath the A-horizon from which it obtains organic matter chiefly by illuviation and is usu. distinguished by less weathering

bhp *abbr* bishop

BHT *abbr* butylated hydroxytoluene

bi \'bī\ *n or adj* **:** BISEXUAL

Bi *symbol* bismuth

[1]**bi-** *prefix* [ME, fr. L; akin to OE *twi-*] **1 a :** two <*bi*parous> **b :** coming or occurring every two <*bi*monthly> <*bi*weekly> **c :** into two parts <*bi*sect> **2 a :** twice **:** doubly **:** on both sides <*bi*convex> <*bi*serrate> **b :** coming or occurring two times <*bi*weekly> — often disapproved in this sense because of the likelihood of confusion with sense 1b; compare SEMI- **3 :** between, involving, or affecting two (specified) symmetrical parts <*bi*aural> **4 a :** containing one (specified) constituent in double the proportion of the other constituent or in double the ordinary proportion <*bi*carbonate> **b :** DI- 2 <*bi*phenyl>

[2]**bi-** *or* **bio-** *comb form* [Gk, fr. *bios* mode of life — more at QUICK] **:** life **:** living organisms or tissue <*bio*ecology> <*bio*luminescence>

BIA *abbr* **1** bachelor of industrial arts **2** Braille Institute of America **3** Bureau of Indian Affairs

Bi·a·fran \bē-'af-rən, bī-, -'äf-\ *n* [*Biafra,* name adopted by Eastern Region of Nigeria during its secession, 1967–70] **:** a native or inhabitant of the secessionist Republic of Biafra — **Biafran** *adj*

bi·an·nu·al \(ˈ)bī-'an-yə(-wə)l\ *adj* **:** occurring twice a year — **bi·an·nu·al·ly** \-ē\ *adv*

[1]**bi·as** \'bī-əs\ *n* [MF *biais*] **1 :** a line diagonal to the grain of a fabric; *esp* **:** a line at a 45° angle to the selvage often utilized in the cutting of garments for smoother fit **2 a :** an inclination of temperament or outlook; *esp* **:** a highly personal and unreasoned distortion of judgment **:** PREJUDICE <a ~ in favor of jolly fat men> **b :** BENT, TENDENCY <a man of antiquarian ~> **c (1) :** deviation of the expected value of a statistical estimate from the quantity it estimates **(2) :** systematic error introduced into sampling or testing by selecting or encouraging one outcome or answer over others **3 a :** a peculiarity in the shape of a bowl that causes it to swerve when rolled on the green **b :** the tendency of a bowl to swerve; *also* **:** the impulse causing this tendency **c :** the swerve of the bowl **4 :** a voltage applied to a device (as the grid of an electron tube) to establish a reference level for operation ***syn*** see PREDILECTION — **on the bias :** ASKEW, OBLIQUELY

[2]**bias** *adj* **:** DIAGONAL, SLANTING — used chiefly of fabrics and their cut — **bi·as·ness** *n*

[3]**bias** *adv* **1 :** in a slanting manner **:** DIAGONALLY <cut cloth ~> **2** *obs* **:** AWRY

[4]**bias** *vt* **bi·ased** *or* **bi·assed; bi·as·ing** *or* **bi·as·sing 1 :** to give a settled and often prejudiced outlook to <his background ~*es* him against foreigners> **2 :** to apply a slight negative or positive voltage to (as an electron-tube grid) ***syn*** see INCLINE

bi·ased *adj* **1 :** exhibiting or characterized by bias **2 :** tending to yield one outcome more frequently than others in a statistical experiment <a ~ coin> **3 :** not having minimum probability of rejecting the null hypothesis when it is true <a ~ statistical test>

bi·ath·lon \bī-'ath-lən, -ˌlän\ *n* [[1]*bi-* + Gk *athlon* contest — more at ATHLETE] **:** a composite athletic contest consisting of cross-country skiing and rifle sharpshooting

bi·ax·i·al \(ˈ)bī-'ak-sē-əl\ *adj* **:** having two axes <a ~ crystal> — **bi·ax·i·al·ly** \-ə-lē\ *adv*

[1]**bib** \'bib\ *vb* **bibbed; bib·bing** [ME *bibben*] **:** DRINK

[2]**bib** *n* **1 :** a cloth or plastic shield tied under a child's chin to protect the clothes **2 :** the part of an apron or of overalls extending above the waist — **bibbed** \'bibd\ *adj* — **bib·less** \'bib-ləs\ *adj*

[3]**bib** *abbr* Bible; biblical

bib and tucker *n* **:** an outfit of clothing — usu. used in the phrase *best bib and tucker*

bibb \ˈbib\ *n* [alter. of [2]*bib*] **:** a side piece of timber bolted to the hounds of a ship's mast to support the trestletrees

bib·ber \ˈbib-ər\ *n* **:** one addicted to drinking **:** TIPPLER — **bib·bery** \ˈbib-ə-rē\ *n*

Bibb lettuce \ˈbib-\ *n* [Major John *Bibb*, 19th cent. Am grower] **:** lettuce of a variety that has a small head and dark green color

bib·cock \ˈbib-ˌkäk\ *also* **bibb cock** *n* **:** a faucet having a bent-down nozzle

bi·be·lot \ˈbē-bə-ˌlō\ *n, pl* **bibelots** \-ˌlō(z)\ [F] **1 :** a small household ornament or decorative object **:** TRINKET **2 :** a miniature book esp. of elegant design or format

bi·ble \ˈbī-bəl\ *n* [ME, fr. OF, fr. ML *biblia*, fr. Gk, pl. of *biblion* book, dim. of *byblos* papyrus, book, fr. *Byblos*, ancient Phoenician city from which papyrus was exported] **1** *cap* **a :** the sacred scriptures of Christians comprising the Old Testament and the New Testament **b :** the sacred scriptures of some other religion (as Judaism) **2** *obs* **:** BOOK **3** *cap* **:** a copy or an edition of the Bible **4 :** a publication that is preeminent esp. in authoritativeness <the fisherman's ~> **5 :** something suggesting a book: as **a :** a small holystone **b :** OMASUM

BOOKS OF THE OLD TESTAMENT

ROMAN CATHOLIC CANON	PROTESTANT CANON	ROMAN CATHOLIC CANON	PROTESTANT CANON
Genesis	Genesis	Wisdom	
Exodus	Exodus	Ecclesiasticus	
Leviticus	Leviticus	Isaias	Isaiah
Numbers	Numbers	Jeremias	Jeremiah
Deuteronomy	Deuteronomy	Lamentations	Lamentations
Josue	Joshua	Baruch	
Judges	Judges	Ezechiel	Ezekiel
Ruth	Ruth	Daniel	Daniel
1 & 2 Kings	1 & 2 Samuel	Osee	Hosea
3 & 4 Kings	1 & 2 Kings	Joel	Joel
1 & 2 Paralipomenon	1 & 2 Chronicles	Amos	Amos
		Abdias	Obadiah
1 Esdras	Ezra	Jonas	Jonah
2 Esdras	Nehemiah	Micheas	Micah
Tobias		Nahum	Nahum
Judith		Habacuc	Habakkuk
Esther	Esther	Sophonias	Zephaniah
Job	Job	Aggeus	Haggai
Psalms	Psalms	Zacharias	Zechariah
Proverbs	Proverbs	Malachias	Malachi
Ecclesiastes	Ecclesiastes	1 & 2 Machabees	
Canticle of Canticles	Song of Solomon		

JEWISH SCRIPTURE

Law	1 & 2 Kings	Nahum	Song of Songs
Genesis	Isaiah	Habakkuk	Ruth
Exodus	Jeremiah	Zephaniah	Lamentations
Leviticus	Ezekiel	Haggai	Ecclesiastes
Numbers	Hosea	Zechariah	Esther
Deuteronomy	Joel	Malachi	Daniel
Prophets	Amos	*Hagiographa*	Ezra
Joshua	Obadiah	Psalms	Nehemiah
Judges	Jonah	Proverbs	1 & 2 Chronicles
1 & 2 Samuel	Micah	Job	

PROTESTANT APOCRYPHA

1 & 2 Esdras	Wisdom of Solomon	Baruch	Susanna
Tobit	Ecclesiasticus or the Wisdom of Jesus Son of Sirach	Prayer of Azariah and the Song of the Three Holy Children	Bel and the Dragon
Judith			The Prayer of Manasses
Additions to Esther			1 & 2 Maccabees

BOOKS OF THE NEW TESTAMENT

Matthew	Romans	1 & 2 Thessalonians	1 & 2 Peter
Mark	1 & 2 Corinthians	1 & 2 Timothy	1, 2, 3 John
Luke	Galatians	Titus	Jude
John	Ephesians	Philemon	Revelation (Roman Catholic canon: Apocalypse)
Acts of the Apostles	Philippians	Hebrews	
	Colossians	James	

Bible Belt *n* **:** an area chiefly in the southern U.S. believed to hold uncritical allegiance to the literal accuracy of the Bible; *broadly* **:** an area characterized by ardent religious fundamentalism

bib·li·cal \ˈbib-li-kəl\ *adj* [ML *biblicus*, fr. *biblia*] **1 :** of, relating to, or being in accord with the Bible **2 :** suggestive of the Bible or Bible times — **bib·li·cal·ly** \-k(ə-)lē\ *adv*

bib·li·cism \ˈbib-lə-ˌsiz-əm\ *n, often cap* **:** adherence to the letter of the Bible — **bib·li·cist** \-lə-səst\ *n, often cap*

biblio- *comb form* [MF, fr. L, fr. Gk, fr. *biblion*] **:** book <*biblio*film>

bib·li·og·ra·pher \ˌbib-lē-ˈäg-rə-fər\ *n* **1 :** an expert in bibliography **2 :** a compiler of bibliographies

bib·lio·graph·ic \ˌbib-lē-ə-ˈgraf-ik\ *adj* **:** of or relating to bibliography — **bib·lio·graph·i·cal** \-i-kəl\ *adj* — **bib·lio·graph·i·cal·ly** \-k(ə-)lē\ *adv*

bib·li·og·ra·phy \ˌbib-lē-ˈäg-rə-fē\ *n, pl* **-phies** [prob. fr. NL *bibliographia*, fr. Gk, the copying of books, fr. *biblio-* + *-graphia* -graphy] **1 :** the history, identification, or description of writings or publications **2 a :** a list often with descriptive or critical notes of writings relating to a particular subject, period, or author **b :** a list of works written by an author or printed by a publishing house **3 :** the works or a list of the works referred to in a text or consulted by the author in its production

bib·li·ol·a·ter \ˌbib-lē-ˈäl-ət-ər\ *n* **1 :** one overly devoted to books **2 :** one having excessive reverence for the letter of the Bible — **bib·li·ol·a·trous** \-ˈäl-ə-trəs\ *adj* — **bib·li·ol·a·try** \-trē\ *n*

bib·lio·ma·nia \ˌbib-lē-ə-ˈmā-nē-ə, -nyə\ *n* [F *bibliomanie*, fr. *biblio-* + *manie* mania, fr. LL *mania*] **:** extreme preoccupation with collecting books — **bib·lio·ma·ni·ac** \-nē-ˌak\ *n or adj* — **bib·lio·ma·ni·a·cal** \-lē-ō-mə-ˈnī-ə-kəl\ *adj*

bib·li·ol·o·gy \ˌbib-lē-ˈäl-ə-jē\ *n* **1 :** the history and science of books as physical objects **:** bibliography in its broadest sense **2** *often cap* **:** the study of the theological doctrine of the Bible

bib·li·op·e·gy \ˌbib-lē-ˈäp-ə-jē\ *n* [deriv. of Gk *biblio-* + *pēgnynai* to fasten together — more at PACT] **:** the art of binding books — **bib·li·o·pe·gic** \ˌbib-lē-ə-ˈpej-ik, -ˈpēj-\ *adj* — **bib·li·o·pe·gi·cal·ly** \-i-k(ə-)lē\ *adv* — **bib·li·op·e·gist** \ˌbib-lē-ˈäp-ə-jəst\ *n* — **bib·li·op·e·gis·tic** \-äp-ə-ˈjis-tik\ *adj*

bib·lio·phile \ˈbib-lē-ə-ˌfīl\ *n* [F, fr. *biblio-* + *-phile*] **:** a lover of books esp. for qualities of format; *also* **:** a book collector — **bib·lio·phil·ic** \ˌbib-lē-ə-ˈfil-ik\ *adj* — **bib·li·oph·i·lism** \-äf-ə-ˌliz-əm\ *n* — **bib·li·oph·i·list** \-ləst\ *n* — **bib·li·oph·i·ly** \-lē\ *n*

bib·li·o·pole \ˈbib-lē-ə-ˌpōl\ *or* **bib·li·op·o·list** \ˌbib-lē-ˈäp-ə-ləst\ *n* [L *bibliopola* bookseller, fr. Gk *bibliopōlēs*, fr. *biblio-* + *pōlein* to sell] **:** a dealer esp. in rare or curious books — **bib·li·o·po·lic** \ˌbib-lē-ə-ˈpō-lik, -ˈpäl-ik\ *adj*

bib·lio·the·ca \ˌbib-lē-ə-ˈthē-kə\ *n, pl* **-cas** *or* **-cae** \-ˌsē, -ˌkē\ [L, fr. Gk *bibliothēkē*, fr. *biblio-* + *thēkē* case; akin to Gk *tithenai* to put, place — more at DO] **1 :** a collection of books **2 :** a list of books — **bib·lio·the·cal** \-ˈthē-kəl\ *adj*

bib·li·ot·ics \ˌbib-lē-ˈät-iks\ *n pl but sing in constr* [*biblio-* + connective *-t-* + *-ics*] **:** the study of handwriting, documents, and writing materials esp. for determining genuineness or authorship — **bib·li·ot·ic** \-ik\ *adj* — **bib·li·o·tist** \ˈbib-lē-ə-təst\ *n*

bib·u·lous \ˈbib-yə-ləs\ *adj* [L *bibulus*, fr. *bibere* to drink — more at POTABLE] **1 :** highly absorbent **2 a :** inclined to drink **b :** of or relating to drink or drinking — **bib·u·lous·ly** *adv* — **bib·u·lous·ness** *n*

bi·cam·er·al \(ˈ)bī-ˈkam-(ə-)rəl\ *adj* **:** having, consisting of, or based on two legislative chambers <a ~ legislature> — **bi·cam·er·al·ism** \-ə-ˌliz-əm\ *n*

bi·cap·su·lar \(ˈ)bī-ˈkap-sə-lər\ *adj* [prob. fr. F *bicapsulaire*, fr. *bi-* + *capsulaire* capsular] **:** having two capsules or a 2-celled capsule

bi·car·bon·ate \(ˈ)bī-ˈkär-bə-ˌnāt, -nət\ *n* [ISV] **:** an acid carbonate

bicarbonate of soda : SODIUM BICARBONATE

bi·cen·te·na·ry \ˌbī-(ˌ)sen-ˈten-ə-rē, (ˈ)bī-ˈsent-ᵊn-ˌer-ē, ˌbī-(ˌ)sen-ˈtē-nə-rē\ *n* **:** BICENTENNIAL — **bicentenary** *adj*

bi·cen·ten·ni·al \ˌbī-(ˌ)sen-ˈten-ē-əl\ *n* **:** a 200th anniversary or its celebration — **bicentennial** *adj*

bi·cen·tric \(ˈ)bī-ˈsen-trik\ *adj* **:** having or involving two centers — **bi·cen·tric·i·ty** \ˌbī-(ˌ)sen-ˈtris-ət-ē\ *n*

bi·ceps \ˈbī-ˌseps\ *n* [NL *bicipit-, biceps*, fr. L, two-headed, fr. *bi-* + *capit-, caput* head — more at HEAD] **:** a muscle having two heads: as **a :** the large flexor muscle of the front of the upper arm **b :** the large flexor muscle of the back of the upper leg

bi·chlo·ride \(ˈ)bī-ˈklō(ə)r-ˌīd, -ˈklȯ(ə)r-\ *n* [ISV] **1 :** DICHLORIDE **2 :** MERCURIC CHLORIDE — called also *bichloride of mercury*

bi·chro·mate \(ˈ)bī-ˈkrō-ˌmāt, ˈbī-krō-\ *n* **:** DICHROMATE; *esp* **:** one of sodium or potassium — **bi·chro·mat·ed** \-ˌmāt-əd\ *adj*

bi·chrome \ˈbī-ˌkrōm\ *adj* **:** two-colored

bi·cip·i·tal \bī-ˈsip-ət-ᵊl\ *adj* **:** of, relating to, or being a biceps

[1]**bick·er** \ˈbik-ər\ *n* [ME *biker*] **1 :** petulant quarreling **:** ALTERCATION **2 :** a sound of or as if of bickering

[2]**bicker** *vi* **bick·ered; bick·er·ing** \-(ə-)riŋ\ **1 :** to contend in petulant or petty altercation **2 a :** to move quickly and unsteadily with a rapidly repeated noise **b :** QUIVER, FLICKER — **bick·er·er** \-ər-ər\ *n*

bi·col·or \ˈbī-ˌkəl-ər\ *adj* [L *bicolor*, fr. *bi-* + *color*] **:** two-colored — **bicolor** *n* — **bi·col·ored** \-ˈkəl-ərd\ *adj*

bi·col·our *chiefly Brit var of* BICOLOR

bicolor lespedeza *n* **:** an Asiatic leguminous shrub (*Lespedeza bicolor*) with purple flowers in axillary racemes widely used as an ornamental, as a source of wild-bird food, and in erosion control

bi·con·cave \ˌbī-(ˌ)kän-ˈkāv, (ˈ)bī-ˈkän-ˌ\ *adj* [ISV] **:** concave on both sides — **bi·con·cav·i·ty** \ˌbī-(ˌ)kän-ˈkav-ət-ē\ *n*

bi·con·di·tion·al \ˌbī-kən-ˈdish-nəl, -ən-ᵊl\ *n* **:** a two-way implication

bi·con·vex \ˌbī-(ˌ)kän-ˈveks, (ˈ)bī-ˈkän-ˌ, ˌbī-kən-ˈ\ *adj* [ISV] **:** convex on both sides — **bi·con·vex·i·ty** \ˌbī-kən-ˈvek-sət-ē, -(ˌ)kän-\ *n*

bi·corne \ˈbī-ˌkȯ(ə)rn\ *n* [F, fr. L *bicornis* two-horned, fr. *bi-* + *cornu* horn — more at HORN] **:** COCKED HAT 2

bi·cor·nu·ate \(ˈ)bī-ˈkȯr-nyə-wət\ *adj* [*bi-* + L *cornu*] **:** having two horns or horn-shaped processes

bi·cul·tur·al·ism \(ˈ)bī-ˈkəlch-(ə-)rə-ˌliz-əm\ *n* **:** the existence of two distinct cultures in one nation <Canada's ~> — **bi·cul·tur·al** \-rəl\ *adj*

[1]**bi·cus·pid** \(ˈ)bī-ˈkəs-pəd\ *also* **bi·cus·pi·date** \-pə-ˌdāt\ *adj* [NL *bicuspid-, bicuspis*, fr. *bi-* + L *cuspid-, cuspis* point] **:** having or ending in two points <~ teeth> <~ leaves>

[2]**bicuspid** *n* **:** a human premolar tooth — see TOOTH illustration

bicuspid valve *n* **:** a cardiac valve that consists of two triangular flaps and guards the orifice between the left auricle and ventricle — called also *mitral valve*

[1]**bi·cy·cle** \ˈbī-ˌsik-əl *also* -ˌsī-k-\ *n* [F, fr. *bi-* + *-cycle* (as in *tricycle*)] **:** a vehicle with two wheels tandem, a steering handle, a saddle seat, and pedals by which it is propelled

[2]**bicycle** *vi* **bi·cy·cled; bi·cy·cling** \(-ə)-liŋ\ **:** to ride a bicycle — **bi·cy·cler** \-lər\ *n* — **bi·cy·clist** \-ləst\ *n*

bi·cy·clic \(ˈ)bī-ˈsī-klik, -ˈsik-lik\ *adj* [ISV] **1 :** consisting of or arranged in two cycles **2 :** containing two usu. fused rings in the structure of the molecule

[1]**bid** \ˈbid\ *vb* **bade** \ˈbad, ˈbād\ *or* **bid; bid·den** \ˈbid-ᵊn\ *or* **bid** *also* **bade; bid·ding** [partly fr. ME *bidden,* fr. OE *biddan;* akin to OHG *bitten* to entreat, Skt *bādhate* he harasses; partly fr. ME *beden* to offer, command, fr. OE *bēodan;* akin to OHG *biotan* to offer, Gk *pynthanesthai* to learn by inquiry] *vt* **1 a** *obs* **:** BESEECH, ENTREAT **b :** to issue an order to **:** TELL **c :** to request to come **:** INVITE **2 :** to give expression to <*bade* a tearful farewell> **3 a :** OFFER — usu. used in the phrase *to bid defiance* **b** *past bid* (1) **:** to offer (a price) whether for payment or acceptance (2) **:** to make a bid of or in (a suit at cards) ~ *vi* **:** to make a bid ***syn*** see COMMAND ***ant*** forbid — **bid·der** *n* — **bid fair :** to seem likely

[2]**bid** *n* **1 a :** the act of one who bids **b :** a statement of what one will give or take for something; *esp* **:** an offer of a price **c :** something offered as a bid **2 :** an opportunity to bid **3 :** INVITATION **4 a :** an announcement of what a cardplayer proposes to undertake **b :** the amount of such a bid **c :** a biddable bridge hand **5 :** an attempt or effort to win, achieve, or attract

BID *abbr* **1** bachelor of industrial design **2** [L *bis in die*] twice a day

bid·da·ble \ˈbid-ə-bəl\ *adj* **1 :** easily led, taught, or controlled **:** DOCILE **2 :** capable of being bid — **bid·da·bil·i·ty** \ˌbid-ə-ˈbil-ət-ē\ *n* — **bid·da·bly** \ˈbid-ə-blē\ *adv*

[1]**bid·dy** \ˈbid-ē\ *n, pl* **biddies** [perh. imit.] **:** HEN 1a; *also* **:** a young chicken

[2]**biddy** *n, pl* **biddies** [dim. of the name *Bridget*] **1 :** a hired girl or cleaning woman **2 :** WOMAN <an eccentric old ~>

Bid·dy Basketball \ˌbit-ē-\ *n* [alter. of [2]*bitty*] **:** basketball designed to be played by youngsters and marked by the use of a smaller ball, a shorter court, and baskets at a height of 8½ feet

bide \ˈbīd\ *vb* **bode** \ˈbōd\ *or* **bid·ed; bided; bid·ing** [ME *biden,* fr. OE *bīdan;* akin to OHG *bītan* to wait, L *fidere* to trust, Gk *peithesthai* to believe] *vi* **1 :** to continue in a state or condition **2 :** to wait awhile **:** TARRY **3 :** to continue in a place **:** SOJOURN ~ *vt* **1** *past usu* **bided :** to wait for — used chiefly in the phrase *bide one's time* **2** *archaic* **:** to await confidently or defiantly **:** WITHSTAND <two men . . . might ~ the winter storm — W. C. Bryant> **3** *chiefly dial* **:** to put up with **:** TOLERATE — **bid·er** *n*

bi·det \bi-ˈdā\ *n* [F, small horse, bidet, fr. MF, fr. *bider* to trot] **:** a fixture about the height of the seat of a chair used esp. for bathing the external genitals and the posterior parts of the body

bi·di·a·lec·tal·ism \ˌbī-ˌdī-ə-ˈlek-tᵊl-ˌiz-əm\ *n* **:** the constant oral use of two dialects of the same language — **bi·di·a·lec·tal** *adj*

bi·don·ville \bē-ˌdōⁿ-ˈvē(ə)l\ *n* [F, fr. *bidon* tin can + *ville* city] **:** a settlement of jerry-built dwellings on the outskirts of a city (as in France)

bid up *vt* **:** to raise the price of (as property at auction) by a succession of offers

BIE *abbr* bachelor of industrial engineering

bield \ˈbē(ə)ld\ *vt or n* [ME *belden* to encourage, protect, fr. OE *bieldan* to encourage; akin to OE *beald* bold] *chiefly Scot* **:** SHELTER

bi·en·ni·al \(ˈ)bī-ˈen-ē-əl\ *adj* **1 :** occurring every two years **2 :** continuing or lasting for two years; *specif* **:** growing vegetatively during the first year and fruiting and dying during the second — **biennial** *n* — **bi·en·ni·al·ly** \-ə-lē\ *adv*

bi·en·ni·um \bī-ˈen-ē-əm\ *n, pl* **-ni·ums** *or* **-nia** \-ē-ə\ [L, fr. *bi-* + *annus* year — more at ANNUAL] **:** a period of two years

bier \ˈbi(ə)r\ *n* [ME *bere,* fr. OE *bǣr;* akin to OE *beran* to carry — more at BEAR] **1** *archaic* **:** a framework for carrying **2 :** a stand on which a corpse or coffin is placed; *also* **:** a coffin together with its stand

bi·fa·cial \(ˈ)bī-ˈfā-shəl\ *adj* **1 :** having opposite surfaces alike <~ leaves> **2 :** having two fronts or faces

biff \ˈbif\ *n* [prob. imit.] *slang* **:** WHACK, BLOW — **biff** *vt, slang*

bi·fid \ˈbī-ˌfid, -fəd\ *adj* [L *bifidus,* fr. *bi-* + *-fidus* -fid] **:** divided into two equal lobes or parts by a median cleft <a ~ leaf> — **bi·fid·i·ty** \bī-ˈfid-ət-ē\ *n* — **bi·fid·ly** \ˈbī-ˌfid-lē, -fəd-\ *adv*

bi·fi·lar \(ˈ)bī-ˈfī-lər\ *adj* [ISV *bi-* + L *filum* thread — more at FILE] **1 :** involving two threads or wires <~ suspension of a pendulum> **2 :** involving a single thread or wire doubled back upon itself <a ~ resistor> — **bi·fi·lar·ly** *adv*

bi·fla·gel·late \(ˈ)bī-ˈflaj-ə-lət, -ˌlāt; ˌbī-flə-ˈjel-ət\ *adj* **:** having two flagella

[1]**bi·fo·cal** \(ˈ)bī-ˈfō-kəl\ *adj* [ISV] **1 :** having two focal lengths **2 :** having one part that corrects for near vision and one for distant vision <a ~ eyeglass lens>

[2]**bifocal** *n* **1 :** a bifocal glass or lens **2** *pl* **:** eyeglasses with bifocal lenses

bi·form \ˈbī-ˌfȯrm\ *adj* [L *biformis,* fr. *bi-* + *forma* form] **:** combining the qualities or forms of two distinct kinds of individuals

bi·fur·cate \ˈbī-(ˌ)fər-ˌkāt, bī-ˈfər-\ *vi* **-cat·ed; -cat·ing** [ML *bifurcatus,* pp. of *bifurcare,* fr. L *bifurcus* two-pronged, fr. *bi-* + *furca* fork] **:** to divide into two branches or parts — **bi·fur·cate** \(ˈ)bī-ˈfər-kət, -ˌkāt; ˈbī-(ˌ)fər-ˌkāt\ *adj* — **bi·fur·cate·ly** *adv*

bi·fur·ca·tion \ˌbī-(ˌ)fər-ˈkā-shən\ *n* **1 :** the act of bifurcating **:** the state of being bifurcated **2 a :** the point at which bifurcating occurs **b :** BRANCH

[1]**big** \ˈbig\ *adj* **big·ger; big·gest** [ME, prob. of Scand origin; akin to Norw dial. *bugge* important man; akin to OE *bȳl* boil, Skt *bhūri* abundant] **1 a** *obs* **:** of great strength **b :** of great force <a ~ storm> **2 a :** large in dimensions, bulk, or extent <a ~ house>; *also* **:** large in quantity, number, or amount <a ~ fleet> **b :** conducted on a large scale <~ government> **3 a :** PREGNANT; *esp* **:** nearly ready to give birth **b :** full to bursting **:** SWELLING <~ with rage> **c** *of the voice* **:** full and resonant **4 a :** CHIEF, PREEMINENT <the ~ issue of the campaign> **b :** outstandingly worthy or able <a truly ~ man> **c :** of great importance or significance <the ~ moment> **d :** IMPOSING, PRETENTIOUS; *also* **:** marked by or given to boasting <~ talk> **e :** MAGNANIMOUS, GENEROUS <a ~ heart> **5 :** POPULAR <soft drinks are very ~ in Mexico — Russ Leadabrand> ***syn*** see LARGE ***ant*** little — **big·ly** *adv* — **big·ness** *n*

[2]**big** *adv* **1 :** to a large amount or extent <eats ~ at noon> **2 a :** in an outstanding manner <made it ~ in New York> **b :** in a pretentious manner <he talks ~> **c :** in a magnanimous manner <took his defeat ~>

big·a·mous \ˈbig-ə-məs\ *adj* **1 :** guilty of bigamy **2 :** involving bigamy — **big·a·mous·ly** *adv*

big·a·my \ˈbig-ə-mē\ *n* [ME *bigamie,* fr. ML *bigamia,* fr. L *bi-* + LL *-gamia* -gamy, fr. Gk, fr. *gamos* marriage; akin to L *gener* son-in-law] **:** the act of entering into a ceremonial marriage with one person while still legally married to another — **big·a·mist** \-məst\ *n*

Big·ar·reau \ˈbig-ə-ˌrō\ *n* [F] **:** any of several cultivated sweet cherries with rather firm often light-colored globular fruits

big bang theory *n* **:** a theory in astronomy: the universe originated billions of years ago from the explosion of a single mass of material so that the pieces are still flying apart — compare STEADY STATE THEORY

big beat *n, often cap both B's* **:** music (as rock 'n' roll) characterized by a heavy persistent beat

Big Ben \-ˈben\ *n* [after Sir *Benjamin* Hall †1867 E Chief Commissioner of Works] **1 :** a large bell in the clock tower of the Houses of Parliament in London **2 :** the tower that houses Big Ben; *also* **:** the clock in the tower

big brother *n* **1 :** an older brother **2 :** a man who befriends a delinquent or friendless boy **3** *cap both Bs* **:** the leader of an authoritarian state or movement

Big Broth·er·ism \-ˈbrət͟h-ə-ˌriz-əm\ *n* **:** authoritarian attempts at complete control (as of a person or a nation)

big deal *n* **:** one that is of exaggerated and usu. doubtful importance

Big Dipper *n* **:** DIPPER 2a

bi·gem·i·ny \bī-ˈjem-ə-nē\ *n* [*bigeminal* (double, paired), fr. LL *bigeminus,* fr. *bi-* + *geminus* twin] **:** the state of having a pulse characterized by two beats close together with a pause following each pair of beats — **bi·gem·i·nal** \-ən-ᵊl\ *adj*

bi·ge·ner·ic \ˌbī-jə-ˈner-ik\ *adj* **:** of, relating to, or involving two genera <a ~ hybrid>

big·eye \ˈbig-ˌī\ *n* **:** either of two small widely distributed reddish to silvery percoid fishes (*Priacanthus cruentatus* and *P. arenatus*) of tropical seas

big game *n* **1 :** large animals sought or taken by hunting or fishing for sport **2 :** an important objective esp. when involving risk

big·ge·ty *or* **big·gi·ty** \ˈbig-ət-ē\ *adj* [prob. irreg. fr. *big* + *-y*] **1** *South & Midland* **:** CONCEITED, VAIN **2** *South & Midland* **:** rudely self-important **:** IMPUDENT <Mama never acted ~ in court, but she would bow her head only so low — Claude Brown>

[1]**big·gin** *or* **big·ging** \ˈbig-ən\ *n* [ME *bigging,* fr. *biggen* to dwell, fr. ON *byggja;* akin to OE *bēon* to be] *archaic* **:** BUILDING

[2]**biggin** *n* [MF *beguin*] *archaic* **:** CAP: **a :** a child's cap **b :** NIGHTCAP

big·gish \ˈbig-ish\ *adj* **:** somewhat big

big·head \ˈbig-ˌhed\ *n* **1 :** any of several diseases of animals marked by swelling about the head **2 :** an exaggerated opinion of one's importance **:** CONCEIT — **big·head·ed** \-ˈhed-əd\ *adj*

big·heart·ed \-ˈhärt-əd\ *adj* **:** being generous and kindly — **big·heart·ed·ly** *adv* — **big·heart·ed·ness** *n*

big·horn \ˈbig-ˌhȯ(ə)rn\ *n, pl* **bighorn** *or* **bighorns :** a usu. grayish brown wild sheep (*Ovis canadensis*) of mountainous western No. America

bighorn

[1]**bight** \ˈbīt\ *n* [ME, fr. OE *byht;* akin to OE *būgan* to bend — more at BOW] **1** *obs* **:** a corner, bend, or angle esp. of a body part **2 a :** the middle part of a slack rope **b :** a loop esp. in a rope **3 a :** a bend esp. in a river or a mountain chain **b :** a bend in a coast forming an open bay; *also* **:** a bay formed by such a bend

[2]**bight** *vt* **1 :** to lay or fasten (a rope) in bights **2 :** to fasten with a bight

big league *n* **1 :** MAJOR LEAGUE **2 :** one that is outstanding of its kind — **big leagu·er** \-ˈlē-gər\ *n*

big·mouthed \ˈbig-ˈmau̇t͟hd, -ˈmau̇tht\ *adj* **1 :** having a large mouth **2 :** LOUDMOUTHED

big–name \-ˈnām\ *adj* **1 :** of top rank in popular recognition **2 :** of or involving a big-name person, organization, or product

big name *n* **:** a big-name performer or personage

big·no·nia \big-ˈnō-nē-ə\ *n* [NL, genus name, fr. J. P. *Bignon* †1743 F royal librarian] **:** any of a genus (*Bignonia*) of American and Japanese woody vines of the trumpet-creeper family with compound leaves and tubular flowers

big·ot \ˈbig-ət\ *n* [MF, hypocrite, bigot] **:** one obstinately or intolerantly devoted to his own church, party, belief, or opinion — **big·ot·ed** \-ət-əd\ *adj* — **big·ot·ed·ly** *adv*

big·ot·ry \ˈbig-ə-trē\ *n, pl* **-ries 1 :** the state of mind of a bigot **2 :** acts or beliefs characteristic of a bigot

big shot \ˈbig-ˌshät\ *n* **:** a person of consequence or prominence

big stick *n* **:** threat esp. of military or political intervention

big–tick·et \ˈbig-ˈtik-ət\ *adj* **:** high-priced

big time \-ˌtīm\ *n* **1 :** a high-paying vaudeville circuit requiring only two performances a day **2 :** the top rank — **big–tim·er** \-ˌtī-mər\ *n*

big toe *n* **:** the innermost and largest digit of the foot

big top *n* **1 :** the main tent of a circus **2 :** CIRCUS 2a, 2b, 2c

big tree *n* : a California evergreen (*Sequoiadendron giganteum*) of the pine family that often exceeds 300 feet in height — called also *giant sequoia, sequoia*
big·wig \'big-,wig\ *n* : an important person
Bi·ha·ri \bi-'här-ē\ *n* : a group of Indic dialects spoken by the inhabitants of Bihar
bi·jou \'bē-,zhü\ *n, pl* **bijous** *or* **bi·joux** \-,zhü(z)\ [F, fr. Bret *bizou* ring, fr. *biz* finger; akin to W *bys* finger] : a small dainty usu. ornamental piece of delicate workmanship : JEWEL — **bijou** *adj*
bi·jou·te·rie \bi-'zhüt-ə-(,)rē\ *n* [F, fr. *bijou*] : a collection of trinkets or ornaments : JEWELS; *also* : DECORATION
¹bike \'bīk\ *n* [ME] **1** *chiefly Scot* : a nest of wild bees, wasps, or hornets **2** *chiefly Scot* : a crowd or swarm of people
²bike *n* [by shortening & alter.] **1** : BICYCLE **2** : MOTORCYCLE **3** : MOTORBIKE — **bik·er** *n*
³bike *vi* **biked; bik·ing** : to ride a bike
bike·way \'bī-,kwā\ *n* : a thoroughfare esp. suitable for bicycles
bi·ki·ni \bə-'kē-nē\ *n* [F, fr. *Bikini,* atoll of the Marshall islands] : a woman's scanty two-piece bathing suit — **bi·ki·nied** \-nēd\ *adj*
¹bi·la·bi·al \(')bī-'lā-bē-əl\ *adj* [ISV] **1** *of a consonant* : produced with both lips **2** : of or relating to both lips
²bilabial *n* : a bilabial consonant
bi·la·bi·ate \-bē-ət\ *adj* : having two lips <a ~ corolla of a mint>
bi·lat·er·al \(')bī-'lat-ə-rəl, -'la-trəl\ *adj* **1** : having two sides **2** : affecting reciprocally two sides or parties <a ~ treaty> **3** : having bilateral symmetry — **bi·lat·er·al·ism** \-,iz-əm\ *n* — **bi·lat·er·al·ly** \-ē\ *adv* — **bi·lat·er·al·ness** *n*
bilateral symmetry *n* : a pattern of animal symmetry in which similar parts are arranged on opposite sides of a median axis so that one and only one plane can divide the individual into essentially identical halves
bi·layer \'bī-,lā-ər, -,le(-ə)r\ *n* : a film or membrane with two molecular layers <a ~ of phospholipid molecules>
bil·ber·ry \'bil-,ber-ē\ *n* [*bil-* (prob. of Scand origin; akin to Dan *bolle* whortleberry) + *berry*] : any of several plants (genus *Vaccinium*) that differ from the typical blueberries in having their flowers arise solitary or in very small clusters from axillary buds; *also* : its sweet edible bluish fruit
¹bil·bo *or* **bil·boa** \'bil-(,)bō\ *n* [*Bilboa, Bilbao,* Spain] : a finely tempered sword
²bilbo *n* [perh. fr. *Bilboa,* Spain] : a long bar of iron with sliding shackles used to confine the feet of prisoners esp. on shipboard
bile \'bī(ə)l\ *n* [F, fr. L *bilis;* akin to W *bustl* bile] **1 a** : a yellow or greenish viscid alkaline fluid secreted by the liver and passed into the duodenum where it aids esp. in the digestion and absorption of fats **b** : either of two humors associated in old physiology with irascibility and melancholy **2** : inclination to anger : SPLEEN
bile acid *n* : a steroid acid (as cholic acid) of or derived from bile
bile duct *n* : a duct by which bile passes from the liver or gallbladder to the duodenum
bile salt *n* **1** : a salt of bile acid **2** : a dry mixture of the principal salts of the gall of the ox used as a liver stimulant and as a laxative
bi–lev·el \'bī-'lev-əl\ *adj* **1** : having two levels of freight or passenger space **2** : divided vertically into two ground-floor levels
¹bilge \'bilj\ *n* [prob. modif. of MF *boulge, bouge* leather bag, curved part — more at BUDGET] **1** : the bulging part of a cask or barrel **2 a** : the part of the underwater body of a ship between the flat of the bottom and the vertical topsides **b** : the lowest point of a ship's inner hull **3** : stale or worthless remarks or ideas
²bilge *vi* **bilged; bilg·ing** **1** : to undergo damage (as a fracture) in the bilge **2** : to rest on the bilge
bilge keel *n* : a longitudinal projection like a fin secured for a distance along a ship near the turn of the bilge on either side to check rolling
bilge water *n* : water that collects by seepage or leakage in the bilge of a ship
bilgy \'bil-jē\ *adj* **bilg·i·er; -est** : resembling bilge water esp. in smell
bil·har·zia \bil-'här-zē-ə, -'härt-sē-\ *n* [NL, fr. Theodor *Bilharz* †1862 G zoologist] **1** : SCHISTOSOME **2** : SCHISTOSOMIASIS — **bil·har·zi·al** \-zē-əl, -sē-\ *adj*
bil·har·zi·a·sis \,bil-,här-'zī-ə-səs, -,härt-'sī-\ *n, pl* **-a·ses** \-,sēz\ [NL, fr. *bilharzia* + *-iasis*] : SCHISTOSOMIASIS
bil·i·ary \'bil-ē-,er-ē\ *adj* [F *biliare,* fr. L *bilis*] : of, relating to, or conveying bile; *also* : affecting the bile-conveying structures <~ disorders>
bi·lin·ear \(')bī-'lin-ē-ər\ *adj* : linear with respect to each of two mathematical variables; *specif* : of or relating to an algebraic form each term of which involves one variable to the first degree from each of two sets of variables
bi·lin·gual \(')bī-'liŋ-g(yə-)wəl\ *adj* [L *bilinguis,* fr. *bi-* + *lingua* tongue — more at TONGUE] **1** : of, containing, or expressed in two languages **2** : using or able to use two languages esp. with the fluency characteristic of a native speaker — **bilingual** *n* — **bi·lin·gual·ly** \-ē\ *adv*
bi·lin·gual·ism \-,iz-əm\ *n* : the constant oral use of two languages
bil·ious \'bil-yəs\ *adj* [MF *bilieux,* fr. L *biliosus,* fr. *bilis*] **1 a** : of or relating to bile **b** : marked by or suffering from disordered liver function and esp. excessive secretion of bile **c** : appearing as though affected by a bilious disorder **2** : of a peevish ill-natured disposition : CHOLERIC — **bil·ious·ly** *adv* — **bil·ious·ness** *n*
bil·i·ru·bin \,bil-i-'rü-bən, 'bil-i-,\ *n* [L *bilis* + *ruber* red — more at RED] : a reddish yellow pigment $C_{33}H_{36}N_4O_6$ occurring in bile, blood, urine, and gallstones
bil·i·ver·din \-'vərd-ᵊn, -,vərd-\ *n* [Sw, fr. L *bilis* + obs. F *verd* green] : a green pigment $C_{33}H_{34}N_4O_6$ occurring in bile
¹bilk \'bilk\ *vt* [perh. alter. of *-balk*] **1** : to block the free development of : FRUSTRATE <fate ~s their hopes> **2 a** : to cheat out of what is due **b** : to evade payment of <~s his creditors> **3** : to slip away from : ELUDE <~ his pursuers> — **bilk·er** *n*
²bilk *n* : an untrustworthy tricky individual : CHEAT
¹bill \'bil\ *n* [ME *bile,* fr. OE; akin to OE *bill* (weapon)] **1** : the jaws of a bird together with their horny covering **2** : a mouthpart (as the beak of a turtle) that resembles a bird's bill **3** : a projection of land like a beak **4** : the end of an anchor fluke or of a sail yard **5** : the visor of a cap

bills of birds: *1* flamingo, *2* hawk, *3* pigeon, *4* thrush, *5* duck (merganser), *6* toucan, *7* finch, *8* spoonbill, *9* pelican

²bill *vi* **1** : to touch and rub bill to bill **2** : to caress affectionately
³bill *n* [ME *bil,* fr. OE *bill;* akin to OHG *bill* pickax, Gk *phitros* log] **1** : a weapon in use up to the 18th century that consists of a long staff terminating in a hook-shaped blade **2** : BILLHOOK
⁴bill *n* [ME, fr. ML *billa,* alter. of *bulla,* fr. L, bubble, boss] **1 a** : a written document **b** : MEMORANDUM **c** : LETTER **2** *obs* : a formal petition **3** : a draft of a law presented to a legislature for enactment **4** : a declaration in writing stating a wrong a complainant has suffered from a defendant or stating a breach of law by some person <a ~ of complaint> **5** : a paper carrying a statement of particulars (as a list of men and their duties as part of a ship's crew) **6 a** : an itemized account of the separate cost of goods sold, services performed, or work done : INVOICE **b** : a statement in gross of a creditor's claim **c** : a statement of charges for food or drink : CHECK **7 a** : a written or printed advertisement posted or otherwise distributed to announce an event of interest to the public; *esp* : an announcement of a theatrical entertainment **b** : a programmed presentation (as a motion picture, play, or concert) **8 a** : a piece of paper money **b** : an individual or commercial note <~*s* receivable> **c** *slang* : one hundred dollars
⁵bill *vt* **1 a** : to enter in a book of accounts : prepare a bill of (charges) **b** : to submit a bill of charges to **c** : to enter (as freight) in a waybill **d** : to issue a bill of lading to or for **2 a** : to announce esp. by posters or placards **b** : to arrange for the presentation of **3** : ADVERTISE <the book is ~*ed* as a "report" —P. G. Altbach>
bil·la·bong \'bil-ə-,bȯŋ, -,bäŋ\ *n* [native name in Australia] **1** *Austral* **a** : a blind channel leading out from a river **b** : a usu. dry stream bed that is filled seasonally **2** *Austral* : a backwater forming a stagnant pool
¹bill·board \'bil-,bō(ə)rd, -,bȯ(ə)rd\ *n* : a projection or ledge fixed on the bow of a vessel for the anchor to rest on
²billboard *n* [⁴*bill* + *board*] : a flat surface (as of a panel, wall, or fence) on which bills are posted; *specif* : a large panel designed to carry outdoor advertising
bill·bug \'bil-,bəg\ *n* [¹*bill* + *bug*] : a weevil (esp. genus *Calendra*) having larvae that eat the roots of cereal and other grasses
-billed \'bild\ *adj comb form* : having (such) a bill <hard-*billed*>
bill·er \'bil-ər\ *n* : one that bills: as **a** : a clerk who makes out bills **b** : a machine for making out bills
¹bil·let \'bil-ət\ *n* [ME *bylet,* fr. MF *billette,* dim. of *bulle* document, fr. ML *bulla*] **1** *archaic* : a brief letter : NOTE **2 a** : an official order directing that a member of a military force be provided with board and lodging (as in a private home) **b** : quarters assigned by or as if by a billet **3** : POSITION, JOB <a lucrative ~>
²billet *vt* **1** : to assign lodging to (as soldiers) by a billet : QUARTER **2** : to serve with a billet <~ a householder> ~ *vi* : to have quarters
³billet *n* [ME *bylet,* fr. MF *billete,* dim. of *bille* log, of Celt origin; akin to OIr *bile* sacred tree] **1 a** : a chunky piece of wood (as for firewood) : BOLT 5 **b** *obs* : CUDGEL **2 a** : a bar of metal **b** : a piece of semifinished iron or steel nearly square in section made by rolling an ingot or bloom **c** : a section of nonferrous metal ingot hot-worked by forging, rolling, or extrusion : a nonferrous casting suitable for rolling or extrusion
bil·let–doux \,bil-(,)ā-'dü\ *n, pl* **billets–doux** \-(,)ā-'dü(z)\ [F *billet doux,* lit., sweet letter] : a love letter
bill·fish \'bil-,fish\ *n* : a fish (as a marlin or gar) with long slender jaws
bill·fold \-,fōld\ *n* [short for earlier *billfolder*] **1** : a folding pocketbook for paper money **2** : WALLET 2b
bill·head \-,hed\ *n* : a printed form usu. headed with a business address and used for billing charges
bill·hook \-,hu̇k\ *n* : a cutting tool consisting of a blade with a hooked point fitted with a handle and used esp. in pruning
bil·liard \'bil-yərd\ *n* [back-formation fr. *billiards*] **1** : CAROM 1a **2** — used as an attributive form of *billiards* <~ ball>
bil·liards \-yərdz\ *n pl but sing in constr* [MF *billard* billiard cue, billiards, fr. *bille*] : any of several games played on an oblong table by driving small balls against one another or into pockets with a cue; *specif* : a game in which one scores by causing a cue ball to hit in succession two object balls — compare POOL
bill·ing \'bil-iŋ\ *n* [⁵*bill*] **1** : ADVERTISING <advance ~> **2** : total amount of business or investments (as of an advertising

agency) within a given period **3 :** the relative prominence given a name (as of an actor) in advertising programs <top ~>

bil·lings·gate \'bil-iŋz-,gāt, *Brit usu* -git\ *n* [*Billingsgate,* old gate and fish market, London, England] **:** coarsely abusive language *syn* see ABUSE

bil·lion \'bil-yən\ *n* [F, fr. *bi-* + *-illion* (as in *million*)] **1** — see NUMBER table **2 :** a very large number — **billion** *adj* — **bil·lionth** \-yən(t)th\ *adj or n*

bil·lion·aire \,bil-yə-'na(ə)r, -'ne(ə)r, 'bil-yə-,\ *n* [*billion* + *-aire* (as in *millionaire*)] **:** one whose wealth is estimated at a billion or more (as of dollars or pounds)

bill of exchange : an unconditional written order from one person to another to pay a specified sum of money to a designated person

bill of fare 1 : MENU **2 :** PROGRAM

bill of goods : a consignment of merchandise

bill of health 1 : a certificate given to the ship's master at the time of leaving port that indicates the state of health of a ship's company and of a port with regard to infectious diseases **2 :** a report about a condition or situation <gave the criticized textbook a clean *bill of health*>

bill of lading : a receipt listing goods shipped that is signed by the agent of the owner of a ship or issued by a common carrier

bill of rights *often cap B&R* **:** a summary of fundamental rights and privileges guaranteed to a people against violation by the state — used esp. of the first 10 amendments to the U.S. Constitution

bill of sale : a formal instrument for the conveyance or transfer of title to goods and chattels

bil·lon \'bil-ən\ *n* [F, fr. MF, fr. *bille* log — more at BILLET] **1 :** an alloy of silver containing more than 50 percent of copper by weight **2 :** gold or silver heavily alloyed with a less valuable metal

¹bil·low \'bil-(,)ō, -ə(-w)\ *n* [prob. fr. ON *bylgja;* akin to OHG *balg* bag — more at BELLY] **1 :** WAVE; *esp* **:** a great wave or surge of water **2 :** a rolling mass (as of flame or smoke) that resembles a high wave — **bil·lowy** \'bil-ə-wē\ *adj*

²billow *vi* **1 :** to rise or roll in waves or surges **2 :** to bulge or swell out (as through action of the wind) ~ *vt* **:** to cause to billow

bill·post·er \'bil-,pō-stər\ *n* **:** one that posts advertising bills — called also *billsticker* — **bill·post·ing** \-stiŋ\ *n*

¹bil·ly \'bil-ē\ *n, pl* **billies** [prob. fr. the name *Billy*] **:** BILLY CLUB

²billy *n, pl* **billies** [prob. short for *billycan* (billy)] *chiefly Austral* **:** a can of metal or enamelware made with a lid and a wire bail and used for outdoor cooking or for carrying food or liquid

billy club *n* [¹*billy*] **:** a heavy usu. wooden club; *specif* **:** a policeman's club

bil·ly·cock \'bil-ē-,käk\ *n* [origin unknown] *Brit* **:** a stiff felt hat

bil·ly goat \'bil-ē-\ *n* [fr. the name *Billy*] **:** a male goat

bi·lobed \'bī-'lōbd\ *adj* **:** divided into two lobes

bi·loc·u·lar \(')bī-'läk-yə-lər\ *or* **bi·loc·u·late** \-lət\ *adj* [*bi-* + NL *loculus*] **:** divided into two cells or compartments <~ ovary>

bil·tong \'bil-,tȯŋ, -,täŋ\ *n* [Afrik, fr. *bil* buttock + *tong* tongue] *chiefly So Afr* **:** jerked meat

bi·man·u·al \(')bī-'man-yə(-wə)l\ *adj* **:** done with or requiring the use of both hands — **bi·man·u·al·ly** \-ē\ *adv*

bi·mes·ter \(')bī-'mes-tər, 'bī-,\ *n* [*bi-* + *-mester* (as in *semester*)] **:** a period of two months

bi·mes·tri·al \bī-'mes-trē-əl\ *adj* [L *bimestris,* fr. *bi-* + *mensis* month — more at MOON] **:** continuing for two months

bi·met·al \'bī-,met-ᵊl\ *adj* **:** BIMETALLIC — **bimetal** *n*

bi·me·tal·lic \,bī-mə-'tal-ik\ *adj* **1 :** relating to, based on, or using bimetallism **2 :** composed of two different metals — often used of devices having a part in which two metals that expand differently are bonded together — **bimetallic** *n*

bi·met·al·lism \(')bī-'met-ᵊl-,iz-əm\ *n* [F *bimétallisme,* fr. *bi-* + *métal* metal] **:** the use of two metals (as gold and silver) jointly as a monetary standard with both constituting legal tender at a predetermined ratio — **bi·met·al·list** \-ᵊl-əst\ *n* — **bi·met·al·lis·tic** \,bī-,met-ᵊl-'is-tik\ *adj*

bi·mil·le·na·ry \(')bī-'mil-ə-,ner-ē, ,bī-mə-'len-ə-rē\ *or* **bi·mil·len·i·al** \,bī-mə-'len-ē-əl\ *n* **1 :** a period of 2000 years **2 :** a 2000th anniversary — **bimillenary** *adj*

bi·mod·al \(')bī-'mōd-ᵊl\ *adj* **:** having two statistical modes — **bi·mo·dal·i·ty** \,bī-mō-'dal-ət-ē\ *n*

bi·mo·lec·u·lar \,bī-mə-'lek-yə-lər\ *adj* [ISV] **1 :** relating to or formed from two molecules **2 :** being two molecules thick — **bi·mo·lec·u·lar·ly** *adv*

¹bi·month·ly \(')bī-'mən(t)th-lē\ *adj* **1 :** occurring every two months **2 :** occurring twice a month **:** SEMIMONTHLY

²bimonthly *n* **:** a bimonthly publication

³bimonthly *adv* **1 :** once every two months **2 :** twice a month

bi·mor·phe·mic \,bī-mȯr-'fē-mik\ *adj* **:** consisting of two morphemes

¹bin \'bin\ *n* [ME *binn,* fr. OE] **:** a box, frame, crib, or enclosed place used for storage

²bin *vt* **binned; bin·ning :** to put into a bin

bin- *comb form* [ME, fr. LL, fr. L *bini* two by two; akin to OE *twīn* twine] **:** ¹BI- <*bin*aural>

¹bi·na·ry \'bī-nə-rē\ *adj* [LL *binarius,* fr. L *bini*] **1 :** compounded or consisting of or marked by two things or parts **2 :** composed of two chemical elements, an element and a radical that acts as an element, or two such radicals **3 a :** relating to, being, or belonging to a system of numbers having 2 as its base <the ~ digits 0 and 1> **b :** involving a choice or condition of two alternatives (as on-off or yes-no) **4 :** relating two logical elements <~ operation> **5 a :** having two musical subjects or two complementary sections **b :** DUPLE — used of measure or rhythm

²binary *n, pl* **-ries :** something made of two things or parts

binary fission *n* **:** reproduction of a cell by division into two approximately equal parts <the *binary fission* of protozoans>

binary star *n* **:** a system of two stars that revolve around each other under their mutual gravitation

bi·na·tion·al \(')bī-'nash-nəl, -ən-ᵊl\ *adj* **:** of or relating to two nations <a ~ board of directors>

bin·au·ral \(')bī-'nȯr-əl, (')bin-'ȯr-\ *adj* [ISV] **1 :** of, relating to, or used with two or both ears **2 :** of, relating to, or characterized by the placement of sound sources (as in sound transmission and recording) to achieve in sound reproduction an effect of hearing the sound sources in their original positions — **bin·au·ral·ly** \-ə-lē\ *adv*

¹bind \'bīnd\ *vb* **bound** \'baund\; **bind·ing** [ME *binden,* fr. OE *bindan;* akin to OHG *bintan* to bind, Gk *peisma* cable] *vt* **1 a :** to make secure by tying **b :** to confine, restrain, or restrict as if with bonds **c :** to put under an obligation <~*s* himself with an oath> **d :** to constrain with legal authority **2 a :** to wrap around with something so as to enclose or cover **b :** BANDAGE **3 :** to fasten round about **4 :** to tie together (as stocks of wheat) **5 a :** to cause to stick together **b :** to take up and hold (as by chemical forces) **:** combine with **6 :** CONSTIPATE **7 :** to make firm or sure **:** SETTLE <a deposit ~*s* the sale> **8 :** to protect, strengthen, or decorate by a band or binding **9 :** to apply the parts of the cover to (a book) **10 :** to set at work as an apprentice **:** INDENTURE **11 :** to cause to be attached (as by gratitude) **12 :** to fasten together **13 :** to effect (an insurance policy) by an oral commitment or a written instrument ~ *vi* **1 :** to form a cohesive mass **2 :** to hamper free movement or natural action **3 :** to become hindered from free operation **4 :** to exert a restraining or compelling effect <a promise that ~*s*>

²bind *n* **1 a :** something that binds **b :** the act of binding **:** the state of being bound **c :** a place where binding occurs **2 a :** TIE 3 **b :** SLUR 1a **3 :** a position that restricts an opponent's freedom of action (as in chess) — **in a bind :** in trouble

bind·er \'bīn-dər\ *n* **1 :** a person that binds something (as books) **2 a :** something used in binding **b :** a usu. detachable cover (as for holding sheets of paper) **c :** the sheet of tobacco that binds the filler in a cigar **3 :** something (as tar or cement) that produces or promotes cohesion in loosely assembled substances **4 :** a receipt for money paid to secure the right to purchase real estate on agreed terms; *also* **:** the money itself

bind·ery \'bīn-d(ə-)rē\ *n, pl* **-er·ies :** a place where books are bound

¹bind·ing \'bīn-diŋ\ *n* **1 :** the action of one that binds **2 :** a material or device used to bind: as **a :** the cover and fastenings of a book **b :** a narrow fabric used to finish raw edges **c :** a set of ski fastenings for holding the boot firm on the ski

²binding *adj* **1 :** that binds **2 :** imposing an obligation — **bind·ing·ly** \-diŋ-lē\ *adv* — **bind·ing·ness** *n*

binding energy *n* **:** the energy required to break up a molecule, atom, or atomic nucleus completely into its constituent particles

bind off *vt* **:** to cast off in knitting

bind over *vt* **:** to put under bonds to do something (as to appear in court)

bind·weed \'bīn-,dwēd\ *n* **:** any of various twining plants (esp. genus *Convolvulus* of the morning-glory family) that mat or interlace with plants among which they grow

bine \'bīn\ *n* [alter. of ²*bind*] **:** a twining stem or flexible shoot (as of the hop); *also* **:** a plant (as woodbine) whose shoots are bines

Bi·net–Si·mon scale \bi-,nā-sē-'mōⁿ-\ *n* [Alfred *Binet* †1911 and Théodore *Simon* †1961 F psychologists] **:** an intelligence test consisting orig. of tasks graded from the level of the average 3-year-old to that of the average 12-year-old but later extended in range

binge \'binj\ *n* [E dial. *binge* (to drink heavily)] **1 a :** a drunken revel **:** SPREE **b :** an unrestrained indulgence <a buying ~> **2 :** a social gathering **:** PARTY

bin·go \'biŋ-(,)gō\ *n, pl* **bingos** [earlier *bingo* (interj. used to announce an unexpected event)] **:** a game of chance played with cards having numbered squares corresponding to numbered balls drawn at random and won by covering five such squares in a row

bin·na·cle \'bin-i-kəl\ *n* [alter. of ME *bitakle,* fr. OPg or OSp; OPg *bitácola* & OSp *bitácula,* fr. L *habitaculum* dwelling place, fr. *habitare* to inhabit — more at HABITATION] **:** a case, box, or stand containing a ship's compass and a lamp

¹bin·oc·u·lar \bī-'näk-yə-lər, bə-\ *adj* **:** of, relating to, using, or adapted to the use of both eyes <~ vision> — **bin·oc·u·lar·i·ty** \(,)bī-,näk-yə-'lar-ət-ē, bə-\ *n* — **bin·oc·u·lar·ly** \bī-'näk-yə-lər-lē, bə-\ *adv*

²bin·oc·u·lar \bə-'näk-yə-lər, bī-\ *n* **1 :** a binocular optical instrument **2 :** FIELD GLASS — usu. used in pl.

bi·no·mi·al \bī-'nō-mē-əl\ *n* [NL *binomium,* fr. ML, neut. of *binomius* having two names, alter. of L *binominis,* fr. *bi-* + *nomin-, nomen* name — more at NAME] **1 :** a mathematical expression consisting of two terms connected by a plus sign or minus sign **2 :** a biological species name consisting of two terms — **binomial** *adj* — **bi·no·mi·al·ly** \-mē-ə-lē\ *adv*

binomial coefficient *n* **:** the coefficient of any term resulting from the expansion of the binomial $(x + y)^n$

binomial distribution *n* **:** a probability function each of whose values gives the probability that an outcome with constant probability of occurrence in a statistical experiment will occur a given number of times in a succession of repetitions of the experiment

binomial nomenclature *n* **:** a system of nomenclature in which each species of animal or plant receives a name of two terms of which the first identifies the genus to which it belongs and the second the species itself

binomial theorem *n* **:** a theorem that specifies the expansion of a binomial of the form $(x + y)^n$ in $n + 1$ terms of which the general term is of the form

$$\frac{n!}{k!(n-k)!}\,x^k y^{(n-k)}$$

bint \'bint\ *n* [Ar, girl, daughter] *slang Brit* **:** GIRL, WOMAN

bi·nu·cle·ate \(')bī-'n(y)ü-klē-ət\ *also* **bi·nu·cle·at·ed** \-klē-,āt-əd\ *adj* **:** having two nuclei

bio \'bī-(,)ō\ *n, pl* **bi·os :** BIOGRAPHY

bio- — see BI-

bio·as·say \,bī-(,)ō-'as-,ā, -a-'sā\ *n* [*bio*logical *assay*] **:** determination of the relative strength of a substance (as a drug) by comparing its effect on a test organism with that of a standard preparation — **bio·as·say** \-a-'sā, -'as-,ā\ *vt*

bio·as·tro·nau·tics \ˌbī-ō-ˌas-trə-ˈnȯt-iks, -ˈnät-\ *n pl but sing or pl in constr* **:** the medical and biological aspect of astronautics — **bio·as·tro·nau·ti·cal** \-i-kəl\ *adj*

bio·cat·a·lyst \ˌbī-ō-ˈkat-ᵊl-əst\ *n* **:** a substance (as an enzyme or a trace element) that activates or accelerates biological processes — **bio·cat·a·lyt·ic** \-ˌkat-ᵊl-ˈit-ik\ *adj*

bio·ce·no·sis *or* **bio·coe·no·sis** \-sə-ˈnō-səs\ *n, pl* **-no·ses** \-ˌsēz\ [NL, fr. ²*bi-* + Gk *koinōsis* sharing, fr. *koinos* common — more at CO-] **:** an ecological community (as an oyster bed) esp. when forming a self-regulating unit — **bio·ce·not·ic** *or* **bio·coe·not·ic** \-ˈnät-ik\ *adj*

bio·chem·i·cal \ˌbī-ō-ˈkem-i-kəl\ *adj* [ISV] **1 :** of or relating to biochemistry **2 :** characterized by, produced by, or involving chemical reactions in living organisms — **biochemical** *n* — **bio·chem·i·cal·ly** \-k(ə-)lē\ *adv*

biochemical oxygen demand *n* **:** the oxygen used in meeting the metabolic needs of aerobic microorganisms in water rich in organic matter (as water polluted with sewage) — called also *biological oxygen demand*

bio·chem·is·try \ˌbī-ō-ˈkem-ə-strē\ *n* [ISV] **:** chemistry that deals with the chemical compounds and processes occurring in organisms — **bio·chem·ist** \-əst\ *n*

bio·cide \ˈbī-ə-ˌsīd\ *n* **:** a substance (as DDT) that is destructive to many different organisms — **bio·cid·al** \ˌbī-ə-ˈsīd-ᵊl\ *adj*

bio·clean \ˈbī-ō-ˌklēn\ *adj* **:** free or almost free of harmful or potentially harmful organisms (as bacteria) <a ~ room>

bio·cli·mat·ic \ˌbī-ō-klī-ˈmat-ik\ *adj* **:** of or relating to the relations of climate and living matter

bio·de·grad·able \-di-ˈgrād-ə-bəl\ *adj* [²*bi-* + *degrade* + *-able*] **:** capable of being broken down esp. into innocuous products by the action of living beings (as microorganisms) — **bio·de·grad·abil·i·ty** \-ˌgrād-ə-ˈbil-ət-ē\ *n* — **bio·deg·ra·da·tion** \-ˌdeg-rə-ˈdā-shən\ *n* — **bio·de·grade** \-di-ˈgrād\ *vt*

bio·ecol·o·gy \ˌbī-ō-i-ˈkäl-ə-jē\ *n* **:** ecology dealing with the interrelation of plants and animals with their common environment — **bio·eco·log·i·cal** \-ˌē-kə-ˈläj-i-kəl, -ˌek-ə-\ *adj* — **bio·ecol·o·gist** \-i-ˈkäl-ə-jəst\ *n*

bio·elec·tric \-i-ˈlek-trik\ *or* **bio·elec·tri·cal** \-tri-kəl\ *adj* **:** of or relating to electric phenomena in animals and plants — **bio·elec·tric·i·ty** \-ˌlek-ˈtris-ət-ē, -ˈtris-tē\ *n*

bio·en·gi·neer·ing \-ˌen-jə-ˈni(ə)r-iŋ\ *n* **:** application to biological or medical science of engineering principles (as the theory of control systems in models of the nervous system) or engineering equipment (as in the construction of artificial organs)

bio·en·vi·ron·men·tal \-in-ˌvī-rən-ˈment-ᵊl\ *adj* **:** concerned with the environment and esp. with deleterious factors in the environment of living beings

bio·feed·back \-ˈfēd-ˌbak\ *n* **:** the technique of making unconscious or involuntary bodily processes (as heartbeat or brain waves) perceptible to the senses (as by the use of an oscilloscope) in order to manipulate them by conscious mental control

bio·fla·vo·noid \-ˈflā-və-ˌnȯid\ *n* **:** a biologically active flavonoid — called also *vitamin P*

biog *abbr* biographer; biographical; biography

bio·gen·e·sis \ˌbī-ō-ˈjen-ə-səs\ *n* [NL] **1 :** the development of life from preexisting life **2 :** a supposed tendency for stages in the evolutionary history of a race to briefly recur during the development and differentiation of an individual of that race **3 :** BIOSYNTHESIS — **bio·ge·net·ic** \-jə-ˈnet-ik\ *adj* — **bio·ge·net·i·cal·ly** \-i-k(ə-)lē\ *adv*

bio·gen·ic \-ˈjen-ik\ *adj* **:** produced by living organisms

bio·geo·chem·is·try \-ˌjē-ō-ˈkem-ə-strē\ *n* [²*bi-* + *geochemistry*] **:** a science that deals with the relation of earth chemicals to plant and animal life in an area — **bio·geo·chem·i·cal** \-ˈkem-i-kəl\ *adj*

bio·ge·og·ra·phy \-jē-ˈäg-rə-fē\ *n* [ISV] **:** a branch of biology that deals with the geographical distribution of animals and plants — **bio·geo·graph·ic** \-ˌjē-ə-ˈgraf-ik\ *or* **bio·geo·graph·i·cal** \-i-kəl\ *adj*

bi·og·ra·phee \bī-ˌäg-rə-ˈfē, bē-\ *n* **:** a person about whom a biography is written

bi·og·ra·pher \-ˈäg-rə-fər\ *n* **:** a writer of a biography

bio·graph·i·cal \ˌbī-ə-ˈgraf-i-kəl\ *or* **bio·graph·ic** \-ik\ *adj* **1 :** of, relating to, or constituting biography **2 :** consisting of biographies <a ~ dictionary> **3 :** relating to a list briefly identifying persons <~ notes> — **bio·graph·i·cal·ly** \-i-k(ə-)lē\ *adv*

bi·og·ra·phy \bī-ˈäg-rə-fē, bē-\ *n, pl* **-phies** [LGk *biographia,* fr. Gk *bi-* + *-graphia* -graphy] **1 :** a usu. written history of a person's life **2 :** biographical writings in general **3 :** an account of the life of something (as an animal, a coin, or a building)

bio·in·stru·men·ta·tion \ˈbī-ō-ˌin-strə-mən-ˈtā-shən, -ˌmen-\ *n* **:** the development and use of instruments for recording and transmitting physiological data (as from astronauts in flight)

biol *abbr* biologic; biological; biologist; biology

¹bi·o·log·ic \ˌbī-ə-ˈläj-ik\ *adj* **1 :** of or relating to biology or to life and living processes **2 :** used in or produced by applied biology — **bi·o·log·i·cal** \-i-kəl\ *adj* — **bi·o·log·i·cal·ly** \-i-k(ə-)lē\ *adv*

²biologic *n* **:** a biological product used in medicine — **biological** *n*

biological clock *n* **:** an inherent timing mechanism responsible for various cyclical physiological and behavioral responses of living beings

biological control *n* **:** attack upon noxious organisms by interference with their ecological adjustment

biological oxygen demand *n* **:** BIOCHEMICAL OXYGEN DEMAND

biological warfare *n* **:** warfare involving the use of living organisms (as disease germs) or their toxic products against men, animals, or plants; *also* **:** warfare involving the use of synthetic chemicals harmful to plants

bi·ol·o·gism \bī-ˈäl-ə-ˌjiz-əm\ *n* **:** preoccupation with biological explanations in the analysis of social situations — **bi·ol·o·gis·tic** \-ˌäl-ə-ˈjis-tik\ *adj*

bi·ol·o·gy \bī-ˈäl-ə-jē\ *n* [G *biologie,* fr. *bi-* + *-logie* -logy] **1 a :** a branch of knowledge that deals with living organisms and vital processes **b :** ECOLOGY **2 a :** the plant and animal life of a region or environment **b :** the laws and phenomena relating to an organism or group — **bi·ol·o·gist** \-jəst\ *n*

bio·lu·mi·nes·cence \ˌbī-ō-ˌlü-mə-ˈnes-ᵊn(t)s\ *n* [ISV] **:** the emission of light from living organisms; *also* **:** the light so produced — **bio·lu·mi·nes·cent** \-ᵊnt\ *adj*

bio·mass \ˈbī-ō-ˌmas\ *n* **:** the amount of living matter (as in a unit area or volume of habitat)

bio·ma·te·ri·al \ˌbī-ō-mə-ˈtir-ē-əl\ *n* **:** material used for or suitable for use in prostheses that come in direct contact with living tissues

bi·ome \ˈbī-ˌōm\ *n* [²*bi-* + *-ome*] **:** a major ecological community type <the grassland ~>

bio·med·i·cal \ˌbī-ō-ˈmed-i-kəl\ *adj* **1 :** of or relating to biomedicine **2 :** of, relating to, or involving biological, medical, and physical science

bio·med·i·cine \-ˈmed-ə-sən, *Brit usu* -ˈmed-sən\ *n* **:** a branch of medical science concerned esp. with the capacity of human beings to survive and function in abnormal environments and with the protective modification of such environments

bio·met·ric \-ˈme-trik\ *or* **bio·met·ri·cal** \-tri-kəl\ *adj* **:** of, relating to, or concerned with biometry — **bio·met·ri·cal·ly** \-tri-k(ə-)lē\ *adv*

bio·met·rics \-ˈme-triks\ *n pl but sing or pl in constr* **:** BIOMETRY

bi·om·e·try \bī-ˈäm-ə-trē\ *n* [ISV] **:** the statistical analysis of biological observations and phenomena

bi·on·ics \bī-ˈän-iks\ *n pl but sing or pl in constr* [²*bi-* + *-onics* (as in *electronics*)] **:** a science concerned with the application of data about the functioning of biological systems to the solution of engineering problems — **bi·on·ic** \-ik\ *adj*

bi·o·nom·ics \ˌbī-ə-ˈnäm-iks\ *n pl but sing or pl in constr* [*bionomic,* adj., prob. fr. F *bionomique,* fr. *bionomie* ecology, fr. *bi-* + *-nomie* -nomy] **:** ECOLOGY — **bi·o·nom·ic** \-ik\ *adj* — **bi·o·nom·i·cal** \-i-kəl\ *adj* — **bi·o·nom·i·cal·ly** \-i-k(ə-)lē\ *adv*

-bi·ont \ˈbī-ˌänt\ *comb form* [prob. fr. G, modif. of Gk *biount-, biōn,* prp. of *bioun* to live, fr. *bios* life] **:** one having a (specified) mode of life <haplo*biont*>

bio·phys·ics \ˌbī-ō-ˈfiz-iks\ *n* **:** a branch of knowledge concerned with the application of physical principles and methods to biological problems — **bio·phys·i·cal** \-i-kəl\ *adj* — **bio·phys·i·cist** \-ˈfiz-(ə-)səst\ *n*

bio·poly·mer \ˌbī-ō-ˈpäl-ə-mər\ *n* **:** a polymeric substance (as a protein or polysaccharide) formed in a biological system

bi·op·sy \ˈbī-ˌäp-sē\ *n, pl* **-sies** [ISV *bi-* + Gk *opsis* appearance — more at OPTIC] **:** the removal and examination of tissue, cells, or fluids from the living body

bio·sat·el·lite \ˌbī-ō-ˈsat-ᵊl-ˌīt\ *n* **:** an artificial satellite for carrying a living human being, animal, or plant

bio·sci·ence \-ˈsī-ən(t)s\ *n* **:** BIOLOGY 1a — **bio·sci·en·tif·ic** \-ˌsī-ən-ˈtif-ik\ *adj* — **bio·sci·en·tist** \-ˈsī-ənt-əst\ *n*

-bi·o·sis \(ˌ)bī-ˈō-səs, bē-\ *n comb form, pl* **-bi·o·ses** \-sēz\ [NL, fr. Gk *biōsis,* fr. *bioun* to live, fr. *bios*] **:** mode of life <para*biosis*>

bio·sphere \ˈbī-ə-ˌsfi(ə)r\ *n* **1 :** the part of the world in which life can exist **2 :** living beings together with their environment

bio·syn·the·sis \ˌbī-ō-ˈsin(t)-thə-səs\ *n* [NL] **:** the production of a chemical compound by a living organism — **bio·syn·thet·ic** \-sin-ˈthet-ik\ *adj* — **bio·syn·thet·i·cal·ly** \-i-k(ə-)lē\ *adv*

bio·sys·tem·at·ic \-ˌsis-tə-ˈmat-ik\ *adj* **:** of or relating to experimental taxonomy esp. as based on cytogenetics — **bio·sys·tem·a·tist** \-ˈtem-ət-əst\ *n* — **bio·sys·tem·a·ty** \-sis-ˈtem-ət-ē\ *n*

bi·o·ta \bī-ˈōt-ə\ *n* [NL, fr. Gk *biotē* life; akin to Gk *bios*] **:** the flora and fauna of a region

bio·tech·nol·o·gy \ˌbī-ō-tek-ˈnäl-ə-jē\ *n* **:** the aspect of technology concerned with the application of biological and engineering data to problems relating to man and the machine — **bio·tech·no·log·i·cal** \-ˌtek-nə-ˈläj-i-kəl\ *adj*

bio·te·lem·e·try \-tə-ˈlem-ə-trē\ *n* **:** the remote detection and measurement of a condition, activity, or function relating to a man or animal — **bio·tel·e·met·ric** \-ˌtel-ə-ˈme-trik\ *adj*

bi·ot·ic \bī-ˈät-ik\ *adj* [Gk *biōtikos,* fr. *bioun*] **:** of or relating to life; *esp* **:** caused or produced by living beings

-bi·ot·ic \(ˌ)bī-ˈät-ik, bē-\ *adj comb form* [prob. fr. NL *-bioticus,* fr. Gk *biōtikos*] **:** having a (specified) mode of life <endo*biotic*>

biotic potential *n* **:** the inherent capacity of an organism or species to reproduce and survive

bi·o·tin \ˈbī-ə-tən\ *n* [ISV, fr. Gk *biotos* life, sustenance; akin to Gk *bios*] **:** a colorless crystalline growth vitamin $C_{10}H_{16}N_2O_3S$ of the vitamin B complex found esp. in yeast, liver, and egg yolk

bi·o·tite \ˈbī-ə-ˌtīt\ *n* [G *biotit,* fr. Jean B. *Biot* †1862 F mathematician] **:** a generally black or dark green form of mica $K_2(Mg,Fe,Al)_6(Si,Al)_8O_{20}(OH)_4$ forming a constitutent of crystalline rocks and consisting of a silicate of iron, magnesium, potassium, and aluminum — **bi·o·tit·ic** \ˌbī-ə-ˈtit-ik\ *adj*

bio·tope \ˈbī-ə-ˌtōp\ *n* [²*bi-* + Gk *topos* place — more at TOPIC] **:** a region uniform in environmental conditions and in its populations of animals and plants for which it is the habitat

bio·trans·for·ma·tion \ˈbī-ō-ˌtran(t)s-fər-ˈmā-shən, -ˌfȯr-\ *n* **:** the transformation of chemical compounds within a living system

bio·tron \ˈbī-ə-ˌträn\ *n* [²*bi-* + *-tron* (as in *cyclotron*)] **:** a climate control chamber used to study the effect of specific environmental factors on living organisms

bio·type \-ˌtīp\ *n* [ISV] **:** the organisms sharing a specified genotype; *also* **:** the genotype shared or its distinguishing peculiarity — **bio·typ·ic** \ˌbī-ə-ˈtip-ik\ *adj*

bi·ovu·lar \(ˈ)bī-ˈäv-yə-lər, -ˈōv-\ *adj, of fraternal twins* **:** derived from two ova

ə abut	ᵊ kitten	ər further	a back	ā bake	ä cot, cart
au̇ out	ch chin	e less	ē easy	g gift	i trip
ī life	j joke	ŋ sing	ō flow	ȯ flaw	ȯi coin
th thin	t͟h this	ü loot	u̇ foot	y yet	yü few
yu̇ furious	zh vision				

bi·pack \'bī-ˌpak\ *n* **:** a pair of films each sensitive to a different color used by simultaneous exposure one through the other
bi·pa·ren·tal \ˌbī-pə-'rent-ᵊl\ *adj* **:** of, relating to, or derived from two parents — **bi·pa·ren·tal·ly** \-ᵊl-ē\ *adv*
bi·par·ti·san \(ˈ)bī-'pärt-ə-zən, -sən\ *adj* **:** of, relating to, or involving members of two parties <a ~ commission> — **bi·par·ti·san·ism** \-zə-ˌniz-əm, -sə-\ *n* — **bi·par·ti·san·ship** \-zən-ˌship, -sən-\ *n*
bi·par·tite \(ˈ)bī-'pär-ˌtīt\ *adj* [L *bipartitus,* pp. of *bipartire* to divide in two, fr. *bi-* + *partire* to divide, fr. *part-, pars* part] **1 a :** being in two parts **b :** having two correspondent parts one for each party <a ~ contract> **c :** shared by two <a ~ treaty> **2 :** divided into two parts almost to the base <a ~ leaf> — **bi·par·tite·ly** *adv* — **bi·par·ti·tion** \ˌbī-(ˌ)pär-'tish-ən\ *n*
bi·ped \'bī-ˌped\ *n* [L *biped-, bipes,* fr. *bi-* + *ped-, pes* foot — more at FOOT] **:** a two-footed animal — **biped** *or* **bi·ped·al** \(ˈ)bī-'ped-ᵊl\ *adj*
bi·phe·nyl \(ˈ)bī-'fen-ᵊl, -'fēn-\ *n* [ISV] **:** a white crystalline hydrocarbon $C_6H_5C_6H_5$ used esp. as a heat-transfer medium
bi·pin·nate \-'pin-ˌāt\ *adj* **:** twice pinnate — **bi·pin·nate·ly** *adv*
bi·plane \'bī-ˌplān\ *n* **:** an airplane with two main supporting surfaces usu. placed one above the other
bi·pod \'bī-ˌpäd\ *n* [*bi-* + *-pod* (as in *tripod*)] **:** a two-legged support
bi·po·lar \(ˈ)bī-'pō-lər\ *adj* **1 :** having or involving the use of two poles **2 :** relating to or associated with the polar regions **3 :** having or marked by two mutually repellent forces or diametrically opposed natures or views — **bi·po·lar·i·ty** \ˌbī-pō-'lar-ət-ē\ *n* — **bi·po·lar·iza·tion** \(ˌ)bī-ˌpō-lə-rə-'zā-shən\ *n* — **bi·po·lar·ize** \(ˈ)bī-'pō-lə-ˌrīz\ *vt*
bi·pro·pel·lant \ˌbī-prə-'pel-ənt\ *n* **:** a rocket propellant consisting of separate fuel and oxidizer that come together only in a combustion chamber
bi·qua·drat·ic \ˌbī-kwä-'drat-ik\ *n* **:** a fourth power or equation involving a fourth power in mathematics — **biquadratic** *adj*
bi·ra·cial \(ˈ)bī-'rā-shəl\ *adj* **:** of, relating to, or involving members of two races — **bi·ra·cial·ism** \-shə-ˌliz-əm\ *n*
bi·ra·di·al \(ˈ)bī-'rād-ē-əl\ *adj* **:** having both bilateral and radial symmetry
bi·ra·mous \(ˈ)bī-'rā-məs\ *adj* **:** having two branches
[1]**birch** \'bərch\ *n* [ME, fr. OE *beorc;* akin to OHG *birka* birch, L *fraxinus* ash tree, OE *beorht* bright — more at BRIGHT] **1 :** any of a genus (*Betula* of the family Betulaceae, the birch family) of monoecious deciduous usu. short-lived trees or shrubs having simple petioled leaves and typically a layered membranous outer bark that peels readily **2 :** the hard pale close-grained wood of a birch **3 :** a birch rod or bundle of twigs for flogging — **birch** *or* **birch·en** \'bər-chən\ *adj*
[2]**birch** *vt* **:** to beat with or as if with a birch **:** WHIP
birch·bark \'bərch-ˌbärk\ *n* **:** a canoe made of birch bark
Birch·er \'bər-chər\ *n* **:** a member or adherent of the John Birch Society — **Birch·ism** \'bər-ˌchiz-əm\ *n* — **Birch·ist** \-chəst\ *or* **Birch·ite** \-ˌchīt\ *n*
[1]**bird** \'bərd\ *n, often attrib* [ME, fr. OE *bridd*] **1** *archaic* **:** the young of a feathered vertebrate **2 :** any of a class (Aves) of warm-blooded vertebrates distinguished by having the body more or less completely covered with feathers and the forelimbs modified as wings **3 :** a game bird **4 :** CLAY PIGEON **5 a :** FELLOW; *esp* **:** a peculiar person **b** *chiefly Brit* **:** GIRL **6 :** SHUTTLECOCK **7 a :** a hissing or jeering expressive of disapproval **b :** dismissal from employment **8 :** GUIDED MISSILE — **bird·like** \-ˌlīk\ *adj* — **for the birds :** WORTHLESS, RIDICULOUS

bird 2 (waxwing): *1* bill, *2* forehead, *3* crown, *4* crest, *5* auricular region, *6* throat, *7* breast, *8* abdomen, *9* under-tail coverts, *10* tail, *11* primaries, *12* secondaries, *13* upper wing coverts, *14* scapulars

[2]**bird** *vi* **:** to observe or identify wild birds in their natural environment
bird·bath \'bərd-ˌbath, -ˌbàth\ *n* **:** a usu. ornamental basin set up for birds to bathe in
bird·brain \-ˌbrān\ *n* **1 :** a stupid person **2 :** SCATTERBRAIN — **bird·brained** \-ˌbrānd\ *adj*
bird·call \-ˌkȯl\ *n* **1 :** the note or cry of a bird; *also* **:** a sound imitative of it **2 :** a device for imitating a birdcall
bird colonel *n* [fr. the eagle serving as his insignia] *slang* **:** COLONEL 1a
bird–dog \'bərd-ˌdȯg\ *vi* **:** to watch closely ~ *vt* **:** to seek out **:** FOLLOW, DETECT
bird dog *n* **1 :** a gundog trained to hunt or retrieve birds **2 a :** one (as a canvasser or talent scout) who seeks out something for another **b :** one who steals another's date
bird–dog·ging *n* **1 :** the action of one that bird-dogs **2 :** the stealing of another's date (as at a party)
bird·er \'bərd-ər\ *n* **1 :** a catcher or hunter of birds esp. for market **2 :** one that birds
bird·house \'bərd-ˌhau̇s\ *n* **:** an artificial nesting site for birds; *also* **:** AVIARY
[1]**bird·ie** \'bərd-ē\ *n* **1 :** a little bird **2 :** a golf score of one stroke less than par on a hole — compare EAGLE
[2]**birdie** *vt* **bird·ied; bird·ie·ing :** to shoot in one stroke under par
bird·lime \'bərd-ˌlīm\ *n* **1 :** a sticky substance usu. made from the bark of a holly (*Ilex aquifolium*) that is smeared on twigs to snare small birds **2 :** something that ensnares — **birdlime** *vt*
bird louse *n* **:** any of numerous wingless insects (order Mallophaga) that are mostly parasitic on birds
bird·man \'bərd-mən, *esp for 1 also* -ˌman\ *n* **1 :** one who deals with birds **2 :** AVIATOR
bird of paradise : any of numerous brilliantly colored plumed oscine birds (family Paradiseidae) of the New Guinea area
bird of passage 1 : a migratory bird **2 :** a person who leads a wandering or unsettled life
bird of prey : a carnivorous bird that feeds wholly or chiefly on meat taken by hunting
bird pepper *n* **:** a capsicum (*Capsicum frutescens*) having very small oblong extremely pungent red fruits
bird·seed \'bərd-ˌsēd\ *n* **:** a mixture of seeds (as of hemp, millet, and sunflowers) used for feeding caged and wild birds
[1]**bird's–eye** \'bərd-ˌzī\ *n* **1 :** any of numerous plants with small bright-colored flowers **2 a :** an allover pattern for textiles consisting of a small diamond with a center dot **b :** a fabric woven with this pattern **3 :** a small spot in wood surrounded with an ellipse of concentric fibers
[2]**bird's–eye** *adj* **1 a :** seen from above as if by a flying bird <a ~ view> **b :** CURSORY **2 :** marked with spots resembling birds' eyes **3 :** of or relating to wood (as maple) containing bird's-eyes
bird's–foot \'bərdz-ˌfu̇t\ *n, pl* **bird's–foots :** any of numerous plants with leaves or flowers resembling the foot of a bird; *esp* **:** any of several legumes (as of the genera *Ornithopus, Lotus,* and *Trigonella*) with bent and jointed pods
bird's–foot trefoil *n* **:** a European legume (*Lotus corniculatus*) having claw-shaped pods and widely used esp. in the U.S. as a forage and fodder plant
bird–watch \'bərd-ˌwäch\ *vi* [back-formation fr. *bird-watcher*] **:** BIRD
bird–watch·er \-ər\ *n* **:** BIRDER 2
birdy·back *or* **bird·ie·back** \'bərd-ē-ˌbak\ *n* [*birdie* + *-back* (as in *piggyback*)] **:** the movement of loaded truck trailers by airplane
bi·re·frin·gence \ˌbī-ri-'frin-jən(t)s\ *n* [ISV] **:** the refraction of light in two slightly different directions to form two rays — **bi·re·frin·gent** \-jənt\ *adj*
bi·reme \'bī-ˌrēm\ *n* [L *biremis,* fr. *bi-* + *remus* oar — more at ROW] **:** a galley with two banks of oars common in the early classical period
bi·ret·ta \bə-'ret-ə\ *n* [It *berretta,* fr. OProv *berret* cap, irreg. fr. LL *birrus* cloak with a hood, of Celt origin; akin to MIr *berr* short] **:** a square cap with three ridges on top worn by clergymen esp. of the Roman Catholic Church

biretta

birk \'bi(ə)rk\ *n* [ME *birch, birk*] *chiefly Scot* **:** BIRCH
birk·ie \'bi(ə)r-kē, 'bər-\ *n* [origin unknown] **1** *Scot* **:** a lively smart assertive person **2** *Scot* **:** FELLOW, BOY
birl \'bər(-ə)l, *Scot also* 'bir(ə)l\ *vb* [ME *birlen,* fr. OE *byrelian;* akin to OE *beran* to carry — more at BEAR] *vt* **1** *chiefly Scot* **a :** POUR **b :** to ply with drink **2 a :** to cause (a floating log) to rotate by treading **b :** SPIN ~ *vi* **1** *chiefly Scot* **:** CAROUSE **2 :** to progress by whirling — **birl·er** \'bər-lər, 'bi(ə)r-lər\ *n*
[1]**birr** \'bər, 'bi(ə)r\ *n* [ME, strong wind, attack, fr. OE *byre* strong wind & ON *byrr* favoring wind; both akin to OE *beran*] **1 a :** force or onward rush (as of the wind) **b :** VIGOR **2 :** a whirring sound
[2]**birr** *vi, chiefly Scot* **:** to make a whirring sound
birse \'bi(ə)rs, 'bərs\ *n* [(assumed) ME *birst,* fr. OE *byrst* — more at BRISTLE] **1** *chiefly Scot* **:** a bristle or tuft of bristles **2** *chiefly Scot* **:** ANGER
[1]**birth** \'bərth\ *n, often attrib* [ME, fr. ON *byrth;* akin to OE *beran*] **1 a :** the emergence of a new individual from the body of its parent **b :** the act or process of bringing forth young from the womb **2 :** a state resulting from being born esp. at a particular time or place <a Southerner by ~> **3 a :** LINEAGE, EXTRACTION <marriage between equals in ~> **b :** high or noble birth **4 a** *archaic* **:** one that is born **b :** BEGINNING, START <the ~ of an idea>
[2]**birth** *vt* **1** *chiefly dial* **:** to bring forth **2 :** to give rise to **:** ORIGINATE ~ *vi, dial* **:** to bring forth a child or young
birth certificate *n* **:** a copy of an official record of a person's date and place of birth and parentage
birth control *n* **:** control of the number of children born esp. by preventing or lessening the frequency of conception
birth·day \'bərth-ˌdā\ *n* **1 a :** the day of a person's birth **b :** a day of origin **2 :** an anniversary of a birth <her 21st ~>
birthday suit *n* **:** unclothed skin **:** NAKEDNESS
birth·mark \'bərth-ˌmärk\ *n* **:** an unusual mark or blemish on the skin at birth **:** NEVUS — **birthmark** *vt*
birth pang *n* **1 :** one of the regularly recurrent pains that are characteristic of childbirth — usu. used in pl. **2** *pl* **:** disorder and distress incident esp. to a major social change
birth·place \'bərth-ˌplās\ *n* **:** place of birth or origin
birth·rate \'bər-ˌthrāt\ *n* **:** the ratio between births and individuals in a specified population and time often expressed as number of live births per hundred or per thousand population per year
birth·right \'bər-ˌthrīt\ *n* **:** a right, privilege, or possession to which a person is entitled by birth *syn* see HERITAGE
birth·root \'bər-ˌthrüt, -ˌthru̇t\ *n* **:** any of several trilliums with astringent roots used in folk medicine
birth·stone \'bərth-ˌstōn\ *n* **:** a gemstone associated symbolically with the month of one's birth
birth·wort \-ˌwərt, -ˌwȯ(ə)rt\ *n* **:** any of several plants (genus *Aristolochia* of the family Aristolochiaceae, the birthwort family) of herbs or woody vines with aromatic roots used in folk medicine to aid childbirth
bis \'bis\ *adv* [L, fr. OL *dvis;* akin to OHG *zwiro* twice, L *duo* two — more at TWO] **1 :** AGAIN — used in music as a direction to

repeat **2 :** TWICE — used to point out the occurrence of an item twice (as in an account)
bis- \(,)bis, 'bis\ *comb form* [L *bis*] **:** twice **:** doubled — esp. in complex chemical expressions <*bis*-dithiocarbamate>
Bi·sa·yan \bə-'sī-ən\ *n* [Bisayan *Bisayâ*] **1 :** a member of any of several peoples in the Visayan islands, Philippines **2 :** the Austronesian language of the Bisayans
bis·cuit \'bis-kət\ *n* [ME *bisquite,* fr. MF *bescuit,* fr. (*pain*) *bescuit* twice-cooked bread] **1 a :** any of various hard or crisp dry baked products: (1) *Brit* **:** CRACKER 4 (2) *Brit* **:** COOKIE **b :** a small quick bread made from dough that has been rolled out and cut or dropped from a spoon **2 :** earthenware or porcelain after the first firing and before glazing **:** BISQUE **3 a :** a light grayish yellowish brown **b :** a grayish yellow
bise \'bēz\ *n* [ME, fr. OF, of Gmc origin] **:** a cold dry north wind of southern France, Switzerland, and Italy
bi·sect \'bī-,sekt, bī-'\ *vt* **:** to divide into two usu. equal parts ~ *vi* **:** CROSS, INTERSECT — **bi·sec·tion** \'bī-,sek-shən, bī-'\ *n* — **bi·sec·tion·al** \-shnəl, -shən-ᵊl\ *adj* — **bi·sec·tion·al·ly** \-ē\ *adv*
bi·sec·tor \'bī-,sek-tər, bī-'\ *n* **:** one that bisects; *esp* **:** a straight line that bisects an angle or a line segment
bi·sex·u·al \(')bī-'seksh-(ə-)wəl, -'sek-shəl\ *adj* **1 a :** possessing characters of both sexes **:** HERMAPHRODITIC **b :** sexually oriented toward both sexes <a ~ person who participates in both heterosexual and homosexual relationships> **2 :** of, relating to, or involving two sexes — **bisexual** *n* — **bi·sex·u·al·i·ty** \,bī-,sek-shə-'wal-ət-ē\ *n* — **bi·sex·u·al·ly** \(')bī-'seksh-(ə-)wə-lē, -(ə-)lē\ *adv*
bish·op \'bish-əp\ *n* [ME *bisshop,* fr. OE *bisceop,* fr. LL *episcopus,* fr. Gk *episkopos,* lit., overseer, fr. *epi-* + *skeptesthai* to look — more at SPY] **1 :** one having spiritual or ecclesiastical supervision: as **a :** an Anglican, Eastern Orthodox, or Roman Catholic clergyman ranking above a priest, having authority to ordain and confirm, and typically governing a diocese **b :** any of various Protestant clerical officials who superintend other clergy **c :** a Mormon high priest presiding over a ward or over all other bishops and over the Aaronic priesthood **2 :** either of two pieces of the same color in a set of chessmen having the power to move diagonally across any number of unoccupied squares **3 :** a mulled beverage of port wine flavored with roasted orange and cloves
bish·op·ric \'bish-ə-(,)prik\ *n* [ME *bisshopriche,* fr. OE *bisceoprice,* fr. *bisceop* + *rice* kingdom — more at RICH] **1 :** DIOCESE **2 :** the office of bishop **3 :** a bishop's seat or residence **4 :** the administrative body of a Mormon ward consisting of a bishop and two high priests as counselors
Bishops' Bible *n* [fr. its production by a number of bishops] **:** an officially commissioned English translation of the Bible published in 1568
bis·muth \'biz-məth\ *n* [obs. G *bismut* (now *wismut*), modif. of *wismut,* fr. *wise* meadow + *mut* claim to a mine] **:** a heavy brittle grayish white chiefly trivalent metallic element that is chemically like arsenic and antimony and that is used in alloys and pharmaceuticals — see ELEMENT table — **bis·mu·thic** \biz-'məth-ik, -'myü-thik\ *adj*
bi·son \'bīs-ᵊn, 'bīz-\ *n, pl* **bison** [L *bisont-, bison,* of Gmc origin; akin to OHG *wisant* aurochs; akin to OPruss *wissambrs* aurochs] **:** any of several large shaggy-maned usu. gregarious recent or extinct bovine mammals (genus *Bison*) having a large head with short horns and heavy forequarters surmounted by a large fleshy hump: as **a :** WISENT **b :** BUFFALO b — **bi·son·tine** \-ᵊn-,tīn\ *adj*

bison

¹bisque \'bisk\ *n* [F] **:** odds allowed an inferior player: as **a :** a point taken when desired in a set of tennis **b :** an extra turn in croquet **c :** one or more strokes off a golf score
²bisque *n* [F] **1 a :** a thick cream soup made of shellfish or of the flesh of birds or rabbits **b :** a cream soup of pureed vegetables **2 :** ice cream containing powdered nuts or macaroons
³bisque *n* [by shortening & alter.] **:** BISCUIT 2; *esp* **:** unglazed ceramic ware that is not to be glazed but is hard-fired and vitreous
bi·state \'bī-,stāt\ *adj* **:** of or relating to two states <a ~ agency>
bis·ter *or* **bis·tre** \'bis-tər\ *n* [F *bistre*] **1 :** a yellowish brown to dark brown pigment used in art **2 :** a grayish to yellowish brown — **bis·tered** \-tərd\ *adj*
bis·tort \'bis-,tȯ(ə)rt, bis-'\ *n* [MF *bistorte,* fr. (assumed) ML *bistorta,* fr. L *bis-* + *torta,* fem. of *tortus,* pp. of *torquēre* to twist — more at TORTURE] **:** any of several polygonums; *esp* **:** a European herb (*Polygonum bistorta*) or a related American plant (*P. bistortoides*) with twisted roots used as astringents
bis·tro \'bēs-(,)trō, 'bis-\ *n, pl* **bistros** [F] **1 :** a small or unpretentious European wineshop or restaurant **2 a :** a small bar or tavern **b :** NIGHTCLUB — **bis·tro·ic** \bēs-'trō-ik, bis-\ *adj*
bi·sul·fate \(')bī-'səl-,fāt\ *n* [ISV] **:** an acid sulfate
bi·sul·fide \-,fīd\ *n* [ISV] **:** DISULFIDE
bi·sul·fite \-,fīt\ *n* [F, fr. *bi-* + *sulfite*] **:** an acid sulfite
¹bit \'bit\ *n* [ME *bitt,* fr. OE *bite* act of biting; akin to OE *bītan*] **1 :** something bitten or held with the teeth: **a :** the usu. steel part of a bridle inserted in the mouth of a horse **b :** the rimmed mouth end on the stem of a pipe or cigar holder **2 a** (1) **:** the biting or cutting edge or part of a tool (2) **:** a replaceable part of a compound tool that actually performs the function (as drilling or boring) for which the whole tool is designed **b** *pl* **:** the jaws or nippers of tongs or pincers **3 :** something that curbs or restrains **4 :** the part of a key that enters the lock and acts on the bolt and tumblers

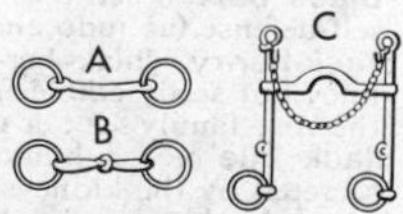

bits 1a: *A* bar bit, *B* snaffle, *C* curb

²bit *vt* **bit·ted; bit·ting 1 a :** to put a bit in the mouth of (a horse) **b :** to control as if with a bit **:** CURB **2 :** to form a bit on (a key)
³bit *n* [ME, fr. OE *bita;* akin to OE *bītan*] **1 :** a small quantity of food: *esp* **:** a small delicacy **2 a :** a small piece or quantity of some material thing **b** (1) **:** a small coin (2) **:** a unit of value equal to ⅛ of a dollar <four ~*s*> **3 :** something small or unimportant of its kind: as **a :** a brief period **:** WHILE **b** (1) **:** an indefinite usu. small degree, extent, or amount <a ~ of a rascal> <every ~ as powerful> (2) **:** the smallest or an insignificant amount or degree <didn't feel a ~ sorry> **c** (1) **:** a small part usu. with spoken lines in a theatrical performance (2) **:** a usu. short theatrical routine <a corny comedy ~> **4 :** the aggregate of items, situations, or activities appropriate to a given style, genre, or role <rejected the whole ~ about love-marriage-motherhood —Vance Packard> — **a bit much :** a little more than one wants to endure — **bit by bit :** little by little **:** by degrees
⁴bit *n* [*bi*nary digi*t*] **1 :** a unit of computer information equivalent to the result of a choice between two alternatives (as *yes* or *no, on* or *off*) **2 :** the physical representation (as in a computer tape or memory) of a bit by an electrical pulse, a magnetized spot, or a hole whose presence or absence indicates data
bi·tar·trate \(')bī-'tär-,trāt\ *n* [ISV] **:** an acid tartrate
¹bitch \'bich\ *n* [ME *bicche,* fr. OE *bicce;* akin to OE *bæc* back] **1 :** the female of the dog or some other carnivorous mammals **2 a :** a lewd or immoral woman **b :** a malicious, spiteful, and domineering woman **3 :** COMPLAINT **4 :** something that is highly objectionable or unpleasant
²bitch *vt* **1 :** SPOIL, BOTCH <I must have ~*ed* up my life —Mavis Gallant> **2 :** to complain of or about <was occasionally quite talkative about his wife . . . mostly he ~*ed* her, but not vehemently —Chandler Brossard> **3 :** CHEAT, DOUBLECROSS ~ *vi* **:** COMPLAIN <wives ~ theatrically at their shrimpy husbands —Fred Powledge>
bitch·ery \'bich-ə-rē\ *n, pl* **-er·ies :** malicious, spiteful, or domineering behavior; *also* **:** an instance of such behavior
bitch goddess *n* **:** SUCCESS; *esp* **:** material or worldly success
bitchy \'bich-ē\ *adj* **bitch·i·er; -est :** characterized by malicious, spiteful, or arrogant behavior — **bitch·i·ly** \'bich-ə-lē\ *adv* — **bitch·i·ness** \'bich-ē-nəs\ *n*
¹bite \'bīt\ *vb* **bit** \'bit\; **bit·ten** \'bit-ᵊn\ *also* **bit; bit·ing** \'bīt-iŋ\ [ME *biten,* fr. OE *bītan;* akin to OHG *bīzan* to bite, L *findere* to split] *vt* **1 a :** to seize esp. with teeth or jaws so as to enter, grip, or wound **b :** to wound, pierce, or sting esp. with a fang or a proboscis **2 :** to cut or pierce with or as if with an edged weapon **3 :** to cause sharp pain or stinging discomfort to **4 :** to take hold of **5 :** to eat into **:** CORRODE **6** *archaic* **:** to take in **:** CHEAT ~ *vi* **1 :** to bite or have the habit of biting something **2** *of a weapon or tool* **:** to cut, pierce, or take hold **3 :** to cause irritation or smarting **4 :** CORRODE **5 a** *of fish* **:** to take a bait **b :** to respond so as to be caught (as by a trick) **6 :** to take or maintain a firm hold — **bit·er** \'bīt-ər\ *n* — **bite off more than one can chew :** to undertake more than one can perform — **bite the dust 1 :** to fall dead esp. in battle **2 :** to suffer humiliation or defeat — **bite the hand that feeds one :** to injure a benefactor maliciously
²bite *n* **1 :** the act or manner of biting **2 :** FOOD: **a :** the amount of food taken at a bite **:** MORSEL **b :** a small amount of food **:** SNACK **c :** a usu. impromptu meal **3** *archaic* **a :** CHEAT, TRICK **b :** SHARPER **4 :** a wound made by biting **5 :** the hold or grip by which friction is created or purchase is obtained **6 :** a surface that creates friction or is brought into contact with another for the purpose of obtaining a hold **7 a :** a keen incisive quality <the ~ of sharp analysis> **b :** a sharp penetrating effect <the ~ of raw whiskey> **8 :** the corroding of an etcher's plate by acid **9 :** an amount taken usu. in one operation for one purpose **:** CUT <the tax ~>
bite·wing \'bīt-,wiŋ\ *n* **:** a dental X-ray film designed to show the crowns of the upper and lower teeth simultaneously
bit·ing \'bīt-iŋ\ *adj* **:** having the power to bite <a ~ wind>; *esp* **:** able to grip and impress deeply <the report is ~ in its intolerance of deceit> *syn* see INCISIVE — **bit·ing·ly** \-iŋ-lē\ *adv*
biting midge *n* **:** any of a family (Ceratopogonidae) of tiny biting two-winged flies of which some are vectors of filarial worms
bit·stock \'bit-,stäk\ *n* **:** a device for turning a bit by hand **:** BRACE
bit·sy \'bit-sē\ *adj* [*itsy-bitsy*] *dial* **:** TINY
¹bitt \'bit\ *n* [perh. fr. ON *biti* beam; akin to OE *bōt* boat] **1 :** a single or double post of metal or wood fixed on the deck of a ship for securing lines **2 :** BOLLARD 1
²bitt *vt* **:** to make (a cable) fast about a bitt
¹bit·ter \'bit-ər\ *adj* [ME, fr. OE *biter;* akin to OHG *bittar* bitter, OE *bītan* to bite] **1 a :** having or being a peculiarly acrid, astringent, or disagreeable taste suggestive of an infusion of hops that is one of the four basic taste sensations — compare SALT, SOUR, SWEET **b :** distasteful or distressing to the mind **:** GALLING <a ~ sense of shame> **2 :** marked by intensity or severity: **a :** accompanied by severe pain or suffering <a ~ death> **b :** being relentlessly determined **:** VEHEMENT <a ~ partisan> **c :** exhibiting intense animosity <~ enemies> **d** (1) **:** harshly reproachful <~ complaints> (2) **:** marked by cynicism and rancor <~ contempt> **e :** intensely unpleasant esp. in coldness or rawness **3 :** expressive of severe pain, grief, or regret <~ tears> — **bit·ter·ish** \'bit-ə-rish\ *adj* — **bit·ter·ly** *adv* — **bit·ter·ness** *n*
²bitter *adv* **:** in a bitter manner <it's ~ cold>
³bitter *n* **1 :** bitter quality **2 a** *pl* **:** a usu. alcoholic solution of bitter and often aromatic plant products used esp. in preparing

ə abut	ᵊ kitten	ər further	a back	ā bake	ä cot, cart
au̇ out	ch chin	e less	ē easy	g gift	i trip	ī life
j joke	ŋ sing	ō flow	ȯ flaw	ȯi coin	th thin	t͟h this
ü loot	u̇ foot	y yet	yü few	yu̇ furious	zh vision

mixed drinks or as a mild tonic **b** *Brit* : a very dry heavily hopped ale

[4]**bitter** *vt* : to make bitter <~*ed* ale>

bit·ter·brush \'bit-ər-ˌbrəsh\ *n* : a much-branched silvery shrub (*Purshia tridentata*) of arid western No. America that has 3-toothed leaves and yellow flowers and is valuable for forage

[1]**bitt·er end** \ˌbit-ə-'rend\ *n* [*bitter* (a turn of cable around the bitts)] : the inboard end of a ship's anchoring cable

[2]**bit·ter end** \ˌbit-ə-'rend\ *n* [prob. fr. [1]*bitter end*] : the last extremity however painful or calamitous — **bit·ter–end·er** \-'ren-dər\ *n*

[1]**bit·tern** \'bit-ərn\ *n* [ME *bitoure,* fr. MF *butor*] : any of various small or medium-sized nocturnal herons (*Botaurus* and related genera) with a characteristic booming cry

[2]**bittern** *n* [irreg. fr. [1]*bitter*] : the bitter mother liquor that remains in saltworks after the salt has crystallized out

bitter principle *n* : any of various neutral substances of strong bitter taste (as aloin) extracted from plants

bit·ter·root \'bit-ə(r)-ˌrüt, -ˌru̇t\ *n* : a succulent Rocky mountain herb (*Lewisia rediviva*) of the purslane family with fleshy farinaceous roots and pink flowers

[1]**bit·ter·sweet** \'bit-ər-ˌswēt\ *n* **1** : something that is bittersweet; *esp* : pleasure alloyed with pain **2 a** : a sprawling poisonous weedy nightshade (*Solanum dulcamara*) with purple flowers and oval reddish orange berries **b** : a No. American woody climbing plant (*Celastrus scandens* of the family Celastraceae) having clusters of small greenish flowers succeeded by yellow capsules that open when ripe and disclose the scarlet aril

[2]**bittersweet** *adj* **1** : being at once bitter and sweet; *esp* : pleasant but including or marked by elements of suffering or regret <a ~ ballad> **2** : of or relating to a prepared chocolate containing little sugar — **bit·ter·sweet·ly** *adv* — **bit·ter·sweet·ness** *n*

bit·ter·weed \'bit-ər-ˌwēd\ *n* : any of several American plants containing a bitter principle: as **a** : HORSEWEED 1, 2 **b** : a sneezeweed (genus *Helenium*) **c** : an erect composite herb (*Actinea odorata*) of the southwestern U.S. having chiefly yellow terminal flowerheads and causing poisoning of livestock

bit·tock \'bit-ək\ *n, chiefly Scot* : a little bit

[1]**bit·ty** \'bit-ē\ *adj* : made up of or containing bits <the contributors are given space to develop their thoughts, and it is not a ~ anthology —*Times Lit. Supp.*>

[2]**bitty** *adj, dial* : SMALL, TINY

bi·tu·men \bə-'t(y)ü-mən, bī-, *esp Brit also* 'bit-yə-\ *n* [ME *bithumen* mineral pitch, fr. L *bitumin-, bitumen*] **1** : an asphalt of Asia Minor used in ancient times as a cement and mortar **2** : any of various mixtures of hydrocarbons (as tar) often together with their nonmetallic derivatives that occur naturally or are obtained as residues after heat-refining naturally occurring substances (as petroleum); *specif* : such a mixture soluble in carbon disulfide — **bi·tu·mi·ni·za·tion** \bə-ˌt(y)ü-mə-nə-'zā-shən, bī-\ *n* — **bi·tu·mi·nize** \-t(y)ü-mə-ˌnīz\ *vt* — **bi·tu·mi·noid** \-ˌnȯid\ *adj*

bi·tu·mi·nous \bə-'t(y)ü-mə-nəs, bī-\ *adj* **1** : resembling, containing, or impregnated with bitumen **2** : of or relating to bituminous coal

bituminous coal *n* : a coal that when heated yields considerable volatile bituminous matter — called also *soft coal*

[1]**bi·va·lent** \(ˈ)bī-'vā-lənt\ *adj* **1** : having a valence of two **2** : associated in pairs in synapsis

[2]**bivalent** *n* : a pair of synaptic chromosomes

[1]**bi·valve** \'bī-ˌvalv\ *also* **bi·valved** \-ˌvalvd\ *adj* **1** : having a shell composed of two valves **2** : having or consisting of two corresponding movable pieces

[2]**bivalve** *n* : an animal (as a clam) with a 2-valved shell

bi·var·i·ate \(ˈ)bī-'ver-ē-ət, -'var-\ *adj* : of, relating to, or involving two variables <a ~ frequency distribution>

[1]**biv·ouac** \'biv(-ə)-ˌwak\ *n* [F, fr. LG *biwake,* fr. *bi* at + *wake* guard] **1** : a usu. temporary encampment under little or no shelter **2 a** : a camping out for a night **b** : a temporary shelter or settlement

[2]**bivouac** *vi* **-ouacked; -ouack·ing** : to make a bivouac : CAMP

[1]**bi·week·ly** \(ˈ)bī-'wē-klē\ *adj* **1** : occurring every two weeks : FORTNIGHTLY **2** : occurring twice a week — **biweekly** *adv*

[2]**biweekly** *n* **1** : a publication issued every two weeks **2** : SEMIWEEKLY

bi·year·ly \(ˈ)bī-'yi(ə)r-lē\ *adj* **1** : BIENNIAL **2** : BIANNUAL

[1]**bi·zarre** \bə-'zär\ *adj* [F, fr. It *bizzarro*] : strikingly out of the ordinary: as **a** : odd, extravagant, or eccentric in style or mode **b** : involving sensational contrasts or incongruities ***syn*** see FANTASTIC ***ant*** chaste, subdued — **bi·zarre·ly** *adv* — **bi·zarre·ness** *n*

[2]**bizarre** *n* : a flower with atypical striped marking

bi·zon·al \(ˈ)bī-'zōn-ᵊl\ *adj* : of or relating to the affairs of a zone governed or administered by two powers acting together — **bi·zone** \'bī-ˌzōn\ *n*

BJ *abbr* bachelor of journalism

bk *abbr* **1** bank **2** book **3** break **4** brook

Bk *symbol* berkelium

bkg *abbr* **1** banking **2** bookkeeping **3** breakage

bkgd *abbr* background

bks *abbr* barracks

bkt *abbr* **1** basket **2** bracket

bl *abbr* **1** bale **2** barrel **3** black **4** block **5** blue

BL *abbr* **1** bachelor of law **2** bachelor of letters **3** baseline **4** bats left **5** bill of lading **6** breath-length

[1]**blab** \'blab\ *n* [ME *blabbe;* akin to ME *blaberen*] **1** *archaic* : one that blabs : TATTLETALE **2** : idle or excessive talk : CHATTER — **blab·by** \'blab-ē\ *adj*

[2]**blab** *vb* **blabbed; blab·bing** *vt* : to reveal esp. by talking without reserve or discretion ~ *vi* **1** : to reveal a secret esp. by indiscreet chatter **2** : to talk idly or thoughtlessly : PRATTLE

[1]**blab·ber** \'blab-ər\ *vb* **blab·bered; blab·ber·ing** \-(ə-)riŋ\ [ME *blaberen*] *vi* : to talk foolishly or excessively : BABBLE ~ *vt* : to say indiscreetly

[2]**blabber** *n* : idle talk : BABBLE

[3]**blabber** *n* [[2]*blab*] : one that blabs

blab·ber·mouth \'blab-ər-ˌmau̇th\ *n* : one who talks too much; *esp* : TATTLETALE

[1]**black** \'blak\ *adj* [ME *blak,* fr. OE *blæc;* akin to OHG *blah* black, L *flagrare* to burn, Gk *phlegein,* OE *bǣl* fire — more at BALD] **1 a** : of the color black **b** (1) : very dark in color <his face was ~ with rage> (2) : having a very deep or low register <a bass with a ~ voice> (3) : HEAVY, SERIOUS <the play was a ~ intrigue> **2 a** : having dark skin, hair, and eyes : SWARTHY <a ~ Irishman> **b** (1) : of or relating to a group or race characterized by dark pigmentation; *esp* : of or relating to the Negro race <~ Americans> (2) : of or relating to the Afro-American people or culture <~ literature> <~ theater> <~ pride> **3** : dressed in black **4** : DIRTY, SOILED <hands ~ with grime> **5 a** : characterized by the absence of light <a ~ night> **b** : reflecting or transmitting little or no light <~ water> **c** : served without milk or cream <~ coffee> **6 a** : thoroughly sinister or evil : WICKED <a ~ deed> **b** : indicative of condemnation or discredit <got a ~ mark for being late> **7** : connected with or invoking the supernatural and esp. the devil <a ~ curse> **8 a** : very sad, gloomy, or calamitous <~ despair> **b** : marked by the occurrence of disaster <~ Friday> **9** : characterized by hostility or angry discontent : SULLEN <~ resentment filled his heart> **10** *chiefly Brit* : subject to boycott by trade-union members as employing or favoring nonunion workers or as operating under conditions considered unfair by the trade union <declare a fish market ~> **11** : showing a profit <a ~ financial statement> — compare RED **12 a** *of propaganda* : conducted so as to appear to originate within an enemy country and designed to weaken enemy morale — compare WHITE **b** : characterized by or connected with the use of black propaganda <~ radio> **13** : characterized by grim, distorted, or grotesque satire <~ comedy> <~ humor> — **black·ish** \'blak-ish\ *adj* — **black·ly** *adv* — **black·ness** *n*

[2]**black** *n* **1** : a black pigment or dye; *esp* : one consisting largely of carbon **2** : the achromatic object color of least lightness characteristically perceived to belong to objects that neither reflect nor transmit light **3** : something that is black: as **a** : black clothing <looks good in ~> **b** : a black animal (as a horse) **4 a** : a person belonging to a dark-skinned race or one stemming in part from such a race; *esp* : NEGRO **b** : AFRO-AMERICAN **5** : the pieces of a dark color in a two-handed board game (as chess) **6** : total or nearly total absence of light <the ~ of night> **7** : the condition of making a profit — usu. used with *the* <operating in the ~> — compare RED

[3]**black** *vi* : to become black ~ *vt* **1** : to make black **2** *chiefly Brit* : to declare (as a business or industry) subject to boycott by trade-union members

black·a·moor \'blak-ə-ˌmu̇(ə)r\ *n* [irreg. fr. *black* + *Moor*] : a dark-skinned person; *esp* : NEGRO

black–and–blue \ˌblak-ən-'blü\ *adj* : darkly discolored from blood effused by bruising

black–and–tan \-ən-'tan\ *adj* **1** : having a predominantly black color pattern with deep red or rusty tan on the feet, breeching, and cheek patches, above the eyes, and inside the ears **2** : favoring or practicing proportional representation of whites and blacks in politics — compare LILY-WHITE **3** : frequented by both blacks and whites <a ~ bar>

black and tan *n* **1** : a member of a black-and-tan political organization (as in the southern U.S.) — compare LILY-WHITE **2** *cap B&T* [fr. the color of his uniform] : a recruit enlisted in England in 1920–21 for service in the Royal Irish Constabulary against the armed movement for Irish independence

black–and–tan coonhound *n* : any of an American breed of strong vigorous coonhounds that have black-and-tan markings

black–and–white \ˌblak-ən-'hwīt, -'wīt\ *adj* **1** : being in writing or print <a ~ statement of the problem> **2** : partly black and partly white in color <a ~ cat> **3** : executed in dark pigment on a light background or in light pigment on a dark ground <a ~ drawing> **4** : characterized by the reproduction or transmission of visual images in tones of gray rather than in colors <~ film> <~ television> **5 a** : sharply divided into good and evil groups, sides, or ideas **b** : evaluating or viewing things as either all good or all bad <~ morality> <~ thinkers>

black and white *n* **1** : WRITING, PRINT **2** : a drawing or print done in black and white or in monochrome **3** : monochrome reproduction of visual images (as by photography or television)

black art *n* : magic practiced by or as if by conjurers and witches

black–a–vised \'blak-ə-ˌvīst\ *adj* [*black* + F *à vis* as to face] : dark-complexioned

[1]**black·ball** \'blak-ˌbȯl\ *n* **1** : a small black ball for use as a negative vote in a ballot box **2** : an adverse vote esp. against admitting someone to membership in an organization

[2]**blackball** *vt* **1** : to vote against; *esp* : to exclude from membership by casting a negative vote **2 a** : to exclude socially : OSTRACIZE **b** : BOYCOTT

black bass *n* : any of several highly prized freshwater sunfishes (genus *Micropterus*) native to eastern and central No. America

black beast *n* : BÊTE NOIRE

[1]**black belt** \'blak-ˌbelt\ *n* **1** : an area characterized by rich black soil **2** *cap both Bs* : an area densely populated by blacks

[2]**black belt** \-'belt\ *n* **1** : a rating of expert in various arts of self-defense (as judo and karate) **2** : one who holds a black belt

black·ber·ry \'blak-ˌber-ē\ *n* **1** : the usu. black or dark purple juicy but seedy edible fruit of various brambles (genus *Rubus*) of the rose family **2** : a plant that bears blackberries

black bile *n* : a humor of medieval physiology believed to be secreted by the kidneys or spleen and to cause melancholy

[1]**black·bird** \'blak-ˌbərd\ *n* **1** : any of various birds of which the males are largely or entirely black: as **a** : a common and familiar British thrush (*Turdus merula*) that is black with orange bill and eye rim **b** : any of several American birds (family Icteridae) **2** : a Pacific islander kidnapped for use as a plantation laborer

[2]**blackbird** *vi* : to engage in the slave trade

black·bird·er *n* **1 :** a person that blackbirds **2 :** a ship used in blackbirding

black·board \'blak-ˌbō(ə)rd, -ˌbȯ(ə)rd\ *n* **:** a hard smooth usu. dark surface used for writing or drawing on with chalk

black·body \'blak-'bäd-ē\ *n* **:** an ideal body or surface that completely absorbs all radiant energy falling upon it with no reflection

black book *n* **:** a book containing a blacklist

black box *n* **1 :** a usu. complicated electronic device that can be inserted in or removed as a unit from a larger assembly of parts (as those constituting a spacecraft) **2 :** a usu. electronic device whose internal mechanism is hidden from or mysterious to the user

black·cap \'blak-ˌkap\ *n* **1 :** BLACK RASPBERRY **2 :** any of several birds with black heads or crowns: as **a :** a small European warbler (*Sylvia atricapilla*) with a black crown **b :** CHICKADEE

black–capped \-'kapt\ *adj, of a bird* **:** having the top of the head black

black·cock \-ˌkäk\ *n* **:** BLACK GROUSE: *specif* **:** the male black grouse

black cohosh *n* **:** a bugbane (*Cimicifuga racemosa*) of the eastern U.S.

black crappie *n* **:** a silvery black-mottled sunfish (*Pomoxis nigromaculatus*) of the Mississippi drainage and eastern U.S. having seven or eight protruding spines on the dorsal fins

black·damp \'blak-'damp\ *n* **:** a carbon dioxide mixture occurring as a mine gas and incapable of supporting life or flame

black death *n, often cap B&D* [fr. the black patches formed on the skin of its victims] **:** a form of plague epidemic in Europe and Asia in the 14th century

black diamond *n* **1** *pl* **:** COAL 3a **2 :** 3CARBONADO **3 :** dense black hematite

black·en \'blak-ən\ *vb* **black·ened; black·en·ing** \-(ə-)niŋ\ *vi* **:** to become dark or black <the sky ~*s*> ~ *vt* **1 :** to make black **2 :** DEFAME, SULLY — **black·en·er** \-(ə-)nər\ *n*

black·en·ing \-(ə-)niŋ\ *n* **:** BLACKING

black eye *n* **1 :** a discoloration of the skin around the eye from bruising **2 :** a bad reputation

black–eyed pea \ˌblak-ˌīd-\ *n* **:** COWPEA

black–eyed Su·san \-'süz-ᵊn\ *n* **:** either of two No. American coneflowers (*Rudbeckia hirta* and *R. serotina*) having flower heads with deep yellow to orange rays and dark conical disks

black·face \'blak-ˌfās\ *n* **1 :** makeup for a Negro role esp. in a minstrel show; *also* **:** an actor who plays this role **2 :** BOLDFACE

black·fin \-ˌfin\ *n* **:** a whitefish (*Leucichthys nigripinnis*) of the Great Lakes used as a food fish

black·fish \-ˌfish\ *n* **1 :** any of numerous dark-colored fishes: as **a :** TAUTOG **b :** a small food fish (*Dallia pectoralis*) of Alaska and Siberia that is remarkable for its ability to revive after being frozen for a long time **2 :** any of several small toothed whales (genus *Globicephala*) related to the dolphins and found in the warmer seas

black–flag \-'flag\ *vt* **:** to signal (a race-car driver) to go immediately to the pits

black flag *n* **:** a pirate's flag usu. bearing a skull and crossbones

black·fly \'blak-ˌflī\ *n, pl* **-flies** *or* **-fly :** any of several small dark-colored insects; *esp* **:** a two-winged biting fly (*Simulium* or related genera) whose larvae usu. live in clear flowing streams

Black·foot \'blak-ˌfu̇t\ *n, pl* **Blackfeet** *or* **Blackfoot 1 a** *pl* **:** an Amerindian confederacy of Montana, Alberta, and Saskatchewan **b :** a member of any of the Blackfoot peoples **2 :** the Algonquian language of the Blackfeet

black–foot·ed albatross \ˌblak-ˌfu̇t-əd-\ *n* **:** an albatross (*Diomedea nigripes*) of the Pacific that is chiefly blackish with dusky bill and black feet and legs — called also *gooney, gooney bird*

black–footed ferret *n* **:** an American weasel (*Mustela nigripes*) that is related to the European polecat and resembles a yellow mink with dark feet, tail, and mask

black gold *n* **:** PETROLEUM

black grouse *n* **:** a large grouse (*Lyrurus tetrix*) of western Asia and Europe of which the male is black with white wing patches and the female is barred and mottled

1**black·guard** \'blag-ərd, -ˌärd; 'blak-ˌgärd\ *n* **1** *obs* **:** the kitchen servants of a large household **2 a :** a rude or unscrupulous person **:** SCOUNDREL **b :** one who uses foul or abusive language — **black·guard·ism** \-ˌiz-əm\ *n* — **black·guard·ly** \-lē\ *adj or adv*

2**blackguard** *vt* **:** to talk about or address in abusive terms

black gum *n* **:** a tupelo (*Nyssa sylvatica*) of the eastern U.S. with light and soft but tough wood

black hand *n, often cap B&H* [*Black Hand,* a Sicilian and Italian-American society of the late 19th and 20th centuries] **:** a lawless secret society engaged in criminal activities (as terrorism or extortion) — **black·hand·er** \'blak-ˌhan-dər\ *n*

black·head \'blak-ˌhed\ *n* **1 :** a small plug of sebum blocking the duct of a sebaceous gland esp. on the face **2 :** a destructive disease of turkeys and related birds caused by a protozoan (*Histomonas meleagridis*) that invades the intestinal ceca and liver **3 :** a larval clam or mussel attached to the skin or gills of a freshwater fish

black·heart \-ˌhärt\ *n* **:** a plant disease in which the central tissues blacken

black hole *n* **:** a hypothetical celestial body with a small diameter and intense gravitational field that is held to be a collapsed star

black·ing \'blak-iŋ\ *n* **:** a substance (as a paste or polish) that is applied to an object to make it black

1**black·jack** \-ˌjak\ *n* **1** [*black* + *jack* (vessel)] **:** a tankard for beer or ale usu. of tar-coated leather **2 :** SPHALERITE **3 :** a hand weapon typically consisting of a piece of leather-enclosed metal with a strap or springy shaft for a handle **4 :** a common often scrubby oak (*Quercus marilandica*) of the southeastern and southern U.S. with black bark **5 :** a card game the object of which is to be dealt cards having a higher count than those of the dealer up to but not exceeding 21 — called also *twenty-one, vingt-et-un*

2**blackjack** *vt* **1 :** to strike with a blackjack **2 :** to coerce with threats or pressure

black knot *n* **:** a destructive disease of plum and cherry trees characterized by black excrescences on the branches and caused by a fungus (*Dibotryon morbosa*)

black·land \'blak-ˌland\ *n* **1 :** a heavy sticky black soil such as that covering large areas in Texas **2** *pl* **:** a region of blackland

black lead *n* **:** GRAPHITE

black·leg \'blak-ˌleg, -ˌläg\ *n* **1 :** an enzootic usu. fatal toxemia esp. of young cattle **2 :** a cheating gamester **:** SWINDLER **3** *chiefly Brit* **:** a worker hostile to trade unionism or acting in opposition to union policies **:** SCAB

black letter *n* **:** a style of type or lettering with a heavy face and angular outlines used esp. by the earliest European printers — called also *Gothic, Old English*

Black Letter

black light *n* **:** invisible ultraviolet or infrared light

black·light trap \ˌblak-ˌlīt-\ *n* **:** a trap for insects that uses a form of black light perceptible to particular insects as an attractant

1**black·list** \'blak-ˌlist\ *n* **:** a list of persons who are disapproved of or are to be punished or boycotted

2**blacklist** *vt* **:** to put on a blacklist — **black·list·er** *n*

black locust *n* **:** a tall tree (*Robinia pseudoacacia*) of eastern No. America with pinnately compound leaves, drooping racemes of fragrant white flowers, and strong stiff wood

black lung *n* **:** a disease of the lungs caused by habitual inhalation of coal dust

black magic *n* **:** WITCHCRAFT

black·mail \'blak-ˌmāl\ *n* [*black* + 1*mail*] **1 :** a tribute anciently exacted on the Scottish border by freebooting chiefs for immunity from pillage **2 a :** extortion by threats esp. of public exposure or criminal prosecution **b :** the payment that is extorted — **blackmail** *vt* — **black·mail·er** *n*

Black Ma·ria \ˌblak-mə-'rī-ə\ *n* **:** PATROL WAGON

black–mar·ket *vi* **:** to buy or sell goods in the black market ~ *vt* **:** to sell in the black market — **black marketer** *or* **black marketeer** *n*

black market *n* **:** illicit trade in goods or commodities in violation of official regulations; *also* **:** a place where such trade is carried on

Black Mass *n* **:** a travesty of the Christian mass ascribed to the reputed worshipers of Satan

Black Muslim *n* **:** a member of an exclusively black group that professes Islamic religious belief and advocates a strictly separate black community

black nationalist *n, often cap B&N* **:** a member of a group of militant blacks who advocate separatism from the whites and the formation of self-governing black communities — **black nationalism** *n, often cap B&N*

black·out \'blak-ˌau̇t\ *n* **1 a :** a turning off of the stage lighting to separate scenes in a play, indicate that the play is over, or end a skit; *also* **:** a skit that ends with a blackout **b :** a period of darkness enforced as a precaution against air raids **c :** a period of darkness (as in a city) caused by a lack of illumination due to a failure of electrical power **2 :** a transient dulling or loss of vision, consciousness, or memory <an alcoholic ~> **3 a :** a wiping out or erasure **:** OBLITERATION <a sudden ~ of his policy by the insurance company> **b :** a blotting out by censorship **:** SUPPRESSION <a ~ of news about the invasion> **4 :** a usu. temporary loss of radio signal due to a magnetic storm or to a local effect at the transmitter of a spacecraft upon reentry

black out \(')blak-'au̇t\ *vi* **1 :** to become enveloped in darkness **2 :** to undergo a temporary loss of vision, consciousness, or memory **3 :** to extinguish or screen all lights for protection esp. against air attack ~ *vt* **1 :** to cause to black out <*black out* the stage> **2 :** to make inoperative or temporarily nonexistent **:** DESTROY <falling trees *blacked out* electric power lines> **3 a :** to blot out or erase <*blacked out* the event from his mind> **b :** to suppress by censorship <*black out* the news>

Black Panther *n* **:** a member of an organization of militant American Negroes

black pepper *n* **:** a pungent condiment that consists of the fruit of an East Indian plant (*Piper nigrum*) ground with the black husk still on

black perch *n* **:** any of various dark-colored fishes (as a bass)

black·poll \'blak-ˌpōl\ *n* **:** a No. American warbler (*Dendroica striata*) having the top of the head of the male bird black when in full plumage

black power *n* **:** the mobilization of the political and economic power of American Negroes esp. to further racial equality

black pudding *n, chiefly Brit* **:** BLOOD SAUSAGE

black racer *n* **:** an American blacksnake (*Coluber constrictor constrictor*) common in the eastern U.S.

black raspberry *n* **:** a raspberry (*Rubus occidentalis*) with a purplish black fruit that is native to eastern No. America and is the source of several cultivated varieties — called also *blackcap*

Black Rod *n* **:** the principal usher of the House of Lords

black rot *n* **:** a bacterial or fungous rot of plants marked by dark brown discoloration

black sheep *n* **:** a discreditable member of a respectable group

Black·shirt \'blak-ˌshərt\ *n* **:** a member of a fascist organization having a black shirt as a distinctive part of its uniform; *esp* **:** a member of the Italian Fascist party

black·smith \'blak-ˌsmith\ *n* [fr. his working with iron, known as black metal] **:** a smith who forges iron — **black·smith·ing** \-iŋ\ *n*

black·snake \-ˌsnāk\ *n* **1 :** any of several snakes that are largely black or very dark in color; *esp* **:** either of two harmless snakes

---

ə abut ᵊ kitten ər further a back ā bake ä cot, cart
au̇ out ch chin e less ē easy g gift i trip ī life
j joke ŋ sing ō flow ȯ flaw ȯi coin th thin t͟h this
ü loot u̇ foot y yet yü few yu̇ furious zh vision

(*Coluber constrictor* and *Elaphe obsoleta*) of the U.S. **2 :** a long tapering braided whip of rawhide or leather
black spot *n* **:** any of several plant diseases characterized by black spots or blotches
black studies *n pl* **:** studies (as history and literature) relating to American Negro culture
black·tail \ˈblak-ˌtāl\ *n* **:** BLACK-TAILED DEER
black–tailed deer \ˌblak-ˌtāl- ˈdi(ə)r\ *n* **:** MULE DEER; *specif* **:** one of a subspecies (*Odocoileus hemionus columbianus*) esp. of British Columbia, Oregon, and Washington — see DEER illustration
black tea *n* **:** tea that is dark in color from complete fermentation of the leaf before firing
black·thorn \ˈblak-ˌthȯ(ə)rn\ *n* **1 :** a European spiny plum (*Prunus spinosa*) with hard wood and small white flowers **2 :** any of several American hawthorns
black–tie *adj* **:** characterized by or requiring the wearing of semiformal evening dress by men <a ~ dinner> — compare WHITE-TIE
black·top \ˈblak-ˌtäp\ *n* **:** a bituminous material used esp. for surfacing roads; *also* **:** a surface paved with blacktop — **blacktop** *vt*
black vomit *n* **1 :** vomitus consisting of dark-colored matter **2 :** a condition characterized by black vomit; *esp* **:** YELLOW FEVER
Black·wall hitch \ˌblak-ˌwȯl-\ *n* [*Blackwall*, shipyard in London, England] **:** a hitch for securing a rope to a hook — see KNOT illustration
black walnut *n* **:** a walnut (*Juglans nigra*) of eastern No. America with hard strong heavy dark brown wood and oily edible nuts; *also* **:** its wood or nut
black·wash \ˈblak-ˌwȯsh, -ˌwäsh\ *vt* [*black* + *-wash* (as in *whitewash*)] **:** to uncover or bring to light **:** EXPOSE
black·wa·ter \ˈblak-ˌwȯt-ər, -ˌwät-\ *n* **:** any of several diseases of lower animals or man characterized by dark-colored urine
black widow *n* **:** a venomous New World spider (*Latrodectus mactans*) having the female black with an hourglass-shaped red mark on the underside of the abdomen
blad·der \ˈblad-ər\ *n* [ME, fr. OE *blǣdre;* akin to OHG *blātara* bladder, OE *blāwan* to blow] **1 a :** a membranous sac in animals that serves as the receptacle of a liquid or contains gas; *esp* **:** the urinary bladder **b :** VESICLE **2 :** something (as the rubber bag inside a football) resembling a bladder — **blad·der·like** \-ˌlīk\ *adj*
blad·der·nut \ˈblad-ər-ˌnət\ *n* **:** an ornamental shrub or small tree (genus *Staphylea* of the family Staphyleaceae, the bladdernut family) with panicles of small white flowers followed by inflated capsules; *also* **:** one of the capsules
bladder worm *n* **:** a bladderlike larval tapeworm (as a cysticercus)
blad·der·wort \ˈblad-ər-ˌwərt, -ˌwȯ(ə)rt\ *n* **:** any of a genus (*Utricularia* of the family Lentibulariaceae, the bladderwort family) of chiefly aquatic plants with vesicular floats or insect traps
bladder wrack *n* **:** a common black rockweed (*Fucus vesiculosus*) used in preparing kelp and as a manure
blade \ˈblād\ *n* [ME, fr. OE *blæd;* akin to OHG *blat* leaf, L *folium*, Gk *phyllon*, OE *blōwan* to blossom — more at BLOW] **1 a :** LEAF 1a(1); *esp* **:** the leaf of an herb or a grass **b :** the flat expanded part of a leaf as distinguished from the petiole **2 :** something resembling the blade of a leaf: as **a :** the broad flattened part of an oar or paddle **b :** an arm of a screw propeller, electric fan, or steam turbine **c :** the broad flat or concave part of a machine (as a bulldozer or snowplow) that comes into contact with the material to be moved **d :** a broad flat body part; *specif* **:** SCAPULA — used chiefly in naming cuts of meat **e :** the flat portion of the tongue immediately behind the tip; *also* **:** this portion together with the tip **f :** the expanded rear portion of the comb of a single-comb fowl — see COCK illustration **3 a :** the cutting part of an implement **b** (1) **:** SWORD (2) **:** SWORDSMAN (3) **:** a dashing lively man **c :** the runner of an ice skate
blad·ed \ˈblād-əd\ *adj* **:** having blades — often used in combination <broad-*bladed* leaves>
blae \ˈblā\ *adj* [ME *bla, blo,* fr. ON *blār;* akin to OHG *blāo* blue — more at BLUE] *chiefly Scot* **:** dark blue or bluish gray
1**blah** \ˈblä\ *also* **blah–blah** \-ˌblä\ *n* [imit.] **1 :** silly or pretentious chatter or nonsense **2** *pl* [perh. influenced in meaning by *blasé*] **:** a feeling of boredom, discomfort, or general dissatisfaction
2**blah** *adj* **:** lacking interest **:** MEDIOCRE <a ~ winter day>
blain \ˈblān\ *n* [ME, fr. OE *blegen;* akin to MLG *bleine* blain, OE *blāwan* to blow] **:** an inflammatory swelling or sore
blam·able \ˈblā-mə-bəl\ *adj* **:** deserving blame **:** REPREHENSIBLE ***syn*** see BLAMEWORTHY ***ant*** blameless — **blam·ably** \-blē\ *adv*
1**blame** \ˈblām\ *vt* **blamed; blam·ing** [ME *blamen,* fr. OF *blamer,* fr. LL *blasphemare* to blaspheme, fr. Gk *blasphēmein*] **1 :** to find fault with **:** CENSURE <the right to praise or ~ a literary work> **2 a :** to hold responsible <~ him for everything> **b :** to place responsibility for <~*s* it on me> ***syn*** see CRITICIZE — **blam·er** *n* — **to blame :** at fault **:** RESPONSIBLE
2**blame** *n* **1 :** an expression of disapproval or reproach **:** CENSURE **2 a :** a state of being blameworthy **:** CULPABILITY **b** *archaic* **:** FAULT, SIN **3 :** responsibility for something believed to deserve censure <they must share the ~ for the crime> — **blame·less** \-ləs\ *adj* — **blame·less·ly** *adv* — **blame·less·ness** *n*
blame·ful \ˈblām-fəl\ *adj* **:** BLAMABLE — **blame·ful·ly** \-fə-lē\ *adv*
blame·wor·thy \-ˌwər-t͟hē\ *adj* **:** being at fault **:** deserving blame — **blame·wor·thi·ness** *n*

syn BLAMEWORTHY, BLAMABLE, GUILTY, CULPABLE *shared meaning element* **:** deserving reproach or punishment for some act or course of action. BLAMEWORTHY and BLAMABLE acknowledge the fact of censurable quality in what is described but in themselves imply nothing about the degree of reprehensibility involved <though not criminal, his behavior was certainly *blameworthy*> <a person is only *blamable* for his own faults> GUILTY implies responsibility for or consciousness of crime, sin, or, at the least, grave error or misdoing <found *guilty* of murder> <suspicion always haunts the *guilty* mind; the thief doth fear each bush an officer —Shak.> CULPABLE is weaker than *guilty* and is likely to connote malfeasance or errors of ignorance, omission, or negligence <avaricious victims, almost as *culpable* as the confidence man who tricked them> <*culpable* neglect> ***ant*** blameless

blanc fixe \ˈblaŋk-ˈfiks\ *n* [F, lit., fixed white] **:** barium sulfate prepared as a heavy white powder and used esp. as a filler in paper, rubber, and linoleum or as a pigment
blanch \ˈblanch\ *vb* [ME *blaunchen,* fr. MF *blanchir,* fr. OF *blanche,* fem. of *blanc,* adj., white] *vt* **1 :** to take the color out of: **a :** to bleach by excluding light <~ celery> **b :** to scald or parboil in water or steam in order to remove the skin from, whiten, or stop enzymatic action in (as food for freezing) **c :** to clean (a coin blank) in an acid solution **d :** to cover (sheet iron or steel) with a coating of tin **2 :** to make ashen or pale <fear ~*es* the cheek> ~ *vi* **:** to become white or pale ***syn*** see WHITEN — **blanch·er** *n*
blanc·mange \blə-ˈmänj, -ˈmänzh\ *n* [ME *blancmanger,* fr. MF *blanc manger,* lit., white food] **:** a dessert made from gelatinous or starchy substances and milk usu. sweetened, flavored, and shaped in a mold
bland \ˈbland\ *adj* [L *blandus*] **1 a :** smooth and soothing in manner or quality <a ~ smile> **b :** exhibiting no personal concern or embarrassment **:** UNPERTURBED <a ~ confession of guilt> **2 a :** not irritating, stimulating, or invigorating **:** SOOTHING **b :** DULL, INSIPID <~ stories with little plot or action> ***syn* 1** see SOFT ***ant*** piquant, savory **2** see SUAVE ***ant*** brusque — **bland·ly** \ˈblan-(d)lē\ *adv* — **bland·ness** \ˈblan(d)-nəs\ *n*
blan·dish \ˈblan-dish\ *vb* [ME *blandishen,* fr. MF *blandiss-,* stem of *blandir,* fr. L *blandiri,* fr. *blandus* mild, flattering] *vt* **:** to coax with flattery **:** CAJOLE ~ *vi* **:** to act or speak in a flattering or coaxing manner — **blan·dish·er** *n*
blan·dish·ment \-dish-mənt\ *n* **:** something that tends to coax or cajole **:** ALLUREMENT — often used in pl.
1**blank** \ˈblaŋk\ *adj* [ME, fr. MF *blanc,* of Gmc origin; akin to OHG *blanch* white; akin to L *flagrare* to burn — more at BLACK] **1** *archaic* **:** COLORLESS **2 a :** appearing or causing to appear dazed, confounded, or nonplussed <stared in ~ dismay> **b :** EXPRESSIONLESS <a ~ stare> **3 a :** lacking interest, variety, or change <~ hours> **b :** devoid of covering or content; *esp* **:** free from writing or marks <~ paper> **c :** having spaces to be filled in **d :** lacking any card **:** VOID <a ~ suit at cards> **4 :** ABSOLUTE, UNQUALIFIED <a ~ refusal> **5 :** UNFINISHED; *esp* **:** having a plain or unbroken surface where an opening is usual <a ~ key> <a ~ arch> ***syn*** see EMPTY — **blank·ly** *adv* — **blank·ness** *n*
2**blank** *n* **1 a :** an empty space (as on a paper) **b :** a paper with spaces for the entry of data <a subscription ~> **2 a :** an empty or featureless place or space <my mind was a ~ during the test> **b :** a vacant or uneventful period <a long ~ in history> **c :** something useless, valueless, or undesirable <drew a ~> **3 :** the bull's-eye of a target **4 :** a dash substituting for an omitted word **5 a :** a piece of material prepared to be made into something (as a key) by a further operation **b :** a cartridge loaded with powder but no bullet **6 :** VOID 4
3**blank** *vt* **1 a :** OBSCURE, OBLITERATE <~ out a line> **b :** to stop access to **:** SEAL <~ off a tunnel> **2 :** to keep (an opposing team) from scoring <were ~*ed* for eight innings> **3 :** to cut with a die from a piece of stock ~ *vi* **1 :** FADE — usu. used with *out* <the music ~*ed* out> **2 :** to become confused or abstracted — often used with *out* <his mind ~*ed* out momentarily>
blank check *n* **1 :** a signed check with the amount unspecified **2 :** complete freedom of action or control **:** CARTE BLANCHE
blank endorsement *n* **:** an endorsement of commercial paper without a qualifying phrase thus making the paper payable to the bearer
1**blan·ket** \ˈblaŋ-kət\ *n* [ME, fr. OF *blankete,* fr. *blanc*] **1 a :** a large usu. oblong piece of woven fabric used as a bed covering **b :** a similar piece of fabric used as a body covering (as for an animal) <a horse ~> **2 :** something that resembles a blanket; *esp* **:** a covering or enclosing layer <a ~ of fog> <a ~ of gloom> — **blan·ket·like** \-ˌlīk\ *adj*
2**blanket** *vt* **1 :** to cover with a blanket <new grass ~*s* the slope> **2 a :** to cover so as to obscure, interrupt, suppress, or extinguish <~ a fire with foam> **b :** to apply or cause to apply to uniformly despite wide separation or diversity among the elements included <freight rates that ~ a region> **c :** to cause to be included <automatically ~*ed* into the insurance program> **3** *archaic* **:** to toss in a blanket (as by way of punishment)
3**blanket** *adj* **1 :** covering all members of a group or class <a ~ wage increase> **2 :** effective or applicable in all instances
blan·ket·flow·er \ˈblaŋ-kət-ˌflau̇(-ə)r\ *n* **:** GAILLARDIA
blanket stitch *n* **:** a buttonhole stitch with spaces of variable width used on materials too thick to hem — **blanket–stitch** *vt*
blank verse *n* **:** unrhymed verse; *specif* **:** unrhymed iambic pentameter verse
1**blare** \ˈbla(ə)r, ˈble(ə)r\ *vb* **blared; blar·ing** [ME *bleren;* akin to OE *blǣtan* to bleat] *vi* **:** to sound loud and strident <radios *blaring*> ~ *vt* **1 :** to sound or utter raucously <sat *blaring* the car horn> **2 :** to proclaim flamboyantly <headlines *blared* his defeat>
2**blare** *n* **1 :** a loud strident noise **2 :** dazzling often garish brilliance **3 :** FLAMBOYANCE
blar·ney \ˈblär-nē\ *n* [*Blarney stone,* a stone in Blarney Castle, near Cork, Ireland, held to bestow skill in flattery on those who kiss it] **1 :** skillful flattery **:** BLANDISHMENT **2 :** NONSENSE, HUMBUG <gave her some ~ about why he was late> — **blarney** *vb*
bla·sé \blä-ˈzā\ *adj* [F] **1 :** apathetic to pleasure or excitement as a result of excessive indulgence or enjoyment **:** WORLD-WEARY **2 :** SOPHISTICATED, WORLDLY-WISE
blas·pheme \blas-ˈfēm\ *vb* **blas·phemed; blas·phem·ing** [ME *blasfemen,* fr. LL *blasphemare* — more at BLAME] *vt* **1 :** to speak of or address with irreverence **2 :** REVILE, ABUSE ~ *vi* **:** to utter blasphemy — **blas·phem·er** *n*
blas·phe·mous \ˈblas-fə-məs\ *adj* **:** impiously irreverent **:** PROFANE — **blas·phe·mous·ly** *adv* — **blas·phe·mous·ness** *n*
blas·phe·my \ˈblas-fə-mē\ *n, pl* **-mies 1 a :** the act of insulting or showing contempt or lack of reverence for God **b :** the act of

claiming the attributes of deity **2 :** irreverence toward something considered sacred or inviolable

1blast \'blast\ *n* [ME, fr. OE *blǣst;* akin to OHG *blāst* blast, OE *blāwan* to blow] **1 a :** a violent gust of wind **b :** the effect or accompaniment (as sleet) of such a gust **2 :** the sound produced by an impulsion of air through a wind instrument or whistle **3 :** something resembling a gust of wind: as **a :** a stream of air or gas forced through a hole **b :** a violent outburst <the speaker's ~ against special privileges> **c :** the continuous blowing to which a charge of ore or metal is subjected in a blast furnace **4 a :** a sudden pernicious influence or effect <the ~ of a huge epidemic> **b :** a disease that suggests the effects of a noxious wind; *esp* **:** one of plants that causes the foliage or flowers to wither **5 a :** an explosion or violent detonation **b :** the explosive charge used esp. for shattering rock **c :** the violent effect produced in the vicinity of an explosion that consists of a wave of increased atmospheric pressure followed by a wave of decreased atmospheric pressure **6 :** SPEED, CAPACITY <going full ~ down the road> **7 :** OPERATION, ACTIVITY <the furnace must be kept in continual ~> **8 :** a riotous or exuberant occasion; *esp* **:** an enjoyable party **9 :** HOME RUN

2blast *vi* **1 :** to produce a strident sound <music ~*ing* from the radio> **2 a :** to use an explosive **b :** SHOOT **3 :** to make a vigorous attack **4 :** SHRIVEL, WITHER **5 :** to hit a golf ball out of a sand trap with explosive force ~ *vt* **1 a :** to injure by or as if by the action of wind **b :** to affect with a blighting influence **2 :** to shatter by or as if by an explosive **:** DEMOLISH **3 a :** to apply a forced draft to **b :** to strike with explosive force **4 :** to cause to blast off <will ~ themselves from the moon's surface> **5 :** to hit vigorously and effectively **6 :** to cause to emerge like a blast of wind <the tenor ~*s* out the high C's> — **blast·er** *n* — **blast·ing** *n or adj*

blast- *or* **blasto-** *comb form* [G, fr. Gk, fr. *blastos*] **:** bud **:** budding **:** germ <*blasto*disc> <*blast*ula>

-blast \,blast\ *n comb form* [NL *-blastus,* fr. Gk *blastos* bud, shoot; akin to OE *molda* top of the head, Skt *mūrdhan* head] **:** formative unit esp. of living matter **:** germ **:** cell **:** cell layer <epi*blast*>

blast·ed *adj* **1 a :** BLIGHTED, WITHERED **b :** damaged by or as if by an explosive, lightning, or the wind **:** BATTERED <a ~ apple tree> **2 :** CONFOUNDED, DETESTABLE <this ~ weather>

blas·te·ma \bla-'stē-mə\ *n, pl* **-mas** *or* **-ma·ta** \-mət-ə\ [NL, fr. Gk *blastēma* offshoot, fr. *blastos*] **:** a mass of living substance capable of growth and differentiation — **blas·te·mat·ic** \,blas-tə-'mat-ik\ *or* **blas·te·mic** \bla-'stē-mik, -'stem-ik\ *adj*

blast furnace *n* **:** a furnace in which combustion is forced by a current of air under pressure; *esp* **:** one for the reduction of iron ore

-blas·tic \'blas-tik\ *adj comb form* [ISV, fr. *-blast*] **:** having (such or so many) buds, germs, cells, or cell layers <diplo*blastic*>

blast·ie \'blas-tē\ *n* [Sc *blast* to wither, fr. 2*blast*] *Scot* **:** an ugly little creature

blast·ment \'blas(t)-mənt\ *n, archaic* **:** a blighting influence

blas·to·coel *or* **blas·to·coele** \'blas-tə-,sēl\ *n* [ISV] **:** the cavity of a blastula — see BLASTULA illustration — **blas·to·coe·lic** \,blas-tə-'sē-lik\ *adj*

blas·to·cyst \'blas-tə-,sist\ *n* **:** the modified blastula of a placental mammal

blas·to·derm \-,dərm\ *n* [G, fr. *blast-* + *-derm*] **:** a blastodisc after completion of cleavage and formation of the blastocoel — **blas·to·der·mat·ic** \,blas-tə-,dər-'mat-ik\ *or* **blas·to·der·mic** \-'dər-mik\ *adj*

blas·to·disc \'blas-tə-,disk\ *n* **:** the embryo-forming portion of an egg with discoidal cleavage usu. appearing as a small disc on the upper surface of the yolk mass — see EGG illustration

blast–off \'blas-,tȯf\ *n* **:** a blasting off (as of a rocket)

blast off \(')blas-'tȯf\ *vi* **:** to take off — used esp. of rocket-propelled missiles and vehicles

blas·to·mere \'blas-tə-,mi(ə)r\ *n* [ISV] **:** a cell produced during cleavage of an egg — **blas·to·mer·ic** \,blas-tə-'mi(ə)r-ik, -'mer-\ *adj*

blas·to·my·cete \,blas-tə-'mī-,sēt, -,mī-'sēt\ *n* [deriv. of *blast-* + Gk *mykēt-, mykēs* fungus — more at MYC-] **:** any of a group (Blastomycetes) of pathogenic fungi growing typically like yeasts

blas·to·my·co·sis \-,mī-'kō-səs\ *n* **:** a disease caused by a blastomycete — **blas·to·my·cot·ic** \-'kät-ik\ *adj*

blas·to·pore \'blas-tə-,pō(ə)r, -,pȯ(ə)r\ *n* **:** the opening of the archenteron — **blas·to·por·al** \,blas-tə-'pōr-əl, -'pȯr-\ *or* **blas·to·por·ic** \-'pōr-ik, -'pȯr-\ *adj*

blas·to·sphere \'blas-tə-,sfi(ə)r\ *n* **:** BLASTULA — **blas·to·spher·ic** \,blas-tə-'sfi(ə)r-ik, -'sfer-\ *adj*

blas·tu·la \'blas-chə-lə\ *n, pl* **-las** *or* **-lae** \-,lē\ [NL, fr. Gk *blastos*] **:** an early metazoan embryo typically having the form of a hollow fluid-filled rounded cavity bounded by a single layer of cells — compare GASTRULA, MORULA — **blas·tu·lar** \-lər\ *adj* — **blas·tu·la·tion** \,blas-chə-'lā-shən\ *n*

a mi c ma v

section of blastula: *c* blastocoel, *ma* macromere, *mi* micromere, *a* animal pole, *v* vegetal pole

blat \'blat\ *vb* **blat·ted; blat·ting** [imit.] *vi* **1 :** to cry like a calf or sheep **:** BLEAT **2 a :** to make a raucous noise **b :** BLAB ~ *vt* **:** to utter loudly or foolishly **:** BLURT — **blat** *n*

bla·tan·cy \'blāt-ᵊn-sē\ *n, pl* **-cies** **1 :** the quality or state of being blatant **2 :** something that is blatant

bla·tant \'blāt-ᵊnt\ *adj* [perh. fr. L *blatire* to chatter] **1 :** noisy esp. in a vulgar or offensive manner **:** CLAMOROUS **2 :** completely obvious, conspicuous, or obtrusive esp. in a crass or offensive manner **:** BRAZEN ***syn*** see VOCIFEROUS ***ant*** decorous, reserved — **bla·tant·ly** *adv*

blate \'blāt\ *adj* [ME] *chiefly Scot* **:** TIMID, SHEEPISH

1blath·er \'bla*th*-ər\ *vi* **blath·ered; blath·er·ing** \-(ə-)riŋ\ [ON *blathra;* akin to MHG *blōdern* to chatter] **:** to talk foolishly — **blath·er·er** \-ər-ər\ *n*

2blather *n* **1 :** voluble or nonsensical talk **2 :** STIR, COMMOTION

blath·er·skite \'bla*th*-ər-,skīt\ *n* [*blather* + Sc dial. *skate* a contemptible person] **1 :** a blustering talkative fellow **2 :** NONSENSE, BLATHER

blat·ter \'blat-ər\ *vi* [perh. fr. L *blaterare* to chatter — more at BLATANT] *dial* **:** to talk noisily and fast **:** PRATTLE

blaw \'blȯ\ *vb* **blawed; blawn** \'blȯn\; **blaw·ing** [ME (northern dial.) *blawen,* fr. OE *blāwan*] *chiefly Scot* **:** BLOW

1blaze \'blāz\ *n* [ME *blase,* fr. OE *blæse* torch; akin to OE *bǣl* fire — more at BALD] **1 a :** an intensely burning fire **b :** intense direct light often accompanied by heat <the ~ of noon> **c :** an active burning; *esp* **:** a sudden bursting forth of flame <several ~*s* in the woods> **2 :** something that resembles the blaze of a fire: as **a :** a dazzling display **b :** a sudden outburst <a ~ of fury> **c :** BRILLIANCE <the ~ of autumn>
syn BLAZE, FLAME, FLARE, GLARE, GLOW *shared meaning element* **:** a brightly burning light or fire or something suggesting this

2blaze *vi* **blazed; blaz·ing** **1 a :** to burn brightly <the sun *blazed* overhead> **b :** to flare up **:** FLAME <he suddenly *blazed* with anger> **2 :** to be conspicuously brilliant or resplendent <fields *blazing* with flowers> **3 :** to shoot rapidly and repeatedly <~ away at the target> — **blaz·ing·ly** \'blā-ziŋ-lē\ *adv*

3blaze *vt* **blazed; blaz·ing** [ME *blasen,* fr. MD *blāsen* to blow; akin to OHG *blāst* blast] **:** to make public or conspicuous **:** PROCLAIM

4blaze *n* [G *blas,* fr. OHG *plas;* akin to OE *blæse*] **1 a :** a white mark on the face of an animal **b :** a white or gray streak in the hair of the head **2 :** a trail marker; *esp* **:** a mark made on a tree by chipping off a piece of the bark

5blaze *vt* **blazed; blaz·ing** **1 :** to mark (as a trail) with blazes **2 :** to lead or pioneer in some direction or activity — usu. used in the phrase *blaze the trail*

blaz·er \'blā-zər\ *n* **1 :** one that blazes **2 :** a sports jacket often with notched collar and patch pockets

blazing star *n* **1** *archaic* **:** COMET **2** *archaic* **:** a center of attraction **:** CYNOSURE **3 :** any of several plants having conspicuous flower clusters: as **a :** a plant (*Chamaelirium luteum*) of the bunchflower family **b :** BUTTON SNAKEROOT 1

1bla·zon \'blāz-ᵊn\ *n* [ME *blason,* fr. MF] **1 a :** armorial bearings **:** COAT OF ARMS **b :** the proper description or representation of heraldic or armorial bearings **2 :** DESCRIPTION, SHOW; *esp* **:** ostentatious display

2blazon *vt* **bla·zoned; bla·zon·ing** \'blāz-niŋ, -ᵊn-iŋ\ **1 :** to publish widely **:** PROCLAIM; *esp* **:** to boast of **2 a :** to describe (heraldic or armorial bearings) in technical terms **b :** to represent (armorial bearings) in drawing or engraving **3 a :** to depict or inscribe in colors **b :** DISPLAY **c :** DECK, ADORN <forests ~*ed* with autumn colors> — **bla·zon·er** \-nər, -ᵊn-ər\ *n* — **blazoning** *n*

bla·zon·ry \'blāz-ᵊn-rē\ *n, pl* **-ries** **1 a :** BLAZON 1b **b :** BLAZON 1a **2 :** a dazzling display

bld *abbr* **1** blond **2** blood

bldg *abbr* building

Bldg E *abbr* building engineer

bldr *abbr* builder

1bleach \'blēch\ *vb* [ME *blechen,* fr. OE *blǣcean;* akin to OE *blāc* pale, *bǣl* fire — more at BALD] *vt* **1 :** to remove color or stains from **2 :** to make whiter or lighter esp. by physical or chemical removal of color ~ *vi* **:** to grow white or lose color ***syn*** see WHITEN — **bleach·able** \'blē-chə-bəl\ *adj*

2bleach *n* **1 :** the act or process of bleaching **2 :** a preparation used in bleaching **3 :** the degree of whiteness obtained by bleaching

bleach·er \'blē-chər\ *n* **1 :** one that bleaches or is used in bleaching **2 :** a usu. uncovered stand of tiered planks providing seating space for spectators — usu. used in pl.

bleach·er·ite \'blē-chə-,rīt\ *n* **:** one who sits in the bleachers

bleaching powder *n* **:** a white powder consisting chiefly of calcium hydroxide, calcium chloride, and calcium hypochlorite used as a bleach, disinfectant, or deodorant

1bleak \'blēk\ *adj* [ME *bleke* pale; prob. akin to OE *blāc*] **1 :** exposed and barren and often windswept **2 :** COLD, RAW **3 a :** lacking in warmth or kindliness **b:** not hopeful or encouraging <a ~ outlook> **c :** severely simple or austere — **bleak·ish** \'blē-kish\ *adj* — **bleak·ly** *adv* — **bleak·ness** *n*

2bleak *n* [ME *bleke*] **:** a small European cyprinid river fish (*Alburnus lucidus*) with silvery scale pigment used in making artificial pearls

1blear \'bli(ə)r\ *vt* [ME *bleren*] **1 :** to make (the eyes) sore or watery **2 :** DIM, BLUR

2blear *adj* **1 :** dim with water or tears **2 :** obscure to the view or imagination <clarifies the ~ side of things> — **blear–eyed** \-'īd\ *adj*

bleary \'bli(ə)r-ē\ *adj* **1** *of the eyes or vision* **:** dull or dimmed esp. from fatigue or sleep **2 :** poorly outlined or defined **:** DIM **3 :** tired to the point of exhaustion — **blear·i·ly** \'blir-ə-lē\ *adv* — **blear·i·ness** \'blir-ē-nəs\ *n*

1bleat \'blēt\ *vb* [ME *bleten,* fr. OE *blǣtan;* akin to L *flēre* to weep, OE *bellan* to roar — more at BELLOW] *vi* **1 a :** to utter the natural cry of a sheep or goat **b :** to make a sound resembling this cry **c :** WHIMPER **2 a :** to talk complainingly or with a whine **b :** BLATHER ~ *vt* **:** to utter in a bleating manner — **bleat·er** *n*

2bleat *n* **1 a :** the cry of a sheep or goat **b :** a sound resembling this cry **2 :** whining or foolish talk **:** BLATHER

bleb \'bleb\ *n* [perh. alter. of *blob*] **1 :** a small blister **2 :** BUBBLE — **bleb·by** \'bleb-ē\ *adj*

1bleed \'blēd\ *vb* **bled** \'bled\; **bleed·ing** [ME *bleden,* fr. OE *blēdan,* fr. *blōd* blood] *vi* **1 a :** to emit or lose blood **b :** to sacrifice one's blood esp. in battle **2 :** to feel anguish, pain, or sympathy <a heart that ~*s* at a friend's misfortune> **3 :** to escape by oozing or flowing (as from a wound) **4 :** to give up some constituent (as sap or dye) by exuding or diffusing it **5 a :** to pay out or give money **b :** to have money extorted **6 :** to be printed so as to run off one or more edges of a printed page or sheet after trimming — often used with *off* ~ *vt* **1 :** to remove or draw blood from **2 :** to get or extort money from **3 :** to draw sap from (a tree) **4 a :** to extract or let out some or all of a contained substance from <~ a tire> **b :** to extract or cause to escape from a container **5 :** to cause (as a printed illustration) to bleed; *also* **:** to trim (as a page) so that some of the printing bleeds — **bleed white :** to drain of blood or resources

²**bleed** *n* **:** an illustration or a page that bleeds or is bled; *also* **:** the part trimmed off in bleeding or the corresponding area of the printing plate

bleed·er *n* **:** one that bleeds; *esp* **:** HEMOPHILIAC

bleeding heart *n* **1 :** a garden plant (*Dicentra spectabilis*) of the poppy family with racemes of deep pink drooping heart-shaped flowers; *broadly* **:** any of several plants (genus *Dicentra*) **2 :** one who shows extravagant sympathy esp. for an object of alleged persecution

blel·lum \'blel-əm\ *n* [perh. blend of Sc *bleber* to babble and *skellum* rascal] *Scot* **:** a lazy talkative person

¹**blem·ish** \'blem-ish\ *vt* [ME *blemisshen*, fr. MF *blesmiss-*, stem of *blesmir* to make pale, wound, of Gmc origin; akin to G *blass* pale; akin to OE *blæse* torch — more at BLAZE] **:** to spoil by a flaw

²**blemish** *n* **:** a noticeable imperfection; *esp* **:** one that seriously impairs appearance

syn BLEMISH, DEFECT, FLAW *shared meaning element* **:** an imperfection that mars or damages ***ant*** immaculateness

¹**blench** \'blench\ *vi* [ME *blenchen* to deceive, blench, fr. OE *blencan* to deceive; akin to ON *blekkja* to impose on] **:** to draw back or turn aside from lack of courage **:** FLINCH ***syn*** see RECOIL

²**blench** *vb* [alter. of *blanch*] **:** BLEACH, WHITEN

¹**blend** \'blend\ *vb* **blend·ed** *also* **blent** \'blent\; **blend·ing** [ME *blenden*, modif. of ON *blanda*; akin to OE *blandan* to mix, Lith *blandus* thick (of soup)] *vt* **1 :** MIX; *esp* **:** to combine or associate so that the separate constituents or the line of demarcation cannot be distinguished **2 :** to prepare by thoroughly intermingling different varieties or grades **3 :** to darken the tips of (a fur) with dye ~ *vi* **1 a :** to mingle intimately **b :** to combine into an integrated whole **2 :** to produce a harmonious effect ***syn*** see MIX

²**blend** *n* **:** something produced by blending: as **a :** a product prepared by blending **b :** a word (as *brunch*) produced by combining other words or parts of words

blende \'blend\ *n* [G, fr. *blenden* to blind, fr. OHG *blenten*; akin to OE *blind*] **1 :** SPHALERITE **2 :** any of several minerals (as metallic sulfides) with somewhat bright but nonmetallic luster

blended whiskey *n* **:** whiskey consisting of either a blend of two or more straight whiskeys or a blend of whiskey and neutral spirits

blend·er \'blen-dər\ *n* **:** one that blends; *esp* **:** an electric appliance for grinding or mixing to produce a uniform mixture or a fine suspension <a food ~>

blending inheritance *n* **:** inheritance by the progeny of characters intermediate between those of the parents

blen·ny \'blen-ē\ *n, pl* **blennies** [L *blennius*, a sea fish, fr. Gk *blennos*] **:** any of numerous usu. small and elongated and often scaleless fishes (Blenniidae and related families) living about rocky shores

blephar- *or* **blepharo-** *comb form* [NL, fr. Gk, fr. *blepharon*] **1 :** eyelid <*blepharo*spasm> **2 :** cilium **:** flagellum <*blepharo*plast>

bleph·a·ro·plast \'blef-ə-rō-ˌplast\ n **:** a basal body esp. of a flagellated cell

bles·bok \'bles-ˌbäk\ *n* [Afrik, fr. *bles* blaze + *bok* male antelope] **:** a So. African antelope (*Damaliscus albifrons*) having a large white spot on the face

bless \'bles\ *vt* **blessed** \'blest\ *also* **blest** \'blest\; **bless·ing** [ME *blessen*, fr. OE *blētsian*, fr. *blōd* blood; fr. the use of blood in consecration] **1 :** to hallow or consecrate by religious rite or word **2 :** to hallow with the sign of the cross **3 :** to invoke divine care for **4 a :** PRAISE, GLORIFY <~ his holy name> **b :** to speak gratefully of <~*ed* him for his kindness> **5 :** to confer prosperity or happiness upon **6** *archaic* **:** PROTECT, PRESERVE

bless·ed \'bles-əd\ *or* **blest** \'blest\ *adj* **1 a :** held in reverence **:** VENERATED <the ~ saints> **b :** honored in worship **:** HALLOWED <the ~ Trinity> **c :** BEATIFIC <a ~ visitation> **2 :** of or enjoying happiness; *specif* **:** enjoying the bliss of heaven — used as a title for a beatified person **3 :** bringing pleasure or contentment **:** DELIGHTFUL **4** — used as an intensive <no one gave us a ~ penny — *Saturday Rev.*> — **bless·ed·ly** *adv* — **bless·ed·ness** *n*

Bless·ed Sacrament \ˌbles-əd-\ *n* **:** the Communion elements; *specif* **:** the consecrated Host

bless·ing *n* **1 a :** the act of one that blesses **b :** APPROVAL, ENCOURAGEMENT **2 :** a thing conducive to happiness or welfare **3 :** grace said at a meal

bleth·er \'bleth-ər\ *var of* BLATHER

blew *past of* BLOW

¹**blight** \'blīt\ *n* [origin unknown] **1 a :** a disease or injury of plants resulting in withering, cessation of growth, and death of parts without rotting **b :** an organism that causes blight **2 :** something that frustrates plans or hopes **3 :** something that impairs or destroys **4 :** an impaired condition <urban ~>

²**blight** *vt* **1 :** to affect (as a plant) with blight **2 :** to cause to deteriorate ~ *vi* **:** to suffer from or become affected with blight

blight·er \'blīt-ər\ *n* **1 :** one that blights **2** *chiefly Brit* **a :** one who is held in low esteem **b :** FELLOW, GUY

blimp \'blimp\ *n* [imit.; fr. the sound made by striking the gas bag with the thumb] **1 :** a nonrigid airship **2** *cap* **:** COLONEL BLIMP

blimp·ish \'blim-pish\ *adj, often cap* **:** of, relating to, or suggesting a Blimp <a *Blimpish* colonel and his mousy, neglected wife —*Time*> — **blimp·ish·ly** *adv* — **blimp·ish·ness** *n*

blin \'blin\ *n, pl* **bli·ni** \blə-'nē\ *or* **bli·nis** \blə-'nēz\ [Russ] **:** BLINTZE

¹**blind** \'blīnd\ *adj* [ME, fr. OE; akin to OHG *blint* blind, OE *blandan* to mix — more at BLEND] **1 a** (1) **:** SIGHTLESS (2) **:** having less than 1/10 of normal vision in the more efficient eye when refractive defects are fully corrected by lenses **b :** of or relating to sightless persons **2 a :** unable or unwilling to discern or judge **b :** unsupported by evidence or plausibility <~ faith> **3 a :** having no regard to rational discrimination, guidance, or restriction <~ choice> **b :** lacking a directing or controlling consciousness <~ chance> **c :** marked by complete insensibility **d :** DRUNK **4 :** made or done without sight of certain objects or knowledge of certain facts that could serve for guidance; *esp* **:** performed solely by the aid of instruments within an airplane <a ~ landing> **5 :** DEFECTIVE: as **a :** lacking a growing point or producing leaves instead of flowers **b :** lacking a complete or legible address <~ mail> **6 :** difficult to discern, make out, or discover: as **a :** ILLEGIBLE **b :** hidden from sight **:** COVERED <~ seam> **7 :** having but one opening or outlet <~ sockets> **8 :** having no opening for light or passage **:** BLANK <~ wall> — **blind·ly** \'blīn-(d)lē\ *adv* — **blind·ness** \'blīn(d)-nəs\ *n*

²**blind** *vt* **1 a :** to make blind **b :** DAZZLE **2 a :** to withhold light from **:** DARKEN **b :** HIDE, CONCEAL — **blind·ing·ly** \'blīn-diŋ-lē\ *adv*

³**blind** *n* **1 :** something to hinder sight or keep out light: as **a :** a window shutter **b :** a roller window shade **c :** VENETIAN BLIND **d :** BLINDER **2 :** a place of concealment **3 a :** something put forward for the purpose of misleading **:** SUBTERFUGE **b** (1) **:** a person serving as an agent for another who keeps under cover (2) **:** one who acts as a decoy or distraction

⁴**blind** *adv* **:** BLINDLY: as **a :** to the point of insensibility <~ drunk> **b :** without seeing outside an airplane <fly ~>

blind alley *n* **:** a fruitless or mistaken course or direction

blind date *n* **1 :** a date between two persons who have not previously met **2 :** either participant in a blind date

blind·er \'blīn-dər\ *n* **1 :** either of two flaps on a horse's bridle to prevent sight of objects at his sides **2** *pl* **:** an obstruction to sight or discernment

blind·fish \'blīn(d)-ˌfish\ *n* **:** any of several small fishes with vestigial functionless eyes found usu. in the waters of caves

¹**blind·fold** \-ˌfōld\ *vt* [ME *blindfellen*, *blindfelden* to strike blind, blindfold, fr. *blind* + *fellen* to fell] **1 :** to cover the eyes of with or as if with a bandage **2 :** to hinder from seeing; *esp* **:** to keep from comprehension — **blindfold** *adj*

²**blindfold** *n* **1 :** a bandage for covering the eyes **2 :** something that obscures mental or physical vision

blind gut *n* **:** a digestive cavity open at only one end; *esp* **:** the cecum of the large intestine

blind·man's buff \ˌblīn(d)-ˌmanz-\ *n* **:** a group game in which a blindfolded player tries to catch and identify another player

blind pig *n* **:** BLIND TIGER

blind side *n* **1 :** the side on which one that is blind in one eye cannot see **2 :** the side away from which one is looking

blind spot *n* **1 a :** the point in the retina where the optic nerve enters that is not sensitive to light — see EYE illustration **b :** a portion of a field that cannot be seen or inspected with available equipment **2 :** an area in which one fails to exercise judgment or discrimination **3 :** a locality in which radio reception is markedly poorer than in the surrounding area

blind tiger *n* **:** a place that sells intoxicants illegally

blind·worm \'blīn-ˌdwərm\ n **:** a small burrowing limbless lizard with minute eyes; *esp* **:** a European lizard (*Anguis fragilis*) popularly believed to be blind — called also *slowworm*

¹**blink** \'bliŋk\ *vb* [ME *blinken* to open one's eyes] *vi* **1 a** *obs* **:** to look glancingly **:** PEEP **b :** to look with half-shut eyes **c :** to close and open the eyes involuntarily (as when struggling against drowsiness or when dazzled) **2 :** to shine dimly or intermittently **3 a :** to look with too little concern **b :** to look with surprise or dismay ~ *vt* **1 a :** to cause to blink **b :** to remove (as tears) from the eye by blinking **2 :** to deny recognition to ***syn*** see WINK

²**blink** *n* **1** *chiefly Scot* **:** GLIMPSE, GLANCE **2 :** GLIMMER, SPARKLE **3 :** a usu. involuntary shutting and opening of the eye **4 a :** a whiteness about the horizon caused by the reflection of light from ice at sea **b :** a dark appearance of the sky about the horizon caused by the absence of reflected light due to open water — **on the blink :** in or into a disabled or useless condition

¹**blink·er** \'bliŋ-kər\ *n* **1 :** one that blinks; *esp* **:** a light that flashes off and on (as for the directing of traffic or the coded signaling of messages) **2 a :** BLINDER 1 **b :** a cloth hood with shades projecting at the sides of the eye openings used on skittish racehorses — usu. used in pl. **3** *pl* **:** BLINDER 2

²**blinker** *vt* **:** to put blinders on

blin·tze \'blin(t)-sə\ *or* **blintz** \'blin(t)s\ *n* [Yiddish *blintse*, fr. Russ *blinets*, dim. of *blin* pancake] **:** a thin rolled pancake with a filling usu. of cheese

¹**blip** \'blip\ *n* [imit.] **1 :** a short crisp sound **2 :** an image on a radar screen **3 :** an interruption of the sound received in a television program as a result of blipping

²**blip** *vt* **blipped; blip·ping :** to remove (recorded sound) from a videotape so that there is an interruption of the sound in the received television program <a censor *blipped* the swearwords>

bliss \'blis\ *n* [ME *blisse*, fr. OE *bliss*; akin to OE *blīthe* blithe] **1 :** complete happiness **2 :** PARADISE, HEAVEN

bliss·ful \'blis-fəl\ *adj* **:** full of, marked by, or causing bliss — **bliss·ful·ly** \-fə-lē\ *adv* — **bliss·ful·ness** *n*

¹**blis·ter** \'blis-tər\ *n* [ME, modif. of OF or MD; OF *blostre* boil, fr. MD *bluyster* blister; akin to OE *blǣst* blast] **1 :** an elevation of the epidermis containing watery liquid **2 :** an enclosed raised spot (as in paint) resembling a blister **3 :** an agent that causes blistering **4 :** a disease of plants marked by large swollen patches on the leaves **5 :** any of various structures (as a gunner's compartment on an airplane) that bulge out — **blis·tery** \-t(ə-)rē\ *adj*

[2]**blister** *vb* **blis·tered; blis·ter·ing** \-t(ə-)riŋ\ *vi* **:** to become affected with a blister ~ *vt* **1 :** to raise a blister on **2 :** to deal with severely <~*ed* his opponent with charges of corruption>
blister beetle *n* **:** a beetle (as the Spanish fly) used medicinally dried and powdered to raise blisters on the skin; *broadly* **:** any of numerous soft-bodied beetles (family Meloidae)
blister copper *n* **:** metallic copper of a black blistered surface that is the product of converting copper matte and is about 98.5 to 99.5 percent pure
blis·ter·ing *adj* **:** extremely intense or severe — **blistering** *adv* — **blis·ter·ing·ly** \-t(ə-)riŋ-lē\ *adv*
blister rust *n* **:** any of several diseases of pines that are caused by rust fungi (genus *Cronartium*) in the aecial stage and that affect the sapwood and inner bark and produce blisters externally
blithe \'blīth, 'blīth\ *adj* **blith·er; blith·est** [ME, fr. OE *blīthe;* akin to OHG *blīdi* joyous, OE *bǣl* fire — more at BALD] **1 :** of a happy lighthearted character or disposition <hail to thee, ~ spirit — P. B. Shelley> **2 :** CASUAL, HEEDLESS <~ unconcern> *syn* see MERRY *ant* morose, atrabilious — **blithe·ly** *adv*
blith·er \'blith-ər\ *vi* **:** BLATHER
blithe·some \'blīth-səm, 'blīth-\ *adj* **:** GAY, MERRY — **blithe·some·ly** *adv*
BLitt *or* **BLit** *abbr* [ML *baccalaureus litterarum*] bachelor of letters; bachelor of literature
blitz \'blits\ *n* **1 a :** BLITZKRIEG 1 **b** (1) **:** an intensive aerial campaign (2) **:** AIR RAID **2 a :** an intensive nonmilitary campaign **b :** a rush of the passer by the defensive linebackers in football — **blitz** *vb*
blitz·krieg \-ˌkrēg\ *n* [G, lit., lightning war, fr. *blitz* lightning + *krieg* war] **1 :** war conducted with great speed and force; *specif* **:** a violent surprise offensive by massed air forces and mechanized ground forces in close coordination **2 :** a sudden overpowering bombardment
bliz·zard \'bliz-ərd\ *n* [origin unknown] **1 :** a long severe snowstorm **2 :** an intensely strong cold wind filled with fine snow **3 :** an overwhelming rush or deluge <the ~ of mail at Christmas> — **bliz·zardy** \-ē\ *adj*
blk *abbr* **1** black **2** block **3** bulk
[1]**bloat** \'blōt\ *adj* [alter. of ME *blout*] **:** BLOATED, PUFFY
[2]**bloat** *vt* **1 :** to make turgid or swollen **2 :** to fill to capacity or overflowing ~ *vi* **:** SWELL
[3]**bloat** *n* **1 :** one that is bloated **2 :** a flatulent digestive disturbance of domestic animals and esp. cattle marked by abdominal bloating
bloat·ed *adj* **1 :** being much larger than what is warranted <a ~ estimate> **2 :** obnoxiously vain
[1]**bloat·er** \'blōt-ər\ *n* [obs. *bloat* (to cure)] **:** a large fat herring or mackerel lightly salted and briefly smoked
[2]**bloater** *n* [[2]*bloat*] **:** a small but common cisco (*Coregonus hoyi*) of the Great Lakes
[1]**blob** \'bläb\ *n* [ME] **1 a :** a small drop or lump of something viscid or thick **b :** a daub or spot of color **2 :** something ill-defined or amorphous
[2]**blob** *vt* **blobbed; blob·bing :** to mark with blobs **:** SPLOTCH
bloc \'bläk\ *n* [F, lit., block] **1 a :** a temporary combination of parties in a legislative assembly **b :** a group of legislators (as in a U.S. legislative assembly) who act together for some common purpose irrespective of party lines **2 a :** a combination of persons, groups, or nations forming a unit with a common interest or purpose **b :** a group of nations united by treaty or agreement for mutual support or joint action
[1]**block** \'bläk\ *n, often attrib* [ME *blok,* fr. MF *bloc,* fr. MD *blok;* akin to OHG *bloh* block, MIr *blog* fragment] **1 :** a compact usu. solid piece of substantial material esp. when worked or altered from its natural state to serve a particular purpose: as **a :** the piece of wood on which a person condemned to be beheaded lays his neck for execution **b :** a mold or form on which articles are shaped or displayed **c :** a hollow rectangular building unit usu. of artificial material **d :** a lightweight usu. cubical and solid wooden or plastic building toy that is usu. provided in sets **e :** the casting that contains the cylinders of an internal-combustion engine **2** *slang* **:** HEAD 1 **3 a :** OBSTACLE **b :** an obstruction of an opponent's play in sports; *esp* **:** a halting or impeding of the progress or movement of an opponent in football by use of the body **c :** interruption of normal physiological function of a tissue or organ; *esp* **:** HEART BLOCK **d :** an instance or the result of psychological blockage or blocking **4 :** a wooden or metal case enclosing one or more pulleys and having a hook, eye, or strap by which it may be attached **5 :** a platform from which property is sold at auction; *broadly* **:** sale at auction **6 a :** a quantity, number, or section of things dealt with as a unit **b** (1) **:** a large building divided into separate functional units (2) **:** a line of row houses (3) **:** a part of a building or integrated group of buildings distinctive in some respect **c** (1) **:** a usu. rectangular space (as in a city) enclosed by streets and occupied by or intended for buildings (2) **:** the distance along one of the sides of such a block **d :** a length of railroad track of defined limits the use of which is governed by block signals **7 :** a piece of material (as wood or linoleum) having on its surface a hand-cut design from which impressions are to be printed

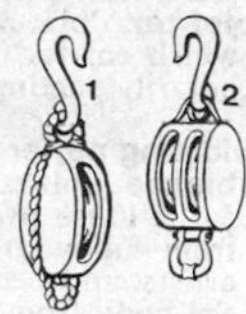

blocks 4: *1* single block, *2* double block

[2]**block** *vt* **1 a :** to make unsuitable for passage or progress by obstruction **b** *archaic* **:** BLOCKADE **c :** to hinder the passage, progress, or accomplishment of by or as if by interposing an obstruction <~ a kick> **d :** to shut off from view <forest canopy ~*ing* the sun> **e :** to interfere usu. legitimately with (as an opponent) in various games or sports **f :** to prevent normal functioning of **g :** to prohibit conversion of (foreign-held funds) into foreign exchange; *also* **:** to limit the use to be made of (such funds) within the country **2 :** to mark or indicate the outline or chief lines of <~ out a design> <~ in a sketched figure> **3 :** to shape on, with, or as if with a block <~ a hat> **4 :** to make (two or more lines of writing or type) flush at the left or at both left and right **5 :** to secure, support, or provide with a block **6 :** to work out or chart the movements of stage performers or of mobile television equipment ~ *vi* **:** to block an opponent in sports *syn* see HINDER — **block·er** *n*
[1]**block·ade** \blä-'kād\ *n* **1 :** the isolation by a warring nation of a particular enemy area (as a harbor) by means of troops or warships to prevent passage of persons or supplies; *broadly* **:** a restrictive measure designed to obstruct the commerce and communications of an unfriendly nation **2 :** something that constitutes an obstacle **3 :** interruption of normal physiological function (as transmission of nerve impulses) of a tissue or organ
[2]**blockade** *vt* **block·ad·ed; block·ad·ing 1 :** to subject to a blockade **2 :** BLOCK, OBSTRUCT — **block·ad·er** *n*
block·ade–run·ner \-'kād-ˌrən-ər\ *n* **:** a ship or person that runs through a blockade — **block·ade–run·ning** \-ˌrən-iŋ\ *n*
block·age \'bläk-ij\ *n* **:** an act or instance of obstructing **:** the state of being blocked <a ~ in the saltshaker>
block and tackle *n* **:** pulley blocks with associated rope or cable for hoisting or hauling
block·bust·er \'bläk-ˌbəs-tər\ *n* **1 :** a huge high-explosive demolition bomb **2 :** one that is notably effective or violent **3 :** one who engages in blockbusting
block·bust·ing \-tiŋ\ *n* **:** profiteering by inducing property owners to sell hastily and often at a loss by appeals to fears of depressed values because of threatened minority encroachment and then reselling at inflated prices
block diagram *n* **:** a diagram (as of a system, process, or program) in which labeled figures (as rectangles) and interconnecting lines represent the relationship of parts
block·head \'bläk-ˌhed\ *n* **:** a stupid person
block·house \-ˌhau̇s\ *n* **1 a :** a structure of heavy timbers formerly used for military defense with sides loopholed and pierced for gunfire and often with a projecting upper story **b :** a small easily defended building for protection from enemy fire **2 :** a building usu. of reinforced concrete serving as an observation point for an operation likely to be accompanied by heat, blast, or radiation hazard
block·ish \-ish\ *adj* **:** resembling a block — **block·ish·ly** *adv*
block letter *n* **:** an often hand-drawn bold simple capital letter composed of strokes of uniform thickness
block plane *n* **:** a small plane made with the blade set at a lower pitch than other planes and used chiefly on end grains of wood
block signal *n* **:** a fixed signal at the entrance of a block to govern railroad trains entering and using that block
block system *n* **:** a system by which a railroad track is divided into short sections and trains are run by guidance signals
blocky \'bläk-ē\ *adj* **block·i·er; -est 1 :** resembling a block in form or massiveness **:** CHUNKY **2 :** filled with or made up of blocks or patches
bloke \'blōk\ *n* [origin unknown] *chiefly Brit* **:** MAN, FELLOW
[1]**blond** *or* **blonde** \'bländ\ *adj* [F *blond,* masc., *blonde,* fem.] **1 a :** of a flaxen, golden, light auburn, or pale yellowish brown color <~ hair> **b :** of a pale white or rosy white color <~ skin> **c :** being a blond <a pretty ~ secretary> **2 a :** of a light color **b :** of the color blond **c :** made light-colored by bleaching <a table of ~ walnut>
[2]**blond** *or* **blonde** *n* **1 :** a person having blond hair and usu. a light complexion and blue or gray eyes **2 :** a light yellowish brown to dark grayish yellow
blond·ish \'blän-dish\ *adj* **:** somewhat blond
[1]**blood** \'bləd\ *n, often attrib* [ME, fr. OE *blōd;* akin to OHG *bluot* blood] **1 a :** the fluid that circulates in the heart, arteries, capillaries, and veins of a vertebrate animal carrying nourishment and oxygen to and bringing away waste products from all parts of the body **b :** a comparable fluid of an invertebrate **c :** a fluid resembling blood **2 a :** LIFEBLOOD; *broadly* **:** LIFE **b :** human stock or lineage; *esp* **:** royal lineage <a prince of the ~> **c :** relationship by descent from a common ancestor **:** KINSHIP **d :** persons related through common descent **:** KINDRED **e** (1) **:** honorable or high birth or descent (2) **:** descent from parents of recognized breed or pedigree **3 :** the shedding of blood; *also* **:** the taking of life **4 a :** blood regarded as the seat of the emotions **:** TEMPER **b** *obs* **:** LUST **c :** a gay showy foppish man **:** RAKE **5 :** PERSONNEL
[2]**blood** *vt* **1 :** BLEED 1a **2 :** to stain or wet with blood **3 :** to expose (a hunting dog) to sight, scent, or taste of the blood of its prey
blood bank *n* **:** a place for storage of or an institution storing blood or plasma; *also* **:** blood so stored
blood·bath \'bləd-ˌbath, -ˌbȧth\ *n* **:** a great slaughter **:** MASSACRE
blood brother *n* **1 :** a brother by birth **2 :** one of two men pledged to mutual loyalty by a ceremonial use of each other's blood — **blood brotherhood** *n*
blood cell *n* **:** a cell normally present in blood

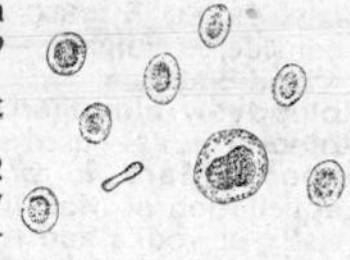
blood cells

blood count *n* **:** the determination of the blood cells in a definite volume of blood; *also* **:** the number of cells so determined
blood·cur·dling \'bləd-ˌkərd-liŋ, -ᵊl-iŋ\ *adj* **:** arousing horror <~ screams> — **blood·cur·dling·ly** \-ˌkərd-liŋ-lē\ *adv*
blood·ed \'bləd-əd\ *adj* **:** being entirely or largely of superior breed <a herd of ~ stock>

ə abut	ᵊ kitten	ər further	a back	ā bake	ä cot, cart
au̇ out	ch chin	e less	ē easy	g gift	i trip ī life
j joke	ŋ sing	ō flow	ȯ flaw	ȯi coin	th thin th this
ü loot	u̇ foot	y yet	yü few	yu̇ furious	zh vision

-blooded *adj comb form* **:** having (such) blood or temperament <cold-*blooded*> <warm-*blooded*>
blood feud *n* **:** a feud between different clans or families
blood·fin \ˈbləd-ˌfin\ *n* **:** a small silvery So. American fish (*Aphyocharax rubripinnis*) with deep-red fins
blood fluke *n* **:** SCHISTOSOME
blood group *n* **:** one of the classes into which human beings can be separated on the basis of the presence or absence in their blood of specific antigens — called also *blood type*
blood·guilt \ˈbləd-ˌgilt\ *n* **:** guilt resulting from bloodshed — **blood·guilt·i·ness** \-ˌgil-tē-nəs\ *n* — **blood·guilty** \-tē\ *adj*
blood heat *n* **:** a temperature approximating that of the human body
blood·hound \ˈbləd-ˌhau̇nd\ *n* **1 :** a large powerful hound of a breed of European origin remarkable for acuteness of smell **2 :** a person keen in pursuit
blood·less \ˈbləd-ləs\ *adj* **1 :** deficient in or free from blood **2 :** not accompanied by loss or shedding of blood <a ~ victory> **3 :** lacking in spirit or vitality <~ young people with no spirit of fun> **4 :** lacking in human feeling <~ statistics> — **blood·less·ly** *adv* — **blood·less·ness** *n*
blood·let·ting \-ˌlet-iŋ\ *n* **1 :** PHLEBOTOMY **2 :** BLOODSHED **3 :** attrition of personnel or resources
blood·line \-ˌlīn\ *n* **:** a sequence of direct ancestors esp. in a pedigree; *also* **:** FAMILY, STRAIN
blood·mo·bile \-mō-ˌbēl\ *n* [*blood* + auto*mobile*] **:** an automobile staffed and equipped for collecting blood from donors
blood money *n* **1 :** money obtained at the cost of another's life **2 :** money paid by a manslayer or members of his family, clan, or tribe to the next of kin of a person killed by him
blood platelet *n* **:** one of the minute protoplasmic disks of vertebrate blood that assist in blood clotting
blood poisoning *n* **:** SEPTICEMIA
blood pressure *n* **:** pressure exerted by the blood upon the walls of the blood vessels and esp. arteries varying with the muscular efficiency of the heart, the blood volume and viscosity, the age and health of the individual, and the state of the vascular wall
blood·red \ˈbləd-ˈred\ *adj* **:** having the color of blood
blood·root \-ˌrüt, -ˌru̇t\ *n* **:** a plant (*Sanguinaria canadensis*) of the poppy family having a red root and sap and bearing a solitary lobed leaf and white flower in early spring
blood sausage *n* **:** very dark sausage containing a large proportion of blood — called also *blood pudding*
blood serum *n* **:** blood plasma from which the fibrin has been removed
blood·shed \ˈbləd-ˌshed\ *n* **1 :** the shedding of blood **2 :** the taking of life **:** SLAUGHTER
blood·shot \-ˌshät\ *adj, of an eye* **:** inflamed to redness
blood·stain \-ˌstān\ *n* **:** a discoloration caused by blood
blood·stained \-ˌstānd\ *adj* **1 :** stained with blood **2 :** involved with slaughter <a ~ chronicle of war>
blood·stock \-ˌstäk\ *n* **:** horses of Thoroughbred breeding esp. when used for racing
blood·stone \-ˌstōn\ *n* **:** a green chalcedony sprinkled with red spots resembling blood
blood·stream \-ˌstrēm\ *n* **1 :** the flowing blood in a circulatory system **2 :** a mainstream of power or vitality <introduce into the economic ~ a large amount of money — *Harper's*>
blood·suck·er \-ˌsək-ər\ *n* **1 :** an animal that sucks blood; *esp* **:** LEECH **2 :** a person who sponges or preys on another — **blood·suck·ing** \-iŋ\ *adj*
blood sugar *n* **:** the glucose in the blood; *also* **:** its concentration (as in milligrams per 100 milliliters)
blood test *n* **:** a test of the blood; *esp* **:** a serologic test for syphilis
blood·thirsty \ˈbləd-ˌthər-stē\ *adj* **:** eager for or marked by the shedding of blood — **blood·thirst·i·ly** \-stə-lē\ *adj* — **blood·thirst·i·ness** \-stē-nəs\ *n*
blood-type \-ˌtīp\ *vt* **:** to determine the blood group of
blood vessel *n* **:** a vessel in which blood circulates in an animal
blood·worm \ˈbləd-ˌwərm\ *n* **1 :** any of various reddish annelid worms often used as bait **2 :** the red aquatic larva of some midges
blood·wort \-ˌwərt, -ˌwȯ(ə)rt\ *n* **:** any of a family (Haemodoraceae, the bloodwort family) of perennial herbs with a deep red coloring matter in the roots
[1]**bloody** \ˈbləd-ē\ *adj*, **-blood·i·er; -est 1 a :** containing or made up of blood **b :** of or contained in the blood **2 :** smeared or stained with blood **3 :** accompanied by or involving bloodshed; *esp* **:** marked by great slaughter **4 a :** MURDEROUS **b :** MERCILESS, CRUEL **5 :** BLOODRED **6** — used as an intensive; sometimes considered vulgar — **blood·i·ly** \ˈbləd-ᵊl-ē\ *adv* — **blood·i·ness** \ˈbləd-ē-nəs\ *n*
[2]**bloody** *vt* **blood·ied; bloody·ing :** to make bloody or bloodred
[3]**bloody** *adv* — used as an intensive; sometimes considered vulgar
Bloody Mary *n, pl* **Bloody Marys** [prob. fr. *Bloody Mary*, appellation of Mary I of England] **:** a cocktail consisting essentially of vodka and tomato juice
bloody-mind·ed·ness \ˌbləd-ē-ˈmīn-dəd-nəs\ *n* **1 :** willingness to accept violence or bloodshed **2 :** CONTRARIETY, CANTANKEROUSNESS — **bloody-minded** *adj*
bloody shirt *n* **:** a means employed to stir up or revive party or sectional animosity
[1]**bloom** \ˈblüm\ *n* [ME *blome* lump of metal, fr. OE *blōma*] **1 :** a mass of wrought iron from the forge or puddling furnace **2 :** a bar of iron or steel hammered or rolled from an ingot
[2]**bloom** *n* [ME *blome*, fr. ON *blōm*; akin to OE *blōwan* to blossom — more at BLOW] **1 a :** FLOWER <green leaves with large yellow ~*s*> <the apple trees had a very light ~ this spring> **b :** the flowering state <the roses in ~> **c :** a period of flowering <the spring ~> **d :** an excessive growth of plankton **2 :** a state or time of beauty, freshness, and vigor **3 :** a surface coating or appearance: as **a :** a delicate powdery coating on some fruits and leaves **b :** a rosy appearance of the cheeks; *broadly* **:** an outward evidence of freshness or healthy vigor **c :** the grainy or powdery surface of a newly minted coin **d :** a cloudiness on a film of varnish or lacquer **e :** glare caused by an object reflecting too much light into a television camera **4 :** BOUQUET 3a
[3]**bloom** *vi* **1 a :** to produce or yield flowers **b :** to support abundant plant life <make the desert ~> **2 a :** to flourish in youthful beauty, freshness or excellence **b :** to shine out **:** GLOW **3 :** to appear or occur unexpectedly or in surprising quantity or degree **4 :** to become densely populated with microorganisms and esp. plankton — used of bodies of water ~ *vt* **1** *obs* **:** to cause to bloom **2 :** to give bloom to
[1]**bloom·er** \ˈblü-mər\ *n* **1 :** a plant that blooms **2 :** a person who reaches full competence or maturity **3 :** a stupid blunder
[2]**bloo·mer** \ˈblü-mər\ *n* [Amelia *Bloomer* †1894 Am pioneer in feminism] **1 :** a costume for women consisting of a short skirt and long loose trousers gathered closely about the ankles **2** *pl* **a :** full loose trousers gathered at the knee formerly worn by women for athletics **b :** underpants of similar design worn chiefly by girls

bloomer 1

bloom·ing \ˈblü-mən, -miŋ\ *adj* [prob. euphemism for *bloody*] *chiefly Brit* — used as a generalized intensive <~ fool>
bloomy \ˈblü-mē\ *adj* **1 :** full of bloom **2 :** covered with bloom <~ red plums — Elizabeth Bowen> **3 :** showing freshness or vitality <all the ~ flush of life is fled — Oliver Goldsmith>
[1]**bloop** \ˈblüp\ *vt* [prob. fr. *bloop* (an unpleasing sound)] **:** to hit (a fly ball) usu. just beyond the infield in baseball <~*ed* a single to center field>
[2]**bloop** *adj, of a baseball* **:** hit in the air just beyond the infield
bloop·er \ˈblü-pər\ *n* [*bloop* (an unpleasing sound)] **1 :** an embarrassing public blunder **2 a :** a high baseball pitch lobbed to the batter **b :** a fly ball hit barely beyond a baseball infield
[1]**blos·som** \ˈbläs-əm\ *n* [ME *blosme*, fr. OE *blōstm*; akin to OE *blōwan*] **1 a :** the flower of a seed plant <apple ~*s*> **b :** the mass of bloom on a single plant; *also* **:** the state of bearing flowers **2 :** a peak period or stage of development — **blos·somy** \-ə-mē\ *adj*
[2]**blossom** *vi* **1 :** BLOOM **2 a :** to come into one's own **:** DEVELOP <a ~*ing* talent> **b :** to become evident **:** make an appearance
[1]**blot** \ˈblät\ *n* [ME] **1 :** a soiling or disfiguring mark **:** SPOT **2 :** a mark of reproach **:** moral flaw
[2]**blot** *vb* **blot·ted; blot·ting** *vt* **1 :** to spot, stain, or spatter with a discoloring substance **2 :** to make obscure **:** ECLIPSE — usu. used with *out* **3** *obs* **:** MAR; *esp* **:** to stain with infamy **4 a :** to dry with an absorbing agent (as blotting paper) **b :** to remove by blotting the surface ~ *vi* **1 :** to make a blot **2 :** to become marked with a blot — **blot one's copybook :** to do something that detracts from one's record or standing
[3]**blot** *n* [origin unknown] **1 :** a backgammon man exposed to capture **2** *archaic* **:** a weak or exposed point
[1]**blotch** \ˈbläch\ *n* [prob. alter. of *botch*] **1 :** IMPERFECTION, BLEMISH **2 :** a spot or mark (as of color or ink) esp. when large or irregular — **blotch·i·ly** \ˈbläch-ə-lē\ — **blotchy** \ˈbläch-ē\ *adj*
[2]**blotch** *vt* **:** to mark or mar with blotches
blot out *vt* **1 :** to make insignificant or inconsequential <this one good act *blots out* many bad ones> **2 :** to wipe out **:** DESTROY <one such bomb can *blot out* a city> **syn** see ERASE
blot·ter \ˈblät-ər\ *n* **1 :** a piece of blotting paper **2 :** a book in which entries (as of transactions or occurrences) are made temporarily pending their transfer to permanent record books <police ~>
blotting paper *n* **:** a soft spongy unsized paper used to absorb ink
[1]**blouse** \ˈblau̇s *also* ˈblau̇z; *many say* ˈblau̇s *but* ˈblau̇-zəz\ *n* [F] **1 :** a loose overgarment that resembles a shirt or smock, varies from hip-length to calf-length, and is worn esp. by workmen, artists, and peasants **2 :** a usu. loose-fitting garment that covers the body from the neck to the waist and is worn esp. by women
[2]**blouse** *vb* **bloused; blous·ing** *vi* **:** to fall in a fold <coats that ~ above the hip> ~ *vt* **:** to cause to blouse <trousers are *bloused* over the boots>
blou·son \ˈblau̇-ˌsän, ˈblü-ˌzän\ *n* [F, fr. *blouse*] **:** a woman's garment (as a dress or blouse) having a close waistband with blousing of material over it
[1]**blow** \ˈblō\ *vb* **blew** \ˈblü\; **blown** \ˈblōn\; **blow·ing** [ME *blowen*, fr. OE *blāwan*; akin to OHG *blāen* to blow, L *flare*, Gk *phallos* penis] *vi* **1** *of air* **:** to move with speed or force **2 :** to send forth a current of air or other gas **3 a :** to make a sound by or as if by blowing **b** *of a wind instrument* **:** SOUND **4 a :** BOAST **b :** to talk windily **5 a :** PANT, GASP <the horse *blew* heavily> **b** *of a cetacean* **:** to eject moisture-laden air from the lungs through the blowhole **6 :** to move or be carried by or as if by wind **7** *of an electric fuse* **:** to melt when overloaded — usu. used with *out* **8** *of a tire* **:** to release the contained air through a spontaneous rupture — usu. used with *out* ~ *vt* **1 a :** to set (gas or vapor) in motion **b :** to act on with a current of gas or vapor **2 :** to play or sound on (a wind instrument) **3 a :** to spread by report **b :** DAMN, DISREGARD <~ the expense> **4 a :** to drive with a current of gas or vapor **b :** to clear of contents by forcible passage of a current of air **5 a :** to distend with or as if with gas **b :** to produce or shape by the action of blown or injected air <~*ing* bubbles> <~*ing* glass> **6** *of insects* **:** to deposit eggs or larvae on or in **7 :** to shatter, burst, or destroy by explosion **8 a :** to put out of breath with exertion **b :** to let (as a horse) pause to catch the breath **9 a :** to spend (money) recklessly **b :** to treat with unusual expenditure <I'll ~ you to a steak> **10 :** to cause (a fuse) to blow **11 :** to rupture by too much pressure <*blew* a gasket> **12 :** to lose by failing to use an advantage **:** MUFF <*blew* his chance> **13 :** to leave hurriedly <*blew* town> **14 :** to propel with great force or speed <*blew* a fast ball by the batter> — **blow hot and cold :** to be favorable at one moment and adverse the next

— **blow into** : to appear or arrive at casually or unexpectedly <*blew* into town today> — **blow one's cool** : to lose one's composure — **blow one's top** *or* **blow one's stack** **1** : to become violently angry **2** : to go crazy — **blow the mind of** : to overwhelm with wonder or bafflement — **blow the whistle on** **1** : to bring (something covert) into the open **2** : to inform against

2**blow** *n* **1** : a blowing of wind esp. when strong or violent **2** : BRAG, BOASTING **3** : an act or instance of blowing **4 a** : the time during which air is forced through molten metal to refine it **b** : the quantity of metal refined during that time

3**blow** *vi* **blew** \'blü\; **blown** \'blōn\; **blow·ing** [ME *blowen,* fr. OE *blōwan;* akin to OHG *bluoen* to bloom, L *florēre* to bloom, *flor-, flos* flower] : FLOWER, BLOOM

4**blow** *n* **1** : 2BLOOM 1b <lilacs in full ~> **2** : BLOSSOMS <peach ~>

5**blow** *n* [ME (northern dial.) *blaw*] **1** : a forcible stroke delivered with a part of the body or with an instrument **2** : a hostile act or state : COMBAT <come to ~*s*> **3** : a forcible or sudden act or effort : ASSAULT **4** : an unfortunate or calamitous happening <failure to land the job came as a ~>

blow–by–blow \-bī-,-bə-\ *adj* : minutely detailed <a ~ account>

blow·er \'blō(-ə)r\ *n* **1** : one that blows **2** : BRAGGART **3** : a device for producing a current of air or gas <snow ~>

blow·fish \'blō-,fish\ *n* : PUFFER 2

blow·fly \-,flī\ *n* : any of various two-winged flies (family Calliphoridae) that deposit their eggs or maggots esp. on meat or in wounds; *esp* : a widely distributed bluebottle (*Calliphora vicina*)

blow·gun \-,gən\ *n* : a tube through which a projectile (as a dart) may be impelled by the force of the breath

blow·hard \-,härd\ *n* : BRAGGART

blow·hole \-,hōl\ *n* **1** : a hole in metal caused by a bubble of gas captured during solidification **2** : a nostril in the top of the head of a whale or other cetacean **3** : a hole in the ice to which aquatic mammals (as seals) come to breathe

blow in *vi* : to arrive casually or unexpectedly

blown \'blōn\ *adj* [ME *blowen,* fr. pp. of *blowen* to blow] **1** : SWOLLEN; *esp* : afflicted with bloat **2** : FLYBLOWN **3** : being out of breath

blow off *vt* : to relieve by vigorous speech or action — **blow off steam** : to release pent-up emotions

blow·out \'blō-,au̇t\ *n* **1** : a festive social affair **2 a** : a bursting of a container (as a tire) by pressure of the contents on a weak spot **b** : a hole made in a container by such bursting **3** : an uncontrolled eruption of an oil or gas well

blow out \(')blō-'au̇t\ *vi* **1** : to become extinguished by a gust **2** : to erupt out of control — used of an oil or gas well ~ *vt* **1** : to extinguish by a gust **2** : to dissipate (itself) by blowing — used of storms

blow over *vi* : to pass away without effect

blow·pipe \'blō-,pīp\ *n* **1** : a small tubular instrument for directing a jet of air or other gas into a flame so as to concentrate and increase the heat **2** : a tubular instrument used for revealing or cleaning a bodily cavity by forcing air into it **3** : BLOWGUN **4** : a long metal tube on the end of which a glassmaker gathers a quantity of molten glass and through which he blows to expand and shape it

blow·sy *also* **blow·zy** \'blau̇-zē\ *adj* [E dial. *blowse, blowze* (wench)] **1** : being coarse and ruddy of complexion **2** : having a sloppy appearance or aspect : FROWZY

blow·torch \'blō-,tȯrch\ *n* : a small burner having a device to intensify combustion by means of a blast of air or oxygen, usu. including a fuel tank pressurized by a hand pump, and used esp. in plumbing

blow·tube \-,t(y)üb\ *n* **1** : BLOWGUN **2** : BLOWPIPE 4

blow·up \'blō-,əp\ *n* : a blowing up: as **a** : EXPLOSION **b** : an outburst of temper **c** : a photographic enlargement

blow up \(')blō-'əp\ *vt* **1** : to rend apart, shatter, or destroy by explosion **2** : to build up or tout to an unreasonable extent <advertisers *blowing up* their products> **3** : to bring into existence by blowing of wind <it may *blow up* a storm> **4** : to fill up with a gas and esp. air <*blow up* a balloon> **5** : to make a photographic enlargement of ~ *vi* **1 a** : EXPLODE **b** : to be disrupted or destroyed (as by explosion) **c** : to lose self-control; *esp* : to become violently angry **2 a** : to become filled with a gas and esp. air **b** : to become expanded to unreasonable proportions **3** : to become or come into being by or as if by blowing of wind

blowy \'blō-ē\ *adj* **1** : WINDY <a ~ March day> **2** : readily blown about <~ desert sand>

BLS *abbr* **1** bachelor of liberal studies **2** bachelor of library science **3** Bureau of Labor Statistics

BLT *n* : a bacon, lettuce, and tomato sandwich

1**blub·ber** \'bləb-ər\ *n* [ME *bluber* bubble, foam, prob. of imit. origin] **1 a** : the fat of whales and other large marine mammals **b** : excessive fat on the body **2** : the action of blubbering

2**blubber** *vb* **blub·bered; blub·ber·ing** \'bləb-(ə-)riŋ\ [ME *blubren* to make a bubbling sound, fr. *bluber*] *vi* : to weep noisily ~ *vt* **1** : to swell, distort, or wet with weeping **2** : to utter while weeping

3**blubber** *adj* : puffed out : THICK <~ lips>

1**blub·bery** \'bləb-(ə-)rē\ *adj* : 3BLUBBER

2**blubbery** *adj* : having or characterized by blubber

blu·cher \'blü-chər *also* -kər\ *n* [G. L. von *Blücher*] : a shoe having the tongue and vamp cut in one piece and the quarters lapped over the vamp and laced together for closing

1**blud·geon** \'bləj-ən\ *n* [origin unknown] **1** : a short stick that usu. has one thick or loaded end and is used as a weapon **2** : something used to attack or bully <the ~ of satire>

2**bludgeon** *vt* **1** : to hit with heavy impact **2** : to overcome by aggressive argument

1**blue** \'blü\ *adj* **blu·er; blu·est** [ME, fr. OF *blou,* of Gmc origin; akin to OHG *blāo* blue; akin to L *flavus* yellow, OE *bǣl* fire — more at BALD] **1** : of the color blue **2 a** : BLUISH **b** : LIVID <~ with cold> **c** : bluish gray <~ cat> **3 a** : low in spirits : MELANCHOLY **b** : marked by low spirits : DEPRESSING <a ~ funk> <things looked ~> **4** : wearing blue **5** *of a woman* : LEARNED, INTELLECTUAL **6** : PURITANICAL **7 a** : PROFANE, INDECENT <~ language> **b** : OFF-COLOR, RISQUÉ <~ jokes> **8** : of or relating to blues singing <a ~ song> — **blue in the face** : extremely exasperated — **blue·ly** *adv* — **blue·ness** *n*

2**blue** *n* **1** : a color whose hue is that of the clear sky or that of the portion of the color spectrum lying between green and violet **2 a** : a pigment or dye that colors blue **b** : BLUING **3 a** : blue clothing or cloth **b** *pl* : a blue costume or uniform **4** : one who wears a blue uniform: as **a** : a soldier in the Union army during the American Civil War **b** : the Union army **5 a** (1) : SKY (2) : the far distance **b** : SEA **6** : a blue object **7** : BLUESTOCKING **8** : any of numerous small chiefly blue butterflies (family Lycaenidae) **9** : BLUEFISH — **out of the blue** : without advance notice : UNEXPECTEDLY <a job offer that came *out of the blue*>

3**blue** *vb* **blued; blue·ing** *or* **blu·ing** *vt* : to make blue ~ *vi* : to turn blue

blue baby *n* : an infant with a bluish tint usu. from a congenital defect of the heart in which mingling of venous and arterial blood occurs

blue·beard \'blü-,bi(ə)rd\ *n* [*Bluebeard,* a fairy-tale character] : a man who marries and kills one wife after another

blue·bell \-,bel\ *n* **1** : any of various bellflowers; *esp* : HAREBELL 1 **2** : any of various plants bearing blue bell-shaped flowers: as **a** : the European wood hyacinth or grape hyacinth **b** : a low tufted New Zealand plant (*Wahlenbergia gracilis,* family Campanulaceae) **3** : a blue-flowered columbine

blue·ber·ry \'blü-,ber-ē, -b(ə-)rē\ *n* : the edible blue or blackish berry of any of several plants (genus *Vaccinium*) of the heath family; *also* : a low or tall shrub producing these berries

blue·bird \-,bərd\ *n* : any of several small No. American songbirds (genus *Sialia*) related to the robin but more or less blue above

blue–black \-'blak\ *adj* : being of a dark bluish hue

blue blood *n* **1** \'blü-'bləd\ : membership in a noble or socially prominent family **2** \-,bləd\ : a member of a noble or socially prominent family — **blue–blood·ed** \-'bləd-əd\ *adj*

blue·bon·net \'blü-,bän-ət\ *n* **1 a** : a wide flat round cap of blue wool formerly worn in Scotland **b** : one that wears such a cap; *specif* : SCOT **2** : a low-growing annual lupine of Texas with silky foliage and blue flowers usu. classified as a single variable species (*Lupinus subcarnosus*)

blue book *n* **1** : a book of specialized information often published under government auspices **2** : a register esp. of socially prominent persons **3** : a blue-covered booklet used for writing examinations

blue·bot·tle \'blü-,bät-ᵊl\ *n* **1 a** : BACHELOR'S BUTTON **b** : GRAPE HYACINTH **2** : any of several blowflies that have the abdomen or the whole body iridescent blue in color and that make a loud buzzing noise in flight

blue cat *n* : a large bluish catfish (*Ictalurus furcatus*) of the Mississippi valley that may exceed 100 pounds in weight

blue cheese *n* : cheese ripened by and marked with veins of greenish blue mold

blue chip *n* **1 a** : a stock issue of high investment quality that usu. pertains to a substantial well-established company and enjoys public confidence in its worth and stability **b** : a consistently successful and profitable venture or enterprise **2** : an outstandingly worthwhile or valuable property or asset — **blue–chip** *adj*

blue·coat \'blü-,kōt\ *n* : one that wears a blue coat: as **a** : a Union soldier during the Civil War **b** : POLICEMAN

blue cohosh *n* : a perennial herb (*Caulophyllum thalictroides*) of the barberry family that has greenish yellow or purplish flowers and large blue fruits like berries

blue–col·lar \'blü-'käl-ər\ *adj* : of, relating to, or constituting the class of wage earners whose duties call for the wearing of work clothes or protective clothing — compare WHITE-COLLAR

blue crab *n* : any of several largely blue swimming crabs; *esp* : an edible crab (*Callinectes sapidus*) of the Atlantic and Gulf coasts

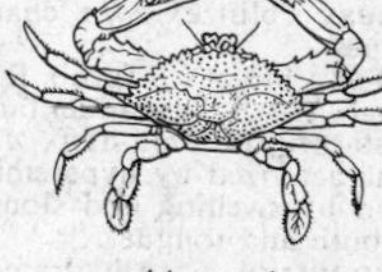

blue crab

blue curls *n pl but sing or pl in constr* : a mint (genus *Trichostema*) with irregular blue flowers

blue devils *n pl* : low spirits : DESPONDENCY

blue–eyed grass \,blü-,īd-\ *n* : a plant (genus *Sisyrinchium*) of the iris family with grasslike foliage and delicate blue flowers

blue·fin \'blü-,fin\ *n* : a very large tuna (*Thunnus thynnus*)

blue·fish \-,fish\ *n* **1** : an active voracious fish (*Pomatomus saltatrix*) related to the pompanos that is bluish above and silvery below **2** : any of various dark or bluish fishes (as the pollack)

blue flag *n* : a blue-flowered iris; *esp* : a common iris (*Iris versicolor*) of the eastern U.S. with a root formerly used medicinally

blue·gill \'blü-,gil\ *n* : a common sunfish (*Lepomis machrochirus*) of the eastern and central U.S. sought for food and sport

blue·grass \-,gras\ *n* **1** : any of several grasses (genus *Poa*) of which some have bluish green culms; *esp* : KENTUCKY BLUEGRASS **2** [fr. the *Blue Grass Boys,* performing group, fr. *Bluegrass state,* nickname of Kentucky] : country music played at a rapid tempo on unamplified stringed instruments (as banjos, guitars, and fiddles) and usu. characterized by free improvisation

blue–green alga \,blü-,grēn-\ *n* : any of a class (Myxophyceae) of algae having the chlorophyll masked by bluish green pigments

blue gum *n* : any of several Australian timber trees (genus *Eucalyptus*)
blue heron *n* : any of various herons with bluish or slaty plumage; *esp* : GREAT BLUE HERON
blue·jack \ˈblü-ˌjak\ *n* [*blue* + *jack* (as in *blackjack*)] : an oak (*Quercus cinerea*) of the southern U.S. with entire leaves and small acorns
blue·jack·et \-ˌjak-ət\ *n* : an enlisted man in the navy : SAILOR
blue jay \-ˌjā\ *n* : JAY 1b
blue jeans *n pl* : pants usu. made of blue denim
blue law *n* **1** : one of numerous extremely rigorous laws designed to regulate morals and conduct in colonial New England **2** : a statute regulating work, commerce, and amusements on Sundays
blue line *n* : either of two blue lines that divide an ice-hockey rink into three equal zones and that separate the offensive and defensive zones from the center-ice neutral zone
blue mold *n* **1** : a fungus (genus *Penicillium*) that produces blue or blue-green surface growths **2** : a disease of tobacco seedlings caused by a fungus (*Peronospora tabacina*) and characterized by yellowish spots and bluish gray mildew on the underside of the leaves
blue moon *n* : a very long period of time <once in a *blue moon*>
blue·nose \ˈblü-ˌnōz\ *n* : one who advocates a rigorous moral code
blue note *n* [fr. its frequent use in blues music] : a flatted third or seventh note in a chord where a major interval would be expected
blue–pen·cil \ˈblü-ˈpen(t)-səl\ *vt* : to edit by corrective change or deletion — **blue pen·cil·ler** *n*
blue pe·ter \-ˈpēt-ər\ *n* : a blue signal flag with a white square in the center used to indicate that a merchant vessel is ready to sail
blue pike *n* : PIKE PERCH; *esp* : WALLEYE
blue plate *adj* : being a main course (as of a meat with vegetables) offered typically at a special price in a restaurant <*blue plate* luncheon>
blue·point \ˈblü-ˌpȯint\ *n* [*Blue Point*, Long Island] : a small oyster typically from the south shore of Long Island
blue point \-ˌpȯint\ *n* : a Siamese cat having a bluish cream body and dark gray points
blue·print \-ˌprint\ *n* **1** : a photographic print in white on a bright blue ground used esp. for copying maps, mechanical drawings, and architects' plans **2** : a program of action <a ~ for victory> — **blueprint** *vt*
blue racer *n* : a blacksnake of a bluish green subspecies (*Coluber constrictor flaviventris*) occurring from Ohio to Texas
blue–ribbon *adj* : selected for quality, reputation, or authority <a ~ committee>
blue ribbon *n* **1** : a blue ribbon awarded the first-place winner in a competition **2** : an honor or award gained for preeminence
blue–ribbon jury *n* : SPECIAL JURY
blues \ˈblüz\ *n pl but sing or pl in constr* **1** : low spirits : MELANCHOLY **2** : a song of lamentation characterized by usu. 12-bar phrases, 3-line stanzas in which the words of the second stanza repeat those of the first, and continual occurrence of blue notes in melody and harmony
blue–sky \ˈblü-ˈskī\ *adj* **1** : having little or no value <~ stock> **2** : having no practical application <~ thinking>
blue–sky law *n* : a law providing for the regulation of the sale of securities (as stock)
blues·man \ˈblüz-mən\ *n* : one who plays or sings the blues
blue·stem \ˈblü-ˌstem\ *n* **1** : an important hay and forage grass (*Andropogon furcatus*) of the western U.S. with smooth bluish leaf sheaths and slender spikes borne in pairs or clusters **2** : LITTLE BLUESTEM
blue·stock·ing \-ˌstäk-iŋ\ *n* [*Bluestocking* society, 18th cent. literary clubs] : a woman having intellectual or literary interests
blue·stone \-ˌstōn\ *n* : a building or paving stone of bluish gray color; *specif* : a sandstone quarried near the Hudson river
blue streak *n* **1** : something that moves very fast **2** : a constant stream of words <talked a *blue streak*>
bluesy \ˈblü-zē\ *adj* : characterized by the musical patterns of the blues
blu·et \ˈblü-ət\ *n* [prob. fr. 1*blue*] : an American plant (*Houstonia caerulea*) of the madder family with bluish flowers and tufted stems
blue·tongue \ˈblü-ˌtəŋ\ *n* : a serious virus disease esp. of sheep characterized by hyperemia, cyanosis, and punctate hemorrhages and by swelling and sloughing of the epithelium esp. about the mouth and tongue
blue vitriol *n* : a hydrated copper sulfate $CuSO_4{\cdot}5H_2O$
blue·weed \ˈblü-ˌwēd\ *n* **1** : a coarse prickly blue-flowered European weed (*Echium vulgare*) of the borage family naturalized in the U.S. **2** : a small perennial (*Helianthus ciliaris*) of the southwestern U.S. with blue-green or gray-green foliage
bluey \ˈblü-ē\ *n* [fr. the blue blanket commonly used to wrap the bundle] *Austral* : a swagman's bundle of personal effects; *broadly* : a bag of clothing carried in travel
1bluff \ˈbləf\ *adj* [obs. D *blaf* flat; akin to MLG *blaff* smooth] **1 a** : having a broad flattened front **b** : rising steeply with a broad flat or rounded front **2** : good-naturedly frank and outspoken — **bluff·ly** *adv* — **bluff·ness** *n*
syn BLUFF, BLUNT, BRUSQUE, CURT, CRUSTY, GRUFF *shared meaning element* : abrupt and unceremonious in manner or speech ***ant*** smooth, suave
2bluff *n* : a high steep bank : CLIFF
3bluff *vb* [prob. fr. D *bluffen* to boast, play a kind of card game] *vt* **1** : to deceive (an opponent) in cards by a bold bet on an inferior hand with the result that the opponent withdraws a winning hand **2 a** : to deter or frighten by pretense or a mere show of strength **b** : DECEIVE **c** : FEIGN ~ *vi* : to bluff someone — **bluff·er** *n*
4bluff *n* **1 a** : an act or instance of bluffing **b** : the practice of bluffing **2** : one who bluffs
blu·ing *or* **blue·ing** \ˈblü-iŋ\ *n* : a preparation used in laundering to counteract yellowing of white fabrics
blu·ish \ˈblü-ish\ *adj* : somewhat blue : having a tinge of blue — **blu·ish·ness** *n*
1blun·der \ˈblən-dər\ *vb* **blun·dered; blun·der·ing** \-d(ə-)riŋ\ [ME *blundren*] *vi* **1** : to move unsteadily or confusedly **2** : to make a mistake through stupidity, ignorance, or carelessness ~ *vt* **1** : to utter stupidly, confusedly, or thoughtlessly **2** : to make a stupid, careless, or thoughtless mistake in — **blun·der·er** \-dər-ər\ *n* — **blun·der·ing·ly** \-d(ə-)riŋ-lē\ *adv*
2blunder *n* : a gross error or mistake resulting usu. from stupidity, ignorance, or carelessness ***syn*** see ERROR
blun·der·buss \ˈblən-dər-ˌbəs\ *n* [by folk etymology fr. obs. D *donderbus*, fr. D *donder* thunder + obs. D *bus* gun] **1** : an obsolete short firearm having a large bore and usu. a flaring muzzle **2** : a blundering person

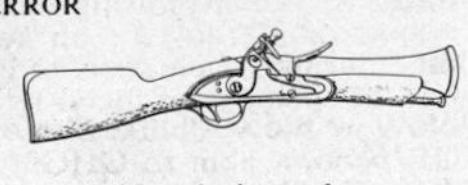
blunderbuss 1

1blunt \ˈblənt\ *adj* [ME] **1 a** : slow or deficient in feeling : INSENSITIVE **b** : obtuse in understanding or discernment : DULL **2** : having an edge or point that is not sharp **3 a** : abrupt in speech or manner : aggressively outspoken **b** : being straight to the point : DIRECT ***syn*** **1** see DULL ***ant*** keen, sharp **2** see BLUFF ***ant*** tactful, subtle — **blunt·ly** *adv* — **blunt·ness** *n*
2blunt *vt* : to make less sharp or definite ~ *vi* : to become blunt
1blur \ˈblər\ *n* [perh. akin to ME *bleren* to blear] **1** : a smear or stain that obscures **2** : something that is vague or lacking definite outline or distinct character
2blur *vb* **blurred; blur·ring** *vt* **1** : to obscure or blemish by smearing **2** : SULLY **3** : to make dim, indistinct, or vague in outline or character **4** : to make cloudy or confused ~ *vi* **1** : to make blurs **2** : to become vague, indistinct, or indefinite — **blur·ring·ly** \ˈblər-iŋ-lē\ *adv*
blurb \ˈblərb\ *n* [coined by Gelett Burgess] : a short publicity notice (as on a book jacket)
blur·ry \ˈblər-ē\ *adj* **blur·ri·er; -est** : marked by blurring — **blur·ri·ly** \ˈblər-ə-lē\ *adv* — **blur·ri·ness** \ˈblər-ē-nəs\ *n*
blurt \ˈblərt\ *vt* [prob. imit.] : to utter abruptly and impulsively — usu. used with *out* — **blurt·er** *n*
1blush \ˈbləsh\ *vi* [ME *blusshen*, fr. OE *blyscan* to redden, fr. *blȳsa* flame; akin to OHG *bluhhen* to burn brightly] **1** : to become red in the face esp. from shame, modesty, or confusion **2** : to feel shame or embarrassment **3** : to have a rosy or fresh color : BLOOM — **blush·er** *n* — **blush·ing·ly** \-iŋ-lē\ *adv*
2blush *n* [ME, prob. fr. *blusshen*] **1** : APPEARANCE, VIEW <at first ~> **2** : a reddening of the face esp. from shame, modesty, or confusion **3** : a red or rosy tint — **blush·ful** \-fəl\ *adj*
1blus·ter \ˈbləs-tər\ *vb* **blus·tered; blus·ter·ing** \-t(ə-)riŋ\ [ME *blustren*, prob. fr. MLG *blüsteren*] *vi* **1 a** : to blow in stormy noisy gusts **b** : to be windy and boisterous **2** : to talk or act with noisy swaggering threats ~ *vt* **1** : to utter with noisy self-assertiveness **2** : to drive or force by blustering — **blus·ter·er** \-tər-ər\ *n* — **blus·ter·ing·ly** \-t(ə-)riŋ-lē\ *adv*
2bluster *n* **1** : a violent boisterous blowing **2** : violent commotion **3** : loudly boastful or threatening speech — **blus·ter·ous** \-t(ə-)rəs\ *adj* — **blus·tery** \-t(ə-)rē\ *adj*
blvd *abbr* boulevard
bm *abbr* beam
BM *abbr* **1** bachelor of medicine **2** bachelor of music **3** basal metabolism **4** bill of material **5** board measure **6** bowel movement **7** bronze medal
BME *abbr* **1** bachelor of mechanical engineering **2** bachelor of mining engineering **3** bachelor of music education
BMOC *abbr* big man on campus
BMR *abbr* basal metabolic rate
BMS *abbr* bachelor of marine science
BMT *abbr* **1** bachelor of medical technology **2** basic military training
bn *abbr* **1** baron **2** battalion **3** beacon **4** been
BN *abbr* **1** bachelor of nursing **2** bank note **3** Bureau of Narcotics
BNDD *abbr* Bureau of Narcotics and Dangerous Drugs
BNS *abbr* bachelor of naval sciences
BO *abbr* **1** bad order **2** body odor **3** box office **4** branch office **5** buyer's option
boa \ˈbō-ə\ *n* [L, a water snake] **1** : a large snake (as the boa constrictor, anaconda, or python) that crushes its prey **2** : a long fluffy scarf of fur, feathers, or delicate fabric
boa constrictor *n* : a tropical American boa (*Constrictor constrictor*) that is light brown barred or mottled with darker brown and reaches a length of 10 feet or more; *broadly* : BOA 1
boar \ˈbō(ə)r, ˈbȯ(ə)r\ *n* [ME *bor*, fr. OE *bār*; akin to OHG & OS *bēr* boar] **1 a** : an uncastrated male swine **b** : the male of any of several mammals (as a guinea pig or raccoon) **2** : the Old World wild hog (*Sus scrofa*) from which most domestic swine derive — **boar·ish** \-ish\ *adj*
1board \ˈbō(ə)rd, ˈbȯ(ə)rd\ *n* [ME *bord* piece of sawed lumber, border, ship's side, fr. OE; akin to OHG *bort* ship's side, Skt *bardhaka* carpenter] **1** *obs* : BORDER, EDGE **2 a** : the side of a ship **b** : the stretch that a ship makes on one tack in beating to windward **3 a** : a piece of sawed lumber of little thickness and a length greatly exceeding its width **b** *pl* : STAGE 2a(2) **4 a** *archaic* : TABLE 3a **b** : a table spread with a meal **c** : daily meals esp. when furnished for pay **d** : a table at which a council or magistrates sit **e** : a group of persons having managerial, supervisory, or investigatory powers <~ of directors> <~ of examiners> **f** : LEAGUE, ASSOCIATION **g (1)** : the exposed hands of all the players in a stud poker game **(2)** : an exposed dummy hand in bridge **5 a** : a flat usu. rectangular piece of material (as wood) designed for a special purpose: as (1) : BACKBOARD (2) : a diving board (3) : SURFBOARD **b** : a surface, frame, or device for posting notices or listing market quotations **c** : BLACKBOARD **d** : SWITCHBOARD **6 a** : any of various wood pulps or composition materials formed into stiff flat rectangular sheets **b** : material of the same general composition as paper but stiffer and thicker **c** : the stiff foundation piece for the side of a book cover **7** : an organized

securities or commodities exchange **8** *pl* : the low wooden wall enclosing a hockey rink — **board·like** \-ˌlīk\ *adj* — **on board** : ABOARD

[2]**board** *vt* **1** *archaic* : to come up against or alongside (a ship) usu. to attack **2** : ACCOST, ADDRESS **3** : to go aboard (as a ship, train, airplane, or bus) **4** : to cover with boards <~ up a window> **5** : to provide with regular meals and often also lodging usu. for compensation **6** : to check (a player) against the rink boards in hockey ~ *vi* : to take one's meals usu. as a paying customer

board check *n* : a body check of an opposing player against the rink boards in ice hockey

board·er \ˈbōrd-ər, ˈbȯrd-\ *n* : one that boards; *esp* : one that is provided with regular meals or regular meals and lodging

board foot *n* : a unit of quantity for lumber equal to the volume of a board 12 x 12 x 1 inches — abbr. *bd ft*

board game *n* : a game of strategy (as checkers, chess, or backgammon) played by moving pieces on a board

board·ing·house \ˈbōrd-iŋ-ˌhau̇s, ˈbȯrd-\ *n* : a lodging house at which meals are provided

boarding school *n* : a school at which meals and lodging are provided

board·man \ˈbō(ə)rd-mən, ˈbȯ(ə)rd-, *esp for 2* -ˌman\ *n* **1** : one who works at a board **2** : a member of a board — **board·man·ship** *or* **boards·man·ship** \ˈbōrd(z)-mən-ˌship, ˈbȯrd(z)-\ *n*

board measure *n* : measurement in board feet

board of education : SCHOOL BOARD

board of trade **1** *cap B&T* : a British governmental department concerned with commerce and industry **2** : an organization of businessmen for the protection and promotion of business interests **3** : a commodities exchange

board·room \ˈbō(ə)rd-ˌrüm, ˈbȯ(ə)rd-, -ˌru̇m\ *n* **1** : a room that is designated for meetings of a board **2** : a room (as in a broker's office) containing a board for the listing of transactions or prices

board·walk \ˈbō(ə)rd-ˌwȯk, ˈbȯ(ə)rd-\ *n* **1** : a walk constructed of planking **2** : a walk constructed along a beach

boart \ˈbō(ə)rt, ˈbȯ(ə)rt\ *var of* BORT

[1]**boast** \ˈbōst\ *n* [ME *boost*] **1** : the act or an instance of boasting : BRAG **2** : a cause for pride — **boast·ful** \ˈbōst-fəl\ *adj* — **boast·ful·ly** \-fə-lē\ *adv* — **boast·ful·ness** *n*

[2]**boast** *vi* **1** : to puff oneself up in speech : speak vaingloriously **2** *archaic* : GLORY, EXULT ~ *vt* **1** : to speak of or assert with excessive pride **2 a** : to possess and often call attention to (something that is a source of pride) <their home ~*s* all the newest conveniences> **b** : HAVE, CONTAIN <a miserable room ~*ing* no more than a wobbly desk and a single chair>

syn BOAST, BRAG, VAUNT, CROW *shared meaning element* : to express pride in oneself or one's accomplishments. BOAST often suggests ostentation and exaggeration <ready to *boast* of every trivial success> but it may imply a claiming with proper and justifiable pride <the town *boasts* one of the best hospitals in the area> BRAG suggests crudity and artlessness in glorifying oneself <boys *bragging* to each other> VAUNT usually connotes more pomp and bombast than *boast* and less crudity or naiveté than *brag* <charity *vaunteth* not itself, is not puffed up —1 Cor 13:4(AV)> CROW usually implies exultant boasting or bragging <loved to ~ about his ancestors> *ant* depreciate (*as oneself*)

[3]**boast** *vt* [origin unknown] : to shape (stone) roughly with a broad chisel in sculpture and stonecutting as a preliminary to finer work

[1]**boat** \ˈbōt\ *n* [ME *boot*, fr. OE *bāt*; akin to ON *beit* boat] **1** : a small vessel propelled by oars or paddles or by sail or power **2** : SHIP **3** : a boat-shaped utensil or device <a gravy ~> — **in the same boat** : in the same situation or predicament

[2]**boat** *vt* : to place in or bring into a boat <catch and ~ a fish> ~ *vi* : to go by boat

boa·tel \bō-ˈtel\ *n* [blend of *boat* and *hotel*] : a waterside hotel having docks to accommodate persons traveling by boat

boat·er \ˈbōt-ər\ *n* **1** : one who travels in a boat **2** : a stiff straw hat

boat hook *n* : a pole-handled hook with a point or knob on the back used esp. to pull or push a boat, raft, or log into place

boat·man \ˈbōt-mən\ *n* : a man who works on, deals in, or operates boats — **boat·man·ship** \-ˌship\ *or* **boats·man·ship** \ˈbōts-\ *n*

boat·swain \ˈbōs-ᵊn\ *n* [ME *bootswein*, fr. *boot* boat + *swein* boy, servant] **1** : a petty officer on a merchant ship having charge of hull maintenance and related work **2** : a naval warrant officer in charge of the hull and all related equipment

boat train *n* : an express train for transporting passengers between a port and a city

[1]**bob** \ˈbäb\ *vb* **bobbed**; **bob·bing** [ME *boben*] *vt* **1** : to strike with a quick light blow : RAP **2** : to move up and down in a short quick movement <~ the head> **3** : to polish with a bob : BUFF ~ *vi* **1 a** : to move up and down briefly or repeatedly <a cork *bobbed* in the water> **b** : to emerge, arise, or appear suddenly or unexpectedly <the question *bobbed* up again> **2** : to nod or curtsy briefly **3** : to try to seize a suspended or floating object with the teeth <~ for apples>

[2]**bob** *n* **1 a** : a short quick down-and-up motion **b** *Scot* : any of several folk dances **2** *obs* : a blow or tap esp. with the fist **3 a** : a modification of the order in change ringing **b** : a method of change ringing using a bob **4** : a small polishing wheel of solid felt or leather with rounded edges

[3]**bob** *vt* **bobbed**; **bob·bing** [ME *bobben*, fr. MF *bober*] **1** *obs* : DECEIVE, CHEAT **2** *obs* : to take by fraud : FILCH

[4]**bob** *n* [ME *bobbe*] **1 a (1)** : BUNCH, CLUSTER **(2)** *Scot* : NOSEGAY **b** : a knob, knot, twist, or curl esp. of ribbons, yarn, or hair **c** : a short haircut on a woman or child **2** : FLOAT 2a **3** : a hanging ball or weight (as on a plumb line or on the tail of a kite) **4** *archaic* : the refrain of a song; *specif* : a short and abrupt refrain often of two syllables **5** : a small insignificant piece : TRIFLE <~*s* and trinkets>

[5]**bob** *vt* **bobbed**; **bob·bing** **1** : to cut shorter : CROP <~ a horse's tail> **2** : to cut (hair) in the style of a bob

[6]**bob** *n, pl* **bob** [perh. fr. the name *Bob*] *Brit* : SHILLING

[7]**bob** *n* **1** : BOBSLED **2** : SKIBOB

bob·ber \ˈbäb-ər\ *n* **1** : one that bobs **2** : one who rides or races on a bobsled

bob·bery \ˈbäb-ə-rē\ *n, pl* **-ber·ies** [Hindi *bāp re*, lit., oh father!] : HUBBUB

bob·bin \ˈbäb-ən\ *n* [origin unknown] **1 a** : any of various small round devices on which threads are wound for working handmade lace **b** : a cylinder or spindle on which yarn or thread is wound (as in a sewing machine) **c** : a coil of insulated wire or the reel it is wound on **2** : a narrow cotton cord formerly used by dressmakers for piping

bob·bi·net \ˈbäb-ə-ˌnet\ *n* [blend of *bobbin* and *net*] : a machine-made net of cotton, silk, or nylon usu. with hexagonal mesh

[1]**bob·ble** \ˈbäb-əl\ *vb* **bob·bled**; **bob·bling** \-(ə-)liŋ\ [freq. of [1]*bob*] **1** : [1]BOB **2** : FUMBLE

[2]**bobble** *n* **1** : a repeated bobbing movement **2** : a small ball of fabric; *esp* : one in a series used on an edging <curtains . . . with plush ~*s* —H. E. Bates> **3** : ERROR, MISTAKE; *esp* : a fumble in baseball or football

bob·by \ˈbäb-ē\ *n, pl* **bobbies** [*Bobby*, nickname for *Robert*, after Sir *Robert* Peel, who organized the London police force] *Brit* : POLICEMAN

bob·by pin \ˈbäb-ē-\ *n* [[4]*bob*] : a flat wire hairpin with prongs that press close together

bob·by socks *or* **bobby sox** \ˈbäb-ē-\ *n pl* [fr. the name *Bobby*] : girls' socks reaching above the ankle

bob·by–sox·er \-ˌsäk-sər\ *n* : an adolescent girl

bob·cat \ˈbäb-ˌkat\ *n* [[4]*bob*; fr. the stubby tail] : a common No. American lynx (*Lynx rufus*) typically rusty or reddish in base color

bobcat

bo·beche \bō-ˈbesh, -ˈbāsh\ *n* [F *bobèche*] : a usu. glass collar on a candle socket to catch drippings or on a candlestick or chandelier to hold suspended glass prisms

bob·o·link \ˈbäb-ə-ˌliŋk\ *n* [imit.] : an American migratory songbird (*Dolichonyx oryzivorus*)

bob·sled \ˈbäb-ˌsled\ *n* [perh. fr. [4]*bob*] **1** : a short sled usu. used as one of a pair joined by a coupling **2** : a large usu. metal sled used in racing and equipped with two pairs of runners in tandem, a long seat for two or more people, a steering wheel, and a hand brake — **bobsled** *vi* — **bob·sled·der** *n*

bob·sled·ding \-ˌsled-iŋ\ *n* : the act, skill, or sport of riding or racing on a bobsled

bob·stay \ˈbäb-ˌstā\ *n* [prob. fr. [2]*bob*] : a stay to hold a ship's bowsprit down

bob·tail \ˈbäb-ˌtāl\ *n* [[4]*bob*] **1 a** : a bobbed tail **b** : a horse or dog with a bobbed tail; *esp* : OLD ENGLISH SHEEPDOG **2** : something curtailed or abbreviated — **bobtail** *or* **bob·tailed** \-ˌtāld\ *adj*

bob veal \ˈbäb-\ *n* [E dial. *bob* young calf] : the veal of a very young or unborn calf

bob·white \(ˈ)bäb-ˈ(h)wīt\ *n* [imit.] : any of a genus (*Colinus*) of quail; *esp* : a favorite game bird (*C. virginianus*) of the eastern and central U.S. — called also *partridge*

bo·cac·cio \bə-ˈkäch-(ē-ˌ)ō\ *n* [perh. deriv. of Sp *bocacha*, aug. of *boca* mouth] : a large rockfish (*Sebastes paucispinis*) of the Pacific coast locally important as a market fish

boc·cie *or* **boc·ci** *or* **boc·ce** \ˈbäch-ē\ *n* [It *bocce*, pl. of *boccia* ball, fr. (assumed) VL *bottia* boss] : Italian lawn bowling played in a long narrow court

bock \ˈbäk\ *n* [G, short for *bockbier*, by shortening & alter. fr. *Einbecker bier*, lit., beer from Einbeck, fr. *Einbeck*, Germany] : a heavy dark rich beer usu. sold in the early spring

bod \ˈbäd\ *n* : BODY

BOD *abbr* biochemical oxygen demand; biological oxygen demand

bo·da·cious \bō-ˈdā-shəs\ *adj* [back-formation fr. earlier *bodaciously* (thoroughly), alter. of earlier *bodyaciously*, perh. fr. *body* + *-aciously* (as in *graciously*)] **1** *South & Midland* : OUTRIGHT, UNMISTAKABLE **2** *South & Midland* : REMARKABLE, NOTEWORTHY <I got some ~ gossip —Fred Lasswell> — **bo·da·cious·ly** *adv*

[1]**bode** \ˈbōd\ *vt* **bod·ed**; **bod·ing** [ME *boden*, fr. OE *bodian*; akin to OE *bēodan* to proclaim — more at BID] **1** *archaic* : to announce beforehand : FORETELL **2** : to indicate by signs : PRESAGE <this controversy . . . will ~ ill for both of us — A. H. Lowe>

[2]**bode** *past of* BIDE

bo·de·ga \bō-ˈdā-gə\ *n* [Sp, fr. L *apotheca* storehouse — more at APOTHECARY] **1** : a storehouse for wine **2 a** : WINESHOP **b** : a combined wineshop and grocery store **c** : [1]BAR 5

bode·ment \ˈbōd-mənt\ *n* **1** : OMEN, FOREBODING **2** : PREDICTION, PROPHECY

bo·dhi·satt·va *or* **bod·dhi·satt·va** \ˌbōd-i-ˈsət-və\ *n* [Skt *bodhisattva* one whose essence is enlightenment, fr. *bodhi* enlightenment + *sattva* being] : a being that compassionately refrains from entering nirvana in order to save others and is worshiped as a deity in Mahayana Buddhism

bod·ice \ˈbäd-əs\ *n* [alter. of *bodies*, pl. of [1]*body*] **1** *archaic* : CORSET, STAYS **2** : the upper part of a woman's dress

-bodied \ˈbäd-ēd\ *adj comb form* : having a body of a specified nature <full-*bodied*> <glass-*bodied*>

bodi·less \ˈbäd-i-ləs, ˈbäd-ᵊl-əs\ *adj* : having no body : INCORPOREAL

[1]**bodi·ly** \ˈbäd-ᵊl-ē\ *adj* **1** : having a body : PHYSICAL **2** : of or relating to the body <~ comfort> <~ organs>

syn BODILY, PHYSICAL, CORPOREAL, CORPORAL, SOMATIC *shared meaning element* : of or relating to the human body

2**bodily** *adv* **1 :** in the flesh **2 :** as a whole : ALTOGETHER

bod·ing \'bōd-iŋ\ *n* : FOREBODING

bod·kin \'bäd-kən\ *n* [ME] **1 a :** DAGGER, STILETTO **b :** a sharp slender instrument for making holes in cloth **c :** an ornamental hairpin shaped like a stiletto **2 :** a blunt needle with a large eye for drawing tape or ribbon through a loop or hem

1**body** \'bäd-ē\ *n, pl* **bod·ies** [ME, fr. OE *bodig;* akin to OHG *botah* body] **1 a :** the organized physical substance of an animal or plant either living or dead: as (1) **:** the material part or nature of man (2) **:** the dead organism : CORPSE (3) **:** the person of a human being before the law **b :** a human being : PERSON **2 a :** the main part of a plant or animal body esp. as distinguished from limbs and head : TRUNK **b :** the main, central, or principal part: as (1) **:** the nave of a church (2) **:** the bed or box of a vehicle on or in which the load is placed **3 a :** the part of a garment covering the body or trunk **b :** the main part of a literary or journalistic work : TEXT 2b **c :** the sound box or pipe of a musical instrument **4 a :** a mass of matter distinct from other masses <a ~ of water> **b :** one of the seven planets of the old astronomy **c :** something that embodies or gives concrete reality to a thing; *specif* **:** a sensible object in physical space **5 :** a group of persons or things: as **a :** a fighting unit : FORCE **b :** a group of individuals organized for some purpose : CORPORATION <a legislative ~> **6 a :** VISCOSITY, CONSISTENCY — used esp. of oils and grease **b :** compactness or firmness of texture **c :** fullness or resonance of a musical tone **d :** richness of flavor — used of a beverage (as wine) **7 :** the part of a printing type extending from foot to shoulder and underlying the bevel — see TYPE illustration

2**body** *vt* **bod·ied; body·ing 1 a :** to give form or shape to : EMBODY **b :** REPRESENT, SYMBOLIZE — usu. used with *forth* **2 :** to increase the viscosity of (an oil)

body cavity *n* : a cavity within an animal body; *specif* : COELOM

body check *n* : a blocking of an opposing player with the body (as in ice hockey or lacrosse)

body corporate *n* : CORPORATION

body English *n* : the instinctive attempt of a person to influence the movement of a propelled object (as a ball or puck) by contorting his body in the desired direction

body·guard \'bäd-ē-ˌgärd\ *n* : a man or group of men whose duty is to protect a person from bodily harm

body louse *n* : a louse feeding primarily on the body; *esp* : a sucking louse (*Pediculus humanus*) feeding on the body and living in the clothing of man

body mechanics *n pl but sing or pl in constr* : systematic exercises (as for women) designed esp. to develop coordination, endurance, and poise

body politic *n* **1** *archaic* : CORPORATION 2 **2 :** a group of persons politically organized under a single governmental authority **3 :** a people considered as a collective unit

body shirt *n* : a close-fitting high-collared shirt or blouse with curved front and back seams and deep cuffs

body shop *n* : a shop where automotive bodies are made or repaired

body snatcher *n* : one that without authority takes corpses from graves usu. for dissection

body stocking *n* : a sheer close-fitting one-piece garment for the torso that often has sleeves and legs

body·surf \'bäd-ē-ˌsərf\ *vi* : to ride on a wave without a surfboard by planing on the chest and stomach — **body·surf·er** *n*

body wall *n* : the external surface of the body in animals consisting of ectoderm and mesoderm and enclosing the body cavity

body·work \'bäd-ē-ˌwərk\ *n* **1 :** a vehicle body **2 :** the act or process of making or repairing vehicle bodies

boehm·ite \'bām-ˌīt, 'bə(r)m-\ *n* [G *böhmit,* fr. J. *Böhm* (*Boehm*), 20th cent. G scientist] : a mineral consisting of an orthorhombic form of aluminum oxide and hydroxide AlO(OH) found in bauxite

Boer \'bō(ə)r, 'bȯ(ə)r, 'bu̇(ə)r\ *n* [D, lit., farmer — more at BOOR] : a South African of Dutch or Huguenot descent

boff \'bäf\ *or* **bof·fo** \'bäf-(ˌ)ō\ *n, pl* **boffs** *or* **boffos** [prob. fr. *box office*] **1 :** a hearty laugh **2 :** a gag or line that produces a hearty laugh **3 :** something that is conspicuously successful : HIT

bof·fin \'bäf-ən\ *n* [origin unknown] *chiefly Brit* : a scientific expert

bof·fo \'bäf-(ˌ)ō\ *adj* : extraordinarily successful : SENSATIONAL

bof·fo·la \bä-'fō-lə\ *n* [irreg. fr. *boff*] : BOFF

Bo·fors gun \ˌbō-ˌfȯrz-, ˌbü-\ *n* [*Bofors,* munition works in Sweden] : a double-barreled automatic antiaircraft gun

1**bog** \'bäg, 'bȯg\ *n* [of Celt origin; akin to OIr *bocc* soft; akin to OE *būgan* to bend — more at BOW] : wet spongy ground; *esp* : a poorly drained usu. acid area rich in plant residues, frequently surrounding a body of open water, and having a characteristic flora (as of sedges, heaths, and sphagnum) — **bog·gy** \'bäg-ē, 'bȯg-\ *adj*

2**bog** *vb* **bogged; bog·ging** *vt* : to cause to sink into or as if into a bog : IMPEDE — usu. used with *down* ~ *vi* : to become impeded — usu. used with *down*

bog asphodel *n* : either of two bog herbs (*Narthecium ossifragum* of Europe and *N. americanum* of the U.S.) of the lily family

1**bo·gey** *also* **bo·gy** *or* **bo·gie** *n, pl* **bogeys** *also* **bogies** [prob. alter. of *bogle*] **1** \'bu̇g-ē, 'bō-gē, 'bü-gē, 'bu̇g-ər\ **:** SPECTER, PHANTOM **2** \'bō-gē *also* 'bu̇g-ē *or* 'bü-gē\ **:** a source of fear, perplexity, or harassment **3** \'bō-gē\ **a** *chiefly Brit* **:** an average golfer's score used as a standard for a particular hole or course **b :** one stroke over par on a hole in golf **4** \'bō-gē\ **:** a numerical standard of performance set up as a mark to be aimed at in competition **5** \'bu̇g-ē, 'bō-gē, 'bü-gē\ *slang* **:** an unidentified flying object

2**bo·gey** \'bō-gē\ *vt* **bo·geyed; bo·gey·ing :** to shoot (a hole in golf) in one over par

bo·gey·man \'bu̇g-ē-ˌman, 'bō-gē-, 'bü-gē-, 'bu̇g-ər-\ *n* **:** a monstrous imaginary figure used in threatening children; *broadly* **:** a terrifying person or thing : BUGBEAR

bog·gle \'bäg-əl\ *vb* **bog·gled; bog·gling** \-(ə-)liŋ\ [perh. fr. *bogle*] *vi* **1 :** to start with fright or amazement : be overwhelmed <the mind ~*s* at the amount of research yet to be done> **2 :** to hesitate because of doubt, fear, or scruples **3 :** BUNGLE ~ *vt* **:** to overwhelm with wonder or bewilderment — **boggle** *n*

bo·gie *also* **bo·gey** *or* **bo·gy** \'bō-gē\ *n, pl* **bogies** *also* **bogeys** [origin unknown] **1 :** a low strongly built cart **2 a** *chiefly Brit* **:** a swiveling railway truck **b :** the driving-wheel assembly consisting of the rear four wheels of a 6-wheel automotive truck **3 :** one of the weight-carrying wheels on the inside perimeter of the tread of a tank serving to keep the treads in line

bo·gle \'bō-gəl\ *also* **bog·gle** \'bäg-əl\ *n* [E dial. (Sc & northern), terrifying apparition; akin to ME *bugge* scarecrow — more at BUG] *dial Brit* **:** GOBLIN, SPECTER; *also* **:** an object of fear or loathing

Bo·go·mil *also* **Bo·go·mile** \ˌbəg-ə-'mē(ə)l\ *n* [Russ *bogomil,* fr. OSlav *Bogomilŭ* Bogomil, 10th cent. Bulg priest, founder of the sect] **:** a member of a medieval chiefly Bulgarian religious sect teaching that God is the father of two sons, the rebellious Satan and the obedient Jesus

bo·gus \'bō-gəs\ *adj* [*bogus* (a machine for making counterfeit money)] **:** not genuine : COUNTERFEIT, SHAM

bo·hea \bō-'hē\ *n, often cap* [Chin (Pek) wu^3-i^2, hills in China where it was grown] **:** a black tea

bo·he·mia \bō-'hē-mē-ə\ *n, often cap* [trans. of F *bohème*] **:** a community of bohemians **:** the world of bohemians

Bo·he·mi·an \-mē-ən\ *n* **1 a :** a native or inhabitant of Bohemia **b :** the group of Czech dialects used in Bohemia **2** *often not cap* **a :** VAGABOND, WANDERER; *esp* **:** GYPSY **b :** a person (as a writer or an artist) living an unconventional life usu. in a colony with others — **bohemian** *adj, often cap*

Bohemian Brethren *n pl* **:** a Christian body originating in Bohemia in 1467 and forming a parent body of the Moravian Brethren

bo·he·mi·an·ism \bō-'hē-mē-ə-ˌniz-əm\ *n, often cap* **:** the unconventional way of life of bohemians

Bohr theory \'bō(ə)r-, 'bȯ(ə)r-\ *n* [Niels *Bohr*] **:** a theory in physical chemistry: an atom consists of a positively charged nucleus about which revolves one or more electrons

1**boil** \'bȯi(ə)l\ *n* [alter. of ME *bile,* fr. OE *bȳl* — more at BIG] **:** a localized swelling and inflammation of the skin resulting from infection in a skin gland, having a hard central core, and forming pus

2**boil** *vb* [ME *boilen,* fr. OF *boillir,* fr. L *bullire* to bubble, fr. *bulla* bubble] *vi* **1 a :** to generate bubbles of vapor when heated — used of a liquid **b :** to come to the boiling point **2 :** to become agitated like boiling water : SEETHE **3 :** to be moved, excited, or stirred up <his blood ~*s* at the mention of it> **4 a :** to rush headlong <came ~*ing* through the door> **b :** to burst forth : ERUPT <water ~*ing* from a spring> **5 :** to undergo the action of a boiling liquid ~ *vt* **1 :** to subject to the action of a boiling liquid <~ eggs> **2 :** to heat to the boiling point <~ water> **3 :** to form or separate (as sugar or salt) by boiling

3**boil** *n* **1 :** the act or state of boiling **2 :** a swirling upheaval (as of water)

boil down *vt* **1 :** to reduce in bulk by boiling **2 :** CONDENSE, SUMMARIZE <*boil down* a report> ~ *vi* **1 :** to undergo reduction in bulk by boiling **2 :** to be equivalent in summary : AMOUNT <his speech *boiled down* to a plea for more money>

boiled oil *n* **:** a fatty oil (as linseed oil) whose drying properties have been improved by heating usu. with driers

boil·er \'bȯi-lər\ *n* **1 :** one that boils **2 a :** a vessel used for boiling **b :** the part of a steam generator in which water is converted into steam and which consists usu. of metal shells and tubes **c :** a tank in which water is heated or hot water is stored

boil·er·mak·er \'bȯi-lər-ˌmā-kər\ *n* **1 :** a workman who makes, assembles, or repairs boilers **2 :** whiskey with a beer chaser

boiler suit *n* : COVERALL

1**boil·ing** \'bȯi-liŋ\ *adj* **1 a :** heated to the boiling point **b :** TORRID <a ~ sun> **2 :** intensely agitated, excited, or stirred up <a ~ sea>

2**boiling** *adv* **:** to an extreme degree : VERY <~ mad> <~ hot>

boiling point *n* **1 :** the temperature at which a liquid boils **2 a :** the point at which a person loses his temper **b :** the point at which decisive action becomes imperative : HEAD 17b <matters had reached the *boiling point*>

boil over *vi* **1 :** to overflow while boiling **2 :** to become so incensed as to lose one's temper

bois d'arc \'bō-ˌdärk\ *n, pl* **bois d'arcs** *or* **bois d'arc** [F, lit., bow wood] : OSAGE ORANGE

bois·ter·ous \'bȯi-st(ə-)rəs\ *adj* [ME *boistous* rough] **1** *obs* **a :** DURABLE, STRONG **b :** COARSE **c :** MASSIVE **2 a :** noisily turbulent : ROWDY **b :** marked by or expressive of exuberance and high spirits **3 :** STORMY, TUMULTUOUS *syn* see VOCIFEROUS — **bois·ter·ous·ly** *adv* — **bois·ter·ous·ness** *n*

Bok·mål \'bu̇k-ˌmōl, 'bōk-\ *n* [Norw, lit., book language] **:** a literary form of Norwegian developed by the gradual reform of written Danish — compare NYNORSK

bo·la \'bō-lə\ *or* **bo·las** \-ləs\ *n, pl* **bolas** \-ləz\ *also* **bo·las·es** [AmerSp *bolas,* fr. Sp *bola* ball] **:** a weapon consisting of two or more stone or iron balls attached to the ends of a cord for hurling at and entangling an animal

bola

bold \'bōld\ *adj* [ME, fr. OE *beald;* akin to OHG *bald* bold] **1 a :** fearless before danger : INTREPID **b :** showing or requiring a fearless daring spirit <a ~ plan> **2 :** IMPUDENT, PRESUMPTUOUS **3** *obs* **:** ASSURED, CONFIDENT **4 :** SHEER, STEEP <~ cliffs> **5 :** ADVENTUROUS, DARING <a ~ thinker> **6 :** standing out prominently : CONSPICUOUS **7 :** BOLD-FACED 2 — **bold·ly** \'bōl-(d)lē\ *adv* — **bold·ness** \'bōl(d)-nəs\ *n*

bold·face \'bōl(d)-ˌfās\ *n* **:** a heavy-faced type; *also* **:** printing in boldface — compare LIGHTFACE

bold–faced \'bōl(d)-'fāst\ *adj* **1 :** bold in manner or conduct

: IMPUDENT **2** : set in boldface

bole \ˈbōl\ *n* [ME, fr. ON *bolr*] : the trunk of a tree

bo·le·ro \bə-ˈle(ə)r-(ˌ)ō\ *n, pl* **-ros** [Sp] **1** : a Spanish dance characterized by sharp turns, stamping of the feet, and sudden pauses in a position with one arm arched over the head; *also* : music in ¾ time for or suitable for a bolero **2** : a loose waist-length jacket open at the front

bo·le·tus \bō-ˈlēt-əs\ *n, pl* **-tus·es** *or* **-ti** \-ˈlēt-ˌī\ [NL, genus name, fr. L, a fungus, fr. Gk *bōlitēs*] : any of a genus (*Boletus*) of soft pore fungi some of which are poisonous and others edible

bo·li·var \bə-ˈlē-ˌvär, ˈbäl-ə-vər\ *n, pl* **-vars** *or* **-va·res** \ˌbäl-ə-ˈvär-ˌäs, ˌbō-li-\ [AmerSp *bolívar*, fr. Simón *Bolívar*] — see MONEY table

bo·li·vi·a·no \bə-ˌliv-ē-ˈän-(ˌ)ō\ *n, pl* **-nos** [Sp] : a former monetary unit of Bolivia replaced in 1963 by the peso

boll \ˈbōl\ *n* [ME] : the pod or capsule of a plant (as cotton)

bol·lard \ˈbäl-ərd\ *n* [perh. irreg. fr. *bole*] **1** : a post of metal or wood on a wharf around which to fasten mooring lines **2** : BITT 1

bol·lix \ˈbäl-iks\ *vt* [alter. of *ballocks*, pl. of *ballock* (testis), fr. ME, fr. OE *bealluc* — more at BALL] : to throw into disorder; *also* : BUNGLE — usu. used with *up* — **bollix** *n*

boll weevil *n* : a grayish weevil (*Anthonomus grandis*) about ¼ inch long that infests the cotton plant and feeds on the squares and bolls both as a larva and an adult

boll·worm \ˈbōl-ˌwərm\ *n* : CORN EARWORM; *also* : any of several other moth larvae that feed on cotton bolls

bo·lo \ˈbō-(ˌ)lō\ *n, pl* **bolos** [Sp] : a long heavy single-edged knife of Philippine origin

bo·lo·gna \bə-ˈlō-nē *also* -n(y)ə\ *n* [short for *Bologna sausage*, fr. *Bologna*, Italy] : a large smoked sausage of beef, veal, and pork

bo·lom·e·ter \bō-ˈläm-ət-ər\ *n* [Gk *bolē* + E *-o-* + *-meter*] : a very sensitive resistance thermometer used in the detection and measurement of feeble thermal radiation and esp. adapted to the study of infrared spectra — **bo·lo·met·ric** \ˌbō-lə-ˈme-trik\ *adj* — **bo·lo·met·ri·cal·ly** \-tri-k(ə-)lē\ *adv*

bo·lo·ney \bə-ˈlō-nē\ *var of* BALONEY

bo·lo tie \ˌbō-lō-\ *or* **bo·la tie** \-lə-\ *n* [prob. fr. *bola*] : a cord fastened around the neck with an ornamental clasp and worn as a necktie

Bol·she·vik \ˈbōl-shə-ˌvik, ˈbȯl-, ˈbäl-, -ˌvēk\ *n, pl* **Bolsheviks** *also* **Bol·she·vi·ki** \ˌbōl-shə-ˈvik-ē, ˌbȯl-, ˌbäl-, -ˈvē-kē\ [Russ *bol'shevik*, fr. *bol'she* larger] **1** : a member of the extremist wing of the Russian Social Democratic party that seized supreme power in Russia by the Revolution of November 1917 **2** : COMMUNIST 3 — **Bolshevik** *adj*

bol·she·vism \ˈbōl-shə-ˌviz-əm, ˈbȯl-, ˈbäl-\ *n, often cap* **1** : the doctrine or program of the Bolsheviks advocating violent overthrow of capitalism **2** : Russian communism

Bol·she·vist \-vəst\ *n or adj* : BOLSHEVIK

bol·she·vize \-ˌvīz\ *vt* **-vized; -viz·ing** : to make Bolshevist — **Bol·she·vi·za·tion** \ˌbōl-shə-və-ˈzā-shən, ˌbȯl-, ˌbäl-\ *n*

¹bol·ster \ˈbōl-stər\ *n* [ME, fr. OE; akin to OE *belg* bag — more at BELLY] **1** : a long pillow or cushion **2** : a structural part designed to eliminate friction or provide support or bearing; *esp* : the horizontal connection between the volutes of an Ionic capital

²bolster *vt* **bol·stered; bol·ster·ing** \-st(ə-)riŋ\ **1** : to support with or as if with a bolster : REINFORCE **2** : to give a boost to <news that ~*ed* his spirits> — **bol·ster·er** \-stər-ər\ *n*

¹bolt \ˈbōlt\ *n* [ME, fr. OE; akin to OHG *bolz* crossbow bolt, Lith *beldėti* to beat] **1 a** : a shaft or missile designed to be shot from a crossbow or catapult; *esp* : a short stout usu. blunt-headed arrow **b** : a lightning stroke : THUNDERBOLT **2 a** : a wood or metal bar or rod used to fasten a door **b** : the part of a lock that is shot or withdrawn by the key **3 a** : a roll of cloth of specified length **b** : a roll of wallpaper of specified length **4** : a metal rod or pin for fastening objects together that usu. has a head at one end and a screw thread at the other and is secured by a nut **5 a** : a block of timber to be sawed or cut **b** : a short round section of a log **6** : the breech closure of a breech-loading firearm

1 a 4 2 5 6 3 7

bolts 4: *1* stove bolt with cotter pin *a*, *2* carriage bolt, *3* machine bolt, *4* eyebolt, *5* U bolt, *6* plow bolt, *7* expansion bolt

²bolt *vi* **1** : to move suddenly or nervously : START **2** : to move rapidly : DASH **3 a** : to dart off or away : FLEE **b** : to break away from control or a set course **4** : to break away from or oppose one's political party ~ *vt* **1 a** *archaic* : SHOOT, DISCHARGE **b** : FLUSH, START <~ rabbits> **2** : to say impulsively : BLURT **3** : to secure with a bolt **4** : to attach or fasten with bolts **5** : to swallow hastily or without chewing **6** : to break away from

³bolt *adv* **1** : in an erect or straight-backed position : RIGIDLY <sat ~ upright> **2** *archaic* : DIRECTLY, STRAIGHT

⁴bolt *n* : the act or an instance of bolting: as **a** : DASH, RUN **b** : a refusal to support one's usual political party or its candidate or platform

⁵bolt *vt* [ME *bulten*, fr. OF *buleter*, of Gmc origin; akin to MHG *biuteln* to sift, fr. *biutel* bag, fr. OHG *būtil*] **1** : to sift (as flour) usu. through fine-meshed cloth **2** *archaic* : SIFT 2

¹bolt·er \ˈbōl-tər\ *n* : a machine for bolting flour; *also* : the operator of such a machine

²bolter *n* **1** : a horse given to running away **2** : a voter who bolts his party

bolt–operated *adj, of a firearm* : utilizing a sliding bolt to operate the action

bolt·rope \ˈbōlt-ˌrōp\ *n* : a strong rope stitched to the edges of a sail to strengthen it

bo·lus \ˈbō-ləs\ *n* [LL, fr. Gk *bōlos* lump] : a rounded mass: as **a** : a large pill **b** : a soft mass of chewed food

¹bomb \ˈbäm\ *n* [F *bombe*, fr. It *bomba*, prob. fr. L *bombus* deep hollow sound, fr. Gk *bombos*, of imit. origin] **1 a** : an explosive device fused to detonate under specified conditions **b** : ATOM BOMB — usu. used with *the* **2** : a vessel for compressed gases: as **a** : a pressure vessel for conducting chemical experiments **b** : a small dispenser for a substance (as paint or an insecticide) stored under pressure **3** : a rounded mass of lava exploded from a volcano **4** : a lead-lined container for radioactive material **5** : a long pass in football **6** : FAILURE, FLOP <the play was awful — a complete ~> **7** *slang Brit* : a large sum of money

²bomb *vt* **1** : to attack with or as if with bombs : BOMBARD **2 a** : to score heavily against (an opponent) **b** : to defeat decisively ~ *vi* : to fall flat : FAIL

¹bom·bard \ˈbäm-ˌbärd\ *n* [ME *bombarde*, fr. MF, prob. fr. L *bombus*] : a cannon used in late medieval times chiefly to hurl large stones

²bom·bard \bäm-ˈbärd *also* bəm-\ *vt* **1** : to attack esp. with artillery or bombers **2** : to assail vigorously or persistently (as with questions) **3** : to subject to the impact of rapidly moving particles (as electrons or alpha rays) ***syn*** see ATTACK — **bom·bard·ment** \-mənt\ *n*

bom·bar·dier \ˌbäm-bə(r)-ˈdi(ə)r\ *n* **1 a** *archaic* : ARTILLERYMAN **b** : a noncommissioned officer in the British artillery **2** : a bomber-crew member who uses the bombsight and releases the bombs

bom·bar·don \ˈbäm-bər-ˌdōn, bäm-ˈbärd-ᵊn\ *n* [F, fr. It *bombardone*] **1** : the bass member of the shawm family **2** : a bass tuba

bom·bast \ˈbäm-ˌbast\ *n* [MF *bombace*, fr. ML *bombac-*, *bombax* cotton, alter. of L *bombyc-*, *bombyx* silkworm, silk, fr. Gk *bombyk-*, *bombyx*] : pretentious inflated speech or writing — **bombast** *adj* — **bom·bast·er** \-ˌbas-tər\ *n* — **bom·bas·tic** \bäm-ˈbas-tik\ *adj* — **bom·bas·ti·cal·ly** \-ti-k(ə-)lē\ *adv*

syn BOMBAST, RHAPSODY, RANT, FUSTIAN *shared meaning element* : speech or writing marked by high-flown pomposity or pretentiousness

bom·ba·zine \ˌbäm-bə-ˈzēn\ *n* [MF *bombasin*, fr. ML *bombacinum*, *bombycinum* silken texture, fr. L, neut. of *bombycinus* of silk, fr. *bombyc-*, *bombyx*] **1** : a silk fabric in twill weave dyed black **2** : a twilled fabric with silk warp and worsted filling

bomb bay *n* : a bomb-carrying compartment on the underside of a combat airplane

bombe \ˈbäm, ˈbōⁿ(m)b\ *n* [F, lit., bomb] : a frozen dessert made by lining a round or melon-shaped mold with one mixture and filling it with another

bombed \ˈbämd\ *adj, slang* : affected by alcohol or drugs

bomb·er \ˈbäm-ər\ *n* : one that bombs; *specif* : an airplane designed for bombing

bom·bi·nate \ˈbäm-bə-ˌnāt\ *vi* **-nat·ed; -nat·ing** [NL *bombinatus*, pp. of *bombinare*, alter. of L *bombilare*, fr. *bombus*] : BUZZ, DRONE — **bom·bi·na·tion** \ˌbäm-bə-ˈnā-shən\ *n*

bomb·proof \ˈbäm-ˈprüf\ *adj* : safe from the force of bombs

bomb run *n* : the part of a bomber's attack during which the actual sighting for and release of bombs occurs

bomb·shell \ˈbäm-ˌshel\ *n* **1** : BOMB 1a **2** : one that stuns, amazes, or is devastatingly upsetting <the book was a political ~>

bomb·sight \-ˌsīt\ *n* : a sighting device for aiming bombs

bona fide \ˈbō-nə-ˌfīd, ˈbän-ə-; ˌbō-nə-ˈfīd-ē, -ˈfīd-ə\ *adj* [L, in good faith] **1** : made in good faith without fraud or deceit <a *bona fide* offer to purchase a farm> **2** : made with earnest intent : SINCERE **3** : neither specious nor counterfeit : GENIUNE <a *bona fide* antique> ***syn*** see AUTHENTIC ***ant*** counterfeit, bogus

bo·na fi·des \ˌbō-nə-ˈfīd-ˌēz\ *n* [L, good faith] : lack of fraud or deceit : SINCERITY <a man on whom suspicion had never rested and whose *bona fides* was unshakeable —Victor Canning>

bo·nan·za \bə-ˈnan-zə\ *n* [Sp, lit., calm, fr. ML *bonacia*, alter. of L *malacia* calm at sea, fr. Gk *malakia*, lit., softness, fr. *malakos* soft] **1** : an exceptionally large and rich ore shoot or pocket in veins carrying gold and silver **2 a** : something that is considered very valuable, profitable, or rewarding <achieved a box-office ~> **b** : an extremely large amount <expected a ~ of sympathy>

Bo·na·part·ism \ˈbō-nə-ˌpärt-ˌiz-əm\ *n* **1** : support of the French emperors Napoleon I, Napoleon III, or their dynasty **2** : a political movement associated chiefly with authoritarian rule usu. by a military leader ostensibly supported by a popular mandate — **Bo·na·part·ist** \-ˌpärt-əst\ *n or adj*

bon·bon \ˈbän-ˌbän\ *n* [F, (baby talk), redupl. of *bon* good, fr. L *bonus* — more at BOUNTY] : a candy with chocolate or fondant coating and fondant center that sometimes contains fruits and nuts

¹bond \ˈbänd\ *adj* [ME *bonde*, fr. *bonde* peasant, serf, fr. OE *bōnda* householder, fr. ON *bōndi*] *archaic* : bound in slavery

²bond *n* [ME *band*, *bond* — more at BAND] **1** : something that binds or restrains : FETTER **2** : a binding agreement : CONVENANT **3 a** : a band or cord used to tie something **b** : a material or device for binding **c** : a mechanism by means of which atoms, ions, or groups of atoms are held together in a molecule or crystal — usu. represented in formulas by a line or dot **d** : an adhesive, cementing material, or fusible ingredient that combines, unites, or strengthens **4** : a uniting or binding element or force <the ~*s* of friendship> **5 a** : an obligation made binding by a money forfeit; *also* : the amount of the money guarantee **b** : one who acts as bail or surety **c** : an interest-bearing certificate of public or private indebtedness <a 20-year ~ issue to finance a new courthouse> **d** : an insurance agreement pledging surety for financial loss caused to another by the act or default of a third person or by some contingency over which the third person may have no control **6** : the systematic lapping of brick in a wall **7** : the state of goods manufactured, stored, or transported under the care of bonded agencies until the duties or taxes on them are paid **8** : a 100-proof straight whiskey that has been aged at least four years under government supervision before being bottled — called also *bonded whiskey*

3**bond** *vt* **1 :** to lap (as brick) for solidity of construction **2 a :** to secure payment of duties and taxes on (goods) by giving a bond **b :** to convert into a debt secured by bonds **c :** to provide a bond for or cause to provide such a bond <~ an employee> **3 a :** to cause to adhere firmly **b :** to embed in a matrix **c :** to hold together in a molecule or crystal by chemical bonds ~ *vi* **:** to hold together or solidify by or as if by means of a bond or binder **:** COHERE — **bond·able** \'bän-də-bəl\ *adj* — **bond·er** *n*

bond·age \'bän-dij\ *n* **1 :** the tenure or service of a villein, serf, or slave **2 :** a state of being bound usu. by compulsion (as of law or mastery): as **a :** CAPTIVITY, SERFDOM <the ~ of the Israelites in Egypt> **b :** servitude or subjugation to a controlling person or force <young people in ~ to drugs> ***syn*** see SERVITUDE

bond·ed \'bänd-əd\ *adj* **:** composed of two or more layers of the same or different fabrics held together by an adhesive **:** LAMINATED <~ jersey>

bond·er·ize \'bän-də-,rīz\ *vt* **-ized; -iz·ing** [back-formation fr. *Bonderized,* a trademark] **:** to coat (steel) with a patented phosphate solution for protection against corrosion

bond·hold·er \'bänd-,hōl-dər\ *n* **:** one that holds a government or corporation bond

bond·maid \'bän(d)-,mād\ *n, archaic* **:** a female slave or bond servant

bond·man \'bän(d)-mən\ *n* **:** SLAVE, SERF

bond paper *n* **:** a strong durable paper orig. used for documents

bond servant *n* **:** one bound to service without wages; *also* **:** SLAVE

1**bonds·man** \'bän(d)z-mən\ *n* **:** BONDMAN

2**bondsman** *n* **:** one who assumes the responsibility of a bond **:** SURETY

bond·stone \'bän(d)-,stōn\ *n* **:** a stone long enough to extend through the full thickness of a wall to bind it together

bond·wom·an \'bän-,dwu̇m-ən\ *n* **:** a female slave

1**bone** \'bōn\ *n, often attrib* [ME *bon,* fr. OE *bān;* akin to OHG & ON *bein* bone] **1 a :** one of the hard parts of the skeleton of a vertebrate **b :** any of various hard animal substances or structures (as baleen or ivory) akin to or resembling bone **c :** the hard largely calcareous connective tissue of which the adult skeleton of most vertebrates is chiefly composed **2 a :** ESSENCE, CORE <cut expenses to the ~> **b :** the most deeply ingrained part **:** HEART — usu. used in pl. <knew in his ~*s* that it was an evil deed> **3** *pl* **a** (1) **:** SKELETON (2) **:** BODY <ran as fast as his ~*s* would carry him> (3) **:** CORPSE <inter a person's ~*s*> **b :** the basic design or framework (as of a play or novel) **4 :** MATTER, SUBJECT <a ~ of contention> **5 a** *pl* **:** thin bars of bone, ivory, or wood held in pairs between the fingers and used to produce musical rhythms **b :** a strip of whalebone or steel used to stiffen a corset or dress **c** *pl* **:** DICE **6 :** the bow wave of a ship when under way and esp. when traveling at a good speed — usu. used with the phrase *in her teeth* **7** *pl but sing or pl in constr, often cap* **:** an end man in a minstrel show who may perform on the bones **8 :** something that is designed to placate **:** SOP <throw a ~ to angry workers with a small pay increase> **9 :** a light beige — **boned** \'bōnd\ *adj* — **bone·less** \'bōn-ləs\ *adj* — **bone to pick :** a matter to argue or complain about

2**bone** *vb* **boned; bon·ing** *vt* **1 :** to remove the bones from <~ a fish> **2 :** to provide (a garment) with stays ~ *vi* **1 :** to study hard **:** GRIND <~ through medical school> **2 a :** to try to master necessary information in a short time **:** CRAM — used with *up* <better ~ up on those theories before the exam> **b :** to renew one's skill or refresh one's memory — used with *up* <~ up on the libretto before going to the opera>

3**bone** *adv* **:** ABSOLUTELY, UTTERLY <~ tired>

bone ash *n* **:** the white porous residue chiefly of tribasic calcium phosphate from bones calcined in air used esp. in making pottery and glass and in cleaning jewelry

bone black *n* **:** the black residue chiefly of tribasic calcium phosphate and carbon from bones calcined in closed vessels used esp. as a pigment or as a decolorizing adsorbent in sugar manufacturing — called also *bone char*

bone china *n* **:** translucent white china made with bone ash or calcium phosphate and characterized by whiteness

bone–dry \'bōn-'drī\ *adj* **1 :** very dry **2 a :** marked by the absence of intoxicating beverages <the wedding reception was ~> **b :** opposed to the sale of intoxicating beverages

bone·fish \'bōn-,fish\ *n* **1 a :** a slender silvery small-scaled fish (*Albula vulpes*) that is a notable sport and food fish of warm seas **b :** any of several fish of the same family (Albulidae) as the bonefish **2 :** LADYFISH 2

bone·head \-,hed\ *n* **:** a stupid person **:** NUMSKULL — **bone·head·ed** \-'hed-əd\ *adj*

bone meal *n* **:** fertilizer or feed made of crushed or ground bone

bon·er \'bō-nər\ *n* **1 :** one that bones **2 :** BLUNDER, HOWLER

bone·set \'bōn-,set\ *n* **:** any of several composite herbs (genus *Eupatorium*); *esp* **:** a perennial (*E. perfoliatum*) with opposite perfoliate leaves and white-rayed flower heads used in folk medicine

bone·set·ter \-,set-ər\ *n* **:** a person and usu. not a licensed physician who sets broken or dislocated bones

bone·yard \-,yärd\ *n* **:** a place where worn-out or irreparably damaged objects (as cars) are collected to await disposal

bon·fire \'bän-,fī(ə)r\ *n* [ME *bonefire* a fire of bones, fr. *bon* bone + *fire*] **:** a large fire built in the open air

1**bong** \'bäŋ, 'bȯŋ\ *n* [imit.] **:** the deep resonant sound esp. of a bell

2**bong** *vb* **:** RING

bon·go \'bäŋ-(,)gō, 'bȯŋ-\ *n, pl* **bongos** *also* **bongoes** [AmerSp *bongó*] **:** one of a pair of small tuned drums played with the hands — **bon·go·ist** \-,gō-əst\ *n*

bon·ho·mie \,bän-ə-'mē, ,bō-nə-\ *n* [F *bonhomie,* fr. *bonhomme* good-natured man, fr. *bon* good + *homme* man] **:** good-natured easy friendliness **:** GENIALITY

bon·i·face \'bän-ə-fəs, -,fās\ *n* [*Boniface,* innkeeper in *The Beaux' Stratagem* (1707) by George Farquhar] **:** the proprietor of a hotel, nightclub, or restaurant

boning knife *n* **:** a short knife with a narrow blade and a sharp point for boning meat or fish

bo·ni·to \bə-'nēt-(,)ō, -'nēt-ə\ *n, pl* **-tos** *or* **-to** [Sp, fr. *bonito* pretty, fr. L *bonus* good] **:** any of various medium-sized tunas (esp. genera *Sarda* and *Euthynnus*) intermediate between the smaller mackerels and the larger tunas

bon·kers \'bäŋ-kərz\ *adj* [origin unknown] *chiefly Brit* **:** CRAZY, MAD

bon mot \bōⁿ-'mō\ *n, pl* **bons mots** \bōⁿ-'mō(z)\ *or* **bon mots** \-'mō(z)\ [F, lit., good word] **:** a clever remark **:** WITTICISM

bonne \'bȯn\ *n* [F, fr. fem. of *bon*] **:** a French nursemaid or maidservant

1**bon·net** \'bän-ət\ *n* [ME *bonet,* fr. MF, fr. ML *abonnis*] **1 a** (1) *chiefly Scot* **:** a man's or boy's cap (2) **:** a brimless Scotch cap of seamless woolen fabric — compare TAM-O'-SHANTER 2 **b :** a cloth or straw hat tied under the chin and worn by women and small children **2 a :** an additional piece of canvas laced to the foot of a jib or foresail **b** *Brit* **:** an automobile hood **c :** a cover for an open fireplace or a cowl or hood to increase the draft of a chimney **d :** a metal covering for valve chambers, hydrants, or ventilators

2**bonnet** *vt* **:** to provide with or dress in a bonnet

bon·ny \'bän-ē\ *adj* **bon·ni·er; -est** [ME *bonie,* fr. OF *bon* good, fr. L *bonus* — more at BOUNTY] *chiefly Brit* **:** ATTRACTIVE, EXCELLENT — **bon·ni·ly** \'bän-ə-lē\ *adv*

bon·ny·clab·ber \'bän-ē-,klab-ər\ *n* [IrGael *bainne clabair,* fr. *bainne* milk + *clabair,* gen. of *clabar* sour thick milk] *North & Midland* **:** 1CLABBER

bon·sai \(')bōn-'sī, 'bōn-,\ *n, pl* **bonsai** [Jap] **:** a potted plant (as a tree) dwarfed by special methods of culture; *also* **:** the art of growing such a plant

bon·spiel \'bän-,spēl\ *n* [perh. fr. D *bond* league + *spel* game] **:** a match or tournament between curling clubs

bon ton \(')bän-'tän, 'bän-,\ *n* [F, lit., good tone] **1 a :** fashionable manner or style <admired the worldiness and *bon ton* of the characters> **b :** the fashionable or proper thing <it was considered *bon ton* to go to the event> **2 :** high society

bo·nus \'bō-nəs\ *n* [L, good — more at BOUNTY] **1 :** something given in addition to what is usual or strictly due **2 a** *Brit* **:** DIVIDEND 1b **b :** money or an equivalent given in addition to an employee's usual compensation **c :** a premium (as of stock) given by a corporation to a purchaser of its securities, to a promoter, or to an employee **d** (1) **:** a government subsidy to an industry (2) **:** a government payment to war veterans **e :** a sum in excess of salary given an athlete for signing with a professional team **3 :** a sum of money in addition to interest or royalties charged for the granting of a loan or privilege to a company or for the lease or transfer of property

bon vi·vant \,bän-vē-'vänt, ,bōⁿ-vē-'väⁿ\ *n, pl* **bons vivants** \,bän-vē-'vän(t)s, ,bōⁿ-vē-'väⁿ(z)\ *or* **bon vivants** *same*\ [F, lit., good liver] **:** a person having cultivated, refined, and sociable tastes esp. in respect to pleasures of the table ***syn*** see EPICURE

bon voy·age \,bōⁿv-,wi-'äzh, -,wä-'yäzh; ,bōⁿ-,vȯi-'äzh, ,bän-\ *n* [F] **:** FAREWELL — often used interjectionally

bony *or* **bon·ey** \'bō-nē\ *adj* **bon·i·er; -est 1 a :** consisting of bone **b :** resembling bone **2 a :** full of bones <a ~ piece of fish> **b :** having prominent bones <a rugged ~ face> **3 a :** SKINNY, SCRAWNY **b :** BARREN, LEAN

bony fish *n* **:** TELEOST

bony labyrinth *n* **:** the cavity in the temporal bone that contains the membranous labyrinth of the ear

bonze \'bänz\ *n* [F, fr. Pg *bonzo,* fr. Jap *bonsō*] **:** a Buddhist monk

1**boo** \'bü\ *interj* [ME *bo*] — used to express contempt or disapproval or to startle or frighten

2**boo** *n, pl* **boos 1 :** a shout of disapproval or contempt **2 :** any sound at all — usu. used in negative constructions <never said ~>

3**boo** *vi* **:** to deride esp. by uttering *boo* ~ *vt* **:** to express disapproval of by booing <the crowd ~*ed* the referee>

4**boo** *n* [origin unknown] **:** MARIJUANA

boob \'büb\ *n* [short for *booby*] **1 :** a stupid awkward person **:** SIMPLETON **2 :** BOOR, PHILISTINE **3 :** BREAST — often considered vulgar

boob·oi·sie \,büb-,wä-'zē\ *n* [*boob* + *-oisie* (as in *bourgeoisie*)] **:** a class of the general public that is composed of boobs

boo–boo \'bü-(,)bü\ *n, pl* **boo–boos** [prob. baby-talk alter. of *boohoo,* imitation of the sound of weeping] **1 :** a usu. trivial physical injury (as a bruise or scratch) esp. on a child **2 :** a foolish mistake **:** BLUNDER

boob tube *n* **:** TELEVISION; *specif* **:** a television set

1**boo·by** \'bü-bē\ *n, pl* **boobies** [modif. of Sp *bobo,* fr. L *balbus* stammering, prob. of imit. origin] **1 :** an awkward foolish person **:** DOPE **2 :** any of several small gannets (genus *Sula*) of tropical seas **3 :** the poorest performer or lowest scorer in a group

booby 2

2**boo·by** \'bu̇b-ē, 'büb-\ *n, pl* **boobies** [alter. of *bubby,* perh. imit. of the noise made by a sucking infant] **:** BREAST — often considered vulgar

booby hatch *n* **1 :** an insane asylum **2 :** a place thought to resemble a booby hatch

booby prize *n* **1 :** an award for the poorest performance in a game or competition **2 :** an acknowledgment of notable inferiority

booby trap *n* **1 :** a trap for the unwary or unsuspecting **:** PITFALL **2 :** a concealed explosive device contrived to go off when some harmless-looking object is touched — **boo·by–trap** *vt*

boo·dle \'büd-ᵊl\ *n* [D *boedel* estate, lot, fr. MD; akin to ON *būth* booth] **1 :** a collection or lot of persons **:** CABOODLE **2 a :** bribe money **b :** a large amount esp. of money

boog·er \'bu̇g-ər\ *n* [alter. of E dial. *buggard, boggart,* fr. [1]*bug* + *-ard*] : BOGEYMAN

boo·gey·man \'bu̇g-ē-ˌman, 'bü-gē-\ *or* **boog·er·man** \'bu̇g-ər-\ *n* [*boogey,* alter. of *booger* + *man*] : BOGEYMAN

boo·gie–woo·gie \ˌbu̇g-ē-'wu̇g-ē, ˌbü-gē-'wü-gē\ *n* [origin unknown] : a percussive style of playing blues on the piano characterized by a steady rhythmic ground bass of eighth notes in quadruple time and a simple often improvised melody — called also *boogie*

[1]**book** \'bu̇k\ *n* [ME, fr. OE *bōc;* akin to OHG *buoh* book, OE *bōc* beech; prob. fr. the early Germanic practice of carving runic characters on beech wood tablets — more at BEECH] **1 a :** a set of written sheets of skin or paper or tablets of wood or ivory **b :** a set of written, printed, or blank sheets bound together into a volume **c :** a long written or printed literary composition **d :** a major division of a treatise or literary work **e :** a volume of business records (as a ledger or journal) — often used in pl. <their *~s* show a profit> **2** *cap* **:** BIBLE **3 :** something regarded as a source of enlightenment or instruction <her face was an open ~> **4 a :** the total available knowledge and experience that can be brought to bear on a task or problem <tried every trick in the ~ to win the election> **b :** the standards or authority relevant in a situation <the factory is run according to the ~> **5 a :** all the charges that can be made against an accused person <they threw the ~ at him> **b :** a position from which one must answer for certain acts **:** ACCOUNT <the police try to bring criminals to ~> **6 a :** LIBRETTO **b :** the script of a play **c :** the repertory of an orchestra or a musician **7 :** a packet of commodities bound together <a ~ of matches> **8 a** (1) **:** BOOKMAKER (2) **:** a bookmaker's business or base of operations **b :** the bets registered by a bookmaker **9 :** the number of tricks a card player or side must win before any trick can have scoring value — **book·ful** \-ˌfu̇l\ *n* — **in one's book :** in one's own opinion — **in one's good books :** in favor with one — **one for the book :** an act or occurrence worth noting — **on the books :** on the records

[2]**book** *vt* **1 a :** to enter, write, or register so as to engage transportation or reserve lodgings <he is *~ed* to sail Monday> **b :** to schedule engagements for <~ the band for a week> **c :** to set aside time for **d :** to reserve in advance <~ two seats at the theater> **2 :** to enter charges against in a police register ~ *vi* **1 :** to reserve something in advance <~ through your travel agent> **2** *chiefly Brit* **:** to register in a hotel — **book·er** *n*

[3]**book** *adj* **1 :** derived from books and not from practical experience <~ farming> **2 :** shown by books of account

book·bind·ing \'bu̇k-ˌbin-diŋ\ *n* **1 :** the binding of a book **2 :** the art or trade of binding books — **book·bind·er** \-ˌbin-dər\ *n* — **book·bind·ery** \-d(ə-)rē\ *n*

book·case \-ˌkās\ *n* **:** a piece of furniture consisting of shelves to hold books

book·end \-ˌend\ *n* **:** a support placed at the end of a row of books

book·ie \'bu̇k-ē\ *n* [by shortening & alter.] **:** BOOKMAKER 2

book·ing \'bu̇k-iŋ\ *n* **1 :** the act of one that books **2 :** an engagement or scheduled performance <she has *~s* for several concerts> **3 :** RESERVATION; *esp* **:** one for transportation, entertainment, or lodging

booking office *n, chiefly Brit* **:** a ticket office; *esp* **:** one in a railroad station

book·ish \'bu̇k-ish\ *adj* **1 a :** of or relating to books **b :** fond of books and reading **2 a :** inclined to rely on book knowledge rather than practical experience **b :** literary and formal as opposed to colloquial and informal <many English words derived from Latin have a ~ flavor> **c :** given to literary or scholarly pursuits; *also* **:** affectedly learned ***syn*** see PEDANTIC — **book·ish·ly** *adv* — **book·ish·ness** *n*

book·keep·er \'bu̇k-ˌkē-pər\ *n* **:** one who records the accounts or transactions of a business — **book·keep·ing** \-piŋ\ *n*

book·let \'bu̇k-lət\ *n* **:** a little book; *esp* **:** PAMPHLET

book louse *n* **:** a minute wingless insect (order Corrodentia); *esp* **:** an insect (as *Liposcelis divinatorius*) injurious esp. to books

book lung *n* **:** a saccular breathing organ in many arachnids containing numerous thin folds of membrane arranged like the leaves of a book

book·mak·er \'bu̇k-ˌmā-kər\ *n* **1 a :** a printer, binder, or designer of books **b :** one who compiles books from the writings of others **2 :** one who determines odds and receives and pays off bets — **book·mak·ing** \-kiŋ\ *n*

book·man \-mən\ *n* **1 :** one who is interested in books; *esp* **:** LITTERATEUR **2 :** one who sells books

book·mark \-ˌmärk\ *or* **book·mark·er** \-ˌmär-kər\ *n* **:** a marker for finding a place in a book

book–match \-ˌmach\ *vt* **:** to match the grains of (as two sheets of veneer) so that one sheet seems to be the mirrored image of the other

book·mo·bile \'bu̇k-mō-ˌbēl\ *n* [*book* + auto*mobile*] **:** a truck that serves as a traveling library

book of account : a book of business records (as a ledger, journal, or register) that constitutes an integral part of a system of accounts

Book of Common Prayer : the service book of the Anglican Communion

book of original entry : that one of the books of account of an organization (as a cashbook or register of sales) in which transactions are first recorded

book·plate \'bu̇k-ˌplāt\ *n* **:** a book owner's identification label that is usu. pasted to the inside front cover of a book

book review *n* **:** a usu. written critical estimate of a book

book·sell·er \'bu̇k-ˌsel-ər\ *n* **:** one who sells books; *esp* **:** the proprietor of a bookstore — **book·sell·ing** \-ˌsel-iŋ\ *n*

book·shelf \-ˌshelf\ *n* **:** an open shelf for holding books

book·stall \-ˌstȯl\ *n* **1 :** a stall where books are sold **2** *chiefly Brit* **:** NEWSSTAND

book·store \-ˌstō(ə)r, -ˌstȯ(ə)r\ *n* **:** a place of business where books are the main item offered for sale — called also *bookshop*

book value *n* **:** the value of something as shown by the books of account of the business owning it; *esp* **:** a value of a share of capital stock consisting of its equity in corporate assets usu. exclusive of goodwill less its share in corporate liabilities

book·worm \'bu̇k-ˌwərm\ *n* **1 :** any of various insect larvae (as of a beetle) that feed on the binding and paste of books **2 :** a person unusually devoted to reading and study

Bool·ean \'bü-lē-ən\ *adj* [George *Boole* †1860 E mathematician] **:** of, relating to, or being a logical combinatorial system that represents symbolically relationships (as those implied by the linguistic operators AND, OR, and NOT) between entities (as sets, propositions, or on-off computer circuit elements) <~ algebra> <~ expression> <~ search strategy for information retrieval>

[1]**boom** \'büm\ *n* [D, tree, beam; akin to OHG *boum* tree — more at BEAM] **1 :** a long spar used to extend the foot of a sail or facilitate handling of cargo or mooring **2 a :** a long beam projecting from the mast of a derrick to support or guide an object to be lifted or swung **b :** a long movable arm used to manipulate a microphone **3 :** a line of connected floating timbers across a river or enclosing an area of water to keep sawlogs together; *also* **:** the enclosed logs **4 :** a chain cable or line of spars extended across a river or the mouth of a harbor to defend it by obstructing navigation **5 :** a spar or outrigger connecting the tail surfaces and the main supporting structure of an airplane

[2]**boom** *vb* [imit.] *vi* **1 :** to make a deep hollow sound **2 a :** to increase in importance or esteem **b :** to experience a sudden rapid growth and expansion usu. with an increase in prices <business was *~ing*> **c :** to develop rapidly in population and importance <California *~ed* when gold was discovered there> ~ *vt* **1 :** to cause to resound — often used with *out* <his voice *~s* out the lyrics> **2 :** to cause a rapid growth or increase of **:** BOOST

[3]**boom** *n* **1 :** a booming sound or cry **2 :** a rapid expansion or increase: as **a :** a general movement in support of a candidate for office **b :** rapid settlement and development of a town or district **c :** a rapid widespread expansion of economic activity

boom·er *n* **1 :** one that booms **2 :** one that joins a rush of settlers to a boom area **3 :** a transient worker (as a bridge builder)

boo·mer·ang \'bü-mə-ˌraŋ\ *n* [native name in Australia] **1 :** a bent or angular throwing club which can be thrown so as to return near the starting point **2 :** an act or utterance that backfires on its originator — **boomerang** *vi*

boomerangs 1

boom·let \'büm-lət\ *n* **:** a small boom; *specif* **:** a sudden often short-term increase or expansion <a stock market ~>

boomy \'bü-mē\ *adj* **boom·i·er; -est 1 :** of, relating to, or characterized by an economic boom **2 :** having an excessive accentuation on the tones of lower pitch in reproduced sound

[1]**boon** \'bün\ *n* [ME, fr. ON *bōn* petition; akin to OE *bēn* prayer, *bannan* to summon — more at BAN] **1 :** BENEFIT, FAVOR; *esp* **:** one that is given in answer to a request **2 :** a timely benefit **:** BLESSING

[2]**boon** *adj* [ME *bon,* fr. MF, good — more at BONNY] **1** *archaic* **:** BOUNTEOUS, BENIGN **2 :** MERRY, CONVIVIAL <a ~ companion>

boon·docks \'bün-ˌdäks\ *n pl* [Tag *bundok* mountain] **1 :** rough country filled with dense brush **:** JUNGLE **2 :** a rural area **:** STICKS

boon·dog·gle \'bün-ˌdäg-əl, -ˌdȯg-\ *n* [coined by Robert H. Link †1957 Am scoutmaster] **1 :** a handicraft article made of leather or wicker **2 :** a trivial, useless, or wasteful project or activity — **boondoggle** *vi* — **boon·dog·gler** \-(ə-)lər\ *n*

boon·ies \'bü-nēz\ *n pl, slang* **:** BOONDOCKS 2

boor \'bu̇(ə)r\ *n* [D *boer;* akin to OE *būan* to dwell — more at BOWER] **1 :** PEASANT **2 :** BOER **3 a :** YOKEL **b :** a rude or insensitive person

boor·ish \'bu̇(ə)r-ish\ *adj* **:** resembling or befitting a boor (as in crude insensitivity) — **boor·ish·ly** *adv* — **boor·ish·ness** *n*

syn BOORISH, CHURLISH, LOUTISH, CLOWNISH *shared meaning element* **:** uncouth in manner or appearance ***ant*** gentlemanly

[1]**boost** \'büst\ *vb* [origin unknown] *vt* **1 :** to push or shove up from below **2 a :** INCREASE, RAISE <plans to ~ production by 30 percent next year> **b :** to aid or assist esp. towards progress or increase <an extra holiday to ~ morale> **3 :** to promote the cause or interests of **:** PLUG <a campaign to ~ the new fashions> **4 :** to increase in force, pressure, or amount; *esp* **:** to raise the voltage of or across (an electric circuit) **4** *slang* **:** STEAL, SHOPLIFT ~ *vi, slang* **:** SHOPLIFT ***syn*** see LIFT

[2]**boost** *n* **1 :** a push upwards **2 :** an increase in amount **3 :** an act that brings help or encouragement

boost·er \'bü-stər\ *n* **1 :** one that boosts **2 :** an enthusiastic supporter **3 :** an auxiliary device for increasing force, power, or pressure **4 :** a radio-frequency amplifier for a radio or television receiving set **5 :** the first stage of a multistage rocket providing thrust for the launching and the initial part of the flight **6 :** a substance that increases the effectiveness of a medicament; *esp* **:** a supplementary dose of an immunizing agent to increase immunity **7** *slang* **:** SHOPLIFTER

boost·er·ism \-ə-ˌriz-əm\ *n* **:** the activities and attitudes characteristic of boosters

[1]**boot** \'büt\ *n* [ME, fr. OE *bōt* remedy; akin to OE *betera* better] **1** *archaic* **:** DELIVERANCE **2** *chiefly dial* **:** something to equalize a trade **3** *obs* **:** AVAIL — **to boot :** BESIDES

[2]**boot** *vb, archaic* **:** AVAIL, PROFIT

[3]**boot** *n* [ME, fr. MF *bote*] **1 :** a covering of leather or rubber for the foot and leg **2 :** an instrument of torture used to crush the leg and foot **3 :** a sheath or casing resembling a boot that provides a protective covering for the foot or leg or for an object or part resembling a leg; *also* **:** a thick patch for the inside of a tire casing

4 : a sheath enclosing the inflorescence **5** *Brit* **:** an automobile trunk **6 a :** a blow delivered by or as if by a booted foot **:** KICK; *also* **:** a rude discharge or dismissal **b :** pleasure or enjoyment esp. of a momentary kind **:** BANG <got a big ~ out of the joke> **7 :** a navy or marine recruit undergoing basic training

4boot *vt* **1 :** to put boots on **2 a :** KICK **b :** to eject or discharge summarily — often used with *out* <was ~*ed* out of office> **3 :** to make an error on (a grounder in baseball)

5boot *n* [¹*boot*] *archaic* **:** BOOTY, PLUNDER

boot·black \ˈbüt-ˌblak\ *n* **:** one who shines shoes

boot camp *n* **:** a navy or marine camp for basic training

boot·ed \ˈbüt-əd\ *adj* **:** wearing boots

boo·tee *or* **boo·tie** \bü-ˈtē, *of infants' footwear* ˈbüt-ē\ *n* **:** a boot or sock with a short leg; *esp* **:** an infant's knitted or crocheted sock

Bo·ö·tes \bō-ˈōt-ēz\ *n* [L (gen. *Boötis*), fr. Gk *Boōtēs*, lit., plowman, fr. *bous* head of cattle — more at COW] **:** a northern constellation containing the bright star Arcturus

booth \ˈbüth, *esp Brit* ˈbüth\ *n, pl* **booths** \ˈbüthz, ˈbüths\ [ME *bothe*, of Scand origin; akin to ON *būth* booth; akin to OE *būan* to dwell — more at BOWER] **1 :** a temporary shelter for livestock or field workers **2 a :** a stall or stand (as at a fair) for the sale or exhibition of goods **b** (1) **:** a small enclosure affording privacy for one person at a time <a telephone ~> (2) **:** a small enclosure that separates its occupant from patrons or customers <a ticket ~> **c :** a restaurant seating arrangement consisting of a table between two backed benches

boot·jack \ˈbüt-ˌjak\ *n* **:** a metal or wood device shaped like the letter V and used in pulling off boots

boot·lace \-ˌlās\ *n, Brit* **:** SHOELACE

1boot·leg \-ˌleg, -ˌlāg\ *n* **1 :** the upper part of a boot **2 :** something bootlegged; *specif* **:** MOONSHINE **3 :** a football play in which the quarterback fakes a handoff, hides the ball on his hip, and rolls out — compare DRAW 8 — **bootleg** *adj*

2bootleg *vt* **1 a :** to carry (alcoholic liquor) on one's person illegally **b :** to manufacture, sell, or transport for sale (alcoholic liquor) contrary to law **2 a :** to produce or sell illicitly **b** (1) **:** SMUGGLE (2) **:** to obtain secretly or illicitly ~ *vi* **1 :** to engage in bootlegging **2 :** to run a bootleg play in football

boot·less \ˈbüt-ləs\ *adj* **:** USELESS, UNPROFITABLE — **boot·less·ly** *adv* — **boot·less·ness** *n*

boot·lick \-ˌlik\ *vt* **:** to fawn on obsequiously ~ *vi* **:** to attempt to gain favor by a cringing or flattering manner — **bootlick** *n* — **boot·lick·er** *n*

boot·print \-ˌprint\ *n* **:** an impression made by a boot

boots \ˈbüts\ *n pl but sing or pl in constr* [fr. pl. of ³*boot*] *Brit* **:** a servant who shines shoes esp. in a hotel

1boot·strap \ˈbüt-ˌstrap\ *n* **1 :** a looped strap sewed at the side or the rear top of a boot to help in pulling it on **2** *pl* **:** unaided efforts — often used in the phrase *by one's own bootstraps*

2bootstrap *adj* **1 :** carried out with minimum resources or advantages **:** SELF-RELIANT <the city recovered from the flood by the ~ method> **2 :** using its own action to initiate or sustain itself <a ~ operation to load a computer>

boo·ty \ˈbüt-ē\ *n, pl* **booties** [modif. of MF *butin*, fr. MLG *būte* exchange] **1 :** plunder taken (as in war); *esp* **:** plunder taken on land as distinguished from prizes taken at sea **2 :** a rich gain or prize *syn* see SPOIL

1booze \ˈbüz\ *vi* **boozed; booz·ing** [ME *bousen*, fr. MD or MFlem *būsen*; akin to MHG *būs* swelling] **:** to drink intoxicating liquor to excess — **booz·er** \ˈbü-zər\ *n* — **booz·i·ly** \-zə-lē\ *adv* — **boozy** \-zē\ *adj*

2booze *n* **1 :** intoxicating drink; *esp* **:** hard liquor **2 :** a drinking spree

1bop \ˈbäp\ *vt* **bopped; bop·ping** [imit.] **:** HIT, SOCK

2bop *n* **:** a blow (as with the fist or a club) that strikes a person

3bop *n* [short for *bebop*] **:** jazz characterized by unusual chord structures, accents on the upbeat, a lengthened melodic line, and harmonic complexity and innovation — **bop·per** *n*

BOQ *abbr* bachelor officers' quarters

bor *abbr* borough

bo·ra \ˈbōr-ə, ˈbȯr-\ *n* [It. dial., fr. L *boreas*] **:** a violent cold northerly wind of the Adriatic

bo·rac·ic acid \bə-ˌras-ik-\ *n* [ML *borac-*, *borax* borax] **:** BORIC ACID

bor·age \ˈbȯr-ij, ˈbär-\ *n* [ME, fr. MF *bourage*] **:** a coarse hairy blue-flowered European herb (*Borago officinalis* of the family Boraginaceae, the borage family) used medicinally and in salads

bo·rane \ˈbō(ə)r-ˌän, ˈbȯ(ə)r-\ *n* [ISV, fr. *boron*] **:** a compound of boron and hydrogen or a derivative of such a compound

bo·rate \-ˌāt\ *n* **:** a salt or ester of a boric acid

bo·rat·ed \-ˌāt-əd\ *adj* **:** mixed or impregnated with borax or boric acid

bo·rax \ˈbō(ə)r-ˌaks, ˈbȯ(ə)r-, -əks\ *n* [ME *boras*, fr. MF, fr. ML *borac-*, *borax*, fr. Ar *būraq*, fr. Per *būrah*] **:** a white crystalline compound that consists of a hydrated sodium borate $Na_2B_4O_7 \cdot 10H_2O$, that occurs as a mineral or is prepared from other minerals, and that is used esp. as a flux, cleansing agent, and water softener and as a preservative

bo·ra·zon \ˈbōr-ə-ˌzän, ˈbȯr-\ *n* [*boron* + *az-* + *-on*] **:** a substance that consists of a boron nitride BN of cubical crystallization and is as hard as diamond but more resistant to high temperature

Bor·deaux \bȯr-ˈdō\ *n, pl* **Bor·deaux** \-ˈdōz\ **:** white or red wine of the Bordeaux region of France

bor·deaux mixture \bȯr-ˈdō-, ˈbȯrd-ˌō-\ *n, often cap B* **:** a fungicide made by reaction of copper sulfate, lime, and water

bor·del \ˈbȯrd-ᵊl\ *n* [ME, fr. MF, fr. OF, fr. *borde* hut, of Gmc origin; akin to OE *bord* board] *archaic* **:** BROTHEL

bor·del·lo \bȯr-ˈdel-(ˌ)ō\ *n, pl* **-los** [It, fr. OF *bordel*] **:** BROTHEL

1bor·der \ˈbȯrd-ər\ *n* [ME *bordure*, fr. MF, fr. OF, fr. *border* to border, fr. *bort* border, of Gmc origin; akin to OE *bord*] **1 :** an outer part or edge **2 :** BOUNDARY, FRONTIER <crossed the ~ into Italy> **3 :** a narrow bed of planted ground along the edge of a garden or walk <a ~ of tulips> **4 :** an ornamental design at the edge of a fabric or rug **5 :** a plain or decorative margin around printed matter — **bor·dered** \-ərd\ *adj*

syn BORDER, MARGIN, VERGE, EDGE, RIM, BRIM, BRINK *shared meaning element* **:** a line or outer part that marks the limit of something

2border *vb* **bor·dered; bor·der·ing** \ˈbȯrd-(ə-)riŋ\ *vt* **1 :** to put a border on <~ a bedspread with fringe> **2 :** to touch at the edge or boundary **:** BOUND <an airport ~*s* the city on the south> ~ *vi* **1 :** to lie on the border <the U.S. ~*s* on Canada> **2 :** to approach the nature of a specified thing **:** VERGE <his devotion to his dog ~*s* on the ridiculous> — **bor·der·er** \-ər-ər\ *n*

bor·de·reau \ˌbȯrd-ə-ˈrō\ *n, pl* **-reaux** \-ˈrō(z)\ [F] **:** a detailed note or memorandum of account; *esp* **:** one containing an enumeration of documents

bor·der·land \ˈbȯrd-ər-ˌland\ *n* **1 a :** territory at or near a border **:** FRONTIER **b :** an outlying region **:** FRINGE <lives on the ~ of society> **2 :** a vague intermediate state or region <the ~ between fantasy and reality>

bor·der·line \-ˌlīn\ *adj* **1 :** situated at or near a border line **2 a :** situated between two points or states **:** INTERMEDIATE **b :** not quite average, standard, or normal <a person of ~ intelligence> **c :** not quite meeting accepted patterns (as of morality or good taste); *esp* **:** verging on the indecent <a ~ joke> **d :** having only marginal certainty or validity <the new theory is of ~ value>

border line *n* **:** a line of demarcation

Border terrier *n* **:** a small terrier of British origin with a harsh dense coat and close undercoat

bor·dure \ˈbȯr-jər\ *n* [ME] **:** a border surrounding a heraldic shield

1bore \ˈbō(ə)r, ˈbȯ(ə)r\ *vb* **bored; bor·ing** [ME *boren*, fr. OE *borian*; akin to OHG *borōn* to bore, L *forare* to bore, *ferire* to strike] *vt* **1 :** to pierce with or as if with a rotary tool **2 :** to form or construct by boring ~ *vi* **1 a :** to make a hole by boring **b :** to sink a mine shaft or well **2 a :** to make one's way laboriously <we *bored* through the jostling crowd> **b :** to move ahead steadily <the sturdy ship continued to ~ through towering waves>

2bore *n* **1 :** a hole made by or as if by boring **2 a :** an interior lengthwise cylindrical cavity **b :** the interior tube of a gun **3 a :** the size of a hole **b :** the interior diameter of a tube **:** CALIBER, GAUGE **c :** the diameter of an engine cylinder

3bore *past of* BEAR

4bore *n* [(assumed) ME *bore* wave, fr. ON *bāra*] **:** a tidal flood with a high abrupt front

5bore *n* [origin unknown] **:** one that causes boredom: as **a :** a tiresome person **b :** something that is devoid of interest

6bore *vt* **bored; bor·ing :** to weary with ennui or tedium <a good entertainer never ~*s* his audience>

bo·re·al \ˈbōr-ē-əl, ˈbȯr-\ *adj* [ME *boriall*, fr. LL *borealis*, fr. L *boreas* north wind, north, fr. Gk, fr. *Boreas*] **1 :** of, relating to, or located in northern regions **2** *cap* **:** of, relating to, or growing in northern and mountainous parts of the northern hemisphere

Bo·re·as \-ē-əs\ *n* [L, fr. Gk] **1 :** the god of the north wind in Greek mythology **2 :** the north wind personified

bore·dom \ˈbō(ə)rd-əm, ˈbȯ(ə)rd-\ *n* **:** the state of being bored **:** ENNUI

bor·er \ˈbōr-ər, ˈbȯr-\ *n* **:** one that bores: as **a :** a worker who bores holes **b :** a tool used for boring **c** (1) **:** SHIPWORM (2) **:** an insect that as larva or adult bores in the woody parts of plants

bo·ric \ˈbōr-ik, ˈbȯr-\ *adj* **:** of or containing boron

boric acid *n* **:** a white crystalline acid H_3BO_3 easily obtained from its salts and used esp. as a weak antiseptic

bo·ride \ˈbō(ə)r-ˌīd, ˈbȯ(ə)r-\ *n* **:** a binary compound of boron usu. with a more electropositive element or radical

bor·ing \ˈbō(ə)r-iŋ, ˈbȯ(ə)r-\ *adj* **:** causing boredom **:** TIRESOME — **bor·ing·ly** \-iŋ-lē\ *adv* — **bor·ing·ness** *n*

born \ˈbȯ(ə)rn\ *adj* [ME, fr. OE *boren*, pp. of *beran* to carry — more at BEAR] **1 a :** brought into existence by or as if by birth **b :** NATIVE — usu. used in combination <American-*born*> **c :** deriving or resulting from — usu. used in combination <poverty-*born* crime> **2 a :** having from birth specified qualities <a ~ leader> **b :** being in specified circumstances from birth <nobly ~> **3 :** destined from or as if from birth <~ to succeed>

borne *past part of* BEAR

bor·ne·ol \ˈbȯr-nē-ˌȯl, -ˌōl\ *n* [ISV, fr. *Borneo*, island in the Malay archipelago] **:** a cystalline cyclic alcohol $C_{10}H_{17}OH$ that is known in three optically different forms, is found in essential oils, and is used esp. in perfumery

born·ite \ˈbȯ(ə)r-ˌnīt\ *n* [G *bornit*, fr. Ignaz von *Born* †1791 Austrian mineralogist] **:** a brittle metallic-looking mineral Cu_5FeS_4 consisting of a sulfide of copper and iron and constituting a valuable ore of copper

bo·ron \ˈbō(ə)r-ˌän, ˈbȯ(ə)r-\ *n* [*borax* + *-on* (as in *carbon*)] **:** a trivalent metalloid element found in nature only in combination and used in metallurgy and in nucleonics — see ELEMENT table — **bo·ron·ic** \bȯr-ˈän-ik, bōr-\ *adj*

bo·ro·sil·i·cate \ˌbōr-ō-ˈsil-ə-ˌkāt, ˌbȯr-, -ˈsil-i-kət\ *n* [ISV *boron* + *silicate*] **:** a silicate containing boron in the anion and occurring naturally

bor·ough \ˈbər-(ˌ)ō, ˈbə-(ˌ)rō, -ə(-w), -rə(-w)\ *n* [ME *burgh*, fr. OE *burg* fortified town; akin to OHG *burg* fortified place, OE *beorg* mountain — more at BARROW] **1 a :** a medieval fortified group of houses forming a town with special duties and privileges **b :** a town or urban constituency in Great Britain that sends a member to Parliament **c :** an urban area in Great Britain incorporated for purposes of self-government **2 a :** a municipal corporation proper in some states (as New Jersey and Minnesota) corresponding to the incorporated town or village of the other states **b :** one of the five constituent political divisions of New York City **3 :** a civil division of the state of Alaska corresponding to a county in most other states

borough English *n* **:** a custom formerly existing in parts of England by which the lands of a tenant intestate descend to the youngest son

bor·row \ˈbär-(ˌ)ō, ˈbȯr-, -ə(-w)\ *vb* [ME *borwen*, fr. OE *borgian*; akin to OE *beorgan* to preserve — more at BURY] *vt* **1 :** to receive with the implied or expressed intention of returning the same or an equivalent <~ a book> **2 a :** to appropriate for one's own use <~ a metaphor> **b :** DERIVE, ADOPT **3 :** to take (one) from a figure of the minuend in arithmetical subtraction in order to add as 10 to the next lower denomination **4 :** to introduce into one language from another **5 :** to dig from a borrow pit **6** *dial* **:** LEND ~ *vi* **:** to borrow something — **bor·row·er** \-ə-wər\ *n*

bor·row·ing \'bär-ə-wiŋ, 'bȯr-\ *n* **:** something borrowed; *esp* **:** a word or phrase adopted from one language into another

borrow pit *n* **:** an excavated area where material has been dug for use as fill at another location

Bors \'bȯ(ə)rz\ *n* **:** a knight of the Round Table and nephew of Lancelot in Malory's *Morte d'Arthur*

borscht *or* **borsch** \'bȯ(ə)rsh(t)\ *n* [Russ *borshch*] **:** a soup made primarily of beets and served hot or cold often with sour cream

borscht circuit *or* **borsch circuit** *n, often cap B&C* [fr. the popularity of borscht on menus of the resorts] **:** the theaters and nightclubs associated with the Jewish summer resorts in the Catskills — called also *borscht belt*

bor·stal \'bȯr-stᵊl\ *n* [*Borstal,* E village where the first such institution was set up] *Brit* **:** a reformatory for delinquent boys and girls between the ages of 16 and 21

bort \'bȯ(ə)rt\ *n* [prob. fr. D *boort*] **:** imperfectly crystallized diamond or diamond fragments used as an abrasive

bor·zoi \'bȯr-ˌzȯi\ *n* [Russ *borzoĭ,* fr. *borzoĭ* swift; akin to L *festinare* to hasten] **:** any of a breed of large long-haired dogs of greyhound type developed in Russia esp. for pursuing wolves

bos·cage *also* **bosk·age** \'bäs-kij\ *n* [ME *boskage,* fr. MF *boscage,* fr. OF, fr. *bois, bosc* forest, perh. of Gmc origin; akin to ME *bush*] **:** a growth of trees or shrubs **:** THICKET

bosh \'bäsh\ *n* [Turk *boş* empty] **1 :** foolish talk or activity **:** NONSENSE **2 :** something worthless or trifling

bosk *or* **bosque** \'bäsk\ *n* [prob. back-formation fr. *bosky*] **:** a small wooded area

bosk·et *or* **bos·quet** \'bäs-kət\ *n* [F *bosquet,* fr. It *boschetto,* dim of *bosco* forest, perh. of Gmc origin; akin to ME *bush*] **:** THICKET

Bos·kop man \ˌbäs-ˌkäp-\ *n* [*Boskop,* locality in the Transvaal] **:** a late Pleistocene southern African man prob. ancestral to modern Bushmen and Hottentots — **bos·kop·oid** \'bäs-kə-ˌpȯid\ *adj*

bosky \'bäs-kē\ *adj* [E dial. *bosk* bush, fr. ME *bush, bosk*] **1 :** having abundant trees or shrubs **2 :** of or relating to a woods

bo·s'n *or* **bo's'n** *or* **bo·sun** *or* **bo'·sun** \'bōs-ᵊn\ *var of* BOATSWAIN

¹bo·som \'bu̇z-əm *also* 'büz-\ *n* [ME, fr. OE *bōsm;* akin to OHG *buosam* bosom, Skt *bhūri* abundant — more at BIG] **1 :** the front of the human chest; *esp* **:** the female breasts **2 a :** the anatomical center of secret thoughts and emotions **b :** close relationship <lived in the ~ of her family> **3 a :** a broad surface **b :** an inmost recess **4 a :** the part of a garment covering the breast **b :** the space between the breast and the garment covering it

²bosom *vt* **1 :** to enclose or carry in the bosom **2 :** EMBRACE

³bosom *adj* **:** CLOSE, INTIMATE <~ friends>

-bo·somed \-əmd\ *adj comb form* **:** having (such) a bosom <flat-*bosomed*>

bo·somy \-ə-mē\ *adj* **1 :** swelling upward or outward <~ hills> **2 :** having prominent well-developed breasts

bo·son \'bō-ˌsän\ *n* [Satyendranath *Bose* b1894 Indian physicist] **:** a particle (as a photon, meson, or alpha particle) whose spin is zero or an integral number

¹boss \'bäs, 'bȯs\ *n* [ME *boce,* fr. OF, fr. (assumed) VL *bottia*] **1 a :** a protuberant part or body <a ~ of granite> <a ~ on an animal's horn> **b :** a raised ornamentation **:** STUD **c :** an ornamental projecting block used in architecture **2 :** a soft pad used in ceramics and glassmaking **3 a :** the enlarged part of a shaft on which a wheel is mounted **b :** the hub of a propeller

boss 1c

²boss *vt* **1 :** to ornament with bosses **:** EMBOSS **2 :** to treat (as the surface of porcelain) with a boss

³boss \'bȯs\ *n* [D *baas* master; akin to Fris *baes* master] **1 :** one who exercises control or authority; *specif* **:** one who directs or supervises workers **2 a :** a politician who controls votes in a party organization or dictates appointments or legislative measures **b :** an official with dictatorial authority over an organization — **boss·dom** \-dəm\ *n* — **boss·ism** \-ˌiz-əm\ *n*

⁴boss \'bȯs\ *adj* **1 :** being in charge **:** having authority **2** *slang* **:** EXCELLENT <a beautiful blazer, a ~ piece of stitching —*N.Y. Times*>

⁵boss \'bȯs\ *vt* **1 :** to act as director or supervisor of **2 :** ORDER

⁶boss \'bȯs, 'bäs\ *n* [E dial., young cow] **:** COW, CALF

bos·sa no·va \ˌbäs-ə-'nō-və\ *n* [Pg, lit., new trend] **1 :** a Brazilian dance characterized by the sprightly step pattern of the samba and a subtle bounce **2 :** music resembling the samba with jazz interpolations

boss man *n* **:** BOSS

¹bossy \'bäs-ē, 'bȯ-sē\ *adj* **1 :** marked by a swelling or roundness **2 :** marked by bosses **:** STUDDED

²bossy \'bȯ-sē, 'bäs-ē\ *n, pl* **boss·ies :** COW, CALF

³bossy \'bȯ-sē\ *adj* **boss·i·er; -est :** inclined to domineer **:** DICTATORIAL — **boss·i·ness** *n*

Bos·ton \'bȯ-stən\ *n* [F, fr. *Boston,* Massachusetts] **1 :** a card game for four players with two decks of cards **2 :** a dance somewhat like a waltz

Boston bag *n* **:** a traveling bag or utility bag that is held together at the top opening by two handles

Boston cream pie *n* **:** a round cake that is split and filled with a custard or cream filling

Boston fern *n* **:** a luxuriant fern (*Nephrolepis exaltata bostoniensis*) often with drooping much-divided fronds

Boston ivy *n* **:** a woody Asiatic vine (*Parthenocissus tricuspidata*) of the grape family with 3-lobed leaves

Boston terrier *n* **:** any of a breed of small smooth-coated terriers originating as a cross of the bulldog and bullterrier and being brindle or black with white markings — called also *Boston bull*

Bos·well \'bäz-ˌwel, -wəl\ *n* [James *Boswell*] **:** one who records in detail the conversation and activities of a usu. famous contemporary — **Bos·well·ize** \-wə-ˌlīz, -ˌwel-\ *vb*

¹bot *also* **bott** \'bät\ *n* [perh. modif. of ScGael *boiteag* maggot] **:** the larva of a botfly; *esp* **:** one infesting the horse

²bot *abbr* **1** botanical; botany; botanist **2** bottle **3** bottom **4** bought

botan *abbr* botanical

¹bo·tan·i·cal \bə-'tan-i-kəl\ *adj* [F *botanique,* fr. Gk *botanikos* of herbs, fr. *botanē* pasture, herb, fr. *boskein* to feed; akin to Lith *gauja* herd] **1 :** of or relating to plants or botany **2 :** derived from plants **3 :** SPECIES <~ tulips> — **bo·tan·i·cal·ly** \-k(ə-)lē\ *adv*

²botanical *n* **:** a vegetable drug esp. in the crude state

bot·a·nist \'bät-ᵊn-əst, 'bät-nəst\ *n* **:** a specialist in botany or in a branch of botany **:** a professional student of plants

bot·a·nize \-ᵊn-ˌīz\ *vb* **-nized; -niz·ing** *vi* **:** to collect plants for botanical investigation; *also* **:** to study plants esp. on a field trip ~ *vt* **:** to explore for botanical purposes

bot·a·ny \'bät-ᵊn-ē, 'bät-nē\ *n, pl* **-nies** [back-formation fr. *botanical*] **1 :** a branch of biology dealing with plant life **2 a :** plant life **b :** the properties and life phenomena exhibited by a plant, plant type, or plant group **3 :** a botanical treatise or study; *esp* **:** a particular system of botany

¹botch \'bäch\ *n* [ME *boche,* fr. ONF, fr. (assumed) VL *bottia* boss] **:** an inflammatory sore

²botch *vt* [ME *bocchen*] **1 :** to repair or patch ineptly **2 :** to foul up hopelessly **:** BUNGLE **3 :** to assemble or construct in a makeshift way — **botch·er** *n*

³botch *n* **1 :** something that is botched **:** MESS **2 :** PATCHWORK, HODGEPODGE — **botchy** \-ē\ *adj*

botch·work \'bäch-ˌwərk\ *n* **:** clumsy or careless work

bo·tel \bō-'tel\ *var of* BOATEL

bot·fly \'bät-ˌflī\ *n* **:** any of various stout two-winged flies (group Oestroidea) with larvae parasitic in cavities or tissues of various mammals including man

¹both \'bōth\ *adj* [ME *bothe,* fr. ON *bāthir;* akin to OHG *beide* both] **:** being the two **:** affecting or involving the one and the other <~ feet> <~ his eyes> <~ these armies>

²both *pron* **:** the one as well as the other <~ of us> <~ of the books> <we are ~ well>

³both *conj* — used as a function word to indicate and stress the inclusion of each of two or more things specified by coordinated words, phrases, or clauses <~ New York and London> <spoke with ~ kindness and understanding>

¹both·er \'bäth-ər\ *vb* **both·ered; both·er·ing** \-(ə-)riŋ\ [perh. fr. IrGael *bodhar* bothered] *vt* **1 a :** to cause to be nervous **:** FLUSTER **b :** PUZZLE, MYSTIFY **2 a :** to annoy esp. by petty provocation **:** IRK **b :** to intrude upon **:** PESTER **c :** to cause to be anxious or concerned **:** TROUBLE ~ *vi* **1 :** to feel mild concern or anxiety **2 :** to take pains **:** take the trouble **3 :** to stir up petty trouble ***syn*** see ANNOY ***ant*** comfort

²bother *n* **1 a :** a state of petty discomfort, annoyance, or worry **b :** something that causes petty annoyance or worry **2 :** FUSS

both·er·ation \ˌbäth-ə-'rā-shən\ *n* **1 :** the act of bothering **:** the state of being bothered **2 :** something that bothers

both·er·some \'bäth-ər-səm\ *adj* **:** causing bother **:** VEXING

bot·o·née *or* **bot·on·née** \ˌbät-ᵊn-'ā\ *adj* [MF *botonné*] *of a heraldic cross* **:** having a cluster of three balls or knobs at the end of each arm — see CROSS illustration

bo tree \'bō-\ *n* [Sinhalese *bō,* fr. Skt *bodhi*] **:** PIPAL

bot·ry·oi·dal \ˌbä-trē-'ȯid-ᵊl\ *also* **bot·ry·oid** \'bä-trē-ˌȯid\ *adj* [Gk *botryoeidēs,* fr. *botrys* bunch of grapes] **:** having the form of a bunch of grapes <~ garnets>

¹bot·tle \'bät-ᵊl\ *n, often attrib* [ME *botel,* fr. MF *bouteille,* fr. ML *butticula,* dim. of LL *buttis* cask] **1 a :** a rigid or semirigid container typically of glass or plastic having a comparatively narrow neck or mouth and usu. no handle **b :** a bag made of skin **c :** the quantity held by a bottle **2 a :** intoxicating drink <hit the ~> **b :** bottled milk used in place of mother's milk — **bot·tle·ful** \-ˌfu̇l\ *n*

²bottle *vt* **bot·tled; bot·tling** \'bät-liŋ, -ᵊl-iŋ\ **1 :** to put into a bottle **2 :** to confine as if in a bottle **:** RESTRAIN — usu. used with *up* <*bottling* up their anger> — **bot·tler** \-lər, -ᵊl-ər\ *n*

bottle club *n* **:** a usu. private establishment at which patrons are served alcoholic drinks after normal legal closing hours from supplies they have previously purchased or reserved

bottled gas *n* **:** gas under pressure in portable cylinders

bot·tle–feed \'bät-ᵊl-ˌfēd\ *vt* **-fed; -feed·ing :** to feed (as an infant) with a bottle

bottle gourd *n* **:** a common cultivated gourd (*Lagenaria siceraria*) with a variably shaped fruit that is sometimes used as a container

¹bot·tle·neck \'bät-ᵊl-ˌnek\ *n* **1 a :** a narrow route **b :** a point of traffic congestion **2 a :** a condition or situation that retards or halts free movement and progress **b :** IMPASSE **3 :** a style of guitar playing using an object (as a metal bar or the neck of a bottle) pressed against the strings for a glissando effect

²bottleneck *vt* **:** to slow or halt by causing a bottleneck

³bottleneck *adj* **:** NARROW <~ harbors>

bot·tle–nosed dolphin \ˌbät-ᵊl-ˌnōz-\ *n* **:** any of various moderately large stout-bodied toothed whales (genus *Tursiops* and esp. *T. truncatus*) with a prominent beak and falcate dorsal fin — called also *bottle-nosed porpoise*

¹bot·tom \'bät-əm\ *n* [ME *botme,* fr. OE *botm;* akin to OHG *bodam* bottom, L *fundus,* Gk *pythmēn*] **1 a :** the undersurface of something : UNDERSIDE **b :** a surface designed to support something resting on it **c :** the posterior end of the trunk : BUTTOCKS, RUMP **2 :** the surface on which a body of water lies **3 a :** the part of a ship's hull lying below the water **b :** BOAT, SHIP **4 a :** the lowest part or place **b :** the remotest or inmost point **c :** the lowest or last place in point of precedence <started work at the ~> **d :** the trousers or short pants of pajamas — usu. used in pl. **e :** the last half of an inning of baseball **5 :** low-lying grassland along a watercourse — usu. used in pl. **6 :** BASIS, SOURCE **7 :** capacity (as of a horse) to endure strain **8 :** the main plowing mechanism of a plow **9 :** a foundation color applied to textile fibers before dyeing — **bot·tomed** \-əmd\ *adj* — **at bottom :** REALLY, BASICALLY

²bottom *vt* **1 :** to furnish with a bottom **2 :** to provide a foundation for **3 :** to bring to the bottom **4 :** to get to the bottom of ~ *vi* **1 :** to become based **2 :** to reach the bottom — **bot·tom·er** *n*

³bottom *adj* **1 :** of, relating to, or situated at the bottom <~ rock> **2 :** frequenting the bottom <~ fishes>

bot·tom·land \'bät-əm-ˌland\ *n* : BOTTOM 5

bot·tom·less \-ləs\ *adj* **1 :** having no bottom <a ~ chair> **2 a :** extremely deep **b :** impossible to comprehend : UNFATHOMABLE <a ~ mystery> **c :** BOUNDLESS, UNLIMITED **3 a** [fr. the absence of lower as well as upper garments] **:** NUDE <~ dancers> **b :** featuring nude entertainers <a ~ nighclub> — **bot·tom·less·ly** *adv* — **bot·tom·less·ness** *n*

bot·tom·most \'bät-əm-ˌmōst\ *adj* **1 a :** situated at the very bottom : LOWEST, DEEPEST **b :** LAST <the ~ part of the day —Alfred Kazin> **2 :** most basic <the ~ problems facing the world>

bottom out *vi, of a security market* **:** to decline to a point where demand begins to exceed supply and a rise in prices is imminent

bottom round *n* **:** meat (as steak) from the outer part of a round of beef

bot·tom·ry \'bät-əm-rē\ *n, pl* **-ries** [modif. of D *bodmerij,* fr. *bodem* bottom, ship; akin to OHG *bodam*] **:** a contract by which a ship is hypothecated as security for repayment of a loan at the end of a successful voyage

bot·u·lin \'bäch-ə-lən\ *n* [prob. fr. NL *botulinus*] **:** a toxin that is formed by the botulinum and is the direct cause of botulism

bot·u·li·num \ˌbäch-ə-'lī-nəm\ *also* **bot·u·li·nus** \-nəs\ *n* [NL, fr. L *botulus* sausage] **:** a spore-forming bacterium (*Clostridium botulinum*) that secrets botulin — **bot·u·li·nal** \-'līn-ᵊl\ *adj*

bot·u·lism \'bäch-ə-ˌliz-əm\ *n* **:** acute food poisoning caused by botulin in food

bou·clé *or* **bou·cle** \bü-'klā\ *n* [F *bouclé* curly, fr. pp. of *boucler* to curl, fr. *bocle* buckle, curl] **1 :** an uneven yarn of three plies one of which forms loops at intervals **2 :** a textile fabric of bouclé yarn

bou·doir \'büd-ˌwär, 'bu̇d-, -ˌwȯ(ə)r\ *n* [F, fr. *bouder* to pout] **:** a woman's dressing room, bedroom, or private sitting room

bouf·fant \bü-'fänt, 'bü-ˌ\ *adj* [F, fr. MF, fr. prp. of *bouffer* to puff] **:** puffed out <~ hairdos> <a ~ veil>

bou·gain·vil·laea *or* **bou·gain·vil·lea** \ˌbüg-ən-'vil-yə, ˌbōg-, ˌbu̇g-, -'vē-(y)ə\ *n* [NL, fr. Louis Antoine de *Bougainville*] **:** any of a genus (*Bougainvillaea*) of the four-o'clock family of ornamental tropical American woody vines with brilliant purple red floral bracts

bough \'bau̇\ *n* [ME, shoulder, bough, fr. OE *bōg;* akin to OHG *buog* shoulder, Gk *pēchys* forearm] **:** a branch of a tree; *esp* **:** a main branch — **boughed** \'bau̇d\ *adj*

bought \'bȯt\ *adj* [pp. of *buy*] **:** READY-MADE <~ clothes>

bought·en \-ᵊn\ *adj* [*bought* + *-en* (as in *forgotten*)] *chiefly dial* **:** BOUGHT <the only ~ carpet in the region —H. W. Thompson>

bou·gie \'bü-ˌzhē, -ˌjē\ *n* [F, fr. *Bougie,* seaport in Algeria] **1 :** a wax candle **2 a :** a tapering cylindrical instrument for introduction into a tubular passage of the body **b :** SUPPOSITORY

bouil·la·baisse \ˌbü-yə-'bās\ *n* [F] **:** a highly seasoned fish stew made of at least two kinds of fish

bouil·lon \'bü-ˌyän; 'bu̇l-ˌyän, -yən\ *n* [F, fr. OF *boillon,* fr. *boillir* to boil] **:** a clear seasoned soup made usu. from lean beef

bouillon cube *n* **:** a cube of evaporated seasoned meat extract

boul·der \'bōl-dər\ *n* [short for *boulder ston,* fr. ME *bulder ston,* part trans. of a word of Scand origin; akin to Sw dial. *bullersten* large stone in a stream, fr. *buller* noise + *sten* stone] **:** a detached and rounded or much-worn mass of rock — **boul·dered** \-dərd\ *adj* — **boul·dery** \-d(ə-)rē\ *adj*

¹bou·le \'bü-(ˌ)lē, bü-'lā\ *n* [Gk *boulē,* lit., will, fr. *boulesthai* to wish] **:** a legislative council of ancient Greece consisting first of an aristocratic advisory body and later of a representative senate

²boule \'bül\ *n* [F, ball — more at BOWL] **:** a pear-shaped mass (as of sapphire) formed synthetically in a special furnace with the atomic structure of a single crystal

bou·le·vard \'bu̇l-ə-ˌvärd, 'bül-\ *n* [F, modif. of MD *bolwerc* bulwark] **:** a broad often landscaped thoroughfare

bou·le·vard·ier \ˌbu̇l-ə-ˌvär-'dyā, ˌbül-, -'di(ə)r\ *n* [F, fr. *boulevard* + *-ier* -er] **:** a frequenter of the Parisian boulevards; *broadly* **:** MAN-ABOUT-TOWN

bou·le·ver·se·ment \bül-(ə-)ver-sə-mä^{n}\ *n* [F] **1 :** REVERSAL **2 :** a violent disturbance : DISORDER

boulle \'bül, 'byü(ə)l\ *n* [André Charles *Boulle* †1732 F cabinetmaker] **:** inlaid decoration of tortoiseshell, yellow metal, and white metal in cabinetwork

¹bounce \'bau̇n(t)s\ *vb* **bounced; bounc·ing** [ME *bounsen*] *vt* **1** *obs* **:** BEAT, BUMP **2 :** to cause to rebound <~ a ball> **3 a :** DISMISS, FIRE **b :** to expel precipitately from a place ~ *vi* **1 :** to rebound after striking **2 :** to recover from a blow or a defeat quickly — usu. used with *back* **3 :** to be returned by a bank as no good <his checks ~> **4 a :** to leap suddenly : BOUND **b :** to walk with springing steps **5 :** to hit a baseball so that it hits the ground before it reaches an infielder

²bounce *n* **1 a :** a sudden leap or bound **b :** REBOUND **2 :** BLUSTER **3 :** VERVE, LIVELINESS

bounc·er \'bau̇n(t)-sər\ *n* **:** one that bounces: as **a :** one employed to restrain or eject disorderly persons **b :** a batted baseball that bounces

bounc·ing \-siŋ\ *adj* **1 :** enjoying good health : ROBUST **2 :** LIVELY, ANIMATED — **bounc·ing·ly** \-siŋ-lē\ *adv*

bouncing bet \-'bet\ *n, often cap 2d B* [fr. *Bet,* nickname for *Elizabeth*] **:** a European perennial herb (*Saponaria officinalis*) of the pink family that is widely naturalized in the U.S. and has pink or white flowers and leaves which yield a detergent when bruised — called also *soapwort*

bouncy \'bau̇n(t)-sē\ *adj* **bounc·i·er; -est 1 :** BUOYANT, EXUBERANT **2 :** RESILIENT **3 :** marked by or producing bounces — **bounc·i·ly** \-sə-lē\ *adv*

¹bound \'bau̇nd\ *adj* [ME *boun,* fr. ON *būinn,* pp. of *būa* to dwell, prepare; akin to OHG *būan* to dwell — more at BOWER] **1** *archaic* **:** READY **2 :** intending to go : GOING <~ for home> <college-*bound*>

²bound *n* [ME, fr. OF *bodne,* fr. ML *bodina*] **1 a :** a limiting line : BOUNDARY — usu. used in pl. **b :** something that limits or restrains <beyond the ~*s* of decency> **2** *usu pl* **a :** BORDERLAND **b :** the land within certain bounds

³bound *vt* **1 :** to set limits to : CONFINE **2 :** to form the boundary of : ENCLOSE **3 :** to name the boundaries of

⁴bound *adj* [ME *bounden,* fr. pp. of *binden* to bind] **1 a :** fastened by or as if by a band : CONFINED <desk-*bound*> **b :** CERTAIN, SURE <~ to rain soon> **2 :** placed under legal or moral restraint or obligation : OBLIGED <duty-*bound*> **3 :** made costive : CONSTIPATED **4** *of a book* **a :** secured to the covers by cords or tapes **b :** cased in **5 :** DETERMINED, RESOLVED **6 :** held in chemical or physical combination <~ water in a molecule> **7 :** always occurring in combination with another linguistic form <*un-* in *unknown* and *-er* in *speaker* are ~ forms> — compare FREE

⁵bound *n* [MF *bond,* fr. *bondir* to leap, fr. (assumed) VL *bombitire* to hum, fr. L *bombus* deep hollow sound — more at BOMB] **1 :** LEAP, JUMP **2 :** the action of rebounding : BOUNCE

⁶bound *vi* **1 :** to move by leaping **2 :** REBOUND, BOUNCE

bound·ary \'bau̇n-d(ə-)rē\ *n, pl* **-aries :** something that indicates or fixes a limit or extent; *specif* **:** a bounding or separating line

boundary layer *n* **:** a region of retarded fluid near the surface of a body which moves through a fluid or past which a fluid moves

bound·en \'bau̇n-dən\ *adj* [ME] **1** *archaic* **:** being under obligation : BEHOLDEN **2 :** made obligatory : BINDING <our ~ duty>

bound·er \-dər\ *n* **1 :** one that bounds **2 :** a man of objectionable social behavior : CAD

bound·er·ish \-də-rish\ *adj* **:** resembling or typical of a bounder — **bound·er·ish·ly** *adv*

bound·less \'bau̇n-dləs\ *adj* **:** having no boundaries : VAST — **bound·less·ly** *adv* — **bound·less·ness** *n*

bound up *adj* **:** closely involved or associated — usu. used with *with*

boun·te·ous \'bau̇nt-ē-əs\ *adj* [ME *bountevous,* fr. MF *bontif* kind, fr. OF, fr. *bonté*] **1 :** giving or disposed to give freely **2 :** liberally bestowed — **boun·te·ous·ly** *adv* — **boun·te·ous·ness** *n*

boun·tied \'bau̇nt-ēd\ *adj* **1 :** having the benefit of a bounty **2 :** rewarded or rewardable by a bounty

boun·ti·ful \'bau̇nt-i-fəl\ *adj* **1 :** liberal in bestowing gifts or favors **2 :** given or provided abundantly : PLENTIFUL <a ~ harvest> ***syn*** see LIBERAL ***ant*** niggardly — **boun·ti·ful·ly** \-f(ə-)lē\ *adv* — **boun·ti·ful·ness** \-fəl-nəs\ *n*

boun·ty \'bau̇nt-ē\ *n, pl* **bounties** [ME *bounte* goodness, fr. OF *bonté,* fr. L *bonitat-, bonitas,* fr. *bonus* good, fr. OL *duenos;* akin to MHG *zwiden* to grant, L *bene* well] **1 :** liberality in giving : GENEROSITY **2 :** something that is given generously **3 :** yield esp. of a crop **4 :** a reward, premium, or subsidy esp. when offered or given by a government: as **a :** an extra allowance to induce entry into the armed services **b :** a grant to encourage an industry **c :** a payment to encourage the destruction of noxious animals **d :** a payment for the capture of an outlaw

bounty hunter *n* **1 :** one that hunts predatory animals for the reward offered **2 :** one that tracks down and captures outlaws for whom a reward is offered

bou·quet \bō-'kā, bü-\ *n* [F, fr. MF, thicket, fr. ONF *bosquet,* fr. OF *bosc* forest — more at BOSCAGE] **1 a :** flowers picked and fastened together in a bunch : NOSEGAY **b :** a large flight of fireworks **2 :** COMPLIMENT **3 a :** a distinctive and characteristic fragrance (as of wine) **b :** a subtle aroma or quality (as of an artistic performance or a piece of writing) ***syn*** see FRAGRANCE

bour·bon \'bu̇(ə)r-bən, 'bō(ə)r-, 'bȯ(ə)r; *usu* 'bər- *in sense 4*\ *n* [*Bourbon,* seigniory in France] **1** *cap* **:** a member of a French family founded in 1272 to which belong the rulers of France from 1589 to 1793 and from 1814 to 1830, of Spain from 1700 to 1808, from 1814 to 1868, and from 1875 to 1931, of Naples from 1735 to 1805, and of the Two Sicilies from 1815 to 1860 **2** *often cap* **:** a person who clings obstinately to the social and political ideas of the old order of things; *specif* **:** an extremely conservative member of the U.S. Democratic party usu. from the South **3** [*Bourbon* (now Réunion), French island in the Indian ocean] **:** a rose (*Rosa borboniana*) of compact upright growth with shining leaves, prickly branches, and clustered flowers **4** [*Bourbon* county, Kentucky] **:** a whiskey distilled from a mash made up of not less than 51 percent corn plus malt and rye — compare CORN WHISKEY — **bour·bon·ism** \-bə-ˌniz-əm\ *n, often cap*

bour·don \'bu̇(ə)rd-ᵊn\ *n* [ME *burdoun,* fr. MF *bourdon* bass pipe, of imit. origin] **:** a drone bass (as in a bagpipe)

bourg \'bu̇(ə)r(g)\ *n* [ME, fr. MF, fr. OF *borc,* fr. L *burgus* fortified place, of Gmc origin; akin to OHG *burg* fortified place — more at BOROUGH] **:** TOWN, VILLAGE; as **a :** one neighboring a castle **b :** a market town

¹bour·geois \'bu̇(ə)rzh-ˌwä, bu̇rzh-'\ *n, pl* **bourgeois** \-ˌwä(z), -'wä(z)\ [MF, fr. OF *borjois,* fr. *borc*] **1 a :** BURGHER **b :** a middle-class person **2 :** one with social behavior and political views held to be influenced by private-property interest : CAPITALIST **3** *pl* **:** BOURGEOISIE

2**bourgeois** *adj* **1 :** of, relating to, or characteristic of the townsman or of the social middle class **2 :** marked by a concern for material interests and respectability and a tendency toward mediocrity **3 :** dominated by commercial and industrial interests : CAPITALISTIC — **bour·geois·ify** \bu̇rzh-'wäz-ə-ˌfī\ *vb*

bour·geoise \'bu̇(ə)rzh-ˌwäz, bu̇rzh-'wä\ *n* [F, fem. of *bourgeois*] **1 :** a woman of the middle class **2 :** BOURGEOIS

bour·geoi·sie \ˌbu̇rzh-ˌwä-'zē\ *n, pl* **bourgeoisie** [F, fr. *bourgeois*] **1 :** MIDDLE CLASS **2 :** a social order dominated by bourgeois

bour·geon \'bər-jən\ *var of* BURGEON

1**bourn** *or* **bourne** \'bō(ə)rn, 'bȯ(ə)rn, 'bu̇(ə)rn\ *n* [ME *burn, bourne* — more at BURN] : STREAM, BROOK

2**bourn** *or* **bourne** *n* [MF *bourne,* fr. OF *bodne* — more at BOUND] **1** *archaic* : BOUNDARY, LIMIT **2** *archaic* : GOAL, DESTINATION

bour·rée \bu̇-'rā, 'bü-ˌ\ *n* [F] **1 :** a 17th century French dance usu. in duple time with an upbeat; *also* : a musical composition with the rhythm of this dance **2 :** PAS DE BOURRÉE

bourse \'bu̇(ə)rs\ *n* [F, lit., purse, fr. ML *bursa* — more at PURSE] **1 :** EXCHANGE 5a; *specif* : a European stock exchange **2 :** a sale of numismatic or philatelic items on tables (as at a convention)

bour·tree \'bu̇(ə)r-(ˌ)trē\ *n* [ME *bourtre*] *Brit* : the common large black-fruited elder (*Sambucus nigra*) of Europe and Asia

bouse \'bau̇z\ *vb* **boused; bous·ing** [origin unknown] *vt* : to haul by means of a tackle ~ *vi* : to bouse something

bou·stro·phe·don \ˌbü-strə-'fēd-ˌän, -ᵊn\ *adj* [Gk *boustrophēdon,* adv., lit., turning like oxen in plowing, fr. *bous* ox, cow + *strephein* to turn — more at COW, STROPHE] : having alternate lines written in opposite directions (as from left to right and from right to left); *also* : of, relating to, or using boustrophedon writing

bout \'bau̇t\ *n* [E dial., a trip going and returning in plowing, fr. ME *bought* bend] : a spell of activity: as **a :** an athletic match (as of boxing) **b :** OUTBREAK, ATTACK **c :** SESSION

bou·tique \bü-'tēk\ *n* [F, shop] : a small fashionable specialty shop; *also* : a small shop within a large department store

bou·ton·niere \ˌbüt-ᵊn-'i(ə)r, ˌbü-tən-'ye(ə)r\ *n* [F *boutonnière* buttonhole, fr. MF, fr. *bouton* button] : a flower or bouquet worn in a buttonhole

Bou·vi·er des Flan·dres \ˌbü-vē-ˌād-ə-'flan-dərz, -'flä^ndrᵊ\ *n* [F, lit., cowherd of Flanders] : any of a breed of large powerfully built rough-coated dogs originating in Belgium and used esp. for herding and in guard work

bou·zou·ki *also* **bou·sou·ki** \bu̇-'zü-kē\ *n* [NGk *mpouzouki;* prob. fr. Turk *büyük* large] : a long-necked stringed instrument of Greek origin that resembles a mandolin

1**bo·vine** \'bō-ˌvīn, -ˌvēn\ *adj* [LL *bovinus,* fr. L *bov-, bos* ox, cow — more at COW] **1 :** of, relating to, or resembling the ox or cow **2 :** having qualities (as sluggishness or patience) characteristic of oxen or cows — **bo·vine·ly** *adv* — **bo·vin·i·ty** \bō-'vin-ət-ē\ *n*

2**bovine** *n* : an ox (genus *Bos*) or a closely related animal

1**bow** \'bau̇\ *vb* [ME *bowen,* fr. OE *būgan;* akin to OHG *biogan* to bend, Skt *bhujati* he bends] *vt* **1 :** to suffer defeat in a contest : SUBMIT, YIELD **2 :** to bend the head, body, or knee in reverence, submission, or shame **3 :** to incline the head or body in salutation or assent or to acknowledge applause ~ *vt* **1 :** to cause to incline **2 :** to incline (as the head) esp. in respect or submission **3 :** to crush with a heavy burden **4 a :** to express by bowing **b :** to usher in or out with a bow

2**bow** *n* : a bending of the head or body in respect, submission, assent, or salutation

3**bow** \'bō\ *n* [ME *bowe,* fr. OE *boga;* akin to OE *būgan*] **1 a :** something bent into a simple curve : BEND, ARCH **b :** RAINBOW **2 :** a weapon that is made of a strip of flexible material (as wood) with a cord connecting the two ends and holding the strip bent and that is used to propel an arrow **3 :** ARCHER **4 a :** a metal ring or loop forming a handle (as of a key) **b :** a knot formed by doubling a ribbon or string into two or more loops **c :** BOW TIE **d :** a frame for the lenses of eyeglasses; *also* : the curved sidepiece of the frame passing over the ear **5 a :** a resilient wooden rod with horsehairs stretched from end to end used in playing an instrument of the viol or violin family **b :** a stroke of such a bow

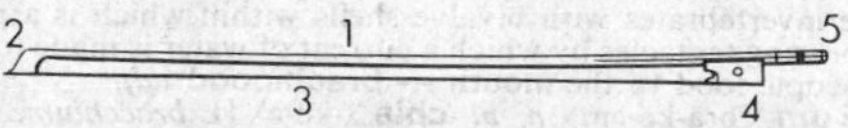

violin bow: *1* stick, *2* head, *3* hair, *4* frog, *5* screw

4**bow** \'bō\ *vi* **1 :** to bend into a curve **2 :** to play a stringed musical instrument with a bow ~ *vt* **1 :** to cause to bend into a curve **2 :** to play (a stringed instrument) with a bow

5**bow** \'bau̇\ *n* [prob. fr. Dan *bov* shoulder, bow, fr. ON *bōgr;* akin to OE *bōg* bough] **1 :** the forward part of a ship **2 :** 2BOWMAN

Bow bells \'bō-\ *n pl* : the bells of the Church of St. Mary-le-Bow in London

bowd·ler·iza·tion \ˌbōd-lə-rə-'zā-shən, ˌbau̇d-\ *n* : the act or result of bowdlerizing

bowd·ler·ize \'bōd-lə-ˌrīz, 'bau̇d-\ *vt* **-ized; -iz·ing** [Thomas *Bowdler* †1825 E editor] : to expurgate (as a book) by omitting or modifying parts considered vulgar — **bowd·ler·iz·er** *n*

1**bowed** \'bau̇d\ *adj* [pp. of 1*bow*] **1 :** bent downward and forward <listened with ~ heads> **2 :** having the back and head inclined

2**bowed** \'bōd\ *adj* [partly fr. 3*bow* + *-ed;* partly fr. pp. of 4*bow*] : furnished with or shaped like a bow

bow·el \'bau̇(-ə)l\ *n* [ME, fr. OF *boel,* fr. MF *botellus,* fr. L, dim. of *botulus* sausage] **1 :** INTESTINE : one of the divisions of the intestines : GUT — usu. used in pl. except in medical use <the large ~> <move your ~*s*> **2** *archaic* : the seat of pity, tenderness, or courage — usu. used in pl. **3** *pl* : the interior parts; *esp* : the deep or remote parts <~*s* of the earth> — **bow·el·less** \'bau̇(-ə)l-ləs\ *adj*

1**bow·er** \'bau̇(-ə)r\ *n* [ME *bour* dwelling, fr. OE *būr;* akin to OE & OHG *būan* to dwell, OE *bēon* to be] **1 :** an attractive dwelling or retreat **2 :** a lady's private apartment in a medieval hall or castle **3 :** a shelter (as in a garden) made with tree boughs or vines twined together : ARBOR — **bow·ery** \-ē\ *adj*

2**bower** *vt* : EMBOWER, ENCLOSE

3**bower** *n* : an anchor carried at the bow of a ship

bow·er·bird \'bau̇(-ə)r-ˌbərd\ *n* : any of various passerine birds (family Paradisaeidae) of the Australian region in which the male builds a chamber or passage arched over with twigs and grasses, often adorned with bright-colored objects, and used esp. to attract the female

bow·ery \'bau̇(-ə-)rē\ *n, pl* **-er·ies** [D *bouwerij,* fr. *bouwer* farmer, fr. *bouwen* to till; akin to OHG *būan* to dwell] **1 :** a colonial Dutch plantation or farm **2** [*Bowery,* street in New York City] : a city district notorious for cheap bars and homeless derelicts

bow·fin \'bō-ˌfin\ *n* : a predaceous dull-green iridescent American freshwater ganoid fish (*Amia calva*) of little value for food or sport

bow·front \-ˌfrənt\ *adj* **1 :** having an outward curving front <~ furniture> **2 :** having a bow window in front <~ houses>

bow·head \-ˌhed\ *n* : the whalebone whale (*Balaena mysticetus*) of the Arctic

bow·ie knife \'bü-ē-, 'bō-\ *n* [James *Bowie* †1836 Am soldier] : a stout single-edged hunting knife with part of the back edge curved concavely to a point and sharpened

bow·ing \'bō-iŋ\ *n* : the technique of managing the bow in playing a stringed musical instrument

bow·knot \'bō-ˌnät, -'nät\ *n* : a knot with decorative loops

1**bowl** \'bōl\ *n* [ME *bolle,* fr. OE *bolla;* akin to OHG *bolla* blister, OE *blāwan* to blow] **1 :** a concave usu. hemispherical vessel used esp. for holding liquids; *specif* : a drinking vessel (as for wine) **2 :** the contents of a bowl **3 :** a bowl-shaped or concave part: as **a :** the hollow of a spoon or tobacco pipe **b :** the receptacle of a toilet **4 a :** a natural formation or geographical region shaped like a bowl **b :** a bowl-shaped structure; *esp* : an athletic stadium **5 :** a postseasonal football game between specially invited teams — **bowled** \'bōld\ *adj* — **bowl·ful** \-ˌfu̇l\ *n*

2**bowl** *n* [ME *boule,* fr. MF, fr. L *bulla* bubble] **1 a :** a ball (as of lignum vitae) weighted or shaped to give it a bias when rolled in lawn bowling **b** *pl but sing in constr* : LAWN BOWLING **2 :** a delivery of the ball in bowling **3 :** a cylindrical roller or drum (as for a mechanical device)

3**bowl** *vi* **1 a :** to participate in a game of bowling **b :** to roll a ball in bowling **2 :** to travel in a vehicle smoothly and rapidly ~ *vt* **1 a :** to roll (a ball) in bowling **b (1) :** to complete by bowling <~ a string> **(2) :** to score by bowling <~*s* 150> **2 :** to strike with a swiftly moving object **3 :** to overwhelm with surprise

bowlder *var of* BOULDER

bow·leg \'bō-ˌleg, -ˌläg, 'bō-'\ *n* : a leg bowed outward at or below the knee — **bow·legged** \'bō-'leg(-ə)d, -'läg(-ə)d\ *adj*

1**bowl·er** \'bō-lər\ *n* : one that bowls; *specif* : the player that delivers the ball to the batsman in cricket

2**bow·ler** \'bō-lər\ *n* [*Bowler,* 19th cent. family of E hatters] : a derby hat

bow·line \'bō-lən, -ˌlīn\ *n* [ME *bouline,* perh. fr. *bowe* bow + *line*] **1 :** a rope used to keep the weather edge of a square sail taut forward **2 :** a knot used to form a loop that neither slips nor jams — see KNOT illustration

bowl·ing \'bō-liŋ\ *n* : any of several games in which balls are rolled on a green or down an alley at an object or group of objects

1**bow·man** \'bō-mən\ *n* : ARCHER

2**bow·man** \'bau̇-mən\ *n* : a boatman, oarsman, or paddler stationed in the front of a boat

Bow·man's capsule \ˌbō-mənz-\ *n* [Sir William *Bowman* †1892 E surgeon] : a thin membranous double-walled capsule surrounding the glomerulus of a vertebrate nephron

bow out \(ˈ)bau̇-\ *vi* : RETIRE, WITHDRAW

bow saw \'bō-\ *n* : a saw having a narrow blade held under tension by a light bow-shaped frame

bowse \'bau̇z\ *var of* BOUSE

bow·sprit \'bau̇-ˌsprit, 'bō-\ *n* [ME *bouspret,* prob. fr. MLG *bōchsprēt,* fr. *bōch* bow + *sprēt* pole] : a large spar projecting forward from the stem of a ship

bow·string \'bō-ˌstriŋ\ *n* : a waxed or sized cord joining the ends of a shooting bow

bowstring hemp *n* : any of various Asiatic and African sansevierias; *also* : its soft tough leaf fiber used esp. in cordage

bow tie \'bō-\ *n* : a short necktie tied in a bowknot

bow window \'bō-\ *n* : a usu. curved bay window

bow·wow \'bau̇-ˌwau̇, bau̇-'\ *n* [imit.] **1 :** the bark of a dog; *also* : DOG **2 :** noisy clamor **3 :** arrogant dogmatic manner

bow·yer \'bō-yər\ *n* : one that makes shooting bows

1**box** \'bäks\ *n, pl* **box** *or* **box·es** [ME, fr. OE, fr. L *buxus,* fr. Gk *pyxos*] : an evergreen shrub or small tree (genus *Buxus* of the family Buxaceae, the box family) with opposite entire leaves and capsular fruits; *esp* : a widely cultivated shrub (*B. sempervirens*) used for hedges, borders, and topiary figures

2**box** *n* [ME, fr. OE, fr. LL *buxis,* fr. Gk *pyxis,* fr. *pyxos*] **1 a :** a rigid typically rectangular receptacle often with a cover **b :** something having a flat bottom and four upright sides **c :** the contents of a box as a measure of quantity **d :** the driver's seat on a carriage or coach **e** *slang* : GUITAR **f** *slang* : RECORD PLAYER **2** *Brit* : a gift in a box **3 a :** a small compartment (as for a group of spectators in a theater) **b :** PENALTY BOX **4 a :** a boxlike receptacle (as for a bearing) **b :** a signaling apparatus with its enclosing case <a police ~> **5 :** a square or oblong division or compartment **6 :** a square or oblong hollow space or recess **7**

: a small simple sheltering or enclosing structure **8 a :** printed matter enclosed by rules or white space **b :** FRAME 6b(1) **9 :** any of six spaces on a baseball diamond where the batter, coaches, pitcher, and catcher stand **10 :** PREDICAMENT, FIX — **box·ful** \-ˌfu̇l\ *n*

[3]box *vt* **1 :** to furnish (as a wheel hub) with a box **2 :** to enclose in or as if in a box **3 :** BOXHAUL **4 :** to enclose with boarding or lathing so as to bring to a required form **5 :** to mix (paint) by pouring back and forth between two containers **6 :** to hem in (as an opponent) — usu. used with *in, out,* or *up* <~*ed* out the opposing tackle> — **box the compass 1 :** to name the 32 points of the compass in their order **2 :** to make a complete reversal

[4]box *n* [ME] **:** a punch or slap esp. on the ear

[5]box *vt* **1 :** to hit (as the ears) with the hand **2 :** to engage in boxing with ~ *vi* **:** to fight with the fists **:** engage in boxing

box calf *n* **:** calfskin that is tanned with chromium salts and has square markings on the grain

box camera *n* **:** a camera of simple box shape with a simple lens and rotary shutter

box·car \'bäk-ˌskär\ *n* **:** a roofed freight car usu. with sliding doors in the sides

box coat *n* **1 :** a heavy overcoat formerly worn for driving **2 :** a loose coat usu. fitted at the shoulders

box elder *n* **:** a No. American maple (*Acer negundo*) with compound leaves

[1]box·er \'bäk-sər\ *n* **:** one that engages in the sport of boxing

[2]boxer *n* **:** one that makes boxes or packs things in boxes

[3]boxer *n* [G, fr. E [1]*boxer*] **:** a compact medium-sized short-haired usu. fawn or brindle dog of a breed originating in Germany

Box·er \'bäk-sər\ *n* [approx. trans. of Chin (Pek.) *i⁴ hê² ch'üan²*, lit., righteous harmonious fist] **:** a member of a Chinese secret society that in 1900 attempted by violence to drive foreigners out of China and to force native converts to renounce Christianity

boxer shorts *n pl* **:** SHORT 4b

box·haul \'bäks-ˌhȯl\ *vt* **:** to put (a square-rigged ship) on the other tack by luffing and then veering short round on the heel

[1]box·ing \'bäk-siŋ\ *n* **1 :** an act of enclosing in a box **2 :** a boxlike enclosure **:** CASING **3 :** material used for boxes and casings

[2]boxing *n* **:** the art of attack and defense with the fists practiced as a sport

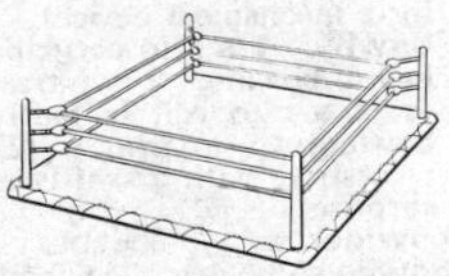

boxing ring

Boxing Day *n* **:** the first weekday after Christmas observed as a legal holiday in parts of the British Commonwealth and marked by the giving of Christmas boxes to service workers (as postmen)

boxing glove *n* **:** one of a pair of leather mittens heavily padded on the back and worn in boxing

box kite *n* **:** a tailless kite consisting of two or more open-ended connected boxes

box·like \'bäk-ˌslik\ *adj* **:** resembling a box esp. in shape

box lunch *n* **:** a lunch packed in a container (as a box)

box office *n* **1 :** an office (as in a theater) where tickets of admission are sold **2 :** success (as of a show) in attracting ticket buyers; *also* **:** something that enhances such success

box pleat *n* **:** a pleat made by forming two folded edges one facing right and the other left

box score *n* [fr. its arrangement in a newspaper box] **:** a printed score of a game (as baseball) giving the names and positions of the players and a record of the play arranged in tabular form; *broadly* **:** total count **:** SUMMARY

box seat *n* **1 :** the driver's seat on a coach **2 a :** a seat in a box (as in a theater or grandstand) **b :** a position favorable for viewing something

box social *n* **:** a fund-raising affair at which box lunches or suppers are auctioned to the highest bidder

box spring *n* **:** a bedspring that consists of spiral springs attached to a foundation and enclosed in a cloth-covered frame

box stall *n* **:** an individual enclosure within a barn or stable in which an animal may move about freely without a restraining device (as a tether)

box·thorn \'bäks-ˌthȯ(ə)rn\ *n* **:** MATRIMONY VINE

box turtle *n* **:** any of several No. American land tortoises (genus *Terrapene*) capable of withdrawing entirely within the shell and closing it by hinged joints in the lower shell — called also *box tortoise*

box·wood \'bäk-ˌswu̇d\ *n* **1 :** the very close-grained heavy tough hard wood of the box (*Buxus*); *also* **:** a wood of similar properties **2 :** a plant producing boxwood

boxy \'bäk-sē\ *adj* **box·i·er; -est :** resembling a box — **box·i·ness** *n*

boy \'bȯi\ *n, often attrib* [ME; akin to Fris *boi* boy] **1 a :** a male child from birth to puberty **b :** SON **c :** an immature male **:** YOUTH **d :** SWEETHEART, BEAU **2 a :** one native to a given place <local ~> **b :** FELLOW, PERSON <the ~*s* at the office> — often used interjectionally <~, what a game> **3 :** a male servant — sometimes taken to be offensive — **boy·hood** \-ˌhu̇d\ *n* — **boy·ish** \-ish\ *adj* — **boy·ish·ly** *adv* — **boy·ish·ness** *n*

bo·yar *also* **bo·yard** \bō-'yär\ *n* [Russ *boyarin*, fr. OSlav *boljarinŭ*] **:** a member of a Russian aristocratic order next in rank below the ruling princes until its abolition by Peter the Great

[1]boy·cott \'bȯi-ˌkät\ *vt* [Charles C. *Boycott* †1897 E land agent in Ireland who was ostracized for refusing to reduce rents] **:** to engage in a concerted refusal to have dealings (as with a person, store, or organization) usu. to express disapproval or to force acceptance of certain conditions — **boy·cot·ter** *n*

[2]boycott *n* **:** the process or an instance of boycotting

boy·friend \'bȯi-ˌfrend\ *n* **1 :** a male friend **2 :** a frequent or regular male companion of a girl or woman **3 :** a male lover

Boyg \'bȯig\ *n* [Norw *boig* bugbear] **:** a formless or pervasive obstacle, problem, or enemy

boyo \'bȯi-(ˌ)ō\ *n, pl* **boy·os** [*boy* + *-o*] *Irish* **:** BOY, LAD

boy scout *n* **1 :** a member of the Boy Scouts of America **2 :** one who performs a service for or gives assistance to others

boy·sen·ber·ry \'bȯiz-ᵊn-ˌber-ē, 'bȯis-\ *n* [Rudolph *Boysen fl*1923 Am horticulturist + E *berry*] **:** a large bramble fruit with a raspberry flavor; *also* **:** the trailing hybrid bramble yielding this fruit and developed by crossing several blackberries and raspberries

boy wonder *n* **:** a young man whose achievements arouse admiration

bo·zo \'bō-(ˌ)zō\ *n, pl* **bozos** [origin unknown] *slang* **:** FELLOW, GUY

bp *abbr* **1** baptized **2** birthplace **3** bishop

BP *abbr* **1** before the present **2** blood pressure **3** blueprint **4** boiling point

BPD *abbr* barrels per day

BPE *abbr* **1** bachelor of petroleum engineering **2** bachelor of physical education

BPh *abbr* bachelor of philosophy

bpi *abbr* bits per inch; bytes per inch

bpl *abbr* birthplace

BPOE *abbr* Benevolent and Protective Order of Elks

BPW *abbr* **1** Board of Public Works **2** Business and Professional Women's Clubs

br *abbr* **1** branch **2** brass **3** brown

[1]Br *abbr* British

[2]Br *symbol* bromine

BR *abbr* **1** bats right **2** bedroom **3** bills receivable

bra \'brä\ *n* **:** BRASSIERE

brab·ble \'brab-əl\ *vi* **brab·bled; brab·bling** \-(ə-)liŋ\ [MD *brabbelen*, of imit. origin] **:** SQUABBLE — **brabble** *n*

[1]brace \'brās\ *n, pl* **brac·es** [ME, pair, clasp, fr. MF, two arms, fr. L *bracchia*, pl. of *bracchium* arm, fr. Gk *brachiōn*, fr. compar. of *brachys* short — more at BRIEF] **1** *or pl* **brace :** two of a kind <several ~ of quail> **2 :** something (as a clasp) that connects or fastens **3 :** a crank-shaped instrument for turning a bit **4 :** something that transmits, directs, resists, or supports weight or pressure: as **a :** a diagonal piece of structural material that serves to strengthen something (as a framework) **b :** a rope rove through a block at the end of a ship's yard to swing it horizontally **c** *pl* **:** SUSPENDERS **d :** an appliance for supporting a body part **e :** a dental appliance worn on the teeth to correct irregularities of growth and position **5 a :** a mark { or } used to connect words or items to be considered together **b (1) :** this mark connecting two or more musical staffs the parts on which are to be performed simultaneously **(2) :** the staffs so connected **c :** BRACKET 3a **6 :** an exaggerated position of rigidly erect bearing **7 :** something that arouses energy or strengthens morale

[2]brace *vb* **braced; brac·ing** *vt* **1** *archaic* **:** to fasten tightly **:** BIND **2 a :** to prepare for use by making taut **b :** PREPARE, STEEL <~ yourself for the shock> **c :** INVIGORATE, FRESHEN **3 :** to turn (a sail yard) by means of a brace **4 a :** to furnish or support with a brace <heavily *braced* because of polio> **b :** to make stronger **:** REINFORCE **5 :** to put or plant firmly <~*s* his foot in the stirrup> **6 :** to waylay esp. with demands or questions ~ *vi* **1 :** to take heart — used with *up* **2 :** to get ready (as for an attack)

brace·let \'brā-slət\ *n* [ME, fr. MF, dim. of *bras* arm, fr. L *bracchium*] **1 :** an ornamental band or chain worn around the wrist **2 :** something (as handcuffs) resembling a bracelet

[1]bra·cer \'brā-sər\ *n* [ME, fr. MF *braciere*, fr. OF, fr. *braz* arm, fr. L *bracchium*] **:** an arm or wrist protector esp. for use by an archer

[2]brac·er \'brā-sər\ *n* **1 :** one that braces, binds, or makes firm **2 :** a drink (as of liquor) taken as a stimulant

bra·ce·ro \brä-'se(ə)r-(ˌ)ō\ *n, pl* **-ros** [Sp, laborer, fr. *brazo* arm, fr. L *brachium*] **:** a Mexican laborer admitted to the U.S. esp. for seasonal contract labor in agriculture — compare WETBACK

brace root *n* **:** PROP ROOT

bra·chi·ate \'brā-kē-ˌāt\ *vi* **-at·ed; -at·ing** [L *bracchium*] **:** to progress by swinging from one hold to another by the arms <*brachiating* gibbon> — **bra·chi·a·tion** \ˌbrā-kē-'ā-shən\ *n*

bra·chio·pod \'brā-kē-ə-ˌpäd\ *n* [deriv. of L *bracchium* + Gk *pod-, pous* foot — more at FOOT] **:** any of a phylum (Brachiopoda) of marine invertebrates with bivalve shells within which is a pair of arms bearing tentacles by which a current of water is made to bring microscopic food to the mouth — **brachiopod** *adj*

bra·chi·um \'brā-kē-əm\ *n, pl* **-chia** \-kē-ə\ [L *bracchium, brachium* arm] **1 :** the upper part of the arm or forelimb from shoulder to elbow **2 :** a process of an invertebrate comparable to an arm — **bra·chi·al** \-əl\ *adj*

brachy- *comb form* [Gk, fr. *brachys* — more at BRIEF] **:** short <*brachy*dactylous>

brachy·ce·phal·ic \ˌbrak-i-sə-'fal-ik\ *adj* [NL *brachycephalus*, fr. Gk *brachy-* + *kephalē* head — more at CEPHALIC] **:** short-headed or broad-headed with a cephalic index of over 80 — **brachy·ceph·a·ly** \-'sef-ə-lē\ *n*

brachy·ceph·a·li·za·tion \-ˌsef-ə-lə-'zā-shən\ *n* **:** transition toward a more brachycephalic condition <the increasing ~ of Europe>

brachy·dac·ty·lous \ˌbrak-i-'dak-tə-ləs\ *adj* **:** having abnormally short digits — **brachy·dac·ty·ly** \-lē\ *n*

bra·chyp·ter·ous \bra-'kip-tə-rəs\ *adj* [Gk *brachypteros*, fr. *brachy-* + *pteron* wing — more at FEATHER] **:** having rudimentary or abnormally small wings <~ insects>

brachy·uran \ˌbrak-ē-'yu̇r-ən\ *n* [deriv. of Gk *brachy-* + *oura* tail — more at SQUIRREL] **:** any of a tribe or suborder (Brachyura) of crustaceans (as the typical crabs) having the abdomen greatly reduced — **brachyuran** *adj* — **brachy·urous** \-'yu̇r-əs\ *adj*

brac·ing \'brā-siŋ\ *adj* **:** giving strength, vigor, or freshness <a ~ breeze>

brack·en \'brak-ən\ *n* [ME *braken*, prob. of Scand origin; akin to OSw *bräkne* fern] **1 :** a large coarse fern; *esp* **:** a common brake (*Pteridium aquilinum*) **2 :** a growth of brakes

[1]brack·et \'brak-ət\ *n* [MF *braguette* codpiece, fr. dim. of *brague* breeches, fr. OProv *braga*, fr. L *braca*, fr. Gaulish *brāca*, of Gmc origin; akin to OHG *bruoh* breeches — more at BREECH] **1 :** an overhanging member that projects from a structure (as a wall) and is usu. designed to support a vertical load or to strengthen an angle **2 a :** a short wall shelf **b :** a fixture (as for holding a lamp) projecting from a wall or column **3 a :** one of a pair of marks [ ] used in writing and printing to enclose matter or in mathematics and logic as signs of aggregation — called also *square bracket* **b :** one of the pair of marks < > used to enclose matter — called also *angle bracket* **c :** PARENTHESIS 3 **d :** BRACE 5b **4 :** a pair of shots fired (as in front of and beyond a target) to aid in determining the exact distance from gun to target **5 a :** a section of a continuously numbered or graded series <the 18 to 22 age ~> **b :** one of a graded series of income groups <the $20,000 income ~>

²bracket *vt* **1 a :** to place within or as if within brackets **b :** to eliminate from consideration <his approach to moral questions ~*s* off religion> **2 :** to furnish or fasten with brackets **3 a :** to put in the same category : ASSOCIATE **b :** to assign to a group : CLASSIFY **4 a :** to get the range on (a target) by firing over and short **b :** to establish a margin on either side of (as an estimation)

brack·et·ed *adj, of a serif* **:** joined to the stroke by a curved line

bracket fungus *n* **:** a basidiomycete that forms shelflike sporophores

brack·ish \ˈbrak-ish\ *adj* [D *brac* salty; akin to MLG *brac* salty] **1 :** somewhat salty **2 a :** not appealing to the taste <~ tea> **b :** REPULSIVE — **brack·ish·ness** *n*

bract \ˈbrakt\ *n* [NL *bractea,* fr. L, thin metal plate] **1 :** a leaf from the axil of which a flower or floral axis arises **2 :** a leaf borne on a floral axis; *esp* **:** one subtending a flower or flower cluster — see COMPOSITE illustration — **brac·te·al** \ˈbrak-tē-əl\ *adj* — **brac·te·ate** \-tē-ət, -ˌāt\ *adj* — **bract·ed** \-təd\ *adj*

brac·te·ole \ˈbrak-tē-ˌōl\ *n* [NL *bracteola,* fr. L, dim. of *bractea*] **:** a small bract esp. on a floral axis — **brac·te·o·late** \ brak-ˈtē-ə-lət, ˈbrak-tē-ə-ˌlāt\ *adj*

¹brad \ˈbrad\ *n* [ME, fr. ON *broddr* spike; akin to OE *byrst* bristle — more at BRISTLE] **1 :** a thin nail of the same thickness throughout but tapering in width and having a slight projection at the top of one side instead of a head **2 :** a slender wire nail with a small barrel-shaped head

²brad *vt* **brad·ded; brad·ding :** to fasten with brads

brad·awl \ˈbrad-ˌȯl\ *n* **:** an awl with chisel edge used to make holes for brads or screws

bra·dy·car·dia \ˌbrād-i-ˈkärd-ē-ə *also* ˌbrad-\ *n* [NL, fr. Gk *bradys* slow + NL *-cardia*] **:** relatively slow heart action whether physiological or pathological — compare TACHYCARDIA

bra·dy·ki·nin \-ˈkī-nən\ *n* [Gk *bradys* slow] **:** a kinin that is formed in injured tissue, acts in vasodilation of small arterioles, is considered to play a part in inflammatory processes, and is composed of nine amino acids

brae \ˈbrā\ *n* [ME *bra,* fr. ON *brā* eyelash; akin to OE *bregdan* to move quickly — more at BRAID] *chiefly Scot* **:** a hillside esp. along a river

¹brag \ˈbrag\ *adj* **brag·ger; brag·gest** [ME] **:** FIRST-RATE

²brag *n* **1 :** a pompous or boastful statement **2 :** arrogant talk or manner **:** COCKINESS **3 :** BRAGGART

³brag *vb* **bragged; brag·ging** *vi* **:** to talk boastfully **:** engage in self-glorification ~ *vt* **:** to assert boastfully ***syn*** see BOAST ***ant*** apologize — **brag·ger** \ˈbrag-ər\ *n* — **brag·gy** \ˈbrag-ē\ *adj*

brag·ga·do·cio \ˌbrag-ə-ˈdō-s(h)ē-ˌō, -(ˌ)shō\ *n, pl* **-cios** [*Braggadocchio,* personification of boasting in *Faerie Queene* by Edmund Spenser] **1 :** BRAGGART **2 a :** empty boasting **b :** arrogant pretension **:** COCKINESS

brag·gart \ˈbrag-ərt\ *n* **:** a loud arrogant boaster — **braggart** *adj*

brah·ma \ˈbräm-ə, ˈbräm-, ˈbram-\ *n* [*Brahmaputra* river, India] **:** any of an Asian breed of large domestic fowls with feathered legs

¹Brah·ma \ˈbräm-ə\ *n* [Skt *brahman*] **1 :** the ultimate ground of all being in Hinduism **2 :** the creator god of the Hindu sacred triad — compare SIVA, VISHNU

²Brah·ma \ˈbrā-mə, ˈbräm-ə, ˈbram-\ *n* **:** BRAHMAN 2

Brah·man *or* **Brah·min** \ˈbräm-ən; *2 is* ˈbrām-, ˈbräm-, ˈbram-\ *n* [Skt *brāhmana,* lit., having to do with prayer, fr. *brahman,* neut., prayer] **1 a :** a Hindu of the highest caste traditionally assigned to the priesthood **b :** ¹BRAHMA 1 **2 :** any of an Indian breed of humped cattle **:** ZEBU; *esp* **:** a large vigorous heat-resistant and tick-resistant usu. silvery gray animal developed in the southern U.S. by interbreeding Indian cattle and used chiefly for crossbreeding — **Brah·man·ic** \brä-ˈman-ik\ *adj*

Brah·man·ism \ˈbräm-ə-ˌniz-əm\ *n* **:** orthodox Hinduism adhering to the pantheism of the Vedas and to the ancient sacrifices and family ceremonies

Brah·min \ˈbräm-ən\ *n* [var. of *Brahman*] **:** an intellectually and socially cultivated person regarded as aloof; *esp* **:** such a person from one of the older New England families <Boston ~*s*> — **Brah·min·i·cal** \brä-ˈmin-i-kəl\ *adj* — **Brah·min·ism** \ˈbräm-ə-ˌniz-əm\ *n*

¹braid \ˈbrād\ *vt* [ME *breyden,* lit., to move suddenly, fr. OE *bregdan;* akin to OHG *brettan* to draw (a sword), Gk *phorkon* something white or wrinkled] **1 a :** to form (three or more strands) into a braid **b :** to make by braiding **2 :** to do up (the hair) by interweaving three or more strands **3 :** INTERMINGLE, MIX <~ fact with fiction> **4 :** to ornament esp. with ribbon or braid — **braid·er** *n*

²braid *n* **1 a :** a cord or ribbon having usu. three or more component strands forming a regular diagonal pattern down its length; *esp* **:** a narrow fabric of intertwined threads used esp. for trimming **b :** a length of braided hair **2 :** high-ranking naval officers

braid·ed *adj* **1 a :** ornamented with braid **b :** made by intertwining three or more strands **2 :** forming an interlacing network of channels <a ~ river>

braid·ing \ˈbrād-iŋ\ *n* **:** something made of braided material

¹brail \ˈbrā(ə)l\ *n* [ME *brayle,* fr. AF *braiel,* fr. OF, strap] **1 :** a rope fastened to the leech of a sail and used for hauling the sail up or in **2 :** a dip net with which fish are hauled aboard a boat from a purse seine or trap

²brail *vt* **1 :** to take in (a sail) by the brails **2 :** to hoist (fish) by means of a brail

braille \ˈbrā(ə)l\ *n, often cap* [Louis *Braille*] **:** a system of writing for the blind that uses characters made up of raised dots — **braille** *vt*

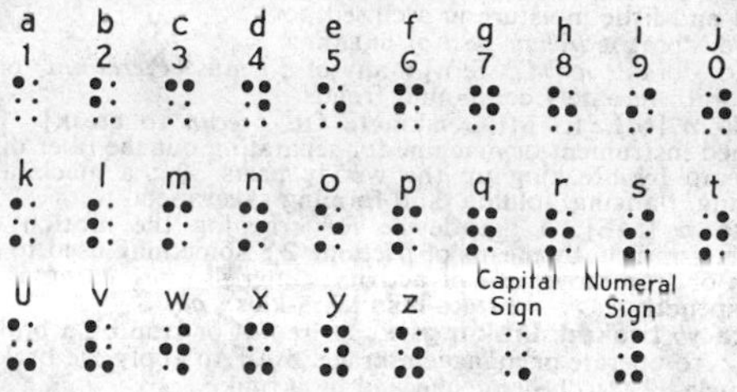

a b c d e f g h i j
1 2 3 4 5 6 7 8 9 0
k l m n o p q r s t
u v w x y z Capital Sign Numeral Sign

braille alphabet

braille·writ·er \-ˌrīt-ər\ *n, often cap* **:** a machine for writing braille

¹brain \ˈbrān\ *n* [ME, fr. OE *brægen;* akin to MLG *bregen* brain, Gk *brechmos* front part of the head] **1 a :** the portion of the vertebrate central nervous system that constitutes the organ of thought and neural coordination, includes all the higher nervous centers receiving stimuli from the sense organs and interpreting and correlating them to formulate the motor impulses, is made up of neurons and supporting and nutritive structures, is enclosed within the skull, and is continuous with the spinal cord through the foramen magnum **b :** a nervous center in invertebrates comparable in position and function to the vertebrate brain **2 a** (1) **:** INTELLECT, MIND <has a clever ~> (2) **:** intellectual endowment **:** INTELLIGENCE — often used in pl. <plenty of ~*s* in that family> **b** (1) **:** a very intelligent or intellectual person (2) **:** the chief planner of an organization or enterprise — usu. used in pl. **3 :** an automatic device (as a computer) that performs one or more of the functions of the human brain for control or computation

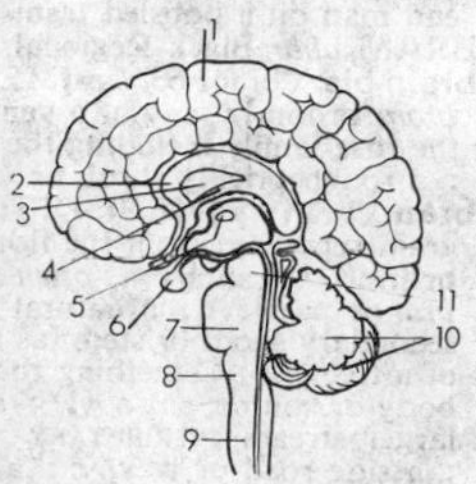

brain 1a: *1* cerebral hemisphere, *2* corpus callosum, *3* ventricle, *4* fornix, *5* thalamus, *6* pituitary gland, *7* pons, *8* medulla oblongata, *9* spinal cord, *10* cerebellum, *11* midbrain

²brain *vt* **1 :** to kill by smashing the skull **2 :** to hit on the head

brain·case \ˈbrān-ˌkās\ *n* **:** the cranium enclosing the brain

brain·child \-ˌchīld\ *n* **:** a product of one's creative imagination

brain drain *n* **:** a migration of professional people (as scientists, professors, or physicians) from one country to another usu. for higher salaries or better living conditions

-brained \ˈbrānd\ *adj comb form* **:** having (such) a brain <bigbrained> <feather*brained*>

brain hormone *n* **:** a hormone that is secreted by neurosecretory cells of the insect brain and that stimulates the prothoracic glands to secrete ecdysone

brain·ish \ˈbrā-nish\ *adj, archaic* **:** IMPETUOUS, HOTHEADED <and in this ~ apprehension kills the unseen good old man —Shak.>

brain·less \ˈbrān-ləs\ *adj* **:** devoid of intelligence **:** STUPID — **brain·less·ly** *adv* — **brain·less·ness** *n*

brain·pan \ˈbrān-ˌpan\ n **:** BRAINCASE

brain–pick·ing \-ˌpik-iŋ\ *n* **:** the act of picking information from another's mind — **brain–pick·er** *n*

brain·pow·er \-ˌpau̇(-ə)r\ *n* **1 :** intellectual ability **2 :** people with developed intellectual ability

brain·sick \-ˌsik\ *adj* **1 :** mentally disordered **2 :** arising from mental disorder <a ~ frenzy> — **brain·sick·ly** *adv*

brain stem *n* **:** the part of the brain composed of the mesencephalon, pons, and medulla oblongata and connecting the spinal cord with the forebrain and cerebrum

brain·storm \-ˌstȯ(ə)rm\ *n* **1 :** a violent transient fit of insanity **2 a :** a sudden bright idea **b :** a harebrained idea

brain·storm·ing \-ˌstȯr-miŋ\ *n* **:** a group problem-solving technique that involves the spontaneous contribution of ideas from all members of the group — **brain·storm** *vi* — **brain·storm·er** *n*

brains trust *n, chiefly Brit* **:** BRAIN TRUST

brain·teas·er \-ˌtē-zər\ *n* **:** something (as a puzzle) that demands mental effort and acuity for its solution

brain trust *n* **:** expert advisers concerned esp. with planning and strategy who often lack official or acknowledged status — **brain trust·er** \-ˌtrəs-tər\ *n*

brain·wash·ing \ˈbrān-ˌwȯsh-iŋ, -ˌwäsh-\ *n* [trans. of Chin (Pek) *hsi*[3] *nao*[3]] **1 :** a forcible indoctrination to induce someone to give up basic political, social, or religious beliefs and attitudes and to accept contrasting regimented ideas **2 :** persuasion by propaganda or salesmanship — **brain·wash** *vt* — **brainwash** *n* — **brain·wash·er** *n*

brain wave *n* **1 a :** rhythmic fluctuations of voltage between parts of the brain resulting in the flow of an electric current **b :** a current produced by brain waves **2 :** BRAINSTORM 2a

brainy \ˈbrā-nē\ *adj* **brain·i·er; -est :** having a well-developed intellect : INTELLIGENT — **brain·i·ness** *n*

braise \ˈbrāz\ *vt* **braised; brais·ing** [F *braiser*] **:** to cook slowly in fat and little moisture in a closed pot

¹brake \ˈbrāk\ *archaic past of* BREAK

²brake \ˈbrāk\ *n* [ME, fern] **:** any of a genus (*Pteridium*) of tall ferns with ternately compound fronds

³brake *n* [ME, fr. MLG; akin to OE *brecan* to break] **1 :** a toothed instrument or machine for separating out the fiber of flax or hemp by breaking up the woody parts **2 :** a machine for bending, flanging, folding, and forming sheet metal

⁴brake *n* [ME] **1 :** a device for arresting the motion of a mechanism usu. by means of friction **2 :** something used to slow down or stop movement or activity <interest rates acting as a ~ on expenditures> — **brake·less** \ˈbrā-kləs\ *adj*

⁵brake *vb* **braked; brak·ing** *vt* **:** to retard or stop by a brake ~ *vi* **1 :** to operate or manage a brake; *esp* **:** to apply the brake on a vehicle **2 :** to become checked by a brake

⁶brake *n* [ME *-brake*] **:** rough or marshy land overgrown usu. with one kind of plant — **braky** \ˈbrā-kē\ *adj*

brake·man \ˈbrāk-mən\ *n* **1 :** a freight or passenger train crew member who inspects the train and assists the conductor **2 :** the end man on a bobsled team who operates the brake

BRAM *abbr* Black Regional Action Movement

bram·ble \ˈbram-bəl\ *n* [ME *brembel,* fr. OE *brēmel;* akin to OE *brōm* broom] **:** any of a genus (*Rubus*) of usu. prickly shrubs of the rose family including the raspberries and blackberries; *broadly* **:** a rough prickly shrub or vine — **bram·bly** \-b(ə-)lē\ *adj*

bran \ˈbran\ *n* [ME, fr. OF] **:** the broken coat of the seed of cereal grain separated from the flour or meal by sifting or bolting

¹branch \ˈbranch\ *n, often attrib* [ME, fr. OF *branche,* fr. LL *branca* paw] **1 :** a natural subdivision of a plant stem; *esp* **:** a secondary shoot or stem (as a bough) arising from a main axis (as of a tree) **2 :** something that extends from or enters into a main body or source: as **a** (1) **:** a stream that flows into another usu. larger stream **:** TRIBUTARY (2) *South & Midland* **:** CREEK 2 **b :** a side road or way **c :** a slender projection (as the tine of an antler) **d :** a part of a mathematical curve separated from others **e :** a part of a computer program executed as a result of a program decision **3 :** a part of a complex body: as **a :** a division of a family descending from a particular ancestor **b :** an area of knowledge that may be considered apart from related areas <pathology is a ~ of medicine> **c** (1) **:** a division of an organization (2) **:** a separate but dependent part of a central organization <the neighborhood ~ of the city library> **d :** a language group less inclusive than a family <the Germanic ~ of the Indo-European language family> — **branched** \ˈbrancht\ *adj* — **branch·less** \ˈbranch-ləs\ *adj* — **branchy** \ˈbran-chē\ *adj*

²branch *vi* **1 :** to put forth branches **:** RAMIFY **2 :** to spring out (as from a main stem) **:** DIVERGE **3 :** to be an outgrowth — used with *from* <poetry that ~*ed* from religious prose> **4 :** to extend activities — usu. used with *out* <the business is ~*ing* out all over the state> **5 :** to follow one of two or more branches (as in a computer program) ~ *vt* **:** to ornament with designs of branches **2 :** to divide up **:** SECTION

bran·chia \ˈbraŋ-kē-ə\ *n, pl* **-chi·ae** \-kē-ˌē, -ˌī\ [L, sing., fr. Gk, pl. of *branchion* gill; akin to Gk *bronchos* trachea — more at CRAW] **:** ²GILL — **bran·chi·al** \-kē-əl\ *adj* — **bran·chi·ate** \-kē-ət, -ˌāt\ *adj*

bran·chio·pod \ˈbraŋ-kē-ə-ˌpäd\ *n* [deriv. of Gk *branchia* gills + *pod-, pous* foot — more at FOOT] **:** any of a group (Branchiopoda) of aquatic crustaceans typically having a long body, a carapace, and many pairs of leaflike appendages — **branchiopod** *adj* — **bran·chi·op·o·dan** \ˌbraŋ-kē-ˈäp-əd-ən\ *adj* — **bran·chi·op·o·dous** \-əd-əs\ *adj*

branch·let \ˈbranch-lət\ *n* **:** a small usu. terminal branch

branch water *n* [¹*branch* (creek)] **:** plain water <bourbon and *branch water*>

¹brand \ˈbrand\ *n* [ME, torch, sword, fr. OE; akin to OE *bærnan* to burn] **1 a :** a charred piece of wood **b :** FIREBRAND **1 c :** something (as lightning) that resembles a firebrand **2 :** SWORD **3 a** (1) **:** a mark made by burning with a hot iron to attest manufacture or quality or to designate ownership (2) **:** a mark made with a stamp or stencil for similar purposes **:** TRADEMARK **b** (1) **:** a mark put on criminals with a hot iron (2) **:** a mark of disgrace **:** STIGMA <the ~ of poverty> **4 a :** a class of goods identified by name as the product of a single firm or manufacturer **:** MAKE **b :** a characteristic or distinctive kind **:** VARIETY <a lively ~ of theater> **5 :** a tool used to produce a brand

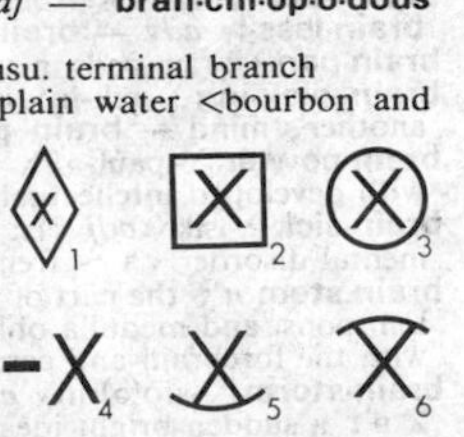

brands 3a(1) for cattle: *1* diamond X, *2* box X, *3* circle X, *4* bar X, *5* rocking X, *6* swinging X, *7* tumbling X, *8* walking X, *9* flying X, *10* crazy P, *11* lazy P, *12* reverse P

²brand *vt* **1 :** to mark with a brand **2 :** to mark with disapproval **:** STIGMATIZE **3 :** to impress indelibly <~ the lesson on his mind> — **brand·er** *n*

¹bran·dish \ˈbran-dish\ *vt* [ME *braundisshen,* fr. MF *brandiss-,* stem of *brandir,* fr. OF, fr. *brand* sword, of Gmc origin; akin to OE *brand*] **1 :** to shake or wave (as a weapon) menacingly **2 :** to exhibit in an ostentatious or aggressive manner ***syn*** see SWING

²brandish *n* **:** an act or instance of brandishing

brand·ling \ˈbran-(d)liŋ\ *n* **:** a small yellowish earthworm (*Eisenia foetida*) with brownish purple rings that is found in dunghills

brand name *n* **:** TRADE NAME 1b

brand-new \ˈbran-ˈn(y)ü\ *adj* **:** conspicuously new and unused

¹bran·dy \ˈbran-dē\ *n, pl* **brandies** [short for *brandywine,* fr. D *brandewijn,* fr. MD *brantwijn,* fr. *brant* distilled + *wijn* wine] **:** an alcoholic liquor distilled from wine or fermented fruit juice (as of apples)

²brandy *vt* **bran·died; bran·dy·ing :** to flavor, blend, or preserve with brandy

brank \ˈbraŋk\ *n* [origin unknown] **:** an instrument made of an iron frame surrounding the head and a sharp metal bit entering the mouth and formerly used to punish scolds — usu. used in pl.

bran·ni·gan \ˈbran-i-gən\ *n* [prob. fr. the name *Brannigan*] **1 :** a drinking spree **2 :** SQUABBLE

brant \ˈbrant\ *n, pl* **brant** *or* **brants** [origin unknown] **:** a wild goose; *esp* **:** any of several small dark geese (genus *Branta*) that breed in the Arctic and migrate southward

¹brash \ˈbrash\ *n* [obs. E *brash* to breach a wall] **:** a mass of fragments (as of ice)

²brash *adj* [origin unknown] **1 :** BRITTLE <~ wood> **2 a :** tending to act in headlong fashion **:** IMPETUOUS <the ~ young man darted into the traffic> **b :** done in haste without regard for consequences **:** RASH <~ acts> **3 :** uninhibitedly energetic or demonstrative **:** BUMPTIOUS <a delightfully ~ comedian> **4 a :** lacking restraint and discernment **:** TACTLESS <made a ~ speech about his wife's bad habits> **b :** aggressively self-assertive **:** IMPUDENT <a man ~ to the point of arrogance> **5 :** piercingly sharp **:** HARSH <a ~ squeal of brakes> — **brash·ly** *adv* — **brash·ness** *n*

brass \ˈbras\ *n* [ME *bras,* fr. OE *bræs;* akin to MLG *bras* metal] **1 :** an alloy consisting essentially of copper and zinc in variable proportions **2 a :** the brass instruments of an orchestra or band — often used in pl. **b :** a usu. brass memorial tablet **c :** bright metal fittings or utensils **d :** a brass, bronze, or gunmetal lining for a bearing **e :** empty fired cartridge shells **3 :** brazen self-assurance **:** GALL **4 :** BRASS HATS — **brass** *adj*

bras·sard \brə-ˈsärd, ˈbras-ˌärd\ *n* [F *brassard,* fr. MF *brassal,* fr. OIt *bracciale,* fr. *braccio* arm, fr. L *bracchium* — more at BRACE] **1 :** armor for protecting the arm — see ARMOR illustration **2 :** a cloth band worn around the upper arm usu. bearing an identifying mark

brass band *n* **:** a band consisting chiefly or solely of brass and percussion instruments

brass·bound \ˈbras-ˌbau̇nd, -ˈbau̇nd\ *adj* **1 :** having trim made of brass or a metal resembling brass **2 a** (1) **:** tradition-bound and opinionated (2) **:** making no concessions **:** INFLEXIBLE **b :** BRAZEN, PRESUMPTUOUS

brass–collar \-ˈkäl-ər\ *adj* **:** invariably voting the straight party ticket <~ Democrats>

bras·se·rie \ˌbras-(ə-)ˈrē\ *n* [F, fr. MF *brasser* to brew, fr. OF *bracier,* fr. L *braces* spelt] **:** a restaurant that sells beer

brass hat *n* **1 :** a high-ranking military officer **2 :** a person in a high position in civilian life

bras·si·ca \ˈbras-i-kə\ *n* [NL, genus name, fr. L, cabbage] **:** any of a large genus (*Brassica*) of Old World temperate zone herbs (as cabbages) with beaked cylindrical pods

bras·siere \brə-ˈzi(ə)r *also* ˌbras-ē-ˈe(ə)r\ *n* [obs. F *brassière* bodice, fr. OF *braciere* arm protector, fr. *bras* arm — more at BRACELET] **:** a woman's close-fitting undergarment with cups for bust support

brass instrument *n* **:** one of a group of wind instruments (as a French horn, trombone, trumpet, or tuba) that is usu. characterized by a long cylindrical or conical metal tube commonly curved two or more times and ending in a flared bell, that produces tones by the vibrations of the player's lips against a usu. cup-shaped mouthpiece, and that usu. has valves or a slide by which the player may produce all the tones within the instrument's range

brass knuckles *n pl but sing or pl in constr* **:** KNUCKLE 4

brass tacks *n pl* **:** details of immediate practical importance — usu. used in the phrase *get down to brass tacks*

brassy \ˈbras-ē\ *adj* **brass·i·er; -est 1 a :** being shamelessly bold **b :** OBSTREPEROUS **2 :** resembling brass esp. in color **3 :** resembling the sound of a brass instrument — **brass·i·ly** \ˈbras-ə-lē\ *adv* — **brass·i·ness** \ˈbras-ē-nəs\ *n*

brat \ˈbrat\ *n* [perh. fr. E dial. *brat* (ragamuffin)] **:** CHILD; *specif* **:** an ill-mannered annoying child — **brat·ti·ness** \ˈbrat-ē-nəs\ *n* — **brat·tish** \ˈbrat-ish\ *adj* — **brat·ty** \-ē\ *adj*

brat·tice \ˈbrat-əs, ˈbrat-ish\ *n* [ME *bretais* parapet, fr. OF *bretesche,* fr. ML *breteschia*] **:** an often temporary partition of planks or cloth used esp. in a mine to control ventilation — **brattice** *vt*

¹brat·tle \ˈbrat-ᵊl\ *n* [prob. imit.] *chiefly Scot* **:** CLATTER, SCAMPER

²brattle *vi* **brat·tled; brat·tling** *chiefly Scot* **:** to make a clattering or rattling sound

brat·wurst \ˈbrät-(ˌ)wərst, -ˌvu̇(ə)rst, -ˌvu̇s(h)t\ *n* [G, fr. OHG *brātwurst,* fr. *brāt* meat without waste + *wurst* sausage] **:** fresh pork sausage for frying

braun·schweig·er \ˈbrau̇n-ˌs(h)wī-gər\ *n* [G *Braunschweiger* (*wurst*), lit., Brunswick sausage] **:** smoked liverwurst

bra·va \ˈbräv-(ˌ)ä, brä-ˈvä\ *n* [It, fem. of *bravo*] **:** BRAVO — used interjectionally in applauding a woman

bra·va·do \brə-ˈväd-(ˌ)ō\ *n, pl* **-does** *or* **-dos** [MF *bravade* & OSp *bravata,* fr. OIt *bravata,* fr. *bravare* to challenge, show off, fr. *bravo*] **1 a :** blustering swaggering conduct **b :** a pretense of bravery **2 :** the quality or state of being foolhardy

¹brave \ˈbrāv\ *adj* **brav·er; brav·est** [MF, fr. OIt & OSp *bravo* courageous, wild, fr. L *barbarus* barbarous] **1 :** having courage **:** DAUNTLESS **2 :** making a fine show **:** COLORFUL <~ banners flying in the wind> **3 :** EXCELLENT, SPLENDID <the business collapsed despite a ~ start> — **brave·ly** *adv*

²brave *vb* **braved; brav·ing** *vt* **1 :** to face or endure with courage **2** *obs* **:** to make showy ~ *vi, archaic* **:** to make a brave show — **brav·er** *n*

³brave *n* **1** *archaic* **:** BRAVADO **2 :** one who is brave; *specif* **:** an American Indian warrior **3** *archaic* **:** BULLY, ASSASSIN

brav·ery \ˈbrāv-(ə-)rē\ *n, pl* **-er·ies 1 a :** fine clothes **b :** showy display **2 :** the quality or state of being brave **:** COURAGE

¹bra·vo \ˈbräv-(ˌ)ō\ *n, pl* **bravos** *or* **bravoes** [It, fr. *bravo,* adj.] **:** VILLAIN, DESPERADO; *esp* **:** a hired assassin

2bra·vo \ˈbräv-(ˌ)ō, brä-ˈvō\ *n, pl* **bravos** **:** a shout of approval — often used interjectionally in applauding a performance

3bra·vo \ˈbräv-(ˌ)ō, brä-ˈvō\ *vt* **bra·voed; bra·vo·ing :** to applaud by shouts of *bravo*

Bra·vo \ˈbräv-(ˌ)ō\ — a communications code word for the letter *b*

bra·vu·ra \brə-ˈv(y)u̇r-ə\ *n* [It, lit., bravery, fr. *bravare*] **1 :** a florid brilliant style **2 :** a musical passage requiring exceptional agility and technical skill in execution **3 :** a show of daring or brilliance

braw \ˈbrȯ, ˈbrä\ *adj* [modif. of MF *brave*] **1** *chiefly Scot* **:** GOOD, FINE **2** *chiefly Scot* **:** well dressed

1brawl \ˈbrȯl\ *vi* [ME *brawlen*] **1 :** to quarrel or fight noisily **:** WRANGLE **2 :** to make a loud confused noise <the river ~*ing* by> — **brawl·er** *n*

2brawl *n* **1 :** a noisy quarrel or fight **2 :** a loud tumultuous noise

brawly \ˈbrȯ-lē\ *adj* **brawl·i·er; -est 1 :** inclined to brawl **2 :** characterized by brawls or brawling

brawn \ˈbrȯn\ *n* [ME, fr. MF *braon* muscle, of Gmc origin; akin to OE *brǣd* flesh] **1 a :** full strong muscles esp. of the arm or leg **b :** muscular strength **2 a** *Brit* **:** the flesh of a boar **b :** HEADCHEESE

brawny \ˈbrȯ-nē\ *adj* **brawn·i·er; -est 1 :** MUSCULAR, STRONG **2 :** being swollen and hard <a ~ infected foot> — **brawn·i·ly** \-nə-lē\ *adv* — **brawn·i·ness** \-nē-nəs\ *n*

1bray \ˈbrā\ *vb* [ME *brayen*, fr. OF *braire* to cry, fr. (assumed) VL *bragere*, of Celt origin; akin to MIr *braigid* he breaks wind; akin to L *frangere* to break — more at BREAK] *vi* **:** to utter the characteristic loud harsh cry of a donkey ~ *vt* **:** to utter or play loudly, harshly, or discordantly — **bray** *n*

2bray *vt* [ME *brayen*, fr. MF *broiier*, of Gmc origin; akin to OHG *brehhan* to break — more at BREAK] **1 :** to crush or grind fine <~ seeds in a mortar> **2 :** to spread thin <~ printing ink>

bray·er \ˈbrā-ər\ *n* **:** a printer's hand inking roller

Braz *abbr* Brazil; Brazilian

1braze \ˈbrāz\ *vt* [irreg. fr. *brass*] *archaic* **:** HARDEN

2braze *vt* **brazed; braz·ing** [prob. fr. F *braser*, fr. OF, to burn, fr. *brese* live coals] **:** to solder with a nonferrous alloy that melts at a lower temperature than that of the metals being joined — **braz·er** *n*

1bra·zen \ˈbrāz-ᵊn\ *adj* [ME *brasen*, fr. OE *bræsen*, fr. *bræs* brass] **1 :** made of brass **2 a :** sounding harsh and loud like struck brass **b :** of the color of polished brass **3 :** marked by contemptuous boldness — **bra·zen·ly** *adv* — **bra·zen·ness** \ˈbrāz-ᵊn-(n)əs\ *n*

2brazen *vt* **bra·zened; bra·zen·ing** \ˈbrāz-niŋ, -ᵊn-iŋ\ **:** to face with defiance or impudence — usu. used in the phrase *brazen it out*

bra·zen–faced \ˌbrāz-ᵊn-ˈfāst\ *adj* **:** marked by insolence and bold disrespect <~ assertions>

1bra·zier \ˈbrā-zhər\ *n* [ME *brasier*, fr. *bras* brass] **:** one that works in brass

2brazier *n* [F *brasier*, fr. OF, fire of hot coals, fr. *brese*] **1 :** a pan for holding burning coals **2 :** a utensil in which food is exposed to heat through a wire grill

Bra·zil nut \brə-ˌzil-\ *n* [*Brazil*, So. America] **:** a tall So. American tree (*Bertholletia excelsa* of the family Lecythidaceae) that bears large globular capsules each containing several closely packed roughly triangular oily edible nuts; *also* **:** its nut

bra·zil·wood \brə-ˈzil-ˌwu̇d\ *n* [Sp *brasil*, fr. *brasa* live coals; fr. its color] **:** the heavy wood of any of various tropical leguminous trees (esp. genus *Caesalpinia*) that is used as red and purple dyewood and in cabinetwork

BRE *abbr* bachelor of religious education

1breach \ˈbrēch\ *n* [ME *breche*, fr. OE *bryce*; akin to OE *brecan* to break] **1 :** infraction or violation of a law, obligation, tie, or standard **2 a :** a broken, ruptured, or torn condition or area **b :** a gap (as in a wall) made by battering **3 a :** a break in accustomed friendly relations **b :** a temporary gap in continuity **:** HIATUS **4 :** a leap esp. of a whale out of water

2breach *vt* **1 :** to make a breach in <~ the city walls> **2 :** BREAK, VIOLATE <~ an agreement> ~ *vi* **:** to leap out of water <a whale ~*ing*>

breach of promise : violation of a promise esp. to marry

1bread \ˈbred\ *n* [ME *breed*, fr. OE *brēad*; akin to OHG *brōt* bread, OE *brēowan* to brew] **1 :** a usu. baked and leavened food made of a mixture whose basic constituent is flour or meal **2 :** FOOD, SUSTENANCE <our daily ~> **3 a :** LIVELIHOOD <earns his ~ as a laborer> **b** *slang* **:** MONEY — **bread upon the waters :** resources chanced or charitable deeds performed without expectation of return

2bread *vt* **:** to cover with bread crumbs <a ~*ed* pork chop>

bread–and–butter *adj* **1 a :** being as basic as the earning of one's livelihood <small paychecks, inadequate housing, and other ~ issues> **b :** that can be depended upon <a football team's ~ play> <the ~ repertoire of an orchestra> **2 :** sent or given as thanks for hospitality <a ~ letter>

bread and butter *n* **:** a means of sustenance or livelihood

bread and circuses *n pl* [trans. of L *panis et circenses*] **:** a palliative offered esp. to avert potential discontent

bread·bas·ket \ˈbred-ˌbas-kət\ *n* **1** *slang* **:** STOMACH **2 :** a major cereal-producing region

1bread·board \ˈbred-ˌbō(ə)rd, -ˌbȯ(ə)rd\ *n* **1 :** a board on which dough is kneaded or bread cut **2 :** a board on which electric or electronic circuit diagrams may be laid out

2breadboard *vt* **:** to make an experimental arrangement of (as an electronic circuit or a mechanical system) to test feasibility

bread·fruit \ˈbred-ˌfrüt\ *n* **:** a round usu. seedless fruit that resembles bread in color and texture when baked; *also* **:** a tall tropical tree (*Artocarpus altilis*) of the mulberry family that bears this fruit

bread·stuff \-ˌstəf\ *n* **1 :** a cereal product (as grain or flour) **2 :** BREAD

breadth \ˈbredth, ˈbretth\ *n* [obs. E *brede* breadth (fr. ME, fr. OE *brǣdu*, fr. *brād* broad) + *-th* (as in *length*)] **1 :** distance from side to side **:** WIDTH **2 a :** something of full width **b :** a wide expanse <~*s* of grass> **3 a :** comprehensive quality **:** SCOPE <the remarkable ~ of his learning> **b :** liberality of views or taste

breadth·ways \-ˌwāz\ *adv or adj* **:** in the direction of the breadth <a course of bricks laid ~>

breadth·wise \-ˌwīz\ *adv or adj* **:** BREADTHWAYS

bread·win·ner \ˈbred-ˌwin-ər\ *n* **1 :** a member of a family whose wages supply its livelihood **2 :** a means of livelihood — **bread·win·ning** \-ˌwin-iŋ\ *n*

1break \ˈbrāk\ *vb* **broke** \ˈbrōk\; **bro·ken** \ˈbrō-kən\; **break·ing** [ME *breken*, fr. OE *brecan*; akin to OHG *brehhan* to break, L *frangere*] *vt* **1 a :** to separate into parts with suddenness or violence **b :** FRACTURE <~ an arm> **c :** MAIM, MUTILATE **d :** RUPTURE <~ the skin> **e :** to cut into and turn over the surface of **:** PLOW **2 a :** VIOLATE, TRANSGRESS <~ the law> **b :** to invalidate (a will) by action at law **3 a** *archaic* **:** to force entry into **b :** to burst and force a way through **c :** to escape by force from <~ jail> **d :** to make or effect by cutting, forcing, or pressing through <~ a trail through the woods> **4 :** to make ineffective as a binding force **:** SUNDER <~*ing* his chains> **5 a :** to disrupt the order or compactness of <~ ranks> **b :** to end, close, or destroy by dispersing <~ up the partnership> **6 a :** to defeat utterly and end as an effective force **:** DESTROY **b :** to crush the spirit of **c :** to make tractable or submissive: as (1) **:** to train (an animal) to adjust to the service or convenience of man (2) **:** INURE, ACCUSTOM **d :** to exhaust in health, strength, or capacity **7 a :** to ruin financially **b :** to reduce in rank **8 a :** to check the force or intensity of <the bushes will ~ his fall> **b :** to cause failure and discontinuance of (a strike) by measures outside bargaining processes **9 a :** EXCEED, SURPASS <~ a speed record> **b :** to score less than (a specified total) <golfer trying to ~ 90> **10 :** to ruin the prospects of <could make or ~ her career> **11 :** to demonstrate the falsity of <~ an alibi> **12 :** to cause a sharp reduction in the price of <news likely to ~ the market sharply> **13 a :** to stop or bring to an end suddenly **:** HALT <~ a deadlock> **b :** INTERRUPT, SUSPEND <~ the silence with a cry> **c :** to open and bring about suspension of operation <~ an electric circuit> **d :** to destroy unity or completeness of <~ a dining room set by buying a chair> **e :** to change the appearance of uniformity of <a dormer ~*s* the level roof> **f :** to split the surface of <fish ~*ing* water> **g :** to cause to discontinue a habit <tried to ~ him of smoking> **14 :** to make known **:** TELL <~ the bad news gently> **15 a :** to find an explanation or solution for **:** SOLVE <the detective will ~ the case> **b :** to discover the essentials of (a code or cipher system) **16 :** to split into smaller units, parts, or processes **:** DIVIDE <~ a $5 bill> — often used with *up* or *down* **17 :** to make (a propelled ball) curve, drop, or rise sharply **18 :** to open the action of (a gun) ~ *vi* **1 a :** to escape with sudden forceful effort — often used with *out* <~ out of jail> **b :** to come into being by or as if by bursting forth <day was ~*ing*> **c :** to give vent to expression with abruptness <~*ing* into tears> <his face ~*s* out into a smile> **d :** to effect a penetration <~ through security lines> **e :** to emerge through the surface of the water **f :** to come to pass **:** OCCUR <report news stories as they ~> **g :** to take a different course **:** DEPART <~ away from tradition> **h :** to make a sudden dash <~ for cover> **i :** to separate after a clinch in boxing **2 a :** to come apart or split into pieces **:** BURST, SHATTER **b :** to open spontaneously or by pressure from within <his boil finally *broke*> **c** *of a wave* **:** to curl over and fall apart in surf or foam **3 :** to become fair **:** CLEAR <when the weather ~*s*> **4 :** to give way in disorderly retreat **5 a :** to fail in health, strength, vitality, or control <may ~ under questioning> **b :** to become inoperative because of damage, wear, or strain **6 :** to undergo a sudden marked decrease in price or value <rail stocks may ~ sharply> **7 :** to end a relationship, connection, accord, or agreement — usu. used with *with* **8 a :** to swerve suddenly **b :** to curve, drop, or rise sharply <a fastball that ~*s* away from the batter> **9 a :** to alter sharply in tone, pitch, or intensity <his voice ~*ing* with emotion> **b :** to shift abruptly from one register to another <his voice *broke* from his new bass to his original soprano> **10 :** to fail to keep a prescribed gait — used of a horse **11 :** to interrupt one's activity or occupation for a brief period <~ for lunch> **12 :** to make the opening shot of a game of pool **13 a :** to divide into classes, categories, or types **b :** to fold, bend, lift, or come apart at a seam, groove, or joint **c** *of cream* **:** to separate during churning into liquid and fat **14 :** HAPPEN, DEVELOP <for the team to succeed, everything has to ~ right> — **break a leg :** to be successful in a performance — used in the phrase *I hope you break a leg* — **break camp :** to pack up gear and leave a camp or campsite — **break cover** *or* **break covert :** to start from a covert or lair <the hunted fox *broke cover*> — **break even :** to achieve a balance; *esp* **:** to operate a business or enterprise without either loss or profit — **break ground 1 :** to begin excavating **2 :** to make or show discoveries **:** PIONEER — **break into 1 :** to begin with or as if with a sudden throwing off of restraint <the horse *breaks into* a gallop> **2 :** to make entry or entrance <trying to *break into* show business> **3 :** INTERRUPT <*break into* a TV program with a news flash> — **break one's heart :** to crush emotionally with sorrow — **break one's wrists :** to turn the wrists as part of the swing of a club or bat — **break service** *or* **break one's service :** to win a point against an opponent's service in a racket game — **break the back :** to subdue the main force <*break the back* of inflation> — **break the ice 1 :** to make a beginning **2 :** to get through the first difficulties in starting a conversation or discussion — **break through :** to make a penetration — **break wind :** to expel gas from the intestine

---

ə abut ᵊ kitten ər further a back ā bake ä cot, cart
au̇ out ch chin e less ē easy g gift i trip ī life
j joke ŋ sing ō flow ȯ flaw ȯi coin th thin t͟h this
ü loot u̇ foot y yet yü few yu̇ furious zh vision

[2]**break** *n* **1 a :** an act or action of breaking **b :** the opening shot in a game of pool or billiards **c :** the process of opening a gap in an electrical circuit **2 a :** a condition produced by or as if by breaking : GAP <a ~ in the clouds> **b :** a gap in an otherwise continuous electric circuit **3 :** the action or act of breaking in, out, or forth <convicts planning a jail ~> **4 a :** DASH, RUSH <a base runner making a ~ for home> **b :** FAST BREAK **5 a :** the start of a race **b :** the act of separating after a clinch in boxing **6 :** an interruption in continuity <a ~ in the weather>: as **a :** a notable change of subject matter, attitude, or treatment **b (1) :** an abrupt, significant, or noteworthy change or interruption in a continuous process, trend, or surface **(2) :** a respite from work or duty **(3) :** a planned interruption in a radio or television program <a ~ for the commercial> **c :** deviation of a pitched baseball from a straight line **d** *mining* **:** DISLOCATION, FAULT **e :** failure of a horse to maintain the prescribed gait **f :** an abrupt change in the quality or pitch of musical tone **g :** a notable variation in pitch, intensity, or tone in the voice **h :** the action or an instance of breaking service **7 a :** a rupture in previously agreeable relations <a ~ between the two countries> **b :** an abrupt split or difference with something previously adhered to or followed <a sharp ~ with tradition> **8 :** a sequence of successful shots in billiards : RUN **9 :** a place or situation at which a break occurs: **a :** the point where one musical register changes to another **b :** a short ornamental passage interpolated between phrases in jazz **c :** the place at which a word is divided esp. at the end of a line of print or writing **d :** a pause or interruption (as a caesura or diaeresis) within or at the end of a verse **e :** a failure to make a strike or a spare on a frame in bowling **10 :** a sudden and abrupt decline of prices or values **11 :** an awkward social blunder **12 :** a stroke of luck and esp. of good luck <a bad ~> <got a ~> **13 :** BREAKDOWN b <suffered a mental ~>

break·able \'brā-kə-bəl\ *adj* **:** capable of being broken — **break·able** *n*

break·age \'brā-kij\ *n* **1 a :** the action of breaking **b :** a quantity broken **2 :** allowance for things broken

[1]**break·away** \'brā-kə-ˌwā\ *n* **1 a :** one that breaks away **b :** an act or instance of breaking away (as from a group or tradition) **2 :** an object made to shatter or collapse under pressure or impact

[2]**breakaway** *adj* **1 :** favoring independence from an affiliation : SECEDING <a ~ faction formed a new party> **2 :** made to break, shatter, or bend easily <~ road signs for highway safety>

break ball *n* **:** a ball that must be pocketed before the cue ball breaks the rack in some forms of pool

break·bone fever \ˌbrāk-ˌbōn-\ *n* **:** DENGUE

break·down \'brāk-ˌdau̇n\ *n* **:** the action or result of breaking down: as **a :** a failure to function **b :** a physical, mental, or nervous collapse **c :** failure to progress or have effect : DISINTEGRATION <a ~ of negotiations> **d :** the process of decomposing <~ of food during digestion> **e :** division into categories : CLASSIFICATION; *also* **:** an account analyzed into categories

break down \(ˈ)brāk-'dau̇n\ *vt* **1 a :** to cause to fall or collapse by breaking or shattering **b :** to make ineffective <*break down* legal barriers> **2 a :** to divide into parts or categories **b :** to separate (as a chemical compound) into simpler substances : DECOMPOSE **c :** to take apart esp. for storage or shipment and for later reassembling ~ *vi* **1 a :** to become inoperative through breakage or wear **b :** to become inapplicable or ineffective : DETERIORATE <relations began to *break down*> **2 a :** to be susceptible to analysis or subdivision <the outline *breaks down* into three parts> **b :** to undergo decomposition ***syn*** see ANALYZE

[1]**break·er** \'brā-kər\ *n* **1 a :** one that breaks **b :** a machine or plant for breaking rocks or coal **2 :** a wave breaking into foam (as against the shore) **3 :** a strip of fabric under the tread of a tire for extra protection of the carcass

[2]**brea·ker** \'brā-kər\ *n* [by folk etymology fr. Sp *barrica*] **:** a small water cask

break-even \brā-'kē-vən\ *adj* **:** having equal loss and profit <the ~ point in a business venture>

break·fast \'brek-fəst\ *n* **1 :** the first meal of the day esp. when taken in the morning **2 :** the food prepared for a breakfast <eat your ~> — **breakfast** *vb* — **break·fast·er** *n*

break·front \'brāk-ˌfrənt\ *n* **:** a large cabinet or bookcase whose center section projects beyond the flanking end sections

break-in \'brā-ˌkin\ *n* **1 :** the act or action of breaking in <a rash of ~*s* at the new apartment house> **2 :** a performance or a series of performances serving as a trial run

break in \(ˈ)brā-'kin\ *vi* **1 :** to enter a house or building by force **2 a :** to interrupt in a conversation **b :** INTRUDE <*break in* upon his privacy> **3 :** to start in an activity or enterprise <*breaking in* as a cub reporter> ~ *vt* **1 :** to accustom to a certain activity or occurrence <*break in* the new quarterback> **2 :** to overcome the stiffness of (a new article)

breaking and entering *n* **:** HOUSEBREAKING

breaking point *n* **1 :** the point at which a person gives way under stress **2 :** the point at which a situation becomes crucial

break·neck \ˌbrāk-ˌnek\ *adj* **:** very fast or dangerous <~ speed>

break off *vi* **1 :** to become detached : SEPARATE **2 :** to stop abruptly <*break off* in the middle of a sentence> ~ *vt* **:** DISCONTINUE <*break off* diplomatic relations>

break·out \'brā-ˌkau̇t\ *n* **:** a violent or forceful break from a restraining condition or situation; *esp* **:** a military attack to break from encirclement

break out \(ˈ)brā-'kau̇t\ *vi* **1 :** to become affected with a skin eruption **2 :** to develop or emerge with suddenness and force <a riot *broke out*> ~ *vt* **1 a :** to take from shipboard stowage preparatory to using **b :** to make ready for action or use <*break out* the tents and make camp> **c :** to produce for consumption <*break out* a bottle> **2 a :** to display flying and unfurled **b :** DISLODGE

break·point \'brāk-ˌpȯint\ *n* **:** a point (as in a process) at which an interruption can be made

break·through \-ˌthrü\ *n* **1 :** an act or point of breaking through an obstruction **2 :** an offensive thrust that penetrates and carries beyond a defensive line in warfare **3 :** a sudden advance esp. in knowledge or technique <a medical ~>

break·up \'brā-ˌkəp\ *n* **1 :** DISSOLUTION, DISRUPTION <the ~ of a marriage> **2 :** a division into smaller units <the ~ of the large estates>

break up \(ˈ)brā-'kəp\ *vt* **1 :** to disrupt the continuity or flow of <too many footnotes can *break up* a text> **2 :** DECOMPOSE <*break up* a chemical> **3 :** to bring to an end <a fight *breaks up* the meeting> **4 a :** to break into pieces in scrapping or salvaging : SCRAP **b :** CRUMBLE <*break up* soil around growing plants> **5 :** to do away with : DESTROY <the move to *break up* big school systems —F. H. Vaughn> **6 :** to cause to laugh heartily <that joke *breaks* me *up*> ~ *vi* **1 a :** to cease to exist as a unified whole <their partnership *broke up*> **b :** to end a romance **2 :** to lose morale, composure, or resolution <likely to *break up* under enemy attack>; *esp* **:** to become abandoned to laughter <*breaks up* completely, laughing himself into a coughing fit —Gene Williams>

break·wa·ter \'brā-ˌkwȯt-ər, -ˌkwät-\ *n* **:** an offshore structure (as a wall) used to protect a harbor or beach from the force of waves

[1]**bream** \'brim, 'brēm\ *n, pl* **bream** *or* **breams** [ME *breme*, fr. MF, of Gmc origin; akin to OHG *brahsima* bream, *brettan* to draw (a sword) — more at BRAID] **1 :** a European freshwater cyprinid fish (*Abramis brama*); *broadly* **:** any of various related fishes **2 a :** a porgy or related fish (family Sparidae) **b :** any of various freshwater sunfishes (*Lepomis* and related genera); *esp* **:** BLUEGILL

[2]**bream** \'brēm\ *vt* [prob. fr. D *brem* furze] **:** to clean (a ship's bottom) by heating and scraping

[1]**breast** \'brest\ *n* [ME *brest*, fr. OE *brēost*; akin to OHG *brust* breast, Russ *bryukho* belly] **1 :** either of two protuberant milk-producing glandular organs situated on the front of the chest in the human female and some other mammals; *broadly* **:** a discrete mammary gland **2 :** the fore or ventral part of the body between the neck and the abdomen **3 :** the seat of emotion and thought : BOSOM <caused little concern in official ~*s*> **4 a :** something (as a front, swelling, or curving part) resembling a breast **b :** FACE 6

[2]**breast** *vt* **1 :** to contend with resolutely : CONFRONT <~ the rush traffic> **2** *chiefly Brit* **:** CLIMB, ASCEND **3 :** to thrust the chest against <the sprinter ~*ed* the tape>

breast-beat·ing \'brest-ˌbēt-iŋ\ *n* **:** noisy demonstrative protestation (as of grief, anger, or self-recrimination)

breast·bone \'bres(t)-'bōn, -ˌbōn\ *n* **:** STERNUM

breast drill *n* **:** a portable drill with a plate that is pressed by the breast in forcing the drill against the work

breast-feed \'brest-ˌfēd\ *vt* **:** to feed (a baby) from a mother's breast rather than from a bottle

breast·plate \'bres(t)-ˌplāt\ *n* **1 :** a metal plate worn as defensive armor for the breast — see ARMOR illustration **2 :** a vestment worn in ancient times by a Jewish high priest and set with 12 gems bearing the names of the tribes of Israel **3 :** a piece against which the workman presses his breast in operating a breast drill or similar tool **4 :** PLASTRON 2

breast·stroke \'bres(t)-ˌstrōk\ *n* **:** a swimming stroke executed in a prone position by extending the arms in front of the head while drawing the knees forward and outward and then sweeping the arms back with palms out while kicking outward and backward — **breast·strok·er** \-ˌstrō-kər\ *n*

breast·work \'bres-ˌtwərk\ *n* **:** a temporary fortification

breath \'breth\ *n* [ME *breth*, fr. OE *brǣth*; akin to OHG *brādam* breath, OE *beorma* yeast —more at BARM] **1 a :** air filled with a fragrance or odor **b :** a slight indication : SUGGESTION <the faintest ~ of scandal> **2 a :** the faculty of breathing <recovering his ~ after the race> **b :** an act of breathing <fought to his last ~> **c :** opportunity or time to breathe : RESPITE **3 :** a slight breeze **4 a :** air inhaled and exhaled in breathing <bad ~> **b :** something (as moisture on a cold surface) produced by breath or breathing **5 :** a spoken sound : UTTERANCE **6 :** SPIRIT, ANIMATION **7 :** expiration of air with the glottis wide open (as in the formation of \f\ and \s\ sounds) — **in one breath** *or* **in the same breath :** almost simultaneously — **out of breath :** breathing very rapidly (as from strenuous exercise)

breath·able \'brē-th̲ə-bəl\ *adj* **1 :** suitable for breathing <~ air> **2 :** allowing air to pass through : POROUS <a ~ synthetic fabric> —**breath·abil·i·ty** \ˌbrē-th̲ə-'bil-ət-ē\ *n*

breathe \'brēth̲\ *vb* **breathed; breath·ing** [ME *brethen*, fr. *breth*] *vi* **1 a** *obs* **:** to emit a fragrance or aura **b :** to become perceptible **2 a :** to draw air into and expel it from the lungs : RESPIRE; *broadly* **:** to take in oxygen and give out carbon dioxide through natural processes **b :** to inhale and exhale freely **3 :** LIVE **4 :** to pause and rest before continuing **5 :** to blow softly **6** *of an internal-combustion engine* **:** to use air to support combustion ~ *vt* **1 a :** to send out by exhaling **b :** to instill by or as if by breathing <~ new life into the movement> **2 a :** UTTER, EXPRESS <don't ~ a word of it to anyone> **b :** to make manifest : EVINCE <the novel ~*s* despair> **3 :** to give rest from exertion to **4 :** to take in in breathing <~ the scent of pines> — **breathe down one's neck 1 :** to threaten esp. in attack or pursuit **2 :** to keep one under close or constant surveillance <parents always *breathing down his neck*> — **breathe easily** *or* **breathe freely :** to enjoy relief (as from pressure or danger)

breathed \'bretht\ *adj* **:** VOICELESS 2

breath·er \'brē-th̲ər\ *n* **1 :** one that breathes **2 :** a break in activity for rest or relief **3 :** a small vent in an otherwise airtight enclosure

breath·ing \'brē-th̲iŋ\ *n* **1 :** BREATHER 2 **2 :** either of the marks ʻ and ʼ used in writing Greek to indicate aspiration or its absence

breathing space *n* **:** a period of inactivity esp. for rest and mustering up strength for subsequent efforts

breath·less \'breth-ləs\ *adj* **1 a :** not breathing **b :** DEAD **2 a :** panting or gasping for breath **b :** leaving one breathless <drove at a ~ speed> **c :** holding one's breath from emotion <~ in anticipation> **d :** GRIPPING, INTENSE <~ tension> **3 :** STALE, STUFFY <~ air in the attic> — **breath·less·ly** *adv* — **breath·less·ness** *n*

breath·tak·ing \'breth-,tā-kiŋ\ *adj* **1 :** making one out of breath **2 a :** EXCITING, THRILLING <a ~ stock car race> **b :** ASTONISHING <his ~ ignorance> — **breath·tak·ing·ly** \-kiŋ-lē\ *adv*

breathy \'breth-ē\ *adj* **breath·i·er; -est :** characterized by or accompanied with the audible passage of breath

brec·cia \'brech-(ē-)ə\ *n* [It] **:** a rock consisting of sharp fragments embedded in a fine-grained matrix (as sand or clay)

brec·ci·ate \'brech-ē-,āt\ *vt* **-at·ed; -at·ing 1 :** to break (rock) into fragments **2 :** to form (rock) into breccia — **brec·ci·a·tion** \,brech-ē-'ā-shən\ *n*

Breck *abbr* Brecknockshire

brede \'brēd\ *n* [alter. of *braid*] *archaic* **:** EMBROIDERY

bred–in–the–bone \,bred-ᵊn-t͟hə-'bōn\ *adj* **1 :** very deeply inculcated <~ honesty> **2 :** marked by an inveterate or lasting quality <a ~ gambler>

bree \'brē\ *n* [ME *bre*] *chiefly Scot* **:** BROTH, LIQUOR

breech \'brēch; "*breeches*" (*garment*) *is usu* 'brich-əz\ *n* [ME, breeches, fr. OE *brēc*, pl. of *brōc* leg covering; akin to OHG *bruoh* breeches, OE *brecan* to break] **1** *pl* **a :** short trousers covering the hips and thighs and fitting snugly at the lower edges at or just below the knee **b :** TROUSERS **2 :** the hind end of the body **:** BUTTOCKS **3 a :** the part of a firearm at the rear of the bore **b :** the bottom of a pulley block

breech·block \'brēch-,bläk\ *n* **:** the block in breech-loading firearms that closes the rear of the bore against the force of the charge

breech·clout \'brēch-,klau̇t, 'brich-\ *or* **breech·cloth** \-,klȯth\ *n* **:** LOINCLOTH

breech·es buoy \'brē-chəz- *also* 'brich-əz-\ *n* **:** a canvas seat in the form of breeches hung from a life buoy running on a hawser and used to haul persons from one ship to another or from ship to shore esp. in rescue operations

breech·ing \'brē-chiŋ, 'brich-iŋ\ *n* **1 :** the part of a harness that passes around the breech of a draft animal **2 :** the short coarse wool on the breech and hind legs of a sheep or goat; *also* **:** the hair on the corresponding part of a dog

breech·load·er \'brēch-'lōd-ər\ *n* **:** a firearm that receives its ammunition at the breech — **breech–load·ing** \-'lōd-iŋ\ *adj*

1**breed** \'brēd\ *vb* **bred** \'bred\; **breed·ing** [ME *breden*, fr. OE *brēdan*; akin to OE *brōd* brood] *vt* **1 :** to produce (offspring) by hatching or gestation **2 a :** BEGET 1 **b :** PRODUCE, ENGENDER <despair often ~s violence> **3 :** to propagate (plants or animals) sexually and usu. under controlled conditions <*bred* several strains of corn together to produce a new high-lysine variety> **4 a :** to bring up **:** NURTURE <born and *bred* in the country> **b :** to inculcate by training <~ good manners into one's children> **5 a :** to mate with **:** INSEMINATE **b :** IMPREGNATE **6 :** to produce (a fissionable element) by bombarding a nonfissionable element with neutrons from a radioactive element so that more fissionable material is produced than is used up ~ *vi* **1 :** to produce offspring by sexual union **2 :** to propagate animals or plants

2**breed** *n* **1 :** a group of animals or plants presumably related by descent from common ancestors and visibly similar in most characters; *esp* **:** such a group differentiated from the wild type under the influence of man **2 :** a number of persons of the same stock **3 :** CLASS, KIND <a new ~ of radicals>

breed·er *n* **:** one that breeds: as **a :** an animal or plant kept for propagation **b :** one engaged in the breeding of a specified organism

breed·ing *n* **1 :** the action or process of bearing or generating **2 :** ANCESTRY **3 a** *archaic* **:** EDUCATION <she had her ~ at my father's charge —Shak.> **b :** training in or observance of the proprieties **4 :** the sexual propagation of plants or animals

breeding ground *n* **1 :** the place to which animals go to breed **2 :** a place or set of circumstances considered favorable esp. to the propagation of certain ideas or conditions

breed of cat : TYPE, SORT — usu. used with *new* or *different*

breeks \'brēks, 'briks\ *n pl* [ME (northern dial.) *breke*, fr. OE *brēc*] *chiefly Scot* **:** BREECHES

1**breeze** \'brēz\ *n* [ME *brise*] **1 a :** a light gentle wind **b :** a wind of from 4 to 31 miles an hour **2 :** something easily done **:** CINCH — **breeze·less** \-ləs\ *adj* — **in a breeze :** EASILY <won the talent contest *in a breeze*>

2**breeze** *vi* **breezed; breez·ing 1 :** to move swiftly and airily <she *breezed* in wearing chiffon> **2 :** to make progress quickly and easily <~ through the book>

3**breeze** *n* [prob. modif. of F *braise* cinders] **:** residue from the making of coke or charcoal

breeze·way \'brēz-,wā\ *n* **:** a roofed often open passage connecting two buildings (as a house and garage) or halves of a building

breezy \'brē-zē\ *adj* **breez·i·er; -est 1 :** swept by breezes **2 :** BRISK, LIVELY — **breez·i·ly** \-zə-lē\ *adv* — **breez·i·ness** \-zē-nəs\ *n*

breg·ma \'breg-mə\ *n, pl* **-ma·ta** \-mət-ə\ [NL *bregmat-*, *bregma*, fr. LL, front part of the head, fr. Gk; akin to Gk *brechmos* front part of the head — more at BRAIN] **:** the point of junction of the coronal and sagittal sutures of the skull — **breg·mat·ic** \breg-'mat-ik\ *adj*

brems·strah·lung \'brem(p)sh-,shträl-əŋ\ *n* [G, lit., decelerated radiation] **:** the electromagnetic radiation produced by the sudden retardation of an electrical particle in an intense electric field

brent \'brent\ *var of* BRANT

breth·ren \'bret͟h-(ə-)rən, -ərn\ *pl of* BROTHER — used chiefly in formal or solemn address or in referring to the members of a profession, society, or sect

Brethren *n pl* **:** members of various sects originating chiefly in 18th century German Pietism; *esp* **:** DUNKERS

Bret·on \'bret-ᵊn\ *n* [F, fr. ML *Briton-*, *Brito*, fr. L, Briton] **1 :** a native or inhabitant of Brittany **2 :** the Celtic language of the Breton people — **Breton** *adj*

breve \'brēv, 'brev\ *n* [L, neut. of *brevis* brief — more at BRIEF] **1 :** a curved mark ˘ used to indicate a short vowel or a short or unstressed syllable **2 :** a note equivalent to four half notes

1**bre·vet** \bri-'vet, *chiefly Brit* 'brev-it\ *n* [ME, an official message, fr. MF, fr. OF, dim. of *brief* letter — more at BRIEF] **:** a commission giving a military officer higher nominal rank than that for which he receives pay

breve 2

2**brevet** *vt* **bre·vet·ted** *or* **bre·vet·ed; bre·vet·ting** *or* **brev·et·ing :** to confer rank upon by brevet

bre·via·ry \'brē-v(y)ə-rē, -vē-,er-ē\ *n, pl* **-ries** [L *breviarium*, fr. *brevis* — more at BRIEF] **1 :** a brief summary **:** ABRIDGMENT **2** *often cap* [ML *breviarium*, fr. L] **a :** a book containing the prayers, hymns, psalms, and readings for the canonical hours **b :** DIVINE OFFICE

brev·i·ty \'brev-ət-ē\ *n, pl* **-ties** [L *brevitas*, fr. *brevis*] **1 :** shortness of duration **2 :** expression in few words **:** CONCISENESS

1**brew** \'brü\ *vb* [ME *brewen*, fr. OE *brēowan*; akin to L *fervēre* to boil — more at BURN] *vt* **1 :** to prepare (as beer or ale) by steeping, boiling, and fermentation or by infusion and fermentation **2 a :** to bring about **:** FOMENT <~ trouble> **b :** CONTRIVE, PLOT **3 :** to prepare (as tea) by infusion in hot water ~ *vi* **1 :** to brew beer or ale **2 :** to be in the process of formation <a storm is ~*ing* in the east> — **brew·er** \'brü-ər, 'bru̇(-ə)r\ *n*

2**brew** *n* **1 a :** a brewed beverage **b** (1) **:** a cup of coffee or tea (2) **:** a glass of beer **c :** a product of brewing **2 :** the process of brewing

brew·age \'brü-ij\ *n* **:** BREW

brewer's yeast *n* **:** a yeast used or suitable for use in brewing; *specif* **:** the dried pulverized cells of such a yeast (*Saccharomyces cerevisiae*) used esp. as a source of B-complex vitamins

brew·ery \'brü-ə-rē, 'bru̇(-ə)r-ē\ *n, pl* **-er·ies :** a plant where malt liquors are manufactured

brewis \'brüz, 'brü-əs\ *n* [ME *brewes*, fr. OF *broez*, nom. sing. acc. pl. of *broet*, dim. of *breu* broth, of Gmc origin] *dial* **:** BROTH

1**bri·ar** \'brī(-ə)r\ *var of* BRIER

2**briar** *n* **:** a tobacco pipe made from the root of a brier

bri·ard \brē-'är(d)\ *n* [F, fr. *Brie*, district in France] **:** any of an old French breed of large strong usu. black dogs

1**bribe** \'brīb\ *vb* **bribed; brib·ing** *vt* **:** to induce or influence by or as if by bribery ~ *vi* **:** to practice bribery — **brib·able** \'brī-bə-bəl\ *adj* — **brib·er** *n*

2**bribe** *n* [ME, something stolen, fr. MF, bread given to a beggar] **1 :** money or favor given or promised to a person in a position of trust to influence his judgment or conduct **2 :** something that serves to induce or influence

brib·ery \'brī-b(ə-)rē\ *n* **:** the act or practice of giving or taking a bribe

bric–a–brac \'brik-ə-,brak\ *n, pl* **bric–a–brac** [F *bric-à-brac*] **1 :** a miscellaneous collection of small articles commonly of ornamental or sentimental value **:** CURIOS **2 :** something suggesting bric-a-brac esp. in extraneous decorative quality

1**brick** \'brik\ *n, often attrib* [ME *bryke*, fr. MF *brique*, fr. MD *bricke*; akin to OE *brecan* to break] **1** *pl* **bricks** *or* **brick :** a handy-sized unit of building or paving material typically being rectangular and about $2^1/_4$ x $3^3/_4$ x 8 inches and of moist clay hardened by heat **2 :** a good-hearted person **3 :** a rectangular compressed mass (as of ice cream) **4 :** a semisoft cheese with numerous small holes, smooth texture, and usu. mild flavor

2**brick** *vt* **:** to close, face, or pave with bricks — usu. used with *up* <~*ed* up a disused entrance>

brick·bat \'brik-,bat\ *n* **1 :** a fragment of a hard material (as a brick); *esp* **:** one used as a missile **2 :** an uncomplimentary remark

brick·field \-,fēld\ *n. Brit* **:** BRICKYARD

brick·lay·er \'brik-,lā-ər, -,le(-ə)r\ *n* **:** one who lays brick — **brick·lay·ing** \-,lā-iŋ\ *n*

brick·le \'brik-əl\ *adj* [ME *brekyl*] *dial* **:** BRITTLE

brick red *n* **:** a variable color averaging a moderate reddish brown

brick·work \'brik-,wərk\ *n* **:** work of or with bricks and mortar

brick·yard \-,yärd\ *n* **:** a place where bricks are made

1**brid·al** \'brīd-ᵊl\ *n* [ME *bridale*, fr. OE *brȳdealu*, fr. *brȳd* + *ealu* ale — more at ALE] **:** a nuptial festival or ceremony **:** MARRIAGE

2**bridal** *adj* **1 :** of or relating to a bride or a wedding **:** NUPTIAL **2 :** intended for a newly married couple <a ~ suite>

bridal wreath *n* **:** a spirea (*Spiraea prunifolia*) widely grown for its umbels of small white flowers borne in spring

bride \'brīd\ *n* [ME, fr. OE *brȳd*; akin to OHG *brūt* bride] **:** a woman just married or about to be married

bride·groom \'brīd-,grüm, -,gru̇m\ *n* [ME *bridegome*, fr. OE *brȳdguma*; akin to OHG *brūtigomo* bridegroom; both fr. a prehistoric NGmc-WGmc compound whose constituents are represented by OE *brȳd* and by OE *guma* man — more at HOMAGE] **:** a man just married or about to be married

brides·maid \'brīdz-,mād\ *n* **:** a woman attendant of a bride

bride·well \'brī-,dwel, -dwəl\ *n* [*Bridewell*, London jail] **:** PRISON

1**bridge** \'brij\ *n* [ME *brigge*, fr. OE *brycg*; akin to OHG *brucka* bridge, OSlav *brŭvŭno* beam] **1 a :** a structure carrying a pathway or roadway over a depression or obstacle **b :** a time, place, or means of connection or transition **2 :** something resembling a bridge in form or function: as **a :** the upper bony part of the nose; *also* **:** the part of a pair of glasses that rests upon it **b :** an arch serving to raise the strings of a musical instrument **c :** a raised transverse platform on a ship from which it is conned **d :** GANTRY 2b **e :** the hand as a rest for a billiards or pool cue; *also* **:** a device used as a cue rest **f :** the position of a wrestler on his back with his body arched so that he is supported usu. by his head and feet **3 a :** something (as a partial denture anchored to adjacent teeth) that fills a gap **b :** a connection (as an atom or bond) that joins two different parts of a molecule (as opposite sides of a ring) **4** : an electrical instrument or network for measuring or comparing resistances, inductances, capacitances, or impedances by comparing the ratio of two opposing voltages to a known ratio — **bridge·less** \-ləs\ *adj*

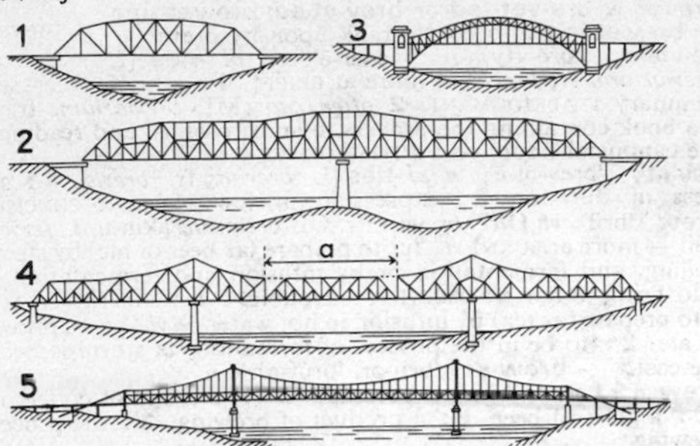

bridges 1a: *1* simple truss, *2* continuous truss, *3* steel arch, *4* cantilever, *a* suspended span, *5* suspension

2**bridge** *vt* **bridged; bridg·ing** **1** : to make a bridge over or across; *also* : to traverse by a bridge **2** : to provide with a bridge — **bridge·able** \-ə-bəl\ *adj*

3**bridge** *n* [alter. of earlier *biritch*, of unknown origin] : any of various card games for usu. four players in two partnerships that bid for the right to name a trump suit, score points for tricks made in excess of six, and play with the hand of declarer's partner exposed and played by declarer; *esp* : CONTRACT BRIDGE

bridge·board \ˈbrij-ˌbō(ə)rd, -ˌbȯ(ə)rd\ *n* : STRING 7a

bridge·head \-ˌhed\ *n* **1 a** : a fortification protecting the end of a bridge nearest an enemy **b** : a fortification protecting a bridge site, ford, or defile from attack from the other side **c** : an area around the end of a bridge **2** : an advanced position seized in hostile territory as a foothold for further advance

bridge·work \-ˌwərk\ *n* : a phase of prosthodontics concerned with the construction of dental bridges; *also* : the resulting structures

1**bri·dle** \ˈbrīd-ᵊl\ *n* [ME *bridel*, fr. OE *bridel;* akin to OE *bregdan* to move quickly — more at BRAID] **1 a** : the headgear with which a horse is governed and which carries a bit and reins **b** : a strip of metal joining two parts of a machine esp. for limiting or restraining motion **2** : something resembling a bridle in shape or function: as **a** : a length of secured cable with a second cable attached to the bight to which force is applied **b** : CURB, RESTRAINT <set a ~ on his power> **c** : FRENUM

2**bridle** *vb* **bri·dled; bri·dling** \ˈbrīd-liŋ, -ᵊl-iŋ\ *vt* **1** : to put a bridle on **2** : to restrain, check, or control with or as if with a bridle; *esp* : to get and keep under restraint <you must learn to ~ your tongue> ~ *vi* : to show hostility or resentment (as to an affront to one's pride or dignity) esp. by drawing back the head and chin ***syn*** **1** see RESTRAIN ***ant*** vent **2** see STRUT

bridle path *n* : a trail suitable for horseback riding

Brie \ˈbrē\ *n* [F, fr. *Brie*, district in France] : a soft perishable surface-ripened cheese somewhat similar to Camembert

1**brief** \ˈbrēf\ *adj* [ME *bref, breve*, fr. MF *brief*, fr. L *brevis;* akin to OHG *murg* short, Gk *brachys*] **1** : short in duration, extent, or length **2 a** : CONCISE <a ~ report> **b** : CURT, ABRUPT <a cold and ~ welcome> — **brief·ness** *n*

2**brief** *n* [ME *bref*, fr. MF, fr. ML *brevis*, fr. LL, summary, fr. L *brevis*, adj.] **1** : an official letter or mandate; *esp* : a papal letter less formal than a bull **2** : a brief written item or document: as **a** : a concise article **b** : SYNOPSIS, SUMMARY **c** : a concise statement of a client's case made out for the instruction of counsel in a trial at law **3** : an outline of an argument; *esp* : a formal outline esp. in law that sets forth the main contentions with supporting statements or evidence **4** *pl* : short snug underpants — **in brief** : in a few words : BRIEFLY

3**brief** *vt* **1** : to make an abstract or abridgment of **2** *Brit* : to retain as legal counsel **3 a** : to give final precise instructions to **b** : to coach thoroughly in advance **c** : to give essential information to — **brief·er** *n*

brief·case \ˈbrēf-ˌkās\ *n* : a flat flexible case for carrying papers or books

brief·ing \ˈbrē-fiŋ\ *n* **1** : an act or instance of giving precise instructions or essential information **2** : the instructions or information given at a briefing

brief·less \ˈbrē-fləs\ *adj* : having no legal clients

brief·ly \ˈbrē-flē\ *adv* **1 a** : in a brief way **b** : in brief **2** : for a short time

1**bri·er** \ˈbrī(-ə)r\ *n* [ME *brere*, fr. OE *brēr*] : a plant (as of the genera *Rosa, Rubus*, and *Smilax*) with a woody thorny or prickly stem; *also* : a mass or twig of these — **bri·ery** \ˈbrī(-ə)r-ē\ *adj*

2**brier** *n* [F *bruyère* heath, fr. (assumed) VL *brucaria*, fr. LL *brucus* heather, of Celt origin; akin to OIr *froech* heather; akin to Gk *ereikē* heather] : a heath (*Erica arborea*) of southern Europe with a root used for making pipes

bri·er·root \ˈbrī(-ə)r-ˌrüt, -ˌru̇t\ *n* : a root (as of the brier *Erica arborea*) used for tobacco pipes

1**brig** \ˈbrig\ *n* [short for *brigantine*] : a 2-masted square-rigged ship — compare HERMAPHRODITE BRIG

2**brig** *n* [prob. fr. 1*brig*] **1** : a place (as on a ship) for temporary confinement of offenders in the U.S. Navy **2** : GUARDHOUSE, PRISON

3**brig** *abbr* brigade; brigadier

1**bri·gade** \brig-ˈād\ *n* [F, fr. It *brigata*, fr. *brigare*] **1 a** : a large body of troops **b** : a tactical and administrative unit composed of a headquarters, one or more units of infantry or armor, and supporting units **2** : a group of people organized for special activity

brig

2**brigade** *vt* **bri·gad·ed; bri·gad·ing** **1** : to form or unite into a brigade **2** : COMBINE <an instance where speech and action are closely *brigaded* —W. O. Douglas>

brig·a·dier \ˌbrig-ə-ˈdi(ə)r\ *n* [F, fr. *brigade*] **1** : BRIGADIER GENERAL **2** : an officer in the British army commanding a brigade and ranking immediately below a major general

brigadier general *n* : a commissioned officer in the army, air force, or marine corps who ranks above a colonel and whose insignia is one star

brig·and \ˈbrig-ənd\ *n* [ME *brigaunt*, fr. MF *brigand*, fr. OIt *brigante*, fr. *brigare* to fight, fr. *briga* strife, of Celt origin; akin to OIr *brig* strength] : one who lives by plunder usu. as a member of a band : BANDIT — **brig·and·age** \-ən-dij\ *n* — **brig·and·ism** \-ˌdiz-əm\ *n*

brig·an·dine \ˈbrig-ən-ˌdēn\ *n* [ME, fr. MF, fr. *brigand*] : medieval body armor of scales or plates

brig·an·tine \ˈbrig-ən-ˌtēn\ *n* [MF *brigantin*, fr. OIt *brigantino*, fr. *brigante*] **1** : a 2-masted square-rigged ship differing from a brig in not carrying a square mainsail **2** : HERMAPHRODITE BRIG

Brig Gen *abbr* brigadier general

bright \ˈbrīt\ *adj* [ME, fr. OE *beorht;* akin to OHG *beraht* bright Skt *bhrājate* it shines] **1 a** : radiating or reflecting light : SHINING **b** : radiant with happiness or good fortune <~ faces> **2** : ILLUSTRIOUS, GLORIOUS **3** : resplendent with charms **4** : of high saturation or brilliance <~ colors> **5 a** : INTELLIGENT, CLEVER <a ~ idea> **b** : LIVELY, CHEERFUL <be ~ and jovial among your guests —Shak.> — **bright** *adv* — **bright·ly** *adv*

syn BRIGHT, BRILLIANT, RADIANT, LUMINOUS, LUSTROUS *shared meaning element* : shining or glowing with light ***ant*** dull, dim

bright·en \ˈbrīt-ᵊn\ *vb* **bright·ened; bright·en·ing** \ˈbrīt-niŋ, -ᵊn-iŋ\ *vt* : to make bright or brighter ~ *vi* : to become bright or brighter — **bright·en·er** \-nər, -ᵊn-ər\ *n*

brightness *n* **1** : the quality or state of being bright; *also* : an instance of such a quality or state **2** : a psychological dimension in which visual stimuli are ordered continuously from light to dark and which is correlated with light intensity

Bright's disease \ˈbrīts-\ *n* [Richard *Bright* †1858 E physician] : any of several kidney diseases marked by albumin in the urine

bright·work \ˈbrīt-ˌwərk\ *n* : polished or plated metalwork

brill \ˈbril\ *n, pl* **brill** [perh. fr. Corn *brythel* mackerel] : a European flatfish (*Bothus rhombus*) related to the turbot; *broadly* : TURBOT

bril·liance \ˈbril-yən(t)s\ *n* : the quality or state of being brilliant

bril·lian·cy \-yən-sē\ *n, pl* **-cies** **1** : BRILLIANCE **2** : an instance of brilliance

1**bril·liant** \ˈbril-yənt\ *adj* [F *brillant*, prp. of *briller* to shine, fr. It *brillare*, fr. *brillo* beryl, fr. L *beryllus*] **1** : very bright : GLITTERING <a ~ light> **2 a** : STRIKING, DISTINCTIVE <a ~ example> **b** : distinguished by unusual mental keenness or alertness ***syn*** see BRIGHT ***ant*** subdued (*of light, color*) — **bril·liant·ly** *adv* — **bril·liant·ness** *n*

2**brilliant** *n* : a gem (as a diamond) cut in a particular form with numerous facets so as to have special brilliance

bril·lian·tine \ˈbril-yən-ˌtēn\ *n* **1** : a preparation for making hair glossy **2** : a light lustrous fabric that is similar to alpaca and is woven usu. with a cotton warp and mohair or worsted filling

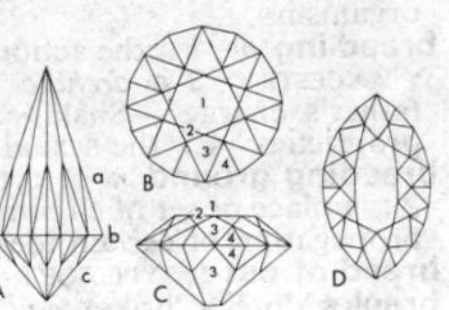

brilliant: *A*, briolette; *B* and *C*, American cut, top and side view; *D*, marquise; *a* bezel, *b* girdle, *c* pavilion: *1* table, *2* star facet, *3* main facet, *4* corner facet, *5* culet

Brill's disease \ˈbrilz-\ *n* [Nathan E. *Brill* †1925 Am physician] : an acute infectious disease milder than epidemic typhus but caused by the same rickettsia

1**brim** \ˈbrim\ *n* [ME *brimme;* akin to MHG *brem* edge] **1 a (1)** : an upper or outer margin : VERGE **(2)** *archaic* : the upper surface of a body of water **b** : the edge or rim of a hollow vessel, a natural depression, or a cavity **2** : the projecting rim of a hat ***syn*** see BORDER — **brim·less** \-ləs\ *adj*

2**brim** *vb* **brimmed; brim·ming** *vt* : to fill to the brim ~ *vi* **1** : to become full to the brim **2** : to reach or overflow a brim

brim·ful \ˈbrim-ˈfu̇l\ *adj* : full to the brim : ready to overflow

-brimmed \ˈbrimd\ *adj comb form* : having a brim of a specified nature <a wide-*brimmed* hat>

brim·mer \ˈbrim-ər\ *n* : a brimming cup or glass

brim·stone \ˈbrim-ˌstōn\ *n* [ME *brinston*, prob. fr. *birnen* to burn + *ston* stone] : SULFUR

brind·ed \ˈbrin-dəd\ *adj* [ME *brended*] *archaic* : BRINDLED

brin·dle \ˈbrin-dᵊl\ *n* [*brindle*, adj.] **1** : a brindled color **2** : a brindled animal

brin·dled \-dᵊld\ *adj* [alter. of *brinded*] : having obscure dark streaks or flecks on a gray or tawny ground

1**brine** \ˈbrīn\ *n* [ME, fr. OE *brȳne;* akin to MD *brīne* brine, L *fricare* to rub — more at FRICTION] **1 a** : water saturated or strongly impregnated with common salt **b** : a strong saline solution (as of calcium chloride) **2** : the water of a sea or salt lake

2**brine** *vt* **brined; brin·ing** : to treat (as by steeping) with brine — **brin·er** *n*

Bri·nell hardness \brə-ˌnel-\ *n* [Johann A. *Brinell* †1925 Sw engineer] : the hardness of a metal or alloy measured by hydraulically pressing a hard ball under a standard load into the specimen

Brinell number *n* : a number expressing Brinell hardness and denoting the load applied in testing in kilograms divided by the spherical area of indentation produced in the specimen in square millimeters

brine shrimp *n* : any of a genus (*Artemia*) of branchiopod crustaceans

bring \'briŋ\ *vb* **brought** \'bròt\; **bring·ing** \'briŋ-iŋ\ [ME *bringen,* fr. OE *bringan;* akin to OHG *bringan* to bring, W *hebrwng* to accompany] *vt* **1 a :** to convey, lead, carry, or cause to come along with one toward the place from which the action is being regarded **b :** to cause to be, act, or move in a special way: as (1) : ATTRACT <her screams *brought* the neighbors> (2) : PERSUADE, INDUCE (3) : FORCE, COMPEL (4) : to cause to come into a particular state or condition <~ water to a boil> **c** *dial* : ESCORT, ACCOMPANY **2 :** to cause to exist or occur: as **a :** PRODUCE <winter will ~ snow and ice> **b :** to result in : EFFECT **c** : INSTITUTE <~ legal action> **d :** ADDUCE <~ an argument> **3** : PREFER <~ a charge> **4 :** to procure in exchange : sell for ~ *vi, chiefly Midland* : YIELD, PRODUCE — **bring home :** to make unmistakably clear — **bring to account 1 :** to bring to book **2** : REPRIMAND — **bring to bear 1 :** to put to use <*bring* knowledge *to bear* on the problem> **2 :** APPLY, EXERT <*bring* pressure *to bear*> — **bring to book :** to compel to give an account — **bring to light :** DISCLOSE, REVEAL — **bring to mind :** to cause to be recalled — **bring to terms :** to compel to agree, assent, or submit — **bring up the rear :** to come last or behind

bring about *vt* : to cause to take place : EFFECT

bring around *vt* **1 :** to cause (someone) to adopt a particular opinion or course of action : PERSUADE **2 :** to restore to consciousness : REVIVE

bring·down \'briŋ-,dau̇n\ *n* : something that is depressing or disappointing

bring down \(')briŋ-'dau̇n\ *vt* **1 :** to cause to fall by or as if by shooting **2 :** to carry (a total) forward — **bring down the house** : to win the enthusiastic approval of the audience

bring forth *vt* **1 :** BEAR <*brought forth* fruit> **2 :** to give birth to : PRODUCE **3 :** ADDUCE <*brought forth* arguments to justify his conduct>

bring forward *vt* **1 :** to produce to view : INTRODUCE **2 :** to carry (a total) forward

bring in *vt* **1 :** to produce as profit or return <each sale *brought in* $5> **2 :** INCLUDE, INTRODUCE **3 :** to enable (a man on base) to reach home plate by a hit **4 :** to report to a court <jury *brought in* a verdict> **5 a :** to cause (as an oil well) to be productive **b** : to win tricks with the long cards of (a suit) in bridge **6 :** EARN <he *brings in* a good salary>

bring off *vt* **1 :** to cause to escape : RESCUE **2 :** to carry to a successful conclusion : ACHIEVE, ACCOMPLISH

bring on *vt* : to cause to appear or occur

bring out *vt* **1 :** to make clear **2 a :** to present to the public **b** : to introduce formally to society **3 :** UTTER

bring to *vt* **1 :** to cause (a boat) to lie to or come to a standstill **2 :** to restore to consciousness : REVIVE

bring up *vt* **1 :** REAR, EDUCATE **2 :** to cause to stop suddenly **3** : to bring to attention : INTRODUCE **4 :** VOMIT ~ *vi* : to stop suddenly

brink \'briŋk\ *n* [ME, prob. of Scand origin; akin to ON *brekka* slope; akin to L *front-, frons* forehead] **1 :** EDGE; *esp* : the edge at the top of a steep place **2 :** a bank esp. of a river **3 :** the point of onset : VERGE <on the ~ of war> ***syn*** see BORDER

brink·man·ship \'briŋk-mən-,ship\ *also* **brinks·man·ship** \'-briŋ(k)-smən-\ *n* [*brink* + *-manship* (as in *horsemanship*)] : the art or practice of pushing a dangerous situation to the limit of safety before stopping

briny \'brī-nē\ *adj* **brin·i·er; -est :** of, relating to, or resembling brine or the sea : SALTY — **brin·i·ness** *n*

brio \'brē-(,)ō\ *n* [It] : enthusiastic vigor : VIVACITY, VERVE

bri·oche \brē-'ōsh, -'òsh\ *n* [F, fr. MF dial., fr. *brier* to knead, of Gmc origin; akin to OHG *brehhan* to break — more at BREAK] : a roll baked from light yeast dough rich with eggs and butter

bri·o·lette \,brē-ə-'let\ *n* [F] : an oval or pear-shaped diamond cut in triangular facets — see BRILLIANT illustration

bri·quette *or* **bri·quet** \brik-'et\ *n* [F *briquette,* dim. of *brique* brick] : a compacted often brick-shaped mass of usu. fine material <a charcoal ~> — **briquette** *vt*

bri·sance \bri-'zän(t)s, -'zä^{n}s\ *n* [F, fr. *brisant,* prp. of *briser* to break, fr. OF *brisier,* of Celt origin; akin to OIr *brissim* I break; akin to L *fricare* to rub — more at FRICTION] : the shattering or crushing effect of an explosive — **bri·sant** \-'zänt, -'zä^n\ *adj*

Bri·se·is \brī-'sē-əs\ *n* [L, fr. Gk *Brisēis*] : a woman captive of Achilles taken away from him by Agamemnon

[1]**brisk** \'brisk\ *adj* [prob. modif. of MF *brusque*] **1 :** keenly alert : LIVELY **2 a :** pleasingly tangy <~ tea> **b :** FRESH, INVIGORATING <~ weather> **3 :** sharp in tone or manner **4 :** ENERGETIC, QUICK <a ~ pace> ***syn*** see AGILE ***ant*** sluggish — **brisk·ly** *adv* — **brisk·ness** *n*

[2]**brisk** *vt* : to make brisk ~ *vi* : to become brisk — usu. used with *up* <business ~*ed* up>

bris·ket \'bris-kət\ *n* [ME *brusket;* akin to OE *brēost* breast] : the breast or lower chest of a quadruped animal — see BEEF illustration

bris·ling *or* **bris·tling** \'briz-liŋ, 'bris-\ *n* [Norw *brisling,* fr. LG *bretling,* fr. *bret* broad; akin to OE *brād* broad] : a small herring (*Clupea sprattus*) that resembles and is processed like a sardine

[1]**bris·tle** \'bris-əl\ *n* [ME *bristil,* fr. *brust* bristle, fr. OE *bryst;* akin to OHG *burst* bristle, L *fastigium* top] : a short stiff coarse hair or filament — **bris·tle·like** \'bris-əl-,(l)īk\ *adj*

[2]**bristle** *vb* **bris·tled; bris·tling** \'bris-(ə-)liŋ\ *vi* **1 a :** to rise and stand stiffly erect <quills *bristling* in all directions> **b :** to raise the bristles (as in anger) **2 :** to take on an aggressive attitude or appearance (as in response to a slight) **3 :** to be full of or covered with something suggestive of bristles <roofs *bristled* with chimneys> ~ *vt* **1 :** to furnish with bristles **2 :** to make bristly : RUFFLE ***syn*** see STRUT

bris·tle·cone pine \,bris-əl-,kōn-\ *n* : a pine (*Pinus aristata*) of the western U.S. that includes the oldest living trees

bris·tle·tail \'bris-əl-,tāl\ *n* : any of various wingless insects (orders Thysanura and Entotrophi) with two slender caudal bristles

bris·tly \'bris-(ə-)lē\ *adj* **bris·tli·er; -est 1 a :** consisting of or resembling bristles **b :** thickly set with bristles **2 :** tending to bristle easily : BELLIGERENT

bris·tol \'bris-tᵊl\ *n* [*Bristol,* England] : cardboard with a smooth surface suitable for writing or printing — called also *bristol board*

Bristol fashion *adj* [*Bristol,* England, important seaport] : being in good order : SHIPSHAPE <spick-and-span, shipshape and *Bristol fashion* —Jack Lusby>

brit *or* **britt** \'brit\ *n* [Corn *brȳthel* mackerel] **1 :** young or small schooling fishes (as herring) **2 :** minute marine animals (as crustaceans and pteropods) upon which right whales feed

Brit *abbr* Britain; British

Bri·tan·nia metal \bri-,tan-yə-, -,tan-ē-ə-\ *n* [*Britannia,* poetic name for Great Britain, fr. L] : a silver-white alloy largely of tin, antimony, and copper that is similar to pewter

Bri·tan·nic \bri-'tan-ik\ *adj* : BRITISH

britch·es \'brich-əz\ *n pl* [alter. of *breeches*] : BREECHES, TROUSERS

Brith Mi·lah \brit(h)-'mē-(,)lä, bris-\ *n* [LHeb *bĕrīth mīlāh* covenant of circumcision] : the Jewish rite of circumcision

Brit·i·cism \'brit-ə-,siz-əm\ *n* [*Brit*ish + *-icism* (as in *gallicism*)] : a characteristic feature of British English

Brit·ish \'brit-ish\ *n* [ME *Bruttische* of Britain, fr. OE *Brettisc,* of Celt origin; akin to W *Brython* Briton] **1 a :** the Celtic language of the ancient Britons **b :** BRITISH ENGLISH **2** *pl in constr* : the people of Great Britain or the British Commonwealth — **British** *adj* — **Brit·ish·ness** *n*

British English *n* : the native language of most inhabitants of England; *esp* : English characteristic of England and clearly distinguishable from that used elsewhere (as in the U.S. or Australia)

Brit·ish·er \'brit-ish-ər\ *n* : BRITON 2

British thermal unit *n* : the quantity of heat required to raise the temperature of one pound of water one degree Fahrenheit at or near 39.2°F

Brit·on \'brit-ᵊn\ *n* [ME *Breton,* fr. MF & L; MF, fr. L *Briton-, Brito,* of Celt origin; akin to W *Brython*] **1 :** a member of one of the peoples inhabiting Britain prior to the Anglo-Saxon invasions **2 :** a native or subject of Great Britain; *esp* : ENGLISHMAN

Brit·ta·ny spaniel \,brit-ᵊn-ē-\ *n* [*Brittany,* region in France] : a large active spaniel of a French breed developed by interbreeding pointers with spaniels of Brittany

[1]**brit·tle** \'brit-ᵊl\ *adj* **brit·tler** \'brit-lər, -ᵊl-ər\ **brit·tlest** \-ləst, -ᵊl-əst\ [ME *britil;* akin to OE *brēotan* to break, Skt *bhrūṇa* embryo] **1 a :** easily broken, cracked, or snapped <~ clay> <~ glass> **b :** easily disrupted, overthrown, or damaged : FRAIL <a ~ friendship> **2 :** easily hurt or offended : SENSITIVE <a ~ personality> **3 :** SHARP, TENSE <~ staccato of snare drums> **4 a** : PERISHABLE, MORTAL **b :** TRANSITORY, EVANESCENT **5 :** lacking warmth, depth, or generosity of spirit : COLD <a ~ selfish person> ***syn*** see FRAGILE ***ant*** supple — **brit·tle·ly** \'brit-lē, -ᵊl-(l)ē\ *adv* — **brit·tle·ness** \'brit-ᵊl-nəs\ *n*

[2]**brittle** *vi* **brit·tled; brit·tling** \'brit-liŋ, -ᵊliŋ\ : to become brittle : CRUMBLE, DETERIORATE

[3]**brittle** *n* : candy made by caramelizing sugar, adding nuts, and cooling in thin sheets <peanut ~>

brittle star *n* : any of a subclass or class (Ophiuroidea) of echinoderms that have slender flexible arms

Brit·ton·ic \bri-'tän-ik\ *adj* [L *Britton-, Britto* Briton] : BRYTHONIC 2

Brix \'briks\ *adj* : of or relating to a Brix scale

Brix scale *n* [Adolf F. *Brix* †1870 G scientist] : a hydrometer scale for sugar solutions so graduated that its readings at a specified temperature represent percentages by weight of sugar in the solution — called also *Brix*

brl *abbr* barrel

bro *abbr* brother; brothers

[1]**broach** \'brōch\ *n* [ME *broche,* fr. MF, fr. (assumed) VL *brocca,* fr. L, fem. of *broccus* projecting] **1 :** any of various pointed or tapered tools, implements, or parts: as **a :** a spit for roasting meat **b :** a tool for tapping casks **c :** a cutting tool for removing material from metal or plastic to shape an outside surface or a hole **2 :** BROOCH

[2]**broach** *vt* **1 a :** to pierce (as a cask) in order to draw the contents : TAP **b :** to open up or break into (as a mine or stores) **2 :** to shape or enlarge (a hole) with a broach **3 a :** to make known for the first time **b :** to open up (a subject) for discussion ~ *vi* : to break the surface from below ***syn*** see EXPRESS — **broach·er** *n*

[3]**broach** *vb* [perh. fr. [2]*broach*] *vi* : to veer or yaw dangerously esp. in a following sea so as to lie broadside to the waves — used chiefly with *to* ~ *vt* : to cause (a boat) to broach

[1]**broad** \'bròd\ *adj* [ME *brood,* fr. OE *brād;* akin to OHG *breit* broad] **1 a :** having ample extent from side to side or between limits <~ shoulders> **b :** having a specified extension from side to side <made the path 10 feet ~> **2 :** extending far and wide : SPACIOUS <the ~ plains> **3 a :** OPEN, FULL <~ daylight> **b** : PLAIN, OBVIOUS <a ~ hint> **4 :** marked by lack of restraint, delicacy, or subtlety: **a** *obs* : OUTSPOKEN **b :** COARSE, RISQUÉ <~ humor> **5 a :** LIBERAL, TOLERANT <~ views> **b :** widely applicable or applied : GENERAL **6 :** relating to the main or essential points <~ outlines> **7 :** dialectal esp. in pronunciation **8** *of a vowel* : OPEN — used specif. of **a** pronounced as in *father* — **broad·ly** *adv* — **broad·ness** *n*

syn BROAD, WIDE, DEEP *shared meaning element* : having horizontal extent ***ant*** narrow

ə abut	ᵊ kitten	ər further	a back	ā bake	ä cot, cart
au̇ out	ch chin	e less	ē easy	g gift	i trip	ī life
j joke	ŋ sing	ō flow	ȯ flaw	ȯi coin	th thin	t͟h this
ü loot	u̇ foot	y yet	yü few	yu̇ furious	zh vision

[2]**broad** *adv* **:** in a broad manner **:** FULLY

[3]**broad** *n* **1** *Brit* **:** an expansion of a river — often used in pl. **2** *slang* **:** WOMAN

broad arrow *n* **1 :** an arrow with a flat barbed head **2** *Brit* **:** a mark shaped like a broad arrow that identifies government property including clothing formerly worn by convicts

broad·ax \ˈbrȯ-ˌdaks\ *n* **:** a large ax with a broad blade

broad·band \ˈbrȯd-ˌband\ *adj* **:** of, having, or involving operation with uniform efficiency over a wide band of frequencies <a ~ radio antenna>

broad bean *n* **:** the large flat edible seed of an Old World upright vetch (*Vicia faba*); *also* **:** this plant widely grown for its seeds and as fodder

[1]**broad·cast** \ˈbrȯd-ˌkast\ *adj* **1 :** cast or scattered in all directions **2 :** made public by means of radio or television **3 :** of or relating to radio or television broadcasting

[2]**broadcast** *n* **1 :** the act of transmitting sound or images by radio or television **2 :** a single radio or television program

[3]**broadcast** *vb* **broadcast** *also* **broad·cast·ed; broad·cast·ing** *vt* **1 :** to scatter or sow (seed) broadcast **2 :** to make widely known **3 :** to transmit as a broadcast ~ *vi* **1 :** to transmit a broadcast **2 :** to speak or perform on a broadcast program — **broad·cast·er** *n*

[4]**broadcast** *adv* **:** to or over a broad area

Broad Church *adj* **:** of or relating to a liberal party in the Anglican communion esp. in the later 19th century — **Broad Churchman** *n*

broad·cloth \ˈbrȯd-ˌklȯth\ *n* **1 :** a twilled napped woolen or worsted fabric with smooth lustrous face and dense texture **2 :** a fabric usu. of cotton, silk, or rayon made in plain and rib weaves with soft semigloss finish

broad·en \ˈbrȯd-ᵊn\ *vb* **broad·ened; broad·en·ing** \ˈbrȯd-niŋ, -ᵊn-iŋ\ *vi* **:** to become broad ~ *vt* **:** to make broader

broad gauge *n* **:** a railroad gauge wider than standard gauge — **broad–gauged** \ˈbrȯd-ˈgājd\ *adj*

broad jump *n* **:** LONG JUMP — **broad jumper** *n*

broad·leaf \ˈbrȯd-ˌlēf\ *adj* **:** BROAD-LEAVED

broad–leaved \-ˈlēvd\ *or* **broad–leafed** \-ˈlēft\ *adj* **:** having broad leaves; *specif* **:** having leaves that are not needles <~ evergreens>

[1]**broad·loom** \-ˌlüm\ *adj* **:** woven on a wide loom; *also* **:** so woven in solid color

[2]**broadloom** *n* **:** a broadloom carpet

broad–mind·ed \ˈbrȯd-ˈmīn-dəd\ *adj* **1 :** tolerant of varied views **:** CATHOLIC **2 :** inclined to condone minor departures from conventional behavior — **broad–mind·ed·ly** *adv* — **broad–mind·ed·ness** *n*

broad·sheet \-ˌshēt\ *n* **:** BROADSIDE 3b

[1]**broad·side** \-ˌsīd\ *n* **1 :** the side of a ship above the waterline **2 :** a broad or unbroken surface **3 a** *archaic* **:** a sheet of paper printed on one side **b :** a sheet printed on one or both sides and folded; *also* **:** something (as a ballad or an advertisement) printed on a broadside **4 a :** all the guns on one side of a ship; *also* **:** their simultaneous discharge **b :** a volley of verbal abuse or denunciation

[2]**broadside** *adj* **:** directed or placed broadside <a ~ attack>

[3]**broadside** *adv* **1 :** with the broadside toward a given object or point **2 :** in one volley **3 :** at random

broad–spectrum *adj* **:** effective against various insects or microorganisms

broad·sword \ˈbrȯd-ˌsō(ə)rd, -ˌsȯ(ə)rd\ *n* **:** a sword with a broad blade for cutting rather than thrusting

broad·tail \-ˌtāl\ *n* **1 a :** KARAKUL 1 **b :** a fat-tailed sheep **2 :** the fur or skin of a very young or premature karakul lamb having a flat and wavy appearance resembling moiré silk

Broad·way \ˈbrȯd-ˌwā, -ˈwā\ *n* [*Broadway,* street in New York on or near which were once located the majority of the city's legitimate theaters] **:** the New York commercial theater and amusement world; *specif* **:** playhouses located in the area between Fifth Avenue and Ninth Avenue from 34th Street to 56th Street and between Fifth Avenue and the Hudson River from 56th Street to 72d Street — **Broadway** *adj* — **Broad·way·ite** \-ˌīt\ *n*

broad·wife \ˈbrȯd-ˌwīf\ *n* [a*broad* + *wife*] **:** the wife of a slave belonging to another master in the slaveholding states of the U.S.

Brob·ding·nag·ian \ˌbräb-diŋ-ˈnag-ē-ən, -dig-ˈnag-\ *n* **:** an inhabitant of a country in Swift's *Gulliver's Travels* where everything is on a giant scale — **Brobdingnagian** *adj*

bro·cade \brō-ˈkād\ *n* [Sp *brocado,* fr. Catal *brocat,* fr. It *broccato,* fr. *broccare* to spur, brocade, fr. *brocco* small nail, fr. L *broccus* projecting] **1 :** a rich oriental silk fabric with raised patterns in gold and silver **2 :** a fabric characterized by raised designs — **brocade** *vt* — **bro·cad·ed** *adj*

broc·a·telle \ˌbräk-ə-ˈtel\ *n* [F, fr. It *broccatello,* dim. of *broccato*] **:** a stiff decorating fabric with patterns in high relief

broc·co·li *or* **broc·o·li** \ˈbräk-(ə-)lē\ *n* [It, pl. of *broccolo* flowering top of a cabbage, dim. of *brocco* small nail, sprout] **1 :** a large hardy cauliflower **2 :** a branching cauliflower with a head of functional florets at the end of each branch that is cut for food while the florets are tight green or purplish buds — called also *sprouting broccoli*

bro·chette \brō-ˈshet\ *n* [F, fr. OF *brochete,* fr. *broche* pointed tool — more at BROACH] **:** SKEWER; *also* **:** food broiled on a skewer

bro·chure \brō-ˈshů(ə)r\ *n* [F, fr. MF, fr. *brocher* to sew, fr. MF, to prick, fr. OF *brochier,* fr. *broche*] **:** a small pamphlet **:** BOOKLET

brock \ˈbräk\ *n* [ME, fr. OE *broc,* of Celt origin; akin to W *broch* badger] **:** BADGER

brock·age \ˈbräk-ij\ *n* [E dial. *brock* rubbish + E *-age*] **:** an imperfectly minted coin

brock·et \ˈbräk-ət\ *n* [ME *broket*] **1 :** a male red deer two years old — compare PRICKET **2 :** any of several small So. American deer (genus *Mazama*) with unbranched horns

bro·gan \ˈbrō-gən, -ˌgan; brō-ˈgan\ *n* [IrGael *brōgan,* dim. of *brōg*] **:** a heavy shoe; *esp* **:** a coarse work shoe reaching to the ankle

[1]**brogue** \ˈbrōg\ *n* [IrGael & ScGael *brōg,* fr. MIr *brōc,* fr. ON *brōk* leg covering; akin to OE *brōc* leg covering — more at BREECH] **1 :** a stout coarse shoe worn formerly in Ireland and the Scottish Highlands **2 :** a heavy shoe often with a hobnailed sole **:** BROGAN **3 :** a stout oxford shoe with perforations and usu. a wing tip

[2]**brogue** *n* [perh. fr. IrGael *barrōg* wrestling hold; fr. the idea that unfamiliar features of pronunciation must be the result of a physical impediment of the tongue] **:** a dialect or regional pronunciation; *esp* **:** an Irish accent

broi·der \ˈbrȯid-ər\ *vt* [ME *broideren,* modif. of MF *broder* — more at EMBROIDER] **:** EMBROIDER — **broi·dery** \ˈbrȯid-(ə-)rē\ *n*

[1]**broil** \ˈbrȯi(ə)l\ *vb* [ME *broilen,* fr. MF *bruler* to burn, modif. of L *ustulare* to singe, fr. *ustus,* pp. of *urere* to burn] *vt* **:** to cook by direct exposure to radiant heat **:** GRILL ~ *vi* **:** to become broiled

[2]**broil** *n* **1 :** the act or state of broiling **2 :** something broiled **:** GRILL

[3]**broil** *vb* [ME *broilen,* fr. MF *brouiller* to mix, broil, fr. OF *brooilier,* fr. *breu* broth — more at BREWIS] *vt* **:** EMBROIL ~ *vi* **:** BRAWL

[4]**broil** *n* **:** a noisy disturbance **:** TUMULT; *esp* **:** BRAWL

broil·er \ˈbrȯi-lər\ *n* **1 :** one that broils **2 :** a bird fit for broiling; *esp* **:** a young chicken of up to 2½ pounds dressed weight

[1]**broke** \ˈbrōk\ *past of* BREAK

[2]**broke** *adj* [ME, alter. of *broken*] **:** PENNILESS

bro·ken \ˈbrō-kən\ *adj* [ME, fr. OE *brocen,* fr. pp. of *brecan* to break] **1 :** violently separated into parts **:** SHATTERED **2 :** damaged or altered by breaking: as **a :** having undergone or been subjected to fracture <a ~ leg> **b** *of land surfaces* **:** being irregular, interrupted, or full of obstacles **c :** violated by transgression <a ~ promise> **d :** DISCONTINUOUS, INTERRUPTED **e :** disrupted by change **f** *of a flower* **:** having an irregular, streaked, or blotched pattern esp. from virus infection **3 a :** made weak or infirm **b :** subdued completely **:** CRUSHED <a ~ spirit> **c :** BANKRUPT **d :** reduced in rank **4 a :** cut off **:** DISCONNECTED **b :** imperfectly spoken or written <~ English> **5 :** not complete or full — **bro·ken·ly** *adv* — **bro·ken·ness** \-kən-(n)əs\ *n*

bro·ken–down \ˌbrō-kən-ˈdau̇n\ *adj* **:** extremely infirm **:** WORN-OUT

bro·ken–field \ˌbrō-kən-ˌfēld\ *adj* **:** accomplished (as by a ballcarrier in football) against widely scattered opposition

bro·ken·heart·ed \ˌbrō-kən-ˈhärt-əd\ *adj* **:** overcome by grief or despair

broken home *n* **:** a family in which the parents are not living together

broken wind *n* **:** HEAVES — **bro·ken–wind·ed** \ˌbrō-kən-ˈwin-dəd\ *adj*

bro·ker \ˈbrō-kər\ *n* [ME, negotiator, fr. (assumed) AF *brocour;* akin to OF *broche* pointed tool, tap of a cask — more at BROACH] **1 :** one who acts as an intermediary: as **a :** an agent who arranges marriages **b :** an agent who negotiates contracts of purchase and sale (as of real estate, commodities, or securities) **2** *Brit* **:** a dealer in secondhand goods

bro·ker·age \ˈbrō-k(ə-)rij\ *n* **1 :** the business or establishment of a broker **2 :** the fee or commission for transacting business as a broker

brol·ly \ˈbräl-ē\ *n, pl* **brollies** [by shortening & alter.] *chiefly Brit* **:** UMBRELLA

brom- *or* **bromo-** *comb form* [prob. fr. F *brome,* fr. Gk *brōmos* bad smell] **:** bromine <*brom*ide>

[1]**bro·mate** \ˈbrō-ˌmāt\ *n* **:** a salt of bromic acid

[2]**bromate** *vt* **bro·mat·ed; bro·mat·ing :** to treat with a bromate; *broadly* **:** BROMINATE

brome·grass \ˈbrōm-ˌgras\ *n* [NL *Bromus,* genus name, fr. L *bromos* oats, fr. Gk] **:** any of a large genus (*Bromus*) of tall grasses often having drooping spikelets

bro·me·li·ad \brō-ˈmē-lē-ˌad\ *n* [NL *Bromelia,* genus of tropical American plants, fr. Olaf *Bromelius* †1705 Sw botanist] **:** any of a family (Bromeliaceae) of chiefly tropical American and epiphytic herbaceous plants including the pineapple, Spanish moss, and various ornamentals

bro·me·lin \ˈbrō-mə-lən, brō-ˈmē-\ *n* [NL *Bromelia,* genus name of the pineapple in some classifications + E *-in*] **:** a proteinase obtained from the juice of the pineapple

bro·mic \ˈbrō-mik\ *adj* **:** of, relating to, or containing bromine esp. with a valence of five

bromic acid *n* **:** an unstable strongly oxidizing acid $HBrO_3$ known only in solution or in the form of its salts

bro·mide \ˈbrō-ˌmīd\ *n* **1 :** a binary compound of bromine with another element or a radical including some (as potassium bromide) used as sedatives **2 a :** a commonplace or tiresome person **:** BORE **b :** a commonplace or hackneyed statement or notion

bro·mid·ic \brō-ˈmid-ik\ *adj* **:** lacking in originality **:** DULL, TRITE

bro·mi·nate \ˈbrō-mə-ˌnāt\ *vt* **-nat·ed; -nat·ing :** to treat or cause to combine with bromine or a compound of bromine — **bro·mi·na·tion** \ˌbrō-mə-ˈnā-shən\ *n*

bro·mine \ˈbrō-ˌmēn\ *n* [F *brome* bromine + E *-ine*] **:** a nonmetallic element normally a deep red corrosive toxic liquid giving off an irritating reddish brown vapor of disagreeable odor — see ELEMENT table

bro·mism \ˈbrō-ˌmiz-əm\ *n* **:** an abnormal state due to excessive or prolonged use of bromides

bro·mo \ˈbrō-(ˌ)mō\ *n, pl* **bromos** [*brom-*] **:** a proprietary effervescent mixture used as a headache remedy, sedative, and alkalinizing agent; *also* **:** a dose of such a mixture

bro·mo·ura·cil \ˌbrō-mō-ˈyu̇r-ə-ˌsil, -səl\ *n* [*bromo-* + *uracil*] **:** a uracil derivative $C_4H_3N_2O_2Br$ that is readily incorporated during bacterial or phage DNA synthesis in place of thymine

bronc \ˈbräŋk\ *n* **:** BRONCO

bronch- *or* **broncho-** *comb form* [prob. fr. F, throat, fr. LL, fr. Gk, fr. *bronchos* — more at CRAW] **:** bronchial tube **:** bronchial <*bronch*itis>

bronchi- *or* **bronchio-** *comb form* [NL, fr. *bronchia,* pl., branches of the bronchi, fr. Gk, dim. of *bronchos* bronchus] **:** bronchial tubes <*bronchi*ectasis>

bron·chi·al \'bräŋ-kē-əl\ *adj* : of or relating to the bronchi or their ramifications in the lungs — **bron·chi·al·ly** \-ə-lē\ *adv*
bronchial asthma *n* : asthma resulting from spasmodic contraction of bronchial muscles
bronchial pneumonia *n* : BRONCHOPNEUMONIA
bronchial tube *n* : a primary bronchus or any of its branches
bron·chi·ec·ta·sis \,bräŋ-kē-'ek-tə-səs\ *n* [NL] : a chronic dilatation of bronchi or bronchioles
bron·chi·ole \'bräŋ-kē-,ōl\ *n* [NL *bronchiolum*, dim. of *branchia*] : a minute thin-walled branch of a bronchus — **bron·chi·o·lar** \,bräŋ-kē-'ō-lər\ *adj*
bron·chi·tis \brän-'kīt-əs, bräŋ-\ *n* : acute or chronic inflammation of the bronchial tubes or a disease marked by this — **bron·chit·ic** \-'kit-ik\ *adj*
bron·cho·gen·ic \,bräŋ-kə-'jen-ik\ *adj* : of, relating to, or arising in or by way of the air passages of the lungs
bron·chog·ra·phy \brän-'käg-rə-fē, bräŋ-\ *n* : the roentgenographic visualization of the bronchi and their branches after injection of a radiopaque substance — **bron·cho·graph·ic** \,bräŋ-kə-'graf-ik\ *adj*
bron·cho·pneu·mo·nia \,bräŋ-(,)kō-n(y)ù-'mō-nyə\ *n* [NL] : pneumonia involving many relatively small areas of lung tissue
bron·cho·scope \'bräŋ-kə-,skōp\ *n* [ISV] : a tubular illuminated instrument used for inspecting or passing instruments into the bronchi — **bron·cho·scop·ic** \,bräŋ-kə-'skäp-ik\ *adj* — **bron·cho·scop·i·cal·ly** \-i-k(ə-)lē\ *adv* — **bron·chos·co·pist** \brän-'käs-kə-pəst, bräŋ-\ *n* — **bron·chos·co·py** \-pē\ *n*
bron·chus \'bräŋ-kəs\ *n, pl* **bron·chi** \'bräŋ-,kī, -,kē\ [NL, fr. Gk *bronchos*] : either of the two primary divisions of the trachea that lead respectively into the right and the left lung; *broadly* : BRONCHIAL TUBE
bron·co \'bräŋ-(,)kō\ *n, pl* **broncos** [MexSp, fr. Sp, rough, wild] : an unbroken or imperfectly broken range horse of western No. America; *broadly* : MUSTANG
bron·co·bust·er \-kō-,bəs-tər\ *n* : one who breaks wild horses to the saddle
bron·to·saur \'bränt-ə-,sȯ(ə)r\ *also* **bron·to·sau·rus** \,bränt-ə-'sȯr-əs\ *n* [deriv. of Gk *brontē* thunder + *sauros* lizard; akin to Gk *bremein* to roar — more at SAURIAN] : any of various large quadrupedal and prob. herbivorous dinosaurs (genus *Apatosaurus*)
Bronx cheer \'bräŋ(k)s-\ *n* [*Bronx*, borough of New York City] : RASPBERRY 2
¹bronze \'bränz\ *vt* **bronzed; bronz·ing** : to give the appearance of bronze to — **bronz·er** *n*
²bronze *n, often attrib* [F, fr. It *bronzo*] **1 a** : an alloy of copper and tin and sometimes other elements **b** : any of various copper-base alloys with little or no tin **2** : a sculpture or artifact of bronze **3** : a moderate yellowish brown — **bronzy** \'brän-zē\ *adj*
Bronze Age *n* : the period of human culture characterized by the use of bronze tools that began in Europe about 3500 B.C. and in western Asia and Egypt somewhat earlier
Bronze Star Medal *n* : a U.S. military decoration awarded for heroic or meritorious service not involving aerial flights
bronz·ing *n* : a bronze coloring or discoloration (as of leaves)
brooch \'brōch, 'brüch\ *n* [ME *broche* pointed tool, brooch — more at BROACH] : an ornament that is held by a pin or clasp and is worn at or near the neck
¹brood \'brüd\ *n* [ME, fr. OE *brōd*; akin to OE *beorma* yeast — more at BARM] **1** : the young of an animal or a family of young; *esp* : the young (as of a bird or insect) hatched or cared for at one time **2** : a group having a common nature or origin
²brood *vt* **1 a** : to sit on or incubate (eggs) **b** : to produce by or as if by incubation : HATCH **2** *of a bird* : to cover (young) with the wings **3** : to think anxiously or gloomily about : PONDER ~ *vi* **1 a** *of a bird* : to brood eggs or young **b** : to sit quietly and thoughtfully : MEDITATE **2** : HOVER, LOOM **3 a** : to dwell gloomily on a subject : WORRY **b** : to be in a state of depression — **brood·ing·ly** \-iŋ-lē\ *adv*
³brood *adj* : kept for breeding <a ~ mare> <a ~ flock>
brood·er \'brüd-ər\ *n* **1** : one that broods **2** : a heated structure used for raising young fowl
broody \'brüd-ē\ *adj* **1 a** : being in a state of readiness to brood eggs that is characterized by cessation of laying and by marked changes in behavior and physiology **b** : suitable for producing offspring <a strong ~ mare> **2** : given or conducive to introspection : CONTEMPLATIVE, MOODY — **brood·i·ness** *n*
¹brook \'brùk\ *vt* [ME *brouken* to use, enjoy, fr. OE *brūcan*; akin to OHG *brūhhan* to use, L *frui* to enjoy] : to stand for : TOLERATE <he would ~ no interference with his plans> *syn* see BEAR
²brook *n* [ME, fr. OE *brōc*; akin to OHG *bruoh* marshy ground] : CREEK 2
brook·ite \'brùk-,īt\ *n* [Henry J. *Brooke* †1857 E mineralogist] : titanium dioxide TiO_2 occurring as a mineral in orthorhombic crystals commonly translucent brown or opaque brown to black
brook·let \'brùk-lət\ *n* : a small brook
brook trout *n* : the common speckled cold-water char (*Salvelinus fontinalis*) of eastern No. America
¹broom \'brüm, 'brùm\ *n* [ME, fr. OE *brōm*; akin to OHG *brāmo* bramble, MF *brimme* brim] **1** : any of various leguminous shrubs (esp. genera *Cytisus* and *Genista*) with long slender branches, small leaves, and usu. showy yellow flowers **2** : a bundle of firm stiff twigs or fibers bound together on a long handle for sweeping and brushing
²broom *vt* **1** : to sweep with or as if with a broom **2** : to finish (as a concrete surface) by means of a broom
broom·ball \-,bȯl\ *n* : a variation of ice hockey played on ice without skates and with brooms and a soccer ball used instead of sticks and a puck — **broom·ball·er** \-,bȯ-lər\ *n*
broom·corn \-,kȯ(ə)rn\ *n* : any of several tall cultivated sorghums whose stiff-branched panicle is used in brooms and brushes
broom·rape \-,rāp\ *n* **1** : any of various leafless herbs (family Orobanchaceae, the broomrape family) growing as parasites on the roots of other plants **2** : INDIAN PIPE
broom·stick \-,stik\ *n* : the long thin handle of a broom
brose \'brōz\ *n* [perh. alter. of Sc *bruis* broth, fr. ME *brewes* — more at BREWIS] : a chiefly Scottish dish made with a boiling liquid and meal
broth \'brȯth\ *n, pl* **broths** \'brȯths, 'brȯt͟hz\ [ME, fr. OE; akin to OHG *brod* broth, L *fervēre* to boil — more at BURN] **1** : liquid in which meat, fish, cereal grains, or vegetables have been cooked : STOCK **2** : a fluid culture medium
broth·el \'bräth-əl, 'brȯth-\ *n* [ME, worthless fellow, prostitute, fr. *brothen*, pp. of *brethen* to waste away, go to ruin, fr. OE *brēothan* to waste away; akin to OE *brēotan* to break — more at BRITTLE] : WHOREHOUSE
broth·er \'brət͟h-ər\ *n, pl* **brothers** *also* **breth·ren** \'bret͟h-(ə-)rən, 'bret͟h-ərn\ [ME, fr. OE *brōthor*; akin to OHG *bruodor* brother, L *frater*, Gk *phratēr* member of the same clan] **1** : a male who has the same parents as another or one parent in common with another **2 a** : KINSMAN **b** : one who shares with another a common national or racial origin **3** : a fellow member — used as a title for ministers in some evangelical denominations **4** : one related to another by common ties or interests **5 a** *cap* : a member of a congregation of men not in holy orders and usu. in hospital or school work **b** : a member of a men's religious order who is not preparing for or is not ready for holy orders <a lay ~>
broth·er·hood \'brət͟h-ər-,hùd\ *n* [ME *brotherhede, brotherhod*, alter. of *brotherrede*, fr. OE *brōthorrǣden*, fr. *brōthor* + *rǣden* condition — more at KINDRED] **1** : the quality or state of being brothers **2** : an association (as a labor union) for a particular purpose **3** : the whole body of persons engaged in business or profession
broth·er-in-law \'brət͟h-(ə-)rən-,lȯ, 'brət͟h-ərn-,lȯ\ *n, pl* **broth·ers-in-law** \'brət͟h-ər-zən-\ **1** : the brother of one's spouse **2 a** : the husband of one's sister **b** : the husband of one's spouse's sister
broth·er·ly \'brət͟h-ər-lē\ *adj* **1** : of or relating to brothers **2** : natural or becoming to brothers : AFFECTIONATE <~ love> — **broth·er·li·ness** *n* — **brotherly** *adv*
brougham \'brü(-ə)m, 'brō(-ə)m\ *n* [Henry Peter *Brougham*, Baron Brougham and Vaux †1868 Sc jurist] **1** : a light closed horse carriage with the driver outside in front **2** : a coupe automobile; *esp* : one driven electrically **3** : a sedan automobile having no roof over the driver's seat

brougham 1

brought *past of* BRING
brou·ha·ha \brü-'(h)ä-(,)hä, 'brü-,(h)ä-,hä\ *n* [F] : HUBBUB, UPROAR
brow \'braù\ *n* [ME, fr. OE *brū*; akin to ON *brūn* eyebrow, Gk *ophrys*] **1 a** : EYEBROW **b** : the ridge on which the eyebrow grows **c** : FOREHEAD **2** : the projecting upper part or margin of a steep place **3** : EXPRESSION, MIEN
brow antler *n* : the first branch of a stag's antler — see ANTLER illustration
brow·beat \'braù-,bēt\ *vt* **-beat; -beat·en** \-'bēt-ᵊn\ *or* **-beat; -beat·ing** : to intimidate or disconcert by a stern manner or arrogant speech : BULLY
-browed \'braùd\ *adj comb form* : having brows of a specified nature <smooth-*browed*>
¹brown \'braùn\ *adj* [ME *broun*, fr. OE *brūn*; akin to OHG *brūn* brown, Gk *phrynē* toad] : of the color brown; *esp* : of dark or tanned complexion
²brown *n* **1** : any of a group of colors between red and yellow in hue, of medium to low lightness, and of moderate to low saturation **2** : a brown-skinned person — **brown·ish** \'braù-nish\ *adj* — **browny** \-nē\ *adj*
³brown *vi* : to become brown ~ *vt* : to make brown
brown alga *n* : any of a division (Phaeophyta) of variable mostly marine algae with chlorophyll masked by brown pigment
brown bag·ging \-'bag-iŋ\ *n* [fr. the brown paper bag in which the bottle is carried] **1** : the practice of carrying a bottle of liquor into a restaurant or club where setups are available **2** : the practice of carrying (as to work) one's lunch usu. in a brown paper bag — **brown bag·ger** \-'bag-ər\ *n*
brown Bet·ty \-'bet-ē\ *n* : a baked pudding of apples, bread crumbs, and spices
brown bread \-,bred\ *n* **1** : bread made of whole wheat flour **2** : a dark brown steamed bread made usu. of cornmeal, white or whole wheat flours, molasses, soda, and milk or water
brown coal *n* : LIGNITE
brown-eyed Su·san \,braù-,nīd-'süz-ᵊn\ *n* [*brown-eyed* + *Susan* (as in black-eyed *Susan*)] : a dark-centered coneflower (*Rudbeckia triloba*) of eastern No. America distinguished by tripartite lower leaves
brown fat *n* : a heat-producing tissue of hibernating mammals
Brown·ian movement \,braù-nē-ən\ *n* [Robert *Brown* †1858 Sc botanist] : a random movement of microscopic particles suspended in liquids or gases resulting from the impact of molecules of the fluid surrounding the particles — called also *Brownian motion*
brown·ie \'braù-nē\ *n* [¹*brown*] **1** : a good-natured goblin believed to perform helpful services at night **2** *cap* : a member of the Girl Scouts from 7 through 9 years **3** : a small square or rectangle of rich usu. chocolate cake containing nuts
Brownie point *n* [fr. the system of points awarded for achievement to Brownies in the Girl Scouts] : a credit regarded as earned esp. by currying favor with a superior

Brow·ning automatic rifle \'brau̇-niŋ-\ *n* [John N. *Browning* †1926 Am designer of firearms] **:** a .30 caliber gas-operated air-cooled magazine-fed automatic rifle often provided with a rest for the barrel and used by U.S. troops in World War II and the Korean war — abbr. *BAR*
Browning machine gun *n* **:** a .30 or .50 caliber recoil-operated air-or water-cooled machine gun fed by a cartridge belt and used by U.S. troops in World War II and the Korean war
brown–nose \'brau̇n-ˌnōz\ *vt* [fr. the implication that servility is equivalent to kissing the hinder parts of the person from whom advancement is sought] *slang* **:** to ingratiate oneself with **:** curry favor with — **brownnose** *n* — **brown·nos·er** *n*
brown·out \'brau̇-ˌnau̇t\ *n* [*brown* + *-out* (as in *blackout*)] **:** a curtailment of the use of electric power esp. in display lighting; *also* **:** a period of reduced illumination resulting from such curtailment
brown rat *n* **:** the common domestic rat (*Rattus norvegicus*)
brown recluse spider *n* **:** a venomous spider (*Loxosceles reclusa*) introduced into the southern U.S. that has a violin-shaped mark on the cephalothorax and produces a dangerous neurotoxin
brown·shirt \'brau̇n-ˌshərt\ *n, often cap* **:** NAZI; *esp* **:** STORM TROOPER
brown·stone \-ˌstōn\ *n* **1 :** a reddish brown sandstone used for building **2 :** a dwelling faced with brownstone
brown study *n* **:** a state of serious absorption or abstraction
brown sugar *n* **:** soft sugar whose crystals are covered by a film of refined dark syrup
Brown Swiss *n* **:** any of a breed of large hardy brown dairy cattle originating in Switzerland
brown–tail moth \ˌbrau̇n-ˌtāl-\ *n* **:** a tussock moth (*Nygmia phaeorrhoea*) whose larvae feed on foliage and are irritating to the skin
brown trout *n* **:** a speckled European trout (*Salmo trutta*) widely introduced as a game fish
brows·abil·i·ty \ˌbrau̇-zə-'bil-ət-ē\ *n* **:** the property (as of an information retrieval system) of permitting users to browse
1**browse** \'brau̇z\ *n* [prob. modif. of MF *brouts*, pl. of *brout* sprout, fr. OF *brost*, of Gmc origin; akin to OS *brustian* to sprout; akin to OE *brēost* breast] **1 :** tender shoots, twigs, and leaves of trees and shrubs fit for food for cattle **2 :** an act or instance of browsing
2**browse** *vb* **browsed; brows·ing** *vt* **1 a :** to consume as browse **b :** GRAZE **2 :** to look over casually **:** SKIM ~ *vi* **1 a :** to feed on or as if on browse **b :** GRAZE **2 a :** to skim through a book reading at random passages that catch the eye **b :** to look over or through an aggregate of things casually esp. in search of something of interest — **brows·er** *n*
bru·cel·la \brü-'sel-ə\ *n, pl* **-cel·lae** \-'sel-(ˌ)ē\ *or* **-cellas** [NL, genus name, fr. Sir David *Bruce* †1931 Brit bacteriologist] **:** any of a genus (*Brucella*) of nonmotile capsulated bacteria that cause disease in man and domestic animals
bru·cel·lo·sis \ˌbrü-sə-'lō-səs\ *n, pl* **-lo·ses** \-ˌsēz\ **:** infection with or disease caused by brucellae esp. in man or cattle
bru·cine \'brü-ˌsēn\ *n* [prob. fr. F, fr. NL *Brucea* (genus name of *Brucea antidysenterica*, a shrub)] **:** a poisonous alkaloid $C_{23}H_{26}$-N_2O_4 found with strychnine esp. in nux vomica
bru·in \'brü-ən\ *n* [D, name of the bear in *Reynard the Fox*] **:** BEAR
1**bruise** \'brüz\ *vb* **bruised; bruis·ing** [ME *brusen, brisen*, fr. MF & OE; MF *bruisier* to break, of Celt origin; akin to OIr *brūu* I shatter; OE *brȳsan* to bruise; akin to OIr *brūu*, L *frustum* piece] *vt* **1 a** *archaic* **:** DISABLE **b :** BATTER, DENT **2 :** to inflict a bruise on **:** CONTUSE **3 :** to break down (as leaves or berries) by pounding **:** CRUSH **4 :** WOUND, INJURE; *esp* **:** to inflict psychological hurt on ~ *vi* **1 :** to inflict a bruise **2 :** to undergo bruising <tomatoes ~ easily>
2**bruise** *n* **1 a :** an injury involving rupture of small blood vessels and discoloration without a break in the overlying skin **:** CONTUSION **b :** a similar injury to plant tissue **2 :** ABRASION, SCRATCH **3 :** an injury esp. to the feelings
bruis·er \'brü-zər\ *n* **:** a big husky man
1**bruit** *n* [ME, fr. MF, fr. OF, noise] **1** \'brüt\ *archaic* **a :** NOISE, DIN **b :** REPORT, RUMOR **2** \'brü-ē\ [F, lit., noise] **:** any of several generally abnormal sounds heard on auscultation
2**bruit** \'brüt\ *vt* **:** to noise abroad **:** REPORT
bru·mal \'brü-məl\ [L *brumalis*, fr. L *bruma* winter] *adj, archaic* **:** indicative of or occurring in the winter
brum·by \'brəm-bē\ *n, pl* **brumbies** [prob. native name in Queensland, Australia] *Austral* **:** a wild or unbroken horse
brume \'brüm\ *n* [F, mist, winter, fr. OProv *bruma*, fr. L, winter, fr. *brevis* short — more at BRIEF] **:** MIST, FOG — **bru·mous** \'brü-məs\ *adj*
1**brum·ma·gem** \'brəm-i-jəm\ *adj* [alter. of *Birmingham*, England, the source in the 17th cent. of counterfeit groats] **:** having a cheaply contrived and showy quality
2**brummagem** *n* **:** something cheap or inferior **:** TINSEL
brunch \'brənch\ *n* [*breakfast* + *lunch*] **:** a late breakfast, an early lunch, or a combination of the two
1**bru·net** *or* **bru·nette** \brü-'net\ *adj* [F *brunet*, masc., *brunette*, fem., brownish, fr. OF, fr. *brun* brown, fr. ML *brunus*, of Gmc. origin; akin to OHG *brūn*, brown] **1 :** being a brunet <his ~ wife> **2 :** of a dark-brown or black color <~ hair>
2**brunet** *or* **brunette** *n* **:** a person having brown or black hair and usu. a relatively dark complexion
Brun·hild \'brün-ˌhilt\ *n* [G] **:** a queen in Germanic legend won by Siegfried for Gunther
bru·ni·zem \ˌbrü-nə-'zem, -'zhȯm\ *n* [*bruni-* (fr. ML *brunus* brown) + *-zem* earth (as in *chernozem*)] **:** any of a zonal group of deep dark prairie soils developed from loess
Bruns·wick stew \ˌbrənz-(ˌ)wik-\ *n* [*Brunswick* county, Va.] **:** a stew made of vegetables and usu. of two meats (as chicken and squirrel)
brunt \'brənt\ *n* [ME] **1 :** the principal force, shock, or stress (as of an attack) **2 :** the greater part **:** BURDEN
1**brush** \'brəsh\ *n* [ME *brusch*, fr. MF *broce*] **1 :** BRUSHWOOD **2 a :** scrub vegetation **b :** land covered with scrub vegetation
2**brush** *n* [ME *brusshe*, fr. MF *broisse*, fr. OF *broce*] **1 :** a device composed of bristles set into a handle and used esp. for sweeping, scrubbing, or painting **2 :** something resembling a brush: as **a :** a bushy tail **b :** a feather tuft worn on a hat **3 a :** an electrical conductor (as of copper strips or carbon) that makes sliding contact between a stationary and a moving part of a generator or a motor **b :** BRUSH DISCHARGE **4 a :** an act of brushing **b :** a quick light touch or momentary contact in passing
3**brush** *vt* **1 a :** to apply a brush to **b :** to apply with a brush **2 a :** to remove with passing strokes (as of a brush) <~*ed* the dirt off his coat> **b :** to dispose of in an offhand way **:** DISMISS <~*ed* him off> **3 :** to pass lightly over or across **:** touch gently against in passing — **brush·er** *n*
4**brush** *vi* [ME *bruschen* to rush, fr. MF *brosser* to dash through underbrush, fr. *broce*] **:** to move lightly or heedlessly <~*ed* by the well-wishers in his path>
5**brush** *n* [ME *brusche* rush, hostile collision, fr. *bruschen*] **:** a brief encounter or skirmish
brush·abil·i·ty \ˌbrəsh-ə-'bil-ət-ē\ *n* **:** ease of application with a brush <~ of a paint>
brush·back \'brəsh-ˌbak\ *n* **:** a fastball thrown near the batter's head in baseball in an attempt to make him move back from home plate
brush border *n* **:** microvilli on the plasma membrane of an epithelial cell (as in a kidney tubule) that is specialized for absorption
brush discharge *n* **:** a faintly luminous relatively slow electrical discharge having no spark
brushed \'brəsht\ *adj* **:** finished with a nap <a ~ fabric>
brush·fire \'brəsh-ˌfī(ə)r\ *adj* [*brush fire* (a fire involving brush but not full-sized trees)] **:** involving mobilization only on a small and local scale <~ border wars>
brush·land \-ˌland\ *n* **:** an area covered with brush growth
brush–off \-ˌȯf\ *n* **:** a quietly curt or disdainful dismissal
brush up \(ˈ)brəsh-'əp\ *vt* **1 :** to polish by eliminating small imperfections **2 :** to renew one's skill in ~ *vi* **:** to refresh one's memory **:** renew one's skill <*brush up* on his math> — **brush·up** \'brəsh-ˌəp\ *n*
brush·wood \'brəsh-ˌwu̇d\ *n* **1 :** wood of small branches esp. when cut or broken **2 :** a thicket of shrubs and small trees
brush·work \-ˌwərk\ *n* **:** work done with a brush (as in painting); *esp* **:** the characteristic work of an artist using a brush
1**brushy** \'brəsh-ē\ *adj* **brush·i·er; -est :** SHAGGY, ROUGH
2**brushy** *adj* **brush·i·er; -est :** covered with or abounding in brush or brushwood
brusque *also* **brusk** \'brəsk\ *adj* [F *brusque*, fr. It *brusco*, fr. ML *bruscus* butcher's-broom] **1 :** markedly short and abrupt **2 :** blunt in manner or speech often to the point of ungracious harshness ***syn*** see BLUFF ***ant*** unctuous, bland — **brusque·ly** *adv* — **brusque·ness** *n*
brus·que·rie \ˌbrəs-kə-'rē\ *n* [F, fr. *brusque*] **:** abruptness of manner
Brus·sels carpet \ˌbrəs-əlz-\ *n* [*Brussels*, Belgium] **:** a carpet made of colored worsted yarns first fixed in a foundation web of strong linen thread and then drawn up in loops to form the pattern
Brussels griffon *n* **:** any of a breed of short-faced compact rough- or smooth-coated toy dogs of Belgian origin — called also *griffon*
Brussels lace *n* **1 :** any of various fine needlepoint or bobbin laces with floral designs made orig. in or near Brussels **2 :** a machine-made net of hexagonal mesh
brussels sprout *n, often cap B* **1 :** any of the edible small green heads borne on the stem of a plant (*Brassica oleracea gemmifera*) — usu. used in pl. **2** *pl* **:** the plant that bears brussels sprouts

brussels sprouts

brut \'brüt, 'brü̅t\ *adj* [F, lit., rough] *of champagne* **:** very dry; *specif* **:** containing less than 1.5 percent sugar by volume
bru·tal \'brüt-ᵊl\ *adj* **1** *archaic* **:** typical of beasts **:** ANIMAL **2 :** befitting a brute: as **a :** grossly ruthless or unfeeling <a ~ slander> **b :** CRUEL, COLD-BLOODED <a ~ attack> **c :** HARSH, SEVERE <~ weather> **d :** unpleasantly accurate and incisive <the ~ truth> — **bru·tal·ly** \-ᵊl-ē\ *adv*
bru·tal·i·ty \brü-'tal-ət-ē\ *n, pl* **-ties 1 :** the quality or state of being brutal **2 :** a brutal act or course of action
bru·tal·ize \'brüt-ᵊl-ˌīz\ *vt* **-ized; -iz·ing 1 :** to make brutal, unfeeling, or inhuman <people *brutalized* by poverty and disease> **2 :** to treat brutally <an accord not to ~ prisoners of war> — **bru·tal·iza·tion** \ˌbrüt-ᵊl-ə-'zā-shən\ *n*
1**brute** \'brüt\ *adj* [ME, fr. MF *brut* rough, fr. L *brutus* stupid, lit., heavy; akin to L *gravis* heavy — more at GRIEVE] **1 :** of or relating to beasts <the ways of the ~ world> **2 :** INANIMATE 1a **3 :** characteristic of an animal in quality, action, or instinct: as **a :** CRUEL, SAVAGE <~ force> **b :** not working by reason <~ instinct> **4 :** purely physical <~ strength> **5 :** being of unrelieved severity <~ necessity>
2**brute** *n* **1 :** BEAST **2 :** a brutal person
brut·ish \'brüt-ish\ *adj* **1 :** befitting beasts <lived a short and ~ life as a slave> **2 a :** strongly and grossly sensual <~ gluttony> **b :** showing little intelligence or sensibility <a ~ lack of understanding> — **brut·ish·ly** *adv* — **brut·ish·ness** *n*
brux·ism \'brək-ˌsiz-əm\ *n* [irreg. fr. Gk *brychein* to gnash the teeth + E *-ism*] **:** the habit of unconsciously gritting or grinding the teeth esp. in situations of stress or during sleep
Bryn·hild \'brin-ˌhild\ *n* [ON *Brynhildr*] **:** a Valkyrie waked from an enchanted sleep by Sigurd who later forgets her and is killed through her agency
bry·ol·o·gy \brī-'äl-ə-jē\ *n* [Gk *bryon* moss + ISV *-logy*] **1 :** a branch of botany that deals with the bryophytes **2 :** moss life or biology
bry·o·ny \'brī-ə-nē\ *n, pl* **-nies** [L *bryonia*, fr. Gk *bryōnia*; akin to Gk *bryon*] **:** any of a genus (*Bryonia*) of tendril-bearing vines of the gourd family with large leaves and red or black fruit

bryo·phyte \ˈbrī-ə-ˌfīt\ *n* [deriv. of Gk *bryon* + *phyton* plant; akin to Gk *phyein* to bring forth — more at BE] **:** any of a division (Bryophyta) of nonflowering plants comprising the mosses and liverworts — **bryo·phyt·ic** \ˌbrī-ə-ˈfit-ik\ *adj*

bryo·zo·an \ˌbrī-ə-ˈzō-ən\ *n* [NL *Bryozoa*, class name, fr. Gk *bryon* + NL *-zoa*] **:** any of a phylum or class (Bryozoa) of aquatic mostly marine invertebrate animals that reproduce by budding and usu. form permanently attached branched or mossy colonies — **bryozoan** *adj*

Bryth·on \ˈbrith-ˌän, -ən\ *n* **1 :** a member of the British branch of Celts **2 :** a speaker of a Brythonic language

1Bry·thon·ic \brith-ˈän-ik\ *adj* **1 :** of, relating to, or characteristic of the Brythons **2 :** of, relating to, or characteristic of the division of the Celtic languages that includes Welsh, Cornish, and Breton

2Brythonic *n* **:** the Brythonic branch of the Celtic languages — see INDO-EUROPEAN LANGUAGES table

BS *abbr* **1** bachelor of science **2** balance sheet **3** bill of sale **4** British standard

BSA *abbr* **1** bachelor of science in agriculture **2** Boy Scouts of America

BSAA *abbr* bachelor of science in applied arts

BSArch *abbr* bachelor of science in architecture

BSAE *abbr* **1** bachelor of science in aeronautical engineering **2** bachelor of science in agricultural engineering **3** bachelor of science in architectural engineering

BSAg *abbr* bachelor of science in agriculture

BSB *abbr* bachelor of science in business

BSc *abbr* bachelor of science

BSCh *abbr* bachelor of science in chemistry

BSEc *or* **BSEcon** *abbr* bachelor of science in economics

BSEd *or* **BSE** *abbr* bachelor of science in education

BSEE *abbr* bachelor of science in elementary education

BSFor *abbr* bachelor of science in forestry

BSFS *abbr* bachelor of science in foreign service

BSI *abbr* British Standards Institution

bskt *abbr* basket

BSL *abbr* **1** bachelor of sacred literature **2** bachelor of science in languages **3** bachelor of science in law **4** bachelor of science in linguistics

BSN *abbr* bachelor of science in nursing

btry *abbr* battery

Btu *abbr* British thermal unit

bu *abbr* **1** bureau **2** bushel

1bub·ble \ˈbəb-əl\ *vb* **bub·bled; bub·bling** \ˈbəb-(ə-)liŋ\ [ME *bublen*] *vi* **1 :** to form or produce bubbles **2 :** to flow with a gurgling sound <a brook *bubbling* over rocks> **3 a :** to become lively or effervescent <*bubbling* with good humor> **b :** to speak in a lively and fluent manner <*bubbled* excitedly about his prize> ~ *vt* **1 :** to utter (as words) effervescently **2 :** to cause to bubble

2bubble *n, often attrib* **1 :** a small globule typically hollow and light: as **a :** a small body of gas within a liquid **b :** a thin film of liquid inflated with air or gas **c :** a globule in a transparent solid **d :** something that is hemispherical or semicylindrical **2 a :** something that lacks firmness, solidity, or reality **b :** a delusive scheme **3 :** a sound like that of bubbling

bubble and squeak *n, chiefly Brit* **:** a dish consisting of potatoes, cabbage, and sometimes meat fried together

bubble chamber *n* **:** a chamber of heated liquid in which the path of an ionizing particle is made visible by a string of vapor bubbles

bubble gum *n* **1 :** a chewing gum that can be blown into large bubbles **2 :** rock music characterized by simple repetitive phrasings and intended esp. for young teenagers

bub·bler \ˈbəb-(ə-)lər\ *n* **1 :** one that bubbles **2 :** a drinking fountain from which a stream of water bubbles upward

1bub·bly \ˈbəb-(ə-)lē\ *adj* **bub·bli·er; -est 1 :** full of bubbles **:** EFFERVESCENT <a ~ bottle of pop> **2 :** showing lively good spirits <a ~ group at the celebration> **3 :** resembling a bubble <a ~ dome>

2bubbly *n* **:** CHAMPAGNE

bubby *var of* BOOBY

bu·bo \ˈb(y)ü-(ˌ)bō\ *n, pl* **buboes** [ML *bubon-*, *bubo*, fr. Gk *boubōn*] **:** an inflammatory swelling of a lymph gland esp. in the groin — **bu·bon·ic** \b(y)ü-ˈbän-ik\ *adj*

bubonic plague *n* **:** plague in which the formation of buboes is a prominent feature

buc·cal \ˈbək-əl\ *adj* [L *bucca* cheek — more at POCK] **:** of, relating to, or involving the cheeks or the cavity of the mouth

buc·ca·neer \ˌbək-ə-ˈni(ə)r\ *n* [F *boucanier*] **1 :** one of the freebooters preying on Spanish ships and settlements esp. in the West Indies in the 17th century; *broadly* **:** PIRATE **2 :** an unscrupulous adventurer esp. in politics or business — **buccaneer** *vi* — **buc·ca·neer·ish** \-ish\ *adj*

Bu·ceph·a·lus \byü-ˈsef-ə-ləs\ *n* [L, fr. Gk *Boukephalos*] **:** the war-horse of Alexander the Great

1buck \ˈbək\ *n, pl* **bucks** [ME, fr. OE *bucca* stag, he-goat; akin to OHG *boc* he-goat, MIr *bocc*] **1** *or pl* **buck :** a male animal; *esp* **:** a male deer or antelope **2 a :** a male human being **:** MAN **b :** a dashing fellow **:** DANDY **3** *or pl* **buck :** ANTELOPE **4 a :** BUCKSKIN; *also* **:** an article (as a shoe) made of buckskin **b** *slang* **:** DOLLAR 3b **5** [short for *sawbuck*] **:** SAWHORSE **6 a :** a supporting rack or frame **b :** a short thick leather-covered block for gymnastic vaulting

2buck *vi* **1** *of a horse or mule* **:** to spring with a quick plunging leap **2 :** to charge against something (as an obstruction) **3 a :** to move or react jerkily **b :** to refuse assent **:** BALK **4 :** to strive for advancement sometimes without regard to ethical behavior ~ *vt* **1 :** to throw (as a rider) by bucking **2 a** *archaic* **:** 1BUTT **b :** OPPOSE, RESIST <~*ing* a trend> **3 :** to charge into (as the opponent's line in football) **4 a :** to pass esp. from one person to another <~*ed* the question on to someone else> **b :** to move or load (as heavy objects) esp. with mechanical equipment — **buck·er** *n*

3buck *adj* [prob. fr. 1*buck*] **:** of the lowest grade within a military category <~ private>

4buck *n* [short for earlier *buckhorn knife*] **:** an object formerly used in poker to mark the next player to deal; *broadly* **:** a token used as a mark or reminder

5buck *adv* [origin unknown] *South & Midland* **:** STARK <~ naked>

buck–and–wing \ˌbək-ən-ˈwiŋ\ *n* **:** a solo tap dance with sharp foot accents, springs, leg flings, and heel clicks

buck·a·roo *or* **buck·er·oo** \ˌbək-ə-ˈrü, ˈbək-ə-ˌ\ *n, pl* **-aroos** *or* **-eroos** [by folk etymology fr. Sp *vaquero*, fr. *vaca* cow, fr. L *vacca* — more at VACCINE] **1 :** COWBOY **2 :** BRONCOBUSTER

buck·bean \ˈbək-ˌbēn\ *n* **:** a plant (*Menyanthes trifoliata* of the family Menyanthaceae) growing in bogs and having racemes of white or purplish flowers

buck·board \-ˌbō(ə)rd, -ˌbȯ(ə)rd\ *n* [obs. E *buck* body of a wagon + E *board*] **:** a four-wheeled vehicle with a springy platform

buckboard

1buck·et \ˈbək-ət\ *n* [ME, fr. AF *buket*, fr. OE *būc* pitcher, belly; akin to OHG *būh* belly, Skt *bhūri* abundant — more at BIG] **1 :** a typically round vessel for catching, holding, or carrying liquids or solids **2 :** something resembling a bucket: as **a :** the scoop of an excavating machine **b :** one of the receptacles on the rim of a waterwheel **c :** one of the cups of an endless-belt conveyor **d :** one of the vanes of a turbine rotor **3 :** a large quantity **4 :** BUCKET SEAT

2bucket *vt* **1 :** to draw or lift in buckets **2** *Brit* **a :** to ride (a horse) hard **b :** to drive hurriedly or roughly **3 :** to deal with in a bucket shop ~ *vi* **1 :** HUSTLE, HURRY **2 a :** to move about haphazardly or irresponsibly **b :** to move roughly or jerkily <~*ing* over the rocky road>

bucket brigade *n* **:** a chain of persons acting to put out a fire by passing buckets of water from hand to hand

buck·et·ful \ˈbək-ət-ˌfu̇l\ *n, pl* **bucketfuls** \-ˌfu̇lz\ *or* **buck·ets·ful** \-əts-ˌfu̇l\ **:** as much as a bucket will hold

bucket seat *n* **:** a low separate seat for one person (as in automobiles and airplanes)

bucket shop *n* **1 :** a saloon in which liquor was formerly sold from or dispensed in open containers (as buckets or pitchers) **2 a :** an establishment in which security and commodity options and uncompleted purchases and sales at trivial margins are handled like bets **b :** a dishonest brokerage house; *esp* **:** one that fleeces customers by failing to execute orders on margin in anticipation of market fluctuations adverse to their interest

buck·eye \ˈbək-ˌī\ *n* **1 :** a shrub or tree (genus *Aesculus*) of the horse-chestnut family; *also* **:** its large nutlike seed **2** *cap* **:** a native or resident of Ohio — used as a nickname

buck fever *n* **:** nervous excitement of an inexperienced hunter at the sight of game

1buck·le \ˈbək-əl\ *n* [ME *bocle*, fr. MF, boss of a shield, buckle, fr. L *buccula*, dim. of *bucca* cheek — more at POCK] **1 :** a fastening for two loose ends that is attached to one and holds the other by a catch **2 :** an ornamental device that suggests a buckle **3** *archaic* **:** a crisp curl

2buckle *vb* **buck·led; buck·ling** \ˈbək-(ə-)liŋ\ *vt* **1 :** to fasten with a buckle **2 :** to prepare with vigor <*buckled* himself to the task> **3 :** to cause to bend, give way, or crumple ~ *vi* **1 :** to apply oneself with vigor <~*s* down to the job> **2 :** to bend, heave, warp, or kink usu. under the influence of some external agency <cornstalk *buckling* in the high wind> **3 :** COLLAPSE <the supports *buckled* under the strain> **4 :** to give way **:** YIELD <one who does not ~ under pressure>

3buckle *n* **:** a product of buckling

1buck·ler \ˈbək-lər\ *n* [ME *bocler*, fr. OF, shield with a boss, fr. *bocle*] **1 a :** a small round shield held by a handle at arm's length **b :** a shield worn on the left arm **2 :** one that shields and protects

2buckler *vt* **:** to shield or defend with a buckler

bucko \ˈbək-(ˌ)ō\ *n, pl* **buck·oes 1 :** one who is domineering and bullying **:** SWAGGERER **2** *chiefly Irish* **:** young fellow **:** LAD

buck passer *n* [4*buck*] **:** a person who habitually passes the buck — **buck–pass·ing** \ˈbək-ˌpas-iŋ\ *n*

1buck·ram \ˈbək-rəm\ *n* [ME *bukeram*, fr. OF *boquerant*, fr. OProv *bocaran*, fr. *Bokhara*, city of central Asia] **1 :** a stiff-finished heavily sized fabric of cotton or linen used for interlinings in garments, for stiffening in millinery, and in bookbinding **2** *archaic* **:** STIFFNESS, RIGIDITY

2buckram *adj* **:** suggesting buckram esp. in stiffness or formality

3buckram *vt* **1 :** to give strength or stiffness to (as with buckram) **2** *archaic* **:** to make pretentious

Bucks *abbr* Buckinghamshire

buck·saw \ˈbək-ˌsȯ\ *n* **:** a saw set in a usu. H-shaped frame that is used for sawing wood

buck·shee \ˈbək-(ˌ)shē\ *n* [Hindi *bakhśiś*] **1** *Brit* **:** something extra obtained free; *esp* **:** extra rations **2** *Brit* **:** WINDFALL, GRATUITY

buck·shot \ˈbək-ˌshät\ *n* **:** a coarse lead shot

buck·skin \-ˌskin\ *n* **1 a :** the skin of a buck **b :** a soft pliable usu. suede-finished leather **2 a** *pl* **:** buckskin breeches **b** *archaic* **:** a person dressed in buckskin; *esp* **:** an early American backwoodsman **3 :** a horse of a light yellowish dun color usu. with dark mane and tail — **buckskin** *adj*

buck·tail \-ˌtāl\ *n* **:** an angler's lure made typically of hairs from the tail of a deer

buck·thorn \-ˌthȯ(ə)rn\ *n* **1 :** any of a genus (*Rhamnus* of the family Rhamnaceae, the buckthorn family) of often thorny trees or shrubs some of which yield purgatives or pigments **2 :** a tree (*Bumelia lycioides*) of the sapodilla family of the southern U.S.
buck·tooth \-ˈtüth\ *n* **:** a large projecting front tooth — **buck-toothed** \-ˈtütht\ *adj*
buck up *vb* [[1]*buck*] *vi* **:** to become encouraged ~ *vt* **1 :** IMPROVE, SMARTEN **2 :** to raise the morale of
buck·wheat \ˈbək-ˌ(h)wēt\ *n* [D *boekweit*, fr. MD *boecweit*, fr. *boec-* (akin to OHG *buohha* beech tree) + *weit* wheat — more at BEECH] **1 :** any of a genus (*Fagopyrum* of the family Polygonaceae, the buckwheat family) of herbs with alternate leaves, clusters of apetalous pinkish white flowers and triangular seeds; *esp* **:** either of two plants (*F. esculentum* and *F. tartaricum*) cultivated for their edible seeds **2 :** the seed of a buckwheat used as a cereal grain
1bu·col·ic \byü-ˈkäl-ik\ *adj* [L *bucolicus*, fr. Gk *boukolikos*, fr. *boukolos* cowherd, fr. *bous* head of cattle + *-kolos* (akin to L *colere* to cultivate) — more at COW, WHEEL] **1 :** of or relating to shepherds or herdsmen **:** PASTORAL **2 :** relating to or typical of rural life ***syn*** see RURAL — **bu·col·i·cal·ly** \-i-k(ə-)lē\ *adv*
2bucolic *n* **:** a pastoral poem **:** ECLOGUE
1bud \ˈbəd\ *n* [ME *budde;* akin to OE *budda* beetle, Skt *bhūri* abundant — more at BIG] **1 :** a small lateral or terminal protuberance on the stem of a plant that may develop into a flower, leaf, or shoot **2 :** something not yet mature or at full development: as **a :** an incompletely opened flower **b :** CHILD, YOUTH **c :** an outgrowth of an organism that differentiates into a new individual **:** GEMMA; *also* **:** PRIMORDIUM — **in the bud :** in an early stage of development <nipped the rebellion *in the bud*>
2bud *vb* **bud·ded; bud·ding** *vi* **1** *of a plant* **a :** to set or put forth buds **b :** to commence growth from buds **2 :** to develop by way of outgrowth **3 :** to reproduce asexually esp. by the pinching off of a small part of the parent ~ *vt* **1 :** to produce or develop from buds **2 :** to cause (as a plant) to bud **3 :** to insert a bud from a plant of one kind into an opening in the bark of (a plant of another kind) usu. in order to propagate a desired variety — **bud·der** *n*
Bud·dha \ˈbüd-ə, ˈbůd-\ *n* [Skt, enlightened] **1 :** a person who has attained Buddhahood **2 :** a representation of Gautama Buddha
Bud·dha·hood \-ˌhůd\ *n* **:** a state of perfect enlightenment sought in Buddhism
Bud·dhism \ˈbü-ˌdiz-əm, ˈbů-ˌiz-\ *n* **:** a religion of eastern and central Asia growing out of the teaching of Gautama Buddha that suffering is inherent in life and that one can be liberated from it by mental and moral self-purification — **Bud·dhist** \ˈbüd-əst, ˈbůd-\ *n or adj* — **Bud·dhis·tic** \bü-ˈdis-tik, bů-\ *adj*
bud·ding \ˈbəd-iŋ\ *adj* **:** being in an early stage of development <~ novelists>
bud·dle \ˈbəd-ᵊl\ *n* [origin unknown] **:** an apparatus on which crushed ore is washed
bud·dle·ia \ˈbəd-lē-ə, ˌbəd-ˈlē-\ *n* [NL, genus name, fr. Adam *Buddle* †1715 E botanist] **:** any of a genus (*Buddleia* of the family Loganiaceae) of shrubs or trees of warm regions with showy terminal clusters of usu. yellow or violet flowers
bud·dy \ˈbəd-ē\ *n, pl* **buddies** [prob. baby talk alter. of *brother*] **1 :** COMPANION, PARTNER **2 :** FELLOW — used esp. in informal address
buddy system *n* **:** an arrangement in which two individuals are paired (as for mutual safety in a hazardous situation)
1budge \ˈbəj\ *n* [ME *bugee*, fr. AF *bogee*] **:** a fur formerly prepared from lambskin dressed with the wool outward
2budge *vb* **budged; budg·ing** [MF *bouger*, fr. (assumed) VL *bullicare*, fr. L *bullire* to boil — more at BOIL] *vi* **1 :** MOVE, SHIFT <the mule wouldn't ~> **2 :** to give way **:** YIELD <wouldn't ~ on the issue> ~ *vt* **:** to cause to move
3budge *adj* [origin unknown] *archaic* **:** POMPOUS, SOLEMN
bud·ger·i·gar \ˈbəj-(ə-)rē-ˌgär, ˌbəj-ə-ˈrē-\ *n* [native name in Australia] **:** a small Australian parrot (*Melopsittacus undulatus*) usu. light green with black and yellow markings in the wild but bred under domestication in many colors
1bud·get \ˈbəj-ət\ *n* [ME *bowgette*, fr. MF *bougette*, dim. of *bouge* leather bag, fr. L *bulga*, of Gaulish origin; akin to MIr *bolg* bag; akin to OE *bælg* bag — more at BELLY] **1** *chiefly dial* **:** a usu. leather pouch, wallet, or pack; *also* **:** its contents **2 :** STOCK, SUPPLY **3 a :** a statement of the financial position of an administration for a definite period of time based on estimates of expenditures during the period and proposals for financing them **b :** a plan for the coordination of resources and expenditures **c :** the amount of money that is available for, required for, or assigned to a particular purpose — **bud·get·ary** \ˈbəj-ə-ˌter-ē\ *adj*

budgerigar

2budget *vt* **1 a :** to put or allow for in a budget **b :** to require to adhere to a budget <~*ed* shoppers> **2 a :** to allocate funds for in a budget <~*ing* a new hospital> **b :** to plan or provide for the use of in detail <~*ing* manpower in a tight labor market> ~ *vi* **:** to put oneself on a budget <~*ing* for a vacation>
bud·ge·teer \ˌbəj-ə-ˈti(ə)r\ *or* **bud·get·er** \ˈbəj-ət-ər\ *n* **1 :** one who prepares a budget **2 :** one who is restricted to a budget
bud·gie \ˈbəj-ē\ *n* [by shortening and alter.] **:** BUDGERIGAR
bud scale *n* **:** one of the leaves resembling scales that form the sheath of a plant bud
bud sport *n* **:** a mutation arising in a plant bud
1buff \ˈbəf\ *n* [MF *buffle* wild ox, fr. OIt *bufalo*] **1 :** a garment (as a uniform) made of buff leather **2 :** the bare skin **3 a :** a moderate orange yellow **b :** a light to moderate yellow **4 :** a device (as a stick or block) having a soft absorbent surface (as of cloth) by which polishing material is applied **5** [earlier *buff* (an enthusiast about going to fires); fr. the buff overcoats worn by volunteer firemen in New York City *ab*1820] **:** FAN, ENTHUSIAST
2buff *adj* **:** of the color buff
3buff *vt* **1 :** POLISH, SHINE <waxed and ~*ed* the floor> **2 :** to give a buff or velvety surface to (leather)
1buf·fa·lo \ˈbəf-ə-ˌlō\ *n, pl* **-lo** *or* **-loes** *also* **-los** [It *bufalo* & Sp *búfalo*, fr. LL *bufalus*, alter. of L *bubalus*, fr. Gk *boubalos* African gazelle, irreg. fr. *bous* head of cattle — more at COW] **1 :** any of several wild oxen: as **a :** WATER BUFFALO **b :** any of a genus (*Bison*); *esp* **:** a large shaggy-maned No. American wild ox (*B. bison*) with short horns and heavy forequarters with a large muscular hump **2 :** any of several suckers (genus *Ictiobus*) found mostly in the Mississippi valley — called also *buffalofish*
2buffalo *vt* **-loed; -lo·ing :** BEWILDER, BAFFLE
buffalo berry *n* **:** either of two western U.S. shrubs (*Shepherdia argentea* and *S. canadensis*) of the oleaster family with silvery foliage; *also* **:** their edible scarlet berry
buffalo bug *n* **:** CARPET BEETLE
buffalofish *n* **:** BUFFALO 2
buffalo grass *n* **:** a low-growing grass (*Buchloë dactyloides*) of former feeding grounds of the American buffalo; *also* **:** GRAMA
buffalo robe *n* **:** the hide of an American buffalo lined on the skin side with fabric and used as a coverlet or rug
1buff·er \ˈbəf-ər\ *n* **:** one that buffs
2buffer *n* [*buff* (to react like a soft body when struck)] **1 :** any of various devices or pieces of material for reducing shock due to contact **2 :** a means or device used as a cushion against the shock of fluctuations in business or financial activity **3 :** something that serves to separate two items: as **a :** BUFFER STATE **b :** a person who shields another esp. from annoying routine matters **4 :** a substance capable in solution of neutralizing both acids and bases and thereby maintaining the original acidity or basicity of the solution; *also* **:** such a solution **5 :** a temporary storage unit (as in a computer); *esp* **:** one that accepts information at one rate and delivers it at another
3buffer *vt* **1 :** to lessen the shock of **:** CUSHION **2 :** to treat (as a solution) with a buffer; *also* **:** to prepare (aspirin) with an antacid
buffer state *n* **:** a small neutral state lying between two larger potentially rival powers
buffer zone *n* **:** a neutral area separating conflicting forces; *broadly* **:** an area designed to separate
1buf·fet \ˈbəf-ət\ *n* [ME, fr. MF, fr. OF, dim. of *buffe*] **1 :** a blow esp. with the hand **2 :** something that strikes with telling force
2buffet *vt* **1 :** to strike sharply esp. with the hand **:** CUFF **2 a :** to strike repeatedly **:** BATTER <the waves ~*ed* the shore> **b :** to contend against ~ *vi* **:** to make one's way esp. under difficult conditions
3buf·fet \(ˌ)bə-ˈfā, bü-ˈ, ˈbü-ˌ\ *n* [F] **1 :** a sideboard often without a mirror **2 :** a cupboard or set of shelves for the display of tableware **3 a :** a counter for refreshments **b** *chiefly Brit* **:** a restaurant operated as a public convenience (as in a railway station) **c :** a meal set out on a buffet or table for ready access and informal service
4buffet *like*[3]\ *adj* **:** served informally (as from a buffet)
buffing wheel *n* **:** a wheel covered with material for polishing
buff leather *n* **:** a strong supple oil-tanned leather produced chiefly from cattle hides
buf·fle·head \ˈbəf-əl-ˌhed\ *n* [archaic E *buffle* buffalo + E *head*] **:** a small No. American diving duck (*Bucephala albeola*)
buf·fo \ˈbü-(ˌ)fō\ *n, pl* **buf·fi** \-(ˌ)fē\ *or* **buffos** [It, fr. *buffone*] **:** CLOWN, BUFFOON; *specif* **:** a male singer of comic roles in opera
buf·foon \(ˌ)bə-ˈfün\ *n* [MF *bouffon*, fr. OIt *buffone*, fr. ML *bufon-*, *bufo*, fr. L, toad] **1 :** a ludicrous figure **:** CLOWN **2 :** a gross and usu. ill-educated or stupid person — **buf·foon·ish** \-ish\ *adj*
buf·foon·ery \-ˈfün-(ə-)rē\ *n, pl* **-er·ies :** coarse loutish behavior or practice
1bug \ˈbəg\ *n* [ME *bugge* scarecrow; akin to Norw dial. *bugge* important man — more at BIG] **1** *obs* **:** BOGEY, BUGBEAR **2 a :** an insect or other creeping or crawling invertebrate **b :** any of several insects commonly considered esp. obnoxious: as (1) **:** BEDBUG (2) **:** COCKROACH (3) **:** HEAD LOUSE **c :** any of an order (Hemiptera and esp. its suborder Heteroptera) of insects that have sucking mouthparts, fore wings thickened at the base, and incomplete metamorphosis and are often economic pests — called also *true bug* **3 :** an unexpected defect, fault, flaw, or imperfection **4 :** a disease-producing germ; *also* **:** a disease caused by it **5 :** a temporary enthusiasm **6 :** ENTHUSIAST, HOBBYIST <a camera ~> **7 :** a prominent person **8 :** a concealed listening device **9** [fr. its designation by an asterisk on race programs] **:** a weight allowance given apprentice jockeys **:** HANDICAP
2bug *vt* **bugged; bug·ging 1 :** BOTHER, ANNOY <don't ~ me with petty details> **2 :** to plant a concealed microphone in
bug·a·boo \ˈbəg-ə-ˌbü\ *n, pl* **-boos** [origin unknown] **1 :** an imaginary object of fear **:** BUGBEAR, BOGEY **2 :** a source of concern <the national ~ of inflation>
bug·bane \ˈbəg-ˌbān\ *n* **:** any of several perennial herbs (esp. genus *Cimicifuga*) of the buttercup family that have two or three ternately divided serrate leaves and white flowers in long racemes; *esp* **:** BLACK COHOSH
bug·bear \-ˌba(ə)r, -ˌbe(ə)r\ *n* **1 :** an imaginary goblin or specter used to excite fear **2 :** an object or source of dread
bug·eye \-ˌī\ *n* **:** a small boat with a flat bottom, a centerboard, and two raked masts
bug·ger \ˈbüg-ər, ˈbəg-\ *n* [ME *bougre* heretic, sodomite, fr. MF, fr. ML *Bulgarus*, lit., Bulgarian] **1 :** SODOMITE **2 a :** a worthless person **:** RASCAL **b :** FELLOW, CHAP
bug·gery \-ə-rē\ *n* **:** SODOMY
1bug·gy \ˈbəg-ē\ *adj* **:** infested with bugs
2buggy *n, pl* **buggies** [origin unknown] **1 :** a light one-horse carriage made with two wheels in England and with four wheels in the U.S. **2 :** a small cart or truck for short transportations of heavy materials **3 :** BABY CARRIAGE
1bug·house \ˈbəg-ˌhaůs\ *n* **:** an insane asylum
2bughouse *adj* **:** mentally deranged **:** CRAZY

[1]bu·gle \'byü-gəl\ *n* [ME, fr. OF, fr. LL *bugula*] **:** any of a genus (*Ajuga*) of plants of the mint family; *esp* **:** a European annual (*A. reptans*) that has spikes of blue flowers and is naturalized in the U.S.
[2]bugle *n* [ME, buffalo, instrument made of buffalo horn, bugle, fr. OF, fr. L *buculus,* dim. of *bos* head of cattle — more at COW] **:** a valveless brass instrument that resembles a trumpet and is used esp. for military calls

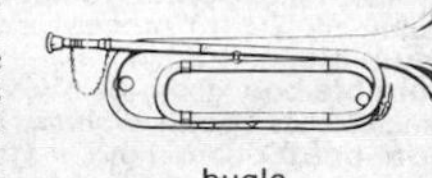
bugle

[3]bugle *vi* **bu·gled; bu·gling** \-g(ə-)liŋ\ **1 :** to sound a bugle **2 :** to utter a prolonged cry that is the characteristic rutting call of the bull elk
[4]bugle *n* [perh. fr. [2]*bugle*] **:** a small cylindrical bead of glass or plastic used for trimming esp. on women's clothing — **bugle** *adj*
bu·gler \'byü-glər\ *n* **:** one who sounds a bugle
bu·gle·weed \'byü-gəl-,wēd\ *n* **:** any of a genus (*Lycopus*) of mints; *esp* **:** one (*L. virginicus*) that is mildly narcotic and astringent
bu·gloss \'byü-,gläs, -,glòs\ *n* [MF *buglosse,* fr. L *buglossa,* irreg. fr. Gk *bouglōssos,* fr. *bous* head of cattle + *glōssa* tongue — more at COW, GLOSS] **:** any of several coarse hairy plants (genera *Lycopsis* and *Anchusa,* esp. *A. officinalis*) of the borage family
bug·seed \'bəg-,sēd\ *n* **:** a fleshy annual herb (*Corispermum hyssopifolium*) of the goosefoot family with flat oval seeds
buhl \'bül, 'byü(ə)l\ *var of* BOULLE
buhr \'bər\ *n* **:** BUHRSTONE 2
buhr·stone \-,stōn\ *n* [prob. fr. *burr* + *stone*] **1 :** a siliceous rock used for millstones **2 :** a millstone cut from buhrstone
[1]build \'bild\ *vb* **built** \'bilt\; **build·ing** [ME *bilden,* fr. OE *byldan;* akin to OE *būan* to dwell — more at BOWER] *vt* **1 :** to form by ordering and uniting materials by gradual means into a composite whole **:** CONSTRUCT **2 :** to cause to be constructed **3 :** to develop according to a systematic plan, by a definite process, or on a particular base **4 :** INCREASE, ENLARGE ~ *vi* **1 :** to engage in building **2 a :** to increase in intensity <~ to a climax> **b :** to develop in extent <a line of people ~*ing* along the avenue>
[2]build *n* **:** form or mode of structure **:** MAKE; *esp* **:** bodily conformation of a person or lower animal ***syn*** see PHYSIQUE
build·ed *archaic past of* BUILD
build·er \'bil-dər\ *n* **1 :** one that builds; *esp* **:** one that contracts to build and supervises building operations **2 :** a substance added to or used with detergents to increase their cleansing action
builder's knot *n* **:** CLOVE HITCH
build in *vt* **:** to construct or develop as an integral part of something
build·ing \'bil-diŋ\ *n* **1 :** a usu. roofed and walled structure built for permanent use (as for a dwelling) **2 :** the art or business of assembling materials into a structure
building block *n* **:** a unit of construction or composition
build·up \'bil-,dəp\ *n* **1 :** the act or process of building up **2 :** something produced by building up
build up \(')bil-'dəp\ *vt* **1 :** to develop gradually by increments <*building up* his endurance> <*built up* a library> **2 :** to promote the esteem of <a salesman *building up* his product> ~ *vi* **:** to accumulate or develop appreciably <clouds *building up* on the horizon>
built \'bilt\ *adj* **:** formed as to physique or bodily contours <a slimly ~ girl>
built-in \'bil-'tin\ *adj* **1 :** forming an integral part of a structure; *esp* **:** constructed as or in a recess in a wall **2 :** INHERENT
built-up \'bil-'təp\ *adj* **1 :** made of several sections or layers fastened together **2 :** covered with buildings
buird·ly \'bü(ə)r(d)-lē\ *adj* [prob. alter. of *burly*] *Scot* **:** STURDY
bulb \'bəlb\ *n* [L *bulbus,* fr. Gk *bolbos* bulbous plant; akin to Arm *bolk* radish] **1 a :** a resting stage of a plant (as the lily, onion, hyacinth, or tulip) that is usu. formed underground and consists of a short stem base bearing one or more buds enclosed in overlapping membranous or fleshy leaves **b :** a fleshy structure (as a tuber or corm) resembling a bulb in appearance **c :** a plant having or developing from a bulb **2 :** a bulb-shaped part; *specif* **:** a rounded glass envelope enclosing the light source of an electric lamp or such an envelope together with the light source it encloses **3 :** a rounded or swollen anatomical structure **4 :** a camera setting that indicates that the shutter can be opened by pressing on the release and closed by ending the pressure — **bul·ba·ceous** \,bəl-'bā-shəs\ *adj* — **bulbed** \'bəlbd\ *adj*
bul·bar \'bəl-bər, -,bär\ *adj* **:** of or relating to a bulb; *specif* **:** involving the medulla oblongata
bul·bil \'bəl-bəl, -,bil\ *n* [F *bulbille,* dim. of *bulbe* bulb, fr. L *bulbus*] **:** a small or secondary bulb; *esp* **:** an aerial deciduous bud produced in a leaf axil or replacing the flowers
bul·bous \'bəl-bəs\ *adj* **1 :** having a bulb **:** growing from or bearing bulbs **2 :** resembling a bulb esp. in roundness <a ~ nose> — **bul·bous·ly** *adv*
bul·bul \'bůl-,bůl\ *n* [Per, fr. Ar] **1 :** a Persian songbird frequently mentioned in poetry that is prob. a nightingale (*Luscinia golzii*) **2 :** any of a group of gregarious passerine birds (family Pycnonotidae) of Asia and Africa
Bulg *abbr* Bulgaria; Bulgarian
Bul·gar \'bəl-,gär, 'bůl-\ *n* [ML *Bulgarus*] **:** BULGARIAN
Bul·gar·i·an \,bəl-'gar-ē-ən, bůl-, -'ger-\ *n* **1 :** a native or inhabitant of Bulgaria **2 :** the Slavic language of the Bulgarians — **Bulgarian** *adj*
[1]bulge \'bəlj\ *n* [MF *boulge, bouge* leather bag, curved part — more at BUDGET] **1 :** BILGE 1, 2 **2 :** a usu. localized swelling of a surface caused by pressure from within or below **3 :** ADVANTAGE, UPPER HAND **4 :** sudden expansion ***syn*** see PROJECTION
[2]bulge *vb* **bulged; bulg·ing** *vt* **:** to cause to bulge ~ *vi* **1** *archaic* **:** BILGE 1 **2 a :** to jut out **:** SWELL **b :** to bend outward **c :** to become swollen or protuberant
bul·gur \bůl-'gů(ə)r\ *n* [Turk] **:** parched crushed wheat prepared for human consumption
bulgy \'bəl-jē\ *adj* **:** showing a bulge **:** BULGING — **bulg·i·ness** *n*
bu·lim·ia \byü-'lim-ē-ə\ *n* [NL, fr. Gk *boulimia* great hunger, fr. *bous* head of cattle + *limos* hunger — more at COW, LESS] **:** an abnormal and constant craving for food
[1]bulk \'bəlk\ *n* [ME, heap, bulk, fr. ON *bulki* cargo] **1 a :** spatial dimension **:** MAGNITUDE **b :** material (as indigestible fibrous residues of food) that forms a mass in the intestine **2 a :** BODY; *esp* **:** a large or corpulent human body **b :** an organized structure esp. when viewed primarily as a mass of material <the shrouded ~*s* of snow-covered cars> **c :** a ponderous shapeless mass of material <on the living sea rolls an inanimate ~ —P. B. Shelley> **3 :** the main or greater part
syn BULK, MASS, VOLUME *shared meaning element* **:** the aggregate that forms a body or unit
— **in bulk 1 :** not divided into parts **2 :** not packaged in separate units
[2]bulk *vt* **1 :** to cause to swell or bulge **:** STUFF **2 :** to gather into a mass or aggregate **3 :** to have a bulk of ~ *vi* **1 :** SWELL, EXPAND **2 :** to appear as a factor **:** LOOM <a consideration that ~*s* large in everyone's thinking>
[3]bulk *adj* **1 :** being in bulk <~ cement> **2 :** of or relating to materials in bulk
bulk·head \'bəlk-,hed, 'bəl-,ked\ *n* [*bulk* (structure projecting from a building) + *head*] **1 :** an upright partition separating compartments **2 :** a structure or partition to resist pressure or to shut off water, fire, or gas **3 :** a retaining wall along a waterfront **4 :** a projecting framework with a sloping door giving access to a cellar stairway or a shaft
bulky \'bəl-kē\ **bulk·i·er; -est** *adj* **1 a :** having bulk **b** (1) **:** large of its kind (2) **:** CORPULENT **2 :** having great volume in proportion to weight <a ~ knit sweater> — **bulk·i·ly** \-kə-lē\ *adv* — **bulk·i·ness** \-kē-nəs\ *n*
[1]bull \'bůl\ *n* [ME *bule,* fr. OE *bula;* akin to OE *blāwan* to blow] **1 a :** an adult male bovine animal; *also* **:** a usu. adult male of various large animals **b :** ELEPHANT **c :** a draft ox **2 :** one who buys securities or commodities in expectation of a price rise or who acts to effect such a rise — compare BEAR **3 :** one that resembles a bull (as in brawny physique) **4 :** BULLDOG **5** *slang* **:** POLICEMAN, DETECTIVE **6** *cap* **:** TAURUS
[2]bull *adj* **1 a :** MALE **b :** of or relating to a bull **c :** suggestive of a bull **2 :** large of its kind **3 :** RISING <a ~ market>
[3]bull *vi* **:** to advance forcefully ~ *vt* **1 :** to try to raise the price of (as stocks) or in (a market) **2 a :** to act on with violence **b :** FORCE <~*ed* his way through the crowd>
[4]bull *n* [ME *bulle,* fr. ML *bulla,* fr. L, bubble, amulet] **1 :** a solemn papal letter sealed with a bulla or with a red-ink imprint of the device on the bulla **2 :** EDICT, DECREE
[5]bull *n* [perh. fr. obs. *bull* to mock] **:** a grotesque blunder in language
[6]bull *n* [short for *bullshit*] **1** *slang* **:** empty boastful talk **2** *slang* **:** NONSENSE
[7]bull *vi, slang* **:** to engage in idle and often boastful talk ~ *vt, slang* **:** to fool esp. by fast boastful talk
[8]bull *abbr* bulletin
bul·la \'bůl-ə\ *n, pl* **bul·lae** \'bůl-,ē, -,ī\ **1** [ML] **:** the round usu. lead seal attached to a papal bull **2** [NL, fr. L] **:** a hollow thin-walled rounded bony prominence **3 :** a large vesicle or blister
bul·lace \'bůl-əs\ *n* [ME *bolace,* fr. MF *beloce,* fr. ML *bolluca*] **:** a European plum (*Prunus domestica insititia*) with small ovoid fruit in clusters
bull·bait·ing \'bůl-,bāt-iŋ\ *n* **:** the former practice of baiting bulls with dogs
bull·bat \'bůl-,bat\ *n* **:** NIGHTHAWK 1a
[1]bull·dog \'bůl-,dòg\ *n* **1 :** a compact muscular short-haired dog of an English breed that is marked by vigor and sagacity and has widely separated forelegs and an undershot lower jaw **2 :** a revolver of large caliber and short barrel **3 :** a proctor's attendant at an English university
[2]bulldog *adj* **:** suggestive of a bulldog <~ tenacity>
[3]bulldog *vt* **:** to throw (a steer) by seizing the horns and twisting the neck — **bull·dog·ger** *n*
bull·doze \'bůl-,dōz\ *vt* [perh. fr. [1]*bull* + alter. of *dose*] **1 :** BULLY **2 :** to move, clear, gouge out, or level off by pushing with a bulldozer **3 :** to force insensitively or ruthlessly
bull·doz·er \-,dō-zər\ *n* **1 :** one that bulldozes **2 :** a tractor-driven machine having a broad blunt horizontal blade or ram for clearing land, road building, or comparable activities
bul·let \'bůl-ət\ *n, often attrib* [MF *boulette* small ball & *boulet* missile, dims. of *boule* ball — more at BOWL] **1 :** a round or elongated missile (as of lead) designed to be fired from a firearm; *broadly* **:** CARTRIDGE 1a **2 :** something resembling a bullet (as in curved form) **3 :** a very fast and accurately thrown ball **4 :** a ballot cast for a straight ticket — **bul·let·proof** \,bůl-ət-'prüf\ *adj*
[1]bul·le·tin \'bůl-ət-ᵊn\ *n* [F, fr. It *bullettino,* dim. of *bulla* papal edict, fr. ML] **1 :** a brief public notice issuing usu. from an authoritative source; *specif* **:** a brief news item intended for immediate publication **2 :** PERIODICAL; *esp* **:** the organ of an institution or association
[2]bulletin *vt* **:** to make public by bulletin
bulletin board *n* **:** a board for posting notices (as at a school)
bull fiddle *n* **:** DOUBLE BASS — **bull fiddler** *n*
bull·fight \'bůl-,fīt\ *n* **:** a spectacle in which men ceremonially excite, fight with, and in Hispanic tradition kill bulls in an arena for public amusement — **bull·fight·er** \-ər\ *n*
bull·fight·ing \-iŋ\ *n* **:** the action involved in a bullfight

bull·finch \ˈbu̇l-ˌfinch\ *n* **:** a European finch (*Pyrrhula pyrrhula*) having in the male rosy red underparts, blue-gray back, and black cap, chin, tail, and wings; *also* **:** any of several other finches
bull·frog \-ˌfrȯg, -ˌfräg\ *n* **:** FROG; *esp* **:** a heavy-bodied deep-voiced frog (as of the genus *Rana*)
bull·head \-ˌhed\ *n* **:** any of various large-headed fishes (as a miller's-thumb or sculpin); *esp* **:** any of several common freshwater catfishes (genus *Ictalurus*) of the U.S.
bull·head·ed \ˈbu̇l-ˈhed-əd\ *adj* **:** stupidly stubborn **:** HEADSTRONG — **bull·head·ed·ly** *adv* — **bull·head·ed·ness** *n*
bull·horn \ˈbu̇l-ˌhȯ(ə)rn\ *n* **1 :** a loudspeaker on a naval ship **2 :** a hand-held combined microphone and loudspeaker
bul·lion \ˈbu̇l-yən\ *n* [ME, fr. Af, mint] **1 a :** gold or silver considered as so much metal; *specif* **:** uncoined gold or silver in bars or ingots **b :** metal in the mass <lead ~> **2 :** lace, braid, or fringe of gold or silver threads
bull·ish \ˈbu̇l-ish\ *adj* **1 :** suggestive of a bull (as in brawniness) **2 a :** marked by, tending to cause, or hopeful of rising prices (as in a stock market) **b :** OPTIMISTIC — **bull·ish·ly** *adv* — **bull·ish·ness** *n*
bull mastiff *n* **:** a large powerful dog of a breed developed by crossing bulldogs with mastiffs
Bull Moose *n* [*bull moose,* emblem of the Progressive party of 1912] **:** a follower of Theodore Roosevelt in the U.S. presidential campaign of 1912
Bull Moos·er \-ˈmü-sər\ *n* **:** BULL MOOSE
bull neck *n* **:** a thick short powerful neck — **bull·necked** \ˈbu̇l-ˈnekt\ *adj*
bull·ock \ˈbu̇l-ək\ *n* **1 :** a young bull **2 :** a castrated bull **:** STEER — **bull·ocky** \-ə-kē\ *adj*
bul·lous \ˈbu̇l-əs\ *adj* **:** resembling or characterized by bullae **:** VESICULAR <~ lesions>
bull pen *n* **1 :** a large detention cell where prisoners are held until brought into court **2 a :** a place on a baseball field where relief pitchers warm up during a game **b :** the relief pitchers of a baseball team
bull·pout \ˈbu̇l-ˌpau̇t\ *n* [*bull*head + *pout*] **:** BULLHEAD; *esp* **:** the common dark bullhead (*Ictalurus nebulosus*)
bull·ring \ˈbu̇l-ˌriŋ\ *n* **:** an arena for bullfights
bull session *n* [6*bull*] **:** an informal discursive group discussion
bull's–eye \ˈbu̇l-ˌzī\ *n, pl* **bull's–eyes** **1 :** a small thick disk of glass inserted (as in a deck) to let in light **2 :** a very hard globular candy **3 a :** the center of a target; *also* **:** something central or crucial **b :** a shot that hits the bull's-eye; *broadly* **:** something that precisely attains a desired end **4 :** a simple lens of short focal distance; *also* **:** a lantern with such a lens — see LANTERN illustration **5 :** a circular opening for air or light
bull·shit \ˈbu̇l-ˌshit\ *n* [1*bull* + *shit*] **:** NONSENSE; *esp* **:** foolish insolent talk — usu. considered vulgar
bull snake *n* **:** any of several large harmless No. American snakes (genus *Pituophis*) that feed chiefly on rodents — called also *gopher snake, pine snake*
bull·ter·ri·er \ˈbu̇l-ˈter-ē-ər\ *n* [*bull*dog + *terrier*] **:** a short-haired terrier of a breed originated in England by crossing the bulldog with terriers
bull tongue *n* **:** a wide blade attached to a cultivator or plow to stir the soil, kill weeds, or mark furrows
bull·whip \ˈbu̇l-ˌhwip, -ˌwip\ *n* **:** a rawhide whip with plaited lash 15 to 25 feet long
1bul·ly \ˈbu̇l-ē\ *n, pl* **bullies** [prob. modif. of D *boel* lover, fr. MHG *buole*] **1** *archaic* **a :** SWEETHEART **b :** a fine chap **2 a :** a blustering browbeating fellow; *esp* **:** one habitually cruel to others weaker than himself **b :** the protector of a prostitute **:** PIMP **3 :** a hired ruffian
2bully *adj* **1 :** EXCELLENT, FIRST-RATE — often used in interjectional expressions <~ for you> **2 :** resembling or characteristic of a bully
3bully *vb* **bul·lied; bul·ly·ing** *vt* **:** to treat abusively ~ *vi* **:** to use browbeating language or behavior **:** BLUSTER
4bully *n* [prob. modif. of F (*bœuf*) *bouilli* boiled beef] **:** pickled or canned usu. corned beef
bul·ly·boy \ˈbu̇l-ē-ˌbȯi\ *n* **:** a swaggering tough
bul·ly·rag \-ˌrag\ *vt* [origin unknown] **1 :** to intimidate by bullying **2 :** to vex by teasing **:** BADGER
bul·rush *also* **bull·rush** \ˈbu̇l-ˌrəsh\ *n* [ME *bulrysche*] **:** any of several large rushes or sedges growing in wetlands: as **a :** any of a genus of annual or perennial sedges (*Scirpus,* esp. *S. lacustris*) that bear solitary or much-clustered spikelets containing perfect flowers with a perianth of six bristles **b** *Brit* **:** either of two cattails (*Typha latifolia* and *T. angustifolia*) **c :** PAPYRUS
1bul·wark \ˈbu̇l-(ˌ)wərk, -ˌwȯrk; ˈbəl-(ˌ)wərk\ *n* [ME *bulwerke,* fr. MD *bolwerc,* fr. MHG, fr. *bole* plank + *werc* work] **1 a :** a solid wall-like structure raised for defense **:** RAMPART **b :** BREAKWATER, SEAWALL **2 :** a strong support or protection <education as a ~ of democracy> **3 :** the side of a ship above the upper deck — usu. used in pl.
2bulwark *vt* **:** to fortify or safeguard with a bulwark
1bum \ˈbəm\ *n* [ME *bom*] *chiefly Brit* **:** BUTTOCKS — sometimes considered vulgar
2bum *vb* **bummed; bumming** [prob. back-formation fr. 1*bummer*] *vi* **1 :** LOAF **2 :** to spend time unemployed and often wandering ~ *vt* **:** to obtain by begging **:** CADGE
3bum *n* [prob. short for *bummer*] **1 a :** one who sponges off others and avoids work **b :** one who performs a function poorly <called the umpire a ~> **c :** one who devotes his time to a recreational activity <a beach ~> <ski ~*s*> **2 :** VAGRANT, TRAMP
4bum *adj* **1 a :** INFERIOR, WORTHLESS <~ advice> **b :** acutely disagreeable <a ~ trip> **2 :** not functioning because of damage or injury **:** DISABLED <a ~ knee>
5bum *n* [prob. fr. 2*bum*] **:** a drinking spree **:** BENDER — **on the bum :** with no settled residence or means of support
bum·ber·shoot \ˈbəm-bər-ˌshüt\ *n* [*bumber-* (alter. of *umbr-* in *umbrella*) + *-shoot* (alter. of *-chute* in *parachute*)] **:** UMBRELLA

1bum·ble \ˈbəm-bəl\ *vi* **bum·bled; bum·bling** \-b(ə-)liŋ\ [ME *bomblen* to boom, of imit. origin] **1 :** BUZZ **2 :** DRONE, RUMBLE
2bumble *vb* **bumbled; bumbling** [prob. alter. of *bungle*] *vi* **1 :** BLUNDER; *specif* **:** to speak ineptly in a stuttering and faltering manner **2 :** to proceed unsteadily **:** STUMBLE ~ *vt* **:** BUNGLE — **bum·bler** \-b(ə-)lər\ *n* — **bum·bling·ly** \-b(ə-)liŋ-lē\ *adv*
bum·ble·bee \ˈbəm-bəl-ˌbē\ *n* **:** any of numerous large robust hairy social bees (genus *Bombus*)
bum·boat \ˈbəm-ˌbōt\ *n* [prob. fr. LG *bumboot,* fr. *bum* tree + *boot* boat] **:** a boat that brings provisions and commodities for sale to larger ships in port or offshore
bumf \ˈbəm(p)f\ *n* [Brit. slang *bumf* toilet paper, short for *bumfodder,* fr. 1*bum*] *Brit* **:** PAPERWORK
1bum·mer \ˈbəm-ər\ *n* [prob. modif. of G *bummler* loafer, fr. *bummel* to dangle, loaf] **:** one that bums
2bummer *n* [4*bum* + *-er*] *slang* **:** an unpleasant experience (as a bad reaction to a hallucinogenic drug)
1bump \ˈbəmp\ *vb* [imit.] *vt* **1 :** to strike or knock with force or violence **2 :** to collide with **3 a** (1) **:** to dislodge with a jolt (2) **:** to subject to a scalar change <rates being ~*ed* up> **b :** to oust usu. by virtue of seniority or priority <was ~*ed* from the flight> **4 :** to apply pressure to (as sheet metal) so as to make or remove a concavity or convexity ~ *vi* **1 :** to knock against something with a forceful jolt **2 :** to proceed in a series of bumps — **bump into :** to encounter esp. by chance
2bump *n* **1 a :** a sudden forceful blow, impact, or jolt **b :** DEMOTION **2 :** a relatively abrupt convexity or protuberance on a surface: as **a :** a swelling of tissue **b :** a cranial protuberance **3 :** an act of thrusting the hips forward in an erotic manner
1bum·per \ˈbəm-pər\ *n* [prob. fr. *bump* (to bulge)] **1 :** a brimming cup or glass **2 :** something unusually large
2bumper *adj* **:** unusually large <a ~ crop>
3bump·er \ˈbəm-pər\ *n* **1 :** one that bumps **2 :** a device for absorbing shock or preventing damage (as in collision); *specif* **:** a metal bar at either end of an automobile
bumper–to–bumper *adj* **:** marked by long closed lines of cars <~ traffic>
1bump·kin \ˈbəm(p)-kən\ *n* [perh. fr. Flem *bommekijn* small cask, fr. MD, fr. *bomme* cask] **:** an awkward and unsophisticated rustic — **bump·kin·ish** \-kə-nish\ *adj* — **bump·kin·ly** \-kən-lē\ *adj*
2bump·kin *or* **bum·kin** \ˈbəm(p)-kən\ *n* [prob. fr. Flem *boomken,* dim. of *boom* tree] **:** a spar projecting from the stern of a ship
bump off *vt* **:** to murder casually or cold-bloodedly
bump·tious \ˈbəm(p)-shəs\ *adj* [1*bump* + *-tious* (as in *fractious*)] **:** presumptuously, obtusely, and often noisily self-assertive **:** OBTRUSIVE — **bump·tious·ly** *adv* — **bump·tious·ness** *n*
bumpy \ˈbəm-pē\ *adj* **bump·i·er; -est** **1 a :** having or covered with bumps <a ~ road> **b :** marked by ups and downs **:** UNEVEN **2 a :** marked by bumps or jolts <a ~ ride> **b :** rhythmically jerky <~ dance music> — **bump·i·ly** \-pə-lē\ *adv* — **bump·i·ness** \-pē-nəs\ *n*
1bun \ˈbən\ *n* [ME *bunne*] **1 :** any of various sweet or plain small breads; *esp* **:** a round roll **2 :** a knot of hair shaped like a bun
2bun *n* [perh. alter. of E dial. *bung* (intoxicated)] **:** LOAD 4
Bu·na \ˈb(y)ü-nə\ *trademark* — used for any of several rubbers made by polymerization or copolymerization of butadiene
1bunch \ˈbənch\ *n* [ME *bunche*] **1 :** PROTUBERANCE, SWELLING **2 a :** a number of things of the same kind **:** CLUSTER <a ~ of grapes> **b :** a homogeneous group **syn** see GROUP — **bunch·i·ly** \ˈbən-chə-lē\ *adv* — **bunchy** \-chē\ *adj*
2bunch *vi* **1 :** SWELL, PROTRUDE **2 :** to form a group or cluster — often used with *up* ~ *vt* **:** to form into a bunch
bunch·ber·ry \ˈbənch-ˌber-ē\ *n* **:** a creeping perennial herb (*Cornus canadensis*) that has whorled leaves and white floral bracts and bears red berries in capitate cymes
bunch·flow·er \ˈbənch-ˌflau̇(-ə)r\ *n* **:** a tall summer-blooming herb (*Melanthium virginicum*) of the lily family that is found in the eastern and southern U.S. and bears a panicle of small greenish flowers
bun·co *or* **bun·ko** \ˈbəŋ-(ˌ)kō\ *n, pl* **buncos** *or* **bunkos** [perh. alter. of Sp *banca* bench, bank, fr. It — more at BANK] **:** a swindling game or scheme — **bunco** *vt*
1bund \ˈbənd\ *n* [Hindi *band,* fr. Per; akin to OE *binden* to bind] **1 :** an embankment used esp. in India to control the flow of water **2 :** an embanked thoroughfare along a river or the sea esp. in the Far East
2bund \ˈbu̇nd, ˈbənd\ *n, often cap* [G, fr. MHG *bunt;* akin to OE *byndel* bundle] **:** a political association; *specif* **:** a pro-Nazi German-American organization of the 1930s — **bund·ist** \-əst\ *n, often cap*
1bun·dle \ˈbən-dᵊl\ *n* [ME *bundel,* fr. MD; akin to OE *byndel* bundle, *bindan* to bind] **1 a :** a group of things fastened together for convenient handling **b :** PACKAGE, PARCEL **c :** a considerable number of things **:** LOT <a ~ of contradictions> **d :** a sizable sum of money **2 a :** a small band of mostly parallel fibers (as of nerve) **b :** VASCULAR BUNDLE
2bundle *vb* **bun·dled; bun·dling** \ˈbən-(d)liŋ, -dᵊl-iŋ\ *vt* **1 :** to make into a bundle or package **:** WRAP **2 :** to hustle or hurry unceremoniously <*bundled* the children off to school> ~ *vi* **1 :** HUSTLE, HURRY **2 :** to practice bundling — **bun·dler** \-dlər, -dᵊl-ər\ *n*
bundle of nerves : a very nervous person
bundle up *vi* **:** to dress warmly ~ *vt* **:** to dress (someone) warmly
bun·dling \ˈbən-(d)liŋ, -dᵊl-iŋ\ *n* **:** a former custom of an unmarried couple's occupying the same bed without undressing esp. during courtship
1bung \ˈbəŋ\ *n* [ME, fr. MD *bonne, bonghe,* fr. LL *puncta* puncture, fr. L, fem. of *punctus,* pp. of *pungere* to prick — more at PUNGENT] **1 :** the stopper in the bunghole of a cask; *also* **:** BUNGHOLE **2 :** the cecum or anus esp. of a slaughtered animal
2bung *vt* **:** to plug with or as if with a bung
bun·ga·low \ˈbəŋ-gə-ˌlō\ *n* [Hindi *baṅglā,* lit., (house) in the Bengal style] **:** a usu. one-storied house with a low-pitched roof
bung·hole \ˈbəŋ-ˌhōl\ *n* **:** a hole for emptying or filling a cask

bun·gle \'bəŋ-gəl\ *vb* **bun·gled; bun·gling** \-g(ə-)liŋ\ [perh. of Scand origin; akin to Icel *banga* to hammer] *vi* **:** to act or work clumsily and awkwardly ~ *vt* **:** MISHANDLE, BOTCH — **bun·gler** \-g(ə-)lər\ *n* — **bun·gling** *adj or n* — **bun·gling·ly** \-g(ə-)liŋ-lē\ *adv*

bun·gle·some \-gəl-səm\ *adj* **:** AWKWARD, CLUMSY

bung up *vt* **:** BATTER

bun·ion \'bən-yən\ *n* [prob. irreg. fr. *bunny* (swelling)] **:** an inflamed swelling of the small sac on the first joint of the big toe

1bunk \'bəŋk\ *n* [prob. short for *bunker*] **1 a :** a built-in bed (as on a ship) that is often one of a tier of berths **b :** a sleeping place **2 :** a feeding trough for cattle

2bunk *vi* **:** to occupy a bunk or bed **:** stay the night <~ *ed* with a friend for the night> ~ *vt* **:** to provide with a bunk or bed

3bunk *n* **:** BUNKUM, NONSENSE

bunk bed *n* **:** one of two single beds usu. placed one above the other

1bun·ker \'bəŋ-kər\ *n* [Sc *bonker* chest, box] **1 :** a bin or compartment for storage; *esp* **:** one on shipboard for the ship's fuel **2 a :** a protective embankment or dugout; *esp* **:** a fortified chamber mostly below ground often built of reinforced concrete and provided with embrasures **b :** a sand trap or embankment constituting a hazard on a golf course

2bunker *vb* **bun·kered; bun·ker·ing** \-k(ə-)riŋ\ *vi* **:** to fill a ship's bunker with coal or oil ~ *vt* **:** to place or store in a bunker

bunk·house \'bəŋk-ˌhau̇s\ *n* **:** a rough simple building providing sleeping quarters

bun·kum *or* **bun·combe** \'bəŋ-kəm\ *n* [*Buncombe* county, N.C.; fr. the defense of a seemingly irrelevant speech made by its congressional representative that he was speaking to Buncombe] **:** insincere or foolish talk **:** NONSENSE

bun·ny \'bən-ē\ *n, pl* **bunnies** [E dial. *bun* (rabbit)] **1 :** RABBIT **2 :** a young woman who frequents recreational areas (as beaches or ski resorts) usu. only for social reasons — **bunny** *adj*

Bun·ra·ku \bün-'räk-(ˌ)ü\ *n* [Jap] **:** Japanese puppet theater featuring large costumed wooden puppets, puppeteers who are onstage, and a chanter who speaks all the lines

Bun·sen burner \ˌbən(t)-sən-\ *n* [Robert W. *Bunsen*] **:** a gas burner consisting typically of a straight tube with small holes at the bottom where air enters and mixes with the gas to produce an intensely hot blue flame

1bunt \'bənt\ *n* [perh. fr. LG, bundle, fr. MLG; akin to OE *byndel* bundle] **1 a :** the middle part of a square sail **b :** the part of a furled sail gathered up in a bunch at the center of the yard **2 :** the bagging part of a fishing net

2bunt *n* [origin unknown] **:** a destructive covered smut of wheat caused by a fungus (*Tilletia foetida* or *T. caries*)

3bunt *vb* [alter. of *butt*] *vt* **1 :** to strike or push with or as if with the head **:** BUTT **2 :** to push or tap (a baseball) lightly without swinging the bat ~ *vi* **:** to bunt a baseball — **bunt·er** *n*

4bunt *n* **1 :** an act or instance of bunting **2 :** a bunted ball

1bun·ting \'bənt-iŋ\ *n* [ME] **:** any of various stout-billed birds (*Emberiza* and related genera) usu. included with the finches

2bunting *n* [perh. fr. E dial. *bunt* (to sift)] **1 :** a lightweight loosely woven fabric used chiefly for flags and festive decorations **2 a :** FLAGS **b :** decorations esp. in the colors of the national flag

bunt·line \'bənt-ˌlīn, -lən\ *n* **:** one of the ropes attached to the foot of a square sail to haul the sail up to the yard for furling

Bun·yan·esque \ˌbən-yə-'nesk\ *adj* **1** [John *Bunyan* †1688 E preacher & author] **:** of, relating to, or suggestive of the allegorical writings of John Bunyan **2** [Paul *Bunyan*, legendary giant lumberjack of U.S. & Canada] **:** of, relating to, or suggestive of the tales of Paul Bunyan; *esp* **:** of fantastically large size

1buoy \'bü-ē, 'bȯi\ *n* [ME *boye*, fr. (assumed) MF *boie*, of Gmc origin; akin to OE *bēacen* sign — more at BEACON] **1 :** FLOAT 2; *esp* **:** a floating object moored to the bottom to mark a channel or something (as a shoal) lying under the water **2 :** LIFE BUOY

2buoy *vt* **1 :** to mark by or as if by a buoy **2 a :** to keep afloat **b :** SUPPORT, SUSTAIN <an economy ~*ed* by the dramatic postwar growth of industry—*Time*> **3 :** to raise the spirits of — usu. used with *up* <hope ~*s* him up> ~ *vi* **:** FLOAT

buoy·ance \-ən(t)s, -yən(t)s\ *n* **:** BUOYANCY

buoy·an·cy \'bȯi-ən-sē, 'bü-yən-\ *n* **1 a :** the tendency of a body to float or to rise when submerged in a fluid **b :** the power of a fluid to exert an upward force on a body placed in it **2 :** the ability to recover quickly from depression or discouragement **:** RESILIENCE, VIVACITY

buoy·ant \'bȯi-ənt, 'bü-yənt\ *adj* **:** having buoyancy: as **a :** capable of floating **b :** CHEERFUL, GAY — **buoy·ant·ly** *adv*

buq·sha \'bük-shə\ *n* [Ar] — see *rial* at MONEY table

1bur *var of* BURR

2bur *abbr* bureau

Bur·ber·ry \'bər-bə-rē, 'bər-ˌber-ē\ *trademark* — used for various fabrics used esp. for coats for outdoor wear

1bur·ble \'bər-bəl\ *vi* **bur·bled; bur·bling** \-b(ə-)liŋ\ [ME *burblen*] **1 :** BUBBLE **2 :** BABBLE, PRATTLE — **bur·bler** \-b(ə-)lər\ *n*

2burble *n* **1 :** PRATTLE **2 :** the breaking up of the streamline flow of air about the body (as an airplane wing) — **bur·bly** \-b(ə-)lē\ *adj*

bur·bot \'bər-bət\ *n, pl* **burbot** *also* **burbots** [ME *borbot*, fr. MF *bourbotte*, fr. *bourbeter* to burrow in the mud] **:** a freshwater fish (*Lota lota*) of the cod family having barbels on the nose and chin and existing in the northern parts of the New and the Old World

1bur·den \'bərd-ᵊn\ *n* [ME, fr. OE *byrthen*; akin to OE *beran* to carry — more at BEAR] **1 a :** something that is carried **:** LOAD **b :** DUTY, RESPONSIBILITY **2 :** something oppressive or worrisome **:** ENCUMBRANCE **3 a :** the bearing of a load — usu. used in the phrase *beast of burden* **b :** capacity for carrying cargo <a ship of a hundred tons ~>

2burden *vt* **bur·dened; bur·den·ing** \'bərd-niŋ, -ᵊn-iŋ\ **:** LOAD, OPPRESS <the numerous petty things . . . which ~ the tables —Herbert Spencer> <I will not ~ you with a lengthy account>

3burden *n* [alter. of *bourdon*] **1** *archaic* **:** a bass or accompanying part **2 a :** CHORUS, REFRAIN **b :** a central topic **:** THEME

burden of proof : the duty of proving a disputed assertion or charge

bur·den·some \'bərd-ᵊn-səm\ *adj* **:** imposing or constituting a burden **:** OPPRESSIVE <~ restrictions> *syn* see ONEROUS — **bur·den·some·ly** *adv* — **bur·den·some·ness** *n*

bur·dock \'bər-ˌdäk\ *n* **:** any of a genus (*Arctium*) of coarse composite herbs bearing globular flower heads with prickly bracts

bu·reau \'byu̇(ə)r-(ˌ)ō\ *n, pl* **bureaus** *also* **bu·reaux** \-(ˌ)ōz\ [F, desk, cloth covering for desks, fr. OF *burel* woolen cloth, fr. (assumed) OF *bure*, fr. LL *burra* shaggy cloth] **1 a** *Brit* **:** WRITING DESK; *esp* **:** one having drawers and a slant top **b :** a low chest of drawers for use in a bedroom **2 a :** a specialized administrative unit; *esp* **:** a subdivision of an executive department of a government **b :** a business establishment for exchanging information, making contacts, or coordinating activities **c :** a branch of a newspaper, newsmagazine, or wire service in an important news center

bu·reau·cra·cy \byu̇-'räk-rə-sē\ *n, pl* **-cies** [F *bureaucratie*, fr. *bureau* + *-cratie* -cracy] **1 a :** a body of nonelective government officials **b :** an administrative policy-making group **2 :** government characterized by specialization of functions, adherence to fixed rules, and a hierarchy of authority **3 :** a system of administration marked by officialism, red tape, and proliferation

bu·reau·crat \'byu̇r-ə-ˌkrat\ *n* **:** a member of a bureaucracy; *esp* **:** a government official who follows a narrow rigid formal routine or who is established with great authority in his own department

bu·reau·crat·ic \ˌbyu̇r-ə-'krat-ik\ *adj* **:** of, relating to, or having the characteristics of a bureaucracy or a bureaucrat <~ government> — **bu·reau·crat·i·cal·ly** \-i-k(ə-)lē\ *adv*

bu·reau·cra·tize \byu̇-'räk-rə-ˌtīz\ *vt* **-tized; -tiz·ing :** to make bureaucratic **:** subject to bureaucracy — **bu·reau·cra·ti·za·tion** \-ˌräk-rət-ə-'zā-shən\ *n*

bu·rette *or* **bu·ret** \byu̇-'ret\ *n* [F *burette*, fr. MF, cruet, fr. *buire* pitcher, alter. of OF *buie*, of Gmc origin; akin to OE *būc* pitcher — more at BUCKET] **:** a graduated glass tube with a small aperture and stopcock for delivering measured quantities of liquid or for measuring the liquid or gas received or discharged

burg \'bərg\ *n* [OE — more at BOROUGH] **1 :** an ancient or medieval fortress or walled town **2 :** CITY, TOWN

bur·gage \'bər-gij\ *n* [ME, property held by burgage tenure, fr. MF *bourgage*, lit., burgage, fr. OF, fr. *bourg*, *borc* town — more at BOURG] **:** a tenure by which real property in England and Scotland was held under the king or a lord for a yearly rent or for watching and warding

bur·gee \ˌbər-'jē, 'bər-ˌ\ *n* [perh. fr. F dial. *bourgeais* shipowner] **:** a swallow-tailed flag used esp. by ships for signals or identification

bur·geon \'bər-jən\ *vi* [ME *burjonen*, fr. *burjon* bud, fr. OF, fr. (assumed) VL *burrion-*, *burrio*, fr. LL *burra* shaggy cloth] **1 a :** to send forth new growth (as buds or branches) **:** SPROUT **b :** BLOSSOM, BLOOM **2 :** to grow and expand rapidly **:** FLOURISH <one of Africa's great problems is to get well-educated people out of the ~*ing* cities . . . and into the backward rural areas —P. R. Gould>

-burg·er \-ˌbər-gər\ *n comb form* [*hamburger*] **:** a fried or grilled patty usu. served in a sandwich

bur·gess \'bər-jəs\ *n* [ME *burgeis*, fr. OF *borjois*, fr. *borc*] **1 a :** a citizen of a British borough **b :** a representative of a borough, corporate town, or university in the British Parliament **2 :** a representative in the popular branch of the legislature of colonial Maryland and Virginia

burgh \'bər-(ˌ)ō, 'bə-(ˌ)rō, -ə(-w), -rə(-w)\ *n* [ME — more at BOROUGH] **:** BOROUGH; *specif* **:** an incorporated town in Scotland having local jurisdiction of certain services

bur·gher \'bər-gər\ *n* **:** an inhabitant of a borough or a town

bur·glar \'bər-glər\ *n* [AF *burgler*, fr. ML *burglator*, prob. alter. of *burgator*, fr. *burgatus*, pp. of *burgare* to commit burglary, fr. L *burgus* fortified place — more at BOURG] **:** one who commits burglary **:** THIEF

bur·glar·i·ous \ˌbər-'glar-ē-əs, -'gler-\ *adj* **:** of, relating to, or resembling burglary — **bur·glar·i·ous·ly** *adv*

bur·glar·ize \'bər-glə-ˌrīz\ *vb* **ized; -iz·ing** *vt* **1 :** to break into and steal from **2 :** to commit burglary against ~ *vi* **:** to commit burglary

bur·glar·proof \ˌbər-glər-'prüf\ *adj* **:** protected against or designed to afford protection against burglary

bur·glary \'bər-glə-rē\ *n, pl* **-glar·ies :** the act of breaking into a building esp. with intent to steal; *specif* **:** the act of breaking into and entering the dwelling house of another at night with intent to commit a felony

bur·gle \'bər-gəl\ *vt* **bur·gled; bur·gling** \-g(ə-)liŋ\ [back-formation fr. *burglar*] **:** BURGLARIZE

bur·go·mas·ter \'bər-gə-ˌmas-tər\ *n* [part modif., part trans. of D *burgemeester*, fr. *burg* town + *meester* master] **:** the chief magistrate of a town in certain European countries **:** MAYOR

bur·go·net \'bər-gə-nət, ˌbər-gə-'net\ *n* [modif. of MF *bourguignotte*] **:** either of two 16th century helmets

bur·goo \'bər-ˌgü, (ˌ)bər-'\ *n, pl* **burgoos** [origin unknown] **1 :** oatmeal gruel **2 :** hardtack and molasses cooked together **3 a :** a stew or thick soup of meat and vegetables orig. served at outdoor gatherings (as a political rally or barbecue) **b :** a picnic at which burgoo is served

Bur·gun·dy \'bər-gən-dē\ *n, pl* **-dies** [*Burgundy*, region in France] **:** a red or white table wine from the vineyards of Côte d'Or, Yonne, and Saône-et-Loire, France; *also* **:** a similar wine made elsewhere

buri·al \ˈber-ē-əl\ *n, often attrib* [ME *beriel, berial,* back-formation fr. *beriels* (taken as a plural), fr. OE *byrgels;* akin to OS *burgisli* tomb, OE *byrgan* to bury — more at BURY] **1 :** GRAVE, TOMB **2 :** the act or process of burying

buri·er \ˈber-ē-ər\ *n* **:** one that buries

bu·rin \ˈbyu̇r-ən, ˈbər-\ *n* [F] **1 :** an engraver's steel cutting tool having the blade ground obliquely to a sharp point **2 :** a prehistoric flint tool with a beveled point

burke \ˈbərk\ *vt* **burked; burk·ing** [William *Burke* †1829 Ir criminal executed for this crime] **1 :** to suffocate or strangle in order to obtain a body to be sold for dissection **2 a :** to suppress quietly or indirectly <~ an inquiry> **b :** BYPASS, AVOID <~ an issue>

[1]**burl** \ˈbər(-ə)l\ *n* [ME *burle,* fr. (assumed) MF *bourle* tuft of wool, fr. (assumed) VL *burrula,* dim. of LL *burra* shaggy cloth] **1 :** a knot or lump in thread or cloth **2 a :** a hard woody often flattened hemispherical outgrowth on a tree **b :** veneer made from burls

[2]**burl** *vt* **:** to finish (cloth) esp. by repairing loose threads and knots — **burl·er** *n*

bur·la·de·ro \ˌbu̇r-lə-ˈde(ə)r-(ˌ)ō, ˌbər-\ *n, pl* **-ros** [Sp, fr. *burlar* to make fun of, elude, fr. *burla* joke] **:** a wooden shield set parallel to the wall in a bullring and behind which bullfighters can take shelter if pursued

bur·lap \ˈbər-ˌlap\ *n* [alter. of earlier *borelapp*] **1 :** a coarse heavy plain-woven fabric usu. of jute or hemp used for bagging and wrapping and in furniture and linoleum manufacture **2 :** a lightweight material resembling burlap used in interior decoration or for clothing

burled \ˈbər(-ə)ld\ *adj* **:** having a distorted grain due to burls

[1]**bur·lesque** \(ˌ)bər-ˈlesk\ *n* [*burlesque,* adj. (comic, droll), fr. F, fr. It *burlesco,* fr. *burla* joke, fr. Sp] **1 :** a literary or dramatic work that seeks to ridicule by means of grotesque exaggeration or comic imitation **2 :** mockery usu. by caricature **3 :** theatrical entertainment of a broadly humorous often earthy character consisting of short turns, comic skits, and sometimes striptease acts ***syn*** see CARICATURE — **burlesque** *adj* — **bur·lesque·ly** *adv*

[2]**burlesque** *vb* **bur·lesqued; bur·lesqu·ing** *vt* **:** to imitate in a humorous or derisive manner **:** MOCK ~ *vi* **:** to employ burlesque — **bur·lesqu·er** *n*

bur·ley \ˈbər-lē\ *n* [prob. fr. the name *Burley*] **:** a thin-bodied air-cured tobacco grown mainly in Kentucky

bur·ly \ˈbər-lē\ *adj* **bur·li·er; -est** [ME] **1 :** strongly and heavily built **:** HUSKY **2 :** heartily direct and frank **:** BLUFF, FORTHRIGHT <an evocative story less ~ than the real thing but entertaining—E. A. Weeks> — **bur·li·ly** \-lə-lē\ *adv* — **bur·li·ness** \-lē-nəs\ *n*

bur marigold *n* **:** any of a genus (*Bidens*) of coarse composite herbs with prickly flattened achenes that adhere to clothing

Bur·mese \ˌbər-ˈmēz, -ˈmēs\ *n, pl* **Burmese 1 :** a native or inhabitant of Burma **2 :** the Tibeto-Burman language of the Burmese people — **Burmese** *adj*

Burmese cat *n* **:** any of a breed of cats resembling the Siamese cat but of solid and darker color and with orange eyes

[1]**burn** \ˈbərn\ *n* [ME, fr. OE; akin to OHG *brunno* spring of water, L *fervēre* to boil] *Brit* **:** CREEK 2

[2]**burn** \ˈbərn\ *vb* **burned** \ˈbərnd, ˈbərnt\ *or* **burnt** \ˈbərnt\; **burn·ing** [ME *birnan,* fr. OE *byrnan,* v.i., *bærnan,* v.t.; akin to OHG *brinnan* to burn, L *fervēre* to boil] *vi* **1 a :** to consume fuel and give off heat, light, and gases <a small fire ~*s* on the hearth> **b :** to undergo combustion; *also* **:** to undergo nuclear fission or nuclear fusion **c :** to contain a fire <little stove ~*ing* in the corner> **d :** to give off light **:** SHINE, GLOW <a light ~*ing* in the window> **2 a :** to be hot <the ~*ing* sand> **b :** to produce or undergo discomfort or pain <iodine ~*s* so> <ears ~*ing* from the cold> **c :** to become emotionally excited or agitated: as (1) **:** to yearn ardently <~*ing* to tell the story> (2) **:** to be or become very angry or disgusted <that remark really made him ~ > **3 a :** to undergo alteration or destruction by the action of fire or heat <watched their house ~ down> <the potatoes ~*ed* to a crisp> **b :** to die in the electric chair **4 :** to force or make a way by or as if by burning <her words ~*ed* into his heart> **5 :** to receive sunburn <she ~*s* easily> ~ *vt* **1 a :** to cause to undergo combustion; *esp* **:** to destroy by fire <~*ed* the trash> **b :** to use as fuel <this furnace ~*s* gas> **2 a :** to transform by exposure to heat or fire <~ clay to bricks> **b :** to produce by burning <~*ed* a hole in his sleeve> **3 a :** to injure or damage by exposure to fire, heat, or radiation **:** SCORCH <~*ed* his hand> **b :** to execute by burning <heretics ~*ed* at the stake> ; *also* **:** ELECTROCUTE **4 a :** IRRITATE, ANNOY — usu. used with *up* <really ~*s* me up> **b :** to take advantage of **:** DECEIVE, CHEAT — often used in passive **5 :** to wear out **:** EXHAUST — **burn·able** \ˈbər-nə-bəl\ *adj* — **burn one's bridges** *also* **burn one's boats :** to cut off all means of retreat — **burn one's ears :** to rebuke strongly — **burn the candle at both ends :** to use one's resources or energies to excess — **burn the midnight oil :** to work or study far into the night

[3]**burn** *n* **1 :** the act, process, or result of burning: as **a :** injury or damage resulting from exposure to fire, heat, caustics, electricity, or certain radiations **b :** a burned area <a ~ on the table top> **c :** an abrasion (as of the skin) having the appearance of a burn <rope ~*s*> **d :** a burning sensation <the ~ of iodine on a cut> **2 :** the firing of a spacecraft rocket engine in flight **3 :** ANGER; *esp* **:** increasing fury — used chiefly in the phrase *slow burn*

burned–out \ˈbərn-ˈdau̇t, ˈbərnt-ˈau̇t\ *or* **burnt–out** \ˈbərnt-ˈau̇t\ *adj* **:** worn out by excessive or improper use <~ bearings>; *also* **:** EXHAUSTED <died a ~ man>

burn·er \ˈbər-nər\ *n* **:** one that burns; *esp* **:** the part of a fuel-burning device (as a stove or furnace) where the flame is produced

bur·net \(ˌ)bər-ˈnet, ˈbər-nət\ *n* [ME, fr. OF *burnete,* fr. *brun* brown — more at BRUNET] **:** any of a genus (*Sanguisorba*) of herbs of the rose family with odd-pinnate stipulate leaves and spikes of apetalous flowers

burn in *vt* **:** to increase the density of (portions of a photographic print) during enlarging by giving extra exposure — compare DODGE

burn·ing \ˈbər-niŋ\ *adj* **1 a :** being on fire **b :** ARDENT, INTENSE <~ enthusiasm> **2 a :** affecting with or as if with heat <a ~ fever> **b :** resembling that produced by a burn <a ~ sensation on the tongue> **3 :** of fundamental importance **:** URGENT <one of the ~ issues of our time> — **burn·ing·ly** \-niŋ-lē\ *adv*

burning bush *n* **:** any of several plants associated with fire (as by redness): as **a :** [2]WAHOO **b :** SUMMER CYPRESS

burning ghat *n* **:** a level space at the head of a ghat for cremation

[1]**bur·nish** \ˈbər-nish\ *vt* [ME *burnischen,* fr. MF *bruniss-,* stem of *brunir,* lit., to make brown, fr. *brun*] **1 :** to make shiny or lustrous esp. by rubbing **:** POLISH **2 :** to rub (a material) with a tool for compacting or smoothing or for turning an edge — **bur·nish·er** *n* — **bur·nish·ing** *adj or n*

[2]**burnish** *n* **:** LUSTER, GLOSS

bur·noose *or* **bur·nous** \(ˌ)bər-ˈnüs\ *n* [F *burnous,* fr. Ar *burnus*] **:** a one-piece hooded cloak worn by Arabs and Moors

burn·out \ˈbər-ˌnau̇t\ *n* **:** the cessation of operation of a jet or rocket engine; *also* **:** the point at which burnout occurs

burn·sides \ˈbərn-ˌsīdz\ *n pl* [Ambrose E. *Burnside*] **:** SIDE-WHISKERS; *esp* **:** full muttonchop whiskers

[1]**burp** \ˈbərp\ *n* [imit.] **:** BELCH

[2]**burp** *vi* **:** BELCH ~ *vt* **:** to help (a baby) expel gas from the stomach esp. by patting or rubbing the back

burp gun *n* **:** a small submachine gun

[1]**burr** \ˈbər\ *n* [ME *burre;* akin to OE *byrst* bristle — more at BRISTLE] **1** *usu* **bur a :** a rough or prickly envelope of a fruit **b :** a plant that bears burs **2 a :** something that sticks or clings <a ~ in the throat> **b :** HANGER-ON **3** [ME *burwhe* circle] **:** a small washer put on the end of a rivet before swaging it down **4 :** an irregular rounded mass; *esp* **:** a tree burl **5 :** a thin ridge or area of roughness produced in cutting or shaping metal **6 a :** a trilled uvular *r* as used by some speakers of English esp. in northern England and in Scotland **b :** a tongue-point trill that is the usual Scottish *r* **7 a :** a small rotary cutting tool **b** *usu* **bur :** a bit used on a dental drill **8 :** a rough humming sound **:** WHIR — **burred** \ˈbərd\ *adj*

[2]**burr** *vi* **1 :** to speak with a burr **2 :** to make a whirring sound ~ *vt* **1 :** to pronounce with a burr **2 a :** to form into a projecting edge **b :** to remove burrs from — **burr·er** *n*

[3]**burr** *n* [perh. fr. [1]*burr*] **:** BUHRSTONE

bur reed *n* **:** any of a genus (*Sparganium,* family Sparganiaceae) of plants with globose fruits resembling burs

bur·ro \ˈbər-(ˌ)ō, ˈbu̇r-, -ə(-w); ˈbə-(ˌ)rō, -rə(-w)\ *n, pl* **burros** [Sp, irreg. fr. *borrico,* fr. LL *burricus* small horse] **:** DONKEY; *esp* **:** a small one used as a pack animal

[1]**bur·row** \ˈbər-(ˌ)ō, ˈbə-(ˌ)rō, -ə(-w), -rə(-w)\ *n* [ME *borow*] **:** a hole or excavation in the ground made by an animal (as a rabbit) for shelter and habitation

[2]**burrow** *vt* **1** *archaic* **:** to hide in or as if in a burrow **2 a :** to construct by tunneling **b :** to penetrate by means of a burrow **3 :** to make a motion suggestive of burrowing with **:** NESTLE <she ~*s* her grubby hand into mine> ~ *vi* **1 :** to conceal oneself in or as if in a burrow **2 a :** to make a burrow **b :** to progress by or as if by digging **3 :** to make a motion suggestive of burrowing **:** SNUGGLE, NESTLE <~*ed* against his back for warmth> — **bur·row·er** *n*

burrstone *var of* BUHRSTONE

bur·ry \ˈbər-ē\ *adj* **bur·ri·er; -est 1 :** containing burs **2 :** PRICKLY **3** *of speech* **:** characterized by a burr

bur·sa \ˈbər-sə\ *n, pl* **bur·sas** \-səz\ *or* **bur·sae** \-ˌsē, -ˌsī\ [NL, fr. ML, bag, purse — more at PURSE] **:** a bodily pouch or sac; *esp* **:** a small serous sac between a tendon and a bone — **bur·sal** \-səl\ *adj*

bur·sar \ˈbər-sər, -ˌsär\ *n* [ML *bursarius,* fr. *bursa*] **:** an officer (as of a monastery or college) in charge of funds **:** TREASURER

bur·sa·ry \-s(ə-)rē\ *n, pl* **-ries** [ML *bursaria,* fr. *bursa*] **1 :** the treasury of a college or monastery **2 :** a monetary grant to a needy student **:** SCHOLARSHIP

burse \ˈbərs\ *n* [MF *bourse,* fr. ML *bursa*] **1** *obs* **:** EXCHANGE, BOURSE **2 a :** PURSE **b :** a square cloth case used to carry the corporal in a Communion service

bur·seed \ˈbər-ˌsēd\ *n* **:** STICKSEED

bur·si·tis \(ˌ)bər-ˈsīt-əs\ *n* [NL, fr. *bursa*] **:** inflammation of a bursa esp. of the shoulder or elbow

[1]**burst** \ˈbərst\ *vb* **burst** *or* **burst·ed; burst·ing** [ME *bersten,* fr. OE *berstan;* akin to OHG *brestan* to burst, MIr *brosc* noise] *vi* **1 :** to break open, apart, or into pieces usu. from impact or from pressure from within **2 a :** to give way from an excess of emotion <his heart will ~ with grief> **b :** to give vent suddenly to a repressed emotion <~ into tears > <~ out laughing> **3 a :** to emerge or spring suddenly <~ out of a house> **b :** LAUNCH, PLUNGE <~ into song> **4 :** to be filled to the breaking point ~ *vt* **1 :** to cause to burst **2 :** to force open (as a door) by strong or vigorous action **3 :** to produce by or as if by bursting — **burst·er** *n* — **burst at the seams :** to be larger, fuller, or more crowded than could reasonably have been anticipated

[2]**burst** *n* **1 a :** a sudden outbreak; *esp* **:** a vehement outburst (as of emotion) **b :** EXPLOSION, ERUPTION **c :** a sudden intense effort <a sudden ~ of speed > **d :** a volley of shots **2 :** an act of bursting **3 :** a result of bursting; *specif* **:** a visible puff accompanying the explosion of a shell

bur·then \ˈbər-t͟hən\ *var of* BURDEN

bur·ton \ˈbərt-ᵊn\ *n* [origin unknown] **:** any of several arrangements of hoisting tackle; *esp* **:** one with a single and a double block

bur·weed \ˈbər-ˌwēd\ *n* **:** any of various plants (as a cocklebur or burdock) having burry fruit

bury \ˈber-ē\ *vt* **bur·ied; bury·ing** [ME *burien,* fr. OE *byrgan;* akin to OHG *bergan* to shelter, Russ *berech'* to save] **1 :** to dispose of by depositing in or as if in the earth; *esp* **:** to inter with funeral ceremonies **2 a :** to conceal by or as if by covering with earth <~ a treasure> <the report was *buried* under miscellaneous papers> **b :** to cover from view <*buried* her face in her hands> **3 a :** to put completely out of mind **:** have done with <~*ing* their differences> **b :** to conceal in obscurity <*buried* the retraction

among the classified ads> **c :** SUBMERGE, ENGROSS — usu. used with *in* <*buried* himself in his books> **4 :** to put (a playing card) out of play by placing it in or under the dealer's pack ***syn*** see HIDE — **bury the hatchet :** to settle a disagreement : become reconciled

[1]bus \ˈbəs\ *n, pl* **bus·es** *or* **bus·ses** *often attrib* [short for *omnibus*] **1 a :** a large motor-driven passenger vehicle operating usu. according to a schedule along a fixed route **b :** AUTOMOBILE <not a bad old ~ —A. J. Cronin> **2 :** a small hand truck **3 :** a conductor or an assembly of conductors for collecting electric currents and distributing them to outgoing feeders — called also *bus bar*

[2]bus *vb* **bused** *or* **bussed; bus·ing** *or* **bus·sing** *vi* **1 :** to travel by bus **2 :** to work as a busboy ~ *vt* **:** to transport by bus

[3]bus *abbr* business

bus·boy \ˈbəs-ˌbȯi\ *n* [*omnibus* (busboy)] **:** a waiter's assistant; *specif* **:** one who removes dirty dishes and resets tables in a restaurant

bus·by \ˈbəz-bē\ *n, pl* **busbies** [prob. fr. the name *Busby*] **1 :** a military full-dress fur hat with a pendent bag on one side usu. of the color of regimental facings **2 :** the bearskin worn by British guardsmen

busby 2

[1]bush \ˈbu̇sh\ *n, often attrib* [ME; akin to OHG *busc* forest] **1 a :** SHRUB; *esp* **:** a low densely branched shrub **b :** a close thicket of shrubs suggesting a single plant **2 :** a large uncleared or sparsely settled area (as in Australia) usu. scrub-covered or forested **:** WILDERNESS **3 a** (1) *archaic* **:** a bunch of ivy formerly hung outside a tavern to indicate wine for sale (2) *obs* **:** TAVERN **b :** ADVERTISING <good wine needs no ~ —Shak.> **4 :** a bushy tuft or mass <a ~ of hair —Roger Senhouse> ; *esp* **:** [2]BRUSH 2a

[2]bush *vt* **:** to support, mark, or protect with bushes ~ *vi* **:** to extend like a bush **:** resemble a bush

[3]bush *n* [D *bus* bushing, box, fr. MD *busse* box, fr. LL *buxis* — more at BOX] **1 :** BUSHING **2 :** a threaded socket

[4]bush *vt* **:** to furnish with a bushing

bush baby *n* **:** GALAGO

bush basil *n* **:** a small cultivated annual herb (*Ocimum minimum*) with nearly entire leaves

bush bean *n* **:** any of a variety of the kidney bean with a low-growing compact bushy habit

bush·buck \ˈbu̇sh-ˌbək\ *n, pl* **bushbuck** *or* **bushbucks** [trans. of Afrik *bosbok*] **:** a small southern African striped antelope (*Strepsiceros scriptus* or *Tragelaphus scriptus*) having spirally twisted horns and frequenting forests; *also* **:** any of several related antelopes

bush clover *n* **:** any of several usu. shrubby lespedezas

bushed \ˈbu̇sht\ *adj* **1 :** covered with or as if with a bushy growth **2** *chiefly Austral* **a :** lost esp. in the bush **b :** perplexed or confused esp. by a complexity or variety of considerations <adapting his language to my ~ comprehension —Henry Lawson> **3 :** TIRED, EXHAUSTED

[1]bush·el \ˈbu̇sh-əl\ *n* [ME *busshel*, fr. OF *boissel*, fr. (assumed) OF *boisse* one sixth of a bushel, of Celt origin; akin to MIr *boss* palm of the hand] **1 :** any of various units of dry capacity — see WEIGHT table **2 :** a container holding a bushel **3 :** a large quantity **:** LOTS <always sends them a ~ of love> — **bush·el·age** \-ə-lij\ *n*

[2]bushel *vb* **bush·eled; bush·el·ing** \-(ə-)liŋ\ [prob. fr. G *bosseln* to do poor work, to patch; akin to OE *bēatan* to beat] **:** REPAIR, RENOVATE — **bush·el·man** \-əl-mən\ *n*

bush·fire \ˈbu̇sh-ˌfī(ə)r\ *n, Austral* **:** an uncontrolled fire in a wooded area

Bu·shi·do \ˈbü-shi-ˌdō, ˈbüsh-\ *n* [Jap *bushidō*] **:** a feudal-military Japanese code of chivalry valuing honor above life

bush·ing \ˈbu̇sh-iŋ\ *n* **1 :** a usu. removable cylindrical lining for an opening (as of a mechanical part) used to limit the size of the opening, resist abrasion, or serve as a guide **2 :** an electrically insulating lining for a hole to protect a through conductor

bush jacket *n* [fr. its use in rough country] **:** a long cotton jacket resembling a shirt and having four patch pockets, a belt, and a notched collar

bush–league *adj* **:** belonging to an inferior class or group of its kind **:** MEDIOCRE

bush league *n* **:** MINOR LEAGUE — **bush leaguer** *n*

bush lima *n* **:** a lima bean that resembles a bush bean in growth rather than a vine

bush·man \ˈbu̇sh-mən\ *n* **1** [modif. of obs. Afrik *boschjesman*, fr. *boschje* (dim. of *bosch* forest) + Afrik *man*] *cap* **:** a member of a race of nomadic hunters of southern Africa **2 :** a Khoisan language of the Bushmen **3 a :** WOODSMAN **b** *chiefly Austral* **:** one that lives in the bush; *specif* **:** HICK

bush·mas·ter \-ˌmas-tər\ *n* **:** a tropical American pit viper (*Lachesis mutus*) that is the largest New World venomous snake

bush·rang·er \-ˌrān-jər\ *n* **1 :** FRONTIERSMAN, WOODSMAN **2** *Austral* **:** an outlaw living in the bush — **bush·rang·ing** \-jiŋ\ *n*

bush shirt *n* [fr. its use in rough country] **:** a usu. loose fitting cotton shirt with patch pockets

bush·tit \-ˌtit\ *n* **:** any of several titmice (genus *Psaltriparus*) of western No. America

bush·whack \ˈbu̇sh-ˌhwak, -ˌwak\ *vb* [back-formation fr. *bushwhacker*] *vi* **1 a :** to clear a path through thick woods esp. by chopping down bushes and low branches **b :** to propel a boat by pulling on bushes along the bank **2 a :** to live or hide out in the woods **b :** to fight in or attack from the bush ~ *vt* **:** AMBUSH — **bush·whack·er** *n* — **bush·whack·ing** *n*

bushy \ˈbu̇sh-ē\ *adj* **bush·i·er; -est** **1 :** full of or overgrown with bushes **2 :** resembling a bush; *esp* **:** being thick and spreading — **bush·i·ly** \ˈbu̇sh-ə-lē\ *adv* — **bush·i·ness** \ˈbu̇sh-ē-nəs\ *n*

busi·ness \ˈbiz-nəs, -nəz\ *n, often attrib* **1** *archaic* **:** purposeful activity **:** BUSYNESS **2 a :** ROLE, FUNCTION <how the human mind went about its ~ of learning —H. A. Overstreet> **b :** an immediate task or objective **:** MISSION <what is your ~ here at this hour> **c :** a particular field of endeavor <the best in the ~> **3 a :** a usu. commercial or mercantile activity engaged in as a means of livelihood **:** TRADE, LINE <in the ~ of supplying emergency services to industry> **b :** a commercial or sometimes an industrial enterprise <sold his ~ and retired>; *also* **:** such enterprises <~ seldom acts as a unit> **c :** usu. economic dealings **:** PATRONAGE <ready to take his ~ elsewhere unless service improved> **4 :** AFFAIR, MATTER <a strange ~> **5 :** movement or action (as lighting a cigarette) by an actor intended esp. to establish atmosphere, reveal character or explain a situation — called also *stage business* **6 a :** personal concern <none of your ~> **b :** RIGHT <you have no ~ hitting her> **7 a :** serious activity requiring time and effort and usu. the avoidance of distractions <immediately got down to ~> **b :** maximum effort **8 a :** a damaging assault **b :** a rebuke or tongue-lashing **:** a hard time **c :** DOUBLE CROSS

syn BUSINESS, COMMERCE, INDUSTRY, TRADE, TRAFFIC ***shared meaning element*** **:** activity concerned with the supplying and distribution of commodities

business administration *n* **:** a program of studies in a college or university providing general knowledge of business principles and practices

business card *n* **:** a small card that bears information (as name and address) about a business or a business representative — compare VISITING CARD

business cycle *n* **:** a recurring succession of fluctuations in economic activity

busi·ness·like \ˈbiz-nə-ˌslīk, -nəz-ˌlīk\ *adj* **1 :** exhibiting qualities believed to be advantageous in business **2 :** SERIOUS, PURPOSEFUL

busi·ness·man \ˈbiz-nə-ˌsman\ *n* a man who transacts business; *esp* **:** a business executive

business reply mail *n* **:** printed postal matter (as a postcard) for use in replying, ordering, or subscribing and bearing a statement that postage for its use will be paid by the addressee

business size envelope *n* **:** an envelope measuring usu. 9½ by 4⅛ inches in size — called also *business envelope*

busi·ness·wom·an \ˈbiz-nə-ˌswu̇m-ən\ *n* **:** a woman active in business; *esp* **:** a female business executive

bus·ing *or* **bus·sing** \ˈbəs-iŋ\ *n* **:** the act of transporting by bus; *specif* **:** the transporting of children to a school outside their residential area as a means of establishing racial balance in that school <he opposes most ~ as a tool of desegregation —*Boston Sunday Herald Traveler*>

busk \ˈbəsk\ *vb* [ME *busken*, fr. ON *būask* to prepare oneself, refl. of *būa* to prepare, dwell] *chiefly Scot* **:** PREPARE

busk·er \ˈbəs-kər\ *n* [origin unknown] *chiefly Brit* **:** one who entertains esp. by singing or reciting on the street or in a pub

bus·kin \ˈbəs-kən\ *n* [perh. modif. of Sp *borcegui*] **1 :** a laced boot reaching halfway or more to the knee **2 a :** COTHURNUS **b :** TRAGEDY; *esp* **:** tragedy resembling that of ancient Greek drama

bus·man's holiday \ˌbəs-mənz-\ *n* **:** a holiday spent in following or observing the practice of one's usual occupation

buss \ˈbəs\ *n* [prob. imit.] **:** KISS — **buss** *vt*

[1]bust \ˈbəst\ *n* [F *buste*, fr. It *busto*, fr. L *bustum* tomb] **1 :** a sculptured representation of the upper part of the human figure including the head and neck and usu. part of the shoulders and breast **2 :** the upper part of the human torso between neck and waist; *esp* **:** the breasts of a woman

[2]bust *vb* **bust·ed** *also* **bust; bust·ing** *vt* [alter. of *burst*] **1 :** HIT, SLUG **2 a :** to break or smash esp. with force; *also* **:** to make inoperative <~*ed* my watch this morning> **b :** to bring an end to **:** break up <helped ~ trusts —*Newsweek*> <reached second on a ~*ed* hit-and-run play —*Sporting News*> — often used with *up* <better not try to ~ up his happy marriage —*Forbes*> **c :** to ruin financially **3 :** DEMOTE **4 :** TAME <bronco ~*ing*> **5** *slang* **a :** ARREST <~*ed* for carrying guns — Saul Gottlieb> **b :** RAID <~*ed* the flat below . . . and found a sizable quantity of pot — Robert Courtney> ~ *vi* **1 a :** BURST <laughing fit to ~> **b :** to break down **2 :** to go broke **3 a :** to fail to complete a straight or flush in poker **b :** to lose at cards by exceeding a limit (as the count of 21 in blackjack)

[3]bust *n* **1 :** PUNCH, SOCK **2 a :** a complete failure **:** FLOP **b :** a business depression **3 a :** a hearty drinking session <a beer ~> **b :** SPREE **4** *slang* **:** a police raid <everyone knew of the . . . takeover of University Hall and the administration's decision to call the police, and the ~ in the stillness of the early hours — T.J. Cottle>

bus·tard \ˈbəs-tərd\ *n* [ME, modif. of MF *bistarde*, fr. OIt *bistarda*, fr. L *avis tarda*, lit., slow bird] **:** any of a family (Otididae) of Old World and Australian game birds

bust·er \ˈbəs-tər\ *n* **1 a :** an unusually sturdy child **b** *often cap* **:** FELLOW — usu. used as a noun of address <hey ~, come here> **2 :** one that breaks or breaks up <crime ~*s*> : as **a :** PLOW **b** [short for *broncobuster*] **:** one who breaks horses **3** *Austral* **:** a sudden violent wind often coming from the south **4 :** something having unusual destructive force: as **a :** a jarring fall **b :** BLOCKBUSTER

[1]bus·tle \ˈbəs-əl\ *vi* **bus·tled; bus·tling** \ˈbəs-(ə-)liŋ\ [prob. alter. of obs. *buskle* to prepare, freq. of *busk*] **1 :** to move briskly and often ostentatiously **2 :** to be busily astir **:** TEEM — **bustling** *adj* — **bus·tling·ly** \-(ə-)liŋ-lē\ *adv*

[2]bustle *n* **:** noisy, energetic, and often obtrusive activity <the hustle and ~ of the big city> ***syn*** see STIR

[3]bustle *n* [origin unknown] **:** a pad or framework expanding and supporting the fullness and drapery of the back of a woman's skirt

---

ə abut ᵊ kitten ər further a back ā bake ä cot, cart
au̇ out ch chin e less ē easy g gift i trip ī life
j joke ŋ sing ō flow ȯ flaw ȯi coin th thin t͟h this
ü loot u̇ foot y yet yü few yu̇ furious zh vision

busty \ˈbəs-tē\ *adj* **bust·i·er, -est :** having a large bust

bu·sul·fan \byü-ˈsəl-fən\ *n* [*butane* + *sulf*onyl] **:** an antineoplastic agent $C_6H_{14}O_6S_2$ used in the treatment of chronic myelogenous leukemia

1busy \ˈbiz-ē\ *adj* **busi·er; -est** [ME *bisy,* fr. OE *bisig;* akin to MD & MLG *besich* busy] **1 a :** engaged in action **:** OCCUPIED **b :** being in use <found the telephone ~> **2 :** full of activity **:** BUSTLING <a ~ seaport> **3 :** foolishly or intrusively active **:** MEDDLING **4 :** full of distracting detail <a ~ design> — **busi·ly** \ˈbiz-ə-lē\ *adv* — **busy·ness** \ˈbiz-ē-nəs\ *n*

syn BUSY, INDUSTRIOUS, DILIGENT, ASSIDUOUS, SEDULOUS *shared meaning element* **:** actively engaged or occupied (as in work or in accomplishing an end). BUSY stresses activity as opposed to idleness or leisure <had plenty of work to keep him *busy*> but does not in itself convey anything about the utility or effectiveness of the activity <always too *busy* to get a job finished> INDUSTRIOUS implies habitual or characteristic attentiveness and persistent earnest application (as to work or a business) <an *industrious* boy, always ready to help his father> DILIGENT suggests earnest application to a particular occupation <a *diligent* student> ASSIDUOUS stresses careful and unremitting application <*assiduous* in his attentions to his bride> SEDULOUS implies painstaking and persevering application <taking *sedulous* care of her husband's needs> ***ant*** idle, unoccupied

2busy *vb* **bus·ied; busy·ing** *vt* **:** to make busy **:** OCCUPY ~ *vi* **:** BUSTLE <small boats *busied* to and fro —Quentin Crewe>

busy·body \ˈbiz-ē-ˌbäd-ē\ *n* **:** an officious or inquisitive person

busy·work \-ˌwərk\ *n* **:** work that usu. appears productive or of intrinsic value but actually only keeps one occupied

1but \(ˈ)bət\ *conj* [ME, fr. OE *būtan,* prep. & conj., outside, without, except, except that; akin to OHG *būzan* without, except; both fr. a prehistoric WGmc compound whose constituents are represented by OE *be* by and OE *ūtan* outside; akin to OE ūt out — more at BY, OUT] **1 a :** except for the fact <would have protested ~ that he was afraid> **b :** THAT — used after a negative <there is no doubt ~ he won> **c :** without the concomitant that <it never rains ~ it pours> **d :** if not **:** UNLESS **e** *substand* **:** THAN <no sooner started ~ it stopped> **2 a :** on the contrary **:** on the other hand **:** NOTWITHSTANDING — used to connect coordinate elements <he was called ~ he did not answer> <not peace ~ a sword> **b :** YET <poor ~ proud> **c :** with the exception of — used before a word often taken to be the subject of a clause <none ~ the brave deserve the fair —John Dryden> — **but what :** that ... not <I don't know *but what* I will go>

2but *prep* **1** *Scot* **a :** WITHOUT, LACKING **b :** OUTSIDE **2 a :** with the exception of **:** BARRING <no one there ~ me> — compare 1BUT 2c **b :** other than <this letter is nothing ~ an insult>

3but *adv* **1 :** ONLY, MERELY <he is ~ a child> **2** *Scot* **:** OUTSIDE **3 :** to the contrary <who knows ~ that he may succeed> **4 :** DEFINTELY, POSITIVELY <get there ~ fast>

4but *pron* **:** that not **:** who not <nobody ~ has his fault —Shak.>

5but \ˈbət\ *n* [Sc *but,* adj. (outer)] *Scot* **:** the kitchen or living quarters of a 2-room cottage

bu·ta·di·ene \ˌbyüt-ə-ˈdī-ˌēn, -ˌdī-ˈ\ *n* [ISV *butane* + *di-* + *-ene*] **:** a flammable gaseous hydrocarbon C_4H_6 used in making synthetic rubbers

bu·tane \ˈbyü-ˌtān\ *n* [ISV *buty*ric + *-ane*] **:** either of two isomeric flammable gaseous paraffin hydrocarbons C_4H_{10} obtained usu. from petroleum or natural gas and used as a fuel

bu·ta·nol \ˈbyüt-ᵊn-ˌȯl, -ˌōl\ *n* **:** either of two butyl alcohols $C_4H_{10}O$ derived from normal butane

1butch·er \ˈbu̇ch-ər\ *n* [ME *bocher,* fr. OF *bouchier,* fr. *bouc* he-goat, prob. of Celt origin; akin to MIr *bocc* he-goat — more at BUCK] **1 a :** one who slaughters animals or dresses their flesh **b :** a dealer in meat **2 :** one that kills ruthlessly or brutally **3 :** BOTCHER **4 :** a vendor esp. on trains or in theaters

2butcher *vt* **butch·ered; butch·er·ing** \-(ə-)riŋ\ **1 :** to slaughter and dress for market <~ hogs> **2 :** to kill in a barbarous manner **3 :** BOTCH <~*ed* the play beyond recognition> — **butch·er·er** \-ər-ər\ *n*

butch·er–bird \ˈbu̇ch-ər-ˌbərd\ *n* **:** any of various shrikes

butcher knife *n* **:** a heavy-duty knife usu. six to eight inches long having a broad blade that curves slightly at the tip

butch·er·ly \ˈbu̇ch-ər-lē\ *adj* **:** resembling a butcher **:** SAVAGE

butch·er's–broom \ˈbu̇ch-ərz-ˌbrüm, -ˌbru̇m\ *n* **:** a European leafless plant (*Ruscus aculeatus*) of the lily family with stiff-pointed leaflike twigs used for brooms

butch·ery \ˈbu̇ch-(ə-)rē\ *n, pl* **-er·ies 1** *chiefly Brit* **:** SLAUGHTERHOUSE **2 :** the preparation of meat for sale **3 :** cruel and ruthless slaughter of human beings **4 :** BOTCH ***syn*** see MASSACRE

bu·tene \ˈbyü-ˌtēn\ *n* [ISV *buty*l + *-ene*] **:** a normal butylene

bu·teo \ˈbyüt-ē-ˌō\ *n, pl* **-te·os** [NL, genus name, fr. L, a hawk] **:** any of a genus (*Buteo*) of hawks with broad rounded wings and soaring flight; *broadly* **:** a hawk of similar appearance or habit of flight — **bu·te·o·nine** \byü-ˈtē-ə-ˌnīn, ˈbyüt-ē-\ *adj or n*

but·ler \ˈbət-lər\ *n* [ME *buteler,* fr. OE *bouteillier* bottle bearer, fr. *bouteille* bottle — more at BOTTLE] **1 :** a manservant having charge of the wines and liquors **2 :** the chief male servant of a household who has charge of other employees, receives guests, directs the serving of meals, and performs various personal services

butler's pantry *n* **:** a service room between kitchen and dining room

1butt \ˈbət\ *vb* [ME *butten,* fr. OF *boter,* of Gmc origin; akin to OHG *bozan* to beat — more at BEAT] *vi* **:** to thrust or push head foremost **:** strike with the head or horns ~ *vt* **:** to strike or shove with the head or horns

2butt *n* **:** a blow or thrust usu. with the head or horns

3butt *n* [ME, partly fr. MF *but* target, end, of Gmc origin; akin to ON *būtr* log, LG *butt* blunt; partly fr. MF *bute* backstop, fr. *but* target] **1 a :** a backstop (as a mound or bank) for catching missiles shot at a target **b :** TARGET **c** *pl* **:** RANGE 5b **d :** a blind for shooting birds **2 a** *obs* **:** LIMIT, BOUND **b** *archaic* **:** GOAL <here is my journey's end, here is my ~ —Shak.> **3 :** an object of abuse or ridicule **:** VICTIM <he was the ~ of all their jokes>

4butt *vb* [partly fr. 3*butt,* partly fr. 5*butt*] *vi* **:** ABUT — used with *on* or *against* ~ *vt* **1 a :** to place (as two boards) end to end without overlapping **b :** to join (as strips of wallpaper) along the edges **2 :** to trim or square off (as a log) at the end **3 :** to reduce (as a cigarette) to a butt by stubbing or stamping

5butt *n* [ME; prob. akin to ME *buttok* buttock, LG *butt* blunt, OHG *bōzan* to beat] **1 :** BUTTOCKS **2 a :** the large or thicker end of something **b :** the base of a plant from which the roots spring **c :** the thicker or handle end of a tool or weapon **3 :** an unused remainder **4 :** the part of a hide or skin corresponding to the animal's back and sides

6butt *n* [ME, fr. MF *botte,* fr. OProv *bota,* fr. LL *buttis*] **1 :** a large cask esp. for wine, beer, or water **2 :** any of various units of liquid capacity; *esp* **:** a measure equal to 108 imperial gallons

butte \ˈbyüt\ *n* [F, knoll, fr. MF *bute* mound of earth serving as a backstop] **:** an isolated hill or small mountain with steep or precipitous sides usu. having a smaller summit area than a mesa

1but·ter \ˈbət-ər\ *n* [ME, fr. OE *butere;* akin to OHG *butera* butter; both fr. a prehistoric WGmc word borrowed fr. L *butyrum* butter, fr. Gk *boutyron,* fr. *bous* cow + *tyros* cheese; akin to Av *tūiri-* whey — more at COW] **1 :** a solid emulsion of fat globules, air, and water made by churning milk or cream and used as food **2 :** a buttery substance: as **a :** any of various fatty oils remaining nearly solid at ordinary temperatures **b :** a food spread made from fruit, nuts, or other food <apple ~> **3 :** FLATTERY — **but·ter·less** \-ləs\ *adj*

2butter *vt* **:** to spread with or as if with butter

but·ter–and–eggs \ˌbət-ə-rə-ˈnegz, -ˈnāgz\ *n pl but sing or pl in constr* **:** a common European perennial herb (*Linaria vulgaris*) of the snapdragon family that has showy yellow and orange flowers and is a naturalized weed in much of No. America — called also *toadflax*

but·ter·ball \ˈbət-ər-ˌbȯl\ *n* **1 :** a chubby person **2 :** BUFFLEHEAD

butter bean *n* **1 :** WAX BEAN **2 :** LIMA BEAN: as **a** *chiefly South & Midland* **:** a large dried lima bean **b :** SIEVA BEAN **3 :** a green shell bean esp. as opposed to a snap bean

butter clam *n* **:** either of two large delicately flavored clams (*Saxidomus nuttallii* and *S. giganteus*) of the Pacific coast of No. America

but·ter·cup \ˈbət-ər-ˌkəp\ *n* **:** any of numerous plants (genus *Ranunculus* of the family Ranunculaceae, the buttercup family) with yellow flowers and pedately lobed leaves

but·ter·fat \-ˌfat\ *n* **:** the natural fat of milk and chief constituent of butter consisting essentially of a mixture of glycerides (as butyrin, olein, and palmitin)

but·ter·fin·gered \-ˌfiŋ-gərd\ *adj* **:** apt to let things fall or slip through the fingers **:** CARELESS — **but·ter·fin·gers** \-gərz\ *n pl but sing or pl in constr*

but·ter·fish \-ˌfish\ *n* **:** any of numerous mostly percoid fishes with a slippery coating of mucus

1but·ter·fly \-ˌflī\ *n, often attrib* **1 :** any of numerous slender-bodied diurnal insects (order Lepidoptera) with large broad often brightly colored wings **2 :** something that resembles or suggests a butterfly; *esp* **:** a person chiefly occupied with the pursuit of pleasure **3 :** a swimming stroke executed in a prone position by moving both arms in a circular motion while kicking the legs up and down simultaneously **4** *pl* **:** a feeling of hollowness or queasiness caused esp. by emotional or nervous tension or anxious anticipation

2butterfly *vt* **-flied; -fly·ing :** to split almost entirely and spread apart <a *butterflied* steak> <*butterflied* shrimp>

butterfly bush *n* **:** BUDDLEIA

butterfly chair *n* **:** a chair for lounging consisting of a cloth sling supported by a frame of metal tubing or bars

but·ter·fly·er \ˈbət-ər-ˌflī(-ə)r\ *n* **:** a swimmer who specializes in the butterfly

butterfly fish *n* **:** a fish having variegated colors, broad expanded fins, or both: as **a :** a European blenny (*Blennius ocellaris*) **b :** FLYING GURNARD **c :** any of a family (Chaetodontidae) of small brilliantly colored spiny-finned fishes of tropical seas with a narrow deep body and fins partly covered with scales

butterfly valve *n* **1 :** a double clack valve **2 :** a damper or valve in a pipe consisting of a disk turning on a diametral axis

butterfly weed *n* **:** an orange-flowered showy milkweed (*Asclepias tuberosa*) of eastern No. America

but·ter·milk \ˈbət-ər-ˌmilk\ *n* **1 :** the liquid left after butter has been churned from milk or cream **2 :** cultured milk made by the addition of suitable bacteria to sweet milk

but·ter·nut \-ˌnət\ *n* **1 a :** the edible oily nut of an American tree (*Juglans cinerea*) of the walnut family **b :** a tree that bears butternuts **2 a :** a light yellowish brown **b** *pl* **:** homespun overalls dyed brown with a butternut extract **c :** a soldier or partisan of the Confederacy during the Civil War

but·ter·scotch \-ˌskäch\ *n* **1 :** a candy made from brown sugar, corn syrup, and water; *also* **:** the flavor of such candy **2 :** a moderate yellowish brown

butter up *vt* **:** to charm or beguile with lavish flattery or praise **:** CAJOLE

but·ter·weed \ˈbət-ər-ˌwēd\ *n* **:** any of several plants having yellow flowers or smooth soft foliage: as **a :** HORSEWEED 1 **b :** an American ragwort (*Senecio glabellus*)

but·ter·wort \-ˌwərt, -ˌwȯ(ə)rt\ *n* **:** any of a genus (*Pinguicula*) of herbs of the bladderwort family with fleshy greasy leaves that produce a viscid secretion serving to capture and digest insects

1but·tery \ˈbət-ə-rē, ˈbə-trē\ *n, pl* **-ter·ies** [ME *boterie,* fr. MF, fr. *botte* cask, butt — more at BUTT] **1 :** a storeroom for liquors **2 a** *chiefly dial* **:** PANTRY **b :** a room (as in an English college) stocking provisions for sale to students

2but·tery \ˈbət-ə-rē\ *adj* **1 a :** having the qualities, consistency, or appearance of butter **b :** containing or spread with butter **2 :** marked by flattery

butt hinge *n* **:** a hinge usu. mortised flush into the edge of a door

butt in *vi* **:** to meddle in the affairs of others **:** INTERFERE, INTRUDE

butt·in·sky *also* **butt·in·ski** \ˌbət-ˈin-skē\ *n, pl* **-skies** [*butt in* + *-sky, -ski* (last element in many Slavic names)] **:** one given to butting in **:** a troublesome meddler

[1]c \'sē\ *n, pl* **c's** *or* **cs** \'sēz\ **1 a :** the 3d letter of the English alphabet **b :** a graphic representation of this letter **c :** a speech counterpart of orthographic *c* **2 a :** one hundred — see NUMBER table **b** *slang* **:** a sum of $100 **3 :** the keynote of a C-major scale **4 :** a graphic device for reproducing the letter *c* **5 :** one designated *c* esp. as the 3d in order or class **6 a :** a grade rating a student's work as fair or mediocre in quality **b :** one graded or rated with a C **7 :** something shaped like the letter C

[2]c *abbr, often cap* **1** calm **2** calorie **3** Canadian **4** canceled **5** candle **6** carat **7** case **8** castle **9** catcher **10** Catholic **11** cedi **12** Celsius **13** cent **14** centavo **15** center **16** centi- **17** centigrade **18** centime **19** centimeter **20** centum **21** century **22** chairman **23** chapter **24** circa **25** circuit **26** circumference **27** clockwise **28** cloudy **29** cobalt **30** cocaine **31** codex **32** coefficient **33** college **34** colon **35** color **36** colt **37** [L *congius*] gallon **38** congress **39** conservative **40** contralto **41** copyright **42** cost **43** cubic

[3]c *symbol* speed of light

C *symbol* **1** capacitance **2** carbon

ca *abbr* **1** centare **2** circa

Ca *symbol* calcium

CA *abbr* **1** California **2** chartered accountant **3** chief accountant **4** chronological age **5** commercial agent **6** controller of accounts **7** current account

ca' \'kȯ, 'kä\ *Scot var of* CALL

[1]cab \'kab\ *n* [Heb *qabh*] **:** an ancient Hebrew unit of capacity equal to about two quarts

[2]cab \'kab\ *n* [short for *cabriolet*] **1 a** (1) **:** CABRIOLET (2) **:** a similar light closed carriage (as a hansom) **b :** a carriage for hire **2 :** TAXICAB **3** [short for *cabin*] **a :** the part of a locomotive that houses the engineer and operating controls **b :** a comparable shelter on a truck, tractor, or crane

CAB *abbr* Civil Aeronautics Board

[1]ca·bal \kə-'bal\ *n* [F *cabale* cabala, intrigue, cabal, fr. ML *cabbala* cabala, fr. LHeb *qabbālāh*, lit., received (lore)] **1 :** a number of persons secretly united to bring about an overturn or usurpation esp. in public affairs **2 :** the artifices and intrigues of such a group

[2]cabal *vi* **ca·balled; ca·bal·ling :** to unite in or form a cabal

ca·ba·la *or* **cab·ba·la** *or* **cab·ba·lah** \'kab-ə-lə, kə-'bäl-ə\ *n, often cap* [ML *cabbala*] **1 :** a medieval and modern system of Jewish theosophy, mysticism, and thaumaturgy marked by belief in creation through emanation and a cipher method of interpreting Scripture **2 a :** a traditional, esoteric, occult, or secret matter **b :** esoteric doctrine or mysterious art — **cab·a·lism** \'kab-ə-ˌliz-əm\ *n* — **cab·a·lis·tic** \ˌkab-ə-'lis-tik\ *adj*

ca·ba·let·ta \ˌkab-ə-'let-ə, ˌkäb-\ *n* [It]**:** an operatic song in simple popular style characterized by a uniform rhythm

[1]ca·ba·list \'kab-ə-ləst, kə-'bäl-əst\ *n* **1** *often cap* **:** a student, interpreter, or devotee of the Jewish cabala **2 :** one skilled in esoteric doctrine or mysterious art

[2]ca·bal·ist \kə-'bal-əst\ *n* **:** a member of a cabal

ca·bal·le·ro \ˌkab-ə-'le(ə)r-(ˌ)ō, -ə(l)-'ye(ə)r-\ *n, pl* **-ros** [Sp, fr. LL *caballarius* hostler — more at CAVALIER] **1 :** KNIGHT, CAVALIER **2** *chiefly Southwest* **:** HORSEMAN

ca·bana \kə-'ban-(y)ə\ *n* [Sp *cabaña*, lit., hut, fr. ML *capanna*] **1 :** a shelter resembling a cabin usu. with an open side facing a beach or swimming pool **2 :** a lightweight structure with living facilities

cabana set *n* **:** a two-piece beachwear ensemble for men consisting of loosely fitting shorts and a short-sleeved jacket

cab·a·ret \ˌkab-ə-'rā\ *n* [F, fr. ONF] **1** *archaic* **:** a shop selling wines and liquors **2 :** a restaurant serving liquor and providing entertainment (as by singers or dancers); *also* **:** the show provided

[1]cab·bage \'kab-ij\ *n, often attrib* [ME *caboche*, fr. ONF, head] **1 :** a leafy garden plant (*Brassica oleracea capitata*) of European origin that has a short stem and a dense globular head of usu. green leaves and is used as a vegetable **2 :** a terminal bud of a palm tree that resembles a head of cabbage and is eaten as a vegetable **3** *slang* **:** paper money or bank notes

[2]cabbage *n* [perh. by folk etymology fr. MF *cabas* cheating, theft] *Brit* **:** pieces of cloth left in cutting out garments and traditionally kept by tailors as perquisites

[3]cabbage *vt* **cab·baged; cab·bag·ing :** to take surreptitiously **:** STEAL, FILCH

cabbage butterfly *n* **:** any of several largely white butterflies (family Pieridae) whose green larvae are cabbageworms; *esp* **:** a small cosmopolitan butterfly (*Pieris rapae*) that is a universal pest on cabbage

cabbage looper *n* **:** a moth (*Trichoplusia ni*) whose pale green white-striped larva is a measuring worm that feeds on cruciferous plants (as the cabbage)

cabbage palm *n* **:** a palm with terminal buds used as a vegetable

cabbage palmetto *n* **:** a fan-leaved cabbage palm (*Sabal palmetto*) native to coastal southern U.S. and the Bahamas

cab·bage·worm \'kab-ij-ˌwərm\ *n* **:** an insect larva (as of a cabbage butterfly) that feeds on cabbages

cab·by *or* **cab·bie** \'kab-ē\ *n, pl* **cabbies :** CABDRIVER

cab·driv·er \'kab-ˌdrī-vər\ *n* **:** a driver of a cab

ca·ber \'käb-ər, 'kā-bər\ *n* [ScGael *cabar*] **:** POLE; *esp* **:** a young tree trunk used for tossing as a trial of strength in a Scottish sport

[1]cab·in \'kab-ən\ *n* [ME *cabane*, fr. MF, fr. OProv *cabana* hut, fr. ML *capanna*] **1 a :** a private room on a ship for one or a few persons — compare CABIN CLASS **b :** a compartment below deck on a small boat for passengers or crew **c :** an airplane or airship compartment for cargo, crew, or passengers **2 :** a small one-story dwelling usu. of simple construction **3 a** *chiefly Brit* **:** CAB 3 **b :** the part of a passenger trailer used for living quarters

[2]cabin *vi* **:** to live in or as if in a cabin ~ *vt* **:** CONFINE

cabin boy *n* **:** a boy acting as servant on a ship

cabin car *n* **:** CABOOSE

cabin class *n* **:** a class of accommodations on a passenger ship superior to tourist class and inferior to first class

cabin cruiser *n* **:** CRUISER 3

[1]cab·i·net \'kab-(ə-)nət\ *n* [MF, small room, dim. of ONF *cabine* gambling house] **1 a :** a case or cupboard usu. having doors and shelves **b :** a collection of specimens esp. of mineralogical, biological, or numismatic interest **c :** an upright case housing a radio or television receiver **:** CONSOLE **d :** a chamber having temperature and humidity controls and used esp. for incubating biological samples **2 a** *archaic* **:** a small room providing seclusion **b :** a small exhibition room in a museum **3 a** *archaic* (1) **:** the private room serving as council chamber of the chief councillors or ministers of a sovereign (2) **:** the consultations and actions of these councillors **b** (1) *often cap* **:** a body of advisers of a head of state (as a sovereign or president) (2) **:** a similar advisory council of a governor of a state or a mayor **c** *Brit* **:** a meeting of a cabinet

[2]cabinet *adj* **1 :** suitable by reason of size for a small room or by reason of attractiveness or perfection for preservation and display in a cabinet **2 :** of or relating to a governmental cabinet **3 a :** used or adapted for cabinetmaking **b :** done or used by a cabinetmaker

cab·i·net·mak·er \-ˌmā-kər\ *n* **:** a skilled woodworker who makes fine furniture — **cab·i·net·mak·ing** \-ˌmā-kiŋ\ *n*

cab·i·net·work \-ˌwərk\ *n* **:** finished woodwork made by a cabinetmaker

cabin fever *n* **:** extreme irritability and restlessness resulting from the boredom of living in a remote region alone or with only a few companions; *also* **:** the same emotions resulting from living in a small enclosed space

[1]ca·ble \'kā-bəl\ *n, often attrib* [ME, fr. ONF, fr. ML *capulum* lasso, fr. L *capere* to take — more at HEAVE] **1 a :** a strong rope esp. of 10 or more inches in circumference **b :** a cable-laid rope **c :** a wire rope or metal chain of great tensile strength **d :** a wire or wire rope by which force is exerted to control or operate a mechanism **2 :** CABLE LENGTH **3 a :** an assembly of electrical conductors insulated from each other but laid up together usu. by being twisted around a central core **b :** CABLEGRAM **4 :** something resembling or fashioned like a cable

cable 3a

[2]cable *vb* **ca·bled; ca·bling** \'kā-b(ə-)liŋ\ *vt* **1 :** to fasten with or as if with a cable **2 :** to provide with cables **3 :** to telegraph by submarine cable **4 :** to make into a cable or into a form resembling a cable ~ *vi* **:** to communicate by a submarine cable

cable car *n* **:** a car made to be moved on a railway by an endless cable operated by a stationary motor or along an overhead cable

ca·ble·gram \'kā-bəl-ˌgram\ *n* **:** a message sent by a submarine telegraph cable

ca·ble–laid \ˌkā-bəl-'lād\ *adj* **:** composed of three ropes laid together left-handed with each containing three strands twisted together <~ rope>

cable length *n* **:** a maritime unit of length variously reckoned as 100 fathoms, 120 fathoms, or 608 feet

ca·blet \'kā-blət\ *n* **:** a small cable; *specif* **:** a cable-laid rope less than 10 inches in circumference

cable TV *n* **:** COMMUNITY ANTENNA TELEVISION — called also *cable television*

ca·ble·way \'kā-bəl-ˌwā\ *n* **:** a suspended cable used as a track along which carriers can be pulled

cab·man \'kab-mən\ *n* **:** CABDRIVER

cab·o·chon \'kab-ə-ˌshän\ *n* [MF, aug. of ONF *caboche* head] **:** a gem or bead cut in convex form and highly polished but not faceted; *also* **:** this style of cutting — **cabochon** *adv*

ca·boo·dle \kə-'büd-ᵊl\ *n* [prob. fr. *ca-* (intensive prefix, prob. of imit. origin) + *boodle*] **:** COLLECTION, LOT <sell the whole ~>

ca·boose \kə-'büs\ *n* [prob. fr. D *kabuis*, fr. MLG *kabūse*] **1 a :** a ship's galley **b :** an open-air cooking oven **2 :** a freight-train car attached usu. to the rear mainly for the use of the train crew **3 :** one that follows or brings up the rear

cab·o·tage \'kab-ə-ˌtäzh\ *n* [F, fr. *caboter* to sail along the coast] **1 :** trade or transport in coastal waters or between two points within a country **2 :** the right to engage in cabotage

ca·bret·ta \kə-'bret-ə\ *n* [modif. of Pg and Sp *cabra* goat]**:** a light soft leather from hair sheepskins

ca·bril·la \kə-'brē-(y)ə, -'bril-ə\ *n* [Sp, fr. dim. of *cabra* goat, fr. L *capra* she-goat, fem. of *caper* he-goat — more at CAPRIOLE]**:** any of various sea basses of the Mediterranean, the California coast, and the warmer parts of the western Atlantic

cab·ri·ole \'kab-rē-ˌōl\ *n* [F, caper] **1 :** a curved furniture leg ending in an ornamental foot **2 :** a ballet leap in which one leg is extended in mid-air and the other struck against it

1 2 3 4

cabrioles 1: *1* early 18th century, *2* mid-18th century, *3* early Georgian, *4* second half of 18th century

cab·ri·o·let \ˌkab-rē-ə-'lā\ *n* [F, fr. dim. of *cabriole* caper, alter. of MF *capriole*] **1 :** a light 2-wheeled one-horse carriage with a folding leather hood, a large apron, and upward-curving shafts **2 :** a convertible coupe

cab·stand \'kab-ˌstand\ *n* **:** a place where cabs await hire

cac- *or* **caco-** *comb form* [NL, fr. Gk *kak-*, *kako-*, fr. *kakos* bad] **:** bad <cacogenics>

ca' can·ny \kȯ-'kan-ē\ *n, Brit* **:** SLOWDOWN — **ca' canny** *vi, Brit*

ca·cao \kə-ˈkau̇, kə-ˈkā-(ˌ)ō\ *n, pl* **cacaos** [Sp, fr. Nahuatl *cacahuatl* cacao beans] **1 :** a So. American tree (*Theobroma cacao* of the family Sterculiaceae) with small yellowish flowers followed by fleshy yellow pods with many seeds — called also *chocolate tree* **2 :** the dried partly fermented fatty seeds of the cacao used in making cocoa, chocolate, and cocoa butter — called also *cacao bean, cocoa bean*

cacao butter *var of* COCOA BUTTER

cac·cia·to·re \ˌkäch-ə-ˈtōr-ē, -ˈtȯr-\ *adj* [It, fr. *cacciatore* hunter] **:** cooked with tomatoes and herbs and sometimes with wine <veal ~>

cach·a·lot \ˈkash-ə-ˌlät, -ˌlō\ *n* [F] **:** SPERM WHALE

¹cache \ˈkash\ *n* [F, fr. *cacher* to press, hide, fr. (assumed) VL *coacticare* to press together, fr. L *coactare* to compel, fr. *coactus,* pp. of *cogere* to compel — more at COGENT] **1 a :** a hiding place esp. for concealing and preserving provisions or implements **b :** a secure place of storage **2 :** something hidden or stored in a cache

²cache *vt* **cached; cach·ing :** to place, hide, or store in a cache

ca·chec·tic \kə-ˈkek-tik, ka-\ *adj* [F *cachectique,* fr. L *cachecticus,* fr. Gk *kachektikos,* fr. *kak-* + *echein*] **:** affected by cachexia

cache·pot \ˈkash-ˌpät, ˈkash-(ə-)ˌpō\ *n* [F, fr. *cacher* to hide + *pot* pot] **:** an ornamental receptacle to hold and usu. to conceal a flowerpot

ca·chet \ka-ˈshā\ *n* [MF, fr. *cacher* to press, hide] **1 a :** a seal used esp. as a mark of official approval **b :** an indication of approval carrying great prestige **2 a :** a characteristic feature or quality conferring prestige **b :** PRESTIGE **3 :** a flour-paste case in which an unpleasant medicine is swallowed **4 a :** a design or inscription on an envelope to commemorate a postal or philatelic event **b :** an advertisement forming part of a postal meter impression **c :** a motto or slogan included in a postal cancellation

ca·chex·ia \kə-ˈkek-sē-ə, ka-\ *also* **ca·chexy** \kə-ˈkek-sē, ka-; ˈkak-ˌek-\ *n* [LL *cachexia,* fr. Gk *kachexia* bad condition, fr. *kak-* cac- + *hexis* condition, fr. *echein* to have, be disposed — more at SCHEME] **:** general physical wasting and malnutrition usu. associated with chronic disease

cach·in·nate \ˈkak-ə-ˌnāt\ *vi* **-nat·ed; -nat·ing** [L *cachinnatus,* pp. of *cachinnare,* of imit. origin] **:** to laugh loudly or immoderately — **cach·in·na·tion** \ˌkak-ə-ˈnā-shən\ *n*

ca·chou \ka-ˈshü, ˈkash-(ˌ)ü\ *n* [F, fr. Pg *cachu,* fr. Malayalam *kāccu*] **1 :** CATECHU **2 :** a pill or pastille used to sweeten the breath

ca·chu·cha \kə-ˈchü-chə\ *n* [Sp, small boat, cachucha] **:** a gay Andalusian solo dance in triple time done with castanets

ca·cique \kə-ˈsēk\ *n* [Sp, of Arawakan origin; akin to Taino *cacique* chief] **1 a :** a native Indian chief in areas dominated primarily by a Spanish culture **b :** a local political boss in Spain and Latin America **2** [AmerSp, fr. Sp] **:** any of numerous tropical American orioles (as of the genus *Cacicus*) having the base of the bill expanded into a frontal shield — **ca·ciqu·ism** \-ˈsē-ˌkiz-əm\ *n*

cack·le \ˈkak-əl\ *vi* **cack·led; cack·ling** \-(ə-)liŋ\ [ME *cakelen,* of imit. origin] **1 :** to make the sharp broken noise or cry characteristic of a hen esp. after laying **2 :** to laugh in a way suggestive of a hen's cackle **3 :** CHATTER — **cackle** *n* — **cack·ler** \-(ə-)lər\ *n*

caco·de·mon \ˌkak-ə-ˈdē-mən\ *n* [Gk *kakodaimōn,* fr. *kak-* cac- + *daimōn* spirit] **:** DEMON — **caco·de·mon·ic** \-di-ˈmän-ik\ *adj*

cac·o·dyl \ˈkak-ə-ˌdil\ *n* [ISV, fr. Gk *kakōdēs* ill smelling, fr. *kak-* + *-ōdēs* (akin to Gk *ozein* to smell) — more at ODOR] **1 :** an arsenical radical $As(CH_3)_2$ whose compounds have a vile smell and are usu. poisonous **2 :** a colorless liquid $As_2(CH_3)_4$ consisting of two cacodyl radicals

cac·o·dyl·ic acid \ˌkak-ə-ˌdil-ik-\ *n* **:** a toxic crystalline compound of arsenic $C_2H_7AsO_2$ used esp. as an herbicide

caco·ë·thes \ˌkak-ə-ˈwē-(ˌ)thēz\ *n* [L, fr. Gk *kakoēthes* wickedness, fr. neut. of *kakoēthēs* malignant, fr. *kak-* cac- + *ēthos* character — more at ETHICAL] **:** an insatiable desire **:** MANIA

caco·gen·e·sis \ˌkak-ə-ˈjen-ə-səs\ *n* [NL] **:** racial deterioration esp. when due to the retention of inferior breeding stock — **caco·gen·ic** \-ˈjen-ik\ *adj*

caco·gen·ics \-ˈjen-iks\ *n pl but sing or pl in constr* [*cac-* + *-genics* (as in *eugenics*)] **1 :** DYSGENICS **2 :** CACOGENESIS

ca·cog·ra·phy \ka-ˈkäg-rə-fē\ *n* **1 :** bad handwriting — compare CALLIGRAPHY **2 :** bad spelling — compare ORTHOGRAPHY — **caco·graph·i·cal** \ˌkak-ə-ˈgraf-i-kəl\ *adj*

cac·o·mis·tle \ˈkak-ə-ˌmis-əl, ˌkak-ə-ˈmis(t)-lē\ *n* [MexSp, fr. Nahuatl *tlacomiztli,* fr. *tlaco* half + *miztli* mountain lion] **:** a carnivore (*Bassariscus astutus*) related to and resembling the raccoon; *also* **:** its fur or pelt

ca·coph·o·nous \ka-ˈkäf-ə-nəs\ *adj* [Gk *kakophōnos,* fr. *kak-* + *phōnē* voice, sound — more at BAN] **:** marked by cacophony **:** harsh-sounding — **ca·coph·o·nous·ly** *adv*

ca·coph·o·ny \-nē\ *n, pl* **-nies :** harsh or discordant sound **:** DISSONANCE; *specif* **:** harshness in the sound of words or phrases

cac·tus \ˈkak-təs\ *n, pl* **cac·ti** \-ˌtī, -(ˌ)tē\ *or* **cac·tus·es** [NL, genus name, fr. L, cardoon, fr. Gk *kaktos*] **:** any of a family (Cactaceae, the cactus family) of plants that have fleshy stems and branches with scales or spines instead of leaves and are found esp. in dry areas (as deserts)

ca·cu·mi·nal \ka-ˈkyü-mən-ᵊl, kə-\ *adj* [ISV, fr. L *cacumin-, cacumen* top, point] **:** RETROFLEX

cad \ˈkad\ *n* [E dial., unskilled assistant, short for Sc *caddie*] **1** *obs* **:** an omnibus conductor **2 :** a person without gentlemanly instincts

ca·das·tral \kə-ˈdas-trəl\ *adj* **1 :** of or relating to a cadastre **2 :** showing or recording property boundaries, subdivision lines, buildings, and related details — **ca·das·tral·ly** \-trə-lē\ *adv*

ca·das·tre \kə-ˈdas-tər\ *n* [F, fr. It *catastro,* fr. OIt *catastico,* fr. LGk *katastichon* notebook, fr. Gk *kata* by + *stichos* row, line — more at CATA-, DISTICH] **:** an official register of the quantity, value, and ownership of real estate used in apportioning taxes

ca·dav·er \kə-ˈdav-ər\ *n* [L, fr. *cadere* to fall] **:** a dead body usu. intended for dissection — **ca·dav·er·ic** \-(ə-)rik\ *adj*

ca·dav·er·ine \kə-ˈdav-ə-ˌrēn\ *n* **:** a syrupy colorless poisonous ptomaine $C_5H_{14}N_2$ formed by decarboxylation of lysine esp. in putrefaction of flesh

ca·dav·er·ous \kə-ˈdav-(ə-)rəs\ *adj* **1 a :** of or relating to a corpse **b :** suggestive of corpses or tombs **2 a :** PALLID, LIVID **b :** GAUNT, EMACIATED — **ca·dav·er·ous·ly** *adv*

cad·die *or* **cad·dy** \ˈkad-ē\ *n, pl* **caddies** [F *cadet* military cadet] **1** *Scot* **:** one that waits about for odd jobs **2 a :** one that assists a golfer esp. by carrying his clubs **b :** a wheeled device for conveying things not readily carried by hand — **caddie** *or* **caddy** *vi*

¹cad·dis *also* **cad·dice** \ˈkad-əs\ *n* [ME *cadas* cotton wool, prob. fr. MF *cadaz,* fr. OProv *cadarz*] **:** worsted yarn; *specif* **:** a worsted ribbon or binding formerly used for garters and girdles

²caddis *or* **caddice** *n* **:** CADDISWORM

caddis fly *n* **:** any of an order (Trichoptera) of insects with four membranous wings, vestigial mouthparts, slender many-jointed antennae, and aquatic larvae — compare CADDISWORM

cad·dish \ˈkad-ish\ *adj* **:** resembling a cad — **cad·dish·ly** *adv* — **cad·dish·ness** *n*

cad·dis·worm \ˈkad-ə-ˌswərm\ *n* [prob. alter. of obs. *codworm;* fr. the case or tube in which it lives] **:** the larva of a caddis fly that lives in and carries around a silken case covered with bits of debris

caddisworm

Cad·do \ˈkad-(ˌ)ō\ *n, pl* **Caddo** *or* **Cad·dos :** a member of an Amerindian people ranging from No. Dakota south to Texas

cad·dy \ˈkad-ē\ *n, pl* **caddies** [Malay *kati* catty] **1 :** a small box, can, or chest used esp. to keep tea in **2 :** a container or device for storing or holding objects when they are not in use

¹cade \ˈkād\ *adj* [E dial. *cade* pet lamb, fr. ME *cad*] **:** left by its mother and reared by hand **:** PET <a ~ lamb> <a ~ colt>

²cade *n* [MF, fr. OProv, fr. ML *catanus*] **:** a European juniper (*Juniperus oxycedrus*) whose wood yields by distillation a dark tarry liquid used locally in treating skin diseases

-cade \ˌkād, ˈkād\ *n comb form* [*cavalcade*] **:** procession <*motorcade*>

ca·delle \kə-ˈdel\ *n* [F, fr. Prov *cadello,* fr. L *catella,* fem. of *catellus* little dog, dim. of *catulus* young animal] **:** a small cosmopolitan black beetle (*Tenebroides mauritanicus*) destructive to stored grain

ca·dence \ˈkād-ᵊn(t)s\ *n* [ME, fr. OIt *cadenza,* fr. *cadere* to fall, fr. L — more at CHANCE] **1 a :** a rhythmic sequence or flow of sounds in language **b :** the beat, time, or measure of rhythmical motion or activity **2 a :** a falling inflection of the voice **b :** a concluding and usu. falling strain; *specif* **:** a musical chord sequence moving to a harmonic close or point of rest and giving the sense of harmonic completion **3 :** the modulated and rhythmic recurrence of a sound esp. in nature — **ca·denced** \-ᵊn(t)st\ *adj* — **ca·den·tial** \kā-ˈden-chəl\ *adj*

ca·den·cy \ˈkād-ᵊn-sē\ *n* **:** CADENCE

ca·dent \ˈkād-ᵊnt\ *adj* [L *cadent-, cadens,* prp. of *cadere*] **1** *archaic* **:** being in the process of falling <with ~ tears fret channels in her cheeks—Shak.> **2 :** having rhythmic fall

ca·den·za \kə-ˈden-zə\ *n* [It, cadence, cadenza] **1 :** a parenthetic flourish in an aria or other solo piece commonly just before a final or other important cadence **2 :** a technically brilliant sometimes improvised solo passage toward the close of a concerto

ca·det \kə-ˈdet\ *n, often attrib* [F, fr. F dial. *capdet* chief, fr. LL *capitellum,* dim. of L *capit-, caput* head — more at HEAD] **1 a :** a younger brother or son **b :** youngest son **c :** a younger branch of a family or a member of it **2 :** one in training for a military or naval commission; *esp* **:** a student in a service academy **3 :** a junior in a business or occupation who is engaged principally in learning **4** *slang* **:** PIMP — **ca·det·ship** \-ˌship\ *n*

Ca·dette scout \kə-ˌdet-\ *n* [fr. *cadet,* after such pairs as F *brunet* male brunet: *brunette* female brunet] **:** a member of the Girl Scouts from 12 through 14 years of age

cadge \ˈkaj\ *vb* **cadged; cadg·ing** [back-formation fr. Sc *cadger* carrier, huckster, fr. ME *cadgear,* fr. *caggen* to tie] **:** BEG, SPONGE — **cadg·er** *n*

cad·mi·um \ˈkad-mē-əm\ *n* [NL, fr. L *cadmia* calamine; fr. the occurrence of its ores together with calamine — more at CALAMINE] **:** a bluish white malleable ductile toxic bivalent metallic element used esp. in protective platings and in bearing metals — see ELEMENT table

Cad·mus \ˈkad-məs\ *n* [L, fr. Gk *Kadmos*] **:** the legendary founder of Thebes

CADO *abbr* Central Air Documents Office

cad·re \ˈkad-rē\ *n* [F, fr. It *quadro,* fr. L *quadrum* square — more at QUARREL] **1 :** FRAME, FRAMEWORK **2 :** a nucleus esp. of trained personnel capable of assuming control and of training others

ca·du·ceus \kə-ˈd(y)ü-sē-əs, -shəs\ *n, pl* **-cei** \-sē-ˌī\ [L, modif. of Gk *karykeion,* fr. *karyx, kēryx* herald; akin to OE *hrēth* glory] **1 :** the symbolic staff of a herald; *specif* **:** a representation of a staff with two entwined snakes and two wings at the top **2 :** an insignia bearing a caduceus and symbolizing a physician — **ca·du·cean** \-sē-ən, -shən\ *adj*

ca·du·ci·ty \kə-ˈd(y)ü-sət-ē\ *n* [F *caducité,* fr. *caduc* transitory, fr. L *caducus*] **1 :** the quality of being transitory or perishable **2 :** SENILITY

ca·du·cous \kə-ˈd(y)ü-kəs\ *adj* [L *caducus* tending to fall, transitory, fr. *cadere* to fall — more at CHANCE] **:** falling off easily or before the usual time — used esp. of floral organs

cae·cal, cae·cum *var of* CECAL, CECUM

cae·ci·lian \si-ˈsil-yən, -ˈsēl-, -ē-ən\ *n* [deriv. of L *caecilia,* a lizard, fr. *caecus* blind] **:** any of an order (Gymnophiona) of chiefly tropical burrowing amphibians resembling worms — **caecilian** *adj*

caen- *or* **caeno-** — see CEN-

Caer·phil·ly \kär-ˈfil-ē\ *n* [*Caerphilly,* urban district in Wales]

: a mild white whole-milk Welsh cheese
Cae·sar \'sē-zər\ *n* [Gaius Julius *Caesar*] **1 :** any of the Roman emperors succeeding Augustus Caesar — used as a title **2 a** *often not cap* **:** a powerful ruler: (1) **:** EMPEROR (2) **:** AUTOCRAT, DICTATOR **b** [fr. the reference in Mt 22:21] **;** the civil power **:** a temporal ruler — **Cae·sar·e·an** *or* **Cae·sar·i·an** \si-'zar-ē-ən, -'zer-\ *adj*
Cae·sar·ism \'sē-zə-,riz-əm\ *n* **:** imperial authority or system **:** political absolutism **:** DICTATORSHIP — **Cae·sar·ist** \-zə-rəst\ *n*
Cae·sar salad \,sē-zər-\ *n* [*Caesar's*, restaurant in Tijuana, Mexico] **:** a tossed salad made typically with romaine, garlic, anchovies, and croutons and served with a dressing of olive oil, coddled egg, lemon juice, and grated cheese

caduceus 2

cae·si·um *var of* CESIUM
caes·pi·tose \'ses-pə-,tōs\ *adj* [NL *caespitosus*, fr. L *caespit-, caespes* turf] **1 :** forming a dense turf or sod **2 :** growing in clusters or tufts
cae·su·ra \si-'z(h)ůr-ə\ *n, pl* **-suras** *or* **-su·rae** \-'z(h)ů(ə)r-(,)ē\ [LL, fr. L, act of cutting, fr. *caedere* to cut — more at CONCISE] **1** *in Greek and Latin prosody* **:** a break in the flow of sound in a verse caused by the ending of a word within a foot **2** *in modern prosody* **:** a usu. rhetorical break in the flow of sound in the middle of a line of verse **3 :** BREAK, INTERRUPTION **4 :** a pause marking a rhythmic point of division in a melody — **cae·su·ral** \-'z(h)ůr-əl\ *adj*
CAF *abbr* cost and freight
ca·fé *also* **ca·fe** \ka-'fā, kə-\ *n, often attrib* [F *café* coffee, café, fr. Turk *kahve* — more at COFFEE] **1 :** COFFEE **2 :** RESTAURANT **3 :** BARROOM **4 :** CABARET, NIGHTCLUB
ca·fé au lait \(,)ka-,fā-ō-'lā\ *n* [F, coffee with milk] **1 :** coffee with usu. hot milk in about equal parts **2 :** the color of coffee with milk
ca·fé noir \(,)ka-,fān-(ə-)'wär\ *n* [F, black coffee] **:** coffee without milk or cream; *also* **:** DEMITASSE
caf·e·te·ria \,kaf-ə-'tir-ē-ə\ *n* [AmerSp *cafetería* retail coffee store, fr. Sp *café* coffee] **:** a restaurant in which the customers serve themselves or are served at a counter and take the food to tables to eat
caf·e·to·ri·um \-'tōr-ē-əm, -'tȯr-\ *n* [blend of *cafeteria* and *auditorium*] **:** a large room (as in a school building) designed for use both as a cafeteria and an auditorium
caf·feine \ka-'fēn, 'ka-,; 'kaf-ē-ən\ *n* [G *kaffein*, fr. *kaffee* coffee, fr. F *café*] **:** a bitter compound $C_8H_{10}N_4O_2$ found esp. in coffee, tea, and kola nuts and used medicinally as a stimulant and diuretic — **caf·fein·ic** \ka-'fē-nik, ,kaf-ē-'in-ik\ *adj*
caf·tan \kaf-'tan, 'kaf-,\ *n* [Russ *kaftan*, fr. Turk, fr. Per *qaftān*] **:** a usu. cotton or silk ankle-length garment with long sleeves that is common throughout the Levant
[1]**cage** \'kāj\ *n* [ME, fr. OF, fr. L *cavea* cavity, cage, fr. *cavus* hollow — more at CAVE] **1 :** a box or enclosure having some openwork for confining or carrying animals (as birds) **2 a :** a barred cell for confining prisoners **b :** a fenced area for prisoners of war **3 :** a framework serving as support <the steel ~ of a skyscraper> **4 :** an enclosure resembling a cage in form or purpose **5 a :** a screen placed behind home plate to stop baseballs during batting practice **b :** a goal structure consisting of posts or a frame with a net attached (as in ice hockey) **c :** FIELD HOUSE 2; *also* **:** a basketball court **6 :** a large building with unobstructed area for practicing outdoor sports and often adapted for indoor events **7 :** a sheer one-piece dress that has no waistline, is often gathered at the neck, and is worn over a close-fitting underdress or slip
[2]**cage** *vt* **caged; cag·ing 1 :** to confine or keep in or as if in a cage **2 :** to put (as a puck) into a cage and score a goal
cage bird *n* **:** a bird adaptable to being kept in a cage
cage·ling \'kāj-liŋ\ *n* **:** a caged bird
ca·gey *also* **ca·gy** \'kā-jē\ *adj* **ca·gi·er; -est** [origin unknown] **1 :** hesitant about committing oneself **2 :** wary of being trapped or deceived **:** SHREWD — **ca·gi·ly** \-jə-lē\ *adv* — **ca·gi·ness** *also* **ca·gey·ness** \-jē-nəs\ *n*
CAGS *abbr* Certificate of Advanced Graduate Study
ca·hier \kä-'yā, kī-'ā\ *n* [F, fr. MF *quaer, caier* quire — more at QUIRE] **1 :** a report or memorial concerning policy esp. of a parliamentary body **2 :** a number of sheets of paper put together for binding or bound loosely
ca·hoot \kə-'hüt\ *n* [perh. fr. F *cahute* cabin, hut] **:** PARTNERSHIP, LEAGUE — usu. used in pl. <in ~*s* with the devil>
ca·how \kə-'hau̇\ *n* [imit.] **:** a brown-and-white earth-burrowing nocturnal bird (*Pterodroma cahow*) formerly abundant in Bermuda but now nearly extinct
CAI *abbr* computer-aided instruction; computer-assisted instruction
cai·man \kā-'man, kī-; 'kā-mən\ *n* [Sp *caimán*, prob. fr. Carib *caymán*] **:** any of several Central and So. American crocodilians similar to alligators but often superficially resembling crocodiles
Cain \'kān\ *n* [Heb *Qayin*] **:** the brother and murderer of Abel
-caine \,kān, 'kān\ *n comb form* [G *-kain*, fr. *kokain* cocaine] **:** synthetic alkaloid anesthetic <pro*caine*>
ca·ique \kä-'ēk, 'kīk\ *n* [Turk *kayik*] **1 :** a light skiff used on the Bosporus **2 :** a Levantine sailing vessel
caird \'ke(ə)rd\ *n* [ScGael *ceard*; akin to Gk *kerdos* profit] *Scot* **:** a traveling tinker; *also* **:** TRAMP, GYPSY
cairn \'ka(ə)rn, 'ke(ə)rn\ *n* [ME *carne*, fr. ScGael *carn*; akin to OIr & W *carn* cairn] **:** a heap of stones piled up as a memorial or as a landmark — **cairned** \'ka(ə)rnd, 'ke(ə)rnd\ *adj*
cairn·gorm \'ka(ə)rn-,gȯ(ə)rm, 'ke(ə)rn-\ *n* [*Cairngorm*, mountain in Scotland] **:** a yellow or smoky-brown crystalline quartz
cairn terrier *n* [fr. its use in hunting among cairns] **:** a small compactly built hard-coated terrier of Scottish origin
cais·son \'kā-,sän, 'kās-ᵊn\ *n* [F, aug. of *caisse* box, fr. OProv *caisa*, fr. L *capsa* chest, case — more at CASE] **1 a :** a chest to hold ammunition **b :** a usu. 2-wheeled vehicle for artillery ammunition attachable to a horse-drawn limber **2 a :** a watertight chamber used in construction work under water or as a foundation **b :** a float for raising a sunken vessel **c :** a hollow floating box or a boat used as a floodgate for a dock or basin **3 :** COFFER 4

caisson 1b

caisson disease *n* **:** a sometimes fatal disorder that is marked by neuralgic pains and paralysis, distress in breathing, and often collapse and that is caused by the release of gas bubbles in tissue upon too rapid decrease in air pressure after a stay in a compressed atmosphere — called also *bends*
Caith *abbr* Caithness
cai·tiff \'kāt-əf\ *adj* [ME *caitif*, fr. ONF, captive, vile, fr. L *captivus* captive] **:** being base, cowardly, or despicable — **caitiff** *n*
ca·jole \kə-'jōl\ *vt* **ca·joled; ca·jol·ing** [F *cajoler* to chatter like a jay in a cage, cajole, alter. of MF *gaioler*, fr. ONF *gaiole* birdcage, fr. LL *caveola*, dim. of L *cavea* cage — more at CAGE] **1 :** to persuade with deliberate flattery esp. in the face of reluctance <the women ~ their husbands into giving them a vote —Kathleen Karr> **2 :** to deceive with soothing words or false promises — **ca·jole·ment** \-'jōl-mənt\ *n* — **ca·jol·er** *n* — **ca·jol·ery** \-'jōl-(ə-)rē\ *n*
Ca·jun *also* **Ca·jan** \'kā-jən\ *n* [by alter. of *Acadian*] **1 :** ACADIAN 2a **2 :** one of a people of mixed white, Indian, and Negro ancestry in southwest Alabama and southeast Mississippi
[1]**cake** \'kāk\ *n* [ME, fr. ON *kaka*; akin to OHG *kuocho* cake] **1 a :** batter that may be fried or baked into a usu. small round flat shape **b :** sweet batter or dough usu. containing a leaven (as baking powder) that is first baked and then often coated with an icing **c :** a flattened usu. round mass of food that is baked or fried <a codfish ~> **2 a :** a block of compacted or congealed matter <a ~ of ice> **b :** a hard or brittle layer or deposit <~ formed in a pipe>
[2]**cake** *vb* **caked; cak·ing** *vt* **1 :** ENCRUST <*caked* with dust> **2 :** to fill (a space) with a packed mass ~ *vi* **:** to form or harden into a mass
cake·walk \'kā-,kwȯk\ *n* **1 :** an American Negro entertainment having a cake as prize for the most accomplished steps and figures in walking **2 :** a stage dance developed from walking steps and figures typically involving a high prance with backward tilt **3 :** a one-sided contest — **cakewalk** *vi* — **cake·walk·er** *n*
cal *abbr* **1** calendar **2** caliber **3** calorie
Cal *abbr* **1** California **2** large calorie
Cal·a·bar bean \,kal-ə-,bär-\ *n* [*Calabar*, Nigeria] **:** the dark brown highly poisonous seed of a tropical African woody vine (*Physostigma venenosum*) that is used as a source of physostigmine and as an ordeal poison in native witchcraft trials
cal·a·bash \'kal-ə-,bash\ *n* [F & Sp; F *calebasse* gourd, fr. Sp *calabaza*, prob. fr. Ar *qar'ah yābisah* dry gourd] **1 :** GOURD; *esp* **:** one whose hard shell is used for a utensil (as a bottle) **2 :** a tropical American tree (*Crescentia cujete*) of the trumpet-creeper family; *also* **:** its hard globose fruit **3 :** a utensil made from the shell of a calabash
cal·a·boose \'kal-ə-,büs\ *n* [Sp *calabozo* dungeon] *dial* **:** JAIL; *esp* **:** a local jail
ca·la·di·um \kə-'lād-ē-əm\ *n* [NL, genus name, fr. Malay *kĕladi*, an aroid plant] **:** any of a genus (*Caladium*, esp. *C. bicolor*) of tropical American ornamental plants of the arum family with showy variously colored leaves
cal·a·man·der \'kal-ə-,man-dər, ,kal-ə-'\ *n* [prob. fr. D *kalamanderhout* calamander wood] **:** the hazel-brown black-striped wood of an East Indian tree (genus *Diospyros*, esp. *D. quaesita*) that is used in furniture manufacturing
cal·a·mary \'kal-ə-,mer-ē\ *or* **cal·a·mar** \-,mär\ *n, pl* **-maries** *or* **-mars** [L *calamarius* of a pen, fr. *calamus* reed; fr. the shape of its inner shell] **:** SQUID
cal·a·mine \'kal-ə-,mīn, -mən\ *n* [F, ore of zinc, fr. ML *calamina*, alter. of L *cadmia*, fr. Gk *kadmeia*, lit., Theban (earth), fr. fem. of *kadmeios* Theban, fr. *Kadmos* Cadmus, founder of Thebes] **:** a mixture of zinc oxide with a small amount of ferric oxide used in lotions, liniments, and ointments
cal·a·mint \'kal-ə-,mint\ *n* [ME *calament*, fr. OF, fr. ML *calamentum*, fr. Gk *kalaminthē*] **:** any of a genus (*Satureja*, esp. *S. calamintha*) of mints — called also *basil thyme*
cal·a·mite \'kal-ə-,mīt\ *n* [NL *Calamites*, genus of fossil plants, fr. L *calamus*] **:** a Paleozoic fossil plant (esp. genus *Calamites*) resembling a giant horsetail
ca·lam·i·tous \kə-'lam-ət-əs\ *adj* **:** causing or accompanied by calamity **:** DISASTROUS — **ca·lam·i·tous·ly** *adv* — **ca·lam·i·tous·ness** *n*
ca·lam·i·ty \kə-'lam-ət-ē\ *n, pl* **-ties** [MF *calamité*, fr. L *calamitat-, calamitas*; akin to L *clades* destruction — more at HALT] **1 :** a state of deep distress or misery caused by major misfortune or loss **2 :** an extraordinarily grave event marked by great loss and lasting distress and affliction ***syn*** see DISASTER
cal·a·mon·din \,kal-ə-'män-dən\ *n* [Tag *kalamunding*] **:** a small spiny citrus tree (*Citrus mitis*) of the Philippines; *also* **:** its fruit
cal·a·mus \'kal-ə-məs\ *n, pl* **-mi** \-,mī, -,mē\ [L, reed, reed pen, fr. Gk *kalamos* — more at HAULM] **1 a :** SWEET FLAG **b :** the aromatic peeled and dried rhizome of the calamus that is the source of a carcinogenic essential oil **2 :** the barrel of a feather **:** QUILL

ca·lash \kə-ˈlash\ *n* [F *calèche,* fr. G *kalesche,* fr. Czech *kolesa* wheels, carriage; akin to Gk *kyklos* wheel — more at WHEEL] **1 a** : a light small-wheeled 4-passenger carriage with a folding top **b** : CALÈCHE 2 **2 a** : a large hood worn by women in the 18th century **b** : a folding carriage top

cal·a·thos \ˈkal-ə-ˌthäs\ *or* **cal·a·thus** \-thəs\ *n, pl* **-thi** \-ˌthī, -ˌthē\ [Gk *kalathos* basket] : a flared fruit basket borne on the head as a symbol of fruitfulness in Greek and Egyptian art

calc *abbr* calculate; calculated

calc- *or* **calci-** *or* **calco-** *comb form* [L *calc-, calx* lime — more at CHALK] : calcium : calcium salt <*calc*ic> <*calci*fy>

cal·ca·ne·al \kal-ˈkā-nē-əl\ *adj* : relating to the heel or calcaneus

cal·ca·ne·um \-nē-əm\ *n, pl* **-nea** \-nē-ə\ [L, heel — more at CALK] **1** : CALCANEUS **2** : a process of the tarsometatarsus of a bird analogous to the calcaneus

cal·ca·ne·us \-nē-əs\ *n, pl* **-nei** \-nē-ˌī\ [LL, heel, alter. of L *calcaneum*] : a tarsal bone that in man is the great bone of the heel

cal·car \ˈkal-ˌkär\ *n, pl* **cal·car·ia** \kal-ˈkar-ē-ə, -ˈker-\ [L, fr. *calc-, calx* heel — more at CALK] : a spurred prominence (as of the calcaneum of a bat)

cal·car·e·ous \kal-ˈkar-ē-əs, -ˈker-\ *adj* [L *calcarius* of lime, fr. *calc-, calx* lime] **1 a** : resembling calcite or calcium carbonate esp. in hardness **b** : consisting of or containing calcium carbonate; *also* : containing calcium **2** : growing on limestone or in soil impregnated with lime — **cal·car·e·ous·ly** *adv* — **cal·car·e·ous·ness** *n*

cal·ce·o·lar·ia \ˌkal-sē-ə-ˈlar-ē-ə, -ˈler-\ *n* [NL, genus name, fr. L *calceolus* small shoe, dim. of *calceus* shoe, fr. *calc-, calx* heel] : any of a genus (*Calceolaria*) of tropical American plants of the snapdragon family with showy pouch-shaped flowers

calces *pl of* CALX

cal·cic \ˈkal-sik\ *adj* : derived from or containing calcium or lime : rich in calcium

cal·ci·cole \ˈkal-sə-ˌkōl\ *n* [F, calcicolous, fr. *calc-* + *-cole* -colous] : a plant normally growing on calcareous soils — **cal·cic·o·lous** \kal-ˈsik-ə-ləs\ *adj*

cal·cif·er·ol \kal-ˈsif-ə-ˌrȯl, -ˌrōl\ *n* [blend of *calciferous* + *ergosterol*] : VITAMIN D_2

cal·cif·er·ous \kal-ˈsif-(ə-)rəs\ *adj* : producing or containing calcium carbonate

cal·cif·ic \kal-ˈsif-ik\ *adj* [*calcify*] : involving or caused by calcification <~ lesions>

cal·ci·fi·ca·tion \ˌkal-sə-fə-ˈkā-shən\ *n* **1** : the process of calcifying; *specif* : deposition of insoluble lime salts (as in tissue) **2** : a calcified structure

cal·ci·fuge \ˈkal-sə-ˌfyüj\ *n* [F, calcifugous, fr. *calc-* + L *fugere* to flee — more at FUGITIVE] : a plant not normally growing on calcareous soils — **cal·cif·u·gous** \kal-ˈsif-yə-gəs\ *adj*

cal·ci·fy \ˈkal-sə-ˌfī\ *vb* **-fied; -fy·ing** *vt* **1** : to make calcareous by deposit of calcium salts **2** : to make inflexible or unchangeable ~ *vi* **1** : to become calcareous **2** : to become inflexible and changeless : HARDEN

cal·ci·mine \ˈkal-sə-ˌmīn\ *n* [alter. of *kalsomine,* of unknown origin] : a white or tinted wash that consists of glue, whiting or zinc white, and water and that is used esp. on plastered surfaces — **calcimine** *vt*

cal·ci·na·tion \ˌkal-sə-ˈnā-shən\ *n* : the act or process of calcining : the state of being calcined

[1]**cal·cine** \kal-ˈsīn\ *vb* **cal·cined; cal·cin·ing** [ME *calcenen,* fr. MF *calciner,* fr. L *calc-, calx* lime — more at CHALK] *vt* : to heat (as inorganic materials) to a high temperature but without fusing in order to drive off volatile matter or to effect changes (as oxidation or pulverization) ~ *vi* : to undergo calcination

[2]**cal·cine** \ˈkal-ˌsīn\ *n* : a product (as a metal oxide) of calcination or roasting

cal·ci·no·sis \ˌkal-sə-ˈnō-səs\ *n, pl* **-no·ses** \-ˌsēz\ [NL, irreg. (influenced by ISV *calcine*) fr. *calc-* + *-osis*] : the abnormal deposition of calcium salts in a part or tissue of the body

cal·ci·phy·lax·is \ˌkal-sə-fə-ˈlak-səs\ *n, pl* **-lax·es** \-ˌsēz\ [NL, fr. *calc-* + ana*phylaxis*] : an adaptive response that follows systemic sensitization by a calcifying factor (as a vitamin D) and a challenge (as with a metallic salt) and that involves local inflammation and sclerosis with calcium deposition — **cal·ci·phy·lac·tic** \-ˈlak-tik\ *adj* — **cal·ci·phy·lac·ti·cal·ly** \-ti-k(ə-)lē\ *adv*

cal·cite \ˈkal-ˌsīt\ *n* : a mineral $CaCO_3$ consisting of calcium carbonate crystallized in hexagonal form and including common limestone, chalk, and marble — **cal·cit·ic** \kal-ˈsit-ik\ *adj*

cal·ci·to·nin \ˌkal-sə-ˈtō-nən\ *n* [*calci-* + [1]*tonic* + *-in*] : THYROCALCITONIN

cal·ci·um \ˈkal-sē-əm\ *n, often attrib* [NL, fr. L *calc-, calx* lime] : a silver-white bivalent metallic element of the alkaline-earth group occurring only in combination — see ELEMENT table

calcium carbide *n* : a usu. dark gray crystalline compound CaC_2 used esp. for the generation of acetylene and for making calcium cyanamide

calcium carbonate *n* : a compound $CaCO_3$ found in nature as calcite and aragonite and in plant ashes, bones, and shells and used in making lime and portland cement

calcium chloride *n* : a white deliquescent salt $CaCl_2$ used in its anhydrous state as a drying and dehumidifying agent and in a hydrated state for controlling dust and ice on roads

calcium cyanamide *n* : a compound $CaCN_2$ used as a fertilizer and a weed killer and as a source of other nitrogen compounds

calcium hypochlorite *n* : a white powder $CaCl_2O_2$ used esp. as a bleaching agent and disinfectant

calcium light *n* : LIMELIGHT 1a, 1b

calcium phosphate *n* : any of various phosphates of calcium: as **a** : the phosphate $CaH_4P_2O_8$ used as a fertilizer and in baking powder **b** : the phosphate $CaHPO_4$ used in pharmaceutical preparations and animal feeds **c** : the phosphate $Ca_3P_2O_8$ used as a fertilizer **d** : a naturally occurring phosphate of calcium $Ca_5(F,Cl,OH,\frac{1}{2}CO_3)(PO_4)_3$ that contains other elements or radicals and is the chief constituent of phosphate rock, bones, and teeth

calcium silicate *n* : any of several silicates of calicum; *esp* : either of two Ca_3SiO_5 or Ca_2SiO_4 that are essential constituents of portland cement

calc·spar \ˈkalk-ˌspär\ *n* [part trans. of Sw *kalkspat,* fr. *kalk* lime + *spat* spar] : CALCITE

cal·cu·la·bil·i·ty \ˌkal-kyə-lə-ˈbil-ət-ē\ *n* : the quality of being calculable

cal·cu·la·ble \ˈkal-kyə-lə-bəl\ *adj* **1** : subject to or ascertainable by calculation **2** : that may be counted on : DEPENDABLE <a systematic man, as ~ as the stars> — **cal·cu·la·ble·ness** *n* — **cal·cu·la·bly** \-blē\ *adv*

cal·cu·late \ˈkal-kyə-ˌlāt\ *vb* **-lat·ed; -lat·ing** [L *calculatus,* pp. of *calculare,* fr. *calculus* pebble (used in reckoning), dim. of *calc-, calx* stone used in gaming, lime — more at CHALK] *vt* **1 a** : to determine by mathematical processes **b** : to reckon by exercise of practical judgment : ESTIMATE **c** : to solve or probe the meaning of : figure out <trying to ~ his expression —Hugh MacLennan> **2** : to design or adapt for a purpose **3** *chiefly North* **a** : to judge to be true or probable **b** : INTEND ~ *vi* **1 a** : to make a calculation **b** : to forecast consequences **2** : COUNT, RELY

cal·cu·lat·ed \-ˌlāt-əd\ *adj* **1 a** : worked out by mathematical calculation **b** : engaged in, undertaken, or displayed after reckoning or estimating the statistical probability of success or failure <a ~ risk> **2** : planned or contrived to accomplish a purpose **3** : brought about by deliberate intent **4** : APT, LIKELY — **cal·cu·lat·ed·ly** *adv* — **cal·cu·lat·ed·ness** *n*

cal·cu·lat·ing \-ˌlāt-iŋ\ *adj* **1** : making calculations <~ machine> **2** : marked by prudent and deliberate analysis or by shrewd consideration of self-interest : SCHEMING — **cal·cu·lat·ing·ly** \-iŋ-lē\ *adv*

cal·cu·la·tion \ˌkal-kyə-ˈlā-shən\ *n* **1 a** : the process or an act of calculating **b** : the result of an act of calculating **2 a** : studied care in analyzing or planning **b** : cold heartless planning to promote self-interest <by every effort of subterfuge and ~ —Hilaire Belloc> — **cal·cu·lat·ive** \ˈkal-kyə-ˌlāt-iv\ *adj*

cal·cu·la·tor \ˈkal-kyə-ˌlāt-ər\ *n* **1** : one that calculates: as **a** : a machine for performing mathematical operations mechanically **b** : a person who operates a mechanical calculator **2** : a set or book of tables for facilitating computations

cal·cu·lous \ˈkal-kyə-ləs\ *adj* : caused or characterized by a calculus or calculi

cal·cu·lus \-ləs\ *n, pl* **-li** \-ˌlī, -ˌlē\ *also* **-lus·es** [L, pebble, stone in the bladder or kidney, stone used in reckoning] **1** : a concretion usu. of mineral salts around organic material found esp. in hollow organs or ducts **2** *archaic* : CALCULATION **3 a** : a method of computation or calculation in a special symbolic notation **b** : the mathematical methods comprising differential and integral calculus

calculus of variations : a branch of mathematics dealing with maxima and minima of definite integrals which have an integrand that is a function of independent variables and of dependent variables and their derivatives

cal·de·ra \kal-ˈder-ə, kȯl-, -ˈdir-\ *n* [Sp, lit., caldron, fr. LL *caldaria*] : a crater with a diameter many times that of the volcanic vent formed by collapse of the central part of a volcano or by explosions of extraordinary violence

cal·dron \ˈkȯl-drən\ *n* [ME, alter. of *cauderon,* fr. ONF, dim. of *caudiere,* fr. LL *caldaria,* fr. L, warm bath, fr. fem. of *caldarius* suitable for warming, fr. *calidus* warm, fr. *calēre* to be warm — more at LEE] **1** : a large kettle or boiler **2** : something resembling a boiling caldron <a ~ of intense emotions>

ca·lèche *or* **ca·leche** \kə-ˈlesh, -ˈlash\ *n* [F *calèche* — more at CALASH] **1** : CALASH 1a **2** : a 2-wheeled horse-drawn vehicle with a driver's seat on the splashboard used in Quebec **3** : CALASH 2a

cal·e·fac·to·ry \ˌkal-ə-ˈfak-t(ə-)rē\ *n, pl* **-ries** [ML *calefactorium,* fr. L *calefactus,* pp. of *calefacere* to warm — more at CHAFE] : a monastery room warmed and used as a sitting room

[1]**cal·en·dar** \ˈkal-ən-dər\ *n* [ME *calender,* fr. AF or ML; AF *calender,* fr. ML *kalendarium,* fr. L, moneylender's account book, fr. *kalendae* calends] **1** : a system for fixing the beginning, length, and divisions of the civil year and arranging days and longer divisions of time (as weeks and months) in a definite order — see MONTH table **2** : a tabular register of days according to a system usu. covering one year and referring the days of each month to the days of the week **3** : an orderly list: as **a** : a list of cases to be tried in court **b** : a list of bills or other items reported out of committee for consideration by a legislative assembly **c** : a list of events or activities giving dates and details **4** *Brit* : a university catalog

[2]**calendar** *vt* **-dared; -dar·ing** \-d(ə-)riŋ\ : to enter in a calendar

calendar year *n* **1** : a period of a year beginning and ending with the dates that are conventionally accepted as marking the beginning and end of a numbered year (as January 1 and December 31 in the Gregorian calendar) **2** : a period of time equal in length to that of the year in the calendar conventionally in use (as 365 days in the Gregorian calendar or when a Feb. 29 is included 366 days)

[1]**cal·en·der** \ˈkal-ən-dər\ *vt* **-dered; -der·ing** \-d(ə-)riŋ\ [MF *calandrer,* fr. *calandre* machine for calendering, modif. of Gk *kylindros* cylinder — more at CYLINDER] : to press (as cloth, rubber, or paper) between rollers or plates in order to smooth and glaze or to thin into sheets — **cal·en·der·er** \-dər-ər\ *n*

[2]**calender** *n* : a machine for calendering something

[3]**calender** *n* [Per *qalandar,* fr. Ar, fr. Per *kalandar* uncouth man] : one of a Sufic order of wandering mendicant dervishes

ca·len·dri·cal \kə-ˈlen-dri-kəl, ka-\ *also* **ca·len·dric** \-drik\ *adj* : of, relating to, characteristic of, or used in a calendar

cal·ends \ˈkal-ən(d)z, ˈkāl-\ *n pl but sing or pl in constr* [ME *kalendes,* fr. L *kalendae, calendae*] : the 1st day of the ancient Roman month from which days were counted backward to the ides

ca·len·du·la \kə-ˈlen-jə-lə\ *n* [NL, genus name, fr. ML, fr. L *calendae* calends] : any of a small genus (*Calendula*) of yellow-rayed composite herbs of temperate regions

cal·en·ture \ˈkal-ən-ˌchü(ə)r\ *n* [Sp *calentura,* fr. *calentar* to heat, fr. L *calent-, calens,* prp. of *calēre* to be warm — more at LEE] : a tropical fever caused by exposure to heat

[1]**calf** \'kaf, 'kȧf\ *n, pl* **calves** \'kavz, 'kȧvz\ *also* **calfs** *often attrib* [ME, fr. OE *cealf;* akin to OHG *kalb* calf, ON *kālfi* calf of the leg, L *galla* gallnut] **1 a :** the young of the domestic cow; *also* **:** that of a closely related mammal (as a bison or water buffalo) **b :** the young of various large animals (as the elephant and whale) **2** *pl calfs* **:** the hide of the domestic calf; *esp* **:** CALFSKIN **3 :** an awkward or silly boy or youth **4 :** a small mass of ice set free from a coast glacier or from an iceberg or floe — **calf·like** \'kaf-ˌlīk, 'kȧf-\ *adj* — **in calf :** PREGNANT — used of a cow

[2]**calf** *n, pl* **calves** \'kavz, 'kȧvz\ [ME, fr. ON *kālfi*] **:** the fleshy hinder part of the leg below the knee

calf love *n* **:** PUPPY LOVE

calf's–foot jelly \ˌkavz-ˌfu̇t-, ˌkȧvz-, ˌkafs-, ˌkȧfs-\ *n* **:** jelly made from gelatin obtained by boiling calves' feet

calf·skin \'kaf-ˌskin, 'kȧf-\ *n* **:** leather made of the skin of a calf

Cal·gon \'kal-ˌgän\ *trademark* — used for a water softener that is essentially a complex phosphate of sodium

Cal·i·ban \'kal-ə-ˌban\ *n* **:** a savage and deformed slave in Shakespeare's *The Tempest*

cal·i·ber *or* **cal·i·bre** \'kal-ə-bər, *Brit also* kə-'lē-\ *n* [MF *calibre,* fr. OIt *calibro,* fr. Ar *qālib* shoemaker's last] **1 a :** the diameter of a bullet or other projectile **b :** the diameter of a bore of a gun usu. expressed in modern U.S. and British usage in hundredths or thousandths of an inch and typically written as a decimal fraction <.32 ~> **2 :** the diameter of a round body; *esp* **:** the internal diameter of a hollow cylinder **3 a :** degree of mental capacity or moral quality **b :** degree of excellence or importance ***syn*** see QUALITY

cal·i·brate \'kal-ə-ˌbrāt\ *vt* **-brat·ed; -brat·ing 1 :** to ascertain the caliber of (as a thermometer tube) **2 :** to determine, rectify, or mark the graduations of (as a thermometer tube) **3 :** to standardize (as a measuring instrument) by determining the deviation from a standard so as to ascertain the proper correction factors — **cal·i·bra·tor** \-ˌbrāt-ər\ *n*

cal·i·bra·tion \ˌkal-ə-'brā-shən\ *n* **1 :** the act or process of calibrating **:** the state of being calibrated **2 :** a set of graduations to indicate values or positions — usu. used in pl. <~*s* on a gauge> <~*s* on a radio dial>

ca·li·che \kə-'lē-chē\ *n* [AmerSp, fr. Sp, flake of lime, fr. *cal* lime, fr. L *calx* — more at CHALK] **1 :** the nitrate-bearing gravel or rock of the sodium nitrate deposits of Chile and Peru **2 :** a crust of calcium carbonate that forms on the stony soil of arid regions

cal·i·co \'kal-i-ˌkō\ *n, pl* **-coes** *or* **-cos** [*Calicut,* India] **1 a :** cotton cloth imported from India **b** *Brit* **:** a plain white cotton fabric that is heavier than muslin **c :** any of various cheap cotton fabrics with figured patterns **2 :** a blotched or spotted animal (as a piebald horse) — **calico** *adj*

calico bass *n* **1 :** BLACK CRAPPIE **2 :** KELP BASS

calico bush *n* **:** MOUNTAIN LAUREL

calico printing *n* **:** the process of making fast-color designs on cotton fabrics (as calico)

Calif *abbr* California

Cal·i·for·nia condor \ˌkal-ə-ˌfȯr-nyə-\ *n* [*California,* state of U.S.] **:** a large nearly extinct vulture (*Gymnogyps californianus*) that is related to the condor of So. America and is found in the mountains of southern California

California laurel *n* **:** a Pacific coast tree (*Umbellularia californica*) of the laurel family with evergreen foliage and small umbellate flowers

California poppy *n* **:** any of a genus (*Eschscholtzia*) of herbs of the poppy family; *esp* **:** one (*E. californica*) widely cultivated for its pale yellow to red flowers

California rosebay *n* **:** a usu. pink-flowered rhododendron (*Rhododendron macrophyllum*) of the Pacific coast

Cal·i·for·nio \ˌkal-ə-'fȯr-nē-ˌō\ *n, pl* **-nios** [Sp, fr. *California*] **:** one of the original Spanish colonists of California or their descendants

cal·i·for·ni·um \ˌkal-ə-'fȯr-nē-əm\ *n* [NL, fr. *California,* U.S.] **:** a radioactive element discovered by bombarding curium 242 with alpha particles — see ELEMENT table

ca·lig·i·nous \kə-'lij-ə-nəs\ *adj* [MF or L; MF *caligineux,* fr. L *caliginosus,* fr. *caligin-, caligo* darkness; akin to Gk *kelainos* black — more at COLUMBINE] **:** MISTY, DARK

Ca·li·na·go \ˌkal-ə-'nä-(ˌ)gō\ *n* **:** an Arawakan language of the Lesser Antilles and Central America

cal·i·pash \'kal-ə-ˌpash, ˌkal-ə-'\ *n* **:** a fatty gelatinous dull greenish edible substance next to the upper shell of a turtle

cal·i·pee \'kal-ə-ˌpē, ˌkal-ə-'\ *n* **:** a fatty gelatinous light yellow edible substance attached to the lower shell of a turtle

[1]**cal·i·per** *or* **cal·li·per** \'kal-ə-pər\ *n* [alter. of *caliber*] **1 a :** a measuring instrument with two legs or jaws that can be adjusted to determine thickness, diameter, and distance between surfaces — usu. used in pl. <a pair of ~*s*> **b :** an instrument for measuring diameters (as of logs or trees) consisting of a graduated beam and at right angles to it a fixed arm and a movable arm **c :** a device consisting of two plates lined with a frictional material that press against the sides of a rotating wheel or disk in certain brake systems **2 :** thickness esp. of paper, paperboard, or a tree

calipers 1a: *1* outside, *2* inside

[2]**caliper** *or* **calliper** *vt* **-pered; -per·ing** \-p(ə-)riŋ\ **:** to measure by or as if by calipers

ca·liph *or* **ca·lif** \'kā-ləf, 'kal-əf\ *n* [ME *caliphe,* fr. MF *calife,* fr. Ar *khalīfah* successor] **:** a successor of Muhammad as temporal and spiritual head of Islam — used as a title — **ca·liph·al** \-əl\ *adj*

ca·liph·ate \-ˌāt, -ət\ *n* **:** the office or dominion of a caliph

cal·is·then·ic \ˌkal-əs-'then-ik\ *adj* **:** of or relating to calisthenics

cal·is·then·ics \-iks\ *n pl but sing or pl in constr* [Gk *kalos* beautiful + *sthenos* strength — more at CALLIGRAPHY] **1 :** systematic rhythmic bodily exercises performed usu. without apparatus **2** *usu sing in constr* **:** the art or practice of calisthenics

ca·lix \'kā-liks, 'kal-iks\ *n, pl* **ca·li·ces** \'kā-lə-ˌsēz, 'kal-ə-\ [L *calic-, calix* — more at CHALICE] **:** CUP

[1]**calk** \'kȯk\, **calk·er** \'kȯ-kər\ *var of* CAULK, CAULKER

[2]**calk** \'kȯk\ *n* [prob. alter. of *calkin,* fr. ME *kakun,* fr. MD or ONF; MD *calcoen* horse's hoof, fr. ONF *calcain* heel, fr. L *calcaneum,* fr. *calc-, calx* heel; akin to Gk *kōlon* limb, *skelos* leg] **:** a tapered piece projecting downward on the shoe of a horse to prevent slipping; *also* **:** a similar device worn on the sole of a shoe

[3]**calk** *vt* **1 :** to furnish with calks **2 :** to wound with a calk

[1]**call** \'kȯl\ *vb* [ME *callen,* prob. fr. ON *kalla;* akin to OE *hildecalla* battle herald, OHG *kallōn* to talk loudly, OSlav *glasŭ* voice] *vi* **1 a :** to speak in a loud distinct voice so as to be heard at a distance **:** SHOUT <~ for help> **b :** to make a request or demand <~ for an investigation> **c** *of an animal* **:** to utter a characteristic note or cry **d :** to get or try to get into communication by telephone — often used with *up* **e :** to make a demand in card games (as for a particular card or for a show of hands) **f :** to give the calls for a square dance **2** *Scot* **:** DRIVE **3 :** to make a brief visit <~*ed* to pay his respects> <~*ed* on a friend> ~ *vt* **1 a** (1) **:** to utter in a loud distinct voice — often used with *out* <~ out a number> (2) **:** to announce or read loudly or authoritatively <~ the roll> <~ off a row of figures> **b** (1) **:** to command or request to come or be present <~*ed* to testify> (2) **:** to cause to come **:** BRING <~*s* to mind an old saying> **c :** to summon to a particular activity, employment, or office <was ~*ed* to active duty> **d :** to invite or command to meet **:** CONVOKE <~ a meeting> **e :** to rouse from sleep or summon to get up **f** (1) **:** to give the order for **:** bring into action <~ a strike against the company> (2) **:** to manage (as an offensive game) by giving the signals or orders <that catcher ~*s* a good game> **g** (1) **:** to make a demand in bridge for (a card or suit) (2) **:** to require (a player) to show the hand in poker by making an equal bet (3) **:** to challenge to make good on a statement (4) **:** to charge with or censure for an offense <deserves to be ~*ed* on that> **h :** to attract (as game) by imitating the characteristic cry **i :** to halt (as a baseball game) because of unsuitable conditions **j :** to rule on the status of (as a pitched ball or a player's action) <~ balls and strikes> <~ a base runner safe> **k :** to give the calls for (a square dance) — often used with *off* **l** (1) **:** to get or try to get in communication with by telephone (2) **:** to deliver (a message) by telephone (3) **:** to make a signal to in order to transmit a message <~ the flagship> **m :** SUSPEND <time was ~*ed* while the field was cleared> **n** (1) **:** to demand payment of esp. by formal notice <~ a loan> (2) **:** to demand presentation of (a bond issue) for redemption **2 a :** to speak of or address by a specified name **:** give a name to <~ her Kitty> **b** (1) **:** to regard or characterize as of a certain kind **:** CONSIDER <can hardly be ~*ed* generous> (2) **:** to estimate or consider for purposes of an estimate or for convenience <~ it an even dollar> **c** (1) **:** to describe correctly in advance of or without knowledge of the event **:** PREDICT (2) **:** to name or specify in advance <~ the toss of a coin> ***syn*** see SUMMON — **call a spade a spade :** to speak frankly — **call for 1 :** to call (as at one's house) to get <I'll *call for* you after dinner> **2a :** to require as necessary or appropriate <lifting the box *called for* all her strength> **b :** to make necessary **3a :** to give an order for **:** DIRECT <legislation *calling for* the establishment of new schools> **b :** to provide for <the design *calls for* three windows> — **call forth :** to bring into being or action **:** ELICIT <these events *call forth* great emotions> — **call in question :** to cast doubt upon — **call it a day :** to stop at least for the present whatever one has been doing — **call it quits :** to call it a day — **call names :** to address or speak of a person or thing contemptuously or offensively — **call on 1 :** to call upon **2 :** to cause (as a student) to recite <the teacher always *called on* her first> — **call one's bluff :** to challenge and expose an empty pretense or threat — **call one's shot :** to predict the result of a shot in a game or sport — **call the shots :** to be in charge or control **:** determine the policy or procedure — **call the tune :** to call the shots — **call to account :** to hold responsible **:** REPRIMAND <*called to account* for violation of the rules> — **call to the colors :** to summon for active military duty — **call upon 1 :** REQUIRE, OBLIGE <may be *called upon* to do several jobs> **2 :** to make a demand on **:** depend on <universities are *called upon* to produce trained men>

[2]**call** *n* **1 a :** an act of calling with the voice **:** SHOUT **b :** an imitation of the cry of a bird or other animal made to attract it **c :** an instrument used for calling <a duck ~> **d :** the cry of an animal (as a bird) **2 a :** a request or command to come or assemble **b :** a summons or signal on a drum, bugle, or pipe **c :** admission to the bar as a barrister **d :** an invitation to become the minister of a church or to accept a professional appointment **e :** a divine vocation or strong inner prompting to a particular course of action **f :** a summoning of actors to rehearsal <the ~ is for 11 o'clock> **g :** the attraction or appeal of a particular activity, condition, or place <the ~ of the wild> **h :** an order specifying the number of men to be inducted into the armed services during a specified period **i :** the selection of a play in football **3 a :** DEMAND, CLAIM **b :** NEED, JUSTIFICATION **c :** a demand for payment of money **d :** an option to buy a specified amount of a security (as stock) or commodity (as wheat) at a fixed price at or within a specified time — compare [2]PUT 2 **e :** an instance of asking for something **:** REQUEST <many ~*s* for Christmas stories> **4 :** ROLL CALL **5 :** a short usu. formal visit **6 :** the name or thing called <the ~ was heads> **7 :** the act of calling in a card game **8 :** the act of calling on the telephone **9 :** the score at any given time in a tennis game **10 :** a direction or a succession of directions for a square dance rhythmically called to the dancers **11 :** a decision or ruling made by an official of a sports contest ***syn*** see VISIT — **at call** *or* **on call 1a :** available for use **:** at the service of <thousands of men *at* his *call*> **b :** ready to respond to a

summons or command <a doctor *on call*> **2 :** subject to demand for payment or return without previous notice <money lent *at call*> — **within call :** within hearing or reach of a summons : subject to summons

cal·la \'kal-ə\ *n* [NL, genus name, modif. of Gk *kallaia* rooster's wattles] **1 :** a house or greenhouse plant (*Zantedeschia aethiopica*) of the arum family with a white showy spathe and yellow spadix **2 :** a plant resembling the calla

call·able \'kȯ-lə-bəl\ *adj* **:** capable of being called; *specif* **:** subject to a demand for presentation for payment <~ bond>

cal·lant \'kal-ənt, 'käl-\ *or* **cal·lan** \-ən\ *n* [D or ONF; D *kalant* customer, fellow, fr. ONF *calland* customer, fr. L *calent-, calens,* prp. of *calēre* to be warm — more at LEE] *chiefly Scot* **:** BOY, LAD

call·back \'kȯl-ˌbak\ *n* **:** a recall by a manufacturer of a recently sold product (as an automobile) for correction of a defect

call–board \-ˌbō(ə)rd, -ˌbȯ(ə)rd\ *n* **:** a bulletin board

call box *n* **1** *Brit* **:** a public telephone booth **2 :** a telephone usu. located on the side of a road for reporting emergencies (as fires or automobile breakdowns)

call·boy \'kȯl-ˌbȯi\ *n* **1 :** BELLHOP, PAGE **2 :** a boy who summons actors to go on stage

call down *vt* **1 :** to cause or entreat to descend <*call down* a blessing on the crops> **2 :** REPRIMAND <*called* me *down* for coming in late>

called strike *n* **:** a pitched baseball not struck at by the batter that passes through the strike zone

¹cal·ler \'kal-ər\ *adj* [ME *callour*] **1** *Scot* **:** FRESH **2** *Scot* **:** COOL <blessed by the ~ upland air —R. P. Kennedy>

²call·er \'kȯ-lər\ *n* **:** one that calls

cal·let \'kal-ət\ *n* [perh. fr. MF *caillette* frivolous person, fr. *Caillette fl* 1500 F court fool] *chiefly Scot* **:** PROSTITUTE

call girl *n* **:** a prostitute with whom an appointment may be made by telephone

call house *n* **:** a house or apartment where call girls may be procured

cal·lig·ra·pher \kə-'lig-rə-fər\ *n* **1 :** one that writes a beautiful hand **2 :** PENMAN <a fair ~> **3 :** a professional copyist or engrosser

cal·lig·ra·phist \-fəst\ *n* **:** CALLIGRAPHER

cal·lig·ra·phy \-fē\ *n* [F or Gk; F *calligraphie,* fr. Gk *kalligraphia,* fr. *kalli-* beautiful (fr. *kallos* beauty) + *-graphia* -graphy; akin to Gk *kalos* beautiful, Skt *kalya* healthy] **1 a :** beautiful or elegant handwriting — compare CACOGRAPHY **b :** the art of producing such writing **2 :** PENMANSHIP — **cal·li·graph·ic** \ˌkal-ə-'graf-ik\ *adj* — **cal·li·graph·i·cal·ly** \-i-k(ə-)lē\ *adv*

call in *vt* **1 :** to order to return or to be returned: as **a :** to withdraw from an advanced position <*call in* the outposts> **b :** to withdraw from circulation <*call in* bank notes and issue new ones> **2 :** to summon to one's aid or for consultation <*call in* a mediator to settle the dispute> ~ *vi* **:** to communicate with a person by telephone — **call in sick :** to report by telephone that one will be absent because of illness

call·ing \'kȯ-liŋ\ *n* **1 :** a strong inner impulse toward a particular course of action esp. when accompanied by conviction of divine influence **2 :** the vocation or profession in which one customarily engages **3 :** the characteristic cry of a female cat during heat; *also* **:** the period of heat

calling card *n* **:** VISITING CARD

cal·li·ope \kə-'lī-ə-(ˌ)pē, *in sense 2 also* 'kal-ē-ˌōp\ *n* [L, fr. Gk *Kalliopē*] **1** *cap* **:** the Greek Muse of heroic poetry **2 :** a keyboard musical instrument resembling an organ and consisting of a series of whistles sounded by steam or compressed air

cal·li·op·sis \ˌkal-ē-'äp-səs\ *n* [NL, fr. Gk *kalli-* + *opsis* appearance — more at OPTIC] **:** COREOPSIS — used esp. of annual forms

Cal·lis·to \kə-'lis-(ˌ)tō\ *n* [*Callisto,* Gk nymph] **1 :** a nymph loved by Zeus, changed into a she-bear by Hera, and subsequently changed into the Great Bear constellation **2 :** the so-called fourth but really fifth satellite of Jupiter

cal·li·thump \'kal-ə-ˌthəmp\ *n* [back-formation fr. *callithumpian,* adj., alter. of E dial. *gallithumpian* disturber of order at elections in 18th cent.] **:** a noisy boisterous parade — **cal·li·thump·ian** \ˌkal-ə-'thəm-pē-ən\ *adj*

call letters *n pl* **:** CALL SIGN

call loan *n* **:** a loan payable on demand of either party

call number *n* **:** a combination of characters assigned to a library book to indicate its place on a shelf

call off *vt* **1 :** to draw away **:** DIVERT <her attention was *called off* by a new arrival> **2 :** to give up **:** CANCEL <*call* the trip *off*>

call of nature : the need to expel body wastes

cal·lose \'kal-ˌōs, -ˌōz\ *n* [L *callosus* callous] **:** a carbohydrate component of plant cell walls

cal·los·i·ty \ka-'läs-ət-ē, kə-\ *n, pl* **-ties 1 :** the quality or state of being callous: as **a :** marked or abnormal hardness and thickness **b :** lack of feeling or capacity for emotion **2 :** CALLUS 1

¹cal·lous \'kal-əs\ *adj* [MF *calleux,* fr. L *callosus,* fr. *callum, callus* callous skin; akin to Skt *kiṇa* callosity] **1 a :** being hardened and thickened **b :** having calluses **2 a :** feeling no emotion **b :** feeling no sympathy for others — **cal·lous·ly** *adv* — **cal·lous·ness** *n*

²callous *vt* **:** to make callous

call out *vt* **1 :** to summon into action <*call out* troops> **2 :** to challenge to a duel **3 :** to order on strike <*call out* the steelworkers>

cal·low \'kal-(ˌ)ō, -ə(-w)\ *adj* [ME *calu* bald, fr. OE; akin to OHG *kalo* bald] **1** *of a bird* **:** not yet having enough feathers to fly **2 :** lacking adult sophistication **:** IMMATURE <~ youth> ***syn*** see RUDE — **cal·low·ness** \'kal-ō-nəs, -ə-nəs\ *n*

call sign *n* **:** the combination of identifying letters or letters and numbers assigned to an operator, office, activity, or station for use in communication (as in the address of a message sent by radio)

call slip *n* **:** a form filled out by a library patron for a desired book

call to quarters : a bugle call usu. shortly before taps that summons soldiers to their quarters

call–up \'kȯ-ˌləp\ *n* **:** an order to report for military service

call up \(')kȯ-'ləp\ *vt* **1 :** to bring to mind **:** EVOKE **2 :** to summon before an authority **3 :** to summon together or collect (as for a united effort) <*call up* all his forces for the attack> **4 :** to summon for active military duty **5 :** to bring forward for consideration or action <*call up* a bill for senate approval>

¹cal·lus \'kal-əs\ *n* [L] **1 :** a thickening of or a hard thickened area on skin or bark **2 :** a mass of exudate and connective tissue that forms around a break in a bone and is converted into bone in the healing of the break **3 :** soft tissue that forms over a wounded or cut plant surface

²callus *vi* **:** to form callus ~ *vt* **:** to cause callus to form on

¹calm \'käm, 'kälm\ *n* [ME *calme,* fr. MF, fr. OIt *calma,* fr. LL *cauma* heat, fr. Gk *kauma,* fr. *kaiein* to burn — more at CAUSTIC] **1 a :** a period or condition of freedom from storms, high winds, or rough activity of water **b :** complete absence of wind or presence of wind having a speed no greater than one mile per hour **2 :** a state of repose and freedom from turmoil or agitation

²calm *adj* **1 :** marked by calm **:** STILL <a ~ sea> **2 :** free from agitation, excitement, or disturbance <a ~ manner> — **calm·ly** *adv* — **calm·ness** *n*

syn CALM, TRANQUIL, SERENE, PLACID, PEACEFUL *shared meaning element* **:** quiet and free from whatever disturbs or hurts ***ant*** stormy, agitated

³calm *vi* **:** to become calm ~ *vt* **:** to make calm

calm·ative \'käm-ət-iv, 'käl-mət-\ *n or adj* [³*calm* + *-ative* (as in *sedative*)] **:** SEDATIVE

cal·o·mel \'kal-ə-məl, -ˌmel\ *n* [prob. fr. (assumed) NL *calomelas,* fr. Gk *kalos* beautiful + *melas* black — more at CALLIGRAPHY, MULLET] **:** a white tasteless compound Hg_2Cl_2 used in medicine esp. as a purgative and fungicide — called also *mercurous chloride*

¹ca·lo·ric \kə-'lȯr-ik, -'lōr-, -'lär-; 'kal-ə-rik\ *n* [F *calorique,* fr. L *calor*] **1 :** a supposed form of matter formerly held responsible for the phenomena of heat and combustion **2** *archaic* **:** HEAT

²caloric *adj* **1 :** of or relating to heat **2 :** of or relating to calories — **ca·lo·ri·cal·ly** \kə-'lȯr-i-k(ə-)lē, -'lōr-, -'lär-\ *adv*

cal·o·rie *also* **cal·o·ry** \'kal-(ə-)rē\ *n, pl* **-ries** [F *calorie,* fr. L *calor* heat, fr. *calēre* to be warm — more at LEE] **1 a :** the amount of heat required at a pressure of one atmosphere to raise the temperature of one gram of water one degree centigrade — called also *gram calorie, small calorie;* abbr. *cal* **b :** the amount of heat required to raise the temperature of one kilogram of water one degree centigrade **:** 1000 gram calories or 3.968 Btu — called also *kilogram calorie, large calorie;* abbr. *Cal* **2 a :** a unit equivalent to the large calorie expressing heat-producing or energy-producing value in food when oxidized in the body **b :** an amount of food having an energy-producing value of one large calorie

cal·o·rif·ic \ˌkal-ə-'rif-ik\ *adj* [F or L; F *calorifique,* fr. L *calorificus,* fr. *calor*] **1 :** CALORIC **2 :** of or relating to the production of heat

cal·o·rim·e·ter \ˌkal-ə-'rim-ət-ər\ *n* [ISV, fr. L *calor*] **:** any of several apparatuses for measuring quantities of absorbed or evolved heat or for determining specific heats — **ca·lo·ri·met·ric** \ˌkal-ə-rə-'me-trik; kə-ˌlȯr-ə-, -ˌlōr, -ˌlär-\ *adj* — **ca·lo·ri·met·ri·cal·ly** \-tri-k(ə-)lē\ *adv* — **cal·o·rim·e·try** \ˌkal-ə-'rim-ə-trē\ *n*

ca·lotte \kə-'lät\ *n* [F] **:** SKULLCAP; *esp* **:** ZUCCHETTO

ca·loy·er \kə-'lȯi(-ə)r, 'kal-ə-yər\ *n* [It & F; F *caloyer,* fr. obs. It *caloiero,* fr. MGk *kalogēros* venerable, fr. *kalos* beautiful + *gēras* old age] **:** a monk of the Eastern Church

cal·pac *or* **cal·pack** \'kal-ˌpak, kal-'\ *n* [Turk *kalpak*] **:** a high-crowned cap worn in Turkey, Iran, and neighboring countries

calque \'kalk\ *n* [F, lit., copy, fr. *calquer* to trace, fr. It *calcare* to trample, trace, fr. L, to trample — more at CAULK] **:** LOAN TRANSLATION

cal·trop \'kal-trəp, 'kȯl-\ *also* **cal·throp** \-thrəp\ *n* [ME *calketrappe* star thistle, fr. OE *calcatrippe,* fr. ML *calcatrippa*] **1 a** *pl but sing in constr* **:** STAR THISTLE 1 **b :** PUNCTURE VINE; *also* **:** any of various related herbs (genera *Tribulus* and *Kallstroemia*) **c :** WATER CHESTNUT 1 **2 :** a device with four metal points so arranged that when any three are on the ground the fourth projects upward as a hazard to the hoofs of horses or to pneumatic tires

caltrop 2

cal·trops \-trəps\ *n pl but sing or pl in constr* **:** a widely naturalized spiny European weed (*Centaurea calcitrapa*) with purple flowers

cal·u·met \'kal-yə-ˌmet, -mət\ *n* [AmerF, fr. F dial., straw, fr. LL *calamellus,* dim. of L *calamus* reed — more at CALAMUS] **:** a highly ornamented ceremonial pipe of the American Indians

ca·lum·ni·ate \kə-'ləm-nē-ˌāt\ *vt* **-at·ed; -at·ing 1 :** to utter maliciously false statements, charges, or imputations about **2 :** to injure the reputation of by calumny ***syn*** see MALIGN ***ant*** eulogize, vindicate — **ca·lum·ni·a·tion** \-ˌləm-nē-'ā-shən\ *n* — **ca·lum·ni·a·tor** \-'ləm-nē-ˌāt-ər\ *n*

ca·lum·ni·ous \kə-'ləm-nē-əs\ *adj* **:** constituting or marked by calumny **:** SLANDEROUS — **ca·lum·ni·ous·ly** *adv*

cal·um·ny \'kal-əm-nē *also* -yəm-\ *n, pl,* **-nies** [MF & L; MF *calomnie,* fr. L *calumnia,* fr. *calvi* to deceive; akin to OE *hōl* calumny, Gk *kēlein* to beguile] **1 :** the act of uttering false charges or misrepresentations maliciously calculated to damage another's reputation <a circle of false friends spending their time in *calumnies*> **2 :** a misrepresentation intended to blacken another's reputation

cal·va·dos \ˌkal-və-'dōs\ *n, often cap* [F, fr. *Calvados,* Normandy, France] **:** a dry brown apple brandy

cal·var·i·um \kal-'var-ē-əm, -'ver-\ *n, pl* **-ia** \-ē-ə\ [NL, fr. L *calvaria* skull, fr. *calvus* bald; akin to Skt *ati kulva* completely bald] **:** a skull lacking the lower jaw or lower jaw and facial portion

cal·va·ry \'kalv-(ə-)rē\ *n, pl* **-ries** [*Calvary,* the hill near Jerusalem where Jesus was crucified] **1 :** an open-air representation of the crucifixion of Christ **2 :** an experience of usu. intense mental suffering

Calvary cross *n* **:** a Latin cross usually mounted on three steps — see CROSS illustration

calve \'kav, 'kȧv\ *vb* **calved; calv·ing** [ME *calven,* fr. OE *cealfian,* fr. *cealf* calf] *vi* **1 :** to give birth to a calf; *also* **:** to produce offspring **2** *of an ice mass* **:** to separate or break so that a part becomes detached ~ *vt* **1 :** to produce by birth **2 :** *of an ice mass* **:** to let become detached

calves *pl of* CALF

Cal·vin·ism \ˈkal-və-ˌniz-əm\ *n* [John *Calvin*] **:** the theological system of Calvin and his followers marked by strong emphasis on the sovereignty of God and esp. by the doctrine of predestination — **Cal·vin·ist** \-və-nəst\ *n or adj* — **Cal·vin·is·tic** \ˌkal-və-ˈnis-tik\ *adj* — **Cal·vin·is·ti·cal·ly** \-ti-k(ə-)lē\ *adv*

calx \ˈkalks\ *n, pl* **calx·es** *or* **cal·ces** \ˈkal-ˌsēz\ [ME *cals,* fr. L *calx* lime — more at CHALK] **:** the crumbly residue left when a metal or other mineral has been subjected to calcination or combustion

ca·lyc·u·late \kə-ˈlik-yə-ˌlāt, -lət\ *adj* **:** having a calyculus

ca·lyc·u·lus \-ləs\ *n, pl* **-li** \-ˌlī, -ˌlē\ [NL, modif. of E *calicle*] **:** a small cup-shaped structure (as a taste bud)

[1]**ca·lyp·so** \kə-ˈlip-(ˌ)sō\ *n* [L, fr. Gk *Kalypsō*] **1** *cap* **:** a sea nymph in Homer's *Odyssey* who kept Odysseus seven years on the island of Ogygia **2** *pl* **calypsos** [NL, genus name, prob. fr. L] **:** a bulbous bog orchid (genus *Cytherea*) of northern regions bearing a single white flower variegated with purple, pink, and yellow

[2]**calypso** *n, pl* **-sos** *also* **-soes** [prob. fr. *Calypso*] **:** an improvised ballad usu. satirizing current events in a style originating in the West Indies — **ca·lyp·so·ni·an** \kə-ˌlip-ˈsō-nē-ən, ˌkal-(ˌ)ip-\ *n or adj*

ca·lyp·tra \kə-ˈlip-trə\ *n* [NL, fr. Gk *kalyptra* veil, fr. *kalyptein* to cover — more at HELL] **1 :** the archegonium of a liverwort or moss; *esp* **:** one forming a membranous hood over the capsule in a moss **2 :** a covering (as the calyx of a California poppy) of a flower or fruit suggestive of a cap or hood **3 :** ROOT CAP — **ca·lyp·trate** \kə-ˈlip-ˌtrāt, ˈkal-əp-\ *adj*

ca·lyx \ˈkā-liks, *also* ˈkal-iks\ *n, pl* **ca·lyx·es** *or* **ca·ly·ces** \ˈkā-lə-ˌsēz *also* ˈkal-ə-\ [L *calyc-, calyx,* fr. Gk *kalyx* — more at CHALICE] **1 :** the external usu. green or leafy part of a flower consisting of sepals **2 :** a cuplike animal structure — **ca·ly·ce·al** \ˌkā-lə-ˈsē-əl, ˌkal-ə-\ *adj*

cam \ˈkam\ *n* [perh. fr. F *came,* fr. G *kamm,* lit., comb, fr. OHG *kamb*] **:** a rotating or sliding piece that imparts motion to a roller moving against its edge or to a pin free to move in a groove on its face or that receives motion from such a roller or pin

ca·ma·ra·de·rie \ˌkam-(ə-)ˈrad-ə-rē, ˌkäm-(ə-)ˈräd-\ *n* [F, fr. *camarade* comrade] **:** friendly good-fellowship among comrades

cam·a·ril·la \ˌkam-ə-ˈril-ə, -ˈrē-(y)ə\ *n* [Sp, lit., small room] **:** a group of unofficial often secret and scheming advisers; *also* **:** CABAL

cam·as *or* **cam·ass** \ˈkam-əs\ *n* [Chinook Jargon *kamass*] **:** any of a genus (*Camassia*) of plants of the lily family of the western U.S. with edible bulbs — compare DEATH CAMAS

[1]**cam·ber** \ˈkam-bər\ *vb* **cam·bered; cam·ber·ing** \-b(ə-)riŋ\ [F *cambrer,* fr. MF *cambre* curved, fr. L *camur* — more at CHAMBER] *vi* **:** to curve upward in the middle ~ *vt* **1 :** to arch slightly **2 :** to impart camber to

[2]**camber** *n* **1 :** a slight convexity, arching, or curvature (as of a beam, deck, or road) **2 :** the convexity of the curve of an airfoil from the leading edge to the trailing edge **3 :** a setting of the wheels of an automotive vehicle closer together at the bottom than at the top

cam·bi·um \ˈkam-bē-əm\ *n, pl* **-bi·ums** *or* **-bia** \-bē-ə\ [NL, fr. ML, exchange, fr. L *cambiare* to exchange — more at CHANGE] **:** a thin formative layer between the xylem and phloem of most vascular plants that gives rise to new cells and is responsible for secondary growth — **cam·bi·al** \-bē-əl\ *adj*

Cam·bo·di·an \kam-ˈbōd-ē-ən\ *n* **1 :** a native or inhabitant of Cambodia **2 :** KHMER 2 — **Cambodian** *adj*

Cam·bri·an \ˈkam-brē-ən\ *adj* [ML *Cambria* Wales, fr. W *Cymry* Welshmen] **1 :** WELSH **2 :** of, relating to, or being the earliest geologic period of the Paleozoic era or the corresponding system of rocks marked by fossils of every great animal type except the vertebrate and by scarcely recognizable plant fossils — **Cambrian** *n*

cam·bric \ˈkām-brik\ *n* [obs. Flem *Kameryk* Cambrai, city of France] **1 :** a fine thin white linen fabric **2 :** a cotton fabric that resembles cambric

cambric tea *n* **:** a hot drink of water, milk, sugar, and often a small amount of tea

Cambs *abbr* Cambridgeshire

[1]**came** *past of* COME

[2]**came** \ˈkām\ *n* [origin unknown] **:** a slender grooved lead rod used to hold together panes of glass esp. in a stained-glass window

cam·el \ˈkam-əl\ *n* [ME, fr. OE & ONF, fr. L *camelus,* fr. Gk *kamēlos,* of Sem origin; akin to Heb & Phoenician *gāmāl* camel] **1 :** either of two large ruminant mammals used as draft and saddle animals in desert regions esp. of Africa and Asia: **a :** the Arabian camel (*Camelus dromedarius*) with a single large hump on the back **b :** the camel (*C. bactrianus*) with two humps — called also *Bactrian camel* **2 :** a watertight structure used esp. to lift submerged ships **3 :** a variable color averaging a light yellowish brown

camels 1: *1* Arabian, *2* Bactrian

cam·el·back \ˈkam-əl-ˌbak\ *n* **1 :** the back of a camel **2 :** a steam locomotive with the cab astride the boiler **3 :** an uncured compound chiefly of reclaimed or synthetic rubber used for retreading or recapping pneumatic tires

cam·el·eer \ˌkam-ə-ˈli(ə)r\ *n* **:** a camel driver

ca·mel·lia *also* **ca·me·lia** \kə-ˈmēl-yə\ *n* [NL *Camellia,* genus name, fr. *Camellus* (Georg Josef Kamel †1706 Moravian Jesuit missionary)] **:** any of several shrubs or trees (genus *Camellia*) of the tea family; *esp* **:** an ornamental greenhouse shrub (*C. japonica*) with glossy evergreen leaves and showy roselike flowers

ca·mel·o·pard \kə-ˈmel-ə-ˌpärd\ *n* [LL *camelopardus,* alter. of L *camelopardalis,* fr. Gk *kamēlopardalis,* fr. *kamēlos* + *pardalis* leopard] **1 :** GIRAFFE **2** *cap* **:** CAMELOPARDALIS

Ca·mel·o·par·da·lis \kə-ˌmel-ə-ˈpärd-ᵊl-əs\ *n* [L (gen. *Camelopardalis*), camelopard] **:** a northern constellation between Cassiopeia and Ursa Major

Cam·e·lot \ˈkam-ə-ˌlät\ *n* **1 :** the site of King Arthur's palace and court in Arthurian legend **2 :** a time, place, or atmosphere of idyllic happiness

camel's hair *n* **1 :** the hair of the camel or a substitute for it (as hair from squirrels' tails) **2 :** cloth made of camel's hair or a mixture of camel's hair and wool usu. light tan and of soft silky texture

Cam·em·bert \ˈkam-əm-ˌbe(ə)r\ *n* [F, fr. *Camembert,* Normandy, France] **:** a soft surface-ripened cheese with a thin grayish white rind and a yellow interior

cam·eo \ˈkam-ē-ˌō\ *n, pl* **-eos** [It] **1 a :** a gem carved in relief; *esp* **:** a small piece of sculpture on a stone or shell cut in relief in one layer with another contrasting layer serving as background **b :** a small medallion with a profiled head in relief **2 :** a carving or sculpture made in the manner of a cameo **3 :** a usu. brief literary or filmic piece that brings into delicate or sharp relief the character of a person, place, or event **4 :** a small theatrical role (as in television) performed by a well-known actor and often limited to a single scene — **cameo** *adj* — **cameo** *vt*

cam·era \ˈkam(ə-)rə\ *n* [LL, room — more at CHAMBER] **1 :** the treasury department of the papal curia **2 a :** CAMERA OBSCURA **b :** a lightproof box fitted with a lens through the aperture of which the image of an object is recorded on a light-sensitive material **c :** the part of a television transmitting apparatus in which the image to be televised is formed for conversion into electrical impulses — **on camera :** before a live televising camera

cam·er·a·lism \ˈkam-(ə-)rə-ˌliz-əm\ *n* [G *kameralismus,* fr. ML *cameralis* of the royal treasury, fr. *camera* royal treasury, fr. LL, chamber] **:** the mercantilism of a group of 18th century German public administrators emphasizing economic policies designed to strengthen the power of the ruler — **cam·er·a·list** \-ləst\ *n*

camera lu·ci·da \ˌkam-(ə-)rə-ˈlü-səd-ə\ *n* [NL, lit., light chamber] **:** an instrument that by means of a prism or mirrors and often a microscope causes a virtual image of an object to appear as if projected upon a plane surface so that an outline may be traced

cam·era·man \ˈkam-(ə-)rə-ˌman, -mən\ *n* **1 :** one who operates a camera **2 :** one who sells photographic equipment

camera ob·scu·ra \ˌkam-(ə-)rə-əb-ˈskyůr-ə\ *n* [NL, lit., dark chamber] **:** a darkened enclosure having an aperture usu. provided with a lens through which light from external objects enters to form an image of the objects on the opposite surface

cam·er·len·go \ˌkam-ər-ˈleŋ-(ˌ)gō\ *n, pl* **-gos** [It *camarlingo*] **:** a cardinal who heads the Apostolic Camera

ca·mion \kȧ-myōⁿ\ *n* [F] **:** MOTORTRUCK; *also* **:** BUS

cam·i·sa·do \ˌkam-ə-ˈsäd-(ˌ)ō, -ˈsād-\ *n, pl* **-does** [prob. fr. obs. Sp. *camisada*] *archaic* **:** an attack by night

ca·mise \kə-ˈmēz, -ˈmēs\ *n* [Ar *qamīṣ,* fr. LL *camisia*] **:** a light loose long-sleeved shirt, gown, or tunic

cam·i·sole \ˈkam-ə-ˌsōl\ *n* [F, prob. fr. OProv *camisolla,* dim. of *camisa* shirt, fr. LL *camisia*] **1 :** a short negligee jacket for women **2 :** a short sleeveless undergarment for women

cam·let \ˈkam-lət\ *n* [ME *cameloit,* fr. MF *camelot,* fr. Ar *hamlat* woolen plush] **1 a :** a medieval Asian fabric of camel's hair or angora wool **b :** a European fabric of silk and wool **c :** a fine lustrous woolen **2 :** a garment made of camlet

camomile *var of* CHAMOMILE

ca·mor·ra \kə-ˈmȯr-ə, -ˈmär-\ *n* [It] **:** a group of persons united for dishonest or dishonorable ends; *esp* **:** a secret organization formed about 1820 at Naples, Italy

ca·mor·ris·ta \ˌkäm-ō-ˈrē-stə\ *n, pl* **-ti** \-(ˌ)stē\ [It, fr. *camorra* + *-ista* -ist] **:** a member of a camorra

[1]**cam·ou·flage** \ˈkam-ə-ˌfläzh, -ˌfläj\ *n* [F, fr. *camoufler* to disguise, fr. It *camuffare*] **1 :** the disguising esp. of military equipment or installations with paint, nets, or foliage; *also* **:** the disguise so applied **2 a :** concealment by means of disguise **b :** behavior or artifice designed to deceive or hide — **cam·ou·flag·ic** \ˌkam-ə-ˈfläzh-ik, -ˈfläj-\ *adj*

[2]**camouflage** *vb* **-flaged; -flag·ing** *vt* **:** to conceal or disguise by camouflage ~ *vi* **:** to practice camouflage — **cam·ou·flage·able** \ˈkam-ə-ˌfläzh-ə-bəl, -ˈfläj-\ *adj*

[1]**camp** \ˈkamp\ *n, often attrib* [MF, prob. fr. ONF or OProv, fr. L *campus* plain, field; akin to OHG *hamf* crippled, Gk *kampē* bend] **1 a :** ground on which temporary shelters (as tents) are erected **b :** a group of shelters erected on such ground **c :** a temporary shelter (as a cabin or tent) **d :** an open-air location where one or more persons camp **e :** a settlement newly sprung up in a lumbering or mining region **2 a :** a body of persons encamped **b** (1) **:** a group or body of persons; *esp* **:** a group engaged in promoting or defending a theory, doctrine, or position <liberal and

conservative ~*s*> (2) : an ideological position **3** : military service or life

²**camp** *vi* **1** : to pitch or occupy a camp **2** : to live temporarily in a camp or outdoors — often used with *out* **3** : to take up one's quarters : LODGE **4** : to take up one's position : settle down ~ *vt* : to put into a camp; *also* : ACCOMMODATE

³**camp** *n* [origin unknown] **1** : HOMOSEXUAL **2** : exaggerated effeminate mannerisms exhibited esp. by homosexuals **3** : something so outrageously artificial, affected, inappropriate, or out-of-date as to be considered amusing — **camp** *adj* — **camp·i·ly** \-pə-lē\ *adv* — **camp·i·ness** \-pē-nəs\ *n* — **campy** \ˈkam-pē\ *adj*

⁴**camp** *vi* : to engage in camp : exhibit the qualities of camp <he . . . was ~*ing*, hands on hips, with a quick eye to notice every man who passed by —R. M. McAlmon>

¹**cam·paign** \(ˈ)kam-ˈpān\ *n* [F *campagne*, prob. fr. It *campagna* level country, campaign, fr. LL *campania* level country, fr. L, the level country around Naples] **1** : a connected series of military operations forming a distinct phase of a war **2** : a connected series of operations designed to bring about a particular result <election ~>

²**campaign** *vi* : to go on, engage in, or conduct a campaign — **cam·paign·er** *n*

campaign ribbon *n* : a narrow ribbon-covered bar or a strip of ribbon whose distinctive coloring indicates a military campaign in which the wearer has taken part

cam·pa·nile \ˌkam-pə-ˈnē-lē, *esp of U.S. structures also* -ˈnē(ə)l\ *n*, *pl* **-ni·les** *or* **-ni·li** \-ˈnē-lē\ [It, fr. *campana* bell, fr. LL] : a usu. freestanding bell tower

cam·pa·nol·o·gist \ˌkam-pə-ˈnäl-ə-jəst\ *n* : one that practices or is skilled in campanology

cam·pa·nol·o·gy \-jē\ *n* [NL *campanologia*, fr. LL *campana* + NL *-o-* + *-logia* -logy] : the art of bell ringing

cam·pan·u·la \kam-ˈpan-yə-lə\ *n* [NL, dim. of LL *campana*] : BELLFLOWER

cam·pan·u·late \-lət, -ˌlāt\ *adj* [NL *campanula* bell-shaped part, dim. of LL *campana*] : shaped like a bell

Camp·bell·ite \ˈkam-(b)ə-ˌlīt\ *n* [Alexander *Campbell* †1866 Am preacher] : DISCIPLE 2 — often taken to be offensive

camp·craft \ˈkamp-ˌkraft\ *n* : skill and practice in the activities relating to camping

camp·er \ˈkam-pər\ *n* **1** : one that camps **2** : a portable dwelling (as a specially equipped trailer or automotive vehicle) for use during casual travel and camping

camp·er·ship \-ˌship\ *n* [*camper* + *ship* (as in *scholarship*)] : a grant that enables a youngster to attend a summer camp

cam·pe·si·no \ˌkam-pə-ˈsē-(ˌ)nō\ *n*, *pl* **-nos** [Sp, fr. *campo* field, country, fr. L *campus* field — more at CAMP] : a native of a Latin-American rural area; *esp* : a Latin-American Indian farmer or farm laborer

cam·pes·tral \kam-ˈpes-trəl\ *adj* [L *campestr-, campester*, fr. *campus*] : of or relating to fields or open country : RURAL

camp fire girl *n* [fr. *Camp Fire Girls*, Inc.] : a member of a national organization of girls from 7 to 18

camp follower *n* **1** : a civilian who follows a military unit to attend or exploit military personnel; *specif* : PROSTITUTE **2** : a disciple or follower who is not of the main body of members or adherents; *esp* : a politician who joins the party or movement solely for personal gain

camp·ground \ˈkamp-ˌgraůnd\ *n* : the area or place (as a field or grove) used for a camp, for camping, or for a camp meeting

cam·phene \ˈkam-ˌfēn\ *n* : any of several terpenes related to camphor; *esp* : a colorless crystalline terpene $C_{10}H_{16}$ used in insecticides

cam·phine *or* **cam·phene** \ˈkam-ˌfēn\ *n* [ISV, fr. *camphor*] : an explosive mixture of turpentine and alcohol formerly used as an illuminant

cam·phor \ˈkam(p)-fər\ *n* [ME *caumfre*, fr. AF, fr. ML *camphora*, fr. Ar *kāfūr*, fr. Malay *kāpūr*] : a tough gummy volatile fragrant crystalline compound $C_{10}H_{16}O$ obtained esp. from the wood and bark of the camphor tree and used as a carminative and stimulant in medicine, as a plasticizer, and as an insect repellent; *also* : any of several similar compounds (as some terpene alcohols and ketones) — **cam·pho·ra·ceous** \ˌkam(p)-fə-ˈrā-shəs\ *adj* — **cam·phor·ic** \kam-ˈfȯr-ik, -ˈfär-\ *adj*

cam·phor·ate \ˈkam(p)-fə-ˌrāt\ *vt* **-at·ed; -at·ing** : to impregnate or treat with camphor

camphor tree *n* : a large evergreen tree (*Cinnamomum camphora*) of the laurel family grown in most warm countries

cam·pi·on \ˈkam-pē-ən\ *n* [prob. fr. obs. *campion* (champion)] : any of various plants (genera *Lychnis* and *Silene*) of the pink family: as **a** : a European crimson-flowered plant (*L. coronaria*) **b** : an herb (*S. cucubalus*) with white flowers

camp meeting *n* : a series of evangelistic meetings usu. held outdoors or in a tent or wooden structure and attended by families who often camp nearby

cam·po \ˈkam-(ˌ)pō, ˈkäm-\ *n*, *pl* **campos** [AmerSp, fr. Sp, field, fr. L *campus*] : a grassland plain in So. America with scattered perennial herbs

campong *var of* KAMPONG

camp·o·ree \ˌkam-pə-ˈrē\ *n* [*camp* + *jamboree*] : a gathering of boy scouts or girl scouts from a given geographic area

camp–out \ˈkam-ˌpaůt\ *n* : an occasion on which a group camps out

camp·site \ˈkamp-ˌsīt\ *n* : a place suitable for or used as the site of a camp

camp·stool \-ˌstül\ *n* : a small portable backless folding stool

cam·pus \ˈkam-pəs\ *n* [L, plain — more at CAMP] : the grounds and buildings of a university, college, or school; *also* : the grassy area in the central part of the grounds

cam·py·lot·ro·pous \ˌkam-pi-ˈlä-trə-pəs\ *adj* [Gk *kampylos* bent + ISV *-tropous*; akin to Gk *kampē* bend — more at CAMP] : having the ovule curved

cam·shaft \ˈkam-ˌshaft\ *n* : a shaft to which a cam is fastened or of which a cam forms an integral part

cam wheel *n* : a wheel set or shaped to act as a cam

¹**can** \kən, (ˌ)kan *sometimes* kᵊŋ\ *vb, past* **could** \kəd, (ˈ)kůd\; *pres sing & pl* **can** [ME (1st & 3d sing. pres. indic.), fr. OE; akin to OHG *kan* (1st & 3d sing. pres. indic.) know, am able, OE *cnāwan* to know — more at KNOW] *vt* **1** *obs* : KNOW, UNDERSTAND **2** : to be able to do, make, or accomplish ~ *vi, archaic* : to have knowledge or skill ~ *verbal auxiliary* **1 a** : know how to <he ~ read> **b** : be physically or mentally able to <he ~ lift 200 pounds> **c** : may perhaps <do you think he ~ still be living> **d** : be permitted by conscience or feeling to <~ hardly blame him> **e** : be made possible or probable by circumstances to <he ~ hardly have meant that> **f** : be inherently able or designed to <everything that money ~ buy> **g** : be logically or axiologically able to <2 + 2 ~ also be written 3 + 1> **h** : be enabled by law, agreement, or custom to **2** : have permission to — used interchangeably with *may* <you ~ go now if you like>

²**can** \ˈkan\ *n* [ME *canne*, fr. OE; akin to OHG *channa*] **1** : a usu. cylindrical receptacle: **a** : a vessel for holding liquids; *specif* : a drinking vessel **b** : a typically cylindrical metal receptacle usu. with an open top, often with a removable cover, and sometimes with a spout or side handles (as for holding milk, oil, coffee, tobacco, ashes, or garbage) **c** : a container (as of tinplate) in which perishable foods or other products are hermetically sealed for preservation until use **d** : a jar for packing or preserving fruit or vegetables **2** *slang* : JAIL **3** : TOILET **4** : BUTTOCKS **5** : DEPTH CHARGE **6** : DESTROYER 2 **7** *slang* : an ounce of marijuana — **can·ful** \ˈkan-ˌfůl\ *adj* — **in the can** *of a film or videotape* : completed and ready for release

³**can** \ˈkan\ *vt* **canned; can·ning** **1 a** : to put in a can : preserve by sealing in airtight cans or jars **b** : to hit (a golf ball) into the cup **2** *slang* : to expel from school : discharge from employment **3** *slang* : to put a stop or end to <~ that racket —Nathaniel Burt> **4** : to record on discs or tape <they *canned* the music for the broadcast> — **can·ner** *n*

⁴**can** *abbr* **1** canceled; cancellation **2** cannon **3** canto

Can *or* **Canad** *abbr* Canada; Canadian

Ca·naan·ite \ˈkā-nə-ˌnīt\ *n* [Gk *Kananitēs*, fr. *Kanaan* Canaan] : a member of a Semitic people inhabiting ancient Palestine and Phoenicia from about 3000 B.C. — **Canaanite** *adj*

Can·a·da balsam \ˌkan-əd-ə-\ *n* [*Canada*, country in No. America] : a viscid yellowish to greenish oleoresin exudate of the balsam fir (*Abies balsamea*) that solidifies to a transparent mass and is used as a transparent cement esp. in microscopy

Canada goose *n* : the common wild goose (*Branta canadensis*) of No. America that is chiefly gray and brownish with black head and neck and a white patch running from the sides of the head under the throat

Canada goose

Canada lynx *n* : LYNX c

Canada thistle *n* : a European thistle (*Cirsium arvense*) that is a naturalized weed in No. America

Ca·na·di·an \kə-ˈnād-ē-ən\ *n* : a native or inhabitant of Canada — **Canadian** *adj*

Ca·na·di·an bacon \kə-ˌnād-ē-ən-\ *n* : bacon cut from the loin of a pig

Canadian football *n* : a game resembling both American football and rugby that is played on a turfed field between two teams of 12 players each

Canadian French *n* : the language of the French Canadians

ca·naille \kə-ˈnī, -ˈnā(ə)l\ *n* [F, fr. It *canaglia*, fr. *cane* dog, fr. L *canis* — more at HOUND] **1** : RABBLE, RIFFRAFF **2** : PROLETARIAN

¹**ca·nal** \kə-ˈnal\ *n* [ME, fr. L *canalis* pipe, channel, fr. *canna* reed — more at CANE] **1** : CHANNEL, WATERCOURSE **2** : a tubular anatomical passage or channel : DUCT **3** : an artificial waterway for navigation or for draining or irrigating land **4** : any of various faint narrow markings on the planet Mars

²**canal** *vt* **-nalled** *or* **-naled; -nal·ling** *or* **-nal·ing** : to construct a canal through or across

ca·nal·boat \kə-ˈnal-ˌbōt\ *n* : a boat for use on a canal

can·a·lic·u·late \ˌkan-ᵊl-ˈik-yə-lət, -ˌlāt\ *adj* : grooved or channeled longitudinally <a ~ leafstalk>

can·a·lic·u·lus \-yə-ləs\ *n*, *pl* **-li** \-ˌlī, -ˌlē\ [L, dim. of *canalis*] : a minute canal in a bodily structure

can·a·li·za·tion \ˌkan-ᵊl-ə-ˈzā-shən\ *n* **1** : an act or instance of canalizing **2** : a system of channels

can·a·lize \ˈkan-ᵊl-ˌīz\ *vb* **-lized; -liz·ing** *vt* **1 a** : to provide with a canal or channel **b** : to make into or similar to a canal **2** : to provide with an outlet; *esp* : to direct into preferred channels ~ *vi* **1** : to flow in or into a channel **2** : to establish new channels

can·a·pé \ˈkan-ə-pē, -ˌpā\ *n* [F, lit., sofa, fr. ML *canopeum*, *canapeum* mosquito net — more at CANOPY] : an appetizer consisting of a piece of bread or toast or a cracker topped with a savory spread (as caviar or cheese) — compare HORS D'OEUVRE

ca·nard \kə-ˈnärd *also* -ˈnär\ *n* [F, lit., duck, fr. MF *vendre des canards à moitié* to cheat, lit., to half-sell ducks] : a false or unfounded report or story; *esp* : a fabricated report

ca·nary \kə-ˈne(ə)r-ē\ *n*, *pl* **ca·nar·ies** [MF *canarie*, fr. OSp *canario*, fr. *Islas Canarias* Canary islands] **1** : a lively 16th century court dance **2** : a Canary islands usu. sweet wine similar to Madeira **3 a** : a small finch (*Serinus canarius*) of the Canary islands that is usu. greenish to yellow and is kept as a cage bird and singer **b** : any of various small birds largely yellow in color **4** [fr. his singing] *slang* : INFORMER 2

canary seed *n* **1** : seed of a Canary island grass (*Phalaris canariensis*) used as food for cage birds **2** : seed of a common plantain (*Plantago major*)

canary yellow *n* : a light to a moderate or vivid yellow

ca·nas·ta \kə-ˈnas-tə\ *n* [Sp, lit., basket] **1** : a form of rummy using two full decks in which players or partnerships try to meld groups of three or more cards of the same rank and score bonuses for 7-card melds **2 :** a meld of seven cards of the same rank in canasta

canc *abbr* canceled

can·can \ˈkan-ˌkan\ *n* [F] **:** a woman's dance of French origin characterized by high kicking usu. while holding up the front of a full ruffled skirt

[1]can·cel \ˈkan(t)-səl\ *vb* **-celed** *or* **-celled; -cel·ing** *or* **-cel·ling** \-s(ə-)liŋ\ [ME *cancellen,* fr. MF *canceller,* fr. LL *cancellare,* fr. L, to make like a lattice, fr. *cancelli* (pl.), dim. of *cancer* lattice, alter. of *carcer* prison] *vt* **1 a :** to mark or strike out for deletion **b :** OMIT, DELETE **2 a :** to destroy the force, effectiveness, or validity of **:** ANNUL <~ a magazine subscription> **b :** to bring to nothingness **:** DESTROY **c :** to match in force or effect **:** OFFSET — often used with *out* <his irritability ~*ed* out his natural kindness — Osbert Sitwell> **d :** to call off usu. without expectation of conducting or performing at a later time <~ a football game> **3 a :** to remove (a common divisor) from numerator and denominator **b :** to remove (equivalents) on opposite sides of an equation or account **4 :** to deface (a postage or revenue stamp) esp. with a set of parallel lines so as to invalidate for reuse ~ *vi* **:** to neutralize each other's strength or effect **:** COUNTERBALANCE ***syn*** see ERASE — **can·cel·able** *or* **can·cel·la·ble** \-s(ə-)lə-bəl\ *adj* — **can·cel·er** *or* **can·cel·ler** \-s(ə)lər\ *n*

[2]cancel *n* **1 :** CANCELLATION **2 a :** a deleted part or passage **b :** a passage or page from which something has been deleted **c** (1) **:** a leaf containing deleted matter (2) **:** a new leaf or slip substituted for matter already printed

can·cel·late \kan-ˈsel-ət, ˈkan(t)-sə-ˌlāt\ *adj* [L *cancellatus,* pp. of *cancellare*] **:** RETICULATE, CHAMBERED <~ leaves>; *specif* **:** CANCELLOUS

can·cel·la·tion *also* **can·cel·ation** \ˌkan(t)-sə-ˈlā-shən\ *n* **1 :** the act or an instance of canceling **2 :** a released accommodation **3 :** a mark made to cancel something (as a postage stamp)

can·cel·lous \kan-ˈsel-əs, ˈkan(t)-sə-ləs\ *adj* [NL *cancelli* intersecting osseous plates and bars in cancellous bone, fr. L, lattice] *of bone* **:** having a porous structure

can·cer \ˈkan(t)-sər\ *n* [ME, fr. L (gen. *Cancri*), lit., crab; akin to Gk *karkinos* crab, cancer] **1** *cap* **a :** a northern zodiacal constellation between Gemini and Leo **b** (1) **:** the 4th sign of the zodiac in astrology — see ZODIAC table (2) **:** one born under this sign **2** [L, crab, cancer] **a :** a malignant tumor of potentially unlimited growth that expands locally by invasion and systemically by metastasis **b :** an abnormal state marked by such tumors **3 :** a source of evil or anguish <the ~ of hidden resentment — *Irish Digest*> **4 a :** an enlarged tumorlike growth **b :** a disease marked by such growths — **can·cer·ous** \ˈkan(t)s-(ə-)rəs\ *adj* — **can·cer·ous·ly** *adv*

can·cha \ˈkän-(ˌ)chä\ *n* [Sp, yard, court, fr. Quechua, yard] **:** a jai alai court

can·croid \ˈkaŋ-ˌkrȯid\ *adj* [L *cancr-, cancer* crab, cancer] **1 :** resembling a crab **2 :** resembling a cancer

can·de·la \kan-ˈdē-lə, -ˈdel-ə\ *n* [L, candle] **:** CANDLE 3

can·de·la·bra \ˌkan-də-ˈläb-rə, -ˈlab-, -ˈlāb-\ *n* **:** CANDELABRUM

can·de·la·brum \-rəm\ *n, pl* **-bra** \-rə\ *also* **-brums** [L, fr. *candela*] **:** a branched candlestick or lamp with several lights

candelabrum

can·dent \ˈkan-dənt\ *adj* [L *candent-, candens,* prp. of *candēre*] **:** heated to whiteness **:** GLOWING

can·des·cence \kan-ˈdes-ᵊn(t)s\ *n* **:** a candescent state **:** glowing whiteness

can·des·cent \-ᵊnt\ *adj* [L *candescent-, candescens,* prp. of *candescere* incho. of *candēre*] **:** glowing or dazzling esp. from great heat

C and F *abbr* cost and freight

can·did \ˈkan-dəd\ *adj* [F & L; F *candide,* fr. L *candidus* bright, white, fr. *candēre* to shine, glow; akin to LGk *kandaros* ember] **1 :** WHITE <~ flames> **2 :** free from bias, prejudice, or malice **:** FAIR <a ~ observer> **3 a :** marked by honest sincere expression **b :** indicating or suggesting sincere honesty and absence of deception **c :** disposed to criticize severely **:** BLUNT **4 :** relating to photography of subjects acting naturally or spontaneously without being posed <~ picture> ***syn*** see FRANK ***ant*** evasive — **can·did·ly** *adv* — **can·did·ness** *n*

can·di·da \ˈkan-dəd-ə\ *n* [NL, genus name, fr. L, fem. of *candidus,* white] **:** any of a genus (*Candida*) of parasitic imperfect fungi that resemble yeasts, produce small amounts of mycelium, and include the causative agent of thrush

can·di·da·cy \ˈkan-(d)əd-ə-sē\ *n, pl* **-cies :** the state of being a candidate

can·di·date \ˈkan-(d)ə-ˌdāt, -(d)əd-ət\ *n* [L *candidatus,* fr. *candidatus* clothed in white, fr. *candidus* white; fr. the white toga worn by candidates for office in ancient Rome] **:** one that aspires to or is nominated or qualified for an office, membership, or award

can·di·da·ture \ˈkan-(d)əd-ə-ˌchu̇(ə)r, -chər\ *n, chiefly Brit* **:** CANDIDACY

candid camera *n* **1 :** a usu. small camera equipped with a fast lens and used for taking informal photographs of unposed subjects often without their knowledge **2 :** a miniature camera

can·di·di·a·sis \ˌkan-də-ˈdī-ə-səs\ *n, pl* **-a·ses** \-ˌsēz\ **:** infection with a disease caused by a candida

can·died \ˈkan-dēd\ *adj* **1 :** encrusted or coated with sugar **2 :** baked with sugar or syrup until translucent

[1]can·dle \ˈkan-dᵊl\ *n* [ME *candel,* fr. OE, fr. L *candela,* fr. *candēre*] **1 :** a usu. long slender cylindrical mass of tallow or wax containing a loosely twisted linen or cotton wick that is burned to give light **2 :** something resembling a candle in shape or use <a sulfur ~ for fumigating> **3 :** a unit of luminous intensity equal to one sixtieth of the luminous intensity of one square centimeter of a blackbody surface at the solidification temperature of platinum — called also *candela, new candle*

[2]candle *vt* **can·dled; can·dling** \ˈkan-(d)liŋ, -dᵊl-iŋ\ **:** to examine by holding between the eye and a light; *esp* **:** to test (eggs) in this way for staleness, blood clots, fertility, and growth — **can·dler** \-(d)lər, -dᵊl-ər\ *n*

can·dle·ber·ry \ˈkan-dᵊl-ˌber-ē\ *n* **1 a :** CANDLENUT **b :** WAX MYRTLE **2 :** the fruit of a candleberry

can·dle·fish \-ˌfish\ *n* **1 :** EULACHON **2 :** SABLEFISH

can·dle–foot \-ˈfu̇t\ *n* **:** FOOTCANDLE

can·dle·hold·er \-ˌhōl-dər\ *n* **:** CANDLESTICK

can·dle·light \ˈkan-dᵊl-(l)īt\ *n* **1 a :** the light of a candle **b :** a soft artificial light **2 :** the time for lighting up **:** TWILIGHT

can·dle·light·er \-ər\ *n* **1 :** a long-handled implement with a taper and a snuffer that is used for the ceremonial lighting and extinguishing of candles **2 :** one who lights the candles for a ceremony (as a wedding)

Can·dle·mas \ˈkan-dᵊl-məs\ *n* [ME *candelmasse,* fr. OE *candelmæsse,* fr. *candel* + *mæsse* mass, feast; fr. the candles blessed and carried in celebration of the feast] **:** February 2 observed as a church festival in commemoration of the presentation of Christ in the temple and the purification of the Virgin Mary

can·dle·nut \-ˌnət\ *n* **:** the oily seed of a tropical tree (*Aleurites moluccana*) of the spurge family used locally to make candles and commercially as a source of oil; *also* **:** this tree

can·dle·pin \-ˌpin\ *n* **1 :** a slender bowling pin tapering toward top and bottom **2** *pl but sing in constr* **:** a bowling game using candlepins and a smaller ball than that used in tenpins

can·dle·pow·er \-ˌpau̇(-ə)r\ *n* **:** luminous intensity expressed in candles

can·dle·snuff·er \-ˌsnəf-ər\ *n* **:** an implement for snuffing candles that consists of a small hollow cone attached to a handle

can·dle·stick \-ˌstik\ *n* **:** a holder with a socket for a candle

can·dle·wick \-ˌwik\ *n* **1 :** the wick of a candle **2 :** a soft cotton embroidery yarn; *also* **:** embroidery made with this yarn usu. in tufts

can·dle·wood \-ˌwu̇d\ *n* **1 :** any of several trees or shrubs (as ocotillo) chiefly of resinous character **2 :** slivers of resinous wood burned for light

can·dor \ˈkan-dər, -ˌdȯ(ə)r\ *n* [F&L; F *candeur,* fr. L *candor,* fr. *candēre* — more at CANDID] **1 a :** WHITENESS, BRILLIANCE **b** *obs* **:** unstained purity **2 :** freedom from prejudice or malice **:** FAIRNESS **3** *archaic* **:** KINDLINESS **4 :** unreserved, honest, or sincere expression **:** FORTHRIGHTNESS

can·dour \ˈkan-dər\ *chiefly Brit var of* CANDOR

C and W *abbr* country and western

[1]can·dy \ˈkan-dē\ *n, pl* **candies** [ME *sugre candy,* part trans. of MF *sucre candi,* part trans. of OIt *zucchero candi,* fr. *zucchero* sugar + Ar *qandī* candied, fr. *qand* cane sugar] **1 :** crystallized sugar formed by boiling down sugar syrup **2 a :** a confection made of sugar often with flavoring and filling **b :** a piece of such confection — **candy** *adj*

[2]candy *vb* **can·died; can·dy·ing** *vt* **1 :** to encrust in or coat with sugar often by cooking to a thicker consistency in a heavy syrup **2 :** to make attractive **:** SWEETEN **3 :** to crystallize into sugar ~ *vi* **:** to become coated or encrusted with sugar crystals **:** become crystallized into sugar

candy strip·er \-ˌstrī-pər\ *n* [fr. the striped uniform worn suggesting the stripes on some sticks of candy] **:** a teenage volunteer nurse's aide

can·dy·tuft \ˈkan-dē-ˌtəft\ *n* [*Candy* (now *Candia*) Crete, Greek island + E *tuft*] **:** any of a genus (*Iberis*) of plants of the mustard family cultivated for their white, pink, or purple flowers

[1]cane \ˈkān\ *n* [ME, fr MF, fr. OProv *cana,* fr. L *canna,* fr. Gk *kanna,* of Sem origin; akin to Ar *qanāh* hollow stick, reed] **1 a** (1) **:** a hollow or pithy and usu. slender and flexible jointed stem (as of a reed) (2) **:** any of various slender woody stems; *esp* **:** an elongated flowering or fruiting stem (as of a rose) usu. arising directly from the ground **b :** any of various tall woody grasses or reeds: as (1) **:** any of a genus (*Arundinaria*) of coarse grasses (2) **:** SUGARCANE (3) **:** SORGHUM **2 :** cane dressed for use: as **a :** a cane walking stick; *broadly* **:** WALKING STICK **b :** a cane or rod for flogging **c :** RATTAN; *esp* **:** split rattan for wickerwork or basketry

[2]cane *vt* **caned; can·ing 1 :** to beat with a cane **2 :** to weave or furnish with cane <~ the seat of a chair>

cane·brake \ˈkān-ˌbrāk\ *n* **:** a thicket of cane

can·er \ˈkā-nər\ *n* **:** one that weaves cane seats and backs of chairs

ca·nes·cent \kə-ˈnes-ᵊnt, ka-\ *adj* [L *canescent-, canescens,* prp. of *canescere,* incho. of *canēre* to be gray, be white, fr. *canus* white, hoary — more at HARE] **:** growing white, whitish, or hoary; *esp* **:** having a fine grayish white pubescence <~ leaves>

cane sugar *n* **:** sugar from sugarcane

cane·ware \ˈkān-ˌwa(ə)r, -ˌwe(ə)r\ *n* [fr. its color] **:** a buff or yellowish stoneware

ca·nic·o·la fever \kə-ˌnik-ə-lə-\ *n* [NL *canicola* (specific epithet of *Leptospira canicola*) fr. L *canis* dog + *-cola* inhabitant — more at HOUND, -COLOUS] **:** an acute disease in man and dogs characterized by gastroenteritis and mild jaundice and caused by a spirochete (*Leptospira canicola*)

Ca·nic·u·la \kə-ˈnik-yə-lə\ *n* [L, dim. of *canis*] **:** SIRIUS

ca·nic·u·lar \kə-ˈnik-yə-lər\ *adj* **1 :** of or relating to the Dog Star or its rising **2 :** of or relating to the dog days

[1]ca·nine \ˈkā-ˌnīn\ *adj* [L *caninus,* fr. *canis* dog — more at HOUND] **1 :** of or relating to dogs or to the family (Canidae) including the dogs, wolves, jackals, and foxes **2 :** of, relating to, or resembling a dog

[2]**canine** *n* **1 :** a conical pointed tooth; *esp* **:** one situated between the lateral incisor and the first premolar — see TOOTH illustration **2 :** DOG

Ca·nis Ma·jor \ˌkā-nə-ˈsmā-jər, ˌkan-ə-\ *n* [L (gen. *Canis Majoris*), lit., greater dog] **:** a constellation to the southeast of Orion containing the Dog Star

Canis Mi·nor \-ˈsmī-nər\ *n* [L, (gen. *Canis Minoris*), lit., lesser dog] **:** a constellation to the east of Orion containing Procyon

can·is·ter *also* **can·nis·ter** \ˈkan-ə-stər\ *n* [L *canistrum* basket, fr. Gk *kanastron*, fr. *kanna* reed — more at CANE] **1 :** a small box or can for holding a dry product **2 :** encased shot for close-range artillery fire **3 :** a light perforated metal box for gas masks that contains material to adsorb, filter, or detoxify poisons and irritants in the air

[1]**can·ker** \ˈkaŋ-kər\ *n* [ME, fr. ONF *cancre*, fr. L *cancer* crab, cancer] **1 a** (1) **:** an erosive or spreading sore (2) *obs* **:** GANGRENE 1 (3) **:** an area of necrosis in a plant **b :** any of various disorders of animals marked by chronic inflammatory changes **2** *archaic* **:** a caterpillar destructive to plants **3** *chiefly dial* **a :** RUST **b :** VERDIGRIS 2 **4 :** a source of corruption or debasement **5** *chiefly dial* **:** a common European wild rose (*Rosa canina*) — **can·ker·ous** \-kaŋ-k(ə-)rəs\ *adj*

[2]**canker** *vb* **can·kered; can·ker·ing** \ˈkaŋ-k(ə-)riŋ\ *vt* **1** *obs* **:** to infect with a spreading sore **2 :** to corrupt with a malignancy of mind or spirit <God help that country, ~*ed* deep by doubt —Archibald MacLeish> ~ *vi* **1 :** to become infested with canker **2 :** to undergo corruption

canker sore *n* **:** a small painful ulcer esp. of the mouth

can·ker·worm \ˈkaŋ-kər-ˌwərm\ *n* **:** any of various insect larvae that injure plants esp. by feeding on buds and foliage

can·na \ˈkan-ə\ *n* [NL, genus name, fr. L, reed — more at CANE] **:** any of a genus (*Canna* of the family Cannaceae) of tropical herbs with simple stems, large leaves, and a terminal raceme of irregular flowers

can·na·bin \ˈkan-ə-bən\ *n* [L *cannabis*] **:** a dark resin from pistillate hemp plants that contains the physiologically active principles of cannabis

can·na·bis \-bəs\ *n* [L, hemp, fr. Gk *kannabis*, fr. the source of OE *hænep* hemp] **:** the dried flowering spikes of the pistillate plants of the hemp — compare HASHISH, MARIJUANA

canned \ˈkand\ *adj* **1 :** sealed in a can or jar **2 :** recorded for mechanical or electronic reproduction; *also* **:** prerecorded for addition to a sound track or a videotape <~ laughter> **3 a :** prepared in identical form for wide or repeated use **:** SYNDICATED <~ editorials> **b :** made trite by overuse **:** HACKNEYED <~ phrases> **4** *slang* **:** DRUNK

can·nel coal \ˌkan-ᵊl-\ *n* [prob. fr. E dial. *cannel* candle, fr. ME *candel*] **:** a bituminous coal containing much volatile matter that burns brightly

can·nery \ˈkan-(ə-)rē\ *n, pl* **-ner·ies :** a factory for the canning of foods

can·ni·bal \ˈkan-ə-bəl\ *n* [NL *Canibalis* Carib, fr. Sp *Caníbal*, fr. Arawakan *Caniba, Carib*, of Cariban origin; akin to Carib *Galibi* Caribs, lit., strong men] **1 :** a human being who eats human flesh **2 :** an animal that devours its own kind — **cannibal** *adj* — **can·ni·bal·ic** \ˌkan-ə-ˈbal-ik\ *adj* — **can·ni·bal·ism** \ˈkan-ə-bə-ˌliz-əm\ *n* — **can·ni·bal·is·tic** \ˌkan-ə-bə-ˈlis-tik\ *adj*

can·ni·bal·ize \ˈkan-ə-bə-ˌlīz\ *vb* **-ized; iz·ing** *vt* **1 :** to dismantle (a machine) for parts to be used as replacements in other machines **2 :** to deprive of parts or men in order to repair or strengthen another unit ~ *vi* **1 :** to practice cannibalism **2 :** to cannibalize one unit for the sake of another of the same kind — **can·ni·bal·iza·tion** \ˌkan-ə-bə-lə-ˈzā-shən\ *n*

can·ni·kin \ˈkan-i-kən\ *n* [prob. fr. obs. D *kanneken*, fr. MD *canneken*, dim. of *canne* can; akin to OE *canne* can] **:** a small can or drinking vessel

[1]**can·non** \ˈkan-ən\ *n, pl* **cannons** *or* **cannon** [MF *canon*, fr. It *cannone*, lit., large tube, aug. of *canna* reed, tube, fr. L, cane, reed — more at CANE] **1** *pl usu* **cannon a :** an artillery piece **:** big gun **b :** a heavy-caliber automatic aircraft gun firing explosive shells **2 :** a smooth round horse bit **3** *or* **can·on :** the projecting part of a bell by which it is hung **:** EAR **4 :** the part of the leg in which the cannon bone is found

[2]**cannon** *vi* **:** to discharge cannon ~ *vt* **:** CANNONADE

[3]**cannon** *n* [alter. of *carom*] *Brit* **:** a carom in billiards and bagatelle

[4]**cannon** *vi, Brit* **:** to carom in billiards ~ *vt, Brit* **:** to carom into

[1]**can·non·ade** \ˌkan-ə-ˈnād\ *n* **:** a heavy fire of artillery

[2]**cannonade** *vb* **-ad·ed; -ad·ing** *vt* **:** to attack with artillery ~ *vi* **:** to deliver artillery fire

[1]**can·non·ball** \ˈkan-ən-ˌbȯl\ *n* **1 a :** a round solid missile made for firing from a cannon **b :** a missile of a solid or hollow shape made for cannon **2 :** a jump into water made with the arms holding the knees tight against the chest **3 :** a hard straight tennis service **4 :** a fast train

[2]**cannonball** *vi* **:** to travel with great speed

cannon bone *n* [F *canon*, lit., cannon] **:** a bone in hoofed mammals that supports the leg from the hock joint to the fetlock

can·non·eer \ˌkan-ə-ˈni(ə)r\ *n* **:** an artillery gunner

cannon fodder *n* **:** soldiers subject to the risk of being wounded or killed by artillery fire

can·non·ry \ˈkan-ən-rē\ *n, pl* **-ries 1 :** CANNONADE **2 :** ARTILLERY

can·not \ˈkan-(ˌ)ät; kə-ˈnät, ka-\ **:** can not — **cannot but :** to be bound to **:** MUST

can·nu·la \ˈkan-yə-lə\ *n, pl* **-las** *or* **-lae** \-ˌlē, -ˌlī\ [NL, fr. L, dim. of *canna* reed — more at CANE] **:** a small tube for insertion into a body cavity or into a duct or vessel

can·nu·lar \ˈkan-yə-lər\ *adj* **:** TUBULAR

can·nu·la·tion \ˌkan-yə-ˈlā-shən\ *n* **:** the act or process of inserting a cannula — **can·nu·late** \ˈkan-yə-ˌlāt\ *vt*

[1]**can·ny** \ˈkan-ē\ *adj* **can·ni·er; -est** [[1]*can*] **1 :** being cautious and shrewd **:** CLEVER **2** *Scot* **a :** FORTUNATE, LUCKY **b :** free from unnatural powers or unfavorable aspects **c :** skilled in the supernatural or occult **3 a** *Scot* **:** CAREFUL, STEADY **b** *Scot* **:** QUIET, SNUG <then ~, in some cozy place, they close the day — Robert Burns> **c** *dial Brit* **:** agreeable to the eyes **:** PLEASANT — **can·ni·ly** \ˈkan-ᵊl-ē\ *adv* — **can·ni·ness** \ˈkan-ē-nəs\ *n*

[2]**canny** *adv, Scot* **:** in a canny manner

[1]**ca·noe** \kə-ˈnü\ *n* [F, fr. NL *canoa*, fr. Sp, fr. Arawakan, of Cariban origin; akin to Galibi *canaoua*] **:** a long light narrow boat with both ends sharp and sides curved that is usu. propelled by hand-driven paddles

[2]**canoe** *vb* **ca·noed; ca·noe·ing** *vi* **1 :** to paddle a canoe **2 :** to go or travel in a canoe ~ *vt* **:** to transport in a canoe — **ca·noe·ist** *n*

can of worms : PANDORA'S BOX

[1]**canon** \ˈkan-ən\ *n* [ME, fr. OE, fr. LL, fr. L, ruler, rule, model, standard, fr. Gk *kanōn*; akin to Gk *kanna* reed — more at CANE] **1 a :** a regulation or dogma decreed by a church council **b :** a provision of canon law **2** [ME, prob. fr. OF, fr. LL, fr. L, model] **:** the most solemn and unvarying part of the Mass including the consecration of the bread and wine **3** [ME, fr. LL, fr. L, standard] **a :** an authoritative list of books accepted as Holy Scripture **b :** the authentic works of a writer **4 a :** an accepted principle or rule **b :** a criterion or standard of judgment **c :** a body of principles, rules, standards, or norms **5** [LGk *kanōn*, fr. Gk, model] **:** a contrapuntal musical composition in two or more voice parts in which the melody is imitated exactly and completely by the successive voices though not always at the same pitch

[2]**canon** *n* [ME *canoun*, fr. AF *canunie*, fr. LL *canonicus* one living under a rule, fr. L, according to rule, fr. Gk *kanonikos*, fr. *kanōn*] **1 :** a clergyman belonging to the chapter or the staff of a cathedral or collegiate church **2 :** CANON REGULAR

ca·ñon \ˈkan-yən\ *var of* CANYON

can·on·ess \ˈkan-ə-nəs\ *n* **1 :** a woman living in community under a religious rule but not under a perpetual vow **2 :** a member of a Roman Catholic congregation of women corresponding to canons regular

ca·non·ic \kə-ˈnän-ik\ *adj* **1 :** CANONICAL **2 :** of or relating to musical canon

ca·non·i·cal \-i-kəl\ *adj* **1 :** of or relating to a canon **2 :** conforming to a general rule **:** ORTHODOX **3 :** accepted as forming the canon of scripture **4 :** of or relating to a clergyman who is a canon **5 :** reduced to the simplest or clearest schema possible <a ~ matrix> — **ca·non·i·cal·ly** \-k(ə-)lē\ *adv*

canonical form *n* **:** the simplest form of a matrix; *specif* **:** the form of a square matrix that has zero elements everywhere except along the principal diagonal

canonical hour *n* **1 :** a time of day canonically appointed for an office of devotion **2 :** one of the daily offices of devotion that compose the Divine Office and include matins with lauds, prime, terce, sext, none, vespers, and compline

ca·non·i·cals \kə-ˈnän-i-kəlz\ *n pl* **:** the vestments prescribed by canon for an officiating clergyman

can·on·ic·i·ty \ˌkan-ə-ˈnis-ət-ē\ *n* **:** the quality or state of being canonical

can·on·ist \ˈkan-ə-nəst\ *n* **:** a specialist in canon law

can·on·ize \ˈkan-ə-ˌnīz\ *vt* **can·on·ized** \-ˌnīzd; *in "Hamlet", usu* kə-ˈnän-ˌīzd\; **can·on·iz·ing** [ME *canonizen*, fr. ML *canonizare*, fr. LL *canon* catalog of saints, fr. L, standard] **1 :** to declare (a deceased person) an officially recognized saint **2 :** to make canonical **3 :** to sanction by ecclesiastical authority **4 :** to attribute authoritative sanction or approval to — **can·on·iza·tion** \ˌkan-ə-nə-ˈzā-shən\ *n*

canon law *n* **:** the usu. codified law governing a church

canon lawyer *n* **:** CANONIST

canon regular *n, pl* **canons regular :** a member of one of several Roman Catholic religious institutes of regular priests living in community under a usu. Augustinian rule

can·on·ry \ˈkan-ən-rē\ *n, pl* **-ries :** the office of a canon; *also* **:** the endowment that financially supports a canon

ca·no·pic jar \kə-ˌnō-pik-, -ˌnäp-ik-\ *n, often cap C* [*Canopus*, Egypt] **:** a jar in which the ancient Egyptians preserved the viscera of a deceased person usu. for burial with the mummy

canopic jars

Ca·no·pus \kə-ˈnō-pəs\ *n* [L, fr. Gk *Kanōpos*] **:** a star of the first magnitude in the constellation Argo not visible north of 37° latitude

[1]**can·o·py** \ˈkan-ə-pē\ *n, pl* **-pies** [ME *canope*, fr. ML *canopeum* mosquito net, fr. L *conopeum*, fr. Gk *kōnōpion*, fr. *kōnōps* mosquito] **1 a :** a cloth covering suspended over a bed **b :** a cover (as of cloth) fixed or carried above a person of high rank or a sacred object **:** BALDACHIN **c :** the uppermost spreading branchy layer of a forest **d :** AWNING, MARQUEE **2 :** an ornamental rooflike structure **3 a :** the transparent enclosure over an airplane cockpit **b :** the lifting or supporting surface of a parachute

[2]**canopy** *vt* **-pied; -py·ing :** to cover with or as if with a canopy

ca·no·rous \kə-ˈnōr-əs, -ˈnȯr-; ˈkan-ə-rəs\ *adj* [L *canorus*, fr. *canor* melody, fr. *canere* to sing — more at CHANT] **:** sounding pleasantly **:** MELODIOUS — **ca·no·rous·ly** *adv* — **ca·no·rous·ness** *n*

canst \kən(t)st, (ˈ)kan(t)st\ *archaic pres 2d sing of* CAN

[1]**cant** \ˈkant\ *adj* [ME, prob. fr. (assumed) MLG *kant*] *dial Eng* **:** LIVELY, LUSTY

[2]**cant** *n* [ME, prob. fr. MD or ONF; MD, edge, corner, fr. ONF, fr. L *canthus, cantus* iron tire, perh. of Celt origin; akin to W *cant* rim; akin to Gk *kanthos* corner of the eye] **1** *obs* **:** CORNER, NICHE **2 :** an external angle (as of a building) **3 :** a log slabbed on one or more sides **4 a :** a sudden thrust producing a bias **b :** the bias so caused **5 :** an oblique or slanting surface **6 :** an inclination from a given line **:** SLOPE

[3]**cant** *vt* **1 :** to give a cant or oblique edge to **:** BEVEL **2 :** to set at an angle **:** tip or tilt up or over **3 :** to turn or throw off or out

by tilting or rotating <~ a rifle> **4** *chiefly Brit* **:** to give a sudden turn or new direction to ~ *vi* **1 :** to pitch to one side **:** LEAN **2 :** SLOPE

[4]**cant** *adj* **1 :** having canted corners or sides **2 :** slanting with respect to a particular straight line

[5]**cant** *vi* [prob. fr. ONF *canter* to tell, lit., to sing, fr. L *cantare* — more at CHANT] **1 :** BEG **2 :** to speak in cant or technical terms **3 :** to talk hypocritically

[6]**cant** *n* **1 :** affected singsong speech **2 a :** the argot of the underworld **b** *obs* **:** the phraseology peculiar to a religious class or sect **c :** JARGON 2 **3 :** a set or stock phrase **4 :** the expression or repetition of conventional, trite, or unconsidered opinions or sentiments; *esp* **:** the insincere use of pious phraseology ***syn*** see DIALECT

can't \(ˈ)kant, (ˈ)kȧnt, (ˈ)känt, *esp South* (ˈ)kānt\ **:** can not

Cant *abbr* **1** Canticle of Canticles **2** Cantonese

Can·tab \ˈkan-ˌtab\ *n* [L *Cantabrigiensis*] **:** CANTABRIGIAN

can·ta·bi·le \kän-ˈtäb-ə-ˌlā, kan-ˈtab-ə-lē\ *adv or adj* [It, fr. LL *cantabilis* worthy to be sung, fr. L *cantare*] **:** in a singing manner — often used as a direction in music

Can·ta·bri·gian \ˌkant-ə-ˈbrij-(ē-)ən\ *n* [ML *Cantabrigia* Cambridge] **1 :** a student or graduate of Cambridge University **2 :** a native or resident of Cambridge, Mass. — **Cantabrigian** *adj*

can·ta·la \kan-ˈtäl-ə\ *n* [origin unknown] **:** a hard fiber produced from the leaves of an agave (*Agave cantala*)

can·ta·loupe \ˈkant-ᵊl-ˌōp\ *n* [*Cantalupo*, former papal villa near Rome, Italy] **1 :** a muskmelon (*Cucumis melo cantalupensis*) with a hard ridged or warty rind and reddish orange flesh **2 :** any of several muskmelons resembling the cantaloupe; *broadly* **:** MUSKMELON

can·tan·ker·ous \kan-ˈtaŋ-k(ə-)rəs, kən-\ *adj* [perh. irreg. fr. obs. *contack* (contention)] **:** ILL-NATURED, QUARRELSOME — **can·tan·ker·ous·ly** *adv* — **can·tan·ker·ous·ness** *n*

can·ta·ta \kən-ˈtät-ə\ *n* [It, fr. L, sung mass, ecclesiastical chant, fr. fem. of *cantatus*, pp. of *cantare*] **:** a usu. sacred choral composition comprising choruses, solos, recitatives, and interludes usu. accompanied by organ, piano, or orchestra

can·ta·trice \ˌkänt-ə-ˈtrē-(ˌ)chä, ˌkä^{n}-tə-ˈtrēs\ *n, pl* **can·ta·trices** \-ˈtrē-(ˌ)chäz, -ˈtrēs(-əz)\ *or* **can·ta·tri·ci** \ˌkänt-ə-ˈtrē-(ˌ)chē\ [It & F, fr. It, fr. LL *cantatric-, cantatrix*, fem. of L *cantator* singer, fr. *cantatus*, pp.] **:** a female singer; *esp* **:** an opera singer

cant dog *n* [[2]*cant*] **:** PEAVEY

can·teen \kan-ˈtēn\ *n* [F *cantine* bottle case, sutler's shop, fr. It *cantina* wine cellar, fr. *canto* corner, fr. L *canthus* iron tire — more at CANT] **1 :** POST EXCHANGE **2 :** a place of refreshment and recreation maintained by civilians for servicemen **3 :** a temporary or mobile restaurant **4 a :** a partitioned chest or box for holding cutlery **b :** a soldier's mess kit **5 :** a usu. cloth-jacketed flask for carrying liquids and esp. water

[1]**can·ter** \ˈkant-ər\ *n* **:** one that uses cant: as **a :** BEGGAR, VAGABOND **b :** a user of professional or religious cant

[2]**can·ter** \ˈkant-ər\ *vb* [short for obs. *canterbury*, fr. *canterbury*, n. (canter), fr. *Canterbury*, England; fr. the supposed gait of pilgrims to Canterbury] *vi* **1 :** to move at or as if at a canter **:** LOPE **2 :** to ride or go on a cantering horse ~ *vt* **:** to cause to go at a canter

[3]**can·ter** *n* **1 :** a 3-beat gait resembling but smoother and slower than the gallop **2 :** a ride at a canter

Can·ter·bury bell \ˌkant-ə(r)-ˌber-ē-\ *n* [*Canterbury*, England] **:** any of several bellflowers (as *Campanula medium*) cultivated for their showy flowers

can·tha·ris \ˈkan(t)-thə-rəs\ *n, pl* **can·thar·i·des** \kan-ˈthar-ə-ˌdēz\ [ME & L; ME *cantharide*, fr. L *cantharid-, cantharis*, fr. Gk *kantharid-, kantharis*] **1 :** SPANISH FLY 1 **2** *pl but sing or pl in constr* **:** a preparation of dried beetles (as Spanish flies) used in medicine as a counterirritant and formerly as an aphrodisiac

cant hook *n* [[2]*cant*] **:** a stout wooden lever used esp. in handling logs that has a blunt usu. metal-clad end and a movable metal arm with a sharp spike

can·thus \ˈkan(t)-thəs\ *n, pl* **can·thi** \ˈkan-ˌthī, -ˌthē\ [LL, fr. Gk *kanthos* — more at CANT] **:** either of the angles formed by the meeting of the upper and lower eyelids

can·ti·cle \ˈkant-i-kəl\ *n* [ME, fr. L *canticulum*, dim. of *canticum* song, fr. *cantus*, pp. of *canere* to sing] **:** SONG; *specif* **:** one of several liturgical songs (as the Magnificat) taken from the Bible

Canticle of Canticles : SONG OF SOLOMON

Canticles *n pl but sing in constr* **:** SONG OF SOLOMON

can·ti·le·ver \ˈkant-ᵊl-ˌē-vər *also* -ˌev-ər\ *n* [perh. fr. [2]*cant* + *-i-* + *lever*] **:** a projecting beam or member supported at only one end: as **a :** a bracket-shaped member supporting a balcony or a cornice **b :** either of the two beams or trusses that project from piers toward each other and that when joined directly or by a suspended connecting member form a span of a cantilever bridge — see BRIDGE illustration

can·til·late \ˈkant-ᵊl-ˌāt\ *vt* **-lat·ed; -lat·ing** [L *cantillatus*, pp. of *cantillare* to sing low, fr. *cantare* to sing — more at CHANT] **:** to recite with usu. improvised musical tones — **can·til·la·tion** \ˌkant-ᵊl-ˈā-shən\ *n*

can·ti·na \kan-ˈtē-nə\ *n* [AmerSp, fr. Sp, canteen, fr. It, wine cellar — more at CANTEEN] **1** *Southwest* **:** a pouch or bag at the pommel of a saddle **2** *Southwest* **:** a small barroom **:** SALOON

cant·ing \ˈkant-iŋ\ *adj* [[5]*cant*] **:** affectedly pious or righteous ***syn*** see HYPOCRITICAL

can·tle \ˈkant-ᵊl\ *n* [ME *cantel*, fr. ONF, dim. of *cant* edge, corner — more at CANT] **1 :** a segment cut off or out of something **:** PART, PORTION **2 :** the upward projecting rear part of a saddle

can·to \ˈkan-(ˌ)tō\ *n, pl* **cantos** [It, fr. L *cantus* song, fr. *cantus*, pp. of *canere* to sing — more at CHANT] **:** one of the major divisions of a long poem

[1]**can·ton** \ˈkant-ᵊn, ˈkan-ˌtän\ *n* [MF, fr. OProv, fr. *cant* edge, corner fr. L *canthus* iron tire — more at CANT] **1** *obs* **:** DIVISION, SECTION **2** [MF, fr. It *cantone*, fr. *canto* corner, fr. L *canthus*] **:** a small territorial division of a country: as **a :** one of the states of the Swiss confederation **b :** a division of a French arrondissement **3 :** the top inner quarter of a flag **4 :** the dexter chief region of a heraldic field — **can·ton·al** \ˈkant-ᵊn-əl, kan-ˈtän-ᵊl\ *adj*

[2]**can·ton** \ˈkant-ᵊn, ˈkan-ˌtän, *in sense 2 usu.* kan-ˈtōn *or* -ˈtän\ *vt* **1 :** to divide into parts; *specif* **:** to divide into cantons **2 :** to allot quarters to (as a body of troops)

can·ton crepe \ˌkan-ˌtän-\ *n, often cap 1st C* [*Canton*, China] **:** a soft thick dress crepe made in plain weave with fine crosswise ribs

Can·ton·ese \ˌkant-ᵊn-ˈēz, -ˈēs\ *n, pl* **Cantonese 1 :** a native or inhabitant of Canton, China **2 :** the dialect of Chinese spoken in and around Canton — **Cantonese** *adj*

can·ton flannel \ˌkan-ˌtän-\ *n, often cap C* [*Canton*, China] **:** FLANNEL 1b

can·ton·ment \kan-ˈtōn-mənt, -ˈtän-\ *n* **1 :** the quartering of troops **2 a :** a group of more or less temporary structures for housing troops **b :** a permanent military station in India

Can·ton ware \ˈkan-ˌtän-\ *n* **:** ceramic ware exported from China esp. during the 18th and 19th centuries by way of Canton and including blue-and-white and enameled porcelain and various ornamented stonewares

can·tor \ˈkant-ər\ *n* [L, singer, fr. *cantus*, pp. of *canere* to sing] **1 :** a choir leader **:** PRECENTOR **2 :** a synagogue official who sings or chants liturgical music and leads the congregation in prayer

can·trip \ˈkan-trəp\ *n* [prob. alter. of *caltrop*] **1** *chiefly Brit* **:** a witch's trick **:** SPELL **2** *chiefly Brit* **:** a mischievous or whimsically eccentric act

can·tus \ˈkant-əs\ *n, pl* **can·tus** \ˈkant-əs, ˈkan-ˌtüs\ **1 :** CANTUS FIRMUS **2 :** the principal melody or voice

can·tus fir·mus \ˌkant-əs-ˈfi(ə)r-məs, -ˈfər-\ *n* [ML, lit., fixed song] **1 :** the plainchant or simple Gregorian melody orig. sung in unison and prescribed as to form and use by ecclesiastical tradition **2 :** a melodic theme or subject; *esp* **:** one for contrapuntal treatment

canty \ˈkant-ē\ *adj* [[1]*cant*] *dial Brit* **:** CHEERFUL, SPRIGHTLY

Ca·nuck \kə-ˈnək\ *n* [prob. alter. of *Canadian*] **1 :** CANADIAN **2** *chiefly Canad* **:** FRENCH CANADIAN **3 :** CANADIAN FRENCH — usu. used disparagingly

[1]**can·vas** *also* **can·vass** \ˈkan-vəs\ *n, often attrib* [ME *canevas*, fr. ONF, fr. (assumed) VL *cannabaceus* hempen, fr. L *cannabis* hemp — more at CANNABIS] **1 :** a firm closely woven cloth usu. of linen, hemp, or cotton used for clothing and sails **2 :** a set of sails **:** SAIL **3 :** a piece of canvas used for a particular purpose **4 :** a military or camping tent; *also* **:** a group of such tents **5 a :** a cloth surface prepared to receive an oil painting; *also* **:** the painting on such a surface **b :** the background, setting, or scope of an historical or fictional account or narrative <the crowded ~ of history> **6 :** a coarse cloth so woven as to form regular meshes for working with the needle **7 :** the floor of a boxing or wrestling ring — **can·vas·like** \-və-ˌslīk\ *adj*

[2]**canvas** *vt* **-vased** *or* **-vassed; -vas·ing** *or* **-vass·ing :** to cover, line, or furnish with canvas

can·vas·back \ˈkan-vəs-ˌbak\ *n* **:** a No. American wild duck (*Aythya valisineria*) characterized esp. by the elongate sloping profile of the bill and head

[1]**can·vass** *also* **can·vas** \ˈkan-vəs\ *vt* **1** *obs* **:** to toss in a canvas sheet in sport or punishment **2 a** *obs* **:** BEAT, TROUNCE **b** *archaic* **:** CASTIGATE **3 a :** to examine in detail; *specif* **:** to examine (votes) officially for authenticity **b :** DISCUSS, DEBATE **4 :** to go through (a district) or go to (persons) in order to solicit orders or political support or to determine opinions or sentiments ~ *vi* **:** to seek orders or votes **:** SOLICIT — **can·vass·er** *also* **can·vas·er** *n*

[2]**canvass** *n* **1 a :** a detailed examination or discussion **b :** a scrutiny esp. of votes **2 :** the act of canvassing <a house-to-house ~>: as **a :** the personal solicitation of votes **b :** a survey to ascertain the probable vote before an election

can·yon \ˈkan-yən\ *n* [AmerSp *cañón*, prob. alter. of obs. Sp *callón*, aug. of *calle* street, fr. L *callis* footpath] **:** a deep narrow valley with precipitous sides often with a stream flowing through it

can·zo·ne \kan-ˈzō-nē, känt-ˈsō-(ˌ)nā\ *n, pl* **-nes** \-nēz, -(ˌ)nāz\ *or* **-ni** \-nē\ [It, fr. L *cantion-, cantio* song, fr. *cantus*, pp. of *canere* to sing — more at CHANT] **1 :** a medieval Italian or Provençal lyric poem **2 :** the melody of a canzone

can·zo·net \ˌkan-zə-ˈnet\ *n* [It *canzonetta*, dim. of *canzone*] **1 :** a part-song resembling but less elaborate than a madrigal **2 :** a light and graceful song

caou·tchouc \ˈkau̇-ˌchu̇k, -ˌchük, -ˌchü\ *n* [F, fr. obs. Sp *cauchuc* (now *caucho*) fr. Quechua] **:** [1]RUBBER 2a

[1]**cap** \ˈkap\ *n, often attrib* [ME *cappe*, fr. OE *cæppe*, fr. LL *cappa* head covering, cloak] **1 :** a head covering; *esp* **:** one for men and boys that has a visor and no brim **2 :** a natural cover or top: as **a :** an overlying rock layer that is usu. hard to penetrate **b** (1) **:** PILEUS (2) **:** CALYPTRA **c :** the top of a bird's head or a patch of distinctively colored feathers in this area **3 a :** something that serves as a cover or protection esp. for a tip, knob, or end <a bottle ~> **b :** a fitting for closing the end of a tube (as a water pipe or electric conduit) **c :** a layer of new rubber fused onto the worn surface of a pneumatic tire **4 a :** a cardinal's biretta **b :** MORTARBOARD **5 :** an overlying or covering structure <the gallery ~ of the old water tower is open to visitors> **6 :** a paper or metal container holding an explosive charge (as for a toy pistol)

[2]**cap** *vt* **capped; cap·ping 1 a :** to provide or protect with a cap **b :** to give a cap to as a symbol of honor or rank **2 :** to form a cap over **:** CROWN <the mountains were *capped* with mist —John Buchan> **3 a :** to follow with something more noticeable or more significant **:** OUTDO **b :** MATCH **c :** CLIMAX

[3]**cap** *abbr* **1** capacity **2** capital **3** capitalize; capitalized

---

ə abut	ᵊ kitten	ər further	a back	ā bake	ä cot, cart
au̇ out	ch chin	e less	ē easy	g gift	i trip	ī life
j joke	ŋ sing	ō flow	ȯ flaw	ȯi coin	th thin	t͟h this
ü loot	u̇ foot	y yet	yü few	yu̇ furious	zh vision

CAP *abbr* Civil Air Patrol
ca·pa·bil·i·ty \ˌkā-pə-ˈbil-ət-ē\ *n, pl* **-ties** **1 :** the quality or state of being capable **2 :** a feature or faculty capable of development **:** POTENTIALITY **3 :** the capacity for an indicated use or development <the ~ of a metal to be fused>
ca·pa·ble \ˈkā-pə-bəl, ˈkāp-bəl\ *adj* [MF or LL; MF *capable,* fr. LL *capabilis,* irreg. fr. L *capere* to take — more at HEAVE] **1 :** SUSCEPTIBLE <a remark ~ of being misunderstood> **2** *obs* **:** COMPREHENSIVE **3 :** having attributes (as physical or mental power) required for performance or accomplishment <a man ~ of intense concentration> **4 :** having traits conducive to or admitting of <this woman is ~ of murder by violence —Robert Graves> **5 :** having general efficiency and ability **6** *obs* **:** having legal right to own, enjoy, or perform ***syn*** see ABLE ***ant*** incapable — **ca·pa·ble·ness** \ˈkā-pə-bəl-nəs\ *n* — **ca·pa·bly** \-pə-blē\ *adv*
ca·pa·cious \kə-ˈpā-shəs\ *adj* [L *capac-, capax* capacious, capable, fr. L *capere*] **:** able to contain a great deal ***syn*** see SPACIOUS — **ca·pa·cious·ly** *adv* — **ca·pa·cious·ness** *n*
ca·pac·i·tance \kə-ˈpas-ət-ən(t)s\ *n* [*capacity*] **1 a :** the property of an electric nonconductor that permits the storage of energy as a result of electric displacement when opposite surfaces of the nonconductor are maintained at a difference of potential **b :** the measure of this property equal to the ratio of the charge on either surface to the potential difference between the surfaces **2 :** a part of a circuit or network that possesses capacitance — **ca·pac·i·tive** \-ˈpas-ət-iv\ *adj* — **ca·pac·i·tive·ly** *adv*
ca·pac·i·tate \kə-ˈpas-ə-ˌtāt\ *vt* **-tat·ed; -tat·ing** *archaic* **:** to make capable **:** QUALIFY
ca·pac·i·tor \kə-ˈpas-ət-ər\ *n* **:** a device giving capacitance and usu. consisting of conducting plates or foils separated by thin layers of dielectric (as air or mica) with the plates on opposite sides of the dielectric layers oppositely charged by a source of voltage and the electrical energy of the charged system stored in the polarized dielectric
[1]**ca·pac·i·ty** \kə-ˈpas-ət-ē, -ˈpas-tē\ *n, pl* **-ties** [ME *capacite,* fr. MF *capacité,* fr. L *capacitat-, capacitas,* fr. *capac-, capax*] **1 a :** the ability to hold, receive, store, or accommodate **b :** a measure of content **:** the measured ability to contain **:** VOLUME <a jug with a ~ of one gallon> — see METRIC SYSTEM table, WEIGHT table **c :** maximum production or output **d** (1) **:** CAPACITANCE (2) **:** the quantity of electricity that a battery can deliver under specified conditions **2 :** legal qualification, competency, power, or fitness **3 a :** ABILITY, CALIBER **b :** power to grasp and analyze ideas and cope with problems **c :** POTENTIALITY **4 :** a position or character assigned or assumed <in his ~ as a judge>
[2]**capacity** *adj* **:** attaining to or equaling maximum capacity <a ~ crowd> <~ production of electricity>
cap-a-pie *or* **cap-à-pie** \ˌkap-ə-ˈpē, -ˈpā\ *adv* [MF *(de) cap a pé* from head to foot] **:** from head to foot **:** at all points <armed ~>
ca·par·i·son \kə-ˈpar-ə-sən\ *n* [MF *caparaçon,* fr. OSp *caparazón*] **1 a :** an ornamental covering for a horse **b :** decorative trappings and harness **2 :** rich clothing **:** ADORNMENT — **caparison** *vt*
[1]**cape** \ˈkāp\ *n, often attrib* [ME *cap,* fr. MF, fr. OProv, fr. L *caput* head — more at HEAD] **:** a point or extension of land jutting out into water as a peninsula or as a projecting point
[2]**cape** *n* [prob. fr. Sp *capa* cloak, fr. LL *cappa* head covering, cloak] **1 :** a sleeveless outer garment or part of a garment that fits closely at the neck and hangs loosely from the shoulders **2 :** the short feathers covering the shoulders of a fowl below the hackle — see COCK illustration; see DUCK illustration
Cape buffalo \ˈkāp-\ *n* [*Cape* of Good Hope, Africa] **:** a large dangerous and often savage buffalo (*Syncerus caffer*) of southern Africa
Cape Cod cottage \(ˌ)kāp-ˌkäd-\ *n* [*Cape Cod,* Mass.] **:** a compact rectangular dwelling of one or one-and-a-half stories usu. with a central chimney and steep gable roof
Cape crawfish *n* [*Cape* of Good Hope] **:** the common edible spiny lobster (*Jasus lalandii*) of southern Africa
Cape Horn·er \kāp-ˈhȯr-nər\ *n* **:** a ship that voyages around Cape Horn
cape·let \ˈkāp-lət\ *n* **:** a small cape usu. covering the shoulders
cap·e·lin \ˈkap-(ə-)lən\ *n* [CanF *capelan,* fr. F, codfish, fr. OProv, chaplain, codfish, fr. ML *cappellanus* chaplain — more at CHAPLAIN] **:** a small northern sea fish (*Mallotus villosus*) related to the smelts
Ca·pel·la \kə-ˈpel-ə\ *n* [L, lit., she-goat, fr. *caper* he-goat — more at CAPRIOLE] **:** a star of the first magnitude in Auriga
Cape marigold *n* [*Cape* of Good Hope] **:** DIMORPHOTHECA
[1]**ca·per** \ˈkā-pər\ *n* [back-formation fr. earlier *capers* (taken as a plural), fr. ME *caperis,* fr. L *capparis,* fr. Gk *kapparis*] **1 :** any of a genus (*Capparis* of the family Capparidaceae, the caper family) of low prickly shrubs of the Mediterranean region; *esp* **:** one (*C. spinosa*) cultivated for its buds **2 :** one of the greenish flower buds or young berries of the caper pickled for use as a relish
[2]**caper** *vi* **ca·pered; ca·per·ing** \-p(ə-)riŋ\ [prob. by shortening & alter. fr. *capriole*] **:** to leap about in a gay frolicsome way **:** PRANCE
[3]**caper** *n* **1 :** a gay bounding leap **2 :** a capricious escapade **:** PRANK **3 :** an illegal enterprise **:** CRIME
cap·er·cail·lie \ˌkap-ər-ˈkāl-(y)ē\ *or* **cap·er·cail·zie** \-ˈkāl-zē\ *n* [ScGael *capalcoille,* lit., horse of the woods] **:** the largest Old World grouse (*Tetrao urogallus*)
cape·skin \ˈkāp-ˌskin\ *n* [*Cape* of Good Hope] **:** a light flexible leather made from sheepskins with the natural grain retained and used esp. for gloves and garments
Ca·pe·tian \kə-ˈpē-shən\ *adj* [Hugh *Capet*] **:** of or relating to the French royal house that ruled from 987–1328 — **Capetian** *n*
cape·work \ˈkāp-ˌwərk\ *n* **:** the art of the bullfighter in working a bull with the cape
cap·ful \ˈkap-ˌfu̇l\ *n* **1 :** as much as a cap will hold <a ~ of detergent> **2 :** a light puff <a ~ of wind>
cap gun *n* **:** CAP PISTOL
ca·pi·as \ˈkā-pē-əs\ *n* [ME, fr. L, you should seize, fr. *capere* to take — more at HEAVE] **:** a legal writ or process commanding the officer to arrest the person named in it
cap·il·lar·i·ty \ˌkap-ə-ˈlar-ət-ē\ *n, pl* **-ties** **1 :** the property or state of being capillary **2 :** the action by which the surface of a liquid where it is in contact with a solid (as in a capillary tube) is elevated or depressed depending on the relative attraction of the molecules of the liquid for each other and for those of the solid
[1]**cap·il·lary** \ˈkap-ə-ˌler-ē, *Brit usu* kə-ˈpil-ə-rē\ *adj* [F or L; F *capillaire,* fr. L *capillaris,* fr. *capillus* hair] **1 :** resembling a hair esp. in slender elongated form; *esp* **:** having a very small bore <a ~ tube> **2 :** involving, held by, or resulting from surface tension <~ water in the soil> **3 :** of or relating to capillaries or capillarity
[2]**capillary** *n, pl* **-lar·ies** **:** a capillary tube; *esp* **:** any of the smallest vessels of the blood-vascular system connecting arterioles with venules and forming networks throughout the body
capillary attraction *n* **:** the force of adhesion between a solid and a liquid in capillarity
[1]**cap·i·tal** \ˈkap-ət-ᵊl, ˈkap-tᵊl\ *adj* [ME, fr. L *capitalis,* fr. *capit-, caput* head — more at HEAD] **1 a :** punishable by death <a ~ crime> **b :** involving execution <~ punishment> **c :** most serious <a ~ error> **2** *of a letter* **:** of or conforming to the series A, B, C, etc. rather than a, b, c, etc. **3 a :** chief in importance or influence <the ~ importance of criticism in the work of creation itself —T. S. Eliot> **b :** being the seat of government **4 :** of or relating to capital **5 :** EXCELLENT <a ~ book>
[2]**capital** *n* [F or It; F, fr. It *capitale,* fr. *capitale,* adj., chief, principal, fr. L *capitalis*] **1 a** (1) **:** a stock of accumulated goods esp. at a specified time and in contrast to income received during a specified period; *also* **:** the value of these accumulated goods (2) **:** accumulated goods devoted to the production of other goods (3) **:** accumulated possessions calculated to bring in income **b** (1) **:** net worth (2) **:** CAPITAL STOCK **c :** persons holding capital **d :** ADVANTAGE, GAIN **2** [[1]*capital*] **a :** a capital letter; *esp* **:** an initial capital letter **b :** a letter belonging to a style of alphabet modeled on the style customarily used in inscriptions **3** [[1]*capital*] **a :** a city serving as a seat of government **b :** a city preeminent in some special activity
[3]**capital** *n* [ME *capitale,* modif. of ONF *capitel,* fr. LL *capitellum* small head, top of column, dim. of L *capit-, caput*] **:** the uppermost member of a column or pilaster crowning the shaft and taking the weight of the entablature — see COLUMN illustration
capital assets *n pl* **:** tangible or intangible long-term assets
capital expenditure *n* **:** an expenditure for long-term additions or betterments properly chargeable to a capital assets account
capital gains distribution *n* **:** the part of a payment made by an investment company to its shareholders that consists of realized profits from the sale of securities and technically is not income
capital goods *n pl* **:** [2]CAPITAL 1a(1), 1a(2)
cap·i·tal·ism \ˈkap-ət-ᵊl-ˌiz-əm, ˈkap-tᵊl-\ *n* **:** an economic system characterized by private or corporate ownership of capital goods, by investments that are determined by private decision rather than by state control, and by prices, production, and the distribution of goods that are determined mainly by competition in a free market
[1]**cap·i·tal·ist** \-əst\ *n* **1 :** a person who has capital esp. invested in business; *broadly* **:** a person of wealth **:** PLUTOCRAT **2 :** a person who favors capitalism
[2]**capitalist** *or* **cap·i·tal·is·tic** \ˌkap-ət-ᵊl-ˈis-tik, ˌkap-tᵊl-\ *adj* **1 :** owning capital <the ~ class> **2 a :** practicing or advocating capitalism <~ nations> **b :** marked by capitalism <the modern ~ period of history from 1815 to 1914 —Norman Thomas> — **cap·i·tal·is·ti·cal·ly** \-ti-k(ə-)lē\ *adv*
cap·i·tal·iza·tion \ˌkap-ət-ᵊl-ə-ˈzā-shən, ˌkap-tᵊl-\ *n* **1 a :** the act or process of capitalizing **b :** a sum resulting from a process of capitalizing **c :** the total liabilities of a business including both ownership capital and borrowed capital **d :** the total par value or the stated value of no-par issues of authorized capital stock **2 :** the use of a capital letter in writing or printing
cap·i·tal·ize \ˈkap-ət-ᵊl-ˌīz, ˈkap-tᵊl-\ *vb* **-ized; -iz·ing** *vt* **1 :** to write or print with an initial capital or in capitals **2 :** to convert into capital <~ the company's reserve fund> **3 a :** to compute the present value of (an income extended over a period of time) **b :** to convert (a periodic payment) into an equivalent capital sum <*capitalized* annuities> **4 :** to supply capital for ~ *vi* **:** to gain by turning something to advantage **:** PROFIT <~ on an opponent's mistake>
capital levy *n* **:** a levy on personal or industrial capital in addition to income tax and other taxes **:** a general property tax
cap·i·tal·ly \ˈkap-ət-ᵊl-ē, ˈkap-tᵊl-\ *adv* **1 :** in a manner involving capital punishment **2 :** in a capital manner **:** EXCELLENTLY, ADMIRABLY
capital ship *n* **:** a warship of the first rank in size and armament
capital sin *n* **:** DEADLY SIN
capital stock *n* **1 :** the outstanding shares of a joint-stock company considered as an aggregate **2 :** CAPITALIZATION 1d **3 :** the ownership element of a corporation divided into shares and represented by certificates
capital structure *n* **:** the makeup of the capitalization of a business in terms of the amounts and kinds of equity and debt securities **:** the equity and debt securities of a business together with its surplus and reserves
cap·i·tate \ˈkap-ə-ˌtāt\ *adj* [L *capitatus* headed, fr. *capit-, caput* head] **1 :** forming a head **2 :** abruptly enlarged and globose
cap·i·ta·tion \ˌkap-ə-ˈtā-shən\ *n* [LL *capitation-, capitatio* poll tax, fr. L *capit-, caput*] **1 :** a direct uniform tax imposed upon each head or person **:** POLL TAX **2 :** a uniform per capita payment or fee
cap·i·tol \ˈkap-ət-ᵊl, ˈkap-tᵊl\ *n* [L *Capitolium,* temple of Jupiter at Rome on the Capitoline hill] **1 a :** a building in which a state legislative body meets **b :** a group of buildings in which the functions of state government are carried out **2** *cap* **:** the building in which the U.S. Congress meets at Washington
Capitol Hill *n* [*Capitol Hill,* Washington, site of the U.S. Capitol] **:** the legislative branch of the U.S. government
Cap·i·to·line \ˈkap-ət-ᵊl-ˌīn, *Brit usu* kə-ˈpit-ə-ˌlīn\ *adj* [L *capitolinus,* fr. *Capitolium*] **:** of or relating to the smallest of the seven hills of ancient Rome, the temple on it, or the gods worshiped there

ca·pit·u·lar \kə-ˈpich-ə-lər\ *adj* [ML *capitularis*, fr. *capitulum* chapter] **:** of or relating to an ecclesiastical chapter

ca·pit·u·lary \-ˌler-ē\ *n, pl* **-lar·ies** [ML *capitulare*, lit., document divided into sections, fr. LL *capitulum* section, chapter — more at CHAPTER] **:** a civil or ecclesiastical ordinance; *also* **:** a collection of ordinances

ca·pit·u·late \kə-ˈpich-ə-ˌlāt\ *vi* **-lat·ed; -lat·ing** [ML *capitulatus*, pp. of *capitulare* to distinguish by heads or chapters, fr. LL *capitulum*] **1** *archaic* **:** PARLEY, NEGOTIATE **2 a :** to surrender often after negotiation of terms **b :** to cease resisting **:** ACQUIESCE ***syn*** see YIELD

ca·pit·u·la·tion \kə-ˌpich-ə-ˈlā-shən\ *n* **1 :** a set of terms or articles constituting an agreement between governments **2 :** the act or agreement of one that surrenders upon stipulated terms **3 :** a giving over of resistance usu. to something that presses or dominates ***syn*** see SURRENDER

ca·pit·u·lum \kə-ˈpich-ə-ləm\ *n, pl* **-la** \-lə\ [NL, fr. L, small head — more at CHAPTER] **1 :** a rounded protuberance of an anatomical part (as a bone) **2 :** a racemose inflorescence (as of the buttonbush) with the axis shortened and dilated to form a rounded or flattened cluster of sessile flowers — see INFLORESCENCE illustration

ca·po \ˈkā-(ˌ)pō\ *n, pl* **capos** [short for *capotasto*, fr. It, lit., head of fingerboard] **:** a movable bar attached to the fingerboard esp. of a guitar to uniformly raise the pitch of all the strings

ca·pon \ˈkā-ˌpän, -pən\ *n* [ME, fr. OE *capūn*, prob. fr. ONF *capon*, fr. L *capon-, capo*; akin to Gk *koptein* to cut] **:** a castrated male chicken — **ca·pon·ize** \-pə-ˌnīz\ *vt*

cap·o·ral \ˈkap-(ə-)rəl, ˌkap-ə-ˈral\ *n* [F, lit., corporal — more at CORPORAL] **:** a coarse tobacco

ca·pote \kə-ˈpōt\ *n* [F, fr. *cape* cloak, fr. LL *cappa*] **:** a usu. long and hooded cloak or overcoat

cap·per \ˈkap-ər\ *n* **1 :** one that caps; *esp* **:** an operator or a machine that applies the closure or cap **2 :** a lure or decoy esp. in an illicit or questionable activity **:** SHILL

cap·ping \ˈkap-iŋ\ *n* **:** something that caps

cap pistol *n* **:** a toy pistol that fires caps

cap·ric acid \ˌkap-rik-\ *n* [ISV, fr. L *capr-, caper* goat; fr. its odor — more at CAPRIOLE] **:** a fatty acid $C_{10}H_{20}O_2$ found in fats and oils and used in flavors and perfumes

ca·pric·cio \kə-ˈprē-ch(ē-ˌ)ō\ *n, pl* **-cios** [It] **1 :** WHIMSY, FANCY **2 :** CAPER, PRANK **3 :** an instrumental piece in free form usu. lively in tempo and brilliant in style

ca·price \kə-ˈprēs\ *n* [F, fr. It *capriccio*, lit., head with hair standing on end, shudder, fr. *capo* head (fr. L *caput*) + *riccio* hedgehog, fr. L *ericius* — more at HEAD, URCHIN] **1 a :** a sudden, impulsive, and seemingly unmotivated change of mind **b :** a sudden change or series of changes hard to explain or predict <the ~*s* of the weather> **2 :** a disposition to change one's mind impulsively **3 :** CAPRICCIO 3

syn CAPRICE, FREAK, WHIM, VAGARY, CROTCHET *shared meaning element* **:** an arbitrary and typically fanciful or impracticable notion. CAPRICE emphasizes lack of evident motivation and suggests willfulness <my cousin's pet *caprice* is to affect a distaste for art, to which she is passionately devoted —G. B. Shaw> FREAK suggests an impulsive causeless change of mind befitting a child or a lunatic <chose to work or loaf as the *freak* took him> WHIM often implies a quaint, fantastic, or humorous turn of mind that may lead to freakish or capricious acts or behavior <had a *whim* to dress only in white> <a man subject to sudden *whims* and moods> VAGARY stresses the erratic, irresponsible, or extravagant quality of a notion or impulse <the *vagaries* of fashion> <straight they changed their minds, flew off, and into strange *vagaries* fell —John Milton> CROTCHET implies a perversely heretical or eccentric opinion or preference, especially on some trivial matter <she was eccentric . . . full of *crotchets*. She never drank water without some vinegar in it —to cleanse it, she said —Robert Henderson>

ca·pri·cious \kə-ˈprish-əs, -ˈprē-shəs\ *adj* **:** governed or characterized by caprice **:** apt to change suddenly or unpredictably ***syn*** see INCONSTANT ***ant*** steadfast — **ca·pri·cious·ly** *adv* — **ca·pri·cious·ness** *n*

Cap·ri·corn \ˈkap-ri-ˌkȯ(ə)rn\ *n* [ME *Capricorne*, fr. L *Capricornus* (gen. *Capricorni*), fr. *caper* goat + *cornu* horn — more at HORN] **1 :** a southern zodiacal constellation between Sagittarius and Aquarius **2 a :** the 10th sign of the zodiac in astrology — see ZODIAC table **b :** one born under this sign

cap·ri·fi·ca·tion \ˌkap-rə-fə-ˈkā-shən\ *n* [L *caprification-, caprificatio*, fr. *caprificatus*, pp. of *caprificare* to pollinate by caprification, fr. *caprificus*] **:** artificial pollination of figs that usu. bear only pistillate flowers by hanging male flowering branches of the caprifig in the trees to facilitate pollen transfer by a wasp to the edible figs

cap·ri·fig \ˈkap-rə-ˌfig\ *n* [ME *caprifige*, part trans. of L *caprificus*, fr. *capr-, caper* goat + *ficus* fig — more at FIG] **:** a wild fig (*Ficus carica sylvestris*) of southern Europe and Asia Minor used for caprification of the edible fig; *also* **:** its fruit

cap·rine \ˈkap-ˌrīn\ *adj* [L *caprinus*, fr. *capr-, caper*] **:** of, relating to, or being a goat

cap·ri·ole \ˈkap-rē-ˌōl\ *n* [MF or OIt; MF *capriole*, fr. OIt *capriola*, fr. *capriolo* roebuck, fr. L *capreolus* goat, roebuck, fr. *capr-, caper* he-goat; akin to OE *hæfer* goat, Gk *kapros* wild boar] **1 :** CAPER **2** *of a trained horse* **:** a vertical leap with a backward kick of the hind legs at the height of the leap — **capriole** *vi*

ca·pri pants \kə-ˌprē-\ *n pl, often cap C* [*Capri*, Italy] **:** close-fitting pants that have tapered legs with a slit on the outside of the leg bottom, extend almost to the ankle, and are used for informal wear esp. by women

ca·pro·ic acid \kə-ˌprō-ik-\ *n* [ISV, fr. L *capr-, caper*] **:** a liquid fatty acid $C_6H_{12}O_2$ that is found as a glycerol ester in fats and oils or made synthetically and used in pharmaceuticals and flavors

ca·pryl·ic acid \kə-ˌpril-ik-\ *n* [ISV *capryl*, a radical contained in it] **:** a fatty acid $C_8H_{16}O_2$ of rancid odor occurring in fats and oils and used in perfumes

caps *abbr* **1** capitals **2** capsule

cap·sa·icin \kap-ˈsā-ə-sən\ *n* [irreg. fr. NL *Capsicum*] **:** a colorless irritant phenolic amide $C_{18}H_{27}NO_3$ obtained from various capsicums

Cap·si·an \ˈkap-sē-ən\ *adj* [F *capsien*, fr. L *Capsa* Gafsa, Tunisia] **:** of or relating to a Paleolithic culture of northern Africa and southern Europe

cap·si·cum \ˈkap-si-kəm\ *n* [NL, genus name] **1 :** any of a genus (*Capsicum*) of tropical herbs and shrubs of the nightshade family widely cultivated for their many-seeded usu. fleshy-walled berries — called also *pepper* **2 :** the dried ripe fruit of some capsicums (as *C. frutescens*) used as a gastric and intestinal stimulant

cap·sid \ˈkap-səd\ *n* [L *capsa* case + E [2]*-id* — more at CASE] **:** the outer protein shell of a virus particle — **cap·sid·al** \-səd-ᵊl\ *adj*

cap·size \ˈkap-ˌsīz, kap-ˈ\ *vb* **cap·sized; cap·siz·ing** [origin unknown] *vt* **:** to cause to overturn <~ a canoe> ~ *vi* **:** to turn over **:** UPSET <the canoe *capsized*>

cap·stan \ˈkap-stən, -ˌstan\ *n* [ME] **1 :** a machine for moving or raising heavy weights by winding cable around a vertical spindle-mounted drum that is rotated manually or driven by steam or electric power **2 :** a rotating shaft that drives tape at a constant speed in a recorder

capstan 1

cap·stone \ˈkap-ˌstōn\ *n* [[1]*cap*] **1 :** a coping stone **:** COPING **2 :** the crowning point **:** ACME

cap·su·lar \ˈkap-sə-lər\ *adj* **1 :** of, relating to, or resembling a capsule **2 :** CAPSULATE

cap·su·late \-ˌlāt, -lət\ *or* **cap·su·lat·ed** \-ˌlāt-əd\ *adj* **:** enclosed in a capsule

[1]**cap·sule** \ˈkap-səl, -(ˌ)sül\ *n* [F, fr. L *capsula*, dim. of *capsa* box — more at CASE] **1 a :** a membrane or sac enclosing a body part **b :** either of two layers of white matter in the cerebrum **2 :** a closed receptacle containing spores or seeds: as **a :** a dry dehiscent usu. many-seeded fruit composed of two or more carpels **b :** the spore sac of a moss **3 :** a gelatin shell enclosing medicine **4 :** an often polysaccharide envelope surrounding a microorganism **5 :** an extremely brief condensation **:** OUTLINE, SURVEY **6 :** a compact usu. detachable receptacle **7 :** a small pressurized compartment for an aviator or astronaut for flight or emergency escape; *specif* **:** SPACECRAFT

[2]**capsule** *vt* **cap·suled; cap·sul·ing 1 :** to equip with or enclose in a capsule **2 :** to condense into or formulate in a very brief compact form <*capsuled* the news>

[3]**capsule** *adj* **1 :** extremely brief **2 :** small and very compact

cap·sul·ize \ˈkap-sə-ˌlīz\ *vt* **-ized; -iz·ing :** CAPSULE

Capt *abbr* captain

[1]**cap·tain** \ˈkap-tən\ *n* [ME *capitane*, fr. MF *capitain*, fr. LL *capitaneus*, adj. & n., chief, fr. L *capit-, caput* head — more at HEAD] **1 a :** the commander of a body of troops or of a military establishment **b :** a commander under a sovereign or general **c** (1) **:** an officer in charge of a ship (2) **:** a commissioned officer in the navy or coast guard ranking above a commander and below a rear admiral **d :** a commissioned officer in the army, air force, or marine corps ranking above a first lieutenant and below a major **e :** a distinguished military leader **f :** a leader of a side or team in a sports contest **g :** a fire or police department officer usu. ranking between a lieutenant and a chief **h** (1) **:** a restaurant functionary in charge of waiters (2) **:** a hotel functionary in charge of bellboys — called also *bell captain* **2 :** a dominant figure <~*s* of commerce> — **cap·tain·cy** \-sē\ *n* — **cap·tain·ship** \-ˌship\ *n*

[2]**captain** *vt* **:** to be captain of **:** LEAD <~*ed* the football team>

captain of industry : the head of a great industrial enterprise **:** ENTREPRENEUR

captain's chair *n* **:** an armchair with a low curved back with vertical spindles and a saddle seat

captain's mast *n* **:** MAST 3

cap·tan \ˈkap-ˌtan\ *n* [origin unknown] **:** a fungicide $C_9H_8Cl_3NO_2S$ used on agricultural crops

[1]**cap·tion** \ˈkap-shən\ *n* [ME *capcioun*, fr. L *caption-, captio* act of taking, fr. *captus*, pp. of *capere* to take — more at HEAVE] **1 :** the part of a legal instrument that shows where, when, and by what authority it was taken, found, or executed **2 a :** the heading esp. of an article or document **:** TITLE **b :** the explanatory comment or designation accompanying a pictorial illustration **c :** a motion-picture subtitle — **cap·tion·less** \-ləs\ *adj*

[2]**caption** *vt* **cap·tioned; cap·tion·ing** \-sh(ə-)niŋ\ **:** to furnish with a caption **:** ENTITLE

cap·tious \ˈkap-shəs\ *adj* [ME *capcious*, fr. MF or L; MF *captieux* fr. L *captiosus*, fr. *captio* act of taking, deception] **1 :** calculated to confuse, entrap, or entangle in argument **2 :** marked by an often ill-natured inclination to stress faults and raise objections ***syn*** see CRITICAL ***ant*** appreciative — **cap·tious·ly** *adv* — **cap·tious·ness** *n*

cap·ti·vate \ˈkap-tə-ˌvāt\ *vt* **-vat·ed; -vat·ing 1** *archaic* **:** SEIZE, CAPTURE **2 :** to influence and dominate by some special charm, art, or trait and with an irresistible appeal ***syn*** see ATTRACT ***ant*** repulse — **cap·ti·va·tion** \ˌkap-tə-ˈvā-shən\ *n* — **cap·ti·va·tor** \ˈkap-tə-ˌvāt-ər\ *n*

cap·tive \ˈkap-tiv\ *adj* [ME, fr. L *captivus*, fr. *captus*, pp. of *capere*] **1 a :** taken and held as prisoner esp. by an enemy in war **b :** kept within bounds **:** CONFINED **c** (1) **:** held under control (2)

: owned or controlled by another concern and operated for its needs rather than for an open market <a ~ mine> **2 :** of or relating to captivity **3 :** extremely pleased or gratified : CAPTIVATED **4 :** being in a situation that makes departure or inattention difficult <a ~ audience> — **captive** *n*

cap·tiv·i·ty \kap-'tiv-ət-ē\ *n* **1 :** the state of being captive <some birds thrive in ~> **2** *obs* **:** a group of captives

cap·tor \'kap-tər, -ˌtȯ(ə)r\ *n* [LL, fr. L *captus*] : one that has captured a person or thing

[1]**cap·ture** \'kap-chər\ *n* [MF, fr. L *captura,* fr. *captus,* pp. of *capere*] **1 :** the act of catching or gaining control by force, stratagem, or guile **2 :** one that has been taken; *esp* **:** a prize ship **3 :** a move in various board games (as checkers or chess) that gains an opponent's man **4 :** the coalescence of an atomic nucleus with an elementary particle that may result in an emission from or fission of the nucleus

[2]**capture** *vt* **cap·tured; cap·tur·ing** \'kap-chə-riŋ, 'kap-shriŋ\ **1 a :** to take captive : WIN, GAIN <~ a city> **b :** to preserve in a relatively permanent form <at any such moment as a photograph might ~ —C. E. Montague> **c :** to captivate and hold the interest of <*captured* her> **2 :** to take according to the rules of a game **3 :** to bring about the capture of (an elementary particle)

capture the flag : a game in which players on each of two teams seek to capture the other team's flag and return it to their side without being captured and imprisoned

ca·puche \kə-'püch, -'püsh\ *n* [It *cappuccio,* fr. *cappa* cloak, fr. LL] : HOOD; *esp* **:** the cowl of a Capuchin friar

ca·pu·chin \'kap-(y)ə-shən, *esp for 3 also* kə-'p(y)ü-\ *n* [MF, fr. OIt *cappuccino,* fr. *cappuccio;* fr. his cowl] **1** *cap* **:** a member of the Order of Friars Minor Capuchin forming since 1529 an austere branch of the first order of St. Francis of Assisi engaged in missionary work and preaching **2 :** a hooded cloak for women **3 :** any of a genus (*Cebus*) of So. American monkeys; *esp* **:** one (*C. capucinus*) with the hair on its crown resembling a monk's cowl

Cap·u·let \'kap-yə-lət\ *n* **:** the family of Juliet in Shakespeare's *Romeo and Juliet*

cap·y·bara \ˌkap-i-'bar-ə, -'bär-\ *n* [Pg *capibara,* fr. Tupi] : a tailless largely aquatic So. American rodent (*Hydrochoerus capybara*) often exceeding four feet in length

capybara

car \'kär\ *n* [ME *carre,* fr. AF, fr. L *carra,* pl. of *carrum,* alter. of *carrus,* of Celt origin; akin to OIr & MW *carr* vehicle; akin to L *currere* to run] **1 :** a vehicle moving on wheels: **a** *archaic* **:** CARRIAGE, CART, WAGON **b :** a chariot of war or of triumph **c :** a vehicle adapted to the rails of a railroad or street railway **d :** AUTOMOBILE **2 :** the cage of an elevator **3 :** the part of an airship or balloon that carries the power plant, personnel, and cargo

Car *abbr* Carlow

CAR *abbr* civil air regulations

ca·ra·bao \ˌkar-ə-'bau̇, ˌkär-\ *n* [PhilSp, fr. Eastern Bisayan *karabáw*] : WATER BUFFALO

ca·ra·bid \'kar-ə-bəd, kə-'rab-əd\ *n* [deriv. of Gk *karabos* horned beetle] **:** any of a large family (Carabidae) of usu. carnivorous and often shining black or metallic beetles — **carabid** *adj*

car·a·bi·neer *or* **car·a·bi·nier** \ˌkar-ə-bə-'ni(ə)r\ *n* [F *carabinier,* fr. *carabine* carbine] : a soldier armed with a carbine

car·a·bi·ner \ˌkar-ə-'bē-nər\ *n* [G *karabiner*] **:** an oblong ring that snaps to the eye or link of a piton to hold a freely running rope

ca·ra·bi·ne·ro \ˌkar-ə-bə-'ne(ə)r-(ˌ)ō, ˌkär-\ *n, pl* **-ros** [Sp, fr. *carabina* carbine, fr. F *carabine*] **1 :** a member of a Spanish national police force serving esp. as frontier guards **2 :** a customs or coast guard officer in the Philippines

ca·ra·bi·nie·re \ˌkar-ə-bən-'ye(ə)r-(ˌ)ā, ˌkär-\ *n, pl* **-nie·ri** \-'ye(ə)r-ē\ [It, fr. F *carabinier*] : a member of the Italian national police force

ca·ra·ca·ra \ˌkar-ə-'kar-ə, -ə-kə-'rä\ *n* [Sp *caracara* & Pg *caracará,* fr. Tupi *caracará,* of imit. origin] **:** any of various large long-legged mostly So. American hawks resembling vultures in habits

car·a·cole \'kar-ə-ˌkōl\ *n* [F, fr. Sp *caracol* snail, spiral stair, caracole] **1 :** a half turn to right or left executed by a mounted horse **2 :** a turning or capering movement — **caracole** *vb*

car·a·cul \'kar-ə-kəl\ *n* [alter. of *karakul*] **:** the pelt of a karakul lamb after the curl begins to loosen

ca·rafe \kə-'raf, -'räf\ *n* [F, fr. It *caraffa,* fr. Ar *gharrāfah*] **:** a bottle with a flaring lip used to hold water or beverages

car·a·ga·na \ˌkar-ə-'gän-ə\ *n* [NL, genus name, of Turkic origin; akin to Kirghiz *karaghan* Siberian pea tree] **:** any of a genus (*Caragana*) of Asiatic leguminous shrubs or small trees extensively used in dry areas for hedges and in shelterbelts

car·a·geen *var of* CARRAGEEN

car·a·mel \'kar-ə-məl, -ˌmel; 'kär-məl\ *n* [F, fr. Sp *caramelo,* fr. Pg, icicle, caramel, fr. LL *calamellus* small reed — more at SHAWM] **1 :** an amorphous brittle brown and somewhat bitter substance obtained by heating sugar and used as a coloring and flavoring agent **2 :** a firm chewy usu. caramel-flavored candy

car·a·mel·ize \-mə-ˌlīz\ *vb* **-ized; -iz·ing** *vt* **:** to change (sugar or the sugar content of a food) into caramel ~ *vi* **:** to change to caramel

ca·ran·gid \kə-'ran-jəd, -'raŋ-gəd\ *adj* [deriv. of F *carangue* shad, horse mackerel, fr. Sp *caranga*] **:** of or relating to a large family (Carangidae) of marine spiny-finned fishes including important food fishes — **carangid** *n*

car·a·pace \'kar-ə-ˌpās\ *n* [F, fr. Sp *carapacho*] **1 :** a bony or chitinous case or shield covering the back or part of the back of an animal (as a turtle or crab) **2 :** a hard protective outer covering; *esp* **:** an attitude or state of mind (as indifference) serving to protect or isolate from external influence

[1]**carat** *var of* KARAT

[2]**car·at** \'kar-ət\ *n* [prob. fr. ML *carratus,* fr. Ar *qīrāt* bean pod, a small weight, fr. Gk *keration* carob bean, a small weight, fr. dim. of *kerat-, keras* horn — more at HORN] **:** a unit of weight for precious stones equal to 200 milligrams

[1]**car·a·van** \'kar-ə-ˌvan\ *n* [It *caravana,* fr. Per *kārwān*] **1 a :** a company of travelers on a journey through desert or hostile regions; *also* **:** a train of pack animals **b :** a group of vehicles traveling together in a file **2 :** a covered vehicle: as **a :** a vehicle equipped as traveling living quarters **b** *Brit* **:** a nonautomotive vehicle designed to be hauled and to serve as a dwelling

[2]**caravan** *vi* **-vanned** *or* **-vaned** \-ˌvand\; **-van·ning** *or* **-van·ing** **:** to travel in a caravan

car·a·van·ner \-ˌvan-ər\ *n* **1** *or* **car·a·van·er** \-ˌvan-\ **:** one that travels in a caravan **2** *Brit* **:** one that goes camping with a trailer

car·a·van·sa·ry \ˌkar-ə-'van(t)-sə-rē\ *or* **car·a·van·se·rai** \-sə-ˌrī\ *n, pl* **-ries** *or* **-rais** *or* **-rai** [Per *kārwānsarāī,* fr. *kārwān* caravan + *sarāī* palace, inn] **1 :** a usu. large bare building surrounding a court in eastern countries where caravans rest at night **2 :** HOTEL, INN

car·a·vel \'kar-ə-ˌvel, -vəl\ *n* [MF *caravelle,* fr. OPg *caravela*] **:** any of several sailing ships; *specif* **:** a small 15th and 16th century ship with broad bows, high narrow poop, and lateen sails

car·a·way \'kar-ə-ˌwā\ *n* [ME, prob. fr. ML *carvi,* fr. Ar *karawyā,* fr. Gk *karon*] **:** a biennial usu. white-flowered aromatic herb (*Carum carvi*) of the carrot family with pungent fruits

carb- *or* **carbo-** *comb form* [F, fr. *carbone*] **:** carbon : carbonic : carbonyl : carboxyl <*carb*ide> <*carbo*hydrate>

car·ba·chol \'kär-bə-ˌkȯl, -ˌkōl\ *n* [*carba*mic acid + *chol*ine] **:** a synthetic parasympathomimetic drug $C_6H_{15}ClN_2O_2$ that is used in veterinary medicine and topically in glaucoma

car·ba·mate \'kär-bə-ˌmāt, kär-'bam-ˌāt\ *n* **:** a salt or ester of carbamic acid; *esp* **:** one that is a synthetic organic insecticide

car·bam·ic acid \(ˌ)kär-ˌbam-ik-\ *n* [ISV *carb-* + *am*ide + *-ic*] **:** an acid CH_3NO_2 known in the form of salts and esters that is a half amide of carbonic acid

carb·amide \'kär-bə-ˌmīd, kär-'bam-əd\ *n* [ISV *carb-* + *amide*] **:** UREA

carb·ami·no \ˌkär-bə-'mē-(ˌ)nō\ *adj* **:** relating to any carbamic acid derivative formed by reaction of carbon dioxide with an amino acid or a protein (as hemoglobin)

car·ba·myl \'kär-bə-ˌmil\ *or* **car·bam·o·yl** \kär-'bam-ə-ˌwil\ *n* **:** the radical NH_2CO of carbamic acid

carb·an·ion \kär-'ban-ˌī-ən, -ˌī-ˌän\ *n* **:** an organic ion carrying a negative charge at a carbon position — compare CARBONIUM

car·barn \'kär-ˌbärn\ *n* **:** a building that houses the cars of a street railway or the buses of a bus system

car·ba·ryl \'kär-bə-ˌril\ *n* [*carb*amate + *ar*omatic + *-yl*] **:** a carbamate insecticide effective against numerous crop, forage, and forest pests

car·ba·zole \'kär-bə-ˌzōl\ *n* [ISV] **:** a crystalline slightly basic cyclic compound $C_{12}H_9N$ found in anthracene and used in making dyes

car bed *n* [fr. its use in carrying infants in cars] **:** a portable bed for an infant

car·bide \'kär-ˌbīd\ *n* [ISV] **:** a binary compound of carbon with a more electropositive element; *esp* **:** CALCIUM CARBIDE

car·bine \'kär-ˌbēn, -ˌbīn\ *n* [F *carabine,* fr. MF *carabin* carabineer] **1 :** a short-barreled lightweight firearm orig. used by cavalry **2 :** a .30 caliber gas-operated magazine fed semiautomatic or automatic rifle that is shorter and lighter and fires lighter ammunition than the M1 rifle and that was used by U.S. troops in World War II and the Korean war

car·bi·nol \'kär-bə-ˌnȯl, -ˌnōl\ *n* [ISV, fr. obs. G *karbin* methyl, fr. G *karb-* carb-] **:** METHANOL; *also* **:** an alcohol derived from it

car·bo·cy·clic \ˌkär-bō-'sī-klik, -'sik-lik\ *adj* [ISV] **:** being or having an organic ring composed of carbon atoms

car·bo·hy·drase \ˌkär-bō-'hī-ˌdrās, -bə-, -ˌdrāz\ *n* [ISV *carbohydrate* + *-ase*] **:** any of a group of enzymes (as amylase) that promote hydrolysis or synthesis of a carbohydrate (as a disaccharide)

car·bo·hy·drate \-ˌdrāt, -drət\ *n* **:** any of various neutral compounds of carbon, hydrogen, and oxygen (as sugars, starches, and celluloses) most of which are formed by green plants and which constitute a major class of animal foods

car·bo·lat·ed \'kär-bə-ˌlāt-əd\ *adj* **:** impregnated with carbolic acid

car·bol·ic acid \(ˌ)kär-ˌbäl-ik-\ *n* [ISV *carb-* + L *oleum* oil — more at OIL] **:** PHENOL 1

car·bo·line \'kär-bə-ˌlēn\ *n* [*carb-* + ind*ole* + pyrid*ine*] **:** any of various isomers $C_{11}H_8N_2$ whose tricyclic structure is related to indole and pyridine and is found in many alkaloids

car·bon \'kär-bən\ *n, often attrib* [F *carbone,* fr. L *carbon-, carbo* ember, charcoal] **1 :** a nonmetallic chiefly tetravalent element found native (as in the diamond and graphite) or as a constituent of coal, petroleum, and asphalt, of limestone and other carbonates, and of organic compounds or obtained artificially in varying degrees of purity esp. as carbon black, lampblack, activated carbon, charcoal, and coke — see ELEMENT table **2 a :** a sheet of carbon paper **b :** CARBON COPY **3 a :** a carbon rod used in an arc lamp **b :** a piece of carbon used as an element in a voltaic cell — **car·bon·less** \-ləs\ *adj*

car·bo·na·ceous \ˌkär-bə-'nā-shəs\ *adj* **1 :** rich in carbon **2 :** relating to, containing, or composed of carbon **3 :** CARBONOUS 2

[1]**car·bo·na·do** \ˌkär-bə-'näd-(ˌ)ō, -'nād-\ *n, pl* **-dos** *or* **-does** [Sp *carbonada*] *archaic* **:** a broiled or grilled piece of meat scored before cooking

[2]**carbonado** *vt* **1** *archaic* **:** to make a carbonado of **2** *archaic* **:** CUT

[3]**carbonado** *n, pl* **-dos** [Pg, lit., carbonated] **:** an impure opaque dark-colored fine-grained aggregate of diamond particles valuable for its superior toughness

[1]**car·bon·ate** \'kär-bə-ˌnāt, -nət\ *n* **:** a salt or ester of carbonic acid

²car·bon·ate \-ˌnāt\ *vt* **-at·ed; -at·ing 1 :** to convert into a carbonate **2 :** to impregnate with carbon dioxide <*carbonated* beverage> — **car·bon·ation** \ˌkär-bə-ˈnā-shən\ *n*

carbon black *n* **:** any of various colloidal black substances consisting wholly or principally of carbon obtained usu. as soot and used esp. as pigments

carbon copy *n* **1 :** a copy made by carbon paper **2 :** DUPLICATE

carbon cycle *n* **1 :** a cycle of thermonuclear reactions in which four hydrogen atoms synthesize into a helium atom with the release of nuclear energy and which is held to be the source of most of the energy radiated by the sun and stars **2 :** the cycle of carbon in living beings in which carbon dioxide is fixed by photosynthesis to form organic nutrients and is ultimately restored to the inorganic state by respiration and protoplasmic decay

carbon dating *n* **:** the determination of the age of old material (as an archaeological or paleontological specimen) by means of the content of carbon 14

carbon dioxide *n* **:** a heavy colorless gas CO_2 that does not support combustion, dissolves in water to form carbonic acid, is formed esp. by the combustion and decomposition of organic substances, is absorbed from the air by plants in photosynthesis, and is used in the carbonation of beverages

carbon disulfide *n* **:** a colorless flammable poisonous liquid CS_2 used as a solvent for rubber and as an insect fumigant — called also *carbon bisulfide*

carbon 14 \-(ˈ)fōr(t)-ˈtēn, -(ˈ)fȯr(t)-\ *n* **:** a heavy radioactive isotope of carbon of mass number 14 used esp. in tracer studies and in dating archaeological and geological materials

car·bon·ic \kär-ˈbän-ik\ *adj* **:** of, relating to, or derived from carbon, carbonic acid, or carbon dioxide

carbonic acid *n* **:** a weak dibasic acid H_2CO_3 known only in solution that reacts with bases to form carbonates

carbonic acid gas *n* **:** CARBON DIOXIDE

carbonic an·hy·drase \-an-ˈhī-ˌdrās, -ˌdrāz\ *n* [*carbonic* + *anhydrous* + *-ase;* fr. its promotion of dehydration] **:** a zinc-containing enzyme that occurs in living tissues (as red blood cells) and aids carbon-dioxide transport from the tissues and its release from the blood in the lungs by catalyzing the reversible hydration of carbon dioxide to carbonic acid

car·bon·if·er·ous \ˌkär-bə-ˈnif-(ə-)rəs\ *adj* **1 :** producing or containing carbon or coal **2** *cap* **:** of, relating to, or being the period of the Paleozoic era between the Devonian and the Permian or the corresponding system of rocks that includes coal beds — **Carboniferous** *n*

car·bo·ni·um \kär-ˈbō-nē-əm\ *n* [*carb-* + *-onium*] **:** an organic ion carrying a positive charge at a carbon position — compare CARBANION

car·bon·iza·tion \ˌkär-bə-nə-ˈzā-shən\ *n* **:** the process of carbonizing; *esp* **:** destructive distillation (as of coal)

car·bon·ize \ˈkär-bə-ˌnīz\ *vb* **-ized; -iz·ing** *vt* **1 :** to convert into carbon or a carbonic residue **2 :** CARBURIZE 1 ~ *vi* **:** to become carbonized **:** CHAR

carbon monoxide *n* **:** a colorless odorless very toxic gas CO that burns to carbon dioxide with a blue flame and is formed as a product of the incomplete combustion of carbon

car·bon·ous \ˈkär-bə-nəs\ *adj* **1 :** derived from, containing, or resembling carbon **2 :** brittle and dark in color

carbon paper *n* **1 :** a thin paper faced with a waxy pigmented coating so that when placed between two sheets of paper the pressure of writing or typing on the top sheet causes transfer of pigment to the bottom sheet **2 :** gelatin-coated paper used in the carbon process

carbon process *n* **:** a photographic printing process utilizing a sheet of paper coated with bichromated gelatin mixed with a pigment

carbon tetrachloride *n* **:** a colorless nonflammable toxic liquid CCl_4 that has an odor resembling that of chloroform and is used as a solvent (as in dry cleaning) and a fire extinguisher

car·bon·yl \ˈkär-bə-ˌnil, -ˌnēl\ *n* **1 :** a bivalent radical CO occurring in aldehydes, ketones, carboxylic acids, esters, acid halides, and amides **2 :** a compound of the carbonyl radical with a metal — **car·bon·yl·ic** \ˌkär-bə-ˈnil-ik\ *adj*

Car·bo·run·dum \ˌkär-bə-ˈrən-dəm\ *trademark* — used for various abrasives

carboxy- *or* **carbox-** *comb form* **:** carboxyl

car·box·yl \kär-ˈbäk-səl\ *n* [ISV] **:** a univalent radical COOH typical of organic acids — **car·box·yl·ic** \ˌkär-(ˌ)bäk-ˈsil-ik\ *adj*

car·box·yl·ase \kär-ˈbäk-sə-ˌlās, -ˌlāz\ *n* [ISV] **:** an enzyme that catalyzes decarboxylation or carboxylation

¹car·box·yl·ate \-ˌlāt, -lət\ *n* **:** a salt or ester of a carboxylic acid

²car·box·yl·ate \-ˌlāt\ *vt* **-at·ed; -at·ing :** to introduce carboxyl or carbon dioxide into (a compound) with formation of a carboxylic acid — **car·box·yl·ation** \(ˌ)kär-ˌbäk-sə-ˈlā-shən\ *n*

carboxylic acid *n* **:** an organic acid (as acetic acid) containing one or more carboxyl groups

car·boxy·pep·ti·dase \kär-ˌbäk-sē-ˈpep-tə-ˌdās, -ˌdāz\ *n* **:** an enzyme that hydrolyzes peptides and esp. polypeptides by splitting off the amino acids containing free carboxyl groups

car·boy \ˈkär-ˌbȯi\ *n* [Per *qarāba,* fr. Ar *qarrābah* demijohn] **:** a bottle or rectangular container of about 5 to 15 gallons capacity for liquids that is made of glass, plastic, or metal and is often cushioned in a special container

car·bun·cle \ˈkär-ˌbəŋ-kəl\ *n* [ME, fr. MF, fr. L *carbunculus* small coal, carbuncle, dim. of *carbon-, carbo* charcoal, ember — more at CARBON] **1 a** *obs* **:** any of several red precious stones **b :** the garnet cut cabochon **2 :** a painful local purulent inflammation of the skin and deeper tissues with multiple openings for the discharge of pus and usu. necrosis and sloughing of dead tissue — **car·bun·cled** \-kəld\ *adj* — **car·bun·cu·lar** \kär-ˈbəŋ-kyə-lər\ *adj*

car·bu·ret \ˈkär-b(y)ə-ˌrāt, *esp by chemists* -ˌret\ *vt* **-ret·ed** *also* **-ret·ted; -ret·ing** *also* **-ret·ting** [obs. *carburet* (carbide)] **1 :** to combine chemically with carbon **2 :** to enrich (as gas) by mixing with volatile carbon compounds (as hydrocarbons) — **car·bu·re·tion** \ˌkär-b(y)ə-ˈrā-shən\ *n*

car·bu·re·tor \ˈkär-b(y)ə-ˌrāt-ər\ *n* **:** an apparatus for supplying an internal-combustion engine with atomized and vaporized fuel mixed with air in an explosive mixture

car·bu·rize \ˈkär-b(y)ə-ˌrīz\ *vt* **-rized; -riz·ing** [obs. *carburet* (carbide)] **1 :** to combine or impregnate (as metal) with carbon **2 :** CARBURET 2 — **car·bu·ri·za·tion** \ˌkär-b(y)ə-rə-ˈzā-shən\ *n*

car·ca·jou \ˈkär-kə-ˌjü, -ˌzhü\ *n* [CanF, of AmerInd origin] **:** WOLVERINE

car·ca·net \ˈkär-kə-nət\ *n* [MF *carcan*] *archaic* **:** an ornamental necklace or headband

car card *n* **:** a small cardboard placard for advertising esp. in or on streetcars and buses

car·case \ˈkär-kəs\ *Brit var of* CARCASS

car·cass \ˈkär-kəs\ *n* [MF *carcasse,* fr. OF *carcois*] **1 :** a dead body **:** CORPSE; *esp* **:** the dressed body of a meat animal **2 :** the living, material, or physical body **3 :** the decaying or worthless remains of a structure <the ~ of an abandoned automobile> **4 :** the foundation structure of something (as a tire)

carcin- *or* **carcino-** *comb form* [Gk *karkin-, karkino-,* fr. *karkinos* — more at CANCER] **1 :** crab <*carcino*logy> **2 :** tumor **:** cancer <*carcino*genic>

car·cin·o·gen \kär-ˈsin-ə-jən, ˈkärs-ᵊn-ə-ˌjen\ *n* **:** a substance or agent producing or inciting cancer — **car·ci·no·gen·e·sis** \ˌkärs-ᵊn-ō-ˈjen-ə-səs\ *n* — **car·ci·no·gen·ic** \-ˈjen-ik\ *adj* — **car·ci·no·ge·nic·i·ty** \-jə-ˈnis-ət-ē\ *n*

car·ci·noid \ˈkärs-ᵊn-ˌȯid\ *n* **:** a usu. benign tumor arising esp. from the mucosa of the gastrointestinal tract (as in the stomach or appendix)

car·ci·no·ma \ˌkärs-ᵊn-ˈō-mə\ *n, pl* **-mas** *or* **-ma·ta** \-mət-ə\ [L, fr. Gk *karkinōma* cancer, fr. *karkinos*] **:** a malignant tumor of epithelial origin — **car·ci·no·ma·tous** \-ˈō-mət-əs\ *adj*

car·ci·no·ma·to·sis \-ˌō-mə-ˈtō-səs\ *n* [NL, fr. L *carcinomat-, carcinoma*] **:** a condition in which multiple carcinomas are developing simultaneously usu. after dissemination from a primary source

car·ci·no·sar·co·ma \ˈkärs-ᵊn-ō-(ˌ)sär-ˈkō-mə\ *n, pl* **-mas** *or* **-ma·ta** \-mət-ə\ **:** a malignant tumor combining elements of carcinoma and sarcoma

car coat *n* **:** a three-quarter-length overcoat

¹card \ˈkärd\ *vt* **:** to cleanse, disentangle, and collect together (as fibers) by the use of a card preparatory to spinning — **card·er** *n*

²card *n* [ME *carde,* fr. MF, fr. LL *cardus* thistle, fr. L *carduus* — more at CHORD] **1 :** an implement for raising a nap on cloth **2 :** an instrument or machine for carding fibers that consists usu. of bent wire teeth set closely in rows in a thick piece of leather fastened to a back

³card *n* [ME *carde,* modif. of MF *carte,* prob. fr. OIt *carta,* lit., leaf of paper, fr. L *charta* leaf of papyrus, fr. Gk *chartēs*] **1 :** PLAYING CARD **2** *pl but sing or pl in constr* **a :** a game played with cards **b :** card playing **3 :** something compared to a valuable playing card in one's hand **4 :** a usu. clownishly amusing person **:** WAG **5 :** COMPASS CARD **6 a :** a flat stiff usu. small and rectangular piece of paper or thin paperboard: as (1) **:** POSTCARD (2) **:** VISITING CARD **b :** PROGRAM; *esp* **:** a sports program **c** (1) **:** a wine list (2) **:** MENU **d :** GREETING CARD

⁴card *vt* **1 :** to place or fasten on or by means of a card **2 :** to provide with a card **3 :** to list or record on a card **4 :** SCORE

⁵card *abbr* cardinal

Card *abbr* Cardiganshire

car·da·mom \ˈkärd-ə-məm, -ˌmäm\ *n* [L *cardamomum,* fr. Gk *kardamōmon,* blend of *kardamon* peppergrass & *amōmon,* an Indian spice plant] **:** the aromatic capsular fruit of an East Indian herb (*Elettaria cardamomum*) of the ginger family with seeds used as a condiment and in medicine; *also* **:** this plant

¹card·board \ˈkärd-ˌbō(ə)rd, -ˌbȯ(ə)rd\ *n* **:** a stiff moderately thick paperboard

²cardboard *adj* **1 a :** made of or as if of cardboard **b :** FLAT, TWO-DIMENSIONAL **2 :** UNREAL, STEREOTYPED <the story has too many ~ characters>

card–car·ry·ing \ˈkärd-ˌkar-ē-iŋ\ *adj* [fr. the assumption that such a person carries a card identifying him as a member] **:** being a regularly enrolled member of an organized group and esp. of the Communist party and not merely a sympathizer with its ideals and programs

card catalog *n* **:** a catalog (as of books) in which the entries are arranged systematically on cards

cardi- *or* **cardio-** *comb form* [Gk *kardi-, kardio-,* fr. *kardia* — more at HEART] **:** heart **:** cardiac **:** cardiac and <*cardio*gram> <*cardio*vascular>

-car·dia \ˈkärd-ē-ə\ *n comb form* [NL, fr. Gk *kardia*] **:** heart action or location (of a specified type) <dextro*cardia*> <tachy*cardia*>

¹car·di·ac \ˈkärd-ē-ˌak\ *adj* [L *cardiacus,* fr. Gk *kardiakos,* fr. *kardia*] **1 a :** of, relating to, situated near, or acting on the heart **b :** of or relating to the part of the stomach into which the esophagus opens or to the stomach exclusive of the pyloric end **2 :** of or relating to heart disease

²cardiac *n* **:** a person with heart disease

car·di·al·gia \ˌkärd-ē-ˈal-j(ē-)ə\ *n* [NL, fr. Gk *kardialgia,* fr. *kardia* + *-algia*] **1 :** HEARTBURN **2 :** pain in the heart

car·di·gan \ˈkärd-i-gən\ *n* [James Thomas Brudenell, 7th Earl of *Cardigan* †1868 E soldier] **:** a usu. collarless sweater or jacket that opens the full length of the center front

Cardigan *n* [*Cardigan* county, Wales] **:** a Welsh corgi with rounded ears, slightly bowed forelegs, and long tail — called also *Cardigan Welsh corgi*

cham·ber·lain \'chām-bər-lən\ *n* [ME, fr. OF *chamberlayn,* of Gmc origin; akin to OHG *chamarling* chamberlain, fr. *chamara* chamber, fr. LL *camera*] **1 :** an attendant on a sovereign or lord in his bedchamber **2 a :** a chief officer in the household of a king or nobleman **b :** TREASURER **3 :** an often honorary papal attendant; *specif*: a priest having a rank of honor below domestic prelate

cham·ber·maid \-ˌmād\ *n* **:** a maid who makes beds and does general cleaning of bedrooms (as in a hotel)

chamber music *n* **:** music and esp. instrumental ensemble music intended for performance in a private room or small auditorium and usu. having one performer for each part

chamber of commerce : an association of businessmen to promote commercial and industrial interests in the community

chamber of horrors : a hall in which objects of macabre interest (as instruments of torture) are exhibited; *also* **:** a collection of such exhibits

chamber orchestra *n* **:** a small orchestra usu. with one player for each instrumental part

chamber pot *n* **:** a bedroom vessel for urine and feces

cham·bray \'sham-ˌbrā, -brē\ *n* [irreg. fr. *Cambrai,* France] **:** a lightweight clothing fabric with colored warp and white filling yarns

cha·me·leon \kə-'mēl-yən\ *n* [ME *camelion,* fr. MF, fr. L *chamaeleon,* fr. Gk *chamaileōn,* fr. *chamai* on the ground + *leōn* lion — more at HUMBLE] **1 :** any of a group (Rhiptoglossa) of Old World lizards with granular skin, prehensile tail, independently movable eyeballs, and unusual ability to change the color of the skin **2 :** a fickle or changeable person or thing **3 :** any of various American lizards (as of the genus *Anolis*) capable of changing their color; *esp* **:** AMERICAN CHAMELEON — **cha·me·le·on·ic** \-ˌmē-lē-'än-ik\ *adj*

[1]**cham·fer** \'cham(p)-fər, 'cham-pər\ *n* [MF *chanfreint,* fr. pp. of *chanfraindre* to bevel, fr. *chant* edge (fr. L *canthus* iron tire) + *fraindre* to break, fr. L *frangere* — more at CANT, BREAK] **:** a beveled edge

[2]**chamfer** *vt* **cham·fered; cham·fer·ing** \-f(ə-)riŋ, -p(ə-)riŋ\ **1 :** to cut a furrow in (as a column) **:** GROOVE **2 :** to make a chamfer on **:** BEVEL

cham·fron \'sham-frən, 'cham-\ *n* [ME *shamfron,* fr. MF *chanfrein*] **:** the headpiece of a horse's bard

cham·ois \'sham-ē, *in sense 1 also* sham-'wä\ *n, pl* **cham·ois** *also* **cham·oix** *in sense 1* 'sham-ē(z) *or* sham-'wä(z), *in sense 2* 'sham-ēz\ [MF, fr. LL *camox*] **1 :** a small goatlike antelope (*Rupicapra rupicapra*) of Europe and the Caucasus **2** *also* **cham·my** \'sham-ē\ **:** a soft pliant leather prepared from the skin of the chamois or from sheepskin

chamois 1

cham·o·mile \'kam-ə-ˌmīl, -ˌmēl\ *n* [ME *camemille,* fr. ML *camomilla,* modif. of L *chamaemelon,* fr. Gk *chamaimēlon,* fr. *chamai* + *mēlon* apple] **:** any of a genus (*Anthemis,* esp. the common European *A. nobilis*) of composite herbs with strong-scented foliage and flower heads that contain a bitter medicinal principle; *also* **:** a similar plant of a related genus (*Matricaria*)

[1]**champ** \'champ, 'chämp, 'chȯmp\ *vb* [perh. imit.] *vt* **1 :** CHOMP **2 :** MASH, TRAMPLE ~ *vi* **1 :** to make biting or gnashing movements **2 :** to show impatience of delay or restraint — usu. used in the phrase *champing at the bit* <the children were ~*ing* at the bit to get on board>

[2]**champ** \'champ\ *n* **:** CHAMPION

cham·pac *or* **cham·pak** \'cham-ˌpak, 'chəm-(ˌ)pək\ *n* [Hindi & Skt; Hindi *campak,* fr. Skt *campaka*] **:** an East Indian tree (*Michelia champaca*) of the magnolia family with yellow flowers

cham·pagne \sham-'pān\ *n* [F, fr. *Champagne,* France] **1 :** a white sparkling wine made in the old province of Champagne, France; *also* **:** a similar wine made elsewhere **2 :** a pale orange yellow to light grayish yellowish brown

cham·paign \sham-'pān\ *n* [ME *champaine,* fr. MF *champagne,* fr. LL *campania* — more at CAMPAIGN] **1 :** an expanse of level open country **:** PLAIN **2** *archaic* **:** BATTLEFIELD — **champaign** *adj*

cham·per·ty \'cham-pərt-ē\ *n* [ME *champartie,* fr. MF *champart* field rent, fr. *champ* field (fr. L *campus*) + *part* portion — more at CAMP, PART] **:** a proceeding by which a person not a party in a suit bargains to aid in or carry on its prosecution or defense in consideration of a share of the matter in suit — **cham·per·tous** \-pərt-əs\ *adj*

cham·pi·gnon \sham-'pin-yən, cham-\ *n* [MF, fr. *champagne*] **:** an edible fungus; *esp* **:** the common meadow mushroom (*Agaricus campestris*)

[1]**cham·pi·on** \'cham-pē-ən\ *n* [ME, fr. OF, fr. ML *campion-, campio,* of WGmc origin] **1 :** WARRIOR, FIGHTER **2 :** a militant advocate or defender <an outspoken ~ of civil rights> **3 :** one that does battle for another's rights or honor <God will raise me up a ~ —Sir Walter Scott> **4 :** a winner of first prize or first place in competition; *also* **:** one who shows marked superiority <a ~ at telling stories>

[2]**champion** *vt* **1** *archaic* **:** CHALLENGE, DEFY **2 :** to protect or fight for as a champion **3 :** to act as militant supporter of **:** UPHOLD <always ~*s* the cause of the underdog> ***syn*** see SUPPORT

cham·pi·on·ship \-ˌship\ *n* **1 :** designation as champion **2 :** the act of championing **:** DEFENSE <his ~ of freedom of speech> **3 :** a contest held to determine a champion

champ·le·vé \ˌshäⁿl-ə-'vā\ *adj* [F] **:** of, relating to, or being a style of enamel decoration in which the enamel is applied and fired in cells depressed (as by incising) into a metal background — compare CLOISONNÉ — **champlevé** *n*

chan *abbr* channel

[1]**chance** \'chan(t)s\ *n* [ME, fr. OF, fr. (assumed) VL *cadentia* fall, fr. L *cadent-, cadens,* prp. of *cadere* to fall; akin to Skt *śad* to fall] **1 a :** something that happens unpredictably without discernible human intention or observable cause **b :** the assumed impersonal purposeless determiner of unaccountable happenings **:** LUCK **c :** the fortuitous or incalculable element in existence **:** CONTINGENCY **2 :** a situation favoring some purpose **:** OPPORTUNITY <the weekend gives him a ~ to relax> **3 :** a fielding opportunity in baseball **4 a :** the possibility of an indicated or a favorable outcome in an uncertain situation; *also* **:** the degree of likelihood of such an outcome <we have almost no ~ of winning> **b** *pl* **:** the more likely indications <~*s* are he's already heard the news> **5 a :** RISK <took a ~ and guessed at the answer> **b :** a ticket in a raffle — **chance** *adj* — **by chance :** in the haphazard course of events <they met *by chance* but parted by design>

[2]**chance** *vb* **chanced; chanc·ing** *vi* **1 a :** to take place or come about by chance **:** HAPPEN **b :** to be found by chance **c :** to have the good or bad luck **2 :** to come or light by chance ~ *vt* **1 :** to leave the outcome of to chance **2 :** to accept the hazard of **:** RISK ***syn*** see HAPPEN

chance·ful \'chan(t)s-fəl\ *adj* **1** *archaic* **:** CASUAL **2 :** EVENTFUL

chan·cel \'chan(t)-səl\ *n* [ME, fr. MF, fr. LL *cancellus* lattice, fr. L *cancelli;* fr. the latticework enclosing it] **:** the part of a church containing the altar and seats for the clergy and choir

chan·cel·lery *or* **chan·cel·lory** \'chan(t)-s(ə-)lə-rē, -səl-rē\ *n, pl* **-ler·ies** *or* **-lor·ies** **1 a :** the position, court, or department of a chancellor **b :** the building or room where a chancellor has his office **2 :** the office of secretary of the court of a person high in authority **3 :** the office or staff of an embassy or consulate

chan·cel·lor \'chan(t)-s(ə-)lər\ *n* [ME *chanceler,* fr. OF *chancelier,* fr. LL *cancellarius* doorkeeper, secretary, fr. *cancellus*] **1 a :** the secretary of a nobleman, prince, or king **b :** the lord chancellor of Great Britain **c** *Brit* **:** the chief secretary of an embassy **d :** a Roman Catholic priest heading the office in which diocesan business is transacted and recorded **2 a :** the titular head of a British university **b (1) :** a university president **(2) :** the chief executive officer in some state systems of higher education **3 a :** a lay legal officer or adviser of an Anglican diocese **b :** a judge in a court of chancery or equity in various states of the U.S. **4 :** the chief minister of state in some European countries — **chan·cel·lor·ship** \-ˌship\ *n*

chancellor of the exchequer *often cap C&E* **:** a member of the British cabinet in charge of the public income and expenditure

chance–med·ley \'chan(t)-'smed-lē\ *n* [AF *chance medlée* mingled chance] **1 :** accidental homicide not entirely without fault of the killer but without evil intent **2 :** haphazard action **:** CONFUSION

chance music *n* **:** music in which the elements of chance are introduced by the composer (as by selecting tempo, pitch, or dynamics by the throw of dice) or by the performer (as by choosing what parts to perform and the manner and order in which they are performed)

chan·cery \'chan(t)s-(ə-)rē\ *n, pl* **-cer·ies** [ME *chancerie,* alter. of *chancellerie* chancellery, fr. OF, fr. *chancelier*] **1 a** *cap* **:** a high court of equity in England and Wales with common-law functions and jurisdiction over causes in equity **b :** a court of equity in the American judicial system **c :** the principles and practice of judicial equity **2 :** a record office for public archives or those of ecclesiastical, legal, or diplomatic proceedings **3 a :** a chancellor's court or office or the building in which he has his office **b :** the office in which the business of a Roman Catholic diocese is transacted and recorded **c :** the office of an embassy **:** CHANCELLERY 3 — **in chancery 1 :** in litigation in a court of chancery; *also* **:** under the superintendence of the lord chancellor <a ward *in chancery*> **2 :** in a hopeless predicament

chan·cre \'shaŋ-kər\ *n* [F, fr. L *cancer*] **:** a primary sore or ulcer at the site of entry of a pathogen (as in tularemia); *esp* **:** the initial lesion of syphilis — **chan·crous** \-k(ə-)rəs\ *adj*

chan·croid \'shaŋ-ˌkrȯid\ *n* **:** a venereal disease caused by a hemophilic bacterium (*Hemophilus ducreyi*) and characterized by chancres that differ from those of syphilis in lacking firm indurated margins — called also *soft chancre* — **chan·croi·dal** \shaŋ-'krȯid-ᵊl\ *adj*

chancy \'chan(t)-sē\ *adj* **chanc·i·er; -est** **1** *Scot* **:** bringing good luck **:** AUSPICIOUS **2 :** uncertain in outcome or prospect **:** RISKY **3 :** occurring by chance **:** HAPHAZARD — **chanc·i·ness** *n*

chan·de·lier \ˌshan-də-'li(ə)r\ *n* [F, lit., candlestick, modif. of L *candelabrum*] **:** a branched often ornate lighting fixture suspended from a ceiling

chandelier

chan·delle \shan-'del, shäⁿ-\ *n* [F, lit., candle] **:** an abrupt climbing turn of an airplane in which the momentum of the plane is used to attain a higher rate of climb — **chandelle** *vi*

chan·dler \'chan-(d)lər\ *n* [ME *chandeler,* fr. MF *chandelier,* fr. OF, fr. *chandelle* candle, fr. L *candela*] **1 :** a maker or seller of tallow or wax candles and usu. soap **2 :** a retail dealer in provisions and supplies or equipment of a specified kind <a yacht ~>

chan·dlery \-(d)lə-rē\ *n, pl* **-dler·ies** **1 :** a place where candles are kept **2 :** the business of a chandler **3 :** the commodities sold by a chandler

[1]**change** \'chānj\ *vb* **changed; chang·ing** [ME *changen,* fr. OF *changier,* fr. L *cambiare* to exchange, of Celt origin; akin to OIr *camm* crooked; akin to Gk *skambos* crooked] *vt* **1 a :** to make

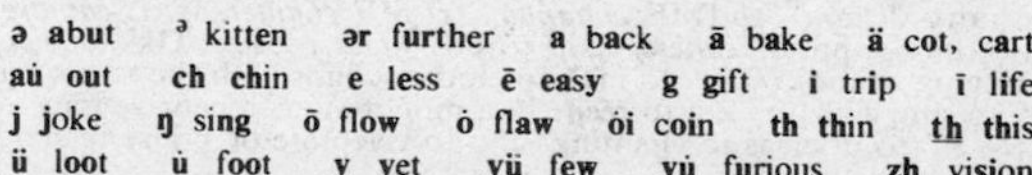

1car·di·nal \ˈkärd-nəl, -ᵊn-əl\ *adj* [ME, fr. OF, fr. LL *cardinalis*, fr. L, of a hinge, fr. *cardin-*, *cardo* hinge; akin to OE *hratian* to rush, Gk *skairein* to gambol] **:** of basic importance **:** MAIN, CHIEF, PRIMARY <the ~ virtue in the Shavian scale . . . is responsibility; every creed he has attacked Shaw has attacked on the grounds of irresponsibility —E. R. Bentley> ***syn*** see ESSENTIAL — **car·di·nal·ly** \-ē\ *adv*

2cardinal *n* **1 :** a high ecclesiastical official of the Roman Catholic Church who ranks next below the pope and is appointed by him to assist him as a member of the college of cardinals **2 :** CARDINAL NUMBER — usu. used in pl. **3 :** a woman's short hooded cloak orig. of scarlet cloth **4** [fr. its color, resembling that of the cardinal's robes] **:** any of several American finches (genus *Richmondena*) of the southern and middle U.S. of which the male is bright red with a black face and pointed crest — **car·di·nal·ship** \-ˌship\ *n*

car·di·nal·ate \-ət, -ˌāt\ *n* **:** the office, rank, or dignity of a cardinal

cardinal flower *n* **:** a No. American lobelia (*Lobelia cardinalis*) that bears a spike of brilliant red flowers

car·di·nal·i·ty \ˌkärd-ᵊn-ˈal-ət-ē\ *n, pl* **-ties** [2*cardinal* + *-ity*] **:** the number of elements in a given mathematical set

cardinal number *n* **1 :** a number (as 1, 5, 15) that is used in simple counting and that indicates how many elements there are in an assemblage — see NUMBER table **2 :** the property that a mathematical set has in common with all sets that can be put in one-to-one correspondence with it

cardinal point *n* **:** one of the four principal compass points north, south, east, and west

cardinal virtue *n* **1 :** one of the four classically defined natural virtues prudence, justice, temperance, or fortitude **2 :** a quality designated as a major virtue

car·dio·gram \ˈkärd-ē-ə-ˌgram\ *n* [ISV] **:** the curve or tracing made by a cardiograph

car·dio·graph \-ˌgraf\ *n* [ISV] **:** an instrument that registers graphically movements of the heart — **car·di·og·ra·pher** \ˌkärd-ē-ˈäg-rə-fər\ *n* — **car·dio·graph·ic** \ˌkärd-ē-ə-ˈgraf-ik\ *adj* — **car·di·og·ra·phy** \ˌkärd-ē-ˈäg-rə-fē\ *n*

car·di·oid \ˈkärd-ē-ˌȯid\ *n* **:** a heart-shaped curve that is traced by a point on the circumference of a circle rolling completely around an equal fixed circle and has the general equation $\rho = a(1 + \cos \theta)$ in polar coordinates

car·di·ol·o·gy \ˌkärd-ē-ˈäl-ə-jē\ *n* [ISV] **:** the study of the heart and its action and diseases — **car·di·o·log·i·cal** \-ē-ə-ˈläj-i-kəl\ *adj* — **car·di·ol·o·gist** \-ē-ˈäl-ə-jəst\ *n*

car·dio·my·op·a·thy \ˈkärd-ē-ō-(ˌ)mī-ˈäp-ə-thē\ *n, pl* **-thies** [*cardi-* + *my-* + *-pathy*] **:** a typically chronic disorder of heart muscle that may involve hypertrophy and obstructive damage to the heart

car·di·op·a·thy \ˌkärd-ē-ˈäp-ə-thē\ *n, pl* **-thies :** a disease of the heart

car·dio·pul·mo·nary \ˈkärd-ē-ō-ˈpu̇l-mə-ˌner-ē, -ˈpəl-\ *adj* **:** of or relating to the heart and lungs

car·dio·re·spi·ra·to·ry \ˈkärd-ē-ō-ˈres-p(ə-)rə-ˌtōr-ē, -ri-ˈspī-rə-, -ˌtȯr-\ *adj* **:** of or relating to the heart and the respiratory system **:** CARDIOPULMONARY

car·dio·ton·ic \ˌkärd-ē-ō-ˈtän-ik\ *adj* **:** tending to increase the tonus of heart muscle — **cardiotonic** *n*

car·dio·vas·cu·lar \-ˈvas-kyə-lər\ *adj* [ISV] **:** of, relating to, or involving the heart and blood vessels

-car·di·um \ˈkärd-ē-əm\ *n comb form, pl* **car·dia** \-ē-ə\ [NL, fr. Gk *kardia*] **:** heart <epi*cardium*>

car·doon \kär-ˈdün\ *n* [F *cardon*, fr. LL *cardon-*, *cardo* thistle, fr. *cardus*, fr. L *carduus* thistle, artichoke — more at CHARD] **:** a large perennial plant (*Cynara cardunculus*) related to the artichoke and cultivated for its edible root and leafstalks

card·play·er \ˈkärd-ˌplā-ər\ *n* **:** one that plays cards

card·sharp·er \-ˌshär-pər\ *or* **card·sharp** \-ˌshärp\ *n* **:** one who habitually cheats at cards

1care \ˈke(ə)r, ˈka(ə)r\ *n* [ME, fr. OE *caru*; akin to OHG *kara* lament, L *garrire* to chatter] **1 :** suffering of mind **:** GRIEF **2 a :** a disquieted state of blended uncertainty, apprehension, and responsibility **b :** a cause for such anxiety **3 :** painstaking or watchful attention **4 :** regard coming from desire or esteem **5 :** CHARGE, SUPERVISION <under a doctor's ~> **6 :** a person or thing that is an object of attention, anxiety, or solicitude <the flower garden was her special ~>

syn CARE, CONCERN, SOLICITUDE, ANXIETY, WORRY *shared meaning element* **:** a troubled or engrossed state of mind or the thing that causes this

2care *vb* **cared; car·ing** *vi* **1 a :** to feel trouble or anxiety **b :** to feel interest or concern <~ about freedom> **2 :** to give care <~ for the sick> **3 a :** to have a liking, fondness, or taste <don't ~ for her> **b :** to have an inclination <would you ~ for some pie> ~ *vt* **1 :** to be concerned about or to the extent of **2 :** WISH — **car·er** *n*

CARE *abbr* Cooperative for American Relief to Everywhere

1ca·reen \kə-ˈrēn\ *n* [MF *carène* keel, fr. OIt *carena*, fr. L *carina* keel, lit., nutshell; akin to Gk *karyon* nut] *archaic* **:** the act or process of careening **:** the state of being careened

2careen *vt* **1 a :** to cause (a boat) to lean over on one side **b :** to clean, caulk, or repair (a boat) in this position **2 :** to cause to heel over ~ *vi* **1 a :** to careen a boat **b :** to undergo this process **2 :** to heel over **3 :** to sway from side to side **:** LURCH <a ~*ing* carriage being pulled wildly along a street by a team of runaway horses —J. P. Getty>

1ca·reer \kə-ˈri(ə)r\ *n* [MF *carrière*, fr. OProv *carriera* street, fr. ML *carraria* road for vehicles, fr. L *carrus* car] **1 a :** COURSE, PASSAGE **b :** full speed or exercise of activity <he was now in the full ~ of conquest—T. B. Macaulay> **2 :** ENCOUNTER, CHARGE **3 :** a field for or pursuit of consecutive progressive achievement esp. in public, professional, or business life <Washington's ~ as a soldier> **4 :** a profession for which one trains and which is undertaken as a permanent calling <a ~ diplomat>

2career *vi* **:** to go at top speed esp. in a headlong manner <a car ~*ed* off the road>

ca·reer·ism \-ˌiz-əm\ *n* **:** the policy or practice of advancing one's career often at the cost of one's integrity — **ca·reer·ist** \-əst\ *n*

care·free \ˈke(ə)r-ˌfrē, ˈka(ə)r-\ *adj* **:** free from care **:** IRRESPONSIBLE <is ~ with his money> <a ~ vacation>

care·ful \-fəl\ *adj* **care·ful·ler; care·ful·lest 1** *archaic* **a :** SOLICITOUS, ANXIOUS **b :** filling with care or solicitude **2 :** exercising or taking care **3 a :** marked by attentive concern and solicitude **b :** marked by wary caution or prudence <be very ~ with knives> **c :** marked by painstaking effort to avoid errors or omissions — often used with *of* or an infinitive <~ of money> <~ to adjust the machine> — **care·ful·ly** \-f(ə-)lē\ *adv* — **care·ful·ness** \-fəl-nəs\ *n*

syn CAREFUL, METICULOUS, SCRUPULOUS, PUNCTILIOUS *shared meaning element* **:** showing close attention to detail (as of behavior or performance) ***ant*** careless

care·less \-ləs\ *adj* **1 a :** free from care **:** UNTROUBLED <~ days> **b :** INDIFFERENT, UNCONCERNED <~ of the consequences> **2 :** not taking care **3 :** not showing or receiving care: **a :** NEGLIGENT, SLOVENLY <writing that is ~ and full of errors> **b :** UNSTUDIED, SPONTANEOUS <~ grace> **c** *obs* **:** UNVALUED, DISREGARDED — **care·less·ly** *adv* — **care·less·ness** *n*

1ca·ress \kə-ˈres\ *n* [F *caresse*, fr. It *carezza*, fr. *caro* dear, fr. L *carus* — more at CHARITY] **1 :** an act or expression of kindness or affection **:** ENDEARMENT **2 a :** a light stroking, rubbing, or patting **b :** KISS — **ca·res·sive** \-ˈres-iv\ *adj* — **ca·res·sive·ly** *adv*

2caress *vt* **1 :** to treat with tokens of fondness, affection, or kindness **:** CHERISH **2 a :** to touch or stroke lightly in a loving or endearing manner **b :** to touch or affect as if with a caress <echoes that ~ the ear> — **ca·ress·er** *n* — **ca·ress·ing·ly** \-iŋ-lē\ *adv*

syn CARESS, FONDLE, PET, CUDDLE *shared meaning element* **:** to show affection by touching or handling

car·et \ˈkar-ət\ *n* [L, there is lacking, fr. *carēre* to lack, be without — more at CASTE] **:** a wedge-shaped mark made on written or printed matter to indicate the place where something is to be inserted

care·tak·er \ˈke(ə)r-ˌtā-kər, ˈka(ə)r-\ *n* **1 :** one that takes care of the house or land of an owner who may be absent **2 :** one temporarily fulfilling the function of office <a ~ government>

care·worn \-ˌwō(ə)rn, -ˌwȯ(ə)rn\ *adj* **:** showing the effect of grief or anxiety <a ~ face>

car·ex \ˈka(ə)r-ˌeks\ *n, pl* **car·i·ces** \ˈkar-ə-ˌsēz\ [NL, genus name, fr. L, sedge] **:** any of a genus (*Carex* of the family Cyperaceae) of perennial sedges that have seedlike achenes enclosed in a sac in the axil of a bract

car·fare \ˈkär-ˌfa(ə)r, -ˌfe(ə)r\ *n* **:** passenger fare (as on a bus)

car·ful \ˈkär-ˌfu̇l\ *n* **:** as much or as many as a car will hold

car·go \ˈkär-(ˌ)gō\ *n, pl* **cargoes** *or* **cargos** [Sp, load, charge, fr. *cargar* to load, fr. LL *carricare* — more at CHARGE] **:** the goods or merchandise conveyed in a ship, airplane, or vehicle **:** FREIGHT

car·hop \ˈkär-ˌhäp\ *n* [*car* + *-hop* (as in *bellhop*)] **:** one who serves customers at a drive-in restaurant

Car·ib \ˈkar-əb\ *n* [NL *Caribes* (pl.), fr. Sp *Caribe*, fr. Arawakan *Carib* — more at CANNIBAL] **1 :** a member of an American Indian people of northern So. America and the Lesser Antilles **2 :** the language of the Caribs

Ca·ri·ban \ˈkar-ə-bən, kə-ˈrē-bən\ *n* **1 :** a member of a group of American Indian peoples of northern So. America, the Lesser Antilles, and the Caribbean coast of Honduras, Guatemala, and British Honduras **2 :** the language family comprising the languages of the Cariban peoples

Ca·rib·be·an \ˌkar-ə-ˈbē-ən, kə-ˈrib-ē-\ *adj* [NL *Caribbaeus*, fr. *Caribes*] **:** of or relating to the Caribs, the eastern and southern West Indies, or the Caribbean sea

ca·ri·be \kə-ˈrē-bē\ *n* [AmerSp, fr. Sp, Carib, cannibal] **:** PIRANHA

car·i·bou \ˈkar-ə-ˌbü\ *n, pl* **caribou** *or* **caribous** [CanF, of Algonquian origin] **:** any of several large palmate-antlered deer (genus *Rangifer*) of northern No. America that are related to the reindeer

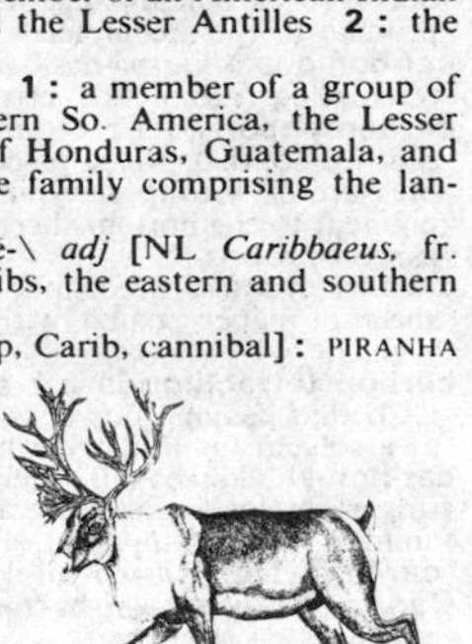

caribou

1car·i·ca·ture \ˈkar-i-kə-ˌchu̇(ə)r, -ˌt(y)u̇(ə)r\ *n* [It *caricatura*, lit., act of loading, fr. *caricare* to load, fr. LL *carricare*] **1 :** exaggeration by means of often ludicrous distortion of parts or characteristics **2 :** a representation esp. in literature or art that has the qualities of caricature **3 :** a distortion so gross as to seem like caricature — **car·i·ca·tur·al** \ˌkar-i-kə-ˈchu̇r-əl, -ˈt(y)u̇r-\ *adj* — **car·i·ca·tur·ist** \ˈkar-i-kə-ˌchu̇r-əst, -ˌt(y)u̇r-\ *n*

syn CARICATURE, BURLESQUE, PARODY, TRAVESTY *shared meaning element* **:** a comic or grotesque imitation

2caricature *vt* **-tured; -tur·ing :** to make or draw a caricature of **:** represent in caricature <his face has often been *caricatured* in the newspapers>

car·ies \ˈka(ə)r-ēz, ˈke(ə)r-\ *n, pl* **caries** [L, decay; akin to Gk *kēr* death] **:** a progressive destruction of bone or tooth; *esp* **:** tooth decay

car·il·lon \ˈkar-ə-ˌlän, -lən\ *n* [F, alter. of OF *quarregnon*, fr. LL *quaternion-*, *quaternio* set of four — more at QUATERNION] **1 a :** a set of fixed chromatically tuned bells sounded by hammers controlled from a keyboard **b :** an electronic instrument imitating a carillon **2 :** a composition for the carillon

car·il·lon·neur \ˌkar-ə-lə-ˈnər, ˌkar-ē-ə-ˈnər\ *n* [F, fr. *carillon*] **:** a carillon player

ca·ri·na \kə-ˈrī-nə, -ˈrē-\ *n, pl* **-ri·nas** *or* **-ri·nae** \-ˈrī-ˌnē, -ˈrē-ˌnī\ [NL, fr. L, keel — more at CAREEN] **:** a keel-shaped anatomical part, ridge, or process; *esp* **:** the part of a papilionaceous flower that encloses the stamens and pistil — **ca·ri·nal** \-ˈrīn-ᵊl\ *adj*

car·i·nate \ˈkar-ə-ˌnāt, -nət\ *also* **car·i·nat·ed** \-ˌnāt-əd\ *adj* **:** shaped like the keel or prow of a ship **:** KEELED, RIDGED <a ~ sepal>

ca·ri·o·ca \ˌkar-ē-ˈō-kə\ *n* [Pg, fr. Tupi] **1** *cap* **:** a native or resident of Rio de Janeiro **2 a :** a variation of the samba **b :** the music for this dance

car·i·ole \ˈkar-ē-ˌōl\ *n* [F *carriole,* fr. OProv *carriola,* deriv. of L *carrus* car] **1 :** a light one-horse carriage **2 :** a dog-drawn toboggan

car·i·ous \ˈkar-ē-əs, ˈker-\ *adj* [L *cariosus,* fr. *caries*] **:** affected with caries

1**cark** \ˈkärk\ *vb* [ME *carken,* lit., to load, burden, fr. ONF *carquier,* fr. LL *carricare*] *vt* **:** WORRY ~ *vi* **:** to be anxious

2**cark** *n* **:** TROUBLE, DISTRESS

carl *or* **carle** \ˈkär(ə)l\ *n* [ME, fr. OE *-carl,* fr. ON *karl* man, carl; akin to OE *ceorl* churl — more at CHURL] **1 :** a man of the common people **2** *chiefly dial* **:** CHURL, BOOR

car·line *or* **car·lin** \ˈkär-lən\ *n* [ME *kerling,* fr. ON, fr. *karl* man] *chiefly Scot* **:** WOMAN; *esp* **:** an old woman

car·ling \ˈkär-liŋ, -lən\ *n* [F *carlingue,* fr. ONF *calingue,* fr. ON *kerling,* lit., old woman] **:** a fore-and-aft member supporting a deck of a ship or framing a deck opening

Car·list \ˈkär-ləst\ *n* [Sp *carlista,* fr. Don *Carlos* claimant to the Spanish throne under the Salic law] **:** a supporter of Don Carlos or his successors as having rightful title to the Spanish throne — **Carlist** *adj*

car·load \ˈkär-ˈlōd, -ˌlōd\ *n* **1 :** a load that fills a car **2 :** the minimum number of tons required for shipping at carload rates

carload rate *n* **:** a rate for large shipments lower than that quoted for less-than-carload lots of the same class

Car·lo·vin·gian \ˌkär-lə-ˈvin-j(ē-)ən\ *adj* [F *carlovingien,* prob. fr. ML *Carl*us Charles + F *-ovingien* (as in *mérovingien* Merovingian)] **:** CAROLINGIAN

Carm *abbr* Carmarthenshire

car·ma·gnole \ˈkär-mən-ˌyōl\ *n* [F] **1 :** a lively song popular at the time of the first French Revolution **2 :** a street dance in a meandering course to the tune of the carmagnole

car·mak·er \ˈkär-ˌmā-kər\ *n* **:** an automobile manufacturer

Car·mel·ite \ˈkär-mə-ˌlīt\ *n* [ME, fr. ML *carmelita,* fr. *Carmel* Mount Carmel, Palestine] **:** a member of the Roman Catholic mendicant Order of Our Lady of Mount Carmel founded in the 12th century — **Carmelite** *adj*

car·mi·na·tive \kär-ˈmin-ət-iv, ˈkär-mə-ˌnāt-\ *adj* [F *carminatif,* fr. L *carminatus,* pp. of *carminare* to card, fr. *carmin-, carmen* card, fr. *carrere* to card — more at CHARD] **:** expelling gas from the alimentary canal so as to relieve colic or griping — **carminative** *n*

car·mine \ˈkär-mən, -ˌmīn\ *n* [F *carmin,* fr. ML *carminium,* irreg. fr. Ar *qirmiz* kermes + L *minium* — more at MINIUM] **1 :** a rich crimson or scarlet lake made from cochineal **2 :** a vivid red

Carn *abbr* Caernarvonshire

car·nage \ˈkär-nij\ *n* [MF, fr. ML *carnaticum* tribute consisting of animals or meat, fr. L *carn-, caro*] **1 :** the flesh of slain animals or men **2 :** great and bloody slaughter (as in battle) ***syn*** see MASSACRE

car·nal \ˈkärn-ᵊl\ *adj* [ME, fr. ONF or LL; ONF, fr. LL *carnalis,* fr. L *carn-, caro* flesh; akin to Gk *keirein* to cut — more at SHEAR] **1 :** BODILY, CORPOREAL **2 a :** marked by sexuality **b :** relating to or given to crude bodily pleasures and appetites **3 a :** TEMPORAL **b :** WORLDLY — **car·nal·i·ty** \kär-ˈnal-ət-ē\ *n* — **car·nal·ly** \ˈkärn-ᵊl-ē\ *adv*

syn CARNAL, FLESHLY, SENSUAL, ANIMAL *shared meaning element* **:** having or showing a physical rather than an intellectual or spiritual orientation or origin ***ant*** spiritual, intellectual

car·nall·ite \ˈkärn-ᵊl-ˌīt\ *n* [G *carnallit,* fr. Rudolf von *Carnall* †1874 G mining engineer] **:** a mineral $KMgCl_3 \cdot 6H_2O$ consisting of hydrous potassium-magnesium chloride important as a source of potassium

car·nas·si·al \kär-ˈnas-ē-əl\ *adj* [F *carnassier* carnivorous, deriv. of L *carn-, caro*] **:** of, relating to, or being teeth of a carnivore larger and longer than adjacent teeth and adapted for cutting rather than tearing — **carnassial** *n*

car·na·tion \kär-ˈnā-shən\ *n* [MF, fr. OIt *carnagione,* fr. *carne* flesh, fr. L *carn-, caro*] **1 a (1) :** the variable color of human flesh **(2) :** a pale to grayish yellow **b :** a moderate red **2 :** any of numerous cultivated usu. double-flowered pinks derived from the common gillyflower

car·nau·ba \kär-ˈnō-bə, -ˈnau̇-; ˌkär-nə-ˈü-bə\ *n* [Pg] **:** a fan-leaved palm (*Copernicia cerifera*) of Brazil that has an edible root and yields a useful leaf fiber and carnauba wax

carnauba wax *n* **:** a hard brittle high-melting wax from the leaves of the carnauba palm used chiefly in polishes

Car·ne·gie unit \ˌkär-nə-gē-, (ˌ)kär-ˌneg-ē-\ *n* [fr. its having been first defined by the Carnegie Foundation for the Advancement of Teaching] **:** the credit given for the successful completion of a year's study of one subject in a secondary school

car·ne·lian \kär-ˈnēl-yən\ *n* [alter. of *cornelian* fr. ME *corneline,* fr. MF, perh. fr. *cornelle* cornel] **:** a hard tough chalcedony that has a reddish color and is used in jewelry

car·ni·tine \ˈkär-nə-ˌtēn\ *n* [ISV, deriv. of L *carn-, caro* meat, flesh] **:** a white betaine that is an essential vitamin for some insect larvae (as a mealworm) and that occurs in vertebrate muscle

car·ni·val \ˈkär-nə-vəl\ *n* [It *carnevale,* alter. of earlier *carnelevare,* lit., removal of meat, fr. *carne* flesh (fr. L *carn-, caro*) + *levare* to remove, fr. L, to raise] **1 :** a season or festival of merrymaking before Lent **2 :** an instance of merrymaking, feasting, or masquerading **3 a :** a traveling enterprise offering amusements **b :** an organized program of entertainment or exhibition **:** FESTIVAL <a winter ~>

car·ni·vore \ˈkär-nə-ˌvō(ə)r, -ˌvȯ(ə)r\ *n* [deriv. of L *carnivorus*] **1 :** a flesh-eating animal; *esp* **:** any of an order (Carnivora) of flesh-eating mammals **2 :** an insectivorous plant

car·niv·o·rous \kär-ˈniv-(ə-)rəs\ *adj* [L *carnivorus,* fr. *carn-, caro* flesh + *-vorus* -vorous — more at CARNAL] **1 :** subsisting or feeding on animal tissues **2** *of a plant* **:** subsisting on nutrients obtained from the breakdown of animal protoplasm **3 :** of or relating to the carnivores — **car·niv·o·rous·ly** *adv* — **car·niv·o·rous·ness** *n*

car·no·tite \ˈkär-nə-ˌtīt\ *n* [F, fr. M. A. *Carnot* †1920 F inspector general of mines] **:** a mineral $K_2(UO_2)_2(VO_4)_2 \cdot 3H_2O$ consisting of a hydrous radioactive vanadate of uranium and potassium that is a source of radium and uranium

car·ny *or* **car·ney** *or* **car·nie** \ˈkär-nē\ *n, pl* **carnies** *or* **carneys** **1 :** CARNIVAL 3a **2 :** one who works with a carnival — **carny** *adj*

car·ob \ˈkar-əb\ *n* [MF *carobe,* fr. ML *carrubium,* fr. Ar *kharrūbah*] **1 :** a Mediterranean evergreen leguminous tree (*Ceratonia siliqua*) with racemose red flowers **2 :** a carob pod; *also* **:** its sweet pulp

ca·roche \kə-ˈrōch, -ˈrōsh\ *n* [MF *carroche,* fr. OIt *carroccio,* aug. of *carro* car, fr. L *carrus*] **:** a luxurious or stately horse-drawn carriage

1**car·ol** \ˈkar-əl\ *n* [ME *carole,* fr. OF, modif. of LL *choraula* choral song, fr. L, choral accompanist, fr. Gk *choraulēs,* fr. *choros* chorus + *aulein* to play a reed instrument, fr. *aulos,* a reed instrument — more at ALVEOLUS] **1 :** an old round dance with singing **2 :** a song of joy or mirth <the ~ of a bird —Lord Byron> **3 :** a popular song or ballad of religious joy

2**carol** *vb* **-oled** *or* **-olled; -ol·ing** *or* **-ol·ling** *vi* **1 :** to sing esp. in a joyful manner **2 :** to sing carols; *specif* **:** to go about outdoors in a group singing Christmas carols ~ *vt* **1 :** to praise in or as if in song **2 :** to sing esp. in a cheerful manner **:** WARBLE

Car·o·line \ˈkar-ə-ˌlīn, -lən\ *or* **Car·o·le·an** \ˌkar-ə-ˈlē-ən\ *adj* [NL *carolinus,* fr. ML *Carolus* Charles] **:** of or relating to Charles — used esp. with reference to Charles I and Charles II of England

Car·o·lin·gian \ˌkar-ə-ˈlin-j(ē-)ən\ *adj* [F *carolingien,* fr. ML *karolingi* French people, prob. fr. (assumed) OHG *karling* Frenchman, fr. *Karl* Charles] **:** of or relating to a Frankish dynasty dating from about A.D. 613 and including among its members the rulers of France from 751 to 987, of Germany from 752 to 911, and of Italy from 774 to 961 — **Carolingian** *n*

1**car·om** \ˈkar-əm\ *n* [by shortening & alter. fr. obs. *carambole,* fr. Sp *carambola*] **1 a :** a shot in billiards in which the cue ball strikes each of two object balls **b :** a shot in pool in which an object ball strikes another ball before falling into a pocket — compare COMBINATION SHOT **2 :** a rebounding esp. at an angle

2**carom** *vi* **1 :** to make a carom **2 :** to strike and rebound **:** GLANCE <the car ~*ed* off several trees>

car·o·tene \ˈkar-ə-ˌtēn\ *n* [ISV, fr. LL *carota* carrot] **:** any of several orange or red crystalline hydrocarbon pigments (as $C_{40}H_{56}$) that occur in the chromoplasts of plants and in the fatty tissues of plant-eating animals and are convertible to vitamin A

ca·rot·enoid *also* **ca·rot·i·noid** \kə-ˈrät-ᵊn-ˌȯid\ *n* **:** any of various usu. yellow to red pigments (as carotenes) found widely in plants and animals and characterized chemically by a long aliphatic polyene chain composed of isoprene units — **carotenoid** *adj*

ca·rot·id \kə-ˈrät-əd\ *adj* [F or Gk; F *carotide,* fr. Gk *karōtides* carotid arteries, fr. *karoun* to stupefy; akin to Gk *kara* head — more at CEREBRAL] **:** of, relating to, or being the chief artery or pair of arteries that pass up the neck and supply the head — **carotid** *n*

carotid body *n* **:** a small body of vascular tissue that adjoins the carotid sinus, functions as a chemoreceptor sensitive to change in the oxygen tension of blood, and mediates reflex changes in respiratory activity

carotid sinus *n* **:** a small but richly innervated arterial enlargement that is located at the point in the neck where either carotid artery forms its main branches and that functions in the regulation of heart rate and blood pressure

ca·rous·al \kə-ˈrau̇-zəl\ *n* **:** CAROUSE 2

1**ca·rouse** \kə-ˈrau̇z\ *n* [MF *carrousse,* fr. *carous,* adv., all out (in *boire carous* to empty the cup), fr. G *garaus*] **1** *archaic* **:** a large draft of liquor **:** TOAST **2 :** a drunken revel

2**carouse** *vb* **ca·roused; ca·rous·ing** *vi* **1 :** to drink liquor deeply or freely **2 :** to take part in a carouse ~ *vt, obs* **:** to drink up **:** QUAFF — **ca·rous·er** *n*

car·ou·sel \ˌkar-ə-ˈsel *also* -ˈzel; ˈkar-ə-ˌ\ *n* [F *carrousel,* fr. It *carosello*] **1 :** a tournament or exhibition in which horsemen execute evolutions **2 a :** MERRY-GO-ROUND **b :** a circular conveyer on which objects are placed <the luggage ~ at the airport>

1**carp** \ˈkärp\ *vi* [ME *carpen,* of Scand origin; akin to Icel *karpa* to dispute] **:** to find fault or complain querulously — **carp·er** *n*

2**carp** *n, pl* **carp** *or* **carps** [ME *carpe,* fr. MF, fr. LL *carpa,* prob. of Gmc origin; akin to OHG *karpfo* carp] **1 :** a large variable Old World soft-finned freshwater fish (*Cyprinus carpio*) of sluggish waters often raised for food; *also* **:** any of various related cyprinid fishes **2 :** a fish (as the European sea bream) resembling a carp

carp- *or* **carpo-** *comb form* [F & NL, fr. Gk *karp-, karpo-,* fr. *karpos* — more at HARVEST] **:** fruit <*carpo*logy>

-carp \ˌkärp\ *n comb form* [NL *-carpium,* fr. Gk *-karpion,* fr. *karpos*] **:** part of a fruit <meso*carp*> **:** fruit <schizo*carp*>

1**car·pal** \ˈkär-pəl\ *adj* [NL *carpalis,* fr. *carpus*] **:** relating to the carpus

2**carpal** *n* **:** a carpal element **:** CARPALE

car·pa·le \kär-ˈpal-(ˌ)ē, -ˈpāl-, -ˈpäl-\ *n, pl* **-lia** \-ē-ə\ [NL, neut. of *carpalis*] **:** a carpal bone

car park *n, chiefly Brit* **:** an area set apart for the parking of motor vehicles **:** PARKING LOT

car·pe di·em \ˌkär-pe-ˈdē-ˌem, -ˈdī-, -əm\ *n* [L, enjoy the day] **:** the enjoyment of the pleasures of the moment without concern for the future <the *carpe diem* theme in poetry>

car·pel \ˈkär-pəl\ *n* [NL *carpellum,* fr. Gk *karpos* fruit] **:** one of the structures in a seed plant comprising the innermost whorl of a flower, functioning as megasporophylls, and collectively constituting the gynoecium — **car·pel·lary** \-pə-ˌler-ē\ *adj* — **car·pel·late** \-ˌlāt, -lət\ *adj*

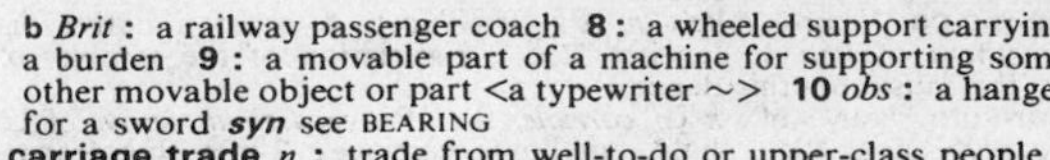

carpels: flower cut away: *1* petals; *2* stamens: *3* carpels: *4* sepals

¹car·pen·ter \ˈkär-pən-tər, ˈkärp-ᵊm-tər\ *n* [ME, fr. ONF *carpentier,* fr. L *carpentarius* carriage maker, fr. *carpentum* carriage, of Celt origin; akin to OIr *carr* vehicle — more at CAR] **:** a workman who builds or repairs wooden structures or their structural parts

²carpenter *vb* **car·pen·tered; car·pen·ter·ing** \-t(ə-)riŋ\ *vi* **:** to follow the trade of a carpenter <~*ed* when he was young> ~ *vt* **1 :** to make by or as if by carpentry **2 :** to put together often in a mechanical manner <~*ed* many television scripts>

carpenter ant *n* **:** an ant (esp. genus *Campanotus*) that gnaws galleries in dead or decayed wood

carpenter bee *n* **:** any of various solitary bees (*Xylocopa* and related genera) that gnaw galleries in sound timber

car·pen·try \-trē\ *n* **1 :** the art or trade of a carpenter; *specif* **:** the art of shaping and assembling structural woodwork **2 :** timberwork constructed by a carpenter **3 :** the form or manner of putting together the parts (as of a literary or musical composition) **:** STRUCTURE, ARRANGEMENT

car·pet \ˈkär-pət\ *n* [ME, fr. MF *carpite,* fr. OIt *carpita,* fr. *carpire* to pluck, modif. of L *carpere* to pluck — more at HARVEST] **1 :** a heavy woven or felted fabric used as a floor covering; *also* **:** a floor covering made of this fabric **2 :** a surface resembling or suggesting a carpet — **carpet** *vt* — **on the carpet :** before an authority for censure or reproof

¹car·pet·bag \-ˌbag\ *n* **:** a traveling bag made of carpet and widely used in the U.S. in the 19th century

²carpetbag *adj* **:** of, relating to, or characteristic of carpetbaggers <a ~ government>

car·pet·bag·ger \-ˌbag-ər\ *n* [fr. their carrying all their belongings in carpetbags] **1 :** a Northerner in the South after the American Civil War usu. seeking private gain under the reconstruction governments **2 :** a nonresident who meddles in politics — **car·pet·bag·gery** \-ˌbag-(ə-)rē\ *n*

carpet beetle *n* **:** a small beetle (*Bothynus gibbosus*) whose larva damages woolen goods; *broadly* **:** any beetle of similar habits

car·pet·ing \ˈkär-pət-iŋ\ *n* **:** material for carpets; *also* **:** CARPETS

carpet knight *n* [fr. the carpet's having been a symbol of luxury] **:** a knight devoted to idleness and luxury

car·pet·weed \ˈkär-pət-ˌwēd\ *n* **:** a No. American mat-forming weed (*Mollugo verticillata* of the family Aizoaceae, the carpetweed family)

-car·pic \ˈkär-pik\ *adj comb form* [prob. fr. NL *-carpicus,* fr. Gk *karpos* fruit] **:** -CARPOUS <poly*carpic*>

carp·ing \ˈkär-piŋ\ *adj* **:** marked by or inclined to querulous and often perverse criticism ***syn*** see CRITICAL ***ant*** fulsome — **carp·ing·ly** \-piŋ-lē\ *adv*

car·po·go·ni·um \ˌkär-pə-ˈgō-nē-əm\ *n, pl* **-nia** \-nē-ə\ [NL] **1 :** the flask-shaped egg-bearing portion of the female reproductive branch in some thallophytes **2 :** ASCOGONIUM — **car·po·go·ni·al** \-nē-əl\ *adj*

car·pol·o·gy \kär-ˈpäl-ə-jē\ *n* [ISV] **:** a branch of plant morphology dealing with fruit and seeds

car pool *n* **:** a joint arrangement by a group of private automobile owners in which each in turn drives his own car and carries the other passengers; *also* **:** the group entering into such an agreement

car·poph·a·gous \kär-ˈpäf-ə-gəs\ *adj* [Gk *karpophagos,* fr. *karp-* carp- + *-phagos* -phagous] **:** feeding on fruits

car·po·phore \ˈkär-pə-ˌfō(ə)r, -ˌfȯ(ə)r\ *n* [prob. fr. NL *carpophorum,* fr. *carp-* + *-phorum* -phore] **1 :** the stalk of a fungal fruiting body; *also* **:** the entire fruiting body **2 :** a slender prolongation of a floral axis from which the carpels are suspended

car·port \ˈkär-ˌpō(ə)rt, -ˌpȯ(ə)rt\ *n* **:** an open-sided automobile shelter sometimes formed by extension of a roof from the side of a building

car·po·spore \ˈkär-pə-ˌspō(ə)r, -ˌspȯ(ə)r\ *n* **:** a diploid spore of a red alga — **car·po·spor·ic** \ˌkär-pə-ˈspōr-ik, -ˈspȯr-\ *adj*

-car·pous \ˈkär-pəs\ *adj comb form* [NL *-carpus,* fr. Gk *-karpos,* fr. *karpos* fruit — more at HARVEST] **:** having (such) fruit or (so many) fruits <poly*carpous*> — **-car·py** \ˌkär-pē\ *n comb form*

car·pus \ˈkär-pəs\ *n, pl* **car·pi** \-ˌpī, -(ˌ)pē\ [NL, fr. Gk *karpos* — more at WHARF] **1 :** WRIST **2 :** the bones of the wrist

car·rack \ˈkar-ək, -ik\ *n* [ME *carrake,* fr. MF *caraque,* fr. OSp *carraca,* fr. Ar *qarāqir,* pl. of *qurqūr* merchant ship] **:** a large galleon

car·ra·geen *also* **car·ra·gheen** \ˈkar-ə-ˌgēn\ *n* [*Carragheen,* near Waterford, Ireland] **1 :** a dark purple branching cartilaginous seaweed (*Chondrus crispus*) found on the coasts of northern Europe and No. America — called also *Irish moss* **2 :** CARRAGEENAN

car·ra·geen·an *or* **car·ra·geen·in** *also* **car·ra·gheen·in** \ˌkar-ə-ˈgē-nən\ *n* [*carrageen* + ³*-an* or *-in*] **:** a colloid extracted esp. from carrageen and used esp. as a suspending agent (as in foods) and as a clarifying agent (as for beverages) and in controlling crystal growth in frozen confections

car·re·four \ˌkar-ə-ˈfu̇(ə)r\ *n* [MF, fr. LL *quadrifurcum,* neut. of *quadrifurcus* having four forks, fr. L *quadri-* + *furca* fork] **1 :** CROSSROADS **2 :** SQUARE, PLAZA <the farmers . . . preferred the open ~ for their transactions —Thomas Hardy>

car·rel \ˈkar-əl\ *n* [alter. of ME *carole* round dance, ring — more at CAROL] **:** a table that is often partitioned or enclosed and is used for individual study esp. in a library

car·riage \ˈkar-ij\ *n* [ME *cariage,* fr. ONF, fr. *carier* to transport in a vehicle — more at CARRY] **1 :** the act of carrying **2 a** *archaic* **:** DEPORTMENT **b :** manner of bearing the body **:** POSTURE **3** *archaic* **:** MANAGEMENT **4 :** the price or expense of carrying **5** *obs* **:** BURDEN, LOAD **6** *obs* **:** IMPORT, SENSE **7 a :** a wheeled vehicle; *esp* **:** a horse-drawn vehicle designed for private use and comfort **b** *Brit* **:** a railway passenger coach **8 :** a wheeled support carrying a burden **9 :** a movable part of a machine for supporting some other movable object or part <a typewriter ~> **10** *obs* **:** a hanger for a sword ***syn*** see BEARING

carriage trade *n* **:** trade from well-to-do or upper-class people

car·riage·way \ˈkar-ij-ˌwā\ *n, Brit* **:** a road used by vehicular traffic **:** HIGHWAY; *specif* **:** LANE 2b

car·rick bend \ˌkar-ik-\ *n* [prob. fr. obs. E *carrick* carrack, fr. ME *carrake, carryk*] **:** a knot used to join the ends of two large ropes — see KNOT illustration

car·ri·er \ˈkar-ē-ər\ *n* **1 :** one that carries **:** BEARER, MESSENGER **2 a :** an individual or organization engaged in transporting passengers or goods for hire **b :** a transportation line carrying mail between post offices **c :** a postal employee who delivers or collects mail **d :** one that delivers newspapers **e :** an entity (as a hole or an electron) capable of carrying an electric charge **3 a :** a container for carrying **b :** a device or machine that carries **:** CONVEYER **4 :** AIRCRAFT CARRIER **5 :** a bearer and transmitter of a causative agent of disease; *esp* **:** one who carries in his system the causative agent of a disease (as typhoid fever) to which he is immune **6 a :** a usu. inactive accessory substance **:** VEHICLE <a ~ for a drug or an insecticide> **b :** a substance (as a catalyst) by whose agency some element or group is transferred from one compound to another **7 :** an electric wave or alternating current whose modulations are used as signals in radio, telephonic, or telegraphic transmission **8 :** an organization acting as an insurer

carrier pigeon *n* **1 :** a pigeon used to carry messages; *esp* **:** HOMING PIGEON **2 :** any of a breed of large long-bodied show pigeons

car·ri·ole *var of* CARIOLE

car·ri·on \ˈkar-ē-ən\ *n* [ME *caroine,* fr. AF, fr. (assumed) VL *caronia,* irreg. fr. L *carn-, caro* flesh — more at CARNAL] **:** dead and putrefying flesh; *also* **:** flesh unfit for food

carrion crow *n* **:** a common European black crow (*Corvus corone*)

car·ron·ade \ˌkar-ə-ˈnād\ *n* [*Carron,* Scotland] **:** an obsolete short light iron cannon

car·rot \ˈkar-ət\ *n* [MF *carotte,* fr. LL *carota,* fr. Gk *karōton*] **1 :** a biennial herb (*Daucus carota* of the family Umbelliferae, the carrot family) with a usu. orange spindle-shaped edible root; *also* **:** its root **2 :** a promised often illusory reward or advantage

car·roty \-ət-ē\ *adj* **1 :** resembling carrots in color **2 :** having hair the color of carrots

car·rou·sel *var of* CAROUSEL

¹car·ry \ˈkar-ē\ *vb* **car·ried; car·ry·ing** [ME *carien,* fr. ONF *carier* to transport in a vehicle, fr. *car* vehicle, fr. L *carrus* — more at CAR] *vt* **1 :** to move while supporting (as a package) **:** TRANSPORT <her legs refused to ~ her further —Ellen Glasgow> **2 :** to convey by direct communication <~ tales about a friend> **3** *chiefly dial* **:** CONDUCT, ESCORT **4 :** to influence by mental or emotional appeal **:** SWAY **5 :** to get possession or control of **:** CAPTURE <*carried* off the prize> **6 :** to transfer from one place to another <~ a number in adding> **7 :** to contain and direct the course of <the drain *carries* sewage> **8 a :** to wear or have on one's person **b :** to bear upon or within one <is ~*ing* an unborn child> **9 a :** to have as a mark, attribute, or property <~ a scar> **b :** IMPLY, INVOLVE <the crime *carried* a heavy penalty> **10 :** to hold or comport (as one's person) in a specified manner **11 :** to sustain the weight or burden of <pillars ~ an arch> **12 :** to bear as a crop **13 :** to sing with reasonable correctness of pitch <~ a tune> **14 a :** to keep in stock for sale; *also* **:** to provide sustenance for <land ~*ing* 10 head of cattle> **b :** to have or maintain on a list or record <~ a person on a payroll> **15 :** to maintain and cause to continue through financial support or personal effort <he *carried* the magazine singlehandedly> **16 :** to prolong in space, time, or degree <~ a principle too far> **17 a :** to gain victory for; *esp* **:** to secure the adoption or passage of **b :** to win a majority of votes in (as a legislative body or a state) **18 :** PUBLISH <newspapers ~ weather reports> **19 a :** to bear the charges of holding or having (as stocks or merchandise) from one time to another **b :** to keep on one's books as a debtor <a merchant *carries* a customer> **20 :** to hold to and follow after (as a scent) **21 :** to hoist and maintain (a sail) in use **22 :** to cover (a distance) or pass (an object) at a single stroke in golf **23 :** to allow (an opponent) to make a good showing by lessening one's opposition ~ *vi* **1 :** to act as a bearer **2 a :** to reach or penetrate to a distance <voices ~ well> **b :** to convey itself to a reader or audience **3 :** to undergo or admit of carriage in a specified way **4** *of a hunting dog* **:** to keep and follow the scent **5 :** to win adoption <the motion *carried* by a vote of 71-25>
syn CARRY, BEAR, CONVEY, TRANSPORT *shared meaning element* **:** to move something from one place to another
— **carry a torch** *or* **carry the torch 1 :** CRUSADE **2 :** to be in love esp. without reciprocation **:** cherish a longing or devotion <she still *carries a torch* for him even though their engagement is broken> — **carry the ball :** to perform or assume the chief role **:** bear the major portion of work or responsibility — **carry the day :** WIN, PREVAIL

²carry *n* **1 :** carrying power; *esp* **:** the range of a gun or projectile or of a struck or thrown ball **2 a :** the act or method of carrying <fireman's ~> **b :** PORTAGE **3 :** the position assumed by a color-bearer with the flag or guidon held in position for marching **4 :** a quantity that is transferred in addition from one number place to the adjacent one of higher place value

car·ry·all \ˈkar-ē-ˌȯl\ *n* **1** [by folk etymology fr. F *carriole* — more at CARIOLE] **a :** a light covered carriage for four or more persons **b :** a passenger automobile similar to a station wagon but with a higher body often on a truck chassis **2** [¹*carry* + *all*] **:** a capacious bag or carrying case **3 :** a self-loading carrier esp. for hauling earth and crushed rock

carry away *vt* **1 :** to carry off **2 :** to arouse to a high and often excessive degree of emotion or enthusiasm

carrying capacity *n* **:** the population (as of deer) that an area will support without undergoing deterioration

carrying charge *n* **1 :** expense incident to ownership or use of property **2 :** a charge added to the price of merchandise sold on the installment plan

car·ry·ing–on \ˌkar-ē-iŋ-ˈȯn, -ˈän\ *n, pl* **carryings–on :** foolish, excited, or improper behavior; *also* **:** an instance of such behavior <scandalous *carryings-on*>

carry off *vt* **1 :** to cause the death of <the plague *carried off* thousands> **2 :** to perform easily or successfully <the actress *carried off* her part brilliantly in spite of only a few rehearsals> **3 :** to brave out

car·ry·on \ˈkar-ē-ˌȯn, -ˌän\ *n* **:** a piece of luggage suitable for being carried aboard an airplane by a passenger

carry on *vt* **:** CONDUCT, MANAGE <*carried on* the business> ~ *vi* **1 :** to behave in a foolish, excited, or improper manner <embarrassed by the way he *carries on*> **2 :** to continue one's course or activity in spite of hindrance or discouragement

car·ry·out \ˈkar-ē-ˌau̇t\ *n* **:** a food product packaged to be carried away from its place of sale rather than consumed on the premises — **carryout** *adj*

carry out \ˌkar-ē-ˈau̇t\ *vt* **1 :** to put into execution <*carry out* a plan> **2 :** to bring to a successful issue **:** COMPLETE, ACCOMPLISH <you will be paid when you have *carried out* the assignment> **3 :** to continue to an end or stopping point

car·ry–over \ˈkar-ē-ˌō-vər\ *n* **1 :** the act or process of carrying over **2 :** something carried over

carry over \ˌkar-ē-ˈō-vər\ *vt* **1 a :** to hold over (as goods) for another season **b :** to transfer (an amount) to the succeeding column, page, or book relating to the same account **2 :** to deduct (a loss or an unused credit) for taxable income of a subsequent period ~ *vi* **:** to persist from one stage or sphere of activity to another

carry through *vt* **:** to carry out ~ *vi* **:** PERSIST, SURVIVE <feelings that *carry through* to the present>

car·sick \ˈkär-ˌsik\ *adj* **:** affected with motion sickness esp. in an automobile — **car sickness** *n*

¹cart \ˈkärt\ *n* [ME, prob. fr. ON *kartr;* akin to OE *cræt* cart, OE *cradol* cradle] **1 :** a heavy usu. horse-drawn 2-wheeled vehicle used for farming or transporting freight **2 :** a lightweight 2-wheeled vehicle drawn by a horse, pony, or dog **3 :** a small wheeled vehicle

²cart *vt* **1 :** to carry or convey in or as if in a cart <buses to ~ the kids to and from school —L. S. Gannett> **2 :** to take or drag away without ceremony or by force — usu. used with *off* <they ~*ed* him off to jail> — **cart·er** *n*

cart·age \ˈkärt-ij\ *n* **:** the act of or rate charged for carting

carte blanche \ˈkärt-ˈbläⁿsh, -ˈblänch\ *n, pl* **cartes blanches** \ˈkärt-ˈbläⁿsh(-əz), -ˈblänch(-əz)\ [F, lit., blank document] **:** full discretionary power <was given *carte blanche* to build, landscape, and furnish the house>

carte du jour \ˌkärt-də-ˈzhu̇(ə)r\ *n, pl* **cartes du jour** \ˌkärt(s)-\ [F, lit., card of the day] **:** MENU

car·tel \kär-ˈtel\ *n* [MF, letter of defiance, fr. OIt *cartello,* lit., placard, fr. *carta* leaf of paper — more at CARD] **1 :** a written agreement between belligerent nations **2 :** a combination of independent commercial enterprises designed to limit competition **3 :** a combination of political groups for common action

Car·te·sian \kär-ˈtē-zhən\ *adj* [NL *cartesianus,* fr. *Cartesius* Descartes] **:** of or relating to René Descartes or his philosophy — **Cartesian** *n* — **Car·te·sian·ism** \-zhə-ˌniz-əm\ *n*

Cartesian coordinate *n* **1 :** either of two coordinates that locate a point on a plane and measure its distance from either of two intersecting straight-line axes along a line parallel to the other axis **2 :** any of three coordinates that locate a point in space and measure its distance from any of three intersecting coordinate planes measured parallel to that one of three straight-line axes that is the intersection of the other two planes

Cartesian plane *n* **:** a plane whose points are labeled with Cartesian coordinates

Cartesian product *n* **:** a set that is constructed from two given sets and comprises all pairs of elements such that one element of the pair is from the first set and the other element is from the second set

Car·thu·sian \kär-ˈth(y)ü-zhən\ *n* [ML *cartusiensis,* irreg. fr. OF *Chartrouse,* motherhouse of the Carthusian order, near Grenoble, France] **:** a member of an austere contemplative religious order founded by St. Bruno in 1084 — **Carthusian** *adj*

car·ti·lage \ˈkärt-ᵊl-ij, ˈkärt-lij\ *n* [L *cartilagin-, cartilago;* akin to L *cratis* wickerwork — more at HURDLE] **1 :** a translucent elastic tissue that composes most of the skeleton of the embryos and very young of vertebrates and becomes for the most part converted into bone in the higher vertebrates **2 :** a part or structure composed of cartilage

car·ti·lag·i·nous \ˌkärt-ᵊl-ˈaj-ə-nəs\ *adj* **:** composed of, relating to, or resembling cartilage

cartilaginous fish *n* **:** any of the fishes (esp. class Chondrichthyes) having the skeleton wholly or largely composed of cartilage; *also* **:** CYCLOSTOME

cart·load \ˈkärt-ˈlōd, -ˌlōd\ *n* **1 :** as much as a cart will hold **2 :** one third of a cubic yard (as of dirt)

car·to·gram \ˈkärt-ə-ˌgram\ *n* [F *cartogramme,* fr. *carte* + *-gramme* -gram] **:** a map showing statistics geographically

car·tog·ra·pher \kär-ˈtäg-rə-fər\ *n* **:** one that makes maps

car·tog·ra·phy \-fē\ *n* [F *cartographie,* fr. *carte* card, map + *-graphie* -graphy — more at CARD] **:** the science or art of making maps — **car·to·graph·ic** \ˌkärt-ə-ˈgraf-ik\ *or* **car·to·graph·i·cal** \-i-kəl\ *adj*

car·to·man·cy \ˈkärt-ə-ˌman(t)-sē\ *n* [F *cartomancie,* fr. *carte* card + *-o-* + *-mancie* -mancy] **:** fortune-telling by the use of playing cards

¹car·ton \ˈkärt-ᵊn\ *n* [F, fr. It *cartone* pasteboard] **:** a cardboard box or container

²carton *vt* **:** to pack or enclose in a carton ~ *vi* **:** to shape cartons from cardboard sheets

car·toon \kär-ˈtün\ *n* [It *cartone* pasteboard, cartoon, aug. of *carta* leaf of paper — more at CARD] **1 :** a preparatory design, drawing, or painting (as for a fresco) **2 a :** a satirical drawing commenting on public and usu. political matters **b :** COMIC STRIP **3 :** ANIMATED CARTOON — **cartoon** *vb* — **car·toon·ist** \-ˈtü-nəst\ *n*

car·top \ˈkär-ˌtäp\ *adj* **:** suitable in size and weight for carrying on top of an automobile <a ~ fishing boat>

car·top·per \-ˌtäp-ər\ *n* **:** a small boat that may be transported on top of a car

car·touche *also* **car·touch** \kär-ˈtüsh\ *n* [F *cartouche,* fr. It *cartoccio,* fr. *carta*] **1 :** a gun cartridge with a paper case **2 :** an ornate or ornamental frame **3 :** an oval or oblong figure (as on ancient Egyptian monuments) enclosing a sovereign's name

car·tridge \ˈkär-trij, *dial or archaic* ˈka-trij\ *n* [alter. of earlier *cartage,* modif. of MF *cartouche*] **1 a :** a tube of metal, paper, or both containing a complete charge for a firearm and usu. an initiating device (as a cap) **b :** a case containing an explosive charge for blasting **2 :** an often cylindrical container of material for insertion into a larger mechanism or apparatus **3 :** a small case in a phonograph pickup containing the needle and the mechanism for translating stylus motion into electrical voltage **4 :** a case containing a reel of magnetic tape arranged for insertion into a tape recorder

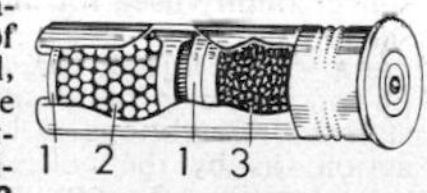

cartridge for shotgun: *1* wads, *2* shot, *3* powder

cartridge belt *n* **1 :** a belt having a series of loops for holding cartridges **2 :** a belt worn around the waist and designed for carrying various attachable equipment (as a cartridge case, canteen, or compass)

car·tu·lary \ˈkär-chə-ˌler-ē\ *n, pl* **-lar·ies** [ML *chartularium,* fr. *chartula* charter — more at CHARTER] **:** a collection of charters; *esp* **:** a book containing duplicates of the charters and title deeds of an estate

¹cart·wheel \ˈkärt-ˌhwēl, -ˌwēl\ *n* **1 :** a large coin (as a silver dollar) **2 :** a lateral handspring with arms and legs extended

²cartwheel *vi* **:** to move like a turning wheel; *specif* **:** to perform cartwheels — **cart·wheel·er** *n*

ca·run·cle \ˈkar-ˌəŋ-kəl, kə-ˈrəŋ-\ *n* [obs. F *caruncule,* fr. L *caruncula* little piece of flesh, dim. of *caro* flesh — more at CARNAL] **1 :** a naked fleshy outgrowth (as a bird's wattle) **2 :** an outgrowth on a seed adjacent to the micropyle — **ca·run·cu·lar** \kə-ˈrəŋ-kyə-lər\ *adj* — **ca·run·cu·late** \-lət, -ˌlāt\ *or* **ca·run·cu·lat·ed** \-ˌlāt-əd\ *adj*

car·va·crol \ˈkär-və-ˌkrōl, -ˌkrōl\ *n* [ISV, fr. NL *carvi* (specific epithet of *Carum carvi* caraway) + L *acr-, acer* sharp — more at CARAWAY, EDGE] **:** a liquid phenol $C_{10}H_{14}O$ found in essential oils of various mints (as thyme) and used as an antiseptic

carve \ˈkärv\ *vb* **carved; carv·ing** [ME *kerven,* fr. OE *ceorfan;* akin to MHG *kerben* to notch, Gk *graphein* to scratch, write] *vt* **1 :** to cut with care or precision <*carved* fretwork> **2 :** to make or get by or as if by cutting — often used with *out* <~ out a fortune> **3 :** to cut into pieces or slices <*carved* the turkey> ~ *vi* **1 :** to cut up and serve meat **2 :** to work as a sculptor or engraver — **carv·er** *n*

car·vel \ˈkär-vəl, -ˌvel\ *n* [ME *carvile,* fr. MF *caravelle, carvelle*] **:** CARAVEL

car·vel–built \-ˌbilt\ *adj* [prob. fr. D *karveel-,* fr. *karveel* caravel, fr. MF *carvelle*] **:** built with the planks meeting flush at the seams <a ~ boat>

carv·en \ˈkär-vən\ *adj* **:** wrought or ornamented by carving **:** CARVED

carv·ing \ˈkär-viŋ\ *n* **1 :** the act or art of one who carves **2 :** a carved object, design, or figure

car wash *n* **:** an area or structure equipped with facilities for washing automobiles

cary- *or* **caryo-** — see KARY-

cary·at·id \ˌkar-ē-ˈat-əd\ *n, pl* **-ids** *or* **-i·des** \-ə-ˌdēz\ [L *caryatides,* pl., fr. Gk *karyatides* priestesses of Artemis at Caryae, caryatids, fr. *Karyai* Caryae in Laconia] **:** a draped female figure supporting an entablature

cary·op·sis \ˌkar-ē-ˈäp-səs\ *n, pl* **-op·ses** \-ˌsēz\ *or* **-si·des** \-sə-ˌdēz\ [NL] **:** a small one-seeded dry indehiscent fruit (as of Indian corn or wheat) in which the fruit and seed fuse in a single grain

CAS *abbr* certificate of advanced study

ca·sa \ˈkäs-ə\ *n* [Sp & It, fr. L, cabin] *Southwest* **:** DWELLING

ca·sa·ba \kə-ˈsäb-ə\ *n* [*Kasaba* (now Turgutlu), Turkey] **:** any of several winter melons with yellow rind and sweet flesh

Ca·sa·no·va \ˌkaz-ə-ˈnō-və, ˌkas-\ *n* [Giacomo Girolamo *Casanova*] **:** LOVER; *esp* **:** a man who is a promiscuous and unscrupulous lover

Cas·bah \ˈkaz-ˌbä, ˈkäz-\ *n* [F, fr. Ar dial. *qaṣbah*] **1 :** a No. African castle or fortress **2 :** the native section of a No. African city

cas·ca·bel \ˈkas-kə-ˌbel\ *n* [Sp, lit., small bell like a sleigh bell] **1 :** a projection behind the breech of a muzzle-loading cannon **2 :** a small hollow perforated spherical bell enclosing a loose pellet

¹cas·cade \(ˈ)kas-ˈkād\ *n* [F, fr. It *cascata,* fr. *cascare* to fall, fr. (assumed) VL *casicare,* fr. L *casus* pp. of *cadere* to fall] **1 :** a steep usu. small fall of water; *esp* **:** one of a series **2 a :** something arranged in a series or in a succession of stages so that each stage derives from or acts upon the product of the preceding **b :** a fall of material (as lace) that hangs in a zigzag line **3 :** something falling or rushing forth in quantity <a ~ of sound> <a ~ of roses and daisies>

ə abut ᵊ kitten ər further a back ā bake ä cot, cart
au̇ out ch chin e less ē easy g gift i trip ī life
j joke ŋ sing ō flow ȯ flaw ȯi coin th thin th this
ü loot u̇ foot y yet yü few yu̇ furious zh vision

2**cascade** *vb* **cas·cad·ed; cas·cad·ing** *vi* **:** to fall or pour in or as if in a cascade ~ *vt* **1 :** to cause to fall like a cascade **2 :** to connect in a cascade arrangement

cas·cara \ka-ˈskar-ə\ *n* [Sp *cáscara* bark, fr. *cascar* to crack, break, fr. (assumed) VL *quassicare* to shake, break, fr. L *quassare* — more at QUASH] **1 :** CASCARA BUCKTHORN **2 :** CASCARA SAGRADA

cascara buckthorn *n* **:** a buckthorn (*Rhamnus purshiana*) of the Pacific coast of the U.S. yielding cascara sagrada

cascara sa·gra·da \-sə-ˈgräd-ə\ *n* [AmerSp *cáscara sagrada*, lit., sacred bark] **:** the dried bark of cascara buckthorn used as a mild laxative

cas·ca·ril·la \ˌkas-kə-ˈril-ə, -ˈrē-(y)ə\ *n* [Sp, dim. of *cáscara*] **:** the aromatic bark of a West Indian shrub (*Croton eluteria*) of the spurge family used for making incense and as a tonic; *also* **:** this shrub

1**case** \ˈkās\ *n* [ME *cas*, fr. OF, fr. L *casus* fall, chance, fr. *casus*, pp. of *cadere* to fall — more at CHANCE] **1 a :** a set of circumstances or conditions **b** (1) **:** a situation requiring investigation or action (as by the police) (2) **:** the object of investigation or consideration **2 :** CONDITION; *specif* **:** condition of body or mind **3** [ME *cas*, fr. MF, fr. L *casus*, trans. of Gk *ptōsis*, lit., fall] **a :** an inflectional form of a noun, pronoun, or adjective indicating its grammatical relation to other words **b :** such a relation whether indicated by inflection or not **4 :** what actually exists or happens **:** FACT **5 a :** a suit or action in law or equity **b** (1) **:** the evidence supporting a conclusion or judgment (2) **:** ARGUMENT; *esp* **:** a convincing argument **6 a :** an instance of disease or injury; *also* **:** PATIENT **b :** an instance that directs attention to a situation or exhibits it in action **:** EXAMPLE **c :** a peculiar person **:** CHARACTER ***syn*** see INSTANCE — **in any case :** without regard to or in spite of other considerations **:** whatever else is done or is the case <war is inevitable *in any case*> <*in any case* the seminar agreed that teachers of literature had to be concerned with . . . values —H. J. Muller> — **in case 1 :** IF **2 :** as a precaution **3 :** as a precaution against the event that — **in case of :** in the event of <*in case of* trouble, yell>

2**case** *n* [ME *cas*, fr. ONF *casse*, fr. L *capsa* chest, case, fr. *capere* to take — more at HEAVE] **1 a :** a box or receptacle for holding something **b :** a box together with its contents **c :** SET; *specif* **:** PAIR **2 :** an outer covering or housing **3 :** a shallow divided tray for holding printing type **4 :** the frame of a door or window **:** CASING

3**case** *vt* **cased; cas·ing 1 :** to enclose in or cover with a case **:** ENCASE **2 :** to line (as a well) with supporting material (as metal pipe) **3 :** to inspect or study esp. with intent to rob

ca·se·ate \ˈkā-sē-ˌāt\ *vi* **-at·ed; -at·ing** [L *caseus* cheese — more at CHEESE] **:** to undergo caseation

ca·se·ation \ˌkā-sē-ˈā-shən\ *n* **:** necrosis with conversion of damaged tissue into a soft cheesy substance

case·bear·er \ˈkās-ˌbar-ər, -ˌber-\ *n* **:** an insect larva that forms a protective case (as of silk)

case·book \-ˌbu̇k\ *n* **1 :** a book containing records of illustrative cases that is used for reference and instruction (as in law or medicine) **2 :** a compilation of primary and secondary documents relating to a central topic together with scholarly comment, exercises, and study aids that is designed to serve as a source book for short papers (as in a course in composition) or as a point of departure for a research paper

cased glass \ˈkāst-\ *n* **:** glass consisting of two or more fused layers of different colors often decorated by cutting so that the inner layers show through — called also *case glass*

case goods *n pl* **1 :** furniture (as bureaus or bookcases) that provides interior storage space; *also* **:** dining-room and bedroom furniture sold as sets **2 :** products (as liquor or canned milk) often sold by the case

case hard·en \ˈkās-ˌhärd-ᵊn\ *vt* **1 :** to harden (a ferrous alloy) so that the surface layer is harder than the interior **2 :** to make callous — **case–hard·ened** *adj*

case history *n* **:** a record of history, environment, and relevant details (as of individual behavior or condition) esp. for use in analysis or illustration

ca·sein \kā-ˈsēn, ˈkā-sē-ən\ *n* [prob. fr. F *caséine*, fr. L *caseus*] **:** a phosphoprotein of milk: as **a :** one that is precipitated from milk by heating with an acid or by the action of lactic acid in souring and is used in making paints and adhesives **b :** one that is produced when milk is curdled by rennet, is the chief constituent of cheese, and is used in making plastics

case knife *n* **1 :** SHEATH KNIFE **2 :** a table knife

case law *n* **:** law established by judicial decision in cases

case load *n* **:** the number of cases handled in a particular period (as by a court or clinic)

case·mate \ˈkā-ˌsmāt\ *n* [MF, fr. OIt *casamatta*] **:** a fortified position or chamber or an armored enclosure on a warship from which guns are fired through embrasures

case·ment \ˈkā-smənt\ *n* [ME, hollow molding, prob. fr. ONF *encassement* frame, fr. *encasser* to enchase, frame, fr. *en-* + *casse*] **:** a window sash that opens on hinges at the side; *also* **:** a window with such a sash

ca·se·ous \ˈkā-sē-əs\ *adj* [L *caseus* cheese] **:** marked by caseation; *also* **:** CHEESY

ca·sern *or* **ca·serne** \kə-ˈzərn\ *n* [F *caserne*] **:** a military barracks in a garrison town

case shot *n* **:** an artillery projectile consisting of a number of balls or metal fragments enclosed in a case

case study *n* **1 :** an intensive analysis of an individual unit (as a person or community) stressing developmental factors in relation to environment **2 :** CASE HISTORY

case system *n* **:** a system of teaching law in which instruction is chiefly on the basis of leading or selected cases as primary authorities instead of from textbooks

case·work \ˈkā-ˌswərk\ *n* **:** social work involving direct consideration of the problems, needs, and adjustments of the individual case (as a person or family) — **case·work·er** \-ˌswər-kər\ *n*

1**cash** \ˈkash\ *n* [MF or OIt; MF *casse* money box, fr. OIt *cassa*, fr. L *capsa* chest — more at CASE] **1 :** ready money **2 :** money or its equivalent paid promptly after purchasing — **cash·less** \-ləs\ *adj*

2**cash** *vt* **1 :** to pay or obtain cash for <~ a check> **2 :** to lead and win a bridge trick with (a card that is the highest remaining card of its suit) — **cash·able** \-ə-bəl\ *adj*

3**cash** *n, pl* **cash** [Pg *caixa* fr. Tamil *kācu*, a small copper coin, fr. Skt *karsa*, a weight of gold or silver; akin to OPer *karsha-*, a weight] **1 :** any of various coins of small value in China and southern India; *esp* **:** a Chinese coin usu. of copper alloy that has a square hole in the center **2 :** a unit of value equivalent to one cash

1**cash–and–car·ry** \ˌkash-ən-ˈkar-ē\ *adj* **:** sold or provided for cash and usu. without delivery service

2**cash–and–carry** *n* **:** the policy of selling on a cash-and-carry basis

cash·book \ˈkash-ˌbu̇k\ *n* **:** a book in which record is kept of all cash receipts and disbursements

cash crop *n* **:** a readily salable crop (as cotton or tobacco) produced or gathered primarily for market

cash discount *n* **:** a discount granted in consideration of immediate payment or payment within a prescribed time

ca·shew \ˈkash-(ˌ)ü, kə-ˈshü\ *n* [Pg *acajú*, *cajú*, fr. Tupi *acajú*] **:** a tropical American tree (*Anacardium occidentale*) of the sumac family grown for its edible kidney-shaped nut and receptacle and the gum it yields; *also* **:** its nut

cashew

cash flow *n* **:** a measure of corporate worth that consists of net income after taxes plus certain noncash charges against income (as allowances for depreciation and depletion) and that is usu. figured in dollars per share of common stock outstanding

1**ca·shier** \ka-ˈshi(ə)r, kə-\ *vt* [D *casseren*, fr. MF *casser* to discharge, annul — more at QUASH] **1 :** to dismiss from service; *esp* **:** to dismiss dishonorably **2 :** REJECT, DISCARD

2**cash·ier** \ka-ˈshi(ə)r\ *n* [D or MF; D *kassier*, fr. MF *cassier*, fr. *casse* money box] **:** one that has charge of money: as **a :** a high officer in a bank or trust company responsible for moneys received and expended **b :** one who collects and records payments

cashier's check *n* **:** a check drawn by a bank on its own funds and signed by the cashier

cash in *vt* **:** to convert into cash <*cashed in* all his bonds> ~ *vi* **1 a :** to retire from a gambling game **b :** to settle accounts and withdraw from an involvement (as a business deal) **2 :** to obtain financial profit or advantage <fly-by-night promoters trying to *cash in* — Tom McSloy> — often used with *on* <the chance of *cashing in* on a best-seller>

cash·mere \ˈkazh-ˌmi(ə)r, ˈkash-\ *n* [*Cashmere* (Kashmir)] **1 :** fine wool from the undercoat of the Kashmir goat; *also* **:** a yarn of this wool **2 :** a soft twilled fabric made orig. from cashmere

cash register *n* **:** a business machine that usu. has a money drawer, indicates the amount of each sale, and records the amount of money received and often automatically makes change

cas·ing \ˈkā-siŋ\ *n* **1 :** something that encases **:** material for encasing: as **a :** an enclosing frame esp. around a door or window opening **b :** a metal pipe used to case a well **c :** TIRE 2b **d :** a membranous case for processed meat **2 :** a space formed between two parallel lines of stitching through at least two layers of cloth into which something (as a rod or string) may be inserted

ca·si·no \kə-ˈsē-(ˌ)nō\ *n, pl* **-nos** [It, fr. *casa* house, fr. L, cabin] **1 :** a building or room used for social amusements; *specif* **:** one used for gambling **2 :** SUMMERHOUSE **3** *also* **cas·si·no :** a card game in which each player wins cards by matching or combining cards in his hand with those exposed on the table

cask \ˈkask\ *n* [MF *casque* helmet, fr. Sp *casco* potsherd, skull, helmet, fr. *cascar* to break — more at CASCARA] **1 :** a barrel-shaped vessel of staves, headings, and hoops usu. for liquids **2 :** a cask and its contents; *also* **:** the quantity contained in a cask — **casky** \ˈkas-kē\ *adj*

cas·ket \ˈkas-kət\ *n* [ME, modif. of MF *cassette*] **1 :** a small chest or box (as for jewels) **2 :** a usu. fancy coffin — **casket** *vt*

casque \ˈkask\ *n* [MF — more at CASK] **1 :** a piece of armor for the head **:** HELMET **2 :** an anatomic structure suggestive of a helmet

cas·sa·ba *var of* CASABA

Cas·san·dra \kə-ˈsan-drə\ *n* [L, fr. Gk *Kassandra*] **1 :** a daughter of Priam endowed with the gift of prophecy but fated never to be believed **2 :** one that predicts misfortune or disaster

cas·sa·va \kə-ˈsäv-ə\ *n* [Sp *cazabe* cassava bread, fr. Taino *caçábi*] **:** any of several plants (genus *Manihot*) of the spurge family grown in the tropics for their fleshy edible rootstocks which yield a nutritious starch; *also* **:** the rootstock

cas·se·role \ˈkas-ə-ˌrōl *also* ˈkaz-\ *n* [F, saucepan, fr. MF, irreg. fr. *casse* ladle, dripping pan, deriv. of Gk *kyathos* ladle] **1 :** a deep round usu. porcelain dish with a handle used for heating substances in the laboratory **2 :** a dish in which food may be baked and served **3 :** the food cooked and served in a casserole <a tuna ~>

cas·sette *or* **ca·sette** \kə-ˈset, ka-\ *n* [F, fr. MF, dim. of ONF *casse* case] **1 :** CASKET 1 **2 :** a lighttight magazine for holding film or plates for use in a camera **3 :** a small plastic cartridge containing magnetic tape with the tape on one reel passing to the other

cas·sia \ˈkash-ə\ *n* [ME, fr. OE, fr. L, fr. Gk *kassia*, of Sem origin; akin to Heb *qĕṣīʿāh* cassia] **1 :** a coarse cinnamon bark (as from *Cinnamomum cassia*) **2 :** any of a genus (*Cassia*) of leguminous herbs, shrubs, and trees of warm regions

cas·si·mere \ˈkaz-ə-ˌmi(ə)r, ˈkas-\ *n* [obs. *Cassimere* (Kashmir)] **:** CASHMERE

Cas·si·o·pe·ia \ˌkas-ē-ə-ˈpē-(y)ə\ *n* [L, fr. Gk *Kassiopeia*] **1 :** the wife of the Ethiopian King Cepheus who became mother of Andromeda by him and was later changed into a constellation **2** [L (gen. *Cassiopeiae*), fr. Gk *Kassiopeia*] **:** a northern constellation between Andromeda and Cepheus

Cassiopeia's Chair *n* **:** a group of stars in the constellation Cassiopeia resembling a chair

cas·sit·er·ite \kə-ˈsit-ə-ˌrīt\ *n* [F *cassitérite,* fr. Gk *kassiteros* tin] **:** a brown or black mineral that consists of tin dioxide SnO_2 and is the chief source of metallic tin

cas·sock \ˈkas-ək\ *n* [MF *casaque,* fr. Per *kazhāghand* padded jacket, fr. *kazh* raw silk + *āghand* stuffed] **:** an ankle-length garment with close-fitting sleeves worn esp. in Roman Catholic and Anglican churches by the clergy and by laymen assisting in services

cas·so·wary \ˈkas-ə-ˌwer-ē\ *n, pl* **-war·ies** [Malay *kĕsuari*] **:** any of several large ratite birds (genus *Casuarius*) esp. of New Guinea and Australia closely related to the emu

[1]**cast** \ˈkast\ *vb* **cast; cast·ing** [ME *casten,* fr. ON *kasta;* akin to ON *kös* heap and perh. to L *gerere* to carry, wage] *vt* **1 a :** to cause to move by throwing <~ a fishing lure> **b :** DIRECT <~ a glance> **c** (1) **:** to put forth <the fire ~*s* a warm glow> (2) **:** to place as if by throwing <~ doubt on their reliability> **d :** to deposit (a ballot) formally **e** (1) **:** to throw off or away <the horse ~ a shoe> (2) **:** to get rid of **:** DISCARD <~ off all restraint> (3) **:** SHED, MOLT (4) **:** to bring forth; *esp* **:** to give birth to prematurely **f :** to throw to the ground esp. in wrestling **g :** to build by throwing up earth **2 a** (1) **:** to perform arithmetical operations on **:** ADD (2) **:** to calculate by means of astrology **b** *archaic* **:** DECIDE, INTEND **3 a :** to dispose or arrange into parts or into a suitable form or order **b** (1) **:** to assign the parts of (a dramatic production) to actors (2) **:** to assign (an actor) to a role or part **4 a :** to give a shape to (a substance) by pouring in liquid or plastic form into a mold and letting harden without pressure <~ steel> **b :** to form by this process <~ machine parts> **5 :** TURN <~ the scale slightly> **6 :** to make (a knot or stitch) by looping or catching up **7 :** TWIST, WARP <a beam ~ by age> ~ *vi* **1 :** to throw something; *specif* **:** to throw out a lure with a fishing rod **2** *dial Brit* **:** VOMIT **3** *dial Eng* **:** to bear fruit **:** YIELD **4 a :** to perform addition **b** *obs* **:** ESTIMATE, CONJECTURE **5 :** WARP **6 :** to range over land in search of a trail — used of hunting dogs or trackers **7 a :** VEER **b :** to wear ship **8 :** to take form in a mold ***syn*** see THROW, DISCARD — **cast lots :** to draw lots to determine a matter by chance

[2]**cast** *n* **1 a :** an act of casting **b :** something that happens as a result of chance **c :** a throw of dice **d :** a throw of a line (as a fishing line) or net **2 a :** the form in which a thing is constructed **b :** the set of actors in a play or narrative **c :** the arrangement of draperies in a painting **3 :** the distance to which a thing can be thrown; *specif* **:** the distance a bow can shoot **4 a :** a turning of the eye in a particular direction; *also* **:** EXPRESSION <this freakish, elfish ~ came into the child's eye —Nathaniel Hawthorne> **b :** a slight strabismus **5 :** something that is thrown or the quantity thrown: as **a :** the number of hawks released by a falconer at one time **b** *Brit* **:** the leader of a fishing line **c :** the quantity of metal cast at a single operation **6 a :** something that is formed by casting in a mold or form: as (1) **:** a reproduction (as of a statue) in metal or plaster **:** CASTING (2) **:** a fossil reproduction of the details of a natural object by mineral infiltration **b :** an impression taken from an object with a liquid or plastic substance **:** MOLD **c :** a rigid dressing of gauze impregnated with plaster of paris for immobilizing a diseased or broken part **7 :** FORECAST, CONJECTURE **8 a :** an overspread of a color or modification of the appearance of a substance by a trace of some added hue **:** SHADE <gray with a greenish ~> **b :** TINGE, SUGGESTION **9 a :** a ride on one's way in a vehicle **:** LIFT **b** *Scot* **:** HELP, ASSISTANCE **10 a :** SHAPE, APPEARANCE <the delicate ~ of her features> **b :** characteristic quality <modern science . . . was in conflict with the humanist ~ of mind —T. F. O'Dea> **11 :** something that is shed, ejected, or thrown out or off: as **a :** the excrement of an earthworm **b :** a mass of plastic matter formed in cavities of diseased organs and discharged from the body **c :** the skin of an insect **12 :** the ranging in search of a trail by a dog, hunting pack, or tracker

cast about *vt* **:** to lay plans concerning **:** CONTRIVE <*cast about* how he was to go> ~ *vi* **:** to look around **:** SEEK <he *casts about* uncertainly for a place to sit>

cas·ta·net \ˌkas-tə-ˈnet\ *n* [Sp *castañeta,* fr. *castaña* chestnut, fr. L *castanea* — more at CHESTNUT] **:** a rhythm instrument used esp. by dancers that consists of two small shells of ivory, hard wood, or plastic fastened to the thumb and clicked together by the other fingers — usu. used in pl.

castanets

cast·away \ˈkas-tə-ˌwā\ *adj* **1 :** thrown away **:** REJECTED **2 a :** cast adrift or ashore as a survivor of a shipwreck **b :** thrown out or left without friends or resources — **castaway** *n*

caste \ˈkast\ *n* [Pg *casta,* lit., race, lineage, fr. fem. of *casto* pure, chaste, fr. L *castus;* akin to L *carēre* to be without, Gk *keazein* to split, Skt *śasati* he cuts to pieces] **1 :** one of the hereditary social classes in Hinduism that restrict the occupation of their members and their association with the members of other castes **2 a :** a division of society based on differences of wealth, inherited rank or privilege, profession, or occupation **b :** the position conferred by caste standing **:** PRESTIGE **3 :** a system of rigid social stratification characterized by hereditary status, endogamy, and social barriers sanctioned by custom, law, or religion **4 :** a specialized form (as the soldier or worker of an ant) of a polymorphic social insect that carries out a particular function in the colony — **caste·ism** \ˈkas-ˌtiz-əm\ *n*

cas·tel·lan \ˈkas-tə-lən\ *n* [ME *castelleyn,* fr. ONF *castelain,* fr. L *castellanus* occupant of a castle, fr. *castellanus* of a castle, fr. *castellum* castle] **:** a governor or warden of a castle or fort

cas·tel·lat·ed \ˈkas-tə-ˌlāt-əd\ *adj* [ML *castellatus,* pp. of *castellare* to fortify, fr. L *castellum*] **1 :** having battlements like a castle **2 :** having or supporting a castle

cast·er \ˈkas-tər\ *n* **1 :** one that casts; *esp* **:** a machine that casts type **2** *or* **cas·tor** \-tər\ **a :** a usu. silver table vessel with a perforated top for sprinkling a seasoning (as sugar or spice) **b :** a usu. revolving metal stand bearing condiment containers (as cruets, mustard pot, and often shakers) for table use **:** a cruet stand **3** *or* **castor :** a wheel or set of wheels mounted in a swivel frame and used for supporting furniture, trucks, and portable machines

cas·ti·gate \ˈkas-tə-ˌgāt\ *vt* **-gat·ed; -gat·ing** [L *castigatus,* pp. of *castigare* — more at CHASTEN] **:** to subject to severe punishment, reproof, or criticism ***syn*** see PUNISH — **cas·ti·ga·tion** \ˌkas-tə-ˈgā-shən\ *n* — **cas·ti·ga·tor** \ˈkas-tə-ˌgāt-ər\ *n*

cas·tile soap \(ˌ)kas-ˌtēl-\ *n, often cap C* [*Castile,* region of Spain] **:** a fine hard bland soap made from olive oil and sodium hydroxide; *also* **:** any of various similar soaps

Cas·til·ian \ka-ˈstil-yən\ *n* **1 :** a native or inhabitant of Castile; *broadly* **:** SPANIARD **2 a :** the dialect of Castile **b :** the official and literary language of Spain based on this dialect — **Castilian** *adj*

cast·ing *n* **1 :** the act of one that casts: as **a :** the throwing of a fishing line by means of a rod and reel **b :** the assignment of parts and duties to actors or performers **2 :** something cast in a mold **3 :** something that is cast out or off

casting director *n* **:** one who supervises the casting of dramatic productions (as films and plays)

casting vote *n* **:** a deciding vote cast by a presiding officer to break a tie

cast–iron *adj* **1 :** made of cast iron **2 :** resembling cast iron: as **a :** capable of withstanding great strain <a ~ stomach> **b :** not admitting change, adaptation, or exception **:** RIGID <a man of ~ will>

cast iron *n* **:** a commercial alloy of iron, carbon, and silicon that is cast in a mold and is hard, brittle, nonmalleable, and incapable of being hammer-welded but more easily fusible than steel

[1]**cas·tle** \ˈkas-əl\ *n* [ME *castel,* fr. OE, fr. ONF, fr. L *castellum* fortress, castle, dim. of *castrum* fortified place; akin to L *castrare* to castrate] **1 a :** a large fortified building or set of buildings **b :** a massive or imposing house **2 :** a retreat safe against intrusion or invasion **3 :** ROOK

[2]**castle** *vb* **cas·tled; cas·tling** \ˈkas-(ə-)liŋ\ *vt* **1 :** to establish in a castle **2 :** to move (the chess king) in castling ~ *vi* **:** to move a chess king two squares toward a rook and in the same move the rook to the square next past the king

cas·tled \ˈkas-əld\ *adj* **:** CASTELLATED

castle in the air : an impracticable project **:** DAYDREAM — called also *castle in Spain*

cast–off \ˈkas-ˌtȯf\ *adj* **:** thrown away or aside — **cast·off** *n*

cast off \(ˈ)kas-ˈtȯf\ *vt* **1 :** LOOSE <*cast off* a hunting dog> **2 :** UNFASTEN <*cast off* a boat> **3 :** to remove (a stitch) from a knitting needle in such a way as to prevent unraveling ~ *vi* **1 :** to unfasten or untie a boat or a line **2 :** to turn one's partner in a square dance and pass around the outside of the set and back **3 :** to finish a knitted fabric by casting off all stitches

cast on *vt* **:** to place (stitches) on a knitting needle for beginning or enlarging knitted work

cas·tor \ˈkas-tər\ *n* [ME, fr. L, fr. Gk *kastōr,* fr. *Kastōr* Castor] **1 :** BEAVER 1a **2 :** a bitter strong-smelling creamy orange-brown substance consisting of the dried perineal glands of the beaver and their secretion used esp. by perfumers **3 :** a beaver hat

Cas·tor \ˈkas-tər\ *n* [L, fr. Gk *Kastōr*] **1 :** one of the Dioscuri **2 :** the more northern of the two bright stars in Gemini

castor bean *n* **:** the very poisonous seed of the castor-oil plant; *also* **:** CASTOR-OIL PLANT

castor oil *n* [prob. fr. its former use as a substitute for castor in medicine] **:** a pale viscous fatty oil from castor beans used esp. as a cathartic or lubricant

castor–oil plant *n* **:** a tropical Old World herb (*Ricinus communis*) widely grown as an ornamental or for its oil-rich castor beans

cast out *vt* **:** to drive out **:** EXPEL

cas·trate \ˈkas-ˌtrāt\ *vt* **cas·trat·ed; cas·trat·ing** [L *castratus,* pp. of *castrare;* akin to Skt *śasati* he cuts to pieces — more at CASTE] **1 a :** to deprive of the testes **:** GELD **b :** to deprive of the ovaries **:** SPAY **2 :** to deprive of vitality or effect **:** EMASCULATE — **castrate** *n* — **cas·trat·er** *n* — **cas·tra·tion** \ka-ˈstrā-shən\ *n* — **cas·tra·to·ry** \ˈkas-trə-ˌtōr-ē, -ˌtȯr-\ *adj*

cas·tra·to \ka-ˈsträt-(ˌ)ō, kə-\ *n, pl* **-ti** \-ē\ [It, fr. pp. of *castrare* to castrate, fr. L] **:** a singer castrated in boyhood to preserve the soprano or contralto range of his voice

Cas·tro·ism \ˈkas-(ˌ)trō-ˌiz-əm\ *n* **:** the political, economic, and social principles and policies of Fidel Castro — **Cas·tro·ite** \-ˌīt\ *n*

[1]**ca·su·al** \ˈkazh-(ə-)wəl, ˈkazh-əl\ *adj* [ME, fr. MF & LL; MF *casuel,* fr. LL *casualis,* fr. L *casus* fall, chance — more at CASE] **1 :** subject to, resulting from, or occurring by chance **2 a :** occurring without regularity **:** OCCASIONAL **b :** employed for irregular periods **3 a :** feeling or showing little concern **:** NONCHALANT **b** (1) **:** INFORMAL, NATURAL (2) **:** designed for informal use ***syn* 1** see ACCIDENTAL **2** see RANDOM ***ant*** deliberate — **ca·su·al·ly** \-ē\ *adv* — **ca·su·al·ness** *n*

[2]**casual** *n* **1 :** a casual or migratory worker **2 :** an officer or enlisted man awaiting assignment or transportation to his unit

ca·su·al·ty \ˈkazh-əl-tē, ˈkazh-(ə-)wəl-\ *n, pl* **-ties 1 :** serious or fatal accident **:** DISASTER **2 a :** a military person lost through death, wounds, injury, sickness, internment, or capture or through

being missing in action **b :** a person or thing injured, lost, or destroyed <the ex-senator was a ~ of the last election>
casual water *n* **:** a temporary accumulation of water not forming a regular hazard of a golf course
ca·su·a·ri·na \ˌkazh-ə-(wə-)ˈrē-nə\ *n* [NL, genus name, fr. Malay (*pohon*) *kĕsuari,* lit., cassowary tree; fr. the resemblance of its twigs to cassowary feathers] **:** any of a genus (*Casuarina* of the family Casuarinaceae) of dicotyledonous chiefly Australian trees which have whorls of scalelike leaves and jointed stems resembling horsetails and some of which yield a heavy hard wood
ca·su·ist \ˈkazh-(ə-)wəst\ *n* [prob. fr. Sp *casuista,* fr. L *casus* fall, chance — more at CASE] **:** one skilled in or given to casuistry — **ca·su·is·tic** \ˌkazh-ə-ˈwis-tik\ *or* **ca·su·is·ti·cal** \-ti-kəl\ *adj*
ca·su·ist·ry \ˈkazh-(ə-)wə-strē\ *n, pl* **-ries** **1 :** a method or doctrine dealing with cases of conscience and the resolution of questions of right or wrong in conduct **2 :** false application of principles esp. with regard to morals or law <no ~ will convince us that this serious loss is really a victory>
ca·sus bel·li \ˌkäs-əs-ˈbel-ˌē, ˌkā-səs-ˈbel-ˌī\ *n, pl* **ca·sus belli** \ˌkäs-ˌüs-, ˌkā-ˌsüs-\ [NL, occasion of war] **:** an event or action that justifies or allegedly justifies war or conflict
[1]cat \ˈkat\ *n, often attrib* [ME, fr. OE *catt;* akin to OHG *kazza* cat; both fr. a prehistoric NGmc-WGmc word prob. borrowed fr. LL *cattus, catta* cat] **1 a :** a carnivorous mammal (*Felis catus*) long domesticated and kept by man as a pet or for catching rats and mice **b :** any of a family (Felidae) including the domestic cat, lion, tiger, leopard, jaguar, cougar, wildcat, lynx, and cheetah **c :** the fur or pelt of the domestic cat **2 :** a malicious woman **3 :** a strong tackle used to hoist an anchor to the cathead of a ship **4 a :** CATBOAT **b :** CATAMARAN **5 :** CAT-O'-NINE-TAILS **6 :** CATFISH **7** *slang* **a :** a player or devotee of hot jazz **b :** GUY **8 :** a burglar who is esp. adept at entering and leaving the place he burglarizes without attracting notice
[2]cat *vb* **cat·ted; cat·ting** *vt* **:** to bring (an anchor) up to the cathead ~ *vi* **:** to search for a sexual mate — often used with *around;* often considered vulgar
[3]cat *abbr* **1** catalog **2** catalyst
Cat \ˈkat\ *trademark* — used for a Caterpillar tractor
CAT *abbr* **1** clear-air turbulence **2** college ability test
cata- *or* **cat-** *or* **cath-** *prefix* [Gk *kata-, kat-, kath-,* fr. *kata* down, in accordance with, by; akin to L *com-* with — more at CO-] **:** down <*cata*clinal>
cat·a·bol·ic \ˌkat-ə-ˈbäl-ik\ *adj* **:** of or relating to catabolism — **cat·a·bol·i·cal·ly** \-i-k(ə-)lē\ *adv*
ca·tab·o·lism \kə-ˈtab-ə-ˌliz-əm\ *n* [Gk *katabolē* throwing down, fr. *kataballein* to throw down, fr. *kata-* + *ballein* to throw — more at DEVIL] **:** destructive metabolism involving the release of energy and resulting in the breakdown of complex materials within the organism
ca·tab·o·lite \-ˌlīt\ *n* **:** a substance (as nectar or a waste product) produced in catabolism
ca·tab·o·lize \-ˌlīz\ *vb* **-lized; -liz·ing** *vt* **:** to subject to catabolism ~ *vi* **:** to undergo catabolism
cat·a·chre·sis \ˌkat-ə-ˈkrē-səs\ *n, pl* **-chre·ses** \-ˌsēz\ [L, fr. Gk *katachrēsis* misuse, fr. *katachrēsthai* to use up, misuse, fr. *kata-* + *chrēsthai* to use] **1 :** use of the wrong word for the context **2 :** use of a forced and esp. paradoxical figure of speech (as *blind mouths*) — **cat·a·chres·tic** \-ˈkres-tik\ *or* **cat·a·chres·ti·cal** \-ti-kəl\ *adj* — **cat·a·chres·ti·cal·ly** \-ti-k(ə-)lē\ *adv*
cat·a·clysm \ˈkat-ə-ˌkliz-əm\ *n* [F *cataclysme,* fr. L *cataclysmos,* fr. Gk *kataklysmos,* fr. *kataklyzein* to inundate, fr. *kata-* + *klyzein* to wash — more at CLYSTER] **1 :** FLOOD, DELUGE **2 :** a violent geologic change of the earth's surface **3 :** a momentous and violent event marked by overwhelming upheaval and demolition ***syn*** see DISASTER — **cat·a·clys·mal** \ˌkat-ə-ˈkliz-məl\ *or* **cat·a·clys·mic** \-mik\ *adj*
cat·a·comb \ˈkat-ə-ˌkōm\ *n* [MF *catacombe,* prob. fr. OIt *catacomba,* fr. LL *catacumbae,* pl.] **1 :** a subterranean cemetery of galleries with recesses for tombs — usu. used in pl. **2 :** something resembling a catacomb: as **a :** an underground passageway or group of passageways <the ~*s* of the Old Senate Office Building> **b :** a complex set of interrelated things <the endless ~*s* of formal education —Kingman Brewster, Jr.> — **cat·a·comb·ic** \ˌkat-ə-ˈkō-mik\ *adj*
ca·tad·ro·mous \kə-ˈtad-rə-məs\ *adj* [prob. fr. NL *catadromus,* fr. *cata-* + *-dromus* -dromous] **:** living in fresh water and going to the sea to spawn <~ eels>
cat·a·falque \ˈkat-ə-ˌfalk, -ˌfȯ(l)k\ *n* [It *catafalco,* fr. (assumed) VL *catafalicum* scaffold, fr. *cata-* + L *fala* siege tower] **1 :** an ornamental structure sometimes used in funerals for the lying in state of the body **2 :** a pall-covered coffin-shaped structure used at requiem masses celebrated after burial
Cat·a·lan \ˈkat-ᵊl-ən, -ˌan\ *n* [Sp *Catalán*] **1 :** a native or inhabitant of Catalonia **2 :** the Romance language of Catalonia, Valencia, and the Balearic islands — **Catalan** *adj*
cat·a·lase \ˈkat-ᵊl-ˌās, -ˌāz\ *n* [*catalysis*] **:** a red crystalline enzyme that consists of a protein complex with hematin groups and catalyzes the decomposition of hydrogen peroxide into water and oxygen — **cat·a·lat·ic** \ˌkat-ᵊl-ˈat-ik\ *adj*
cat·a·lec·tic \ˌkat-ᵊl-ˈek-tik\ *adj* [LL *catalecticus,* fr. Gk *katalēktikos,* fr. *katalēgein* to leave off, fr. *kata-* + *lēgein* to stop — more at SLACK] **:** lacking a syllable at the end or ending in an imperfect foot — **catalectic** *n*
cat·a·lep·sy \ˈkat-ᵊl-ˌep-sē\ *n, pl* **-sies** [ME *catalempsi,* fr. ML *catalepsia,* fr. LL *catalepsis,* fr. Gk *katalēpsis,* lit., act of seizing, fr. *katalambanein* to seize, fr. *kata-* + *lambanein* to take — more at LATCH] **:** a condition of suspended animation and loss of voluntary motion in which the limbs remain in whatever position they are placed — **cat·a·lep·tic** \ˌkat-ᵊl-ˈep-tik\ *adj or n* — **cat·a·lep·ti·cal·ly** \-ti-k(ə-)lē\ *adv*
cat·a·lex·is \ˌkat-ᵊl-ˈek-səs\ *n, pl* **-lex·es** \-ˌsēz\ [NL, fr. Gk *katalēxis* close, cadence, fr. *katalēgein*] **:** omission or incompleteness usu. in the last foot of a line in metrical verse
[1]cat·a·log *or* **cat·a·logue** \ˈkat-ᵊl-ˌȯg, -ˌäg\ *n* [ME *cateloge,* fr. MF *catalogue,* fr. LL *catalogus,* fr. Gk *katalogos,* fr. *katalegein* to list, enumerate, fr. *kata-* + *legein* to gather, speak — more at LEGEND] **1 :** LIST, REGISTER **2 a :** a complete enumeration of items arranged systematically with descriptive details **b :** a pamphlet or book that contains such a list **c :** material in such a list
[2]catalog *or* **catalogue** *vb* **-loged** *or* **-logued; -log·ing** *or* **-logu·ing** *vt* **1 :** to make a catalog of **2 :** to enter in a catalog; *esp* **:** to classify (books or information) descriptively ~ *vi* **1 :** to make or work on a catalog **2 :** to become listed in a catalog at a specified price <this stamp ~*s* at two dollars> — **cat·a·log·er** *or* **cat·a·logu·er** *n*
cat·a·logue rai·son·né \-ˌrāz-ᵊn-ˈā\ *n, pl* **cat·a·logues rai·son·nes** \-ˌȯg(z)-ˌrāz-ᵊn-ˈā\ [F, lit., reasoned catalog] **:** a systematic annotated catalog; *esp* **:** a critical bibliography
ca·tal·pa \kə-ˈtal-pə, -ˈtȯl-\ *n* [Creek *kutuhlpa,* lit., head with wings] **:** any of a small genus (*Catalpa*) of American and Asiatic trees of the trumpet-creeper family with cordate leaves and pale showy flowers in terminal racemes
ca·tal·y·sis \kə-ˈtal-ə-səs\ *n, pl* **-y·ses** \-ˌsēz\ [Gk *katalysis* dissolution, fr. *katalyein* to dissolve, fr. *kata-* cata- + *lyein* to dissolve, release — more at LOSE] **1 :** a modification and esp. increase in the rate of a chemical reaction induced by material unchanged chemically at the end of the reaction **2 :** an action or reaction between two or more persons or forces precipitated by a separate agent and esp. by one that is essentially unaltered by the reaction <a representative list of questions . . . valuable for the ~ of class discussions —B. S. Meyer & D. B. Anderson>
cat·a·lyst \ˈkat-ᵊl-əst\ *n* **1 :** an agent that induces catalysis <he was rumored to be the ~ in a native uprising —H. W. Wind> <the housing program is intended to become the ~ of the new French economy —Edmond Taylor> **2 :** a substance (as an enzyme) that initiates a chemical reaction and enables it to proceed under milder conditions (as at a lower temperature) than otherwise possible
cat·a·lyt·ic \ˌkat-ᵊl-ˈit-ik\ *adj* **:** causing, involving, or relating to catalysis <a ~ reaction > <a ~ personality> — **cat·a·lyt·i·cal·ly** \-ˈit-i-k(ə-)lē\ *adv*
catalytic cracker *n* **:** the unit in a petroleum refinery in which cracking is carried out in the presence of a catalyst
cat·a·lyze \ˈkat-ᵊl-ˌīz\ *vt* **-lyzed; -lyz·ing** **1 :** to bring about the catalysis of (a chemical reaction) **2 :** to bring about **:** INSPIRE **3 :** to alter significantly by catalysis <innovations in basic chemical theory that have *catalyzed* the field and its technology — *Newsweek*> — **cat·a·lyz·er** *n*
cat·a·ma·ran \ˌkat-ə-mə-ˈran\ *n* [Tamil *kattumaram,* fr. *kattu* to tie + *maram* tree] **1 :** a raft consisting of logs or pieces of wood lashed together and propelled by paddles or sails **2 :** a boat with twin hulls or planing surfaces side by side
cata·me·nia \ˌkat-ə-ˈmē-nē-ə\ *n pl* [NL, fr. Gk *katamēnia,* fr. neut. pl. of *katamēnios* monthly, fr. *kata* by + *mēn* month — more at CATA-, MOON] **:** MENSES — **cata·me·ni·al** \-nē-əl\ *adj*
cat·a·mite \ˈkat-ə-ˌmīt\ *n* [L *catamitus,* fr. *Catamitus* Ganymede, fr. Etruscan *Catmite,* fr. Gk *Ganymēdēs*] **:** a boy kept by a pederast
cat·a·mount \ˈkat-ə-ˌmau̇nt\ *n* [short for *cat-a-mountain*] **:** any of various wild cats: as **a :** COUGAR **b :** LYNX
cat–a–moun·tain \ˌkat-ə-ˈmau̇nt-ᵊn\ *n* [ME *cat of the mountaine*] **:** any of various wild cats: as **a :** the European wildcat **b :** LEOPARD
cat–and–mouse \ˌkat-ᵊn-ˈmau̇s\ *adj* **:** consisting of constant torment, continuous pursuit, near captures, repeated escapes, or watchful waiting for the best opportunity to attack <the ~ technique of handling an opponent>
cat and mouse *n* **:** behavior like that of a cat with a mouse; *esp* **:** the act of toying with something before tormenting or destroying it
cat·a·pho·re·sis \ˌkat-ə-fə-ˈrē-səs\ *n, pl* **-re·ses** \-ˌsēz\ [NL] **:** ELECTROPHORESIS — **cat·a·pho·ret·ic** \-ˈret-ik\ *adj* — **cat·a·pho·ret·i·cal·ly** \-i-k(ə-)lē\ *adv*
cat·a·pla·sia \ˌkat-ə-ˈplā-zh(ē-)ə\ *n* [NL] **:** reversion of cells or tissues to a more embryonic condition — **cat·a·plas·tic** \-ˈplas-tik\ *adj*
cat·a·plasm \ˈkat-ə-ˌplaz-əm\ *n* [MF *cataplasme,* fr. L *cataplasma,* fr. Gk *kataplasma,* fr. *kataplassein* to plaster over — more at PLASTER] **:** POULTICE
cat·a·plexy \ˈkat-ə-ˌplek-sē\ *n, pl* **-plex·ies** \-sēz\ [G *kataplexie,* fr. Gk *kataplēxis,* fr. *kataplēssein* to strike down, terrify, fr. *kata-* + *plēssein* to strike — more at PLAINT] **:** sudden loss of muscle power following a strong emotional stimulus
[1]cat·a·pult \ˈkat-ə-ˌpəlt, -ˌpu̇lt\ *n* [MF or L; MF *catapulte,* fr. L *catapulta,* fr. Gk *katapaltēs,* fr. *kata-* + *pallein* to hurl — more at POLEMIC] **1 :** an ancient military device for hurling missiles **2 :** a device for launching an airplane at flying speed (as from an aircraft carrier)
[2]catapult *vt* **:** to throw or launch by or as if by a catapult ~ *vi* **:** to become catapulted
cat·a·ract \ˈkat-ə-ˌrakt\ *n* [L *cataracta* waterfall, portcullis, fr. Gk *kataraktēs,* fr. *katarassein* to dash down, fr. *kata-* cata- + *arassein* to strike, dash] **1** [MF or ML; MF *cataracte,* fr. ML *cataracta,* fr. L, portcullis] **:** a clouding of the lens of the eye or of its capsule obstructing the passage of light **2 a** *obs* **:** WATERSPOUT **b :** WATERFALL; *esp* **:** a large one over a precipice **c :** steep rapids in a river **d :** DOWNPOUR, FLOOD — **cat·a·rac·tal** \ˌkat-ə-ˈrak-tᵊl\ *adj*
ca·tarrh \kə-ˈtär\ *n* [MF or LL; MF *catarrhe,* fr. LL *catarrhus,* fr. Gk *katarrhous,* fr. *katarrhein* to flow down, fr. *kata-* + *rhein* to flow — more at STREAM] **:** inflammation of a mucous membrane; *esp* **:** one chronically affecting the human nose and air passages — **ca·tarrh·al** \-əl\ *adj* — **ca·tarrh·al·ly** \-ə-lē\ *adv*
ca·tas·ta·sis \kə-ˈtas-tə-səs\ *n, pl* **-ta·ses** \-ˌsēz\ [Gk *katastasis* settlement, fr. *kathistanai* to set in order, fr. *kata-* + *histanai* to cause to stand — more at STAND] **1 :** the complication immediately preceding the climax of a play **2 :** the climax of a play
ca·tas·tro·phe \kə-ˈtas-trə-(ˌ)fē\ *n* [Gk *katastrophē,* fr. *katastrephein* to overturn, fr. *kata-* + *strephein* to turn — more at STROPHE] **1 :** the final event of the dramatic action esp. of a tragedy **2**

: a momentous tragic event ranging from extreme misfortune to utter overthrow or ruin **3** : a violent and sudden change in a feature of the earth **4** : utter failure : FIASCO ***syn*** see DISASTER — **cat·a·stroph·ic** \ˌkat-ə-ˈsträf-ik\ *adj* — **cat·a·stroph·i·cal·ly** \-i-k(ə-)lē\ *adv*

cata·to·nia \ˌkat-ə-ˈtō-nē-ə\ *n* [NL, fr. G *katatonie,* fr. *kata-* cata- + NL *tonus*] **1** : CATALEPSY **2** : a disorder marked by catalepsy — **cata·ton·ic** \-ˈtän-ik\ *adj or n*

Ca·taw·ba \kə-ˈtȯ-bə\ *n* **1** *pl* **Catawba** *or* **Catawbas** : a member of an Amerindian people of No. Carolina and So. Carolina **2** : the language of the Catawba people **3** : a dry white wine produced from a native American grape; *also* : a sweet fortified wine made from this grape

cat·bird \ˈkat-ˌbərd\ *n* : an American songbird (*Dumetella carolinensis*) dark gray in color with black cap and reddish coverts under the tail

catbird seat *n* : a position of great prominence or advantage

cat·boat \ˈkat-ˌbōt\ *n* : a sailboat having a cat rig and usu. a centerboard and being of light draft and broad beam

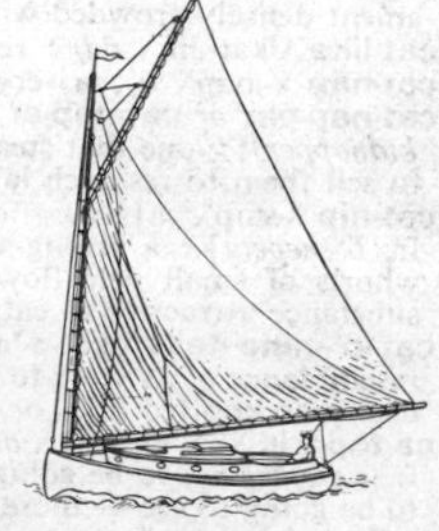
catboat

cat·bri·er \-ˌbrī(-ə)r\ *n* : any of several prickly climbers (genus *Smilax*) of the lily family

cat·call \-ˌkȯl\ *n* : a loud or raucous cry made to express disapproval (as at a sports event) — **catcall** *vb*

[1]**catch** \ˈkach, ˈkech\ *vb* **caught** \ˈkȯt\; **catch·ing** [ME *cacchen,* fr. ONF *cachier* to hunt, fr. (assumed) VL *captiare,* alter. of L *captare* to chase, fr. *captus,* pp. of *capere* to take — more at HEAVE] *vt* **1 a** : to capture or seize esp. after pursuit **b** : to take or entangle in or as if in a snare **c** : DECEIVE **d** : to discover unexpectedly : FIND <*caught* in the act> **e** : to check suddenly or momentarily **f** : to become suddenly aware of **2 a** : to take hold of : SEIZE **b** : to affect suddenly **c** : SNATCH, INTERCEPT **d** : to avail oneself of : TAKE **e** : to obtain through effort : GET **f** : to get entangled <~ a sleeve on a nail> **3** : to become affected by <the grease *caught* fire>: as **a** : CONTRACT <~ a cold> **b** : to respond sympathetically to the point of being imbued with <~ the spirit of an occasion> **c** : to be struck by **4 a** : to seize and hold firmly **b** : FASTEN **5** : to take or get usu. momentarily or quickly <~ a glimpse of a friend> **6 a** : OVERTAKE **b** : to get aboard in time <~ the bus> **7** : ATTRACT, ARREST **8** : to make contact with **9** : to grasp by the senses or the mind : APPREHEND ~ *vi* **1** : to grasp hastily or try to grasp **2** : to become caught **3** *of a crop* : to come up and become established **4** : to play the position of catcher on a baseball team — **catch·able** \ˈkach-ə-bəl, ˈkech-\ *adj*

syn **1** CATCH, TRAP, SNARE, ENTRAP, ENSNARE, BAG ***shared meaning element*** : to get into one's possession or under one's control by or as if by taking or seizing ***ant*** miss
2 see INCUR

— **catch fire** **1** : to become ignited **2** : to become fired with enthusiasm <the poet *caught fire* from the philosopher's talk> **3** : to increase greatly in scope, interest, or effectiveness <this stock has not *caught fire* — yet —*Forbes*> — **catch it** : to incur blame, reprimand, or punishment — **catch one's breath** : to rest long enough to restore normal breathing

[2]**catch** *n* **1** : something caught; *esp* : the total quantity caught at one time <a large ~ of fish> **2 a** : the act, action, or fact of catching **b** : a game in which a ball is thrown and caught **3** : something that checks or holds immovable <the safety ~ of her pin broke> **4** : one worth catching esp. as a spouse **5** : a round for three or more unaccompanied voices written out as one continuous melody with each succeeding singer taking up a part in turn **6** : FRAGMENT, SNATCH **7** : a concealed difficulty <there must be a ~ to it somewhere> **8** : the germination of a field crop to such an extent that replanting is unnecessary

catch·all \ˈkach-ˌȯl, ˈkech-\ *n* : something to hold various odds and ends

catch–as–catch–can \ˌkach-əz-ˌkach-ˈkan, ˌkech-əz-ˌkech-\ *adj* : using any available means or method : UNPLANNED <a ~ existence begging and running errands —*Time*>

catch·er \ˈkach-ər, ˈkech-\ *n* : one that catches; *specif* : a baseball player stationed behind home plate

catch·fly \-ˌflī\ *n* : any of various plants (as of the genera *Lychnis* and *Silene*) with viscid stems to which small insects adhere

catch·ing *adj* **1** : INFECTIOUS, CONTAGIOUS **2** : CATCHY, ALLURING

catch·ment \ˈkach-mənt, ˈkech-\ *n* **1** : the action of catching water **2** : something that catches water; *also* : the amount of water caught

catch on *vi* **1** : UNDERSTAND, LEARN <the police *caught on* to what he was doing> **2** : to become popular <this movement has already *caught on* in other states — Bernard Smith>

catch out *vt* : to detect in error or wrongdoing : ENTRAP <the Court . . . is now *caught out* by history — Ed Yoder>

catch·pen·ny \ˈkach-ˌpen-ē, ˈkech-\ *adj* : designed esp. to appeal to the ignorant or unwary through sensationalism or cheapness <a ~ newspaper with many lurid photographs>

catch·pole *or* **catch·poll** \-ˌpōl\ *n* [ME *cacchepol,* fr. OE *cæcepol,* fr. (assumed) ONF *cachepol,* lit., chicken chaser, fr. ONF *cachier* + *pol* chicken, fr. L *pullus* — more at CATCH, PULLET] : a sheriff's deputy; *esp* : one who makes arrests for debt

catch·up \ˈkech-əp, ˈkach-; ˈkat-səp\ *var of* CATSUP

catch up *vt* **1 a** : to pick up often abruptly <the thief *caught* the purse *up* and ran> **b** : ENSNARE, ENTANGLE <education has been *caught up* in a stultifying mythology, largely of its own devising — N. M. Pusey> **c** : ENTHRALL <the . . . public was *caught up* in the car's magic — D. A. Jedlicka> **2** : to provide with the latest information <*catch* me *up* on the news> ~ *vi* **1** : to travel fast enough to overtake an advance party <*catch up* with the group ahead> **2** : to bring about arrest for illicit activities <the police *caught up* with the thieves> **3 a** : to bring something to completion <*catch up* on the bookkeeping> **b** : to acquire belated information <*catch up* on the news>

catch·word \ˈkach-ˌwərd, ˈkech-\ *n* **1 a** : a word under the right-hand side of the last line on a book page that repeats the first word on the following page **b** : GUIDE WORD **2** : a word or expression repeated until it becomes representative of a party, school, or point of view

catchy \-ē\ *adj* **catch·i·er; -est** **1** : tending to catch the interest or attention <a ~ title> **2** : TRICKY <a ~ question> **3** : FITFUL, IRREGULAR <~ breathing>

cat distemper *n* : PANLEUCOPENIA

cate \ˈkāt\ *n* [ME, article of purchased food, short for *acate,* fr. ONF *acat* purchase, fr. *acater* to buy, fr. (assumed) VL *accaptare,* fr. L *acceptare* to accept] *archaic* : a dainty or choice food

cat·e·che·sis \ˌkat-ə-ˈkē-səs\ *n, pl* **-che·ses** \-ˌsēz\ [LL, fr. Gk *katēchēsis,* fr. *katēchein* to teach] : oral instruction of catechumens — **cat·e·chet·i·cal** \-ˈket-i-kəl\ *adj*

cat·e·chin \ˈkat-ə-ˌkin\ *n* [ISV *catechu* + *-in*] : a crystalline compound $C_{15}H_{14}O_6$ that is related chemically to the flavones, is found in catechu, and is used in dyeing and tanning

cat·e·chism \ˈkat-ə-ˌkiz-əm\ *n* **1** : oral instruction **2** : a manual for catechizing; *specif* : a summary of religious doctrine often in the form of questions and answers **3** : a set of formal questions put as a test — **cat·e·chis·mal** \ˌkat-ə-ˈkiz-məl\ *adj* — **cat·e·chis·tic** \-ˈkis-tik\ *adj*

cat·e·chist \ˈkat-ə-ˌkist, ˈkat-i-kəst\ *n* : one that catechizes: as **a** : a teacher of catechumens **b** : a native in a missionary district who does Christian teaching — **cat·e·chis·tic** \ˌkat-ə-ˈkis-tik\ *adj*

cat·e·chize \ˈkat-ə-ˌkīz\ *vt* **-chized; -chiz·ing** [LL *catechizare,* fr. Gk *katēchein* to teach, lit., to din into, fr. *kata-* cata- + *ēchein* to resound, fr. *ēchē* sound — more at ECHO] **1** : to instruct systematically esp. by questions, answers, and explanations and corrections; *specif* : to give religious instruction in such a manner **2** : to question systematically or searchingly — **cat·e·chi·za·tion** \ˌkat-i-kə-ˈzā-shən\ *n* — **cat·e·chiz·er** \ˈkat-ə-ˌkī-zər\ *n*

cat·e·chol \ˈkat-ə-ˌkȯl, -ˌkōl\ *n* **1** : CATECHIN **2** : PYROCATECHOL

cat·e·chol·amine \ˌkat-ə-ˈkō-lə-ˌmēn, -ˈkȯ-\ *n* : any of various substances (as epinephrine and dopamine) that are related to pyrocatechol but have one or more amine side groups some of which are sympathomimetic agents

cat·e·chu \ˈkat-ə-ˌchü, -ˌshü\ *n* [prob. fr. Malay *kachu,* of Dravidian origin; akin to Tamil & Kannada *kācu* catechu] : any of several dry, earthy, or resinous astringent substances obtained from tropical Asiatic plants: as **a** : an extract of the heartwood of an East Indian acacia (*Acacia catechu*) **b** : GAMBIER

cat·e·chu·men \ˌkat-ə-ˈkyü-mən\ *n* [ME *cathecumyn,* fr. MF *cathecumine,* fr. LL *catechumenus,* fr. Gk *katēchoumenos,* pres. pass. part. of *katēchein* to teach] **1** : a convert to Christianity receiving training in doctrine and discipline before baptism **2** : one receiving instruction in the basic doctrines of Christianity before admission to communicant membership in a church

cat·e·gor·i·cal \ˌkat-ə-ˈgȯr-i-kəl, -ˈgär-\ *also* **cat·e·gor·ic** \-ik\ *adj* [LL *categoricus, fr.* Gk *katēgorikos,* fr. *katēgoria* affirmation, category] **1** : ABSOLUTE, UNQUALIFIED <a ~ denial> **2** : of, relating to, or constituting a category — **cat·e·gor·i·cal·ly** \-i-k(ə-)lē\ *adv*

categorical imperative *n* : a moral obligation or command that is unconditionally and universally binding

cat·e·go·rize \ˈkat-i-gə-ˌrīz\ *vt* **-rized; -riz·ing** : to put into a category : CLASSIFY — **cat·e·go·ri·za·tion** \ˌkat-i-gə-rə-ˈzā-shən\ *n*

cat·e·go·ry \ˈkat-ə-ˌgōr-ē, -ˌgȯr-\ *n, pl* **-ries** [LL *categoria,* fr. Gk *katēgoria* predication, category, fr. *katēgorein* to accuse, affirm, predicate, fr. *kata-* + *agora* public assembly — more at GREGARIOUS] **1 a** : a general class to which a logical predicate or that which it predicates belongs **b** : one of the underlying forms to which any object of experience must conform **c** : one of the fundamental or ultimate classes of entities or of language **2** : a division within a system of classification

ca·te·na \kə-ˈtē-nə\ *n, pl* **-nae** \-(ˌ)nē\ *or* **-nas** [ML, fr. L, chain — more at CHAIN] : a connected series of related things

cat·e·nary \ˈkat-ə-ˌner-ē, *esp Brit* kə-ˈtē-nə-rē\ *n, pl* **-nar·ies** [NL *catenaria,* fr. L, fem. of *catenarius* of a chain, fr. *catena*] **1** : the curve assumed by a perfectly flexible inextensible cord of uniform density and cross section hanging freely from two fixed points **2** : something in the form of a catenary — **catenary** *adj*

cat·e·nate \ˈkat-ə-ˌnāt\ *vt* **-nat·ed; -nat·ing** [L *catenatus,* pp. of *catenare,* fr. *catena*] : to connect in a series : LINK — **cat·e·na·tion** \ˌkat-ə-ˈnā-shən\ *n*

ca·ten·u·late \kə-ˈten-yə-lət\ *adj* [ISV, fr. LL *catenula,* dim. of L *catena*] : shaped like a chain <~ colonies of bacteria>

ca·ter \ˈkāt-ər\ *vb* [obs. *cater* (buyer of provisions), fr. ME *catour,* short for *acatour,* fr. AF, fr. ONF *acater* to buy — more at CATE] *vi* **1** : to provide a supply of food **2** : to supply what is required or desired <~*ed* to her whims all day long> ~ *vt* : to provide food and service for <~*ed* the banquet> — **ca·ter·er** \-ər-ər\ *n* — **ca·ter·ess** \ˈkāt-ə-rəs\ *n*

cat·er·an \ˈkat-ə-rən\ *n* [ME *ketharan,* prob. fr. ScGael *ceathairneach* freebooter, robber] : a former military irregular or brigand of the Scottish Highlands

cat·er·cor·ner \ˌkat-ē-ˈkȯ(r)-nər, ˌkat-ə-, ˌkit-ē-\ *or* **cat·er–cor·nered** \-nərd\ *adv or adj* [obs. *cater* (four-spot) + E *corner*] : in a diagonal or oblique position : on a diagonal or oblique line <the house stood ~ across the square>

ə abut ᵊ kitten ər further a back ā bake ä cot, cart
au̇ out ch chin e less ē easy g gift i trip ī life
j joke ŋ sing ō flow ȯ flaw ȯi coin th thin t͟h this
ü loot u̇ foot y yet yü few yu̇ furious zh vision

ca·ter–cous·in \ˈkāt-ər-ˌkəz-ᵊn\ *n* [perh. fr. obs. *cater* (buyer of provisions)] : an intimate friend

cat·er·pil·lar \ˈkat-ə(r)-ˌpil-ər\ *n, often attrib* [ME *catyrpel,* fr. ONF *catepelose,* lit., hairy cat] : the elongated wormlike larva of a butterfly or moth; *also* : any of various similar larvae

Caterpillar *trademark* — used for a tractor made for use on rough or soft ground and moved on two endless metal belts

cat·er·waul \ˈkat-ər-ˌwȯl\ *vi* [ME *caterwawen*] **1** : to make a harsh cry **2** : to quarrel noisily — **caterwaul** *n*

cat·fac·ing \ˈkat-ˌfā-siŋ\ *n* : a disfigurement or malformation of fruit suggesting a cat's face in appearance

cat·fish \-ˌfish\ *n* : any of numerous usu. stout-bodied large-headed fishes (order Ostariophysi) with long tactile barbels

cat·gut \-ˌgət\ *n* : a tough cord made usu. from sheep intestines

cath *abbr* **1** cathedral **2** cathode

cath- — see CATA-

Cath·ar \ˈkath-ˌär\ *n, pl* **Cath·a·ri** \ˈkath-ə-ˌrī, -ˌrē\ *or* **Cathars** [LL *cathari* (pl.), fr. LGk *katharoi,* fr. Gk, pl. of *katharos,* adj.] : a member of one of various ascetic and dualistic Christian sects flourishing in the later Middle Ages teaching that matter is evil and professing faith in an angelic Christ who did not really undergo human birth or death — **Cath·a·rism** \ˈkath-ə-ˌriz-əm\ *n* — **Cath·a·rist** \-rəst\ *or* **Cath·a·ris·tic** \ˌkath-ə-ˈris-tik\ *adj*

ca·thar·sis \kə-ˈthär-səs\ *n, pl* **ca·thar·ses** \-ˌsēz\ [NL, fr. Gk *katharsis,* fr. *kathairein* to cleanse, purge, fr. *kartharos* pure] **1** : PURGATION **2 a** : purification or purgation of the emotions (as pity and fear) primarily through art **b** : a purification or purgation that brings about spiritual renewal or release from tension **3** : elimination of a complex by bringing it to consciousness and affording it expression

1**ca·thar·tic** \kə-ˈthärt-ik\ *adj* [LL *or* Gk; LL *catharticus,* fr. Gk *kathartikos,* fr. *kathairein*] : of, relating to, or producing catharsis

2**carthartic** *n* : a cathartic medicine : PURGATIVE

cat·head \ˈkat-ˌhed\ *n* : a projecting piece of timber or iron near the bow of a ship to which the anchor is hoisted and secured

ca·thect \kə-ˈthekt, ka-\ *vt* [back-formation fr. *cathectic*] : to invest with libidinal energy

ca·thec·tic \kə-ˈthek-tik, ka-\ *adj* [NL *cathexis*] : of, relating to, or invested with libidinal energy

ca·the·dra \kə-ˈthē-drə\ *n* [L, chair — more at CHAIR] : a bishop's official throne

1**ca·the·dral** \kə-ˈthē-drəl\ *adj* **1** : of, relating to, or containing a cathedra **2** : emanating from a chair of authority **3** : suggestive of a cathedral

2**cathedral** *n* **1** : a church that is the official seat of a diocesan bishop **2** : something that resembles or suggests a cathedral <higher education has been . . . the secular ~ of our time — David Riesman>

ca·thep·sin \kə-ˈthep-sən\ *n* [Gk *kathepsein* to digest (fr. *kata-* cata- + *hepsein* to boil) + E *-in*] : any of several intracellular proteinases of animal tissue that aid in autolysis in certain diseased conditions and after death

cath·er·ine wheel \ˌkath-(ə-)rən-\ *n, often cap C* [St. *Catherine* of Alexandria †*ab*307 Christian martyr] **1** : a wheel with spikes projecting from the rim **2** : PINWHEEL 2 **3** : CARTWHEEL 2

cath·e·ter \ˈkath-ət-ər, ˈkath-tər\ *n* [LL, fr. Gk *kathetēr,* fr. *kathienai* to send down, fr. *kata-* cata- + *hienai* to send — more at JET] : a tubular medical device for insertion into canals, vessels, passageways, or body cavities usu. to permit injection or withdrawal of fluids or to keep a passage open

cath·e·ter·ize \ˈkath-ət-ə-ˌrīz, ˈkath-tə-\ *vt* **-ized; -iz·ing** : to introduce a catheter into — **cath·e·ter·iza·tion** \ˌkath-ət-ə-rə-ˈzā-shən, ˌkath-tə-rə-\ *n*

ca·thex·is \kə-ˈthek-səs, ka-\ *n, pl* **ca·thex·es** \-ˌsēz\ [NL (intended as trans. of G *besetzung*), fr. Gk *kathexis* holding, fr. *katerchein* to hold fast, occupy, fr. *kata-* + *echein* to have, hold — more at SCHEME] : investment of libidinal energy in a person, object, or idea

cath·ode \ˈkath-ˌōd\ *n* [Gk *kathodos* way down, fr. *kata-* + *hodos* way — more at CEDE] **1** : the negative terminal of an electrolytic cell — compare ANODE **2** : the positive terminal of a primary cell or of a storage battery that is delivering current **3** : the electron-emitting electrode of an electron tube — **ca·thod·ic** \ka-ˈthäd-ik\ *adj* — **ca·thod·i·cal·ly** \-i-k(ə-)lē\ *adv*

cathode ray *n* **1** : one of the high-speed electrons projected in a stream from the heated cathode of a vacuum tube under the propulsion of a strong electric field **2** : a stream of cathode-ray electrons

cathode–ray tube *n* : a vacuum tube in which cathode rays usu. in the form of a slender beam are projected on a fluorescent screen and produce a luminous spot

cath·o·lic \ˈkath-(ə-)lik\ *adj* [MF & LL; MF *catholique,* fr. LL *catholicus,* fr. Gk *katholikos* universal, general, fr. *katholou* in general, fr. *kata* by + *holos* whole — more at CATA-, SAFE] **1** : COMPREHENSIVE, UNIVERSAL; *esp* : broad in sympathies, tastes, or interests **2** *cap* **a** : of, relating to, or forming the church universal **b** : of, relating to, or forming the ancient undivided Christian church or a church claiming historical continuity from it; *specif* : Roman Catholic — **ca·thol·i·cal·ly** \kə-ˈthäl-i-k(ə-)lē\ *adv* — **ca·thol·i·cize** \kə-ˈthäl-ə-ˌsīz\ *vb*

Cath·o·lic \ˈkath-(ə-)lik\ *n* **1** : a person who belongs to the universal Christian church **2** : a member of a Catholic church; *specif* : ROMAN CATHOLIC

Catholic Apostolic *adj* : of or relating to a Christian sect founded in 19th century England in anticipation of Christ's second coming

ca·thol·i·cate \kə-ˈthäl-ə-ˌkāt, -ˈthäl-i-kət\ *n* : the jurisdiction of a catholicos

Catholic Epistles *n pl* : the five New Testament letters including James, I and II Peter, I John, and Jude addressed to the early Christian churches at large rather than to particular churches or persons

Ca·thol·i·cism \kə-ˈthäl-ə-ˌsiz-əm\ *n* **1** : the faith, practice, or system of Catholic Christianity **2** : ROMAN CATHOLICISM

cath·o·lic·i·ty \ˌkath-ə-ˈlis-ət-ē\ *n, pl* **-ties** **1** *cap* : the character of being in conformity with a Catholic church **2 a** : liberality of sentiments or views <~ of viewpoint — W. V. O'Connor> **b** : UNIVERSALITY **c** : comprehensive range <the ~ of subjects represented by the press's trade list — *Current Biog.*>

ca·thol·i·con \kə-ˈthäl-ə-ˌkän\ *n* [F or ML; F, fr. ML, fr. Gk *katholikon,* neut. of *katholikos*] : CURE-ALL, PANACEA

ca·thol·i·cos \kə-ˈthäl-i-kəs\ *n, pl* **ca·thol·i·cos·es** \-kə-səz\ *or* **ca·thol·i·coi** \-ˈthäl-ə-ˌkȯi\ *often cap* [LGk *katholikos,* fr. Gk. general] : a primate of certain Eastern churches and esp. of the Armenian or of the Nestorian church

cat·house \ˈkat-ˌhau̇s\ *n* : a house of prostitution

cat·ion \ˈkat-ˌī-ən\ *n* [Gk *kation,* neut. of *katiōn,* prp. of *katienai* to go down, fr. *kata-* cata- + *ienai* to go — more at ISSUE] : the ion in an electrolized solution that migrates to the cathode; *broadly* : a positively charged ion

cat·ion·ic \ˌkat-(ˌ)ī-ˈän-ik\ *adj* **1** : of or relating to cations **2** : characterized by an active and esp. surface-active cation <a ~ dye> — **cat·ion·i·cal·ly** \-i-k(ə-)lē\ *adv*

cat·kin \ˈkat-kən\ *n* [fr. its resemblance to a cat's tail] : a usu. long ament densely crowded with bracts — **cat·kin·ate** \-kə-ˌnāt\ *adj*

cat·like \ˈkat-ˌlīk\ *adj* : resembling a cat : STEALTHY

cat·nap \-ˌnap\ *n* : a very short light nap — **catnap** *vi*

cat·nap·per *or* **cat·nap·er** \ˈkat-ˌnap-ər\ *n* [1cat + *-napper* (as in *kidnapper*)] : one that steals cats; *esp* : one that does so in order to sell them to research laboratories

cat·nip \-ˌnip\ *n* [1*cat* + obs. *nep* (catnip), fr. ME, fr. OE *nepte,* fr. L *nepeta*] : a strong-scented mint (*Nepeta cataria*) that has whorls of small pale flowers in terminal spikes and contains a substance attractive to cats

cat–o'–nine–tails \ˌkat-ə-ˈnīn-ˌtālz\ *n, pl* **cat–o'–nine–tails** [fr. the resemblance of its scars to the scratches of a cat] : a whip made of usu. nine knotted lines or cords fastened to a handle

ca·top·tric \kə-ˈtäp-trik\ *adj* [Gk *katoptrikos,* fr. *katoptron* mirror, fr. *katopsesthai* to be going to observe, fr. *kata-* cata- + *opsesthai* to be going to see — more at OPTIC] : of or relating to a mirror or reflected light; *also* : produced by reflection — **ca·top·tri·cal·ly** \-tri-k(ə-)lē\ *adv*

cat rig *n* : a rig consisting of a single mast far forward carrying a single large sail extended by a boom — **cat–rigged** \ˈkat-ˈrigd\ *adj*

cat's cradle *n* **1** : a game in which a string looped in a pattern like a cradle on the fingers of one person's hands is transferred to the hands of another so as to form a different figure **2** : INTRICACY <the socioreligious *cat's cradle* of small Greek communities — *Times Lit. Supp.*>

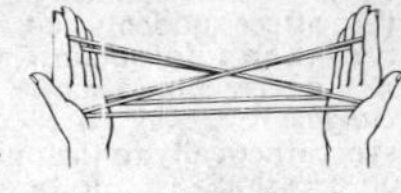

cat's cradle 1, first figure

cat's–eye \ˈkat-ˌsī\ *n, pl* **cat's–eyes** **1 a** : any of various gems (as a chrysoberyl or a chalcedony) exhibiting opalescent reflections from within **b** : a marble with eyelike concentric circles **2** : a small reflector placed to reflect beams from automobile headlights

cat's–foot \ˈkats-ˌfu̇t\ *n, pl* **cat's–feet** \-ˌfēt\ **1** : GROUND IVY **2** : any of several woolly composite plants (genus *Antennaria,* esp. *A. neodioica*) with small whitish discoid flower heads

cat's–paw \ˈkat-ˌspȯ\ *n, pl* **cat's–paws** **1** : a light air that ruffles the surface of the water in irregular patches during a calm **2** [fr. the fable of the monkey that used a cat's paw to draw chestnuts from the fire] : one used by another as a tool : DUPE **3** : a hitch in the bight of a rope so made as to form two eyes into which a tackle may be hooked — see KNOT illustration

cat·sup \ˈkech-əp, ˈkach-; ˈkat-səp\ *n* [Malay *kĕchap* spiced fish sauce] : a seasoned tomato puree

cat·tail \ˈkat-ˌtāl\ *n* : any of a genus (*Typha* of the family Typhaceae, the cattail family) of tall reedy marsh plants with brown furry fruiting spikes; *esp* : a plant (*Typha latifolia*) with long flat leaves used for making mats and chair seats

cat·ta·lo \ˈkat-ᵊl-ˌō\ *n, pl* **-loes** *or* **-los** [blend of *cattle* and *buffalo*] : a hybrid between the American buffalo and domestic cattle that is hardier than the latter

cat·tle \ˈkat-ᵊl\ *n pl* [ME, *catel,* fr. ONF, personal property, fr. ML *capitale,* fr. L, neut. of *capitalis* of the head — more at CAPITAL] **1** : domesticated quadrupeds held as property or raised for use; *specif* : bovine animals kept on a farm or ranch **2** : human beings esp. en masse

cattle grub *n* : any of several heel flies esp. in the larval stage; *esp* : COMMON CATTLE GRUB

cat·tle·man \-mən, -ˌman\ *n* : a man who tends or raises cattle

cattle tick *n* : a tick (*Boophilus annulatus*) that infests cattle in the southern U.S. and tropical America and transmits the causative agent of Texas fever

cat·tleya \ˈkat-lē-ə; kat-ˈlā-ə, -ˈlē-\ *n* [NL, fr. Wm. *Cattley* †1832 E patron of botany] : any of a genus (*Cattleya*) of tropical American epiphytic orchids with showy hooded flowers

1**cat·ty** \ˈkat-ē\ *n, pl* **catties** [Malay *kati*] : any of various units of weight of China and southeast Asia varying around 1⅓ pounds; *also* : a standard Chinese unit equal to 1.1023 pounds

2**catty** *adj* **cat·ti·er; -est** **1 a** : resembling a cat: as (1) : STEALTHY (2) : AGILE **b** : slyly spiteful : MALICIOUS **2** : of or relating to a cat — **cat·ti·ly** \ˈkat-ᵊl-ē\ *adv* — **cat·ti·ness** \ˈkat-ē-nəs\ *n*

cat·ty–cor·ner *or* **cat·ty–cor·nered** *var of* CATERCORNER

CATV *abbr* community antenna television

cat·walk \ˈkat-ˌwȯk\ *n* : a narrow walkway (as along a bridge)

Cau·ca·sian \ˈ ȯ-ˈkā-zhən, -ˈkazh-ən\ *adj* **1** : of or relating to the Caucasus or its inhabitants **2 a** : of or relating to the white race of mankind as classified according to physical features **b** : of or relating to the white race as defined by law specif. as composed of persons of European, No. African, or southwest Asia ancestry — **Caucasian** *n* — **Cau·ca·soid** \ˈkȯ-kə-ˌsȯid\ *adj or n*

1**cau·cus** \ˈkȯ-kəs\ *n* [prob. of Algonquian origin] : a closed meeting of a group of persons belonging to the same political party or faction usu. to select candidates or to decide on policy

2**caucus** *vi* : to hold or meet in a caucus

cau·dad \ˈkȯ-ˌdad\ *adv* [L *cauda*] **:** toward the tail or posterior end

cau·dal \ˈkȯd-ᵊl\ *adj* [NL *caudalis*, fr. L *cauda* tail — more at COWARD] **1 :** of, relating to, or being a tail **2 :** situated in or directed toward the hind part of the body — **cau·dal·ly** \-ᵊl-ē\ *adv*

cau·date \ˈkȯ-ˌdāt\ *also* **cau·dat·ed** \-ˌdāt-əd\ *adj* **:** having a tail or a taillike appendage **:** TAILED — **cau·da·tion** \kȯ-ˈdā-shən\ *n*

cau·dex \ˈkȯ-ˌdeks\ *n, pl* **cau·di·ces** \ˈkȯd-ə-ˌsēz\ *or* **cau·dex·es** [L, tree trunk or stem — more at CODE] **1 :** the stem of a palm or tree fern **2 :** the woody base of a perennial plant

cau·di·llo \kau̇-ˈt͟hē-(ˌ)(y)ō, -ˈt͟hēl-(ˌ)yō\ *n, pl* **-llos** [Sp. fr. LL *capitellum* small head — more at CADET] **:** a Spanish or Latin-American military dictator

cau·dle \ˈkȯd-ᵊl\ *n* [ME *caudel*, fr. ONF, fr. *caut* warm, fr. L *calidus* — more at CALDRON] **:** a drink (as for invalids) usu. of warm ale or wine mixed with bread or gruel, eggs, sugar, and spices

[1]**caught** \ˈkȯt\ *past of* CATCH

[2]**caught** *adj* **:** PREGNANT — often used in the phrase *get caught*

caul \ˈkȯl\ *n* [ME *calle*, fr. MF *cale*] **1 :** the large fatty omentum covering the intestines **2 :** the inner fetal membrane of higher vertebrates esp. when covering the head at birth

cauldron *var of* CALDRON

cau·les·cent \kȯ-ˈles-ᵊnt\ *adj* [ISV, fr. L *caulis*] **:** having a stem evident above ground

cau·li·cle \ˈkȯ-li-kəl\ *n* [L *cauliculus*, dim. of *caulis*] **:** a rudimentary stem (as of an embryo or seedling)

cau·li·flow·er \ˈkȯ-li-ˌflau̇(-ə)r, ˈkäl-i-\ *n, often attrib* [It *cavolfiore*, fr. *cavolo* cabbage (fr. LL *caulus*, fr. L *caulis* stem, cabbage) + *fiore* flower, fr. L *flor-, flos* — more at HOLE, BLOW] **:** a garden plant (*Brassica oleracea botrytis*) related to the cabbage and grown for its compact edible head of usu. white undeveloped flowers; *also* **:** its flower cluster

cauliflower ear *n* **:** an ear deformed from injury and excessive growth of reparative tissue

cau·line \ˈkȯ-ˌlīn\ *adj* [prob. fr. NL *caulinus*, fr. L *caulis*] **:** of, relating to, or growing on a stem; *specif* **:** growing on the upper part of a stem

[1]**caulk** \ˈkȯk\ *vt* [ME *caulken*, fr. ONF *cauquer* to trample, fr. L *calcare*, fr. *calc-, calx* heel — more at CALK] **1 :** to stop up and make watertight the seams of (as a boat) by filling with a waterproofing compound or material **2 :** to stop up and make tight against leakage (as the seams of a boat, the cracks in a window frame, or the joints of a pipe) — **caulk·er** *n*

[2]**caulk** *var of* CALK

caus *abbr* causative

caus·al \ˈkȯ-zəl\ *adj* **1 :** expressing or indicating cause **:** CAUSATIVE <a ~ clause introduced by *since* or *because*> **2 :** of, relating to, or constituting a cause <the ~ agent of a disease> **3 :** involving causation or a cause <the relationship . . . was not one of ~ antecedence so much as one of analogous growth — H. O. Taylor> **4 :** arising from a cause <a ~ development> — **caus·al·ly** \-zə-lē\ *adv*

cau·sal·i·ty \kȯ-ˈzal-ət-ē\ *n, pl* **-ties 1 :** a causal quality or agency **2 :** the relation between a cause and its effect or between regularly correlated events or phenomena

cau·sa·tion \kȯ-ˈzā-shən\ *n* **1 a :** the act or process of causing **b :** the act or agency by which an effect is produced **2 :** CAUSALITY

caus·ative \ˈkȯ-zət-iv\ *adj* **1 :** effective or operating as a cause or agent **2 :** expressing causation — **causative** *n* — **caus·ative·ly** *adv*

[1]**cause** \ˈkȯz\ *n* [ME, fr. OF, fr. L *causa*] **1 a :** something that brings about an effect or a result **b :** a person or thing that is the occasion of an action or state; *esp* **:** an agent that brings something about **c :** a reason for an action or condition **:** MOTIVE **2 a :** a ground of legal action **b :** CASE **3 :** a matter or question to be decided **4 :** a principle or movement militantly defended or supported — **cause·less** \-ləs\ *adj*

syn CAUSE, DETERMINANT, ANTECEDENT, REASON, OCCASION *shared meaning element* **:** something that precedes and usually induces an effect or result. CAUSE applies to anything (as an event, circumstance, or condition) that brings about or helps bring about an effect <water and soil pollution are the root *causes* of mortality in the tropics — V. G. Heiser> DETERMINANT applies to a cause that fixes the nature of what results <the quality of education provided is a *determinant* of the quality of the child's later life> ANTECEDENT stresses the fact of priority and usually suggests some degree of responsibility for what follows <the *antecedents* and consequences of the war> REASON applies to a traceable or explainable cause of a known effect <trying to figure out the *reason* for her failure> OCCASION applies to a precipitating cause and especially to a time or situation at which underlying causes become effective; thus, the *cause* of a war may be a longtime deep-rooted antipathy between peoples, its *occasion* some trivial incident

[2]**cause** *vt* **caused; caus·ing 1 :** to serve as a cause or occasion of **2 :** to effect by command, authority, or force — **caus·er** *n*

'cause \(ˈ)kȯz, (ˈ)kəz\ *conj* **:** BECAUSE

cause cé·lè·bre \ˌkōz-sā-ˈlebrᵊ, ˌkȯz-\ *n, pl* **causes cé·lè·bres** *same*\ [F, lit., celebrated case] **1 :** a legal case that excites widespread interest **2 :** a notorious incident or episode

cau·se·rie \ˌkōz-(ə-)ˈrē\ *n* [F, fr. *causer* to chat, fr. L *causari* to plead, discuss, fr. *causa*] **1 :** an informal conversation **:** CHAT **2 :** a short informal composition

cause·way \ˈkȯz-ˌwā\ *n* [ME *cauciwey*, fr. *cauci* causey + *wey* way] **1 :** a raised way across wet ground or water **2 :** HIGHWAY; *esp* **:** one of ancient Roman construction in Britain — **causeway** *vt*

cau·sey \ˈkȯ-zē\ *n, pl* **causeys** [ME *cauci*, fr. ONF *caucie*, fr. ML *calciata* paved highway, fr. fem. of *calciatus* paved with limestone, fr. L *calc-, calx* limestone — more at CHALK] **1 :** CAUSEWAY 1 **2** *obs* **:** CAUSEWAY 2

caus·tic \ˈkȯ-stik\ *adj* [L *causticus*, fr. Gk *kaustikos*, fr. *kaiein* to burn; akin to Lith *kūlė* smut of plants] **1 :** capable of destroying or eating away by chemical action **:** CORROSIVE **2 :** INCISIVE, BITING <~ wit> **3 :** relating to or being the envelope of rays emanating from a point and reflected or refracted by a curved surface — **caustic** *n* — **caus·ti·cal·ly** \-sti-k(ə-)lē\ *adv* — **caus·tic·i·ty** \kȯ-ˈstis-ət-ē\ *n*

caustic lime *n* **:** [1]LIME 2a

caustic potash *n* **:** POTASSIUM HYDROXIDE

caustic soda *n* **:** SODIUM HYDROXIDE

cau·ter·i·za·tion \ˌkȯt-ə-rə-ˈzā-shən\ *n* **:** the act or effect of cauterizing

cau·ter·ize \ˈkȯt-ə-ˌrīz\ *vt* **-ized; -iz·ing :** to sear with a cautery or caustic

cau·tery \ˈkȯt-ə-rē\ *n, pl* **-ter·ies** [L *cauterium*, fr. Gk *kautērion* branding iron, fr. *kaiein*] **1 :** CAUTERIZATION **2 :** a hot iron, caustic, or other agent used to burn, sear, or destroy tissue

[1]**cau·tion** \ˈkȯ-shən\ *n* [L *caution-, cautio* precaution, fr. *cautus*, pp. of *cavēre* to be on one's guard — more at HEAR] **1 :** WARNING, ADMONISHMENT **2 :** PRECAUTION **3 :** prudent forethought to minimize risk **4 :** one that arouses astonishment or commands attention <some shoes you see . . . these days are a ~ — *Esquire*> — **cau·tion·ary** \-shə-ˌner-ē\ *adj*

[2]**caution** *vt* **cau·tioned; cau·tion·ing** \ˈkȯ-sh(ə-)niŋ\ **:** to advise caution to ***syn*** see WARN

cau·tious \ˈkȯ-shəs\ *adj* **:** marked by or given to caution — **cau·tious·ly** *adv* — **cau·tious·ness** *n*

syn CAUTIOUS, CIRCUMSPECT, WARY, CHARY *shared meaning element* **:** prudently watchful and discreet in the face of danger or risk ***ant*** adventurous, temerarious

cav *abbr* **1** cavalry **2** cavity

cav·al·cade \ˌkav-əl-ˈkād, ˈkav-əl-ˌ\ *n* [MF, ride on horseback, fr. OIt *cavalcata*, fr. *cavalcare* to go on horseback, fr. LL *caballicare*, fr. L *caballus* horse; akin to Gk dial. *kaballeion* horse-drawn vehicle] **1 a :** a procession of riders or carriages **b :** a procession of vehicles or ships **2 :** a dramatic sequence or procession **:** SERIES

[1]**cav·a·lier** \ˌkav-ə-ˈli(ə)r\ *n* [MF, fr. OIt *cavaliere*, fr. OProv *cavalier*, fr. LL *caballarius* horseman, fr. L *caballus*] **1 :** a gentleman trained in arms and horsemanship **2 :** a mounted soldier **:** KNIGHT **3** *cap* **:** an adherent of Charles I of England **4 :** GALLANT

[2]**cavalier** *adj* **1 :** DEBONAIR **2 :** given to offhand dismissal of important matters **:** DISDAINFUL **3 a** *cap* **:** of or relating to the party of Charles I of England in his struggles with the Puritans and Parliament **b :** ARISTOCRATIC **c** *cap* **:** of or relating to the English Cavalier poets of the mid-17th century — **ca·va·lier·ism** \-ˌiz-əm\ *n* — **cav·a·lier·ly** *adv*

ca·val·la \kə-ˈval-ə\ *n, pl* **-la** *or* **-las** [Sp *caballa*, a fish, fr. LL, mare, fem. of L *caballus*] **1 :** CERO **2** *also* **ca·val·ly** \-ˈval-ē\ **:** any of various carangid fishes (esp. genus *Caranx*)

cav·al·ry \ˈkav-əl-rē\ *n, pl* **-ries** [It *cavalleria* cavalry, chivalry, fr. *cavaliere*] **1 :** HORSEMEN <a thousand ~ in flight> **2 :** an army component mounted on horseback or moving in motor vehicles and assigned to combat missions that require great mobility

cav·al·ry·man \-rē-mən, -ˌman\ *n* **:** a cavalry soldier

cav·a·ti·na \ˌkav-ə-ˈtē-nə, ˌkäv-\ *n* [It, fr. *cavata* production of sound from an instrument, fr. *cavare* to dig out, fr. L, to make hollow, fr. *cavus*] **1 :** an operatic solo simpler and briefer than an aria **2 :** a sustained melody

[1]**cave** \ˈkāv\ *n* [ME, fr. OF, fr. L *cava*, fr. *cavus* hollow; akin to ON *hūnn* cub, Gk *kyein* to be pregnant, *koilos* hollow, Skt *śvayati* he swells] **1 :** a natural underground chamber open to the surface **2** [short for *cave of Adullam*; fr. the story in I Sam 22:1, 2 of David's being joined by malcontents in the cave of that name] *Brit* **:** a secession or a group of seceders from a political party

[2]**cave** *vt* **caved; cav·ing :** to form a cave in or under **:** HOLLOW, UNDERMINE — **cav·er** *n*

[3]**cave** \ˈkāv\ *vb* **caved; cav·ing** [prob. alter. of *calve*] *vi* **1 :** to fall in or down esp. from being undermined **2 :** to cease to resist **:** SUBMIT — usu. used with *in* ~ *vt* **:** to cause to fall or collapse — usu. used with *in*

ca·ve·at \ˈkā-vē-ˌat, ˈkav-ē-, -ət; ˈkäv-ē-ˌät, -ət\ *n* [L, let him beware, fr. *cavēre* — more at HEAR] **1 a :** a warning enjoining one from certain acts or practices **b :** an explanation to prevent misinterpretation **2 :** a legal warning to a judicial officer to suspend a proceeding until the opposition has a hearing

caveat emp·tor \-ˈem(p)-tər, -ˌtȯ(ə)r\ *n* [NL, let the buyer beware] **:** a principle in commerce: without a warranty the buyer takes the risk of quality upon himself

cave dweller *n* **1 :** one (as a prehistoric man) that dwells in a cave **2 :** one that lives in a city apartment building

cave–in \ˈkā-ˌvin\ *n* **1 :** the action of caving in **2 :** a place where earth has caved in

cave·man \ˈkāv-ˌman\ *n* **1 :** a cave dweller esp. of the Stone Age **2 :** one who acts in a rough primitive manner esp. toward women

[1]**cav·ern** \ˈkav-ərn\ *n* [ME *caverne*, fr. MF, fr. L *caverna*, fr. *cavus*] **:** an underground chamber often of large or indefinite extent **:** CAVE

[2]**cavern** *vt* **1 :** to place in or as if in a cavern **2 :** to form a cavern of **:** HOLLOW — used with *out*

cav·er·nic·o·lous \ˌkav-ər-ˈnik-ə-ləs\ *adj* **:** inhabiting caves <a ~ fauna>

cav·ern·ous \ˈkav-ər-nəs\ *adj* **1 :** having caverns or cavities **2 :** constituting or suggesting a cavern **3** *of animal tissue* **:** composed largely of vascular sinuses and capable of dilating with blood to bring about the erection of a body part — **cav·ern·ous·ly** *adv*

ca·vet·to \kə-ˈvet-(ˌ)ō, kä-\ *n, pl* **-ti** \-ē\ [It, fr. *cavo* hollow, fr. L *cavus*] **:** a concave molding having a curve that roughly approximates a quarter circle — see MOLDING illustration

cav·i·ar *or* **cav·i·are** \'kav-ē-ˌär *also* 'käv-\ *n* [earlier *cavery, caviarie,* fr. obs. It *caviari,* pl. of *caviaro,* fr. Turk *havyar*] **1** : processed salted roe of large fish (as sturgeon) prepared as an appetizer **2** : something considered too delicate or lofty for mass appreciation <the play, I remember, pleased not the million; 'twas ~ to the general — Shak.>

cav·il \'kav-əl\ *vb* **-iled** *or* **-illed; -il·ing** *or* **-il·ling** \-(ə-)liŋ\ [L *cavillari* to jest, cavil, fr. *cavilla* raillery] *vi* : to raise trivial and frivolous objection ~ *vt* : to raise trivial objections to — **cavil** *n* — **cav·il·er** *or* **cav·il·ler** \-(ə-)lər\ *n*

cav·i·tary \'kav-ə-ˌter-ē\ *adj* : of, relating to, or characterized by bodily cavitation <~ tuberculosis>

cav·i·tate \'kav-ə-ˌtāt\ *vb* **-tat·ed; -tat·ing** *vi* : to form cavities or bubbles ~ *vt* : to cavitate in

cav·i·ta·tion \ˌkav-ə-'tā-shən\ *n* [*cavity* + *-ation*] : the process of cavitating: as **a** : the formation of partial vacuums in a liquid by a swiftly moving solid body (as a propeller) or by high-frequency sound waves; *also* : the pitting and wearing away of solid surfaces (as of metal or concrete) as a result of the collapse of these vacuums in surrounding liquid **b** : the formation of cavities in an organ or tissue esp. in disease

cav·i·ty \'kav-ət-ē\ *n, pl* **-ties** [MF *cavité,* fr. LL *cavitas,* fr. L *cavus* hollow] : an unfilled space within a mass; *esp* : a hollowed out space

ca·vort \kə-'vȯ(ə)rt\ *vi* [perh. alter. of *curvet*] **1** : PRANCE **2** : to engage in extravagant behavior

CAVU *abbr* ceiling and visibility unlimited

ca·vy \'kā-vē\ *n, pl* **cavies** [NL *Cavia,* genus name, fr. obs. Pg *çavia* (now *savía*), fr. Tupi *sawiya* rat] **1** : any of several short-tailed roughhaired So. American rodents (family Caviidae); *esp* : GUINEA PIG **2** : any of several rodents related to the cavies

caw \'kȯ\ *vi* [imit.] : to utter the harsh raucous natural call of the crow or a similar cry — **caw** *n*

cay \'kē, 'kā\ *n* [Sp *cayo* — more at KEY] : a low island or reef of sand or coral

cay·enne pepper \(ˌ)kī-ˌen-, (ˌ)kā-\ *n* [by folk etymology fr. earlier *cayan,* modif. of Tupi *kyinha*] **1** : a pungent condiment consisting of the ground dried fruits or seeds of hot peppers **2** : HOT PEPPER 2; *esp* : a cultivated pepper with very long twisted pungent red fruits **3** : the fruit of a cayenne pepper

cay·man *var of* CAIMAN

Ca·yu·ga \kē-'ü-gə, 'kyü-, kā-'(y)ü-\ *n, pl* **Cayuga** *or* **Cayugas** **1 a** : an Amerindian people of New York **b** : a member of this people **2** : the language of the Cayuga people

Cay·use \'kī-ˌ(y)üs, kī-'\ *n, pl* **Cayuse** *or* **Cayuses** **1** : a member of an Amerindian people of Oregon and Washington **2** *pl cayuses, not cap, West* : a native range horse

[1]**Cb** *abbr* cumulonimbus

[2]**Cb** *symbol* columbium

CB *abbr* **1** confined to barracks **2** county borough

C battery *n* : a battery used to maintain the potential of a grid-controlled electron tube at a desired value constant except for signals superposed upon it

CBC *abbr* Canadian Broadcasting Corporation

CBD *abbr* cash before delivery

CBI *abbr* **1** computer-based instruction **2** Cumulative Book Index

CBS *abbr* Columbia Broadcasting System

CBW *abbr* chemical and biological warfare

cc *abbr* cubic centimeter

Cc *abbr* cirrocumulus

CC *abbr* **1** carbon copy **2** chief clerk **3** common carrier

CCAT *abbr* Cooperative College Ability Test

CCC *abbr* **1** Civilian Conservation Corps **2** Commodity Credit Corporation

CCCO *abbr* Central Committee for Conscientious Objectors

CCD *abbr* Confraternity of Christian Doctrine

CCF *abbr* **1** Chinese communist forces **2** Cooperative Commonwealth Federation (of Canada)

cckw *abbr* counterclockwise

C clef *n* : a movable clef indicating middle C by its placement on one of the lines of the staff

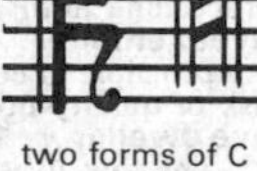

two forms of C clef

CCTV *abbr* closed-circuit television

ccw *abbr* counterclockwise

cd *abbr* cord

Cd *symbol* cadmium

CD *abbr* **1** carried down **2** certificate of deposit **3** civil defense **4** [F *corps diplomatique*] diplomatic corps **5** current density

CDD *abbr* certificate of disability for discharge

CDR *abbr* commander

Ce *symbol* cerium

CE *abbr* **1** chemical engineer **2** civil engineer **3** (International Society of) Christian Endeavor

CEA *abbr* **1** College English Association **2** Council of Economic Advisors

[1]**cease** \'sēs\ *vb* **ceased; ceas·ing** [ME *cesen,* fr. OF *cesser,* fr. L *cessare* to delay, fr. *cessus,* pp. of *cedere*] *vt* : to bring to an end : TERMINATE <the dying man soon *ceased* to breathe> ~ *vi* **1 a** : to come to an end <when will this quarreling ~?> **b** : to bring an activity or action to an end : DISCONTINUE <cried for hours without *ceasing*> **2** *obs* : to die out : become extinct ***syn*** see STOP

[2]**cease** *n* : CESSATION — usu. used with *without*

cease and desist order *n* : an order from an administrative agency to refrain from a method of competition or a labor practice found by the agency to be unfair

cease–fire \'sēs-'fī(ə)r\ *n* **1** : a military order to cease firing **2** : a suspension of active hostilities

cease·less \'sē-sləs\ *adj* : continuing without cease : CONSTANT — **cease·less·ly** *adv* — **cease·less·ness** *n*

ce·cro·pia moth \si-ˌkrō-pē-ə-\ *n* [NL *cecropia,* fr. L, fem. of *Cecropius* Athenian, fr. Gk *Kekropios,* fr. *Kekrops* Cecrops, legendary king of Athens] : a large silkworm moth (*Samia cecropia*) of the eastern U.S.

ce·cum \'sē-kəm\ *n, pl* **ce·ca** \-kə\ [NL, fr. L *intestinum caecum,* lit., blind intestine] : a cavity open at one end (as the blind end of a duct); *esp* : the blind pouch in which the large intestine begins and into which the ileum opens from one side — **ce·cal** \-kəl\ *adj* — **ce·cal·ly** \-kə-lē\ *adv*

CED *abbr* Committee for Economic Development

ce·dar \'sēd-ər\ *n* [ME *cedre,* fr. OF, fr. L *cedrus,* fr. Gk *kedros;* akin to Lith *kadagys* juniper] **1 a** : any of a genus (*Cedrus*) of usu. tall coniferous trees (as the cedar of Lebanon or the deodar) of the pine family noted for their fragrant durable wood **b** : any of numerous coniferous trees (as of the genera *Juniperus, Chamaecyparis,* or *Thuja*) that resemble the true cedars esp. in the fragrance and durability of their wood **2** : the wood of a cedar

ce·darn \'sēd-ərn\ *adj, archaic* : made or suggestive of cedar

cedar of Leb·a·non \-'leb(-ə)-nən\ : a long-lived evergreen tree (*Cedrus libani*) with short fascicled leaves and erect cones that is native to Asia Minor

cedar waxwing *n* : a long-crested brown waxwing (*Bombycilla cedrorum*) of temperate No. America with a yellow band on the tip of the tail — called also *cedarbird*

ce·dar·wood \'sēd-ər-ˌwu̇d\ *n* : the wood of a cedar that is esp. repellent to insects

cede \'sēd\ *vt* **ced·ed; ced·ing** [F or L; F *céder,* fr. L *cedere* to go, withdraw, yield; prob. akin to L *cis* on this side and to Gk *hodos* road, way, L *sedēre* to sit — more at HE, SIT] **1** : to yield or grant typically by treaty **2** : ASSIGN, TRANSFER — **ced·er** *n*

ce·di \'sād-ē\ *n* [Akan *sedie* cowry] — see MONEY table

ce·dil·la \si-'dil-ə\ *n* [Sp, the obs. letter *ç* (actually a medieval form of the letter *z*), cedilla, fr. dim. of *ceda, zeda* the letter *z,* fr. LL *zeta* — more at ZED] : the diacritical mark ¸ placed under a letter (as *ç* in French) to indicate an alteration or modification of its usual phonetic value (as in the French word *façade*)

cee \'sē\ *n* : the letter *c*

CEEB *abbr* College Entrance Examination Board

cei·ba \'sā-bə\ *n* [Sp] **1** : a massive tropical tree (*Ceiba pentandra*) of the silk-cotton family with large pods filled with seeds invested with a silky floss that yields the fiber kapok **2** : KAPOK

ceil \'sē(ə)l\ *vt* [ME *celen,* prob. fr. (assumed) MF *celer,* fr. L *caelare* to carve, fr. *caelum* chisel, fr. *caedere* to cut — more at CONCISE] **1** : to furnish (as a wooden ship) with a lining **2** : to furnish with a ceiling

ceil·ing \'sē-liŋ\ *n* **1 a** : the overhead inside lining of a room **b** : material used to ceil a wall or roof of a room **2** : something thought of as an overhanging shelter or a lofty canopy <a ~ of stars> **3 a** : the height above the ground from which prominent objects on the ground can be seen and identified **b** : the height above the ground of the base of the lowest layer of clouds when over half of the sky is obscured **4 a** : ABSOLUTE CEILING **b** : SERVICE CEILING **5** : an upper usu. prescribed limit <a ~ on prices, rents, and wages> — **ceil·inged** \-liŋd\ *adj*

ceil·om·e·ter \sē-'läm-ət-ər\ *n* [*ceiling* + *-o-* + *-meter*] : a photoelectric instrument for determining by triangulation the height of the cloud ceiling above the earth

cein·ture \sa^n(n)-'t(y)u̇(ə)r, 'san-chər\ *n* [F, fr. L *cinctura* — more at CINCTURE] : a belt or sash for the waist

cel·an·dine \'sel-ən-ˌdīn, -ˌdēn\ *n* [ME *celidoine,* fr. MF, fr. L *chelidonia,* fr. fem. of *chelidonius* of the swallow, fr. Gk *chelidonios,* fr. *chelidon-, chelidōn* swallow] **1** : a yellow-flowered biennial herb (*Chelidonium majus*) of the poppy family **2** : a European perennial herb (*Ranunculus ficaria*) of the buttercup family that has been introduced locally into the U.S. — called also *lesser celandine*

-cele \ˌsēl\ *n comb form* [MF, fr. L, fr. Gk *kēlē;* akin to OE *hēala* hernia, OSlav *kyla*] : tumor : hernia <varico*cele*>

cel·e·brant \'sel-ə-brənt\ *n* : one who celebrates; *specif* : the priest officiating at the Eucharist

cel·e·brate \'sel-ə-ˌbrāt\ *vb* **-brat·ed; -brat·ing** [L *celebratus,* pp. of *celebrare* to frequent, celebrate, fr. *celebr-, celeber* much frequented, famous; akin to L *celer*] *vt* **1** : to perform (a sacrament or solemn ceremony) publicly and with appropriate rites <~ the mass> **2 a** : to honor (as a holy day or feast day) by solemn ceremonies or by refraining from ordinary business **b** : to demonstrate satisfaction in (as an anniversary) by festivities or other deviation from routine **3** : to hold up or play up for public acclaim : EXTOL <his poetry ~*s* the glory of nature> <~ life> ~ *vi* **1** : to observe a holiday, perform a religious ceremony, or take part in a festival **2** : to observe a notable occasion with festivities ***syn*** see KEEP — **cel·e·bra·tion** \ˌsel-ə-'brā-shən\ *n* — **cel·e·bra·tor** \'sel-ə-ˌbrāt-ər\ *n* — **cel·e·bra·to·ry** \-brə-ˌtōr-ē, -ˌtȯr-\ *adj*

cel·e·brat·ed *adj* : widely known and often referred to ***syn*** see FAMOUS ***ant*** obscure — **cel·e·brat·ed·ness** *n*

ce·leb·ri·ty \sə-'leb-rət-ē\ *n, pl* **-ties** **1** : the state of being celebrated **2** : a celebrated person

ce·le·ri·ac \sə-'ler-ē-ˌak, -'lir-\ *n* [irreg. fr. *celery*] : a celery grown for its thickened edible root

ce·ler·i·ty \sə-'ler-ət-ē\ *n* [ME *celerite,* fr. MF *célérité,* fr. L *celeritat-, celeritas,* fr. *celer* swift — more at HOLD] : rapidity of motion or action

syn CELERITY, ALACRITY, LEGERITY *shared meaning element* : quickness in movement or action ***ant*** leisureliness

cel·ery \'sel-(ə-)rē\ *n, pl* **-er·ies** [prob. fr. It dial. *seleri,* pl. of *selero,* modif. of LL *selinon,* fr. Gk] : a European herb (*Apium graveolens*) of the carrot family; *specif* : one of a cultivated variety (*A. graveolens dulce*) with leafstalks eaten raw or cooked

ce·les·ta \sə-'les-tə\ *n* [F *célesta,* alter. of *céleste,* lit., heavenly, fr. L *caelestis*] : a keyboard instrument with hammers that strike steel plates producing a tone similar to that of a glockenspiel

[1]**ce·les·tial** \sə-'les(h)-chəl\ *adj* [ME, fr. MF, fr. L *caelestis* celestial, fr. *caelum* sky; akin to Skt *citra* bright] **1** : of, relating to, or suggesting heaven or divinity **2** : of or relating to the sky or visible heavens <the sun, moon, and stars are ~ bodies> **3 a** : ETHEREAL, OTHERWORLDLY **b** : OLYMPIAN, SUPREME **4** [*Celestial* Empire, old name for China] *cap* : of or relating to China or the Chinese — **ce·les·tial·ly** \-chə-lē\ *adv*

[2]**celestial** *n* **1** : a heavenly or mythical being **2** *cap* : CHINESE 1a
celestial equator *n* : the great circle on the celestial sphere midway between the celestial poles
celestial globe *n* : a globe depicting the celestial bodies
celestial hierarchy *n* : a traditional hierarchy of angels ranked from lowest to highest into the following nine orders: angels, archangels, principalities, powers, virtues, dominions, thrones, cherubim, and seraphim
celestial marriage *n* : a special order of Mormon marriage solemnized in a Mormon temple and held to be binding for a future life as well as the present one
celestial navigation *n* : navigation by observation of the positions of celestial bodies
celestial pole *n* : one of the two points on the celestial sphere around which the diurnal rotation of the stars appears to take place
celestial sphere *n* : an imaginary sphere of infinite radius against which the celestial bodies appear to be projected and of which the apparent dome of the visible sky forms half
ce·les·tite \'sel-ə-ˌstīt, sə-'les-ˌtīt\ *n* [G *zölestin,* fr. L *caelestis*] : a usu. white mineral $SrSO_4$ consisting of the sulfate of strontium
ce·li·ac \'sē-lē-ˌak\ *adj* [L *coeliacus,* fr. Gk *koiliakos,* fr. *koilia* cavity, fr. *koilos* hollow — more at CAVE] : of or relating to the abdominal cavity
celiac disease *n* : a chronic nutritional disturbance in young children characterized by defective digestion and utilization of fats and by abdominal distention, diarrhea, and fatty stools
cel·i·ba·cy \'sel-ə-bə-sē\ *n* **1** : the state of not being married **2 a** : abstention from sexual intercourse **b** : abstention by vow from marriage
cel·i·bate \'sel-ə-bət\ *n* [L *caelibatus,* fr. *caelib-, caelebs* unmarried; akin to Skt *kevala* alone and to OE *libban* to live] : one who lives in celibacy — **celibate** *adj*
cell \'sel\ *n* [ME, fr. OE, religious house and OF *celle* hermit's cell, fr. L *cella* small room; akin to L *celare* to conceal — more at HELL] **1** : a small religious house dependent on a monastery or convent **2 a** : a one-room dwelling occupied by a solitary person (as a hermit) **b** : a single room (as in a convent or prison) usu. for one person **3** : a small compartment (as in a honeycomb), receptacle (as the calyculus of a polyp), cavity (as in a plant ovary), or bounded space (as in an insect wing) **4** : a small usu. microscopic mass of protoplasm bounded externally by a semipermeable membrane, usu. including one or more nuclei and various nonliving products, capable alone or interacting with other cells of performing all the fundamental functions of life, and forming the least structural unit of living matter capable of functioning independently **5 a (1)** : a receptacle (as a cup or jar) containing electrodes and an electrolyte either for generating electricity by chemical action or for use in electrolysis **(2)** : FUEL CELL **b** : a single unit in a device for converting radiant energy into electrical energy or for varying the intensity of an electrical current in accordance with radiation **6** : a set of points in one-to-one correspondence with a set in a euclidean space of any number of dimensions **7** : the basic and usu. smallest unit of an organization or movement; *esp* : the primary unit of a Communist organization **8** : a portion of the atmosphere that behaves as a unit **9** : a basic subdivision of a computer memory that is addressable and can hold one unit of a computer's basic operating data unit (as a word)

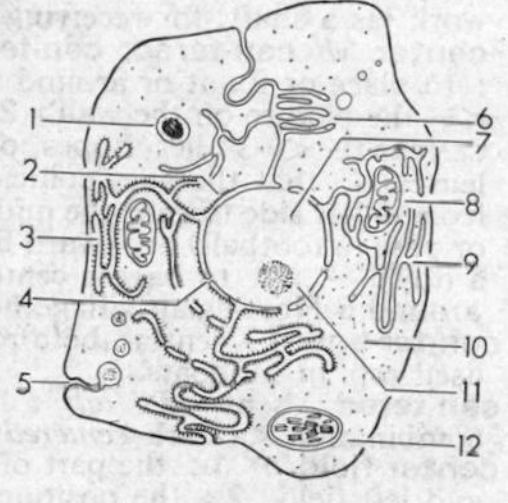

a schematic cell 4: *1* lysosome, *2* nuclear membrane, *3* endoplasmic reticulum with associated ribosomes, *4* nuclear pore, *5* intrusion of cell membrane, *6* Golgi apparatus, *7* nucleus, *8* mitochondrion, *9* endoplasmic reticulum, *10* cytoplasm and ribosomes, *11* nucleolus, *12* chloroplast

cel·lar \'sel-ər\ *n* [ME *celer,* fr. AF, fr. L *cellarium* storeroom, fr. *cella*] **1 a** : BASEMENT **b** : the lowest rank; *esp* : the lowest place in the standings (as of an athletic league) **2** : a stock of wines
cel·lar·age \'sel-ə-rij\ *n* **1** : cellar space esp. for storage **2** : charge for storage in a cellar
cel·lar·er \'sel-ər-ər\ *n* [ME *celerer,* fr. OF, fr. LL *cellariarius,* fr. L *cellarium*] : an official (as in a monastery) in charge of provisions
cel·lar·ette *or* **cel·lar·et** \ˌsel-ə-'ret\ *n* : a case or sideboard for holding bottles of wine or liquor
cell body *n* : the nucleus-containing central part of a neuron exclusive of its axons and dendrites
cell division *n* : the process by which cells multiply involving both nuclear and cytoplasmic division — compare MEIOSIS, MITOSIS
-celled \'seld\ *adj comb form* : having (such or so many) cells <single-*celled* organisms>
cell membrane *n* **1** : PLASMA MEMBRANE **2** : a cell wall
cel·lo \'chel-(ˌ)ō\ *n, pl* **cellos** [short for *violoncello*] : the bass member of the violin family tuned an octave below the viola — **cel·list** \'chel-əst\ *n*
cel·lo·bi·ose \ˌsel-ə-'bī-ˌōs, -ˌōz\ *n* [ISV *cell*ulose + *-o-* + *biose* (disaccharide), fr. [1]*bi-* + *-ose*] : a faintly sweet disaccharide $C_{12}H_{22}O_{11}$ obtained by partial hydrolysis of cellulose
cel·loi·din \se-'lȯid-ᵊn\ *n* [*cell*ulose + *-oid* + *-in*] : a purified pyroxylin used chiefly in microscopy
cel·lo·phane \'sel-ə-ˌfān\ *n* [F, fr. *cellulose* + *-phane* (as in *diaphane* diaphanous, fr. ML *diaphanus*)] : regenerated cellulose in thin transparent sheets used esp. for packaging
cell plate *n* : a disk formed in the phragmoplast of a dividing plant cell that eventually forms the middle lamella of the wall between the daughter cells
cell sap *n* **1** : the liquid contents of a plant cell vacuole **2** : HYALOPLASM
cell theory *n* : a theory in biology that includes one or both of the statements that the cell is the fundamental structural and functional unit of living matter and that the organism is composed of autonomous cells with its properties being the sum of those of its cells
cel·lu·lar \'sel-yə-lər\ *adj* [NL *cellularis,* fr. *cellula* living cell, fr. L, dim. of *cella* small room] **1** : of, relating to, or consisting of cells **2** : containing cavities : having a porous texture <~ rocks> — **cel·lu·lar·i·ty** \ˌsel-yə-'lar-ət-ē\ *n* — **cel·lu·lar·ly** \'sel-yə-lər-lē\ *adv*

cello

cel·lu·lase \'sel-yə-ˌlās, -ˌlāz\ *n* [ISV *cellulose* + *-ase*] : an enzyme that hydrolyzes cellulose
cel·lule \'sel-(ˌ)yü(ə)l\ *n* [L *cellula*] : a small cell
cel·lu·li·tis \ˌsel-yə-'līt-əs\ *n* [NL, fr. *cellula*] : diffuse and esp. subcutaneous inflammation of connective tissue
cel·lu·loid \'sel-(y)ə-ˌlȯid\ *n* [fr. *Celluloid,* a trademark] : motion-picture film — **celluloid** *adj*
Celluloid *trademark* — used for a tough flammable thermoplastic composed essentially of cellulose nitrate and camphor
cel·lu·lo·lyt·ic \ˌsel-yə-lō-'lit-ik\ *adj* [*cellul*ose + *-o-* + *-lytic*] : hydrolyzing or having the capacity to hydrolyze cellulose <~ bacteria> <~ activity>
cel·lu·lose \'sel-yə-ˌlōs, -ˌlōz\ *n* [F, fr. *cellule* living cell, fr. NL *cellula*] : a polysaccharide $(C_6H_{10}O_5)_x$ of glucose units that constitutes the chief part of the cell walls of plants, occurs naturally in such fibrous products as cotton and kapok, and is the raw material of many manufactured goods (as paper, rayon, and cellophane)
cellulose acetate *n* : any of several compounds insoluble in water that are formed esp. by the action of acetic acid, anhydride of acetic acid, and sulfuric acid on cellulose and are used for making textile fibers, packaging sheets, photographic films, and varnishes
cellulose nitrate *n* : any of several esters of nitric acid formed by the action of nitric acid on cellulose (as paper, linen, or cotton) and used for making explosives, plastics, rayon, and varnishes
[1]**cel·lu·los·ic** \ˌsel-yə-'lō-sik, -zik\ *adj* : of, relating to, or made from cellulose <~ fibers>
[2]**cellulosic** *n* : a substance made from cellulose or a derivative of cellulose
cell wall *n* : the firm nonliving and usu. chiefly cellulose wall that encloses and supports most plant cells
Cel·sius \'sel-sē-əs, -shəs\ *adj* [Anders *Celsius*] : CENTIGRADE <10° ~>
celt \'selt\ *n* [LL *celtis* chisel] : a prehistoric stone or metal implement shaped like a chisel or ax head
Celt \'selt, 'kelt\ *n* [F *Celte,* sing. of *Celtes,* fr. L *Celtae*] **1** : a member of a division of the early Indo-European peoples distributed from the British Isles and Spain to Asia Minor **2** : a modern Gael, Highland Scot, Irishman, Welshman, Cornishman, or Breton
[1]**Celt·ic** \'sel-tik, 'kel-\ *adj* : of, relating to, or characteristic of the Celts or their languages
[2]**Celtic** *n* : a group of Indo-European languages usu. subdivided into Brythonic and Goidelic and confined to Brittany, Wales, western Ireland, and the Scottish Highlands — see INDO-EUROPEAN LANGUAGES table
Celtic cross *n* : a cross having essentially the form of a Latin cross with a ring about the intersection of the crossbar and upright shaft — see CROSS illustration
Celt·i·cist \'sel-tə-səst, 'kel-\ *n* : a specialist in Celtic languages or cultures
cem *abbr* cement
cem·ba·lo \'chem-bə-ˌlō\ *n, pl* **-ba·li** \-(ˌ)lē\ *or* **-balos** [It] : HARPSICHORD
[1]**ce·ment** \si-'ment\ *n* [ME *sement,* fr. OF *ciment,* fr. L *caementum* stone chips used in making mortar, fr. *caedere* to cut — more at CONCISE] **1** : a powder of alumina, silica, lime, iron oxide, and magnesia burned together in a kiln and finely pulverized and used as an ingredient of mortar and concrete **2** : a binding element or agency: as **a** : a substance to make objects adhere to each other **b** : something serving to unite firmly <justice is the ~ that holds a political community together —R. M. Hutchins> **3** : CEMENTUM **4** : a plastic composition usu. made of zinc, copper, or silica for filling dental cavities **5** : the fine-grained groundmass or glass of a porphyry
[2]**cement** *vt* **1** : to unite or make firm by or as if by cement **2** : to overlay with concrete ~ *vi* : to become cemented — **ce·ment·er** *n*
ce·men·ta·tion \ˌsē-ˌmen-'tā-shən\ *n* **1** : the act or process of cementing : the state of being cemented **2** : a process of surrounding a solid with a powder and heating the whole so that the solid is changed by chemical combination with the powder
ce·ment·ite \si-'ment-ˌīt\ *n* [[1]*cement*] : a hard brittle iron carbide Fe_3C in steel, cast iron, and iron-carbon alloys
ce·men·ti·tious \ˌsē-ˌmen-'tish-əs\ *adj* : having the properties of cement
ce·men·tum \si-'ment-əm\ *n* [NL, fr. L *caementum*] : a specialized external bony layer of the part of a tooth normally within the gum — see TOOTH illustration
cem·e·tery \'sem-ə-ˌter-ē\ *n, pl* **-ter·ies** [ME *cimitery,* fr. MF *cimitere,* fr. LL *coemeterium,* fr. Gk *koimētērion* sleeping chamber, burial place, fr. *koiman* to put to sleep; akin to L *cunae* cradle] : a burial ground
CEMF *abbr* counter electromotive force

cen *abbr* central

cen- *or* **ceno-** *or* **caen-** *or* **caeno-** *comb form* [Gk *kain-, kaino-,* fr. *kainos* — more at RECENT] : new : recent <*Cenozoic*>

cen·a·cle \'sen-i-kəl\ *n* [LL *cenaculum,* the room where Christ and his disciples had the Last Supper, fr. L, dining room, fr. *cena* dinner] : a retreat house; *esp* : one for Roman Catholic women directed by nuns of the Society of Our Lady of the Cenacle

-cene \ˌsēn\ *adj comb form* [Gk *kainos*] : recent — in names of geologic periods <Eo*cene*>

cen·o·bite \'sen-ə-ˌbīt, *esp Brit* 'sēn-\ *n* [LL *coenobita,* fr. *coenobium* monastery, fr. LGk *koinobion,* deriv. of Gk *koin-* coen- + *bios* life — more at QUICK] : a member of a religious group living together in a monastic community — **cen·o·bit·ic** \ˌsen-ə-'bit-ik, ˌsēn-\ *or* **cen·o·bit·i·cal** \-i-kəl\ *adj*

ce·no·ge·net·ic \ˌsē-nə-jə-'net-ik, ˌsen-ə-\ *adj* [G *zänogenetisch,* fr. *zän-* cen- + *genetisch* genetic] : relating to or being a specialized adaptive character (as the amnion or chorion surrounding the embryo of higher vertebrates) that is not represented in primitive ancestral forms — **ce·no·ge·net·i·cal·ly** \-i-k(ə-)lē\ *adv*

ce·no·spe·cies \'sē-nə-ˌspē-(ˌ)shēz, 'sen-ə-, -(ˌ)sēz\ *n* [*coen-* + *species*] **1** : the sum of the possible expressions of a complex genotype **2** : a group of biological units capable by reason of closely related genotypes of essentially free gene interchange

ceno·taph \'sen-ə-ˌtaf\ *n* [F *cénotaphe,* fr. L *cenotaphium,* fr. Gk *kenotaphion,* fr. *kenos* empty + *taphos* tomb; akin to Arm *sin* empty — more at EPITAPH] : a tomb or a monument erected in honor of a person or group of persons whose remains are elsewhere

ce·no·te \si-'nōt-ē\ *n* [Sp, fr. Maya *tzonot*] : a deep sinkhole in limestone with a pool at the bottom that is found esp. in Yucatán

Ce·no·zo·ic \ˌsē-nə-'zō-ik, ˌsen-ə-\ *adj* : of, relating to, or being an era of geological history that extends from the beginning of the Tertiary period to the present time and is marked by a rapid evolution of mammals and birds and of grasses, shrubs, and higher flowering plants and by little change in the invertebrates; *also* : relating to the system of rocks formed in this era — see GEOLOGIC TIME table — **Cenozoic** *n*

cense \'sen(t)s\ *vt* **censed; cens·ing** [ME *censen,* prob. short for *encensen* to incense, fr. MF *encenser,* fr. LL *incensare,* fr. *incensum* incense] : to perfume esp. with a censer

cen·ser \'sen(t)-sər\ *n* : a vessel for burning incense; *esp* : a covered incense burner swung on chains in a religious ritual

censer

[1]cen·sor \'sen(t)-sər\ *n* [L, fr. *censēre* to assess, tax; akin to Skt *śaṃsati* he recites] **1** : one of two magistrates of early Rome acting as census takers, assessors, and inspectors of morals and conduct **2** : one who supervises conduct and morals: as **a** : an official who examines publications or films for objectionable matter **b** : an official (as in time of war) who reads communications (as letters) and deletes material considered harmful to the interests of his organization **3** : a hypothetical psychic agency that represses unacceptable notions before they reach consciousness — **cen·so·ri·al** \sen-'sōr-ē-əl, -'sór-\ *adj*

[2]censor *vt* **cen·sored; cen·sor·ing** \'sen(t)s-(ə-)riŋ\ : to subject to censorship

cen·so·ri·ous \sen-'sōr-ē-əs, -'sór-\ *adj* [L *censorius* of a censor, fr. *censor*] : marked by or given to censure ***syn*** see CRITICAL ***ant*** eulogistic — **cen·so·ri·ous·ly** *adv* — **cen·so·ri·ous·ness** *n*

cen·sor·ship \'sen(t)-sər-ˌship\ *n* **1 a** : the institution, system, or practice of censoring **b** : the actions or practices of censors; *esp* : censorial control exercised repressively **2** : the office, power, or term of a Roman censor **3** : exclusion from consciousness by the psychic censor

cen·sur·able \'sench-(ə-)rə-bəl\ *adj* : deserving or open to censure

[1]cen·sure \'sen-chər\ *n* [L *censura,* fr. *censēre*] **1** : a judgment involving condemnation **2** *archaic* : OPINION, JUDGMENT **3** : the act of blaming or condemning sternly **4** : an official reprimand

[2]censure *vt* **cen·sured; cen·sur·ing** \'sench-(ə-)riŋ\ **1** *obs* : ESTIMATE, JUDGE **2** : to find fault with and criticize as blameworthy ***syn*** see CRITICIZE — **cen·sur·er** \'sen-chər-ər\ *n*

cen·sus \'sen(t)-səs\ *n* [L, fr. *censēre*] **1** : a count of the population and a property evaluation in early Rome **2** : a usu. complete enumeration of a population; *specif* : a periodic governmental enumeration of population **3** : COUNT, TALLY — **census** *vt*

[1]cent \'sent\ *n* [MF, hundred, fr. L *centum* — more at HUNDRED] **1** : a monetary unit equal to 1/100 of a basic unit of value — see *dollar, gulden, leone, piaster, rand, rupee, shilling* at MONEY table **2** : a coin, token, or note representing one cent

[2]cent *abbr* **1** centigrade **2** central **3** centum **4** century

cen·tal \'sent-ᵊl\ *n* [L *centum* + E *-al* (as in *quintal*)] *chiefly Brit* : a short hundredweight

cent·are \'sen-ˌta(ə)r, -ˌte(ə)r, -ˌtär\ *or* **cen·ti·are** \'sent-ē-ˌa(ə)r, 'sänt-, -ˌe(ə)r, -ˌär\ *n* [F *centiare,* fr. *centi-* hundred + *are*] — see METRIC SYSTEM table

cen·taur \'sen-ˌtȯ(ə)r\ *n* [ME, fr. L *Centaurus,* fr. Gk *Kentauros*] : one of a race fabled to be half man and half horse and to live in the mountains of Thessaly

cen·tau·rea \sen-'tȯr-ē-ə\ *n* [NL, genus name, fr. ML] : any of a large genus (*Centaurea*) of composite herbs (as knapweed) including several cultivated for their showy heads of tubular florets

Cen·tau·rus \-'tȯr-əs\ *n* [L (gen. *Centauri*)] : a southern constellation between the Southern Cross and Hydra

cen·tau·ry \'sen-ˌtȯr-ē\ *n, pl* **-ries** [ME *centaure,* fr. MF *centaurée,* fr. ML *centaurea,* fr. L *centaureum,* fr. Gk *kentaureion,* fr. *Kentauros*] **1** : any of a genus (*Centaurium*) of low herbs of the gentian family; *esp* : an Old World herb (*C. umbellatum*) formerly used as a tonic **2** : an American plant (*Sabatia angularis*) closely related to centaury

[1]cen·ta·vo \sen-'täv-(ˌ)ō\ *n, pl* **-vos** [Sp, lit., hundredth, fr. L *centum* hundred] — see *colon, cordoba, lempira, peso, quetzal, sol, sucre* at MONEY table

[2]cen·ta·vo \-'täv-(ˌ)ü, -(ˌ)ō\ *n, pl* **-vos** [Pg, fr. Sp] — see *cruzeiro, escudo* at MONEY table

cen·te·nar·i·an \ˌsent-ᵊn-'er-ē-ən\ *n* : one that is 100 years old or older — **centenarian** *adj*

cen·te·na·ry \sen-'ten-ə-rē, 'sent-ᵊn-ˌer-ē, *esp Brit* sen-'tē-nə-rē\ *n, pl* **-ries** [LL *centenarium,* fr. L *centenarius* of a hundred, fr. *centeni* one hundred each, fr. *centum* hundred — more at HUNDRED] : CENTENNIAL — **centenary** *adj*

cen·ten·ni·al \sen-'ten-ē-əl\ *n* [L *centum* + E *-ennial* (as in *biennial*)] : a 100th anniversary or its celebration — **centennial** *adj* — **cen·ten·ni·al·ly** \-ə-lē\ *adv*

[1]cen·ter \'sent-ər\ *n* [ME *centre,* fr. MF, fr. L *centrum,* fr. Gk *kentron* sharp point, center of a circle, fr. *kentein* to prick; akin to OHG *hantag* pointed, Latvian *sits* hunting spear] **1 a** : the point around which a circle or sphere is described; *broadly* : a point that is related to a geometrical figure in such a way that for any point on the figure there is another point on the figure such that a straight line joining the two points is bisected by the original point — called also *center of symmetry* **b** *of a regular polygon* : the center of the inscribed circle **2 a** : a point, area, person, or thing that is most important or pivotal in relation to an indicated activity, interest, or condition <a shopping ~> <the ~ of the controversy> **b** : a source from which something originates <a propaganda ~> **c** : a group of nerve cells having a common function <respiratory ~> **d** : a region of concentrated population <an urban ~> **3 a** : the middle part (as of the forehead or a stage) **b** *often cap* (1) : a grouping of political figures holding moderate views esp. between those of conservatives and liberals (2) : the views of such politicians (3) : the adherents of such views **4** : a player occupying a middle position on a team: as **a** : the football player in the middle of a line who passes the ball between his legs to a back to start a down **b** : the usu. tallest player on a basketball team who usu. plays near the basket **5 a** : one of two tapered rods which support work in a lathe or grinding machine and about or with which the work revolves **b** : a conical recess in the end of work (as a shaft) for receiving such a center

[2]center *vb* **cen·tered; cen·ter·ing** \'sent-ə-riŋ, 'sen-triŋ\ *vt* **1** : to place or fix at or around a center or central area or position <~ the picture on the wall> **2** : to gather to a center : CONCENTRATE <~*s* her hopes on her son> **3** : to adjust (as lenses) so that the axes coincide **4 a** : to pass (a ball or puck) from either side toward the middle of the playing area **b** : to hand or pass (a football) backward between one's legs to a back to start a down ~ *vi* : to have a center : FOCUS <the novel itself is ~*ed* around a Norwegian village hostelry —Maxwell Geismar>

cen·ter·board \'sent-ər-ˌbō(ə)rd, -ˌbȯ(ə)rd\ *n* : a retractable keel used esp. in sailboats

cen·tered \'sent-ərd\ *adj* : having a center — often used in combination <a dark-*centered* coneflower>

center field *n* **1** : the part of the baseball outfield between right and left field **2** : the position of the player for defending center field — **center fielder** *n*

cen·ter·line \ˌsent-ər-'līn\ *n* : a real or imaginary line that is equidistant from the surface or sides of something (as a machine part or a roadway)

center of curvature : the center of the osculating circle at a given point of a curve

center of gravity **1** : CENTER OF MASS **2** : the point at which the entire weight of a body may be considered as concentrated so that if supported at this point the body would remain in equilibrium in any position **3** : CENTER 2a

center of mass : the point in a body or system of bodies at which the whole mass may be considered as concentrated

cen·ter·piece \'sent-ər-ˌpēs\ *n* : an object occupying a central position; *specif* : an adornment in the center of a table

center punch *n* : a hand punch consisting of a short steel bar with a hardened conical point at one end used for marking the centers of holes to be drilled

cen·tes·i·mal \sen-'tes-ə-məl\ *adj* [L *centesimus* hundredth, fr. *centum*] : marked by or relating to division into hundredths

[1]cen·tes·i·mo \chen-'tez-ə-ˌmō\ *n, pl* **-mi** \-(ˌ)mē\ [It] — see *lira* at MONEY table

[2]cen·tes·i·mo \sen-'tes-ə-ˌmō\ *n, pl* **-mos** [Sp *centésimo*] — see *balboa, escudo, peso* at MONEY table

centi- *comb form* [F&L; F, hundredth, fr. L, hundred, fr. *centum* — more at HUNDRED] **1** : hundred <*centi*pede> **2** : hundredth part <*centi*second>

cen·ti·grade \'sent-ə-ˌgrād, 'sänt-\ *adj* [F, fr. L *centi-* hundred + F *grade*] : relating to, conforming to, or having a thermometric scale on which the interval between the freezing point and the boiling point of water is divided into 100 degrees with 0° representing the freezing point and 100° the boiling point <10° ~> — abbr. *C*

cen·ti·gram \-ˌgram\ *n* — see METRIC SYSTEM table

cen·ti·li·ter \'sent-i-ˌlēt-ər, 'sänt-\ *n* — see METRIC SYSTEM table

cen·til·lion \sen-'til-yən\ *n, often attrib* [L *centum* + E *-illion* (as in *million*)] — see NUMBER table

cen·time \'sän-ˌtēm, 'sen-\ *n* [F, fr. *cent* hundred, fr. L *centum*] — see *dinar, franc, gourde* at MONEY table

cen·ti·me·ter \'sent-ə-ˌmēt-ər, 'sänt-\ *n* — see METRIC SYSTEM table

centimeter-gram-second *adj* : of, relating to, or being a system of units based on the centimeter as the unit of length, the gram as the unit of mass, and the mean solar second as the unit of time — abbr. *cgs*

cen·ti·mo \'sent-ə-ˌmō\ *n, pl* **-mos** [Sp *céntimo*] — see *bolivar, colon, guarani, peseta* at MONEY table

cen·ti·pede \'sent-ə-ˌpēd\ *n* [L *centipeda,* fr. *centi-* + *ped-, pes* foot — more at FOOT] : any of a class (Chilopoda) of long flattened many-segmented predaceous arthropods with each segment bearing one pair of legs of which the foremost pair is modified into poison fangs

cent·ner \'sent-nər\ *n* [prob. fr. LG] : a unit of weight used in Germany and Scandinavia usu. equal to 110.23 pounds; *also* : a unit used in the U.S.S.R. equal to 220.46 pounds

cen·to \'sen-(ˌ)tō\ *n, pl* **cen·to·nes** \sen-'tō-(ˌ)nēz\ [LL, fr. L, patchwork garment; akin to OHG *hadara* rag, Skt *kanthā* patched garment] : a literary work made up of parts from other works

CENTO *abbr* Central Treaty Organization
centr- *or* **centri-** *or* **centro-** *comb form* [Gk *kentr-, kentro-,* fr. *kentron* center — more at CENTER] **:** center <*centri*fugal> <*cen-troid*>
1cen·tral \'sen-trəl\ *adj* [L *centralis,* fr. *centrum* center — more at CENTER] **1 :** containing or constituting a center **2 :** of cardinal importance **:** ESSENTIAL, PRINCIPAL <the ~ character of the novel> **3 a :** situated at, in, or near the center <the plains of ~ North America> **b :** easily accessible from outlying districts <a ~ location for the new theater> **4 a :** centrally placed and superseding separate scattered units <~ heating> **b :** controlling or directing local or branch activities <decided by the ~ committee> **5 :** holding to a middle between extremes **:** MODERATE **6 :** of, relating to, or comprising the brain and spinal cord; *also* **:** originating within the central nervous system <~ deafness> — **cen·tral·ly** \-trə-lē\ *adv*
2central *n* **1 :** a telephone exchange or operator **2 :** a central office or bureau usu. controlling others <weather ~>
central angle *n* **:** an angle formed by two radii of a circle
central city *n* **:** a city that constitutes the densely populated center of a metropolitan area and is characterized by a concentration of cultural and commercial facilities serving the area and by a population disproportionately high in disadvantaged persons
cen·tral·ism \'sen-trə-ˌliz-əm\ *n* **:** the concentration of power and control in the central authority of an organization (as a political or educational system) — compare FEDERALISM — **cen·tral·ist** \-ləst\ *n or adj* — **cen·tral·is·tic** \ˌsen-trə-'lis-tik\ *adj*
cen·tral·i·ty \sen-'tral-ət-ē\ *n, pl* **-ties** **1 :** the quality or state of being central **2 :** central situation **3 :** tendency to remain in or at the center
cen·tral·ize \'sen-trə-ˌlīz\ *vb* **-ized; -iz·ing** *vi* **:** to form a center **:** cluster around a center ~ *vt* **1 :** to bring to a center **:** CONSOLIDATE <~ all the data in one file> **2 :** to concentrate by placing power and authority in a center or central organization — **cen·tral·iza·tion** \ˌsen-trə-lə-'zā-shən\ *n* — **cen·tral·iz·er** \'sen-trə-ˌlī-zər\ *n*
central limit theorem *n* **:** any of several fundamental theorems of probability and statistics that state the conditions under which the distribution of a sum of independent random variables is approximated by the normal distribution; *esp* **:** a special case of the central limit theorem which is much applied in sampling and which states that the distribution of a mean of a sample from a population with finite variance is approximated by the normal distribution as the number in the sample becomes large
central nervous system *n* **:** the part of the nervous system which in vertebrates consists of the brain and spinal cord, to which sensory impulses are transmitted and from which motor impulses pass out, and which supervises and coordinates the activity of the entire nervous system
central processing unit *n* **:** PROCESSOR 2a(2)
central tendency *n* **:** clustering of the values of a statistical distribution that is usu. measured by the arithmetic mean, mode, or median
central time *n, often cap C* **:** the time of the 6th time zone west of Greenwich that includes the central U.S. — see TIME ZONE illustration
cen·tre *chiefly Brit var of* CENTER
cen·tric \'sen-trik\ *adj* [Gk *kentrikos* of the center, fr. *kentron*] **1 :** located in or at a center **:** CENTRAL <a ~ point> **2 :** concentrated about or directed to a center <a ~ activity> **3 :** of or relating to a nerve center **4 :** of, relating to, or having a centromere **5 :** of, relating to, or resembling an order (Centrales) of diatoms having the surface markings centrally arranged — **cen·tri·cal·ly** \-tri-k(ə-)lē\ *adv* — **cen·tric·i·ty** \sen-'tris-ət-ē\ *n*
-cen·tric \'sen-trik\ *adj comb form* [ML *-centricus,* fr. L *centrum* center] **:** having (such) a center or (such or so many) centers <poly*centric*> **:** having (something specified) as its center <helio*centric*>
1cen·trif·u·gal \sen-'trif-yə-gəl, -'trif-i-gəl\ *adj* [NL *centrifugus,* fr. *centr-* + L *fugere* to flee — more at FUGITIVE] **1 :** proceeding or acting in a direction away from a center or axis **2 :** using or acting by centrifugal force <a ~ pump> **3 :** EFFERENT **4 :** tending away from centralization **:** SEPARATIST <~ tendencies in modern society> — **cen·trif·u·gal·ly** \-gə-lē\ *adv*
2centrifugal *n* **:** a centrifugal machine or a drum in such a machine
centrifugal force *n* **1 :** the force that tends to impel a thing or parts of a thing outward from a center of rotation **2 :** the force that an object moving along a circular path exerts on the body constraining the object and that acts outwardly away from the center of rotation <a stone whirled about on the end of a string exerts *centrifugal force* on the string>
cen·trif·u·ga·tion \ˌsen-trə-fyü-'gā-shən\ *n* **:** the process of centrifuging
1cen·tri·fuge \'sen-trə-ˌfyüj\ *n* [F, fr. *centrifuge* centrifugal, fr. NL *centrifugus*] **:** a machine using centrifugal force for separating substances of different densities, for removing moisture, or for simulating gravitational effects
2centrifuge *vt* **-fuged; -fug·ing** **:** to subject to centrifugal action esp. in a centrifuge
cen·tri·ole \'sen-trē-ˌōl\ *n* [G *zentriol,* fr. *zentrum* center] **:** one of a pair of cellular organelles that are adjacent to the nucleus, function in the formation of the mitotic apparatus, and consist of a cylinder with nine microtubules arranged peripherally in a circle
cen·trip·e·tal \sen-'trip-ət-ᵊl\ *adj* [NL *centripetus,* fr. *centr-* + L *petere* to go to, seek — more at FEATHER] **1 :** proceeding or acting in a direction toward a center or axis **2 :** AFFERENT **3 :** tending toward centralization **:** UNIFYING <~ tendencies in Western society> — **cen·trip·e·tal·ly** \-ᵊl-ē\ *adv*
centripetal force *n* **:** the force that is necessary to keep an object moving in a circular path and that is directed inward toward the center of rotation <a string on the end of which a stone is whirled about exerts *centripetal force* on the stone>
cen·trist \'sen-trəst\ *n* **1** *often cap* **:** a member of a center party **2 :** one who holds moderate views — **cen·trism** \-ˌtriz-əm\ *n*
cen·troid \'sen-ˌtrȯid\ *n* **:** CENTER OF MASS — **cen·troi·dal** \sen-'trȯid-ᵊl\ *adj*
cen·tro·mere \'sen-trə-ˌmi(ə)r\ *n* [ISV] **:** the point on a chromosome by which it appears to attach to the spindle in mitosis — **cen·tro·mer·ic** \ˌsen-trə-'mi(ə)r-ik, -'mer-\ *adj*
cen·tro·some \'sen-trə-ˌsōm\ *n* [G *zentrosom,* fr. *zentr-* centr- + *-som* -some] **1 :** the centriole-containing region of clear cytoplasm adjacent to the cell nucleus **2 :** CENTRIOLE — **cen·tro·so·mic** \ˌsen-trə-'sō-mik\ *adj*
cen·tro·sphere \'sen-trə-ˌsfi(ə)r\ *n* [ISV] **1 :** the differentiated layer of cytoplasm surrounding the centriole within the centrosome **2 :** the central part of the earth composed of very dense material
cen·trum \'sen-trəm\ *n, pl* **centrums** *or* **cen·tra** \-trə\ [L — more at CENTER] **1 :** CENTER **2 :** the body of a vertebra — see VERTEBRA illustration
cen·tum \'kent-əm, 'ken-ˌtu̇m\ *adj* [L, hundred; fr. the fact that its initial sound (a velar stop) is the representative of an IE palatal stop — more at HUNDRED] **:** of, relating to, or constituting an Indo-European language group characterized by the retention of the Proto-Indo-European stops *k, g,* and *gh* in certain environments — compare SATEM
cen·tu·ri·on \sen-'t(y)u̇r-ē-ən\ *n* [ME, fr. MF & L; MF, fr. L *centurion-, centurio,* fr. *centuria*] **:** an officer commanding a Roman century
cen·tu·ry \'sench-(ə-)rē\ *n, pl* **-ries** [L *centuria,* irreg. fr. *centum* hundred] **1 :** a subdivision of the Roman legion **2 :** a group, sequence, or series of 100 like things **3 :** a period of 100 years esp. of the Christian era or of the preceding period of human history **4 :** a race over a hundred units (as yards or miles)
century plant *n* **:** a Mexican agave (*Agave americana*) maturing and flowering only once in many years and then dying
ceorl \'chā-ˌȯr(ə)l\ *n* [OE — more at CHURL] **:** a freeman of the lowest rank in Anglo-Saxon England
cephal- *or* **cephalo-** *comb form* [L, fr. Gk *kephal-, kephalo-,* fr. *kephalē*] **:** head <*cephal*ad> <*Cephalo*poda>
ceph·a·lad \'sef-ə-ˌlad\ *adv* **:** toward the head or anterior end of the body
ce·phal·ic \sə-'fal-ik\ *adj* [MF *céphalique,* fr. L *cephalicus,* fr. Gk *kephalikos,* fr. *kephalē* head; akin to OHG *gebal* skull, ON *gafl* gable, Toch A *spāl-* head] **1 :** of or relating to the head **2 :** directed toward or situated on or in or near the head — **ce·phal·i·cal·ly** \-i-k(ə-)lē\ *adv*
cephalic index *n* **:** the ratio multiplied by 100 of the maximum breadth of the head to its maximum length

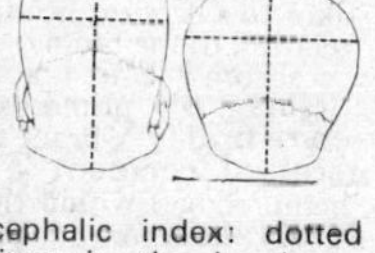

cephalic index: dotted lines in the brachycephalic (right) and dolichocephalic (left) skulls above indicate measurements taken

ceph·a·lin \'kef-ə-lən, 'sef-\ *n* [ISV] **:** any of various acidic phosphatides of living tissues (as of the brain) with marked thromboplastic activity
ceph·a·li·za·tion \ˌsef-ə-lə-'zā-shən\ *n* **:** an evolutionary tendency to specialization of the body with concentration of sensory and neural organs in an anterior head
ceph·a·lom·e·try \ˌsef-ə-'läm-ə-trē\ *n* [ISV] **:** the science of measuring the head — **ceph·a·lo·met·ric** \-lō-'me-trik\ *adj*
ceph·a·lo·pod \'sef-ə-lə-ˌpäd\ *n* [deriv. of *cephal-* + Gk *pod-, pous* foot — more at FOOT] **:** any of a class (Cephalopoda) of mollusks including the squids, cuttlefishes, and octopuses that have a tubular siphon under the head, a group of muscular arms around the front of the head which are usu. furnished with suckers, highly developed eyes, and usu. a bag of inky fluid which can be ejected for defense or concealment — **cephalopod** *adj* — **ceph·a·lop·o·dan** \ˌsef-ə-'läp-əd-ən\ *adj or n*
ceph·a·lor·i·dine \ˌsef-ə-'lȯr-ə-ˌdēn, -'lär-\ *n* [prob. fr. *cephalosporin* + *-idine*] **:** a broad-spectrum antibiotic $C_{19}H_{17}N_3O_4S_2$ derived from cephalosporin and used esp. in the treatment of gonorrhea
ceph·a·lo·spo·rin \ˌsef-ə-lə-'spōr-ən, -'spȯr-\ *n* [*Cephalosporium,* genus of fungi + *-in*] **:** any of several antibiotics produced by an imperfect fungus (genus *Cephalosporium*)
ceph·a·lo·tho·rax \ˌsef-ə-lə-'thō(ə)r-ˌaks, -'thȯ(ə)r-\ *n* [ISV] **:** the united head and thorax of an arachnid or higher crustacean
Ce·phe·id \'sē-fē-əd, 'sef-ē-\ *n* **:** one of a class of pulsating stars whose intrinsic light variations are very regular
Ce·pheus \'sē-ˌfyüs; 'sē-fē-əs, 'sef-ē-\ *n* [L (gen. *Cephei*), fr. Gk *Kēpheus*] **:** a constellation between Cygnus and the north pole
CER *abbr* conditioned emotional response
ce·ra·ceous \sə-'rā-shəs\ *adj* [L *cera* wax — more at CERUMEN] **:** resembling wax
ce·ra·mal \sə-'ram-əl, 'ser-ə-ˌmal\ *n* [*ceram*ic + *al*loy] **:** CERMET
1ce·ram·ic \sə-'ram-ik, *esp Brit* kə-\ *adj* [Gk *keramikos,* fr. *keramos* potter's clay, pottery] **:** of or relating to the manufacture of any product (as earthenware, porcelain, brick, glass, vitreous enamels) made essentially from a nonmetallic mineral by firing at high temperatures; *also* **:** of or relating to such a product
2ceramic *n* **1** *pl but sing in constr* **:** the art or process of making ceramic articles **2 :** a product of ceramic manufacture
ce·ra·mist \sə-'ram-əst, 'ser-ə-məst\ *or* **ce·ram·i·cist** \sə-'ram-ə-səst\ *n* **:** one who engages in ceramics
ce·ras·tes \sə-'ras-(ˌ)tēz\ *n* [ME, fr. L, fr. Gk *kerastēs,* lit., horned, fr. *keras*] **:** a venomous viper (*Cerastes cornutus*) of the Near East having a horny process over each eye — called also *horned viper*
cerat- *or* **cerato-** *or* **kerat-** *or* **kerato-** *comb form* [NL, fr. Gk *kerat-, kerato-,* fr. *keras* horn — more at HORN] **1 :** horn **:** horny

<*cerat*odus> <*kerat*in> **2** *usu kerat- or kerato-* **:** cornea <*kerati*tis>

ce·rate \'si(ə)r-,āt\ *n* [L *ceratum* wax salve, fr. *cera* wax — more at CERUMEN] **:** an unctuous preparation for external use consisting of wax or resin or spermaceti mixed with oil, lard, and medicinal ingredients

ce·rat·odus \sə-'rat-əd-əs\ *n* [NL, genus name, fr. *cerat-* + Gk *odous* tooth — more at TOOTH] **:** any of various recent or fossil dipnoan fishes (as of the genus *Ceratodus*); *esp* **:** BARRAMUNDA a

Cer·ber·us \'sər-b(ə-)rəs\ *n* [L, fr. Gk *Kerberos*] **:** a 3-headed dog that in Greek myth guards the entrance to Hades — **Cer·ber·e·an** \,sər-bə-'rē-ən\ *adj*

-cer·cal \'sər-kəl\ *adj comb form* [F *-cerque,* fr. Gk *kerkos* tail] **:** -tailed <homo*cercal*>

cer·car·ia \(,)sər-'kar-ē-ə, -'ker-\ *n, pl* **-i·ae** \-ē-,ē\ [NL, fr. Gk *kerkos* tail] **:** a usu. tadpole-shaped larval trematode worm produced in a molluscan host by a redia — **cer·car·i·al** \-ē-əl\ *adj*

cer·cis \'sər-səs\ *n* [NL, genus name, fr. Gk *kerkis* Judas tree] **:** any of a small genus (*Cercis*) of leguminous shrubs or low trees (as a red bud)

cer·cus \'sər-kəs\ *n, pl* **cer·ci** \'sər-,sī, -,kī\ [NL, fr. Gk *kerkos* tail] **:** either of a pair of simple or segmented appendages at the posterior end of various arthropods

1cere \'si(ə)r\ *vt* **cered; cer·ing** [ME *ceren* to wax, fr. MF *cirer,* fr. L *cerare,* fr. *cera*] **:** to wrap in or as if in a cerecloth

2cere *n* [ME *sere,* fr. MF *cere,* fr. ML *cera,* fr. L, wax] **:** a usu. waxy protuberance or tumid area at the base of the bill of a bird

1ce·re·al \'sir-ē-əl\ *adj* [F or L; F *céréale,* fr. L *cerealis* of Ceres, of grain, fr. *Ceres*] **:** relating to grain or to the plants that produce it; *also* **:** made of grain

2cereal *n* **1 :** a plant (as a grass) yielding farinaceous grain suitable for food; *also* **:** its grain **2 :** a prepared foodstuff of grain

cereal leaf beetle *n* **:** a small reddish brown black-headed Old World chrysomelid beetle (*Oulema melanopa*) that feeds on cereal grasses and is a serious threat to U.S. grain crops

cer·e·bel·lum \,ser-ə-'bel-əm\ *n, pl* **-bellums** *or* **-bel·la** \-'bel-ə\ [ML, fr. L, dim. of *cerebrum*] **:** a large dorsally projecting part of the brain concerned esp. with the coordination of muscles and the maintenance of bodily equilibrium, situated anterior to and above the medulla which it partly overlaps, and formed in man of two lateral lobes and a median lobe — see BRAIN illustration — **cer·e·bel·lar** \-'bel-ər\ *adj*

cerebr- *or* **cerebro-** *comb form* [*cerebrum*] **1 :** brain **:** cerebrum <*cerebr*ation> **2 :** cerebral and <*cerebro*spinal>

ce·re·bral \sə-'rē-brəl, 'ser-ə-\ *adj* [F *cérébral,* fr. L *cerebrum* brain; akin to Gk *kara* head, *keras* horn — more at HORN] **1 a :** of or relating to the brain or the intellect **b :** of, relating to, or being the cerebrum **2 a :** appealing to intellectual appreciation <~ drama> **b :** primarily intellectual in nature <a ~ society> — **ce·re·bral·ly** \-brə-lē\ *adv*

cerebral accident *n* **:** a sudden damaging occurrence (as of hemorrhage) within the cerebrum — compare APOPLEXY

cerebral cortex *n* **:** the surface layer of gray matter of the cerebral hemisphere that functions chiefly in coordination of higher nervous activity

cerebral hemisphere *n* **:** either of the two hollow convoluted lateral halves of the cerebrum — see BRAIN illustration

cerebral palsy *n* **:** a disability resulting from damage to the brain before or during birth and outwardly manifested by muscular incoordination and speech disturbances — **cerebral palsied** *adj*

cer·e·brate \'ser-ə-,brāt\ *vi* **-brat·ed; -brat·ing** [back-formation fr. *cerebration,* fr. *cerebrum*] **:** to use the mind **:** THINK — **cer·e·bra·tion** \,ser-ə-'brā-shən\ *n*

cer·e·bro·side \'ser-ə-brə-,sīd, sə-'rē-\ *n* [*cerebrose* (galactose)] **:** any of various lipids found esp. in nerve tissue

ce·re·bro·spi·nal \sə-,rē-brō-'spīn-ᵊl, ,ser-ə-brō-\ *adj* **:** of or relating to the brain and spinal cord or to these together with the cranial and spinal nerves that innervate voluntary muscles

cerebrospinal fluid *n* **:** a liquid that is comparable to serum and is secreted from the blood into the lateral ventricles of the brain

cerebrospinal meningitis *n* **:** inflammation of the meninges of both brain and spinal cord; *specif* **:** an infectious epidemic and often fatal meningitis caused by the meningococcus

ce·re·bro·vas·cu·lar \sə-,rē-brō-'vas-kyə-lər, ,ser-ə-brō-\ *adj* **:** of or involving the cerebrum and the blood vessels supplying it <~ disease>

ce·re·brum \sə-'rē-brəm, 'ser-ə-brəm\ *n, pl* **-brums** *or* **-bra** \-brə\ [L] **1 :** BRAIN 1a **2 :** an enlarged anterior or upper part of the brain: **a :** the forebrain and midbrain with their derivatives **b :** FOREBRAIN 2a **c :** the expanded anterior portion of the brain that in higher mammals overlies the rest of the brain, consists of cerebral hemispheres and connecting structures, and is considered to be the seat of conscious mental processes **:** TELENCEPHALON

cere·cloth \'si(ə)r-,klȯth\ *n* [alter. of earlier *cered cloth* (waxed cloth)] **:** cloth treated with melted wax or gummy matter and formerly used esp. for wrapping a dead body

cere·ment \'ser-ə-mənt, 'si(ə)r-mənt\ *n* **:** a shroud for the dead; *esp* **:** CERECLOTH — usu. used in pl.

1cer·e·mo·ni·al \,ser-ə-'mō-nē-əl\ *adj* **:** marked by, involved in, or belonging to ceremony **:** stressing careful attention to form and detail — **cer·e·mo·ni·al·ism** \-ə-,liz-əm\ *n* — **cer·e·mo·ni·al·ist** \-ə-ləst\ *n* — **cer·e·mo·ni·al·ly** \-ə-lē\ *adv*

syn CEREMONIAL, CEREMONIOUS, FORMAL, CONVENTIONAL *shared meaning element* **:** marked by attention to or adhering strictly to prescribed forms, procedures, and details. CEREMONIAL and CEREMONIOUS both imply strict attention to what is prescribed (as by custom, code, or ritual) but CEREMONIAL more often applies to things that are or are pertinent to ceremonies <read the service in a nasal *ceremonial* drawl> and CEREMONIOUS to persons addicted to ceremony or to acts attended by ceremony <an ever precise, utterly proper, and extremely *ceremonious* old gentleman> FORMAL applies equally to things prescribed by and persons obedient to custom and often conveys a notion of stiff, restrained, or old-fashioned behavior <paying *formal* attention to his hostess> <the committee made a *formal* report to the president> CONVENTIONAL implies accord with general custom and usage and may suggest lack of originality or independence <a *conventional* courtesy> <they are not moral; they are only *conventional*—G. B. Shaw>

2ceremonial *n* **:** a ceremonial act, action, or system

cer·e·mo·ni·ous \,ser-ə-'mō-nē-əs\ *adj* **1 :** of, relating to, or constituting a ceremony **2 :** devoted to forms and ceremony **:** PUNCTILIOUS **3 :** according to formal usage or prescribed procedures **4 :** marked by ceremony ***syn*** see CEREMONIAL ***ant*** unceremonious, informal — **cer·e·mo·ni·ous·ly** *adv* — **cer·e·mo·ni·ous·ness** *n*

cer·e·mo·ny \'ser-ə-,mō-nē\ *n, pl* **-nies** [ME *ceremonie,* fr. MF *cérémonie,* fr. L *caerimonia*] **1 :** a formal act or series of acts prescribed by ritual, protocol, or convention <the marriage ~> **2 a :** a conventional act of politeness or etiquette <the ~ of introduction> **b :** an action performed only formally with no deep significance **c :** a routine action performed with elaborate pomp **3 a :** prescribed procedures **:** USAGES <the ~ attending an inauguration> **b :** observance of an established code of civility or politeness <the door opened without ~ and the man strode in>

Ce·ren·kov radiation \chər-'(y)eŋ-kəf-\ *n* [P. A. *Cherenkov b* 1904 Russ physicist] **:** light produced by charged particles (as electrons) traversing a transparent medium at a speed greater than that of light in the same medium

Ce·res \'si(ə)r-(,)ēz\ *n* [L] **1 :** the Roman goddess of agriculture — compare DEMETER **2 :** the largest asteroid and the one first discovered

ce·re·us \'sir-ē-əs\ *n* [NL, genus name, fr. L, wax candle, fr. *cera* wax — more at CERUMEN] **:** any of various cacti (as of the genus *Cereus*) of the western U.S. and tropical America

ce·ric \'si(ə)r-ik, 'ser-\ *adj* **:** of, relating to, or containing cerium esp. with a valence of four

ce·rise \sə-'rēs, -'rēz\ *n* [F, lit., cherry, fr. LL *ceresia* — more at CHERRY] **:** a moderate red

ce·ri·um \'sir-ē-əm\ *n* [NL, fr. *Ceres*] **:** a malleable ductile metallic element that is the most abundant of the rare-earth group — see ELEMENT table

cerium metal *n* **:** any of a group of related rare-earth metals comprising cerium, lanthanum, praseodymium, neodymium, promethium, samarium, and sometimes europium

cer·met \'sər-,met\ *n* [*ceramic* + *metal*] **:** a strong alloy of a heat-resistant compound (as titanium carbide) and a metal (as nickel) used esp. for turbine blades — called also *ceramal*

cer·nu·ous \'sər-nyə-wəs\ *adj* [L *cernuus* with the face turned earthward; akin to L *cerebrum*] **:** PENDULOUS, NODDING <a ~ flower>

cero \'se(ə)r-(,)ō\ *n, pl* **cero** *or* **ceros** [modif. of Sp *sierra* saw, cero] **:** either of two large food and sport fishes (*Scomberomorus cavalla* and *S. regalis*) of the warmer parts of the western Atlantic ocean

ce·ro·tic acid \sə-,rōt-ik-, -,rät-\ *n* [L *cerotum,* a pomade, fr. Gk *kērōton,* fr. *kēros* wax — more at CERUMEN] **:** a solid fatty acid $C_{26}H_{52}O_2$ occurring in waxes (as beeswax) and some fats

ce·rous \'sir-əs\ *adj* **:** of, relating to, or containing cerium esp. with a valence of three

cert *abbr* certificate; certification; certified; certify

1cer·tain \'sərt-ᵊn\ *adj* [ME, fr. OF, fr. (assumed) VL *certanus,* fr. L *certus,* fr. pp. of *cernere* to sift, discern, decide; akin to Gk *krinein* to separate, decide, judge, *keirein* to cut — more at SHEAR] **1 a :** FIXED, SETTLED <guaranteed a ~ percentage of the profit> **b :** proved to be true **2 :** of a specific but unspecified character, quantity, or degree **:** PARTICULAR <the house has a ~ charm> <everyone has a ~ amount of success> **3 a :** DEPENDABLE, RELIABLE <a ~ remedy for the disease> **b :** INDISPUTABLE <it is ~ that we exist> **4 a :** INEVITABLE <the ~ advance of age and decay> **b :** incapable of failing **:** DESTINED — used with a following infinitive <she is ~ to do well> **5 :** assured in mind or action ***syn*** see SURE ***ant*** uncertain — **cer·tain·ly** *adv* — **for certain** **:** as a certainty **:** ASSUREDLY

2certain *pron, pl in constr* **:** certain ones

cer·tain·ty \'sərt-ᵊn-tē\ *n, pl* **-ties** **1 :** something that is certain **2 :** the quality or state of being certain esp. on the basis of objective evidence

syn CERTAINTY, CERTITUDE, ASSURANCE, CONVICTION *shared meaning element* **:** a state of being free from doubt ***ant*** uncertainty

cer·tes \'sərt-ēz, 'sərts\ *adv* [ME, fr. OF, fr. *cert* certain, fr. L *certus*] *archaic* **:** in truth **:** CERTAINLY

1cer·tif·i·cate \(,)sər-'tif-i-kət\ *n* [ME *certificat,* fr. MF, fr. ML *certificatum,* fr. LL, neut. of *certificatus,* pp. of *certificare* to certify] **1 :** a document containing a certified statement esp. as to the truth of something; *specif* **:** a document certifying that one has fulfilled the requirements of and may practice in a field **2 :** something serving the same end as a certificate **3 :** a document evidencing ownership or debt <a ~ of deposit>

2cer·tif·i·cate \-'tif-ə-,kāt\ *vt* **-cat·ed; -cat·ing** **:** to testify to or authorize by a certificate — **cer·tif·i·ca·to·ry** \-'tif-i-kə-,tōr-ē, -,tȯr-\ *adj*

cer·ti·fi·ca·tion \,sərt-ə-fə-'kā-shən\ *n* **1 :** the act of certifying **:** the state of being certified **2 :** a certified statement

certified check *n* **:** a check certified to be good by the bank on which it is drawn

certified mail *n* **:** first class mail for which proof of delivery is secured but no indemnity value is claimed

certified milk *n* **:** milk produced in dairies that operate under the rules and regulations of an authorized medical milk commission

certified public accountant *n* **:** an accountant who has met the requirements of a state law and has been granted a state certificate

cer·ti·fy \'sərt-ə-,fī\ *vt* **-fied; -fy·ing** [ME *certifien,* fr. MF *certifier,* fr. LL *certificare,* fr. L *certus* certain — more at CERTAIN] **1 :** to attest authoritatively: as **a :** CONFIRM **b :** to present in formal communication **c :** to attest as being true or as represented or as meeting a standard **d :** to attest officially to the insanity of **2 :** to inform with certainty **:** ASSURE **3 :** to guarantee (a personal check) as to signature and amount by so indicating on the face **4** : CERTIFICATE, LICENSE ***syn*** see APPROVE — **cer·ti·fi·able** \-ˌfī-ə-bəl\ *adj* — **cer·ti·fi·ably** \-blē\ *adv* — **cer·ti·fi·er** \-ˌfī(-ə)r\ *n*

cer·tio·ra·ri \ˌsər-sh(ē-)ə-'ra(ə)r-ē, -'rär-ē\ *n* [ME, fr. L, to be informed; fr. the use of the word in the writ] : a writ of a superior court to call up the records of an inferior court or a body acting in a quasi-judicial capacity

cer·ti·tude \'sərt-ə-ˌt(y)üd\ *n* [ME, fr. LL *certitudo*, fr. L *certus*] **1** : the state of being or feeling certain **2** : unfailingness of act or event ***syn*** see CERTAINTY ***ant*** doubt

ce·ru·le·an \sə-'rü-lē-ən\ *adj* [L *caeruleus* dark blue] : resembling the blue of the sky

ce·ru·lo·plas·min \sə-ˌrü-lō-'plaz-mən\ *n* [ISV *cerulo* (fr. L *caeruleus* dark blue) + *plasma* + *-in*] : a plasma oxidase active in copper storage and transport

ce·ru·men \sə-'rü-mən\ *n* [NL, irreg. fr. L *cera* wax, prob. fr. Gk *kēros*; akin to Lith *korys* honeycomb] : the yellow waxy secretion from the glands of the external ear — called also *earwax* — **ce·ru·mi·nous** \-mə-nəs\ *adj*

ce·ruse \sə-'rüs, 'si(ə)r-ˌüs\ *n* [ME, fr. MF *céruse*, fr. L *cerussa*] **1** : white lead as a pigment **2** : a cosmetic containing white lead

ce·rus·site \sə-'rəs-ˌīt\ *n* [G *zerussit*, fr. L *cerussa*] : a mineral $PbCO_3$ consisting of lead carbonate occurring in colorless transparent crystals and also massive

cer·ve·lat \'sər-və-ˌlat, -ˌlä\ *n* [obs. F (now *cervelas*)] : smoked sausage made of varying proportions of pork and beef

cervic- *or* **cervici-** *or* **cervico-** *comb form* [L *cervic-*, *cervex* neck] : neck : cervix of an organ <*cervicitis*> : cervical and <*cervicothoracic*>

cer·vi·cal \'sər-vi-kəl\ *adj* : of or relating to a neck or cervix

cer·vi·ci·tis \ˌsər-və-'sīt-əs\ *n* : inflammation of the uterine cervix

cer·vine \'sər-ˌvīn\ *adj* [L *cervinus* of a deer, fr. *cervus* stag, deer — more at HART] : of, relating to, or resembling deer

cer·vix \'sər-viks\ *n, pl* **cer·vi·ces** \'sər-və-ˌsēz, (ˌ)sər-'vī-(ˌ)sēz\ *or* **cer·vix·es** [L *cervic-*, *cervix*] **1** : NECK; *esp* : the back part of the neck **2** : a constricted portion of an organ or part; *esp* : the narrow outer end of the uterus

ce·sar·e·an *also* **ce·sar·i·an** \si-'zar-ē-ən, -'zer-\ *n* [fr. the belief that Julius Caesar was born this way] : surgical incision of the walls of the abdomen and uterus for delivery of offspring — **cesarean** *also* **cesarian** *adj*

ce·si·um \'sē-zē-əm\ *n* [NL, fr. L *caesius* bluish gray] : a silver-white soft ductile element of the alkali metal group that is the most electropositive element known and that is used esp. in photoelectric cells — see ELEMENT table

[1]**cess** \'ses\ *n* [ME *cessen* to tax, short for *assessen* — more at ASSESS] : LEVY, TAX

[2]**cess** *n* [prob. short for *success*] *chiefly Irish* : LUCK — usu. used in the phrase *bad cess to you*

ces·sa·tion \se-'sā-shən\ *n* [ME *cessacioun*, fr. MF *cessation*, fr. L *cessation-*, *cessatio* delay, idleness, fr. *cessatus*, pp. of *cessare* to delay, be idle — more at CEASE] : a temporary or final ceasing (as of action) : STOP

ces·sion \'sesh-ən\ *n* [ME, fr. MF, fr. L *cession-*, *cessio*, fr. *cessus*, pp. of *cedere* to withdraw — more at CEDE] : a yielding to another : CONCESSION

cess·pit \'ses-ˌpit\ *n* [*cesspool* + *pit*] : a pit for the disposal of refuse (as sewage)

cess·pool \-ˌpül\ *n* [by folk etymology fr. ME *suspiral* vent, cesspool, fr. MF *souspirail* ventilator, fr. *soupirer* to sigh, fr. L *suspirare*, lit., to draw a long breath — more at SUSPIRE] : an underground catch basin for liquid waste (as household sewage)

ces·ta \'ses-tə\ *n* [Sp, lit., basket, fr. L *cista* box, basket] : a narrow curved wicker basket used to catch and propel the ball in jai alai

ces·tode \'ses-ˌtōd\ *n* [deriv. of Gk *kestos* girdle] : any of a subclass (Cestoda) of internally parasitic flatworms comprising the tapeworms — **cestode** *adj*

[1]**ces·tus** \'ses-təs\ *n, pl* **ces·ti** \-ˌtī\ [L, girdle, belt, fr. Gk *kestos*, fr. *kestos* stitched; akin to Gk *kentron* sharp point — more at CENTER] : a woman's belt; *esp* : a symbolic one worn by a bride

[2]**cestus** *n* [L *caestus*, fr. *caedere* to strike — more at CONCISE] : a hand covering of leather bands often loaded with lead or iron and used by boxers in ancient Rome

ce·su·ra *var of* CAESURA

ce·ta·cean \si-'tā-shən\ *n* [deriv. of L *cetus* whale, fr. Gk *kētos*] : any of an order (Cetacea) of aquatic mostly marine mammals including the whales, dolphins, porpoises, and related forms with large head, fishlike nearly hairless body, and paddle-shaped forelimbs — **cetacean** *adj* — **ce·ta·ceous** \-shəs\ *adj*

ce·tane \'sē-ˌtān\ *n* [fr. *cetyl* (the radical $C_{16}H_{33}$)] : a colorless oily hydrocarbon $C_{16}H_{34}$ found in petroleum

cetane number *n* : a measure of the ignition value of a diesel fuel that represents the percentage by volume of cetane in a mixture of liquid methylnaphthalene that gives the same ignition lag as the oil being tested — called also *cetane rating* — compare OCTANE NUMBER

ce·te·ris pa·ri·bus \ˌkāt-ə-rə-'spar-ə-bəs\ *adv* [NL, other things being equal] : if all other relevant things, factors, or elements remain unaltered

Ce·tus \'sēt-əs\ *n* [L (gen. *Ceti*), lit., whale] : an equatorial constellation south of Pisces and Aries

cetyl alcohol \'sēt-ᵊl-\ *n* [ISV *cet-* (fr. L *cetus* whale) + *-yl*; fr. its occurrence in spermaceti] : a waxy crystalline alcohol $C_{16}H_{34}O$ found in the form of its ester in spermaceti and used in pharmaceutical and cosmetic preparations and in making detergents

ce·vi·tam·ic acid \ˌsē-(ˌ)vī-ˌtam-ik-\ *n* [*cee* + *vitamin*] : VITAMIN C

cf *abbr* **1** calf **2** [L *confer*, imper. of *conferre* to compare — more at CONFER] compare

Cf *symbol* californium

CF *abbr* **1** carried forward **2** centrifugal force **3** cost and freight **4** cystic fibrosis

CFI *abbr* **1** chief flying instructor **2** cost, freight, and insurance

CFM *abbr* cubic feet per minute

CFS *abbr* cubic feet per second

cg *or* **cgm** *abbr* centigram

CG *abbr* **1** center of gravity **2** coast guard **3** commanding general

cgs *abbr* centimeter-gram-second

CGT *abbr* [F *Confédération Générale du Travail*] General Confederation of Labor

ch *abbr* **1** chain **2** champion **3** chaplain **4** chapter **5** chief **6** child; children **7** church

CH *abbr* **1** clearinghouse **2** courthouse **3** customhouse

Cha·blis \'shab-(ˌ)lē; sha-'blē, shä-\ *n, pl* **Cha·blis** \-(ˌ)lēz, -'blēz\ [F, fr. *Chablis*, France] : a dry white Burgundy table wine

cha–cha \'chä-(ˌ)chä\ *n* [AmerSp *cha-cha-cha*] : a fast rhythmic ballroom dance of Latin-American origin with a basic pattern of three steps and a shuffle

chac·ma \'chak-mə\ *n* [Hottentot] : a large dusky southern African baboon (*Papio comatus*)

cha·conne \shä-'kon, sha-, -'kän, -'kən\ *n* [F & Sp; F *chaconne*, fr. Sp *chacona*] **1** : an old Spanish dance tune resembling the passacaglia **2** : a musical composition in moderate 3/4 time with stress on the second beat and typically consisting of variations on a repeated succession of chords

chad \'chad\ *n* [perh. fr. Sc, gravel] : small pieces of paper or cardboard produced in punching paper tape or data cards; *also* : a piece of chad — **chad·less** \-ləs\ *adj*

Chad \'chad\ *n* : a branch of the Afro-Asiatic language family comprising numerous languages of northern Nigeria and Cameroons

chae·ta \'kēt-ə\ *n, pl* **chae·tae** \'kē-ˌtē\ [NL, fr. Gk *chaitē* long flowing hair] : BRISTLE, SETA — **chae·tal** \kēt-ᵊl\ *adj*

chae·to·gnath \'kēt-äg-ˌnath, -ə(g)-\ *n* [deriv. of Gk *chaitē* + *gnathos* jaw — more at GNATH-] : any of a class or phylum (Chaetognatha) of small free-swimming marine worms with movable curved chaetae on either side of the mouth — **chaetognath** *adj* — **chae·tog·na·than** \kē-'täg-nə-thən\ *adj or n*

[1]**chafe** \'chāf\ *vb* **chafed; chaf·ing** [ME *chaufen* to warm, fr. MF *chaufer*, fr. (assumed) VL *calfare*, alter. of L *calefacere*, fr. *calēre* to be warm + *facere* to make — more at LEE, DO] *vt* **1** : IRRITATE, VEX **2** : to warm by rubbing esp. with the hands **3 a** : to rub so as to wear away : ABRADE <the boat *chafed* her sides against the dock> **b** : to make sore by or as if by rubbing ~ *vi* **1** : to feel irritation or discontent : FRET <~*s* at his restrictive desk job> **2** : to rub and thereby cause wear or irritation

[2]**chafe** *n* **1** : a state of vexation : RAGE **2** : injury or wear caused by friction; *also* : FRICTION, RUBBING

cha·fer \'chā-fər\ *n* [ME *cheaffer*, fr. OE *ceafor*; akin to OE *ceafl* jowl — more at JOWL] : any of various large beetles (esp. family Scarabaeidae)

[1]**chaff** \'chaf\ *n* [ME *chaf*, fr. OE *ceaf*; akin to OHG *cheva* husk] **1** : the seed coverings and other debris separated from the seed in threshing grain **2** : something comparatively worthless **3** : the scales borne on the receptacle among the florets in the heads of many composite plants **4** : material (as strips of foil or clusters of fine wires) ejected into the air for reflecting radar waves (as for confusing an enemy's radar detection or for tracking a descending spacecraft) — **chaffy** \-ē\ *adj*

[2]**chaff** *n* [prob. fr. [1]*chaff*] : light jesting talk : BANTER

[3]**chaff** *vt* : to tease good-naturedly ~ *vi* : JEST, BANTER

[1]**chaf·fer** \'chaf-ər\ *n* [ME *chaffare*, fr. *chep* trade + *fare* journey — more at CHEAP, FARE] *archaic* : a haggling about price

[2]**chaffer** *vb* **chaf·fered; chaf·fer·ing** \'chaf-(ə-)riŋ\ *vi* **1** : HAGGLE **2** *Brit* : to exchange small talk : CHATTER ~ *vt* **1** : EXCHANGE, BARTER **2** : to bargain for — **chaf·fer·er** \-ər-ər\ *n*

chaf·finch \'chaf-(ˌ)inch\ *n* [ME, fr. OE *ceaffinc*, fr. *ceaf* + *finc* finch] : a European finch (*Fringilla coelebs*) of which the male has a reddish breast plumage and a cheerful song

chaf·ing dish \'chā-fiŋ-\ *n* [ME *chafing*, prp. of *chaufen*, *chafen* to warm] : a utensil for cooking or keeping food warm esp. at the table

Cha·gas' disease \'shäg-əs-(əz-)\ *n* [Carlos *Chagas* †1934 Braz. physician] : a tropical American trypanosomiasis marked by prolonged high fever, edema, and enlargement of spleen, liver, and lymph nodes and caused by a flagellate (*Trypanosoma cruzi*)

[1]**cha·grin** \shə-'grin\ *n* [F, fr. *chagrin* sad] : disquietude or distress of mind caused by humiliation, disappointment, or failure

[2]**chagrin** *vt* **cha·grined** \-'grind\; **cha·grin·ing** \-'grin-iŋ\ : to vex acutely by disappointing or humiliating

Chai·ma \'chī-mə\ *n* **1** : a member of a Cariban people of the coast of Venezuela **2** : the language of the Chaima people

[1]**chain** \'chān\ *n, often attrib* [ME *cheyne*, fr. OF *chaeine*, fr. L *catena*; akin to L *cassis* net] **1 a** : a series of usu. metal links or rings connected to or fitted into one another and used for various purposes (as support, restraint, transmission of mechanical power, or measurement) **b** : a series of links used or worn as an ornament or insignia **c** (1) : a measuring instrument of 100 links used in surveying (2) : a unit of length equal to 66 feet **2** : something that confines, restrains or secures **3 a** : a series of things linked, connected, or associated together <a ~ of events> **b** : a number of atoms or chemical groups united like links in a chain

[2]**chain** *vt* **1** : to fasten, bind, or connect with or as if with a chain; *also* : FETTER **2** : to obstruct or protect by a chain

chai·né \shā-'nā\ *n* [F, fr. pp. of *chainer* to chain] : a series of short regular usu. fast turns by which a ballet dancer moves across the stage

chain gang *n* : a gang of convicts chained together esp. as an outside working party

ə abut ᵊ kitten ər further a back ā bake ä cot, cart
aù out ch chin e less ē easy g gift i trip ī life
j joke ŋ sing ō flow ȯ flaw ȯi coin th thin t͟h this
ü loot u̇ foot y yet yü few yu̇ furious zh vision

chain letter *n* **1 :** a social letter sent to a series of persons in succession and often added to by each **2 :** a letter sent to several persons with a request that each send copies of the letter to an equal number of persons
chain mail *n* **:** flexible armor of interlinked metal rings
chain of command : a series of executive positions in order of authority <a military *chain of command*>
chain·omat·ic \ˌchā-nə-ˈmat-ik\ *adj* [fr. *Chainomatic,* a trademark] *of a balance or scale* **:** having suspended from the beam an adjustable fine chain whose length is measured to determine minute weights
chain pickerel *n* [fr. the markings resembling chains on the sides] **:** a large greenish black pickerel (*Esox niger*) with dark markings along the sides that is common in quiet waters of eastern No. America
chain printer *n* **:** a line printer in which the printing element is a continuous chain
chain–reacting pile *n* **:** REACTOR 3b
chain reaction *n* **1 :** a series of events so related to each other that each one initiates the next **2 :** a self-sustaining chemical or nuclear reaction yielding energy or products that cause further reactions of the same kind — **chain–re·act** \ˌchān-rē-ˈakt\ *vi*
chain rule *n* **:** a mathematical rule concerning the differentiation of a function of a function (as $f[u(x)]$) by which under suitable conditions of continuity and differentiability one function is differentiated with respect to the second considered as an independent variable and then the second function is differentiated with respect to the independent variable <if $v = u^2$ and $u = 3x^2 + 2$ the derivative of v is $2u(6x)$ or $12x(3x^2 + 2)$>
chain saw *n* **:** a portable power saw that has teeth linked together to form an endless chain
chain–smoke \ˈchān-ˈsmōk\ *vi* **:** to smoke esp. cigarettes continually often by lighting each from the previous one ~ *vt* **:** to smoke (as cigarettes) almost without interruption
chain stitch *n* **1 :** an ornamental stitch like the links of a chain **2 :** a machine stitch forming a chain on the underside of the work
chain store *n* **:** one of numerous usu. retail stores having the same ownership and selling the same lines of goods
[1]**chair** \ˈche(ə)r, ˈcha(ə)r\ *n* [ME *chaiere,* fr. OF, fr. L *cathedra,* fr. Gk *kathedra,* fr. *kata-* cata- + *hedra* seat — more at SIT] **1 a :** a seat typically having four legs and a back for one person **b :** ELECTRIC CHAIR **2 a :** an official seat or a seat of authority, state, or dignity **b :** an office or position of authority or dignity <holds a university ~> **c :** CHAIRMAN **3 :** a sedan chair **4 :** a position of employment usu. of one occupying a chair or desk; *specif* **:** the position of a player in an orchestra or band **5 :** any of various devices that hold up or support
[2]**chair** *vt* **1 :** to install in office **2** *chiefly Brit* **:** to carry shoulder-high in acclaim <the time you won your town the race we ~*ed* you through the market place —A. E. Housman> **3 :** to preside as chairman of
chair car *n* **1 :** a railroad car having pairs of chairs with individually adjustable backs on each side of the aisle **2 :** PARLOR CAR
chair lift *n* **:** a motor-driven conveyor consisting of a series of seats suspended from an overhead moving cable and used for transporting skiers or sightseers up or down a long slope or mountainside
[1]**chair·man** \ˈche(ə)r-mən, ˈcha(ə)r-\ *n* **1 a :** the presiding officer of a meeting or an organization or committee **b :** the administrative officer of a department of instruction (as in a college) **2 :** a carrier of a sedan chair — **chair·man·ship** \-ˌship\ *n*
[2]**chairman** *vt* **-maned** *or* **-manned; -man·ing** *or* **-man·ning :** CHAIR 3
chair·wom·an \-ˌwu̇m-ən\ *n* **:** a female chairman
chaise \ˈshāz\ *n* [F, chair, chaise, alter. of OF *chaiere*] **1 a :** a 2-wheeled carriage for one or two persons with a calash top and the body hung on leather straps and usu. drawn by one horse **b :** a similar 4-wheeled pleasure carriage **c :** POST CHAISE **2 :** a light carriage or pleasure cart **3 :** CHAISE LONGUE

chaise 1a

chaise longue \ˈshāz-ˈlȯŋ\ *n, pl* **chaise longues** *also* **chaises longues** \ˈshāz-ˈlȯŋ(z)\ [F *chaise longue,* lit., long chair] **:** a long reclining chair
chaise lounge \ˈshāz-ˈlau̇nj, ˈchās-\ *n* [by folk etymology fr. F *chaise longue*] **:** CHAISE LONGUE
Chait \ˈchīt\ *n* [Hindi *Cait,* fr. Skt *Caitra*] **:** a month of the Hindu year — see MONTH table
cha·la·za \kə-ˈlā-zə, -ˈlaz-ə\ *n, pl* **-zae** \-ˌzē\ *or* **-zas** [NL, fr. Gk, hailstone; akin to Per *zhāla* hail] **1 :** either of a pair of spiral bands in the white of a bird's egg that extend from the yolk and attach to opposite ends of the lining membrane — see EGG illustration **2 :** the point at the base of a plant ovule where the seed stalk is attached — **cha·la·zal** \-ˈlā-zəl, -ˈlaz-əl\ *adj*
Chal·ce·do·ni·an \ˌkal-sə-ˈdō-nē-ən\ *adj* **:** of or relating to Chalcedon or the ecumenical council held there in A.D. 451 declaring Monophysitism heretical — **Chalcedonian** *n*
chal·ced·o·ny \kal-ˈsed-ᵊn-ē\ *n, pl* **-nies** [ME *calcedonie,* a precious stone, fr. LL *chalcedonius,* fr. Gk *Chalkēdōn* Chalcedon] **:** a translucent quartz that is commonly pale blue or gray with nearly waxlike luster — **chal·ce·don·ic** \ˌkal-sə-ˈdän-ik\ *adj*
chal·cid \ˈkal-səd\ *n* [deriv. of Gk *chalkos* copper] **:** any of a large superfamily (Chalcidoidea) of mostly minute hymenopterous insects parasitic in the larval state on the larvae or pupae of other insects — **chalcid** *adj*
chal·co·gen \ˈkal-kə-jən\ *n* [prob. fr. G *chalkogen,* fr. *chalk-* bronze, ore (fr. Gk *chalkos* bronze) + *-gen;* fr. the occurrence of oxygen and sulfur in many ores] **:** any of the elements oxygen, sulfur, selenium, and tellurium
chal·co·gen·ide \-jə-ˌnīd\ *n* **:** a binary compound of a chalcogen with a more electropositive element or radical
chal·co·py·rite \ˌkal-kə-ˈpī-ˌrīt\ *n* [NL *chalcopyrites,* fr. Gk *chalkos* + L *pyrites*] **:** a yellow mineral $CuFeS_2$ consisting of copper-iron sulfide and constituting an important ore of copper
Chal·da·ic \kal-ˈdā-ik\ *adj or n* **:** CHALDEAN
Chal·de·an \kal-ˈdē-ən\ *n* [L *Chaldaeus* Chaldean, astrologer, fr. Gk *Chaldaios,* fr. Chaldaia Chaldea, region of ancient Babylonia] **1 a :** a member of an ancient Semitic people that became dominant in Babylonia **b :** the Semitic language of the Chaldeans **2 :** a person versed in the occult arts — **Chaldean** *adj*
Chal·dee \ˈkal-ˌdē\ *n* [ME *Caldey,* prob. fr. MF *chaldée,* fr. L *Chaldaeus*] **1 :** the Aramaic vernacular that was the original language of some parts of the Bible **2 :** CHALDEAN 1a
chal·dron \ˈchȯl-drən\ *n* [MF *chauderon,* fr. *chaudere* pot, fr. LL *caldaria* — more at CALDRON] **:** any of various old units of measure varying from 32 to 72 imperial bushels
cha·let \sha-ˈlā, ˈshal-(ˌ)ā\ *n* [F] **1 :** a remote herdsman's hut in the Alps **2 a :** a Swiss dwelling with unconcealed structural members and a wide overhang at the front and sides **b :** a cottage or house in chalet style

chalet 2a

chal·ice \ˈchal-əs\ *n* [ME, fr. AF, fr. L *calic-, calix;* akin to Gk *kalyx* calyx] **1 :** a drinking cup **:** GOBLET; *esp* **:** the eucharistic cup **2 :** the cup-shaped interior of a flower
[1]**chalk** \ˈchȯk\ *n* [ME, fr. OE *cealc;* akin to OHG & MLG *kalk* lime; all fr. a prehistoric WGmc word borrowed fr. L *calc-, calx* lime, fr. Gk *chalix* pebble; akin to Gk *skallein* to hoe — more at SHELL] **1 a :** a soft white, gray, or buff limestone composed chiefly of the shells of foraminifers **b :** chalk or a chalky material esp. when used in the form of a crayon **2 a :** a mark made with chalk **b** *Brit* **:** a point scored in a game — **chalky** \ˈchȯ-kē\ *adj*
[2]**chalk** *vt* **1 :** to rub or mark with chalk **2 :** to write or draw with chalk **3 a :** to delineate roughly **:** SKETCH <~ out a plan of attack> **b :** to set down or add up with or as if with chalk **:** TOT — usu. used with *up* <~ up the casualties on the bulletin board> ~ *vi* **:** to become chalky
chalk·board \ˈchȯk-ˌbō(ə)rd, -ˌbȯ(ə)rd\ *n* **:** BLACKBOARD
chalk up *vt* **1 :** ASCRIBE, CREDIT <*chalk up* the opened package to someone's curiosity> **2 :** ATTAIN, ACHIEVE <*chalk up* a record score for the season>
[1]**chal·lenge** \ˈchal-ənj\ *vb* **chal·lenged; chal·leng·ing** [ME *chalengen* to accuse, fr. OF *chalengier,* fr. L *calumniari* to accuse falsely, fr. *calumnia* calumny] *vt* **1 :** to demand as of right **:** REQUIRE <an event that ~*s* explanation> **2 :** to order to halt and prove identity <the sentry *challenged* the stranger at the gates> **3 :** to dispute esp. as being unjust, invalid, or outmoded **:** IMPUGN <uncovered new data that ~*s* old assumptions> **4 :** to question formally the legality or legal qualifications of **5 a :** to defy boldly **:** DARE **b :** to call out to duel or combat **c :** to invite into competition **6 :** STIMULATE, EXCITE <math ~*s* him but English bores him> **7 :** to administer an immunologic challenge to (an organism) ~ *vi* **1 :** to make or present a challenge **2 :** to take legal exception — **chal·leng·er** *n*
[2]**challenge** *n* **1 a :** a calling to account or into question **:** PROTEST **b :** an exception taken to a juror before he is sworn **c :** a sentry's command to halt and prove identity **d :** a questioning of the right or validity of a vote or voter **2 a :** a summons that is often threatening, provocative, stimulating, or inciting; *specif* **:** a summons to a duel to answer an affront **b :** an invitation to compete in a sport **3 :** a test of immunity by exposure to virulent infective material after specific immunization
chal·leng·ing \-ən-jiŋ\ *adj* **1 :** arousing competitive interest, thought, or action <the curriculum should have ~ intellectual content> **2 :** invitingly provocative **:** FASCINATING <a ~ personality> — **chal·leng·ing·ly** \-jiŋ-lē\ *adv*
chal·lis \ˈshal-ē\ *n, pl* **chal·lises** \-ēz\ [prob. fr. the name *Challis*] **:** a lightweight soft clothing fabric made of cotton, wool, or synthetic yarns
cha·lone \ˈkā-ˌlōn, ˈkal-ˌōn\ *n* [Gk *chalōn,* prp. of *chalan* to slacken] **:** an internal secretion that depresses activity — compare HORMONE
[1]**cha·ly·be·ate** \kə-ˈlib-ē-ət, -ˈlē-bē-\ *adj* [prob. fr. NL *chalybeatus,* irreg. fr. L *chalybs* steel, fr. Gk *chalyb-, chalyps,* fr. *Chalybes,* ancient people in Asia Minor] **:** impregnated with salts of iron; *also* **:** having a taste due to iron <~ springs>
[2]**chalybeate** *n* **:** a chalybeate liquid or medicine
cham \ˈkam\ *var of* KHAN
cham·ae·phyte \ˈkam-i-ˌfīt\ *n* [Gk *chamai* on the ground + E *-phyte* — more at HUMBLE] **:** a perennial plant that bears its overwintering buds just above the surface of the soil
[1]**cham·ber** \ˈchām-bər\ *n* [ME *chambre,* fr. OF, fr. LL *camera,* fr. L, arched roof, fr. Gk *kamara* vault; akin to L *camur* curved] **1 :** ROOM; *esp* **:** BEDROOM **2 :** a natural or artificial enclosed space or cavity **3 a :** a hall for the meetings of a deliberative, legislative, or judicial body <the senate ~> **b :** a room where a judge transacts business — usu. used in pl. **c :** the reception room of a person of rank or authority **4 a :** a legislative or judicial body; *esp* **:** either of the houses of a bicameral legislature **b :** a voluntary board or council **5 a :** the part of the bore of a gun that holds the charge **b :** a compartment in the cartridge cylinder of a revolver
[2]**chamber** *vt* **cham·bered; cham·ber·ing** \-b(ə-)riŋ\ **1 :** to place in or as if in a chamber **:** HOUSE **2 :** to serve as a chamber for; *esp* **:** to accommodate in the chamber of a firearm
[3]**chamber** *adj* **:** being, relating to, or performing chamber music
cham·bered \ˈchām-bərd\ *adj* **:** having a chamber <the ~ nautilus>
[1]**chamberer** *n, obs* **:** CHAMBERMAID
[2]**cham·ber·er** \ˈchām-bər-ər\ *n* [ME, chamberlain, fr. MF *chamberier,* fr. LL *camerarius,* fr. *camera*] *archaic* **:** GALLANT, LOVER

different in some particular <never bothered to ~ his will> **b** : to make radically different : TRANSFORM <can't ~ human nature> **c** : to give a different position, course, or direction to **d** : REVERSE <~ one's vote> **2 a** : to replace with another <let's ~ the subject> **b** : to make a shift from one to another : SWITCH <always ~*s* sides in an argument> **c** : to exchange for an equivalent sum or comparable item **d** : to undergo a loss or modification of <foliage *changing* color> **e** : to put fresh clothes or covering on <~ a bed> ~ *vi* **1** : to become different <her mood ~*s* every hour> <prices ~ overnight> **2** *of the moon* : to pass from one phase to another **3** : to shift one's means of conveyance : TRANSFER <on the bus trip to New York he *changed* twice> **4** *of the voice* : to shift to lower register : BREAK **5** : to undergo transformation, transition, or substitution <winter *changed* to spring> **6** : to put on different clothes **7** : to engage in giving something and receiving something in return : EXCHANGE <I need a sharper knife, so I'll ~ with you>
syn CHANGE, ALTER, VARY, MODIFY *shared meaning element* : to make or become different
— **change hands** : to pass from the possession of one person to that of another <money *changes hands* many times> — **change one's mind** : to reverse one's intention or opinion <was going to drive but then *changed his mind* and took the bus>

[2]**change** *n* **1** : the act, process, or result of changing: as **a** : ALTERATION <there was little ~ in her daily routine> **b** : TRANSFORMATION <has undergone a great ~ since he was married> **c** : SUBSTITUTION <went to the country for a ~ of air> **d** : the passage of the moon from one monthly revolution to another; *also* : the passage of the moon from one phase to another **2** : a fresh set of clothes **3** *Brit* : EXCHANGE 5a **4 a** : money in small denominations received in exchange for an equivalent sum in larger denominations **b** : money returned when a payment exceeds the amount due **c** : coins of low denominations <a pocketful of ~> **5** : an order in which a set of bells is struck in change ringing
syn CHANGE, MUTATION, PERMUTATION, VICISSITUDE *shared meaning element* : altered state

change·able \'chān-jə-bəl\ *adj* : capable of change: as **a** : able or apt to vary <~ weather> **b** : subject to change : ALTERABLE <a clause in the contract ~ at will> **c** : FICKLE **d** : IRIDESCENT — **change·abil·i·ty** \ˌchān-jə-'bil-ət-ē\ *n* — **change·able·ness** \'chān-jə-bəl-nəs\ *n* — **change·ably** \-blē\ *adv*

change·ful \'chānj-fəl\ *adj* : notably variable : UNCERTAIN — **change·ful·ly** \-fə-lē\ *adv* — **change·ful·ness** *n*

change·less \'chānj-ləs\ *adj* : marked by the absence of change : CONSTANT — **change·less·ly** *adv* — **change·less·ness** *n*

change·ling \'chānj-liŋ\ *n* **1** *archaic* : TURNCOAT **2** : a child secretly exchanged for another in infancy **3** *archaic* : IMBECILE — **changeling** *adj*

change off *vi* **1** : to alternate with another at doing an act **2** : to alternate between two different acts or instruments or between an action and a rest period

change of heart : a full reversal in position or attitude

change of life : [2]CLIMACTERIC 2

change of pace **1** : an interruption of continuity by a sudden shift (as for relief from monotony) to a different activity **2** : CHANGE-UP

change·over \'chān-ˌjō-vər\ *n* : conversion to a different function or use of a different method

chang·er \'chān-jər\ *n* **1** : one that changes **2** *obs* : MONEY CHANGER

change ringing *n* : the art or practice of ringing a set of tuned bells (as in the bell tower of a church) in continually varying order

change–up \'chān-ˌjəp\ *n* : a slow pitch in baseball thrown for deception with the same motion as a fastball

[1]**chan·nel** \'chan-ᵊl\ *n* [ME *chanel,* fr. OF, fr. L *canalis* channel — more at CANAL] **1 a** : the bed where a natural stream of water runs **b** : the deeper part of a river, harbor, or strait **c** : a strait or narrow sea between two close land masses **d** (1) : a means of communication or expression <the ~*s* between government and industry should be kept open> (2) : a path along which data passes or along which data may be stored serially (as in a computer) **e** *pl* : a fixed or official course of communication <went through established military ~*s* with his grievances> **f** : a way, course, or direction of thought or action <new ~*s* of exploration> **g** : a band of frequencies of sufficient width for a single radio or television communication **2** : a usu. tubular enclosed passage : CONDUIT **3** : a long gutter, groove, or furrow **4** : a metal bar of flattened U-shaped section

[2]**channel** *vt* **-neled** *or* **-nelled; -nel·ing** *or* **-nel·ling** **1 a** : to form, cut, or wear a channel in **b** : to make a groove in <~ a chair leg> **2** : to convey into or through a channel <~ his energy into constructive activities>

[3]**channel** *n* [alter. of *chainwale,* fr. *chain* + *wale*] : one of the flat ledges of heavy plank or metal bolted edgewise to the outside of a ship to increase the spread of the shrouds

channel bass *n* : a large coppery drum (*Sciaenops ocellatus*) with a black spot at the base of the tail that is an important game and food fish of the Atlantic coast of No. and So. America — called also *redfish*

chan·nel·ize \'chan-ᵊl-ˌīz\ *vt* **-ized; -iz·ing** : CHANNEL — **chan·nel·iza·tion** \ˌchan-ᵊl-ə-'zā-shən\ *n*

chan·son \shä^{n}-sō^{n}\ *n, pl* **chan·sons** \-sō^{n}(z)\ [F, fr. L *cantion-, cantio,* fr. *cantus,* pp.] : SONG; *specif* : a music-hall or cabaret song

chan·son de geste \-sō^{n}-də-zhest\ *n, pl* **chansons de geste** *same*\ [F, lit., song of heroic deeds] : any of several Old French epic poems of the 11th to the 13th centuries

chan·son·nier \ˌshä^{n}-sō-'nyā\ *n* [F, fr. *chanson*] : a writer or singer of chansons; *esp* : a cabaret singer

[1]**chant** \'chant\ *vb* [ME *chaunten,* fr. MF *chanter,* fr. L *cantare,* fr. *cantus,* pp. of *canere;* akin to OE *hana* rooster, Gk *kanachē* ringing sound] *vi* **1** : to make melodic sounds with the voice; *esp* : to sing a chant **2** : to recite in a monotonous repetitive tone ~ *vt* **1** : to utter as in chanting **2** : to celebrate or praise in song or chant

[2]**chant** *n* **1** : SONG **2 a** : a repetitive liturgical melody in which as many syllables are assigned to each tone as required **b** : a rhythmic monotonous utterance or song <the ~ of an auctioneer> **c** : a composition for chanting

chant·er \'chant-ər\ *n* **1** : one that chants: **a** : CHORISTER **b** : CANTOR **2** : the chief singer in a chantry **3** : the reed pipe of a bagpipe with finger holes on which the melody is played — **chant·ress** \'chan-trəs\ *n*

chan·te·relle \ˌshant-ə-'rel, ˌshänt-\ *n* [F] : an edible mushroom (*Cantharellus cibarius*) of rich yellow color and pleasant aroma

chan·teuse \shä^{n}-'tə̄z, shan-'tüz\ *n, pl* **chan·teuses** \-'tə(r)z(-əz), -'tüz(-əz)\ [F, fem. of *chanteur* singer, fr. *chanter*] : a female concert or nightclub singer

chan·tey *or* **chan·ty** \'shant-ē, 'chant -\ *n, pl* **chanteys** *or* **chanties** [modif. of F *chanter*] : a song sung by sailors in rhythm with their work

chan·ti·cleer \ˌchant-ə-'kli(ə)r, ˌshant-\ *n* [ME *Chantecleer,* rooster in verse narratives, fr. OF *Chantecler,* rooster in the *Roman de Renart*] : [1]COCK 1

Chan·til·ly lace \shan-ˌtil-ē-\ *n* [trans. of F *dentelle de Chantilly,* fr. *Chantilly,* France] : a delicate silk, linen, or synthetic lace having a six-sided mesh ground and a floral or scrolled design — called also *Chantilly*

chan·try \'chan-trē\ *n, pl* **chantries** [ME *chanterie,* fr. MF, singing, fr. *chanter*] **1** : an endowment for the chanting of masses commonly for the founder **2** : a chapel endowed by a chantry

Cha·nu·kah \'kän-ə-kə, 'hän-\ *var of* HANUKKAH

cha·os \'kā-ˌäs\ *n* [L, fr. Gk — more at GUM] **1** *obs* : CHASM, ABYSS **2 a** *often cap* : a state of things in which chance is supreme; *esp* : the confused unorganized state of primordial matter before the creation of distinct forms — compare COSMOS **b** : a state of utter confusion <the citywide blackout caused ~> **c** : a confused mass or heterogeneous agglomeration <a ~ of television antennas> — **cha·ot·ic** \kā-'ät-ik\ *adj* — **cha·ot·i·cal·ly** \-i-k(ə-)lē\ *adv*

[1]**chap** \'chap\ *n* [short for *chapman*] **1** : FELLOW **2** *South & Midland* : BABY, CHILD

[2]**chap** *vb* **chapped; chap·ping** [ME *chappen;* akin to MD *cappen* to cut down] *vt* : to cause to open in slits or cracks <*chapped* lips> ~ *vi* : to open in slits or chinks : CRACK <the hands and lips often ~ in winter>

[3]**chap** *n* : a crack in or a sore roughening of the skin caused by exposure to wind or cold

[4]**chap** \'chäp, 'chap\ *n* [[2]*chap*] **1 a** : the fleshy covering of a jaw; *also* : JAW — usu. used in pl. <the wolf's ~*s* were smeared with blood> **2** : the forepart of the face — usu. used in pl.

[5]**chap** *abbr* chapter

chap·a·ra·jos *or* **chap·a·re·jos** \ˌshap-ə-'rā-(ˌ)ōs, -əs\ *n pl* [MexSp *chaparreras*] : CHAPS

chap·ar·ral \ˌshap-ə-'ral, -'rel\ *n* [Sp, fr. *chaparro* dwarf evergreen oak, fr. Basque *txapar*] **1** : a thicket of dwarf evergreen oaks; *broadly* : a dense impenetrable thicket of shrubs or dwarf trees **2** : an ecological community occurring widely in southern California and comprised of shrubby plants esp. adapted to dry summers and moist winters

chaparral bird *n* : ROADRUNNER — called also *chaparral cock*

chaparral pea *n* **1** : a thorny California leguminous shrub (*Pickeringia montana*) forming dense thickets

chap·book \'chap-ˌbu̇k\ *n* [*chap*man + *book*] : a small book containing ballads, tales, or tracts

chape \'chāp, 'chap\ *n* [ME, scabbard, fr. MF, cape, fr. LL *cappa*] : the metal mounting or trimming of a scabbard or sheath

cha·peau \sha-'pō, shə-\ *n, pl* **cha·peaus** \-'pōz\ *or* **cha·peaux** \-'pō(z)\ [MF, fr. OF *chapel* — more at CHAPLET] : HAT

cha·pel \'chap-əl\ *n* [ME, fr. OF *chapele,* fr. ML *cappella,* fr. dim. of LL *cappa* cloak; fr. the cloak of St. Martin of Tours preserved as a sacred relic in a chapel built for that purpose] **1** : a subordinate or private place of worship: as **a** : a place of worship serving a residence or institution **b** : a small house of worship usu. related to a main church **c** : a room or recess in a church for meditation and prayer or small religious services **2** : a choir of singers belonging to a chapel (as of a prince) **3** : a chapel service or assembly at a school or college **4** : an association of the employees in a printing office **5** : a place of worship used by a Christian group other than an established church <a nonconformist ~> **6 a** : FUNERAL HOME **b** : a room for funeral services in a funeral home

chapel of ease : a chapel or dependent church built to accommodate an expanding parish

[1]**chap·er·on** *or* **chap·er·one** \'shap-ə-ˌrōn\ *n* [F *chaperon,* lit., hood, fr. MF, head covering, fr. *chape*] **1** : a person (as a matron) who for propriety accompanies one or more young unmarried women in public or in mixed company **2** : an older person who accompanies young people at a social gathering to ensure proper behavior; *broadly* : one delegated to ensure proper behavior

[2]**chaperon** *or* **chaperone** *vb* **-oned; -on·ing** *vt* **1** : ESCORT **2** : to act as chaperon to or for ~ *vi* : to act as a chaperon — **chap·er·on·age** \-ˌrō-nij\ *n*

chap·fall·en \'chap-ˌfō-lən, 'chäp-\ *adj* **1** : having the lower jaw hanging loosely **2** : cast down in spirit : DEPRESSED

chap·i·ter \'chap-ət-ər\ *n* [ME *chapitre,* fr. MF, alter. of OF *chapitle,* fr. L *capitulum,* lit., little head] : the capital of a column

chap·lain \'chap-lən\ *n* [ME *chapelain,* fr. OF, fr. ML *cappellanus,* fr. *cappella*] **1** : a clergyman in charge of a chapel **2** : a clergyman officially attached to a branch of the military, to an institution, or to a family or court **3** : a person chosen to conduct religious exercises (as at a meeting of a club or society) **4** : a clergyman appointed to assist a bishop (as at a liturgical function) — **chap·lain·cy** \-sē\ *n* — **chap·lain·ship** \-ˌship\ *n*

chap·let \'chap-lət\ *n* [ME *chapelet,* fr. MF, fr. OF, dim. of *chapel* hat, garland, fr. ML *cappellus* head covering, fr. LL *cappa*] **1** : a wreath to be worn on the head **2 a** : a string of beads **b** : a part of a rosary comprising five decades **3** : a small molding carved with small decorative forms — **chap·let·ed** \-lət-əd\ *adj*

Chap·lin·esque \ˌchap-lə-ˈnesk\ *adj* **:** resembling or suggesting the largely pantomime comedy of the motion-picture comedian Charles Chaplin

chap·man \ˈchap-mən\ *n* [ME, fr. OE *cēapman*, fr. *cēap* trade + *man*] **1** *archaic* **:** MERCHANT, TRADER **2** *Brit* **:** an itinerant dealer **:** PEDDLER

chaps \ˈshaps\ *n pl* [modif. of MexSp *chaparreras*] **:** leather leggings joined together by a belt or lacing, often having flared outer flaps, and worn over the trousers esp. by western ranch hands

chap·ter \ˈchap-tər\ *n* [ME *chapitre* division of a book, meeting of canons, fr. OF, fr. LL *capitulum* division of a book & ML, meeting place of canons, fr. L, dim. of *capit-*, *caput* head — more at HEAD] **1 a :** a main division of a book **b :** something resembling a chapter in being a significant specified unit <with his death a ~ was closed in the history of the industry> **2 a :** a regular meeting of the canons of a cathedral or collegiate church or of the members of a religious house **b :** the body of canons of a cathedral or collegiate church **3 :** a local branch of a society or fraternity

chapter house *n* **1 :** the building or rooms where a chapter meets **2 :** the residence of a local chapter of a fraternity or sorority

1char \ˈchär\ *n, pl* **char** *or* **chars** [origin unknown] **:** any of a genus (*Salvelinus*) of small-scaled trouts

2char *vb* **charred; char·ring** [back-formation fr. *charcoal*] *vt* **1 :** to convert to charcoal or carbon usu. by heat **:** BURN **2 :** to burn slightly or partly **:** SCORCH <the fire *charred* the beams> ~ *vi* **:** to become charred **:** BURN

3char *n* **:** a charred substance **:** CHARCOAL; *specif* **:** a combustible residue remaining after the destructive distillation of coal

4char *vi* **charred; char·ring** [back-formation fr. *charwoman*] **:** to work as a cleaning woman

5char *n* [short for *charwoman*] *Brit* **:** CHARWOMAN

char·a·banc \ˈshar-ə-ˌbaŋ\ *n* [F *char à bancs*, lit., wagon with benches] *Brit* **:** a sightseeing motor coach

char·a·cin \ˈkar-ə-sən\ *n* [deriv. of Gk *charak-*, *charax* pointed stake, a fish] **:** any of a family (Characidae) of usu. small brightly colored tropical fishes — **characin** *adj*

1char·ac·ter \ˈkar-ik-tər\ *n* [ME *caracter*, fr. MF *caractère*, fr. L *character* mark, distinctive quality, fr. Gk *charaktēr*, fr. *charassein* to scratch, engrave; akin to Lith *žerti* to scratch] **1 a :** a conventionalized graphic device placed on an object as an indication of ownership, origin, or relationship **b :** a graphic symbol (as a hieroglyph or alphabet letter) used in writing or printing **c :** a magical or astrological emblem **d :** ALPHABET **e (1) :** WRITING, PRINTING **(2) :** style of writing or printing **(3) :** CIPHER **f :** a symbol (as a letter or number) that represents information; *also* **:** a representation of such a character that may be accepted by a computer **2 a :** one of the attributes or features that make up and distinguish the individual **b (1) :** a feature used to separate distinguishable things into categories; *also* **:** a group or kind so separated <people of this ~> <advertising of a very primitive ~> **(2) :** the detectable expression of the action of a gene or group of genes **(3) :** the aggregate of distinctive qualities characteristic of a breed, strain, or type <a wine of great ~> **c :** the complex of mental and ethical traits marking and often individualizing a person, group, or nation <assess a person's ~ by studying his handwriting> **d :** main or essential nature esp. as strongly marked and serving to distinguish <excess sewage gradually changed the ~ of the lake> **3 :** POSITION, CAPACITY <his ~ as a town official> **4 :** a short literary sketch of the qualities of a social type **5 :** REFERENCE 4b **6 a :** a person marked by notable or conspicuous traits **:** PERSONAGE <a notorious campus ~> **b :** one of the persons of a drama or novel **c :** the personality or part which an actor recreates **d :** characterization esp. in drama or fiction **e :** PERSON, INDIVIDUAL <some ~ just stole her purse> **7 :** REPUTATION **8 :** moral excellence and firmness <a man of sound ~> ***syn*** see DISPOSITION, TYPE — **char·ac·ter·less** \-ləs\ *adj* — **in character :** in accord with a person's usual qualities or traits — **out of character :** not in accord with a person's usual qualities or traits

2character *vt* **1** *archaic* **:** ENGRAVE, INSCRIBE **2 a** *archaic* **:** REPRESENT, PORTRAY **b :** CHARACTERIZE

3character *adj* **1 :** capable of portraying an unusual or eccentric personality often markedly different (as in age) from the player <a ~ actor> **2 :** requiring the qualities of a character actor <a ~ role>

character assassination *n* **:** the slandering of a person (as a public figure) with the intention of destroying public confidence in him

char·ac·ter·ful \ˈkar-ik-tər-fəl\ *adj* **1 :** markedly expressive of character <a ~ face> **2 :** marked by character <a ~ decision>

1char·ac·ter·is·tic \ˌkar-ik-tə-ˈris-tik\ *adj* **:** serving to reveal and distinguish the individual character — **char·ac·ter·is·ti·cal·ly** \-ti-k(ə-)lē\ *adv*

syn CHARACTERISTIC, INDIVIDUAL, PECULIAR, DISTINCTIVE *shared meaning element* **:** revealing a special quality or identity

2characteristic *n* **1 :** a distinguishing trait, quality, or property **2 :** the integral part of a common logarithm **3 :** the smallest positive integer *n* which for an operation in a ring or field yields 0 when any element is used *n* times with the operation

characteristic equation *n* **:** an equation in which the characteristic polynomial of a matrix is set equal to 0

characteristic polynomial *n* **:** the determinant of a square matrix in which an arbitrary variable (as *x*) is subtracted from each of the elements along the principal diagonal

characteristic root *n* **:** a scalar such that for a linear transformation of a vector space there is some nonzero vector that when multiplied by the scalar is equal to the vector obtained by letting the transformation operate on the vector; *esp* **:** a root of the characteristic equation of a matrix — called also *characteristic value, eigenvalue*

characteristic vector *n* **:** a nonzero vector that is mapped by a linear transformation of a vector space onto a vector that is the product of a scalar multiplied by the original vector — called also *eigenvector*

char·ac·ter·iza·tion \ˌkar-ik-t(ə-)rə-ˈzā-shən\ *n* **:** the act of characterizing; *esp* **:** the artistic representation (as in fiction or drama) of human character or motives

char·ac·ter·ize \ˈkar-ik-tə-ˌrīz\ *vt* **-ized; -iz·ing 1 :** to describe the character or quality of **:** DELINEATE <*characterized* him as soft-spoken yet ambitious> **2 :** to be a characteristic of **:** DISTINGUISH <a cool light fragrance ~*s* the cologne>

char·ac·ter·olog·i·cal \ˌkar-ik-t(ə-)rə-ˈläj-i-kəl\ *adj* [*characterology* (study of character)] **:** of, relating to, or based on character or the study of character including its development and its differences in different individuals — **char·ac·ter·olog·i·cal·ly** \-ˈläj-i-k(ə-)lē\ *adv*

character sketch *n* **:** a sketch dealing with a character usu. of marked individuality

character witness *n* **:** one that gives evidence concerning the reputation, conduct, and moral nature of a party to a legal action

char·ac·tery \ˈkar-ik-t(ə-)rē, kə-ˈrak-\ *n, pl* **-ter·ies :** a system of written letters or symbols used in the expression of thought

cha·rade \shə-ˈrād\ *n* [F] **1 :** a word represented in riddling verse or by picture, tableau, or dramatic action **2** *pl* **:** a game in which each syllable of a word or phrase is acted out by some of the persons playing the game while the others try to guess the word or phrase **3 :** an almost transparent pretense

cha·ras \ˈchär-əs\ *n* [Hindi *caras*] **:** HASHISH

char·coal \ˈchär-ˌkōl\ *n* [ME *charcole*] **1 :** a dark or black porous carbon prepared from vegetable or animal substances (as from wood by charring in a kiln from which air is excluded) **2 a :** a piece or pencil of fine charcoal used in drawing **b :** a charcoal drawing

chard \ˈchärd\ *n* [F *carde*, fr. OProv *cardo* edible cardoon, fr. L *carduus* thistle, artichoke; akin to MLG *harst* rake, L *carrere* to card] **:** a beet (*Beta vulgaris cicla*) whose large leaves and succulent stalks are often cooked as a vegetable — called also *Swiss chard*

chare \ˈcha(ə)r, ˈche(ə)r\ *or* **char** \ˈchär\ *n* [ME *char* turn, piece of work, fr. OE *cierr*; akin to OE *cierran* to turn] **:** CHORE <the peasant who does the humblest ~*s* — Thomas De Quincey>

1charge \ˈchärj\ *vb* **charged; charg·ing** [ME *chargen*, fr. OF *chargier*, fr. LL *carricare*, fr. L *carrus* wheeled vehicle — more at CAR] *vt* **1 a** *archaic* **:** to lay or put a load on or in **:** LOAD **b (1) :** to place a charge (as of powder) in **(2) :** to load or fill to capacity **c (1) :** to restore the active materials in (a storage battery) by the passage of a direct current through in the opposite direction to that of discharge **(2) :** to give an electric charge to **d (1) :** to assume as a heraldic bearing **(2) :** to place a heraldic bearing on **e :** to fill or furnish fully <a mind *charged* with fancies> <the music is *charged* with excitement> **2 a :** to impose a task or responsibility on <~ him with the job of finding a new meeting place> **b :** to command, instruct, or exhort with right or authority <I ~ you not to accept the gift> **c :** to give a charge to (a jury) — used of a judge **3 a :** BLAME <~*s* him as the instigator> **b :** to make an assertion against esp. by ascribing guilt for an offense **:** ACCUSE <~*s* him with armed robbery> <~*s* them with hypocrisy> **c :** to place the guilt or blame for <~ her failure to negligence> **d :** to assert as an accusation <~*s* that he distorted the data> **4 a :** to bring (a weapon) into position for attack **:** LEVEL <~ a lance> **b :** to rush against or bear down upon **:** ATTACK; *also* **:** to rush into (an opponent) usu. illegally in various games or sports **5 a (1) :** to impose a pecuniary burden on <~ his estate with debts incurred> **(2) :** to impose or record as pecuniary obligation <~ debts to an estate> **b (1) :** to fix or ask as fee or payment <~*s* $10 for an office visit> **(2) :** to ask payment of (a person) <~ a client for expenses> **c :** to record (an item) as an expense, debt, obligation, or liability <~ a purchase to a customer> <~ a library book to a borrower> ~ *vi* **1 :** to rush forward in or as if in assault **:** ATTACK; *also* **:** to charge an opponent in sports **2 :** to ask or set a price **3 :** to charge an item to an account <~ now, pay later> ***syn*** see COMMAND

2charge *n* **1 a** *obs* **:** a material load or weight **b :** a figure borne on a heraldic field **2 a :** the quantity that an apparatus is intended to receive and fitted to hold **b :** a store or accumulation of impelling force <the deeply emotional ~ of the drama> **c :** a definite quantity of electricity; *esp* **:** an excess or deficiency of electrons in a body **d :** THRILL, KICK <got a ~ out of the game> **3 a :** OBLIGATION, REQUIREMENT **b :** MANAGEMENT, SUPERVISION <has ~ of the home office> **c :** the ecclesiastical jurisdiction (as a parish) committed to a clergyman **d :** a person or thing committed to the care of another **4 a :** INSTRUCTION, COMMAND **b :** instruction in points of law given by a court to a jury **5 a :** EXPENSE, COST <gave the banquet at his own ~> **b :** the price demanded for something <no admission ~> **c :** a debit to an account <the purchase was a ~> **d :** the record of a loan (as of a book from a library) **6 a :** ACCUSATION, INDICTMENT <a ~ of assault with intent to kill> **b :** a statement of complaint or hostile criticism <denied the ~*s* of nepotism that were leveled against him> **7 :** a violent rush forward (as to attack) — **in charge :** having control or custody of something <he is *in charge* of the training program>

charge·able \ˈchär-jə-bəl\ *adj* **1** *archaic* **:** financially burdensome **:** EXPENSIVE **2 a :** liable to be accused or held responsible **b :** suitable to be charged to a particular account **c :** qualified to be made a charge on the county or parish — **charge·able·ness** *n*

charge account *n* **:** a customer's account with a creditor (as a merchant) to which the purchase of goods is charged

charge–a–plate \ˈchär-jə-ˌplāt\ *or* **charge plate** *n* [fr. *Charga-plate*, a trademark] **:** an embossed address plate used by a customer when buying on credit

charged \'chärjd\ *adj* **1 :** possessing strong emotion or vigorous purpose <attacked the author in an emotionally ~ review> **2 :** capable of arousing strong emotion <a highly ~ political theme>
char·gé d'af·faires \(,)shär-,zhād-ə-'fa(ə)r, -'fe(ə)r\ *n, pl* **char·gés d'affaires** \-,zhād-ə-, -,zhāz-də-\ [F, lit., one charged with affairs] **1 :** a subordinate diplomat who substitutes for an ambassador or minister in his absence **2 :** a diplomat inferior in rank to an ambassador or minister and accredited by one government to the foreign minister of another
charge of quarters : an enlisted man designated to handle administrative matters in his unit esp. after duty hours
[1]**char·ger** \'chär-jər\ *n* [ME *chargeour;* akin to ME *chargen* to charge] *archaic* **:** a large flat platter for carrying meat
[2]**charg·er** *n* **1 :** one that charges: as **a :** an appliance for holding or inserting a charge of powder or shot in a gun **b :** a cartridge clip **2 :** a horse for battle or parade
char·i·ness \'char-ē-nəs, 'cher-\ *n* **1 :** the quality or state of being chary **:** CAUTION **2 :** carefully preserved state **:** INTEGRITY
[1]**char·i·ot** \'char-ē-ət\ *n* [ME, fr. MF, fr. OF, fr. *char* wheeled vehicle, fr. L *carrus*] **1 :** a light 4-wheeled pleasure or state carriage **2 :** a 2-wheeled horse-drawn battle car of ancient times used also in processions and races
[2]**chariot** *vt* **:** to carry in or as if in a chariot ~ *vi* **:** to drive or ride in or as if in a chariot

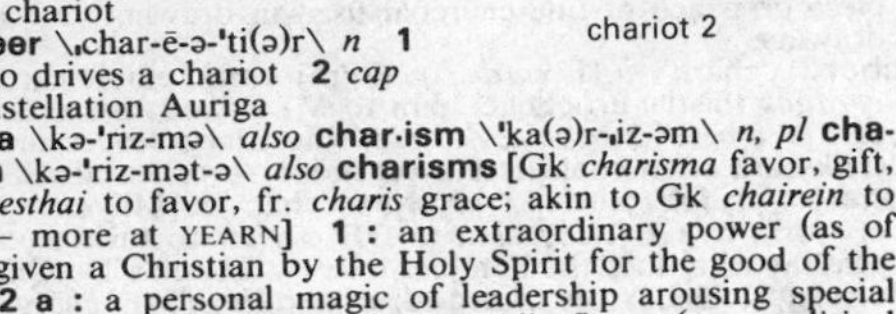
chariot 2

char·i·o·teer \,char-ē-ə-'ti(ə)r\ *n* **1 :** one who drives a chariot **2** *cap* **:** the constellation Auriga
cha·ris·ma \kə-'riz-mə\ *also* **char·ism** \'ka(ə)r-,iz-əm\ *n, pl* **cha·ris·ma·ta** \kə-'riz-mət-ə\ *also* **charisms** [Gk *charisma* favor, gift, fr. *charizesthai* to favor, fr. *charis* grace; akin to Gk *chairein* to rejoice — more at YEARN] **1 :** an extraordinary power (as of healing) given a Christian by the Holy Spirit for the good of the church **2 a :** a personal magic of leadership arousing special popular loyalty or enthusiasm for a public figure (as a political leader or military commander) **b :** a special magnetic charm or appeal <the ~ of a popular actor> — **char·is·mat·ic** \,kar-əz-'mat-ik\ *adj*
char·i·ta·ble \'char-ət-ə-bəl\ *adj* **1 :** full of love for and goodwill toward others **:** BENEVOLENT **2 a :** liberal in benefactions to the poor **:** GENEROUS **b :** of or relating to charity <~ institutions> **3 :** merciful or kind in judging others **:** LENIENT — **char·i·ta·ble·ness** *n* — **char·i·ta·bly** \-blē\ *adv*
char·i·ty \'char-ət-ē\ *n, pl* **-ties** [ME *charite,* fr. OF *charité,* fr. LL *caritat-, caritas* Christian love, fr. L, dearness, fr. *carus* dear; akin to Skt *kāma* love] **1 :** benevolent goodwill toward or love of humanity **2 a :** kindly liberality and helpfulness esp. toward the needy or suffering; *also* **:** aid given to those in need **b :** an institution engaged in relief of the poor **c :** public provision for the relief of the needy **3 a :** a gift for public benevolent purposes **b :** an institution (as a hospital) founded by such a gift **4 :** lenient judgment of others ***syn*** see MERCY ***ant*** malice, ill will
cha·ri·va·ri \,shiv-ə-'rē, 'shiv-ə-,\ *n* [F, fr. LL *caribaria* headache, fr. Gk *karēbaria,* fr. *kara, karē* head + *barys* heavy — more at CEREBRAL, GRIEVE] **:** SHIVAREE
char·ka *or* **char·kha** \'chər-kə, 'chär-\ *n* [Hindi *carkhā*] **:** a domestic spinning wheel used in India chiefly for spinning cotton
char·la·tan \'shär-lə-tən, -lət-ᵊn\ *n* [It *ciarlatano,* alter. of *cerretano,* lit., inhabitant of Cerreto, fr. *Cerreto,* village in Italy] **1 :** QUACK 1 <~*s* killing their patients with empirical procedures> **2 :** one making usu. noisy or showy pretenses to knowledge or ability **:** FRAUD, FAKER — **char·la·tan·ism** \-,iz-əm\ *n* — **char·la·tan·ry** \-rē\ *n*
Charles's Wain \,chärl-zəz-'wān, 'chärlz-'wān\ *n* [*Charlemagne*] **:** the Big Dipper
Charles·ton \'chärl-stən\ *n* [*Charleston,* S. C.] **:** a lively ballroom dance in which the knees are twisted in and out and the heels are swung sharply outward on each step
char·ley horse \'chär-lē-,hȯrs\ *n* [fr. *Charley,* nickname for *Charles*] **:** a muscular strain or bruise esp. of the quadriceps that is characterized by pain and stiffness
Char·lie \'chär-lē\ [fr. the name *Charlie*] — a communications code word for the letter *c*
char·lock \'chär-,läk, -lək\ *n* [ME *cherlok,* fr. OE *cerlic*] **:** a wild mustard (*Brassica kaber*) that is often troublesome in grainfields
char·lotte \'shär-lət\ *n* [F] **:** a dessert consisting of a filling (as of fruit, whipped cream, or custard) placed over cake, ladyfingers, or strips of bread
char·lotte russe \,shär-lət-'rüs\ *n* [F, lit., Russian charlotte] **:** a charlotte made with sponge cake or ladyfingers and a whipped-cream or custard-gelatin filling
[1]**charm** \'chärm\ *n* [ME *charme,* fr. OF, fr. L *carmen* song, fr. *canere* to sing — more at CHANT] **1 a :** the chanting or reciting of a magic spell **:** INCANTATION **b :** an act or expression believed to have magic power **2 :** something worn about the person to ward off evil or ensure good fortune **:** AMULET **3 a :** a trait that fascinates, allures, or delights **b :** a physical grace or attraction — used in pl. **c :** compelling attractiveness <the island possessed great ~> **4 :** a small ornament worn on a bracelet or chain ***syn*** see FETISH — **charm·less** \-ləs\ *adj*
[2]**charm** *vt* **1 a :** to affect by or as if by magic **:** COMPEL **b :** to please, soothe, or delight by compelling attraction <~*s* women with his suave manner> **2 :** to endow with supernatural powers by means of charms; *also* **:** to protect by spells, charms, or supernatural influences **3 :** to control (an animal) typically by charms (as the playing of music) <~ a snake> ~ *vi* **1 :** to practice magic and enchantment **2 :** to have the effect of a charm **:** FASCINATE ***syn*** see ATTRACT ***ant*** disgust
charm·er \'chär-mər\ *n* **1 :** ENCHANTER, MAGICIAN **2 :** one that pleases or fascinates; *esp* **:** an attractive woman
charm·ing \'chär-miŋ\ *adj* **:** extremely pleasing or delightful **:** ENTRANCING — **charm·ing·ly** \-miŋ-lē\ *adv*
charm school *n* **:** a school or course of instruction in which social graces are taught
char·nel \'chärn-ᵊl\ *n* [ME, fr. MF, fr. ML *carnale,* fr. LL, neut. of *carnalis* of the flesh — more at CARNAL] **:** a building or chamber in which bodies or bones are deposited — called also *charnel house* — **charnel** *adj*
Cha·ro·lais \,shar-ə-'lā\ *n* [*Charolais,* district in eastern France] **:** any of a French breed of large white cattle used primarily for beef and crossbreeding
Char·on \'kar-ən, 'ker-\ *n* [L, fr. Gk *Charōn*] **:** a son of Erebus who in Greek myth ferries the souls of the dead over the Styx
char·poy \'chär-,pȯi\ *n, pl* **charpoys** [Hindi *cārpāī*] **:** a bed consisting of a frame strung with tapes or light rope that is used esp. in India
char·qui \'chär-kē, 'shär-\ *n* [Sp, fr. Quechua *ch'arki* dried meat] **:** jerked beef
charr \'chär\ *var of* CHAR
[1]**chart** \'chärt\ *n* [MF *charte,* fr. L *charta* piece of papyrus, document — more at CARD] **1 :** MAP: as **a :** an outline map exhibiting something (as climatic or magnetic variations) in its geographical aspects **b :** a map for the use of navigators **2 a :** a sheet giving information in tabular form **b :** GRAPH **c :** DIAGRAM **d :** a sheet of paper ruled and graduated for use in a recording instrument
[2]**chart** *vt* **1 :** to make a map or chart of **2 :** to lay out a plan for
char·ta·ceous \kär-'tā-shəs\ *adj* **:** resembling or made of paper <a ~ plant part>
[1]**char·ter** \'chärt-ər\ *n* [ME *chartre,* fr. OF, fr. ML *chartula,* fr. L, dim. of *charta*] **1 :** a written instrument or contract (as a deed) executed in due form **2 a :** a grant or guarantee of rights, franchises, or privileges from the sovereign power of a state or country **b :** an instrument in writing creating and defining the franchises of a city, educational institution, or corporation **c :** CONSTITUTION **3 :** an instrument in writing from the authorities of a society creating a lodge or branch **4 :** a special privilege, immunity, or exemption **5 :** a mercantile lease of a ship or some principal part of it
[2]**charter** *vt* **1 a :** to establish, enable, or convey by charter **b** *Brit* **:** CERTIFY <a ~*ed* mechanical engineer> **2 :** to hire, rent, or lease for usu. exclusive and temporary use <~*ed* a boat for deep-sea fishing> ***syn*** see HIRE — **char·ter·er** \-ər-ər\ *n*
[3]**charter** *adj* **:** of, relating to, or being a travel arrangement in which transportation (as a bus or plane) is hired by and for one specific group of people <a ~ flight>
chartered accountant *n, Brit* **:** a member of a chartered institute of accountants
charter member *n* **:** an original member of a society or corporation — **charter membership** *n*
Char·tism \'chärt-,iz-əm\ *n* [ML *charta* charter, fr. L, document] **:** the principles and practices of a body of 19th century English political reformers advocating better social and industrial conditions for the working classes — **Char·tist** \'chärt-əst\ *n*
chart·ist \'chärt-əst\ *n* **1 :** CARTOGRAPHER **2 :** an analyst of market action whose predictions of market courses are based on study of graphic presentations of past market performance
char·treuse \shär-'trüz, -'trüs\ *n* [F, fr. La Grande *Chartreuse,* chief monastery of the Carthusian order] **1 :** a usu. green or yellow liqueur **2 :** a variable color averaging a brilliant yellow green
char·tu·lary \'kär-chə-,ler-ē\ *n, pl* **-lar·ies** [ML *chartularium*] **:** CARTULARY
char·wom·an \'chär-,wu̇m-ən\ *n* [*chare* + *woman*] **1** *Brit* **:** a woman hired to char **2 :** a cleaning woman esp. in a large building
chary \'cha(ə)r-ē, 'che(ə)r-\ *adj* **chari·er; -est** [ME, sorrowful, dear, fr. OE *cearig* sorrowful, fr. *caru* sorrow — more at CARE] **1** *archaic* **:** DEAR, TREASURED **2 :** discreetly cautious: as **a :** hesitant and vigilant about dangers and risks **b :** slow to grant, accept, or expend <a man very ~ of compliments> ***syn*** see CAUTIOUS — **chari·ly** \'char-ə-lē, 'cher-\ *adv*
Cha·ryb·dis \kə-'rib-dəs\ *n* [L, fr. Gk] **:** a daughter of Poseidon and Gaea thrown into the sea off Sicily by Zeus where by swallowing and spewing water she created a whirlpool — compare SCYLLA
[1]**chase** \'chās\ *vb* **chased; chas·ing** [ME *chasen,* fr. MF *chasser,* fr. (assumed) VL *captiare* — more at CATCH] *vt* **1 a :** to follow rapidly **:** PURSUE **b :** HUNT **c :** to follow regularly or persistently with the intention of attracting or alluring <he's too old to be *chasing* women> **2** *obs* **:** HARASS **3 :** to seek out — often used with *down* <detectives *chasing* down clues> **4 :** to cause to depart or flee **:** DRIVE <~ the dog out of the pantry> **5 :** to cause the removal of (a baseball pitcher) by a batting rally ~ *vi* **1 :** to chase an animal, person, or thing <~ after material possessions> **2 :** RUSH, HASTEN <*chased* all over town looking for a place to stay> ***syn*** see FOLLOW
[2]**chase** *n* **1 a :** the act of chasing **:** PURSUIT **b :** the hunting of wild animals — used with *the* **c :** an earnest or frenzied seeking after something desired **2 :** something pursued **:** QUARRY **3 a :** a franchise to hunt within certain limits of land **b :** a tract of unenclosed land used as a game preserve **4 :** a sequence (as in a movie) in which the characters pursue one another
[3]**chase** *vt* **chased; chas·ing** [ME *chassen,* modif. of MF *enchasser* to set] **1 a :** to ornament (metal) by indenting with a hammer and tools without a cutting edge **b :** to make by such indentation **c :** to set with gems **2 a :** GROOVE, INDENT **b :** to cut (a thread) with a chaser
[4]**chase** *n* [F *chas* eye of a needle, fr. LL *capsus* enclosed space, fr. L, pen, alter. of *capsa* box — more at CASE] **1 :** GROOVE, FURROW **2 :** the bore of a cannon **3 a :** TRENCH **b :** a channel (as in a wall) for something to lie in or pass through
[5]**chase** *n* [prob. fr. F *châsse* frame, fr. L *capsa*] **:** a rectangular steel or iron frame into which letterpress matter is locked for printing or plating — compare FORM

1**chas·er** \ˈchā-sər\ *n* **1 :** one that chases **2 :** a mild drink (as beer) taken after hard liquor

2**chaser** *n* **:** a skilled worker who produces ornamental chasing

3**chaser** *n* **:** a tool for cutting screw threads

Cha·sid \ˈhas-əd, ˈkäs-\ *n, pl* **Cha·si·dim** \ˈhas-əd-əm, kä-ˈsēd-\ *var of* HASID

chasm \ˈkaz-əm\ *n* [L *chasma,* fr. Gk; akin to L *hiare* to yawn — more at YAWN] **1 :** a deep cleft in the earth **:** GORGE **2 :** a marked division, separation, or difference <a political ~ between the two countries>

1**chas·sé** \sha-ˈsā\ *vi* **chas·séd; chas·sé·ing** [F, n., fr. pp. of *chasser* to chase] **1 :** to make a chassé **2 :** SASHAY

2**chassé** *n* **:** a sliding dance step resembling the galop

chasse·pot \ˈshas-(ə-)ˌpō\ *n* [F, fr. Antoine A. *Chassepot* †1905 F inventor] **:** a bolt-action rifle firing a paper cartridge

chas·seur \sha-ˈsər\ *n* [F, fr. MF *chasser*] **1 :** HUNTER, HUNTSMAN **2 :** one of a body of light cavalry or infantry trained for rapid maneuvering **3 :** a liveried attendant **:** FOOTMAN

chas·sis \ˈshas-ē, ˈchas-ē *also* ˈchas-əs\ *n, pl* **chas·sis** \-ēz\ [F *châssis,* fr. (assumed) VL *capsicum,* fr. L *capsa* box — more at CASE] **1 :** the frame upon which is mounted the body (as of an automobile or airplane), the working parts (as of a radio), the recoiling parts (of a cannon), or the roof, walls, floors, and facing (as of a building) **2 :** the frame and working parts as opposed to the body (as of an automobile) or cabinet (as of a radio or television set)

chaste \ˈchāst\ *adj* **chast·er; chast·est** [ME, fr. OF, fr. L *castus* pure — more at CASTE] **1 :** innocent of unlawful sexual intercourse **2 :** CELIBATE **3 :** pure in thought and act **:** MODEST **4 :** severely simple in design or execution **:** AUSTERE <the ~ hospital corridor> <~ poetry> — **chaste·ly** *adv* — **chaste·ness** \ˈchās(t)-nəs\ *n*

syn CHASTE, PURE, MODEST, DECENT *shared meaning element* **:** free from all taint of what is lewd or salacious ***ant*** lewd, wanton, immoral

chas·ten \ˈchās-ᵊn\ *vt* **chas·tened; chas·ten·ing** \ˈchās-niŋ, -ᵊn-iŋ\ [alter. of obs. E *chaste* to chasten, fr. ME *chasten,* fr. OF *chastier,* fr. L *castigare,* fr. *castus* + *-igare* (fr. *agere* to drive) — more at ACT] **1 :** to correct by punishment or suffering **:** DISCIPLINE; *also* **:** PURIFY **2 :** to prune (as a work or style of art) of excess, pretense, or falsity **:** REFINE ***syn*** see PUNISH ***ant*** pamper, mollycoddle — **chas·ten·er** \ˈchās-nər, -ᵊn-ər\ *n*

chas·tise \(ˈ)chas-ˈtīz\ *vt* **chas·tised; chas·tis·ing** [ME *chastisen,* alter. of *chasten*] **1 :** to inflict punishment on (as by whipping) **2 :** to censure severely **:** CASTIGATE **3** *archaic* **:** CHASTEN 2 ***syn*** see PUNISH — **chas·tise·ment** \(ˈ)chas-ˈtīz-mənt *also* ˈchas-təz-\ *n* — **chas·tis·er** \(ˈ)chas-ˈtī-zər\ *n*

chas·ti·ty \ˈchas-tət-ē\ *n* **1 :** the quality or state of being chaste: as **a :** abstention from unlawful sexual intercourse **b :** abstention from all sexual intercourse **c :** purity in conduct and intention **d :** restraint and simplicity in design or expression **2 :** personal integrity

chastity belt *n* **:** a belt device (as of medieval times) designed to prevent sexual intercourse on the part of the woman wearing it

cha·su·ble \ˈchaz(h)-ə-bəl, ˈchas-ə-\ *n* [F, fr. LL *casubla* hooded garment] **:** a sleeveless outer vestment worn by the officiating priest at mass

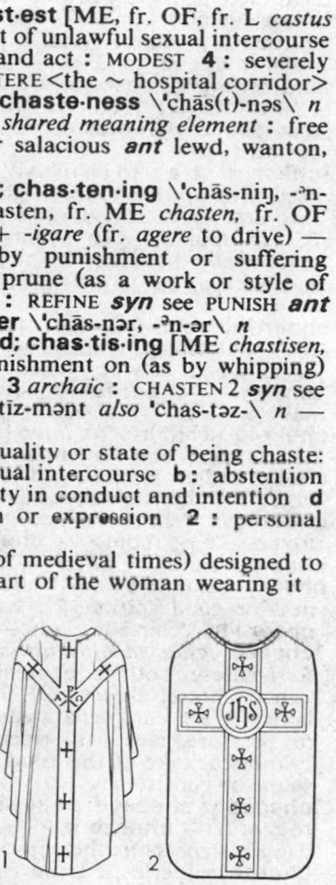

chasubles: *1* Gothic *2* fiddleback

1**chat** \ˈchat\ *vb* **chat·ted; chat·ting** [ME *chatten,* short for *chatteren*] *vi* **1 :** CHATTER, PRATTLE **2 :** to talk in an informal or familiar manner ~ *vt, Brit* **:** to talk to; *esp* **:** to talk lightly or glibly with — often used with *up*

2**chat** *n* **1 :** idle small talk **:** CHATTER **2 :** light familiar talk; *esp* **:** CONVERSATION **3** [imit.] **:** any of several songbirds (as of the genera *Saxicola* or *Icteria*)

châ·teau \sha-ˈtō\ *n, pl* **châ·teaus** \-ˈtōz\ *or* **châ·teaux** \-ˈtō(z)\ [F, fr. L *castellum* castle] **1 :** a feudal castle or fortress in France **2 :** a large country house **:** MANSION **3 :** a French vineyard estate

cha·teau·bri·and \(ˌ)sha-ˌtō-brē-ˈä^{n}\ *n, often cap* [François René de *Chateaubriand*] **:** a large tenderloin steak usu. grilled or broiled and served with a sauce (as béarnaise)

chat·e·lain \ˈshat-ᵊl-ˌān\ *n* [MF *châtelain,* fr. L *castellanus* occupant of a castle] **:** CASTELLAN

chat·e·laine \ˈshat-ᵊl-ˌān\ *n* [F *châtelaine,* fem. of *châtelain*] **1 a :** the wife of a castellan **b :** the mistress of a château **2 :** a clasp or hook for a watch, purse, or bunch of keys

cha·toy·ance \shə-ˈtȯi-ən(t)s\ *n* **:** CHATOYANCY

cha·toy·an·cy \-ən-sē\ *n* **:** the quality or state of being chatoyant

1**cha·toy·ant** \shə-ˈtȯi-ənt\ *adj* [F, fr. prp. of *chatoyer* to shine like a cat's eyes] **:** having a changeable luster or color with an undulating narrow band of white light <a ~ gem>

2**chatoyant** *n* **:** a chatoyant gem

chat·tel \ˈchat-ᵊl\ *n* [ME *chatel* property, fr. OF, fr. ML *capitale* — more at CATTLE] **1 :** an item of tangible movable or immovable property except real estate, freehold, and the things which are parcel of it **:** a piece of personal property **2 :** SLAVE, BONDSMAN

1**chat·ter** \ˈchat-ər\ *vb* [ME *chatteren,* of imit. origin] *vi* **1 :** to utter rapidly succeeding sounds suggestive of language but inarticulate and indistinct <squirrels ~*ed* angrily> <a ~*ing* stream> **2 :** to talk idly, incessantly, or fast **:** JABBER **3 a :** to click repeatedly or uncontrollably <teeth ~*ing* with cold> <machine guns ~*ing* > **b** *of a tool* **:** to vibrate rapidly in cutting **c :** to operate with an irregularity that causes rapid intermittent noise or vibration <~*ing* brakes> ~ *vt* **1 :** to utter rapidly, idly, or indistinctly **2 :** to cut unevenly with a chattering tool

2**chatter** *n* **1 :** the action or sound of chattering **2 :** idle talk **:** PRATTLE

chat·ter·box \ˈchat-ər-ˌbäks\ *n* **:** one who engages in much idle talk

chat·ter·er \ˈchat-ər-ər\ *n* **1 :** one that chatters **2 :** any of various passerine birds (as a waxwing)

chatter mark *n* **1 :** a fine undulation formed on the surface of work by a chattering tool **2 :** one of a series of short curved cracks on a glaciated rock surface transverse to the glacial striae

chat·ty \ˈchat-ē\ *adj* **chat·ti·er; -est 1 :** fond of chatting **:** TALKATIVE <a ~ neighbor> **2 :** having the style and manner of light familiar conversation <a ~ letter> — **chat·ti·ly** \ˈchat-ᵊl-ē\ *adv* — **chat·ti·ness** \ˈchat-ē-nəs\ *n*

1**chauf·feur** \ˈshō-fər, shō-ˈ\ *n* [F, lit., stoker, fr. *chauffer* to heat, fr. MF *chaufer* — more at CHAFE] **1 :** a person employed to drive a motor vehicle **2 :** one that transports others by operating a motor vehicle

2**chauffeur** *vb* **chauf·feured; chauf·feur·ing** \ˈshō-f(ə-)riŋ, shō-ˈfər-iŋ\ *vi* **:** to do the work of a chauffeur ~ *vt* **1 :** to transport in the manner of a chauffeur <~*s* the children to school> **2 :** to operate (as an automobile) as chauffeur

chaul·moo·gra \chȯl-ˈmü-grə\ *n* [Beng *cāulmugrā*] **:** any of several East Indian trees (family Flacourtiaceae) that yield an acrid oil used in treating leprosy and skin diseases

chaunt \ˈchȯnt, ˈchänt\, **chaunter** *var of* CHANT, CHANTER

chaus·sure \shō-ˈsu̇r\ *n, pl* **chaussures** *same*\ [ME *chaucer,* fr. MF *chaussure*] **1 :** FOOTGEAR **2** *pl* **:** SHOES

chau·tau·qua \shə-ˈtȯ-kwə\ *n* [*Chautauqua* lake] **:** an institution of the late 19th and early 20th centuries providing popular education combined with entertainment in the form of lectures, concerts, and plays often presented outdoors or in a tent

chau·vin·ism \ˈshō-və-ˌniz-əm\ *n* [F *chauvinisme,* fr. Nicolas *Chauvin fl* 1815 F soldier of excessive patriotism and devotion to Napoleon] **1 :** excessive or blind patriotism — compare JINGOISM **2 :** undue partiality or attachment to a group or place to which one belongs or has belonged <male ~> — **chau·vin·ist** \-və-nəst\ *n* — **chau·vin·is·tic** \ˌshō-və-ˈnis-tik\ *adj* — **chau·vin·is·ti·cal·ly** \-ti-k(ə-)lē\ *adv*

1**chaw** \ˈchȯ\ *vb* [by alter.] *vt, dial* **:** to grind (as tobacco) with the teeth ~ *vi, dial* **:** CHEW

2**chaw** *n, dial* **:** a chew esp. of tobacco

1**cheap** \ˈchēp\ *n* [ME *chep,* fr. OE *cēap* trade; akin to OHG *kouf* trade; both fr. a prehistoric Gmc stem borrowed fr. L *caupo* tradesman] *obs* **:** BARGAIN — **on the cheap :** at minimum expense **:** CHEAPLY <schools that are run *on the cheap*>

2**cheap** *adj* **1 a :** purchasable below the going price or the real value **b :** charging a low price **c :** depreciated in value (as by currency inflation) <~ dollars> **2 :** gained with little effort <a ~ victory> **3 a :** of inferior quality or worth **:** TAWDRY, SLEAZY **b :** contemptible because of lack of any fine, lofty, or redeeming qualities **c :** STINGY **4 a :** yielding small satisfaction **b :** paying or able to pay less than going prices **5** *of money* **:** obtainable at a low rate of interest **6** *Brit* **:** specially reduced in price ***syn*** see CONTEMPTIBLE ***ant*** noble — **cheap** *adv* — **cheap·ish** \ˈchē-pish\ *adj* — **cheap·ish·ly** *adv* — **cheap·ly** \ˈchēp-lē\ *adv* — **cheap·ness** *n*

cheap·en \ˈchē-pən\ *vb* **cheap·ened; cheap·en·ing** \ˈchēp-(ə-)niŋ\ *vt* **1** [obs. E *cheap* (to price, bid for)] *archaic* **a :** to ask the price of **b :** to bid or bargain for **2 a :** to make cheap in price or value **b :** to lower in general esteem **c :** to make tawdry, vulgar, or inferior ~ *vi* **:** to become cheap

cheap·ie \ˈchē-pē\ *n* **:** one that is cheap <$8 and $15 tires — the ~*s* — *Nat'l Observer*> — **cheapie** *adj*

1**cheap–jack** \ˈchēp-ˌjak\ *n* [*cheap* + the name *Jack*] **1 :** a haggling huckster **2 :** a dealer in cheap merchandise

2**cheap–jack** *adj* **1 :** being inferior, cheap, or worthless <~ movie companies> **2 :** unscrupulously opportunistic <~ speculators>

cheap·skate \-ˌskāt\ *n* **:** a miserly or stingy person; *esp* **:** one who tries to avoid his share of costs or expenses

1**cheat** \ˈchēt\ *n* [earlier *cheat* forfeited property, fr. ME *chet* escheat, short for *eschete* — more at ESCHEAT] **1 :** the act or an instance of fraudulently deceiving **:** DECEPTION, FRAUD **2 :** one that cheats **:** PRETENDER, DECEIVER **3 :** any of several grasses; *esp* **:** the common chess (*Bromus secalinus*) **4 :** the obtaining of property from another by an intentional active distortion of the truth

2**cheat** *vt* **1 :** to deprive of something valuable by the use of deceit or fraud **2 :** to influence or lead by deceit, trick, or artifice **3 :** to defeat the purpose or blunt the effects of <~ winter of its dreariness — Washington Irving> ~ *vi* **1 a :** to practice fraud or trickery **b :** to violate rules dishonestly (as at cards or on an examination) **2 :** to be sexually unfaithful — often used with *on* — **cheat·er** *n*

syn CHEAT, COZEN, DEFRAUD, SWINDLE, OVERREACH *shared meaning element* **:** to get something by dishonest or deceitful means

1**check** \ˈchek\ *n* [ME *chek,* fr. OF *eschec,* fr. Ar *shāh,* fr. Per, lit., king; akin to Gk *ktasthai* to acquire] **1 :** exposure of a chess king to an attack from which he must be protected or moved to safety **2 a :** a sudden stoppage of a forward course or progress **:** ARREST **b :** a checking of an opposing player (as in ice hockey) **3 :** a sudden pause or break in a progression **4** *archaic* **:** REPRIMAND, REBUKE **5 :** one that arrests, limits, or restrains **:** RESTRAINT <against all ~*s,* rebukes, and manners, I must advance — Shak.> **6 a :** a standard for testing and evaluation **:** CRITERION **b :** EXAMINATION **c :** INSPECTION, INVESTIGATION <a loyalty ~ on government employees> **d :** the act of testing or verifying; *also* **:** the sample or unit used for testing or verifying **7 :** a written order directing a bank to pay money as instructed **:** DRAFT **8 a :** a ticket or token showing ownership or identity or indicating payment made <a baggage ~> **b :** a counter in various games **c**

: a slip indicating the amount due : BILL **9** [ME *chek,* short for *cheker* checker] **a :** a pattern in squares that resembles a checkerboard **b :** a fabric woven or printed with such a design **10** : a mark typically √ placed beside an item to show it has been noted, examined, or verified **11 :** CRACK, BREAK **12 :** a rabbet-shaped cutting : RABBET — **check·less** \-ləs\ *adj* — **in check** : under restraint or control <held the enemy *in check*>

[2]**check** *vt* **1 :** to put (a chess king) in check **2** *chiefly dial* : REBUKE, REPRIMAND **3 a :** to slow or bring to a stop : BRAKE <hastily ~*ed* the impulse> **b :** to block the progress of (as a hockey player) **4 a :** to restrain or diminish the action or force of : CONTROL **b :** to slack or ease off and then belay again (as a rope) **5 a :** to compare with a source, original, or authority : VERIFY **b** : to inspect for satisfactory condition, accuracy, safety, or performance — usu. used with *out* **c :** to mark with a check as examined, verified, or satisfactory — often used with *off* <~*ed* off each item> **6 a :** to consign for shipment as a service to the holder of a passenger ticket <~*ed* his bags before boarding> **b :** to ship or accept for shipment under such a consignment **7 :** to mark into squares : CHECKER **8 :** to leave or accept for safekeeping in a checkroom **9 :** to make checks or chinks in : cause to crack <the sun ~*s* timber> ~ *vi* **1 a** *of a dog* **:** to stop in a chase esp. when scent is lost **b :** to halt through caution, uncertainty, or fear : STOP **2 a :** to investigate conditions <~*ed* on the passengers' safety> **b :** to correspond point for point : TALLY <the description ~*s* with the photograph> — often used with *out* <his story ~*ed* out> **3 :** to draw a check on a bank **4 :** to waive the right to initiate the betting in a round of poker **5 :** CRACK, SPLIT ***syn*** see RESTRAIN ***ant*** accelerate (*as speed*), advance (*as a plan*), release (*as feelings*) — **check·able** \ˈchek-ə-bəl\ *adj* — **check into 1 :** to check in at <*check into* a hotel> **2 :** INVESTIGATE <*check into* a rumor> — **check up on :** INVESTIGATE

check·book \ˈchek-ˌbu̇k\ *n* **:** a book containing blank checks to be drawn on a bank

[1]**check·er** \ˈchek-ər\ *n* [ME *cheker,* fr. OF *eschequier,* fr. *eschec*] **1** *archaic* : CHESSBOARD **2 :** a square or spot resembling the markings of a checkerboard **3** [back-formation fr. *checkers*] : a man in checkers

[2]**checker** *vt* **check·ered; check·er·ing** \ˈchek-(ə-)riŋ\ **1 a :** to variegate with different colors or shades **b :** to vary with contrasting elements or situations <had a ~*ed* career as a racer> **2** : to mark into squares

[3]**checker** *n* **:** one that checks; *esp* **:** an employee who checks out purchases in a self-service store (as a supermarket)

check·er·ber·ry \ˈchek-ə(r)-ˌber-ē\ *n* [*checker* (wild service tree) + *berry*] **1 :** any of several reddish berries; *esp* **:** the spicy red berrylike fruit of an American wintergreen (*Gaultheria procumbens*) **2 :** a plant producing checkerberries

check·er·bloom \-ər-ˌblüm\ *n* [prob. fr. [1]*checker* + *bloom*] **:** a purple-flowered mallow (*Sidalcea malvaeflora*) of the western U.S.

check·er·board \-ə(r)-ˌbō(ə)rd, -ˌbȯ(ə)rd\ *n* **1 :** a board used in various games (as checkers) with usu. 64 squares in 2 alternating colors **2 :** something that has a pattern or arrangement like a checkerboard

check·ers \ˈchek-ərz\ *n pl but sing in constr* **:** a checkerboard game for 2 players each with 12 men

check in *vi* **1 :** to register at a hotel **2 :** to report one's presence or arrival by supplying requisite information <*check in* at a convention> ~ *vt* **:** to satisfy all requirements in returning <*check in* the equipment after using>

checking account *n* **:** a bank account against which the depositor can draw checks

check·list \ˈchek-ˌlist\ *n* **:** INVENTORY, CATALOG; *esp* **:** a complete list

check mark *n* **:** CHECK 10 — **check·mark** *vt*

[1]**check·mate** \ˈchek-ˌmāt\ *vt* [ME *chekmaten,* fr. *chekmate,* interj. used to announce checkmate, fr. MF *eschec mat,* fr. Ar *shāh māt,* fr. Per, lit., the king is left unable to escape] **1 :** to arrest, thwart, or counter completely **2 :** to check (a chess opponent's king) so that escape is impossible

[2]**checkmate** *n* **1 a :** the act of checkmating **b :** the situation of a checkmated king **2 :** a complete check

check·off \ˈchek-ˌȯf\ *n* **1 :** the deduction of union dues from a worker's paycheck by the employer **2 :** AUTOMATIC 2

check off \-ˈȯf\ *vt* **1 :** to eliminate from further consideration <robbery was *checked off* as a motive> **2 :** to change (a football play called in the huddle) at the line of scrimmage **3 :** to deduct (union dues) from a worker's paycheck

check·out \ˈchek-ˌau̇t\ *n* **1 :** the action or an instance of checking out **2 :** the time at which a lodger must vacate his room (as in a hotel) or be charged for retaining it **3 :** a counter at which checking out is done **4 a :** the action of examining and testing something for performance, suitability, or readiness **b :** the action of familiarizing oneself with the operation of a mechanical thing (as an airplane)

check out \-ˈau̇t\ *vi* **:** to vacate and pay for one's lodging (as at a hotel) ~ *vt* **1 :** to satisfy all requirements in taking away <*checked out* a library book> **2 a :** to itemize and reckon up the total cost of and receive payment for (outgoing merchandise) esp. in a self-service store **b :** to have the cost totaled and pay for (purchases) at a checkout counter

check over *vt* **:** EXAMINE, INVESTIGATE

check·point \ˈchek-ˌpȯint\ *n* **:** a point at which a check is performed <vehicles were inspected at various ~*s*>

check·rein \-ˌrān\ *n* **1 :** a short rein looped over a hook on the saddle of a harness to prevent a horse from lowering his head **2** : a branch rein connecting the driving rein of one horse of a span or pair with the bit of the other

check·room \-ˌrüm, -ˌru̇m\ *n* **:** a room at which baggage, parcels, or clothing is checked

check·row \-ˌrō\ *vt* **:** to plant (as corn) at the points of intersection of right-angled rows to permit two-way cultivation

check·up \-ˌəp\ *n* **:** EXAMINATION; *esp* **:** a general physical examination

ched·dar \ˈched-ər\ *n, often cap* [*Cheddar,* England] **:** a hard cheese of smooth texture and a flavor ranging from mild to sharp depending on the length of cure

che·der \ˈkād-ər, ˈked-\ *var of* HEDER

chee·cha·ko \chi-ˈchäk-(ˌ)ō, -ˈchȯk-\ *n, pl* **-kos** [Chinook Jargon *chee chahco,* fr. Chinook *t'shi* new + Nootka *chako* to come] *chiefly Northwest* **:** TENDERFOOT 1

[1]**cheek** \ˈchēk\ *n* [ME *cheke,* fr. OE *cēace;* akin to MLG *kāke* jawbone] **1 :** the fleshy side of the face below the eye and above and to the side of the mouth; *broadly* **:** the lateral aspect of the head **2 :** something suggestive of the human cheek in position or form; *esp* **:** one of two laterally paired parts **3 :** insolent boldness and flaunted self-assurance **4 :** BUTTOCK 1 ***syn*** see TEMERITY ***ant*** diffidence — **cheek·ful** \-ˌfu̇l\ *n* — **cheek by jowl :** in close proximity

[2]**cheek** *vt* **:** to speak rudely or impudently to

cheek·bone \ˈchēk-ˈbōn, -ˌbōn\ *n* **:** the prominence below the eye that is formed by the zygomatic bone; *also* **:** ZYGOMATIC BONE

-cheeked \ˈchēkt\ *adj comb form* **:** having cheeks of a specified nature <rosy-*cheeked*>

cheeky \ˈchē-kē\ *adj* **cheek·i·er; -est 1 :** having or showing cheek : IMPUDENT **2 :** having well-developed cheeks — used esp. of a bulldog — **cheek·i·ly** \-kə-lē\ *adv* — **cheek·i·ness** \-kē-nəs\ *n*

cheep \ˈchēp\ *vi* [imit.] **1 :** to utter faint shrill sounds : PEEP **2** : to utter a single word or sound — **cheep** *n*

[1]**cheer** \ˈchi(ə)r\ *n* [ME *chere* face, cheer, fr. OF, face] **1 a** *obs* : FACE **b** *archaic* **:** facial expression **2 :** state of mind or heart : SPIRIT <be of good ~ — Mt 9:2(AV)> **3 :** lightness of mind and feeling : ANIMATION, GAIETY **4 :** hospitable entertainment : WELCOME **5 :** food and drink for a feast : FARE **6 :** something that gladdens <words of ~> **7 :** a shout of applause or encouragement

[2]**cheer** *vt* **1 a :** to instill with hope or courage : COMFORT — usu. used with *up* **b :** to make glad or happy — usu. used with *up* **2** : to urge on or encourage esp. by shouts <*cheered* the team on> **3 :** to applaud with shouts ~ *vi* **1** *obs* **:** to be mentally or emotionally disposed **2 :** to grow or be cheerful : REJOICE — usu. used with *up* **3 :** to utter a shout of applause or triumph — **cheer·er** *n*

cheer·ful \ˈchir-fəl\ *adj* **1 a :** full of good spirits : MERRY **b** : UNGRUDGING <~ obedience> **2 :** conducive to cheer : likely to dispel gloom or worry <sunny ~ room> ***syn*** see GLAD ***ant*** glum, gloomy — **cheer·ful·ly** \-f(ə-)lē\ *adv* — **cheer·ful·ness** \-fəl-nəs\ *n*

cheer·io \ˌchi(ə)r-ē-ˈō\ *interj* [*cheery* + *-o*] *chiefly Brit* — usu. used as a farewell and sometimes as a greeting or toast

cheer·lead·er \ˈchi(ə)r-ˌlēd-ər\ *n* **:** one that calls for and directs organized cheering (as at a football game) — **cheer·lead** \-ˌlēd\ *vt*

cheer·less \ˈchi(ə)r-ləs\ *adj* **:** lacking qualities that cheer : BLEAK, JOYLESS <a ~ room> — **cheer·less·ly** *adv* — **cheer·less·ness** *n*

cheers \ˈchi(ə)rz\ *interj* — used as a toast

cheery \ˈchi(ə)r-ē\ *adj* **cheer·i·er; -est 1 :** marked by cheerfulness or good spirits **2 :** causing or suggesting cheerfulness — **cheer·i·ly** \ˈchir-ə-lē\ *adv* — **cheer·i·ness** \ˈchir-ē-nəs\ *n*

[1]**cheese** \ˈchēz\ *n, often attrib* [ME *chese,* fr. OE *cēse;* akin to OHG *kāsi* cheese; both fr. a prehistoric WGmc word borrowed fr. L *caseus* cheese; akin to OE *hwatherian* to foam, Skt *kvathati* he boils] **1 a :** curd separated from whey, consolidated by molding or pressure, and usu. ripened for use as food **b :** an often cylindrical cake of this food **2 :** something resembling cheese in shape or consistency

[2]**cheese** *vt* **cheesed; chees·ing** [origin unknown] **:** to put an end to : STOP — **cheese it** — used in the imperative as a warning of danger <*cheese it,* the cops>

[3]**cheese** *n* [perh. fr. Urdu *chīz* thing] *slang* **:** someone important : BOSS <the . . . big ~ who bought the program for his network — Neil Hickey>

cheese·burg·er \ˈchēz-ˌbər-gər\ *n* [*cheese* + ham*burger*] **:** a hamburger containing a slice of cheese

cheese·cake \-ˌkāk\ *n* **1 :** a cake made by baking a mixture of cream cheese or cottage cheese, eggs, and sugar or a filling of similar texture in a pastry shell or a mold lined with sweet crumbs **2** : a photographic display of shapely and scantily clothed female figures — compare BEEFCAKE

cheese·cloth \-ˌklȯth\ *n* [fr. its use in cheesemaking] **:** a very lightweight unsized cotton gauze

cheese·mak·er \-ˌmā-kər\ *n* **:** one that makes cheese — **cheese·mak·ing** \-kiŋ\ *n*

cheese·par·ing \-ˌpa(ə)r-iŋ, -ˌpe(ə)r-\ *n* **1 :** something worthless or insignificant **2 :** miserly or petty economizing : STINGINESS — **cheeseparing** *adj*

cheesy \ˈchē-zē\ *adj* **chees·i·er; -est 1 a :** resembling or suggesting cheese esp. in consistency or odor **b :** containing cheese **2** *slang* **:** SHABBY, CHEAP — **chees·i·ness** *n*

chee·tah \ˈchēt-ə\ *n* [Hindi *cītā,* fr. Skt *citrakāya* tiger, fr. *citra* bright + *kāya* body] **:** a long-legged spotted swift-moving African and formerly Asiatic cat (*Acinonyx jubatus*) about the size of a small leopard that has blunt nonretractile claws and is often trained to run down game

chef \ˈshef\ *n* [F, short for *chef de cuisine* head of the kitchen] **1** : a skilled male cook who manages a kitchen **2 :** COOK — **chef·dom** \-dəm\ *n*

chef d'oeu·vre \shā-dœvrᵊ, (ˈ)shā-ˈdə(r)v\ *n, pl* **chefs d'oeuvre** \-dœvrᵊ, -ˈdə(r)v(z)\ [F *chef-d'oeuvre,* lit., leading work] **:** a masterpiece esp. in art or literature

che·la \ˈkē-lə\ *n, pl* **che·lae** \-(ˌ)lē\ [NL, fr. Gk *chēlē* claw] **:** a pincerlike organ or claw borne by a limb of a crustacean or arachnid

[1]**che·late** \ˈkē-ˌlāt\ *adj* **1 :** resembling or having chelae **2** [Gk *chēlē* claw, hoof] **:** of, relating to, or having a ring structure that usu. contains a metal ion held by coordination bonds — **chelate** *n*

[2]**chelate** *vb* **che·lat·ed; che·lat·ing** *vt* **:** to combine with (a metal) so as to form a chelate ring ~ *vi* **:** to react so as to form a chelate

ring — **che·lat·able** \-ˌlāt-ə-bəl\ *adj* — **che·la·tion** \kē-ˈlā-shən\ *n* — **che·la·tor** \-ˌlāt-ər\ *n*

che·lic·era \ki-ˈlis-ə-rə\ *n, pl* **-er·ae** \-ˌrē\ [NL, fr. F *chélicère,* fr. Gk *chēlē* + *keras* horn — more at HORN] : one of the anterior pair of appendages of an arachnid often specialized as fangs — **che·lic·er·al** \-ə-rəl\ *adj*

Chel·le·an *or* **Chel·li·an** \ˈshel-ē-ən\ *adj* [F *chelléen,* fr. *Chelles,* France] : ABBEVILLIAN

che·lo·ni·an \ki-ˈlō-nē-ən\ *adj* [Gk *chelōnē* tortoise] : of, relating to, or being a tortoise or turtle — **chelonian** *n*

chem *abbr* chemical; chemist; chemistry

chem- *or* **chemo-** *also* **chemi-** *comb form* [NL, fr. LGk *chēmeia* alchemy — more at ALCHEMY] **1 :** chemical : chemistry <*chem*osmosis> <*chemo*taxis> **2 :** chemically <*chemi*sorb>

Chem·a·ku·an \ˌchem-ə-ˈkü-ən\ *n* **:** a language stock of the Mosan phylum in the state of Washington

chem·ic \ˈkem-ik\ *adj* [NL *chimicus* alchemist, fr. ML *alchimicus,* fr. *alchymia* alchemy] **1** *archaic* : ALCHEMIC **2 :** CHEMICAL

[1]**chem·i·cal** \ˈkem-i-kəl\ *adj* **1 :** of, relating to, used in, or produced by chemistry **2 a :** acting or operated or produced by chemicals **b :** detectable by chemical means — **chem·i·cal·ly** \-i-k(ə-)lē\ *adv*

[2]**chemical** *n* **:** a substance (as an element or chemical compound) obtained by a chemical process or used for producing a chemical effect

chemical engineering *n* **:** engineering dealing with the industrial application of chemistry

chemical warfare *n* **:** tactical warfare using incendiary mixtures, smokes, or irritant, burning, poisonous, or asphyxiating gases

che·mi·lu·mi·nes·cence \ˌkem-i-ˌlü-mə-ˈnes-ᵊn(t)s, ˌkē-mi-\ *n* [ISV] **:** luminescence due to chemical reaction usu. at low temperatures; *esp* : BIOLUMINESCENCE — **che·mi·lu·mi·nes·cent** \-ˈnes-ᵊnt\ *adj*

che·min de fer \shə-ˌman-də-ˈfe(ə)r\ *n, pl* **che·mins de fer** \-ˌman-də-\ [F, lit., railroad]**:** a card game in which two hands are dealt, any number of players may bet against the dealer, and the winning hand is the one that comes closer to but does not exceed a count of nine on two or three cards

che·mise \shə-ˈmēz\ *n* [ME, fr. OF, shirt, fr. LL *camisia*] **1 :** a woman's one-piece undergarment **2 :** a loose straight-hanging dress

chem·i·sette \ˌshem-i-ˈzet\ *n* [F, dim. of *chemise*] **:** a woman's garment; *esp* **:** one (as of lace) to fill the open front of a dress

che·mism \ˈkem-ˌiz-əm, ˈkē-ˌmiz-\ *n* **1 :** chemical activity or affinity **2 :** operation in obedience to chemical laws

che·mi·sorb \ˈkem-i-ˌsȯ(ə)rb, ˈkē̇mi-, -ˌzȯ(ə)rb\ *or* **che·mo·sorb** \ˈkē-mə-, ˈkem-ə-\ *vt* [*chem-* + *-sorb* (as in *adsorb*)] **:** to take up and hold usu. irreversibly by chemical forces — **che·mi·sorp·tion** \ˌkem-i-ˈsȯrp-shən, ˌkē-mi-, -ˈzȯrp-\ *n*

chem·ist \ˈkem-əst\ *n* [NL *chimista,* short for ML *alchimista*] **1 a** *obs* : ALCHEMIST **b :** one trained in chemistry **2** *Brit* : PHARMACIST

chem·is·try \ˈkem-ə-strē\ *n, pl* **-tries 1 :** a science that deals with the composition, structure, and properties of substances and of the transformations that they undergo **2 a :** the composition and chemical properties of a substance <the ~ of iron> **b :** chemical processes and phenomena (as of an organism) <blood ~>

che·mo·au·to·tro·phic \ˌkē-mō-ˌȯt-ə-ˈtrō-fik *also* ˌkem-ō-\ *adj* **:** being autotrophic and oxidizing some inorganic compound as a source of energy — **chemo·au·to·tro·phi·cal·ly** \-fi-k(ə-)lē\ *adv* — **chemo·au·tot·ro·phy** \-ō-ˈtä-trə-fē\ *n*

che·mo·pro·phy·lax·is \-ˌprō-fə-ˈlak-səs *also* -ˌpräf-ə-\ *n* **:** the prevention of infectious disease by the use of chemical agents — **che·mo·pro·phy·lac·tic** \-ˈlak-tik\ *adj*

che·mo·re·cep·tion \-ri-ˈsep-shən\ *n* [ISV] **:** the physiological reception of chemical stimuli — **che·mo·re·cep·tive** \-ˈsep-tiv\ *adj* — **che·mo·re·cep·tiv·i·ty** \-ˌrē-ˌsep-ˈtiv-ət-ē, -ri-\ *n*

che·mo·re·cep·tor \-ri-ˈsep-tər\ *n* [ISV]**:** a sense organ (as a taste bud) responding to chemical stimuli

che·mo·sphere \ˈkē-mə-ˌsfi(ə)r, ˈkem-ə-\ *n* **:** a stratum of the upper atmosphere in which photochemical reactions are prevalent and which begins about 20 miles above the earth's surface

che·mo·ster·il·ant \ˌkē-mō-ˈster-ə-lənt *also* ˌkem-ō-\ *n* [*chemosterilize* + *-ant*] **:** a substance that produces irreversible sterility (as of an insect) without marked alteration of mating habits or life expectancy

che·mo·sur·gery \-ˈsərj-(ə-)rē\ *n* **:** removal by chemical means of diseased or unwanted tissue — **che·mo·sur·gi·cal** \-ˈsər-ji-kəl\ *adj*

che·mo·syn·the·sis \-ˈsin(t)-thə-səs\ *n* [ISV] **:** synthesis of organic compounds (as in living cells) by energy derived from chemical reactions — **che·mo·syn·thet·ic** \-sin-ˈthet-ik\ *adj*

che·mo·tac·tic \-ˈtak-tik\ *adj* **:** involving or exhibiting chemotaxis — **che·mo·tac·ti·cal·ly** \-ti-k(ə-)lē\ *adv*

che·mo·tax·is \-ˈtak-səs\ *n* [NL]**:** orientation or movement of an organism in relation to chemical agents

che·mo·tax·on·o·my \-(ˌ)tak-ˈsän-ə-mē\ *n* **:** the classification of plants and animals based on similarities and differences in biochemical composition — **che·mo·tax·o·nom·ic** \-ˌtak-sə-ˈnäm-ik\ *adj* — **che·mo·tax·o·nom·i·cal·ly** \-i-k(ə-)lē\ *adv* — **che·mo·tax·on·o·mist** \-(ˌ)tak-ˈsän-ə-məst\ *n*

che·mo·ther·a·peu·tic \-ˌther-ə-ˈpyüt-ik\ *or* **che·mo·ther·a·peu·ti·cal** \-i-kəl\ *adj* **:** of or relating to chemotherapy — **chemo·therapeutic** *n* — **che·mo·ther·a·peu·ti·cal·ly** \-i-k(ə-)lē\ *adv*

che·mo·ther·a·py \-ˈther-ə-pē\ *n* [ISV] **:** the use of chemical agents in the treatment or control of disease

che·mot·ro·pism \ki-ˈmä-trə-ˌpiz-əm, ke-\ *n* [ISV]**:** orientation of cells or organisms in relation to chemical stimuli

chem·ur·gy \ˈkem-(ˌ)ər-jē, kə-ˈmər-\ *n* **:** a branch of applied chemistry that deals with industrial utilization of organic raw materials esp. from farm products — **chem·ur·gic** \kə-ˈmər-jik, ke-\ *adj* — **chem·ur·gi·cal·ly** \-ji-k(ə-)lē\ *adv*

che·nille \shə-ˈnē(ə)l\ *n* [F, lit., caterpillar, fr. L *canicula,* dim. of *canis* dog; fr. its hairy appearance — more at HOUND] **1 :** a wool, cotton, silk, or rayon yarn with protruding pile; *also* **:** a pile-face fabric with a filling of this yarn **2 :** an imitation of chenille yarn or fabric

che·no·pod \ˈkē-nə-ˌpäd, ˈken-ə-\ *n* [deriv. of Gk *chēn* goose + *podion,* dim. of *pod-, pous* foot — more at FOOT] **:** a plant of the goosefoot family

cheong·sam \ˈchȯŋ-ˈsäm\ *n* [Chin (Cant) *ch'eūng shaam,* lit., long gown] **:** a dress with a slit skirt and a mandarin collar worn esp. by oriental women

cheque \ˈchek\ *chiefly Brit var of* [1]CHECK 7

che·quer \ˈchek-ər\ *chiefly Brit var of* CHECKER

cher·i·moya \ˌcher-ə-ˈmȯi-(y)ə, ˌchir-\ *n* [Sp *chirimoya*] **:** a small widely cultivated tropical American tree (*Annona cherimola*) of the custard-apple family with a round, oblong, or heart-shaped fruit that has a pitted rind

cher·ish \ˈcher-ish\ *vt* [ME *cherisshen,* fr. MF *cheriss-,* stem of *cherir* to cherish, fr. OF, fr. *chier* dear, fr. L *carus* — more at CHARITY] **1 a :** to hold dear : feel or show affection for **b :** to keep or cultivate with care and affection : NURTURE **2 :** to entertain or harbor in the mind deeply and resolutely <still ~*es* that memory> *syn* see APPRECIATE *ant* neglect — **cher·ish·able** \-ə-bəl\ *adj* — **cher·ish·er** *n*

cher·no·zem \ˌcher-nə-ˈzhȯm, -ˈzem\ *n* [Russ, lit., black earth] **:** a dark-colored zonal soil with a deep rich humus horizon found in temperate to cool climates of rather low humidity — **cher·no·zem·ic** \-ˈzhȯm-ik, -ˈzem-\ *adj*

Cher·o·kee \ˈcher-ə-(ˌ)kē\ *n, pl* **Cherokee** *or* **Cherokees** [prob. fr. Creek *tciloki* people of a different speech] **1 :** a member of an Amerindian people orig. of Tennessee and No. Carolina **2 :** the language of the Cherokee people

Cherokee rose *n* **:** a Chinese climbing rose (*Rosa laevigata*) with a fragrant white blossom

che·root \shə-ˈrüt, chə-\ *n* [Tamil *curuṭṭu,* lit., roll] **:** a cigar cut square at both ends

cher·ry \ˈcher-ē\ *n, pl* **cherries** [ME *chery,* fr. ONF *cherise* (taken as a plural), fr. LL *ceresia,* fr. L *cerasus* cherry tree, fr. Gk *kerasos* — more at CORNEL] **1 a :** any of numerous trees and shrubs (genus *Prunus*) of the rose family that bear pale yellow to deep red or blackish smooth-skinned drupes enclosing a smooth seed and that belong to any of several varieties including some cultivated for their fruits or ornamental flowers **b :** the fruit of a cherry **c :** the wood of a cherry **2 :** a variable color averaging a moderate red **3 a :** HYMEN **b :** VIRGINITY — **cher·ry·like** \-ē-ˌlīk\ *adj*

cherry bomb *n* **:** a powerful globular red firecracker

cherry picker *n* **:** a traveling crane equipped for holding a passenger at the end of the boom

cherry plum *n* **:** an Asiatic plum (*Prunus cerasifera*) used extensively in Europe as a stock on which to bud domestic varieties

cher·ry·stone \ˈcher-ē-ˌstōn\ *n* **:** a small quahog

cher·so·nese \ˈkər-sə-ˌnēz, -ˌnēs\ *n* [L *chersonesus,* fr. Gk *chersonēsos,* fr. *chersos* dry land + *nēsos* island] **:** PENINSULA

chert \ˈchərt, ˈchat\ *n* [origin unknown] **:** a rock resembling flint and consisting essentially of cryptocrystalline quartz or fibrous chalcedony — **cherty** \-ē\ *adj*

cher·ub \ˈcher-əb\ *n* [L, fr. Gk *cheroub,* fr. Heb *kĕrūbh*] **1** *pl* **cher·u·bim** \ˈcher-(y)ə-ˌbim, ˈker-\ **a :** a biblical attendant of God or of a holy place often represented as a being with large wings, a human head, and an animal body **b** *pl* **:** an order of angels — see CELESTIAL HIERARCHY **2** *pl* **cherubs a :** a beautiful usu. winged child in painting and sculpture **b :** an innocent-looking usu. chubby and rosy person — **che·ru·bic** \chə-ˈrü-bik\ *adj* — **che·ru·bi·cal·ly** \-bi-k(ə-)lē\ *adv* — **cher·ub·like** \ˈcher-əb-ˌlīk\ *adj*

cher·vil \ˈchər-vəl\ *n* [ME *chervile,* fr. OE *cerfille;* akin to OHG *kervila*] **:** an aromatic herb (*Anthriscus cerefolium*) of the carrot family with divided leaves that are often used in soups and salads; *also* **:** any of several related plants

Ches *abbr* Cheshire

Ches·a·peake Bay retriever \ˌches-(ə-)ˌpēk-ˌbā-\ *n* **:** a large powerful sporting dog developed in Maryland by crossing Newfoundlands with native retrievers

Chesh·ire cat \ˌchesh-ər-\ *n* [*Cheshire,* England] **:** a cat with a broad grin in Lewis Carroll's *Alice's Adventures in Wonderland*

chessboard with men arranged as at beginning of game

Cheshire cheese *n* **:** a cheese similar to cheddar made chiefly in Cheshire, England

[1]**chess** \ˈches\ *n* [ME *ches,* fr. OF *esches,* acc. pl. of *eschec* check at chess — more at CHECK] **:** a game for two players each of whom moves his 16 pieces according to fixed rules across a checkerboard and tries to checkmate his opponent's king — **chess·board** \-ˌbō(ə)rd, -ˌbȯ(ə)rd\ *n* — **chess·man** \-ˌman, -mən\ *n*

[2]**chess** *n* [origin unknown] **:** a weedy annual bromegrass (*Bromus secalinus*) widely distributed as a weed esp. in grain; *broadly* **:** any of several weedy bromegrasses

chest \ˈchest\ *n* [ME, fr. OE *cest;* akin to OHG & ON *kista* chest] **1 a :** a container for storage or shipping; *esp* **:** a box with a lid used esp. for the safekeeping of belongings **b :** a cupboard used esp. for the storing of medicines or first-aid supplies **2 :** the place where money of a public institution is kept : TREASURY; *also* : the fund so kept **3** : the part of the body enclosed by the ribs and breastbone — **chest·ful** \-ˌfu̇l\ *n*

-chest·ed \ˈches-təd\ *adj comb form* : having (such) a chest <flat-*chested*> <deep-*chested*>

ches·ter·field \ˈches-tər-ˌfēld\ *n* [fr. a 19th cent. Earl of *Chesterfield*] **1** : a single-breasted or double-breasted semifitted overcoat with velvet collar **2** : a davenport usu. with upright armrests

Ches·ter White \ˌches-tər-\ *n* [*Chester* County, Pa.] : any of a breed of large white swine

¹chest·nut \ˈches-(ˌ)nət\ *n* [ME *chasteine, chesten* chestnut tree, fr. MF *chastaigne*, fr. L *castanea*, fr. Gk *kastanea*] **1 a** : a tree or shrub (genus *Castanea*) of the beech family **b** : the edible nut of a chestnut **c** : the wood of a chestnut **2** : a grayish to reddish brown **3** : HORSE CHESTNUT **4** : a chestnut-colored animal; *specif* : a horse having a body color of any shade of pure or reddish brown with mane, tail, and points of the same or a lighter shade — compare ²BAY 1, ¹SORREL 1a **5** : a callosity on the inner side of the leg of the horse **6 a** : an old joke or story **b** : something (as a musical piece) repeated to the point of staleness

²chestnut *adj* **1** : of, relating to, or resembling a chestnut **2** : of the color chestnut

chestnut blight *n* : a destructive fungous disease of the American chestnut marked by cankers of bark and cambium

chest of drawers : a piece of furniture designed to contain a set of drawers (as for holding clothing)

chesty *adj* **chest·i·er; -est** **1** : marked by a large or well-developed chest **2** : proudly or arrogantly self-assertive

che·val-de-frise \shə-ˌval-də-ˈfrēz\ *n, pl* **che·vaux-de-frise** \shə-ˌvōd-ə-\ [F, lit., horse from Friesland] **1** : a defense consisting of a timber or an iron barrel covered with projecting spikes and often strung with barbed wire **2** : a protecting line (as of spikes) on top of a wall — usu. used in pl.

che·val glass \shə-ˈval-\ *n* [F *cheval* horse, support] : a full-length mirror in a frame by which it may be tilted

che·va·lier \ˌshev-ə-ˈli(ə)r, *esp for 1b & 2 also* shə-ˈval-ˌyā\ *n* [ME, fr. MF, fr. LL *caballarius* horseman] **1 a** : CAVALIER 2 **b** : a member of any of various orders of knighthood or of merit (as the Legion of Honor) **2 a** : a member of the lowest rank of French nobility **b** : a cadet of the French nobility **3** : a chivalrous man

che·ve·lure \shəv-lu̇r\ *n* [F, fr. L *capillatura*, fr. *capillatus* having hair, fr. *capillus* hair] : a head of hair

chev·i·ot \ˈshev-ē-ət, *esp Brit* ˈchev-\ *n, often cap* **1** : any of a breed of hardy hornless medium-wooled meat-type sheep that are a source of quality mutton and have their origin in the Cheviot hills **2 a** : a fabric of cheviot wool **b** : a heavy rough napped plain or twill fabric of coarse wool or worsted **c** : a sturdy soft-finished plain or twill cotton shirting

chev·ron \ˈshev-rən\ *n* [ME, fr. MF, rafter, chevron, fr. (assumed) VL *caprion-, caprio* rafter; akin to L *caper* goat] : a figure, pattern, or object having the shape of a V or an inverted V: as **a** *or* **chev·er·on** \-(ə-)rən\ : a heraldic charge consisting of two diagonal stripes meeting at an angle usu. with the point up **b** : a sleeve badge that usu. consists of one or more chevron-shaped stripes often with arcs or distinctive emblems and that indicates the wearer's rank and service (as in the armed forces) — **chev·roned** \ˈshev-rənd\ *adj*

chevrons b: *1* marine staff sergeant, *2* air force staff sergeant, *3* army staff sergeant

chev·ro·tain \ˈshev-rə-ˌtān\ *n* [F, dim. of *chevrot* kid, fawn, fr. MF, dim. of *chèvre* goat, fr. L *capra* she-goat, fem. of *capr-, caper* he-goat] : any of several very small hornless ruminants (family Tragulidae) of tropical Asia and West Africa

¹chew \ˈchü\ *vb* [ME *chewen*, fr. OE *cēowan*; akin to OHG *kiuwan* to chew, OSlav *živati*] *vt* : to crush, grind, or gnaw (as food) with or as if with the teeth : MASTICATE ~ *vi* : to chew something; *specif* : to chew tobacco — **chew·able** \-ə-bəl\ *adj* — **chew·er** *n* — **chewy** \ˈchü-ē\ *adj* — **chew the rag** *or* **chew the fat** *slang* : to make friendly familiar conversation : CHAT

²chew *n* **1** : the act of chewing **2** : something for chewing <a ~ of tobacco>

chewing gum *n* : a sweetened and flavored insoluble plastic material (as a preparation of chicle) used for chewing

che·wink \chi-ˈwiŋk\ *n* [imit.] : TOWHEE 1

chew out *vt* : to bawl out : REPRIMAND <the sergeant *chewed* him *out* for being late>

chew over *vt* : to meditate on : think about reflectively <*chewed over* the problems of life>

Chey·enne \shi-ˈan, -ˈen\ *n, pl* **Cheyenne** *or* **Cheyennes** [CanF, F, fr. Dakota *Shaiyena*, fr. *shaia* to speak unintelligibly] **1** : a member of an Amerindian people of the western plains of the U.S. **2** : the Algonquian language of the Cheyenne people

chg *abbr* **1** change **2** charge

chi \ˈkī\ *n* [Gk *chei*] : the 22d letter of the Greek alphabet — see ALPHABET table

Chi·an·ti \kē-ˈänt-ē, -ˈant-\ *n* [It, fr. the *Chianti* mt. area, Italy] : a still dry usu. red table wine

Chi·an turpentine \ˈkī-ən-\ *n* [*Chios*, Greece] : TURPENTINE 1a

chiao \ˈtyau̇\ *n, pl* **chiao** [Chin (Pek) *chiao*³] — see *yuan* at MONEY table

chiar·oscu·rist \kē-ˌär-ə-ˈsk(y)u̇r-əst, kē-ˌar-\ *n* : an artist in chiaroscuro

chiar·oscu·ro \-ˈsk(y)u̇(ə)r-(ˌ)ō\ *n, pl* **-ros** [It, fr. *chiaro* clear, light + *oscuro* obscure, dark] **1** : pictorial representation in terms of light and shade without regard to color **2** : the arrangement or treatment of light and dark parts in a pictorial work of art **3** : a 16th century woodcut technique involving the use of several blocks to print different tones of the same color; *also* : a print made by this technique

chi·asm \ˈkī-ˌaz-əm\ *n* [NL *chiasma*] : CHIASMA 1

chi·as·ma \kī-ˈaz-mə\ *n, pl* **-ma·ta** \-mət-ə\ [NL, X-shaped configuration, fr. Gk, crosspiece, fr. *chiazein* to mark with a chi, fr. *chi* (x)] **1** : an anatomical intersection or decussation — compare OPTIC CHIASMA **2** : a cross-shaped configuration of paired chromatids visible in the diplotene of meiotic prophase and considered the cytological equivalent of genetic crossing-over — **chi·as·mat·ic** \ˌkī-əz-ˈmat-ik\ *adj*

chi·as·mus \kī-ˈaz-məs\ *n* [NL, fr. Gk *chiasmos*, fr. *chiazein* to mark with a chi] : an inverted relationship between the syntactic elements of parallel phrases (as in Goldsmith's *to stop too fearful, and too faint to go*)

chiaus \ˈchau̇s(h)\ *n* [Turk *çavus*, fr. *çav* voice, news] : a Turkish messenger or sergeant

Chib·cha \ˈchib-(ˌ)chä\ *n, pl* **Chibcha** *or* **Chibchas** [Sp, of AmerInd origin] **1** : a member of an Amerindian people of central Colombia **2** : the extinct language of the Chibcha people

Chib·chan \-chən\ *adj* : of, relating to, or constituting a language stock of Colombia and Central America

chi·bouk *or* **chi·bouque** \chə-ˈbük, shə-\ *n* [F *chibouque*, fr. Turk *çibuk*] : a long-stemmed Turkish tobacco pipe with a clay bowl

¹chic \ˈshēk\ *n* [F] : smart elegance and sophistication esp. of dress or manner : STYLE <wears her clothes with superb ~>

²chic *adj* **1** : cleverly stylish : SMART <the woman who is ~ adapts fashion to her own personality —Elizabeth L. Post> **2** : currently fashionable : MODISH <a ~ restaurant> — **chic·ly** *adv* — **chic·ness** *n*

chi·ca·lo·te \ˌchik-ə-ˈlōt-ē\ *n* [Sp, fr. Nahuatl *chicalotl*] : a white-flowered prickly poppy (*Argemone platyceras*) of Mexico and the southwestern U.S.

¹chi·cane \shik-ˈān, chik-\ *vb* **chi·caned; chi·can·ing** [F *chicaner*, fr. MF, to quibble, prevent justice] *vi* : to use chicanery <a wretch he had taught to lie and ~ —George Meredith> ~ *vt* : TRICK, CHEAT

²chicane *n* **1** : CHICANERY **2 a** : an obstacle on a racecourse **b** : a series of tight turns in opposite directions in an otherwise straight stretch of a road-racing course **3** : the absence of trumps in a hand of cards

chi·ca·nery \-ˈān-(ə-)rē\ *n, pl* **-ner·ies** **1** : deception by artful subterfuge or sophistry : TRICKERY **2** : a piece of sharp practice (as at law) : TRICK

Chi·ca·no \chi-ˈkän-(ˌ)ō\ *n, pl* **-nos** [modif. of Sp *mejicano* Mexican] : an American of Mexican descent — **Chicano** *adj*

¹chi·chi \ˈshē-(ˌ)shē, ˈchē-(ˌ)chē\ *adj* [F] **1** : elaborately ornamented : SHOWY, FRILLY <a ~ dress> **2** : ARTY, PRECIOUS <~ poetry> **3** : CHIC, FASHIONABLE <a ~ nightclub>

²chichi *n* **1** : frilly or elaborate ornamentation **2** : AFFECTATION, PRECIOSITY **3** : CHIC

chick \ˈchik\ *n* **1 a** : CHICKEN; *esp* : one newly hatched **b** : the young of any bird **2** : CHILD **3** : a young woman

chick·a·dee \ˈchik-ə-(ˌ)dē\ *n* [imit.] : any of several crestless American titmice (genus *Penthestes* or *Parus*) usu. with the crown of the head sharply demarked and darker than the body

chick·a·ree \ˈchik-ə-ˌrē\ *n* [imit.] : an American red squirrel (*Sciurus hudsonicus*); *also* : a related squirrel

Chick·a·saw \ˈchik-ə-ˌsȯ\ *n, pl* **Chickasaw** *or* **Chickasaws** **1** : a member of an Amerindian people of Mississippi and Alabama **2** : a dialect of Choctaw spoken by the Chickasaw

¹chick·en \ˈchik-ən\ *n* [ME *chiken*, fr. OE *cicen* young chicken; akin to OE *cocc* cock] **1 a** : the common domestic fowl (*Gallus gallus*) esp. when young; *also* : its flesh used as food **b** : any of various birds or their young **2** : a young woman **3 a** : COWARD **b** : any of various contests in which the participants risk personal safety in order to see which one will give up first **4** *slang* : the petty details of duty or discipline

²chicken *adj* **1** *slang* : afraid to do something : SCARED **2** *slang* : insistent on petty esp. military discipline

³chicken *vi* **chick·ened; chick·en·ing** \ˈchik-(ə-)niŋ\ : to lose one's nerve — usu. used with *out* <seemed to exhibit courage, manliness, and conviction when others ~*ed* out —J. R. Seeley>

chicken colonel *n* [fr. the eagle serving as his insignia] *slang* : COLONEL 1a

chicken feed *n, slang* : a paltry sum (as in profits or wages)

chicken hawk *n* : a hawk that preys or is believed to prey on chickens

chick·en·heart·ed \ˌchik-ən-ˈhärt-əd\ *adj* : TIMID, COWARDLY

chick·en-liv·ered \-ˈliv-ərd\ *adj* : FAINTHEARTED, COWARDLY

chicken pox *n* : an acute contagious virus disease esp. of children that is marked by low-grade fever and formation of vesicles

chicken snake *n* : RAT SNAKE

chicken wire *n* [fr. its use for making enclosures for chickens] : a light galvanized wire netting of hexagonal mesh

chick-pea \ˈchik-ˌpē\ *n* [by folk etymology fr. ME *chiche*, fr. MF, fr. L *cicer*] : an Asiatic leguminous herb (*Cicer arietinum*) cultivated for its short pods with one or two seeds; *also* : its seed

chick·weed \ˈchik-ˌwēd\ *n* : any of various low-growing small-leaved weedy plants of the pink family (esp. genera *Arenaria*, *Cerastium*, and *Stellaria*) several of which are relished by birds or used as potherbs

chi·cle \ˈchik-əl, -lē\ *n* [Sp, fr. Nahautl *chictli*] : a gum from the latex of the sapodilla used as the chief ingredient of chewing gum

chi·co \ˈchē-(ˌ)kō, ˈchik-(ˌ)ō\ *n, pl* **chicos** [modif. of Sp *chicalote*] : a common greasewood (*Sarcobatus vermiculatus*) of the western U.S.

chic·o·ry \ˈchik-(ə-)rē\ *n, pl* **-ries** [ME *cicoree*, fr. MF *cichorée*, *chicorée*, fr. L *cichoreum*, fr. Gk *kichoreia*] **1** : a thick-rooted usu. blue-flowered European perennial composite herb (*Cichorium intybus*) widely grown for its roots and as a salad plant **2** : the dried ground roasted root of chicory used to flavor or adulterate coffee

chide \ˈchīd\ *vb* **chid** \ˈchid\ *or* **chid·ed** \ˈchīd-əd\; **chid** *or* **chid·den** \ˈchid-ᵊn\ *or* **chided; chid·ing** \ˈchīd-iŋ\ [ME *chiden*, fr. OE *cīdan* to quarrel, chide, fr. *cīd* strife] *vi* : to speak out in angry or displeased rebuke ~ *vt* : to voice disapproval to : reproach in a usu. mild and constructive manner : SCOLD ***syn*** see REPROVE

[1]**chief** \ˈchēf\ *n* [ME, fr. OF, head, chief, fr. L *caput* head — more at HEAD] **1 :** the upper part of a heraldic field **2 :** the head of a body of persons or an organization : LEADER <~ of police> **3 :** the principal or most valuable part — **chief·dom** \-dəm\ *n* — **chief·ship** \-ˌship\ *n* — **in chief :** in the chief position or place — often used in titles <commander *in chief*>

[2]**chief** *adj* **1 :** accorded highest rank or office <~ librarian> **2 :** of greatest importance, significance, or influence <the ~ reasons>

[3]**chief** *adv, archaic* : CHIEFLY

chief executive *n* **:** a principal executive officer: as **a :** the president of a republic **b :** the governor of a state

chief justice *n* **:** the presiding or principal judge of a court of justice

[1]**chief·ly** \ˈchē-flē\ *adv* **1 :** most importantly : PRINCIPALLY, ESPECIALLY **2 :** for the most part : MOSTLY, MAINLY

[2]**chiefly** *adj* **:** of or relating to a chief <~ duties>

chief master sergeant *n* **:** a noncommissioned officer in the air force ranking above a senior master sergeant

chief master sergeant of the air force : the ranking noncommissioned officer in the air force serving as adviser to the chief of staff

chief of naval operations : the commanding officer of the navy and a member of the Joint Chiefs of Staff

chief of staff 1 : the ranking officer of a staff in the armed forces serving as principal adviser to a commander **2 :** the commanding officer of the army or air force and a member of the Joint Chiefs of Staff

chief of state : the formal head of a national state as distinguished from the head of the government

chief petty officer *n* **:** an enlisted man in the navy or coast guard ranking above a petty officer first class and below a senior chief petty officer

chief·tain \ˈchēf-tən\ *n* [ME *chieftaine,* fr. MF *chevetain,* fr. LL *capitaneus* chief — more at CAPTAIN] **:** a chief esp. of a band, tribe, or clan — **chief·tain·ship** \-ˌship\ *n*

chief·tain·cy \-sē\ *n, pl* **-cies 1 :** the rank, dignity, office, or rule of a chieftain **2 :** a region or a people ruled by a chief : CHIEFDOM

chief warrant officer *n* **:** a warrant officer of senior rank in the armed forces; *also* **:** a commissioned officer in the navy or coast guard ranking below an ensign

chiel \ˈchē(ə)l\ *or* **chield** \ˈchē(ə)ld\ *n* [ME (Sc) *cheld,* alter. of ME *child* child] *chiefly Scot* : FELLOW, LAD

chiff·chaff \ˈchif-ˌchaf\ *n* [imit.] **:** a small grayish European warbler (*Phylloscopus collybita*)

[1]**chif·fon** \shif-ˈän, ˈshif-ˌ\ *n* [F, lit., rag, fr. *chiffe* old rag, alter. of MF *chipe,* fr. ME *chip* chip] **1 :** an ornamental addition (as a knot of ribbons) to a woman's dress **2 :** a sheer fabric esp. of silk

[2]**chiffon** *adj* **1 :** resembling chiffon in sheerness or softness **2 :** having a light delicate texture achieved usu. by adding whipped egg whites or whipped gelatin <lemon ~ pie>

chif·fo·nier \ˌshif-ə-ˈni(ə)r\ *n* [F *chiffonnier,* fr. *chiffon*] **:** a high narrow chest of drawers

chif·fo·robe \ˈshif-ə-ˌrōb\ *n* [*chiffo*nier + ward*robe*] **:** a combination of wardrobe and chest of drawers

chiffonier

chig·ger \ˈchig-ər, ˈjig-\ *n* **1 :** CHIGOE 1 **2** [of African origin; akin to Wolof *jiga* insect] **:** a 6-legged mite larva (family Trombiculidae) that sucks the blood of vertebrates and causes intense irritation

chi·gnon \ˈshēn-ˌyän\ *n* [F, fr. MF *chaignon* chain, collar, nape] **:** a knot of hair that is worn at the back of the head and esp. at the nape of the neck

chi·goe \ˈchig-(ˌ)ō, ˈchē-(ˌ)gō\ *n* [of Cariban origin; akin to Galibi *chico* chigoe] **1 :** a tropical flea (*Tunga penetrans*) of which the fertile female causes great discomfort by burrowing under the skin— called also *chigger* **2 :** CHIGGER 2

Chi·hua·hua \chə-ˈwä-(ˌ)wä, shə-, -wə\ *n* [MexSp, fr. *Chihuahua,* Mexico] **:** a very small round-headed large-eared short-coated dog believed to antedate Aztec civilization

chil·blain \ˈchil-ˌblān\ *n* [[3]*chill*] **:** an inflammatory swelling or sore caused by exposure (as of the feet or hands) to cold

child \ˈchī(ə)ld\ *n, pl* **chil·dren** \ˈchil-drən, -dərn\ *often attrib* [ME, fr. OE *cild;* akin to Goth *kilthei* womb, Skt *jathara* belly] **1 a :** an unborn or recently born person **b** *dial* **:** a female infant **2 a :** a young person esp. between infancy and youth **b :** a childlike or childish person **c :** a person not yet of age **3** *usu* **childe** \ˈchī(ə)ld\ *archaic* **:** a youth of noble birth **4 a :** a son or daughter of human parents **b :** DESCENDANT **5 :** one strongly influenced by another or by a place or state of affairs **6 :** PRODUCT, RESULT <barbed wire . . . is truly a ~ of the plains —W. P. Webb> — **child·less** \ˈchī(ə)l-(d)ləs\ *adj* — **child·less·ness** *n* — **with child :** PREGNANT

child·bear·ing \ˈchīl(d)-ˌbar-iŋ, -ˌber-\ *n* **:** the act of bringing forth children : PARTURITION — **childbearing** *adj*

child·bed \-ˌbed\ *n* **:** the condition of a woman in childbirth

childbed fever *n* : PUERPERAL FEVER

childbirth \ˈchīl(d)-ˌbərth\ *n* : PARTURITION

child·hood \ˈchīld-ˌhu̇d\ *n* **1 :** the state or period of being a child **2 :** the early period in the development of something <in the ~ of our culture —Michael Novak>

child·ish \ˈchīl-dish\ *adj* **1 :** of, relating to, or befitting a child or childhood <a clear ~ voice> <calling back ~ memories> **2 a :** marked by or suggestive of immaturity and lack of poise <a ~ spiteful remark> **b :** lacking complexity : SIMPLE <it's a ~ device, but it works> **c :** deteriorated with age esp. in mind : SENILE <the old man was becoming ~> — **child·ish·ly** *adv* — **child·ish·ness** *n*

syn CHILDISH, CHILDLIKE *shared meaning element* **:** having qualities natural or suitable to a child. CHILDISH tends to suggest unpleasing qualities (as fretful impatience or undeveloped taste and mentality) that are appropriate to children but deplorable in adults <a *childish* determination to excel> CHILDLIKE usu. suggests such attractive and admirable qualities of childhood as innocence, straightforwardness, or trust <had a *childlike* faith>

child·like \ˈchī(ə)l-ˌ(d)līk\ *adj* **:** of, relating to, or resembling a child or childhood; *esp* **:** marked by innocence, trust, and ingenuousness **syn** see CHILDISH — **child·like·ness** *n*

child·ly \ˈchī(ə)l-(d)lē\ *adj* : CHILDLIKE

child's play *n* **1 :** an extremely simple task or act **2 :** something that is insignificant <his injury was *child's play* compared with the damage he inflicted>

Chile–bells \ˈchil-ē-ˌbelz\ *n pl but sing or pl in constr* : COPIHUE

Chile saltpeter \ˈchil-ē-\ *n* [*Chile,* So. America] **:** sodium nitrate esp. occurring naturally (as in caliche) — called also *Chile niter*

chili *or* **chile** *or* **chil·li** \ˈchil-ē\ *n, pl* **chil·ies** *or* **chil·es** *or* **chil·lies** [Sp *chile,* fr. Nahuatl *chilli*] **1 a :** HOT PEPPER **b** *usu chilli, chiefly Brit* **:** a pepper whether hot or sweet **2 a :** a thick sauce of meat and chilies **b :** CHILI CON CARNE

chil·i·ad \ˈkil-ē-ˌad, -əd\ *n* [LL *chiliad-, chilias,* fr. Gk, fr. *chilioi* thousand — more at MILE] **1 :** a group of 1000 **2 :** a period of 1000 years : MILLENNIUM

chil·i·asm \ˈkil-ē-ˌaz-əm\ *n* [NL *chiliasmus,* fr. LL *chiliastes* one that believes in chiliasm, fr. *chilias*] : MILLENARIANISM — **chil·i·ast** \-ē-ˌast, -ē-əst\ *n* — **chil·i·as·tic** \ˌkil-ē-ˈas-tik\ *adj*

chili con car·ne \ˌchil-ē-ˌkän-ˈkär-nē, -kən-\ *n* [Sp *chile con carne* chili with meat] **:** a spiced stew of ground beef and minced chilies or chili powder usu. with beans

chili sauce *n* **:** a spiced tomato sauce usu. made with red and green peppers

[1]**chill** \ˈchil\ *vb* [ME *chillen,* fr. *chile* cold, frost, fr. OE *cele;* akin to OE *ceald* cold] *vi* **1 a :** to become cold **b :** to shiver or quake with or as if with cold **2 :** to become taken with a chill **3** *of a metal* **:** to become surface-hardened by sudden cooling ~ *vt* **1 a :** to make cold or chilly **b :** to make cool esp. without freezing **2 :** to affect as if with cold : DISPIRIT <were ~*ed* by the drab austerity and the police-state atmosphere — William Attwood> **3 :** to harden the surface of (metal) by sudden cooling — **chill·ing·ly** \-iŋ-lē\ *adv*

[2]**chill** *adj* **1 a :** moderately cold **b :** COLD, RAW **2 :** affected by cold <~ travelers> **3 :** DISTANT, FORMAL <a ~ reception> **4 :** DEPRESSING, DISPIRITING <~ penury —Thomas Gray> — **chill·ness** *n*

[3]**chill** *n* **1 a :** a sensation of cold accompanied by shivering **b :** a disagreeable sensation of coldness **2 :** a moderate but disagreeable degree of cold **3 :** a check to enthusiasm or warmth of feeling <felt the ~ of his opponent's stare>

chill·er \ˈchil-ər\ *n* **1 :** one that chills **2 :** an eerie or frightening story of murder, violence, or the supernatural

chill factor *n* : WINDCHILL

chil·lum \ˈchil-əm\ *n* [Hindi *cilam,* fr. Per *chilam*] **1 :** the part of a water pipe that contains the substance (as tobacco or hashish) which is smoked; *also* **:** a quantity of a substance thus smoked **2 :** a funnel-shaped clay pipe for smoking

chilly \ˈchil-ē\ *adj* **chill·i·er; -est 1 :** noticeably cold : CHILLING **2 :** unpleasantly affected by cold **3 :** lacking warmth of feeling **4 :** tending to arouse fear or apprehension <~ suspicions> — **chill·i·ly** \ˈchil-ə-lē\ *adv* — **chill·i·ness** \ˈchil-ē-nəs\ *n*

chi·mae·ra \kī-ˈmir-ə, kə-\ *n* [NL, genus name, fr. L, chimera] **:** any of a family (Chimaeridae) of marine elasmobranch fishes with a tapering or threadlike tail and usu. no anal fin

[1]**chime** \ˈchīm\ *n* [ME, cymbal, fr. OF *chimbe,* fr. L *cymbalum* cymbal] **1 :** an apparatus for chiming a bell or set of bells **2 a :** a musically tuned set of bells **b :** one of a set of objects giving a bell-like sound when struck **3 a :** the sound of a set of bells — usu. used in pl. **b :** a musical sound suggesting that of bells **4 :** ACCORD, HARMONY <such happy ~ of fact and theory —Henry Maudsley>

[2]**chime** *vb* **chimed; chim·ing** *vi* **1 a :** to make a musical and esp. a harmonious sound **b :** to make the sounds of a chime **2 :** to be or act in accord <the music and the mood *chimed* well together> ~ *vt* **1 :** to cause to sound musically by striking **2 :** to produce by chiming **3 :** to call or indicate by chiming <the clock *chimed* midnight> **4 :** to utter repetitively : DIN 2 — **chim·er** *n*

[3]**chime** \ˈchīm\ *n* [ME *chimbe,* fr. OE *cimb-;* akin to OE *camb* comb] **:** the edge or rim of a cask

chime in *vi* **1 :** to break into a conversation or discussion esp. to express an opinion **2 :** to combine harmoniously <the artist's illustrations *chime in* perfectly with the text —*Book Production*> ~ *vt* **:** to remark while chiming in

chi·me·ra *or* **chi·mae·ra** \kī-ˈmir-ə, kə-\ *n* [L *chimaera,* fr. Gk *chimaira* she-goat, chimera; akin to Gk *cheimōn* winter — more at HIBERNATE] **1 a** *cap* **:** a fire-breathing she-monster in Greek mythology having a lion's head, a goat's body, and a serpent's tail **b :** an imaginary monster compounded of incongruous parts **2 :** an illusion or fabrication of the mind; *esp* **:** an unrealizable dream <a fancy, a ~ in my brain, troubles me in my prayer —John Donne> **3 :** an individual, organ, or part consisting of tissues of diverse genetic constitution and occurring esp. in plants and most frequently at a graft union

chi·mere \shə-ˈmi(ə)r, chə-\ *n* [ME *chimmer, chemeyr*] **:** a loose sleeveless robe (as of black satin) worn by Anglican bishops over the rochet

chi·me·ri·cal \kī-ˈmer-i-kəl, kə-, -ˈmir-\ *or* **chi·me·ric** \-ik\ *adj* [*chimera*] **1 :** existing only as the product of unrestrained imagination : fantastically visionary or improbable **2 :** inclined to fantastic schemes or projects ***syn*** see IMAGINARY ***ant*** feasible — **chi·me·ri·cal·ly** \-i-k(ə-)lē\ *adv*

chi·me·rism \kī-'mi(ə)r-,iz-əm, kə-; 'kī-mə-,riz-\ *n* : the state of being a genetic chimera

chim·ney \'chim-nē\ *n, pl* **chimneys** [ME, fr. MF *cheminée,* fr. LL *caminata,* fr. L *caminus* furnace, fireplace, fr. Gk *kaminos;* akin to Gk *kamara* vault] **1** *dial* : FIREPLACE, HEARTH **2** : a vertical structure incorporated into a building and enclosing a flue or flues that carry off smoke; *esp* : the part of such a structure extending above a roof **3** : SMOKESTACK **4** : a tube usu. of glass placed around a flame (as of a lamp) **5** : something (as a narrow cleft in rock) resembling a chimney

chim·ney·piece \'chim-nē-,pēs\ *n* : an ornamental construction over and around a fireplace that includes the mantel

chimney pot *n* : a usu. earthenware pipe placed at the top of a chimney

chimney sweep *n* : one whose occupation is cleaning soot from chimney flues — called also *chimney sweeper*

chimney swift *n* : a small sooty-gray bird (*Chaetura pelagica*) with long narrow wings that often builds its nest inside an unused chimney — called also *chimney swallow*

chimp \'chimp, 'shimp\ *n* : CHIMPANZEE

chim·pan·zee \,chim-,pan-'zē, ,shim-, -pən-; chim-'pan-zē, shim-\ *n* [Kongo dial. *chimpenzi*] : an anthropoid ape (*Pan troglodytes*) of equatorial Africa that is smaller, more arboreal, and less fierce than the gorilla

1**chin** \'chin\ *n* [ME, fr. OE *cinn;* akin to OHG *kinni* chin, L *gena* cheek, Gk *genys* jaw, cheek] **1** : the lower portion of the face lying below the lower lip and including the prominence of the lower jaw **2** : the surface beneath or between the branches of the lower jaw — **chin·less** \-ləs\ *adj*

2**chin** *vb* **chinned; chin·ning** *vt* **1** : to bring to or hold with the chin <*chinned* his violin> **2** : to raise (oneself) while hanging by the hands until the chin is level with the support ~ *vi, slang* : to talk idly : CHATTER

Chin *abbr* Chinese

chi·na \'chī-nə\ *n* [Per *chīnī* Chinese porcelain] **1** : PORCELAIN; *also* : vitreous porcelain wares (as dishes, vases, or ornaments) for domestic use **2** : earthenware or porcelain tableware <set the table with the good ~> **3** : CROCKERY

China aster *n* : a common annual garden aster (*Callistephus chinensis*) native to northern China that occurs in many showy forms

chi·na·ber·ry \'chī-nə-,ber-ē, *South also* 'chā-nē-,ber-ē\ *n* **1** : a soapberry (*Sapindus saponaria*) of the southern U.S. and Mexico **2** : a small Asiatic tree (*Melia azedarach* of the mahogany family) naturalized in the southern U.S. where it is widely planted for shade or ornament

china clay *n* : KAOLIN

china closet *n* : a cabinet or cupboard for the storage or display of household china

Chi·na·man \'chī-nə-mən\ *n* : a native of China : CHINESE — often taken to be offensive

China rose *n* **1** : any of numerous garden roses derived from a shrubby Chinese rose (*Rosa chinensis*) **2** : a large showy-flowered Asiatic hibiscus (*Hibiscus rosa-sinensis*)

Chi·na·town \'chī-nə-,taun\ *n* : the Chinese quarter of a city

China tree *n* : CHINABERRY

chi·na·ware \'chī-nə-,wa(ə)r, -,we(ə)r\ *n* : tableware made of china

chin·bone \'chin-'bōn, -,bōn\ *n* : MANDIBLE; *esp* : the median anterior part of the human mandible

chinch \'chinch\ *n* [Sp *chinche,* fr. L *cimic-, cimex*] : BEDBUG

chinch bug *n* : a small black-and-white bug (*Blissus leucopterus*) very destructive to cereal grasses

chin·che·rin·chee \,chin-chə-ri(n)-'chē, ,chiŋ-kə-\ *n, pl* **chincherinchee** *or* **chincherinchees** [origin unknown] : a southern African perennial bulbous herb (*Ornithogalum thyrsoides*) with long-lasting spikes of starry white blossoms

chin·chil·la \chin-'chil-ə\ *n* [Sp] **1** : a small rodent (*Chinchilla laniger*) that is the size of a large squirrel, has very soft fur of a pearly gray color, is native to the mountains of Peru and Chile, and is extensively bred in captivity; *also* : its fur **2** : a heavy twilled woolen coating

1**chine** \'chīn\ *n* [ME, fr. MF *eschine,* of Gmc origin; akin to OHG *scina* shinbone, needle — more at SHIN] **1** : BACKBONE, SPINE; *also* : a cut of meat or fish including the backbone or part of it and the surrounding flesh **2** : RIDGE, CREST **3** : the intersection of the bottom and the sides of a flat or V-bottomed boat

2**chine** *vt* **chined; chin·ing** : to cut through the backbone of (as in butchering)

Chi·nese \chī-'nēz, -'nēs\ *n, pl* **Chinese** **1 a** : a native or inhabitant of China **b** : a person of Chinese descent **2** : a group of related languages used by the people of China that are often mutually unintelligible in their spoken form but share a single system of writing and that constitute a branch of the Sino-Tibetan language family; *specif* : MANDARIN — **Chinese** *adj*

Chinese boxes *n pl* : a set of boxes graduated in size so that each fits into the next larger one

Chinese cabbage *n* : either of two Asiatic brassicas (*Brassica pekinensis* and *B. chinensis*) widely used as greens

Chinese checkers *n pl but sing or pl in constr* : a game in which each player seeks to be the first to transfer a set of marbles from a home point to the opposite point of a pitted 6-pointed star by single moves or jumps

Chinese chestnut *n* : an Asiatic chestnut (*Castanea mollissima*) that is resistant to chestnut blight

Chinese copy *n* : an exact imitation or duplicate that includes defects as well as desired qualities

Chinese date *n* : an Asiatic jujube (*Ziziphus jujuba*)

Chinese lacquer *n* : LACQUER 1b

Chinese lantern *n* : a collapsible lantern of thin colored paper

Chinese puzzle *n* **1** : an intricate or ingenious puzzle **2** : something intricate and obscure

Chinese wall *n* [*Chinese Wall,* a defensive wall built in the 3d cent. B.C. between China and Mongolia] : a strong barrier; *esp* : a serious obstacle to understanding

Ching *or* **Ch'ing** \'chiŋ\ *n* [Chin (Pek) *ch'ing*[1]] : a Manchu dynasty in China dated 1644–1912 and the last imperial dynasty

1**chink** \'chiŋk\ *n* [prob. alter. of ME *chin* crack, fissure, fr. OE *cine;* akin to OE *cīnan* to gape, OHG *chīnan* to split open] **1** : a small cleft, slit, or fissure <a ~ in the curtain> **2** : a means of evasion or escape : LOOPHOLE <a ~ in the law> **3** : a narrow beam of light shining through a chink

2**chink** *vt* : to fill the chinks of (as by caulking) <~ a log cabin>

3**chink** *n* [imit.] **1** : a short sharp sound **2** *archaic* : COIN, MONEY

4**chink** *vi* : to make a slight sharp metallic sound ~ *vt* : to cause to make a chink

chi·no \'chē-(,)nō, 'shē-\ *n, pl* **chinos** [AmerSp] **1** : a usu. khaki cotton twill of the type used for military uniforms **2** *pl* : an article of clothing made of chino

Chi·no- \,chī-(,)nō\ *comb form* : Chinese and <*Chino*-Japanese>

chi·noi·se·rie \shēn-'wäz-(ə-)rē, ,shēn-,wäz-(ə-)'rē\ *n* [F, fr. *chinois* Chinese, fr. *Chine* China] : a style in art (as in decoration) reflecting Chinese qualities or motifs; *also* : an object or decoration in this style

Chi·nook \shə-'nuk, chə-, -'nük\ *n, pl* **Chinook** *or* **Chinooks** [Chehalis *Tsinúk*] **1** : a member of an Amerindian people of Oregon **2** : a Chinookan language of the Chinook and other nearby peoples **3** *not cap* **a** : a warm moist southwest wind of the coast from Oregon northward **b** : a warm dry wind that descends the eastern slopes of the Rocky mountains

Chi·nook·an \-ən\ *n* : a language family of Washington and Oregon — **Chinookan** *adj*

Chinook Jargon *n* : a pidgin language based on Chinook and other Indian languages, French, and English and formerly used as a lingua franca in the northwestern U.S. and on the Pacific coast of Canada and Alaska

Chinook salmon *n* : a large commercially important salmon (*Oncorhynchus tshawytscha*) that occurs in the northern Pacific ocean and usu. has red flesh

chin·qua·pin \'chiŋ-ki-,pin\ *n* [alter. of earlier *chincomen,* of Algonquian origin] **1** : any of several trees (genera *Castanea* or *Castanopsis*); *esp* : a dwarf chestnut (*Castanea pumila*) of the U.S. **2** : the edible nut of a chinquapin

chintz \'chin(t)s\ *n* [earlier *chints,* pl. of *chint,* fr. Hindi *chīṭ*] **1** : a printed calico from India **2** : a usu. glazed printed cotton fabric

chintzy \'chin(t)-sē\ *adj* **chintz·i·er; -est** **1** : decorated with or as if with chintz **2** : GAUDY, CHEAP <~ toys>

chin–up \'chin-,əp\ *n* : the act or an instance of chinning oneself performed esp. as a conditioning exercise

chin–wag \-,wag\ *n, slang* : CONVERSATION, CHAT

1**chip** \'chip\ *n* [ME] **1 a** : a small usu. thin and flat piece (as of wood or stone) cut, struck, or flaked off **b** (1) : a small thin slice of food; *esp* : POTATO CHIP (2) : FRENCH FRY **2** : something small, worthless, or trivial **3 a** : one of the counters used as a token for money in poker and other games **b** *pl* : MONEY — used esp. in the phrase *in the chips* **4** : a piece of dried dung — usu. used in combination <cow ~> **5** : a flaw left after a chip is removed **6** : INTEGRATED CIRCUIT **7** : CHIP SHOT — **chip off the old block** : a child that resembles his parent — **chip on one's shoulder** : a challenging or belligerent attitude

2**chip** *vb* **chipped; chip·ping** *vt* **1 a** : to cut or hew with an edged tool **b** (1) : to cut or break (a small piece) from something (2) : to cut or break a fragment from **2** *Brit* : CHAFF, BANTER ~ *vi* **1** : to break off in small pieces **2** : to play a chip shot

chip·board \'chip-,bō(ə)rd, -,bȯ(ə)rd\ *n* : a paperboard made from waste paper

chip in *vb* : CONTRIBUTE <everyone *chipped in* for the gift>

chip·munk \'chip-,məŋk\ *n* [alter. of earlier *chitmunk,* of Algonquian origin; akin to Ojibwa *atchitamō̃* squirrel] : any of numerous small striped semiterrestrial American squirrels (genera *Tamias* and *Eutamias*) — called also *ground squirrel*

chipped beef \'chip(t)-\ *n* : smoked dried beef sliced thin

Chip·pen·dale \'chip-ən-,dāl\ *adj* [Thomas *Chippendale*] : of or relating to an 18th century English furniture style characterized by graceful outline and often ornate rococo ornamentation

1**chip·per** \'chip-ər\ *n* : one that chips

2**chipper** *adj* [perh. alter. of E dial. *kipper* (lively)] : GAY, SPRIGHTLY

Chip·pe·wa \'chip-ə-,wȯ, -,wä, -,wā, -wə\ *n, pl* **Chippewa** *or* **Chippewas** : OJIBWA

chip shot *n* : a short usu. low approach shot in golf that lofts the ball to the green and allows it to roll

chir- *or* **chiro-** *comb form* [L, fr. Gk *cheir-, cheiro-,* fr. *cheir;* akin to Hitt *kesar* hand] : hand <*chiro*practic>

Chi–Rho \'kī-'rō, 'kē-\ *n, pl* **Chi–Rhos** [*chi* + *rho*] : a Christian monogram and symbol formed from the first two letters X and P of the Greek word for *Christ* — called also *Christogram*

Chir·i·ca·hua \,chir-ə-'kä-wə\ *n, pl* **Chiricahua** *or* **Chiricahuas** : a member of an Apache people of Arizona

chirk \'chərk\ *vb* [ME *charken, chirken* to creak, chirp, fr. OE *cearcian* to creak; akin to OE *cracian* to crack] : CHEER <play with her and ~ her up a little —Harriet B. Stowe>

chi·rog·ra·pher \kī-'räg-rə-fər\ *n* : one who studies or practices chirography

chi·rog·ra·phy \-fē\ *n* **1** : HANDWRITING, PENMANSHIP **2** : CALLIGRAPHY 1 — **chi·ro·graph·ic** \,kī-rə-'graf-ik\ *or* **chi·ro·graph·i·cal** \-i-kəl\ *adj*

chi·ro·man·cy \'kī-rə-,man(t)-sē\ *n* [prob. fr. MF *chiromancie,* fr. ML *chiromantia,* fr. Gk *cheir-* chir- + *-manteia* -mancy — more at -MANCY] : PALMISTRY — **chi·ro·man·cer** \-,man(t)-sər\ *n*

chi·ron·o·mid \kī-'rän-ə-məd\ *n* [deriv. of Gk *cheironomos* one who gestures with his hands] : any of a family (Chironomidae) of midges that lack piercing mouthparts

chi·rop·o·dy \kə-'räp-əd-ē, shə- *also* kī-\ *n* [*chir-* + *pod-,* fr. its original concern with both hands and feet] : PODIATRY — **chi·rop·o·dist** \-əd-əst\ *n*

chi·ro·prac·tic \ˈkī-rə-ˌprak-tik\ *n* [*chir-* + Gk *praktikos* practical, operative — more at PRACTICAL] : a system of healing which holds that disease results from a lack of normal nerve function and which employs manipulation and specific adjustment of body structures (as the spinal column) — **chi·ro·prac·tor** \-tər\ *n*

chi·rop·ter \kī-ˈräp-tər, ˈkī-ˌ\ *n* [deriv. of Gk *cheir* hand + *pteron* wing — more at FEATHER] : ³BAT — **chi·rop·ter·an** \kī-ˈräp-tə-rən\ *adj or n*

chirp \ˈchərp\ *n* [imit.] : the characteristic short sharp sound esp. of a small bird or insect — **chirp** *vi* — **chirp·i·ly** \ˈchər-pə-lē\ *adv* — **chirpy** \ˈchər-pē\ *adj*

chirr \ˈchər\ *n* [imit.] : the short vibrant or trilled sound characteristic of an insect (as a grasshopper or cicada) — **chirr** *vi*

¹**chir·rup** \ˈchər-əp, ˈchir-\ *vi* [imit.] **1** : CHIRP **2** : to make a sound like a chirrup ~ *vt* : to utter by chirruping

²**chirrup** *n* : CHIRP

chi·rur·geon \kī-ˈrər-jən\ *n* [ME *cirurgian*, fr. OF *cirurgien*, fr. *cirurgie* surgery] *archaic* : SURGEON

¹**chis·el** \ˈchiz-əl\ *n* [ME, fr. ONF, prob. alter. of *chisoir* goldsmith's chisel, fr. (assumed) VL *caesorium* cutting instrument, fr. L *caesus*, pp. of *caedere* to cut — more at CONCISE] : a metal tool with a cutting edge at the end of a blade used in dressing, shaping, or working a solid material (as wood, stone, or metal)

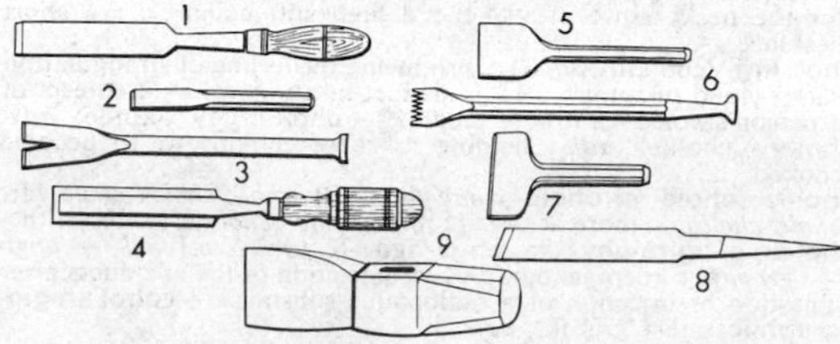

chisels: *1* socket paring chisel, *2* cold chisel, *3* box chisel, *4* beveled firmer chisel, *5* floor chisel, *6* stonecutter's chisel, *7* bricklayer's chisel, *8* turning chisel, *9* blacksmith's chisel

²**chisel** *vb* **-eled** *or* **-elled; -el·ing** *or* **-el·ling** \ˈchiz-(ə-)liŋ\ *vt* **1** : to cut or work with or as if with a chisel **2** : to employ shrewd or unfair practices on in order to obtain one's end; *also* : to obtain by such practices <~ a job> ~ *vi* **1** : to work with a chisel **2 a** : to employ shrewd or unfair practices **b** : to thrust oneself : INTRUDE <~ in on a racket> — **chis·el·er** \-(ə-)lər\ *n*

chis·eled *or* **chis·elled** \ˈchiz-əld\ *adj* **1** : cut or wrought with a chisel **2** : appearing as if chiseled : CLEAR-CUT <sharply ~ features>

chi–square \ˈkī-ˈskwa(ə)r, -ˈskwe(ə)r\ *n* : a statistic that is a sum of terms each of which is a quotient obtained by dividing the square of the difference between the observed and theoretical values of a quantity by the theoretical value

chi–square distribution *n* : a probability density function that gives the distribution of the sum of the squares of a number of independent random variables each with a normal distribution with zero mean and unit variance, that has the property that the sum of two random variables with such a distribution also has one, and that is widely used in testing statistical hypotheses esp. about the theoretical and observed values of a quantity and about population variances and standard deviations

¹**chit** \ˈchit\ *n* [ME *chitte* kitten, cub] **1** : CHILD **2** : a pert young woman

²**chit** *n* [Hindi *ciṭṭhī*] **1** : a short letter or note; *esp* : a signed voucher of a small debt (as for food) **2** : a small slip of paper with writing on it

chit·chat \ˈchit-ˌchat\ *n* [redupl. of *chat*] : SMALL TALK, GOSSIP — **chitchat** *vi*

chi·tin \ˈkīt-ᵊn\ *n* [F *chitine*, fr. Gk *chitōn* chiton, tunic] : a horny polysaccharide that forms part of the hard outer integument esp. of insects and crustaceans — **chi·tin·ous** \ˈkīt-ᵊn-əs, ˈkīt-nəs\ *adj*

chi·ton \ˈkīt-ᵊn, ˈkī-ˌtän\ *n* [NL, genus name, fr. Gk *chitōn* tunic; of Sem origin; akin to Heb *kuttōneth* tunic] **1** : any of an order (Polyplacophora) of elongated bilaterally symmetrical marine mollusks with a dorsal shell of calcareous plates **2** [Gk *chitōn*] : the basic garment of ancient Greece worn usu. knee-length by men and full-length by women

chit·ter \ˈchit-ər\ *vi* [ME *chiteren*, prob. of imit. origin] : TWITTER, CHIRP; *also* : CHATTER

chit·ter·lings *or* **chit·lings** *or* **chit·lins** \ˈchit-lənz\ *n pl* [ME *chiterling*] : the intestines of hogs esp. when prepared as food

chi·val·ric \shə-ˈval-rik\ *adj* : relating to chivalry : CHIVALROUS

chiv·al·rous \ˈshiv-əl-rəs\ *adj* **1** : VALIANT **2** : of, relating to, or characteristic of chivalry and knight-errantry **3 a** : marked by honor, generosity, and courtesy **b** : marked by gracious courtesy and high-minded consideration esp. to women ***syn*** see CIVIL ***ant*** unchivalrous, churlish — **chiv·al·rous·ly** *adv* — **chiv·al·rous·ness** *n*

chiv·al·ry \ˈshiv-əl-rē\ *n, pl* **-ries** [ME *chivalrie*, fr. OF *chevalerie*, fr. *chevalier*] **1** : mounted men-at-arms **2** *archaic* **a** : martial valor **b** : knightly skill **3** : gallant or distinguished gentlemen **4** : the system, spirit, or customs of medieval knighthood **5** : the qualities (as bravery, honor, protection of the weak, and generous treatment of foes) of the ideal knight : chivalrous conduct

chive \ˈchīv\ *n* [ME, fr. ONF, fr. L *cepa* onion] : a perennial plant (*Allium schoenoprasum*) related to the onion

chivy *or* **chiv·vy** \ˈchiv-ē\ *vt* **chiv·ied** *or* **chiv·vied; chivy·ing** *or* **chiv·vy·ing** [*chivy*, n. (chase, hunt), prob. fr. E dial. *Chevy Chase* chase, confusion, fr. the name of a ballad describing the battle of Otterburn (1388)] **1** : to tease or annoy with persistent petty attacks : HARRY, HARASS **2** : MANEUVER, MANIPULATE ***syn*** see BAIT

chlam·ydo·mo·nas \ˌklam-əd-ə-ˈmō-nəs\ *n* [NL, genus name, fr. L *chlamyd-*, *chlamys* + NL *monas* monad] : any of a genus (*Chlamydomonas*) of single-celled photosynthetic flagellates or algae that have two flagella and are common in fresh water and damp soil

chla·mydo·spore \klə-ˈmid-ə-ˌspō(ə)r, -ˌspȯ(ə)r\ *n* [L *chlamyd-*, *chlamys* + ISV *spore*] : a thick-walled usu. resting spore — **chla·mydo·spor·ic** \klə-ˌmid-ə-ˈspōr-ik, -ˈspȯr-\ *adj*

chla·mys \ˈklam-əs, ˈklām-əs\ *n, pl* **chla·mys·es** *or* **chla·my·des** \-ə-ˌdēz\ [L *chlamyd-*, *chlamys*, fr. Gk] : a short oblong mantle worn by young men of ancient Greece

Chloe \ˈklō-ē\ *n* [L, fr. Gk *Chloē*] : a lover of Daphnis in a Greek pastoral romance

chlor- *or* **chloro-** *comb form* [NL, fr. Gk, fr. *chlōros* greenish yellow — more at YELLOW] **1** : green <*chlor*ine> <*chlor*osis> **2** : chlorine : containing chlorine <*chlor*ic> <*chloro*prene>

chlo·ral \ˈklōr-əl, ˈklȯr-\ *n* [F, fr. *chlor-* + *al*cool alcohol] **1** : a pungent colorless oily aldehyde CCl_3CHO used in making DDT and chloral hydrate **2** : CHLORAL HYDRATE

chloral hydrate *n* : a bitter white crystalline drug $C_2H_3Cl_3O_2$ used as a hypnotic or in knockout drops

chlo·ral·ose \ˈklōr-ə-ˌlōs, ˈklȯr-, -ˌlōz\ *n* : a bitter crystalline compound $C_8H_{11}Cl_3O_6$ used as a hypnotic — **chlo·ral·osed** \-ˌlōst, -ˌlōzd\ *adj*

chlo·ram·bu·cil \klōr-ˈam-byə-ˌsil, klȯr-\ *n* [*chlor-* + *amin-* + *bu*tyric + *-cil* (of unknown origin)] : a nitrogen mustard derivative $C_{14}H_{19}Cl_2NO_2$ used esp. to treat leukemias and Hodgkin's disease

chlo·ra·mine \ˈklōr-ə-ˌmēn, ˈklȯr-\ *n* [ISV] : any of various compounds containing nitrogen and chlorine

chlor·am·phen·i·col \ˌklōr-ˌam-ˈfen-i-ˌkȯl, ˌklȯr-, -ˌkōl\ *n* [*chlor-* + *am*id- + *phen-* + *nitr-* + gly*col*] : a broad-spectrum antibiotic $C_{11}H_{12}Cl_2N_2O_5$ isolated from cultures of a soil microorganism (*Streptomyces venezuelae*) or prepared synthetically

chlo·rate \ˈklō(ə)r-ˌāt, ˈklȯ(ə)r-\ *n* : a salt containing the radical ClO_3 <~ of potassium>

chlor·dane \ˈklō(ə)r-ˌdān\ *or* **chlor·dan** \-ˌdan\ *n* [*chlor-* + in*dane*, in*dan* (C_9H_{10})] : a highly chlorinated viscous volatile liquid insecticide $C_{10}H_6Cl_8$

chlor·di·az·epox·ide \ˌklōr-dī-ˌaz-ə-ˈpäk-ˌsīd, ˌklȯr-\ *n* [*chlor-* + *di-* + *az-* + *epoxide*] : a compound $C_{16}H_{14}ClN_3O$ the hydrochloride of which is used as a tranquilizer in the treatment of various psychoneuroses

chlo·rel·la \klə-ˈrel-ə\ *n* [NL, genus name, fr. Gk *chlōros*] : any of a genus (*Chlorella*) of unicellular green algae potentially a cheap source of high-grade protein and B-complex vitamins

chlo·ric \ˈklōr-ik, ˈklȯr-\ *adj* : relating to or obtained from chlorine esp. with a valence of five

chlo·ride \ˈklō(ə)r-ˌīd, ˈklȯ(ə)r-\ *n* [G *chlorid*, fr. *chlor-* + *-id* -ide] : a compound of chlorine with another element or radical; *esp* : a salt or ester of hydrochloric acid

chloride of lime : BLEACHING POWDER

chlo·ri·nate \ˈklōr-ə-ˌnāt, ˈklȯr-\ *vt* **-nat·ed; -nat·ing** : to treat or cause to combine with chlorine or a chlorine compound — **chlo·ri·na·tion** \ˌklōr-ə-ˈnā-shən, ˌklȯr-\ *n* — **chlo·ri·na·tor** \ˈklōr-ə-ˌnāt-ər, ˈklȯr-\ *n*

chlorinated lime *n* : BLEACHING POWDER

chlo·rine \ˈklō(ə)r-ˌēn, ˈklȯ(ə)r-, -ən\ *n* : a halogen element that is isolated as a heavy greenish yellow gas of pungent odor and is used esp. as a bleach, oxidizing agent, and disinfectant in water purification — see ELEMENT table

chlo·rin·i·ty \klōr-ˈin-ət-ē, klȯr-\ *n* [*chlorine* + *-ity*] : a measure of the amount of halides present in one kilogram of seawater

¹**chlo·rite** \ˈklō(ə)r-ˌīt, ˈklȯ(ə)r-\ *n* [G *chlorit*, fr. L *chloritis*, a green stone, fr. Gk *chlōritis*, fr. *chlōros*] : any of a group of monoclinic usu. green minerals associated with and resembling the micas — **chlo·rit·ic** \klōr-ˈit-ik, klȯr-\ *adj*

²**chlorite** *n* [prob. fr. F, fr. *chlor-*] : a salt containing the group ClO_2 <~ of sodium>

chloro- — see CHLOR-

chlo·ro·ben·zene \ˌklōr-ō-ˈben-ˌzēn, ˌklȯr-, -ben-ˈ\ *n* [ISV] : a colorless flammable volatile toxic liquid C_6H_5Cl used in organic synthesis (as of DDT) and as a solvent

¹**chlo·ro·form** \ˈklōr-ə-ˌfȯrm, ˈklȯr-\ *n* [F *chloroforme*, fr. *chlor-* + *formyle* formyl; fr. its having been regarded as a trichloride of this radical] : a colorless volatile heavy toxic liquid $CHCl_3$ with an ether odor used esp. as a solvent or as a general anesthetic

²**chloroform** *vt* : to treat with chloroform esp. so as to produce anesthesia or death

chlo·ro·gen·ic acid \ˌklōr-ə-ˌjen-ik-, ˌklȯr-\ *n* : a crystalline acid $C_{16}H_{18}O_9$ occurring in various plant parts (as potatoes or coffee beans)

chlo·ro·hy·drin \ˌklōr-ə-ˈhī-drən, ˌklȯr-\ *n* [ISV, fr. *chlor-* + *hydr-*] : any of various organic compounds derived from glycols or polyhydroxy alcohols by substitution of chlorine for part of the hydroxyl groups

Chlo·ro·my·ce·tin \ˌklōr-ō-mī-ˈsēt-ᵊn, ˌklȯr-\ *trademark* — used for chloramphenicol

chlo·ro·phyll \ˈklōr-ə-ˌfil, ˈklȯr-, -fəl\ *n* [F *chlorophylle*, fr. *chlor-* + Gk *phyllon* leaf — more at BLADE] **1** : the green photosynthetic coloring matter of plants found in chloroplasts and made up chiefly of a blue-black ester $C_{55}H_{72}MgN_4O_5$ and a dark green ester $C_{55}H_{70}MgN_4O_6$ — called also respectively *chlorophyll a*, *chlorophyll b* **2** : a waxy green chlorophyll-containing substance extracted from green plants and used as a coloring agent or deodorant —

chlo·ro·phyl·lose \ˌklōr-ə-ˈfil-ˌōs, ˌklȯr-, -(ˌ)fil-ˈ\ *adj* — **chlo·ro·phyl·lous** \-ˈfil-əs\ *adj*

chlo·ro·pic·rin \ˌklōr-ə-ˈpik-rən, ˌklȯr-\ *n* [G *chlorpikrin,* fr. *chlor-* + Gk *pikros* bitter]: a heavy colorless liquid CCl_3NO_2 that causes tears and vomiting and is used esp. as a soil fumigant

chlo·ro·plast \ˈklōr-ə-ˌplast, ˈklȯr-\ *n* [ISV] : a plastid that contains chlorophyll and is the site of photosynthesis and starch formation — see CELL illustration

chlo·ro·prene \-ˌprēn\ *n* [*chlor-* + iso*prene*] : a colorless liquid C_4H_5Cl used esp. in making neoprene by polymerization

chlo·ro·quine \ˈklōr-ə-ˌkwēn, ˈklȯr-\ *n* [*chlor-* + *quinoline*] : an antimalarial drug $C_{18}H_{26}ClN_3$ administered as the bitter crystalline diphosphate

chlo·ro·sis \klə-ˈrō-səs\ *n* **1** : an iron-deficiency anemia in young girls characterized by a greenish color of the skin — called also *greensickness* **2** : a diseased condition in green plants marked by yellowing or blanching — **chlo·rot·ic** \-ˈrät-ik\ *adj* — **chlo·rot·i·cal·ly** \-i-k(ə-)lē\ *adv*

chlo·rous \ˈklōr-əs, ˈklȯr-\ *adj* : relating to or obtained from chlorine esp. with a valence of three

chlor·prom·a·zine \klōr-ˈpräm-ə-ˌzēn, klȯr-\ *n* [*chlor-* + *propyl* + *methyl* + phenothi*azine*] : a phenothiazine derivative $C_{17}H_{19}ClN_2S$ used as a tranquilizer in the form of its hydrochloride

chlor·prop·amide \-ˈpräp-ə-ˌmīd, -ˈprōp-\ *n* [*chlor-* + *propane* + *amide*] : a sulfonyl urea compound $C_{10}H_{13}ClN_2O_3S$ used to reduce blood sugar in the treatment of mild diabetes

chlor·tet·ra·cy·cline \ˌklōr-ˌte-trə-ˈsī-ˌklēn, ˌklȯr-\ *n* : a yellow crystalline antibiotic $C_{22}H_{23}ClN_2O_8$ produced by a soil actinomycete (*Streptomyces aureofaciens*), used in the treatment of diseases, and added to animal feeds for stimulating growth

chm *abbr* **1** chairman **2** checkmate

cho·ano·cyte \kō-ˈan-ə-ˌsīt\ *n* [ISV *choan-* (funnel-shaped) (fr. Gk *choanē* funnel) + *-cyte*] : COLLAR CELL

1chock \ˈchäk\ *n* [origin unknown] **1** : a wedge or block for steadying a body (as a cask) and holding it motionless, for filling in an unwanted space, or for blocking the movement of a wheel **2** : a heavy metal casting (as on the bow or stern of a ship) with two short horn-shaped arms curving inward between which ropes or hawsers may pass for mooring or towing

2chock *vt* **1** : to provide, stop, or make fast with or as if with chocks **2** : to raise or support on chocks

3chock *adv* : as close or as completely as possible

1chock·a·block \ˈchäk-ə-ˌbläk\ *adj* **1** : brought close together **2** : very full : CROWDED

2chockablock *adv* : in a crowded manner or condition <families living ~>

chock–full \ˈchək-ˈfu̇l, ˈchäk-\ *adj* [ME *chokkefull,* prob. fr. *choken* to choke + *full*] : full to the limit : CRAMMED

choc·o·late \ˈchäk-(ə-)lət, ˈchȯk-\ *n* [Sp, fr. Nahuatl *xocoatl*] **1** : a food prepared from ground roasted cacao beans **2** : a beverage of chocolate in water or milk **3** : a small candy with a center (as a fondant) and a chocolate coating **4** : a variable color averaging a brownish gray — **chocolate** *adj*

chocolate–box *adj* [fr. the pictures formerly commonly seen on boxes of chocolates] : superficially pretty or sentimental <his fiancée wanted him to paint her, and always in a ~ pose —L. S. Gannett>

chocolate tree *n* : CACAO 1

choc·o·laty *or* **choc·o·lat·ey** \ˈchäk-(ə-)lət-ē, ˈchȯk-\ *adj* : made of or resembling chocolate

Choc·taw \ˈchäk-(ˌ)tȯ\ *n, pl* **Choctaw** *or* **Choctaws** [Choctaw *Chahta*] **1** : a member of an Amerindian people of Mississippi, Alabama, and Louisiana **2** : the language of the Choctaw and Chickasaw people

1choice \ˈchȯis\ *n* [ME *chois,* fr. OF, fr. *choisir* to choose, of Gmc origin; akin to OHG *kiosan* to choose — more at CHOOSE] **1** : the act of choosing : SELECTION **2** : power of choosing : OPTION **3 a** : a person or thing chosen **b** : the best part : CREAM **4** : a sufficient number and variety to choose among **5** : care in selecting **6** : a grade of meat between prime and good
syn CHOICE, OPTION, ALTERNATIVE, PREFERENCE, SELECTION, ELECTION *shared meaning element* : the act or opportunity of choosing or the thing chosen

2choice *adj* **choic·er; choic·est 1** : worthy of being chosen : SELECT **2** : selected with care : well chosen **3 a** : of high quality **b** : of a grade between prime and good <~ meat> — **choice·ly** *adv* — **choice·ness** *n*
syn CHOICE, EXQUISITE, ELEGANT, RARE, DAINTY, DELICATE *shared meaning element* : having qualities that appeal to a cultivated taste *ant* indifferent

1choir \ˈkwī(-ə)r\ *n* [ME *quer,* fr. OF *cuer,* fr. ML *chorus,* fr. L, chorus] **1** : an organized company of singers esp. in church service **2** : a group of instruments of the same class <a brass ~> **3** : an organized group of persons or things **4** : a division of angels **5** : the part of a church occupied by the singers or by the clergy; *specif* : the part of the chancel between sanctuary and nave **6** : a group organized for ensemble speaking

2choir *vi* : to sing or sound in chorus or concert

3choir *adj* : of the class in a religious order bound to recite the Divine Office and devoted chiefly to the order's special work

choir·boy \ˈkwī(-ə)r-ˌbȯi\ *n* : a boy member of a choir

choir loft *n* : a gallery occupied by a church choir

choir·mas·ter \-ˌmas-tər\ *n* : the director of a choir (as in a church) <served as organist and ~>

1choke \ˈchōk\ *vb* **choked; chok·ing** [ME *choken,* alter. of *achoken,* fr. OE *aceōcian*] *vt* **1** : to check normal breathing of by compressing or obstructing the windpipe or by poisoning or adulterating available air **2** : to check or suppress expression of or by : SILENCE <a cloture rule designed to ~ off discussion> **3 a** : to check the growth, development, or activity of <the flowers were *choked* by the weeds> **b** : to obstruct by filling up or clogging <leaves *choked* the drain> **c** : to fill completely : JAM <dandelions *choked* the strips of lawn dividing the auto lanes —Herman Wouk> **4** : to enrich the fuel mixture of (a motor) by partially shutting off the air intake of the carburetor **5** : to grip (as a baseball bat) some distance from the end of the handle ~ *vi* **1** : to become choked in breathing **2 a** : to become obstructed or checked **b** : to become or feel constricted in the throat (as from strong emotion) — usu. used with *up* <he *choked* up and couldn't finish his speech> **3** : to shorten one's grip esp. on the handle of a bat — usu. used with *up* **4** : to lose one's composure and fail to perform effectively in a critical situation

2choke *n* **1** : the act of choking **2** : something that obstructs passage or flow: as **a** : a valve for choking a gasoline engine **b** : a constriction in an outlet (as of an oil well) that restricts flow **c** : REACTOR 2 **d** : a narrowing toward the muzzle in the bore of a gun **e** : an attachment that allows variation of muzzle constriction of a shotgun

choke·ber·ry \-ˌber-ē\ *n* : a small berrylike astringent fruit; *also* : a shrub (genus *Aronia*) of the rose family bearing chokeberries

choke·cher·ry \-ˌcher-ē, -ˈcher-\ *n* : any of several American wild cherries with bitter or astringent fruit; *also* : this fruit

choke coil *n* : REACTOR 2

choke collar *n* : a collar that may be tightened as a noose and that is used esp. in training and controlling powerful or stubborn dogs

choke·damp \ˈchōk-ˌdamp\ *n* : BLACKDAMP

chok·er \ˈchō-kər\ *n* **1** : one that chokes **2** : something worn closely about the throat or neck; as **a** : a wide ornamental cloth for the neck; *esp* : STOCK **b** : a high stiff collar **c** : a short necklace

chok·ing \ˈchō-kiŋ\ *adj* **1** : producing the feeling of strangulation <a ~ cloud of smog> **2** : indistinct in utterance — used esp. of a person's voice <a low ~ laugh> — **chok·ing·ly** \-kiŋ-lē\ *adv*

choky \ˈchō-kē\ *adj* : tending to cause choking or to become choked

chol- *or* **chole-** *or* **cholo-** *comb form* [Gk *chol-, cholē-, cholo-,* fr. *cholē, cholos* — more at GALL] : bile : gall <*chol*ate> <*chole*lith>

chol·an·gi·og·ra·phy \kə-ˌlan-jē-ˈäg-rə-fē, (ˌ)kō-\ *n* [*chol-* + *angi-* + *-graphy*] : roentgenographic visualization of the bile ducts after ingestion or injection of a radiopaque substance — **chol·an·gio·graph·ic** \-jē-ə-ˈgraf-ik\ *adj*

cho·late \ˈkō-ˌlāt\ *n* : a salt or ester of cholic acid

cho·le·cys·tec·to·my \ˌkō-lə-(ˌ)sis-ˈtek-tə-mē\ *n, pl* **-mies** [NL *cholecystis* gallbladder (fr. *chol-* + Gk *kystis* bladder) + ISV *-ectomy* — more at CYST] : surgical excision of the gallbladder

cho·le·cys·ti·tis \-ˈtīt-əs\ *n, pl* **-tit·i·des** \-ˈtit-ə-ˌdēz\ [NL, fr. *cholecystis*] : inflammation of the gallbladder

cho·le·cys·to·ki·nin \-ˌsis-tə-ˈkī-nən\ *n* [NL *cholecystis* + E *-o-* + *kinin*] : a hormone secreted by the duodenal mucosa that regulates the emptying of the gallbladder

cho·le·li·thi·a·sis \ˌkō-li-lith-ˈī-ə-səs\ *n* [NL *chol-* + *lithiasis*] : production of gallstones; *also* : the resulting abnormal condition

chol·er \ˈkäl-ər, ˈkō-lər\ *n* [ME *coler,* fr. MF *colere,* fr. L *cholera* bilious disease, fr. Gk, fr. *cholē*] **1 a** *archaic* : YELLOW BILE **b** *obs* : BILE 1a **2** *obs* : the quality or state of being bilious **3** : the quality or state of being irascible

chol·era \ˈkäl-ə-rə\ *n* [ME *colera* bile, fr. L *cholera*] : any of several diseases of man and domestic animals usu. marked by severe gastrointestinal symptoms; *esp* : ASIATIC CHOLERA — **chol·e·ra·ic** \ˌkäl-ə-ˈrā-ik\ *adj*

chol·era mor·bus \ˌkäl-ə-rə-ˈmȯr-bəs\ *n* [NL, lit., the disease cholera] : a gastrointestinal disturbance characterized by griping, diarrhea, and sometimes vomiting — not used technically

cho·ler·ic \ˈkäl-ə-rik, kə-ˈler-ik\ *adj* **1** : easily moved to often unreasonable or excessive anger : hot-tempered **2** : ANGRY, IRATE
syn see IRASCIBLE *ant* placid, imperturbable

cho·les·ter·ol \kə-ˈles-tə-ˌrōl, -ˌrōl\ *n* [F *cholésterine,* fr. *chol-* + Gk *stereos* solid] : a steroid alcohol $C_{27}H_{45}OH$ present in animal cells and body fluids, important in physiological processes, and implicated experimentally as a factor in arteriosclerosis

cho·lic acid \ˌkō-lik-\ *n* [Gk *cholikos* bilious, fr. *cholē*] : a crystalline bile acid $C_{24}H_{40}O_5$

cho·line \ˈkō-ˌlēn\ *n* [ISV] : a base $C_5H_{15}NO_2$ that occurs in many animal and plant products and is a vitamin of the B complex essential to the liver function

cho·lin·er·gic \ˌkō-lə-ˈnər-jik\ *adj* [ISV acetyl*choline* + Gk *ergon* work — more at WORK] **1** *of autonomic nerve fibers* : liberating or activated by acetylcholine **2** : resembling acetylcholine esp. in physiologic action

cho·lin·es·ter·ase \ˌkō-lə-ˈnes-tə-ˌrās, -ˌrāz\ *n* **1** : ACETYLCHOLINESTERASE **2** : an enzyme that hydrolyzes choline esters and that is found esp. in blood plasma — called also *pseudocholinesterase*

cho·li·no·lyt·ic \ˌkō-lə-nō-ˈlit-ik\ *adj* [*choline* + *-o-* + *-lytic*] : interfering with the action of acetylcholine or cholinergic agents — **cholinolytic** *n*

chol·la \ˈchȯi-(y)ə\ *n* [MexSp, fr. Sp, head] : any of several arborescent very spiny cacti (genus *Opuntia*) of the southwestern U.S. and Mexico

chomp \ˈchämp, ˈchȯmp\ *vb* [alter. of *champ*] *vt* : to chew or bite on <he ~*ed* his cigar in anger —J. A. Michener> ~ *vi* : to chew or bite on something

chon \ˈchän\ *n, pl* **chon** [Korean] — see *won* at MONEY table

chondr- *or* **chondri-** *or* **chondro-** *comb form* [NL, fr. Gk *chondr-, chondro-,* fr. *chondros* grain, cartilage] : cartilage <*chondro*cranium>

chon·drio·some \ˈkän-drē-ə-ˌsōm\ *n* [Gk *chondrion,* dim. of *chondros,* + ISV *-some*] : MITOCHONDRION

chon·drite \ˈkän-ˌdrīt\ *n* [ISV, fr. Gk *chondros* grain] : a meteoric stone characterized by the presence of chondrules — **chon·drit·ic** \kän-ˈdrit-ik\ *adj*

chon·dro·cra·ni·um \ˌkän-drō-ˈkrā-nē-əm\ *n* : the embryonic cartilaginous cranium; *also* : the part of the adult skull derived therefrom

chon·droi·tin \kän-ˈdrȯit-ᵊn, -ˈdrō-ət-ᵊn\ *n* [ISV *chondroitic* acid (an acid found in cartilage) (fr. *chondr-*) + *-in*] : a mucopolysaccharide occurring in sulfated form in various animal tissues (as cartilage and tendons)

chon·drule \ˈkän-(ˌ)drül\ *n* [Gk *chondros* grain] **:** a rounded granule of cosmic origin often found embedded in meteoric stones and sometimes free in marine sediments
choose \ˈchüz\ *vb* **chose** \ˈchōz\; **cho·sen** \ˈchōz-ᵊn\; **choos·ing** \ˈchü-ziŋ\ [ME *chosen,* fr. OE *cēosan;* akin to OHG *kiosan* to choose, L *gustare* to taste] *vt* **1 a :** to select freely and after consideration **b :** to decide on esp. by vote **:** ELECT <*chosen* to serve as senator> **2 a :** to have a preference for **b** (1) **:** DECIDE <*chose* to go by train> (2) **:** PREFER ~ *vi* **1 :** to make a selection **2 :** to take an alternative — used after *cannot* and usu. followed by *but* <when earth is so kind, men cannot ~ but be happy —J. A. Froude> — **choos·er** \ˈchü-zər\ *n*
choose up *vt* **:** to form (sides) esp. for a game by having opposing captains choose their players ~ *vi* **:** to form sides for a game <let's *choose up* and play ball>
choosy *or* **choos·ey** \ˈchü-zē\ *adj* **choos·i·er; -est :** fastidiously selective **:** PARTICULAR
1chop \ˈchäp\ *vb* **chopped; chop·ping** [ME *chappen, choppen* — more at CHAP] *vt* **1 a :** to cut into or sever usu. by repeated blows of a sharp instrument <~ down a tree> **b :** to cut into pieces **:** MINCE — often used with *up* <~ up the vegetables> **c :** to weed and thin out (young cotton) **2 :** to strike (a ball) with a short quick downward stroke **3 :** to subject to the action of a chopper <~ a beam of light> ~ *vi* **1 :** to make a quick stroke or repeated strokes with or as if with a sharp instrument (as an ax) **2** *archaic* **:** to move or act suddenly or violently
2chop *n* **1 a :** a forceful usu. slanting blow with or as if with an ax or cleaver **b :** a sharp downward blow or stroke **2 :** a small cut of meat often including part of a rib — see LAMB illustration **3 :** a mark made by or as if by chopping **4 :** material that has been chopped up **5 a :** a short abrupt motion (as of a wave) **b :** a stretch of choppy sea **6 :** CHOPPER 4
3chop *vi* **chopped; chop·ping** [ME *chappen, choppen* to barter, fr. OE *cēapian*] **1 :** to change direction **2 :** to veer with or as if with wind — **chop logic :** to argue with sophistical reasoning and minute distinctions
4chop *n* [Hindi *chāp* stamp] **1 a :** a seal or official stamp or its impression **b :** a license validated by a seal **2 a :** a mark on goods or coins to indicate nature or quality **b :** a kind, brand, or lot of goods bearing the same chop **c :** QUALITY, GRADE <first-*chop* tea>
chop–chop \ˈchäp-ˌchäp\ *adv* [Pidgin E, redupl. of *chop* fast — more at CHOPSTICK] **:** without delay **:** QUICKLY
chop·fall·en \ˈchäp-ˌfō-lən\ *var of* CHAPFALLEN
chop·house \ˈchäp-ˌhau̇s\ *n* **:** RESTAURANT
cho·pine \shä-ˈpēn, chä-\ *n* [MF *chapin,* fr. OSp] **:** a woman's shoe of the 16th and 17th centuries with a very high sole designed to increase stature and protect the feet from mud and dirt
1chop·log·ic \ˈchäp-ˌläj-ik\ *n* [obs. *chop* (to exchange, trade), fr. ME *choppen* to barter — more at CHOP] **:** involved and often specious argumentation
2choplogic *adj* **:** given to complex and often erroneous or absurd argumentation <a ~ speech>
chop mark *n* **:** an indentation made on a coin to attest weight, silver content, or legality — **chop–marked** \ˈchäp-ˌmärkt\ *adj*
chop·per \ˈchäp-ər\ *n* **1 :** one that chops **2 :** HELICOPTER **3 :** a device that interrupts an electric current or a beam of radiation (as light) at short regular intervals **4 :** a high-bouncing batted baseball **5 :** a customized motorcycle
chop·pi·ness \ˈchäp-ē-nəs\ *n* **:** the quality or state of being choppy
chopping block *n* **:** a wooden block on which material (as meat, wood, or vegetables) is cut, split, or diced
1chop·py \ˈchäp-ē\ *adj* **chop·pi·er; -est** [2*chop*] **:** being roughened **:** CHAPPED
2choppy *adj* **chop·pi·er; -est** [3*chop*] *of the wind* **:** CHANGEABLE, VARIABLE
3choppy *adj* **choppier; -est** [1*chop*] **1 :** rough with small waves **2 :** JERKY, DISCONNECTED <criticized for his ~ novel> — **chop·pi·ly** \ˈchäp-ə-lē\ *adv*
chops \ˈchäps\ *n pl* [alter. of 4*chap*] **1 :** JAW **2 a :** MOUTH **b :** the fleshy covering of the jaws <the hungry dog licked his ~>
chop·stick \ˈchäp-ˌstik\ *n* [Pidgin E, fr. *chop* fast (of Chinese origin; akin to Cant *kap*) + E *stick*] **:** one of a pair of slender sticks held between thumb and fingers and used chiefly in oriental countries to lift food to the mouth
chop su·ey \chäp-ˈsü-ē\ *n, pl* **chop sueys** [Chin (Cant) *shap sui* odds and ends, fr. *shap* miscellaneous + *sui* bits] **:** a dish prepared chiefly from bean sprouts, bamboo shoots, water chestnuts, onions, mushrooms, and meat or fish and served with rice and soy sauce

chopsticks

cho·ra·gus \kə-ˈrā-gəs\ *or* **cho·re·gus** \-ˈrē-, -ˈrā-\ *n* [L & Gk; L *choragus,* fr. Gk *choragos, chorēgos,* fr. *choros* chorus + *agein* to lead — more at AGENT] **1 :** the leader of a chorus or choir; *broadly* **:** the leader of any group or movement **2 :** a leader of a dramatic chorus in ancient Greece — **cho·rag·ic** \-ˈraj-ik\ *adj*
cho·ral \ˈkōr-əl, ˈkȯr-\ *adj* [F or ML; F *choral,* fr. ML *choralis,* fr. L *chorus*] **1 a :** of or relating to a chorus or choir <a ~ group> **b :** accompanied with song <a ~ dance> **2 :** sung or designed for singing by a choir <a ~ arrangement> — **cho·ral·ly** \-ə-lē\ *adv*
cho·rale *also* **cho·ral** \kə-ˈral, -ˈräl\ *n* [G *choral,* short for *choralgesang* choral song] **1 :** a hymn or psalm sung to a traditional or composed melody in church; *also* **:** a hymn tune or a harmonization of a traditional melody <a Bach ~> **2 :** CHORUS, CHOIR
chorale prelude *n* **:** a composition usu. for organ based on a chorale
choral speaking *n* **:** ensemble speaking of poetry or prose by a group often using various voice combinations and contrasts
1chord \ˈkȯ(ə)rd\ *n* [alter. of ME *cord,* short for *accord*] **:** a combination of tones that blend harmoniously when sounded together
2chord *vi* **1 :** ACCORD **2 :** to play chords esp. on a stringed instrument ~ *vt* **1 :** to make chords on **2 :** HARMONIZE
3chord *n* [alter. of 1*cord*] **1 :** CORD 3a **2 :** a straight line joining two points on a curve; *specif* **:** the segment of a secant between its intersections with a curve **3 :** an individual emotion or disposition **4 :** either of the two outside members of a truss connected and braced by the web members **5 :** the straight line joining the leading and trailing edges of an airfoil
chord·al \ˈkȯrd-ᵊl\ *adj* **1 :** of, relating to, or suggesting a chord **2 :** relating to music characterized more by harmony than by counterpoint
chor·da·meso·derm \ˌkȯrd-ə-ˈmez-ə-ˌdərm *also* -ˈmes-\ *n* [NL *chorda* cord + E *mesoderm*] **:** the portion of the embryonic mesoderm that forms notochord and related structures and serves as an inductor of neural structures — **chor·da·meso·der·mal** \-ˌmez-ə-ˈdər-məl, -ˌmes-\ *adj*
chor·date \ˈkȯrd-ət, ˈkȯ(ə)r-ˌdāt\ *n* [deriv. of L *chorda* cord] **:** any of a phylum or subkingdom (Chordata) of animals having at least at some stage of development a notochord, dorsally situated central nervous system, and gill clefts and including the vertebrates, lancelets, and tunicates — **chordate** *adj*
chord organ *n* **:** an electronic or reed organ with buttons to produce simple chords
chore \ˈchō(ə)r, ˈchȯ(ə)r\ *n* [alter. of *chare*] **1** *pl* **:** the regular or daily light work of a household or farm **2 :** a routine task or job **3 :** a difficult or disagreeable task ***syn*** see TASK
-chore \ˌkō(ə)r, ˌkȯ(ə)r\ *n comb form* [Gk *chōrein* to withdraw, go; akin to Gk *chēros* bereaved — more at HEIR] **:** plant distributed by (such) an agency <zoo*chore*> — **-cho·rous** \ˈkōr-əs, ˈkȯr-\ *adj comb form* — **-cho·ry** \ˌkōr-ē, ˌkȯr-\ *n comb form*
cho·rea \kə-ˈrē-ə\ *n* [NL, fr. L, dance, fr. Gk *choreia,* fr. *choros* chorus] **:** a nervous disorder (as of man or dogs) marked by spasmodic movements of limbs and facial muscles and by incoordination
chore boy *n* **1 :** one who does chores; *esp* **:** a man who does the domestic maintenance tasks and helps the cook in a lumber camp **2 :** a person who assumes responsibility for onerous detail in an undertaking
chore·man \ˈchō(ə)r-mən, ˈchȯ(ə)r-\ *n* **:** a worker who performs menial jobs in a factory or camp (as a logging or construction camp)
cho·reo·dra·ma \ˌkōr-ē-ō-ˈdräm-ə, -ˈdram-\ *n* [Gk *choreia* dance + E *drama*] **:** a dance drama for large groups
cho·reo·graph \ˈkōr-ē-ə-ˌgraf, ˈkȯr-\ *vt* **:** to compose the choreography of ~ *vi* **:** to engage in choreography — **cho·re·og·ra·pher** \ˌkōr-ē-ˈäg-rə-fər, ˌkȯr-\ *n*
cho·re·og·ra·phy \ˌkōr-ē-ˈäg-rə-fē, ˌkȯr-\ *n, pl* **-phies** [F *chorégraphie,* fr. Gk *choreia* + F *-graphie* -graphy] **1 :** the art of symbolically representing dancing **2 :** stage dancing as distinguished from social or ballroom dancing **3 a :** the composition and arrangement of dances esp. for ballet **b :** a composition created by this art — **cho·reo·graph·ic** \ˌkōr-ē-ə-ˈgraf-ik, ˌkȯr-\ *adj* — **cho·reo·graph·i·cal·ly** \-i-k(ə-)lē\ *adv*
chor·iamb \ˈkōr-ē-ˌam(b), ˈkȯr-\ *n, pl* **-iambs** \-ˌamz\ [LL *choriambus,* fr. Gk *choriambos,* fr. *choreios* of a chorus, (fr. *choros*) + *iambos* iambus] **:** a prosodic foot consisting of a trochee followed by an iamb — **chor·iam·bic** \ˌkōr-ē-ˈam-bik, ˌkȯr-\ *adj*
cho·ric \ˈkōr-ik, ˈkȯr-, ˈkär-\ *adj* **:** of, relating to, or being in the style of a chorus and esp. a Greek chorus — **cho·ri·cally** \-i-k(ə-)lē\ *adv*
cho·rine \ˈkō(ə)r-ˌēn, ˈkȯ(ə)r-\ *n* [*chorus* + *-ine*] **:** CHORUS GIRL
cho·rio·al·lan·to·is \ˌkōr-ē-ō-ə-ˈlant-ə-wəs, ˌkȯr-\ *n* [NL, fr. Gk *chorion* + NL *allantois*] **:** a vascular fetal membrane composed of the fused chorion and adjacent wall of the allantois that in the hen's egg is used as a living culture medium for viruses and for tissues — **cho·rio·al·lan·to·ic** \-ˌal-ən-ˈtō-ik\ *adj*
cho·rio·car·ci·no·ma \-ˌkärs-ᵊn-ˈō-mə\ *n* [NL, fr. *chorion* + *carcinoma*] **:** a malignant tumor developing in the uterus from trophoblast and rarely in the testes from a neoplasm
cho·ri·on \ˈkōr-ē-ˌän, ˈkȯr-\ *n* [NL, fr. Gk] **:** the highly vascular outer embryonic membrane of higher vertebrates that in placental mammals is associated with the allantois in the formation of the placenta — **cho·ri·on·ic** \ˌkōr-ē-ˈän-ik, ˌkȯr-\ *adj*
cho·ris·ter \ˈkōr-ə-stər, ˈkȯr-, ˈkär-\ *n* [ME *querister,* fr. AF *cueristre,* fr. ML *chorista,* fr. L *chorus*] **1 :** a singer in a choir; *specif* **:** CHOIRBOY **2 :** the singer in a church choir who leads the singing and in the absence of instrumental accompaniment sets the pitch and tempo
cho·ri·zo \chə-ˈrē-(ˌ)zō, -(ˌ)sō\ *n, pl* **-zos** [Sp] **:** pork sausage that is highly seasoned with cayenne pepper, pimientos, garlic, and paprika
C–horizon *n* **:** the layer of a soil profile lying beneath the B-horizon and consisting essentially of more or less weathered parent rock
cho·rog·ra·phy \kə-ˈräg-rə-fē\ *n* [L *chorographia,* fr. Gk *chōrographia,* fr. *chōros* place + *-graphia* -graphy] **1 :** the art of describing or mapping a region or district **2 :** a description or map of a region; *also* **:** the physical conformation and features of such a region — **cho·ro·graph·ic** \ˌkȯr-ə-ˈgraf-ik, ˌkär-\ *adv*
cho·roid \ˈkō(ə)r-ˌȯid, ˈkȯ(ə)r-\ *also* **cho·ri·oid** \ˈkōr-ē-ˌȯid, ˈkȯr-\ *n* [*choroid coat*] **:** a vascular membrane containing large branched pigment cells that lies between the retina and the sclerotic coat of the vertebrate eye — see EYE illustration — **choroid** *adj* — **cho·roi·dal** \kə-ˈrȯid-ᵊl\ *adj*

choroid coat *n* [NL *choroides* resembling the chorion, fr. Gk *chorioeidēs*, fr. *chorion*] : CHOROID
chor·tle \'chȯrt-ᵊl\ *vb* **chor·tled; chor·tling** \'chȯrt-liŋ, -ᵊl-iŋ\ [blend of *chuckle* and *snort*] *vi* **1 :** to sing or chant exultantly <he *chortled* in his joy —Lewis Carroll> **2 :** to laugh or chuckle esp. in satisfaction or exultation ~ *vt* **:** to express effervescently or with a chortling intonation — **chortle** *n* — **chor·tler** \'chȯrt-lər, -ᵊl-ər\ *n*
[1]**chorus** \'kōr-əs, 'kȯr-\ *n* [L, ring dance, chorus, fr. Gk *choros*] **1 a :** a company of singers and dancers in Athenian drama participating in or commenting on the action; *also* **:** a similar company in later plays **b :** a character in Elizabethan drama who speaks the prologue and epilogue and comments on the action **c :** an organized company of singers who sing in concert : CHOIR: *specif* **:** a body of singers who sing the choral parts of a work (as in opera) **d :** a group of dancers and singers supporting the featured players in a musical comedy or revue **2 a :** a part of a song or hymn recurring at intervals **b :** the part of a drama sung or spoken by the chorus **c :** a composition to be sung by a number of voices in concert **d :** the main part of a popular song **3 :** something performed, sung, or uttered simultaneously by a number of persons or animals; *also* **:** sounds so uttered **4 :** a unanimous utterance by members of a group <a ~ of boos> — **in chorus :** in unison
[2]**chorus** *vt* **:** to sing or utter in chorus
chorus boy *n* **:** a young man who sings or dances in the chorus of a theatrical production (as a musical comedy or revue)
chorus girl *n* **:** a young woman who sings or dances in the chorus of a theatrical production (as a musical comedy or revue) — called also *chorine*
[1]**chose** *past of* CHOOSE
[2]**chose** \'shōz\ *n* [F, fr. L *causa* cause, reason] **:** a piece of personal property : THING
[1]**cho·sen** \'chōz-ᵊn\ *adj* [ME, fr. pp. of *chosen* to choose] **1 :** selected or marked for favor or special privilege <an hour granted to a ~ few> **2 :** ELECT
[2]**chosen** *n, pl* **chosen :** one who is the object of choice or of divine favor : an elect person
chott \'shät\ *n* [F *chott,* fr. Ar *shaṭṭ*] **:** a shallow saline lake of northern Africa; *also* **:** the dried bed of such a lake
Chou \'jō\ *n* [Chin (Pek) *Chou*[1]] **:** a Chinese dynasty traditionally dated 1122 to about 256 B.C. and marked by the development of the philosophical schools of Confucius, Mencius, Lao-tzu, and Mo Ti
chough \'chəf\ *n* [ME] **:** a bird of an Old World genus (*Pyrrhocorax*) that is related to the crows and has red legs and glossy black plumage
[1]**chouse** \'chau̇s\ *vt* **choused; chous·ing** [Turk *çavuş* doorkeeper, messenger] **:** CHEAT, TRICK
[2]**chouse** *vt* **choused; chous·ing** [origin unknown] *West* **:** to drive or herd roughly
[1]**chow** \'chau̇\ *n* [perh. fr. Chin (Pek) *chiao*[3] meat dumpling] **:** FOOD, VICTUALS
[2]**chow** *vi* **:** EAT — often used with *down*
[3]**chow** *n* **:** CHOW CHOW
chow·chow \'chau̇-ˌchau̇\ *n* [Pidgin E] **1 :** a Chinese preserve of ginger, fruits, and peels in heavy syrup **2 :** a relish of chopped mixed pickles in mustard sauce
chow chow \'chau̇-ˌchau̇\ *n, often cap both Cs* [fr. a Chin dial. word akin to Cant *kaú* dog] **:** a heavy-coated blocky dog with a broad head and muzzle, a very full ruff of long hair, and a distinctive blue-black tongue and black-lined mouth — called also *chow*

chow chow

[1]**chow·der** \'chau̇d-ər\ *n* [F *chaudière* kettle, contents of a kettle, fr. LL *caldaria* — more at CALDRON] **:** a thick soup or stew of seafood (as clams or mussels) usu. made with milk, salt pork or bacon, onions and other vegetables (as potatoes); *also* **:** a soup resembling chowder <corn ~>
[2]**chowder** *vt* **:** to make chowder of
chow·der·head \-ˌhed\ *n* **:** DOLT, BLOCKHEAD — **chow·der·head·ed** \ˌchau̇d-ər-'hed-əd\ *adj*
chow·hound \'chau̇-ˌhau̇nd\ *n* **:** one excessively fond of food : GLUTTON
chow line *n* **:** a line of people waiting to be served food (as in a military mess)
chow mein \'chau̇-'mān\ *n* [Chin (Pek) *ch'ao*[3] *mien*[4], fr. *ch'ao*[3] to fry + *mien*[4] dough] **:** a thick stew of shredded or diced meat, mushrooms, vegetables, and seasonings that is usu. served with fried noodles
chow·time \'chau̇-ˌtīm\ *n* **:** MEALTIME
chres·tom·a·thy \kre-'stäm-ə-thē\ *n, pl* **-thies** [NL *chrestomathia,* fr. Gk *chrēstomatheia,* fr. *chrēstos* useful + *manthanein* to learn; akin to Skt *hrasva* small — more at MATHEMATICAL] **1 :** a selection of passages compiled as an aid to learning a language **2 :** a volume of selections from an author
chrism \'kriz-əm\ *n* [ME *crisme,* fr. OE *crisma,* fr. LL *chrisma,* fr. Gk, ointment, fr. *chriein* to anoint; akin to OE *grēot* grit, sand] **:** consecrated oil used in Greek and Latin churches esp. in baptism, confirmation, and ordination
chris·mon \'kriz-ˌmän\ *n, pl* **chris·ma** \-mə\ *or* **chrismons** [ML, fr. L *Chris*tus Christ + LL *mon*ogramma monogram] **:** CHI-RHO
chris·om \'kriz-əm\ *n* [ME *crisom,* short for *crisom cloth,* fr. *crisom* chrism + *cloth*] **:** a white cloth or robe put on a person at baptism as a symbol of innocence
chrisom child *n* **:** a child that dies in its first month
Christ \'krīst\ *n* [ME *Crist,* fr. OE, fr. L *Christus,* fr. Gk *Christos,* lit., anointed, fr. *chriein* to anoint] **1 :** MESSIAH **2 :** JESUS **3 :** an ideal type of humanity **4** *Christian Science* **:** the ideal truth that comes as a divine manifestation of God to destroy incarnate error
chris·ten \'kris-ᵊn\ *vt* **chris·tened; chris·ten·ing** \'kris-niŋ, -ᵊn-iŋ [ME *cristnen,* fr. OE *cristnian,* fr. *cristen* Christian, fr. L *christianus*] **1 a :** BAPTIZE **b :** to name at baptism **2 :** to name or dedicate (as a ship) by a ceremony suggestive of baptism **3 :** NAME **4 :** to use for the first time
Chris·ten·dom \'kris-ᵊn-dəm\ *n* [ME *cristendom,* fr. OE *cristendōm,* fr. *cristen*] **1 :** CHRISTIANITY **2 :** the part of the world in which Christianity prevails
chris·ten·ing *n* **:** the ceremony of baptizing and naming a child
[1]**Chris·tian** \'kris(h)-chən\ *n* [L *christianus,* adj. & n., fr. Gk *christianos,* fr. *Christos*] **1 a :** an adherent of Christianity **b** (1) **:** DISCIPLE 2 (2) **:** a member of one of the Churches of Christ separating from the Disciples of Christ in 1906 (3) **:** a member of the Christian denomination having part in the union of the United Church of Christ concluded in 1961 **2 :** the hero in Bunyan's *Pilgrim's Progress*
[2]**Christian** *adj* **1 a :** of or relating to Christianity <~ scriptures> **b :** based on or conforming with Christianity <~ ethics> **2 a :** of or relating to a Christian <~ responsibilities> **b :** professing Christianity <a ~ affirmation> **3 :** commendably decent or generous <has a very ~ concern for others> — **Chris·tian·ly** *adv*
Christian Brother *n* **:** a member of the Roman Catholic institute of Brothers of the Christian Schools founded by St. John Baptist de la Salle in France in 1684 and dedicated to education
Christian era *n* **:** the period dating from the birth of Christ
chris·ti·ania \ˌkris(h)-chē-'an-ē-ə, ˌkris-tē-, -'än-\ *n* [*Christiania,* former name of Oslo, Norway] **:** CHRISTIE
Chris·tian·i·ty \ˌkris(h)-chē-'an-ət-ē, ˌkris-tē-'an-, kris(h)-'chan-\ *n* **1 :** the religion derived from Jesus Christ, based on the Bible as sacred scripture, and professed by Eastern, Roman Catholic, and Protestant bodies **2 :** conformity to the Christian religion
Chris·tian·ize \'kris(h)-chə-ˌnīz\ *vt* **-ized; -iz·ing :** to make Christian — **Chris·tian·iza·tion** \ˌkris(h)-chə-nə-'zā-shən\ *n* — **Chris·tian·iz·er** \'kris(h)-chə-ˌnī-zər\ *n*
Christian name *n* **1 :** a name given at christening or confirmation **2 :** a name that precedes one's surname; *esp* **:** FIRST NAME
Christian Science *n* **:** a religion discovered by Mary Baker Eddy in 1866 that was organized under the official name of the Church of Christ, Scientist, that derives its teachings from the Scriptures as understood by its adherents, and that includes a practice of spiritual healing based on the teaching that cause and effect are mental and that sin, sickness, and death will be destroyed by a full understanding of the divine principle of Jesus's teaching and healing — **Christian Scientist** *n*
chris·tie *or* **chris·ty** \'kris-tē\ *n, pl* **christies** [by shortening & alter. fr. *christiania*] **:** a skiing turn used for altering the direction of hill descent or for stopping and executed usu. at high speed by shifting the body weight forward and skidding into a turn with parallel skis — called also *christiania*
Christ·like \'krīst-ˌlīk\ *adj* **:** resembling Christ in character, spirit, or action — **Christ·like·ness** *n*
Christ·ly \'krīst-lē\ *adj* **:** of, relating to, or resembling Christ
Christ·mas \'kris-məs\ *n* [ME *Christemasse,* fr. OE *Cristes mæsse,* lit., Christ's mass] **1 :** a Christian feast on December 25 or among the Eastern Orthodox on January 6 that commemorates the birth of Christ and is usu. observed as a legal holiday **2 :** CHRISTMASTIDE — **Christ·mas·sy** \-mə-sē\ *adj*
Christmas cactus *n* [fr. its annual blooming around Christmastime] **:** a branching So. American cactus (*Zygocactus truncatus*) with flat stems, short joints, and showy red zygomorphic flowers — called also *crab cactus*
Christmas card *n* **:** an ornamental card with a greeting sent at Christmas
Christmas club *n* **:** a savings account in which regular deposits are made throughout the year to provide money for Christmas shopping
Christmas Eve *n* **:** the eve of Christmas
Christmas fern *n* **:** a No. American evergreen fern (*Polystichum acrostichoides*) used for decoration in winter — see FERN illustration
Christmas rose *n* **:** a European herb (*Helleborus niger*) of the buttercup family that has white or purplish flowers produced in winter
Christ·mas·tide \'kris-mə-ˌstīd\ *n* **:** the festival season from Christmas Eve till after New Year's Day or esp. in England till Epiphany
Christ·mas·time \-mə-ˌstīm\ *n* **:** the Christmas season
Christmas tree *n* **1 :** a usu. evergreen tree decorated at Christmas **2 :** an oil-well control device consisting of an assembly of fittings placed at the top of the well **3 :** a set of flashing red, yellow, and green lights used to start drag races
Chris·to·cen·tric \ˌkris-tə-'sen-trik, ˌkrīs-\ *adj* [Gk *Christos* Christ + E *-centric*] **:** centering theologically on Christ
Chris·to·gram \'kris-tə-ˌgram, 'krīs-\ *n* [Gk *Christos* Christ + E *-gram*] **:** a graphic symbol of Christ; *esp* **:** CHI-RHO
Chris·tol·o·gy \kris-'täl-ə-jē, krīs-\ *n* [Gk *Christos* Christ + E *-logy*] **:** theological interpretation of the person and work of Christ — **Chris·to·log·i·cal** \ˌkris-tə-'läj-i-kəl, ˌkrīs-\ *adj*
Christ's-thorn \'krīs(ts)-ˌthȯ(ə)rn\ *n* **:** any of several prickly or thorny shrubs of Palestine (esp. the shrub *Paliurus spina-christi* or the jujube *Ziziphus jujuba*)
chrom- *or* **chromo-** *comb form* [F, fr. Gk *chrōma* color] **1 :** chromium <*chrom*ize> **2 a :** color **:** colored <*chromo*sphere> **b :** pigment <*chromo*gen>
chro·ma \'krō-mə\ *n* [Gk *chrōma*] **1 :** SATURATION 4a **2 :** a quality of color combining hue and saturation
chro·maf·fin \'krō-mə-fən\ *adj* [ISV *chrom-* + L *affinis* bordering on, related — more at AFFINITY] **:** staining deeply with chromium salts <~ cells of the adrenal medulla>
chromat- *or* **chromato-** *comb form* [Gk *chrōmat-, chrōma*] **1 :** color <*chromat*id> **2 :** chromatin <*chromato*lysis>

chro·mate \'krō-ˌmāt\ *n* [F, fr. Gk *chrōma*] **:** a salt or ester of chromic acid

[1]**chro·mat·ic** \krō-'mat-ik\ *adj* [Gk *chrōmatikos,* fr. *chrōmat-, chrōma* skin, color, modified tone; akin to OE *grēot* sand — more at GRIT] **1 a :** of or relating to color or color phenomena or sensations **b :** highly colored **2 :** of or relating to chroma **3 a :** of, relating to, or giving all the tones of the chromatic scale **b :** characterized by frequent use of nonharmonic tones or of harmonies based on nonharmonic tones — **chro·mat·i·cal·ly** \-i-k(ə-)lē\ *adv* — **chro·mat·i·cism** \-'mat-ə-ˌsiz-əm\ *n*

[2]**chromatic** *n* **:** ACCIDENTAL 2

chromatic aberration *n* **:** aberration caused by the differences in refraction of the colored rays of the spectrum

chro·ma·tic·i·ty \ˌkrō-mə-'tis-ət-ē\ *n* **1 :** the quality or state of being chromatic **2 :** the quality of color characterized by its dominant or complementary wavelength and purity taken together

chro·mat·ics \krō-'mat-iks\ *n pl but sing in constr* **:** the branch of colorimetry that deals with hue and saturation

chromatic scale *n* **:** a musical scale consisting entirely of half steps

chro·ma·tid \'krō-mə-təd\ *n* **:** one of the paired complex constituent strands of a chromosome — compare CHROMONEMA

chro·ma·tin \'krō-mət-ən\ *n* **:** the part of a cell nucleus that stains intensely with basic dyes; *specif* **:** a complex of a polymerized nucleic acid with basic proteins of protamine or histone type present in chromosomes and carrying the genes — **chro·ma·tin·ic** \ˌkrō-mə-'tin-ik\ *adj*

chro·mato·gram \krō-'mat-ə-ˌgram, krə-\ *n* **:** the pattern formed on the adsorbent medium by the layers of components separated by chromatography

chro·ma·tog·ra·phy \ˌkrō-mə-'täg-rə-fē\ *n* **:** a process of separating esp. a solution of closely related compounds by allowing a solution to seep through an adsorbent (as clay or paper) so that each compound becomes adsorbed in a separate often colored layer — **chro·mato·graph** \krō-'mat-ə-ˌgraf, krə-\ *vt* — **chro·mato·graph·ic** \-ˌmat-ə-'graf-ik\ *adj* — **chro·mato·graph·i·cal·ly** \-i-k(ə-)lē\ *adv*

chro·ma·tol·y·sis \ˌkrō-mə-'täl-ə-səs\ *n* [NL] **:** the dissolution and breaking up of chromophil material (as chromatin) of a cell — **chro·mato·lyt·ic** \krō-ˌmat-ᵊl-'it-ik, krə-\ *adj*

chro·mato·phore \krō-'mat-ə-ˌfō(ə)r, krə-, -ˌfȯ(ə)r\ *n* [ISV] **1 :** a pigment-bearing cell; *esp* **:** one of the integumental cells of an animal capable of causing skin color changes by expanding or contracting **2 :** the organelle of photosynthesis in blue-green algae and photosynthetic bacteria; *broadly* **:** CHROMOPLAST, CHLOROPLAST

[1]**chrome** \'krōm\ *n* [F, fr. Gk *chrōma*] **1 a :** CHROMIUM **b :** a chromium pigment **2 :** something plated with an alloy of chromium

[2]**chrome** *vt* **chromed; chrom·ing 1 :** to treat with a compound of chromium (as in dyeing) **2 :** CHROMIZE

-chrome \ˌkrōm\ *n comb form or adj comb form* [ML *-chromat-, -chroma* colored thing, fr. Gk *chrōmat-, chrōma*] **1 :** colored thing <helio*chrome*> **:** colored <hetero*chrome*> **2 :** coloring matter <uro*chrome*>

chrome alum *n* **:** an alum with trivalent chromium; *esp* **:** a dark violet salt $KCr(SO_4)_2 \cdot 12H_2O$ used in tanning, in photography, and as a mordant in dyeing

chrome green *n* **:** any of various brilliant green pigments containing or consisting of chromium compounds

chrome red *n* **:** a red pigment consisting of basic lead chromate $PbCrO_4 \cdot PbO$

chrome yellow *n* **:** a yellow pigment consisting essentially of neutral lead chromate $PbCrO_4$

chro·mic \'krō-mik\ *adj* **:** of, relating to, or derived from chromium esp. with a valence of three

chromic acid *n* **:** an acid H_2CrO_4 analogous to sulfuric acid but known only in solution and esp. in the form of its salts

chro·mide \'krō-ˌmīd\ *n* [deriv. of Gk *chromis,* a sea fish] **:** any of several small brightly colored African fishes (family Cichlidae)

chro·mi·nance \'krō-mən-ən(t)s\ *n* [*chrom-* + lum*inance*] **:** the difference between a color and a chosen reference color of the same luminous intensity in color television

chro·mite \'krō-ˌmīt\ *n* [G *chromit,* fr. *chrom-*] **1 :** a mineral $FeCr_2O_4$ that consists of an oxide of iron and chromium **2 :** an oxide of bivalent chromium

chro·mi·um \'krō-mē-əm\ *n* [NL, fr. F *chrome*] **:** a blue-white metallic element found naturally only in combination and used esp. in alloys and in electroplating — see ELEMENT table

chro·mize \'krō-ˌmīz\ *vt* **chro·mized; chro·miz·ing :** to treat (metal) with chromium in order to form a protective surface alloy

chro·mo \'krō(ˌ)mō\ *n, pl* **chromos :** CHROMOLITHOGRAPH

chro·mo·gen \'krō-mə-jən\ *n* [ISV] **1 a :** a precursor of a biochemical pigment **b :** a compound not itself a dye but containing a chromophore and so capable of becoming one **2 :** a pigment-producing microorganism — **chro·mo·gen·ic** \ˌkrō-mə-'jen-ik\ *adj*

chro·mo·litho·graph \ˌkrō-mə-'lith-ə-ˌgraf\ *n* **:** a picture printed in colors from a series of stones prepared by the lithographic process — **chro·mo·litho·graph·ic** \-ˌlith-ə-'graf-ik\ *adj* — **chro·mo·li·thog·ra·phy** \-lith-'äg-rə-fē\ *n*

chro·mo·mere \'krō-mə-ˌmi(ə)r\ *n* [ISV] **:** one of the small bead-shaped and heavily staining concentrations of chromatin that are linearly arranged along the chromosome — **chro·mo·mer·ic** \ˌkrō-mə-'mer-ik, -'mi(ə)r-\ *adj*

chro·mo·ne·ma \ˌkrō-mə-'nē-mə\ *n, pl* **-ne·ma·ta** \-'nē-mət-ə\ [NL, fr. *chrom-* + Gk *nēmat-, nēma* thread — more at NEMAT-] **:** the coiled filamentous core of a chromatid — **chro·mo·ne·mal** \-'nē-məl\ *or* **chro·mo·ne·ma·tal** \-'nē-mət-ᵊl, -'nem-ət-\ *or* **chro·mo·ne·mat·ic** \-ni-'mat-ik\ *adj*

chro·mo·phil \'krō-mə-ˌfil\ *or* **chro·mat·o·phil** \krō-'mat-ə-ˌfil\ *adj* [ISV] **:** staining readily with dyes

chro·mo·phore \'krō-mə-ˌfō(ə)r, -ˌfȯ(ə)r\ *n* [ISV] **:** a chemical group that gives rise to color in molecule — **chro·mo·phor·ic** \ˌkrō-mə-'fȯr-ik, -'fär-\ *adj*

chro·mo·plast \'krō-mə-ˌplast\ *n* [ISV] **:** a colored plastid usu. containing red or yellow pigment (as carotene)

chro·mo·pro·tein \ˌkrō-mə-'prō-ˌtēn, -'prōt-ē-ən\ *n* **:** a compound (as hemoglobin) of a protein with a metal-containing pigment (as heme) or a carotenoid

chro·mo·some \'krō-mə-ˌsōm, -ˌzōm\ *n* [ISV] **:** one of the usu. linear nucleoprotein-containing basophilic bodies of the cell nucleus made up of chromatids — **chro·mo·som·al** \ˌkrō-mə-'sō-məl, -'zō\ *adj* — **chro·mo·som·al·ly** \-mə-lē\ *adv* — **chro·mo·so·mic** \-mik\ *adj*

chromosome number *n* **:** the usu. constant number of chromosomes characteristic of a particular kind of animal or plant

chro·mo·sphere \'krō-mə-ˌsfi(ə)r\ *n* **:** the lower part of the atmosphere of the sun that is thousands of miles thick and is composed chiefly of hydrogen gas; *also* **:** a similar part of the atmosphere of any star — **chro·mo·spher·ic** \ˌkrō-mə-'sfi(ə)r-ik, -'sfer-\ *adj*

chro·mous \'krō-məs\ *adj* **:** of, relating to, or derived from chromium esp. with a valence of two

chron *abbr* **1** chronicle **2** chronological; chronology

Chron *abbr* Chronicles

chron- *or* **chrono-** *comb form* [Gk, fr. *chronos*] **:** time <*chrono*gram>

chron·ax·ie *or* **chron·axy** \'krōn-ˌak-sē, 'krän-\ *n* [F *chronaxie,* fr. *chron-* + Gk *axia* value, fr. *axios* worthy] **:** the minimum time required for excitation of a structure (as a nerve cell) by a constant electric current of twice the threshold voltage

chron·ic \'krän-ik\ *adj* [F *chronique,* fr. Gk *chronikos* of time, fr. *chronos*] **1 a :** marked by long duration or frequent recurrence **:** not acute <~ indigestion> <~ experiments> **b :** suffering from a chronic disease <the special needs of ~ patients> **2 a :** always present or encountered; *esp* **:** constantly vexing, weakening, or troubling <~ petty warfare> **b :** being such habitually <a ~ grumbler> ***syn*** see INVETERATE — **chronic** *n* — **chron·i·cal** \-i-kəl\ *adj* — **chron·i·cal·ly** \-i-k(ə-)lē\ *adv* — **chro·nic·i·ty** \krä-'nis-ət-ē, krō-\ *n*

[1]**chron·i·cle** \'krän-i-kəl\ *n* [ME *cronicle,* fr. AF, alter. of OF *chronique,* fr. L *chronica,* fr. Gk *chronika,* fr. neut. pl. of *chronikos*] **1 :** a usu. continuous and detailed historical account of events arranged in order of time without analysis or interpretation **2 :** NARRATIVE ***syn*** see HISTORY

[2]**chronicle** *vt* **-cled; -cling** \-k(ə-)liŋ\ **1 :** to record in or as if in a chronicle **2 :** LIST, DESCRIBE — **chron·i·cler** \-k(ə-)lər\ *n*

chronicle play *n* **:** a play with a theme from history consisting usu. of rather loosely connected episodes chronologically arranged

Chron·i·cles \'krän-i-kəlz\ *n pl but sing in constr* **:** either of two historical books of canonical Jewish and Christian Scripture — see BIBLE table

chro·no·gram \'krän-ə-ˌgram, 'krō-nə-\ *n* **1 :** an inscription, sentence, or phrase in which certain letters express a date or epoch **2 :** the record made by a chronograph — **chro·no·gram·mat·ic** \ˌkrän-ə-grə-'mat-ik, ˌkrō-nə-\ *or* **chro·no·gram·mat·i·cal** \-i-kəl\ *adj*

chro·no·graph \'krän-ə-ˌgraf, 'krō-nə-\ *n* **:** an instrument for measuring and recording time intervals: as **a :** an instrument having a revolving drum on which a stylus makes marks **b :** a watch with a sweep-second hand **c :** an instrument for measuring the time of flight of projectiles — **chro·no·graph·ic** \ˌkrän-ə-'graf-ik, ˌkrō-nə\ *adj* — **chro·nog·ra·phy** \krə-'näg-rə-fē\ *n*

chro·nol·o·ger \krə-'näl-ə-jər\ *n* **:** CHRONOLOGIST

chro·no·log·i·cal \ˌkrän-ᵊl-'äj-i-kəl, ˌkrōn-\ *also* **chro·no·log·ic** \-ik\ *adj* **:** of, relating to, or arranged in or according to the order of time <~ tables of American history> — **chro·no·log·i·cal·ly** \-i-k(ə-)lē\ *adv*

chro·nol·o·gist \krə-'näl-ə-jəst\ *n* **:** an expert in chronology

chro·nol·o·gize \krə-'näl-ə-ˌjīz\ *vt* **-gized; -giz·ing :** to arrange chronologically **:** establish the order in time of (as events or documents)

chro·nol·o·gy \-jē\ *n, pl* **-gies** [NL *chronologia,* fr. *chron-* + *-logia* -logy] **1 :** the science that deals with measuring time by regular divisions and that assigns to events their proper dates **2 :** a chronological table or list **3 :** an arrangement in order of occurrence

chro·nom·e·ter \krə-'näm-ət-ər\ *n* **:** an instrument for measuring time **:** TIMEPIECE; *esp* **:** one designed to keep time with great accuracy

chro·no·met·ric \ˌkrän-ə-'me-trik, ˌkrō-nə-\ *or* **chro·no·met·ri·cal** \-tri-kəl\ *adj* **:** of or relating to a chronometer or chronometry — **chro·no·met·ri·cal·ly** \-tri-k(ə-)lē\ *adj*

chro·nom·e·try \-ə-trē\ *n* **1 :** the science of measuring time **2 :** the measuring of time by periods or divisions

chro·no·scope \'krän-ə-ˌskōp, 'krō-nə-\ *n* **:** an instrument for precise measurement of small time intervals

chrys- *or* **chryso-** *comb form* [Gk, fr. *chrysos*] **:** gold **:** yellow <*chrys*arobin>

chrys·a·lid \'kris-ə-ləd\ *n* **:** CHRYSALIS — **chrysalid** *adj*

chrys·a·lis \'kris-ə-ləs\ *n, pl* **chry·sal·i·des** \kris-'al-ə-ˌdēz\ *or* **chrys·a·lis·es** [L *chrysallid-, chrysallis* gold-colored pupa of butterflies, fr. Gk, fr. *chrysos* gold, of Sem origin] **1 :** a pupa of a butterfly; *broadly* **:** an insect pupa **2 :** a protecting covering **:** a sheltered state or stage of being or growth <a budding writer could not emerge from his ~ too soon —William Du Bois>

ə abut ᵊ kitten ər further a back ā bake ä cot, cart
aú out ch chin e less ē easy g gift i trip ī life
j joke ŋ sing ō flow ȯ flaw ȯi coin th thin t͟h this
ü loot ú foot y yet yü few yú furious zh vision

chry·san·the·mum \kris-'an(t)-thə-məm *also* kriz-\ *n* [L, fr. Gk *chrysanthemon*, fr. *chrys-* + *anthemon* flower; akin to Gk *anthos* flower] **1 :** any of various composite plants (genus *Chrysanthemum*) including weeds, ornamentals grown for their brightly colored often double flower heads, and others important as sources of medicinals and insecticides **2 :** a flower head of an ornamental chrysanthemum

chrys·a·ro·bin \ˌkris-ə-'rō-bən\ *n* [*chrys-* + araroba + *-in*] **:** a powder obtained from Goa powder and used to treat skin diseases

Chry·se·is \krī-'sē-əs\ *n* [L, fr. Gk *Chryseïs*] **:** a daughter of a priest of Apollo in the *Iliad* narrative taken at Troy by Agamemnon but later restored to her father

chryso·ber·yl \'kris-ə-ˌber-əl\ *n* [L *chrysoberyllus*, fr. Gk *chrysobēryllos*, fr. *chrys-* + *bēryllos* beryl] **1** *obs* **:** a yellowish beryl **2 :** a usu. yellow or pale green mineral $BeAl_2O_4$ consisting of beryllium aluminum oxide with a little iron and sometimes used as a gem

chrys·o·lite \'kris-ə-ˌlīt\ *n* [ME *crisolite*, fr. OF, fr. L *chrysolithos*, fr. Gk, fr. *chrys-* + *-lithos* -lite] **:** OLIVINE

chrys·o·me·lid \ˌkris-ə-'mel-əd, -'mēl-\ *n* [deriv. of Gk *chrysomēlolonthē* golden cockchafer] **:** any of a large family (Chrysomelidae) of small, usu. oval and smooth, shining, and brightly colored beetles (as the Colorado potato beetle) — **chrysomelid** *adj*

chryso·phyte \'kris-ə-ˌfīt\ *n* [deriv. of Gk *chrysos* + *phyton* plant — more at PHYT-] **:** any of a major group (Chrysophyta) of algae (as diatoms) with yellowish green to golden brown pigments

chrys·o·prase \'kris-ə-ˌprāz\ *n* [ME *crisopace*, fr. OF, fr. L *chrysoprasus*, fr. Gk *chrysoprasos*, fr. *chrys-* + *prason* leek; akin to L *porrum* leek] **:** an apple-green chalcedony valued as a gem

chrys·o·tile \-ˌtīl\ *n* [G *chrysotil*, fr. *chrys-* + *-til* fiber, fr. Gk *tillein* to pluck] **:** a mineral consisting of a fibrous silky serpentine and constituting a kind of asbestos

chthon·ic \'thän-ik\ *or* **chtho·ni·an** \'thō-nē-ən\ *adj* [Gk *chthon-*, *chthōn* earth — more at HUMBLE] **:** INFERNAL <~ deities>

chub \'chəb\ *n, pl* **chub** *or* **chubs** [ME *chubbe*] **1 :** any of various freshwater cyprinid fishes (esp. of the genera *Gila*, *Hybopsis*, and *Nocomis*) **2 :** any of several marine or freshwater fishes not closely related to the true chub

chub·bi·ly \'chəb-ə-lē\ *adv* **:** in the manner of one that is chubby

chub·by \'chəb-ē\ *adj* **chub·bi·er; -est** [*chub*] **:** PLUMP <a ~ boy> — **chub·bi·ness** \'chəb-ē-nəs\ *n*

1chuck \'chək\ *vb* [ME *chukken*] **:** CLUCK

2chuck *n* — used as a term of endearment

3chuck *vt* [origin unknown] **1 :** PAT, TAP **2 a :** TOSS **b :** DISCARD <~*ed* his old shirt> **c :** DISMISS, OUST — used esp. with *out* <was ~*ed* out of office> **3 :** to have done with <~*ed* up his job> — **chuck it :** QUIT, YIELD

4chuck *n* **1 :** a pat or nudge under the chin **2 :** TOSS, JERK

5chuck *n* [E dial. *chuck* (lump)] **1 a :** a portion of a side of dressed beef including most of the neck, the parts about the shoulder blade, and those about the first three ribs — see BEEF illustration **b :** a similar cut of dressed veal or lamb **2** *chiefly West* **:** FOOD **3 :** an attachment for holding a workpiece or tool in a machine (as a drill press or lathe)

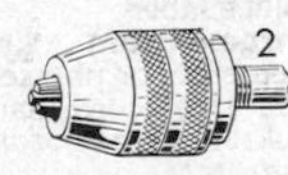

chucks 3: *1* with setscrew, *2* drill chuck

chuck·hole \'chək-ˌhōl, 'chəg-\ *n* [3*chuck* + *hole*] **:** a hole or rut in a road

chuck·le \'chək-əl\ *vi* **chuck·led; chuck·ling** \-(ə-)liŋ\ [prob. freq. of 1*chuck*] **1 :** to laugh inwardly or quietly **2 :** to make a continuous gentle sound resembling suppressed mirth <the clear bright water *chuckled* over gravel —B. A. Williams> — **chuckle** *n* — **chuck·le·some** \-əl-səm\ *adj* — **chuck·ling·ly** \-(ə-)liŋ-lē\ *adv*

chuck·le·head \'chək-əl-ˌhed\ *n* [*chuckle* (lumpish) + *head*] **:** BLOCKHEAD — **chuck·le·head·ed** \ˌchək-əl-'hed-əd\ *adj*

chuck wagon *n* [5*chuck*] **:** a wagon carrying a stove and provisions for cooking (as on a ranch)

chuck·wal·la \'chək-ˌwäl-ə\ *or* **chuck·a·wal·la** \'chək-ə-ˌwäl-ə\ *n* [MexSp *chacahuala*] **:** a large edible herbivorous lizard (*Sauromalus obesus* of the family Iguanidae) of desert regions of the southwestern U.S.

chuck–will's–wid·ow \ˌchək-ˌwilz-'wid-(ˌ)ō, -'wid-ə(-w)\ *n* [imit.] **:** a goatsucker (*Caprimulgus carolinensis*) of the southern U.S.

1chuff \'chəf\ *n* [ME *chuffe*] **:** BOOR, CHURL

2chuff *n* [imit.] **:** the sound of noisy exhaust or exhalations

3chuff *vi* **:** to produce noisy exhaust or exhalations **:** proceed or operate with chuffs <the ~*ing* and snorting of switch engines —Paul Gallico>

chuf·fy \'chəf-ē\ *adj* **chuf·fi·er; -est** [perh. fr. E dial. *chuff* chubby] **:** FAT, CHUBBY

1chug \'chəg\ *n* [imit.] **:** a dull explosive sound made by or as if by a laboring engine

2chug *vi* **chugged; chug·ging :** to move or go with chugs <a locomotive *chugging* along> — **chug·ger** *n*

chug·a·lug \'chəg-ə-ˌləg\ *vb* **-lugged; -lug·ging** [imit.] *vt* **:** to drink a whole container of without pause ~ *vi* **:** to drink a whole container (as of beer) without pause

chu·kar \chə-'kär\ *n, pl* **chukar** *or* **chukars** [Hindi *cakor*] **:** a largely gray and black Indian partridge (*Alectoris graeca chukar*) introduced into dry parts of the western U.S.

chuk·ka \'chək-ə\ *n* [*chukka*, alter. of *chukker*; fr. a similar polo player's boot] **:** a usu. ankle-length leather boot with two pairs of eyelets or a buckle and strap

chuk·ker *or* **chuk·kar** \'chək-ər\ *or* **chuk·ka** \'chək-ə\ *n* [Hindi *cakkar* circular course, fr. Skt *cakra* wheel, circle — more at WHEEL] **:** a playing period of a polo game

1chum \'chəm\ *n* [perh. by shortening & alter. fr. *chamber fellow* (roommate)] **:** a close friend **:** PAL — **chum·ship** \-ˌship\ *n*

2chum *vi* **chummed; chum·ming 1 :** to room together **2 a :** to be a close friend **b :** to show affable friendliness

3chum *n* [origin unknown] **:** chopped fish or other matter thrown overboard to attract fish

4chum *vb* **chummed; chumming** *vi* **:** to throw chum overboard to attract fish ~ *vt* **:** to attract with chum <*chumming* the fish with cut-up shrimp>

chum·my \'chəm-ē\ *adj* **chum·mi·er; -est :** INTIMATE, SOCIABLE — **chum·mi·ly** \'chəm-ə-lē\ *adv* — **chum·mi·ness** \'chəm-ē-nəs\ *n*

chump \'chəmp\ *n* [perh. blend of *chunk* and *lump*] **:** FOOL, DUPE

1chunk \'chəŋk\ *n* [perh. alter. of *chuck* (short piece of wood)] **1 :** a short thick piece or lump (as of wood or coal) **2 :** a large noteworthy quantity <bet a sizable ~ of money on the race> **3 :** a strong thickset horse usu. smaller than a draft horse

2chunk *vi* [imit.] **:** to make a dull plunging or explosive sound <the rhythmic ~*ing* of thrown quoits —John Updike>

chunky \'chəŋ-kē\ *adj* **chunk·i·er; -est 1 :** STOCKY **2 :** filled with chunks <breakfast . . . with toast and ~ marmalade —*The People*> — **chunk·i·ly** \-kə-lē\ *adv*

chun·ter \'chənt-ər\ *vi* [prob. of imit. origin] *Brit* **:** to talk in a low inarticulate way **:** MUTTER

1church \'chərch\ *n* [ME *chirche*, fr. OE *cirice*; akin to OHG *kirihha* church; both fr. a prehistoric WGmc word derived fr. LGk *kyriakon*, fr. Gk, neut. of *kyriakos* of the lord, fr. *kyrios* lord, master, fr. *kyros* power; akin to L *cavus* hollow — more at CAVE] **1 :** a building for public and esp. Christian worship **2 :** the clergy or officialdom of a religious body **3 :** a body or organization of religious believers: as **a :** the whole body of Christians **b :** DENOMINATION **c :** CONGREGATION **4 :** a public divine worship <goes to ~ every Sunday> **5 :** the clerical profession <considered the ~ as a possible career>

2church *vt* **:** to bring to church to receive one of its rites

3church *adj* **1 :** of or relating to a church <~ government> **2** *chiefly Brit* **:** of or relating to the established church

churched \'chərcht\ *adj* **:** affiliated with a church

church father *n* **:** FATHER 4

church·go·er \'chərch-ˌgō(-ə)r\ *n* **:** one who frequently attends church — **church·go·ing** \-ˌgō-iŋ, -ˌgȯ(-)iŋ\ *adj or n*

church·ian·i·ty \ˌchər-chē-'an-ət-ē\ *n* [*church* + *-ianity* (as in *Christianity*)] **:** the usu. excessive or sectarian attachment to the practices and interests of a particular church

church·ing *n* **:** the administration or reception of a rite of the church; *specif* **:** a ceremony in some churches by which women after childbirth are received in the church with prayers, blessings, and thanksgiving

church key *n* **:** an implement with a triangular pointed head for piercing the tops of cans (as of beer)

church·less \'chərch-ləs\ *adj* **:** not affiliated with a church

church·ly \'chərch-lē\ *adj* **1 :** of or relating to a church **2 :** suitable to or suggestive of a church **3 :** adhering to a church **4 :** CHURCHY 2 — **church·li·ness** *n*

church·man \'chərch-mən\ *n* **1 :** CLERGYMAN **2 :** a member of a church

church·man·ship \-mən-ˌship\ *n* **:** the attitude, belief, or practice of a churchman

church mode *n* **:** one of several usu. 8-tone scales prevalent in medieval music each utilizing a different pattern of intervals and each beginning on a different tone

Church of England : the established episcopal church of England

church register *n* **:** a parish register of baptisms, marriages, and deaths

church school *n* **1 :** a school providing a general education but supported by a particular church in contrast to a public school or a nondenominational private school **2 :** an organization of officers, teachers, and pupils for purposes of moral and religious education under the supervision of a local church

Church Slavic *n* **:** OLD CHURCH SLAVONIC

church·war·den \'chərch-ˌwȯrd-ᵊn\ *n* **1 :** one of two lay parish officers in Anglican churches with responsibility esp. for parish property and alms **2 :** a long-stemmed clay pipe

church·wom·an \-ˌwu̇m-ən\ *n* **:** a woman who is a member of a church

churchy \'chər-chē\ *adj* **1 :** of or suggesting a church **2 :** marked by strict conformity or zealous adherence to the forms or beliefs of a church

church·yard \-ˌyärd\ *n* **:** a yard that belongs to a church and is often used as a burial ground

churl \'chər(-ə)l\ *n* [ME, fr. OE *ceorl* man, ceorl; akin to Gk *gēras* old age — more at CORN] **1 :** CEORL **2 :** a medieval peasant **3 :** RUSTIC, COUNTRYMAN **4 a :** a rude ill-bred person **b :** a stingy morose person

churl·ish \'chər-lish\ *adj* **1 :** of or resembling a churl **:** VULGAR **2 :** resembling or befitting a churl (as in lack of refinement or delicacy of feelings) **3 :** difficult to work with or deal with **:** INTRACTABLE <~ soil> *syn* see BOORISH — **churl·ish·ly** *adv* — **churl·ish·ness** *n*

1churn \'chərn\ *n* [ME *chyrne*, fr. OE *cyrin*; akin to OE *corn* grain; fr. the granular appearance of cream as it is churned — more at CORN] **:** a vessel in which milk or cream is agitated to separate the oily globules from the other parts and thus to obtain butter

2churn *vt* **1 :** to agitate (milk or cream) in a churn in order to make butter **2 a :** to stir or agitate violently <an old sternwheeler ~*ing* the muddy river> **b :** to make (as foam) by so doing **3 :** to make (the account of a client) excessively active by frequent purchases and sales primarily in order to generate commissions ~ *vi* **1 :** to work a churn **2 a :** to produce or be in violent motion **b :** to proceed by means of rotating members (as wheels)

churn out *vt* **:** to produce mechanically **:** grind out <generators . . . able to *churn out* 2,100,000 kilowatts —Lawrence Mosher>

churr \'chər\ *vi* [imit.] **:** to make a vibrant or whirring noise like that made by some insects (as the cockchafer) or by some birds (as the partridge) — **churr** *n*

chur·ri·gue·resque \ˌchu̇r-i-gə-'resk\ *adj, often cap* [Sp *churrigueresco*, fr. José *Churriguera* †1723 Sp architect] **:** of or relating to a Spanish baroque architectural style characterized by elaborate surface decoration or its Latin-American adaptation

[1]**chute** \'shüt\ *n* [F, fr. OF, fr. *cheoir* to fall, fr. L *cadere* — more at CHANCE] **1 a :** FALL 6b **b :** a quick descent (as in a river) : RAPID **2 :** an inclined plane, sloping channel, or passage down or through which things may pass : SLIDE **3 :** PARACHUTE
[2]**chute** *vb* **chut·ed; chut·ing** *vt* **:** to convey by a chute ~ *vi* **1 :** to go in or as if in a chute **2 :** to utilize a chute (as by passing ore down it)
chut·ist \'shüt-əst\ *n* **:** PARACHUTIST
chut·ney \'chət-nē\ *n, pl* **chutneys** [Hindi *caṭnī*] **:** a condiment that is made of acid fruits with added raisins, dates, and onions and seasoned with spices
chutz·pah *or* **chutz·pa** \'hu̇t-spə, 'k̲u̇t-, -(,)spä\ *n* [Yiddish, fr. L Heb *ḥuṣpāh*] **:** supreme self-confidence **:** NERVE, GALL
chyle \'kī(ə)l\ *n* [LL *chylus,* fr. Gk *chylos* juice, chyle, fr. *chein* to pour — more at FOUND] **:** lymph that is milky from emulsified fats, characteristically present in the lacteals, and most apparent during intestinal absorption of fats — **chy·lous** \'kī-ləs\ *adj*
chy·lo·mi·cron \,kī-lō-'mī-,krän\ *n* [Gk *chylos* + *mikron,* neut. of *mikros* small] **:** a microscopic lipid particle common in the blood during fat digestion and assimilation
chyme \'kīm\ *n* [NL *chymus,* fr. LL, chyle, fr. Gk *chymos* juice, fr. *chein*] **:** the semifluid mass of partly digested food expelled by the stomach into the duodenum — **chy·mous** \'kī-məs\ *adj*
chy·mo·tryp·sin \,kī-mō-'trip-sən\ *n* [*chyme* + *-o-* + *trypsin*] **:** a pancreatic proteinase acting on proteins by breaking internal peptide bonds
chy·mo·tryp·sin·o·gen \-,trip-'sin-ə-jən\ *n* **:** a zymogen that is converted by trypsin to chymotrypsin
Ci *abbr* **1** cirrus **2** curie
CI *abbr* **1** cast iron **2** certificate of insurance **3** cost and insurance
CIA *abbr* Central Intelligence Agency
cia *abbr* [Sp *compañía*] company
CIAA *abbr* Central Intercollegiate Athletic Association
ciao \'chau̇\ *interj* [It, fr. It dial., alter. of *schiavo* (I am your) slave, fr. ML *sclavus*] — used conventionally as an utterance at meeting or parting
ci·bo·ri·um \sə-'bōr-ē-əm, -'bȯr-\ *n, pl* **-ria** \-ē-ə\ [ML, fr. L, cup, fr. Gk *kibōrion*] **1 :** a goblet-shaped vessel for holding eucharistic bread **2 :** BALDACHIN; *specif* **:** a freestanding vaulted canopy supported by four columns over a high altar
ci·ca·da \sə-'kād-ə, -'käd-; sī-'kād-\ *n* [NL, genus name, fr. L, cicada] **:** any of a family (Cicadidae) of homopterous insects with a stout body, wide blunt head, and large transparent wings
ci·ca·la \sə-'käl-ə\ *n* [It, fr. ML, alter. of L *cicada*] **:** CICADA
cic·a·tri·cial \,sik-ə-'trish-əl\ *adj* **:** of or relating to a cicatrix
cic·a·tri·cle \'sik-ə-,trik-əl\ *n* [L *cicatricula*] **1 :** CICATRIX 2a **2 :** BLASTODISC
ci·ca·trix \'sik-ə-,triks, sə-'kā-triks\ *n, pl* **ci·ca·tri·ces** \,sik-ə-'trī-(,)sēz, sə-'kā-trə-,sēz\ [L *cicatric-, cicatrix*] **1 :** a scar resulting from formation and contraction of fibrous tissue in a flesh wound **2 :** a mark resembling a scar esp. when caused by the previous attachment of a part or organ: as **a :** a mark left on a stem after the fall of a leaf or bract **b :** HILUM 1a
cic·a·trize \'sik-ə-,trīz\ *vb* **-trized; -triz·ing** *vt* **1 :** to induce the formation of a scar in **2 :** SCAR ~ *vi* **:** to heal by forming a scar — **cic·a·tri·za·tion** \,sik-ə-trə-'zā-shən\ *n*
ci·ce·ro·ne \,sis-ə-'rō-nē, ,chē-chə-\ *n, pl* **-ni** \-(,)nē\ [It, fr. *Cicerone* Cicero] **:** a guide who conducts sightseers
cich·lid \'sik-ləd\ *n* [deriv. of Gk *kichlē* thrush, a kind of wrasse; akin to Gk *chelidōn* swallow — more at CELANDINE] **:** any of a family (Cichlidae) of mostly tropical spiny-finned freshwater fishes including several kept in tropical aquariums — **cichlid** *adj*
ci·cis·beo \,chē-chəz-'bā-(,)ō\ *n, pl* **-bei** \-'bā-,ē\ [It] **:** LOVER, GALLANT — **ci·cis·be·ism** \-'bā-,iz-əm\ *n*
CID *abbr* **1** Criminal Investigation Department **2** cubic inch displacement
-cid·al \'sīd-ᵊl\ *adj comb form* [LL *-cidalis,* fr. L *-cida*] **:** killing **:** having power to kill <filari*cidal*>
-cide \,sīd\ *n comb form* [MF, fr. L *-cida,* fr. *caedere* to cut, kill — more at CONCISE] **1 :** killer <insecti*cide*> **2** [MF, fr. L *-cidium,* fr. *caedere*] **:** killing <sui*cide*>
ci·der \'sīd-ər\ *n* [ME *sidre, fr. OF, fr. LL sicera* strong drink, fr. Gk *sikera,* fr. Heb *shēkhār*] **1 :** the expressed juice of fruit (as apples) used as a beverage or for making other products (as applejack) **2** *Brit* **:** fermented apple juice often made sparkling by carbonation or fermentation in a sealed container
cider vinegar *n* **:** vinegar made from fermented cider
ci–de·vant \,sēd-ə-'väⁿ\ *adj* [F, lit., formerly] **:** FORMER
cie *abbr* [F *compagnie*] company
CIF *abbr* **1** central information file **2** cost, insurance, and freight
ci·gar \sig-'är\ *n* [Sp *cigarro*] **:** a small roll of tobacco leaf for smoking
cig·a·rette *also* **cig·a·ret** \,sig-ə-'ret, 'sig-ə-,\ *n* [F *cigarette,* dim. of *cigare* cigar, fr. Sp *cigarro*] **:** a narrow tube of cut tobacco enclosed in paper and designed for smoking
cig·a·ril·lo \,sig-ə-'ril-(,)ō, -'rē-(,)(y)ō\ *n, pl* **-los** [Sp *cigarrillo* cigaret, dim. of *cigarro* cigar] **1 :** a very small cigar **2 :** a cigarette wrapped in tobacco rather than paper
cil·i·ary \'sil-ē-,er-ē\ *adj* **1 :** of or relating to cilia **2 :** of, relating to, or being the annular suspension of the lens of the eye
[1]**cil·i·ate** \'sil-ē-ət, -ē-,āt\ *or* **cil·i·at·ed** \-,āt-əd\ *adj* **:** provided with cilia — **cil·i·ate·ly** *adv*
[2]**ciliate** *n* **:** any of a subphylum (Ciliophora) of ciliate protozoans
cil·i·um \'sil-ē-əm\ *n, pl* **-ia** \-ē-ə\ [NL, fr. L, eyelid] **1 :** EYELASH **2 :** a minute short hairlike process often forming part of a fringe; *esp* **:** one of a cell that is capable of lashing movement and serves esp. in free unicellular organisms to produce locomotion or in higher forms a current of fluid
ci·mex \'sī-,meks\ *n, pl* **ci·mi·ces** \'sī-mə-,sēz, 'sim-ə-\ [L *cimic-, cimex* — more at CHINCH] **:** BEDBUG
[1]**Cim·me·ri·an** \sə-'mir-ē-ən\ *adj* **:** very dark or gloomy **:** STYGIAN <there under ebon shades . . . in dark ~ desert ever dwell —John Milton>
[2]**Cimmerian** *n* [L *Cimmerii,* a mythical people, fr. Gk *Kimmerioi*] **:** one of a mythical people described by Homer as dwelling in a remote realm of mist and gloom
C in C *abbr* commander in chief
[1]**cinch** \'sinch\ *n* [Sp *cincha,* fr. L *cingula* girdle, girth, fr. *cingere*] **1 :** a strong girth for a pack or saddle **2 :** a tight grip **3 a :** a thing done with ease **b :** a certainty to happen
[2]**cinch** *vt* **1 :** to put a cinch on **2 :** to make certain **:** ASSURE ~ *vi* **:** to perform the act of cinching **:** tighten the cinch — often used with *up*
cin·cho·na \siŋ-'kō-nə, sin-'chō-\ *n* [NL, genus name, fr. the countess of *Chinchón* †1641 wife of the Peruvian viceroy] **1 :** any of a genus (*Cinchona*) of So. American trees and shrubs of the madder family **2 :** the dried bark of a cinchona (as *C. ledgeriana*) containing alkaloids (as quinine) and used as a specific in malaria
cin·cho·nine \'siŋ-kə-,nēn, 'sin-chə-\ *n* **:** a bitter white crystalline alkaloid $C_{19}H_{22}N_2O$ found esp. in cinchona bark and used like quinine
cin·cho·nism \'siŋ-kə-,niz-əm, 'sin-chə-\ *n* **:** a disorder due to excessive or prolonged use of cinchona or its alkaloids and marked by temporary deafness, ringing in the ears, headache, dizziness, and rash
cinc·ture \'siŋ(k)-chər\ *n* [L *cinctura* girdle, fr. *cinctus,* pp. of *cingere* to gird; akin to Skt *kāñcī* girdle] **1 :** the act of encircling **2 a :** an encircling area **b :** GIRDLE, BELT; *esp* **:** a cord or sash of cloth worn around an ecclesiastical vestment (as an alb) or the habit of a religious
cin·der \'sin-dər\ *n* [ME *sinder,* fr. OE; akin to OHG *sintar* dross, slag, OSlav *sędra* stalactite] **1 :** the slag from a metal furnace **:** DROSS **2 a** *pl* **:** ASHES **b :** a fragment of ash **3 a :** a partly burned combustible in which fire is extinct **b :** a hot coal without flame **c :** a partly burned coal capable of further burning without flame **4 :** a fragment of lava from an erupting volcano — **cinder** *vt* — **cin·dery** \-d(ə-)rē\ *adj*
cinder block *n* **:** a hollow rectangular building block made of cement and coal cinders
Cin·der·el·la \,sin-də-'rel-ə\ *n* **1 :** a fairy-tale heroine who is used as a drudge by her stepmother but ends up happily married to a prince through the intervention of her fairy godmother **2 :** one resembling the fairy-tale Cinderella: as **a :** one suffering undeserved neglect **b :** one suddenly lifted from obscurity to honor or significance
cine \'sin-ē\ *n* [short for *cinema*] **:** MOTION PICTURE
cine- *comb form* [*cinema*] **:** motion picture <*cine*camera> <*cine*film> <*cine*-X ray>
cine·an·gio·car·di·og·ra·phy \,sin-ē-'an-jē-ō-,kärd-ē-'äg-rə-fē\ *n* [*cine-* + *angi-* + *cardi-* + *-graphy*] **:** motion-picture photography of a fluoroscopic screen recording passage of a contrasting medium through the chambers of the heart and large blood vessels — **cine·an·gio·car·dio·graph·ic** \-,kärd-ē-ə-'graf-ik\ *adj*
cine·an·gi·og·ra·phy \-,an-jē-'äg-rə-fē\ *n* [*cine-* + *angi-* + *-graphy*] **:** motion-picture photography of a fluorescent screen recording passage of a contrasting medium through the blood vessels — **cine·an·gio·graph·ic** \-jē-ə-'graf-ik\ *adj*
cine·ast \'sin-ē-,ast, -ē-əst\ *or* **cine·aste** \'sin-ē-,ast\ *n* [F *cinéaste,* fr. *ciné* cine + *-aste* (as in *enthousiaste* enthusiast)] **:** a devotee of motion pictures
cin·e·ma \'sin-ə-mə\ *n* [short for *cinematograph*] **1** *chiefly Brit* **a :** MOTION PICTURE **b :** a motion-picture theater **2 a :** MOVIES; *esp* **:** the motion-picture industry **b :** the art or technique of making motion pictures
cin·e·ma·go·er \-,gō(-ə)r\ *n* **:** MOVIEGOER
cin·e·ma·theque \,sin-ə-mə-'tek\ *n* [F *cinémathèque* film library, fr. *cinéma* cinema + *-thèque* (as in *bibliothèque* library)] **:** a small movie house specializing in avant-garde films
cin·e·mat·ic \,sin-ə-'mat-ik\ *adj* **1 :** filmed and presented as a motion picture <~ fantasies> **2 :** of, relating to, or suitable for motion pictures or the filming of motion pictures <~ principles and techniques> — **cin·e·mat·i·cal·ly** \-'mat-i-k(ə-)lē\ *adv*
cin·e·ma·tize \'sin-ə-mə-,tīz\ *vt* **-tized; -tiz·ing :** to make a motion picture of (as a novel) **:** adapt for motion pictures
cin·e·mat·o·graph \,sin-ə-'mat-ə-,graf\ *n* [F *cinématographe,* fr. Gk *kinēmat-, kinēma* movement (fr. *kinein* to move) + *-o-* + *-graphe* -graph — more at HIGHT] **1** *chiefly Brit* **:** a motion-picture camera, projector, theater, or show **2** *chiefly Brit* **:** CINEMA 2b
cin·e·ma·tog·ra·pher \,sin-ə-mə-'täg-rə-fər\ *n* **1 :** a motion-picture cameraman **2 :** a motion-picture projectionist
cin·e·ma·tog·ra·phy \,sin-ə-mə-'täg-rə-fē\ *n* **:** the art or science of motion-picture photography — **cin·e·mat·o·graph·ic** \-,mat-ə-'graf-ik\ *also* **cin·e·mat·o·graph·i·cal** \-i-kəl\ *adj* — **cin·e·mat·o·graph·i·cal·ly** \-i-k(ə-)lē\ *adv*
ci·ne·ma ve·ri·té \'sin-ə-mə-,ver-ə-'tā\ *n* [F *cinéma-vérité,* lit., truth cinema] **:** the art or technique of filming a motion picture so as to convey candid realism
cin·e·ole \'sin-ē-,ōl\ *n* [ISV, by transposition fr. NL *oleum cinae* wormseed oil] **:** a liquid $C_{10}H_{18}O$ with a camphor odor contained in many essential oils (as of eucalyptus) and used esp. as an expectorant
cin·er·ar·ia \,sin-ə-'rer-ē-ə, -'rar-\ *n* [NL, fr. L, fem. of *cinerarius* of ashes, fr. *ciner-, cinis*] **:** any of several pot plants deriving from a perennial composite herb (*Senecio cruentus*) of the Canary islands and having heart-shaped leaves and clusters of bright flower heads
cin·er·ar·i·um \-ē-əm\ *n, pl* **-ia** \-ē-ə\ [L, fr. *ciner-, cinis*] **:** a place to receive the ashes of the cremated dead — **cin·er·ary** \'sin-ə-,rer-ē\ *adj*

ci·ne·re·ous \sə-'nir-ē-əs\ *adj* [L *cinereus,* fr. *ciner-, cinis* ashes] **1** : gray tinged with black **2** : resembling or consisting of ashes

cin·er·in \'sin-ə-rən\ *n* [L *ciner-, cinis* ashes] : either of two compounds $C_{20}H_{28}O_3$ and $C_{21}H_{28}O_5$ of high insecticidal properties

cin·gu·lum \'siŋ-gyə-ləm\ *n, pl* **-la** \-lə\ [NL, fr. L, girdle, fr. *cingere* to gird — more at CINCTURE] : a differentiated band or a girdle (as of color) — **cin·gu·late** \-lət\ *adj*

cin·na·bar \'sin-ə-ˌbär\ *n* [ME *cynabare,* fr. MF & L; MF *cenobre,* fr. L *cinnabaris,* fr. Gk *kinnabari* of non-IE origin; akin to Ar *zinjafr* cinnabar] **1** : native red mercuric sulfide HgS that is the only important ore of mercury **2** : artificial red mercuric sulfide used esp. as a pigment **3** : a European moth (*Tyria jacobeae*) with grayish black fore wings marked with red and clear reddish pink hind wings that has been introduced into the U.S. in attempts to control ragwort on the leaves of which its larvae feed — called also *cinnabar moth* — **cin·na·bar·ine** \-ˌbär-ˌīn, ˌsin-ə-'bär-ən\ *adj*

cin·nam·ic \sə-'nam-ik\ *adj* [F *cinnamique,* fr. *cinname* cinnamon, fr. L *cinnamon*] : of, relating to, or obtained from cinnamon

cinnamic acid *n* : a white crystalline odorless acid $C_9H_8O_2$ found esp. in cinnamon oil and storax

cin·na·mon \'sin-ə-mən\ *n, often attrib* [ME *cynamone,* fr. L *cinnamomum, cinnamon,* fr. Gk *kinnamōmon, kinnamon,* of non-IE origin; akin to Heb *qinnāmōn* cinnamon] **1 a** : the highly aromatic bark of any of several trees (genus *Cinnamomum*) of the laurel family used as a spice **b** : a tree that yields cinnamon **2** : a light yellowish brown

cinnamon fern *n* : a large No. American fern (*Osmunda cinnamomea*) with cinnamon-colored spore-bearing fronds shorter than and separate from the green foliage fronds

cinnamon stone *n* : ESSONITE

cin·quain \'siŋ-ˌkān, 'saŋ-\ *n* [F, fr. *cinq* five, fr. L *quinque* — more at FIVE] : a five-line stanza

cin·que·cen·tist \ˌchiŋ-kwi-'chent-əst\ *n* : an Italian of the cinquecento; *esp* : a poet or artist of this period

cin·que·cen·to \ˌchiŋ-kwi-'chen-(ˌ)tō\ *n* [It, lit., five hundred, fr. *cinque* five (fr. L *quinque*) + *cento* hundred, fr. L *centum* — more at HUNDRED] : the 16th century esp. in Italian art

cinque·foil \'siŋk-ˌfȯil, 'saŋk-\ *n* [ME *sink foil,* fr. MF *cincfoille,* fr. L *quinquefolium,* fr. *quinque* five + *folium* leaf — more at BLADE] **1** : any of a genus (*Potentilla*) of plants of the rose family with 5-lobed leaves **2** : a design enclosed by five joined foils

ci·on *var of* SCION

¹ci·pher \'sī-fər\ *n, often attrib* [ME, fr. MF *cifre,* fr. ML *cifra,* fr. Ar *ṣifr* empty, cipher, zero] **1 a** : ZERO 3a **b** : one that has no weight, worth, or influence : NONENTITY **2 a** : a method of transforming a text in order to conceal its meaning — compare CODE 3b **b** : a message in code **3** : an arabic numeral **4** : a combination of symbolic letters; *esp* : the interwoven initials of a name

²cipher *vb* **ci·phered; ci·pher·ing** \-f(ə-)riŋ\ *vi* : to use figures in a mathematical process ~ *vt* **1** : ENCIPHER **2** : to compute arithmetically

cipher alphabet *n* : a set of one-to-one equivalences between a sequence of plaintext letters and the sequence of their cipher substitutes used in cryptography

ci·pher·text \'sī-fər-ˌtekst\ *n* : the enciphered form of a text or of its elements — compare PLAINTEXT

ci·pho·ny \'sī-fə-nē\ *n* [*cipher* + *telephony*] : the electronic scrambling of voice transmissions

cir *or* **circ** *abbr* circular

cir·ca \'sər-kə, 'ki(ə)r-(ˌ)kä\ *prep* [L, fr. *circum* around — more at CIRCUM-] : at, in, or of approximately — used esp. with dates <born ~ 1600>

cir·ca·di·an \(ˌ)sər-'kad-ē-ən, -'kād-; ˌsər-kə-'dī-ən, -'dē-\ *adj* [L *circa* about + *dies* day + E *-an* — more at DEITY] **1** : based on or involving approximately 24 hour periods <~ periodicity of blood cell production> **2** : of, relating to, or being a biological activity that recurs at approximately 24 hour intervals <a ~ rhythm in hatching>

Cir·cas·sian \(ˌ)sər-'kash-ən\ *n* [*Circassia,* Russia] **1** : a member of a group of peoples of the Caucasus of Caucasian race but not of Indo-European speech **2** : the language of the Circassian peoples — **Circassian** *adj*

Circassian walnut *n* : the light brown irregularly black-veined wood of the English walnut much used for veneer and cabinetwork

Cir·ce \'sər-(ˌ)sē\ *n* [L, fr. Gk *Kirkē*] : a sorceress who changed Odysseus' men into swine but was forced by Odysseus to change them back

cir·ci·nate \'sərs-ᵊn-ˌāt\ *adj* [L *circinatus,* pp. of *circinare* to round, fr. *circinus* pair of compasses, fr. *circus*] : ROUNDED, COILED; *esp* : rolled up on the axis with the apex as a center <~ fern fronds unfolding> — **cir·ci·nate·ly** *adv*

¹cir·cle \'sər-kəl\ *n, often attrib* [ME *cercle,* fr. OF, fr. L *circulus,* dim. of *circus* circle, circus, fr. or akin to Gk *krikos, kirkos* ring] **1 a** : RING, HALO **b** : a closed plane curve every point of which is equidistant from a fixed point within the curve **c** : the plane surface bounded by such a curve **2** : the orbit or period of revolution of a heavenly body **3** : something in the form of a circle or section of a circle: as **a** : CIRCLET, DIADEM **b** : an instrument of astronomical observation the graduated limb of which consists of an entire circle **c** : a balcony or tier of seats in a theater **d** : a circle formed on the surface of a sphere by the intersection of a plane that passes through it <~ of latitude> **e** : ROTARY **4** : an area of action or influence : REALM **5 a** : CYCLE, ROUND <the wheel has come full ~> **b** : fallacious reasoning in which something to be demonstrated is covertly assumed **6** : a group of persons sharing a common interest or revolving about a common center <joined the sewing ~ of her church> <the gossip of court ~*s*> **7** : a territorial or administrative division or district ***syn*** see SET

²circle *vb* **cir·cled; cir·cling** \-k(ə-)liŋ\ *vt* **1** : to enclose in or as if in a circle **2** : to move or revolve around ~ *vi* **1 a** : to move in or as if in a circle **b** : CIRCULATE **2** : to describe or extend in a circle — **cir·cler** \-k(ə-)lər\ *n*

circle graph *n* : PIE CHART

cir·clet \'sər-klət\ *n* : a little circle; *esp* : a circular ornament

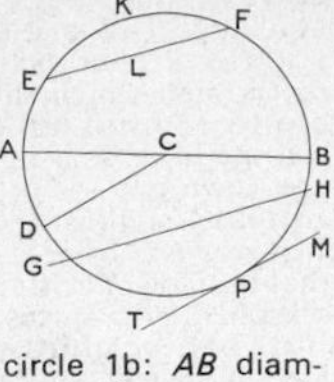

circle 1b: *AB* diameter: *C* center; *CD, CA, CB,* radii; *EKF* arc on chord *EF; EFKL* (area) segment on chord *EF; ACD* (area) sector; *GH* secant; *TPM* tangent at point *P; EKFBPDA* circumference

¹cir·cuit \'sər-kət\ *n, often attrib* [ME, fr. MF *circuite,* fr. L *circuitus,* fr. pp. of *circumire, circuire* to go around, fr. *circum-* + *ire* to go — more at ISSUE] **1 a** : a usu. circular line encompassing an area **b** : the space enclosed within such a line **2 a** : a course around a periphery **b** : a circuitous or indirect route **3 a** : a regular tour (as by a traveling judge or preacher) around an assigned district or territory **b** : the route traveled **c** : a group of church congregations ministered to by one pastor **4 a** : the complete path of an electric current including usu. the source of electric energy **b** : an assemblage of electronic elements : HOOKUP **c** : a two-way communication path between points (as in a computer) **5 a** : an association of similar groups : LEAGUE **b** : a group of establishments offering similar entertainment or presenting a series of contests; *esp* : a chain of theaters at which productions are successively presented — **cir·cuit·al** \-kət-ᵊl\ *adj*

²circuit *vt* : to make a circuit about ~ *vi* : to make a circuit

circuit breaker *n* : a switch that automatically interrupts an electric circuit under an infrequent abnormal condition

circuit court *n* : a court that sits at two or more places within one judicial district

circuit judge *n* : a judge who holds a circuit court

cir·cu·itous \(ˌ)sər-'kyü-ət-əs\ *adj* **1** : marked by a circular or winding course <a ~ route> **2** : marked by roundabout or indirect procedure — **cir·cu·itous·ly** *adv* — **cir·cu·itous·ness** *n*

circuit rider *n* : a clergyman assigned to a circuit esp. in a rural area

cir·cuit·ry \'sər-kə-trē\ *n, pl* **-ries** **1** : the detailed plan of an electric circuit **2** : the components of an electric circuit

cir·cu·ity \(ˌ)sər-'kyü-ət-ē\ *n, pl* **-ities** [irreg. fr. *circuit*] : lack of straightforwardness : INDIRECTION <mired so deeply in its own complicated ~ of words —C. O. Gregory>

¹cir·cu·lar \'sər-kyə-lər\ *adj* [ME *circuler,* fr. MF, fr. LL *circularis,* fr. L *circulus* circle] **1** : having the form of a circle : ROUND **2** : moving in or describing a circle or spiral **3** : CIRCUITOUS, INDIRECT <a ~ explanation> **4** : characterized by reasoning in a circle <~ arguments> **5** : marked by or moving in a cycle **6** : intended for circulation — **cir·cu·lar·i·ty** \ˌsər-kyə-'lar-ət-ē\ *n* — **cir·cu·lar·ly** \'sər-kyə-lər-lē\ *adv* — **cir·cu·lar·ness** *n*

²circular *n* : a paper (as a leaflet) intended for wide distribution

circular file *n* : WASTEBASKET

circular function *n* : TRIGONOMETRIC FUNCTION

cir·cu·lar·ize \'sər-kyə-lə-ˌrīz\ *vt* **-ized; -iz·ing** **1 a** : to send circulars to **b** : to poll by questionnaire **2** : PUBLICIZE — **cir·cu·lar·iza·tion** \ˌsər-kyə-lə-rə-'zā-shən\ *n*

circular measure *n* : the measure of an angle in radians

cir·cu·late \'sər-kyə-ˌlāt\ *vb* **-lat·ed; -lat·ing** [L *circulatus,* pp. of *circulare,* fr. *circulus* circle] *vi* **1** : to move in a circle, circuit, or orbit; *esp* : to follow a course that returns to the starting point <blood ~*s* through the body> **2** : to pass from person to person or place to place: as **a** : to flow without obstruction **b** : to become well known or widespread <rumors *circulated* through the town> **c** : to go from group to group at a social gathering **d** : to come into the hands of readers; *specif* : to become sold or distributed ~ *vt* : to cause to circulate — **cir·cu·lat·able** \-ˌlāt-ə-bəl\ *adj* — **cir·cu·la·tive** \-ˌlāt-iv\ *adj* — **cir·cu·la·tor** \-ˌlāt-ər\ *n* — **cir·cu·la·to·ry** \-lə-ˌtōr-ē, -ˌtȯr-\ *adj*

circulating decimal *n* : REPEATING DECIMAL

cir·cu·la·tion \ˌsər-kyə-'lā-shən\ *n* **1** : FLOW **2** : orderly movement through a circuit; *esp* : the movement of blood through the vessels of the body induced by the pumping action of the heart **3 a** : passage or transmission from person to person or place to place; *esp* : the interchange of currency <coins in ~> **b** : the extent of dissemination: as (1) : the average number of copies of a publication sold over a given period (2) : the total number of items taken by borrowers from a library

circulatory system *n* : the system of blood, blood vessels, lymphatics, and heart concerned with the circulation of the blood and lymph

circum- *prefix* [OF or L; OF, fr. L, fr. *circum,* fr. *circus* circle — more at CIRCLE] : around : about <*circum*polar>

cir·cum·am·bi·ent \ˌsər-kə-'mam-bē-ənt\ *adj* [LL *circumambient-, circumambiens,* prp. of *circumambire* to surround in a circle, fr. L *circum-* + *ambire* to go around — more at AMBIENT] : being on all sides : ENCOMPASSING — **cir·cum·am·bi·ent·ly** *adv*

cir·cum·am·bu·late \-byə-ˌlāt\ *vt* **-lat·ed; -lat·ing** [LL *circumambulatus,* pp. of *circumambulare,* fr. L *circum-* + *ambulare* to walk] : to circle on foot esp. ritualistically

cir·cum·cise \'sər-kəm-ˌsīz\ *vt* **-cised; -cis·ing** [ME *circumcisen,* fr. L *circumcisus,* pp. of *circumcidere,* fr. *circum-* + *caedere* to cut — more at CONCISE] : to cut off the prepuce of (a male) or the clitoris of (a female) — **cir·cum·cis·er** *n*

cir·cum·ci·sion \ˌsər-kəm-'sizh-ən\ *n* **1 a** : the act of circumcising; *specif* : a Jewish rite performed on male infants as a sign of inclusion in the Jewish religious community **b** : the condition of being circumcised **2** *cap* : January 1 observed as a church festival in commemoration of the circumcision of Jesus

cir·cum·fer·ence \sə(r)-'kəm(p)-fərn(t)s, -f(ə-)rən(t)s\ *n* [ME, fr. MF, fr. L *circumferentia,* fr. *circumferre* to carry around, fr. *circum-* + *ferre* to carry — more at BEAR] **1** : the perimeter of a circle **2** : the external boundary or surface of a figure or object : PERIPHERY — **cir·cum·fer·en·tial** \-ˌkəm(p)-fə-'ren-chəl\ *adj*

¹cir·cum·flex \'sər-kəm-ˌfleks\ *adj* [L *circumflexus,* pp. of *circumflectere* to bend around, mark with a circumflex, fr. *circum-* + *flectere* to bend] **1 a** : characterized by the pitch, quantity, or quality indicated by a circumflex **b :** marked with a circumflex **2 :** bending around <a ~ artery>

[2]**circumflex** *n* **:** a mark ^, ˘, or ~ orig. used in Greek over long vowels to indicate a rising-falling tone and in other languages to mark length, contraction, or a particular vowel quality

cir·cum·flu·ent \(ˌ)sər-ˈkəm-flə-wənt, ˌsər-kəm-ˈflü-ənt\ *adj* [fr. L *circumfluent-, circumfluens,* prp. of *circumfluere* to flow around, fr. *circum-* + *fluere* to flow] **:** flowing round or surrounding in the manner of a fluid — **cir·cum·flu·ous** \(ˌ)sər-ˈkəm-flə-wəs\ *adj*

cir·cum·fuse \ˌsər-kəm-ˈfyüz\ *vt* **-fused; -fus·ing** [L *circumfusus,* pp. of *circumfundere* to pour around, fr. *circum-* + *fundere* to pour — more at FOUND] **:** SURROUND, ENVELOP — **cir·cum·fu·sion** \-ˈfyü-zhən\ *n*

cir·cum·ja·cent \ˌsər-kəm-ˈjās-ᵊnt\ *adj* [L *circumjacent-, circumjacens,* prp. of *circumjacēre* to lie around, fr. *circum-* + *jacēre* to lie — more at ADJACENT] **:** lying adjacent on all sides **:** SURROUNDING

cir·cum·lo·cu·tion \ˌsər-kəm-lō-ˈkyü-shən\ *n* [L *circumlocution-, circumlocutio,* fr. *circum-* + *locutio* speech, fr. *locutus,* pp. of *loqui* to speak] **1 :** the use of an unnecessarily large number of words to express an idea **2 :** evasion in speech — **cir·cum·loc·u·to·ry** \-ˈläk-yə-ˌtōr-ē, -ˌtȯr-\ *adj*

cir·cum·lu·nar \ˌsər-kəm-ˈlü-nər\ *adj* **:** revolving about or surrounding the moon

cir·cum·nav·i·gate \-ˈnav-ə-ˌgāt\ *vt* [L *circumnavigatus,* pp. of *circumnavigare* to sail around, fr. *circum-* + *navigare* to navigate] **:** to go completely around (as the earth) esp. by water; *also* **:** to go around instead of through **:** BYPASS <~ a congested area> — **cir·cum·nav·i·ga·tion** \-ˌnav-ə-ˈgā-shən\ *n* — **cir·cum·nav·i·ga·tor** \-ˈnav-ə-ˌgāt-ər\ *n*

cir·cum·po·lar \ˌsər-kəm-ˈpō-lər\ *adj* **1 :** continually visible above the horizon <a ~ star> **2 :** surrounding or found in the vicinity of a terrestrial pole

cir·cum·scis·sile \-ˈsis-əl, -ˌīl\ *adj* [L *circumscissus,* pp. of *circumscindere* to tear around, fr. *circum-* + *scindere* to cut, split — more at SHED] **:** dehiscing by fissure around the circumference of the pyxidium

cir·cum·scribe \ˈsər-kəm-ˌskrīb\ *vt* [L *circumscribere,* fr. *circum-* + *scribere* to write, draw — more at SCRIBE] **1 a :** to draw a line around **b :** to surround by a boundary **2 a :** to constrict the range or activity of definitely and clearly **b :** to define or mark off carefully **3 :** to encircle (a geometrical figure) so as to touch at as many points as possible *syn* see LIMIT *ant* expand, dilate

cir·cum·scrip·tion \ˌsər-kəm-ˈskrip-shən\ *n* [L *circumscription-, circumscriptio,* fr. *circumscriptus,* pp. of *circumscribere*] **1 :** something that circumscribes: as **a :** LIMIT, BOUNDARY **b :** RESTRICTION **2 :** the act of circumscribing **:** the state of being circumscribed: as **a :** DEFINITION, DELIMITATION **b :** LIMITATION **3 :** a circumscribed area or district

cir·cum·spect \ˈsər-kəm-ˌspekt\ *adj* [ME, fr. MF or L; MF *circonspect,* fr. L *circumspectus,* fr. pp. of *circumspicere* to look around, be cautious, fr. *circum-* + *specere* to look — more at SPY] **:** careful to consider all circumstances and possible consequences **:** PRUDENT *syn* see CAUTIOUS *ant* audacious — **cir·cum·spec·tion** \ˌsər-kəm-ˈspek-shən\ *n* — **cir·cum·spect·ly** \ˈsər-kəm-ˌspek-tlē\ *adv*

cir·cum·stance \ˈsər-kəm-ˌstan(t)s, -stən(t)s\ *n* [ME, fr. MF, fr. L *circumstantia,* fr. *circumstant-, circumstans,* prp. of *circumstare* to stand around, fr. *circum-* + *stare* to stand — more at STAND] **1 a :** a condition, fact, or event accompanying, conditioning, or determining another **:** an essential or inevitable concomitant <the weather is a ~ to be taken into consideration> **b :** a subordinate or accessory fact or detail <cost is a minor ~ in this case> **c :** a piece of evidence that indicates the probability or improbability of an event (as a crime) <the ~ of the missing weapon told against him> <the ~*s* suggest murder> **2 a :** the sum of essential and environmental factors (as of an event or situation) <constant and rapid change in economic ~ —G. M. Trevelyan> **b :** state of affairs **:** EVENTUALITY <open rebellion was a rare ~> — often used in pl. <a victim of ~*s*> **c** *pl* **:** situation with regard to wealth <he was in easy ~*s*> **3 :** attendant formalities and ceremonial <pride, pomp, and ~ of glorious war —Shak.> **4 :** an event that constitutes a detail (as of a narrative or course of events) <considering each ~ in turn> *syn* see OCCURRENCE

cir·cum·stanced \-ˌstan(t)st, -stən(t)st\ *adj* **:** placed in particular circumstances esp. in regard to property or income

cir·cum·stan·tial \ˌsər-kəm-ˈstan-chəl\ *adj* **1 :** belonging to, consisting in, or dependent on circumstances **2 :** pertinent but not essential **:** INCIDENTAL **3 :** marked by careful attention to detail **:** abounding in factual details <a ~ account of the fight> **4 :** CEREMONIAL — **cir·cum·stan·ti·al·i·ty** \-ˌstan-chē-ˈal-ət-ē\ *n* — **cir·cum·stan·tial·ly** \-ˈstanch-(ə-)lē\ *adv*

syn CIRCUMSTANTIAL, MINUTE, PARTICULAR, DETAILED *shared meaning element* **:** dealing with a matter carefully and fully and usu. point by point *ant* abridged, summary

circumstantial evidence *n* **:** evidence that tends to prove a fact by proving other events or circumstances which afford a basis for a reasonable inference of the occurrence of the fact in issue

cir·cum·stan·ti·ate \ˌsər-kəm-ˈstan-chē-ˌāt\ *vt* **-at·ed; -at·ing :** to supply with circumstantial evidence or support

cir·cum·stel·lar \ˌsər-kəm-ˈstel-ər\ *adj* **:** surrounding or occurring in the vicinity of a star

[1]**cir·cum·val·late** \-ˈval-ˌāt, -ˈval-ət\ *adj* **:** surrounded by or as if by a rampart; *esp* **:** enclosed by a ridge of tissue <~ papilla>

[2]**cir·cum·val·late** \-ˈval-ˌāt\ *vt* **-lat·ed; -lat·ing** [L *circumvallatus,* pp. of *circumvallare,* fr. *circum-* + *vallum* rampart — more at WALL] **:** to surround by or as if by a rampart — **cir·cum·val·la·tion** \-ˌval-ˈā-shən\ *n*

cir·cum·vent \ˌsər-kəm-ˈvent\ *vt* [L *circumventus,* pp. of *circumvenire,* fr. *circum-* + *venire* to come — more at COME] **1 a :** to hem in **b :** to make a circuit around **2 :** to check or defeat esp. by ingenuity or stratagem *syn* see FRUSTRATE *ant* conform (*as to laws*), cooperate (*with persons*) — **cir·cum·ven·tion** \-ˈven-chən\ *n*

cir·cum·vo·lu·tion \(ˌ)sər-ˌkəm-və-ˈlü-shən, ˌsər-kəm-vō-\ *n* [ME *circumvolucioun,* fr. ML *circumvolution-, circumvolutio,* fr. L *circumvolutus,* pp. of *circumvolvere* to revolve, fr. *circum-* + *volvere* to roll — more at VOLUBLE] **:** an act or instance of turning around an axis

cir·cus \ˈsər-kəs\ *n, often attrib* [L, circle, circus — more at CIRCLE] **1 a :** a large arena enclosed by tiers of seats on three or all four sides and used esp. for sports or spectacles (as athletic contests, exhibitions of horsemanship, or in ancient times chariot racing) **b :** a public spectacle **2 a :** an arena often covered by a tent and used for variety shows usu. including feats of physical skill and daring, wild animal acts, and performances by jugglers and clowns **b :** a circus performance **c :** the physical plant, livestock, and personnel of such a circus **d :** an activity suggesting a circus <huge political clambakes, outsize chowder parties and other eating ~*es* —Thomas Mario> **3 a** *obs* **:** CIRCLE, RING **b** *Brit* **:** a usu. circular area at an intersection of streets — **cir·cusy** \-kə-sē\ *adj*

cirque \ˈsərk\ *n* [F, fr. L *circus*] **1** *archaic* **:** CIRCUS **2 :** CIRCLE, CIRCLET **3 :** a deep steep-walled basin on a mountain shaped like half a bowl

cirr- *or* **cirri-** *or* **cirro-** *comb form* [NL *cirrus*] **:** cirrus <*cirri*ped> <*cirr*ose> <*cirro*stratus>

cir·rho·sis \sə-ˈrō-səs\ *n, pl* **-rho·ses** \-ˌsēz\ [NL, fr. Gk *kirrhos* orange-colored] **:** fibrosis esp. of the liver with hardening caused by excessive formation of connective tissue followed by contraction — **cir·rhot·ic** \-ˈrät-ik\ *adj or n*

cir·ri·ped \ˈsir-ə-ˌped\ *or* **cir·ri·pede** \-ˌpēd\ *n* [deriv. of NL *cirr-* + L *ped-, pes* foot — more at FOOT] **:** any of a subclass (Cirripedia) of specialized marine crustaceans (as barnacles) free-swimming as larvae but permanently attached or parasitic as adults — **cirriped** *adj*

cir·ro·cu·mu·lus \ˌsir-ō-ˈkyü-myə-ləs\ *n* [NL] **:** a cloud form of small white rounded masses at a high altitude usu. in regular groupings forming a mackerel sky — see CLOUD illustration

cir·ro·stra·tus \ˌsir-ō-ˈstrāt-əs, -ˈstrat-\ *n* [NL] **:** a fairly uniform layer of high stratus darker than cirrus — see CLOUD illustration

cir·rous \ˈsir-əs\ *adj* **:** resembling cirrus clouds

cir·rus \ˈsir-əs\ *n, pl* **cir·ri** \ˈsi(ə)r-ˌī\ [NL, fr. L, curl] **1 :** TENDRIL **2 :** a slender usu. flexible animal appendage: as **a :** an arm of a barnacle — see BARNACLE illustration **b :** a filament of a crinoid **c :** a fused group of cilia functioning like a limb on some protozoans **d :** the male copulatory organ of various invertebrate animals **3 :** a wispy white cloud usu. of minute ice crystals formed at altitudes of 20,000 to 40,000 feet — see CLOUD illustration

cis- *prefix* [L, fr. *cis* — more at HE] **1 :** on this side <*cis*-border> <*cis*atlantic> **2** *usu ital* **:** characterized by having such atoms or groups on the same side of the molecule <*cis*-dichloroethylene>

cis·al·pine \(ˈ)sis-ˈal-ˌpīn\ *adj* **:** situated on the south side of the Alps <*Cisalpine* Gaul> — compare TRANSALPINE

cis·co \ˈsis-(ˌ)kō\ *n, pl* **ciscoes** [short for CanF *ciscoette*] **:** any of various whitefishes (genus *Coregonus*) including important food fishes (esp. *C. artedii*) of the Great Lakes region

cis·lu·nar \(ˈ)sis-ˈlü-nər\ *adj* **:** lying between the earth and the moon or the moon's orbit <~ space>

cist \ˈsist, ˈkist\ *n* [W, chest, fr. L *cista*] **:** a neolithic or Bronze Age burial chamber typically lined with stone

Cis·ter·cian \sis-ˈtər-shən\ *n* [ML *Cistercium* Cîteaux] **:** a member of a monastic order founded by St. Robert of Molesme in 1098 at Cîteaux, France, under an austere Benedictine rule — **Cistercian** *adj*

cis·tern \ˈsis-tərn\ *n* [ME, fr. OF *cisterne,* fr. L *cisterna,* fr. *cista* box, chest — more at CHEST] **1 :** an artificial reservoir for storing liquids and esp. water; *specif* **:** an often underground tank for storing rainwater **2 :** a large usu. silver vessel formerly used (as in cooling wine) at the dining table **3 :** a fluid-containing sac or cavity in an organism

cis·ter·na \sis-ˈtər-nə\ *n, pl* **-nae** \-ˌnē\ [NL, fr. L, reservoir] **:** CISTERN 3: as **a :** one of the large spaces under the arachnoid membrane **b :** one of the interconnected vesicles or tubules comprising the endoplasmic reticulum

cis·tron \ˈsis-ˌträn\ *n* [*cis-* + *trans-* + [2]*-on*] **:** a segment of DNA which specifies a single functional unit (as a protein or enzyme) and within which two heterozygous and closely linked recessive mutations are expressed in the phenotype when on different chromosomes but not when on the same chromosome — **cis·tron·ic** \sis-ˈträn-ik\ *adj*

cit *abbr* **1** citation; cited **2** citizen

cit·a·del \ˈsit-əd-ᵊl, -ə-ˌdel\ *n* [MF *citadelle,* fr. OIt *cittadella,* dim. of *cittade* city, fr. ML *civitat-, civitas* — more at CITY] **1 :** a fortress that commands a city **2 :** STRONGHOLD

ci·ta·tion \sī-ˈtā-shən\ *n* **1 :** an official summons to appear (as before a court) **2 a :** an act of quoting; *esp* **:** the citing of a previously settled case at law **b :** EXCERPT, QUOTE **3 :** MENTION: as **a :** a formal statement of the achievements of a person receiving an academic honor **b :** specific reference in a military dispatch to meritorious performance of duty *syn* see ENCOMIUM — **ci·ta·tion·al** \-shnəl, -shən-ᵊl\ *adj*

cite \ˈsīt\ *vt* **cit·ed; cit·ing** [MF *citer* to cite, summon, fr. L *citare* to put in motion, rouse, summon, fr. *citus,* pp. of *ciēre* to stir, move — more at HIGHT] **1 :** to call upon officially or authoritatively to appear (as before a court) **2 :** to quote by way of example, authority, or proof **3 a :** to refer to; *esp* **:** to mention formally in commendation or praise **b :** to name in a citation **4 :** to bring forward or call to another's attention esp. as an example, proof, or precedent *syn* see SUMMON, QUOTE, ADDUCE — **cit·able** \ˈsīt-ə-bəl\ *adj*

cith·a·ra \'sith-ə-rə, 'kith-\ *n* [L, fr. Gk *kithara*] **:** an ancient Greek stringed instrument of the lyre class with a wooden sounding board

cith·er \'sith-ər, 'sith-\ *n* [F *cithare,* fr. L *cithara*] **:** CITTERN

cit·ied \'sit-ēd\ *adj* **:** occupied by cities

citi·fy \'sit-i-,fī\ *vt* **-fied; -fy·ing :** URBANIZE

cit·i·zen \'sit-ə-zən\ *n* [ME *citizein,* fr. AF *citezein,* alter. of OF *citeien,* fr. *cité* city] **1 :** an inhabitant of a city or town; *esp* **:** one entitled to the rights and privileges of a freeman **2 a :** a member of a state **b :** a native or naturalized person who owes allegiance to a government and is entitled to reciprocal protection from it **3 :** a civilian as distinguished from a specialized servant of the state — **cit·i·zen·ess** \-zə-nəs\ *n* — **cit·i·zen·ly** \-zən-lē\ *adj*

syn CITIZEN, SUBJECT, NATIONAL *shared meaning element* **:** a person owing allegiance to and entitled to the protection of a sovereign state

cit·i·zen·ry \-zən-rē\ *n, pl* **-ries :** a whole body of citizens

citizen's arrest *n* **:** an arrest made by a citizen who derives his authority from the fact that he is a citizen

cit·i·zen·ship \'sit-ə-zən-,ship\ *n* **1 :** the status of being a citizen **2 :** the quality of an individual's response to membership in a community

citr- *or* **citri-** *or* **citro-** *comb form* [NL, fr. *Citrus,* genus name] **1 :** citrus <*citri*culture> **2 :** citric acid <*citr*ate>

cit·ral \'si-,tral\ *n* [ISV] **:** an unsaturated liquid isomeric aldehyde $C_{10}H_{16}O$ of many essential oils that has a strong lemon and verbena odor and is used esp. in perfumery and as a flavoring

ci·trate \'si-,trāt\ *n* [ISV] **:** a salt or ester of citric acid

cit·ric acid \,si-trik-\ *n* [ISV] **:** a tricarboxylic acid $C_6H_8O_7$ occurring in cellular metabolism, obtained esp. from lemon and lime juices or by fermentation of sugars, and used as a flavoring

citric acid cycle *n* **:** KREBS CYCLE

cit·ri·cul·ture \'si-trə-,kəl-chər\ *n* **:** the cultivation of citrus fruits — **cit·ri·cul·tur·ist** \,si-trə-'kəlch-(ə-)rəst\ *n*

¹cit·rine \'si-,trīn\ *adj* [ME, fr. MF *citrin,* fr. ML *citrinus,* fr. L *citrus* citron tree] **:** resembling a citron or lemon esp. in color

²ci·trine \si-'trēn\ *n* **:** a black quartz changed in color by heating into a semiprecious yellow stone resembling topaz

cit·ron \'si-trən\ *n* [ME, fr. MF, fr. OProv, modif. of L *citrus* citron tree] **1 a :** a fruit like the lemon in appearance and structure but larger **b :** a small shrubby citrus tree (*Citrus medica*) that produces citrons **c :** the preserved rind of the citron used esp. in cakes and puddings **2 :** a small hard-fleshed watermelon used esp. in pickles and preserves

cit·ro·nel·la \,si-trə-'nel-ə\ *n* [NL, fr. F *citronnelle* lemon balm, fr. *citron*] **:** a fragrant grass (*Cymbopogon nardus*) of southern Asia that yields an oil used in perfumery and as an insect repellent

cit·ro·nel·lal \-'nel-,al\ *n* [ISV, fr. NL *citronella*] **:** a lemon-odored aldehyde $C_{10}H_{18}O$ found in many essential oils and used in perfumery

cit·rul·line \'si-trə-,lēn\ *n* [ISV, fr. NL *Citrullus,* genus name of the watermelon] **:** a crystalline amino acid $C_6H_{13}N_3O_3$ formed esp. as an intermediate in the conversion of ornithine to arginine in the living system

cit·rus \'si-trəs\ *n, pl* **citrus** *or* **cit·rus·es** *often attrib* [NL, genus name, fr. L, citron tree] **:** any of a genus (*Citrus*) of often thorny trees and shrubs of the rue family grown in warm regions for their edible fruit (as the orange) with firm usu. thick rind and pulpy flesh

citrus red mite *n* **:** a comparatively large mite (*Panonychus citri*) that is a destructive pest on the foliage of citrus — called also *citrus red spider*

cit·tern \'sit-ərn\ *or* **cith·ern** \'sith-ərn, 'sith-\ *or* **cith·ren** \'sith-rən\ *n* [blend of *cither* and *gittern*] **:** a guitar with a pear-shaped flat-backed body popular esp. in Renaissance England

city \'sit-ē\ *n, pl* **cit·ies** *often attrib* [ME *citie* large or small town, fr. OF *cité* capital city, fr. ML *civitat-, civitas,* fr. L, citizenship, state, city of Rome, fr. *civis* citizen — more at HOME] **1 a :** an inhabited place of greater size, population, or importance than a town or village **b :** an incorporated British town usu. of major size or importance having the status of an episcopal see **c :** a usu. large or important municipality in the U.S. governed under a charter granted by the state **d :** an incorporated municipal unit of the highest class in Canada **2 :** CITY-STATE **3 :** the people of a city

city council *n* **:** the legislative body of a city

city edition *n* **:** an edition of a usu. metropolitan newspaper that is designed for sale within the city and that is distinguished from a suburban edition or mail edition

city editor *n* **:** a newspaper editor with varying functions but usu. in charge of local news and staff assignments

city father *n* **:** a member (as an alderman or councilman) of the governing body of a city

city hall *n* **1 :** the chief administrative building of a city **2 a :** a municipal government **b :** city officialdom or bureaucracy <you can't fight *city hall*>

city manager *n* **:** an official employed by an elected council to direct the administration of a city government

city plan *n* **:** an organized arrangement (as of streets, parks, and business and residential areas) of a city with a view to convenience, appearance, healthful environment, and future growth — **city planning** *n*

city planner *n* **:** one that makes city plans; *esp* **:** a professional who participates in such activity

city room *n* **:** the department where local news is handled in a newspaper editorial office

city·scape \'sit-ē-,skāp\ *n* **1 :** a pictorial representation of a city **2 :** a city viewed as a scene <the skyscrapers which now bedizen the American ~ —*Amer. Mercury*> **3 :** a pictorial composition of urban elements

city slicker *n* **:** SLICKER 2b

city–state \'sit-ē-'stāt, -,stāt\ *n* **:** an autonomous state consisting of a city and surrounding territory

civ *abbr* civil; civilian

civ·et \'siv-ət\ *n* [MF *civette,* fr. OIt *zibetto,* fr. Ar *zabād* civet perfume] **:** a thick yellowish musky-odored substance found in a pouch near the sexual organs of the civet cat and used in perfume

civet cat *n* **1 a :** any of several carnivorous mammals (family Viverridae); *esp* **:** a long-bodied short-legged African animal (*Civettictis civetta*) that produces most of the civet of commerce **b :** CACOMISTLE **c :** any of the small spotted skunks (genus *Spilogale*) of western No. America **2 :** the fur of a civet cat

civet cat 1a

civ·ic \'siv-ik\ *adj* [L *civicus,* fr. *civis* citizen] **:** of or relating to a citizen, a city, citizenship, or civil affairs — **civ·i·cal·ly** \'siv-i-k(ə-)lē\ *adv*

civ·ic–mind·ed \,siv-ik-'mīn-dəd\ *adj* **:** disposed to look after civic needs and interests — **civ·ic–mind·ed·ness** *n*

civ·ics \'siv-iks\ *n pl but sing or pl in constr* **:** a social science dealing with the rights and duties of citizens

civ·il \'siv-əl\ *adj* [ME, fr. MF, fr. L *civilis,* fr. *civis*] **1 a :** of or relating to citizens <~ liberties> **b :** of or relating to the state or its citizenry **2 a :** CIVILIZED <~ society> **b :** adequate in courtesy and politeness **:** MANNERLY **3 a :** of, relating to, or based on civil law **b :** relating to private rights and to remedies sought by action or suit distinct from criminal proceedings **c :** established by law **4** *of time* **:** based on the mean sun and legally recognized for use in ordinary affairs **5 :** of, relating to, or involving the general public, their activities, needs, or ways, or civic affairs as distinguished from special (as military or religious) affairs

syn CIVIL, POLITE, COURTEOUS, GALLANT, CHIVALROUS *shared meaning element* **:** observant of the forms required by good breeding. CIVIL is feeble in force, often suggesting little more than avoidance of overt rudeness. POLITE is more positive and commonly implies polish of manners and address more than warmth and cordiality <the cultured, precise tone, *polite* but faintly superior —William Styron> COURTEOUS implies an actively considerate and sometimes rather stately politeness <listened with *courteous* attention> *Gallant* and *chivalrous* imply courteous attentiveness esp. to women but GALLANT is likely to suggest dashing behavior and ornate expression <ever ready with *gallant* remarks of admiration> while CHIVALROUS tends to suggest high-minded and disinterested attentions <felt at once *chivalrous* and paternal to the lost girl> *ant* uncivil, rude

civil death *n* **:** the status of a living person equivalent in its legal consequences to natural death; *specif* **:** deprivation of civil rights

civil defense *n* **:** the complex of protective measures and emergency relief activities conducted by civilians in case of hostile attack, sabotage, or natural disaster

civil disobedience *n* **:** refusal to obey governmental demands or commands esp. as a nonviolent and usu. collective means of forcing concessions from the government

civil engineer *n* **:** an engineer whose training or occupation is in the designing and construction of public works (as roads or harbors) and of various private works — **civil engineering** *n*

ci·vil·ian \sə-'vil-yən\ *n* **1 :** a specialist in Roman or modern civil law **2 :** one not on active duty in a military, police, or fire-fighting force — **civilian** *adj*

ci·vil·ian·ize \-yə-,nīz\ *vt* **-ized; -iz·ing :** to convert from military to civilian status or control — **ci·vil·ian·iza·tion** \-,vil-yə-nə-'zā-shən\ *n*

civ·i·li·sa·tion, civ·i·lise *chiefly Brit var of* CIVILIZATION, CIVILIZE

ci·vil·i·ty \sə-'vil-ət-ē\ *n, pl* **-ties 1** *archaic* **:** training in the humanities **2 a :** COURTESY, POLITENESS **b :** a polite act or expression

civ·i·li·za·tion \,siv-ə-lə-'zā-shən\ *n* **1 a :** a relatively high level of cultural and technological development; *specif* **:** the stage of cultural development at which writing and the keeping of written records is attained **b :** the culture characteristic of a particular time or place **2 :** the process of becoming civilized **3 a :** refinement of thought, manners, or taste **b :** a situation of urban comfort

civ·i·lize \'siv-ə-,līz\ *vb* **-lized; -liz·ing** *vt* **1 :** to cause to develop out of a primitive state; *specif* **:** to bring to a technically advanced and rationally ordered stage of cultural development **2 a :** EDUCATE, REFINE **b :** SOCIALIZE 1 ~ *vi* **:** to acquire the customs and amenities of a civil community — **civ·i·liz·able** \-,lī-zə-bəl\ *adj* — **civ·i·liz·er** *n*

civ·i·lized *adj* **:** of or relating to peoples or nations in a state of civilization

civil law *n, often cap C&L* **1 :** Roman law esp. as set forth in the Justinian code **2 :** the body of private law developed from Roman law and used in Louisiana and in many countries outside the English-speaking world **3 :** the law established by a nation or state for its own jurisdiction **4 :** the law of civil or private rights

civil liberty *n* **:** freedom from arbitrary governmental interference (as with the right of free speech) specif. by denial of governmental power and in the U.S. esp. as guaranteed by the Bill of Rights — usu. used in pl. — **civil lib·er·tar·i·an** \-,lib-ər-'ter-ē-ən\ *n*

civ·il·ly \'siv-ə(l)-lē\ *adv* **1 :** in a civil manner **:** POLITELY **2 :** in terms of civil rights, law, or matters <~ dead>

civil marriage *n* **:** a marriage performed by a magistrate

civil right·er \-'rīt-ər\ *n* **:** an advocate of civil rights; *esp* **:** one who works to gain civil rights for minority groups

civil right·ist \-'rīt-əst\ *n* **:** CIVIL RIGHTER

civil rights *n pl* **:** the nonpolitical rights of a citizen; *esp* **:** the rights of personal liberty guaranteed to U.S. citizens by the 13th and 14th amendments to the Constitution and by acts of Congress

civil servant *n* **1 :** a member of a civil service **2 :** a member of the administrative staff of an international agency (as the United Nations)

civil service *n* : the administrative service of a government or international agency exclusive of the armed forces; *esp* : one in which appointments are determined by competitive examination
civil war *n* : a war between opposing groups of citizens of the same country
Civ·i·tan \'siv-ə-,tan\ *n* [*Civitan (club)*] : a member of a major national and international service club
civ·vy *also* **civ·ie** \'siv-ē\ *n, pl* **civvies** *also* **civies** **1** *pl* : civilian clothes as distinguished from a military uniform **2** : CIVILIAN
CJ *abbr* chief justice
ck *abbr* **1** cask **2** check
cl *abbr* **1** centiliter **2** class **3** clause **4** close **5** closet **6** cloth
Cl *symbol* chlorine
CL *abbr* **1** carload **2** center line **3** civil law **4** common law
Cla *abbr* Clackmannanshire
CLA *abbr* College Language Association
1clab·ber \'klab-ər\ *n* [short for *bonnyclabber*] *chiefly dial* : sour milk that has thickened or curdled
2clabber *vi, chiefly dial* : CURDLE
clach·an \'klak-ən\ *n* [ME, fr. ScGael] *Scot & Irish* : HAMLET
1clack \'klak\ *vb* [ME *clacken*, of imit. origin] *vi* **1** : CHATTER, PRATTLE **2** : to make an abrupt striking sound or series of sounds **3** *of fowl* : CACKLE, CLUCK ~ *vt* **1** : to cause to make a clatter **2** : to produce with a chattering sound; *specif* : BLAB — **clack·er** *n*
2clack *n* **1 a** : rapid continuous talk : CHATTER **b** : TONGUE **2** *archaic* : an object (as a clack valve) that produces clapping or rattling noises usu. in regular rapid sequence **3** : a sound of clacking <the ~ of a typewriter>
clack valve *n* : a valve usu. hinged at one edge that permits flow of fluid in one direction only and that closes with a clacking sound
Clac·to·ni·an \klak-'tō-nē-ən\ *adj* [*Clacton*-on-Sea, England] : of or relating to a Lower Paleolithic culture characterized by stone flakes with a half cone at the point of striking
1clad \'klad\ *adj* [pp. of *clothe*] **1** : being covered or clothed <ivy-*clad* buildings> **2** *of a coin* : consisting of outer layers of one metal bonded to a core of a different metal
2clad *vt* **clad; clad·ding** : SHEATHE, FACE; *specif* : to cover (a metal) with another metal by bonding
3clad *n* **1** : a composite material formed by cladding; *specif* : a clad coin **2** : something that overlays : CLADDING; *specif* : the outer layer of a clad coin
clad·ding \'klad-iŋ\ *n* : something that covers or overlays <stone ~ on a building wall>; *specif* : metal coating bonded to a metal core
clad·ode \'klad-,ōd\ *n* [NL *cladodium*, fr. Gk *klados*] : CLADOPHYLL — **cla·do·di·al** \kla-'dōd-ē-əl\ *adj*
clado·gen·e·sis \,klad-ə-'jen-ə-səs\ *n* [NL, fr. Gk *klados* branch + L *genesis*] : evolutionary change characterized by treelike branching of taxa — **clado·ge·net·ic** \,klad-ō-jə-'net-ik\ *adj* — **clado·ge·net·i·cal·ly** \-i-k(ə-)lē\ *adv*
clado·phyll \'klad-ə-,fil\ *n* [NL *cladophyllum*, fr. Gk *klados* branch + *phyllon* leaf —more at GLADIATOR, BLADE] : a branch assuming the form of and closely resembling an ordinary foliage leaf and often bearing leaves or flowers on its margins
1claim \'klām\ *vt* [ME *claimen*, fr. OF *clamer*, fr. L *clamare* to cry out, shout; akin to L *calare* to call — more at LOW] **1 a** : to ask for esp. as a right <~*ed* the inheritance> **b** : to call for : REQUIRE <this matter ~*s* our attention> **2** : to take as the rightful owner <went to ~ his bags at the station> **3** : to assert in the face of possible contradiction : MAINTAIN <~*ed* that he'd been cheated> **syn** see DEMAND — **claim·able** \'klā-mə-bəl\ *adj* — **claim·er** *n*
2claim *n* **1** : a demand for something due or believed to be due <insurance ~> **2 a** : a right to something; *specif* : a title to a debt, privilege, or other thing in the possession of another **b** : an assertion open to challenge <a ~ of authenticity> **3** : something that is claimed; *esp* : a tract of land staked out
claim·ant \'klā-mənt\ *n* : one that asserts a right or title <a ~ to an estate>
claiming race *n* : a horse race in which each entry is offered for sale for a specified price to a purchaser who pledges the selling price before the race
clair·au·di·ence \kla(ə)r-'ȯd-ē-ən(t)s, kle(ə)r-, -'äd-\ *n* [*clair-* (as in *clairvoyance*) + *audience* (act of hearing)] : the power or faculty of hearing something not present to the ear but regarded as having objective reality
clair·au·di·ent \-ənt\ *adj* : of or relating to clairaudience — **clair·au·di·ent·ly** *adv*
clair·voy·ance \kla(ə)r-'vȯi-ən(t)s, kle(ə)r-\ *n* **1** : the power or faculty of discerning objects not present to the senses **2** : ability to perceive matters beyond the range of ordinary perception : PENETRATION
1clair·voy·ant \-ənt\ *adj* [F, fr. *clair* clear (fr. L *clarus*) + *voyant*, prp. of *voir* to see, fr. L *vidēre*] **1** : unusually perceptive : DISCERNING **2** : of or relating to clairvoyance — **clair·voy·ant·ly** *adv*
2clairvoyant *n* : one having the power of clairvoyance
1clam \'klam\ *n* [ME, fr. OE *clamm* bond, fetter; akin to OHG *klamma* constriction, L *glomus* ball] : CLAMP, CLASP
2clam *n, often attrib* [1*clam*; fr. the clamping action of the shells] **1 a** : any of numerous edible marine bivalve mollusks living in sand or mud **b** : a freshwater mussel **2** : a stolid or close-mouthed person **3** : CLAMSHELL
3clam *vi* **clammed; clam·ming** : to gather clams esp. by digging
cla·mant \'klā-mənt, 'klam-ənt\ *adj* [L *clamant-*, *clamans*, prp. of *clamare* to cry out] **1** : CLAMOROUS, BLATANT **2** : demanding attention : URGENT — **cla·mant·ly** *adv*
clam·bake \'klam-,bāk\ *n* **1 a** : an outdoor party; *esp* : a seashore outing where food is cooked on heated rocks covered by seaweed **b** : the food served at a clambake **2** : a gathering characterized by noisy sociability; *esp* : a political rally
clam·ber \'klam-(b)ər\ *vi* **clam·bered; clam·ber·ing** \'klam-b(ə-)riŋ, 'klam-(ə-)riŋ\ [ME *clambren*; akin to OE *climban* to climb] : to climb awkwardly (as by scrambling) <~*ed* over the rocks> — **clam·ber·er** \-(b)ər-ər\ *n*

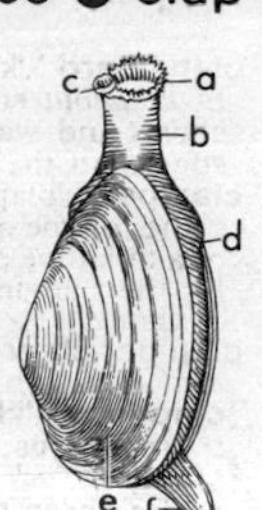

clam 1a: *a* incurrent orifice, *b* siphon, *c* excurrent orifice, *d* mantle, *e* shell, *f* foot

clam·my \'klam-ē\ *adj* **clam·mi·er; -est** [ME, prob. fr. *clammen* to smear, stick, fr. OE *clǣman*; akin to OE *clǣg* clay] **1** : being damp, soft, sticky, and usu. cool <a ~ and intensely cold mist —Charles Dickens> **2 a** : lacking normal human warmth <the ~ atmosphere of an institution> **b** : ALOOF, REPELLENT — **clam·mi·ly** \'klam-ə-lē\ *adv* — **clam·mi·ness** \'klam-ē-nəs\ *n*
1clam·or \'klam-ər\ *n* [ME, fr. MF *clamour*, fr. L *clamor*, fr. *clamare* to cry out — more at CLAIM] **1 a** : noisy shouting **b** : a loud continuous noise **2** : insistent public expression (as of support or protest) <a ~ against increased taxes>
2clamor *vb* **clam·ored; clam·or·ing** \'klam-(ə-)riŋ\ *vi* **1** : to make a din **2** : to become loudly insistent <~*ed* for his impeachment> ~ *vt* **1** : to utter or proclaim insistently and noisily **2** : to influence by means of clamor
3clamor *vt* [origin unknown] *obs* : SILENCE
clam·or·ous \'klam-(ə-)rəs\ *adj* **1** : marked by confused din or outcry : TUMULTUOUS <the busy ~ market> **2** : noisily insistent **syn** see VOCIFEROUS **ant** taciturn — **clam·or·ous·ly** *adv* — **clam·or·ous·ness** *n*
clam·our \'klam-ər\ *chiefly Brit var of* CLAMOR
1clamp \'klamp\ *n* [ME, prob. fr. (assumed) MD *klampe*; akin to OE *clamm* bond, fetter — more at CLAM] **1** : a device designed to bind or constrict or to press two or more parts together so as to hold them firmly **2** : any of various instruments or appliances having parts brought together for holding or compressing something
2clamp *vt* **1** : to fasten with or as if with a clamp **2 a** : to place by decree : IMPOSE — often used with *on* <~*ed* on a curfew after the riots> **b** : to hold tightly
clamp·down \'klamp-,daun\ *n* : the act or action of making regulations and restrictions more stringent : CRACKDOWN <a ~ on charge accounts, bank loans, and other inflationary influences —*Time*>
clamp down \(')klamp-'daun\ *vi* : to impose restrictions : become repressive <the police are *clamping down* on speeders>
clam·shell \'klam-,shel\ *n* **1** : a bucket or grapple (as on a dredge) having two hinged jaws **2** : an excavating machine having a clamshell
clam up *vi* : to become silent <he *clammed up* when asked for details>
clam worm *n* : any of several large burrowing polychaete worms (as a nereis) often used as bait
clan \'klan\ *n* [ME, fr. ScGael *clann* offspring, clan, fr. OIr *cland* plant, offspring, fr. L *planta* plant] **1 a** : a Celtic group esp. in the Scottish Highlands comprising a number of households whose heads claim descent from a common ancestor **b** : SIB 3 **2** : a group united by a common interest or common characteristics
clan·des·tine \klan-'des-tən *also* -,tīn *or* -,tēn *or* 'klan-dəs-\ *adj* [MF or L; MF *clandestin*, fr. L *clandestinus*, irreg. fr. *clam* secretly; akin to L *celare* to hide — more at HELL] : held in or conducted with secrecy : SURREPTITIOUS **syn** see SECRET **ant** open — **clan·des·tine·ly** *adv* — **clan·des·tine·ness** *n*
1clang \'klaŋ\ *vb* [L *clangere*; akin to Gk *klazein* to scream, bark, OE *hlōwan* to low] *vi* **1 a** : to make a loud metallic ringing sound <anvils ~*ed*> **b** : to go with a clang **2** : to utter the characteristic harsh cry of a bird ~ *vt* : to cause to clang <~ a bell>
2clang *n* **1** : a loud ringing metallic sound <the ~ of a fire alarm> **2** : a harsh cry of a bird (as a crane or goose)
1clan·gor \'klaŋ-ər *also* -gər\ *n* [L *clangor*, fr. *clangere*] : a resounding clang or medley of clangs <the ~ of hammers> — **clan·gor·ous** \-(g)ə-rəs\ *adj* — **clan·gor·ous·ly** *adv*
2clangor *vi* : to make a clangor
clan·gour \'klaŋ-ər, -gər\ *chiefly Brit var of* CLANGOR
1clank \'klaŋk\ *vb* [prob. imit.] *vi* **1** : to make a clank or series of clanks <the radiator hissed and ~*ed*> **2** : to go with a clank <tanks ~*ing* through the streets> ~ *vt* : to cause to clank — **clank·ing·ly** \'klaŋ-kiŋ-lē\ *adv*
2clank *n* : a sharp brief metallic ringing sound
clan·nish \'klan-ish\ *adj* **1** : of or relating to a clan **2** : tending to associate only with a select group of similar background or status <~ immigrants> — **clan·nish·ly** *adv* — **clan·nish·ness** *n*
clans·man \'klanz-mən\ *n* : a member of a clan
1clap \'klap\ *vb* **clapped** *also* **clapt; clap·ping** [ME *clappen*, fr. OE *clæppan*; akin to OHG *klaphōn* to beat, L *glēba* clod — more at CLIP] *vt* **1** : to strike (as two flat hard surfaces) together so as to produce a sharp percussive noise **2 a** : to strike (the hands) together repeatedly usu. in applause **b** : APPLAUD **3** : to strike with the flat of the hand in a friendly way <*clapped* his friend on the shoulder> **4** : to place, put, or set esp. energetically <~ him into jail> **5** : to improvise hastily ~ *vi* **1** : to produce a percussive sound; *esp* : SLAM **2** : to go abruptly or briskly **3** : APPLAUD
2clap *n* **1** : a device that makes a clapping noise **2** *obs* : a sudden stroke of fortune and esp. ill fortune **3** : a loud percussive noise; *specif* : a sudden crash of thunder **4 a** : a sudden blow **b** : a friendly slap <a ~ on the shoulder> **5** : the sound of clapping hands; *esp* : APPLAUSE
3clap *n* [MF *clapoir* bubo] : GONORRHEA

ə abut   ə kitten   ər further   a back   ā bake   ä cot, cart
au̇ out   ch chin   e less   ē easy   g gift   i trip   ī life
j joke   ŋ sing   ō flow   ȯ flaw   ȯi coin   th thin   t͟h this
ü loot   u̇ foot   y yet   yü few   yu̇ furious   zh vision

clap·board \'klab-ərd; 'kla(p)-ˌbō(ə)rd, -ˌbȯ(ə)rd\ *n* [part trans. of D *klaphout* stave wood] **1** *archaic* : a size of board for making staves and wainscoting **2** : a narrow board usu. thicker at one edge than the other used for siding — **clapboard** *vt*

clap·per \'klap-ər\ *n* : one that makes a clapping sound: as **a** : the tongue of a bell — see BELL illustration **b** *slang* : the tongue of a talkative person **c** : a mechanical device that makes noise esp. by the banging of one part against another **d** : a person who applauds

clap·per·claw \'klap-ər-ˌklȯ\ *vt* [perh. fr. *clapper* + *claw* (v.)] **1** *dial Eng* : to claw with the nails **2** *dial Eng* : SCOLD, REVILE

1clap·trap \'klap-ˌtrap\ *n* [2*clap;* fr. its attempt to win applause] : pretentious nonsense : TRASH

2claptrap *adj* : characterized by or suggestive of claptrap; *esp* : of a cheap showy nature <~ sentiment>

claque \'klak\ *n* [F, fr. *claquer* to clap, of imit. origin] **1** : a group hired to applaud at a performance **2** : a group of sycophants

cla·queur \kla-'kər\ *n* [F, fr. *claquer* to clap] : a member of a claque

clar·ence \'klar-ən(t)s\ *n* [duke of *Clarence,* later William IV of England] : a closed four-wheeled four-passenger carriage

clar·et \'klar-ət\ *n* [ME, fr. MF (*vin*) *claret* clear wine, fr. *claret* clear, fr. *cler* clear] **1** : a dry red table wine from the Bordeaux district of France; *also* : a similar wine produced elsewhere **2** : a dark purplish red — **claret** *adj*

Cla·re·tian \klə-'rē-shən, kla-\ *n* [St. Anthony *Claret* †1870 Sp priest] : a member of the Congregation of the Missionary Sons of the Immaculate Heart of Mary founded by St. Anthony Claret in Vich, Spain, in 1849 — **Claretian** *adj*

clar·i·fy \'klar-ə-ˌfī\ *vb* **-fied; fy·ing** [ME *clarifien,* fr. MF *clarifier,* fr. LL *clarificare,* fr. L *clarus* clear — more at CLEAR] *vt* **1** : to make (as a liquid) clear or pure usu. by freeing from suspended matter **2** : to free of confusion **3** : to make understandable ~ *vi* : to become clear — **clar·i·fi·ca·tion** \ˌklar-ə-fə-'kā-shən\ *n* — **clar·i·fi·er** \'klar-ə-ˌfī(-ə)r\ *n*

clar·i·net \ˌklar-ə-'net, 'klar-ə-nət\ *n* [F *clarinette,* prob. deriv. of ML *clarion-, clario*] : a single-reed woodwind instrument having a cylindrical tube with a moderately flared bell and a usual range from D below middle C upward for 3½ octaves — **clar·i·net·ist** *or* **clar·i·net·tist** \ˌklar-ə-'net-əst\ *n*

clarinet

1clar·i·on \'klar-ē-ən\ *n* [ME, fr. MF & ML; MF *clairon,* fr. ML *clarion-, clario,* fr. L *clarus* clear] **1** : a medieval trumpet with clear shrill tones **2** : the sound of or as if of a clarion

2clarion *adj* : brilliantly clear; *esp* : STENTORIAN <a ~ call to action>

clar·i·ty \'klar-ət-ē\ *n* [ME *clarite,* fr. L *claritat-, claritas,* fr. *clarus*] : the quality or state of being clear : LUCIDITY <the ~ of her voice>

clark·ia \'klär-kē-ə\ *n* [NL, fr. William *Clark* †1838 Am explorer] : a showy annual herb (genus *Clarkia*) of the evening-primrose family of the Pacific slope of No. America

cla·ro \'klär-(ˌ)ō\ *n, pl* **claroes** [Sp, fr. *claro* light, fr. L *clarus*] : a light-colored generally mild cigar

clary \'kla(ə)r-ē, 'kle(ə)r-\ *n, pl* **clar·ies** [ME *clarie,* fr. MF *sclaree,* fr. ML *sclareia*] : an aromatic mint (*Salvia sclarea*) of southern Europe grown as a potherb and ornamental

1clash \'klash\ *vb* [imit.] *vi* **1** : to make a clash <cymbals ~*ed*> **2** : to come into conflict <where ignorant armies ~ by night —Matthew Arnold> ~ *vt* : to cause to clash — **clash·er** *n*

2clash *n* **1** : a noisy usu. metallic sound of collision **2 a** : a hostile encounter : SKIRMISH <a ~ between the two armies> **b** : a sharp conflict <a ~ of opinions>

clas·mato·cyte \klaz-'mat-ə-ˌsīt\ *n* [ISV, fr. Gk *klasmat-, klasma* fragment (fr. *klan* to break) + ISV *-cyte* — more at HALT] : HISTIOCYTE — **clas·mato·cyt·ic** \(ˌ)klaz-ˌmat-ə-'sit-ik\ *adj*

1clasp \'klasp\ *n* [ME *claspe*] **1 a** : a device (as a hook) for holding objects or parts together **b** : a device (as a bar) attached to a military medal to indicate an additional award of the medal or the action or service for which it was awarded **2** : a holding or enveloping with or as if with the hands or arms ***syn*** see HOLD

2clasp *vt* **1** : to fasten with or as if with a clasp <a robe ~*ed* with a brooch> **2** : to enclose and hold with the arms; *specif* : EMBRACE **3** : to seize with or as if with the hand : GRASP

clasp·er \'klas-pər\ *n* : a male copulatory structure: **a** : one of a pair of external anal processes of an insect **b** : one of a pair of organs on the pelvic fins of elasmobranch fishes

clasp knife *n* : POCKETKNIFE; *esp* : a large one-bladed folding knife having a catch to hold the blade open

1class \'klas\ *n, often attrib* [F *classe,* fr. L *classis* group called to arms, class of citizens; akin to L *calare* to call — more at LOW] **1 a** : a group sharing the same economic or social status <the working ~> **b** : social rank; *esp* : high social rank **c** : high quality : ELEGANCE **2 a** : a course of instruction **b** : a body of students meeting regularly to study the same subject **c** : the period during which such a body meets **d** : a body of students or alumni whose year of graduation is the same **3** : a group, set, or kind sharing common attributes: as **a** : a major category in biological taxonomy ranking above the order and below the phylum or division **b** : a group of adjacent and discrete or continuous values of a random variable **c** : SET 19 **4** : a division or rating based on grade or quality

2class *vt* : CLASSIFY

class action *n* : a legal action undertaken by one or more plaintiffs on behalf of themselves and all other persons having an identical interest in the alleged wrong

class–con·scious *adj* **1** : actively aware of one's common status with others in a particular economic or social level of society **2** : believing in and actively aware of class struggle — **class consciousness** *n*

1clas·sic \'klas-ik\ *adj* [F or L; F *classique,* fr. L *classicus* of the highest class of Roman citizens, of the first rank, fr. *classis*] **1 a** : of recognized value : serving as a standard of excellence **b** : TRADITIONAL, ENDURING **c** : characterized by simple tailored lines in fashion year after year <a ~ suit> **2** : of or relating to the ancient Greeks and Romans or their culture : CLASSICAL **3 a** : historically memorable **b** : noted because of special literary or historical associations <Paris is the ~ refuge of expatriates> **4 a** : AUTHENTIC, AUTHORITATIVE **b** : TYPICAL <a ~ example of guilt by association>

2classic *n* **1** : a literary work of ancient Greece or Rome **2 a** : a work of enduring excellence; *also* : its author **b** : an authoritative source **3** : a typical example **4** : a traditional event <a football ~>

clas·si·cal \'klas-i-kəl\ *adj* [L *classicus*] **1** : STANDARD, CLASSIC **2 a** : of or relating to the ancient Greek and Roman world and esp. to its literature, art, architecture, or ideals **b** : versed in the classics **3 a** : of or relating to music of the late 18th and early 19th centuries characterized by an emphasis on simplicity, objectivity, and proportion; *also* : of or relating to a composer of this music **b** : of, relating to, or being music in the educated European tradition that includes such forms as art song, chamber music, opera, and symphony as distinguished from folk or popular music or jazz **4 a** : AUTHORITATIVE, TRADITIONAL **b** (1) : of or relating to a form or system considered of first significance in earlier times <~ Mendelian genetics versus modern molecular genetics> (2) : not involving relativity, wave mechanics, or quantum theory <~ physics> **c** : conforming to a pattern of usage sanctioned by a body of literature rather than by everyday speech **5** : concerned with or giving instruction in the humanities, the fine arts, and the broad aspects of science <a ~ curriculum>

clas·si·cal·ism \'klas-i-kə-ˌliz-əm\ *n* : CLASSICISM — **clas·si·cal·ist** \-ləst\ *n*

clas·si·cal·i·ty \ˌklas-ə-'kal-ət-ē\ *n* **1** : the quality or state of being classic **2** : classical scholarship

clas·si·cal·ly \'klas-i-k(ə-)lē\ *adv* : in a classic or classical manner

clas·si·cism \'klas-ə-ˌsiz-əm\ *n* **1 a** : the principles or style embodied in the literature, art, or architecture of ancient Greece and Rome **b** : classical scholarship **c** : a classical idiom or expression **2** : adherence to traditional standards (as of simplicity, restraint, and proportion) that are universally and enduringly valid

clas·si·cist \-səst\ *n* **1** : an advocate or follower of classicism **2** : a classical scholar — **clas·si·cis·tic** \ˌklas-ə-'sis-tik\ *adj*

clas·si·cize \'klas-ə-ˌsīz\ *vb* **-cized; -ciz·ing** *vt* : to make classic or classical ~ *vi* : to follow classic style

clas·si·fi·ca·tion \ˌklas-(ə-)fə-'kā-shən\ *n* **1** : the act or process of classifying **2 a** : systematic arrangement in groups or categories according to established criteria; *specif* : TAXONOMY **b** : CLASS, CATEGORY — **clas·si·fi·ca·to·ri·ly** \ˌklas-(ə-)fə-kə-'tōr-ə-lē, kla-ˌsif-ə-, -'tȯr-\ *adv* — **clas·si·fi·ca·to·ry** \'klas-(ə-)fə-kə-ˌtōr-ē, kla-'sif-ə-, -ˌtȯr-; 'klas-(ə-)fə-ˌkāt-ə-rē\ *adj*

clas·si·fied \'klas-ə-ˌfīd\ *adj* **1** : divided into classes or placed in a class <~ ads> **2** : withheld from general circulation for reasons of national security <~ information>

clas·si·fi·er \'klas-ə-ˌfī(-ə)r\ *n* **1** : one that classifies; *specif* : a machine for sorting out the constituents of a substance (as ore) **2** : a word or morpheme used with numerals or with nouns designating countable or measurable objects

clas·si·fy \'klas-ə-ˌfī\ *vt* **-fied; -fy·ing** **1** : to arrange in classes <~*ing* books according to subject matter> **2** : to assign (as a document) to a category — **clas·si·fi·able** \-ˌfī-ə-bəl\ *adj*

class interval *n* : CLASS 3b; *also* : the width of a statistical class

clas·sis \'klas-əs\ *n, pl* **clas·ses** \'klas-ˌēz\ [NL, fr. L, class] **1** : a governing body in some Reformed churches (as in the former Reformed Church in the U. S.) corresponding to a presbytery **2** : the district governed by a classis

class·less \'klas-ləs\ *adj* **1** : free from distinctions of social class <a ~ society> **2** : belonging to no particular social class — **class·less·ness** *n*

class·mate \-ˌmāt\ *n* : a member of the same class in a school or college

class·room \-ˌrüm, -ˌru̇m\ *n* : a place where classes meet

classy \'klas-ē\ *adj* **class·i·er; -est** : ELEGANT, STYLISH — **class·i·ness** *n*

clast \'klast\ *n* [Gk *klastos* broken] : a fragment of rock

clas·tic \'klas-tik\ *adj* [ISV, fr. Gk *klastos* broken, fr. *klan* to break — more at HALT] : made up of fragments of preexisting rocks <a ~ sediment> — **clastic** *n*

clath·rate \'klath-ˌrāt\ *adj* [L *clathratus,* fr. *clathri* (pl.) lattice, fr. Gk *klēithron* bar, fr. *kleiein* to close — more at CLOSE] **1** : resembling a lattice **2** : relating to or being a compound formed by the inclusion of molecules of one kind in cavities of the crystal lattice of another — **clathrate** *n*

1clat·ter \'klat-ər\ *vb* [ME *clatren,* fr. (assumed) OE *clatrian;* of imit. origin] *vi* **1** : to make a rattling sound <the dishes ~*ed* on the shelf> **2** : to move or go with a clatter <~*ed* down the stairs> **3** : PRATTLE ~ *vt* : to cause to clatter — **clat·ter·er** \-ər-ər\ *n* — **clat·ter·ing·ly** \'klat-ə-riŋ-lē\ *adv*

2clatter *n* **1** : a rattling sound (as of hard bodies striking together) <the ~ of pots and pans> **2** : COMMOTION <the midday ~ of the business district> **3** : noisy chatter — **clat·tery** \'klat-ə-rē\ *adj*

clau·di·ca·tion \ˌklȯd-ə-'kā-shən\ *n* [L *claudication-, claudicatio,* fr. *claudicatus,* pp. of *claudicare* to limp, fr. *claudus* lame; akin to L *claudere* to close — more at CLOSE] : the quality or state of being lame : LIMPING

claus·al \'klȯ-zəl\ *adj* : relating to or of the nature of a clause

clause \'klȯz\ *n* [ME, fr. OF, clause, fr. ML *clausa* close of a rhetorical period, fr. L, fem. of *clausus,* pp. of *claudere* to close] **1** : a separate section of a discourse or writing; *specif* : a distinct article in a formal document **2** : a group of words containing a subject and predicate and functioning as a member of a complex or compound sentence

claus·tral \'klȯ-strəl\ *adj* [ME, fr. ML *claustralis,* fr. *claustrum* cloister — more at CLOISTER] : CLOISTRAL

claus·tro·pho·bia \ˌklȯ-strə-ˈfō-bē-ə\ *n* [NL, fr. L *claustrum* bar, bolt + NL *phobia* — more at CLOISTER] **:** abnormal dread of being in closed or narrow spaces — **claus·tro·pho·bic** \-bik\ *adj*

cla·vate \ˈklā-ˌvāt\ *adj* [NL *clavatus*, fr. L *clava* club, fr. *clavus* nail, knot in wood] **:** gradually thickening near the distal end **:** CLAVIFORM — **cla·vate·ly** *adv* — **cla·va·tion** \klā-ˈvā-shən\ *n*

clave *past of* CLEAVE

cla·ver \ˈklā-vər\ *vi* [prob. of Celt origin; akin to ScGael *clabaire* babbler] *chiefly Scot* **:** PRATE, GOSSIP — **claver** *n*, *chiefly Scot*

clav·i·chord \ˈklav-ə-ˌkȯ(ə)rd\ *n* [ML *clavichordium*, fr. L *clavis* key + *chorda* string — more at CORD] **:** an early keyboard instrument having strings pressed by tangents attached directly to the key ends — **clav·i·chord·ist** \-əst\ *n*

clav·i·cle \ˈklav-i-kəl\ *n* [F *clavicule*, fr. NL *clavicula*, fr. L, dim. of L *clavis* key; akin to Gk *kleid-*, *kleis* key, L *claudere* to close — more at CLOSE] **:** a bone of the vertebrate shoulder girdle typically serving to link the scapula and sternum — **cla·vic·u·lar** \kla-ˈvik-yə-lər, klə-\ *adj*

cla·vier \klə-ˈvi(ə)r; ˈklāv-ē-ər, ˈklav-\ *n* [F, fr. OF, key bearer, fr. L *clavis* key] **1 :** the keyboard of a musical instrument **2** [G *klavier*, fr. F *clavier*] **:** an early keyboard instrument — **cla·vier·ist** \klə-ˈvir-əst; ˈklāv-ē-ə-rəst, ˈklav-\ *n* — **cla·vier·is·tic** \klə-ˌvi(ə)r-ˈis-tik, ˌklāv-ē-ə-ˈris-tik, ˌklav-\ *adj*

clav·i·form \ˈklav-ə-ˌfȯrm\ *adj* [L *clava* club] **:** shaped like a club

[1]**claw** \ˈklȯ\ *n*, *often attrib* [ME *clawe*, fr. OE *clawu* hoof, claw; akin to ON klō claw, OE *cliewen* ball — more at CLEW] **1 :** a sharp usu. slender and curved nail on the toe of an animal **2 :** any of various similar sharp curved processes esp. if at the end of a limb (as of an insect); *also* **:** a limb ending in such a process **3 :** one of the pincerlike organs terminating some limbs of various arthropods (as a lobster or scorpion) **4 :** something that resembles a claw; *specif* **:** the forked end of a tool (as a hammer) **5 :** a wound from or as if from a claw — **clawed** \ˈklȯd\ *adj*

[2]**claw** *vt* **:** to rake, seize, dig, or progress with or as if with claws ~ *vi* **:** to scrape, scratch, dig, or pull with or as if with claws

claw hammer *n* **1 :** a hammer with one end of the head forked for pulling out nails **2 :** TAILCOAT

[1]**clay** \ˈklā\ *n*, *often attrib* [ME, fr. OE *clæg*; akin to OHG *klīwa* bran, LL *glut-*, *glus* glue, MGk *glia*] **1 a :** an earthy material that is plastic when moist but hard when fired, that is composed mainly of fine particles of hydrous aluminum silicates and other minerals, and that is used for brick, tile, and pottery; *specif* **:** soil composed chiefly of this material having particles less than a specified size **b :** EARTH, MUD **2 a :** a substance that resembles clay in plasticity and is used for modeling **b :** the human body as distinguished from the spirit **3 :** CLAY COURT — **clay·ey** \ˈklā-ē\ *adj* — **clay·ish** \ˈklā-ish\ *adj*

[2]**clay** *vt* **:** to treat or cover with clay; *also* **:** to filter through clay

clay·bank \ˈklā-ˌbaŋk\ *n* **:** a horse of yellowish color

clay court *n* **:** a tennis court with a clay surface

clay loam *n* **:** a loam containing from 20 to 30 percent clay

clay mineral *n* **:** any of a group of hydrous silicates of aluminum and sometimes other metals formed chiefly in weathering processes and occurring esp. in clay and shale

clay·more \ˈklā-ˌmō(ə)r, -ˌmȯ(ə)r\ *n* [ScGael *claidheamh mōr*, lit., great sword] **:** a large 2-edged sword formerly used by Scottish Highlanders; *also* **:** their basket-hilted broadsword

clay·pan \-ˌpan\ *n* **:** hardpan consisting mainly of clay

clay pigeon *n* **:** a saucer-shaped target usu. made of baked clay and pitch and thrown from a trap in skeet and trapshooting

clay·ware \ˈklā-ˌwa(ə)r, -ˌwe(ə)r\ *n* **:** articles made of fired clay

cld *abbr* **1** called **2** cleared

[1]**clean** \ˈklēn\ *adj* [ME *clene*, fr. OE *clǣne*; akin to OHG *kleini* delicate, dainty, Gk *glainoi* ornaments] **1 a :** free from dirt or pollution <changed to ~ clothes> <ship with a ~ bottom> **b :** free from contamination or disease **c :** relatively free from radioactive fallout <a ~ atomic explosion> **2 a :** UNADULTERATED, PURE <the ~ thrill of one's first flight> **b** *of a precious stone* **:** having no interior flaws visible **c :** free from growth that hinders tillage **3 a :** free from moral corruption or sinister connections of any kind <a candidate with a ~ record> **b :** free from offensive treatment of sexual subjects and from the use of obscenity <do you know a ~ joke> **c :** observing the rules **:** FAIR <a ~ fight> **4 :** ceremonially or spiritually pure <and all who are ~ may eat flesh — Lev 7:19 (RSV)> **5 a :** THOROUGH, COMPLETE <a ~ break with the past> **b :** deftly executed **:** SKILLFUL <~ ballet technique> **6 a :** relatively free from error or blemish **:** CLEAR; *specif* **:** LEGIBLE <~ copy> **b :** UNENCUMBERED <~ bill of sale> **7 a :** characterized by clarity and precision **:** TRIM <a ~ prose style> <architecture with ~ almost austere lines> **b :** EVEN, SMOOTH <a ~ edge> <a sharp blow causing a ~ break> **8 a :** EMPTY <the whaling ship returned with a ~ hold> **b** *slang* **:** carrying no concealed weapons **9 :** habitually neat — **clean·ness** \ˈklēn-nəs\ *n*

[2]**clean** *adv* **1 a :** so as to clean <a new broom sweeps ~> **b :** in a clean manner <play the game ~> **2 :** all the way **:** COMPLETELY <the bullet went ~ through his arm>

[3]**clean** *vt* **1 :** to rid of dirt, impurities, or extraneous matter **2 a :** STRIP, EMPTY <the tree was ~*ed* of fruit by hurricane winds> <the hungry men quickly ~*ed* the platter> **b :** to deprive of money or possessions — often used with *out* <they ~*ed* him out completely> ~ *vi* **:** to undergo or perform a process of cleaning <~ up before dinner> — **clean·able** \ˈklē-nə-bəl\ *adj* — **clean·er** *n* — **clean house 1 :** to clean a house and its furniture **2 :** to eradicate whatever is obstructive, thwarting, or degrading

[4]**clean** *n* **:** an act of cleaning dirt esp. from the surface of something

clean and jerk *n* **:** a lift in weight lifting in which the weight is raised to shoulder height, held momentarily, and then quickly thrust overhead usu. with a lunge or a spring from the legs — compare PRESS, SNATCH

clean–cut \ˈklēn-ˈkət\ *adj* **1 :** cut so that the surface or edge is smooth and even **2 :** sharply defined **3 :** of wholesome appearance

clean·er \ˈklē-nər\ *n* **1 :** one whose work is cleaning **2 :** a preparation for cleaning **3 :** an implement or machine for cleaning — **to the cleaners** *slang* **:** to or through the experience of being deprived of all one's money

clean·hand·ed \ˈklēn-ˈhan-dəd\ *adj* **:** innocent of wrongdoing

cleaning woman *n* **:** a woman who hires herself out for housecleaning

clean–limbed \ˈklēn-ˈlimd\ *adj* **:** well proportioned **:** TRIM <~ youths>

[1]**clean·ly** \ˈklen-lē\ *adj* **clean·li·er; -est 1 :** careful to keep clean **:** FASTIDIOUS **2 :** habitually kept clean — **clean·li·ness** *n*

[2]**clean·ly** \ˈklēn-lē\ *adv* **:** in a clean manner

clean room \ˈklēn-ˌ\ *n* **:** a room for the manufacture or assembly of objects (as precision parts) that is maintained at a high level of cleanliness by special means

cleanse \ˈklenz\ *vb* **cleansed; cleans·ing** [ME *clensen*, fr. OE *clǣnsian* to purify, fr. *clǣne* clean] **:** CLEAN

cleans·er \ˈklen-zər\ *n* **1 :** one that cleanses **2 :** a preparation (as a scouring powder or a skin cream) used for cleaning

[1]**clean·up** \ˈklē-ˌnəp\ *n* **1 :** an act or instance of cleaning **2 :** an exceptionally large profit **:** KILLING

[2]**cleanup** *adj* **:** being in the fourth position in the batting order of a baseball team

clean up \(ˈ)klē-ˈnəp\ *vi* **:** to make a spectacular profit in a business enterprise or a killing in speculation or gambling

[1]**clear** \ˈkli(ə)r\ *adj* [ME *clere*, fr. OF *cler*, fr. L *clarus* clear, bright; akin to L *calare* to call — more at LOW] **1 a :** BRIGHT, LUMINOUS **b :** CLOUDLESS; *specif* **:** less than one-tenth covered <a ~ sky> **c :** free from mist, haze, or dust <a ~ day> **d :** UNTROUBLED, SERENE <a ~ gaze> **2 :** CLEAN, PURE: as **a :** free from blemishes **b :** easily seen through **:** TRANSPARENT **c :** free from abnormal sounds on auscultation **3 a :** easily heard **b :** easily visible **:** PLAIN **c :** free from obscurity or ambiguity **:** easily understood **:** UNMISTAKABLE **4 a :** capable of sharp discernment **:** KEEN **b :** free from doubt **:** SURE **5 :** free from guile or guilt **:** INNOCENT **6 :** unhampered by restriction or limitation: as **a :** unencumbered by debts or charges **b :** NET <a ~ profit> **c :** UNQUALIFIED, ABSOLUTE **d :** free from obstruction **e :** emptied of contents or cargo **f :** free from entanglement **g :** BARE, DENUDED — **clear·ly** *adv* — **clear·ness** *n*

syn **1** CLEAR, PERSPICUOUS, LUCID *shared meaning element* **:** quickly and easily understood ***ant*** unintelligible, abstruse **2** see EVIDENT

[2]**clear** *adv* **1 :** in a clear manner <to cry loud and ~> **2 :** all the way <can see ~ to the mountains on a day like this>

[3]**clear** *vt* **1 a :** to make clear or translucent **b :** to free from pollution or cloudiness **2 a :** to free from accusation or blame **:** VINDICATE <the opportunity to ~ himself> **b :** to certify as trustworthy <~ a man for top secret military work> **3 a :** to give insight to **:** ENLIGHTEN **b :** to make intelligible **:** EXPLAIN <~ up the mystery> **4 a :** to free from obstruction: as (1) **:** OPEN (2) **:** DISENTANGLE <~ a fishing line> (3) **:** to rid or make a rasping noise as if ridding (the throat) of phlegm (4) **:** to erase accumulated totals or stored data from (as a business machine or computer memory) **b** (1) **:** to submit for approval (2) **:** AUTHORIZE <the chairman ~*ed* the article for publication> **5 a :** to free from obligation or encumbrance **b :** SETTLE, DISCHARGE <~ an account> **c** (1) **:** to free (a ship or shipment) by payment of duties or harbor fees (2) **:** to pass through (customs) **d :** to gain without deduction **:** NET <~ a profit> **e :** to put through a clearinghouse **6 a :** to get rid of **:** REMOVE <~ the land of trees and brush> **b :** TRANSMIT, DISPATCH **7 a :** to go over, under, or by without touching **b :** PASS <the bill ~*ed* the legislature> ~ *vi* **1 a :** to become clear <it ~*ed* up quickly after the rain> **b :** to go away **:** VANISH <the symptoms ~*ed* gradually> **c :** SELL **2 a :** to obtain permission to discharge cargo **b :** to conform to regulations or pay requisite fees prior to leaving port **3 :** to pass through a clearinghouse **4 :** to go to an authority (as for approval) before becoming effective — **clear·able** \ˈklir-ə-bəl\ *adj* — **clear·er** \ˈklir-ər\ *n* — **clear the air** *also* **clear the atmosphere :** to remove elements of hostility, tension, confusion, or uncertainty from the mood or temper of the time

[4]**clear** *n* **1 :** a clear space or part **2 :** a high arcing shot over an opponent's head in badminton — **in the clear 1 :** in inside measurement **2 :** free from guilt or suspicion **3 :** in plaintext **:** not in code or cipher <a message sent *in the clear*>

clear–air turbulence *n* **:** sudden severe turbulence occurring in cloudless regions that causes violent jarring or buffeting of aircraft — abbr. *CAT*

clear·ance \ˈklir-ən(t)s\ *n* **1 :** an act or process of clearing: as **a :** the act of clearing a ship at the customhouse; *also* **:** the papers showing that a ship has cleared **b :** the offsetting of checks and other claims among banks through a clearinghouse **c :** certification as clear of objection **:** AUTHORIZATION **d :** a sale to clear out stock **2 :** the distance by which one object clears another or the clear space between them

[1]**clear–cut** \ˈkli(ə)r-ˈkət\ *adj* **1 :** sharply outlined **:** DISTINCT **2 :** free from ambiguity or uncertainty **:** UNAMBIGUOUS ***syn*** see INCISIVE

[2]**clear–cut** *vt* **-cut; -cut·ting :** to cut all the trees in (a stand of timber)

clear–eyed \ˈkli(ə)r-ˈīd\ *adj* **1 :** having clear eyes **2 :** DISCERNING

clear·head·ed \-ˈhed-əd\ *adj* **:** having a clear understanding **:** PERCEPTIVE — **clear·head·ed·ly** *adv* — **clear·head·ed·ness** *n*

clear·ing \'kli(ə)r-iŋ\ *n* **1 :** the act or process of making or becoming clear **2 :** a tract of land cleared of wood and brush **3 a :** a method of exchanging and offsetting commercial papers or accounts with cash settlement only of the balances due after the clearing **b** *pl* **:** the gross amount of balances so adjusted
clear·ing·house \-ˌhau̇s\ *n* **1 :** an establishment maintained by banks for settling mutual claims and accounts **2 :** a central agency for the collection, classification, and distribution esp. of information
clear-sight·ed \'kli(ə)r-'sīt-əd\ *adj* **1 :** having clear vision **2 :** DISCERNING — **clear-sight·ed·ly** *adv* — **clear-sight·ed·ness** *n*
clear·wing \-ˌwiŋ\ *n* **:** a moth (as of the families Aegeriidae or Sphingidae) having the wings largely transparent and devoid of scales
[1]**cleat** \'klēt\ *n* [ME *clete* wedge, fr. (assumed) OE *clēat;* akin to MHG *klōz* lump — more at CLOUT] **1 a :** a wedge-shaped piece fastened to or projecting from something and serving as a support or check **b :** a wooden or metal fitting usu. with two projecting horns around which a rope may be made fast **2 a :** a strip fastened across something to give strength or hold in position **b** (1) **:** a projecting piece (as on the bottom of a shoe) that furnishes a grip (2) *pl* **:** shoes equipped with cleats
[2]**cleat** *vt* **1 :** to secure to or by a cleat **2 :** to provide with a cleat
cleav·able \'klē-və-bəl\ *adj* **:** capable of being split
cleav·age \'klē-vij\ *n* **1 a :** the quality of a crystallized substance or rock of splitting along definite planes **b :** a fragment (as of a diamond) obtained by splitting **2 :** the action of cleaving **:** the state of being cleft **3 :** cell division; *esp* **:** the series of mitotic divisions of the egg that results in the formation of the blastomeres and changes the single-celled zygote into a multicellular embryo **4 :** the splitting of a molecule into simpler molecules **5 :** the depression between a woman's breasts esp. when made visible by the wearing of a low-cut dress
[1]**cleave** \'klēv\ *vi* **cleaved** \'klēvd\ *or* **clove** \'klōv\ *also* **clave** \'klāv\; **cleav·ing** [ME *clevien,* fr. OE *clifian*] **:** to adhere firmly and closely or loyally and unwaveringly ***syn*** see STICK
[2]**cleave** *vb* **cleaved** \'klēvd\ *also* **cleft** \'kleft\ *or* **clove** \'klōv\; **cleaved** *also* **cleft** *or* **clo·ven** \'klō-vən\; **cleav·ing** [ME *cleven,* fr. OE *clēofan;* akin to ON *kljūfa* to split, L *glubere* to peel, Gk *glyphein* to carve] *vt* **1 :** to divide by or as if by a cutting blow **:** SPLIT **2 :** to separate into distinct parts and esp. into groups having divergent views ~ *vi* **1 :** to split esp. along the grain **2 :** to penetrate or pass through something by or as if by cutting ***syn*** see TEAR
cleav·er \'klē-vər\ *n* **1 :** one that cleaves; *esp* **:** a butcher's implement for cutting animal carcasses into joints or pieces **2 :** a rock ridge protruding from a glacier or snowfield
cleav·ers \'klē-vərz\ *n pl but sing or pl in constr* [ME *clivre,* alter. of OE *clife* burdock, cleavers; akin to OE *clifian* to cleave, adhere] **1 :** an annual plant (*Galium aparine*) of the madder family that has numerous stalked white flowers, stems covered with curved prickles, and whorls of bristle-tipped leaves **2 :** a plant related to cleavers
cleek \'klēk\ *n* [ME (northern) *cleke,* fr. *cleken* to clutch] *chiefly Scot* **:** a large hook (as for a pot over a fire)
clef \'klef\ *n* [F, lit., key, fr. L *clavis* — more at CLAVICLE] **:** a sign placed at the beginning of a musical staff to determine the position of the notes
[1]**cleft** \'kleft\ *n* [ME *clift,* fr. OE *geclyft;* akin to OE *clēofan* to cleave] **1 :** a space or opening made by splitting **:** FISSURE **2 :** a usu. V-shaped indented formation **:** a hollow between ridges or protuberances <the anal ~ of the human body>
[2]**cleft** *adj* [ME, fr. pp. of *cleven*] **:** partially split or divided; *specif* **:** divided about halfway to the midrib <a ~ leaf>
cleft palate *n* **:** congenital fissure of the roof of the mouth
cleis·tog·a·my \klī-'stäg-ə-mē\ *n* [Gk *kleistos* closed (fr. *kleiein* to close) + ISV *-gamy* — more at CLOSE] **:** the production (as in violets) of small inconspicuous closed self-pollinating flowers additional to and often more fruitful than the showier type — **cleis·tog·a·mous** \-məs\ *or* **cleis·to·gam·ic** \ˌklī-stə-'gam-ik\ *adj* — **cleis·tog·a·mous·ly** *adv*
cle·ma·tis \'klem-ət-əs; kli-'mat-əs, -'māt-, -'mät-\ *n* [NL, genus name, fr. L, fr. Gk *klēmatis* brushwood, clematis, fr. *klēmat-, klēma* twig, fr. Gk *klan* to break — more at HALT] **:** a vine or herb (genera *Clematis, Atragene,* or *Viorna*) of the buttercup family having three leaflets on each leaf and usu. white or purple flowers
clem·en·cy \'klem-ən-sē\ *n, pl* **-cies 1 a :** disposition to be merciful and esp. to moderate the severity of punishment due **b :** an act or instance of leniency **2 :** pleasant mildness of weather ***syn*** see MERCY ***ant*** harshness
clem·ent \'klem-ənt\ *adj* [ME, fr. L *clement-, clemens*] **1 :** inclined to be merciful **:** LENIENT <a ~ judge> **2 :** MILD <~ weather for November> — **clem·ent·ly** *adv*
[1]**clench** \'klench\ *vt* [ME *clenchen,* fr. OE *-clencan;* akin to OE *clingan* to cling] **1 :** CLINCH 1 **2 :** to hold fast **:** CLUTCH <he ~*ed* the arms of his chair> **3 :** to set or close tightly <~*ed* his teeth> <~*ed* his fists>
[2]**clench** *n* **1 :** the end of a nail that is turned back in clinching it **2 :** an act or instance of clenching
clepe \'klēp\ *vt* **cleped** \'klēpt, 'klept\; **cleped** *or* **ycleped** \i-\ *or* **yclept** \i-'klept \; **clep·ing** \'klē-piŋ\ [ME *clepen,* fr. OE *clipian* to speak, call; akin to OFris *kleppa* to ring, knock] *archaic* **:** NAME, CALL
clep·sy·dra \'klep-sə-drə\ *n, pl* **-dras** *or* **-drae** \-ˌdrē, -ˌdrī\ [L, fr. Gk *klepsydra,* fr. *kleptein* to steal + *hydōr* water — more at KLEPT-, WATER] **:** WATER CLOCK
clere·sto·ry *or* **clear·sto·ry** \'kli(ə)r-ˌstōr-ē, -ˌstȯr-\ *n* [ME, fr. *clere* clear + *story*] **1 :** an outside wall of a room or building that rises above an adjoining roof and contains windows **2 :** GALLERY **3 :** a ventilating section of a railroad car roof
cler·gy \'klər-jē\ *n* [ME *clergie,* fr. OF, knowledge, learning, fr. *clerc* clergyman] **1 :** a group ordained to perform pastoral or sacerdotal functions in a Christian church **2 :** the official or sacerdotal class of a non-Christian religion
cler·gy·man \-ji-mən\ *n* **:** a member of the clergy
cler·ic \'kler-ik\ *n* [LL *clericus*] **:** a member of the clergy; *specif* **:** one in orders below the grade of priest

clerestory 1

[1]**cler·i·cal** \'kler-i-kəl\ *adj* **1 :** of, relating to, or characteristic of the clergy, a clergyman, or a cleric **2 :** of or relating to a clerk or office worker — **cler·i·cal·ly** \-i-k(ə-)lē\ *adv*
[2]**clerical** *n* **1 :** CLERGYMAN **2 :** CLERICALIST **3 :** CLERK
clerical collar *n* **:** a narrow stiffly upright white collar worn buttoned at the back of the neck by clergymen
cler·i·cal·ism \'kler-i-kə-ˌliz-əm\ *n* **:** a policy of maintaining or increasing the power of a religious hierarchy
cler·i·cal·ist \-ləst\ *n* **:** one that favors maintained or increased ecclesiastical power and influence
cler·i·hew \'kler-i-ˌhyü\ *n* [Edmund *Clerihew* Bentley †1956 E writer] **:** a light verse quatrain rhyming *aabb* and usu. dealing with a person named in the initial rhyme
cler·i·sy \'kler-ə-sē\ *n* [G *klerisei* clergy, fr. ML *clericia,* fr. LL *clericus* cleric] **:** INTELLIGENTSIA
[1]**clerk** \'klərk, *Brit usu rhymes with "lark"*\ *n* [ME, fr. OF *clerc* & OE *cleric, clerc,* both fr. LL *clericus,* fr. LGk *klērikos,* fr. Gk *klēros* lot, inheritance (in allusion to Deut 18:2); akin to Gk *klan* to break — more at HALT] **1 :** CLERIC **2** *archaic* **:** SCHOLAR **3 a :** an official responsible for correspondence, records, and accounts <city ~> **b :** one employed to keep records or accounts or to perform general office work **c :** one who works at a sales or service counter
[2]**clerk** *vi* **:** to act or work as a clerk <~*ed* in his father's store>
clerk·ly \'klər-klē\ *adj* **1 :** of, relating to, or characteristic of a clerk **2** *archaic* **:** SCHOLARLY — **clerkly** *adv*
clerk regular *n, pl* **clerks regular :** a Roman Catholic religious combining life in a monastic community with the ministry of a diocesan priest
clerk·ship \'klərk-ˌship\ *n* **:** the office or business of a clerk
clev·er \'klev-ər\ *adj* [ME *cliver,* prob. of Scand origin; akin to ON *kljūfa* to split — more at CLEAVE] **1 a :** skillful or adroit in using the hands or body **:** NIMBLE **b :** mentally quick and resourceful but often lacking in depth and soundness **2 :** marked by wit or ingenuity **3** *dial* **a :** GOOD **b :** easy to use or handle — **clev·er·ish** \-(ə-)rish\ *adj* — **clev·er·ly** \-ər-lē\ *adv* — **clev·er·ness** \-ər-nəs\ *n*
syn* 1** see INTELLIGENT ***ant dull
2 CLEVER, ADROIT, CUNNING, INGENIOUS *shared meaning element* **:** having or showing practical wit or skill in contriving
clev·is \'klev-əs\ *n* [earlier *clevi,* prob. of Scand origin; akin to ON *kljūfa* to split] **:** a usu. U-shaped metal shackle that has the ends drilled to receive a pin or bolt and that is used for attaching or suspending parts
[1]**clew** *or* **clue** \'klü\ *n* [ME *clewe,* fr. OE *cliewen;* akin to OHG *kliuwa* ball, Skt *glau* lump] **1 :** a ball of thread, yarn, or cord **2** *usu clue* **:** something that guides through an intricate procedure or maze of difficulties; *specif* **:** a piece of evidence that leads one toward the solution of a problem **3 a :** a lower corner or only the after corner of a sail **b :** a metal loop attached to the lower corner of a sail **c** *pl* **:** a combination of lines by which a hammock is suspended
[2]**clew** *or* **clue** *vt* **clewed** *or* **clued; clew·ing** *or* **clue·ing** *or* **clu·ing 1 :** to roll into a ball **2** *usu clue* **a :** to provide with a clue **b :** to give reliable information to <~ me in on how it happened> **3 :** to haul (a sail) up or down by ropes through the clews
cli·ché \kli-'shā\ *n* [F, lit., stereotype, fr. pp. of *clicher* to stereotype, of imit. origin] **1 :** a trite phrase or expression; *also* **:** the idea expressed by it **2 :** a hackneyed theme or situation — **cliché** *adj*
cli·chéd \-'shād\ *adj* **1 :** marked by or abounding in clichés **2 :** HACKNEYED
[1]**click** \'klik\ *n* [prob. imit.] **1 a :** a slight sharp noise **b :** a speech sound in some languages made by enclosing air between two stop articulations of the tongue, enlarging the enclosure to rarefy the air, and suddenly opening the enclosure **2 :** DETENT
[2]**click** *vt* **:** to strike, move, or produce with a click <~*ed* his heels together> ~ *vi* **1 :** to make a click <the Geiger counter was ~*ing* furiously> **2 a :** to fit or agree exactly **b :** to fit together **:** hit it off <they did not ~ as friends> **c :** to function smoothly **d :** SUCCEED <a movie that ~*s*>
click beetle *n* **:** any of a family (Elateridae) of beetles able to right themselves with a click when inverted
click stop *n* **:** a turnable control device (as for a camera diaphragm opening) that engages with a definite click at specific setting positions
cli·ent \'klī-ənt\ *n* [ME, fr. MF & L; MF *client,* fr. L *client-, cliens;* akin to L *clinare* to lean — more at LEAN] **1 :** a person under the protection of another **:** DEPENDENT **2 a :** a person who engages the professional advice or services of another <a lawyer's ~*s*> **b :** CUSTOMER <hotel ~*s*> **c :** a person served by or utilizing the services of a social agency <a welfare ~> — **cli·ent·age** \-ən-tij\ *n* — **cli·en·tal** \klī-'ent-ᵊl, 'klī-ənt-\ *adj*
cli·en·tele \ˌklī-ən-'tel, ˌklē-ən- *also* ˌklē-ˌän-\ *n* [F *clientèle,* fr. L *clientela,* fr. *client-, cliens*] **:** a body of clients <a shop that caters to an exclusive ~>
cliff \'klif\ *n* [ME *clif,* fr. OE; akin to OE *clifian* to adhere to] **:** a very steep, vertical, or overhanging face of rock, earth, or ice **:** PRECIPICE — **cliffy** \'klif-ē\ *adj*
cliff dweller *n* **1** *often cap C&D* **a :** a member of a prehistoric Amerindian people of the southwestern U.S. who built their homes on rock ledges or in the natural recesses of canyon walls and cliffs **b :** a member of any cliff-dwelling people **2 :** a person who lives in a large usu. metropolitan apartment building — **cliff dwelling** *n*

cliff–hang \ˈklif-ˌhaŋ\ *vi* [back-formation fr. *cliff-hanger*] **:** to end an installment of a cliff-hanger with a suspenseful melodramatic unresolved conflict; *also* **:** to await the outcome of a suspenseful situation

cliff–hang·er \-ˌhaŋ-ər\ *n* **1 :** an adventure serial or melodrama; *esp* **:** one presented in installments each ending in suspense **2 :** a contest whose outcome is in doubt up to the very end

[1]**cli·mac·ter·ic** \klī-ˈmak-t(ə-)rik, ˌklī-ˌmak-ˈter-ik\ *adj* [L *climactericus,* fr. Gk *klimaktērikos,* fr. *klimaktēr* critical point, lit., rung of a ladder, fr. *klimak-, klimax* ladder] **1 :** constituting or relating to a critical period (as of life) **2 :** CRITICAL, CRUCIAL

[2]**climacteric** *n* **1 :** a major turning point or critical stage **2 :** MENOPAUSE; *also* **:** a corresponding period in the male during which sexual activity and competence are reduced **3 :** the maximum to which the respiratory rate of fruit rises just prior to full ripening

cli·mac·tic \klī-ˈmak-tik\ *adj* **:** of, relating to, or constituting a climax — **cli·mac·ti·cal·ly** \-ti-k(ə-)lē\ *adv*

cli·mate \ˈklī-mət\ *n* [ME *climat,* fr. MF, fr. LL *climat-, clima,* fr. Gk *klimat-, klima* inclination, latitude, climate, fr. *klinein* to lean — more at LEAN] **1 :** a region of the earth having specified climatic conditions **2 :** the average course or condition of the weather at a place over a period of years as exhibited by temperature, wind velocity, and precipitation **3 :** the prevailing temper or environmental conditions characterizing a group or period **:** MILIEU <a ~ of fear> — **cli·mat·ic** \klī-ˈmat-ik\ *adj* — **cli·mat·i·cal·ly** \-i-k(ə-)lē\ *adv*

cli·ma·tol·o·gy \ˌklī-mə-ˈtäl-ə-jē\ *n* **:** the science that deals with climates and their phenomena — **cli·ma·to·log·i·cal** \ˌklī-mət-ᵊl-ˈäj-i-kəl\ *adj* — **cli·ma·to·log·i·cal·ly** \-k(ə-)lē\ *adv* — **cli·ma·tol·o·gist** \-mə-ˈtäl-ə-jəst\ *n*

[1]**cli·max** \ˈklī-ˌmaks\ *n* [L, fr. Gk *klimax* ladder, fr. *klinein* to lean] **1 :** a figure of speech in which a series of phrases or sentences is arranged in ascending order of rhetorical forcefulness **2 a :** the highest point **:** CULMINATION **b :** the point of highest dramatic tension or a major turning point in the action (as of a play) **c :** ORGASM **d :** MENOPAUSE **3 :** a relatively stable stage or community esp. of plants that is achieved through successful adjustment to an environment; *esp* **:** the final stage in ecological succession *syn* see SUMMIT

[2]**climax** *vi* **:** to come to a climax <a riot ~*ing* in the destruction of several houses> ~ *vt* **:** to bring to a climax <~*ed* his boxing career with a knockout>

[1]**climb** \ˈklīm\ *vb* [ME *climben,* fr. OE *climban;* akin to OE *clamm* bond, fetter — more at CLAM] *vi* **1 a :** to go upward with gradual or continuous progress **:** RISE <watching the smoke ~> <the airplane ~*ed* slowly> **b :** to slope upward <the road ~*s* steadily> **2 a :** to go upward or raise oneself esp. by grasping or clutching with the hands <~*ed* upon her father's knee> **b** *of a plant* **:** to ascend in growth (as by twining) **3 :** to go about or down usu. by grasping or holding with the hands <~ down the ladder> **4 :** to get into or out of clothing usu. with some haste or effort <the firemen ~*ed* into their clothes> ~ *vt* **1 :** to go upward on or along, to the top of, or over <~ a hill> **2 :** to draw or pull oneself up, over, or to the top of by using hands and feet <children ~*ing* the tree> **3 :** to grow up or over *syn* see ASCEND *ant* descend — **climb·able** \ˈklī-mə-bəl\ *adj*

[2]**climb** *n* **1 :** a place where climbing is necessary to progress **2 :** the act or an instance of climbing **:** ascent by climbing

climb·er \ˈklī-mər\ *n* **:** one that climbs or helps in climbing

climbing iron *n* **:** a steel framework with spikes attached that may be affixed to one's boots for climbing

climbing iron

clime \ˈklīm\ *n* [L *clima*] **:** CLIMATE <traveled to warmer ~*s*>

clin *abbr* clinical

clin- *or* **clino-** *comb form* [NL, fr. Gk *klinein* to lean — more at LEAN] **:** lean **:** slant <*clino*meter>

-cli·nal \ˈklīn-ᵊl\ *adj comb form* [ISV, fr. Gk *klinein*] **:** sloping <mono*clinal*>

[1]**clinch** \ˈklinch\ *vb* [prob. alter. of [1]*clench*] *vt* **1 a :** to turn over or flatten the protruding pointed end of (a driven nail); *also* **:** to treat (a screw, bolt, or rivet) in a similar way **b :** to fasten in this way **2 :** CLENCH 3 **3 :** to make final or irrefutable **:** SETTLE <that ~*ed* the argument> ~ *vi* **1 :** to hold an opponent (as in boxing) at close quarters with one or both arms **2 :** to hold fast or firmly — **clinch·ing·ly** \ˈklin-chiŋ-lē\ *adv*

[2]**clinch** *n* **1 :** a fastening by means of a clinched nail, rivet, or bolt; *also* **:** the clinched part of a nail, rivet, or bolt **2** *archaic* **:** PUN **3 :** an act or instance of clinching in boxing

clinch·er \ˈklin-chər\ *n* **:** one that clinches: as **a :** a decisive fact, argument, act, or remark <the expense was the ~ that persuaded us to give up the enterprise> **b :** an automobile tire with flanged beads fitting into the wheel rim

cline \ˈklīn\ *n* [Gk *klinein* to lean] **:** a graded series of morphological or physiological differences exhibited by a group of related organisms usu. along a line of environmental or geographic transition — **clin·al** \ˈklīn-ᵊl\ *adj* — **clin·al·ly** \-ᵊl-ē\ *adv*

-cline \ˌklīn\ *n comb form* [back-formation fr. *-clinal*] **:** slope <mono*cline*>

[1]**cling** \ˈkliŋ\ *vi* **clung** \ˈkləŋ\; **cling·ing** [ME *clingen,* fr. OE *clingan;* akin to OHG *klunga* tangled ball of thread, MIr *glacc* hand] **1 a :** to hold together **b :** to adhere as if glued firmly **c :** to hold or hold on tightly or tenaciously **2 a :** to have a strong emotional attachment or dependence **b :** to remain or linger as if resisting complete dissipation or dispersal <the odor *clung* to the room for hours> *syn* see STICK — **clingy** \ˈkliŋ-ē\ *adj*

[2]**cling** *n* **:** an act or instance of clinging **:** ADHERENCE

cling·stone \ˈkliŋ-ˌstōn\ *n* **:** a fruit (as a peach) whose flesh adheres strongly to the pit

clin·ic \ˈklin-ik\ *n* [F *clinique,* fr. Gk *klinikē* medical practice at the sickbed, fr. fem. of *klinikos* of a bed, fr. *klinē* bed, fr. *klinein* to lean, recline — more at LEAN] **1 :** a class of medical instruction in which patients are examined and discussed **2 :** a group meeting devoted to the analysis and solution of concrete problems or to the acquiring of specific skills or knowledge in a particular field <writing ~*s*> <golf ~*s*> **3 a :** a facility (as of a hospital) for diagnosis and treatment of outpatients **b :** a group practice in which several physicians work cooperatively

-clin·ic \ˈklin-ik\ *adj comb form* [ISV, fr. Gk *klinein*] **1 :** inclining **:** dipping <iso*clinic*> **2 :** having (so many) oblique intersections of the axes <mono*clinic*> <tri*clinic*>

clin·i·cal \ˈklin-i-kəl\ *adj* **1 :** of, relating to, or conducted in or as if in a clinic: as **a :** involving direct observation of the patient **b :** apparent to or based on clinical observation **2 :** analytical, detached, or coolly dispassionate <a ~ attitude> — **clin·i·cal·ly** \-k(ə-)lē\ *adv*

clinical thermometer *n* **:** a thermometer for measuring body temperature that has a constriction in the tube where the column of liquid breaks and continues to indicate the maximum temperature to which the thermometer was exposed until reset by shaking

cli·ni·cian \klin-ˈish-ən\ *n* **:** one qualified in the clinical practice of medicine, psychiatry, or psychology as distinguished from one specializing in laboratory or research techniques

clinico- *comb form* **:** clinical and <*clinico*pathological> <*clinico*statistical>

clin·i·co·path·o·log·ic \ˈklin-i-(ˌ)kō-ˌpath-ə-ˈläj-ik\ *or* **clin·i·co·path·o·log·i·cal** \-ˈläj-i-kəl\ *adj* **:** involving both clinical and pathologic factors, aspects, or approaches — **clin·i·co·path·o·log·i·cal·ly** \-i-k(ə-)lē\ *adv*

[1]**clink** \ˈkliŋk\ *vb* [ME *clinken,* of imit. origin] *vi* **:** to give out a slight sharp short metallic sound ~ *vt* **:** to cause to clink

[2]**clink** *n* **:** a clinking sound

[3]**clink** *n* [*Clink,* a prison in Southwark, London, England] *slang* **:** a prison cell **:** JAIL

[1]**clin·ker** \ˈkliŋ-kər\ *n* [alter. of earlier *klincard* (a hard yellowish Dutch brick)] **1 :** a brick that has been burned too much in the kiln **2 :** stony matter fused together **:** SLAG

[2]**clinker** *vb* **clin·kered; clin·ker·ing** \ˈkliŋ-k(ə-)riŋ\ *vt* **1 :** to cause to form clinker **2 :** to clear out the clinkers from ~ *vi* **:** to turn to clinker under heat

[3]**clink·er** \ˈkliŋ-kər\ *n* [[1]*clink*] **1** *Brit* **:** something first-rate **2 a :** a wrong note **b :** a serious mistake or error **:** BONER **c :** an utter failure **:** FLOP <the play turned out to be a ~>

clink·er–built \-ˌbilt\ *adj* [*clinker,* n. (clinch)] **:** having the external planks or plates overlapping like the clapboards on a house <a ~ boat>

clink·ety–clank \ˌkliŋ-kət-ē-ˈklaŋk\ *n* [imit.] **:** a repeated usu. rhythmic clanking sound <the ~ of a loose tire chain>

cli·nom·e·ter \klī-ˈnäm-ət-ər\ *n* **:** any of various instruments for measuring angles of elevation or inclination — **cli·no·met·ric** \ˌklī-nə-ˈme-trik\ *adj* — **cli·nom·e·try** \klī-ˈnäm-ə-trē\ *n*

-cli·nous \ˈklī-nəs\ *adj comb form* [prob. fr. NL *-clinus,* fr. Gk *klinē* bed — more at CLINIC] **:** having the androecium and gynoecium in a (single or different) flower or (two separate) flowers <di*clinous*>

[1]**clin·quant** \ˈkliŋ-kənt, klaⁿ-ˈkäⁿ\ *adj* [MF, fr. prp. of *clinquer* to glitter, lit., to clink, of imit. origin] **:** glittering with gold or tinsel

[2]**clinquant** *n* [F, fr. *clinquant,* adj.] **:** imitation gold leaf **:** TINSEL

clin·to·nia \klin-ˈtō-nē-ə\ *n* [NL, genus name, fr. DeWitt *Clinton*] **:** any of a genus (*Clintonia*) of herbs of the lily family with yellow or white flowers

Clio \ˈklī-(ˌ)ō, ˈklē-\ *n* [L, fr. Gk *Kleiō*] **1 :** the Greek Muse of history **2** *pl* **Cli·os :** a statuette awarded annually by a professional organization for notable achievement in radio and television commercials

[1]**clip** \ˈklip\ *vb* **clipped; clip·ping** [ME *clippen,* fr. OE *clyppan;* akin to OHG *klāftra* fathom, L *gleba* clod, *globus* globe] *vt* **1 :** ENCOMPASS **2 a :** to hold in a tight grip **:** CLUTCH **b :** to clasp or fasten with a clip **3 :** to illegally block (an opposing player) in football ~ *vi* **:** to clip an opposing player in football

[2]**clip** *n* **1 :** any of various devices that grip, clasp, or hook **2 :** a device to hold cartridges for charging the magazines of some rifles; *also* **:** a magazine from which ammunition is fed into the chamber of a firearm **3 :** a piece of jewelry held in position by a spring clip

[3]**clip** *vb* **clipped; clip·ping** [ME *clippen,* fr. ON *klippa*] *vt* **1 a :** to cut or cut off with or as if with shears <~ a dog's hair> <~ an hour off traveling time> **b :** to cut off the distal or outer part of **c** (1) **:** [3]EXCISE (2) **:** to cut items out of (as a newspaper) **2 a :** CURTAIL, DIMINISH <tried to ~ his influence> **b :** to abbreviate in speech or writing **3 :** HIT, PUNCH **4 :** to take money from unfairly or dishonestly esp. by overcharging <the nightclub *clipped* the diner for $23> ~ *vi* **1 :** to clip something **2 :** to travel or pass rapidly

[4]**clip** *n* **1 a** *pl, Scot* **:** SHEARS **b :** a 2-bladed instrument for cutting esp. the nails **2 :** something that is clipped: as **a :** the product of a single shearing (as of sheep) **b :** a crop of wool of a sheep, a flock, or a region **c :** a section of filmed material **d :** a clipping esp. from a newspaper **3 :** an act of clipping **4 :** a sharp blow **5 :** a rapid pace **6 :** a single instance or occasion **:** TIME <he charged $10 a ~> — often used in the phrase *at a clip* <trained 1000 workers at a clip>

clip·board \ˈklip-ˌbō(ə)rd, -ˌbȯ(ə)rd\ *n* **:** a small writing board with a spring clip at the top for holding papers

ə abut ᵊ kitten ər further a back ā bake ä cot, cart
au̇ out ch chin e less ē easy g gift i trip ī life
j joke ŋ sing ō flow ȯ flaw ȯi coin th thin t͟h this
ü loot u̇ foot y yet yü few yu̇ furious zh vision

clip joint *n* **1** *slang* **:** a place of public entertainment (as a nightclub) that makes a practice of defrauding patrons (as by overcharging) **2** *slang* **:** a business establishment that makes a practice of overcharging

clip–on \ˌklip-ˌȯn, -ˌän\ *adj* **:** of or relating to something that clips on <a ~ tie> <~ earrings>

clip on \(ˈ)klip-ˈȯn, -ˈän\ *vi* **:** to be capable of being fastened by an attached clip <the medal *clips on* to the coat lapel>

clip·per \ˈklip-ər\ *n* **1 :** one that clips something **2 :** an implement for clipping esp. hair, fingernails, or toenails — usu. used in pl. **3 a :** one that moves swiftly **b :** a fast sailing ship; *esp* **:** one with long slender lines, an overhanging bow, tall raking masts, and a large sail area

clip·ping \ˈklip-iŋ\ *n* **:** something that is clipped off or out of something; *esp* **:** an item clipped from a publication

clip·sheet \ˈklip-ˌshēt\ *n* **:** a sheet of newspaper material issued by an organization and usu. printed on only one side to facilitate clipping and reprinting

clique \ˈklēk, ˈklik\ *n* [F] **:** a narrow exclusive circle or group of persons; *esp* **:** one held together by a presumed identity of interests, views, or purposes ***syn*** see SET — **cliqu·ey** *or* **cliquy** \ˈklē-kē, ˈklik-\ *adj* — **cliqu·ish** \-ish\ *adj* — **cliqu·ish·ly** *adv* — **cliqu·ish·ness** *n*

cli·tel·lum \klī-ˈtel-əm\ *n, pl* **-la** \-ə\ [NL, modif. of L *clitellae* packsaddle] **:** a thickened glandular section of the body wall of some annelids that secretes a viscid sac in which the eggs are deposited

cli·to·ris \ˈklit-ə-rəs, ˈklīt-\ *n* [NL, fr. Gk *kleitoris*] **:** a small organ at the anterior or ventral part of the vulva homologous to the penis — **cli·to·ral** \ˈklit-ə-rəl, ˈklīt-\ *or* **cli·tor·ic** \kli-ˈtȯr-ik, klī-, -ˈtär-\ *adj*

clk *abbr* clerk

clo *abbr* clothing

clo·aca \klō-ˈā-kə\ *n, pl* **-acae** \-ˌkē, -ˌsē\ [L; akin to Gk *klyzein* to wash] **1 :** 3SEWER **2** [NL, fr. L] **:** the common chamber into which the intestinal, urinary, and generative canals discharge in birds, reptiles, amphibians, and many fishes; *also* **:** a comparable chamber of an invertebrate — **clo·acal** \-ˈā-kəl\ *adj*

1cloak \ˈklōk\ *n* [ME *cloke*, fr. ONF *cloque* bell, cloak, fr. ML *clocca* bell; fr. its shape] **1 :** a loose outer garment **2 :** something that conceals **:** PRETENSE, DISGUISE

2cloak *vt* **:** to cover or hide with a cloak ***syn*** see DISGUISE

cloak–and–dag·ger *adj* **:** dealing in or suggestive of melodramatic intrigue and action usu. involving secret agents and espionage

cloak·room \ˈklō-ˌkrüm, -ˌkru̇m\ *n* **1 a :** a room in which outdoor clothing may be placed during one's stay **b :** a room or cubicle where garments, parcels, and luggage may be checked for temporary safekeeping (as in a theater) **2 :** an anteroom of a legislative chamber where members may keep their wraps, rest, and confer with colleagues

clob·ber \ˈkläb-ər\ *vt* **clob·bered; clob·ber·ing** \-(ə-)riŋ\ [origin unknown] **1 :** to pound mercilessly; *also* **:** to hit with force **:** SMASH **2 :** to defeat overwhelmingly

cloche \ˈklōsh\ *n* [F, lit., bell, fr. ML *clocca*] **:** a woman's small helmetlike hat usu. with deep rounded crown and very narrow brim

1clock \ˈkläk\ *n, often attrib* [ME *clok*, fr. MD *clocke* bell, clock, fr. ONF or ML; ONF *cloque* bell, fr. ML *clocca*, of Celt origin; akin to MIr *clocc* bell] **1 :** a device other than a watch for indicating or measuring time commonly by means of hands moving on a dial **2 :** a registering device with a dial and indicator attached to a mechanism to measure or gauge its functioning or to record its output; *specif* **:** SPEEDOMETER **3 :** TIME CLOCK **4 :** a synchronizing device (as in a computer) that produces pulses at regular intervals — **around the clock 1 :** continuously for 24 hours **:** day and night without cessation **2 :** without relaxation and heedless of time — **kill the clock** *or* **run out the clock :** to use up as much as possible of the playing time remaining in a game (as football) while retaining possession of the ball or puck esp. to protect a lead

2clock *vt* **1 :** to time with a stopwatch or by an electric timing device **2 :** to register on a mechanical recording device <wind velocities were ~*ed* at 80 miles per hour> ~ *vi* **:** to register on a time sheet or time clock **:** PUNCH — used with *in, out, on, off* <he ~*ed* in late> — **clock·er** *n*

3clock *n* [prob. fr. *clock* (bell); fr. its original bell-like shape] **:** an ornamental figure on the ankle or side of a stocking or sock

clock·like \ˈkläk-ˌlīk\ *adj* **:** unusually regular, undeviating, and precise <does his job with ~ efficiency>

clock–watcher \-ˌwäch-ər\ *n* **:** a person (as a worker or student) who displays lack of zeal or interest esp. by keeping close watch on the passage of time — **clock–watch·ing** \-iŋ\ *n*

clock·wise \ˈkläk-ˌwīz\ *adv* **:** in the direction in which the hands of a clock rotate as viewed from in front — **clockwise** *adj*

clock·work \-ˌwərk\ *n* **1 :** machinery containing a train of wheels of small size (as in a mechanical toy or a bomb-actuating device) **2 :** something that seems to perform in response to clockwork or to be controlled by clockwork

clod \ˈkläd\ *n* [ME, alter. of *clot*] **1 a :** a lump or mass esp. of earth or clay **b :** SOIL, EARTH **2 :** OAF, DOLT — **clod·dish** \ˈkläd-ish\ *adj* — **clod·dish·ness** *n* — **clod·dy** \ˈkläd-ē\ *adj*

clod·hop·per \ˈkläd-ˌhäp-ər\ *n* **1 :** a clumsy and uncouth rustic **2 :** a large heavy shoe

clod·hop·ping \-ˌhäp-iŋ\ *adj* **:** BOORISH, RUDE

clod·poll *or* **clod·pole** \ˈkläd-ˌpōl\ *n* **:** BLOCKHEAD

clo·fi·brate \klō-ˈfī-ˌbrāt, -ˈfib-\ *n* [perh. fr. *ch*l*or-* + *fibr-* + *propion*ate] **:** a compound $C_{12}H_{15}ClO_3$ used esp. in the treatment of hypercholesterolemia

1clog \ˈkläg\ *n* [ME *clogge* short thick piece of wood] **1 a :** a weight attached esp. to an animal to hinder motion **b :** something that shackles or impedes **:** ENCUMBRANCE 1 **2 :** a shoe, sandal, or overshoe having a thick typically wooden sole

2clog *vb* **clogged; clog·ging** *vt* **1 :** ENCUMBER **2 a :** to impede with a clog **:** HINDER **b :** to halt or retard the progress, operation, or growth of <restraints that have been *clogging* the market —T. W. Arnold> **3 :** to fill beyond capacity **:** OVERLOAD <cars *clogged* the main street for hours> ~ *vi* **1 :** to become filled with extraneous matter <the heater *clogged* with dust> **2 :** to unite in a mass **:** CLOT **3 :** to dance a clog dance ***syn*** see HAMPER ***ant*** expedite, facilitate

clog dance *n* **:** a dance in which the performer wears clogs and beats out a clattering rhythm on the floor — **clog dancer** *n* — **clog dancing** *n*

cloi·son·né \ˌklȯiz-ᵊn-ˈā, klə-ˌwäz-\ *adj* [F, fr. pp. of *cloisonner* to partition] **:** of, relating to, or being a style of enamel decoration in which the enamel is applied and fired in raised cells (as of soldered wires) on a usu. metal background — compare CHAMPLEVÉ— **cloisonné** *n*

1clois·ter \ˈklȯi-stər\ *n* [ME *cloistre*, fr. OF, fr. ML *claustrum*, fr. L, bar, bolt, fr. *claudere* to close — more at CLOSE] **1 a :** an area within a monastery or convent to which the religious are normally restricted **b :** a monastic establishment **c :** monastic life **2 :** a covered passage on the side of a court usu. having one side walled and the other an open arcade or colonnade

2cloister *vt* **clois·tered; clois·ter·ing** \-st(ə-)riŋ\ **1 :** to seclude from the world in or as if in a cloister <a scientist who ~*s* himself in a laboratory> **2 :** to surround with a cloister <~*ed* gardens>

clois·tral \ˈklȯi-strəl\ *adj* **:** of, relating to, or suggestive of a cloister

clois·tress \ˈklȯi-strəs\ *n, obs* **:** NUN

clo·mi·phene \ˈkläm-ə-ˌfēn, ˈklōm-\ *n* [*ch*l*or-* + *amine* + *-phene* (fr. *phenyl*)] **:** an ovulation-inducing synthetic drug $C_{26}H_{28}ClNO$

1clone \ˈklōn\ *n* [Gk *klōn* twig, slip; akin to Gk *klan* to break] **:** the aggregate of the asexually produced progeny of an individual — **clon·al** \ˈklōn-ᵊl\ *adj* — **clon·al·ly** \-ᵊl-ē\ *adv*

2clone *vt* **cloned; clon·ing :** to cause to grow as a clone

clo·nus \ˈklō-nəs\ *n* [NL, fr. Gk *klonos* agitation; akin to L *celer* swift] **:** a forced series of alternating contractions and partial relaxations of a muscle occurring in some nervous diseases — **clon·ic** \ˈklän-ik\ *adj* — **clo·nic·i·ty** \klō-ˈnis-ət-ē, klä-\ *n*

1clonk \ˈkläŋk, ˈklȯŋk\ *vi* [imit.] **:** to make a dull thumping sound as if from impact of a hard object on a hard but hollow surface ~ *vt* **:** to produce a clonk

2clonk *n* **:** a clonking sound

cloot \ˈklüt\ *n* [prob. of Scand origin; akin to ON *klō* claw] **1** *Scot* **:** a cloven hoof **2** *pl, cap, Scot* **:** CLOOTIE

Cloot·ie \ˈklüt-ē\ *n* [dim. of *cloot*] *chiefly Scot* — used as a name of the devil

clop \ˈkläp\ *n* [imit.] **:** a sound made by or as if by a hoof or wooden shoe against the pavement — **clop** *vi*

clop–clop \ˈkläp-ˌkläp\ *n* **:** a sound of rhythmically repeated clops — **clop–clop** *vi*

1close \ˈklōz\ *vb* **closed; clos·ing** [ME *closen*, fr. OF *clos-*, stem of *clore*, fr. L *claudere*] *vt* **1 a :** to move so as to bar passage through something <~ the gate> **b :** to block against entry or passage <~ a street> **c :** to deny access to <because of drought the governor *closed* the woodlands> **d :** SCREEN, EXCLUDE <~ a view> **e :** to suspend or stop the operations of <~ school> **2** *archaic* **:** ENCLOSE, CONTAIN **3 a :** to bring to an end or period <~ a charge account> **b :** to conclude discussion or negotiation about <the question is *closed*>; *also* **:** to consummate by performing something previously agreed <~ a transfer of real estate title> **4 a :** to bring or bind together the parts or edges of <a *closed* fist> **b :** to fill up (as an opening) <~ a crack with patching plaster> ~ *vi* **1 a :** to contract, fold, swing, or slide so as to leave no opening <the door *closed* quietly> **b :** to cease operation <the factory *closed* down> <the stores ~ at 9 p.m.> **2 a :** to draw near <the ship was *closing* with the island> **b :** to engage in a struggle at close quarters **:** GRAPPLE <~ with the enemy> **3 :** to come together **:** MEET **4 :** to enter into or complete an agreement **5 :** to come to an end or period — **clos·able** *or* **close·able** \ˈklō-zə-bəl\ *adj* — **clos·er** *n*

syn CLOSE, END, CONCLUDE, FINISH, COMPLETE, TERMINATE *shared meaning element* **:** to bring or come to a stopping point or limit. CLOSE usually carries over from another sense the idea of action on something that is in some way open as well as unfinished <*close* an account> <*close* a debate> END conveys a stronger sense of finality and usually implies a progress or development which is felt as having been carried to a conclusion <the harvest is past, the summer is *ended*, and we are not saved —Jer 8:20 (AV)> CONCLUDE can imply a formal closing (as of a meeting) and often stresses less the fact than the form of that closing <*concluded* his speech with a plea for unity> or it can be very close to *close* or *end* <*concluded* their game and went home> FINISH implies that something proposed or begun has been done and may stress completion of a final step in a process <*finished* the dress by carefully pressing the seams> COMPLETE implies the removal of all deficiencies or a successful finishing of what has been undertaken <[his] education was ended, if not *completed* —J. T. Farrell> TERMINATE implies the setting of a limit in time or space <the path *terminates* near the lake>

— **close one's doors 1 :** to refuse admission <the nation *closed its doors* to immigrants> **2 :** to go out of business <after nearly 40 years he had to *close his doors* for lack of trade> — **close one's eyes to :** to ignore deliberately — **close ranks :** to unite in a concerted stand esp. to meet a challenge — **close the door :** to be uncompromisingly obstructive <his attitude *closed the door* to further negotiation>

2close \ˈklōz\ *n* **1 a :** a coming or bringing to a conclusion <at the ~ of the party> **b :** a conclusion or end in time or existence **:** CESSATION <the decade drew to a ~> **c :** the concluding passage (as of a speech or play) **2 :** the conclusion of a musical strain or period **:** CADENCE **3** *archaic* **:** a hostile encounter **4 :** the movement of the free foot in dancing toward or into contact with the supporting foot with or without a transfer of weight

3close \ˈklōs, *U.S. also* ˈklōz\ *n* [ME *clos*, lit., enclosure, fr. OF *clos*, fr. L *clausum*, fr. neuter of *clausus*, pp.] **1 a :** an enclosed area **b** *Brit* **:** the precinct of a cathedral **2** *chiefly Brit* **a :** a narrow passage leading from a street to a court and the houses within or to the common stairway of tenements **b :** a road closed at one end

[4]**close** \ˈklōs\ *adj* **clos·er; clos·est** [ME *clos,* fr. MF, fr. L *clausus,* pp. of *claudere* to shut, close; akin to Gk *kleiein* to close, OHG *sliozan*] **1 :** having no openings : CLOSED **2 a :** confined or confining strictly <five days of ~ arrest> **b** (1) *of a vowel* : HIGH 12 (2) : formed with the tongue in a higher position than for the other vowel of a pair **3 :** restricted to a privileged class **4 a :** SECLUDED, SECRET **b :** SECRETIVE <she could tell us something if she would . . . but she was as ~ as wax —A. Conan Doyle> **5 :** STRICT, RIGOROUS <keep ~ watch> **6 :** hot and stuffy **7 :** reluctant to part with money or possessions : cautious and often stingy in expenditure **8 :** having little space between items or units **9 a :** fitting tightly or exactly **b :** very short or near to the surface <the barber gave him a ~ shave> **c :** matching or blending without gap **10 :** being near in time, space, effect, or degree **11 :** INTIMATE, FAMILIAR **12 a :** ACCURATE, PRECISE <a ~ study> **b :** marked by fidelity to an original <a ~ copy of an old master> **c :** TERSE, COMPACT **13 :** decided by a narrow margin <a ~ baseball game> **14 :** difficult to obtain <money is ~> **15** *of punctuation* : characterized by liberal use esp. of commas — **close·ly** *adv* — **close·ness** *n*

syn **1** CLOSE, DENSE, COMPACT, THICK *shared meaning element* : having constituent parts that are massed or gathered tightly together ***ant*** open
2 see STINGY ***ant*** liberal

— **close to home :** within one's personal interests so that one is strongly affected <the audience felt that the speaker's remarks hit pretty *close to home*>

[5]**close** \ˈklōs\ *adv* : in a close position or manner : NEAR

close call \ˈklōs-\ *n* : a narrow escape

close corporation \ˈklōs-\ *n* : a corporation whose stock is held by a few persons who are often those active in the management

close–cropped \ˈklō-ˌskräpt\ *adj* **1 :** clipped short **2 :** having the hair clipped short

closed \ˈklōzd\ *adj* **1 a :** not open **b :** ENCLOSED <a ~ porch> **2 a :** forming a self-contained unit allowing no additions <~ association> **b** (1) : traced by a moving point that returns to an arbitrary starting point <~ curve>; *also* : so formed that every plane section is a closed curve <~ surface> (2) : characterized by mathematical elements that when subjected to an operation produce only elements of the same set <the set of whole numbers is ~ under addition and multiplication> (3) : containing all the limit points of every possible subset <a ~ set> **c :** characterized by continuous return and reuse of the working substance <a ~ cooling system> **d** *of a racecourse* : having the same starting and finishing point **3 a :** confined to a few <~ membership> **b :** excluding participation of outsiders or witnesses : conducted in strict secrecy **c :** rigidly excluding outside influence <~ economy> <a ~ mind> **4 :** ending in a consonant <~ syllable>

closed chain *n* : RING 10

closed circuit *n* : a television installation in which the signal is transmitted by wire to a limited number of receivers

closed couplet *n* : a rhymed couplet in which the sense is complete

closed–door \ˌklōz-ˌdō(ə)r, -ˌdȯ(ə)r\ *adj* : done or carried on in a closed session barring public and press <a ~ session of the investigating committee>

closed–end \ˌklōz-ˌdend\ *adj* : having a fixed capitalization of shares that are traded on the market at prices determined by the operation of the law of supply and demand <a ~ investment company> — compare OPEN-END

closed loop *n* : an automatic control system for an operation or process in which feedback in a closed path or group of paths acts to maintain output at a desired level

close down \(ˈ)klōz-\ *vi* : to settle or appear close around so as to block any outward view <fog presently *closed down*>

closed shop *n* : an establishment in which the employer by agreement hires only union members in good standing

closed stance *n* : a preparatory position (as in baseball batting or golf) in which the forward foot (as the left foot of a right-handed person) is closer to the line of play than the back foot — compare OPEN STANCE

close·fist·ed \ˈklōs-ˈfis-təd\ *adj* : STINGY, TIGHTFISTED

close–grained \-ˈgrānd\ *adj* : having a closely compacted smooth texture; *esp* : having narrow annual rings or small wood elements

close–hauled \-ˈhȯld\ *adj* : having the sails set for sailing as nearly against the wind as the ship will go

close in \(ˈ)klō-ˈzin\ *vi* **1 :** to gather in close all around with an oppressing or isolating effect <despair *closed in* on her> **2 :** to approach from various directions to close quarters esp. for an attack, raid, or arrest <intelligence agents *closed in* on him> **3 :** to grow dark <the short November day was already *closing in* —Ellen Glasgow> ~ *vt* **1 :** to encircle closely and isolate **2 :** to enshroud to such an extent as to preclude entrance or exit <the airport is *closed in*>

close–knit \ˈklō-ˈsnit\ *adj* : bound together by imtimate social or cultural ties or by close economic or political ties <the immigrants had left their ~ little villages —Oscar Handlin>

close–lipped \ˈklō-ˈslipt\ *adj* : TIGHT-LIPPED

close·mouthed \ˈklō-ˈsmau̇t͟hd, -ˈsmau̇tht\ *adj* : cautious in speaking : UNCOMMUNICATIVE; *also* : SECRETIVE <is ~ about her personal life>

close order *n* : an arrangement of troops for formations, drill, or marching according to an exact scheme prescribing fixed distances and intervals

close·out \ˈklō-ˌzau̇t\ *n* **1 :** a clearing out by a sale usu. at reduced prices of the whole remaining stock (as of a business) **2 :** an article offered or bought at a closeout

close out \(ˈ)klō-ˈzau̇t\ *vt* **1 a :** EXCLUDE **b :** PRECLUDE <*close out* his chances> **2 a :** to dispose of a whole stock of by sale **b :** to dispose of (a business) **c :** SELL <*closed out* his share of the business> **d :** to put (an account) in order for disposal or transfer **3 a :** TERMINATE **b :** to discontinue operation ~ *vi* **1 :** to sell out a business **2 :** to buy or sell securities or commodities in order to terminate an account (as when margin is exhausted)

close quarters \ˈklōs-\ *n pl* : immediate contact or close range <fought at *close quarters*>

close shave \ˈklōs(h)-\ *n* : a narrow escape

close·stool \ˈklōs-ˌstül\ *n* : a stool holding a chamber pot

[1]**clos·et** \ˈkläz-ət, ˈklȯz-\ *n* [ME, fr. MF, dim. of *clos* enclosure] **1 a :** an apartment or small room for privacy **b :** a monarch's or official's private chamber for counsel or devotions **2 :** a cabinet or recess for china, household utensils, or clothing : CUPBOARD **3 :** a place of retreat or privacy **4 :** WATER CLOSET — **clo·set·ful** \-ˌfu̇l\ *n*

[2]**closet** *adj* **1 :** closely private **2 :** working in or suited to the closet as the place of seclusion or study : THEORETICAL

[3]**closet** *vt* **1 :** to shut up in or as if in a closet **2 :** to take into a closet for a secret interview

closet drama *n* : drama suited primarily for reading rather than production

closet queen *n* : one who secretly engages in homosexual activities while leading an ostensibly heterosexual life

close–up \ˈklō-ˌsəp *also* -ˌzəp\ *n* **1 :** a photograph or movie shot taken at close range **2 :** an intimate view or examination of something

clos·ing \ˈklō-ziŋ\ *n* **1 :** a concluding part (as of a speech) **2 :** a closable gap (as in an article of wear)

clos·trid·i·um \klä-ˈstrid-ē-əm\ *n, pl* **-ia** \-ē-ə\ [NL, genus name, fr. Gk *klōstēr* spindle, fr. *klōthein* to spin] : any of various spore-forming mostly anaerobic soil or intestinal bacteria (esp. genus *Clostridium*) — compare BOTULISM — **clos·trid·i·al** \-ē-əl\ *adj*

[1]**clo·sure** \ˈklō-zhər\ *n* [ME, fr. MF, fr. L *clausura,* fr. *clausus,* pp. of *claudere* to close — more at CLOSE] **1** *archaic* : means of enclosing : ENCLOSURE **2 :** an act of closing : the condition of being closed <~ of the eyelids> **3 :** something that closes <pocket with zipper ~> **4** [trans. of F *clôture*] : CLOTURE **5 :** the property that a number system or a set has when it is mathematically closed under an operation **6 :** a set that contains a set and all limit points of the set

[2]**closure** *vt* **clo·sured; clo·sur·ing** \ˈklōzh-(ə-)riŋ\ : CLOTURE

[1]**clot** \ˈklät\ *n* [ME, fr. OE *clott;* akin to MHG *klōz* lump, ball — more at CLOUT] **1 :** a portion of a substance cleaving together in a thick nondescript mass (as of clay or gum) **2 a :** a roundish viscous lump formed by coagulation of a portion of liquid or by melting **b :** the coagulum produced by clotting of blood **3** *Brit* : BLOCKHEAD **4 :** CLUSTER

[2]**clot** *vb* **clot·ted; clot·ting** *vi* **1 :** to become a clot : form clots **2 :** to undergo a sequence of complex chemical and physical reactions that results in conversion of fluid blood into a coagulum : COAGULATE ~ *vt* **1 :** to cause to clot **2 :** to fill with clots

cloth \ˈklȯth\ *n, pl* **cloths** \ˈklȯt͟hz, ˈklȯths\ *often attrib* [ME, fr. OE *clāth;* akin to OE *clīthan* to adhere to, LL *glut-, glus* glue] **1 a :** a pliable material made usu. by weaving, felting, or knitting natural or synthetic fibers and filaments **b :** a similar material (as of glass) **2 :** a piece of cloth adapted for a particular purpose; *esp* : TABLECLOTH **3 a :** a distinctive dress of a profession or calling **b :** the dress of the clergy; *also* : CLERGY

clothe \ˈklōt͟h\ *vt* **clothed** *or* **clad** \ˈklad\; **cloth·ing** [ME *clothen,* fr. OE *clāthian,* fr. *clāth* cloth, garment] **1 a :** to cover with or as if with cloth or clothing : DRESS **b :** to provide with clothes **2 :** to express or enhance by suitably significant language : COUCH <treaties *clothed* in stately phraseology> **3 :** to endow esp. with power or a quality <an act *clothing* Indians with United States citizenship>

clothes \ˈklō(t͟h)z\ *n pl, often attrib* [ME, fr. OE *clāthas,* pl. of *clāth* cloth, garment] **1 :** CLOTHING **2 :** BEDCLOTHES **3 :** all the cloth articles of personal and household use that can be washed

clothes·horse \-ˌhȯ(ə)rs\ *n* **1 :** a frame on which to hang clothes **2 :** a conspicuously dressy person

[1]**clothes·line** \-ˌlīn\ *n* **1 :** a line (as of cord) on which clothes may be hung to dry **2 :** a tackle in football in which a defensive player's outstretched arm catches the ballcarrier by the head and neck unawares

[2]**clothesline** *vt* : to hit (a football player) with an outstretched arm

clothes moth *n* : any of several small yellowish moths (esp. genera *Tinea* and *Tineola* of the family Tineidae) whose larvae eat wool, fur, or feathers

clothes·pin \ˈklō(t͟h)z-ˌpin\ *n* : a forked piece of wood or plastic or a small spring clamp used for fastening clothes on a clothesline

clothes·press \-ˌpres\ *n* : a receptacle for clothes

clothes tree *n* : an upright post-shaped stand with hooks or pegs around the top on which to hang clothes

cloth·ier \ˈklōt͟h-yər, ˈklō-t͟hē-ər\ *n* [ME, alter. of *clother,* fr. *cloth*] : one who makes or sells cloth or clothing

cloth·ing \ˈklō-t͟hiŋ\ *n* : garments in general; *also* : COVERING

cloth yard *n* : a yard esp. for measuring cloth; *specif* : a unit of 37 inches equal to the Scotch ell and used also as a length for arrows

clotted cream *n* : a thick cream made chiefly in England by slowly heating whole milk on which the cream has been allowed to rise and then skimming the cooled cream from the top — called also *Cornish cream, Devonshire cream*

clo·ture \ˈklō-chər\ *n* [F *clôture,* lit., closure, alter. of MF *closure*] : the closing or limitation of debate in a legislative body esp. by calling for a vote <attempted to end the filibuster by ~> — **cloture** *vt*

[1]**cloud** \ˈklau̇d\ *n, often attrib* [ME rock, cloud, fr. OE *clūd;* akin to Gk *gloutos* buttock] **1 a :** a visible mass of particles of water or ice in the form of fog, mist, or haze suspended usu. at a considerable height in the air **b :** a light filmy, puffy, or billowy

mass seeming to float in the air **2 a** : a usu. visible mass of minute particles suspended in the air or in a gas; *also* : one of the masses of obscuring matter in interstellar space **b** : an aggregate of charged particles (as electrons) **3** : a great crowd or multitude : SWARM <~*s* of mosquitoes> **4** : something that has a dark, lowering, or threatening aspect <~*s* of another war began to loom over the horizon> **5** : something that obscures or blemishes <worked under ~*s* of secrecy> **6** : a dark or opaque vein or spot (as in marble)

2cloud *vi* **1** : to grow cloudy — usu. used with *over* or *up* <~*ed* over before the storm> **2 a** *of facial features* : to become troubled, apprehensive, or distressed in appearance **b** : to become blurry, dubious, or ominous **3** : to billow up in the form of a cloud ~ *vt* **1 a** : to envelop or hide with or as if with a cloud <smog ~*ed* our view> **b** : to make opaque esp. by condensation of moisture **c** : to make murky esp. with smoke or mist **2** : to make unclear or confused **3** : TAINT, SULLY <a ~*ed* reputation> **4** : to cast gloom over

cloud·ber·ry \ˈklau̇d-ˌber-ē\ *n* : a creeping herbaceous raspberry (*Rubus chamaemorus*) of north temperate regions; *also* : its pale amber-colored edible fruit

cloud·burst \-ˌbərst\ *n* **1** : a sudden copious rainfall **2** : DELUGE 2

cloud chamber *n* : a vessel containing saturated water vapor whose sudden expansion reveals the passage of an ionizing particle by a trail of visible droplets

cloud·land \ˈklau̇d-ˌland\ *n* **1** : the region of the clouds **2** : the realm of visionary speculation or poetic imagination

cloud·less \-ləs\ *adj* : free from clouds : CLEAR — **cloud·less·ly** *adv* — **cloud·less·ness** *n*

cloud·let \ˈklau̇d-lət\ *n* : a small cloud

cloud nine *n* [perh. fr. the ninth and highest heaven of Dante's Paradise, whose inhabitants are most blissful because nearest to God] : a feeling of extreme well-being or elation— usu. used with *on* <was on *cloud nine* after his victory>

clouds 1a: *1* cirrus, *2* cirrostratus, *3* cirrocumulus, *4* altostratus, *5* altocumulus, *6* stratocumulus, *7* nimbostratus, *8* cumulus, *9* cumulonimbus, *10* stratus

cloudy \ˈklau̇d-ē\ *adj* **cloud·i·er; -est** **1** : of, relating to, or resembling cloud **2** : darkened by gloom or anxiety **3 a** : overcast with clouds; *specif* : six tenths to nine tenths covered with clouds **b**: having a cloudy sky **4**: obscure in meaning <~ issues> **5** : dimmed or dulled as if by clouds <a ~ mirror> **6** : uneven in color or texture **7** : having visible material in suspension : MURKY — **cloud·i·ly** \ˈklau̇d-ᵊl-ē\ *adv* — **cloud·i·ness** \ˈklau̇d-ē-nəs\ *n*

1clout \ˈklau̇t\ *n* [ME, fr. OE *clūt;* akin to MHG *klōz* lump, Russ *gluda*] **1 a** *dial chiefly Brit* : a piece of cloth or leather : RAG **b** : a household cloth **c** : an article of clothing (as for infants) **2** : a blow esp. with the hand; *also* : a hit in baseball **3** : a white cloth on a stake or frame used as a target in archery **4** : PULL, INFLUENCE <had a lot of ~ with the governor>

2clout *vt* **1** : to cover or patch with a clout **2** : to hit forcefully <~*ed* the ball into the bleachers> <whose mother has just ~*ed* his head —G. B. Shaw>

1clove \ˈklōv\ *n* [ME, fr. OE *clufu;* akin to OE *clēofan* to cleave] : one of the small bulbs (as in garlic) developed in the axils of the scales of a large bulb

2clove *past of* CLEAVE

3clove \ˈklōv\ *n* [alter. of ME *clowe,* fr. OF *clou* (*de girofle*), lit., nail of clove, fr. L *clavus* nail] : the dried flower bud of a tropical tree (*Eugenia aromatica*) of the myrtle family that is used as a spice and is the source of an oil; *also* : this tree

clove hitch \ˈklōv-\ *n* [ME *cloven, clove* divided, fr. pp. of *clevien* to cleave] : a knot securing a rope temporarily to an object (as a post or spar) and consisting of a turn around the object, over the standing part, around the object again, and under the last turn — see KNOT illustration

clo·ven \ˈklō-vən\ *past part of* CLEAVE

cloven foot *n* **1** : a foot (as of a sheep) divided into two parts at its distal extremity — called also *cloven hoof* **2** [fr. the traditional representation of Satan as cloven-footed] : the sign of devilish character — **clo·ven–foot·ed** \ˌklō-vən-ˈfu̇t-əd\ *adj*

clove pink *n* : GILLYFLOWER 1

clo·ver \ˈklō-vər\ *n* [ME, fr. OE *clāfre;* akin to OHG *klēo* clover] : any of a genus (*Trifolium*) of low leguminous herbs having trifoliolate leaves and flowers in dense heads and including many that are valuable for forage and attractive to bees; *also* : any of various other leguminous plants (as of the genera *Melilotus, Lespedeza,* or *Medicago*) — **in clover** *or* **in the clover** : in prosperity or in pleasant circumstances

1clo·ver·leaf \-ˌlēf\ *adj* : resembling a clover leaf in shape

2cloverleaf *n, pl* **cloverleafs** \-ˌlēfs\ *or* **clo·ver·leaves** \-ˌlēvz\ : a road plan passing one highway over another and routing turning traffic onto connecting roadways which branch only to the right and lead around in a circle to enter the other highway from the right and thus merge traffic without left-hand turns or direct crossings

1clown \ˈklau̇n\ *n* [perh. fr. MF *coulon* settler, fr. L *colonus* colonist, farmer — more at COLONY] **1** : FARMER, COUNTRYMAN **2** : a rude ill-bred person : BOOR **3 a** : a fool, jester, or comedian in an entertainment (as a play); *specif* : a grotesquely dressed comedy performer in a circus **b** : one who habitually plays the buffoon : JOKER

2clown *vi* : to act as a clown

clown·ery \ˈklau̇-nə-rē\ *n, pl* **-er·ies** : clownish behavior or an instance of clownishness : BUFFOONERY

cloverleaf

clown·ish \ˈklau̇-nish\ *adj* : resembling or befitting a clown (as in ignorance and lack of sophistication) ***syn*** see BOORISH — **clown·ish·ly** *adv* — **clown·ish·ness** *n*

clox·a·cil·lin \ˌkläk-sə-ˈsil-ən\ *n* [*chl*or- + *oxacillin*] : a synthetic oral penicillin $C_{19}H_{17}ClN_3NaO_5S$ esp. effective against staphylococci

cloy \ˈklȯi\ *vb* [ME *acloien* to lame, fr. MF *encloer* to drive in a nail, fr. ML *inclavare,* fr. L *in* + *clavus,* nail] *vt* : to surfeit with an excess usu. of something orig. pleasing ~ *vi* : to cause surfeit ***syn*** see SATIATE — **cloy·ing·ly** \-iŋ-lē\ *adv*

cloze \ˈklōz\ *adj* [by shortening and alter. fr. *closure*] : of, relating to, or being a test of reading comprehension that involves having the person being tested supply words which have been systematically deleted from a text

clr *abbr* clear; clearance

CLU *abbr* chartered life underwriter

1club \ˈkləb\ *n* [ME *clubbe,* fr. ON *klubba;* akin to OHG *kolbo* club, OE *clamm* bond] **1 a** : a heavy usu. tapering staff esp. of wood wielded as a weapon **b** : a stick or bat used to hit a ball in any of various games **c** : something resembling a club **d** : a light spar **e** : INDIAN CLUB **2 a** : a figure that resembles a stylized clover leaf on each playing card of one of the four suits; *also* : a card marked with this figure **b** : *pl but sing or pl in constr* : the suit comprising cards marked with a club **3 a** : an association of persons for some common object usu. jointly supported and meeting periodically **b** : the meeting place of a club **c** : an association of persons participating in a plan by which they agree to make regular payments or purchases in order to secure some advantage **d** : NIGHTCLUB

2club *vb* **clubbed; club·bing** *vt* **1 a** : to beat or strike with or as if with a club **b** : to gather into a club-shaped mass <*clubbed* her hair> **c** : to hold like a club **2 a** : to unite or combine for a common cause **b** : to contribute to a common fund ~ *vi* **1** : to form a club : COMBINE **2** : to pay a share of a common expense : CONTRIBUTE

3club *adj* **1** : of or relating to a club **2** : consisting of foods in a fixed combination offered on a menu at a set price <~ breakfast>

club·ba·ble *or* **club·able** \ˈkləb-ə-bəl\ *adj* : SOCIABLE

club bag *n* : a rectangular and usu. leather traveling bag that tapers to a purselike opening at the top and that is often zippered

clubbed \ˈkləbd\ *adj* : shaped like a club <~ antennae>

club·ber \ˈkləb-ər\ *n* : a member of a club

club·by \ˈkləb-ē\ *adj* **club·bi·er; -est** : characteristic of a club or club members: as **a** : SOCIABLE **b** : open only to qualified or approved persons : SELECT — **club·bi·ness** *n*

club car *n* : LOUNGE CAR

club chair *n* : a deep low thickly upholstered easy chair often with rather low back and heavy sides and arms

club cheese *n* : a process cheese made by grinding cheddar and other cheeses usu. with added condiments and seasoning

club coupe *n* : an automobile resembling a coupe in having only two doors but with a full-width rear seat accessible by tilting the front-seat backs forward

club·foot \ˈkləb-ˈfu̇t\ *n* : a misshapen foot twisted out of position from birth; *also* : this deformity — **club·foot·ed** \-ˈfu̇t-əd\ *adj*

club fungus *n* : any of a family (Clavariaceae) of basidiomycetes with a simple or branched often club-shaped sporophore

club·house \ˈkləb-ˌhau̇s\ *n* **1** : a house occupied by a club or used for club activities **2** : locker rooms used by an athletic team

club moss *n* : any of an order (Lycopodiales) of primitive vascular plants (as ground pine) often with the sporangia borne in club-shaped strobiles

club·root \ˈkləb-ˌrüt, -ˌru̇t\ *n* : a disease of cabbages and related plants caused by a slime mold (*Plasmodiophora brassicae*) producing swellings or distortions of the root

club sandwich *n* : a sandwich of three slices of bread with two layers of various meats (as chicken or turkey) and lettuce, tomato, and mayonnaise

club soda *n* : SODA WATER 2a

club steak *n* : a small steak cut from the end of the short loin — see BEEF illustration

club moss

1cluck \ˈklək\ *vb* [imit.] *vi* **1** : to make a cluck **2** : to make a clicking sound with the tongue **3** : to express interest or concern <critics ~*ed* over the new developments> ~ *vt* **1** : to call with a cluck **2** : to express with interest or concern

2cluck *n* **1** : the characteristic sound made by a hen esp. in calling her chicks **2** : a broody fowl **3** : a stupid or naive person

clue *var of* CLEW

clum·ber spaniel \ˌkləm-bər-\ *n, often cap C & S* [*Clumber,* estate in Nottinghamshire, England] : a large massive heavyset spaniel with a dense silky largely white coat

1clump \ˈkləmp\ *n* [prob. fr. LG *klump;* akin to OE *clamm*] **1** : a group of things clustered together <a ~ of bushes> **2** : a compact mass **3 :** a heavy tramping sound — **clumpy** \'kləm-pē\ *adj*

[2]**clump** *vi* **1 :** to tread clumsily and noisily **2 :** to form clumps ~ *vt* **:** to arrange in or cause to form clumps <the serum ~*s* the bacteria>

clum·sy \'kləm-zē\ *adj* **clum·si·er; -est** [prob. fr. obs. E *clumse* (benumbed with cold)] **1 a :** lacking dexterity, nimbleness, or grace <~ fingers> **b :** lacking tact or subtlety <a ~ joke> **2 :** awkwardly or poorly made : UNWIELDY *syn* see AWKWARD *ant* adroit, facile — **clum·si·ly** \-zə-lē\ *adv* — **clum·si·ness** \-zē-nəs\ *n*

clung *past of* CLING

[1]**clunk** \'kləŋk\ *n* [imit.] **1 :** a blow or the sound of a blow : THUMP **2 :** a dull or stupid person

[2]**clunk** *vi* **1 :** to make a clunk **2 :** to hit something with a clunk ~ *vt* **:** to strike or hit with a clunk

clunk·er \'kləŋ-kər\ *n* **:** a dilapidated rattling old machine; *esp* : JALOPY

clu·pe·id \'klü-pē-əd\ *n* [deriv. of L *clupea,* a small river fish] **:** any of a large family (Clupeidae) of soft-finned teleost fishes (as herrings) having a laterally compressed body and a forked tail — **clupeid** *adj*

[1]**clus·ter** \'kləs-tər\ *n* [ME, fr. OE *clyster;* akin to OE *clott* clot] **1 :** a number of similar things growing together or of things or persons collected or grouped closely together : BUNCH **2 :** two or more consecutive consonants or vowels in a segment of speech **3 :** a group of buildings and esp. houses built close together on a sizable tract in order to preserve open spaces larger than the individual yard for common recreation *syn* see GROUP — **clus·tery** \-t(ə-)rē\ *adj*

[2]**cluster** *vb* **clus·tered; clus·ter·ing** \-t(ə-)riŋ\ *vt* **1 :** to collect into a cluster <~ the tents together> **2 :** to furnish with clusters ~ *vi* **:** to grow or assemble in a cluster <men ~*ed* around the stove>

cluster college *n* **:** a small residential college constituting a semiautonomous division of a university and usu. specializing in one area of knowledge (as history and the social sciences)

[1]**clutch** \'kləch\ *vb* [ME *clucchen,* fr. OE *clyccan;* akin to MIr *glacc* hand — more at CLING] *vt* **1 :** to grasp or hold with or as if with the hand or claws usu. strongly, tightly, or suddenly **2** *obs* : CLENCH ~ *vi* **1 :** to seek to grasp and hold **2 :** to operate an automobile clutch *syn* see TAKE

[2]**clutch** *n* **1 a :** the claws or a hand in the act of grasping or seizing firmly **b :** an often cruel or unrelenting control, power, or possession <the fell ~ of circumstance —W. E. Henley> **c :** the act of grasping, holding, or restraining **2 :** a device for gripping an object (as at the end of a chain or tackle) **3 a :** a coupling used to connect and disconnect a driving and a driven part of a mechanism **b :** a lever operating such a clutch **4 :** a tight or critical situation : PINCH <the batter came through with a hit in the ~> **5 :** CLUTCH BAG *syn* see HOLD

[3]**clutch** *adj* **1 :** made or done in a crucial situation <a ~ hit drove in the winning run> **2 :** successful in a crucial situation <a ~ pitcher>

[4]**clutch** *n* [alter. of dial. E *cletch* (hatching, brood)] **1 :** a nest of eggs or a brood of chicks **2 :** GROUP, BUNCH <a ~ of gossipy matrons>

clutch bag *n* **:** a woman's small usu. strapless handbag — called also *clutch purse*

[1]**clut·ter** \'klət-ər\ *vb* [ME *clotteren* to clot, fr. *clot*] *vt* **:** to fill or cover with scattered or disordered things that impede movement or reduce effectiveness — often used with *up* <~*ed* up his room> ~ *vi, chiefly dial* **:** to run in disorder

[2]**clutter** *n* **1 a :** a crowded or confused mass or collection <a ~ of shops and tenements> **b :** LITTER, DISORDER <the ~ in her room> **2 :** interfering echoes visible on a radar screen caused by reflection from objects other than the target **3** *chiefly dial* : DISTURBANCE, HUBBUB

Clydes·dale \'klīdz-,dāl\ *n* **:** a heavy feathered-legged draft horse of a breed orig. from Clydesdale, Scotland

Clydesdale terrier *n* **:** a small terrier of a breed distinguished by erect ears, long silky coat, and short legs

clyp·e·ate \'klip-ē-āt\ *or* **clyp·e·at·ed** \-ē-,āt-əd\ *adj* [L & NL *clypeus* + E *-ate*] **1 :** shaped like a shield or buckler **2 :** having a clypeus

clyp·e·us \'klip-ē-əs\ *n, pl* **clyp·ei** \-ē-,ī, -ē-,ē\ [NL, fr. L, round shield] **:** a plate on the anterior median aspect of an insect's head

clys·ter \'klis-tər\ *n* [ME, fr. MF or L; MF *clistere,* fr. L *clyster,* fr. Gk *klystēr,* fr. *klyzein* to wash out] **:** ENEMA

Cly·tem·nes·tra \,klīt-əm-'nes-trə\ *n* [L, fr. Gk *Klytaimnēstra*] **:** the wife and murderess of Agamemnon

cm *abbr* **1** centimeter **2** cumulative

Cm *symbol* curium

CM *abbr* **1** center matched **2** circular mil **3** common meter **4** Congregation of the Mission

cmd *abbr* command

cmdg *abbr* commanding

cmdr *abbr* commander

CMG *abbr* Companion of the Order of St. Michael and St. George

c–mitosis \,sē-\ *n* [colchicine + *mitosis*] **:** an artificially induced abortive nuclear division in which the chromosome number is doubled — **c–mitotic** *adj*

cml *abbr* commercial

CMSgt *abbr* chief master sergeant

CN *abbr* credit note

cni·do·blast \'nīd-ə-,blast\ *n* [NL *cnida* nematocyst, fr. Gk *knidē* nettle] **:** a cell that develops a nematocyst or develops into a nematocyst

CNO *abbr* chief of naval operations

CNS *abbr* central nervous system

co *abbr* **1** company **2** county

Co *symbol* cobalt

CO *abbr* **1** cash order **2** Colorado **3** commanding officer **4** conscientious objector

co- *prefix* [ME, fr. L, fr. *com-;* akin to OE *ge-,* perfective and collective prefix, Gk *koinos* common] **1 :** with : together : joint : jointly <*co*exist> <*co*heir> **2 :** in or to the same degree <*co*extensive> **3 a :** one that is associated in an action with another : fellow : partner <*co*author> <*co*-worker> **b :** having a usu. lesser share in duty or responsibility : alternate : deputy <*co*pilot> **4 :** of, relating to, or constituting the complement of an angle <*co*sine> <*co*declination>

c/o *abbr* care of

co·ac·er·vate \kō-'as-ər-,vāt\ *n* [L *coacervatus,* pp. of *coacervare* to heap up, fr. *co-* + *acervus* heap] **:** an aggregate of colloidal droplets held together by electrostatic attractive forces — **co·acer·vate** \,kō-ə-'sər-vət\ *adj* — **co·ac·er·va·tion** \(,)kō-,as-ər-'vā-shən\ *n*

coach 1a

[1]**coach** \'kōch\ *n, often attrib* [ME *coche,* fr. MF, fr. G *kutsche*] **1 a :** a large usu. closed four-wheeled carriage having doors in the sides and an elevated seat in front for the driver **b :** a railroad passenger car intended primarily for day travel **c** : BUS 1a **d :** a house trailer **e :** an automobile body esp. of a closed model **f :** a class of passenger air transportation at a lower fare than first class **2** [fr. the concept that the tutor conveys the student through his examinations] **a :** a private tutor **b :** one who instructs or trains a performer or a team of performers; *specif* **:** one who instructs players in the fundamentals of a competitive sport and directs team strategy <football ~>

[2]**coach** *vt* **1 :** to train intensively by instruction, demonstration, and practice **2 :** to act as coach to **3 :** to direct the movements of (a player) ~ *vi* **1 :** to go in a coach **2 :** to instruct, direct, or prompt as a coach — **coach·er** *n*

coach dog *n* **:** DALMATIAN

coach·man \'kōch-mən\ *n* **1 :** a man whose business is to drive a coach or carriage **2 :** an artifical fishing fly with white wings, peacock feather body, brown hackle, and gold tag

co·act \kō-'akt\ *vi* **:** to act or work together — **co·ac·tive** \-'ak-tiv\ *adj*

co·ac·tion \-'ak-shən\ *n* **1 :** joint action **2 :** the interaction between individuals or kinds (as species) in an ecological community

co·adapt·ed \,kō-ə-'dap-təd\ *adj* **:** mutually adapted esp. by natural selection <~ gene complexes>

co·ad·ju·tor \,kō-ə-'jüt-ər, kō-'aj-ət-ər\ *n* [ME *coadjutour,* fr. MF *coadjuteur,* fr. L *coadjutor,* fr. *co-* + *adjutor* aid, fr. *adjutus,* pp. of *adjuvare* to help — more at AID] **1 :** one who works together with another : ASSISTANT **2 :** a bishop assisting a diocesan bishop and often having the right of succession — **coadjutor** *adj*

co·ad·ju·trix \,kō-ə-'jü-triks, kō-'aj-ə-(,)triks\ *n, pl* **co·ad·ju·tri·ces** \,kō-ə-'jü-trə-,sēz, (,)kō-,aj-ə-'trī-(,)sēz\ [NL, fem. of *coadjutor*] **:** a female coadjutor

co·ad·u·nate \kō-'aj-ə-nət, -,nāt\ *adj* [LL *coadunatus,* pp. of *coadunare* to combine, fr. L *co-* + *adunare* to unite, fr. *ad-* + *unus* one — more at ONE] **:** UNITED; *esp* **:** grown together — **co·ad·u·na·tion** \(,)kō-,aj-ə-'nā-shən\ *n*

co·ag·u·lant \kō-'ag-yə-lənt\ *n* **:** something that produces coagulation

co·ag·u·lase \kō-'ag-yə-,lās, -,lāz\ *n* **:** an enzyme that causes coagulation

[1]**co·ag·u·late** \-lət, -,lāt\ *adj, archaic* **:** being clotted or congealed

[2]**co·ag·u·late** \kō-'ag-yə-,lāt\ *vb* **-lat·ed; -lat·ing** [L *coagulatus,* pp. of *coagulare* to curdle, fr. *coagulum* curdling agent, fr. *cogere* to drive together — more at COGENT] *vt* **1 :** to cause to become viscous or thickened into a coherent mass : CURDLE, CLOT **2 :** to gather together or form into a mass or group ~ *vi* **:** to become coagulated — **co·ag·u·la·bil·i·ty** \kō-,ag-yə-lə-'bil-ət-ē\ *n* — **co·ag·u·la·ble** \-'ag-yə-lə-bəl\ *adj* — **co·ag·u·la·tion** \-,ag-yə-'lā-shən\ *n*

co·ag·u·lum \kō-'ag-yə-ləm\ *n, pl* **-u·la** \-lə\ *or* **-ulums** [L, coagulant] **:** a coagulated mass or substance : CLOT

[1]**coal** \'kōl\ *n, often attrib* [ME *col,* fr. OE; akin to OHG & ON *kol* burning ember, IrGael *gual* coal] **1 :** a piece of glowing carbon or charred wood : EMBER **2 :** CHARCOAL 1 **3 a :** a black or brownish black solid combustible substance formed by the partial decomposition of vegetable matter without free access of air and under the influence of moisture and often increased pressure and temperature that is widely used as a natural fuel **b** *pl, Brit* **:** pieces or a quantity of the fuel broken up for burning

[2]**coal** *vt* **1 :** to burn to charcoal : CHAR **2 :** to supply with coal ~ *vi* **:** to take in coal

coal·er \'kō-lər\ *n* **:** something (as a ship) employed in transporting or supplying coal

co·alesce \,kō-ə-'les\ *vi* **co·alesced; co·alesc·ing** [L *coalescere,* fr. *co-* + *alescere* to grow — more at OLD] **1 :** to grow together **2 a :** to unite into a whole : FUSE <allowing the new community to ~ . . . into a major city —J. A. Michener> **b :** to unite for a common end : join forces <people with different points of view ~ into opposing factions — I. L. Horowitz> *syn* see MIX — **co·ales·cence** \-'les-ᵊn(t)s\ *n* — **co·ales·cent** \-ᵊnt\ *adj*

coal·field \'kōl-,fēld\ *n* **:** a region in which deposits of coal occur

coal·fish \-,fish\ *n* **:** any of several blackish or dark-backed fishes (as a pollack or sablefish)

coal gas *n* **:** gas made from coal: as **a :** the mixture of gases thrown off by burning coal **b :** gas made by carbonizing bituminous coal in retorts and used for heating and lighting
coal·hole \ˈkōl-ˌhōl\ *n* **1 :** a hole for coal (as a trap or opening in a sidewalk leading to a coal bin) **2** *Brit* **:** a compartment for storing coal
coal·ifi·ca·tion \ˌkō-lə-fə-ˈkā-shən\ *n* **:** a process in which vegetable matter becomes converted into coal of increasingly higher rank with anthracite as the final product — **coal·ify** \ˈkō-lə-ˌfī\ *vt*
coaling station *n* **:** a port at which ships may coal
co·ali·tion \ˌkō-ə-ˈlish-ən\ *n* [MF, fr. L *coalitus,* pp. of *coalescere*] **1 a :** the act of coalescing **:** UNION **b :** a body formed by the coalescing of orig. distinct elements **:** COMBINATION **2 :** a temporary alliance of distinct parties, persons, or states for joint action — **co·ali·tion·ist** \-ˈlish-(ə-)nəst\ *n*
coal measures *n pl* **:** beds of coal with the associated rocks
coal oil *n* **1 :** petroleum or a refined oil prepared from it **2 :** KEROSINE
Coal·sack \ˈkōl-ˌsak\ *n* **:** either of two dark nebulae in the Milky Way located one near the Northern Cross and the other near the Southern Cross
coal seam *n* **:** a bed of coal usu. thick enough to be mined with profit
coal tar *n* **:** tar obtained by distillation of bituminous coal and used esp. in making dyes and drugs
coam·ing \ˈkō-miŋ\ *n* [prob. irreg. fr. *comb*] **:** a raised frame (as around a hatchway in the deck of a ship) to keep out water
co·apt \kō-ˈapt\ *vt* [LL *coaptare,* fr. L *co-* + *aptus* fastened, fit — more at APT] **:** to fit together and make fast — **co·ap·ta·tion** \(ˌ)kō-ˌap-ˈtā-shən\ *n*
co·arc·tate \kō-ˈärk-ˌtāt\ *adj* [L *coarctatus,* pp. of *coartare* to press together, fr. *co-* + *artus* narrow, confined; akin to L *artus* joint — more at ARTICLE] **:** CONSTRICTED; *specif* **:** enclosed in a rigid case <~ insect pupae> — **co·arc·ta·tion** \(ˌ)kō-ˌärk-ˈtā-shən\ *n*
coarse \ˈkō(ə)rs, ˈkȯ(ə)rs\ *adj* **coars·er; coars·est** [ME *cors,* fr. *course,* n.] **1 :** of ordinary or inferior quality or value **:** COMMON **2 a** (1) **:** composed of relatively large parts or particles <~ sand> (2) **:** loose or rough in texture <~ cloth> **b :** adjusted or designed for heavy, fast, or less delicate work <a ~ saw with large teeth> **c :** not precise or detailed with respect to adjustment or discrimination **3 :** crude or unrefined in taste, manners, or language **4 :** harsh, raucous, or rough in tone — **coarse·ly** *adv* — **coarse·ness** *n*
syn COARSE, VULGAR, GROSS, OBSCENE, RIBALD *shared meaning element* **:** offensive to good taste or moral principles ***ant*** fine, refined
coarse–grained \ˈkō(ə)rs-ˈgrānd, ˈkȯ(ə)rs-\ *adj* **1 :** having a coarse grain **2 :** CRUDE
coars·en \ˈkōrs-ᵊn, ˈkȯrs-\ *vb* **coars·ened; coars·en·ing** \ˈkōrs-niŋ, ˈkȯrs-, -ᵊn-iŋ\ *vt* **:** to make coarse ~ *vi* **:** to become coarse
1coast \ˈkōst\ *n* [ME *cost,* fr. MF *coste,* fr. L *costa* rib, side; akin to OSlav *kostĭ* bone] **1** *obs* **:** BORDER, FRONTIER **2 :** the land near a shore **:** SEASHORE **3 a :** a hill or slope suited to coasting **b :** a slide down a slope (as on a sled) **4** *often cap* **:** the Pacific coast of the U.S. — **coast·al** \ˈkōs-tᵊl\ *adj* — **coast·wise** \ˈkōs-ˌtwīz\ *adv or adj*
2coast *vt* **1** *obs* **:** to move along or past the side of **:** SKIRT **2 :** to sail along the shore of ~ *vi* **1 a** *archaic* **:** to travel on land along a coast or along or past the side of something **b :** to sail along the shore **2 a :** to slide, run, or glide downhill by the force of gravity **b :** to move along without or as if without further application of propulsive power (as by momentum or gravity) **c :** to proceed easily without special application of effort or concern
coast artillery *n* **:** artillery for defending a coast
coast·er \ˈkō-stər\ *n* **1 :** one that coasts: as **a :** a person engaged in coastal traffic or commerce **b :** a ship sailing along a coast or engaged in trade between ports of the same country **2 :** a resident of a seacoast **3 a :** a tray or decanter stand usu. of silver and sometimes on wheels that is used for circulating a decanter after a meal **b :** a shallow container or a plate or mat to protect a surface **4 a :** a small vehicle (as a sled or wagon) used in coasting **b :** ROLLER COASTER
coaster brake *n* **:** a brake in the hub of the rear wheel of a bicycle operated by reverse pressure on the pedals
coaster wagon *n* **:** a child's toy wagon often used for coasting
coast guard *n* **1 :** a military or naval force employed in guarding a coast or responsible for the safety, order, and operation of maritime traffic in neighboring waters **2** *usu* **coast·guard** *chiefly Brit* **:** COASTGUARDSMAN
coast·guards·man \ˈkōs(t)-ˌgärdz-mən\ *or* **coast·guard·man** \-ˌgärd-mən\ *n* **:** a member of a coast guard
coast·land \-ˌland\ *n* **:** land bordering the sea
coast·line \ˈkōst-ˌlīn\ *n* **1 :** a line that forms the boundary between the land and the ocean or a lake **2 :** the outline or shape of a coast
coast·ward \ˈkōs-twərd\ *or* **coast·wards** \-twərdz\ *adv* **:** toward the coast — **coastward** *adj*
1coat \ˈkōt\ *n, often attrib* [ME *cote,* fr. OF, of Gmc origin; akin to OHG *kozza* coarse mantle] **1 a :** an outer garment varying in length and style according to fashion and use **b :** something resembling a coat **2 :** the external growth on an animal **3 :** a layer of one substance covering another — **coat·ed** \-əd\ *adj*
2coat *vt* **1 :** to cover with a coat **2 :** to cover or spread with a finishing, protecting, or enclosing layer — **coat·er** *n*
coat·dress \ˈkōt-ˌdres\ *n* **:** a dress styled like a coat usu. with a front buttoning from neckline to hemline
coat hanger *n* **:** a slender arched device (as of wood, metal, or plastic) which is shaped typically somewhat like a person's shoulders and over which garments may be hung
co·ati \kə-ˈwät-ē, kwä-ˈtē\ *n* [Pg *coatí,* fr. Tupi] **:** a tropical American mammal (genus *Nasua*) related to the raccoon but with a longer body and tail and a long flexible snout
co·ati·mun·di \kə-ˌwät-i-ˈmən-dē, ˌkwät-, -ˈmün-\ *n* [Tupi] **:** COATI
coat·ing \ˈkōt-iŋ\ *n* **1 :** COAT, COVERING **2 :** cloth for coats
coat of arms [trans. of F *cotte d'armes*] **1 :** a tabard or surcoat embroidered with armorial bearings **2 a :** the particular heraldic bearings (as of a person) usu. depicted on an escutcheon often with accompanying adjuncts (as a crest, motto, and supporters) **b :** a similar symbolic emblem

coati

coat of mail : a garment of metal scales or chain mail worn as armor
coat·rack \ˈkōt-ˌrak\ *n* **:** a stand or rack fitted with pegs, hooks, or hangers and used for the temporary storage of garments
coat·room \-ˌrüm, -ˌru̇m\ *n* **:** CLOAKROOM
coat·tail \ˈkōt-ˌtāl\ *n* **1 :** the rear flap of a man's coat **2** *pl* **:** the skirts of a dress coat, cutaway, or frock coat — **on one's coattails :** with the help of another; *esp* **:** with the benefit of another's political prestige <congressmen riding into office *on the coattails* of the president>
coat tree *n* **:** CLOTHES TREE
1co·au·thor \(ˈ)kō-ˈȯ-thər\ *n* **:** a joint or associate author
2coauthor *vt* **:** to be coauthor of <the two ~*ed* a novel>
coax \ˈkōks\ *vt* [earlier *cokes,* fr. *cokes,* n. (simpleton)] **1** *obs* **:** FONDLE, PET **2 :** to influence or gently urge by caressing or flattering **:** WHEEDLE **3 :** to draw, gain, or persuade by means of gentle urging or flattery <~*ed* an answer out of her> **4 :** to manipulate with great perseverance and usu. with considerable effort toward a desired state or activity <~ a fire to burn>
co·ax·i·al \(ˈ)kō-ˈak-sē-əl\ *adj* **1 :** having coincident axes **2 :** mounted on concentric shafts — **co·ax·i·al·ly** \-sē-ə-lē\ *adv*
coaxial cable *n* **:** a transmission line that consists of a tube of electrically conducting material surrounding a central conductor held in place by insulators and that is used to transmit telegraph, telephone, and television signals of high frequency — called also *coaxial line*
1cob \ˈkäb\ *n* [ME *cobbe* leader; akin to OE *cot* cottage — more at COT] **1 :** a male swan **2** *dial Eng* **:** a rounded mass, lump, or heap **3 :** CORNCOB 1 **4 :** a short-legged stocky horse usu. with an artificially high stylish action — **cob·by** \ˈkäb-ē\ *adj*
2cob *n* [Sp *caba de barra,* lit., end of the bar] **:** a crudely struck old Spanish coin of irregular shape
3cob *n* [prob. fr. 1*cob*] **:** a mixture that consists of unburned clay usu. with straw as a binder and that is used for constructing walls of small buildings
co·bal·a·min \kō-ˈbal-ə-mən\ *also* **co·bal·a·mine** \-ˌmēn\ *n* [*cobalt* + vit*amin*] **:** a member of the vitamin B_{12} group; *broadly* **:** the vitamin B_{12} group
co·balt \ˈkō-ˌbȯlt\ *n* [G *kobalt,* alter. of *kobold,* lit., goblin, fr. MHG *kobolt;* fr. its occurrence in silver ore, believed to be due to goblins] **:** a tough lustrous silver-white magnetic metallic element that is related to and occurs with iron and nickel and is used esp. in alloys — see ELEMENT table
cobalt blue *n* **:** a greenish blue pigment consisting essentially of cobalt oxide and alumina
co·bal·tic \kō-ˈbȯl-tik\ *adj* **:** of, relating to, or containing cobalt esp. with a valence of three
co·balt·ite \ˈkō-ˌbȯl-ˌtīt, kō-ˈ-\ *or* **co·balt·ine** \-ˌtēn\ *n* [*cobaltite,* alter. of *cobaltine,* fr. F, fr. *cobalt*] **:** a mineral consisting of a grayish to silver-white cobalt sulfarsenide CoAsS used in making smalt
co·bal·tous \kō-ˈbȯl-təs\ *adj* **:** of, relating to, or containing cobalt esp. with a valence of two
cobalt 60 *n* **:** a heavy radioactive isotope of cobalt of the mass number 60 produced in nuclear reactors and used as a source of gamma rays (as for radiotherapy)
cob·ber \ˈkäb-ər\ *n* [origin unknown] *Austral* **:** BUDDY
1cob·ble \ˈkäb-əl\ *vt* **cob·bled; cob·bling** \-(ə-)liŋ\ [ME *coblen,* perh. back-formation fr. *cobelere* cobbler] **1** *chiefly Brit* **:** to mend or patch coarsely **2 :** REPAIR, MAKE <*cobbled* shoes> **3 :** to make or put together roughly or hastily
2cobble *n* [back-formation fr. *cobblestone*] **1 :** a naturally rounded stone larger than a pebble and smaller than a boulder; *esp* **:** such a stone used in paving a street or in construction **2** *pl, chiefly Brit* **:** lump coal about the size of small cobblestones
3cobble *vt* **cob·bled; cob·bling** \-(ə-)liŋ\ **:** to pave with cobblestones
cob·bler \ˈkäb-lər\ *n* [ME *cobelere*] **1 :** a mender or maker of shoes and often of other leather goods **2** *archaic* **:** a clumsy workman **3 :** a tall iced drink consisting usu. of wine, rum, or whiskey and sugar garnished with mint or a slice of lemon or orange **4 :** a deep-dish fruit pie with a thick top crust
cob·ble·stone \ˈkäb-əl-ˌstōn\ *n* [ME, fr. *cobble-* (prob. fr. *cob*) + *stone*] **:** 2COBBLE 1 — **cob·ble·stoned** \-ˌstōnd\ *adj*
co·bel·lig·er·ent \ˌkō-bə-ˈlij-(ə-)rənt\ *n* **:** a country fighting with another power against a common enemy — **cobelligerent** *adj*
co·bia \ˈkō-bē-ə\ *n* [origin unknown] **:** a large percoid fish (*Rachycentron canadum*) of warm seas that is a popular food and sport fish
co·ble \ˈkō-bəl\ *n* [ME] **1** *Scot* **:** a short flat-bottomed rowboat **2 :** a flat-floored fishing boat with a rudder extending below the keel and a lugsail on a raking mast
cob·nut \ˈkäb-ˌnət\ *n* **:** the fruit of a European hazel (*Corylus avellana grandis*); *also* **:** the plant bearing this fruit
CO·BOL *or* **Co·bol** \ˈkō-ˌbȯl\ *n* [*common business oriented language*] **:** a standardized business language for programming a computer
co·bra \ˈkō-brə\ *n* [Pg *cobra (de capello),* lit., hooded snake, fr. L *colubra* snake] **:** any of several venomous Asiatic and African elapid snakes (genus *Naja*) that when excited expand the skin of the

neck into a hood by movement of the anterior ribs; *also* : any of several related African snakes

cob·web \'käb-ˌweb\ *n* [ME *coppeweb,* fr. *coppe* spider (fr. OE *ātorcoppe*) + *web;* akin to MD *coppe* spider] **1** : the network spread by a spider **2** : a single thread spun by a spider or insect larva **3** : something resembling a spider web <filled with the ~*s* of bigotry, suspicion and restraint —Robert Smylie> — **cob·webbed** \-ˌwebd\ *adj* — **cob·web·by** \-ˌweb-ē\ *adj*

co·ca \'kō-kə\ *n* [Sp, fr. Quechua *kúka*] **1** : any of several So. American shrubs (genus *Erythroxylon,* family Erythroxylaceae); *esp* : one (*E. coca*) with leaves resembling tea **2** : dried leaves of a coca (as *E. coca*) containing alkaloids including cocaine

co·caine \kō-'kān, 'kō-ˌ\ *n* : a bitter crystalline alkaloid $C_{17}H_{21}NO_4$ that is obtained from coca leaves, is used as a local anesthetic, can result in psychological dependence, and in large doses produces intoxication like that from hemp

co·cain·ism \kō-'kā-ˌniz-əm\ *n* : habituation to cocaine

co·cain·ize \kō-'kā-ˌnīz\ *vt* **-ized; -iz·ing** : to treat or anesthetize with cocaine

co·car·box·yl·ase \ˌkō-kär-'bäk-sə-ˌlās, -ˌlāz\ *n* [*co-* + *carboxylase*] : a coenzyme $C_{12}H_{19}ClN_4O_7P_2S{\cdot}H_2O$ that is a pyrophosphate of thiamine and is important in metabolic reactions (as decarboxylation in the Krebs cycle)

coc·cid \'käk-səd\ *n* [NL *Coccus,* genus of scales, fr. Gk *kokkos* grain, kermes berry] : SCALE INSECT, MEALYBUG

coc·cid·i·oi·do·my·co·sis \(ˌ)käk-ˌsid-ē-ˌȯid-ō-(ˌ)mī-'kō-səs\ *n* [NL, fr. *Coccidioides,* genus of fungi, (fr. *coccidium*) + *mycosis*] : a disease of man and lower animals caused by a fungus (*Coccidioides immitis*) and marked esp. by fever and localized pulmonary symptoms

coc·cid·i·o·sis \(ˌ)käk-ˌsid-ē-'ō-səs\ *n, pl* **-oses** \-ˌsēz\ : infestation with or disease caused by coccidia

coc·cid·i·um \käk-'sid-ē-əm\ *n, pl* **-ia** \-ē-ə\ [NL, dim. of *coccus*] : any of an order (Coccidia) of protozoans usu. parasitic in the digestive epithelium of vertebrates

coc·coid \'käk-ˌȯid\ *adj* : related to or resembling a coccus : GLOBOSE — **coccoid** *n*

coc·cus \'käk-əs\ *n, pl* **coc·ci** \'käk-ˌ(s)ī, 'käk-(ˌ)(s)ē\ [NL, fr. Gk *kokkos*] **1** : one of the separable carpels of a schizocarp **2** : a spherical bacterium — **coc·cal** \'käk-əl\ *adj*

-coccus *n comb form, pl* **-cocci** [NL, fr. Gk *kokkos*] : berry-shaped organism <Micro*coccus*>

coc·cy·geal \käk-'sij-(ē-)əl\ *adj* [ML *coccygeus* of the coccyx, fr. Gk *kokkyk-, kokkyx*] : of or relating to the coccyx

coc·cyx \'käk-siks\ *n, pl* **coc·cy·ges** \'käk-sə-ˌjēz\ *also* **coc·cyx·es** \'käk-sik-səz\ [NL, fr. Gk *kokkyx* cuckoo, coccyx; fr. its resemblance to a cuckoo's beak] : the end of the vertebral column beyond the sacrum in man and tailless apes

co·chair \(')kō-'che(ə)r, -'cha(ə)r\ *vt* : to serve as cochairman of

co·chair·man \(')kō-'che(ə)r-mən, -'cha(ə)r-\ *n* : a joint chairman, vice-chairman, or assistant chairman

Co·chin Chi·na \ˌkō-chən-'chī-nə\ *n* [*Cochin China,* So. Vietnam] : any of an Asian breed of large domestic fowl with thick plumage, small wings and tail, and densely feathered legs and feet

co·chi·neal \'käch-ə-ˌnēl, 'kō-chə-\ *n* [MF & Sp; MF *cochenille,* fr. OSp *cochinilla* wood louse, cochineal] : a red dyestuff consisting of the dried bodies of female cochineal insects used esp. as a biological stain and as an indicator

cochineal insect *n* : a small bright red insect (*Dactylopius coccus*) that is related to and resembles the mealybug and feeds on cactus

co·chlea \'kō-klē-ə, 'käk-lē-\ *n pl* **co·chle·as** *or* **co·chle·ae** \-(k)lē-ˌē, -ˌī\ [NL, fr. L, snail, snail shell, fr. Gk *kochlias,* fr. *kochlos* land snail; akin to Gk *konchē* mussel] : a division of the labyrinth of the ear of higher vertebrates that is usu. coiled like a snail shell and is the seat of the hearing organ — see EAR illustration — **coch·le·ar** \-lē-ər\ *adj*

co·chle·ate \'kō-klē-ət, -ˌāt, 'käk-lē-\ *or* **co·chle·at·ed** \-ˌāt-əd\ *adj* : having the form of a snail shell

co·chro·ma·tog·ra·phy \ˌkō-ˌkrō-mə-'täg-rə-fē\ *n* : chromatography of two or more samples together; *esp* : identification of an unknown substance by chromatographic comparison with a known substance

[1]cock \'käk\ *n* [ME *cok,* fr. OE *cocc,* of imit. origin] **1 a** : the adult male of the domestic fowl (*Gallus gallus*) **b** : the male of birds other than the domestic fowl **c** : WOODCOCK **d** *archaic* : the crowing of a cock; *also* : COCKCROW **e** : WEATHERCOCK **2** : a device (as a faucet or valve) for regulating the flow of a liquid **3 a** : a chief person : LEADER **b** : a person of spirit and often of a certain swagger or arrogance **4 a** : the hammer in the lock of a firearm **b** : the cocked position of the hammer **5** : PENIS — usu. considered vulgar — **cock of the walk** : one that dominates a group or situation esp. overbearingly

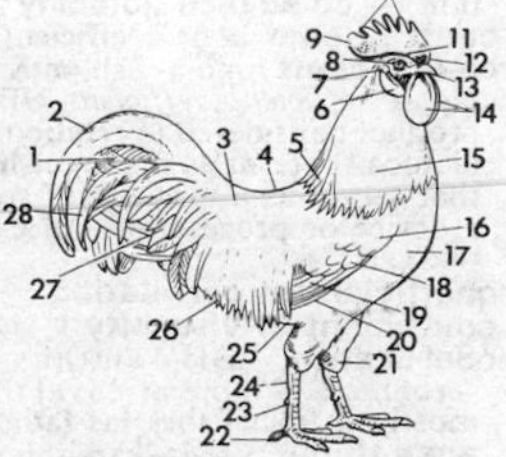

cock 1a: *1* main tail, *2* sickle feathers, *3* saddle, *4* back, *5* cape, *6* ear lobe, *7* ear, *8* eye, *9* blade, *10* points, *11* base, *12* comb, *13* beak, *14* wattles, *15* hackle, *16* wing bow, *17* breast, *18* wing bar, *19* secondaries, *20* primaries, *21* hock, *22* claw, *23* spur, *24* shank, *25* fluff, *26* saddle feathers, *27* tail coverts, *28* lesser sickle feathers

[2]cock *vi* **1** : STRUT, SWAGGER **2** : to turn, tip, or stick up **3** : to position the hammer of a firearm for firing ~ *vt* **1 a** : to draw the hammer of (a firearm) back and set for firing; *also* : to set (the trigger) for firing **b** : to draw or bend back in preparation for throwing or hitting **c** : to set a mechanism (as a camera shutter) for tripping **2 a** : to set erect **b** : to turn, tip, or tilt usu. to one side **c** : to lift and place high <sat down and ~*ed* his feet up on the desk> **3** : to turn up (as a hat brim) — **cock a snook** *or* **cock snooks** \-'snu̇k(s), -'snüks\ : to thumb the nose

[3]cock *n* : TILT, SLANT <~ of the head>

[4]cock *n* [ME *cok,* of Scand origin] : a small pile (as of hay)

[5]cock *vt* : to put (as hay) into cocks

cock·ade \kä-'kād\ *n* [modif. of F *cocarde,* fr. fem. of *cocard* vain, fr. *coq* cock, fr. OF *coc,* of imit. origin] : a rosette or a similar ornament worn on the hat as a badge — **cock·ad·ed** \-'kād-əd\ *adj*

cock–a–hoop \ˌkäk-ə-'hüp, -'hu̇p\ *adj* [fr. the phrase *to set cock a hoop* to be festive] **1** : triumphantly boastful : EXULTING **2** : AWRY

Cock·aigne \kä-'kān\ *n* [ME *cokaygne,* fr. MF (*pais de*) *cocaigne* land of plenty] : an imaginary land of great luxury and ease

cock–a–leek·ie \ˌkäk-i-'lē-kē\ *n* [alter. of *cockie* (dim. of [1]*cock*) + *leekie,* dim. of *leek*] : a soup made of chicken boiled with leeks

cock·a·lo·rum \ˌkäk-ə-'lōr-əm, -'lȯr-\ *n, pl* **-rums** [prob. modif. of obs. Flem *kockeloeren* to crow, of imit. origin] **1** : a self-important little man **2** : the game of leapfrog **3** : boastful talk

cock·a·ma·my *or* **cock·a·ma·mie** \ˌkäk-ə-'mā-mē\ *adj* [E dial. *cockamamy* decal, alter. of E *decalcomania*] : RIDICULOUS, INCREDIBLE <of all the ~ excuses I ever heard —Leo Rosten>

cock–and–bull story \ˌkäk-ən-'bu̇l-\ *n* : an incredible story told as true

cock·a·tiel \ˌkäk-ə-'tē(ə)l\ *n* [D *kaketielje,* deriv. of Malay *kakatua*] : a small crested gray Australian parrot (*Nymphicus hollandicus*) with a yellow head

cock·a·too \'käk-ə-ˌtü\ *n, pl* **-toos** [D *kaketoe,* fr. Malay *kakatua,* fr. *kakak* elder sibling + *tua* old] : any of numerous large noisy usu. showy and crested chiefly Australasian parrots (esp. genus *Kakatoe*)

cock·a·trice \'käk-ə-trəs, -ˌtrīs\ *n* [ME *cocatrice,* fr. MF *cocatris* ichneumon, cockatrice, fr. ML *cocatric-, cocatrix* ichneumon] : a legendary serpent that is hatched by a reptile from a cock's egg and that has a deadly glance

cock·boat \'käk-ˌbōt\ *n* : a small boat; *esp* : one used as a tender to a larger boat

cock·cha·fer \'käk-ˌchā-fər\ *n* [[1]*cock* + *chafer*] : a large European beetle (*Melolontha melolontha*) destructive to vegetation as an adult and to roots as a larva; *also* : any of various related beetles

cock·crow \'käk-ˌkrō\ *n* **1** : DAWN **2** : an utterance suggesting the triumphant crowing of a cock

cocked hat \'käkt-\ *n* **1** : a hat with brim turned up to give a three-cornered appearance **2** : a hat with brim turned up on two sides and worn either front to back or sideways

[1]cock·er \'käk-ər\ *vt* [ME *cokeren*] : INDULGE, PAMPER

[2]cocker *n* : a keeper or handler of fighting cocks

cock·er·el \'käk-(ə-)rəl\ *n* [ME *cokerelle,* fr. OF dial. *kokerel,* dim. of OF *coc*] : a young male domestic fowl

cock·er spaniel \ˌkäk-ər-\ *n* [*cocking* (woodcock hunting)] : a small spaniel with long ears, square muzzle, and silky coat

cock·eye \'käk-'ī, -ˌī\ *n* : a squinting eye

cock·eyed \'käk-'īd\ *adj* **1** : having a cockeye **2 a** : ASKEW, AWRY **b** : slightly crazy : TOPSY-TURVY <a ~ scheme> **c** : DRUNK — **cock·eyed·ly** \(')käk-'ī(-ə)d-lē\ *adv* — **cock·eyed·ness** \-'īd-nəs\ *n*

cock·fight \'käk-ˌfīt\ *n* : a contest of gamecocks usu. fitted with metal spurs — **cock·fight·ing** \-ˌfīt-iŋ\ *adj or n*

cockfight chair *n* [fr. its use for viewing sports] : READING CHAIR

cock·horse \'käk-ˌhȯ(ə)rs\ *n* [perh. fr. *cock,* adj., (male) + *horse*] : ROCKING HORSE

[1]cock·le \'käk-əl\ *n* [ME, fr. OE *coccel*] : any of several grainfield weeds; *esp* : CORN COCKLE

[2]cockle *n* [ME *cokille,* fr. MF *coquille* shell, modif. of L *conchylia,* pl. of *conchylium,* fr. Gk *konchylion,* fr. *konchē* conch] **1** : a bivalve mollusk (family Cardiidae) having a shell with convex radially ribbed valves; *esp* : a common edible European bivalve (*Cardium edule*) **2** : COCKLESHELL

[3]cockle *n* [MF *coquille*] : PUCKER, WRINKLE — **cockle** *vb*

cock·le·bur \'käk-əl-ˌbər, 'kək-\ *n* : any of a genus (*Xanthium*) of prickly-fruited composite plants; *also* : one of its stiff-spined fruits

cock·le·shell \'käk-əl-ˌshel\ *n* **1 a** : the shell or one of the shell valves of a cockle **b** : a shell (as a scallop shell) suggesting a cockleshell **2** : a light flimsy boat

cockleshell 1a

cock·les of the heart \ˌkäk-əlz-\ [perh. fr. [2]*cockle*] : the core of one's being — usu. used in the phrase *warm the cockles of the heart*

cock·loft \'käk-ˌlȯft\ *n* [prob. fr. [1]*cock*] : a small garret

cock·ney \'käk-nē\ *n, pl* **cockneys** [ME *cokeney,* lit., cocks' egg, fr. *coken* (gen. pl. of *cok* cock) + *ey* egg, fr. OE *ǣg*] **1** *obs* **a** : a spoiled child **b** : a squeamish woman **2 a** : a native of London and esp. of the East End of London **b** : the dialect of London or of the East End of London — **cockney** *adj* — **cock·ney·ish** \-ish\ *adj* — **cock·ney·ism** \-ˌiz-əm\ *n*

cock·ney·fy \'käk-ni-ˌfī\ *vt* **-fied; -fy·ing** : to make cockney or similar to a cockney

cock·pit \'käk-ˌpit\ *n* **1 a** : a pit or enclosure for cockfights **b** : a place noted for esp. bloody, violent, or long-continued conflict <in the ~ of Southeast Asia —James Morris> **2** *obs* : the pit of a theater **3 a** : an apartment of an old sailing warship used as quarters for junior officers and for treatment of the wounded in an engagement **b** : an open space aft of a decked area from which a small ship is steered **c** : a space in the fuselage of an airplane for the pilot or the pilot and passengers or in large passenger planes the pilot and crew — see AIRPLANE illustration **d :** the driver's compartment in an automobile

cock·roach \'käk-ˌrōch\ *n* [by folk etymology fr. Sp *cucaracha* cockroach, irreg. fr. *cuca* caterpillar] **:** any of an order (Blattaria) of chiefly nocturnal insects including some that are domestic pests

cocks·comb \'käk-ˌskōm\ *n* **1 :** COXCOMB **2 :** a garden plant (genus *Celosia*) of the amaranth family grown for its flowers

cocks·foot \-ˌfu̇t\ *n* **:** a tall hay and pasture grass (*Dactylis glomerata*) that grows in tufts with loose open panicles

cock·shut \'käk-ˌshət\ *n* [fr. the time poultry are shut in to rest] *dial Eng* **:** evening twilight

cock·shy \-ˌshī\ *n, pl* **cockshies** [¹*cock* + *shy,* n.] **1 a :** a throw at an object set up as a mark **b :** a mark or target so set up **2 :** an object or person taken as a butt (as of constant criticism or ridicule)

cock·sure \'käk-'shu̇(ə)r\ *adj* [prob. fr. ¹*cock* + *sure*] **1 :** feeling perfect assurance sometimes on inadequate grounds **2 :** marked by overconfidence or presumptuousness **:** COCKY ***syn*** see SURE ***ant*** dubious, doubtful — **cock·sure·ly** *adv* — **cock·sure·ness** *n*

¹cock·tail \'käk-ˌtāl\ *n* [¹*cock* + *tail*] **1 :** a horse with its tail docked **2 :** a horse not of pure breed

²cocktail *n* [prob. fr. ¹*cock* + *tail*] **1 a :** an iced drink of distilled liquor mixed with flavoring ingredients **b :** something resembling or suggesting such a drink; *esp* **:** a mixture of diverse elements <fog and smoke in equal parts — a city ~ familiar to all —*New Yorker*> **2 :** an appetizer (as tomato juice) served as a first course at a meal

³cocktail *adj* **1 :** of, relating to, or set aside for cocktails <a ~ hour> **2 :** designed for semiformal wear <~ dress>

cocktail glass *n* **:** a bell-shaped drinking glass usu. having a foot and stem and holding about three ounces

cocktail lounge *n* **:** a public room (as in a hotel, club, or restaurant) where cocktails and other drinks are served

cocktail party *n* **:** an informal or semiformal party or gathering at which cocktails are served

cocktail table *n* **:** COFFEE TABLE

cocky \'käk-ē\ *adj* **cock·i·er; -est 1 :** PERT, ARROGANT **2 :** JAUNTY — **cock·i·ly** \'käk-ə-lē\ *adv* — **cock·i·ness** \'käk-ē-nəs\ *n*

¹co·co \'kō-(ˌ)kō\ *n, pl* **cocos** [Sp & Pg; Sp, fr. Pg *côco,* lit., bogeyman] **:** the coconut palm; *also* **:** its fruit

²coco *adj* **:** made from the fibrous husk of the coconut <~ matting>

co·coa \'kō-(ˌ)kō\ *n* [modif. of Sp *cacao*] **1 :** CACAO 1 **2 a :** chocolate deprived of a portion of its fat and pulverized **b :** a beverage prepared by heating powdered cocoa with water or milk

cocoa bean *n* **:** CACAO 2

cocoa butter *n* **:** a pale vegetable fat with a low melting point obtained from cacao beans

¹co·con·scious \(ˈ)kō-'kän-chəs\ *adj* **1 :** experiencing or aware of the same things <a ~ people> **2 :** of or relating to the coconscious

²coconscious *n* **:** mental processes outside the main stream of consciousness but sometimes available to it

co·con·scious·ness *n* **:** COCONSCIOUS

co·con·spir·a·tor \ˌkō-kən-'spir-ət-ər\ *n* **:** a fellow conspirator

co·co·nut \'kō-kə-(ˌ)nət\ *n* **1 :** the drupaceous fruit of the coconut palm whose outer fibrous husk yields coir and whose nut contains thick edible meat and coconut milk **2 :** the edible meat of the coconut

coconut crab *n* **:** PURSE CRAB

coconut oil *n* **:** a nearly colorless fatty oil or white semisolid fat extracted from fresh coconuts and used esp. in making soaps and food products

coconut palm *n* **:** a tall pinnate-leaved tropical palm (*Cocos nucifera*) prob. of American origin

¹co·coon \kə-'kün\ *n* [F *cocon,* fr. Prov *coucoun,* fr. *coco* shell, fr. L *coccum* excrescence on a tree, fr. Gk *kokkos* grain, seed, kermes berry] **1 a :** an envelope often largely of silk which an insect larva forms about itself and in which it passes the pupa stage — see SILKWORM illustration **b :** any of various other protective coverings produced by animals **2 a :** a covering suggesting a cocoon **b :** a protective covering placed or sprayed over military or naval equipment in storage

²cocoon *vt* **:** to wrap or envelop esp. tightly in or as if in a cocoon

co·cotte \kō-kȯt\ *n, pl* **cocottes** \-kȯt(s)\ [F] **:** PROSTITUTE

coc·o·zel·le \ˌkäk-ə-'zel-ē\ *n* [prob. deriv. of It *cocuzza* squash] **:** a summer squash resembling the zucchini

co·cur·ric·u·lar \ˌkō-kə-'rik-yə-lər\ *adj* **:** being outside of but usu. complementing the regular curriculum

¹cod \'käd\ *n, pl* **cod** *also* **cods** [ME] **1 a :** a soft-finned fish (*Gadus morrhua*) of the colder parts of the No. Atlantic that is a major food fish **b :** a fish of the cod family (Gadidae); *esp* **:** a Pacific fish (*Gadus macrocephalus*) closely related to the Atlantic cod **2 :** any of various spiny-finned fishes resembling the true cods

²cod *abbr* codex

COD *abbr* **1** cash on delivery **2** collect on delivery

co·da \'kōd-ə\ *n* [It, lit., tail, fr. L *cauda*] **1 a :** a concluding musical section that is formally distinct from the main structure **b :** a concluding part of a literary or dramatic work **2 :** something that serves to round out, conclude, or summarize and that has an interest of its own

cod·dle \'käd-ᵊl\ *vt* **cod·dled; cod·dling** \'käd-liŋ, -ᵊl-iŋ\ [perh. fr. *caudle*] **1 :** to cook (as eggs) in liquid slowly and gently just below the boiling point **2 :** to treat with extreme care **:** PAMPER — **cod·dler** \'käd-lər, -ᵊl-ər\ *n*

¹code \'kōd\ *n* [ME, fr. MF, fr. L *caudex, codex* trunk of a tree, tablet of wood covered with wax for writing on, book; akin to L *cudere* to beat — more at HEW] **1 :** a systematic statement of a body of law; *esp* **:** one given statutory force **2 :** a system of principles or rules <moral ~> **3 a :** a system of signals for communication **b :** a system of symbols (as letters, numbers, or words) used to represent assigned and often secret meanings **4 :** GENETIC CODE — **code·less** \-ləs\ *adj*

²code *vt* **cod·ed; cod·ing :** to put in or into the form or symbols of a code — **cod·able** \'kōd-ə-bəl\ *adj* — **cod·er** *n*

code book *n* **:** a book containing an alphabetical list of words or expressions with their code group equivalents for use in secret communications

co·dec·li·na·tion \(ˌ)kō-ˌdek-lə-'nā-shən\ *n* **:** the complement of the declination

co·de·fen·dant \ˌkō-di-'fen-dənt\ *n* **:** a joint defendant

code group *n* **:** one of the constituent groups of letters or numbers in an encoded text

co·deine \'kō-ˌdēn, 'kōd-ē-ən\ *n* [F *codéine,* fr. Gk *kōdeia* poppyhead, fr. *kōos* cavity; akin to Gk *koilos* hollow] **:** a morphine derivative $C_{18}H_{21}NO_3{\cdot}H_2O$ that is found in opium, is weaker in action than morphine, and is used esp. in cough remedies

co·den \'kō-ˌden\ *n* [irreg. fr. ¹*code*] **:** a code classification assigned to a library item (as a book, document, or periodical)

code name *n* **:** a word made to serve as a code designation

co·de·ter·mi·na·tion \ˌkō-di-ˌtər-mə-'nā-shən\ *n* **:** the participation of labor with management in the determination of business policy

code word *n* **1 :** CODE NAME **2 :** CODE GROUP

co·dex \'kō-ˌdeks\ *n, pl* **co·di·ces** \'kōd-ə-ˌsēz, 'käd-\ [L] **:** a manuscript book esp. of Scripture, classics, or ancient annals

cod·fish \'käd-ˌfish\ *n* **:** COD; *also* **:** its flesh used as food

cod·ger \'käj-ər\ *n* [prob. alter. of *cadger*] **:** a mildly eccentric or disreputable fellow

cod·i·cil \'käd-ə-səl, -ˌsil\ *n* [MF *codicille,* fr. L *codicillus,* dim. of *codic-, codex* book] **1 :** a legal instrument made subsequently to a will and modifying it **2 :** APPENDIX, SUPPLEMENT — **cod·i·cil·la·ry** \ˌkäd-ə-'sil-ə-rē\ *adj*

cod·i·fy \'käd-ə-ˌfī, 'kōd-\ *vt* **-fied; -fy·ing 1 :** to reduce to a code **2 a :** SYSTEMATIZE **b :** CLASSIFY — **cod·i·fi·abil·i·ty** \ˌkäd-ə-ˌfī-ə-'bil-ət-ē, ˌkōd-\ *n* — **cod·i·fi·ca·tion** \-fə-'kā-shən\ *n*

¹cod·ling \'käd-liŋ\ *n* **1 :** a young cod **2 :** any of several hakes (esp. genus *Urophycis*)

²cod·ling \'käd-liŋ\ *or* **cod·lin** \-lən\ *n* [alter. of ME *querdlyng*] **:** a small immature apple; *also* **:** any of several elongated greenish English cooking apples

codling moth *n* **:** a small moth (*Laspeyresia pomonella*) whose larva lives in apples, pears, quinces, and English walnuts

cod–liver oil *n* **:** an oil obtained from the liver of the cod and closely related fishes and used as a source of vitamins A and D

co·dom·i·nant \(ˈ)kō-'däm-ə-nənt\ *adj* **1 a :** forming part of the main canopy of a forest <~ trees> **b :** sharing in the controlling influence of a biotic community **2 :** being fully expressed in the heterozygous condition <two ~ alleles> — **codominant** *n*

co·don \'kō-ˌdän\ *n* [¹*code* + ²*-on*] **:** a triplet of nucleotides that is part of the genetic code and that specifies a particular amino acid in a protein or starts or stops protein synthesis

cod·piece \'käd-ˌpēs\ *n* [ME *codpese,* fr. *cod* bag, scrotum (fr. OE *codd*) + *pese* piece] **:** a flap or bag concealing an opening in the front of men's breeches esp. in the 15th and 16th centuries

1 codpiece

cods·wal·lop \'kädz-ˌwäl-əp\ *n* [origin unknown] *Brit* **:** NONSENSE

¹co·ed \'kō-ˌed\ *n* [short for *coeducational student*] **:** a female student in a coeducational institution

²coed *adj* **1 :** COEDUCATIONAL **2 :** of or relating to a coed **3 :** open to both men and women

co–edi·tion \ˌkō-ə-'dish-ən\ *n* **:** an edition of a book published simultaneously by more than one publisher usu. in different countries and in different languages

co·ed·i·tor \(ˈ)kō-'ed-ət-ər\ *n* **:** one who collaborates with another in editing a newspaper, magazine, or book

co·ed·u·ca·tion \(ˌ)kō-ˌej-ə-'kā-shən\ *n* **:** the education of students of both sexes at the same institution

co·ed·u·ca·tion·al \-shnəl, -shən-ᵊl\ *adj* **:** of or relating to coeducation — **co·ed·u·ca·tion·al·ly** \-ē\ *adv*

coeff *or* **coef** *abbr* coefficient

co·ef·fi·cient \ˌkō-ə-'fish-ənt\ *n* [NL *coefficient-, coefficiens,* fr. L *co-* + *efficient-, efficiens* efficient] **1 :** any of the factors of a product considered in relation to a specific factor; *esp* **:** a constant factor of a term as distinguished from a variable **2 a :** a number that serves as a measure of some property or characteristic (as of a device or process) <~ of expansion of a metal> **b :** MEASURE, DEGREE

coefficient of correlation : CORRELATION COEFFICIENT

coefficient of viscosity : VISCOSITY 3

coel·acanth \'sē-lə-ˌkan(t)th\ *n* [deriv. of Gk *koilos* hollow + NL *-acanthus* — more at CAVE] **:** any of a family (Coelacanthidae) of mostly extinct fishes (as latimeria) — **coelacanth** *adj* — **coel·acan·thine** \ˌsē-lə-'kan-ˌthin, -'kan(t)-thən\ *adj* — **coel·acan·thous** \-'kan(t)-thəs\ *adj*

-coele *or* **-coel** \ˌsēl\ *n comb form* [prob. fr. NL *-coela,* fr. neut. pl. of *-coelus* hollow, concave, fr. Gk *-koilos,* fr. *koilos*] **:** cavity **:** chamber **:** ventricle <blasto*coel*> <entero*coele*>

coel·en·ter·ate \si-'lent-ə-ˌrāt, -rət\ *n* [deriv. of Gk *koilos* + *enteron* intestine — more at INTER-] **:** any of a phylum (Coelenterata) of basically radially symmetrical invertebrate animals including the corals, sea anemones, jellyfishes, and hydroids — **coelenterate** *adj*

coel·en·ter·on \-ˌrän, -rən\ *n, pl* **-tera** \-rə\ [NL, fr. Gk *koilos* + *enteron*] **:** the internal cavity of a coelenterate

coe·li·ac \'sē-lē-ˌak\ *var of* CELIAC

coe·lom \'sē-ləm\ *n, pl* **coeloms** *or* **coe·lo·ma·ta** \si-'lō-mət-ə\ [G, fr. Gk *koilōma* cavity, fr. *koilos*] **:** the usu. epithelium-lined space between the body wall and the digestive tract of metazoans above the lower worms — **coe·lo·mate** \'sē-lə-ˌmāt\ *adj or n* — **coe·lo·mic** \si-'läm-ik, -'lō-mik\ *adj*

coen- *or* **coeno-** *comb form* [NL, fr. Gk *koin-, koino-*, fr. *koinos* — more at CO-] : common : general <*coeno*cyte>

coe·no·bite \'sē-nə-ˌbīt\ *var of* CENOBITE

coe·no·cyte \'sē-nə-ˌsīt\ *n* [ISV] **1 a :** a multinucleate mass of protoplasm resulting from repeated nuclear division unaccompanied by cell fission **b :** an organism consisting of such a structure **2 :** SYNCYTIUM 1 — **coe·no·cyt·ic** \ˌsē-nə-'sit-ik\ *adj*

coe·no·ge·net·ic \ˌsē-nə-jə-'net-ik\ *var of* CENOGENETIC

coe·nu·rus \si-'n(y)u̇r-əs\ *n, pl* **-nu·ri** \-'n(y)u̇(ə)r-ˌī\ [NL, fr. *coen-* + Gk *oura* tail] : a complex tapeworm larva consisting of a sac from the inner wall of which numerous scolices develop

co·en·zyme \(ˈ)kō-'en-ˌzīm\ *n* : a thermostable nonprotein compound that forms the active portion of an enzyme system after combination with an apoenzyme — **co·en·zy·mat·ic** \(ˌ)kō-ˌen-zə-'mat-ik, -(ˌ)zī-\ *adj* — **co·en·zy·mat·i·cal·ly** \-i-k(ə-)lē\ *adv*

coenzyme A *n* : a coenzyme $C_{21}H_{36}N_7O_{16}P_3S$ that occurs in all living cells and is essential to the metabolism of carbohydrates, fats, and some amino acids

coenzyme Q *n* : UBIQUINONE

co·equal \(ˈ)kō-'ē-kwəl\ *adj* : equal with one another — **co·equal·i·ty** \ˌkō-ē-'kwäl-ət-ē\ *n* — **co·equal·ly** \(ˈ)kō-'ē-kwə-lē\ *adv*

co·erce \kō-'ərs\ *vt* **co·erced; co·erc·ing** [L *coercēre*, fr. *co-* + *arcēre* to shut up, enclose — more at ARK] **1 :** to restrain or dominate by nullifying individual will **2 :** to compel to an act or choice <they could ~ the citizens by threats but not persuade their agreement> **3 :** to enforce or bring about by force or threat ***syn*** see FORCE — **co·erc·ible** \-'ər-sə-bəl\ *adj*

co·er·cion \-'ər-zhən, -shən\ *n* : the act, process, or power of coercing

co·er·cive \-'ər-siv\ *adj* : serving or intended to coerce — **co·er·cive·ly** *adv* — **co·er·cive·ness** *n*

coercive force *n* : the opposing magnetic intensity that must be applied to a magnetized material to remove the residual magnetism

co·er·civ·i·ty \ˌkō-ˌər-'siv-ət-ē\ *n* : the property of a material determined by the value of the coercive force when the material has been magnetized to saturation

co·eta·ne·ous \ˌkō-ə-'tā-nē-əs\ *adj* [L *coaetaneus*, fr. *co-* + *aetas* age — more at AGE] : COEVAL

co·eter·nal \ˌkō-i-'tərn-ᵊl\ *adj* : equally or jointly eternal — **co·eter·nal·ly** \-ᵊl-ē\ *adv* — **co·eter·ni·ty** \-'tər-nət-ē\ *n*

co·eval \kō-'ē-vəl\ *adj* [L *coaevus*, fr. *co-* + *aevum* age, lifetime — more at AGE] : of the same or equal age, antiquity, or duration ***syn*** see CONTEMPORARY — **coeval** *n* — **co·eval·i·ty** \ˌkō-(ˌ)ē-'val-ət-ē\ *n*

co·ex·ist \ˌkō-ig-'zist\ *vi* **1 :** to exist together or at the same time **2 :** to live in peace with each other esp. as a matter of policy — **co·ex·is·tence** \-'zis-tən(t)s\ *n* — **co·ex·is·tent** \-tənt\ *adj*

co·ex·ten·sive \ˌkō-ik-'sten(t)-siv\ *adj* : having the same spatial or temporal scope or boundaries — **co·ex·ten·sive·ly** *adv*

co·fac·tor \'kō-ˌfak-tər\ *n* **1 :** the signed minor of an element of a square matrix or of a determinant with the sign positive if the sum of the column number and row number of the element is even and with the sign negative if it is odd **2 :** a substance that acts with another substance to bring about certain effects; *esp* : COENZYME

C of C *abbr* Chamber of Commerce

co·fea·ture \'kō-ˌfē-chər\ *n* : a feature (as in an entertainment) accompanying a main attraction

cof·fee \'kȯ-fē, 'käf-ē\ *n, often attrib* [It & Turk; It *caffè*, fr. Turk *kahve*, fr. Ar *qahwa*] **1 a :** a drink made by percolation, infusion, or decoction from the roasted and ground or pounded seeds of a coffee tree; *also* : these seeds either green or roasted **b :** COFFEE TREE 1 **2 :** a cup of coffee <two ~*s*> **3 :** COFFEE HOUR

coffee: *1* flowering and fruiting branch with leaves, *2* fruit with pericarp partly removed to show seeds

coffee break *n* : a short rest period (as in mid-morning or mid-afternoon) during which refreshments are often consumed

coffee cake *n* : a sweet rich bread often with added fruit, nuts, and spices that is sometimes glazed after baking

coffee hour *n* **1 :** a usu. fixed occasion of informal meeting and chatting at which refreshments are served **2 :** COFFEE BREAK

cof·fee·house \-ˌhau̇s\ *n* : an establishment that sells coffee and usu. other refreshments and that commonly serves its habitués as an informal club

coffee klatch \-ˌklach\ *n* [part trans. of G *kaffeeklatsch*] : KAFFEEKLATSCH

coffee maker *n* : a utensil in which coffee is brewed

coffee mill *n* : a mill for grinding coffee beans

cof·fee·pot \-ˌpät\ *n* : a utensil for preparing or serving coffee

coffee ring *n* : coffee cake in the shape of a ring

coffee roll *n* : a roll made from sweet raised dough (as coffee cake dough)

coffee room *n* : a room where refreshments are served

coffee royal *n* : a drink of black coffee and a liquor (as brandy or rum) often sweetened with sugar

coffee service *n* : a usu. sterling silver or silverplate service consisting of coffeepot, sugar bowl, creamer, and tray

coffee set *n* **1 :** COFFEE SERVICE **2 :** a set of porcelain or pottery for the serving of coffee consisting typically of coffeepot, sugar bowl, cream pitcher, and matching cups and saucers

coffee shop *n* : a small restaurant

coffee table *n* : a low table customarily placed in front of a sofa — called also *cocktail table*

coffee–ta·bler \-ˌtā-blər\ *n* : an expensive illustrated oversize book suitable for display on a coffee table — called also *coffee-table book*

coffee tree *n* **1 a :** a large evergreen shrub or small tree (*Coffea arabica*) of the madder family that is native to Africa but is now widely cultivated in warm regions for its seeds which form most of the coffee of commerce — called also *Arabian coffee* **b :** a tree (genus *Coffea*) related to the coffee tree **2 :** KENTUCKY COFFEE TREE

[1]**cof·fer** \'kȯ-fər, 'käf-ər\ *n* [ME *coffre*, fr. OF, fr. L *cophinus* basket, fr. Gk *kophinos*] **1 :** CHEST, BOX; *esp* : STRONGBOX **2 :** TREASURY, EXCHEQUER — usu. used in pl. **3 a :** the chamber of a canal lock **b :** CAISSON **c :** COFFERDAM **4 :** a recessed panel in a vault, ceiling, or soffit

[2]**coffer** *vt* **1 :** to store or hoard up in a coffer **2 :** to form (as a ceiling) with recessed panels

cof·fer·dam \-ˌdam\ *n* **1 :** a watertight enclosure from which water is pumped to expose the bottom of a body of water and permit construction (as of a pier) **2 :** a watertight structure for making repairs below the waterline of a ship

[1]**cof·fin** \'kȯ-fən\ *n* [ME, basket, receptacle, fr. MF *cofin*, fr. L *cophinus*] **1 :** a box or chest for burying a corpse **2 :** the horny body forming the hoof of a horse's foot

[2]**coffin** *vt* : to enclose in or as if in a coffin

coffin bone *n* : the bone enclosed within the hoof of the horse

coffin corner *n* : one of the corners formed by a goal line and a sideline on a football field into which a punt is often aimed so that it may go out of bounds close to the defender's goal line

coffin nail *n, slang* : CIGARETTE

cof·fle \'kȯ-fəl, 'käf-əl\ *n* [Ar *qāfila* caravan] : a train of slaves or animals fastened together

C of S *abbr* chief of staff

co·func·tion \(ˈ)kō-'fəŋ(k)-shən\ *n* : a trigonometric function whose value for the complement of an angle is equal to the value of a given trigonometric function for the angle itself <the sine is the ~ of the cosine>

[1]**cog** \'käg\ *n* [ME *cogge*, of Scand origin; akin to Norw *kug* cog; akin to OE *cycgel* cudgel] **1 :** a tooth on the rim of a wheel or gear **2 :** a subordinate person or part — **cogged** \'kägd\ *adj*

[2]**cog** *vb* **cogged; cog·ging** [*cog* (a trick)] *vi* **1** *obs* **:** to cheat in throwing dice **2** *obs* **:** DECEIVE **3** *obs* **:** to use venal flattery ~ *vt* **1 :** to direct the fall of (dice) fraudulently **2** *obs* **:** WHEEDLE

[3]**cog** *vt* **cogged; cog·ging** [prob. alter. of *cock* (cog)] : to connect (as timbers or joists) by means of tenons

[4]**cog** *n* : a tenon on a beam or timber received into a mortise in another beam to secure the two together

[5]**cog** *abbr* cognate

co·gen·cy \'kō-jən-sē\ *n* : the quality or state of being cogent

co·gent \'kō-jənt\ *adj* [L *cogent-, cogens*, prp. of *cogere* to drive together, collect, fr. *co-* + *agere* to drive — more at AGENT] **1 :** having power to compel or constrain <~ forces of nature> **2 a :** appealing forcibly to the mind or reason : CONVINCING <~ evidence> **b :** presented in a way that brings out pertinent and fundamental points <a ~ analysis of a problem> ***syn*** see VALID — **co·gent·ly** *adv*

cog·i·ta·ble \'käj-ət-ə-bəl\ *adj* : capable of being brought before the mind as a thought or idea : THINKABLE

cog·i·tate \'käj-ə-ˌtāt\ *vb* **-tat·ed; -tat·ing** [L *cogitatus*, pp. of *cogitare* to think, think about, fr. *co-* + *agitare* to drive, agitate — more at AGITATE] *vt* **1 :** to ponder or meditate on usu. with intentness and objectivity **2 :** PLAN, PLOT ~ *vi* **:** to think deeply : PONDER ***syn*** see THINK

cog·i·ta·tion \ˌkäj-ə-'tā-shən\ *n* **1 a :** the act of cogitating : MEDITATION **b :** the capacity to think or reflect **2 :** THOUGHT

cog·i·ta·tive \'käj-ə-ˌtāt-iv\ *adj* **1 :** of or relating to cogitation **2 :** capable of or given to cogitation

co·gi·to \'kō-gi-ˌtō\ *n* [NL *cogito, ergo sum* I think, therefore I am, principle stated by René Descartes] **1 :** the philosophic principle that one's existence is demonstrated by the fact that one thinks **2 :** the intellectual processes of the self or ego

co·gnac \'kōn-ˌyak\ *n* [F, fr. *Cognac*, France] **1 :** a brandy from the departments of Charente and Charente-Maritime distilled from white wine **2 :** a French brandy

[1]**cog·nate** \'käg-ˌnāt\ *adj* [L *cognatus*, fr. *co-* + *gnatus, natus*, pp. of *nasci* to be born; akin to L *gignere* to beget — more at KIN] **1 a :** related by blood **b :** related on the mother's side **2 a :** related by descent from the same ancestral language **b** *of a word or morpheme* : related by derivation, borrowing, or descent **c** *of a substantive* : related usu. in derivation to the verb of which it is the object **3 :** of the same or similar nature : generically alike ***syn*** see RELATED — **cog·nate·ly** *adv*

[2]**cognate** *n* : one that is cognate with another

cog·na·tion \käg-'nā-shən\ *n* : cognate relationship

cog·ni·tion \käg-'nish-ən\ *n* [ME *cognicioun*, fr. L *cognition-, cognitio*, fr. *cognitus*, pp. of *cognoscere* to become acquainted with, know, fr. *co-* + *gnoscere* to come to know — more at KNOW] : the act or process of knowing including both awareness and judgment; *also* : a product of this act — **cog·ni·tion·al** \-'nish-nəl, -'nish-ən-ᵊl\ *adj*

cog·ni·tive \'käg-nət-iv\ *adj* **1 :** of, relating to, or involving cognition <the ~ elements of perception —C. H. Hamburg> **2 :** based on or capable of being reduced to empirical factual knowledge — **cog·ni·tive·ly** *adv* — **cog·ni·tiv·i·ty** \ˌkäg-nə-'tiv-ət-ē\ *n*

cognitive dissonance *n* : psychological conflict resulting from incongruous beliefs and attitudes held simultaneously

ə abut	ᵊ kitten	ər further	a back	ā bake	ä cot, cart	
au̇ out	ch chin	e less	ē easy	g gift	i trip	ī life
j joke	ŋ sing	ō flow	ȯ flaw	ȯi coin	th thin	th this
ü loot	u̇ foot	y yet	yü few	yu̇ furious	zh vision	

cog·ni·za·ble \'käg-nə-zə-bəl, käg-'nī-\ *adj* **1 :** capable of being known **2 :** capable of being judicially heard and determined — **cog·ni·za·bly** \-blē\ *adv*

cog·ni·zance \'käg-nə-zən(t)s\ *n* [ME *conisaunce,* fr. OF *conoissance,* fr. *conoistre* to know, fr. L *cognoscere*] **1 :** a distinguishing mark or emblem (as a heraldic bearing) **2 a :** SURVEILLANCE, CONTROL **b :** APPREHENSION, PERCEPTION **c :** range of apprehension **d :** NOTICE, OBSERVANCE **3 a :** the right and power to hear and decide controversies : JURISDICTION **b :** the judicial hearing of a matter

cog·ni·zant \-zənt\ *adj* **:** having cognizance; *esp* **:** having special or certain knowledge often from firsthand sources ***syn*** see AWARE ***ant*** ignorant

cog·nize \käg-'nīz\ *vt* **cog·nized; cog·niz·ing** [back-formation fr. *cognizance*] **:** KNOW — **cog·niz·er** *n*

cog·no·men \käg-'nō-mən, 'käg-nə-\ *n, pl* **cognomens** *or* **cog·no·mi·na** \käg-'näm-ə-nə, -'nō-mə-\ [L, irreg. fr. *co-* + *nomen* name — more at NAME] **1 :** SURNAME; *esp* **:** the third of usu. three names of a person among the ancient Romans **2 :** NAME; *esp* **:** a distinguishing nickname or epithet — **cog·nom·i·nal** \käg-'näm-ən-ᵊl\ *adj*

co·gno·scen·te \ˌkän-(y)ə-'shent-ē, ˌkäg-nə\ *n, pl* **-scen·ti** \-ē\ [obs. It (now *conoscente*), fr. *cognoscente,* adj., wise, fr. L *cognoscent-, cognoscens,* prp. of *cognoscere*] **:** a person having or claiming expert knowledge (as of fine arts or fashion) **:** CONNOISSEUR

cog·nos·ci·ble \käg-'näs-ə-bəl\ *adj* [LL *cognoscibilis,* fr. L *cognoscere*] **:** COGNIZABLE, KNOWABLE

co·gon \kō-'gōn\ *n* [Sp *cogón,* fr. Tag, Bisayan, & Bikol *kugon*] **:** any of several coarse tall grasses (genus *Imperata*) used esp. in the Philippines for thatching

cog railway *n* **:** a steep mountain railroad that has a rail with cogs which engages a cogwheel on the locomotive to ensure traction

cogs·well chair \ˌkägz-ˌwel-, -wəl-\ *n, often cap 1st C* [fr. the name *Cogswell*] **:** an upholstered easy chair with inclined back, thin open arms, and cabriole legs

cog·wheel \'käg-ˌhwēl, -ˌwēl\ *n* **:** a wheel with cogs or teeth

co·hab·it \kō-'hab-ət\ *vi* [LL *cohabitare,* fr. L *co-* + *habitare* to inhabit, fr. *habitus,* pp. of *habēre* to have] **1 :** to live together as husband and wife **2 a :** to live together or in company <buffaloes ~*ing* with crossbred cows —*Biol. Abstracts*> **b :** to exist together <two strains in his philosophy . . . ~ in each of his major works — Justus Buchler> — **co·hab·i·tant** \-ət-ənt\ *n* — **co·hab·i·ta·tion** \(ˌ)kō-ˌhab-ə-'tā-shən\ *n*

co·heir \(')kō-'a(ə)r, -'e(ə)r\ *n* **:** a joint heir

co·heir·ess \-əs\ *n* **:** a joint heiress

co·here \kō-'hi(ə)r\ *vb* **co·hered; co·her·ing** [L *cohaerēre,* fr. *co-* + *haerēre* to stick — more at HESITATE] *vi* **1 a :** to hold together firmly as parts of the same mass; *broadly* **:** STICK, ADHERE **b :** to display cohesion of plant parts **2 :** to consist of parts that cohere **3 a :** to become united in principles, relationships, or interests **b :** to be logically or aesthetically consistent ~ *vt* **:** to make (parts or components) fit or stick together in a suitable or orderly way ***syn*** see STICK

co·her·ence \-ən(t)s\ *n* **1 :** the quality or state of cohering; *esp* **:** systematic connection esp. in logical discourse **2 :** the property of being coherent

co·her·en·cy \kō-'hir-ən-sē, -'her-\ *n, pl* **-cies :** COHERENCE

co·her·ent \-ənt\ *adj* [MF or L; MF *cohérent,* fr. L *cohaerent-, cohaerens,* prp. of *cohaerēre*] **1 :** having the quality of cohering **2 :** logically consistent <a ~ argument> **3 :** relating to electromagnetic waves that have a definite relationship to each other: as **a :** composed of wave trains in phase with each other <~ light> **b :** producing coherent light <a ~ source> — **co·her·ent·ly** *adv*

co·her·er \kō-'hir-ər\ *n* **:** a radio detector in which an imperfectly conducting contact between pieces of conductive material loosely resting against each other is materially improved in conductance by the passage of high-frequency current

co·he·sion \kō-'hē-zhən\ *n* [L *cohaesus,* pp. of *cohaerēre*] **1 :** the act or process of sticking together tightly <social and economic ~ . . . in a small city —J. B. Conant> **2 :** union between similar plant parts or organs **3 :** molecular attraction by which the particles of a body are united throughout the mass — **co·he·sion·less** \-ləs\ *adj*

co·he·sive \kō-'hē-siv, -ziv\ *adj* **:** exhibiting or producing cohesion or coherence <a ~ social unit> <~ soils> — **co·he·sive·ly** *adv* — **co·he·sive·ness** *n*

co·ho \'kō-(ˌ)hō\ *n, pl* **cohos** *or* **coho** [origin unknown] **:** a rather small salmon (*Oncorhynchus kisutch*) with light-colored flesh that is native to both coasts of the No. Pacific and is stocked in the Great Lakes

co·hort \'kō-ˌhȯ(ə)rt\ *n* [MF & L; MF *cohorte,* fr. L *cohort-, cohors* — more at COURT] **1 a :** one of 10 divisions of an ancient Roman legion **b :** a group of warriors or soldiers **c :** BAND, GROUP **d :** a group of individuals having a statistical factor (as age or class membership) in common in a demographic study <a ~ of premedical students> **2 a :** COMPANION, ACCOMPLICE **b :** FOLLOWER, SUPPORTER

co·hosh \'kō-ˌhäsh\ *n* [of Algonquian origin; akin to Natick *kôshki* it is rough] **:** any of several American medicinal or poisonous plants: **a :** BLACK COHOSH **b :** BLUE COHOSH **c :** BANEBERRY

co·iden·ti·ty \ˌkō-ī-'den(t)-ət-ē, ˌkō-ə-'den(t)-\ *n* **:** identity between two or more things

[1]**coif** \'kȯif, *in sense 2 usu* 'kwäf\ *n* [ME *coife,* fr. MF, fr. LL *cofea*] **1 :** a close-fitting cap: as **a :** a hoodlike cap worn by nuns under a veil **b :** a protective usu. metal skullcap formerly worn under a hood of mail **c :** a white cap formerly worn by English lawyers and esp. by serjeants-at-law; *also* **:** the order or rank of a serjeant-at-law **2 :** COIFFURE

[2]**coif** *vt* **coiffed; coif·fing 1 :** to cover or dress with or as if with a coif **2 :** to arrange (hair) by brushing, combing, or curling

coif·feur \kwä-'fər\ *n* [F, fr. *coiffer*] **:** a male hairdresser

coif·feuse \kwä-'fə(r)z, -'f(y)üz\ *n* [F, fem. of *coiffeur*] **:** a female hairdresser

coif·fure \kwä-'fyu̇(ə)r\ *n* [F, fr. *coiffer* to cover with a coif, arrange (hair), fr. *coife*] **:** a style or manner of arranging the hair

coiffured *adj* **1 :** being dressed <beautifully ~ hair> **2 :** having the hair brushed, combed, and curled <stylishly ~ women>

coign of van·tage \ˌkȯi-nə-'vant-ij\ [*coign,* earlier spelling of [1]*coin* (corner)] **:** an advantageous position

[1]**coil** \'kȯi(ə)l\ *n* [origin unknown] **1 :** TURMOIL **2 :** TROUBLE

[2]**coil** *vb* [MF *coillir, cuillir* to gather — more at CULL] *vt* **1 :** to wind into rings or spirals **2 :** to roll or twist into a shape resembling a coil ~ *vi* **1 :** to move in a circular, spiral, or winding course **2 :** to form or lie in a coil — **coil·abil·i·ty** \ˌkȯi-lə-'bil-ət-ē\ *n*

[3]**coil** *n* **1 a** (1) **:** a series of loops (2) **:** SPIRAL **b :** a single loop of such a coil **2 :** a number of turns of wire esp. in spiral form usu. for electromagnetic effect or for providing electrical resistance **3 :** a series of connected pipes in rows, layers, or windings **4 :** a roll of postage stamps; *also* **:** a stamp from such a roll

[1]**coin** \'kȯin\ *n* [ME, fr. MF, wedge, corner, fr. L *cuneus* wedge] **1** *archaic* **a :** CORNER, CORNERSTONE **b :** WEDGE **2 a :** a usu. flat round piece of metal issued by governmental authority as money **b :** metal money **c :** something resembling a coin esp. in shape **3 :** something accepted as having value or validity <perhaps wisecracks . . . are respectable literary ~ in the U.S. —*Times Lit. Supp.*> **4 :** something having two different and usu. opposing sides **5 :** MONEY <I'm in it for the ~ —Sinclair Lewis>

[2]**coin** *vt* **1 a :** to make (a coin) esp. by stamping **:** MINT **b :** to convert (metal) into coins **c :** to shape (a piece of metal) in a mold or die **2 :** CREATE, INVENT <~ a phrase> **3 :** to make or earn (money) rapidly and in large quantity — **coin·er** *n*

[3]**coin** *adj* **1 :** of or relating to coins <a ~ show> **2 :** operated by coins <a ~ laundry>

coin·age \'kȯi-nij\ *n* **1 :** the act or process of coining **2 a :** COINS **b :** something (as a word) made up or invented

co·in·cide \ˌkō-ən-'sīd, 'kō-ən-ˌ\ *vi* **-cid·ed; -cid·ing** [ML *coincidere,* fr. L *co-* + *incidere* to fall on, fr. *in-* + *cadere* to fall — more at CHANCE] **1 a :** to occupy the same place in space or time **b :** to occupy exactly corresponding or equivalent positions on a scale or in a series **2 :** to correspond in nature, character, or function **3 :** to be in accord or agreement **:** CONCUR ***syn*** see AGREE ***ant*** differ

co·in·ci·dence \kō-'in(t)-səd-ən(t)s, -sə-ˌden(t)s\ *n* **1 :** the act or condition of coinciding **:** CORRESPONDENCE **2 :** the occurrence of events that happen at the same time by accident but seem to have some connection; *also* **:** any of these happenings

co·in·ci·dent \-səd-ənt, -sə-ˌdent\ *adj* [F *coincident,* fr. ML *coincident-, coincidens,* prp. of *coincidere*] **1 :** occupying the same space or time <~ events> **2 :** of similar nature **:** HARMONIOUS <a theory ~ with the facts> ***syn*** see CONTEMPORARY — **co·in·ci·dent·ly** *adv*

co·in·ci·den·tal \(ˌ)kō-ˌin(t)-sə-'dent-ᵊl\ *adj* **1 :** resulting from a coincidence <similarity between the two texts is too consistent to be ~> **2 :** occurring or existing at the same time <rebellion in Burma was ~ with . . . insurrection in Malaya —W. B. Hamilton>

coin lock *n* **:** a lock released by the insertion of a coin

coin machine *n* **:** SLOT MACHINE

coin–op \'kȯi-ˌnäp\ *n* **:** a self-service laundry where the machines are operated by coins

co·in·sur·ance \ˌkō-ən-'shu̇r-ən(t)s, *chiefly South* (')kō-'in-ˌ\ *n* **1 :** joint assumption of risk (as by two underwriters) with another **2 :** a system of insurance (as fire insurance) in which the insured is obligated to maintain coverage on a risk at a stipulated percentage of its total value or in the event of loss suffer a penalty in proportion to the deficiency

co·in·sure \ˌkō-ən-'shu̇(ə)r\ *vt* **:** to insure jointly — **co·in·sur·er** *n*

coir \'kȯi(-ə)r\ *n* [Tamil *kayiru* rope] **:** a stiff coarse fiber from the outer husk of a coconut

cois·trel \'kȯi-strəl\ *n* [MF *coustillier* soldier carrying a short sword, fr. *coustille* short sword, fr. L *cultellus* knife — more at CUTLASS] *archaic* **:** a mean fellow **:** VARLET

co·ition \kō-'ish-ən\ *n* [LL, fr. L *coition-, coitio* a coming together, fr. *coitus,* pp. of *coire* to come together, fr. *co-* + *ire* to go — more at ISSUE] **:** COITUS — **co·ition·al** \-'ish-nəl, -ən-ᵊl\ *adj*

co·itus \'kō-ət-əs, kō-'ēt-\ *n* [L, fr. *coitus,* pp.] **:** the natural conveying of semen to the female reproductive tract; *broadly* **:** SEXUAL INTERCOURSE — **co·ital** \-ət-ᵊl, -'ēt-\ *adj* — **co·ital·ly** \-ᵊl-ē\ *adv*

coitus in·ter·rup·tus \-ˌint-ə-'rəp-təs\ *n* [NL, interrupted coitus] **:** coitus which is purposely interrupted in order to prevent ejaculation of sperm into the vagina

coitus re·ser·va·tus \-ˌrez-ər-'vät-əs, -'vät-\ *n* [NL, reserved coitus] **:** COITUS INTERRUPTUS

[1]**coke** \'kōk\ *n* [ME; akin to Sw *kälk* pith, Gk *gelgis* bulb of garlic] **:** the residue of coal left after destructive distillation and used as fuel; *also* **:** a similar residue left by other materials (as petroleum) distilled to dryness

[2]**coke** *vb* **coked; cok·ing** *vt* **:** to change into coke ~ *vi* **:** to become coked

[3]**coke** *n* [by shortening & alter.] **:** COCAINE

[1]**col** \'käl\ *n* [F, fr. MF, neck, fr. L *collum*] **1 :** a pass in a mountain range **2 :** a saddle-shaped depression in the crest of a ridge

[2]**col** *abbr* **1** colonial; colony **2** color; colored **3** column **4** counsel

[3]**col** *or* **coll** *abbr* **1** collateral **2** collect; collected; collection **3** college; collegiate

Col *abbr* **1** colonel **2** Colorado **3** Colossians

COL *abbr* cost of living

[1]**col-** — see COM-

[2]**col-** *or* **coli-** *or* **colo-** *comb form* [NL, fr. L *colon*] **1 :** colon <*col*itis> <*colo*stomy> **2 :** colon bacillus <*coli*form>

[1]**cola** *pl of* COLON

[2]**co·la** \'kō-lə\ *n* [fr. *Coca-Cola,* a trademark] **:** a carbonated soft drink flavored with extract from coca leaves, kola nut, sugar, caramel, and acid and aromatic substances

col·an·der \'kəl-ən-dər, 'käl-\ *n* [ME *colyndore,* prob. modif. of OProv *colador,* fr. ML *colatorium,* fr. L *colatus,* pp. of *colare* to sieve, fr. *colum* sieve] **:** a perforated utensil for washing or draining food

co·lat·i·tude \(ˈ)kō-'lat-ə-ˌt(y)üd\ *n* **:** the complement of the latitude

col·can·non \käl-'kan-ən\ *n* [IrGael *cāl ceannan,* lit., white-headed cabbage] **:** potatoes and cabbage boiled and mashed together with butter and seasoning

col·chi·cine \'käl-chə-ˌsēn, 'käl-kə-\ *n* **:** a poisonous alkaloid $C_{22}H_{25}NO_6$ extracted from the corms or seeds of the meadow saffron (*Colchicum autumnale*) and used on mitotic cells to induce polyploidy and in the treatment of gout

col·chi·cum \'käl-chi-kəm, 'käl-ki-\ *n* [NL, genus name, fr. L, a kind of plant with a poisonous root, fr. Gk *kolchikon,* lit., product of Colchis] **1 :** any of a genus (*Colchicum*) of Old World corm-producing herbs of the lily family with flowers that resemble crocuses **2 :** the dried corm or dried ripe seeds of autumn crocus containing colchicine, possessing emetic, diuretic, and cathartic action, and used for gout and rheumatism

col·co·thar \'käl-kə-ˌthär\ *n* [ML, fr. MF or OSp; MF *colcotar,* fr. OSp *colcotar,* fr. Ar dial. *qulquṭār*] **:** a reddish brown oxide of iron left as a residue when ferrous sulfate is heated and used as glass polish and as a pigment

¹cold \'kōld\ *adj* [ME, fr. OE *ceald, cald;* akin to OHG *kalt* cold, L *gelu* frost, *gelare* to freeze] **1 :** having a low temperature often below that compatible with human comfort **2 a :** marked by lack of warm feeling **:** UNEMOTIONAL **b :** marked by deliberation or calculation <a ~ act of aggression> **3 a :** previously cooked but served cold **b :** heated insufficiently <the soup was ~> **c :** not heated <stored in a ~ cellar> **d :** made cold <~ drinks> **e :** unheated while being worked <~ conditioning of steel prior to rolling> **4 a :** DEPRESSING, CHEERLESS **b :** producing a sensation of cold **:** CHILLING <~ blank walls> **c :** COOL 6a **5 a :** DEAD **b :** UNCONSCIOUS <knocked out ~> **c :** CERTAIN, SURE <the actors had their lines ~ a week before opening night> **6 :** made uncomfortable by cold **7 a :** retaining only faint scents, traces, or clues <a ~ trail> **b :** STALE, UNINTERESTING <~ news> **8 :** not illegal or suspect <traded the hot car for a ~ one> **9 :** presented or regarded in a straightforward way **:** IMPERSONAL <the ~ facts> **10 :** UNPREPARED **11 :** intense and barely controlled <a ~ fury> — **cold·ish** *adj* — **cold·ly** \'kōl-(d)lē\ *adv* — **cold·ness** \'kōl(d)-nəs\ *n* — **in cold blood :** with premeditation **:** DELIBERATELY

²cold *n* **1 a :** a condition of low temperature **b :** cold weather **2 :** bodily sensation produced by loss or lack of heat **:** CHILL **3 :** a bodily disorder popularly associated with chilling; *specif* **:** COMMON COLD — **in the cold :** without heating — **out in the cold :** deprived of benefits given others **:** NEGLECTED <the plan benefits management but leaves labor *out in the cold*>

³cold *adv* **:** with utter finality **:** TOTALLY, ABSOLUTELY <he was turned down ~>

cold–blood·ed \'kōl(d)-'bləd-əd\ *adj* **1 a :** done or acting without consideration, compunction, or clemency <~ murder> **b :** MATTER-OF-FACT, EMOTIONLESS **2 :** having cold blood; *specif* **:** having a body temperature not internally regulated but approximating that of the environment **3** *or* **cold·blood** \-'bləd\ **:** of mixed or inferior breeding **4 :** noticeably sensitive to cold — **cold–blood·ed·ly** *adv* — **cold–blood·ed·ness** *n*

cold cash *n* **:** money in hand <enough *cold cash* to close the deal>

cold chisel *n* **:** a chisel made of tool steel of a strength, shape, and temper suitable for chipping or cutting cold metal — see CHISEL illustration

cold comfort *n* **:** scant consolation **:** quite limited sympathy or encouragement

cold cream *n* **:** a soothing and cleansing cosmetic basically consisting of a perfumed emulsion of a bland vegetable oil or heavy mineral oil

cold cuts *n pl* **:** sliced assorted cold meats

cold duck *n* [trans. of G *kalte ente,* a drink made of a mixture of fine wines] **:** a beverage that consists of a blend of sparkling burgundy and champagne

cold feet *n pl* **:** apprehension or doubt strong enough to prevent a planned course of action

cold fish *n* **:** a cold aloof person

cold frame *n* **:** a usu. glass-covered frame without artificial heat used to protect plants and seedlings

cold front *n* **:** an advancing edge of a cold air mass

cold·heart·ed \'kōld-'härt-əd\ *adj* **:** marked by lack of sympathy, interest, or sensitivity — **cold·heart·ed·ly** *adv* — **cold·heart·ed·ness** *n*

cold rubber *n* **:** a wear-resistant synthetic rubber made at a low temperature (as 41° F.) and used esp. for tire treads

cold shoulder *n* **:** intentionally cold or unsympathetic treatment — **cold–shoul·der** *vt*

cold sore *n* **:** the group of blisters appearing about or within the mouth in herpes simplex

cold storage *n* **1 :** storage (as of food) in a cold place for preservation **2 :** a condition of being held or continued without being acted on **:** ABEYANCE <the second world war effectively put the question into *cold storage* —Leo Marquard>

cold store *n* **:** a building for cold storage

cold sweat *n* **:** concurrent perspiration and chill usu. associated with fear, pain, or shock

cold turkey *n* **1 :** unrelieved blunt language or procedure <I'm talking *cold turkey* to you . . . I think it wise if your relationship has ended —J. B. Clayton> **2 :** abrupt complete cessation of the use of an addictive drug either voluntarily or under medical supervision **3 :** a cold aloof person

cold type *n* **:** composition or typesetting (as photocomposition) done without the casting of metal; *specif* **:** such composition produced directly on paper by a typewriter mechanism

cold war *n* **1 :** a conflict carried on by methods short of sustained overt military action and usu. without breaking off diplomatic relations — compare HOT WAR **2 :** a conflict short of violence esp between power groups (as labor and management) — **cold warrior** *n*

cold–water *adj* **1 :** of or relating to temperance groups **2 a :** provided only with running cold water **b :** not having all modern plumbing or heating facilities <a ~ flat>

cold water *n* **:** depreciation of something as being ill-advised, unwarranted, or worthless <throw *cold water* on our hopes>

cold wave *n* **1 :** a period of unusually cold weather **2 :** a permanent wave set by a chemical preparation without the use of curlers attached to a heating unit

cole \'kōl\ *n* [ME, fr. OE *cāl,* fr. L *caulis* stem, cabbage — more at HOLE] **:** any of a genus (*Brassica*) of herbaceous plants (as broccoli, Brussel sprouts, cabbage, cauliflower, kohlrabi, and rape)

cole·man·ite \'kōl-mə-ˌnīt\ *n* [William T. *Coleman* †1893 Am businessman and mine owner] **:** a mineral $Ca_2B_6O_{11}\cdot 5H_2O$ consisting of a hydrous calcium borate occurring in brilliant colorless or white massive monoclinic crystals

co·le·op·tera \ˌkō-lē-'äp-tə-rə\ *n pl* [NL, deriv. of Gk *koleon* sheath + *pteron* wing — more at FEATHER] **:** insects that are beetles — **co·le·op·ter·ist** \-tə-rəst\ *n* — **co·le·op·ter·ous** \-tə-rəs\ *adj*

co·le·op·ter·an \-tə-rən\ *n* **:** ¹BEETLE 1 — **coleopteran** *adj*

co·le·op·tile \-'äp-tᵊl\ *n* [NL *coleoptilum,* fr. Gk *koleon* + *ptilon* down; akin to Gk *pteron*] **:** the first leaf of a monocotyledon forming a protective sheath about the plumule

co·leo·rhi·za \ˌkō-lē-ə-'rī-zə\ *n, pl* **-zae** \-(ˌ)zē\ [NL, fr. Gk *koleon* + NL *-rhiza*] **:** the sheath investing the hypocotyl in some plants through which the roots burst

cole·slaw \'kōl-ˌslȯ\ *n* [D *koolsla,* fr. *kool* cabbage + *sla* salad] **:** a salad made of raw sliced or chopped cabbage

co·le·us \'kō-lē-əs\ *n* [NL, genus name, fr. Gk *koleos, koleon* sheath] **:** any of a large genus (*Coleus*) of herbs of the mint family

cole·wort \'kōl-ˌwərt, -ˌwȯ(ə)rt\ *n* **:** COLE; *esp* **:** one (as kale) that forms no head

coli- — see COL-

¹col·ic \'käl-ik\ *n* [ME, fr. MF *colique,* fr. L *colicus* colicky, fr. Gk *kōlikos,* fr. *kōlon,* alter. of *kolon* colon] **:** a paroxysm of acute abdominal pain localized in a hollow organ and caused by spasm, obstruction, or twisting

²colic *adj* **:** of or relating to colic **:** COLICKY <~ crying>

³co·lic \'kō-lik, 'käl-ik\ *adj* **:** of or relating to the colon <~ lymph glands>

co·li·cin \'kō-lə-sən\ *also* **co·li·cine** \-ˌsēn\ *n* [³*colic* + *-in* or *-ine*] **:** any of various antibacterial substances that are produced by some strains of intestinal bacteria and inhibit macromolecular synthesis (as of DNA or proteins)

colicky \'käl-i-kē\ *adj* **1 :** relating to or associated with colic <~ pain> **2 :** suffering from colic <~ babies>

col·ic·root \'käl-ik-ˌrüt, -ˌrůt\ *n* **:** any of several plants having roots used in folk medicine to treat colic: as **a :** either of two bitter herbs (*Aletris farinosa* and *A. aurea*) of the lily family **b :** a wild yam (*Dioscorea paniculata*)

col·ic·weed \-ˌwēd\ *n* **:** SQUIRREL CORN

co·li·form \'kō-lə-ˌfȯrm, 'käl-ə-\ *adj* [NL *Escherichia coli* colon bacillus + E *-form*] **:** relating to, resembling, or being the colon bacillus — **coliform** *n*

co·lin \kō-'lēn\ *n* [Sp *colín,* modif. of Nahuatl *çolin*] **:** BOBWHITE; *also* **:** a related New World game bird

co·lin·ear \(ˈ)kō-'lin-ē-ər\ *n* **1 :** COLLINEAR **2 :** having corresponding parts arranged in the same linear order <a gene and the protein it determines are ~> — **co·lin·ear·i·ty** \(ˌ)kō-ˌlin-ē-'ar-ət-ē\ *n*

co·li·phage \'kō-lə-ˌfāj, -ˌfäzh\ *n* [NL *Escherichia coli* colon bacillus + E *-phage*] **:** a bacteriophage active against the colon bacillus

col·i·se·um \ˌkäl-ə-'sē-əm\ *n* [ML *Colosseum, Colisseum*] **1** *cap* **:** COLOSSEUM 1 **2 :** a large structure for public entertainments

co·lis·tin \kə-'lis-tən, kō-\ *n* [NL *colistinus,* specific epithet of the bacterium producing it] **:** a polymyxin produced by a bacterium (*Bacillus colistinus*) from Japanese soil

co·li·tis \kō-'līt-əs, kə-\ *n* **:** inflammation of the colon

coll *abbr* — see COL

coll- *or* **collo-** *comb form* [NL, fr. Gk *koll-, kollo-,* fr. *kolla* — more at PROTOCOL] **1 :** glue <*coll*enchyma> **2 :** colloid <*collo*type>

col·lab·o·rate \kə-'lab-ə-ˌrāt\ *vi* **-rat·ed; -rat·ing** [LL *collaboratus,* pp. of *collaborare* to labor together, fr. L *com-* + *laborare* to labor] **1 :** to work jointly with others esp. in an intellectual endeavor **2 :** to cooperate with or willingly assist an enemy of one's country and esp. an occupying force **3 :** to cooperate with an agency or instrumentality with which one is not immediately connected — **col·lab·o·ra·tion** \-ˌlab-ə-'rā-shən\ *n* — **col·lab·o·ra·tive** \-'lab-ə-ˌrāt-iv, -(ə-)rət-\ *adj* — **col·lab·o·ra·tor** \-'lab-ə-ˌrāt-ər\ *n*

col·lab·o·ra·tion·ism \kə-ˌlab-ə-'rā-shə-ˌniz-əm\ *n* **:** the advocacy or practice of collaboration with an enemy — **col·lab·o·ra·tion·ist** \-sh(ə-)nəst\ *adj or n*

col·lage \kə-'läzh, kō-, kō-\ *n* [F, gluing, fr. *coller* to glue, fr. *colle* glue, fr. (assumed) VL *colla,* fr. Gk *kolla*] **1 :** an artistic composition made of various materials (as paper, cloth, or wood) glued on a picture surface **2 :** the art of making collages **3 :** an assembly of diverse fragments <a ~ of ideas> **4 :** a film showing disparate scenes in rapid succession without transitions — **col·lag·ist** \-'läzh-əst\ *n*

col·la·gen \'käl-ə-jən\ *n* [Gk *kolla* + ISV *-gen*] **:** an insoluble fibrous protein that occurs in vertebrates as the chief constituent of connective tissue fibrils and in bones and yields gelatin and glue on prolonged heating with water — **col·la·gen·ic** \ˌkäl-ə-'jen-ik\ *adj* — **col·lag·e·nous** \kə-'laj-ə-nəs\ *adj*

col·la·ge·nase \kə-ˈlaj-ə-ˌnās, ˈkäl-ə-jə-, -ˌnāz\ *n* : any of a group of proteolytic enzymes that decompose collagen and gelatin

[1]**col·lapse** \kə-ˈlaps\ *vb* **col·lapsed; col·laps·ing** [L *collapsus*, pp. of *collabi*, fr. *com-* + *labi* to fall, slide — more at SLEEP] *vi* **1** : to break down completely : DISINTEGRATE <his case had *collapsed* in a mass of legal wreckage —Erle Stanley Gardner> **2** : to fall or shrink together abruptly and completely : fall into a jumbled or flattened mass through the force of external pressure <a blood vessel that *collapsed*> **3** : to cave or fall in or give way **4** : to suddenly lose force, significance, effectiveness, or worth **5** : to break down in vital energy, stamina, or self-control through exhaustion or disease; *esp* : to fall helpless or unconscious **6** : to fold down into a more compact shape <a telescope that ~*s*> ~ *vt* : to cause to collapse — **col·laps·ibil·i·ty** \-ˌlap-sə-ˈbil-ət-ē\ *n* — **col·laps·ible** \-ˈlap-sə-bəl\ *adj*

[2]**collapse** *n* **1 a** : a breakdown in vital energy, strength, or stamina **b** : a state of extreme prostration and physical depression (as from circulatory failure or great loss of body fluids) **c** : an airless state of all or part of a lung originating spontaneously or induced surgically **2** : the act or action of collapsing <the cutting of many tent ropes, the ~ of the canvas —Rudyard Kipling> **3** : a sudden failure : DISINTEGRATION, RUIN <the widespread ~ of moral standards —Robert Gordis> **4** : a sudden loss of force, value, or effect <the ~ of respect for ancient law and custom —L. S. B. Leakey>

[1]**col·lar** \ˈkäl-ər\ *n* [ME *coler*, fr. OF, fr. L *collare*, fr. *collum* neck; akin to ON & OHG *hals* neck, OE *hwēol* wheel — more at WHEEL] **1** : a band, strip, or chain worn around the neck: as **a** : a band that serves to finish or decorate the neckline of a garment **b** : a short necklace **c** : a band about the neck of an animal **d** : a part of the harness of draft animals fitted over the shoulders and taking strain when a load is drawn **e** : an indication of control : a token of subservience <refused to wear another man's ~> **f** : a protective or supportive device (as a brace or cast) worn around the neck **2** : something resembling a collar in shape or use (as a ring or round flange to restrain motion or hold something in place) **3** : any of various animal structures or markings similar to a collar **4** : an act of collaring : ARREST, CAPTURE — **col·lared** \-ərd\ *adj* — **col·lar·less** \-ər-ləs\ *adj*

[2]**collar** *vt* **1 a** : to seize by the collar or neck **b** : APPREHEND, GRAB **c** : to get control of : PREEMPT <with our machine . . . we can ~ nearly the whole of this market —Roald Dahl> **d** : to stop and detain in unwilling conversation <~*ed* the guest of honor> **2** : to put a collar on

col·lar·bone \ˈkäl-ər-ˌbōn, ˌkäl-ər-ˈ\ *n* : CLAVICLE

collar cell *n* : a flagellated endodermal cell that lines the cavity of a sponge and has a contractile protoplasmic cup surrounding the flagellum — called also *choanocyte*

col·lard \ˈkäl-ərd\ *n* [alter. of *colewort*] : a stalked smooth-leaved kale — usu. used in pl.

collat *abbr* collateral

col·late \kə-ˈlāt, kä-, kō-; ˈkäl-ˌāt, ˈkōl-ˌ\ *vt* **col·lat·ed; col·lat·ing** [back-formation fr. *collation*] **1 a** : to compare critically **b** : to collect, compare carefully in order to verify, and often to integrate or arrange in order **2** [L *collatus*, pp.] : to institute (a cleric) to a benefice **3 a** : to verify the order of (printed sheets) **b** : to assemble in proper order; *esp* : to assemble (as printed sheets) in order for binding ***syn*** see COMPARE — **col·la·tor** \-ˈlāt-ər, -ˌāt-\ *n*

[1]**col·lat·er·al** \kə-ˈlat-ə-rəl, -ˈla-trəl\ *adj* [ME, prob. fr. MF, fr. ML *collateralis*, fr. L *com-* + *lateralis* lateral] **1 a** : accompanying as secondary or subordinate : CONCOMITANT <digress into ~ matters> **b** : INDIRECT **c** : serving to support or reinforce : ANCILLARY **2** : belonging to the same ancestral stock but not in a direct line of descent **3** : parallel, coordinate, or corresponding in position, order, time, or significance <~ states like Athens and Sparta> **4 a** : of, relating to, or being collateral used as security (as for payment of a debt or performance of a contract) **b** : secured by collateral — **col·lat·er·al·i·ty** \-ˌlat-ə-ˈral-ət-ē\ *n* — **col·lat·er·al·ly** \-ˈlat-ə-rə-lē, -ˈla-trə-\ *adv*

[2]**collateral** *n* **1** : a collateral relative **2** : property (as securities) pledged by a borrower to protect the interests of the lender **3** : a branch of a bodily part (as a vein)

col·lat·er·al·ize \kə-ˈlat-ə-rə-ˌlīz, -ˈla-trə-\ *vt* **-ized; -iz·ing** **1** : to make (a loan) secure with collateral **2** : to use (as securities) for collateral

col·la·tion \kə-ˈlā-shən, kä-, kō-\ *n* **1** [ME, fr. ML *collation-, collatio*, fr. LL, conference, fr. L, bringing together, comparison, fr. *collatus* (pp. of *conferre* to bring together, bestow upon), fr. *com-* + *latus*, pp. of *ferre* to carry] **a** : a light meal allowed on fast days in place of lunch or supper **b** : a light meal **2** [ME, fr. L *collation-, collatio*] : the act, process, or result of collating

col·league \ˈkäl-ˌēg *also* -ig\ *n* [MF *collegue*, fr. L *collega*, fr. *com-* + *legare* to appoint, depute — more at LEGATE] : an associate in a profession or in a civil or ecclesiastical office — **col·league·ship** \-ˌship\ *n*

col·leagues·man·ship \kə-ˈlēgz-mən-ˌship, kä-; ˈkäl-ˌēgz-, -igz-\ *n* : the theory or practice of attracting (as to a university) competent personnel by emphasizing the advantages to be gained by association with distinguished colleagues

[1]**col·lect** \ˈkäl-ikt *also* -ˌekt\ *n* [ME *collecte*, fr. OF, fr. ML *collecta*, short for *oratio ad collectam* prayer upon assembly] **1** : a short prayer comprising an invocation, petition, and conclusion; *specif*, *often cap* : one preceding the eucharistic Epistle and varying with the day **2** : COLLECTION

[2]**col·lect** \kə-ˈlekt\ *vb* [L *collectus*, pp. of *colligere* to collect, fr. *com-* + *legere* to gather] *vt* **1 a** : to bring together into one body or place **b** : to gather or exact from a number of persons or sources <~ taxes> **2** : INFER, DEDUCE **3** : to gain or regain control of <~ his thoughts> **4** : to claim as due and receive payment for **5** : to call for : pick up : ESCORT <~ his girl and bring her in to the cinema —F. T. B. Macartney> ~ *vi* **1** : to come together in a band, group, or mass : GATHER **2 a** : to collect objects **b** : to receive payment <~*ing* on his insurance> ***syn*** see GATHER — **col·lect·ible** *or* **col·lect·able** \-ˈlek-tə-bəl\ *adj*

[3]**col·lect** \kə-ˈlekt\ *adv or adj* : to be paid for by the receiver <send the package ~> <a ~ telephone call>

col·lec·ta·nea \ˌkäl-ˌek-ˈtā-nē-ə\ *n pl* [L, neut. pl. of *collectaneus* collected, fr. *collectus*, pp.] : collected writings; *also* : literary items forming a collection

col·lect·ed \kə-ˈlek-təd\ *adj* **1** : gathered together <the ~ works of Scott> **2** : possessed of calmness and composure often through concentrated effort **3** *of a gait* : performed or performable by a horse from a state of collection ***syn*** see COOL ***ant*** distracted, distraught — **col·lect·ed·ly** *adv* — **col·lect·ed·ness** *n*

col·lect·ible \kə-ˈlek-tə-bəl\ *n* : a cultural object other than an antique or such traditionally collectible items as stamps, coins, or works of art that is the subject of fancier interest

col·lec·tion \kə-ˈlek-shən\ *n* **1** : the act or process of collecting **2** : something collected; *esp* : an accumulation of objects gathered for study, comparison, or exhibition **3** : a standard pose of a well-handled saddle horse in which it is responsive to the bit and has its head arched at the poll and the hocks well under the body so that the center of gravity is toward the rear quarters

[1]**col·lec·tive** \kə-ˈlek-tiv\ *adj* **1** : denoting a number of persons or things considered as one group or whole <*flock* is a ~ word> **2 a** : formed by collecting : AGGREGATED **b** *of a fruit* : MULTIPLE **3 a** : of, relating to, or being a group of individuals **4** : marked by similarity among or with the members of a group **5** : collectivized or characterized by collectivism **6** : shared or assumed by all members of the group <~ leadership> — **col·lec·tive·ly** *adv*

[2]**collective** *n* **1** : a collective body : GROUP **2** : a cooperative unit or organization; *specif* : COLLECTIVE FARM

collective bargaining *n* : negotiation between an employer and union representatives usu. on wages, hours, and working conditions

collective farm *n* : a farm esp. in a communist country formed from many small holdings collected into a single unit for joint operation under governmental supervision

collective security *n* : the maintenance by common action of the security of all members of an association of nations

col·lec·tiv·isa·tion, col·lec·tiv·ise *chiefly Brit var of* COLLECTIVIZATION, COLLECTIVIZE

col·lec·tiv·ism \kə-ˈlek-ti-ˌviz-əm\ *n* : a political or economic theory advocating collective control esp. over production and distribution or a system marked by such control — **col·lec·tiv·ist** \-vəst\ *adj or n* — **col·lec·tiv·is·tic** \-ˌlek-ti-ˈvis-tik\ *adj* — **col·lec·tiv·is·ti·cal·ly** \-ti-k(ə-)lē\ *adv*

col·lec·tiv·i·ty \kə-ˌlek-ˈtiv-ət-ē, ˌkäl-ˌek-\ *n*, *pl* **-ties** **1** : the quality or state of being collective **2** : a collective whole; *esp* : the people as a body

col·lec·tiv·iza·tion \kə-ˌlek-ti-və-ˈzā-shən\ *n* : the act or process of collectivizing : the state of being collectivized

col·lec·tiv·ize \kə-ˈlek-ti-ˌvīz\ *vt* **-ized; -iz·ing** : to organize under collective control

col·lec·tor \kə-ˈlek-tər\ *n* **1** : an official who collects funds or moneys **2** : one that makes a collection <stamp ~> **3** : an object or device that collects <the statuette was a dust ~> **4** : a conductor maintaining contact between moving and stationary parts of an electric circuit — **col·lec·tor·ship** \-ˌship\ *n*

collector's item *n* : COLLECTIBLE

col·leen \kä-ˈlēn, ˈkäl-ˌēn\ *n* [IrGael *cailín*] : an Irish girl

col·lege \ˈkäl-ij\ *n* [ME, fr. MF, fr. L *collegium* society, fr. *collega* colleague — more at COLLEAGUE] **1** : a body of clergy living together and supported by a foundation **2** : a building used for an educational or religious purpose **3 a** : a self-governing constituent body of a university offering living quarters and instruction but not granting degrees <Balliol and Magdalen *Colleges* at Oxford> **b** : a preparatory or high school **c** : an independent institution of higher learning offering a course of general studies leading to a bachelor's degree **d** : a part of a university offering a specialized group of courses **e** : an institution offering instruction usu. in a professional, vocational, or technical field <war ~> <business ~> <barber ~> **4** : COMPANY, GROUP; *specif* : an organized body of persons engaged in a common pursuit or having common interests or duties **5 a** : a group of persons considered by law to be a unit **b** : a body of electors — compare ELECTORAL COLLEGE **6** : the faculty, students, or administration of a college — **college** *adj*

college boards *n pl* : a set of examinations given by a college entrance examination board and required by some colleges of all candidates for admission and by others of all those whose academic records are below a certain standard

col·le·gial \kə-ˈlē-j(ē-)əl, *esp for 2a also* -ˈlē-gē-əl\ *adj* **1** : COLLEGIATE **2 a** : marked by power or authority vested equally in each of a number of colleagues **b** : characterized by equal sharing of authority esp. by Roman Catholic bishops — **col·le·gial·ly** \-ē\ *adv*

col·le·gi·al·i·ty \-ˌlē-jē-ˈal-ət-ē, -ˌlē-gē-\ *n* : the relationship of colleagues; *specif* : parity among bishops sharing collegial authority in the Roman Catholic Church

col·le·gian \kə-ˈlē-j(ē-)ən\ *n* : a student or recent graduate of a college

col·le·giate \kə-ˈlē-jət, -jē-ət\ *adj* [ML *collegiatus*, fr. L *collegium*] **1** : of or relating to a collegiate church **2** : of, relating to, or comprising a college **3** : COLLEGIAL 2 **4** : designed for or characteristic of college students — **col·le·giate·ly** *adv*

collegiate church *n* **1** : a church other than a cathedral that has a chapter of canons **2** : a church or corporate group of churches under the joint pastorate of two or more ministers

col·le·gi·um \kə-ˈleg-ē-əm, -ˈläg-\ *n*, *pl* **-gia** \-ē-ə\ *or* **-gi·ums** [modif. of Russ *kollegya*, fr. L *collegium*] : a group in which each member has approximately equal power and authority; *esp* : one in a soviet organization

col·lem·bo·lan \kə-ˈlem-bə-lən\ *n* [deriv. of *coll-* + Gk *embolos* wedge, stopper — more at EMBOLUS] : any of an order (Collembola) of small primitive wingless arthropods related to or classed among the insects — called also *springtail* — **collembolan** *or* **col·lem·bo·lous** \-ləs\ *adj*

col·len·chy·ma \kə-ˈleŋ-kə-mə, kä-\ *n* [NL] **:** a plant tissue of living usu. elongated cells with walls variously thickened esp. at the angles but capable of further growth — compare SCLERENCHYMA — **col·len·chy·ma·tous** \ˌkäl-ən-ˈkim-ət-əs, -ˈkī-mət-\ *adj*

col·let \ˈkäl-ət\ *n* [MF, dim. of *col* collar, fr. L *collum* neck — more at COLLAR] **:** a metal band, collar, ferrule, or flange; as **a :** a small collar pierced to receive the inner end of a balance spring on a timepiece **b :** a circle or flange in which a gem is set

col·lide \kə-ˈlīd\ *vi* **col·lid·ed; col·lid·ing** [L *collidere*, fr. *com-* + *laedere* to injure by striking] **1 :** to come together with solid impact **2 :** CLASH

col·lie \ˈkäl-ē\ *n* [prob. fr. E dial. *colly* (black)] **:** a large dog of a breed developed in Scotland esp. for use in herding sheep

col·lier \ˈkäl-yər\ *n* [ME *colier*, fr. *col* coal] **1 :** one that produces charcoal **2 :** a coal miner **3 :** a ship employed in transporting coal

col·liery \ˈkäl-yə-rē\ *n, pl* **-lier·ies :** a coal mine and its connected buildings

col·lie·shang·le \ˈkäl-ē-ˌshaŋ-ē, ˈkəl-\ *n* [perh. fr. *collie* + *shang* (kind of meal)] *Scot* **:** SQUABBLE, BRAWL

col·li·gate \ˈkäl-ə-ˌgāt\ *vb* **-gat·ed; -gat·ing** [L *colligatus*, pp. of *colligare*, fr. *com-* + *ligare* to tie — more at LIGATURE] *vt* **1 :** to bind, unite, or group together **2 :** to subsume (isolated facts) under a general concept ~ *vi* **:** to be or become a member of a group or unit — **col·li·ga·tion** \ˌkäl-ə-ˈgā-shən\ *n*

col·li·ga·tive \ˈkäl-ə-ˌgāt-iv\ *adj* **:** depending on the number of particles (as molecules) and not on the nature of the particles <pressure is a ~ property>

col·li·mate \ˈkäl-ə-ˌmāt\ *vt* **-mat·ed; -mat·ing** [L *collimatus*, pp. of *collimare*, MS var. of *collineare* to make straight, fr. *com-* + *linea* line] **1 :** to make (as rays of light) parallel **2 :** to adjust the line of sight of (a transit or level) — **col·li·ma·tion** \ˌkäl-ə-ˈmā-shən\ *n*

col·li·ma·tor \ˈkäl-ə-ˌmāt-ər\ *n* **1 :** a device for producing a beam of parallel rays of light or other radiation or for forming an infinitely distant virtual image that can be viewed without parallax **2 :** a device for obtaining a beam of molecules, atoms, or nuclear particles of limited cross section

col·lin·ear \kə-ˈlin-ē-ər, kä-\ *adj* [ISV] **1 :** lying on or passing through the same straight line **2 :** having axes lying end to end in a straight line <~ antenna elements> — **col·lin·ear·i·ty** \-ˌlin-ē-ˈar-ət-ē\ *n*

col·lins \ˈkäl-ənz\ *n* [prob. fr. the name *Collins*] **:** a tall iced drink that usu. has lemon juice added to a base of distilled liquor (as gin)

col·lin·sia \kə-ˈlin-zē-ə, kä-\ *n* [NL, genus name, fr. Zaccheus *Collins* †1831 Am botanist] **:** any of a genus (*Collinsia*) of U.S. biennial or annual herbs of the figwort family

col·li·sion \kə-ˈlizh-ən\ *n* [ME, fr. L *collision-*, *collisio*, fr. *collisus*, pp. of *collidere*] **1 :** an act or instance of colliding **:** CLASH **2 :** an encounter between particles (as atoms or molecules) resulting in exchange or transformation of energy — **col·li·sion·al** \-ˈlizh-nəl, -ən-ᵊl\ *adj*

collision course *n* **:** a course (as of moving bodies or antithetical philosophies) that will result in collision or conflict if continued unaltered <Roosevelt's idealism was on a *collision course* with Stalin's spheres-of-interest realpolitik —M. F. Harrington>

collo- — see COLL-

col·lo·cate \ˈkäl-ə-ˌkāt\ *vb* **-cat·ed; -cat·ing** [L *collocatus*, pp. of *collocare*, fr. *com-* + *locare* to place, fr. *locus* place — more at STALL] *vt* **:** to set or arrange in a place or position; *esp* **:** to set side by side ~ *vi* **:** to occur in conjunction with

col·lo·ca·tion \ˌkäl-ə-ˈkā-shən\ *n* **:** the act or result of placing or arranging together; *specif* **:** a noticeable arrangement or conjoining of linguistic elements (as words) — **col·lo·ca·tion·al** \-shnəl, -shən-ᵊl\ *adj*

col·lo·di·on \kə-ˈlōd-ē-ən\ *n* [modif. of NL *collodium*, fr. Gk *kollōdēs* glutinous, fr. *kolla* glue] **:** a viscous solution of pyroxylin used esp. as a coating for wounds or for photographic films

col·logue \kə-ˈlōg\ *vi* **col·logued; col·logu·ing** [origin unknown] **1** *dial* **:** INTRIGUE, CONSPIRE **2 :** to talk privately **:** CONFER

col·loid \ˈkäl-ˌȯid\ *n* [ISV *coll-* + *-oid*] **1 a :** a substance that is in a state of division preventing passage through a semipermeable membrane, consists of particles too small for resolution with an ordinary light microscope, and in suspension or solution fails to settle out and diffracts a beam of light **b :** a system consisting of a colloid together with the gaseous, liquid, or solid medium in which it is dispersed **2 :** a gelatinous or mucinous substance found in tissues in disease or normally (as in the thyroid) — **col·loi·dal** \kə-ˈlȯid-ᵊl, kä-\ *adj* — **col·loi·dal·ly** \-ᵊl-ē\ *adv*

col·lop \ˈkäl-əp\ *n* [ME] **1 :** a small piece or slice esp. of meat **2 :** a fold of fat flesh

colloq *abbr* colloquial

col·lo·qui·al \kə-ˈlō-kwē-əl\ *adj* **1 :** of or relating to conversation **:** CONVERSATIONAL **2 a :** used in or characteristic of familiar and informal conversation **b :** using conversational style — **colloquial** *n* — **col·lo·qui·al·i·ty** \-ˌlō-kwē-ˈal-ət-ē\ *n* — **col·lo·qui·al·ly** \-ˈlō-kwē-ə-lē\ *adv*

col·lo·qui·al·ism \-ˈlō-kwē-ə-ˌliz-əm\ *n* **1 a :** a colloquial expression **b :** a local or regional dialect expression **2 :** colloquial style

col·lo·quist \ˈkäl-ə-kwəst\ *n* **:** SPEAKER

col·lo·qui·um \kə-ˈlō-kwē-əm\ *n, pl* **-qui·ums** *or* **-quia** \-kwē-ə\ [L, colloquy] **:** a usu. academic meeting at which one or more specialists deliver addresses on a topic or on related topics and then answer questions relating thereto

col·lo·quy \ˈkäl-ə-kwē\ *n, pl* **-quies** [L *colloquium*, fr. *colloqui* to converse, fr. *com-* + *loqui* to speak] **1 :** CONVERSATION, DIALOGUE **2 :** a high-level serious discussion **:** CONFERENCE

col·lo·type \ˈkäl-ə-ˌtīp\ *n* [ISV] **1 :** a photomechanical process for making prints directly from a hardened film of gelatin or other colloid that has ink-receptive and ink-repellent parts **2 :** a print made by collotype

col·lude \kə-ˈlüd\ *vi* **col·lud·ed; col·lud·ing** [L *colludere*, fr. *com-* + *ludere* to play, fr. *ludus* game — more at LUDICROUS] **:** CONSPIRE, PLOT

col·lu·sion \kə-ˈlü-zhən\ *n* [ME, fr. MF, fr. L *collusion-*, *collusio*, fr. *collusus*, pp. of *colludere*] **:** secret agreement or cooperation for an illegal or deceitful purpose — **col·lu·sive** \-ˈlü-siv, -ziv\ *adj* — **col·lu·sive·ly** *adv*

col·lu·vi·um \kə-ˈlü-vē-əm\ *n, pl* **-via** \-vē-ə\ *or* **-vi·ums** [NL, fr. ML, offscourings, alter. of L *colluvies*, fr. *colluere* to wash, fr. *com-* + *lavere* to wash — more at LYE] **:** rock detritus and soil accumulated at the foot of a slope — **col·lu·vi·al** \-vē-əl\ *adj*

col·ly \ˈkäl-ē\ *vt* **col·lied; col·ly·ing** [alter. of ME *colwen*, fr. (assumed) OE *colgian*, fr. OE *col* coal] *dial chiefly Brit* **:** to blacken with or as if with soot

col·lyr·i·um \kə-ˈlir-ē-əm\ *n, pl* **-ia** \-ē-ə\ *or* **-i·ums** [L, fr. Gk *kollyrion* pessary, eye salve, fr. dim. of *kollyra* roll of bread] **:** an eye lotion **:** EYEWASH

col·ly·wob·bles \ˈkäl-ē-ˌwäb-əlz\ *n pl but sing or pl in constr* [prob. by folk etymology, fr. NL *cholera morbus*, lit., the disease cholera] **:** BELLYACHE

Colo *abbr* Colorado

colo- — see COL-

co·lo·cate \(ˈ)kō-ˈlō-ˌkāt, ˈkō-lō-\ *vt* **:** to place two or more units in close proximity so as to share common facilities

col·o·cynth \ˈkäl-ə-ˌsin(t)th\ *n* [L *colocynthis*] **:** a Mediterranean and African herbaceous vine (*Citrullus colocynthis*) related to the watermelon; *also* **:** its spongy fruit from which a powerful cathartic is prepared

colog *abbr* cologarithm

co·log·a·rithm \(ˈ)kō-ˈlȯg-ə-ˌrith-əm, -ˈläg-\ *n* **:** the logarithm of the reciprocal

co·logne \kə-ˈlōn\ *n* [*Cologne*, Germany] **1 :** a perfumed toilet water **2 :** a cream or paste of cologne sometimes formed into a semisolid stick — **co·logned** \-ˈlōnd\ *adj*

1**co·lon** \ˈkō-lən\ *n, pl* **colons** *or* **co·la** \-lə\ [L, fr. Gk *kolon*] **:** the part of the large intestine that extends from the cecum to the rectum — **co·lon·ic** \kō-ˈlän-ik\ *adj*

2**colon** *n, pl* **colons** *or* **co·la** \-lə\ [L, part of a poem, fr. Gk *kōlon* limb, part of a strophe — more at CALK] **1** *pl* **cola :** a rhythmical unit of an utterance; *specif, in Greek or Latin verse* **:** a system or series of from two to not more than six feet having a principal accent and forming part of a line **2** *pl* **colons a :** a punctuation mark : used chiefly to direct attention to matter (as a list, explanation, or quotation) that follows **b :** the sign : used between the parts of a numerical expression of time in hours and minutes (as in 1:15) or in hours, minutes, and seconds (as in 8:25:30), in a bibliographical reference (as in *Nation* 130:20), in a ratio where it is usu. read as "to" (as in 4:1 read "four to one"), or in a proportion where it is usu. read as "is to" or when doubled as "as" (as in 2:1::8:4 read "two is to one as eight is to four")

3**co·lon** \kō-lō^{n}, kə-ˈlōn\ *n* [F, fr. L *colonus*] **:** a colonial farmer or plantation owner

4**co·lon** \kə-ˈlōn\ *n, pl* **co·lo·nes** \-ˈlō-ˌnās\ [Sp *colón*] — see MONEY table

colon bacillus *n* **:** any of various bacilli (esp. genera *Escherichia* and *Aerobacter*) that are normally commensal in vertebrate intestines; *esp* **:** one (*E. coli*) used extensively in genetic research

col·o·nel \ˈkərn-ᵊl\ *n* [alter. of *coronel*, fr. MF, modif. of OIt *colonnello* column of soldiers, colonel, dim. of *colonna* column, fr. L *columna*] **1 a :** a commissioned officer in the army, air force, or marine corps ranking above a lieutenant colonel and below a brigadier general **b :** LIEUTENANT COLONEL **2 :** a minor titular official of a state esp. in southern or midland U.S. — used as an honorific title — **col·o·nel·cy** \-ᵊl-sē\ *n*

Colonel Blimp \ˌkərn-ᵊl-ˈblimp\ *n* [*Colonel Blimp*, cartoon character created by David Low] **:** a pompous person with out-of-date or ultraconservative views; *broadly* **:** REACTIONARY — **Colonel Blimp·ism** \-ˈblim-ˌpiz-əm\ *n*

1**co·lo·nial** \kə-ˈlō-nē-əl, -nyəl\ *adj* **1 :** of, relating to, or characteristic of a colony **2** *often cap* **:** of or relating to the original 13 colonies forming the United States: as **a :** made or prevailing in America during the colonial period <~ architecture was a modification of English Georgian> **b :** adapted from or reminiscent of an American colonial mode of design <~ furniture> **3 :** possessing or composed of colonies <Britain's ~ empire> — **co·lo·nial·ize** \-ˌīz\ *vt* — **co·lo·nial·ly** \-ē\ *adv* — **co·lo·nial·ness** *n*

2**colonial** *n* **1 :** a member or inhabitant of a colony **2 a :** a product made for use in a colony **b :** a product exhibiting colonial style

co·lo·nial·ism \-ˌiz-əm\ *n* **1 :** the quality or state of being colonial **2 :** something characteristic of a colony **3 a :** control by one power over a dependent area or people **b :** a policy advocating or based on such control — **co·lo·nial·ist** \-əst\ *n or adj* — **co·lo·nial·is·tic** \-ˌlō-nē-ə-ˈlis-tik, -nyə-ˈlis-\ *adj*

col·o·nist \ˈkäl-ə-nəst\ *n* **1 :** a member or inhabitant of a colony **2 :** one that colonizes or settles in a new country

col·o·ni·za·tion \ˌkäl-ə-nə-ˈzā-shən\ *n* **:** an act or instance of colonizing or of being colonized — **col·o·ni·za·tion·ist** \-sh(ə-)nəst\ *n*

col·o·nize \ˈkäl-ə-ˌnīz\ *vb* **-nized; -niz·ing** *vt* **1 a :** to establish a colony in or on or of **b :** to establish in a colony **2 :** to send illegal or irregularly qualified voters into <the machine was *colonizing* doubtful districts> **3 :** to infiltrate with usu. subversive militants for propaganda and strategy reasons <~ industries> ~ *vi* **:** to make or establish a colony **:** SETTLE — **col·o·niz·er** *n*

col·on·nade \ˌkäl-ə-ˈnād\ *n* [F, fr. It *colonnato*, fr. *colonna* column] **:** a series of columns set at regular intervals and usu. supporting the base of a roof structure — **col·on·nad·ed** \-ˈnād-əd\ *adj*

co·lo·nus \kə-ˈlō-nəs\ *n, pl* **-ni** \-ˌnī, -(ˌ)nē\ [L, lit., farmer] : a free-born serf in the later Roman Empire who could sometimes own property but who was bound to the land and obliged to pay a rent usu. in produce

col·o·ny \ˈkäl-ə-nē\ *n, pl* **-nies** [ME *colonie,* fr. MF & L; MF, fr. L *colonia,* fr. *colonus* farmer, colonist, fr. *colere* to cultivate — more at WHEEL] **1 a :** a body of people living in a new territory but retaining ties with the parent state **b :** the territory inhabited by such a body **2 :** a distinguishable localized population within a species <~ of termites> **3 a :** a circumscribed mass of microorganisms usu. growing in or on a solid medium **b :** the aggregation of zooids of a compound animal **4 a :** a group of individuals or things with common characteristics or interests situated in close association <an artist ~> <the growing ~ of off-Broadway satires —*Current Biog.*> **b :** the section occupied by such a group **5 :** a group of persons institutionalized away from others (as for care or correction) <a leper ~> <a penal ~>; *also* **:** the land or buildings occupied by such a group

col·o·phon \ˈkäl-ə-fən, -ˌfän\ *n* [L, fr. Gk *kolophōn* summit, finishing touch] **1 :** an inscription placed at the end of a book or manuscript usu. with facts relative to its production **2 :** an identifying device used by a printer or a publisher

colophon 2, of printer Peter Schöffer

co·lo·pho·ny \kə-ˈläf-ə-nē, ˈkäl-ə-ˌfō-\ *n, pl* **-nies** [ME *colophonie,* deriv. of Gk *Kolophōn* Colophon, an Ionian city] **:** ROSIN

¹col·or \ˈkəl-ər\ *n, often attrib* [ME *colour,* fr. OF, fr. L *color;* akin to L *celare* to conceal — more at HELL] **1 a :** a phenomenon of light (as red, brown, pink, or gray) or visual perception that enables one to differentiate otherwise identical objects **b :** the aspect of objects and light sources that may be described in terms of hue, lightness, and saturation for objects and hue, brightness, and saturation for light sources — used in this sense as the psychological basis for definitions of color in this dictionary **c :** a hue as contrasted with black, white, or gray **2 a :** an outward often deceptive show **:** APPEARANCE <his story has the ~ of truth> **b :** a legal claim to or appearance of a right, authority, or office **c :** a pretense offered as justification **:** PRETEXT <she could have drawn from the Versailles treaty the ~ of legality for any action she chose —*Yale Rev.*> **d :** an appearance of authenticity **:** PLAUSIBILITY <lending ~ to this notion> **3 :** complexion tint: **a :** the tint characteristic of good health **b :** BLUSH **4 a :** vividness or variety of effects of language <that ~ and force of style which were later to make him outstanding —Arthur Krock> **b :** LOCAL COLOR **5 a :** an identifying badge, pennant, or flag — usu. used in pl. <a ship sailing under Swedish ~*s*> **b :** colored clothing distinguishing one as a member of a particular group or representative of a particular person or thing — usu. used in pl. <a jockey riding under the ~*s* of his stable> **6 a** *pl* **:** position as to a question or course of action **:** STAND <the USSR changed neither its ~*s* nor its stripes during all of this —Norman Mailer> **b :** CHARACTER, NATURE — usu. used in pl. <showed himself in his true ~*s*> **7 :** the use or combination of colors **8** *pl* **a :** a naval or nautical salute to a flag being hoisted or lowered **b :** ARMED FORCES **9 :** VITALITY, INTEREST <the play had a good deal of ~ to it> **10 :** something used to give color **:** PIGMENT **11 :** tonal quality in music <the ~ and richness of the instrument> **12 :** skin pigmentation other than white characteristic of race **13 :** a small particle of gold in a gold miner's pan after washing **14 :** analysis of game action or strategy, statistics and background information on participants, and often anecdotes provided by a sportscaster to give variety and interest to the broadcast of a game or contest — **color** *adj* — **col·or·ism** \-ə-ˌriz-əm\ *n*

²color *vb* **col·ored; col·or·ing** \ˈkəl-(ə-)riŋ\ *vt* **1 a :** to give color to **b :** to change the color of (as by dyeing, staining, or painting) **2 :** to change as if by dyeing or painting: as **a :** MISREPRESENT, DISTORT **b :** GLOSS, EXCUSE <~ a lie> **c :** INFLUENCE, AFFECT <the lives of most of us have been ~*ed* by politics —Christine Weston> **3 :** CHARACTERIZE, LABEL <call it progress; ~ it inevitable with shades of job security —C. E. Price> ~ *vi* **:** to take on color; *specif* **:** BLUSH — **col·or·er** \ˈkəl-ər-ər\ *n*

col·or·able \ˈkəl-(ə-)rə-bəl\ *adj* **1 :** seemingly valid or genuine **2 :** intended to deceive **:** COUNTERFEIT <~ piety> *syn* see PLAUSIBLE — **col·or·ably** \-blē\ *adv*

Col·o·ra·do potato beetle \ˌkäl-ə-ˈrad-ō-, -ˈräd-\ *n* [*Colorado,* state of U.S.] **:** a black-and-yellow striped beetle (*Leptinotarsa decimlineata*) that feeds on the leaves of the potato — called also *potato beetle, potato bug*

col·or·ation \ˌkəl-ə-ˈrā-shən\ *n* **1 a :** the state of being colored <the dark ~ of his skin> **b :** use or choice of colors (as by an artist <Millet's subdued ~> **c :** arrangement of colors <the brilliant ~ of a butterfly's wing> **2 a :** characteristic quality <the newspapers . . . took on the former ~ of the magazine —L. B. Seltzer> **b :** aspect suggesting an attitude **:** PERSUASION <the chameleon talent for taking on the intellectual ~ of whatever idea he happened to fasten onto —Budd Schulberg> **3 :** subtle variation of intensity or quality of tone <a wide range of ~ from the orchestra>

col·or·a·tu·ra \ˌkəl-ə-rə-ˈt(y)u̇r-ə\ *n* [obs. It, lit., coloring, fr. LL, fr. L *coloratus,* pp. of *colorare* to color, fr. *color*] **1 :** elaborate embellishment in vocal music; *broadly* **:** music with ornate figuration **2 :** a soprano with a light, agile voice specializing in coloratura

color bar *n* **:** a barrier preventing colored persons from participating with whites in various activities — called also *color line*

col·or–bear·er \ˈkəl-ər-ˌbar-ər, -ˌber-\ *n* **:** one that carries a color or standard esp. in a military parade or drill

col·or–blind \-ˌblīnd\ *adj* **1 :** affected with partial or total inability to distinguish one or more chromatic colors **2 :** INSENSITIVE, OBLIVIOUS **3 :** not recognizing differences of race <tried to get the welfare establishment in Washington to abandon its ~ policy —D. P. Moynihan>; *esp* **:** free from racial prejudice <a white man with an invisible black skin in a ~ community —James Farmer> — **color blindness** *n*

col·or·breed \-ˌbrēd\ *vt* **-bred; -breed·ing :** to breed selectively for the development of particular colors <~*ing* canaries for red>

col·or·cast \-ˌkast\ *n* [*color* + tele*cast*] **:** a television broadcast in color — **colorcast** *vb*

col·or·cast·er \-ˌkas-tər\ *n* [*color* + broad*caster*] **:** a broadcaster (as of a sports contest) who supplies vivid or picturesque details and often gives statistical or analytical information

¹col·ored \ˈkəl-ərd\ *adj* **1 :** having color **2 a :** COLORFUL **b :** marked by exaggeration or bias **3 a :** of a race other than the white; *esp* **:** NEGRO **b :** of mixed race **4 :** of or relating to colored persons

²colored *n, pl* **colored** *or* **coloreds** *often cap* **:** a colored person

col·or·fast \ˈkəl-ər-ˌfast\ *adj* **:** having color that retains its original hue without fading or running — **col·or·fast·ness** \-ˌfas(t)-nəs\ *n*

color filter *n* **:** FILTER 3b

col·or·ful \ˈkəl-ər-fəl\ *adj* **1 :** having striking colors **2 :** full of variety or interest — **col·or·ful·ly** \-f(ə-)lē\ *adv* — **col·or·ful·ness** \-fəl-nəs\ *n*

color guard *n* **:** a guard of honor for the colors of an organization

col·or·if·ic \ˌkəl-ə-ˈrif-ik\ *adj* **:** capable of communicating color

col·or·im·e·ter \ˌkəl-ə-ˈrim-ət-ər\ *n* [ISV] **:** an instrument or device for determining and specifying colors; *specif* **:** one used for chemical analysis by comparison of a liquid's color with standard colors — **col·or·i·met·ric** \ˌkəl-ə-rə-ˈme-trik\ *adj* — **col·or·i·met·ri·cal·ly** \-tri-k(ə-)lē\ *adv* — **col·or·im·e·try** \ˌkəl-ə-ˈrim-ə-trē\ *n*

col·or·ing \ˈkəl-(ə-)riŋ\ *n* **1 a :** the act of applying colors **b :** something that produces color or color effects **c (1) :** the effect produced by applying or combining colors **(2) :** natural color **(3) :** COMPLEXION, COLORATION **d :** change of appearance (as by adding color) **2 :** INFLUENCE, BIAS **3 :** COLOR 4 **4 :** TIMBRE, QUALITY

col·or·ist \ˈkəl-ə-rəst\ *n* **:** one that colors or deals with color — **col·or·is·tic** \ˌkəl-ə-ˈris-tik\ *adj* — **col·or·is·ti·cal·ly** \-ti-k(ə-)lē\ *adv*

col·or·less \ˈkəl-ər-ləs\ *adj* **:** lacking color: as **a :** PALLID, BLANCHED **b :** DULL, UNINTERESTING — **col·or·less·ly** *adv* — **col·or·less·ness** *n*

color phase *n* **1 a :** a genetic variant manifested by the occurrence of a skin or pelage color unlike the wild type of the animal group in which it appears **b :** an individual marked by such a variant **2 :** a seasonally variant pelage color

color photography *n* **:** photographic reproduction of images in nearly natural colors

color temperature *n* **:** the temperature at which a blackbody emits radiant energy competent to evoke a color the same as that evoked by radiant energy from a given source (as a lamp)

co·los·sal \kə-ˈläs-əl\ *adj* **1 :** of, relating to, or resembling a colossus **2 :** of a bulk, extent, power, or effect approaching or suggesting the stupendous or incredible **3 :** of an exceptional or astonishing degree *syn* see HUGE — **co·los·sal·ly** \-ə-lē\ *adv*

col·os·se·um \ˌkäl-ə-ˈsē-əm\ *n* [ML, fr. L, neut. of *colosseus* colossal, fr. *colossus*] **1** *cap* **:** an amphitheater built in Rome in the first century A.D. **2 :** COLISEUM 2

Co·los·sians \kə-ˈläsh-ənz *also* -ˈläs(h)-ē-ənz\ *n pl but sing in constr* **:** a letter written by St. Paul to the Christians of Colossae and included as a book in the New Testament — see BIBLE table

co·los·sus \kə-ˈläs-əs\ *n, pl* **co·los·sus·es** \-ˈläs-ə-səz\ *or* **co·los·si** \-ˈläs-ˌī\ [L, fr. Gk *kolossos*] **1 :** a statue of gigantic size and proportions **2 :** one that resembles a colossus in size or scope: **a :** a nation vastly larger and more powerful than those near it **b :** a huge industrial concern **c :** one remarkably outstanding and preeminent over others <such an artistic ~ as Michelangelo —Hunter Mead>

co·los·to·my \kə-ˈläs-tə-mē\ *n, pl* **-mies** [ISV ²*col-* + *-stomy*] **:** surgical formation of an artificial anus

co·los·trum \kə-ˈläs-trəm\ *n* [L, beastings] **:** milk secreted for a few days after parturition and characterized by high protein and immune body content — **co·los·tral** \-trəl\ *adj*

col·our \ˈkəl-ər\ *chiefly Brit var of* COLOR

-c·o·lous \k-ə-ləs\ *adj comb form* [L *-cola* inhabitant; akin to L *colere* to inhabit — more at WHEEL] **:** living or growing in or on <areni*colous*>

col·por·tage \ˈkäl-ˌpōrt-ij, -ˌpȯrt-; ˌkäl-pōr-ˈtäzh, -pȯr-\ *n* **:** a colporteur's work

col·por·teur \ˈkäl-ˌpōrt-ər, -ˌpȯrt-; ˌkäl-pōr-ˈtər, -pȯr-\ *n* [F, alter. of MF *comporteur,* fr. *comporter* to bear, peddle] **:** a peddler of religious books

colt \ˈkōlt\ *n* [ME, fr. OE; akin to OE *cild* child] **1 a :** FOAL **b :** a young male horse that is either sexually immature or has not attained an arbitrarily designated age **2 :** a young untried person **:** NOVICE

colter *var of* COULTER

colt·ish \ˈkōl-tish\ *adj* **1 a :** not subjected to discipline **b :** FRISKY, PLAYFUL **2 :** of, relating to, or resembling a colt — **colt·ish·ly** *adv* — **colt·ish·ness** *n*

colts·foot \ˈkōlts-ˌfu̇t\ *n, pl* **coltsfoots :** any of various plants with large rounded leaves resembling the foot of a colt; *esp* **:** a perennial composite herb (*Tussilago farfara*) with yellow flower heads appearing before the leaves

col·u·brid \ˈkäl-(y)ə-brəd\ *n* [deriv. of L *colubra* snake] **:** any of a large cosmopolitan family (Colubridae) of nonvenomous snakes — **colubrid** *adj*

col·u·brine \-ˌbrīn\ *adj* **1 :** of, relating to, or resembling a snake **2 :** COLUBRID

co·lu·go \kə-ˈlü-(ˌ)gō\ *n, pl* **-gos** [prob. native name in Malaya] **:** FLYING LEMUR

col·um·bar·i·um \ˌkäl-əm-ˈbar-ē-əm, -ˈber-\ *n, pl* **-ia** \-ē-ə\ [L, lit., dovecote, fr. *columba* dove] **1 :** a structure of vaults lined with recesses for cinerary urns **2 :** a recess in a columbarium

Co·lum·bia \kə-ˈləm-bē-ə\ *n* [NL, fr. Christopher *Columbus*] **:** the United States

Co·lum·bi·an \-bē-ən\ *adj* **:** of or relating to the United States or to Christopher Columbus

col·um·bine \ˈkäl-əm-ˌbīn\ *n* [ME, fr. ML *columbina*, fr. L, fem. of *columbinus* dovelike, fr. *columba* dove; akin to OHG *holuntar* elder tree, Gk *kolymbos* a bird, *kelainos* black] **:** any of a genus (*Aquilegia*) of plants of the buttercup family with irregular showy spurred flowers: as **a :** a red-flowered plant (*A. canadensis*) of eastern No. America **b :** a blue-flowered plant (*A. coerulea*) of the Rocky mountains

Col·um·bine \-ˌbīn, -ˌbēn\ *n* [It *Colombina*] **:** the saucy sweetheart of Harlequin in comedy and pantomime

co·lum·bite \kə-ˈləm-ˌbīt, ˈkäl-əm-\ *n* [NL *columbium*] **:** a black mineral $(Fe,Mn)(Cb,Ta)_2O_6$ consisting essentially of iron and columbium

co·lum·bi·um \kə-ˈləm-bē-əm\ *n* [NL, fr. *Columbia*] **:** NIOBIUM

Columbus Day *n* **1 :** October 12 formerly observed as a legal holiday in many states of the U.S. in commemoration of the landing of Columbus in the Bahamas in 1492 **2 :** the second Monday in October observed as a legal holiday in many states of the U.S.

col·u·mel·la \ˌkäl-(y)ə-ˈmel-ə\ *n, pl* **-mel·lae** \-ˈmel-(ˌ)ē, -ˌī\ [NL, fr. L, dim. of *columna*] **1 a :** the bony or partly cartilaginous rod connecting the tympanic membrane with the internal ear in birds and in many reptiles and amphibians **b :** the bony central axis of the cochlea **2 :** the central column or axis of a spiral univalve shell **3 :** the axis of the capsule in mosses and in some liverworts **4 :** the central sterile portion of the sporangium in various fungi (*Mucor* and related genera) — **col·u·mel·lar** \-ˈmel-ər\ *adj* — **col·u·mel·late** \-ət, -ˌāt\ *adj*

col·umn \ˈkäl-əm\ *n* [ME *columne*, fr. MF *colomne*, fr. L *columna*, fr. *columen* top; akin to L *collis* hill — more at HILL] **1 a :** a vertical arrangement of items printed or written on a page **b :** one of two or more vertical sections of a printed page separated by a rule or blank space **c :** an accumulation arranged vertically **:** STACK **d :** a special department or feature in a newspaper or periodical **2 :** a supporting pillar; *esp* **:** one consisting of a usu. round shaft, a capital, and a base **3 :** something resembling a column in form, position, or function <a ~ of water> **4 :** a long row (as of soldiers) **5 :** one of the vertical lines of elements of a determinant or matrix — **col·umned** \-əmd\ *adj*

CORNICE / FRIEZE / ARCHITRAVE / ENTABLATURE / CAPITAL / SHAFT / COLUMN / BASE / PEDESTAL

column 2 with pedestal and entablature

co·lum·nar \kə-ˈləm-nər\ *adj* **1 :** of, relating to, or characterized by columns **2 :** of, relating to, being, or composed of tall narrow somewhat cylindrical or prismatic epithelial cells

co·lum·ni·a·tion \kə-ˌləm-nē-ˈā-shən\ *n* [modif. of L *columnation-, columnatio*, fr. *columna*] **:** the employment or the arrangement of columns in a structure

column inch *n* **:** a unit of measure for printed matter one column wide and one inch deep

col·um·nist \ˈkäl-əm-(n)əst *also* ˈkäl-yəm-\ *n* **:** one who writes a newspaper or magazine column — **col·um·nis·tic** \ˌkäl-əm-ˈnis-tik *also* -yəm-\ *adj*

col·za \ˈkäl-zə, ˈkōl-\ *n* [F, fr. D *koolzaad*, fr. MD *coolsaet*, fr. *coole* cabbage + *saet* seed] **1 :** any of several coles; *esp* **:** one (as rape) producing seed used as a source of oil **2 :** RAPESEED

¹com *abbr* **1** comedy; comic **2** comma

²com *or* **comm** *abbr* **1** command; commandant; commander; commanding **2** commentary **3** commerce; commercial **4** commission; commissioned; commissioner **5** committee **6** common; commoner **7** commonwealth **8** commune **9** communication **10** communist **11** community

COM *abbr* computer output microfilm; computer output microfilmer

com- *or* **col-** *or* **con-** *prefix* [ME, fr. OF, fr. L, with, together, thoroughly — more at CO-] **:** with **:** together **:** jointly — usu. *com-* before *b, p,* or *m* <*com*mingle>, *col-* before *l* <*col*linear>, and *con-* before other sounds <*con*centrate>

¹co·ma \ˈkō-mə\ *n* [NL, fr. Gk *kōma* deep sleep] **1 :** a state of profound unconsciousness caused by disease, injury, or poison **2 :** a state of mental or physical sluggishness **:** TORPOR

²coma *n, pl* **co·mae** \-ˌmē, -ˌmī\ [L, hair, fr. Gk *komē*] **1 :** a tufted bunch (as of branches, bracts, or seed hairs) **2 :** the head of a comet usu. containing a nucleus **3 :** spherical aberration in which the image of a point source is a comet-shaped blur — **co·mat·ic** \kō-ˈmat-ik\ *adj*

Co·ma Ber·e·ni·ces \ˈkō-mə-ˌber-ə-ˈnī-(ˌ)sēz\ *n* [L (gen. *Comae Berenices*), lit., Berenice's hair] **:** a constellation north of Virgo and between Boötes and Leo

co·mak·er \(ˈ)kō-ˈmā-kər\ *n* **:** one that participates in an agreement; *specif* **:** one who stands to meet a financial obligation in case of another's default

Co·man·che \kə-ˈman-chē\ *n, pl* **Comanche** *or* **Comanches** [Sp, of Shoshonean origin; perh. akin to Hopi *kománči* scalp lock] **:** a member of an Amerindian people ranging from Wyoming and Nebraska south into New Mexico and northwestern Texas

Co·man·che·an \-chē-ən\ *adj* [*Comanche*, Texas] **:** of, relating to, or being the period of the Mesozoic era between the Jurassic and the Cretaceous or the corresponding system of rocks — **Comanchean** *n*

co·mate \(ˈ)kō-ˈmāt, ˈkō-ˌ\ *n* **:** COMPANION

co·ma·tose \ˈkō-mə-ˌtōs, ˈkäm-ə-\ *adj* [F *comateux*, fr. Gk *kōmat-, kōma*] **1 :** of, resembling, or affected with coma **2 :** characterized by lethargic inertness **:** TORPID <a ~ economy> ***syn*** see LETHARGIC ***ant*** awake

co·mat·u·lid \kō-ˈmach-ə-ləd\ *n* [deriv. of LL *comatulus* having hair neatly curled, fr. L *comatus* hairy, fr. *coma*] **:** any of an order (Comatulida) of free-swimming stalkless crinoids — called also *feather star*

¹comb \ˈkōm\ *n* [ME, fr. OE *camb*; akin to OHG *kamb* comb, Gk *gomphos* tooth] **1 a :** a toothed instrument used esp. for adjusting, cleaning, or confining hair **b :** a structure resembling such a comb; *esp* **:** any of several toothed devices used in handling or ordering textile fibers **c :** CURRYCOMB **2 a :** a fleshy crest on the head of the domestic fowl and other gallinaceous birds — see COCK illustration **b :** something (as the ridge of a roof) resembling the comb of a cock **3 :** HONEYCOMB — **combed** \ˈkōmd\ *adj* — **comb·like** \ˈkōm-ˌlīk\ *adj*

²comb *vt* **1 :** to draw a comb through for the purpose of arranging or cleaning **2 :** to pass across with a scraping or raking action **3 a :** to eliminate (as with a comb) by a thorough going over **b :** to search or examine systematically **4 :** to use in a combing action ~ *vi* **:** to roll over or break into foam <waves ~>

³comb *abbr* **1** combination; combined; combining **2** combustion

¹com·bat \kəm-ˈbat, ˈkäm-ˌ\ *vb* **-bat·ed** *or* **-bat·ted**; **-bat·ing** *or* **-bat·ting** [MF *combattre*, fr. (assumed) VL *combattere*, fr. L *com-* + *battuere* to beat — more at BATTLE] *vi* **:** to engage in combat **:** FIGHT ~ *vt* **1 :** to fight with **:** BATTLE **2 :** to struggle against; *esp* **:** to strive to reduce or eliminate <~ inflation> ***syn*** see OPPOSE

²com·bat \ˈkäm-ˌbat\ *n* **1 :** a fight or contest between individuals or groups **2 :** CONFLICT, CONTROVERSY **3 :** active fighting in a war **:** ACTION <casualties suffered in ~>

³com·bat \ˈkäm-ˌbat\ *adj* **1 :** relating to combat <~ missions> **2 :** designed or destined for combat <~ troops>

com·bat·ant \kəm-ˈbat-ᵊnt *also* ˈkäm-bət-ənt\ *n* **:** one that is engaged in or ready to engage in combat — **combatant** *adj*

combat fatigue *n* **:** a traumatic psychoneurotic reaction or an acute psychotic reaction occurring under conditions (as wartime combat) that cause intense stress

com·bat·ive \kəm-ˈbat-iv\ *adj* **:** marked by eagerness to fight or contend <the ~ element in human nature> ***syn*** see BELLIGERENT ***ant*** pacifistic — **com·bat·ive·ly** *adv* — **com·bat·ive·ness** *n*

combe \ˈküm, ˈkōm\ *n* [of Celt origin; akin to W *cwm* valley] **1** *Brit* **:** a deep narrow valley **2** *Brit* **:** a valley or basin on the flank of a hill

comb·er \ˈkō-mər\ *n* **1 :** one that combs **2 :** a long curling wave of the sea

com·bin·abil·i·ty \kəm-ˌbī-nə-ˈbil-ət-ē\ *n* **:** ability to enter into combination — **com·bin·able** \-ˈbī-nə-bəl\ *adj*

com·bi·nate \ˈkäm-bə-ˌnāt\ *vt* **-nat·ed; -nat·ing** **1** [L *combinatus*, pp. of *combinare*] **:** COMBINE **2** [back-formation fr. *combination*] **:** to set up the combination of (a lock)

com·bi·na·tion \ˌkäm-bə-ˈnā-shən\ *n, often attrib* **1 a :** a result or product of combining; *esp* **:** an alliance of individuals, corporations, or states united to achieve a social, political, or economic end **b :** two or more persons working as a team <a double-play ~> **2 :** an ordered sequence: as **a :** a sequence of letters or numbers chosen in setting a lock; *also* **:** the mechanism operating or moved by the sequence **b :** any of the different sets of k individuals (as letters) that can be chosen from a population of size n and are considered without regard to order within the set **3 :** any of various one-piece undergarments for the upper and lower parts of the body **4 :** an instrument designed to perform two or more tasks **5 a :** the act or process of combining; *esp* **:** that of uniting to form a chemical compound **b :** the quality or state of being combined — **com·bi·na·tion·al** \-shnəl, -shən-ᵊl\ *adj*

combination shot *n* **:** a shot in pool in which a ball is pocketed by an object ball

com·bi·na·tive \ˈkäm-bə-ˌnāt-iv, kəm-ˈbī-nət-\ *adj* **1 :** tending or able to combine **2 :** resulting from combination

com·bi·na·to·ri·al \kəm-ˌbī-nə-ˈtōr-ē-əl, ˌkäm-bə-nə-, -ˈtȯr-\ *adj* **1 :** of, relating to, or involving combinations **2 :** of or relating to the arrangement, operation, and selection of mathematical elements within finite sets and configurations <~ mathematics>

combinatorial topology *n* **:** a study that deals with geometric forms based on their decomposition into combinations of the simplest geometric figures

com·bi·na·tor·ics \-ˈtōr-iks, -ˈtär-\ *n pl but sing in constr* **:** combinatorial mathematics

com·bi·na·to·ry \kəm-ˈbī-nə-ˌtōr-ē, -ˌtȯr-\ *adj* **:** COMBINATIVE

¹com·bine \kəm-ˈbīn\ *vb* **com·bined; com·bin·ing** [ME *combinen*, fr. MF *combiner*, fr. LL *combinare*, fr. L *com-* + *bini* two by two — more at BIN-] *vt* **1 a :** to bring into such close relationship as to obscure individual characters **:** MERGE **b :** to cause to unite into a chemical compound **2 :** INTERMIX, BLEND **3 :** to possess in combination ~ *vi* **1 a :** to become one **b :** to unite to form a chemical compound **2 :** to act together ***syn*** see JOIN ***ant*** separate — **com·bin·er** *n*

²com·bine \ˈkäm-ˌbīn\ *n* **1 :** a combination esp. of industrial interests **2 :** a harvesting machine that heads, threshes, and cleans grain while moving over a field

³com·bine \ˈkäm-ˌbīn\ *vt* **com·bined; com·bin·ing :** to harvest with a combine

comb·ing \ˈkō-miŋ\ *var of* COAMING

comb·ings \ˈkō-miŋz\ *n pl* **:** loose hair removed by a comb

combing wool *n* **:** long-staple strong-fibered wool found suitable for combing and used esp. in the manufacture of worsteds

com·bin·ing form \kəm-ˌbī-niŋ-\ *n* **:** a linguistic form that occurs only in compounds or derivatives and can be distinguished descriptively from an affix by its ability to occur as one immediate constituent of a form whose only other immediate constituent is an affix (as *cephal-* in *cephalic*) or by its being an allomorph of a morpheme having another allomorph that may occur alone or can be distinguished historically from an affix by the fact that it is borrowed from another language in which it is descriptively a word or a combining form

comb jelly *n* **:** CTENOPHORE

com·bo \'käm-(,)bō\ *n, pl* **combos** [*comb*ination + *-o*] **1** : COMBINATION **2** : a usu. small jazz or dance band

com·bust \kəm-'bəst\ *vb* [L *combustus,* pp. of *comburere* to burn up, irreg. fr. *com-* + *urere* to burn — more at EMBER] : BURN

com·bus·ti·ble \kəm-'bəs-tə-bəl\ *adj* **1** : capable of combustion **2** : easily excited — **com·bus·ti·bil·i·ty** \-,bəs-tə-'bil-ət-ē\ *n* — **combustible** *n* — **com·bus·ti·bly** \-'bəs -tə-blē\ *adv*

com·bus·tion \kəm-'bəs-chən\ *n* **1** : an act or instance of burning **2 a** : a chemical process (as an oxidation) accompanied by the evolution of light and heat **b** : a slower oxidation **3** : violent agitation : TUMULT <he is seething with inner ~ —*Current Biog.*> — **com·bus·tive** \-'bəs-tiv\ *adj*

com·bus·tor \-'bəs-tər\ *n* : a chamber (as in a gas turbine or a jet engine) in which combustion occurs

comd *abbr* command

comdg *abbr* commanding

comdr *abbr* commander

comdt *abbr* commandant

come \'kəm, *sometimes without stress when a stress follows*\ *vb* **came** \'kām\; **come; com·ing** \'kəm-iŋ\ [ME *comen,* fr. OE *cuman;* akin to OHG *queman* to come, L *venire,* Gk *bainein* to walk, go] *vi* **1 a** : to move toward something : APPROACH <~ here> **b** : to move or journey to a vicinity with a specified purpose <he *came* to see us> <~ see us> <~ and see what's going on> **c** (1) : to reach a particular station in a series <now we ~ to the section on health> (2) : to arrive in due course <the time has ~> **d** (1) : to approach in kind or quality <this ~*s* near perfection> (2) : to reach a condition <*came* to regard him as a friend> **e** (1) : to advance toward accomplishment <learning new ways doesn't ~ easy> <the job is *coming* nicely> (2) : to advance in a particular manner <~ running when I call> (3) : to advance, rise, or improve in rank or condition <has ~ a long way> **f** : to get along : FARE — often used with *along* **g** : EXTEND <her dress *came* to her ankles> **2 a** (1) : to arrive at a particular place, end, result, or conclusion <*came* to his senses> <~ untied> (2) : AMOUNT <taxes ~ to more than it's worth> **b** (1) : to appear to the mind <the answer *came* to him> (2) : to appear on a scene : make an appearance <children ~ equipped to learn any language> **c** : HAPPEN, OCCUR <no harm will ~ to you> **d** : ORIGINATE, ARISE <wine ~*s* from grapes><~ of sturdy stock> <the best play to ~ out of Europe this year> **e** : to enter or assume a condition <artillery *came* into action> **f** : to fall within a field of view or a range of application <this ~*s* within the terms of the treaty> **g** : to issue forth <a sob *came* from her throat> **h** : to take form <churn till the butter ~*s*> **i** : to be available <this model ~*s* in several sizes> <as good as they ~> **j** : to experience orgasm **3** : to fall to a person in a division or inheritance of property **4** *obs* : to become moved favorably : RELENT **5** : to turn out to be <good clothes ~ high> <*came* short of his goal> **6** : BECOME <a dream that *came* true> <things will ~ clear if we are patient> ~ *vt* **1** : to approach or be near (an age) <a child *coming* eight years old> **2** : to take on the aspect of <~ the stern parent> — **come a cropper** : to fail completely — **come across** : to meet or find by chance <*came across* a long lost friend today> — **come alive** : to become animated or responsive — **come apart** : to disintegrate physically or mentally — **come at** : to accomplish an understanding or mastery of : ATTAIN <art is not something to *come at* by dint of study —Clive Bell> — **come between** : to cause to be estranged <parents *came between* the lovers> — **come by** : to get possession of : ACQUIRE <a good job can be hard to *come by*> — **come clean** : to tell the whole story : CONFESS — **come from** : to be or have been a native or resident of — **come into** : to acquire as a possession or achievement <*come into* a fortune> — **come into one's own** : to achieve one's potential; *also* : to gain recognition — **come off it** : to cease foolish or pretentious talk or behavior — **come over** : to seize suddenly and strangely <what's *come over* you> — **come to** : to be a question of <when it *comes to* pitching horseshoes, he's the champ> — **come to grips with** : to wrestle with : meet firmly <*coming to grips with* the problem> — **come to life 1** : to regain consciousness or vitality **2** : to take on a real or lifelike quality <a writer whose characters *come to life*> — **come to oneself** : to get hold of oneself : regain self-control — **come to pass** : HAPPEN — **come upon** : to come across — **come with** : to be a concomitant of : accompany or follow upon as a matter of course <the increase of traffic that *comes with* new roads>

come about *vi* **1** : to come to pass : HAPPEN **2** : to change direction <the wind has *come about* into the north> **3** : to shift to a new tack

come across *vi* **1** : to give over or furnish something demanded; *esp* : to pay over money **2** : to produce an impression <*comes across* as a persuasive speaker>

come along *vi* **1** : to accompany someone who leads the way <asked me to *come along* to keep him company> **2** : to make progress : SUCCEED <the work is *coming along* quite well> **3** : to make an appearance <wouldn't just marry the first man that *came along*>

come around *vi* **1** : to come round **2** : MENSTRUATE

come·back \'kəm-,bak\ *n* **1 a** : a sharp or witty reply : RETORT **b** : a cause for complaint **2** : RECOVERY

come back \(,)kəm-'bak\ *vi* **1** : to return to life or vitality **2** : to return to memory <it's all *coming back* to me now> **3** : REPLY, RETORT **4** : to regain a former favorable condition or position

come by *vi* : to make a visit

co·me·di·an \kə-'mēd-ē-ən\ *n* **1** *archaic* **a** : a writer of comedies **b** : an actor who plays comic roles **2** : a comical individual; *specif* : a professional entertainer who uses any of various physical or verbal means to be amusing

co·me·dic \-'mēd-ik, -'med-\ *adj* **1** : of or relating to comedy **2** : COMICAL 2

co·me·di·enne \-,mēd-ē-'en\ *n* [F *comédienne,* fem. of *comédien* comedian, fr. *comédie*] : a female comedian

com·e·do \'käm-ə-,dō\ *n, pl* **com·e·do·nes** \,käm-ə-'dō-(,)nēz\ [NL, fr. L, glutton, fr. *comedere* to eat — more at COMESTIBLE] : BLACKHEAD 1

come·down \'kəm-,daùn\ *n* : a descent in rank or dignity

come down \(,)kəm-'daùn\ *vi* **1** : to pass by tradition <a story that has *come down* from medieval times> **2 a** : to reduce itself : AMOUNT <it *comes down* to this> **b** : to deal directly with <when you *come down* to it, we all depend on others> **3** : to lose or fall in estate or condition <he has *come down* in the world> **4** : to place oneself in opposition <the judge *came down* hard on gambling> **5** : to become ill <they *came down* with measles> **6** : to recover from the effects of a stimulant drug

com·e·dy \'käm-əd-ē\ *n, pl* **-dies** [ME, fr. MF *comedie,* fr. L *comoedia,* fr. Gk *kōmōidia,* fr. *kōmos* revel + *aeidein* to sing — more at ODE] **1 a** : a drama of light and amusing character and typically with a happy ending **b** : the genre of dramatic literature dealing with the comic or with the serious in a light or satirical manner — compare TRAGEDY **2 a** : a medieval narrative that ends happily <Dante's Divine *Comedy*> **b** : a literary work written in a comic style or treating a comic theme **3** : a ludicrous or farcical event or series of events **4** : the comic element <the ~ of many life situations>

comedy drama *n* : serious drama that is interspersed with comedy

comedy of manners : comedy that satirically portrays the manners and fashions of a particular class or set

come–hith·er \(,)kəm-'hith-ər, (,)kə-'mith-\ *adj* : sexually provocative <that ~ look in her eyes>

come in *vi* **1 a** : to arrive on a scene <new models *coming in*> **b** : to become available <data began *coming in*> **2** : to place among those finishing <*came in* second> **3 a** : to function in an indicated manner <*come in* handy> **b** : to make reply to a signal or call <*came in* loud and clear> **4** : to assume a role or function <that's where you *come in*> **5** : to attain maturity, fruitfulness, or production — **come in for** : to become subject to <*coming in for* increasing criticism>

come·ly \'kəm-lē *also* 'kōm- *or* 'käm-\ *adj* **come·li·er, -est** [ME *comly,* alter. of OE *cȳmlic* glorious, fr. *cȳme* lively, fine; akin to OHG *kūmig* weak, Gk *goan* to lament] **1** : having a generally pleasing appearance : not homely or plain **2** : pleasurably conforming to notions of good appearance, fitness, or proportion : SEEMLY <everything in neat and ~ arrangement> ***syn*** see BEAUTIFUL ***ant*** homely — **come·li·ness** *n*

come off *vi* **1** : to acquit oneself <*came off* well in the contest> **2** : SUCCEED <a television series that never *came off* —*TV Guide*> **3** : HAPPEN, OCCUR

come–on \'kəm-,ȯn, -,än\ *n* : an attraction used esp. in sales promotion

come on \(,)kəm-'ȯn, -'än\ *vi* **1 a** : to advance by degrees <as darkness *came on,* it got harder to see> **b** : to begin by degrees <rain *came on* toward noon> **2** : PLEASE — used in cajoling or pleading **3** : to project an indicated personal image <*comes on* as a liberal in his political speeches>

come out *vi* **1 a** : to come into public view : make a public appearance <a new magazine has *come out*> **b** : to become evident <his pride *came out* in his refusal to accept help> **2** : to declare oneself esp. in public utterance <*came out* in favor of the popular candidate> **3** : to turn out in an outcome : end up <everything will *come out* all right> **4** : to make a debut — **come out with 1** : to give expression to <he *came out with* an interesting proposal> **2** : PUBLISH

come–out·er \(,)kə-'maùt-ər\ *n* : RADICAL, REFORMER

come over *vi* **1 a** : to change from one side (as of a controversy) to the other **b** : to visit casually : drop in <*come over* anytime; we're always in> **2** *Brit* : BECOME

com·er \'kəm-ər\ *n* **1** : one that comes or arrives <all ~*s*> **2** : one making rapid progress or showing promise

come round *vi* **1** : to return to a former condition; *esp* : to come to **2** : to accede to a particular opinion or course of action <the rest of the world has *come round* to his way of living —David Halberstam> **3** : to change in direction <the wind *came round* at dawn>

[1]**co·mes·ti·ble** \kə-'mes-tə-bəl\ *adj* [MF, fr. ML *comestibilis,* fr. L *comestus,* pp. of *comedere* to eat, fr. *com-* + *edere* to eat — more at EAT] : EDIBLE

[2]**comestible** *n* : FOOD — usu. used in pl.

com·et \'käm-ət\ *n* [ME *comete,* fr. OE *cometa,* fr. L, fr. Gk *komētēs,* lit., long-haired, fr. *koman* to wear long hair, fr. *komē* hair] : a celestial body that consists of a fuzzy head usu. surrounding a bright nucleus, that often when in the part of its orbit near the sun develops a long tail which points away from the sun, and that has an orbit varying in eccentricity between nearly round and parabolic — **com·e·tary** \-ə-,ter-ē\ *adj* — **co·met·ic** \kə-'met-ik, kä-\ *adj*

come through *vi* **1** : to do what is needed or expected **2** : to become communicated

come to *vi* **1** : to recover consciousness **2 a** : to bring a ship's head nearer the wind : LUFF **b** : to come to anchor or to a stop

come up *vi* **1** : to come near : make an approach <*came up* and introduced himself> **2** : to rise in rank or status <an officer who *came up* from the ranks> **3 a** : to come to attention or consideration <the question never *came up* in discussion> **b** : to occur in the course of time <any problem that may *come up*> **4** : to get up — used typically in a command to a horse — **come up with** : to produce esp. in dealing with a problem or challenge <*came up with* a better solution>

come·up·pance \(,)kə-'məp-ən(t)s\ *n* [*come up* + *-ance*] : a deserved rebuke or penalty : DESERTS

com·fit \'kəm(p)-fət, 'käm(p)-\ *n* [ME *confit,* fr. MF, fr. pp. of *confire* to prepare, fr. L *conficere,* fr. *com-* + *facere* to make — more at DO] : a confection consisting of a piece of fruit, a root, or a seed coated and preserved with sugar

[1]**com·fort** \'kəm(p)-fərt\ *n* **1** : strengthening aid : **a** : ASSISTANCE, SUPPORT <accused of giving aid and *comfort* to the enemy> **b** : consolation in time of trouble or worry : SOLACE **2 a** : a feeling

of relief or encouragement **b :** contented well-being **3 :** a satisfying or enjoyable experience <the ~ of a good meal after hard work> **4 :** one that gives or brings comfort <the ~*s* of civilization> — **com·fort·less** \-ləs\ *adj*

[2]**comfort** *vt* [ME *comforten,* fr. OF *conforter,* fr. LL *confortare* to strengthen greatly, fr. L *com-* + *fortis* strong] **1 :** to give strength and hope to : CHEER **2 :** to ease the grief or trouble of : CONSOLE — **com·fort·ing·ly** \-iŋ-lē\ *adv*

syn COMFORT, CONSOLE, SOLACE *shared meaning element* **:** to act to ease the griefs or sufferings of (another) ***ant*** afflict, bother

com·fort·able \'kəm(p)-fərt-ə-bəl, 'kəm(p)(f)-tə(r)-bəl\ *adj* **1 a :** affording or enjoying contentment and security <a ~ income> **b :** affording or enjoying physical comfort <a ~ chair> <was too ~ to move> **2 a :** free from vexation or doubt <~ assumptions that require no thought> **b :** free from stress or tension <a ~ routine> — **com·fort·able·ness** *n* — **com·fort·ably** \-blē\ *adv*

syn COMFORTABLE, COZY, SNUG, EASY, RESTFUL *shared meaning element* **:** enjoying or providing circumstances that make for contentment and security ***ant*** uncomfortable, miserable

com·fort·er \'kəm(p)-fə(r)t-ər\ *n* **1 a** *cap* **:** HOLY SPIRIT **b :** one that gives comfort **2 a :** a long narrow usu. knitted neck scarf **b :** a warm bed covering : QUILT

comfort station *n* **:** REST ROOM

com·frey \'kəm(p)-frē\ *n, pl* **comfreys** [ME *cumfirie,* fr. OF, fr. L *conferva*] **:** any of a genus (*Symphytum*) of plants of the borage family with coarse hairy entire leaves and flowers in one-sided racemes

com·fy \'kəm(p)-fē\ *adj* **com·fi·er; -est** [by shortening & alter.] **:** COMFORTABLE

[1]**com·ic** \'käm-ik\ *adj* [L *comicus,* fr. Gk *kōmikos,* fr. *kōmos* revel] **1 :** of, relating to, or marked by comedy **2 :** causing laughter or amusement : FUNNY **3 :** of or relating to comic strips ***syn*** see LAUGHABLE

[2]**comic** *n* **1 :** COMEDIAN **2 :** the comic element **3 a :** COMIC STRIP **b** (1) **:** COMIC BOOK (2) *pl* **:** the part of a newspaper devoted to comic strips

com·i·cal \'käm-i-kəl\ *adj* **1** *obs* **:** of or relating to comedy **2 :** being of a kind to excite laughter esp. because of a startlingly or unexpectedly humorous impact ***syn*** see LAUGHABLE — **com·i·cal·i·ty** \ˌkäm-i-'kal-ət-ē\ *n* — **com·i·cal·ly** \'käm-i-k(ə-)lē\ *adv*

comic book *n* **:** a magazine containing sequences of comic strips

comic–opera *adj* **:** not to be taken seriously <a ~ state where the regime changes every few months>

comic opera *n* **:** opera having a usu. sentimental plot and characterized by spoken dialogue, humorous episodes, and usu. a happy ending

comic relief *n* **:** a relief from the emotional tension of a drama that is provided by the interposition of a comic episode

comic strip *n* **:** a group of cartoons in narrative sequence

[1]**com·ing** \'kəm-iŋ\ *n* **:** an act or instance of arriving

[2]**coming** *adj* **1 :** immediately due in sequence or development <~ year> **2 :** gaining importance

Com·in·tern \'käm-ən-ˌtərn\ *n* [Russ *Komintern,* fr. *Kommunisticheskiĭ Intern*atsional Communist International] **:** an international of Socialist organizations established in 1929

co·mi·tia \kə-'mish-(ē-)ə\ *n, pl* **comitia** [L, pl. of *comitium,* fr. *com-* + *itus,* pp. of *ire* to go — more at ISSUE] **:** one of several public assemblies of the people in ancient Rome for the exercise of legislative, judicial, and electoral functions — **co·mi·tial** \-'mish-əl\ *adj*

co·mi·ty \'käm-ət-ē, 'kō-mət-\ *n, pl* **-ties** [L *comitat-, comitas,* fr. *comis* courteous, fr. OL *cosmis,* fr. *com-* + *-smis* (akin to Skt *smayate* he smiles) — more at SMILE] **1 a :** friendly quality of social atmosphere : social harmony <group activities promoting ~> **b :** a loose widespread community based on common social institutions <the ~ of civilization> **c :** COMITY OF NATIONS **d :** the informal and voluntary recognition by courts of one jurisdiction of the laws and judicial decisions of another **2 :** avoidance of proselytizing members of another religious denomination

comity of nations 1 : the courtesy and friendship of nations marked esp. by mutual recognition of executive, legislative, and judicial acts **2 :** the group of nations practicing international comity

coml *abbr* commercial

comm *abbr* — see COM

com·ma \'käm-ə\ *n* [LL, fr. L, part of a sentence, fr. Gk *komma* segment, clause, fr. *koptein* to cut — more at CAPON] **1 :** a punctuation mark , used esp. as a mark of separation within the sentence **2 :** PAUSE, INTERVAL **3 :** any of several nymphalid butterflies (genus *Polygonia*) with a silvery comma-shaped mark on the underside of the hind wings

comma bacillus *n* **:** a bacterium (*Vibrio comma*) that causes Asiatic cholera

comma fault *n* **:** the careless or unjustified use of a comma between coordinate main clauses not connected by a conjunction

[1]**com·mand** \kə-'mand\ *vb* [ME *comanden,* fr. OF *comander,* fr. (assumed) VL *commandare,* alter. of L *commendare* to commit to one's charge — more at COMMEND] *vt* **1 :** to direct authoritatively : ORDER **2 :** to exercise a dominating influence over: as **a :** to have at one's immediate disposal **b :** to demand as one's due : EXACT <~*s* a high fee> **c :** to overlook or dominate from a strategic position **d :** to have military command of as senior officer **3** *obs* **:** to order or request to be given ~ *vi* **1 :** to have or exercise direct authority : GOVERN **2 :** to give orders **3 :** to be commander **4 :** to have an overlook — **com·mand·able** \-'man-də-bəl\ *adj*

syn COMMAND, ORDER, BID, ENJOIN, DIRECT, INSTRUCT, CHARGE *shared meaning element* **:** to issue orders or issue an order to ***ant*** comply, obey

[2]**command** *n* **1 :** the act of commanding **2 a :** an order given **b :** an electrical signal that actuates a device (as a control mechanism in a spacecraft or one step in a computer); *also* **:** the activation of a device by means of such a signal **3 a :** the ability to control : MASTERY **b :** the authority or right to command <an air of ~> <the officer in ~> **c** (1) **:** the power to dominate (2) **:** scope of vision **d :** facility in use <a good ~ of French> **4 :** the personnel, area, or organization under a commander <troops of the southern ~>; *specif* **:** a unit of the U.S. Air Force higher than an air force **5 :** a position of highest usu. military authority

[3]**command** *adj* **:** done on command or request <a ~ performance>

com·man·dant \'käm-ən-ˌdant, -ˌdänt\ *n* **:** COMMANDING OFFICER

command car *n* **:** an open armored car designed esp. for military reconnaissance and capable of traveling over rough terrain

com·man·deer \ˌkäm-ən-'di(ə)r\ *vt* [Afrik *kommandeer,* fr. F *commander* to command, fr. OF *comander*] **1 a :** to compel to perform military service **b :** to seize for military purposes **2 :** to take arbitrary or forcible possession of

com·mand·er \kə-'man-dər\ *n* **1 :** one in an official position of command or control: as **a :** COMMANDING OFFICER **b :** the presiding officer of a society or organization **2 :** a commissioned officer in the navy or coast guard ranking above a lieutenant commander and below a captain — **com·mand·er·ship** \-ˌship\ *n*

commander in chief : one who holds the supreme command of an armed force

com·mand·ery \kə-'man-d(ə-)rē\ *n, pl* **-er·ies 1 :** a district under the control of a commander of an order of knights **2 :** an assembly or lodge in a secret order

com·mand·ing \kə-'man-diŋ\ *adj* **:** drawing attention or priority — **com·mand·ing·ly** \-diŋ-lē\ *adv*

commanding officer *n* **:** an officer in command; *esp* **:** an officer in the armed forces in command of an organization or installation

com·mand·ment \kə-'man(d)-mənt\ *n* **1 :** the act or power of commanding **2 :** something that is commanded; *specif* **:** one of the biblical Ten Commandments

command module *n* **:** a space vehicle module designed to carry the crew, the chief communication equipment, and the equipment for reentry

com·man·do \kə-'man-(ˌ)dō\ *n, pl* **-dos** *or* **-does** [Afrik *kommando,* fr. D *commando* command, fr. Sp *comando,* fr. *comandar* to command, fr. F *commander*] **1** *So Afr* **a :** a military unit or command of the Boers **b :** a raiding expedition **2 a :** a military unit trained and organized as shock troops esp. for hit-and-run raids into enemy territory **b :** a member of such a specialized raiding unit

command post *n* **:** a post at which the commander of a unit in the field receives orders from his headquarters and exercises command over his unit

command sergeant major *n* **:** a noncommissioned officer in the army ranking above a first sergeant

comma splice *n* **:** COMMA FAULT

com·me·dia del·l'ar·te \kə-ˌmād-ē-ə-(ˌ)del-'ärt-ē, -ˌmed-\ *n* [It, lit., comedy of art] **:** Italian comedy of the 16th to 18th centuries improvised from standardized situations and stock characters

comme il faut \ˌkəm-ē(l)-'fō\ *adj* [F, lit., as it should be] **:** conforming to accepted standards : PROPER

com·mem·o·rate \kə-'mem-ə-ˌrāt\ *vt* **-rat·ed; -rat·ing** [L *commemoratus,* pp. of *commemorare,* fr. *com-* + *memorare* to remind of, fr. *memor* mindful — more at MEMORY] **1 :** to call to remembrance **2 :** to mark by some ceremony or observation : OBSERVE **3 :** to serve as a memorial of <a plaque that ~*s* the battle> ***syn*** see KEEP — **com·mem·o·ra·tor** \-ˌrāt-ər\ *n*

com·mem·o·ra·tion \kə-ˌmem-ə-'rā-shən\ *n* **1 :** the act of commemorating **2 :** something that commemorates

com·mem·o·ra·tive \kə-'mem-(ə-)rət-iv, -'mem-ə-ˌrāt-iv\ *adj* **:** intended as a commemoration : COMMEMORATING — **commemorative** *n* — **com·mem·o·ra·tive·ly** *adv*

com·mence \kə-'men(t)s\ *vb* **com·menced; com·menc·ing** [ME *comencen,* fr. MF *comencer,* fr. (assumed) VL *cominitiare,* fr. L *com-* + LL *initiare* to begin, fr. L, to initiate] *vt* **1 :** to enter upon : BEGIN **2 :** to initiate formally by performing the first act of <~ proceedings> ~ *vi* **1 :** to have or make a beginning : START **2** *chiefly Brit* **:** to begin to be or to act as **3** *chiefly Brit* **:** to take a degree at a university ***syn*** see BEGIN — **com·menc·er** *n*

com·mence·ment \kəm-'men(t)-smənt\ *n* **1 :** an act, instance, or time of commencing **2 a :** the ceremonies or the day for conferring degrees or diplomas **b :** the period of activities at this time

com·mend \kə-'mend\ *vb* [ME *commenden,* fr. L *commendare,* fr. *com-* + *mandare* to entrust — more at MANDATE] *vt* **1 :** to entrust for care or preservation **2 :** to recommend as worthy of confidence or notice **3 :** to mention with approbation : PRAISE ~ *vi* **:** to commend or serve as a commendation of something — **com·mend·able** \-'men-də-bəl\ *adj* — **com·mend·ably** \-blē\ *adv* — **com·mend·er** *n*

com·men·da·tion \ˌkäm-ən-'dā-shən, -ˌen-\ *n* **1 a :** an act of commending **b :** something (as a formal citation) that commends **2** *archaic* **:** COMPLIMENT

com·men·da·to·ry \kə-'men-də-ˌtōr-ē, -ˌtȯr-\ *adj* **:** serving to commend

com·men·sal \kə-'men(t)-səl\ *adj* [ME, fr. ML *commensalis,* fr. L *com-* + LL *mensalis* of the table, fr. L *mensa* table] **1 :** of or relating to those who habitually eat together **2 :** living in a state of commensalism — **commensal** *n* — **com·men·sal·ly** \-sə-lē\ *adv*

com·men·sal·ism \-sə-ˌliz-əm\ *n* **:** a relation between two kinds of organisms in which one obtains food or other benefits from the other without damaging or benefiting it

com·men·su·ra·ble \kə-'men(t)s(-ə)-rə-bəl, -'mench(-ə)-\ *adj* **1 :** having a common measure; *specif* **:** divisible by a common unit an integral number of times **2 :** COMMENSURATE 2 — **com·men-**

ə abut   ᵊ kitten   ər further   a back   ā bake   ä cot, cart
au̇ out   ch chin   e less   ē easy   g gift   i trip   ī life
j joke   ŋ sing   ō flow   ȯ flaw   ȯi coin   th thin   t͟h this
ü loot   u̇ foot   y yet   yü few   yu̇ furious   zh vision

su·ra·bil·i·ty \-ˌmen(t)s(-ə)-rə-ˈbil-ət-ē, -ˈmench(-ə)-\ *n* — **com·men·su·ra·bly** \-ˈmen(t)s(-ə)-rə-blē, -ˈmench(-ə)-\ *adv*

com·men·su·rate \kə-ˈmen(t)s(-ə)-rət, -ˈmench (-ə)-\ *adj* [LL *commensuratus,* fr. L *com-* + LL *mensuratus,* pp. of *mensurare* to measure, fr. L *mensura* measure — more at MEASURE] **1 :** equal in measure or extent **:** COEXTENSIVE <lived a life ~ with the early years of the republic> **2 :** corresponding in size, extent, amount, or degree **:** PROPORTIONATE <was given a job ~ with his abilities> **3 :** COMMENSURABLE 1 — **com·men·su·rate·ly** *adv* — **com·men·su·ra·tion** \-ˌmen(t)-sə-ˈrā-shən, -ˌmen-chə-\ *n*

1com·ment \ˈkäm-ˌent\ *n* [ME, fr. LL *commentum,* fr. L, invention, fr. neut. of *commentus,* pp. of *comminisci* to invent, fr. *com-* + *-minisci* (akin to *ment-, mens* mind) — more at MIND] **1 :** COMMENTARY **2 :** a note explaining, illustrating, or criticizing the meaning of a writing <~*s* printed in the margin> **3 a :** an observation or remark expressing an opinion or attitude <had no ~ for the press> **b :** a judgment expressed indirectly <this film is a ~ on current moral standards>

2comment *vi* **:** to explain or interpret something by comment <~*ing* on recent developments> ~ *vt* **:** to make a comment on <the discovery . . . is hardly ~*ed* by the press —*Nation*> ***syn*** see REMARK

com·men·tary \ˈkäm-ən-ˌter-ē\ *n, pl* **-tar·ies** **1 a :** an explanatory treatise — usu. used in pl. **b :** a record of events usu. written by a participant — usu. used in pl. **2 a :** a systematic series of explanations or interpretations (as of a writing) **b :** COMMENT 2 **3 a :** something that serves for illustration or explanation <the dark, airless apartments and sunless factories . . . are a sad ~ upon our civilization —H. A. Overstreet> **b :** an expression of opinion <a scene that is a gem of satiric ~ on the world of art —Rose Feld>

com·men·tate \ˈkäm-ən-ˌtāt\ *vb* **-tat·ed; -tat·ing** [back-formation fr. *commentator*] *vt* **:** to give a commentary on ~ *vi* **:** to comment in a usu. expository or interpretive manner; *also* **:** to act as a commentator ***syn*** see REMARK

com·men·ta·tor \-ˌtāt-ər\ *n* **:** one who gives a commentary; *specif* **:** one who reports and discusses news on radio or television

1com·merce \ˈkäm-(ˌ)ərs\ *n* [MF, fr. L *commercium,* fr. *com-* + *merc-, merx* merchandise] **1 :** social intercourse **:** interchange of ideas, opinions, or sentiments **2 :** the exchange or buying and selling of commodities on a large scale involving transportation from place to place **3 :** SEXUAL INTERCOURSE ***syn*** see BUSINESS

2com·merce \ˈkäm-(ˌ)ərs, kə-ˈmərs\ *vi* **com·merced; com·merc·ing** *archaic* **:** COMMUNE

1com·mer·cial \kə-ˈmər-shəl\ *adj* **1 a** (1) **:** engaged in work designed for the market <a ~ artist> (2) **:** of or relating to commerce <~ regulations> (3) **:** characteristic of commerce <~ weights> (4) **:** suitable, adequate, or prepared for commerce <found oil in ~ quantities> **b** (1) **:** being of an average or inferior quality <~ oxalic acid> (2) **:** producing artistic work of low standards for quick market success **2 a :** viewed with regard to profit <a ~ success> **b :** designed for a large market **3 :** emphasizing skills and subjects useful in business **4 :** supported by advertisers <~ TV> — **com·mer·cial·ly** \-ˈmərsh-(ə-)lē\ *adv*

2commercial *n* **:** an advertisement broadcast on radio or television

commercial bank *n* **:** a bank including in its functions the acceptance of demand deposits subject to withdrawal by check

com·mer·cial·ism \kə-ˈmər-shə-ˌliz-əm\ *n* **1 :** commercial spirit, institutions, or methods **2 :** excessive emphasis on profit — **com·mer·cial·ist** \-ˈmərsh-(ə-)ləst\ *n* — **com·mer·cial·is·tic** \-ˌmər-shə-ˈlis-tik\ *adj*

com·mer·cial·ize \kə-ˈmər-shə-ˌlīz\ *vt* **-ized; -iz·ing** **1 a :** to manage on a business basis for profit **b :** to develop commerce in **2 :** to exploit for profit <~ Christmas> **3 :** to debase in quality for more profit — **com·mer·cial·iza·tion** \-ˌmərsh-(ə-)lə-ˈzā-shən\ *n*

commercial paper *n* **:** short-term negotiable instruments arising out of commercial transactions

commercial traveler *n* **:** TRAVELING SALESMAN

com·mie \ˈkäm-ē\ *n, often cap* [by shortening and alter.] **:** COMMUNIST

com·mi·na·tion \ˌkäm-ə-ˈnā-shən\ *n* [ME, fr. MF or L; MF, fr. L *commination-, comminatio,* fr. *comminatus,* pp. of *comminari* to threaten, fr. *com-* + *minari* to threaten] **:** DENUNCIATION — **com·mi·na·to·ry** \ˈkäm-ə-nə-ˌtōr-ē, -ˌtȯr-; kə-ˈmin-ə-, -ˈmin-\ *adj*

com·min·gle \kə-ˈmiŋ-gəl, kä-\ *vt* **1 :** to blend thoroughly into a harmonious whole **2 :** to combine (funds or properties) into a common fund or stock <~ accounts> ~ *vi* **:** to become commingled ***syn*** see MIX

com·mi·nute \ˈkäm-ə-ˌn(y)üt\ *vt* **-nut·ed; -nut·ing** [L *comminutus,* pp. of *comminuere,* fr. *com-* + *minuere* to lessen] **:** to reduce to minute particles **:** PULVERIZE — **com·mi·nu·tion** \ˌkäm-ə-ˈn(y)ü-shən\ *n*

com·mis·er·ate \kə-ˈmiz-ə-ˌrāt\ *vb* **-at·ed; -at·ing** [L *commiseratus,* pp. of *commiserari,* fr. *com-* + *miserari* to pity, fr. *miser* wretched] *vt* **:** to feel or express sorrow or compassion for ~ *vi* **:** to feel or express sympathy **:** CONDOLE <~ over their hard luck> — **com·mis·er·a·tive** \-ˈmiz-ə-ˌrāt-iv\ *adj*

com·mis·er·a·tion \-ˌmiz-ə-ˈrā-shən\ *n* **:** the act of commiserating

com·mis·sar \ˈkäm-ə-ˌsär\ *n* [Russ *komissar,* fr. G *kommissar,* fr. ML *commissarius*] **1 a :** a Communist party official assigned to a military unit to teach party principles and policies and to ensure party loyalty **b :** one that attempts to control public opinion or its expression **2 :** the head of a government department in the U.S.S.R. until 1946

com·mis·sar·i·at \ˌkäm-ə-ˈser-ē-ət, -ˈsar-, *esp for 3* -ˈsär-\ *n* [NL *commissariatus,* fr. ML *commissarius*] **1 :** a system for supplying an army with food **2 :** food supplies **3** [Russ *komissariat,* fr. G *kommissariat,* fr. NL *commissariatus*] **:** a government department in the U.S.S.R. until 1946

com·mis·sary \ˈkäm-ə-ˌser-ē\ *n, pl* **-sar·ies** [ME *commissarie,* fr. ML *commissarius,* fr. L *commissus,* pp.] **1 :** one delegated by a superior to execute a duty or an office **2 a :** a store for equipment and provisions; *specif* **:** a supermarket operated for military personnel **b :** food supplies **c :** a lunchroom esp. in a motion-picture studio

1com·mis·sion \kə-ˈmish-ən\ *n* [ME, fr. MF, fr. L *commission-, commissio* act of bringing together, fr. *commissus,* pp. of *committere*] **1 a :** a formal written warrant granting the power to perform various acts or duties **b :** a certificate conferring military rank and authority; *also* **:** the rank and authority so conferred **2 :** an authorization or command to act in a prescribed manner or to perform prescribed acts **:** CHARGE **3 a :** authority to act for, in behalf of, or in place of another **b :** a task or matter entrusted to one as an agent for another <executed a ~ for me abroad> **4 a :** a group of persons directed to perform some duty **b :** a government agency having administrative, legislative, or judicial powers **c :** a city council having legislative and executive functions **5 :** an act of committing something <charged with ~ of felonies> **6 :** a fee paid to an agent or employee for transacting a piece of business or performing a service; *esp* **:** a percentage of the money received from a total paid to the agent responsible for the business **7 :** an act of entrusting or giving authority — **in commission** *or* **into commission** **1 :** under the authority of commissioners **2** *of a ship* **:** ready for active service **3 :** in use or in condition for use — **on commission :** with commission serving as partial or full pay for work done — **out of commission** **1 :** out of active service or use **2 :** out of working order

2commission *vt* **com·mis·sioned; com·mis·sion·ing** \-ˈmish-(ə-)niŋ\ **1 :** to furnish with a commission: as **a :** to confer a formal commission on <was ~*ed* lieutenant> **b :** to appoint or assign to a task or function <the writer who was ~*ed* to do the biography> **2 :** to order to be made <wealthy persons who ~*ed* portraits of themselves> **3 :** to put (a ship) in commission

com·mis·sion·aire \kə-ˌmish-ə-ˈna(ə)r, -ˈne(ə)r\ *n* [F *commissionnaire,* fr. *commission*] *chiefly Brit* **:** a uniformed attendant

commissioned officer *n* **:** an officer of the armed forces holding rank by virtue of a commission from the president

com·mis·sion·er \kə-ˈmish-(ə-)nər\ *n* **:** a person with a commission: as **a :** a member of a commission **b :** the representative of the governmental authority in a district, province, or other unit often having both judicial and administrative powers **c :** the officer in charge of a department or bureau of the public service **d :** the administrative head of a professional sport — **com·mis·sion·er·ship** \-ˌship\ *n*

commission merchant *n* **:** one who buys or sells another's goods for a commission

commission plan *n* **:** a method of municipal government under which a small elective commission exercises both executive and legislative powers and each commissioner directly administers one or more municipal departments

com·mis·sure \ˈkäm-ə-ˌshu̇(ə)r\ *n* [ME, fr. MF or L; MF, fr. L *commissura* a joining, fr. *commissus,* pp.] **1 :** the place where two bodies or parts unite **:** CLOSURE **2 :** a connecting band of nerve tissue in the brain or spinal cord — **com·mis·sur·al** \ˌkäm-ə-ˈshu̇r-əl\ *adj*

com·mit \kə-ˈmit\ *vb* **com·mit·ted; com·mit·ting** [ME *committen,* fr. L *committere* to connect, entrust, fr. *com-* + *mittere* to send] *vt* **1 a :** to put into charge or trust **:** ENTRUST **b :** to place in a prison or mental institution **c :** to consign or record for preservation <~ it to memory> **d :** to put into a place for disposal or safekeeping **e :** to refer (as a legislative bill) to a committee for consideration and report **2 :** to carry into action deliberately <~ a crime> **3 a :** OBLIGATE, BIND **b :** to pledge or assign to some particular course or use <all available troops were *committed* to the attack> **c :** to reveal the views of <refused to ~ himself on the issue> ~ *vi, obs* **:** to perpetrate an offense — **com·mit·ta·ble** \-ˈmit-ə-bəl\ *adj*

syn COMMIT, ENTRUST, CONFIDE, CONSIGN, RELEGATE *shared meaning element* **:** to assign (as to a person or place) esp. for care or safekeeping

com·mit·ment \kə-ˈmit-mənt\ *n* **1 a :** an act of committing to a charge or trust: as (1) **:** a consignment to a penal or mental institution (2) **:** an act of referring a matter to a legislative committee **b :** MITTIMUS **2 a :** an agreement or pledge to do something in the future; *specif* **:** an engagement to assume a financial obligation at a future date **b :** something pledged **c :** the state of being obligated or emotionally impelled <his ~ to unpopular causes>

com·mit·tal \kə-ˈmit-ᵊl\ *n* **:** COMMITMENT, CONSIGNMENT

com·mit·tee \kə-ˈmit-ē, *sense* 1 *also* ˌkäm-ə-ˈtē\ *n* **1** *archaic* **:** a person to whom a charge or trust is committed **2 a :** a body of persons delegated to consider, investigate, take action on, or report on some matter; *specif* **:** a group of fellow legislators chosen by a legislative body to give consideration to legislative matters **b :** a self-constituted organization for the promotion of a common object

com·mit·tee·man \kə-ˈmit-ē-mən, -ˌman\ *n* **1 :** a member of a committee **2 :** a party leader of a ward or precinct

committee of the whole : the whole membership of a legislative house sitting as a committee and operating under informal rules

com·mit·tee·woman \-ˌwu̇m-ən\ *n* **:** a female member of a committee

com·mix \kə-ˈmiks, kä-\ *vb* [back-formation fr. ME *comixt* blended, fr. L *commixtus,* pp. of *commiscēre* to mix together, fr. *com-* + *miscēre* to mix — more at MIX] *vt* **:** MINGLE, BLEND ~ *vi* **:** to become mingled or blended

com·mix·ture \-chər\ *n* [L *commixtura,* fr. *commixtus*] **1 :** the act or process of mixing **:** the state of being mixed **2 :** COMPOUND, MIXTURE

commo *abbr* commodore

com·mode \kə-ˈmōd\ *n* [F, fr. *commode,* adj., suitable, convenient, fr. L *commodus,* fr. *com-* + *modus* measure — more at METE] **1 :** a woman's ornate cap popular in the late 17th and early 18th centuries **2 a :** a low chest of drawers **b :** a movable washstand with a cupboard underneath **c :** a boxlike structure holding a chamber pot under an open seat; *also* **:** CHAMBER POT **d :** TOILET 3b

com·mo·di·ous \kə-ˈmōd-ē-əs\ *adj* [ME, useful, fr. MF *commodieux,* fr. ML *commodiosus,* irreg. fr. L *commodum* convenience, fr. neut. of *commodus*] **1** *archaic* : HANDY, SERVICEABLE **2** : comfortably or conveniently spacious : ROOMY <one ~ drawer held all his clothes> ***syn*** see SPACIOUS — **com·mo·di·ous·ly** *adv* — **com·mo·di·ous·ness** *n*

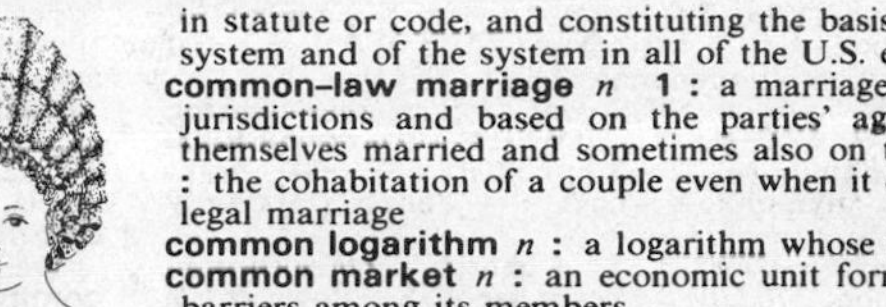
commode 1

com·mod·i·ty \kə-ˈmäd-ət-ē\ *n, pl* **-ties** [ME *commoditee,* fr. MF *commodité,* fr. L *commoditat-, commoditas,* fr. *commodus*] **1 a** : CONVENIENCE, ADVANTAGE **b** : something useful or valuable **2** : an economic good: as **a** : a product of agriculture or mining **b** : an article of commerce esp. when delivered for shipment **3** *obs* : QUANTITY, LOT

com·mo·dore \ˈkäm-ə-ˌdō(ə)r, -ˌdȯ(ə)r\ *n* [prob. modif. of D *commandeur* commander, fr. F, fr. OF *comandeor,* fr. *comander* to command] **1 a** : a former captain in the navy in command of a squadron **b** : a former commissioned officer in the navy ranking above captain and below rear admiral and having an insignia of one star **2** : the ranking officer commanding a body of merchant ships **3** : the chief officer of a yacht club or boating association

¹com·mon \ˈkäm-ən\ *adj* [ME *commun,* fr. OF, fr. L *communis* — more at MEAN] **1 a** : of or relating to a community at large : PUBLIC <work for the ~ good> **b** : known to the community <~ nuisances> **2 a** : belonging to or shared by two or more individuals or by all members of a group <all destined to the ~ grave> **b** : belonging equally to two or more quantities **c** : having two or more branches <~ carotid artery> **3 a** : occurring or appearing frequently : FAMILIAR <a ~ sight> **b** : of the best known kind <~ salt> **4 a** : WIDESPREAD, GENERAL <being ~ knowledge> **b** : characterized by a lack of privilege or special status <~ people> **c** : just satisfying accustomed criteria : ELEMENTARY <~ decency> **5 a** : falling below ordinary standards : SECOND-RATE **b** : lacking refinement <~ manners> **c** : completely unprincipled **6 a** : either masculine or feminine in gender **b** : denoting relations by a single case form that in a more highly inflected language might be denoted by two or more different case forms — **com·mon·ly** *adv* — **com·mon·ness** \-ən-nəs\ *n*

syn **1** see RECIPROCAL ***ant*** individual

2 COMMON, ORDINARY, PLAIN, FAMILIAR, POPULAR, VULGAR *shared meaning element* : being what is generally met with and not in any way special, strange, or unusual. COMMON implies usual everyday quality or frequency of occurrence <a *common* error> <lacked *common* honesty> and may additionally suggest inferiority or coarseness <O hard is the bed . . . and *common* the blanket and cheap —A. E. Housman> ORDINARY stresses conformance in quality or kind with the regular order of things <an *ordinary* pleasant summer day> <a very *ordinary* sort of man> PLAIN is likely to suggest homely simplicity <the *plain* people everywhere . . . wish to live in peace — F. D. Roosevelt> FAMILIAR stresses the fact of being generally known and easily recognized <a *familiar* melody> POPULAR applies to what is accepted by or prevalent among people in general sometimes in contrast to upper classes or special groups <a *popular* tune> VULGAR, otherwise similar to *popular,* is likely to carry derogatory connotations (as of inferiority or coarseness) <goods designed to appeal to the *vulgar* taste> ***ant*** uncommon, exceptional

²common *n* **1** *pl* : the common people **2** *pl but sing in constr* : a dining hall **3** *pl but sing or pl in constr, often cap* **a** : the political group or estate comprising the commoners **b** : the parliamentary representatives of the commoners **c** : HOUSE OF COMMONS **4** : the legal right of taking a profit in another's land in common with the owner **5** : a piece of land subject to common use: as **a** : undivided land used esp. for pasture **b** : a public open area in a municipality **6 a** : a religious service suitable for any of various festivals **b** : the ordinary of the Mass — **in common** : shared together

com·mon·age \ˈkäm-ə-nij\ *n* **1** : community land **2** : COMMONALTY 1a(2)

com·mon·al·i·ty \ˌkäm-ə-ˈnal-ət-ē\ *n, pl* **-ties** [ME *communalitie,* alter. of *communalte*] **1 a** : possession of common features or attributes : COMMONNESS **b** : a common feature or attribute <can see *commonalities* as well as differences> **2** : the common people

com·mon·al·ty \ˈkäm-ən-ᵊl-tē\ *n, pl* **-ties** [ME *communalte,* fr. OF *comunalté,* fr. *comunal* communal] **1 a** (1) : the common people (2) : the political estate formed by the common people **b** : a usage or practice common to members of a group **2** : a general group or body

common carrier *n* : an individual or corporation undertaking to transport for compensation persons, goods, or messages

common cattle grub *n* : a heel fly (*Hypoderma lineatum*) which is found throughout the U.S. and whose larva is particularly destructive to cattle

common chord *n* : TRIAD 2

common cold *n* : an acute virus disease of the upper respiratory tract marked by inflammation of mucous membranes

common denominator *n* **1** : a common multiple of the denominators of a number of fractions **2** : a common trait or theme

common divisor *n* : a number or expression that divides two or more numbers or expressions without remainder — called also *common factor*

com·mon·er \ˈkäm-ə-nər\ *n* **1 a** : one of the common people **b** : one who is not of noble rank **2** : a student (as at Oxford) who pays for his own board

common fraction *n* : a fraction in which both the numerator and denominator are expressed as numbers and are separated by a horizontal or slanted line — compare DECIMAL

common informer *n* : INFORMER 2

common–law *adj* **1** : of, relating to, or based on the common law **2** : relating to or based on a common-law marriage <his ~ wife>

common law *n* : the body of law developed in England primarily from judicial decisions based on custom and precedent, unwritten in statute or code, and constituting the basis of the English legal system and of the system in all of the U.S. except Louisiana

common–law marriage *n* **1** : a marriage recognized in some jurisdictions and based on the parties' agreement to consider themselves married and sometimes also on their cohabitation **2** : the cohabitation of a couple even when it does not constitute a legal marriage

common logarithm *n* : a logarithm whose base is 10

common market *n* : an economic unit formed to remove trade barriers among its members

common measure *n* : a meter consisting chiefly of iambic lines of 7 accents each arranged in alternately rhymed pairs usu. printed in 4-line stanzas — called also *common meter*

common multiple *n* : a multiple of each of two or more numbers or expressions

common noun *n* : a noun that may occur with limiting modifiers (as *a* or *an, some, every,* and *my*) and that designates any one of a class of beings or things

¹com·mon·place \ˈkäm-ən-ˌplās\ *n* [trans. of L *locus communis* widely applicable argument, trans. of Gk *koinos topos*] **1** *archaic* : a striking passage entered in a commonplace book **2 a** : an obvious or trite observation **b** : something taken for granted

²commonplace *adj* : routinely found : ORDINARY, UNREMARKABLE — **com·mon·place·ness** *n*

commonplace book *n* : a book of memorabilia

common pleas *n* **1** *pl* **a** : actions over which the English crown did not claim exclusive jurisdiction **b** : civil actions between English subjects **2** *pl but sing in constr* : COURT OF COMMON PLEAS

common room *n* **1** : a lounge available to all members of a residential community **2** : a room in a college for the use of the faculty

common salt *n* : SALT 1a

common school *n* : a free public school

common sense *n* **1** : sound and prudent but often unsophisticated judgment **2** : the unreflective opinions of ordinary men ***syn*** see SENSE — **com·mon·sense** \ˌkäm-ən-ˌsen(t)s\ *adj* — **com·mon·sen·si·ble** \-ˈsen(t)-sə-bəl\ *adj* — **com·mon·sen·si·bly** \-blē\ *adv* — **com·mon·sen·si·cal** \-ˈsen(t)-si-kəl\ *adj*

common stock *n* : capital stock other than preferred stock

common time *n* : the musical tempo marked by four beats per measure

common touch *n* : the gift of appealing to or arousing sympathetic interest

com·mon·weal \ˈkäm-ən-ˌwēl\ *n* **1** : the general welfare **2** *archaic* : COMMONWEALTH

com·mon·wealth \-ˌwelth\ *n* **1** *archaic* : COMMONWEAL 1 **2** : a nation, state, or other political unit: as **a** : one founded on law and united by compact or tacit agreement of the people for the common good **b** : one in which supreme authority is vested in the people **c** : REPUBLIC **3** *cap* **a** : the English state from the death of Charles I in 1649 to the Restoration in 1660 **b** : PROTECTORATE 1b **4** : a state of the U.S. — used officially of Kentucky, Massachusetts, Pennsylvania, and Virginia **5** *cap* : a federal union of constituent states — used officially of Australia **6** *often cap* : an association of self-governing autonomous states more or less loosely associated in a common allegiance (as to the British crown) **7** *often cap* : a political unit having local autonomy but voluntarily united with the U.S. — used officially of Puerto Rico

Commonwealth Day *n* : May 24 observed in parts of the British Commonwealth as the anniversary of Queen Victoria's birthday

common year *n* : a calendar year containing no intercalary period

com·mo·tion \kə-ˈmō-shən\ *n* [ME, fr. MF, fr. L *commotion-, commotio,* fr. *commotus,* pp. of *commovēre*] **1** : a condition of civil unrest or insurrection **2** : steady or recurrent motion **3** : mental excitement or confusion **4 a** : a flurried disturbance : TO-DO <a crowd raising a ~ in the street> **b** : noisy confusion : AGITATION

com·move \kə-ˈmüv, kä-\ *vt* **com·moved; com·mov·ing** [ME *commoeven,* fr. MF *commuev-,* pres. stem of *commovoir,* fr. L *commovēre,* fr. *com-* + *movēre* to move] **1** : to move violently : AGITATE **2** : to rouse intense feeling in : excite to passion

com·mu·nal \kə-ˈmyün-ᵊl, ˈkäm-yən-ᵊl\ *adj* [F, fr. LL *communalis,* fr. L *communis*] **1** : of or relating to one or more communes **2** : of or relating to a community **3 a** : characterized by collective ownership and use of property **b** : participated in, shared, or used in common by members of a group or community **4** : of, relating to, or based on racial or cultural groups

com·mu·nal·ism \-ᵊl-ˌiz-əm\ *n* **1** : social organization on a communal basis **2** : loyalty to a sociopolitical grouping based on religious affiliation — **com·mu·nal·ist** \-ᵊl-əst\ *n or adj*

com·mu·nal·i·ty \ˌkäm-yü-ˈnal-ət-ē\ *n, pl* **-ties** **1** : communal state or character **2** : a feeling of group solidarity

com·mu·nal·ize \kə-ˈmyün-ᵊl-ˌīz, ˈkäm-yən-\ *vt* **-ized; -iz·ing** : to make communal

com·mu·nard \ˌkäm-yü-ˈnär(d)\ *n* [F] **1** *cap* : one who supported or participated in the Commune of Paris in 1871 **2** : one that lives in a commune

¹com·mune \kə-ˈmyün\ *vb* **com·muned; com·mun·ing** [ME *communen* to converse, administer Communion, fr. MF *comunier* to converse, administer or receive Communion, fr. LL *communicare,* fr. L] *vt, obs* : to talk over : DISCUSS <have more to ~ — Shak.> ~ *vi* **1** : to receive Communion **2** : to communicate intimately <~ with nature>

²com·mune \ˈkäm-ˌyün; kə-ˈmyün, kä-\ *n* [F, alter. of MF *comugne,* fr. ML *communia,* fr. L, neut. pl. of *communis*] **1** : the smallest administrative district of many countries esp. in

Europe **2 :** COMMONALTY 1a **3 :** COMMUNITY: as **a :** a medieval usu. municipal corporation **b** (1) **:** MIR (2) **:** an often rural community organized on a communal basis

com·mu·ni·ca·ble \kə-ˈmyü-ni-kə-bəl\ *adj* **1 :** capable of being communicated **:** TRANSMITTABLE <~ disease> **2 :** COMMUNICATIVE — **com·mu·ni·ca·bil·i·ty** \-ˌmyü-ni-kə-ˈbil-ət-ē\ *n* — **com·mu·ni·ca·ble·ness** \-ˈmyü-ni-kə-bəl-nəs\ *n* — **com·mu·ni·ca·bly** \-blē\ *adv*

com·mu·ni·cant \-ˈmyü-ni-kənt\ *n* **1 :** a church member entitled to receive Communion; *broadly* **:** a member of a fellowship **2 :** one that communicates; *specif* **:** INFORMANT — **communicant** *adj*

com·mu·ni·cate \kə-ˈmyü-nə-ˌkāt\ *vb* **-cat·ed; -cat·ing** [L *communicatus,* pp. of *communicare* to impart, participate, fr. *communis* common — more at MEAN] *vt* **1** *archaic* **:** SHARE **2 a :** to convey knowledge of or information about **:** make known <~ a story> **b :** to reveal by clear signs <his fear *communicated* itself to his friends> **3 :** to cause to pass from one to another <some diseases are easily *communicated*> ~ *vi* **1 :** to receive Communion **2 :** to transmit information, thought, or feeling so that it is satisfactorily received or understood **3 :** to open into each other **:** CONNECT <the rooms ~>

syn COMMUNICATE, IMPART *shared meaning element* **:** to convey or transmit something intangible (as information, feelings, or a flavor)

com·mu·ni·ca·tee \-ˌmyü-ni-kə-ˈtē\ *n* **:** one that receives a communication

com·mu·ni·ca·tion \kə-ˌmyü-nə-ˈkā-shən\ *n* **1 :** an act or instance of transmitting **2 a :** information communicated **b :** a verbal or written message **3 a :** a process by which information is exchanged between individuals through a common system of symbols, signs, or behavior <the function of pheromones in insect ~>; *also* **:** exchange of information **b :** personal rapport <a lack of ~ between old and young persons> **4** *pl* **a :** a system (as of telephones) for communicating **b :** a system of routes for moving troops, supplies, and vehicles **c :** personnel engaged in communicating **5** *pl but sing or pl in constr* **a :** a technique for expressing ideas effectively (as in speech) **b :** the technology of the transmission of information (as by the printed word, telecommunication, or the computer) — **com·mu·ni·ca·tion·al** \-shnəl, -shən-ᵊl\ *adj*

com·mu·ni·ca·tive \kə-ˈmyü-nə-ˌkāt-iv, -ni-kət-iv\ *adj* **1 :** tending to communicate **:** TALKATIVE **2 :** of or relating to communication — **com·mu·ni·ca·tive·ly** *adv* — **com·mu·ni·ca·tive·ness** *n*

com·mu·ni·ca·tor \-ˌkāt-ər\ *n* **:** one that communicates

com·mu·ni·ca·to·ry \kə-ˈmyü-ni-kə-ˌtōr-ē, -ˌtȯr-\ *adj* **:** designed to communicate information <~ letters>

com·mu·nion \kə-ˈmyü-nyən\ *n* [ME, fr. L *communion-, communio* mutual participation, fr. *communis*] **1 :** an act or instance of sharing **2 a** *cap* **:** a Christian sacrament in which bread and wine are partaken of as a commemoration of the death of Christ **b :** the act of receiving the sacrament **c** *cap* **:** the part of the Mass in which the sacrament is received **d** *cap* **:** a variable verse of scripture traditionally said or sung at mass during the people's communion — called also *Communion Verse* **3 :** intimate fellowship or rapport **:** COMMUNICATION **4 :** a body of Christians having a common faith and discipline

Communion Sunday *n* **:** a Sunday (as the first Sunday of the month) on which a Protestant church regularly holds a Communion service

com·mu·ni·qué \kə-ˈmyü-nə-ˌkā, -ˌmyü-nə-ˈ\ *n* [F, fr. pp. of *communiquer* to communicate, fr. L *communicare*] **:** BULLETIN 1

com·mu·nism \ˈkäm-yə-ˌniz-əm\ *n* [F *communisme,* fr. *commun* common] **1 a :** a theory advocating elimination of private property **b :** a system in which goods are owned in common and are available to all as needed **2** *cap* **a :** a doctrine based on revolutionary Marxian socialism and Marxism-Leninism that is the official ideology of the U.S.S.R. **b :** a totalitarian system of government in which a single authoritarian party controls state-owned means of production with the professed aim of establishing a stateless society **c :** a final stage of society in Marxist theory in which the state has withered away and economic goods are distributed equitably

com·mu·nist \ˈkäm-yə-nəst\ *n* **1 :** an adherent or advocate of communism **2** *cap* **:** COMMUNARD **3 a** *cap* **:** a member of a Communist party or movement **b** *often cap* **:** an adherent or advocate of a Communist government, party, or movement **4** *often cap* **:** one held to engage in left-wing, subversive, or revolutionary activities — **communist** *adj, often cap* — **com·mu·nis·tic** \ˌkäm-yə-ˈnis-tik\ *adj, often cap* — **com·mu·nis·ti·cal·ly** \-ti-k(ə-)lē\ *adv*

com·mu·ni·tar·i·an \kə-ˌmyü-nə-ˈter-ē-ən\ *adj* **:** of or relating to social organization in small cooperative partially collectivist communities — **communitarian** *n* — **com·mu·ni·tar·i·an·ism** \-ē-ə-ˌniz-əm\ *n*

com·mu·ni·ty \kə-ˈmyü-nət-ē\ *n, pl* **-ties** [ME *comunete,* fr. MF *comuneté,* fr. L *communitat-, communitas,* fr. *communis*] **1 :** a unified body of individuals: as **a :** STATE, COMMONWEALTH **b :** the people with common interests living in a particular area; *broadly* **:** the area itself <the problems of a large ~> **c :** an interacting population of various kinds of individuals (as species) in a common location **d :** a group of people with a common characteristic or interest living together within a larger society <a ~ of retired persons> **e :** a group linked by a common policy **f :** a body of persons or nations having a common history or common social, economic, and political interests <the international ~> **g :** a body of persons of common and esp. professional interests scattered through a larger society <the academic ~> **2 :** society at large **3 a :** joint ownership or participation <asserts that ~ of goods would be the ideal institution —G. L. Dickinson> **b :** common character **:** LIKENESS <bound by ~ of interests> **c :** social activity **:** FELLOWSHIP **d :** a social state or condition

community antenna television *n* **:** a system of television reception in which signals from distant stations are picked up by a tall or elevated antenna and sent by cable to the individual receivers of paying subscribers

community center *n* **:** a building or group of buildings for a community's educational and recreational activities

community chest *n* **:** a general fund accumulated from individual subscriptions to defray demands on a community for charity and social welfare

community college *n* **:** a nonresidential junior college that is usu. government-supported

community property *n* **:** property held jointly by husband and wife

com·mu·ni·ty·wide \kə-ˌmyü-nət-ē-ˈwīd\ *adj* **:** operative or effective throughout a community

com·mu·nize \ˈkäm-yə-ˌnīz\ *vt* **-nized; -niz·ing** [back-formation fr. *communization*] **1 a :** to make common **b :** to make into state-owned property **2 :** to subject to Communist principles of organization — **com·mu·ni·za·tion** \ˌkäm-yə-nə-ˈzā-shən\ *n*

com·mu·tate \ˈkäm-yə-ˌtāt\ *vt* **-tat·ed; -tat·ing** [back-formation fr. *commutation*] **:** to reverse every other cycle of (an alternating current) so as to form a unidirectional current

com·mu·ta·tion \ˌkäm-yə-ˈtā-shən\ *n* [ME, fr. MF, fr. L *commutation-, commutatio,* fr. *commutatus,* pp. of *commutare*] **1 :** EXCHANGE, TRADE **2 :** REPLACEMENT; *specif* **:** a substitution of one form of payment or charge for another **3 :** a change of a legal penalty or punishment to a lesser one **4 :** an act or process of commuting **5 :** the action of commutating

commutation ticket *n* **:** a transportation ticket sold for a fixed number of trips over the same route during a limited period

com·mu·ta·tive \ˈkäm-yə-ˌtāt-iv, kə-ˈmyüt-ət-\ *adj* **1 :** of, relating to, or showing commutation **2 :** combining elements or having elements that combine in such a manner that the result is independent of the order in which the elements are taken <a ~ group> <addition of the positive integers is ~>

com·mu·ta·tiv·i·ty \kə-ˌmyüt-ə-ˈtiv-ət-ē, ˌkäm-yə-tə-\ *n* **:** the property of being commutative <the ~ of a mathematical operation>

com·mu·ta·tor \ˈkäm-yə-ˌtāt-ər\ *n* **1 :** a switch for reversing the direction of an electric current **2 :** a series of bars or segments so connected to armature coils of a dynamo that rotation of the armature will in conjunction with fixed brushes result in unidirectional current output in the case of a generator and in the reversal of the current into the coils in the case of a motor **3 :** an element of a mathematical group that when multiplied by the product of two given elements yields the product of the elements in reverse order

[1]**com·mute** \kə-ˈmyüt\ *vb* **com·mut·ed; com·mut·ing** [L *commutare* to change, exchange, fr. *com-* + *mutare* to change] *vt* **1 a :** to give in exchange for another **:** EXCHANGE **b :** CHANGE, ALTER **2 :** to convert (as a payment) into another form **3 :** to exchange (a penalty) for another less severe **4 :** COMMUTATE ~ *vi* **1 :** to make up **:** COMPENSATE **2 :** to pay in gross **3 :** to travel back and forth regularly (as between a suburb and a city) — **com·mut·able** \-ˈmyüt-ə-bəl\ *adj* — **com·mut·er** *n*

[2]**commute** *n* **:** a trip made in commuting

co·mo·no·mer \(ˈ)kō-ˈmän-ə-mər, -ˈmō-nə-\ *n* [*co-* + *monomer*] **:** one of the constituents of a copolymer

co·mose \ˈkō-ˌmōs\ *adj* [L *comosus* hairy, fr. *coma* hair — more at COMA] **:** bearing a tuft of soft hairs

[1]**comp** \ˈkämp, ˈkämp\ *vi* [short for *accompany*] **:** to play an irregularly rhythmic jazz accompaniment

[2]**comp** *abbr* **1** comparative; compare **2** compensation **3** compiled; compiler **4** composition **5** compound **6** comprehensive **7** comptroller

[1]**com·pact** \kəm-ˈpakt, käm-ˈ, ˈkäm-ˌ\ *adj* [ME, firmly put together, fr. L *compactus,* fr. pp. of *compingere* to put together, fr. *com-* + *pangere* to fasten — more at PACT] **1 :** COMPOSED, MADE **2 a :** having parts or units closely packed or joined <a ~ woolen> **b :** not diffuse or verbose <a ~ statement> **c :** occupying a small volume by reason of efficient use of space <a ~ camera> <a ~ formation of troops> ***syn*** see CLOSE — **com·pact·ly** *adv* — **com·pact·ness** *n*

[2]**compact** *vt* **1 a :** to knit or draw together **:** COMBINE, CONSOLIDATE **b :** to press together **:** COMPRESS **2 :** to make up by connecting or combining **:** COMPOSE ~ *vi* **:** to become compacted — **com·pact·ible** \-ˈpak-tə-bəl, -ˌpak-\ *adj* — **com·pac·tor** *or* **com·pact·er** \-ˈpak-tər, -ˌpak-\ *n*

[3]**com·pact** \ˈkäm-ˌpakt\ *n* **:** something that is compact or compacted: as **a :** a small cosmetic case (as for compressed powder) **b :** an automobile smaller than an intermediate but larger than a subcompact

[4]**com·pact** \ˈkäm-ˌpakt\ *n* [L *compactum,* fr. neut. of *compactus,* pp. of *compacisci* to make an agreement, fr. *com-* + *pacisci* to contract] **:** an agreement or covenant between two or more parties

com·pac·tion \kəm-ˈpak-shən, käm-\ *n* **:** the act or process of compacting **:** the state of being compacted

[1]**com·pan·ion** \kəm-ˈpan-yən\ *n* [ME *compainoun,* fr. OF *compagnon,* fr. LL *companion-, companio,* fr. L *com-* + *panis* bread, food] **1 :** COMRADE, ASSOCIATE **2** *obs* **:** RASCAL **3 a :** one of a pair or set of matching things **b :** one employed to live with and serve another

[2]**companion** *vt* **:** ACCOMPANY ~ *vi* **:** to keep company **:** ASSOCIATE

[3]**companion** *n* [by folk etymology fr. D *kampanje* poop deck] **1 :** a hood covering at the top of a companionway **2 :** COMPANIONWAY

com·pan·ion·able \kəm-ˈpan-yə-nə-bəl\ *adj* **:** marked by, conducive to, or suggestive of companionship **:** SOCIABLE <tells her story calmly in a quiet ~ voice —Edward Callan> — **com·pan·ion·able·ness** *n* — **com·pan·ion·ably** \-blē\ *adv*

com·pan·ion·ate \kəm-ˈpan-yə-nət\ *adj* **:** relating to or in the manner of companions; *specif* **:** harmoniously or suitably accompanying

companionate marriage *n* **:** a proposed form of marriage in which legalized birth control would be practiced, the divorce of childless couples by mutual consent permitted, and neither party would have any financial or economic claim on the other

companion cell *n* **:** a living nucleated cell that is closely associated in origin, position, and probably function with a cell making up part of a sieve tube of a vascular plant

companion piece *n* **:** an object (as a literary work) that is associated with and complements another

com·pan·ion·ship \kəm-ˈpan-yən-ˌship\ *n* **:** the fellowship existing among companions

com·pan·ion·way \-yən-ˌwā\ *n* [[3]*companion*] **:** a ship's stairway from one deck to another

[1]**com·pa·ny** \ˈkəmp-(ə-)nē\ *n, pl* **-nies** *often attrib* [ME *companie,* fr. OF *compagnie,* fr. *compain* companion, fr. LL *companio*] **1 a :** association with another **:** FELLOWSHIP <enjoy a person's ~> **b :** COMPANIONS, ASSOCIATES <know a person by the ~ he keeps> **c :** VISITORS, GUESTS <having ~ for dinner> **2 a :** a group of persons or things <a ~ of horsemen> **b :** a body of soldiers; *specif* **:** a unit (as of infantry) consisting usu. of a headquarters and two or more platoons **c :** an organization of musical or dramatic performers <an opera ~> **d :** the officers and men of a ship **e :** a fire-fighting unit **3 a :** a chartered commercial organization or medieval trade guild **b :** an association of persons for carrying on a commercial or industrial enterprise **c :** those members of a partnership firm whose names do not appear in the firm name <John Doe and *Company*>

[2]**company** *vt* **-nied; -ny·ing :** ACCOMPANY <may . . . fair winds ~ your safe return —John Masefield> ~ *vi* **:** ASSOCIATE

company officer *n* **:** a commissioned officer in the army, air force, or marine corps of the rank of captain, first lieutenant, or second lieutenant — called also *company grade officer;* compare FIELD OFFICER, GENERAL OFFICER

company town *n* **:** a community that is dependent on one firm for all or most of the necessary services or functions of town life (as employment, housing, and stores)

company union *n* **:** an unaffiliated labor union of the employees of a single firm; *esp* **:** one dominated by the employer

com·pa·ra·bil·i·ty \ˌkäm-p(ə-)rə-ˈbil-ət-ē\ *n* **:** the quality or state of being comparable

com·pa·ra·ble \ˈkäm-p(ə-)rə-bəl\ *adj* **1 :** capable of or suitable for comparison **2 :** EQUIVALENT, SIMILAR <fabrics of ~ quality> — **com·pa·ra·ble·ness** *n* — **com·pa·ra·bly** \-blē\ *adv*

com·par·a·tist \kəm-ˈpar-ət-əst\ *n* [*comparative* + *-ist*] **:** one that uses a comparative method (as in the study of literature)

[1]**com·par·a·tive** \kəm-ˈpar-ət-iv\ *adj* **1 :** of, relating to, or constituting the degree of comparison in a language that denotes increase in the quality, quantity, or relation expressed by an adjective or adverb **2 :** considered as if in comparison to something else as a standard not quite attained **:** RELATIVE <~ stranger> **3 :** characterized by the systematic comparison of phenomena and esp. of likenesses and dissimilarities <~ anatomy> — **com·par·a·tive·ly** *adv* — **com·par·a·tive·ness** *n*

[2]**comparative** *n* **1 a :** one that compares with another esp. on equal footing **:** RIVAL **b :** one that makes witty or mocking comparisons **2 :** the comparative degree or form in a language

com·par·a·tiv·ist \kəm-ˈpar-ət-i-vəst\ *n* **:** COMPARATIST

com·par·a·tor \kəm-ˈpar-ət-ər\ *n* **:** a device for comparing something with a similar thing or with a standard measure

[1]**com·pare** \kəm-ˈpa(ə)r, -ˈpe(ə)r\ *vb* **com·pared; com·par·ing** [ME *comparen,* fr. MF *comparer,* fr. L *comparare* to couple, compare, fr. *compar* like, fr. *com-* + *par* equal] *vt* **1 :** to represent as similar **:** LIKEN **2 :** to examine the character or qualities of esp. in order to discover resemblances or differences **3 :** to inflect or modify (an adjective or adverb) according to the degrees of comparison ~ *vi* **1 :** to bear being compared **2 :** to make comparisons **3 :** to be equal or alike

syn COMPARE, CONTRAST, COLLATE *shared meaning element* **:** to set side by side in order to show likenesses and differences

[2]**compare** *n* **:** COMPARISON <beauty beyond ~>

com·par·i·son \kəm-ˈpar-ə-sən\ *n* [ME, fr. MF *comparaison,* fr. L *comparation-, comparatio,* fr. *comparatus,* pp. of *comparare*] **1 :** the act or process of comparing: **a :** the representing of one thing or person as similar to or like another <a ~ of man to monkey> **b :** an examination of two or more items to establish similarities and dissimilarities **2 :** identity of features **:** SIMILARITY <several points of ~ between two authors> **3 :** the modification of an adjective or adverb to denote different levels of quality, quantity, or relation

com·part \kəm-ˈpärt\ *vt* [It *compartire,* fr. LL *compartiri* to share out, fr. L *com-* + *partiri* to share, fr. *part-, pars* part, share] **:** to mark out into parts; *specif* **:** to lay out in parts according to a plan

[1]**com·part·ment** \kəm-ˈpärt-mənt\ *n* [MF *compartiment,* fr. It *compartimento,* fr. *compartire*] **1 :** one of the parts into which an enclosed space is divided **2 :** a separate division or section — **com·part·men·tal** \kəm-ˌpärt-ˈment-ᵊl, ˌkäm-\ *adj*

[2]**com·part·ment** \-ˌment, -mənt\ *vt* **:** COMPARTMENTALIZE

com·part·men·tal·ize \kəm-ˌpärt-ˈment-ᵊl-ˌīz, ˌkäm-\ *vt* **-ized; -iz·ing :** to separate into isolated compartments or categories <*compartmentalized* knowledge —H. M. McLuhan> — **com·part·men·tal·iza·tion** \-ˌment-ᵊl-ə-ˈzā-shən\ *n*

com·part·men·ta·tion \kəm-ˌpärt-mən-ˈtā-shən, -ˌmen-\ *n* **:** division into separate sections or units

[1]**com·pass** \ˈkəm-pəs *also* ˈkäm-\ *vt* [ME *compassen,* fr. OF *compasser* to measure, fr. (assumed) VL *compassare* to pace off, fr. L *com-* + *passus* pace] **1 :** to devise or contrive often with craft or skill **2 a :** ENCOMPASS **b :** to travel entirely around <~ the earth> **3 a :** to bring about **:** ACHIEVE **b :** to get into one's possession or power **:** OBTAIN **4 :** COMPREHEND ***syn*** see REACH — **com·pass·able** \-pə-sə-bəl\ *adj*

[2]**compass** *n* **1 a :** BOUNDARY, CIRCUMFERENCE <within the ~ of the city walls> **b :** a circumscribed space <within the narrow ~ of 21 pages —V. L. Parrington> **c :** RANGE, SCOPE <the ~ of a voice> **2 :** a curved or roundabout course <a ~ of seven days' journey — 2 Kings 3:9 (AV)> **3 a :** a device for determining directions by means of a magnetic needle or group of needles turning freely on a pivot and pointing to the magnetic north **b :** any of various nonmagnetic devices that serve the same purpose as the magnetic compass **c :** an instrument for describing circles or transferring measurements that consists of two pointed branches joined at the top by a pivot — usu. used in pl.; called also *pair of compasses*

[3]**compass** *adj* **1 :** forming a curve <a ~ timber> **2 :** semicircular in plan — used of a bow window

compass card *n* **:** the circular card attached to the needles of a mariner's compass on which are marked 32 points of the compass and the 360° of the circle

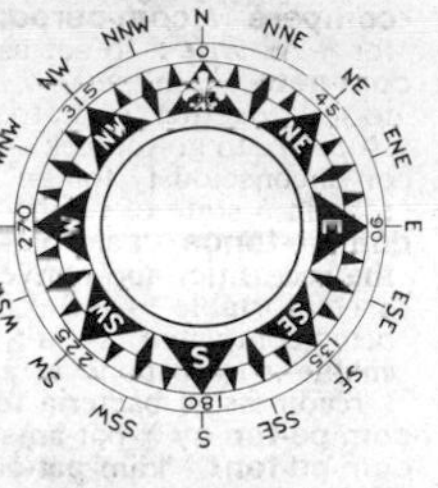

compass card

com·pas·sion \kəm-ˈpash-ən\ *n* [ME, fr. MF or LL; MF, fr. LL *compassion-, compassio,* fr *compassus,* pp. of *compati* to sympathize, fr. L *com-* + *pati* to bear, suffer — more at PATIENT] **:** sympathetic consciousness of others' distress together with a desire to alleviate it ***syn*** see SYMPATHY — **com·pas·sion·less** \-ləs\ *adj*

[1]**com·pas·sion·ate** \kəm-ˈpash-(ə-)nət\ *adj* **1 :** having or showing compassion **:** SYMPATHETIC **2 :** granted because of unusual distressing circumstances affecting an individual — used of leaves and other military privileges — **com·pas·sion·ate·ly** *adv* — **com·pas·sion·ate·ness** *n*

[2]**com·pas·sion·ate** \-ˈpash-ə-ˌnāt\ *vt* **-at·ed; -at·ing :** PITY

compass plant *n* **:** any of several plants whose leaves or branches grow on the axis so as to indicate the cardinal points of the compass

com·pat·i·ble \kəm-ˈpat-ə-bəl\ *adj* [MF, fr. ML *compatibilis,* lit., sympathetic, fr. LL *compati*] **1 :** capable of existing together in harmony **2 :** capable of cross-fertilizing freely or uniting vegetatively **3 :** being or relating to a system in which color television broadcasts may be received in black and white on receivers without special modification **4 :** capable of forming a homogeneous mixture that neither separates nor is altered by chemical interaction ***syn*** see CONSONANT ***ant*** incompatible — **com·pat·i·bil·i·ty** \-ˌpat-ə-ˈbil-ət-ē\ *n* — **com·pat·i·ble·ness** \-ˈpat-ə-bəl-nəs\ *n* — **com·pat·i·bly** \-blē\ *adv*

com·pa·tri·ot \kəm-ˈpā-trē-ət, käm-, -trē-ˌät, *chiefly Brit* -ˈpa-\ *n* [F *compatriote,* fr. LL *compatriota,* fr. L *com-* + LL *patriota* fellow countryman — more at PATRIOT] **1 :** a fellow countryman **2 :** COMPEER, COLLEAGUE — **com·pa·tri·ot·ic** \kəm-ˌpā-trē-ˈät-ik, ˌkäm-, *chiefly Brit* -ˌpa-\ *adj*

compd *abbr* compound

[1]**com·peer** \ˈkäm-ˌpi(ə)r, käm-ˈ, kəm-ˈ\ *n* **1** [ME, fr. OF *compere,* lit., godfather, fr. ML *compater,* fr. L *com-* + *pater* father — more at FATHER] **:** COMPANION **2** [modif. of L *compar,* fr. *compar,* adj., like — more at COMPARE] **:** EQUAL, PEER

[2]**compeer** *vt, obs* **:** EQUAL, MATCH

com·pel \kəm-ˈpel\ *vt* **com·pelled; com·pel·ling** [ME *compellen,* fr. MF *compellir,* fr. L *compellere,* fr. *com-* + *pellere* to drive — more at FELT] **1 :** to drive or urge forcefully or irresistibly <poverty *compelled* him to work> **2 :** to cause to do or occur by overwhelming pressure <exhaustion of ammunition *compelled* their surrender> **3** *archaic* **:** to drive together ***syn*** see FORCE — **com·pel·la·ble** \-ˈpel-ə-bəl\ *adj* — **com·pel·ler** *n*

com·pel·la·tion \ˌkäm-pə-ˈlā-shən, -ˌpel-ˈā-\ *n* [L *compellation-, compellatio,* fr. *compellatus,* pp. of *compellare* to address, fr. *com-* + *-pellare* (as in *appellare* to accost, appeal to)] **1 :** an act or action of addressing someone **2 :** APPELLATION 2

com·pend \ˈkäm-ˌpend\ *n* [ML *compendium*] **:** COMPENDIUM

com·pen·di·ous \kəm-ˈpen-dē-əs\ *adj* **:** marked by brief expression of a comprehensive matter ***syn*** see CONCISE — **com·pen·di·ous·ly** *adv* — **com·pen·di·ous·ness** *n*

com·pen·di·um \kəm-ˈpen-dē-əm\ *n, pl* **-di·ums** *or* **-dia** \-dē-ə\ [ML, fr. L, saving, shortcut, fr. *compendere* to weigh together, fr. *com-* + *pendere* to weigh — more at PENDANT] **:** a brief summary of a larger work or of a field of knowledge **:** ABSTRACT

com·pen·sa·ble \kəm-ˈpen(t)-sə-bəl\ *adj* **:** that is to be or can be compensated — **com·pen·sa·bil·i·ty** \kəm-ˌpen(t)-sə-ˈbil-ət-ē, ˌkäm-\ *n*

com·pen·sate \ˈkäm-pən-ˌsāt, -ˌpen-\ *vb* **-sat·ed; -sat·ing** [L *compensatus,* pp. of *compensare,* fr. *compensus,* pp. of *compendere*] *vt* **1 :** to be equivalent to **:** COUNTERBALANCE **2 :** to make an appropriate and usu. counterbalancing payment to <~ a neighbor for damage to his property> **3 a :** to provide with means of counteracting variation **b :** to neutralize the effect of (variations) ~ *vi* **1 :** to supply an equivalent — used with *for* **2 :** to offset an error, defect, or undesired effect — **com·pen·sa·tive** \ˈkäm-pən-ˌsāt-iv, -ˌpen-; kəm-ˈpen(t)-sət-\ *adj* — **com·pen·sa·tor** \ˈkäm-pən-ˌsāt-ər, -ˌpen-\ *n* — **com·pen·sa·to·ry** \kəm-ˈpen(t)-sə-ˌtōr-ē, -ˌtȯr-\ *adj*

syn **1** COMPENSATE, COUNTERVAIL, BALANCE, OFFSET *shared meaning element* **:** to make up for what is excessive or deficient or helpful or harmful
2 see PAY

com·pen·sa·tion \ˌkäm-pən-ˈsā-shən, -ˌpen-\ *n* **1 a (1) :** correction of an organic inferiority or loss by hypertrophy or by increased functioning of another organ or unimpaired parts of the same organ **(2) :** a psychological mechanism by which feelings of inferiority, frustration, or failure in one field are counterbalanced by achievement in another **b :** adjustment of the phase retardation of one light ray with respect to that of another **2 a :** something that constitutes an equivalent or recompense <age has its ~*s*>; *specif* : payment to an unemployed or injured worker or his dependents **b** : PAYMENT, REMUNERATION — **com·pen·sa·tion·al** \-shnəl, -shən-ᵊl\ *adj*

[1]**com·pere** \'käm-ˌpe(ə)r\ *n* [F *compère,* lit. godfather — more at COMPEER] *Brit* : the master of ceremonies of an entertainment (as a television program)

[2]**compere** *vb* **com·pered; com·per·ing** *vt, Brit* : to act as compere for ~ *vi, Brit* : to act as a compere

com·pete \kəm-'pēt\ *vi* **com·pet·ed; com·pet·ing** [LL *competere* to seek together, fr. L, to come together, agree, be suitable, fr. *com-* + *petere* to go to, seek — more at FEATHER] : to strive consciously or unconsciously for an objective (as position, profit, or a prize) : be in a state of rivalry ***syn*** see RIVAL

com·pe·tence \'käm-pət-ən(t)s\ *n* **1** : a sufficiency of means for the necessities and conveniences of life <provided his family with a comfortable ~—Rex Ingamells> **2** : the quality or state of being competent: as **a** : the properties of an embryonic field that enable it to respond in a characteristic manner to an inductor **b** : readiness of bacteria to undergo genetic transformation

com·pe·ten·cy \-pət-ən-sē\ *n, pl* **-cies** : COMPETENCE

com·pe·tent \'käm-pət-ənt\ *adj* [ME, suitable, fr. MF & L; MF, fr. L *competent-, competens,* fr. prp. of *competere* to be suitable] **1** : having requisite or adequate ability or qualities : FIT <a ~ workman> <a ~ and well constructed novel —Elaine Bender> **2** : proper or rightly pertinent **3** : legally qualified or adequate <a ~ witness> **4** : having the capacity to function or develop in a particular way; *specif* : having the capacity to respond (as by producing an antibody) to an antigenic determinant <immunologically ~ cells> ***syn*** **1** see ABLE **2** see SUFFICIENT ***ant*** incompetent — **com·pe·tent·ly** *adv*

com·pe·ti·tion \ˌkäm-pə-'tish-ən\ *n* [LL *competition-, competitio,* fr. L *competitus,* pp. of *competere*] **1** : the act or process of competing : RIVALRY **2** : a contest between rivals <a high-diving ~>; *also* : the person competing <keep ahead of the ~ > **3** : the effort of two or more parties acting independently to secure the business of a third party by offering the most favorable terms **4** : active demand by two or more organisms or kinds of organisms for some environmental resource in short supply — **com·pet·i·to·ry** \kəm-'pet-ə-ˌtōr-ē, -ˌtór-\ *adj*

com·pet·i·tive \kəm-'pet-ət-iv\ *adj* **1** : relating to, characterized by, or based on competition <~ sports> <~ examinations> **2** : inclined, desiring, or suited to compete <a ~ breed of men—Ken Purdy> <salary benefits must be ~—M. S. Eisenhower> **3** : depending for effectiveness on the relative concentration of two or more substances <~ inhibition of an enzyme> — **com·pet·i·tive·ly** *adv* — **com·pet·i·tive·ness** *n*

com·pet·i·tor \kəm-'pet-ət-ər\ *n* : one that competes: *as* **a** : RIVAL **b** : one selling or buying goods or services in the same market as another **c** : an organism that lives in competition with another

com·pi·la·tion \ˌkäm-pə-'lā-shən *also* -ˌpī-\ *n* **1** : the act or process of compiling **2** : something compiled <a ~ of statistics>

com·pile \kəm-'pī(ə)l\ *vt* **com·piled; com·pil·ing** [ME *compilen,* fr. MF *compiler,* fr. L *compilare* to plunder] **1** : to collect into a volume **2** : to compose out of materials from other documents

com·pil·er \kəm-'pī-lər\ *n* **1** : one that compiles **2** : a computer program that translates instructions written in a higher-level symbolic language (as COBOL) into machine language

com·pla·cence \kəm-'plās-ᵊn(t)s\ *n* **1** : calm or secure satisfaction with one's self or lot : SELF-SATISFACTION **2** *obs* : COMPLAISANCE **3** : UNCONCERN

com·pla·cen·cy \-ᵊn-sē\ *n, pl* **-cies** **1** : COMPLACENCE; *esp* : self-satisfaction accompanied by unawareness of actual dangers or deficiencies **2** : an instance of complacency <a book which broke up . . . theological *complacencies* — *Times Lit. Supp.*>

com·pla·cent \kəm-'plās-ᵊnt\ *adj* [L *complacent-, complacens,* prp. of *complacēre* to please greatly, fr. *com-* + *placēre* to please — more at PLEASE] **1** : SELF-SATISFIED <a ~ smile> **2** : COMPLAISANT 1 **3** : UNCONCERNED <~ about inflation —N. H. Jacoby> — **com·plai·sant·ly** *adv*

com·plain \kəm-'plān\ *vi* [ME *compleynen,* fr. MF *complaindre,* fr. (assumed) VL *complangere,* fr. L *com-* + *plangere* to lament — more at PLAINT] **1** : to express grief, pain, or discontent **2** : to make a formal accusation or charge — **com·plain·er** *n* — **com·plain·ing·ly** \-'plā-niŋ-lē\ *adv*

com·plain·ant \kəm-'plā-nənt\ *n* : the party who makes the complaint in a legal action or proceeding

com·plaint \kəm-'plānt\ *n* [ME *compleynte,* fr. MF *complainte,* fr. OF, fr. *complaindre*] **1** : expression of grief, pain, or resentment **2 a** : something that is the cause or subject of protest or outcry **b** : a bodily ailment or disease **3** : a formal allegation against a party

com·plai·sance \kəm-'plās-ᵊn(t)s, -'plāz-; ˌkäm-plā-'zan(t)s, -plə-, -'zän(t)s\ *n* : disposition to please or comply : AFFABILITY

com·plai·sant \-ᵊnt, -'zant, -'zänt\ *adj* [F, fr. MF, fr. prp. of *complaire* to gratify, acquiesce, fr. L *complacēre* to please greatly] **1** : marked by an inclination to please or oblige **2** : tending to consent to others' wishes ***syn*** see AMIABLE ***ant*** contrary, perverse — **com·plai·sant·ly** *adv*

com·pleat \kəm-'plēt\ *adj* [archaic variant of *complete* in *The Compleat Angler* (1653) by Izaak Walton] : COMPLETE 3 <the ~ conductor, experienced in opera as well as in the symphonic repertoire —Winthrop Sargeant>

com·plect·ed \kəm-'plek-təd\ *adj* [irreg. fr. *complexion*] : having a specified facial complexion <a tall, thin man, fairly dark ~ —E. J. Kahn>

[1]**com·ple·ment** \'käm-plə-mənt\ *n* [ME, fr. L *complementum,* fr. *complēre*] **1 a** : something that fills up, completes, or makes perfect **b** : the quantity or number required to make a thing complete <he had the usual ~ of eyes and ears—Francis Parkman>; *specif* : the whole force or personnel of a ship **c** : one of two mutually completing parts : COUNTERPART **2 a** : an angle or arc that when added to a given angle or arc equals a right angle **b** : the set of all elements that do not belong to a given set and are contained in a particular mathematical set containing the given set **c** : a number that when added to another number of the same sign yields zero if the significant digit farthest to the left is discarded **3** : the interval in music required with a given interval to complete the octave **4** : an added word or expression by which a predication is made complete <*president* and *beautiful* in "they elected him president" and "he thought her beautiful" are ~*s*> **5** : the thermolabile substance in normal blood serum and plasma that in combination with antibodies causes the destruction of bacteria, foreign blood corpuscles, and other antigens

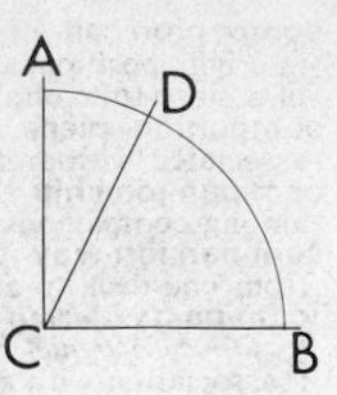

complement 2a: *ACB* right angle; *ACD* complement of *DCB* (and vice versa); *AD* complement of *DB* (and vice versa)

[2]**com·ple·ment** \-ˌment\ *vt* **1** : to be complementary to **2** *obs* : COMPLIMENT ~ *vi, obs* : to exchange formal courtesies

com·ple·men·tal \ˌkäm-plə-'ment-ᵊl\ *adj* **1** : relating to or being a complement **2** *obs* : CEREMONIOUS, COMPLIMENTARY

com·ple·men·tar·i·ty \ˌkäm-plə-(ˌ)men-'tar-ət-ē, -mən-\ *n* : the quality or state of being complementary

com·ple·men·ta·ry \ˌkäm-plə-'ment-ə-rē, -'men-trē\ *adj* **1** : serving to fill out or complete **2** : mutually supplying each other's lack **3** : relating to or constituting one of a pair of contrasting colors that produce a neutral color when combined in suitable proportions **4** : of or relating to the precise pairing of purine and pyrimidine bases between strands of DNA and sometimes RNA such that the structure of one strand determines the other — **com·ple·men·ta·ri·ly** \-'men-trə-lē, -(ˌ)men-'ter-ə-lē, -'ment-ə-rə-lē\ *adv* — **com·ple·men·ta·ri·ness** \-'ment-ə-rē-nəs, -'men-trē-\ *n* — **complementary** *n*

complementary angles *n pl* : two angles whose sum is 90 degrees

com·ple·men·ta·tion \ˌkäm-plə-(ˌ)men-'tā-shən, -mən-\ *n* **1** : the determination of the complement of a given mathematical set **2** : production of normal phenotype in an individual heterozygous for two closely related mutations with one on each homologous chromosome and at a slightly different position

complement fixation *n* : the absorption of complement to the product of the union of an antibody and the antigen for which it is specific when added to a mixture of such antibody and antigen

[1]**com·plete** \kəm-'plēt\ *adj* **com·plet·er; -est** [ME *complet,* fr. MF, fr. L *completus,* fr. pp. of *complēre* to fill up, complete, fr. *com-* + *plēre* to fill — more at FULL] **1 a** : having all necessary parts, elements, or steps <~ diet> <~ analysis of a problem> **b** : having all four sets of floral organs : MONOCLINOUS **c** *of a subject or predicate* : including modifiers, complements, or objects **2** : brought to an end : CONCLUDED <a ~ period of time> **3** : highly proficient <a ~ artist> **4 a** : fully carried out : THOROUGH <a ~ renovation> **b** : TOTAL, ABSOLUTE <~ silence> ***syn*** see FULL ***ant*** incomplete — **com·plete·ly** *adv* — **com·plete·ness** *n* — **com·ple·tive** \-'plēt-iv\ *adj*

[2]**complete** *vt* **com·plet·ed; com·plet·ing** **1** : to bring to an end and esp. into a perfected state <~ a painting> **2 a** : to make whole or perfect <its song ~*s* the charm of this bird> **b** : to mark the end of <a rousing chorus ~*s* the show> **c** : EXECUTE, FULFILL <~ a contract> **3** : to carry out (a forward pass) successfully

complete fertilizer *n* : a fertilizer that contains the three chief plant nutrients nitrogen, phosphoric acid, and potash

com·ple·tion \kəm-'plē-shən\ *n* **1** : the act or process of completing **2** : the quality or state of being complete

[1]**com·plex** \käm-'pleks, kəm-', 'käm-ˌ\ *adj* [L *complexus,* pp. of *complecti* to embrace, comprise (a multitude of objects), fr. *com-* + *plectere* to braid — more at PLY] **1 a** : composed of two or more parts : COMPOSITE **b** (1) *of a word* : having a bound form as one or both of its immediate constituents <*unmanly* is a ~ word> (2) *of a sentence* : consisting of a main clause and one or more subordinate clauses **2** : hard to separate, analyze, or solve — **com·plex·ly** *adv* — **com·plex·ness** *n*

syn COMPLEX, COMPLICATED, INTRICATE, INVOLVED, KNOTTY *shared meaning element* : having confusingly interrelated parts ***ant*** simple

[2]**com·plex** \'käm-ˌpleks\ *n* **1** : a whole made up of complicated or interrelated parts <a ~ of university buildings> <a ~ of welfare programs> <the military-industrial ~ > **2 a** : a group of culture traits relating to a single activity (as hunting), process (as use of flint), or culture unit **b** (1) : a group of repressed desires and memories that exerts a dominating influence upon the personality (2) : an exaggerated reaction to a subject or situation **c** : a group of obviously related units of which the degree and nature of the relationship is imperfectly known **3** : a complex substance (as a coordination complex) in which the constituents are more intimately associated than in a simple mixture

[3]**com·plex** *like* [1]\ *vt* **1** : to make complex or into a complex **2** : CHELATE — **com·plex·ation** \ˌkäm-ˌplek-'sā-shən, kəm-\ *n*

complex fraction *n* : a fraction with a fraction or mixed number in the numerator or denominator or both — compare SIMPLE FRACTION

com·plex·ion \kəm-'plek-shən\ *n* [ME, fr. MF, fr. ML *complexion-, complexio,* fr. L, combination, fr. *complexus,* pp] **1** : the combination of the hot, cold, moist, and dry qualities held in medieval physiology to determine the quality of a body **2 a** : an individual complex of ways of thinking or feeling **b** : a complex of attitudes and inclinations **3** : the hue or appearance of the skin and esp. of the face <a dark ~> **4** : overall aspect or impression <by changing the ~ of the legislative branch—Trevor Armbrister> — **com·plex·ion·al** \-shnəl, -shən-ᵊl\ *adj* — **com·plex·ioned** \-shənd\ *adj*

com·plex·i·ty \kəm-'plek-sət-ē, käm-\ *n, pl* **-ties** **1** : the quality or state of being complex **2** : something complex <the *complexities* of today's society —John J. Gallagher>

complex number *n* **:** a number of the form $a + b\sqrt{-1}$ where *a* and *b* are real numbers
com·plex·om·e·try \ˌkäm-ˌplek-ˈsäm-ə-trē, kəm-\ *n* **:** a titrimetric technique involving the use of a complexing agent (as EDTA) as the titrant — **com·plex·o·met·ric** \(ˌ)käm-ˌplek-sə-ˈme-trik, kəm-\ *adj*
complex plane *n* **:** a plane whose points are identified by means of complex numbers
com·pli·ance \kəm-ˈplī-ən(t)s\ *n* **1 :** the act or process of complying to a desire, demand, or proposal or to coercion **2 :** a disposition to yield to others **3 a :** the ability of an object to yield elastically when a force is applied **:** FLEXIBILITY **b :** the force required to move a phonograph stylus a given distance
com·pli·an·cy \-ən-sē\ *n* **:** COMPLIANCE
com·pli·ant \-ənt\ *adj* **:** ready or disposed to comply **:** SUBMISSIVE — **com·pli·ant·ly** *adv*
com·pli·ca·cy \ˈkäm-pli-kə-sē\ *n, pl* **-cies** [[2]*complicate*] **1 :** the quality or state of being complicated **2 :** something that is complicated
[1]**com·pli·cate** \ˈkäm-plə-ˌkāt\ *vb* **-cat·ed; -cat·ing** *vt* **1 :** to combine esp. in an involved or inextricable manner **2 :** to make complex or difficult **3 :** INVOLVE; *esp* **:** to cause to be more complex or severe <a virus disease *complicated* by bacterial infection ~ *vi* **:** to become complicated
[2]**com·pli·cate** \-pli-kət\ *adj* [L *complicatus,* pp. of *complicare* to fold together, fr. *com-* + *plicare* to fold — more at PLY] **1 :** COMPLEX, INTRICATE **2 :** CONDUPLICATE
com·pli·cat·ed \ˈkäm-plə-ˌkāt-əd\ *adj* **1 :** consisting of parts intricately combined **2 :** difficult to analyze, understand, or explain ***syn*** see COMPLEX ***ant*** simple — **com·pli·cat·ed·ly** *adv* — **com·pli·cat·ed·ness** *n*
com·pli·ca·tion \ˌkäm-plə-ˈkā-shən\ *n* **1 a :** COMPLEXITY, INTRICACY; *specif* **:** a situation or a detail of character complicating the main thread of a plot **b :** a making difficult, involved, or intricate **c :** a complex or intricate feature or element **d :** a difficult factor or issue often appearing unexpectedly and changing existing plans, methods, or attitudes **2 :** a secondary disease or condition developing in the course of a primary disease
com·plice \ˈkäm-pləs, ˈkəm-\ *n* [ME, fr. MF, fr. LL *complic-, complex,* fr. L *com-* + *plicare* to fold] *archaic* **:** ASSOCIATE
com·plic·i·ty \kəm-ˈplis-ət-ē, -ˈplis-tē\ *n, pl* **-ties 1 :** association or participation in or as if in a wrongful act **2 :** an instance of complicity
com·pli·er \-ˈplī(-ə)r\ *n* **:** one that complies
[1]**com·pli·ment** \ˈkäm-plə-mənt\ *n* [F, fr. It *complimento,* fr. Sp *cumplimiento,* fr. *cumplir* to be courteous — more at COMPLY] **1 a :** an expression of esteem, respect, affection, or admiration; *esp* **:** a flattering remark **b :** formal and respectful recognition **:** HONOR <a party in ~ of house guests> **2** *pl* **:** best wishes **:** REGARDS <accept my ~*s*> <~*s* of the season>
[2]**com·pli·ment** \-ˌment\ *vt* **1 :** to pay a compliment to **2 :** to present with a token of esteem
com·pli·men·ta·ry \ˌkäm-plə-ˈment-ə-rē, -ˈmen-trē\ *adj* **1 a :** expressing or containing a compliment **b :** FAVORABLE <the novel received ~ reviews> **2 :** given free as a courtesy or favor <~ tickets> — **com·pli·men·ta·ri·ly** \-ˈmen-trə-lē, -(ˌ)men-ˈter-ə-lē, -ˈment-ə-rə-lē\ *adv*
complimentary close *n* **:** the words (as *sincerely yours*) that conventionally come immediately before the signature of a letter and express the sender's regard for the receiver — called also *complimentary closing*
com·pline \ˈkäm-plən, -ˌplīn\ *n, often cap* [ME *complie, compline,* fr. OF *complie,* modif. of LL *completa,* fr. L, fem. of *completus* complete] **:** the seventh and last of the canonical hours
[1]**com·plot** \ˈkäm-ˌplät\ *n* [MF *complot* crowd, plot] *archaic* **:** PLOT, CONSPIRACY
[2]**com·plot** \kəm-ˈplät, käm-\ *vb, archaic* **:** PLOT
com·ply \kəm-ˈplī\ *vi* **com·plied; com·ply·ing** [It *complire,* fr. Sp *cumplir* to complete, perform what is due, be courteous, fr. L *complēre* to complete] **1** *obs* **:** to be ceremoniously courteous **2 :** to conform or adapt one's actions to another's wishes, to a rule, or to necessity ***syn*** see OBEY
com·po \ˈkäm-(ˌ)pō\ *n, pl* **compos** [short for *composition*] **:** any of various composition materials
[1]**com·po·nent** \kəm-ˈpō-nənt, ˈkäm-ˌ, käm-ˈ\ *n* [L *component-, componens,* prp. of *componere* to put together — more at COMPOUND] **1 :** a constituent part **:** INGREDIENT **2 a :** any one of the vector terms added to form a vector sum or resultant **b :** a coordinate of a vector ***syn*** see ELEMENT ***ant*** composite, complex — **com·po·nen·tial** \ˌkäm-pə-ˈnen-chəl\ *adj*
[2]**component** *adj* **:** serving or helping to constitute **:** CONSTITUENT
[1]**com·port** \kəm-ˈpō(ə)rt, -ˈpȯ(ə)rt\ *vb* [MF *comporter* to bear, conduct, fr. L *comportare* to bring together, fr. *com-* + *portare* to carry — more at PORT] *vi* **:** to be fitting **:** ACCORD <acts that ~ with ideals> ~ *vt* **:** BEHAVE; *esp* **:** to behave in a manner conformable to what is right, proper, or expected <~*ed* himself well in the emergency> ***syn*** see AGREE, BEHAVE
[2]**com·port** \ˈkäm-ˌpō(ə)rt, -ˌpȯ(ə)rt\ *n* **:** COMPOTE 2
com·port·ment \kəm-ˈpōrt-mənt, -ˈpȯrt-\ *n* **:** BEARING, DEMEANOR
com·pose \kəm-ˈpōz\ *vb* **com·posed; com·pos·ing** [MF *composer,* fr. L *componere* (perf. indic. *composui*) — more at COMPOUND] *vt* **1 a :** to form by putting together **:** FASHION <a committee *composed* of three representatives—*Current Biog.*> **b :** to form the substance of **:** CONSTITUTE <*composed* of many ingredients> **c :** ARRANGE, SET, PHOTOCOMPOSE **2 a :** to create by mental or artistic labor **:** PRODUCE <~ a sonnet sequence> **b (1) :** to formulate and write (a piece of music) **(2) :** to compose music for **3 :** to deal with or act on so as to reduce to a minimum <~ their differences> **4 :** to arrange in proper or orderly form <~ her clothing> **5 :** to free from agitation **:** CALM, SETTLE <~ a patient> ~ *vi* **:** to practice composition
com·posed \-ˈpōzd\ *adj* **:** free from agitation **:** CALM; *esp* **:** SELF-POSSESSED ***syn*** see COOL ***ant*** discomposed, anxious — **com·pos·ed·ly** \-ˈpō-zəd-lē\ *adv* — **com·pos·ed·ness** \-ˈpō-zəd-nəs\ *n*
com·pos·er \kəm-ˈpō-zər\ *n* **:** one that composes; *esp* **:** a person who writes music
composing room *n* **:** the department in a printing office where typesetting and related operations are performed
composing stick *n* **:** a tray with an adjustable slide that is held in one hand by a compositor as he sets type into it with the other hand
[1]**com·pos·ite** \käm-ˈpäz-ət, kəm-ˈ, *esp Brit* ˈkäm-pə-zit\ *adj* [L *compositus,* pp. of *componere*] **1 :** made up of distinct parts: as **a** *cap* **:** relating to or being a modification of the Corinthian order combining angular Ionic volutes with the acanthus-circled bell of the Corinthian **b :** of or relating to a very large family (Compositae) of dicotyledonous herbs, shrubs, and trees often considered to be the most highly evolved plants and characterized by florets arranged in dense heads that resemble single flowers **c :** factorable into two or more prime factors other than 1 and itself <8 is a positive~ integer> **2 :** combining the typical or essential characteristics of individuals making up a group <the ~ man called the Poet —Richard Poirier> **3** *of a statistical hypothesis* **:** specifying a range of values for one or more statistical parameters — compare SIMPLE 10 — **com·pos·ite·ly** *adv*
[2]**composite** *n* **1 :** something composite **:** COMPOUND **2 :** a composite plant
[3]**composite** *vt* **-it·ed; -it·ing :** to make composite or into something composite <*composited* four soil samples>

composite 2: section of a composite flower head: *1* disk flower, *2* ray flower, *3* bracts

com·po·si·tion \ˌkäm-pə-ˈzish-ən\ *n* [ME *composicioun,* fr. MF *composition,* fr. L *composition-, compositio,* fr. *compositus*] **1 a :** the act or process of composing; *specif* **:** arrangement into proper proportion or relation and esp. into artistic form **b (1) :** the arrangement of type for printing <hand ~> **(2) :** the production of type or typographic characters (as in photocomposition) arranged for printing **2 a :** the manner in which something is composed **b :** general makeup <the changing ethnic ~ of the city —Leonard Buder> **c :** the qualitative and quantitative makeup of a chemical compound **3 :** mutual settlement or agreement **4 :** a product of mixing or combining various elements or ingredients **5 :** an intellectual creation: as **a :** a piece of writing; *esp* **:** a school exercise in the form of a brief essay **b :** a written piece of music esp. of considerable size and complexity **6 :** the quality or state of being compound — **com·po·si·tion·al** \-ˈzish-nəl, -ən-ᵊl\ *adj* — **com·po·si·tion·al·ly** \-ē\ *adv*
com·pos·i·tor \kəm-ˈpäz-ət-ər\ *n* **:** one who sets type
com·pos men·tis \ˌkäm-pə-ˈsment-əs\ *adj* [L, lit., having mastery of one's mind] **:** of sound mind, memory, and understanding
[1]**com·post** \ˈkäm-ˌpōst, *esp Brit* -ˌpäst\ *n* [MF, fr. ML *compostum,* fr. L, neut. of *compositus, compostus,* pp. of *componere* to put together] **1 :** a mixture that consists largely of decayed organic matter and is used for fertilizing and conditioning land **2 :** MIXTURE, COMPOUND
[2]**compost** *vt* **:** to convert (as plant debris) to compost
com·po·sure \kəm-ˈpō-zhər\ *n* **:** a calmness or repose esp. of mind, bearing, or appearance **:** SELF-POSSESSION ***syn*** see EQUANIMITY ***ant*** discomposure, perturbation
com·pote \ˈkäm-ˌpōt\ *n* [F, fr. OF *composte,* fr. L *composta,* fem. of *compostus,* pp.] **1 :** whole fruits cooked in syrup **2 :** a bowl of glass, porcelain, or metal usu. with a base and stem from which compotes, fruits, nuts, or sweets are served
[1]**com·pound** \käm-ˈpau̇nd, kəm-ˈ, ˈkäm-ˌ\ *vb* [ME *compounen,* fr. MF *compondre,* fr. L *componere,* fr. *com-* + *ponere* to put — more at POSITION] *vt* **1 :** to put together (parts) so as to form a whole **:** COMBINE <~ ingredients> **2 :** to form by combining parts <~ a medicine> **3 :** to settle amicably **:** adjust by agreement <~ a debt> **4 a :** to pay (interest) on both the accrued interest and the principal **b :** to add to **:** AUGMENT <we ~*ed* our error in later policy—Robert Lekachman> **5 :** to agree for a consideration not to prosecute (an offense) <~ a felony> ~ *vi* **1 :** to become joined in a compound **2 :** to come to terms of agreement — **com·pound·able** \-ə-bəl\ *adj* — **com·pound·er** *n*
[2]**com·pound** \ˈkäm-ˌpau̇nd, käm-ˈ, kəm-ˈ\ *adj* [ME *compouned,* pp. of *compounen*] **1 :** composed of or resulting from union of separate elements, ingredients, or parts; *specif* **:** composed of united similar elements esp. of a kind usu. independent <a ~ plant ovary> **2 :** involving or used in a combination **3 a** *of a word* **:** constituting a compound **b** *of a sentence* **:** having two or more main clauses
[3]**com·pound** \ˈkäm-ˌpau̇nd\ *n* **1 a :** a word consisting of components that are words (as *rowboat, high school, devil-may-care*) **b :** a word consisting of any of various combinations of words, combining forms, or affixes (as *anthropology, kilocycle, builder*) **2 :** something formed by a union of elements or parts; *specif* **:** a distinct substance formed by chemical union of two or more ingredients in definite proportion by weight
[4]**com·pound** \ˈkäm-ˌpau̇nd\ *n* [by folk etymology fr. Malay *kampong* group of buildings, village] **:** a fenced or walled-in area containing a group of buildings and esp. residences
compound–complex *adj, of a sentence* **:** having two or more main clauses and one or more subordinate clauses
compound eye *n* **:** an eye (as of an insect) made up of many separate visual units
compound fracture *n* **:** a bone fracture produced in such a way as to form an open wound through which bone fragments usu. protrude

compound interest *n* : interest computed on the sum of an original principal and accrued interest
compound leaf *n* : a leaf in which the blade is divided to the midrib forming two or more leaflets on a common axis
compound microscope *n* : a microscope consisting of an objective and an eyepiece mounted in a drawtube
compound number *n* : a number (as 2 ft. 5 in.) involving different denominations or more than one unit
com·pra·dor \ˌkäm-prə-ˈdȯ(ə)r\ *or* **com·pra·dore** \-ˈdō(ə)r, -ˈdȯ(ə)r\ *n* [Pg *comprador*, lit., buyer] : a Chinese agent engaged by a foreign establishment in China to have charge of its Chinese employees and to act as an intermediary in business affairs
com·pre·hend \ˌkäm-pri-ˈhend\ *vt* [ME *comprehenden*, fr. L *comprehendere*, fr. *com-* + *prehendere* to grasp — more at PREHENSILE] **1** : to grasp the nature, significance, or meaning of **2** : to include as an integral part <philosophy's scope ~*s* the truth of everything which man may understand —H. O. Taylor> **3** : to include by construction or implication : COMPRISE ***syn*** see UNDERSTAND, INCLUDE — **com·pre·hend·ible** \-ˈhen-də-bəl\ *adj*
com·pre·hen·si·ble \-ˈhen(t)-sə-bəl\ *adj* : capable of being comprehended : INTELLIGIBLE — **com·pre·hen·si·bil·i·ty** \-ˌhen(t)-sə-ˈbil-ət-ē\ *n* — **com·pre·hen·si·ble·ness** \-ˈhen(t)-sə-bəl-nəs\ *n* — **com·pre·hen·si·bly** \-blē\ *adv*
com·pre·hen·sion \ˌkäm-pri-ˈhen-chən\ *n* [MF & L; MF, fr. L *comprehension-, comprehensio*, fr. *comprehensus*, pp. of *comprehendere* to understand, comprise] **1 a** : the act or process of comprising **b** : the faculty or capability of including : COMPREHENSIVENESS **2 a** : the act or action of grasping with the intellect : UNDERSTANDING **b** : knowledge gained by comprehending **c** : the capacity for understanding fully **3** : CONNOTATION 3
com·pre·hen·sive \-ˈhen(t)-siv\ *adj* **1** : covering completely or broadly : INCLUSIVE <~ examinations> <~ insurance> **2** : having or exhibiting wide mental grasp <~ knowledge> — **com·pre·hen·sive·ly** *adv* — **com·pre·hen·sive·ness** *n*
[1]**com·press** \kəm-ˈpres\ *vb* [ME *compressen*, fr. LL *compressare* to press hard, fr. L *compressus*, pp. of *comprimere* to compress, fr. *com-* + *premere* to press] *vt* **1** : to press or squeeze together **2** : to reduce in size or volume as if by squeezing ~ *vi* : to undergo compression ***syn*** see CONTRACT ***ant*** stretch, spread
[2]**com·press** \ˈkäm-ˌpres\ *n* [MF *compresse*, fr. *compresser* to compress, fr. LL *compressare*] **1** : a folded cloth or pad applied so as to press upon a body part **2** : a machine for compressing
com·pressed \kəm-ˈprest *also* ˈkäm-,\ *adj* **1** : pressed together : reduced in size or volume (as by pressure) **2** : flattened as though subjected to compression: **a** : flattened laterally <petioles ~> **b** : narrow from side to side and deep in a dorsoventral direction — **com·pressed·ly** \kəm-ˈprest-lē, -ˈpres-əd-lē\ *adv*
compressed air *n* : air under pressure greater than that of the atmosphere
com·press·ible \kəm-ˈpres-ə-bəl\ *adj* : capable of being compressed — **com·press·ibil·i·ty** \-ˌpres-ə-ˈbil-ət-ē\ *n*
com·pres·sion \kəm-ˈpresh-ən\ *n* **1 a** : the act, process, or result of compressing **b** : the state of being compressed **2** : the process of compressing the fuel mixture in a cylinder of an internal-combustion engine (as in an automobile) **3** : a much compressed fossil plant — **com·pres·sion·al** \-ˈpresh-nəl, -ən-ᵊl\ *adj*
compressional wave *n* : a longitudinal wave (as a sound wave) propagated by the elastic compression of the medium — called also *compression wave*
com·pres·sive \kəm-ˈpres-iv\ *adj* **1** : of or relating to compression **2** : tending to compress — **com·pres·sive·ly** *adv*
com·pres·sor \-ˈpres-ər\ *n* : one that compresses: as **a** : a muscle that compresses a part **b** : a machine that compresses gases
com·prise \kəm-ˈprīz\ *vt* **com·prised; com·pris·ing** [ME *comprisen*, fr. MF *compris*, pp. of *comprendre*, fr. L *comprehendere*] **1** : INCLUDE, CONTAIN **2** : to be made up of **3** : to make up : CONSTITUTE
[1]**com·pro·mise** \ˈkäm-prə-ˌmīz\ *n* [ME, mutual promise to abide by an arbiter's decision, fr. MF *compromis*, fr. L *compromissum*, fr. neut. of *compromissus*, pp. of *compromittere* to promise mutually, fr. *com-* + *promittere* to promise — more at PROMISE] **1 a** : settlement of differences by arbitration or by consent reached by mutual concessions **b** : something blending qualities of two different things **2** : a concession to something derogatory or prejudicial <a ~ of principles>
[2]**compromise** *vb* **-mised; -mis·ing** *vt* **1** *obs* : to bind by mutual agreement **2** : to adjust or settle by mutual concessions **3** : to expose to discredit or mischief ~ *vi* **1** : to come to agreement by mutual concession **2** : to make a shameful or disreputable concession — **com·pro·mis·er** *n*
compt \ˈkau̇nt, ˈkäm(p)t\ *archaic var of* COUNT
comp·trol·ler \kən-ˈtrō-lər, ˈkäm(p)-ˌ, käm(p)-ˈ\ *n* [ME, alter. of *conterroller* controller] **1** : a royal-household official who examines and supervises expenditures **2** : a public official who audits government accounts and sometimes certifies expenditures **3** : CONTROLLER 1c — **comp·trol·ler·ship** \-ˌship\ *n*
com·pul·sion \kəm-ˈpəl-shən\ *n* [ME, fr. MF or LL; MF, fr. LL *compulsion-, compulsio*, fr. L *compulsus*, pp. of *compellere* to compel] **1 a** : an act of compelling : the state of being compelled **b** : a force or agency that compels **2** : an irresistible impulse to perform an irrational act
com·pul·sive \-ˈpəl-siv\ *adj* **1** : having power to compel <a strangely ~, resonant voice—L. C. Douglas> **2** : of, relating to, caused by, or suggestive of psychological compulsion or obsession <~ actions> — **com·pul·sive·ly** *adv* — **com·pul·sive·ness** *n* — **com·pul·siv·i·ty** \kəm-ˌpəl-ˈsiv-ət-ē, ˌkäm-\ *n*
com·pul·so·ry \kəm-ˈpəls-(ə-)rē\ *adj* **1** : MANDATORY, ENFORCED <~ arbitration> **2** : COERCIVE, COMPELLING — **com·pul·so·ri·ly** \-(ə-)rə-lē\ *adv*
com·punc·tion \kəm-ˈpəŋ(k)-shən\ *n* [ME *compunccioun*, fr. MF *componction*, fr. LL *compunction-, compunctio*, fr. L *compunctus*, pp. of *compungere* to prick hard, sting, fr. *com-* + *pungere* to prick — more at PUNGENT] **1 a** : anxiety arising from awareness of guilt <~*s* of conscience> **b** : distress of mind over an anticipated action or result <he showed no ~ in planning devilish engines of . . . destruction —Havelock Ellis> **2** : a twinge of misgiving : SCRUPLE <cheated without ~> ***syn*** see PENITENCE, QUALM — **com·punc·tious** \-shəs\ *adj*
com·pur·ga·tion \ˌkam(ˌ)pər-ˈgā-shən\ *n* [LL *compurgation-, compurgatio*, fr. L *compurgatus*, pp. of *compurgare* to clear completely, fr. *com-* + *purgare* to purge] : the clearing of an accused person by oaths of persons who swear to his veracity or innocence
com·pur·ga·tor \ˈkäm-(ˌ)pər-ˌgāt-ər\ *n* : one that under oath vouches for the character or conduct of an accused person
com·put·able \kəm-ˈpyüt-ə-bəl\ *adj* : capable of being computed — **com·put·abil·i·ty** \-ˌpyüt-ə-ˈbil-ət-ē\ *n*
com·pu·ta·tion \ˌkäm-pyu̇-ˈtā-shən\ *n* **1 a** : the act or action of computing : CALCULATION **b** : the use or operation of a computer **2** : a system or reckoning **3** : an amount computed — **com·pu·ta·tion·al** \-shnəl, -shən-ᵊl\ *adj*
[1]**com·pute** \kəm-ˈpyüt\ *n* : COMPUTATION <numbers beyond ~>
[2]**compute** *vb* **com·put·ed; com·put·ing** [L *computare* — more at COUNT] *vt* : to determine esp. by mathematical means <~ your income tax>; *also* : to determine or calculate by means of a computer ~ *vi* **1** : to make calculation : RECKON **2** : to use a computer
com·put·er \kəm-ˈpyüt-ər\ *n* : one that computes; *specif* : an automatic electronic machine for performing calculations — **com·put·er·like** \-ˌlīk\ *adj*
com·put·er·ese \-ˌpyüt-ə-ˈrēz, -ˈrēs\ *n* **1** : MACHINE LANGUAGE **2** : jargon used by computer technologists
com·put·er·ise *chiefly Brit var of* COMPUTERIZE
com·put·er·ite \-ˈpyüt-ə-ˌrīt\ *n* : COMPUTERNIK
com·put·er·ize \kəm-ˈpyüt-ə-ˌrīz\ *vt* **-ized; -iz·ing** **1** : to carry out, control, or conduct by means of a computer **2** : to equip with computers — **com·put·er·iz·able** \-ˌrī-zə-bəl\ *adj* — **com·put·er·iza·tion** \-ˌpyüt-ə-rə-ˈzā-shən\ *n*
com·put·er·nik \kəm-ˈpyüt-ər-ˌnik\ *n* [*computer* + *-nik*] : a person who works with or has a deep interest in computers
comr *abbr* commissioner
com·rade \ˈkäm-ˌrad, -rəd, *esp Brit* -ˌräd\ *n* [MF *comarade* group sleeping in one room, roommate, companion, fr. OSp *camarada*, fr. *cámara* room, fr. LL *camera, camara*] **1 a** : an intimate friend or associate : COMPANION **b** : a fellow soldier **2** [fr. its use as a form of address by communists] : COMMUNIST — **com·rade·ship** \-ˌship\ *n*
com·rade·ly \-lē\ *adj* : of or resembling a comrade or partner — **com·rade·li·ness** *n*
com·rad·ery \ˈkäm-ˌrad-(ə-)rē, rəd-rē, -ˌräd-(ə-)rē\ *n* : CAMARADERIE
comsat \ˈkäm-ˌsat\ *n* [*com*munication *sat*ellite] : an artificial satellite of the earth used for reflecting or relaying radio waves (as for intercontinental communication)
Com·stock·ery \ˈkäm-ˌstäk-ə-rē *also* ˈkəm-\ *n* [Anthony *Comstock* + E *-ery*] **1** : strict censorship of materials (as books and plays) considered obscene **2** : censorious opposition to alleged immorality in art, literature, and the theater
Com·stock·ian \käm-ˈstäk-ē-ən *also* ˌkəm-\ *adj* : of or relating to Comstockery
Comt·ian *or* **Comt·ean** \ˈkäm(p)-tē-ən, ˈkōⁿ(n)t-ē-\ *adj* : of or relating to Auguste Comte or his doctrines — **Comt·ism** \ˈkäm(p)-ˌtiz-əm, ˈkōⁿ(n)t-ˌiz-\ *n* — **Comt·ist** \ˈkäm(p)-təst, ˈkōⁿ(n)t-əst\ *adj or n*
[1]**con** \ˈkän\ *vt* **conned; con·ning** [ME *connen* to know, learn, study, alter. of *cunnen* to know, infin. of *can* — more at CAN] **1** : to study or examine closely : PERUSE **2** : to commit to memory
[2]**con** *var of* CONN
[3]**con** *adv* [ME, short for *contra*] : on the negative side : in opposition <so much has been written pro and ~>
[4]**con** *n* **1** : an argument or evidence in opposition **2** : the negative position or one holding it <an appraisal of the pros and ~*s*>
[5]**con** *adj* : CONFIDENCE
[6]**con** *vt* **conned; con·ning** [[5]*con*] **1** : SWINDLE **2** : PERSUADE, CAJOLE
[7]**con** *n* : CONVICT
[8]**con** *n* [short for *consumption*] *slang* : a destructive disease of the lungs; *esp* : TUBERCULOSIS
[9]**con** *abbr* **1** [L *conjunx*] consort **2** consolidated **3** consul **4** continued
con- — see COM-
con amo·re \ˌkän-ə-ˈmōr-ē, ˌkō-nə-ˈmōr-(ˌ)ā, -ˈmȯr-\ *adv* [It] **1** : with love, devotion, or zest **2** : in a tender manner — used as a direction in music
con ani·ma \kä-ˈnan-ə-ˌmä, kō-ˈnän-i-\ *adv* [It, lit., with spirit] : in a spirited manner : with animation — used as a direction in music
co·na·tion \kō-ˈnā-shən\ *n* [L *conation-, conatio* act of attempting, fr. *conatus*, pp. of *conari* to attempt — more at DEACON] : an inclination (as an instinct, a drive, a wish, or a craving) to act purposefully : IMPULSE 3 — **co·na·tion·al** \-shnəl, -shən-ᵊl\ *adj* — **co·na·tive** \ˈkō-nət-iv, -ˌnāt-; ˈkän-ət-\ *adj*
co·na·tus \kō-ˈnāt-əs, -ˈnät-\ *n, pl* **co·na·tus** \-əs; -ˈnä-ˌtüs, -ˈnä-\ [NL, fr. L, attempt, effort, fr. *conatus*, pp.] : a natural tendency, impulse, or striving
con brio \kän-ˈbrē-(ˌ)ō, kōn-\ *adv* [It, lit., with vigor] : in a vigorous or brisk manner — used as a direction in music
conc *abbr* **1** concentrate; concentrated; concentration **2** concrete
con·ca·nav·a·lin \ˌkän-kə-ˈnav-ə-lən\ *n* [*com-* + *canavalin* (a noncrystalline globulin found in the jack bean), fr. NL *Canavalia*, genus name of the jack bean] : either of two crystalline globulins occurring in the jack bean; *esp* : one that is a potent hemagglutinin
[1]**con·cat·e·nate** \kän-ˈkat-ə-nət, kən-\ *adj* [ME, fr. LL *concatenatus*, pp. of *concatenare* to link together, fr. L *com-* + *catena* chain — more at CHAIN] : linked together
[2]**concatenate** *vt* **-nat·ed; -nat·ing** : to link together in a series or chain — **con·cat·e·na·tion** \(ˌ)kän-ˌkat-ə-ˈnā-shən, kən-\ *n*

[1]**con·cave** \kän-'kāv, 'kän-,\ *adj* [MF, fr. L *concavus*, fr. *com-* + *cavus* hollow — more at CAVE] **1 :** hollowed or rounded inward like the inside of a bowl **2 :** arched in : curving in — used of the side of a curve or surface on which neighboring normals to the curve or surface converge and on which lies the chord joining two neighboring points of the curve or surface

[2]**con·cave** \'kän-,kāv\ *n* : a concave line or surface

con·cav·i·ty \kän-'kav-ət-ē\ *n, pl* **-ties** **1 :** a concave line, surface, or space : HOLLOW **2 :** the quality or state of being concave

con·ca·vo–con·cave \kän-,kā-(,)vō-\ *adj* : concave on both sides

concavo–convex *adj* **1 :** concave on one side and convex on the other **2 :** having the concave side curved more than the convex

con·ceal \kən-'sē(ə)l\ *vt* [ME *concelen*, fr. MF *conceler*, fr. L *concelare*, fr. *com-* + *celare* to hide — more at HELL] **1 :** to prevent disclosure or recognition of **2 :** to place out of sight ***syn*** see HIDE — **con·ceal·able** \-'sē-lə-bəl\ *adj* — **con·ceal·er** \-'sē-lər\ *n* — **con·ceal·ing·ly** \-'sē-liŋ-lē\ *adv* — **con·ceal·ment** \-'sē(ə)l-mənt\ *n*

con·cede \kən-'sēd\ *vb* **con·ced·ed; con·ced·ing** [F or L; F *concéder*, fr. L *concedere*, fr. *com-* + *cedere* to yield — more at CEDE] *vt* **1 :** to grant as a right or privilege **2 a :** to accept as true, valid, or accurate <the right of the state to tax is generally *conceded*> **b :** to acknowledge grudgingly or hesitantly ~ *vi* : to make concession : YIELD ***syn*** see GRANT ***ant*** deny — **con·ced·ed·ly** \-'sēd-əd-lē\ *adv* — **con·ced·er** *n*

[1]**con·ceit** \kən-'sēt\ *n* [ME, fr. *conceiven*] **1 a (1) :** a result of mental activity : THOUGHT **(2) :** individual opinion **b :** favorable opinion; *esp* : excessive appreciation of one's own worth or virtue **2 a :** a fanciful idea **b :** an elaborate or strained metaphor **c :** use or presence of such conceits in poetry **3 :** a fancy article

[2]**conceit** *vt* **1** *obs* : CONCEIVE, UNDERSTAND **2** *dial* : IMAGINE **3** *dial Brit* : to take a fancy to

con·ceit·ed \-'sēt-əd\ *adj* [[1]*conceit*] **1 :** ingeniously contrived : FANCIFUL **2 :** having an excessively high opinion of oneself — **con·ceit·ed·ly** *adv* — **con·ceit·ed·ness** *n*

con·ceiv·able \kən-'sē-və-bəl\ *adj* : capable of being conceived : IMAGINABLE — **con·ceiv·abil·i·ty** \kən-,sē-və-'bil-ət-ē\ *n* — **con·ceiv·able·ness** \-'sē-və-bəl-nəs\ *n* — **con·ceiv·ably** \-blē\ *adv*

con·ceive \kən-'sēv\ *vb* **con·ceived; con·ceiv·ing** [ME *conceiven*, fr. OF *conceivre*, fr. L *concipere* to take in, conceive, fr. *com-* + *capere* to take — more at HEAVE] *vt* **1 a :** to become pregnant with (young) **b :** to cause to begin : ORIGINATE **2 a :** to take into one's mind <~ a prejudice against him> **b :** to form a conception of : IMAGINE, IMAGE **3 :** to apprehend by reason or imagination : UNDERSTAND **4 :** to be of the opinion ~ *vi* **1 :** to become pregnant **2 :** to have a conception — usu. used with *of* <he ~*s* of death as emptiness> ***syn*** see THINK — **con·ceiv·er** *n*

con·cel·e·brant \kən-'sel-ə-brant, kän-\ *n* : one that concelebrates a Eucharist or Mass

con·cel·e·brate \kən-'sel-ə-,brāt, kän-\ *vb* [L *concelebratus*, pp. of *concelebrare* to celebrate in great numbers, fr. *com-* + *celebrare* to celebrate] *vt* : to participate in (a Eucharist) as a joint celebrant who recites the canon in unison with other celebrants ~ *vi* : to participate as a celebrant in a concelebrated Eucharist — **con·cel·e·bra·tion** \(,)kän-,sel-ə-'brā-shən, kən-\ *n*

con·cent \kən-'sent\ *n* [L *concentus*, fr. *concentus*, pp. of *concinere* to sing together, fr. *com-* + *canere* to sing] *archaic* : HARMONY

con·cen·ter \kən-'sent-ər, kän-\ *vb* [MF *concentrer*, fr. *com-* + *centre* center] *vt* : to draw or direct to a common center : CONCENTRATE ~ *vi* : to come to a common center

[1]**con·cen·trate** \'kän(t)-sən-,trāt, -,sen-\ *vb* **-trat·ed; -trat·ing** [*com-* + L *centrum* center] *vt* **1 a :** to bring or direct toward a common center or objective : FOCUS **b :** to gather into one body, mass, or force <power was *concentrated* in a few able hands> **2 a :** to make less dilute <~ syrup> **b :** to separate a valuable material from <~ an ore> **c :** to express or exhibit in condensed form ~ *vi* **1 :** to draw forward or meet in a common center **2 :** GATHER, COLLECT **3 :** to concentrate one's powers, efforts, or attention <~ on a problem> — **con·cen·tra·tive** \-,trāt-iv\ *adj* — **con·cen·tra·tor** \-,trāt-ər\ *n*

[2]**concentrate** *n* : something concentrated

con·cen·tra·tion \,kän(t)-sən-'trā-shən, -,sen-\ *n* **1 :** the act or process of concentrating : the state of being concentrated; *specif* : direction of attention to a single object **2 :** a concentrated mass or thing **3 :** the relative content of a component : STRENGTH

concentration camp *n* : a camp where persons (as prisoners of war, political prisoners, or refugees) are detained or confined

con·cen·tric \kən-'sen-trik, (')kän-\ *adj* [ML *concentricus*, fr. L *com-* + *centrum* center] **1 :** having a common center <~ circles> **2 :** having a common axis : COAXIAL — **con·cen·tri·cal·ly** \-tri-k(ə-)lē\ *adv* — **con·cen·tric·i·ty** \,kän-,sen-'tris-ət-ē\ *n*

con·cept \'kän-,sept\ *n* [L *conceptum*, neut. of *conceptus*, pp. of *concipere* to conceive] **1 :** something conceived in the mind : THOUGHT, NOTION **2 :** an abstract or generic idea generalized from particular instances ***syn*** see IDEA

con·cep·ta·cle \kən-'sep-ti-kəl\ *n* [NL *conceptaculum*, fr. L, receptacle, fr. *conceptus*, pp. of *concipere* to take in] : an external cavity containing reproductive cells in algae (as of the genus *Fucus*)

con·cep·tion \kən-'sep-shən\ *n* [ME *concepcioun*, fr. OF *conception*, fr. L *conception-*, *conceptio*, fr. *conceptus*, pp. of *concipere* to take in, conceive] **1 a (1) :** the act of becoming pregnant : the state of being conceived **(2) :** EMBRYO, FETUS **b** *archaic* : BEGINNING <joy had the like ~ in our eyes —Shak.> **2 a :** the capacity, function, or process of forming or understanding ideas or abstractions or their symbols **b :** a general idea : CONCEPT **c :** a complex product of abstract or reflective thinking **d :** the sum of a person's ideas and beliefs concerning something **3 :** the originating of something in the mind ***syn*** see IDEA — **con·cep·tion·al** \-shnəl, -shən-ᵊl\ *adj* — **con·cep·tive** \-'sep-tiv\ *adj*

con·cep·tu·al \kən-'sep-chə(-wə)l, kän-, -'sepsh-wəl\ *adj* [ML *conceptualis* of thought, fr. LL *conceptus* act of conceiving, thought, fr. L *conceptus*, pp.] : of, relating to, or consisting of concepts — **con·cep·tu·al·i·ty** \-,sep-chə-'wal-ət-ē, -shə-\ *n* — **con·cep·tu·al·ly** *adv*

con·cep·tu·al·ism \-'sep-chə(-wə)-,liz-əm, -'sepsh-wə-\ *n* : a theory intermediate between realism and nominalism that universals exist in the mind as concepts of discourse or as predicates which may be properly affirmed of reality — **con·cep·tu·al·ist** \-ləst\ *n* — **con·cep·tu·al·is·tic** \-,sep-chə(-wə)-lis-tik, -,sepsh-wə-\ *adj* — **con·cep·tu·al·is·ti·cal·ly** \-ti-k(ə-)lē\ *adv*

con·cep·tu·al·iza·tion \-,sep-chə(-wə)-lə-'zā-shən, -,sepsh-wə-\ *n* : the act or process of conceptualizing

con·cep·tu·al·ize \-'sep-chə(-wə)-,līz, -'sepsh-wə-\ *vt* **-ized; -iz·ing** : to form a concept of; *esp* : to interpret conceptually — **con·cep·tu·al·iz·er** *n*

con·cep·tus \kən-'sep-təs\ *n* [L, one conceived, fr. pp. of *concipere* to conceive] : FETUS

[1]**con·cern** \kən-'sərn\ *vb* [ME *concernen*, fr. MF & ML; MF *concerner*, fr. ML *concernere*, fr. LL, to sift together, mingle, fr. L *com-* + *cernere* to sift — more at CERTAIN] *vt* **1 a :** to relate to : be about <the novel ~*s* three soldiers> **b :** to bear on **2 :** to have an influence on : INVOLVE; *also* : to be the business or affair of <the problem ~*s* us all> **3 :** to be a care, trouble, or distress to <his ill health ~*s* me> **4 :** ENGAGE, OCCUPY <he ~*s* himself with trivia> ~ *vi, obs* : to be of importance : MATTER

[2]**concern** *n* **1 :** something that relates or belongs to one : AFFAIR **2 :** matter for consideration **3 a :** marked interest or regard usu. arising through a personal tie or relationship **b :** an uneasy state of blended interest, uncertainty, and apprehension **4 :** an organization or establishment for business or manufacture **5 :** CONTRIVANCE, GADGET ***syn*** see CARE ***ant*** unconcern

con·cerned *adj* **1 :** DISTURBED, ANXIOUS <~ for his safety> **2 a :** interestedly engaged <~ with books and music> **b :** culpably involved : IMPLICATED <arrested all ~>

con·cern·ing *prep* : relating to : REGARDING

con·cern·ment \kən-'sərn-mənt\ *n* **1 :** something in which one is concerned **2 :** IMPORTANCE, CONSEQUENCE **3** *archaic* : INVOLVEMENT, PARTICIPATION **4 :** SOLICITUDE, ANXIETY

[1]**con·cert** \kən-'sərt\ *vb* [MF *concerter*, fr. OIt *concertare*, fr. LL, fr. L, to contend, fr. *com-* + *certare* to strive, fr. *certus* decided, determined — more at CERTAIN] *vt* **1 :** to settle or adjust by conferring and reaching an agreement <got together to ~ their differences> **2 :** to make a plan for <~ measures for aiding the poor> ~ *vi* : to act in harmony or conjunction ***syn*** see NEGOTIATE

[2]**con·cert** \'kän(t)-sərt, 'kän-,sərt\ *n* [F, fr. It *concerto*, fr. *concertare*] **1 a :** agreement in design or plan : union formed by mutual communication of opinion and views **b :** a concerted action <the sacrifice was hailed with a ~ of praise> **2 :** musical harmony : CONCORD **3 :** a public performance of music or dancing; *esp* : a performance usu. by a group of musicians (as a chorus, band, or orchestra) that is made up of several individual compositions not joined in an integrated whole — compare BALLET, OPERA — **in concert** : TOGETHER <he worked *in concert* with others>

con·cert·ed \kən-'sərt-əd\ *adj* **1 a :** mutually contrived or agreed on <a ~ effort> **b :** performed in unison <~ artillery fire> **2 :** arranged in parts for several voices or instruments — **con·cert·ed·ly** *adv* — **con·cert·ed·ness** *n*

con·cert·go·er \'kän(t)-sərt-,gō(-ə)r, 'kän-,sərt-\ *n* : one who frequently attends concerts

con·cert grand \,kän(t)-sərt-, ,kän-,sərt-\ *n* : a grand piano of the largest size adapted in volume, timbre, and brilliance of tone to concert use

con·cer·ti·na \,kän(t)-sər-'tē-nə\ *n* **1 :** a musical instrument of the accordion family **2 :** a coiled barbed wire for use as an obstacle

concertina 1

con·cer·ti·no \,kän-chər-'tē-(,)nō\ *n, pl* **-nos** [It, dim. of *concerto*] **1 :** the solo instruments in a concerto grosso **2 :** a short concerto

con·cert·ize \'kän(t)-sər-,tīz\ *vi* **-ized; -iz·ing** : to perform professionally in concerts

con·cert·mas·ter \'kän(t)-sərt-,mas-tər\ *or* **con·cert·meis·ter** \-,mī-stər\ *n* [G *konzertmeister*, fr. *konzert* concert + *meister* master] : the leader of the first violins of an orchestra and by custom usu. the assistant to the conductor

con·cer·to \kən-'chert-(,)ō\ *n, pl* **-ti** \-(,)ē\ *or* **-tos** [It, fr. *concerto* concert] : a piece for one or more soloists and orchestra usu. in symphonic form with three contrasting movements

concerto gros·so \-'grō-(,)sō\ *n, pl* **concerti gros·si** \-(,)sē\ [It, lit., big concerto] : a baroque orchestral composition featuring a small group of solo instruments contrasting with the full orchestra

concert pitch *n* **1** *archaic* : a tuning standard for use in a concert **2 :** a high state of fitness, tension, or readiness

con·ces·sion \kən-'sesh-ən\ *n* [F or L; F, fr. L *concession-*, *concessio*, fr. *concessus*, pp. of *concedere* to concede] **1 a :** the act or an instance of conceding **b :** the admitting of a point claimed in argument **2 :** something conceded: **a :** ACKNOWLEDGMENT, ADMISSION **b :** GRANT **c (1) :** a grant of land or property esp. by a government in return for services or for a particular use **(2) :** a right to undertake and profit by a specified activity **(3) :** a lease of a portion of premises for a particular purpose; *also* : the portion leased or the activities carried on — **con·ces·sion·al** \-'sesh-nəl, -ən-ᵊl\ *adj* — **con·ces·sion·ary** \-'sesh-ə-,ner-ē\ *adj*

con·ces·sion·aire \kən-,sesh-ə-'na(ə)r, -'ne(ə)r\ *n* [F *concessionnaire*, fr. *concession*] : the owner or operator of a concession; *esp* : one that operates a refreshment stand at a recreational center

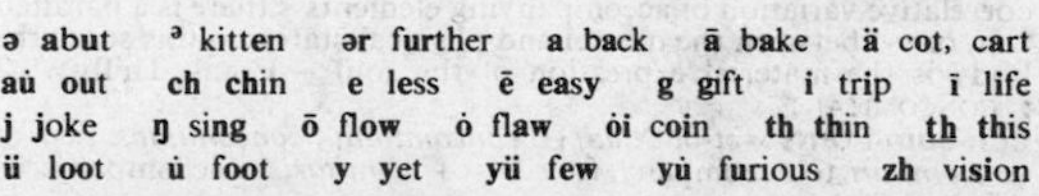

ə abut	ᵊ kitten	ər further	a back	ā bake	ä cot, cart
au̇ out	ch chin	e less	ē easy	g gift	i trip	ī life
j joke	ŋ sing	ō flow	ȯ flaw	ȯi coin	th thin	th this
ü loot	u̇ foot	y yet	yü few	yu̇ furious	zh vision

con·ces·sion·er \kən-ˈsesh-(ə-)nər\ *n* : CONCESSIONAIRE

con·ces·sive \kən-ˈses-iv\ *adj* **1 :** making for or being a concession **2 :** denoting concession <a ~ clause> — **con·ces·sive·ly** *adv*

[1]**conch** \ˈkäŋk, ˈkänch, ˈkȯŋk\ *n, pl* **conchs** \ˈkäŋks, ˈkȯŋks\ *or* **conch·es** \ˈkän-chəz\ [L *concha* mussel, mussel shell, fr. Gk *konchē*; akin to Skt *śaṅkha* conch shell] **1 :** any of various large spiral-shelled marine gastropod mollusks (as of the genera *Strombus* and *Cassis*); *also* **:** its shell used esp. for cameos **2 :** CONCHA 2

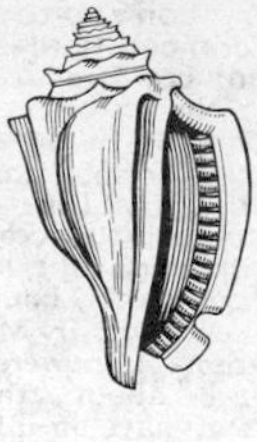

conch 1

[2]**conch** *or* **conchol** *abbr* conchology

conch- *or* **concho-** *comb form* [Gk *konch-*, *koncho-*, fr. *konchē*] : shell <*concho*logy> <*conch*iolin>

con·cha \ˈkäŋ-kə\ *n, pl* **con·chae** \-ˌkē, -ˌkī\ [It & L; It *conca* semidome, apse, fr. LL *concha*, fr. L, shell] **1 a :** the plain semidome of an apse **b :** APSE **2 :** something shaped like a shell; *esp* **:** the largest and deepest concavity of the external ear — **con·chal** \-kəl\ *adj*

con·chi·o·lin \käŋ-ˈkī-ə-lən, kän-\ *n* [*conch-* + *-i-* + *-ol* + *-in*] **:** a scleroprotein forming the organic basis of mollusk shells

con·choi·dal \käŋ-ˈkȯid-ᵊl, kän-\ *adj* [Gk *konchoeidēs* like a mussel, fr. *konchē*] **:** having elevations or depressions shaped like the inside surface of a bivalve shell — **con·choi·dal·ly** \-ᵊl-ē\ *adv*

con·chol·o·gy \käŋ-ˈkäl-ə-jē\ *n* **1 :** a branch of zoology that deals with shells **2 :** a treatise on shells — **con·chol·o·gist** \-jəst\ *n*

con·cierge \kōⁿ-ˈsyerzh\ *n, pl* **con·cierges** \-ˈsyerzh(-əz)\ [F, modif. of L *conservus* fellow slave, fr. *com-* + *servus* slave] **1 :** a resident in an apartment building esp. in France who serves as doorkeeper, landlord's representative, and janitor **2 :** a usu. multilingual hotel staff member esp. in Europe who handles luggage and mail, makes reservations, and arranges tours for the guests

con·cil·i·ar \kən-ˈsil-ē-ər\ *adj* [L *concilium* council] **:** of, relating to, or issued by a council — **con·cil·i·ar·ly** *adv*

con·cil·i·ate \kən-ˈsil-ē-ˌāt\ *vb* **-at·ed; -at·ing** [L *conciliatus*, pp. of *conciliare* to assemble, unite, win over, fr. *concilium* assembly, council — more at COUNCIL] *vt* **1 :** to gain (as goodwill) by pleasing acts **2 :** to make compatible **:** RECONCILE **3 :** APPEASE ~ *vi* **:** to become friendly or agreeable — **con·cil·i·a·tion** \-ˌsil-ē-ˈā-shən\ *n* — **con·cil·i·a·tive** \-ˈsil-ē-ˌāt-iv\ *adj* — **con·cil·i·a·tor** \-ˌāt-ər\ *n* — **con·cil·ia·to·ry** \-ˈsil-yə-ˌtōr-ē, -ˈsil-ē-ə-, -ˌtȯr-\ *adj*

con·cin·ni·ty \kən-ˈsin-ət-ē\ *n, pl* **-ties** [L *concinnitas*, fr. *concinnus* skillfully put together] **:** harmony and often elegance of design esp. of literary style in adaptation of parts to a whole or to each other

con·cise \kən-ˈsīs\ *adj* [L *concisus*, fr. pp. of *concidere* to cut up, fr. *com-* + *caedere* to cut, strike; akin to MHG *heie* mallet, Arm *xaitʻ* to prick] **1 :** marked by brevity of expression or statement **:** free from all elaboration and superfluous detail **2 :** cut short **:** BRIEF — **con·cise·ly** *adv* — **con·cise·ness** *n*

syn CONCISE, TERSE, SUCCINCT, LACONIC, SUMMARY, PITHY, COMPENDIOUS *shared meaning element* **:** very brief in statement or expression ***ant*** redundant

con·ci·sion \kən-ˈsizh-ən\ *n* [ME, fr. L *concision-*, *concisio*, fr. *concisus*, pp.] **1** *archaic* **:** a cutting up or off **2 :** the quality or state of being concise <the commentary is exemplary in its ~ and lucidity>

con·clave \ˈkän-ˌklāv\ *n* [ME, fr. MF or ML; MF, fr. ML, fr. L, room that can be locked up, fr. *com-* + *clavis* key — more at CLAVICLE] **1 :** a private meeting or secret assembly; *esp* **:** a meeting of Roman Catholic cardinals secluded continuously while choosing a pope **2 :** a gathering of a group or association **:** CONVENTION

con·clude \kən-ˈklüd\ *vb* **con·clud·ed; con·clud·ing** [ME *concluden*, fr. L *concludere* to shut up, end, infer, fr. *com-* + *claudere* to shut — more at CLOSE] *vt* **1** *obs* **:** to shut up **:** ENCLOSE **2 :** to bring to an end esp. in a particular way or with a particular action <~ a meeting with a prayer> **3 a :** to reach as a logically necessary end by reasoning **:** infer on the basis of evidence <*concluded* that her argument was sound> **b :** to make a decision about **:** DECIDE <*concluded* he would wait a little longer> **c :** to come to an agreement on **:** EFFECT <~ a sale> **4 :** to bring about as a result **:** COMPLETE ~ *vi* **1 :** END **2 a :** to form a final judgment **b :** to reach a decision or agreement ***syn* 1** see CLOSE ***ant*** open **2** see INFER — **con·clud·er** *n*

con·clu·sion \kən-ˈklü-zhən\ *n* [ME, fr. MF, fr. L *conclusion-*, *conclusio*, fr. *conclusus*, pp. of *concludere*] **1 a :** a reasoned judgment **:** INFERENCE **b :** the necessary consequence of two or more propositions taken as premises; *esp* **:** the inferred proposition of a syllogism **2 :** the last part of something: as **a :** RESULT, OUTCOME **b** *pl* **:** trial of strength or skill — used in the phrase *try conclusions* **c :** a final summation **d :** the final decision in a law case **e :** the final part of a pleading in law **3 :** an act or instance of concluding

con·clu·sive \-ˈklü-siv, -ziv\ *adj* **1 :** of or relating to a conclusion **2 :** putting an end to debate or question esp. by reason of irrefutability — **con·clu·sive·ly** *adv* — **con·clu·sive·ness** *n*

syn CONCLUSIVE, DECISIVE, DETERMINATIVE, DEFINITIVE *shared meaning element* **:** bringing to an end ***ant*** inconclusive

concn *abbr* concentration

con·coct \kən-ˈkäkt, kän-\ *vt* [L *concoctus*, pp. of *concoquere* to cook together, fr. *com-* + *coquere* to cook] **1 :** to prepare by combining crude materials **2 :** DEVISE, FABRICATE — **con·coct·er** *n* — **con·coc·tion** \-ˈkäk-shən\ *n* — **con·coc·tive** \-ˈkäk-tiv\ *adj*

con·com·i·tance \kən-ˈkäm-ət-ən(t)s, kän-\ *n* **1 :** ACCOMPANIMENT; *esp* **:** a conjunction that is regular and is marked by correlative variation of accompanying elements <there is a parallelism, or ~, between the mental and physical states: in this sense the body is the material expression of the soul —Frank Thilly> **2 :** CONCOMITANT

[1]**con·com·i·tant** \-ət-ənt\ *adj* [L *concomitant-*, *concomitans*, prp. of *concomitari* to accompany, fr. *com-* + *comitari* to accompany, fr. *comit-*, *comes* companion — more at COUNT] **:** accompanying esp. in a subordinate or incidental way — **con·com·i·tant·ly** *adv*

[2]**concomitant** *n* **:** something that accompanies or is collaterally connected with something else **:** ACCOMPANIMENT

con·cord \ˈkän-ˌkȯ(ə)rd, ˈkäŋ-\ *n* [ME, fr. OF *concorde*, fr. L *concordia*, fr. *concord-*, *concors* agreeing, fr. *com-* + *cord-*, *cor* heart — more at HEART] **1 a :** a state of agreement **:** HARMONY **b :** a harmonious combination of simultaneously heard tones — compare DISCORD **2 :** agreement by stipulation, compact, or covenant **3 :** grammatical agreement

con·cor·dance \kən-ˈkȯrd-ᵊn(t)s, kän-\ *n* [ME, fr. MF, fr. ML *concordantia*, fr. L *concordant-*, *concordans*] **1 :** an alphabetical index of the principal words in a book or the works of an author with their immediate contexts **2 :** CONCORD, AGREEMENT

con·cor·dant \-ᵊnt\ *adj* [ME, fr. MF, fr. L *concordant-*, *concordans*, prp. of *concordare* to agree, fr. *concord-*, *concors*] **:** CONSONANT, AGREEING — **con·cor·dant·ly** *adv*

con·cor·dat \kən-ˈkȯr-ˌdat\ *n* [F, fr. ML *concordatum*, fr. L, neut. of *concordatus*, pp. of *concordare*] **:** COMPACT, COVENANT; *specif* **:** an agreement between a pope and a sovereign or government for the regulation of ecclesiastical matters

con·cours d'é·lé·gance \(ˌ)kōⁿ-ˌkü(ə)r-ˌdā-lā-ˈgäⁿs\ *n* [F *concours d'élégance*, lit., competition of elegance] **:** a show or contest of vehicles and accessories in which the entries are judged chiefly on excellence of appearance and turnout

con·course \ˈkän-ˌkō(ə)rs, ˈkäŋ-, -ˌkȯ(ə)rs\ *n* [ME, fr. MF & L; MF *concours*, fr. L *concursus*, fr. *concursus*, pp. of *concurrere* to run together — more at CONCUR] **1 :** an act or process of coming together and merging **2 :** a meeting produced by voluntary or spontaneous coming together **3 a :** an open space where roads or paths meet **b :** an open space or hall (as in a railroad terminal) where crowds gather ***syn*** see JUNCTION

con·cres·cence \kən-ˈkres-ᵊn(t)s, kän-\ *n* [L *concrescentia*, fr. *concrescent-*, *concrescens*, prp. of *concrescere*] **1 :** increase by the addition of particles **2 :** a growing together **:** COALESCENCE; *esp* **:** convergence and fusion of the lateral lips of the blastopore to form the primordium of an embryo — **con·cres·cent** \-ᵊnt\ *adj*

[1]**con·crete** \kän-ˈkrēt, ˈkän-ˌ\ *adj* [ME, fr. L *concretus*, fr. pp. of *concrescere* to grow together, fr. *com-* + *crescere* to grow — more at CRESCENT] **1 :** formed by coalition of particles into one solid mass **2 :** naming a real thing or class of things <the word *poem* is ~, *poetry* is abstract> **3 a :** characterized by or belonging to immediate experience of actual things or events **b :** SPECIFIC, PARTICULAR **c :** REAL, TANGIBLE **4 :** relating to or made of concrete — **con·crete·ly** *adv* — **con·crete·ness** *n*

[2]**con·crete** \ˈkän-ˌkrēt, kän-ˈ\ *n* **1 :** a mass formed by concretion or coalescence of separate particles of matter in one body **2 :** a hard strong building material made by mixing a cementing material (as portland cement) and a mineral aggregate (as sand and gravel) with sufficient water to cause the cement to set and bind the entire mass **3 :** a waxy essence of flowers prepared by extraction and evaporation and used in perfumery

[3]**con·crete** \ˈkän-ˌkrēt, kän-ˈ\ *vb* **con·cret·ed; con·cret·ing** *vt* **1 a :** to form into a solid mass **:** SOLIDIFY **b :** COMBINE, BLEND <art *concreted* with nature to produce a gracious whole> **2 :** to make actual or real **:** cause to take on the qualities of reality **3 :** to cover with, form of, or set in concrete ~ *vi* **:** to become concreted

concrete music *n* **:** MUSIQUE CONCRÈTE

concrete poetry *n* **:** poetry in which the poet's intent is conveyed by the graphic patterns of letters, words, or symbols rather than by the conventional arrangement of words

con·cre·tion \kän-ˈkrē-shən, kən-\ *n* **1 :** the act or process of concreting **:** the state of being concreted <~ of ideas in an hypothesis> **2 :** something concreted: as **a :** a hard usu. inorganic mass (as a bezoar or tophus) formed in a living body **b :** a mass of mineral matter found generally in rock of a composition different from its own and produced by deposition from aqueous solution in the rock — **con·cre·tion·ary** \-shə-ˌner-ē\ *adj*

con·cret·ism \kän-ˈkrēt-ˌiz-əm, ˈkän-ˌ\ *n* **:** representation of abstract things as concrete; *esp* **:** the theory or practice of emphasizing graphic rather than linguistic effects in poetry — **con·cret·ist** \-ˈkrēt-əst, -ˌkrēt-\ *n*

con·cret·ize \-ˌīz\ *vb* **-ized; -iz·ing** *vt* **:** to make concrete, specific, or definite <tried to ~ his ideas> ~ *vi* **:** to become concrete — **con·cret·i·za·tion** \(ˌ)kän-ˌkrēt-ə-ˈzā-shən\ *n*

con·cu·bi·nage \kän-ˈkyü-bə-nij, kən-\ *n* **1 :** cohabitation of persons not legally married **2 :** the state of being a concubine

con·cu·bine \ˈkäŋ-kyü-ˌbīn, ˈkän-\ *n* [ME, fr. OF, fr. L *concubina*, fr. *com-* + *cubare* to lie — more at HIP] **1 :** a woman living in a socially recognized state of concubinage **2 :** MISTRESS

con·cu·pis·cence \kän-ˈkyü-pə-sən(t)s, kən-\ *n* [ME, fr. MF, fr. LL *concupiscentia*, fr. L *concupiscent-*, *concupiscens*, prp. of *concupiscere* to desire ardently, fr. *com-* + *cupere* to desire — more at COVET] **:** strong desire; *esp* **:** sexual desire — **con·cu·pis·cent** \-sənt\ *adj*

con·cu·pis·ci·ble \-ˈkyü-pə-sə-bəl\ *adj* [ME, fr. MF or LL; MF, fr. LL *concupiscibilis*, fr. L *concupiscere*] **:** motivated by concupiscence **:** LUSTFUL

con·cur \kən-ˈkər, kän-\ *vi* **con·curred; con·cur·ring** [ME *concurren*, fr. L *concurrere*, fr. *com-* + *currere* to run] **1** *obs* **:** to come together **:** MEET **2 :** to happen together **:** COINCIDE **3 :** to act together to a common end or single effect **4 a :** APPROVE <~ in a statement> **b :** to express agreement <~ with an opinion> ***syn*** see AGREE ***ant*** contend, altercate

con·cur·rence \-ˈkər-ən(t)s, -ˈkə-rən(t)s\ *n* **1 a :** agreement or union in action **:** COOPERATION **b (1) :** agreement in opinion or design **(2) :** CONSENT **2 :** a coming together **:** CONJUNCTION **3 :** a coincidence of equal powers in law

con·cur·rent \-ˈkər-ənt, -ˈkə-rənt\ *adj* [ME, fr. MF & L; MF, fr. L *concurrent-*, *concurrens*, prp. of *concurrere*] **1 a :** CONVERGENT; *specif* **:** a meeting or intersecting in a point **b :** running parallel **2 :** operating or occurring at the same time **3 :** acting in conjunction **4 :** exercised over the same matter or area by two different authorities <~ jurisdiction> — **concurrent** *n* — **con·cur·rent·ly** *adv*

concurrent resolution *n* **:** a resolution passed by both houses of a legislative body that lacks the force of law

con·cuss \kən-ˈkəs\ *vt* [L *concussus,* pp.] **:** to affect with concussion

con·cus·sion \kən-ˈkəsh-ən\ *n* [MF or L; MF, fr. L *concussion-, concussio,* fr. *concussus,* pp. of *concutere* to shake violently, fr. *com-* + *quatere* to shake] **1 :** AGITATION, SHAKING **2 a :** a hard blow or collision **b :** a stunning, damaging, or shattering effect from a hard blow; *esp* **:** a jarring injury of the brain resulting in disturbance of cerebral function — **con·cus·sive** \-ˈkəs-iv\ *adj* — **con·cus·sive·ly** *adv*

cond *abbr* conductivity

con·demn \kən-ˈdem\ *vt* [ME *condemnen,* fr. OF *condemner,* fr. L *condemnare,* fr. *com-* + *damnare* to condemn — more at DAMN] **1 :** to declare to be reprehensible, wrong, or evil usu. after weighing evidence and without reservation **2 a :** to pronounce guilty **:** CONVICT **b :** SENTENCE, DOOM **3 :** to adjudge unfit for use or consumption **4 :** to declare convertible to public use under the right of eminent domain ***syn*** see CRITICIZE — **con·dem·nable** \-ˈdem-(n)ə-bəl\ *adj* — **con·dem·na·tory** \-nə-ˌtōr-ē, -ˌtȯr-\ *adj* — **con·demn·er** \-ˈdem-ər\ *or* **con·dem·nor** \kən-ˈdem-ər; kən-ˌdem-ˈnȯ(ə)r, ˌkän-\ *n*

con·dem·na·tion \ˌkän-ˌdem-ˈnā-shən, -dəm-\ *n* **1 :** CENSURE, BLAME **2 :** the act of judicially condemning **3 :** the state of being condemned **4 :** a reason for condemning

con·den·sate \ˈkän-dən-ˌsāt, -ˌden-; kən-ˈden-\ *n* **:** a product of condensation; *esp* **:** a liquid obtained by condensation of a gas or vapor <steam ~>

con·den·sa·tion \ˌkän-ˌden-ˈsā-shən, -dən-\ *n* **1 :** the act or process of condensing: as **a :** a chemical reaction involving union between molecules often with elimination of a simple molecule (as water) to form a new more complex compound of often greater molecular weight **b :** a reduction to a denser form (as from steam to water) **c :** compression of a written or spoken work into more concise form **2 :** the quality or state of being condensed **3 :** a product of condensing; *specif* **:** an abridgment of a literary work — **con·den·sa·tion·al** \-shnəl, -shən-ᵊl\ *adj*

con·dense \kən-ˈden(t)s\ *vb* **con·densed; con·dens·ing** [ME *condensen,* fr. MF *condenser,* fr. L *condensare,* fr. *com-* + *densare* to make dense, fr. *densus* dense] *vt* **:** to make denser or more compact; *esp* **:** to subject to condensation ~ *vi* **:** to undergo condensation ***syn*** see CONTRACT ***ant*** amplify (*as a speech*) — **con·dens·able** *also* **con·dens·ible** \-ˈden(t)-sə-bəl\ *adj*

con·densed *adj* **:** reduced to a more compact form; *specif* **:** having a face that is narrower than that of a typeface not so characterized

condensed milk *n* **:** evaporated milk with sugar added

con·dens·er \kən-ˈden(t)-sər\ *n* **1 :** one that condenses: as **a :** a lens or mirror used to concentrate light on an object **b :** an apparatus in which gas or vapor is condensed **2 :** CAPACITOR

con·de·scend \ˌkän-di-ˈsend\ *vi* [ME *condescenden,* fr. MF *condescendre,* fr. LL *condescendere,* fr. L *com-* + *descendere* to descend] **1 a :** to descend to a less formal or dignified level **:** UNBEND **b :** to waive the privileges of rank **2 :** to assume an air of superiority ***syn*** see STOOP

con·de·scen·dence \-ˈsen-dən(t)s\ *n* **:** CONDESCENSION

con·de·scend·ing *adj* **:** showing or characterized by condescension **:** PATRONIZING — **con·de·scend·ing·ly** \-ˈsen-diŋ-lē\ *adv*

con·de·scen·sion \ˌkän-di-ˈsen-chən\ *n* [LL *condescension-, condescensio,* fr. *condescensus,* pp. of *condescendere*] **1 :** voluntary descent from one's rank or dignity in relations with an inferior **2 :** a patronizing attitude

con·dign \kən-ˈdīn, ˈkän-ˌ\ *adj* [ME *condigne,* fr. MF, fr. L *condignus* very worthy, fr. *com-* + *dignus* worthy — more at DECENT] **:** DESERVED, APPROPRIATE <~ punishment> — **con·dign·ly** *adv*

con·di·ment \ˈkän-də-mənt\ *n* [ME, fr. MF, fr. L *condimentum,* fr. *condire* to pickle, fr. *condere* to build, store up, fr. *com-* + *-dere* to put — more at DO] **:** something used to enhance the flavor of food; *esp* **:** a pungent seasoning — **con·di·men·tal** \ˌkän-də-ˈment-ᵊl\ *adj*

¹con·di·tion \kən-ˈdish-ən\ *n* [ME *condicion,* fr. MF, fr. L *condicion-, condicio* terms of agreement, condition, fr. *condicere* to agree, fr. *com-* + *dicere* to say, determine — more at DICTION] **1 a :** a premise upon which the fulfillment of an agreement depends **:** STIPULATION **b** *obs* **:** COVENANT **c :** a provision making the effect of a legal instrument contingent upon an uncertain event; *also* **:** the event itself **2 :** something essential to the appearance or occurrence of something else **:** PREREQUISITE: as **a :** an environmental requirement <available oxygen is an essential ~ for animal life> **b :** the subordinate clause of a conditional sentence **3 a :** a restricting or modifying factor **:** QUALIFICATION **b :** a state of affairs that hampers or impedes or requires correction <delayed by the ~ of the road> **c :** an unsatisfactory academic grade that may be raised by doing additional work **4 a :** a state of being **b :** social status **:** RANK **c :** a usu. defective state of health <a serious heart ~> **d :** a state of physical fitness or readiness for use <the car was in good ~> <exercising to get into ~> **e** *pl* **:** attendant circumstances **5 a** *obs* **:** temper of mind **b** *obs* **:** TRAIT **c** *pl, archaic* **:** MANNERS, WAYS ***syn*** see STATE

²condition *vb* **con·di·tioned; con·di·tion·ing** \-ˈdish-(ə-)niŋ\ *vi, archaic* **:** to make stipulations ~ *vt* **1 :** to agree by stipulating **2 :** to make conditional **3 a :** to put into a proper state for work or use **b :** AIR-CONDITION **4 :** to give a grade of condition to **5 a :** to adapt, modify, or mold so as to conform to an environing culture **b :** to modify so that an act or response previously associated with one stimulus becomes associated with another ***syn*** see PREPARE — **con·di·tion·able** \-(ə-)nə-bəl\ *adj* — **con·di·tion·er** \-(ə-)nər\ *n*

con·di·tion·al \kən-ˈdish-nəl, -ən-ᵊl\ *adj* **1 :** subject to, implying, or dependent upon a condition <a ~ promise> **2 :** expressing, containing, or implying a supposition <the ~ clause *if he speaks*> **3 a :** true only for certain values of the variables or symbols involved <~ equations> **b :** stating the case when one or more random variables are fixed or one or more events are known <~ frequency distribution> **4 a :** CONDITIONED 3 <~ reflex> <~ response> **b :** established by conditioning as the stimulus eliciting a conditional response — **conditional** *n* — **con·di·tion·al·i·ty** \-ˌdish-ə-ˈnal-ət-ē\ *n* — **con·di·tion·al·ly** \-ˈdish-nə-lē, -ən-ᵊl-ē\ *adv*

conditional probability *n* **:** the probability that a given event will occur if it is certain that another event has taken place or will take place

con·di·tioned *adj* **1 :** CONDITIONAL **2 :** brought or put into a specified state **3 :** determined or established by conditioning

con·dole \kən-ˈdōl\ *vb* **con·doled; con·dol·ing** [LL *condolēre,* fr. L *com-* + *dolēre* to feel pain; akin to Gk *daidalos* ingeniously formed] *vi* **1** *obs* **:** GRIEVE **2 :** to express sympathetic sorrow <we ~ with you in your misfortune> ~ *vt, archaic* **:** LAMENT, GRIEVE — **con·do·la·to·ry** \-ˈdō-lə-ˌtōr-ē, -ˌtȯr-\ *adj*

con·do·lence \kən-ˈdō-lən(t)s, ˈkän-də-\ *n* **1 :** sympathy with another in sorrow **2 :** an expression of sympathy

con·dom \ˈkən-dəm, ˈkän-\ *n* [after Dr. *Condom* or Conton, 18th cent. Eng. physician, its reputed inventor] **:** a sheath commonly of rubber worn over the penis (as to prevent conception or venereal infection during coitus)

con·do·min·i·um \ˌkän-də-ˈmin-ē-əm\ *n, pl* **-ums** [NL, fr. L *com-* + *dominium* domain] **1 a :** joint dominion; *esp* **:** joint sovereignty by two or more nations **b :** a government operating under joint rule **2 :** a politically dependent territory under condominium **3 :** individual ownership of a unit in a multi-unit structure (as an apartment building); *also* **:** a unit so owned — **con·do·min·i·al** \-ē-əl\ *adj*

con·do·na·tion \ˌkän-də-ˈnā-shən, -dō-\ *n* **:** implied pardon of an offense by treating the offender as if it had not been committed

con·done \kən-ˈdōn\ *vt* **con·doned; con·don·ing** [L *condonare* to forgive, fr. *com-* + *donare* to give — more at DONATE] **:** to pardon or overlook voluntarily; *esp* **:** to treat as if trivial, harmless, or of no importance <~ corruption in politics> ***syn*** see EXCUSE — **con·don·able** \-ˈdō-nə-bəl\ *adj* — **con·don·er** *n*

con·dor \ˈkän-dər, -ˌdȯ(ə)r\ *n* [Sp *cóndor,* fr. Quechua *kúntur*] **1 :** a very large American vulture (*Vultur gryphus*) of the high Andes having the head and neck bare and the plumage dull black with a downy white neck ruff and white patches on the wings **2** *pl* **condors** *or* **con·do·res** \kən-ˈdōr-ˌās, -ˈdȯr-\ **:** a coin (as the centesimo of Chile) bearing the picture of a condor

condor 1

con·dot·tie·re \ˌkän-də-ˈtye(ə)r-ē, ˌkän-ˌdät-ē-ˈe(ə)r-\ *n, pl* **-tie·re** \-ē\ [It *condottiere*] **1 :** a leader of a band of mercenaries common in Europe between the 14th and 16th centuries; *also* **:** a member of such a band **2 :** a mercenary soldier

con·duce \kən-ˈd(y)üs\ *vi* **con·duced; con·duc·ing** [ME *conducen* to conduct, fr. L *conducere* to conduct, conduce, fr. *com-* + *ducere* to lead — more at TOW] **:** to lead or tend to a particular and usu. desirable result **:** CONTRIBUTE

syn CONDUCE, CONTRIBUTE, REDOUND *shared meaning element* **:** to lead to an end ***ant*** ward off

con·du·cive \-ˈd(y)ü-siv\ *adj* **:** tending to promote or assist **:** CONTRIBUTIVE <an atmosphere ~ to education> — **con·du·cive·ness** *n*

¹con·duct \ˈkän-(ˌ)dəkt\ *n* [alter. of ME *conduit,* fr. OF, act of leading, escort, fr. ML *conductus,* fr. L *conductus,* pp. of *conducere*] **1** *obs* **:** ESCORT, GUIDE **2 :** the act, manner, or process of carrying on **:** MANAGEMENT **3 :** a mode or standard of personal behavior esp. as based on moral principles

²con·duct \kən-ˈdəkt\ *vt* **1 :** to bring by or as if by leading **:** GUIDE <~ tourists through a museum> **2 :** to carry on or out usu. from a position of command or control <~ a siege> <~ an experiment> **3 a :** to convey in a channel **b :** to act as a medium for conveying **4 :** to act or behave in a particular and esp. in a

controlled or directed manner ~ *vi* **1** *of a road or passage* : to show the way : LEAD **2 a** : to act as leader or director **b** : to have the quality of transmitting light, heat, sound, or electricity — **con·duct·i·bil·i·ty** \kən-ˌdək-tə-ˈbil-ət-ē\ *n* — **con·duct·ible** \-ˈdək-tə-bəl\ *adj*
syn **1** CONDUCT, MANAGE, CONTROL, DIRECT *shared meaning element* : to use one's powers to lead, guide, or dominate
2 see BEHAVE

con·duc·tance \kən-ˈdək-tən(t)s\ *n* **1** : conducting power **2 a** : the readiness with which a conductor transmits an electric current **b** : the reciprocal of electrical resistance

con·duc·tion \kən-ˈdək-shən\ *n* **1** : the act of conducting or conveying **2** : transmission through or by means of a conductor; *also* : CONDUCTIVITY **3** : the transmission of excitation through living tissue and esp. nervous tissue

con·duc·tive \kən-ˈdək-tiv\ *adj* : having conductivity : relating to conduction (as of electricity)

con·duc·tiv·i·ty \ˌkän-ˌdək-ˈtiv-ət-ē, kən-\ *n, pl* **-ties** : the quality or power of conducting or transmitting: as **a** : the reciprocal of electrical resistivity **b** : the quality of living matter responsible for the transmission of and progressive reaction to stimuli

con·duc·to·met·ric *or* **con·duc·ti·met·ric** \kən-ˌdək-tə-ˈme-trik\ *adj* **1** : of or relating to the measurement of conductivity **2** : being or relating to titration based on determination of changes in the electrical conductivity of the solution

con·duc·tor \kən-ˈdək-tər\ *n* : one that conducts: as **a** : GUIDE **b** : a collector of fares in a public conveyance **c** : the leader of a musical ensemble **d** : a substance or body capable of transmitting electricity, heat, or sound — **con·duc·to·ri·al** \ˌkän-ˌdək-ˈtōr-ē-əl, kən-, -ˈtȯr-\ *adj* — **con·duc·tress** \kən-ˈdək-trəs\ *n*

con·duit \ˈkän-ˌd(y)ü-ət *also* -d(w)ət\ *n* [ME, fr. MF, lit., act of leading] **1** : a natural or artificial channel through which something (as a fluid) is conveyed **2** *archaic* : FOUNTAIN **3** : a pipe, tube, or tile for protecting electric wires or cables

con·du·pli·cate \(ˈ)kän-ˈd(y)ü-pli-kət\ *adj* [L *conduplicatus*, pp. of *conduplicare* to double, fr. *com-* + *duplic-, duplex* double — more at DUPLEX] : folded lengthwise — used of leaves or petals in the bud — **con·du·pli·ca·tion** \ˌkän-ˌd(y)ü-pli-ˈkā-shən\ *n*

con·dy·lar \ˈkän-də-lər\ *adj* : of or relating to a condyle

con·dyle \ˈkän-ˌdīl *also* -dᵊl\ *n* [F & L; F, fr. L *condylus* knuckle, fr. Gk *kondylos*] : an articular prominence of a bone; *esp* : one of a pair that resembles knuckles — **con·dy·loid** \-də-ˌlȯid\ *adj*

con·dy·lo·ma \ˌkän-də-ˈlō-mə\ *n* [NL, fr. Gk *kondylōma*, fr. *kondylos*] : a warty growth on the skin or adjoining mucous membrane usu. near the anus and genital organs — **con·dy·lo·ma·tous** \-mət-əs\ *adj*

¹cone \ˈkōn\ *n* [MF or L; MF, fr. L *conus*, fr. Gk *kōnos* — more at HONE] **1 a** : a mass of ovule-bearing or pollen-bearing scales or bracts in trees of the pine family or in cycads that are arranged usu. on a somewhat elongated axis **b** : any of several flower or fruit clusters suggesting a cone **2 a** : a solid generated by rotating a right triangle about one of its legs — called also *right circular cone* **b** : a solid bounded by a circular or other closed plane base and the surface formed by line segments joining every point of the boundary of the base to a common vertex — see VOLUME table **c** : a surface traced by a moving straight line passing through a fixed vertex **3** : something that resembles a cone in shape: as **a** : one of the short sensory end organs of the vertebrate retina that function in color vision **b** : any of numerous somewhat conical tropical gastropod mollusks (family Conidae) **c** : the apex of a volcano **d** : a crisp cone-shaped wafer for holding ice cream

cones 1a: *1* stone pine, *2* cluster pine, *3* big-cone pine, *4* sugar pine, *5* deodar, *6* red spruce, *7* Santa Lucia fir, *8* Nordmann's fir, *9* giant sequoia

²cone *vt* **coned; con·ing** **1** : to make cone-shaped **2** : to bevel like the slanting surface of a cone <~ a tire>

cone·flow·er \ˈkōn-ˌflau̇(-ə)r\ *n* : any of several composite plants having cone-shaped flower disks; *esp* : RUDBECKIA

cone·nose \ˈkōn-ˌnōz\ *n* : any of various large bloodsucking bugs (esp. genus *Triatoma*) including some capable of inflicting painful bites — called also *assassin bug, kissing bug*

con es·pres·sio·ne \ˌkän-ˌes-(ˌ)pres-ē-ˈō-nē, ˌkōn-, -ˈō-(ˌ)nā\ *adv* [It, lit., with expression] : with feeling — used as a direction in music

Con·es·to·ga \ˌkän-ə-ˈstō-gə\ *n* [*Conestoga*, Pa.] : a broad-wheeled covered wagon drawn usu. by six horses and used esp. for transporting freight across the prairies

co·ney \ˈkō-nē\ *n, pl* **coneys** [ME *conies*, pl., fr. OF *conis*, pl. of *conil*, fr. L *cuniculus*] **1 a** (1) : RABBIT; *esp* : the European rabbit (*Oryctolagus cuniculus*) (2) : PIKA **b** : HYRAX **c** : rabbit fur **2** *obs* : DUPE **3** : any of several fishes; *esp* : a dusky black-spotted reddish-finned grouper (*Cephalopholis fulvus*) of the tropical Atlantic

conf *abbr* **1** conference **2** confidential

con·fab \kən-ˈfab, ˈkän-ˌ\ *vi* **con·fabbed; con·fab·bing** : CONFABULATE — **con·fab** \ˈkän-ˌfab, kən-ˈ\ *n*

con·fab·u·late \kən-ˈfab-yə-ˌlāt\ *vi* **-lat·ed; -lat·ing** [L *confabulatus*, pp. of *confabulari*, fr. *com-* + *fabulari* to talk, fr. *fabula* story — more at FABLE] **1** : CHAT **2** : to hold a discussion : CONFER — **con·fab·u·la·tion** \kən-ˌfab-yə-ˈlā-shən, ˌkän-\ *n* — **con·fab·u·la·tor** \kən-ˈfab-yə-ˌlāt-ər\ *n* — **con·fab·u·la·to·ry** \-lə-ˌtōr-ē, -ˌtȯr-\ *adj*

con·fect \kən-ˈfekt\ *vt* [L *confectus*, pp. of *conficere* to prepare — more at COMFIT] **1** : to put together from varied material <writers ~*ing* best sellers> **2 a** : PREPARE **b** : PRESERVE — **con·fect** \ˈkän-ˌ\ *n*

con·fec·tion \kən-ˈfek-shən\ *n* **1** : the act or process of confecting **2** : something confected: as **a** : a fancy dish or sweetmeat : DELICACY; *esp* : a fruit or nut preserve **b** : a medicinal preparation usu. made with sugar, syrup, or honey **c** : a piece of fine craftsmanship

con·fec·tion·ary \-shə-ˌner-ē\ *n, pl* **-ar·ies** **1** *archaic* : CONFECTIONER **2** : CONFECTIONERY 3 **3** : SWEETS — **confectionary** *adj*

con·fec·tion·er \-sh(ə-)nər\ *n* : a manufacturer of or dealer in confections

con·fec·tion·ery \-shə-ˌner-ē\ *n, pl* **-er·ies** **1** : sweet edibles (as candy or pastry) **2** : the confectioner's art or business **3** : a confectioner's shop

Confed *abbr* Confederate

con·fed·er·a·cy \kən-ˈfed-(ə-)rə-sē\ *n, pl* **-cies** **1** : a league or compact for mutual support or common action : ALLIANCE **2** : a combination of persons for unlawful purposes : CONSPIRACY **3** : the body formed by persons, states, or nations united by a league; *specif, cap* : the 11 southern states seceding from the U.S. in 1860 and 1861 — **con·fed·er·al** \-(ə-)rəl\ *adj* — **con·fed·er·al·ist** \-əst\ *n*

¹con·fed·er·ate \kən-ˈfed-(ə-)rət\ *adj* [ME *confederat*, fr. LL *confoederatus*, pp. of *confoederare* to unite by a league, fr. L *com-* + *foeder-, foedus* compact — more at FEDERAL] **1** : united in a league : ALLIED **2** *cap* : of or relating to the Confederate States of America

²confederate *n* **1** : ALLY, ACCOMPLICE **2** *cap* : an adherent of the Confederate States of America or their cause

³con·fed·er·ate \-ˈfed-ə-ˌrāt\ *vb* **-at·ed; -at·ing** *vt* : to unite in a confederacy ~ *vi* : to band together — **con·fed·er·a·tive** \-ˈfed-(ə-)rət-iv, -ə-ˌrāt-\ *adj*

Confederate Memorial Day *n* : any of several days appointed for the commemoration of servicemen of the Confederacy: **a** : April 26 in Florida and Georgia **b** : the last Monday in April in Alabama and Mississippi **c** : May 10 in No. and So. Carolina **d** : the last Monday in May in Virginia **e** : June 3 in Kentucky, Louisiana, and Texas

confederate rose *n, often cap C* : a Chinese mallow (*Hibiscus mutabilis*) with white or pink flowers that become deep red at night

con·fed·er·a·tion \kən-ˌfed-ə-ˈrā-shən\ n **1** : an act of confederating : a state of being confederated : ALLIANCE **2** : LEAGUE

con·fer \kən-ˈfər\ *vb* **con·ferred; con·fer·ring** [L *conferre* to bring together, fr. *com-* + *ferre* to carry — more at BEAR] *vi* **1** *obs* : to call into comparison **2** : to bestow from or as if from a position of superiority <your trust ~*s* an honor on me> ~ *vi* : to come together to compare views or take counsel : CONSULT *syn* see GIVE — **con·fer·ment** \-ˈfər-mənt\ *n* — **con·fer·ra·ble** \-ˈfər-ə-bəl\ *adj* — **con·fer·ral** \-ˈfər-əl\ *n* — **con·fer·rer** \-ˈfər-ər\ *n*

con·fer·ee \ˌkän-fə-ˈrē\ *n* **1** : one conferred with **2** : one on whom something (as a degree) is conferred

con·fer·ence \ˈkän-f(ə-)rən(t)s, -fərn(t)s, *for 2 usu* kən-ˈfər-ən(t)s\ *n* **1 a** : a usu. formal interchange of views : CONSULTATION **b** : a meeting of two or more persons for discussing matters of common concern **c** : a meeting of members of the two branches of a legislature to adjust differences **2** *also* **con·fer·rence** \kən-ˈfər-ən(t)s\ : BESTOWAL, CONFERMENT **3 a** : a representative assembly or administrative organization of a denomination **b** : a territorial division of a denomination **4** : an association of athletic teams — **con·fer·en·tial** \ˌkän-fə-ˈren-chəl\ *adj*

con·fer·va \kən-ˈfər-və\ *n, pl* **-vae** \-(ˌ)vē, -ˌvī\ *also* **-vas** [L, a water plant, fr. *confervēre* to boil together, heal, fr. *com-* + *fervēre* to boil — more at BURN] : any of a genus (*Tribonema*) of filamentous freshwater yellow-green algae; *broadly* : any of various filamentous algae forming scums on still water — **con·fer·void** \-ˌvȯid\ *adj or n*

con·fess \kən-ˈfes\ *vb* [ME *confessen*, fr. MF *confesser*, fr. OF, fr. *confes* having confessed, fr. L *confessus*, pp. of *confitēri* to confess, fr. *com-* + *fatēri* to confess; akin to L *fari* to speak — more at BAN] *vt* **1** : to tell or make known (as something wrong or damaging to oneself) : ADMIT **2 a** : to acknowledge (sin) to God or to a priest **b** : to receive the confession of (a penitent) **3** : to declare faith in or adherence to : PROFESS **4** : to give evidence of ~ *vi* **1 a** : to disclose one's faults; *specif* : to unburden one's sins or the state of one's conscience to God or to a priest **b** : to hear a confession **2** : ADMIT, OWN *syn* see ACKNOWLEDGE — **con·fess·able** \-ə-bəl\ *adj*

con·fessed·ly \-ˈfes-əd-lē, -ˈfest-lē\ *adv* : by confession : ADMITTEDLY

con·fes·sion \kən-ˈfesh-ən\ *n* **1** : an act of confessing; *specif* : a disclosure of one's sins in the sacrament of penance **2** : a statement of what is confessed: as **a** : a written acknowledgment of guilt by a party accused of an offense **b** : a formal statement of religious beliefs : CREED **3** : an organized religious body having a common creed — **con·fes·sion·al** \-ˈfesh-nəl, -ən-ᵊl\ *adj* — **con·fes·sion·al·ism** \-ˌiz-əm\ *n* — **con·fes·sion·al·ist** \-əst\ *n* — **con·fes·sion·al·ly** \-ē\ *adv*

confessional *n* **1** : a place where a priest hears confessions **2** : the practice of confessing to a priest

con·fes·sor \kən-ˈfes-ər *also (for 2 & 3)* ˈkän-ˌfes-ər *& (for 3)* ˈkän-fə-ˌsȯ(ə)r\ *n* **1** : one that confesses **2** : one who gives heroic evidence of faith but does not suffer martyrdom **3 a** : a priest who hears confessions **b** : a priest who is one's regular spiritual guide

con·fet·ti \kən-ˈfet-ē\ *n* [It, pl. of *confetto* sweetmeat, fr. ML *confectum*, fr. L, neut. of *confectus*, pp. of *conficere* to prepare] : small bits or streamers of brightly colored paper made for throwing (as at weddings)

con·fi·dant \ˈkän-fə-ˌdant, -ˌdänt, ˌkän-fə-ˈ\ *n* [F *confident*, fr. It *confidente*, fr. *confidente* confident, trustworthy, fr. L *confident-, confidens*] : one to whom secrets are entrusted; *esp* : INTIMATE

con·fi·dante \like CONFIDANT\ *n* [F *confidente,* fem. of *confident*] : a female confidant

con·fide \kən-ˈfīd\ *vb* **con·fid·ed; con·fid·ing** [ME *confiden,* fr. MF or L; MF *confider,* fr. L *confidere,* fr. *com-* + *fidere* to trust — more at BIDE] *vi* **1** : to have confidence : TRUST **2** : to show confidence by imparting secrets ~ *vt* **1** : to tell confidentially **2** : ENTRUST *syn* see COMMIT — **con·fid·er** *n*

[1]**con·fi·dence** \ˈkän-fəd-ən(t)s, -fə-ˌden(t)s\ *n* **1** : FAITH, TRUST <their ~ in God's mercy> **2** : a feeling or consciousness of one's powers or of reliance on one's circumstances <he had perfect ~ in his ability to succeed> <met the risk with brash ~> **3** : the quality or state of being certain : CERTITUDE <they had every ~ of success> **4 a** : a relation of trust or intimacy <took his friend into his ~> **b** : reliance on another's discretion <their story was told in strictest ~> **c** : legislative support <vote of ~> **5** : a communication made in confidence : SECRET

syn CONFIDENCE, ASSURANCE, SELF-POSSESSION, APLOMB *shared meaning element* : a state of mind or a manner marked by easy coolness and freedom from uncertainty, diffidence, or embarrassment. CONFIDENCE stresses faith in oneself and one's powers without any suggestion of conceit or arrogance <had the *confidence* that comes only from long experience> ASSURANCE carries a stronger implication of certainty and may suggest arrogance or lack of objectivity in assessing one's own powers <had a conceited *assurance* of his own worth> SELF-POSSESSION implies an ease or coolness under stress that reflects perfect self-control and command of one's powers <he answered the insolent question with complete *self-possession*> APLOMB applies to the bearing or behavior under difficulties of a person with marked assurance or self-possession but usually carries none of the unpleasant connotations often felt in *assurance* <meet a challenge with *aplomb*> ***ant*** diffidence

[2]**confidence** *adj* : of or relating to swindling by false promises

confidence interval *n* : a group of continuous or discrete adjacent values that is used to estimate a statistical parameter (as a mean or variance) and that tends to include the true value of the parameter a predetermined proportion of the time if the process of finding the group of values is repeated a number of times

confidence limits *n pl* : the end points of a confidence interval

con·fi·dent \ˈkän-fəd-ənt, -fə-ˌdent\ *adj* [L *confident-, confidens,* fr. prp. of *confidere*] **1** *obs* : TRUSTFUL, CONFIDING **2** : characterized by assurance; *esp* : SELF-RELIANT **3 a** : full of conviction : CERTAIN **b** : COCKSURE — **con·fi·dent·ly** *adv*

con·fi·den·tial \ˌkän-fə-ˈden-chəl\ *adj* **1** : PRIVATE, SECRET **2** : marked by intimacy or willingness to confide <a ~ tone> **3** : entrusted with confidences <~ clerk> **4** : containing information whose unauthorized disclosure could be prejudicial to the national interest — compare SECRET, TOP SECRET — **con·fi·den·ti·al·i·ty** \-ˌden-chē-ˈal-ət-ē\ *n* — **con·fi·den·tial·ly** \-ˈdench-(ə-)lē\ *adv* — **con·fi·den·tial·ness** \-ˈden-chəl-nəs\ *n*

con·fid·ing \kən-ˈfīd-iŋ\ *adj* : tending to confide : TRUSTFUL — **con·fid·ing·ly** \-iŋ-lē\ *adv* — **con·fid·ing·ness** *n*

con·fig·u·rat·ed \kən-ˈfig-(y)ə-ˌrāt-əd\ *adj* : having a patterned surface — used of glass or metal

con·fig·u·ra·tion \kən-ˌfig-(y)ə-ˈrā-shən, ˌkän-\ *n* [LL *configuration-, configuratio,* similar formation, fr. L *configuratus,* pp. of *configurare* to form from or after, fr. *com-* + *figurare* to form, fr. *figura* figure] **1 a** : relative arrangement of parts **b** (1) : something (as a figure, contour, pattern, or apparatus) produced by such arrangement (2) : a set of interconnected equipment forming a computer system **c** : the stable structural makeup of a chemical compound esp. with reference to the space relations of the constituent atoms **2** : GESTALT <personality ~> ***syn*** see FORM — **con·fig·u·ra·tion·al** \-shnəl, -shən-ᵊl\ *adj* — **con·fig·u·ra·tion·al·ly** \-ē\ *adv* — **con·fig·u·ra·tive** \-ˈfig-(y)ə-rət-iv\ *adj*

con·fig·ure \kən-ˈfig-yər, *esp Brit* -ˈfig-ər\ *vt* **-ured; -ur·ing** : to give a configuration to : SHAPE <a society *configured* by reliance on a few commodities —H. M. McLuhan>

[1]**con·fine** \kən-ˈfīn\ *vb* **con·fined; con·fin·ing** *vi, archaic* : BORDER ~ *vt* **1** : to keep within limits : RESTRICT **2 a** : to shut up : IMPRISON **b** : to keep indoors ***syn*** see LIMIT — **con·fin·er** *n*

[2]**con·fine** \ˈkän-ˌfīn *also* kən-ˈ\ *n* [MF or L; MF *confines,* pl., fr. L *confine* border, fr. neut. of *confinis* adjacent, fr. *com-* + *finis* end] **1** *pl* **a** : BOUNDS, BORDERS <in the ~*s* of the big city slums —J. B. Conant> **b** : outlying parts : LIMITS <feel more comfortable within the protective ~*s* of the system —Paul Potter> **c** : TERRITORY <the future of the city lies in the eastern corner of its ~*s* — *Springfield (Mass.) Daily News*> **2 a** *archaic* : RESTRICTION **b** *obs* : PRISON

con·fined \kən-ˈfīnd\ *adj* **1** : kept within confines **2** : restricted to quarters; *esp* : undergoing childbirth

con·fine·ment \kən-ˈfīn-mənt\ *n* : an act of confining : the state of being confined; *esp* : LYING-IN

con·firm \kən-ˈfərm\ *vt* [ME *confirmen,* fr. OF *confirmer,* fr. L *confirmare,* fr. *com-* + *firmare* to make firm, fr. *firmus* firm] **1** : to make firm or firmer : STRENGTHEN **2** : to give approval to : RATIFY **3** : to administer the rite of confirmation to **4** : to give new assurance of the validity of : remove doubt about by authoritative act or indisputable fact **5** : ASSERT, MAINTAIN — **con·firm·abil·i·ty** \-ˌfər-mə-ˈbil-ət-ē\ *n* — **con·firm·able** \-ˈfər-mə-bəl\ *adj*

syn CONFIRM, CORROBORATE, SUBSTANTIATE, VERIFY, AUTHENTICATE, VALIDATE *shared meaning element* : to attest the truth or validity of something ***ant*** deny, contradict

con·fir·ma·tion \ˌkän-fər-ˈmā-shən\ *n* **1** : an act or process of confirming: as **a** (1) : a Christian rite conferring the gift of the Holy Spirit and among Protestants full church membership (2) : a ceremony confirming Jewish youths in their ancestral faith **b** : the ratification of an executive act by a legislative body **2 a** : confirming proof : CORROBORATION **b** : the process of supporting a statement by evidence — **con·fir·ma·tion·al** \-shnəl, -shən-ᵊl\ *adj*

con·fir·ma·to·ry \kən-ˈfər-mə-ˌtōr-ē, -ˌtȯr-\ *adj* : serving to confirm : CORROBORATIVE

con·firmed \kən-ˈfərmd\ *adj* **1 a** : made firm : STRENGTHENED **b** : being so fixed in habit as to be unlikely to change <a ~ bachelor> **c** : marked by long continuance and likely to persist <a ~ habit> **2** : having received the rite of confirmation ***syn*** see INVETERATE — **con·firm·ed·ly** \-ˈfər-məd-lē\ *adv* — **con·firmed·ness** \-ˈfər-məd-nəs, -ˈfərm(d)-nəs\ *n*

con·fis·ca·ble \kən-ˈfis-kə-bəl\ *adj* : liable to confiscation

con·fis·cat·able \ˈkän-fə-ˌskāt-ə-bəl\ *adj* : CONFISCABLE

[1]**con·fis·cate** \ˈkän-fə-ˌskāt, kən-ˈfis-kət\ *adj* [L *confiscatus,* pp. of *confiscare* to confiscate, fr. *com-* + *fiscus* treasury — more at FISCAL] **1** : appropriated by the government : FORFEITED **2** : deprived of property by confiscation

[2]**con·fis·cate** \ˈkän-fə-ˌskāt\ *vt* **-cat·ed; -cat·ing** **1** : to seize as forfeited to the public treasury **2** : to seize by or as if by authority ***syn*** see APPROPRIATE — **con·fis·ca·tion** \ˌkän-fə-ˈskā-shən\ *n* — **con·fis·ca·tor** \ˈkän-fə-ˌskāt-ər\ *n* — **con·fis·ca·to·ry** \kən-ˈfis-kə-ˌtōr-ē, -ˌtȯr-\ *adj*

con·fi·te·or \kən-ˈfēt-ē-ər, -ē-ˌȯ(ə)r\ *n* [ME, fr. L, I confess, fr. *confitēri* to confess — more at CONFESS] : a liturgical form in which sinfulness is acknowledged and intercession for God's mercy requested

con·fi·ture \ˈkän-fə-ˌchu̇(ə)r, -ˌt(y)u̇(ə)r\ *n* [F, fr. MF, fr. *confit* comfit] : preserved or candied fruit : JAM

con·fla·grant \kən-ˈflā-grənt\ *adj* [L *conflagrant-, conflagrans,* prp. of *conflagrare* to burn, fr. *com-* + *flagrare* to burn — more at BLACK] : BURNING, BLAZING

con·fla·gra·tion \ˌkän-flə-ˈgrā-shən\ *n* [L *conflagration-, conflagratio,* fr. *conflagratus,* pp. of *conflagrare*] **1** : FIRE; *esp* : a large disastrous fire **2** : CONFLICT

con·flate \kən-ˈflāt\ *vt* **con·flat·ed; con·flat·ing** [L *conflare* to blow together, fuse, fr. *com-* + *flare* to blow — more at BLOW] **1 a** : to bring together : FUSE **b** : CONFUSE **2** : to combine (as two readings of a text) into a composite whole

con·fla·tion \-ˈflā-shən\ *n* : BLEND, FUSION; *esp* : a composite reading or text

[1]**con·flict** \ˈkän-ˌflikt\ *n* [ME, fr. L *conflictus* act of striking together, fr. *conflictus* pp. of *confligere* to strike together, fr. *com-* + *fligere* to strike — more at PROFLIGATE] **1 a** : competitive or opposing action of incompatibles : antagonistic state or action (as of divergent ideas, interests, or persons) **b** : mental struggle resulting from incompatible or opposing needs, drives, wishes, or external or internal demands **2** : hostile encounter : FIGHT, BATTLE, WAR **3** : COLLISION **4** : the opposition of persons or forces that gives rise to the dramatic action in a drama or fiction ***syn*** see DISCORD ***ant*** harmony — **con·flict·ful** \ˈkän-ˌflikt-fəl\ *adj* — **con·flict·less** \-flik-tləs\ *adj* — **con·flic·tu·al** \kän-ˈflik-ch(ə-w)əl, kən-\ *adj*

[2]**con·flict** \kən-ˈflikt, ˈkän-ˌ\ *vi* **1** *archaic* : to contend in warfare **2** : to show antagonism or irreconcilability — **con·flic·tion** \kən-ˈflik-shən, kän-\ *n* — **con·flic·tive** \kən-ˈflik-tiv, ˈkän-ˌ\ *adj*

con·flict·ing *adj* : being in conflict, collision, or opposition : INCOMPATIBLE — **con·flict·ing·ly** \-ˈflik-tiŋ-lē, -ˌflik-\ *adv*

conflict of interest : a conflict between the private interests and the official responsibilities of a person in a position of trust (as a government official)

con·flu·ence \ˈkän-ˌflü-ən(t)s, kən-ˈ\ *n* **1** : a coming or flowing together, meeting, or gathering at one point <the ~ of scholarship that produced the atomic bomb> **2 a** : the flowing together of two or more streams **b** : the place of meeting of two streams **c** : the combined stream formed by conjunction ***syn*** see JUNCTION

[1]**con·flu·ent** \-ənt\ *adj* [L *confluent-, confluens,* prp. of *confluere* to flow together, fr. *com-* + *fluere* to flow — more at FLUID] **1** : flowing or coming together; *also* : run together <~ pustules> **2** : characterized by confluent lesions <~ smallpox>

[2]**confluent** *n* : a confluent stream; *broadly* : TRIBUTARY

con·flux \ˈkän-ˌfləks\ *n* [ML *confluxus,* fr. L *confluxus,* pp. of *confluere*] : CONFLUENCE

con·fo·cal \(ˈ)kän-ˈfō-kəl\ *adj* : having the same foci <~ ellipses> <~ lenses> — **con·fo·cal·ly** \-kə-lē\ *adv*

[1]**con·form** \kən-ˈfȯ(ə)rm\ *vb* [ME *conformen,* fr. MF *conformer,* fr. L *conformare,* fr. *com-* + *formare* to form, fr. *forma* form] *vt* : to give the same shape, outline, or contour to : bring into harmony or accord <~ furrows to the slope of the land> ~ *vi* **1** : to be similar or identical **2** : to be obedient or compliant; *esp* : to adapt oneself to prevailing standards or customs ***syn*** **1** see ADAPT **2** see AGREE ***ant*** diverge — **con·form·er** *n* — **con·form·ism** \-ˈfȯr-ˌmiz-əm\ *n* — **con·form·ist** \-məst\ *n*

[2]**conform** *adj* : CONFORMABLE

con·form·able \kən-ˈfȯr-mə-bəl\ *adj* **1** : corresponding in form or character : SIMILAR — usu. used with *to* <decisions ~ to the will and desire of the people —David Fromkin> **2** : SUBMISSIVE, COMPLIANT **3** : following in unbroken sequence — used of geologic strata formed under uniform conditions — **con·form·ably** \-blē\ *adv*

con·for·mal \kən-ˈfȯr-məl, (ˈ)kän-\ *adj* [LL *conformalis* having the same shape, fr. L *com-* + *formalis* formal, fr. *forma*] : leaving the size of the angle between corresponding curves unchanged <~ transformation>; *esp, of a map* : representing small areas in their true shape

con·for·mance \kən-ˈfȯr-mən(t)s\ *n* : CONFORMITY

con·for·ma·tion \ˌkän-(ˌ)fȯr-ˈmā-shən, -fər-\ *n* **1** : the act of conforming or producing conformity : ADAPTATION **2** : formation of something by appropriate arrangement of parts or elements : an assembling into a whole <the gradual ~ of the embryo> **3 a** : correspondence esp. to a model or plan **b** : STRUCTURE **c** : the proportionate shape or contour esp. of an animal **d** : any of the spatial arrangements of a molecule that can be obtained by rotation of the atoms about a single bond ***syn*** see FORM — **con·for·ma·tion·al** \-shnəl, -shən-ᵊl\ *adj*

con·for·mi·ty \kən-ˈfȯr-mət-ē\ *n, pl* **-ties** **1 :** correspondence in form, manner, or character : AGREEMENT <behaved in ~ with his beliefs> **2 :** an act or instance of conforming **3 :** action in accordance with some specified standard or authority : OBEDIENCE <~ to social custom>

con·found \kən-ˈfau̇nd, kän-\ *vt* [ME *confounden*, fr. OF *confondre*, fr. L *confundere* to pour together, confuse, fr. *com-* + *fundere* to pour — more at FOUND] **1** *archaic* **:** to bring to ruin : DESTROY **2** *obs* **:** CONSUME, WASTE **3 a :** to put to shame : DISCOMFIT <a performance that ~*ed* his critics> **b :** REFUTE <sought to ~ his arguments> **4 :** DAMN **5 :** to throw (a person) into confusion or perplexity **6 a :** to fail to discern differences between : mix up **b :** to increase the confusion of ***syn*** **1** see PUZZLE **2** see MISTAKE ***ant*** distinguish, discriminate — **con·found·er** *n*

con·found·ed \kən-ˈfau̇n-dəd, (ˈ)kän-ˈ, ˈkän-ˌ\ *adj* **1 :** CONFUSED, PERPLEXED **2 :** DAMNED — **con·found·ed·ly** *adv*

con·fra·ter·ni·ty \ˌkän-frə-ˈtər-nət-ē\ *n* [ME *confraternite*, fr. MF *confraternité*, fr. ML *confraternitat-, confraternitas*, fr. *confrater* fellow, brother, fr. L *com-* + *frater* brother — more at BROTHER] **1 :** a society devoted to a religious or charitable cause **2 :** fraternal union

con·frere \ˈkän-ˌfre(ə)r, kōⁿ-ˌ, kän-ˈ, kōⁿ-ˈ, kən-ˈ\ *n* [ME, fr. MF, trans. of ML *confrater*] **:** COLLEAGUE, COMRADE

con·front \kən-ˈfrənt\ *vt* [MF *confronter* to border on, confront, fr. ML *confrontare* to bound, fr. L *com-* + *front-, frons* forehead, front — more at BRINK] **1 :** to face esp. in challenge : OPPOSE <scholars must ~ society, often in conflict —Paul Goodman> **2 a :** to cause to meet : bring face to face <~ a reader with statistics> **b :** ENCOUNTER <the problems that one ~*s* are enormous> — **con·front·al** \-ˈfrənt-ᵊl\ *n* — **con·front·er** *n*

con·fron·ta·tion \ˌkän-(ˌ)frən-ˈtā-shən\ *n* **:** the act of confronting : the state of being confronted: as **a :** a face-to-face meeting **b :** the clashing of forces or ideas : CONFLICT **c :** COMPARISON <the flashbacks bring into meaningful ~ present and past, near and far —R. J. Clements> — **con·fron·ta·tion·al** \-shnəl, -shən-ᵊl\ *adj* — **con·fron·ta·tion·ism** \-shə-ˌniz-əm\ *n* — **con·fron·ta·tion·ist** \-sh(ə-)nəst\ *n*

Con·fu·cian \kən-ˈfyü-shən\ *adj* **:** of or relating to the Chinese philosopher Confucius or his teachings or followers — **Confucian** *n* — **Con·fu·cian·ism** \-shə-ˌniz-əm\ *n*

con·fuse \kən-ˈfyüz\ *vt* **con·fused; con·fus·ing** [back-formation fr. ME *confused* perplexed, fr. MF *confus*, fr. L *confusus*, pp. of *confundere*] **1** *archaic* **:** to bring to ruin **2 a :** to make embarrassed : ABASH **b :** to disturb in mind or purpose : throw off <interrogators who do their best to frighten, ~ and bewilder him —Aldous Huxley> **3 a :** to make indistinct : BLUR <stop *confusing* the issue> **b :** to mix indiscriminately : JUMBLE **c :** to fail to differentiate from an often similar or related other <~ money with comfort> ***syn*** see MISTAKE ***ant*** differentiate — **con·fus·ing** \-ˈfyü-ziŋ\ *adj* — **con·fus·ing·ly** \-ziŋ-lē\ *adv*

con·fused \-ˈfyüzd\ *adj* **1 :** being perplexed or disconcerted <the ~ students> **2 :** INDISTINGUISHABLE <a zigzag, crisscross, ~ trail —Harry Hervey> **3 :** being disordered or mixed up <a contradictory and often ~ philosophy> — **con·fused·ly** \-ˈfyüz(-ə)d-lē\ *adv* — **con·fused·ness** \-ˈfyü-zəd-nəs, -ˈfyüz(d)-\ *n*

con·fu·sion \kən-ˈfyü-zhən\ *n* **1 :** an act or instance of confusing **2 :** the quality or state of being confused — **con·fu·sion·al** \-ˈfyüzh-nəl, -ˈfyü-zhən-ᵊl\ *adj*

con·fu·ta·tion \ˌkän-fyu̇-ˈtā-shən\ *n* **1 :** the act or process of confuting : REFUTATION **2 :** something (as an argument or statement) that confutes — **con·fu·ta·tive** \kən-ˈfyüt-ət-iv\ *adj*

con·fute \kən-ˈfyüt\ *vt* **con·fut·ed; con·fut·ing** [L *confutare*, fr. *com-* + *-futare* to beat — more at BEAT] **1 :** to overwhelm in argument : refute conclusively <Elijah . . . *confuted* the prophets of Baal . . . with . . . bitter mockery —G. B. Shaw> **2** *obs* **:** CONFOUND ***syn*** see DISPROVE — **con·fut·er** *n*

cong *abbr* congress; congressional

con·ga \ˈkäŋ-gə\ *n* [AmerSp, fr. Sp, fem. of *congo* of the Congo, fr. *Congo*, region in Africa] **1 :** a Cuban dance of African origin involving three steps followed by a kick and performed by a group usu. in single file **2 :** a tall narrow bass drum beaten with the hands

con·gé \kōⁿ-ˈzhā, ˈkän-ˌjā\ *n* [F, fr. L *commeatus* going back and forth, leave, fr. *commeatus*, pp. of *commeare* to go back and forth, fr. *com-* + *meare* to go — more at PERMEATE] **1 a :** a formal permission to depart **b :** DISMISSAL **2 :** a ceremonious bow **3 :** FAREWELL **4 :** an architectural molding of concave profile — see MOLDING illustration

con·geal \kən-ˈjē(ə)l\ *vb* [ME *congelen*, fr. MF *congeler*, fr. L *congelare*, fr. *com-* + *gelare* to freeze — more at COLD] *vt* **1 :** to change from a fluid to a solid state by or as if by cold **2 :** to make viscid or curdled : COAGULATE **3 :** to make rigid, inflexible, or immobile ~ *vi* **:** to become congealed — **con·geal·ment** \-mənt\ *n*

con·gee \ˈkän-(ˌ)jē\ *n* **:** CONGÉ

con·ge·la·tion \ˌkän-jə-ˈlā-shən\ *n* **:** the process or result of congealing

con·ge·ner \ˈkän-jə-nər, kən-ˈjē-\ *n* [L, of the same kind, fr. *com-* + *gener-, genus* kind — more at KIN] **1 :** a member of the same taxonomic genus as another plant or animal **2 :** a person or thing resembling another in nature or action <the New England private schools and their ~*s* west of the Alleghenies —Oliver La Farge> — **con·ge·ner·ic** \ˌkän-jə-ˈner-ik\ *adj* — **con·ge·ner·ous** \kən-ˈjē-nə-rəs, -ˈjen-ə-, (ˈ)kän-\ *adj*

con·ge·nial \kən-ˈjē-nyəl\ *adj* [*com-* + *genius*] **1 :** having the same nature, disposition, or tastes : KINDRED **2 a :** existing or associated together harmoniously **b :** PLEASANT; *esp* **:** agreeably suited to one's nature, tastes, or outlook **c :** SOCIABLE, GENIAL ***syn*** see CONSONANT ***ant*** uncongenial, antipathetic (*of persons*), abhorrent (*of tasks, duties*) — **con·ge·nial·i·ty** \-ˌjē-nē-ˈal-ət-ē, -ˌjen-ˈyal-\ *n* — **con·ge·nial·ly** \-ˈjē-nyə-lē\ *adv*

con·gen·i·tal \kän-ˈjen-ə-tᵊl\ *adj* [L *congenitus*, fr. *com-* + *genitus* pp. of *gignere* to bring forth — more at KIN] **1 a :** existing at or dating from birth <~ idiocy> **b :** constituting an essential characteristic : INHERENT <~ fear of snakes> **c :** acquired during development in the uterus and not through heredity <~ syphilis> **2 :** being such by nature <~ liar> ***syn*** see INNATE — **con·gen·i·tal·ly** \-tᵊl-ē\ *adv*

con·ger eel \ˈkäŋ-gər-\ *n* [ME *congre*, fr. OF, fr. L *congr-, conger*, fr. Gk *gongros*; akin to ON *kökkr* ball, L *gingiva* gum] **:** a large strictly marine scaleless eel (*Conger oceanicus*) important as a food fish; *broadly* **:** any of various related eels (family Congridae)

con·ge·ries \ˈkän-jə-(ˌ)rēz\ *n, pl* **congeries** *same*\ [L, fr. *congerere*] **:** AGGREGATION, COLLECTION <the alternative was to turn linguistics into a ~ of meaningless guesses —C. A. Ladd>

con·gest \kən-ˈjest\ *vb* [L *congestus*, pp. of *congerere* to bring together, fr. *com-* + *gerere* to bear — more at CAST] *vt* **1 :** to cause an excessive fullness of the blood vessels of (as an organ) **2 :** CLOG <traffic ~*ed* the highways> **3 :** to concentrate in a small or narrow space ~ *vi* **:** to become congested — **con·ges·tion** \-ˈjes(h)-chən\ *n* — **con·ges·tive** \-ˈjes-tiv\ *adj*

con·glo·bate \kän-ˈglō-ˌbāt, kən-\ *vt* **-bat·ed; -bat·ing** [L *conglobatus*, pp. of *conglobare*, fr. *com-* + *globus* globe] **:** to form into a round compact mass — **con·glo·bate** \-bət, -ˌbāt\ *adj* — **con·glo·ba·tion** \ˌkän-(ˌ)glō-ˈbā-shən\ *n*

con·globe \kän-ˌglōb, kən-\ *vt* **con·globed; con·glob·ing** **:** CONGLOBATE

¹con·glom·er·ate \kən-ˈgläm-(ə-)rət\ *adj* [L *conglomeratus*, pp. of *conglomerare* to roll together, fr. *com-* + *glomerare* to wind into a ball, fr. *glomer-, glomus* ball — more at CLAM] **:** made up of parts from various sources or of various kinds <an ethnically ~ culture>

²con·glom·er·ate \-ə-ˌrāt\ *vb* **-at·ed; -at·ing** *vt* **:** ACCUMULATE ~ *vi* **:** to gather into a mass or coherent whole <numbers of dull people *conglomerated* round her —Virginia Woolf> — **con·glom·er·a·tive** \-ˈgläm-(ə-)rət-iv, -ə-ˌrāt-\ *adj* — **con·glom·er·a·tor** \-ˈgläm-ə-ˌrāt-ər\ *n*

³con·glom·er·ate \-(ə-)rət\ *n* **1 :** a composite mass or mixture; *specif* **:** rock composed of rounded fragments varying from small pebbles to large boulders in a cement (as of hardened clay) **2 :** a widely diversified corporation — **con·glom·er·at·ic** \kən-ˌgläm-ə-ˈrat-ik, ˌkän-\ *adj*

con·glom·er·a·tion \kən-ˌgläm-ə-ˈrā-shən, ˌkän-\ *n* **1 :** the act of conglomerating : the state of being conglomerated **2 :** something conglomerated : a mixed coherent mass

con·glu·ti·nate \kən-ˈglüt-ᵊn-ˌāt, kän-\ *vb* **-nat·ed; -nat·ing** [L *conglutinatus*, pp. of *conglutinare* to glue together, fr. *com-* + *glutin-, gluten* glue] *vt* **:** to unite by or as if by a glutinous substance ~ *vi* **:** to become conglutinated <blood platelets ~ in blood clotting> — **con·glu·ti·na·tion** \kən-ˌglü t-ᵊn-ˈā-shən, ˌkän-\ *n*

Con·go dye \ˌkäŋ-(ˌ)gō-\ *n* [*Congo*, territory in Africa] **:** any of various direct azo dyes mostly derived from benzidine

Congo red *n* **:** an azo dye $C_{32}H_{22}N_6Na_2O_6S_2$ that is red in alkaline and blue in acid solution and that is used esp. as an indicator and as a biological stain

congo snake *n* **:** an elongated bluish black amphibian (*Amphiuma means*) of the southeastern U.S. that has two pairs of very short limbs each with two or three toes — called also *congo eel*

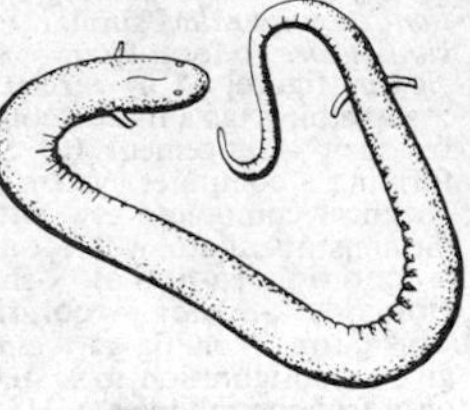

congo snake

con·gou \ˈkäŋ-(ˌ)gō, -(ˌ)gü\ *n* [prob. fr. Chin (Amoy) *kong-hu* pains taken] **:** a black tea from China

con·grat·u·late \kən-ˈgrach-ə-ˌlāt, *nonstand* -ˈgraj-\ *vt* **-lat·ed; -lat·ing** [L *congratulatus*, pp. of *congratulari* to wish joy, fr. *com-* + *gratulari* to wish joy, fr. *gratus* pleasing — more at GRACE] **1 :** to express pleasure to (a person) on account of success or good fortune **2** *archaic* **:** to express sympathetic pleasure at (an event) **3** *obs* **:** SALUTE, GREET — **con·grat·u·la·tor** \-ə-ˌlāt-ər\ *n* — **con·grat·u·la·to·ry** \-(ə-)lə-ˌtōr-ē, -ˌtȯr-\ *adj*

con·grat·u·la·tion \kən-ˌgrach-ə-ˈlā-shən, *nonstand* -ˌgraj-\ *n* **1 :** the act of congratulating **2 :** a congratulatory expression — usu. used in pl.

con·gre·gant \-gənt\ *n* **:** one that congregates; *specif* **:** a member of a congregation

con·gre·gate \ˈkäŋ-gri-ˌgāt\ *vb* **-gat·ed; -gat·ing** [ME *congregaten*, fr. L *congregatus*, pp. of *congregare*, fr. *com-* + *greg-, grex* flock — more at GREGARIOUS] *vt* **:** to collect into a group or crowd : ASSEMBLE ~ *vi* **:** to come together into a group, crowd, or assembly ***syn*** see GATHER — **con·gre·ga·tor** \-ˌgāt-ər\ *n*

con·gre·ga·tion \ˌkäŋ-gri-ˈgā-shən\ *n* **1 a :** an assembly of persons : GATHERING; *esp* **:** an assembly of persons met for worship and religious instruction **b :** a religious community: as **(1) :** an organized body of believers in a particular locality **(2) :** a Roman Catholic religious institute with only simple vows **(3) :** a group of monasteries forming an independent subdivision of an order **2 :** the act or an instance of congregating or bringing together : the state of being congregated **3 :** a body of cardinals and officials forming an administrative division of the papal curia

con·gre·ga·tion·al \-shnəl, -shən-ᵊl\ *adj* **1 :** of or relating to a congregation **2** *cap* **:** of or relating to a body of Protestant churches deriving from the English Independents of the 17th century and affirming the essential importance and the autonomy of the local congregation **3 :** of or relating to church government placing final authority in the assembly of the local congregation — **con·gre·ga·tion·al·ism** \-shnə-ˌliz-əm, -shən-ᵊl-ˌiz-\ *n, often cap* — **con·gre·ga·tion·al·ist** \-shnə-ləst, -shən-ᵊl-əst\ *n or adj, often cap*

con·gress \ˈkäŋ-grəs\ *n* [L *congressus*, fr. *congressus*, pp. of *congredi* to come together, fr. *com-* + *gradi* to go — more at

GRADE] **1 a :** the act or action of coming together and meeting **b :** COITUS **2 :** a formal meeting of delegates for discussion and usu. action on some question **3 :** the supreme legislative body of a nation and esp. of a republic **4 :** an association usu. made up of delegates from constituent organizations **5 :** a single meeting or session of a group — **con·gres·sio·nal** \kən-ˈgresh-nəl, -ən-ᵊl\ *adj* — **con·gres·sio·nal·ly** \-ē\ *adv*

congress gaiter *n, often cap C* [fr. its former popularity with U.S. congressmen] **:** an ankle-high shoe with elastic gussets in the sides — called also *congress shoe*

congressional district *n* **:** a territorial division of a state from which a member of the U.S. House of Representatives is elected

Congressional Medal *n* **:** MEDAL OF HONOR

con·gress·man \ˈkäŋ-grə-smən\ *n* **:** a member of a congress; *esp* **:** a member of the U.S. House of Representatives

con·gress·wom·an \-grə-ˌswu̇m-ən\ *n* **:** a female member of a congress; *esp* **:** a female member of the U.S. House of Representatives

con·gru·ence \kən-ˈgrü-ən(t)s, ˈkäŋ-grə-wən(t)s\ *n* **1 :** the quality or state of agreeing or coinciding **2 :** a statement that two numbers are congruent with respect to a modulus

con·gru·en·cy \-ən-sē, -wən-\ *n, pl* **-cies :** CONGRUENCE

con·gru·ent \kən-ˈgrü-ənt, ˈkäŋ-grə-wənt\ *adj* [L *congruent-, congruens,* prp. of *congruere*] **1 :** CONGRUOUS **2 :** superposable so as to be coincident throughout **3 :** having the difference divisible by a given modulus <12 is ~ to 2 (modulo 5) since 12−2=2·5> **4 :** relating to the melting point at which there coexist for a compound both liquid and solid phases having the same composition — **con·gru·ent·ly** *adv*

con·gru·ity \kən-ˈgrü-ət-ē, kän-\ *n, pl* **-ities 1 :** the quality or state of being congruent or congruous **2 :** a point of agreement

con·gru·ous \ˈkäŋ-grə-wəs\ *adj* [L *congruus,* fr. *congruere* to come together, agree, fr. *com-* + *-gruere* (akin to Gk *zachrēēs* attacking violently)] **1 a :** being in agreement, harmony, or correspondence **b :** conforming to the circumstances or requirements of a situation **:** APPROPRIATE <a ~ room to work in —G. B. Shaw> **2 :** marked or enhanced by harmonious agreement among constituent elements <a ~ theme in music> ***syn*** see CONSONANT ***ant*** incongruous — **con·gru·ous·ly** *adv* — **con·gru·ous·ness** *n*

¹con·ic \ˈkän-ik\ *adj* **1 :** CONICAL **2 :** of or relating to a cone — **co·nic·i·ty** \kō-ˈnis-ət-ē\ *n*

²conic *n* **:** CONIC SECTION

con·i·cal \ˈkän-i-kəl\ *adj* **:** resembling a cone esp. in shape <~ roots> — **con·i·cal·ly** \-k(ə-)lē\ *adv* — **con·i·cal·ness** \-kəl-nəs\ *n*

conic section *n* **1 :** a plane section of a right circular conical surface **2 :** a curve generated by a point which always moves so that the ratio of its distance from a fixed point to its distance from a fixed line is constant

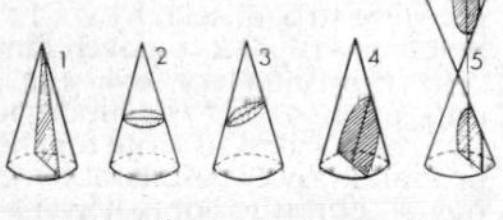

1 2 3 4 5

conic sections: *1* straight lines, *2* circle, *3* ellipse, *4* parabola, *5* hyperbola

co·nid·io·phore \kə-ˈnid-ē-ə-ˌfō(ə)r, -ˌfȯ(ə)r\ *n* [NL *conidium* + ISV *-phore*] **:** a structure that bears conidia; *specif* **:** a specialized hyphal branch that produces successive conidia usu. by abstriction — **co·nid·i·oph·o·rous** \-ˌnid-ē-ˈäf-(ə-)rəs\ *adj*

co·nid·i·um \kə-ˈnid-ē-əm\ *n, pl* **-ia** \-ē-ə\ [NL, fr. Gk *konis* dust — more at INCINERATE] **:** an asexual spore produced on a conidiophore — **co·nid·i·al** \-ē-əl\ *adj*

co·ni·fer \ˈkän-ə-fər *also* ˈkō-nə-\ *n* [deriv. of L *conifer* cone-bearing, fr. *conus* cone + *-fer*] **:** any of an order (Coniferales) of mostly evergreen trees and shrubs including forms (as pines) with true cones and others (as yews) with an arillate fruit — **co·nif·er·ous** \kō-ˈnif-(ə-)rəs, kə-\ *adj*

co·ni·ine \ˈkō-nē-ˌēn\ *n* [G *koniin,* fr. LL *conium*] **:** a poisonous alkaloid $C_8H_{17}N$ found in poison hemlock (*Conium maculatum*)

co·ni·um \kō-ˈnī-əm, ˈkō-nē-\ *n* [NL, genus name, fr. LL, hemlock, fr. Gk *kōneion*] **:** any of a genus (*Conium*) of poisonous herbs of the carrot family

conj *abbr* conjunction; conjunctive

con·jec·tur·al \kən-ˈjek-chə-rəl, -ˈjeksh-rəl\ *adj* **1 :** of the nature of or involving or based on conjecture **2 :** given to conjectures — **con·jec·tur·al·ly** \-ē\ *adv*

¹con·jec·ture \kən-ˈjek-chər\ *n* [ME, fr. MF or L; MF, fr. L *conjectura,* fr. *conjectus,* pp. of *conicere,* lit., to throw together, fr. *com-* + *jacere* to throw — more at JET] **1** *obs* **a :** interpretation of omens **b :** SUPPOSITION **2 a :** inference from defective or presumptive evidence **b :** a conclusion deduced by surmise or guesswork

²conjecture *vb* **-tured; -tur·ing** \-ˈjek-chə-riŋ, -ˈjek-shriŋ\ *vt* **1 :** to arrive at by conjecture **2 :** to make conjectures as to ~ *vi* **:** to form conjectures — **con·jec·tur·er** \-ˈjek-chər-ər\ *n*

syn CONJECTURE, SURMISE, GUESS *shared meaning element* **:** to draw an inference from slight evidence

con·join \kən-ˈjȯin, kän-\ *vb* [ME *conjoinen,* fr. MF *conjoindre,* fr. L *conjungere,* fr. *com-* + *jungere* to join — more at YOKE] *vt* **:** to join together (as separate entities) for a common purpose ~ *vi* **:** to join together for a common purpose

con·joined \-ˈjȯind\ *adj* **:** being, coming, or brought together so as to meet, touch, or overlap <~ heads on a coin>

con·joint \-ˈjȯint\ *adj* [ME, fr. MF, pp. of *conjoindre*] **1 :** UNITED, CONJOINED **2 :** related to, made up of, or carried on by two or more in combination **:** JOINT — **con·joint·ly** *adv*

con·ju·gal \ˈkän-ji-gəl, kən-ˈjü-\ *adj* [MF or L; MF, fr. L *conjugalis,* fr. *conjug-, conjux* husband, wife, fr. *conjungere* to join, unite in marriage] **:** of or relating to the married state or to married persons and their relations **:** CONNUBIAL ***syn*** see MATRIMONIAL — **con·ju·gal·i·ty** \ˌkän-ji-ˈgal-ət-ē, -jü-\ *n* — **con·ju·gal·ly** \ˈkän-ji-gə-lē, kən-ˈjü-\ *adv*

conjugal rights *n pl* **:** the sexual rights or privileges implied by and involved in the marriage relationship **:** the right of sexual intercourse between husband and wife

con·ju·gant \ˈkän-ji-gənt\ *n* **:** either of a pair of conjugating gametes or organisms

¹con·ju·gate \ˈkän-ji-gət, -jə-ˌgāt\ *adj* [ME *conjugat,* fr. L *conjugatus,* pp. of *conjugare* to unite, fr. *com-* + *jugare* to join, fr. *jugum* yoke — more at YOKE] **1 a :** joined together esp. in pairs **:** COUPLED **b :** acting or operating as if joined **2 :** having features in common but opposite or inverse in some particular **3** *of an acid or base* **:** related by the difference of a proton <the acid NH_4 and the base NH_3 are ~ to each other> **4 :** having the same derivation and therefore usu. some likeness in meaning <~ words> **5** *of two leaves of a book* **:** forming a single piece — **con·ju·gate·ly** *adv* — **con·ju·gate·ness** *n*

²con·ju·gate \-jə-ˌgāt\ *vb* **-gat·ed; -gat·ing** *vt* **1 :** to give in prescribed order the various inflectional forms of — used esp. of a verb **2 :** to join together ~ *vi* **1 :** to become joined together **2 a :** to pair and fuse in conjugation **b :** to pair in synapsis

³conjugate *like* ¹CONJUGATE\ *n* **1 :** something conjugate **:** a product of conjugating **2 :** an element of a mathematical group that is equal to a given element of the group multiplied on the right by another element and on the left by the inverse of the latter element

conjugate complex number *n* **:** one of two complex numbers (as $a + bi$ and $a - bi$) differing only in the sign of the imaginary part

con·ju·gat·ed *adj* **1 :** formed by the union of two compounds or united with another compound <~ bile acids> **2 :** relating to or containing a system of two double bonds separated by a single bond <~ fatty acids>

conjugated protein *n* **:** a compound of a protein with a nonprotein <hemoglobin is a *conjugated protein* of heme and globin>

con·ju·ga·tion \ˌkän-jə-ˈgā-shən\ *n* **1 :** the act of conjugating **:** the state of being conjugated **2 a :** a schematic arrangement of the inflectional forms of a verb **b :** verb inflection **c :** a class of verbs having the same type of inflectional forms <the weak ~> **d :** a set of the simple or derivative inflectional forms of a verb esp. in Sanskrit or the Semitic languages <the causative ~> **3 a :** fusion of usu. similar gametes with ultimate union of their nuclei that among lower thallophytes replaces the typical fertilization of higher forms **b :** temporary cytoplasmic union with exchange of nuclear material that is the usual sexual process in ciliated protozoans **c :** the one-way transfer of DNA between bacteria in cellular contact — **con·ju·ga·tion·al** \-shnəl, -shən-ᵊl\ *adj* — **con·ju·ga·tion·al·ly** \-ē\ *adv* — **con·ju·ga·tive** \ˈkän-jə-ˌgāt-iv\ *adj*

¹con·junct \kən-ˈjəŋ(k)t, kän-\ *adj* [ME, fr. L *conjunctus,* pp. of *conjungere*] **1 :** JOINED, UNITED **2 :** JOINT **3 :** relating to melodic progression by diatonic degrees — compare DISJUNCT

²con·junct \ˈkän-ˌjəŋ(k)t\ *n* **:** something joined or associated with another; *specif* **:** one of the components of a conjunction

con·junc·tion \kən-ˈjəŋ(k)-shən\ *n* **1 :** the act or an instance of conjoining **:** the state of being conjoined **2 :** occurrence together in time or space **:** CONCURRENCE **3 a :** the apparent meeting or passing of two or more celestial bodies in the same degree of the zodiac **b :** a configuration in which two celestial bodies have their least apparent separation **4 :** an uninflected linguistic form that joins together sentences, clauses, phrases, or words **:** CONNECTIVE **5 :** a complex sentence in logic true if and only if each of its components is true — **con·junc·tion·al** \-shnəl, -shən-ᵊl\ *adj* — **con·junc·tion·al·ly** \-ē\ *adv*

con·junc·ti·va \ˌkän-ˌjəŋ(k)-ˈtī-və, kən-\ *n, pl* **-vas** *or* **-vae** \-(ˌ)vē\ [NL, fr. LL, fem. of *conjunctivus* conjoining, fr. L *conjunctus*] **:** the mucous membrane that lines the inner surface of the eyelids and is continued over the forepart of the eyeball — see EYE illustration — **con·junc·ti·val** \-vəl\ *adj*

con·junc·tive \kən-ˈjəŋ(k)-tiv\ *adj* **1 :** CONNECTIVE **2 :** CONJUNCT, CONJOINED **3 :** being or functioning like a conjunction **4 :** COPULATIVE 1a — **conjunctive** *n* — **con·junc·tive·ly** *adv*

con·junc·ti·vi·tis \kən-ˌjəŋ(k)-ti-ˈvīt-əs\ *n* **:** inflammation of the conjunctiva

con·junc·ture \kən-ˈjəŋ(k)-chər\ *n* **1 :** CONJUNCTION, UNION **2 :** a combination of circumstances or events usu. producing a crisis **:** JUNCTURE

con·ju·ra·tion \ˌkän-jü-ˈrā-shən, ˌkən-\ *n* **1 :** the act or process of conjuring **:** INCANTATION **2 :** an expression or trick used in conjuring **3 :** a solemn appeal **:** ADJURATION

con·jure *in vt 2 & vi senses* ˈkän-jər *also* ˈkən-; *in vt 1 sense* kən-ˈju̇(ə)r\ *vb* **con·jured; con·jur·ing** \ˈkänj-(ə-)riŋ, ˈkənj-; kən-ˈju̇(ə)r-iŋ\ [ME *conjuren,* fr. OF *conjurer,* fr. L *conjurare* to swear together, fr. *com-* + *jurare* to swear — more at JURY] *vt* **1 :** to charge or entreat earnestly or solemnly **2 a :** to summon by invocation or incantation **b (1) :** to affect or effect by or as if by magic **(2) :** IMAGINE, CONTRIVE — often used with *up* <we ~ up our own metaphors for our own needs —R. J. Kaufmann> ~ *vi* **1 a :** to summon a devil or spirit by invocation or incantation **b :** to practice magical arts **2 :** to use a conjurer's tricks **:** JUGGLE

con·jur·er *or* **con·ju·ror** \ˈkän-jər-ər, ˈkən-\ *n* **1 :** one that practices magic arts **:** WIZARD **2 :** one that performs feats of sleight of hand and illusion **:** MAGICIAN, JUGGLER

¹conk \ˈkäŋk, ˈkȯŋk\ *vt* [slang *conk* (head); prob. alter. of *conch*] **:** to hit esp. on the head **:** knock out

²conk *n* [prob. alter. of *conch*] **:** the visible fruiting body of a tree fungus; *also* **:** decay caused by such a fungus — **conky** \-ē\ *adj*

³conk *vi* [prob. imit.] **1 :** to break down; *esp* **:** STALL — usu. used with *out* <the motor suddenly ~*ed* out> **2 a :** FAINT **b :** to go to sleep — usu. used with *off* or *out* <~*ed* out for a while after lunch> **c :** DIE <I caught pneumonia. I almost ~*ed* —Truman Capote>

4conk *vt* [prob. by shortening & alter. fr. *congolene* (a hydrocarbon produced from Congo copal and used for straightening hair), fr. *Congol*ese + *-ene*] **:** to straighten out (hair) usu. by the use of chemicals

5conk *n* **:** a hairstyle in which the hair is straightened out and flattened down or lightly waved — called also *process*

conk·er \ˈkäŋ-kər\ *n* [*conch* + *-er*; fr. the original use of a snail shell on a string in the game] **1** *pl* **:** a game popular in England in which each player swings a horse chestnut on a string to try to break one held by his opponent **2 :** a horse chestnut esp. when used in conkers

con mo·to \kän-ˈmō-(ˌ)tō, kōn-\ *adv* [It] **:** with movement **:** in a spirited manner — used as a direction in music

1conn \ˈkän\ *vt* [alter. of ME *condien* to conduct, fr. MF *conduire,* fr. L *conducere*] **:** to conduct or direct the steering of (as a ship)

2conn *n* **:** the control exercised by one who conns a ship

Conn *abbr* Connecticut

con·nate \kä-ˈnāt, ˈkän-ˌāt\ *adj* [LL *connatus,* pp. of *connasci* to be born together, fr. L *com-* + *nasci* to be born — more at NATION] **1 :** INNATE, INBORN **2 :** AKIN, CONGENIAL **3 :** born or originated together **4 :** congenitally or firmly united <~ leaves> **5 :** entrapped in sediments at the time of their deposition <~ water> — **con·nate·ly** *adv*

con·nat·u·ral \kä-ˈnach-(ə-)rəl, kə-\ *adj* [ML *connaturalis,* fr. L *com-* + *naturalis* natural] **1 :** connected by nature **:** INBORN **2 :** of the same nature — **con·nat·u·ral·i·ty** \-ˌnach-ə-ˈral-ət-ē\ *n* — **con·nat·u·ral·ly** \-ˈnach-(ə-)rə-lē\ *adv*

con·nect \kə-ˈnekt\ *vb* [L *conectere, connectere,* fr. *com-* + *nectere* to bind] *vt* **1 :** to join or fasten together usu. by something intervening **2 :** to place or establish in relationship ~ *vi* **1 :** to become joined <the two rooms ~ by a hallway> <ideas that ~ easily to form a theory> **2 :** to make a successful hit, shot, or throw <~*ed* for a home run> <~*ed* on 60 percent of his shots and on 10 of 11 free throws —*N.Y. Times*> <~*ed* with a right to the jaw> ***syn*** see JOIN ***ant*** disconnected — **con·nect·able** *also* **con·nect·ible** \-ˈnek-tə-bəl\ *adj* — **con·nec·tor** *also* **con·nect·er** \-ˈnek-tər\ *n*

con·nect·ed *adj* **1 :** joined or linked together **2 :** having the parts or elements logically linked together <presented a thoroughly ~ view of the problem> **3 :** related by blood or marriage **4 :** having a social, professional, or commercial relationship <for the well ~, there are elegantly overdone parties —John Griffin> — **con·nect·ed·ly** *adv* — **con·nect·ed·ness** *n*

connecting rod *n* **:** a rod that transmits power from one rotating part of a machine to another in reciprocating motion

con·nec·tion \kə-ˈnek-shən\ *n* [L *connexion-, connexio,* fr. *conexus,* pp. of *conectere*] **1 :** the act of connecting **:** the state of being connected: as **a :** causal or logical relation or sequence <the ~ between two ideas> **b :** contextual relations or associations <in this ~ the word has a different meaning> **c :** a relation of personal intimacy (as of family ties) **d :** COHERENCE, CONTINUITY **2 a :** something that connects **:** LINK <a loose ~ in the wiring> **b :** a means of communication or transport **3 :** a person connected with others esp. by marriage, kinship, or common interest <has powerful ~*s* in high places> **4 :** a social, professional, or commercial relationship: as **a :** POSITION, JOB **b :** an arrangement to execute orders or advance interests of another <a firm's foreign ~*s*> **c :** a source of contraband (as illegal drugs) **5 :** a set of persons associated together: as **a :** DENOMINATION **b :** CLAN — **con·nec·tion·al** \-shnəl, -shən-ᵊl\ *adj*

1con·nec·tive \kə-ˈnek-tiv\ *adj* **:** tending to connect — **con·nec·tive·ly** *adv* — **con·nec·tiv·i·ty** \(ˌ)kä-ˌnek-ˈtiv-ət-ē, kə-\ *n*

2connective *n* **:** something that connects: as **a :** the tissue connecting the pollen sacs of an anther **b :** a linguistic form that connects words or word groups

connective tissue *n* **:** a tissue of mesodermal origin rich in intercellular substance or interlacing processes with little tendency for the cells to come together in sheets or masses; *specif* **:** connective tissue of stellate or spindle-shaped cells with interlacing processes that pervades, supports, and binds together other tissues and forms ligaments, tendons, and aponeuroses

con·nex·ion \kə-ˈnek-shən\ *chiefly Brit var of* CONNECTION

conning tower *n* **1 :** an armored pilothouse (as on a battleship) **2 :** a raised structure on the deck of a submarine used as an observation post and often as an entrance to the vessel

conning tower 2

con·nip·tion \kə-ˈnip-shən\ *n* [origin unknown] **:** a fit of rage, hysteria, or alarm

con·niv·ance \kə-ˈnī-vən(t)s\ *n* **:** the act of conniving; *esp* **:** knowledge of and active or passive consent to wrongdoing

con·nive \kə-ˈnīv\ *vi* **con·nived; con·niv·ing** [F or L; F *conniver,* fr. L *conivēre, connivēre* to close the eyes, connive, fr. *com-* + *-nivēre* (akin to *nictare* to wink); akin to OE & OHG *hnīgan* to bow, L *nicere* to beckon] **1 :** to pretend ignorance of or fail to take action against something one ought to oppose **2 a :** to be indulgent or in secret sympathy **:** WINK **b :** to cooperate secretly or have a secret understanding **3 :** CONSPIRE, INTRIGUE — **con·niv·er** *n*

con·ni·vent \-ˈnī-vənt\ *adj* [L *conivent-, conivens,* prp. of *conivēre*] **:** converging but not fused <~ stamens>

con·niv·ery \-ˈnīv-(ə-)rē\ *n* **:** the practice of conniving

con·nois·seur \ˌkän-ə-ˈsər *also* -ˈsu̇(ə)r\ *n* [obs. F (now *connaisseur*), fr. OF *connoisseor,* fr. *connoistre* to know, fr. L *cognoscere* — more at COGNITION] **1 :** EXPERT; *esp* **:** one who understands the details, technique, or principles of an art and is competent to act as a critical judge **2 :** one who enjoys with discrimination and appreciation of subtleties <a ~ of fine wines> — **con·nois·seur·ship** \-ˌship\ *n*

con·no·ta·tion \ˌkän-ə-ˈtā-shən\ *n* **1 a :** the suggesting of a meaning by a word apart from the thing it explicitly names or describes **b :** something suggested by a word or thing **:** IMPLICATION <the ~*s* of comfort that surrounded that old chair> **2 :** the signification of something <that abuse of logic which consists in moving counters about as if they were known entities with a fixed ~ —W. R. Inge> **3 :** the property or properties connoted by a term in logic — **con·no·ta·tion·al** \-shnəl, -shən-ᵊl\ *adj*

con·no·ta·tive \ˈkän-ə-ˌtāt-iv, kə-ˈnōt-ət-iv\ *adj* **1 :** connoting or tending to connote **2 :** relating to connotation — **con·no·ta·tive·ly** *adv*

con·note \kə-ˈnōt, kä-\ *vt* **con·not·ed; con·not·ing** [ML *connotare,* fr. L *com-* + *notare* to note] **1 :** to convey in addition to exact explicit meaning <all the misery that poverty ~*s*> **2 :** to be associated with or inseparable from as a consequence or concomitant <the remorse so often *connoted* by guilt> **3 :** to imply or indicate as a logically essential attribute of something denoted ***syn*** see DENOTE

con·nu·bi·al \kə-ˈn(y)ü-bē-əl\ *adj* [L *conubialis,* fr. *conubium, connubium* marriage, fr. *com-* + *nubere* to marry — more at NUPTIAL] **:** of or relating to the married state **:** CONJUGAL ***syn*** see MATRIMONIAL — **con·nu·bi·al·ism** \-bē-ə-ˌliz-əm\ *n* — **con·nu·bi·al·i·ty** \-ˌn(y)ü-bē-ˈal-ət-ē\ *n* — **con·nu·bi·al·ly** \-ˈn(y)ü-bē-ə-lē\ *adv*

con·odont \ˈkō-nə-ˌdänt\ *n* [ISV *con-* (fr. Gk *kōnos* cone) + *-odont*] **:** a Paleozoic fossil that may consist of the teeth of an extinct cyclostome or more probably the remains of an invertebrate

co·noid \ˈkō-ˌnȯid\ *or* **co·noi·dal** \kō-ˈnȯid-ᵊl\ *adj* **:** shaped like or nearly like a cone — **conoid** *n*

con·quer \ˈkäŋ-kər\ *vb* **con·quered; con·quer·ing** \-k(ə-)riŋ\ [ME *conqueren* to acquire, conquer, fr. OF *conquerre,* fr. (assumed) VL *conquaerere,* fr. L *conquirere* to search for, collect, fr. *com-* + *quaerere* to ask, search] *vt* **1 :** to gain or acquire by force of arms **:** SUBJUGATE **2 :** to overcome by force of arms **:** VANQUISH **3 :** to gain mastery over or win by overcoming obstacles or opposition <~*ed* the mountain> <after ~*ing* movies and television, he decided to write for the stage> **4 :** to overcome by mental or moral power **:** SURMOUNT <~*ed* her fear> ~ *vi* **:** to be victorious — **con·quer·or** \-kər-ər\ *n*

con·quest \ˈkän-ˌkwest, ˈkäŋ-; ˈkäŋ-kwəst\ *n* [ME, fr. OF, fr. (assumed) VL *conquaesitus,* alter. of L *conquisitus,* pp. of *conquirere*] **1 :** the act or process of conquering **2 a :** something conquered; *esp* **:** territory appropriated in war **b :** a person whose favor or hand has been won ***syn*** see VICTORY

con·qui·an \ˈkäŋ-kē-ən\ *n* [MexSp *con quien* — more at COONCAN] **:** a card game for two played with 40 cards from which all games of rummy developed

con·quis·ta·dor \kȯŋ-ˈkēs-tə-ˌdȯ(ə)r, kän-ˈk(w)is-, kən-\ *n, pl* **con·quis·ta·do·res** \(ˌ)kȯŋ-ˌkēs-tə-ˈdȯr-ēz, -ˈdȯr-ˌās, -ˈdōr-, (ˌ)kän-ˌk(w)is-, kən-\ *or* **con·quis·ta·dors** [Sp, deriv. of L *conquirere*] **:** one that conquers; *specif* **:** a leader in the Spanish conquest of America and esp. of Mexico and Peru in the 16th century

cons *abbr* **1** consecrated **2** conservative **3** consigned; consignment **4** consol; consolidated **5** consonant **6** constable **7** constitution **8** construction **9** consul **10** consulting

con·san·guine \kän-ˈsaŋ-gwən, kən-\ *adj* **:** CONSANGUINEOUS

con·san·guin·e·ous \ˌkän-ˌsan-ˈgwin-ē-əs, -ˌsaŋ-\ *adj* [L *consanguineus,* fr. *com-* + *sanguin-, sanguis* blood — more at SANGUINE] **:** of the same blood or origin; *specif* **:** descended from the same ancestor — **con·san·guin·e·ous·ly** *adv*

con·san·guin·i·ty \-ˈgwin-ət-ē\ *n, pl* **-ties** **1 :** the quality or state of being consanguineous **2 :** a close relation or connection **:** AFFINITY

con·science \ˈkän-chən(t)s\ *n* [ME, fr. OF, fr. L *conscientia,* fr. *conscient-, consciens,* prp. of *conscire* to be conscious, be conscious of guilt, fr. *com-* + *scire* to know — more at SCIENCE] **1 a :** the sense or consciousness of the moral goodness or blameworthiness of one's own conduct, intentions, or character together with a feeling of obligation to do right or be good **b :** a faculty, power, or principle enjoining good acts **c :** the part of the superego in psychoanalysis that transmits commands and admonitions to the ego **2** *archaic* **:** CONSCIOUSNESS **3 :** conformity to the dictates of conscience **:** CONSCIENTIOUSNESS **4 :** sensitive regard for fairness or justice **:** SCRUPLE — **con·science·less** \-ləs\ *adj* — **in all conscience** *or* **in conscience :** in all fairness

conscience money *n* **:** money paid usu. anonymously to relieve the conscience by restoring what has been wrongfully acquired

con·sci·en·tious \ˌkän-chē-ˈen-chəs\ *adj* **1 :** governed by or conforming to the dictates of conscience **:** SCRUPULOUS <a ~ public servant> **2 :** METICULOUS, CAREFUL <a ~ listener> ***syn*** see UPRIGHT ***ant*** unconscientious, unscrupulous — **con·sci·en·tious·ly** *adv* — **con·sci·en·tious·ness** *n*

conscientious objection *n* **:** objection on moral or religious grounds (as to service in the armed forces or to bearing arms)

conscientious objector *n* **:** one who refuses to serve in the armed forces or bear arms on the grounds of moral or religious principles

con·scio·na·ble \ˈkänch-(ə-)nə-bəl\ *adj* [irreg. fr. *conscience*] **:** CONSCIENTIOUS

[1]con·scious \ˈkän-chəs\ *adj* [L *conscius,* fr. *com-* + *scire* to know] **1** *archaic* **:** sharing another's knowledge or awareness of an inward state or outward fact **2 :** perceiving, apprehending, or noticing with a degree of controlled thought or observation **3 :** personally felt <~ guilt> **4 :** capable of or marked by thought, will, design, or perception **5 :** SELF-CONSCIOUS **6 :** having mental faculties undulled by sleep, faintness, or stupor **:** AWAKE <became ~ after the anesthesia wore off> **7 :** done or acting with critical awareness <made a ~ effort to avoid the same mistakes> **8 a :** likely to notice, consider, or appraise <a bargain-*conscious* shopper> **b :** being concerned or interested <a budget-*conscious* businessman> **c :** marked by strong feelings or notions <a race-*conscious* society> ***syn*** see AWARE ***ant*** unconscious — **con·scious·ly** *adv*

[2]conscious *n* **:** CONSCIOUSNESS 5

con·scious·ness \ˈkän-chə-snəs\ *n* **1 a :** the quality or state of being aware esp. of something within oneself **b :** the state or fact of being conscious of an external object, state, or fact **c :** CONCERN, AWARENESS <race ~> **2 :** the state of being characterized by sensation, emotion, volition, and thought **:** MIND **3 :** the totality of conscious states of an individual **4 :** the normal state of conscious life **5 :** the upper level of mental life of which the person is aware as contrasted with unconscious processes

con·scribe \kən-ˈskrīb\ *vt* **con·scribed; con·scrib·ing** [L *conscribere* to enroll] **1 :** LIMIT, CIRCUMSCRIBE <ill-health . . . *conscribed* the force of his intentions —*Times Lit. Supp.*> **2 :** to enlist forcibly **:** CONSCRIPT

[1]con·script \ˈkän-ˌskript\ *adj* [MF, fr. L *conscriptus,* pp. of *conscribere* to enroll, fr. *com-* + *scribere* to write — more at SCRIBE] **1 :** enrolled into service by compulsion **:** DRAFTED **2 :** made up of conscripted persons

[2]conscript *n* **:** a conscripted person (as a military recruit)

[3]con·script \kən-ˈskript\ *vt* **:** to enroll into service by compulsion **:** DRAFT <was ~*ed* into the army>

con·scrip·tion \kən-ˈskrip-shən\ *n* **1 :** compulsory enrollment of persons esp. for military service **:** DRAFT **2 :** a forced contribution (as of money) imposed by a government in time of emergency (as war)

[1]con·se·crate \ˈkän(t)-sə-ˌkrāt\ *adj* **:** dedicated to a sacred purpose **:** HALLOWED

[2]consecrate *vt* **-crat·ed; -crat·ing** [ME *consecraten,* fr. L *consecratus,* pp. of *consecrare,* fr. *com-* + *sacrare* to consecrate — more at SACRED] **1 :** to induct (a person) into a permanent office with a religious rite; *specif* **:** to ordain to the office of bishop **2 a :** to make or declare sacred; *specif* **:** to devote irrevocably to the worship of God by a solemn ceremony **b :** to effect the liturgical transubstantiation of (eucharistic bread and wine) **c :** to devote to a purpose with deep solemnity or dedication **3 :** to make inviolable or venerable <principles *consecrated* by the weight of history> ***syn*** see DEVOTE — **con·se·cra·tive** \-ˌkrāt-iv\ *adj* — **con·se·cra·tor** \-ˌkrāt-ər\ *n* — **con·se·cra·to·ry** \ˈkän(t)-si-krə-ˌtōr-ē, -ˌtȯr-\ *adj*

con·se·cra·tion \ˌkän(t)-sə-ˈkrā-shən\ *n* **1 :** the act or ceremony of consecrating **2 :** the state of being consecrated **3** *cap* **:** the part of a Communion rite in which the bread and wine are consecrated

con·se·cu·tion \ˌkän(t)-si-ˈkyü-shən\ *n* [L *consecution-, consecutio,* fr. *consecutus,* pp. of *consequi* to follow along — more at CONSEQUENT] **:** SEQUENCE

con·sec·u·tive \kən-ˈsek-(y)ət-iv\ *adj* **:** following one after the other in order without gaps **:** CONTINUOUS — **con·sec·u·tive·ly** *adv* — **con·sec·u·tive·ness** *n*

syn CONSECUTIVE, SUCCESSIVE *shared meaning element* **:** following one after the other ***ant*** inconsecutive

con·sen·su·al \kən-ˈsench-(ə-)wəl, -ˈsen-chəl\ *adj* [L *consensus* + E *-al*] **1 :** existing or made by mutual consent without an act of writing <a ~ contract> **2 :** relating to or being the constrictive pupillary response of an eye that is covered when the other eye is exposed to light — **con·sen·su·al·ly** \-ē\ *adv*

con·sen·sus \kən-ˈsen(t)-səs\ *n* [L, fr. *consensus,* pp. of *consentire*] **1 :** group solidarity in sentiment and belief **2 a :** general agreement **:** UNANIMITY <the ~ of their opinion, based on reports that had drifted back from the border —John Hersey> **b :** the judgment arrived at by most of those concerned <the ~ was to abandon the project>

[1]con·sent \kən-ˈsent\ *vi* [ME *consenten,* fr. L *consentire,* fr. *com-* + *sentire* to feel — more at SENSE] **1** *archaic* **:** to be in concord in opinion or sentiment **2 :** to give assent or approval **:** AGREE ***syn*** see ASSENT ***ant*** dissent — **con·sent·ing·ly** \-iŋ-lē\ *adv*

[2]consent *n* **1 :** compliance in or approval of what is done or proposed by another **:** ACQUIESCENCE <he shall have power, by and with the advice and ~ of the Senate, to make treaties —*U.S. Constitution*> **2 :** agreement as to action or opinion; *specif* **:** voluntary agreement by a people to organize a civil society and give authority to the government — **con·sent·er** *n*

con·sen·ta·ne·ous \ˌkän(t)-sən-ˈtā-nē-əs, ˌkän-ˌsen-\ *adj* [L *consentaneus,* fr. *consentire* to agree] **1 :** expressing agreement **:** SUITED **2 :** done or made by the consent of all — **con·sen·ta·ne·ous·ly** *adv*

con·se·quence \ˈkän(t)-sə-ˌkwen(t)s, -si-kwən(t)s\ *n* **1 :** something produced by a cause or necessarily following from a set of conditions **2 :** a conclusion that results from reason or argument **3 a :** importance with respect to power to produce an effect **:** MOMENT **b :** social importance **4 :** the appearance of importance; *esp* **:** SELF-IMPORTANCE ***syn* 1** see EFFECT ***ant*** antecedent **2** see IMPORTANCE — **in consequence :** as a result **:** CONSEQUENTLY

[1]con·se·quent \-kwənt, -ˌkwent\ *n* **1 a :** DEDUCTION 2b **b :** the conclusion of a conditional sentence **2 :** the second term of a ratio

[2]consequent *adj* [MF, fr. L *consequent-, consequens,* prp. of *consequi* to follow along, fr. *com-* + *sequi* to follow — more at SUE] **1 :** following as a result or effect <removal of the trees and ~ exposure to sun, rain and wind . . . may cause serious degradation of the soil —C. J. Taylor> **2 :** observing logical sequence **:** RATIONAL

con·se·quen·tial \ˌkän(t)-sə-ˈkwen-chəl\ *adj* **1 :** CONSEQUENT **2 :** of the nature of a secondary result **:** INDIRECT **3 :** having significant consequences **:** IMPORTANT <a grave and ~ event> **4 :** SELF-IMPORTANT — **con·se·quen·ti·al·i·ty** \-ˌkwen-chē-ˈal-ət-ē\ *n* — **con·se·quen·tial·ly** \-ˈkwench-(ə-)lē\ *adv* — **con·se·quen·tial·ness** \-ˈkwen-chəl-nəs\ *n*

con·se·quent·ly \-ˌkwent-lē, -kwənt-\ *adv* **:** as a result **:** in view of the foregoing **:** ACCORDINGLY

con·ser·van·cy \kən-ˈsər-vən-sē\ *n, pl* **-cies** [alter. of obs. *conservacy* conservation, fr. AF *conservacie,* fr. ML *conservatia,* fr. L *conservatus,* pp.] **1** *Brit* **:** a board regulating fisheries and navigation in a river or port **2 a :** CONSERVATION **b :** an organization or area designated to conserve and protect natural resources

con·ser·va·tion \ˌkän(t)-sər-ˈvā-shən\ *n* [ME, fr. MF, fr. L *conservation-, conservatio,* fr. *conservatus,* pp. of *conservare*] **1 :** a careful preservation and protection of something; *esp* **:** planned management of a natural resource to prevent exploitation, destruction, or neglect **2 :** the process of conserving a quantity — **con·ser·va·tion·al** \-shnəl, -shən-ᵊl\ *adj*

con·ser·va·tion·ist \-sh(ə-)nəst\ *n* **:** one who advocates conservation esp. of natural resources

conservation of charge : a principle in physics: the total electric charge of an isolated system remains constant irrespective of whatever internal changes may take place

conservation of energy : a principle in physics: the total energy of an isolated system remains constant irrespective of whatever internal changes may take place with energy disappearing in one form reappearing in another

conservation of mass : a principle in classical physics: the total mass of any material system is neither increased nor diminished by reactions between the parts — called also *conservation of matter*

con·ser·va·tism \kən-ˈsər-və-ˌtiz-əm\ *n* **1 a :** disposition in politics to preserve what is established **b :** a political philosophy based on tradition and social stability, stressing established institutions, and preferring gradual development to abrupt change **2** *cap* **a :** the principles and policies of a Conservative party **b :** the Conservative party **3 :** the tendency to prefer an existing situation to change

[1]con·ser·va·tive \kən-ˈsər-vət-iv\ *adj* **1 :** PRESERVATIVE **2 a :** of or relating to a philosophy of conservatism **b** *cap* **:** of or constituting a political party professing the principles of conservatism: as (1) **:** of or constituting a party of the United Kingdom advocating support of established institutions (2) **:** Progressive Conservative **3 a :** tending or disposed to maintain existing views, conditions, or institutions **:** TRADITIONAL **b :** MODERATE, CAUTIOUS **c :** marked by or relating to traditional norms of taste, elegance, style, or manners <a ~ suit> **4 :** of or relating to Conservative Judaism — **con·ser·va·tive·ly** *adv* — **con·ser·va·tive·ness** *n*

[2]conservative *n* **1 a :** an adherent or advocate of political conservatism **b** *cap* **:** a member or supporter of a conservative political party **2 a :** one who adheres to traditional methods or views **b :** a cautious or discreet person

Conservative Judaism *n* **:** Judaism as practiced esp. among some U.S. Jews with adherence to the Torah and Talmud but with allowance for some departures in keeping with differing times and circumstances — compare ORTHODOX JUDAISM

con·ser·va·tize \-ˌtīz\ *vb* **-tized; -tiz·ing** *vi* **:** to grow conservative ~ *vt* **:** to make conservative <unions are being *conservatized* —Theodore Levitt>

con·ser·va·toire \kən-ˈsər-və-ˌtwär\ *n* [F, fr. It *conservatorio*] **:** CONSERVATORY 2

con·ser·va·tor \kən-ˈsər-vət-ər, -və-ˌtȯ(ə)r; ˈkän(t)-sər-ˌvāt-ər\ *n* **1 a :** one that preserves from injury or violation **:** PROTECTOR **b :** one that is responsible for the care, restoration, and repair of museum articles **2 :** a person, official, or institution designated to take over and protect the interests of an incompetent **3 :** an official charged with the protection of something affecting public welfare and interests — **con·ser·va·to·ri·al** \kən-ˌsər-və-ˈtōr-ē-əl, (ˌ)kän-, -ˈtȯr-\ *adj*

con·ser·va·to·ry \kən-ˈsər-və-ˌtōr-ē, -ˌtȯr-\ *n, pl* **-ries** **1 :** a greenhouse for growing or displaying plants **2** [It *conservatorio* home for foundlings, music school, fr. L *conservatus,* pp.] **:** a school specializing in one of the fine arts <a music ~>

[1]con·serve \kən-ˈsərv\ *vt* **con·served; con·serv·ing** [ME *conserven,* fr. MF *conserver,* fr. L *conservare,* fr. *com-* + *servare* to keep, guard, observe; akin to OE *searu* armor, Av *haurvaiti* he guards] **1 :** to keep in a safe or sound state <he *conserved* and enlarged the estate he inherited>; *esp* **:** to avoid wasteful or destructive use of <~ natural resources> **2 :** to preserve with sugar **3 :** to maintain (a quantity) constant during a process of chemical or physical change ***syn*** see SAVE — **con·serv·er** *n*

[2]con·serve \ˈkän-ˌsərv\ *n* **1 :** SWEETMEAT; *esp* **:** a candied fruit **2 :** PRESERVE; *specif* **:** one prepared from a mixture of fruits

con·sid·er \kən-ˈsid-ər\ *vb* **con·sid·ered; con·sid·er·ing** \-(ə-)riŋ\ [ME *consideren,* fr. MF *considerer,* fr. L *considerare,* lit., to observe the stars, fr. *com-* + *sider-, sidus* star — more at SIDEREAL] *vt* **1 :** to think about with care or caution **2 :** to regard or treat in an attentive, solicitous, or kindly way <he ~*ed* her every wish> **3 :** to gaze on steadily or reflectively **4 :** to come to judge or classify <~ thrift essential> **5 :** REGARD <his works are well ~*ed* abroad> **6 :** SUPPOSE ~ *vi* **:** REFLECT, DELIBERATE <paused a moment to ~>

ə abut ᵊ kitten ər further a back ā bake ä cot, cart
au̇ out ch chin e less ē easy g gift i trip ī life
j joke ŋ sing ō flow ȯ flaw ȯi coin th thin t͟h this
ü loot u̇ foot y yet yü few yu̇ furious zh vision

syn CONSIDER, STUDY, CONTEMPLATE, WEIGH *shared meaning element* : to apply one's mind to something in order to increase one's knowledge or understanding of it or to reach a decision about it

1**con·sid·er·able** \-'sid-ər(-ə)-bəl, -'sid-rə-bəl\ *adj* **1 :** worth consideration : SIGNIFICANT **2 :** large in extent or degree <a ~ number> — **con·sid·er·a·bly** \-blē\ *adv*

2**considerable** *n* : a considerable amount, degree, or extent

con·sid·er·ate \kən-'sid-(ə-)rət\ *adj* **1 :** marked by or given to careful consideration : CIRCUMSPECT **2 :** thoughtful of the rights and feelings of others ***syn*** see THOUGHTFUL ***ant*** inconsiderate — **con·sid·er·ate·ly** *adv* — **con·sid·er·ate·ness** *n*

con·sid·er·ation \kən-ˌsid-ə-'rā-shən\ *n* **1 :** continuous and careful thought <after long ~ he agreed to their requests> **2 a :** something considered as a ground : REASON **b :** a taking into account **3 :** thoughtful and sympathetic regard **4 :** an opinion obtained by reflection **5 :** ESTEEM, REGARD <the family built themselves a large, ugly villa . . . and became people of ~ —V. S. Pritchett> **6 a :** RECOMPENSE, PAYMENT **b :** the inducement to a contract or other legal transaction; *specif* : an act or forbearance or the promise thereof done or given by one party in return for the act or promise of another — **in consideration of :** as payment or recompense for <a small fee *in consideration of* many kind services>

con·sid·ered \kən-'sid-ərd\ *adj* **1 :** matured by extended deliberative thought <his ~ opinion> **2 :** regarded with respect or esteem

1**con·sid·er·ing** \-(ə-)riŋ\ *prep* : in view of : taking into account <he did well ~ his limitations>

2**considering** *conj* : inasmuch as <~ he was new at the job, he did quite well>

con·sign \kən-'sīn\ *vb* [MF *consigner*, fr. L *consignare*, fr. *com-* + *signum* sign, mark, seal] *vt* **1 :** to give over to another's care **2 :** to give, transfer, or deliver into the hands or control of another; *also* : to assign as a destination or end <~*ed* his books to the devil> **3 :** to send or address to an agent to be cared for or sold ~ *vi, obs* : AGREE, SUBMIT ***syn*** see COMMIT — **con·sign·able** \-'sī-nə-bəl\ *adj* — **con·sig·na·tion** \ˌkän-ˌsī-'nā-shən, ˌkän(t)-sig-\ *n* — **con·sign·or** \ˌkän(t)-sə-'nȯ(ə)r, ˌkän-ˌsī-, kən-ˌsī-\ *n*

con·sign·ee \ˌkän(t)-sə-'nē, ˌkän-ˌsī-, kən-ˌsī-\ *n* : one to whom something is consigned or shipped

1**con·sign·ment** \kən-'sīn-mənt\ *n* **1 :** the act or process of consigning **2 :** something consigned esp. in a single shipment — **on consignment :** shipped to a dealer who pays only for what he sells and who may return what is unsold <goods shipped *on consignment*>

2**consignment** *adj* : of, relating to, or received as goods on consignment <a ~ sale>

1**con·sist** \kən-'sist\ *vi* [MF & L; MF *consister*, fr. L *consistere*, lit., to stand together, fr. *com-* + *sistere* to take a stand; akin to L *stare* to stand — more at STAND] **1 :** LIE, RESIDE — used with *in* <liberty ~*s* in the absence of obstructions —A. E. Housman> **2** *archaic* **a :** EXIST, BE **b :** to be capable of existing **3 :** to become made up — used with *of* <breakfast ~*ed* of cereal, milk, and fruit> **4 :** to be consistent <it ~*s* with the facts>

2**con·sist** \'kän-ˌsist\ *n* : makeup or composition (as of coal sizes or a railroad train) by classes, types, or grades and arrangement

con·sis·tence \kən-'sis-tən(t)s\ *n* : CONSISTENCY

con·sis·ten·cy \kən-'sis-tən-sē\ *n, pl* **-cies 1 a** *archaic* : condition of adhering together : firmness of material substance **b :** firmness of constitution or character : PERSISTENCY **2 :** degree of firmness, density, viscosity, or resistance to movement or separation of constituent particles <boil the juice to the ~ of a thick syrup> **3 a :** agreement or harmony of parts or features to one another or a whole : CORRESPONDENCE; *specif* : ability to be asserted together without contradiction **b :** harmony of conduct or practice with profession <followed his own advice with ~>

con·sis·tent \kən-'sis-tənt\ *adj* [L *consistent-, consistens*, prp. of *consistere*] **1** *archaic* : possessing firmness or coherence **2 a :** marked by harmonious regularity or steady continuity : free from irregularity, variation, or contradiction <a ~ style in painting> **b :** showing steady conformity to character, profession, belief, or custom <a very ~ man, consistently bad-tempered> **3 :** tending to be arbitrarily close to the true value of the parameter estimated as the sample becomes large <a ~ statistical estimator> ***syn*** see CONSONANT ***ant*** inconsistent — **con·sis·tent·ly** *adv*

con·sis·to·ri·al \ˌkän-ˌsis-'tōr-ē-əl, -'tȯr-, kən-\ *adj* : of or relating to a consistory

con·sis·to·ry \kən-'sis-t(ə-)rē\ *n, pl* **-ries** [ME *consistorie*, fr. MF, fr. ML & LL; ML *consistorium* church tribunal, fr. LL, imperial council, fr. L *consistere* to stand together] **1 :** a solemn assembly : COUNCIL **2 :** a church tribunal or governing body: as **a :** a solemn meeting of Roman Catholic cardinals convoked and presided over by the pope **b :** a church session in some Reformed churches **3 :** the organization that confers the degrees of the Ancient and Accepted Scottish Rite of Freemasonry usu. from the 19th to the 32d inclusive; *also* : a meeting of such an organization

con·so·ci·ate \kən-'sō-s(h)ē-ˌāt\ *vb* **-at·ed; -at·ing** [L *consociatus*, pp. of *consociare*, fr. *com-* + *socius* companion — more at SOCIAL] *vt* : to bring into association ~ *vi* : to associate esp. in fellowship or partnership

con·so·ci·a·tion \-ˌsō-sē-'ā-shən, -shē-\ *n* **1 :** association in fellowship or alliance **2 :** an association of churches or religious societies **3 :** an ecological community with a single dominant — **con·so·ci·a·tion·al** \-shnəl, -shən-ᵊl\ *adj*

1**con·sol** \kən-'säl, 'kän-ˌ\ *n* [short for *Consolidated Annuities*, British government securities] : an interest-bearing government bond having no maturity date but redeemable on call; *specif* : one first issued by the British government in 1751 — usu. used in pl.

2**consol** *abbr* consolidated

con·so·la·tion \ˌkän(t)-sə-'lā-shən\ *n* **1 :** the act or an instance of consoling : the state of being consoled : COMFORT **2 :** something that consoles; *specif* : a contest held for those who have lost early in a tournament <the losers met in a ~ game> — **con·so·la·to·ry** \kən-'sō-lə-ˌtōr-ē, -'säl-ə-, -ˌtȯr-\ *adj*

consolation prize *n* : a prize given to a runner-up or a loser in a contest

1**con·sole** \kən-'sōl\ *vt* **con·soled; con·sol·ing** [F *consoler*, fr. L *consolari*, fr. *com-* + *solari* to console — more at SILLY] : to alleviate the grief or sense of loss of <~ a widow> ***syn*** see COMFORT — **con·sol·ing·ly** \-'sō-liŋ-lē\ *adv*

2**con·sole** \'kän-ˌsōl\ *n* [F, fr. MF, short for *consolateur* bracket in human shape, lit., consoler, fr. L *consolator*, fr. *consolatus*, pp. of *consolari*] **1 :** an architectural member projecting from a wall to form a bracket or from a keystone for ornament **2 a :** the desk from which an organ is played and which contains the keyboards, pedal board, and other controlling mechanisms **b :** a panel or cabinet on which are mounted dials, switches, and other apparatus used in centrally monitoring and controlling electrical or mechanical devices; *specif* : the part of a computer used for communication between the operator and the computer **3 a :** a cabinet (as for a radio or television set) designed to rest directly on the floor **b :** a small storage cabinet between bucket seats in an automobile

console 1

console table *n* : a table fixed to a wall with its top supported by consoles or front legs; *broadly* : a table designed to fit against a wall

con·so·lette \ˌkän(t)-sə-'let\ *n* [2*console* + *-ette*] : a small cabinet containing a radio, television, or record player

con·sol·i·date \kən-'säl-ə-ˌdāt\ *vb* **-dat·ed; -dat·ing** [L *consolidatus*, pp. of *consolidare* to make solid, fr. *com-* + *solidus* solid] *vt* **1 :** to join together into one whole : UNITE <~ several small school districts> **2 :** to make firm or secure : STRENGTHEN <~ their hold on first place> **3 :** to form into a compact mass ~ *vi* : to become consolidated; *specif* : MERGE <the two companies *consolidated*> — **con·sol·i·da·tor** \-ˌdāt-ər\ *n*

consolidated school *n* : a public school formed by merging other schools

con·sol·i·da·tion \kən-ˌsäl-ə-'dā-shən\ *n* **1 :** the act or process of consolidating : the state of being consolidated **2 :** the process of uniting : the quality or state of being united; *specif* : the unification of two or more corporations by dissolution of existing ones and creation of a single new corporation — compare MERGER **3 :** alteration of lung tissue from an aerated condition to one of solid consistency

con·som·mé \ˌkän(t)-sə-'mā\ *n* [F, fr. pp. of *consommer* to complete, boil down, fr. L *consummare* to complete — more at CONSUMMATE] : a clear soup made from well-seasoned meat broth

con·so·nance \'kän(t)-s(ə-)nən(t)s\ *n* **1 :** harmony or agreement among components **2 a :** correspondence or recurrence of sounds esp. in words; *specif* : recurrence or repetition of consonants esp. at the end of stressed syllables without the similar correspondence of vowels <the final sounds of "stroke" and "luck" exhibit ~> **b :** an agreeable combination of musical tones **c :** SYMPATHETIC VIBRATION, RESONANCE

con·so·nan·cy \-s(ə-)nən-sē\ *n, pl* **-cies :** CONSONANCE 1

1**con·so·nant** \'kän(t)-s(ə-)nənt\ *n* [ME, fr. L *consonant-, consonans*, fr. prp. of *consonare*] **1 :** one of a class of speech sounds (as \p\, \g\, \n\, \l\, \s\, \r\) characterized by constriction or closure at one or more points in the breath channel **2 :** a letter representing a consonant; *esp* : any letter of the English alphabet except *a, e, i, o,* and *u*

2**consonant** *adj* [MF, fr. L *consonant-, consonans* prp. of *consonare* to sound together, agree, fr. *com-* + *sonare* to sound] **1 :** being in agreement or harmony : free from elements making for discord **2 :** marked by musical consonances **3 :** having similar sounds <~ words> **4 :** relating to or exhibiting consonance : RESONANT — **con·so·nant·ly** *adv*

syn CONSONANT, CONSISTENT, COMPATIBLE, CONGRUOUS, CONGENIAL, SYMPATHETIC *shared meaning element* : being in agreement one with another or agreeable one to another ***ant*** inconsonant

con·so·nan·tal \ˌkän(t)-sə-'nant-ᵊl\ *adj* : relating to, being, or marked by a consonant or group of consonants

consonant shift *n* : a set of regular changes in consonant articulation in the history of a language or dialect: **a :** such a set affecting the Indo-European stops and distinguishing the Germanic languages from the other Indo-European languages — called also *first consonant shift* **b :** such a set affecting the Germanic stops and distinguishing High German from the other Germanic languages — called also *second consonant shift*

1**con·sort** \'kän-ˌsȯ(ə)rt\ *n* [ME, fr. MF, fr. L *consort-, consors*, lit., one who shares a common lot, fr. *com-* + *sort-, sors* lot, share] **1 :** ASSOCIATE **2 :** a ship accompanying another **3 :** SPOUSE — compare PRINCE CONSORT

2**consort** *n* [MF *consorte*, fr. *consort*] **1 :** GROUP, ASSEMBLY <a ~ of specialists> **2 :** CONJUNCTION, ASSOCIATION <he ruled in ~ with his father> **3 a :** a group of musicians entertaining by voice or instrument **b :** a set of musical instruments of the same family

3**con·sort** \kən-'sȯ(ə)rt, kän-', 'kän-ˌ\ *vt* **1 :** UNITE, ASSOCIATE **2** *obs* : ESCORT ~ *vi* **1 :** to keep company <~*ing* with criminals> **2** *obs* : to make harmony : PLAY **3 :** ACCORD, HARMONIZE <the illustrations ~ admirably with the text — *Times Lit. Supp.*>

con·sor·tium \kən-'sȯrt-ē-əm, -'sȯr-sh(ē-)əm\ *n, pl* **-sor·tia** \-'sȯrt-ē-ə, -'sȯr-sh(ē-)ə\ *also* **-sortiums** [L, fellowship, fr. *consort-, consors*] **1 :** an international business or banking agreement or combination **2 :** ASSOCIATION, SOCIETY **3 :** the legal right of one spouse to the company, affection, and service of the other

con·spe·cif·ic \ˌkän(t)-spi-'sif-ik\ *adj* : of the same species

con·spec·tus \kən-'spek-təs\ *n* [L, fr. *conspectus*, pp. of *conspicere*] **1 :** a usu. brief survey or summary often providing an overall view **2 :** OUTLINE, SYNOPSIS ***syn*** see ABRIDGMENT

con·spi·cu·ity \ˌkän(t)-spə-'kyü-ət-ē\ *n* : CONSPICUOUSNESS

con·spic·u·ous \kən-'spik-yə-wəs\ *adj* [L *conspicuus*, fr. *conspicere* to get sight of, fr. *com-* + *specere* to look — more at SPY] **1 :** obvious to the eye or mind **2 :** attracting attention : STRIKING

3 : marked by a noticeable violation of good taste ***syn*** see NOTICEABLE ***ant*** inconspicuous — **con·spic·u·ous·ly** *adv*
conspicuous consumption *n* **:** lavish or wasteful spending thought to enhance social prestige
con·spic·u·ous·ness *n* **:** the quality or state of being conspicuous
con·spir·a·cy \kən-ˈspir-ə-sē\ *n, pl* **-cies** [ME *conspiracie,* fr. L *conspiratus,* pp. of *conspirare*] **1 :** the act of conspiring together **2 a :** an agreement among conspirators **b :** a group of conspirators
conspiracy of silence : a secret agreement to keep silent about an occurrence, situation, or subject esp. in order to promote or protect selfish interests
con·spi·ra·tion \ˌkän(t)-spə-ˈrā-shən, -(ˌ)spir-ˈā-\ *n* **1 :** the act or action of plotting or secretly combining **2 :** a joint effort toward a particular end — **con·spi·ra·tion·al** \-shnəl, -shən-ᵊl\ *adj*
con·spir·a·tor \kən-ˈspir-ət-ər\ *n* **:** one that conspires **:** PLOTTER
con·spir·a·to·ri·al \kən-ˌspir-ə-ˈtōr-ē-əl, -ˈtȯr-\ *adj* **:** of, relating to, or suggestive of a conspiracy — **con·spir·a·to·ri·al·ly** \-ē-ə-lē\ *adv*
con·spire \kən-ˈspī(ə)r\ *vb* **con·spired; con·spir·ing** [ME *conspiren,* fr. MF *conspirer,* fr. L *conspirare* to breathe together, agree, conspire, fr. *com-* + *spirare* to breathe — more at SPIRIT] *vt* **:** PLOT, CONTRIVE ~ *vi* **1 a :** to join in a secret agreement to do an unlawful or wrongful act or to use such means to accomplish a lawful end **b :** SCHEME **2 :** to act in harmony <circumstances *conspired* to defeat his efforts>
con spi·ri·to \kän-ˈspir-ə-ˌtō, kōn-\ *adv* [It] **:** with spirit or animation — used as a direction in music
const *abbr* **1** constant **2** constitution; constitutional **3** construction
con·sta·ble \ˈkän(t)-stə-bəl, ˈkən(t)-\ *n* [ME *conestable,* fr. OF, fr. LL *comes stabuli,* lit., officer of the stable] **1 :** a high officer of a medieval royal or noble household **2 :** the warden or governor of a royal castle or a fortified town **3 a :** a public officer usu. of a town or township responsible for keeping the peace and for minor judicial duties **b** *Brit* **:** POLICEMAN; *esp* **:** one ranking below sergeant
[1]**con·stab·u·lary** \kən-ˈstab-yə-ˌler-ē\ *n, pl* **-lar·ies** **1 :** the organized body of constables of a particular district or country **2 :** an armed police force organized on military lines but distinct from the regular army
[2]**constabulary** *adj* **:** of or relating to a constable or constabulary
con·stan·cy \ˈkän(t)-stən-sē\ *n, pl* **-cies** **1 a :** steadfastness of mind under duress **:** FORTITUDE **b :** FIDELITY, LOYALTY **2 :** freedom from change
[1]**con·stant** \ˈkän(t)-stənt\ *adj* [ME, fr. MF, fr. L *constant-, constans,* fr. prp. of *constare* to stand firm, be consistent, fr. *com-* + *stare* to stand — more at STAND] **1 :** marked by firm steadfast revolution or faithfulness **:** exhibiting constancy of mind or attachment **2 :** INVARIABLE, UNIFORM **3 :** continually occurring or recurring **:** REGULAR ***syn* 1** see FAITHFUL ***ant*** inconstant, fickle **2** see CONTINUOUS ***ant*** fitful — **con·stant·ly** *adv*
[2]**constant** *n* **:** something invariable or unchanging: as **a :** a number that has a fixed value in a given situation or universally or that is characteristic of some substance or instrument **b :** a number that is assumed not to change value in a given mathematical discussion **c :** a term in logic with a fixed designation
con·stan·tan \ˈkän(t)-stən-ˌtan\ *n* [fr. the fact that its resistance remains constant under change of temperature] **:** an alloy of copper and nickel used for electrical resistors and in thermocouples
con·stel·late \ˈkän(t)-stə-ˌlāt\ *vb* **-lat·ed; -lat·ing** *vt* **1 :** to unite in a cluster **2 :** to set or adorn with or as if with constellations ~ *vi* **:** CLUSTER
con·stel·la·tion \ˌkän(t)-stə-ˈlā-shən\ *n* [ME *constellacioun,* fr. MF *constellation,* fr. LL *constellation-, constellatio,* fr. *constellatus* studded with stars, fr. L *com-* + *stella* star — more at STAR] **1 a :** the configuration of stars esp. at one's birth **b** *obs* **:** character or constitution as determined by the stars **2 :** any of 88 arbitrary configurations of stars or an area of the celestial sphere covering one of these configurations **3 :** an assemblage, collection, or gathering of usu. related persons, qualities, or things <a ~ of . . . relatives, friends, and hangers-on —Brendan Gill> **4 :** PATTERN, ARRANGEMENT <taking advantage of the shifting ~ of power throughout the known world —H. D. Lasswell> — **con·stel·la·to·ry** \kən-ˈstel-ə-ˌtōr-ē, -ˌtȯr-\ *adj*
con·ster·nate \ˈkän(t)-stər-ˌnāt\ *vt* **-nat·ed; -nat·ing :** to fill with consternation
con·ster·na·tion \ˌkän(t)-stər-ˈnā-shən\ *n* [F or L; F, fr. L *consternation-, consternatio,* fr. *consternatus,* pp. of *consternare* to bewilder, alarm, fr. *com-* + *-sternare* (akin to OE *starian* to stare)] **:** amazement or dismay that hinders or throws into confusion <the two . . . stared at each other in ~, and neither knew what to do —Pearl Buck>
con·sti·pate \ˈkän(t)-stə-ˌpāt\ *vt* **-pat·ed; -pat·ing** [ML *constipatus,* pp. of *constipare,* fr. L, to crowd together, fr. *com-* + *stipare* to press together — more at STIFF] **1 :** to make costive **:** cause constipation in **2 :** to make immobile, inactive, or dull **:** STULTIFY <so much clutter . . . will tend to ~ the novel's working order —*Times Lit. Supp.*>
con·sti·pa·tion \ˌkän(t)-stə-ˈpā-shən\ *n* **1 :** abnormally delayed or infrequent passage of dry hardened feces **2 :** STULTIFICATION
con·stit·u·en·cy \kən-ˈstich-(ə-)wən-sē\ *n, pl* **-cies** **1 a :** a body of citizens entitled to elect a representative to a legislative or other public body **b :** the residents in an electoral district **c :** an electoral district **2 a :** a group or body that patronizes, supports, or offers representation <there was no ~ of millionaires to back him> **b :** the people involved in or served by an organization (as a business or institution) <the big dailies and urban TV stations are not in touch with the special problems of their own *constituencies* —J. P. Lyford>
[1]**con·stit·u·ent** \kən-ˈstich-(ə-)wənt\ *n* [F *constituant,* fr. MF, fr. prp. of *constituer* to constitute, fr. L *constituere*] **1 :** one who authorizes another to act for him **:** PRINCIPAL **2 :** an essential part **:** COMPONENT, ELEMENT **3 :** one of two or more linguistic forms that enter into a construction or a compound and are either immediate (as *he* and *writes reviews* in the construction "he writes reviews") or ultimate (as *he, write, -s, review,* and *-s* in the same construction) **4 a :** one of a group who elects another to represent him in a public office **b :** a resident in a constituency ***syn*** see ELEMENT ***ant*** whole, aggregate
[2]**constituent** *adj* [L *constituent-, constituens,* prp. of *constituere*] **1 :** serving to form, compose, or make up a unit or whole **:** COMPONENT **2 :** having the power to create a government or frame or amend a constitution <a ~ assembly> — **con·stit·u·ent·ly** *adv*
con·sti·tute \ˈkän(t)-stə-ˌt(y)üt\ *vt* **-tut·ed; -tut·ing** [L *constitutus,* pp. of *constituere* to set up, constitute, fr. *com-* + *statuere* to set — more at STATUTE] **1 :** to appoint to an office, function, or dignity **2 :** to set up **:** ESTABLISH: as **a :** ENACT **b :** FOUND **c** (1) **:** to give due or lawful form to (2) **:** to legally process **3 :** to make up **:** FORM, COMPOSE <twelve months ~ a year> <high school dropouts who ~ a major problem in large city slums —J. B. Conant>
con·sti·tu·tion \ˌkän(t)-stə-ˈt(y)ü-shən\ *n* **1 :** an established law or custom **:** ORDINANCE **2 :** the act of establishing, making, or setting up **3 a :** the physical makeup of the individual comprising inherited qualities modified by environment **b :** the structure, composition, physical makeup, or nature of something **4 :** the mode in which a state or society is organized; *esp* **:** the manner in which sovereign power is distributed **5 a :** the basic principles and laws of a nation, state, or social group that determine the powers and duties of the government and guarantee certain rights to the people in it **b :** a written instrument embodying the rules of a political or social organization ***syn*** see PHYSIQUE — **con·sti·tu·tion·less** \-ləs\ *adj*
[1]**con·sti·tu·tion·al** \-shnəl, -shən-ᵊl\ *adj* **1 :** relating to, inherent in, or affecting the constitution of body or mind **2 :** of, relating to, or entering into the fundamental makeup of something **:** ESSENTIAL **3 :** being in accordance with or authorized by the constitution of a state or society <a ~ government> **4 :** regulated by or ruling according to a constitution <a ~ monarchy> **5 :** of or relating to a constitution **6 :** loyal to or supporting an established constitution or form of government
[2]**constitutional** *n* **:** a walk taken for one's health
con·sti·tu·tion·al·ism \-ˌiz-əm\ *n* **:** adherence to or government according to constitutional principles; *also* **:** a constitutional system of government — **con·sti·tu·tion·al·ist** \-əst\ *n*
con·sti·tu·tion·al·i·ty \-ˌt(y)ü-shə-ˈnal-ət-ē\ *n* **:** the quality or state of being constitutional; *esp* **:** accordance with the provisions of a constitution <questioned the ~ of the law>
con·sti·tu·tion·al·ize \-ˈt(y)ü-shnəl-ˌīz, -shən-ᵊl-\ *vt* **-ized; -iz·ing** **:** to provide with a constitution **:** organize along constitutional principles — **con·sti·tu·tion·al·iza·tion** \-ˌt(y)ü-shnəl-ə-ˈzā-shən, -shən-ᵊl-\ *n*
con·sti·tu·tion·al·ly \-ˈt(y)ü-shnə-lē, -shən-ᵊl-ē\ *adv* **1 a :** in accordance with one's constitution <~ unable to grasp subtleties> **b :** in structure, composition, or constitution <despite repeated heatings the material remained ~ the same> **2 :** in accordance with a political constitution <was not ~ eligible to fill the office>
con·sti·tu·tive \ˈkän(t)-stə-ˌt(y)üt-iv, kən-ˈstich-ət-iv\ *adj* **1 :** having the power to enact or establish **:** CONSTRUCTIVE **2 :** CONSTITUENT, ESSENTIAL **3 :** relating to or dependent on constitution <a ~ property of all electrolytes> — **con·sti·tu·tive·ly** *adv*
constr *abbr* construction
con·strain \kən-ˈstrān\ *vt* [ME *constrainen,* fr. MF *constraindre,* fr. L *constringere* to constrict, constrain, fr. *com-* + *stringere* to draw tight — more at STRAIN] **1 a :** to force by imposed stricture, restriction, or limitation **b :** to restrict the motion of (a mechanical body) to a particular mode **2 :** to force or produce in an unnatural or strained manner <a ~*ed* smile> **3 :** to secure by or as if by bonds **:** CONFINE <when winter frosts ~ the field with cold —John Dryden> **4 :** to bring into narrow compass; *also* **:** to clasp tightly **5 :** to hold back by or as if by force <~*ing* my mind not to wander from the task —Charles Dickens> ***syn*** see FORCE — **con·strained·ly** \-ˈstrā-nəd-lē, -ˈstrān-dlē\ *adv*
con·straint \kən-ˈstrānt\ *n* [ME, fr. MF *constrainte,* fr. *constraindre*] **1 a :** the act of constraining **b :** the state of being checked, restricted, or compelled to avoid or perform some action <the ~ and monotony of a monastic life —Matthew Arnold> **c :** a constraining agency or force **:** CHECK <put legal ~*s* on the board's activities> **2 a :** repression of one's own feelings, behavior, or actions **b :** a sense of being constrained **:** EMBARRASSMENT
con·strict \kən-ˈstrikt\ *vb* [L *constrictus,* pp. of *constringere*] *vt* **1 a :** to make narrow by drawing together or squeezing **b :** COMPRESS, SQUEEZE <~ a nerve> **2 :** to stultify, stop, or cause to falter **:** INHIBIT ~ *vi* **:** to become constricted ***syn*** see CONTRACT — **con·stric·tive** \-ˈstrik-tiv\ *adj*
con·stric·tion \-ˈstrik-shən\ *n* **1 :** an act or product of constricting **2 :** the quality or state of being constricted **3 :** something that constricts
con·stric·tor \-ˈstrik-tər\ *n* **1 :** one that constricts **2 :** a muscle that contracts a cavity or orifice or compresses an organ **3 :** a snake (as a boa constrictor) that kills prey by compression in its coils
con·stringe \kən-ˈstrinj\ *vt* **con·stringed; con·string·ing** [L *constringere*] **1 :** CONSTRICT **2 :** to cause to shrink <cold ~*s* the pores> — **con·strin·gent** \-ˈstrin-jənt\ *adj*
con·stru·able \kən-ˈstrü-ə-bəl\ *adj* **:** that may be construed
[1]**con·struct** \kən-ˈstrəkt\ *vt* [L *constructus,* pp. of *construere,* fr. *com-* + *struere* to build — more at STRUCTURE] **1 :** to make or form by combining parts **:** BUILD **2 :** to set in logical order **3 :** to draw (a geometrical figure) with suitable instruments and

under specified conditions — **con·struct·ible** \-'strək-tə-bəl\ *adj* — **con·struc·tor** \-tər\ *n*

[2]**con·struct** \'kän-ˌstrəkt\ *n* **:** something constructed esp. by mental synthesis <form a ~ of a physical object by mentally assembling and integrating sense-data>

con·struc·tion \kən-'strək-shən\ *n* **1 :** the arrangement and connection of words or groups of words in a sentence **:** syntactical arrangement **2 :** the process, art, or manner of constructing; *also* **:** a thing constructed **3 :** the act or result of construing, interpreting, or explaining **4 :** a sculptural creation that is put together out of separate pieces of often disparate materials — **con·struc·tion·al** \-shnəl, -shən-ᵊl\ *adj* — **con·struc·tion·al·ly** \-ē\ *adv*

con·struc·tion·ist \-sh(ə-)nəst\ *n* **:** one who construes a legal document (as the U.S. Constitution) in a specific way <a strict ~>

construction paper *n* **:** colored paper suitable for crayon or ink drawings and watercolors and for making cutouts

con·struc·tive \kən-'strək-tiv\ *adj* **1 :** declared such by judicial construction or interpretation <~ fraud> **2 :** of or relating to construction **3 :** promoting improvement or development <~ criticism> — **con·struc·tive·ly** *adv* — **con·struc·tive·ness** *n*

con·struc·tiv·ism \kən-'strək-ti-ˌviz-əm\ *n* **1 :** a nonobjective art movement originating in Russia and concerned with formal organization of planes and expression of volume in terms of modern industrial materials (as glass and plastic) **2 :** an abstract style of stage setting that employs skeletal structures instead of realistic props — **con·struc·tiv·ist** \-ti-vəst\ *adj or n*

[1]**con·strue** \kən-'strü\ *vb* **con·strued; con·stru·ing** [ME *construen,* fr. LL *construere,* fr. L, to construct] *vt* **1 :** to analyze the arrangement and connection of words in (a sentence or sentence part) **2 :** to understand or explain the sense or intention of usu. in a particular way or with respect to a given set of circumstances <*construed* my actions as hostile> ~ *vi* **:** to construe a sentence or sentence part esp. in connection with translating

[2]**con·strue** \'kän-ˌstrü\ *n* **:** an act of construing esp. by piecemeal translation; *also* **:** the translated version resulting from such an act

con·sub·stan·tial \ˌkän(t)-səb-'stan-chəl\ *adj* [LL *consubstantialis,* fr. L *com-* + *substantia* substance] **:** of the same substance

con·sub·stan·ti·a·tion \ˌkän(t)-səb-ˌstan-chē-'ā-shən\ *n* **:** the actual substantial presence and combination of the body of Christ with the eucharistic bread and wine according to a teaching associated with Martin Luther

con·sue·tude \'kän(t)-swi-ˌt(y)üd, kən-'sü-ə-\ *n* [ME, fr. L *consuetudo* — more at CUSTOM] **:** social usage **:** CUSTOM — **con·sue·tu·di·nary** \ˌkän(t)-swi-'t(y)üd-ᵊn-ˌer-ē, kən-ˌsü-ə-\ *adj*

con·sul \'kän(t)-səl\ *n* [ME, fr. L, fr. *consulere* to consult] **1 a :** either of two annually elected chief magistrates of the Roman republic **b :** one of three chief magistrates of the French republic from 1799 to 1804 **2 :** an official appointed by a government to reside in a foreign country to represent the commercial interests of citizens of the appointing country — **con·sul·ar** \-s(ə-)lər\ *adj* — **con·sul·ship** \-səl-ˌship\ *n*

con·sul·ate \-s(ə-)lət\ *n* **1 :** a government by consuls **2 :** the office, term of office, or jurisdiction of a consul **3 :** the residence or official premises of a consul

consulate general *n, pl* **consulates general :** the residence, office, or jurisdiction of a consul general

consul general *n, pl* **consuls general :** a consul of the first rank stationed in an important place or having jurisdiction in several places or over several consuls

[1]**con·sult** \kən-'səlt\ *vb* [MF or L; MF *consulter,* fr. L *consultare,* fr. consultus, pp. of *consulere* to deliberate, counsel, consult] *vt* **1 a :** to ask the advice or opinion of <~ a doctor> **b :** to refer to <~ a dictionary> **2 :** to have regard to **:** CONSIDER ~ *vi* **1 :** to consult an individual **2 :** to deliberate together **:** CONFER **3 :** to serve as a consultant <was ~*ing* for three large companies> — **con·sult·er** *n*

[2]**con·sult** \kən-'səlt, 'kän-ˌ\ *n* **:** CONSULTATION

con·sul·tan·cy \kən-'səlt-ᵊn-sē\ *n, pl* **-cies 1 :** an agency that provides consulting services **2 :** CONSULTATION

con·sul·tant \kən-'səlt-ᵊnt\ *n* **1 :** one who consults another **2 :** one who gives professional advice or services **:** EXPERT — **con·sul·tant·ship** \-ˌship\ *n*

con·sul·ta·tion \ˌkän(t)-səl-'tā-shən\ *n* **1 :** COUNCIL, CONFERENCE; *specif* **:** a deliberation between physicians on a case or its treatment **2 :** the act of consulting or conferring

con·sul·ta·tive \kən-'səl-tət-iv, 'kän(t)-səl-ˌtāt-iv\ *adj* **:** of, relating to, or intended for consultation **:** ADVISORY <~ committee>

con·sult·ing \kən-'səl-tiŋ\ *adj* **1 :** providing professional or expert advice <a ~ architect> **2 :** of or relating to consultation or a consultant <the ~ room of a psychiatrist>

con·sul·tive \kən-'səl-tiv\ *adj* **:** CONSULTATIVE

con·sul·tor \kən-'səl-tər\ *n* **:** one that consults or advises; *esp* **:** an adviser to a Roman Catholic bishop, provincial, or sacred congregation

[1]**con·sum·able** \kən-'sü-mə-bəl\ *adj* **:** capable of being consumed

[2]**consumable** *n* **:** something that is consumable — usu. used in pl. <the ~*s* on board their ship are adequate for the 14-day mission —R. C. Cowen>

con·sume \kən-'süm\ *vb* **con·sumed; con·sum·ing** [ME *consumen,* fr. MF or L; MF *consumer,* fr. L *consumere,* fr. *com-* + *sumere* to take up, take, fr. *sub-* up + *emere* to take — more at SUB-, REDEEM] *vt* **1 :** to do away with completely **:** DESTROY <fire *consumed* several buildings> **2 a :** to spend wastefully **:** SQUANDER **b :** to use up <his correspondence *consumed* much of his time> **3 :** to eat or drink esp. in great quantity <*consumed* several kegs of beer> **4 :** to engage fully **:** ENGROSS <she was *consumed* with curiosity> ~ *vi* **:** to waste or burn away **:** PERISH ***syn*** see WASTE, MONOPOLIZE — **con·sum·ing·ly** \-'sü-miŋ-lē\ *adv*

con·sum·ed·ly \-'sü-məd-lē\ *adv* **:** as if consumed **:** EXCESSIVELY

con·sum·er \kən-'sü-mər\ *n, often attrib* **:** one that consumes: as **a :** one that utilizes economic goods **b :** an organism requiring complex organic compounds for food which it obtains by preying on other organisms or by eating particles of organic matter — compare PRODUCER 4 — **con·sum·er·ship** \-ˌship\ *n*

consumer credit *n* **:** credit granted to an individual esp. to finance the purchase of consumer goods or to defray personal or family expenses

consumer goods *n pl* **:** goods that directly satisfy human wants

con·sum·er·ism \kən-'sü-mə-ˌriz-əm\ *n* **:** the promotion of consumers' interests (as against false advertising or shoddy goods) — **con·sum·er·ist** \-rəst\ *n*

consumer price index *n* **:** an index measuring the change in the cost of typical wage-earner purchases of goods and services expressed as a percentage of the cost of these same goods and services in some base period — called also *cost-of-living index*

[1]**con·sum·mate** \kən-'səm-ət, 'kän(t)-sə-mət\ *adj* [ME, fr. L *consummatus,* pp. of *consummare* to sum up, finish, fr. *com-* + *summa* sum] **1 :** complete in every detail **:** PERFECT **2 :** extremely skilled and accomplished <a ~ liar> **3 :** of the highest degree <~ skill> <~ cruelty> — **con·sum·mate·ly** *adv*

[2]**con·sum·mate** \'kän(t)-sə-ˌmāt\ *vb* **-mat·ed; -mat·ing** *vt* **1 a :** FINISH, COMPLETE <~ a business deal> **b :** to make perfect **:** ACHIEVE **2 :** to make (marital union) complete by sexual intercourse <~ a marriage> ~ *vi* **:** to become perfected — **con·sum·ma·tive** \'kän(t)-sə-ˌmāt-iv, kən-'səm-ət-iv\ *adj* — **con·sum·ma·tor** \'kän(t)-sə-ˌmāt-ər\ *n*

con·sum·ma·tion \ˌkän-sə-'mā-shən\ *n* **1 :** the act of consummating <the ~ of a contract by mutual signature>; *specif* **:** the consummating of a marriage **2 :** the ultimate end **:** FINISH

con·sum·ma·to·ry \kən-'səm-ə-ˌtōr-ē, -ˌtȯr-\ *adj* **1 :** of or relating to consummation **:** CONCLUDING **2 :** of, relating to, or being a response or act (as eating or copulating) that terminates a period of usu. goal-directed behavior

con·sump·tion \kən-'səm(p)-shən\ *n* [ME *consumpcioun,* fr. L *consumption-, consumptio,* fr. *consumptus,* pp. of *consumere*] **1 :** the act or process of consuming **2 :** the utilization of economic goods in the satisfaction of wants or in the process of production resulting chiefly in their destruction, deterioration, or transformation **3 a :** a progressive wasting away of the body esp. from pulmonary tuberculosis **b :** TUBERCULOSIS

[1]**con·sump·tive** \-'səm(p)-tiv\ *adj* **1 :** tending to consume **2 :** of, relating to, or affected with consumption — **con·sump·tive·ly** *adv*

[2]**consumptive** *n* **:** a person affected with consumption

cont *abbr* **1** containing **2** contents **3** continent; continental **4** continued **5** control

[1]**con·tact** \'kän-ˌtakt\ *n* [F or L; F, fr. L *contactus,* fr. *contactus,* pp. of *contingere* to have contact with — more at CONTINGENT] **1 a :** union or junction of surfaces **b :** the apparent touching or mutual tangency of the limbs of two celestial bodies or of the disk of one body with the shadow of another during an eclipse, transit, or occultation **c (1) :** the junction of two electrical conductors through which a current passes **(2) :** a special part made for such a junction **2 a :** ASSOCIATION, RELATIONSHIP **b :** CONNECTION, COMMUNICATION **c :** direct visual observation of the earth's surface made from an airplane esp. as an aid to navigation **d :** an establishing of communication with someone or an observing or receiving of a significant signal from a person or object <radar ~ with Mars> **3 :** one serving as a carrier or source **4 :** CONTACT LENS

[2]**con·tact** \'kän-ˌtakt, kən-'\ *vt* **1 :** to bring into contact **2 a :** to enter or be in contact with **:** JOIN **b :** to get in communication with <~ your local dealer> ~ *vi* **:** to make contact

[3]**con·tact** \'kän-ˌtakt\ *adj* **:** maintaining, involving, or activated or caused by contact <~ poisons>

[4]**con·tact** \'kän-ˌtakt\ *adv* **:** by contact flying <the ceiling was so low that the patrol was flown ~ —J. L. Foley>

contact flying \'kän-ˌtakt-\ *n* **:** navigation of an airplane by means of direct observation of landmarks

contact inhibition \'kän-ˌtakt\ *n* **:** cessation of cellular undulating movements upon contact with other cells with accompanying cessation of cell growth and division

contact lens \ˌkän-ˌtakt\ *n* **:** a thin lens designed to fit over the cornea

contact print \ˌkän-ˌtak(t)-\ *n* **:** a photographic print made with the negative in contact with the sensitized paper, plate, or film

con·ta·gion \kən-'tā-jən\ *n* [ME, fr. MF & L; MF, fr. L *contagion-, contagio,* fr. *contingere* to have contact with, pollute] **1 a :** the transmission of a disease by direct or indirect contact **b :** a contagious disease **c :** a disease-producing agent (as a virus) **2 a :** POISON **b :** contagious influence, quality, or nature **c :** corrupting influence or contact **3 a :** rapid communication of an influence (as a doctrine or emotional state) **b :** an influence that spreads rapidly

con·ta·gious \-jəs\ *adj* **1 :** communicable by contact **:** CATCHING **2 :** bearing contagion **3 :** used for contagious diseases <a ~ ward> **4 :** exciting similar emotions or conduct in others <~ enthusiasm> — **con·ta·gious·ly** *adv* — **con·ta·gious·ness** *n*

contagious abortion *n* **:** a contagious or infectious disease (as a brucellosis) of domestic animals characterized by abortion

con·ta·gium \kən-'tā-j(ē-)əm\ *n, pl* **-gia** \-j(ē-)ə\ [L, contagion, fr. *contingere*] **:** a virus or living organism capable of causing a communicable disease

con·tain \kən-'tān\ *vb* [ME *conteinen,* fr. OF *contenir,* fr. L *continēre* to hold together, hold in, contain, fr. *com-* + *tenēre* to hold — more at THIN] *vt* **1 :** to keep within limits **:** hold back or hold down: as **a :** RESTRAIN, CONTROL **b :** CHECK, HALT **c :** to follow successfully a policy of containment toward **d :** to prevent (as an enemy or opponent) from advancing or from making a successful attack **2 a :** to have within **:** HOLD **b :** COMPRISE, INCLUDE **3 a :** to be divisible by usu. without a remainder **b :** ENCLOSE, BOUND ~ *vi* **:** to restrain oneself — **con·tain·able** \-'tā-nə-bəl\ *adj*

contained *adj* **1 :** RESTRAINED, CONTROLLED **2 :** COMPOSED, CALM

con·tain·er \kən-'tā-nər\ *n* **:** one that contains; *esp* **:** a receptacle or a flexible covering for the shipment of goods

con·tain·er·board \-ˌbō(ə)rd, -ˌbȯ(ə)rd\ *n* **:** a paperboard (as corrugated board or fiberboard) from which containers are made

con·tain·er·iza·tion \kən-ˌtā-nə-rə-ˈzā-shən\ *n* : a shipping method in which a large amount of material (as merchandise) is packaged together in one large container

con·tain·er·ize \kən-ˈtā-nə-ˌrīz\ *vt* **-ized; -iz·ing** : to ship by containerization

con·tain·er·ship \-nər-ˌship\ *n* : a ship esp. designed or equipped for carrying containerized cargo

con·tain·ment \kən-ˈtān-mənt\ *n* **1** : the act or process of containing **2** : the policy, process, or result of preventing the expansion of a hostile power or ideology

con·tam·i·nant \kən-ˈtam-ə-nənt\ *n* : something that contaminates

con·tam·i·nate \kən-ˈtam-ə-ˌnāt\ *vt* **-nat·ed; -nat·ing** [L *contaminatus,* pp. of *contaminare;* akin to L *contagio* contagion] **1 a** : to soil, stain, or infect by contact or association <bacteria *contaminated* the wound> **b** : to make inferior or impure by admixture <iron *contaminated* with phosphorus> **2** : to make unfit for use by the introduction of unwholesome or undesirable elements — **con·tam·i·na·tive** \-ˌnāt-iv\ *adj* — **con·tam·i·na·tor** \-ˌnāt-ər\ *n*

syn CONTAMINATE, TAINT, POLLUTE, DEFILE *shared meaning element* : to make impure or unclean. CONTAMINATE implies intrusion of or contact with dirt or foulness from an outside source <water *contaminated* by industrial wastes> <filthy books that *contaminate* young minds> TAINT stresses the loss of purity or cleanliness that follows contamination <*tainted* meat> <his unkindness may defeat my life, but never *taint* my love —Shak.> POLLUTE, sometimes interchangeable with *contaminate,* distinctively may imply that the process which begins with contamination is complete and that what was pure or clean has been made foul, poisoned, or filthy <the *polluted* waters of Lake Erie, in parts no better than an open cesspool> DEFILE implies befouling of what could or should have been kept clean and pure or held sacred and commonly suggests violation or desecration <*defile* a hero's memory with slanderous innuendo>

con·tam·i·na·tion \kən-ˌtam-ə-ˈnā-shən\ *n* **1** : a process of contaminating : a state of being contaminated **2** : something that contaminates

contd *abbr* continued

conte \kō^{n}t\ *n* [F] : a usu. short tale of adventure

con·temn \kən-ˈtem\ *vt* [ME *contempnen,* fr. MF *contempner,* fr. L *contemnere,* fr. *com-* + *temnere* to despise — more at STAMP] : to view or treat with contempt : SCORN ***syn*** see DESPISE — **con·tem·ner** *also* **con·tem·nor** \-ˈtem-(n)ər\ *n*

con·tem·plate \ˈkänt-əm-ˌplāt, ˈkän-ˌtem-\ *vb* **-plat·ed, -plat·ing** [L *contemplatus,* pp. of *contemplari,* fr. *com-* + *templum* space marked out for observation of auguries — more at TEMPLE] *vt* **1** : to view or consider with continued attention : meditate on **2** : to have in view as contingent or probable or as an end or intention ~ *vi* : PONDER, MEDITATE ***syn*** see CONSIDER — **con·tem·pla·tor** \-ˌplāt-ər\ *n*

con·tem·pla·tion \ˌkänt-əm-ˈplā-shən, ˌkän-ˌtem-\ *n* **1 a** : concentration on spiritual things as a form of private devotion **b** : a state of mystical awareness of God's being **2** : an act of considering with attention : STUDY **3** : the act of regarding steadily **4** : INTENTION, EXPECTATION

[1]**con·tem·pla·tive** \kən-ˈtem-plət-iv; ˈkänt-əm-ˌplāt-, ˈkän-ˌtem-\ *adj* : marked by or given to contemplation; *specif* : of or relating to a religious order devoted to prayer and penance — **con·tem·pla·tive·ly** *adv* — **con·tem·pla·tiv·ness** *n*

[2]**contemplative** *n* : one who practices contemplation

con·tem·po·ra·ne·ity \kən-ˌtem-p(ə-)rə-ˈnē-ət-ē, -ˈnā-\ *n* : the quality or state of being contemporaneous

con·tem·po·ra·ne·ous \kən-ˌtem-pə-ˈrā-nē-əs\ *adj* [L *contemporaneus,* fr. *com-* + *tempor-, tempus* time — more at TEMPORAL] : existing, occurring, or originating during the same time ***syn*** see CONTEMPORARY — **con·tem·po·ra·ne·ous·ly** *adv* — **con·tem·po·ra·ne·ous·ness** *n*

[1]**con·tem·po·rary** \kən-ˈtem-pə-ˌrer-ē\ *adj* [*com-* + L *tempor-, tempus*] **1** : happening, existing, living, or coming into being during the same period of time **2 a** : SIMULTANEOUS **b** : marked by characteristics of the present period : MODERN — **con·tem·po·rar·i·ly** \-ˌtem-pə-ˈrer-ə-lē\ *adv*

syn CONTEMPORARY, CONTEMPORANEOUS, COEVAL, SYNCHRONOUS, SIMULTANEOUS, COINCIDENT *shared meaning element* : existing or occurring at the same time

[2]**contemporary** *n, pl* **-rar·ies** **1** : one that is contemporary with another **2** : one of the same or nearly the same age as another

con·tempt \kən-ˈtem(p)t\ *n* [ME, fr. L *contemptus,* fr. *contemptus,* pp. of *contemnere*] **1 a** : the act of despising : the state of mind of one who despises : DISDAIN <had nothing but ~ for his weakness> **b** : lack of respect or reverence for something **2** : the state of being despised **3** : willful disobedience to or open disrespect of a court, judge, or legislative body <~ of court>

con·tempt·ible \kən-ˈtem(p)-tə-bəl\ *adj* **1** : worthy of contempt **2** *obs* : SCORNFUL, CONTEMPTUOUS — **con·tempt·ible·ness** *n* — **con·tempt·ibly** \-blē\ *adv*

syn CONTEMPTIBLE, DESPICABLE, PITIABLE, SORRY, SCURVY, CHEAP, BEGGARLY *shared meaning element* : arousing or deserving scorn or contempt ***ant*** admirable, estimable, formidable

con·temp·tu·ous \-ˈtem(p)-chə(-wə)s, -ˈtem(p)sh-wəs\ *adj* [L *contemptus* contempt] : manifesting, feeling, or expressing contempt — **con·temp·tu·ous·ly** *adv* — **con·temp·tu·ous·ness** *n*

con·tend \kən-ˈtend\ *vb* [MF or L; MF *contendre,* fr. L *contendere,* fr. *com-* + *tendere* to stretch — more at TEND] *vi* **1** : to strive or vie in contest or rivalry or against difficulties **2** : to strive in debate : ARGUE ~ *vt* **1** : MAINTAIN, ASSERT <~*ed* that he was right> **2** : to struggle for — **con·tend·er** *n*

[1]**con·tent** \kən-ˈtent\ *adj* [ME, fr. MF, fr. L *contentus,* fr. pp. of *continēre* to hold in, contain] : CONTENTED, SATISFIED <~ to wait quietly>

[2]**content** *vt* **1** : to appease the desires of **2** : to limit (oneself) in requirements, desires, or actions

[3]**content** *n* : CONTENTMENT; *esp* : freedom from care or discomfort

[4]**con·tent** \ˈkän-ˌtent\ *n* [ME, fr. L *contentus,* pp. of *continēre* to contain] **1 a** : something contained — usu. used in pl <the jar's ~*s*> <the drawer's ~*s*> <the bag's ~*s*> **b** : the topics or matter treated in a written work <table of ~*s*> **2 a** : SUBSTANCE, GIST **b** : essential meaning : SIGNIFICANCE **c** : the events, physical detail, and information in a work of art — compare FORM 10c **3 a** : the matter dealt with in a field of study **b** : a part, element, or complex of parts **4** : the amount of specified material contained : PROPORTION

content analysis *n* : analysis of the manifest and latent content of a body of communicated material (as a book or film) through a classification, tabulation, and evaluation of its key symbols and themes in order to ascertain its meaning and probable effect

con·tent·ed \kən-ˈtent-əd\ *adj* : manifesting satisfaction with one's possessions, status, or situation <a ~ smile> — **con·tent·ed·ly** *adv* — **con·tent·ed·ness** *n*

con·ten·tion \kən-ˈten-chən\ *n* [ME *contencioun,* fr. MF, fr. L *contention-, contentio,* fr. *contentus,* pp. of *contendere* to contend] **1** : an act or instance of contending **2** : a point advanced or maintained in a debate or argument **3** : RIVALRY, COMPETITION ***syn*** see DISCORD

con·ten·tious \kən-ˈten-chəs\ *adj* **1** : exhibiting an often perverse and wearisome tendency to quarrels and disputes <a man of a most ~ nature> **2** : likely to cause contention <a ~ argument> ***syn*** see BELLIGERENT ***ant*** peaceable — **con·ten·tious·ly** *adv* — **con·ten·tious·ness** *n*

con·tent·ment \kən-ˈtent-mənt\ *n* **1** : the quality or state of being contented **2** : something that contents

content word \ˈkän-ˌtent-\ *n* : a word that primarily expresses lexical meaning — compare FUNCTION WORD

con·ter·mi·nous \kən-ˈtər-mə-nəs, kän-\ *adj* [L *conterminus,* fr. *com-* + *terminus* boundary — more at TERM] **1** : having a common boundary **2** : COTERMINOUS **3** : enclosed within one common boundary <the 48 ~ states of the United States> ***syn*** see ADJACENT — **con·ter·mi·nous·ly** *adv*

[1]**con·test** \kən-ˈtest, ˈkän-\ *vb* [MF *contester,* fr. L *contestari* (*litem*) to bring an action at law, fr. *contestari* to call to witness, fr. *com-* + *testis* witness — more at TESTAMENT] *vt* : to make the subject of dispute, contention, or litigation; *esp* : DISPUTE, CHALLENGE ~ *vi* : STRIVE, VIE — **con·test·able** \-ə-bəl\ *adj* — **con·test·er** *n*

[2]**con·test** \ˈkän-ˌtest\ *n* **1** : a struggle for superiority or victory **2** : a competition in which each contestant performs without direct contact with or interference from his competitors

con·tes·tant \kən-ˈtes-tənt, *also* ˈkän-ˌ\ *n* **1** : one that participates in a contest **2** : one that contests an award or decision

con·tes·ta·tion \ˌkän-ˌtes-ˈtā-shən\ *n* : CONTROVERSY

con·text \ˈkän-ˌtekst\ *n* [ME, weaving together of words, fr. L *contextus* connection of words, coherence, fr. *contextus,* pp. of *contexere* to weave together, fr. *com-* + *texere* to weave — more at TECHNICAL] **1** : the parts of a discourse that surround a word or passage and can throw light on its meaning **2** : the interrelated conditions in which something exists or occurs : ENVIRONMENT — **con·tex·tu·al** \kän-ˈteks-chə(-wə)l, kən-\ *adj* — **con·tex·tu·al·ly** \-ē\ *adv*

con·tex·ture \kən-ˈteks-chər, ˈkän-ˌ, kän-ˈ\ *n* [F, fr. L *contextus,* pp.] **1** : the act, process, or manner of weaving parts into a whole; *also* : a structure so formed <a ~ of lies> **2** : CONTEXT

contg *abbr* containing

con·ti·gu·ity \ˌkänt-ə-ˈgyü-ət-ē\ *n, pl* **-ities** : the quality or state of being contiguous : PROXIMITY

con·tig·u·ous \kən-ˈtig-yə-wəs\ *adj* [L *contiguus,* fr. *contingere* to have contact with — more at CONTINGENT] **1** : being in actual contact : touching along a boundary or at a point **2** *of angles* : ADJACENT **3** : next or near in time or sequence **4** : CONTERMINOUS 3 ***syn*** see ADJACENT — **con·tig·u·ous·ly** *adv* — **con·tig·u·ous·ness** *n*

con·ti·nence \ˈkänt-ᵊn-ən(t)s\ *n* **1** : self-restraint from yielding to impulse or desire **2** : ability to refrain from a bodily activity

[1]**con·ti·nent** \ˈkänt-ᵊn-ənt\ *adj* [ME, fr. MF, fr. L *continent-, continens,* fr. prp. of *continēre* to hold in — more at CONTAIN] **1** : exercising continence **2** *obs* : RESTRICTIVE ***syn*** see SOBER ***ant*** incontinent — **con·ti·nent·ly** *adv*

[2]**con·ti·nent** \ˈkänt-ᵊn-ənt, ˈkänt-nənt\ *n* [in senses 1 & 2, fr. L *continent-, continens,* prp. of *continēre,* to hold together, contain; in senses 3 & 4, fr. L *continent-, continens* continuous mass of land, mainland, fr. *continent-, continens,* prp.] **1** *archaic* : CONTAINER, RECEPTACLE **2** *archaic* : a summary example : EPITOME **3** : MAINLAND **4 a** : one of the usu. seven great divisions of land on the globe **b** *cap* : the continent of Europe — used with *the*

[1]**con·ti·nen·tal** \ˌkänt-ᵊn-ˈent-ᵊl\ *adj* **1** : of, relating to, or characteristic of a continent <~ waters>; *specif* : of or relating to the continent of Europe as distinguished from the British Isles **2** *often cap* : of or relating to the colonies later forming the U.S. <*Continental* Congress> — **con·ti·nen·tal·ly** \-ᵊl-ē\ *adv*

[2]**continental** *n* **1 a** *often cap* : an American soldier of the Revolution in the Continental army **b** : a piece of Continental paper currency **c** : an inhabitant of a continent and esp. the continent of Europe **2** : the least bit <not worth a ~>

continental code *n* : the international Morse code

continental divide *n* : a divide separating streams that flow to opposite sides of a continent

continental drift *n* : a hypothetical slow movement of the continents on a deep-seated viscous zone within the earth

continental shelf *n* : a shallow submarine plain of varying width forming a border to a continent and typically ending in a steep slope to the oceanic abyss

con·tin·gence \kən-'tin-jən(t)s\ *n* **1** : TANGENCY **2** : CONTINGENCY

con·tin·gen·cy \kən-'tin-jən-sē\ *n, pl* **-cies** **1** : the quality or state of being contingent **2** : a contingent event or condition: as **a** : an event (as an emergency) that is of possible but uncertain occurrence <trying to provide for every ~> **b** : something liable to happen as an adjunct to something else ***syn*** see JUNCTURE

contingency table *n* : a table that tabulates the frequency distribution of one variable in the rows and that of another variable in the columns and that is used esp. in the study of correlation between the variables

[1]**con·tin·gent** \kən-'tin-jənt\ *adj* [ME, fr. MF, fr. L *contingent-, contingens,* prp. of *contingere* to have contact with, befall, fr. *com-* + *tangere* to touch — more at TANGENT] **1** : likely but not certain to happen : POSSIBLE **2 a** : happening by chance or unforeseen causes **b** : intended for use in circumstances not completely foreseen **c** : UNPREDICTABLE **3** : dependent on or conditioned by something else **4** : not logically necessary; *esp* : EMPIRICAL, FACTUAL **5** : not necessitated : FREE ***syn*** see ACCIDENTAL — **con·tin·gent·ly** *adv*

[2]**contingent** *n* **1** : something contingent : CONTINGENCY **2** : a quota or share esp. of persons supplied from or representative of an area or group

con·tin·u·al \kən-'tin-yə(-wə)l\ *adj* [ME, fr. MF, fr. L *continuus* continuous] **1** : continuing indefinitely in time without interruption <~ fear> **2** : recurring in steady rapid succession **3** : forming a continuous series ***syn*** see CONTINUOUS ***ant*** intermittent — **con·tin·u·al·ly** \-ē\ *adv*

con·tin·u·ance \kən-'tin-yə-wən(t)s\ *n* **1 a** : the act or process of continuing in a state, condition, or course of action **b** : PROLONGATION, DURATION **2** : CONTINUITY **3** : SEQUEL **4** : adjournment of court proceedings to a future day ***syn*** see CONTINUATION

con·tin·u·ant \-yə-wənt\ *n* : something that continues or serves as a continuation (as a consonant that may be prolonged without alteration during one emission of breath) — **continuant** *adj*

continuate *adj, obs* : CONTINUOUS

con·tin·u·a·tion \kən-ˌtin-yə-'wā-shən\ *n* **1** : continuance in or prolongation of a state or activity **2** : resumption after an interruption **3** : something that continues, increases, or adds
syn CONTINUATION, CONTINUANCE, CONTINUITY *shared meaning element* : a persisting in being or continuing or an instance revealing such persistence

con·tin·u·a·tive \kən-'tin-yə-ˌwāt-iv, -wət-iv\ *adj* : relating to, causing, or being in the process of continuation

con·tin·u·a·tor \-ˌwāt-ər\ *n* : one that continues

con·tin·ue \kən-'tin-(ˌ)yü, -yə(-w)\ *vb* **-tin·ued; -tinu·ing** [ME *continuen,* fr. MF *continuer,* fr. L *continuare,* fr. *continuus*] *vi* **1** : to maintain without interruption a condition, course, or action **2** : to remain in existence : ENDURE **3** : to remain in a place or condition : STAY **4** : to resume an activity after interruption ~ *vt* **1 a** : to carry on or keep up : MAINTAIN <~*s* walking> **b** : PROLONG; *specif* : to resume after intermission **2** : to cause to continue **3** : to allow to remain in a place or condition : RETAIN **4** : to postpone (a legal proceeding) by a continuance — **con·tinu·er** \-yə-wər\ *n*
syn CONTINUE, LAST, ENDURE, ABIDE, PERSIST *shared meaning element* : to exist over a period of time or indefinitely

con·tin·ued *adj* **1** : lasting or extending without interruption : CONTINUOUS **2** : resumed after interruption <a ~ story>

continued fraction *n* : a fraction whose numerator is an integer and whose denominator is an integer plus a fraction whose numerator is an integer and whose denominator is an integer plus a fraction and so on

con·tinu·ing \kən-'tin-yə-wiŋ\ *adj* **1** : CONTINUOUS, CONSTANT **2** : needing no renewal : LASTING

continuing education *n* : an educational program designed to update the knowledge and skills of its participants

con·ti·nu·ity \ˌkänt-ᵊn-'(y)ü-ət-ē\ *n, pl* **-ities** **1 a** : uninterrupted connection, succession, or union **b** : persistence without essential change **c** : uninterrupted duration in time **2** : something that has, exhibits, or provides continuity: as **a** : a script or scenario in the performing arts **b** : transitional spoken or musical matter esp. for a radio or television program **c** : the story and dialogue of a comic strip **3** : the property characteristic of a continuous function; *also* : an example of this property ***syn*** see CONTINUATION

con·tin·uo \kən-'tin-(y)ə-ˌwō\ *n, pl* **-u·os** [It, fr. *continuo* continuous, fr. L *continuus*] : a bass part (as for a keyboard or stringed instrument) used esp. in baroque ensemble music and consisting of a succession of bass notes with figures that indicate the required chords — called also *figured bass, thoroughbass*

con·tin·u·ous \kən-'tin-yə-wəs\ *adj* [L *continuus,* fr. *continēre* to hold together — more at CONTAIN] **1** : marked by uninterrupted extension in space, time, or sequence **2** *of a function* : having the numerical difference between the value at a point and the value at any point in a sufficiently small neighborhood of the point arbitrarily small — **con·tin·u·ous·ly** *adv* — **con·tin·u·ous·ness** *n*
syn CONTINUOUS, CONTINUAL, CONSTANT, INCESSANT, PERPETUAL, PERENNIAL *shared meaning element* : characterized by continued occurrence or recurrence ***ant*** interrupted

continuous waves *n pl* **1** : radio waves that continue with unchanging intensity or amplitude without modulation **2** : radio waves whose intensity continues unchanged except for modulation — abbr. *CW*

con·tin·u·um \kən-'tin-yə-wəm\ *n, pl* **-ua** \-yə-wə\ *also* **-ums** [L, neut. of *continuus*] **1** : something absolutely continuous and homogeneous of which no distinction of content can be affirmed except by reference to something else (as duration and extension) **2 a** : something in which a fundamental common character is discernible amid a series of insensible or indefinite variations <the ~ of consciousness> **b (1)** : an uninterrupted ordered sequence **(2)** : a series of ecological communities whose vegetation gradually changes along an environmental gradient **c** : an identity of substance uniting discrete parts; *broadly* : CONTINUITY **3** : a set with the same transfinite cardinal number as the set of real numbers

con·tort \kən-'tȯ(ə)rt\ *vb* [L *contortus,* pp. of *contorquēre,* fr. *com-* + *torquēre* to twist — more at TORTURE] *vt* : to twist in a violent manner <features ~*ed* with fury> ~ *vi* : to twist into a strained shape or expression ***syn*** see DEFORM — **con·tor·tion** \-'tȯr-shən\ *n* — **con·tor·tive** \-'tȯrt-iv\ *adj*

con·tor·tion·ist \kən-'tȯr-sh(ə-)nəst\ *n* : one who contorts; *specif* : an acrobat who specializes in unnatural body postures — **con·tor·tion·is·tic** \-ˌtȯr-shə-'nis-tik\ *adj*

[1]**con·tour** \'kän-ˌtu̇(ə)r\ *n* [F, fr. It *contorno* fr. *contornare* to round off, sketch in outline, fr. L *com-* + *tornare* to turn in a lathe, fr. *tornus* lathe] : an outline esp. of a curving or irregular figure : SHAPE; *also* : the line representing this outline ***syn*** see OUTLINE

[2]**contour** *vt* **1 a** : to shape the contour of **b** : to shape so as to fit contours **2** : to construct (as a road) in conformity to a contour

[3]**contour** *adj* **1** : following contour lines or forming furrows or ridges along them <~ flooding> <~ farming> **2** : made to fit the contour of something <a ~ couch>

contour feather *n* : one of the medium-sized feathers that form the general covering of a bird and determine the external contour

contour line *n* : a line (as on a map) connecting the points on a land surface that have the same elevation

contour map *n* : a map having contour lines

contr *abbr* **1** contract; contraction **2** contralto **3** contrary **4** control; controller

contra- *prefix* [ME, fr. L, fr. *contra* against, opposite — more at COUNTER] **1** : against : contrary : contrasting <*contra*distinction> **2** : pitched below normal bass <*contra*octave>

con·tra·band \'kän-trə-ˌband\ *n* [It *contrabbando,* fr. ML *contrabannum,* fr. *contra-* + *bannus, bannum* decree, of Gmc origin — more at BAN] **1** : illegal or prohibited traffic **2** : goods or merchandise whose importation, exportation, or possession is forbidden; *also* : smuggled goods **3** : a Negro slave who during the Civil War escaped to or was brought within the Union lines — **contraband** *adj*

con·tra·band·ist \-ˌban-dəst\ *n* : SMUGGLER

con·tra·bass \'kän-trə-ˌbās\ *n* [It *contrabbasso,* fr. *contra-* + *basso* bass] : DOUBLE BASS — **con·tra·bass·ist** \-ˌbā-səst\ *n*

con·tra·bas·soon \ˌkän-trə-bə-'sün, -ba-\ *n* : a double-reed woodwind instrument having a range an octave lower that that of the bassoon

contrabassoon

con·tra·cep·tion \ˌkän-trə-'sep-shən\ *n* [*contra-* + *conception*] : voluntary prevention of conception or impregnation — **con·tra·cep·tive** \-'sep-tiv\ *adj or n*

[1]**con·tract** \'kän-ˌtrakt\ *n* [ME, fr. L *contractus,* fr. *contractus,* pp. of *contrahere* to draw together, make a contract, reduce in size, fr. *com-* + *trahere* to draw — more at DRAW] **1 a** : a binding agreement between two or more persons or parties : COVENANT **b** : BETROTHAL **2** : a writing made by the parties to evidence the terms and conditions of a contract **3** : the department or principles of law having to do with contracts **4** : an undertaking to win a specified number of tricks or points in bridge

[2]**con·tract** \ *vt 1a & vi 1 usu* 'kän-ˌtrakt, *others usu* kən-'\ *vb* [partly fr. MF *contracter* to agree upon, fr. L *contractus* n.; partly fr. L *contractus,* pp. of *contrahere* to draw together] *vt* **1 a** : to establish or undertake by contract **b** : BETROTH **2 a** : to acquire usu. involuntarily <~ pneumonia> **b** : to bring on oneself as an obligation : INCUR <~ a debt> **3 a** : LIMIT, RESTRICT **b** : KNIT, WRINKLE <frown ~*ed* his brow> **c** : to draw together : CONCENTRATE **4** : to reduce to smaller size by or as if by squeezing or forcing together **5** : to shorten (as a word) by omitting one or more sounds or letters ~ *vi* **1** : to make a contract **2** : to draw together so as to become diminished in size <metal ~*s* on cooling>; *also* : to become less in compass, duration, or length <muscle ~*s* in tetanus> — **con·tract·ibil·i·ty** \kən-ˌtrak-tə-'bil-ət-ē, ˌkän-\ *n* — **con·tract·ible** \kən-'trak-tə-bəl, 'kän-ˌ\ *adj*
syn **1** see INCUR
2 CONTRACT, SHRINK, CONDENSE, COMPRESS, CONSTRICT, DEFLATE *shared meaning element* : to decrease in bulk or volume ***ant*** expand

contract bridge \ˌkän-ˌtrakt-\ *n* : a bridge game distinguished by the fact that overtricks do not count toward game or slam bonuses

con·trac·tile \kən-'trak-tᵊl, -ˌtīl\ *adj* : having the power or property of contracting <~ proteins of muscle fibrils> — **con·trac·til·i·ty** \ˌkän-ˌtrak-'til-ət-ē\ *n*

contractile vacuole *n* : a vacuole in a unicellular organism that contracts regularly to discharge fluid from the body and that probably has an excretory or hydrostatic function

con·trac·tion \kən-'trak-shən\ *n* **1 a** : the action or process of contracting : the state of being contracted **b** : the shortening and thickening of a functioning muscle or muscle fiber **c** : a reduction in business activity **2** : a shortening of a word, syllable, or word group by omission of a sound or letter; *also* : a form produced by such shortening — **con·trac·tion·al** \-shnəl, -shən-ᵊl\ *adj* — **con·trac·tive** \kən-'trak-tiv, 'kän-ˌ\ *adj*

con·trac·tor \'kän-ˌtrak-tər (*usual for 1*), kən-'\ *n* **1** : one that contracts or is party to a contract: as **a** : one that contracts to perform work or provide supplies on a large scale **b** : one that contracts to erect buildings **2** : something (as a muscle) that contracts or shortens

con·trac·tu·al \kən-'trak-chə(-wə)l, kän-, -'traksh-wəl\ *adj* [L *contractus* contract] : of, relating to, or constituting a contract — **con·trac·tu·al·ly** \-ē\ *adv*

con·trac·ture \kən-'trak-chər\ *n* : a permanent shortening (as of muscle, tendon, or scar tissue) producing deformity or distortion

con·tra·dict \ˌkän-trə-'dikt\ *vt* [L *contradictus,* pp. of *contradicere,* fr. *contra-* + *dicere* to say, speak — more at DICTION] **1** : to resist or oppose in argument **2 a** : to assert the contrary of : GAINSAY **b** : to deny the truth of **3 a** : to be the contradictory of **b**

: to go counter to **c** : to act in a manner contrary to ***syn*** see DENY ***ant*** corroborate — **con·tra·dict·able** \-'dik-tə-bəl\ *adj* — **con·tra·dic·tor** \-'dik-tər\ *n*

con·tra·dic·tion \ˌkän-trə-'dik-shən\ *n* **1** : the act of contradicting **2** : an expression or proposition containing contradictory parts **3 a** : logical incongruity **b** : opposition of factors inherent in a system or situation

con·tra·dic·tious \-shəs\ *adj* **1** : CONTRADICTORY, OPPOSITE **2** : given to or marked by contradiction : CONTRARY

[1]**con·tra·dic·to·ry** \ˌkän-trə-'dik-t(ə-)rē\ *n, pl* **-ries** **1 a** : something that contradicts **b** : OPPOSITE, CONTRARY **2** : a proposition so related to another that if either of the two is true the other is false and if either is false the other must be true — **con·tra·dic·to·ri·ly** \-t(ə-)rə-lē\ *adv* — **con·tra·dic·to·ri·ness** \-t(ə-)rē -nəs\ *n*

[2]**contradictory** *adj* **1** : CONTRADICTIOUS 2 <an irritable ~ nature> **2** : involving, causing, or constituting a contradiction <ill-planned and often ~ proposals> ***syn*** see OPPOSITE

con·tra·dis·tinc·tion \ˌkän-trə-dis-'tiŋ(k)-shən\ *n* : distinction by contrast <painting in ~ to sculpture> — **con·tra·dis·tinc·tive** \-'tiŋ(k)-tiv\ *adj* — **con·tra·dis·tinc·tive·ly** *adv*

con·tra·dis·tin·guish \-'tiŋ-gwish\ *vt* : to distinguish by contrast of qualities

con·trail \'kän-ˌtrāl\ *n* [*con*densation *trail*] : streaks of condensed water vapor created in the air by an airplane or rocket at high altitudes

con·tra·in·di·cate \ˌkän-trə-'in-də-ˌkāt\ *vt* : to make (a treatment or procedure) inadvisable — **con·tra·in·di·ca·tion** \-ˌin-də-'kā-shən\ *n* — **con·tra·in·dic·a·tive** \-in-'dik-ət-iv\ *adj*

con·tra·lat·er·al \-'lat-ə-rəl, -'la-trəl\ *adj* [ISV] : occurring on or acting in conjunction with similar parts on an opposite side

con·tral·to \kən-'tral-(ˌ)tō\ *n, pl* **-tos** [It, fr. *contra-* + *alto*] **1 a** : the lowest female singing voice **b** : a person having this voice **2** : the part sung by a contralto

con·tra·oc·tave \ˌkän-trə-'äk-tiv, -təv, -ˌtāv\ *n* : the musical octave that begins on the third C below middle C — see PITCH illustration

con·tra·po·si·tion \-pə-'zish-ən\ *n* [LL *contraposition-, contrapositio*, fr. L *contrapositus*, pp. of *contraponere* to place opposite, fr. *contra-* + *ponere* to place] **1** : OPPOSITION, ANTITHESIS **2** : the relationship between two propositions when the subject and predicate of one are respectively the negation of the predicate and the negation of the subject of the other

con·tra·pos·i·tive \-'päz-ət-iv, -'päz-tiv\ *n* : a proposition resulting from an operation of immediate inference in which the terms of a given proposition are permuted and negated <"all not-*P* is not-*S*" is the ~ of "all *S* is *P*">

con·trap·tion \kən-'trap-shən\ *n* [perh. blend of *contrivance, trap*, and *invention*] : CONTRIVANCE, GADGET

con·tra·pun·tal \ˌkän-trə-'pənt-ᵊl\ *adj* [It *contrappunto* counterpoint, fr. ML *contrapunctus*] **1** : of or relating to counterpoint **2** : POLYPHONIC — **con·tra·pun·tal·ly** \-ᵊl-ē\ *adv*

con·tra·pun·tist \-'pənt-əst\ *n* : one who writes counterpoint

con·tra·ri·ety \ˌkän-trə-'rī-ət-ē\ *n, pl* **-eties** [ME *contrariete*, fr. MF *contrarieté*, fr. LL *contrarietat-, contrarietas*, fr. L *contrarius* contrary] **1** : the quality or state of being contrary **2** : something contrary

con·trar·i·ous \kən-'trer-ē-əs, kän-\ *adj* : PERVERSE, ANTAGONISTIC

con·trari·wise \'kän-ˌtrer-ē-ˌwīz, kən-'\ *adv* **1** : on the contrary **2** : vice versa : CONVERSELY **3** : in a contrary manner

[1]**con·trary** \'kän-ˌtrer-ē\ *n, pl* **-trar·ies** **1** : a fact or condition incompatible with another : OPPOSITE **2** : one of a pair of opposites **3 a** : a proposition so related to another that though both may be false they cannot both be true **b** : either of two terms (as black and white) that cannot both be affirmed of the same subject — **by contraries** : in a manner opposite to what is logical or expected — **on the contrary** : just the opposite : NO — **to the contrary** : NOTWITHSTANDING

[2]**con·trary** \'kän-ˌtrer-ē, *in sense 4 often* kən-'tre(ə)r-ē\ *adj* [ME *contrarie*, fr. MF *contraire*, fr. L *contrarius*, fr. *contra* opposite] **1 a** : diametrically different <the result was ~ to our plan> **b** : opposite in character : tending to an opposing course <he remained firm in the ~ intention> **c** : mutually opposed : ANTAGONISTIC <they held ~ opinions> **2** : opposite in position, direction, or nature **3** : UNFAVORABLE — used of wind or weather **4** : temperamentally unwilling to accept control or advice <a ~ child> — **con·trari·ly** \-ˌtrer-ə-lē, -'trer-\ *adv* — **con·trari·ness** \-ˌtrer-ē-nəs, -'trer-\ *n*

syn **1** see OPPOSITE

2 CONTRARY, PERVERSE, RESTIVE, BALKY, FROWARD, WAYWARD *shared meaning element* : unwilling or unable to conform to custom or submit to authority ***ant*** complaisant

[3]**con·trary** *like* [2]CONTRARY\ *adv* : CONTRARIWISE, CONTRARILY

contrary to *prep* : in opposition to <*contrary to* orders, he set out alone>

[1]**con·trast** \'kän-ˌtrast\ *n* **1 a** : juxtaposition of dissimilar elements (as color, tone, or emotion) in a work of art **b** : degree of difference between the lightest and darkest parts of a picture **2** : comparison of similar objects to set off their dissimilar qualities **3** : a person or thing that exhibits differences when compared with another

[2]**con·trast** \kən-'trast, 'kän-ˌ\ *vb* [F *contraster*, fr. MF, to oppose, resist, alter. of *contrester*, fr. (assumed) VL *contrastare*, fr. L *contra-* + *stare* to stand — more at STAND] *vi* : to exhibit contrast ~ *vt* **1** : to put in contrast **2** : to compare or appraise in respect to differences <~ European and American manners> ***syn*** see COMPARE — **con·trast·able** \-ə-bəl\ *adj*

con·tras·tive \kən-'tras-tiv, 'kän-ˌ\ *adj* : forming or consisting of a contrast : CONTRASTING — **con·tras·tive·ly** *adv*

con·trasty \'kän-ˌtras-tē\ *adj* : having or producing in photography great contrast between highlights and shadows

con·tra·vene \ˌkän-trə-'vēn\ *vt* **-vened; -ven·ing** [MF or LL; MF *contrevenir*, fr. LL *contravenire*, fr. L *contra-* + *venire* to come — more at COME] **1** : to go or act contrary to <~ a law> **2** : to oppose in argument : CONTRADICT <~ a proposition> ***syn*** see DENY ***ant*** uphold (*as a law or principle*), allege (*as a right or claim*) — **con·tra·ven·er** *n*

con·tra·ven·tion \ˌkän-trə-'ven-chən\ *n* [MF, fr. LL *contraventus*, pp. of *contravenire*] : the act of contravening : VIOLATION

con·tre·danse \'kän-trə-ˌdan(t)s, kōⁿ-trə-däⁿs\ *or* **con·tra dance** \'kän-trə-ˌdan(t)s\ *n* [F *contredanse*, by folk etymology fr. E *country-dance*] **1** : a folk dance in which couples face each other in two lines or in a square **2** : a piece of music for a contredanse

con·tre·temps \'kän-trə-ˌtäⁿ, kōⁿ-trə-täⁿ\ *n, pl* **con·tre·temps** \-(ˌ)täⁿ(z)\ [F, fr. *contre-* counter- + *temps* time, fr. L *tempus* — more at TEMPORAL] : an inopportune and embarrassing occurrence

contrib *abbr* contribution; contributor

con·trib·ute \kən-'trib-yət\ *vb* **-ut·ed; -ut·ing** [L *contributus*, pp. of *contribuere*, fr. *com-* + *tribuere* to grant — more at TRIBUTE] *vt* **1** : to give or supply in common with others **2** : to supply (as an article) for a publication ~ *vi* **1 a** : to give a part to a common fund or store **b** : to play a significant part in bringing about an end or result **2** : to submit articles to a publication ***syn*** see CONDUCE — **con·trib·u·tor** \-yət-ər\ *n*

con·tri·bu·tion \ˌkän-trə-'byü-shən\ *n* **1** : a payment (as a levy or tax) imposed by military, civil, or ecclesiastical authorities usu. for a special or extraordinary purpose **2** : the act of contributing; *also* : the thing contributed **3** : a writing for publication esp. in a periodical — **con·trib·u·tive** \kən-'trib-yət-iv\ *adj* — **con·trib·u·tive·ly** *adv*

con·trib·u·to·ry \kən-'trib-yə-ˌtōr-ē, -ˌtòr-\ *adj* **1 a** : contributing to a common fund or enterprise **b** : subject to a levy of supplies, money, or men **2** : of, relating to, or forming a contribution

con·trite \'kän-ˌtrīt, kən-'\ *adj* [ME *contrit*, fr. MF, fr. ML, fr. L, pp. of *conterere* to grind, bruise, fr. *com-* + *terere* to rub — more at THROW] **1** : grieving and penitent for sin or shortcoming **2** : proceeding from contrition <~ sighs> — **con·trite·ly** *adv* — **con·trite·ness** *n*

con·tri·tion \kən-'trish-ən\ *n* : the state of being contrite : REPENTANCE ***syn*** see PENITENCE

con·triv·ance \kən-'trī-vən(t)s\ *n* **1** : the act or faculty of contriving : the state of being contrived **2** : a thing contrived; *esp* : a mechanical device

con·trive \kən-'trīv\ *vb* **con·trived; con·triv·ing** [ME *controven, contreven*, fr. MF *controver*, fr. LL *contropare* to compare] *vt* **1 a** : DEVISE, PLAN <~ ways of handling the situation> **b** : to form or create in an artistic or ingenious manner <*contrived* household utensils from stone> **2** : to bring about by stratagem or with difficulty : MANAGE ~ *vi* : to make schemes — **con·triv·er** *n*

con·trived *adj* : ARTIFICIAL, LABORED

[1]**con·trol** \kən-'trōl\ *vt* **con·trolled; con·trol·ling** [ME *controllen*, fr. MF *contreroller*, fr. *contrerolle* copy of an account, audit, fr. *contre-* counter- + *rolle* roll, account] **1** : to check, test, or verify by evidence or experiments **2 a** : to exercise restraining or directing influence over : REGULATE **b** : to have power over : RULE ***syn*** see CONDUCT — **con·trol·la·ble** \-'trō-lə-bəl\ *adj* — **con·trol·ment** \-'trōl-mənt\ *n*

[2]**control** *n* **1 a** : an act or instance of controlling; *also* : power or authority to guide or manage **b** : skill in the use of a tool, instrument, technique, or artistic medium **c** : direction, regulation, and coordination of business activities (as production and administration) **2** : RESTRAINT, RESERVE **3** : one that controls: as **a** (1) : an experiment in which the subjects are treated as in a parallel experiment except for omission of the procedure or agent under test and which is used as a standard of comparison in judging experimental effects — called also *control experiment* (2) : one (as an organism, culture, or group) that is part of a control **b** : a mechanism used to regulate or guide the operation of a machine, apparatus, or system **c** : an organization that directs a space flight <mission ~> **d** : a personality or spirit believed to actuate the utterances or performances of a spiritualist medium

control chart *n* : a chart that gives the results of periodic sampling for rejects of a manufactured product and that is used in making decisions concerning the maintenance of product quality

con·trolled \kən-'trōld\ *adj* : RESTRAINED

con·trol·ler \kən-'trō-lər, 'kän-ˌ\ *n* [ME *conterroller*, fr. MF *contrerolleur*, fr. *contrerolle*] **1 a** : COMPTROLLER 1 **b** : COMPTROLLER 2 **c** : the chief accounting officer of a business enterprise or an institution (as a college) **2** : one that controls or has power or authority to control — **con·trol·ler·ship** \-ˌship\ *n*

controlling interest *n* : sufficient stock ownership in a corporation to exert control over policy

control surface *n* : a movable airfoil designed to change the attitude of an aircraft

con·tro·ver·sial \ˌkän-trə-'vər-shəl, -'vər-sē-əl\ *adj* **1** : of, relating to, or arousing controversy <a ~ public figure> **2** : given to controversy : DISPUTATIOUS — **con·tro·ver·sial·ism** \-ˌiz-əm\ *n* — **con·tro·ver·sial·ist** \-əst\ *n* — **con·tro·ver·sial·ly** \-ē\ *adv*

con·tro·ver·sy \'kän-trə-ˌvər-sē\ *n, pl* **-sies** [ME *controversie*, fr. L *controversia*, fr. *controversus* disputable, lit., turned opposite, fr. *contro-* (akin to *contra-*) + *versus*, pp. of *vertere* to turn — more at WORTH] **1** : a discussion marked esp. by the expression of opposing views : DISPUTE **2** : QUARREL, STRIFE

con·tro·vert \'kän-trə-ˌvərt, ˌkän-trə-'\ *vb* [*controversy*] *vt* : to dispute or oppose by reasoning <~ a point in a discussion> ~ *vi* : to engage in controversy ***syn*** see DISPROVE ***ant*** assert — **con·tro·vert·er** \-ər\ *n* — **con·tro·vert·ible** \-ə-bəl\ *adj*

con·tu·ma·cious \ˌkän-t(y)ə-'mā-shəs, ˌkän-chə-\ *adj* : stubbornly disobedient : REBELLIOUS — **con·tu·ma·cious·ly** *adv*

con·tu·ma·cy \kən-'t(y)ü-mə-sē; 'kän-t(y)ə-, 'kän-chə-\ *n* [ME *contumacie*, fr. L *contumacia*, fr. *contumac-, contumax* insubordinate, fr. *com-* + *tumēre* to swell, be proud — more at THUMB]

: stubborn resistance to authority; *specif* : willful contempt of court

con·tu·me·li·ous \ˌkän-t(y)ə-ˈmē-lē-əs, ˌkän-chə-\ *adj* : insolently abusive and humiliating — **con·tu·me·li·ous·ly** *adv*

con·tume·ly \kən-ˈt(y)ü-mə-lē; ˈkän-t(y)ə-ˌmē-lē, ˈkän-chə-; ˈkän-təm-lē\ *n, pl* **-lies** [ME *contumelie,* fr. MF, fr. L *contumelia;* perh. akin to L *contumacia*] : rude language or treatment arising from haughtiness and contempt; *also* : an instance of such language or treatment

con·tuse \kən-ˈt(y)üz\ *vt* **con·tused; con·tus·ing** [MF *contuser,* fr. L *contusus,* pp. of *contundere* to crush, bruise, fr. *com-* + *tundere* to beat — more at STINT] : to injure (tissue) usu. without laceration : BRUISE — **con·tu·sion** \-ˈt(y)ü-zhən\ *n*

co·nun·drum \kə-ˈnən-drəm\ *n* [origin unknown] **1** : a riddle whose answer is or involves a pun **2 a** : a question or problem having only a conjectural answer **b** : an intricate and difficult problem ***syn*** see MYSTERY

con·ur·ba·tion \ˌkän-(ˌ)ər-ˈbā-shən\ *n* [*com-* + L *urb-, urbs* city] : an aggregation or continuous network of urban communities

co·nus ar·te·ri·o·sus \ˈkō-nə-sär-ˌtir-ē-ˈō-səs\ *n, pl* **co·ni ar·te·ri·o·si** \-ˌnī-är-ˌtir-ē-ˈō-ˌsī\ [NL, lit., arterial cone] **1** : a prolongation of the ventricle of amphibians and some fishes that has a spiral valve separating venous blood going to the respiratory arteries from blood going to the aorta and systemic arteries **2** : a conical prolongation of the right ventricle in mammals from which the pulmonary arteries emerge — called also *conus*

conv *abbr* **1** convention; conventional **2** convertible **3** convocation

con·va·lesce \ˌkän-və-ˈles\ *vi* **-lesced; -lesc·ing** [L *convalescere,* fr. *com-* + *valescere* to grow strong, fr. *valēre* to be strong, be well — more at WIELD] : to recover health and strength gradually after sickness or weakness — **con·va·les·cence** \-ˈles-ᵊn(t)s\ *n* — **con·va·les·cent** \-ᵊnt\ *adj or n*

con·vect \kən-ˈvekt\ *vb* [back-formation fr. *convection*] *vi* : to transfer heat by convection ~ *vt* : to circulate (warm air) by convection

con·vec·tion \kən-ˈvek-shən\ *n* [LL *convection-, convectio,* fr. L *convectus,* pp. of *convehere* to bring together, fr. *com-* + *vehere* to carry — more at WAY] **1** : the action or process of conveying **2 a** : the circulatory motion that occurs in a fluid at a nonuniform temperature owing to the variation of its density and the action of gravity **b** : the transfer of heat by this automatic circulation of a fluid — **con·vec·tion·al** \-shnəl, -shən-ᵊl\ *adj* — **con·vec·tive** \-ˈvek-tiv\ *adj*

con·vec·tor \-ˈvek-tər\ *n* : a heating unit in which air heated by contact with a heating device (as a radiator or a tube with fins) in a casing circulates by convection

con·vene \kən-ˈvēn\ *vb* **con·vened; con·ven·ing** [ME *convenen,* fr. MF *convenir* to come together] *vi* : to come together in a body ~ *vt* **1** : to summon before a tribunal **2** : to cause to assemble ***syn*** see SUMMON — **con·ven·er** *n*

con·ve·nience \kən-ˈvē-nyən(t)s\ *n* **1** : fitness or suitability for performing an action or fulfilling a requirement **2** : an appliance, device, or service conducive to comfort **3** : a suitable time : OPPORTUNITY **4** : freedom from discomfort : EASE

con·ve·nien·cy \-nyən-sē\ *n, archaic* : CONVENIENCE

con·ve·nient \kən-ˈvē-nyənt\ *adj* [ME, fr. L *convenient-, conveniens,* fr. prp. of *convenire* to come together, be suitable] **1** *obs* : SUITABLE, PROPER **2 a** : suited to personal comfort or to easy performance **b** : suited to a particular situation **c** : affording accommodation or advantage **3** : being near at hand : HANDY — **con·ve·nient·ly** *adv*

[1]**con·vent** \ˈkän-vənt, -ˌvent\ *n* [ME *covent,* fr. OF, fr. ML *conventus,* fr. L, assembly, fr. *conventus,* pp. of *convenire*] : a local community or house of a religious order or congregation; *esp* : an establishment of nuns

[2]**con·vent** \kən-ˈvent\ *vb* [L *conventus,* pp.] *obs* : CONVENE

con·ven·ti·cle \kən-ˈvent-i-kəl\ *n* [ME, fr. L *conventiculum,* dim. of *conventus* assembly] **1** : ASSEMBLY, MEETING **2** : an assembly of an irregular or unlawful character **3** : an assembly for religious worship; *esp* : a secret meeting for worship not sanctioned by law **4** : MEETINGHOUSE — **con·ven·ti·cler** \-k(ə-)lər\ *n*

con·ven·tion \kən-ˈven-chən\ *n* [ME, fr. MF or L; MF, fr. L *convention-, conventio,* fr. *conventus,* pp. of *convenire* to come together, be suitable, fr. *com-* + *venire* to come — more at COME] **1 a** : AGREEMENT, CONTRACT **b** : an agreement between states for regulation of matters affecting all of them **c** : a compact between opposing commanders esp. concerning prisoner exchange or armistice **d** : a general agreement about basic principles; *also* : a principle that is true by convention **2 a** : the summoning or convening of an assembly **b** : an assembly of persons met for a common purpose; *esp* : a meeting of the delegates of a political party for the purpose of formulating a platform and selecting candidates for office **c** : the usu. state or national organization of a religious denomination **3 a** : usage or custom esp. in social matters **b** : a rule of conduct or behavior **c** : a practice in bidding or playing that conveys information between partners in a card game (as bridge) **d** : an established theatrical technique or practice (as a stage whisper or spotlighting)

con·ven·tion·al \kən-ˈvench-nəl, -ˈven-chən-ᵊl\ *adj* **1** : formed by agreement or compact **2 a** : according with, sanctioned by, or based on convention **b** : lacking originality or individuality : TRITE **3 a** : according with a mode of artistic representation that simplifies or provides symbols or substitutes for natural forms **b** : of traditional design **4** : of, resembling, or relating to a convention, assembly, or public meeting **5** : not making use of nuclear powers <~ warfare> ***syn*** see CEREMONIAL ***ant*** unconventional — **con·ven·tion·al·ism** \-ˌiz-əm\ *n* — **con·ven·tion·al·ist** \-əst\ *n* — **con·ven·tion·al·ly** \-ē\ *adv*

con·ven·tion·al·i·ty \-ˌven-chə-ˈnal-ət-ē\ *n, pl* **-ties** **1** : the quality or state of being conventional; *specif* : adherence to conventions **2** : a conventional usage, practice, or thing

con·ven·tion·al·iza·tion \kən-ˌvench-nə-lə-ˈzā-shən, -ˌven-chən-ᵊl-ə-ˈzā-\ *n* : the act, practice, or product of conventionalizing

con·ven·tion·al·ize \kən-ˈvench-nə-ˌlīz, -ˈven-chən-ᵊl-ˌīz\ *vt* **-ized; -iz·ing** : to make conventional

con·ven·tion·eer \kən-ˌven-chə-ˈni(ə)r\ *n* : a person attending a convention

[1]**con·ven·tu·al** \kən-ˈvench-(ə-)wəl, kän-\ *adj* [ME, fr. MF or ML; MF, fr. ML *conventualis,* fr. *conventus* convent] **1** : of, relating to, or befitting a convent or monastic life : MONASTIC **2** *cap* : of or relating to the Conventuals — **con·ven·tu·al·ly** \-ē\ *adv*

[2]**conventual** *n* **1** : a member of a conventual community **2** *cap* : a member of the Order of Friars Minor Conventual forming a branch of the first order of St. Francis of Assisi under a mitigated rule

con·verge \kən-ˈvərj\ *vb* **con·verged; con·verg·ing** [ML *convergere,* fr. L *com-* + *vergere* to bend, incline — more at WRENCH] *vi* **1** : to tend or move toward one point or one another : come together : MEET **2** : to come together and unite in a common interest or focus **3** : to approach a limit as the number of terms increases without limit ~ *vt* : to cause to converge

con·ver·gence \kən-ˈvər-jən(t)s\ *n* **1** : the act of converging and esp. moving toward union or uniformity; *esp* : coordinated movement of the two eyes resulting in impingement of the image of a point on corresponding retinal areas **2** : the condition of converging; *esp* : independent development of similar characters (as of bodily structure or cultural traits) often associated with similarity of habits or environment

con·ver·gen·cy \-jən-sē\ *n* : CONVERGENCE

con·ver·gent \-jənt\ *adj* **1** : tending to move toward one point or to approach each other : CONVERGING <~ lines> **2** : exhibiting convergence in form, function, or development **3 a** *of an improper integral* : having a value that is a real number **b** : characterized by having the *n*th term or the sum of the first *n* terms approach a finite limit <a ~ sequence> <a ~ series>

convergent lady beetle *n* [fr. the pattern of spots on its back] : a periodically migratory beneficial lady beetle (*Hippodamia convergens*) that feeds on various crop pests (as aphids) — called also *convergent*

con·vers·able \kən-ˈvər-sə-bəl\ *adj* **1** : pleasant and easy to converse with **2** *archaic* : relating to or suitable for social interaction

con·ver·sance \kən-ˈvərs-ᵊn(t)s *also* ˈkän-vər-sən(t)s\ *n* : the quality or state of being conversant

con·ver·san·cy \-ᵊn-sē, -sən-sē\ *n* : CONVERSANCE

con·ver·sant \kən-ˈvərs-ᵊnt *also* ˈkän-vər-sənt\ *adj* **1** *archaic* : OCCUPIED, CONCERNED **2** *archaic* : having frequent, customary, or familiar association **3** : having knowledge or experience — **con·ver·sant·ly** *adv*

con·ver·sa·tion \ˌkän-vər-ˈsā-shən\ *n* [ME *conversacioun,* fr. MF *conversation,* fr. L *conversation-, conversatio,* fr. *conversatus,* pp. of *conversari* to live, keep company with] **1** *obs* : CONDUCT, BEHAVIOR **2 a** (1) : oral exchange of sentiments, observations, opinions, or ideas (2) : an instance of such exchange : TALK **b** : an informal discussion of an issue by representatives of governments, institutions, or groups **c** : an exchange similar to conversation; *esp* : real-time interaction with a computer esp. through a keyboard — **con·ver·sa·tion·al** \-shnəl, -shən-ᵊl\ *adj* — **con·ver·sa·tion·al·ly** \-ē\ *adv*

con·ver·sa·tion·al·ist \-shnə-ləst, -shən-ᵊl-əst\ *n* : one who converses a great deal or who excels in conversation

conversation piece *n* **1** : a painting of a group of persons in their customary surroundings **2** : a novel or striking object that stimulates conversation

con·ver·sa·zi·o·ne \ˌkän-vər-ˌsät-sē-ˈō-nē, ˌkōn-\ *n, pl* **-ones** *or* **-o·ni** \-ˈō(ˌ)nē\ [It, lit. conversation, fr. L *conversation-, conversatio*] : a meeting for conversation esp. about art, literature, or science

[1]**con·verse** \kən-ˈvərs\ *vi* **con·versed; con·vers·ing** [ME *conversen,* fr. MF *converser,* fr. L *conversari* to live, keep company with, fr. *conversus,* pp. of *convertere* to turn around] **1** *archaic* **a** : to become occupied or engaged **b** : to have acquaintance or familiarity **2 a** : to exchange thoughts and opinions in speech : TALK **b** : to carry on an exchange similar to a conversation; *esp* : to interact with a computer ***syn*** see SPEAK — **con·vers·er** *n*

[2]**con·verse** \ˈkän-ˌvərs\ *n* **1** *obs* : social interaction **2** : CONVERSATION

[3]**con·verse** \kən-ˈvərs, ˈkän-ˌ\ *adj* [L *conversus,* pp. of *convertere*] : reversed in order, relation, or action — **con·verse·ly** *adv*

[4]**con·verse** \ˈkän-ˌvərs\ *n* : something converse to another; *esp* : a proposition obtained by interchange of the subject and predicate of a logical proposition <"no *P* is *S*" is the ~ of "no *S* is *P*">

con·ver·sion \kən-ˈvər-zhən, -shən\ *n* [ME, fr. MF, fr. L *conversion-, conversio,* fr. *conversus,* pp. of *convertere*] **1** : the act of converting : the process of being converted **2** : an experience associated with a definite and decisive adoption of religion **3 a** : the operation of finding a converse in logic **b** : reduction of a mathematical expression by clearing of fractions **4** : the making of a score on a try for point after touchdown in football or a free throw in basketball **5** : something converted from one use to another — **con·ver·sion·al** \-ˈvərzh-nəl, -ˈvərsh-, -ən-ᵊl\ *adj*

conversion reaction *n* : a psychoneurosis in which bodily symptoms (as paralysis of the limbs) appear without physical basis — called also *conversion hysteria*

[1]**con·vert** \kən-ˈvərt\ *vb* [ME *converten,* fr. OF *convertir,* fr. L *convertere,* to turn around, transform, convert, fr. *com-* + *vertere* to turn — more at WORTH] *vt* **1 a** : to bring over from one belief, view, or party to another **b** : to bring about a religious conversion in **2 a** : to alter the physical or chemical nature or properties of esp. in manufacturing **b** (1) : to change from one form or function to another (2) : to alter for more effective utilization (3) : to appropriate without right **c** : to exchange for an equivalent **3** *obs* : TURN **4** : to subject to logical conversion **5 a** : to make a goal after receiving (a pass) from a teammate **b** : to make (a spare) in bowling ~ *vi* **1** : to undergo conversion **2** : to make good on a try for point after touchdown or on a free throw ***syn*** see TRANSFORM

²con·vert \'kän-,vərt\ *n* : one that is converted; *esp* : one who has experienced conversion

con·vert·er \kən-'vərt-ər\ *n* : one that converts: as **a** : the furnace used in the Bessemer process **b** *or* **con·ver·tor** \-'vərt-ər\ : a device employing mechanical rotation for changing electrical energy from one form to another; *also* : a radio device for converting one frequency to another **c** : a device for adapting a television receiver to receive channels for which it was not orig. designed **d** : a device that accepts data in one form and converts it to another <analog-digital ~>

¹con·vert·ible \kən-'vərt-ə-bəl\ *adj* **1** : capable of being converted **2** : having a top that may be lowered or removed <~ coupe> **3** : capable of being exchanged for a specified equivalent (as another currency or security) <U.S. currency is no longer ~ to gold> <a bond ~ to 12 shares of common stock> — **con·vert·ibil·i·ty** \-,vərt-ə-'bil-ət-ē\ *n* — **con·vert·ible·ness** \-'vərt-ə-bəl-nəs\ *n* — **con·vert·ibly** \-blē\ *adv*

²convertible *n* : something convertible; *esp* : a convertible automobile

con·verti·plane *or* **con·verta·plane** \kən-'vərt-ə-,plān\ *n* : an aircraft that takes off and lands like a helicopter and is convertible to a fixed-wing configuration for forward flight

con·vex \kän-'veks; 'kän-, kən-'\ *adj* [MF or L; MF *convexe,* fr. L *convexus* vaulted, concave, convex, fr. *com-* + *-vexus* (akin to OE *wōh* crooked, bent — more at PREVARICATE] **1** : curved or rounded like the exterior of a sphere or circle — used of a spherical surface or curved line viewed from without **2** : arched up : bulging out — used of that side of a curve or surface on which the tangent line or plane lies or on which normals at neighboring points diverge

con·vex·i·ty \kən-'vek-sət-ē, kän-\ *n, pl* **-ties** **1** : the quality or state of being convex **2** : a convex surface or part

con·vexo–con·cave \-,vek-(,)sō-\ *adj* **1** : CONCAVO-CONVEX **2** : having the convex side of greater curvature than the concave

con·vey \kən-'vā\ *vt* [ME *conveyen,* fr. OF *conveier* to accompany, escort, fr. (assumed) VL *conviare,* fr. L *com-* + *via* way — more at VIA] **1** *obs* : LEAD, CONDUCT **2 a** : to bear from one place to another; *esp* : to move in a continuous stream or mass **b** : to impart or communicate by statement, suggestion, gesture, or appearance **c** (1) *archaic* : STEAL (2) *obs* : to carry away secretly **d** : to transfer or deliver to another; *specif* : to transfer by a sealed writing **e** : to cause to pass from one place or person to another : TRANSMIT ***syn*** see CARRY, TRANSFER

con·vey·ance \kən-'vā-ən(t)s\ *n* **1** : the action of conveying **2** : a means or way of conveying: as **a** : an instrument by which title to property is conveyed **b** : a means of transport : VEHICLE

con·vey·anc·er \-ən-sər\ *n* : one whose business is conveyancing

con·vey·anc·ing \-ən-siŋ\ *n* : the act or business of drawing deeds, leases, or other writings for transferring the title to property

con·vey·er *or* **con·vey·or** \kən-'vā-ər\ *n* : one that conveys: as **a** : a person who transfers property **b** *usu* *conveyor* : a mechanical apparatus for carrying packages or bulk material from place to place (as by an endless moving belt or a chain of receptacles)

con·vey·or·ize \-ə-,rīz\ *vt* **-ized; -iz·ing** : to equip with a conveyor — **con·vey·or·iza·tion** \-,vā-ə-rə-'zā-shən\ *n*

¹con·vict \kən-'vikt\ *adj, archaic* : CONVICTED

²con·vict \kən-'vikt\ *vt* [ME *convicten,* fr. L *convictus,* pp. of *convincere* to refute, convict] **1** : to find or prove to be guilty **2** : to convince of error or sinfulness

³con·vict \'kän-,vikt\ *n* **1** : a person convicted of and under sentence for a crime **2** : a person serving a prison sentence usu. for a long term

con·vic·tion \kən-'vik-shən\ *n* **1** : the act or process of convicting of a crime esp. in a court of law **2 a** : the act of convincing a person of error or of compelling the admission of a truth **b** : the state of being convinced of error or compelled to admit the truth **3 a** : a strong persuasion or belief **b** : the state of being convinced ***syn*** see CERTAINTY, OPINION

con·vince \kən-'vin(t)s\ *vt* **con·vinced; con·vinc·ing** [L *convincere* to refute, convict, prove, fr. *com-* + *vincere* to conquer — more at VICTOR] **1 a** *obs* : to overcome by argument **b** *obs* : OVERPOWER, OVERCOME **2** *obs* : DEMONSTRATE, PROVE **3** : to bring by argument to assent or belief <*convinced* them to leave the country> — **con·vinc·er** *n*

con·vinc·ing \kən-'vin(t)-siŋ\ *adj* **1** : satisfying or assuring by argument or proof <a ~ test of a new product> **2** : having power to convince of the truth, rightness, or reality of something : PLAUSIBLE <told a very ~ story of his adventures> ***syn*** see VALID ***ant*** unconvincing — **con·vinc·ing·ly** \-siŋ-lē\ *adv* — **con·vinc·ing·ness** *n*

con·viv·ial \kən-'viv-yəl, -'viv-ē-əl\ *adj* [LL *convivialis,* fr. L *convivium* banquet, fr. *com-* + *vivere* to live — more at QUICK] : relating to, occupied with, or fond of feasting, drinking, and good company — **con·viv·i·al·i·ty** \-,viv-ē-'al-ət-ē\ *n* — **con·viv·ial·ly** \-'viv-yə-lē, -'viv-ē-ə-lē\ *adv*

con·vo·ca·tion \,kän-və-'kā-shən\ *n* [ME, fr. MF, fr. L *convocation-, convocatio,* fr. *convocatus,* pp. of *convocare*] **1 a** : an assembly of persons convoked **b** (1) : an assembly of bishops and representative clergy of the Church of England (2) : a consultative assembly of clergy and lay delegates from one part of an Episcopal diocese; *also* : a territorial division of an Episcopal diocese **c** : a ceremonial assembly of members of a college or university **2** : the act or process of convoking — **con·vo·ca·tion·al** \-shnəl, -shən-ᵊl\ *adj*

con·voke \kən-'vōk\ *vt* **con·voked; con·vok·ing** [MF *convoquer,* fr. L *convocare,* fr. *com-* + *vocare* to call — more at VOICE] : to call together to a meeting ***syn*** see SUMMON ***ant*** prorogue, dissolve

¹con·vo·lute \'kän-və-,lüt\ *vb* **-lut·ed; -lut·ing** [L *convolutus,* pp. of *convolvere*] : TWIST, COIL

²convolute *adj* : rolled or wound together with one part upon another : COILED <a ~ shell> — **con·vo·lute·ly** *adv*

con·vo·lut·ed *adj* **1** : folded in curved or tortuous windings; *specif* : having convolutions **2** : INVOLVED, INTRICATE

convoluted tubule *n* **1** : PROXIMAL CONVOLUTED TUBULE **2** : DISTAL CONVOLUTED TUBULE

con·vo·lu·tion \,kän-və-'lü-shən\ *n* **1** : one of the irregular ridges on the surface of the brain and esp. of the cerebrum of higher mammals **2** : a convoluted form or structure — **con·vo·lu·tion·al** \-shnəl, -shən-ᵊl\ *adj*

con·volve \kən-'välv, -'vȯlv\ *vb* **con·volved; con·volv·ing** [L *convolvere,* fr. *com-* + *volvere* to roll — more at VOLUBLE] *vt* : to roll together : WRITHE ~ *vi* : to roll together or circulate involvedly

con·vol·vu·lus \kən-'väl-vyə-ləs, -'vȯl-\ *n, pl* **-lus·es** *or* **-li** \-,lī, -,lē\ [NL, fr. L *convolvere* to roll together, roll up] : any of a genus (*Convolvulus*) of erect, trailing, or twining herbs and shrubs of the morning-glory family

¹con·voy \'kän-,vȯi, kən-'\ *vt* [ME *convoyen,* fr. MF *conveier, convoier* — more at CONVEY] : ACCOMPANY, GUIDE; *esp* : to escort for protection

²con·voy \'kän-,vȯi\ *n* **1** : one that convoys; *esp* : a protective escort (as for ships) **2** : the act of convoying **3** : a group convoyed or organized for convenience or protection in moving

con·vul·sant \kən-'vəl-sənt\ *adj* : causing convulsions : CONVULSIVE 1 — **convulsant** *n*

con·vulse \kən-'vəls\ *vt* **con·vulsed; con·vuls·ing** [L *convulsus,* pp. of *convellere* to pluck up, convulse, fr. *com-* + *vellere* to pluck — more at VULNERABLE] : to shake or agitate violently; *esp* : to shake with or as if with irregular spasms ***syn*** see SHAKE

con·vul·sion \kən-'vəl-shən\ *n* **1** : an abnormal violent and involuntary contraction or series of contractions of the muscles **2 a** : a violent disturbance **b** : an uncontrolled fit : PAROXYSM — **con·vul·sion·ary** \-shə-,ner-ē\ *adj*

con·vul·sive \kən-'vəl-siv\ *adj* **1** : constituting or producing a convulsion **2** : attended or affected with convulsions ***syn*** see FITFUL — **con·vul·sive·ly** *adv* — **con·vul·sive·ness** *n*

cony *var of* CONEY

coo \'kü\ *vi* [imit.] **1** : to make the low soft cry of a dove or pigeon or a similar sound **2** : to talk fondly, amorously, or appreciatively <an album that will be ~*ed* over by condescending classical music critics —Ellen Sander> — **coo** *n*

¹cook \'ku̇k\ *n* [ME, fr. OE *cōc;* akin to OHG *koch;* both fr. a prehistoric WGmc word borrowed fr. L *coquus,* fr. *coquere* to cook; akin to OE *āfigen* fried, Gk *pessein* to cook] **1** : one who prepares food for eating **2** : a technical or industrial process comparable to cooking food; *also* : a substance so processed

²cook *vi* **1** : to prepare food for eating **2** : to undergo the action of being cooked <the rice is ~*ing* now> **3** : OCCUR, HAPPEN <find out what was ~*ing* in the committee> ~ *vt* **1** : CONCOCT, IMPROVISE — usu. used with *up* <~*ed* up a scheme> **2** : to prepare for eating by a heating process **3** : FALSIFY, DOCTOR <an old hand at company manipulation, he prepares to ~ the books —*Punch*> **4** : to subject to the action of heat or fire — **cook one's goose** : to ruin (one) irretrievably

cook·book \-,bu̇k\ *n* : a book of cooking directions and recipes; *broadly* : a book of detailed instructions

cook cheese *n* : a soft unripened cheese made from curd that has been heated to the consistency of honey and poured into containers

cooked cheese \'ku̇k-'chēz\ *n* : COOK CHEESE

cook·er \'ku̇k-ər\ *n* : one that cooks: as **a** : a utensil, device, or apparatus for cooking **b** : one who tends a cooking process : COOK **c** *Brit* : STOVE

cook·ery \'ku̇k-(ə-)rē\ *n, pl* **-er·ies** **1** : the art or practice of cooking **2** : an establishment for cooking

cookery book *n, chiefly Brit* : COOKBOOK

cook·ie *or* **cooky** \'ku̇k-ē\ *n, pl* **cook·ies** [D *koekje,* dim. of *koek* cake] **1** : any of various small sweet flat or slightly raised cakes **2 a** : an attractive woman <a buxom French ~ who haunts the . . . colony's one night spot —*Newsweek*> **b** : PERSON, GUY <a very tough ~ indeed, who can break a man's wrist without a quiver of distaste —John Crosby>

cookie sheet *n* : a flat rectangle of metal with at least one rolled edge used esp. for the baking of cookies or biscuits

cook·ing *adj* : suitable for or used in cooking <~ apples> <~ sherry> <~ utensils>

cooking top *n* : a built-in cabinet-top cooking apparatus consisting usu. of four heating units for gas or electricity

cook off *vi, of a cartridge* : to fire as a result of being allowed to rest in the chamber of an overheated weapon

cook·out \'ku̇k-,au̇t\ *n* : an outing at which a meal is cooked and served in the open; *also* : the meal cooked

cook·shack \-,shak\ *n* : a shack used for cooking

cook·shop \-,shäp\ *n* : a shop supplying or serving cooked food

Cook's tour \'ku̇ks-\ *n* [Thomas *Cook* & Son, E travel agency] : a quick tour in which attractions are viewed briefly and cursorily

cook·ware \'ku̇k-,wa(ə)r, -,we(ə)r\ *n* : utensils used in cooking

¹cool \'kül\ *adj* [ME *col,* fr. OE *cōl;* akin to OHG *kuoli* cool, OE *ceald* cold] **1** : moderately cold : lacking in warmth <warm days and ~ nights> **2 a** : marked by steady dispassionate calmness and self-control <a ~ and calculating administrator —*Current Biog.*> **b** : lacking ardor or friendliness <the ~, impersonal manner of some of the bright young men . . . who administer the antipoverty programs —J. C. Cort> **c** (1) : marked by restrained emotion or excitement <~ jazz> (2) : free from racial tensions or violence <meeting with minority groups in an attempt to keep the city ~> **3** — used as an intensive <a ~ million dollars> **4** : marked by deliberate effrontery or lack of due respect or discretion <a ~ reply> **5** : facilitating or suggesting relief from heat <a ~ dress> **6 a** *of a color* : producing an impression of being cool; *specif* : of a hue in the range violet through blue to green **b** *of a musical tone* : relatively lacking in timbre or resonance **7** *slang* : very good : EXCELLENT **8** : employing understatement and a minimum of detail to convey information and usu. requiring the listener, viewer, or reader to complete the message <another indication of the very ~ . . . character of this medium —H. M. McLuhan> — **cool·ish** \'kü-lish\ *adj* — **cool·ly** *also* **cooly** \-'kül-(l)ē\ *adv* — **cool·ness** \'kül-nəs\ *n*

syn COOL, COMPOSED, COLLECTED, UNRUFFLED, IMPERTURBABLE, NONCHALANT *shared meaning element* : actually or apparently free from agitation or excitement ***ant*** ardent, agitated

2**cool** *vi* **1** : to become cool : lose heat or warmth <placed the pie in the window to ~> — sometimes used with *off* or *down* **2** : to lose ardor or passion <his anger ~*ed*> ~ *vt* **1** : to make cool : impart a feeling of coolness to <~*ed* the room with a fan> — often used with *off* or *down* <a swim ~*ed* us off a little> **2 a** : to moderate the heat, excitement, or force of : CALM <~*ed* her growing anger> **b** : to slow or lessen the growth or activity of — usu. used with *off* or *down* <wants to ~ off the economy without freezing it —*Newsweek*> — **cool it** : to calm down : go easy <the word went out to the young to *cool it* — W. M. Young> — **cool one's heels** : to wait or be kept waiting for a long time esp. from or as if from disdain or discourtesy

3**cool** *n* **1** : a cool time, place, or situation <the ~ of the evening> **2 a** : a lack of excitement or enthusiasm : INDIFFERENCE <wears her ~ like perfume, without a . . . single expression to disturb her aristocratic unconcern —Hubert Saal> **b** : SELF-ASSURANCE, SOPHISTICATION <girls, from 9 to 12, who are only beginning to awaken to the world around and have not yet developed any ~ about themselves —J. K. Sale & Ben Apfelbaum> **3** : POISE, COMPOSURE <press questions . . . seemed to rattle him and he lost his ~ —*New Republic*>

4**cool** *adv* : in a casual and nonchalant manner <they learn to play it ~, not really involve themselves —Marilyn B. Noble>

cool·ant \'kü-lənt\ *n* : a usu. fluid cooling agent

cool·er \'kü-lər\ *n* **1** : one that cools: as **a** : a container for cooling liquids **b** : REFRIGERATOR **2** : LOCK-UP, JAIL; *esp* : a cell for violent or unmanageable prisoners **3** : an iced drink usu. with an alcoholic beverage as base

Coo·ley's anemia \ˌkü-lēz-\ *n* [Thomas B. *Cooley* †1945 Amer pediatrician] : THALASSEMIA

cool·head·ed \'kül-'hed-əd\ *adj* : free from passion : not easily excited : LEVELHEADED

coo·lie \'kü-lē\ *n* [Hindi *kulī*] : an unskilled laborer or porter usu. in or from the Far East hired for low or subsistence wages

coolie hat *n* : a conical-shaped usu. straw hat worn esp. to protect the head from the heat of the sun

cool·ing-off \ˌkü-liŋ-'ȯf\ *adj* : designed to allow passions to cool or to permit negotiation between parties <a ~ period>

coombe *or* **coomb** \'küm\ *var of* COMBE

coon \'kün\ *n* : RACCOON

coon·can \'kün-ˌkan\ *n* [by folk etymology fr. MexSp *conquián* conquian, fr. Sp *¿con quién?* with whom?] : a game of rummy played with two packs including two jokers

coon cat *n, chiefly NewEng* : ANGORA CAT

coon cheese \'kün-\ *n* [prob. fr. *coon* (Negro), fr. *coon* (raccoon)] : a sharp cheddar cheese that has been cured at higher than usual temperature and humidity and that is usu. coated with black wax

coon·hound \'kün-ˌhau̇nd\ *n* : a sporting dog trained to hunt raccoons; *esp* : BLACK AND TAN COONHOUND

coon's age *n* : a long while <best fried chicken I've tasted for a *coon's age* —Sinclair Lewis>

coon·skin \'kün-ˌskin\ *n* **1** : the skin or pelt of the raccoon **2** : an article (as a cap or coat) made of coonskin

coon·tie \'künt-ē\ *n* [Seminole *kunti* coontie flour] : any of several tropical American woody plants (genus *Zamia*) of the cycad family whose roots and stems yield a starchy foodstuff — called also *arrowroot*

1**coop** \'küp, 'ku̇p\ *n* [ME *cupe*; akin to OE *cȳpe* basket, *cot* cot] **1** : a cage or small enclosure (as for poultry); *also* : a small building for housing poultry **2 a** : a confined area **b** : JAIL

2**coop** *vt* **1** : to confine in a restricted and often crowded area — usu. used with *up* **2** : to place or keep in a coop : PEN — often used with *up*

co–op \'kō-ˌäp, kō-'; 'küp\ *n* : COOPERATIVE

1**coo·per** \'kü-pər, 'ku̇p-ər\ *n* [ME *couper, cowper*, fr. MD *cūper* (fr. *cūpe* cask) or MLG *kūper*, fr. *kūpe* cask; MD *cūpe* & MLG *kūpe*, fr. L *cupa*; akin to Gk *kypellon* cup — more at HIVE] : one that makes or repairs wooden casks or tubs

2**cooper** *vb* **coo·pered; coo·per·ing** \'kü-p(ə-)riŋ, 'ku̇p-(ə-)riŋ\ *vt* : to work as a cooper on ~ *vi* : to work at or do coopering

coo·per·age \'kü-p(ə-)rij, 'ku̇p-(ə-)\ *n* **1** : a cooper's place of business **2** : a cooper's work or products

co·op·er·ate \kō-'äp(-ə)-ˌrāt\ *vi* [LL *cooperatus*, pp. of *cooperari*, fr. L *co-* + *operari* to work — more at OPERATE] **1** : to act or work with another or others : act together **2** : to associate with another or others for mutual benefit — **co·op·er·a·tor** \-ˌrāt-ər\ *n*

co·op·er·a·tion \(ˌ)kō-ˌäp-ə-'rā-shən\ *n* **1** : the action of cooperating : common effort **2** : association of persons for common benefit **3** : a dynamic social process in ecological aggregations (as communities or colonies) in which mutual benefits outweigh the disadvantages (as competition) of crowding — **co·op·er·a·tion·ist** \-sh(ə-)nəst\ *n*

1**co·op·er·a·tive** \kō-'äp-(ə-)rət-iv, -'äp-ə-ˌrāt-\ *adj* **1 a** : marked by cooperation <~ efforts> **b** : marked by a willingness and ability to work with others <~ neighbors> **2** : of, relating to, or organized as a cooperative **3** : relating to or comprising a program of combined usu. liberal arts and technical studies at different schools — **co·op·er·a·tive·ly** *adv* — **co·op·er·a·tive·ness** *n*

2**cooperative** *n* : an enterprise or organization owned by and operated for the benefit of those using its services

co–opt \kō-'äpt\ *vt* [L *cooptare*, fr. *co-* + *optare* to choose] **1 a** : to choose or elect as a member **b** : to appoint as a colleague or assistant **2 a** : to take into a group (as a faction, movement, or culture) : ABSORB, ASSIMILATE <the students are ~*ed* by a system they serve even in their struggle against it —A. C. Danto> **b** : to take over : APPROPRIATE — **co–op·ta·tion** \ˌkō-ˌäp-'tā-shən\ *n* — **co–op·ta·tive** \kō-'äp-tət-iv\ *adj* — **co–op·tion** \-'äp-shən\ *n* — **co–op·tive** \-'äp-tiv\ *adj*

1**co·or·di·nate** \kō-'ȯrd-nət, -ᵊn-ət, -ᵊn-ˌāt\ *adj* [back-formation fr. *coordination*] **1 a** : equal in rank, quality, or significance **b** : being of equal rank in a sentence <~ clauses> **2** : relating to or marked by coordination **3 a** : being a university that awards degrees to men and women taught usu. by the same faculty but attending separate classes often on separate campuses **b** : being one of the colleges and esp. the women's branch of a coordinate university **4** : of, relating to, or being a system of indexing by two or more terms so that documents may be retrieved through the intersection of index terms — **co·or·di·nate·ly** *adv* — **co·or·di·nate·ness** *n*

2**coordinate** *n* **1** : one who is of equal rank, authority, or importance with another **2 a** : any of a set of numbers used in specifying the location of a point on a line, on a surface, or in space **b** : any one of a set of variables used in specifying the state of a substance or the motion of a particle or momentum **3** *pl* : articles (as of clothing or furniture) designed to be used together and to attain their effect through pleasing contrast (as of color, material, or texture)

3**co·or·di·nate** \kō-'ȯrd-ᵊn-ˌāt\ *vb* **-nat·ed; -nat·ing** [back-formation fr. *coordination*] *vt* **1** : to put in the same order or rank **2** : to bring into a common action, movement, or condition : HARMONIZE **3** : to attach so as to form a coordination complex ~ *vi* **1** : to be or become coordinate esp. so as to act together in a smooth concerted way **2** : to combine by means of a coordinate bond — **co·or·di·na·tive** \kō-'ȯrd-nət-iv, -ᵊn-ət-, -ᵊn-ˌāt-\ *adj* — **co·or·di·na·tor** \-ᵊn-ˌāt-ər\ *n*

coordinate bond *n* : a covalent bond held to consist of a pair of electrons supplied by only one of the two atoms it joins

co·or·di·nat·ed \-ᵊn-ˌāt-əd\ *adj* : able to use more than one set of muscle movements to a single end <a well-*coordinated* athlete>

coordinate geometry *n* : ANALYTIC GEOMETRY

coordinating conjunction *n* : a conjunction that joins together words or word groups of equal grammatical rank

co·or·di·na·tion \(ˌ)kō-ˌȯrd-ᵊn-'ā-shən\ *n* [F or LL; F, fr. LL *coordination-, coordinatio*, fr. L *co-* + *ordination-, ordinatio* arrangement] **1** : the act or action of coordinating **2** : the state of being coordinate or coordinated

coordination complex *n* : a compound or ion with a central usu. metallic atom or ion combined by coordinate bonds with a definite number of surrounding ions, groups, or molecules

coot \'küt\ *n* [ME *coote*; akin to D *koet* coot] **1** : any of various sluggish slow-flying slaty-black birds (genus *Fulica*) of the rail family that somewhat resemble ducks and have lobed toes and the upper mandible prolonged on the forehead as a horny frontal shield **2** : any of several No. American scoters **3** : a harmless simple person; *broadly* : FELLOW <not a bad ~ when you get him on the cricket field —Rex Ingamells>

coo·tie \'küt-ē\ *n* [perh. modif. of Malay *kutu*] : BODY LOUSE

1**cop** \'käp\ *n* [ME, fr. OE *copp*] **1** *dial chiefly Eng* : TOP, CREST **2** : a cylindrical or conical mass of thread, yarn, or roving wound on a quill or tube; *also* : a quill or tube upon which it is wound

2**cop** *vt* **copped; cop·ping** [perh. fr. D *kapen* to steal, fr. Fris *kāpia* to take away; akin to OHG *kouf* trade — more at CHEAP] **1** *slang* : to get hold of : CATCH, CAPTURE; *also* : PURCHASE **2** *slang* : STEAL, SWIPE — **cop a plea** : to plead guilty to a lesser charge in order to avoid standing trial for a more serious one; *broadly* : to admit fault and plead for mercy

3**cop** *n* [short for 3*copper*] : POLICEMAN

4**cop** *abbr* **1** copper **2** copulative **3** copy **4** copyright

Cop *abbr* Coptic

co·pa·ce·tic *or* **co·pe·se·tic** \ˌkō-pə-'set-ik, -'sēt-\ *adj* [origin unknown] : very satisfactory

co·pai·ba \kō-'pī-bə, -'pā-; ˌkō-pə-'ē-bə\ *n* [Sp & Pg; Sp, fr. Pg *copaíba*, of Tupian origin; akin to Guarani *cupaiba* copaiba] : a stimulant oleoresin obtained from several pinnate-leaved So. American leguminous trees (genus *Copaifera*); *also* : one of these trees

co·pal \'kō-pəl, -ˌpal; kō-'pal\ *n* [Sp, fr. Nahuatl *copalli* resin] : a recent or fossil resin from various tropical trees

co·par·ce·nary \kō-'pärs-ᵊn-ˌer-ē\ *n, pl* **-nar·ies** **1** : joint heirship **2** : joint ownership

co·par·ce·ner \-'pärs-nər, -ᵊn-ər\ *n* : a joint heir

co·part·ner \(')kō-'pärt-nər\ *n* : PARTNER — **co·part·ner·ship** \-ˌship\ *n*

1**cope** \'kōp\ *n* [ME, fr. OE *-cāp*, fr. LL *cappa* head covering] **1** : a long enveloping ecclesiastical vestment **2 a** : something resembling a cope (as by concealing or covering) <the dark sky's starry ~ —P. B. Shelley> **b** : COPING

2**cope** *vt* **coped; cop·ing** : to cover or furnish with a cope or coping

3**cope** *vb* **coped; cop·ing** [ME *copen*, fr. MF *couper* to strike, cut, fr. OF, fr. *coup* blow, fr. LL *colpus*, alter. of L *colaphus*, fr. Gk *kolaphos* buffet] *vi* **1** *obs* : STRIKE, FIGHT **2 a** : to maintain a contest or combat usu. on even terms or with success — used with *with* **b** : to deal with and attempt to overcome problems and difficulties — usu. used with *with* **3** *archaic* : MEET, ENCOUNTER ~ *vt* **1** *obs* : to meet in combat **2** *obs* : to come in contact with **3** *obs* : MATCH

4**cope** *vt* **coped; cop·ing** [prob. fr. F *couper* to cut] **1** : NOTCH **2** : to shape (a structural member) to fit a coping or conform to the shape of another member

copeck *var of* KOPECK

copemate *or* **copesmate** *n* [3*cope* + *mate*] **1** *obs* : ANTAGONIST **2** *obs* : PARTNER, COMRADE

co·pen \'kō-pən\ *n* [short for *copenhagen blue*, fr. *Copenhagen*, Denmark] : a variable color averaging a moderate blue — called also *copen blue*

co·pe·pod \ˈkō-pə-ˌpäd\ *n* [deriv. of Gk *kōpē* oar + *pod-, pous* foot] : any of a large subclass (Copepoda) of usu. minute freshwater and marine crustaceans — **copepod** *adj*

cop·er \ˈkō-pər\ *n* [E dial. *cope* (to trade)] *Brit* : a horse dealer; *esp* : a dishonest one

Co·per·ni·can \kō-ˈpər-ni-kən\ *adj* **1** : of or relating to Copernicus or the belief that the earth rotates daily on its axis and the planets revolve in orbits around the sun **2** : of radical or major importance or degree <effected a ~ revolution in philosophy —*Times Lit. Supp.*> — **Copernican** *n* — **Co·per·ni·can·ism** \-kə-ˌniz-əm\ *n*

cope·stone \ˈkōp-ˌstōn\ *n* **1** : a stone forming a coping **2** : a finishing touch : CROWN

copi·er \ˈkäp-ē-ər\ *n* : one that copies; *specif* : a machine for making copies of graphic matter (as printing, drawings, or pictures)

co·pi·hue \kō-ˈpē-(ˌ)wā\ *n* [AmerSp, fr. Araucan *copiu*] : a showy climbing vine (*Lapageria rosea*) with deep rosy red trumpet-shaped flowers and oval edible yellowish fruits that is the national flower of Chile — called also *Chile-bells*

co·pi·lot \ˈkō-ˌpī-lət\ *n* : a qualified pilot who assists or relieves the pilot but is not in command

cop·ing \ˈkō-piŋ\ *n* : the covering course of a wall usu. with a sloping top

cop·ing saw \ˈkō-piŋ-\ *n* [fr. prp. of [4]*cope*] : a saw of ribbon shape under tension in a U-shaped frame for use in cutting intricate patterns in wood

cop·ing·stone \ˈkō-piŋ-ˌstōn\ *n, chiefly Brit* : COPESTONE

co·pi·ous \ˈkō-pē-əs\ *adj* [ME, fr. L *copiosus,* fr. *copia* abundance, fr. *co-* + *ops* wealth — more at OPULENT] **1** : yielding something abundantly <a ~ harvest> <~ springs> **2 a** : full of thought, information, or matter **b** : profuse or exuberant in words, expression, or style <she was evidently a ~ talker, and now poured forth a breathless stream of anecdote and comment —W. S. Maugham> **3** : present in large quantity : taking place on a large scale <~ rainfall> <~ eating and still more ~ drinking —Aldous Huxley> ***syn*** see PLENTIFUL ***ant*** meager — **co·pi·ous·ly** *adv* — **co·pi·ous·ness** *n*

co·pla·nar \(ˈ)kō-ˈplā-nər, -ˌnär\ *adj* : lying or acting in the same plane — **co·pla·nar·i·ty** \ˌkō-plā-ˈnar-ət-ē\ *n*

co·pol·y·mer \(ˈ)kō-ˈpäl-ə-mər\ *n* : a product of copolymerization — **co·pol·y·mer·ic** \ˌkō-ˌpäl-ə-ˈmer-ik\ *adj*

co·po·ly·mer·ize \ˌkō-pə-ˈlim-ə-ˌrīz, (ˈ)kō-ˈpäl-ə-mə-\ *vb* : to polymerize (as two different monomers) together — **co·po·ly·mer·iza·tion** \ˌkō-pə-ˌlim-ə-rə-ˈzā-shən, ˌkō-ˌpäl-ə-mə-\ *n*

cop–out \ˈkäp-ˌau̇t\ *n* **1** : an excuse for copping out : PRETEXT **2** : the means for copping out **3** : one who cops out **4** : the act or an instance of copping out

cop out \(ˈ)käp-ˈau̇t\ *vi* : to back out (as of an unwanted responsibility) — often used with *on* or *of* <young Americans who *cop out* on society —*Christian Science Monitor*> <*copping out* of jury duty through a variety of machinations —H. F. Waters>

[1]**cop·per** \ˈkäp-ər\ *n, often attrib* [ME *coper,* fr. OE; akin to OHG *kupfar* copper; both fr. a prehistoric WGmc-NGmc word borrowed fr. LL *cuprum* copper, fr. L (*aes*) *Cyprium,* lit., Cyprian metal] **1** : a common reddish metallic element that is ductile and malleable and one of the best conductors of heat and electricity — see ELEMENT table **2** : a coin or token made of copper or bronze **3** *chiefly Brit* : a large boiler (as for cooking) **4** : any of various small butterflies (family Lycaenidae) with usu. copper-colored wings — **cop·pery** \ˈkäp-(ə-)rē\ *adj*

[2]**copper** *vt* **cop·pered; cop·per·ing** \ˈkäp-(ə-)riŋ\ **1** : to coat or sheathe with or as if with copper **2 a** : to bet against (as in faro) **b** : HEDGE

[3]**copper** *n* [[2]*cop*] : POLICEMAN

cop·per·as \ˈkäp-(ə-)rəs\ *n* [alter. of ME *coperose,* fr. MF, fr. (assumed) VL *cuprirosa,* fr. LL *cuprum* + L *rosa* rose] : a green hydrated ferrous sulfate $FeSO_4 \cdot 7H_2O$ used esp. in making inks and pigments

cop·per·head \ˈkäp-ər-ˌhed\ *n* **1** : a common largely coppery brown pit viper (*Agkistrodon contortrix*) found esp. in uplands of the eastern U.S. **2** : a person in the northern states who sympathized with the South during the Civil War

cop·per·plate \ˌkäp-ər-ˈplāt\ *n* : an engraved or etched copper printing plate; *also* : a print made from such a plate

copper pyrites *n* : CHALCOPYRITE

cop·per·smith \ˈkäp-ər-ˌsmith\ *n* : a worker in copper

copper sulfate *n* : a sulfate of copper; *esp* : the normal sulfate that is white in the anhydrous form but blue in the crystalline hydrous form $CuSO_4 \cdot 5H_2O$ and that is often used as an algicide and fungicide

cop·pice \ˈkäp-əs\ *n* [MF *copeiz,* fr. *couper* to cut — more at COPE] **1** : a thicket, grove, or growth of small trees **2** : forest originating mainly from shoots or root suckers rather than seed

copr- *or* **copro-** *comb form* [NL, fr. Gk *kopr-, kopro-,* fr. *kopros* akin to Skt *śakṛt* dung] : dung : feces <*copro*lite>

co·pra \ˈkō-prə *also* ˈkäp-rə\ *n* [Pg, fr. Malayalam *koppara*] : dried coconut meat yielding coconut oil

co·pro·duce \ˌkō-prə-ˈd(y)üs\ *vt* : to produce in cooperation with another producer — **co·pro·duc·er** *n* — **co·pro·duc·tion** \-ˈdək-shən\ *n*

co·prod·uct \(ˈ)kō-ˈpräd-(ˌ)əkt\ *n* : BY-PRODUCT 1

cop·ro·lite \ˈkäp-rə-ˌlīt\ *n* : fossil excrement — **cop·ro·lit·ic** \ˌkäp-rə-ˈlit-ik\ *adj*

co·proph·a·gous \kä-ˈpräf-ə-gəs\ *adj* [Gk *koprophagos,* fr. *kopr-* + *-phagos* -phagous] : feeding on dung — **co·proph·a·gy** \-ə-jē\ *n*

cop·ro·phil·ia \ˌkäp-rə-ˈfil-ē-ə\ *n* [NL] : marked interest in excrement; *esp* : the use of feces or filth for sexual excitement — **cop·ro·phil·i·ac** \-ē-ˌak\ *n*

co·proph·i·lous \kä-ˈpräf-ə-ləs\ *adj* : growing or living on dung <~ fungi>

copse \ˈkäps\ *n* [by alter.] : COPPICE 1

[1]**Copt** \ˈkäpt\ *n* [Ar *qubṭ* Copts, fr. Coptic *gyptios* Egyptian, fr. Gk *aigyptios*] **1** : a member of a people descended from the ancient Egyptians **2** : a member of the traditional Monophysite Christian church originating and centering in Egypt

[2]**Copt** *abbr* Coptic

cop·ter \ˈkäp-tər\ *n* : HELICOPTER

[1]**Cop·tic** \ˈkäp-tik\ *adj* : of or relating to the Copts, their liturgical language, or their church

[2]**Coptic** *n* : an Afro-Asiatic language descended from ancient Egyptian and used as the liturgical language of the Coptic church

co–pub·lish \(ˈ)kō-ˈpəb-lish\ *vt* : to publish in cooperation with another publisher — **co–pub·lish·er** *n*

cop·u·la \ˈkäp-yə-lə\ *n* [L, bond] : something that connects: as **a** : the connecting link between subject and predicate of a proposition **b** : a word or expression (as a form of *be, become, feel,* or *seem*) that links a subject with its predicate

cop·u·late \ˈkäp-yə-ˌlāt\ *vi* **-lat·ed; -lat·ing** [L *copulatus,* pp. of *copulare* to join, fr. *copula*] **1** : to engage in sexual intercourse **2** *of gametes* : to fuse permanently — **cop·u·la·tion** \ˌkäp-yə-ˈlā-shən\ *n* — **cop·u·la·to·ry** \ˈkäp-yə-lə-ˌtōr-ē, -ˌtȯr-\ *adj*

[1]**cop·u·la·tive** \ˈkäp-yə-ˌlāt-iv\ *adj* **1 a** : joining together coordinate words or word groups and expressing addition of their meanings <a ~ conjunction> **b** : functioning as a copula **2** : relating to or serving for copulation **3** : of or relating to coupling of chemical compounds or radicals — **cop·u·la·tive·ly** *adv*

[2]**copulative** *n* : a copulative word

[1]**copy** \ˈkäp-ē\ *n, pl* **cop·ies** [ME *copie,* fr. MF, fr. ML *copia,* fr. L, abundance — more at COPIOUS] **1** : an imitation, transcript, or reproduction of an original work (as a letter, a painting, a piece of furniture, or a dress) **2** : one of a series of esp. mechanical reproductions of an original impression; *also* : an individual example of such a reproduction <a presentation ~> **3** *archaic* : something to be imitated : MODEL **4 a** : matter to be set up for printing or photoengraving **b** : something considered printable or newsworthy — used in the singular and without an article <at the mercy of newsmen . . . who found anything she did to be good ~ —*Current Biog.*>

[2]**copy** *vb* **cop·ied; copy·ing** *vt* **1** : to make a copy of **2** : to model oneself on ~ *vi* **1** : to make a copy **2** : to undergo copying <the document did not ~ well>

syn COPY, IMITATE, MIMIC, APE, MOCK *shared meaning element* : to make something so that it resembles an existing thing ***ant*** originate

copy·book \ˈkäp-ē-ˌbu̇k\ *n* : a book formerly used in teaching penmanship and containing models for imitation

copy·boy \-ˌbȯi\ *n* : one who carries copy and runs errands

[1]**copy·cat** \-ˌkat\ *n* : one who slavishly imitates or adopts the behavior or practices of another

[2]**copycat** *vb* **copy·cat·ted; copy·cat·ting** *vi* : to act as a copycat ~ *vt* : IMITATE

copy·desk \-ˌdesk\ *n* : the desk at which newspaper copy is edited

copy editor *n* **1** : COPYREADER **2 a** : an editor who prepares copy for the printer **b** : an editor in charge of a copydesk and the copyreaders on a newspaper

copy·hold \ˈkäp-ē-ˌhōld\ *n* **1** : a former tenure of land in England and Ireland by right of being recorded in the court of the manor **2** : an estate held by copyhold

copy·hold·er \-ˌhōl-dər\ *n* **1** : a device for holding copy esp. for a typesetter **2** : one who reads copy for a proofreader

copy·ist \ˈkäp-ē-əst\ *n* **1** : one who makes copies **2** : IMITATOR

copy·read·er \-ˌrēd-ər\ *n* : a publishing-house editor who reads and corrects manuscript copy; *also* : one who edits and headlines newspaper copy

[1]**copy·right** \-ˌrīt\ *n* : the exclusive legal right to reproduce, publish, and sell the matter and form of a literary, musical, or artistic work — **copyright** *adj*

[2]**copyright** *vt* : to secure a copyright on

copy·writ·er \ˈkäp-ē-ˌrīt-ər\ *n* : a writer of advertising or publicity copy

[1]**co·quet** *n* [F, dim. of *coq* cock] **1** \kō-ˈket, -ˈkā\ *obs* : a man who indulges in coquetry **2** \-ˈket\ : COQUETTE

[2]**co·quet** \kō-ˈket\ *adj* : COQUETTISH

[3]**co·quet** *or* **co·quette** \-ˈket\ *vi* **co·quet·ted; co·quet·ting** **1** : to play the coquette : FLIRT **2** : to deal with something playfully rather than seriously ***syn*** see TRIFLE

co·que·try \ˈkō-kə-trē, kō-ˈke-trē\ *n, pl* **-tries** : a flirtatious act or attitude

co·quette \kō-ˈket\ *n* [F, fem. of *coquet*] : a woman who endeavors without sincere affection to gain the attention and admiration of men

co·quett·ish \kō-ˈket-ish\ *adj* : having the air or nature of a coquette or of coquetry — **co·quett·ish·ly** *adv* — **co·quett·ish·ness** *n*

co·quil·la nut \kō-ˌkē-(y)ə-, -ˌkēl-yə-\ *n* [Pg *coquilho,* dim. of *côco* coconut] : the nut of a piassava palm (*Attalea funifera*) of Brazil having a hard brown shell much used by turners

co·qui·na \kō-ˈkē-nə\ *n* [Sp, prob. irreg. dim. of *concha* shell] **1** : a small marine clam (genus *Donax*) used for broth or chowder **2** : a soft whitish limestone formed of broken shells and corals cemented together and used for building

[1]**cor** *abbr* **1** corner **2** coroner **3** corpus

[2]**cor** *or* **corr** *abbr* **1** correct; corrected; correction **2** correspondence; correspondent; corresponding **3** corrupt; corruption

Cor *abbr* Corinthians

co·rac·ii·form \kə-ˈras-ē-ə-ˌfȯrm\ *adj* [deriv. of Gk *korak-, korax* raven + L *forma* form — more at RAVEN] : of or relating to an order (Coraciiformes) of arboreal nonpasserine birds including the rollers, kingfishers, and hornbills

cor·a·cle \'kȯr-ə-kəl, 'kär-\ *n* [W *corwgl*] **1 :** a small boat made by covering a wicker frame with hide or leather and used by the ancient Britons **2 :** a boat made of broad hoops covered with horsehide or tarpaulin and used in parts of the British Isles

cor·a·coid \'kȯr-ə-ˌkȯid, 'kär-\ *adj* [NL *coracoides,* fr. Gk *korakoeidēs,* lit., like a raven, fr. *korak-, korax*] **:** of, relating to, or being a process or cartilage bone of many vertebrates that extends from the scapula to or toward the sternum — **coracoid** *n*

cor·al \'kȯr-əl, 'kär-\ *n* [ME, fr. MF, fr. L *corallium,* fr. Gk *korallion*] **1 a :** the calcareous or horny skeletal deposit produced by anthozoan or rarely hydrozoan polyps; *esp* **:** a richly red precious coral secreted by a gorgonian (*Corallium nobile*) **b :** a polyp or polyp colony together with its membranes and skeleton **2 :** a piece of coral and esp. of red coral **3 a :** a bright reddish ovary (as of a lobster or scallop) **b :** a variable color averaging a deep pink — **coral** *adj* — **cor·al·loid** \-ə-ˌlȯid\ *or* **cor·al·loi·dal** \ˌkȯr-ə-'lȯid-ᵊl, ˌkär-\ *adj*

coral 1b

cor·al·bells \'kȯr-əl-ˌbelz, 'kär-\ *n pl but sing or pl in constr* **:** a perennial alumroot (*Heuchera sanguinea*) widely cultivated for its feathery spikes of tiny coral flowers

cor·al·ber·ry \-ˌber-ē\ *n* **:** an American dwarf shrub (*Symphoricarpos orbiculatus*) that bears clusters of small flowers succeeded by red berries

¹**cor·al·line** \'kȯr-ə-ˌlīn, 'kär-\ *adj* [F *corallin,* fr. LL *corallinus,* fr. L *corallium*] **:** of, relating to, or resembling coral or a coralline

²**coralline** *n* **1 :** any of a family (Corallinaceae) of calcareous red algae **2 :** a bryozoan or hydroid that resembles a coral

coral pink *n* **:** a moderate yellowish pink

coral snake *n* **1 :** any of several venomous chiefly tropical New World elapid snakes (genus *Micrurus*) brilliantly banded in red, black, and yellow or white that include two (*M. fulvius* and *M. euryxanthus*) ranging northward into the southern U.S. **2 :** any of several harmless snakes resembling the coral snakes

co·ran·to \kə-'rant-(ˌ)ō\ *n, pl* **-tos** *or* **-toes** [modif. of F *courante*] **:** COURANTE

cor·ban \'kȯ(ə)r-ˌban\ *n* [Heb *qorbān* offering] **:** a sacrifice or offering to God among the ancient Hebrews

cor·beil *or* **cor·beille** \'kȯr-bəl, kȯr-'bā\ *n* [F *corbeille,* lit., basket, fr. LL *corbicula,* dim. of *corbis* basket] **:** a sculptured basket of flowers or fruit as an architectural decoration

¹**cor·bel** \'kȯr-bəl\ *n* [ME, fr. MF, fr. dim. of *corp* raven, fr. L *corvus* — more at RAVEN] **:** an architectural member that projects from within a wall and supports a weight; *esp* **:** one that is stepped upward and outward from a vertical surface

²**corbel** *vt* **-beled** *or* **-belled; -bel·ing** *or* **-bel·ling :** to furnish with or make into a corbel

corbeling *n* **1 :** corbel work **2 :** the construction of a corbel

cor·bic·u·la \kȯr-'bik-yə-lə\ *n, pl* **-lae** \-(ˌ)lē, -ˌlī\ [LL, basket] **:** POLLEN BASKET

cor·bie \'kȯr-bē\ *n* [ME, modif. of OF *corbin,* fr. L *corvinus* of a raven] *chiefly Scot* **:** a carrion crow; *also* **:** RAVEN

corbie gable *n* **:** a gable having corbiesteps

cor·bie·step \'kȯr-bē-ˌstep\ *n* **:** one of a series of steps terminating the upper part of a gable wall

cor·bi·na \kȯr-'bē-nə\ *n* [MexSp, fr. Sp, an acanthopterygian fish, fr. fem. of *corvino* of a raven, fr. L *corvinus*] **:** any of several American marine fishes; *esp* **:** a spotted whiting (*Menticirrhus undulatus*) favored by surf casters along the California coast

¹**cord** \'kȯ(ə)rd\ *n* [ME, fr. OF *corde,* fr. L *chorda* string, fr. Gk *chordē* — more at YARN] **1 a :** a long slender flexible material usu. consisting of several strands (as of thread or yarn) woven or twisted together **b :** the hangman's rope **2 :** a moral, spiritual, or emotional bond **3 a :** an anatomical structure (as a nerve) resembling a cord **b :** a small flexible insulated electrical cable having a plug at one or both ends used to connect a lamp or other appliance with a receptacle **4 :** a unit of wood cut for fuel equal to a stack 4x4x8 feet or 128 cubic feet **5 a :** a rib like a cord on a textile **b** (1) **:** a fabric made with such ribs or a garment made of such a fabric (2) *pl* **:** trousers made of such a fabric

²**cord** *vt* **1 :** to furnish, bind, or connect with a cord **2 :** to pile up (wood) in cords — **cord·er** *n*

cord·age \'kȯrd-ij\ *n* **1 :** ropes or cords; *esp* **:** the ropes in the rigging of a ship **2 :** the number of cords (as of wood) on a given area

cor·date \'kȯ(ə)r-ˌdāt\ *adj* [NL *cordatus,* fr. L *cord-, cor*] **:** shaped like a heart <a ~ leaf> — **cor·date·ly** *adv*

cord·ed \'kȯrd-əd\ *adj* **1 a :** made of or provided with cords or ridges; *specif* **:** muscled in ridges **b** *of a muscle* **:** TENSE, TAUT **2 :** bound, fastened, or wound about with cords **3 :** striped or ribbed with or as if with cord **:** TWILLED

¹**cor·dial** \'kȯr-jəl\ *adj* [ME, fr. ML *cordialis,* fr. L *cord-, cor* heart — more at HEART] **1** *obs* **:** of or relating to the heart **:** VITAL **2 :** tending to revive, cheer, or invigorate **3 :** warmly and genially affable **:** HEARTFELT <she received a most ~ welcome> *syn* see GRACIOUS *ant* uncordial — **cor·dial·ly** \'kȯrj-(ə-)lē\ *adv* — **cor·dial·ness** \'kȯr-jəl-nəs\ *n*

²**cordial** *n* **1 :** a stimulating medicine or drink **2 :** LIQUEUR

cor·dial·i·ty \ˌkȯr-jē-'al-ət-ē, kȯr-'jal *also* kȯrd-'yal-\ *n* **:** sincere affection and kindness **:** cordial regard

cordia pulmonalia *pl of* COR PULMONALE

cor·di·er·ite \'kȯrd-ē-ə-ˌrīt\ *n* [F, fr. Pierre L. A. *Cordier* †1861 F geologist] **:** a blue mineral $(Mg,Fe)_2Al_4Si_5O_{18}$ with vitreous luster and strong dichroism consisting of a silicate of aluminum, iron, and magnesium

cor·di·form \'kȯrd-ə-ˌfȯrm\ *adj* [F *cordiforme,* fr. L *cord-, cor* + F *-iforme* -iform] **:** shaped like a heart

cor·dil·le·ra \ˌkȯrd-ᵊl-'(y)er-ə, kȯr-'dil-ə-rə\ *n* [Sp] **:** a system of mountain ranges often consisting of a number of more or less parallel chains — **cor·dil·le·ran** \-'(y)er-ən, -ə-rən\ *adj*

cord·ite \'kȯ(ə)r-ˌdīt\ *n* **:** a smokeless powder composed of nitroglycerin, guncotton, and a petroleum substance usu. gelatinized by addition of acetone and pressed into cords resembling brown twine

cord·less \'kȯrd-ləs\ *adj* **:** having no cord; *esp* **:** powered by a battery <~ tools>

cor·do·ba \'kȯrd-ə-bə, -ə-və\ *n* [Sp *córdoba,* fr. Francisco Fernández de *Córdoba* †1526 Sp explorer] — see MONEY table

¹**cor·don** \'kȯrd-ᵊn, 'kȯ(ə)r-ˌdän\ *n* [F, dim. of *corde* cord] **1 a :** an ornamental cord used esp. on costumes **b :** a cord or ribbon worn as a badge of honor or as a decoration **c :** STRINGCOURSE **2 a :** a line of troops or of military posts enclosing an area to prevent passage **b :** a line of persons or objects around a person or place <a ~ of police>

²**cordon** *vt* **1 :** to ornament with a cordon **2 :** to form a protective or restrictive cordon around — often used with *off*

¹**cor·do·van** \'kȯrd-ə-vən\ *adj* [OSp *cordovano,* fr. *Córdova* (now *Córdoba*), Spain] **1** *cap* **:** of or relating to Córdoba and esp. Córdoba, Spain **2 :** made of cordovan leather

²**cordovan** *n* **1 :** a soft fine-grained colored leather **2 :** leather tanned from the inner layer of horsehide and characterized by nonporosity and density

¹**cor·du·roy** \'kȯrd-ə-ˌrȯi\ *n, pl* **-roys** [perh. alter. of the name *Corderoy*] **1 a :** a durable usu. cotton pile fabric with vertical ribs or wales **b** *pl* **:** trousers of corduroy **2 :** a road built of logs laid side by side transversely

²**corduroy** *vt* **-royed; -roy·ing :** to build (a road) of logs laid side by side transversely

cord·wain \'kȯ(ə)r-ˌdwān\ *n* [ME *cordwane,* fr. MF *cordoan,* fr. OSp *cordovano, cordován*] *archaic* **:** cordovan leather

cord·wain·er \-ˌdwā-nər\ *n* **1** *archaic* **:** a worker in cordovan leather **2 :** SHOEMAKER — **cord·wain·ery** \-ˌdwā-nə-rē\ *n*

cord·wood \'kȯ(ə)r-ˌdwu̇d\ *n* **:** wood piled or sold in cords; *also* **:** standing timber suitable for use as fuel

¹**core** \'kō(ə)r, 'kȯ(ə)r\ *n* [ME] **1 :** a central and often foundational part usu. distinct from the enveloping part by a difference in nature <~ of the city>: as **a :** the usu. inedible central part of some fruits (as a pineapple); *esp* **:** the papery or leathery carpels composing the ripened ovary in a pome fruit **b :** the portion of a foundry mold that shapes the interior of a hollow casting **c :** a part removed from the interior of a mass esp. to determine the interior composition or a hidden condition **d :** the central strand around which other strands twist in some ropes **e** (1) **:** a mass of iron serving to concentrate and intensify the magnetic field resulting from a current in a surrounding coil (2) **:** a tiny doughnut-shaped piece of magnetic material (as ferrite) used in computer memories — called also *magnetic core* (3) **:** a computer memory consisting of an array of cores strung on fine wires — called also *core memory, core storage* **f :** the central part of the earth having a radius of about 2100 miles and physical properties different from those of the surrounding parts **g :** a nodule of stone (as flint or obsidian) from which flakes have been struck for making implements **h :** the conducting wire with its insulation in an electric cable **i :** a layer of wood on which veneers are glued (as in making plywood) **j :** an arrangement of a course of studies that combines under certain basic topics material from subjects conventionally separated and aims to provide a common background for all students **2 a :** a basic, essential, or enduring part (as of an individual, a class, or an entity) **b :** the essential meaning **:** GIST <the ~ of the book is thus an attempt to comprehend the nature of total war — *Times Lit. Supp.*> **c :** the inmost or most intimate part <he was honest to the ~>

²**core** *vt* **cored; cor·ing :** to remove a core from — **cor·er** *n*

³**core** *n* [ME *chore* chorus, company, fr. L *chorus*] *chiefly Scot* **:** a group of people

CORE \'kō(ə)r, 'kȯ(ə)r\ *abbr* Congress of Racial Equality

co·re·cip·i·ent \ˌkō-ri-'sip-ē-ənt\ *n* **:** a joint recipient (as of an honor or a prize)

core city *n* **:** INNER CITY

co·re·late \ˌkō-ri-'lāt\ *vt* **-lat·ed; -lat·ing** [back-formation fr. *correlation*] *chiefly Brit* **:** CORRELATE — **co·re·la·tion** \-'lā-shən\ *n* — **co·rel·a·tive** \kō-'rel-ət-iv, kə-\ *adj* — **co·rel·a·tive·ly** *adv*

co·re·li·gion·ist \ˌkō-ri-'lij-(ə-)nəst\ *n* **:** one of the same religion

co·re·mi·um \kə-'rē-mē-əm\ *n, pl* **-mia** \-mē-ə\ [NL, fr. Gk *korēma* broom, fr. *korein* to sweep] **:** a fruiting body characteristic of certain imperfect fungi (as the Stilbellaceae) that consists of a sterile stalk of parallel or fascicled hyphae and a terminal head of fertile or spore-bearing branches

co·re·op·sis \ˌkōr-ē-'äp-səs, ˌkȯr-\ *n* [NL, genus name, fr. Gk *koris* bedbug + NL *-opsis;* akin to Gk *keirein* to cut — more at SHEAR] **:** any of a genus (*Coreopsis*) of composite herbs widely grown for their showy flower heads

co·re·pres·sor \ˌkō-ri-'pres-ər\ *n* **:** a substance that activates a particular genetic repressor by combining with it

co·req·ui·site \kō-'rek-wə-zət\ *n* **:** a formal course of study required to be taken simultaneously with another

co·re·spon·dent \ˌkō-ri-'spän-dənt\ *n* **:** a person named as guilty of adultery with the defendant in a divorce suit

corf \'kȯ(ə)rf\ *n, pl* **corves** \'kȯ(ə)rvz\ [ME, basket, fr. MD *corf* or MLG *korf*] *Brit* **:** a basket, tub, or truck used in a mine

cor·gi \'kȯr-gē\ *n, pl* **corgis** [W, fr. *cor* dwarf + *ci* dog; akin to OI *cū* dog, OE *hund* — more at HOUND] **:** WELSH CORGI

co·ri·a·ceous \ˌkōr-ē-'ā-shəs, ˌkȯr-\ *adj* [LL *coriaceus* — more at CUIRASS] **:** resembling leather

co·ri·an·der \'kōr-ē-ˌan-dər, ˌkōr-ē-', 'kȯr-, ˌkȯr-\ *n* [ME *coriandre,* fr. OF, fr. L *coriandrum,* fr. Gk *koriandron*] **1 :** an Old World herb (*Coriandrum sativum*) of the carrot family with aromatic fruits **2 :** the ripened dried fruit of coriander used as a flavoring — called also *coriander seed*

1Co·rin·thi·an \kə-ˈrin(t)-thē-ən\ *n* **1 :** a native or resident of Corinth, Greece **2 a :** a gay profligate man **b :** a fashionable man-about-town; *esp* **:** SPORTSMAN **c :** an amateur yachtsman
2Corinthian *adj* **1 :** of, relating to, or characteristic of Corinth or Corinthians **2 :** of or relating to the lightest and most ornate of the three Greek orders of architecture characterized esp. by its bell-shaped capital enveloped with acanthuses
Co·rin·thi·ans \-thē-ənz\ *n pl but sing in constr* **:** either of two letters written by St. Paul to the Christians of Corinth and included as books in the New Testament — see BIBLE table
Co·ri·o·lis force \ˌkōr-ē-ˈō-ləs-, ˌkȯr-, -ē-ə-ˌlēs-\ *n* [Gaspard G. *Coriolis* †1843 F civil engineer] **:** an apparent force that as a result of the earth's rotation deflects moving objects (as projectiles or air currents) to the right in the northern hemisphere and to the left in the southern hemisphere
co·ri·um \ˈkōr-ē-əm, ˈkȯr-\ *n, pl* **co·ria** \-ē-ə\ [NL, fr. L, leather — more at CUIRASS] **:** DERMIS
1cork \ˈkȯ(ə)rk\ *n* [ME, cork, bark, prob. fr. Ar *qurq,* fr. L *cortic-, cortex*] **1 a :** the elastic tough outer tissue of the cork oak that is used esp. for stoppers and insulation **b :** PHELLEM **2 :** a usu. cork stopper for a bottle or jug **3 :** an angling float
2cork *vt* **1 :** to furnish or fit with cork or a cork **2 :** to stop up with a cork **3 :** to blacken with burnt cork
cork·board \ˈkȯ(ə)rk-ˌbō(ə)rd, -ˌbȯ(ə)rd\ *n* **:** a heat-insulating material made of compressed granulated cork
cork cambium *n* **:** PHELLOGEN
cork·er \ˈkȯr-kər\ *n* **1 :** one that corks containers (as bottles) **2 :** one that is excellent or remarkable
cork·ing \ˈkȯr-kiŋ\ *adj or adv* **:** extremely fine — often used as an intensive esp. before *good* <had a ~ good time>
cork oak *n* **:** an oak (*Quercus suber*) of southern Europe and northern Africa that is the source of the cork of commerce
1cork·screw \ˈkȯrk-ˌskrü\ *n* **:** a pointed spiral piece of metal with a handle used for drawing corks from bottles
2corkscrew *vt* **1 :** WIND **2 :** to draw out with difficulty **3 :** to twist into a spiral ~ *vi* **:** to move in a winding course
3corkscrew *adj* **:** resembling a corkscrew **:** SPIRAL <the single ~ staircase that connected the two floors —G. K. Chesterton>
cork·wood \ˈkȯr-ˌkwu̇d\ *n* **:** any of several trees having light or corky wood; *esp* **:** a small or shrubby tree (*Leitneria floridana*) of the southeastern U.S. that has extremely light soft wood
corky \ˈkȯr-kē\ *adj* **cork·i·er; -est :** resembling cork
corm \ˈkȯ(ə)rm\ *n* [NL *cormus,* fr. Gk *kormos* tree trunk, fr. *keirein* to cut — more at SHEAR] **:** a rounded thick modified underground stem base bearing membranous or scaly leaves and buds and acting as a vegetative reproductive structure — compare BULB, TUBER
corm·el \ˈkȯr-məl, kȯr-ˈmel\ *n* [dim. of *corm*] **:** a small or secondary corm produced by a larger corm
cor·mo·rant \ˈkȯrm-(ə-)rənt, ˈkȯr-mə-ˌrant\ *n* [ME *cormeraunt,* fr. MF *cormorant,* fr. OF *cormareng,* fr. *corp* raven + *marenc* of the sea, fr. L *marinus*] **1 :** any of various dark-colored web-footed seabirds (family Phalacrocoracidae) that have a long neck, wedge-shaped tail, hooked bill, and a patch of bare often brightly colored distensible skin under the mouth and are used in eastern Asia for catching fish **2 :** a gluttonous, greedy, or rapacious person
1corn \ˈkȯ(ə)rn\ *n, often attrib* [ME, fr. OE; akin to OHG & ON *korn* grain, L *granum,* Gk *gēras* old age] **1** *chiefly dial* **:** a small hard particle **:** GRAIN **2 :** a small hard seed **3 a :** the seeds of a cereal grass and esp. of the important cereal crop of a particular region (as wheat in Britain, oats in Scotland and Ireland, and Indian corn in the New World and Australia) **b :** the kernels of sweet corn served as a vegetable while still soft and milky **4 :** a plant that produces corn **5 :** CORN WHISKEY **6 :** something (as writing, music, or acting) that is corny
2corn *vt* **1 :** to form into grains **:** GRANULATE **2 a :** to preserve or season with salt in grains **b :** to cure or preserve in brine containing preservatives and often seasonings <~*ed* beef> **3 :** to feed with corn <~ the horses>
3corn *n* [ME *corne,* fr. MF, horn, corner, fr. L *cornu* horn, point] **:** a local hardening and thickening of epidermis (as on a toe)
Corn *abbr* **1** Cornish **2** Cornwall
1corn·ball \ˈkȯ(ə)rn-ˌbȯl\ *n* [*corn ball* (ball of popcorn and molasses); influenced in meaning by *1corn* 5] **:** an unsophisticated person **:** HICK
2cornball *adj* **:** CORNY <terrible ~ cliches —Bosley Crowther>
corn borer *n* **:** any of several insects that bore in maize: as **a :** EUROPEAN CORN BORER **b :** SOUTHWESTERN CORN BORER
corn bread *n* **:** bread made with cornmeal
corn·cob \ˈkȯ(ə)rn-ˌkäb\ *n* **1 :** the axis on which the kernels of Indian corn are arranged **2 :** an ear of Indian corn
corncob pipe *n* **:** a tobacco pipe with a bowl made from a corncob
corn cockle *n* **:** an annual hairy weed (*Agrostemma githago*) with purplish red flowers that is found in grainfields
corn·crake \ˈkȯ(ə)rn-ˌkrāk\ *n* **:** a common Eurasian short-billed rail (*Crex crex*) that frequents grainfields — called also *land rail*
corn·crib \-ˌkrib\ *n* **:** a crib for storing ears of Indian corn
corn dodger *n, chiefly South & Midland* **:** a cake of corn bread that is fried, baked, or boiled as a dumpling
cor·nea \ˈkȯr-nē-ə\ *n* [ML, fr. L, fem. of *corneus* horny, fr. *cornu*] **:** the transparent part of the coat of the eyeball that covers the iris and pupil and admits light to the interior — see EYE illustration — **cor·ne·al** \-əl\ *adj*
corn earworm *n* **:** a noctuid moth (*Heliothis zea*) whose large striped yellow-headed larva is esp. destructive to the ear of Indian corn
cor·nel \ˈkȯrn-ᵊl, ˈkȯr-ˌnel\ *n* [deriv. of L *cornus* cornel cherry tree; akin to Gk *kerasos* cherry tree] **:** any of various shrubs or trees (*Cornus* and related genera) with very hard wood and perfect flowers; *specif* **:** DOGWOOD
cor·ne·lian \kȯr-ˈnēl-yən\ *n* **:** CARNELIAN
cor·ne·ous \ˈkȯr-nē-əs\ *adj* [L *corneus*] **:** HORNY
1cor·ner \ˈkȯ(r)-nər\ *n* [ME, fr. OF *cornere,* fr. *corne* horn, corner] **1 a :** the point where converging lines, edges, or sides meet **:** ANGLE **b :** the place of intersection of two streets or roads **c :** a piece (as a leather or metal cap for the corner of a book) designed to form, mark, or protect a corner **2 :** the angular part or space between meeting lines, edges, or borders near the vertex of the angle <the southwest ~ of the state is hilly> <lift up the ~*s* of the tablecloth>: as **a :** the area of a playing field or court near the intersection of the sideline and the goal line or baseline <hit four for six from the ~> **b (1) :** either of the four angles of a boxing ring; *esp* **:** the angle in which a boxer rests or is worked on by his seconds during periods between rounds **(2) :** a group of supporters, well-wishers, or adherents associated esp. with a contestant **c :** the side of home plate nearest to or farthest from a batter <a fast ball over the outside ~> **d :** CORNER KICK **e :** the outside of a football formation **3 a :** a private, secret, or remote place <a quiet ~ of a small New England town> <to every ~ of the earth> **b :** a difficult or embarrassing situation **:** a position from which escape or retreat is difficult or impossible <talked himself into a ~> **4 :** control or ownership of enough of the available supply of a commodity or security esp. to permit manipulation of the price **5 :** a point at which significant change occurs — often used in the phrase *turn a corner* — **cor·nered** \-nərd\ *adj* — **around the corner :** at hand **:** IMMINENT <promised that good times were just *around the corner*>
2cor·ner *vb* **cor·nered; cor·ner·ing** \ˈkȯ(r)n-(ə-)riŋ\ *vt* **1 a :** to drive into a corner <the animal is dangerous when ~*ed*> <the prosecutor ~*ed* the witness and forced out the truth> **b :** to catch and hold the attention of esp. so as to force an interview <he ~*s* the secretary on his way to lunch . . . and says what he has to say right in his ear —Clarence Woodbury> **2 :** to get a corner on <~ the wheat market> ~ *vi* **1 :** to meet or converge at a corner or angle **2 :** to turn a corner <a car that ~*s* well>
3corner *adj* **1 :** situated at a corner <the ~ drugstore> **2 :** used or fitted for use in or on a corner <a ~ table> **3 :** of or relating to the corners of a playing area
cor·ner·back \ˈkȯ(r)-nər-ˌbak\ *n* **:** a defensive halfback in football who defends the flank and whose duties include covering a pass receiver
corner kick *n* **:** a free kick in soccer from close to the point of intersection of the goal line and touchline allowed to the attacking team when a member of the defending team has sent the ball behind his own goal line
cor·ner·man \ˈkȯ(r)-nər-ˌman\ *n* **:** one who plays in or near the corner: as **a :** CORNERBACK **b :** a basketball forward
cor·ner·stone \ˈkȯ(r)-nər-ˌstōn\ *n* **1 :** a stone forming a part of a corner or angle in a wall; *specif* **:** such a stone laid at a formal ceremony **2 :** the most basic element **:** FOUNDATION <a ~ of foreign policy>
cor·ner·ways \-ˌwāz\ *adv* **:** DIAGONALLY
cor·ner·wise \-ˌwīz\ *adv* **:** DIAGONALLY
cor·net \kȯr-ˈnet, *Brit usu* ˈkȯr-nit\ *n* [ME, fr. MF, fr. dim. of *corn* horn, fr. L *cornu*] **1 :** a valved brass instrument resembling a trumpet in design and range but having a shorter tube and less brilliant tone **2 :** something shaped like a cone: as **a :** a piece of paper twisted for use as a container **b :** a cone-shaped pastry shell that is often filled with whipped cream **c** *Brit* **:** an ice-cream cone — **cor·net·ist** *or* **cor·net·tist** \-ˈnet-əst, -ni-tist\ *n*

cornet 1

corn–fed \ˈkȯ(ə)rn-ˌfed\ *adj* **1 :** fed or fattened on grain (as corn) <~ hogs> **2 :** PLUMP <she was gorgeous. A little ~, but gorgeous. —Albert Morgan>
corn·field \-ˌfēld\ *n* **:** a field in which corn is grown
corn·flakes \-ˌflāks\ *n pl* **:** toasted flakes made from the coarse meal of hulled corn for use as a breakfast cereal
corn flour *n, Brit* **:** CORNSTARCH
corn·flow·er \ˈkȯ(ə)rn-ˌflau̇(-ə)r\ *n* **1 :** CORN COCKLE **2 :** BACHELOR'S BUTTON
cornflower blue *n* **:** a variable color averaging a moderate purplish blue
corn·husk·ing \ˈkȯrn-ˌhəs-kiŋ\ *n* **:** the husking of corn; *specif* **:** HUSKING
1cor·nice \ˈkȯr-nəs, -nish\ *n* [MF, fr. It] **1 a :** the molded and projecting horizontal member that crowns an architectural composition **b :** a top course that crowns a wall **2 :** a decorative band of metal or wood used to conceal curtain fixtures **3 :** an overhanging mass of snow, ice, or rock usu. on a ridge
2cornice *vt* **cor·niced; cor·nic·ing :** to furnish or crown with a cornice
cor·niche \kȯr-ˈnēsh\ *n* [F *cornice, corniche,* lit., cornice] **:** a road built along a coast and esp. along the face of a cliff
cor·nic·u·late cartilage \kȯr-ˌnik-yə-lət-\ *n* [L *corniculatus* horned, fr. *corniculum,* dim. of *cornu* horn] **:** a small nodule of yellow elastic cartilage articulating with the apex of the arytenoid

1, cornice 1a

cor·ni·fi·ca·tion \ˌkȯr-nə-fə-ˈkā-shən\ *n* [L *cornu* horn + E *-i-* + *-fication*] **1 :** conversion into horn or a horny substance or tissue **2 :** the conversion of the vaginal epithelium from the columnar to the squamous type
1Cor·nish \ˈkȯr-nish\ *adj* [*Corn*wall, England + E *-ish*] **:** of, relating to, or characteristic of Cornwall, Cornishmen, or Cornish

[2]**Cornish** *n* **1 :** a Celtic language of Cornwall extinct since the late 18th century **2 :** any of an English breed of domestic fowls much used in crossbreeding for meat production

Cor·nish·man \-mən\ *n* **:** a native or resident of Cornwall, England

Corn Law *n* **:** one of a series of laws in force in Great Britain before 1846 prohibiting or discouraging the importation of foreign grain

corn leaf aphid *n* **:** a dusky greenish or brownish aphid (*Rhopalosiphum maidis*) that feeds on the flowers and foliage of various commercially important grasses (as Indian corn)

corn·meal \ˈkȯ(ə)rn-ˈmē(ə)l, -ˌmēl\ *n* **:** meal ground from corn

corn pone *n, South & Midland* **:** corn bread often made without milk or eggs and baked or fried

corn poppy *n* **:** an annual red-flowered poppy (*Papaver rhoeas*) common in European grainfields and cultivated in several varieties

corn rootworm *n* **:** any of several beetles (genus *Diabrotica* of the family Galerucidae) whose root-eating larvae are pests esp. of Indian corn

corn silk *n* **:** the silky styles on an ear of Indian corn

corn snow *n* **:** granular snow formed by alternate thawing and freezing

corn·stalk \ˈkȯ(ə)rn-ˌstȯk\ *n* **:** a stalk of Indian corn

corn·starch \-ˌstärch\ *n* **:** starch made from corn and used in foods as a thickening agent, in making corn syrup and sugars, and in the manufacture of adhesives and sizes for paper and textiles

corn sugar *n* **:** DEXTROSE; *esp* **:** that made by hydrolysis of cornstarch

corn syrup *n* **:** a syrup containing dextrins, maltose, and dextrose that is obtained by partial hydrolysis of cornstarch

cor·nu \ˈkȯr-(ˌ)n(y)ü\ *n, pl* **cor·nua** \-n(y)ə-wə\ [L] **:** HORN; *esp* **:** a horn-shaped anatomical structure — **cor·nu·al** \-n(y)ə-wəl\ *adj*

cor·nu·co·pia \ˌkȯr-n(y)ə-ˈkō-pē-ə\ *n* [LL, fr. L *cornu copiae* horn of plenty] **1 :** a curved goat's horn overflowing with fruit and ears of grain that is used as a decorative motif emblematic of abundance **2 :** an inexhaustible store **:** ABUNDANCE <a pair of books that . . . add up to a 550-page ~ of humor —Bernard Kalb> **3 :** a receptacle shaped like a horn or cone — **cor·nu·co·pi·an** \-pē-ən\ *adj*

cor·nu·to \kȯr-ˈn(y)üt-(ˌ)ō\ *n, pl* **-tos** [It, fr. L *cornutus* having horns, fr. *cornu*] **:** CUCKOLD

corn whiskey *n* **:** whiskey distilled from a mash made up of not less than 80 percent corn — compare BOURBON

[1]**corny** \ˈkȯr-nē\ *adj* **corn·i·er; -est** **1** *archaic* **:** tasting strongly of malt **2 :** of or relating to corn **3 :** mawkishly old-fashioned **:** tiresomely simple and sentimental **:** TRITE — **corn·i·ly** \ˈkȯrn-ᵊl-ē\ *adv* — **corn·i·ness** \ˈkȯr-nē-nəs\ *n*

[2]**corny** *adj* **corn·i·er; -est :** relating to or having corns on the feet

cor·o·dy \ˈkȯr-əd-ē, ˈkär-\ *n, pl* **-dies** [ME *corrodie,* fr. ML *corrodium*] **:** an allowance of provisions for maintenance dispensed as a charity

co·rol·la \kə-ˈräl-ə\ *n* [NL, fr. L, dim. of *corona*] **:** the petals of a flower constituting the inner floral envelope surrounding the sporophylls — **co·rol·late** \kə-ˈräl-ət; ˈkȯr-ə-ˌlāt, ˈkär-\ *adj*

cor·ol·lary \ˈkȯr-ə-ˌler-ē, ˈkär-, *Brit* kə-ˈräl-ə-rē\ *n, pl* **-lar·ies** [ME *corolarie,* fr. LL *corollarium,* fr. L, money paid for a garland, gratuity, fr. *corolla*] **1 :** an immediate inference from a proved proposition **2 a :** something that naturally follows **:** RESULT **b :** something that incidentally or naturally accompanies or parallels — **corollary** *adj*

cor·o·man·del \ˌkȯr-ə-ˈman-dᵊl, ˌkär-\ *n* [*Coromandel* coast region, India] **:** an East Indian timber tree (*Diospyros melanoxylon*) with a hard dark-colored wood — called also *coromandel ebony*

co·ro·na \kə-ˈrō-nə\ *n* [L, garland, crown, cornice — more at CROWN] **1 :** the projecting part of a classic cornice **2 a :** a usu. colored circle often seen around and close to a luminous body (as the sun or moon) caused by diffraction produced by suspended droplets or occas. particles of dust **b :** the tenuous outermost part of the atmosphere of the sun appearing as a halo around the moon's black disk during a total eclipse of the sun; *also* **:** a similar portion of the atmosphere of a star **c :** a circle of light made by the apparent convergence of the streamers of the aurora borealis **d :** the upper portion of a bodily part (as a tooth or the skull) **e :** an appendage on the inner side of the corolla in some flowers (as the daffodil, jonquil, or milkweed) **f :** a faint glow adjacent to the surface of an electrical conductor at high voltage **3** [fr. *La Corona,* a trademark] **:** a long cigar having the sides straight to the unsealed end and being roundly blunt at the sealed end

Corona Aus·tra·lis \-ō-ˈstrā-ləs, -ä-\ *n* [L (gen. *Coronae Australis*), lit., southern crown] **:** a southern constellation adjoining Sagittarius on the south

Corona Bo·re·al·is \-ˌbōr-ē-ˈal-əs, -ˌbȯr-\ *n* [L (gen. *Coronae Borealis*), lit., northern crown] **:** a northern constellation between Hercules and Boötes

cor·o·nach \ˈkȯr-ə-nək, ˈkär-\ *n* [ScGael *corranach* & IrGael *coránach*] **:** a funeral dirge sung or played on the bagpipes in Scotland and Ireland

co·ro·na·graph *also* **co·ro·no·graph** \kə-ˈrō-nə-ˌgraf\ *n* **:** a telescope for observation of the sun's corona

[1]**cor·o·nal** *also* **cor·o·nel** \ˈkȯr-ən-ᵊl, ˈkär-\ *n* [ME *coronal,* fr. AF, fr. L *coronalis* of a crown, fr. *corona*] **:** a circlet for the head usu. implying rank or dignity

[2]**co·ro·nal** \ˈkȯr-ən-ᵊl, ˈkär-; kə-ˈrōn-\ *adj* **1 :** of or relating to a corona or crown **2 a :** lying in the direction of the coronal suture **b :** of or relating to the frontal plane that passes through the long axis of the body

coronal suture *n* **:** a suture extending across the skull between the parietal and frontal bones

co·ro·na ra·di·a·ta \kə-ˈrō-nə-ˌrād-ē-ˈät-ə, -ˈāt-\ *n, pl* **co·ro·nae ra·di·a·tae** \-(ˌ)nē-ˌrād-ē-ˈät-(ˌ)ē, -ˈāt-\ [NL, lit., crown with rays] **:** the zone of small follicular cells immediately surrounding the ovum in the Graafian follicle and accompanying the ovum on its discharge from the follicle

[1]**cor·o·nary** \ˈkȯr-ə-ˌner-ē, ˈkär-\ *adj* **1 :** of, relating to, resembling, or being a crown or coronal **2 :** relating to or being the coronary arteries or veins of the heart; *broadly* **:** of or relating to the heart

[2]**coronary** *n, pl* **-nar·ies** **1 a :** CORONARY ARTERY **b :** CORONARY VEIN **2 :** CORONARY THROMBOSIS

coronary artery *n* **:** either of two arteries, one on the right and one on the left, that arise from the aorta immediately above the semilunar valves and supply the tissues of the heart itself

coronary occlusion *n* **:** the partial or complete blocking (as by a thrombus, by spasm, or by sclerosis) of a coronary artery

coronary sinus *n* **:** a venous channel that is derived from the sinus venosus, is continuous with the largest of the cardiac veins, receives most of the blood from the walls of the heart, and empties into the right atrium

coronary thrombosis *n* **:** the blocking of a coronary artery of the heart by a thrombus

coronary vein *n* **:** any of several veins that drain the tissues of the heart and empty into the coronary sinus

cor·o·na·tion \ˌkȯr-ə-ˈnā-shən, ˌkär-\ *n* [ME *coronacion,* fr. MF *coronation,* fr. *coroner* to crown] **:** the act or ceremony of investing a sovereign or his consort with the royal crown

cor·o·ner \ˈkȯr-ə-nər, ˈkär-\ *n* [ME, an officer of the crown, fr. AF, fr. OF *corone* crown, fr. L *corona*] **:** a public officer whose principal duty is to inquire by an inquest into the cause of any death which there is reason to suppose is not due to natural causes

cor·o·net \ˌkȯr-ə-ˈnet, ˌkär-\ *n* [MF *coronette,* fr. OF *coronete,* fr. *corone*] **1 :** a small or lesser crown usu. signifying a rank below that of a sovereign **2 :** an ornamental wreath or band for the head usu. for wear by women on formal occasions **3 :** the lower part of a horse's pastern where the horn terminates in skin — see HORSE illustration

co·ro·tate \(ˈ)kō-ˈrō-ˌtāt\ *vi* **:** to rotate in conjunction with or at the same rate as another rotating body — **co·ro·ta·tion** \ˌkō-rō-ˈtā-shən\ *n*

corp *abbr* **1** corporal **2** corporation

corpora *pl of* CORPUS

[1]**cor·po·ral** \ˈkȯr-p(ə-)rəl\ *n* [ME, fr. MF, fr. ML *corporale,* fr. L, neut. of *corporalis;* fr. the doctrine that the bread of the Eucharist becomes or represents the body of Christ] **:** a linen cloth on which the eucharistic elements are placed

[2]**corporal** *adj* [ME, fr. MF, fr. L *corporalis,* fr. *corpor-, corpus* body] **1 :** of, relating to, or affecting the body <~ punishment> **2** *obs* **:** CORPOREAL, PHYSICAL ***syn*** see BODILY — **cor·po·ral·ly** \-p(ə-)rə-lē\ *adv*

[3]**corporal** *n* [MF, lowest noncommissioned officer, alter. of *caporal,* fr. OIt *caporale,* fr. *capo* head, fr. L *caput* — more at HEAD] **:** a noncommissioned officer ranking in the army above a private first class and below a sergeant and in the marine corps above a lance corporal and below a sergeant

cor·po·ral·i·ty \ˌkȯr-pə-ˈral-ət-ē\ *n, pl* **-ties :** the quality or state of being or having a body or a material or physical existence

corporal's guard *n* **1 :** the small detachment commanded by a corporal **2 :** a small group

cor·po·rate \ˈkȯr-p(ə-)rət\ *adj* [L *corporatus,* pp. of *corporare* to make into a body, fr. *corpor-, corpus*] **1 a :** formed into an association and endowed by law with the rights and liabilities of an individual **:** INCORPORATED **b :** of or realting to a corporation <a plan to reorganize the ~ structure> **2 :** of, relating to, or formed into a unified body of individuals <human law arises by the ~ action of a people —G. H. Sabine> <the yeomen . . . were a ~ society like the country gentry —Adrian Bell> **3 :** CORPORATIVE 2 — **cor·po·rate·ly** *adv*

cor·po·ra·tion \ˌkȯr-pə-ˈrā-shən\ *n* **1 a** *obs* **:** a group of merchants or traders united in a trade guild **b :** the municipal authorities of a town or city **2 :** a body formed and authorized by law to act as a single person although constituted by one or more persons and legally endowed with various rights and duties including the capacity of succession **3 :** an association of employers and employees in a basic industry or of members of a profession organized as an organ of political representation in a corporative state **4 :** POTBELLY 1

cor·po·rat·ism \ˈkȯr-p(ə-)rət-ˌiz-əm\ *n* **:** the organization of a society into industrial and professional corporations serving as organs of political representation and exercising some control over persons and activities within their jurisdiction — **cor·po·rat·ist** \-p(ə-)rət-əst\ *adj*

cor·po·ra·tive \ˈkȯr-pə-ˌrāt-iv, -p(ə-)rət-\ *adj* **1 :** of or relating to a corporation **2 :** of or relating to corporatism <a ~ state>

cor·po·ra·tiv·ism \ˈkȯr-pə-ˌrāt-i-ˌviz-əm, -p(ə-)rət-\ *n* **:** CORPORATISM

cor·po·ra·tor \ˈkȯr-pə-ˌrāt-ər\ *n* **:** a corporation organizer, member, or stockholder

cor·po·re·al \kȯr-ˈpōr-ē-əl, -ˈpȯr-\ *adj* [L *corporeus* of the body, fr. *corpor-, corpus*] **1 :** having, consisting of, or relating to a physical material body: as **a :** not spiritual **b :** not immaterial or intangible **:** SUBSTANTIAL **2** *archaic* **:** CORPORAL ***syn*** **1** see MATERIAL ***ant*** incorporeal **2** see BODILY — **cor·po·re·al·ly** \-ē-ə-lē\ *adv* — **cor·po·re·al·ness** *n*

cor·po·re·al·i·ty \(ˌ)kȯr-ˌpōr-ē-ˈal-ət-ē, -ˌpȯr-\ *n, pl* **-ties :** corporeal existence

cor·po·re·ity \ˌkȯr-pə-ˈrē-ət-ē, -ˈrā-\ *n, pl* **-ities :** the quality or state of having or being a body **:** MATERIALITY

cor·po·sant \ˈkȯr-pə-ˌsant, -ˌzant\ *n* [Pg *corpo-santo,* lit., holy body] **:** SAINT ELMO'S FIRE

corps \ˈkō(ə)r, ˈkȯ(ə)r\ *n, pl* **corps** \ˈkō(ə)rz, ˈkȯ(ə)rz\ [F, fr. L *corpus* body] **1 a :** an organized subdivision of the military establishment <Marine *Corps*> <Signal *Corps*> **b :** a tactical unit usu. consisting of two or more divisions and auxiliary arms and services **2 a :** a group of persons associated together or acting under common direction; *esp* **:** a body of persons having a common activity or occupation <the press ~> **b :** an association of German university students **3 :** CORPS DE BALLET

corps area *n* : a former territorial division of the U. S. for purposes of military administration and training

corps de bal·let \ˌkȯrd-ə-(ˌ)ba-ˈlā, ˌkȯrd-\ *n, pl* **corps de ballet** *same, or* ˌkȯrz-də-, ˌkȯrz-\ [F] : the ensemble of a ballet company

corps d'elite \ˌkȯr-dā-ˈlēt, ˌkȯr-\ *n, pl* **corps d'elite** *same, or* ˌkȯrz-dā-, ˌkȯrz-\ [F *corps d'élite*] **1** : a body of picked troops **2** : a group of the best people in a category <thirteen reporters — the *corps d'elite* of a great newspaper —*N.Y. Herald Tribune*>

corpse \ˈkȯ(ə)rps\ *n* [ME *corps,* fr. MF, fr. L *corpus* — more at MIDRIFF] **1** *obs* : a human or animal body whether living or dead **2 a** : a dead body esp. of a human being **b** : something discarded or defunct <it was an awful thing to look at the ~ of a city —*Nat'l Geographic*>

corps·man \ˈkō(ə)r(z)-mən, ˈkȯ(ə)r(z)-\ *n* **1** : an enlisted man trained to give first aid and minor medical treatment **2** : a member of a government-sponsored service corps

cor·pu·lence \ˈkȯr-pyə-lən(t)s\ *n* : the state of being excessively fat

cor·pu·len·cy \-lən-sē\ *n, pl* **-cies** : CORPULENCE

cor·pu·lent \-lənt\ *adj* [ME, fr. L *corpulentus,* fr. *corpus*] : having a large bulky body : OBESE — **cor·pu·lent·ly** *adv*

cor pul·mo·na·le \ˌkȯr-ˌpu̇l-mə-ˈnäl-ē, -ˌpəl-, -ˈnal-\ *n, pl* **cor·dia pul·mo·na·lia** \ˈkȯrd-ē-ə- . . . -ˈnäl-ē-ə, -ˈnal-\ [NL, lit., pulmonary heart] : disease of the heart characterized by hypertrophy and dilatation of the right ventricle and secondary to disease of the lungs or their blood vessels

cor·pus \ˈkȯr-pəs\ *n, pl* **cor·po·ra** \-p(ə-)rə\ [ME, fr. L] **1** : the body of a man or animal esp. when dead **2 a** : the main part or body of a bodily structure or organ <the ~ of the uterus> **b** : the main body or corporeal substance of a thing; *specif* : the principal of a fund or estate as distinct from income or interest **3** : all the writings of a particular kind or on a particular subject; *esp* : the complete works of an author

corpus al·la·tum \-ə-ˈlāt-əm, -ˈlät-\ *n, pl* **corpora al·la·ta** \-ˈlāt-ə, -ˈlät-ə\ [NL, lit., applied body] : one of a pair of separate or fused bodies in many insects that are sometimes closely associated with the corpora cardiaca and that secrete hormones (as juvenile hormone)

corpus cal·lo·sum \-ka-ˈlō-səm\ *n, pl* **corpora cal·lo·sa** \-sə\ [NL, lit., callous body] : the great band of commissural fibers uniting the cerebral hemispheres in man and in the higher mammals — see BRAIN illustration

corpus car·di·a·cum \-kär-ˈdī-ə-kəm\ *n, pl* **corpora car·di·a·ca** \-ə-kə\ [NL, lit., cardiac body] : one of a pair of separate or fused bodies of nervous tissue in many insects that lie posterior to the brain and dorsal to the esophagus and that function in the storage and secretion of brain hormone

Cor·pus Chris·ti \ˌkȯr-pə-ˈskris-tē\ *n* [ME, fr. ML, lit., body of Christ] : the Thursday after Trinity Sunday observed as a Roman Catholic festival in honor of the Eucharist

cor·pus·cle \ˈkȯr-(ˌ)pəs-əl\ *n* [L *corpusculum,* dim. of *corpus*] **1** : a minute particle **2 a** : a living cell; *esp* : one (as a red or white blood cell or a cell in cartilage or bone) not aggregated into continuous tissues **b** : a small circumscribed multicellular body — **cor·pus·cu·lar** \kȯr-ˈpəs-kyə-lər\ *adj*

cor·pus de·lic·ti \-di-ˈlik-ˌtī, -(ˌ)tē\ *n, pl* **corpora delicti** [NL, lit., body of the crime] **1** : the substantial and fundamental fact necessary to prove the commission of a crime **2** : the material substance (as the body of the victim of a murder) upon which a crime has been committed

corpus lu·te·um \-ˈlüt-ē-əm\ *n, pl* **corpora lu·tea** \-ē-ə\ [NL, lit., yellowish body] : a reddish yellow mass of endocrine tissue that forms a ruptured Graafian follicle in the mammalian ovary

corr *abbr* — see COR

cor·rade \kə-ˈrād\ *vb* **cor·rad·ed; cor·rad·ing** [L *corradere* to scrape together, fr. *com-* + *radere* to scrape — more at RAT] *vt* : to wear away by abrasion ~ *vi* : to crumble away through abrasion — **cor·ra·sion** \-ˈrā-zhən\ *n* — **cor·ra·sive** \-ˈrā-siv, -ziv\ *adj*

¹cor·ral \kə-ˈral, -ˈrel\ *n* [Sp, fr. (assumed) VL *currale* enclosure for vehicles, fr. L *currus* cart, fr. *currere* to run — more at CURRENT] **1** : a pen or enclosure for confining or capturing livestock **2** : an enclosure made with wagons for defense of an encampment

²corral *vt* **cor·ralled; cor·ral·ling** **1** : to enclose in a corral **2** : to arrange (wagons) so as to form a corral **3** : COLLECT, GATHER <helped elect certain municipal council members by *corralling* the necessary votes —R. L. Maullin>

¹cor·rect \kə-ˈrekt\ *vt* [ME *correcten,* fr. L *correctus,* pp. of *corrigere,* fr. *com-* + *regere* to lead straight — more at RIGHT] **1 a** : to make or set right : AMEND **b** : COUNTERACT, NEUTRALIZE **c** : to alter or adjust so as to bring to some standard or required condition <~ a lens for spherical aberration> **2 a** : to punish (as a child) with a view to reforming or improving **b** : to point out for amendment the errors or faults of <spent the whole day ~*ing* examination papers> — **cor·rect·able** \-ˈrek-tə-bəl\ *adj* — **cor·rec·tor** \-ˈrek-tər\ *n*

syn **1** CORRECT, RECTIFY, EMEND, REMEDY, REDRESS, AMEND, REFORM, REVISE *shared meaning element* : to make right what is wrong
2 see PUNISH

²correct *adj* [ME, corrected, fr. L *correctus,* fr. pp. of *corrigere*] **1** : conforming to an approved or conventional standard <relations . . . were ~ but not very friendly —W. L. Shirer> <find him a courteous, ~, if not always candid, subject —Robert Neville> **2** : conforming to or agreeing with fact, logic, or known truth **3** : conforming to a set figure <enclosed the ~ return postage> — **cor·rect·ly** \kə-ˈrek-(t)lē\ *adv* — **cor·rect·ness** *n*

syn CORRECT, ACCURATE, EXACT, PRECISE, NICE, RIGHT *shared meaning element* : conforming to fact, truth, or a standard ***ant*** incorrect

corrected time *n* : a boat's elapsed time less her time allowance in yacht racing

cor·rec·tion \kə-ˈrek-shən\ *n* **1** : the action or an instance of correcting: as **a** : AMENDMENT, RECTIFICATION **b** : REBUKE, PUNISHMENT **c** : a bringing into conformity with a standard **d** : NEUTRALIZATION, COUNTERACTION <~ of acidity> **2** : a decline in market price or business activity following and counteracting a rise **3 a** : something substituted in place of what is wrong <marking ~*s* on the students' papers> **b** : a quantity applied by way of correcting (as for adjustment or inaccuracy of an instrument) **4** : the treatment and rehabilitation of offenders through a program involving penal custody, parole, and probation; *also* : the administration of such treatment as a matter of public policy — usu. used in pl. — **cor·rec·tion·al** \-shnəl, -shən-ᵊl\ *adj*

cor·rec·ti·tude \kə-ˈrek-tə-ˌt(y)üd\ *n* [blend of *correct* and *rectitude*] : correctness or propriety of conduct

cor·rec·tive \kə-ˈrek-tiv\ *adj* : tending to correct <~ lenses> <~ punishment> — **corrective** *n* — **cor·rec·tive·ly** *adv* — **cor·rec·tive·ness** *n*

¹cor·re·late \ˈkȯr-ə-lət, ˈkär-, -ˌlāt\ *n* [back-formation fr. *correlation*] **1** : either of two things so related that one directly implies or is complementary to the other (as husband and wife) **2** : a phenomenon (as brain activity) that accompanies another phenomenon (as behavior), and is usu. parallel to it (as in form, type, development, or distribution), and is related in some way to it ***syn*** see PARALLEL — **correlate** *adj*

²cor·re·late \-ˌlāt\ *vb* **-lat·ed; -lat·ing** *vi* : to bear reciprocal or mutual relations ~ *vt* **1 a** : to establish a mutual or reciprocal relation of **b** : to show a causal relationship between **2** : to relate so that to each member of one set or series a corresponding member of another is assigned **3** : to present or set forth so as to show relationship <he ~*s* the findings of the scientists, the psychologists, and the mystics —Eugene Exman> — **cor·re·lat·able** \-ˌlāt-ə-bəl\ *adj*

cor·re·la·tion \ˌkȯr-ə-ˈlā-shən, ˌkär-\ *n* [ML *correlation-, correlatio,* fr. L *com-* + *relation-, relatio* relation] **1 a** : the act of correlating **b** : the state of being correlated; *specif* : a relation of phenomena as invariable accompaniments of each other <the assumption that there is a positive ~ between performance and pay —Kermit Eby> **2** : reciprocal relation in the occurrence of different structures, characteristics, or processes in organisms **3** : an interdependence between mathematical variables esp. in statistics — **cor·re·la·tion·al** \-shnəl, -shən-ᵊl\ *adj*

correlation coefficient *n* : a number or function that indicates the degree of correlation between two sets of data or between two random variables and that is equal to their covariance divided by the product of their standard deviations

cor·rel·a·tive \kə-ˈrel-ət-iv\ *adj* **1** : naturally related : CORRESPONDING **2** : reciprocally related **3** : regularly used together but typically not adjacent <the ~ conjunctions *either . . . or*> — **correlative** *n* — **cor·rel·a·tive·ly** *adv*

cor·re·spond \ˌkȯr-ə-ˈspänd, ˌkär-\ *vi* [MF or ML; MF *correspondre,* fr. ML *correspondēre,* fr. L *com-* + *respondēre* to respond] **1 a** : to be in conformity or agreement : SUIT <fulfillment seldom ~*s* to anticipation> **b** : to compare closely : MATCH — usu. used with *to* or *with* **c** : to be equivalent or parallel **2** : to communicate with a person by exchange of letters <frequently ~*s* with his cousin> ***syn*** see AGREE

cor·re·spon·dence \-ˈspän-dən(t)s\ *n* **1 a** : the agreement of things with one another **b** : a particular similarity **c** : association of members of one set with each member of a second and of members of the second with each member of the first **2 a** : communication by letters; *also* : the letters exchanged **b** : the news, information, or opinion contributed by a correspondent to a newspaper or periodical

correspondence school *n* : a school that teaches nonresident students by mailing them lessons and exercises which upon completion are returned to the school for grading

cor·re·spon·den·cy \ˌkȯr-ə-ˈspän-dən-sē, ˌkär-\ *n, pl* **-cies** : CORRESPONDENCE

¹cor·re·spon·dent \ˌkȯr-ə-ˈspän-dənt, ˌkär-\ *adj* [ME, fr. MF or ML; MF, fr. ML *correspondent-, correspondens,* prp. of *correspondēre*] **1** : CORRESPONDING <each advantage having ~ disadvantages> **2** : FITTING, CONFORMING — used with *with* or *to* <the outcome was entirely ~ with my wishes>

²correspondent *n* **1** : something that corresponds **2 a** : one who communicates with another by letter **b** : one who has regular commercial relations with another **c** : one who contributes news or comment to a publication (as a newspaper) often from a distant place <a war ~>

cor·re·spond·ing *adj* **1 a** : agreeing in some respect (as kind, degree, position, or function) <the figures are large but the ~ totals next year will be larger> **b** : RELATED, ACCOMPANYING <all rights carry with them ~ responsibilites —W. P. Paepcke> **2 a** : charged with the duty of writing letters <~ secretary> **b** : participating or serving at a distance and by mail <a ~ member of the society> — **cor·re·spond·ing·ly** \-ˈspän-diŋ-lē\ *adv*

cor·re·spon·sive \ˌkȯr-ə-ˈspän(t)-siv, ˌkär-\ *adj* : mutually responsive

cor·ri·da \kō-ˈrē-t͟hə\ *n* [Sp, lit., act of running] : BULLFIGHT

cor·ri·dor \ˈkȯr-əd-ər, ˈkär-, -ə-ˌdȯ(ə)r\ *n* [MF, fr. OIt *corridore,* fr. *correre* to run, fr. L *currere* — more at CURRENT] **1** : a passageway (as in a hotel) into which compartments or rooms open **2** : a usu. narrow passageway or route: as **a** : a narrow strip of land through foreign-held territory **b** (1) : a restricted lane for air traffic (2) : a restricted path a spacecraft must follow to accomplish its mission : WINDOW 3 **c** : a major transportation route through a densely populated area <high-speed rail lines were also seen as the most practical means of travel in megalopolitan ~*s* —*Engineering News-Record*>

cor·rie \ˈkȯr-ē, ˈkär-ē\ *n* [ScGael *coire,* lit., kettle] : CIRQUE 3

Cor·rie·dale \-ˌdāl\ *n* [*Corriedale,* ranch in New Zealand] **:** any of a dual-purpose breed of rather large usu. hornless sheep developed in New Zealand

cor·ri·gen·dum \ˌkȯr-ə-ˈjen-dəm, ˌkär-\ *n, pl* **-da** \-də\ [L, neut. of *corrigendus,* gerundive of *corrigere* to correct] **:** an error in a printed work discovered after printing and shown with its correction on a separate sheet bound with the original

cor·ri·gi·ble \ˈkȯr-ə-jə-bəl, ˈkär-\ *adj* [ME, fr. MF, fr. ML *corrigibilis,* fr. L *corrigere*] **:** capable of being set right **:** REPARABLE <a ~ defect> — **cor·ri·gi·bil·i·ty** \ˌkȯr-ə-jə-ˈbil-ət-ē, ˈkär-\ *n* — **cor·ri·gi·bly** \ˈkȯr-ə-jə-blē, ˈkär-\ *adv*

cor·ri·val \kə-ˈrī-vəl, kȯ-, kō-\ *n* [MF, fr. L *corrivalis,* fr. *com-* + *rivalis* rival] **:** RIVAL, COMPETITOR — **corrival** *adj*

cor·rob·o·rant \kə-ˈräb-ə-rənt\ *adj, archaic* **:** having an invigorating effect — used of a medicine

cor·rob·o·rate \kə-ˈräb-ə-ˌrāt\ *vt* **-rat·ed; -rat·ing** [L *corroboratus,* pp. of *corroborare,* fr. *com-* + *robor-, robur* strength] **:** to support with evidence or authority **:** make more certain ***syn*** see CONFIRM ***ant*** contradict — **cor·rob·o·ra·tion** \-ˌräb-ə-ˈrā-shən\ *n* — **cor·rob·o·ra·tive** \-ˈräb-ə-ˌrāt-iv, -ˈräb-(ə-)rət-\ *adj* — **cor·rob·o·ra·tor** \-ˈräb-ə-ˌrāt-ər\ *n* — **cor·rob·o·ra·to·ry** \-ˈräb-(ə-)rə-ˌtōr-ē, -ˌtȯr-\ *adj*

cor·rob·o·ree \kə-ˈräb-ə-rē\ *n* [fr. native name in New South Wales, Australia] **1 :** a nocturnal festivity with songs and symbolic dances by which the Australian aborigines celebrate events of importance **2** *Austral* **a :** a noisy festivity **b :** TUMULT

cor·rode \kə-ˈrōd\ *vb* **cor·rod·ed; cor·rod·ing** [ME *corroden,* fr. L *corrodere* to gnaw to pieces, fr. *com-* + *rodere* to gnaw — more at RAT] *vt* **1 :** to eat away by degrees as if by gnawing; *esp* **:** to wear away gradually usu. by chemical action <the metal was *corroded* beyond repair> **2 :** to weaken or destroy gradually <manners and miserliness that ~ the human spirit —Bernard DeVoto> ~ *vi* **:** to undergo corrosion <the bare metal will ~ after a few weeks of exposure to the weather> — **cor·rod·ible** \-ˈrōd-ə-bəl\ *adj*

cor·ro·dy *var of* CORODY

cor·ro·sion \kə-ˈrō-zhən\ *n* [ME, fr. LL *corrosion-, corrosio* act of gnawing, fr. L *corrosus,* pp. of *corrodere*] **1 :** the action, process, or effect of corroding **2 :** a product of corroding

cor·ro·sive \-ˈrō-siv, -ziv\ *adj* **1 :** tending or having the power to corrode <~ acids> <~ action> **2 a :** weakening or destroying by a gradual process <the ~ influence of industrialization —Louise C. Hunter> **b :** bitingly sarcastic <~ satire> — **corrosive** *n* — **cor·ro·sive·ly** *adv* — **cor·ro·sive·ness** *n*

corrosive sublimate *n* **:** MERCURIC CHLORIDE

cor·ru·gate \ˈkȯr-ə-ˌgāt, ˈkär-\ *vb* **-gat·ed; -gat·ing** [L *corrugatus,* pp. of *corrugare,* fr. *com-* + *ruga* wrinkle — more at ROUGH] *vt* **:** to form or shape into wrinkles or folds or into alternating ridges and grooves **:** FURROW <*corrugated* his brows in thought —John Buchan> ~ *vi* **:** to become corrugated

corrugated iron *n* **:** usu. galvanized sheet iron or sheet steel shaped into straight parallel regular and equally curved ridges and hollows

cor·ru·ga·tion \ˌkȯr-ə-ˈgā-shən, ˌkär-\ *n* **1 :** the act of corrugating **2 :** a ridge or groove of a corrugated surface

[1]**cor·rupt** \kə-ˈrəpt\ *vb* [ME *corrupten,* fr. L *corruptus,* pp. of *corrumpere,* fr. *com-* + *rumpere* to break — more at REAVE] *vt* **1 a :** to change from good to bad in morals, manners, or actions; *also* **:** BRIBE **b :** to degrade with unsound principles or moral values **2 :** ROT, SPOIL **3 :** to subject (a person) to corruption of blood **4 :** to alter from the original or correct form or version ~ *vi* **1 a :** to become tainted or rotten **b :** to become morally debased **2 :** to cause disintegration or ruin ***syn*** see DEBASE — **cor·rupt·er** *or* **cor·rup·tor** \-ˈrəp-tər\ *n* — **cor·rupt·ibil·i·ty** \-ˌrəp-tə-ˈbil-ət-ē\ *n* — **cor·rupt·ible** \-ˈrəp-tə-bəl\ *adj* — **cor·rupt·ibly** \-blē\ *adv*

[2]**corrupt** *adj* [ME, fr. MF or L; MF, fr. L *corruptus,* fr. pp. of *corrumpere*] **1 a :** morally degenerate and perverted **:** DEPRAVED **b :** characterized by bribery, the selling of political favors, or other improper conduct <~ judges> **2** *archaic* **:** PUTRID, TAINTED ***syn*** see VICIOUS — **cor·rupt·ly** \-ˈrəp-(t)lē\ *adv* — **cor·rupt·ness** \-ˈrəp(t)-nəs\ *n*

cor·rup·tion \kə-ˈrəp-shən\ *n* **1 a :** impairment of integrity, virtue, or moral principle **:** DEPRAVITY **b :** DECAY, DECOMPOSITION **c :** inducement to wrong by bribery or other unlawful or improper means **d :** a departure from what is pure or correct **2** *archaic* **:** an agency or influence that corrupts **3** *chiefly dial* **:** PUS

cor·rup·tion·ist \-sh(ə-)nəst\ *n* **:** one who practices or defends corruption esp. in politics

corruption of blood : the effect of an attainder upon a person which bars him from inheriting, retaining, or transmitting any estate, rank, or title

cor·rup·tive \kə-ˈrəp-tiv\ *adj* **:** producing or tending to produce corruption — **cor·rup·tive·ly** *adv*

cor·sage \kȯr-ˈsäzh, -ˈsäj, ˈkȯr-ˌ\ *n* [F, bust, bodice, fr. OF, bust, fr. *cors* body, fr. L *corpus*] **1 :** the waist or bodice of a woman's dress **2 :** an arrangement of flowers to be worn by a woman

cor·sair \ˈkȯr-ˌsa(ə)r, -ˌse(ə)r\ *n* [MF & OIt; MF *corsaire* pirate, fr. OProv *corsari,* fr. OIt *corsaro,* fr. ML *cursarius,* fr. L *cursus* course — more at COURSE] **:** PIRATE; *esp* **:** a privateer of the Barbary coast

corse \ˈkȯ(ə)rs\ *n* [ME *cors,* fr. OF, body] *archaic* **:** CORPSE

corse·let *for 1* ˈkȯr-slət, *for 2* ˌkȯr-sə-ˈlet\ *n* **1** *or* **corslet** [MF, dim. of *cors* body, bodice] **a :** a piece of armor covering the trunk but usu. not the arms or legs **b :** a pikeman's armor including helmet **2** *or* **cor·se·lette** [fr. *Corselette,* a trademark] **:** an undergarment combining girdle and brassiere

[1]**cor·set** \ˈkȯr-sət\ *n* [ME, fr. OF, dim. of *cors*] **1 :** a usu. close-fitting and often laced medieval jacket **2 :** a woman's close-fitting boned supporting undergarment that is often hooked and laced and that extends from above or beneath the bust or from the waist to below the hips and has garters attached

[2]**corset** *vt* **1 :** to dress in or fit with a corset **2 :** to restrict closely **:** control rigidly

corset cover *n* **:** a woman's undergarment worn over a corset

cor·se·tiere \ˌkȯr-sə-ˈti(ə)r, -ˈtye(ə)r\ *n* [F *corsetière,* fem. of *corsetier,* fr. *corset*] **:** one who makes, fits, or sells corsets, girdles, or brassieres

cor·tege *also* **cor·tège** \kȯr-ˈtezh, ˈkȯr-ˌ\ *n* [F *cortège,* fr. It *corteggio,* fr. *corteggiare* to court, fr. *corte* court, fr. L *cohort-, cohors* throng — more at COURT] **1 :** a train of attendants **:** RETINUE **2 :** PROCESSION; *esp* **:** a funeral procession

cor·tex \ˈkȯr-ˌteks\ *n, pl* **cor·ti·ces** \ˈkȯrt-ə-ˌsēz\ *or* **cor·tex·es** [L *cortic-, cortex* bark — more at CUIRASS] **1 :** a plant bark or rind (as cinchona) used medicinally **2 a :** the outer or superficial part of an organ or body structure (as the kidney, adrenal gland, or a hair); *esp* **:** the outer layer of gray matter of the cerebrum and cerebellum **b :** the outer part of some organisms (as paramecia) **3 a :** the typically parenchymatous layer of tissue external to the vascular tissue and internal to the corky or epidermal tissues of a green plant; *broadly* **:** all tissues external to the xylem **b :** an outer or investing layer of various algae, lichens, or fungi

cor·ti·cal \ˈkȯrt-i-kəl\ *adj* **1 :** of, relating to, or consisting of cortex **2 :** involving or resulting from the action or condition of the cerebral cortex — **cor·ti·cal·ly** \-k(ə-)lē\ *adv*

cor·ti·cate \ˈkȯrt-ə-ˌkāt\ *adj* **:** having a cortex

cortico- *comb form* **1 :** cortex <*cortico*adrenal> **2 :** cortical and <*cortico*spinal>

cor·ti·coid \ˈkȯrt-i-ˌkȯid\ *n* **:** any of various adrenal-cortex steroids

cor·ti·co·ste·roid \ˌkȯrt-i-kō-ˈsti(ə)r-ˌȯid *also* -ˈste(ə)r-\ *n* **:** CORTICOID

cor·ti·co·ste·rone \ˌkȯrt-ə-ˈkäs-tə-ˌrōn, -i-kō-stə-ˈ\ *n* **:** a colorless crystalline steroid hormone $C_{21}H_{30}O_4$ of the adrenal cortex that is important in protein and carbohydrate metabolism

cor·ti·co·tro·pin \-ˈtrō-pən\ *or* **cor·ti·co·tro·phin** \-fən\ *n* [*corticotropic* + *-in*] **:** ADRENOCORTICOTROPHIC HORMONE; *also* **:** a preparation of ACTH that is used esp. in the treatment of rheumatoid arthritis and rheumatic fever

cor·tin \ˈkȯrt-ᵊn\ *n* **:** the active principle of the adrenal cortex

cor·ti·sol \ˈkȯrt-ə-ˌsȯl, -ˌzȯl, -ˌsōl, -ˌzōl\ *n* [*cortisone* + *-ol*] **:** a crystalline hormone $C_{21}H_{30}O_5$ of the adrenal cortex that is a dihydro derivative of cortisone and is used in the treatment of rheumatoid arthritis — called also *hydrocortisone*

cor·ti·sone \-ˌsōn, -ˌzōn\ *n* [alter. of *corticosterone*] **:** a steroid hormone $C_{21}H_{28}O_5$ of the adrenal cortex used esp. in the treatment of rheumatoid arthritis

co·run·dum \kə-ˈrən-dəm\ *n* [Tamil *kuruntam,* fr. Skt *kuruvinda* ruby] **:** a very hard mineral Al_2O_3 that consists of aluminum oxide occurring massive and as variously colored crystals which include the ruby and sapphire, that can be synthesized, and that is used as an abrasive (hardness 9, sp. gr. 3.95–4.10)

co·rus·cant \kə-ˈrəs-kənt\ *adj* **:** SHINING, GLITTERING

cor·us·cate \ˈkȯr-ə-ˌskāt, ˈkär-\ *vi* **-cat·ed; -cat·ing** [L *coruscatus,* pp. of *coruscare*] **1 :** to give off or reflect light in bright beams or flashes **:** SPARKLE **2 :** to be brilliant or showy in technique or style ***syn*** see FLASH

cor·us·ca·tion \ˌkȯr-ə-ˈskā-shən, ˌkär-\ *n* **1 :** GLITTER, SPARKLE **2 :** a flash of wit

cor·vée \ˈkȯr-ˌvā, kȯr-ˈ\ *n* [ME *corvee,* fr. MF, fr. ML *corrogata,* fr. L, fem. of *corrogatus,* pp. of *corrogare* to collect, requisition, fr. *com-* + *rogare* to ask — more at RIGHT] **1 :** unpaid labor (as on roads) due from a feudal vassal to his lord **2 :** labor exacted in lieu of taxes by public authorities esp. for highway construction or repair

corves *pl of* CORF

cor·vette \kȯr-ˈvet\ *n* [F] **1 :** a warship ranking in the old sailing navies next below a frigate **2 :** a highly maneuverable armed escort ship that is smaller than a destroyer

cor·vi·na \kȯr-ˈvē-nə\ *var of* CORBINA

cor·vine \ˈkȯr-ˌvīn\ *adj* [L *corvinus,* fr. *corvus* raven — more at RAVEN] **:** of or relating to the crows **:** resembling a crow

Cor·vus \ˈkȯr-vəs\ *n* [L (gen. *Corvi*), lit., raven] **:** a small constellation adjoining Virgo on the south

Cor·y·bant \ˈkȯr-ə-bant, ˈkär-\ *n, pl* **Cor·y·bants** \-ˌban(t)s\ *or* **Cor·y·ban·tes** \ˌkȯr-ə-ˈbant-ēz, ˌkär-\ [F *Corybante,* fr. L *Corybas,* fr. Gk *Korybas*] **:** one of the attendants or priests of Cybele noted for orgiastic processions and rites — **cor·y·ban·tic** \ˌkȯr-ə-ˈbant-ik, ˌkär-\ *adj*

co·ryd·a·lis \kə-ˈrid-ᵊl-əs\ *n* [NL, genus name, fr. Gk *korydallis* crested lark; akin to L *cornu* horn — more at HORN] **:** any of a large genus (*Corydalis*) of herbs of the fumitory family with racemose irregular flowers

cor·ymb \ˈkȯr-ˌim(b), ˈkär-, -əm(b)\ *n, pl* **cor·ymbs** \-ˌimz, -əmz\ [F *corymbe,* fr. L *corymbus* cluster of fruit or flowers, fr. Gk *korymbos*] **:** a flat-topped inflorescence; *specif* **:** one in which the flower stalks arise at different levels on the main axis and reach about the same height and in which the outer flowers open first and the inflorescence is indeterminate — **cory·mbed** \-ˌimd, -əmd\ *adj* — **cor·ym·bose** \-əm-ˌbōs\ *adj* — **cor·ym·bose·ly** *adv*

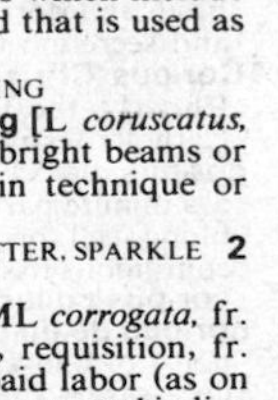

corymb of cherry: *1* peduncle, *2* pedicels, *3* bracts

co·ry·ne·bac·te·ri·um \ˌkȯr-ə-(ˌ)nē-bak-ˈtir-ē-əm, kə-ˌrim-ə-\ *n* [NL, genus name, fr. Gk *korynē* club; akin to L *cornu* horn] **:** any of a large genus (*Corynebacterium*) of usu. gram-positive nonmotile bacteria that occur as irregular or branching rods and include numerous important parasites of man, lower animals, and plants — **co·ry·ne·bac·te·ri·al** \-ē-əl\ *adj*

co·ryne·form \kə-ˈrin-ə-ˌfȯrm\ *adj* **:** being or resembling coryne-bacteria

cor·y·phae·us \ˌkȯr-ə-ˈfē-əs, ˌkär-\ *n, pl* **-phaei** \-ˈfē-ˌī\ [L, leader, fr. Gk *koryphaios,* fr. *koryphē* summit; akin to L *cornu*] **1 :** the leader of a chorus **2 :** the leader of a party or school of thought

co·ry·phée \ˌkȯr-i-ˈfā\ *n* [F, fr. L *coryphaeus*] **:** a ballet dancer who dances in a small group instead of in the corps de ballet or as a soloist

co·ry·za \kə-ˈrī-zə\ *n* [LL, fr. Gk *koryza* nasal mucus; akin to OHG *hroz* nasal mucus, Skt *kardama* mud] **:** an acute inflammatory contagious disease involving the upper respiratory tract; *esp* **:** COMMON COLD — **co·ry·zal** \-zəl\ *adj*

1cos *abbr* consul; consulship

2cos *symbol* cosine

COS *abbr* **1** cash on shipment **2** chief of staff

cosec *abbr* cosecant

co·se·cant \(ˈ)kō-ˈsē-ˌkant, -kənt\ *n* [NL *cosecant-, cosecans,* fr. *co-* + *secant-, secans* secant] **:** the trigonometric function that for an acute angle is the ratio between the hypotenuse of a right triangle of which the angle is considered part and the side opposite the angle

co·set \ˈkō-ˌset\ *n* **:** a subset of a mathematical group that consists of all the products obtained by multiplying either on the right or the left a fixed element of the group by each of the elements of a given subgroup

1cosh \ˈkäsh\ *n* [perh. fr. Romany *kosh* stick] *chiefly Brit* **:** a weighted weapon similar to a blackjack; *also* **:** an attack with a cosh

2cosh *vt, chiefly Brit* **:** to strike or assault with or as if with a cosh

co·sig·na·to·ry \(ˈ)kō-ˈsig-nə-ˌtōr-ē, -ˌtȯr-\ *n* **:** a joint signer

co·sign·er \ˈkō-ˌsī-nər\ *n* **:** COSIGNATORY; *esp* **:** a joint signer of a promissory note

co·sine \ˈkō-ˌsīn\ *n* [NL *cosinus,* fr. *co-* + ML *sinus* sine] **:** the trigonometric function that for an acute angle is the ratio between the side adjacent to the angle when it is considered part of a right triangle and the hypotenuse

cos lettuce \ˈkäs-, ˈkōs-\ *n* [*Kos, Cos,* Gk island] **:** a lettuce (*Lactuca sativa longifolia*) with long crisp leaves and columnar heads

1cos·met·ic \käz-ˈmet-ik\ *n* **:** a cosmetic preparation for external use

2cosmetic *adj* [Gk *kosmētikos* skilled in adornment, fr. *kosmein* to arrange, adorn, fr. *kosmos* order] **1 :** of, relating to, or making for beauty esp. of the complexion **:** BEAUTIFYING <~ salves> **2 :** correcting defects esp. of the face <~ surgery>

cosmetic case *n* **:** a small piece of luggage esp. for cosmetics

cos·me·ti·cian \ˌkäz-mə-ˈtish-ən\ *n* **:** one who is professionally trained in the use of cosmetics

cos·me·tol·o·gist \-ˈtäl-ə-jəst\ *n* **:** one who gives beauty treatments (as to skin and hair) — called also *beautician*

cos·me·tol·o·gy \-jē\ *n* [F *cosmétologie,* fr. *cosmétique* cosmetic (fr. E *cosmetic*) + *-logie* -logy] **:** the cosmetic treatment of the skin, hair, and nails

cos·mic \ˈkäz-mik\ *also* **cos·mi·cal** \-mi-kəl\ *adj* [Gk *kosmikos,* fr. *kosmos* order, universe] **1 :** of or relating to the cosmos, the extraterrestrial vastness, or the universe in contrast to the earth alone **2 :** characterized by greatness esp. in extent, intensity, or comprehensiveness <an abiding illness of the 20th century . . . — a ~ boredom —Albert Hubbell> — **cos·mi·cal·ly** \-mi-k(ə-)lē\ *adv*

cosmic dust *n* **:** very fine particles of solid matter in any part of the universe

cosmic noise *n* **:** GALACTIC NOISE

cosmic ray *n* **:** a stream of atomic nuclei of heterogeneous extremely penetrating character that enter the earth's atmosphere from outer space at speeds approaching that of light and bombard atmospheric atoms to produce mesons as well as secondary particles possessing some of the original energy

cos·mo·chem·is·try \ˌkäz-mō-ˈkem-ə-strē\ *n* [Gk *kosmos* universe] **:** a branch of chemistry that deals with the chemical composition and changes in the universe — **cos·mo·chem·i·cal** \-ˈkem-i-kəl\ *adj*

cos·mo·gen·ic \ˌkäz-mə-ˈjen-ik\ *adj* [*cosmic* ray + *-o-* + *-genic*] **:** produced by the action of cosmic rays <~ carbon 14>

cos·mog·o·ny \käz-ˈmäg-ə-nē\ *n, pl* **-nies** [NL *cosmogonia,* fr. Gk *kosmogonia,* fr. *kosmos* + *gonos* offspring] **1 :** the creation or origin of the world or universe **2 :** a theory of the origin of the universe — **cos·mo·gon·ic** \ˌkäz-mə-ˈgän-ik\ *or* **cos·mo·gon·i·cal** \-i-kəl\ *adj* — **cos·mog·o·nist** \käz-ˈmäg-ə-nəst\ *n*

cos·mog·ra·phy \käz-ˈmäg-rə-fē\ *n, pl* **-phies** [ME *cosmographie,* fr. LL *cosmographia,* fr. Gk *kosmographia,* fr. *kosmos* + *-graphia* -graphy] **1 :** a general description of the world or of the universe **2 :** the science that deals with the constitution of the whole order of nature — **cos·mog·ra·pher** \-fər\ *n* — **cos·mo·graph·ic** \ˌkäz-mə-ˈgraf-ik\ *or* **cos·mo·graph·i·cal** \-i-kəl\ *adj* — **cos·mo·graph·i·cal·ly** \-i-k(ə-)lē\ *adv*

Cosmoline \ˈkaz-mə-ˌlēn\ *trademark* — used for petrolatum

cos·mol·o·gy \käz-ˈmäl-ə-jē\ *n, pl* **-gies** [NL *cosmologia,* fr. Gk *kosmos* + NL *-logia* -logy] **1 :** a branch of metaphysics that deals with the universe as an orderly system **2 :** a branch of astronomy that deals with the origin, structure, and space-time relationships of the universe — **cos·mo·log·ic** \ˌkäz-mə-ˈläj-ik\ *or* **cos·mo·log·i·cal** \-i-kəl\ *adj* — **cos·mo·log·i·cal·ly** \-i-k(ə-)lē\ *adv* — **cos·mol·o·gist** \käz-ˈmäl-ə-jəst\ *n*

cos·mo·naut \ˈkäz-mə-ˌnȯt, -ˌnät\ *n* [part trans. of Russ *kosmonavt,* fr. Gk *kosmos* + Russ *-navt* (as in *aeronavt* aeronaut)] **:** a Soviet traveler beyond the earth's atmosphere **:** ASTRONAUT

cos·mop·o·lis \käz-ˈmäp-ə-ləs\ *n* [NL, back-formation fr. *cosmopolites*] **:** cosmopolitan city

1cos·mo·pol·i·tan \ˌkäz-mə-ˈpäl-ət-ᵊn\ *adj* **1 :** having worldwide rather than limited or provincial scope or bearing **2 :** having wide international sophistication **3 :** composed of persons, constituents, or elements from all or many parts of the world **4 :** found in most parts of the world and under varied ecological conditions <a ~ herb> — **cos·mo·pol·i·tan·ism** \-ᵊn-ˌiz-əm\ *n*

2cosmopolitan *n* **:** COSMOPOLITE

cos·mop·o·lite \käz-ˈmäp-ə-ˌlīt\ *n* [NL *cosmopolites,* fr. Gk *kosmopolitēs,* fr. *kosmos* + *politēs* citizen] **:** a cosmopolitan person or organism — **cos·mo·pol·i·tism** \käz-ˈmäp-ə-ˌlīt-ˌiz-əm, -lə-ˌtiz-; ˌkäz-mə-ˈpäl-ə-ˌtiz-\ *n*

cos·mos \ˈkäz-məs, *1 & 2 also* -ˌmōs, -ˌmäs\ *n* [G *kosmos,* fr. Gk] **1 a :** an orderly harmonious systematic universe — compare CHAOS **b :** ORDER, HARMONY **2 :** a complex orderly self-inclusive system **3** *pl* **cosmos** \-məs, -məz\ *also* **cos·mos·es** \-mə-səz\ [NL, genus name, fr. Gk *kosmos*] **:** any of a genus (*Cosmos*) of tropical American composite herbs; *esp* **:** a widely cultivated tall fall-blooming annual (*C. bipinnatus*) with yellow or red disks and showy ray flowers

co·spon·sor \ˈkō-ˌspän(t)-sər, -ˈspän(t)-\ *n* **:** a joint sponsor — **cosponsor** *vt* — **co·spon·sor·ship** \-ˌship\ *n*

cos·sack \ˈkäs-ˌak, -ək\ *n* [Russ *kazak* & Ukrainian *kozak,* fr. Turk *kazak* free person] **:** a member of a group of frontiersmen of southern Russia organized as cavalry in the czarist army

1cos·set \ˈkäs-ət\ *n* [origin unknown] **:** a pet lamb; *broadly* **:** PET

2cosset *vt* **:** to treat as a pet **:** PAMPER

1cost \ˈkȯst\ *n* **1 a :** the amount or equivalent paid or charged for something **:** PRICE **b :** the outlay or expenditure (as of effort or sacrifice) made to achieve an object **2 :** loss or penalty incurred in gaining something **3** *pl* **:** expenses incurred in litigation; *esp* **:** those given by the law or the court to the prevailing party against the losing party — **cost·less** \-ləs\ *adj* — **cost·less·ly** *adv*

2cost *vb* **cost; cost·ing** [ME *costen,* fr. MF *coster,* fr. L *constare* to stand firm, to cost — more at CONSTANT] *vi* **1 :** to require expenditure or payment <the best goods ~ more> **2 :** to require effort, suffering, or loss ~ *vt* **1 :** to have a price of **2 :** to cause (someone) to pay, suffer, or lose something <frequent absences ~ him his job> **3 :** to estimate or set the cost of

cos·ta \ˈkäs-tə\ *n, pl* **cos·tae** \-(ˌ)tē, -ˌtī\ [L — more at COAST] **1 :** 1RIB 1a **2 :** a part (as the midrib of a leaf or the anterior vein of an insect wing) that resembles a rib — **cos·tal** \-tᵊl\ *adj* — **cos·tate** \-ˌtāt\ *adj*

cost accountant *n* **:** a specialist in cost accounting

cost accounting *n* **:** the systematic recording and analysis of the costs of material, labor, and overhead incident to production

1co–star \ˈkō-ˌstär\ *n* **:** a star whose role in a motion picture or play is equal in importance to that of another leading player

2co–star *vi* **:** to appear as a co-star in a motion picture or play ~ *vt* **:** to feature (a player) as a co-star

cos·tard \ˈkäs-tərd\ *n* [ME] **1 :** any of several large English cooking apples **2** *archaic* **:** NODDLE, PATE

cost–ef·fec·tive \ˌkȯs-tə-ˈfek-tiv\ *adj* **:** economical in terms of tangible benefits produced by money spent <~ measures to combat poverty> — **cost–ef·fec·tive·ness** *n*

cos·ter \ˈkäs-tər\ *n, Brit* **:** COSTERMONGER

cos·ter·mon·ger \-ˌməŋ-gər, -ˌmäŋ-\ *n* [*costard* + *monger*] *Brit* **:** a hawker of fruit or vegetables

cos·tive \ˈkäs-tiv\ *adj* [ME, fr. MF *costivé,* pp. of *costiver* to constipate, fr. L *constipare*] **1 a :** affected with constipation **b :** causing constipation **2 :** slow in action or expression **3 :** NIGGARDLY — **cos·tive·ly** *adv* — **cos·tive·ness** *n*

cost·ly \ˈkȯs(t)-lē\ *adj* **cost·li·er; -est** **1 :** commanding a high price usu. because of intrinsic worth <~ gems> **2 :** GORGEOUS, SPLENDID **3 :** made at heavy expense or sacrifice — **cost·li·ness** *n*

syn COSTLY, EXPENSIVE, DEAR, VALUABLE, PRECIOUS, INVALUABLE, PRICELESS *shared meaning element* **:** having a high value or valuation esp. in terms of money ***ant*** cheap

cost·mary \ˈkȯst-ˌmer-ē, ˈkäst-\ *n, pl* **-mari·es** [ME *costmarie,* fr. *coste* costmary (fr. OE *cost,* fr. L *costum,* fr. Gk *kostos,* a fragrant root) + *Marie* the Virgin Mary] **:** a tansy-scented composite herb (*Chrysanthemum majus*) used as a potherb and in flavoring

cost of living : the cost of purchasing those goods and services which are included in an accepted standard level of consumption

cost–of–living index *n* **:** CONSUMER PRICE INDEX

cost–plus \ˈkȯs(t)-ˈpləs\ *adj* **:** paid on the basis of a fixed fee or a percentage added to actual cost <a ~ contract>

cost–push \ˈkȯs(t)-ˌpu̇sh\ *n* **:** an increase or upward trend in production costs (as wages) that tends to result in increased consumer prices irrespective of the level of demand — compare DEMAND-PULL — **cost–push** *adj*

cos·trel \ˈkäs-trəl\ *n* [ME, fr. MF *costerel,* fr. *costier* at the side, fr. *coste* rib, side — more at COAST] **:** a flat usu. earthenware container for liquids with loops through which a belt or cord may be passed for easy carrying — called also *pilgrim bottle*

1cos·tume \ˈkäs-ˌt(y)üm *also* -təm *or* -ˌchüm\ *n* [F, fr. It, custom, dress, fr. L *consuetudin-, consuetudo* custom — more at CUSTOM] **1 :** the prevailing fashion in coiffure, jewelry, and apparel of a period, country, or class **2 :** a suit or dress characteristic of a period, country, or class **3 :** a person's ensemble of outer garments; *esp* **:** a woman's ensemble of dress with coat or jacket — **cos·tum·ey** *adj*

2cos·tume \käs-ˈt(y)üm *also* -ˈchüm; *or like* 1\ *vt* **cos·tumed; cos·tum·ing** **1 :** to provide with a costume **2 :** to design costumes for a <~ a play>

3costume *like* 1\ *adj* **1 :** characterized by the use of costumes <a ~ ball> <a ~ drama> **2 :** suitable for or enhancing the effect of a particular costume <a ~ handbag>

costume jewelry *n* **:** inexpensive jewelry designed for wear with current fashions

cos·tum·er \ˈkäs-ˌt(y)ü-mər *also* -ˌchü-; käs-ˈ\ *n* **1 :** one that deals in or makes costumes **2 :** CLOTHES TREE

cos·tum·ery \-mə-rē\ *n* **1 :** articles of costume **2 :** the art of costuming

cos·tu·mi·er \käs-ˈt(y)ü-mē-ˌā, -mē-ər\ *n* [F] **:** COSTUMER 1

co·sy \ˈkō-zē\ *var of* COZY

1cot \ˈkät\ *n* [ME, fr. OE; akin to ON *kot* small hut, L *guttur* throat] **1 :** a small house **2 :** COVER, SHEATH; *esp* **:** STALL 4

2cot *n* [Hindi *khāṭ* bedstead, fr. Skt *khaṭvā,* of Dravidian origin; akin to Tamil *kaṭṭil* bedstead] **:** a small usu. collapsible bed often of fabric stretched on a frame

3cot *symbol* cotangent

co·tan·gent \(ˈ)kō-ˈtan-jənt\ *n* [NL *cotangent-, cotangens,* fr. *co-* + *tangent-, tangens* tangent] **:** the trigonometric function that for an acute angle is the ratio between the side adjacent to the angle when it is considered part of a right triangle and the side opposite

1cote \ˈkōt, ˈkät\ *n* [ME, fr. OE] **1** *dial Eng* **:** 1COT 1 **2 :** a shed or coop for small domestic animals and esp. pigeons

2cote \ˈkōt\ *vt* [prob. fr. MF *cotoyer*] *obs* **:** to pass by

co·te·rie \ˈkōt-ə-(ˌ)rē, ˌkōt-ə-ˈ\ *n* [F, fr. MF, tenants, fr. (assumed) MF *cotier* cotter, fr. ML *cotarius*] **:** an intimate and often exclusive group of persons with a unifying common interest or purpose ***syn*** see SET

co·ter·mi·nous \(ˈ)kō-ˈtər-mə-nəs\ *adj* [alter. of *conterminous*] **1 :** having the same or coincident boundaries <~ states> **2 :** coextensive in scope or duration <~ interests> — **co·ter·mi·nous·ly** *adv*

co·thur·nus \kō-ˈthər-nəs\ *n, pl* **-ni** \-ˌnī, -(ˌ)nē\ [L, fr. Gk *kothornos*] **1 :** a high thick-soled laced boot worn by actors in Greek and Roman tragic drama — called also *cothurn* **2 :** the dignified somewhat stylized spirit of ancient tragedy

co·tid·al \(ˈ)kō-ˈtīd-ᵊl\ *adj* **:** indicating equality in the tides or a coincidence in the time of high or low tide

co·til·lion \kō-ˈtil-yən\ *also* **co·til·lon** \kō-ˈtil-yən, kò-tē-(y)ō^{n}\ *n* [F *cotillon,* lit., petticoat, fr. OF, fr. *cote* coat] **1 :** a ballroom dance for couples that resembles the quadrille **2 :** an elaborate dance with frequent changing of partners carried out under the leadership of one couple at formal balls **3 :** a formal ball

co·to·neas·ter \kə-ˈtō-nē-ˌas-tər, ˈkät-ᵊn-ˌēs-\ *n* [NL, genus name, fr. L *cydonia, cotoneum* quince + NL *-aster*] **:** any of a genus (*Cotoneaster*) of Old World flowering shrubs of the rose family

cot·quean \ˈkät-ˌkwēn\ *n* **1** *archaic* **:** a coarse masculine woman **2** *archaic* **:** a man who busies himself with women's work or affairs

Cots·wold \ˈkät-ˌswōld\ *n* [*Cotswold* hills, England] **:** a sheep of an English breed of large long-wooled sheep

cot·ta \ˈkät-ə\ *n* [ML, of Gmc origin; akin to OHG *kozza* coarse mantle — more at COAT] **:** a waist-length surplice

cot·tage \ˈkät-ij\ *n* [ME *cotage,* fr. (assumed) AF, fr. ME *cot*] **1 :** the dwelling of a farm laborer or small farmer **2 :** a small usu. frame one-family house **3 :** a small detached dwelling unit at an institution **4 :** a small house for vacation use — **cot·tag·ey** \-ij-ē\ *adj*

cottage cheese *n* **:** a soft uncured cheese made from soured skim milk — called also *Dutch cheese, pot cheese, smearcase*

cottage curtains *n pl* **:** a double set of upper and lower straight-hanging window curtains

cottage industry *n* **:** an industry whose labor force consists of family units working at home with their own equipment

cottage pudding *n* **:** plain cake covered with a hot sweet sauce

cot·tag·er \ˈkät-ij-ər\ *n* **:** one who lives in a cottage (as at a vacation resort)

cottage tulip *n* **:** any of various tall-growing tulips that flower in the middle of the tulip-flowering season

1cot·ter *or* **cot·tar** \ˈkät-ər\ *n* [ME *cottar,* fr. ML *cotarius,* fr. ME *cot*] **:** a peasant or farm laborer who occupies a cottage and sometimes a small holding of land usu. in return for services

2cotter *n* [origin unknown] **1 :** a wedge-shaped or tapered piece used to fasten together parts of a structure **2 :** COTTER PIN

cotter pin *n* **:** a half-round metal strip bent into a pin whose ends can be flared after insertion through a slot or hole

1cot·ton \ˈkät-ᵊn\ *n, often attrib* [ME *coton,* fr. MF, fr. Ar *quṭn*] **1 a :** a soft usu. white fibrous substance composed of the hairs surrounding the seeds of various erect freely branching tropical plants (genus *Gossypium*) of the mallow family **b :** a plant producing cotton; *esp* **:** one grown for its cotton **c :** a crop of cotton **2 a :** fabric made of cotton **b :** yarn spun from cotton **3 :** a downy cottony substance produced by various plants (as the cottonwood)

cotton: *1* flowering branch, *2* fruit, unopened, *3* fruit, partly opened

2cotton *vi* **cot·toned; cot·ton·ing** \ˈkät-niŋ, -ᵊn-iŋ\ **1 :** to take a liking <~*s* to people easily> **2 :** to come to understand **:** catch on **:** TUMBLE <~*ed* on to the fact that our children work furiously —H. M. McLuhan>

cotton candy *n* **:** a candy made of spun sugar

cotton gin *n* **:** a machine that separates the seeds, hulls, and foreign material from cotton

cotton grass *n* **:** any of a genus (*Eriophorum*) of sedges with tufted spikes

cot·ton·mouth \ˈkät-ᵊn-ˌmau̇th\ *n* **:** WATER MOCCASIN

cottonmouth moccasin *n* **:** WATER MOCCASIN

cot·ton–pick·ing \ˌkät-ᵊn-ˌpik-iŋ, -ˌpik-ən\ *adj* **1 :** DAMNED — used as a generalized expression of disapproval <a ~ hypocrite> **2 :** DAMNED — used as an intensive <out of his ~ mind —Irving Kristol>

cot·ton·seed \ˈkät-ᵊn-ˌsēd\ *n* **:** the seed of the cotton plant

cottonseed oil *n* **:** a pale yellow semidrying fatty oil that is obtained from the cottonseed and is used chiefly in salad and cooking oils and after hydrogenation in shortenings and margarine

cotton stainer *n* **:** any of several red and black or dark brown bugs (genus *Dysdercus*) that damage and stain the lint of developing cotton; *specif* **:** a red and brown bug (*D. suturellus*) that attacks cotton in the southern U.S.

cot·ton·tail \ˈkät-ᵊn-ˌtāl\ *n* **:** any of several rather small No. American rabbits (genus *Sylvilagus*) sandy brown in color with a white-tufted underside of the tail

cot·ton·weed \-ˌwēd\ *n* **:** any of various weedy plants (as cudweed) with hoary pubescence or cottony seeds

cot·ton·wood \-ˌwu̇d\ *n* **:** a poplar with a tuft of cottony hairs on the seed; *esp* **:** one (*Populus deltoides*) of the eastern and central U.S. often cultivated for its rapid growth and luxuriant foliage

cotton wool *n* **:** raw cotton; *esp* **:** cotton batting

cot·tony \ˈkät-nē, -ᵊn-ē\ *adj* **:** resembling cotton in appearance or character: as **a :** covered with hairs or pubescence **b :** SOFT

cotyl- *or* **cotyli-** *or* **cotylo-** *comb form* [Gk *kotyl-, kotylo-,* fr. *kotylē*] **:** cup **:** organ or part like a cup <*cotyl*oid> <*cotyli*form>

-cot·yl \ˌkät-ᵊl\ *n comb form* [*cotyledon*] **:** cotyledon <di*cotyl*>

cot·y·le·don \ˌkät-ᵊl-ˈēd-ᵊn\ *n* [NL, fr. Gk *kotylēdōn* cup-shaped hollow, fr. *kotylē* cup] **1 :** a placental lobule **2 :** the first leaf or one of the first pair or whorl of leaves developed by the embryo of a seed plant or of some lower plants (as ferns) — see PLUMULE illustration — **cot·y·le·don·al** \-ˈēd-nəl, -ᵊn-əl\ *adj* — **cot·y·le·don·ary** \-ˈēd-ᵊn-ˌer-ē\ *or* **cot·y·le·don·ous** \-ˈēd-nəs, -ᵊn-əs\ *adj*

co·ty·lo·saur \ˈkät-ᵊl-ō-ˌsȯ(ə)r, kə-ˈtil-ə-\ *n* [NL *Cotylosauria,* group name, deriv. of Gk *kotylē* cup & *sauros* lizard] **:** any of an order (Cotylosauria) of extinct ancient primitive reptiles with short legs and massive bodies that were prob. the earliest truly terrestrial vertebrate animals

co·type \ˈkō-ˌtīp\ *n* **:** any of several secondary taxonomic types

1couch \ˈkau̇ch\ *vb* [ME *couchen,* fr. MF *coucher,* fr. L *collocare* to set in place — more at COLLOCATE] *vt* **1 :** to lay (oneself) down for rest or sleep **2 :** to embroider (a design) by laid threads fastened by small stitches at regular intervals **3 :** to place or hold level and pointed forward ready for use **4 :** to phrase in a specified manner <the memorandum was ~*ed* in strong language —W. L. Shirer> **5 :** to treat (a cataract) by displacing the lens of the eye into the vitreous humor ~ *vi* **1 :** to lie down or recline for sleep or rest **2 :** to lie in ambush

2couch *n* **1 a :** an article of furniture (as a bed or sofa) for sitting or reclining **b :** a couch on which a patient reclines when undergoing psychoanalysis **2 :** the den of an animal (as an otter) — **on the couch :** receiving psychiatric treatment

couch·ant \ˈkau̇-chənt\ *adj* [ME, fr. MF, fr. prp. of *coucher*] **:** lying down esp. with the head up <a heraldic lion ~>

couch grass \ˈkau̇ch-, ˈküch-\ *n* [alter. of *quitch grass*] **1 :** QUACK GRASS **2 :** any of several grasses that resemble quack grass in spreading by creeping rhizomes

cou·dé \kü-ˈdā\ *adj* [F *coudé* bent like an elbow, fr. *coude* elbow, fr. L *cubitum* — more at HIP] **1** *of a telescope* **:** constructed so that the light is reflected along the polar axis to come to a focus at a fixed place where the holder for a photographic plate or a spectrograph may be mounted **2 :** of or relating to a coudé telescope

cou·gar \ˈkü-gər, -ˌgär\ *n, pl* **cougars** *also* **cougar** [F *couguar,* fr. NL *cuguacuarana,* modif. of Tupi *suasuarana,* lit., false deer, fr. *suasú* deer + *rana* false] **:** a large powerful tawny brown cat (*Felis concolor*) formerly widespread in the Americas but now extinct in many areas — called also *catamount, mountain lion, panther, puma*

cougar

1cough \ˈkȯf\ *vb* [ME *coughen,* fr. (assumed) OE *cohhian;* akin to MHG *kūchen* to breathe heavily] *vi* **1 :** to expel air from the lungs suddenly with an explosive noise **2 :** to make a noise like that of coughing ~ *vt* **:** to expel by coughing — often used with *up* <~ up mucus>

2cough *n* **1 :** a condition marked by repeated or frequent coughing **2 :** an act or sound of coughing

cough drop *n* **:** a lozenge or troche used to relieve coughing

cough syrup *n* **:** any of various sweet usu. medicated liquids used to relieve coughing

cough up *vt* **:** to hand over **:** DELIVER, PAY <*cough up* the money>

could \kəd, (ˈ)ku̇d\ [ME *couthe, coude,* fr. OE *cūthe;* akin to OHG *konda* could] *past of* CAN — used in auxiliary function in the past <he found he ~ go>, in the past conditional <he said he would go if he ~>, and as an alternative to *can* suggesting less force or certainty or as a polite form in the present <~ you do this for me> <if you ~ come we would be pleased>

could·est \ˈku̇d-əst\ *archaic past 2d sing of* CAN

couldn't \ˈku̇d-ᵊnt\ **:** could not

couldst \kədst, (ˈ)ku̇dst, kətst, (ˈ)ku̇tst\ *archaic past 2d sing of* CAN

cou·lee \ˈkü-lē\ *n* [CanF *coulée,* fr. F, flowing, flow of lava, fr. *couler* to flow, fr. L *colare* to strain, fr. *colum* sieve] **1 a :** a small stream **b :** a dry stream bed **c :** a usu. small or shallow ravine **:** GULLY **2 :** a thick sheet or stream of lava

cou·lisse \kü-ˈlēs, -ˈlis\ *n* [F] **1 a :** a side scene of a theater stage; *also* **:** the space between the side scenes **b :** a backstage area **c :** HALLWAY **2 :** a piece of timber having a groove in which something glides

cou·loir \kül-ˈwär\ *n* [F, lit., strainer, fr. LL *colatorium,* fr. L *colatus,* pp. of *colare*] **:** a mountainside gorge esp. in the Swiss Alps

1cou·lomb \ˈkü-ˌläm, -ˌlōm, kü-ˈ\ *n* [Charles A. de *Coulomb*] **:** the practical mks unit of electric charge equal to the quantity of electricity transferred by a current of one ampere in one second

2coulomb *or* **cou·lom·bic** \kü-ˈläm-(b)ik, -ˈlōm-\ *adj* **:** of, relating to, or being the electrostatic force of attraction or repulsion between charged particles

cou·lom·e·try \kü-ˈläm-ə-trē\ *n* [alter. of earlier *coulombmeter*] **:** chemical analysis performed by determining the amount of a substance released in an electrolysis by measuring the number of coulombs used — **cou·lo·met·ric** \ˌkü-lə-ˈme-trik\ *adj* — **cou·lo·met·ri·cal·ly** \-tri-k(ə-)lē\ *adv*

coul·ter \ˈkōl-tər\ *n* [ME *colter,* fr. OE *culter* & OF *coltre,* both fr. L *culter* plowshare] **:** a cutting tool (as a knife or sharp disc) that is attached to the beam of a plow, makes a vertical cut in the surface, and permits clean separation and effective covering of the soil and materials being turned under

cou·ma·phos \ˈkü-mə-ˌfäs\ *n* [*coumar*in + *phos*phorus] **:** an organophosphorus systemic insecticide $C_{14}H_{16}ClO_5PS$ used esp. on cattle and poultry

cou·ma·rin \ˈkü-mə-rən\ *n* [F *coumarine,* fr. *coumarou* tonka bean tree, fr. Sp or Pg; Sp *coumarú,* fr. Pg, fr. Tupi] **:** a toxic white crystalline lactone $C_9H_6O_2$ with an odor of new-mown hay found in plants or made synthetically and used esp. in perfumery

cou·ma·rone \-ˌrōn\ *n* [ISV *coumarin* + *-one*] **:** a compound C_8H_6O found in coal tar and polymerized with indene to form thermoplastic resins used esp. in coatings and printing inks — called also *benzofuran*

¹coun·cil \ˈkau̇n(t)-səl\ *n* [ME *counceil,* fr. OF *concile,* fr. L *concilium,* fr. *com-* + *calare* to call — more at LOW] **1 :** an assembly or meeting for consultation, advice, or discussion **2 :** a group elected or appointed as an advisory or legislative body **3 a :** a usu. administrative body **b :** an executive body whose members are equal in power and authority **c :** a governing body of delegates from local units of a federation **4 :** deliberation in a council **5 a :** a federation of or a central body uniting a group of organizations **b :** a local chapter of an organization **c :** CLUB, SOCIETY

²council *adj* **1 :** used for councils esp. by or with No. American Indians <a ~ ground> **2** *Brit* **:** built, maintained, or operated by a local governing agency <a ~ house> <~ flats>

coun·cil·lor *or* **coun·cil·or** \ˈkau̇n(t)-s(ə-)lər\ *n* **:** a member of a council — **coun·cil·lor·ship** \-ˌship\ *n*

coun·cil·man \ˈkau̇n(t)-səl-mən\ *n* **:** a member of a council (as of a town or city) — **coun·cil·man·ic** \ˌkau̇n(t)-səl-ˈman-ik\ *adj*

council of ministers *often cap C&M* **:** CABINET 3b

coun·cil·wom·an \ˈkau̇n(t)-səl-ˌwu̇m-ən\ *n* **:** a female member of a council

¹coun·sel \ˈkau̇n(t)-səl\ *n* [ME *conseil,* fr. OF, fr. L *consilium,* fr. *consulere* to consult] **1 a :** advice given esp. as a result of consultation **b :** a policy or plan of action or behavior **2 :** DELIBERATION, CONSULTATION **3 a** *archaic* **:** PURPOSE **b :** guarded thoughts or intentions **4 a** *pl* **counsel (1) :** a lawyer engaged in the trial or management of a case in court **(2) :** a lawyer appointed to advise and represent in legal matters an individual client or a corporate and esp. a public body **b :** CONSULTANT 2

²counsel *vb* **-seled** *or* **-selled; -sel·ing** *or* **-sel·ling** \-s(ə-)liŋ\ *vt* **:** ADVISE <~*ed* them to avoid rash actions —George Orwell> ~ *vi* **:** CONSULT <~*ed* with her husband>

coun·sel·ee \ˌkau̇n(t)-sə-ˈlē\ *n* **:** one who is being counseled

coun·sel·ing *n* **:** professional guidance of the individual by utilizing psychological methods esp. in collecting case history data, using various techniques of the personal interview, and testing interests and aptitudes

coun·sel·or *or* **coun·sel·lor** \ˈkau̇n(t)-s(ə-)lər\ *n* **1 :** ADVISER **2 :** LAWYER; *specif* **:** one that gives advice in law and manages cases for clients in court **3 :** one who has supervisory duties at a summer camp — **coun·sel·or·ship** \-ˌship\ *n*

counselor–at–law *n, pl* **counselors–at–law :** COUNSELOR 2

¹count \ˈkau̇nt\ *vb* [ME *counten,* fr. MF *compter,* fr. L *computare,* fr. *com-* + *putare* to consider — more at PAVE] *vt* **1 a :** to indicate or name by units or groups so as to find the total number of units involved **:** NUMBER **b :** to name the numbers in order up to and including <~ ten> **c :** to include in a tallying and reckoning <about 100 present, ~*ing* children> **d :** to call aloud (beats or time units) <~ cadence > <~ eighth notes> **2 a :** CONSIDER, ACCOUNT <~ oneself lucky> **b :** ESTIMATE, ESTEEM **c :** to record as of an opinion or persuasion <~ me as uncommitted> **3 :** to include or exclude by or as if by counting <~ me in> ~ *vi* **1 a :** to recite or indicate the numbers in order by units or groups <~ by fives> **b :** to count the units in a group **2 :** to rely or depend on someone or something <~*ed* on his brother to help with the expenses> **3 :** ADD, TOTAL <it ~*s* up to a sizable amount> **4 :** to have value or significance <these are the men who really ~> ***syn*** see RELY — **count heads** *or* **count noses :** to count the number present — **count on :** to look forward to as certain **:** ANTICIPATE <*counted on* winning>

²count *n* **1 a :** the action or process of counting **b :** a total obtained by counting **:** TALLY **2** *archaic* **a :** RECKONING, ACCOUNT **b :** CONSIDERATION, ESTIMATION **3 a :** ALLEGATION, CHARGE; *specif* **:** one separately stating the cause of action or prosecution in a legal declaration or indictment <guilty on all ~*s*> **b :** a specific point under consideration **:** ISSUE **4 :** the total number of individual things in a given unit or sample <blood ~> **5 a :** the calling off of the seconds from one to ten when a boxer has been knocked down **b :** the number of balls and strikes charged to a baseball batter during one turn <the ~ stood at 3 and 2> **c :** SCORE <tied the ~ with a minute to play>

³count *n* [MF *comte,* fr. LL *comit-, comes,* fr. L, companion, one of the imperial court, fr. *com-* + *ire* to go — more at ISSUE] **:** a European nobleman whose rank corresponds to that of a British earl

count·able \ˈkau̇nt-ə-bəl\ *adj* **:** capable of being counted; *esp* **:** DENUMERABLE <a ~ set> — **count·abil·i·ty** \ˌkau̇nt-ə-ˈbil-ət-ē\ *n* — **count·ably** \ˈkau̇nt-ə-blē\ *adv*

count·down \ˈkau̇nt-ˌdau̇n\ *n* **:** an audible backward counting in fixed units (as seconds) from an arbitrary starting number to mark the time remaining before an event; *also* **:** preparations carried on during such a count — **count down** \-ˈdau̇n\ *vi*

¹coun·te·nance \ˈkau̇nt-ᵊn-ən(t)s, ˈkau̇nt-nən(t)s\ *n* [ME *contenance,* fr. MF, fr. ML *continentia,* fr. L, restraint, fr. *continent-, continens,* prp. of *continēre* to hold together — more at CONTAIN] **1** *obs* **:** BEARING, DEMEANOR **2 a :** calm expression **b :** mental composure **c :** LOOK, EXPRESSION **3** *archaic* **a :** ASPECT, SEMBLANCE **b :** PRETENSE **4 :** FACE, VISAGE; *esp* **:** the face as an indication of mood, emotion, or character **5 :** bearing or expression that offers approval or sanction **:** moral support ***syn*** see FAVOR

²countenance *vt* **-nanced; -nanc·ing :** to extend approval or toleration to **:** SANCTION <he never *countenanced* violence> — **coun·te·nanc·er** *n*

¹count·er \ˈkau̇nt-ər\ *n* [ME *countour,* fr. MF *comptouer,* fr. ML *computatorium* computing place, fr. L *computatus,* pp. of *computare*] **1 :** a piece (as of metal or ivory) used in reckoning or in games **2 :** something of value in bargaining **:** ASSET **3 :** a level surface (as a table) over which transactions are conducted or food is served or on which goods are displayed or work is conducted <a lunch ~> — **over the counter 1 :** in or through a broker's office rather than through a stock exchange <stock bought *over the counter*> **2 :** without a prescription <drugs available *over the counter*> — **under the counter :** by surreptitious means **:** in an illicit and private manner

²count·er *n* [ME, fr. MF *conteor,* fr. *compter* to count] **:** one that counts; *esp* **:** a device for indicating a number or amount

³coun·ter \ˈkau̇nt-ər\ *vb* [ME *countren,* fr. MF *contre*] *vt* **1 a :** to act in opposition to **:** OPPOSE **b :** OFFSET, NULLIFY <tried to ~ the trend toward depersonalization> **2 :** to adduce in answer <he ~*ed* that his warnings had been ignored> ~ *vi* **:** to meet attacks or arguments with defensive or retaliatory steps

⁴coun·ter *adv* [ME *contre,* fr. MF, fr. L *contra* against, opposite; akin to L *com-* with, together — more at CO-] **1 :** in an opposite or wrong direction **2 :** to or toward a different or opposite direction, result, or effect <values that run ~ to those of established society>

⁵coun·ter *n* **1 :** CONTRARY, OPPOSITE **2 :** the after portion of a boat from the waterline to the extreme outward swell or stern overhang **3 a :** the act of making an attack while parrying one (as in boxing or fencing); *also* **:** a blow thus given in boxing **b :** an agency or force that offsets **:** CHECK **4 :** a stiffener to give permanent form to a boot or shoe upper around the heel **5 :** an area in the face of a letter that is less than type-high and enclosed by the strokes — see TYPE illustration **6 :** a football play in which the ballcarrier goes in a direction opposite to the movement of the play

⁶coun·ter *adj* **1 :** marked by or tending toward or in an opposite direction or effect **2 :** given to or marked by opposition, hostility, or antipathy **3 :** situated or lying opposite <the ~ side> **4 :** recalling or ordering back by a superseding contrary order **:** COUNTERMANDING <~ orders from the colonel> ***syn*** see ADVERSE

coun·ter- *prefix* [ME *contre-,* fr. MF, fr. *contre*] **1 a :** contrary **:** opposite <*counter*clockwise> <*counter*march> **b :** opposing **:** retaliatory <*counter*irritant> <*counter*offensive> **2 :** complementary **:** corresponding <*counter*weight> <*counter*part> **3 :** duplicate **:** substitute <*counter*foil>

coun·ter·act \ˌkau̇nt-ə-ˈrakt\ *vt* **:** to make ineffective or restrain or neutralize the usu. ill effects of by an opposite force — **coun·ter·ac·tion** \-ˈrak-shən\ *n*

coun·ter·ac·tive \-ˈrak-tiv\ *adj* **:** tending to counteract ***syn*** see ADVERSE

¹coun·ter·at·tack \ˈkau̇nt-ə-rə-ˌtak\ *n* **:** an attack made to counter an enemy's attack

²counterattack *vi* **:** to make a counterattack ~ *vt* **:** to make a counterattack against — **coun·ter·at·tack·er** *n*

¹coun·ter·bal·ance \ˈkau̇nt-ər-ˌbal-ən(t)s, ˌkau̇nt-ər-ˈ\ *n* **1 :** a weight that balances another **2 :** a force or influence that offsets or checks an opposing force

²counterbalance \ˌkau̇nt-ər-ˈ, ˈkau̇nt-ər-ˌ\ *vt* **1 :** to oppose or balance with an equal weight or force **2 :** to equip with counterbalances

coun·ter·blow \ˈkau̇nt-ər-ˌblō\ *n* **:** a retaliatory blow

coun·ter·change \-ˌchānj\ *vt* **1 :** INTERCHANGE, TRANSPOSE **2 :** CHECKER 1a

¹coun·ter·check \-ˌchek\ *n* **:** a check or restraint often operating against something that is itself a check

²countercheck *vt* **1 :** CHECK, COUNTERACT **2 :** to check a second time for verification

counter check *n* **:** a check obtainable at a bank usu. to be cashed only at the bank by the drawer

¹coun·ter·claim \ˈkau̇nt-ər-ˌklām\ *n* **:** an opposing claim esp. in law

²counterclaim *vi* **:** to enter or plead a counterclaim ~ *vt* **:** to ask in a counterclaim

coun·ter·clock·wise \ˌkau̇nt-ər-ˈkläk-ˌwīz\ *adv* **:** in a direction opposite to that in which the hands of a clock rotate as viewed from in front — **counterclockwise** *adj*

coun·ter·con·di·tion·ing \-kən-ˈdish-(ə-)niŋ\ *n* **:** conditioning in order to replace an undesirable response (as fear) to a stimulus (as an engagement in public speaking) by a favorable one

coun·ter·coup \ˈkau̇nt-ər-ˌkü\ *n* **:** a coup directed toward overthrowing a government which seized power by a coup

coun·ter·cul·ture \-ˌkəl-chər\ *n* **:** a culture esp. of the young with values and mores that run counter to those of established society — **coun·ter·cul·tur·al** \ˌkau̇nt-ər-ˈkəlch-(ə-)rəl\ *adj* — **coun·ter·cul·tur·ist** \-(ə-)rəst\ *n*

¹coun·ter·cur·rent \ˈkau̇nt-ər-ˌkər-ənt, -ˌkə-rənt\ *n* **:** a current flowing in a direction opposite that of another current

²countercurrent \ˌkau̇nt-ər-ˈ\ *adj* **1 :** flowing in an opposite direction **2 :** involving flow of materials in opposite directions <~ dialysis> — **coun·ter·cur·rent·ly** *adv*

coun·ter·dem·on·stra·tion \ˈkau̇nt-ər-ˌdem-ən-ˈstrā-shən\ *n* **:** a demonstration opposing another demonstration — **coun·ter·dem·on·strate** \ˌkau̇nt-ər-ˈdem-ən-ˌstrāt\ *vi* — **coun·ter·dem·on·stra·tor** \-ˌstrāt-ər\ *n*

coun·ter·es·pi·o·nage \ˌkau̇nt-ə-ˈres-pē-ə-ˌnäzh, -nij, -ˌnäj; -rə-ˈspē-ə-nij\ *n* **:** espionage directed toward detecting and thwarting enemy espionage

ə abut ᵊ kitten ər further a back ā bake ä cot, cart
au̇ out ch chin e less ē easy g gift i trip ī life
j joke ŋ sing ō flow ȯ flaw ȯi coin th thin th this
ü loot u̇ foot y yet yü few yu̇ furious zh vision

coun·ter·ex·am·ple \'kau̇nt-ə-rig-ˌzam-pəl\ *n* **:** an example that disproves a theorem or proposition

1**coun·ter·feit** \'kau̇nt-ər-ˌfit\ *vt* **:** to imitate or copy closely esp. with intent to deceive <~*ed* interest that she did not feel> ~ *vi* **1 :** to try to deceive by pretense or dissembling **2 :** to engage in counterfeiting something of value ***syn*** see ASSUME — **coun·ter·feit·er** *n*

2**counterfeit** *adj* [ME *countrefet,* fr. MF *contrefait,* fr. pp. of *contrefaire* to imitate, fr. *contre-* + *faire* to make, fr. L *facere* — more at DO] **1 :** made in imitation of something else with intent to deceive **:** FORGED <~ money> **2 a :** INSINCERE, FEIGNED <~ sympathy> **b :** marked by false pretense **:** SHAM, PRETENDED

3**counterfeit** *n* **1 :** something counterfeit **:** FORGERY **2 :** something likely to be mistaken for something of higher value <pity was a ~ of love —Harry Hervey> ***syn*** see IMPOSTURE

coun·ter·foil \'kau̇nt-ər-ˌfȯil\ *n* **:** a detachable stub (as on a check or ticket) usu. serving as a record or receipt

coun·ter·force \-ˌfōrs, -ˌfȯrs\ *n* **:** a force or trend that runs counter to another force or trend

coun·ter·guer·ril·la *also* **coun·ter·gue·ril·la** \ˌkau̇nt-ər-gə-'ril-ə, -g(y)i-, -ge-\ *n* **:** a guerrilla who is trained to thwart enemy guerrilla operations

coun·ter·in·sur·gen·cy \ˌkau̇nt-ə-rin-'sər-jən-sē\ *n* **:** organized military activity designed to counter insurgency — **coun·ter·in·sur·gent** \-jənt\ *n*

coun·ter·in·tel·li·gence \ˌkau̇nt-ə-rin-'tel-ə-jən(t)s\ *n* **:** organized activity of an intelligence service designed to block an enemy's sources of information, to deceive the enemy, to prevent sabotage, and to gather political and military information

coun·ter·ir·ri·tant \-'rir-ə-tənt\ *n* **1 :** an agent applied locally to produce superficial inflammation with the object of reducing inflammation in deeper adjacent structures **2 :** an irritation or discomfort that diverts attention from another — **counterirritant** *adj*

count·er·man \'kau̇nt-ər-ˌman, -mən\ *n* **:** one who tends a counter

1**coun·ter·mand** \'kau̇nt-ər-ˌmand, ˌkau̇nt-ər-'\ *vt* [ME *countermaunden,* fr. MF *contremander,* fr. *contre-* counter- + *mander* to command, fr. L *mandare*] **1 :** to revoke (a command) by a contrary order **2 :** to recall or order back by a superseding contrary order <~ reinforcements>

2**coun·ter·mand** \'kau̇nt-ər-ˌmand\ *n* **1 :** a contrary order **2 :** the revocation of an order or command

coun·ter·march \'kau̇nt-ər-ˌmärch\ *n* **1 :** a marching back; *specif* **:** a movement in marching by which a unit of troops reverses direction while marching but keeps the same order **2 :** a march (as of political demonstrators) designed to counter the effect of another march — **countermarch** *vi*

coun·ter·mea·sure \-ˌmezh-ər, -ˌmā-zhər\ *n* **:** a measure designed to counter another measure

1**coun·ter·mine** \-ˌmīn\ *n* **1 :** a tunnel for intercepting an enemy mine **2 :** a stratagem for defeating an attack **:** COUNTERPLOT

2**countermine** *vt* **1 :** to thwart by secret measures **2 :** to oppose or intercept with a countermine ~ *vi* **:** to make or lay down countermines

coun·ter·move \'kau̇nt-ər-ˌmüv\ *n* **:** a move designed to counter another move

coun·ter·move·ment \-mənt\ *n* **:** a movement in an opposite direction

coun·ter·of·fen·sive \'kau̇nt-ə-rə-ˌfen(t)-siv\ *n* **:** a large-scale military offensive undertaken by a force previously on the defensive

coun·ter·of·fer \-ˌrȯf-ər, -ˌräf-\ *n* **:** a return offer made by one who has rejected an offer

coun·ter·pane \'kau̇nt-ər-ˌpān\ *n* [alter. of ME *countrepointe,* modif. of MF *coute pointe,* lit., embroidered quilt] **:** BEDSPREAD

coun·ter·part \-ˌpärt\ *n* **1 :** one of two corresponding copies of a legal instrument **:** DUPLICATE **2 a :** a thing that fits another perfectly **b :** something that completes **:** COMPLEMENT **3 a :** one remarkably similar to another **b :** one having the same function or characteristics as another **:** EQUIVALENT <college presidents and their ~*s* in business> ***syn*** see PARALLEL

coun·ter·plan \'kau̇nt-ər-ˌplan\ *n* **1 :** a plan designed to counter another plan **2 :** an alternate or substitute plan

coun·ter·plea \-ˌplē\ *n* **:** a replication to a legal plea **:** an answering plea

1**coun·ter·plot** \-ˌplät\ *vt* **:** to intrigue against **:** foil with a plot

2**counterplot** *n* **:** a plot designed to thwart an opponent's plot

1**coun·ter·point** \'kau̇nt-ər-ˌpȯint\ *n* [MF *contrepoint,* fr. ML *contrapunctus,* fr. L *contra-* counter- + ML *punctus* musical note, melody, fr. L, act of pricking, fr. *punctus,* pp. of *pungere* to prick — more at POINT] **1 a :** one or more independent melodies added above or below a given melody **b :** the combination of two or more independent melodies into a single harmonic texture in which each retains its linear character **:** POLYPHONY **2 a :** a complementing or contrasting item **:** OPPOSITE **b :** use of contrast or interplay of elements in a work of art (as a drama)

2**counterpoint** *vt* **1 :** to compose or arrange in counterpoint **2 :** to set off or emphasize by contrast or juxtaposition **:** set in contrast <~*s* opposing themes ... hope and apathy —Curt Leviant>

1**coun·ter·poise** \-ˌpȯiz\ *vt* [ME *countrepesen,* fr. MF *contrepeser,* fr. *contre-* + *peser* to weigh — more at POISE] **:** COUNTERBALANCE

2**counterpoise** *n* **1 :** COUNTERBALANCE **2 :** an equivalent power or force acting in opposition **3 :** a state of balance

coun·ter·pose \ˌkau̇nt-ər-'pōz\ *vt* [*counter-* + *-pose* (as in *compose*)] **:** to place in opposition, contrast, or equilibrium <*counterposed* an alternative solution to the problem>

coun·ter·pro·duc·tive \-prə-'dək-tiv\ *adj* **:** tending to hinder the attainment of a desired goal <violence as a means to achieve an end is ~ —W. E. Brock *b*1930>

coun·ter·pro·gram·ming \ˌkau̇nt-ər-'prō-ˌgram-iŋ, -grəm-\ *n* **:** the scheduling of programs by television networks so as to attract audiences away from simultaneously telecast programs of competitors

coun·ter·pro·pa·gan·da \-ˌpräp-ə-'gan-də, -ˌprō-pə-\ *n* **:** propaganda designed to counter enemy propaganda

coun·ter·pro·pos·al \'kau̇nt-ər-prə-ˌpō-zəl\ *n* **:** a return proposal made by one who has rejected a proposal

coun·ter·punch \'kau̇nt-ər-ˌpənch\ *n* **:** a counter in boxing; *also* **:** a countering blow or attack — **coun·ter·punch·er** \-ˌpən-chər\ *n*

coun·ter·ref·or·ma·tion \ˌkau̇nt-ə(r)-ˌref-ər-'mā-shən\ *n* **1 :** a reformation designed to counter the effects of a previous reformation **2** *usu* **Counter-Reformation :** the reform movement in the Roman Catholic Church following the Reformation

coun·ter·rev·o·lu·tion \-ˌrev-ə-'lü-shən\ *n* **:** a revolution directed toward overthrowing a government or social system established by a previous revolution — **coun·ter·rev·o·lu·tion·ary** \-shə-ˌner-ē\ *adj or n* — **coun·ter·rev·o·lu·tion·ist** \-sh(ə-)nəst\ *n*

coun·ter·shaft \'kau̇nt-ər-ˌshaft\ *n* **:** a shaft that receives motion from a main shaft and transmits it to a working part

1**coun·ter·sign** \-ˌsīn\ *n* **1 :** a signature attesting the authenticity of a document already signed by another **2 :** a sign given in reply to another; *specif* **:** a military secret signal that must be given by one wishing to pass a guard

2**countersign** *vt* **1 :** to add one's signature to (a document) after another's so as to attest authenticity **2 :** CONFIRM, CORROBORATE — **coun·ter·sig·na·ture** \ˌkau̇nt-ər-'sig-nə-ˌchu̇(ə)r, -chər, -ˌt(y)u̇(ə)r\ *n*

1**coun·ter·sink** \'kau̇nt-ər-ˌsiŋk\ *vt* **-sunk** \-ˌsəŋk\; **-sink·ing 1 :** to make a countersink on **2 :** to set the head of (as a screw) at or below the surface

2**countersink** *n* **1 :** a funnel-shaped enlargement at the outer end of a drilled hole **2 :** a bit or drill for making a countersink

coun·ter·spy \'kau̇nt-ər-ˌspī\ *n* **:** a spy engaged in counterespionage

coun·ter·state·ment \-ˌstāt-mənt\ *n* **:** a statement opposing or denying another statement **:** REJOINDER

coun·ter·ten·or \-ˌten-ər\ *n* [ME *countretenour,* fr. MF *contreteneur,* fr. *contre-* + *teneur* tenor] **:** a tenor with an unusually high range and tessitura

coun·ter·ter·ror·ism \ˌkau̇nt-ər-'ter-ər-ˌiz-əm\ *n* **:** retaliatory terrorism — **coun·ter·ter·ror·ist** \-ər-əst\ *adj*

coun·ter·trend \'kau̇nt-ər-ˌtrend\ *n* **:** a trend that runs counter to another trend

coun·ter·vail \ˌkau̇nt-ər-'vā(ə)l\ *vb* [ME *countrevailen,* fr. MF *contrevaloir,* fr. *contre-* counter- + *valoir* to be worth, fr. L *valēre* — more at WIELD] *vt* **1 :** to compensate for **2** *archaic* **:** EQUAL, MATCH **3 :** to exert force against **:** COUNTERACT ~ *vi* **:** to exert force against an opposing and often bad or harmful force or influence ***syn*** see COMPENSATE

coun·ter·view \'kau̇nt-ər-ˌvyü\ *n* **1** *archaic* **:** CONFRONTATION **2 :** an opposite point of view

coun·ter·weight \-ˌwāt\ *n* **:** an equivalent weight **:** COUNTERBALANCE — **counterweight** *vt*

count·ess \'kau̇nt-əs\ *n* **1 :** the wife or widow of an earl or count **2 :** a woman who holds in her own right the rank of earl or count

coun·ti·an \'kau̇nt-ē-ən\ *n* **:** a native or resident of a usu. specified county

count·ing·house \'kau̇nt-iŋ-ˌhau̇s\ *n* **:** a building, room, or office used for keeping books and transacting business

counting room *n* **:** COUNTINGHOUSE

counting tube *n* **:** an ionization chamber designed to respond to passage through it of fast-moving ionizing particles and usu. connected to some device for counting the particles — called also *counter tube*

count·less \'kau̇nt-ləs\ *adj* **:** too numerous to be counted **:** MYRIAD — **count·less·ly** *adv*

count noun *n* **:** a noun (as *bean* or *sheet*) that forms a plural and is used with a numeral, with words such as *many* or *few,* or with the indefinite article *a* or *an* — compare MASS NOUN

count palatine *n* **1 a :** a high judicial official in the Holy Roman Empire **b :** a count of the Holy Roman Empire having imperial powers in his own domain **2 :** the proprietor of a county palatine in England or Ireland

coun·tri·fied *also* **coun·try·fied** \'kən-tri-ˌfīd\ *adj* [*country* + *-fied* (as in *glorified*)] **1 :** RURAL, RUSTIC **2 :** UNSOPHISTICATED

1**coun·try** \'kən-trē\ *n, pl* **countries** [ME *contree,* fr. OF *contrée,* fr. ML *contrata,* fr. L *contra* against, on the opposite side] **1 :** an indefinite usu. extended expanse of land **:** REGION **2 a :** the land of a person's birth, residence, or citizenship **b :** a political state or nation or its territory **3 a :** the people of a state or district **:** POPULACE **b :** JURY **c :** ELECTORATE **4 :** rural as distinguished from urban areas **5 :** COUNTRY MUSIC — **coun·try·ish** \-trē-ish\ *adj*

2**country** *adj* **1 :** of, relating to, or characteristic of the country **2 :** prepared or processed with farm supplies and procedures **3 :** of or relating to country music <~ singers>

country and western *n* **:** COUNTRY MUSIC

country club *n* **:** a suburban club for social life and recreation

coun·try–dance \'kən-trē-ˌdan(t)s\ *n* **:** any of various native English dances in which partners face each other esp. in rows

country gentleman *n* **1 :** a well-to-do country resident **:** an owner of a country estate **2 :** one of the English landed gentry

country house *n* **:** a house in the country; *specif* **:** COUNTRYSEAT

coun·try·man \'kən-trē-mən, *3 often* -ˌman\ *n* **1 :** an inhabitant or native of a specified country **2 :** COMPATRIOT **3 :** one living in the country or marked by country ways **:** RUSTIC

country music *n* **:** music derived from or imitating the folk style of the southern U.S. or of the Western cowboy

coun·try·seat \ˌkən-trē-'sēt\ *n* **:** a mansion or estate in the country

coun·try·side \'kən-trē-ˌsīd\ *n* **1 :** a rural area **2 :** the inhabitants of a countryside

country singer *n* **:** one who sings country music or in the style of country music

coun·try·wom·an \'kən-trē-ˌwu̇m-ən\ *n* **1 :** a woman compatriot **2 :** a woman resident of the country

1coun·ty \ˈkau̇nt-ē\ *n, pl* **counties** [ME *counte*, fr. OF *conté*, fr. ML *comitatus*, fr. LL, office of a count, fr. *comit-, comes* count — more at COUNT] **1 :** the domain of a count **2 a :** one of the territorial divisions of Great Britain and Ireland constituting the chief units for administrative, judicial, and political purposes **b** (1) **:** the people of a county (2) *Brit* **:** the gentry of a county **3 :** the largest territorial division for local government within a state of the U.S. **4 :** the largest local administrative unit in various countries — **county** *adj*

2county *n, pl* **counties** [modif. of MF *comte*] *obs* **:** 3COUNT

county agent *n* **:** a consultant employed jointly by federal and state governments to provide information about agriculture and home economics by means of lectures, demonstrations, and discussions in rural areas

county court *n* **:** a court in some states that has a designated jurisdiction usu. both civil and criminal within the limits of a county

county fair *n* **:** a fair usu. held annually at a set location in a county esp. to exhibit local agricultural products and livestock

county palatine *n* **:** the territory of a count palatine

county seat *n* **:** a town that is the seat of county administration

county town *n, chiefly Brit* **:** COUNTY SEAT

1coup \ˈkōp\ *vb* [ME *coupen* to strike, fr. MF *couper* — more at COPE] *chiefly Scot* **:** OVERTURN, UPSET

2coup \ˈkü\ *n, pl* **coups** \ˈküz\ [F, blow, stroke — more at COPE] **1 :** a brilliant, sudden, and usu. highly successful stroke or act **2 :** COUP D'ETAT

coup de grace \ˌküd-ə-ˈgräs\ *n, pl* **coups de grace** \ˌküd-ə-\ [F *coup de grâce*, lit., stroke of mercy] **1 :** a death blow or shot administered to end the suffering of one mortally wounded **2 :** a decisive finishing blow, act, or event

coup de main \-ˈmaⁿ\ *n, pl* **coups de main** \ˌküd-ə-\ [F, lit., hand stroke] **:** a sudden attack in force

coup d'etat \ˌküd-ə-ˈtä, ˌküd-(ˌ)ā-\ *n, pl* **coups d'etat** \ˌküd-ə-ˈtä(z), ˌküd-(ˌ)ā-\ [F *coup d'état*, lit., stroke of state] **:** a sudden decisive exercise of force in politics; *esp* **:** the violent overthrow or alteration of an existing government by a small group

coup de the·atre \ˌküd-ə-tā-ˈätrᵊ\ *n, pl* **coups de theatre** \ˌküd-ə-\ [F *coup de théâtre*, lit., stroke of theater] **1 :** a sudden sensational turn in a play; *also* **:** a sudden dramatic turn of events **2 :** a theatrical success

coup d'oeil \kü-ˈdə(r), -ˈdəi\ *n, pl* **coups d'oeil** *same*\ [F, lit., stroke of the eye] **:** a brief survey **:** GLANCE

cou·pé *or* **coupe** \kü-ˈpā, *2 often* ˈküp\ *n* [F *coupé*, fr. pp. of *couper* to cut] **1 :** a four-wheeled closed horse-drawn carriage for two persons inside with an outside seat for the driver in front **2** *usu* *coupe* **a :** a closed 2-door automobile for usu. two persons **b :** a usu. closed 2-door automobile with a full-width rear seat

1cou·ple \ˈkəp-əl\ *vb* **cou·pled; cou·pling** \-(ə-)liŋ\ *vt* **1 :** to connect for consideration together <*coupled* his praise with a request> **2 a :** to fasten together **:** LINK **b :** to bring (two electric circuits) into such close proximity as to permit mutual influence **3 :** to join in marriage or sexual union ~ *vi* **1 :** to unite in sexual union **2 :** JOIN **3 :** to unite chemically usu. with elimination of a simple molecule

2couple \ˈkəp-əl; *"couple of" is often* ˌkəp-lə(v)\ *n* [ME, pair, bond, fr. OF *cople*, fr. L *copula* bond, fr. *co-* + *apere* to fasten — more at APT] **1 a :** a man and woman married, engaged, or otherwise paired **b :** two persons paired together **2 :** PAIR, BRACE **3 :** something that joins or links two things together: as **a :** two equal and opposite forces that act along parallel lines **b :** GALVANIC COUPLE **4 :** an indefinite small number **:** FEW <a ~ of days ago>

3couple *adj* **:** TWO — used with *a* <a ~ more drinks>

cou·ple·ment \ˈkəp-əl-mənt\ *n* [MF, fr. *coupler* to join, fr. L *copulare*, fr. *copula*] *archaic* **:** the act or result of coupling

cou·pler \ˈkəp-(ə-)lər\ *n* **1 :** one that couples **2 :** a contrivance on a keyboard instrument by which keyboards or keys are connected to play together

cou·plet \ˈkəp-lət\ *n* [MF, dim. of *cople*] **1 :** two successive lines of verse forming a unit marked usu. by rhythmic correspondence, rhyme, or the inclusion of a self-contained utterance **:** DISTICH **2 :** COUPLE **3 :** one of the musical episodes alternating with the main theme (as in a rondo)

cou·pling \ˈkəp-liŋ (*usual for 2*), -ə-liŋ\ *n* **1 :** the act of bringing or coming together **:** PAIRING; *specif* **:** sexual union **2 :** a device that serves to connect the ends of adjacent parts or objects **3 :** the joining of or the part of the body that joins the hindquarters to the forequarters of a quadruped **4 :** means of electric connection of two electric circuits by having a part common to both

cou·pon \ˈk(y)ü-ˌpän\ *n* [F, fr. OF, piece, fr. *couper* to cut — more at COPE] **1 :** a statement of due interest to be cut from a bearer bond when payable and presented for payment **2 :** a form surrendered in order to obtain an article, service, or accommodation: as **a :** one of a series of attached tickets or certificates often to be detached and presented as needed **b :** a ticket or form authorizing purchases of rationed commodities **c :** a certificate or similar evidence of a purchase redeemable in premiums **d :** a part of a printed advertisement to be cut off for use as an order blank or inquiry form

cour·age \ˈkər-ij, ˈkə-rij\ *n* [ME *corage*, fr. OF, fr. *cuer* heart, fr. L *cor* — more at HEART] **:** mental or moral strength to venture, persevere, and withstand danger, fear, or difficulty

syn COURAGE, METTLE, SPIRIT, RESOLUTION, TENACITY *shared meaning element* **:** mental or moral strength to resist opposition, danger, or hardship. COURAGE implies firmness of mind and will in the face of danger or extreme difficulty <but screw your *courage* to the sticking place, and we'll not fail —Shak.> METTLE suggests an ingrained capacity for meeting strain or stress with fortitude and resilience <a situation to try the *mettle* of the most resolute man> SPIRIT suggests a quality of temperament that enables one to hold one's own against opposition, interference, or temptation <constant unremitting drudgery had slowly broken his *spirit*> RESOLUTION stresses firmness of character and determination to achieve one's ends <approach an unpleasant task with *resolution*> TENACITY adds an implication of stubborn persistence and unwillingness to acknowledge defeat <the *tenacity* of the bulldog breed> ***ant*** cowardice

cou·ra·geous \kə-ˈrā-jəs\ *adj* **:** having or characterized by courage **:** BRAVE — **cou·ra·geous·ly** *adv* — **cou·ra·geous·ness** *n*

cou·rante \ku̇-ˈränt, -ˈrant\ *n* [MF, fr. *courir* to run, fr. L *currere*] **1 :** a dance of Italian origin marked by quick running steps **2 :** music in quick triple time or in a mixture of 3/2 and 6/4 time

cou·reur de bois \ku̇-ˌrərd-əb-ˈwä\ *n, pl* **coureurs de bois** *same*\ [CanF, lit., woods runner] **:** a French or half-breed trapper of No. America and esp. of Canada

cour·gette \ku̇r-ˈzhet\ *n* [F dial., dim. of *courge* gourd, fr. L *cucurbita*] *chiefly Brit* **:** ZUCCHINI

cou·ri·er \ˈku̇r-ē-ər, ˈkər-ē-, ˈkə-rē-\ *n* [MF *courrier*, fr. OIt *corriere*, fr. *correre* to run, fr. L *currere*] **1 :** MESSENGER; as **a :** a member of a diplomatic service entrusted with bearing messages **b** (1) **:** an espionage agent transferring secret information (2) **:** a runner of contraband **c :** a member of the armed services whose duties include carrying mail, information, or supplies **2 :** a traveler's paid attendant; *esp* **:** a tourists' guide employed by a travel agency

cour·lan \ˈku̇(ə)r-lən\ *n* [F, modif. of Galibi *kurliri*] **:** a long-billed bird (*Aramus guarauna*) that is intermediate in some respects between the cranes and rails and occurs in So. and Central America

1course \ˈkō(ə)rs, ˈkȯ(ə)rs\ *n* [ME, fr OF, fr. L *cursus*, fr. *cursus*, pp. of *currere* to run — more at CAR] **1 a :** the act or action of moving in a path from point to point **b :** LIFE HISTORY, CAREER **2 :** the path over which something moves: as **a :** RACECOURSE **b** (1) **:** the direction of flight of an airplane usu. measured as a clockwise angle from north (2) **:** a point of the compass **c :** WATERCOURSE **d :** GOLF COURSE **3 a :** accustomed procedure or normal action <the law taking its ~> **b :** a chosen manner of conducting oneself **:** BEHAVIOR <our wisest ~ is to retreat> **c :** progression through a series of acts or events or a development or period **4 :** an ordered process or succession: as **a :** a series of lectures or other matter dealing with a subject; *also* **:** a series of such courses constituting a curriculum **b :** a series of doses or medicaments administered over a designated period **5 a :** a part of a meal served at one time **b :** ROW, LAYER; *esp* **:** a continuous level range of brick or masonry throughout a wall **c :** the lowest sail on a square-rigged mast — **in due course :** after a normal passage of time **:** in the expected or allotted time — **of course 1 :** following the ordinary way or procedure **2 :** as might be expected

2course *vb* **coursed; cours·ing** *vt* **1 a :** to hunt or pursue (game) with hounds **b :** to cause (dogs) to run (as after game) **2 :** to follow close upon **:** PURSUE **3 :** to run or move swiftly through or over **:** TRAVERSE <jets *coursed* the area daily> ~ *vi* **:** to run or pass rapidly along or as if along an indicated path <blood *coursing* through his veins>

course of study 1 : the total number of courses offered by a school **:** CURRICULUM **2 :** COURSE 4a

1cours·er \ˈkōr-sər, ˈkȯr-\ *n* [ME, fr. OF *coursier*, fr. *course* course, run] **:** a swift or spirited horse **:** CHARGER

2courser *n* **1 :** a dog for coursing **2 :** one that courses **:** HUNTSMAN **3 :** any of various birds (subfamily Cursoriinae of the family Glareolidae) of Africa and southern Asia related to the plovers and noted for their speed in running

cours·ing *n* **1 :** the act of one that courses **2 :** the pursuit of running game with dogs that follow by sight instead of by scent

1court \ˈkō(ə)rt, ˈkȯ(ə)rt\ *n, often attrib* [ME, fr. OF, fr. L *cohort-, cohors* enclosure, throng, cohort, fr. *co-* + *-hort-, -hors* (akin to *hortus* garden) — more at YARD] **1 a :** the residence or establishment of a sovereign or similar dignitary **b :** a sovereign's formal assembly of his councillors and officers **c :** the sovereign and his officers and advisers who are the governing power **d :** the family and retinue of a sovereign **e :** a reception held by a sovereign **2 a** (1) **:** a manor house or large building surrounded by usu. enclosed grounds (2) **:** MOTEL **b :** an open space enclosed wholly or partly by buildings or circumscribed by a single building **c :** a quadrangular space walled or marked off for playing one of various games with a ball (as lawn tennis, racquets, handball, or basketball) or a division of such a court **d :** a wide alley with only one opening onto a street **3 a :** an official assembly for the transaction of judicial business **b :** a session of such a court <~ is now adjourned> **c :** a place (as a chamber) for the administration of justice **d :** a judge or judges in session **e :** a faculty or agency of judgment or evaluation <rest our case in the ~ of world opinion —L. H. Marks> **4 a :** an assembly or board with legislative or administrative powers **b :** PARLIAMENT, LEGISLATURE **5 :** conduct or attention intended to win favor or dispel hostility **:** HOMAGE <pay ~ to the king>

2court *vt* **1 a :** to seek to gain or achieve **b** (1) **:** ALLURE, TEMPT (2) **:** to act so as to invite or provoke <~*s* disaster> **2 a :** to seek the affections of **b** *of an animal* **:** to perform actions in order to attract for mating **3 :** to seek to attract by attentions and flatteries ~ *vi* **1 :** to engage in social activities leading to engagement and marriage **2** *of an animal* **:** to engage in activity leading to mating ***syn*** see INVITE

cour·te·ous \ˈkərt-ē-əs, *esp Brit* ˈkȯrt-\ *adj* [ME *corteis*, fr. OF, fr. *court*] **1 :** marked by polished manners, gallantry, or ceremonial usage of a court **2 :** marked by respect for and consideration of others ***syn*** see CIVIL ***ant*** discourteous — **cour·te·ous·ly** *adv* — **cour·te·ous·ness** *n*

cour·te·san \ˈkōrt-ə-zən, ˈkȯrt-, -ˌzan *also* ˈkərt-\ *n* [MF *courtisane*, fr. OIt *cortigiana* woman courtier, fem. of *cortigiano* courtier, fr.

corte court, fr. L *cohort-, cohors*] : a prostitute with a courtly, wealthy, or upper-class clientele

[1]**cour·te·sy** \'kərt-ə-sē, *esp Brit* 'kȯrt-\ *n, pl* **-sies** [ME *corteisie,* fr. OF, fr. *corteis*] **1 a :** courteous behavior **b :** a courteous act or expression **2 a :** general allowance despite facts : INDULGENCE <hills called mountains by ~ only> **b :** consideration, cooperation, and generosity in providing; *also* : AGENCY, MEANS

[2]**courtesy** *adj* : granted, provided, or performed as a courtesy or by way of courtesy <made a ~ call on the ambassador>

courtesy card *n* : a card entitling its holder to some special privilege

courtesy title *n* **1 :** a title (as "Lord" added to the Christian name of a peer's younger son) used in addressing certain lineal relatives of British peers **2 :** a title (as "Professor" for any teacher) taken by the user and commonly accepted without consideration of official right

court game *n* : an athletic game (as tennis, handball, or basketball) played on a court

court·house \'kō(ə)rt-ˌhau̇s, 'kȯ(ə)rt-\ *n* **1 a :** a building in which courts of law are regularly held **b :** the principal building in which county offices are housed **2 :** COUNTY SEAT

court·ier \'kōrt-ē-ər, 'kōrt-yər, 'kȯrt-; 'kōr-chər, 'kȯr-\ *n* **1 :** one in attendance at a royal court **2 :** one who practices flattery

[1]**court·ly** \'kō(ə)rt-lē, 'kȯ(ə)rt-\ *adj* **court·li·er; -est 1 a :** of a quality befitting the court : ELEGANT **b :** insincerely flattering **2 :** favoring the policy or party of the court — **court·li·ness** *n*

[2]**courtly** *adv* : in a courtly manner : POLITELY

courtly love *n* : a late medieval conventionalized code prescribing conduct and emotions of ladies and their lovers

[1]**court–mar·tial** \'kōrt-ˌmär-shəl, 'kȯrt-, -'mär-\ *n, pl* **courts–martial** *also* **court–martials 1 :** a court consisting of commissioned officers and in some instances enlisted personnel for the trial of members of the armed forces or others within its jurisdiction **2 :** a trial by court-martial

[2]**court–martial** *vt* **–mar·tialed** *also* **–mar·tialled; –mar·tial·ing** *also* **–mar·tial·ling** \-ˌmärsh-(ə-)liŋ, -'märsh-\ : to subject to trial by court-martial

court of appeal : a court hearing appeals from the decisions of lower courts — called also *court of appeals*

court of claims : a court that has jurisdiction over claims (as against a government)

court of common pleas 1 : a former English superior court having civil jurisdiction **2 :** an intermediate court in some American states that usu. has civil and criminal jurisdiction

court of domestic relations : a court that has jurisdiction and often special advisory powers over family disputes involving the rights and duties of husband, wife, parent, or child esp. in matters affecting the support, custody, and welfare of children

court of honor : a tribunal (as a military court) for investigating questions of personal honor

court of inquiry : a military court that inquires into and reports on some military matter (as an officer's questionable conduct)

court of law : a court that hears cases and decides them on the basis of statutes or the common law

court of record : a court whose acts and proceedings are kept on permanent record

Court of St. James's \-sānt-'jāmz, -sənt-\ [fr. *St. James's* Palace, London, former seat of the British court] : the British court

court of sessions : any of various state criminal courts of record

court order *n* : an order issuing from a competent court that requires a person to do or abstain from doing a specified act

court plaster *n* [fr. its use for beauty spots by ladies at royal courts] : an adhesive plaster esp. of silk coated with isinglass and glycerin

court reporter *n* : a stenographer who records and transcribes a verbatim report of all proceedings in a court of law

court·room \'kō(ə)rt-ˌrüm, 'kȯ(ə)rt-, -ˌru̇m\ *n* : a room in which a court of law is held

court·ship \-ˌship\ *n* : the act, process, or period of courting

court·side \-ˌsīd\ *n* : the area at the edge of a court (as for tennis or basketball)

court tennis *n* : a game played with a ball and racket in an enclosed court divided by a net

court·yard \'kō(ə)rt-ˌyärd, 'kȯ(ə)rt-\ *n* : a court or enclosure adjacent to a building (as a house or palace)

cous·in \'kəz-ᵊn\ *n* [ME *cosin,* fr. OF, fr. L *consobrinus,* fr. *com-* + *sobrinus* cousin on the mother's side, fr. *soror* sister — more at SISTER] **1 a :** a child of one's uncle or aunt **b :** a relative descended from one's grandparent or more remote ancestor in a different line **c :** KINSMAN, RELATIVE <a distant ~> **2 :** one associated with another : EQUIVALENT **3 —** used as a title by a sovereign in addressing a nobleman **4 :** a person of a race or people ethnically or culturally related <our English ~*s*> — **cous·in·hood** \-ˌhu̇d\ *n* — **cous·in·ship** \-ˌship\ *n*

cous·in·age \'kəz-ᵊn-ij\ *n* **1 :** relationship of cousins : KINSHIP **2 :** a collection of cousins : KINFOLK

cous·in–ger·man \ˌkəz-ᵊn-'jər-mən\ *n, pl* **cous·ins–ger·man** \-ᵊnz-\ [ME *cosin germain,* fr. MF, fr. OF, fr. *cosin* + *germain* german] : COUSIN 1a

Cousin Jack \ˌkəz-ᵊn-'jak\ *n* : CORNISHMAN; *esp* : a Cornish miner

[1]**couth** \'küth\ *adj* [back-formation fr. *uncouth*] : SOPHISTICATED, POLISHED

[2]**couth** *n* : POLISH, REFINEMENT <lacks ~ but has ample energy and acting talent —*Newsweek*>

couth·ie \'kü-thē\ *adj* [ME *couth*] *chiefly Scot* : PLEASANT, KINDLY

cou·ture \kü-'tu̇(ə)r, -'tu̇r\ *n* [F, fr. OF *cousture* sewing, fr. (assumed) VL *consutura,* fr. L *consutus,* pp. of *consuere* to sew together, fr. *com-* + *suere* to sew — more at SEW] : the business of designing, making, and selling fashionable custom-made women's clothing; *also* : the designers and establishments engaged in this business

cou·tu·ri·er \kü-'tu̇r-ē-ər, -ē-ˌā\ *n* [F, dressmaker, fr. OF *cousturier* tailor's assistant, fr. *cousture*] : an establishment engaged in couture; *also* : the proprietor of or designer for such an establishment

cou·tu·ri·ere \kü-'tu̇r-ē-ər, -ē-ˌe(ə)r\ *n* [F *couturière,* fr. OF *cousturiere,* fem. of *cousturier*] : a female couturier

cou·vade \kü-'väd\ *n* [F, fr. MF, cowardly inactivity, fr. *cover* to sit on, brood over — more at COVEY] : a custom among some primitive peoples in accordance with which when a child is born the father takes to bed as if bearing the child, cares for it, and submits himself to fasting, purification, or taboos

co·va·lence \(ˈ)kō-'vā-lən(t)s\ *n* : valence characterized by the sharing of electrons; *also* : the number of pairs of electrons an atom can share with its neighbors — compare ELECTROVALENCE — **co·va·lent** \-lənt\ *adj* — **co·va·lent·ly** *adv*

co·va·len·cy \-lən-sē\ *n* : COVALENCE

covalent bond *n* : a nonionic chemical bond formed by shared electrons

co·vari·ance \(ˈ)kō-'ver-ē-ən(t)s, -'var-\ *n* **1 :** the expected value of the product of the deviations of two random variables from their respective means **2 :** the arithmetic mean of the products of the deviations of corresponding values of two quantitative variables from their respective means

co·var·i·ant \-ənt\ *adj* [ISV] : varying with something else so as to preserve certain mathematical interrelations

[1]**cove** \'kōv\ *n* [ME, den, fr. OE *cofa;* akin to OE *cot*] **1 :** a recessed place : CONCAVITY; as **a :** an architectural member with a concave cross section **b :** a trough for concealed lighting at the upper part of a wall **2 :** a small sheltered inlet or bay **3 a :** a deep recess or small valley in the side of a mountain **b :** a level area sheltered by hills or mountains

[2]**cove** *vt* **coved; cov·ing :** to make in a hollow concave form

[3]**cove** *n* [Romany *kova* thing, person] *Brit* : MAN, FELLOW

co·ven \'kəv-ən, 'kō-vən\ *n* [ME *covin* band, fr. MF, fr. ML *convenium* agreement, fr. L *convenire* to agree — more at CONVENTION] : an assembly or band of usu. 13 witches

[1]**cov·e·nant** \'kəv-(ə-)nənt\ *n* [ME, fr. OF, fr. prp. of *covenir* to agree, fr. L *convenire*] **1 :** a usu. formal, solemn, and binding agreement : COMPACT **2 a :** a written agreement or promise usu. under seal between two or more parties esp. for the performance of some action **b :** the common-law action to recover damages for breach of such a contract — **cov·e·nan·tal** \ˌkəv-ə-'nant-ᵊl\ *adj*

[2]**cov·e·nant** \'kəv-(ə-)nənt, -ə-ˌnant\ *vt* : to promise by a covenant : PLEDGE ~ *vi* : to enter into a covenant : CONTRACT

cov·e·nan·tee \ˌkəv-ə-ˌnan-'tē, -nən-\ *n* : the person to whom a promise in the form of a covenant is made

cov·e·nant·er \'kəv-ə-ˌnant-ər, *2 also* ˌkəv-ə-'\ *n* **1 :** one that makes a covenant **2** *cap* : a signer or adherent of the Scottish National Covenant of 1638

cov·e·nan·tor \'kəv-ə-ˌnant-ər; ˌkəv-ə-ˌnan-'tȯ(ə)r, -nən-\ *n* : the party to a covenant bound to perform the obligation expressed in it

Cov·en·try \'kəv-ən-trē, 'käv-\ *n* [*Coventry,* England] : a state of ostracism or exclusion <sent to ~>

[1]**cov·er** \'kəv-ər\ *vb* **cov·ered; cov·er·ing** \'kəv-(ə-)riŋ [ME *coveren,* fr. OF *covrir,* fr. L *cooperire,* fr. *co-* + *operire* to close, cover — more at WEIR] *vt* **1 a :** to guard from attack **b (1) :** to have within the range of one's guns : COMMAND **(2) :** to hold within range of an aimed firearm **c (1) :** to afford protection or security to : INSURE **(2) :** to afford protection against or compensation for **d (1) :** to guard (an opponent) in order to obstruct a play **(2) :** to be in position to receive a throw to (a base in baseball) **e (1) :** to make provision for (a demand or charge) by means of a reserve or deposit <his balance was insufficient to ~ his check> **(2) :** to maintain a check on esp. by patrolling **(3) :** to protect by contrivance or expedient **2 a :** to hide from sight or knowledge : CONCEAL <~ up a scandal> **b :** to lie over : ENVELOP **3 :** to lay or spread something over : OVERLAY **4 a :** to spread over **b :** to appear here and there on the surface of **5 :** to place or set a cover or covering over **6 a :** to copulate with (a female animal) <a horse ~*s* a mare> **b :** to sit on and incubate (eggs) **7 :** to invest with a large or excessive amount of something <~*s* himself with glory> **8 :** to play a higher-ranking card on (a previously played card) **9 :** to have sufficient scope to include or take into account **10 :** to deal with : TREAT **11 a :** to have as one's territory or field of activity <one salesman ~*s* the whole state> **b :** to report news about **12 :** to pass over : TRAVERSE **13 :** to place one's stake in equal jeopardy with in a bet **14 :** to buy securities or commodities for delivery against (an earlier short sale) ~ *vi* **1 :** to conceal something illicit, blameworthy, or embarrassing from notice <~ up for a friend> **2 :** to act as a substitute or replacement during an absence — **cov·er·able** \'kəv-(ə-)rə-bəl\ *adj* — **cov·er·er** \-ər-ər\ *n* — **cover one's tracks :** to conceal traces in order to elude pursuers — **cover the ground** *or* **cover ground 1 :** to traverse a course or distance with satisfying speed **2 :** to handle an assignment thoroughly and efficiently

[2]**cover** *n, often attrib* **1 :** something that protects, shelters, or guards: as **a :** natural shelter for an animal; *also* : the factors that provide such shelter **b (1) :** a position or situation affording protection from enemy fire **(2) :** the protection offered by airplanes in tactical support of a military operation **2 :** something that is placed over or about another thing: **a :** LID, TOP **b :** a binding or case for a book; *also* : the front or back of such a binding **c :** an overlay or outer layer esp. for protection <a mattress ~> **d :** a tablecloth and the other table fittings **e :** COVER CHARGE **f :** ROOF **g :** a cloth used on a bed **h :** something (as vegetation or snow) that covers the ground **i :** the extent to which clouds obscure the sky **3 a :** something that conceals or obscures <under ~ of darkness> **b :** a masking device : PRETEXT <the project was a ~ for intelligence operations> **4 :** an envelope or wrapper for mail **5 :** one who substitutes for another during an absence — **cov·er·less** \-ər-ləs\ *adj* — **under cover 1 :** in an envelope or wrapper **2 :** under concealment : in secret

cov·er·age \'kəv-(ə-)rij\ *n* **1 :** the act or fact of covering **2 :** something that covers: as **a :** inclusion within the scope of an insurance policy or protective plan : INSURANCE **b :** the amount available to meet liabilities **c :** inclusion within the scope of discussion or reporting <the news ~ of the trial> **3 :** the total group covered : SCOPE: as **a :** all the risks covered by the terms of an insurance contract **b :** the number or percentage of persons reached by a communications medium

cov·er·all \ˈkəv-ə-ˌrȯl\ *n* **:** a one-piece outer garment worn to protect other garments — usu. used in pl. — **cov·er·alled** \-ˌrȯld\ *adj*

cover–all \ˈkəv-ə-ˌrȯl\ *adj* : COMPREHENSIVE <~ provisions>

cover charge *n* **:** a charge made by a restaurant or nightclub in addition to the charge for food and drink

cover crop *n* **:** a crop planted to prevent soil erosion and to provide humus

covered bridge *n* **:** a bridge that has its roadway protected by a roof and enclosing sides

covered smut *n* **:** a smut disease of grains in which the spore masses are held together by the persistent grain membrane and glumes

covered wagon *n* **:** a wagon with a canvas top supported by bowed strips of wood or metal

cover girl *n* **:** an attractive girl whose picture appears on a magazine cover

cover glass *n* **1 :** a piece of very thin glass used to cover material on a glass microscope slide **2 :** a sheet of plain glass applied to a transparency for protection

[1]**cov·er·ing** \ˈkəv-(ə-)riŋ\ *n* **:** something that covers or conceals

[2]**covering** *adj* **:** containing explanation of or additional information about an accompanying communication <a ~ letter>

cov·er·let \ˈkəv-ər-lət, -(ˌ)lid\ *n* [ME, alter. of *coverlite,* fr. AF *coverelyth,* fr. OF *covrir* + *lit* bed, fr. L *lectus* — more at LIE] **:** BEDSPREAD

cover shot *n* **:** a wide-angle photographic shot that includes a whole scene

cov·er·slip \ˈkəv-ər-ˌslip\ *n* : COVER GLASS 1

cover story *n* **:** a story accompanying a magazine-cover illustration

[1]**co·vert** \ˈkō-(ˌ)vərt, kō-ˈ; ˈkəv-ərt\ *adj* [ME, fr. OF, pp. of *covrir* to cover] **1 :** not openly shown, engaged in, or avowed : VEILED <a ~ alliance> <~ dislike concealed under apparent goodwill> **2 :** covered over : SHELTERED **3 :** being married and under the authority or protection of one's husband ***syn*** see SECRET ***ant*** overt — **co·vert·ly** *adv* — **co·vert·ness** *n*

[2]**co·vert** \ˈkəv-ər(t), ˈkō-vərt\ *n* **1 a :** hiding place : SHELTER **b :** a thicket affording cover for game **c :** a masking or concealing device **2 :** a feather covering the bases of the quills of the wings and tail of a bird — see BIRD illustration **3 :** a firm durable twilled sometimes waterproofed cloth usu. of mixed-color yarns

cover text *n* **:** a text in plain language within which a ciphertext is concealed

cov·er·ture \ˈkəv-ər-ˌchu̇(ə)r, -chər, -ˌt(y)u̇(ə)r\ *n* **1 a :** COVERING **b :** SHELTER **2 :** the status a woman acquires upon marriage under common law

cov·er–up \ˈkəv-ə-ˌrəp\ *n* **:** a device or stratagem for masking or concealing <indifference to others . . . is a ~ for a lack of easy sociability —Marguerite Barze>

cov·et \ˈkəv-ət\ *vb* [ME *coveiten,* fr. OF *coveitier,* fr. *coveitié* desire, modif. of L *cupiditat-, cupiditas,* fr. *cupidus* desirous, fr. *cupere* to desire; akin to L *vapor* steam, vapor, Gk *kapnos* smoke] *vt* **1 :** to wish for enviously **2 :** to desire (what belongs to another) inordinately or culpably ~ *vi* **:** to feel inordinate desire for what belongs to another ***syn*** see DESIRE — **cov·et·able** \-ə-bəl\ *adj* — **cov·et·er** \-ər\ *n* — **cov·et·ing·ly** \-iŋ-lē\ *adv*

cov·et·ous \-əs\ *adj* **1 :** marked by inordinate desire for wealth or possessions or for another's possessions **2 :** having a craving for possession <~ of power> — **cov·et·ous·ly** *adv* — **cov·et·ous·ness** *n*

syn COVETOUS, GREEDY, ACQUISITIVE, GRASPING, AVARICIOUS ***shared meaning element*** **:** having or showing a strong desire for possessions and esp. material possessions

cov·ey \ˈkəv-ē\ *n, pl* **coveys** [ME, fr. MF *covee,* fr. OF, fr. *cover* to sit on, brood over, fr. L *cubare* to lie — more at HIP] **1 :** a mature bird or pair of birds with a brood of young; *also* **:** a small flock **2 :** COMPANY, GROUP

[1]**cow** \ˈkau̇\ *n* [ME *cou,* fr. OE *cū;* akin to OHG *kuo* cow, L *bos* head of cattle, Gk *bous,* Skt *go*] **1 :** the mature female of cattle

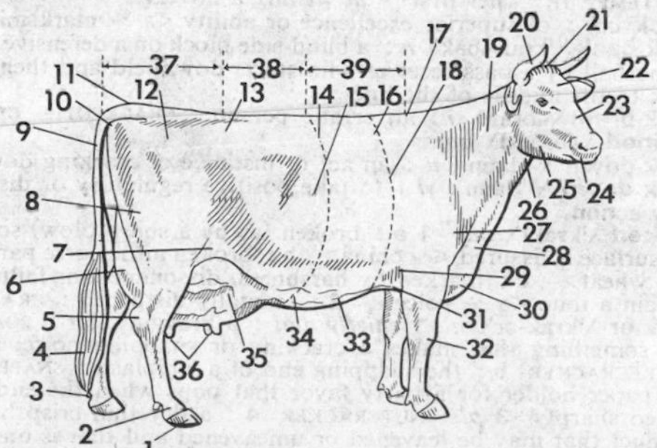

cow: *1* hoof, *2* pastern, *3* dewclaw, *4* switch, *5* hock, *6* rear udder, *7* flank, *8* thigh, *9* tail, *10* pinbone, *11* tail head, *12* thurl, *13* hip, *14* barrel, *15* ribs, *16* crops, *17* withers, *18* heart girth, *19* neck, *20* horn, *21* poll, *22* forehead, *23* bridge of nose, *24* muzzle, *25* jaw, *26* throat, *27* point of shoulder, *28* dewlap, *29* point of elbow, *30* brisket, *31* chest floor, *32* knee, *33* milk well, *34* milk vein, *35* fore udder, *36* teats, *37* rump, *38* loin, *39* chine

(genus *Bos*) or of any animal the male of which is called *bull* (as the moose) **2 :** a domestic bovine animal regardless of sex or age — **cowy** \-ē\ *adj*

[2]**cow** *vt* [alter. of *coll* (to poll)] *chiefly Scot* **:** to cut short : POLL

[3]**cow** *vt* [prob. of Scand origin; akin to Dan *kue* to subdue] **:** to intimidate with threats or show of strength : DAUNT <~*ed* them with his hard, intelligent eyes —Arthur Morrison> — **cowed·ly** \ˈkau̇(-ə)d-lē\ *adv*

cow·age *or* **cow·hage** \ˈkau̇-ij\ *n* [Hindi *kavāc*] **:** a tropical leguminous woody vine (*Mucuna pruritum*) with crooked pods covered with barbed hairs that cause severe itching; *also* **:** these hairs sometimes used as a vermifuge

cow·ard \ˈkau̇(-ə)rd\ *n* [ME, fr. OF *coart,* fr. *coe* tail, fr. L *cauda*] **:** one who shows disgraceful fear or timidity — **coward** *adj*

cow·ard·ice \-əs\ *n* [ME *cowardise,* fr. OF *coardise,* fr. *coart*] **:** lack of courage or resolution

[1]**cow·ard·ly** \-lē\ *adv* **:** in a cowardly manner

[2]**cowardly** *adj* **:** resembling or befitting a coward <a ~ retreat> — **cow·ard·li·ness** *n*

cow·bane \ˈkau̇-ˌbān\ *n* **:** any of several poisonous plants (as a water hemlock) of the carrot family

cow·bell \-ˌbel\ *n* **:** a bell hung around the neck of a cow to make a sound by which it can be located

cow·ber·ry \-ˌber-ē\ *n* **:** any of several pasture shrubs (as mountain cranberry); *also* **:** the fruit of a cowberry

cow·bird \-ˌbərd\ *n* **:** a small No. American blackbird (*Molothrus ater*) that lays its eggs in the nests of other birds

cow·boy \-ˌbȯi\ *n* **:** one who tends or drives cattle; *esp* **:** a usu. mounted cattle ranch hand

cowboy boot *n* **:** a boot made with a high arch, a high Cuban heel, and usu. fancy stitching

cowboy hat *n* **:** a wide-brimmed hat with a large soft crown — called also *ten-gallon hat*

cow·catch·er \ˈkau̇-ˌkach-ər, -ˌkech-\ *n* **:** an inclined frame on the front of a railroad locomotive for throwing obstacles off the track

cow college *n* **1 :** a college that specializes in agriculture **2 :** a provincial college or university that lacks culture, sophistication, and tradition

cow·er \ˈkau̇(-ə)r\ *vi* [ME *couren,* of Scand origin; akin to Norw *kura* to cower; akin to Gk *gyros* circle, OE *cot*] **:** to shrink away or crouch quivering (as in abject fear or grave distress) from something that menaces, domineers, or dismays <~*ing* in their huts . . . listening in fear —Charles Kingsley>

cow·fish \ˈkau̇-ˌfish\ *n* **1 a :** any of various small cetaceans **b :** SIRENIAN **2 :** any of various small bright-colored fishes (family Ostraciidae) with projections resembling horns over the eyes

cow·girl \-ˌgər(-ə)l\ *n* **:** a female cowboy

cow·hand \-ˌhand\ *n* : COWBOY

cow·herd \-ˌhərd\ *n* **:** one who tends cows

[1]**cow·hide** \-ˌhīd\ *n* **1 :** the hide of a cow; *also* **:** leather made from this hide **2 :** a coarse whip of rawhide or braided leather

[2]**cowhide** *vt* **cow·hid·ed; cow·hid·ing :** to flog with a cowhide whip

cow horse *n* : COW PONY

[1]**cowl** \ˈkau̇(ə)l\ *n* [ME *cowle,* fr. OE *cugele,* fr. LL *cuculla* monk's hood, fr. L *cucullus* hood] **1 :** a hood or long hooded cloak esp. of a monk **2 a :** a chimney covering designed to improve the draft **b :** the top portion of the front part of an automobile body forward of the two front doors to which are attached the windshield and instrument board **c :** COWLING

[2]**cowl** *vt* **:** to cover with or as if with a cowl

cowled \ˈkau̇(ə)ld\ *adj* **:** shaped like a hood : HOODED <a ~ flower>

cow·lick \ˈkau̇-ˌlik\ *n* [fr. its appearance of having been licked by a cow] **:** a lock or tuft of hair growing in a different direction from the rest of the hair

cowl·ing \ˈkau̇-liŋ\ *n* **:** a removable metal covering that houses the engine and sometimes a part of the fuselage or nacelle of an airplane; *also* **:** a metallic cover for an engine

cowl·staff \ˈkōl-ˌstaf, ˈkau̇(ə)l-\ *n* [ME *cuvelstaff,* fr. *cuvel* vessel (fr. OE *cȳfel,* fr. ONF *cuvele* small vat) + *staff*] *archaic* **:** a staff from which a vessel is suspended and carried between two persons

cow·man \ˈkau̇-mən, -ˌman\ *n* **1 :** COWHERD, COWBOY **2 :** a cattle owner or rancher

co–work·er \ˈkō-ˌwər-kər\ *n* **:** a fellow worker

cow parsnip *n* **:** a tall perennial No. American plant (*Heracleum maximum*) of the carrot family with large compound leaves and broad umbels of white or purplish flowers; *also* **:** a related plant (*H. sphondylium*) naturalized in the U.S. from the Old World

cow·pat \ˈkau̇-ˌpat\ *n* **:** a dropping of cow dung

cow·pea \ˈkau̇-ˌpē\ *n* **:** a sprawling leguminous herb (*Vigna sinensis*) related to the bean and widely cultivated in southern U.S. esp. for forage and green manure; *also* **:** its edible seed — called also *black-eyed pea*

Cow·per's gland \ˌkau̇-pərz-, ˌkü-pərz-, ˌku̇p-ərz-\ *n* [William *Cowper* †1709 E surgeon] **:** either of two small glands discharging into the male urethra

cow·poke \ˈkau̇-ˌpōk\ *n* : COWBOY

cow pony *n* **:** a light saddle horse trained for herding cattle

cow·pox \ˈkau̇-ˌpäks\ *n* **:** a mild eruptive disease of the cow that when communicated to man protects against smallpox

cow·punch·er \-ˌpən-chər\ *n* : COWBOY

cow·rie *or* **cow·ry** \ˈkau̇(ə)r-ē\ *n, pl* **cowries** [Hindi *kaurī*] **:** any of numerous marine gastropods (family Cypraeidae) widely distributed in warm seas with glossy and often brightly colored shells

cow·slip \\ˈkau̇-ˌslip\\ *n* [ME *cowslyppe,* fr. OE *cūslyppe,* lit., cow dung, fr. *cū* cow + *slypa, slyppe* paste] **1 :** a common British primrose (*Primula veris*) with fragrant yellow or purplish flowers **2 :** MARSH MARIGOLD **3 :** SHOOTING STAR **4 :** VIRGINIA COWSLIP

cow town *n* **1 :** a town or city that serves as a market center or shipping point for cattle **2 :** a small unsophisticated town within a cattle-raising area

1cox \\ˈkäks\\ *n* **:** COXSWAIN

2cox *vb* **:** COXSWAIN

coxa \\ˈkäk-sə\\ *n, pl* **cox·ae** \\-ˌsē, -ˌsī\\ [L, hip; akin to OHG *hāhsina* hock, Skt *kakṣa* armpit] **:** the basal segment of a limb of various arthropods (as an insect) — **cox·al** \\-səl\\ *adj*

cox·comb \\ˈkäk-ˌskōm\\ *n* [ME *cokkes comb,* lit., cock's comb] **1 a** *obs* **:** a jester's cap adorned with a strip of red **b** *archaic* **:** PATE, HEAD **2 a** *obs* **:** FOOL **b :** a conceited foolish person **:** FOP — **cox·comb·ical** \\käk-ˈskō-mi-kəl, -ˈskäm-i-\\ *adj*

cox·comb·ry \\ˈkäk-skəm-rē, -ˌskōm-\\ *n, pl* **-ries :** behavior that is characteristic of a coxcomb **:** FOPPERY

Cox·sack·ie virus \\(ˌ)ku̇k-ˌsäk-ē-, -ˌsak-; (ˌ)käk-ˌsak-ē-\\ *n* [*Coxsackie,* N.Y.] **:** any of several viruses related to that of poliomyelitis and associated with human diseases

1cox·swain \\ˈkäk-sən, -ˌswān\\ *n* [ME *cokswayne,* fr. *cok* cockboat + *swain* servant] **1 :** a sailor who has charge of a ship's boat and its crew and who usu. steers **2 :** a steersman of a racing shell who usu. directs the crew

2coxswain *vt* **:** to steer or direct as coxswain ~ *vi* **:** to act as coxswain

1coy \\ˈkȯi\\ *adj* [ME, quiet, shy, fr. MF *coi* calm, fr. L *quietus* quiet] **1 a :** shrinking from contact or familiarity **b :** marked by cute, coquettish, or artful playfulness **2 :** showing reluctance to make a definite commitment ***syn*** see SHY ***ant*** pert — **coy·ly** *adv* — **coy·ness** *n*

2coy *vt, obs* **:** CARESS ~ *vi, archaic* **:** to act coyly

coy·ote \\ˈkī-ˌōt, kī-ˈōt-ē\\ *n, pl* **coyotes** *or* **coyote** [MexSp, fr. Nahuatl *coyotl*] **:** a small wolf (*Canis latrans*) native to western No. America

coyote

coy·o·til·lo \\ˌkī-ə-ˈtil-(ˌ)ō, ˌkȯi-ə-, -ˈtē-(ˌ)(y)ō\\ *n* [MexSp, dim. of *coyote*] **:** a low poisonous shrub (*Karwinskia humboldtiana*) of the buckthorn family of the southwestern U.S. and Mexico

coy·pu \\ˈkȯi-(ˌ)pü, kȯi-ˈ\\ *n* [AmerSp *coipú,* fr. Araucan *coypu*] **1 :** a So. American aquatic rodent (*Myocastor coypus*) with webbed feet and dorsal mammae that has been introduced into the U.S. on the Gulf coast and in the Pacific Northwest **2 :** NUTRIA 2

coz \\ˈkəz\\ *n* [by shortening & alter.] **:** COUSIN

coz·en \\ˈkəz-ᵊn\\ *vt* **coz·ened; coz·en·ing** \\ˈkəz-niŋ, -ᵊn-iŋ\\ [obs. It *cozzonare,* fr. It *cozzone* horse trader, fr. L *cocion-, cocio* trader] **1 :** to deceive, win over, or induce to do something by artful coaxing and wheedling or shrewd trickery <tried to ~ his opponent's supporters> **2 :** to gain by cozening someone <~*ed* his supper out of the old woman> ***syn*** see CHEAT — **coz·en·er** \\ˈkəz-nər, -ᵊn-ər\\ *n*

coz·en·age \\ˈkəz-nij, -ᵊn-ij\\ *n* **1 :** the art or practice of cozening **:** FRAUD **2 :** an act or an instance of cozening

1co·zy \\ˈkō-zē\\ *adj* **co·zi·er; -est** [prob. of Scand origin; akin to Norw *koselig* cozy] **1 :** enjoying or affording warmth and ease **:** SNUG **2 a :** marked by the intimacy of the family or a close group **b :** suggesting close association or connivance <a ~ agreement> **3 :** marked by a discreet and cautious attitude or procedure ***syn*** see COMFORTABLE — **co·zi·ly** \\-zə-lē\\ *adv* — **co·zi·ness** \\-zē-nəs\\ *n*

2cozy *adv* **:** in a cautious manner <play it ~ and wait for the other team to make a mistake —Bobby Dodd>

3cozy *n, pl* **cozies :** a padded covering esp. for a teapot to keep the contents hot

cozy up *vi* **:** to attain or try to attain familiarity, friendship, or intimacy **:** ingratiate onself <*cozying up* to the party leaders>

cp *abbr* **1** compare **2** coupon

CP *abbr* **1** candlepower **2** Cape Province **3** center of pressure **4** charter party **5** chemically pure **6** command post **7** communist party **8** Congregation of the Passion **9** custom of port

CPA *abbr* **1** Catholic Press Association **2** certified public accountant

cpd *abbr* compound

CPFF *abbr* cost plus fixed fee

CPI *abbr* consumer price index

cpl *abbr* **1** complete **2** compline

Cpl *abbr* corporal

CPM *abbr* **1** cost per thousand **2** cycles per minute

CPO *abbr* chief petty officer

CPOM *abbr* master chief petty officer

CPOS *abbr* senior chief petty officer

CPS *abbr* **1** cards per second **2** certified professional secretary **3** characters per second **4** Civilian Public Service **5** cycles per second

CPT *abbr* captain

cpu *abbr* central processing unit

1CQ \\ˌsē-ˈkyü\\ [abbr. for *call to quarters*] — communication code letters used at the beginning of radiograms of general information or safety notices or by shortwave amateurs as an invitation to talk to other shortwave amateurs

2CQ *abbr* **1** call to quarters **2** charge of quarters **3** commercial quality

CQT *abbr* College Qualification Test

cr *abbr* **1** center **2** circular **3** commander **4** cream **5** creased **6** credit; creditor **7** crescendo **8** cruzeiro

Cr *symbol* chromium

CR *abbr* **1** carrier's risk **2** cathode ray **3** class rate **4** conditioned reflex; conditioned response **5** current rate

1crab \\ˈkrab\\ *n, often attrib* [ME *crabbe,* fr. OE *crabba;* akin to OHG *krebiz* crab, OE *ceorfan* to carve] **1 :** any of numerous chiefly marine broadly built crustaceans: **a :** any of a tribe (Brachyura) with a short broad usu. flattened carapace, a small abdomen that curls forward beneath the body, short antennae, and the anterior pair of limbs modified as grasping pincers **b :** any of various crustaceans (tribe Anomura) resembling true crabs in the more or less reduced condition of the abdomen **2** *cap* **:** CANCER 1 **3 :** any of various machines for raising or hauling heavy weights **4 :** failure to raise an oar clear of the water on recovery of a stroke or missing the water altogether when attempting a stroke <catch a ~> **5** *pl* **:** infestation with crab lice **6 :** apparent sideways motion of an airplane headed into a crosswind

2crab *vb* **crabbed; crab·bing** *vt* **1 :** to cause to move sideways or in an indirect or diagonal manner; *specif* **:** to head (an airplane) by means of the rudder into a crosswind to counteract drift **2 :** to subject to crabbing ~ *vi* **1 a** (1) **:** to move sideways indirectly or diagonally (2) **:** to crab an airplane **b :** to scuttle or scurry sideways **2 :** to fish for crabs — **crab·ber** *n*

3crab *n* [ME *crabbe,* perh. fr. *crabbe* ¹crab] **:** CRAB APPLE

4crab *vb* **crabbed; crab·bing** [ME *crabben,* prob. back-formation fr. *crabbed*] *vt* **1 :** to make sullen **:** SOUR <old age has *crabbed* his nature> **2 :** to complain about peevishly **3 :** SPOIL, RUIN ~ *vi* **:** CARP, GROUSE <always ~*s* about the weather> — **crab·ber** *n*

5crab *n* **:** an ill-tempered person **:** CROSSPATCH

crab apple *n* [³*crab*] **1 :** a small wild sour apple **2 :** a cultivated apple with small usu. highly colored acid fruit

crab·bed \\ˈkrab-əd\\ *adj* [ME, partly fr. *crabbe* ¹crab, partly fr. *crabbe* ³crab] **1 :** MOROSE, PEEVISH **2 :** difficult to read or understand <~ handwriting> — **crab·bed·ly** *adv* — **crab·bed·ness** *n*

crab·by \\ˈkrab-ē\\ *adj* **crab·bi·er; -est** [⁵crab] **:** CROSS, ILL-NATURED

crab cactus *n* **:** CHRISTMAS CACTUS

crab·grass \\ˈkrab-ˌgras\\ *n* **:** a grass (esp. *Digitaria sanguinalis*) that has creeping or decumbent stems which root freely at the nodes and that is often a pest in turf or cultivated lands

crab louse *n* **:** a louse (*Phthirus pubis*) infesting the pubic region of the human body

crab·stick \\ˈkrab-ˌstik\\ *n* **1 :** a stick, cane, or cudgel of crab apple tree wood **2 :** a crabbed ill-natured person

crab·wise \\-ˌwīz\\ *adv* **1 :** SIDEWAYS **2 :** in a sidling or cautiously indirect manner

1crack \\ˈkrak\\ *vb* [ME *crakken,* fr. OE *cracian;* akin to Skt *jarate* it crackles — more at CRANE] *vi* **1 :** to make a very sharp explosive sound <the whip ~*s* through the air> **2 :** to break, split, or snap apart <the friendly atmosphere began to ~> **3 :** FAIL: as **a :** to lose control or effectiveness under pressure — often used with *up* **b :** to fail in tone <his voice ~*ed*> **4 :** to go at good speed; *specif* **:** to proceed under full sail or steam **5 :** to break up into simpler chemical compounds usu. as a result of heating ~ *vt* **1 a :** to break so that fissures appear on the surface <~ a mirror> **b :** to break with a sudden sharp sound <~ nuts> **2 :** to utter esp. suddenly or strikingly <~ a joke> **3 :** to strike with a sharp noise **:** RAP <then ~*s* him over the head> <~*ed* a two-run homer in the fifth —*N. Y. Times*> **4 a** (1) **:** to open (as a bottle) for drinking (2) **:** to open (a book) for studying **b :** to puzzle out and expose, solve, or reveal the mystery of <~ a code> **c :** to break into <~ a safe> **d :** to open slightly <~ the throttle> **e :** to break through (as a barrier) so as to gain acceptance or recognition **5 a :** to impair seriously or irreparably **:** WRECK <~ a car up> **b :** to destroy the tone of (a voice) **c :** DISORDER, CRAZE **d :** to interrupt sharply or abruptly <the criticism ~*ed* our complacency> **6 :** to cause to make a sharp noise <~ one's knuckles> **7 a** (1) **:** to subject (hydrocarbons) to cracking (2) **:** to produce by cracking <~*ed* gasoline> **b :** to break up (chemical compounds) into simpler compounds by means of heat

2crack *n* **1 a :** a loud roll or peal <a ~ of thunder> **b :** a sudden sharp noise <the ~ of rifle fire> **2 :** a sharp witty remark **:** QUIP **3 a :** a narrow break **:** FISSURE <a ~ in the ice> **b :** a narrow opening <leave the door open a ~> **4 a :** a weakness or flaw caused by decay, age, or deficiency **:** UNSOUNDNESS **b :** a broken tone of the voice **c :** CRACKPOT **5 :** MOMENT, INSTANT <the ~ of dawn> <the ~ of doom> **6 :** HOUSEBREAKING, BURGLARY **7 :** a sharp resounding blow <gave him a ~ on the head> **8 :** ATTEMPT, TRY <her first ~ at writing a novel>

3crack *adj* **:** of superior excellence or ability <a ~ marksman>

crack·back \\ˈkrak-ˌbak\\ *n* **:** a blind-side block on a defensive back in football by a pass receiver who starts downfield and then cuts back to the middle of the line

crack·brain \\-ˌbrān\\ *n*: an erratic person **:** CRACKPOT — **crack·brained** \\-ˈbrānd\\ *adj*

crack·down \\-ˌdau̇n\\ *n* **:** an act or instance of cracking down

crack down \\-ˈdau̇n\\ *vi* **:** to take positive regulatory or disciplinary action

cracked \\ˈkrakt\\ *adj* **1 a :** broken (as by a sharp blow) so that the surface is fissured <~ china> **b :** broken into coarse particles <~ wheat> **c :** marked by harshness, dissonance, or failure to sustain a tone <a ~ voice> **2 :** mentally disturbed **:** CRAZY

crack·er \\ˈkrak-ər\\ *n* **1** *chiefly dial* **:** a bragging liar **:** BOASTER **2 :** something that makes a cracking or snapping noise: as **a :** FIRECRACKER **b :** the snapping end of a whiplash **:** SNAPPER **c :** a paper holder for a party favor that pops when the ends are pulled sharply **3** *pl* **:** NUTCRACKER **4 :** a dry thin crisp bakery product that may be leavened or unleavened and that is made in various shapes **5 a :** a poor usu. Southern white — usu. used disparagingly **b** *cap* **:** a native or resident of Florida or Georgia — used as a nickname **6 :** the equipment in which cracking (as of petroleum) is carried out

crack·er–bar·rel \\-ˌbar-əl\\ *adj* [*cracker barrel,* a barrel in which crackers were kept in country stores and around which customers lounged for informal conversation] **:** suggestive of the friendly homespun character of a country store <a ~ philosopher>

crack·er·jack \ˈkrak-ər-ˌjak\ *also* **crack·a·jack** \-ə-ˌjak\ *n* [[1]*crack* + *-er* + *jack*] **:** a person or thing of marked excellence — **crackerjack** *adj*

Cracker Jack *trademark* — used for a candied popcorn confection

crack·ers \ˈkrak-ərz\ *adj* [prob. alter. of *cracked*] *chiefly Brit* **:** CRAZY

[1]**crack·ing** \ˈkrak-iŋ\ *adj* **:** very impressive or effective **:** GREAT

[2]**cracking** *adv* **:** VERY, EXTREMELY <a ~ good book>

[3]**cracking** *n* **:** a process in which relatively heavy hydrocarbons are broken up by heat into lighter products (as gasoline)

[1]**crack·le** \ˈkrak-əl\ *vb* **crack·led; crack·ling** \-(ə-)liŋ\ [freq. of [1]*crack*] *vi* **1 a :** to make small sharp sudden repeated noises <the fire ~*s* on the hearth> **b :** to show animation **:** SPARKLE <the essays ~ with wit> **2 :** to develop a surface network of fine cracks ~ *vt* **:** to crush or crack with snapping noises

[2]**crackle** *n* **1 a :** the noise of repeated small cracks or reports **b :** SPARKLE, EFFERVESCENCE **2 :** a network of fine cracks on an otherwise smooth surface

crack·le·ware \ˈkrak-əl-ˌwa(ə)r, -ˌwe(ə)r\ *n* **:** ceramic ware with a designedly crackled glaze

crack·ling *n* **1** \ˈkrak-(ə-)liŋ\ **:** a series of small sharp cracks or reports <the ~ of frozen snow as we walk> **2** \ˈkrak-lən, -liŋ\ **:** the crisp residue left after the rendering of lard from meat or the frying or roasting of the skin (as of pork or goose) — usu. used in pl.

crack·ly \ˈkrak-(ə-)lē\ *adj* **:** inclined to crackle **:** CRISP

crack·nel \ˈkrak-nᵊl\ *n* [ME *krakenelle*] **1 :** a hard brittle biscuit **2 :** CRACKLING 2 — usu. used in pl.

crack·pot \ˈkrak-ˌpät\ *n* **:** one given to eccentric or lunatic notions — **crackpot** *adj*

cracks·man \ˈkrak-smən\ *n* **:** BURGLAR; *also* **:** SAFECRACKER

crack–up \ˈkrak-ˌəp\ *n* **1 a :** a mental collapse **:** NERVOUS BREAKDOWN <his wife's death brought on his ~> **b :** COLLAPSE, BREAKDOWN **2 :** CRASH, WRECK <an automobile ~>

crack up \-ˈəp\ *vi* **:** to smash up a vehicle (as by losing control) <*cracked up* on a curve> ~ *vt* **1 :** EXTOL, PRAISE <wasn't all that it was *cracked up* to be> **2 :** to cause much amusement to <that joke really *cracks* him *up*>

-c·ra·cy \k-rə-sē\ *n comb form* [MF & LL; MF *-cratie,* fr. LL *-cratia,* fr. Gk *-kratia,* fr. *kratos* strength, power — more at HARD] **1 :** form of government; *also* **:** state having such a form <monoc*racy*> **2 :** social or political class (as of powerful persons) <mobo*cracy*> **3 :** theory of social organization <techno*cracy*>

[1]**cra·dle** \ˈkrād-ᵊl\ *n* [ME *cradel,* fr. OE *cradol;* akin to OHG *kratto* basket, Skt *grantha* knot] **1 a :** a bed or cot for a baby usu. on rockers or pivots **b :** a framework or support suggestive of a baby's cradle: as (1) **:** a framework of bars and rods (2) **:** the support for a telephone receiver or handset **c** (1) **:** an implement with rods like fingers attached to a scythe and used formerly for harvesting grain (2) **:** a low frame on casters on which mechanics lie while working under an automobile **d :** a frame to keep the bedclothes from contact with an injured part of the body **2 a :** the earliest period of life **:** INFANCY <from the ~ to the grave> **b :** a place of origin <believed that the Nile valley was the ~ of civilization> **3 :** a rocking device used in panning for gold

[2]**cradle** *vb* **cra·dled; cra·dling** \ˈkrād-liŋ, -ᵊl-iŋ\ *vt* **1 a :** to place or keep in or as if in a cradle **b :** SHELTER, REAR **c :** to support protectively or intimately <*cradling* the injured man's head in her arms> **2 :** to cut (grain) with a cradle scythe **3 :** to place, raise, support, or transport on a cradle **4 :** to wash in a miner's cradle ~ *vi, obs* **:** to rest in or as if in a cradle

cra·dle·song \ˈkrād-ᵊl-ˌsȯŋ\ *n* **:** LULLABY, BERCEUSE

[1]**craft** \ˈkraft\ *n* [ME, strength, skill, fr. OE *cræft;* akin to OHG *kraft* strength] **1 :** skill in planning, making, or executing **:** DEXTERITY — often used in combination <wine*craft*> **2 :** an occupation or trade requiring manual dexterity or artistic skill <the carpenter's ~> **3 :** skill in deceiving to gain an end <used ~ and guile to close the deal> **4 :** the members of a trade or trade association **5** *pl usu* **craft a :** a boat esp. of small size **b :** AIRCRAFT **c :** SPACECRAFT ***syn*** see ART

[2]**craft** *vt* **:** to make by or as if by hand <is ~*ing* a new sculpture> <a carefully ~*ed* story>

crafts·man \ˈkraf(t)-smən\ *n* **1 :** a workman who practices a trade or handicraft **:** ARTISAN **2 :** one who creates or performs with skill or dexterity esp. in the manual arts <jewelry made by European *craftsmen*> — **crafts·man·like** \-ˌlīk\ *adj* — **crafts·man·ship** \-ˌship\ *n*

crafts·wom·an \ˈkraf(t)-ˌswu̇m-ən\ *n* **:** a female craftsman

craft union *n* **:** a labor union with membership limited to workmen of the same craft — compare INDUSTRIAL UNION

crafty \ˈkraf-tē\ *adj* **craft·i·er; -est 1** *dial chiefly Brit* **:** SKILLFUL, CLEVER **2 a :** adept in the use of subtlety and cunning **b :** marked by subtlety and guile <a ~ scheme> ***syn*** see SLY — **craft·i·ly** \ˈkraf-tə-lē\ *adv* — **craft·i·ness** \-tē-nəs\ *n*

[1]**crag** \ˈkrag\ *n* [ME, of Celt origin; akin to OIr *crec* crag] **1 :** a steep rugged rock or cliff **2** *archaic* **:** a sharp detached fragment of rock — **crag·ged** \ˈkrag-əd\ *adj*

[2]**crag** *n* [ME, fr. MD *craghe*] *chiefly Scot* **:** NECK, THROAT

crag·gy \ˈkrag-ē\ *adj* **crag·gi·er; -est 1 :** full of crags <~ slopes> **2 :** ROUGH, RUGGED <a ~ face> — **crag·gi·ly** \ˈkrag-ə-lē\ *adv* — **crag·gi·ness** \ˈkrag-ē-nəs\ *n*

crags·man \ˈkragz-mən\ *n* **:** one that is expert in climbing crags or cliffs

crake \ˈkrāk\ *n* [ME, prob. fr. ON *krāka* crow or *krākr* raven; akin to OE *crāwan* to crow] **1 :** any of various rails; *esp* **:** a short-billed rail (as the corncrake) **2 :** the corncrake's cry

[1]**cram** \ˈkram\ *vb* **crammed; cram·ming** [ME *crammen,* fr. OE *crammian;* akin to Gk *ageirein* to collect] *vt* **1 :** to pack tight **:** JAM <~ a suitcase with clothes> **2 a :** to fill (as poultry) with food to satiety **:** STUFF **b :** to eat voraciously **:** BOLT <the child ~*s* his food> **3 :** to thrust in or as if in a rough or forceful manner <*crammed* the letters angrily into his pocket> **4 :** to prepare hastily for an examination <~ the students for the test> ~ *vi* **1 :** to eat greedily or to satiety **:** STUFF **2 :** to study hastily for an imminent examination — **cram·mer** *n*

[2]**cram** *n* **1 :** a compressed multitude or crowd **:** CRUSH **2 :** last-minute study for an examination

cram·be \ˈkram-(ˌ)bē\ *n* [NL, genus name, fr. L, cabbage, fr. Gk *krambē*] **:** an annual Mediterranean crucifer (*Crambe abyssinica*) cultivated as an oilseed crop

cram·bo \ˈkram-(ˌ)bō\ *n, pl* **cramboes** [alter. of earlier *crambe,* fr. L, cabbage] **1 :** a game in which one player gives a word or line of verse to be matched in rhyme by other players **2 :** sloppy rhyme

cram·oi·sie *or* **cram·oi·sy** \ˈkram-ˌȯi-zē, ˈkram-ə-zē\ *n, pl* **-sies** [ME *crammassy,* fr. MF *cramoisi,* fr. *cramoisi* crimson] **:** crimson cloth

[1]**cramp** \ˈkramp\ *n* [ME *crampe,* fr. MF, of Gmc origin; akin to LG *krampe* hook] **1 :** a painful involuntary spasmodic contraction of a muscle **2 :** a temporary paralysis of muscles from overuse — compare WRITER'S CRAMP **3 :** sharp abdominal pain — usu. used in pl.

[2]**cramp** *n* [LG or obs. D *krampe* hook; akin to OE *cradol* cradle] **1 a :** a usu. iron device bent at the ends and used to hold timbers or blocks of stone together **b :** [1]CLAMP **2 a :** something that confines **:** SHACKLE **b :** the state of being confined — **cramp** *adj*

[3]**cramp** *vt* **1 :** to affect with or as if with cramp **2 a :** CONFINE, RESTRAIN <felt ~*ed* in the tiny apartment> **b :** to restrain from free expression — used esp. in the phrase *cramp one's style* **3 :** to turn (the front wheels of a vehicle) to right or left **4 :** to fasten or hold with a cramp ~ *vi* **:** to suffer from cramps

cramp·fish \ˈkramp-ˌfish\ *n* **:** ELECTRIC RAY

cram·pit \ˈkram-pət\ *n* [alter. of *crampette* (chape), fr. ME, fr. MD *crampe* hook] **:** a sheet of iron on which a player stands to deliver his stone in curling

cram·pon \ˈkram-ˌpän\ *n* [MF *crampon,* of Gmc origin; akin to LG *krampe*] **1 :** a hooked clutch or dog for raising heavy objects — usu. used in pl. **2 :** CLIMBING IRON — usu. used in pl.

cran·ber·ry \ˈkran-ˌber-ē, -b(ə-)rē\ *n* [part trans. of LG *kraanbere,* fr. *kraan* crane + *bere* berry] **1 :** the red acid berry produced by some plants (as *Vaccinium oxycoccos* and *V. macrocarpon*) of the heath family; *also* **:** a plant producing these **2 :** any of various plants with a fruit that resembles a cranberry

cranberry bush *n* **:** a shrubby or arborescent viburnum (*Viburnum trilobum*) of No. America and Europe with prominently 3-lobed leaves and red fruit

cranch \ˈkränch\ *var of* CRAUNCH

[1]**crane** \ˈkrān\ *n* [ME *cran,* fr. OE; akin to OHG *krano* crane, Gk *geranos,* L *grus,* Skt *jarate* it crackles] **1 :** any of a family (Gruidae of the order Gruiformes) of tall wading birds superficially resembling the herons but structurally more nearly related to the rails **2 :** any of several herons **3 :** an often horizontal projection swinging about a vertical axis: as **a :** a machine for raising, shifting, and lowering heavy weights by means of a projecting swinging arm or with the hoisting apparatus supported on an overhead track **b :** an iron arm in a fireplace for supporting kettles **c :** a boom for holding a motion-picture or television camera

[2]**crane** *vb* **craned; cran·ing** *vt* **1 :** to raise or lift by or as if by a crane **2 :** to stretch (as the neck) toward an object of attention <*craning* her neck to get a better view> ~ *vi* **1 :** to stretch one's neck toward an object of attention <I *craned* out of the window of my compartment —Webb Waldron> **2 :** HESITATE

crane fly *n* **:** any of numerous long-legged slender two-winged flies (family Tipulidae) that resemble large mosquitoes but do not bite

cranes·bill \ˈkrānz-ˌbil\ *n* **:** GERANIUM 1

crani- *or* **cranio-** *comb form* [ML *cranium*] **:** cranium <*crani*ate> **:** cranial and <*cranio*sacral>

cra·ni·al \ˈkrā-nē-əl\ *adj* **1 :** of or relating to the skull or cranium **2 :** CEPHALIC — **cra·ni·al·ly** \-ə-lē\ *adv*

cranial index *n* **:** the ratio of the maximum breadth of the skull to its maximum height multiplied by 100

cranial nerve *n* **:** any of the paired nerves that arise from the lower surface of the brain and pass through openings in the skull to the periphery of the body and that comprise 12 pairs in reptiles, birds, and mammals and usu. 10 in fishes and amphibians

cra·ni·ate \ˈkrā-nē-ət, -ˌāt\ *adj* **:** having a cranium — **craniate** *n*

cra·nio·ce·re·bral \ˌkrā-nē-ō-sə-ˈrē-brəl, -ˈser-ə-\ *adj* **:** involving both cranium and brain <~ injury>

cra·nio·fa·cial \-ˈfā-shəl\ *adj* **:** of, relating to, or involving both the cranium and the face

cra·ni·ol·o·gy \ˌkrā-nē-ˈäl-ə-jē\ *n* [prob. fr. G *kraniologie,* fr. *kranio-* crani- + *-logie* -logy] **:** a science dealing with variations in size, shape, and proportions of skulls among the races of men

cra·ni·om·e·try \-ˈäm-ə-trē\ *n* [ISV] **:** a science dealing with cranial measurement

cra·nio·sa·cral \-ˈsak-rəl, -ˈsā-krəl\ *adj* **1 :** of or relating to the cranium and the sacrum **2 :** PARASYMPATHETIC

cra·ni·um \ˈkrā-nē-əm\ *n, pl* **-ni·ums** *or* **-nia** \-nē-ə\ [ML, fr. Gk *kranion;* akin to Gk *kara* head — more at CEREBRAL] **:** SKULL; *specif* **:** the part that encloses the brain

[1]**crank** \ˈkraŋk\ *n* [ME *cranke,* fr. OE *cranc-* (as in *crancstaef,* a weaving instrument); akin to OE *cradol* cradle] **1 :** a bent part of an axle or shaft or an arm keyed at right angles to the end of a shaft by which circular motion is imparted to or received from the shaft or by which reciprocating motion is changed into circular motion or vice versa **2 a** *archaic* **:** BEND **b :** a twist or turn of speech **:** CONCEIT — used esp. in the phrase *quips and cranks* **c** (1) **:** CAPRICE, CROTCHET (2) **:** an eccentric person; *also* **:** one that is

overly enthusiastic about a particular subject or activity **d** : a bad-tempered person : GROUCH

[2]crank *vi* **1** : to move with a winding course : ZIGZAG **2 a** : to turn a crank (as in starting an automobile engine) **b** : to come into being or get started by or as if by the turning of a crank <as the political season *~s* up, with barbecues . . . in the offing — *Newsweek*> ~ *vt* **1** : to bend into the shape of a crank **2** : to furnish or fasten with a crank **3 a** : to move or operate by or as if by a crank <~ the window down> **b** : to start by use of a crank — often used with *up*

[3]crank *adj* [Sc, bent, distorted, prob. fr. [1]*crank*] : out of kilter : LOOSE <~ machinery>

[4]crank *adj* [ME *cranke*, of unknown origin] **1** *chiefly dial* : MERRY, HIGH-SPIRITED **2** *chiefly dial* : COCKY, CONFIDENT

[5]crank *adj* [short for *crank-sided* (easily tipped)] *of a boat* : easily tipped by an external force

crank·case \ˈkraŋk-ˌkās\ *n* : the housing of a crankshaft

[1]cran·kle \ˈkraŋ-kəl\ *vb* **cran·kled; cran·kling** \-k(ə-)liŋ\ [freq. of [2]*crank*] *vt, obs* : to break into turns, bends, or angles : CRINKLE ~ *vi, archaic* : WIND, ZIGZAG

[2]crankle *n* : BEND, CRINKLE

crank out *vt* : to produce esp. in a mechanical manner <*cranks out* two novels a year>

crank·pin \ˈkraŋk-ˌpin\ *n* : the cylindrical piece which forms the handle of a crank or to which the connecting rod is attached

crank·shaft \ˈkraŋk-ˌshaft\ *n* : a shaft driven by or driving a crank

[1]cranky \ˈkraŋ-kē\ *adj* **crank·i·er; -est** [[1]*crank* & [3]*crank*] **1** *dial* : IMBECILE, CRAZY **2** : working erratically : UNPREDICTABLE <a ~ old tractor> **3 a** : marked by eccentricity **b** : given to fretful fussiness : readily angered when opposed : CROTCHETY **4** : full of twists and turns : TORTUOUS <a ~ road> ***syn*** see IRASCIBLE — **crank·i·ly** \-kə-lē\ *adv* — **crank·i·ness** \-kē-nəs\ *n*

[2]cranky *adj* [[5]*crank*] *of a boat* : liable to heel or tip

cran·nog \ˈkran-ˌȯg, kra-ˈnōg\ *n* [ScGael *crannag* & IrGael *crannōg*] : an artificial fortified island constructed in a lake or marsh orig. in prehistoric Ireland and Scotland

cran·ny \ˈkran-ē\ *n, pl* **crannies** [ME *crany*, fr. MF *cren, cran* notch] **1** : a small break or slit : CREVICE **2** : an obscure nook or corner — **cran·nied** \-ēd\ *adj*

cran·reuch \ˈkran-ˌrůk\ *n* [prob. modif. of ScGael *crannreotha*] *Scot* : HOARFROST, RIME

[1]crap \ˈkrap\ *n* [ME *crappe* chaff, residue from rendered fat, fr. MD, piece torn off, fr. *crappen* to break off] **1 a** : EXCREMENT — usu. considered vulgar **b** : DEFECATION — usu. considered vulgar **2** : NONSENSE, RUBBISH — sometimes considered vulgar

[2]crap *vi* **crapped; crap·ping** : DEFECATE — usu. considered vulgar

[3]crap *n* [back-formation fr. *craps*] **1** : a throw of 2, 3, or 12 in the game of craps losing the shooter his bet unless he has a point — called also *craps;* compare NATURAL **2** — used as an attributive form of *craps* <~ game> <~ table>

[4]crap *vi* **crapped; crap·ping** **1** : to throw a crap **2** : to throw a seven while trying to make a point — usu. used with *out*

[1]crape \ˈkrāp\ *n* [alter. of F *crêpe*, fr. MF *crespe*, fr. *crespe* curly, fr. L *crispus* — more at CRISP] **1** : CREPE **2** : a band of crepe worn on a hat or sleeve as a sign of mourning

[2]crape *vt* **craped; crap·ing** : to cover or shroud with or as if with crape

[3]crape *vt* **craped; crap·ing** [F *crêper*, fr. L *crispare*, fr. *crispus*] : to make (the hair) curly

crape myrtle *n* : an East Indian shrub (*Lagerstroemia indica*) of the loosestrife family widely grown in warm regions for its flowers

crap·per \ˈkrap-ər\ *n* [[2]*crap*] : TOILET — usu. considered vulgar

crap·pie \ˈkräp-ē\ *n* [CanF *crapet*] **1** : BLACK CRAPPIE **2** : WHITE CRAPPIE

crap·py \ˈkrap-ē\ *adj* **crap·pi·er; -est** [[1]*crap*] *slang* : markedly inferior in quality : LOUSY

craps \ˈkraps\ *n pl but sing or pl in constr* [LaF, fr. F *crabs, craps*, fr. E *crabs* lowest throw at hazard, fr. pl. of [1]*crab*] **1** : a gambling game played with two dice **2** : [3]CRAP 1

crap·shoot·er \ˈkrap-ˌshüt-ər\ *n* : one who plays craps

crap·u·lous \ˈkrap-yə-ləs\ *adj* [LL *crapulosus*, fr. L *crapula* intoxication, fr. Gk *kraipalē*] **1** : marked by intemperance esp. in eating or drinking **2** : sick from excessive indulgence in liquor

[1]crash \ˈkrash\ *vb* [ME *crasschen*] *vt* **1 a** : to break violently and noisily : SMASH **b** : to damage (an airplane) in landing **2 a** : to cause to make a loud noise <~ the cymbals together> **b** : to force (as one's way) through with loud crashing noises **3** : to enter or attend without invitation or without paying <~ the party> ~ *vi* **1 a** : to break or go to pieces with or as if with violence and noise **b** : to crash an airplane **2** : to make a smashing noise <thunder *~ing* overhead> **3** : to move or force one's way with or as if with a crash <*~es* into the room> **4** *slang* : to spend the night in a particular place : SLEEP <hippies who had . . . been up all night because they couldn't find a place to ~ —Nicholas Von Hoffman> **5** *slang* : to return to a normal state after a drug-induced experience

[2]crash *n* **1** : a loud sound (as of things smashing) <a ~ of thunder> **2** : a breaking to pieces by or as if by collision; *also* : an instance of crashing <a plane ~> **3** : a sudden decline or failure (as of a business) <a stockmarket ~>

[3]crash *adj* : marked by a concerted effort and effected in the shortest possible time <a ~ program to teach dropouts how to read>

[4]crash *n* [prob. fr. Russ *krashenina* colored linen] : a coarse fabric used for draperies, toweling, and clothing

crash dive *n* : a dive made by a submarine in the least possible time — **crash–dive** *vi*

crash helmet *n* : a usu. plastic or leather helmet that is worn (as by motorcyclists) as protection for the head in the event of an accident

crash·ing \ˈkrash-iŋ\ *adj* **1** : UTTER, ABSOLUTE <a ~ bore> **2** : SUPERLATIVE <a ~ effect>

crash–land \ˈkrash-ˈland\ *vt* : to land (an airplane) under emergency conditions usu. with damage to the craft ~ *vi* : to crash-land an airplane — **crash landing** *n*

crash pad *n* **1** : protective padding (as on the inside of an automobile or a military tank) **2** : a place where free temporary lodging is available <a hippie *crash pad*>

crash·wor·thy \ˈkrash-ˌwər-t͟hē\ *adj* : resistant to the effects of collision <~ cars> — **crash·wor·thi·ness** *n*

crass \ˈkras\ *adj* [L *crassus* thick, gross] : having such grossness of mind as precludes delicacy and discrimination : INSENSITIVE ***syn*** see STUPID ***ant*** brilliant — **crass·ly** *adv* — **crass·ness** *n*

cras·si·tude \ˈkras-ə-ˌt(y)üd\ *n* : the quality or state of being crass : GROSSNESS; *also* : an instance of grossness

-crat \ˌkrat\ *n comb form* [F *-crate*, back-formation fr. *-cratie* -cracy] **1** : advocate or partisan of a (specified) theory of government <theo*crat*> **2** : member of a (specified) dominant class <pluto*crat*> — **-crat·ic** \ˈkrat-ik\ *adj comb form*

cratch \ˈkrach\ *n* [ME *cracche*, fr. OF *creche* manger — more at CRÈCHE] **1** *dial Brit* : a crib or rack esp. for fodder; *also* : FRAME **2** *archaic* : MANGER

[1]crate \ˈkrāt\ *n* [L *cratis* wickerwork — more at HURDLE] **1** : an open box of wooden slats or a usu. wooden protective case or framework for shipping **2** : JALOPY

[2]crate *vt* **crat·ed; crat·ing** : to pack in a crate

[1]cra·ter *n* [L, mixing bowl, crater, fr. Gk *kratēr*, fr. *kerannynai* to mix; akin to Skt *āśīrta* mixed] **1** \ˈkrāt-ər\ **a** : the bowl-shaped depression around the orifice of a volcano **b** : a depression formed by the impact of a meteorite **c** : a hole in the ground made by the explosion of a bomb or shell **d** : an eroded lesion **e** : a dimple in a painted surface **2** \ˈkrāt-ər, krä-ˈte(ə)r\ : KRATER

[2]cra·ter \ˈkrāt-ər\ *vi* : to exhibit or form craters ~ *vt* : to form craters in

cra·ter·let \ˈkrāt-ər-lət\ *n* : a small crater

C ration *n* : a canned field ration of the U. S. Army

cra·ton \ˈkrā-ˌtän, ˈkra-\ *n* [G *kraton*, modif. of Gk *kratos* strength — more at HARD] : a stable relatively immobile area of the earth's crust that forms the nuclear mass of a continent or the central basis of an ocean — **cra·ton·ic** \krə-ˈtän-ik, krā-, kra-\ *adj*

craunch \ˈkrȯnch, ˈkränch\ *vb* [prob. imit.] : CRUNCH — **craunch** *n*

cra·vat \krə-ˈvat\ *n* [F *cravate*, fr. *Cravate* Croatian] **1** : a band or scarf formerly worn around the neck **2** : NECKTIE

crave \ˈkrāv\ *vb* **craved; crav·ing** [ME *craven*, fr. OE *crafian;* akin to OHG *krāpfo* hook, OE *cradol* cradle] *vt* **1** : to ask for earnestly : BEG, DEMAND <~ a pardon for neglect> **2 a** : to want greatly : NEED <*~s* drugs> **b** : to yearn for <she *~s* her vanished youth> ~ *vi* : to have a strong or inward desire <*~s* after affection> ***syn*** see DESIRE — **crav·er** *n*

cra·ven \ˈkrā-vən\ *adj* [ME *cravant*] **1** *archaic* : DEFEATED, VANQUISHED **2** : completely lacking courage : contemptibly fainthearted — **craven** *n* — **cra·ven·ly** *adv* — **cra·ven·ness** \-vən-nəs\ *n*

crav·ing \ˈkrā-viŋ\ *n* : a great desire or longing; *esp* : an abnormal desire (as for a habit-forming drug)

craw \ˈkrȯ\ *n* [ME *crawe*, fr. (assumed) OE *crawa;* akin to Gk *bronchos* trachea, throat, L *vorare* to devour — more at VORACIOUS] **1** : the crop of a bird or insect **2** : the stomach esp. of a lower animal

[1]craw·fish \ˈkrȯ-ˌfish\ *n* [by folk etymology fr. ME *crevis, kraveys*] **1** : CRAYFISH **2** : SPINY LOBSTER

[2]crawfish *vi* : to retreat from a position : back out

[1]crawl \ˈkrȯl\ *vb* [ME *crawlen*, fr. ON *krafla;* akin to OE *crabba* crab] *vi* **1** : to move slowly in a prone position without or as if without the use of limbs <the snake *~ed* into its hole> **2** : to move or progress slowly or laboriously <traffic *~s* along at 10 miles an hour> **3** : to advance by guile or servility <*~ing* into favor by toadying to his boss> **4** : to spread by extending stems or tendrils **5 a** : to be alive or swarming with or as if with creeping things <a kitchen *~ing* with ants> **b** : to have the sensation of insects creeping over one <the story made her flesh ~> **6** : to fail to stay evenly spread — used of paint, varnish, or glaze ~ *vt* **1** : to move upon in or as if in a creeping manner <the meanest man who ever *~ed* the earth> **2** *slang* : to reprove harshly <they got no good right to ~ me for what I wrote —Marjorie K. Rawlings> ***syn*** see CREEP

[2]crawl *n* **1 a** : the act or action of crawling **b** : slow or laborious progress **c** *chiefly Brit* : a going from one pub to another **2** : a prone speed swimming stroke consisting of alternating overarm strokes and a flutter kick

[3]crawl *n* [Afrik *kraal* pen —more at KRAAL] : an enclosure in shallow waters (as for confining lobsters)

crawl·er *n* **1** : one that crawls **2 a** : a Caterpillar tractor **b** : a vehicle (as a crane) that travels on endless chain belts like those of such a tractor

crawl·way \ˈkrȯl-ˌwā\ *n* : a low passageway (as in a cave) that can be traversed only by crawling

crawly \ˈkrȯ-lē\ *adj* : CREEPY

cray·fish \ˈkrā-ˌfish\ *n* [by folk etymology fr. ME *crevis*, fr. MF *crevice*, of Gmc origin; akin to OHG *krebiz* crab — more at CRAB] **1** : any of numerous freshwater crustaceans (tribe Astacura) resembling the lobster but usu. much smaller **2** : SPINY LOBSTER

[1]cray·on \ˈkrā-ˌän, -ən; ˈkran\ *n* [F, crayon, pencil, fr. dim. of *craie* chalk, fr. L *creta*] **1** : a stick of white or colored chalk or of colored wax used for writing or drawing **2** : a crayon drawing

[2]crayon *vt* : to draw with a crayon — **cray·on·ist** \ˈkrā-ə-nəst\ *n*

[1]craze \ˈkrāz\ *vb* **crazed; craz·ing** [ME *crasen* to crush, craze, of Scand origin; akin to OSw *krasa* to crush] *vt* **1** *obs* : BREAK, SHATTER **2** : to produce minute cracks on the surface or glaze of **3** : to make insane or as if insane <*crazed* by pain and fear> ~ *vi* **1** *archaic* : SHATTER, BREAK **2** : to become insane **3** : to develop a mesh of fine cracks

[2]craze *n* **1** *obs* **a** : BREAK, FLAW **b** : physical weakness : INFIRMITY **2** : an exaggerated and often transient enthusiasm

: MANIA **3** : a crack in a surface or coating (as of glaze or enamel) ***syn*** see FASHION

cra·zy \ˈkrā-zē\ *adj* **craz·i·er; -est** **1 a** : full of cracks or flaws : UNSOUND **b** : CROOKED, ASKEW **2 a** : MAD, INSANE **b** (1) : IMPRACTICAL (2) : ERRATIC **c** : out of the ordinary : UNUSUAL <a taste for ~ hats> **3 a** : distracted with desire or excitement <a thrill-*crazy* mob> **b** : absurdly fond : INFATUATED <he's ~ about the girl> **c** : passionately preoccupied : OBSESSED <~ about boats> — **cra·zi·ly** \-zə-lē\ *adv* — **cra·zi·ness** \-zē-nəs\ *n* — **like crazy** : to an extreme degree <everyone dancing *like crazy*>

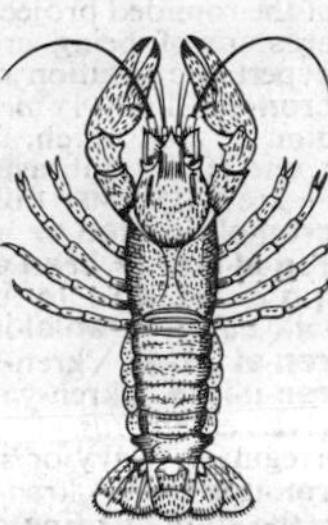
crayfish 1

crazy bone *n* : FUNNY BONE

crazy quilt *n* **1** : a patchwork quilt without a design **2** : JUMBLE, HODGEPODGE

cra·zy·weed \ˈkrā-zē-ˌwēd\ *n* : LOCOWEED

CRC *abbr* Civil Rights Commission

C-re·ac·tive protein \ˌsē-rē-ˌak-tiv-\ *n* [*C-polysaccharide* (a polysaccharide found in the cell wall of pneumococci and precipitated by this protein), fr. *carbohydrate*] : a protein present in blood serum in various abnormal states (as inflammation or neoplasia)

[1]**creak** \ˈkrēk\ *vi* [ME *creken* to croak, of imit. origin] : to make a prolonged grating or squeaking sound

[2]**creak** *n* : a rasping or grating noise

creaky \ˈkrē-kē\ *adj* **creak·i·er; -est** **1** : marked by creaking : SQUEAKY <~ shoes> **2** : DILAPIDATED, DECREPIT <a ~ old house> — **creak·i·ly** \-kə-lē\ *adv*

[1]**cream** \ˈkrēm\ *n, often attrib* [ME *creime, creme,* fr. MF *craime, cresme,* fr. LL *cramum,* of Celt origin; akin to W *cramen* scab] **1** : the yellowish part of milk containing from 18 to about 40 percent butterfat **2 a** : a food prepared with cream **b** : something having the consistency of cream; *esp* : a usu. emulsified medicinal or cosmetic preparation **3** : the choicest part <the ~ of the crop> **4** : CREAMER 2 **5 a** : a pale yellow **b** : a cream-colored animal — **cream·i·ly** \ˈkrē-mə-lē\ *adv* — **cream·i·ness** \-mē-nəs\ *n* — **creamy** \-mē\ *adj*

[2]**cream** *vi* **1** : to form cream or a surface layer like the cream on standing milk **2** : to break into or cause something to break into a creamy froth; *also* : to move like froth ~ *vt* **1 a** : SKIM 1c **b** (1) : to take the choicest part of <got in first with a new blade and ~*ed* the market> (2) : to take off the choicest part of <exporters ~*ed* consumer goods from the market> **2** : to furnish, prepare, or treat with cream; *also* : to dress with a cream sauce **3 a** : to beat into a creamy froth **b** : to work or blend to the consistency of cream <~ butter and sugar together> **c** (1) : to drub thoroughly <was ~*ed* in the first round> (2) : WRECK <~*ed* the car on the turnpike> **4** : to cause to form a surface layer of or like cream

cream cheese *n* : a mild soft unripened cheese made from whole sweet milk enriched with cream

cream·cups \ˈkrēm-ˌkəps\ *n pl but sing or pl in constr* : any of several California annuals (esp. *Platystemon californicus*) of the poppy family

cream·er \ˈkrē-mər\ *n* **1** : a device for separating cream from milk **2** : a small vessel for serving cream

cream·ery \ˈkrēm-(ə-)rē\ *n, pl* **-er·ies** : an establishment where butter and cheese are made or where milk and cream are prepared or sold

cream of tartar : a white crystalline salt $C_4H_5KO_6$ used esp. in baking powder and in certain treatments of metals

cream puff *n* **1** : a round shell of light pastry filled with whipped cream or a cream filling **2** : an ineffectual person **3** : something of little or no consequence

cream soda *n* : a carbonated soft drink flavored with vanilla and sweetened with sugar

[1]**crease** \ˈkrēs\ *n* [prob. alter. of earlier *creaste,* fr. ME *creste* crest] **1** : a line or mark made by or as if by folding a pliable substance **2** : a specially marked area in various sports; *esp* : an area surrounding a goal (as in lacrosse or hockey) forbidden to attacking players unless the ball or puck is in it — **crease·less** \-ləs\ *adj*

[2]**crease** *vb* **creased; creas·ing** *vt* **1** : to make a crease in or on : WRINKLE <old age had *creased* her face> **2** : to wound slightly esp. by grazing ~ *vi* : to become creased — **creas·er** *n*

[1]**cre·ate** \krē-ˈāt, ˈkrē-ˌ\ *adj, archaic* : CREATED

[2]**create** *vt* **cre·at·ed; cre·at·ing** [ME *createn,* fr. L *creatus,* pp. of *creare*] **1** : to bring into existence <God *created* the heaven and the earth —Gen 1:1 (AV)> **2 a** : to invest with a new form, office, or rank <was *created* a lieutenant> **b** : to produce or bring about by a course of action or behavior <her arrival *created* a terrible fuss> <~ new jobs for the unemployed> **3** : CAUSE, OCCASION <famine ~*s* high food prices> **4 a** : to produce through imaginative skill <the actor *created* an entirely new Hamlet> <~ a painting> **b** : DESIGN <~*s* evening dresses> ***syn*** see INVENT

cre·atine \ˈkrē-ə-ˌtēn, -ət-ᵊn\ *n* [ISV, fr. Gk *kreat-, kreas* flesh — more at RAW] : a white crystalline nitrogenous substance $C_4H_9N_3O_2$ found esp. in the muscles of vertebrates free or as phosphocreatine

creatine phosphate *n* : PHOSPHOCREATINE

cre·at·i·nine \krē-ˈat-ᵊn-ˌēn, -ᵊn-ən\ *n* [G *kreatinin,* fr. *kreatin* creatine] : a white crystalline strongly basic compound $C_4H_7N_3O$ formed from creatine and found esp. in muscle, blood, and urine

cre·ation \krē-ˈā-shən\ *n* **1** : the act of creating; *esp* : the act of bringing the world into ordered existence **2** : the act of making, inventing, or producing: as **a** : the act of investing with a new rank or office **b** : the first representation of a dramatic role **3** : something that is created: as **a** : WORLD **b** : creatures singly or in aggregate **c** : an original work of art **d** : a new usu. striking article of clothing

cre·ative \krē-ˈāt-iv\ *adj* **1** : marked by the ability or power to create : given to creating <the ~ impulse> <nature is a ~ agent> **2** : PRODUCTIVE — used with *of* <news ~ of alarm> **3** : having the quality of something created rather than imitated : IMAGINATIVE <the ~ arts> — **cre·ative·ly** *adv* — **cre·ative·ness** *n*

creative evolution *n* [trans. of F *évolution créatrice*] : evolution that is a creative product of a vital force rather than a naturalistically explicable process

cre·ativ·i·ty \ˌkrē-(ˌ)ā-ˈtiv-ət-ē, ˌkrē-ə-\ *n* **1** : the quality of being creative **2** : the ability to create

cre·ator \krē-ˈāt-ər\ *n* : one that creates usu. by bringing something new or original into being; *esp, cap* : GOD 1 ***syn*** see MAKER

crea·ture \ˈkrē-chər\ *n* **1** : something created: as **a** : a lower animal; *esp* : a farm animal **b** : a human being : PERSON **c** : a being of anomalous or uncertain aspect or nature <~*s* of fantasy> **2** : one who is the servile dependent or tool of another — **crea·tur·al** \ˈkrēch-(ə-)rəl\ *adj* — **crea·ture·hood** \ˈkrē-chər-ˌhu̇d\ *n* — **crea·ture·li·ness** \-chər-lē-nəs\ *n* — **crea·ture·ly** \-chər-lē\ *adj*

creature comfort *n* : something (as food or warmth) that gives bodily comfort

crèche \ˈkresh, ˈkrāsh\ *n* [F, fr. OF *creche* manger, crib, of Gmc origin; akin to OHG *krippa* manger — more at CRIB] **1** : DAY NURSERY **2** : a foundling hospital **3** : a representation of the Nativity scene

cre·dence \ˈkrēd-ᵊn(t)s\ *n* [ME, fr. MF or ML; MF, fr. ML *credentia,* fr. L *credent-, credens,* prp. of *credere* to believe trust — more at CREED] **1** : mental acceptance as true or real <give ~ to gossip> **2** : CREDENTIALS — used in the phrase *letters of credence* **3** [MF, fr. OIt *credenza*] : a Renaissance sideboard used chiefly for valuable plate **4** : a small table where the bread and wine rest before consecration ***syn*** see BELIEF

credence 3

cre·dent \ˈkrēd-ᵊnt\ *adj* [L *credent-, credens,* prp.] **1** *archaic* : giving credence : CONFIDING **2** *obs* : CREDIBLE

[1]**cre·den·tial** \kri-ˈden-chəl\ *adj* : warranting credit or confidence — used chiefly in the phrase *credential letters*

[2]**credential** *n* **1** : something that gives a title to credit or confidence **2** *pl* : testimonials showing that a person is entitled to credit or has a right to exercise official power **3** : CERTIFICATE, DIPLOMA

cre·den·za \kri-ˈden-zə\ *n* [It, lit., belief, confidence, fr. ML *credentia*] **1** : CREDENCE 3 **2** : a sideboard, buffet, or bookcase patterned after a Renaissance credence; *esp* : one without legs

credibility gap *n* **1 a** : lack of trust <a special *credibility gap* is likely to open between the generations —Kenneth Keniston> **b** : lack of believability <a *credibility gap* created by contradictory official statements —Samuel Ellenport> **2** : DISCREPANCY <the *credibility gap* between the professed ideals . . . and their actual practices —Jeanne L. Noble>

cred·i·ble \ˈkred-ə-bəl\ *adj* [ME, fr. L *credibilis,* fr. *credere*] : offering reasonable grounds for being believed <a ~ account of an accident> <~ witnesses> ***syn*** see PLAUSIBLE ***ant*** incredible — **cred·i·bil·i·ty** \ˌkred-ə-ˈbil-ət-ē\ *n* — **cred·i·bly** \ˈkred-ə-blē\ *adv*

[1]**cred·it** \ˈkred-ət\ *n* [MF, fr. OIt *credito,* fr. L *creditum* something entrusted to another, loan, fr. neut. of *creditus,* pp. of *credere* to believe, entrust — more at CREED] **1 a** : the balance in a person's favor in an account **b** : an amount or sum placed at a person's disposal by a bank **c** : time given for payment for goods or services sold on trust <long-term ~> **d** (1) : an entry on the right-hand side of an account constituting an addition to a revenue, net worth, or liability account (2) : a deduction from an expense or asset account **e** : any one of or the sum of the items entered on the right-hand side of an account **f** : a deduction from an amount otherwise due **2** : reliance on the truth or reality of something <too ready to give ~ to idle rumors> **3 a** : influence or power derived from enjoying the confidence of another or others **b** : good name : ESTEEM; *also* : financial or commercial trustworthiness **4** *archaic* : CREDIBILITY **5** : a source of honor <he was a ~ to his upbringing> **6 a** : something that gains or adds to reputation or esteem : HONOR <took no ~ for his kindly act> **b** : RECOGNITION, ACKNOWLEDGMENT <quite willing to accept undeserved ~> **7** : recognition by name of a person contributing to a performance (as a film or telecast) **8 a** : recognition by a school or college that a student has fulfilled a requirement leading to a degree **b** : CREDIT HOUR ***syn*** **1** see BELIEF **2** see INFLUENCE ***ant*** discredit

[2]**credit** *vt* [partly fr. [1]*credit;* partly fr. L *creditus,* pp.] **1** : to supply goods on credit to **2** : to trust in the truth of : BELIEVE **3** *archaic* : to bring credit or honor upon **4** : to enter upon the credit side of an account **5 a** : to consider usu. favorably as the source, agent, or performer of an action or the possessor of a trait <~*s* him with an excellent sense of humor> **b** : to attribute to some person <they ~ the invention to him> ***syn*** see ASCRIBE

cred·it·able \ˈkred-ət-ə-bəl\ *adj* **1** : worthy of belief **2** : worthy of esteem or praise **3** : worthy of commercial credit **4** : capable of being assigned <victory was directly ~ to his efforts> — **cred·it·abil·i·ty** \ˌkred-ət-ə-ˈbil-ət-ē\ *n* — **cred·it·able·ness** \ˈkred-ət-ə-bəl-nəs\ *n* — **cred·it·ably** \-blē\ *adv*

credit card *n* : a card authorizing purchases on credit

credit hour *n* **:** the unit of measuring educational credit based on a given number of classroom periods per week throughout a semester <received three *credit hours* for freshman composition>
credit line *n* **1 :** a line, note, or name that acknowledges the source of an item (as a news dispatch or television program) **2 :** the maximum credit allowed a buyer or borrower
cred·i·tor \ˈkred-ət-ər\ *n* **:** one to whom a debt is owed; *esp* **:** a person to whom money or goods are due
credit union *n* **:** a cooperative association that makes small loans to its members at low interest rates
cre·do \ˈkrēd-(ˌ)ō, ˈkrād-\ *n, pl* **credos** [ME, fr. L, I believe] **:** CREED
cre·du·li·ty \kri-ˈd(y)ü-lət-ē\ *n* **:** undue readiness of belief **:** GULLIBILITY
cred·u·lous \ˈkrej-ə-ləs\ *adj* [L *credulus,* fr. *credere*] **1 :** ready to believe esp. on slight or uncertain evidence **2 :** proceeding from credulity — **cred·u·lous·ly** *adv* — **cred·u·lous·ness** *n*
Cree \ˈkrē\ *n, pl* **Cree** *or* **Crees** [short for earlier *Christeno,* fr. CanF *Christino,* prob. modif. of Ojibwa *Kenistenoag*] **1 :** a member of an Amerindian people of Manitoba and Saskatchewan **2 :** the Algonquian language of the Cree Indians
creed \ˈkrēd\ *n* [ME *crede,* fr. OE *crēda,* fr. L *credo* (first word of the Apostles' and Nicene Creeds), fr. *credere* to believe, trust, entrust; akin to OIr *cretim* I believe, Skt *śrad-dadhāti* he believes] **1 :** a brief authoritative formula of religious belief **2 :** a set of fundamental beliefs — **creed·al** *or* **cre·dal** \ˈkrēd-ᵊl\ *adj*
creek \ˈkrēk, ˈkrik\ *n* [ME *crike, creke,* fr. ON *-kriki* bend; akin to ON *krōkr* hook — more at CROOK] **1** *chiefly Brit* **:** a small inlet or bay narrower and extending farther inland than a cove **2 :** a natural stream of water normally smaller than and often tributary to a river **3** *archaic* **:** a narrow or winding passage — **up the creek :** in a difficult or perplexing situation
Creek \ˈkrēk\ *n* **1 :** an Amerindian confederacy of peoples chiefly of Muskogean stock of Alabama, Georgia, and Florida **2 :** a member of any of the Creek peoples **3 :** the Muskogean language of the Creek Indians
creel \ˈkrē(ə)l\ *n* [ME *creille, crele,* prob. fr. (assumed) MF *creille* grill, fr. L *craticula* — more at GRILL] **1 :** a wickerwork receptacle (as for newly caught fish) **2 :** a bar with skewers for holding bobbins in a spinning machine
[1]**creep** \ˈkrēp\ *vi* **crept** \ˈkrept\; **creep·ing** [ME *crepen,* fr. OE *crēopan;* akin to Gk *grypos* curved, bent] **1 a :** to move along with the body prone and close to the ground **b :** to move slowly on hands and knees **2 a :** to go very slowly <the hours *crept* by> **b :** to go timidly or cautiously so as to escape notice <she *crept* away from the festive scene> **c :** to enter or advance stealthily <age ~*s* upon us> <a note of irritation *crept* into her voice> **3 a :** to move or stir slightly by swelling or shrinking <the thought makes his flesh ~> **b** *of a plant* **:** to spread or grow over a surface rooting at intervals or clinging with tendrils, stems, or aerial roots **4 a :** to slip or gradually shift position **b :** to change shape permanently from prolonged stress or exposure to high temperatures
syn CREEP, CRAWL *shared meaning element* **:** to move along a surface in a prone or crouching position
[2]**creep** *n* **1 :** a movement of or like creeping <traffic moving at a ~> **2 :** a distressing sensation like that caused by the creeping of insects over one's flesh; *esp* **:** a feeling of apprehension or horror — usu. used in pl. **3 :** an enclosure that young animals can enter while adults are excluded **4 :** the slow change of dimensions of an object from prolonged exposure to high temperature or stress **5 :** an obnoxious or insignificant person
creep·age \ˈkrē-pij\ *n* **:** gradual movement **:** CREEP
creep·er \ˈkrē-pər\ *n* **1 :** one that creeps: as **a :** a creeping plant **b :** a bird (as of the family Certhiidae) that creeps about on trees or bushes searching for insects **c :** a creeping insect or reptile **2 :** any of various tools or implements: as **a :** a fixture with iron points worn on the shoe to prevent slipping **b :** CLIMBING IRON **c :** a strip (as of sealskin) attachable to the bottom of a ski to prevent sliding backward in uphill climbing **d :** GRAPNEL **3 :** a device for supplying or moving material in a steady flow
creep·ing \ˈkrē-piŋ\ *adj* **:** developing or advancing by slow imperceptible degrees <a period of ~ inflation>
creeping eruption *n* **:** a skin disorder marked by a spreading red line of eruption and caused esp. by larvae (as of hookworms not normally parasitic in man) burrowing beneath the human skin
creepy \ˈkrē-pē\ *adj* **creep·i·er; -est :** producing a nervous shivery apprehension <~ things were crawling over us> <a ~ horror story> — **creep·i·ness** *n*
creese *var of* KRIS
cre·mains \kri-ˈmānz\ *n pl* [blend of *cremated* and *remains*] **:** the ashes of a cremated human body
cre·mate \ˈkrē-ˌmāt, kri-ˈ\ *vt* **cre·mat·ed; cre·mat·ing** [L *crematus,* pp. of *cremare* to burn up, cremate] **:** to reduce (as a dead body) to ashes by burning — **cre·ma·tion** \kri-ˈmā-shən\ *n*
cre·ma·to·ri·um \ˌkrē-mə-ˈtōr-ē-əm, ˌkrem-ə-, -ˈtȯr-\ *n, pl* **-ri·ums** *or* **-ria** \-ē-ə\ **:** CREMATORY
cre·ma·to·ry \ˈkrē-mə-ˌtōr-ē, ˈkrem-ə-, -ˌtȯr-\ *n, pl* **-ries :** a furnace for cremating; *also* **:** an establishment containing such a furnace — **crematory** *adj*
crème \ˈkrem, ˈkrēm\ *n, pl* **crèmes** \ˈkrem(z), ˈkrēmz\ [F, fr. OF *cresme* — more at CREAM] **1 :** cream or cream sauce as used in cookery **2 :** a sweet liqueur **3 :** CREAM 2b
crème de ca·cao \ˌkrēm-də-ˈkō-(ˌ)kō; ˌkrem-də-kə-ˈkaü, -kə-ˈkā-(ˌ)ō\ *n* [F, lit., cream of cacao] **:** a sweet liqueur flavored with cacao beans and vanilla
crème de la crème \ˌkrem-də-lä-ˈkrem, -lə-\ *n* [F, lit., cream of the cream] **:** the very best
crème de menthe \ˌkrēm-də-ˈmint, -ˈmen(t)th; ˌkrem-də-ˈmänt\ *n* [F, lit., cream of mint] **:** a sweet green or white mint-flavored liqueur
cre·nate \ˈkrē-ˌnāt\ *or* **cre·nat·ed** \-ˌnāt-əd\ *adj* [NL *crenatus,* fr. ML *crena* notch] **:** having the margin cut into rounded scallops <a ~ leaf> — **cre·nate·ly** *adv*
cre·na·tion \kri-ˈnā-shən\ *n* **1 a :** a crenate formation; *esp* **:** one of the rounded projections on an edge (as of a coin) **b :** the quality or state of being crenate **2 :** shrinkage of red blood cells in hypertonic solution resulting in crenate margins
[1]**cren·el** \ˈkren-ᵊl\ *or* **cre·nelle** \krə-ˈnel\ *n* [MF *crenel,* fr. OF, dim. of *cren* notch, fr. *crener* to notch; akin to ML *crena* notch] **:** one of the embrasures alternating with merlons in a battlement — see BATTLEMENT illustration
[2]**cren·el** *vt* **-eled** *or* **-elled; -el·ing** *or* **-el·ling :** CRENELLATE
cren·el·late *or* **cren·el·ate** \ˈkren-ᵊl-ˌāt\ *vt* **-lat·ed** *or* **-at·ed; -lat·ing** *or* **-at·ing :** to furnish with battlements — **cren·el·late** \-ˌāt, -ət\ *adj* — **cren·el·la·tion** \ˌkren-ᵊl-ˈā-shən\ *n*
cren·el·lat·ed \ˈkren-ᵊl-ˌāt-əd\ *adj* **:** having battlements
cren·u·late \ˈkren-yə-lət, -ˌlāt\ *also* **cren·u·lat·ed** \-ˌlāt-əd\ *adj* [NL *crenulatus,* fr. *crenula,* dim. of ML *crena*] **:** having an irregularly wavy or serrate outline <a ~ shoreline>
cren·u·la·tion \ˌkren-yə-ˈlā-shən\ *n* **1 :** a minute crenation **2 :** the state of being crenulate
cre·ole \ˈkrē-ˌōl\ *adj* **1** *often cap* **:** of or relating to Creoles or their language **2 :** of, relating to, or being a domestic animal of a native breed or strain esp. in Latin America **3 :** prepared with rice, okra, tomatoes, peppers, and high seasoning <shrimp ~>
Cre·ole \ˈkrē-ˌōl\ *n* [F *créole,* fr. Sp *criollo,* fr. Pg *crioulo* white person born in the colonies] **1 :** a person of European descent born esp. in the West Indies or Spanish America **2 :** a white person descended from early French or Spanish settlers of the U.S. Gulf states and preserving their speech and culture **3 :** a person of mixed French or Spanish and Negro descent speaking a dialect of French or Spanish **4 a :** the French dialect spoken by many Negroes in southern Louisiana **b :** HAITIAN **c** *not cap* **:** a language based on two or more languages that serves as the native language of its speakers
cre·o·sol \ˈkrē-ə-ˌsȯl, -ˌsōl\ *n* [ISV *creos*ote + *-ol*] **:** a colorless aromatic phenol $C_8H_{10}O_2$ obtained from guaiacum resin and the tar made from beech
[1]**cre·o·sote** \ˈkrē-ə-ˌsōt\ *n* [G *kreosot,* fr. Gk *kreas* flesh + *sōtēr* preserver, fr. *sōzein* to preserve, fr. *sōs* safe; fr. its antiseptic properties — more at RAW, THUMB] **1 :** a clear or yellowish oily liquid mixture of phenolic compounds obtained by the distillation of wood tar esp. from beech wood **2 :** a brownish oily liquid consisting chiefly of aromatic hydrocarbons obtained by distillation of coal tar and used esp. as a wood preservative
[2]**creosote** *vt* **-sot·ed; -sot·ing :** to impregnate with creosote
creosote bush *n* **:** a resinous desert shrub (*Covillea mexicana* of the family Zygophyllaceae) found in the southwestern U.S. and Mexico
crepe *or* **crêpe** \ˈkrāp\ *n* [F *crêpe*] **1 :** a light crinkled fabric woven of any of various fibers **2 :** CRAPE 2 **3 :** a small very thin pancake — **crepe** *adj* — **crep·ey** *or* **crepy** \ˈkrā-pē\ *adj*
crepe de chine \ˌkrāp-də-ˈshēn\ *n, often cap 2d C* [F *crêpe de Chine,* lit., China crepe] **:** a soft fine clothing crepe
crepe myrtle *or* **crêpe myrtle** *n* **:** CRAPE MYRTLE
crepe paper *n* **:** paper with a crinkled or puckered texture
crepe rubber *n* **:** crude rubber in the form of nearly white to brown crinkled sheets used esp. for shoe soles
crepe su·zette \ˌkrāp-sü-ˈzet\ *n, pl* **crepes suzette** \ˌkrāp(s)-sü-ˈzet\ *or* **crepe suzettes** \ˌkrāp-sü-ˈzets\ [F *crêpe Suzette,* fr. *crêpe* pancake + *Suzette* Susy] **:** a thin folded or rolled pancake in a hot orange-butter sauce that is sprinkled with a liqueur (as cognac or curaçao) and set ablaze for serving
crep·i·tant \ˈkrep-ət-ənt\ *adj* **:** having or making a crackling sound
crep·i·tate \ˈkrep-ə-ˌtāt\ *vi* **-tat·ed; -tat·ing** [L *crepitatus,* pp. of *crepitare* to crackle, fr. *crepitus,* pp. of *crepare* to rattle, crack — more at RAVEN] **:** to make a crackling sound **:** CRACKLE — **crep·i·ta·tion** \ˌkrep-ə-ˈtā-shən\ *n*
crept *past of* CREEP
cre·pus·cu·lar \kri-ˈpəs-kyə-lər\ *adj* **1 :** of, relating to, or resembling twilight **:** DIM **2 :** active in the twilight <~ insects>
cre·pus·cule \kri-ˈpəs-(ˌ)kyü(ə)l\ *or* **cre·pus·cle** \-ˈpəs-əl\ *n* [L *crepusculum,* fr. *creper* dusky] **:** TWILIGHT
cresc *abbr* crescendo
[1]**cre·scen·do** \krə-ˈshen-(ˌ)dō\ *n, pl* **-dos** *or* **-does 1 a :** a gradual increase; *esp* **:** a gradual increase in volume of a musical passage **b :** the peak of a gradual increase **:** CLIMAX <complaints about stifling smog conditions reach a ~ —*Down Beat*> **2 :** a crescendo musical passage — **crescendo** *vi*
[2]**crescendo** *adv or adj* **:** with an increase in volume — used as a direction in music

mark indicating crescendo 2

[1]**cres·cent** \ˈkres-ᵊnt\ *n* [ME *cressant,* fr. MF *creissant,* fr. prp. of *creistre* to grow, increase, fr. L *crescere;* akin to OHG *hirsi* millet, L *creare* to create, Gk *koros* boy] **1 a :** the moon at any stage between new moon and first quarter and between last quarter and the succeeding new moon when less than half of the illuminated hemisphere is visible **b :** the figure of the moon at such a stage defined by a convex and a concave edge **2 :** something shaped like a crescent — **cres·cen·tic** \kre-ˈsent-ik, krə-\ *adj*
[2]**crescent** *adj* [L *crescent-, crescens,* prp. of *crescere*] **:** marked by an increase
cres·cive \ˈkres-iv\ *adj* [L *crescere* to grow] **:** capable of growth **:** INCREASING — **cres·cive·ly** *adv*
cre·sol \ˈkrē-ˌsȯl, -ˌsōl\ *n* [ISV, irreg. fr. *creosote*] **:** any of three poisonous colorless crystalline or liquid isomeric phenols C_7H_8O
cress \ˈkres\ *n* [ME *cresse,* fr. OE *cærse, cressa;* akin to OHG *kressa* cress] **:** any of numerous crucifers (esp. genera *Rorippa, Arabis,* and *Barbarea*) with moderately pungent leaves used in salads and garnishes
cres·set \ˈkres-ət\ *n* [ME, fr. MF, fr. OF *craisset,* fr. *craisse* grease — more at GREASE] **:** an iron vessel or basket used for holding an

illuminant (as burning oil) and mounted as a torch or suspended as a lantern

Cres·si·da \'kres-əd-ə\ *n* : a Trojan woman of medieval legend who pledges herself to Troilus but while a captive of the Greeks gives herself to Diomedes

[1]crest \'krest\ *n* [ME *creste,* fr. MF, fr. L *crista;* akin to OE *hrisian* to shake, L *curvus* curved — more at CROWN] **1 a :** a showy tuft or process on the head of an animal and esp. a bird — see BIRD illustration **b :** the plume or identifying emblem worn on a knight's helmet **c** (1) **:** a heraldic representation of the crest (2) **:** a heraldic device depicted above the escutcheon but not upon a helmet (3) **:** COAT OF ARMS 2a **2 :** something suggesting a crest esp. in being an upper prominence, edge, or limit: as **a :** PEAK; *esp* **:** the top line of a mountain or hill **b :** the ridge or top of a wave or roof **3 a :** a high point of an action or process **b :** CLIMAX, CULMINATION <at the ~ of his fame> — **crest·al** \'kres-tᵊl\ *adj*

[2]crest *vt* **1 :** to furnish with a crest **:** CROWN **2 :** to reach the crest of <~*ed* the hill and looked about him> ~ *vi* **:** to rise to a crest <waves ~*ing* in the storm>

crest·ed \'kres-təd\ *adj* **:** having a crest <a ~ bird>

crested wheatgrass *n* **:** either of two grasses (*Agropyron cristatum* or *A. desertorum*) that were introduced from Russia and are grown in the U.S. for forage and for erosion control

crest·fall·en \'krest-ˌfȯ-lən\ *adj* **1 :** having a drooping crest or hanging head **2 :** feeling shame or humiliation **:** DEJECTED — **crest·fall·en·ly** *adv* — **crest·fall·en·ness** \-lən-nəs\ *n*

crest·less \'krest-ləs\ *adj* **:** lacking a crest; *specif* **:** LOWBORN

cre·syl \'kres-əl, 'krē-ˌsil\ *n* [ISV *cres*ol + *-yl*] **:** TOLYL

cre·syl·ic \kri-'sil-ik\ *adj* [ISV *cresyl* + *-ic*] **:** of or relating to cresol or creosote

cre·ta·ceous \kri-'tā-shəs\ *adj* [L *cretaceus,* fr. *creta* chalk] **1 :** having the characteristics of or abounding in chalk **2** *cap* **:** of, relating to, or being the last period of the Mesozoic era or the corresponding system of rocks — **cretaceous** *n* — **cre·ta·ceous·ly** *adv*

cre·tin \'krēt-ᵊn\ *n* [F *crétin,* fr. F dial. *cretin* Christian, human being, kind of idiot found in the Alps, fr. L *christianus* Christian] **:** one afflicted with cretinism; *broadly* **:** a person with marked mental deficiency — **cre·tin·ous** \-ᵊn-əs\ *adj*

cre·tin·ism \-ᵊn-ˌiz-əm\ *n* **:** a usu. congenital abnormal condition marked by physical stunting and mental deficiency and caused by severe thyroid deficiency

cre·tonne \'krē-ˌtän, kri-'\ *n* [F, fr *Creton,* Normandy] **:** a strong unglazed cotton or linen cloth used esp. for curtains and upholstery

cre·val·le \kri-'val-ē\ *n* [by alter.] **:** CAVALLA 2; *esp* **:** JACK CREVALLE

cre·vasse \kri-'vas\ *n* [F, fr. OF *crevace*] **1 :** a deep crevice or fissure (as in a glacier or the earth) **2 :** a breach in a levee

crev·ice \'krev-əs\ *n* [ME, fr. MF *crevace,* fr. OF, fr. *crever* to break, fr. L *crepare* to crack — more at RAVEN] **:** a narrow opening resulting from a split or crack **:** FISSURE

[1]crew \'krü\ *chiefly Brit past of* CROW

[2]crew \'krü\ *n* [ME *crue,* lit., reinforcement, fr. MF *creue* increase, fr. *creistre* to grow — more at CRESCENT] **1** *archaic* **:** a band or force of armed men **2 :** a company of people temporarily associated together **:** ASSEMBLAGE **3 a :** a group of people held together by common traits or interests <a wily politician and his ~ of henchmen> **b :** a company of men working on one job or under one foreman or operating a machine **4 a :** the whole company belonging to a ship sometimes including the officers and master **b :** the persons who man an aircraft in flight **c :** the body of men manning a racing shell; *also* **:** ROWING — **crew·less** \-ləs\ *adj* — **crew·man** \-mən\ *n*

[3]crew *vi* **:** to act as a member of a crew <~*ed* on the winning sailboat> ~ *vt* **:** to serve as a crew member on (as a ship or aircraft)

crew cut *n* **:** a very short haircut in which the hair resembles the bristle surface of a brush

crew·el \'krü-əl\ *n* [ME *crule*] **:** slackly twisted worsted yarn used for embroidery

crew·el·work \-ˌwərk\ *n* **:** embroidery worked with crewel

[1]crib \'krib\ *n* [ME, fr. OE *cribb;* akin to OHG *krippa* manger, Gk *griphos* reed basket, OE *cradol* cradle] **1 :** a manger for feeding animals **2 :** an enclosure esp. of framework: as **a :** a stall for a stabled animal **b :** a small child's bedstead with high enclosing usu. slatted sides **c :** any of various devices resembling a crate or framework in structure **d :** a building for storage **:** BIN **3 :** a small narrow room or dwelling **:** HUT, SHACK **4 :** the cards discarded in cribbage for the dealer to use in scoring **5 a :** a small theft **b :** PLAGIARISM **c :** a literal translation; *esp* **:** PONY 3 **d :** something used for cheating in an examination **6 :** CRÈCHE 3

[2]crib *vb* **cribbed; crib·bing** *vt* **1 :** CONFINE, CRAMP **2 :** to provide with or put into a crib; *esp* **:** to line or support with a framework of timber **3 :** PILFER, STEAL; *esp* **:** PLAGIARIZE ~ *vi* **1 a :** STEAL, PLAGIARIZE **b :** to use a crib **:** CHEAT **2 :** to have the vice of crib biting — **crib·ber** *n*

crib·bage \'krib-ij\ *n* [[1]*crib*] **:** a card game for two players in which each player attempts to form various counting combinations of cards

crib·bing \'krib-iŋ\ *n* **:** material for use in a crib

crib biting *n* **:** a vice of horses in which they gnaw (as at the manger) while slobbering and salivating

crib·ri·form \'krib-rə-ˌfȯrm\ *adj* [L *cribrum* sieve; akin to L *cernere* to sift — more at CERTAIN] **:** pierced with small holes

cri·ce·tid \krī-'set-əd, -'set-\ *n* [deriv. of NL *Cricetus,* genus name, of Slav origin; akin to Czech *křeček* hamster] **:** any of a family (Cricetidae) of small rodents including the hamsters — **cricetid** *adj*

[1]crick \'krik\ *n* [ME *cryk*] **:** a painful spasmodic condition of muscles (as of the neck or back)

[2]crick *vt* **1 :** to cause a crick in (as the neck) **2 :** to turn or twist (as the head) esp. into a strained position

[1]crick·et \'krik-ət\ *n* [ME *criket,* fr. MF *criquet,* of imit. origin] **1 :** a leaping orthopteran insect (family Gryllidae) noted for the chirping notes produced by the male by rubbing together specially modified parts of the fore wings **2 :** a low wooden footstool **3 :** a small metal toy or signaling device that makes a sharp click or snap when pressed

[2]cricket *n* [MF *criquet* goal stake in a bowling game] **1 :** a game played with a ball and bat by two sides of usu. 11 players each on a large field centering upon two wickets each defended by a batsman **2 :** fair and honorable behavior

[3]cricket *vi* **:** to play the game of cricket — **crick·et·er** *n*

cri·coid \'krī-ˌkȯid\ *adj* [NL *cricoides,* fr. Gk *krikoeidēs* ring-shaped, fr. *krikos* ring — more at CIRCLE] **:** of, relating to, or being a cartilage of the larynx with which arytenoid cartilages articulate

cri·er \'krī(-ə)r\ *n* **:** one that cries: **a :** an officer who proclaims the orders of a court **b :** TOWN CRIER

crim con *abbr* criminal conversation

crime \'krīm\ *n* [ME, fr. L *crimen* accusation, fault, crime] **1 :** an act or the commission of an act that is forbidden or the omission of a duty that is commanded by a public law and that makes the offender liable to punishment by that law; *esp* **:** a gross violation of law **2 :** a grave offense esp. against morality **3 :** criminal activity **4 :** something reprehensible, foolish, or disgraceful <it's a ~ to waste good food> ***syn*** see OFFENSE

crime against humanity : atrocity (as extermination or enslavement) that is directed esp. against an entire population or part of a population on specious grounds and without regard to individual guilt or responsibility even on such grounds

crime against nature : SODOMY

[1]crim·i·nal \'krim-ən-ᵊl, 'krim-nəl\ *adj* [ME, fr. MF or LL; MF *criminel,* fr. LL *criminalis,* fr. L *crimin-* *crimen* crime] **1 :** involving or being a crime **2 :** relating to crime or its punishment **3 :** guilty of crime **4 :** DISGRACEFUL — **crim·i·nal·ly** \-ē\ *adv*

[2]criminal *n* **1 :** one that has committed a crime **:** MALEFACTOR **2 :** a person who has been convicted of a crime

criminal conversation *n* **:** adultery considered as a tort

criminal court *n* **:** a court that has jurisdiction to try and punish offenders against criminal law

crim·i·nal·i·ty \ˌkrim-ə-'nal-ət-ē\ *n* **:** the quality or state of being criminal

criminal law *n* **:** the law of crimes and their punishments

crim·i·nate \'krim-ə-ˌnāt\ *vt* **-nat·ed; -nat·ing** [L *criminatus,* pp. of *criminari,* fr. *crimin-, crimen* accusation] **1 a :** to accuse of a crime **b :** INCRIMINATE **2 :** to represent as criminal **:** CONDEMN — **crim·i·na·tion** \ˌkrim-ə-'nā-shən\ *n*

criminol *abbr* criminologist; criminology

crim·i·nol·o·gy \ˌkrim-ə-'näl-ə-jē\ *n* [It *criminologia,* fr. L *crimin-, crimen* + It *-o-* + *-logia* -logy] **:** the scientific study of crime as a social phenomenon, of criminals, and of penal treatment — **crim·i·no·log·i·cal** \-ən-ᵊl-'äj-i-kəl\ *adj* — **crim·i·no·log·i·cal·ly** \-k(ə-)lē\ *adv* — **crim·i·nol·o·gist** \ˌkrim-ə-'näl-ə-jəst\ *n*

crim·i·nous \'krim-ə-nəs\ *adj* **:** CRIMINAL

[1]crimp \'krimp\ *vt* [D or LG *krimpen* to shrivel; akin to LG *krampe* hook — more at CRAMP] **1 :** to cause to become wavy, bent, or warped: as **a :** to form (leather) into a desired shape **b :** to draw or pinch in or together in glass manufacturing <~ the neck of a vase> **c :** to roll the edge of **d :** to pinch or press together (as the margins of a pie crust) in order to seal **2 :** to put a crimp in **:** INHIBIT <dealers whose sales had been ~*ed* by credit controls —*Time*>

[2]crimp *n* **1 :** something produced by or as if by crimping: as **a :** a section of hair artificially waved or curled **b :** a succession of waves (as in wool fiber) **2 :** something that cramps or inhibits

[3]crimp *n* [perh. fr. [1]*crimp*] **:** a person who entraps or forces men into shipping as sailors or into enlisting in an army or navy

[4]crimp *vt* **:** to trap into military or sea service **:** IMPRESS

crimpy \'krim-pē\ *adj* **crimp·i·er; -est :** having a crimped appearance **:** FRIZZY

[1]crim·son \'krim-zən\ *n* [ME *crimisin,* fr. OSp *cremesín,* fr. Ar *qirmizī,* fr. *qirmiz* kermes] **:** any of several deep purplish reds

[2]crimson *adj* **:** of the color crimson

[3]crimson *vt* **:** to make crimson ~ *vi* **:** to become crimson

[1]cringe \'krinj\ *vi* **cringed; cring·ing** [ME *crengen;* akin to OE *cringan* to yield, *cradol* cradle] **1 :** to draw in or contract one's muscles involuntarily **2 :** to shrink in fear or servility **3 :** to approach someone with fawning and self-abasement ***syn*** see FAWN — **cring·er** *n*

[2]cringe *n* **:** a cringing act; *specif* **:** a servile bow

crin·gle \'kriŋ-gəl\ *n* [LG *kringel,* dim. of *kring* ring; akin to OE *cradol* cradle] **:** a thimble, grommet, eyelet, or rope loop worked into or attached to the edge of a sail and used for making rope and lines fast

[1]crin·kle \'kriŋ-kəl\ *vb* **crin·kled; crin·kling** \-k(ə-)liŋ\ [ME *crynkelen;* akin to OE *cringan* to yield] *vi* **1 a :** to form many short bends or turns **b :** WRINKLE, RIPPLE **2 :** to give forth a thin crackling sound **:** RUSTLE <*crinkling* silks> ~ *vt* **:** to cause to crinkle

[2]crinkle *n* **1 :** WINDING, WRINKLE **2 :** any of several plant diseases marked by crinkling of leaves — **crin·kly** \-k(ə-)lē\ *adj*

cri·noid \'krī-ˌnȯid\ *n* [deriv. of Gk *krinon* lily] **:** any of a large class (Crinoidea) of echinoderms usu. having a somewhat cup-shaped body with five or more feathery arms — **crinoid** *adj*

crin·o·line \'krin-ᵊl-ən\ *n* [F, fr. It *crinolino,* fr. *crino* horsehair (fr. L *crinis* hair; akin to L *crista* crest) + *lino* flax, linen, fr. L *linum*] **1 :** an open-weave fabric of horsehair or cotton that is usu. stiffened and used esp. for interlinings and millinery **2 a :** HOOPSKIRT **b :** a full stiff skirt or underskirt — **crinoline** *adj*

cri·num \'krī-nəm\ *n* [NL, genus name, fr. L, lily, fr. Gk *krinon*] **:** any of a large genus (*Crinum*) of chiefly tropical bulbous herbs of the amaryllis family (family Amaryllidaceae) grown for their umbels of often fragrant white red-marked flowers

cri·o·llo \krē-'ō(l)-(,)yō\ *n, pl* **-llos** [Sp] **1 a :** a person of pure Spanish descent born in Spanish America **b :** a person born and usu. raised in a Spanish-American country **2 :** a domestic animal of a breed or strain developed in Latin America — **criollo** *adj*

¹crip·ple \'krip-əl\ *n* [ME *cripel,* fr. OE *crypel;* akin to OE *crēopan* to creep — more at CREEP] **1 :** a lame or partly disabled person or animal **2 :** something flawed or imperfect

²cripple *adj* **1 :** being a cripple : LAME **2 :** worn out : INFERIOR

³cripple *vt* **crip·pled; crip·pling** \-(ə-)liŋ\ **1 :** to deprive of the use of a limb and esp. a leg **2 :** to deprive of strength, efficiency, wholeness or capability for service ***syn*** see MAIM, WEAKEN — **crip·pler** \-(ə-)lər\ *n*

cri·sis \'krī-səs\ *n, pl* **cri·ses** \'krī-,sēz\ [L, fr. Gk *krisis,* lit., decision, fr. *krinein* to decide — more at CERTAIN] **1 a :** the turning point for better or worse in an acute disease or fever **b :** a paroxysmal attack of pain, distress, or disordered function **c :** an emotionally significant event or radical change of status in a person's life **2 :** the decisive moment (as in a literary plot) **3 a :** an unstable or crucial time or state of affairs whose outcome will make a decisive difference for better or worse **b :** the period of strain following the culmination of a period of business prosperity when forced liquidation occurs ***syn*** see JUNCTURE

¹crisp \'krisp\ *adj* [ME, fr. OE, fr. L *crispus;* akin to L *curvus* curved — more at CROWN] **1 a :** CURLY, WAVY; *also* **:** having close stiff or wiry curls or waves **b :** having the surface roughened into small folds or curling wrinkles **2 a :** easily crumbled : BRITTLE **b** *of pastry* : SHORT **c :** being desirably firm and fresh <~ lettuce> **3 a :** being sharp, clean-cut, and clear <a ~ illustration> **b :** noticeably neat **c :** SPRIGHTLY, LIVELY <~ banter between the debating opponents> **d :** FROSTY, SNAPPY <~ winter weather>; *also* **:** FRESH, INVIGORATING <~ autumn air> ***syn*** see FRAGILE, INCISIVE — **crisp·ly** *adv* — **crisp·ness** *n*

²crisp *vt* **1 :** CURL, CRIMP **2 :** to cause to ripple : WRINKLE **3 :** to make or keep crisp ~ *vi* **1 :** CURL **2 :** RIPPLE **3 :** to become crisp — **crisp·er** *n*

³crisp *n* **1 :** something crisp or brittle **2** *chiefly Brit* **:** POTATO CHIP

cris·pa·tion \kris-'pā-shən\ *n* **1 :** the act or process of curling : the state of being curled **2 :** a slight spasmodic contraction

crisp·en \'kris-pən\ *vt* **:** to make crisp <celery ~*ed* by refrigeration> ~ *vi* **:** to become crisp <a pastry shell ~*ing* in the oven>

crispy \'kris-pē\ *adj* **crisp·i·er; -est :** CRISP — **crisp·i·ness** *n*

¹criss·cross \'kris-,krȯs\ *n* [obs. *christcross, crisscross* (mark of a cross)] **1 :** a crisscross pattern : NETWORK **2 :** a confused state <there was a ~ of comment in the room, all of it impatient —Eric Goldman>

²crisscross *vt* **1 :** to mark with intersecting lines **2 :** to pass back and forth through or over ~ *vi* **:** to go or pass back and forth

³crisscross *adj* **:** marked or characterized by crisscrossing

⁴crisscross *adv* **1 :** in a way to cross something else **2 :** AWRY

cris·ta \'kris-tə\ *n, pl* **cris·tae** \-,tē, -,tī\ [NL, fr. L, crest] **:** any of the inwardly projecting folds of the inner membrane of a mitochondrion

crit *abbr* critical; criticism; criticized

cri·te·ri·on \krī-'tir-ē-ən *also* krə-\ *n, pl* **-ria** \-ē-ə\ *also* **-rions** [Gk *kritērion,* fr. *krinein* to judge, decide — more at CERTAIN] **1 :** a characterizing mark or trait **2 :** a standard on which a judgment or decision may be based ***syn*** see STANDARD

¹crit·ic \'krit-ik\ *n* [L *criticus,* fr. Gk *kritikos,* fr. *kritikos* able to discern or judge, fr. *krinein* to judge] **1 a :** one who expresses a reasoned opinion on any matter involving a judgment of its value, truth, or righteousness, an appreciation of its beauty or technique, or an interpretation **b :** one who engages often professionally in the analysis, evaluation, or appreciation of works of art **2 :** one given to harsh or captious judgment : CARPER

²critic *adj* **:** CRITICAL <felt that the world was looking at him with a ~ eye —Thomas Wolfe>

³critic *n* [Gk *kritikē* art of the critic, fr. fem. of *kritikos* able to discern] **1** *archaic* **:** CRITICISM **2** *archaic* **:** CRITIQUE

crit·i·cal \'krit-i-kəl\ *adj* **1 a :** inclined to criticize severely and unfavorably **b :** consisting of or involving criticism <~ writings>; *also* **:** of or relating to the judgment of critics <the play was a ~ success> **c :** exercising or involving careful judgment or judicious evaluation **d :** including variant readings and scholarly emendations <a ~ edition> **2 a :** of, relating to, or being a turning point or specially important juncture <~ phase> **b :** relating to or being a state in which or a measurement or point at which some quality, property, or phenomenon suffers a definite change <~ temperature> **c :** CRUCIAL, DECISIVE <~ test> **d :** indispensable for the weathering, solution, or overcoming of a crisis <the stockpiling of strategic and ~ materials —T. P. Neill> **e :** being in or approaching a state of crisis esp. through economic disorders or by virtue of a disaster <remedy a situation made ~ by the increase of the tax burden —Broadus Mitchell> **3 :** characterized by risk or uncertainty **4 a :** of sufficient size to sustain a chain reaction — used of a mass of fissionable material **b :** sustaining a chain reaction — used of a nuclear reactor — **crit·i·cal·i·ty** \,krit-ə-'kal-ət-ē\ *n* — **crit·i·cal·ly** \'krit-i-k(ə-)lē\ *adv* — **crit·i·cal·ness** \-kəl-nəs\ *n*

syn **1** CRITICAL, HYPERCRITICAL, FAULTFINDING, CAPTIOUS, CARPING, CENSORIOUS *shared meaning element* **:** exhibiting the spirit of one who looks for and points out faults and defects ***ant*** uncritical **2** see ACUTE ***ant*** noncritical

critical angle *n* **1 :** the least angle of incidence at which total reflection takes place **2 :** the angle of attack at which the flow about an airfoil changes abruptly with corresponding abrupt changes in the lift and drag

critical point *n* **:** a point on the graph of a function where the derivative is zero or infinite

critical region *n* **:** the set of outcomes of a statistical test for which the null hypothesis is to be rejected

critical value *n* **:** the value of an independent variable corresponding to a critical point of a function

crit·ic·as·ter \'krit-i-,kas-tər\ *n* **:** an inferior or petty critic

crit·i·cism \'krit-ə-,siz-əm\ *n* **1 a :** the act of criticizing usu. unfavorably **b :** a critical observation or remark **c :** CRITIQUE **2 :** the art of evaluating or analyzing with knowledge and propriety works of art or literature **3 :** the scientific investigation of literary documents (as the Bible) in regard to such matters as origin, text, composition, character, or history

crit·i·cize \'krit-ə-,sīz\ *vb* **-cized; -ciz·ing** *vi* **:** to act as a critic ~ *vt* **1 :** to consider the merits and demerits of and judge accordingly : EVALUATE **2 :** to stress the faults of : cavil at — **crit·i·ciz·able** \-,sī-zə-bəl\ *adj* — **crit·i·ciz·er** *n*

syn CRITICIZE, REPREHEND, BLAME, CENSURE, REPROBATE, CONDEMN, DENOUNCE *shared meaning element* **:** to find fault with openly

¹cri·tique \krə-'tēk, kri-\ *n* [alter. of ³*critic*] **:** an act of criticizing; *esp* **:** a critical estimate or discussion

²critique *vt* **cri·tiqued; cri·tiqu·ing :** CRITICIZE, REVIEW

crit·ter \'krit-ər\ *n* [by alter.] *dial* **:** CREATURE

¹croak \'krōk\ *vb* [ME *croken,* of imit. origin] *vi* **1 a :** to make a deep harsh sound **b :** to speak in a hoarse throaty voice **2 :** to grumble dourly : COMPLAIN **3** *slang* **:** DIE ~ *vt* **1 :** to forebode or utter in a hoarse raucous voice **2** *slang* **:** KILL

²croak *n* **:** a hoarse harsh cry (as of a frog) — **croaky** \'krō-kē\ *adj*

croak·er \'krō-kər\ *n* **1 :** an animal that croaks **2 :** any of various fishes (esp. family Sciaenidae) that produce croaking or grunting noises **3 :** one that habitually forbodes evil : GRUMBLER

Croat \'krōt, 'krō-,at\ *n* [NL *Croata,* fr. Serbo-Croatian *Hrvat*] **:** CROATIAN

Cro·atian \krō-'ā-shən\ *n* **1 :** a native or inhabitant of Croatia **2 :** a south Slavic language spoken by the Croatian people and distinct from Serbian chiefly in its use of the Latin alphabet — **Croatian** *adj*

¹cro·chet \krō-'shā\ *n* [F, hook, crochet, fr. MF, dim. of *croche* hook, of Scand origin; akin to ON *krōkr* hook — more at CROOK] **:** needlework consisting of the interlocking of looped stitches formed with a single thread and a hooked needle

²crochet *vt* **:** to make of crochet <~*ed* a doily> ~ *vi* **:** to work with crochet — **cro·chet·er** \-'shā-ər\ *n*

cro·cid·o·lite \krō-'sid-ᵊl-,īt\ *n* [G *krokydolith,* fr. Gk *krokyd-, krokys* nap on cloth + G *-lith* -lite] **:** a lavender-blue or leek-green mineral of the amphibole group that occurs in silky fibers and massively — compare TIGEREYE

¹crock \'kräk\ *n* [ME, fr. OE *crocc;* akin to MHG *krūche* crock] **1 :** a thick earthenware pot or jar **2** [fr. its formation on cooking pots] *dial* **:** SOOT, SMUT **3 :** coloring matter that rubs off from cloth or dyed leather

²crock *vt, dial* **:** to soil with crock : SMUDGE ~ *vi* **:** to transfer color under rubbing <a suede that will not ~>

³crock *n* [ME *crok,* prob. of Scand origin; akin to Norw dial. *krokje* crock] **1 :** one that is broken down, disabled, or impaired **2 :** a complaining medical patient whose illness is largely imaginary or psychosomatic

⁴crock *vt* **:** to cause to become disabled ~ *vi* **:** to break down

crock·ery \'kräk-(ə-)rē\ *n* **:** EARTHENWARE

crock·et \'kräk-ət\ *n* [ME *croket,* fr. ONF *croquet* crook, dim. of *croc* hook, of Scand origin; akin to ON *krōkr* hook] **:** an ornament usu. in the form of curved and bent foliage used on the edge of a gable or spire — **crock·et·ed** \-ət-əd\ *adj*

croc·o·dile \'kräk-ə-,dīl\ *n* [ME & L; ME *cocodrille,* fr. OF, fr. ML *cocodrillus,* alter. of L *crocodilus,* fr. Gk *krokodilos* lizard, crocodile, fr. *krokē* pebble + *drilos* worm; akin to Skt *śarkara* pebble — more at SUGAR] **1 a :** any of several large voracious thick-skinned long-bodied aquatic reptiles (as of the genus *Crocodylus*) of tropical and subtropical waters; *broadly* **:** CROCODILIAN **b :** the skin or hide of a crocodile **2** *archaic* **:** one who hypocritically affects sorrow

crocodile 1a

crocodile bird *n* **:** an African plover (*Pluvianus aegypticus*) that lights on the crocodile and eats its insect parasites

crocodile tears *n pl* **:** false or affected tears : hypocritical sorrow

croc·o·dil·ian \,kräk-ə-'dil-ē-ən, -'dil-yən\ *n* **:** any of an order (Loricata) of reptiles including the crocodiles, alligators, and related extinct forms — **crocodilian** *adj*

croco·ite \'kräk-ə-,wīt\ *or* **croc·oi·site** \'kräk-wə-,zīt\ *n* [G *krokoisit, krokoit,* fr. F *crocoise,* fr. Gk *krokoeis* saffron-colored, fr. *krokos*] **:** a mineral $PbCrO_4$ consisting of lead chromate

cro·cus \'krō-kəs\ *n, pl* **cro·cus·es** [NL, genus name, fr. L, saffron, fr. Gk *krokos,* of Sem origin] **1** *pl also* **cro·ci** \-,kē, -,kī, -,sī\ **:** any of a large genus (*Crocus*) of herbs of the iris family having solitary long-tubed flowers and slender linear leaves **2 a :** a dark red ferric oxide used for polishing metals **b :** SAFFRON 2

croft \'krȯft\ *n* [ME, fr. OE; akin to OE *crēopan* to creep — more at CREEP] **1** *chiefly Brit* **:** a small enclosed field usu. adjoining a house **2** *chiefly Brit* **:** a small farm worked by a tenant — **croft·er** \'krȯf-tər\ *n*

crois·sant \k(rə-,)wä-'säⁿ\ *n, pl* **croissants** \-'säⁿ(z)\ [F, lit., crescent, fr. MF *creissant*] **:** a rich crescent-shaped roll

Croix de Guerre \k(rə-,)wäd-i-'ge(ə)r\ *n* [F, lit., war cross] **:** a French military decoration awarded for gallant action in war

Cro–Ma·gnon \krō-'mag-nən, -'man-yən\ *n* [*Cro-Magnon,* a cave near Les Eyzies, France] **:** a tall erect race of men known from skeletal remains found chiefly in southern France and classified as the same species (*Homo sapiens*) as recent man

crom·lech \'kräm-,lek\ *n* [W, lit., bent stone] **1 :** DOLMEN **2 :** a circle of monoliths usu. enclosing a dolmen or mound

crone \'krōn\ *n* [ME, fr. ONF *carogne,* lit., carrion, fr. (assumed) VL *caronia* — more at CARRION] **:** a withered old woman

Cro·nus \'krō-nəs, 'krän-əs\ *n* [L, fr. Gk *Kronos*] : a Titan dethroned by his son Zeus

cro·ny \'krō-nē\ *n, pl* **cronies** [perh. fr. Gk *chronios* long-lasting, fr. *chronos* time] : a close friend esp. of long standing : CHUM

cro·ny·ism \-nē-ˌiz-əm\ *n* : partiality to cronies esp. as evidenced in the appointment of political hangers-on to office without regard to their qualifications

[1]**crook** \'krůk\ *n* [ME *crok*, fr. ON *krōkr* hook; akin to OE *cradol* cradle] **1** : an implement having a bent or hooked form: as **a** : POTHOOK **b** (1) : a shepherd's staff (2) : CROSIER 1 **2 a** : a person given to fraudulent practices : THIEF **3** : BEND, CURVE **4** : a part of something that is hook-shaped, curved, or bent <the ~ of an umbrella handle>

[2]**crook** *vt* **1** : BEND <~*ed* my neck so I could see> **2** *slang* **a** : CHEAT **b** : STEAL ~ *vi* : CURVE, WIND <a river ~*ing* through a valley>

crook·back \'krůk-ˌbak\ *n* **1** *obs* : a crooked back **2** *obs* : HUNCHBACK — **crook·backed** \-'bakt\ *adj*

crook·ed \'krůk-əd\ *adj* **1** : having or marked by a crook or curve : BENT **2** : deviating from rectitude <~ dealings>; *also* : DISHONEST <a ~ politician> <~ profits> — **crook·ed·ly** *adv* — **crook·ed·ness** *n*

syn CROOKED, DIVIOUS, OBLIQUE *shared meaning element* : not straight or straightforward ***ant*** straight

Crookes tube \'krůks-\ *n* [Sir William *Crookes*] : a vacuum tube evacuated to a high degree for demonstrating the properties of cathode rays

crook·neck \'krůk-ˌnek\ *n* : a squash with a long recurved neck

croon \'krün\ *vb* [ME *croynen*, fr. MD *cronen*; akin to OE *cran* crane] *vi* **1** *chiefly Scot* **a** : BELLOW, BOOM **b** : WAIL, LAMENT **2 a** : to make a continued moaning sound **b** : to sing in a gentle murmuring manner **c** : to sing in half voice ~ *vt* : to sing in a crooning manner <~ a lullaby> — **croon** *n*

croon·er \'krü-nər\ *n* : one that croons; *esp* : a singer of popular songs who uses a soft-voice technique adapted to amplifying systems

[1]**crop** \'kräp\ *n* [ME, craw, head of a plant, yield of a field, fr. OE *cropp* craw, head of a plant; akin to OHG *kropf* goiter, craw, OE *crēopan* to creep — more at CREEP] **1** : the stock or handle of a whip; *also* : a riding whip with a short straight stock and a loop **2** : a pouched enlargement of the gullet of many birds that serves as a receptacle for food and for its preliminary maceration; *also* : an enlargement of the gullet of another animal (as an insect) **3** [[2]*crop*] **a** : an earmark on an animal; *esp* : one made by a straight cut squarely removing the upper part of the ear **b** : a close cut of the hair **4 a** : a plant or animal or plant or animal product that can be grown and harvested extensively for profit or subsistence <an apple ~> <a ~ of wool> **b** : the product or yield of something formed together <the ice ~> **c** : a batch or lot of something produced during a particular cycle <a whole new ~ of college freshmen> **d** : COLLECTION <a ~ of lies> **5** : the total yearly production from a specified area <the county's cotton ~ had never been better>

[2]**crop** *vb* **cropped; crop·ping** *vt* **1 a** : to remove the upper or outer parts of <~ a hedge> **b** : HARVEST <~ trout> **c** : to cut off short : TRIM <~ a photograph> **2** : to cause (land) to bear a crop <planned to ~ another 40 acres>; *also* : to grow as a crop ~ *vi* **1** : to feed by cropping something **2** : to yield or make a crop **3** : to appear unexpectedly or casually <problems ~ up daily>

crop–eared \'kräp-'i(ə)rd\ *adj* **1** : having the ears cropped **2** : having the hair cropped so that the ears are conspicuous

crop·land \-ˌland\ *n* : land that is suited to or used for crops

[1]**crop·per** \'kräp-ər\ *n* **1** : one that crops **2** : one that raises crops; *specif* : SHARECROPPER

[2]**cropper** *n* [prob. fr. E dial. *crop* neck, fr. [1]*crop*] **1** : a severe fall **2** : a sudden or violent failure or collapse

crop rotation *n* : the practice of growing different crops in succession on the same land chiefly to preserve the productive capacity of the soil

cro·quet \krō-'kā\ *n* [F dial., hockey stick, fr. ONF, crook — more at CROCKET] **1** : a game in which players drive wooden balls with mallets through a series of wickets set out on a lawn **2** : the act of driving away an opponent's croquet ball by striking one's own ball placed against it — **croquet** *vt*

cro·quette \krō-'ket\ *n* [F, fr. *croquer* to crunch, of imit. origin] : a small cone-shaped or rounded mass consisting usu. of minced fowl, meat, or vegetable coated with egg and bread crumbs and fried in deep fat

cro·qui·gnole \'krō-kən-ˌ(y)ōl\ *n* [F, a kind of biscuit, fr. *croquer*] : a method used in waving the hair by winding it on curlers from the ends of the hair toward the scalp

cro·quis \krō-'kē\ *n, pl* **cro·quis** \-'kē(z)\ [F, fr. *croquer* to crunch, sketch] : a rough draft : SKETCH

crore \'krō(ə)r, 'krȯ(ə)r\ *n, pl* **crores** *also* **crore** [Hindi *karoṛ*] : ten million; *specif* : a unit of value equal to ten million rupees or 100 lakhs

cro·sier \'krō-zhər\ *n* [ME *croser* crosier bearer, fr. MF *crossier*, fr. *crosse* crosier, of Gmc origin; akin to OE *crycc* crutch — more at CRUTCH] **1** : a staff resembling a shepherd's crook carried by bishops and abbots as a symbol of office — see VESTMENT illustration **2** : a plant structure with a coiled end

[1]**cross** \'krȯs\ *n* [ME, fr. OE, fr. ON or OIr; ON *kross*, fr. (assumed) OIr *cross*, fr. L *cruc-*, *crux* — more at RIDGE] **1 a** : a structure consisting of an upright with a transverse beam used esp. by the ancient Romans for execution **b** *often cap* : the cross on which Jesus was crucified **2 a** : CRUCIFIXION **b** : an affliction that tries one's virtue, steadfastness, or patience **3** : a cruciform sign made to invoke the blessing of Christ esp. by touching the forehead, breast, and shoulders **4 a** : a device composed of an upright bar traversed by a horizontal one; *specif* : one used as a Christian emblem **b** *cap* : the Christian religion **5** : a structure (as a monument) shaped like or surmounted by a cross **6** : a figure or mark formed by two intersecting lines crossing at their midpoints; *specif* : such a mark used as a signature **7** : a cruciform badge, emblem, or decoration **8** : the intersection of two ways or lines : CROSSING **9** : ANNOYANCE, THWARTING <a ~ in love> **10 a** : an act of crossing dissimilar individuals **b** : a crossbred individual or kind **c** : one that combines characteristics of two different types or individuals **11 a** : a fraudulent or dishonest contest **b** : dishonest or illegal practices — used esp. in the phrase *on the cross* **12** : a movement from one part of a theater stage to another **13** : a hook thrown over the opponent's lead in boxing **14** *cap* **a** : NORTHERN CROSS **b** : SOUTHERN CROSS **15** : a security transaction in which a broker acts for both buyer and seller (as in the placing of a large lot of common stock) — called also *cross-trade*

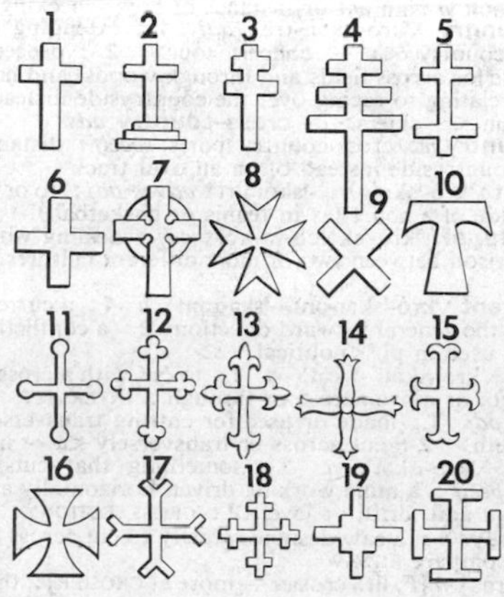

crosses 4a: *1* Latin, *2* Calvary, *3* patriarchal, *4* papal, *5* Lorraine, *6* Greek, *7* Celtic, *8* Maltese, *9* Saint Andrew's, *10* tau, *11* pommée, *12* botonée, *13* fleury, *14* avellan, *15* moline, *16* formée, *17* fourchée, *18* crosslet, *19* quadrate, *20* potent

[2]**cross** *vt* **1 a** : to lie or be situated across **b** : INTERSECT **2** : to make the sign of the cross upon or over **3** : to cancel by marking a cross on or drawing a line through : strike out <~ names off a list> **4** : to place or fold crosswise one over the other <~ the arms> **5 a** (1) : to run counter to : OPPOSE (2) : to deny the validity of : CONTRADICT **b** : to confront in a troublesome manner : OBSTRUCT **c** (1) : to spoil completely : DISRUPT — used with *up* <his failure to appear ~*ed* up the whole program> (2) : to turn against : BETRAY <~*ed* me up on the deal> **6 a** : to extend across : TRAVERSE <a highway ~*ing* the entire state> **b** : REACH, ATTAIN <only two ~*ed* the finish line> **c** : to go from one side of to the other <~ a street> **7 a** : to draw a line across **b** : to mark or figure with lines : STREAK **8** : to cause (an animal or plant) to interbreed with one of a different kind : HYBRIDIZE **9** : to meet and pass on the way <our letters must have ~*ed* each other> **10** : to occur to <it never ~*ed* my mind> **11** : to carry or take across something <~*ed* the children at the intersection> ~ *vi* **1** : to move, pass, or extend across something; *specif* : to pass from one side of the theater stage to another — used with *over* **2** : to lie or be athwart each other **3** : to meet in passing esp. from opposite directions **4** : INTERBREED, HYBRIDIZE — **cross·er** *n* — **cross swords** : to come to grips

[3]**cross** *adj* **1 a** : lying across or athwart **b** : moving across <~ traffic> **2 a** : running counter : OPPOSITE <~ winds> **b** : mutually opposed <~ purposes> **3** : involving mutual interchange : RECIPROCAL **4** : marked by typically transitory bad temper : GRUMPY **5** : extending over or treating several groups or classes <a ~ sample from 25 colleges> **6** : CROSSBRED, HYBRID ***syn*** see IRASCIBLE — **cross·ly** *adv* — **cross·ness** *n*

[4]**cross** *prep* : ACROSS

[5]**cross** *adv* : not parallel : CRISSCROSS, CROSSWISE

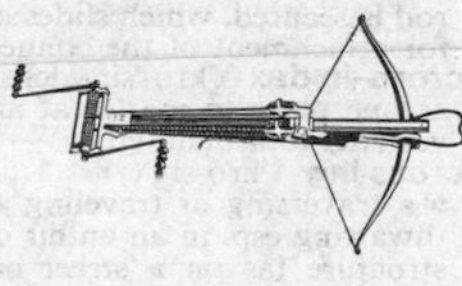

crossbow

cross·abil·i·ty \ˌkrȯ-sə-'bil-ət-ē\ *n* : the ability of different species or varieties to cross with each other

cross·able \'krȯ-sə-bəl\ *adj* : capable of being crossed

cross action *n* : a legal action brought by a defendant in a suit against the person who has sued him and on the same subject matter

cross·bar \'krȯs-ˌbär\ *n* : a transverse bar or stripe

cross·bear·er \'krȯs-ˌbar-ər, -ˌber-\ *n* : CRUCIFER 1

cross·bill \-ˌbil\ *n* : any of a genus (*Loxia*) of finches with strongly curved mandibles that cross each other

cross·bones \-ˌbōnz\ *n pl* : two leg or arm bones placed or depicted crosswise — compare SKULL AND CROSSBONES

cross·bow \-ˌbō\ *n* : a weapon for discharging quarrels and stones that consists chiefly of a short bow mounted crosswise near the end of a wooden stock

---

ə abut ᵊ kitten ər further a back ā bake ä cot, cart
aů out ch chin e less ē easy g gift i trip ī life
j joke ŋ sing ō flow ȯ flaw ȯi coin th thin t͟h this
ü loot ů foot y yet yü few yů furious zh vision

cross·bow·man \-mən\ *n* **:** one (as a soldier or a hunter) whose weapon is a crossbow
cross·bred \'krȯs-'bred\ *adj* **:** HYBRID; *specif* **:** produced by interbreeding two pure but different breeds, strains, or varieties — **cross·bred** \-ˌbred\ *n*
[1]**cross·breed** \'krȯs-ˌbrēd, -'brēd\ *vb* **-bred** \-'bred\; **-breed·ing** *vt* **:** HYBRIDIZE, CROSS; *esp* **:** to interbreed two varieties or breeds of the same species ~ *vi* **:** to engage in or undergo crossbreeding
[2]**cross·breed** \-ˌbrēd\ *n* **:** HYBRID
[1]**cross–check** \-chek\ *vt* **1 :** to obstruct in ice hockey or lacrosse by thrusting one's stick held in both hands across an opponent's face or body **2 :** to check (as data or reports) from various angles or sources to determine validity or accuracy
[2]**cross–check** *n* **:** an act or instance of cross-checking
[1]**cross–coun·try** \'krȯ-'skən-trē\ *adj* **1 :** extending or moving across a country <a ~ concert tour> **2 :** proceeding over countryside (as across fields and through woods) and not by roads **3 :** of or relating to racing over the countryside instead of over a track or run <~ skiers> — **cross–country** *adv*
[2]**cross–country** *n* **:** cross-country sports; *specif* **:** distance running over the countryside instead of on an oval track
cross·court \'krȯ-'skō(ə)rt, -'skȯ(ə)rt\ *adv or adj* **:** to or toward the opposite side of a court (as in tennis or basketball)
cross–cul·tur·al \'krȯ-'skəlch-(ə-)rəl\ *adj* **:** dealing with or offering comparison between two or more different cultures or cultural areas
cross·cur·rent \'krȯ-'skər-ənt, -'skə-rənt\ *n* **1 :** a current running counter to the general forward direction **2 :** a conflicting tendency — usu. used in pl. <political ~*s*>
[1]**cross·cut** \'krȯ-ˌskət, -'skət\ *vt* **1 :** to cut with a crosscut saw **2 :** to cut, go, or move across or through **:** INTERSECT
[2]**crosscut** *adj* **1 :** made or used for cutting transversely <a saw with ~ teeth> **2 :** cut across or transversely <a ~ incision>
[3]**cross·cut** \'krȯ-ˌskət\ *n* **1 :** something that cuts across or through; *specif* **:** a mine working driven horizontally and at right angles to an adit, drift, or level **2 :** CROSS SECTION
crosscut saw *n* **:** a saw designed chiefly to cut across the grain of wood — compare RIPSAW
crosse \'krȯs\ *n* [F, lit., crosier — more at CROSIER] **:** the stick used in lacrosse
crosse–check \-ˌchek\ *vi* **:** to hit an apponent's stick in lacrosse with one's own stick in order to knock the ball loose or to prevent the opponent from picking up the ball
cross–ex·am·i·na·tion \ˌkrȯ-sig-ˌzam-ə-'nā-shən\ *n* **:** the act or process of cross-examining
cross–ex·am·ine \-'zam-ən\ *vt* **:** to examine by a series of questions designed to check or discredit the answers to previous questions — **cross–ex·am·in·er** \-'zam-(ə-)nər\ *n*
cross–eye \'krȯ-ˌsī\ *n* **1 :** strabismus in which the eye turns inward toward the nose **2** *pl* \-'sīz\ **:** eyes affected with cross-eye — **cross–eyed** \-'sīd\ *adj*
cross–fer·tile \'krȯs-'fərt-ᵊl\ *adj* **:** fertile in a cross or capable of cross-fertilization
cross–fer·til·iza·tion \-ˌfərt-ᵊl-ə-'zā-shən\ *n* **1 a :** fertilization in which the gametes are produced by separate individuals or sometimes by individuals of different kinds **b :** CROSS-POLLINATION **2 :** interchange or interaction (as between different ideas, cultures, or categories) esp. of a broadening or productive nature <~ of practical expertise with theoretical learning>
cross–fer·til·ize \-'fərt-ᵊl-ˌīz\ *vt* **:** to accomplish cross-fertilization of ~ *vi* **:** to undergo cross-fertilization
cross–file \-'fī(ə)l\ *vi* **:** to register as a candidate in the primary elections of more than one political party ~ *vt* **:** to register (a person) as a candidate for more than one party
cross fire *n* **1 :** firing (as in combat) from two or more points so that the lines of fire cross; *also* **:** a situation wherein the forces of opposing factions meet or cross **2 :** rapid or heated interchange
cross–grained \'krȯs-'grānd\ *adj* **1 :** having the grain or fibers running diagonally, transversely, or irregularly **2 :** difficult to deal with — **cross–grained·ness** \-'grā-nəd-nəs, -'grān(d)-nəs\ *n*
cross hair *n* **:** one of the fine wires or threads in the focus of the eyepiece of an optical instrument used as a reference line in the field or for marking the instrumental axis
cross·hatch \'krȯs-ˌhach\ *vt* **:** to mark with a series of parallel lines that cross esp. obliquely — **crosshatch** *n* — **cross–hatch·ing** *n*
cross·head \-ˌhed\ *n* **:** a metal block to which one end of a piston rod is secured, which slides on parallel guides, and which has a pin for attachment of the connecting rod
cross–in·dex \'krȯ-'sin-ˌdeks\ *vt* **1 :** to refer by means of a note at one place to matter at another place **2 :** to refer from (as a variant) to a main entry — **cross–index** *n*
cross·ing \'krȯ-siŋ\ *n* **1 :** the act or action of crossing: as **a :** a traversing or traveling across **b :** an opposing, blocking, or thwarting esp. in an unfair or dishonest manner **2 a :** a place or structure (as on a street or over a river) where pedestrians or vehicles cross; *esp* **:** CROSSWALK **b :** a place where a railroad track crosses a highway or street
cross·ing–over \ˌkrȯ-siŋ-'ō-vər\ *n* **:** an interchange of genes or segments between homologous chromosomes
cross–legged \'krȯ-'sleg(-ə)d, -'slāg(-ə)d\ *adv or adj* **1 :** with legs crossed and knees spread wide apart **2 :** with one leg placed over and across the other
cross·let \'krȯ-slət\ *n* **:** a small cross; *esp* **:** one used as a heraldic bearing — see CROSS illustration
cross–link \'krȯ-ˌsliŋk\ *n* **:** a crosswise connecting part (as an atom or group) that connects parallel chains in a complex chemical molecule (as a polymer) — **cross–link** *vb*
cross multiply *vi* **:** to find the two products obtained by multiplying the numerator of each of two fractions by the denominator of the other — **cross multiplication** *n*
cross–na·tion·al \'krȯ-'snash-nəl, -ən-ᵊl\ *adj* **:** of or relating to two or more nations <~ survey of the aged in the United Kingdom, Denmark, and the U.S.A. —Lenore E. Bixby>
cross of Lor·raine \-lə-'rān, -lō-\ [*Lorraine*, France] **:** a cross with two crossbars having the upper one intersecting the upright above its middle and the lower one which is longer than the upper one intersecting the upright below its middle — see CROSS illustration
cross·over \'krȯ-ˌsō-vər\ *n* **1 :** CROSSING 2a **2 :** an instance or product of genetic crossing-over **3 :** interchange of the control group and the experimental group during the course of an experiment **4 :** one who votes in an election for a political party which is not the one he has usu. voted for in past elections
cross·patch \'krȯ-ˌspach\ *n* [[3]*cross* + *patch* (fool)] **:** GROUCH 2
cross·piece \'krȯ-ˌspēs\ *n* **:** a horizontal member (as of a structure)
cross–pol·li·nate \'krȯ-'späl-ə-ˌnāt\ *vt* **:** to subject to cross-pollination
cross–pol·li·na·tion \ˌkrȯ-ˌspäl-ə-'nā-shən\ *n* **:** the transfer of pollen from one flower to the stigma of another
cross–pol·li·nize \'krȯ-'späl-ə-ˌnīz\ *vt* **:** CROSS-POLLINATE
cross product *n* **:** VECTOR PRODUCT
cross–pur·pose \'krȯ-'spər-pəs\ *n* **:** a purpose usu. unintentionally contrary to another purpose of oneself or of someone else <the two men were always working at ~*s*>
cross–ques·tion \'krȯ-'skwes(h)-chən\ *n* **:** a question asked in cross-examination — **cross–question** *vt*
cross–re·ac·tion \ˌkrȯs-rē-'ak-shən\ *n* **:** reaction of one antigen with antibodies developed against another antigen
cross–re·fer \ˌkrȯs-ri-'fər\ *vt* **:** to refer (a reader) by a notation or direction from one place to another (as in a book, list, or catalog) ~ *vi* **:** to make a cross-reference
[1]**cross–ref·er·ence** \'krȯs-'ref-ərn(t)s, -'ref-(ə-)rən(t)s\ *n* **:** a notation or direction at one place (as in a book or filing system) to pertinent information at another place
[2]**cross–reference** *vb* **:** CROSS-REFER
cross–re·sis·tance \ˌkrȯs-ri-'zis-tən(t)s\ *n* **:** tolerance (as of an insect population) to a normally toxic substance (as an insecticide) that is acquired not as a result of direct exposure but by exposure to a related substance
cross·road \'krȯs-ˌrōd, -'rōd\ *n* **1 :** a road that crosses a main road or runs cross-country between main roads **2** *usu pl but sing or pl in constr* **a :** the place of intersection of two or more roads **b (1) :** a small community located at such a crossroads **(2) :** a central meeting place **c :** a crucial point esp. where a decision must be made
cross·ruff \'krȯs-ˌrəf, -'rəf\ *n* **:** a series of plays in a card game in which partners alternately trump different suits and lead to each other for that purpose — **crossruff** *vb*
cross section *n* **1 :** a cutting or piece of something cut off at right angles to an axis; *also* **:** a representation of such a cutting **2 :** a measure of the probability of an encounter between particles such as will result in a specified effect (as ionization or capture) **3 :** a composite representation typifying the constituents of a thing in their relations — **cross–sec·tion·al** *adj*
cross–ster·ile \'krȯs-'(s)ter-əl\ *adj* **:** mutually sterile — **cross–ste·ril·i·ty** \ˌkrȯs-(s)tə-'ril-ət-ē\ *n*
cross–stitch \'krȯs-ˌ(s)tich\ *n* **1 :** a needlework stitch that forms an X **2 :** work having cross-stitch — **cross–stitch** *vb*
cross talk *n* **:** unwanted signals in a communication channel that come from another channel or in one track of a tape recording that come from another track
cross·town \'krȯ-'staun\ *adj* **1 :** situated at opposite points of a town **2 :** extending or running across a town <a ~ street> <a ~ bus>
cross–trade \'krȯ-ˌstrād\ *n* **:** CROSS 15
cross·trees \'krȯ-(ˌ)strēz\ *n* **:** two horizontal crosspieces of timber or metal supported by trestletrees at a masthead that spread the upper shrouds in order to support the mast
cross vault *n* **:** a vault formed by the intersection of two or more simple vaults — called also *cross vaulting*
cross·walk \'krȯ-ˌswȯk\ *n* **:** a specially paved or marked path for pedestrians crossing a street or road
cross·way \'krȯ-ˌswā\ *n* **:** CROSSROAD — often used in pl.
cross·ways \-ˌswāz\ *adv* **:** CROSSWISE, DIAGONALLY
cross·wind \'krȯ-ˌswind\ *n* **:** a wind blowing in a direction not parallel to a course (as of an airplane)
[1]**cross·wise** \'krȯ-ˌswīz\ *adv* **1** *archaic* **:** in the form of a cross **2 :** so as to cross something **:** ACROSS <logs laid ~>
[2]**crosswise** *adj* **:** TRANSVERSE, CROSSING
cross·word puzzle \ˌkrȯ-ˌswərd-\ *n* **:** a puzzle in which words are filled into a pattern of numbered squares in answer to correspondingly numbered clues and in such a way that the words read across and down
crotch \'kräch\ *n* [prob. alter. of [1]*crutch*] **1 :** a pole with a forked end used esp. as a prop **2 :** an angle formed by the parting of two legs, branches, or members — **crotched** \'krächt\ *adj*
crotch·et \'kräch-ət\ *n* [ME *crochet*, fr. MF — more at CROCHET] **1** *obs* **a :** a small hook or hooked instrument **b :** BROOCH **2 a :** a highly individual and usu. eccentric opinion or preference **b :** a peculiar trick, dodge, or device **3 :** QUARTER NOTE ***syn*** see CAPRICE
crotch·ety \'kräch-ət-ē\ *adj* **1 :** given to crotchets **:** subject to whims, crankiness, or ill temper <a ~ old man> **2 :** full of or arising from crotchets — **crotch·et·i·ness** *n*
cro·ton \'krōt-ᵊn\ *n* [NL, genus name, fr. Gk *krotōn* castor-oil plant] **1 :** any of a genus (*Croton*) of herbs and shrubs of the spurge family: as **a :** one (*C. eluteria*) of the Bahamas yielding cascarilla bark **b :** an East Indian plant (*C. tiglium*) yielding a viscid acrid fixed oil used as a drastic cathartic, a vesicant, or a pustulant **2 :** any of a genus (*Codiaeum*) of shrubs related to the crotons
Cro·ton bug \'krōt-ᵊn-\ *n* [*Croton* river, N.Y., used as a water supply for New York City] **:** GERMAN COCKROACH
crouch \'krauch\ *vb* [ME *crouchen*] *vi* **1 a :** to lower the body stance esp. by bending the legs <a sprinter ~*ed* and waited for the gun> **b :** to lie close to the ground with the legs bent <a pair of cats, ~*ing* on the brink of a fight —Aldous Huxley> **2 :** to bend or bow servilely **:** CRINGE ~ *vt* **:** to bow esp. in humility or fear **:** BEND — **crouch** *n*

[1]**croup** \ˈkrüp\ *n* [ME *croupe,* fr. OF, of Gmc origin; akin to OHG *kropf* craw — more at CROP] **:** the rump of a quadruped

[2]**croup** *n* [E dial. *croup* to cry hoarsely, cough, prob. of imit. origin] **:** a spasmodic laryngitis esp. of infants marked by episodes of difficult breathing and hoarse metallic cough — **croup·ous** \ˈkrü-pəs\ *adj* — **croupy** \-pē\ *adj*

crou·pi·er \ˈkrü-pē-ər, -pē-ˌā\ *n* [F, lit., rider on the croup of a horse, fr. *croupe* croup] **:** an employee of a gambling casino who collects and pays bets and assists at the gaming tables

crouse \ˈkrüs\ *adj* [ME] *chiefly Scot* **:** BRISK, LIVELY

crou·ton \ˈkrü-ˌtän, krü-ˈ\ *n* [F *croûton,* dim. of *croûte* crust, fr. MF *crouste*] **:** a small cube of toasted or crisply fried bread

[1]**crow** \ˈkrō\ *n* [ME *crowe,* fr. OE *crāwe;* akin to OHG *krāwa* crow, OE *crāwan* to crow] **1 :** any of various large usu. entirely glossy black oscine birds (family Corvidae and esp. genus *Corvus*) **2 :** CROWBAR **3** *cap* **a :** a member of an Amerindian people of the region between the Platte and Yellowstone rivers **b :** the language of the Crow people **4** *cap* **:** CORVUS — **as the crow flies :** in a straight line

[2]**crow** *vi* **crowed** \ˈkrōd\ *also in sense 1 chiefly Brit* **crew** \ˈkrü\; **crow·ing** [ME *crowen,* fr. OE *crāwan*] **1 :** to make the loud shrill sound characteristic of a cock **2 :** to utter a sound expressive of pleasure **3 a :** to exult gloatingly esp. over the distress of another **b :** to brag exultantly or blatantly ***syn*** see BOAST

[3]**crow** *n* **1 :** the cry of the cock **2 :** a triumphant cry

crow·bar \ˈkrō-ˌbär\ *n* **:** an iron or steel bar that is usu. wedge-shaped at the working end for use as a pry or lever

crow·ber·ry \ˈkrō-ˌber-ē\ *n* **1 :** any of several low shrubby evergreen plants (family Empetraceae); *esp* **:** an undershrub (*Empetrum nigrum*) of arctic and alpine regions with an insipid black berry **2 :** the fruit of a crowberry

[1]**crowd** \ˈkrau̇d\ *vb* [ME *crouden,* fr. OE *crūdan;* akin to MHG *kroten* to crowd, OE *crod* multitude, MIr *gruth* curds] *vi* **1 a :** to press on **:** HURRY **b :** to press close **2 :** to collect in numbers ~ *vt* **1 a :** to fill by pressing or thronging together **b :** to press, force, or thrust into a small space **2 :** PUSH, FORCE <~*ed* us off the sidewalk> **3 a :** to urge on **b :** to put on (sail) in excess of the usual for greater speed **4 :** to put pressure on **5 :** THRONG, JOSTLE **6 :** to press close to

[2]**crowd** *n* **1 :** a large number of persons esp. when collected into a somewhat compact body without order **:** THRONG **2 :** the great body of the people **:** POPULACE **3 :** a large number of things close together **4 :** a group of people having something (as a habit, interest, or occupation) in common <in with the wrong ~>
syn CROWD, THRONG, CRUSH, MOB, HORDE *shared meaning element* **:** an assembled multitude usu. of persons

[3]**crowd** \ˈkrau̇d, ˈkrüd\ *n* [ME *crowde,* fr. (assumed) MW *crwth*] **1 :** an ancient Celtic stringed instrument played by plucking or with a short bow **2** *dial Eng* **:** FIDDLE

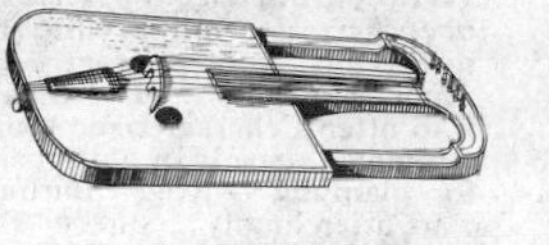

crowd

crowd·ed·ness \ˈkrau̇d-əd-nəs\ *n* **:** the quality or state of being crowded

crow·foot \ˈkrō-ˌfu̇t\ *n, pl* **crow·feet** \-ˌfēt\ **1** *pl usu* **crowfoots :** any of numerous plants having leaves pedately lobed; *esp* **:** any of a genus (*Ranunculus*) of plants of the buttercup family that are mostly yellow-flowered herbs **2 :** CROW'S-FOOT 1 — usu. used in pl. **3 :** a number of small lines of a boat rove through a long block

crow·keep·er \ˈkrō-ˌkē-pər\ *n, Brit* **:** a person employed to scare off crows

[1]**crown** \ˈkrau̇n\ *n, often attrib* [ME *coroune, crowne,* fr. OF *corone,* fr. L *corona* wreath, crown, fr. Gk *korōnē;* akin to Gk *korōnos* curved, L *curvus,* MIr *cruind* round] **1 :** a reward of victory or mark of honor; *esp* **:** the title representing the championship in a sport **2 :** a royal or imperial headdress or cap of sovereignty **:** DIADEM **3 :** the highest part: as **a :** the topmost part of the skull or head **b :** the summit of a mountain **c :** the head of foliage of a tree or shrub **d :** the part of a hat or other headgear covering the crown of the head **e :** the part of a tooth external to the gum or an artificial substitute for this — see TOOTH illustration **4 :** a wreath, band, or circular ornament for the head **5 :** something resembling a wreath or crown **6** *often cap* **a** (1) **:** imperial or regal power **:** SOVEREIGNTY **a** (2) **:** the government under a constitutional monarchy **b :** MONARCH **7 :** something that imparts splendor, honor, or finish **:** CULMINATION **8 a** (1) **:** any of several old gold coins with a crown as part of the device (2) **:** a former usu. silver British coin worth five shillings **b :** a size of paper usu. 15 x 20 in. **9 a :** KORUNA **b :** KRONA **c :** KRONE **10 a :** the region of a seed plant at which stem and root merge **b :** the thick arching end of the shank of an anchor where the arms join it — **crowned** \ˈkrau̇nd\ *adj*

[2]**crown** *vt* [ME *corounen,* fr. OF *coroner,* fr. L *coronare,* fr. *corona*] **1 a :** to place a crown or wreath on the head of; *specif* **:** to invest with regal dignity and power **b :** to recognize officially as <they ~*ed* him athlete of the year> **2 :** to bestow something on as a mark of honor or recompense **:** ADORN **3 :** SURMOUNT, TOP; *esp* **:** to top (a checker) with a checker to make a king **4 :** to bring to a successful conclusion **:** CLIMAX **5 :** to provide with something like a crown: as **a :** to fill so that the surface forms a crown **b :** to put an artifical crown on (a tooth) **6 :** to hit on the head

crown canopy *n* **:** the cover formed by the top branches of trees in a forest

crown colony *n, often cap both Cs* **:** a colony of the British Commonwealth over which the Crown retains some control

crow·ner \ˈkrü-nər, ˈkrau̇-\ *n* [ME, alter. of *coroner*] *chiefly dial* **:** CORONER

crown·et \ˈkrau̇-nət\ *n, archaic* **:** CORONET

crown gall *n* **:** a plant disease that is esp. destructive to stone and pome fruits and that is caused by a bacterium (*Agrobacterium tumefaciens*) which forms tumorous enlargements just below the ground on the stem

crown glass *n* **1 :** a glass blown and whirled into the form of a disk with a center lump left by the worker's rod **2 :** alkali-lime silicate optical glass having relatively low index of refraction and low dispersion value

crown jewels *n pl* **:** the jewels (as crown and scepter) belonging to a sovereign's regalia

crown land *n* **1 :** land belonging to the crown and yielding revenues that the reigning sovereign is entitled to **2 :** public land in some British dominions or colonies

crown lens *n* **:** the crown glass component of an achromatic lens

crown of thorns : a starfish (*Acanthaster planci*) of the Pacific region that is covered with long spines and is destructive to the coral of coral reefs

crown prince *n* **:** an heir apparent to a crown or throne

crown princess *n* **1 :** the wife of a crown prince **2 :** a female heir apparent or heir presumptive to a crown or throne

crown rust *n* **:** a leaf rust of oats and other grasses that is caused by a fungus (*Puccinia coronata*) and is characterized by rounded light-orange uredinia and buried telia

crown saw *n* **:** a saw having teeth at the edge of a hollow cylinder

crown vetch *n* **:** a European herb (*Coronilla varia*) that is naturalized in the eastern U.S. and has umbels of pink-and-white flowers and sharp-angled pods

crow's-foot \ˈkrōz-ˌfu̇t\ *n, pl* **crow's-feet** \-ˌfēt\ **1 :** any of the wrinkles around the outer corners of the eyes — usu. used in pl. **2 :** CROWFOOT 1

crow's nest *n* **:** a partly enclosed platform high on a ship's mast for use as a lookout; *also* **:** a similar lookout (as on a traffic-control tower)

cro·zier *var of* CROSIER

CRT *abbr* cathode-ray tube

cruces *pl of* CRUX

cru·cial \ˈkrü-shəl\ *adj* [F, fr. L *cruc-, crux* cross — more at RIDGE] **1** *archaic* **:** CRUCIFORM **2 a :** important or essential as resolving a crisis **:** DECISIVE **b :** marked by final determination of a doubtful issue **:** TRYING **c :** marked by or possessing importance or significance <what use we make of them will be the ~ question —Stanley Kubrick> ***syn*** see ACUTE — **cru·cial·ly** \ˈkrüsh-(ə-)lē\ *adv*

cru·cian carp \ˌkrü-shən-\ *n* [modif. of LG *karuse,* fr. MHG *karusse,* fr. Lith *karusis*]**:** a European carp (*Carassius carassius*) — called also *crucian*

cru·ci·ate \ˈkrü-shē-ˌāt\ *adj* [NL *cruciatus,* fr. L *cruc-, crux*] **:** cross-shaped **:** CRUCIFORM — **cru·ci·ate·ly** *adv*

cru·ci·ble \ˈkrü-sə-bəl\ *n* [ME *corusible,* fr. ML *crucibulum,* modif. of OF *croiseul*] **1 :** a vessel of a very refractory material (as porcelain) used for melting and calcining a substance that requires a high degree of heat **2 :** a severe test

crucible steel *n* **:** hard cast steel made in pots that are lifted from the furnace before the metal is poured into molds

cru·ci·fer \ˈkrü-sə-fər\ *n* [deriv. of L *cruc-, crux* + *-fer*] **1 :** one who carries a cross esp. at the head of an ecclesiastical procession **2 :** any of a family (*Cruciferae*) of plants including the cabbage and mustard — **cru·cif·er·ous** \krü-ˈsif-(ə-)rəs\ *adj*

cru·ci·fix \ˈkrü-sə-ˌfiks\ *n* [ME, fr. LL *crucifixus* the crucified Christ, fr. *crucifixus,* pp. of *crucifigere* to crucify, fr. L *cruc-, crux* + *figere* to fasten — more at DIKE] **:** a representation of Christ on the cross

cru·ci·fix·ion \ˌkrü-sə-ˈfik-shən\ *n* **1 a :** the act of crucifying **b** *cap* **:** the crucifying of Christ **2 :** extreme and painful punishment, affliction, or suffering

cru·ci·form \ˈkrü-sə-ˌfȯrm\ *adj* [L *cruc-, crux* + E *-form*] **:** forming or arranged in a cross — **cruciform** *n* — **cru·ci·form·ly** *adv*

cru·ci·fy \ˈkrü-sə-ˌfī\ *vt* **-fied; -fy·ing** [ME *crucifien,* fr. OF *crucifier,* fr. LL *crucifigere*] **1 :** to put to death by nailing or binding the hands and feet to a cross **2 :** to destroy the power of **:** MORTIFY <~ the flesh> **3 :** to treat cruelly **:** TORTURE, PERSECUTE

[1]**crud** \ˈkrəd\ *n* [ME *curd, crudd*] **1** *dial* **:** [1]CURD **2 a :** a deposit or incrustation of filth, grease, or refuse **b** *slang* **:** something disagreeable or contemptible **:** RUBBISH, CRAP **3 :** a usu. ill-defined or imperfectly identified bodily disorder — **crud·dy** \ˈkrəd-ē\ *adj*

[2]**crud** *vb* **crud·ded; crud·ding** *dial* **:** [2]CURD

[1]**crude** \ˈkrüd\ *adj* **crud·er; crud·est** [ME, fr. L *crudus* raw — more at RAW] **1 :** existing in a natural state and unaltered by cooking or processing <~ rubber> **2** *archaic* **:** UNRIPE, IMMATURE **3 :** marked by the primitive, gross, or elemental or by uncultivated simplicity or vulgarity **4 :** rough or inexpert in plan or execution <a ~ shelter> **5 :** lacking a covering, glossing, or concealing element **:** OBVIOUS <~ facts> **6 :** tabulated without being broken down into classes <~ death rate> ***syn*** see RUDE ***ant*** finished — **crude·ly** *adv* — **crude·ness** *n*

[2]**crude** *n* **:** a substance in its natural unprocessed state; *esp* **:** unrefined petroleum

cru·di·ty \ˈkrüd-ət-ē\ *n, pl* **-ties 1 :** the quality or state of being crude **2 :** something that is crude

cru·el \ˈkrü-əl\ *adj* **cru·el·er** *or* **cru·el·ler; cru·el·est** *or* **cru·el·lest** [ME, fr. OF, fr. L *crudelis,* irreg. fr. *crudus*] **1 :** disposed to inflict pain or suffering **:** devoid of humane feelings **2 a :** causing or conducive to injury, grief, or pain **b :** unrelieved by leniency ***syn*** see FIERCE ***ant*** pitiful — **cru·el·ly** \ˈkrü-ə-lē\ *adv* — **cru·el·ness** *n*

cru·el·ty \ˈkrü-əl-tē\ *n, pl* **-ties** [ME *cruelte,* fr. OF *cruelté,* fr. L *crudelitat-, crudelitas,* fr. *crudelis*] **1 :** the quality or state of being cruel **2 a :** a cruel action **b :** inhuman treatment **3 :** marital conduct held (as in a divorce action) to endanger life or health or to cause mental suffering or fear

cru·et \'krü-ət\ *n* [ME, fr. AF, dim. of OF *crue*, of Gmc origin; akin to OE *crocc* crock] **1 :** a vessel to hold wine or water for the Eucharist **2 :** a usu. glass bottle used to hold a condiment (as oil or vinegar) for use at the table

[1]**cruise** \'krüz\ *vb* **cruised; cruis·ing** [D *kruisen* to make a cross, cruise, fr. MD *crucen*, fr. *crūce* cross, fr. L *cruc-, crux* — more at RIDGE] *vi* **1 :** to sail about touching at a series of ports **2 :** to be on one's way **:** GO <I'll ~ over to her house to see if she's home> **3 :** to travel for the sake of traveling **4 a :** to go about the streets at random but on the lookout for possible developments <the cabdriver *cruised* for an hour before being hailed> **b :** to search (as in public places) for a sexual partner **5 a** *of an airplane* **:** to fly at the most efficient operating speed **b** *of an automobile* **:** to travel at a speed suitable for being maintained for a long distance ~ *vt* **1 :** to cruise over or about **2 :** to inspect (as land) with reference to possible lumber yield

[2]**cruise** *n* **:** an act or an instance of cruising; *esp* **:** a tour by ship

cruis·er \'krü-zər\ *n* **1 :** a boat or vehicle that cruises; *specif* **:** SQUAD CAR **2 :** a large fast moderately armored and gunned warship usu. of 6000 to 15,000 tons displacement **3 :** a motorboat with cabin, plumbing, and other arrangements necessary for living aboard — called also *cabin cruiser* **4 :** a person who cruises; *specif* **:** one who estimates the volume and value of marketable timber on a tract of land and maps it out for logging

crul·ler \'krəl-ər\ *n* [D *krulle*, a twisted cake, fr. *krul* curly, fr. MD *crul*] **1 :** a small sweet cake in the form of a twisted strip fried in deep fat **2** *North & Midland* **:** an unraised doughnut

[1]**crumb** \'krəm\ *n* [ME *crumme*, fr. OE *cruma*; akin to MHG *krume* crumb] **1 :** a small fragment esp. of bread **2 :** BIT **3 :** the soft part of bread **4** *slang* **:** a worthless person

[2]**crumb** *vt* **1 :** to break into crumbs **2 :** to cover or thicken with crumbs **3 :** to remove crumbs from <~ a table>

crum·ble \'krəm-bəl\ *vb* **crum·bled; crum·bling** \-b(ə-)liŋ\ [alter. of ME *kremelen*, freq. of OE *gecrymian* to crumble, fr. *cruma*] *vt* **:** to break into small pieces ~ *vi* **:** to fall into small pieces **:** DISINTEGRATE — **crumble** *n*

crum·blings \'krəm-b(ə-)liŋz\ *n pl* **:** crumbled particles **:** CRUMBS

crum·bly \-b(ə-)lē\ *adj* **crum·bli·er; -est :** easily crumbled **:** FRIABLE <~ soil> — **crum·bli·ness** *n*

crum·mie *or* **crum·my** \'krəm-ē\ *n, pl* **crummies** [Sc *crumb* crooked, fr. ME, fr. OE] *chiefly Scot* **:** COW; *esp* **:** one with crumpled horns

crum·my *or* **crumby** \'krəm-ē\ *adj* **crum·mi·er** *or* **crumb·i·er; -est** [ME *crumme*] **1** *obs* **:** CRUMBLY **2 a :** MISERABLE, FILTHY **b :** CHEAP, WORTHLESS

[1]**crump** \'krəmp\ *vi* [imit.] **1 :** CRUNCH **2 :** to explode heavily

[2]**crump** *n* **1 :** a crunching sound **2 :** SHELL, BOMB

[3]**crump** *adj* [perh. alter. of *crimp* (friable)] *chiefly Scot* **:** BRITTLE, FRIABLE, CRISP

crum·pet \'krəm-pət\ *n* [perh. fr. ME *crompid* (*cake*) wafer, lit., curled-up cake, fr. *crumped*, pp. of *crumpen* to curl up, fr. *crump*, *crumb* crooked] **:** a small round cake of rich unsweetened batter cooked on a griddle and usu. split and toasted before serving

[1]**crum·ple** \'krəm-pəl\ *vb* **crum·pled; crum·pling** \-p(ə-)liŋ\ [(assumed) ME *crumplen*, freq. of ME *crumpen*] *vt* **1 :** to press, bend, or crush out of shape **:** RUMPLE **2 :** to cause to collapse ~ *vi* **1 :** to become crumpled **2 :** COLLAPSE

[2]**crumple** *n* **:** a wrinkle or crease made by crumpling

[1]**crunch** \'krənch\ *vb* [alter. of *craunch*] *vi* **1 :** to undergo crunching **2 :** to make one's way with crunching <~ through the snow> ~ *vt* **:** to chew, grind, or press with a crushing noise

[2]**crunch** *n* **1 :** an act of crunching **2 :** a sound made by crunching **3 :** a tight or critical situation: as **a :** a critical point in the buildup of pressure between opposing elements **b :** a severe economic squeeze (as on credit)

crunch·er \'krən-chər\ *n* **1 :** one that crunches **2 :** a finishing blow

crunchy \'krən-chē\ *adj* **crunch·i·er; -est :** CRISP — **crunch·i·ness** *n*

crup·per \'krəp-ər, 'krüp-\ *n* [ME *cruper*, fr. OF *crupiere*, fr. *croupe* hindquarters] **1 :** a leather loop passing under a horse's tail and buckled to the saddle **2 :** [1]CROUP; *broadly* **:** BUTTOCKS

cru·ral \'krù(ə)r-əl\ *adj* [L *crur-, crus* leg] **:** of or relating to the thigh or leg; *specif* **:** FEMORAL

crus \'krüs, 'krəs\ *n, pl* **cru·ra** \'krù(ə)r-ə\ [L *crur-, crus*; akin to Arm *srunk* shinbones] **1 :** the part of the hind limb between the femur or thigh and the tarsus or ankle **:** SHANK **2 :** any of various parts that resemble a leg or a pair of legs

[1]**cru·sade** \krü-'sād\ *n* [blend of MF *croisade* & Sp *cruzada*; both derivs. of L *cruc-, crux* cross] **1** *cap* **:** any of the military expeditions undertaken by Christian powers in the 11th, 12th, and 13th centuries to win the Holy Land from the Muslims **2 :** a remedial enterprise undertaken with zeal and enthusiasm

[2]**crusade** *vi* **cru·sad·ed; cru·sad·ing :** to engage in a crusade — **cru·sad·er** *n*

cru·sa·do \krü-'säd-(,)ō\ *also* **cru·za·do** \-'zäd-(,)ō, -(,)ü\ *n, pl* **-does** *or* **-dos** [Pg *cruzado*, lit., marked with a cross] **:** an old gold or silver coin of Portugal having a cross on the reverse

cruse \'krüz, 'krüs\ *n* [ME; akin to OE *crūse* pitcher] **:** a small vessel (as a jar or pot) for holding a liquid (as water or oil)

[1]**crush** \'krəsh\ *vb* [ME *crusshen*, fr. MF *cruisir*, of Gmc origin; akin to MLG *krossen* to crush] *vt* **1 a :** to squeeze or force by pressure so as to alter or destroy structure **b :** to squeeze together into a mass **2 :** HUG, EMBRACE **3 :** to reduce to particles by pounding or grinding **4 a :** to suppress or overwhelm as if by pressure or weight <truth, ~*ed* to earth, shall rise again —W. C. Bryant> **b :** to oppress or burden grievously **c :** to subdue completely **5 :** CROWD, PUSH **6** *archaic* **:** DRINK ~ *vi* **1** *obs* **:** CRASH **2 :** to become crushed **3 :** to advance with or as if with crushing — **crush·able** \-ə-bəl\ *adj* — **crush·er** *n*

syn CRUSH, QUELL, EXTINGUISH, SUPPRESS, QUENCH, QUASH *shared meaning element* **:** to bring to an end by destroying or defeating

[2]**crush** *n* **1 :** an act of crushing **2 :** a crowding together esp. of many people **3 :** an intense and usu. passing infatuation; *also* **:** the object of infatuation ***syn*** see CROWD

crust \'krəst\ *n* [ME, fr. L *crusta*; akin to OE *hrūse* earth, Gk *kryos* icy cold] **1 a :** the hardened exterior or surface part of bread **b :** a piece of this or of bread grown dry or hard **2 :** the pastry cover of a pie **3 :** a hard or brittle external coat or covering: as **a :** a hard surface layer (as of soil or snow) **b :** the outer part of the earth composed essentially of crystalline rocks **c :** a deposit built up on the interior surface of a wine bottle during long aging **d :** an encrusting deposit of dried secretions or exudate; *esp* **:** SCAB **4 :** IMPUDENCE, NERVE — **crust** *vb*

crus·ta·cea \,krəs-'tā-sh(ē)ə\ *n pl* [NL, group name, fr. neut. pl. of *crustaceus*] **:** arthropods that are crustaceans

crus·ta·cean \,krəs-'tā-shən\ *n* **:** any of a large class (Crustacea) of mostly aquatic arthropods that have a chitinous or calcareous and chitinous exoskeleton, a pair of often much modified appendages on each segment, and two pairs of antennae and that include the lobsters, shrimps, crabs, wood lice, water fleas, and barnacles — **crustacean** *adj*

crus·ta·ceous \-shəs\ *adj* [NL *crustaceus*, fr. L *crusta* crust, shell] **:** of, relating to, having, or forming a crust or shell; *esp* **:** CRUSTOSE

crust·al \'krəs-t°l\ *adj* **:** relating to a crust esp. of the earth or the moon

crust·ifi·ca·tion \,krəs-tə-fə-'kā-shən\ *n* **:** INCRUSTATION

crus·tose \'krəs-,tōs\ *adj* [L *crustosus* crusted] **:** having a thin thallus adhering closely to the substratum of rock, bark, or soil <~ lichens> — compare FOLIOSE, FRUTICOSE

crusty \'krəs-tē\ *adj* **crust·i·er; -est 1 :** having or being a crust **2 :** giving an effect of surly incivility in address or disposition ***syn*** see BLUFF — **crust·i·ly** \-tə-lē\ *adv* — **crust·i·ness** \-tē-nəs\ *n*

[1]**crutch** \'krəch\ *n* [ME *crucche*, fr. OE *crycc*; akin to OHG *krucka* crutch, OE *cradol* cradle] **1 a :** a support typically fitting under the armpit for use by the disabled in walking **b :** PROP, STAY **2 :** a forked leg rest constituting the pommel of a sidesaddle **3 :** the crotch of a human being or an animal (as a sheep) **4 :** a forked support

[2]**crutch** *vt* **:** to support on crutches **:** prop up

crux \'krəks, 'krüks\ *n, pl* **crux·es** *also* **cru·ces** \'krü-,sēz\ [L *cruc-, crux* cross, torture — more at RIDGE] **1 :** a puzzling or difficult problem **:** an unsolved question **2 :** an essential point requiring resolution or resolving an outcome <the ~ of the problem> **3 :** a main or central feature (as of an argument)

Cru·zan \krü-'zan\ *n* [(assumed) AmerSp *cruzano*, fr. *Santa Cruz* St. Croix] **:** a native or inhabitant of St. Croix — **Cruzan** *adj*

cru·zei·ro \krü-'ze(ə)r-(,)ō, -(,)ü\ *n, pl* **-ros** [Pg] — see MONEY table

crwth \'krüth\ *n* [W] **:** [3]CROWD 1

[1]**cry** \'krī\ *vb* **cried; cry·ing** [ME *crien*, fr. OF *crier*, fr. L *quiritare* to cry out for help (from a citizen), to scream, fr. *Quirit-, Quiris* Roman citizen] *vi* **1 :** to call loudly **:** SHOUT **2 :** WEEP, SOB **3 :** to utter a characteristic sound or call **4 :** to require or suggest strongly a remedy or a disposition <a hundred things which ~ out for planning —Roger Burlingame> ~ *vt* **1 :** BEG, BESEECH **2 :** to utter loudly **:** SHOUT **3 :** to proclaim publicly **:** ADVERTISE <~ their wares> — **cry havoc :** to sound an alarm — **cry over spilled milk :** to express vain regrets for what cannot be recovered or undone — **cry wolf :** to give alarm unnecessarily

[2]**cry** *n, pl* **cries 1 :** an instance of crying: as **a :** an inarticulate utterance of distress, rage, or pain **b** *obs* **:** OUTCRY, CLAMOR **2 a** *obs* **:** PROCLAMATION **b** *pl, Scot* **:** BANNS **3 :** ENTREATY, APPEAL **4 :** a loud shout **5 :** WATCHWORD, SLOGAN <"death to the invader" was the ~> **6 a :** common report **b :** a general opinion **7 :** the public voice raised in protest or approval **8 a :** a pack of hounds **b :** PURSUIT — used in the phrase *in full cry* **9 :** DISTANCE — usu. used in the phrase *a far cry* <but simple trading is a far ~ from running modern corporations —George Melloan>

cry- *or* **cryo-** *comb form* [G *kryo-*, fr. Gk, fr. *kryos* — more at CRUST] **:** cold **:** freezing <*cry*anesthesia> <*cryo*gen>

cry·ba·by \'krī-,bā-bē\ *n* **:** one who cries or complains easily or often

cry down *vt* **:** DISPARAGE, DEPRECIATE

cry·ing \'krī-iŋ\ *adj* **1 :** calling for notice <a ~ need> **2 :** NOTORIOUS, HEINOUS <a ~ shame>

cry·mo·ther·a·py \,krī-mō-'ther-ə-pē\ *n* [Gk *krymos*, *kryos* icy cold + ISV *therapy*] **:** CRYOTHERAPY

cryo·bi·ol·o·gy \,krī-ō-bī-'äl-ə-jē\ *n* **:** the study of the effects of extremely low temperature on biological systems — **cryo·bi·o·log·i·cal** \-,bī-ə-'läj-i-kəl\ *adj* — **cryo·bi·o·log·i·cal·ly** \-k(ə-)lē\ *adv* — **cryo·bi·ol·o·gist** \-bī-'äl-ə-jəst\ *n*

cry off *vt* **:** to call off (as an agreement) ~ *vi, chiefly Brit* **:** to beg off

cryo·gen \'krī-ə-jən\ *n* **:** a substance for obtaining low temperatures **:** REFRIGERANT — called also *cryogenic*

cryo·gen·ic \,krī-ə-'jen-ik\ *adj* **1 a :** of or relating to the production of very low temperatures **b :** being or relating to very low temperatures **2 a :** requiring or involving the use of a cryogenic temperature **b :** requiring cryogenic storage **c :** suitable for storage of a cryogenic substance — **cryo·gen·i·cal·ly** \-i-k(ə-)lē\ *adv*

cryo·gen·ics \-iks\ *n pl but sing or pl in constr* **:** a branch of physics that deals with the production and effects of very low temperatures

cry·og·e·ny \krī-'äj-ə-nē\ *n* **:** CRYOGENICS

cryo·lite \'krī-ə-,līt\ *n* [ISV] **:** a mineral Na_3AlF_6 consisting of sodium-aluminum fluoride found in Greenland usu. in white cleavable masses and used in making soda and aluminum

cry·on·ics \krī-'än-iks\ *n pl but usu sing in constr* [*cry-* + *-onics* (as in *electronics*)] **:** the practice of freezing a dead diseased human being in hope of bringing him back to life at some future time — **cry·on·ic** \-ik\ *adj*

cryo·phil·ic \,krī-ə-'fil-ik\ *adj* **:** thriving at low temperatures

cryo·probe \'krī-ə-,prōb\ *n* **:** a blunt instrument used to apply cold to tissues in cryosurgery

cryo·pro·tec·tive \,krī-ō-prə-'tek-tiv\ *adj* **:** serving to protect from freezing <an extracellular ~ agent>

cryo·scope \ˈkrī-ə-ˌskōp\ *n* **:** an instrument for determining freezing points

cry·os·co·py \krī-ˈäs-kə-pē\ *n* [ISV] **:** the determination of the lowered freezing points produced in liquid by dissolved substances to determine molecular weights of solutes and various properties of solutions — **cryo·scop·ic** \ˌkrī-ə-ˈskäp-ik\ *adj*

cryo·stat \ˈkrī-ə-ˌstat\ *n* [ISV] **:** an apparatus for maintaining a constant low temperature

cryo·sur·gery \ˌkrī-ō-ˈsərj-(ə-)rē\ *n* **:** surgery in which extreme cold chilling (as by use of liquid nitrogen) produces the desired dissection — **cryo·sur·geon** \-ˈsər-jən\ *n* — **cryo·sur·gi·cal** \-ji-kəl\ *adj*

cryo·ther·a·py \-ˈther-ə-pē\ *n* **:** the therapeutic use of cold

cryo·tron \ˈkrī-ə-ˌträn\ *n* [*cry-* + *-tron*] **:** a device performing some of the functions of an electron tube and utilizing the fact that a changing magnetic field can cause a superconductive element to oscillate between a state of low and high resistance

crypt \ˈkript\ *n* [L *crypta,* fr. Gk *kryptē,* fr. fem. of *kryptos* hidden, fr. *kryptein* to hide; akin to ON *hreysar* heap of stones, Lith *krauti* to pile up] **1 :** a chamber (as a vault) wholly or partly underground; *esp* **:** a vault under the main floor of a church **2 :** a simple gland, glandular cavity, or tube **:** FOLLICLE — **crypt·al** \ˈkrip-tᵊl\ *adj*

crypt- *or* **crypto-** *comb form* [NL, fr. Gk *kryptos*] **1 :** hidden **:** covered <*crypto*genic> **2 :** unavowed <*crypto*fascist> **3 :** CRYPTOGRAPHIC <*crypto*system> <*crypto*security>

crypt·anal·y·sis \ˌkrip-tə-ˈnal-ə-səs\ *n* [*crypt*ogram + *analysis*] **1 :** the solving of cryptograms or cryptographic systems **2 :** the theory of solving cryptograms or cryptographic systems **:** the art of devising methods for this — called also *cryptanalytics* — **crypt·an·a·lyt·ic** \ˌkrip-ˌtan-ᵊl-ˈit-ik\ *also* **crypt·an·a·lyt·i·cal** \-ˈit-i-kəl\ *adj* — **crypt·an·a·lyze** \krip-ˈtan-ᵊl-ˌīz\ *vt*

crypt·an·a·lyst \krip-ˈtan-ᵊl-əst\ *n* **:** a specialist in cryptanalysis

cryp·tic \ˈkrip-tik\ *adj* [LL *crypticus,* fr. Gk *kryptikos,* fr. *kryptos*] **1 :** SECRET, OCCULT **2 :** intended to be obscure or mysterious <a ~ policy> **3 :** serving to conceal <~ coloration in animals> **4 :** UNRECOGNIZED **5 :** employing cipher or code ***syn*** see OBSCURE — **cryp·ti·cal** \-ti-kəl\ *adj* — **cryp·ti·cal·ly** \-ti-k(ə-)lē\ *adv*

[1]**cryp·to** \ˈkrip-(ˌ)tō\ *n, pl* **cryptos** [*crypt-*] **:** one who adheres or belongs secretly to a party, sect, or other group

[2]**crypto** *adj* **:** CRYPTOGRAPHIC

cryp·to·coc·co·sis \ˌkrip-tə-(ˌ)kä-ˈkō-səs\ *n, pl* **-co·ses** \-(ˌ)sēz\ **:** an infectious disease that is caused by a fungus (*Cryptococcus neoformans*) and is characterized by the production of nodular lesions or abscesses in the lungs, subcutaneous tissues, joints, and esp. the brain and meninges

cryp·to·coc·cus \-ˈkäk-əs\ *n, pl* **-coc·ci** \-ˈkäk-ˌ(s)ī, -(ˌ)(s)ē\ [NL, genus name, fr. *crypt-* + *-coccus*] **:** any of a genus (*Cryptococcus*) of budding imperfect fungi that resemble yeasts and include a number of saprophytes and a few serious pathogens — **cryp·to·coc·cal** \-ˈkäk-əl\ *adj*

cryp·to·crys·tal·line \ˌkrip-tō-ˈkris-tə-lən\ *adj* [ISV] **:** having a crystalline structure so fine that no distinct particles are recognizable under the microscope

cryp·to·gam \ˈkrip-tə-ˌgam\ *n* [deriv. of Gk *kryptos* + *-gamia* -gamy] **:** a plant (as a fern, moss, alga, or fungus) reproducing by spores and not producing flowers or seed — **cryp·to·gam·ic** \ˌkrip-tə-ˈgam-ik\ *or* **cryp·tog·a·mous** \krip-ˈtäg-ə-məs\ *adj*

cryp·to·gen·ic \ˌkrip-tə-ˈjen-ik\ *adj* **:** of obscure or unknown origin <a ~ disease>

cryp·to·gram \ˈkrip-tə-ˌgram\ *n* [F *cryptogramme,* fr. *crypt-* + *-gramme* -gram] **1 :** a communication in cipher or code **2 :** a figure or representation having a hidden significance — **cryp·to·gram·mic** \ˌkrip-tə-ˈgram-ik\ *adj*

[1]**cryp·to·graph** \ˈkrip-tə-ˌgraf\ *n* **1 :** CRYPTOGRAM **2 :** a device for enciphering and deciphering

[2]**cryptograph** *vt* **:** ENCRYPT

cryp·tog·ra·pher \-fər\ *n* **:** a specialist in cryptography **:** as **a :** a clerk who enciphers and deciphers messages **b :** one who devises cryptographic methods or systems **c :** CRYPTANALYST

cryp·to·graph·ic \ˌkrip-tə-ˈgraf-ik\ *adj* **:** of, relating to, or using cryptography — **cryp·to·graph·i·cal·ly** \-i-k(ə-)lē\ *adv*

cryp·tog·ra·phy \krip-ˈtäg-rə-fē\ *n* [NL *cryptographia,* fr. *crypt-* + *-graphia* -graphy] **1 :** secret writing **:** cryptic symbolization **2 :** the enciphering and deciphering of messages in secret code **3 :** CRYPTANALYSIS

cryp·tol·o·gy \krip-ˈtäl-ə-jē\ *n* **:** the scientific study of cryptography and cryptanalysis — **cryp·to·log·ic** \ˌkrip-tə-ˈläj-ik\ *or* **cryp·to·log·i·cal** \-i-kəl\ *adj* — **cryp·tol·o·gist** \krip-ˈtäl-ə-jəst\ *n*

cryp·to·me·ria \ˌkrip-tə-ˈmir-ē-ə\ *n* [NL, genus name, fr. *crypt-* + Gk *meros* part] **:** an evergreen tree (*Cryptomeria japonica*) of the pine family that is a valuable timber tree of Japan

crypt·or·chid \krip-ˈtȯr-kəd\ *n* [NL *cryptorchid-, cryptorchis,* fr. *crypt-* + *orchid-, orchis* testicle, fr. Gk *orchis* — more at ORCHIS] **:** one affected with cryptorchidism — **cryptorchid** *adj*

crypt·or·chi·dism \-kə-ˌdiz-əm\ *also* **crypt·or·chism** \-ˌkiz-əm\ *n* **:** a condition in which one or both testes fail to descend normally

cryp·to·zo·ite \ˌkrip-tə-ˈzō-ˌīt\ *n* [*crypt-* + *-zoite* (as in *sporozoite*)] **:** a malaria parasite that develops in tissue cells and gives rise to the forms that invade blood cells

cryst *abbr* crystalline; crystallized

[1]**crys·tal** \ˈkris-tᵊl\ *n* [ME *cristal,* fr. OF, fr. L *crystallum,* fr. Gk *krystallos* — more at CRUST] **1 :** quartz that is transparent or nearly so and that is either colorless or only slightly tinged **2 :** something resembling crystal in transparency and colorlessness **3 :** a body that is formed by the solidification of a chemical element, a compound, or a mixture and has a regularly repeating internal arrangement of its atoms and often external plane faces **4 :** a clear colorless glass of superior quality; *also* **:** objects or ware of such glass **5 :** the glass or transparent plastic cover over a watch or clock dial **6 :** a crystalline material used in electronics as a frequency-determining element or for rectification **7 :** powdered metamphetamine

[2]**crystal** *adj* **1 :** consisting of or resembling crystal **:** CLEAR, LUCID **2 :** relating to or using a crystal <a ~ radio receiver>

crystal ball *n* **1 :** a sphere esp. of quartz crystal traditionally used by fortune-tellers **2 :** a means or method of predicting future events

crystal detector *n* **:** a detector that depends for its operation on the rectifying action of the surface of contact between various crystals (as of galena) and a metallic electrode

crystal gazing *n* **1 :** the art or practice of concentrating on a glass or crystal globe with the aim of inducing a psychic state in which divination can be performed **2 :** the attempt to predict future events or make difficult judgments esp. without adequate data — **crystal gazer** *n*

crystall- *or* **crystallo-** *comb form* [Gk *krystallos*] **:** crystal <*crystall*iferous>

crys·tal·lif·er·ous \ˌkris-tə-ˈlif-(ə-)rəs\ *adj* [ISV] **:** producing or bearing crystals

crys·tal·line \ˈkris-tə-lən *also* -ˌlīn, -ˌlēn\ *adj* [ME *cristallin,* fr. MF & L; MF, fr. L *crystallinus,* fr. Gk *krystallinos,* fr. *krystallos*] **1 :** made of crystal **:** composed of crystals **2 :** resembling crystal: as **a :** TRANSPARENT **b :** CLEAR-CUT **3 :** constituting or relating to a crystal — **crys·tal·lin·i·ty** \ˌkris-tə-ˈlin-ət-ē\ *n*

crystalline lens *n* **:** the lens of the eye in vertebrates

crys·tal·lite \ˈkris-tə-ˌlīt\ *n* [G *kristallit,* fr. Gk *krystallos*] **1 a :** a minute mineral form like those common in glassy volcanic rocks usu. not referable to any mineral species but marking the first step in crystallization **b :** a single grain in a medium composed of many crystals **2 :** MICELLE — **crys·tal·lit·ic** \ˌkris-tə-ˈlit-ik\ *adj*

crys·tal·li·za·tion \ˌkris-tə-lə-ˈzā-shən\ *n* **:** the process of crystallizing; *also* **:** a form resulting from this

crys·tal·lize *also* **crys·tal·ize** \ˈkris-tə-ˌlīz\ *vt* **-lized; -liz·ing 1 :** to cause to form crystals or assume crystalline form **2 :** to cause to take a definite form <tried to ~ his thoughts> **3 :** to coat with crystals esp. of sugar <~ grapes> ~ *vi* **:** to become crystallized — **crys·tal·liz·able** \-ˌlī-zə-bəl\ *adj* — **crys·tal·liz·er** *n*

crys·tal·lized *adj* **1 :** formed into crystals **2 :** coated with crystals esp. of sugar **:** CANDIED **3 :** definite in form <failure to distinguish between ~ and uncrystallized opinion — *Psychological Abstracts*>

crys·tal·log·ra·phy \ˌkris-tə-ˈläg-rə-fē\ *n* **:** the science dealing with the system of forms among crystals, their structure, and their forms of aggregation — **crys·tal·log·ra·pher** \-fər\ *n* — **crys·tal·lo·graph·ic** \-lə-ˈgraf-ik\ *or* **crys·tal·lo·graph·i·cal** \-i-kəl\ *adj* — **crys·tal·lo·graph·i·cal·ly** \-i-k(ə-)lē\ *adv*

crys·tal·loid \ˈkris-tə-ˌlȯid\ *n* **1 :** a substance that forms a true solution and is capable of being crystallized **2 :** a particle of protein that has the properties of crystal and is found esp. in oily seeds — **crystalloid** *adj* — **crys·tal·loi·dal** \ˌkris-tə-ˈlȯid-ᵊl\ *adj*

crystal violet *n* **:** a triphenylmethane dye found in gentian violet

cry up *vt* **:** to enhance in value or repute by public praise **:** EXTOL

cs *abbr* **1** case; cases **2** census **3** consciousness **4** consul

[1]**Cs** *abbr* cirrostratus

[2]**Cs** *symbol* cesium

CS *abbr* **1** capital stock **2** Christian Science practitioner **3** civil service **4** conditioned stimulus **5** county seat

C/S *abbr* cycles per second

CSA *abbr* Confederate States of America

csc *symbol* cosecant

CSC *abbr* **1** Civil Service Commission **2** [L *Congregatio Sanctae Crucis*] Congregation of the Holy Cross

CSF *abbr* cerebrospinal fluid

CSM *abbr* command sergeant major

CSS *abbr* College Scholarship Service

CSsR *abbr* [L *Congregatio Sanctissimi Redemptoris*] Congregation of the Most Holy Redeemer

CST *abbr* **1** central standard time **2** convulsive shock therapy

ct *abbr* **1** carat **2** cent **3** count **4** county **5** court

CT *abbr* **1** central time **2** certificated teacher; certified teacher **3** code telegram **4** Connecticut

CTC *abbr* centralized traffic control

cte·noid \ˈten-ˌȯid, ˈtē-ˌnȯid\ *adj* [ISV, fr. Gk *ktenoeidēs,* fr. *kten-, kteis* comb — more at PECTINATE] **:** having the margin toothed <~ scale>; *also* **:** having or consisting of ctenoid scales <~ fishes> <~ scalation>

cte·noph·o·ran \ti-ˈnäf-ə-rən\ *adj* **:** of or relating to a ctenophore — **ctenophoran** *n*

cteno·phore \ˈten-ə-ˌfō(ə)r, -ˌfȯ(ə)r\ *n* [deriv. of Gk *kten-, kteis* + *pherein* to carry — more at BEAR] **:** any of a phylum (Ctenophora) of marine animals superficially resembling jellyfishes but having decided biradial symmetry and swimming by means of eight meridional bands of transverse ciliated plates — called also *comb jelly*

ctg *or* **ctge** *abbr* cartage

ctn *abbr* **1** carton **2** cotangent

cto *abbr* concerto

c to c *abbr* center to center

ctr *abbr* **1** center **2** counter

cu *abbr* **1** cubic **2** cumulative

[1]**Cu** *abbr* cumulus

[2]**Cu** *symbol* [L *cuprum*] copper

CU *abbr* closeup

cua·dri·lla \kwä-ˈdrē(l)-yə\ *n* [Sp, dim. of *cuadra* square, fr. L *quatra*] **:** the team assisting the matador in the bull ring

cub \ˈkəb\ *n* [origin unknown] **1 a :** a young carnivorous mammal (as a bear or lion) **b :** a young shark **2 :** a young person **3 :** APPRENTICE: *esp* **:** an inexperienced newspaper reporter

---

ə abut	ᵊ kitten	ər further	a back	ā bake	ä cot, cart
aù out	ch chin	e less	ē easy	g gift	i trip ī life
j joke	ŋ sing	ō flow	ȯ flaw	ȯi coin	th thin t͟h this
ü loot	ù foot	y yet	yü few	yù furious	zh vision

cub·age \ˈkyü-bij\ *n* **:** cubic content, volume, or displacement

Cu·ban heel \ˌkyü-bən-\ *n* [*Cuba,* West Indies] **:** a broad medium-high heel with a moderately curved back

cu·ba·ture \ˈkyü-bə-ˌchu̇(ə)r, -ˌchər, -ˌt(y)u̇(ə)r\ *n* [*cube* + *-ature* (as in *quadrature*)] **1 :** determination of cubic contents **2 :** cubic content

cub·by \ˈkəb-ē\ *n, pl* **cubbies** [obs. E *cub* pen, fr. D *kub* thatched roof; akin to OE *cofa* den — more at COVE] **:** a snug place **:** a cramped space

cub·by·hole \ˈkəb-ē-ˌhōl\ *n* **1 :** CUBBY **2 :** PIGEONHOLE 2

[1]**cube** \ˈkyüb\ *n* [ME, fr. L *cubus,* fr. Gk *kybos* cube, vertebra — more at HIP] **1 :** the regular solid of six equal square sides — see VOLUME table **2 :** the product got by taking a number three times as a factor **3** *pl* **:** cubic inches — used of the displacement of an automobile engine

[2]**cube** *vt* **cubed; cub·ing 1 :** to raise to the third power **2 :** to form into a cube **3 :** to cut partly through (a steak) in a checkered pattern to increase tenderness by breaking the fibers — **cub·er** *n*

[3]**cube** *adj* **:** raised to the third power

[4]**cu·be** \ˈkyü-ˌbā, kyü-ˈ\ *n* [AmerSp *cubé*] **:** any of several tropical American plants (genus *Lonchocarpus*) furnishing rotenone

cu·beb \ˈkyü-ˌbeb\ *n* [MF *cubebe,* fr. OF, fr. ML *cubeba,* fr. Ar *kubābah*] **:** the dried unripe berry of a tropical shrub (*Piper cubeba*) of the pepper family that is crushed and smoked in cigarettes for catarrh

cube root *n* **:** a number whose cube is a given number

cube steak *n* **:** a thin slice of beef that has been cubed

[1]**cu·bic** \ˈkyü-bik\ *adj* **1 :** having the form of a cube **:** CUBICAL **2 a :** relating to the cube considered as a crystal form **b :** ISOMETRIC 1b **3 a :** THREE-DIMENSIONAL **b :** being the volume of a cube whose edge is a specified unit <~ inch> **4 :** of third degree, order, or power <a ~ polynomial> — **cu·bic·ly** *adv*

[2]**cubic** *n* **:** a cubic curve, equation, or polynomial

cu·bi·cal \ˈkyü-bi-kəl\ *adj* **1 :** CUBIC; *esp* **:** shaped like a cube **2 :** relating to volume — **cu·bi·cal·ly** \-k(ə-)lē\ *adv*

cubic equation *n* **:** a polynomial equation in which the highest sum of exponents of variables in any term is three

cu·bi·cle \ˈkyü-bi-kəl\ *n* [L *cubiculum,* fr. *cubare* to lie, recline — more at HIP] **1 :** a sleeping compartment partitioned off from a large room **2 :** a small partitioned space; *esp* **:** CARREL

cubic measure *n* **:** a unit (as cubic inch or cubic centimeter) for measuring volume — see METRIC SYSTEM table, WEIGHT table

cu·bi·form \ˈkyü-bə-ˌfȯrm\ *adj* [L *cubus* + E *-form*] **:** having the shape of a cube

cub·ism \ˈkyü-ˌbiz-əm\ *n* **:** a style of art that stresses abstract structure at the expense of other pictorial elements esp. by displaying several aspects of the same object simultaneously and by fragmenting the form of depicted objects — **cub·ist** \-bəst\ *n* — **cubist** *or* **cu·bis·tic** \kyü-ˈbis-tik\ *adj*

cu·bit \ˈkyü-bət\ *n* [ME, fr. L *cubitum* elbow, cubit — more at HIP] **:** any of various ancient units of length based on the length of the forearm from the elbow to the tip of the middle finger and usu. equal to about 18 inches but sometimes to 21 or more

cu·boid \ˈkyü-ˌbȯid\ *adj* **:** approximately cubic in shape; *specif* **:** being the outermost of the distal row of tarsal bones of many higher vertebrates

cu·boi·dal \kyü-ˈbȯid-ᵊl\ *adj* **1 :** somewhat cubical **2 :** composed of nearly cubical elements <~ epithelium>

cub scout *n* **:** a member of the scouting program of the Boy Scouts of America for boys of the age range 8–10

cuck·ing stool \ˈkək-iŋ-\ *n* [ME *cucking stol,* lit., defecating chair] **:** a chair formerly used for punishing offenders (as dishonest tradesmen) by public exposure or ducking in water

[1]**cuck·old** \ˈkək-əld, ˈku̇k-\ *n* [ME *cokewold*] **:** a man whose wife is unfaithful

[2]**cuckold** *vt* **:** to make a cuckold of

cuck·old·ry \-əl-drē\ *n* **1 :** the practice of making cuckolds **2 :** the state of being a cuckold

[1]**cuck·oo** \ˈkük-(ˌ)ü, ˈku̇k-\ *n, pl* **cuckoos** [ME *cuccu,* of imit. origin] **1 :** a largely grayish brown European bird (*Cuculus canorus*) that is a parasite given to laying its eggs in the nests of other birds which hatch them and rear the offspring; *broadly* **:** any of a large family (Cuculidae of the order Cuculiformes) to which this bird belongs **2 :** the call of the cuckoo **3 :** a silly or slightly crackbrained person

[2]**cuckoo** *vt* **:** to repeat monotonously as a cuckoo does its call

[3]**cuckoo** *adj* **1 :** of, relating to, or resembling the cuckoo **2 :** deficient in sense or intelligence **:** SILLY

cuckoo clock *n* **:** a wall or shelf clock that announces the hours by sounds resembling a cuckoo's call

cuck·oo·flow·er \ˈkük-(ˌ)ü-ˌflau̇(-ə)r, ˈku̇k-\ *n* **1 :** a bitter cress (*Cardamine pratensis*) of Europe and America **2 :** RAGGED ROBIN **3 :** WOOD SORREL 1

cuck·oo·pint \-ˌpint\ *n* [ME *cuccupintel,* fr. *cuccu* + *pintel* pintle] **:** a European arum (*Arum maculatum*) with erect spathe and short purple spadix

cuckoo spit *n* **1 :** a frothy secretion exuded on plants by the nymphs of spittle insects **2 :** SPITTLE INSECT

cu·cul·late \ˈkyü-kə-ˌlāt, kyü-ˈkəl-ət\ *also* **cu·cul·lat·ed** \ˈkyü-kə-ˌlāt-əd\ *adj* [ML *cucullatus,* fr. L *cucullus* hood] **:** having the shape of a hood **:** HOODED <a ~ leaf>

cu·cum·ber \ˈkyü-(ˌ)kəm-bər\ *n* [ME, fr. MF *cocombre,* fr. L *cucumer-, cucumis*] **:** the fruit of a vine (*Cucumis sativus*) of the gourd family cultivated as a garden vegetable; *also* **:** this vine

cucumber mosaic *n* **:** a virus disease esp. of cucumbers that is transmitted by an aphid and produces mottled foliage and often pale warty fruits

cucumber tree *n* **:** any of several American magnolias (esp. *Magnolia acuminata*) having fruit resembling a small cucumber

cu·cur·bit \kyü-ˈkər-bət\ *n* [ME *cucurbite,* fr. MF, fr. L *cucurbita* gourd] **1 :** a vessel or flask for distillation used with or forming part of an alembic — see ALEMBIC illustration **2 :** a plant of the gourd family

cud \ˈkəd, ˈku̇d\ *n* [ME *cudde,* fr. OE *cwudu;* akin to OHG *kuti* glue, Skt *jatu* gum] **1 :** food brought up into the mouth by a ruminating animal from its first stomach to be chewed again **2 :** [2]QUID

cud·bear \ˈkəd-ˌba(ə)r, -ˌbe(ə)r\ *n* [irreg. fr. Dr. *Cuthbert* Gordon, 18th cent. Sc chemist] **:** a reddish coloring matter from lichens

[1]**cud·dle** \ˈkəd-ᵊl\ *vb* **cud·dled; cud·dling** \ˈkəd-liŋ, -ᵊl-iŋ\ [origin unknown] *vt* **:** to hold close for warmth or comfort or in affection ~ *vi* **:** to lie close or snug **:** NESTLE, SNUGGLE ***syn*** see CARESS

[2]**cuddle** *n* **:** a close embrace

cud·dle·some \ˈkəd-ᵊl-səm\ *adj* **:** CUDDLY

cud·dly \ˈkəd-lē, -ᵊl-ē\ *adj* **cud·dli·er; -est :** fit for or inviting cuddling

[1]**cud·dy** \ˈkəd-ē\ *n, pl* **cuddies** [origin unknown] **1 a :** a small cabin formerly under the poop deck **b :** the galley or pantry of a small ship **2 :** a small room or cupboard

[2]**cud·dy** *or* **cud·die** \ˈku̇d-ē, ˈkəd-\ *n, pl* **cuddies** [perh. fr. *Cuddy,* nickname for *Cuthbert*] **1** *dial Brit* **:** DONKEY **2** *dial Brit* **:** BLOCKHEAD

[1]**cud·gel** \ˈkəj-əl\ *n* [ME *kuggel,* fr. OE *cycgel;* akin to MHG *kugele* ball, OE *cot* hut — more at COT] **:** a short heavy club

[2]**cudgel** *vt* **-geled** *or* **-gelled; -gel·ing** *or* **-gel·ling** \-(ə-)liŋ\ **:** to beat with or as if with a cudgel — **cudgel one's brains :** to think hard (as for a solution to a problem)

cud·weed \ˈkəd-ˌwēd, ˈku̇d-\ *n* **:** any of several composite plants (as of the genus *Gnaphalium*) with silky or woolly foliage

[1]**cue** \ˈkyü\ *n* [ME *cu*] **:** the letter *q*

[2]**cue** *n* [prob. fr. *qu,* abbr. (used as a direction in actors' copies of plays) of L *quando* when] **1 a :** a signal (as a word, phrase, or bit of stage business) to a performer to begin a specific speech or action **b :** something serving a comparable purpose **:** HINT **2 :** a feature indicating the nature of something perceived **3 :** the part one has to perform in or as if in a play **4** *archaic* **:** MOOD, HUMOR

[3]**cue** *vt* **cued; cu·ing** *or* **cue·ing 1 :** to give a cue to **:** PROMPT **2 :** to insert into a continuous performance <~ in sound effects>

[4]**cue** *n* [F *queue,* lit., tail, fr. L *cauda*] **1 :** QUEUE 2 **2 a :** a leather-tipped tapering rod for striking the cue ball (as in billiards and pool) **b :** a long-handled instrument with a concave head for shoving disks in shuffleboard

[5]**cue** *vb* **cued; cu·ing** *or* **cue·ing** *vt* **1 :** QUEUE **2 :** to strike with a cue ~ *vi* **1 :** QUEUE **2 :** to use a cue

cue ball *n* **:** the ball a player strikes with his cue in billiards and pool

cue bid *n* [[2]*cue*] **:** a bid in contract bridge that usu. indicates an ace or a void in the suit bid — **cue–bid** *vt*

cues·ta \ˈkwes-tə\ *n* [Sp, fr. L *costa* side, rib — more at COAST] **:** a hill or ridge with a steep face on one side and a gentle slope on the other

[1]**cuff** \ˈkəf\ *n* [ME] **1 :** something (as a part of a sleeve or glove) encircling the wrist **2 :** the turned-back hem of a trouser leg **3 :** HANDCUFF — usu. used in pl. **4 :** an inflatable band that is wrapped around an extremity to control the flow of blood through the part when recording blood pressure with a sphygmomanometer — **cuff·less** \-ləs\ *adj* — **off the cuff :** SPONTANEOUS, INFORMAL — **on the cuff :** on credit

[2]**cuff** *vt* **1 :** to furnish with a cuff **2 :** HANDCUFF

[3]**cuff** *vb* [perh. fr. obs. E, glove, fr. ME] *vt* **:** to strike esp. with or as if with the palm of the hand **:** BUFFET ~ *vi* **:** FIGHT, SCUFFLE

[4]**cuff** *n* **:** a blow with the hand esp. when open **:** SLAP

cuff link *n* **:** a usu. ornamental device consisting of two parts joined by a shank, chain, or bar for passing through buttonholes to fasten shirt cuffs — usu. used in pl.

cui bo·no \(ˈ)kwē-ˈbō-(ˌ)nō\ *n* [L, to whose advantage?] **1 :** a principle that probable responsibility for an act or event lies with one having something to gain **2 :** usefulness or utility as a principle in estimating the value of an act or policy

[1]**cui·rass** \kwi-ˈras, kyu̇-\ *n* [ME *curas,* fr. MF *curasse,* fr. LL *coreacea,* fem. of *coreaceus* leathern, fr. L *corium* skin, leather; akin to OE *heortha* deerskin, L *cortex* bark, Gk *keirein* to cut — more at SHEAR] **1 :** a piece of armor covering the body from neck to waist; *also* **:** the breastplate of such a piece **2 :** something (as bony plates covering an animal) resembling a cuirass

[2]**cuirass** *vt* **:** to cover or armor with a cuirass

cui·ras·sier \ˌkwir-ə-ˈsi(ə)r, ˌkyu̇r-\ *n* **:** a mounted soldier wearing a cuirass

cui·sine \kwi-ˈzēn\ *n* [F, lit., kitchen, fr. LL *coquina* — more at KITCHEN] **:** manner of preparing food **:** style of cooking; *also* **:** the food prepared

cuisse \ˈkwis\ *also* **cuish** \ˈkwish\ *n* [ME *cusseis,* pl., fr. MF *cuissaux,* pl. of *cuissel,* fr. *cuisse* thigh, fr. L *coxa* hip — more at COXA] **:** a piece of plate armor for the front of the thigh — see ARMOR illustration

cuit·tle \ˈküt-ᵊl\ *vt* **cuit·tled; cuit·tling** \ˈküt-liŋ, -ᵊl-iŋ\ [origin unknown] *Scot* **:** COAX, WHEEDLE

cuke \ˈkyük\ *n* **:** CUCUMBER

cul–de–sac \ˌkəl-di-ˈsak, ˌku̇l-\ *n, pl* **culs–de–sac** \ˌkəl(z)-, ˌku̇l(z)-\ *also* **cul–de–sacs** \ˌkəl-də-ˈsaks, ˌku̇l-\ [F, lit., bottom of the bag] **1 :** a blind diverticulum or pouch **2 :** a street closed at one end

cu·let \ˈkyü-lət, ˈkəl-ət\ *n* [F, fr. dim. of *cul* backside, fr. L *culus;* akin to OE *hȳdan* to hide] **1 :** the small flat facet at the bottom of a brilliant parallel to the table — see BRILLIANT illustration **2 :** plate armor covering the buttocks

cu·lex \ˈkyü-ˌleks\ *n* [NL, genus name, fr. L, gnat; akin to OIr *cuil* gnat] **:** any of a large cosmopolitan genus (*Culex*) of mosquitoes that includes the common house mosquito (*C. pipiens*) of Europe and No. America — see MOSQUITO illustration — **cu·li·cine** \ˈkyü-lə-ˌsīn\ *adj or n*

cu·li·nary \ˈkəl-ə-ˌner-ē, ˈkyü-lə-\ *adj* [L *culinarius,* fr. *culina* kitchen — more at KILN] **:** of or relating to the kitchen or cookery

[1]**cull** \ˈkəl\ *vt* [ME *cullen,* fr. MF *cuillir,* fr. L *colligere* to bind together — more at COLLECT] **1 :** to select from a group **:** CHOOSE <~*ed* the best passages from the poet's work> **2 :** to identify and remove the culls from — **cull·er** *n*

2cull *n* : something rejected esp. as being inferior or worthless <how to separate good-looking pecans from ~*s* — *Washington Post*>
cul·len·der *var of* COLANDER
cul·let \'kəl-ət\ *n* [perh. fr. F *cueillette* act of gathering, fr. L *collecta,* fr. fem. of *collectus,* pp. of *colligere*] : broken or refuse glass usu. added to new material to facilitate melting in making glass
cul·lion \'kəl-yən\ *n* [ME *coillon* testicle, fr. MF, fr. (assumed) VL *coleon-, coleo,* fr. L *coleus* scrotum] *archaic* : a mean or base fellow
1cul·ly \'kəl-ē\ *n, pl* **cullies** [perh. alter. of *cullion*] : one easily tricked or imposed on : DUPE
2cully *vt* **cul·lied; cul·ly·ing** *archaic* : CHEAT, DECEIVE
1culm \'kəlm\ *n* [ME] **1** : refuse coal screenings : SLACK **2** : a Lower Carboniferous formation in which marine fossil-bearing beds alternate with those containing plant remains
2culm *n* [L *culmus* stalk — more at HAULM] : a monocotyledonous stem
cul·mi·nant \'kəl-mə-nənt\ *adj* **1** : being at greatest altitude or on the meridian **2** : fully developed
cul·mi·nate \'kəl-mə-,nāt\ *vb* **-nat·ed; -nat·ing** [ML *culminatus,* pp. of *culminare,* fr. LL, to crown, fr. L *culmin-, culmen* top — more at HILL] *vi* **1** *of a celestial body* : to reach its highest altitude; *also* : to be directly overhead **2 a** : to rise to or form a summit **b** : to reach the highest or a climactic or decisive point ~ *vt* : to bring to a head or to the highest point
cul·mi·na·tion \,kəl-mə-'nā-shən\ *n* **1** : the action of culminating **2** : culminating position : CLIMAX **syn** see SUMMIT
cu·lotte \'kü-,lät, 'kyü-; k(y)ü-'lät\ *n* [F, breeches, fr. dim. of *cul* backside — more at CULET] : a divided skirt; *also* : a garment having a divided skirt — often used in pl.

culotte

cul·pa·ble \'kəl-pə-bəl\ *adj* [ME *coupable,* fr. MF, fr. L *culpabilis,* fr. *culpare* to blame, fr. *culpa* guilt] **1** *archaic* : GUILTY, CRIMINAL **2** : meriting condemnation or blame esp. as wrong or harmful <~ negligence> **syn** see BLAMEWORTHY — **cul·pa·bil·i·ty** \,kəl-pə-'bil-ət-ē\ *n* — **cul·pa·ble·ness** \'kəl-pə-bəl-nəs\ *n* — **cul·pa·bly** \-blē\ *adv*
cul·prit \'kəl-prət, -,prit\ *n* [AF *cul.* (abbr. of *culpable* guilty) + *prest, prit* ready (i.e. to prove it), fr. L *praestus* — more at PRESTO] **1** : one accused of or charged with a crime **2** : one guilty of a crime or a fault
cult \'kəlt\ *n* [F & L; F *culte,* fr. L *cultus* care, adoration, fr. *cultus,* pp. of *colere* to cultivate — more at WHEEL] **1** : formal religious veneration : WORSHIP **2** : a system of religious beliefs and ritual; *also* : its body of adherents **3** : a religion regarded as unorthodox or spurious; *also* : its body of adherents **4** : a system for the cure of disease based on dogma set forth by its promulgator **5 a** : great devotion to a person, idea, or thing; *esp* : such devotion regarded as a literary or intellectual fad **b** : a usu. small circle of persons united by devotion or allegiance to an artistic or intellectual movement or figure — **cul·tic** \'kəl-tik\ *adj* — **cult·ism** \'kəl-,tiz-əm\ *n* — **cult·ist** \'kəl-təst\ *n*
cultch *or* **culch** \'kəlch\ *n* [perh. fr. a F dial. form of F *couche* couch] **1** : material (as oyster shells) laid down on oyster grounds to furnish points of attachment for the spat **2** *chiefly NewEng* : CLUTTER, TRASH
cul·ti·gen \'kəl-tə-jən\ *n* [*culti*vated + *-gen*] **1** : a cultivated organism (as Indian corn) of a variety or species for which a wild ancestor is unknown **2** : CULTIVAR
cul·ti·va·ble \'kəl-tə-və-bəl\ *adj* : capable of being cultivated — **cul·ti·va·bil·i·ty** \,kəl-tə-və-'bil-ət-ē\ *n*
cul·ti·var \'kəl-tə-,vär, -,ve(ə)r, -,va(ə)r\ *n* [*culti*vated + *var*iety] : an organism of a kind originating and persistent under cultivation
cul·ti·vate \'kəl-tə-,vāt\ *vt* **-vat·ed; -vat·ing** [ML *cultivatus,* pp. of *cultivare,* fr. *cultivus* cultivable, fr. L *cultus,* pp.] **1** : to prepare or prepare and use for the raising of crops; *specif* : to loosen or break up the soil about (growing plants) **2 a** : to foster the growth of <~ vegetables> **b** : CULTURE 2a **c** : to improve by labor, care, or study : REFINE <~ the mind> **3** : FURTHER, ENCOURAGE <~ the arts> **4** : to seek the society of : make friends with — **cul·ti·vat·able** \-,vāt-ə-bəl\ *adj*
cul·ti·vat·ed *adj* : REFINED, EDUCATED <~ speech> <~ tastes>
cul·ti·va·tion \,kəl-tə-'vā-shən\ *n* **1** : the act or art of cultivating; *specif* : TILLAGE **2** : CULTURE, REFINEMENT <a man of charm and ~>
cul·ti·va·tor \'kəl-tə-,vāt-ər\ *n* : one that cultivates; *esp* : an implement to loosen the soil while crops are growing
cul·tur·al \'kəlch(-ə)-rəl\ *adj* **1** : of or relating to culture or culturing **2** : concerned with the fostering of plant or animal growth — **cul·tur·al·ly** \-rə-lē\ *adv*
cultural anthropology *n* : anthropology that deals with the study of culture and that uses the methods, concepts, and data of archaeology, ethnology, and ethnography, folklore and linguistics, and sometimes those of sociology and psychology — compare PHYSICAL ANTHROPOLOGY — **cultural anthropologist** *n*
1cul·ture \'kəl-chər\ *n* [ME, fr. MF, fr. L *cultura,* fr. *cultus,* pp.] **1** : CULTIVATION, TILLAGE **2** : the act of developing the intellectual and moral faculties esp. by education **3** : expert care and training <beauty ~> **4 a** : enlightenment and excellence of taste acquired by intellectual and aesthetic training **b** : acquaintance with and taste in fine arts, humanities, and broad aspects of science as distinguished from vocational and technical skills **5 a** : the integrated pattern of human behavior that includes thought, speech, action, and artifacts and depends upon man's capacity for learning and transmitting knowledge to succeeding generations **b** : the customary beliefs, social forms, and material traits of a racial, religious, or social group **6** : cultivation of living material in prepared nutrient media; *also* : a product of such cultivation
2culture *vt* **cul·tured; cul·tur·ing** \'kəlch-(ə-)riŋ\ **1** : CULTIVATE **2 a** : to grow in a prepared medium **b** : to start a culture from
cul·tured \'kəl-chərd\ *adj* **1** : CULTIVATED **2** : produced under artificial conditions <~ viruses> <~ pearls>
cul·tus \'kəl-təs\ *n* [L, adoration] : CULT
cul·ver \'kəl-vər, 'kul-\ *n* [ME, fr. OE *culfer,* fr. (assumed) VL *columbra,* fr. L *columbula,* dim. of L *columba* dove — more at COLUMBINE] : PIGEON
cul·ver·in \'kəl-və-rən\ *n* [ME, fr. MF *couleuvrine,* fr. *couleuvre* snake, fr. L *colubra*] : an early firearm: **a** : a rude musket **b** : a long cannon (as an 18-pounder) of the 16th and 17th centuries
cul·vert \'kəl-vərt\ *n* [origin unknown] **1** : a transverse drain **2** : a conduit for a culvert **3** : a bridge over a culvert
1cum \(,)kum, (,)kəm\ *prep* [L; akin to L *com-* — more at CO-] : WITH : combined with : along with <served as an office-*cum*-den>
2cum *abbr* cumulative
Cu·ma·na·go·to \(,)kü-,män-ə-'gōt-(,)ō\ *n, pl* **Cumanagoto** *or* **Cumanagotos** [Sp, of AmerInd origin] **1** : a member of a Cariban people of Venezuela **2** : the language of the Cumanagoto people
Cumb *abbr* Cumberland
1cum·ber \'kəm-bər\ *vt* **cum·bered; cum·ber·ing** \-b(ə-)riŋ\ [ME *cumbren*] **1** *archaic* : TROUBLE, HARASS **2 a** : to hinder by being in the way <~*ed* with heavy clothing> **b** : to clutter up <rocks ~*ing* the yard> **c** : to burden needlessly <~ the memory with trival facts>
2cumber *n* : something that cumbers; *esp* : HINDRANCE
cum·ber·some \'kəm-bər-səm\ *adj* **1** *dial* : BURDENSOME, TROUBLESOME **2** : unwieldy because of heaviness and bulk <trying to move a ~ old Victorian sideboard> **3** : slow-moving : PONDEROUS **syn** see HEAVY — **cum·ber·some·ly** *adv* — **cum·ber·some·ness** *n*
cum·brous \'kəm-b(ə-)rəs\ *adj* : CUMBERSOME **syn** see HEAVY — **cum·brous·ly** *adv* — **cum·brous·ness** *n*
cum·in \'kəm-ən\ *n* [ME, fr. OE *cymen;* akin to OHG *kumīn* cumin; both fr. a prehistoric WGmc word borrowed fr. L *cuminum,* fr. Gk *kyminon,* of Sem origin] : a low plant (*Cuminum cyminum*) of the carrot family long cultivated for its aromatic seeds
cum lau·de \kum-'laud-ə, -ē; ,kəm-'lȯd-ē\ *adv or adj* [NL, with praise] : with distinction <graduated *cum laude* > — compare MAGNA CUM LAUDE, SUMMA CUM LAUDE
cum·mer·bund \'kəm-ər-,bənd\ *n* [Hindi *kamarband,* fr. Per, fr. *kamar* waist + *band*] : a broad waistband usu. worn in place of a vest with men's dress clothes and adapted in various styles of women's clothes
cumquat *var of* KUMQUAT
cum·shaw \'kəm-,shȯ\ *n* [Chin (Amoy) *kam sia* grateful thanks (a phrase used by beggars)] : PRESENT, GRATUITY
cumul- *or* **cumuli-** *or* **cumulo-** *comb form* [NL, fr. L *cumulus*] : cumulus and <*cumulo*cirrus>
cu·mu·late \'kyü-myə-,lāt\ *vb* **-lat·ed, -lat·ing** [L *cumulatus,* pp. of *cumulare,* fr. *cumulus* mass] *vt* **1** : to gather or pile in a heap **2** : to combine into one **3** : to build up by addition of new material ~ *vi* : to become massed — **cu·mu·late** \-lət, -,lāt\ *adj* — **cu·mu·la·tion** \,kyü-myə-'lā-shən\ *n*
cu·mu·la·tive \'kyü-myə-lət-iv, -,lāt-\ *adj* **1 a** : made up of accumulated parts **b** : increasing by successive additions **2 a** : tending to prove the same point <~ evidence> **b** : additional rather than repeated <~ legacy> **3 a** : taking effect upon completion of another sentence <~ sentence> **b** : increasing in severity with repetition of the offense <~ penalty> **4** : to be added if not paid when due to the next or a future payment <~ dividends> **5** : formed by the addition of new material of the same kind <~ book index> **6** : summing or integrating over all data or values of a random variable less than or less than and equal to a specified value <~ normal distribution> <~ frequency distribution> — **cu·mu·la·tive·ly** *adv* — **cu·mu·la·tive·ness** *n*
cumulative distribution function *n* : DISTRIBUTION FUNCTION
cumulative voting *n* : a system of voting for corporate directors in which each shareholder is entitled to a number of votes equal to the number of shares he holds multiplied by the number of directors to be elected and has the right to divide his votes among candidates in any way he chooses
cu·mu·lo·cir·rus \,kyü-myə-lō-'sir-əs\ *n* [NL] : a small cumulus cloud at a high altitude having the white delicacy of the cirrus
cu·mu·lo·nim·bus \-'nim-bəs\ *n* [NL] : cumulus cloud often spread out in the shape of an anvil extending to great heights — see CLOUD illustration
cu·mu·lo·stra·tus \-'strāt-əs, -'strat-\ *n* [NL] : a cumulus whose base extends horizontally as a stratus cloud
cu·mu·lous \'kyü-myə-ləs\ *adj* : resembling cumulus
cu·mu·lus \-ləs\ *n, pl* **-li** \-,lī, -,lē\ [L] **1** : HEAP, ACCUMULATION **2** [NL, fr. L] : a massy cloud form having a flat base and rounded outlines often piled up like a mountain — see CLOUD illustration
cunc·ta·tion \,kəŋ(k)-'tā-shən\ *n* [L *cunctation-, cunctatio,* fr. *cunctatus,* pp. of *cunctari* to hesitate; akin to Skt *śaṅkate* he wavers] : DELAY, PROCRASTINATION — **cunc·ta·tive** \'keŋ(k)-,tāt-iv, -tət-\ *adj*
cu·ne·ate \'kyü-nē-,āt, -ət\ *adj* [L *cuneatus,* fr. *cuneus* wedge; akin to Skt *śūla* spear] : narrowly triangular with the acute angle toward the base <a ~ leaf> — **cu·ne·ate·ly** *adv*

ə abut	ᵊ kitten	ər further	a back	ā bake	ä cot, cart
aù out	ch chin	e less	ē easy	g gift	i trip	ī life
j joke	ŋ sing	ō flow	ȯ flaw	ȯi coin	th thin	th this
ü loot	ù foot	y yet	yü few	yù furious	zh vision

[1]cu·ne·i·form \kyu̇-ˈnē-ə-ˌfȯrm, ˈkyü-n(ē-)ə-\ *adj* [prob. fr. F *cunéiforme,* fr. MF, fr. L *cuneus* + MF *-iforme* -iform] **1** : having the shape of a wedge **2** : composed of or written in wedge-shaped characters <~ alphabet>

[2]cuneiform *n* **1** : cuneiform writing **2** : a cuneiform part; *specif* : a cuneiform bone or cartilage

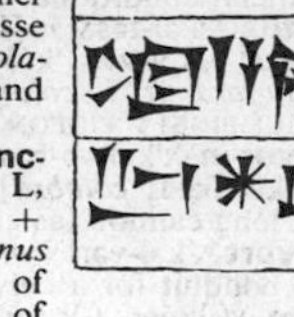

cuneiform 1

cun·ner \ˈkən-ər\ *n* [origin unknown] : either of two wrasses: **a** : an English wrasse (*Crenilabrus melops*) **b** : a wrasse (*Tautogolabrus adspersus*) abundant on the New England shore

cun·ni·lin·gus \ˌkən-i-ˈliŋ-gəs\ *or* **cun·ni·linc·tus** \-ˈliŋ(k)-təs\ *n* [*cunnilingus,* NL, fr. L, one who licks the vulva, fr. *cunnus* vulva + *lingere* to lick; *cunnilinctus,* NL, fr. L *cunnus* + *linctus,* act of licking, fr. *linctus,* pp. of *lingere* — more at LICK] : oral stimulation of the vulva or clitoris

[1]cun·ning \ˈkən-iŋ\ *adj* [ME, fr. prp. of *can* know] **1** : dexterous or crafty in the use of special resources (as skill or knowledge) or in attaining an end <a ~ plotter> **2** : characterized by wiliness and trickery <~ schemes> **3** : prettily appealing : CUTE ***syn* 1** see CLEVER **2** see SLY ***ant*** ingenious — **cun·ning·ly** \-iŋ-lē\ *adv* — **cun·ning·ness** *n*

[2]cunning *n* **1** *obs* **a** : KNOWLEDGE, LEARNING **b** : magic art **2** : dexterous skill and subtlety (as in inventing, devising, or executing) <high-ribbed vault . . . with perfect ~ framed — William Wordsworth> **3** : CRAFT, SLYNESS ***syn*** see ART

cunt \ˈkənt\ *n* [ME *cunte;* akin to MLG *kunte* female pudenda, MHG *kotze* prostitute] : the female pudenda; *also* : COITUS — usu. considered obscene

[1]cup \ˈkəp\ *n* [ME *cuppe,* fr. OE; akin to OHG *kopf* cup; both fr. a prehistoric WGmc word borrowed fr. LL *cuppa* cup, alter. of L *cupa* tub; akin to OE *hȳf* hive] **1** : an open bowl-shaped drinking vessel **2 a** : a drinking vessel and its contents **b** : the consecrated wine of the Communion **3** : something that falls to one's lot **4** : an ornamental cup offered as a prize (as in a championship) **5 a** : something resembling a cup **b** : a cup-shaped plant organ **c** : an athletic supporter reinforced usu. with plastic to provide extra protection to the wearer **d** : either of two parts of a brassiere that are shaped like and fit over the breasts **e** : the metal case inside a hole in golf; *also* : the hole itself **6** : a usu. iced beverage resembling punch but served from a pitcher rather than a bowl **7** : CUPFUL **8** : a food served in a cup-shaped usu. footed vessel <fruit ~> **9** : the symbol ∪ indicating the union of two sets — **cup·like** \-ˌlīk\ *adj* — **in one's cups** : DRUNK

[2]cup *vt* **cupped; cup·ping 1** : to treat by cupping **2 a** : to curve into the shape of a cup <*cupped* his hands around his mouth> **b** : to place in a cup

cup·bear·er \ˈkəp-ˌbar-ər, -ˌber-\ *n* : one who has the duty of filling and handing around the cups in which wine is served

cup·board \ˈkəb-ərd\ *n* : a closet with shelves where dishes, utensils, or food is kept; *also* : a small closet

cup·cake \ˈkəp-ˌkāk\ *n* : a small cake baked in a cuplike mold

[1]cu·pel \kyü-ˈpel, ˈkyü-pəl\ *n* [F *coupelle,* dim. of *coupe* cup, fr. LL *cuppa*] : a small shallow porous cup esp. of bone ash used in assaying to separate precious metals from lead

[2]cupel *vt* **-pelled** *or* **-peled; -pel·ling** *or* **-pel·ing** : to refine by means of a cupel — **cu·pel·ler** *n*

cu·pel·la·tion \ˌkyü-pə-ˈlā-shən, -ˌpe-\ *n* : refinement (as of gold or silver) in a cupel by exposure to high temperature in a blast of air by which the lead, copper, tin, and other unwanted metals are oxidized and partly sink into the porous cupel

cup·ful \ˈkəp-ˌfu̇l\ *n, pl* **cup·fuls** \-ˌfu̇lz\ *also* **cups·ful** \ˈkəps-ˌfu̇l\ **1** : as much as a cup will hold **2** : a half pint : eight ounces

cup fungus *n* : any of an order (Pezizales) of epigeal mostly saprophytic fungi with a fleshy or horny apothecium that is often colored and is typically shaped like a cup, saucer, or disk

Cu·pid \ˈkyü-pəd\ *n* [L *Cupido*] **1** : the Roman god of erotic love — compare EROS **2** *not cap* : a naked usu. winged infantile figure representing Cupid and often holding a bow and arrow

cu·pid·i·ty \kyu̇-ˈpid-ət-ē\ *n, pl* **-ties** [ME *cupidite,* fr. MF *cupidité,* fr. L *cupiditat-, cupiditas* — more at COVET] **1** : strong desire : LUST **2** : inordinate desire for wealth : AVARICE, GREED

Cupid's bow *n* : a bow with two convex curves joined by the handle

Cupid's bow

cup of tea 1 : something one likes or excels in <as for me, I see already that storytelling isn't my *cup of tea* — John Barth> **2** : a thing to be reckoned with : MATTER <poltergeists are a different *cup of tea* — D. B. W. Lewis>

cu·po·la \ˈkyü-pə-lə, -ˌlō\ *n* [It, fr. L *cupula,* dim. of *cupa* tub] **1 a** : a rounded vault resting on a circular or other base and forming a roof or a ceiling **b** : a small structure built on top of a roof **2** : a vertical cylindrical furnace for melting iron in the foundry that has tuyeres and tapping spouts near the bottom

cup·pa \ˈkəp-ə\ *n* [short for *cuppa tea,* pronunciation spelling of *cup of tea*] *chiefly Brit* : a cup of tea

cup·ping *n* : an operation of drawing blood to the surface of the body by use of a glass vessel evacuated by heat

cup·py \ˈkəp-ē\ *adj* **cup·pi·er; -est 1** : resembling a cup **2** : full of small depressions <a ~ racetrack>

cupr- *or* **cupri-** *or* **cupro-** *comb form* [LL *cuprum* — more at COPPER] **1** : copper <*cupri*ferous> **2** : copper and <*cupro*nickel>

cu·pram·mo·nium rayon \ˌk(y)u̇-prə-ˈmō-nē-əm-, -nyəm-\ *n* : a rayon made from cellulose dissolved in an ammoniacal copper solution

cu·pre·ous \ˈk(y)ü-prē-əs\ *adj* [LL *cupreus,* fr. *cuprum*] : containing or resembling copper : COPPERY

cu·pric \-prik\ *adj* : of, relating to, or containing copper with a valence of two

cu·prif·er·ous \k(y)ü-ˈprif-(ə-)rəs\ *adj* : containing copper

cu·prite \ˈk(y)ü-ˌprīt\ *n* [G *kuprit,* fr. LL *cuprum*] : a mineral Cu_2O consisting of copper oxide and constituting an ore of copper

cu·pro·nick·el \ˌk(y)ü-prō-ˈnik-əl\ *n* : an alloy of copper and nickel; *esp* : one containing about 70 percent copper and 30 percent nickel

cu·prous \ˈk(y)ü-prəs\ *adj* : of, relating to, or containing copper with a valence of one

cu·pu·late \ˈkyü-pyə-ˌlāt, -lət\ *also* **cu·pu·lar** \-lər\ *adj* : shaped like, having, or bearing a cupule

cu·pule \ˈkyü-(ˌ)pyü(ə)l\ *n* [NL *cupula,* fr. LL, dim. of L *cupa* tub — more at CUP] : a cup-shaped anatomical structure: as **a** : an involucre characteristic of the oak in which the bracts are indurated and coherent **b** : an outer integument partially enclosing the seed of some seed ferns

[1]cur \ˈkər\ *n* [ME, short for *curdogge,* fr. (assumed) ME *curren* to growl + ME *dogge* dog; akin to OE *cran* crane] **1** : a mongrel or inferior dog **2** : a surly or cowardly fellow

[2]cur *abbr* **1** currency **2** current

cur·able \ˈkyu̇r-ə-bəl\ *adj* : capable of being cured — **cur·abil·i·ty** \ˌkyu̇r-ə-ˈbil-ət-ē\ *n* — **cur·able·ness** \ˈkyu̇r-ə-bəl-nəs\ *n* — **cur·ably** \-blē\ *adv*

cu·ra·çao \ˈk(y)u̇r-ə-ˌsō, -ˌsau̇, ˌk(y)u̇r-ə-ˈ\ *also* **cu·ra·çoa** *same, or* ˌk(y)u̇r-ə-ˈsō-ə\ *n* [D *curaçao,* fr. *Curaçao,* Netherlands Antilles] : a liqueur flavored with the dried peel of the sour orange

cu·ra·cy \ˈkyu̇r-ə-sē\ *n, pl* **-cies** : the office or term of office of a curate

cu·ra·re *or* **cu·ra·ri** \k(y)u̇-ˈrär-ē\ *n* [Pg & Sp *curare,* fr. Carib *kurari*] : a dried aqueous extract esp. of a vine (as *Strychnos toxifera* of the family Loganiaceae or *Chondodendron tomentosum* of the family Menispermaceae) used in arrow poisons by So. American Indians and in medicine to produce muscular relaxation

cu·ra·rine \-ˈrär-ən, -ˌēn\ *n* : any of several alkaloids from curare

cu·ra·rize \-ˈrär-ˌīz\ *vt* **-rized; -riz·ing** : to treat with curare — **cu·ra·ri·za·tion** \-ˌrär-ə-ˈzā-shən\ *n*

cu·ras·sow \ˈk(y)u̇r-ə-ˌsō\ *n* [alter. of *Curaçao*] : any of several large arboreal game birds (esp. genus *Crax*) of So. and Central America related to the domestic fowls

cu·rate \ˈkyu̇r-ət *also* ˈkyu̇(ə)r-ˌāt\ *n* [ME, fr. ML *curatus,* fr. *cura* cure of souls, fr. L, care] **1** : a clergyman in charge of a parish **2** : a clergyman serving as assistant (as to a rector) in a parish

cu·ra·tive \ˈkyu̇r-ət-iv\ *adj* : relating to or used in the cure of diseases — **curative** *n* — **cu·ra·tive·ly** *adv*

cu·ra·tor \kyu̇-ˈrāt-ər, ˈkyu̇r-ət-\ *n* [L, fr. *curatus,* pp. of *curare* to care, fr. *cura* care] : one that has the care and superintendence of something; *esp* : one in charge of a museum, zoo, or other place of exhibit — **cu·ra·to·ri·al** \ˌkyu̇r-ə-ˈtōr-ē-əl, -ˈtȯr-\ *adj* — **cu·ra·tor·ship** \kyu̇-ˈrāt-ər-ˌship, ˈkyu̇r-ət-\ *n*

[1]curb \ˈkərb\ *n* [MF *courbe* curve, curved piece of wood or iron, fr. *courbe* curved, fr. L *curvus*] **1** : a chain or strap on the upper part of the branches of a bit used to restrain a horse — see BIT illustration **2** : an enclosing frame, border, or edging **3** : CHECK, RESTRAINT <a price ~> **4** : a raised edge or margin to strengthen or confine **5** : an edging (as of concrete) built along a street to form part of a gutter **6** [fr. the fact that it orig. transacted its business on the street] : a market for trading in securities not listed on a stock exchange

[2]curb *vt* **1** : to furnish with a curb **2** : to check or control with or as if with a curb <trying to ~ her curiosity> **3** : to lead (a dog) to a suitable place (as a gutter) for defecation ***syn*** see RESTRAIN ***ant*** spur

curb·ing \ˈkər-biŋ\ *n* **1** : the material for a curb **2** : CURB

curb roof *n* : a roof with a ridge at the center and a double slope on each of its two sides

curb service *n* : service extended (as by a restaurant) to persons sitting in parked automobiles

[1]curb·stone \ˈkərb-ˌstōn\ *n* : a stone or edging of concrete forming a curb

[2]curbstone *adj* **1** : operating on the street without maintaining an office <a ~ broker> **2** : not having the benefit of training or experience <a ~ critic>

curch \ˈkərch\ *n* [ME] *Scot* : KERCHIEF 1

cur·cu·lio \(ˌ)kər-ˈkyü-lē-ˌō\ *n, pl* **-li·os** [L, grain weevil] : any of various weevils; *esp* : one that injures fruit

cur·cu·ma \ˈkər-kyə-mə\ *n* [NL, genus name, fr. Ar *kurkum* saffron] : any of a genus (*Curcuma*) of Old World tropical herbs (as the turmeric) of the ginger family with tuberous roots

[1]curd \ˈkərd\ *n* [ME] **1** : the thick casein-rich part of coagulated milk **2** : something suggesting the curd of milk — **curdy** \-ē\ *adj*

[2]curd *vb* : COAGULATE, CURDLE

cur·dle \ˈkərd-ᵊl\ *vb* **cur·dled; cur·dling** \ˈkərd-liŋ, -ᵊl-iŋ\ [freq. of [2]*curd*] *vt* **1** : to cause curds to form in **2** : SPOIL, SOUR ~ *vi* **1** : to form curds : COAGULATE **2** : to go bad or wrong : SPOIL

[1]cure \ˈkyu̇(ə)r\ *n* [ME, fr. OF, fr. ML & L; ML *cura,* cure of souls, fr. L, care] **1 a** : spiritual charge : CARE **b** : pastoral charge of a parish **2 a** : recovery or relief from a disease **b** : something (as a drug or treatment) that cures a disease **c** : a course or period of treatment <take the ~ for alcoholism> **d** : SPA **3** : something that corrects, heals, or permanently alleviates a harmful or troublesome situation <more money is not a certain ~ for the problem> **4** : a process or method of curing — **cure·less** \-ləs\ *adj*

[2]cure *vb* **cured; cur·ing** *vt* **1 a** : to restore to health, soundness, or normality **b** : to bring about recovery from **2 a** : to deal with in a way that eliminates or rectifies <nothing would ~ the unpleasant odor> **b** : to free from something objectionable or harmful **3** : to prepare by chemical or physical processing for keeping or use ~ *vi* **1** : to undergo a curing process **2** : to effect a cure — **cur·er** *n*

syn CURE, HEAL, REMEDY *shared meaning element* : to rectify an unhealthy or undesirable condition

cu·ré \kyu̇-ˈrā, ˈkyu̇(ə)r-ˌā\ *n* [OF, fr. ML *curatus* — more at CURATE] : a parish priest

cure–all \ˈkyu̇(ə)r-ˌȯl\ *n* : a remedy for all ills : PANACEA

cu·ret·tage \ˌkyu̇r-ə-ˈtäzh\ *n* **:** a surgical scraping or cleaning by means of a curette

¹cu·rette *or* **cu·ret** \kyu̇-ˈret\ *n* [F *curette*, fr. *curer* to cure, fr. L *curare*, fr. *cura*] **:** a scoop, loop, or ring used in performing curettage

²curette *or* **curet** *vt* **cu·rett·ed; cu·rett·ing :** to perform curettage on — **cu·rette·ment** \kyu̇-ˈret-mənt\ *n*

cur·few \ˈkər-(ˌ)fyü\ *n* [ME, fr. MF *covrefeu*, signal given to bank the hearth fire, curfew, fr. *covrir* to cover + *feu* fire, fr. L *focus* hearth] **1 :** a regulation enjoining the withdrawal of usu. specified persons (as juveniles or military personnel) from the streets or the closing of business establishments or places of assembly at a stated hour **2 a :** the sounding of a bell or other signal to announce the beginning of a time of curfew **b :** the signal used **3 a :** the hour at which a curfew becomes effective **b :** the period during which a curfew is in effect

cu·ria \ˈk(y)u̇r-ē-ə\ *n, pl* **cu·ri·ae** \ˈkyu̇r-ē-ˌē, ˈku̇r-ē-ˌī\ [L, fr. *co-* + *vir* man — more at VIRILE] **1 a :** a division of the ancient Roman people comprising several gentes of a tribe **b :** the place of assembly of one of these divisions **2 a :** the court of a medieval king **b :** a court of justice **3** *often cap* **:** the body of congregations, tribunals, and offices through which the pope governs the Roman Catholic Church — **cu·ri·al** \ˈkyu̇r-ē-əl\ *adj*

cu·rie \ˈkyu̇(ə)r-(ˌ)ē, kyu̇-ˈrē\ *n* [Mme. Marie *Curie*] **1 :** a unit quantity of any radioactive nuclide in which 3.7×10^{10} disintegrations occur per second **2 :** a unit of radioactivity equal to 3.7×10^{10} disintegrations per second

Curie point *n* [Pierre *Curie*] **1 :** the temperature at which there is a transition between the ferromagnetic and paramagnetic phases **2 :** a temperature at which the anomalies that characterize a ferroelectric substance disappear — called also *Curie temperature*

cu·rio \ˈkyu̇r-ē-ˌō\ *n, pl* **cu·ri·os** [short for *curiosity*] **:** something considered novel, rare, or bizarre **:** CURIOSITY

cu·ri·o·sa \ˌkyu̇r-ē-ˈō-sə, -ˈō-zə\ *n pl* [NL, fr. L, neut. pl. of *curiosus*] **:** CURIOSITIES, RARITIES; *esp* **:** strange or unusual books

cu·ri·os·i·ty \ˌkyu̇r-ē-ˈäs-ət-ē, -ˈäs-tē\ *n, pl* **-ties 1 :** desire to know: **a :** inquisitive interest in others' concerns **:** NOSINESS **b :** interest leading to inquiry <intellectual ~> **2** *archaic* **:** undue nicety or fastidiousness **3 a :** one that arouses interest esp. for uncommon or exotic characteristics **b :** an unusual knickknack **:** CURIO **c :** a curious trait or aspect

cu·ri·ous \ˈkyu̇r-ē-əs\ *adj* [ME, fr. MF *curios*, fr. L *curiosus* careful, inquisitive, fr. *cura* cure] **1 a** *archaic* **:** made carefully **b** *obs* **:** ABSTRUSE **c** *archaic* **:** precisely accurate **2 a :** marked by desire to investigate and learn **b :** marked by inquisitive interest in others' concerns **:** NOSY **3 :** exciting attention as strange or novel **:** ODD — **cu·ri·ous·ly** *adv* — **cu·ri·ous·ness** *n*

syn CURIOUS, INQUISITIVE, PRYING *shared meaning element* **:** interested in what is not one's personal or proper concern. CURIOUS, the most general and the only neutral one of these words, basically implies a lively desire to learn or to know <children are *curious* about everything> <*curious* onlookers got in the way of the firemen> INQUISITIVE applies to impertinent and habitual curiosity and usually suggests quizzing and peering after information <*inquisitive* old women watching from behind drawn curtains> PRYING adds to *inquisitive* the implication of busy meddling and officiousness <I will not bare my soul to their shallow *prying* eyes — Oscar Wilde> ***ant*** incurious, uninterested

cu·rite \ˈkyu̇(ə)r-ˌīt\ *n* [F, fr. Pierre *Curie*] **:** a radioactive mineral $2PbO.5UO_3.4H_2O$ found in orange acicular crystals

cu·ri·um \ˈkyu̇r-ē-əm\ *n* [NL, fr. Marie & Pierre *Curie*] **:** a metallic radioactive trivalent element artificially produced — see ELEMENT table

¹curl \ˈkər(-ə)l\ *vb* [ME *curlen*, fr. *crul* curly, prob. fr. MD; akin to OHG *krol* curly, OE *cradol* cradle] *vt* **1 :** to form into coils or ringlets <~ one's hair> **2 :** to form into a curved shape **:** TWIST <~*ed* his lip in a sneer> **3 :** to furnish with curls ~ *vi* **1 a :** to grow in coils or spirals **b :** to form ripples or crinkles <bacon ~*ing* in a pan> **2 :** to move or progress in curves or spirals **:** WIND <the path ~*ed* along the mountainside> **3 :** TWIST, CONTORT **4 :** to play the game of curling

²curl *n* **1 :** a lock of hair that coils **:** RINGLET **2 :** something having a spiral or winding form **:** COIL **3 :** the action of curling **:** the state of being curled **4 :** an abnormal rolling or curling of leaves **5 :** a curved or spiral marking in the grain of wood **6 :** TENDRIL **7 :** a hollow arch of water formed when the crest of a breaking wave spills forward

curl·er \ˈkər-lər\ *n* **1 :** one that curls; *esp* **:** a device on which hair is wound for curling **2 :** a player of curling

cur·lew \ˈkərl-(ˌ)(y)ü\ *n, pl* **curlews** *or* **curlew** [ME, fr. MF *corlieu*, of imit. origin] **:** any of various largely brownish chiefly migratory birds (esp. genus *Numenius*) related to the woodcocks but distinguished by long legs and a long slender down-curved bill

curlew

¹curli·cue *also* **curly·cue** \ˈkər-li-ˌkyü\ *n* [*curly* + *cue* (a braid of hair)] **:** a fancifully curved or spiral figure (as a flourish in handwriting)

²curlicue *vb* **-cued; -cu·ing** *vi* **:** to form curlicues ~ *vt* **:** to decorate with curlicues

curl·ing \ˈkər-liŋ\ *n* **:** a game in which two teams of four men each slide curling stones over a stretch of ice toward a target circle

curling iron *n* **:** a rod-shaped usu. metal instrument which is heated and around which a lock of hair to be curled or waved is wound

curling stone *n* **:** an ellipsoid stone or occas. piece of iron with a gooseneck handle used in the game of curling

curl·pa·per \ˈkər(-ə)l-ˌpā-pər\ *n* **:** a strip or piece of paper around which a lock of hair is wound for curling

curly \ˈkər-lē\ *adj* **curl·i·er; -est 1 :** tending to curl; *also* **:** having curls **2 :** having the grain composed of fibers that undulate without crossing and that often form alternating light and dark lines <~ maple> — **curl·i·ness** *n*

curly–coat·ed retriever \ˌkər-lē-ˌkōt-əd-\ *n* **:** any of a breed of sporting dogs with a short curly coat

curly top *n* **:** a destructive virus disease esp. of beets that kills young plants and causes curling and puckering of the leaves in older plants

cur·mud·geon \(ˌ)kər-ˈməj-ən\ *n* [origin unknown] **1** *archaic* **:** MISER **2 :** a crusty, ill-tempered, and usu. old man — **cur·mud·geon·ly** *adj*

curn \ˈkərn\ *or* **cur·ran** \ˈkə-rən\ *n* [ME *curn*; akin to ME *corn*] **1** *Scot* **:** GRAIN **2** *Scot* **:** a small number **:** FEW

curr \ˈkər\ *vi* [imit.] **:** to make a murmuring sound (as of doves)

cur·ragh *or* **cur·rach** \ˈkə-rə(k)\ *n* [ScGael *curach* & IrGael *currach*; akin to MIr *curach* coracle] **1** *Irish* **:** marshy wasteland **2** *Irish & Scot* **:** CORACLE

cur·rant \ˈkər-ənt, ˈkə-rənt\ *n* [ME *raison of Coraunte*, lit., raisin of Corinth] **1 :** a small seedless raisin grown chiefly in the Levant **2 :** the acid edible fruit of several shrubs (genus *Ribes*) of the saxifrage family; *also* **:** a plant bearing currants

cur·ren·cy \ˈkər-ən-sē, ˈkə-rən-\ *n, pl* **-cies 1 a :** circulation as a medium of exchange **b :** general use, acceptance, or prevalence **2 a :** something (as coins, government notes, and bank notes) that is in circulation as a medium of exchange **b :** paper money in circulation **c :** a common article for bartering

¹cur·rent \ˈkər-ənt, ˈkə-rənt\ *adj* [ME *curraunt*, fr. OF *curant*, prp. of *courre* to run, fr. L *currere* — more at CAR] **1 a** *archaic* **:** RUNNING, FLOWING **b (1) :** presently elapsing **(2) :** occurring in or belonging to the present time **(3) :** most recent <~ issue> **2 :** used as a medium of exchange **3 :** generally accepted, used, practiced, or prevalent at the moment ***syn*** see PREVAILING — **cur·rent·ly** *adv* — **cur·rent·ness** *n*

²current *n* **1 a :** the part of a fluid body moving continuously in a certain direction **b :** the swiftest part of a stream **c :** a tidal or nontidal movement of lake or ocean water **d :** flow marked by force or strength **2 :** a tendency or course of events that is usu. the resultant of an interplay of forces <~*s* of public opinion that alter with the economic situation> <an increasing ~ of radicalism> **3 :** a flow of electric charge; *also* **:** the rate of such flow ***syn*** see TENDENCY

current assets *n pl* **:** assets of a short-term nature

cur·ri·cle \ˈkər-i-kəl, ˈkə-ri-\ *n* [L *curriculum* running, chariot] **:** a 2-wheeled chaise usu. drawn by two horses

cur·ric·u·lar \kə-ˈrik-yə-lər\ *adj* **:** of or relating to a curriculum

cur·ric·u·lum \-ləm\ *n, pl* **-la** \-lə\ *also* **-lums** [NL, fr. L, running, fr. *currere*] **1 :** the courses offered by an educational institution or one of its branches **2 :** a set of courses constituting an area of specialization

cur·ric·u·lum vi·tae \kə-ˌrik-ə-ləm-ˈwē-ˌtī, -yə-ləm-ˈvīt-ē\ *n, pl* **cur·ric·u·la vitae** \-lə-\ [L, course of (one's) life] **:** a short account of one's career and qualifications prepared typically by an applicant for a position

cur·ri·ery \ˈkər-ē-ə-rē, ˈkə-rē-\ *n, pl* **-er·ies 1 :** the trade of a currier of leather **2 :** a place where currying is done

cur·rish \ˈkər-ish\ *adj* **1 :** resembling a cur **:** MONGREL **2 :** IGNOBLE — **cur·rish·ly** *adv*

¹cur·ry \ˈkər-ē, ˈkə-rē\ *vt* **cur·ried; cur·ry·ing** [ME *curraye*n, fr. OF *correer* to prepare, curry, fr. (assumed) VL *conredare*, fr. L *com-* + a base of Gmc origin; akin to Goth *garaiths* arrayed — more at READY] **1 :** to dress the coat of (as a horse) with a currycomb **2 :** to treat (tanned leather) esp. by incorporating oil or grease **3 :** BEAT, THRASH — **cur·ri·er** *n* — **curry fa·vor** \-ˈfā-vər\ [ME *currayen favel* to curry a chestnut horse] **:** to seek to gain favor by flattery or attention

²cur·ry *also* **cur·rie** \ˈkər-ē, ˈkə-rē\ *n, pl* **curries** [Tamil-Malayalam *kari*] **1 :** CURRY POWDER **2 :** a food or dish seasoned with curry powder <shrimp ~>

³curry *vt* **cur·ried; cur·ry·ing :** to flavor or cook with curry powder

cur·ry·comb \-ˌkōm\ *n* **:** a comb made of rows of metallic teeth or serrated ridges and used esp. to curry horses — **currycomb** *vt*

curry powder *n* **:** a condiment consisting of several pungent ground spices (as cayenne pepper, fenugreek, and turmeric)

¹curse \ˈkərs\ *n* [ME *curs*, fr. OE] **1 :** a prayer or invocation for harm or injury to come upon one **:** IMPRECATION **2 :** something that is cursed or accursed **3 :** evil or misfortune that comes as if in response to imprecation or as retribution **4 :** a cause of great harm or misfortune **:** TORMENT **5 :** MENSTRUATION — used with *the*

²curse *vb* **cursed; curs·ing** *vt* **1 a :** to call upon divine or supernatural power to send injury upon **b :** to execrate in fervent and often profane terms **2 :** to use profanely insolent language against **:** BLASPHEME **3 :** to bring great evil upon **:** AFFLICT ~ *vi* **:** to utter imprecations **:** SWEAR ***syn*** see EXECRATE ***ant*** bless

cursed \ˈkər-səd, ˈkərst\ *also* **curst** \ˈkərst\ *adj* **:** being under or deserving a curse — **cursed·ly** *adv* — **cursed·ness** *n*

¹cur·sive \ˈkər-siv\ *adj* [F or ML; F *cursif*, fr. ML *cursivus*, lit., running, fr. L *cursus*, pp. of *currere* to run] **:** RUNNING, COURSING: as **a** *of writing* **:** flowing often with the strokes of successive characters joined and the angles rounded **b :** having a flowing, easy, impromptu character — **cur·sive·ly** *adv* — **cur·sive·ness** *n*

²cursive *n* **1 :** a manuscript written in cursive writing **2 :** a style of printed letter resembling handwriting

cur·so·ri·al \ˌkər-ˈsōr-ē-əl, -ˈsȯr-\ *adj* **:** adapted to running

cur·so·ry \ˈkərs-(-ə)-rē\ *adj* [LL *cursorius* of running, fr. L *cursus* running, fr. *cursus*, pp.] **:** rapidly and often superficially performed

: HASTY <a ~ glance> ***syn*** see SUPERFICIAL ***ant*** painstaking — **cur·so·ri·ly** \-rə-lē\ *adv* — **cur·so·ri·ness** \-rē-nəs\ *n*

curt \ˈkərt\ *adj* [L *curtus* shortened — more at SHEAR] **1 a :** a sparing of words : TERSE **b :** marked by rude or peremptory shortness : BRUSQUE **2 :** shortened in linear dimension ***syn*** see BLUFF ***ant*** voluble — **curt·ly** *adv* — **curt·ness** *n*

cur·tail \(ˌ)kər-ˈtā(ə)l\ *vt* [alter. of *curtal* to make a curtal of, fr. *curtal,* n.] **:** to make less by or as if by cutting off or away some part <~ the power of the executive branch> <~ inflation> ***syn*** see SHORTEN ***ant*** prolong, enlarge — **cur·tail·er** \-ˈtā-lər\ *n*

cur·tail·ment \-ˈtā(ə)l-mənt\ *n* **:** the act of curtailing **:** the state of being curtailed

[1]**cur·tain** \ˈkərt-ᵊn\ *n* [ME *curtine,* fr. OF, fr. LL *cortina,* fr. L *cohort-, cohors* enclosure, court — more at COURT] **1 :** a hanging screen usu. capable of being drawn back or up; *esp* **:** window drapery **2 :** a device or agency that conceals or acts as a barrier — compare IRON CURTAIN **3 a :** the part of a bastioned front that connects two neighboring bastions **b** (1) **:** a similar stretch of plain wall (2) **:** a nonbearing exterior wall **4 a :** the movable screen separating the stage from the auditorium of a theater **b :** the ascent or opening (as at the beginning of a play) of a stage curtain; *also* **:** its descent or closing (as at the end of an act) **c :** the final situation, line, or scene of an act or play **d :** the time at which a theatrical performance begins **e** *pl* **:** END; *esp* **:** DEATH <it was ~*s* for him when his treason was discovered>

[2]**curtain** *vt* **cur·tained; cur·tain·ing** \ˈkərt-niŋ, -ᵊn-iŋ\ **1 :** to furnish with or as if with curtains **2 :** to veil or shut off with or as if with a curtain

curtain call *n* **:** an appearance by a performer (as after the final curtain of a play) in response to the applause of the audience

curtain lecture *n* [fr. its orig. being given behind the curtains of a bed] **:** a private lecture by a wife to her husband

curtain raiser *n* **1 :** a short play usu. of one scene that is presented before the main full-length drama **2 :** a usu. short preliminary to a main event

[1]**cur·tal** \ˈkərt-ᵊl\ *n, obs* **:** an animal with a docked tail

[2]**curtal** *adj* [MF *courtault,* fr. *court* short, fr. L *curtus*] **1** *obs* **:** having a docked tail **2** *obs* **:** BRIEF, CURTAILED **3** *archaic* **:** wearing a short frock

cur·tal ax *or* **cur·tle ax** \ˈkərt-ᵊl-\ *n* [modif. of MF *coutelas*] **:** CUTLASS

cur·te·sy \ˈkərt-ə-sē\ *n, pl* **-sies** [ME *corteisie* courtesy] **:** the future potential interest that a husband has in the real property of his wife arising upon the birth to them of a child alive and capable for at least an instant of inheriting from her — compare DOWER

cur·ti·lage \ˈkərt-ᵊl-ij\ *n* [ME, fr. OF *cortillage,* fr. *cortil* courtyard, fr. *cort* court] **:** a piece of ground (as a yard or courtyard) within the fence surrounding a house

[1]**curt·sy** *or* **curt·sey** \ˈkərt-sē\ *n, pl* **curtsies** *or* **curtseys** [alter. of *courtesy*] **:** an act of civility, respect, or reverence made mainly by women and consisting of a slight lowering of the body with bending of the knees

[2]**curtsy** *or* **curtsey** *vi* **curt·sied** *or* **curt·seyed; curt·sy·ing** *or* **curt·sey·ing :** to make a curtsy

cu·rule \ˈkyů(ə)r-ˌül\ *adj* [L *curulis* alter. of *currulis* of a chariot, fr. *currus* chariot, fr. *currere* to run] **1 :** of or relating to a seat reserved in ancient Rome for the use of the highest dignitaries and usu. made like a campstool with curved legs **2 :** privileged to sit in a curule chair

cur·va·ceous *also* **cur·va·cious** \ˌkər-ˈvā-shəs\ *adj* **:** having a well-proportioned feminine figure marked by pronounced curves

cur·va·ture \ˈkər-və-ˌchů(ə)r, -chər, -ˌt(y)ů(ə)r\ *n* **1 :** the act of curving **:** the state of being curved **2 :** a measure or amount of curving; *specif* **:** the rate of change of the angle through which the tangent to a curve turns in moving along the curve and which for a circle is equal to the reciprocal of the radius **3 a :** an abnormal curving (as of the spine) **b :** a curved surface of an organ

[1]**curve** \ˈkərv\ *adj* [L *curvus* curved] *archaic* **:** bent or formed into a curve

[2]**curve** *vb* **curved; curv·ing** [L *curvare,* fr. *curvus*] *vi* **:** to have or take a turn, change, or deviation from a straight line without sharp breaks or angularity ~ *vt* **1 :** to cause to curve **2 :** to throw a curveball to (a batter) **3 :** to grade (as an examination) on a curve ***syn*** CURVE, BEND, TURN, TWIST *shared meaning element* **:** to swerve or cause to swerve from a straight line or course

[3]**curve** *n* **1 :** a curving line or surface **:** BEND **2 :** something curved: as **a :** a curving line of the human body **b** *pl* **:** PARENTHESIS **3 a :** CURVEBALL **b :** TRICK, DECEPTION **4 :** a graphical representation of a variable (as one measuring development of progress) affected by conditions **5 a :** a line that may be precisely defined by an equation in such a way that the coordinates of its points are functions of a single independent variable or parameter **b** (1) **:** the intersection of two geometrical surfaces (2) **:** the path of a moving point **6 :** a distribution indicating the relative performance of individuals measured against each other that is used esp. in assigning good, medium, or poor grades to usu. predetermined proportions of students rather than in assigning grades based on predetermined standards of achievement — **curvy** \ˈkər-vē\ *adj*

curve·ball \ˈkərv-ˌbȯl\ *n* **:** a baseball pitch thrown so that it swerves from a normal or expected course; *esp* **:** one that curves to the left when thrown from the right hand or to the right when thrown from the left hand — **curveball** *vb*

[1]**cur·vet** \(ˌ)kər-ˈvet\ *n* [It *corvetta,* fr. MF *courbette,* fr. *courber* to curve, fr. L *curvare*] **:** a prancing leap of a horse in which first the forelegs and then the hind are raised so that for an instant all the legs are in the air

[2]**curvet** *vi* **-vet·ted** *or* **-vet·ed; -vet·ting** *or* **-vet·ing :** to make a curvet; *also* **:** PRANCE, CAPER

cur·vi·lin·eal \ˌkər-və-ˈlin-ē-əl\ *adj* **:** CURVILINEAR

cur·vi·lin·ear \ˌkər-və-ˈlin-ē-ər\ *adj* [L *curvus* + *linea* line] **1 :** consisting of or bounded by curved lines **:** represented by a curved line **2 :** marked by flowing tracery <~ Gothic> — **cur·vi·lin·ear·i·ty** \-ˌlin-ē-ˈar-ət-ē\ *n* — **cur·vi·lin·ear·ly** \-ˈlin-ē-ər-lē\ *adv*

cu·sec \ˈkyü-ˌsek\ *n* [*cu*bic foot per *sec*ond] **:** a volumetric unit of flow equal to a cubic foot per second

cush·at \ˈkəsh-ət\ *n* [ME *cowschote,* fr. OE *cūscote*] *chiefly Scot* **:** RINGDOVE 1

cu·shaw \kü-ˈshȯ, ˈkü-ˌ\ *n* [perh. of Algonquian origin; akin to *escushaw* it is green (in some Algonquian language of Virginia)] **:** WINTER CROOKNECK

Cush·ing's disease \ˈkůsh-iŋz-\ *n* [Harvey *Cushing*] **:** a disease characterized by obesity and muscular weakness associated with adrenal or pituitary dysfunction — called also *Cushing's syndrome*

[1]**cush·ion** \ˈkůsh-ən\ *n* [ME *cusshin,* fr. MF *coissin,* fr. (assumed) VL *coxinus,* fr. L *coxa* hip — more at COXA] **1 :** a soft pillow or pad usu. used for sitting, reclining, or kneeling **2 :** a bodily part resembling a pad **3 :** something resembling a cushion: as **a :** PILLOW 3 **b :** RAT 3 **c :** a pad of springy rubber along the inside of the rim of a billiard table **d :** the head of a drill brace **e :** a padded insert in a shoe **f :** a strip of soft resilient rubber between the breaker and carcass of a pneumatic tire **g :** an artificial pool provided to absorb the kinetic energy of falling water and so prevent erosion **h :** an elastic body for reducing shock **i :** a mat laid under a large rug to ease the effect of wear **4 :** something serving to mitigate the effects of disturbances or disorders: as **a :** a factor that lessens adverse developments in the economy **b :** a medical procedure or drug that eases a patient's discomfort — **cush·ion·less** \-ləs\ *adj* — **cush·iony** \-ə-nē\ *adj*

[2]**cushion** *vt* **cush·ioned; cush·ion·ing** \-(ə-)niŋ\ **1 :** to seat or place on a cushion **2 :** to suppress by ignoring **3 :** to furnish with a cushion **4 a :** to mitigate the effects of **b :** to protect against force or shock **5 :** to check gradually so as to minimize shock of moving parts

Cush·it·ic \ˌkəsh-ˈit-ik, kůsh-\ *n* [*Cush* (Kush), Africa] **:** a subfamily of the Afro-Asiatic language family comprising various languages spoken in East Africa and esp. in Ethiopia and Somaliland — **Cushitic** *adj*

cushy \ˈkůsh-ē\ *adj* **cushi·er; cushi·est** [Hindi *khush* pleasant, fr. Per *khūsh*] **:** entailing little hardship or difficulty **:** EASY <a ~ job with a high salary> — **cushi·ly** \ˈkůsh-ə-lē\ *adv*

cusk \ˈkəsk\ *n, pl* **cusk** *or* **cusks** [prob. alter. of *tusk* (a kind of codfish)] **1 :** a large edible marine fish (*Brosme brosme*) related to the cod **2 :** the New World burbot (*Lota lota maculosa*)

cusp \ˈkəsp\ *n* [L *cuspis* point] **:** POINT, APEX: as **a :** either horn of a crescent moon **b :** a fixed point on a mathematical curve at which a point tracing the curve would exactly reverse its direction of motion **c :** a pointed projection formed by or arising from the intersection of two arcs or foils **d** (1) **:** a point on the grinding surface of a tooth (2) **:** a fold or flap of a cardiac valve — **cus·pate** \ˈkəs-ˌpāt, -pət\ *also* **cus·pat·ed** \-ˌpāt-əd\ *adj*

cus·pid \ˈkəs-pəd\ *n* [back-formation fr. *bicuspid*] **:** a canine tooth

cus·pi·date \ˈkəs-pə-ˌdāt\ *or* **cus·pi·dat·ed** \-ˌdāt-əd\ *adj* [L *cuspidatus,* pp. of *cuspidare* to make pointed, fr. *cuspid-, cuspis* point] **:** having a cusp **:** terminating in a point <a ~ leaf>

cus·pi·da·tion \ˌkəs-pə-ˈdā-shən\ *n* **:** decoration with cusps <the ~ of an arch>

cus·pi·dor \ˈkəs-pə-ˌdȯ(ə)r, -ˌdō(ə)r\ *n* [Pg *cuspidouro* place for spitting, fr. *cuspir* to spit, fr. L *conspuere,* fr. *com-* + *spuere* to spit — more at SPEW] **:** SPITTOON

[1]**cuss** \ˈkəs\ *n* [alter. of *curse*] **1 :** CURSE **2 :** FELLOW <an ornery old ~>

[2]**cuss** *vb* **:** CURSE <~*ed* and decried the generally poor quality of TV newscasting —W. R. Williams> — **cuss·er** *n*

cuss·ed \ˈkəs-əd\ *adj* **1 :** CURSED **2 :** OBSTINATE, CANTANKEROUS — **cuss·ed·ly** *adv*

cuss·ed·ness *n* **:** disposition to willful perversity **:** OBSTINACY

cuss·word \ˈkəs-ˌwərd\ *n* **1 :** SWEARWORD **2 :** a term of abuse **:** a derogatory term

cus·tard \ˈkəs-tərd\ *n* [ME, a kind of pie] **:** a pudding-like usu. sweetened mixture made of eggs and milk

custard apple *n* **1 a :** any of several chiefly tropical American soft-fleshed edible fruits **b :** any of a genus (*Annona* of the family Annonaceae, the custard-apple family) of trees or shrubs bearing this fruit; *esp* **:** a small West Indian tree (*A. reticulata*) **2 :** PAPAW 2

cus·to·di·al \ˌkəs-ˈtōd-ē-əl\ *adj* **:** relating to guardianship; *specif* **:** marked by or given to watching and protecting rather than seeking to cure <~ care>

cus·to·di·an \ˌkəs-ˈtōd-ē-ən\ *n* **:** one that guards and protects or maintains; *esp* **:** one entrusted with guarding and keeping property or records or with custody or guardianship of prisoners or inmates — **cus·to·di·an·ship** \-ˌship\ *n*

cus·to·dy \ˈkəs-təd-ē\ *n, pl* **-dies** [ME *custodie,* fr. L *custodia* guarding, fr. *custod-, custos* guardian] **:** immediate charge and control exercised by a person or an authority (as over a ward or a suspect) **:** SAFEKEEPING

[1]**cus·tom** \ˈkəs-təm\ *n* [ME *custume,* fr. OF, fr. L *consuetudin-, consuetudo,* fr. *consuetus,* pp. of *consuescere* to accustom, fr. *com-* + *suescere* to accustom; akin to *suus* one's own — more at SUICIDE] **1 a :** a usage or practice common to many or to a particular place or class or habitual with an individual **b :** long-established practice considered as unwritten law **c :** repeated practice **d :** the whole body of usages, practices, or conventions that regulate social life **2** *pl* **a :** duties, tolls, or imposts imposed by the sovereign law of a country on imports or exports **b** *usu sing in constr* **:** the agency, establishment, or procedure for collecting such customs **3 a :** business patronage **b :** usu. habitual patrons **:** CUSTOMERS ***syn*** see HABIT

[2]**custom** *adj* **1 :** made or performed according to personal order **2 :** specializing in custom work or operation <a ~ tailor>

cus·tom·ary \ˈkəs-tə-ˌmer-ē\ *adj* **1 :** based on or established by custom **2 :** commonly practiced, used, or observed ***syn*** see USUAL ***ant*** occasional — **cus·tom·ari·ly** \ˌkəs-tə-ˈmer-ə-lē\ *adv* — **cus·tom·ari·ness** \ˈkəs-tə-ˌmer-ē-nəs\ *n*

cus·tom–built \ˌkəs-təm-ˈbilt\ *adj* **:** built to individual specifications

cus·tom·er \ˈkəs-tə-mər\ *n* [ME *custumer,* fr. *custume*] **1 a**

: one that purchases usu. systematically or frequently a commodity or service **b** : one that is a patron (as of a restaurant) or that uses the services (as of a store) **2** : an individual usu. having some specified distinctive trait <a real tough ~>

cus·tom·house \'kəs-təm-ˌhau̇s\ *also* **cus·toms·house** \-təmz-\ *n* : a building where customs and duties are paid or collected and where vessels are entered and cleared

cus·tom·ize \'kəs-tə-ˌmīz\ *vt* **-ized; -iz·ing** : to build, fit, or alter according to individual specifications <~ a car> — **cus·tom·iz·er** *n*

cus·tom–made \ˌkəs-təm-'(m)ād\ *adj* : made to individual specifications

cus·tom–tai·lor \-'tā-lər\ *vt* : to alter, plan, or build according to individual specifications or needs

[1]**cut** \'kət\ *vb* **cut; cut·ting** [ME *cutten*] *vt* **1 a** : to penetrate with or as if with an edged instrument **b** : to hurt the feelings of **c** : to strike sharply with a cutting effect **d** : to strike (a ball) with a glancing blow that imparts a reverse spin **e** : to experience the growth of (a tooth) through the gum **2 a** : TRIM, PARE <~ one's nails> **b** : to shorten by omissions **c** : DISSOLVE, DILUTE, ADULTERATE **d** : to reduce in amount <~ costs> **3 a** : MOW, REAP <~ hay> **b** (1) : to divide into parts with an edged tool <~ bread> (2) : FELL, HEW <~ timber> **c** : to separate from an organization : DETACH **d** : to change the direction of sharply **e** : to go or pass around or about **4 a** : to divide into segments **b** : INTERSECT, CROSS **c** : BREAK, INTERRUPT <~ our supply lines> **d** (1) : to divide (a deck of cards) into two portions (2) : to draw (a card) from the deck **e** : to divide into shares : SPLIT **5 a** : STOP, CEASE <~ the nonsense> **b** : to refuse to recognize (an acquaintance) : OSTRACIZE **c** : to absent oneself from (as a class) **d** : to stop (a motor) by opening a switch **e** : to terminate the filming of (a motion-picture scene) **6 a** : to make by or as if by cutting: as (1) : CARVE <~ stone> (2) : to shape by grinding <~ a diamond> (3) : ENGRAVE (4) : to shear or hollow out **b** : to record sounds (as speech or music) on (a phonograph record) **c** : to type on a stencil **7 a** : to engage in (a frolicsome or mischievous action) <on summer nights strange capers are ~ under the thin guise of a Christian festival —D. C. Peattie> <in his sixty-seventh year with a heart that ~ didoes —H. R. Warfel> **b** : to give the appearance or impression of <~ a fine figure> **8** : to be able to manage or handle a situation — usu. used in negative constructions <can't ~ that kind of work anymore> ~ *vi* **1 a** : to function as or as if as an edged tool **b** : to undergo incision or severance <cheese ~*s* easily> **c** : to perform the operation of dividing, severing, incising, or intersecting **d** : to make a stroke with a whip, sword, or other weapon **e** : to wound feelings or sensibilities **f** : to cause constriction or chafing **g** : to be of effect, influence, or significance <an analysis that ~*s* deep> **2 a** (1) : to divide a pack of cards esp. in order to decide the deal or settle a bet (2) : to draw a card from the pack **b** : to divide spoils : SPLIT **3 a** : to proceed obliquely from a straight course <~ across the yard> **b** : to move swiftly <a yacht *cutting* through the water> **c** : to describe an oblique or diagonal line **d** : to change sharply in direction : SWERVE **e** : to make an abrupt transition from one sound or image to another in motion pictures, radio, or television **4** : to stop photographing motion pictures — **cut corners** : to perform some action in the quickest, easiest, or cheapest way — **cut ice** : to be of importance — usu. used in negative constructions <his opinion *cuts* no *ice* with them> — **cut one's teeth on** : to learn, do, or perform as a beginning or at the start of one's career — **cut short 1** : to check abruptly : INTERRUPT **2** : to terminate usu. in a premature manner : END — **cut the mustard** : to achieve the standard of performance necessary for success

[2]**cut** *n* **1** : something that is cut or cut off: as **a** : a length of cloth varying from 40 to 100 yards in length **b** : the yield of products cut esp. during one harvest **c** : a segment or section of a meat carcass or a part of one **d** : a group of animals selected from a herd **e** : SHARE <took his ~ of the profits> **2** : a product of cutting: as **a** : a creek, channel, or inlet made by excavation or worn by natural action **b** (1) : an opening made with an edged instrument (2) : a wound made by something sharp : GASH **c** : a surface or outline left by cutting **d** : a passage cut as a roadway **e** : a grade or step esp. in a social scale <a ~ above the ordinary person> **f** : a subset of a set such that when it is subtracted from the set the remainder is not connected **g** : a pictorial illustration **3** : the act or an instance of cutting: as **a** : a gesture or expression that hurts the feelings <made an unkind ~> **b** : a straight passage or course **c** : a stroke or blow with the edge of a knife or other edged tool **d** : a lash with or as if with a whip **e** : the act of reducing or removing a part <a ~ in pay> **f** : an act or turn of cutting cards; *also* : the result of cutting **4** : a voluntary absence from a class **5 a** : a stroke that cuts a ball; *also* : the spin imparted by such a stroke **b** : a swing by a batter at a pitched baseball **c** : an exchange of captures in checkers **6** : an abrupt transition from one sound or image to another in motion pictures, radio, or television **7 a** : the shape and style in which a thing is cut, formed, or made <clothes of the latest ~> **b** : PATTERN, TYPE **c** : HAIRCUT **8** : BAND 7 — **cut of one's jib** : the appearance of one's face

cut·abil·i·ty \ˌkət-ə-'bil-ət-ē\ *n* : the proportion of lean salable meat yielded by a carcass

cut–and–dried \ˌkət-ᵊn-'drīd\ *also* **cut–and–dry** \-'drī\ *adj* : being or done according to a plan, set procedure, or formula : ROUTINE

cut–and–try \-ᵊn-'trī\ *adj* : marked by experimental procedure : EMPIRICAL <early development of ships and yachts was achieved by the ~ method —D. F. Hora>

cu·ta·ne·ous \kyu̇-'tā-nē-əs\ *adj* [NL *cutaneus*, fr. L *cutis* skin — more at HIDE] : of, relating to, or affecting the skin — **cu·ta·ne·ous·ly** *adv*

[1]**cut·away** \'kət-ə-ˌwā\ *adj* : having or showing parts cut away

[2]**cutaway** *n* **1** : a coat with skirts tapering from the front waistline to form tails at the back **2 a** : a cutaway picture or representation **b** : a shot that interrupts the main action of a film or television program to take up a related subject or to depict action supposed to be going on at the same time as the main action **3** : a back dive in which the head is lowered toward the board after the takeoff

cut·back \'kət-ˌbak\ *n* **1** : something cut back **2** : REDUCTION

cut back \ˌkət-'bak\ *vt* **1** : to shorten by cutting : PRUNE **2** : REDUCE, DECREASE <*cut back* expenditures> ~ *vi* : to interrupt the sequence of a plot (as of a movie) by introducing events prior to those last presented

cutch \'kəch\ *n* [modif. of Malay *kachu*] : CATECHU a

cut down *vt* **1 a** : to remodel by removing extras or unwanted furnishings and fittings **b** : to remake in a smaller size **2 a** : to strike down and kill or incapacitate **b** : to knock down **3** : REDUCE, CURTAIL <*cut down* expenses> ~ *vi* : to reduce or curtail volume or activity <*cut down* on his smoking> — **cut down to size** : to reduce from an inflated or exaggerated importance to true or suitable stature

cute \'kyüt\ *adj* **cut·er; cut·est** [short for *acute*] **1** : CLEVER, SHREWD **2** : attractive or pretty esp. in a dainty or delicate way **3** : obviously straining for effect — **cute·ly** *adv* — **cute·ness** *n*

cute·sy \'kyüt-sē\ *adj* [*cute* + *-sy* (as in *artsy-craftsy*)] : self-consciously cute : MANNERED <here and there the script is ~, trying for a few mild laughs —H. C. Schonberg>

cut glass *n* : glass ornamented with patterns cut into its surface by an abrasive wheel and polished

cut–grass \'kət-ˌgras\ *n* : a grass (esp. genus *Leersia*) with minute hooked bristles along the edges of the leaf blade

cu·ti·cle \'kyüt-i-kəl\ *n* [L *cuticula*, dim. of *cutis* skin — more at HIDE] **1** : SKIN, PELLICLE: as **a** : an external investment secreted usu. by epidermal cells **b** : the outermost layer of animal integument (as in man) when composed of epidermis **c** : a thin continuous fatty film on the external surface of many higher plants **2** : dead or horny epidermis — **cu·tic·u·lar** \kyu̇-'tik-yə-lər\ *adj*

cut·ie *or* **cut·ey** \'kyüt-ē\ *n, pl* **cuties** *or* **cuteys** [*cute* + *-ie*] : an attractive person; *esp* : a pretty girl

cu·tin \'kyüt-ᵊn\ *n* [ISV, fr. L *cutis*] : an insoluble mixture containing waxes, fatty acids, soaps, and resinous material that forms a continuous layer on the outer epidermal wall of a plant

cut–in \'kət-ˌin\ *n* : something cut in — **cut–in** *adj*

cut in \ˌkət-'in\ *vi* **1** : to thrust oneself into a position between others or belonging to another **2** : to join in something suddenly <*cut in* on the conversation> **3** : to interrupt a dancing couple and take one as one's partner **4** : to become automatically connected or started in operation ~ *vt* **1** : to mix with cutting motions <after sifting the flour into a mixing bowl, *cut* the lard *in*> **2** : to introduce into a number, group, or sequence **3** : to connect into an electrical circuit to a mechanical apparatus so as to permit operation **4** : to include esp. among those benefiting or favored <*cut* them *in* on the profits>

cu·tin·ized \'kyüt-ᵊn-ˌīzd\ *adj* : infiltrated with cutin <~ epidermal cells>

cu·tis \'kyüt-əs\ *n, pl* **cu·tes** \'kyü-ˌtēz\ *or* **cu·tis·es** [L] : DERMIS

cut·lass *also* **cut·las** \'kət-ləs\ *n* [MF *coutelas*, aug. of *coutel* knife, fr. L *cultellus*, dim. of *culter* knife, plowshare] **1** : a short curving sword formerly used by sailors on warships **2** : MACHETE

cutlass 1

cut·ler \'kət-lər\ *n* [ME, fr. MF *coutelier*, fr. LL *cultellarius*, fr. L *cultellus*] : one who makes, deals in, or repairs cutlery

cut·lery \'kət-lə-rē\ *n* **1** : edged or cutting tools; *specif* : implements for cutting and eating food **2** : the business of a cutler

cut·let \'kət-lət\ *n* [F *côtelette*, fr. OF *costelette*, dim. of *coste* rib, side, fr. L *costa* — more at COAST] **1** : a small slice of meat for broiling or frying <a veal ~> **2** : a flat croquette of chopped meat or fish

cut·line \'kət-ˌlīn\ *n* : CAPTION, LEGEND

cut·off \'kət-ˌȯf\ *n* **1** : the act or action of cutting off **2 a** : the new and relatively short channel formed when a stream cuts through the neck of an oxbow **b** : SHORTCUT 1 **c** : a channel made to straighten a stream **3** : a device for cutting off **4** : something cut off **5** : the point, date, or period for a cutoff — **cutoff** *adj*

cut off \ˌkət-'ȯf\ *vt* **1** : to strike off : SEVER **2** : to bring to an untimely end **3** : to stop the passage of **4** : to shut off : BAR **5** : to break off : TERMINATE **6** : SEPARATE, ISOLATE **7** : DISINHERIT **8 a** : to stop the operation of : turn off **b** : to stop or interrupt while in communication <the operator *cut* me *off*> ~ *vi* : to cease operating

cut·out \'kət-ˌau̇t\ *n* **1** : something cut out or off from something else **2** : one that cuts out — **cutout** *adj*

[1]**cut out** \ˌkət-'au̇t\ *vt* **1** : to form by erosion **2** : to form or shape by cutting **3** : to determine or assign through necessity <his work is *cut out* for him> **4** : to take the place of : SUPPLANT **5** : to put an end to : desist from <wasteful expenditures that must be *cut out*> **6** : DEPRIVE, DEFRAUD **7 a** : to remove from a series or circuit : DISCONNECT **b** : to make inoperative ~ *vi* **1** : to depart in haste **2** : to cease operating **3** : to swerve out of a traffic line

[2]**cut out** *adj* : naturally fitted or suited <not *cut out* to be a lawyer>

cut·over \ˌkət-ˌō-vər\ *adj* : having most of the salable timber cut <~ land>

cut·purse \'kət-ˌpərs\ *n* : PICKPOCKET

ə abut	ᵊ kitten	ər further	a back	ā bake	ä cot, cart
au̇ out	ch chin	e less	ē easy	g gift	i trip ī life
j joke	ŋ sing	ō flow	ȯ flaw	ȯi coin	th thin t͟h this
ü loot	u̇ foot	y yet	yü few	yu̇ furious	zh vision

cut–rate \'kət-'rāt\ *adj* **1 :** marked by, offering, or making use of a reduced rate or price <~ stores> **2 :** SECOND-RATE, CHEAP
cut·ta·ble \'kət-ə-bəl\ *adj* **:** capable of being cut **:** ready for cutting
cut·ter \'kət-ər\ *n* **1 :** one that cuts: **a :** one whose work is cutting or involves cutting **b** (1) **:** an instrument, machine, machine part, or tool that cuts (2)**:** a device for vibrating a cutting stylus in disc recording (3) **:** the cutting stylus or its point **2 a :** a ship's boat for carrying stores or passengers **b :** a fore-and-aft rigged sailing boat with a jib, forestaysail, mainsail, and single mast **c :** a small armed boat in government service **3 :** a light sleigh
1cut·throat \'kət-,thrōt\ *n* **1 :** one likely to cut throats **2 :** a cruel unprincipled person
2cutthroat *adj* **1 :** MURDEROUS, CRUEL **2 :** marked by unprincipled practices **:** RUTHLESS <~ competition> **3 :** characterized by each player playing for himself rather than having a permanent partner — used esp. of partnership games adapted for three players <~ bridge>
cutthroat contract *n* **:** contract bridge in which partnerships are determined by the bidding
cutthroat trout *n* **:** a large trout (*Salmo clarki*) native to cold lakes and rivers from northern California to southern Alaska — called also *cutthroat*
cut time *n* **:** duple or quadruple time with the beat represented by a half note
1cut·ting *n* **1 :** something cut or cut off, out, or over: as **a :** a plant section originating from stem, leaf, or root and capable of developing into a new plant **b :** HARVEST **2 :** something made by cutting; *esp* **:** RECORDING
2cutting *adj* **1 :** given to or designed for cutting; *esp* **:** SHARP, EDGED **2 :** marked by sharp piercing cold **3 :** inclined or likely to wound the feelings of others esp. because of a ruthlessly incisive quality <a ~ remark> **4 :** INTENSE, PIERCING <a ~ pain> ***syn*** see INCISIVE — **cut·ting·ly** \-iŋ-lē\ *adv*
cutting board *n* **:** a board on which something (as food or cloth) is placed for cutting
cutting horse *n* **:** a quick light saddle horse trained for use in separating cattle from a herd
cut·tle·bone \'kət-ᵊl-,bōn\ *n* [ME *cotul* cuttlefish (fr. OE *cudele*) + E *bone*]**:** the shell of cuttlefishes used for polishing powder or for supplying cage birds with lime and salts
cut·tle·fish \-,fish\ *n* [ME *cotul* + E *fish*] **:** a 10-armed marine cephalopod mollusk (family Sepiidae) differing from the related squid in having a calcified internal shell

cuttlefish

cut·ty sark \'kət-ē-,särk\ *n* [E dial. *cutty* (short) + *sark*] **1** *chiefly Scot* **:** a short garment; *esp* **:** a woman's short undergarment **2** *chiefly Scot* **:** WOMAN, HUSSY
cutty stool *n* **1** *chiefly Scot* **:** a low stool **2 :** a seat in a Scottish church where offenders formerly sat for public rebuke
cut·up \'kət-,əp\ *n* **:** one that clowns or acts boisterously
cut up \,kət-'əp\ *vt* **1 a :** to cut into parts or pieces **b :** to injure or damage by or as if by cutting **:** GASH, SLASH **2 :** to subject to hostile criticism **:** CENSURE ~ *vi* **1 :** to undergo being cut up **2 :** to behave in a comic, boisterous, or unruly manner **:** CLOWN
cut·wa·ter \'kət-,wȯt-ər, -,wät-\ *n* **:** the forepart of a ship's stem
cut·work \-,wərk\ *n* **:** embroidery usu. on linen in which a design is outlined in buttonhole stitch and the intervening material then cut away
cut·worm \-,wərm\ *n* **:** any of various smooth-bodied chiefly nocturnal caterpillars (family Noctuidae) many of which feed on plant stems near ground level
cu·vette \kyü-'vet\ *n* [F, dim. of *cuve* tub, fr. L *cupa* — more at HIVE]**:** a small often transparent laboratory vessel (as a tube)
cv *or* **cvt** *abbr* convertible
CV *abbr* **1** cardiovascular **2** chief value
CVA *abbr* Columbia Valley Authority
cw *abbr* clockwise
CW *abbr* **1** chemical warfare **2** chief warrant officer **3** continuous waves
cwm \'küm\ *n* [W, valley]**:** CIRQUE 3
CWO *abbr* **1** cash with order **2** chief warrant officer
CWS *abbr* Chemical Warfare Service
cwt *abbr* hundredweight
CY *abbr* calendar year
-cy \sē\ *n suffix* [ME *-cie,* fr. OF, fr. L *-tia,* partly fr. *-t-* (final stem consonant) + *-ia* -y, partly fr. Gk *-tia, -teia,* fr. *-t-* (final stem consonant) + *-ia, -eia* -y] **:** action **:** practice <mendican*cy*> **:** rank **:** office <baronet*cy*> <chaplain*cy*> **:** body **:** class <magistra*cy*> **:** state **:** quality <accura*cy*> <bankrupt*cy*> <normal*cy*> — often replacing a final *-t* or *-te* of the base word
cy·an \'sī-,an, -ən\ *n* [Gk *kyanos*]**:** a greenish blue color — used in photography of one of the primary colors
cyan- *or* **cyano-** *comb form* [G, fr. Gk *kyan-, kyano-,* fr. *kyanos* dark blue enamel] **1 :** dark blue **:** blue <*cyano*type> **2 :** cyanogen <*cyan*ide> **3 :** cyanide <*cyano*genetic>
cy·an·a·mide \sī-'an-ə-məd\ *n* [ISV] **1 :** a caustic acidic compound CH_2N_2 **2 :** CALCIUM CYANAMIDE
cy·a·nate \'sī-ə-,nāt, -nət\ *n* [ISV]**:** a salt (as ammonium cyanate) or ester of cyanic acid
cy·an·ic \sī-'an-ik\ *adj* [ISV] **1 :** relating to or containing cyanogen **2 :** of a blue or bluish color
cyanic acid *n* **:** a strong acid HOCN used to prepare cyanates
1cy·a·nide \'sī-ə-,nīd, -nəd\ *n* [ISV]**:** a compound (as potassium cyanide) of cyanogen usu. with a more electropositive element or radical
2cy·a·nide \-,nīd\ *vt* **-nid·ed; -nid·ing :** to treat with a cyanide; *specif* **:** to treat (iron or steel) with molten cyanide to produce a hard surface
cyanide process *n* **:** a method of extracting gold and silver from ores by treatment with a sodium cyanide or calcium cyanide solution
cy·a·nine \'sī-ə-,nēn, -nən\ *n* [ISV]**:** any of various dyes that sensitize photographic film to light from the green, yellow, red, and infrared regions of the spectrum
cy·a·nite \'sī-ə-,nīt\ *var of* KYANITE
cy·a·no \'sī-ə-(,)nō, sī-'an-(,)ō\ *adj* [*cyan-*]**:** relating to or containing the cyanogen group
cy·a·no·ac·ry·late \sī-ə-nō-'ak-rə-,lāt, sī-,an-ō-\ *n* **:** any of several liquid acrylate monomers that readily polymerize anionically and are used as adhesives in industry and on living tissue in medicine to close wounds as an adjunct to surgery
cy·a·no·co·bal·a·min \-kō-'bal-ə-mən\ *also* **cy·a·no·co·bal·a·mine** \-,mēn\ *n* [*cyan-* + *cobalt* + vit*amin*]**:** VITAMIN B_{12}
cy·a·no·eth·yl·ate \-'eth-ə-,lāt\ *vt* **:** to introduce a cyano-ethyl group CNC_2H_4 into (a compound) usu. by means of acrylonitrile <~ cotton> — **cy·a·no·eth·yl·ation** \-,eth-ə-'lā-shən\ *n*
cy·ano·gen \sī-'an-ə-jən\ *n* [F *cyanogène,* fr. *cyan-* + *gène* -gen] **1 :** a univalent radical CN present in simple and complex cyanides **2 :** a colorless flammable poisonous gas $(CN)_2$
cy·a·no·gen·e·sis \,sī-ə-nō-'jen-ə-səs, sī-,an-ō-\ *n* **:** production of cyanide (as by plants) — **cy·a·no·ge·net·ic** \-jə-'net-ik\ *adj* — **cy·a·no·gen·ic** \-'jen-ik\ *adj*
cy·a·no·hy·drin \-'hī-drən\ *n* [ISV]**:** any of various compounds containing both cyano and alcoholic hydroxyl groups
cy·a·nosed \'sī-ə-,nōst, -,nōzd\ *adj* **:** affected with cyanosis
cy·a·no·sis \,sī-ə-'nō-səs\ *n* [NL, fr. Gk *kyanōsis* dark blue color, fr. *kyan-* cyan-]**:** a bluish or purplish discoloration (as of skin) due to deficient oxygenation of the blood — **cy·a·not·ic** \-'nät-ik\ *adj*
cy·an·urate \,sī-ə-'n(y)u̇(ə)r-,āt, -'n(y)u̇r-ət\ *n* **:** a salt or ester of cyanuric acid
cy·an·uric acid \,sī-ə-,n(y)u̇r-ik-\ *n* [*cyan-* + *urea*]**:** a crystalline weak acid $C_3N_3(OH)_3$ yielding cyanic acid when heated
Cyb·e·le \'sib-ə-(,)lē\ *n* [L, fr. Gk *Kybelē*]**:** a nature goddess of the ancient peoples of Asia Minor
cy·ber·nat·ed \'sī-bər-,nāt-əd\ *adj* **:** characterized by or involving cybernation <a ~ bakery> <a ~ society>
cy·ber·na·tion \,sī-bər-'nā-shən\ *n* [*cyber*netics + *-ation*]**:** the automatic control of a process or operation (as in manufacturing) by means of computers
cy·ber·net·ic \,sī-bər-'net-ik\ *also* **cy·ber·net·i·cal** \-i-kəl\ *adj* **:** of, relating to, or involving cybernetics — **cy·ber·net·i·cal·ly** \-i-k(ə-)lē\ *adv*
cy·ber·ne·ti·cian \,sī-(,)bər-nə-'tish-ən\ *n* **:** a specialist in cybernetics
cy·ber·net·i·cist \,sī-bər-'net-ə-səst\ *n* **:** CYBERNETICIAN
cy·ber·net·ics \,sī-bər-'net-iks\ *n pl but sing or pl in constr* [Gk *kybernētēs* pilot, governor (fr. *kybernan* to steer, govern) + E *-ics*] **:** the science of communication and control theory that is concerned esp. with the comparative study of automatic control systems (as the nervous system and brain and mechanical-electrical communication systems)
cy·borg \'sī-,bȯ(ə)rg\ *n* [*cyb*ernetic + *org*anism]**:** a human being who is linked (as for temporary adaptation to a hostile space environment) to one or more mechanical devices upon which some of his vital physiological functions depend
cyc *or* **cycl** *abbr* cyclopedia
cy·cad \'sī-kəd\ *n* [NL *Cycad-, Cycas*]**:** any of an order (Cycadales) of gymnosperms that are represented by a single surviving family (Cycadaceae) of tropical plants resembling palms but reproducing by means of spermatozoids
cy·cad·e·oid \sī-'kad-ē-,ȯid\ *n* [NL *Cycadeoidales,* group name, deriv. of *Cycad-, Cycas*]**:** any of an extinct order (Cycadeoidales or Bennettitales) of cycadophytes that differ from the cycads chiefly in having the reproductive organs on the trunk embedded in a thick external covering of persistent leaf bases
cy·cado·phyte \sī-'kad-ə-,fīt\ *n* [NL *Cycadophytae,* group name, irreg. fr. *Cycad-, Cycas* + *phyton* plant — more at -PHYTE]**:** any of a subclass (Cycadophytae) of unbranched gymnosperms with pinnate leaves, large pith, little xylem, and a thick cortex that includes the cycads, cycadeoids, and seed ferns
cy·cas \'sī-kəs\ *n* [NL *Cycad-, Cycas* genus name]**:** any of a genus (*Cycas*) of cycads between tree ferns and palms in appearance
cy·ca·sin \'sī-kə-sən\ *n* [*cycas* + *-in*]**:** a glucoside $C_8H_{16}N_2O_7$ that occurs in cycads and results in toxic and carcinogenic effects when introduced into mammals
cycl- *or* **cyclo-** *comb form* [NL, fr. Gk *kykl-, kyklo-,* fr. *kyklos*] **1 :** circle <*cyclo*meter> **2 :** cyclic <*cyclo*hexane>
cy·cla·mate \'sī-klə-,māt, -mət\ *n* [*cyclo*hexyl-sulf*amate*]**:** an artificially prepared salt of sodium or calcium used esp. formerly as a sweetener — compare CYCLOHEXYLAMINE
cy·cla·men \'sī-klə-mən, 'sik-lə-\ *n* [NL, genus name, fr. Gk *kyklaminos*]**:** any of a genus (*Cyclamen*) of plants of the primrose family having showy nodding flowers
cy·clase \'sī-,klās, -,klāz\ *n* [*cycl-* + *-ase*]**:** an enzyme (as adenyl cyclase) that catalyzes cyclization of a compound
cy·claz·o·cine \sī-'klaz-ə-,sēn, -sən\ *n* [*cycl-* + *azocine* (C_7H_7N), of unknown origin]**:** an analgesic $C_{18}H_{25}NO$ that inhibits the effect of morphine and related addictive drugs and is used in the treatment of drug addiction
1cy·cle \'sī-kəl, *6 is also* 'sik-əl\ *n* [F or LL; F, fr. LL *cyclus,* fr. Gk *kyklos* circle, wheel, cycle — more at WHEEL] **1 :** an interval of time during which a sequence of a recurring succession of events or phenomena is completed **2 a :** a course or series of events or operations that recur regularly and usu. lead back to the starting point **b :** one complete performance of a vibration, electric oscillation, current alternation, or other periodic process **c :** a permutation of a set of ordered elements in which each element takes the place of the next and the last becomes first **3 :** a circular or spiral arrangement: as **a :** an imaginary circle or orbit in the heavens **b :** WHORL **c :** RING 10 **4 :** a long period of time **:** AGE **5 a :** a group of poems, plays, novels, or songs treating the same theme **b :** a series of narratives dealing typically with the exploits

of a legendary hero **6 a :** BICYCLE **b :** TRICYCLE **c :** MOTORCYCLE **7 :** the series of a single, double, triple, and home run hit by one player during one baseball game <hit for the ~> — **cy·clic** \ˈsī-klik *also* ˈsik-lik\ *or* **cy·cli·cal** \ˈsī-kli-kəl, ˈsik-li-\ *adj* — **cy·cli·cal·ly** \-k(ə-)lē\ *or* **cy·clic·ly** \ˈsī-kli-klē, ˈsik-li-\ *adv*

[2]**cycle** \ˈsī-kəl, *2 is also* ˈsik-əl\ *vb* **cy·cled; cy·cling** \ˈsī-k(ə-)liŋ, ˈsik(-ə)-\ *vi* **1 a :** to pass through a cycle **b :** to recur in cycles **2 :** to ride a cycle; *specif* **:** BICYCLE ~ *vt* **:** to cause to go through a cycle — **cy·cler** \ˈsī-k(ə-)lər, ˈsik(-ə)-\ *n*

cyclic AMP *n* **:** a cyclic mononucleotide of adenosine that has been implicated in control mechanisms regulating metabolism and function in the nervous system — called also *adenosine monophosphate;* compare ACRASIN

cyclic group *n* **:** a mathematical group that has an element such that every element of the group can be expressed as one of its powers

cyclic poets *n pl* [*Epic Cycle,* the series of epics dealing with the causes, events, and aftermath of the Trojan War] **:** the poets after Homer who composed epics on the Trojan War and its heroes

cy·clist \ˈsī-k(ə-)ləst, ˈsik(-ə)-\ *n* **:** one who rides a cycle

cy·cli·tol \ˈsī-klə-ˌtōl, ˈsik-lə-ˌtōl\ *n* [*cycl-* + *-itol* (as in *inositol*)] **:** an alicyclic polyhydroxy compound (as inositol)

cy·cli·za·tion \ˌsīk-(ə-)lə-ˈzā-shən, ˌsik-\ *n* **:** formation of one or more rings in a chemical compound

cy·clize \ˈsīk-(ə-)ˌlīz, ˈsik-\ *vb* **cy·clized; cy·cliz·ing** *vt* **:** to subject to cyclization ~ *vi* **:** to undergo cyclization

cy·clo \ˈsē-(ˌ)klō, ˈsik-(ˌ)lō\ *n, pl* **cyclos** [prob. fr. F, short for (assumed) *cyclotaxi,* fr. moto*cycl*ette motorcycle + *-o-* + *taxi*] **:** a 3-wheeled motor-driven taxi

cy·clo·ad·di·tion \-ə-ˈdish-ən\ *n* **:** a chemical reaction leading to ring formation in a compound

cy·clo·al·i·phat·ic \ˌsī-klō-ˌal-ə-ˈfat-ik\ *adj* **:** ALICYCLIC

cy·clo·di·ene \-ˈdī-ˌēn, -dī-ˈ\ *n* [*cycl-* + *diene*] **:** an organic insecticide (as aldrin, dieldrin, chlordane, or endosulfan) with a chlorinated methylene group forming a bridge across a 6-membered carbon ring

cy·clo·gen·e·sis \-ˈjen-ə-səs\ *n* [*cyclo*ne + *genesis*] **:** the development or intensification of a cyclone

cy·clo·hex·ane \ˌsī-klō-ˈhek-ˌsān\ *n* [ISV] **:** a pungent saturated cyclic hydrocarbon C_6H_{12} found in petroleum or made synthetically and used chiefly as a solvent and in organic synthesis

cy·clo·hex·a·none \-ˈhek-sə-ˌnōn\ *n* [*cyclohexane* + *-one*] **:** a liquid ketone $C_6H_{10}O$ used esp. as a solvent and in organic synthesis

cy·clo·hex·i·mide \-ˈhek-sə-ˌmīd, -məd\ *n* [*cyclohexane* + *imide*] **:** an agricultural fungicide $C_{15}H_{23}NO_4$ that is obtained from a soil bacterium (*Streptomyces griseus*)

cy·clo·hex·yl·a·mine \-hek-ˈsil-ə-ˌmēn\ *n* [*cyclohexane* + *-yl* + *amine*] **:** an amine $(C_6H_{11}NH_2)$ of cyclohexane that is a probably harmful metabolic breakdown product of cyclamate

[1]**cy·cloid** \ˈsī-ˌklȯid\ *n* [F *cycloïde,* fr. Gk *kykloeidēs* circular, fr. *kyklos*] **1 a :** a curve that is generated by a point on the circumference of a circle as it rolls along a straight line **b :** something having a curved or circular form <a cloud ~> **2 :** CYCLOTHYME — **cy·cloi·dal** \sī-ˈklȯid-ᵊl\ *adj*

cycloid 1a

[2]**cycloid** *adj* **1 :** CIRCULAR; *esp* **:** arranged or progressing in circles **2 :** smooth with concentric lines of growth <~ scales>; *also* **:** having or consisting of cycloid scales **3 :** CYCLOTHYMIC

cy·clom·e·ter \sī-ˈkläm-ət-ər\ *n* **:** a device made for recording the revolutions of a wheel and often used for registering distance traversed by a wheeled vehicle

cy·clone \ˈsī-ˌklōn\ *n* [modif. of Gk *kyklōma* wheel, coil, fr. *kykloun* to go around, fr. *kyklos* circle] **1 a :** a storm or system of winds that rotates about a center of low atmospheric pressure clockwise in the southern hemisphere and counterclockwise in the northern, advances at a speed of 20 to 30 miles an hour, and often brings abundant rain **b :** TORNADO **c :** LOW 1b **2 :** any of various centrifugal devices for separating materials (as solid particles from gases or liquids) — **cy·clon·ic** \sī-ˈklän-ik\ *adj* — **cy·clon·i·cal·ly** \-i-k(ə-)lē\ *adv*

cyclone cellar *n* **:** a cellar or covered excavation designed for protection from dangerous windstorms (as tornadoes)

cy·clo·ole·fin \ˌsī-klō-ˈō-lə-fən\ *n* [ISV] **:** a hydrocarbon (as of the formula C_nH_{2n-2}) containing an unsaturated ring — **cy·clo·ole·fin·ic** \-ˌō-lə-ˈfin-ik\ *adj*

cy·clo·par·af·fin \-ˈpar-ə-fən\ *n* **:** a saturated cyclic hydrocarbon of the formula C_nH_{2n}

cy·clo·pe·an \ˌsī-klə-ˈpē-ən, sī-ˈklō-pē-\ *adj* **1** *often cap* **:** of, relating to, or characteristic of a Cyclops **2 :** HUGE, MASSIVE **3 :** of or relating to a style of stone construction marked typically by the use of large irregular blocks without mortar

cy·clo·pe·dia *or* **cy·clo·pae·dia** \ˌsī-klə-ˈpēd-ē-ə\ *n* **:** ENCYCLOPEDIA — **cy·clo·pe·dic** \-ˈpēd-ik\ *adj*

cy·clo·phos·pha·mide \ˌsī-klō-ˈfäs-fə-ˌmīd\ *n* **:** an immunosuppressive and antineoplastic agent $C_7H_{15}Cl_2N_2O_2P$ used esp. against lymphomas and some leukemias

cy·clo·pro·pane \ˌsī-klə-ˈprō-ˌpān\ *n* [ISV] **:** a saturated cyclic gaseous hydrocarbon C_3H_6 used esp. as an anesthetic

cy·clops \ˈsī-ˌkläps\ *n* [L, fr. Gk *Kyklōps,* fr. *kykl-* cycl- + *ōps* eye] **1** *pl* **cy·clo·pes** \sī-ˈklō-(ˌ)pēz\ *cap* **:** one of a race of giants in Greek mythology with a single eye in the middle of the forehead **2** *pl* **cyclops** [NL, genus name, fr. L] **:** WATER FLEA

cy·clo·ra·ma \ˌsī-klə-ˈram-ə, -ˈräm-\ *n* [*cycl-* + *-orama* (as in *panorama*)] **1 :** a large pictorial representation encircling the spectator and often having real objects as a foreground **2 :** a curved curtain or wall used as a background of a stage set to suggest unlimited space — **cy·clo·ram·ic** \-ˈram-ik\ *adj*

cy·clo·ser·ine \ˌsī-klō-ˈse(ə)r-ˌēn\ *n* **:** an amino antibiotic $C_3H_6N_2O_2$ produced by an actinomycete (*Streptomyces orchidaceus*)

cy·clo·sis \sī-ˈklō-səs\ *n* [NL, fr. Gk *kyklōsis* encirclement, fr. *kykloun* to go around] **:** the streaming of protoplasm within a cell

cy·clos·to·mate \sī-ˈkläs-tə-mət\ *also* **cy·clo·sto·ma·tous** \ˌsī-klə-ˈstäm-ət-əs, -ˈstōm-\ *adj* [*cycl-* + Gk *stomat-, stoma* mouth] **1 :** having a circular mouth **2 :** CYCLOSTOME

cy·clo·stome \ˈsī-klə-ˌstōm\ *n* [deriv. of Gk *kykl-* + *stoma* mouth — more at STOMACH] **:** any of a class (Cyclostomi or Cyclostomata) of lowly craniate vertebrates having a large sucking mouth with no jaws and comprising the hagfishes and lampreys — **cyclostome** *adj*

[1]**cy·clo·style** \-ˌstīl\ *n* [fr. *Cyclostyle,* a trademark] **:** a machine for making multiple copies that utilizes a stencil cut by a graver whose tip is a small rowel

[2]**cyclostyle** *vt* **:** to make multiple copies of by cyclostyle

cy·clo·thyme \ˈsī-klə-ˌthīm\ *n* [back-formation fr. *cyclothymia*] **:** a cyclothymic individual

cy·clo·thy·mia \ˌsī-klə-ˈthī-mē-ə\ *n* [NL, fr. G *zyklothymie,* fr. *zykl-* cycl- + *-thymie* -thymia] **:** a temperament marked by alternate lively and depressed moods — **cy·clo·thy·mic** \-ˈthī-mik\ *adj*

cy·clo·tom·ic \-ˈtäm-ik\ *adj* [*cyclotomy* (mathematical theory of the division of the circle into equal parts), fr. *cycl-* + *-tomy*] **:** relating to, being, or containing a polynomial of the form $x^{p-1} + x^{p-2} + \ldots + x + 1$ where p is a prime number

cy·clo·tron \ˈsī-klə-ˌträn\ *n* [*cycl-* + *-tron;* fr. the circular movement of the particles] **:** an accelerator in which particles (as protons, deuterons, or ions) are propelled by an alternating electric field in a constant magnetic field

cy·der *Brit var of* CIDER

cyg·net \ˈsig-nət\ *n* [ME *sygnett,* fr. MF *cygne* swan, fr. L *cycnus, cygnus,* fr. Gk *kyknos*] **:** a young swan

Cyg·nus \ˈsig-nəs\ *n* [L (gen. *Cygni*), lit., swan] **:** a northern constellation between Lyra and Pegasus in the Milky Way

cyl *abbr* cylinder

cyl·in·der \ˈsil-ən-dər\ *n* [MF or L; MF *cylindre,* fr. L *cylindrus,* fr. Gk *kylindros,* fr. *kylindein* to roll; akin to OE *sceol* squinting, L *scelus* crime, Gk *skelos* leg, *skolios* crooked] **1 a :** the surface traced by a straight line moving parallel to a fixed straight line and intersecting a fixed curve **b :** the space bounded by a cylinder and two parallel planes cutting all its elements — see VOLUME table **2 :** a cylindrical body: as **a :** the turning chambered breech of a revolver **b (1) :** the piston chamber in an engine **(2) :** a chamber in a pump from which the piston expels the fluid **c :** any of various rotating members in printing presses; *esp* **:** one that impresses paper on an inked form **d :** a cylindrical clay object inscribed with cuneiform inscriptions — **cyl·in·dered** \-dərd\ *adj*

cylinder seal *n* **:** a cylinder (as of stone) engraved in intaglio and used esp. in ancient Mesopotamia to roll an impression on wet clay

cy·lin·dri·cal \sə-ˈlin-dri-kəl\ *or* **cy·lin·dric** \-drik\ *adj* **:** relating to or having the form or properties of a cylinder — **cy·lin·dri·cal·ly** \-dri-k(ə-)lē\ *adv*

cylindrical coordinate *n* **:** any of the coordinates in space obtained by constructing in a plane a polar coordinate system and on a line perpendicular to the plane a linear coordinate system

cy·ma \ˈsī-mə\ *n* [Gk *kyma,* lit., wave] **1 :** a projecting molding whose profile is a double curve **2 :** a double curve formed by the union of a concave line and a convex line

cy·ma·tium \sī-ˈmā-sh(ē-)əm\ *n, pl* **-tia** \-sh(ē-)ə\ [L, fr. Gk *kymation,* dim. of *kymat-, kyma*] **:** a crowning molding in classic architecture; *esp* **:** CYMA

cym·bal \ˈsim-bəl\ *n* [ME, fr. OE *cymbal* & MF *cymbale,* fr. L *cymbalum,* fr. Gk *kymbalon,* fr. *kymbē* bowl — more at HUMP] **:** a concave brass plate that produces a brilliant clashing tone and that is struck with a drumstick or is used in pairs struck glancingly together — **cym·bal·ist** \-bə-ləst\ *n*

cym·bid·i·um \sim-ˈbid-ē-əm\ *n* [NL, genus name, fr. L *cymba* boat, fr. Gk *kymbē* bowl, boat] **:** any of a genus (*Cymbidium*) of tropical Old World orchids with showy boat-shaped flowers

cyme \ˈsīm\ *n* [NL *cyma,* fr. L, cabbage sprout, fr. Gk *kyma* swell, wave, cabbage sprout, fr. *kyein* to be pregnant] **:** an inflorescence in which all floral axes terminate in a single flower; *esp* **:** a determinate inflorescence of this type containing several flowers with the first-opening central flower terminating the main axis and subsequent flowers developing from lateral buds — see INFLORESCENCE illustration

cy·mene \ˈsī-ˌmēn\ *n* [F *cymène,* fr. Gk *kyminon* cumin + F *-ène* -ene — more at CUMIN] **:** any of three liquid isomeric hydrocarbons $C_{10}H_{14}$; *esp* **:** a colorless liquid of pleasant odor from essential oils

cym·ling \ˈsim-lən, -liŋ\ *n* [prob. alter. of *simnel*] **:** a summer squash having a scalloped edge

cy·mo·gene \ˈsī-mə-ˌjēn\ *n* [ISV *cym*ene + *-o-* + *-gen*] **:** a flammable gaseous petroleum product consisting chiefly of butane

cy·mo·phane \-ˌfān\ *n* [F, fr. Gk *kyma* wave + F *-phane*] **:** CHRYSOBERYL; *esp* **:** an opalescent chrysoberyl

cy·mose \ˈsī-ˌmōs\ *adj* **:** of, relating to, being, or bearing a cyme — **cy·mose·ly** *adv*

[1]**Cym·ric** \ˈkim-rik, ˈkəm-\ *adj* **:** of, relating to, or characteristic of the non-Gaelic Celtic people of Britain or their language; *specif* **:** WELSH

[2]**Cymric** *n* **:** BRYTHONIC; *specif* **:** the Welsh language

Cym·ry \-rē\ *n pl* [W] **:** the Brythonic Celts; *specif* **:** WELSH

cyn·ic \ˈsin-ik\ *n* [MF or L; MF *cynique,* fr. L *cynicus,* fr. Gk *kynikos,* lit., like a dog, fr. *kyn-, kyōn* dog — more at HOUND] **1** *cap* **:** an adherent of an ancient Greek school of philosophers who held the view that virtue is the only good and that its essence lies in self-control and independence **2 :** a faultfinding captious critic; *esp* **:** one who believes that human conduct is motivated wholly by self-interest — **cynic** *adj*

cyn·i·cal \'sin-i-kəl\ *adj* **1 :** CAPTIOUS, PEEVISH **2 :** having the attitude or temper of a cynic; *esp* **:** contemptuously distrustful of human nature and motives — **cyn·i·cal·ly** \-k(ə-)lē\ *adv*
syn CYNICAL, MISANTHROPIC, PESSIMISTIC, MISOGYNIC *shared meaning element* : deeply distrustful

cyn·i·cism \'sin-ə-ˌsiz-əm\ *n* **1** *cap* **:** the doctrine of the Cynics **2 a :** cynical character or quality **b :** an expression of such quality

cy·no·mol·gus \ˌsī-nə-'mäl-gəs\ *n, pl* **-gi** \-ˌgī, -ˌjī\ [NL, alter. of *cynamolgus,* fr. L, member of an ancient tribe in Africa, fr. Gk *Kynamolgoi,* lit., dog milkers] **:** MACAQUE; *esp* **:** one (*Macaca irus*) of southeastern Asia, Borneo, and the Philippines that is used esp. in medical research

cy·no·sure \'sī-nə-ˌshu̇(ə)r, 'sin-ə-\ *n* [MF & L; MF, Ursa Minor, guide, fr. L *cynosura* Ursa Minor, fr. Gk *kynosoura,* fr. *kynos oura* dog's tail] **1** *cap* **:** the northern constellation Ursa Minor; *also* **:** NORTH STAR **2 :** a center of attraction or attention

Cyn·thia \'sin(t)-thē-ə\ *n* [L, fr. fem. of *Cynthius* of Cynthus, fr. *Cynthus,* mountain on Delos where she was born] **1 :** ARTEMIS **2 :** MOON

CYO *abbr* Catholic Youth Organization

cy·pher *chiefly Brit var of* CIPHER

[1]cy pres \(ˈ)sī-'prā, (ˈ)sē-\ *adv* **:** in accordance with the rule of cy pres

[2]cy pres *n* [AF so near, as near (as may be)] **:** a rule providing for the interpretation of instruments in equity as nearly as possible in conformity to the intention of the testator when literal construction is illegal, impracticable, or impossible — called also *cy pres doctrine*

[1]cy·press \'sī-prəs\ *n* [ME, fr. OF *ciprès,* fr. L *cyparissus,* fr. Gk *kyparissos*] **1 a (1) :** any of a genus (*Cupressus*) of symmetrical mostly evergreen trees of the pine family with overlapping leaves resembling scales **(2) :** any of several trees related to the cypresses; *esp* **:** either of two large swamp trees (*Taxodium distichum* and *T. ascendens*) of the southern U.S. with hard red wood used for shingles **b :** the wood of a cypress tree **2 :** branches of cypress used as a symbol of mourning

[2]cypress *n* [ME *ciprus, cipres,* fr. *Cyprus,* Mediterranean island] **:** a silk or cotton usu. black gauze formerly used for mourning

cypress vine *n* **:** a tropical American vine (*Quamoclit pennata*) of the morning-glory family with red or white tubular flowers and finely dissected leaves

cyp·ri·an \'sip-rē-ən\ *n, often cap* [L *cyprius* of Cyprus, fr. Gk *kyprios,* fr. *Kypros* Cyprus, birthplace of Aphrodite] **:** PROSTITUTE

cyp·ri·nid \'sip-rə-nəd\ *n* [deriv. of L *cyprinus* carp, fr. Gk *kyprinos*] **:** any of a family (Cyprinidae) of soft-finned freshwater fishes including the carps and minnows — **cyprinid** *adj*

cy·prin·odont \sə-'prin-ə-ˌdänt\ *n* [deriv. of L *cyprinus* + Gk *odont-, odous* tooth — more at TOOTH] **:** any of an order (Microcyprini) of soft-finned fishes including the topminnows and killifishes — **cyprinodont** *adj*

cyp·ri·pe·di·um \ˌsip-rə-'pēd-ē-əm\ *n* [NL, genus name, fr. LL *Cypris,* a name for Venus + Gk *pedilon* sandal] **:** any of a genus (*Cypripedium* or *Paphiopedalum*) of leafy-stemmed terrestrial orchids having large usu. showy drooping flowers with the lip inflated or pouched

cy·pro·hep·ta·dine \ˌsī-prō-'hep-tə-ˌdēn\ *n* [cyclic + *-pro-* (of unknown origin) + *hepta-* + piperi*dine*] **:** a drug $C_{21}H_{21}N$ that acts antagonistically to histamine and serotonin and is used esp. in the treatment of asthma

cy·prot·er·one \sī-'prät-ə-ˌrōn\ *n* [perh. fr. *Cypris, Cypria,* epithets of Aphrodite + *-o-* + *-terone* (as in *androsterone*)] **:** a synthetic steroid that inhibits androgenic secretions (as testosterone)

cyp·se·la \'sip-sə-lə\ *n, pl* **-lae** \-ˌlē\ [NL, fr. Gk *kypselē* vessel, box] **:** an achene with two carpels and adherent calyx tube

Cy·re·na·ic \ˌsir-ə-'nā-ik, ˌsī-rə-\ *n* [L *cyrenaicus,* fr Gk *kyrēnaikos,* fr. *Kyrēnē* Cyrene, Africa, home of Aristippus, author of the doctrine] **:** an adherent or advocate of the doctrine that pleasure is the chief end of life — **Cyrenaic** *adj* — **Cy·re·na·icism** \-'nā-ə-ˌsiz-əm\ *n*

Cy·ril·lic \sə-'ril-ik\ *adj* [St. *Cyril* †869, apostle of the Slavs, reputed inventor of the Cyrillic alphabet] **:** of, relating to, or constituting an alphabet used for writing Old Church Slavonic and for Russian and various other Slavic languages

cyst \'sist\ *n* [NL *cystis,* fr. Gk *kystis* bladder, pouch] **1 :** a closed sac having a distinct membrane and developing abnormally in a cavity or structure of the body **2 :** a body resembling a cyst: as **a :** a resting spore of many algae **b :** an air vesicle (as of a rockweed) **c :** a capsule formed about a minute organism going into a resting or spore stage; *also* **:** this capsule with its contents **d :** a resistant cover about a parasite produced by the parasite or the host

cyst- *or* **cysti-** *or* **cysto-** *comb form* [F, fr. Gk *kyst-, kysto-,* fr. *kystis*] **:** bladder <*cysti*tis> **:** sac <*cysto*carp>

-cyst \ˌsist\ *n comb form* [NL *-cystis,* fr. Gk *kystis*] **:** bladder **:** sac <blasto*cyst*>

cys·ta·mine \'sis-tə-ˌmēn\ *n* [*cyst*ine + *amine*] **:** a cystine derivative $C_4H_{12}N_2S_2$ used in the prevention of radiation sickness (as of cancer patients)

cys·ta·thi·o·nine \ˌsis-tə-'thī-ə-ˌnēn\ *n* [irreg. fr. *cyst*eine + me*thionine*] **:** a sulfur-containing amino acid $C_7H_{14}N_2O_4S$ formed as an intermediate in the conversion of methionine to cysteine in animal organisms

cys·te·amine \sis-'tē-ə-mən\ *n* [*cyste*ine + *amine*] **:** a cysteine derivative C_2H_7NS used in the prevention of radiation sickness (as of cancer patients)

cys·te·ine \'sis-tə-ˌēn\ *n* [ISV, fr. *cystine* + *-ein*] **:** a crystalline sulfur-containing amino acid $C_3H_7NO_2S$ readily oxidizable to cystine

cys·tic \'sis-tik\ *adj* **1 :** relating to, composed of, or containing cysts **2 :** of or relating to the urinary bladder or the gallbladder **3 :** enclosed in a cyst

cys·ti·cer·coid \ˌsis-tə-'sər-ˌkȯid\ *n* **:** a tapeworm larva having an invaginated scolex and solid tailpiece

cys·ti·cer·co·sis \ˌsis-tə-(ˌ)sər-'kō-səs\ *n, pl* **-co·ses** \-'kō-ˌsēz\ [NL] **:** infestation with or disease caused by cysticerci

cys·ti·cer·cus \-'sər-kəs\ *n, pl* **-cer·ci** \-'sər-ˌsī, -ˌkī\ [NL, fr. *cyst-* + Gk *kerkos* tail] **:** a tapeworm larva consisting of a scolex invaginated in a fluid-filled sac in tissues of an intermediate host

cystic fibrosis *n* **:** a common hereditary disease esp. in Caucasian populations that appears usu. in early childhood, involves generalized disorder of exocrine glands, and is marked esp. by deficiency of pancreatic enzymes, respiratory symptoms, and excessive loss of salt in the sweat

cys·tine \'sis-ˌtēn\ *n* [fr. its discovery in bladder stones] **:** a crystalline amino acid $C_6H_{12}N_2O_4S_2$ that is widespread in proteins (as keratins) and is a major metabolic sulfur source

cys·tin·uria \ˌsis-tə-'n(y)u̇r-ē-ə\ *n* [NL] **:** a familial metabolic defect characterized by excretion of excessive amounts of cystine in the urine

cys·ti·tis \sis-'tīt-əs\ *n* [NL] **:** inflammation of the urinary bladder

cys·to·carp \'sis-tə-ˌkärp\ *n* [ISV] **:** the fruiting structure produced in the red algae after fertilization

[1]cys·toid \'sis-ˌtȯid\ *adj* [ISV] **:** resembling a bladder

[2]cystoid *n* **:** a cystoid structure; *specif* **:** a mass resembling a cyst but lacking a membrane

cys·to·lith \'sis-tə-ˌlith\ *n* [G *zystolith,* fr. *zyst-* cyst- + *-lith*] **1 :** a calcium carbonate concretion arising from the cellulose wall of cells of higher plants **2 :** a urinary calculus

cys·to·scope \'sis-tə-ˌskōp\ *n* [ISV] **:** an instrument for the visual examination of the bladder and the passage of instruments under visual control — **cys·to·scop·ic** \ˌsis-tə-'skäp-ik\ *adj*

cyt- *or* **cyto-** *comb form* [G *zyt-, zyto-,* fr. Gk *kytos* hollow vessel — more at HIDE] **1 :** cell <*cyto*logy> **2 :** cytoplasm <*cyto*kinesis>

cyt·as·ter \'sīt-ˌas-tər\ *n* [ISV] **:** ASTER 2

-cyte \ˌsīt\ *n comb form* [NL *-cyta,* fr. Gk *kytos* hollow vessel] **:** cell <leuko*cyte*>

Cyth·er·ea \ˌsith-ə-'rē-ə\ *n* [L, fr. Gk *Kythereia,* fr. *Kythēra* Cythera, island associated with Aphrodite] **:** APHRODITE

Cyth·er·e·an \-'rē-ən\ *adj* **:** of or relating to the planet Venus

cy·ti·dine \'sit-ə-ˌdēn, 'sīt-\ *n* [*cyt*osine + *-idine*] **:** a nucleoside containing cytosine

cy·ti·dyl·ic acid \ˌsit-ə-ˌdil-ik-, ˌsīt-\ *n* [*cytid*ine + *-yl* + *-ic*] **:** a nucleotide containing cytosine

cy·to·ar·chi·tec·ture \ˌsīt-ō-'är-kə-ˌtek-chər\ *n* **:** the cellular make-up of a bodily tissue or structure

cy·to·chem·is·try \-'kem-ə-strē\ *n* **1 :** microscopical biochemistry **2 :** the chemistry of cells — **cy·to·chem·i·cal** \-'kem-i-kəl\ *adj*

cy·to·chrome \'sīt-ə-ˌkrōm\ *n* **:** any of several intracellular hemoprotein respiratory pigments that are enzymes functioning as transporters of electrons to molecular oxygen by undergoing alternate oxidation and reduction

cytochrome c *n, often cap 2d C* **:** the most abundant and stable of the cytochromes

cytochrome oxidase *n* **:** an iron-porphyrin enzyme important in cell respiration because of its ability to catalyze the oxidation of reduced cytochrome c in the presence of oxygen

cy·to·dif·fer·en·ti·a·tion \'sīt-ō-ˌdif-ə-ˌren-chē-'ā-shən\ *n* **:** the development of specialized cells (as muscle, blood, or nerve cells) from undifferentiated precursors

cy·to·ge·net·ic \ˌsīt-ō-jə-'net-ik\ *adj* [ISV] **:** of or relating to cytogenetics — **cy·to·ge·net·i·cal** \-i-kəl\ *adj* — **cy·to·ge·net·i·cal·ly** \-i-k(ə-)lē\ *adv* — **cy·to·ge·net·i·cist** \-'net-ə-səst\ *n*

cy·to·ge·net·ics \-jə-'net-iks\ *n pl but sing or pl in constr* [ISV] **:** a branch of biology that deals with the study of heredity and variation by the methods of both cytology and genetics

cy·to·ki·ne·sis \ˌsīt-ō-kə-'nē-səs, -kī-\ *n* [NL, fr. *cyt-* + Gk *kinēsis* motion] **1 :** cytoplasmic changes accompanying karyokinesis **2 :** cleavage of the cytoplasm into daughter cells following nuclear division — **cy·to·ki·net·ic** \-'net-ik\ *adj*

cy·to·ki·nin \ˌsīt-ə-'kī-nən\ *n* [*cyt-* + *kinin*] **:** any of various substituted adenines that are growth substances of plants

cytol *abbr* cytological; cytology

cy·tol·o·gy \sī-'täl-ə-jē\ *n* [ISV] **1 :** a branch of biology dealing with the structure, function, multiplication, pathology, and life history of cells **2 :** the cytological aspects of a process or structure — **cy·to·log·i·cal** \ˌsīt-ᵊl-'äj-i-kəl\ *or* **cy·to·log·ic** \-'äj-ik\ *adj* — **cy·to·log·i·cal·ly** \-i-k(ə-)lē\ *adv* — **cy·tol·o·gist** \sī-'täl-ə-jəst\ *n*

cy·to·ly·sin \ˌsīt-ᵊl-'īs-ᵊn\ *n* [ISV] **:** a substance (as an antibody that lyses bacteria) producing cytolysis

cy·tol·y·sis \sī-'täl-ə-səs\ *n* [NL] **:** the usu. pathologic dissolution or disintegration of cells — **cy·to·lyt·ic** \ˌsīt-ᵊl-'it-ik\ *adj*

cy·to·me·gal·ic \ˌsīt-ō-mi-'gal-ik\ *adj* [NL *cytomegalia* condition of having enlarged cells (fr. *cyt-* + *megal-* + *-ia*) + E *-ic*] **:** characterized by or producing enlarged cells <~ virus>

cy·to·meg·a·lo·vi·rus \ˌsīt-ə-ˌmeg-ə-lō-'vī-rəs\ *n* [NL, fr. *cytomegalia* + *-o-* + *virus*] **:** any of several viruses that cause cellular enlargement and formation of eosinophilic inclusion bodies esp. in the nucleus and include the causative agent of a severe disease esp. of newborns that usu. affects the salivary glands, brain, kidneys, liver, and lungs

cy·to·mor·phol·o·gy \ˌsīt-ə-mȯr-'fäl-ə-jē\ *n* **:** the morphology of cells — **cy·to·mor·pho·log·i·cal** \-ˌmȯr-fə-'läj-i-kəl\ *adj*

cy·to·path·ic \ˌsīt-ə-'path-ik\ *adj* **:** of, relating to, characterized by, or producing pathological changes in cells

cy·to·patho·gen·ic *adj* [*cyt-* + *pathogenic*] **:** pathologic for or destructive to cells — **cy·to·patho·ge·nic·i·ty** \-jə-'nis-ət-ē\ *n*

cy·to·phil·ic \ˌsīt-ə-'fil-ik\ *adj* **:** having an affinity for cells <~ antibodies>

cy·to·plasm \'sīt-ə-ˌplaz-əm\ *n* [ISV] **:** the protoplasm of a cell external to the nuclear membrane — see CELL illustration — **cy·to·plas·mic** \ˌsīt-ə-'plaz-mik\ *adj* — **cy·to·plas·mi·cal·ly** \-mi-k(ə-)lē\ *adv*

cy·to·sine \'sīt-ə-ˌsēn\ *n* [ISV *cyt-* + *-ose* + *-ine*] **:** a pyrimidine base $C_4H_5N_3O$ that codes genetic information in the polynucleotide chain of DNA or RNA — compare ADENINE, GUANINE, THYMINE, URACIL

cy·to·stat·ic \ˌsīt-ə-ˈstat-ik\ *adj* : tending to retard cellular activity and multiplication <~ treatment of tumor cells> — **cytostatic** *n* — **cy·to·stat·i·cal·ly** \-i-k(ə-)lē\ *adv*

cy·to·tax·on·o·my \ˌsīt-ō-(ˌ)tak-ˈsän-ə-mē\ *n* **1** : study of the relationships and classification of organisms using both classical systematic techniques and comparative studies of chromosomes **2** : the nuclear cytologic makeup of a kind of organism — **cy·to·tax·o·nom·ic** \-ˌtak-sə-ˈnäm-ik\ *adj* — **cy·to·tax·o·nom·i·cal·ly** \-i-k(ə-)lē\ *adv*

cy·to·tech·nol·o·gist \ˌsīt-ə-tek-ˈnäl-ə-jəst\ *n* : a medical technician trained in the identification of cells and cellular abnormalities (as in cancer)

cy·to·tox·ic \ˌsīt-ə-ˈtäk-sik\ *adj* **1** : of or relating to a cytotoxin **2** : toxic to cells — **cy·to·tox·ic·i·ty** \-(ˌ)täk-ˈsis-ət-ē\ *n*

cy·to·tox·in \-ˈtäk-sən\ *n* : a substance (as a toxin or antibody) having a toxic effect on cells

cy·to·tro·pic \ˌsīt-ə-ˈtrō-pik, -ˈträp-ik\ *adj* : attracted to cells <a ~ virus>

CZ *abbr* Canal Zone

czar \ˈzär\ *n* [obs. Pol *czar*, fr. Russ *tsar'*, fr. Goth *kaisar*, fr. Gk or L; Gk, fr. L *Caesar* — more at CAESAR] **1** : EMPEROR; *specif* : the ruler of Russia until the 1917 revolution **2** : one having great power or authority <retained the title of undisputed ~ over taxation —Marjorie Hunter> — **czar·dom** \ˈzärd-əm\ *n*

czar·das \ˈchär-ˌdash, -ˌdäsh\ *n, pl* **czardas** *same*\ [Hung *csárdás*] : a Hungarian dance to music in duple time in which the dancers start slowly and finish with a rapid whirl

czar·e·vitch \ˈzär-ə-ˌvich\ *n* [Russ *tsarevich*, fr. *tsar'* + *-evich*, patronymic suffix] : an heir apparent of a Russian czar

cza·ri·na \zä-ˈrē-nə\ *n* [prob. modif of G *zarin*, fr. *zar* czar, fr. Russ *tsar'*] : the wife of a czar

czar·ism \ˈzär-ˌiz-əm\ *n* **1** : the government of Russia under the czars **2** : autocratic rule — **czar·ist** \ˈzär-əst\ *n or adj*

cza·ri·tza \zä-ˈrit-sə, -ˈrēt-\ *n* [Russ *tsaritsa*, fem. of *tsar'*] : CZARINA

Czech \ˈchek\ *n* [Czech *Čech*] **1** : a native or inhabitant of Czechoslovakia; *esp* : a native or inhabitant of Bohemia, Moravia, or Silesia provinces **2** : the Slavic language of the Czechs — **Czech** *adj* — **Czech·ish** \-ish\ *adj*

¹d \ˈdē\ *n, pl* **d's** *or* **ds** \ˈdēz\ *often cap, often attrib* **1 a** : the 4th letter of the English alphabet **b** : a graphic representation of this letter **c** : a speech counterpart of orthographic *d* **2** : 500 — see NUMBER table **3** : the 2d tone of a C-major scale **4** : a graphic device for reproducing the letter *d* **5** : one designated *d* esp. as the 4th in order or class **6 a** : a grade rating a student's work as poor in quality **b** : one graded or rated with a D **7** : something shaped like the letter D; *specif* : a semicircle on a pool table about 22 inches in diameter for use esp. in snooker

²d *abbr, often cap* **1** date **2** daughter **3** day **4** dead **5** deceased **6** deci- **7** degree **8** [L *denarius, denarii*] penny; pence **9** depart; departure **10** diameter **11** dimensional **12** distance **13** dorsal **14** drive; driving **15** Dutch

³d *symbol* differential

D *symbol* **1** derivative **2** deuterium **3** differential coefficient

d- \ˌdē, ˈdē\ *prefix* [ISV, fr. *dextr-*] **1** : dextrorotatory <*d*- tartaric acid> **2** : having a similar configuration at a selected carbon atom to the configuration of dextrorotatory glyceraldehyde — usu. printed as a small capital <D-fructose>

'd \d, əd\ *vb* **1** : HAD **2** : WOULD **3** : DID

DA *abbr* **1** days after acceptance **2** delayed action **3** deposit account **4** Dictionary of Americanisms **5** district attorney **6** doctor of arts **7** documents against acceptance **8** documents for acceptance **9** don't answer

documents against acceptance **7** documents for acceptance **8** don't answer

¹dab \ˈdab\ *n* [ME *dabbe*] **1** : a sudden blow or thrust : POKE **2** : a gentle touch or stroke : PAT

²dab *vb* **dabbed; dab·bing** *vt* **1** : to strike or touch lightly : PAT **2** : to apply lightly or irregularly : DAUB ~ *vi* : to make a dab

³dab *n* **1** : DAUB **2** : a small amount

⁴dab *n* [AF *dabbe*] : FLATFISH *esp* : any of several flounders (genus *Limanda*)

⁵dab *n* [perh. alter. of *adept*] *chiefly Brit* : a skillful person : EXPERT

DAB *abbr* Dictionary of American Biography

dab·ber \ˈdab-ər\ *n* **1** : one that dabs **2** : a pad, brush, or ball used to ink type or engraving plates

dab·ble \ˈdab-əl\ *vb* **dab·bled; dab·bling** \-(ə-)liŋ\ [perh. freq. of *dab*] *vt* : to wet by splashing or by little dips or strokes : SPATTER ~ *vi* **1 a** : to paddle, splash, or play in or as if in water **b** : to reach with the bill to the bottom of shallow water in order to obtain food **2** : to work or concern oneself superficially <~*s* in art>

dab·bler \-(ə-)lər\ *n* : one that dabbles: as **a** : one not deeply engaged in or concerned with something **b** : a duck (as a mallard or shoveler) that feeds by dabbling — called also *dabbling duck, puddle duck, river duck, surface feeder* **syn** see AMATEUR

dab·bling \-(ə-)liŋ\ *n* : a superficial or intermittent interest, investigation, or experiment <his ~*s* in philosophy and art>

dab·chick \ˈdab-ˌchik\ *n* [prob. irreg. fr. obs. E *dop* (to dive) + E *chick*] : any of several small grebes

da ca·po \dä-ˈkäp-(ˌ)ō, də-\ *adv or adj* [It] : from the beginning — used as a direction in music to repeat

dace \ˈdās\ *n, pl* **dace** [ME, fr. MF *dars*, fr. ML *darsus*] **1** : a small freshwater European cyprinid fish (*Leuciscus leuciscus*) **2** : any of various small No. American freshwater cyprinid fishes

da·cha \ˈdäch-ə\ *n* [Russ, lit., gift; fr. its frequently being the gift of a ruler] : a Russian country cottage used esp. in the summer

dachs·hund \ˈdäks-ˌhu̇nt, ˈdäk-sənt\ *n, pl* **dachshunds** *or* **dachs·hun·de** \ˈdäks-ˌhu̇n-də\ [G, fr. *dachs* badger + *hund* dog] : a small dog of a breed of German origin with a long body, short legs, and long drooping ears

dachshund

Da·cron \ˈdā-ˌkrän, ˈdak-ˌrän\ *trademark* — used for a synthetic polyester textile fiber

dac·tyl \ˈdak-tᵊl\ *n* [ME *dactile*, fr. L *dactylus*, fr. Gk *daktylos*, lit., finger; fr. the fact that the three syllables have the first one longest like the joints of the finger] : a metrical foot consisting of one long and two short syllables or of one stressed and two unstressed syllables (as in *tenderly*) — **dac·tyl·ic** \dak-ˈtil-ik\ *adj or n*

dactyl- *or* **dactylo-** *comb form* [Gk *daktyl-, daktylo-*, fr. *daktylos*] : finger : toe : digit <*dactylitis*>

dac·ty·lol·o·gy \ˌdak-tə-ˈläl-ə-jē\ *n* : the art of communicating ideas by signs made with the fingers

-dac·ty·lous \ˈdak-tə-ləs\ *adj comb form* [Gk *-daktylos*, fr. *daktylos*] : having (such or so many) fingers or toes <*didactylous*>

dac·ty·lus \ˈdak-tə-ləs\ *n, pl* **-li** \-ˌlī, -ˌlē\ [NL, fr. Gk *daktylos* finger, toe] : one or more joints of the tarsus of some insects following the enlarged and modified first joint

dad \ˈdad\ *n* [prob. baby talk] : FATHER

da·da \ˈdäd-(ˌ)ä\ *n, often cap* [F] : a movement in art and literature based on deliberate irrationality and negation of traditional artistic values; *also* : the art and literature produced by this movement

da·da·ism \-ˌiz-əm\ *n, often cap* : DADA — **da·da·ist** \-ˌist\ *n, often cap* — **da·da·is·tic** \ˌdäd-ä-ˈis-tik\ *adj, often cap*

dad·dy \ˈdad-ē\ *n, pl* **daddies** : FATHER

dad·dy long·legs \ˌdad-ē-ˈlȯŋ-ˌlegz, -ˌlägz\ *n pl but sing or pl in constr* : any of various animals with long slender legs: as **a** : CRANE FLY **b** : HARVESTMAN

¹da·do \ˈdād-(ˌ)ō\ *n, pl* **dadoes** [It, die, plinth] **1 a** : the part of a pedestal of a column between the base and the surbase **b** : the lower part of an interior wall when specially decorated or faced; *also* : the decoration adorning this part of a wall **2** : a groove made by dadoing **3** : a tool (as a plane) for dadoing

1 2 3

dado 1a: *1* surbase, *2* dado, *3* base

²dado *vt* **da·doed; da·do·ing** **1** : to provide with a dado **2 a** : to set into a groove **b** : to cut a rectangular groove in (as a plank)

DAE *abbr* Dictionary of American English

dae·dal \ˈdēd-ᵊl\ *adj* [L *daedalus*, fr. Gk *daidalos*] **1 a** : INTRICATE <the computer's ~ circuitry> **b** : SKILLFUL, ARTISTIC <words made accessible in a novel and ~ way —*Publisher's*

Weekly> **2 :** adorned with many things <visions of cloud and light and ~ earth are the airman's daily scene —Laurence Binyon>
Dae·da·lus \ˈded-ᵊl-əs, ˈdēd-\ *n* [L, fr. Gk *Daidalos*] **:** the legendary builder of the Cretan labyrinth and the inventor of wings whereby he flew to escape imprisonment — **Dae·da·lian** \di-ˈdāl-yən\ *or* **Dae·da·lean** \di-ˈdāl-yən; ˌded-ᵊl-ˈē-ən, ˌdēd-\ *adj*
dae·mon *var of* DEMON
daff \ˈdaf\ *vt* [alter. of *doff*] **1** *archaic* **:** to thrust aside **2** *obs* **:** to put off (as with an excuse)
daf·fo·dil \ˈdaf-ə-ˌdil\ *n* [prob. fr. D *de affodil* the asphodel, fr. *de* the (fr. MD) + *affodil* asphodel, fr. MF *afrodille*, fr. L *asphodelus*; akin to OHG *thaz* the — more at THAT, ASPHODEL] **:** any of various bulbous herbs (genus *Narcissus*); *esp* **:** a plant whose flowers have a large corona elongated into a trumpet — compare JONQUIL
daf·fy \ˈdaf-ē\ *adj* **daf·fi·er; -est** [obs. E *daff*, n. (fool)] **:** CRAZY, FOOLISH <the story is slight, but it has a ~ kind of logic —*N.Y. Times Bk. Rev.*>
daft \ˈdaft\ *adj* [ME *dafte* gentle, stupid; akin to OE *gedæfte* mild, gentle, ME *defte* deft, L *faber* smith] **1 a :** SILLY, FOOLISH **b :** MAD, INSANE **2** *Scot* **:** frivolously gay — **daft·ly** *adv* — **daft·ness** \ˈdaf(t)-nəs\ *n*
1dag \ˈdag\ *n* [ME *dagge*] **1 :** a hanging end or shred **2 :** matted or manure-coated wool
2dag *abbr* dekagram
dag·ger \ˈdag-ər\ *n* [ME] **1 :** a short weapon for stabbing **2 a :** something that resembles a dagger **b :** a character † used as a reference mark or to indicate a death date
da·go \ˈdā-(ˌ)gō\ *n, pl* **dagos** *or* **dagoes** [alter. of earlier *diego*, fr. *Diego*, a common Sp given name] **:** a person of Italian or Spanish birth or descent — usu. used disparagingly
da·guerre·o·type \də-ˈger-(ē-)ə-ˌtīp\ *n* [F *daguerréotype*, fr. L. J. M. *Daguerre* †1851 F painter + F *-o-* + *type*] **:** an early photograph produced on a silver or a silver-covered copper plate; *also* **:** the process of producing such photographs — **daguerreotype** *vt* — **da·guerre·o·typy** \-ˌtī-pē\ *n*
dah \ˈdä\ *n* [imit.] **:** a dash in radio or telegraphic code
DAH *abbr* Dictionary of American History
dahl·ia \ˈdal-yə, ˈdäl-, *U.S. also & Brit usu* ˈdāl-\ *n* [NL, genus name, fr. Anders *Dahl* †1789 Sw botanist] **:** any of a genus (*Dahlia*) of American tuberous-rooted composite herbs having opposite pinnate leaves and rayed flower heads and including many that are cultivated as ornamentals
1dai·ly \ˈdā-lē\ *adj* **1 a :** occurring, made, or acted upon every day **b :** issued every day or every weekday **c :** of or providing for every day **2 a :** reckoned by the day <average ~ wage> **b :** covering the period of or based on a day < ~ statistics> — **dai·li·ness** *n*

syn DAILY, DIURNAL, QUOTIDIAN, CIRCADIAN *shared meaning element* **:** of each or every day. DAILY is used with reference to the ordinary concerns of the day or daytime <*daily* food> <a *daily* duty> Distinctively, it may refer to weekdays as contrasted with holidays and Sundays and sometimes also Saturdays, and it may imply an opposition to *nightly* <the *daily* anodyne, the nightly draught —Alexander Pope> DIURNAL is used in contrast to *nocturnal* and occurs chiefly in poetic or technical contexts <rolled round in earth's *diurnal* course —William Wordsworth> <*diurnal* mammals, active only by day> QUOTIDIAN emphasizes the quality of daily recurrence <a *quotidian* fever> and may attribute a commonplace, routine, or everyday quality to what it describes <*quotidian* routine> CIRCADIAN, a chiefly technical word of recent coinage, differs from *daily* or *quotidian* in implying only approximate equation with the twenty-four hour day <*circadian* rhythms in insect behavior>

2daily *adv* **:** every day **:** every weekday
3daily *n, pl* **dailies 1 :** a newspaper published every weekday **2** *Brit* **:** a servant who works on a daily basis
daily double *n* **:** a system of betting (as on horse races) in which the bettor must pick the winners of two stipulated races in order to win
daily dozen *n* **1 :** a series of physical exercises to be performed daily **:** WORKOUT **2 :** a set of routine duties or tasks
dai·mon \ˈdī-ˌmōn\ *n, pl* **dai·mo·nes** \ˈdī-mə-ˌnēz\ *or* **daimons** [Gk *daimōn*] **:** DEMON 1, 3 — **dai·mon·ic** \dī-ˈmän-ik\ *adj*
dai·myo *or* **dai·mio** \ˈdī-mē-ˌō, (ˈ)dī-ˈmyō\ *n, pl* **-myos** *or* **-mios** [Jap *daimyō*] **:** a Japanese feudal baron
1dain·ty \ˈdānt-ē\ *n, pl* **dainties** [ME *deinte*, fr. OF *deintié*, fr. L *dignitat-, dignitas* dignity, worth] **1 a :** something delicious to the taste **b :** something choice or pleasing **2** *obs* **:** FASTIDIOUSNESS
2dainty *adj* **dain·ti·er; -est 1 a :** tasting good **:** TASTY **b :** attractively prepared and served **2 :** of a kind to appeal to a fastidious taste esp. because of fragile beauty or diminutive charm and grace **3** *obs* **:** CHARY, RELUCTANT **4 a :** marked by fastidious discrimination or finical taste **b :** showing avoidance of anything rough *syn* **1** see CHOICE *ant* gross **2** see NICE — **dain·ti·ly** \ˈdānt-ᵊl-ē\ *adv* — **dain·ti·ness** \ˈdānt-ē-nəs\ *n*
dai·qui·ri \ˈdī-kə-rē, ˈdak-ə-\ *n* [*Daiquirí*, Cuba] **:** a cocktail made of rum, lime juice, and sugar
dairy \ˈde(ə)r-ē, ˈda(ə)r-\ *n, pl* **dair·ies** [ME *deyerie*, fr. *deye* dairymaid, fr. OE *dǣge* kneader of bread; akin to OE *dāg* dough — more at DOUGH] **1 :** a room, building, or establishment where milk is kept and butter or cheese is made **2 a :** the department of farming or of a farm that is concerned with the production of milk, butter, and cheese **b :** a farm devoted to such production **3 :** an establishment for the sale or distribution chiefly of milk and milk products
dairy breed *n* **:** a cattle breed developed chiefly for milk production
dairy cattle *n pl* **:** cattle of one of the dairy breeds
dairy·ing \ˈder-ē-iŋ\ *n* **:** the business of operating a dairy
dairy·maid \-ē-ˌmād\ *n* **:** a woman employed in a dairy
dairy·man \-ē-mən, -ˌman\ *n* **:** one who operates a dairy farm or works in a dairy
da·is \ˈdā-əs, ˈdī-\ *n* [ME *deis*, fr. OF, fr. L *discus* dish, quoit — more at DISH] **:** a raised platform usu. above the floor of a hall or large room
dai·sy \ˈdā-zē\ *n, pl* **daisies** [ME *dayeseye*, fr. OE *dægesēage*, fr. *dæg* day + *ēage* eye] **1 :** a composite plant (as of the genera *Bellis* or *Chrysanthemum*) having a flower head with well-developed ray flowers usu. arranged in one or a few whorls: as **a :** a low European herb (*Bellis perennis*) with white or pink ray flowers — called also *English daisy* **b :** a leafy-stemmed perennial herb (*Chrysanthemum leucanthemum*) that has long white ray flowers and is often a troublesome weed in parts of the U.S. — called also *oxeye daisy* **2 :** the flower head of a daisy **3 :** a first-rate person or thing
daisy ham *n* **:** a boned and smoked piece of pork from the shoulder
Da·ko·ta \də-ˈkōt-ə\ *n, pl* **Dakotas** *also* **Dakota 1 :** a member of an Amerindian people of the northern Mississippi valley **2 :** the language of the Dakota people
dal *abbr* dekaliter
Da·lai La·ma \ˌdäl-ˌī-ˈläm-ə, ˌdäl-ˌā-, ˌdal-\ *n* [Mongolian *dalai* ocean] **:** the spiritual head of Lamaism
dal·a·pon \ˈdal-ə-ˌpän\ *n* [perh. fr. *di-* + *alpha* + *propionic* acid] **:** an herbicide that kills monocotyledonous plants selectively and is used esp. on unwanted grasses
da·la·si \dä-ˈläs-ē\ *n* [native name in the Gambia] — see MONEY table
dale \ˈdā(ə)l\ *n* [ME, fr. OE *dæl*; akin to OHG *tal* valley, Gk *tholos* rotunda] **:** VALE, VALLEY <went riding over hill and ~>
dales·man \ˈdā(ə)lz-mən\ *n, Brit* **:** one living or born in a dale
da·leth \ˈdäl-ˌeth, -ˌet\ *n* [Heb *dāleth*, fr. *deleth* door] **:** the 4th letter of the Hebrew alphabet — see ALPHABET table
dal·li·ance \ˈdal-ē-ən(t)s\ *n* **:** an act of dallying: as **a :** FOREPLAY **b :** frivolous action **:** TRIFLING
Dal·lis grass \ˈdal-əs-\ *n* [perh. alter. of *Dallas*, Texas] **:** a tall tufted tropical perennial grass (*Paspalum dilatatum*) introduced as a pasture and forage grass in the southern U.S.
Dall sheep \ˈdȯl-\ *or* **Dall's sheep** \ˈdȯlz-\ *n* [William H. *Dall* †1927 Am naturalist] **:** a large white wild sheep (*Ovis montana dalli* or *O. dalli*) of northwestern No. America
dal·ly \ˈdal-ē\ *vi* **dal·lied; dal·ly·ing** [ME *dalyen*, fr. AF *dalier*] **1 a :** to act playfully; *esp* **:** to play amorously **b :** to deal lightly **:** TOY <accused him of ~*ing* with a serious problem> **2 a :** to waste time **b :** LINGER, DAWDLE *syn* see TRIFLE — **dal·li·er** *n*
dal·ma·tian \dal-ˈmā-shən\ *n, often cap* [fr. the supposed origin of the breed in Dalmatia] **:** any of a breed of large dogs having a white short-haired coat with black or brown spots
dal·mat·ic \dal-ˈmat-ik\ *n* [LL *dalmatica*, fr. L, fem. of *dalmaticus* Dalmatian, fr. *Dalmatia*] **:** a wide-sleeved overgarment with slit sides worn by a deacon or prelate; *also* **:** a similar robe worn by a British sovereign at his coronation

dalmatic

dal se·gno \däl-ˈsān-(ˌ)yō\ *adv* [It, from the sign] — used as a direction in music to return to the sign that marks the beginning of a repeat
1dam \ˈdam\ *n* [ME *dam, dame* lady, dam — more at DAME] **:** a female parent — used esp. of a domestic animal
2dam *n* [ME] **1 a :** a barrier preventing the flow of water or of loose solid materials (as soil or snow); *esp* **:** a barrier built across a watercourse for impounding water **b :** a barrier to check the flow of liquid, gas, or air **2 :** a body of water confined by a dam
3dam *vt* **dammed; dam·ming 1 :** to provide or restrain with a dam **2 :** to stop up **:** BLOCK
4dam *abbr* dekameter
1dam·age \ˈdam-ij\ *n* [ME, fr. OF, fr. *dam* damage, fr. L *damnum*] **1 :** loss or harm resulting from injury to person, property, or reputation **2** *pl* **:** compensation in money imposed by law for loss or injury **3 :** EXPENSE, COST <"What's the ~?" he said, asking how much his bill was>
2damage *vt* **dam·aged; dam·ag·ing :** to cause damage to *syn* see INJURE — **dam·ag·er** *n*
dam·ag·ing *adj* **:** causing or able to cause damage **:** INJURIOUS <has a ~ effect on wildlife> — **dam·ag·ing·ly** \ˈdam-ij-iŋ-lē\ *adv*
1dam·a·scene \ˈdam-ə-ˌsēn, ˌdam-ə-ˈ\ *n* **1** *cap* **:** a native or inhabitant of Damascus **2 :** DAMASK 2b
2damascene *adj* **1** *cap* **:** of, relating to, or characteristic of Damascus or the Damascenes **2 :** of or relating to damask or the art of damascening
3damascene *vt* **-scened; -scen·ing** [MF *damasquiner*, fr. *damasquin* of Damascus] **:** to ornament (as iron or steel) with wavy patterns like those of watered silk or with inlaid work of precious metals
Da·mas·cus steel \də-ˌmas-kə(s)-\ *n* **:** hard elastic steel ornamented with wavy patterns and used esp. for sword blades
1dam·ask \ˈdam-əsk\ *n* [ME *damaske*, fr. ML *damascus*, fr. *Damascus*] **1 :** a firm lustrous fabric (as of linen, cotton, silk, or rayon) made with flat patterns in a satin weave on a plain-woven ground on jacquard looms **2 a :** DAMASCUS STEEL **b :** the characteristic markings of this steel **3 :** a grayish red
2damask *adj* **1 :** made of or resembling damask **2 :** of the color damask
damask rose *n* [obs. *Damask* of Damascus, fr. obs. *Damask* Damascus] **:** a large hardy fragrant pink rose (*Rosa damascena*) that is cultivated in Asia Minor as a source of attar of roses and is a parent of many hybrid perpetual roses
dame \ˈdām\ *n* [ME, fr. OF, fr. L *domina*, fem. of *dominus* master; akin to L *domus* house — more at TIMBER] **1 :** a woman of rank, station, or authority: as **a** *archaic* **:** the mistress of a household **b :** the wife or daughter of a lord **c :** a female member of an order of knighthood — used as a title prefixed to the given name **2 a :** an elderly woman **b :** WOMAN

dame school *n* : a school in which the rudiments of reading and writing were taught by a woman in her own home

dame's violet *n* : a Eurasian perennial plant (*Hesperis matronalis*) widely cultivated for its spikes of showy, single or double, and fragrant white or purple flowers — called also *dame's rocket*

dam·mar *or* **dam·ar** *also* **dam·mer** \'dam-ər\ *n* [Malay *damar*] **1 :** any of various hard resins derived esp. from evergreen trees (genus *Agathis*) of the pine family **2 :** a clear to yellow resin obtained in Malaya from several timber trees (family Dipterocarpaceae) and used in varnishes and inks

dam·mit \'dam-ət\ : damn it

[1]**damn** \'dam\ *vb* **damned; damn·ing** \'dam-iŋ\ [ME *dampnen,* fr. OF *dampner,* fr. L *damnare,* fr. *damnum* damage, loss, fine] *vt* **1 :** to condemn to a punishment or fate; *esp* **:** to condemn to hell **2 a :** to condemn vigorously and often irascibly for some real or fancied fault or defect <~*ed* the storm for their delay> **b :** to condemn as a failure by public criticism **3 :** to bring ruin on **4 :** to swear at : CURSE ~ *vi* **:** CURSE, SWEAR ***syn*** see EXECRATE

[2]**damn** *n* **1 :** the utterance of the word *damn* as a curse **2 :** a minimum amount or degree (as of care or consideration) **:** the least bit

[3]**damn** *adj or adv* **:** DAMNED <a ~ nuisance> <ran ~ fast> — **damn well :** beyond doubt or question **:** CERTAINLY <knew *damn well* what would happen>

dam·na·ble \'dam-nə-bəl\ *adj* **1 :** liable to or deserving condemnation **2 :** very bad **:** DETESTABLE <~ weather> — **dam·na·ble·ness** *n* — **dam·na·bly** \-blē\ *adv*

dam·na·tion \dam-'nā-shən\ *n* **:** the act of damning **:** the state of being damned

dam·na·to·ry \'dam-nə-ˌtōr-ē, -ˌtȯr-\ *adj* **:** expressing, imposing, or causing condemnation **:** CONDEMNATORY

[1]**damned** \'dam(d)\ *adj* **damned·er** \'dam-dər\; **damned·est** *or* **damnd·est** \-dəst\ **1 :** DAMNABLE <hoping to get away from this ~ smog> **2 :** COMPLETE, UTTER <~ nonsense> **3 :** EXTRAORDINARY — used in the superlative <the ~*est* contraption he ever saw>

[2]**damned** \'dam(d)\ *adv* **:** EXTREMELY, VERY <a ~ good job>

damned·est *or* **damnd·est** \'dam-dəst\ *n* **:** UTMOST, BEST — used chiefly in the phrase *do one's damnedest* <doing his ~ to succeed>

dam·ni·fy \'dam-nə-ˌfī\ *vt* **-fied; -fy·ing :** to cause loss or damage to <intimidation — the freedom to ~ another person with impunity —Henry Hazlitt>

damn·ing \'dam-iŋ\ *adj* **1 :** bringing damnation <a ~ sin> **2 :** causing or leading to condemnation or ruin <presented some ~ testimony> — **dam·ning·ly** \-iŋ-lē\ *adv*

Dam·o·cles \'dam-ə-ˌklēz\ *n* [L, fr. Gk *Damoklēs*] **:** a courtier of ancient Syracuse held to have been seated at a banquet beneath a sword hung by a single hair — **Dam·o·cle·an** \ˌdam-ə-'klē-ən\ *adj*

Da·mon \'dā-mən\ *n* [L, fr. Gk *Damōn*] **:** a Sicilian who pledges his life for his condemned friend Pythias

[1]**damp** \'damp\ *n* [MD or MLG, vapor; akin to OHG *damph* vapor, OE *dim* dim] **1 :** a noxious gas esp. in a coal mine **2 :** MOISTURE: **a :** HUMIDITY, DAMPNESS **b** *archaic* **:** FOG, MIST **3 a :** DISCOURAGEMENT, CHECK **b** *archaic* **:** DEPRESSION, DEJECTION

[2]**damp** *vt* **1 a :** to affect with a noxious gas **:** CHOKE **b :** to diminish the activity or intensity of — often used with *down* <~*ing* down the causes of inflation> **c :** to check the vibration or oscillation of (as a string or voltage) **2 :** DAMPEN ~ *vi* **:** to diminish progressively in vibration or oscillation

[3]**damp** *adj* **1 a** *archaic* **:** being confused, bewildered, or shocked **:** STUPEFIED **b :** DEPRESSED, DULL **2 :** slightly or moderately wet ***syn*** see WET — **damp·ish** \'dam-pish\ *adj* — **damp·ly** *adv* — **damp·ness** *n*

damp·en \'dam-pən\ *vb* **damp·ened; damp·en·ing** \'damp-(ə-)niŋ\ *vt* **1 :** to check or diminish the activity or vigor of **:** DEADEN <the heat ~*ed* our spirits> **2 :** to make damp <the shower barely ~*ed* the ground> **3 :** DAMP 1c ~ *vi* **1 :** to become damp **2 :** to become deadened or depressed — **damp·en·er** \'damp-(ə-)nər\ *n*

damp·er \'dam-pər\ *n* **1 :** a device that damps: as **a :** a valve or plate (as in the flue of a furnace) for regulating the draft **b :** a small felted block to stop the vibration of a piano string **c :** a device designed to bring a mechanism to rest with minimum oscillation **2 :** a dulling or deadening influence <put a ~ on the celebration>

damp·ing–off \ˌdam-piŋ-'ȯf\ *n* **:** a diseased condition of seedlings or cuttings caused by fungi and marked by wilting or rotting

dam·sel \'dam-zəl\ *also* **dam·o·sel** *or* **dam·o·zel** \'dam-ə-ˌzel\ *n* [ME *damesel,* fr. OF *dameisele,* fr. (assumed) VL *domnicella* young noblewoman, dim. of L *domina* lady] **:** a young woman: **a** *archaic* **:** a young unmarried woman of noble birth **b :** GIRL

dam·sel·fly \'dam-zəl-ˌflī\ *n* **:** any of numerous odonate insects (suborder Zygoptera) distinguished from dragonflies by laterally projecting eyes and petiolate wings folded above the body when at rest

dam·son \'dam-zən\ *n* [ME, fr. L *prunum damascenum,* lit., plum of Damascus] **:** an Asiatic plum (*Prunus insititia* or *P. domestica insititia*) cultivated for its small acid purple fruit; *also* **:** its fruit

[1]**Dan** \'dan\ *n* [Heb *Dān*] **:** a son of Jacob and the traditional eponymous ancestor of one of the tribes of Israel

[2]**Dan** \(')dan\ *n* [ME, title of members of religious orders, fr. MF, fr. ML *domnus,* fr. L *dominus* master] *archaic* **:** MASTER, SIR

[3]**Dan** *abbr* **1** Daniel **2** Danish

Dan·ae \'dan-ə-ˌē\ *n* [L, fr. Gk *Danaē*] **:** a princess of Argos visited by Zeus in the form of a shower of gold and by him the mother of Perseus

[1]**dance** \'dan(t)s\ *vb* **danced; danc·ing** [ME *dauncen,* fr. OF *dancier*] *vi* **1 :** to engage in or perform a dance **2 :** to move quickly up and down or about ~ *vt* **1 :** to perform or take part in as a dancer **2 :** to cause to dance **3 :** to bring into a specified condition by dancing — **dance·able** \'dan(t)-sə-bəl\ *adj* — **danc·er** *n*

[2]**dance** *n, often attrib* **1 :** an act or instance of dancing **2 :** a series of rhythmic and patterned bodily movements usu. performed to music **3 :** a social gathering for dancing **4 :** a piece of music by which dancing may be guided **5 :** the art of dancing

D & C *abbr* dilatation and curettage

dan·de·li·on \'dan-dᵊl-ˌī-ən\ *n* [MF *dent de lion,* lit., lion's tooth] **:** any of a genus (*Taraxacum*) of yellow-flowered composite plants; *esp* **:** an herb (*T. officinale*) sometimes grown as a potherb and nearly cosmopolitan as a weed

dan·der \'dan-dər\ *n* [alter. of *dandruff*] **1 :** minute scales from hair, feathers, or skin that may be allergenic **2 :** ANGER, TEMPER <got his ~ up and shouted at his wife>

dan·di·a·cal \dan-'dī-ə-kəl\ *adj* [[1]*dandy* + *-acal* (as in *demoniacal*)] **:** of, relating to, or suggestive of a dandy — **dan·di·a·cal·ly** \-k(ə-)lē\ *adv*

Dan·die Din·mont terrier \ˌdan-dē-'din-ˌmänt-\ *n* [*Dandie Dinmont,* character owning 2 such dogs in the novel *Guy Mannering* by Sir Walter Scott] **:** a terrier of a breed characterized by short legs, a long body, pendulous ears, a rough coat, and a full silky topknot

dan·di·fy \'dan-di-ˌfī\ *vt* **-fied; -fy·ing :** to cause to resemble a dandy — **dan·di·fi·ca·tion** \ˌdan-di-fə-'kā-shən\ *n*

dan·dle \'dan-dᵊl\ *vt* **dan·dled; dan·dling** \-(d)liŋ, -dᵊl-iŋ\ [origin unknown] **1 :** to move (as a baby) up and down in one's arms or on one's knee in affectionate play **2 :** PAMPER, PET

dan·druff \'dan-drəf\ *n* [prob. fr. *dand-* (origin unknown) + *-ruff,* of Scand origin; akin to ON *hrūfa* scab; akin to OHG *hruf* scurf, Lith *kraupus* rough] **:** a scurf that forms on the scalp and comes off in small white or grayish scales — **dan·druffy** \-ē\ *adj*

[1]**dan·dy** \'dan-dē\ *n, pl* **dandies** [prob. short for *jack-a-dandy,* fr. [1]*jack* + *a* (of) + *dandy* (origin unknown)] **1 :** a man who gives exaggerated attention to dress **2 :** something excellent in its class **3 :** a small 2-masted sailboat with a modified ketch rig — **dan·dy·ish** \-dē-ish\ *adj* — **dan·dy·ish·ly** *adv*

[2]**dandy** *adj* **dan·di·er; -est 1 :** of, relating to, or suggestive of a dandy **:** FOPPISH **2 :** very good **:** FIRST-RATE <a ~ place to stay>

dan·dy·ism \'dan-dē-ˌiz-əm\ *n* **1 :** the style or conduct of a dandy **2 :** a literary and artistic style of the latter part of the 19th century marked by artificiality and excessive refinement

Dane \'dān\ *n* [ME *Dan,* fr. ON *Danr*] **1 :** a native or inhabitant of Denmark **2 :** a person of Danish descent

dane·geld \'dān-ˌgeld\ *n, often cap* **:** an annual tax believed to have been imposed orig. to buy off Danish invaders in England or to maintain forces to oppose them but continued as a land tax

Dane·law \'dān-ˌlȯ\ *n* **1 :** the law in force in the part of England held by the Danes in pre-Conquest times **2 :** the part of England under the Danelaw

[1]**dan·ger** \'dān-jər\ *n* [ME *daunger,* fr. OF *dangier,* alter. of *dongier,* fr. (assumed) VL *dominiarium,* fr. L *dominium* ownership] **1 a** *archaic* **:** JURISDICTION **b** *obs* **:** REACH, RANGE **2** *obs* **:** HARM, DAMAGE **3 :** exposure or liability to injury, pain, or loss <a place where children could play without ~> **4 :** a case or cause of danger <the ~*s* of mining>

[2]**danger** *vt, archaic* **:** ENDANGER

dan·ger·ous \'dānj-(ə-)rəs\ *adj* **1 :** exposing to or involving danger **2 :** able or likely to inflict injury — **dan·ger·ous·ly** *adv* — **dan·ger·ous·ness** *n*

syn DANGEROUS, HAZARDOUS, PRECARIOUS, PERILOUS, RISKY *shared meaning element* **:** bringing or involving the chance of loss or injury ***ant*** safe, secure

[1]**dan·gle** \'daŋ-gəl\ *vb* **dan·gled; dan·gling** \-g(ə-)liŋ\ [prob. of Scand origin; akin to Dan *dangle* to dangle] *vi* **1 :** to hang loosely and usu. so as to be able to swing freely **2 :** to be a hanger-on or a dependent **3 :** to occur in a sentence without having a normally expected syntactic relation to the rest of the sentence <the word *climbing* in "Climbing the mountain the cabin came into view" is *dangling*> ~ *vt* **1 :** to cause to dangle **:** SWING **2 :** to keep hanging uncertainly — **dan·gler** \-g(ə-)lər\ *n* — **dan·gling·ly** \-g(ə-)liŋ-lē\ *adv*

[2]**dangle** *n* **1 :** the action of dangling **2 :** something that dangles

Dan·iel \'dan-yəl *also* 'dan-ᵊl\ *n* [Heb *Dānī'ēl*] **1 :** the Jewish hero of the Book of Daniel who as an exile in Babylon interprets dreams, gives accounts of apocalyptic visions, and is divinely delivered from a den of lions **2 :** a book of narratives, visions, and prophecies in canonical Jewish and Christian Scripture — see BIBLE table

da·nio \'dā-nē-ˌō\ *n, pl* **da·ni·os** [NL, genus name] **:** any of several small brightly colored Asiatic cyprinid fishes

[1]**Dan·ish** \'dā-nish\ *adj* **:** of, relating to, or characteristic of Denmark, the Danes, or the Danish language

[2]**Danish** *n* **1 :** the Germanic language of the Danes **2** *pl* **Danish :** a piece of Danish pastry

Danish pastry *n* **:** a pastry made of a rich yeast-raised dough

dank \'daŋk\ *adj* [ME *danke*] **:** unpleasantly moist or wet ***syn*** see WET — **dank·ly** *adv* — **dank·ness** *n*

dan·seur \däⁿ-'sər, dän-\ *n* [F, fr. *danser* to dance] **:** a male ballet dancer

dan·seuse \däⁿ-'sə(r)z, dän-'süz\ *n* [F, fem. of *danseur*] **:** a female ballet dancer

Dan·te·an \'dant-ē-ən\ *n* **:** a student or admirer of Dante

daph·ne \'daf-nē\ *n* [NL, genus name, fr. L, laurel, fr. Gk *daphnē*] **:** any of a genus (*Daphne*) of Eurasian shrubs of the mezereon family with apetalous flowers whose colored calyx resembles a corolla

Daph·ne \'daf-nē\ *n* [L, fr. Gk *Daphnē*] **:** a nymph transformed into a laurel tree and thus enabled to escape the pursuing Apollo

daph·nia \'daf-nē-ə\ *n* [NL, genus name] **:** any of a genus (*Daphnia*) of minute freshwater branchiopod crustaceans with biramous antennae used as locomotor organs — compare WATER FLEA

Daph·nis \'daf-nəs\ *n* [L, fr. Gk] **:** a son of Hermes who gained renown as a musician and a reputation for being the father of pastoral poetry

dap·per \'dap-ər\ *adj* [ME *dapyr*, fr. MD *dapper* quick, strong; akin to OHG *tapfar* heavy, OSlav *debelŭ* thick] **1 a :** neat and trim in appearance **b :** excessively spruce and stylish **2 :** alert and lively in movement and manners — **dap·per·ly** *adv* — **dap·per·ness** *n*

[1]dap·ple \'dap-əl\ *n* [ME *dappel-gray*, adj., gray variegated with spots of a different color] **1 :** any of numerous usu. cloudy and rounded spots or patches of a color or shade different from their background **2 :** the quality or state of being dappled <the ~ of the leaf-filtered light —Anthony West> **3 :** a dappled animal

[2]dapple *vb* **dap·pled; dap·pling** \-(ə-)liŋ\ *vt* **:** to mark with dapples ~ *vi* **:** to become marked with dapples

DAR *abbr* Daughters of the American Revolution

darb \'därb\ *n* [perh. alter. of [5]*dab*] **:** one that is extremely attractive or desirable

Dar·by and Joan \ˌdär-bē-ən-'jō(-ə)n, -jō-'an\ *n* [prob. fr. *Darby & Joan*, couple in an 18th cent. song] **:** a happily married usu. elderly couple

Dard \'därd\ *n* **:** a complex of Indic languages spoken in the upper valley of the Indus — see INDO-EUROPEAN LANGUAGES table

Dar·dan \'därd-ᵊn\ *adj or n* [L *Dardanus*, fr. Gk *Dardanos*] *archaic* **:** TROJAN

Dar·da·ni·an \där-'dā-nē-ən\ *adj* **:** TROJAN

Dar·dic \'därd-ik\ *n* **:** DARD

[1]dare \'da(ə)r, 'de(ə)r\ *vb* **dared; dar·ing** [ME *dar* (1st & 3d sing. pres. indic.), fr. OE *dear;* akin to OHG gi*tar* (1st & 3d sing. pres. indic.) dare, L in*festus* hostile] *verbal auxiliary* **:** to be sufficiently courageous to <no one *dared* say a word> ~ *vi* **:** to have sufficient courage <try it if you ~> ~ *vt* **1 a :** to challenge to perform an action esp. as a proof of courage <*dared* him to jump> **b :** to confront boldly **:** DEFY <*dared* the anger of his family> **2 :** to have the courage to contend against, venture, or try <the actress *dared* a new interpretation of this classic role> — **dar·er** \'dar-ər, 'der-\ *n*

[2]dare *n* **1 :** an act or instance of daring **:** CHALLENGE <foolishly took a ~> **2 :** imaginative or vivacious boldness **:** DARING

[1]dare·dev·il \'da(ə)r-ˌdev-əl, 'de(ə)r-\ *n* **:** a recklessly bold person — **dare·dev·il·ry** \-əl-rē\ *n* — **dare·dev·il·try** \-əl-trē\ *n*

[2]daredevil *adj* **:** recklessly and often ostentatiously daring ***syn*** see ADVENTUROUS

dareful *adj, obs* **:** DARING

dare·say \(ˈ)da(ə)r-'sā, (ˈ)de(ə)r-\ *vt* **:** venture to say **:** think probable — used in pres. 1st sing. ~ *vi* **:** SUPPOSE, AGREE — used in pres. 1st sing.

[1]dar·ing *adj* **:** venturesomely bold in action or thought ***syn*** see ADVENTUROUS — **dar·ing·ly** \-iŋ-lē\ *adv* — **dar·ing·ness** *n*

[2]daring *n* **:** venturesome boldness

Dar·jee·ling \där-'jē-liŋ\ *n* [*Darjeeling*, India] **:** a tea of high quality grown esp. in the mountainous districts of northern India

[1]dark \'därk\ *adj* [ME *derk*, fr. OE *deorc;* akin to OHG *tarchannen* to hide, Gk *thrassein* to trouble] **1 a :** devoid or partially devoid of light **:** not receiving, reflecting, transmitting, or radiating light **b :** transmitting only a portion of light **2 a :** wholly or partially black **b** *of a color* **:** of low or very low lightness **3 a :** arising from or showing evil traits or desires **:** EVIL <the ~ powers that lead to war> **b :** DISMAL, SAD <had a ~ view of the future> **c :** lacking knowledge or culture **4 :** not clear to the understanding **5 :** not fair **:** SWARTHY <her ~ good looks> **6 :** SECRET <kept his plans ~> **7 :** possessing depth and richness <the ~, voluminous abundance of his voice —Irving Kolodin> **8 :** closed to the public <the theater is ~ in the summer> — **dark·ish** \'där-kish\ *adj* — **dark·ly** *adv* — **dark·ness** *n*

syn **1** DARK, DIM, DUSKY, MURKY, GLOOMY *shared meaning element* **:** more or less destitute of light ***ant*** light
2 see OBSCURE ***ant*** lucid

[2]dark *n* **1 a :** absence of light **:** DARKNESS **b :** a place or time of little or no light **:** NIGHT, NIGHTFALL **2 :** a dark or deep color — **in the dark 1 :** in secrecy <most of his dealings were done *in the dark*> **2 :** in ignorance <kept the public *in the dark* about the agreement>

[3]dark *vi, obs* **:** to grow dark ~ *vt* **:** to make dark

dark adaptation *n* **:** the phenomena including dilatation of the pupil, increase in retinal sensitivity, shift of the region of maximum luminosity toward the blue, and regeneration of visual purple by which the eye adapts to conditions of reduced illumination — **dark–adapt·ed** \ˌdär-kə-'dap-təd\ *adj*

Dark Ages *n pl* **:** the period from about A.D. 476 to about 1000; *broadly* **:** MIDDLE AGES

dark·en \'där-kən\ *vb* **dark·ened; dark·en·ing** \'därk-(ə-)niŋ\ *vi* **:** to grow dark **:** become obscured ~ *vt* **1 :** to make dark **2 :** to make less clear **:** OBSCURE <the financial crisis ~*ed* the future of the company> **3 :** TAINT, TARNISH **4 :** to cast a gloom over **5 :** to make of darker color — **dark·en·er** \'därk-(ə-)nər\ *n*

dark field *n* **:** the dark area that serves as the background for objects viewed in an ultramicroscope

dark–field microscope *n* **:** ULTRAMICROSCOPE

dark horse *n* **1 :** a usu. little known contestant (as a racehorse) that makes an unexpectedly good showing **2 :** a political candidate unexpectedly nominated usu. as a compromise between factions

dark lantern *n* **:** a lantern that can be closed to conceal the light

dar·kle \'där-kəl\ *vi* **dar·kled; dar·kling** \-k(ə-)liŋ\ [back-formation fr. *darkling*] **1 :** to become concealed in the dark **2 a :** to grow dark **b :** to become clouded or gloomy

[1]dark·ling \'där-kliŋ\ *adv* [ME *derkelyng*, fr. *derk* dark + *-lyng* -ling] **:** in the dark

[2]dark·ling *adj* **1 :** DARK **2 :** done or taking place in the dark

darkling beetle *n* **:** a usu. hard-bodied black sluggish terrestrial plant-eating beetle (family Tenebrionidae)

dark reaction *n* **:** the synthetic phase of photosynthesis that does not require the presence of light and that involves the reduction of carbon dioxide to form carbohydrate

dark·room \'där-ˌkrüm, -ˌkrům\ *n* **:** a room with no light or with a safelight for handling and processing light-sensitive photographic materials

dark·some \'därk-səm\ *adj* **:** gloomily somber **:** DARK

[1]dar·ling \'där-liŋ\ *n* [ME *derling*, fr. OE *dēorling*, fr. *dēore* dear] **1 :** a dearly loved person **2 :** FAVORITE

[2]darling *adj* **1 :** dearly loved **:** FAVORITE **2 :** very pleasing **:** CHARMING — **dar·ling·ly** \-liŋ-lē\ *adv* — **dar·ling·ness** *n*

[1]darn \'därn\ *vb* [prob. fr. F dial. *darner*] *vt* **1 :** to mend with interlacing stitches **2 :** to embroider by filling in with long running or interlacing stitches ~ *vi* **:** to do darning — **darn·er** *n*

[2]darn *n* **:** a place that has been darned <a sweater full of ~*s*>

[3]darn *vb* [euphemism] **:** DAMN — **darned** \'därn(d)\ *adj or adv*

[4]darn *adj or adv* **:** DAMNED

[5]darn *n* **:** DAMN

dar·nel \'därn-ᵊl\ *n* [ME] **:** any of several usu. weedy grasses (genus *Lolium*)

darning needle *n* **1 :** a long needle with a large eye for use in darning **2 :** DRAGONFLY, DAMSELFLY

[1]dart \'därt\ *n* [ME, fr. MF, of Gmc origin; akin to OHG *tart* dart] **1 a** *archaic* **:** a light spear **b** (1) **:** a small missile usu. with a pointed shaft at one end and feathers at the other (2) *pl but sing in constr* **:** a game in which darts are thrown at a target **2 a :** something projected with sudden speed; *esp* **:** a sharp glance **b :** something causing sudden pain or distress <~*s* of sarcasm> **3 :** something with a slender pointed shaft or outline; *specif* **:** a stitched tapering fold in a garment **4 :** a quick movement <made a ~ for the door>

[2]dart *vt* **1 :** to throw with a sudden movement **2 :** to thrust or move with sudden speed ~ *vi* **:** to move suddenly or rapidly <~*ed* across the street>

dart board *n* **:** a usu. circular board (as of cork) used as a target in the game of darts

dart·er \'därt-ər\ *n* **1 :** SNAKEBIRD **2 :** any of numerous small American freshwater percoid fishes (esp. genera *Ammocrypta*, *Etheostoma*, and *Percina* of the family Percidae)

Dar·win·ian \där-'win-ē-ən\ *adj* **:** of or relating to Charles Darwin, his theories, or his followers — **Darwinian** *n*

Dar·win·ism \'där-wə-ˌniz-əm\ *n* **:** a theory of the origin and perpetuation of new species of animals and plants that offspring of a given organism vary, that natural selection favors the survival of some of these variations over others, that new species have arisen and may continue to arise by these processes, and that widely divergent groups of plants and animals have arisen from the same ancestors; *broadly* **:** biological evolutionism — **Dar·win·ist** \-wə-nəst\ *n* — **darwinist** *or* **dar·win·is·tic** \ˌdär-wə-'nis-tik\ *adj, often cap*

Dar·win's finches \ˌdär-wənz-\ *n pl* [Charles *Darwin*] **:** finches of a subfamily (Geospizinae) having great variation in bill shape and confined mostly to the Galapagos islands

Dar·win tulip \ˌdär-wən-\ *n* **:** a tall late-flowering tulip with the flowers single and of one color

das *abbr* dekastere

[1]dash \'dash\ *vb* [ME *dasshen*] *vt* **1 :** to knock, hurl, or thrust violently **2 :** to break by striking or knocking **3 :** SPLASH, SPATTER **4 a :** DESTROY, RUIN <the news ~*ed* his hopes> **b :** DEPRESS, SADDEN **c :** to make ashamed **5 :** to affect by mixing in something different <milk ~*ed* with brandy> <his delight was ~*ed* with bitterness over the delay> **6 :** to complete, execute, or finish off hastily — used with *down* or *off* <~*ed* down a drink> <~ off a letter> ~ *vi* **1 :** to move with sudden speed <~*ed* through the rain> **2 :** SMASH

[2]dash *n* **1 a** *archaic* **:** BLOW **b** (1) **:** a sudden burst or splash (2) **:** the sound produced by such a burst **2 a :** a stroke of a pen **b :** a punctuation mark — used esp. to indicate a break in the thought or structure of a sentence **3 :** a small usu. distinctive addition <a ~ of salt> **4 :** flashy display **5 :** animation in style and action **6 a :** a sudden onset, rush, or attempt **b :** a short fast race **7 :** a long click or buzz forming a letter or part of a letter (as in Morse code) **8 :** DASHBOARD 2

dash·board \'dash-ˌbō(ə)rd, -ˌbȯ(ə)rd\ *n* **1 :** a screen on the front of a vehicle to intercept water, mud, or snow **2 :** a panel extending across an automobile, airplane, or motorboat below the windshield and usu. containing dials and controls

dash·er \'dash-ər\ *n* **1 :** a dashing person **2 :** one that dashes; *specif* **:** a device having blades for agitating a liquid or semisolid

da·shi·ki \də-'shē-kē\ *or* **dai·shi·ki** \dī-\ *n* [alter. of Yoruba *danshiki*] **:** a usu. brightly colored loose-fitting pullover garment

dash·ing *adj* **1 :** marked by vigorous action **:** SPIRITED <a ~ young horse> **2 :** marked by smartness esp. in dress and manners — **dash·ing·ly** \-iŋ-lē\ *adv*

dash·pot \'dash-ˌpät\ *n* **:** a device for cushioning or damping a movement (as of a mechanical part) to avoid shock

das·sie \'däs-ē\ *n* [Afrik] **:** a hyrax (genus *Procavia*) of southern Africa

das·tard \'das-tərd\ *n* [ME] **:** COWARD; *esp* **:** one who commits malicious acts

das·tard·ly \-lē\ *adj* **:** despicably mean or cowardly — **das·tard·li·ness** *n*

dasy·ure \'das-ē-ˌ(y)ů(ə)r\ *n* [deriv. of Gk *dasys* thick with hair + *oura* tail] **:** any of a genus (*Dasyurus*) of arboreal carnivorous marsupial mammals of Australia and Tasmania resembling martens

dat *abbr* dative

DAT *abbr* differential aptitude test

da·ta \'dāt-ə, 'dat-, 'dät-\ *n pl but sing or pl in constr* [pl. of *datum*] **:** factual information (as measurements or statistics) used as a basis for reasoning, discussion, or calculation <the ~ is plentiful and easily available —H. A. Gleason, Jr.> <comprehensive ~ on economic growth have been published —N. H. Jacoby>

data bank *n* **1 :** a collection of data organized esp. for rapid search and retrieval (as by computer) **2 :** an institution whose chief concern is building and maintaining a data bank
da·ta·ma·tion \ˌdāt-ə-ˈmā-shən, ˌdat-, ˌdät-\ *n* [*data* + auto*mation*] **:** automatic data processing; *also* **:** the enterprises engaged in manufacturing, selling, and servicing data-processing equipment
data processing *n* **:** the converting (as by computer) of crude information into usable or storable form — **data processor** *n*
1date \ˈdāt\ *n* [ME, fr. OF, deriv. of L *dactylus,* fr. Gk *daktylos,* lit., finger] **1 :** the oblong edible fruit of a palm (*Phoenix dactylifera*) **2 :** the tall palm with pinnate leaves that yields the date
2date *n* [ME, fr. MF, fr. LL *data,* fr. *data* (as in *data Romae* given at Rome), fem. of L *datus,* pp. of *dare* to give; akin to Gk *didonai* to give] **1 a :** the time at which an event occurs <the ~ of his birth> **b :** a statement of the time of execution or making <the ~ on the letter> **2 :** DURATION **3 :** the period of time to which something belongs **4 a :** an appointment for a specified time; *esp* **:** a social engagement between two persons of opposite sex **b :** a person of the opposite sex with whom one has a social engagement **5 :** an engagement for a professional performance (as of a dance band) — **to date :** up to the present moment
3date *vb* **dat·ed; dat·ing** *vt* **1 :** to determine the date of <~ an antique> **2 :** to record the date of **3 a :** to mark with characteristics typical of a particular period **b :** to show up plainly the age of **4 :** to make or have a date with ~ *vi* **1 :** to reckon chronologically **2 :** to become dated and written **3 a :** ORIGINATE **b :** EXTEND <a friendship *dating* from college days> — **dat·able** *or* **date·able** \ˈdāt-ə-bəl\ *adj* — **dat·er** \ˈdāt-ər\ *n*
dat·ed *adj* **1 :** provided with a date <a ~ document> **2 :** OUT-OF-DATE, OLD-FASHIONED <~ formalities> — **dat·ed·ly** *adv* — **dat·ed·ness** *n*
date·less \ˈdāt-ləs\ *adj* **1 :** ENDLESS **2 :** having no date **3 :** too ancient to be dated **4 :** TIMELESS <the play's ~ theme>
date·line \ˈdāt-ˌlīn\ *n* **1 :** a line in a written document or a printed publication giving the date and place of composition or issue **2** *usu* **date line :** a hypothetical line approximately along the 180th meridian designated as the place where each calendar day begins — **dateline** *vt*
dating bar *n* **:** a bar that caters esp. to young unmarried men and women
1da·tive \ˈdāt-iv\ *adj* [ME *datif,* fr. L *dativus,* lit., relating to giving, fr. *datus*] **:** of, relating to, or being the grammatical case that marks typically the indirect object of a verb, the object of some prepositions, or a possessor
2dative *n* **:** a dative case or form
dative bond *n* [fr. the donation of electrons by one of the atoms] **:** COORDINATE BOND
da·tum \ˈdāt-əm, ˈdat-, ˈdät-\ *n* [L, fr. neut. of *datus*] **1** *pl* **da·ta** \-ə\ **:** something given or admitted esp. as a basis for reasoning or inference **2** *pl* **datums :** something used as a basis for calculating or measuring
da·tu·ra \də-ˈt(y)ür-ə\ *n* [NL, genus name, fr. Hindi *dhatūrā* jimsonweed] **:** any of a genus (*Datura*) of widely distributed strong-scented herbs, shrubs, or trees of the nightshade family
1daub \ˈdȯb, ˈdäb\ *vb* [ME *dauben,* fr. OF *dauber*] *vt* **1 :** to cover or coat with soft adhesive matter **:** PLASTER **2 :** to coat with a dirty substance **3 a :** to apply coloring material crudely to **b :** to apply (as paint) crudely ~ *vi* **1** *archaic* **:** to put on a false exterior **2 :** to apply colors crudely — **daub·er** *n*
2daub *n* **1 :** material used to daub walls **2 :** an act or instance of daubing **3 :** something daubed on **:** SMEAR **4 :** a crude picture
1daugh·ter \ˈdȯt-ər\ *n* [ME *doughter,* fr. OE *dohtor;* akin to OHG *tohter* daughter, Gk *thygatēr*] **1 a (1) :** a human female having the relation of child to parent **(2) :** a female offspring of a lower animal **b :** a human female having a specified ancestor or belonging to a group of common ancestry **2 :** something considered as a daughter <the United States is a ~ of Great Britain> **3 :** an atomic species that is the immediate product of the radioactive decay of a given element — **daugh·ter·less** \-ləs\ *adj*
2daughter *adj* **1 :** having the characteristics or relationship of a daughter **2 :** belonging to the first generation of offspring, organelles, or molecules produced by reproduction, division, or replication <~ cell> <~ DNA molecules>
daugh·ter–in–law \ˈdȯt-ə-rən-ˌlȯ, -ərn-ˌlȯ\ *n, pl* **daugh·ters–in–law** \-ər-zən-\ **:** the wife of one's son
dau·no·my·cin \ˌdȯ-nə-ˈmīs-ᵊn, ˌdaù-\ *n* [(assumed) It *daunomicina,* fr. *Daunia,* ancient region of Apulia, Italy + It *-o-* + *-micina* (as in *streptomicina* streptomycin)] **:** an antibiotic $C_{27}H_{29}NO_{10}$ that is a nitrogenous glycoside and is used experimentally as an antineoplastic agent
daunt \ˈdȯnt, ˈdänt\ *vt* [ME *daunten,* fr. OF *danter,* alter. of *donter,* fr. L *domitare* to tame, fr. *domitus,* pp. of *domare* — more at TAME] **:** to lessen the courage of **:** COW, SUBDUE ***syn*** see DISMAY
daunt·less \-ləs\ *adj* **:** FEARLESS, UNDAUNTED <a ~ hero> — **daunt·less·ly** *adv* — **daunt·less·ness** *n*
dau·phin \ˈdȯ-fən\ *n, often cap* [MF *dalfin,* fr. OF, title of lords of the Dauphiné, fr. *Dalfin,* a surname] **:** the eldest son of a king of France
dau·phine \dō-ˈfēn\ *n, often cap* [F] **:** the wife of the dauphin
DAV *abbr* Disabled American Veterans
da·ven \ˈdäv-ən\ *vi* [Yiddish *davnen*] **:** to utter Jewish prayers esp. of a ritual character
dav·en·port \ˈdav-ən-ˌpō(ə)rt, ˈdav-ᵊm-, -ˌpȯ(ə)rt\ *n* [prob. fr. the name *Davenport*] **1 :** a small compact writing desk **2 :** a large upholstered sofa often convertible into a bed
Da·vid \ˈdā-vəd\ *n* [Heb *Dāwīdh*] **:** a Hebrew shepherd who became the second king of Israel in succession to Saul according to Biblical accounts — **Da·vid·ic** \də-ˈvid-ik, dā-\ *adj*
da·vit \ˈdā-vət, ˈdav-ət\ *n* [prob. fr. the name *David*] **:** a crane that projects over the side of a ship or a hatchway and is used esp. for boats, anchors, or cargo
Da·vy Jones \ˌdā-vē-ˈjōnz\ *n* **:** the bottom of the sea personified
Da·vy Jones's locker \ˌdā-vē-ˌjōnz(əz)-\ *n* **:** the bottom of the ocean

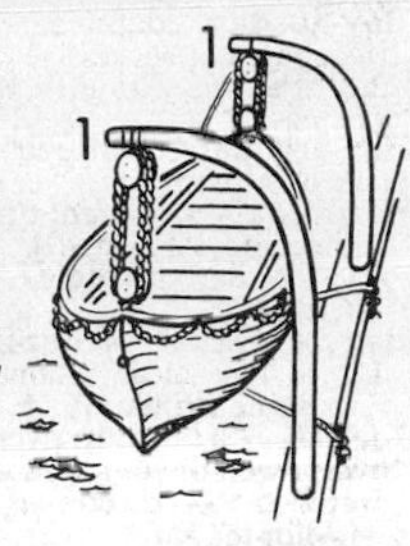

1 davits

1daw \ˈdȯ, ˈdä\ *vi* [ME *dawen,* fr. OE *dagian;* akin to OHG *tagēn* to dawn, OE *dæg* day] *chiefly Scot* **:** DAWN
2daw \ˈdȯ\ *n* [ME *dawe;* akin to OHG *taha* jackdaw] **:** JACKDAW
daw·dle \ˈdȯd-ᵊl\ *vb* **daw·dled; daw·dling** \ˈdȯd-liŋ, -ᵊl-iŋ\ [origin unknown] *vi* **1 :** to spend time idly <*dawdled* over my coffee waiting for him —Max Steele> **2 :** to move lackadaisically <*dawdled* up the hill> ~ *vt* **:** to spend fruitlessly or lackadaisically **:** WASTE — **daw·dler** \ˈdȯd-lər, -ᵊl-ər\ *n*
1dawn \ˈdȯn, ˈdän\ *vi* [ME *dawnen,* prob. back-formation fr. *dawning* daybreak, alter. of *dawing,* fr. OE *dagung,* fr. *dagian*] **1 :** to begin to grow light as the sun rises **2 :** to begin to appear or develop **3 :** to begin to be perceived or understood <the truth finally ~*ed* on him>
2dawn *n* **1 :** the first appearance of light in the morning followed by sunrise **2 :** a first appearance **:** BEGINNING <the ~ of the space age>
day \ˈdā\ *n* [ME, fr. OE *dæg;* akin to OHG *tag* day] **1 a :** the time of light between one night and the next **b :** DAYLIGHT **2 a :** the period of the earth's rotation on its axis **b :** the time required by a celestial body to turn once on its axis **3 :** the mean solar day of 24 hours beginning at mean midnight **4 :** a specified day or date **5 :** a specified time or period **:** AGE <in grandfather's ~> **6 :** the conflict or contention of the day <played hard and won the ~> **7 :** the time established by usage or law for work, school, or business **8 :** BEGINNING <a new ~ for black people> — **day after day :** for an indefinite or seemingly endless number of days — **day in, day out :** for an indefinite number of successive days
Day·ak \ˈdī-ˌak\ *n* [Malay, up-country] **1 :** a member of any of several Indonesian peoples of the interior of Borneo **2 :** the language of the Dayak peoples
day·bed \ˈdā-ˌbed\ *n* **1 :** a chaise longue of a type made 1680–1780 **2 :** a couch that can be converted into a bed
day·book \-ˌbu̇k\ *n* **1 :** DIARY, JOURNAL **2 :** a book formerly used in accounting for recording the transactions of the day
day·break \-ˌbrāk\ *n* **:** DAWN
day–care \ˈdā-ˌke(ə)r, -ˌka(ə)r\ *adj* **:** of, relating to, or providing supervision and facilities for preschool children during the day <~ centers>
1day·dream \ˈdā-ˌdrēm\ *n* **:** a pleasant visionary usu. wishful creation of the imagination — **day·dream·like** \-ˌlīk\ *adj*
2daydream *vi* **:** to have a daydream — **day·dream·er** *n*
day·glow \ˈdā-ˌglō\ *n* **:** airglow seen during the day
day in court 1 : a day or opportunity for appearance in a lawsuit **2 :** an opportunity to present one's point of view
day laborer *n* **:** one who works for daily wages esp. as an unskilled laborer
day letter *n* **:** a telegram sent during the day that has a lower priority than a regular telegram
1day·light \ˈdā-ˌlīt\ *n* **1 :** the light of day **2 :** DAWN **3 a :** knowledge or understanding of something that has been obscure <began to see ~ on the problem> **b :** the quality or state of being open **:** OPENNESS **4** *pl* **a :** CONSCIOUSNESS **b :** mental soundness or stability **:** WITS <scared the ~*s* out of him>
2daylight *vt* **1 :** to provide with daylight **2 :** to remove obstructions (as trees and brush) from in order to provide greater visibility <~ an intersection> ~ *vi* **:** to supply daylight
daylight saving time *n* **:** time usu. one hour ahead of standard time — called also *daylight time*
day lily *n* **1 :** any of various Eurasian plants (genus *Hemerocallis*) of the lily family that have short-lived flowers resembling lilies and are widespread in cultivation and as escapes **2 :** PLANTAIN LILY
day·long \ˌdā-ˌlȯŋ\ *adj* **:** lasting all day <a ~ tour>
day·mare \ˈdā-ˌma(ə)r, -ˌme(ə)r\ *n* [*day* + *-mare* (as in *nightmare*)] **:** a nightmarish fantasy experienced while awake
day–neutral *adj* **:** developing and maturing regardless of relative length of alternating exposures to light and dark periods — compare LONG-DAY, SHORT-DAY
day nursery *n* **:** a public center for the care and training of young children; *specif* **:** NURSERY SCHOOL
Day of Atonement : YOM KIPPUR
day of reckoning : a time when the consequences of a course of mistakes or misdeeds are felt
day·room \ˈdā-ˌrüm, -ˌru̇m\ *n* **:** a room (as in a military barracks) equipped for reading, writing, and recreation
days \ˈdāz\ *adv* **:** in the daytime repeatedly **:** on any day
day school *n* **:** an elementary or secondary school held on weekdays; *specif* **:** a private school without boarding facilities
days of grace : the days allowed for payment of a note or an insurance premium after it becomes due
day·star \ˈdā-ˌstär\ *n* **1 :** MORNING STAR **2 :** SUN 1a
day student *n* **:** a student who attends regular classes at a college or preparatory school but does not live at the institution
1day·time \ˈdā-ˌtīm\ *n* **:** the time during which there is daylight
2daytime *adj* **:** taking place, existing, or presented during the daytime <~ flights> <~ soap operas>

ə abut ᵊ kitten ər further a back ā bake ä cot, cart
au̇ out ch chin e less ē easy g gift i trip ī life
j joke ŋ sing ō flow ȯ flaw ȯi coin th thin t͟h this
ü loot u̇ foot y yet yü few yu̇ furious zh vision

day–to–day \ˌdāt-ə-ˌdā\ *adj* **1 :** taking place, made, or done in the course of successive days <~ problems> **2 :** providing for a day at a time with little thought for the future <lived an aimless ~ existence>

day–trip·per \ˈdā-ˌtrip-ər\ *n* **:** one who takes a trip that does not last overnight

daze \ˈdāz\ *vt* **dazed; daz·ing** [ME *dasen,* fr. ON *dasa* (in *dasask* to become exhausted)] **1 :** to stupefy esp. by a blow **:** STUN **2 :** to dazzle with light — **daze** *n* — **dazed·ness** \ˈdā-zəd-nəs, ˈdāz(d)-\ *n*

daz·zle \ˈdaz-əl\ *vb* **daz·zled; daz·zling** \-(ə-)liŋ\ [freq. of *daze*] *vi* **1 :** to lose clear vision esp. from looking at bright light **2 a :** to shine brilliantly **b :** to arouse admiration by an impressive display ~ *vt* **1 :** to overpower with light **2 :** to impress deeply, overpower, or confound with brilliance <*dazzled* the crowd with his oratory> — **dazzle** *n* — **daz·zler** \-(ə-)lər\ *n* — **daz·zling·ly** \-(ə-)liŋ-lē\ *adv*

db *abbr* **1** debenture **2** decibel

DB *abbr* daybook

DBA *abbr* **1** doctor of business administration **2** doing business as

DBE *abbr* Dame Commander of the Order of the British Empire

DBH *abbr* diameter at breast height

dbl *abbr* double

DC *abbr* **1** [It *da capo*] from the beginning **2** decimal classification **3** direct current **4** District of Columbia **5** doctor of chiropractic **6** double crochet

DChE *abbr* doctor of chemical engineering

DCL *abbr* **1** doctor of canon law **2** doctor of civil law

dd *abbr* **1** dated **2** delivered

DD *abbr* **1** days after date **2** demand draft **3** dishonorable discharge **4** doctor of divinity **5** due date

D day *n* [*D,* abbr. for *day*] **:** a day set for launching an operation; *specif* **:** June 6, 1944, on which the Allies began the invasion of France in World War II

DDC *abbr* Dewey Decimal Classification

DDD \ˌdēd-(ˌ)ē-ˈdē\ *n* [*d*ichloro-*d*iphenyl-*d*ichloro-ethane] **:** an insecticide $(ClC_6H_4)_2CHCHCl_2$ closely related chemically and similar in properties to DDT

DDS *abbr* **1** doctor of dental science **2** doctor of dental surgery

DDT \ˌdēd-(ˌ)ē-ˈtē\ *n* [*d*ichloro-*d*iphenyl-*t*richloro-ethane] **:** a colorless odorless water-insoluble crystalline insecticide $C_{14}H_9Cl_5$ that tends to accumulate in ecosystems and has toxic effects on many vertebrates

DDVP \ˌdēd-(ˌ)ē-ˌvē-ˈpē\ *n* [*d*imethyl + *d*ichlor- + *v*inyl + *p*hosphate] **:** a volatile organophosphate insecticide

DE *abbr* **1** defensive end **2** Delaware **3** doctor of engineering

de- *prefix* [ME, fr. OF *de-, des-,* partly fr. L *de-* from, down, away (fr. *de*) and partly fr. L *dis-;* L *de* akin to OIr *di* from, OE *tō* to — more at TO, DIS-] **1 a :** do the opposite of <*de*vitalize> <*de*activate> **b :** reverse of <*de*-emphasis> **2 a :** remove (a specified thing) from <*de*louse> <*de*hydrogenate> **b :** remove from (a specified thing) <*de*throne> **3 :** reduce <*de*value> **4 :** something derived from (a specified thing) <*de*compound> **:** derived from something (of a specified nature) <*de*nominative> **5 :** get off of (a specified thing) <*de*train> **6 :** having a molecule characterized by the removal of one or more atoms (of a specified element) <*de*oxy->

de·acid·i·fy \ˌdē-ə-ˈsid-ə-ˌfī\ *vt* **:** to remove acid from **:** reduce the acidity of (as by neutralization) — **de·acid·i·fi·ca·tion** \-ˌsid-ə-fə-ˈkā-shən\ *n*

dea·con \ˈdē-kən\ *n* [ME *dekene,* fr. OE *dēacon,* fr. LL *diaconus,* fr. Gk *diakonos,* lit., servant, fr. *dia-* + *-konos* (akin to en*konein* to be active); akin to L *conari* to attempt] **:** a subordinate officer in a Christian church: as **a :** Roman Catholic cleric ranking below a priest and above a subdeacon **b :** one of the laymen elected by a church with congregational polity to serve in worship, in pastoral care, and on administrative committees **c :** a Mormon in the lowest grade of the Aaronic priesthood

dea·con·ess \ˈdē-kə-nəs\ *n* **:** a woman chosen to assist in the church ministry; *specif* **:** one in a Protestant order

deacon's bench *n* **:** a bench with usu. spindled arms and back

de·ac·ti·vate \(ˈ)dē-ˈak-tə-ˌvāt\ *vt* **:** to make inactive or ineffective — **de·ac·ti·va·tion** \(ˌ)dē-ˌak-tə-ˈvā-shən\ *n* — **de·ac·ti·va·tor** \(ˈ)dē-ˈak-tə-ˌvāt-ər\ *n*

[1]**dead** \ˈded\ *adj* [ME *deed,* fr. OE *dēad;* akin to ON *dauthr* dead, *deyja* to die — more at DIE] **1 :** deprived of life **:** having died **2 a** (1) **:** having the appearance of death **:** DEATHLY <in a ~ faint> (2) **:** lacking power to move, feel, or respond **:** NUMB **b :** very tired **c** (1) **:** incapable of being stirred emotionally or intellectually **:** UNRESPONSIVE <~ to pity> (2) **:** grown cold **:** EXTINGUISHED <~ coals> **3 a :** INANIMATE, INERT <~ matter> **b :** BARREN, INFERTILE <~ soil> **c :** no longer producing or functioning **:** EXHAUSTED <a ~ battery> **4 a** (1) **:** lacking power or effect <a ~ law> (2) **:** no longer having interest, relevance, or significance <a ~ issue> **b :** no longer in use **:** OBSOLETE <a ~ language> **c :** no longer active **:** EXTINCT <a ~ volcano> **d :** lacking in gaiety or animation <a ~ party> **e** (1) **:** lacking in commercial activity **:** QUIET (2) **:** commercially idle or unproductive <~ capital> **f :** lacking elasticity <a ~ tennis ball> **g :** being out of action or out of use; *specif* **:** free from any connection to a source of voltage and free from electric charges **h** (1) **:** being out of play <a ~ ball> <~ cards> (2) *of a player* **:** temporarily forbidden to play or to make a certain play **5 a :** not running or circulating **:** STAGNANT <~ water> **b :** not turning <a ~ lathe center> **c :** not imparting motion or power although otherwise functioning <a ~ rear axle> **d :** lacking warmth, vigor, or taste **6 a :** absolutely uniform <a ~ level> **b** (1) **:** UNERRING (2) **:** EXACT <~ center of the target> (3) **:** DOOMED <a ~ duck> (4) **:** IRREVOCABLE <a ~ loss> **c :** ABRUPT <brought to a ~ stop> **d :** COMPLETE, ABSOLUTE <a ~ silence> **7 :** DESERTED <~ villages> — **dead·ness** *n*

syn DEAD, DEFUNCT, DECEASED, DEPARTED, LATE *shared meaning element* **:** devoid of life ***ant*** alive

[2]**dead** *n, pl* **dead** **1 :** one that is dead — usu. used collectively **2 :** the state of being dead <raised him from the ~ —Col 2:12(RSV)> **3 :** the time of greatest quiet <the ~ of night>

[3]**dead** *adv* **1 :** ABSOLUTELY, UTTERLY <~ certain > **2 :** suddenly and completely <stopped ~> **3 :** DIRECTLY <~ ahead>

dead air *n* **:** a period of silence esp. during a radio or television broadcast

dead–air space *n* **:** a sealed or unventilated air space

[1]**dead·beat** \ˈded-ˌbēt\ *adj* **:** having a pointer that gives a reading with little or no oscillation

[2]**deadbeat** *n* **1 :** one who persistently fails to pay his debts or his way **2 :** LOAFER

dead center *n* **:** either of the two positions at the ends of a stroke in a crank and connecting rod when the crank and rod are in the same straight line — called also *dead point*

dead·en \ˈded-ᵊn\ *vb* **dead·ened; dead·en·ing** \ˈded-niŋ, -ᵊn-iŋ\ *vt* **1 :** to impair in vigor or sensation **:** BLUNT <~*ed* his enthusiasm> **2 a :** to deprive of brilliance **b :** to make vapid or spiritless **c :** to make (as a wall) impervious to sound **3 :** to deprive of life **:** KILL ~ *vi* **:** to become dead **:** lose life or vigor — **dead·en·er** \ˈded-nər, -ᵊn-ər\ *n* — **dead·en·ing·ly** \-niŋ-lē, -ᵊn-iŋ-\ *adv*

[1]**dead–end** \ˌded-ˌend\ *adj* **1 a :** lacking opportunities for advancement <a ~ job> **b :** lacking an exit <a ~ street> **2 :** TOUGH <~ kids> — **dead–end·ed·ness** \(ˈ)ded-ˈen-dəd-nəs\ *n*

[2]**dead–end** \ˈded-ˈend\ *vi* **:** to come to a dead end **:** TERMINATE

dead end \ˈded-ˈend\ *n* **1 :** an end (as of a street) without an exit **2 :** a position, situation, or course of action that leads to nothing further

dead·en·ing *n* **:** material used to soundproof walls or floors

dead·eye \ˈded-ˌī\ *n* **1 :** a rounded wood block that is encircled by a rope or an iron band and pierced with holes to receive the lanyard and that is used esp. to set up shrouds and stays **2 :** an unerring marksman

dead·fall \-ˌfȯl\ *n* **:** a trap so constructed that a weight (as a heavy log) falls on an animal and kills or disables it

dead hand *n* **1 :** MORTMAIN 2 **2 :** the oppressive influence of the past

[1]**dead·head** \ˈded-ˌhed\ *n* **1 :** one who has not paid for a ticket **2 :** a dull or stupid person

[2]**deadhead** *vi* **:** to make a return trip without a load — used esp. of a truck

dead heat *n* **:** a tie with no single winner of a race

dead horse *n* [fr. the proverbial futility of flogging a dead horse to make him go] **:** an exhausted or profitless topic or issue

dead-eyes 1

dead letter *n* **1 :** something that has lost its force or authority without being formally abolished **2 :** a letter that is undeliverable and unreturnable by the post office

dead·light \ˈded-ˌlīt\ *n* **1 a :** a metal cover or shutter fitted to a port to keep out light and water **b :** a heavy glass set in a ship's deck or hull to admit light **2 :** a skylight made so as not to open

dead·line \-ˌlīn\ *n* **1 :** a line drawn within or around a prison that a prisoner passes at the risk of being shot **2 :** a date or time before which something must be done; *specif* **:** the time after which copy is not accepted for a particular issue of a publication

dead load *n* **:** a constant load that in structures (as a bridge, building, or machine) is due to the weight of the members, the supported structure, and permanent attachments or accessories

dead·lock \ˈded-ˌläk\ *n* **1 :** a state of inaction or neutralization resulting from the opposition of equally powerful uncompromising persons or factions **:** STANDSTILL **2 :** a tie score — **deadlock** *vt*

[1]**dead·ly** \ˈded-lē\ *adj* **dead·li·er; -est** **1 :** likely to cause or capable of producing death <a ~ disease> <a ~ instrument> **2 a :** aiming to kill or destroy **:** IMPLACABLE <a ~ enemy> **b :** highly effective <a ~ exposé> **c :** UNERRING <a ~ marksman> **d :** marked by determination or extreme seriousness **3 a :** tending to deprive of force or vitality <a ~ habit> **b:** suggestive of death esp. in dullness or lack of animation <~ bores> <a ~ conversation> **4 :** very great **:** EXTREME — **dead·li·ness** *n*

syn DEADLY, MORTAL, FATAL, LETHAL *shared meaning element* **:** causing or capable of causing death. DEADLY applies to whatever is certain or extremely likely to cause death <a *deadly* poison> <*deadly* weapons> MORTAL applies distinctively to what has caused or is about to cause death <a *mortal* wound> FATAL, which stresses the inevitability of eventual death, may be preferred when considerable time intervenes between the causative event and death <his injuries were ultimately *fatal*> and is regularly used in predictions <there is little doubt that his injuries will prove *fatal*> LETHAL applies to something that by its very nature is bound to cause death or which exists for the purpose of destroying life <took a *lethal* dose of poison> <a *lethal* weapon> All these terms are capable of extension in which they are less weighty and typically imply a disconcerting, oppressing, or disturbing that may cause fear, dread, or distress rather than physical or spiritual death; thus, a *deadly* shaft of irony causes complete discomfiture; *mortal* terror is the most extreme terror; a *fatal* error is one that leads to the destruction of one's plans or hopes; a *lethal* verbal attack is utterly devastating to one's composure or position

[2]**deadly** *adv* **1** *archaic* **:** in a manner to cause death **:** MORTALLY **2 :** suggesting death **3 :** EXTREMELY <~ serious>

deadly nightshade *n* **:** BELLADONNA 1

deadly sin *n* **:** one of seven sins of pride, covetousness, lust, anger, gluttony, envy, and sloth held to be fatal to spiritual progress — called also *capital sin*

dead man's float *n* **:** a prone floating position with the arms extended forward

dead march *n* **:** a solemn march for a funeral

dead metaphor *n* **:** a word or phrase (as *time is running out*) that has lost its metaphoric force through common usage

[1]**dead·pan** \ˈded-ˌpan\ *adj* **:** marked by an impassive matter-of-fact manner, style, or expression <a ~ commentary>

[2]**deadpan** *adv* **:** in a deadpan manner <played the role completely ~>

[3]**deadpan** *vt* : to express in a deadpan manner — **dead·pan·ner** *n*

dead point *n* : DEAD CENTER

dead reckoning *n* **1** : the determination without the aid of celestial observations of the position of a ship or aircraft from the record of the courses sailed or flown, the distance made, and the known or estimated drift **2** : GUESSWORK — **dead reckon** *vb* — **dead reckoner** *n*

dead set *adj* : firmly determined : RESOLUTE <*dead set* on winning> <*dead set* against it>

dead space *n* : the portion of the respiratory system which is external to the bronchioles and through which air must pass to reach the bronchioles and alveoli

dead·weight \'ded-'wāt\ *n* **1** : the unrelieved weight of an inert mass **2** : DEAD LOAD

dead·wood \-ˌwu̇d\ *n* **1** : wood dead on the tree **2** : useless personnel or material **3** : solid timbers built in at the extreme bow and stern of a ship when too narrow to permit framing **4** : bowling pins that have been knocked down but remain on the alley

de·aer·ate \(ˈ)dē-'a(-ə)r-ˌāt, -'e(-ə)r-\ *vt* : to remove air or gas from — **de·aer·a·tion** \ˌdē-ˌa(-ə)r-'ā-shən, -ˌe(-ə)r-\ *n*

deaf \'def\ *adj* [ME *deef*, fr. OE *dēaf*; akin to Gk *typhlos* blind, *typhein* to smoke, L *fumus* smoke — more at FUME] **1** : lacking or deficient in the sense of hearing **2** : unwilling to hear or listen : not to be persuaded <was overwrought and ~ to reason> — **deaf·ish** \'def-ish\ *adj* — **deaf·ly** *adv* — **deaf·ness** *n*

deaf·en \'def-ən\ *vb* **deaf·ened**; **deaf·en·ing** \-(ə-)niŋ\ *vt* **1** : to make deaf **2** : to make (as a wall) soundproof ~ *vi* : to cause deafness or stun one with noise — **deaf·en·ing·ly** \-(ə-)niŋ-lē\ *adv*

deaf-mute \'def-ˌmyüt\ *n* : a deaf person who cannot speak — **deaf-mute** *adj*

[1]**deal** \'dē(ə)l\ *n* [ME *deel*, fr. OE *dǣl*; akin to OE *dāl* division, portion, OHG *teil* part] **1** *obs* : PART, PORTION **2** : a usu. large or indefinite quantity or degree <the search was thorough . . . and a ~ of money was spent —J. F. Dobie> <a great ~ of support> <a good ~ faster> **3 a** : the act or right of distributing cards to players in a card game **b** : HAND 9b **4 a** : an extensive governmental program — compare NEW DEAL **b** : the period of such a program

[2]**deal** *vb* **dealt** \'delt\; **deal·ing** \'dē-liŋ\ *vt* **1 a** : to give as one's portion : APPORTION <tried to ~ justice to all men> <*dealt* out three sandwiches apiece> **b** : to distribute (playing cards) to players in a game **2** : ADMINISTER, BESTOW <*dealt* him a blow> **3** : SELL <~*s* marijuana> ~ *vi* **1** : to distribute the cards in a card game **2** : to concern oneself or itself <the book ~*s* with education> **3 a** : to engage in bargaining : TRADE **b** : to sell or distribute something as a business <~ in insurance> **4** : to take action with regard to someone or something <~ with an offender> ***syn*** see DISTRIBUTE, TREAT — **deal·er** \'dē-lər\ *n*

[3]**deal** *n* **1** : an act of dealing : TRANSACTION **2** : PACKAGE DEAL **3** : treatment received <a dirty ~> **4** : an arrangement for mutual advantage

[4]**deal** *n* [MD or MLG *dele* plank; akin to OHG *dili* plank — more at THILL] **1 a** *Brit* : a board of fir or pine **b** : sawed yellow-pine lumber nine inches or wider and three, four, or five inches thick **2** : pine or fir wood — **deal** *adj*

de·alate \(ˈ)dē-'ā-ˌlāt\ *n* : a dealated insect

de·alat·ed \-ˌlāt-əd\ *adj* : divested of the wings — used of postnuptial adults of insects (as ants) that drop their wings after a nuptial flight — **de·ala·tion** \ˌdē-(ˌ)ā-'lā-shən\ *n*

deal·er·ship \'dē-lər-ˌship\ *n* : an authorized sales agency <an automobile ~>

deal·fish \'dē(ə)l-ˌfish\ *n* [[4]*deal*] : any of several long thin fishes (genus *Trachipterus* of the family Trachipteridae) inhabiting the deep sea

deal·ing *n* **1** *pl* : friendly or business interactions **2** : method of business : manner of conduct

dealing box *n* : a case that holds a deck of playing cards so that they may be dealt one by one

de·am·i·nase \(ˈ)dē-'am-ə-ˌnās, -ˌnāz\ *n* [*de-* + *amino* + *-ase*] : an enzyme that hydrolyzes amino compounds (as amino acids) with removal of the amino group

de·am·i·nate \-ˌnāt\ *vt* **-nat·ed**; **-nat·ing** : to remove the amino group from (a compound) — **de·am·i·na·tion** \(ˌ)dē-ˌam-ə-'nā-shən\ *n*

de·am·i·nize \(ˈ)dē-'am-ə-ˌnīz\ *vt* **-nized**; **-niz·ing** : DEAMINATE

dean \'dēn\ *n* [ME *deen*, fr. MF *deien*, fr. LL *decanus*, lit., chief of ten, fr. L *decem* ten — more at TEN] **1 a** : the head of the chapter of a collegiate or cathedral church **b** : a Roman Catholic priest who supervises one district of a diocese **2 a** : the head of a division, faculty, college, or school of a university **b** : a college or secondary school administrator in charge of counseling and disciplining students <~ of men> **3** : DOYEN 1 — **dean** *vi* — **dean·ship** \-ˌship\ *n*

dean·ery \'dēn-(ə-)rē\ *n, pl* **-er·ies** : the office, jurisdiction, or official residence of a clerical dean

dean's list *n* : a list of students receiving special recognition from the dean of a college because of superior scholarship

[1]**dear** \'di(ə)r\ *adj* [ME *dere*, fr. OE *dēor*] : SEVERE, SORE <in our ~ peril —Shak.>

[2]**dear** *adj* [ME *dere*, fr. OE *dēore*] **1** *obs* : NOBLE **2** : highly valued : PRECIOUS <a ~ friend> **3** : AFFECTIONATE, FOND **4** : high or exorbitant in price : exceedingly expensive <eggs are very ~ just now> **5** : HEARTFELT ***syn*** see COSTLY ***ant*** cheap — **dear** *adv* — **dear·ly** *adv* — **dear·ness** *n*

[3]**dear** *n* **1** : a loved one : SWEETHEART **2** : a lovable person

Dear John \-'jän\ *n* : a letter (as to a soldier) in which a wife asks for a divorce or a girl friend breaks off an engagement or a friendship

dearth \'dərth\ *n* [ME *derthe*, fr. *dere* dear, costly] **1** : scarcity that makes dear; *specif* : FAMINE **2** : an inadequate supply : LACK

dea·sil \'dē-zəl\ *adv* [ScGael *deiseil*; akin to L *dexter*] : CLOCKWISE — compare WIDDERSHINS

death \'deth\ *n* [ME *deeth*, fr. OE *dēath*; akin to ON *dauthi* death, *deyja* to die — more at DIE] **1** : a permanent cessation of all vital functions : the end of life **2** : the cause or occasion of loss of life <drinking was the ~ of him> **3** *cap* : the destroyer of life represented usu. as a skeleton with a scythe **4** : the state of being dead **5 a** : the passing or destruction of something inanimate <the ~ of vaudeville> **b** : EXTINCTION **6** : CIVIL DEATH **7** : SLAUGHTER **8** *Christian Science* : the lie of life in matter : that which is unreal and untrue : ILLUSION — **to death** : beyond endurance : EXCESSIVELY

death·bed \'deth-'bed\ *n* **1** : the bed in which a person dies **2** : the last hours of life — **on one's deathbed** : near the point of death

death benefit *n* : money payable to the beneficiary of a deceased

death·blow \'deth-'blō\ *n* : a destructive or killing stroke or event

death camas *n* : any of several plants (genus *Zigadenus*) of the lily family that cause poisoning of livestock in the western U. S.

death camp *n* : a camp where large numbers of persons (as prisoners) are put to death

death cup *n* : a destroying angel (*Amanita phalloides*)

death duty *n, chiefly Brit* : DEATH TAX

death instinct *n* : an innate and unconscious tendency toward self-destruction postulated in psychoanalytic theory to explain aggressive and destructive behavior not satisfactorily explained by the pleasure principle

death·less \'deth-ləs\ *adj* : IMMORTAL, IMPERISHABLE <~ fame> — **death·less·ly** *adv* — **death·less·ness** *n*

death·ly \'deth-lē\ *adj* **1** : FATAL **2** : of, relating to, or suggestive of death <a ~ pallor> — **deathly** *adv*

death mask *n* : a cast taken from the face of a dead person

death point *n* : a limit (as of degree of heat or cold) beyond which an organism or living protoplasm cannot survive

death rattle *n* : a rattling or gurgling sound produced by air passing through mucus in the lungs and air passages of a dying person

death's-head \'deths-ˌhed\ *n* : a human skull emblematic of death

deaths·man \'deth-smən\ *n, archaic* : EXECUTIONER

death tax *n* : a tax arising on the transmission of property after the owner's death; *esp* : ESTATE TAX

death trap *n* : a structure or situation that is potentially very dangerous to life <the risk of going on in a boat that was a *death trap* —Ken Gardner>

death warrant *n* **1** : a warrant for the execution of a death sentence **2** : DEATHBLOW

[1]**death·watch** \'deth-ˌwäch\ *n* [*death* + *watch* (timepiece); fr. the superstition that its ticking presages death] : a small insect that makes a ticking sound: as **a** : any of various small beetles (family Anobiidae) that are common in old houses where they bore in woodwork and furniture — called also *deathwatch beetle* **b** : BOOK LOUSE

[2]**deathwatch** *n* [*death* + *watch* (vigil)] **1** : a vigil kept with the dead or dying **2** : the guard set over a criminal before his execution

death wish *n* : the conscious or unconscious desire for the death of another or of oneself

deb *abbr* debenture

de·ba·cle \di-'bäk-əl, -'bak-; dā-'bäk(lᵊ), 'dā-ˌ ; *also* 'deb-i-kəl\ *n* [F *débâcle*, fr. *débâcler* to unbar, fr. MF *desbacler*, fr. *des-* de- + *bacler* to bar, fr. OProv *baclar*, fr. (assumed) VL *bacculare*, fr. L *baculum* staff — more at BACTERIUM] **1** : a tumultuous breakup of ice in a river **2** : a violent disruption (as of an army) : ROUT **3 a** : a great disaster **b** : a complete failure : FIASCO

de·bar \di-'bär\ *vt* [ME *debarren*, fr. MF *desbarrer* to unbar, fr. *des-* de- + *barrer* to bar] : to bar from having or doing something : PRECLUDE ***syn*** see EXCLUDE — **de·bar·ment** \-mənt\ *n*

de·bark \di-'bärk\ *vb* [MF *debarquer*, fr. *de-* + *barque* bark] : DISEMBARK — **de·bar·ka·tion** \ˌdē-ˌbär-'kā-shən\ *n*

de·base \di-'bās\ *vt* **1** : to lower in status, esteem, quality, or character **2 a** : to reduce the intrinsic value of (a coin) by increasing the base-metal content **b** : to reduce the exchange value of (a monetary unit) — **de·base·ment** \-'bā-smənt\ *n* — **de·bas·er** \-'bā-sər\ *n*

syn* 1** DEBASE, VITIATE, DEPRAVE, CORRUPT, DEBAUCH, PERVERT *shared meaning element* : to cause to become lowered or impaired in quality or character ***ant elevate (*as taste*), amend (*as morals*) **2** see ABASE

de·bat·able \di-'bāt-ə-bəl\ *adj* **1** : claimed by more than one country <~ border territory> **2 a** : open to dispute : QUESTIONABLE <a ~ conclusion> **b** : open to debate **3** : capable of being debated

[1]**de·bate** \di-'bāt\ *n* : a contention by words or arguments: as **a** : the formal discussion of a motion before a deliberative body according to the rules of parliamentary procedure **b** : a regulated discussion of a proposition between two matched sides

[2]**debate** *vb* **de·bat·ed**; **de·bat·ing** [ME *debaten*, fr. MF *debatre*, fr. OF, fr. *de-* + *batre* to beat, fr. L *battuere* — more at BATTLE] *vi* **1** *obs* : FIGHT, CONTEND **2 a** : to contend in words **b** : to discuss a question by considering opposed arguments **3** : to participate in a debate ~ *vt* **1 a** : to argue about **b** : to engage (an opponent) in debate **2** : to turn over in one's mind ***syn*** see DISCUSS — **de·bate·ment** \-'bāt-mənt\ *n* — **de·bat·er** *n*

[1]**de·bauch** \di-'bȯch, -'bäch\ *vt* [MF *debaucher*, fr. OF *desbauchier* to scatter, rough-hew (timber), fr. *des-* de- + *bauch* beam, of Gmc origin; akin to OHG *balko* beam — more at BALK] **1 a** *archaic*

: to make disloyal **b** : to seduce from chastity **2 a** : to lead away from virtue or excellence **b** : to corrupt by intemperance or sensuality ***syn*** see DEBASE — **de·bauch·er** *n*

[2]**debauch** *n* **1** : an act or occasion of debauchery **2** : ORGY

de·bauch·ee \di-ˌbȯch-ˈē, -ˌbäch-; ˌdeb-ə-ˈshē, -ˈshā\ *n* [F *débauché,* fr. pp. of *débaucher*] : one given to debauchery

de·bauch·ery \di-ˈbȯch-(ə-)rē, -ˈbäch-\ *n, pl* **-er·ies** **1 a** : extreme indulgence in sensuality **b** *pl* : ORGIES **2** *archaic* : seduction from virtue or duty

de·ben·ture \di-ˈben-chər\ *n* [ME *debentur,* fr. L, they are due, 3d pl. pres. pass. of *debēre* to owe] **1** : a writing or certificate signed by a public officer as evidence of a debt or of a right to demand a sum of money **2 a** *Brit* : a corporate security other than an equity security : BOND **b** : a bond backed by the general credit of a corporation rather than a specific lien on particular assets

de·bil·i·tate \di-ˈbil-ə-ˌtāt\ *vt* **-tat·ed; -tat·ing** [L *debilitatus,* pp. of *debilitare* to weaken, fr. *debilis*] : to impair the strength of : ENFEEBLE ***syn*** see WEAKEN ***ant*** invigorate — **de·bil·i·ta·tion** \-ˌbil-ə-ˈtā-shən\ *n*

de·bil·i·ty \di-ˈbil-ət-ē\ *n, pl* **-ties** [MF *debilité,* fr. L *debiltat-, debilitas,* fr. *debilis* weak] : WEAKNESS, INFIRMITY

[1]**deb·it** \ˈdeb-ət\ *n* [L *debitum* debt] **1** : a record of an indebtedness; *specif* : an entry on the left-hand side of an account constituting an addition to an expense or asset account or a deduction from a revenue, net worth, or liability account **2** : the sum of the items so entered **3** : a charge against a bank deposit account **4** : DRAWBACK, SHORTCOMING <a film of almost equally divided merits and ~*s* —Richard Corliss>

[2]**debit** *vt* : to enter on the left-hand side of an account : charge with a debit

deb·o·nair \ˌdeb-ə-ˈna(ə)r, -ˈne(ə)r\ *adj* [ME *debonere,* fr. OF *debonaire,* fr. *de bonne aire* of good family or nature] **1** *archaic* : GENTLE, COURTEOUS **2 a** : SUAVE, URBANE **b** : LIGHTHEARTED, NONCHALANT — **deb·o·nair·ly** *adv* — **deb·o·nair·ness** *n*

de·bone \(ˈ)dē-ˈbōn\ *vt* : BONE <*deboned* the meat> — **de·bon·er** *n*

Deb·o·rah \ˈdeb-(ə-)rə\ *n* [Heb *Dĕbhōrāh*] : a Hebrew prophetess who rallied the Israelites in their early struggles against the Canaanites

de·bouch \di-ˈbau̇ch, -ˈbüsh\ *vb* [F *déboucher,* fr. *dé-* de- + *bouche* mouth, fr. L *bucca* cheek — more at POCK] *vi* **1** : to march out (as from a defile) into open ground **2** : EMERGE, ISSUE ~ *vt* : to cause to emerge : let out

de·bouch·ment \-mənt\ *n* **1** : the act or process of debouching **2** : a mouth or outlet esp. of a river

de·bou·chure \di-ˌbü-ˈshu̇(ə)r\ *n* : DEBOUCHMENT 2

de·bride·ment \di-ˈbrēd-mənt, dā-, -ˌmänt, -ˌmän\ *n* [F *débridement,* fr. *débrider* to remove unhealthy tissue, lit., to unbridle, fr. MF *desbrider,* fr. *des-* de- + *bride* bridle, fr. MHG *brīdel* — more at BRIDLE] : the surgical removal of lacerated, devitalized, or contaminated tissue

de·brief \di-ˈbrēf, ˈdē-\ *vt* **1** : to interrogate (as a pilot) in order to obtain useful information **2** : to instruct not to reveal any classified information after release from a senstive position

de·bris \də-ˈbrē, dā-ˈ, ˈdā-ˌ, *Brit usu* ˈdeb-(ˌ)rē\ *n, pl* **de·bris** \-ˈbrēz, -ˌbrēz, -(ˌ)rēz\ [F *débris,* fr. MF, fr. *debriser* to break to pieces, fr. OF *debrisier,* fr. *de-* + *brisier* to break — more at BRISANCE] **1** : the remains of something broken down or destroyed : RUINS **2** : an accumulation of fragments of rock

debt \ˈdet\ *n* [ME *dette, debte,* fr. OF *dette* something owed, fr. (assumed) VL *debita,* fr. L, pl. of *debitum* debt, fr. neut. of *debitus,* pp. of *debēre* to owe, fr. *de-* + *habēre* to have — more at HABIT] **1** : SIN, TRESPASS **2** : a state of owing **3** : something owed : OBLIGATION **4** : the common-law action for the recovery of money held to be due — **debt·less** \-ləs\ *adj*

debt·or \ˈdet-ər\ *n* **1** : one guilty of neglect or violation of duty **2** : one who owes a debt

de·bug \(ˈ)dē-ˈbəg\ *vt* **1** : to eliminate errors in or malfunctions of <~ a computer program> **2** : to remove a concealed microphone or wiretapping device from

de·bunk \(ˈ)dē-ˈbəŋk\ *vt* : to expose the sham or falseness of <~ a hero legend> — **de·bunk·er** *n*

de·but \ˈdā-ˌbyü, dā-ˈ\ *n* [F *début,* fr. *débuter* to begin, fr. MF *desbuter* to play first, fr. *des-* de- + *but* starting point, goal — more at BUTT] **1** : a first public appearance **2** : a formal entrance into society — **debut** *vi*

deb·u·tant \ˈdeb-yu̇-ˌtänt\ *n* [F *débutant,* fr. prp. of *débuter*] : one making a debut

deb·u·tante \ˈdeb-yu̇-ˌtänt\ *n* [F *débutante,* fem. of *débutant*] : a young woman making her formal entrance into society

dec *abbr* **1** deceased **2** declaration **3** declared **4** declination **5** decorated **6** decorative **7** decrease **8** decrescendo

Dec *abbr* December

deca- *or* **dec-** *or* **deka-** *or* **dek-** *comb form* [ME, fr. L, fr. Gk *deka-, dek-,* fr. *deka* — more at TEN] : ten <*decamerous*> <*dekavolt*>

de·cade \ˈdek-ˌād, -əd; de-ˈkād; *3 is usually* ˈdek-əd\ *n* [ME, fr. MF *décade,* fr. LL *decad-, decas,* fr. Gk *dekad-, dekas,* fr. *deka*] **1** : a group or set of 10 **2** : a period of 10 years **3** : a division of the rosary that consists primarily of 10 Hail Marys

dec·a·dence \ˈdek-əd-ən(t)s *also* di-ˈkād-ən(t)s\ *n* [MF, fr. ML *decadentia,* fr. LL *decadent-, decadens,* prp. of *decadere* to fall, sink — more at DECAY] **1** : the process of becoming decadent : the quality or state of being decadent **2** : a period of decline ***syn*** see DETERIORATION ***ant*** rise, flourishing

dec·a·den·cy \-ən-sē, -ən-sē\ *n* : DECADENCE 1

[1]**dec·a·dent** \ˈdek-əd-ənt *also* di-ˈkād-ənt\ *adj* [back-formation fr. *decadence*] **1** : marked by decay or decline **2** : of, relating to, or having the characteristics of the decadents — **dec·a·dent·ly** *adv*

[2]**decadent** *n* **1** : one that is decadent **2** : one of a group of late 19th century French and English writers tending toward artificial and unconventional subjects and subtilized style

de·caf·fein·ate \(ˈ)dē-ˈkaf-(ē-)ə-ˌnāt\ *vt* **-at·ed; -at·ing** : to remove caffeine from <*decaffeinated* coffee>

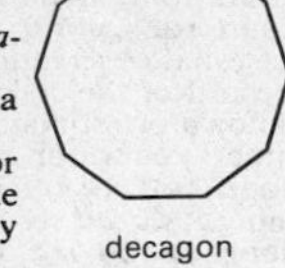

decagon

deca·gon \ˈdek-ə-ˌgän\ *n* [NL *decagonum,* fr. Gk *dekagōnon,* fr. *deka-* deca- + *-gōnon* -gon] : a plane polygon of 10 angles and 10 sides

deca·gram \-ˌgram\ *n* [F *décagramme,* fr. *déca-* deca- + *gramme* gram] : DEKAGRAM

deca·he·dron \ˌdek-ə-ˈhē-drən\ *n* [ISV] : a polyhedron of 10 faces

de·cal \ˈdē-ˌkal, di-ˈkal, ˈdek-əl\ *n* [short for *decalcomania*] : a picture, design, or label made to be transferred (as to glass) from specially prepared paper

de·cal·ci·fi·ca·tion \(ˌ)dē-ˌkal-sə-fə-ˈkā-shən\ *n* : the removal or loss of calcium or calcium compounds (as from bones or soil)

de·cal·ci·fy \(ˈ)dē-ˈkal-sə-ˌfī\ *vt* [ISV] : to remove calcium or calcium compounds from

de·cal·co·ma·nia \di-ˌkal-kə-ˈmā-nē-ə\ *n* [F *décalcomanie,* fr. *décalquer* to copy by tracing (fr. *dé-* de- + *calquer* to trace, fr. It *calcare,* lit., to trample, fr. L) + *manie* mania, fr. LL *mania* — more at CAULK] **1** : the art or process of transferring pictures and designs from specially prepared paper (as to glass) **2** : DECAL

de·ca·les·cence \ˌdē-kə-ˈles-ən(t)s, ˌdek-ə-\ *n* [ISV *de-* + *-calescence* (as in *recalescence*)] : a decrease in temperature that occurs while heating metal through a range in which change in structure occurs

deca·li·ter \ˈdek-ə-ˌlēt-ər\ *n* [F *décalitre,* fr. *déca-* + *litre* liter] : DEKALITER

deca·logue \ˈdek-ə-ˌlȯg, -ˌläg\ *n* [ME *decaloge,* fr. LL *decalogus,* fr. Gk *dekalogos,* fr. *deka-* + *logos* word — more at LEGEND] **1** *cap* : TEN COMMANDMENTS **2** : a basic set of rules carrying binding authority

[1]**de·cam·e·ter** \de-ˈkam-ət-ər, də-\ *n* [Gk *dekametron,* fr. *deka-* + *metron* measure, meter] : a line of verse consisting of 10 metrical feet

[2]**deca·me·ter** \ˈdek-ə-ˌmēt-ər\ *n* [F *décamètre,* fr. *déca-* + *mètre* meter] : DEKAMETER

deca·me·tho·ni·um \ˌdek-ə-mə-ˈthō-nē-əm\ *n* [*decamethonium* (an ammonium ion), fr. *deca-* + *meth*ylene + *-onium*] : any of several halogen salts of a synthetic ion whose curarizing effect produces relaxation of skeletal muscles

deca·met·ric \ˌdek-ə-ˈme-trik\ *adj* [*decameter* + *-ic;* fr. the wavelength range being between 1 and 10 dekameters] : of, relating to, or being a radio wave of high frequency

de·camp \di-ˈkamp\ *vi* [F *décamper,* fr. MF *descamper,* fr. *des-* de- + *camper* to camp] **1** : to break up a camp **2** : to depart suddenly : ABSCOND — **de·camp·ment** \-mənt\ *n*

dec·ane \ˈdek-ˌān\ *n* [ISV *deca-*] : any of several isomeric liquid hydrocarbons $C_{10}H_{22}$ of the methane series

dec·a·no·ic acid \ˌdek-ə-ˌnō-ik-\ *n* [ISV, fr. *decane*] : CAPRIC ACID

de·cant \di-ˈkant\ *vt* [NL *decantare,* fr. L *de-* + ML *cantus* side, fr. L, iron ring round a carriage wheel — more at CANT] **1** : to pour from one vessel into another **2** : to draw off without disturbing the sediment or the lower liquid layers — **de·can·ta·tion** \ˌdē-ˌkan-ˈtā-shən\ *n*

de·cant·er \di-ˈkant-ər\ *n* : a vessel used to decant or to receive decanted liquids; *esp* : an ornamental glass bottle used for serving wine

de·cap·i·tate \di-ˈkap-ə-ˌtāt\ *vt* **-tat·ed; -tat·ing** [LL *decapitatus,* pp. of *decapitare,* fr. L *de-* + *capit-, caput* head — more at HEAD] : to cut off the head of : BEHEAD — **de·cap·i·ta·tion** \-ˌkap-ə-ˈtā-shən\ *n* — **de·cap·i·ta·tor** \-ˈkap-ə-ˌtāt-ər\ *n*

deca·pod \ˈdek-ə-ˌpäd\ *n* [NL *Decapoda,* order name] **1** : any of an order (Decapoda) of highly organized crustaceans (as shrimps, lobsters, and crabs) with five pairs of thoracic appendages one or more of which are modified into pincers, stalked eyes, and the head and thorax fused into a cephalothorax and covered by a carapace **2** : any of an order (Decapoda) of cephalopod mollusks including the cuttlefishes, squids, and related forms that have 10 arms — **decapod** *adj* — **de·cap·o·dal** \di-ˈkap-əd-əl\ *adj* — **de·cap·o·dan** \-əd-ən\ *adj or n* — **de·cap·o·dous** \-əd-əs\ *adj*

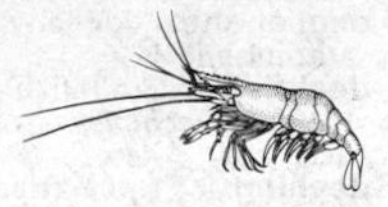

decapod 1: a prawn of the Atlantic coast of America

de·car·bon·ate \(ˈ)dē-ˈkär-bə-ˌnāt\ *vt* : to remove carbon dioxide or carbonic acid from — **de·car·bon·ation** \(ˌ)dē-ˌkär-bə-ˈnā-shən\ *n* — **de·car·bon·ator** \(ˈ)dē-ˈkär-bə-ˌnāt-ər\ *n*

de·car·bon·ize \(ˈ)dē-ˈkär-bə-ˌnīz\ *vt* [ISV] : to remove carbon from — **de·car·bon·iz·er** *n*

de·car·box·yl·ase \ˌdē-kär-ˈbäk-sə-ˌlās, -ˌlāz\ *n* : any of a group of enzymes that accelerate decarboxylation esp. of amino acids

de·car·box·yl·ate \-sə-ˌlāt\ *vt* : to remove carboxyl from — **de·car·box·yl·ation** \-ˌbäk-sə-ˈlā-shən\ *n*

de·car·bu·rize \(ˈ)dē-ˈkär-b(y)ə-ˌrīz\ *vt* : DECARBONIZE — **de·car·bu·ri·za·tion** \(ˌ)dē-ˌkär-b(y)ə-rə-ˈzā-shən\ *n*

dec·are \ˈdek-ˌa(ə)r, -ˌe(ə)r, -ˌär\ *n* [F *décare,* fr. *déca-* deca- + *are*] : a metric unit of area equal to 10 ares or 0.2471 acre

deca·stere \ˈdek-ə-ˌsti(ə)r, -ˌste(ə)r\ *n* [F *décastère,* fr. *déca-* + *stère* stere] : DEKASTERE

de·ca·su·al·iza·tion \(ˌ)dē-ˌkazh-(ə-)wə-lə-ˈzā-shən, -ˌkazh-ə-lə-\ *n* : the process of eliminating the employment of casual workers in order to stabilize the work force

deca·syl·lab·ic \ˌdek-ə-sə-ˈlab-ik\ *adj* [prob. fr. F *décasyllabique,* fr. Gk *dekasyllabos* decasyllabic, fr. *deka-* deca- + *syllabē* syllable] : consisting of 10 syllables or composed of verses of 10 syllables — **decasyllabic** *n* — **deca·syl·la·ble** \ˈdek-ə-ˌsil-ə-bəl, ˌdek-ə-ˈ\ *n*

de·cath·lon \di-ˈkath-lən, -ˌlän\ *n* [F *décathlon,* fr. *déca-* deca- + Gk *athlon* contest — more at ATHLETE] : a 10-event composite athletic contest consisting of the 100-meter, 400-meter, and 1500-meter runs, the 110-meter high hurdles, the javelin and discus throws, shot put, pole vault, high jump, and long jump

[1]**de·cay** \di-ˈkā\ *vb* [ME *decayen,* fr. ONF *decair,* fr. LL *decadere* to fall, sink, fr. L *de-* + *cadere* to fall — more at CHANCE] *vi* **1** : to decline from a sound or prosperous condition **2** : to decrease

gradually in quantity, activity, or force **3 :** to fall into ruin **4 :** to decline in health, strength, or vigor **5 :** to undergo decomposition ~ *vt* **1** *obs* **:** to cause to decay **:** IMPAIR <infirmity that ~*s* the wise —Shak.> **2 :** to destroy by decomposition — **de·cay·er** *n*

syn DECAY, DECOMPOSE, ROT, PUTREFY, SPOIL *shared meaning element* **:** to undergo destructive changes

[2]**decay** *n* **1 :** gradual decline in strength, soundness, or prosperity or in degree of excellence or perfection **2 :** a wasting or wearing away **:** RUIN **3** *obs* **:** DESTRUCTION, DEATH **4 a :** ROT; *specif* **:** aerobic decomposition of proteins chiefly by bacteria **b :** the product of decay **5 :** a decline in health or vigor **6 :** decrease in quantity, activity, or force: as **a :** spontaneous decrease in the number of radioactive atoms in radioactive material **b :** spontaneous disintegration (as of an atom or a meson)

Dec·ca \ˈdek-ə\ *n* [*Decca* Co., British firm which developed it] **:** a system of long-range navigation utilizing the phase differences of continuous-wave signals from synchronized ground transmitters

decd *abbr* deceased

de·cease \di-ˈsēs\ *n* [ME *deces,* fr. MF, fr. L *decessus* departure, death, fr. *decessus,* pp. of *decedere* to depart, die, fr. *de-* + *cedere* to go — more at CEDE] **:** departure from life **:** DEATH — **decease** *vi*

[1]**de·ceased** \-ˈsēst\ *adj* **:** no longer living; *esp* **:** recently dead — used of persons ***syn*** see DEAD

[2]**deceased** *n, pl* **deceased :** a dead person <the will of the ~>

de·ce·dent \di-ˈsēd-ᵊnt\ *n* [L *decedent-, decedens,* prp. of *decedere*] **:** a deceased person — used chiefly in law

de·ceit \di-ˈsēt\ *n* [ME *deceite,* fr. OF, fr. L *decepta,* fem. of *deceptus,* pp. of *decipere*] **1 :** the act or practice of deceiving **:** DECEPTION **2 :** an attempt or device to deceive **:** TRICK **3 :** the quality of being deceitful **:** DECEITFULNESS

de·ceit·ful \-fəl\ *adj* **:** having a tendency or disposition to deceive: **a :** not honest <a ~ child> **b :** DECEPTIVE, MISLEADING ***syn*** see DISHONEST ***ant*** trustworthy — **de·ceit·ful·ly** \-fə-lē\ *adv* — **de·ceit·ful·ness** *n*

de·ceiv·able \di-ˈsē-və-bəl\ *adj* **1** *archaic* **:** DECEITFUL, DECEPTIVE **2** *archaic* **:** capable of being deceived — **de·ceiv·able·ness** *n, archaic*

de·ceive \di-ˈsēv\ *vb* **de·ceived; de·ceiv·ing** [ME *deceiven,* fr. OF *deceivre,* fr. L *decipere,* fr. *de-* + *capere* to take — more at HEAVE] *vt* **1** *archaic* **:** ENSNARE **2 a** *obs* **:** to be false to **b** *archaic* **:** to fail to fulfill **3** *obs* **:** CHEAT **4 :** to cause to accept as true or valid what is false or invalid **5** *archaic* **:** to while away ~ *vi* **:** to practice deceit — **de·ceiv·er** *n* — **de·ceiv·ing·ly** \-ˈsē-viŋ-lē\ *adv*

syn DECEIVE, MISLEAD, DELUDE, BEGUILE *shared meaning element* **:** to lead astray ***ant*** undeceive, enlighten

de·cel·er·ate \(ˈ)dē-ˈsel-ə-ˌrāt\ *vb* **-at·ed; -at·ing** [*de-* + *accelerate*] *vt* **1 :** to reduce the speed of **:** slow down **2 :** to decrease the rate of progress of ~ *vi* **:** to move at decreasing speed — **de·cel·er·a·tion** \(ˌ)dē-ˌsel-ə-ˈrā-shən\ *n* — **de·cel·er·a·tor** \(ˈ)dē-ˈsel-ə-ˌrāt-ər\ *n*

De·cem·ber \di-ˈsem-bər\ *n* [ME *Decembre,* fr. OF, fr. L *December* (tenth month), fr. *decem* ten — more at TEN] **:** the 12th month of the Gregorian calendar

De·cem·brist \-brəst\ *n* **:** one taking part in the unsuccessful uprising against the Russian emperor Nicholas I in December 1825

de·cem·vir \di-ˈsem-vər\ *n* [L, back-formation fr. *decemviri,* pl., fr. *decem* + *viri,* pl. of *vir* man — more at VIRILE] **:** one of a ruling body of 10; *specif* **:** one of a body of 10 magistrates in ancient Rome — **de·cem·vi·ral** \-və-rəl\ *adj* — **de·cem·vi·rate** \-rət\ *n*

de·cen·cy \ˈdēs-ᵊn-sē\ *n, pl* **-cies 1** *archaic* **a :** FITNESS **b :** ORDERLINESS **2 a :** the quality or state of being decent **:** PROPRIETY **b :** conformity to standards of taste, propriety, or quality **3 :** standard of propriety — usu. used in pl. **4** *pl* **:** conditions or services considered essential for a proper standard of living **5 :** literary decorum

de·cen·ni·al \di-ˈsen-ē-əl\ *adj* **1 :** consisting of or lasting for 10 years **2 :** occurring or being done every 10 years — **decennial** *n* — **de·cen·ni·al·ly** \-ē-ə-lē\ *adv*

de·cen·ni·um \-ē-əm\ *n, pl* **-ni·ums** *or* **-nia** \-ē-ə\ [L, fr. *decem* + *annus* year — more at ANNUAL] **:** a period of 10 years **:** DECADE

de·cent \ˈdēs-ᵊnt\ *adj* [MF or L; MF, fr. L *decent-, decens,* prp. of *decēre* to be fitting; akin to L *decus* honor, *dignus* worthy, Gk *dokein* to seem, seem good] **1** *archaic* **a :** APPROPRIATE **b :** well-formed **:** HANDSOME **2 a :** conforming to standards of propriety, good taste, or morality **b :** modestly clothed **3 :** free from immodesty or obscenity **4 :** conforming to current standards of living <~ wages> <~ housing> **5 :** having praiseworthy qualities ***syn*** see CHASTE ***ant*** indecent, obscene — **de·cent·ly** *adv*

de·cen·tral·iza·tion \(ˌ)dē-ˌsen-trə-lə-ˈzā-shən\ *n* **1 :** the dispersion or distribution of functions and powers from a central authority to regional and local authorities **2 :** the redistribution of population and industry from urban centers to outlying areas — **de·cen·tral·iza·tion·ist** \(ˌ)dē-ˌsen-trə-lə-ˈzā-sh(ə-)nəst\ *n*

de·cen·tral·ize \(ˈ)dē-ˈsen-trə-ˌlīz\ *vt* **:** to bring about the decentralization of ~ *vi* **:** to undergo decentralization

de·cep·tion \di-ˈsep-shən\ *n* [ME *decepcioun,* fr. MF *deception,* fr. LL *deception-, deceptio,* fr. L *deceptus,* pp. of *decipere* to deceive] **1 a :** the act of deceiving **b :** the fact or condition of being deceived **2 :** something that deceives **:** TRICK — **de·cep·tion·al** \-shnəl, -shən-ᵊl\ *adj*

de·cep·tive \di-ˈsep-tiv\ *adj* **:** tending or having power to deceive **:** MISLEADING — **de·cep·tive·ly** *adv* — **de·cep·tive·ness** *n*

[1]**de·cer·e·brate** \(ˈ)dē-ˈser-ə-ˌbrāt\ *vt* **:** to remove the cerebrum from; *also* **:** to make incapable of cerebral activity — **de·cer·e·bra·tion** \(ˌ)dē-ˌser-ə-ˈbrā-shən\ *n*

[2]**de·cer·e·brate** \(ˈ)dē-ˈser-ə-brət, -ˌbrāt; ˌdē-sə-ˈrē-brət\ *adj* **1 :** having the cerebrum removed or made inactive **2 :** characteristic of decerebration <~ rigidity>

de·cer·ti·fy \(ˈ)dē-ˈsərt-ə-ˌfī\ *vt* **:** to withdraw or revoke the certification of — **de·cer·ti·fi·ca·tion** \(ˌ)dē-ˌsərt-ə-fə-ˈkā-shən\ *n*

de·chlo·ri·nate \(ˈ)dē-ˈklōr-ə-ˌnāt, -ˈklȯr-\ *vt* **:** to remove chlorine from <~ water> — **de·chlo·ri·na·tion** \(ˌ)dē-ˌklōr-ə-ˈnā-shən, -ˌklȯr-\ *n*

deci- *comb form* [F *déci-,* fr. L *decimus* tenth, fr. *decem* ten — more at TEN] **:** tenth part <*deci*normal>

deci·are \ˈdes-ē-ˌa(ə)r, -ˌe(ə)r, -ˌär\ *n* [F *déciare,* fr. *déci-* + *are*] **:** a metric unit of area equal to 10 square meters or 11.96 square yards

deci·bel \ˈdes-ə-ˌbel, -bəl\ *n* [ISV *deci-* + *bel*] **1 a :** a unit for expressing the ratio of two amounts of electric or acoustic signal power equal to 10 times the common logarithm of this ratio **b :** a unit for expressing the ratio of the magnitudes of two electric voltages or currents or analogous acoustic quantities equal to 20 times the common logarithm of the voltage or current ratio **2 :** a unit for expressing the relative intensity of sounds on a scale from zero for the average least perceptible sound to about 130 for the average pain level

de·cide \di-ˈsīd\ *vb* **de·cid·ed; de·cid·ing** [ME *deciden,* fr. MF *decider,* fr. L *decidere,* lit., to cut off, fr. *de-* + *caedere* to cut — more at CONCISE] *vt* **1 :** to arrive at a solution that ends uncertainty or dispute about <important . . . that we ~ borderline cases in favor of individual freedom —Milton Friedman> **2 :** to bring to a definitive end <one blow *decided* the fight> **3 :** to induce to come to a choice <her pleas *decided* him to help> ~ *vi* **:** to make a choice or judgment — **de·cid·abil·i·ty** \-ˌsīd-ə-ˈbil-ət-ē\ *n* — **de·cid·able** \-ˈsīd-ə-bəl\ *adj* — **de·cid·er** *n*

syn DECIDE, DETERMINE, SETTLE, RULE, RESOLVE *shared meaning element* **:** to come or cause to come to a conclusion

de·cid·ed *adj* **1 :** UNQUESTIONABLE <a ~ advantage> **2 :** free from doubt or wavering — **de·cid·ed·ly** *adv* — **de·cid·ed·ness** *n*

de·cid·ing *adj* **:** that decides **:** DECISIVE <drove in the ~ run>

de·cid·ua \di-ˈsij-ə-wə\ *n, pl* **-u·ae** \-ə-ˌwē\ [NL, fr. L, fem. of *deciduus*] **1 :** the part of the mucous membrane lining the uterus that in higher placental mammals undergoes special modifications in preparation for and during pregnancy and is cast off at parturition **2 :** the part of the mucous membrane of the uterus cast off in the process of menstruation — **de·cid·u·al** \-wəl\ *adj*

de·cid·u·ate \-wət\ *adj* **:** having the fetal and maternal tissues firmly interlocked so that a layer of maternal tissue is torn away at parturition and forms a part of the afterbirth

de·cid·u·ous \di-ˈsij-ə-wəs\ *adj* [L *deciduus,* fr. *decidere* to fall off, fr. *de-* + *cadere* to fall — more at CHANCE] **1 :** falling off or shed seasonally or at a certain stage of development in the life cycle <~ leaves> <~ teeth> **2 :** having deciduous parts <~ trees> **3 :** EPHEMERAL — **de·cid·u·ous·ly** *adv* — **de·cid·u·ous·ness** *n*

deci·gram \ˈdes-ə-ˌgram\ *n* [F *décigramme,* fr. *déci-* + *gramme* gram] — see METRIC SYSTEM table

dec·ile \ˈdes-ˌīl, -əl\ *n* [L *decem* ten — more at TEN] **:** any one of nine numbers in a series dividing the distribution of the individuals in the series into 10 groups of equal frequency; *also* **:** any one of these 10 groups — **decile** *adj*

deci·li·ter \ˈdes-ə-ˌlēt-ər\ *n* [F *décilitre,* fr. *déci-* + *litre* liter] — see METRIC SYSTEM table

de·cil·lion \di-ˈsil-yən\ *n, often attrib* [L *decem* + E *-illion* (as in *million*)] — see NUMBER table

[1]**dec·i·mal** \ˈdes(-ə)-məl\ *adj* [(assumed) NL *decimalis,* fr. ML, of a tithe, fr. L *decima* tithe — more at DIME] **:** numbered or proceeding by tens: **a :** based on the number 10 **b :** subdivided into 10th or 100th units **c :** expressed in a decimal fraction — **dec·i·mal·ly** \-mə-lē\ *adv*

[2]**decimal** *n* **:** a proper fraction in which the denominator is a power of 10 usu. not expressed but signified by a point placed at the left of the numerator (as .2=2/10, .25=25/100, .025=25/1000) — called also *decimal fraction*

dec·i·mal·ize \ˈdes(-ə)-mə-ˌlīz\ *vt* **-ized; -iz·ing :** to convert to a decimal system <~ currency> — **dec·i·mal·iza·tion** \ˌdes(-ə)-mə-lə-ˈzā-shən\ *n*

decimal point *n* **:** the dot at the left of a decimal fraction

dec·i·mate \ˈdes-ə-ˌmāt\ *vt* **-mat·ed; -mat·ing** [L *decimatus,* pp. of *decimare,* fr. *decimus* tenth, fr. *decem* ten] **1 :** to select by lot and kill every tenth man of **2 :** to take a tenth from **:** TITHE **3 :** to destroy a large part of — **dec·i·ma·tion** \ˌdes-ə-ˈmā-shən\ *n*

deci·me·ter \ˈdes-ə-ˌmēt-ər\ *n* [F *décimètre,* fr. *déci-* deci- + *mètre* meter] — see METRIC SYSTEM table

de·ci·pher \di-ˈsī-fər\ *vt* **1 a :** to convert into intelligible form **b :** DECODE **2** *obs* **:** DEPICT **3 :** to make out the meaning of despite indistinctness or obscurity — **de·ci·pher·able** \-f(ə-)rə-bəl\ *adj* — **de·ci·pher·er** \-fər-ər\ *n* — **de·ci·pher·ment** \-fər-mənt\ *n*

de·ci·sion \di-ˈsizh-ən\ *n* [MF, fr. L *decision-, decisio,* fr. *decisus,* pp. of *decidere* to decide] **1 a :** the act or process of deciding **b :** a determination arrived at after consideration **:** CONCLUSION **2 :** a report of a conclusion **3 :** promptness and firmness in deciding **:** DETERMINATION <a man of courage and ~> — **de·ci·sion·al** \-ˈsizh-nəl, -ən-ᵊl\ *adj*

de·ci·sive \di-ˈsī-siv\ *adj* **1 :** having the power or quality of deciding **2 :** marked by or indicative of determination or firmness **:** RESOLUTE **3 :** UNMISTAKABLE, UNQUESTIONABLE <a ~ superiority> ***syn*** see CONCLUSIVE ***ant*** indecisive — **de·ci·sive·ly** *adv* — **de·ci·sive·ness** *n*

deci·stere \ˈdes-ə-ˌsti(ə)r, -ˌste(ə)r\ *n* [F *décistère,* fr. *déci-* + *stère* stere] — see METRIC SYSTEM table

[1]**deck** \ˈdek\ *n* [prob. modif. of (assumed) LG *verdeck* (whence G *verdeck*), fr. (assumed) MLG *vordeck,* fr. MLG *vordecken* to cover, fr. *vor-* (akin to OHG *fur-* for-) + *decken* to cover; akin to OHG *decken* to cover — more at THATCH] **1 :** a platform in a ship serving usu. as a structural element and forming the floor for its

ə abut	ᵊ kitten	ər further	a back	ā bake	ä cot, cart
aù out	ch chin	e less	ē easy	g gift	i trip	ī life
j joke	ŋ sing	ō flow	ȯ flaw	ȯi coin	th thin	t͟h this
ü loot	ù foot	y yet	yü few	yù furious	zh vision

compartments **2 :** something resembling the deck of a ship: as **a** : a story or tier of a building **b :** the roadway of a bridge **c** : a flat floored roofless area adjoining a house **d :** the lid of the compartment at the rear of the body of an automobile; *also* : the compartment **e :** a layer of clouds **f :** TAPE DECK **3 a :** a pack of playing cards **b :** a packet of narcotics **c :** a group of usu. punched data processing cards — **on deck 1 :** ready for duty **2** : next in line

[2]**deck** *vt* [D *dekken* to cover; akin to OHG *decken*] **1** *obs* : COVER **2 a :** to clothe elegantly : ARRAY <~*ed* out in furs> **b :** DECORATE <~ the halls with boughs of holly —English carol> **3** [[1]*deck*] : to furnish with or as if with a deck **4** [[1]*deck*] : to knock down forcibly : FLOOR <~*ed* his opponent with a left hook> *syn* see ADORN

deck chair *n* : a folding chair often having an adjustable leg rest

deck·er \'dek-ər\ *n* : something having a deck or a specified number of levels, floors, or layers — often used in combination <many of the city's buses are double-*deckers*>

deck·hand \'dek-ˌhand\ *n* : a seaman who performs manual duties

deck·house \-ˌhau̇s\ *n* : a superstructure on a ship's upper deck

deck·ing \'dek-iŋ\ *n* : DECK; *also* : material for a deck

deck·le \'dek-əl\ *n* [G *deckel,* lit., cover, fr. *decken* to cover, fr. OHG] **1 :** a detachable wooden frame around the outside edges of a hand mold used in making paper **2 :** either of the bands that run longitudinally on the edges of the wire of a paper machine and determine the width of the web

deckle edge *n* : the rough untrimmed edge of paper left by a deckle or produced artificially — **deck·le–edged** \ˌdek-ə-'lejd\ *adj*

deck tennis *n* [fr. its being played chiefly on the decks of ocean liners] : a game in which players toss a ring or quoit back and forth over a net stretched across a small court

de·claim \di-'klām\ *vb* [ME *declamen,* fr. L *declamare,* fr. *de-* + *clamare* to cry out; akin to L *calare* to call — more at LOW] *vi* **1** : to speak rhetorically; *specif* : to recite something as an exercise in elocution **2 :** to speak pompously or bombastically : HARANGUE ~ *vt* : to deliver rhetorically; *specif* : to recite in elocution — **de·claim·er** *n* — **dec·la·ma·tion** \ˌdek-lə-'mā-shən\ *n*

de·clam·a·to·ry \di-'klam-ə-ˌtōr-ē, -ˌtȯr-\ *adj* : of, relating to, or marked by declamation or rhetorical display

de·clar·ant \di-'klar-ənt, -'kler-\ *n* : one that makes a declaration; *specif* : an alien who has declared his intention of becoming a citizen of the U.S. by signing his first papers

dec·la·ra·tion \ˌdek-lə-'rā-shən\ *n* **1 :** the act of declaring : ANNOUNCEMENT **2 a :** the first pleading in a common-law action **b :** a statement made by a party to a legal transaction usu. not under oath **3 a :** something that is declared **b :** the document containing such a declaration

de·clar·a·tive \di-'klar-ət-iv, -'kler-\ *adj* : making a declaration : DECLARATORY <~ sentence> — **de·clar·a·tive·ly** *adv*

de·clar·a·to·ry \-ə-ˌtōr-ē, -ˌtȯr-\ *adj* **1 :** serving to declare, set forth, or explain **2 a :** declaring what is the existing law <~ statute> **b :** declaring a legal right or interpretation <a ~ judgment>

de·clare \di-'kla(ə)r, -'kle(ə)r\ *vb* **de·clared; de·clar·ing** [ME *declaren,* fr. MF *declarer,* fr. L *declarare,* fr. *de-* + *clarare* to make clear, fr. *clarus* clear — more at CLEAR] *vt* **1** *obs* : to make clear **2 :** to make known formally or explicitly **3 :** to make evident : SHOW **4 :** to state emphatically : AFFIRM <~*s* his innocence> **5 :** to make a full statement of (one's taxable or dutiable property) **6 a :** to announce (as a trump suit) in a card game **b :** MELD **7** : to make payable ~ *vi* **1 :** to make a declaration **2 :** to avow one's support — **de·clar·able** \-'klar-ə-bəl, -'kler-\ *adj*

***syn* 1** DECLARE, ANNOUNCE, PUBLISH, ADVERTISE, PROCLAIM, PROMULGATE *shared meaning element* : to make known publicly **2** see ASSERT

de·clar·er \di-'klar-ər, -'kler-\ *n* : one that declares; *specif* : the bridge player who names the trump and plays both his own hand and that of the dummy

de·class \(ˈ)dē-'klas\ *vt* : to remove from a class; *esp* : to assign to a lower social status ***syn*** see DEGRADE

dé·clas·sé \ˌdā-ˌklas-'ā, -ˌkläs-\ *adj* [F, fr. pp. of *déclasser* to declass] **1 :** fallen or lowered in class, rank, or social position **2** : of inferior status

de·clas·si·fy \(ˈ)dē-'klas-ə-ˌfī\ *vt* : to remove or reduce the security classification of <~ a secret document>

de·clen·sion \di-'klen-chən\ *n* [prob. alter. of earlier *declenson,* modif. of MF *declinaison,* fr. LL *declination-, declinatio,* fr. L, grammatical inflection, turning aside, fr. *declinatus,* pp. of *declinare* to inflect, turn aside] **1 a :** noun, adjective, or pronoun inflection esp. in some prescribed order of the forms **b :** a class of nouns or adjective having the same type of inflectional forms **2 :** a falling off or away : DETERIORATION **3 :** DESCENT, SLOPE — **de·clen·sion·al** \-'klench-nəl, -'klen-chən-ᵊl\ *adj*

dec·li·nate \'dek-lə-ˌnāt, -nət\ *adj* : bent or curved down or aside

dec·li·na·tion \ˌdek-lə-'nā-shən\ *n* [ME *declinacioun,* fr. MF *declination,* fr. L *declination-, declinatio* turning aside, altitude of the pole] **1 :** angular distance north or south from the celestial equator measured along a great circle passing through the celestial poles **2 :** a turning aside or swerving **3 :** DETERIORATION <moral ~> **4 :** a bending downward : INCLINATION **5 :** a formal refusal **6 :** the angle formed between a magnetic needle and the geographical meridian — **dec·li·na·tion·al** \-shnəl, -shən-ᵊl\ *adj*

[1]**de·cline** \di-'klīn\ *vb* **de·clined; de·clin·ing** [ME *declinen,* fr. MF *decliner,* fr. L *declinare* to turn aside, inflect, fr. *de-* + *clinare* to incline — more at LEAN] *vi* **1 :** to turn from a straight course : STRAY **2 a :** to slope downward : DESCEND **b :** to bend down : DROOP **c :** to stoop to what is unworthy **3 a** *of a celestial body* : to sink toward setting **b :** to draw toward a close : WANE **4** : to withhold consent ~ *vt* **1 :** to give in prescribed order the grammatical forms of (a noun, pronoun, or adjective) **2** *obs* **4 a** : AVERT **b :** AVOID **3 :** to cause to bend or bow downward **4 a** : to refuse to undertake, engage in, or comply with **b :** to refuse courteously <~ an invitation> — **de·clin·able** \-'klī-nə-bəl\ *adj*

syn DECLINE, REFUSE, REJECT, REPUDIATE, SPURN *shared meaning element* : to turn away by not accepting, receiving, or considering ***ant*** accept

[2]**decline** *n* **1 :** the process of declining: **a :** a gradual physical or mental sinking and wasting away **b :** a change to a lower state or level **2 :** the period during which something is approaching its end **3 :** a downward slope : DECLIVITY **4 :** a wasting disease; *esp* : pulmonary tuberculosis ***syn*** see DETERIORATION

de·cliv·i·tous \di-'kliv-ət-əs\ *adj* : moderately steep

de·cliv·i·ty \-ət-ē\ *n, pl* **-ties** [L *declivitat-, declivitas,* fr. *declivis* sloping down, fr. *de-* + *clivus* slope, hill; akin to L *clinare*] **1** : downward inclination **2 :** a descending slope

de·coct \di-'käkt\ *vt* [L *decoctus,* pp. of *decoquere,* fr. *de-* + *coquere* to cook — more at COOK] **1 :** to extract the flavor of by boiling **2 :** to boil down : CONCENTRATE

de·coc·tion \di-'käk-shən\ *n* **1 :** the act or process of decocting **2 :** an extract obtained by decocting

de·code \(ˈ)dē-'kōd\ *vt* : to convert (a coded message) into intelligible language — **de·cod·er** *n*

de·col·late \di-'käl-ˌāt\ *vt* **-lat·ed; -lat·ing** [L *decollatus,* pp. of *decollare,* fr. *de-* + *collum* neck — more at COLLAR] : BEHEAD — **de·col·la·tion** \ˌdē-ˌkä-'lā-shən\ *n*

dé·col·le·tage \(ˌ)dā-ˌkäl-ə-'täzh, ˌdek-(ə-)lə-\ *n* [F, action of cutting or wearing a low neckline, fr. *décolleter*] **1 :** the low-cut neckline of a dress **2** : a décolleté dress

décolletage 1

dé·col·le·té \-'tā\ *adj* [F, fr. pp. of *décolleter* to give a low neckline to, fr. *dé-* de- + *collet* collar, fr. OF *colet,* fr. *col* collar, neck, fr. L *collum* neck] **1** : wearing a strapless or low-necked dress **2 :** having a low-cut neckline

de·col·o·nize \(ˈ)dē-'käl-ə-ˌnīz\ *vt* : to free from colonial status — **de·col·o·ni·za·tion** \(ˌ)dē-ˌkäl-ə-nə-'zā-shən\ *n*

de·col·or·ize \(ˈ)dē-'kəl-ə-ˌrīz\ *vt* **-ized; -iz·ing** : to remove color from <~ vinegar by adsorption of impurities on activated charcoal> — **de·col·or·iza·tion** \(ˌ)dē-ˌkəl-ə-rə-'zā-shən\ *n* — **de·col·or·iz·er** \(ˈ)dē-'kəl-ə-ˌrī-zər\ *n*

de·com·mis·sion \ˌdē-kə-'mish-ən\ *vt* : to remove (as a ship) from service

de·com·pen·sate \(ˈ)dē-'käm-pən-ˌsāt, -ˌpen-\ *vi* [prob. back-formation fr. *decompensation*] : to undergo decompensation — **de·com·pen·sa·to·ry** \ˌdē-kəm-'pen(t)-sə-ˌtōr-ē, -ˌtȯr-\ *adj*

de·com·pen·sa·tion \(ˌ)dē-ˌkäm-pən-'sā-shən, -pen-\ *n* [ISV] : loss of compensation; *esp* : inability of the heart to maintain adequate circulation

de·com·pose \ˌdē-kəm-'pōz\ *vb* [F *décomposer,* fr. *dé-* de + *composer* to compose] *vt* **1 :** to separate into constituent parts or elements or into simpler compounds <~ water by electrolysis> **2** : ROT ~ *vi* : to undergo chemical breakdown : DECAY, ROT <fruit ~*s*> ***syn*** see DECAY — **de·com·pos·abil·i·ty** \-ˌpō-zə-'bil-ət-ē\ *n* — **de·com·pos·able** \-'pō-zə-bəl\ *adj* — **de·com·po·si·tion** \(ˌ)dē-ˌkäm-pə-'zish-ən\ *n* — **de·com·po·si·tion·al** \-'zish-nəl, -'zish-ən-ᵊl\ *adj*

de·com·pos·er \ˌdē-kəm-'pō-zər\ *n* : any of various organisms (as many bacteria and fungi) that return constituents of organic substances to ecological cycles by feeding on and breaking down dead protoplasm

de·com·pound \'dē-'käm-ˌpau̇nd; ˌdē-ˌkäm-', -kəm-'\ *adj, of a leaf* : having divisions that are themselves compound

de·com·press \ˌdē-kəm-'pres\ *vt* : to release from pressure or compression — **de·com·pres·sion** \-'presh-ən\ *n*

de·con·cen·trate \(ˈ)dē-'kän(t)-sən-ˌtrāt, -ˌsen-\ *vt* : DECENTRALIZE

de·con·di·tion \ˌdē-kən-'dish-ən\ *vt* **1 :** to cause to lose physical fitness <inactivity ~*s* a bedridden person> **2 :** to cause extinction of (a conditioned response)

de·con·gest \ˌdē-kən-'jest\ *vt* : to relieve the congestion of — **de·con·ges·tion** \-'jes(h)-chən\ *n* — **de·con·ges·tive** \-'jes-tiv\ *adj*

de·con·ges·tant \ˌdē-kən-'jes-tənt\ *n* : an agent that relieves congestion (as of mucous membranes)

de·con·se·crate \(ˈ)dē-'kän(t)-sə-ˌkrāt\ *vt* : to remove the sacred character of <~ a church> — **de·con·se·cra·tion** \(ˌ)dē-ˌkän(t)-sə-'krā-shən\ *n*

de·con·tam·i·nate \ˌdē-kən-'tam-ə-ˌnāt\ *vt* : to rid of contamination — **de·con·tam·i·na·tion** \-ˌtam-ə-'nā-shən\ *n* — **de·con·tam·i·na·tor** \-'tam-ə-ˌnāt-ər\ *n*

de·con·trol \ˌdē-kən-'trōl\ *vt* : to end control of — **decontrol** *n*

de·cor *or* **dé·cor** \dā-'kȯ(ə)r, di-'; 'dek-ˌȯ(ə)r, 'dāk-ˌ\ *n* [F *décor,* fr. *décorer* to decorate, fr. L *decorare*] **1 a :** DECORATION **b :** the style and layout of interior furnishings **2 :** a stage setting

dec·o·rate \'dek-ə-ˌrāt\ *vt* **-rat·ed; -rat·ing** [L *decoratus,* pp. of *decorare,* fr. *decor-, decus* ornament — more at DECENT] **1 :** to add honor to **2 :** to furnish with something ornamental **3 :** to award a mark of honor to ***syn*** see ADORN

dec·o·ra·tion \ˌdek-ə-'rā-shən\ *n* **1 :** the act or process of decorating **2 :** ORNAMENT **3 :** a badge of honor (as a U.S. military award)

Decoration Day *n* [fr. the custom of decorating graves on this day] : MEMORIAL DAY

dec·o·ra·tive \'dek-(ə-)rət-iv, 'dek-ə-ˌrāt-\ *adj* : serving to decorate; *esp* : purely ornamental — **dec·o·ra·tive·ly** *adv* — **dec·o·ra·tive·ness** *n*

[1]**dec·o·ra·tor** \'dek-ə-ˌrāt-ər\ *n* : one that decorates; *esp* : one that designs or executes interiors and their furnishings

[2]**decorator** *adj* : suitable for interior decoration <~ fabrics>

dec·o·rous \'dek-ə-rəs *also* di-'kōr-əs *or* -'kȯr-\ *adj* [L *decorus,* fr. *decor* beauty, grace; akin to L *decēre* to be fitting — more at DECENT] : marked by propriety and good taste : CORRECT <~ conduct> — **dec·o·rous·ly** *adv* — **dec·o·rous·ness** *n*

de·cor·ti·cate \(ˈ)dē-'kȯrt-ə-ˌkāt\ *vt* **-cat·ed; -cat·ing** [L *decorticatus,* pp. of *decorticare* to remove the bark from, fr. *de-* + *cortic-, cortex* bark — more at CORTEX] **1 :** to peel the outer covering from **2 :** to remove all or part of the cortex from (as the brain) — **de·cor·ti·ca·tion** \(,)dē-,kȯrt-ə-'kā-shən\ *n* — **de·cor·ti·ca·tor** \(')dē-'kȯrt-ə-,kāt-ər\ *n*

de·co·rum \di-'kōr-əm, -'kȯr-\ *n* [L, fr. neut. of *decorus*] **1 :** literary and dramatic propriety : FITNESS **2 :** propriety and good taste in conduct or appearance **3 :** ORDERLINESS **4** *pl* **:** the conventions of polite behavior

de·cou·page *or* **dé·cou·page** \,dā-(,)kü-'päzh\ *n* [F *découpage*, lit., act of cutting out, fr. MF, fr. *decouper* to cut out, fr. *de-* + *couper* to cut — more at COPE] **1 :** the art of decorating surfaces by applying cutouts (as of paper) and then coating with usu. several layers of finish (as lacquer or varnish) **2 :** work produced by decoupage

1de·coy \'dē-,kȯi, di-'\ *n* [prob. fr. D *de kooi*, lit., the cage, fr. *de*, masc. def. art. (akin to OE *thæt*, neut. def. article) + *kooi* cage, fr. L *cavea* — more at THAT, CAGE] **1 :** a pond into which wild fowl are lured for capture **2 :** one that is used to lure or lead another into a trap; *esp* **:** an artificial bird used to attract live birds within shot

2de·coy \di-'kȯi, 'dē-,\ *vt* **:** to lure by or as if by a decoy : ENTICE ***syn*** see LURE

1de·crease \di-'krēs, 'dē-,\ *vb* **de·creased; de·creas·ing** [ME *decreessen*, fr. (assumed) AF *decreistre*, fr. L *decrescere*, fr. *de-* + *crescere* to grow — more at CRESCENT] *vi* **:** to grow progressively less (as in size, amount, number, or intensity) ~ *vt* **:** to cause to decrease — **de·creas·ing·ly** \di-'krē-siŋ-lē\ *adv*

syn DECREASE, LESSEN, DIMINISH, REDUCE, ABATE, DWINDLE *shared meaning element* **:** to grow or make less ***ant*** increase

2de·crease \'dē-,krēs, di-'\ *n* **1 :** the process of decreasing **2 :** an amount of diminution : REDUCTION

1de·cree \di-'krē\ *n* [ME, fr. MF *decré*, fr. L *decretum*, fr. neut. of *decretus*, pp. of *decernere* to decide, fr. *de-* + *cernere* to sift, decide — more at CERTAIN] **1 :** an order usu. having the force of law **2 a :** a religious ordinance enacted by council or titular head **b :** a foreordaining will **3 a :** a judicial decision of the Roman emperor **b :** a judicial decision esp. in an equity or probate court

2decree *vb* **de·creed; de·cree·ing** *vt* **1 :** to command or enjoin by decree <~ an amnesty> **2 :** to determine or order judicially <~ a punishment> ~ *vi* **:** ORDAIN — **de·cre·er** \-'krē-ər\ *n*

de·cree–law \di-'krē-,lȯ\ *n* **:** a decree of a ruler or ministry having the force of a law enacted by the legislature

dec·re·ment \'dek-rə-mənt\ *n* [L *decrementum*, fr. *decrescere*] **1 :** a gradual decrease in quality or quantity **2 a :** the quantity lost by diminution or waste **b :** a negative mathematical increment — **dec·re·men·tal** \,dek-rə-'ment-ᵊl\ *adj*

de·crep·it \di-'krep-ət\ *adj* [ME, fr. MF, fr. L *decrepitus*] **1 :** wasted and weakened by or as if by the infirmities of old age **2 a :** impaired by use or wear : WORN-OUT **b :** fallen into ruin or disrepair **3 :** DILAPIDATED, RUN-DOWN ***syn*** see WEAK ***ant*** sturdy — **de·crep·it·ly** *adv*

de·crep·i·tate \di-'krep-ə-,tāt\ *vb* [prob. fr. (assumed) NL *decrepitatus*, pp. of *decrepitare*, fr. L *de-* + *crepitare* to crackle — more at CREPITATE] *vt* **:** to roast or calcine (as salt) so as to cause crackling or until crackling stops ~ *vi* **:** to become decrepitated — **de·crep·i·ta·tion** \-,krep-ə-'tā-shən\ *n*

de·crep·i·tude \di-'krep-ə-,t(y)üd\ *n* **:** the quality or state of being decrepit

1de·cre·scen·do \,dā-krə-'shen-(,)dō\ *adv or adj* [It, lit., decreasing, fr. L *decrescendum*, gerund of *decrescere*] **:** with a decrease in volume — used as a direction in music

2decrescendo *n, pl* **-dos 1 :** a gradual decrease in volume of a musical passage **2 :** a decrescendo musical passage

mark indicating decrescendo 2

de·cres·cent \di-'kres-ᵊnt\ *adj* [alter. of earlier *decressant*, prob. fr. AF, prp. of (assumed) AF *decreistre* to decrease] **:** becoming less by gradual diminution : DECREASING, WANING

de·cre·tal \di-'krēt-ᵊl\ *n* [ME *decretale*, fr. MF, fr. LL *decretalis* of a decree, fr. L *decretum* decree] **:** DECREE; *esp* **:** a papal letter giving an authoritative decision on a point of canon law

de·cre·tive \-'krēt-iv\ *adj* **:** having the force of a decree : DECRETORY

de·cre·to·ry \'dek-rə-,tōr-ē, -,tȯr-; di-'krēt-ə-rē\ *adj* **:** relating to or fixed by a decree or decision

de·cry \di-'krī\ *vt* [F *décrier*, fr. OF *descrier*, fr. *des-* de- + *crier* to cry] **1 :** to depreciate (as a coin) officially or publicly **2 :** to express strong disapproval of <~ the emphasis on sex> — **de·cri·er** \-'krī(-ə)r\ *n*

syn DECRY, DEPRECIATE, DISPARAGE, BELITTLE, MINIMIZE *shared meaning element* **:** to give expression to one's low opinion of something ***ant*** extol

de·crypt \(')dē-'kript\ *vt* [ISV *de-* + *crypt*ogram, *crypt*ograph] **1 :** DECIPHER **2 :** DECODE — **de·cryp·tion** \-'krip-shən\ *n*

de·cryp·to·graph \-'krip-tə-,graf\ *vt* **:** DECRYPT

de·cum·bent \di-'kəm-bənt\ *adj* [L *decumbent-*, *decumbens*, prp. of *decumbere* to lie down, fr. *de-* + *-cumbere* to lie down — more at SUCCUMB] **1 :** lying down **2** *of a plant* **:** reclining on the ground but with ascending apex or extremity

dec·u·ple \'dek-yə-pəl\ *adj* [F *décuple*, fr. MF, fr. LL *decuplus*, fr. L *decem* ten + *-plus* multiplied by — more at TEN, DOUBLE] **1 :** TENFOLD **2 :** taken in groups of 10

de·cu·ri·on \di-'kyu̇r-ē-ən\ *n* [ME *decurioun*, fr. L *decurion-*, *decurio*, fr. *decuria* division of ten, fr. *decem*] **1 :** a Roman cavalry officer in command of 10 men **2 :** a member of a Roman senate

de·curved \(')dē-'kərvd\ *adj* [part trans. of LL *decurvatus*, fr. L *de-* + *curvatus* curved] **:** curved downward : bent down

1de·cus·sate \'dek-ə-,sāt, di-'kəs-,āt\ *vb* **-sat·ed; -sat·ing** [L *decussatus*, pp. of *decussare*, fr. *decussis* the number ten, numeral X, intersection, fr. *decem* + *ass-*, *as* unit — more at ACE] **:** INTERSECT

2de·cus·sate \'dek-ə-,sāt, di-'kəs-ət\ *adj* **1 :** shaped like an X **2 :** arranged in pairs each at right angles to the next pair above or below <~ leaves> — **de·cus·sate·ly** *adv*

de·cus·sa·tion \,dek-ə-'sā-shən, ,dē-,kə-\ *n* **1 :** an intersection in the form of an X **2 :** a band of nerve fibers that connects unlike centers of opposite sides of the central nervous system

de·dans \də-'däⁿ\ *n, pl* **dedans** \-'däⁿ(z)\ [F, lit., interior] **1 :** an open gallery at the service end of the court in court tennis **2 :** the spectators at a court-tennis match

1ded·i·cate \'ded-i-kət\ *adj* [ME, fr. L *dedicatus*, pp. of *dedicare* to dedicate, fr. *de-* + *dicare* to proclaim, dedicate — more at DICTION] **:** DEDICATED

2ded·i·cate \'ded-i-,kāt\ *vt* **-cat·ed; -cat·ing 1 :** to devote to the worship of a divine being; *specif* **:** to set apart (a church) to sacred uses with solemn rites **2 a :** to set apart to a definite use <money *dedicated* to their vacation fund> **b :** to become committed to as a goal or way of life <ready to ~ his life to public service> **3 :** to inscribe or address by way of compliment <~ a book to a friend> **4 :** to open to public use ***syn*** see DEVOTE — **ded·i·ca·tor** \-,kāt-ər\ *n*

ded·i·cat·ed *adj* **1 :** devoted to a cause, ideal, or purpose : ZEALOUS <a ~ scholar> **2 :** given over to a particular purpose <a ~ process control computer> — **ded·i·cat·ed·ly** *adv*

ded·i·ca·tion \,ded-i-'kā-shən\ *n* **1 :** an act or rite of dedicating to a divine being or to a sacred use **2 :** a devoting or setting aside for a particular purpose **3 :** a name and often a message prefixed to a literary, musical, or artistic production in tribute to a person or cause **4 :** self-sacrificing devotion — **ded·i·ca·tive** \'ded-i-,kāt-iv, -kət-\ *adj* — **ded·i·ca·to·ry** \'ded-i-kə-,tōr-ē, -,tȯr-\ *adj*

de·dif·fer·en·ti·a·tion \(')dē-,dif-ə-,ren-chē-'ā-shən\ *n* **:** reversion of specialized structures (as cells) to a more generalized or primitive condition often as a preliminary to major change

de·duce \di-'d(y)üs\ *vt* **de·duced; de·duc·ing** [L *deducere*, lit., to lead away, fr. *de-* + *ducere* to lead — more at TOW] **1 :** to trace the course of **2 :** to determine by deduction; *specif* **:** to infer from a general principle — compare INDUCE ***syn*** see INFER — **de·duc·ible** \-'d(y)ü-sə-bəl\ *adj*

de·duct \di-'dəkt\ *vt* [L *deductus*, pp. of *deducere*] **1 :** to take away (an amount) from a total : SUBTRACT **2 :** DEDUCE, INFER

1de·duct·ible \di-'dək-tə-bəl\ *adj* **:** capable of being deducted — **de·duct·ibil·i·ty** \-,dək-tə-'bil-ət-ē\ *n*

2deductible *n* **:** a clause in an insurance policy that relieves the insurer of responsibility for an initial specified loss of the kind insured against

de·duc·tion \di-'dək-shən\ *n* **1 a :** an act of taking away <~ of legitimate business expenses> **b :** something that is or may be subtracted <~*s* from his taxable income> **2 a :** the deriving of a conclusion by reasoning; *specif* **:** inference in which the conclusion follows necessarily from the premises **b :** a conclusion reached by logical deduction

de·duc·tive \di-'dək-tiv\ *adj* **1 a :** of or relating to deduction **b :** employing deduction in reasoning **2 :** capable of being deduced from premises : INFERENTIAL — **de·duc·tive·ly** *adv*

dee \'dē\ *n* **:** the letter *d*

1deed \'dēd\ *n* [ME *dede*, fr. OE *dǣd*; akin to OE *dōn* to do] **1 :** something that is done <evil ~*s*> **2 :** a usu. illustrious act or action : FEAT, EXPLOIT **3 :** the act of performing <a righteous man who never mistook the word for the ~> **4 :** a signed and usu. sealed instrument containing some legal transfer, bargain, or contract ***syn*** see ACTION — **deed·less** \-ləs\ *adj*

2deed *vt* **:** to convey or transfer by deed ***syn*** see TRANSFER

deed poll \-'pōl\ *n, pl* **deeds poll** [1*deed* + *poll*, adj. (having the edges cut even rather than indented), fr. 2*poll*] **:** a deed made and executed by only one party

deedy \'dēd-ē\ *adj* **deed·i·er; -est** *dial chiefly Eng* **:** INDUSTRIOUS

dee·jay \'dē-'jā\ *n* [*d*isc *j*ockey] **:** DISC JOCKEY

deem \'dēm\ *vb* [ME *demen*, fr. OE *dēman*; akin to OHG *tuomen* to judge, OE *dōm* doom] *vt* **:** to come to think or judge : HOLD <~*ed* it wise to go slow> ~ *vi* **:** to have an opinion : BELIEVE

de–em·pha·size \(')dē-'em(p)-fə-,sīz\ *vt* **:** to play down — **de–em·pha·sis** \-fə-səs\ *n*

1deep \'dēp\ *adj* [ME, fr. OE *dēop*; akin to OHG *tiof* deep, OE *dyppan* to dip — more at DIP] **1 :** extending far from some surface or area: as **a :** extending far downward <a ~ well> **b** (1) **:** extending well inward from an outer surface <a ~ gash> <a *deep*-chested animal> (2) **:** not located superficially within the body <~ pressure receptors in muscles> **c :** extending well back from a front surface <a ~ closet> **d :** extending far laterally from the center <~ borders of lace> **e :** occurring or located near the outer limits of the playing area <hit to ~ right field> **2 :** having a specified extension in an implied direction usu. downward or backward <shelf 20 inches ~> <cars parked three-*deep*> **3 a :** difficult to penetrate or comprehend : RECONDITE <~ mathematical problems> **b :** MYSTERIOUS, OBSCURE <a ~ dark secret> **c :** grave in nature or effect : GRIEVOUS <in ~*est* disgrace> **d :** of penetrating intellect : WISE <a ~ thinker> **e :** ENGROSSED, INVOLVED <a man ~ in debt> **f :** characterized by profundity of feeling or quality <a ~ sleep>; *also* **:** DEEP-SEATED <~ religious beliefs> **4 a** *of color* **:** high in saturation and low in lightness **b :** having a low musical pitch or pitch range <a ~ voice> **5 a :** situated well within the boundaries <a house ~ in the woods> **b :** remote in time or space <had its roots ~ in the Middle Ages —Roy Lewis & Angus Maude> **c :** being below the level of the

conscious <~ neuroses> **d** : covered, enclosed, or filled to a specified degree — usu. used in combination <she was ankle-*deep* in mud> — **deep·ly** *adv* — **deep·ness** *n*
***syn* 1** DEEP, PROFOUND, ABYSMAL *shared meaning element* : having great extension downward or inward
2 see BROAD ***ant*** shallow
— **in deep water** : in difficulty or distress

[2]deep *adv* **1** : to a great depth : DEEPLY <still waters run ~> **2** : far on : LATE <danced ~ into the night> **3** : near the outer limits of the playing area <the shortstop was playing ~>

[3]deep *n* **1** : any of the fathom points on a sounding line that is not a mark **2 a** : a vast or immeasurable extent : ABYSS **b** (1) : the extent of surrounding space or time (2) : OCEAN **3** : the middle or most intense part <the ~ of winter> **4** : one of the deep portions of any body of water; *specif* : a generally long and narrow area in the ocean where the depth exceeds 3000 fathoms

deep–dish pie *n* : a pie usu. with a fruit filling and no bottom crust that is baked in a deep dish

deep·en \ˈdē-pən, ˈdēp-ᵊn\ *vb* **deep·ened; deep·en·ing** \ˈdēp-(ə-)niŋ\ *vt* : to make deep or deeper ~ *vi* : to become deeper or more profound

deep fat *n* : hot fat or oil deep enough in a cooking utensil to cover the food to be fried

deep–freeze \ˈdēp-ˈfrēz\ *vt* **-froze** \-ˈfrōz\; **-fro·zen** \-ˈfrōz-ᵊn\ **1** : QUICK-FREEZE **2** : CHILL, REFRIGERATE

deep–go·ing \ˈdēp-ˈgō-iŋ, -ˈgȯ(-)iŋ\ *adj* : FUNDAMENTAL <a ~ theory>

deep kiss *n* : FRENCH KISS

deep–root·ed \ˈdē-ˈprüt-əd, -ˈprůt-\ *adj* : deeply implanted or established <a ~ loyalty> ***syn*** see INVETERATE

deep–sea \ˌdēp-ˌsē\ *adj* : of, relating to, or occurring in the deeper parts of the sea <~ fishing>

deep–seat·ed \ˈdēp-ˈsēt-əd\ *adj* **1** : situated far below the surface <a ~ inflammation> **2** : firmly established <a ~ tradition> ***syn*** see INVETERATE

deep–six *vt* **1** *slang* : to throw overboard **2** *slang* : to throw away : DISCARD

deep six *n* [naval slang for "burial at sea"; perh. fr. the tradition of burying bodies six feet under ground] *slang* : a place of disposal or abandonment — used esp. in the phrase *give it the deep six*

deep space *n* : space well beyond the limits of the earth's atmosphere including space outside the solar system

deep structure *n* : a formal representation of the underlying semantic content of a sentence; *also* : the structure which such a representation specifies

deer \ˈdi(ə)r\ *n, pl* **deer** *also* **deers** [ME, deer, animal, fr. OE *dēor* beast; akin to OHG *tior* wild animal, Skt *dhvaṁsati* he perishes] **1** *archaic* : ANIMAL; *esp* : a small mammal **2** : a ruminant mammal (family Cervidae, the deer family) having two large and two small hoofs on each foot and antlers borne by the males of nearly all and by the females of a few forms

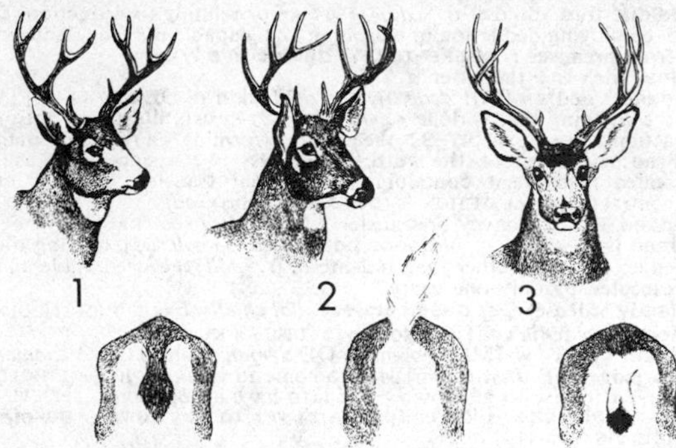

deer 2: *1* blacktailed deer, *2* whitetail, *3* mule deer

deer·ber·ry \-ˌber-ē\ *n* **1** : either of two shrubs (*Vaccinium stamineum* or *V. caesium*) of dry woods and scrub of the eastern U.S. **2** : the edible fruit of a deerberry

deer·fly \ˈdi(ə)r-ˌflī\ *n* : any of numerous small horseflies (as of the genus *Chrysops*) that include important vectors of tularemia

deer·hound \-ˌhau̇nd\ *n* : SCOTTISH DEERHOUND

deer mouse *n* [fr. its agility] : WHITE-FOOTED MOUSE

deer·skin \ˈdi(ə)r-ˌskin\ *n* : leather made from the skin of a deer; *also* : a garment of this leather

deer·stalk·er hat \-ˌstȯ-kər-\ *n* : a close-fitting hat with a visor at the front and the back and with earflaps that may be worn up or down — called also *deerstalker*

deer·yard \ˈdi(ə)r-ˌyärd\ *n* : a place where deer herd in winter

de–es·ca·late \(ˈ)dē-ˈes-kə-ˌlāt, *nonstand* -kyə-\ *vi* : to decrease in extent, volume, or scope ~ *vt* : LIMIT 2 — **de–es·ca·la·tion** \(ˌ)dē-ˌes-kə-ˈlā-shən, *nonstand* -kyə-\ *n* — **de–es·ca·la·to·ry** \(ˈ)dē-ˈes-kə-lə-ˌtōr-ē, -ˌtȯr-, *nonstand* -kyə-\ *adj*

def *abbr* **1** defendant **2** defense **3** deferred **4** defined **5** definite **6** definition

de·face \di-ˈfās\ *vt* [ME *defacen*, fr. MF *desfacier*, fr. OF, fr. *des-* de- + *face*] **1** : to mar the external appearance of : injure by effacing significant details <~ an inscription> **2** : IMPAIR **3** *obs* : DESTROY — **de·face·ment** \-ˈfā-smənt\ *n* — **de·fac·er** *n*
syn DEFACE, DISFIGURE *shared meaning element* : to mar the appearance of

[1]de fac·to \di-ˈfak-(ˌ)tō, dā-\ *adv* [NL] : in reality : ACTUALLY

[2]de facto *adj* **1** : exercising power as if legally constituted <a *de facto* government> **2** : ACTUAL <a *de facto* state of war> — compare DE JURE

de·fal·cate \di-ˈfal-ˌkāt, di-ˈfȯl-, ˈdef-əl-\ *vb* **-cat·ed; -cat·ing** [ML *defalcatus*, pp. of *defalcare*, fr. L *de-* + *falc-, falx* sickle] *vt, archaic* : DEDUCT, CURTAIL ~ *vi* : to engage in embezzlement — **de·fal·ca·tor** \-ˌkāt-ər\ *n*

de·fal·ca·tion \ˌdē-ˌfal-ˈkā-shən, ˌdē-ˌfȯl-, di-; ˌdef-əl-\ *n* **1** *archaic* : DEDUCTION **2** : the act or an instance of embezzling **3** : a failure to meet a promise or an expectation

def·a·ma·tion \ˌdef-ə-ˈmā-shən\ *n* : the act of defaming another : CALUMNY — **de·fam·a·to·ry** \di-ˈfam-ə-ˌtōr-ē, -ˌtȯr-\ *adj*

de·fame \di-ˈfām\ *vt* **de·famed; de·fam·ing** [ME *diffamen, defamen*, fr. MF & L; ME *diffamen* fr. MF *diffamer*, fr. L *diffamare*, fr. *dis-* + *fama* fame; ME *defamen* fr. MF *defamer*, fr. ML *defamare*, fr. L *de-* + *fama*] **1** *archaic* : DISGRACE **2** : to harm the reputation of by libel or slander **3** *archaic* : ACCUSE ***syn*** see MALIGN — **de·fam·er** *n*

de·fat \(ˈ)dē-ˈfat\ *vt* : to remove fat from

[1]de·fault \di-ˈfȯlt\ *n* [ME *defaute, defaulte*, fr. OF *defaute*, fr. (assumed) VL *defallita*, fr. fem. of *defallitus*, pp. of *defallere* to be lacking, fail, fr. L *de-* + *fallere* to deceive] **1** : failure to do something required by duty or law : NEGLECT **2** *archaic* : FAULT **3** : a failure to pay financial debts **4 a** : failure to appear at the required time in a legal proceeding **b** : failure to compete in or to finish an appointed contest — **in default of** : in the absence of

[2]default *vi* : to fail to fulfill a contract, agreement, or duty: as **a** : to fail to meet a financial obligation **b** : to fail to appear in court **c** : to fail to compete in or to finish an appointed contest; *also* : to forfeit a contest by such failure ~ *vt* **1** : to fail to perform, pay, or make good **2** : FORFEIT — **de·fault·er** *n*

de·fea·sance \di-ˈfēz-ᵊn(t)s\ *n* [ME *defesance*, fr. AF, fr. OF *deffesant*, prp. of *deffaire*] **1 a** : a rendering null or void **b** (1) : the termination of a property interest in accordance with stipulated conditions (as in a deed) (2) : an instrument stating such conditions of limitation **2** : DEFEAT, OVERTHROW

de·fea·si·ble \di-ˈfē-zə-bəl\ *adj* : capable of being annulled or made void <a ~ claim to an estate> — **de·fea·si·bil·i·ty** \-ˌfē-zə-ˈbil-ət-ē\ *n*

[1]de·feat \di-ˈfēt\ *vt* [ME *deffeten*, fr. MF *deffait*, pp. of *deffaire* to destroy, fr. ML *disfacere*, fr. L *dis-* + *facere* to do — more at DO] **1** *obs* : DESTROY **2 a** : NULLIFY <~ an estate> **b** : FRUSTRATE <~ a hope> **3** : to win victory over : BEAT <~ the opposing team>

[2]defeat *n* **1** *obs* : DESTRUCTION **2** : frustration by nullification or by prevention of success <the bill suffered ~ in the Senate> **3 a** : an overthrow esp. of an army in battle **b** : the loss of a contest

de·feat·ism \-ˌiz-əm\ *n* : acceptance of or resignation to defeat — **de·feat·ist** \-əst\ *n or adj*

[1]de·fea·ture \di-ˈfē-chər\ *n* [prob. fr. *de-* + *feature*] *archaic* : DISFIGUREMENT

[2]defeature *n* [ˈ*defeat*] *archaic* : DEFEAT

def·e·cate \ˈdef-i-ˌkāt\ *vb* **-cat·ed; -cat·ing** [L *defaecatus*, pp. of *defaecare*, fr. *de-* + *faec-, faex* dregs, lees] *vt* **1** : to free from impurity or corruption : REFINE **2** : to discharge through the anus ~ *vi* : to discharge feces from the bowels — **def·e·ca·tion** \ˌdef-i-ˈkā-shən\ *n*

[1]de·fect \ˈdē-ˌfekt, di-ˈ\ *n* [ME *defaicte*, fr. MF *defect*, fr. L *defectus* lack, fr. *defectus*, pp. of *deficere* to desert, fail, fr. *de-* + *facere* to do — more at DO] **1 a** : an imperfection that impairs worth or utility : SHORTCOMING <the grave ~*s* in our foreign policy> **b** : an imperfection (as a vacancy or a foreign atom) in a crystal lattice **2** [L *defectus*] : a lack of something necessary for completeness, adequacy, or perfection : DEFICIENCY <a hearing ~> ***syn*** see BLEMISH

[2]de·fect \di-ˈfekt\ *vi* [L *defectus*, pp.] : to desert a cause or party often in order to espouse another — **de·fec·tor** \-ˈfek-tər\ *n*

de·fec·tion \di-ˈfek-shən\ *n* : conscious abandonment of allegiance or duty (as to a person, cause, or doctrine) : DESERTION

[1]de·fec·tive \di-ˈfek-tiv\ *adj* **1** : lacking something essential : FAULTY <a ~ pane of glass> <~ eyesight> **2** : lacking one or more of the usual forms of grammatical inflection <*must* is a ~ verb> **3** : markedly subnormal mentally or physically — **de·fec·tive·ly** *adv* — **de·fec·tive·ness** *n*

[2]defective *n* : a person who is subnormal physically or mentally

defective year *n* : a common year of 353 days or a leap year of 383 days in the Jewish calendar

de·fem·i·nize \(ˈ)dē-ˈfem-ə-ˌnīz\ *vt* : to divest of feminine qualities or characteristics : MASCULINIZE

de·fend \di-ˈfend\ *vb* [ME *defenden*, fr. OF *defendre*, fr. L *defendere*, fr. *de-* + *-fendere* to strike; akin to OE *gūth* battle, war, Gk *theinein* to strike] *vt* **1** *archaic* : PREVENT, FORBID **2 a** : to drive danger or attack away from **b** : to maintain in the face of argument or hostile criticism **c** : to attempt to prevent an opponent from scoring at <elects to ~ the south goal> **3** : to act as attorney for **4** : to deny or oppose the right of a plaintiff in regard to (a suit or a wrong charged) : CONTEST ~ *vi* **1** : to take action against attack or challenge <couldn't fight back, could only ~> **2** : to play or be on defense <playing deep to ~ against a pass> **3** : to play against the high bidder in a card game
syn* 1** DEFEND, PROTECT, SHIELD, GUARD, SAFEGUARD *shared meaning element* : to keep secure (as from danger or against attack) ***ant combat, attack
2 see MAINTAIN

de·fend·able \di-ˈfen-də-bəl\ *adj* : DEFENSIBLE

[1]de·fen·dant \di-ˈfen-dənt\ *n* : a person required to make answer in a legal action or suit — compare PLAINTIFF

[2]defendant *adj* : being on the defensive : DEFENDING

de·fend·er \di-ˈfen-dər\ *n* **1** : one that defends **2** : a player in a sport (as football) assigned to a defensive position

de·fen·es·tra·tion \(ˌ)dē-ˌfen-ə-ˈstrā-shən\ *n* [*de-* + L *fenestra* window] : a throwing of a person or thing out of a window — **de·fen·es·trate** \(ˈ)dē-ˈfen-ə-ˌstrāt\ *vt*

1de·fense *or* **de·fence** \di-ˈfen(t)s; *as antonym of "offense," often* ˈdē-ˌ\ *n* [ME, fr. OF, fr. (assumed) VL *defensa,* fr. L, fem. of *defensus,* pp. of *defendere*] **1 a :** the act or action of defending <the ~ of one's country> <to speak out in ~ of justice> **b :** a defendant's denial, answer, or plea **2 :** capability of resisting attack **3 a :** means or method of defending or protecting oneself or another; *also* **:** a defensive structure **b :** an argument in support or justification **c :** the collected facts and method adopted by a defendant to protect himself against a plaintiff's action **d :** a sequence of moves available in chess to the second player in the opening **4 a :** a defending party or group (as in a court of law) <the ~ rested its case> **b :** a defensive team **5 :** the military, governmental, and industrial aggregate esp. in its capacity of authorizing and supervising arms production <~ budget> < ~ contract> — **de·fense·less** \-ləs\ *adj* — **de·fense·less·ly** *adv* — **de·fense·less·ness** *n*

2defense *vt* **de·fensed; de·fens·ing :** to take specific defensive action against (an opposing team or player)

de·fense·man \-mən, -ˌman\ *n* **:** a player in a sport (as hockey) assigned to a defensive zone or position

defense mechanism *n* **1 :** a defensive reaction by an organism **2 :** an often unconscious mental process (as repression, projection, or sublimation) that enables the ego to reach compromise solutions to problems

de·fen·si·ble \di-ˈfen(t)-sə-bəl\ *adj* **:** capable of being defended — **de·fen·si·bil·i·ty** \di-ˌfen(t)-sə-ˈbil-ət-ē, ˌdē-\ *n* — **de·fen·si·bly** \-blē\ *adv*

1de·fen·sive \di-ˈfen(t)-siv, ˈdē-ˌ\ *adj* **1 :** serving to defend or protect **2 a :** devoted to resisting or preventing aggression or attack **b :** of or relating to the attempt to keep an opponent from scoring in a game or contest **3 a :** valuable in defensive play <a ~ card in bridge> **b :** designed to keep an opponent from being the highest bidder <a ~ bid> — **de·fen·sive·ly** *adv* — **de·fen·sive·ness** *n*

2defensive *n* **:** a defensive position — **on the defensive :** in the state or condition of being prepared for an expected aggression or attack

1de·fer \di-ˈfər\ *vt* **de·ferred; de·fer·ring** [ME *deferren, differren,* fr. MF *differer,* fr. L *differre* to postpone, be different — more at DIFFER] **:** to put off **:** DELAY <forced to ~ college because of financial problems> — **de·fer·rer** *n*
syn DEFER, POSTPONE, INTERMIT, SUSPEND, STAY *shared meaning element* **:** to delay an action or proceeding

2defer *vb* **deferred; deferring** [ME *deferren, differren,* fr. MF *deferer, defferer,* fr. LL *deferre,* fr. L, to bring down, bring, fr. *de-* + *ferre* to carry — more at BEAR] *vt* **:** to delegate to another <he could ~ his job to no one —J. A. Michener> ~ *vi* **:** to submit to another's wishes, opinion, or governance usu. through deference or respect <a man who *deferred* only to God> *syn* see YIELD

def·er·ence \ˈdef-(ə-)rən(t)s\ *n* **:** respect and esteem due a superior or an elder; *also* **:** affected or ingratiating regard for another's wishes *syn* see HONOR *ant* disrespect — **in deference to :** in consideration of

1def·er·ent \ˈdef-ə-rənt, -ˌer-ənt\ *adj* [L *deferent-, deferens,* prp. of *deferre*] **:** serving to carry down or out <a ~ conduit>

2def·er·ent \ˈdef-(ə-)rənt\ *adj* [back-formation fr. *deference*] **:** DEFERENTIAL

def·er·en·tial \ˌdef-ə-ˈren-chəl\ *adj* **:** showing or expressing deference <~ attention> — **def·er·en·tial·ly** \-ˈrench-, -rench-(ə-)lē\ *adv*

de·fer·ment \di-ˈfər-mənt\ *n* **:** the act of delaying or postponing; *specif* **:** official postponement of military service

de·fer·ra·ble \di-ˈfər-ə-bəl\ *adj* **:** capable of or suitable or eligible for being deferred — **deferrable** *n*

de·fer·ral \di-ˈfər-əl\ *n* **:** DEFERMENT

de·ferred *adj* **1 :** withheld for or until a stated time <a ~ payment> **2 :** charged in cases of delayed handling <a ~ rate>

de·fer·ves·cence \ˌdē-(ˌ)fər-ˈves-ᵊn(t)s, ˌdef-ər-\ *n* [G *deferveszenz,* fr. L *defervescent-, defervescens,* prp. of *defervescere* to stop boiling, fr. *de-* + *fervescere* to begin to boil — more at EFFERVESCE] **:** the subsidence of a fever

de·fi·ance \di-ˈfī-ən(t)s\ *n* **1 :** the act or an instance of defying **:** CHALLENGE **2 :** disposition to resist or contempt of opposition — **in defiance of :** contrary to **:** DESPITE <worked *in defiance of* doctor's orders>

de·fi·ant \-ənt\ *adj* [F *défiant,* fr. OF, prp. of *defier* to defy] **:** full of defiance **:** BOLD — **de·fi·ant·ly** *adv*

de·fi·bril·late \(ˈ)dē-ˈfib-rə-ˌlāt, -ˈfīb-\ *vt* **:** to restore the rhythm of (a fibrillating heart) — **de·fi·bril·la·tion** \(ˌ)dē-ˌfib-rə-ˈlā-shən, -ˌfīb-\ *n* — **de·fi·bril·la·tive** \(ˈ)dē-ˈfib-rə-ˌlāt-iv, -ˈfīb-\ *adj* — **de·fi·bril·la·tor** \-ˌlāt-ər\ *n* — **de·fi·bril·la·to·ry** \(ˈ)dē-ˈfib-rə-lə-ˌtōr-ē, -ˈfīb-; ˌdē-fī-ˈbril-ə-\ *adj*

de·fi·brin·ate \(ˈ)dē-ˈfib-rə-ˌnāt, -ˈfīb-\ *vt* **-at·ed; -at·ing :** to remove fibrin from (blood) — **de·fi·brin·ation** \(ˌ)dē-ˌfib-rə-ˈnā-shən, -ˌfīb-\ *n*

de·fi·cien·cy \di-ˈfish-ən-sē\ *n, pl* **-cies 1 :** the quality or state of being deficient **:** INADEQUACY **2 a :** a shortage of substances necessary to health **b :** absence of one or more genes from a chromosome

deficiency disease *n* **:** a disease (as scurvy) caused by a lack of essential dietary elements and esp. a vitamin or mineral

1de·fi·cient \di-ˈfish-ənt\ *adj* [L *deficient-, deficiens,* prp. of *deficere* to be wanting — more at DEFECT] **1 :** lacking in some necessary quality or element <~ in judgment> **2 :** not up to a normal standard or complement **:** DEFECTIVE <~ strength> — **de·fi·cient·ly** *adv*

2deficient *n* **:** one that is deficient <a mental ~>

def·i·cit \ˈdef-ə-sət *also, esp Brit,* di-ˈfis-ət *or* ˈdē-fə-sət\ *n* [F *déficit,* fr. L *deficit* it is wanting, 3d sing. pres. indic. of *deficere*] **1 a :** deficiency in amount or quality <a ~ in rainfall> **b :** DISADVANTAGE <a two-run homer in the sixth that overcame a 2-1 ~> **2 a :** an excess of expenditure over revenue **b :** a loss in business operations

deficit spending *n* **:** the spending of public funds raised by borrowing rather than by taxation

de·fi·er \di-ˈfī(-ə)r\ *n* **:** one that defies

1def·i·lade \ˈdef-ə-ˌlād, -ˌläd\ *vt* **-lad·ed; -lad·ing** [prob. fr. *de-* + *-filade* (as in *enfilade*)] **:** to arrange (fortifications) so as to protect the lines from frontal or enfilading fire and the interior of the works from plunging or reverse fire

2defilade *n* **:** the act or process of defilading

1de·file \di-ˈfī(ə)l\ *vt* **de·filed; de·fil·ing** [ME *defilen,* alter. of *defoulen* to trample, defile, fr. OF *defouler* to trample, fr. *de-* + *fouler* to trample, lit., to full — more at FULL] **:** to make unclean or impure **:** BEFOUL, BESMIRCH: as **a :** to corrupt the purity or perfection of **:** DEBASE <the countryside *defiled* by billboards> **b :** to denude of chastity **:** DEFLOWER **c :** to make physically unclean esp. with something unpleasant or contaminating <boots *defiled* with blood> **d :** to make ceremonially unclean <~ a sanctuary> **e :** SULLY, DISHONOR *syn* see CONTAMINATE — **de·file·ment** \-ˈfī(ə)l-mənt\ *n* — **de·fil·er** \-ˈfī-lər\ *n*

2de·file \di-ˈfī(ə)l, ˈdē-ˌfīl\ *vi* **de·filed; de·fil·ing** [F *défiler,* fr. *dé-* de- + *filer* to move in a column — more at FILE] **:** to march off in a line

3de·file \di-ˈfī(ə)l, ˈdē-ˌfīl\ *n* [F *défilé,* fr. pp. of *défiler*] **:** a narrow passage or gorge

de·fin·able \di-ˈfī-nə-bəl\ *adj* **:** capable of being defined, limited, or explained — **de·fin·ably** \-blē\ *adv*

de·fine \di-ˈfīn\ *vb* **de·fined; de·fin·ing** [ME *definen,* fr. MF & L; MF *definer,* fr. L *definire,* fr. *de-* + *finire* to limit, end, fr. *finis* boundary, end — more at FINAL] *vt* **1 a :** to fix or mark the limits of **:** DEMARCATE <rigidly *defined* property lines> **b :** to make distinct, clear, or detailed in outline <the issues aren't too well *defined*> **2 a :** to determine or identify the essential qualities or meaning of <~ a powerful position by salary and prestige> <whatever ~*s* us as human> **b :** to discover and set forth the meaning of (as a word) **3 :** CHARACTERIZE, DISTINGUISH <good manners ~ the gentleman> ~ *vi* **:** to make a definition — **de·fine·ment** \-ˈfīn-mənt\ *n* — **de·fin·er** \-ˈfī-nər\ *n*

de·fin·i·en·dum \di-ˌfin-ē-ˈen-dəm\ *n, pl* **-da** \-də\ [L, something to be defined, neut. of *definiendus,* gerundive of *definire*] **:** an expression that is being defined

de·fin·i·ens \di-ˈfin-ē-ˌenz\ *n, pl* **de·fin·i·en·tia** \di-ˌfin-ē-ˈen-ch(ē-)ə\ [L, prp. of *definire*] **:** an expression that defines **:** DEFINITION

def·i·nite \ˈdef-(ə-)nət\ *adj* [L *definitus,* pp. of *definire*] **1 :** having distinct or certain limits <set ~ standards for pupils to meet> **2 a :** free of all ambiguity, uncertainty, or obscurity <demanded a ~ answer> **b :** UNQUESTIONABLE, DECIDED <the quarterback was a ~ hero today> **3 :** typically designating an identified or immediately identifiable person or thing <the ~ article *the*> **4 a :** being constant in number, usu. less than 20, and occurring in multiples of the petal number <stamens ~> **b :** CYMOSE *syn* see EXPLICIT *ant* indefinite, equivocal — **def·i·nite·ly** *adv* — **def·i·nite·ness** *n*

definite integral *n* **:** a number that is the difference between the values of the indefinite integral of a given function for two values of the independent variable

def·i·ni·tion \ˌdef-ə-ˈnish-ən\ *n* **1 :** an act of determining; *specif* **:** the formal proclamation of a Roman Catholic dogma **2 :** a word or phrase expressing the essential nature of a person or thing **:** MEANING <the confinement of God within our human ~> **3 a :** a statement of the meaning of a word or word group or a sign or symbol <dictionary ~*s*> **b :** the action or process of stating such a meaning **4 a :** the action or the power of describing, explaining, or making definite and clear <the ~ of a telescope> <her comic genius is beyond ~> **b** (1) **:** distinctness of outline or detail (as in a photograph) (2) **:** clarity esp. of musical sound in reproduction **c :** sharp demarcation of outlines or limits <a jacket with definite waist ~> — **def·i·ni·tion·al** \-ˈnish-nəl, -ˈnish-ən-ᵊl\ *adj*

1de·fin·i·tive \di-ˈfin-ət-iv\ *adj* **1 :** serving to provide a final solution <a ~ victory> **2 :** authoritative and apparently exhaustive <a ~ biography> **3 :** serving to define or specify precisely <~ laws> **4 :** fully differentiated or developed **5** *of a postage stamp* **:** issued as a regular stamp for the country or territory in which it is to be used *syn* see CONCLUSIVE *ant* tentative, provisional — **de·fin·i·tive·ly** *adv* — **de·fin·i·tive·ness** *n*

2definitive *n* **:** a definitive postage stamp — compare PROVISIONAL

definitive host *n* **:** the host in which the sexual reproduction of a parasite takes place

de·fi·ni·tize \ˈdef-(ə-)nə-ˌtīz, di-ˈfin-ə-\ *vt* **-tized; -tiz·ing :** to make definite

de·fi·ni·tude \di-ˈfin-ə-ˌt(y)üd, -ˈfi-nə-\ *n* [irreg. fr. *definite*] **:** PRECISION, DEFINITENESS

def·la·grate \ˈdef-lə-ˌgrāt\ *vb* **-grat·ed; -grat·ing** [L *deflagratus,* pp. of *deflagrare* to burn down, fr. *de-* + *flagrare* to burn — more at BLACK] *vi* **:** to burn rapidly with intense heat and sparks being given off ~ *vt* **:** to cause to deflagrate — compare DETONATE — **def·la·gra·tion** \ˌdef-lə-ˈgrā-shən\ *n*

de·flate \di-ˈflāt, ˈdē-\ *vb* **de·flat·ed; de·flat·ing** [*de-* + *-flate* (as in *inflate*)] *vt* **1 :** to release air or gas from **2 :** to reduce in size or importance <~ his ego with cutting remarks> **3 :** to reduce (a price level) or cause (a volume of credit) to contract ~ *vi* **:** to lose firmness through or as if through the escape of contained gas *syn* see CONTRACT *ant* inflate — **de·fla·tor** \-ˈflāt-ər\ *n*

de·fla·tion \di-ˈflā-shən, ˈdē-\ *n* **1 :** an act or instance of deflating **:** the state of being deflated **2 :** a contraction in the volume of available money or credit that results in a decline of the general price level **3 :** the erosion of soil by the wind — **de·fla·tion·ary** \-shə-ˌner-ē\ *adj*

ə abut	ᵊ kitten	ər further	a back	ā bake	ä cot, cart
aù out	ch chin	e less	ē easy	g gift	i trip	ī life
j joke	ŋ sing	ō flow	ȯ flaw	ȯi coin	th thin	t͟h this
ü loot	ù foot	y yet	yü few	yù furious	zh vision

de·flect \di-'flekt\ *vb* [L *deflectere* to bend down, turn aside, fr. *de-* + *flectere* to bend] *vt* : to turn from a straight course or fixed direction : BEND ~ *vi* : to turn aside : DEVIATE — **de·flec·tive** \-'flek-tiv\ *adj* — **de·flec·tor** \-tər\ *n*

de·flec·tion \di-'flek-shən\ *n* **1** : a turning aside or off course : DEVIATION **2** : the departure of an indicator or pointer from the zero reading on the scale of an instrument

de·flexed \'dē-,flekst, di-'\ *adj* [L *deflexus,* pp. of *deflectere*] : turned abruptly downward <a ~ leaf>

de·flo·ra·tion \,def-lə-'rā-shən, ,dē-flə-\ *n* [ME *defloracioun,* fr. LL *defloration-, defloratio,* fr. *defloratus,* pp. of *deflorare*] : rupture of the hymen

de·flow·er \(')dē-'flau̇(-ə)r\ *vt* [ME *deflouren,* fr. MF or LL; MF *deflorer,* fr. LL *deflorare,* fr. L *de-* + *flor-, flos* flower — more at BLOW] **1** : to deprive of virginity : RAVISH **2** : to take away the prime beauty of — **de·flow·er·er** *n*

de·foam \(')dē-'fōm\ *vt* : to remove foam from : prevent the formation of foam in — **de·foam·er** *n*

de·fog \(')dē-'fȯg, -'fäg\ *vt* : to remove fog or condensed moisture from — **de·fog·ger** *n*

de·fo·li·ant \(')dē-'fō-lē-ənt\ *n* : a chemical spray or dust applied to plants in order to cause the leaves to drop off prematurely

de·fo·li·ate \-lē-,āt\ *vt* [LL *defoliatus,* pp. of *defoliare,* fr. L *de-* + *folium* leaf — more at BLADE] : to deprive of leaves esp. prematurely — **de·fo·li·ate** \-lē-ət\ *adj* — **de·fo·li·a·tion** \(,)dē-,fō-lē-'ā-shən\ *n* — **de·fo·li·a·tor** \(')dē-'fō-lē-,āt-ər\ *n*

de·force \(')dē-'fō(ə)rs, -'fȯ(ə)rs\ *vt* [ME *deforcen,* fr. OF *deforcier,* fr. *de-* + *forcier* to force] **1** : to keep (as lands) by force from the rightful owner **2** : to eject (a person) from possession by force — **de·force·ment** \-'fōr-smənt, -'fȯr-\ *n*

de·for·ciant \di-'fōr-shənt, -'fȯr-\ *n* [AF, fr. OF, prp. of *deforcier*] : one who deforces the rightful owner

de·for·est \(')dē-'fȯr-əst, -'fär-\ *vt*: to clear of forests — **de·for·es·ta·tion** \(,)dē-,fȯr-ə-'stā-shən, -,fär-\ *n* — **de·for·est·er** \(')dē-'fȯr-ə-stər,-'fär-\ *n*

de·form \di-'fȯ(ə)rm, 'dē-\ *vb* [ME *deformen,* fr. MF or L; MF *deformer,* fr. L *deformare,* fr. *de-* + *formare* to form, fr. *forma* form] *vt* **1** : to spoil the form of **2 a** : to spoil the looks of : DISFIGURE <a face ~*ed* by bitterness> **b** : to make hideous or monstrous **3** : to alter the shape of by stress ~ *vi* : to become misshapen or changed in shape

syn DEFORM, DISTORT, CONTORT, WARP *shared meaning element* : to mar or spoil by or as if by twisting

de·for·mal·ize \(')dē-'fȯr-mə-,līz\ *vt* : to make less formal <~ a group learning situation>

de·for·ma·tion \,dē-,fȯr-'mā-shən, ,def-ər-\ *n* **1** : the action of deforming : the state of being deformed **2** : change for the worse <a most extensive ecclesiastical reformation (or ~, as it may turn out) —Richard Whately> **3** : alteration of form or shape; *also* : the product of such alteration — **de·for·ma·tion·al** \-shnəl, -shən-ᵊl\ *adj*

de·for·ma·tive \di-'fȯr-mət-iv\ *adj* : tending to deform

de·formed *adj* : distorted or unshapely in form : MISSHAPEN

de·for·mi·ty \di-'fȯr-mət-ē\ *n, pl* **-ties** [ME *deformite,* fr. MF *deformité,* fr. L *deformitat-, deformitas,* fr. *deformis* deformed, fr. *de-* + *forma*] **1** : the state of being deformed **2** : a physical blemish or distortion : DISFIGUREMENT **3** : a moral or aesthetic flaw or defect

de·fraud \di-'frȯd\ *vt* [ME *defrauden,* fr. MF *defrauder,* fr. L *defraudare,* fr. *de-* + *fraudare* to cheat, fr. *fraud-, fraus* fraud] : to deprive of something by deception or fraud ***syn*** see CHEAT — **de·frau·da·tion** \,dē-,frȯ-'dā-shən\ *n* — **de·fraud·er** \di-'frȯd-ər\ *n*

de·fray \di-'frā\ *vt* [MF *deffrayer,* fr. *des-* de- + *frayer* to expend, fr. OF, fr. (assumed) OF *frai* expenditure, lit., damage by breaking, fr. L *fractum,* neut. of *fractus,* pp. of *frangere* to break — more at BREAK] **1** : to provide for the payment of : PAY **2** *archaic* : to bear the expenses of — **de·fray·able** \-ə-bəl\ *adj* — **de·fray·al** \-'frā(-ə)l\ *n*

de·frock \(')dē-'fräk\ *vt* : UNFROCK

de·frost \di-'frȯst, 'dē-\ *vt* **1** : to release from a frozen state <~ meat> **2** : to free from ice <~ the refrigerator> ~ *vi* : to thaw out esp. from a deep-frozen state — **de·frost·er** *n*

deft \'deft\ *adj* [ME *defte*] : marked by facility and skill ***syn*** see DEXTEROUS ***ant*** awkward — **deft·ly** *adv* — **deft·ness** \'def(t)-nəs\ *n*

de·funct \di-'fəŋ(k)t\ *adj* [L *defunctus,* fr. pp. of *defungi* to finish, die, fr. *de-* + *fungi* to perform — more at FUNCTION] : having finished the course of life or existence <her ~ aunt's will> <a ~ philosophy> ***syn*** see DEAD ***ant*** alive, live

de·fuse \(')dē-'fyüz\ *vt* **1** : to remove the fuse from (as a mine or bomb) **2** : to make less harmful, potent, or tense : CALM <~ the crisis>

[1]**de·fy** \di-'fī\ *vt* **de·fied; de·fy·ing** [ME *defyen* to renounce faith in, challenge, fr. OF *defier,* fr. *de-* + *fier* to entrust, fr. (assumed) VL *fidare,* alter. of L *fidere* to trust — more at BIDE] **1** *archaic* : to challenge to combat **2** : to challenge to do something considered impossible : DARE **3** : to confront with assured power of resistance : DISREGARD <~ public opinion> **4** : to resist attempts at : WITHSTAND <the paintings ~ classification>

[2]**de·fy** \di-'fī, 'dē-,\ *n, pl* **defies** : CHALLENGE, DEFIANCE

deg *abbr* degree

dé·ga·gé \,dā-,gä-'zhā\ *adj* [F, fr. pp. of *dégager* to redeem a pledge, free, fr. OF *desgagier,* fr. *des-* de- + *gage* pledge — more at GAGE] **1** : free of constraint : NONCHALANT **2** : being free and easy <clothes with a ~ look> **3** : extended with toe pointed in preparation for a ballet step

de·gas \(')dē-'gas\ *vt* : to remove gas from <~ an electron tube>

de Gaull·ism \di-'gō-,liz-əm, -'gȯ-\ *n* : GAULLISM — **de Gaull·ist** \-ləst\ *n*

de·gauss \(')dē-'gau̇s\ *vt* **1** : DEMAGNETIZE **2** : to make (a steel ship) effectively nonmagnetic by means of electrical coils carrying currents that neutralize the magnetism of the ship — **de·gauss·er** *n*

de·gen·er·a·cy \di-'jen-(ə-)rə-sē\ *n, pl* **-cies** **1** : the state of being degenerate **2** : the process of becoming degenerate **3** : sexual perversion **4** : the coding of an amino acid by more than one codon of the genetic code

[1]**de·gen·er·ate** \di-'jen-(ə-)rət\ *adj* [ME *degenerat,* fr. L *degeneratus,* pp. of *degenerare* to degenerate, fr. *de-* + *gener-, genus* race, kind — more at KIN] **1 a** : having declined (as in nature, character, structure, or function) from an ancestral or former state **b** : having sunk to a condition below that which is normal to a type; *esp* : having sunk to a lower and usu. peculiarly corrupt and vicious state **c** : DEGRADED **2** : being mathematically simpler (as by having a factor or constant equal to zero) than the typical case <the graph of a second degree equation yielding two intersecting lines is a ~ hyperbola> **3** : characterized by atoms stripped of their electrons and by very great density <~ matter>; *also* : consisting of degenerate matter <a ~ star> **4** : having two or more states or subdivisions <~ energy level> **5** : having more than one codon representing an amino acid; *also* : being such a codon ***syn*** see VICIOUS — **de·gen·er·ate·ly** *adv* — **de·gen·er·ate·ness** *n*

[2]**degenerate** *n* : one that is degenerate: as **a** : one degraded from the normal moral standard **b** : one debased by a psychopathic tendency **c** : a sexual pervert **d** : one showing signs of reversion to an earlier culture stage

[3]**de·gen·er·ate** \di-'jen-ə-,rāt\ *vi* **1** : to pass from a higher to a lower type or condition : DETERIORATE <the road *degenerated* into a bumpy brush-filled path> **2** : to sink into a low intellectual or moral state **3** : to decline in quality <his poetry gradually *degenerated* into jingles> **4** : to decline from a condition or from standards proper to a species, race, or breed **5** : to evolve or develop into a less autonomous or less functionally active form <*degenerated* into dependent parasites> <the digestive system *degenerated*> ~ *vt* : to cause to degenerate

de·gen·er·a·tion \di-,jen-ə-'rā-shən, ,dē-\ *n* **1** : a lowering of effective power, vitality, or essential quality to an enfeebled and worsened kind or state **2 a** : intellectual or moral decline **b** : degenerate condition **3 a** : progressive deterioration of physical characters from a level representing the norm of earlier generations or forms **b** : deterioration of a tissue or an organ in which its function is diminished or its structure is impaired **4** : marked decline in excellence (as of workmanship or originality) ***syn*** see DETERIORATION

de·gen·er·a·tive \di-'jen-ə-,rāt-iv, -'jen-(ə-)rət-\ *adj* : of, relating to, or tending to cause degeneration <a ~ disease>

de·glu·ti·tion \,dē-glü-'tish-ən, ,deg-lü-\ *n* [F *déglutition,* fr. L *deglutitus,* pp. of *deglutire* to swallow down, fr. *de-* + *glutire, gluttire* to swallow — more at GLUTTON] : the act or process of swallowing

de·grad·able \di-'grād-ə-bəl\ *adj* : capable of being chemically degraded <~ detergents> — compare BIODEGRADABLE

deg·ra·da·tion \,deg-rə-'dā-shən\ *n* **1** : the act or process of degrading **2 a** : decline to a low, destitute, or demoralized state **b** : moral or intellectual decadence : DEGENERATION

de·grade \di-'grād\ *vb* [ME *degraden,* fr. MF *degrader,* fr. LL *degradare,* fr. L *de-* + *gradus* step, grade] *vt* **1 a** : to lower in grade, rank, or status : DEMOTE **b** : to strip of rank or honors **c** : to deprive of standing or true function : PERVERT **d** : to scale down in desirability or salability **2 a** : to bring to low esteem or into disrepute **b** : to drag down in moral or intellectual character : CORRUPT <*degraded* his office as president> **3** : to impair in respect to some physical property **4** : to wear down by erosion **5** : to reduce the complexity of (a chemical compound) : DECOMPOSE ~ *vi* **1** : to pass from a higher grade or class to a lower **2** *of a chemical compound* : to become reduced in complexity — **de·grad·er** *n*

syn **1** DEGRADE, DEMOTE, DECLASS, DISRATE *shared meaning element* : to lower in station, rank, or grade ***ant*** elevate
2 see ABASE ***ant*** uplift

de·grad·ed *adj* **1** : reduced far below ordinary standards of civilized life and conduct **2** : characterized by degeneration of structure or function — **de·grad·ed·ly** *adv* — **de·grad·ed·ness** *n*

de·grad·ing *adj* : that degrades : DEBASING — **de·grad·ing·ly** \-'grād-iŋ-lē\ *adv*

de·gran·u·la·tion \(,)dē-,gran-yə-'lā-shən\ *n* : the process of losing granules <~ of leukocytes>

de·gree \di-'grē\ *n* [ME, fr. OF *degré,* fr. (assumed) VL *degradus,* fr. L *de-* + *gradus*] **1 a** *obs* : STEP, STAIR **b** *archaic* : a member of a series arranged in steps **2** : a step or stage in a process, course, or order of classification <advanced by ~*s*> **3** : a measure of damage to tissue caused esp. by disease **4 a** : the extent, measure, or scope of an action, condition, or relation <the company's ~ of expansion was small> **b** : relative intensity **c** : one of the forms or sets of forms used in the comparison of an adjective or adverb **d** : a legal measure of guilt or negligence <found guilty of robbery in the first ~> **5 a** : a rank or grade of official, ecclesiastical, or social position <people of low ~> **b** *archaic* : a particular standing esp. as to dignity or worth **c** : the civil condition or status of a person **6** : a step in a direct line of descent or in the line of ascent to a common ancestor **7 a** : a grade of membership attained in a ritualistic order or society **b** : the formal ceremonies observed in the conferral of such a distinction **c** : a title conferred on students by a college, university, or professional school on completion of a unified program of study **d** : an academic title conferred honorarily **8** *archaic* : a position or space on the earth or in the heavens as measured by degrees of latitude **9** : one of the divisions or intervals marked on a scale of a measuring instrument; *specif* : any of various units for measuring temperature **10** : a 360th part of the circumference of a circle **11 a** : the sum of the exponents of the variable factors of a monomial **b** : the sum of the exponents of the variable factors of the term of highest degree in a polynomial **c** : the greatest power of the derivative of highest order in a differential equation after the equation has been rationalized and cleared of fractions with respect to the derivative **12 a** : a line or space of the musical staff **b** : a step, note, or tone of a musical scale — **de·greed** \-ˈgrēd\ *adj* — **to a degree** **1** : to a remarkable extent **2** : in a small way

de·gree–day \di-ˈgrē-ˈdā\ *n* : a unit that represents one degree of declination from a given point (as 65°) in the mean daily outdoor temperature and that is used to measure heat requirements

degree of freedom **1** : any of a limited number of ways in which a body may move or in which a dynamic system may change **2** : one of the capabilities of a statistic for variation of which there are as many as the number of unrestricted and independent variables determining its value

de·gres·sive \di-ˈgres-iv, ˈdē-\ *adj* [*degression* (downward motion), (fr. ME, fr. ML *degression-, degressio,* fr. L *degressus,* pp. of *degredi* to step down, fr. *de-* + *gradi* to step) + *-ive* — more at GRADE] : tending to descend or decrease — **de·gres·sive·ly** *adv*

dé·grin·go·lade \ˌdā-ˌgraⁿ(ŋ)-gə-ˈläd\ *n* [F, fr. *dégringoler* to tumble down, fr. *dé-* de- + *gringoler* to tumble] : a rapid decline or deterioration (as in strength, position, or condition) : DOWNFALL

de·gum \(ˈ)dē-ˈgəm\ *vt* : to free from gum, a gummy substance, or sericin

de·gust \di-ˈgəst\ *vt* [L *degustare,* fr. *de-* + *gustare* to taste — more at CHOOSE] : TASTE, SAVOR

de·gus·ta·tion \ˌdē-ˌgəs-ˈtā-shən, di-\ *n* : the action or an instance of degusting

de haut en bas \də-ō-täⁿ-bä\ *adj or adv* [F, lit., from top to bottom] : having a superior or condescending manner <there is a *de haut en bas* tone about such a judgment —*Times Lit. Supp.*> <the landlady looked at him *de haut en bas* —D. H. Lawrence>

de·hisce \di-ˈhis\ *vi* **de·hisced; de·hisc·ing** [L *dehiscere* to split open, fr. *de-* + *hiscere* to gape; akin to L *hiare* to yawn — more at YAWN] : to split along a natural line; *also* : to discharge contents by so splitting <seedpods *dehiscing* at maturity>

de·his·cence \di-ˈhis-ᵊn(t)s\ *n* [NL *dehiscentia,* fr. L *dehiscent-, dehiscens,* prp. of *dehiscere*] : an act or instance of dehiscing <pollen freed by ~ of the anther> — **de·his·cent** \-ᵊnt\ *adj*

de·horn \(ˈ)dē-ˈhȯ(ə)rn\ *vt* **1** : to deprive of horns **2** : to prevent the growth of the horns of — **de·horn·er** *n*

de·hu·man·iza·tion \(ˌ)dē-ˌhyü-mə-nə-ˈzā-shən, (ˌ)dē-ˌyü-\ *n* : the act or process or an instance of dehumanizing

de·hu·man·ize \(ˈ)dē-ˈhyü-mə-ˌnīz, (ˈ)dē-ˈyü-\ *vt* : to divest of human qualities or personality <fear that the machines will ~ education —J. G. Miller>

de·hu·mid·i·fy \ˌdē-hyü-ˈmid-ə-ˌfī, ˌdē-yü-\ *vt* : to remove moisture from (as air) — **de·hu·mid·i·fi·ca·tion** \-ˌmid-ə-fə-ˈkā-shən\ *n* — **de·hu·mid·i·fi·er** \-ˈmid-ə-ˌfī(-ə)r\ *n*

dehydr- *or* **dehydro-** *comb form* **1** : dehydrated **2** : dehydrogenated

de·hy·drase \(ˈ)dē-ˈhī-ˌdrās, -ˌdrāz\ *n* **1** : DEHYDRATASE **2** : DEHYDROGENASE

de·hy·dra·tase \-drə-ˌtās, -ˌtāz\ *n* : an enzyme that catalyzes the removal of oxygen and hydrogen from metabolites in the proportion in which they form water

de·hy·drate \(ˈ)dē-ˈhī-ˌdrāt\ *vt* **1 a** : to remove bound water or hydrogen and oxygen from (a chemical compound) in the proportion in which they form water **b** : to remove water from (as foods) **2** : to deprive of vitality or savor ~ *vi* : to lose water or body fluids — **de·hy·dra·tor** \-ˌdrāt-ər\ *n*

de·hy·dra·tion \ˌdē-hī-ˈdrā-shən\ *n* : the process of dehydrating; *esp* : an abnormal depletion of body fluids

de·hy·dro·chlo·ri·nase \(ˌ)dē-ˌhī-drə-ˈklōr-ə-ˌnās, -ˈklȯr-, -ˌnāz\ *n* : an enzyme that dehydrochlorinates a chlorinated hydrocarbon (as DDT) and is found esp. in some DDT resistant insects

de·hy·dro·chlo·ri·nate \-ˌnāt\ *vt* [*de-* + *hydr-* + *chlorine*] : to remove hydrogen and chlorine or hydrogen chloride from (a compound) — **de·hy·dro·chlo·ri·na·tion** \-ˌklōr-ə-ˈnā-shən, -ˌklȯr-\ *n*

de·hy·dro·ge·nase \ˌdē-(ˌ)hī-ˈdräj-ə-ˌnās, (ˈ)dē-ˈhī-drə-jə-, -ˌnāz\ *n* [ISV] : an enzyme that accelerates the removal of hydrogen from metabolites and its transfer to other substances <succinic ~>

de·hy·dro·ge·nate \ˌdē-(ˌ)hī-ˈdräj-ə-ˌnāt, (ˈ)dē-ˈhī-drə-jə-\ *vt* : to remove hydrogen from — **de·hy·dro·ge·na·tion** \ˌdē-(ˌ)hī-ˌdräj-ə-ˈnā-shən, (ˌ)dē-ˌhī-drə-jə-\ *n*

de·hyp·no·tize \(ˈ)dē-ˈhip-nə-ˌtīz\ *vt* : to remove from hypnosis

de·ice \(ˈ)dē-ˈīs\ *vt* : to keep free or rid of ice — **de·ic·er** *n*

de·i·cide \ˈdē-ə-ˌsīd, ˈdā-ə-\ *n* [deriv. of L *deus* god & *-cidium, -cida* -cide] **1** : the act of killing a divine being or a symbolic substitute of such a being **2** : the killer or destroyer of a god

deic·tic \ˈdīk-tik, ˈdāk-; dē-ˈik-\ *adj* [Gk *deiktikos,* fr. *deiktos,* verbal of *deiknynai* to show] : showing or pointing out directly <the words *this, that,* and *those* have a ~ function>

de·i·fi·ca·tion \ˌdē-ə-fə-ˈkā-shən, ˌdā-\ *n* **1** : the act or an instance of deifying **2** : absorption of the soul into deity

de·i·fy \ˈdē-ə-ˌfī, ˈdā-\ *vt* **-fied; -fy·ing** [ME *deifyen,* fr. MF *deifier,* fr. LL *deificare,* fr. L *deus* god] **1 a** : to make a god of **b** : to take as an object of worship **2** : to glorify as of supreme worth

deign \ˈdān\ *vb* [ME *deignen,* fr. OF *deignier,* fr. L *dignare, dignari,* fr. *dignus* worthy — more at DECENT] *vi* : to condescend reluctantly and with a strong sense of the affront to one's superiority that is involved <he barely ~*ed* to acknowledge their greeting> ~ *vt* : to condescend to give or offer *syn* see STOOP

deil \ˈdē(ə)l\ *n* [ME *devel, del*] *Scot* : DEVIL

de·in·dus·tri·al·iza·tion \ˌdē-in-ˌdəs-trē-ə-lə-ˈzā-shən\ *n* : the act or process of reducing or destroying the industrial organization and potential esp. of a defeated nation

de–in·sti·tu·tion·al·ize \(ˌ)dē-ˌin(t)-stə-ˈt(y)üsh-nə-ˌlīz, -ˈt(y)ü-shən-ᵊl-ˌīz\ *vt* : to remove the status or character of an institution from — **de–in·sti·tu·tion·al·iza·tion** \-ˌt(y)üsh-nə-lə-ˈzā-shən, -ˌt(y)ü-shən-ᵊl-ə-ˈzā-\ *n*

de·ion·ize \(ˈ)dē-ˈī-ə-ˌnīz\ *vt* : to remove ions from <~ water by ion exchange> — **de·ion·iza·tion** \(ˌ)dē-ˌī-ə-nə-ˈzā-shən\ *n*

de·ism \ˈdē-ˌiz-əm, ˈdā-\ *n, often cap* : a movement or system of thought advocating natural religion based on human reason rather than revelation, emphasizing morality, and in the 18th century denying the interference of the Creator with the laws of the universe

de·ist \ˈdē-əst, ˈdā-\ *n, often cap* : an adherent of deism *syn* see ATHEIST — **de·is·tic** \dē-ˈis-tik, dā-\ *adj* — **de·is·ti·cal** \-ti-kəl\ *adj* — **de·is·ti·cal·ly** \-ti-k(ə-)lē\ *adv*

de·i·ty \ˈdē-ət-ē, ˈdā-\ *n, pl* **-ties** [ME *deitee,* fr. MF *deité,* fr. LL *deitat-, deitas,* fr. L *deus* god; akin to OE *Tīw,* god of war, L *divus* god, *dies* day, Gk *dios* heavenly] **1 a** : the rank or essential nature of a god : DIVINITY **b** *cap* : SUPREME BEING, GOD 1 **2** : a god or goddess <the *deities* of ancient Greece> **3** : one exalted or revered as supremely good or powerful

dé·jà vu \ˌdā-ˌzhä-ˈv(y)ü, dā-zhä-vüᵉ\ *n* [F *déjà vu,* adj., already seen] **1** : PARAMNESIA b **2** : something overly or unpleasantly familiar <the appointment seems like a case of *déjà vu* —E. B. Fiske>

[1]**de·ject** \di-ˈjekt\ *vt* [ME *dejecten* to throw down, fr. L *dejectus,* pp. of *deicere,* fr. *de-* + *jacere* to throw — more at JET] : to make gloomy

[2]**deject** *adj, archaic* : DEJECTED

de·jec·ta \di-ˈjek-tə\ *n pl* [NL, fr. L, neut. pl. of *dejectus*] : EXCREMENTS

de·ject·ed *adj* **1** : cast down in spirits : DEPRESSED **2 a** *obs, of the eyes* : DOWNCAST **b** *archaic* : thrown down **3** *obs* : lowered in rank or condition — **de·ject·ed·ly** *adv* — **de·ject·ed·ness** *n*

de·jec·tion \di-ˈjek-shən\ *n* : lowness of spirits

de ju·re \(ˈ)dē-ˈjü(ə)r-ē, (ˈ)dā-ˈyü(ə)r-\ *adv or adj* [NL] : by right : of right <recognition extended *de jure* to the new government>

deka- *or* **dek-** — see DECA-

deka·gram \ˈdek-ə-ˌgram\ *n* — see METRIC SYSTEM table

deka·li·ter \-ˌlēt-ər\ *n* — see METRIC SYSTEM table

deka·me·ter \-ˌmēt-ər\ *n* — see METRIC SYSTEM table

deka·stere \-ˌsti(ə)r, -ˌste(ə)r\ *n* — see METRIC SYSTEM table

del *abbr* **1** delegate; delegation **2** delete

Del *abbr* Delaware

de·lam·i·nate \(ˈ)dē-ˈlam-ə-ˌnāt\ *vi* : to undergo delamination

de·lam·i·na·tion \(ˌ)dē-ˌlam-ə-ˈnā-shən\ *n* **1** : separation into constituent layers **2** : gastrulation in which the endoderm is split off as a layer from the inner surface of the blastoderm and the archenteron is represented by the space between this endoderm and the yolk mass

de·late \di-ˈlāt\ *vt* **de·lat·ed; de·lat·ing** [L *delatus* (pp. of *deferre* to bring down, report, accuse), fr. *de-* + *latus,* pp. of *ferre* to bear — more at TOLERATE, BEAR] **1** : ACCUSE, DENOUNCE **2** *archaic* : REPORT, RELATE **3** *archaic* : REFER — **de·la·tion** \-ˈlā-shən\ *n* — **de·la·tor** \-ˈlāt-ər\ *n*

Del·a·ware \ˈdel-ə-ˌwa(ə)r, -ˌwe(ə)r, -wər\ *n, pl* **Delaware** *or* **Delawares** [*Delaware* river] **1** : a member of an Amerindian people orig. of the Delaware valley **2** : the Algonquian language of the Delaware

[1]**de·lay** \di-ˈlā\ *n* **1 a** : the act of delaying : the state of being delayed **b** : an instance of being delayed **2** : the time during which something is delayed **3** : a football play in which an offensive back delays momentarily as if to block and then runs his prescribed pattern

[2]**delay** *vb* [ME *delayen,* fr. OF *delaier,* fr. *de-* + *laier* to leave, alter. of *laissier,* fr. L *laxare* to slacken — more at RELAX] *vt* **1** : to put off : POSTPONE <decided to ~ our vacation until next month> **2** : to stop, detain, or hinder for a time ~ *vi* **1** : to move or act slowly **2** : to pause momentarily — **de·lay·er** *n* — **de·lay·ing** *adj*
syn DELAY, RETARD, SLOW, SLACKEN, DETAIN *shared meaning element* : to cause to be late or behind in movement or progress *ant* expedite, hasten

[1]**de·le** \ˈdē-(ˌ)lē\ *vt* **de·led; de·le·ing** [L, imper. sing. of *delēre*] **1** : to remove (as a word or character) from typeset matter **2** : to mark with a dele

[2]**dele** *n* : a mark indicating that something is to be deled

[1]**de·lec·ta·ble** \di-ˈlek-tə-bəl\ *adj* [ME, fr. MF, fr. L *delectabilis,* fr. *delectare* to delight — more at DELIGHT] **1** : highly pleasing : DELIGHTFUL **2** : DELICIOUS — **de·lec·ta·bil·i·ty** \-ˌlek-tə-ˈbil-ət-ē\ *n* — **de·lec·ta·ble·ness** \-ˈlek-tə-bəl-nəs\ *n* — **de·lec·ta·bly** \-blē\ *adv*

[2]**delectable** *n* : something that is delectable <~*s* from the bakery>

de·lec·ta·tion \ˌdē-ˌlek-ˈtā-shən, di-; ˌdel-ək-\ *n* **1** : DELIGHT **2** : ENJOYMENT

del·e·ga·ble \ˈdel-i-gə-bəl\ *adj* : capable of being delegated

del·e·ga·cy \-gə-sē\ *n, pl* **-cies** **1 a** : the act of delegating **b** : appointment as delegate **2** : a body of delegates : BOARD

[1]**del·e·gate** \ˈdel-i-gət, -ˌgāt\ *n* [ME *delegat,* fr. ML *delegatus,* fr. L, pp. of *delegare* to delegate, fr. *de-* + *legare* to send — more at LEGATE] : a person acting for another: as **a** : a representative to a convention or conference **b** : a representative of a U.S. territory in the House of Representatives **c** : a member of the lower house of the legislature of Maryland, Virginia, or West Virginia

[2]**del·e·gate** \-ˌgāt\ *vb* **-gat·ed; -gat·ing** *vt* **1** : to entrust to another <~ one's authority> **2** : to appoint as one's representative : DEPUTIZE ~ *vi* : to assign responsibility or authority

del·e·ga·tion \ˌdel-i-ˈgā-shən\ *n* **1** : the act of empowering to act for another **2** : a group of persons chosen to represent others

de·lete \di-ˈlēt\ *vt* **de·let·ed; de·let·ing** [L *deletus,* pp. of *delēre* to wipe out, destroy, fr. *de-* *-lēre* (akin to L *linere* to smear) — more at LIME] : to eliminate esp. by blotting out, cutting out, or erasing <*deleted* his name from the list> *syn* see ERASE

del·e·te·ri·ous \ˌdel-ə-ˈtir-ē-əs\ *adj* [Gk *dēlētērios,* fr. *dēleisthai* to hurt — more at CONDOLE] : having an often obscure or unexpected harmful effect <the controversial question as to whether prolonged weightlessness has ~ effects —*The Sciences*> *syn* see PERNICIOUS *ant* salutary — **del·e·te·ri·ous·ly** *adv* — **del·e·te·ri·ous·ness** *n*

de·le·tion \di-'lē-shən\ *n* [L *deletion-, deletio* destruction, fr. *deletus*] **1 :** an act of deleting **2 a :** something deleted **b :** DEFICIENCY 2b; *esp* **:** a large deficiency not including either end of a chromosome

delft \'delft\ *n* [*Delft,* Netherlands] **1 :** tin-glazed Dutch earthenware with blue and white or polychrome decoration **2 :** a ceramic ware resembling or imitative of Dutch delft

delft·ware \'delf-ˌtwa(ə)r, -ˌtwe(ə)r\ *n* **:** DELFT

deli \'del-ē\ *n, pl* **del·is :** DELICATESSEN

1de·lib·er·ate \di-'lib-(ə-)rət\ *adj* [L *deliberatus,* pp. of *deliberare* to weigh in mind, ponder, irreg. fr. *de-* + *libra* scale, pound] **1 :** characterized by or resulting from careful and thorough consideration **2 :** characterized by awareness of the consequences **:** WILLFUL **3 :** slow, unhurried, and steady as though allowing time for decision on each individual action involved <walked with a ~ step> ***syn*** see VOLUNTARY ***ant*** impulsive — **de·lib·er·ate·ly** *adv* — **de·lib·er·ate·ness** *n*

2de·lib·er·ate \di-'lib-ə-ˌrāt\ *vb* **-at·ed; -at·ing** *vt* **:** to think about deliberately and often with formal discussion before reaching a decision ~ *vi* **:** to ponder issues and decisions carefully ***syn*** see THINK

de·lib·er·a·tion \di-ˌlib-ə-'rā-shən\ *n* **1 :** the act of deliberating **2 :** a discussion and consideration by a group of persons of the reasons for and against a measure **3 :** the quality or state of being deliberate — **de·lib·er·a·tive** \-'lib-ə-ˌrāt-iv, -'lib-(ə-)rət-\ *adj* — **de·lib·er·a·tive·ly** *adv* — **de·lib·er·a·tive·ness** *n*

del·i·ca·cy \'del-i-kə-sē\ *n, pl* **-cies 1** *obs* **a :** the quality or state of being luxurious **b :** INDULGENCE **2 :** something pleasing to eat that is considered rare or luxurious <considered caviar a ~> **3 a :** the quality or state of being dainty **:** FINENESS <lace of great ~> **b :** FRAILTY **4 :** fineness or subtle expressiveness of touch (as in painting or music) **5 a :** precise and refined perception and discrimination **b :** extreme sensitivity **:** PRECISION <an electronic instrument of great ~> **6 a :** refined sensibility in feeling or conduct **b :** the quality or state of being squeamish **7 :** the quality or state of requiring delicate treatment

1del·i·cate \'del-i-kət\ *adj* [ME *delicat,* fr. L *delicatus* delicate, addicted to pleasure; akin to L *delicere* to allure] **1 :** pleasing to the senses: **a :** generally pleasant **b :** pleasing to the sense of taste or smell esp. in a mild or subtle way **c :** marked by daintiness or charm of color, lines, or proportions **2 a :** marked by keen sensitivity or fine discrimination **b :** FASTIDIOUS, SQUEAMISH **c :** SCRUPULOUS **3 a :** marked by minute precision **b :** exhibiting extreme sensitivity <a ~ instrument> **4 :** calling for or involving meticulously careful treatment <the ~ balance of power> **5 a :** marked by meticulous technique or operation or by execution with adroit finesse <a ~ pirouette> **b :** marked by fineness of structure, workmanship, or texture <~ handwriting> **c** (1) **:** easily torn or hurt <a ~ butterfly wing> (2) **:** WEAK, SICKLY **d :** marked by fine subtlety <~ irony> **e :** marked by tact; *also* **:** requiring tact ***syn*** see CHOICE ***ant*** gross — **del·i·cate·ly** *adv* — **del·i·cate·ness** *n*

2delicate *n* **1** *obs* **:** DELIGHT, LUXURY **2** *archaic* **:** a table delicacy

del·i·ca·tes·sen \ˌdel-i-kə-'tes-ᵊn\ *n pl* [obs. G (now *delikatessen*), pl. of *delicatesse* delicacy, fr. F *délicatesse,* prob. fr. OIt *delicatezza,* fr. *delicato* delicate, fr. L *delicatus*] **1 :** ready-to-eat food products (as cooked meats and prepared salads) **2** *sing, pl* **delicatessens** [*delicatessen* (*store*)] **:** a store where delicatessen are sold

1de·li·cious \di-'lish-əs\ *adj* [ME, fr. OF, fr. LL *deliciosus,* fr. L *deliciae* delight, fr. *delicere* to allure] **1 :** affording great pleasure **:** DELIGHTFUL **2 :** appealing to one of the bodily senses esp. of taste or smell — **de·li·cious·ly** *adv* — **de·li·cious·ness** *n*

2delicious *n, pl* **de·li·cious·es** *or* **delicious** *often cap* **:** a largely red apple of American origin that has a crown of five rounded prominences on the blossom end and is an important market apple

de·lict \di-'likt\ *n* [L *delictum* fault, fr. neut. of *delictus,* pp. of *delinquere*] **:** an offense against the law

1de·light \di-'līt\ *n* **1 :** a high degree of gratification **:** JOY; *also* **:** extreme satisfaction **2 :** something that gives great pleasure <the new puppy was a ~> **3** *archaic* **:** the power of affording pleasurable emotion

2delight *vb* [ME *deliten,* fr. OF *delitier,* fr. L *delectare,* fr. *delectus,* pp. of *delicere* to allure, fr. *de-* + *lacere* to allure; akin to OE *lǣl* switch] *vi* **1 :** to take great pleasure <he ~*ed* in playing his guitar> **2 :** to give keen enjoyment <a book certain to ~> ~ *vt* **:** to give joy or satisfaction to <~*ed* the audience with his performance> — **de·light·er** *n*

de·light·ed *adj* **1** *obs* **:** DELIGHTFUL **2 :** highly pleased — **de·light·ed·ly** *adv* — **de·light·ed·ness** *n*

de·light·ful \di-'līt-fəl\ *adj* **:** highly pleasing — **de·light·ful·ly** \-fə-lē\ *adv* — **de·light·ful·ness** *n*

de·light·some \-'līt-səm\ *adj* **:** very pleasing **:** DELIGHTFUL — **de·light·some·ly** *adv*

De·li·lah \di-'lī-lə\ *n* [Heb *Dĕlīlāh*] **:** the mistress and betrayer of Samson in the book of Judges

de·lim·it \di-'lim-ət\ *vt* [F *délimiter,* fr. L *delimitare,* fr. *de-* + *limitare* to limit, fr. *limit-, limes* boundary, limit — more at LIMB] **1 :** to fix the limits of <~ a boundary> **2 :** to spell out **:** DELINEATE <the problems can be defined and the solutions to the problems explicitly ~*ed* as to generality —Eugene Wall>

de·lim·i·tate \di-'lim-ə-ˌtāt\ *vt* **-tat·ed; -tat·ing :** DELIMIT — **de·lim·i·ta·tion** \di-ˌlim-ə-'tā-shən, ˌdē-\ *n* — **de·lim·i·ta·tive** \di-'lim-ə-ˌtāt-iv\ *adj*

de·lim·it·er \di-'lim-ət-ər\ *n* **:** a character that marks the beginning or end of a unit of data (as on a magnetic tape)

de·lin·eate \di-'lin-ē-ˌāt\ *vt* **-eat·ed; -eat·ing** [L *delineatus,* pp. of *delineare,* fr. *de-* + *linea* line] **1 a :** to indicate by lines drawn in the form or figure of **:** PORTRAY **b :** to represent accurately **2 :** to describe in usu. sharp or vivid detail <~*s* the complexity of the large urban university —J. M. Hester> — **de·lin·ea·tor** \-ē-ˌāt-ər\ *n*

de·lin·ea·tion \di-ˌlin-ē-'ā-shən\ *n* **1 :** the act of representing, portraying, or describing graphically or verbally **2 :** something made by delineating — **de·lin·ea·tive** \-'lin-ē-ˌāt-iv\ *adj*

de·lin·quen·cy \di-'liŋ-kwən-sē, -'lin-\ *n, pl* **-cies 1 :** the quality or state of being delinquent **2 :** conduct that is out of accord with accepted behavior or the law; *also* **:** a tendency to engage or the practice of engaging in such conduct — used esp. when emphasis is placed on social or psychological maladjustment rather than criminal intent **3 :** a debt on which payment is overdue

1de·lin·quent \-kwənt\ *n* **:** a delinquent person

2delinquent *adj* [L *delinquent-, delinquens,* prp. of *delinquere* to fail, offend, fr. *de-* + *linquere* to leave — more at LOAN] **1 :** offending by neglect or violation of duty or of law **2 :** being overdue in payment <a ~ charge account> **3 :** of, relating to, or characteristic of delinquents **:** marked by delinquency — **de·lin·quent·ly** *adv*

del·i·quesce \ˌdel-i-'kwes\ *vi* **-quesced; -quesc·ing** [L *deliquescere,* fr. *de-* + *liquescere,* incho. of *liquēre* to be fluid — more at LIQUID] **1 :** to melt away: **a :** to dissolve gradually and become liquid by attracting and absorbing moisture from the air **b :** to become soft or liquid with age — used of plant structures (as mushrooms) **2 :** to divide repeatedly and so end in fine divisions — used esp. of the veins of a leaf — **del·i·ques·cence** \-'kwes-ᵊn(t)s\ *n* — **del·i·ques·cent** \-ᵊnt\ *adj*

de·lir·i·ous \di-'lir-ē-əs\ *adj* **1 :** of, relating to, or characteristic of delirium **2 :** affected with or marked by delirium — **de·lir·i·ous·ly** *adv* — **de·lir·i·ous·ness** *n*

de·lir·i·um \di-'lir-ē-əm\ *n* [L, fr. *delirare* to be crazy, fr. *de-* + *lira* furrow — more at LEARN] **1 :** a mental disturbance characterized by confusion, disordered speech, and hallucinations **2 :** frenzied excitement <he would stride about his room in a ~ of joy —Thomas Wolfe>

delirium tre·mens \-'trē-mənz, -'trem-ənz\ *n* [NL, lit., trembling delirium] **:** a violent delirium with tremors that is induced by excessive and prolonged use of alcoholic liquors — called also *D.T.'s*

de·list \(ˈ)dē-'list\ *vt* **:** to remove from a list; *esp* **:** to remove (a security) from the list of securities that may be dealt in on a particular exchange

de·liv·er \di-'liv-ər\ *vb* **de·liv·ered; de·liv·er·ing** \-(ə-)riŋ\ [ME *deliveren,* fr. OF *delivrer,* fr. LL *deliberare,* fr. L *de-* + *liberare* to liberate] *vt* **1 :** to set free <and lead us not into temptation, but ~ us from evil —Mt 6:13 (AV)> **2 :** to hand over **:** CONVEY <~*ed* the stolen goods to the police> **3 a :** to assist in giving birth **b :** to aid in the birth of **4 :** UTTER, RELATE <~*ed* his speech effectively> **5 :** to send (something aimed or guided) to an intended target or destination <~*ed* a left hook to the jaw> **6 :** to bring (as votes) to the support of a candidate or cause ~ *vi* **:** to produce the promised, desired, or expected results **:** come through <make sure he ~*s* on his promise> ***syn*** see RESCUE — **de·liv·er·abil·i·ty** \-ˌliv-(ə-)rə-'bil-ət-ē\ *n* — **de·liv·er·able** \-'liv-(ə-)rə-bəl\ *adj* — **de·liv·er·er** \-'liv-ər-ər\ *n*

de·liv·er·ance \di-'liv-(ə-)rən(t)s\ *n* **1 :** the act of delivering **:** the state of being delivered: as **a :** LIBERATION, RESCUE **b** *archaic* **:** the act of speaking **2 :** something delivered or communicated; *esp* **:** an opinion or decision (as the verdict of a jury) expressed publicly

de·liv·ery \di-'liv-(ə-)rē\ *n, pl* **-er·ies 1 :** a delivering from restraint **2 a :** the act of handing over **b :** the physical and legal transfer of a shipment from consignor to consignee <every ~ of perishables was insured against loss> **c :** the act of putting into the legal possession of another **d :** something delivered at one time or in one unit <got my morning ~ of milk> **3 :** the act of giving birth **4 :** a delivering esp. of a speech; *also* **:** manner or style of uttering in speech or song **5 :** the act or manner of sending forth or throwing <a hitch in the pitcher's ~>

delivery boy *n* **:** a person employed by a retail store to deliver small orders to customers on call

de·liv·ery·man \-(ə-)rē-mən, -ˌman\ *n* **:** a person who delivers wholesale or retail goods to customers usu. over a regular local route

dell \'del\ *n* [ME *delle;* akin to MHG *telle* ravine, OE *dæl* valley — more at DALE] **:** a secluded hollow or small valley usu. covered with trees or turf

delly *var of* DELI

de·lo·cal·ize \(ˈ)dē-'lō-kə-ˌlīz\ *vt* **:** to free from the limitations of locality; *specif* **:** to remove (electrons) from a particular position — **de·lo·cal·iza·tion** \(ˌ)dē-ˌlō-kə-lə-'zā-shən\ *n*

de·louse \(ˈ)dē-'laủs, -'laủz\ *vt* **:** to remove lice from

Del·phi·an \'del-fē-ən\ *adj* **:** DELPHIC

Del·phic \'del-fik\ *adj* **1 :** of or relating to ancient Delphi or its oracle **2 :** AMBIGUOUS, OBSCURE — **del·phi·cal·ly** \-fi-k(ə-)lē\ *adv*

del·phin·i·um \del-'fin-ē-əm\ *n* [NL, genus name, fr. Gk *delphinion* larkspur, dim. of *delphin-, delphis* dolphin — more at DOLPHIN] **:** any of a large genus (*Delphinium*) of the buttercup family that comprises chiefly perennial erect branching herbs with palmately divided leaves and irregular flowers in showy spikes and includes several that are poisonous

Del·phi·nus \del-'fī-nəs, -'fē-\ *n* [L (gen. *Delphini*), lit., dolphin — more at DOLPHIN] **:** a northern constellation nearly west of Pegasus

1del·ta \'del-tə\ *n* [ME *deltha,* fr. Gk *delta,* of Sem origin; akin to Heb *dāleth* daleth] **1 :** the 4th letter of the Greek alphabet — see ALPHABET table **2 :** something shaped like a capital Greek delta; *esp* **:** the alluvial deposit at the mouth of a river **3 :** an increment of a variable — symbol Δ — **del·ta·ic** \del-'tā-ik\ *adj*

2delta *or* δ- *adj* **:** fourth in position in the structure of an organic molecule from a particular group or atom

Delta — a communications code word for the letter *d*

delta ray *n* **:** an electron ejected by an ionizing particle in its passage through matter

delta wing *n* ['*delta;* fr. its shape] **:** a triangular swept-back airplane wing with straight trailing edge

1del·toid \'del-ˌtȯid\ *n* [NL *deltoides,* fr. Gk *deltoeidēs* shaped like a delta, fr. *delta*] **:** a large triangular muscle that covers the shoulder joint and serves to raise the arm laterally

2deltoid *adj* **:** shaped like a capital delta **:** TRIANGULAR <a ~ leaf>

del·toi·de·us \del-ˈtȯid-ē-əs\ *n, pl* **del·toi·dei** \-ē-ˌī\ [NL, alter. of *deltoides*] : DELTOID

de·lude \di-ˈlüd\ *vt* **de·lud·ed; de·lud·ing** [ME *deluden,* fr. L *deludere,* fr. *de-* + *ludere* to play — more at LUDICROUS] **1** : to mislead the mind or judgment of : impose on : DECEIVE, TRICK **2** *obs* **a** : FRUSTRATE, DISAPPOINT **b** : EVADE, ELUDE ***syn*** see DECEIVE ***ant*** enlighten — **de·lud·er** *n* — **de·lud·ing·ly** \-ˈlüd-iŋ-lē\ *adv*

¹del·uge \ˈdel-(ˌ)yüj\ *n* [ME, fr. MF, fr. L *diluvium,* fr. *diluere* to wash away, fr. *dis-* + *lavere* to wash — more at LYE] **1 a** : an overflowing of the land by water **b** : a drenching rain **2** : an overwhelming amount or number <a ~ of criticism> <a ~ of letters>

delphinium

²deluge *vt* **del·uged; del·ug·ing** **1** : to overflow with water : INUNDATE **2** : OVERWHELM, SWAMP

de·lu·sion \di-ˈlü-zhən\ *n* [ME, fr. L *delusion-, delusio,* fr. *delusus* pp. of *deludere*] **1 a** : the act of deluding : the state of being deluded **b** : an abnormal mental state characterized by the occurrence of delusions **2 a** : something that is falsely or delusively believed or propagated **b** : a false belief regarding the self or persons or objects outside the self that persists despite the facts and is common in some psychotic states — **de·lu·sion·al** \-ˈlüzh-nəl, -ˈlü-zhən-ᵊl\ *adj* — **de·lu·sion·ary** \-zhə-ˌner-ē\ *adj*

syn DELUSION, ILLUSION, HALLUCINATION, MIRAGE *shared meaning element* : something accepted as true that is actually false or unreal

de·lu·sive \-ˈlü-siv, -ˈlü-ziv\ *adj* **1** : likely to delude **2** : constituting a delusion — **de·lu·sive·ly** *adv* — **de·lu·sive·ness** *n*

de·lu·so·ry \-sə-rē, -zə-\ *adj* : DECEPTIVE, DELUSIVE

de·lus·ter \(ˈ)dē-ˈləs-tər\ *vt* : to reduce the sheen of (as yarn or fabric)

de·luxe \di-ˈlu̇ks, -ˈləks, -ˈlüks\ *adj* [F *de luxe,* lit., of luxury] : notably luxurious or elegant <a ~ edition> <~ hotels>

¹delve \ˈdelv\ *vb* **delved; delv·ing** [ME *delven,* fr. OE *delfan;* akin to OHG *telban* to dig] *vt, archaic* : EXCAVATE ~ *vi* **1** : to dig or labor with a spade **2** : to make a careful or detailed search for information <*delved* into the past> — **delv·er** *n*

²delve *n, archaic* : CAVE, HOLLOW

dely *abbr* delivery

dem *abbr* **1** demonstrative **2** demurrage

Dem *abbr* Democrat; Democratic

de·mag·ne·tize \(ˈ)dē-ˈmag-nə-ˌtīz\ *vt* : to deprive of magnetic properties — **de·mag·ne·ti·za·tion** \(ˌ)dē-ˌmag-nət-ə-ˈzā-shən\ *n* — **de·mag·ne·tiz·er** \(ˈ)dē-ˈmag-nə-ˌtī-zər\ *n*

dem·a·gog·ic \ˌdem-ə-ˈgäg-ik *also* -ˈgäj- *or* -ˈgōj-\ *adj* : of, relating to, or characteristic of a demagogue : employing demagoguery — **dem·a·gog·i·cal** \-i-kəl\ *adj* — **dem·a·gog·i·cal·ly** \-i-k(ə-)lē\ *adv*

dem·a·gog·ism \ˈdem-ə-ˌgäg-ˌiz-əm\ *n* : DEMAGOGUERY

dem·a·gogue *or* **dem·a·gog** \ˈdem-ə-ˌgäg\ *n* [Gk *dēmagōgos,* fr. *dēmos* people (akin to Gk *daiesthai* to divide) + *agōgos* leading, fr. *agein* to lead — more at TIDE, AGENT] **1** : a leader championing the cause of the common people in ancient times **2** : a leader who makes use of popular prejudices and false claims and promises in order to gain power

dem·a·gogu·ery \-ˌgäg-(ə-)rē\ *n* : the principles or practices of a demagogue

dem·a·gogy \-ˌgäg-ē, -ˌgäj-ē, -ˌgō-jē\ *n* : DEMAGOGUERY

¹de·mand \di-ˈmand\ *n* **1 a** : an act of demanding or asking esp. with authority **b** : something claimed as due **2** *archaic* : QUESTION **3 a** : an expressed desire for ownership or use **b** : willingness and ability to purchase a commodity or service **c** : the quantity of a commodity or service wanted at a specified price and time **4 a** : a seeking or state of being sought after <gold is in great ~> **b** : urgent need **5** : the requirement of work or of the expenditure of a resource — **on demand** : upon presentation and request for payment

²demand *vb* [ME *demaunden,* fr. MF *demander,* fr. ML *demandare,* fr. L *de-* + *mandare* to enjoin — more at MANDATE] *vi* : to make a demand : ASK ~ *vt* **1** : to ask or call for with authority : claim as due or just <~ payment of a debt> **2** : to call for urgently, peremptorily, or insistently <~*ed* that the rioters disperse> **3 a** : to ask authoritatively or earnestly to be informed of **b** : to require to come : SUMMON **4** : to call for as useful or necessary — **de·mand·able** \-ˈman-də-bəl\ *adj* — **de·mand·er** *n*

syn DEMAND, CLAIM, REQUIRE, EXACT *shared meaning element* : to ask or call for something as or as if one's right or due

de·man·dant \di-ˈman-dənt\ *n* **1** : the plaintiff in a real action **2** : one who makes a demand or claim

demand deposit *n* : a bank deposit that can be withdrawn without advance notice

de·mand·ing *adj* : EXACTING — **de·mand·ing·ly** \-ˈman-diŋ-lē\ *adv*

demand loan *n* : CALL LOAN

demand note *n* : a note payable on demand

de·mand–pull \di-ˈman(d)-ˌpu̇l\ *n* : an increase or upward trend in spendable money that tends to result in increased competition for available goods and services and a corresponding increase in consumer prices — compare COST-PUSH — **demand–pull** *adj*

dem·an·toid \ˈdem-ən-ˌtȯid\ *n* [G, fr. obs. G *demant* diamond, fr. MHG *diemant,* fr. OF *diamant*] : a green andradite used as a gem

de·mar·cate \di-ˈmär-ˌkāt, ˈdē-ˌ\ *vt* **-cat·ed; -cat·ing** [back-formation fr. *demarcation,* fr. Sp *demarcación* & Pg *demarcação,* fr. *demarcar* to delimit, fr. *de-* + *marcar* to mark, fr. It *marcare,* of Gmc origin; akin to OHG *marha* boundary — more at MARCH] **1** : to mark the limits of **2** : to set apart : SEPARATE — **de·mar·ca·tion** *also* **de·mar·ka·tion** \ˌdē-ˌmär-ˈkā-shən\ *n*

de·marche \dā-ˈmärsh, di-ˈ, ˈdā-ˌ\ *n* [F *démarche,* lit., gait, fr. MF, fr. *demarcher* to march, fr. OF *demarchier,* fr. *de-* + *marchier* to march] **1 a** : a course of action : MANEUVER **b** : a diplomatic move or maneuver **2 a** : a diplomatic representation **b** : a representation of views to a public official

de·mark \di-ˈmärk\ *vt* : DEMARCATE

deme \ˈdēm\ *n* [Gk *dēmos,* lit., people] **1** : a unit of local government in ancient Attica **2** : a local population of closely related organisms; *esp* : GAMODEME

¹de·mean \di-ˈmēn\ *vt* **de·meaned; de·mean·ing** [ME *demenen,* fr. OF *demener* to conduct, fr. *de-* + *mener* to drive, fr. L *minare,* fr. *minari* to threaten — more at MOUNT] : to conduct or behave (oneself) usu. in a proper manner

²demean *vt* **de·meaned; de·mean·ing** [*de-* + *mean*] : DEGRADE, DEBASE ***syn*** see ABASE

de·mean·or \di-ˈmē-nər\ *n* : behavior toward others : outward manner ***syn*** see BEARING

de·ment·ed \di-ˈment-əd\ *adj* : MAD, INSANE — **de·ment·ed·ly** *adv* — **de·ment·ed·ness** *n*

de·men·tia \di-ˈmen-chə\ *n* [L, fr. *dement-, demens* mad, fr. *de-* + *ment-, mens* mind — more at MIND] **1** : a condition of deteriorated mentality **2** : MADNESS, INSANITY — **de·men·tial** \-chəl\ *adj*

dementia prae·cox \-ˈprē-ˌkäks\ *n* [NL, lit., premature dementia] : SCHIZOPHRENIA

de·mer·it \di-ˈmer-ət\ *n* [ME, fr. MF *demerite,* fr. *de-* + *merite* merit] **1** *obs* : OFFENSE **2 a** : a quality that deserves blame or lacks merit : FAULT, DEFECT **b** : lack of merit **3** : a mark usu. entailing a loss of privilege given to an offender

de·mesne \di-ˈmān, -ˈmēn\ *n* [ME, alter. of *demeyne,* fr. OF *demaine* — more at DOMAIN] **1** : legal possession of land as one's own **2** : manorial land actually possessed by the lord and not held by tenants **3 a** : the land attached to a mansion **b** : landed property : ESTATE **c** : REGION, TERRITORY **4** : REALM, DOMAIN

De·me·ter \di-ˈmēt-ər\ *n* [L, fr. Gk *Dēmētēr*] : the Greek goddess of agriculture — compare CERES

demi- *prefix* [ME, fr. *demi,* fr. MF, fr. L *dimidius,* prob. back-formation fr. *dimidiare* to halve, fr. *dis-* + *medius* mid — more at MID] **1** : half <*demi*bastion> **2** : one that partly belongs to (a specified type or class) <*demi*god>

demi·god \ˈdem-i-ˌgäd\ *n* **1** : a mythological being with more power than a mortal but less than a god **2** : a person so outstanding that he seems to approach the divine — **demi·god·dess** \-ˌgäd-əs\ *n*

demi·john \ˈdem-i-ˌjän\ *n* [by folk etymology fr. F *dame-jeanne,* lit., Lady Jane] : a narrow-necked bottle of glass or stoneware enclosed in wickerwork and holding from 1 to 10 gallons

de·mil·i·ta·rize \(ˈ)dē-ˈmil-ə-tə-ˌrīz, di-\ *vt* **1 a** : to do away with the military organization and potential of **b** : to prohibit (as a zone or frontier area) from being used for military purposes **2** : to deprive of military characteristics or purposes — **de·mil·i·tar·i·za·tion** \(ˌ)dē-ˌmil-ə-t(ə-)rə-ˈzā-shən, di-\ *n*

demi·mon·daine \ˌdem-i-ˌmän-ˈdān, -ˈmän-ˌ\ *n* [F *demi-mondaine,* fr. fem. of *demi-mondain,* fr. *demi-monde*] : a woman of the demimonde

demi·monde \ˈdem-i-ˌmänd\ *n* [F *demi-monde,* fr. *demi-* + *monde* world, fr. L *mundus* — more at MUNDANE] **1 a** : a class of women on the fringes of respectable society supported by wealthy lovers **b** : PROSTITUTES **2** : DEMIMONDAINE **3** : a group engaged in activity of doubtful legality or propriety

de·min·er·al·ize \(ˈ)dē-ˈmin-(ə-)rə-ˌlīz\ *vt* : to remove the mineral matter from : DESALT — **de·min·er·al·iza·tion** \(ˌ)dē-ˌmin-(ə-)rə-lə-ˈzā-shən\ *n* — **de·min·er·al·iz·er** \(ˈ)dē-ˈmin-(ə-)rə-ˌlī-zər\ *n*

demi·rep \ˈdem-i-ˌrep\ *n* [*demi-* + *rep* (reprobate)] : DEMIMONDAINE

¹de·mise \di-ˈmīz\ *vb* **de·mised; de·mis·ing** *vt* **1** : to convey (as an estate) by will or lease **2** *obs* : CONVEY, GIVE **3** : to transmit by succession or inheritance ~ *vi* **1** : DIE, DECEASE **2** : to pass by descent or bequest <the property *demised* to the king>

²demise *n* [MF, fem. of *demis,* pp. of *demettre* to dismiss, fr. L *demittere* to send down, fr. *de-* + *mittere* to send — more at SMITE] **1** : the conveyance of an estate **2** : transfer of the sovereignty to a successor **3 a** : DEATH **b** : a cessation of existence or activity

demi·semi·qua·ver \ˌdem-i-ˈsem-i-ˌkwā-vər\ *n* : THIRTY-SECOND NOTE

de·mis·sion \di-ˈmish-ən\ *n* [MF, fr. L *demission-, demissio* lowering, fr. *demissus,* pp. of *demittere*] : RESIGNATION, ABDICATION

de·mit \di-ˈmit\ *vb* **de·mit·ted; de·mit·ting** [MF *demettre*] *vt* **1** *archaic* : DISMISS **2** : RESIGN ~ *vi* : to withdraw from office or membership

demi·tasse \ˈdem-i-ˌtas, -ˌtäs\ *n* [F *demi-tasse,* fr. *demi-* + *tasse* cup, fr. MF, fr. Ar *ṭass,* fr. Per *tast*] : a small cup of black coffee; *also* : the cup used to serve it

demi·urge \ˈdem-ē-ˌərj\ *n* [LL *demiurgus,* fr. Gk *dēmiourgos,* lit., one who works for the people, fr. *dēmios* of the people (fr. *dēmos* people) + *-ourgos* worker (fr. *ergon* work) — more at DEMAGOGUE, WORK] **1** *cap* **a** : a Platonic subordinate deity who fashions the sensible world in the light of eternal ideas **b** : a Gnostic subordinate deity who is the creator of the material world **2** : something that is an autonomous creative force or decisive power — **demi·ur·geous** \ˌdem-ē-ˈər-jəs\ *adj* — **demi·ur·gic** \-jik\ *or* **demi·ur·gi·cal** \-ji-kəl\ *adj* — **demi·ur·gi·cal·ly** \-ji-k(ə-)lē\ *adv*

demi·world \ˈdem-i-ˌwərld\ *n* [part trans. of F *demi-monde*] : DEMIMONDE 3

demo \ˈdem-(ˌ)ō\ *n, pl* **dem·os** **1** *cap* : DEMOCRAT 2 **2** : DEMONSTRATION **3** : DEMONSTRATOR 2

¹de·mob \(ˈ)dē-ˈmäb, di-\ *vt, chiefly Brit* : DEMOBILIZE

2**demob** *n, chiefly Brit* : the act or process of demobilizing : DEMOBILIZATION

de·mo·bi·lize \di-ˈmō-bə-ˌlīz, (ˈ)dē-\ *vt* **1** : DISBAND **2** : to discharge from military service — **de·mo·bi·li·za·tion** \di-ˌmō-bə-lə-ˈzā-shən, (ˌ)dē-\ *n*

de·moc·ra·cy \di-ˈmäk-rə-sē\ *n, pl* **-cies** [MF *democratie,* fr. LL *democratia,* fr. Gk *dēmokratia,* fr. *dēmos* + *-kratia* -cracy] **1 a** : government by the people; *esp* : rule of the majority **b** : a government in which the supreme power is vested in the people and exercised by them directly or indirectly through a system of representation usu. involving periodically held free elections **2** : a political unit that has a democratic government **3** *cap* : the principles and policies of the Democratic party in the U.S. **4** : the common people esp. when constituting the source of political authority **5** : the absence of hereditary or arbitrary class distinctions or privileges

dem·o·crat \ˈdem-ə-ˌkrat\ *n* **1 a** : an adherent of democracy **b** : one who practices social equality **2** *cap* : a member of the Democratic party of the U.S.

dem·o·crat·ic \ˌdem-ə-ˈkrat-ik\ *adj* **1** : of, relating to, or favoring democracy **2** *often cap* : of or relating to one of the two major political parties in the U.S. evolving in the early 19th century from the anti-Federalists and the Democratic-Republican party and associated in modern times with policies of broad social reform and internationalism **3** : of, relating to, or appealing to the broad masses of the people <~ art> **4** : favoring social equality : not snobbish — **dem·o·crat·i·cal·ly** \-i-k(ə-)lē\ *adv*

democratic centralism *n* : participation of Communist party members in discussion of policy and election of higher party organizations and strict obedience of members and lower party bodies to decisions of the higher units

Democratic–Republican *adj* : of or relating to a major American political party of the early 19th century favoring a strict interpretation of the constitution to restrict the powers of the federal government and emphasizing states' rights

de·moc·ra·tize \di-ˈmäk-rə-ˌtīz\ *vt* **-tized; -tiz·ing** : to make democratic — **de·moc·ra·ti·za·tion** \-ˌmäk-rət-ə-ˈzā-shən\ *n* — **de·moc·ra·tiz·er** \-ˈmäk-rə-ˌtī-zər\ *n*

dé·mo·dé \ˌdā-mō-ˈdā\ *adj* [F, fr. *dé-* de- + *mode*] : no longer fashionable : OUT-OF-DATE

de·mod·ed \(ˈ)dē-ˈmōd-əd\ *adj* : DÉMODÉ

de·mod·u·late \(ˈ)dē-ˈmäj-ə-ˌlāt\ *vt* : to extract the intelligence from (a modulated radio, laser, or computer signal) — **de·mod·u·la·tor** \-ˌlāt-ər\ *n*

de·mod·u·la·tion \(ˌ)dē-ˌmäj-ə-ˈlā-shən\ *n* : the process of demodulating

De·mo·gor·gon \ˌdē-mə-ˈgȯr-gən, ˈdē-mə-ˌ\ *n* [LL] : a mysterious spirit or deity often explained as a primeval creator god who antedates the gods of Greek mythology

de·mo·graph·ic \ˌdē-mə-ˈgraf-ik, ˌdem-ə-\ *adj* **1** : of or relating to demography **2** : relating to the dynamic balance of a population esp. with regard to density and capacity for expansion or decline — **de·mo·graph·i·cal·ly** \-i-k(ə-)lē\ *adv*

de·mog·ra·phy \di-ˈmäg-rə-fē\ *n* [F *démographie,* fr. Gk *dēmos* people + F *-graphie* -graphy] : the statistical study of human populations esp. with reference to size and density, distribution, and vital statistics — **de·mog·ra·pher** \-fər\ *n*

dem·oi·selle \ˌdem-(w)ə-ˈzel\ *n* [F, fr. OF *dameisele* — more at DAMSEL] **1** : a young lady **2** : a small Old World crane (*Anthropoides virgo*) with long secondaries and breast feathers **3** : DAMSELFLY

demoiselle 2

De·Moi·vre's theorem \di-ˈmȯi-vərz-, -ˈmwäv(-rə)z-\ *n* [Abraham *De Moivre* †1754 F mathematician] : a theorem of complex numbers: the *n*th power of a complex number has for its absolute value and its argument respectively the *n*th power of the absolute value and *n* times the argument of the complex number

de·mol·ish \di-ˈmäl-ish\ *vt* [MF *demoliss-,* stem of *demolir,* fr. L *demoliri,* fr. *de-* + *moliri* to construct, fr. *moles* mass — more at MOLE] **1 a** : to tear down : RAZE **b** : to break to pieces : SMASH **2 a** : to do away with : DESTROY **b** : to put into a very weak position : DISCREDIT — **de·mol·ish·er** *n* — **de·mol·ish·ment** \-ish-mənt\ *n*

de·mo·li·tion \ˌdem-ə-ˈlish-ən, ˌdē-mə-\ *n* **1** : the act of demolishing; *esp* : destruction in war by means of explosives **2** *pl* : explosives for destruction in war — **de·mo·li·tion·ist** \-ˈlish-(ə-)nəst\ *n*

demolition derby *n* : a contest in which skilled drivers ram old cars into one another until only one car remains running

de·mon *or* **dae·mon** \ˈdē-mən\ *n* [ME *demon,* fr. LL & L; LL *daemon* evil spirit, fr. L, divinity, spirit, fr. Gk *daimōn*] **1** *usu daemon* : an attendant power or spirit : GENIUS **2 a** : an evil spirit **b** : an evil or undesirable emotion, trait, or state **3** *usu daemon* : a supernatural being of Greek mythology intermediate between gods and men **4** : one that has unusual drive or effectiveness <a ~ for work> — **de·mon·ess** \-mə-nəs\ *n* — **de·mo·ni·an** \di-ˈmō-nē-ən\ *adj* — **de·mon·iza·tion** \ˌdē-mə-nə-ˈzā-shən\ *n* — **de·mon·ize** \ˈdē-mə-ˌnīz\ *vt*

de·mon·e·tize \(ˈ)dē-ˈmän-ə-ˌtīz, -ˈmən-\ *vt* [F *démonétiser,* fr. *dé-* de- + L *moneta* coin — more at MINT] **1** : to stop using (a metal) as a monetary standard **2** : to deprive of value for official payment — **de·mon·e·ti·za·tion** \(ˌ)dē-ˌmän-ət-ə-ˈzā-shən, -ˌmən-\ *n*

1**de·mo·ni·ac** \di-ˈmō-nē-ˌak\ *also* **de·mo·ni·a·cal** \ˌdē-mə-ˈnī-ə-kəl\ *adj* [ME *demoniak,* fr. LL *daemoniacus,* fr. Gk *daimoniakos,* fr. *daimon-, daimōn*] **1** : possessed or influenced by a demon **2** : of, relating to, or suggestive of a demon : FIENDISH <~ cruelty> — **de·mo·ni·a·cal·ly** \ˌdē-mə-ˈnī-ə-k(ə-)lē\ *adv*

2**demoniac** *n* : one regarded as possessed by a demon

de·mon·ic \di-ˈmän-ik\ *also* **de·mon·i·cal** \-i-kəl\ *adj* : DEMONIAC 2 — **de·mon·i·cal·ly** \-i-k(ə-)lē\ *adv*

de·mon·ol·o·gy \ˌdē-mə-ˈnäl-ə-jē\ *n* **1** : the study of demons or evil spirits **2** : belief in demons : a doctrine of evil spirits **3** : a catalog of enemies <the liberal creed at that time put Big Business in a central place in its ~ —Carl Kaysen>

de·mon·stra·ble \di-ˈmän(t)-strə-bəl\ *adj* **1** : capable of being demonstrated **2** : APPARENT, EVIDENT — **de·mon·stra·bil·i·ty** \-ˌmän(t)-stə-ˈbil-ət-ē\ *n* — **de·mon·stra·ble·ness** \-ˈmän(t)-strə-bəl-nəs\ *n* — **de·mon·stra·bly** \-blē\ *adv*

dem·on·strate \ˈdem-ən-ˌstrāt\ *vb* **-strat·ed; -strat·ing** [L *demonstratus,* pp. of *demonstrare,* fr. *de-* + *monstrare* to show — more at MUSTER] *vt* **1** : to show clearly **2 a** : to prove or make clear by reasoning or evidence **b** : to illustrate and explain esp. with many examples **3** : to show or prove the value or efficiency of to a prospective buyer ~ *vi* : to make a demonstration ***syn*** see SHOW

dem·on·stra·tion \ˌdem-ən-ˈstrā-shən\ *n* **1** : an outward expression or display **2** : an act, process, or means of demonstrating to the intelligence: as **a** (1) : conclusive evidence : PROOF (2) : a proof in which the conclusion is the immediate sequence of reasoning from premises **b** : a showing to a prospective buyer of the merits of a product **3** : a show of armed force **4** : a public display of group feelings toward a person or cause — **dem·on·stra·tion·al** \-shnəl, -shən-ᵊl\ *adj* — **dem·on·stra·tion·ist** \-sh(ə-)nəst\ *n*

1**de·mon·stra·tive** \di-ˈmän(t)-strət-iv\ *adj* **1 a** : demonstrating as real or true **b** : characterized or established by demonstration **2** : pointing out the one referred to and distinguishing it from others of the same class <~ pronouns> **3 a** : marked by display of feeling **b** : inclined to display feelings openly — **de·mon·stra·tive·ly** *adv* — **de·mon·stra·tive·ness** *n*

2**demonstrative** *n* : a demonstrative word or morpheme

dem·on·stra·tor \ˈdem-ən-ˌstrāt-ər\ *n* **1** : one that demonstrates **2** : a product (as an automobile) used to demonstrate performance or merits to prospective buyers

de·mor·al·ize \di-ˈmȯr-ə-ˌlīz, ˈdē-, -ˈmär-\ *vt* **1** : to corrupt the morals of **2 a** : to weaken the morale of : DISCOURAGE, DISPIRIT **b** : to upset or destroy the normal functioning of **c** : to throw into disorder — **de·mor·al·iza·tion** \di-ˌmȯr-ə-lə-ˈzā-shən, ˌdē-, -ˌmär-\ *n* — **de·mor·al·iz·er** \di-ˈmȯr-ə-ˌlī-zər, ˈdē-, -ˈmär-\ *n* — **de·mor·al·iz·ing·ly** \-ziŋ-lē\ *adv*

de·mos \ˈdē-ˌmäs\ *n* [Gk *dēmos* — more at DEMAGOGUE] **1** : the common people of an ancient Greek state **2** : POPULACE

de·mote \di-ˈmōt, ˈdē-\ *vt* **de·mot·ed; de·mot·ing** [*de-* + *-mote* (as in *promote*)] : to reduce to a lower grade or rank ***syn*** see DEGRADE — **de·mo·tion** \-ˈmō-shən\ *n*

de·mot·ic \di-ˈmät-ik\ *adj* [Gk *dēmotikos,* fr. *dēmotēs* commoner, fr. *dēmos*] **1** : POPULAR 1 **2** : of, relating to, or written in a simplified form of the ancient Egyptian hieratic writing **3** : of or relating to the form of Modern Greek that is based on colloquial use

de·mount \(ˈ)dē-ˈmau̇nt\ *vt* **1** : to remove from a mounted position **2** : DISASSEMBLE — **de·mount·able** \-ə-bəl\ *adj*

1**de·mul·cent** \di-ˈməl-sənt\ *adj* [L *demulcent-, demulcens,* prp. of *demulcēre* to soothe, fr. *de-* + *mulcēre* to soothe] : SOOTHING

2**demulcent** *n* : a usu. mucilaginous or oily substance (as tragacanth) capable of soothing or protecting an abraded mucous membrane

1**de·mur** \di-ˈmər\ *vi* **de·murred; de·mur·ring** [ME *demeoren* to linger, fr. OF *demorer,* fr. L *demorari,* fr. *de-* + *morari* to linger, fr. *mora* delay — more at MEMORY] **1** : to file a demurrer **2** : to take exception : OBJECT <he *demurred* at the horseplay> **3** *archaic* : DELAY, HESITATE

2**demur** *n* **1** : hesitation (as in doing or accepting) usu. based on doubt of the acceptability of something offered or proposed <women who follow fashion without ~> **2** : OBJECTION, PROTEST ***syn*** see QUALM

de·mure \di-ˈmyu̇(ə)r\ *adj* [ME] **1** : RESERVED, MODEST **2** : affectedly modest, reserved, or serious : COY — **de·mure·ly** *adv* — **de·mure·ness** *n*

de·mur·rage \di-ˈmər-ij, -ˈmə-rij\ *n* **1** : the detention of a ship by the freighter beyond the time allowed for loading, unloading, or sailing **2** : a charge for detaining a ship, freight car, or truck

de·mur·ral \di-ˈmər-əl, -ˈmə-rəl\ *n* : an act or instance of demurring

1**de·mur·rer** \di-ˈmər-ər, -ˈmə-rər\ *n* [MF *demorer,* v.] **1** : a pleading by a party to a legal action that assumes the truth of the matter alleged by the opposite party and sets up that it is insufficient in law to sustain his claim or that there is some other defect on the face of the pleadings constituting a legal reason why the opposing party should not be allowed to proceed further **2** : OBJECTION

2**de·mur·rer** \-ˈmər-ər\ *n* [1*demur*] : one that demurs

de·my \di-ˈmī\ *n* [ME *demi* half — more at DEMI-] : a size of paper typically 16 x 21 inches

de·my·e·lin·ate \(ˈ)dē-ˈmī-ə-lə-ˌnāt\ *vt* **-at·ed; -at·ing** : to remove or destroy the myelin of — **de·my·e·lin·ation** \(ˌ)dē-ˌmī-ə-lə-ˈnā-shən\ *n*

de·mys·ti·fy \(ˈ)dē-ˈmis-tə-ˌfī\ *vt* : to remove the mystery from : EXPLICATE — **de·mys·ti·fi·ca·tion** \(ˌ)dē-ˌmis-tə-fə-ˈkā-shən\ *n*

de·my·thol·o·gize \ˌdē-mith-ˈäl-ə-ˌjīz\ *vt* **1** : to divest of mythological forms in order to uncover the meaning underlying them <~ the Gospels> **2** : to divest of mythical elements or associations — **de·my·thol·o·gi·za·tion** \-ˌäl-ə-jə-ˈzā-shən\ *n* — **de·my·thol·o·giz·er** \-ˈäl-ə-ˌjī-zər\ *n*

1**den** \ˈden\ *n* [ME, fr. OE *denn;* akin to OE *denu* valley, OHG *tenni* threshing floor, Gk *thenar* palm of the hand] **1** : the lair of a wild usu. predatory animal **2 a** (1) : a hollow or cavern used esp. as a hideout (2) : a center of secret activity **b** : a small usu. squalid dwelling **3** : a comfortable usu. secluded room **4** : a subdivision of a cub-scout pack made up of two or more boys

2**den** *vb* **denned; den·ning** *vi* : to live in or retire to a den ~ *vt* : to drive into a den

1**Den** *abbr* Denmark

²**Den** *or* **Denb** *abbr* Denbighshire
de·nar·i·us \di-ˈnar-ē-əs, -ˈner-\ *n, pl* **de·nar·ii** \-ē-ˌī, -ē-ˌē\ [ME, fr. L — more at DENIER] **1 :** a small silver coin of ancient Rome **2 :** a gold coin of the Roman Empire equivalent to 25 denarii
de·na·tion·al·ize \(ˈ)dē-ˈnash-nə-ˌlīz, -ˈnash-ən-ᵊl-ˌīz\ *vt* **1 :** to divest of national character or rights **2 :** to remove from ownership or control by the national government — **de·na·tion·al·iza·tion** \(ˌ)dē-ˌnash-nə-lə-ˈzā-shən, -ˌnash-ən-ᵊl-ə-ˈzā-\ *n*
de·nat·u·ral·ize \(ˈ)dē-ˈnach-(ə-)rə-ˌlīz\ *vt* **1 :** to make unnatural **2 :** to deprive of the rights and duties of a citizen — **de·nat·u·ral·iza·tion** \(ˌ)dē-ˌnach-(ə-)rə-lə-ˈzā-shən\ *n*
de·na·tur·ant \(ˈ)dē-ˈnāch-(ə-)rənt\ *n* **:** a denaturing agent
de·na·tur·ation \(ˌ)dē-ˌnā-chə-ˈrā-shən\ *n* **:** the process of denaturing — **de·na·tur·ation·al** \-shnəl, -shən-ᵊl\ *adj*
de·na·ture \(ˈ)dē-ˈnā-chər\ *vt* **de·na·tured; de·na·tur·ing** \-ˈnāch-(ə-)riŋ\ **1 :** to deprive of natural qualities: as **a :** to make (alcohol) unfit for drinking (as by adding an obnoxious substance) without impairing usefulness for other purposes **b :** to modify (as a native protein) esp. by heat, acid, alkali, or ultraviolet radiation so that all the original properties are removed, diminished, or changed **c :** to add nonfissionable material to (fissionable material) so as to make unsuitable for use in an atomic bomb **2 :** DEHUMANIZE
de·na·zi·fy \(ˈ)dē-ˈnät-si-ˌfī, -ˈnat-\ *vt* **-fied; -fy·ing :** to rid of Nazism and its influence — **de·na·zi·fi·ca·tion** \(ˌ)dē-ˌnät-si-fə-ˈkā-shən, -ˌnat-\ *n*
dendr- *or* **dendro-** *comb form* [Gk, fr. *dendron;* akin to Gk *drys* tree — more at TREE] **:** tree <*dendro*philous> **:** resembling a tree <*dendr*ite>
den·dri·form \ˈden-drə-ˌfȯrm\ *adj* **:** resembling a tree in structure
den·drite \ˈden-ˌdrīt\ *n* **1 :** a branching treelike figure produced on or in a mineral by a foreign mineral; *also* **:** the mineral so marked **2 :** a crystallized arborescent form **3 :** any of the usu. branching protoplasmic processes that conduct impulses toward the body of a nerve cell — see NEURON illustration — **den·drit·ic** \den-ˈdrit-ik\ *also* **den·drit·i·cal** \-i-kəl\ *adj* — **den·drit·i·cal·ly** \-i-k(ə-)lē\ *adv*
den·dro·chro·nol·o·gy \ˌden-(ˌ)drō-krə-ˈnäl-ə-jē\ *n* **:** the science of dating events and variations in environment in former periods by comparative study of growth rings in trees and aged wood — **den·dro·chro·no·log·i·cal** \-ˌkrän-ᵊl-ˈäj-i-kəl, -ˌkrōn-\ *adj* — **den·dro·chro·no·log·i·cal·ly** \-i-k(ə-)lē\ *adv*
den·droid \ˈden-ˌdrȯid\ *adj* [Gk *dendroeidēs,* fr. *dendron*] **:** resembling a tree in form **:** ARBORESCENT
den·drol·o·gy \den-ˈdräl-ə-jē\ *n* **:** the study of trees — **den·dro·log·ic** \ˌden-drə-ˈläj-ik\ *or* **den·dro·log·i·cal** \-i-kəl\ *adj* — **den·drol·o·gist** \den-ˈdräl-ə-jəst\ *n*
dene \ˈdēn\ *n* [ME, fr. OE *denu*] *Brit* **:** VALLEY
Dé·né \ˈden-ē\ *n, pl* **Déné** *or* **Dénés** \-ēz\ [F, fr. Déné] **1 :** a member of an Athapaskan people of the interior of Alaska and northwestern Canada **2 :** the language of the Déné people
Den·eb \ˈden-ˌeb, -əb\ *n* [Ar *dhanab al-dajāja,* lit., the tail of the hen] **:** a star of the first magnitude in Cygnus
den·e·ga·tion \ˌden-i-ˈgā-shən\ *n* [ME *denegacioun,* fr. MF or L; MF *denegation,* fr. L *denegation-, denegatio,* fr. *denegatus,* pp. of *denegare* to deny — more at DENY] **:** DENIAL
de·ner·vate \ˈdē-(ˌ)nər-ˌvāt\ *vt* **-vat·ed; -vat·ing :** to deprive of a nerve supply (as by cutting a nerve) — **de·ner·va·tion** \ˌdē-(ˌ)nər-ˈvā-shən\ *n*
den·gue \ˈdeŋ-gē, -ˌgā\ *n* [Sp] **:** an acute infectious viral disease characterized by headache, severe joint pain, and a rash
de·ni·able \di-ˈnī-ə-bəl\ *adj* **:** capable of being denied
de·ni·al \di-ˈnī(-ə)l\ *n* **1 :** refusal to satisfy a request or desire **2 a** (1) **:** refusal to admit the truth or reality (as of a statement or charge) (2) **:** assertion that an allegation is false **b :** refusal to acknowledge a person or a thing **:** DISAVOWAL **3 :** the opposing by the defendant of an allegation of the opposite party in a lawsuit **4 :** SELF-DENIAL **5 :** negation in logic
de·nic·o·tin·ize \(ˈ)dē-ˈnik-ə-ˌtē-ˌnīz\ *vt* **-ized; -iz·ing :** to remove part of the nicotine from (tobacco)
¹**de·ni·er** \di-ˈnī(-ə)r\ *n* **:** one that denies
²**de·nier** *n* [ME *denere,* fr. MF *denier,* fr. L *denarius,* coin worth ten asses, fr. *denarius* containing ten, fr. *deni* ten each, fr. *decem* ten — more at TEN] **1** \də-ˈni(ə)r, dən-ˈyā\ **:** a small orig. silver coin of France and western Europe from the 8th to the 19th century **2** \ˈden-yər\ **:** a unit of fineness for silk, rayon, or nylon yarn equal to the fineness of a yarn weighing one gram for each 9000 meters
den·i·grate \ˈden-i-ˌgrāt\ *vt* **-grat·ed; -grat·ing** [L *denigratus,* pp. of *denigrare,* fr. *de-* + *nigrare* to blacken, fr. *nigr-, niger* black] **1 :** to cast aspersions on **:** DEFAME <expatriates whom we are in the habit of *denigrating* —Henry Miller> **2 :** to deny the importance or validity of **:** BELITTLE <he was a philosopher and inclined to ~ ideas in literature —W. C. DeVane> — **den·i·gra·tion** \ˌden-i-ˈgrā-shən\ *n* — **den·i·gra·tive** \-ˌgrāt-iv\ *adj* — **den·i·gra·tor** \-ˌgrāt-ər\ *n* — **den·i·gra·to·ry** \ˈden-i-grə-ˌtōr-ē, -ˌtȯr-\ *adj*
den·im \ˈden-əm\ *n* [F (*serge*) *de Nîmes* serge of Nîmes, France] **1 a :** a firm durable twilled usu. cotton fabric woven with colored warp and white filling threads **b :** a similar fabric woven in colored stripes **2** *pl* **:** overalls or trousers usu. of blue denim
de·ni·tri·fi·ca·tion \(ˌ)dē-ˌnī-trə-fə-ˈkā-shən\ *n* **:** an act or process of denitrifying; *specif* **:** reduction of nitrates or nitrites commonly by bacteria and usu. resulting in the escape of nitrogen into the air
de·ni·tri·fy \(ˈ)dē-ˈnī-trə-ˌfī\ *vt* **1 :** to remove nitrogen or its compound from **2 :** to convert (a nitrate or a nitrite) into a compound of a lower state of oxidation
den·i·zen \ˈden-ə-zən\ *n* [ME *denysen,* fr. MF *denzein,* fr. OF, inner, fr. *denz* within, fr. LL *deintus,* fr. L *de-* + *intus* within — more at ENT-] **1 :** INHABITANT **2 :** one admitted to residence in a foreign country; *esp* **:** an alien admitted to rights of citizenship **3 a :** a naturalized plant or animal **b :** one that frequents a place
den mother *n* **:** a female adult leader of a cub-scout den

de·nom·i·nate \di-ˈnäm-ə-ˌnāt\ *vt* [L *denominatus,* pp. of *denominare,* fr. *de-* + *nominare* to name — more at NOMINATE] **:** to give a name to **:** DESIGNATE
de·nom·i·nate number \di-ˌnäm-ə-nət-\ *n* [L *denominatus*] **:** a number (as *7* in *7 feet*) that specifies a quantity in terms of a unit of measurement
de·nom·i·na·tion \di-ˌnäm-ə-ˈnā-shən\ *n* **1 :** an act of denominating **2 :** NAME, DESIGNATION; *esp* **:** a general name for a category **3 :** a religious organization uniting in a single legal and administrative body a number of local congregations **4 :** a value or size of a series of values or sizes (as of money) — **de·nom·i·na·tion·al** \-shnəl, -shən-ᵊl\ *adj* — **de·nom·i·na·tion·al·ly** \-ē\ *adv*
de·nom·i·na·tion·al·ism \-shnəl-ˌiz-əm, -shən-ᵊl-\ *n* **1 :** devotion to denominational principles or interests **2 :** the emphasizing of denominational differences to the point of being narrowly exclusive **:** SECTARIANISM — **de·nom·i·na·tion·al·ist** \-shnə-ləst, -shən-ᵊl-əst\ *n*
de·nom·i·na·tive \di-ˈnäm-(ə-)nət-iv\ *adj* [L *de* from + *nomin-, nomen* name] **:** derived from a noun or adjective — **denominative** *n*
de·nom·i·na·tor \di-ˈnäm-ə-ˌnāt-ər\ *n* **1 :** the part of a fraction that is below the line signifying division and that in fractions with 1 as the numerator indicates into how many parts the unit is divided **:** DIVISOR **2 a :** a common trait **b :** the average level (as of taste or opinion) **:** STANDARD
de·no·ta·tion \ˌdē-nō-ˈtā-shən\ *n* **1 :** an act or process of denoting **2 :** MEANING; *esp* **:** a direct specific meaning as distinct from connotations **3 a :** a denoting term **:** NAME **b :** SIGN, INDICATION <visible ~*s* of divine wrath> **4 :** the totality of things to which a term is applicable esp. in logic
de·no·ta·tive \ˈdē-nō-ˌtāt-iv, di-ˈnōt-ət-iv\ *adj* **1 :** denoting or tending to denote **2 :** relating to denotation
de·note \di-ˈnōt\ *vt* [MF *denoter,* fr. L *denotare,* fr. *de-* + *notare* to note] **1 :** to serve as an indication of **:** BETOKEN <the swollen bellies that ~ starvation> **2 :** to serve as an arbitrary mark for <red flares *denoting* danger> **3 :** to make known **:** ANNOUNCE <his crestfallen look *denoted* his distress> **4 a :** to serve as a linguistic expression of the notion of **:** MEAN **b :** to stand for **:** signify by way of logical denotation — **de·note·ment** \-ˈnōt-mənt\ *n* — **de·no·tive** \-ˈnōt-iv\ *adj*
syn DENOTE, CONNOTE *shared meaning element* **:** to mean. In spite of this shared element of meaning, these terms are complementary rather than strictly synonymous and cannot be interchanged without significant loss of precision. DENOTE applies to the definitive meaning content of a term: in a noun, the thing or the definable class of things or ideas which it names; in a verb, the act or state which is affirmed. CONNOTE applies to the ideas or associations that are added to a term and cling to it, often as a result of personal experience but sometimes as a result of something extraneous (as a widely known context or connection with a widely known event). "Home", for example, *denotes* the place where one lives, but to one person it may *connote* comforts, intimacy, and affection and to another misery, estrangement, and abuse
de·noue·ment \ˌdā-ˌnü-ˈmäⁿ, dā-nü-ˌ\ *n* [F *dénouement,* lit., untying, fr. MF *desnouement,* fr. *desnouer* to untie, fr. OF *desnoer,* fr. *des-* de- + *noer* to tie, fr. L *nodare,* fr. *nodus* knot — more at NET] **1 :** the final outcome of the main dramatic complication in a literary work **2 :** the outcome of a complex sequence of events
de·nounce \di-ˈnaůn(t)s\ *vt* **de·nounced; de·nounc·ing** [ME *denouncen,* fr. OF *denoncier* to proclaim, fr. L *denuntiare,* fr. *de-* + *nuntiare* to report — more at ANNOUNCE] **1 :** to pronounce esp. publicly to be blameworthy or evil **2** *archaic* **a :** PROCLAIM **b :** to announce threateningly **3 :** to inform against **:** ACCUSE **4** *obs* **:** PORTEND **5 :** to announce formally the termination of (as a treaty) ***syn*** see CRITICIZE ***ant*** eulogize — **de·nounce·ment** \-ˈnaůn(t)-smənt\ *n* — **de·nounc·er** *n*
de no·vo \di-ˈnō-(ˌ)vō, dā-\ *adv* [L] **:** over again **:** ANEW <a case tried *de novo*>
dense \ˈden(t)s\ *adj* **dens·er; dens·est** [L *densus;* akin to Gk *dasys* thick with hair or leaves] **1 :** marked by compactness or crowding together of parts **2 a :** marked by a stupid imperviousness to ideas or impressions **:** THICKHEADED **b :** EXTREME <~ ignorance> **3 :** having between any two elements at least one element <the rational numbers are ~> **4 :** demanding concentration to follow or comprehend <~ prose> **5 :** possessing relatively great retarding power upon light waves and consequently relatively high density <a ~ glass> **6 :** having high or relatively high opacity <a ~ fog> <a ~ photographic negative>
syn **1** see CLOSE ***ant*** sparse (*as of forests, population*), tenuous (*as of clouds*) **2** see STUPID ***ant*** subtle, bright — **dense·ly** *adv* — **dense·ness** \ˈden(t)-snəs\ *n*
den·si·fy \ˈden(t)-sə-ˌfī\ *vt* **-fied; -fy·ing :** to make denser; *specif* **:** to increase the density of (wood) by pressure usu. with impregnation of a resin — **den·si·fi·ca·tion** \ˌden(t)-sə-fə-ˈkā-shən\ *n*
den·sim·e·ter \den-ˈsim-ət-ər\ *n* [L *densus* + ISV *-meter*] **:** an instrument for determining density or specific gravity — **den·si·met·ric** \ˌden(t)-sə-ˈme-trik\ *adj*
den·si·tom·e·ter \ˌden(t)-sə-ˈtäm-ət-ər\ *n* **:** an instrument for determining optical or photographic density — **den·si·to·met·ric** \ˌden(t)-sət-ə-ˈme-trik\ *adj* — **den·si·tom·e·try** \ˌden(t)-sə-ˈtäm-ə-trē\ *n*
den·si·ty \ˈden(t)-sət-ē, -stē\ *n, pl* **-ties 1 :** the quality or state of being dense **2 :** the quantity per unit volume, unit area, or unit length: as **a :** the mass of a substance per unit volume **b :** the distribution of a quantity (as mass, electricity, or energy) per unit

usu. of space **c :** the average number of individuals or units per space unit <a population ~ of 500 persons per square mile> <a housing ~ of 10 houses per acre> **3 :** STUPIDITY **4 a :** the degree of opacity of a translucent medium **b :** the common logarithm of the opacity

1dent \ˈdent\ *n* [ME, blow, alter. of *dint*] **1 :** a depression or hollow made by a blow or by pressure **2 a :** an impression or effect often made against resistance and usu. having a weakening effect **b :** initial progress : HEADWAY

2dent *vt* **1 :** to make a dent in **2 :** to have a weakening effect on ~ *vi* **:** to form a dent by sinking inward : become dented

3dent *n* [F, lit., tooth, fr. L *dent-, dens*] **:** TOOTH 3a

4dent *abbr* dental; dentist; dentistry

dent- *or* **denti-** *or* **dento-** *comb form* [ME *denti-*, fr. L, fr. *dent-, dens* tooth — more at TOOTH] **1 :** tooth : teeth <*dent*algia> <*denti*form> **2 :** dental and <*dento*surgical>

1den·tal \ˈdent-ᵊl\ *adj* [L *dentalis*, fr. *dent-, dens*] **1 :** of or relating to the teeth or dentistry **2 :** articulated with the tip or blade of the tongue against or near the upper front teeth — **den·tal·ly** \-ē\ *adv*

2dental *n* **:** a dental consonant

dental floss *n* **:** a waxed thread used to clean between the teeth

dental hygienist *n* **:** one who assists a dentist esp. in cleaning teeth

den·ta·li·um \den-ˈtā-lē-əm\ *n, pl* **-lia** \-lē-ə\ [NL, genus name, fr. L *dentalis*] **:** any of a genus (*Dentalium*) of widely distributed tooth shells; *broadly* **:** TOOTH SHELL

dental technician *n* **:** a technician who makes dental appliances

den·tate \ˈden-ˌtāt\ *or* **den·tat·ed** \-ˌtāt-əd\ *adj* [L *dentatus*, fr. *dent-, dens*] **:** having teeth or pointed conical projections <multi*dentate*> <~ leaves> — **den·tate·ly** *adv* — **den·ta·tion** \den-ˈtā-shən\ *n*

dent corn *n* **:** an Indian corn having kernels that contain both hard and soft starch and that become indented at maturity

den·ti·cle \ˈdent-i-kəl\ *n* [ME, fr. L *denticulus*, dim. of *dent-, dens*] **:** a small tooth or other conical pointed projection

den·tic·u·late \den-ˈtik-yə-lət\ *or* **den·tic·u·lat·ed** \-ˌlāt-əd\ *adj* **1 a :** covered with small pointed projections <a ~ shell>; *esp* **:** SERRATE **b :** finely dentate **2 :** cut into dentils — **den·tic·u·late·ly** *adv* — **den·tic·u·la·tion** \(ˌ)den-ˌtik-yə-ˈlā-shən\ *n*

den·ti·form \ˈdent-ə-ˌfȯrm\ *adj* **1 :** shaped like a tooth **2 :** divided into dentate processes

den·ti·frice \ˈdent-ə-frəs\ *n* [MF, fr. L *dentifricium*, fr. *denti-* + *fricare* to rub — more at FRICTION] **:** a powder, paste, or liquid for cleaning the teeth

den·tig·er·ous \den-ˈtij-ə-rəs\ *adj* **:** bearing dentate structures

den·til \ˈdent-ᵊl, ˈden-ˌtil\ *n* [obs. F *dentille*, fr. MF, dim. of *dent*] **:** one of a series of small projecting rectangular blocks esp. under a cornice

den·tin \ˈdent-ᵊn\ *or* **den·tine** \ˈden-ˌtēn, den-ˈ\ *n* **:** a calcareous material similar to but harder and denser than bone that composes the principal mass of a tooth — **den·tin·al** \den-ˈtēn-ᵊl, ˈdent-ᵊn-əl\ *adj*

den·tist \ˈdent-əst\ *n* [F *dentiste*, fr. *dent*] **:** one who is skilled in and licensed to practice the prevention, diagnosis, and treatment of diseases, injuries, and malformations of the teeth, jaws, and mouth and who makes and inserts false teeth

den·tist·ry \ˈdent-ə-strē\ *n* **:** the art or profession of a dentist

den·ti·tion \den-ˈtish-ən\ *n* [L *dentition-, dentitio*, fr. *dentitus*, pp. of *dentire* to cut teeth, fr. *dent-, dens*] **1 :** the development and cutting of teeth **2 :** the number, kind, and arrangement of teeth — see TOOTH illustration **3 :** the character of the teeth as determined by their form and arrangement

den·tu·lous \ˈden-chə-ləs\ *adj* [back-formation fr. *edentulous*] **:** having teeth

den·ture \ˈden-chər\ *n* [F, fr. MF, fr. *dent*] **1 :** a set of teeth **2 :** an artificial replacement for one or more teeth; *esp* **:** a set of false teeth

de·nu·cle·ar·ize \(ˈ)dē-ˈn(y)ü-klē-ə-ˌrīz\ *vt* **-ized; -iz·ing :** to remove nuclear arms from **:** prohibit the use of nuclear arms in — **de·nu·cle·ar·iza·tion** \(ˌ)dē-ˌn(y)ü-klē-ə-rə-ˈzā-shən\ *n*

de·nu·da·tion \ˌdē-(ˌ)n(y)ü-ˈdā-shən, ˌden-yu̇-\ *n* **:** an act or process of denuding — **de·nu·da·tion·al** \-shnəl, -shən-ᵊl\ *adj*

de·nude \di-ˈn(y)üd\ *vt* **de·nud·ed; de·nud·ing** [L *denudare*, fr. *de-* + *nudus* bare — more at NAKED] **1 a :** to strip of all covering **b :** to lay bare by erosion **c :** to strip (land) of forests **2 :** to divest of something important — **de·nude·ment** \-ˈn(y)üd-mənt\ *n* — **de·nud·er** *n*

de·nu·mer·a·ble \di-ˈn(y)üm-(ə-)rə-bəl\ *adj* **:** capable of being put into one-to-one correspondence with the positive integers — **de·nu·mer·a·bil·i·ty** \-ˌn(y)üm-(ə-)rə-ˈbil-ət-ē\ *n* — **de·nu·mer·a·bly** \-ˈn(y)üm-(ə-)rə-blē\ *adv*

de·nun·ci·a·tion \di-ˌnən(t)-sē-ˈā-shən\ *n* **:** an act of denouncing; *esp* **:** a public condemnation — **de·nun·ci·a·tive** \-ˈnən(t)-sē-ˌāt-iv\ *adj* — **de·nun·ci·a·to·ry** \-sē-ə-ˌtōr-ē, -ˌtȯr-\ *adj*

de·ny \di-ˈnī\ *vt* **de·nied; de·ny·ing** [ME *denyen*, fr. OF *denier*, fr. L *denegare*, fr. *de-* + *negare* to deny — more at NEGATE] **1 :** to declare untrue **2 :** to disclaim connection with or responsibility for **:** DISAVOW **3 a :** to give a negative answer to **b :** to refuse to grant **c :** to restrain (oneself) from gratification of desires **4** *archaic* **:** DECLINE **5 :** to refuse to accept the existence, truth, or validity of — **de·ny·ing·ly** \-ˈnī-iŋ-lē\ *adv*

syn DENY, GAINSAY, CONTRADICT, NEGATIVE, IMPUGN, CONTRAVENE *shared meaning element* **:** to refuse to accept as true, valid, or worthy of consideration ***ant*** confirm, concede

de·o·dar \ˈdē-ə-ˌdär\ *or* **de·o·da·ra** \ˌdē-ə-ˈdär-ə\ *n* [Hindi *deodār*, fr. Skt *devadāru*, lit., timber of the gods, fr. *deva* god + *dāru* wood] **:** an East Indian cedar (*Cedrus deodara*)

de·odor·ant \dē-ˈōd-ə-rənt\ *n* **:** a preparation that destroys or masks unpleasant odors — **deodorant** *adj*

de·odor·ize \dē-ˈōd-ə-ˌrīz\ *vt* **1 :** to eliminate or prevent the offensive odor of **2 :** to make (something unpleasant) more acceptable <their buccaneering was *deodorized* by the fact that their victims were Madagascar pirates —*N.Y. Herald Tribune Bk. Rev.*> — **de·odor·iza·tion** \-ˌōd-ə-rə-ˈzā-shən\ *n* — **de·odor·iz·er** *n*

de·on·tol·o·gy \ˌdē-ˌän-ˈtäl-ə-jē\ *n* [Gk *deont-, deon* that which is obligatory, fr. neut. of prp. of *dein* to lack, be needful — more at DEUTER-] **:** the theory or study of moral obligation — **de·on·to·log·i·cal** \ˌdē-ˌänt-ᵊl-ˈäj-i-kəl\ *adj* — **de·on·tol·o·gist** \ˌdē-ˌän-ˈtäl-ə-jəst\ *n*

Deo vo·len·te \ˌdā-(ˌ)ō-və-ˈlent-ē, ˌdē-\ [L] **:** God being willing

de·ox·i·dize \(ˈ)dē-ˈäk-sə-ˌdīz\ *vt* **:** to remove oxygen from — **de·ox·i·da·tion** \(ˌ)dē-ˌäk-sə-ˈdā-shən\ *n* — **de·ox·i·diz·er** \(ˈ)dē-ˈäk-sə-ˌdī-zər\ *n*

deoxy- *or* **desoxy-** *comb form* [ISV] **:** containing less oxygen in the molecule than the compound to which it is closely related <*deoxy*ribonucleic acid>

de·oxy·cor·ti·co·ste·rone \dē-ˌäk-si-ˌkȯrt-i-ˈkäs-tə-ˌrōn, -i-kō-stə-ˈrōn\ *n* [ISV] **:** a steroid hormone $C_{21}H_{30}O_3$ of the adrenal cortex

de·ox·y·gen·ate \(ˈ)dē-ˈäk-si-jə-ˌnāt, ˌdē-äk-ˈsij-ə-\ *vt* **:** to remove oxygen from — **de·ox·y·gen·ation** \(ˌ)dē-ˌäk-si-jə-ˈnā-shən, ˌdē-äk-ˌsij-ə-\ *n*

de·ox·y·gen·at·ed *adj* **:** having the hemoglobin in the reduced state

de·oxy·ri·bo·nu·cle·ase \(ˈ)dē-ˈäk-si-ˌrī-bō-ˈn(y)ü-klē-ˌās, -ˌāz\ *n* [*deoxyribonucle*ic acid + *-ase*] **:** an enzyme that hydrolyzes DNA to nucleotides — called also *DNase*

de·oxy·ri·bo·nu·cle·ic acid \(ˈ)dē-ˈäk-si-ˌrī-bō-n(y)u̇-ˌklē-ik-, -ˌklā-\ *n* [*deoxyribose* + *nucleic acid*] **:** DNA

de·oxy·ri·bo·nu·cle·o·tide \-ˈn(y)ü-klē-ə-ˌtīd\ *n* **:** a nucleotide that contains deoxyribose and is a constituent of DNA

de·oxy·ri·bose \(ˌ)dē-ˌäk-si-ˈrī-ˌbōs, -ˌbōz\ *n* [ISV *deoxy-* + *ribose*] **:** a pentose sugar $C_5H_{10}O_4$ that is a structural element of DNA

dep *abbr* **1** depart **2** department **3** departure **4** deponent **5** deposed **6** deposit **7** depot **8** deputy

de·part \di-ˈpärt\ *vb* [ME *departen* to divide, go away, fr. OF *departir*, fr. *de-* + *partir* to divide, fr. L *partire*, fr. *part-, pars* part] *vi* **1 a :** to go away **:** LEAVE **b :** DIE **2 :** to turn aside **:** DEVIATE ~ *vt* **:** to go away from **:** LEAVE ***syn*** **1** see GO ***ant*** arrive, remain, abide **2** see SWERVE

de·part·ed *adj* **1 :** BYGONE **2 :** having died, esp. recently <mourning our ~ friend> ***syn*** see DEAD

de·part·ment \di-ˈpärt-mənt\ *n* [F *département*; fr. MF, fr. *departir*] **1 :** a distinct sphere **:** PROVINCE **2 :** a functional or territorial division: as **a :** a major administrative division of a government **b :** a major territorial administrative subdivision **c :** a division of a college or school giving instruction in a particular subject **d :** a major division of a business **e :** a section of a department store **f :** a territorial subdivision made for the administration and training of military units — **de·part·men·tal** \di-ˌpärt-ˈment-ᵊl, ˌdē-\ *adj* — **de·part·men·tal·ly** \-ᵊl-ē\ *adv*

de·part·men·tal·ize \di-ˌpärt-ˈment-ᵊl-ˌīz, ˌdē-\ *vt* **-ized; -iz·ing :** to divide into departments — **de·part·men·tal·iza·tion** \-ˌment-ᵊl-ə-ˈzā-shən\ *n*

department store *n* **:** a store selling a wide variety of goods arranged in several departments

de·par·ture \di-ˈpär-chər\ *n* **1 a (1) :** the act of going away **(2)** *archaic* **:** DEATH **b :** a ship's position in latitude and longitude at the beginning of a voyage as a point from which to begin dead reckoning **c :** a setting out (as on a new course) **2 :** the distance due east or west made by a ship in its course **3 :** DIVERGENCE

de·pau·per·ate \di-ˈpȯ-pə-rət\ *adj* [ME *depauperat*, fr. ML *depauperatus*, pp. of *depauperare* to impoverish, fr. L *de-* + *pauperare* to impoverish, fr. *pauper* poor — more at POOR] **:** falling short of natural development or size — **de·pau·per·ation** \-ˌpȯ-pə-ˈrā-shən\ *n*

de·pend \di-ˈpend\ *vi* [ME *dependen*, fr. MF *dependre*, modif. of L *dependēre*, fr. *de-* + *pendēre* to hang — more at PENDANT] **1 a :** to be contingent **b :** to exist by virtue of a necessary relation **2 :** to be pending or undecided **3 a :** to place reliance or trust **b :** to be dependent esp. for financial support **4 :** to hang down ***syn*** see RELY

de·pend·able \di-ˈpen-də-bəl\ *adj* **:** capable of being depended on **:** RELIABLE — **de·pend·abil·i·ty** \-ˌpen-də-ˈbil-ət-ē\ *n* — **de·pend·able·ness** *n* — **de·pend·ably** \-blē\ *adv*

de·pen·dence *also* **de·pen·dance** \di-ˈpen-dən(t)s\ *n* **1 :** the quality or state of being dependent; *esp* **:** the quality or state of being influenced by or subject to another **2 :** RELIANCE, TRUST **3 :** one that is relied on <he was her sole ~> **4 a :** drug addiction **b :** HABITUATION 2b

de·pen·den·cy \-dən-sē\ *n, pl* **-cies 1 :** DEPENDENCE 1 **2 :** something that is dependent on something else; *specif* **:** a territorial unit under the jurisdiction of a nation but not formally annexed by it

1de·pen·dent \di-ˈpen-dənt\ *adj* [ME *dependant*, fr. MF, prp. of *dependre*] **1 :** hanging down **2 a :** determined or conditioned by another **:** CONTINGENT **b :** relying on another for support **c :** subject to another's jurisdiction **d :** SUBORDINATE 3a — **de·pen·dent·ly** *adv*

2dependent *also* **de·pen·dant** \-dənt\ *n* **1** *archaic* **:** DEPENDENCY **2 :** one that is dependent; *esp* **:** a person who relies on another for support

dependent variable *n* **:** a mathematical variable whose value is determined by that of one or more other variables in a function <in $z = x^2 + 3xy + y^2$, *z* is the *dependent variable*>

de·perm \(ˈ)dē-ˈpərm\ *vt* [*de-* + *perm*anent magnetism] **:** to reduce the magnetism of (a ship's steel hull) as a precaution against magnetic operated mines

de·per·son·al·iza·tion \(ˌ)dē-ˌpər-snə-lə-ˈzā-shən, -ˌpərs-ᵊn-ə-lə-\ *n* **1 a :** an act or process of depersonalizing **b :** the quality or state of being depersonalized **2 :** loss of the sense of personal identity

de·per·son·al·ize \(ˈ)dē-ˈpər-snə-ˌlīz, -ˈpərs-ᵊn-ə-\ *vt* **1 :** to deprive of personality <schools that ~ students> **2 :** to make impersonal

de·pict \di-ˈpikt\ *vt* [L *depictus*, pp. of *depingere*, fr. *de-* + *pingere* to paint — more at PAINT] **1 :** to represent by a picture **2 :** DESCRIBE — **de·pic·ter** \-ˈpik-tər\ *n* — **de·pic·tion** \-ˈpik-shən\ *n*

de·pig·men·ta·tion \(,)dē-,pig-mən-'tā-shən, -,men-\ *n* : loss of normal pigmentation

dep·i·late \'dep-ə-,lāt\ *vt* **-lat·ed; -lat·ing** [L *depilatus*, pp. of *depilare*, fr. *de-* + *pilus* hair — more at PILE] : to remove hair from — **dep·i·la·tion** \,dep-ə-'lā-shən\ *n*

de·pil·a·to·ry \di-'pil-ə-,tōr-ē, -,tȯr-\ *n, pl* **-ries** : an agent for removing hair, wool, or bristles — **depilatory** *adj*

de·plane \(')dē-'plān\ *vi* : to get off an airplane

de·plete \di-'plēt\ *vt* **de·plet·ed; de·plet·ing** [L *depletus*, pp. of *deplēre*, fr. *de-* + *plēre* to fill — more at FULL] **1** : to empty of a principal substance **2** : to lessen markedly in quantity, content, power, or value — **de·plet·able** \-'plēt-ə-bəl\ *adj* — **de·ple·tion** \-'plē-shən\ *n* — **de·ple·tive** \-'plēt-iv\ *adj*

syn DEPLETE, DRAIN, EXHAUST, IMPOVERISH, BANKRUPT *shared meaning element* : to deprive of something essential to existence or potency

de·plor·able \di-'plōr-ə-bəl, -'plȯr-\ *adj* **1** : LAMENTABLE **2** : BAD, WRETCHED — **de·plor·able·ness** *n* — **de·plor·ably** \-blē\ *adv*

de·plore \di-'plō(ə)r, -'plȯ(ə)r\ *vt* **de·plored; de·plor·ing** [MF or L; MF *deplorer*, fr. L *deplorare*, fr. *de-* + *plorare* to wail] **1 a** : to feel or express grief for **b** : to regret strongly **2** : to consider unfortunate or deserving of deprecation — **de·plor·er** \-'plōr-ər\ *n* — **de·plor·ing·ly** \-iŋ-lē\ *adv*

syn DEPLORE, LAMENT, BEWAIL, BEMOAN *shared meaning element* : to manifest grief or sorrow for something

de·ploy \di-'plȯi\ *vb* [F *déployer*, fr. L *displicare* to scatter — more at DISPLAY] *vt* **1 a** : to extend (a military unit) esp. in width **b** : to place in battle formation or appropriate positions **2** : to spread out, utilize, or arrange esp. strategically ~ *vi* : to move in being deployed — **de·ploy·able** \-ə-bəl\ *adj* — **de·ploy·ment** \-mənt\ *n*

de·plume \(')dē-'plüm\ *vt* [ME *deplumen*, fr. MF *deplumer*, fr. ML *deplumare*, fr. L *de-* + *pluma* feather — more at FLEECE] **1** : to pluck off the feathers of **2** : to strip of possessions, honors, or attributes

de·po·lar·ize \(')dē-'pō-lə-,rīz\ *vt* **1** : to cause to become partially or wholly unpolarized **2** : to prevent or remove polarization of (as a dry cell or cell membrane) **3** : DEMAGNETIZE — **de·po·lar·iza·tion** \(,)dē-,pō-lə-rə-'zā-shən\ *n* — **de·po·lar·iz·er** \(')dē-'pō-lə-,rī-zər\ *n*

de·po·lit·i·cize \,dē-pə-'lit-ə-,sīz\ *vt* : to remove the political character of : take out of the realm of politics <~ our foreign aid program>

de·pone \di-'pōn\ *vb* **de·poned; de·pon·ing** [ML *deponere*, fr. L, to put down, fr. *de-* + *ponere* to put — more at POSITION] : TESTIFY

[1]**de·po·nent** \di-'pō-nənt\ *adj* [LL *deponent-*, *deponens*, fr. L, prp. of *deponere*] : occurring with passive or middle voice forms but with active voice meaning <the ~ verbs in Latin and Greek>

[2]**deponent** *n* **1** : a deponent verb **2** : one who gives evidence

de·pop·u·late \(')dē-'päp-yə-,lāt\ *vt* [L *depopulatus*, pp. of *depopulari*, fr. *de-* + *populari* to ravage] **1** *obs* : RAVAGE **2** : to reduce greatly the population of — **de·pop·u·la·tion** \(,)dē-,päp-yə-'lā-shən\ *n* — **de·pop·u·la·tor** \(')dē-'päp-yə-,lāt-ər\ *n*

de·port \di-'pō(ə)rt, -'pȯ(ə)rt\ *vt* [MF *deporter*, fr. L *deportare* to carry away, fr. *de-* + *portare* to carry — more at FARE] **1** : to behave or comport (oneself) esp. in accord with a code **2** [L *deportare*] **a** : to carry away **b** : to send out of the country by legal deportation ***syn*** see BANISH, BEHAVE

de·port·able \di-'pōrt-ə-bəl, -'pȯrt-\ *adj* **1** : subject to deportation <~ aliens> **2** : punishable by deportation <~ offenses>

de·por·ta·tion \,dē-,pōr-'tā-shən, -,pȯr-, -pər-\ *n* **1** : an act or instance of deporting **2** : the removal from a country of an alien whose presence is unlawful or prejudicial

de·por·tee \,dē-,pōr-'tē, di-, -,pȯr-\ *n* : one who has been deported or is under sentence of deportation

de·port·ment \di-'pōrt-mənt, -'pȯrt-\ *n* : the manner in which one conducts oneself : BEHAVIOR ***syn*** see BEARING

de·pos·al \di-'pō-zəl\ *n* : an act of deposing from office

de·pose \di-'pōz\ *vb* **de·posed; de·pos·ing** [ME *deposen*, fr. OF *deposer*, fr. LL *deponere* (perf. indic. *deposui*), fr. L, to put down] *vt* **1** : to remove from a throne or other high position **2** : to put down : DEPOSIT **3 a** [ME *deposen*, fr. ML *deponere*, fr. LL] : to testify to under oath or by affidavit **b** : AFFIRM, ASSERT ~ *vi* : to bear witness

[1]**de·pos·it** \di-'päz-ət\ *vb* **de·pos·it·ed** \-'päz-ət-əd, -'päz-təd\; **de·pos·it·ing** \-'päz-ət-iŋ, -'päz-tiŋ\ [L *depositus*, pp. of *deponere*] *vt* **1** : to place esp. for safekeeping or as a pledge; *esp* : to put in a bank **2 a** : to lay down : PLACE **b** : to let fall (as sediment) ~ *vi* : to become deposited : SETTLE — **de·pos·i·tor** \-'päz-ət-ər, -'päz-tər\ *n*

[2]**deposit** *n* **1** : the state of being deposited **2** : something placed for safekeeping: as **a** : money deposited in a bank **b** : money given as a pledge or down payment **3** : a place of deposit : DEPOSITORY **4** : an act of depositing **5 a** : something laid down; *esp* : matter deposited by a natural process **b** : a natural accumulation (as of iron ore, coal, or gas)

de·pos·i·tary \di-'päz-ə-,ter-ē\ *n, pl* **-tar·ies** **1** : a person to whom something is entrusted **2** : DEPOSITORY 2

de·po·si·tion \,dep-ə-'zish-ən, ,dē-pə-\ *n* **1** : an act of removing from a position of authority **2 a** : a testifying esp. before a court **b** : DECLARATION; *specif* : testimony taken down in writing under oath **3** : an act or process of depositing **4** : something deposited : DEPOSIT — **de·po·si·tion·al** \-'zish-nəl, -ən-ᵊl\ *adj*

de·pos·i·to·ry \di-'päz-ə-,tōr-ē, -,tȯr-\ *n, pl* **-ries** **1** : DEPOSITARY 1 **2** : a place where something is deposited esp. for safekeeping

depository library *n* : a library designated to receive U.S. government publications

deposit slip *n* : a slip listing and accompanying bank deposits

de·pot *1 & 2 are* 'dep-(,)ō *also* 'dēp-, *3 is* 'dēp- *sometimes* 'dep-\ *n* [F *dépôt*, fr. ML *depositum*, fr. L, neut. of *depositus*] **1 a** : a place for the storage of military supplies **b** : a place for the reception and forwarding of military replacements **2 a** : a place for storing goods or motor vehicles **b** : STORE, DEPOSIT, COLLECTION, CACHE **3** : a building for railroad or bus passengers or freight : STATION

depr *abbr* **1** depreciation **2** depression

de·prave \di-'prāv\ *vt* **de·praved; de·prav·ing** [ME *depraven*, fr. MF *depraver*, fr. L *depravare* to pervert, fr. *de-* + *pravus* crooked, bad — more at PRAIRIE] **1** *archaic* : to speak ill of : MALIGN **2** : to make bad : CORRUPT; *esp* : to corrupt morally ***syn*** see DEBASE — **de·pra·va·tion** \,dep-rə-'vā-shən, ,dē-,prā-\ *n* — **de·prave·ment** \di-'prāv-mənt\ *n* — **de·prav·er** \di-'prā-vər\ *n*

de·praved \di-'prāvd\ *adj* : marked by corruption or evil; *esp* : PERVERTED — **de·praved·ly** \-'prā-vəd-lē, -'prāv-dlē\ *adv* — **de·praved·ness** \-'prā-vəd-nəs, -'prāv(d)-nəs\ *n*

de·prav·i·ty \di-'prav-ət-ē *also* -'prāv-\ *n, pl* **-ties** **1** : the quality or state of being depraved **2** : a corrupt act or practice

dep·re·cate \'dep-ri-,kāt\ *vt* **-cat·ed; -cat·ing** [L *deprecatus*, pp. of *deprecari* to avert by prayer, fr. *de-* + *precari* to pray — more at PRAY] **1** : to express mild or regretful disapproval of **2** : DEPRECIATE ***syn*** see DISAPPROVE ***ant*** endorse — **dep·re·cat·ing·ly** \-,kāt-iŋ-lē\ *adv* — **dep·re·ca·tion** \,dep-ri-'kā-shən\ *n*

dep·re·ca·to·ry \'dep-ri-kə-,tōr-ē, -,tȯr-\ *adj* **1** : seeking to avert disapproval : APOLOGETIC **2** : serving to deprecate : DISAPPROVING — **dep·re·ca·to·ri·ly** \,dep-ri-kə-'tōr-ə-lē, -'tȯr-\ *adv*

de·pre·ci·ate \di-'prē-shē-,āt\ *vb* **-at·ed; -at·ing** [LL *depretiatus*, pp. of *depretiare*, fr. L *de-* + *pretium* price — more at PRICE] *vt* **1** : to lower the price or estimated value of **2** : to represent as of little value and esp. as of less value than usu. assigned : DISPARAGE ~ *vi* : to fall in value ***syn*** see DECRY ***ant*** appreciate — **de·pre·cia·ble** \-shə-bəl\ *adj* — **de·pre·ci·at·ing·ly** \-shē-,āt-iŋ-lē\ *adv* — **de·pre·ci·a·tion** \-,prē-shē-'ā-shən\ *n* — **de·pre·ci·a·tive** \-'prē-shət-iv, -shē-,āt-iv\ *adj* — **de·pre·ci·a·tor** \-shē-,āt-ər\ *n* — **de·pre·cia·to·ry** \-shə-,tōr-ē, -,tȯr-\ *adj*

dep·re·date \'dep-rə-,dāt\ *vb* **-dat·ed; -dat·ing** [LL *depraedatus*, pp. of *depraedari*, fr. L *de-* + *praedari* to plunder — more at PREY] *vt* : to lay waste : PLUNDER, RAVAGE ~ *vi* : to engage in plunder — **dep·re·da·tion** \,dep-rə-'dā-shən\ *n* — **de·pre·da·tor** \'dep-rə-,dāt-ər, di-'pred-ət-\ *n* — **de·pre·da·to·ry** \di-'pred-ə-,tōr-ē, 'dep-ri-də-, -,tȯr-\ *adj*

de·press \di-'pres\ *vt* [ME *depressen*, fr. MF *depresser*, fr. L *depressus*, pp. of *deprimere* to press down, fr. *de-* + *premere* to press — more at PRESS] **1** *obs* : REPRESS, SUBJUGATE **2 a** : to press down <~ a typewriter key> **b** : to cause to sink to a lower position **3** : to lessen the activity or strength of **4** : SADDEN, DISCOURAGE **5** : to decrease the market value or marketability of — **de·press·ible** \-ə-bəl\ *adj* — **de·press·ing·ly** \-iŋ-lē\ *adv*

de·pres·sant \di-'pres-ᵊnt\ *n* : one that depresses; *specif* : an agent that reduces bodily functional activity — **depressant** *adj*

de·pressed *adj* **1** : low in spirits : SAD **2 a** : vertically flattened <a ~ cactus> **b** : having the central part lower than the margin **c** : lying flat or prostrate **d** : dorsoventrally flattened **3** : suffering from economic depression; *esp* : UNDERPRIVILEGED **4** : being below the standard <his reading achievement is ~>

de·press·ing *adj* : that depresses; *esp* : causing emotional depression <a ~ story> — **de·press·ing·ly** \-iŋ-lē\ *adv*

de·pres·sion \di-'presh-ən\ *n* **1 a** : the angular distance of a celestial object below the horizon **b** : the size of an angle of depression **2** : an act of depressing or a state of being depressed: as **a** : a pressing down : LOWERING **b** (1) : a state of feeling sad : DEJECTION (2) : a psychoneurotic or psychotic disorder marked by sadness, inactivity, difficulty in thinking and concentration, and feelings of dejection **c** (1) : a reduction in activity, amount, quality, or force (2) : a lowering of vitality or functional activity **3** : a depressed place or part : HOLLOW **4** : LOW 1b **5** : a period of low general economic activity marked esp. by rising levels of unemployment

[1]**de·pres·sive** \di-'pres-iv\ *adj* **1** : tending to depress **2** : of or relating to psychological depression — **de·pres·sive·ly** *adv*

[2]**depressive** *n* : one who is psychologically depressed

de·pres·sor \di-'pres-ər\ *n* [LL, fr. L *depressus*] : one that depresses: as **a** : a muscle that draws down a part — compare LEVATOR **b** : a device for pressing a part down or aside **c** : a nerve or nerve fiber that decreases the activity or the tone of the organ or part it innervates

de·pri·va·tion \,dep-rə-'vā-shən, ,dē-,prī-\ *n* **1** : an act or instance of depriving : LOSS **2** : the state of being deprived : PRIVATION; *specif* : removal from an office, dignity, or benefice

de·prive \di-'prīv\ *vt* **de·prived; de·priv·ing** [ME *depriven*, fr. ML *deprivare*, fr. L *de-* + *privare* to deprive — more at PRIVATE] **1** *obs* : REMOVE **2** : to take something away from <a reorganization of the school . . . *deprived* him of his professorship —J. M. Phalen> **3** : to remove from office **4** : to withhold something from <a citizen *deprived* by accident of birth of one of his . . . rights —L. M. Chamberlain>

de·prived *adj* : marked by deprivation esp. of the necessities of life or of healthful environmental influences <culturally ~ children>

dept *abbr* department

depth \'depth\ *n, pl* **depths** \'dep(t)s, 'depths\ [ME, prob. fr. *dep* deep] **1 a** (1) : a deep place in a body of water (2) : a part that is far from the outside or surface <the ~*s* of the woods> (3) : ABYSS **b** (1) : a profound or intense state (as of thought or feeling) <the ~*s* of reflection>; *also* : a reprehensibly low condition <hadn't realized that standards had fallen to such ~*s*> (2) : the middle of a time (as winter) (3) : an extreme state (as of misery) (4) : the worst part **2 a** : the perpendicular measurement downward from a surface **b** : the direct linear measurement from the point of viewing usu. from front to back **3** : the quality of being deep **4** : the degree of intensity <~ of a color>; *also* : the quality of being profound (as in insight) or full (as of knowledge) **5 :** the quality or state of being complete or thorough : THOROUGHNESS <~ of indexing> — **depth·less** \'depth-ləs\ *adj* — **beyond one's depth** *or* **out of one's depth** **1 :** in water that is deeper than one's height **2 :** beyond one's ability to understand — **in depth** **1 :** extending over a considerable distance <these fortifications are built *in depth* —Max Werner> **2 :** with great thoroughness <a study *in depth* of the poems>

depth charge *n* **:** an explosive projectile for use underwater esp. against submarines — called also *depth bomb*

depth interview *n* **:** an interview designed to probe attitudes, feelings, or motives not usu. tapped by the asking of standard questions

depth perception *n* **:** the ability to judge the distance of objects and the spatial relationship of objects at different distances

depth psychology *n* **:** PSYCHOANALYSIS

dep·u·ta·tion \ˌdep-yə-'tā-shən\ *n* **1 :** the act of appointing a deputy **2 :** a group of people appointed to represent others

de·pute \di-'pyüt\ *vt* **de·put·ed; de·put·ing** [ME *deputen* to appoint, fr. MF *deputer,* fr. LL *deputare* to assign, fr. L, to consider (as), fr. *de-* + *putare* to consider — more at PAVE] **:** DELEGATE, ASSIGN

dep·u·tize \'dep-yə-ˌtīz\ *vb* **-tized; -tiz·ing** *vt* **:** to appoint as deputy ~ *vi* **:** to act as deputy — **dep·u·ti·za·tion** \ˌdep-yət-ə-'zā-shən\ *n*

dep·u·ty \'dep-yət-ē\ *n, pl* **-ties** [ME, fr. MF *deputé,* pp. of *deputer*] **1 a :** a person appointed as a substitute with power to act **b :** a second-in-command or assistant who usu. takes charge when his superior is absent **2 :** a member of the lower house of some legislative assemblies

der *or* **deriv** *abbr* derivation; derivative

de·rac·i·nate \(ˈ)dē-'ras-ᵊn-ˌāt\ *vt* **-nat·ed; -nat·ing** [F *déraciner,* fr. MF *desraciner,* fr. *des-* de- + *racine* root, fr. LL *radicina,* fr. L *radic-, radix* — more at ROOT] **:** UPROOT — **de·rac·i·na·tion** \(ˌ)dē-ˌras-ᵊn-'ā-shən\ *n*

de·rail \di-'rā(ə)l\ *vb* [F *dérailler,* fr. *dé-* de- + *rail,* fr. E] *vt* **1 :** to cause to run off the rails **2 :** to throw off course ~ *vi* **:** to leave the rails — **de·rail·ment** \-mənt\ *n*

de·rail·leur \di-'rā-lər\ *n* [F *dérailleur,* fr. *dérailler* to throw off the track, fr. *dé-* de- + *rail* rail, fr. E] **:** a mechanism for shifting gears on a bicycle that operates by moving the chain from one set of exposed gears to another; *also* **:** a bicycle having such a mechanism

de·range \di-'rānj\ *vt* **de·ranged; de·rang·ing** [F *déranger,* fr. OF *desrengier,* fr. *de-* + *reng* place — more at RANK] **1 :** DISARRANGE <hatless, with tie *deranged* —G. W. Stonier> **2 :** to disturb the operation or functions of **3 :** to make insane — **de·range·ment** \-mənt\ *n*

der·by \'dər-bē, *esp Brit* 'där-\ *n, pl* **derbies** [Edward Stanley †1834, 12th earl of *Derby*] **1 :** any of several horse races held annually and usu. restricted to three-year-olds **2 :** a race or contest open to all comers or to a specified category of contestants <bicycle ~> **3 :** a man's stiff felt hat with dome-shaped crown and narrow brim

derby 3

Derbys *abbr* Derbyshire

de·re·al·iza·tion \(ˌ)dē-ˌrē-ə-lə-'zā-shən, -ˌri-ə-\ *n* **:** a feeling of altered reality that occurs often in schizophrenia and in some drug reactions

de·reg·u·la·tion \(ˌ)dē-ˌreg-yə-'lā-shən\ *n* **:** the act or process of removing restrictions and regulations (as on the taxi industry) — **de·reg·u·late** \(ˈ)dē-'reg-yə-ˌlāt\ *vt*

[1]**der·e·lict** \'der-ə-ˌlikt\ *adj* [L *derelictus,* pp. of *derelinquere* to abandon, fr. *de-* + *relinquere* to leave — more at RELINQUISH] **1 :** abandoned esp. by the owner or occupant **:** RUN-DOWN **2 :** lacking a sense of duty **:** NEGLIGENT

[2]**derelict** *n* **1 a :** something voluntarily abandoned; *specif* **:** a ship abandoned on the high seas **b :** a tract of land left dry by receding water **2 :** a person no longer able to support himself **:** BUM

der·e·lic·tion \ˌder-ə-'lik-shən\ *n* **1 a :** an intentional abandonment **b :** the state of being abandoned **2 :** a recession of water leaving permanently dry land **3 a :** intentional or conscious neglect **:** DELINQUENCY <~ of duty> **b :** FAULT, SHORTCOMING

de·re·press \ˌdē-ri-'pres\ *vt* **:** to activate (a gene) by releasing from a blocked state — **de·re·pres·sion** \-'presh-ən\ *n*

de·ride \di-'rīd\ *vt* **de·rid·ed; de·rid·ing** [L *deridēre,* fr. *de-* + *ridēre* to laugh — more at RIDICULOUS] **1 :** to laugh at contemptuously **2 :** to subject to usu. bitter or contemptuous ridicule ***syn*** see RIDICULE — **de·rid·er** *n* — **de·rid·ing·ly** \-'rīd-iŋ-lē\ *adv*

de ri·gueur \də-(ˌ)rē-'gər\ *adj* [F] **:** prescribed or required by fashion, etiquette, or custom **:** PROPER <instructions as to when and where a tuxedo is *de rigueur*>

de·ri·sion \di-'rizh-ən\ *n* [ME, fr. MF, fr. LL *derision-, derisio,* fr. L *derisus,* pp. of *deridēre*] **1 a :** an act of deriding **b :** a state of being derided **2 :** an object of ridicule or scorn **:** LAUGHINGSTOCK

de·ri·sive \di-'rī-siv, -ziv; -'riz-iv, -'ris-\ *adj* **:** expressing or causing derision — **de·ri·sive·ly** *adv* — **de·ri·sive·ness** *n*

de·ri·so·ry \di-'rī-sə-rē, -zə-\ *adj* **1 :** expressing derision **:** DERISIVE <scornful ~ smiles —Katherine A. Porter> **2 :** worthy of derision **:** RIDICULOUS

de·riv·able \di-'rī-və-bəl\ *adj* **:** capable of being derived

der·i·vate \'der-ə-ˌvāt\ *n* **:** DERIVATIVE

der·i·va·tion \ˌder-ə-'vā-shən\ *n* **1 a (1) :** the formation of a word from another word or base (as by the addition of a usu. noninflectional affix) **(2) :** an act of ascertaining or stating the derivation of a word **(3) :** ETYMOLOGY 1 **b :** the relation of a word to its base **2 a :** SOURCE, ORIGIN **b :** DESCENT, ORIGINATION **3 :** something derived **:** DERIVATIVE **4 :** an act or process of deriving **5 :** a sequence of statements (as in logic or mathematics) showing that a result (as a formula) is a necessary consequence of previously accepted statements — **der·i·va·tion·al** \-shnəl, -shən-ᵊl\ *adj*

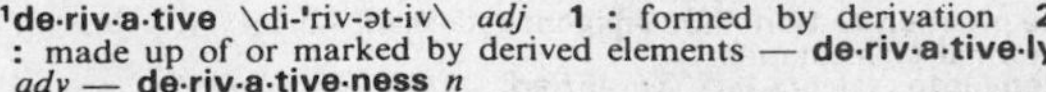

[1]**de·riv·a·tive** \di-'riv-ət-iv\ *adj* **1 :** formed by derivation **2 :** made up of or marked by derived elements — **de·riv·a·tive·ly** *adv* — **de·riv·a·tive·ness** *n*

[2]**derivative** *n* **1 :** a word formed by derivation **2 :** something derived **3 :** the limit of the ratio of the change in a function to the corresponding change in its independent variable as the latter change approaches zero **4 a :** a chemical substance related structurally to another substance and theoretically derivable from it **b :** a substance that can be made from another substance in one or more steps

de·rive \di-'rīv\ *vb* **de·rived; de·riv·ing** [ME *deriven,* fr. MF *deriver,* fr. L *derivare,* fr. *de-* + *rivus* stream — more at RISE] *vt* **1 a :** to take or receive esp. from a specified source **b :** to obtain from a specified source; *specif* **:** to obtain (a chemical substance) actually or theoretically from a parent substance **2 :** INFER, DEDUCE **3** *archaic* **:** BRING **4 :** to trace the derivation of ~ *vi* **:** to have or take origin **:** come as a derivative ***syn*** see SPRING — **de·riv·er** *n*

[1]**derm** \'dərm\ *n* [NL *derma* & *dermis*] **1 :** DERMIS **2 :** SKIN 2a **3 :** CUTICLE 1a

[2]**derm** *abbr* dermatologist; dermatology

derm- *or* **derma-** *or* **dermo-** *comb form* [NL, fr. Gk *derm-, dermo-,* fr. *derma,* fr. *derein* to skin — more at TEAR] **:** skin <*derm*al> <*dermo*tropic>

-derm \ˌdərm\ *n comb form* [prob. fr. F *-derme,* fr. Gk *derma*] **:** skin **:** covering <ecto*derm*>

der·ma \'dər-mə\ *n* [NL, fr. Gk] **:** DERMIS

-der·ma \'dər-mə\ *n comb form, pl* **-dermas** *or* **-der·ma·ta** \-mət-ə\ [NL, fr. Gk *dermat-, derma* skin] **:** skin or skin ailment of a (specified) type <sclero*derma*>

der·mal \'dər-məl\ *adj* **1 :** of or relating to skin and esp. to the dermis **:** CUTANEOUS **2 :** EPIDERMAL

der·map·ter·an \(ˌ)dər-'map-tə-rən\ *n* [NL *Dermaptera,* order name, fr. *derm-* + Gk *pteron* wing — more at FEATHER] **:** any of an order (Dermaptera) of insects consisting of the earwigs and usu. a few related forms — **dermapteran** *adj* — **der·map·ter·ous** \-tə-rəs\ *adj*

dermat- *or* **dermato-** *comb form* [Gk, fr. *dermat-, derma*] **:** skin <*dermat*itis> <*dermato*logy>

der·ma·ti·tis \ˌdər-mə-'tīt-əs\ *n* **:** inflammation of the skin

der·mat·o·gen \(ˌ)dər-'mat-ə-jən\ *n* [ISV] **:** the outer primary meristem of a plant or plant part

der·ma·to·glyph·ics \ˌdər-mət-ə-'glif-iks\ *n pl but sing or pl in constr* [*dermat-* + Gk *glyphein* to carve + E *-ics* — more at CLEAVE] **1 :** skin patterns; *esp* **:** patterns of the specialized skin of the inferior surfaces of the hands and feet **2 :** the science of the study of skin patterns — **der·ma·to·glyph·ic** \-ik\ *adj*

der·ma·toid \'dər-mə-ˌtȯid\ *adj* **:** resembling skin

der·ma·tol·o·gy \ˌdər-mə-'täl-ə-jē\ *n* **:** a branch of science dealing with the skin, its structure, functions, and diseases — **der·ma·to·log·ic** \-mət-ᵊl-'äj-ik\ *or* **der·ma·to·log·i·cal** \-i-kəl\ *adj* — **der·ma·tol·o·gist** \-mə-'täl-ə-jəst\ *n*

der·ma·tome \'dər-mə-ˌtōm\ *n* [ISV *dermat-* + *-ome*] **:** the lateral wall of a somite from which the dermis is produced — **der·ma·to·mic** \ˌdər-mə-'tō-mik, -'täm-ik\ *adj*

der·ma·to·phyte \(ˌ)dər-'mat-ə-ˌfīt, 'dər-mət-\ *n* [ISV] **:** a fungus parasitic on the skin or skin derivatives (as hair or nails) — **der·ma·to·phyt·ic** \(ˌ)dər-ˌmat-ə-'fit-ik, ˌdər-mət-\ *adj*

der·ma·to·sis \ˌdər-mə-'tō-səs\ *n, pl* **-to·ses** \-ˌsēz\ **:** a disease of the skin

-der·ma·tous \'dər-mət-əs\ *adj comb form* [Gk *dermat-, derma* skin] **:** having a (specified) type of skin <sclero*dermatous*>

der·mes·tid \(ˌ)dər-'mes-təd\ *n* [deriv. of Gk *dermēstēs,* a leather-eating worm, lit., skin eater, fr. *derm-* + *edmenai* to eat — more at EAT] **:** any of a family (Dermestidae) of beetles with clubbed antennae that are very destructive to dried meat, fur, wool, and insect collections — **dermestid** *adj*

der·mis \'dər-məs\ *n* [NL, fr. LL *-dermis*] **:** the sensitive vascular inner mesodermic layer of the skin — called also *corium, cutis*

-der·mis \'dər-məs\ *n comb form* [LL, fr. Gk, fr. *derma*] **:** layer of skin or tissue <endo*dermis*>

der·moid \'dər-ˌmȯid\ *also* **der·moi·dal** \(ˌ)dər-'mȯid-ᵊl\ *adj* **1 :** made up of cutaneous elements and esp. ectodermal derivatives <a ~ tumor> **2 :** resembling skin

der·mop·ter·an \(ˌ)dər-'mäp-tə-rən\ *n* [NL *Dermoptera,* order of mammals, fr. *derm-* + Gk *pteron*] **:** FLYING LEMUR — **dermopteran** *adj* — **der·mop·ter·ous** \-tə-rəs\ *adj*

der·mo·tro·pic \ˌdər-mə-'trō-pik, -'träp-ik\ *adj* **:** attracted to, localizing in, or entering by way of the skin <~ viruses>

der·nier cri \ˌdern-ˌyā-'krē\ *n* [F, lit., last cry] **:** the newest fashion

der·o·gate \'der-ə-ˌgāt\ *vb* **-gat·ed; -gat·ing** [LL *derogatus,* pp. of *derogare,* fr. L, to annul (a law), detract, fr. *de-* + *rogare* to ask, propose (a law) — more at RIGHT] *vt* **:** to cause to seem inferior **:** DISPARAGE ~ *vi* **1 :** to take away a part so as to impair **:** DETRACT **2 :** to act beneath one's position or character — **der·o·ga·tion** \ˌder-ə-'gā-shən\ *n* — **de·rog·a·tive** \di-'räg-ət-iv, 'der-ə-ˌgāt-\ *adj*

de·rog·a·to·ry \di-'räg-ə-ˌtōr-ē, -ˌtȯr-\ *adj* **1 :** DEGRADING, DETRACTING **2 :** expressive of a low opinion **:** DISPARAGING — **de·rog·a·to·ri·ly** \-ˌrag-ə-'tor-ə-lē, -'tor-\ *adv*

der·rick \'der-ik\ *n* [obs. *derrick* hangman, gallows, fr. *Derick,* name of 17th cent. E hangman] **1 :** a hoisting apparatus employing a tackle rigged at the end of a beam **2 :** a framework or tower over a deep drill hole (as of an oil well) for supporting boring tackle or for hoisting and lowering

der·ri·ere *or* **der·ri·ère** \ˌder-ē-'e(ə)r\ *n* [F *derrière,* fr. *derrière,* adj., hinder, fr. OF *deriere* adv., behind, fr. L *de retro,* fr. *de* from + *retro* back — more at DE-, RETRO-] **:** BUTTOCKS

der·ring–do \ˌder-iŋ-'dü\ *n* [ME *dorring don* daring to do, fr. *dorring* (gerund of *dorren* to dare) + *don* to do] **:** daring action **:** DARING <deeds of ~>

der·rin·ger \'der-ən-jər\ *n* [Henry *Deringer,* 19th cent. Am inventor] **:** a short-barreled pocket pistol

der·ris \'der-əs\ *n* [NL, genus name, fr. Gk, skin, fr. *derein* to skin — more at TEAR] **1 :** any of a large genus (*Derris*) of leguminous tropical Old World shrubs and woody vines including sources of poisons and esp. commercial sources of rotenone **2 :** a preparation of derris roots and stems used as an insecticide

der·vish \'dər-vish\ *n* [Turk *dervis,* lit., beggar, fr. Per *darvēsh*] **1 :** a member of a Muslim religious order noted for devotional exercises (as bodily movements leading to a trance) **2 :** one that whirls or dances with or as if with the abandonment of a dervish

des- *prefix* [F *dés-,* fr. OF *des-* — more at DE-] **:** DE- 6 — esp. before vowels <*des*oxy->

de·sa·cral·ize \(ˈ)dē-'sā-krə-ˌlīz, -'sak-rə-\ *vt* **-ized; -iz·ing :** to divest ceremonially of supernatural qualities

de·sa·li·nate \(ˈ)dē-'sal-ə-ˌnāt *also* -'sā-lə-\ *vt* **-nat·ed; -nat·ing :** DESALT — **de·sa·li·na·tion** \(ˌ)dē-ˌsal-ə-'nā-shən *also* -ˌsā-lə-\ *n* — **de·sa·li·na·tor** \(ˈ)dē-'sal-ə-ˌnāt-ər *also* -'sā-lə-\ *n*

de·sa·li·nize \(ˈ)dē-'sal-ə-ˌnīz *also* -'sā-lə-\ *vt* **-nized; -niz·ing :** DESALT — **de·sa·li·ni·za·tion** \(ˌ)dē-ˌsal-ə-nə-'zā-shən *also* -ˌsā-lə-\ *n*

de·salt \(ˈ)dē-'sȯlt\ *vt* **:** to remove salt from — **de·salt·er** *n*

1des·cant \'des-ˌkant\ *n* [ME *dyscant,* fr. ONF & ML; ONF *descant,* fr. ML *discantus,* fr. L *dis-* + *cantus* song — more at CHANT] **1 a :** a melody or counterpoint sung above the plainsong of the tenor **b :** the art of composing or improvising contrapuntal part music; *also* **:** the music so composed or improvised **c :** SOPRANO, TREBLE **d :** a superimposed counterpoint to a simple melody sung typically by some or all of the sopranos **2 a :** a song or strain of melody **b :** a musical prelude in which a theme is varied **3 :** discourse or comment on a theme

2des·cant \'des-ˌkant, des-', dis-'\ *vi* **1 a :** to sing or play a descant **b :** SING, WARBLE **2 :** to talk or write at considerable length **:** DILATE <he ~*ed* to his heart's content on his favorite topic —G. B. Shaw>

de·scend \di-'send\ *vb* [ME *descenden,* fr. OF *descendre,* fr. L *descendere,* fr. *de-* + *scandere* to climb — more at SCAN] *vi* **1 :** to pass from a higher place or level to a lower one <~*ed* from the platform> **2 :** to pass in discussion from what is logically prior or more comprehensive **3 a :** to come down from a stock or source **:** DERIVE — usu. used in passive <was ~*ed* from an ancient family> **b :** to pass by inheritance <an heirloom that has ~*ed* in the family> **c :** to pass by transmission <songs ~*ed* from early ballads> **4 :** to incline, lead, or extend downward <the road ~*s* to the river> **5 :** to swoop or pounce down or make a sudden attack <the plague ~*ed* upon them> **6 :** to proceed in a sequence or gradation from higher to lower or from more remote to nearer or more recent **7 a :** to sink in status or dignity **:** STOOP **b :** to worsen and sink in condition or estimation ~ *vt* **1 :** to pass, move, or climb down or down along **2 :** to extend down along — **de·scend·ible** \-'sen-də-bəl\ *adj*

1de·scen·dant *or* **de·scen·dent** \di-'sen-dənt\ *adj* [MF & L; MF *descendant,* fr. L *descendent-, descendens,* prp. of *descendere*] **1 :** moving or directed downward **2 :** proceeding from an ancestor or source

2descendant *or* **descendent** *n* [F & L; F *descendant,* fr. LL *descendent-, descendens,* fr. L, prp. of *descendere*] **1 :** one descended from another or from a common stock **2 :** one deriving directly from a precursor or prototype

de·scend·er \di-'sen-dər, 'dē-ˌ\ *n* **:** the part of a lowercase letter (as p) that descends below the main body of the letter; *also* **:** a letter that has such a part

descending rhythm *n* **:** FALLING RHYTHM

de·scen·sion \di-'sen-chən\ *n, archaic* **:** DESCENT 1

de·scent \di-'sent\ *n* [ME, fr. MF *descente,* fr. *descendre*] **1 :** the act or process of descending from a higher to a lower level or state **2 :** a downward step (as in station or value) **:** DECLINE <~ of the family to actual poverty> **3 a :** derivation from an ancestor **:** BIRTH, LINEAGE <of French ~> **b :** transmission or devolution of an estate by inheritance usu. in the descending line **c :** the fact or process of originating from an ancestral stock **d :** the shaping or development in nature and character by transmission from a source **:** DERIVATION **4 a :** an inclination downward **:** SLOPE **b :** a descending way (as a downgrade or stairway) **c** *obs* **:** the lowest part **5 a :** a sudden disconcerting appearance **b :** a hostile raid or predatory assault **6 :** a step downward in a scale of gradation; *specif* **:** one generation in an ancestral line or genealogical scale

de·scribe \di-'skrīb\ *vt* **de·scribed; de·scrib·ing** [L *describere,* fr. *de-* + *scribere* to write — more at SCRIBE] **1 :** to represent or give an account of in words <~ a picture> **2 :** to represent by a figure, model, or picture **:** DELINEATE **3 :** to trace or traverse the outline of <~ a circle> **4** *obs* **:** DISTRIBUTE **5** *archaic* **:** OBSERVE, PERCEIVE — **de·scrib·able** \-'skrī-bə-bəl\ *adj* — **de·scrib·er** *n*

de·scrip·tion \di-'skrip-shən\ *n* [ME *descripcioun,* fr. MF & L; MF *description,* fr. L *description-, descriptio,* fr. *descriptus,* pp. of *describere*] **1 a :** an act of describing; *specif* **:** discourse intended to give a mental image of something experienced (as a scene, person, or sensation) **b :** a descriptive statement or account <a fascinating ~ of his adventures> **2 :** kind or character esp. as determined by salient features <opposed to any tax of so radical a ~> ***syn*** see TYPE

de·scrip·tive \di-'skrip-tiv\ *adj* **1 :** serving to describe <a ~ account> **2 :** referring to, constituting, or grounded in matters of observation or experience <the ~ basis of science> **3** *of a modifier* **a :** expressing the quality, kind, or condition of what is denoted by the modified term <*hot* in "hot water" is a ~ adjective> **b :** NONRESTRICTIVE **4 :** of, relating to, or dealing with the structure of a language at a particular time usu. with exclusion of historical and comparative data <~ linguistics> — **de·scrip·tive·ly** *adv* — **de·scrip·tive·ness** *n*

de·scrip·tor \di-'skrip-tər\ *n* **:** a word or phrase (as an index term) used to identify an item (as a subject or document) esp. in an information retrieval system; *also* **:** an alphanumeric symbol used similarly

1de·scry \di-'skrī\ *vt* **de·scried; de·scry·ing** [ME *descrien,* fr. OF *descrier* to proclaim, decry] **1 a :** to catch sight of **b :** to find out **:** DISCOVER **2** *obs* **:** to make known **:** REVEAL

2descry *n, obs* **:** discovery or view from afar

Des·de·mo·na \ˌdez-də-'mō-nə\ *n* **:** the wife of Othello in Shakespeare's *Othello*

des·e·crate \'des-i-ˌkrāt\ *vt* **-crat·ed; -crat·ing** [*de-* + *-secrate* (as in *consecrate*)] **1 :** to violate the sanctity of **:** PROFANE **2 :** to treat irreverently or contemptuously — **des·e·crat·er** *or* **des·e·cra·tor** \-ˌkrāt-ər\ *n*

des·e·cra·tion \ˌdes-i-'krā-shən\ *n* **:** an act or instance of desecrating **:** the state of being desecrated ***syn*** see PROFANATION

de·seg·re·gate \(ˈ)dē-'seg-ri-ˌgāt\ *vt* **:** to eliminate segregation in; *specif* **:** to free of any law, provision, or practice requiring isolation of the members of a particular race in separate units ~ *vi* **:** to bring about desegregation

de·seg·re·ga·tion \(ˌ)dē-ˌseg-ri-'gā-shən\ *n* **1 :** the act or process or an instance of desegregating **2 :** the state of being desegregated

de·se·lect \ˌdē-sə-'lekt\ *vt* **:** to dismiss (a trainee) from a training program

de·sen·si·tize \(ˈ)dē-'sen(t)-sə-ˌtīz\ *vt* **1 :** to make (a sensitized or hypersensitive individual) insensitive or nonreactive to a sensitizing agent **2 :** to make (a photographic material) less sensitive or completely insensitive to radiation **3 :** to make emotionally insensitive or callous — **de·sen·si·ti·za·tion** \(ˌ)dē-ˌsen-sət-ə-'zā-shən, -ˌsen-stə-'zā-\ *n* — **de·sen·si·tiz·er** \(ˈ)de-'sen-sə-ˌtī-zər\ *n*

1des·ert \'dez-ərt\ *n* [ME, fr. OF, fr. LL *desertum,* fr. L, neut. of *desertus,* pp. of *deserere* to desert, fr. *de-* + *serere* to join together — more at SERIES] **1** *archaic* **:** a wild uninhabited and uncultivated tract **2 a :** an arid barren tract incapable of supporting any considerable population without an artificial water supply **b :** an area of ocean apparently devoid of marine life **3 :** a desolate or forbidding area <lost in a ~ of doubt> <tiny figures lost in an immense ~ of darkness —Beverley Nichols> — **de·ser·tic** \de-'zərt-ik\ *adj*

2des·ert \'dez-ərt\ *adj* **1** *archaic* **:** FORSAKEN **2 :** desolate and sparsely occupied or unoccupied <a ~ island> **3 :** of or relating to a desert

3de·sert \di-'zərt\ *n* [ME *deserte,* fr. OF, fr. fem. of *desert,* pp. of *deservir* to deserve] **1 :** the quality or fact of deserving reward or punishment **2 :** deserved reward or punishment — usu. used in plural <got his just ~*s*> **3 :** EXCELLENCE, WORTH

4de·sert \di-'zərt\ *vb* [F *déserter,* fr. LL *desertare,* fr. *desertus*] *vt* **1 :** to withdraw from or leave usu. without intent to return **2 a :** to leave in the lurch <~ a friend in trouble> **b :** to abandon (military service) without leave ~ *vi* **:** to quit one's post, allegiance, or service without leave or justification; *esp* **:** to absent oneself from military duty without leave and without intent to return ***syn*** see ABANDON ***ant*** stick (with *to*), cleave (with *to*) — **de·sert·er** *n*

desert boot *n* **:** an ankle-high shoe of tan or brown suede with a rubber sole

de·ser·tion \di-'zər-shən\ *n* **1 :** an act of deserting; *esp* **:** the abandonment without consent or legal justification of a person, post, or relationship and the duties and obligations connected therewith <sued for divorce on grounds of ~> **2 :** a state of being deserted or forsaken **:** DESOLATION

desert locust *n* **:** a destructive migratory locust (*Schistocerca gregaria*) of southwestern Asia and parts of northern Africa

desert soil *n* **:** a soil that develops under sparse shrub vegetation in warm to cool arid climates with a light-colored surface soil usu. underlain by calcareous material and a hardpan layer

de·serve \di-'zərv\ *vb* **de·served; de·serv·ing** [ME *deserven,* fr. OF *deservir,* fr. L *deservire* to serve zealously, fr. *de-* + *servire* to serve] *vt* **:** to be worthy of **:** MERIT <~*s* another chance> ~ *vi* **:** to be worthy, fit, or suitable for some reward or requital <have become recognized as they ~ —T. S. Eliot> — **de·serv·er** *n*

de·served \-'zərvd\ *adj* **:** of, relating to, or being that which one deserves <a ~ reputation> — **de·served·ly** \-'zər-vəd-lē, -'zərv-dlē\ *adv* — **de·served·ness** \-'zər-vəd-nəs, -'zərv(d)-nəs\ *n*

1de·serv·ing \-'zər-viŋ\ *n* **:** DESERT, MERIT <reward the proud according to their ~*s* —Charles Kingsley>

2deserving *adj* **:** MERITORIOUS, WORTHY; *specif* **:** meriting financial aid <scholarships for ~ students>

de·sex \(ˈ)dē-'seks\ *vt* **:** DESEXUALIZE 1

de·sex·u·al·ize \(ˈ)dē-'seksh-(ə-)wə-ˌlīz, -'sek-shə-ˌlīz\ *vt* **1 :** to deprive of sexual characters or power **2 :** to divest of sexual quality — **de·sex·u·al·iza·tion** \(ˌ)dē-ˌseksh-(ə-)wə-lə-'zā-shən, -ˌsek-shə-lə-\ *n*

des·ha·bille \ˌdes-ə-'bē(ə)l, -'bil, -'bē\ *var of* DISHABILLE

des·ic·cant \'des-i-kənt\ *n* **:** a drying agent (as calcium chloride)

des·ic·cate \'des-i-ˌkāt\ *vb* **-cat·ed; -cat·ing** [L *desiccatus,* pp. of *desiccare* to dry up, fr. *de-* + *siccare* to dry, fr. *siccus* dry — more at SACK] *vt* **1 :** to dry up **2 :** to preserve (a food) by drying **:** DEHYDRATE **3 :** to drain of emotional or intellectual vitality ~ *vi* **:** to become dried up — **des·ic·ca·tion** \ˌdes-i-'kā-shən\ *n* — **de·sic·ca·tive** \'des-i-ˌkāt-iv, di-'sik-ət-\ *adj* — **des·ic·ca·tor** \'des-i-ˌkāt-ər\ *n*

de·sid·er·ate \di-'sid-ə-ˌrāt, -'zid-\ *vt* **-at·ed; -at·ing** [L *desideratus,* pp. of *desiderare* to desire] **:** to entertain or express a wish to have or attain — **de·sid·er·a·tion** \-ˌsid-ə-'rā-shən, -ˌzid-\ *n* — **de·sid·er·a·tive** \-'sid-ə-ˌrāt-iv, -'sid-(ə-)rət-, -'zid-\ *adj*

de·sid·er·a·tum \-ˌsid-ə-'rät-əm, -ˌzid-, -'rāt-\ *n, pl* **-ta** \-ə\ [L, neut. of *desideratus*] **:** something desired as essential

1de·sign \di-'zīn\ *vb* [MF *designer,* fr. L *designare,* fr. *de-* + *signare* to mark, mark out — more at SIGN] *vt* **1 a :** to conceive and plan out in the mind <he ~*ed* the perfect crime> **b :** to have as a purpose : INTEND <he ~*ed* to excel in his studies> **c :** to devise for a specific function or end <a book ~*ed* primarily as a college textbook> **2** *archaic* : to indicate with a distinctive mark, sign, or name **3 a :** to make a drawing, pattern, or sketch of **b :** to draw the plans for **c :** to create, fashion, execute, or construct according to plan : DEVISE, CONTRIVE ~ *vi* **1 :** to conceive or execute a plan **2 :** to draw, lay out, or prepare a design — **de·sign·ed·ly** \-'zī-nəd-lē\ *adv* — **de·sign·er** \-'zī-nər\ *n*

2design *n* **1 :** a mental project or scheme in which means to an end are laid down **2 a :** a particular purpose held in view by an individual or group <he has ambitious ~*s* for his son> **b :** deliberate purposive planning <battle was joined . . . more by accident than ~ —John Buchan> **3 a :** a deliberate undercover project or scheme : PLOT **b** *pl* : aggressive or evil intent — used with *on* or *against* <he has ~*s* on the money> **4 :** a preliminary sketch or outline showing the main features of something to be executed : DELINEATION **5 :** an underlying scheme that governs functioning, developing, or unfolding : PATTERN, MOTIF <the general ~ of the epic> **6 :** the arrangement of elements that go into human productions (as of art or machinery) **7 :** a decorative pattern ***syn*** see PLAN, INTENTION

1des·ig·nate \'dez-ig-ˌnāt, -nət\ *adj* [L *designatus,* pp. of *designare*] : chosen for an office but not yet installed <ambassador ~>

2des·ig·nate \-ˌnāt\ *vt* **-nat·ed; -nat·ing 1 a :** to point out the location of <a marker *designating* the crest of the flood waters> **b :** INDICATE <any task *designated* by the employer> **c :** to distinguish as to class <the area we ~ as that of spiritual values —J. B. Conant> **d :** SPECIFY, STIPULATE **2 :** to call by a distinctive title, term, or expression **3 :** to indicate and set apart for a specific purpose, office, or duty **4 :** DENOTE — **des·ig·na·tive** \-ˌnāt-iv\ *adj* — **des·ig·na·tor** \-ˌnāt-ər\ *n* — **des·ig·na·to·ry** \-nə-ˌtōr-ē, -ˌtȯr-\ *adj*

designated hitter *n* : a baseball player designated at the start of the game to bat in place of the pitcher without causing the pitcher to be removed from the game

des·ig·na·tion \ˌdez-ig-'nā-shən\ *n* **1 :** the act of indicating or identifying **2 :** a distinguishing name, sign, or title **3 :** appointment to or selection for an office, post, or service **4 :** the relation between a sign and the thing signified

des·ig·nee \ˌdez-ig-'nē\ *n* : one who is designated

de·sign·ing \di-'zī-niŋ\ *adj* **1 :** practicing forethought **2 :** CRAFTY, SCHEMING <~ widows>

de·sign·ment \di-'zīn-mənt\ *n, obs* : PLAN, PURPOSE

de·si·pra·mine \ˌdez-ə-'pram-ən, də-'zip-rə-ˌmēn\ *n* [*des*methyl + *imipramine*] : a tricyclic drug $C_{18}H_{22}N_2$ used as a psychic stimulant

de·sir·abil·i·ty \di-ˌzī-rə-'bil-ət-ē\ *n, pl* **-ties 1 :** the quality, fact, or degree of being desirable **2** *pl* : desirable conditions <had understood and studied certain *desirabilities* —D. D. Eisenhower>

1de·sir·able \di-'zī-rə-bəl\ *adj* **1 :** having pleasing qualities or properties : ATTRACTIVE <a ~ woman> **2 :** worth seeking or doing as advantageous, beneficial, or wise : ADVISABLE <~ legislation> — **de·sir·able·ness** *n* — **de·sir·ably** \-blē\ *adv*

2desirable *n* : one that is desirable

1de·sire \di-'zī(ə)r\ *vb* **de·sired; de·sir·ing** [ME *desiren,* fr. OF *desirer,* fr. L *desiderare,* fr. *de-* + *sider-, sidus* star] *vt* **1 :** to long or hope for **2 a :** to express a wish for : REQUEST **b :** to express a wish to : ASK **3** *obs* : INVITE **4** *archaic* : to feel the loss of ~ *vi* : to have or feel desire

syn DESIRE, WISH, WANT, CRAVE, COVET *shared meaning element* : to have a longing for something

2desire *n* **1 :** conscious impulse toward an object or experience that promises enjoyment or satisfaction in its attainment **2 a :** LONGING, CRAVING **b :** sexual attraction or appetite **3 :** a usu. formal request or petition for some action **4 :** something desired

de·sir·ous \di-'zī(ə)r-əs\ *adj* : impelled or governed by desire <~ of fame> — **de·sir·ous·ly** *adv* — **de·sir·ous·ness** *n*

de·sist \di-'zist, -'sist\ *vi* [MF *desister,* fr. L *desistere,* fr. *de-* + *sistere* to stand, stop; akin to L *stare* to stand — more at STAND] : to cease to proceed or act ***syn*** see STOP ***ant*** persist — **de·sis·tance** \-'zis-tən(t)s, -'sis-\ *n*

desk \'desk\ *n* [ME *deske,* fr. ML *desca,* modif. of OIt *desco* table, fr. L *discus* dish, disc — more at DISH] **1 a :** a table, frame, or case with a sloping or horizontal surface esp. for writing and reading and often with drawers, compartments, and pigeonholes **b :** a reading table or lectern to support the book from which the liturgical service is read **c :** a table, counter, stand, or booth at which a person performs his duties **d :** a music stand **2 :** a division of an organization specializing in a particular phase of activity <the Russian ~ in the Department of State>

desk·man \'desk-ˌman, -mən\ *n* : one that works at a desk; *specif* : a newspaperman who processes news and prepares copy

desm- *or* **desmo-** *comb form* [NL, fr. Gk, fr. *desmos,* fr. *dein* to bind — more at DIADEM] : bond : ligament <*desmo*cyte>

des·man \'dez-mən\ *n, pl* **desmans** [short for Sw *desmansratta,* fr. *desman* musk + *ratta* rat] : an aquatic insectivorous mammal (*Desmana moschata*) of Russia that resembles a mole

des·mid \'dez-məd\ *n* [deriv. of Gk *desmos*] : any of numerous unicellular or colonial green algae (order Zygnematales)

des·mo·some \'dez-mə-ˌsōm\ *n* [*desm-* + *-some*] : a specialized local thickening of the cell membrane of an epithelial cell that serves to anchor contiguous cells together

1des·o·late \'des-ə-lət, 'dez-\ *adj* [ME *desolat,* fr. L *desolatus,* pp. of *desolare* to abandon, fr. *de-* + *solus* alone — more at SOLE] **1 :** devoid of inhabitants and visitors : DESERTED **2 :** joyless, disconsolate, and sorrowful through or as if through separation from a loved one **3 a :** showing the effects of abandonment and neglect : DILAPIDATED **b :** BARREN, LIFELESS <a ~ landscape> **c :** devoid of warmth, comfort, or hope : GLOOMY <~ memories> ***syn*** see ALONE — **des·o·late·ly** *adv* — **des·o·late·ness** *n*

2des·o·late \-ˌlāt\ *vt* **-lat·ed; -lat·ing :** to make desolate: **a :** to deprive of inhabitants **b :** to lay waste **c :** FORSAKE **d :** to make wretched — **des·o·lat·er** *or* **des·o·la·tor** \-ˌlāt-ər\ *n* — **des·o·lat·ing·ly** \-ˌlāt-iŋ-lē\ *adv*

des·o·la·tion \ˌdes-ə-'lā-shən, ˌdez-\ *n* **1 :** the action of desolating **2 :** the condition of being desolated : DEVASTATION, RUIN <the flood left ~ in its wake> **3 :** barren wasteland **4 a :** GRIEF, SADNESS **b :** LONELINESS

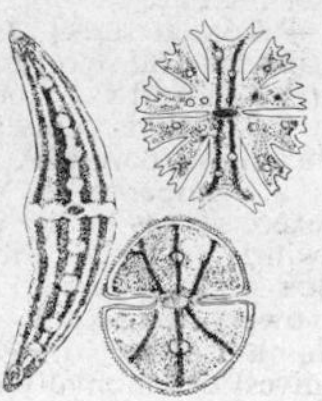
desmids

de·sorb \(ˈ)dē-'sȯ(ə)rb, -'zȯ(ə)rb\ *vt* : to remove (a sorbed substance) by the reverse of adsorption or absorption

de·sorp·tion \-'sȯrp-shən, -'zȯrp-\ *n* : the process of desorbing

desoxy- — see DEOXY-

des·oxy·cor·ti·co·ste·rone \de-ˌzäk-sē-ˌkȯrt-i-'käs-tə-ˌrōn, de-ˌsäk-, -i-kō-stə-'rōn\ *n* : DEOXYCORTICOSTERONE

des·oxy·ri·bo·nu·cle·ic acid \-'rī-bō-n(y)u̇-ˌklē-ik-, -ˌklā-\ *n* : DNA

1de·spair \di-'spa(ə)r, -'spe(ə)r\ *vb* [ME *despeiren,* fr. MF *desperer,* fr. L *desperare,* fr. *de-* + *sperare* to hope; akin to L *spes* hope — more at SPEED] *vi* : to lose all hope or confidence <~ of winning> ~ *vt, obs* : to lose hope for — **de·spair·er** *n*

2despair *n* **1 :** utter loss of hope <~, which may find expression in . . . suicide —Rudyard Kipling> **2 :** a cause of hopelessness <an incorrigible child is the ~ of his parents>

de·spair·ing *adj* : given to, arising from, or marked by despair : devoid of hope ***syn*** see DESPONDENT ***ant*** hopeful — **de·spair·ing·ly** \-iŋ-lē\ *adv*

des·patch \dis-'pach\ *var of* DISPATCH

des·per·a·do \ˌdes-pə-'räd-(ˌ)ō, -'rād-\ *n, pl* **-does** *or* **-dos** [prob. alter. of obs. *desperate* desperado, fr. *desperate,* adj.] : a bold or violent criminal; *esp* : a bandit of the western U.S. in the 19th century

des·per·ate \'des-p(ə-)rət, -pərt\ *adj* [L *desperatus,* pp. of *desperare*] **1 a :** having lost hope <a ~ spirit crying for relief> **b :** giving no ground for hope <his situation was ~> **2 a :** moved by despair <men made ~ by abuse> **b :** involving or employing extreme measures in an attempt to escape defeat or frustration <the bitter, ~ striving unto death of the oppressed race —Rose Macaulay> **3 :** suffering extreme need or anxiety <~ for money> <~ for something to do> **4 :** of extreme intensity : OVERPOWERING **5 :** SHOCKING, OUTRAGEOUS ***syn*** see DESPONDENT — **des·per·ate·ly** *adv* — **des·per·ate·ness** *n*

des·per·a·tion \ˌdes-pə-'rā-shən\ *n* **1 :** loss of hope and surrender to despair **2 :** a state of hopelessness leading to rashness

de·spi·ca·ble \di-'spik-ə-bəl, 'des-(ˌ)pik-\ *adj* [LL *despicabilis,* fr. L *despicari* to despise] : deserving to be despised : so worthless or obnoxious as to rouse moral indignation <a ~ excuse of a father> ***syn*** see CONTEMPTIBLE ***ant*** praiseworthy, laudable — **de·spi·ca·ble·ness** *n* — **de·spi·ca·bly** \-blē\ *adv*

de·spir·i·tu·al·ize \(ˈ)de-'spir-ich-(ə-)wə-ˌlīz, -ich-ə-ˌlīz\ *vt* : to deprive of spiritual character or influence <~ education and you devitalize life —W. L. Sullivan>

de·spise \di-'spīz\ *vt* **de·spised; de·spis·ing** [ME *despisen,* fr. OF *despis-,* stem of *despire,* fr. L *despicere,* fr. *de-* + *specere* to look — more at SPY] **1 :** to look down on with contempt or aversion <*despised* the weak> **2 :** to regard as negligible, worthless, or distasteful — **de·spise·ment** \-'spīz-mənt\ *n* — **de·spis·er** \-'spī-zər\ *n*

syn DESPISE, CONTEMN, SCORN, DISDAIN, SCOUT *shared meaning element* : to regard as beneath one's notice and unworthy of consideration or interest ***ant*** appreciate

1de·spite \di-'spīt\ *n* [ME, fr. OF *despit,* fr. L *despectus,* fr. *despectus,* pp. of *despicere*] **1 :** the feeling or attitude of despising : CONTEMPT **2 :** MALICE, SPITE **3 a :** an act showing contempt or defiance **b :** HARM, INJURY <I know of no government which stands to its obligations, even in its own ~, more solidly —Sir Winston Churchill> — **in despite of :** in spite of

2despite *vt* **de·spit·ed; de·spit·ing 1** *archaic* : to treat with contempt **2** *obs* : to provoke to anger : VEX

3despite *prep* : in spite of : NOTWITHSTANDING <ran ~ his injury>

de·spite·ful \di-'spīt-fəl\ *adj* : expressing malice or hate — **de·spite·ful·ly** \-fə-lē\ *adv* — **de·spite·ful·ness** *n*

de·spit·eous \dis-'pit-ē-əs\ *adj, archaic* : feeling or showing despite : MALICIOUS — **de·spit·eous·ly** *adv, archaic*

de·spoil \di-'spȯi(ə)l\ *vt* [ME *despoylen,* fr. OF *despoillier,* fr. L *despoliare,* fr. *de-* + *spoliare* to strip, rob — more at SPOIL] : to strip of belongings, possessions, or value : PILLAGE — **de·spoil·er** *n* — **de·spoil·ment** \-'spȯi(ə)l-mənt\ *n*

de·spo·li·a·tion \di-ˌspō-lē-'ā-shən\ *n* [LL *despoliation-, despoliatio,* fr. *despoliatus,* pp. of *despoliare*] : the act of plundering : the condition of being despoiled : SPOLIATION

1de·spond \di-'spänd\ *vi* [L *despondēre,* fr. *de-* + *spondēre* to promise solemnly — more at SPOUSE] : to become discouraged or disheartened

2despond *n* : DESPONDENCY

de·spon·dence \di-'spän-dən(t)s\ *n* : DESPONDENCY

de·spon·den·cy \-dən-sē\ *n* : the state of being despondent : DEJECTION, HOPELESSNESS

de·spon·dent \-dənt\ *adj* [L *despondent-, despondens,* prp. of *despondēre*] : feeling extreme discouragement, dejection, or depression <~ about his health> — **de·spon·dent·ly** *adv*

syn DESPONDENT, DESPAIRING, DESPERATE, HOPELESS *shared meaning element* : having lost all or nearly all hope ***ant*** lighthearted

des·pot \'des-pət, -ˌpät\ *n* [MF *despote,* fr. Gk *despotēs;* akin to Skt *dampati* lord of the house; both fr. a prehistoric IE compound whose constituents are akin to L *domus* house and to L *potis* able — more at TIMBER, POTENT] **1 a :** a Byzantine emperor or prince **b :** a bishop or patriarch of the Eastern Orthodox Church **c :** an Italian hereditary prince or military leader during the Renaissance **2 a :** a ruler with absolute power and authority : AUTOCRAT **b :** a person exercising power abusively, oppressively, or tyrannically

des·pot·ic \des-'pät-ik, dis-\ *adj* : of, relating to, or having the characteristics of a despot — **des·pot·i·cal·ly** \-i-k(ə-)lē\ *adv*

des·po·tism \ˈdes-pə-ˌtiz-əm\ *n* **1 a :** rule by a despot **b :** despotic exercise of power **2 a :** a system of government in which the ruler has unlimited power : ABSOLUTISM **b :** a despotic state

des·qua·mate \ˈdes-kwə-ˌmāt\ *vi* **-mat·ed; -mat·ing** [L *desquamatus*, pp. of *desquamare*, fr. *de-* + *squama* scale — more at SQUALOR] **:** to peel off in scales — **des·qua·ma·tion** \ˌdes-kwə-ˈmā-shən\ *n*

des·sert \di-ˈzərt\ *n* [MF, fr. *desservir* to clear the table, fr. *des-* de- + *servir* to serve, fr. L *servire*] **1 :** a course of fruit, pastry, pudding, ice cream, or cheese served at the close of a meal **2** *Brit* **:** a fresh fruit served after a sweet course

des·sert·spoon \-ˌspün\ *n* **:** a spoon intermediate in size between a teaspoon and a tablespoon for use in eating dessert

des·sert·spoon·ful \di-ˌzərt-ˈspün-ˌfu̇l, -ˈzərt-ˌ\ *n* **1 :** as much as a dessertspoon will hold **2 :** a unit of measure equal to about 2½ fluidrams

dessert wine *n* **:** a usu. sweet wine containing over 14 percent alcohol by volume and often served with dessert or between meals

de·sta·bi·lize \(ˈ)dē-ˈstā-bə-ˌlīz\ *vt* **:** to make unstable — **de·sta·bi·li·za·tion** \(ˌ)dē-ˌstā-bə-lə-ˈzā-shən\ *n*

de·stain \(ˈ)dē-ˈstān\ *vt* **:** to selectively remove stain from (a specimen for microscopic study)

de·sta·lin·iza·tion \(ˌ)dē-ˌstäl-ə-nə-ˈzā-shən, -ˌstal-\ *n* **:** the deflation of Stalin and his policies

de·ster·il·ize \(ˈ)dē-ˈster-ə-ˌlīz\ *vt* **:** to release (gold) from an insulated condition in the treasury to useful service

de Stijl \də-ˈstī(ə)l, -ˈstā(ə)l\ *n* [D *De Stijl*, lit., the style, magazine published by members of the school] **:** an influential school of art founded in Holland in 1917 typically using rectangular forms and the primary colors plus black and white and asymmetric balance

des·ti·na·tion \ˌdes-tə-ˈnā-shən\ *n* **1 :** an act of appointing, setting aside for a purpose, or predetermining **2 :** the purpose for which something is destined <a ~ above the objects . . . of this world —J. B. Mozley> **3 :** a place which is set for the end of a journey or to which something is sent <the couple kept their ~ secret>

des·tine \ˈdes-tən\ *vt* **des·tined; des·tin·ing** [ME *destinen*, fr. OF *destiner*, fr. L *destinare*, fr. *de-* + *-stinare* (akin to L *stare* to stand) — more at STAND] **1 :** to decree beforehand : PREDETERMINE **2 a :** to designate, assign, or dedicate in advance <the younger son was *destined* for the church> **b :** to direct, devise, or set apart for a specific purpose or end <freight *destined* for English ports>

des·ti·ny \ˈdes-tə-nē\ *n, pl* **-nies** [ME *destinee*, fr. MF, fr. fem. of *destiné*, pp. of *destiner*] **1 :** something to which a person or thing is destined : FORTUNE **2 :** a predetermined course of events often held to be a resistless power or agency ***syn*** see FATE

des·ti·tute \ˈdes-tə-ˌt(y)üt\ *adj* [ME, fr. L *destitutus*, pp. of *destituere* to abandon, deprive, fr. *de-* + *statuere* to set up — more at STATUTE] **1 :** lacking something needed or desirable <a lake ~ of fish> **2 :** lacking possessions and resources; *esp* **:** suffering extreme want <a ~ old man> — **des·ti·tute·ness** *n*

des·ti·tu·tion \ˌdes-tə-ˈt(y)ü-shən\ *n* **:** the state of being destitute; *esp* **:** such extreme want as threatens life unless relieved ***syn*** see POVERTY

des·trier \ˈdes-trē-ər, də-ˈstri(ə)r\ *n* [ME, fr. OF, fr. *destre* right hand, fr. L *dextra*, fr. fem. of *dexter*] *archaic* **:** WAR-HORSE; *also* **:** a charger used esp. in medieval tournaments

de·stroy \di-ˈstrȯi\ *vb* [ME *destroyen*, fr. OF *destruire*, fr. (assumed) VL *destrugere*, alter. of L *destruere*, fr. *de-* + *struere* to build — more at STRUCTURE] *vt* **1 :** to ruin the structure, organic existence, or condition of : DEMOLISH <priceless art ~*ed* by water> **2 a :** to put out of existence : KILL **b :** NEUTRALIZE <the moon ~*s* the light of the stars> **c :** to subject to a crushing defeat : ANNIHILATE <armies had been crippled but not ~*ed* —W. L. Shirer> ~ *vi* **:** to cause destruction

de·stroy·er \di-ˈstrȯi(-ə)r\ *n* **1 :** one that destroys **2 :** a small fast warship usu. armed with 5-inch guns, depth charges, torpedoes, mines, and sometimes guided missiles

destroyer escort *n* **:** a warship similar to but smaller than a destroyer

destroying angel *n* **:** a very poisonous mushroom (*Amanita phalloides*) varying in color from pure white to olive or yellow and having a prominent volva at the base; *also* **:** a related poisonous mushroom (*A. verna*)

¹de·struct \di-ˈstrəkt\ *vt* [back-formation fr. *destruction*] **:** DESTROY

²de·struct \di-ˈstrəkt, ˈdē-ˌ\ *n* **:** the deliberate destruction of a rocket after launching esp. during a test; *also* **:** the deliberate destruction of a device or material (as to prevent its falling into enemy hands)

de·struc·ti·ble \di-ˈstrək-tə-bəl\ *adj* **:** capable of being destroyed — **de·struc·ti·bil·i·ty** \di-ˌstrək-tə-ˈbil-ət-ē\ *n*

de·struc·tion \di-ˈstrək-shən\ *n* [ME *destruccioun*, fr. MF *destruction*, fr. L *destruction-, destructio*, fr. *destructus*, pp. of *destruere*] **1 :** the action or process of destroying something **2 :** the state or fact of being destroyed : RUIN **3 :** a destroying agency ***syn*** see RUIN

de·struc·tion·ist \-sh(ə-)nəst\ *n* **:** one who delights in or advocates destruction

de·struc·tive \di-ˈstrək-tiv\ *adj* **1 :** causing destruction : RUINOUS <~ storm> **2 :** designed or tending to destroy <~ criticism> — **de·struc·tive·ly** *adv* — **de·struc·tive·ness** *n*

destructive distillation *n* **:** decomposition of a substance (as wood, coal, or oil) by heat in a closed container and collection of the volatile products produced

de·struc·tiv·i·ty \di-ˌstrək-ˈtiv-ət-ē, ˌdē-\ *n* **:** capacity for destruction

de·struc·tor \di-ˈstrək-tər\ *n* **1 :** a furnace for burning refuse : INCINERATOR **2 :** a device for destroying a missile in flight

de·sue·tude \ˈdes-wi-ˌt(y)üd, di-ˈsü-ə-ˌt(y)üd\ *n* [F or L; F *désuétude*, fr. L *desuetudo*, fr. *desuetus*, pp. of *desuescere* to become unaccustomed, fr. *de-* + *suescere* to become accustomed; akin to L *sui* of oneself — more at SUICIDE] **:** discontinuance from use or exercise : DISUSE <after . . . twenty years of innocuous ~ these laws are brought forth —Grover Cleveland>

de·sul·fur·ize \(ˈ)dē-ˈsəl-fə-ˌrīz\ *vt* **:** to remove sulfur or sulfur compounds from — **de·sul·fur·iza·tion** \(ˈ)dē-ˌsəl-fə-rə-ˈzā-shən\ *n*

des·ul·to·ry \ˈdes-əl-ˌtōr-ē, -ˌtȯr- *also* ˈdez-\ *adj* [L *desultorius*, fr. *desultus*, pp. of *desilire* to leap down, fr. *de-* + *salire* to leap — more at SALLY] **1 :** marked by lack of definite plan, regularity, or purpose <a dragged-out ordeal of . . . ~ shopping —Herman Wouk> **2 :** not connected with the main subject ***syn*** see RANDOM ***ant*** assiduous (*as study*), methodical — **des·ul·to·ri·ly** \ˌdes-əl-ˈtōr-ə-lē, ˌdez-, -ˈtȯr-\ *adv* — **des·ul·to·ri·ness** \ˈdes-əl-ˌtōr-ē-nəs, ˈdez-, -ˌtȯr-\ *n*

det *abbr* **1** detached; detachment **2** detail **3** determine

de·tach \di-ˈtach\ *vt* [F *détacher*, fr. OF *destachier*, fr. *des-* de- + *-tachier* (as in *atachier* to attach)] **1 :** to separate esp. from a larger mass and usu. without violence or damage **2 :** DISENGAGE, WITHDRAW — **de·tach·abil·i·ty** \-ˌtach-ə-ˈbil-ət-ē\ *n* — **de·tach·able** \-ˈtach-ə-bəl\ *adj* — **de·tach·ably** \-blē\ *adv*

de·tached \di-ˈtacht\ *adj* **1 :** standing by itself : SEPARATE, UNCONNECTED; *specif* **:** not sharing any wall with another building <~ house> **2 :** exhibiting an aloof objectivity usu. free from prejudice or self-interest <a ~ observer> ***syn*** see INDIFFERENT ***ant*** interested — **de·tached·ly** \-ˈtach-əd-lē, -ˈtach-tlē\ *adv* — **de·tached·ness** \-ˈtach-əd-nəs, -ˈtach(t)-nəs\ *n*

detached service *n* **:** military service away from one's assigned organization

de·tach·ment \di-ˈtach-mənt\ *n* **1 :** the action or process of detaching : SEPARATION **2 a :** the dispatch of a body of troops or part of a fleet from the main body for a special mission or service **b :** the part so dispatched **c :** a permanently organized separate unit usu. smaller than a platoon and different in composition from normal units **3 a :** indifference to worldly concerns : ALOOFNESS **b :** freedom from bias or prejudice

¹de·tail \di-ˈtā(ə)l, ˈdē-ˌtāl\ *n* [F *détail*, fr. OF *detail* slice, piece, fr. *detaillier* to cut in pieces, fr. *de-* + *taillier* to cut — more at TAILOR] **1 :** extended treatment of or attention to particular items **2 :** a part of a whole: as **a :** a small and subordinate part : PARTICULAR; *also* **:** a reproduction of such a part of a work of art **b :** a part considered or requiring to be considered separately from the whole **c :** the small elements that collectively constitute a work of art **d :** the small elements of a photographic image corresponding to those of the subject **3 a :** selection for a particular task (as in military service) of a person or a body of persons **b (1) :** the person or body selected **(2) :** the task to be performed ***syn*** see ITEM

²detail *vt* **1 :** to report minutely and distinctly : SPECIFY <~*ed* his petty grievances> **2 :** to assign to a particular task **3 :** to furnish with the smaller elements of design and finish <trimmings that ~ slips and petticoats> ~ *vi* **:** to make detail drawings — **de·tail·er** *n*

de·tailed \di-ˈtā(ə)ld, ˈdē-ˌtāld\ *adj* **:** marked by abundant detail or by thoroughness in treating small items or parts <the ~ study of history> ***syn*** see CIRCUMSTANTIAL — **de·tailed·ly** \di-ˈtāl(-ə)d-lē, ˈdē-ˌ\ *adv* — **de·tailed·ness** \di-ˈtā-ləd-nəs, -ˈtāl(d)-, ˈdē-ˌ\ *n*

detail man *n* **:** a representative of a drug manufacturer who introduces new drugs esp. to pharmacists and physicians

de·tain \di-ˈtān\ *vt* [ME *deteynen*, fr. MF *detenir*, fr. L *detinēre*, fr. *de-* + *tenēre* to hold — more at THIN] **1 :** to hold or keep in or as if in custody **2** *obs* **:** to keep back (as something due) : WITHHOLD **3 :** to restrain esp. from proceeding : STOP ***syn*** see KEEP, DELAY — **de·tain·ment** \-mənt\ *n*

de·tain·ee \di-ˌtā-ˈnē, ˌdē-\ *n* **:** a person held in custody esp. for political reasons

de·tain·er \di-ˈtā-nər\ *n* [AF *detener*, fr. *detener* to detain, fr. L *detinēre*] **1 :** the act of keeping something in one's possession; *specif* **:** the withholding from the rightful owner of something which has lawfully come into the possession of the holder **2 :** detention in custody **3 :** a writ authorizing the keeper of a prison to continue to hold a person in custody

detd *abbr* determined

de·tect \di-ˈtekt\ *vt* [ME *detecten*, fr. L *detectus*, pp. of *detegere* to uncover, detect, fr. *de-* + *tegere* to cover — more at THATCH] **1 :** to discover the true character of **2 :** to discover or determine the existence, presence, or fact of <~ alcohol in the blood> **3 :** DEMODULATE — **de·tect·abil·i·ty** \-ˌtek-tə-ˈbil-ət-ē\ *n* — **de·tect·able** \-ˈtek-tə-bəl\ *adj*

de·tect·a·phone \-ˈtek-tə-ˌfōn\ *n* **:** a telephonic apparatus with an attached microphone transmitter used esp. for secret listening

de·tec·tion \di-ˈtek-shən\ *n* **1 :** the act of detecting : the state or fact of being detected **2 :** DEMODULATION

¹de·tec·tive \di-ˈtek-tiv\ *adj* **1 :** fitted for or used in detecting something <a ~ device for coal gas> **2 :** of or relating to detectives or their work <a ~ novel>

²detective *n* **:** one employed or engaged in detecting lawbreakers or in getting information that is not readily or publicly accessible

de·tec·tor \di-ˈtek-tər\ *n* **:** one that detects: as **a :** a device for detecting the presence of electric waves or of radioactivity **b :** a rectifier of high-frequency current used esp. for extracting the intelligence from a radio signal

de·tent \ˈdē-ˌtent, di-ˈ\ *n* [F *détente*, fr. MF *destente*, fr. *destendre* to slacken, fr. OF, fr. *des-* de- + *tendre* to stretch, fr. L *tendere* — more at THIN] **:** a device (as a catch, dog, or spring-operated ball) for positioning and holding one mechanical part in relation to another so that the device can be released by force applied to one of the parts

dé·tente \dā-tä^{n}(n)t\ *n* [F] **:** a relaxation of strained relations or tensions (as between nations)
de·ten·tion \di-'ten-chən\ *n* [MF or LL; MF, fr. LL *detention-, detentio,* fr. L *detentus,* pp. of *detinēre* to detain] **1 :** the act or fact of detaining or holding back; *esp* **:** a holding in custody **2 :** the state of being detained; *esp* **:** a period of temporary custody prior to disposition by a court
detention home *n* **:** a house of detention for juvenile delinquents usu. under the supervision of a juvenile court
de·ter \di-'tər\ *vt* **de·terred; de·ter·ring** [L *deterrēre,* fr. *de-* + *terrēre* to frighten — more at TERROR] **1 :** to turn aside, discourage, or prevent from acting (as by fear) **2 :** INHIBIT — **de·ter·ment** \-'tər-mənt\ *n* — **de·ter·rer** \-'tər-ər\ *n*
de·terge \di-'tərj\ *vt* **de·terged; de·terg·ing** [F or L; F *déterger,* fr. L *detergēre,* fr. *de-* + *tergēre* to wipe — more at TERSE] **:** to wash off **:** CLEANSE — **de·terg·er** *n*
de·ter·gen·cy \di-'tər-jən-sē\ *n* **:** cleansing quality or power
[1]de·ter·gent \-jənt\ *adj* **:** that cleanses **:** CLEANSING
[2]detergent *n* **:** a cleansing agent: as **a :** SOAP **b :** any of numerous synthetic water-soluble or liquid organic preparations that are chemically different from soaps but are able to emulsify oils, hold dirt in suspension, and act as wetting agents **c :** an oil-soluble substance that holds insoluble foreign matter in suspension and is used in lubricating oils and dry-cleaning solvents
de·te·ri·o·rate \di-'tir-ē-ə-ˌrāt\ *vb* **-rat·ed; -rat·ing** [LL *deterioratus,* pp. of *deteriorare,* fr. L *deterior* worse, fr. *de-* + *-ter* (suffix as in L *uter* which of two) + *-ior* (compar. suffix) — more at WHETHER, -ER] *vt* **1 :** to make inferior in quality or value **:** IMPAIR **2 :** DISINTEGRATE ~ *vi* **1 :** to grow worse in quality or state <allowed a tradition of academic excellence to ~> **2 :** DEGENERATE
de·te·ri·o·ra·tion \di-ˌtir-ē-ə-'rā-shən\ *n* **:** the action or process of deteriorating **:** the state of having deteriorated
syn DETERIORATION, DEGENERATION, DECADENCE, DECLINE *shared meaning element* **:** a falling from a higher to a lower level (as of quality, character, or vitality) ***ant*** improvement, amelioration
de·te·ri·o·ra·tive \di-'tir-ē-ə-ˌrāt-iv\ *adj* **:** tending to deteriorate
de·ter·min·able \-'tərm-(ə-)nə-bəl\ *adj* **1 :** capable of being determined, definitely ascertained, or decided upon **2 :** liable to be terminated **:** TERMINABLE — **de·ter·min·able·ness** *n* — **de·ter·min·ably** \-blē\ *adv*
de·ter·mi·na·cy \di-'tər-mə-nə-sē\ *n, pl* **-cies 1 :** the quality or state of being determinate **2 a :** the state of being definitely and unequivocally characterized **:** EXACTNESS **b :** the state of being determined or necessitated
de·ter·mi·nant \di-'tərm-(ə-)nənt\ *n* **1 :** an element that identifies or determines the nature of something or that fixes or conditions an outcome **2 :** a square array of numbers bordered on either side by a straight line with a value that is the algebraic sum of all the products that can be formed by taking as factors one element in succession from each row and column and giving to each product a positive or negative sign depending upon whether the number of permutations necessary to place the indices representing each factor's position in its row or column in the order of the natural numbers is odd or even **3 :** GENE; *broadly* **:** a comparable subordinate agent (as a plasmagene) ***syn*** see CAUSE — **de·ter·mi·nan·tal** \-ˌtər-mə-'nant-ᵊl\ *adj*
de·ter·mi·nate \di-'tərm-(ə-)nət\ *adj* [ME, fr. L *determinatus,* pp. of *determinare*] **1 :** having defined limits **:** ESTABLISHED **2 :** definitely settled **:** ARBITRARY **3 :** conclusively determined **:** DEFINITIVE **4 :** CYMOSE **5** *of an egg* **:** undergoing determinate cleavage — **de·ter·mi·nate·ly** *adv* — **de·ter·mi·nate·ness** *n*
determinate cleavage *n* **:** cleavage of an egg in which each division irreversibly separates portions of the zygote with specific potencies for further development
de·ter·mi·na·tion \di-ˌtər-mə-'nā-shən\ *n* **1 a :** a judicial decision settling and ending a controversy **b :** the resolving of a question by argument or reasoning **2** *archaic* **:** TERMINATION **3 a :** the act of deciding definitely and firmly; *also* **:** the result of such an act of decision **b :** the power or habit of deciding definitely and firmly **4 :** a fixing of the position, magnitude, or character of something: as **a :** the act, process, or result of an accurate measurement **b :** an identification of the taxonomic position of a plant or animal **5 a :** the definition of a concept in logic by its essential constituents **b :** the addition of a differentia to a concept to limit its denotation **6 :** direction or tendency to a certain end **:** IMPULSION **7 :** the fixation of the destiny of undifferentiated embryonic tissue
[1]de·ter·mi·na·tive \-'tər-mə-ˌnāt-iv, -'tərm-(ə-)nət-\ *adj* **:** having power or tendency to determine **:** tending to fix, settle, or define something <regard experiments as ~ of the principles from which deductions could be made —S. F. Mason> ***syn*** see CONCLUSIVE — **de·ter·mi·na·tive·ly** *adv* — **de·ter·mi·na·tive·ness** *n*
[2]determinative *n* **:** one that serves to determine
de·ter·mi·na·tor \di-'tər-mə-ˌnāt-ər\ *n* **:** DETERMINER
de·ter·mine \di-'tər-mən\ *vb* **de·ter·mined; de·ter·min·ing** \-'tərm-(ə-)niŋ\ [ME *determinen,* fr. MF *determiner,* fr. L *determinare,* fr. *de-* + *terminare* to limit, fr. *terminus* boundary, limit — more at TERM] *vt* **1 a :** to fix conclusively or authoritatively **b :** to decide by judicial sentence **c :** to settle or decide by choice of alternatives or possibilities **d :** RESOLVE **2 a :** to fix the form or character of beforehand **:** ORDAIN <two points ~ a straight line> **b :** to bring about as a result **:** REGULATE <demand ~*s* the price> **3 a :** to fix the boundaries of **b :** to limit in extent or scope **c :** to put or set an end to **:** TERMINATE <~ an estate> **4 a :** to obtain definite and firsthand knowledge of <~ a position at sea> **b :** to discover the taxonomic position or the generic and specific names of **5 :** to bring about the determination of <~ the fate of a cell> ~ *vi* **1 :** to come to a decision **2 :** to come to an end or become void ***syn*** see DECIDE, DISCOVER
de·ter·mined \-'tər-mənd\ *adj* **1 :** DECIDED, RESOLVED **2 :** FIRM, RESOLUTE — **de·ter·mined·ly** \-mən-dlē, -mə-nəd-lē\ *adv* — **de·ter·mined·ness** \-mən(d)-nəs\ *n*
de·ter·min·er \-'tərm-(ə-)nər\ *n* **:** one that determines: as **a :** GENE, DETERMINANT **b :** a word (as *his* in "his new car") belonging to a group of limiting noun modifiers characterized by occurrence before descriptive adjectives modifying the same noun
de·ter·min·ism \di-'tər-mə-ˌniz-əm\ *n* **1 a :** a doctrine that acts of the will, occurrences in nature, or social or psychological phenomena are determined by antecedent causes **b :** a belief in predestination **2 :** the quality or state of being determined — **de·ter·min·ist** \-(ə-)nəst\ *n or adj* — **de·ter·min·is·tic** \-ˌtər-mə-'nis-tik\ *adj* — **de·ter·min·is·ti·cal·ly** \-ti-k(ə-)lē\ *adv*
de·ter·ra·ble \di-'tər-ə-bəl\ *adj* **:** capable of being deterred — **de·ter·ra·bil·i·ty** \-ˌtər-ə-'bil-ət-ē\ *n*
de·ter·rence \di-'tər-ən(t)s, -'ter-; -'tə-rən(t)s\ *n* **1 :** the act or process of deterring <the penalty for the crime of perjury is often no ~ to lying under oath —*New Republic*> **2 :** the maintaining of vast military power and weaponry in order to discourage war
de·ter·rent \-ənt, -rənt\ *adj* [L *deterrent-, deterrens,* prp. of *deterrēre* to deter] **1 :** serving to deter **2 :** relating to deterrence — **deterrent** *n* — **de·ter·rent·ly** *adv*
de·ter·sive \di-'tər-siv, -ziv\ *adj* [MF *detersif,* fr. L *detersus,* pp. of *detergēre* to deterge] **:** DETERGENT, CLEANSING — **detersive** *n*
de·test \di-'test\ *vt* [ME *detesten,* fr. L *detestari,* lit., to curse while calling a deity to witness, fr. *de-* + *testari* to call to witness — more at TESTAMENT] **1 :** to feel intense and often violent antipathy toward **:** LOATHE **2** *obs* **:** CURSE, DENOUNCE ***syn*** see HATE ***ant*** adore — **de·test·er** *n*
de·test·able \di-'tes-tə-bəl\ *adj* **:** arousing or meriting intense dislike **:** ABOMINABLE — **de·test·able·ness** *n* — **de·test·ably** \-blē\ *adv*
de·tes·ta·tion \ˌdē-ˌtes-'tā-shən, di-\ *n* **1 :** extreme hatred or dislike **:** ABHORRENCE, LOATHING <had a ~ of hypocrites> **2 :** an object of hatred or contempt
de·throne \di-'thrōn\ *vt* **:** to remove from a throne or place of power or prominence **:** DEPOSE — **de·throne·ment** \-mənt\ *n* — **de·thron·er** *n*
de·tick \(')dē-'tik\ *vt* **:** to remove ticks from <dogs should be ~*ed* and sprayed> — **de·tick·er** *n*
det·i·nue \'det-ᵊn-ˌ(y)ü\ *n* [ME *detenewe,* fr. MF *detenue* detention, fr. fem. of *detenu,* pp. of *detenir* to detain] **1 :** detention of something due; *esp* **:** the unlawful detention of a personal chattel from another **2 :** a common-law action for the recovery of a personal chattel wrongfully detained or of its value
detn *abbr* **1** detention **2** determination
det·o·na·ble \'det-ᵊn-ə-bəl, -ə-nə-\ *adj* **:** capable of being detonated — **det·o·na·bil·i·ty** \ˌdet-ᵊn-ə-'bil-ət-ē, ˌdet-ə-nə-\ *n*
det·o·nate \'det-ᵊn-ˌāt, 'det-ə-ˌnāt\ *vb* **-nat·ed; -nat·ing** [L *detonatus,* pp. of *detonare* to thunder down, fr. *de-* + *tonare* to thunder — more at THUNDER] *vi* **:** to explode with sudden violence ~ *vt* **1 :** to cause to detonate <~ an atom bomb> — compare DEFLAGRATE **2 :** to set off in a burst of activity **:** ACTIVATE <has *detonated* a . . . Puerto Rican tourist boom —Horace Sutton> — **det·o·nat·able** \-ˌāt-ə-bəl, -ˌnāt-\ *adj* — **det·o·na·tive** \'det-ᵊn-ˌāt-iv, 'det-ə-ˌnāt-\ *adj*
det·o·na·tion \ˌdet-ᵊn-'ā-shən, ˌdet-ə-'nā-\ *n* **1 :** the action or process of detonating **2 :** rapid combustion in an internal-combustion engine that results in knocking — **det·o·na·tion·al** \-shnəl, -shən-ᵊl\ *adj*
det·o·na·tor \'det-ᵊn-ˌāt-ər, -ə-ˌnāt-\ *n* **:** a device or small quantity of explosive used for detonating a high explosive
[1]de·tour \'dē-ˌtu̇(ə)r *also* di-'\ *n* [F *détour,* fr. OF *destor,* fr. *destorner* to divert, fr. *des-* de- + *torner* to turn — more at TURN] **:** a deviation from a direct course or the usual procedure; *specif* **:** a roundabout way temporarily replacing part of a route
[2]detour *vi* **:** to proceed by a detour <~ around road construction> ~ *vt* **1 :** to send by a circuitous route **2 :** to avoid by going around **:** BYPASS
de·tox·i·cate \(')dē-'täk-sə-ˌkāt\ *vt* **-cat·ed; -cat·ing** [*de-* + L *toxicum* poison — more at TOXIC] **:** DETOXIFY — **de·tox·i·cant** \-si-kənt\ *n* — **de·tox·i·ca·tion** \(ˌ)dē-ˌtäk-sə-'kā-shən\ *n*
de·tox·i·fy \(')dē-'täk-sə-ˌfī\ *vt* **-fied; -fy·ing :** to remove a poison or toxin or the effect of such from — **de·tox·i·fi·ca·tion** \(ˌ)dē-ˌtäk-sə-fə-'kā-shən\ *n*
de·tract \di-'trakt\ *vb* [ME *detracten,* fr. L *detractus,* pp. of *detrahere* to withdraw, disparage, fr. *de-* + *trahere* to draw — more at DRAW] *vt* **1** *archaic* **:** to speak ill of **2** *archaic* **:** to take away **3 :** DIVERT <~ attention> ~ *vi* **:** to take away something — **de·trac·tor** \-'trak-tər\ *n*
de·trac·tion \di-'trak-shən\ *n* **1 :** a lessening of reputation or esteem esp. by envious, malicious, or petty criticism **:** BELITTLING, DISPARAGEMENT **2 :** a taking away <it is no ~ from its dignity or prestige —J. F. Golay> — **de·trac·tive** \-'trak-tiv\ *adj* — **de·trac·tive·ly** *adv*
de·train \(')dē-'trān\ *vi* **:** to get off a railroad train ~ *vt* **:** to remove from a railroad train — **de·train·ment** \-mənt\ *n*
de·trib·al·ize \(')dē-'trī-bə-ˌlīz\ *vt* **-ized; -iz·ing :** to cause to relinquish tribal customs **:** ACCULTURATE — **de·trib·al·iza·tion** \(ˌ)dē-ˌtrī-bə-lə-'zā-shən\ *n*
det·ri·ment \'de-trə-mənt\ *n* [ME, fr. MF or L; MF, fr. L *detrimentum,* fr. *deterere* to wear away, impair, fr. *de-* + *terere* to rub — more at THROW] **1 :** INJURY, DAMAGE <did hard work without ~ to his health> **2 :** a cause of injury or damage <the long strike was a ~ to the industry>
[1]det·ri·men·tal \ˌde-trə-'ment-ᵊl\ *adj* **:** obviously harmful **:** DAMAGING <the ~ effects of heroin> ***syn*** see PERNICIOUS ***ant*** beneficial — **det·ri·men·tal·ly** \-ᵊl-ē\ *adv*
[2]detrimental *n* **:** an undesirable or harmful person or thing
de·tri·tion \di-'trish-ən\ *n* **:** a wearing off or away
de·tri·tus \di-'trīt-əs\ *n, pl* **de·tri·tus** \-'trīt-əs, -'trī-ˌtüs\ [F *détritus,* fr. L *detritus,* pp. of *deterere*] **1 :** loose material (as rock fragments or organic particles) that results directly from disintegration **2 :** a product of disintegration or wearing away — **de·tri·tal** \-'trīt-ᵊl\ *adj*
de trop \də-'trō\ *adj* [F] **:** too much or too many **:** SUPERFLUOUS <a topcoat was *de trop* with the thermometer standing at 72 degrees —Irving Kolodin>

de·tu·mes·cence \ˌdē-t(y)ü-ˈmes-ᵊn(t)s\ *n* : subsidence or diminution of swelling — **de·tu·mes·cent** \-ᵊnt\ *adj*

Deu·ca·lion \d(y)ü-ˈkāl-yən\ *n* [L, fr. Gk *Deukaliōn*] : a survivor with his wife Pyrrha of a great flood by which according to Greek mythology Zeus destroyed the rest of the human race

[1]**deuce** \ˈd(y)üs\ *n* [MF *deus* two, fr. L *duos*, acc. masc. of *duo* two — more at TWO] **1 a** (1) : the face of a die that bears two spots (2) : a playing card bearing an index number two **b** : a throw of the dice yielding two points **2** : a tie in tennis after each side has scored 40 and requiring two consecutive points by one side to win **3** [obs. E *deuce* bad luck] **a** : DEVIL, DICKENS — used chiefly as a mild oath <what the ~ is he up to now> **b** : something notable of its kind <a ~ of a mess>

[2]**deuce** *vt* **deuced; deuc·ing** : to bring the score of (a tennis game or set) to deuce

deuc·ed \ˈd(y)ü-səd\ *adj* : DAMNED, CONFOUNDED <in a ~ fix> — **deuc·ed** *or* **deuc·ed·ly** *adv*

deuces wild *n* : a card game (as poker) in which each deuce may represent any card designated by its holder

de·us ex ma·chi·na \ˌdā-ə-ˌsek-ˈsmäk-i-nə, -ˌnä; -ˈsmak-ə-nə\ *n* [NL, a god from a machine, trans. of Gk *theos ek mēchanēs*] **1** : a god introduced by means of a crane in ancient Greek and Roman drama to decide the final outcome **2** : a person or thing (as in fiction or drama) that appears or is introduced suddenly and unexpectedly and provides a contrived solution to an apparently insoluble difficulty

Deut *abbr* Deuteronomy

deut- *or* **deuto-** *comb form* [ISV, fr. *deuter-*] : second : secondary <*deuto*nymph>

[1]**deuter-** *or* **deutero-** *comb form* [alter. of ME *deutro-*, modif. of LL *deutero-*, fr. Gk *deuter-*, *deutero-*, fr. *deuteros*; prob. akin to L *dudum* formerly, Gk *dein* to lack] : second : secondary <*deutero*genesis>

[2]**deuter-** *or* **deutero-** *comb form* [ISV] : deuterium : containing deuterium <*deuter*ated> <*deutero*alkanes>

deu·ter·ag·o·nist \ˌd(y)üt-ə-ˈrag-ə-nəst\ *n* [Gk *deuteragōnistēs*, fr. *deuter-* + *agōnistēs* combatant, actor — more at PROTAGONIST] **1** : the actor taking the part of second importance in a classical Greek drama **2** : a person who serves as a foil to another

deu·ter·an·ope \ˈd(y)üt-ə-rə-ˌnōp\ *n* : an individual affected with deuteranopia

deu·ter·an·opia \ˌd(y)üt-ə-rə-ˈnō-pē-ə\ *n* [NL, fr. [1]*deuter-* + [2]*a-* + *-opia*; fr. the blindness to green, regarded as the second primary color] : color blindness marked by confusion of purplish red and green — **deu·ter·an·opic** \-ˈnō-pik, -ˈnäp-ik\ *adj*

deu·ter·ate \ˈd(y)üt-ə-ˌrāt\ *vt* **-at·ed; -at·ing** : to introduce deuterium into (a compound) — **deu·ter·a·tion** \ˌd(y)üt-ə-ˈrā-shən\ *n*

deu·te·ri·um \d(y)ü-ˈtir-ē-əm\ *n* [NL, fr. Gk *deuteros* second] : the hydrogen isotope that is of twice the mass of ordinary hydrogen and that occurs in water — called also *heavy hydrogen*

deuterium oxide *n* : heavy water D_2O composed of deuterium and oxygen

deu·tero·ca·non·i·cal \ˌd(y)üt-ə-rō-kə-ˈnän-i-kəl\ *adj* [NL *deuterocanonicus*, fr. [1]*deuter-* + LL *canonicus* canonical] : of, relating to, or constituting the books of Scripture contained in the Septuagint but not in the Hebrew canon

deu·ter·og·a·my \ˌd(y)üt-ə-ˈräg-ə-mē\ *n* [LGk *deuterogamia*, fr. Gk *deuter-* + *-gamia* -gamy] : DIGAMY

deu·tero·gen·e·sis \ˌd(y)üt-ə-rō-ˈjen-ə-səs\ *n* : the appearance of a new adaptive character late in life

deu·ter·on \ˈd(y)üt-ə-ˌrän\ *n* [*deuterium*] : the nucleus of the deuterium atom consisting of one proton and one neutron

Deu·ter·o·nom·ic \ˌd(y)üt-ə-rə-ˈnäm-ik\ *adj* **1** : of or relating to the book of Deuteronomy **2** : marked by the literary style or theological content of Deuteronomy

Deu·ter·on·o·mist \ˌd(y)üt-ə-ˈrän-ə-məst\ *n* : one of the writers or editors of a Deuteronomic body of source material often distinguished in the earlier books of the Old Testament — **Deu·ter·on·o·mis·tic** \-ˌrän-ə-ˈmis-tik\ *adj*

Deu·ter·on·o·my \ˌd(y)üt-ə-ˈrän-ə-mē\ *n* [ME *Deutronomie*, fr. LL *Deuteronomium*, fr. Gk *Deuteronomion*, fr. *deuter-* + *nomos* law — more at NIMBLE] : the fifth book of canonical Jewish and Christian Scripture containing Mosaic laws and narrative material — see BIBLE table

deu·tero·stome \ˈd(y)üt-ə-rə-ˌstōm\ *n* [NL *Deuterostomia*, group name, fr. *deuter-* + Gk *stoma* mouth — more at STOMACH] : any of a major division (Deuterostomia) of the animal kingdom that includes the bilaterally symmetrical animals (as the chordates) with indeterminate cleavage and a mouth that does not arise from the blastopore

deu·to·plasm \ˈd(y)üt-ə-ˌplaz-əm\ *n* [ISV] : the nutritive inclusions of protoplasm; *esp* : the yolk reserves of an egg — **deu·to·plas·mic** \ˌd(y)üt-ə-ˈplaz-mik\ *adj*

deut·sche mark \ˌdȯi-chə-ˈmärk\ *n* [G, German mark] — see MONEY table

deut·zia \ˈd(y)üt-sē-ə\ *n* [NL, fr. Jean *Deutz* †1784? D patron of botanical research] : any of a genus (*Deutzia*) of the saxifrage family of ornamental shrubs with white or pink flowers

dev *abbr* deviation

de·val·u·ate \(ˈ)dē-ˈval-yə-ˌwāt\ *vb* : DEVALUE

de·val·u·a·tion \(ˌ)dē-ˌval-yə-ˈwā-shən\ *n* **1** : an official reduction in the exchange value of a currency by a lowering of its gold equivalency **2** : a lessening esp. of status or stature : DECLINE

de·val·ue \(ˈ)dē-ˈval-(ˌ)yü, -yə(-w)\ *vt* **1** : to institute the devaluation of (money) **2** : to cause or be responsible for a devaluation of (as a person or a literary work) ~ *vi* : to institute devaluation

De·va·na·ga·ri \ˌdā-və-ˈnäg-ə-rē\ *n* [Skt *devanāgarī*, fr. *deva* divine + *nāgarī* script of the city; akin to L *divus* divine — more at DEITY] : an alphabet usu. employed for Sanskrit and also used as a literary hand for various modern languages of India — see ALPHABET table

dev·as·tate \ˈdev-ə-ˌstāt\ *vt* **-tat·ed; -tat·ing** [L *devastatus*, pp. of *devastare*, fr. *de-* + *vastare* to lay waste — more at WASTE] **1** : to bring to ruin or desolation by violent action **2** : to reduce to chaos or disorder : OVERWHELM <her answer *devastated* the class> ***syn*** see RAVAGE — **dev·as·tat·ing·ly** \-ˌstāt-iŋ-lē\ *adv* — **dev·as·tat·ive** \-ˌstāt-iv\ *adj* — **dev·as·ta·tor** \-ˌstāt-ər\ *n*

dev·as·ta·tion \ˌdev-ə-ˈstā-shən\ *n* : the action of devastating : the state of being devastated : DESOLATION ***syn*** see RUIN

de·vel·op \di-ˈvel-əp\ *vb* [F *développer*, fr. OF *desvoloper*, fr. *des-* de- + *voloper* to wrap] *vt* **1 a** : to set forth or make clear by degrees or in detail : EXPOUND **b** : to make visible or manifest **c** : to treat (as in dyeing) with an agent to cause the appearance of color **d** : to subject (exposed photograph material) esp. to chemicals in order to produce a visible image; *also* : to make visible by such a method **e** : to elaborate by the unfolding of a musical idea and by the working out of rhythmic and harmonic changes in the theme **2** : to evolve the possibilities of **3 a** (1) : to make active (2) : to promote the growth of <~*ed* his muscles> **b** : to make available or usable <~ its resources> **c** : to move (a chess piece) from the original position to one providing more opportunity for effective use **4 a** : to cause to unfold gradually <~*ed* his argument> **b** : to expand by a process of growth <~*ed* mature breasts in her early teens> **c** : to cause to grow and differentiate along lines natural to its kind <rain and sun ~ the grain> **5** : to acquire gradually <~ an appreciation for ballet> **6** : to superimpose (a three-dimensional surface) on a plane without stretching ~ *vi* **1 a** : to go through a process of natural growth, differentiation, or evolution by successive changes <a blossom ~*s* from a bud> **b** : to acquire secondary sex characters **c** : EVOLVE, DIFFERENTIATE; *broadly* : GROW **2 a** : to become gradually manifest **b** : to become apparent **3** : to develop one's pieces in chess — **de·vel·op·able** \-ˈvel-ə-pə-bəl\ *adj*

de·vel·op·er \-ə-pər\ *n* : one that develops: as **a** : a chemical used to develop exposed photographic materials **b** : a person who develops real estate; *esp* : one that improves and subdivides land and builds and sells houses thereon

de·vel·op·ment \di-ˈvel-əp-mənt\ *n* **1** : the act, process, or result of developing **2** : the state of being developed **3** : a developed tract of land; *esp* : one that has houses built thereon — **de·vel·op·men·tal** \-ˌvel-əp-ˈment-ᵊl\ *adj* — **de·vel·op·men·tal·ly** \-ᵊl-ē\ *adv*

de·verb·a·tive \(ˈ)dē-ˈvər-bət-iv\ *adj* **1** : derived from a verb <the ~ noun *developer* is derived from *develop*> **2** : used in derivation from a verb <the ~ suffix *-er* in *developer*> — **deverbative** *n*

de·vest \di-ˈvest\ *vt* [MF *desvestir*, fr. ML *disvestire*, fr. L *dis-* + *vestire* to clothe — more at VEST] : DIVEST

de·vi·ance \ˈdē-vē-ən(t)s\ *n* : deviant quality, state, or behavior

de·vi·an·cy \-ən-sē\ *n, pl* **-cies** : DEVIANCE

de·vi·ant \-ənt\ *adj* **1** : deviating esp. from an accepted norm <~ behavior> **2** : characterized by deviation <a ~ child> — **deviant** *n*

[1]**de·vi·ate** \ˈdē-vē-ˌāt\ *vb* **-at·ed; -at·ing** [LL *deviatus*, pp. of *deviare*, fr. L *de-* + *via* way — more at VIA] *vi* **1** : to turn aside esp. from a norm **2** : to stray esp. from a standard, principle, or topic ~ *vt* : to cause to turn out of a previous course ***syn*** see SWERVE — **de·vi·a·tor** \-ˌāt-ər\ *n* — **de·vi·a·to·ry** \-ə-ˌtōr-ē, -ˌtȯr-\ *adj*

[2]**de·vi·ate** \-vē-ət, -vē-ˌāt\ *adj* : characterized by or given to significant departure from the behavioral norms of a particular society

[3]**de·vi·ate** \-vē-ət, -vē-ˌāt\ *n* **1** : one that deviates from a norm; *esp* : a person who differs markedly from his group norm **2** : a statistical variable that gives the deviation of another variable from a fixed value (as the mean)

de·vi·a·tion \ˌdē-vē-ˈā-shən\ *n* : an act or instance of deviating: as **a** : deflection of the needle of a compass caused by local magnetic influences (as in a ship) **b** : the difference between a value in a frequency distribution and a fixed number **c** : evolutionary differentiation involving interpolation of new stages in the ancestral pattern of morphogenesis **d** : departure from an established ideology or party line **e** : noticeable or marked departure from accepted norms of behavior — **de·vi·a·tion·ism** \-shə-ˌniz-əm\ *n* — **de·vi·a·tion·ist** \-sh(ə-)nəst\ *n*

de·vice \di-ˈvīs\ *n* [ME *devis*, *devise*, fr. OF, division, intention, fr. *deviser* to divide, regulate, tell — more at DEVISE] **1** : something devised or contrived: as **a** : a scheme to deceive : STRATEGEM **b** : something fanciful, elaborate, or intricate in design **c** : something (as a figure of speech) in a literary work designed to achieve a particular artistic effect **d** *archaic* : MASQUE, SPECTACLE **e** : a conventional stage practice or means (as a stage whisper) used to achieve a particular dramatic effect **f** : a piece of equipment or a mechanism designed to serve a special purpose or perform a special function **2** : DESIRE, WILL <left to his own ~*s*> **3** : an emblematic design used esp. as a heraldic bearing

[1]**dev·il** \ˈdev-əl\ *n* [ME *devel*, fr. OE *dēofol*, fr. LL *diabolus*, fr. Gk *diabolos*, lit., slanderer, fr. *diaballein* to throw across, slander, fr. *dia-* + *ballein* to throw; akin to OHG *quellan* to well, gush] **1** *often cap* : the personal supreme spirit of evil often represented in Jewish and Christian belief as the tempter of mankind, the leader of all apostate angels, and the ruler of hell — often used as an interjection, an intensive, or a generalized term of abuse **2** : a malignant spirit : DEMON **3 a** : an extremely and malignantly wicked person : FIEND **b** *archaic* : a great evil **4** : a person of notable energy, recklessness, and dashing spirit <a ~ with the ladies> **5 a** : FELLOW, MAN — usu. used in the phrase *poor devil* **b** : PRINTER'S DEVIL **6** : any of various machines or devices (as a paper shredder) **7** *Christian Science* : the opposite of Truth : a belief in sin, sickness, and death : EVIL, ERROR

[2]**devil** *vb* **-iled** *or* **-illed; -il·ing** *or* **-il·ling** \ˈdev-(ə-)liŋ\ *vt* **1** : TEASE, ANNOY **2 :** to season highly <~*ed* eggs> **3 :** to tear to pieces in a devil <~ rags> ~ *vi* : to serve or function as a devil

dev·il·fish \ˈdev-əl-ˌfish\ *n* **1 :** any of several extremely large rays (genera *Manta* and *Mobula*) widely distributed in warm seas **2 :** OCTOPUS; *broadly* : any large cephalopod

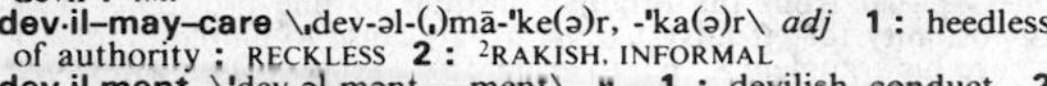

devilfish 1

dev·il·ish \ˈdev-(ə-)lish\ *adj* **1 :** of, relating to, or characteristic of the devil <~ tricks> **2 :** EXTREME, EXCESSIVE <in a ~ hurry> — **dev·il·ish** *adv* — **dev·il·ish·ly** *adv* — **dev·il·ish·ness** *n*

dev·il·kin \ˈdev-əl-kən\ *n* : a little devil : IMP

dev·il–may–care \ˌdev-əl-(ˌ)mā-ˈke(ə)r, -ˈka(ə)r\ *adj* **1 :** heedless of authority ; RECKLESS **2 :** [2]RAKISH, INFORMAL

dev·il·ment \ˈdev-əl-mənt, -ˌment\ *n* **1 :** devilish conduct **2** : reckless mischief

dev·il·ry \ˈdev-əl-rē\ *or* **dev·il·try** \-əl-trē\ *n, pl* **-ilries** *or* **-iltries** **1 a :** action performed with the help of the devil : WITCHCRAFT **b** : gross or malignant cruelty : WICKEDNESS **c :** reckless unrestrained conduct : MISCHIEF **2 :** an act of devilry

devil's advocate *n* [trans. of NL *advocatus diaboli*] **1 :** a Roman Catholic official whose duty is to examine critically the evidence on which a demand for beatification or canonization rests **2 :** a person who champions the less accepted or approved cause for the sake of argument

devil's darning needle *n* **1 :** DRAGONFLY **2 :** DAMSELFLY

dev·il's food cake \ˈdev-əlz-ˌfüd-ˌkāk\ *n* : a rich chocolate cake

devil's paintbrush *n* : ORANGE HAWKWEED; *broadly* : any of various hawkweeds that are naturalized weeds in the eastern U.S.

dev·il·wood \ˈdev-əl-ˌwu̇d\ *n* : a small tree (*Osmanthus americanus*) of the southern U.S. that is related to the olive

de·vi·ous \ˈdē-vē-əs\ *adj* [L *devius*, fr. *de* from + *via* way — more at DE-, VIA] **1 :** OUT-OF-THE-WAY, REMOTE **2 a :** deviating from a straight line : ROUNDABOUT **b :** moving without a fixed course : ERRANT <~ breezes> **3 a :** deviating from a right, accepted, or common course : ERRING **b :** not straightforward **c :** TRICKY ***syn*** see CROOKED ***ant*** straightforward — **de·vi·ous·ly** *adv* — **de·vi·ous·ness** *n*

de·vis·al \di-ˈvī-zəl\ *n* : the act of devising

[1]**de·vise** \di-ˈvīz\ *vt* **de·vised; de·vis·ing** [ME *devisen*, fr. OF *deviser* to divide, regulate, tell, modif. of (assumed) VL *divisare*, fr. L *divisus*, pp. of *dividere* to divide] **1 a :** to form in the mind by new combinations or applications of ideas or principles : INVENT **b** *archaic* : SUPPOSE **c :** to plan to obtain or bring about : PLOT **2 :** to give (real estate) by will — compare BEQUEATH — **de·vis·able** \-ˈvī-zə-bəl\ *adj* — **de·vis·er** *n*

[2]**devise** *n* **1 :** the act of giving or disposing of real property by will **2 :** a will or clause of a will disposing of real property **3** : property devised by will

de·vi·see \ˌdev-ə-ˈzē, di-ˌvī-ˈzē\ *n* : one to whom a devise of property is made

de·vi·sor \ˌdev-ə-ˈzȯ(ə)r; di-ˈvī-zər, -ˌvī-ˈzȯ(ə)r\ *n* : one who devises property in a will

de·vi·tal·ize \(ˈ)dē-ˈvīt-ᵊl-ˌīz\ *vt* : to deprive of life, vigor, or effectiveness <malaria seizes and ~*s* many more people than it actually kills —R. S. Shiwalkar>

de·vit·ri·fy \(ˈ)dē-ˈvi-trə-ˌfī\ *vt* [F *dévitrifier*, fr. *dé-* de- + *vitrifier* to vitrify] : to deprive of glassy luster and transparency; *esp* : to change (as a glass) from a vitreous to a crystalline condition — **de·vit·ri·fi·able** \-ˌfī-ə-bəl\ *adj* — **de·vit·ri·fi·ca·tion** \(ˌ)dē-ˌvi-trə-fə-ˈkā-shən\ *n*

de·vo·cal·ize \(ˈ)dē-ˈvō-kə-ˌlīz\ *vt* : DEVOICE

de·voice \(ˈ)dē-ˈvȯis\ *vt* : to pronounce (as a sometimes or formerly voiced sound) without vibration of the vocal cords

de·void \di-ˈvȯid\ *adj* [ME, prob. short for *devoided*, pp. of *devoiden* to vacate, fr. MF *desvuidier* to empty, fr. OF, fr. *des-* dis- + *vuidier* to empty — more at VOID] : not having or using : DESTITUTE <a poem totally ~ of real quality>

de·voir \dəv-ˈwär, ˈdev-ˌ\ *n* [ME, alter. of *dever*, fr. OF *deveir*, fr. *devoir, deveir* to owe, be obliged, fr. L *debēre* — more at DEBT] **1** : DUTY, RESPONSIBILITY **2 :** a formal act of civility or respect

de·vo·lu·tion \ˌdev-ə-ˈlü-shən *also* ˌdē-və-\ *n* [ML *devolution-, devolutio*, fr. L *devolutus*, pp. of *devolvere*] **1 :** transference from one individual to another: as **a :** a passing or devolving (as of rights) upon a successor **b :** delegation or conferral to a subordinate **c :** the surrender of powers to local authorities by a central government **2 :** retrograde evolution : DEGENERATION — **de·vo·lu·tion·ary** \-shə-ˌner-ē\ *adj* — **de·vo·lu·tion·ist** \-sh(ə-)nəst\ *n*

de·volve \di-ˈvälv, -ˈvȯlv\ *vb* **de·volved; de·volv·ing** [ME *devolven*, fr. L *devolvere*, fr. *de-* + *volvere* to roll — more at VOLUBLE] *vt* **1** *archaic* : to cause to roll onward or downward **2 :** to transfer from one person to another : hand down ~ *vi* **1 :** to pass by transmission or succession **2 :** to flow or roll onward or downward

dev·on \ˈdev-ən\ *n, often cap* [*Devon*, England] : any of a breed of vigorous red dual-purpose cattle of English origin

Devon *abbr* Devonshire

De·vo·ni·an \di-ˈvō-nē-ən\ *adj* [*Devon*, England] **1 :** of or relating to Devonshire, England **2 :** of, relating to, or being the period of the Paleozoic era between the Silurian and the Mississippian or the corresponding system of rocks — **Devonian** *n*

Dev·on·shire cream \ˌdev-ən-ˌshi(ə)r-, -shər-\ *n* : CLOTTED CREAM

de·vote \di-ˈvōt\ *vt* **de·vot·ed; de·vot·ing** [L *devotus*, pp. of *devovēre*, fr. *de-* + *vovēre* to vow] **1 :** to dedicate by a solemn act <Christians are by their baptism *devoted* to God —William Law> **2 a :** to give over (as to a cause, use, or end) wholly or purposefully <land *devoted* to agriculture> **b :** to center the attention or activities of (oneself) <*devoting* herself to the care of her family> — **de·vote·ment** \-ˈvōt-mənt\ *n*

syn DEVOTE, DEDICATE, CONSECRATE, HALLOW *shared meaning element* : to set apart for a particular and often a better or higher use or end. DEVOTE is likely to imply compelling motives and often attachment to an objective <*devoted* his evenings to study> <*devote* money to charity> DEDICATE implies solemn and exclusive devotion to a sacred or serious use or purpose <we Americans are *dedicated* to improvement —Louis Kronenberger> CONSECRATE stresses investment with a solemn or sacred quality <*consecrate* a church to the worship of God> and even in general use carries a strong connotation of intense devotion <rules . . . *consecrated* by time —Edmund Burke> HALLOW, often differing little from *dedicate* or *consecrate*, may distinctively imply an attribution of intrinsic sanctity <the Lord blessed the sabbath day, and *hallowed* it —Exod 20:11 (AV)>

de·vot·ed *adj* **1 :** ARDENT, DEVOUT **2 :** AFFECTIONATE — **de·vot·ed·ly** *adv* — **de·vot·ed·ness** *n*

dev·o·tee \ˌdev-ə-ˈtē, -ˈtā; di-ˌvō-ˈtē\ *n* **1 :** a person preoccupied with religious duties and ceremonies **2 :** an ardent follower, supporter, or enthusiast <a ~ of opera>

de·vo·tion \di-ˈvō-shən\ *n* **1 a :** religious fervor : PIETY **b :** an act of prayer or supplication — usu. used in pl. **c :** a religious exercise or practice other than the regular corporate worship of a congregation; *specif* : one directed in Roman Catholic piety to a particular object of faith **2 a :** the act of devoting or quality of being devoted **b :** ardent love or affection ***syn*** see FIDELITY

[1]**de·vo·tion·al** \-shnəl, -shən-ᵊl\ *adj* : of, relating to, or characterized by devotion — **de·vo·tion·al·ly** \-ē\ *adv*

[2]**devotional** *n* : a short worship service

de·vour \di-ˈvau̇(ə)r\ *vt* [ME *devouren*, fr. MF *devourer*, fr. L *devorare*, fr. *de-* + *vorare* to devour — more at VORACIOUS] **1** : to eat up greedily or ravenously **2 :** to seize upon and destroy : CONSUME <~*ed* by fire> **3 :** to prey upon <a man ~*ed* by guilt> **4 :** to enjoy avidly <~*s* books> — **de·vour·er** *n*

de·vout \di-ˈvau̇t\ *adj* [ME *devot*, fr. OF, fr. LL *devotus*, fr. L, pp. of *devovēre*] **1 :** devoted to religion or to religious duties or exercises **2 :** expressing devotion or piety **3 :** warmly devoted : SINCERE — **de·vout·ly** *adv* — **de·vout·ness** *n*

syn DEVOUT, RELIGIOUS, PIOUS, PIETISTIC, SANCTIMONIOUS *shared meaning element* : showing fervor in the practice of religion

dew \ˈd(y)ü\ *n* [ME, fr. OE *dēaw*; akin to OHG *tou* dew, Gk *thein* to run] **1 :** moisture condensed upon the surfaces of cool bodies esp. at night **2 :** something resembling dew in purity, freshness, or power to refresh **3 :** moisture esp. when appearing in minute droplets: as **a :** TEARS **b :** SWEAT **c :** droplets of water produced by a plant in transpiration — **dew** *vt* — **dew·less** \-ləs\ *adj*

DEW *abbr* distant early warning

de·wan \di-ˈwän\ *n* [Hindi *dīwān*, fr. Per, account book] : an Indian official; *esp* : the prime minister of an Indian state

Dew·ar flask \ˌd(y)ü-ər-\ *n* [Sir James *Dewar*] : a glass or metal container that has an evacuated space between the walls, is often silvered on the innermost surface to prevent heat transfer, and is used esp. for storing liquefied gases — compare VACUUM BOTTLE

de·wa·ter \(ˈ)dē-ˈwȯt-ər, -ˈwät-\ *vt* : to remove water from — **de·wa·ter·er** *n*

dew·ber·ry \ˈd(y)ü-ˌber-ē\ *n* **1 :** any of several sweet edible berries related to and resembling blackberries **2 :** a trailing or decumbent bramble (genus *Rubus*) that bears dewberries

dew·claw \ˈd(y)ü-ˌklȯ\ *n* : a vestigial digit not reaching to the ground on the foot of a mammal; *also* : a claw or hoof terminating such a digit — see COW illustration — **dew·clawed** \-ˌklȯd\ *adj*

dew·drop \ˈd(y)ü-ˌdräp\ *n* : a drop of dew

Dew·ey decimal classification \ˌd(y)ü-ē-\ *n* [Melvil *Dewey*] : a system of classifying books and other publications whereby main classes are designated by a three-digit number and subdivisions are shown by numbers after a decimal point

dew·fall \ˈd(y)ü-ˌfȯl\ *n* : formation of dew; *also* : the time when dew begins to deposit

dew·lap \ˈd(y)ü-ˌlap\ *n* : a hanging fold of skin under the neck esp. of a bovine animal — see COW illustration — **dew·lapped** \-ˌlapt\ *adj*

de·worm \(ˈ)de-ˈwərm\ *vt* : to rid (as a dog) of worms : WORM 1

dew point *n* : the temperature at which a vapor begins to condense

dew worm *n* : NIGHT CRAWLER

dewy \ˈd(y)ü-ē\ *adj* **dew·i·er; -est :** moist with, affected by, or suggestive of dew — **dew·i·ly** \ˈd(y)ü-ə-lē\ *adv* — **dew·i·ness** \ˈd(y)ü-ē-nəs\ *n*

dewy–eyed \ˌd(y)ü-ē-ˈīd\ *adj* : naively credulous

dex \ˈdeks\ *n* : the sulfate of dextroamphetamine

dexa·meth·a·sone \ˌdek-sə-ˈmeth-ə-ˌsōn, -ˌzōn\ *n* [perh. fr. *Dexa*myl, a trademark + *meth*yl + *-sone* (as in *cortisone*)] : a synthetic adrenocortical steroid $C_{22}H_{29}FO_5$ used esp. as an anti-inflammatory agent

Dex·e·drine \ˈdek-sə-ˌdrēn, -drən\ *trademark* — used for a preparation of the sulfate of dextroamphetamine

dex·ies \ˈdek-sēz\ *n pl* [*dex* + *-ie* + *-s*] : tablets or capsules of the sulfate of dextroamphetamine

dex·io·tro·pic \ˌdek-sē-ə-ˈtrō-pik, -ˈträp-ik\ *or* **dex·i·ot·ro·pous** \-sē-ˈä-trə-pəs\ *adj* [Gk *dexios* situated on the right + E *-tropic* or *-tropous*] : turning to the right : DEXTRAL

dex·ter \ˈdek-stər\ *adj* [L; akin to Gk *dexios* situated on the right, L *decēre* to be fitting — more at DECENT] **1 :** relating to or situated on the right **2 :** being or relating to the side of a heraldic shield at the right of the person bearing it **3 :** appearing or facing toward the right and considered of good omen — **dexter** *adv*

dex·ter·i·ty \dek-ˈster-ət-ē\ *n, pl* **-ties** [MF or L; MF *dexterité*, fr. L *dexteritat-, dexteritas*, fr. *dexter*] **1 :** readiness and grace in physical activity; *esp* : skill and ease in using the hands **2** : mental skill or quickness : ADROITNESS

dex·ter·ous *or* **dex·trous** \ˈdek-st(ə-)rəs\ *adj* [L *dextr-, dexter* dextral, skillful] **1 :** skillful and competent with the hands **2** : mentally adroit and skillful : EXPERT **3 :** done with dexterity : ARTFUL — **dex·ter·ous·ly** *adv* — **dex·ter·ous·ness** *n*

syn DEXTEROUS, ADROIT, DEFT *shared meaning element* **:** ready and skilled in physical movements or, sometimes, mental activity ***ant*** clumsy

dextr- *or* **dextro-** *comb form* [LL, fr. L *dextr-, dexter*] **1 :** right **:** on or toward the right <*dextro*rotatory> **2** *usu dextro-* **:** dextrorotatory <*dextro*-tartaric acid>

dex·tral \'dek-strəl\ *adj* **:** of or relating to the right **:** inclined to the right: as **a :** RIGHT-HANDED **b** *of a flatfish* **:** having the right side uppermost **c** *of a gastropod shell* **:** having the whorls turning from the left toward the right as viewed with the apex toward the observer or having the aperture open toward the observer to the right of the axis when held with the spire uppermost — **dex·tral·i·ty** \dek-'stral-ət-ē\ *n* — **dex·tral·ly** \'dek-strə-lē\ *adv*

dex·tran \'dek-stran, -strən\ *n* [*dextr*ose + *-an*] **:** any of numerous polysaccharides $(C_6H_{10}O_5)_n$ that yield only glucose on hydrolysis: as **a :** any such compound of high molecular weight obtained by fermentation of sugar **b :** any such compound of reduced molecular weight obtained by acid hydrolysis of native dextran and used as a plasma substitute

dex·tran·ase \-strə-ˌnās, -ˌnāz\ *n* **:** a hydrolase that breaks down dextran and is effective in attacking dental plaque

dex·trin \'dek-strən\ *also* **dex·trine** \-ˌstrēn, -strən\ *n* [F *dextrine,* fr. *dextr-*] **:** any of various soluble gummy polysaccharides $(C_6H_{10}O_5)_n$ obtained from starch by the action of heat, acids, or enzymes and used as adhesives, as sizes for paper and textiles, and in syrups and beer

dex·tro \'dek-(ˌ)strō\ *adj* [*dextr-*] **:** DEXTROROTATORY

dex·tro·am·phet·amine \ˌdek-(ˌ)strō-am-'fet-ə-ˌmēn, -mən\ *n* **:** AMPHETAMINE 2b

dex·tro–glu·cose \ˌdek-strə-'glü-ˌkōs, -ˌkōz\ *n* **:** DEXTROSE

dex·tro·ro·ta·tion \ˌdek-strə-rō-'tā-shən\ *n* **:** right-handed or clockwise rotation — used of the plane of polarization of light

dex·tro·ro·ta·to·ry \-'rōt-ə-ˌtōr-ē, -ˌtȯr-\ *also* **dex·tro·ro·ta·ry** \-'rōt-ə-rē\ *adj* **:** turning clockwise or toward the right; *esp* **:** rotating the plane of polarization of light toward the right <~ crystals> — compare LEVOROTATORY

dex·trorse \'dek-ˌstrȯ(ə)rs\ *adj* [NL *dextrorsus,* fr. L, toward the right, fr. *dextr-* + *versus,* pp. of *vertere* to turn — more at WORTH] **1** *of a plant or its parts* **:** twining spirally upward around an axis from left to right — compare SINISTRORSE **2 :** DEXTRAL c — **dex·trorse·ly** *adv*

dex·trose \'dek-ˌstrōs, -ˌstrōz\ *n* **:** dextrorotatory glucose

dey \'dā\ *n* [F, fr. Turk *dayı,* lit., maternal uncle] **:** a ruling official of the Ottoman empire in northern Africa

DF *abbr* **1** damage free **2** direction finder; direction finding **3** doctor of forestry

DFA *abbr* doctor of fine arts

DFC *abbr* Distinguished Flying Cross

DFM *abbr* distinguished flying medal

dft *abbr* **1** defendant **2** draft

dg *abbr* decigram

DG *abbr* **1** [LL *Dei gratia*] by the grace of God **2** director general

DH *abbr* **1** designated hitter **2** doctor of humanities

dhar·ma \'dər-mə\ *n* [Skt, fr. *dhārayati* he holds; akin to L *firmus* firm] **1** *Hinduism* **:** an individual's duty fulfilled by observance of custom or law **2** *Hinduism & Buddhism* **a :** the basic principles of cosmic or individual existence **:** NATURE **b :** conformity to one's duty and nature — **dhar·mic** \-mik\ *adj*

DHL *abbr* doctor of Hebrew letters; doctor of Hebrew literature

dhole \'dōl\ *n* [perh. fr. Kanarese *tōla* wolf] **:** a fierce wild dog (*Cuon dukhunensis*) of India that hunts in packs

dho·ti \'dōt-ē\ *or* **dhoo·tie** \'düt-ē\ *n* [Hindi *dhotī*] **1 :** a loincloth worn by Hindu men **2 :** a fabric used for dhotis

dhow \'dau̇\ *n* [Ar *dāwa*] **:** an Arab lateen-rigged boat usu. having a long overhang forward, a high poop, and an open waist

Dhu'l–Hij·ja \ˌdü(-ə)l-'hij-(ˌ)ä\ *n* [Ar *Dhū-l-ḥijjah,* lit., the one of the pilgrimage] **:** the 12th month of the Muhammadan year — see MONTH table

Dhu'l–Qa'·dah \-'käd-(ˌ)ä\ *n* [Ar *Dhū-l-qa'dah,* lit., the one of the sitting] **:** the 11th month of the Muhammadan year — see MONTH table

di- *comb form* [ME, fr. MF, fr. L, fr. Gk; akin to OE *twi-*] **1 :** twice **:** twofold **:** double <*di*chromatic> **2 :** containing two atoms, radicals, or groups <*di*chloride>

dia *abbr* diameter

dia- *also* **di-** *prefix* [ME, fr. OF, fr. L, fr. Gk, through, apart, fr. *dia;* akin to L *dis-*] **:** through <*dia*positive> **:** across <*dia*dromous>

di·a·base \'dī-ə-ˌbās\ *n* [F, fr. Gk *diabasis* act of crossing over, fr. *diabainein* to cross over, fr. *dia-* + *bainein* to go — more at COME] **1** *archaic* **:** DIORITE **2** *chiefly Brit* **:** an altered basalt **3 :** a fine-grained rock of the composition of gabbro but with an ophitic texture — **di·a·ba·sic** \ˌdī-ə-'bā-sik\ *adj*

di·a·be·tes \ˌdī-ə-'bēt-ēz, -'bēt-əs\ *n* [L, fr. Gk *diabētēs,* fr. *diabainein*] **:** any of various abnormal conditions characterized by the secretion and excretion of excessive amounts of urine

diabetes in·sip·i·dus \-in-'sip-əd-əs\ *n* [NL, lit., insipid diabetes] **:** a disorder of the pituitary gland characterized by intense thirst and by the excretion of large amounts of urine

diabetes mel·li·tus \-'mel-ət-əs\ *n* [NL, lit., honey-sweet diabetes] **:** a familial constitutional disorder of carbohydrate metabolism characterized by inadequate secretion or utilization of insulin, by polyuria and excessive amounts of sugar in the blood and urine, and by thirst, hunger, and loss of weight

¹di·a·bet·ic \ˌdī-ə-'bet-ik\ *adj* **1 :** of or relating to diabetes or diabetics **2 :** affected with diabetes

²diabetic *n* **:** a person affected with diabetes

di·a·ble·rie \dē-'äb-lə-(ˌ)rē, -'ab-\ *n* [F, fr. OF, fr. *diable* devil, fr. LL *diabolus* — more at DEVIL] **1 :** black magic **:** SORCERY **2 a :** a representation in words or pictures of black magic or of dealings with the devil **b :** demon lore **3 a :** mischievous conduct or manner **b :** the quality or state of being wicked

diabol- *or* **diabolo-** *comb form* [ME *deabol-,* fr. MF *diabol-,* fr. LL, fr. Gk, fr. *diabolos* — more at DEVIL] **:** devil <*diabol*ism>

di·a·bol·ic \ˌdī-ə-'bäl-ik\ *or* **di·a·bol·i·cal** \-'bäl-i-kəl\ *adj* [ME *deabolik,* fr. MF *diabolique,* fr. LL *diabolicus,* fr. *diabolus*] **:** of, relating to, or characteristic of the devil **:** FIENDISH — **di·a·bol·i·cal·ly** \-i-k(ə-)lē\ *adv* — **di·a·bol·i·cal·ness** \-i-kəl-nəs\ *n*

di·ab·o·lism \dī-'ab-ə-ˌliz-əm\ *n* **1 :** dealings with or possession by the devil **2 :** evil character or conduct **3 :** belief in or worship of devils — **di·ab·o·list** \-ləst\ *n*

di·ab·o·lize \-ˌlīz\ *vt* **-lized; liz·ing :** to represent as or make diabolical

dia·chron·ic \ˌdī-ə-'krän-ik\ *adj* **:** of, relating to, or dealing with phenomena *esp.* of language as they occur or change over a period of time — **dia·chron·i·cal·ly** \-'krän-i-k(ə-)lē\ *adv* — **dia·chron·ic·ness** \-ik-nəs\ *n*

di·ach·ro·ny \dī-'ak-rə-nē\ *n* [ISV *dia-* + *-chrony* (as in *synchrony*)] **1 :** diachronic analysis **2 :** change extending through time

¹di·ac·id \(ˈ)dī-'as-əd\ *or* **di·acid·ic** \ˌdī-ə-'sid-ik\ *adj* **1 :** able to react with two molecules of a monobasic acid or one of a dibasic acid to form a salt or ester — used esp. of bases **2 :** containing two replaceable hydrogen atoms — used esp. of acid salts

²diacid *n* [ISV] **:** an acid with two acid hydrogen atoms

di·ac·o·nal \dī-'ak-ən-ᵊl, dē-\ *adj* [LL *diaconalis,* fr. *diaconus* deacon — more at DEACON] **:** of or relating to a deacon or deaconess

di·ac·o·nate \-'ak-ə-nət, -ˌnāt\ *n* **1 :** the office or period of office of a deacon or deaconess **2 :** an official body of deacons

di·a·crit·ic \ˌdī-ə-'krit-ik\ *n* **:** a modifying mark near or through an orthographic or phonetic character or combination of characters indicating a phonetic value different from that given the unmarked or otherwise marked element

DIACRITICS

´	(é)	acute accent	˘	(ŭ)	breve
`	(è)	grave accent	ˇ	(č)	haček
^	(ô) *or* ⌢ *or* ~	circumflex	¨	(oö)	diaeresis
~	(ñ)	tilde	¸	(ç)	cedilla
¯	(ō)	macron			

di·a·crit·i·cal \ˌdī-ə-'krit-i-kəl\ *also* **di·a·crit·ic** \-'krit-ik\ *adj* [Gk *diakritikos* separative, fr. *diakrinein* to distinguish, fr. *dia-* + *krinein* to separate — more at CERTAIN] **1 :** serving as a diacritic **2 a :** serving to distinguish **:** DISTINCTIVE <the ~ elements in culture — S. F. Nadel> **b :** capable of distinguishing <students of superior ~ powers>

di·adel·phous \ˌdī-ə-'del-fəs\ *adj* [*di-* + *-adelphous*] **:** united by filaments into two fascicles — used of stamens

di·a·dem \'dī-ə-ˌdem, -əd-əm\ *n* [ME *diademe,* fr. OF, fr. L *diadema,* fr. Gk *diadēma,* fr. *diadein* to bind around, fr. *dia-* + *dein* to bind; akin to Alb *duai* sheaf, Skt *dāman* rope] **1 :** CROWN; *specif* **:** a headband worn as a badge of royalty **2 :** regal power or dignity

di·ad·ro·mous \dī-'ad-rə-məs\ *adj, of a fish* **:** migratory between salt and fresh waters

di·aer·e·sis \dī-'er-ə-səs\ *n, pl* **-e·ses** \-ˌsēz\ [LL *diaeresis,* fr. Gk *diairesis,* fr. *diairein* to divide, fr. *dia-* + *hairein* to take] **1 :** a mark ¨ placed over a vowel to indicate that the vowel is pronounced in a separate syllable (as in *naïve* or *Brontë*) **2 :** the break in a verse caused by the coincidence of the end of a foot with the end of a word — **di·ae·ret·ic** \ˌdī-ə-'ret-ik\ *adj*

diag *abbr* **1** diagonal **2** diagram

dia·gen·e·sis \ˌdī-ə-'jen-ə-səs\ *n* [NL] **1 :** recombination or rearrangement of constituents (as of a chemical or mineral) resulting in a new product **2 :** the conversion (as by compaction or chemical reaction) of sediment into rock — **dia·ge·net·ic** \ˌdī-ə-jə-'net-ik\ *adj* — **dia·ge·net·i·cal·ly** \-'net-i-k(ə-)lē\ *adv*

dia·ge·ot·ro·pism \ˌdī-ə-jē-'ä-trə-ˌpiz-əm\ *or* **dia·ge·ot·ro·py** \-pē\ *n* **:** the tendency of growing organs (as branches or roots) to extend the axis at right angles to the line of gravity — **dia·geo·tro·pic** \-ˌjē-ə-'trō-pik, -'träp-ik\ *adj*

di·ag·nose \'dī-ig-ˌnōs, -ˌnōz, ˌdī-ig-', -əg-\ *vb* **-nosed; -nos·ing** [back-formation fr. *diagnosis*] *vt* **:** to recognize (as a disease) by signs and symptoms ~ *vi* **:** to make a diagnosis — **di·ag·nos·able** *or* **di·ag·nose·able** \ˌdī-ig-'nō-sə-bəl, -əg-, -zə- \ *adj*

di·ag·no·sis \ˌdī-ig-'nō-səs, -əg-\ *n, pl* **-no·ses** \-ˌsēz\ [NL, fr. Gk *diagnōsis,* fr. *diagignōskein* to distinguish, fr. *dia-* + *gignōskein* to know — more at KNOW] **1 :** the art or act of identifying a disease from its signs and symptoms **2 :** a concise technical description of a taxon **3 a :** investigation or analysis of the cause or nature of a condition, situation, or problem <~ of engine trouble> **b :** a statement or conclusion concerning the nature or cause of some phenomenon

¹di·ag·nos·tic \-'näs-tik\ *also* **di·ag·nos·ti·cal** \-ti-kəl\ *adj* **:** of or relating to diagnosis — **di·ag·nos·ti·cal·ly** \-ti-k(ə-)lē\ *adv*

²diagnostic *n* **1 :** the art or practice of diagnosis — often used in pl. **2 :** a distinguishing mark — **di·ag·nos·ti·cian** \-(ˌ)näs-'tish-ən\ *n*

¹di·ag·o·nal \dī-'ag-ən-ᵊl, -'ag-nəl\ *adj* [L *diagonalis,* fr. Gk *diagōnios* from angle to angle, fr. *dia-* + *gōnia* angle; akin to Gk *gony* knee — more at KNEE] **1 a :** joining two nonadjacent vertices of a rectilinear or polyhedral figure **b :** passing through two nonadjacent edges of a polyhedron **2 a :** inclined obliquely from a reference line (as the vertical) <wood with a ~ grain> **b :** having diagonal markings or parts <a ~ weave>

[2]**diagonal** *n* **1 :** a diagonal straight line or plane **2 a** (1) **:** a diagonal direction (2) **:** a diagonal row, arrangement, or pattern **b :** a twilled fabric esp. of wool **c :** something placed diagonally **3 :** a mark / used typically to denote "or" (as in *and/or*), "and or" (as in *straggler/deserter*), or "per" (as in *feet/second*) — called also *solidus, virgule*

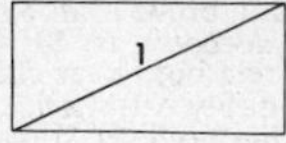

1, diagonal 1

di·ag·o·nal·ize \-ˌīz\ *vt* **-ized; -iz·ing :** to put (a matrix) in a form with all the nonzero elements along the diagonal from upper left to lower right — **di·ag·o·nal·iz·able** \-ˌī-zə-bəl\ *adj* — **di·ag·o·nal·iza·tion** \-ə-gən-ᵊl-ə-'zā-shən, -ˌag-nə-lə-'zā-\ *n*

di·ag·o·nal·ly \dī-'ag-ən-ᵊl-ē, -'ag-nə-lē\ *adv* **:** in a diagonal manner

diagonal matrix *n* **:** a matrix that has all the nonzero elements located along the diagonal from upper left to lower right

[1]**di·a·gram** \'dī-ə-ˌgram\ *n* [Gk *diagramma,* fr. *diagraphein* to mark out by lines, fr. *dia-* + *graphein* to write — more at CARVE] **1 :** a line drawing made for mathematical or scientific purposes **2 a :** a graphic design that explains rather than represents **b :** a drawing that shows arrangement and relations (as of parts) **:** CHART — **di·a·gram·ma·ble** \-ˌgram-ə-bəl\ *adj* — **di·a·gram·mat·ic** \ˌdī-ə-grə-'mat-ik\ *also* **di·a·gram·mat·i·cal** \-'mat-i-kəl\ *adj* — **di·a·gram·mat·i·cal·ly** \-i-k(ə-)lē\ *adv*

[2]**diagram** *vt* **-gramed** \-ˌgramd\ *or* **-grammed; -gram·ing** \-ˌgram-iŋ\ *or* **-gram·ming :** to represent by or put into the form of a diagram

dia·ki·ne·sis \ˌdī-ə-kə-'nē-səs, -(ˌ)kī-\ *n, pl* **-ne·ses** \-ˌsēz\ [NL, fr. *dia-* + Gk *kinēsis* motion, fr. *kinein* to move; akin to L *ciēre* to move — more at HIGHT] **:** the final stage of the meiotic prophase marked by contraction of the bivalents — **dia·ki·net·ic** \-'net-ik\ *adj*

[1]**di·al** \'dī(-ə)l\ *n* [ME, fr. L *dies* day — more at DEITY] **1 :** the face of a sundial **2** *obs* **:** TIMEPIECE **3 :** the graduated face of a timepiece **4 a :** a face upon which some measurement is registered usu. by means of graduations and a pointer <the thermometer ~ reads 70°F> **b :** a device (as a disk) that may be operated to make electrical connections or to regulate the operation of a machine and that usu. has guiding marks around its border <a radio ~> <a telephone ~>

[2]**dial** *vb* **di·aled** *or* **di·alled; di·al·ing** *or* **di·al·ling** *vt* **1 :** to measure with a dial **2 :** to manipulate a device (as a dial) so as to operate, regulate, or select <~ your favorite program> <he *~ed* the wrong number> ~ *vi* **1 :** to manipulate a dial **2 :** to make a call on a dial telephone — **di·al·er** *n*

[3]**dial** *abbr* **1** dialect **2** dialectical

di·a·lect \'dī-ə-ˌlekt\ *n, often attrib* [MF *dialecte,* fr. L *dialectus,* fr. Gk *dialektos* conversation, dialect, fr. *dialegesthai* to converse — more at DIALOGUE] **1 a :** a regional variety of language distinguished by features of vocabulary, grammar, and pronunciation from other regional varieties and constituting together with them a single language of which no one variety is construed as standard <the Doric ~ of ancient Greek> **b :** one of two or more cognate languages <French and Italian are Romance *~s*> **c :** a regional variety of a language usu. transmitted orally and differing distinctively from the standard language <the Lancashire ~ of English> **d :** a variety of a language used by the members of an occupational group <the ~ of the atomic physicist> **e :** a variety of language whose identity is fixed by a factor (as social class or educational level of its habitual users) other than geography <spoke a rough peasant ~> **2 :** manner or means of expressing oneself **:** PHRASEOLOGY — **di·a·lec·tal** \ˌdī-ə-'lek-tᵊl\ *adj* — **di·a·lec·tal·ly** \-tᵊl-ē\ *adv*

syn DIALECT, VERNACULAR, LINGO, JARGON, CANT, ARGOT, SLANG *shared meaning element* **:** a form of language that is not recognized as standard

dialect atlas *n* **:** LINGUISTIC ATLAS

dialect geography *n* **:** LINGUISTIC GEOGRAPHY

di·a·lec·tic \ˌdī-ə-'lek-tik\ *n* [ME *dialetik,* fr. MF *dialetique,* fr. L *dialectica,* fr. Gk *dialektikē,* fr. fem. of *dialektikos* of conversation, fr. *dialektos*] **1 a :** discussion and reasoning by dialogue as a method of intellectual investigation; *specif* **:** the Socratic techniques of exposing false beliefs and eliciting truth **b :** the Platonic investigation of the eternal ideas **2 :** LOGIC 1a(1) **3 :** the logic of fallacy **4 a :** the Hegelian process of change in which a concept or its realization passes over into and is preserved and fulfilled by its opposite; *also* **:** the critical investigation of this process **b** (1) *usu pl but sing or pl in constr* **:** development through the stages of thesis, antithesis, and synthesis in accordance with the laws of dialectical materialism (2) **:** the investigation of this process (3) **:** the theoretical application of this process esp. in the social sciences **5** *usu pl but sing or pl in constr* **a :** any systematic reasoning, exposition, or argument that juxtaposes opposed or contradictory ideas and usu. seeks to resolve their conflict **b :** an intellectual exchange of ideas **6 :** the dialectical tension or opposition between two interacting forces or elements

di·a·lec·ti·cal \ˌdī-ə-'lek-ti-kəl\ *also* **di·a·lec·tic** \-tik\ *adj* **1 a :** of, relating to, or in accordance with dialectic <~ method> **b :** practicing, devoted to, or employing dialectic <a ~ philosopher> **2 :** of, relating to, or characteristic of a dialect — **di·a·lec·ti·cal·ly** \-ti-k(ə-)lē\ *adv*

dialectical materialism *n* **:** the Marxian theory that maintains the material basis of a reality constantly changing in a dialectical process and the priority of matter over mind — compare HISTORICAL MATERIALISM

di·a·lec·ti·cian \ˌdī-ə-ˌlek-'tish-ən\ *n* **1 :** one who is skilled in or practices dialectic **2 :** a student of dialects

di·a·lec·tol·o·gist \-'täl-ə-jəst\ *n* **:** a specialist in dialectology

di·a·lec·tol·o·gy \-jē\ *n* [ISV] **1 :** the systematic study of dialect **2 :** the body of data available for study of a dialect — **di·a·lec·to·log·i·cal** \-ˌlek-tə-'läj-i-kəl\ *adj* — **di·a·lec·to·log·i·cal·ly** \-k(ə-)lē\ *adv*

di·al·lel \'dī-ə-ˌlel\ *adj* [Gk *diallēlos* reciprocating, confused, fr. *di'allēlōn* through or across one another] **:** relating to or being the crossing of each of several individuals with two or more others in order to determine the relative genetic contribution of each parent to certain characters in the offspring

di·a·log·ic \ˌdī-ə-'läj-ik\ *adj* **:** of, relating to, or characterized by dialogue <~ writing> — **di·a·log·i·cal** \-'läj-i-kəl\ *adj* — **di·a·log·i·cal·ly** \-i-k(ə-)lē\ *adv*

di·a·lo·gist \dī-'al-ə-jəst; 'dī-ə-ˌlȯg-əst, -ˌläg-\ *n* **1 :** one who participates in a dialogue **2 :** a writer of dialogues — **di·a·lo·gis·tic** \(ˌ)dī-ˌal-ə-'jis-tik; ˌdī-ə-ˌlȯ-'gis-, -ˌlä-'gis-\ *adj*

[1]**di·a·logue** *or* **di·a·log** \'dī-ə-ˌlȯg, -ˌläg\ *n* [MF, fr. OF, fr. L *dialogus,* fr. Gk *dialogos,* fr. *dialegesthai* to converse, fr. *dia-* + *legein* to speak] **1 :** a written composition in which two or more characters are represented as conversing **2 a :** a conversation between two or more persons; *also* **:** a similar exchange between a person and something else (as a computer) **b :** an exchange of ideas and opinions **3 :** the conversational element of literary or dramatic composition **4 :** a musical composition for two or more parts suggestive of a conversation

[2]**dialogue** *vb* **-logued; -logu·ing** *vi* **:** to take part in a dialogue ~ *vt* **:** to express in dialogue

dial tone *n* **:** a tone emitted by a telephone as a signal that the system is ready for dialing

di·al·y·sate \dī-'al-ə-ˌzāt, -ˌsāt\ *or* **di·al·y·zate** \-ˌzāt\ *n* [*dialysis* or *dialyze* + *-ate*] **:** the material that passes through the membrane in dialysis; *also* **:** the liquid into which this material passes

di·al·y·sis \dī-'al-ə-səs\ *n, pl* **-y·ses** \-ˌsēz\ [NL, fr. Gk, separation, fr. *dialyein* to dissolve, fr. *dia-* + *lyein* to loosen — more at LOSE] **:** the separation of substances in solution by means of their unequal diffusion through semipermeable membranes; *esp* **:** such a separation of colloids from soluble substances — **di·a·lyt·ic** \ˌdī-ə-'lit-ik\ *adj*

di·a·lyze \'dī-ə-ˌlīz\ *vb* **-lyzed; -lyz·ing** *vt* **:** to subject to dialysis ~ *vi* **:** to undergo dialysis — **di·a·lyz·abil·i·ty** \ˌdī-ə-ˌlī-zə-'bil-ət-ē\ *n* — **di·a·lyz·able** \'dī-ə-ˌlī-zə-bəl\ *adj* — **di·a·lyz·er** \-ˌlī-zər\ *n*

diam *abbr* diameter

dia·mag·net \'dī-ə-ˌmag-nət\ *or* **dia·mag·net·ic** \ˌdī-ə-mag-'net-ik\ *n* [*diamagnet* back-formation fr. *diamagnetic,* adj.] **:** a diamagnetic substance

diamagnetic *adj* **:** having a magnetic permeability less than that of a vacuum **:** slightly repelled by a magnet — **dia·mag·ne·tism** \-'mag-nə-ˌtiz-əm\ *n*

di·am·e·ter \dī-'am-ət-ər\ *n* [ME *diametre,* fr. MF, fr. L *diametros,* fr. Gk, fr. *dia-* + *metron* measure — more at MEASURE] **1 :** a chord passing through the center of a figure or body **2 :** the length of a straight line through the center of an object **3 :** a unit of magnification of observations with a magnifying device equal to the number of times the linear dimensions of the object are increased <a microscope magnifying 60 *~s*> — **di·am·e·tral** \-'am-ə-trəl\ *adj*

di·a·met·ric \ˌdī-ə-'me-trik\ *or* **di·a·met·ri·cal** \-tri-kəl\ *adj* **1 :** of, relating to, or constituting a diameter **:** located at the diameter **2 :** completely opposed or opposite <in ~ contradiction to his claims> — **di·a·met·ri·cal·ly** \-tri-k(ə-)lē\ *adv*

di·amide \'dī-ə-ˌmīd, dī-'am-əd\ *n* **:** a compound containing two amido groups

di·amine \'dī-ə-ˌmēn, dī-'am-ən\ *n* [ISV] **:** a compound containing two amino groups

di·am·mo·ni·um phosphate \-ə-ˌmō-nē-əm-, -nyəm-\ *n* **:** an ammonium phosphate $(NH_4)_2HPO_4$

[1]**di·a·mond** \'dī-(ə-)mənd\ *n, often attrib* [ME *diamaunde,* fr. MF *diamant,* fr. LL *diamant-, diamas,* alter. of L *adamant-, adamas,* hardest metal, diamond, fr. Gk] **1 a :** a native crystalline carbon that is usu. nearly colorless, that when transparent and free from flaws is highly valued as a precious stone, and that is used industrially as an abrasive powder and in rock drills because of its great hardness; *also* **:** a piece of this substance **b :** crystallized carbon produced artificially **2 :** something that resembles a diamond **3 :** a square or rhombus-shaped configuration usu. having a distinctive orientation **4 a :** a red diamond-shaped mark impressed on a playing card; *also* **:** a card so marked **b** *pl but sing or pl in constr* **:** the suit comprising cards so marked **5 a :** INFIELD 2a **b :** the entire playing field in baseball

[2]**diamond** *vt* **:** to adorn with or as if with diamonds

[1]**di·a·mond·back** \'dī-(ə-)mən(d)-ˌbak\ *also* **di·a·mond–backed** \ˌdī-(ə-)mən(d)-'bakt\ *adj* **:** having marks like diamonds or lozenges on the back

[2]**diamondback** *n* **:** a large and deadly rattlesnake (*Crotalus adamanteus*) of the southern U.S.

diamondback terrapin *n* **:** any of several edible terrapins (genus *Malaclemys*) formerly widely distributed in salt marshes along the Atlantic and Gulf coasts but now much restricted

di·a·mond·if·er·ous \ˌdī-(ə-)mən-'dif-(ə-)rəs\ *adj* **:** yielding diamonds <~ earth>

Di·ana \dī-'an-ə\ *n* [L] **:** an ancient Italian goddess of the forest and of childbirth who was identified with Artemis by the Romans

di·an·drous \(')dī-'an-drəs\ *adj* **:** having two stamens

di·an·thus \dī-'an(t)-thəs\ *n* [NL, genus name, fr. Gk *dios* heavenly + *anthos* flower — more at DEITY, ANTHOLOGY] **:** [3]PINK 1

di·a·pa·son \ˌdī-ə-'pāz-ᵊn, -'pās-\ *n* [ME, fr. L, fr. Gk (*hē*) *dia pasōn* (*chordōn symphōnia*) the concord through all the notes, fr. *dia* through + *pasōn,* gen. fem. pl. of *pas* all — more at DIA-, PAN-] **1 a** (1) **:** a burst of harmonious sound (2) **:** a full deep outburst of sound **b :** the principal foundation stop in the organ extending through the complete range of the instrument **c** (1) **:** the entire compass of musical tones (2) **:** RANGE, SCOPE <the vast ~ of his poetic talent> **2 a :** TUNING FORK **b :** a standard of pitch

dia·pause \'dī-ə-ˌpȯz\ *n* [Gk *diapausis* pause, fr. *diapauein* to pause, fr. *dia-* + *pauein* to stop — more at PAUSE] **:** a period of physiologically enforced dormancy (as developmental arrest in an insect) between periods of activity

dia·paus·ing \-ˌpȯ-ziŋ\ *adj* **:** undergoing diapause

di·a·pe·de·sis \ˌdī-ə-pə-'dē-səs\ *n, pl* **-de·ses** \-ˌsēz\ [NL, fr. Gk *diapēdēsis* act of oozing through, fr. *diapēdan* to ooze through, fr. *dia-* + *pēdan* to leap] **:** the passage of blood cells through capillary walls into the tissues — **di·a·pe·det·ic** \-'det-ik\ *adj*

1di·a·per \ˈdī(-ə)-pər\ *n* [ME *diapre,* fr. MF, fr. ML *diasprum*] **1 :** a fabric with a distinctive pattern: **a :** a rich silk fabric **b :** a soft usu. white linen or cotton fabric used for tablecloths or towels **2 :** a basic garment for infants consisting of a folded cloth or other absorbent material drawn up between the legs and fastened about the waist **3 :** an allover pattern consisting of one or more small repeated units of design (as geometric figures) connecting with one another or growing out of one another with continuously flowing or straight lines

diaper 3

2diaper *vt* **di·a·pered; di·a·per·ing** \-p(ə-)riŋ\ **1 :** to ornament with diaper designs **2 :** to put on or change the diaper of (an infant)

di·a·pha·ne·ity \(ˌ)dī-ˌaf-ə-ˈnē-ət-ē, ˌdī-ə-fə-, -ˈnā-\ *n* **:** the quality or state of being diaphanous

di·aph·a·nous \dī-ˈaf-ə-nəs\ *adj* [ML *diaphanus,* fr. Gk *diaphanēs,* fr. *diaphainein* to show through, fr. *dia-* + *phainein* to show — more at FANCY] **1 :** characterized by such fineness of texture as to permit seeing through **2 :** characterized by extreme delicacy of form **:** ETHEREAL <painted ~ landscapes> **3 :** INSUBSTANTIAL, VAGUE <had only a ~ hope of success> — **di·aph·a·nous·ly** *adv* — **di·aph·a·nous·ness** *n*

dia·phone \ˈdī-ə-ˌfōn\ *n* **:** a fog signal similar to a siren but producing a blast of two tones

di·aph·o·rase \dī-ˈaf-ə-ˌrās, -ˌrāz\ *n* [Gk *diaphoros* different + E *-ase*]**:** a flavoprotein enzyme capable of oxidizing the reduced form of NAD

di·a·pho·re·sis \ˌdī-ə-fə-ˈrē-səs, (ˌ)dī-ˌaf-ə-\ *n, pl* **-re·ses** \-ˌsēz\ [LL, fr. Gk *diaphorēsis,* fr. *diaphorein* to dissipate by perspiration, fr. *dia-* + *pherein* to carry — more at BEAR]**:** PERSPIRATION; *esp* **:** profuse perspiration artificially induced

di·a·pho·ret·ic \-ˈret-ik\ *adj* **:** having the power to increase perspiration — **diaphoretic** *n*

1di·a·phragm \ˈdī-ə-ˌfram\ *n* [ME *diafragma,* fr. LL *diaphragma,* fr. Gk, fr. *diaphrassein* to barricade, fr. *dia-* + *phrassein* to enclose — more at FARCE] **1 :** a body partition of muscle and connective tissue; *specif* **:** the partition separating the chest and abdominal cavities in mammals **2 :** a dividing membrane or thin partition esp. in a tube **3 a :** a more or less rigid partition in the body or shell of an invertebrate **b :** a transverse septum in a plant stem **4 :** a device that limits the aperture of a lens or optical system — compare IRIS DIAPHRAGM **5 :** a thin flexible disk that vibrates (as in a microphone) **6 :** a molded cap usu. of thin rubber fitted over the uterine cervix to act as a mechanical contraceptive barrier — **di·a·phrag·mat·ic** \ˌdī-ə-frə(g)-ˈmat-ik, -ˌfrag-\ *adj* — **di·a·phrag·mat·i·cal·ly** \-ˈmat-i-k(ə-)lē\ *adv*

2diaphragm *vt* **1 :** to equip with a diaphragm **2 :** to cut down the aperture of (as a lens) by a diaphragm

di·aph·y·sis \dī-ˈaf-ə-səs\ *n, pl* **-y·ses** \-ˌsēz\ [NL, fr. Gk, spinous process of the tibia, fr. *diaphyesthai* to grow between, fr. *dia-* + *phyein* to bring forth — more at BE]**:** the shaft of a long bone — **di·aph·y·se·al** \(ˌ)dī-ˌaf-ə-ˈsē-əl\ *or* **di·a·phys·i·al** \ˌdī-ə-ˈfiz-ē-əl\ *adj*

di·a·pir \ˈdī-ə-ˌpi(ə)r\ *n* [Gk *diapeirein* to drive through, fr. *dia-* + *peirein* to pierce; akin to Gk *poros* passage — more at FARE] **:** an anticlinal fold in which a mobile core has broken through brittle overlying rocks — **di·a·pir·ic** \ˌdī-ə-ˈpir-ik\ *adj*

di·apoph·y·sis \ˌdī-ə-ˈpäf-ə-səs\ *n, pl* **-y·ses** \-ˌsēz\ [NL, fr. *dia-* + *apophysis*]**:** a transverse process of a vertebra that is an outgrowth of the neural arch on the dorsal side; *esp* **:** one of the dorsal pair of such processes when two or more pairs are present

dia·pos·i·tive \ˌdī-ə-ˈpäz-ət-iv, -ˈpäz-tiv\ *n* **:** a transparent photographic positive (as a transparency)

di·ap·sid \dī-ˈap-səd\ *adj* [deriv. of Gk *di-* + *hapsid-, hapsis* arch — more at APSIS]**:** of, relating to, or including reptiles (as the crocodiles) with two pairs of temporal openings in the skull

di·ar·chy *var of* DYARCHY

di·a·rist \ˈdī-ə-rəst\ *n* **:** one who keeps a diary

di·ar·rhea *or* **di·ar·rhoea** \ˌdī-ə-ˈrē-ə\ *n* [ME *diaria,* fr. LL *diarrhoea,* fr. Gk *diarrhoia,* fr. *diarrhein* to flow through, fr. *dia-* + *rhein* to flow — more at STREAM]**:** abnormally frequent intestinal evacuations with more or less fluid stools — **di·ar·rhe·al** \-ˈrē-əl\ *or* **di·ar·rhe·ic** \-ˈrē-ik\ *also* **di·ar·rhet·ic** \-ˈret-ik\ *adj*

di·ar·thro·sis \ˌdī-är-ˈthrō-səs\ *n, pl* **-thro·ses** \-ˌsēz\ [NL, fr. Gk *diarthrōsis,* fr. *diarthroun* to joint, fr. *dia-* + *arthroun* to fasten by a joint, fr. *arthron* joint — more at ARTHR-]**:** articulation that permits free movement **2 :** a freely movable joint

di·a·ry \ˈdī-(ə-)rē\ *n, pl* **-ries** [L *diarium,* fr. *dies* day — more at DEITY] **1 :** a record of events, transactions, or observations kept daily or at frequent intervals **:** JOURNAL; *esp* **:** a daily record of personal activities, reflections, or feelings **2 :** a book intended or used for a diary

di·as·po·ra \dī-ˈas-p(ə-)rə\ *n* [Gk, dispersion, fr. *diaspeirein* to scatter, fr. *dia-* + *speirein* to sow — more at SPROUT] **1** *cap* **a :** the settling of scattered colonies of Jews outside Palestine after the Babylonian exile **b :** the area outside Palestine settled by Jews **c :** the Jews living outside Palestine or modern Israel **2 :** MIGRATION <the great black ~ to the cities of the North and West in the 1940s and 1950s —*Newsweek*>

di·a·spore \ˈdī-ə-ˌspō(ə)r, -ˌspȯ(ə)r\ *n* [F, fr. Gk *diaspora*] **:** a mineral consisting of aluminum hydrogen oxide $HAlO_2$

di·a·stase \ˈdī-ə-ˌstās, -ˌstāz\ *n* [F, fr. Gk *diastasis* separation, interval, fr. *diistanai* to separate, fr. *dia-* + *histanai* to cause to stand — more at STAND] **1 :** AMYLASE; *esp* **:** a mixture of amylases from malt **2 :** ENZYME

di·as·ta·sis \dī-ˈas-tə-səs\ *n, pl* **-ta·ses** \-ˌsēz\ [NL, fr. Gk, interval]**:** the rest phase of cardiac diastole occurring between the filling of the ventricle and the start of auricular contraction

di·a·stat·ic \ˌdī-ə-ˈstat-ik\ *adj* **:** relating to or having the properties of diastase; *esp* **:** converting starch into sugar

di·a·ste·ma \ˌdī-ə-ˈstē-mə\ *n, pl* **-ma·ta** \-mət-ə\ [NL, fr. LL, interval, fr. Gk *diastēma,* fr. *diistanai*]**:** a space between teeth in a jaw — **di·a·ste·mat·ic** \-sti-ˈmat-ik\ *adj*

di·a·ste·reo·iso·mer \ˌdī-ə-ˌster-ē-ō-ˈī-sə-mər, -ˌstir-\ *or* **di·a·ste·reo·mer** \-ˈster-ē-ə-(ˌ)mər, -ˈstir-\ *n* **:** a stereoisomer that does not have a mirror image — compare ENANTIOMORPH — **di·a·ste·reo·iso·mer·ic** \-ˈster-ē-ō-ˌī-sə-ˈmer-ik, -ˈstir-\ *adj* — **di·a·ste·reo·isom·er·ism** \-ī-ˈsäm-ə-ˌriz-əm\ *n*

di·as·to·le \dī-ˈas-tə-(ˌ)lē\ *n* [Gk *diastolē* dilatation, fr. *diastellein* to expand, fr. *dia-* + *stellein* to send — more at STALL]**:** a rhythmically recurrent expansion; *esp* **:** the dilatation of the cavities of the heart during which they fill with blood — **di·a·stol·ic** \ˌdī-ə-ˈstäl-ik\ *adj*

di·as·tro·phism \dī-ˈas-trə-ˌfiz-əm\ *n* [Gk *diastrophē* twisting, fr. *diastrephein* to distort, fr. *dia-* + *strephein* to twist — more at STROPHE]**:** the process of deformation that produces in the earth's crust its continents and ocean basins, plateaus and mountains, folds of strata, and faults — **di·a·stroph·ic** \ˌdī-ə-ˈsträf-ik\ *adj* — **di·a·stroph·i·cal·ly** \-i-k(ə-)lē\ *adv*

di·a·tes·sa·ron \ˌdī-ə-ˈtes-ə-rən\ *n* [ME, fr. L, fr. Gk (*hē*) *dia tessarōn* (*chordōn symphōnia*) the concord through four notes, fr. *dia* through + *tessarōn,* gen. of *tessares* four — more at DIA-, FOUR]**:** a harmony of the four Gospels edited and arranged into a single connected narrative

dia·ther·ma·nous \ˌdī-ə-ˈthər-mə-nəs\ *adj* [Gk *diatherman-,* stem of *diathermainein* to heat through]**:** DIATHERMIC 1

dia·ther·mic \ˌdī-ə-ˈthər-mik\ *adj* **1 :** transmitting infrared radiation **2 :** of or relating to diathermy <~ treatment>

dia·ther·my \ˈdī-ə-ˌthər-mē\ *n* [ISV]**:** the generation of heat in tissue by electric currents for medical or surgical purposes

di·ath·e·sis \dī-ˈath-ə-səs\ *n, pl* **-e·ses** \-ˌsēz\ [NL, fr. Gk, lit., arrangement, fr. *diatithenai* to arrange, fr. *dia-* + *tithenai* to set — more at DO] **1 :** a constitutional predisposition toward an abnormality or disease **2 :** a disposition toward or aptitude for a particular mental development — **di·a·thet·ic** \ˌdī-ə-ˈthet-ik\ *adj*

di·a·tom \ˈdī-ə-ˌtäm\ *n* [deriv. of Gk *diatomos* cut in half, fr. *diatemnein* to cut through, fr. *dia-* + *temnein* to cut — more at TOME]**:** any of a class (Bacillariophyceae) of minute planktonic unicellular or colonial algae with silicified skeletons that form diatomite

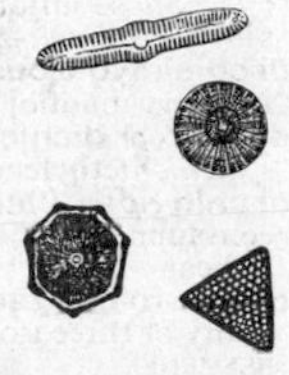

diatoms

di·a·to·ma·ceous \ˌdī-ət-ə-ˈmā-shəs, (ˌ)dī-ˌat-\ *adj* **:** consisting of or abounding in diatoms or their siliceous remains <~ silica>

diatomaceous earth *n* **:** DIATOMITE

di·atom·ic \ˌdī-ə-ˈtäm-ik\ *adj* [ISV] **1 :** consisting of two atoms **:** having two atoms in the molecule **2 :** having two replaceable atoms or radicals

di·at·o·mite \dī-ˈat-ə-ˌmīt\ *n* **:** a light friable siliceous material derived chiefly from diatom remains and used esp. as a filter

dia·ton·ic \ˌdī-ə-ˈtän-ik\ *adj* [LL *diatonicus,* fr. Gk *diatonikos,* fr. *diatonos* stretching, fr. *diateinein* to stretch out, fr. *dia-* + *teinein* to stretch — more at THIN]**:** relating to a musical scale having eight tones to the octave and using a fixed pattern of intervals without chromatic deviation — **dia·ton·i·cal·ly** \-ˈtän-i-k(ə-)lē\ *adv*

di·a·tribe \ˈdī-ə-ˌtrīb\ *n* [L *diatriba,* fr. Gk *diatribē* pastime, discourse, fr. *diatribein* to spend (time), wear away, fr. *dia-* + *tribein* to rub — more at THROW] **1** *archaic* **:** a prolonged discourse **2 :** a bitter and abusive speech or writing **3 :** ironical or satirical criticism

di·at·ro·pism \dī-ˈa-trə-ˌpiz-əm\ *n* [ISV]**:** the tropistic tendency of plant organs to place themselves transversely to the line of action of a stimulus — **dia·tro·pic** \ˌdī-ə-ˈtrō-pik, -ˈträp-ik\ *adj*

di·az·e·pam \dī-ˈaz-ə-ˌpam\ *n* [*di-* + *az-* + *epoxide* + *-am* (of unknown origin)]**:** a tranquilizer $C_{16}H_{13}ClN_2O$ used esp. to relieve anxiety and tension and as a muscle relaxant

di·a·zine \ˈdī-ə-ˌzēn, dī-ˈaz-ᵊn\ *n* [ISV *di-* + *az-* + *-ine*]**:** any of three compounds $C_4H_4N_2$ containing a ring that is composed of four carbon atoms and two nitrogen atoms

di·azo \dī-ˈaz-(ˌ)ō\ *adj* [ISV *diaz-, diazo-,* fr. *di-* + *az-*] **1 :** relating to or containing the group N_2 composed of two nitrogen atoms united to a single carbon atom of an organic radical **2 :** relating to or containing diazonium **3 :** of or relating to a photograph or photocopy whose production involves the use of a coating of a diazo compound that is decomposed by exposure to light

di·a·zo·ni·um \ˌdī-ə-ˈzō-nē-əm\ *n* [ISV *di-* + *az-* + *-onium*]**:** the univalent cation N_2^+ that is composed of two nitrogen atoms united to carbon in an organic radical and that usu. exists in salts used in the manufacture of azo dyes

di·az·o·tize \dī-ˈaz-ə-ˌtīz\ *vt* **-tized; -tiz·ing** [*di-* + *azote* + *-ize*] **:** to convert (a compound) into a diazo compound (as a diazonium salt) — **di·az·o·ti·za·tion** \-ˌaz-ət-ə-ˈzā-shən\ *n*

di·ba·sic \(ˈ)dī-ˈbā-sik\ *adj* **1 :** having two replaceable hydrogen atoms — used of acids **2 :** containing two atoms of a univalent metal <~ sodium phosphate Na_2HPO_4> **3 :** having two hydroxyl groups — used of bases and basic salts

dib·ber \ˈdib-ər\ *n* **:** DIBBLE

1dib·ble \ˈdib-əl\ *n* [ME *debylle*]**:** a small hand implement used to make holes in the ground for plants, seeds, or bulbs

2dibble *vt* **dib·bled; dib·bling** \ˈdib-(ə-)liŋ\ **1 :** to plant with a dibble **2 :** to make holes in (soil) with or as if with a dibble

ə abut	ᵊ kitten	ər further	a back	ā bake	ä cot, cart
aů out	ch chin	e less	ē easy	g gift	i trip	ī life
j joke	ŋ sing	ō flow	ȯ flaw	ȯi coin	th thin	t͟h this
ü loot	ů foot	y yet	yü few	yů furious	zh vision

di·bran·chi·ate \(ˈ)dī-ˈbraŋ-kē-ət\ *adj* [deriv. of Gk *di-* + *branchia*] **:** of or relating to a group (Dibranchia) of cephalopod mollusks including the squids and octopuses and having 2 gills, 2 auricles, 2 nephridia, an apparatus for emitting an inky fluid, and either 8 or 10 cephalic arms bearing suckers or hooks

dibs \ˈdibz\ *n pl* [short for *dibstones* (jacks), fr. obs. *dib* (to dab)] **1** *slang* **:** money esp. in small amounts **2 :** CLAIM, RIGHTS <I have ~ on that piece of cake>

di·bu·tyl phthal·ate \ˌdī-ˌbyüt-ᵊl-ˈthal-ˌāt\ *n* [*di-* + *butyl* + *phthalic* acid + *-ate*] **:** a colorless oily ester $C_{16}H_{22}O_4$ used chiefly as a solvent and plasticizer

di·car·box·yl·ic \ˌdī-ˌkär-ˌbäk-ˈsil-ik\ *adj* **:** containing two carboxyl groups in the molecule

di·cast \ˈdī-ˌkast, ˈdik-ˌast\ *n* [Gk *dikastēs*, fr. *dikazein* to judge, fr. *dikē* judgment — more at DICTION] **:** an ancient Athenian performing the functions of both judge and juror at a trial

[1]**dice** \ˈdīs\ *n, pl* **dice** [ME *dyce*, fr. *dees, dyce*, pl. of *dee* die — more at DIE] **1 a :** DIE 1 **b :** a gambling game played with dice **2** *pl also* **dices :** a small cubical piece (as of food) **3 :** a close contest between two racing-car drivers for position during a race — **no dice :** of no avail **:** no use **:** FUTILE

[2]**dice** *vb* **diced; dic·ing** [ME *dycen*, fr. *dyce*] *vt* **1 a :** to cut into small cubes **b :** to ornament with square markings <*diced* leather> **2 a :** to bring by playing dice <~ himself into debt> **b :** to lose by dicing <~ his money away> ~ *vi* **1 :** to play games with dice <~ for drinks in the bar —Malcolm Lowry> **2 :** to take a chance <the temptation to ~ with death —*Newsweek*> — **dic·er** *n*

di·cen·tra \dī-ˈsen-trə\ *n* [NL *Dicentra*, genus name, fr. *di-* + Gk *kentron* sharp point — more at CENTER] **:** any of a genus (*Dicentra*) of herbs of the fumitory family with dissected leaves and irregular flowers

dic·ey \ˈdī-sē\ *adj* **dic·i·er; -est** [[1]*dice* + *-y*] **:** RISKY, UNPREDICTABLE

dich- *or* **dicho-** *comb form* [LL, fr. Gk, fr. *dicha*; akin to Gk *di-*] **:** in two **:** apart <*dicho*gamous>

di·cha·sium \dī-ˈkā-z(h)ē-əm, -zhəm\ *n, pl* **-sia** \-z(h)ē-ə, -zhə\ [NL, fr. Gk *dichasis* halving, fr. *dichazein* to halve, fr. *dicha*] **:** a cymose inflorescence that produces two main axes — **di·cha·sial** \-z(h)ē-əl, -zhəl\ *adj*

di·chla·myd·e·ous \ˌdī-klə-ˈmid-ē-əs\ *adj* [*di-* + Gk *chlamyd-, chlamys* mantle] **:** having both calyx and corolla

dichlor- *or* **dichloro-** *comb form* **:** containing two atoms of chlorine <*dichloro*ethylene>

di·chlo·ride \(ˈ)dī-ˈklō(ə)r-ˌīd, -ˈklȯ(ə)r-\ *n* **:** a binary compound containing two atoms of chlorine combined with an element or radical

di·chlo·ro·ben·zene \(ˌ)dī-ˌklōr-ə-ˈben-ˌzēn, -ˌklȯr-, -(ˌ)ben-ˈ\ *n* **:** any of three isomeric compounds $C_6H_4Cl_2$; *esp* **:** PARADICHLOROBENZENE

di·chlo·ro·di·flu·o·ro·meth·ane \-ˌflu̇r-ə-ˈmeth-ˌān\ *n* [*dichlor-* + *di-* + *fluor-* + *methane*] **:** a nontoxic nonflammable easily liquefiable gas CCl_2F_2 used as a refrigerant and as a propellant **:** a Freon gas

di·chlor·vos \(ˈ)dī-ˈklō(ə)r-ˌväs, -ˈklȯ(ə)r-, -vəs\ *n* [*dichlor-* + *v*inyl + ph*os*phate] **:** a nonpersistent organophosphorus pesticide $C_4H_7Cl_2O_4P$ that is used esp. against insects and is of low toxicity to man

di·chog·a·mous \dī-ˈkäg-ə-məs\ *or* **di·cho·gam·ic** \ˌdī-kə-ˈgam-ik\ *adj, of a hermaphroditic organism* **:** characterized by production at different times of male and female reproductive elements that ensures cross-fertilization — **di·chog·a·my** \dī-ˈkäg-ə-mē\ *n*

di·chon·dra \dī-ˈkän-drə\ *n* [NL, genus name, fr. *di-* + Gk *chondros* grain] **:** any of a genus (*Dichondra*) of chiefly tropical perennial herbs of the morning glory family that includes some (esp *D. repens* or its varieties) used as a ground cover and a substitute for lawn grasses in warmer parts of the U.S.

dich·otic \(ˈ)dī-ˈkōt-ik\ *adj* [*dich-* + [2]*-otic*] **:** affecting or relating to the two ears differently in regard to a conscious aspect (as pitch or loudness) or a physical aspect (as frequency or energy) of sound — **dich·oti·cal·ly** \-i-k(ə-)lē\ *adv*

di·chot·o·mist \dī-ˈkät-ə-məst *also* də-\ *n* **:** one that dichotomizes

di·chot·o·mize \-ˌmīz\ *vb* **-mized; -miz·ing** [LL *dichotomos*] *vt* **:** to divide into two parts, classes, or groups ~ *vi* **:** to exhibit dichotomy — **di·chot·o·mi·za·tion** \-ˌkät-ə-mə-ˈzā-shən\ *n*

di·chot·o·mous \dī-ˈkät-ə-məs *also* də-\ *adj* [LL *dichotomos*, fr. Gk, fr. *dich-* + *temnein* to cut — more at TOME] **1 :** dividing into two parts **2 :** relating to, involving, or proceeding from dichotomy — **di·chot·o·mous·ly** *adv* — **di·chot·o·mous·ness** *n*

di·chot·o·my \dī-ˈkät-ə-mē *also* də-\ *n, pl* **-mies** [Gk *dichotomia*, fr. *dichotomos*] **1 :** a division or the process of dividing into two esp. mutually exclusive or contradictory groups **2 :** the phase of the moon or an inferior planet in which half its disk appears illuminated **3 a :** FORKING; *esp* **:** repeated bifurcation **b :** a system of branching in which the main axis forks repeatedly into two branches **c :** branching of an ancestral line into two equal diverging branches

di·chro·ic \dī-ˈkrō-ik\ *also* **di·chro·it·ic** \ˌdī-(ˌ)krō-ˈit-ik\ *adj* [Gk *dichroos* two-colored, fr. *di-* + *chrōs* color — more at CHROMATIC] **1 :** having the property of dichroism <a ~ crystal> <a ~ mirror> **2 :** DICHROMATIC

di·chro·ism \ˈdī-(ˌ)krō-ˌiz-əm\ *n* **1 :** the property according to which the colors are unlike when a crystal is viewed in the direction of two different axes **2 a :** the property of a solid of differing in color with the thickness of the transmitting layer or of a liquid with the degree of concentration of the solution **b :** the property of a surface of reflecting light of one color and transmitting light of other colors **3 :** DICHROMATISM

di·chro·mat \ˈdī-krō-ˌmat, (ˈ)dī-ˈ\ *n* [back-formation fr. *dichromatic*] **:** one affected with dichromatism

di·chro·mate \(ˈ)dī-ˈkrō-ˌmāt, ˈdī-krō-\ *n* [ISV] **:** a usu. orange to red chromium salt containing the radical Cr_2O_7 <~ of potassium> — called also *bichromate*

di·chro·mat·ic \ˌdī-krō-ˈmat-ik\ *adj* [*di-* + *chromatic*] **1 :** having or exhibiting two colors **2 :** having two color varieties or color phases independently of age or sex <a ~ bird> **3 :** of, relating to, or exhibiting dichromatism

di·chro·ma·tism \dī-ˈkrō-mə-ˌtiz-əm\ *n* **1 :** the state or condition of being dichromatic **2 :** partial color blindness in which only two colors are perceptible

di·chro·scope \ˈdī-krə-ˌskōp\ *n* **:** an instrument for examining crystals for dichroism

dick \ˈdik\ *n* [*Dick*, nickname for *Richard*] **1** *chiefly Brit* **:** FELLOW, CHAP **2 :** PENIS — usu. considered vulgar **3** [by shortening & alter.] **:** DETECTIVE

dick·cis·sel \dik-ˈsis-əl, ˈdik-ˌ\ *n* [imit.] **:** a common migratory black-throated finch (*Spiza americana*) of the central U.S.

dick·ens \ˈdik-ənz\ *n* [euphemism] **:** DEVIL, DEUCE

[1]**dick·er** \ˈdik-ər\ *n* [ME *dyker*; akin to MHG *techer*; both fr. a prehistoric WGmc word borrowed fr. L *decuria* quantity of ten, fr. *decem* ten — more at TEN] **:** the number or quantity of 10 esp. of hides or skins

[2]**dicker** *vi* **dick·ered; dick·er·ing** \ˈdik-(ə-)riŋ\ [origin unknown] **:** BARGAIN

[3]**dicker** *n* **1 :** BARTER **2 :** an act or session of haggling or bargaining

dick·ey *or* **dicky** *also* **dick·ie** \ˈdik-ē\ *n, pl* **dickeys** *or* **dick·ies** [*Dicky*, nickname for *Richard*] **1 :** any of various articles of clothing: as **a :** a man's separate or detachable shirtfront **b :** a small fabric insert worn to fill in the neckline **2 :** a small bird **3** *chiefly Brit* **a :** the driver's seat in a carriage **b :** a seat at the back of a carriage or automobile

Dick test \ˈdik-\ *n* [George F. *Dick* †1967 and Gladys H. *Dick* †1963 Am physicians] **:** a test to determine susceptibility or immunity to scarlet fever by an injection of scarlet fever toxin

di·cli·nous \(ˈ)dī-ˈklī-nəs\ *adj* **:** having the stamens and pistils in separate flowers — **di·cli·ny** \ˈdī-ˌklī-nē\ *n*

di·cot \ˈdī-ˌkät\ *also* **di·cot·yl** \-ˌkät-ᵊl\ *n* **:** DICOTYLEDON

di·cot·y·le·don \ˌdī-ˌkät-ᵊl-ˈēd-ᵊn\ *n* [deriv. of NL *di-* + *cotyledon*] **:** a plant with two seed leaves **:** a member of the one (Dicotyledones) of the two subclasses of angiospermous plants that comprises those with two cotyledons — **di·cot·y·le·don·ous** \-ᵊn-əs\ *adj*

di·cou·ma·rin \(ˈ)dī-ˈkü-mə-rən\ *n* [fr. *di-* + *coumarin*] **:** a crystalline compound $C_{19}H_{12}O_6$ orig. obtained from spoiled sweet clover hay and used to delay clotting of blood

di·crot·ic \dī-ˈkrät-ik\ *adj* [Gk *dikrotos* having a double beat] **:** being or relating to the second expansion of the artery that occurs during the diastole of the heart — **di·cro·tism** \ˈdī-krə-ˌtiz-əm\ *n*

dict *abbr* dictionary

Dic·ta·phone \ˈdik-tə-ˌfōn\ *trademark* — used for a dictating machine

[1]**dic·tate** \ˈdik-ˌtāt, dik-ˈ\ *vb* [L *dictatus*, pp. of *dictare* to assert, dictate, fr. *dictus*, pp. of *dicere* to say — more at DICTION] *vi* **1 :** to give dictation **2 :** to speak or act domineeringly **:** PRESCRIBE ~ *vt* **1 :** to speak or read for a person to transcribe or for a machine to record **2 a :** to issue as an order **b :** to impose, pronounce, or specify authoritatively

[2]**dic·tate** \ˈdik-ˌtāt\ *n* **1 a :** an authoritative rule, prescription, or injunction **b :** a ruling principle <according to the ~*s* of his conscience> **2 :** a command by one in authority

dictating machine *n* **:** a machine used esp. for the recording of dictated matter

dic·ta·tion \dik-ˈtā-shən\ *n* **1 a :** PRESCRIPTION **b :** arbitrary command **2 a** (1) **:** the act or manner of uttering words to be transcribed (2) **:** material that is dictated or transcribed **b** (1) **:** the performing of music to be reproduced by a student (2) **:** music so reproduced

dic·ta·tor \ˈdik-ˌtāt-ər, dik-ˈ\ *n* [L, fr. *dictatus*] **1 a :** a person granted absolute emergency power; *esp* **:** one appointed by the senate of ancient Rome **b :** one holding complete autocratic control **c :** one ruling absolutely and often oppressively **2 :** one that dictates — **dic·ta·tress** \ˈdik-ˌtā-trəs, dik-ˈ\ *n*

dic·ta·to·ri·al \ˌdik-tə-ˈtōr-ē-əl, -ˈtȯr-\ *adj* **1 a :** of, relating to, or befitting a dictator <~ power> **b :** ruled by a dictator **2 :** oppressive to or contemptuously overbearing toward others **:** arrogantly domineering — **dic·ta·to·ri·al·ly** \-ē-ə-lē\ *adv* — **dic·ta·to·ri·al·ness** *n*

syn DICTATORIAL, MAGISTERIAL, DOGMATIC, DOCTRINAIRE, ORACULAR *shared meaning element* **:** imposing one's will or opinions on others

dic·ta·tor·ship \dik-ˈtāt-ər-ˌship, ˈdik-ˌ\ *n* **1 :** the office of dictator **2 :** autocratic rule, control, or leadership **3 a :** a form of government in which absolute power is concentrated in a dictator or a small clique **b :** a government organization or group in which absolute power is so concentrated **c :** a despotic state

dictatorship of the proletariat : the assumption of political power by the proletariat held in Marxism to be an essential part of the transition from capitalism to communism

dic·tion \ˈdik-shən\ *n* [L *diction-, dictio* speaking, style, fr. *dictus*, pp. of *dicere* to say; akin to OE *tēon* to accuse, L *dicare* to proclaim, dedicate, Gk *deiknynai* to show, *dikē* judgment, right] **1** *obs* **:** verbal description **2 :** choice of words esp. with regard to correctness, clearness, or effectiveness **3 a :** vocal expression **:** ENUNCIATION **b :** pronunciation and enunciation of words in singing — **dic·tion·al** \-shnəl, -shən-ᵊl\ *adj* — **dic·tion·al·ly** \-ē\ *adv*

dic·tio·nary \ˈdik-shə-ˌner-ē\ *n, pl* **-nar·ies** [ML *dictionarium*, fr. LL *diction-, dictio* word, fr. L, speaking] **1 :** a reference book containing words usu. alphabetically arranged along with information about their forms, pronunciations, functions, etymologies, meanings, and syntactical and idiomatic uses **2 :** a reference book listing alphabetically terms or names important to a particular subject or activity along with discussion of their meanings and applications **3 :** a reference book giving for words of one language equivalents in another **4 :** a list (as of phrases, synonyms, or hyphenation instructions) stored in machine-readable form (as on a disk) for reference by an automatic system (as for information retrieval or computerized typesetting)

Dic·to·graph \ˈdik-tə-ˌgraf\ *trademark* — used for a telephonic device for recording sounds or for picking them up in one room and transmitting them to another

dic·tum \ˈdik-təm\ *n, pl* **dic·ta** \-tə\ *also* **dictums** [L, fr. neut. of *dictus*] **1 :** a formal authoritative pronouncement of a principle, proposition, or opinion **2 :** a judicial opinion on a point other than the precise issue involved in determining a case

dicty- *or* **dictyo-** *comb form* [NL, fr. Gk *dikty-*, *diktyo-*, fr. *diktyon*, fr. *dikein* to throw] **:** net <*dictyo*stele> <*dictyo*some>

dic·tyo·some \ˈdik-tē-ə-ˌsōm\ *n* **:** GOLGI BODY

dic·tyo·stele \ˈdik-tē-ə-ˌstēl, ˌdik-tē-ə-ˈstē-lē\ *n* **:** a stele in which the vascular cylinder is broken up into a longitudinal series or network of vascular strands around a central pith (as in many ferns)

di·cy·clic \(ˈ)dī-ˈsī-klik, -ˈsik-lik\ *adj* **1 :** BICYCLIC 2 **2 :** having two maxima of population each year — **di·cy·cly** \ˈdī-ˌsī-klē\ *n*

did *past of* DO

di·dact \ˈdī-ˌdakt\ *n* [back-formation fr. *didactic*] **:** a didactic person

di·dac·tic \dī-ˈdak-tik, də-\ *adj* [Gk *didaktikos*, fr. *didaskein* to teach] **1 a :** designed or intended to teach **b :** intended to convey instruction and information as well as pleasure and entertainment **2 :** making moral observations — **di·dac·ti·cal** \-ti-kəl\ *adj* — **di·dac·ti·cal·ly** \-ti-k(ə-)lē\ *adv* — **di·dac·ti·cism** \-tə-ˌsiz-əm\ *n*

di·dac·tics \-tiks\ *n pl but sing or pl in constr* **:** systematic instruction **:** PEDAGOGY, TEACHINGS

di·dap·per \ˈdī-ˌdap-ər\ *n* [ME *dydoppar*] **:** a dabchick or other small grebe

did·dle \ˈdid-ᵊl\ *vb* **did·dled; did·dling** \ˈdid-liŋ, -ᵊl-iŋ\ [origin unknown] *vi* **:** DAWDLE, FOOL ~ *vt* **1** *chiefly dial* **:** to move with short rapid motions **2 :** to waste (as time) in trifling **3 :** HOAX, SWINDLE — **did·dler** \ˈdid-lər, -ᵊl-ər\ *n*

di·del·phic \(ˈ)dī-ˈdel-fik\ *adj* [*di-* + Gk *delphys* womb — more at DOLPHIN] **1 a :** having or relating to a double uterus **b :** having the female genital tract doubled — used esp. of some worms **2** [NL *Didelphia*, genus name, fr. Gk *di-* + *delphys*] **:** MARSUPIAL

didn't \ˈdid-ᵊnt\ **:** did not

di·do \ˈdīd-(ˌ)ō\ *n, pl* **didoes** *or* **didos** [origin unknown] **1 :** a mischievous or unconventional act **:** PRANK, ANTIC — often used in the phrase *cut didoes* **2 :** something that is frivolous or showy

Di·do \ˈdīd-(ˌ)ō\ *n* [L, fr. Gk *Deidō*] **:** a queen of Carthage in Vergil's *Aeneid* who entertains Aeneas, falls in love with him, and on his departure stabs herself

didst \(ˈ)didst, (ˈ)ditst\ *archaic past 2d sing of* DO

di·dym·i·um \dī-ˈdim-ē-əm\ *n* [NL, fr. Gk *didymos*] **:** a mixture of rare-earth elements made up chiefly of neodymium and praseodymium and used esp. for coloring glass for optical filters

did·y·mous \ˈdid-ə-məs\ *adj* [Gk *didymos* double, twin (adj. & n.), testicle, fr. *dyo* two — more at TWO] **:** growing in pairs **:** TWIN

di·dyn·a·mous \(ˈ)dī-ˈdin-ə-məs\ *adj* [deriv. of Gk *di-* + *dynamis* power — more at DYNAMIC] **:** having four stamens disposed in pairs of unequal length — **di·dyn·a·my** \-mē\ *n*

¹die \ˈdī\ *vi* **died; dy·ing** \ˈdī-iŋ\ [ME *dien*, fr. or akin to ON *deyja* to die; akin to OHG *touwen* to die, OIr *duine* human being] **1 :** to pass from physical life **:** EXPIRE **2 :** to pass out of existence **:** CEASE <their anger *died* at these words> **3 a :** to suffer or face the pains of death **b :** SINK, LANGUISH <*dying* from fatigue> **c :** to long keenly or desperately <*dying* to go> **4 :** to cease to be subject <let them ~ to sin> **5 a :** to pass into an inferior state or situation <they have developed competence which we . . . must utilize lest it wither and ~ —Ruth G. Strickland> **b :** STOP <the motor *died*>

²die \ˈdī\ *n, pl* **dice** \ˈdīs\ *or* **dies** \ˈdīz\ [ME *dee*, fr. MF *dé*] **1** *pl dice* **:** a small cube marked on each face with from one to six spots and used usu. in pairs in various games and in gambling by being shaken and thrown to come to rest at random on a flat surface **2** *pl usu dice* **:** something determined by or as if by a cast of dice **:** CHANCE **3** *pl dies* **:** DADO 1a **4** *pl dies* **:** any of various tools or devices for imparting a desired shape, form, or finish to a material or for impressing an object or material: as **a** (1) **:** the larger of a pair of cutting or shaping tools that when moved toward each other produce a desired form in or impress a desired device on an object by pressure or by a blow (2) **:** a device composed of a pair of such tools **b :** a hollow internally threaded screw-cutting tool used for forming screw threads **c :** a cutter to cut out blanks **d :** a mold into which molten metal or other material is forced **e :** a perforated block through which metal or plastic is drawn or extruded for shaping

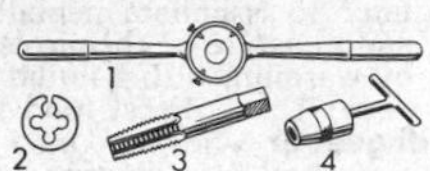

die 4b: four pieces of a tap-and-die set: *1* diestock, *2* adjustable round split die, *3* tap, *4* tap wrench

³die *vt* **died; die·ing :** to cut or shape with a die

die·back \ˈdī-ˌbak\ *n* **:** a condition in woody plants in which peripheral parts are killed esp. by parasites

di·ecious *var of* DIOECIOUS

die down *vi* **1 :** to undergo death of the aboveground portions **2 :** DIMINISH, SUBSIDE <the storm *died down*>

die·hard \ˈdī-ˌhärd\ *n* **:** an irreconcilable opponent of change <party ~*s* who insisted that no concession of any kind be made>

die–hard \ˈdī-ˌhärd\ *adj* **:** strongly resisting change **:** completely and determinedly fixed <a ~ conservative> — **die–hard·ism** \-ˌiz-əm\ *n*

di·el \ˈdī-əl, -ˌel\ *adj* [irreg. fr. L *dies* day + E *-al*] **:** involving a 24-hour period that usu. includes a day and the adjoining night <~ fluctuations in temperature>

diel·drin \ˈdē(ə)l-drən\ *n* [*Diels*-Al*der* reaction, after Otto *Diels* & Kurt *Alder*] **:** a white crystalline persistent chlorinated hydrocarbon insecticide $C_{12}H_8Cl_6O$

di·elec·tric \ˌdī-ə-ˈlek-trik\ *n* [*dia-* + *electric*] **:** a nonconductor of direct electric current — **dielectric** *adj*

dielectric heating *n* **:** the rapid and uniform heating throughout a nonconducting material by means of a high-frequency electromagnetic field

di·en·ceph·a·lon \ˌdī-ən-ˈsef-ə-ˌlän, ˌdī-(ˌ)en-, -lən\ *n* [NL, fr. *dia-* + *encephalon*] **:** the posterior subdivision of the forebrain — **di·en·ce·phal·ic** \-sə-ˈfal-ik\ *adj*

di·ene \ˈdī-ˌēn\ *n* [*di-* + *-ene*] **:** a compound containing two double bonds; *esp* **:** DIOLEFIN

die–off \ˈdī-ˌȯf\ *n* **:** a sudden sharp decline of a population (as rabbits) that is not caused directly by human activity (as hunting)

die out *vi* **:** to become extinct

di·er·e·sis *var of* DIAERESIS

die·sel \ˈdē-zəl, -səl\ *n* [Rudolph *Diesel*] **1 :** DIESEL ENGINE **2 :** a vehicle driven by a diesel engine

diesel–electric *adj* **:** of, relating to, or employing the combination of a diesel engine driving an electric generator <a ~ locomotive>

diesel engine *n* **:** an internal-combustion engine in which air is compressed to a temperature sufficiently high to ignite fuel injected into the cylinder where the combustion actuates a piston

die·sel·ize \ˈdē-zə-ˌlīz, ˈdē-sə-\ *vt* **-ized; -iz·ing :** to equip with a diesel engine or with electric locomotives having electric generators powered by diesel engines

die·sink·er \ˈdī-ˌsiŋ-kər\ *n* **:** one that makes cutting and shaping dies — **die·sink·ing** *n*

Di·es Irae \ˌdē-(ˌ)ā-ˈsē-ˌrā\ *n* [ML, day of wrath; fr. the first words of the hymn] **:** a medieval Latin hymn on the Day of Judgment sung in requiem masses

di·esis \ˈdī-ə-səs\ *n, pl* **di·eses** \-ˌsēz\ [NL, sharp (in music), fr. small interval, fr. Gk, fr. *diienai* to send through, fr. *dia-* + *hienai* to send — more at JET] **:** DOUBLE DAGGER

di·es·ter \ˈdī-ˌes-tər\ *n* **:** a compound containing two ester groupings

die·stock \ˈdī-ˌstäk\ *n* **:** a stock to hold dies used for cutting threads

di·es·trous \(ˈ)dī-ˈes-trəs\ *or* **di·es·tru·al** \-trə-wəl\ *adj* [NL *diestrus* period of sexual quiescence, fr. *dia-* + *estrus*] **:** of, relating to, or having a period of sexual quiescence that intervenes between two periods of estrus — **di·es·trus** \-trəs\ *n*

¹di·et \ˈdī-ət\ *n* [ME *diete*, fr. OF, fr. L *diaeta* prescribed diet, fr. Gk *diaita*, lit., manner of living, fr. *dia-* + *-aita* (akin to Gk *aisa* share)] **1 a :** food and drink regularly provided or consumed **b :** habitual nourishment **c :** the kind and amount of food prescribed for a person or animal for a special reason **2 :** something provided esp. habitually (as for use or enjoyment) <a ~ of Broadway shows and nightclubs —Frederick Wyatt>

²diet *vt* **1 :** to cause to take food **:** FEED **2 :** to cause to eat and drink sparingly or according to prescribed rules ~ *vi* **:** to eat sparingly or according to prescribed rules — **di·et·er** *n*

³diet *n* [ML *dieta*, day's journey, assembly, fr. L *dies* day — more at DEITY] **1 :** a formal deliberative assembly of princes or estates **2 :** any of various national or provincial legislatures

¹di·etary \ˈdī-ə-ˌter-ē\ *n, pl* **di·etar·ies :** the kinds and amounts of food available to or eaten by an individual, group, or population

²dietary *adj* **:** of or relating to a diet or to the rules of a diet — **di·etari·ly** \ˌdī-ə-ˈter-ə-lē\ *adv*

dietary law *n* **:** one of the laws observed by Orthodox Jews that permit or prohibit certain foods

di·etet·ic \ˌdī-ə-ˈtet-ik\ *adj* **1 :** of or relating to diet **2 :** adapted for use in special diets — **di·etet·i·cal·ly** \-i-k(ə-)lē\ *adv*

di·etet·ics \-ˈtet-iks\ *n pl but sing or pl in constr* **:** the science or art of applying the principles of nutrition to feeding

di·eth·yl ether \(ˌ)dī-ˌeth-əl-\ *n* **:** ETHER 3a

di·eth·yl·stil·bes·trol \-stil-ˈbes-ˌtrōl, -ˌtrȯl\ *n* [ISV] **:** a colorless crystalline synthetic compound $C_{18}H_{20}O_2$ used as a potent estrogen — called also *stilbestrol*

di·eti·tian *or* **di·eti·cian** \ˌdī-ə-ˈtish-ən\ *n* [*dietitian* irreg. fr. ¹*diet*] **:** a specialist in dietetics

dif *or* **diff** *abbr* difference

dif·fer \ˈdif-ər\ *vi* **dif·fered; dif·fer·ing** \-(ə-)riŋ\ [ME *differen*, fr. MF or L; MF *differer* to postpone, be different, fr. L *differre*, fr. *dis-* + *ferre* to carry — more at BEAR] **1 a :** to be unlike or distinct in nature, form, or characteristics <the law of one state ~*s* from that of another> **b :** to change from time to time or from one instance to another **:** VARY **2 :** to be of unlike or opposite opinion **:** DISAGREE <men who ~ on religious matters>

¹dif·fer·ence \ˈdif-ərn(t)s, ˈdif-(ə-)rən(t)s\ *n* **1 a :** the quality or state of being different **b :** an instance of differing in nature, form, or quality **c** *archaic* **:** a characteristic that distinguishes one from another or from the average **d :** the element or factor that separates or distinguishes contrasting situations **2 :** distinction or discrimination in preference **3 a :** disagreement in opinion **:** DISSENSION **b :** an instance or cause of disagreement **4 :** the degree or amount by which things differ in quantity or measure; *specif* **:** REMAINDER b(1) **5 :** a significant change in or effect on a situation *syn* see DISCORD

²difference *vt* **-enced; -enc·ing 1 :** DIFFERENTIATE, DISTINGUISH **2 :** to compute the difference between

dif·fer·ent \ˈdif-ərnt, ˈdif-(ə-)rənt\ *adj* [MF, fr. L *different-*, *differens*, prp. of *differre*] **1 :** partly or totally unlike in nature, form, or quality **:** DISSIMILAR <could hardly be more ~> — often followed by *from*, *than*, or chiefly Brit. *to* <small, neat hand, very ~ from the captain's tottery characters —R. L. Stevenson> <vastly ~ in size than it was twenty-five years ago —N. M. Pusey> <a very ~ situation to the . . . one under which we live —Sir Winston Churchill> **2 :** not the same: as **a :** DISTINCT <~ age groups> **b :** VARIOUS <~ members of the class> **c :** ANOTHER <did not like

the TV program so switched to a ~ channel> **3 :** UNUSUAL, SPECIAL <she was ~ and superior> — **dif·fer·ent·ness** *n*
syn DIFFERENT, DIVERSE, DIVERGENT, DISPARATE, VARIOUS *shared meaning element* **:** unlike in kind or character ***ant*** identical, alike, same

dif·fer·en·tia \ˌdif-ə-ˈren-ch(ē-)ə\ *n, pl* **-ti·ae** \-chē-ˌē, -chē-ˌī\ [L, difference, fr. *different-, differens*] **:** the element, feature, or factor that distinguishes one entity, state, or class from another; *esp* **:** a characteristic trait distinguishing a species from other species of the same genus

[1]dif·fer·en·tial \ˌdif-ə-ˈren-chəl\ *adj* **1 a :** of, relating to, or constituting a difference **:** DISTINGUISHING **b :** making a distinction between individuals or classes **c :** based on or resulting from a differential **d :** functioning or proceeding differently or at a different rate **2 :** relating to or involving a differential or differentiation **3 a :** relating to quantitative differences **b :** producing effects by reason of quantitative differences — **dif·fer·en·tial·ly** \-ˈrench-(ə-)lē\ *adv*

[2]differential *n* **1 a :** the product of the derivative of a function of one variable by the increment of the independent variable **b :** the sum of the products of each partial derivative of a function of several variables by the arbitrary increments of the corresponding variables **2 :** a difference between comparable individuals or classes <the price ~ between nationally advertised and private brands of staple food items>; *also* **:** the amount of such a difference <the ~ between regular and high-test gasoline may exceed five cents a gallon> **3 a :** DIFFERENTIAL GEAR **b :** a case covering a differential gear

differential calculus *n* **:** a branch of mathematics dealing chiefly with the rate of change of functions with respect to their variables

differential equation *n* **:** an equation containing differentials or derivatives of functions

differential gear *n* **:** an arrangement of gears forming an epicyclic train for connecting two shafts or axles in the same line, dividing the driving force equally between them, and permitting one shaft to revolve faster than the other — called also *differential gearing*

dif·fer·en·ti·ate \ˌdif-ə-ˈren-chē-ˌāt\ *vb* **-at·ed; -at·ing** *vt* **1 :** to obtain the mathematical derivative of **2 :** to mark or show a difference in **3 :** to develop differential characteristics in **4 :** to cause differentiation of in the course of development **5 :** to express the specific difference of **:** DISCRIMINATE ~ *vi* **1 :** to recognize a difference **2 :** to become distinct or different in character **3 :** to undergo differentiation — **dif·fer·en·tia·bil·i·ty** \-ˌren-ch(ē-)ə-ˈbil-ət-ē\ *n* — **dif·fer·en·tia·ble** \-ˈren-ch(ē-)ə-bəl\ *adj*

dif·fer·en·ti·a·tion \-ˌren-chē-ˈā-shən\ *n* **1 :** the act or process of differentiating **2 :** development from the one to the many, the simple to the complex, or the homogeneous to the heterogeneous **3 a :** modification of body parts for performance of particular functions **b :** the sum of the processes whereby apparently indifferent cells, tissues, and structures attain their adult form and function **4 :** the processes by which various rock types are produced from a common magma

dif·fer·ent·ly \ˈdif-ərnt-lē, ˈdif-(ə-)rənt-\ *adv* **1 :** in a different manner **2 :** OTHERWISE

dif·fi·cile *adj* [MF, fr. L *difficilis,* fr. *dis-* + *facilis* easy — more at FACILE] **1** \də-ˈfis-əl\ *obs* **:** DIFFICULT **2** \ˌdē-fi-ˈsē(ə)l\ [F, lit., difficult] **:** STUBBORN, UNREASONABLE

dif·fi·cult \ˈdif-i-(ˌ)kəlt\ *adj* [back-formation fr. *difficulty*] **1 :** hard to do, make, or carry out **:** ARDUOUS <a ~ climb> **2 a :** hard to deal with, manage, or overcome <a ~ child> **b :** hard to understand **:** PUZZLING <~ reading> ***syn*** see HARD ***ant*** simple — **dif·fi·cult·ly** *adv*

dif·fi·cul·ty \-ˌkəl-tē, -kəl-\ *n, pl* **-ties** [ME *difficulte,* fr. L *difficultas,* irreg. fr. *difficilis*] **1 :** the quality or state of being difficult **2 :** something difficult **:** IMPEDIMENT **3 :** OBJECTION **4 :** EMBARRASSMENT, TROUBLE — usu. used in pl. **5 :** CONTROVERSY, DISAGREEMENT
syn DIFFICULTY, HARDSHIP, RIGOR, VICISSITUDE *shared meaning element* **:** something obstructing one's course and demanding effort and endurance if one's end is to be attained

dif·fi·dence \ˈdif-əd-ən(t)s, -ə-ˌden(t)s\ *n* **:** the quality or state of being diffident

dif·fi·dent \-əd-ənt, -ə-ˌdent\ *adj* [L *diffident-, diffidens,* prp. of *diffidere* to distrust, fr. *dis-* + *fidere* to trust — more at BIDE] **1** *archaic* **:** DISTRUSTFUL **2 :** hesitant in acting or speaking through lack of self-confidence **3 :** RESERVED, UNASSERTIVE ***syn*** see SHY ***ant*** confident — **dif·fi·dent·ly** *adv*

dif·fract \dif-ˈrakt\ *vt* [back-formation fr. *diffraction*] **:** to cause to undergo diffraction

dif·frac·tion \dif-ˈrak-shən\ *n* [NL *diffraction-, diffractio,* fr. L *diffractus,* pp. of *diffringere* to break apart, fr. *dis-* + *frangere* to break — more at BREAK] **:** a modification which light undergoes in passing by the edges of opaque bodies or through narrow slits or in being reflected from ruled surfaces and in which the rays appear to be deflected and to produce fringes of parallel light and dark or colored bands; *also* **:** a similar modification of other waves (as sound waves)

diffraction grating *n* **:** GRATING 3

[1]dif·fuse \dif-ˈyüs\ *adj* [L *diffusus,* pp. of *diffundere* to spread out, fr. *dis-* + *fundere* to pour — more at FOUND] **1 :** not concentrated or localized **:** SCATTERED **2 :** being at once verbose and ill-organized ***syn*** see WORDY ***ant*** succinct — **dif·fuse·ly** *adv* — **dif·fuse·ness** *n*

[2]dif·fuse \dif-ˈyüz\ *vb* **dif·fused; dif·fus·ing** [MF or L; MF *diffuser,* fr. L *diffusus,* pp.] *vt* **1 a :** to pour out and permit or cause to spread freely **b :** EXTEND, SCATTER **c :** to spread thinly or wastefully **2 :** to subject to diffusion; *esp* **:** to break up and distribute (incident light) by reflection ~ *vi* **1 :** to spread out or become transmitted esp. by contact **2 :** to undergo diffusion

dif·fuse–po·rous \dif-ˌyüs-ˈpōr-əs, -ˈpȯr-\ *adj* [[1]*diffuse*] **:** having vessels more or less evenly distributed throughout an annual ring and not varying greatly in size — compare RING-POROUS

dif·fus·er \dif-ˈyü-zər\ *n* **1 :** one that diffuses: as **a :** a device (as a reflector) for distributing the light of a lamp evenly **b :** a screen (as of cloth or frosted glass) for softening lighting (as in photography) **c :** a device (as slats at different angles) for deflecting air from an outlet in various directions **2 :** a device for reducing the velocity and increasing the static pressure of a fluid passing through a system

dif·fus·ible \dif-ˈyü-zə-bəl\ *adj* **:** capable of diffusing or of being diffused

dif·fu·sion \dif-ˈyü-zhən\ *n* **1 :** the action of diffusing **:** the state of being diffused **2 :** PROLIXITY, DIFFUSENESS **3 a :** the process whereby particles of liquids, gases, or solids intermingle as the result of their spontaneous movement caused by thermal agitation and in dissolved substances move from a region of higher to one of lower concentration **b (1) :** reflection of light by a rough reflecting surface **(2) :** transmission of light through a translucent material **:** SCATTERING **4 :** the softening of sharp outlines in a photographic image — **dif·fu·sion·al** \-ˈyüzh-nəl, -ən-ᵊl\ *adj*

dif·fu·sive \dif-ˈyü-siv, -ziv\ *adj* **:** tending to diffuse **:** characterized by diffusion <~ motion of atoms> — **dif·fu·sive·ly** *adv* — **dif·fu·sive·ness** *n*

di·func·tion·al \(ˈ)dī-ˈfəŋ(k)-shnəl, -shən-ᵊl\ *adj* **:** of, relating to, or being a compound with two sites in the molecule that are highly reactive

[1]dig \ˈdig\ *vb* **dug** \ˈdəg\; **dig·ging** [ME *diggen*] *vi* **1 :** to turn up, loosen, or remove earth **:** DELVE **2 :** to work hard or laboriously **3 :** to advance by or as if by removing or pushing aside material ~ *vt* **1 a :** to break up, turn, or loosen (earth) with an implement **b :** to prepare the soil of <~ a garden> **2 :** to bring to the surface by digging **:** UNEARTH **3 :** to hollow out or form by removing earth **:** EXCAVATE **4 :** to drive down so as to penetrate **:** THRUST **5 :** POKE, PROD **6 a :** to pay attention to **:** NOTICE <~ that fancy hat> **b :** UNDERSTAND, APPRECIATE <if you . . . do something subtle . . . only one tenth of the audience will ~ it —Nat Hentoff> **c :** LIKE, ADMIRE <high school students ~ short poetry —David Burmester>

[2]dig *n* **1 a :** THRUST, POKE **b :** a cutting remark **2** *pl, chiefly Brit* **:** DIGGINGS 3 **3 :** an archaeological excavation site; *also* **:** the excavation itself

[3]dig *abbr* digest

di·ga·met·ic \ˌdī-gə-ˈmet-ik\ *adj* **:** forming two kinds of germ cells

dig·a·my \ˈdig-ə-mē\ *n, pl* **-mies** [LL *digamia,* fr. LGk, fr. Gk *digamos* married to two people, fr. *di-* + *-gamos* -gamous] **:** a second marriage after the termination of the first

di·gas·tric \(ˈ)dī-ˈgas-trik\ *adj* [NL *digastricus,* fr. *di-* + *gastricus* gastric] **:** of, relating to, or being a muscle with two bellies separated by a median tendon

di·gen·e·sis \(ˈ)dī-ˈjen-ə-səs\ *n* [NL] **:** successive reproduction by sexual and asexual methods

di·ge·net·ic \ˌdī-jə-ˈnet-ik\ *adj* **1 :** of or relating to digenesis **2 :** of or relating to a subclass (Digenea) of trematode worms in which sexual reproduction as an internal parasite of a vertebrate alternates with asexual reproduction in a mollusk

[1]di·gest \ˈdī-ˌjest\ *n* [ME *Digest* compilation of Roman laws ordered by Justinian, fr. LL *Digesta,* pl., fr. L, collection of writings arranged under headings, fr. neut. pl. of *digestus,* pp. of *digerere* to arrange, distribute, digest, fr. *dis-* + *gerere* to carry — more at CAST] **1 :** a summation or condensation of a body of information: as **a :** a systematic compilation of legal rules, statutes, or decisions **b :** a literary abridgment **2 :** a product of digestion

[2]di·gest \dī-ˈjest, də-\ *vb* [ME *digesten,* fr. L *digestus*] *vt* **1 :** to distribute or arrange systematically **:** CLASSIFY **2 :** to convert (food) into absorbable form **3 :** to take into the mind or memory; *esp* **:** to assimilate mentally **4 a :** to soften or decompose by heat and moisture or chemicals **b :** to extract soluble ingredients from by warming with a liquid **5 :** to compress into a short summary ~ *vi* **1 :** to digest food **2 :** to become digested

di·gest·er \-ˈjes-tər\ *n* **1 :** one that digests or makes a digest **2 :** a vessel for digesting esp. plant or animal materials

di·gest·ibil·i·ty \-ˌjes-tə-ˈbil-ət-ē\ *n, pl* **-ties 1 :** the fitness of something for digestion **2 :** the percentage of a foodstuff taken into the digestive tract that is absorbed into the body

di·gest·ible \-ˈjes-tə-bəl\ *adj* **:** capable of being digested

di·ges·tion \dī-ˈjes(h)-chən, də-\ *n* **:** the action, process, or power of digesting: as **a :** the process of making food absorbable by dissolving it and breaking it down into simpler chemical compounds that occurs in the living body chiefly through the action of enzymes secreted into the alimentary canal **b :** the process in sewage treatment by which organic matter in sludge is decomposed by anaerobic bacteria with the release of a burnable mixture of gases

[1]di·ges·tive \-ˈjes-tiv\ *n* **:** something that aids digestion

[2]digestive *adj* **1 :** relating to digestion **2 :** having the power to cause or promote digestion <~ enzymes> — **di·ges·tive·ly** *adv* — **di·ges·tive·ness** *n*

digestive gland *n* **:** a gland secreting digestive enzymes

dig·ger \ˈdig-ər\ *n* **1 a :** one that digs **b :** a tool or machine for digging **2** *cap* **:** a No. American Indian (as a Paiute) who digs roots for food **3** *Austral* **:** SOLDIER **4 :** a theater ticket speculator

digger wasp *n* **:** a burrowing wasp; *esp* **:** a usu. solitary wasp (superfamily Sphecoidea) that digs nest burrows in the soil and provisions them with insects or spiders paralyzed by stinging

dig·gings *n pl* **1 :** material dug out **2 :** a place of excavating esp. for ore, metals, or precious stones **3 a :** PREMISES, QUARTERS **b** *chiefly Brit* **:** lodgings for a student

dight \ˈdīt\ *vt* **dight·ed** *or* **dight; dight·ing** [ME *dighten,* fr. OE *dihtan* to arrange, compose, fr. a prehistoric WGmc word borrowed fr. L *dictare* to dictate, compose] *archaic* **:** DRESS, ADORN

dig in *vt* **:** to cover or incorporate by burying <*dig in* compost> ~ *vi* **1 :** to dig defensive trenches **2 :** to hold stubbornly to a position **3 a :** to go resolutely to work **b :** to begin eating **4 :** to run hard **5 :** to make and stand in small depressions in the ground for added stability and leverage while batting (as in baseball)

dig·it \ˈdij-ət\ *n* [ME, fr. L *digitus* finger, toe — more at TOE] **1 a :** any of the Arabic numerals 1 to 9 and usu. the symbol 0 **b :** one of the elements that combine to form numbers in a system other than the decimal system **2 :** a unit of length based on the breadth of a finger and equal in English measure to ¾ inch **3 :** one of the divisions in which the limbs of amphibians and all higher vertebrates terminate, which are typically five in number but may be reduced (as in the horse), and which typically have a series of phalanges bearing a nail, claw, or hoof at the tip **:** FINGER, TOE

1**dig·i·tal** \ˈdij-ət-ᵊl\ *adj* **1 :** of or relating to the fingers or toes **:** DIGITATE **2 :** done with a finger **3 :** of or relating to calculation by numerical methods or by discrete units **4 :** of or relating to data in the form of numerical digits **5 :** providing a readout in numerical digits <a ~ voltmeter> — **dig·i·tal·ly** \-ᵊl-ē\ *adv*

2**digital** *n* **:** a part (as a key of an organ) that is depressed with a finger to produce a mechanical effect (as the moving of a lever or the closing of a circuit)

digital computer *n* **:** a computer that operates with numbers expressed directly as digits — compare ANALOG COMPUTER, HYBRID COMPUTER

dig·i·tal·in \ˌdij-ə-ˈtal-ən *also* -ˈtāl-\ *n* [NL *Digitalis*] **1 :** a white crystalline steroid glycoside $C_{36}H_{56}O_{14}$ obtained from seeds of the common foxglove **2 :** a mixture of the glycosides of digitalis leaves or seeds

dig·i·tal·is \-ˈtal-əs *also* -ˈtāl-\ *n* [NL, genus name, fr. L, of a finger, fr. *digitus;* fr. its finger-shaped corolla] **1 :** FOXGLOVE **2 :** the dried leaf of the common foxglove containing important glycosides and serving as a powerful cardiac stimulant and a diuretic

1**dig·i·ta·lize** \ˈdij-ət-ᵊl-ˌīz\ *vt* **-lized; -liz·ing** [*digitalis*] **:** to subject to the administration of digitalis until the desired physiologic adjustment is obtained — **dig·i·ta·li·za·tion** \ˌdij-ət-ᵊl-ə-ˈzā-shən\ *n*

2**dig·i·tal·ize** \ˈdij-ət-ᵊl-ˌīz\ *vt* **-ized; -iz·ing** [1*digital*] **:** DIGITIZE

dig·i·tate \ˈdij-ə-ˌtāt\ *adj* **1 :** having digits **2 :** resembling a finger; *specif* **:** having divisions arranged like the fingers of a hand <~ leaf> — **dig·i·tate·ly** *adv* — **dig·i·ta·tion** \ˌdij-ə-ˈtā-shən\ *n*

digiti- *comb form* [F, fr. L *digitus*] **:** digit **:** finger <*digiti*form>

dig·i·ti·grade \ˈdij-ət-ə-ˌgrād\ *adj* [F, fr. *digiti-* + *-grade*] **:** walking on the digits with the posterior of the foot more or less raised

dig·i·tize \ˈdij-ə-ˌtīz\ *vt* **-tized; -tiz·ing :** to put (as data) into digital notation — **dig·i·ti·za·tion** \ˌdij-ət-ə-ˈzā-shən\ *n* — **dig·i·tiz·er** \ˈdij-ə-ˌtī-zər\ *n*

dig·i·to·nin \ˌdij-ə-ˈtō-nən\ *n* [ISV *digit-* (fr. NL *Digitalis*) + sap*onin*] **:** a steroid saponin $C_{56}H_{92}O_{29}$ occurring in the leaves and seeds of foxglove

digi·toxi·gen·in \ˌdij-ə-ˌtäk-sə-ˈjen-ən\ *n* [ISV, blend of *digitoxin* and *-gen*] **:** a steroid lactone $C_{23}H_{34}O_4$ obtained esp. by hydrolysis of digitoxin

digi·tox·in \ˌdij-ə-ˈtäk-sən\ *n* [ISV, blend of NL *Digitalis* and ISV *toxin*] **:** a poisonous glycoside $C_{41}H_{64}O_{13}$ occurring as the most active principle of digitalis; *also* **:** a mixture of digitalis glycosides consisting chiefly of digitoxin

dig·ni·fied \ˈdig-nə-ˌfīd\ *adj* **:** showing or expressing dignity

dig·ni·fy \ˈdig-nə-ˌfī\ *vt* **-fied; -fy·ing** [MF *dignifier,* fr. LL *dignificare,* fr. L *dignus* worthy — more at DECENT] **1 :** to give distinction to **:** ENNOBLE **2 :** to confer dignity upon by changing name, appearance, or character

dig·ni·tary \ˈdig-nə-ˌter-ē\ *n, pl* **-tar·ies :** one who possesses exalted rank or holds a position of dignity or honor — **dignitary** *adj*

dig·ni·ty \ˈdig-nət-ē\ *n, pl* **-ties** [ME *dignete,* fr. OF *digneté,* fr. L *dignitat-, dignitas,* fr. *dignus*] **1 :** the quality or state of being worthy, honored, or esteemed **2 a :** high rank, office, or position **b :** a legal title of nobility or honor **3** *archaic* **:** DIGNITARY **4 :** formal reserve of manner or language

dig out *vt* **1 :** to make hollow by digging **2 :** FIND, UNEARTH

di·gox·in \dij-ˈäk-sən, dig-\ *n* [ISV *dig-* (fr. NL *Digitalis*) + *toxin*] **:** a poisonous cardiotonic steroid $C_{41}H_{64}O_{14}$ obtained from a foxglove (*Digitalis lanata*) and used similarly to digitalis

di·graph \ˈdī-ˌgraf\ *n* **1 :** a group of two successive letters whose phonetic value is a single sound (as *ea* in *bread* or *ng* in *sing*) or whose value is not the sum of a value borne by each in other occurrences (as *ch* in *chin* where the value is /t/ + /sh/) **2 :** a group of two successive letters **3 :** LIGATURE 4 — **di·graph·ic** \dī-ˈgraf-ik\ *adj* — **di·graph·i·cal·ly** \-i-k(ə-)lē\ *adv*

di·gress \dī-ˈgres, də-\ *vi* [L *digressus,* pp. of *digredi,* fr. *dis-* + *gradi* to step — more at GRADE] **:** to turn aside esp. from the main subject of attention or course of argument in writing or speaking ***syn*** see SWERVE

di·gres·sion \-ˈgresh-ən\ *n* **1** *archaic* **:** a going aside **2 :** the act or an instance of digressing in a discourse or other usu. organized literary work — **di·gres·sion·al** \-ˈgresh-nəl, -ən-ᵊl\ *adj* — **di·gres·sion·ary** \-ˈgresh-ə-ˌner-ē\ *adj*

di·gres·sive \-ˈgres-iv\ *adj* **:** characterized by digressions <a ~ book> — **di·gres·sive·ly** *adv* — **di·gres·sive·ness** *n*

dihal- *or* **dihalo-** *comb form* **:** containing two atoms of a halogen

1**di·he·dral** \(ˈ)dī-ˈhē-drəl\ *adj* **1** *of an airplane* **:** having wings that make with one another a dihedral angle esp. when the angle between the upper sides is less than 180° **2** *of airplane wing pairs* **:** inclined at a dihedral angle to each other

2**dihedral** *n* **1 :** DIHEDRAL ANGLE **2 :** the angle between an aircraft supporting surface and a horizontal transverse line; *esp* **:** the angle between either an upwardly inclined wing or a downwardly inclined wing and such a line

dihedral angle *n* [*di-* + *-hedral*] **:** a figure formed by two intersecting planes

di·hy·brid \(ˌ)dī-ˈhī-brəd\ *adj* [ISV] **:** of, relating to, or being an individual or strain that is heterozygous at two genetic loci — **dihybrid** *n*

dihydr- *or* **dihydro-** *comb form* **:** combined with two atoms of hydrogen

di·hy·dro·er·got·a·mine \(ˌ)dī-ˌhī-drō-ˌər-ˈgät-ə-ˌmēn\ *n* **:** a hydrogenated derivative $C_{33}H_{37}N_5O_5$ of ergotamine that is used in the treatment of migraine

di·hy·dro·strep·to·my·cin \-ˌstrep-tə-ˈmīs-ᵊn\ *n* **:** an antibiotic $C_{21}H_{41}N_7O_{12}$ used esp. in the treatment of tuberculosis and tularemia

dihydroxy- *comb form* **:** containing two hydroxyl groups

di·hy·droxy·ac·e·tone \ˌdī-hī-ˌdräk-sē-ˈas-ə-ˌtōn\ *n* **:** a triose $C_3H_6O_3$ that is used esp. to produce artificial tanning of the skin

dik–dik \ˈdik-ˌdik\ *n* [native name in East Africa] **:** any of several small East African antelopes (genera *Madoqua, Rhynchotragus*)

1**dike** \ˈdīk\ *n* [ME, fr. OE *dīc* ditch, dike; akin to MHG *tīch* pond, dike, L *figere* to fasten, pierce] **1 :** an artificial watercourse **:** DITCH **2 a** *dial Brit* **:** a wall or fence of turf or stone **b :** a bank usu. of earth constructed to control or confine water **:** LEVEE **c :** a barrier preventing passage esp. of something undesirable **3 a :** a raised causeway **b :** a tabular body of igneous rock that has been injected while molten into a fissure

2**dike** *vt* **diked; dik·ing 1 :** to surround or protect with a dike **2 :** to drain by a dike — **dik·er** *n*

3**dike** \ˈdīk\ *n* [origin unknown] **:** LESBIAN

dik·tat \dik-ˈtät\ *n* [G, lit., something dictated, fr. NL *dictatum,* fr. L, neut. of *dictatus,* pp. of *dictare* to dictate] **:** a harsh settlement unilaterally imposed (as on a defeated nation)

dil *abbr* dilute

Di·lan·tin \dī-ˈlant-ᵊn, də-\ *trademark* — used for diphenylhydantoin

di·lap·i·date \də-ˈlap-ə-ˌdāt\ *vb* **-dat·ed; -dat·ing** [L *dilapidatus,* pp. of *dilapidare* to squander, destroy, fr. *dis-* + *lapidare* to throw stones, fr. *lapid-, lapis* stone — more at LAPIDARY] *vt* **1 :** to bring into a condition of decay or partial ruin <furniture is *dilapidated* by use —Janet Flanner> **2** *archaic* **:** SQUANDER ~ *vi* **:** to become dilapidated ***syn*** see RUIN — **di·lap·i·da·tion** \-ˌlap-ə-ˈdā-shən\ *n* — **di·lap·i·da·tor** \-ˈlap-ə-ˌdāt-ər\ *n*

di·lap·i·dat·ed *adj* **:** decayed, deteriorated, or fallen into partial ruin esp. through neglect or misuse <a junkyard filled with ~ autos>

di·lat·an·cy \dī-ˈlāt-ᵊn-sē\ *n* **:** the property of being dilatant

di·lat·ant \-ᵊnt\ *adj* **:** increasing in viscosity and setting to a solid as a result of deformation by expansion, pressure, or agitation

di·la·ta·tion \ˌdil-ə-ˈtā-shən, ˌdī-lə-\ *n* **1 :** amplification in writing or speech **2 a :** the condition of being stretched beyond normal dimensions esp. as a result of overwork or disease or of abnormal relaxation <~ of the heart> <~ of the stomach> **b :** DILATION 2 **3 :** the action of expanding **:** the state of being expanded **4 :** a dilated part or formation — **di·la·ta·tion·al** \-shnəl, -shən-ᵊl\ *adj*

di·late \dī-ˈlāt, ˈdī-ˌ\ *vb* **di·lat·ed; di·lat·ing** [ME *dilaten,* fr. MF *dilater,* fr. L *dilatare,* lit., to spread wide, fr. *dis-* + *latus* wide — more at LATITUDE] *vt* **1** *archaic* **:** to describe or set forth at length or in detail **2 :** to enlarge or expand in bulk or extent **:** DISTEND ~ *vi* **1 :** to comment at length **:** DISCOURSE <~ on a topic> **2 :** to become wide **:** SWELL ***syn*** see EXPAND ***ant*** constrict, circumscribe, attenuate — **di·lat·abil·i·ty** \(ˌ)dī-ˌlāt-ə-ˈbil-ət-ē\ *n* — **di·lat·able** \dī-ˈlāt-ə-bəl, ˈdī-ˌ\ *adj* — **di·la·tor** \dī-ˈlāt-ər, ˈdī-ˌ\ *n*

di·lat·ed *adj* **1 :** expanded laterally **2** *of an insect part* **:** having a broad expanded border **3 :** expanded normally or abnormally in all dimensions — **di·lat·ed·ly** *adv* — **di·lat·ed·ness** *n*

di·la·tion \dī-ˈlā-shən\ *n* **1 :** the act or action of dilating **:** the state of being dilated **:** EXPANSION, DILATATION **2 :** the action of stretching or enlarging an organ or part of the body

di·la·tive \dī-ˈlāt-iv, ˈdī-ˌ\ *adj* **:** causing dilation **:** tending to dilate

di·la·tom·e·ter \ˌdil-ə-ˈtäm-ət-ər, ˌdī-lə-\ *n* [ISV] **:** an instrument for measuring expansion — **di·la·to·met·ric** \-tō-ˈme-trik\ *adj* — **di·la·tom·e·try** \-ˈtäm-ə-trē\ *n*

dil·a·to·ry \ˈdil-ə-ˌtōr-ē, -ˌtȯr-\ *adj* [LL *dilatorius,* fr. L *dilatus* (pp. of *differre* to postpone, differ), fr. *dis-* + *latus,* pp. of *ferre* to carry — more at DIFFER, TOLERATE] **1 :** tending or intended to cause delay <~ tactics> **2 :** characterized by procrastination **:** TARDY <~ in answering letters> — **dil·a·to·ri·ly** \ˌdil-ə-ˈtōr-ə-lē, -ˈtȯr-\ *adv* — **dil·a·to·ri·ness** \ˈdil-ə-ˌtōr-ē-nəs, -ˌtȯr-\ *n*

dil·do \ˈdil-(ˌ)dō\ *n, pl* **dildos** [origin unknown] **:** an object serving as a penis substitute for vaginal insertion

di·lem·ma \də-ˈlem-ə *also* dī-\ *n* [LL, fr. LGk *dilēmmat-, dilēmma,* prob. back-formation fr. Gk *dilēmmatos* involving two assumptions, fr. *di-* + *lēmmat-, lēmma* assumption — more at LEMMA] **1 :** an argument presenting two or more equally conclusive alternatives against an opponent **2 a :** a choice or a situation involving choice between equally unsatisfactory alternatives **b :** a problem seemingly incapable of a satisfactory solution <unemployment . . . the great central ~ of our advancing technology —August Heckscher> — **dil·em·mat·ic** \ˌdil-ə-ˈmat-ik *also* ˌdī-lə-\ *adj*

dil·et·tante \ˌdil-ə-ˈtänt(-ē), -ˈtant(-ē)\ *n, pl* **-tantes** *or* **-tan·ti** \-ˈtänt-ē, -ˈtant-ē\ [It, fr. prp. of *dilettare* to delight, fr. L *dilectare* — more at DELIGHT] **1 :** an admirer or lover of the arts **2 :** a person having a superficial interest in an art or a branch of knowledge **:** DABBLER ***syn*** see AMATEUR — **dilettante** *adj*

dil·et·tant·ish \-ˈtänt-ish, -ˈtant-\ *adj* **:** of, relating to, or characteristic of a dilettante

dil·et·tan·tism \-ˈtän-ˌtiz-əm, -ˈtan-\ *n* **:** dilettantish quality or procedure — **dil·et·tan·tist** \-ˈtänt-əst, -ˈtant-\ *adj*

1**dil·i·gence** \ˈdil-ə-jən(t)s\ *n* [MF, fr. L *diligentia,* fr. *diligent-, diligens*] **1 a :** persevering application **:** ASSIDUITY **b** *obs* **:** SPEED, HASTE **2 :** the attention and care legally expected or required of a person

2di·li·gence \'dil-ə-ˌzhäns, 'dil-ə-jən(t)s\ *n* [F, lit., haste, fr. MF, persevering application] **:** STAGECOACH

dil·i·gent \'dil-ə-jənt\ *adj* [ME, fr. MF, fr. L *diligent-, diligens,* fr. prp. of *diligere* to esteem, love, fr. *di-* + *legere* to select — more at LEGEND] **:** characterized by steady, earnest, and energetic application and effort **:** PAINSTAKING ***syn*** see BUSY ***ant*** dilatory — **dil·i·gent·ly** *adv*

dill \'dil\ *n* [ME *dile,* fr. OE; akin to OHG *tilli* dill] **1 :** any of several plants of the carrot family; *esp* **:** a European herb (*Anethum graveolens*) with aromatic foliage and seeds both of which are used in flavoring foods and esp. pickles **2 :** DILL PICKLE

dill pickle *n* **:** a pickle seasoned with fresh dill or dill juice

dil·ly \'dil-ē\ *n, pl* **dillies** [obs. slang *dilly,* adj. (delightful), irreg. fr. E *delightful*] **:** one that is remarkable or outstanding <always comes up with some *dillies* in his newspaper column —R. M. Rennick>

dil·ly bag \'dil-ē-\ *n* [Australian *dhilla* hair] **:** an Australian mesh bag of native fibers

dil·ly·dal·ly \'dil-ē-ˌdal-ē\ *vi* [redupl. of *dally*] **:** to waste time by loitering **:** DAWDLE

1dil·u·ent \'dil-yə-wənt\ *n* [L *diluent-, diluens,* prp. of *diluere*] **:** a diluting agent

2diluent *adj* [L *diluent-, diluens*] **:** making thinner or less concentrated by admixture **:** DILUTING

1di·lute \dī-'lüt, də-\ *vt* **di·lut·ed; di·lut·ing** [L *dilutus,* pp. of *diluere* to wash away, dilute, fr. *di-* + *lavere* to wash — more at LYE] **1 :** to make thinner or more liquid by admixture **2 :** to diminish the strength, flavor, or brilliance of by admixture **3 :** ATTENUATE — **di·lut·er** *or* **di·lu·tor** \-'lüt-ər\ *n* — **di·lu·tive** \-'lüt-iv\ *adj*

2dilute *adj* **:** WEAK, DILUTED — **di·lute·ness** *n*

di·lu·tion \dī-'lü-shən, də-\ *n* **1 :** the action of diluting **:** the state of being diluted **2 :** something (as a solution) that is diluted **3 :** a lessening of real value (as of a stockholder's equity) by a diminishing of relative worth through attrition <~ of savings by inflation>

di·lu·vi·al \də-'lü-vē-əl, dī-\ *or* **di·lu·vi·an** \-vē-ən\ *adj* [LL *diluvialis,* fr. L *diluvium* deluge — more at DELUGE] **:** of, relating to, or effected by a flood

1dim \'dim\ *adj* **dim·mer; dim·mest** [ME, fr. OE; akin to OHG *timber* dark, Skt *dhamati* he blows] **1 a :** emitting a limited or insufficient amount of light **b :** DULL, LUSTERLESS **c :** lacking pronounced, clear-cut, or vigorous quality or character **2 a :** seen indistinctly or without clear outlines or details **b :** perceived by the senses or mind indistinctly or weakly **:** FAINT <had only a ~ notion of what was going on> **c :** having little prospect of favorable result or outcome <a ~ future> **d :** characterized by an unfavorable, skeptical, or pessimistic attitude — usu. used in the phrase *take a dim view of* **3 :** not perceiving clearly and distinctly <peered at her with ~ eyes —Louis Bromfield> ***syn*** see DARK ***ant*** bright, distinct — **dim·ly** *adv* — **dim·ma·ble** \'dim-ə-bəl\ *adj*

2dim *vb* **dimmed; dim·ming** *vt* **1 :** to make dim or lusterless **2 :** to reduce the light from (headlights) by switching to the low beam ~ *vi* **:** to become dim

3dim *n* **1** *archaic* **:** DUSK, DIMNESS **2 a :** a small light on an automobile for use in parking **b :** LOW BEAM

4dim *abbr* **1** dimension **2** diminished **3** diminuendo **4** diminutive

dime \'dīm\ *n* [ME, tenth part, tithe, fr. MF, fr. L *decima,* fr. fem. of *decimus* tenth, fr. *decem* ten — more at TEN] **1 a :** a coin of the U.S. worth $^1/_{10}$ dollar **b :** a petty sum of money **2 :** a Canadian 10-cent piece — **a dime a dozen :** so plentiful or commonplace as to be of little esteem or slight value — **on a dime :** in a very small area <these cars can turn *on a dime*>

di·men·hy·dri·nate \ˌdī-ˌmen-'hī-drə-ˌnāt\ *n* [*di-* + *me*thyl + ami*ne* + *hydr-* + ami*ne* + *-ate*] **:** a crystalline compound $C_{24}H_{28}ClN_5O_3$ used esp. as an antihistaminic and to prevent nausea

dime novel *n* **:** a usu. paperback melodramatic novel — **dime novelist** *n*

1di·men·sion \də-'men-chən *also* dī-\ *n* [ME, fr. MF, fr. L *dimension-, dimensio,* fr. *dimensus,* pp. of *dimetiri* to measure out, fr. *dis-* + *metiri* to measure — more at MEASURE] **1 a (1) :** measure in one direction; *specif* **:** one of three or four coordinates determining a position in space or space and time **(2) :** one of a group of properties whose number is necessary and sufficient to determine uniquely each element of a system of usu. mathematical entities (as an aggregate of points in real or abstract space) <the surface of a sphere has two ~*s*>; *also* **:** a parameter or coordinate variable assigned to such a property <the three ~*s* of momentum> **(3) :** the number of elements in a basis of a vector space **b :** the quality of spatial extension **:** MAGNITUDE, SIZE **c :** the range over which or the degree to which something extends **:** SCOPE **d :** one of the elements or factors making up a complete personality or entity **:** ASPECT **2** *obs* **:** bodily form or proportions **3 :** wood or stone cut to pieces of specified size — **di·men·sion·al** \-'mench-nəl, -'men-chən-ᵊl\ *adj* — **di·men·sion·al·i·ty** \-ˌmen-chə-'nal-ət-ē\ *n* — **di·men·sion·al·ly** \'mench-nə-lē, -'men-chen-ᵊl-ē\ *adv*

2dimension *vt* **di·men·sioned; di·men·sion·ing** \-'mench-(ə-)niŋ\ **1 :** to form to the required dimensions **2 :** to indicate the dimensions on (a drawing)

di·men·sion·less \-'men-chən-ləs\ *adj* **:** having no dimensions <a ratio of two lengths is a ~ quantity>

di·mer \'dī-mər\ *n* [ISV *di-* + *-mer* (as in *polymer*)] **:** a compound formed by the union of two radicals or two molecules of a simpler compound; *specif* **:** a polymer formed from two molecules of a monomer — **di·mer·iza·tion** \ˌdī-mə-rə-'zā-shən\ *n* — **di·mer·ize** \'dī-mə-ˌrīz\ *vt*

di·mer·ic \(ˈ)dī-'mer-ik\ *adj* [NL *dimerus*] **1 :** consisting of two parts <a ~ chromosome> **2 :** involving or mediated by two factors **3 :** of or relating to a dimer

dim·er·ous \'dim-ə-rəs\ *adj* [NL *dimerus,* fr. L *di-* + NL *-merus* -merous] **:** consisting of two parts: as **a** *of an insect* **:** having the tarsi two-jointed **b** *of a flower* **:** having two members in each whorl — **dim·er·ism** \-ə-ˌriz-əm\ *n*

dime store *n* **:** FIVE-AND-TEN

dim·e·ter \'dim-ət-ər\ *n* [LL, fr. Gk *dimetros,* adj., being a dimeter, fr. *di-* + *metron* measure — more at MEASURE] **:** a line of verse consisting of two metrical feet or of two dipodies

di·meth·o·ate \dī-'meth-ə-ˌwāt\ *n* [*dime*thyl- + *thio* acid + [1]*-ate*] **:** an insecticide $C_5H_{12}NO_3PS_2$ used on livestock and various crops

dimethyl- *comb form* **:** containing two methyl groups

di·meth·yl·hy·dra·zine \ˌdī-ˌmeth-əl-'hī-drə-ˌzēn\ *n* **:** either of two flammable corrosive isomeric liquids $C_2H_8N_2$ which are methylated derivatives of hydrazine and of which one is used in rocket fuels

di·meth·yl·sulf·ox·ide \-ˌsəl-'fäk-ˌsīd\ *n* [*dimethyl-* + *sulf-* + *oxide*] **:** a compound $(CH_3)_2SO$ obtained as a by-product in wood-pulp manufacture and used as a solvent and in experimental medicine — called also *DMSO*

di·meth·yl·tryp·ta·mine \-'trip-tə-ˌmēn\ *n* [*dimethyl-* + *tryptophan* + *amine*] **:** an easily synthesized hallucinogenic drug $C_{12}H_{16}N_2$ that is chemically similar to but shorter than psilocybin

dimin *abbr* diminuendo

di·min·ish \də-'min-ish\ *vb* [ME *deminishen,* alter. of *diminuen,* fr. MF *diminuer,* fr. LL *diminuere,* alter. of L *deminuere,* fr. *de-* + *minuere* to lessen — more at MINOR] *vt* **1 :** to make less or cause to appear less **2 :** to lessen the authority, dignity, or reputation of **:** BELITTLE **3 :** to cause to taper ~ *vi* **1 :** to become gradually less (as in size or importance) **:** DWINDLE **2 :** TAPER ***syn*** see DECREASE — **di·min·ish·able** \-ə-bəl\ *adj* — **di·min·ish·ment** \-mənt\ *n*

di·min·ished *adj, of a musical interval* **:** made one half step less than perfect or minor <a ~ fifth>

diminishing returns *n pl* **:** a rate of yield that beyond a certain point fails to increase in proportion to additional investments of labor or capital

di·min·u·en·do \də-ˌmin-(y)ə-'wen-(ˌ)dō\ *adv or adj* [It, lit., diminishing, fr. LL *diminuendum,* gerund of *diminuere*] **:** DECRESCENDO — **diminuendo** *n*

dim·i·nu·tion \ˌdim-ə-'n(y)ü-shən\ *n* [ME *diminucioun,* fr. MF *diminution,* fr. ML *diminution-, diminutio,* alter. of L *deminution-, deminutio,* fr. *deminutus,* pp. of *deminuere*] **:** the act, process, or an instance of diminishing **:** DECREASE — **dim·i·nu·tion·al** \-shnəl, -shən-ᵊl\ *adj*

1di·min·u·tive \də-'min-yət-iv\ *n* [ME *diminutif,* fr. ML *diminutivum,* alter. of LL *deminutivum,* fr. neut. of *deminutivus*] **1 :** a diminutive word, affix, or name **2 :** a diminutive individual

2diminutive *adj* **1 :** indicating small size and sometimes the state or quality of being familiarly known, lovable, pitiable, or contemptible — used of affixes (as *-ette, -kin, -ling*) and of words formed with them (as *kitchenette, manikin, duckling*), of clipped forms (as *Jim*), and of altered forms (as *Peggy*); compare AUGMENTATIVE **2 :** exceptionally or abnormally small **:** MINUTE ***syn*** see SMALL — **di·min·u·tive·ly** *adv* — **di·min·u·tive·ness** *n*

dim·i·ty \'dim-ət-ē\ *n, pl* **-ties** [alter. of ME *demyt,* prob. fr. MGk *dimitos* of double thread, fr. Gk *di-* + *mitos* warp thread] **:** a sheer usu. corded cotton fabric of plain weave in checks or stripes

dim·mer \'dim-ər\ *n* **1 :** a device for regulating the intensity of an electric lighting unit **2** *pl* **: a :** small lights on an automobile for use in parking **b :** headlights on low beam

dimness *n* **1 :** the quality or state of being dim **2 :** something dim

di·mor·phic \(ˈ)dī-'mȯr-fik\ *adj* **1 a :** DIMORPHOUS 1 **b :** occurring in two distinct forms <~ leaves of emergent plants> <a sexually ~ butterfly> **2 :** combining qualities of two kinds of individuals in one

di·mor·phism \-ˌfiz-əm\ *n* [ISV] **:** the condition or property of being dimorphic or dimorphous: as **a (1) :** the existence of two different forms (as of color or size) of a species esp. in the same population **(2) :** the existence of an organ (as the leaves of a plant) in two different forms **b :** crystallization of a chemical compound in two different forms

di·mor·pho·the·ca \(ˌ)dī-ˌmȯr-fə-'thē-kə\ *n* [NL *Dimorphotheca,* genus name, fr. Gk *dimorphos* + NL *theca*] **:** any of a genus (*Dimorphotheca*) of southern African composite herbs or subshrubs with showy terminal solitary flower heads and conspicuously toothed leaves

di·mor·phous \(ˈ)dī-'mȯr-fəs\ *adj* [Gk *dimorphos* having two forms, fr. *di-* + *-morphos* -morphous] **1 :** crystallizing in two different forms **2 :** DIMORPHIC 1b

dim·out \'dim-ˌau̇t\ *n* **:** a restriction limiting the use or showing of lights at night esp. during the threat of an air raid; *also* **:** a condition of partial darkness produced by this restriction

1dim·ple \'dim-pəl\ *n* [ME *dympull;* akin to OHG *tumphilo* whirlpool, OE *dyppan* to dip — more at DIP] **1 :** a slight natural indentation in the surface of some part of the human body **2 :** a depression or indentation on a surface (as of a golf ball) — **dim·ply** \-p(ə-)lē\ *adj*

2dimple *vb* **dim·pled; dim·pling** \-p(ə-)liŋ\ *vt* **:** to mark with dimples ~ *vi* **:** to exhibit or form dimples

dim·wit \'dim-ˌwit\ *n* **:** a stupid or mentally slow person

dim–wit·ted \-'wit-əd\ *adj* **:** not mentally bright **:** STUPID — **dim–wit·ted·ly** *adv* — **dim–wit·ted·ness** *n*

1din \'din\ *n* [ME, fr. OE *dyne;* akin to ON *dynr* din, Skt *dhvanati* it roars] **:** a loud continued noise; *esp* **:** a welter of discordant sounds <a world of savage violence and incessant ~ —Thomas Wolfe>

2din *vb* **dinned; din·ning** *vt* **1 :** to assail or deafen with loud continued noise **2 :** to impress by insistent repetition ~ *vi* **:** to make a loud noise

3din *abbr* dinar

di·nar \di-'när, 'dē-ˌ\ *n* [Ar *dīnār,* fr. Gk *dēnarion* denarius, fr. L *denarius*] **1 :** a gold coin formerly used in Muslim countries **2 a** —see MONEY table **b** —see *rial* at MONEY table

1dine \'dīn\ *vb* **dined; din·ing** [ME *dinen,* fr. OF *diner,* fr. (assumed) VL *disjejunare* to break one's fast, fr. L *dis-* + LL *jejunare* to fast, fr. L *jejunus* fasting] *vi* **:** to take dinner ~ *vt* **:** to give a dinner to **:** FEED <wined and *dined* his friends>

2dine *n, Scot* **:** DINNER

din·er \'dī-nər\ *n* **1 :** one that dines **2 a :** DINING CAR **b :** a restaurant usu. resembling a dining car in shape
din·er–out \ˌdī-nə-'rau̇t\ *n, pl* **diners–out :** one who dines away from home esp. in the course of an active social life
di·nette \dī-'net\ *n* **:** a small space usu. off a kitchen used for informal dining; *also* **:** furniture for such a space
1**ding** \'diŋ\ *vb* [prob. imit.] *vt* **:** to dwell on with tiresome repetition <keeps ~*ing* it into him that the less he smokes the better —Samuel Butler †1902> ~ *vi* **1 :** to make a ringing sound **:** CLANG **2 :** to speak with tiresome reiteration
2**ding** *n* [*ding* (to strike), fr. ME *dingen*] **:** a damaged area esp. on the surface of a surfboard
ding–a–ling *n* [prob. euphemism for *damn fool*] **:** NITWIT, KOOK
ding·bat \'diŋ-ˌbat\ *n* [origin unknown] **:** a typographical ornament (as an asterisk) used typically to call attention to an opening sentence or to make a break between two paragraphs
1**ding·dong** \'diŋ-ˌdȯŋ, -ˌdäŋ\ *n* [imit.] **:** the ringing sound produced by repeated strokes esp. on a bell
2**dingdong** *vi* **1 :** to make a dingdong sound **2 :** to repeat a sound or action tediously or insistently
3**dingdong** *adj* **1 :** of, relating to, or resembling the ringing sound made by a bell **2 :** marked by a rapid exchange or alternation (as of blows or words)
din·ghy \'diŋ-(k)ē, -gē\ *n, pl* **dinghies** [Bengali *dingi* & Hindi *dīngī*] **1 :** an East Indian rowboat or sailboat **2 :** a small boat propelled by oars, sails, or motor that is often carried on a larger boat as a tender or a lifeboat **3 :** a rubber life raft
din·gle \'diŋ-gəl\ *n* [ME, abyss] **:** a small wooded valley **:** DELL
din·gle·ber·ry \'diŋ-gəl-ˌber-ē\ *n* [origin unknown] **:** a shrub (*Vaccinium erythrocarpus*) of the southeastern U.S.; *also* **:** its globose dark red edible berry
din·go \'diŋ-(ˌ)gō\ *n, pl* **dingoes** [native name in Australia] **:** a reddish brown wild dog (*Canis dingo*) of Australia
din·gus \'diŋ-(g)əs\ *n* [D or G; D *dinges,* prob. fr. G *dings,* fr. gen. of *ding* thing, fr. OHG — more at THING] **:** something (as a gadget) whose common name is unknown or forgotten
din·gy \'din-jē\ *adj* **din·gi·er; -est** [origin unknown] **1 :** DIRTY, DISCOLORED **2 :** SHABBY, SQUALID — **din·gi·ly** \-jə-lē\ *adv* — **din·gi·ness** \-jē-nəs\ *n*

dingo

dining car *n* **:** a railroad car in which meals are served
dining room *n* **:** a room used for the taking of meals
dinitro- *comb form* **:** containing two nitro groups
di·ni·tro·ben·zene \(ˌ)dī-ˌnī-trō-'ben-ˌzēn, -(ˌ)ben-'\ *n* [ISV] **:** any of three isomeric toxic compounds $C_6H_4(NO_2)_2$; *esp* **:** the yellow meta-isomer used chiefly as a dye intermediate
di·ni·tro·phe·nol \-'fē-ˌnōl, -fi-'\ *n* **:** any of six isomeric crystalline compounds $C_6H_4N_2O_5$ some of whose derivatives are pesticides; *esp* **:** a highly toxic compound that increases fat metabolism and was formerly used in weight control
1**dink** \'diŋk\ *n* [*dink* (to hit with a drop shot), prob. of imit. origin] **:** DROP SHOT
2**dink** *n* [prob. alter. of *dick*] **:** PENIS — usu. considered vulgar
din·key *or* **din·ky** \'diŋ-kē\ *n, pl* **dinkeys** *or* **dinkies** [prob. fr. *dinky*] **:** a small locomotive used esp. for hauling freight, logging, and shunting
1**din·kum** \'diŋ-kəm\ *adj* [prob. fr. E dial. *dinkum,* n., work] *Austral* **:** AUTHENTIC, GENUINE
2**dinkum** *adv, Austral* **:** TRULY, HONESTLY
din·ky \'diŋ-kē\ *adj* **din·ki·er; -est** [Sc *dink* neat] **:** SMALL, INSIGNIFICANT
din·ner \'din-ər\ *n, often attrib* [ME *diner,* fr. OF, fr. *diner* to dine] **1 a :** the principal meal of the day **b :** a formal feast or banquet **2 :** TABLE D'HÔTE 2 **3 :** the food prepared for a dinner <eat your ~> **4 :** a packaged meal usu. for quick preparation <warmed up a frozen Chinese ~> — **din·ner·less** \-ləs\ *adj*
dinner jacket *n* **:** a jacket for formal evening wear
din·ner·ware \'din-ər-ˌwa(ə)r, -ˌwe(ə)r\ *n* **:** tableware other than flatware
di·no·fla·gel·late \ˌdī-nō-'flaj-ə-lət, -ˌlāt; -flə-'jel-ət\ *n* [deriv. of Gk *dinos* rotation, eddy + NL *flagellum*] **:** any of an order (Dinoflagellata) of chiefly marine planktonic usu. solitary plantlike flagellates that include luminescent forms, forms important in marine food chains, and forms causing red tide
di·no·saur \'dī-nə-ˌsȯ(ə)r\ *n* [deriv. of Gk *deinos* terrible + *sauros* lizard — more at DIRE, SAURIAN] **1 :** any of a group (Dinosauria) of extinct chiefly terrestrial carnivorous or herbivorous reptiles **2 :** any of various large extinct reptiles — **di·no·sau·ri·an** \ˌdī-nə-'sȯr-ē-ən\ *adj or n* — **di·no·sau·ric** \-'sȯr-ik\ *adj*
di·no·there \'dī-nə-ˌthi(ə)r\ *n* [NL *Deinotherium,* genus name, fr. Gk *deinos* + NL *-therium*] **:** any of a genus (*Deinotherium*) of extinct proboscidean mammals with a pair of downward-directed tusks
1**dint** \'dint\ *n* [ME, fr. OE *dynt*] **1** *archaic* **:** BLOW, STROKE **2 :** FORCE, POWER **3 :** 1DENT — **by dint of :** by force of **:** because of
2**dint** *vt* **1 :** to make a dint in **2 :** to impress or drive in with force
di·nu·cle·o·tide \(ˌ)dī-'n(y)ü-klē-ə-ˌtīd\ *n* **:** a nucleotide consisting of two units each composed of a phosphate, a pentose, and a nitrogen base
di·oc·e·san \dī-'äs-ə-sən *also* ˌdī-ə-'sēz-ᵊn\ *n* **:** a bishop having jurisdiction over a diocese
di·o·cese \'dī-ə-səs, -ˌsēz, -ˌsēs\ *n, pl* **-ces·es** \-sə-səz, -ˌsē-zəz, -ˌsē-səz, -ə-ˌsēz\ [ME *diocise,* fr. MF, fr. LL *diocesis,* alter. of *dioecesis,* fr. L, administrative division, fr. Gk *dioikēsis* administration, administrative division, fr. *dioikein* to keep house, govern, fr. *dia-* + *oikein* to dwell, manage, fr. *oikos* house — more at VICINITY] **:** the territorial jurisdiction of a bishop — **di·oc·e·san** \dī-'äs-ə-sən *also* ˌdī-ə-'sēz-ᵊn\ *adj*
di·ode \'dī-ˌōd\ *n* [ISV] **1 :** a 2-electrode electron tube having a cathode and an anode **2 :** a rectifier that consists of a semiconducting crystal with two terminals and that is analogous in use to an electron tube diode
di·oe·cious \(ˈ)dī-'ē-shəs\ *adj* [deriv. of Gk *di-* + *oikos* house] **1 :** having male reproductive organs in one individual and female in another **2 :** having staminate and pistillate flowers borne on different individuals — **di·oe·cious·ly** *adv* — **di·oe·cism** \-'ē-ˌsiz-əm\ *n*
di·oi·cous \-'ȯi-kəs\ *adj* [NL *dioicus,* fr. *di-* + Gk *oikos*] **:** having archegonia and antheridia on separate plants
di·ol \'dī-ˌōl, -ˌȯl\ *n* [ISV *di-* + 1*-ol*] **:** a compound (as glycol) containing two hydroxyl groups
di·ole·fin \dī-'ō-lə-fən\ *n* [ISV *di-* + *olefin*] **:** any of a series of aliphatic hydrocarbons containing two double bonds — called also *diene*
Di·o·me·des \ˌdī-ə-'mēd-ēz\ *n* [L, fr. Gk *Diomēdēs*] **:** one of the Greek heroes of the Trojan War
Di·o·ny·sia \ˌdī-ə-'niz(h)-ē-ə, -'nis(h)-; -'nizh-ə, -'nish-; -'nī-sē-ə, -'nē-, -zē-\ *n pl* [L, fr. Gk, fr. neut. pl. of *dionysios* of Dionysus fr. *Dionysos*] **:** ancient Greek festival observances held in seasonal cycles in honor of Dionysus; *esp* **:** such observances marked by dramatic performances
Di·o·ny·si·ac \-'niz(h)-ē-ˌak, -'nis(h)-; -'nī-zē-, -'nē-, -sē-\ *adj* [L *dionysiacus,* fr. Gk *dionysiakos,* fr. *Dionysos*] **:** DIONYSIAN 2 — **Dionysiac** *n*
Di·o·ny·sian \-'niz(h)-ē-ən, -'nis(h)-; -'nizh-ən, -'nish-; -'nī-sē-ən, -'nē-, -zē-\ *adj* **1 a :** of or relating to Dionysius **b :** of or related to the theological writings once mistakenly attributed to Dionysius the Areopagite **2 a :** devoted to the worship of Dionysus **b :** being of a frenzied or orgiastic character
Di·o·ny·sus \ˌdī-ə-'nī-səs, -'nē-\ *n* [L, fr. Gk *Dionysos*] **:** the Greek god of wine **:** BACCHUS
Di·o·phan·tine equation \ˌdī-ə-'fan-ˌtīn-, -'fant-ᵊn-\ *n* [*Diophantus,* 3d cent. A.D. Gk mathematician] **:** an indeterminate polynomial equation with integral coefficients for which it is required to find all integral solutions
di·op·side \dī-'äp-ˌsīd\ *n* [F, fr. *di-* + Gk *opsis* appearance — more at OPTIC] **:** a green to white mineral that consists of pyroxene containing little or no aluminum — **diopsidic** *adj*
di·op·ter *also* **di·op·tre** \dī-'äp-tər\ *n* [*diopter* (an optical instrument), fr. MF *dioptre,* fr. L *dioptra,* fr. Gk, fr. *dia-* + *opsesthai* to be going to see] **:** a unit of measurement of the refractive power of lenses equal to the reciprocal of the focal length in meters
di·op·tom·e·ter \(ˌ)dī-ˌäp-'täm-ət-ər\ *n* **:** an instrument used in measuring the accommodation and refraction of the eye — **di·op·tom·e·try** \-'täm-ə-trē\ *n*
di·op·tric \dī-'äp-trik\ *adj* [Gk *dioptrikos* of a diopter (instrument), fr. *dioptra*] **1 :** that effects or serves in refraction of a beam of light **:** REFRACTIVE: *specif* **:** that assists vision by refracting and focalizing light **2 :** produced by means of refraction
di·ora·ma \ˌdī-ə-'ram-ə, -'räm-\ *n* [F, fr. *dia-* + *-orama* (as in *panorama,* fr. E)] **1 :** a scenic representation in which a partly translucent painting is seen from a distance through an opening **2 a :** a scenic representation in which sculptured figures and lifelike details are displayed usu. in miniature so as to blend indistinguishably with a realistic painted background **b :** a life-size exhibit of a wildlife specimen or scene with realistic natural surroundings and a painted background — **di·oram·ic** \-'ram-ik\ *adj*
di·o·rite \'dī-ə-ˌrīt\ *n* [F, irreg. fr. Gk *diorizein* to distinguish, fr. *dia-* + *horizein* to define — more at HORIZON] **:** a granular crystalline igneous rock commonly of acid plagioclase and hornblende, pyroxene, or biotite — **di·o·rit·ic** \ˌdī-ə-'rit-ik\ *adj*
Di·os·cu·ri \ˌdī-əs-'kyu̇(ə)r-ˌī, dī-'äs-kyə-ˌrī\ *n pl* [NL, fr. Gk *Dioskouroi,* lit., sons of Zeus, fr. *Dios* (gen. of *Zeus;* akin to L *divus* divine) + *kouroi,* pl. of *koros, kaoros* boy — more at DEITY, CRESCENT] **:** the twins Castor and Pollux reunited as stars in the sky by Zeus after Castor's death and regarded as patrons of athletes, soldiers, and mariners
di·ox·ane \dī-'äk-ˌsān\ *n* [ISV *di-* + *ox-* + *-ane*] **:** a flammable toxic liquid diether $C_4H_8O_2$ used esp. as a solvent
di·ox·ide \(ˈ)dī-'äk-ˌsīd\ *n* [ISV] **:** an oxide (as carbon dioxide) containing two atoms of oxygen in the molecule
1**dip** \'dip\ *vb* **dipped; dip·ping** [ME *dippen,* fr. OE *dyppan;* akin to OHG *tupfen* to wash, Lith *dubus* deep] *vt* **1 a :** to plunge or immerse momentarily or partially under the surface (as of a liquid) so as to moisten, cool, or coat <~ candles> **b :** to thrust in a way to suggest immersion **c :** to immerse (as a hog) in an antiseptic or parasiticidal solution **2 :** to lift a portion of by reaching below the surface with something shaped to hold liquid **:** LADLE **3 a** *archaic* **:** INVOLVE **b :** MORTGAGE **4 :** to lower and then raise again <~ a flag in salute> ~ *vi* **1 a :** to plunge into a liquid and quickly emerge **b :** to immerse something into a processing liquid or finishing material **2 a :** to suddenly drop down or out of sight **b** *of an airplane* **:** to drop suddenly before climbing **c :** to decline or decrease moderately and usu. temporarily <prices *dipped*> **3 a :** to reach down inside or below a surface esp. to withdraw a part of the contents **b :** to make inroads for funds — used with *into* <*dipped* into the family's savings> **4 :** to examine something casually or tentatively; *specif* **:** to read superficially **5 :** to incline downward from the plane of the horizon — **dip·pa·ble** \'dip-ə-bəl\ *adj*

ə abut ᵊ kitten ər further a back ā bake ä cot, cart
au̇ out ch chin e less ē easy g gift i trip ī life
j joke ŋ sing ō flow ȯ flaw ȯi coin th thin t͟h this
ü loot u̇ foot y yet yü few yu̇ furious zh vision

[2]dip *n* **1 :** an act of dipping; *esp* **:** a brief plunge into the water for sport or exercise **2 :** inclination downward: **a :** PITCH **b :** a sharp downward course **:** DROP **c :** the angle that a stratum or similar geological feature makes with a horizontal plane **3 :** the angle formed with the horizon by a magnetic needle free to rotate in the vertical plane **4 :** HOLLOW, DEPRESSION **5 :** something obtained by or used in dipping **6 a :** a sauce or soft mixture into which food may be dipped **b :** a liquid preparation into which an object may be dipped (as for cleansing or coloring) **7** *slang* **:** PICKPOCKET

di·pep·ti·dase \dī-ˈpep-tə-ˌdās, -ˌdāz\ *n* **:** any of various enzymes that hydrolyze dipeptides but not polypeptides

di·pep·tide \(ˈ)dī-ˈpep-ˌtīd\ *n* **:** a peptide that yields two molecules of amino acid on hydrolysis

di·phase \ˈdī-ˌfāz\ *or* **di·pha·sic** \(ˈ)dī-ˈfā-zik\ *adj* **:** having two phases

di·phe·nyl \(ˈ)dī-ˈfen-ᵊl, -ˈfēn-\ *n* **:** BIPHENYL

di·phe·nyl·amine \(ˌ)dī-ˌfen-ᵊl-ə-ˈmēn, -ˌfēn-, -ᵊl-ˈam-ən\ *n* [ISV] **:** a crystalline pleasant-smelling compound $(C_6H_5)_2NH$ used chiefly in the manufacture of dyes and in stabilizing explosives

di·phe·nyl·hy·dan·to·in \-hī-ˈdant-ə-wən\ *n* [*diphenyl* + *hyd*rogen + all*antoin* (a chemical found in the allantoic liquid of cows)] **:** a crystalline compound $C_{15}H_{12}N_2O_2$ used in the form of its sodium salt in the treatment of epilepsy

di·phos·gene \(ˈ)dī-ˈfäz-ˌjēn\ *n* [ISV] **:** a liquid compound $C_2Cl_4O_2$ used as a poison gas in World War I

di·phos·phate \(ˈ)dī-ˈfäs-ˌfāt\ *n* **:** a phosphate containing two phosphate groups

di·phos·pho·gly·cer·ic acid \(ˈ)dī-ˈfäs-fō-glis-ˌer-ik-\ *n* **:** a diphosphate of glyceric acid that is an important intermediate in photosynthesis and in glycolysis and fermentation

di·phos·pho·pyr·i·dine nucleotide \-ˌpir-ə-ˌdēn-\ *n* [*di-* + *phosph-* + *pyridine*] **:** NAD

diph·the·ria \dif-ˈthir-ē-ə, dip-\ *n* [NL, fr. F *diphthérie*, fr. Gk *diphthera* leather; fr. the toughness of the false membrane] **:** an acute febrile contagious disease marked by the formation of a false membrane esp. in the throat and caused by a bacterium which produces a toxin causing inflammation of the heart and nervous system — **diph·the·ri·al** \-ē-əl\ *or* **diph·the·ri·an** \-ē-ən\ *adj* — **diph·the·rit·ic** \ˌdif-thə-ˈrit-ik, ˌdip-\ *adj*

[1]diph·the·roid \ˈdif-thə-ˌrȯid\ *adj* **:** resembling diphtheria

[2]diphtheroid *n* **:** a bacterium that resembles the bacterium of diphtheria but does not produce diphtheria toxin

diph·thong \ˈdif-ˌthȯŋ, ˈdip-\ *n* [ME *diptonge*, fr. MF *diptongue*, fr. LL *dipthongus*, fr. Gk *diphthongos*, fr. *di-* + *phthongos* voice, sound] **1 :** a gliding monosyllabic speech sound (as the vowel combination that forms the last part of *toy*) that starts at or near the articulatory position for one vowel and moves to or toward the position of another **2 :** DIGRAPH **3 :** a form of the ligature æ or œ — **diph·thon·gal** \dif-ˈthȯŋ-(g)əl, dip-\ *adj*

diph·thong·iza·tion \(ˌ)dif-ˌthȯŋ-ə-ˈzā-shən, (ˌ)dip-\ *n* **:** the act of diphthongizing **:** the state of being diphthongized

diph·thong·ize \ˈdif-ˌthȯŋ-ˌīz, ˈdip-\ *vb* **-ized; -iz·ing** *vi, of a simple vowel* **:** to change into a diphthong ~ *vt* **:** to pronounce as a diphthong

diphy- *or* **diphyo-** *comb form* [NL, fr. Gk *diphy-*, fr. *diphyēs*, fr. *di-* + *phyein* to bring forth — more at BE] **:** double **:** bipartite <*diphy*odont>

diphy·cer·cal \ˌdif-i-ˈsər-kəl\ *adj* [*diphy-* + *-cercal*] **1** *of a tail fin* **:** having the upper and lower portions alike or nearly so and the vertebral column extending to the tip **2 :** having a diphycercal tail fin — **diphy·cer·cy** \ˈdif-i-ˌsər-sē, -ˌsər-kē\ *n*

di·phy·let·ic \ˌdī-fī-ˈlet-ik\ *adj* [*di-* + *phyletic*] **:** derived from two lines of evolutionary descent <~ dinosaurs>

di·phyl·lous \(ˈ)dī-ˈfil-əs\ *adj* [NL *diphyllus*, fr. *di-* + *-phyllus* -phyllous] **:** having two leaves

di·phy·odont \(ˈ)dī-ˈfī-ə-ˌdänt\ *adj* [ISV] **:** marked by the successive development of deciduous and permanent sets of teeth

dipl- *or* **diplo-** *comb form* [Gk, fr. *diploos* — more at DOUBLE] **1 :** double **:** twofold <*diplo*pia> **2 :** diploid <*diplo*phase>

di·ple·gia \dī-ˈplē-j(ē-)ə\ *n* [NL] **:** paralysis of corresponding parts on both sides of the body

di·plex \ˈdī-ˌpleks\ *adj* [alter. of *duplex*] **:** relating to or being simultaneous transmission or reception of two radio signals

dip·lo·ba·cil·lus \ˌdip-lō-bə-ˈsil-əs\ *n* [NL] **:** any of various small aerobic gram-negative bacilli parasitic on mucous membranes

dip·lo·blas·tic \-ˈblas-tik\ *adj* **:** having two germ layers — used of an embryo or lower invertebrate that lacks a true mesoderm

dip·lo·coc·cus \-ˈkäk-əs\ *n* [NL, genus name] **:** any of a genus (*Diplococcus*) of gram-positive encapsulated bacteria that occur usu. in pairs, are parasitic, and include serious pathogens — **dip·lo·coc·cal** \-ˈkäk-əl\ *or* **dip·lo·coc·cic** \-ˈkäk-(s)ik\ *adj*

di·plod·o·cus \də-ˈpläd-ə-kəs, dī-\ *n* [NL, genus name, fr. *dipl-* + Gk *dokos* beam, fr. *dekesthai*, *dechesthai* to receive; akin to L *decēre* to be fitting — more at DECENT] **:** any of a genus (*Diplodocus*) of very large herbivorous dinosaurs from Colorado and Wyoming

dip·loe \ˈdip-lə-ˌwē\ *n* [NL, fr. Gk *diploē*, fr. *diploos* double] **:** cancellous bony tissue between the external and internal layers of the skull — **di·plo·ic** \də-ˈplō-ik, dī-\ *adj*

[1]dip·loid \ˈdip-ˌlȯid\ *adj* **:** having the basic chromosome number doubled — **dip·loi·dy** \-ˌlȯid-ē\ *n*

[2]diploid *n* **1 :** a diploid cell **2 :** an individual or generation characterized by the diploid chromosome number

di·plo·ma \də-ˈplō-mə\ *n, pl* **diplomas** [L, passport, diploma, fr. Gk *diplōma* folded paper, passport, fr. *diploun* to double, fr. *diploos*] **1** *pl also* **di·plo·ma·ta** \-mət-ə\ **:** an official or state document **:** CHARTER **2 :** a writing usu. under seal conferring some honor or privilege **3 :** a document bearing record of graduation from or of a degree conferred by an educational institution

di·plo·ma·cy \də-ˈplō-mə-sē\ *n* **1 :** the art and practice of conducting negotiations between nations **2 :** skill in handling affairs without arousing hostility **:** TACT

diploma mill *n* **1 :** an institution of higher education operating without supervision of a state or professional agency and granting diplomas without the usual required courses and attendance **2 :** an institution of higher education whose academic demands are minimal

dip·lo·mat \ˈdip-lə-ˌmat\ *n* [F *diplomate*, back-formation fr. *diplomatique*] **:** one employed or skilled in diplomacy

dip·lo·mate \ˈdip-lə-ˌmāt\ *n* [*diploma* + [1]*-ate*] **:** one who holds a diploma; *esp* **:** a physician qualified to practice in a medical specialty by advanced training and experience in the specialty followed by passing an intensive examination by a national board of senior specialists

dip·lo·mat·ic \ˌdip-lə-ˈmat-ik\ *adj* [in sense 1, fr. NL *diplomaticus*, fr. L *diplomat-*, *diploma*; in other senses, fr. F *diplomatique* connected with documents regulating international relations, fr. NL *diplomaticus*] **1 a :** PALEOGRAPHIC **b :** exactly reproducing the original <a ~ edition> **2 a :** concerned with or skilled in international relations **b :** of or relating to those conducting international relations <~ immunity> **3 :** employing tact and conciliation esp. in situations of stress ***syn*** see SUAVE — **dip·lo·mat·i·cal·ly** \-i-k(ə-)lē\ *adv*

di·plo·ma·tist \də-ˈplō-mət-əst\ *n* **:** DIPLOMAT

dip·lont \ˈdip-ˌlänt\ *n* [ISV] **:** an organism with somatic cells having the diploid chromosome number — compare HAPLONT — **dip·lon·tic** \dip-ˈlänt-ik\ *adj*

dip·lo·phase \ˈdip-lə-ˌfāz\ *n* **:** a diploid phase in a life cycle

dip·lo·pia \dip-ˈlō-pē-ə\ *n* [NL] **:** a disorder of vision in which two images of a single object are seen because of unequal action of the eye muscles — **dip·lo·pic** \-ˈlō-pik, -ˈläp-ik\ *adj*

dip·lo·pod \ˈdip-lə-ˌpäd\ *n* [deriv. of Gk *dipl-* + *pod-*, *pous* foot — more at FOOT] **:** MILLIPEDE — **dip·lop·o·dous** \dip-ˈläp-əd-əs\ *adj*

dip·lo·sis \dip-ˈlō-səs\ *n* [NL, fr. Gk *diplōsis* action of doubling, fr. *diploun*] **:** restoration of the somatic chromosome number by fusion of two gametes in fertilization

dip·lo·tene \ˈdip-lə-ˌtēn\ *n* [ISV] **:** a stage of meiotic prophase which follows the pachytene and during which the paired homologous chromosomes begin to separate and chiasmata become visible — **diplotene** *adj*

dip net *n* **:** a small bag net with a handle that is used esp. to scoop small fish from the water

dip·no·an \ˈdip-nə-wən\ *adj* [deriv. of Gk *dipnoos*, fr. *di-* + *pnoē* breath, fr. *pnein* to breathe — more at SNEEZE] **:** of or relating to a group (Dipnoi) of fishes with pulmonary circulation, gills, and lungs — **dipnoan** *n*

dip·o·dy \ˈdip-əd-ē\ *n, pl* **-dies** [LL *dipodia*, fr. Gk, fr. *dipod-*, *dipous* having two feet, fr. *di-* + *pod-*, *pous*] **:** a prosodic unit or measure of two feet — **di·pod·ic** \dī-ˈpäd-ik\ *adj*

di·po·lar \ˈdī-ˌpō-lər, -ˈpō-\ *adj* **:** of, relating to, or having a dipole

di·pole \ˈdī-ˌpōl\ *n* [ISV] **1 a :** a pair of equal and opposite electric charges or magnetic poles of opposite sign separated by a small distance **b :** a body or system (as a molecule) having such charges **2 :** a radio antenna consisting of two horizontal rods in line with each other with their ends slightly separated

dip·per \ˈdip-ər\ *n* **1 :** one that dips: as **a :** a worker who dips articles **b :** something (as a long-handled cup) used for dipping **2** *cap* **a :** the seven principal stars in the constellation of Ursa Major arranged in a form resembling a dipper — called also *Big Dipper* **b :** the seven principal stars in Ursa Minor similarly arranged with the North Star forming the outer end of the handle — called also *Little Dipper* **3 :** any of several birds (as a bufflehead or water ouzel) skilled in diving — **dip·per·ful** \-ˌfu̇l\ *n*

di·pro·pel·lant \ˌdī-prə-ˈpel-ənt\ *n* **:** BIPROPELLANT

dip·so·ma·nia \ˌdip-sə-ˈmā-nē-ə, -nyə\ *n* [NL, fr. Gk *dipsa* thirst + LL *mania*] **:** an uncontrollable craving for alcoholic liquors — **dip·so·ma·ni·ac** \-nē-ˌak\ *n* — **dip·so·ma·ni·a·cal** \ˌdip-sō-mə-ˈnī-ə-kəl\ *adj*

dip·stick \ˈdip-ˌstik\ *n* **:** a graduated rod for indicating depth (as of oil in a crankcase)

dip·ter·an \ˈdip-tə-rən\ *adj* [deriv. of Gk *dipteros*] **:** of, relating to, or being a two-winged fly — **dipteran** *n*

dip·tero·carp \ˈdip-tə-rō-ˌkärp\ *n* [NL *Dipterocarpaceae*, group name, fr. *Dipterocarpus*, genus name, fr. *dipterus* dipterous + *-carpus* -carpous] **:** any of a family (Dipterocarpaceae) of tall trees of tropical Asia, Indonesia, and the Philippines that have a 2-winged fruit and are the source of valuable timber, aromatic oils, and resins; *esp* **:** a member of the type genus (*Dipterocarpus*)

dip·ter·on \ˈdip-tə-ˌrän\ *n, pl* **-tera** \-rə\ [Gk, neut. of *dipteros*] **:** TWO-WINGED FLY

dip·ter·ous \ˈdip-tə-rəs\ *adj* [NL *dipterus*, fr. Gk *dipteros*, fr. *di-* + *pteron* wing — more at FEATHER] **1 :** having two wings or winglike appendages **2 :** of or relating to the two-winged flies

dip·tych \ˈdip-(ˌ)tik\ *n* [LL *diptycha*, pl., fr. Gk, fr. neut. pl. of *diptychos* folded in two, fr. *di-* + *ptychē* fold] **1 :** a 2-leaved hinged tablet folding together to protect writing on its waxed surfaces **2 :** a picture or series of pictures (as an altarpiece) painted or carved on two hinged tablets **3 :** a work made up of two matching parts

di·quat \ˈdī-ˌkwät\ *n* [*di-* + *quat*ernary] **:** a powerful nonpersistent herbicide $C_{12}H_{12}Br_2N_2$ that has been used to control water weeds (as the water hyacinth)

dir *abbr* director

dir·dum \ˈdi(ə)rd-əm, ˈdərd-\ *n* [ME (northern dial.) *durdan*, fr. ScGael, grumbling, hum, dim. of *durd* hum] *Scot* **:** BLAME

dire \ˈdī(ə)r\ *adj* **dir·er; dir·est** [L *dirus*; akin to Gk *deinos* terrible, Skt *dvesti* he hates] **1 a :** exciting horror <~ suffering> **b :** DISMAL, OPPRESSIVE <~ days> **2 :** warning of disaster <a ~ forecast> **3 a :** desperately urgent <~ need> **b :** EXTREME <~ poverty> — **dire·ly** *adv* — **dire·ness** *n*

[1]di·rect \də-ˈrekt, dī-\ *vb* [ME *directen*, fr. L *directus*, pp. of *dirigere* to set straight, direct — more at DRESS] *vt* **1 a** *obs* **:** to write (a letter) to a person **b :** to mark with the name and address of the intended recipient **c :** to impart orally **d :** to adapt in expression so as to have particular applicability <a lawyer who ~*s*

his appeals to intelligence and character> **2 :** to cause to turn, move, or point undeviatingly or to follow a straight course <X rays are ~*ed* through the body> **3 :** to point, extend, or project in a specified line or course **4 :** to show or point out the way for **5 a :** to regulate the activities or course of **b :** to carry out the organizing, energizing, and supervising of **c :** to dominate and determine the course of **d :** to train and lead performances of **6 :** to request or enjoin with authority ~ *vi* **1 :** to point out, prescribe, or determine a course or procedure **2 :** to act as director **syn** see CONDUCT, COMMAND

diptych 2

[2]**direct** *adj* [ME, fr. L *directus,* fr. pp. of *dirigere*] **1 a :** proceeding from one point to another in time or space without deviation or interruption : STRAIGHT **b :** proceeding by the shortest way <the ~ route> **2 a :** stemming immediately from a source <~ result> **b :** being or passing in a straight line or descent from parent to offspring : LINEAL <~ ancestor> **c :** having no compromising or impairing element <~ insult> **3 :** characterized by close logical, causal, or consequential relationship <~ evidence> **4 :** NATURAL, STRAIGHTFORWARD <~ manner> **5 a :** marked by absence of an intervening agency, instrumentality, or influence **b :** effected by the action of the people or the electorate and not by representatives **c :** consisting of or reproducing the exact words of a speaker or writer **6 :** capable of dyeing without the aid of a mordant : SUBSTANTIVE **7** *of a celestial body* **:** moving in the general planetary direction from west to east : not retrograde — **di·rect·ness** \-'rek(t)-nəs\ *n*

[3]**direct** *adv* **:** in a direct way: as **a :** from point to point without deviation : by the shortest way <suggesting I write to her ~ —John Willett> **b :** from the source without interruption or diversion <the writer must take his material ~ from life —Douglas Stewart> **c :** without an intervening agency or step <those who did go ~ to the people . . . rallied a considerable majority of the voters —H. S. Ashmore>

direct action *n* **:** action that seeks to achieve an end directly and by the most immediately effective means (as boycott or strike)

direct current *n* **:** an electric current flowing in one direction only and substantially constant in value — abbr. *DC*

di·rect·ed *adj* **1 :** having a positive or negative sense <~ line segment> **2 :** subject to supervision or regulation <a ~ reading program for students>

di·rec·tion \də-'rek-shən, dī-\ *n* **1 :** guidance or supervision of action or conduct : MANAGEMENT **2 a :** the art and technique of directing an orchestra or theatrical production **b :** a word, phrase, or sign indicating the appropriate tempo, mood, or intensity of a passage or movement in music **3** *archaic* **:** SUPERSCRIPTION **4 a :** something imposed as authoritative instruction or bidding : ORDER **b :** an explicit instruction **5 :** the line or course on which something is moving or is aimed to move or along which something is pointing or facing **6 a :** a channel or direct course of thought or action **b :** TENDENCY, TREND **c :** a guiding, governing, or motivating purpose **7** *archaic* **:** DIRECTORATE 1 — **di·rec·tion·less** \-ləs\ *adj*

di·rec·tion·al \-shnəl, -shən-ᵊl\ *adj* **1 :** of, relating to, or indicating direction in space: **a :** suitable for detecting the direction from which radio signals come or for sending out radio signals in one direction only **b :** operating most effectively in a particular direction **2 :** relating to direction or guidance esp. of thought or effort — **di·rec·tion·al·i·ty** \-,rek-shə-'nal-ət-ē\ *n*

direction angle *n* **:** an angle made by a given line with an axis of reference; *specif* **:** one of these angles made by a straight line with the three axes of a rectangular Cartesian coordinate system — usu. used in pl.

direction cosine *n* **:** one of the cosines of the three angles between a directed line in space and the positive direction of the axes of a rectangular Cartesian coordinate system — usu. used in pl.

direction finder *n* **:** a radio receiving device for determining the direction of incoming radio waves that typically consists of a coil antenna rotating freely on a vertical axis

[1]**di·rec·tive** \də-'rek-tiv, dī-\ *adj* **1 :** serving or intended to guide, govern, or influence **2 :** serving to point direction; *specif* **:** DIRECTIONAL 1b **3 :** of or relating to psychotherapy or counseling in which the counselor introduces information, content, or attitudes not previously expressed by the client

[2]**directive** *n* **:** something that serves to direct, guide, and usu. impel toward an action or goal; *esp* **:** an authoritative instrument issued by a high-level body or official

di·rec·tiv·i·ty \də-,rek-'tiv-ət-ē, (,)dī-\ *n* **:** the property of being directional

direct lighting *n* **:** lighting in which the greater part of the light goes directly from the source to the area lit

[1]**di·rect·ly** \də-'rek-(t)lē, dī-, *in sense 2* də-'rek-lē *or* 'drek-lē\ *adv* **1 :** in a direct manner <~ relevant> <the road runs ~ east and west> **2 a :** without delay : IMMEDIATELY **b :** in a little while : SHORTLY **syn** see PRESENTLY

[2]**di·rect·ly** \də-'rek-(t)lē, dī-; 'drek-lē\ *conj, chiefly Brit* **:** immediately after : as soon as <~ I received it I rang up the shipping company —F. W. Crofts>

di·rect·ness \də-'rek(t)-nəs, dī-\ *n* **1 :** the character of being accurate in course or aim **2 :** strict pertinence : STRAIGHTFORWARDNESS

direct object *n* **:** a grammatical object representing the primary goal or the result of the action of a verb <*me* in "he hit me" and *house* in "we built a house" are *direct objects*>

di·rec·tor \də-'rek-tər, dī-\ *n* **:** one that directs: as **a :** the head of an organized group or administrative unit (as a bureau or school) **b :** one of a group of persons entrusted with the overall direction of a corporate enterprise **c :** one that supervises the production of a show (as for stage or screen) with responsibility for action, lighting, music, and rehearsals **d :** CONDUCTOR c — **di·rec·tor·ship** \-,ship\ *n*

di·rec·tor·ate \də-'rek-t(ə-)rət, dī-\ *n* **1 :** the office of director **2 a :** a board of directors (as of a corporation) **b :** membership on a board of directors **3 :** an executive staff (as of a program, bureau, or department)

di·rec·to·ri·al \də-,rek-'tōr-ē-əl, (,)dī-, -'tȯr-\ *adj* **1 :** serving to direct **2 :** of or relating to a director or to theatrical direction **3 :** of, relating to, or administered by a directory

director's chair *n* [fr. its use by motion picture directors on the set] **:** a lightweight folding armchair with a back and seat usu. of cotton duck

[1]**di·rec·to·ry** \də-'rek-t(ə-)rē, dī-\ *adj* **:** serving to direct *specif* **:** providing advisory but not compulsory guidance

[2]**directory** *n, pl* **-ries** [ML *directorium,* fr. neut. of LL *directorius* directorial, fr. L *directus,* pp.] **1 a :** a book or collection of directions, rules, or ordinances **b :** an alphabetical or classified list (as of names and addresses) **2 :** a body of directors

direct primary *n* **:** a primary in which nominations of candidates for office are made by direct vote

di·rec·tress \də-'rek-trəs, dī-\ *n* **:** a female director

di·rec·trix \-triks\ *n, pl* **-trix·es** \-trik-səz\ *also* **-tri·ces** \-trə-,sēz\ [ML, fem. of LL *director,* fr. L *directus,* pp.] **1** *archaic* **:** DIRECTRESS **2 :** a fixed curve with which a generatrix maintains a given relationship in generating a geometric figure; *specif* **:** a straight line the distance to which from any point of a conic section is in fixed ratio to the distance from the same point to a focus

direct tax *n* **:** a tax exacted directly from the person on whom the ultimate burden of the tax is expected to fall

dire·ful \'dī(ə)r-fəl\ *adj* **1 :** DREADFUL **2 :** OMINOUS — **dire·ful·ly** \-fə-lē\ *adv*

dire wolf *n* **:** a large lupine mammal (*Canis dirus* or *Aenocyon dirus*) found in Pleistocene deposits of No. America

dirge \'dərj\ *n* [ME *dirige,* the Office of the Dead, fr. the first word of a LL antiphon, fr. L, imper. of *dirigere*] **1 :** a song or hymn of grief or lamentation; *esp* **:** one intended to accompany funeral or memorial rites **2 :** a slow, solemn, and mournful piece of music

dir·ham \də-'ram\ *n* [Ar, fr. L *drachma* drachma] **1** — see MONEY table **2** — see *dinar* at MONEY table

[1]**di·ri·gi·ble** \'dir-ə-jə-bəl, də-'rij-ə-\ *adj* [L *dirigere*] **:** capable of being steered

[2]**dirigible** *n* [*dirigible* (*balloon*)] **:** AIRSHIP

[1]**dirk** \'dərk\ *n* [Sc *durk*] **:** a long straight-bladed dagger

[2]**dirk** *vt* **:** to stab with a dirk

dirl \'dir(ə)l, 'dərl\ *vi* [prob. alter. of *thirl*] *Scot* **:** TREMBLE, QUIVER

dirndl \'dərn-dᵊl\ *n* [short for G *dirndlkleid,* fr. G dial. *dirndl* girl + G *kleid* dress] **1 :** a dress style with tight bodice, short sleeves, low neck, and gathered skirt **2 :** a full skirt with a tight waistband

dirt \'dərt\ *n* [ME *drit,* fr. ON; akin to OE *drītan* to defecate, L *foria* diarrhea] **1 a :** EXCREMENT **b :** a filthy or soiling substance (as mud, dust, or grime) **c** *archaic* **:** something worthless **d :** a contemptible person **2 a :** loose or packed soil or sand : EARTH **b** (1) **:** alluvial earth in placer mining (2) **:** slate and waste in coal mines **3 a :** an abject or filthy state : SQUALOR **b :** CORRUPTION, CHICANERY **c :** licentiousness of language or theme **d :** scandalous or malicious gossip

dirt farmer *n* **:** a farmer who earns his living by farming his own land; *esp* **:** one who farms without the help of hired hands or tenants

dirt road *n* **:** an unpaved road

[1]**dirty** \'dərt-ē\ *adj* **dirt·i·er; -est 1 a :** not clean or pure <~ clothes> **b :** likely to befoul or defile with dirt <~ jobs> **c :** tedious, disagreeable, and unrecognized or thankless <undertook the ~ tasks that no one else wanted to bother with> **d :** contaminated with infecting organisms <~ wounds> **2 a :** BASE, SORDID <war is a ~ business> **b :** UNSPORTSMANLIKE <a ~ trick> <~ players> **c :** highly regrettable : GRIEVOUS <a ~ shame> **3 :** INDECENT, SMUTTY <~ language> **4 :** FOGGY, STORMY **5 a** *of color* **:** not clear and bright : DULLISH <drab *dirty*-pink walls> **b :** characterized by a husky, rasping, or raw tonal quality — used esp. of jazz **6 :** conveying ill-natured resentment <gave him a ~ look> **7 :** having considerable fallout <~ bombs> — **dirt·i·ly** \'dərt-ᵊl-ē\ *adv* — **dirt·i·ness** \'dərt-ē-nəs\ *n*

syn DIRTY, FILTHY, FOUL, NASTY, SQUALID *shared meaning element* **:** conspicuously unclean or impure. DIRTY emphasizes the fact of the presence of dirt more than an emotional reaction to it <children *dirty* from play> <a *dirty* littered street> FILTHY carries a strong suggestion of offensiveness and typically of gradually accumulated dirt that begrimes and besmears <a stained greasy floor, utterly *filthy*> FOUL implies extreme offensiveness and an accumulation of what is rotten or stinking <the *foul* oil-and-garbage whiffs from the river —Herman Wouk> NASTY applies to what is actually foul or is repugnant to one used to or expecting freshness, cleanliness, or sweetness <it's a *nasty* job to clean up after a sick cat> In practice, *nasty* is often weakened to the point of being no more than a synonym of *unpleasant* or *disagreeable* <had a *nasty* fall> <his answer gave her a *nasty* shock> SQUALID adds to the idea of dirtiness and filth that of slovenly neglect <living in *squalid* poverty> <*squalid* slums> All these terms are applicable to moral uncleanness or baseness or obscenity. DIRTY then stresses meanness or despicableness <the creature's at his *dirty* work again —Alexander Pope> while FILTHY and FOUL describe disgusting obscenity or loathsome behavior <*filthy* language> <a *foul* story> and NASTY implies a peculiarly offensive unpleasantness <a cheap and *nasty* imitation of the real

thing —Robert Wilkes> Distinctively, SQUALID implies sordidness as well as baseness and dirtiness <her life was a series of *squalid* affairs> ***ant*** clean

2**dirty** *vb* **dirt·ied; dirty·ing** *vt* **1 :** to make dirty **2 a :** to stain with dishonor : SULLY **b :** to debase by distorting the real nature of ~ *vi* : to become soiled

dirty linen *n* : private matters whose public exposure brings distress and embarrassment

dirty old man *n* : a lecherous mature man

dirty pool *n* : underhanded or unsportsmanlike conduct

dirty word *n* : a word or expression that is inappropriate, opprobrious, or derogatory in a particular frame of reference

dirty work *n* : behavior or an act that is mean, treacherous, or unfair <the *dirty work* in general elections is often pale by contrast with the primaries —B. L. Felknor>

dis *abbr* **1** discharge **2** discount **3** distance

Dis \ˈdis\ *n* [L] : the Roman god of the underworld — compare PLUTO

dis- *prefix* [ME *dis-, des-,* fr. OF & L; OF *des-, dis-,* fr. L *dis-,* lit., apart; akin to OE *te-* apart, L *duo* two — more at TWO] **1 a :** do the opposite of <*dis*establish> **b :** deprive of (a specified quality, rank, or object) <*dis*able> <*dis*prince> <*dis*frock> **c :** exclude or expel from <*dis*bar> **2 :** opposite or absence of <*dis*union> <*dis*affection> **3 :** not <*dis*agreeable> **4 :** completely <*dis*annul> **5** [by folk etymology] : DYS- <*dis*function>

dis·abil·i·ty \ˌdis-ə-ˈbil-ət-ē\ *n* **1 a :** the condition of being disabled **b :** inability to pursue an occupation because of physical or mental impairment **2 a :** lack of legal qualification to do something **b :** a nonlegal disqualification, restriction, or disadvantage

dis·able \dis-ˈā-bəl, diz-\ *vt* **dis·abled; dis·abling** \-b(ə-)liŋ\ **1 :** to deprive of legal right, qualification, or capacity **2 :** to make incapable or ineffective; *esp* : to deprive of physical, moral, or intellectual strength : CRIPPLE ***syn*** see WEAKEN ***ant*** rehabilitate — **dis·able·ment** \-bəl-mənt\ *n*

dis·abuse \ˌdis-ə-ˈbyüz\ *vt* [F *désabuser,* fr. *dés-* dis- + *abuser* to abuse] : to free from error or fallacy

di·sac·cha·ri·dase \(ˈ)dī-ˈsak-ə-rə-ˌdās, -ˌdāz\ *n* : an enzyme (as maltase or lactase) that hydrolyzes disaccharides

di·sac·cha·ride \(ˈ)dī-ˈsak-ə-ˌrīd\ *n* : any of a class of sugars (as sucrose) that yields on hydrolysis two monosaccharide molecules

1**dis·ac·cord** \ˌdis-ə-ˈkȯ(ə)rd\ *vi* [ME *disacorden,* fr. MF *desacorder,* fr. *desacort* disagreement, fr. *des-* dis- + *acort* accord] : CLASH, DISAGREE

2**disaccord** *n* : lack of harmony : DISAGREEMENT

dis·ac·cus·tom \ˌdis-ə-ˈkəs-təm\ *vt* [MF *desaccoustumer,* fr. OF *desacostumer,* fr. *des-* + *acostumer* to accustom] : to free from a habit

1**dis·ad·van·tage** \ˌdis-əd-ˈvant-ij\ *n* [ME *disavauntage,* fr. MF *desavantage,* fr. OF, fr. *des-* + *avantage* advantage] **1 :** loss or damage esp. to reputation, credit, or finances : DETRIMENT **2 a :** an unfavorable, inferior, or prejudicial condition <we were at a ~> **b :** HANDICAP <it put us under a serious ~>

2**disadvantage** *vt* : to place at a disadvantage : HARM

1**dis·ad·van·taged** *adj* : lacking in the basic resources or conditions (as standard housing, medical and educational facilities, and civil rights) believed to be necessary for an equal position in society — **dis·ad·van·taged·ness** \-ij(d)-nəs\ *n*

2**disadvantaged** *n, pl* **disadvantaged** : one that is deprived and underprivileged (as in cultural, economic, and social matters)

dis·ad·van·ta·geous \(ˌ)dis-ˌad-ˌvan-ˈtā-jəs, -vən-\ *adj* **1 :** constituting a disadvantage **2 :** DEROGATORY, DISPARAGING — **dis·ad·van·ta·geous·ly** *adv* — **dis·ad·van·ta·geous·ness** *n*

dis·af·fect \ˌdis-ə-ˈfekt\ *vt* : to alienate the affection or loyalty of ***syn*** see ESTRANGE ***ant*** win (*as to a cause*) — **dis·af·fec·tion** \-ˈfek-shən\ *n*

dis·af·fect·ed *adj* : discontented and resentful esp. against authority : REBELLIOUS

dis·af·fil·i·ate \ˌdis-ə-ˈfil-ē-ˌāt\ *vt* : DISASSOCIATE ~ *vi* : to terminate an affiliation — **dis·af·fil·i·a·tion** \-ˌfil-ē-ˈā-shən\ *n*

dis·af·firm \ˌdis-ə-ˈfərm\ *vt* **1 :** CONTRADICT **2 :** to refuse to confirm : ANNUL, REPUDIATE — **dis·af·fir·mance** \-ˈfər-mən(t)s\ *n* — **dis·af·fir·ma·tion** \(ˌ)dis-ˌaf-ər-ˈmā-shən\ *n*

dis·ag·gre·gate \(ˈ)dis-ˈag-ri-ˌgāt\ *vt* : to separate into component parts <~ sandstone> <~ demographic data> ~ *vi* : to break up or apart <the molecules of a gel ~ to form a sol> — **dis·ag·gre·ga·tion** \(ˌ)dis-ˌag-ri-ˈgā-shən\ *n* — **dis·ag·gre·ga·tive** \(ˈ)dis-ˈag-ri-ˌgāt-iv\ *adj*

dis·agree \ˌdis-ə-ˈgrē\ *vi* [ME *disagreen,* fr. MF *desagreer,* fr. *des-* + *agreer* to agree] **1 :** to fail to agree <the two accounts ~> **2 :** to differ in opinion <he *disagreed* with me on every topic> **3 :** to be unsuitable <fried foods ~ with me>

dis·agree·able \-ə-bəl\ *adj* **1 :** causing discomfort : UNPLEASANT, OFFENSIVE **2 :** marked by ill temper : PEEVISH — **dis·agree·abil·i·ty** \-ˌgrē-ə-ˈbil-ət-ē\ *n* — **dis·agree·able·ness** *n* — **dis·agree·ably** \-blē\ *adv*

dis·agree·ment \ˌdis-ə-ˈgrē-mənt\ *n* **1 :** the act of disagreeing **2 a :** the state of being at variance : DISPARITY **b :** QUARREL

dis·al·low \ˌdis-ə-ˈlau̇\ *vt* **1 :** to deny the force, truth, or validity of **2 :** to refuse to allow — **dis·al·low·ance** \-ən(t)s\ *n*

dis·am·big·u·ate \ˌdis-am-ˈbig-yə-ˌwāt\ *vt* **-ated; -at·ing :** to establish a single semantic or grammatical interpretation for — **dis·am·big·u·a·tion** \-ˌbig-yə-ˈwā-shən\ *n*

dis·an·nul \ˌdis-ə-ˈnəl\ *vt* : ANNUL, CANCEL

dis·ap·pear \ˌdis-ə-ˈpi(ə)r\ *vi* **1 :** to pass from view suddenly or gradually **2 :** to cease to be — **dis·ap·pear·ance** \-ˈpir-ən(t)s\ *n*

dis·ap·point \ˌdis-ə-ˈpȯint\ *vb* [MF *desapointier,* fr. *des-* dis- + *apointier* to arrange — more at APPOINT] *vt* : to fail to meet the expectation or hope of : FRUSTRATE ~ *vi* : to cause disappointment <where the show ~*s* most is in the work of the younger generation —John Ashbery>

dis·ap·point·ed *adj* **1 :** defeated in expectation or hope : THWARTED **2** *obs* : not adequately equipped — **dis·ap·point·ed·ly** *adv*

dis·ap·point·ing *adj* : failing to meet expectations — **dis·ap·point·ing·ly** \-iŋ-lē\ *adv*

dis·ap·point·ment \ˌdis-ə-ˈpȯint-mənt\ *n* **1 :** the act or an instance of disappointing : the state or emotion of being disappointed **2 :** one that disappoints

dis·ap·pro·ba·tion \(ˌ)dis-ˌap-rə-ˈbā-shən\ *n* : the act or state of disapproving : the state of being disapproved : CONDEMNATION

dis·ap·prov·al \ˌdis-ə-ˈprü-vəl\ *n* : DISAPPROBATION, CENSURE

dis·ap·prove \-ˈprüv\ *vt* **1 :** to pass unfavorable judgment on : CONDEMN **2 :** to refuse approval to : REJECT ~ *vi* : to feel or express disapproval — **dis·ap·prov·er** *n* — **dis·ap·prov·ing·ly** \-ˈprü-viŋ-lē\ *adv*

syn DISAPPROVE, DEPRECATE *shared meaning element* : to feel or express an objection ***ant*** approve

dis·arm \(ˈ)dis-ˈärm, diz-\ *vb* [ME *desarmen,* fr. MF *desarmer,* fr. OF, fr. *des-* + *armer* to arm] *vt* **1 a :** to divest of arms **b :** to deprive of a means of attack or defense **c :** to make harmless **2 a :** to deprive of means, reason, or disposition to be hostile **b :** to win over ~ *vi* **1 :** to lay aside arms **2 :** to give up or reduce armed forces — **dis·ar·ma·ment** \-ˈär-mə-mənt\ *n* — **dis·arm·er** *n*

dis·arm·ing *adj* : allaying criticism or hostility : INGRATIATING — **dis·arm·ing·ly** \-ˈär-miŋ-lē\ *adv*

dis·ar·range \ˌdis-ə-ˈrānj\ *vt* : to disturb the arrangement or order of — **dis·ar·range·ment** \-mənt\ *n*

1**dis·ar·ray** \ˌdis-ə-ˈrā\ *n* **1 :** a lack of order or sequence : CONFUSION, DISORDER **2 :** disorderly dress : DISHABILLE

2**disarray** *vt* [ME *disarayen,* fr. MF *desarroyer,* fr. OF *desareer,* fr. *des-* + *areer* to array] **1 :** to throw into disorder **2 :** UNDRESS

dis·ar·tic·u·late \ˌdis-är-ˈtik-yə-ˌlāt\ *vi* : to become disjointed ~ *vt* : DISJOINT — **dis·ar·tic·u·la·tion** \-ˌtik-yə-ˈlā-shən\ *n*

dis·as·sem·ble \ˌdis-ə-ˈsem-bəl\ *vt* : to take apart <~ a watch> ~ *vi* **1 :** to come apart <the automobile parts ~ into sections> **2 :** DISPERSE, SCATTER <the crowd began to ~> — **dis·as·sem·bla·ble** \-b(ə-)lə-bəl\ *adj* — **dis·as·sem·bly** \-blē\ *n*

dis·as·so·ci·ate \ˌdis-ə-ˈsō-s(h)ē-ˌāt\ *vt* : to detach from association : DISSOCIATE — **dis·as·so·ci·a·tion** \-ˌsō-sē-ˈā-shən, -shē-\ *n*

di·sas·ter \diz-ˈas-tər, dis-\ *n* [MF & OIt; MF *desastre,* fr. OIt *disastro,* fr. *dis-* (fr. L) + *astro* star, fr. L *astrum* — more at ASTRAL] **1** *obs* : an unfavorable aspect of a planet or star **2 :** a sudden calamitous event bringing great damage, loss, or destruction; *broadly* : a sudden or great misfortune

syn DISASTER, CALAMITY, CATASTROPHE, CATACLYSM *shared meaning element* : an event or situation that is regarded as a terrible misfortune

disaster area *n* : an area officially declared to be the scene of an emergency created by a disaster and therefore qualified to receive certain types of governmental aid (as emergency loans and relief supplies)

di·sas·trous \diz-ˈas-trəs *also* dis-\ *adj* : attended by or causing suffering or disaster : CALAMITOUS — **di·sas·trous·ly** *adv*

dis·avow \ˌdis-ə-ˈvau̇\ *vt* [ME *desavowen,* fr. MF *desavouer,* fr. OF, fr. *des-* dis- + *avouer* to avow] **1 :** to refuse to acknowledge : DISCLAIM **2 :** to deny responsibility for : REPUDIATE — **dis·avow·able** \-ə-bəl\ *adj* — **dis·avow·al** \-ˈvau̇(-ə)l\ *n*

dis·band \dis-ˈband\ *vb* [MF *desbander,* fr. *des-* + *bande* band] *vt* : to break up the organization of : DISSOLVE ~ *vi* : to break up as an organization : DISPERSE — **dis·band·ment** \-ˈban(d)-mənt\ *n*

dis·bar \dis-ˈbär\ *vt* : to expel from the bar or the legal profession : deprive (an attorney) of legal status and privileges — **dis·bar·ment** \-mənt\ *n*

dis·be·lief \ˌdis-bə-ˈlēf\ *n* : the act of disbelieving : mental rejection of something as untrue ***syn*** see UNBELIEF ***ant*** belief

dis·be·lieve \-ˈlēv\ *vt* : to hold not to be true or real ~ *vi* : to withhold or reject belief <~*s* in the sanctity of the status quo —W. C. Brownell> — **dis·be·liev·er** *n*

dis·bound \dis-ˈbau̇nd\ *adj* : no longer having a binding <a ~ pamphlet>

dis·branch \(ˈ)dis-ˈbranch\ *vt* [MF *desbrancher,* fr. *des-* + *branche* branch] : to tear off (as a branch)

dis·bud \(ˈ)dis-ˈbəd\ *vt* **1 :** to thin out flower buds in order to improve the quality of bloom of **2 :** to dehorn (cattle) by destroying the undeveloped horn bud

dis·bur·den \(ˈ)dis-ˈbərd-ᵊn\ *vt* **1 a :** to rid of a burden <~ a pack animal> **b :** UNBURDEN <~ your conscience> **2 :** UNLOAD <~*ed* their merchandise in the town square> ~ *vi* : DISCHARGE <the vessels ~*ed* at the dock> — **dis·bur·den·ment** \-mənt\ *n*

dis·burse \dis-ˈbərs\ *vt* **dis·bursed; dis·burs·ing** [MF *desbourser,* fr. OF *desborser,* fr. *des-* + *borser* to get money, fr. *borse* purse, fr. ML *bursa* — more at PURSE] **1 a :** to pay out : expend esp. from a fund **b :** to make a payment in settlement of : DEFRAY **2 :** DISTRIBUTE <~ property by will> — **dis·burs·er** *n*

dis·burse·ment \-ˈbər-smənt\ *n* : the act of disbursing; *also* : funds paid out

1**disc** *var of* DISK

2**disc** *abbr* discount

disc- *or* **disci-** *or* **disco-** *comb form* [L, fr. Gk *disk-, disko-,* fr. *diskos*] **1 :** disk <*disci*gerous> **2 :** phonograph record <*disco*phile>

dis·calced \(ˈ)dis-ˈkalst\ *adj* [part trans. of L *discalceatus,* fr. *dis-* + *calceatus,* pp. of *calceare* to put on shoes, fr. *calceus* shoe, fr. *calc-, calx* heel — more at CALK] : UNSHOD, BAREFOOT <~ friars>

dis·cant \ˈdis-ˌkant\ *var of* DESCANT

1**dis·card** \dis-ˈkärd, ˈdis-ˌ\ *vt* **1 a :** to remove (a playing card) from one's hand **b :** to play (any card except a trump) from a suit different from the one led **2 :** to get rid of as useless or unpleasant ~ *vi* : to discard a playing card — **dis·card·able** \-ə-bəl\ *adj* — **dis·card·er** *n*

syn DISCARD, CAST, SHED, SLOUGH, SCRAP, JUNK *shared meaning element* : to get rid of as of no further use, value, or service

2**dis·card** \ˈdis-ˌkärd\ *n* **1 a :** the act of discarding in a card game **b :** a card discarded **2 :** one that is cast off or rejected

disc brake *n* : a brake that operates by the friction of a caliper pressing against the sides of a rotating disc

dis·cern \dis-ˈərn, diz-\ *vb* [ME *discernen,* fr. MF *discerner,* fr. L *discernere* to separate, distinguish between, fr. *dis-* apart + *cernere* to sift — more at DIS-, CERTAIN] *vt* **1 a :** to detect with the eyes **b :** to detect with other senses than vision **2 :** to come to know or recognize mentally **3 :** to recognize or identify as separate and distinct : DISCRIMINATE ~ *vi* **:** to see or understand the difference — **dis·cern·er** *n* — **dis·cern·ible** *also* **dis·cern·able** \-ˈər-nə-bəl\ *adj* — **dis·cern·ibly** \-blē\ *adv*

dis·cern·ing *adj* **:** revealing insight and understanding : DISCRIMINATING <a ~ critic> — **dis·cern·ing·ly** \-ˈər-niŋ-lē\ *adv*

dis·cern·ment \dis-ˈərn-mənt, diz-\ *n* **1 :** an act of discerning **2 :** the quality of being able to grasp and comprehend what is obscure : skill in discerning

syn DISCERNMENT, DISCRIMINATION, PERCEPTION, PENETRATION, INSIGHT, ACUMEN *shared meaning element* : keen intellectual vision. DISCERNMENT stresses skill and accuracy (as in reading character or appreciating art) <a man of great intelligence and *discernment*> <the *discernment* revealed in her novels> DISCRIMINATION emphasizes a capacity for distinguishing and selecting the excellent, the appropriate, or the true <nobody should reproach them for reading indiscriminately . . . only by so doing can they learn *discrimination* —*Times Lit. Supp.*> PERCEPTION implies quick acute discernment and delicacy of feeling <persecutors were ordinary, reasonably well-intentioned people lacking in keen *perception* —C. H. Sykes> PENETRATION implies a searching mind that goes beyond the obvious or superficial <analyzed the underlying causes of the discontent with great *penetration*> INSIGHT emphasizes depth of discernment coupled with understanding sympathy <the ecstasy of imaginative vision, the sudden *insight* into the nature of things —Edmund Wilson> ACUMEN suggests consistent penetration accompanied by shrewd soundness of judgment <it is clear and bold, reflecting astute scholarship and logical *acumen* —L. L. Gerson>

¹dis·charge \dis(h)-ˈchärj, ˈdis(h)-ˌ\ *vb* [ME *dischargen,* fr. MF *descharger,* fr. LL *discarricare,* fr. L *dis-* + LL *carricare* to load — more at CHARGE] *vt* **1 :** to relieve of a charge, load, or burden: **a :** UNLOAD **b :** to release from an obligation **2 a :** to let go **:** clear out **b :** SHOOT <~ an arrow> **c :** to release from confinement, custody, or care <~ a prisoner> **d :** to give outlet or vent to : EMIT **3 a (1) :** to dismiss from employment **(2) :** to release from service or duty <~ a soldier> **b :** to get rid of (as a debt or obligation) by performing an appropriate action (as payment) : FULFILL **c :** to set aside : ANNUL **d :** to order (a legislative committee) to end consideration of a bill in order to bring it before the house for action **4 :** to bear and distribute (as the weight of a wall above an opening) **5 :** to bleach out or remove (color or dye) in dyeing and printing textiles **6 :** to cancel the record of the loan of (a library book) upon return ~ *vi* **1 :** to throw off or deliver a load, charge, or burden **2 a :** to go off : FIRE — used of a gun **b :** RUN <some dyes ~> **c :** to pour forth fluid or other contents ***syn*** see FREE, PERFORM — **dis·charge·able** \-ə-bəl\ *adj* — **dis·charg·ee** \(ˌ)dis(h)-ˌchär-ˈjē\ *n* — **dis·charg·er** \dis(h)-ˈchär-jər, ˈdis(h)-ˌ\ *n*

²dis·charge \ˈdis(h)-ˌchärj, dis(h)-ˈ\ *n* **1 a :** the act of relieving of something that oppresses : RELEASE **b :** something that discharges or releases; *esp* **:** a certification of release or payment **2 :** the state of being discharged or relieved **3 :** the act of discharging or unloading **4 :** legal release from confinement **5 :** a firing off **6 a :** a flowing or issuing out <a ~ of spores>; *also* **:** a rate of flow **b :** something that is emitted <a purulent ~> **7 :** the act of removing an obligation or liability **8 a :** release or dismissal esp. from an office or employment **b :** complete separation from military service **9 a :** the equalization of a difference of electric potential between two points **b :** the conversion of the chemical energy of a battery into electrical energy

discharge lamp *n* **:** an electric lamp in which discharge of electricity between electrodes causes luminosity of the enclosed vapor or gas or in which the luminosity of the enclosed gas is enhanced by phosphors

discharge tube *n* **:** an electron tube which contains gas or vapor at low pressure and through which conduction takes place when a high voltage is applied

dis·ci·flo·ral \ˌdis-(k)i-ˈflōr-əl, -ˈflȯr-\ *adj* **:** having flowers with the receptacle enlarged into a conspicuous disc

dis·ci·form \ˈdis-(k)ə-ˌfȯrm\ *adj* **:** round or oval in shape

dis·ci·ple \dis-ˈī-pəl\ *n* [ME, fr. OE *discipul* & OF *desciple,* fr. LL and L; LL *discipulus* follower of Jesus Christ in his lifetime, fr. L, pupil] **1 :** one who accepts and assists in spreading the doctrines of another: as **a :** one of the twelve in the inner circle of Christ's followers according to the Gospel accounts **b :** a convinced adherent of a school or individual **2** *cap* **:** a member of the Disciples of Christ founded in the U.S. in 1809 that holds the Bible alone to be the rule of faith and practice, baptizes by immersion, and has a congregational polity ***syn*** see FOLLOWER — **dis·ci·ple·ship** \-ˌship\ *n*

dis·ci·plin·able \ˌdis-ə-ˈplin-ə-bəl; ˈdis-ə-plən-\ *adj* **1 :** DOCILE, TEACHABLE **2 :** subject to or deserving discipline <a ~ offense>

dis·ci·pli·nar·i·an \ˌdis-ə-plə-ˈner-ē-ən\ *n* **:** one who disciplines or enforces order — **disciplinarian** *adj*

dis·ci·plin·ary \ˈdis-ə-plə-ˌner-ē, *esp Brit* ˌdis-ə-ˈplin-ə-rē\ *adj* **1 a :** of or relating to discipline **b :** designed to correct or punish breaches of discipline <took ~ action> **2 :** of or relating to a particular field of study — **dis·ci·plin·ar·i·ly** \ˌdis-ə-plə-ˈner-ə-lē\ *adv* — **dis·ci·plin·ar·i·ty** \-ˈnar-ət-ē\ *n*

¹dis·ci·pline \ˈdis-ə-plən\ *n* [ME, fr. MF & L; MF, fr. L *disciplina* teaching, learning, fr. *discipulus* pupil] **1** *obs* **:** INSTRUCTION **2 :** a subject that is taught : a field of study **3 :** training that corrects, molds, or perfects the mental faculties or moral character **4 :** PUNISHMENT **5 a :** control gained by enforcing obedience or order **b :** orderly or prescribed conduct or pattern of behavior **c :** SELF-CONTROL **6 :** a rule or system of rules governing conduct or activity — **dis·ci·plin·al** \-plən-ᵊl\ *adj*

²discipline *vt* **-plined; plin·ing 1 :** to punish or penalize for the sake of discipline **2 :** to train or develop by instruction and exercise esp. in self-control **3 a :** to bring (a group) under control <~ troops> **b :** to impose order upon <the writer ~*s* and refines his style> ***syn*** see TEACH, PUNISH — **dis·ci·plin·er** *n*

dis·ci·plined *adj* **:** marked by or possessing discipline <a ~ mind>

disc jockey *n* **:** an announcer of a radio or TV show of popular recorded music who often intersperses comments not related to the music

dis·claim \dis-ˈklām\ *vb* [AF *disclaimer,* fr. *dis-* + *claimer* to claim, fr. OF *clamer*] *vi* **1 :** to make a disclaimer **2 a** *obs* **:** to disavow all part or share **b :** to utter denial ~ *vt* **1 :** to renounce a legal claim to **2 :** DENY, DISAVOW

dis·claim·er \-ˈklā-mər\ *n* [AF, fr. *disclaimer,* v.] **1 a :** a denial or disavowal of legal claim : relinquishment of or formal refusal to accept an interest or estate **b :** a writing that embodies a legal disclaimer **2 a :** DENIAL, DISAVOWAL **b :** REPUDIATION

dis·cla·ma·tion \ˌdis-klə-ˈmā-shən\ *n* **:** RENUNCIATION, DISAVOWAL

disc·like *var of* DISKLIKE

dis·cli·max \(ˈ)dis-ˈklī-ˌmaks\ *n* **:** a relatively stable ecological community often including kinds of organisms foreign to the region and displacing the climax because of disturbance esp. by man

¹dis·close \dis-ˈklōz\ *vt* [ME *disclosen,* fr. MF *desclos-,* stem of *desclore* to disclose, fr. ML *disclaudere* to open, fr. L *dis-* + *claudere* to close — more at CLOSE] **1** *obs* **:** to open up **2 a :** to expose to view **b** *archaic* **:** HATCH **c :** to make known or public (something previously held close or secret) <demands that politicians ~ the sources of their income> ***syn*** see REVEAL — **dis·clos·er** *n*

²disclose *n, obs* **:** DISCLOSURE

dis·clo·sure \dis-ˈklō-zhər\ *n* **1 :** the act or an instance of disclosing : EXPOSURE **2 :** something disclosed : REVELATION

dis·co \ˈdis-(ˌ)kō\ *n, pl* **discos :** DISCOTHEQUE

disco- — see DISC-

dis·cog·ra·pher \dis-ˈkäg-rə-fər\ *n* **:** one that compiles discographies

dis·cog·ra·phy \-fē\ *n, pl* **-phies** [F *discographie,* fr. *disc-* + *-graphie* -graphy] **1 :** a descriptive list of phonograph records by category, composer, performer, or date of release **2 :** the history of recorded music — **dis·co·graph·i·cal** \ˌdis-kə-ˈgraf-i-kəl\ *also* **dis·co·graph·ic** \-ik\ *adj* — **dis·co·graph·i·cal·ly** \-i-k(ə-)lē\ *adv*

dis·coid \ˈdis-ˌkȯid\ *adj* [LL *discoides* quoit-shaped, fr. Gk *diskoeidēs,* fr. *diskos* disk] **1 :** resembling a disk or discus : being flat and circular **2 :** relating to or having a disk: as **a** *of a composite floret* **:** situated in the floral disk **b** *of a composite flower head* **:** having only tubular florets

dis·coi·dal \dis-ˈkȯid-ᵊl\ *adj* **:** of, resembling, or producing a disk: as **a** *of a gastropod shell* **:** having the whorls form a flat coil **b :** having the villi restricted to one or more disklike areas

dis·col·or \(ˈ)dis-ˈkəl-ər\ *vb* [ME *discolouren,* fr. MF *descolourer,* fr. LL *discolorari,* fr. L *discolor* of another color, fr. *dis-* + *color*] *vt* **:** to alter or change the hue or color of ~ *vi* **:** to change color **:** STAIN, FADE

dis·col·or·ation \(ˌ)dis-ˌkəl-ə-ˈrā-shən\ *n* **1 :** the act of discoloring **:** the state of being discolored **2 :** a discolored spot or formation **:** STAIN

dis·com·bob·u·late \ˌdis-kəm-ˈbäb-(y)ə-ˌlāt\ *vt* **-lat·ed; -lat·ing** [prob. alter. of *discompose*] **:** UPSET, CONFUSE <the offensive had *discombobulated* all the German defensive arrangements —A. J. Liebling> — **dis·com·bob·u·la·tion** \-ˌbäb-(y)ə-ˈlā-shən\ *n*

¹dis·com·fit \dis-ˈkəm(p)-fət, *esp South* ˌdis-kəm-ˈfit\ *vt* [ME *discomfiten,* fr. OF *desconfit,* pp. of *desconfire,* fr. *des-* + *confire* to prepare — more at COMFIT] **1 a** *archaic* **:** to defeat in battle **b :** to frustrate the plans of : THWART **2 :** to put into a state of perplexity and embarrassment : DISCONCERT ***syn*** see EMBARRASS

²discomfit *n* **:** DISCOMFITURE

dis·com·fi·ture \dis-ˈkəm(p)-fə-ˌchu̇(ə)r, -chər, -ˌt(y)u̇(ə)r\ *n* **:** the act of discomfiting : the state of being discomfited

¹dis·com·fort \dis-ˈkəm(p)-fərt\ *vt* [ME *discomforten,* fr. MF *desconforter,* fr. OF, fr. *des-* + *conforter* to comfort] **1** *archaic* **:** DISMAY **2 :** to make uncomfortable or uneasy — **dis·com·fort·able** \-ˈkəm(p)-fərt-ə-bəl, -ˈkəm(p)(f)-tə(r)-bəl\ *adj* — **dis·com·fort·er** \-ˈkəm(p)-fərt-ər\ *n*

²discomfort *n* **1** *archaic* **:** DISTRESS, GRIEF **2 :** mental or physical uneasiness : ANNOYANCE <he gave every sign of intense ~>

dis·com·mend \ˌdis-kə-ˈmend\ *vt* **1 :** DISAPPROVE, DISPARAGE **2 :** to cause to be viewed unfavorably — **dis·com·mend·able** \-ˈmen-də-bəl\ *adj* — **dis·com·men·da·tion** \(ˌ)dis-ˌkäm-ən-ˈdā-shən, -ˌkäm-ˌen-\ *n*

dis·com·mode \ˌdis-kə-ˈmōd\ *vt* **-mod·ed; -mod·ing** [MF *discommoder,* fr. *dis-* + *commode* convenient — more at COMMODE] **:** to cause inconvenience to : TROUBLE

dis·com·pose \ˌdis-kəm-ˈpōz\ *vt* **1 :** to destroy the composure or serenity of **2 :** to disturb the order of — **dis·com·po·sure** \-ˈpō-zhər\ *n*

syn DISCOMPOSE, DISQUIET, DISTURB, PERTURB, AGITATE, UPSET, FLUSTER, FLURRY *shared meaning element* : to destroy or impair one's capacity for collected thought or decisive action ***ant*** compose

dis·con·cert \ˌdis-kən-ˈsərt\ *vt* [obs. F *disconcerter,* alter. of MF *desconcerter,* fr. *des-* + *concerter* to concert] **1 :** to throw into confusion **2 :** to disturb the composure of ***syn*** see EMBARRASS — **dis·con·cert·ing** *adj* — **dis·con·cert·ing·ly** \-iŋ-lē\ *adv*

dis·con·firm \ˌdis-kən-ˈfərm\ *vt* **:** to establish as invalid : DISPROVE

dis·con·form·able \ˌdis-kən-ˈfȯr-mə-bəl\ *adj* **:** of or relating to a disconformity in rocks — **dis·con·form·ably** \-blē\ *adv*

dis·con·for·mi·ty \ˌdis-kən-ˈfȯr-mət-ē\ *n* **1** *archaic* **:** NONCONFORMITY **2 :** a break in a sequence of sedimentary rocks all of which have approximately the same dip

dis·con·nect \ˌdis-kə-ˈnekt\ *vt* : to sever the connection of or between ~ *vi* **1** : to terminate a connection **2** : to become detached or withdrawn <he has periods when he ~*s* into silences —*Current Biog.*>
dis·con·nect·ed *adj* : not connected : INCOHERENT — **dis·con·nect·ed·ly** *adv* — **dis·con·nect·ed·ness** *n*
dis·con·so·late \dis-ˈkän(t)-s(ə-)lət\ *adj* [ME, fr. ML *disconsolatus*, fr. L *dis-* + *consolatus*, pp. of *consolari* to console] **1** : DEJECTED, DOWNCAST <the team returned ~ from three losses> **2** : CHEERLESS <a clutch of ~ houses —D. H. Lawrence> — **dis·con·so·late·ly** *adv* — **dis·con·so·late·ness** *n* — **dis·con·so·la·tion** \(ˌ)dis-ˌkän(t)-sə-ˈlā-shən\ *n*
1dis·con·tent \ˌdis-kən-ˈtent\ *adj* : DISCONTENTED
2discontent *n* : one who is discontented : MALCONTENT
3discontent *vt* : to make discontented — **dis·con·tent·ment** \-mənt\ *n*
4discontent *n* : lack of contentment: **a** : a sense of grievance : DISSATISFACTION <the winter of our ~ —Shak.> **b** : restless aspiration for improvement
dis·con·tent·ed *adj* : DISSATISFIED, MALCONTENT — **dis·con·tent·ed·ly** *adv* — **dis·con·tent·ed·ness** *n*
dis·con·tin·u·ance \ˌdis-kən-ˈtin-yə-wən(t)s\ *n* **1** : the act or an instance of discontinuing **2** : the interruption or termination of a legal action by failure to continue or by the plaintiff's entry of a discontinuing order
dis·con·tin·ue \ˌdis-kən-ˈtin-(ˌ)yü, -yə(-w)\ *vb* [ME *discontinuen*, fr. MF *discontinuer*, fr. ML *discontinuare*, fr. L *dis-* + *continuare* to continue] *vt* **1** : to break the continuity of : cease to operate, administer, use, or take **2** : to abandon or terminate by a legal discontinuance ~ *vi* : to come to an end; *specif* : to cease publication ***syn*** see STOP ***ant*** continue
dis·con·ti·nu·i·ty \(ˌ)dis-ˌkänt-ᵊn-ˈ(y)ü-ət-ē\ *n* **1** : lack of continuity or cohesion **2** : GAP 5 **3** : a value of an argument at which a function is not continuous
dis·con·tin·u·ous \ˌdis-kən-ˈtin-yə-wəs\ *adj* **1 a** (1) : not continuous <a ~ series of events> (2) : not continued : DISCRETE <~ features of terrain> **b** : lacking sequence or coherence <this ~ style> **2** : having one or more discontinuities — used of a variable or a function — **dis·con·tin·u·ous·ly** *adv*
dis·co·phile \ˈdis-kə-ˌfīl\ *n* : one who studies and collects phonograph records
1dis·cord \ˈdis-ˌkȯ(ə)rd\ *n* **1 a** : lack of agreement or harmony (as between persons, things, or ideas) **b** : active quarreling or conflict resulting from discord among persons or factions : STRIFE **2 a** (1) : a combination of musical sounds that strike the ear harshly (2) : DISSONANCE **b** : a harsh or unpleasant sound
syn DISCORD, STRIFE, CONFLICT, CONTENTION, DISSENSION, DIFFERENCE, VARIANCE *shared meaning element* : the state of those who disagree and lack harmony or the acts and circumstances marking such a state
2dis·cord \ˈdis-ˌkȯ(ə)rd, dis-ˈ\ *vi* [ME *discorden*, fr. OF *discorder*, fr. L *discordare*, fr. *discord-*, *discors* discordant, fr. *dis-* + *cord-*, *cor* heart — more at HEART] : DISAGREE, CLASH
dis·cor·dance \dis-ˈkȯrd-ᵊn(t)s\ *n* **1** : the state or an instance of being discordant **2** : DISSONANCE
dis·cor·dan·cy \-ᵊn-sē\ *n, pl* **-cies** : DISCORDANCE
dis·cor·dant \-ᵊnt\ *adj* **1 a** : being at variance : DISAGREEING **b** : QUARRELSOME **2** : relating to a discord — **dis·cor·dant·ly** *adv*
dis·co·theque \ˈdis-kə-ˌtek, ˌdis-kə-ˈ\ *n* [F *discothèque*, fr. *disque* disk, record + *-o-* + *-thèque* (as in *bibliothèque* library)] : a small intimate nightclub for dancing to live or recorded music; *broadly* : a nightclub often featuring psychedelic and mixed-media attractions (as slides, movies, special lighting effects, and kinetic sound)
1dis·count \ˈdis-ˌkau̇nt\ *n* **1** : a reduction made from the gross amount or value of something: as **a** (1) : a reduction made from a regular or list price (2) : a proportionate deduction from a debt account usu. made for cash or prompt payment **b** : a deduction made for interest in advancing money upon or purchasing a bill or note not due **2** : the act or practice of discounting **3** : a deduction taken or allowance made
2dis·count \ˈdis-ˌkau̇nt, dis-ˈ\ *vb* [modif. of F *décompter*, fr. OF *desconter*, fr. ML *discomputare*, fr. L *dis-* + *computare* to count — more at COUNT] *vt* **1 a** : to make a deduction from usu. for cash or prompt payment **b** : to sell or offer for sale at a discount **2** : to lend money on after deducting the discount **3 a** : to leave out of account : DISREGARD **b** : to underestimate the importance of : MINIMIZE **c** (1) : to make allowance for bias or exaggeration in (2) : to view with doubt : DISBELIEVE **d** : to take into account (as a future event) in present calculations ~ *vi* : to give or make discounts
dis·count·able \dis-ˈkau̇nt-ə-bəl, ˈdis-ˌ\ *adj* **1** : capable of being discounted <a ~ note> **2** : set apart for discounting <within the ~ period>
1dis·coun·te·nance \dis-ˈkau̇nt-ᵊn-ən(t)s, -ˈkau̇nt-nən(t)s\ *vt* **1** : ABASH, DISCONCERT **2** : to look with disfavor on : discourage by evidence of disapproval
2discountenance *n* : DISFAVOR, DISAPPROVAL
dis·count·er \ˈdis-ˌkau̇nt-ər, dis-ˈ\ *n* : one that discounts; *specif* : DISCOUNT STORE
discount house *n* : DISCOUNT STORE
discount rate *n* **1** : the interest on an annual basis deducted in advance on a bank or other loan **2** : the charge levied by a central bank for advances and rediscounts
discount store *n* : a store where merchandise (as consumer durable goods) is sold at a discount from suggested list price
dis·cour·age \dis-ˈkər-ij, -ˈkə-rij\ *vt* **-aged; -ag·ing** [MF *descorager*, fr. OF *descoragier*, fr. *des-* dis- + *corage* courage] **1** : to deprive of courage or confidence : DISHEARTEN **2 a** : to hinder by disfavoring : DETER **b** : to attempt to dissuade — **dis·cour·age·able** \-ə-bəl\ *adj* — **dis·cour·ag·er** *n*
dis·cour·age·ment \-mənt\ *n* **1** : the act of discouraging : the state of being discouraged **2** : something that discourages : DETERRENT
dis·cour·ag·ing *adj* : lessening courage : DISHEARTENING — **dis·cour·ag·ing·ly** \-ij-iŋ-lē\ *adv*
1dis·course \ˈdis-ˌkō(ə)rs, -ˌkȯ(ə)rs, dis-ˈ\ *n* [ME *discours*, fr. ML & LL *discursus*; ML, argument, fr. LL, conversation, fr. L, act of running about, fr. *discursus*, pp. of *discurrere* to run about, fr. *dis-* + *currere* to run — more at CAR] **1** *archaic* : the capacity of orderly thought or procedure : RATIONALITY **2** : verbal interchange of ideas; *esp* : CONVERSATION **3 a** : formal and orderly and usu. extended expression of thought on a subject **b** : connected speech or writing **4** *obs* : social familiarity
2dis·course \dis-ˈkō(ə)rs, -ˈkō(ə)rs, ˈdis-ˌ\ *vb* **dis·coursed; dis·cours·ing** *vi* **1** : to express oneself esp. in oral discourse **2** : TALK, CONVERSE ~ *vt, archaic* : to give forth : UTTER — **dis·cours·er** *n*
dis·cour·te·ous \(ˈ)dis-ˈkərt-ē-əs\ *adj* : lacking courtesy : RUDE — **dis·cour·te·ous·ly** *adv* — **dis·cour·te·ous·ness** *n*
dis·cour·te·sy \-ˈkərt-ə-sē\ *n* **1** : RUDENESS **2** : a rude act
dis·cov·er \dis-ˈkəv-ər\ *vb* **dis·cov·ered; dis·cov·er·ing** \-ˈkəv-(ə-)riŋ\ [ME *discoveren*, fr. OF *descovrir*, fr. LL *discooperire*, fr. L *dis-* + *cooperire* to cover — more at COVER] *vt* **1 a** : to make known or visible : EXPOSE **b** *archaic* : DISPLAY **2** : to obtain sight or knowledge of for the first time : FIND <~ the solution of a puzzle> ~ *vi* : to make a discovery — **dis·cov·er·able** \-ˈkəv-(ə-)rə-bəl\ *adj* — **dis·cov·er·er** \-ər-ər\ *n*
***syn* 1** see REVEAL
2 DISCOVER, ASCERTAIN, DETERMINE, UNEARTH, LEARN *shared meaning element* : to find out something not previously known to one
3 see INVENT
dis·cov·ery \dis-ˈkəv-(ə-)rē\ *n, pl* **-er·ies** **1 a** : the act or process of discovering **b** (1) *archaic* : DISCLOSURE (2) *obs* : DISPLAY **c** *obs* : EXPLORATION **2** : something discovered
Discovery Day *n* : COLUMBUS DAY
1dis·cred·it \(ˈ)dis-ˈkred-ət\ *vt* **1** : to refuse to accept as true or accurate : DISBELIEVE **2** : to cause disbelief in the accuracy or authority of **3** : to deprive of good repute : DISGRACE
2discredit *n* **1** : loss of credit or reputation <I knew stories to the ~ of England —W. B. Yeats> **2** : lack or loss of belief or confidence : DOUBT <contradictions cast ~ on his testimony>
dis·cred·it·able \-ə-bəl\ *adj* : injurious to reputation — **dis·cred·it·ably** \-blē\ *adv*
dis·creet \dis-ˈkrēt\ *adj* [ME, fr. MF *discret*, fr. ML *discretus*, fr. L, pp. of *discernere* to separate, distinguish between — more at DISCERN] **1** : having or showing discernment or good judgment in conduct and esp. in speech : PRUDENT; *esp* : capable of preserving prudent silence **2** : UNPRETENTIOUS, MODEST <the warmth and ~ elegance of a civilized home —Joseph Wechsberg> — **dis·creet·ly** *adv* — **dis·creet·ness** *n*
dis·crep·an·cy \dis-ˈkrep-ən-sē\ *n, pl* **-cies** **1** : the quality or state of being discrepant : DIFFERENCE **2** : an instance of being discrepant
dis·crep·ant \-ənt\ *adj* [L *discrepant-*, *discrepans*, prp. of *discrepare* to sound discordantly, fr. *dis-* + *crepare* to rattle, creak — more at RAVEN] : being at variance : DISAGREEING <widely ~ conclusions> — **dis·crep·ant·ly** *adv*
dis·crete \dis-ˈkrēt, ˈdis-ˌ\ *adj* [ME, fr. L *discretus*] **1** : constituting a separate entity : individually distinct **2 a** : consisting of distinct or unconnected elements : NONCONTINUOUS **b** : taking on or having a finite or countably infinite number of values : not mathematically continuous <a ~ random variable> ***syn*** see DISTINCT — **dis·crete·ly** *adv* — **dis·crete·ness** *n*
dis·cre·tion \dis-ˈkresh-ən\ *n* **1** : the quality of being discreet : CIRCUMSPECTION; *esp* : cautious reserve in speech **2** : ability to make responsible decisions **3 a** : individual choice or judgment <left the decision to his ~> **b** : power of free decision or latitude of choice within certain legal bounds <reached the age of ~> **4** : the result of separating or distinguishing <breaking down every operation into discrete parts, and then making verbal the ~*s* that are made —Elinor Langer>
dis·cre·tion·ary \-ˈkresh-ə-ˌner-ē\ *adj* **1** : left to discretion : exercised at one's own discretion **2** : available for discretionary use <~ purchasing power>
discretionary account *n* : a security or commodity market account in which an agent (as a broker) is given power of attorney allowing him to make independent decisions and buy and sell for the account of his principal
dis·crim·i·na·bil·i·ty \-ˌkrim-(ə-)nə-ˈbil-ət-ē\ *n, pl* **-ties** **1** : the quality of being discriminable <the ~ of the various senses of a word> **2** : the ability to discriminate
dis·crim·i·na·ble \dis-ˈkrim-(ə-)nə-bəl\ *adj* : capable of being discriminated — **dis·crim·i·na·bly** \-blē\ *adv*
dis·crim·i·nant \-ˈkrim-(ə-)nənt\ *n* : a mathematical expression providing a criterion for the behavior of another more complicated expression, relation, or set of relations
dis·crim·i·nate \dis-ˈkrim-ə-ˌnāt\ *vb* **-nat·ed; -nat·ing** [L *discriminatus*, pp. of *discriminare*, fr. *discrimin-*, *discrimen* distinction, fr. *discernere* to distinguish between — more at DISCERN] *vt* **1 a** : to mark or perceive the distinguishing or peculiar features of **b** : DISTINGUISH, DIFFERENTIATE <~ hundreds of colors> **2** : to distinguish by discerning or exposing differences; *esp* : to distinguish (one like object) from another ~ *vi* **1 a** : to make a distinction <~ among the methods which should be used> **b** : to use good judgment **2** : to make a difference in treatment or favor on a basis other than individual merit <~ in favor of your friends> <~ against a certain nationality>
dis·crim·i·nat·ing *adj* **1** : making a distinction : DISTINGUISHING **2** : marked by discrimination: **a** : DISCERNING, JUDICIOUS **b** : DISCRIMINATORY — **dis·crim·i·nat·ing·ly** \-ˌnāt-iŋ-lē\ *adv*
dis·crim·i·na·tion \dis-ˌkrim-ə-ˈnā-shən\ *n* **1 a** : the act of discriminating **b** : the process by which two stimuli differing in some aspect are responded to differently : DIFFERENTIATION **2** : the quality or power of finely distinguishing **3 a** : the act, practice, or an instance of discriminating categorically rather than individually **b** : prejudiced or prejudicial outlook, action, or treatment <provided major opportunities for Negro advancement on purely equal

terms involving neither ~ nor preference —D. P. Moynihan> ***syn*** see DISCERNMENT — **dis·crim·i·na·tion·al** \-shnəl, -shən-ᵊl\ *adj*
dis·crim·i·na·tive \dis-ˈkrim-ə-ˌnāt-iv, -ˈkrim-(ə-)nət-\ *adj* **1** : making distinctions **2** : DISCRIMINATORY 1 <permitted tariffs which were grossly ~ —Mabel R. Gillis>
dis·crim·i·na·tor \dis-ˈkrim-ə-ˌnāt-ər\ *n* : one that discriminates; *specif* : a circuit that can be adjusted to accept or reject signals of different characteristics (as amplitude or frequency)
dis·crim·i·na·to·ry \dis-ˈkrim-(ə-)nə-ˌtōr-ē, -ˌtȯr-\ *adj* **1** : applying or favoring discrimination in treatment **2** : DISCRIMINATIVE 1 — **dis·crim·i·na·to·ri·ly** \-ˌkrim-(ə-)nə-ˈtōr-ə-lē, -ˈtȯr-\ *adv*
dis·cur·sive \dis-ˈkər-siv\ *adj* [ML *discursivus*, fr. L *discursus*, pp. of *discurrere* to run about — more at DISCOURSE] **1** : passing from one topic to another : DIGRESSIVE **2** : marked by analytical reasoning — **dis·cur·sive·ly** *adv* — **dis·cur·sive·ness** *n*
dis·cus \ˈdis-kəs\ *n, pl* **dis·cus·es** [L — more at DISH] **1 a** : a disk (as of wood, rubber, or metal) that is thicker in the center than at the perimeter and that is hurled for distance **b** : a field event in which a discus of about $4^1/_2$ pounds is hurled **2** : DISK 2, 3

1, discus 1a

dis·cuss \dis-ˈkəs\ *vt* [ME *discussen*, fr. L *discussus*, pp. of *discutere*, fr. *dis-* apart + *quatere* to shake — more at DIS-, QUASH] **1** *obs* : DISPEL **2 a** : to investigate by reasoning or argument **b** : to present in detail for examination or consideration <~*ed* plans for the party> **c** : to talk about **3** *obs* : DECLARE — **dis·cuss·able** *or* **dis·cuss·ible** \-ə-bəl\ *adj* — **dis·cuss·er** *n*
syn DISCUSS, ARGUE, DEBATE, DISPUTE *shared meaning element* : to discourse about something in order to arrive at the truth or to convince others of the validity of one's position
dis·cus·sant \dis-ˈkəs-ᵊnt\ *n* : one who takes part in a formal discussion or symposium
dis·cus·sion \dis-ˈkəsh-ən\ *n* **1** : consideration of a question in open and usu. informal debate **2** : a formal treatment of a topic
¹dis·dain \dis-ˈdān\ *n* [ME *desdeyne*, fr. OF *desdeign*, fr. *desdeignier*] : a feeling of contempt for what is beneath one : SCORN
²disdain *vt* [ME *desdeynen*, fr. MF *desdeignier*, fr. (assumed) VL *disdignare*, fr. L *dis-* + *dignare* to deign — more at DEIGN] **1** : to look with scorn on **2** : to refuse or abstain from because of disdain **3** : to treat disdainfully ***syn*** see DESPISE ***ant*** favor
dis·dain·ful \-fəl\ *adj* : full of or expressing disdain ***syn*** see PROUD — **dis·dain·ful·ly** \-fə-lē\ *adv* — **dis·dain·ful·ness** *n*
dis·ease \diz-ˈēz\ *n* [ME *disese*, fr. MF *desaise*, fr. *des-* dis- + *aise* ease] **1** *obs* : TROUBLE **2** : a condition of the living animal or plant body or of one of its parts that impairs the performance of a vital function : SICKNESS, MALADY **3** : a harmful development (as in a social institution) <the various ~*s* of civilization> — **dis·eased** \-ˈēzd\ *adj*
dis·econ·o·my \ˌdis-i-ˈkän-ə-mē\ *n* **1** : a lack of economy **2** : a factor responsible for an increase in cost
dis·em·bark \ˌdis-əm-ˈbärk\ *vb* [MF *desembarquer*, fr. *des-* + *embarquer* to embark] *vt* : to put ashore from a ship ~ *vi* **1** : to go ashore out of a ship **2** : to get out of a vehicle — **dis·em·bar·ka·tion** \(ˌ)dis-ˌem-ˌbär-ˈkā-shən, -bər-\ *n*
dis·em·bar·rass \ˌdis-əm-ˈbar-əs\ *vt* : to free from something troublesome or superfluous ***syn*** see EXTRICATE
dis·em·body \ˌdis-əm-ˈbäd-ē\ *vt* : to divest of a body, of corporeal existence, or of reality
dis·em·bogue \ˌdis-əm-ˈbōg\ *vb* **-bogued; -bogu·ing** [modif. of Sp *desembocar*, fr. *des-* dis- (fr. L *dis-*) + *embocar* to put into the mouth, fr. *en* in (fr. L *in*) + *boca* mouth, fr. L *bucca* — more at POCK] *vi* : to flow or come forth from or as if from a channel ~ *vt* : to pour out : EMPTY
dis·em·bow·el \ˌdis-əm-ˈbau̇(-ə)l\ *vt* **1** : to take out the bowels of : EVISCERATE **2** : to remove the substance of — **dis·em·bow·el·ment** \-mənt\ *n*
dis·en·chant \ˌdis-ᵊn-ˈchant\ *vt* [MF *desenchanter*, fr. *des-* + *enchanter* to enchant] : to free from illusion — **dis·en·chant·er** *n* — **dis·en·chant·ing** *adj* — **dis·en·chant·ing·ly** \-iŋ-lē\ *adv* — **dis·en·chant·ment** \-mənt\ *n*
dis·en·cum·ber \ˌdis-ᵊn-ˈkəm-bər\ *vt* [MF *desencombrer*, fr. *des-* + *encombrer* to encumber] : to free from encumbrance : DISBURDEN ***syn*** see EXTRICATE
dis·en·dow \ˌdis-ᵊn-ˈdau̇\ *vt* : to strip of endowment — **dis·en·dow·er** \-ˈdau̇(-ə)r\ *n* — **dis·en·dow·ment** \-ˈdau̇-mənt\ *n*
dis·en·fran·chise \ˌdis-ᵊn-ˈfran-ˌchīz\ *vt* : DISFRANCHISE — **dis·en·fran·chise·ment** \-ˌchīz-mənt, -chəz-\ *n*
dis·en·gage \ˌdis-ᵊn-ˈgāj\ *vb* [F *désengager*, fr. MF, fr. *des-* + *engager* to engage] *vt* : to release from something that engages ~ *vi* : to release or detach oneself : WITHDRAW — **dis·en·gage·ment** \-mənt\ *n*
dis·en·tail \ˌdis-ᵊn-ˈtā(ə)l\ *vt* : to free from entail
dis·en·tan·gle \ˌdis-ᵊn-ˈtaŋ-gəl\ *vt* : to free from entanglement : UNRAVEL ~ *vi* : to become disentangled ***syn*** see EXTRICATE ***ant*** entangle — **dis·en·tan·gle·ment** \-mənt\ *n*
dis·en·thrall *also* **dis·en·thral** \ˌdis-ᵊn-ˈthrȯl\ *vt* : to free from bondage : LIBERATE
dis·equil·i·brate \ˌdis-i-ˈkwil-ə-ˌbrāt\ *vt* : to put out of balance — **dis·equil·i·bra·tion** \-ˌkwil-ə-ˈbrā-shən\ *n*
dis·equi·lib·ri·um \(ˌ)dis-ˌē-kwə-ˈlib-rē-əm, -ˌek-wə-\ *n* : loss or lack of equilibrium
dis·es·tab·lish \ˌdis-ə-ˈstab-lish\ *vt* : to deprive of an established status; *esp* : to deprive of the status and privileges of an established church — **dis·es·tab·lish·ment** \-mənt\ *n*
dis·es·tab·lish·men·tar·i·an \-ˌstab-lish-ˌmen-ˈter-ē-ən, -mən-\ *n, often cap* [*disestablishment*] : one who opposes an established order — **disestablishmentarian** *adj, often cap*
¹dis·es·teem \ˌdis-ə-ˈstēm\ *vt* : to regard with disfavor
²disesteem *n* : DISFAVOR, DISREPUTE

di·seuse \dē-ˈzə(r)z, -ˈzüz\ *n, pl* **di·seuses** \-ˈzə(r)z(-əz), -ˈzüz(-əz)\ [F, fem. of *diseur*, fr. OF, fr. *dire* to say, fr. L *dicere* — more at DICTION] : a skilled and usu. professional woman reciter
¹dis·fa·vor \(ˈ)dis-ˈfā-vər\ *n* [prob. fr. MF *desfaveur*, fr. *des-* dis- + *faveur* favor, fr. OF *favor*] **1** : DISAPPROVAL, DISLIKE <practices looked upon with ~> **2** : the state or fact of being deprived of favor <fell into ~> **3** : DISADVANTAGE
²disfavor *vt* : to withhold or withdraw favor from
dis·fea·ture \(ˈ)dis-ˈfē-chər\ *vt* : to mar the features of ***syn*** see DEFACE — **dis·fea·ture·ment** \-mənt\ *n*
dis·fig·ure \dis-ˈfig-yər, *esp Brit* -ˈfig-ər\ *vt* [ME *disfiguren*, fr. MF *desfigurer*, fr. *des-* + *figure*] **1** : to impair (as in beauty) by deep and persistent injuries <a girl *disfigured* by smallpox> **2** *obs* : DISGUISE ***syn*** see DEFACE — **dis·fig·ure·ment** \-mənt\ *n*
dis·fran·chise \(ˈ)dis-ˈfran-ˌchīz\ *vt* : to deprive of a franchise, of a legal right, or of some privilege or immunity; *esp* : to deprive of the right to vote — **dis·fran·chise·ment** \-ˌchīz-mənt, -chəz-\ *n*
dis·frock \(ˈ)dis-ˈfräk\ *vt* : UNFROCK
disfunction *var of* DYSFUNCTION
dis·fur·nish \(ˈ)dis-ˈfər-nish\ *vt* [MF *desfourniss-*, stem of *desfournir*, fr. *des-* + *fournir* to furnish — more at FURNISH] : to make destitute of possessions : DIVEST — **dis·fur·nish·ment** \-mənt\ *n*
dis·gorge \(ˈ)dis-ˈgȯ(ə)rj\ *vb* [MF *desgorger*, fr. *des-* + *gorge*] *vt* **1 a** : to discharge by the throat and mouth : VOMIT **b** : to discharge violently, confusedly, or as a result of force **c** : to give up on request or under pressure <refused to ~ his ill-gotten gains> **2** : to discharge the contents of (as the stomach) ~ *vi* : to discharge contents <where the river ~*s* into the sea>
¹dis·grace \dis-ˈgrās\ *vt* **1** *archaic* : to humiliate by a superior showing **2** : to bring reproach or shame to <*disgraced* his family> **3** : to cause to lose favor or standing <was *disgraced* by the hint of scandal> — **dis·grac·er** *n*
²disgrace *n* [MF, fr. OIt *disgrazia*, fr. *dis-* (fr. L) + *grazia* grace, fr. L *gratia* — more at GRACE] **1 a** : loss of grace, favor, or honor **b** : the condition of one fallen from grace or honor **2** : something that disgraces <that boy's manners are a ~>
syn DISGRACE, DISHONOR, DISREPUTE, SHAME, INFAMY, IGNOMINY, OPPROBRIUM *shared meaning element* : loss of esteem and good repute and the resulting denigration and contempt ***ant*** respect, esteem
dis·grace·ful \dis-ˈgrās-fəl\ *adj* : bringing or involving disgrace — **dis·grace·ful·ly** \-fə-lē\ *adv* — **dis·grace·ful·ness** *n*
dis·grun·tle \dis-ˈgrənt-ᵊl\ *vt* **dis·grun·tled; dis·grun·tling** \-ˈgrənt-liŋ, -ᵊl-iŋ\ [*dis-* + *gruntle* (to grumble), fr. ME *gruntlen*, freq. of *grunten* to grunt] : to make ill-humored or discontented <the workers are *disgruntled* with their wages> — **dis·grun·tle·ment** \-ᵊl-mənt\ *n*
¹dis·guise \dis-ˈgīz\ *vt* **dis·guise; dis·guis·ing** [ME *disgisen*, fr. MF *desguiser*, fr. OF, fr. *des-* + *guise*] **1 a** : to change the customary dress or appearance of **b** : to furnish with a false appearance or an assumed identity **2** *obs* : DISFIGURE **3** : to obscure the existence or true state or character of : CONCEAL — **dis·guised·ly** \-ˈgīz(-ə)d-lē\ *adv* — **dis·guise·ment** \-ˈgīz-mənt\ *n* — **dis·guis·er** *n*
syn DISGUISE, CLOAK, MASK, DISSEMBLE *shared meaning element* : to alter so as to hide the true appearance, identity, intention, meaning, or feelings
²disguise *n* **1** : apparel assumed to conceal one's identity or counterfeit another's **2 a** : form misrepresenting the true nature of something <blessings in ~> **b** : an artificial manner : PRETENSE <threw off all ~> **3** : the act of disguising
¹dis·gust \dis-ˈgəst\ *n* : marked aversion aroused by something highly distasteful : REPUGNANCE
²disgust *vb* [MF *desgouster*, fr. *des-* dis- + *goust* taste, fr. L *gustus*; akin to L *gustare* to taste — more at CHOOSE] *vt* **1** : to provoke to loathing, repugnance, or aversion : be offensive to **2** : to cause (one) to lose an interest or intention <his failures ~*ed* him to the point that he stopped trying> ~ *vi* : to cause disgust — **dis·gust·ed** *adj* — **dis·gust·ed·ly** *adv*
dis·gust·ful \-ˈgəst-fəl\ *adj* **1** : provoking disgust **2** : full of or accompanied by disgust — **dis·gust·ful·ly** \-fə-lē\ *adv*
dis·gust·ing *adj* : exciting disgust — **dis·gust·ing·ly** \-ˈgəs-tiŋ-lē\ *adv*
¹dish \ˈdish\ *n* [ME, fr. OE *disc* plate; akin to OHG *tisc* plate, table; both fr. a prehistoric WGmc word borrowed fr. L *discus* quoit, disk, dish, fr. Gk *diskos*, fr. *dikein* to throw] **1 a** : a more or less concave vessel from which food is served **b** : the contents of a dish <a ~ of strawberries> **2** : food prepared in a particular way **3 a (1)** : any of various shallow concave vessels; *broadly* : something shallowly concave **(2)** : a directional microwave antenna having a concave usu. parabolic reflector **b** : the state of being concave or the degree of concavity **4 a** : something that is favored <entertainment that is just his ~> **b** : an attractive woman
²dish *vt* **1** : to put (as food for serving) into a dish — often used with *up* **2** : PRESENT — usu. used with *up* **3** : to make concave like a dish
dis·ha·bille \ˌdis-ə-ˈbē(ə)l, -ˈbil, -ˈbē\ *n* [F *déshabillé*, fr. pp. of *déshabiller* to undress, fr. *dés-* dis- + *habiller* to dress — more at HABILIMENT] **1 a** *archaic* : NEGLIGEE **b** : the state of being dressed in a casual or careless style **2** : a deliberately careless or casual manner
dis·har·mon·ic \ˌdis-(ˌ)här-ˈmän-ik\ *adj* **1** : having a combination of bodily characters that results in an unusual form or appearance **2** : exhibiting or marked by allometry
dis·har·mo·ni·ous \-ˈmō-nē-əs\ *adj* **1** : lacking in harmony **2**

: DISHARMONIC
dis·har·mo·nize \(ˈ)dis-ˈhär-mə-ˌnīz\ *vt* : to make disharmonious
dis·har·mo·ny \-nē\ *n* : lack of harmony : DISCORD
dish·cloth \ˈdish-ˌklȯth\ *n* : a cloth for washing dishes
dishcloth gourd *n* : the fruit of any of several gourds (genus *Luffa*) having a fibrous interior that is dried and used like a sponge
dish·clout \ˈdish-ˌklau̇t\ *n, Brit* : DISHCLOTH
dis·heart·en \(ˈ)dis-ˈhärt-ᵊn\ *vt* : to cause to lose spirit or morale — **dis·heart·en·ing·ly** \-ˈhärt-niŋ-lē, -ᵊn-iŋ-\ *adv* — **dis·heart·en·ment** \-ˈhärt-ᵊn-mənt\ *n*
dished \ˈdisht\ *adj* **1** : CONCAVE **2** *of a pair of vehicle wheels* : nearer together at the bottom than at the top
di·shev·el \dish-ˈev-əl\ *vt* **di·shev·eled** *or* **di·shev·elled; di·shev·el·ing** *or* **di·shev·el·ling** \-ˈev-(ə-)liŋ\ [back-formation fr. *disheveled*] : to throw into disorder or disarray
di·shev·eled *or* **di·shev·elled** *adj* [ME *discheveled,* part trans. of MF *deschevelé,* fr. pp. of *descheveler* to disarrange the hair, fr. *des-* + *chevel* hair, fr. L *capillus*] : marked by disorder or disarray
dis·hon·est \(ˈ)dis-ˈän-əst\ *adj* [ME, fr. MF *deshoneste,* fr. *des-* + *honeste* honest] **1** *obs* : SHAMEFUL, UNCHASTE **2** : characterized by lack of truth, honesty, or trustworthiness — **dis·hon·est·ly** *adv*
syn DISHONEST, DECEITFUL, LYING, MENDACIOUS, UNTRUTHFUL *shared meaning element* : unworthy of trust or belief ***ant*** honest
dis·hon·es·ty \-ə-stē\ *n* **1** : lack of honesty or integrity : disposition to defraud or deceive **2** : a dishonest act : FRAUD
1dis·hon·or \(ˈ)dis-ˈän-ər\ *n* [ME *dishonour,* fr. OF *deshonor,* fr. *des-* + *honor*] **1** : lack or loss of honor or reputation **2** : the state of one who has lost honor or prestige : SHAME <would rather die than live in ~> **3** : a cause of disgrace <became a ~ to his family> **4** : the nonpayment or nonacceptance of commercial paper by the party on whom it is drawn ***syn*** see DISGRACE ***ant*** honor — **dis·hon·or·er** \-ˈän-ər-ər\ *n*
2dishonor *vt* **1 a** : to treat in a degrading manner **b** : to bring shame on **2** : to refuse to accept or pay (as a draft, bill, check, or note)
dis·hon·or·able \(ˈ)dis-ˈän-(ə-)rə-bəl, -ˈän-ər-bəl\ *adj* **1** : lacking honor : SHAMEFUL <~ conduct> **2** *archaic* : not honored — **dis·hon·or·able·ness** *n* — **dis·hon·or·ably** \-blē\ *adv*
dish out *vt* **1** : to serve (food) from a dish **2** : to give freely <the blatant picturing of crime and disorder *dished out* by the cinema —R. T. Flewelling>
dish·pan \ˈdish-ˌpan\ *n* : a large flat-bottomed pan used for washing dishes
dishpan hands *n pl but sing or pl in constr* : a condition of dryness, redness, and scaling of the hands that results typically from repeated exposure to, sensitivity to, or overuse of cleaning materials (as detergents) used in housework
dish·rag \ˈdish-ˌrag\ *n* : DISHCLOTH
dish towel *n* : a cloth for drying dishes
dish·ware \ˈdish-ˌwa(ə)r, -ˌwe(ə)r\ *n* : tableware (as of china) used in serving food
dish·wash·er \-ˌwȯsh-ər, -ˌwäsh-\ *n* **1** : a worker employed to wash dishes **2** : a machine for washing dishes
dish·wa·ter \-ˌwȯt-ər, -ˌwät-\ *n* : water in which dishes have been or are to be washed
dishy \ˈdish-ē\ *adj, chiefly Brit* : ATTRACTIVE
1dis·il·lu·sion \ˌdis-ə-ˈlü-zhən\ *n* : the condition of being disenchanted
2disillusion *vt* **dis·il·lu·sioned; dis·il·lu·sion·ing** \-ˈlüzh-(ə-)niŋ\ : to leave without illusion — **dis·il·lu·sion·ment** \-ˈlü-zhən-mənt\ *n*
dis·in·cen·tive \ˌdis-ᵊn-ˈsent-iv\ *n* : DETERRENT
dis·in·cli·na·tion \(ˌ)dis-ˌin-klə-ˈnā-shən, -ˌiŋ-\ *n* : a preference for avoiding something : slight aversion
dis·in·cline \ˌdis-ᵊn-ˈklīn\ *vt* : to make unwilling
dis·in·clined *adj* : unwilling because of mild dislike or disapproval
syn DISINCLINED, HESITANT, RELUCTANT, LOATH, AVERSE *shared meaning element* : lacking the will or desire to do something indicated
dis·in·fect \ˌdis-ᵊn-ˈfekt\ *vt* [MF *desinfecter,* fr. *des-* + *infecter* to infect] : to free from infection esp. by destroying harmful microorganisms; *broadly* : CLEANSE — **dis·in·fec·tion** \-ˈfek-shən\ *n*
dis·in·fec·tant \-ˈfek-tənt\ *n* : an agent that frees from infection; *esp* : a chemical that destroys vegetative forms of harmful microorganisms but not ordinarily bacterial spores
dis·in·fest \ˌdis-ᵊn-ˈfest\ *vt* : to rid of small animal pests (as insects or rodents) — **dis·in·fes·ta·tion** \(ˌ)dis-ˌin-ˌfes-ˈtā-shən\ *n*
dis·in·fes·tant \ˌdis-ᵊn-ˈfes-tənt\ *n* : a disinfesting agent
dis·in·fla·tion \ˌdis-ᵊn-ˈflā-shən\ *n* : a reversal of inflationary pressures — **dis·in·fla·tion·ary** \-shə-ˌner-ē\ *adj*
dis·in·gen·u·ous \ˌdis-ᵊn-ˈjen-yə-wəs\ *adj* : lacking in candor; *also* : giving a false appearance of simple frankness : CALCULATING — **dis·in·gen·u·ous·ly** *adv* — **dis·in·gen·u·ous·ness** *n*
dis·in·her·it \ˌdis-ᵊn-ˈher-ət\ *vt* **1** : to prevent deliberately (as by making a will) from inheriting **2** : to deprive of natural or human rights or of previously held special privileges — **dis·in·her·i·tance** \-ˈher-ət-ən(t)s\ *n*
dis·in·hi·bi·tion \(ˌ)dis-ˌin-(h)ə-ˈbish-ən\ *n* : loss of a conditioned reflex (as by the action of interfering stimuli)
dis·in·sec·tion \ˌdis-ᵊn-ˈsek-shən\ *n* [*dis-* + *insect* + *-ion*] : DISINSECTIZATION
dis·in·sect·iza·tion \-ˌsek-tə-ˈzā-shən\ *n* : removal of insects (as from an aircraft)
dis·in·te·grate \(ˈ)dis-ˈint-ə-ˌgrāt\ *vt* **1** : to break or decompose into constituent elements, parts, or small particles **2** : to destroy the unity or integrity of ~ *vi* **1** : to break or separate into constituent elements or parts **2** : to lose unity or integrity by or as if by breaking into parts **3** : to undergo a change in composition <an atomic nucleus that ~*s* because of radioactivity> — **dis·in·te·gra·tion** \(ˌ)dis-ˌint-ə-ˈgrā-shən\ *n* — **dis·in·te·gra·tive** \(ˈ)dis-ˈint-ə-ˌgrāt-iv\ *adj* — **dis·in·te·gra·tor** \-ˌgrāt-ər\ *n*
dis·in·ter \ˌdis-ᵊn-ˈtər\ *vt* **1** : to take out of the grave or tomb **2** : to bring to light : UNEARTH — **dis·in·ter·ment** \-mənt\ *n*
1dis·in·ter·est \(ˈ)dis-ˈin-trəst; -ˈint-ə-rəst, -ə-ˌrest, -ərst; -ˈin-ˌtrest\ *vt* : to divest of interest
2disinterest *n* **1** : DISADVANTAGE **2** : lack of self-interest : DISINTERESTEDNESS **3** : lack of interest : APATHY
dis·in·ter·est·ed *adj* **1** : not having the mind or feelings engaged : UNINTERESTED <is supremely ~ in all efforts to find a peaceful solution —C. L. Sulzberger> **2** : free from selfish motive or interest : UNBIASED <a ~ decision> <~ intellectual curiosity is the lifeblood of real civilization —G. M. Trevelyan> ***syn*** see INDIFFERENT ***ant*** interested — **dis·in·ter·est·ed·ly** *adv* — **dis·in·ter·est·ed·ness** *n*
dis·in·tox·i·cate \ˌdis-ᵊn-ˈtäk-sə-ˌkāt\ *vt* : to free (as a drug user or an alcoholic) from an intoxicating agent in the body or from dependence on such an agent — **dis·in·tox·i·ca·tion** \-ˌtäk-sə-ˈkā-shən\ *n*
dis·in·vest·ment \ˌdis-ᵊn-ˈves(t)-mənt\ *n* : consumption of capital
dis·join \(ˈ)dis-ˈjȯin\ *vb* [MF *desjoindre,* fr. L *disjungere,* fr. *dis-* + *jungere* to join — more at YOKE] *vt* : to end the joining of ~ *vi* : to become detached
1dis·joint \-ˈjȯint\ *adj* [ME *disjoynt,* fr. MF *desjoint,* pp. of *desjoindre*] **1** *obs* : DISJOINTED 2a **2** : having no elements in common <~ mathematical sets>
2disjoint *vt* **1** : to disturb the orderly structure or arrangement of **2** : to take apart at the joints ~ *vi* : to come apart at the joints
dis·joint·ed *adj* **1** : separated at or as if at the joint **2 a** : being thrown out of orderly function <a ~ society> **b** : lacking coherence or orderly sequence <an incomplete and ~ history> — **dis·joint·ed·ly** *adv* — **dis·joint·ed·ness** *n*
1dis·junct \dis-ˈjəŋ(k)t\ *adj* [L *disjunctus,* pp. of *disjungere* to disjoin] : marked by separation of or from usu. contiguous parts or individuals: as **a** : DISCONTINUOUS **b** : relating to melodic progression by intervals larger than a major second — compare CONJUNCT **c** *of an insect* : having head, thorax, and abdomen separated by deep constrictions
2dis·junct \ˈdis-ˌjəŋ(k)t, dis-ˈ\ *n* : any of the alternatives comprising a logical disjunction
dis·junc·tion \dis-ˈjəŋ(k)-shən\ *n* **1** : a sharp cleavage : DISUNION, SEPARATION <the ~ between theory and practice> **2 a** : a complex sentence in logic that is true when either one or both of its constituent sentences are true — compare INCLUSIVE DISJUNCTION **b** : a complex sentence in logic that is true when one and only one of its constituent sentences is true — compare EXCLUSIVE DISJUNCTION
1dis·junc·tive \-ˈjəŋ(k)-tiv\ *n* : a disjunctive conjunction
2disjunctive *adj* **1** : marked by breaks or disunity <a ~ narrative sequence> **2 a** : being or belonging to a complex proposition one or both of whose terms are true **b** : expressing an alternative or opposition between the meanings of the words connected <the ~ conjunction *or*> **c** : expressed by mutually exclusive alternatives joined by *or* <~ pleading> **3** *of a pronoun form* : stressed and not attached to the verb as an enclitic or proclitic — **dis·junc·tive·ly** *adv*
dis·junc·ture \-ˈjəŋ(k)-chər\ *n* : DISJUNCTION
1disk *or* **disc** \ˈdisk\ *n, often attrib* [L *discus* — more at DISH] **1 a** *archaic* : DISCUS 1 **b** : the seemingly flat figure of a celestial body <the solar ~> **2 a** : the central part of the flower head of a typical composite made up of closely packed tubular flowers **b** *usu disc* : an enlargement of the torus around, beneath, or above the pistil of a flower **3** : any of various rounded and flattened animal anatomical structures **4 a** : a thin circular object **b** *usu disc* : a phonograph record **c** : a round flat plate coated with a magnetic substance on which data for a computer is stored **5** *usu disc* : one of the concave circular steel tools with sharpened edge making up the working part of a disc harrow or plow; *also* : an implement employing such tools — **disk·like** \-ˌlīk\ *adj*
2disk *or* **disc** *vt* **1** : to cultivate with an implement (as a harrow or plow) that turns and loosens the soil with a series of disks **2** *usu disc* : to record on a phonograph disc
disk flower *n* : one of the tubular flowers in the disk of a composite plant — called also *disk floret*

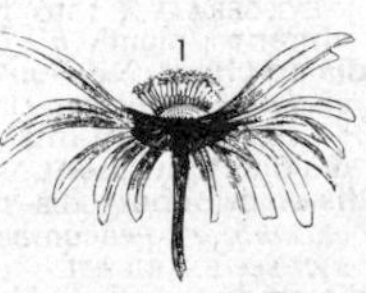

1 disk flowers

disk wheel *n* : a wheel presenting a solid surface from hub to rim
dis·lik·able *also* **dis·like·able** \(ˈ)dis-ˈlī-kə-bəl\ *adj* : easy to dislike
1dis·like \(ˈ)dis-ˈlīk\ *vt* **1** *archaic* : DISPLEASE **2** : to regard with dislike : DISAPPROVE **3** *obs* : to show aversion to — **dis·lik·er** *n*
2dislike *n* **1** : a feeling of aversion or disapproval **2** *obs* : DISCORD
dis·limn \(ˈ)dis-ˈlim\ *vb* : DIM
dis·lo·cate \ˈdis-lō-ˌkāt, -lə-; (ˈ)dis-ˈlō-\ *vt* [ML *dislocatus,* pp. of *dislocare,* fr. L *dis-* + *locare* to locate] **1** : to put out of place; *specif* : to displace (a bone) from normal connections with another bone **2** : DISRUPT
dis·lo·ca·tion \ˌdis-(ˌ)lō-ˈkā-shən, -lə-\ *n* : the act of dislocating : the state of being dislocated: as **a** : displacement of one or more bones at a joint **b** : a discontinuity in the otherwise normal lattice structure of a crystal **c** : disruption of an established order
dis·lodge \(ˈ)dis-ˈläj\ *vb* [ME *disloggen,* fr. MF *desloger,* fr. *des-* + *loger* to lodge, fr. *loge* lodge] *vt* **1** : to force out of a secure or settled position <*dislodged* the rock with a shovel> **2** : to drive from a position of hiding, defense, or advantage ~ *vi* : to leave a lodging place
dis·loy·al \(ˈ)dis-ˈlȯi(-ə)l\ *adj* [MF *desloial,* fr. OF, fr. *des-* + *loial* loyal] : lacking in loyalty : untrue to personal obligations or allegiance <his ~ refusal to help his friend> ***syn*** see FAITHLESS ***ant*** loyal — **dis·loy·al·ly** \-ˈlȯi-ə-lē\ *adv*
dis·loy·al·ty \-ˈlȯi(-ə)l-tē\ *n* : lack of loyalty
dis·mal \ˈdiz-məl\ *adj* [ME, fr. *dismal,* n., days marked as unlucky in medieval calendars, fr. AF, fr. ML *dies mali,* lit., evil days] **1** *obs* : DISASTROUS, DREADFUL **2** : showing or causing gloom or

depression **3 :** lacking interest or merit — **dis·mal·ly** \-mə-lē\ *adv* — **dis·mal·ness** *n*

dis·man·tle \(ˈ)dis-ˈmant-ᵊl\ *vt* **dis·man·tled; dis·man·tling** \-ˈmant-liŋ, -ᵊl-iŋ\ [MF *desmanteler,* fr. *des-* + *mantel* mantle] **1 :** to strip of dress or covering : DIVEST **2:** to strip of furniture and equipment **3 :** to take to pieces — **dis·man·tle·ment** \-ˈmant-ᵊl-mənt\ *n*

dis·mast \(ˈ)dis-ˈmast\ *vt* **:** to remove or break off the mast of

[1]dis·may \dis-ˈmā, diz-\ *vt* [ME *dismayen,* fr. (assumed) OF *desmaiier,* fr. OF *des-* + *-maiier* (as in *esmaiier* to dismay), fr. (assumed) VL *-magare,* of Gmc origin] **:** to deprive of courage, resolution, and initiative through the pressure of sudden fear or anxiety or great perplexity <~*ed* at the size of his adversary> — **dis·may·ing·ly** \-iŋ-lē\ *adv*

syn DISMAY, APPALL, HORRIFY, DAUNT *shared meaning element* **:** to unnerve and check by arousing fear, apprehension, or aversion ***ant*** cheer

[2]dismay *n* **1 :** sudden loss of courage or resolution from alarm or fear **2 a :** sudden disappointment **b :** PERTURBATION

disme \ˈdīm\ *n* [obs. E, tenth, fr. obs. F, fr. MF *disme, dime* — more at DIME] **:** a U.S. 10-cent coin struck in 1792

dis·mem·ber \(ˈ)dis-ˈmem-bər\ *vt* **dis·mem·bered; dis·mem·ber·ing** \-b(ə-)riŋ\ [ME *dismembren,* fr. OF *desmembrer,* fr. *des-* + *membre* member] **1 :** to cut off or disjoin the limbs, members, or parts of **2 :** to break up or tear into pieces — **dis·mem·ber·ment** \-bər-mənt\ *n*

dis·miss \dis-ˈmis\ *vt* [modif. of L *dimissus,* pp. of *dimittere,* fr. *dis-* apart + *mittere* to send — more at DIS-, SMITE] **1 :** to permit or cause to leave <~*ed* his visitor> **2 :** to remove from position or service : DISCHARGE **3 a :** to bar from attention or serious consideration <~*ed* the thought> **b :** to put out of judicial consideration <~*ed* all charges> ***syn*** see EJECT

dis·miss·al \-ˈmis-əl\ *n* **:** the act of dismissing **:** the fact or state of being dismissed

dis·mis·sion \-ˈmish-ən\ *n* **:** DISMISSAL

dis·mis·sive \dis-ˈmis-iv\ *adj* **:** giving dismissal **:** serving to dismiss

[1]dis·mount \(ˈ)dis-ˈmau̇nt\ *vb* [prob. modif. of MF *desmonter,* fr. *des-* + *monter* to mount] *vi* **1** *obs* **:** DESCEND **2 :** to alight from an elevated position (as on a horse) ~ *vt* **1 :** to throw down or remove from a mount or an elevated position; *esp* **:** UNHORSE **2 :** DISASSEMBLE

[2]dismount *n* **:** the act of dismounting

dis·obe·di·ence \ˌdis-ə-ˈbēd-ē-ən(t)s\ *n* **:** refusal or neglect to obey

dis·obe·di·ent \-ənt\ *adj* [ME, fr. MF *desobedient,* fr. *des-* + *obedient*] **:** refusing or neglecting to obey — **dis·obe·di·ent·ly** *adv*

dis·obey \ˌdis-ə-ˈbā\ *vb* [ME *disobeyen,* fr. MF *desobeir,* fr. *des-* + *obeir* to obey] *vt* **:** to fail to obey ~ *vi* **:** to be disobedient — **dis·obey·er** *n*

dis·oblige \ˌdis-ə-ˈblīj\ *vt* [F *désobliger,* fr. MF, fr. *des-* + *obliger* to oblige] **1 :** to go counter to the wishes of **2 :** to put out **:** INCONVENIENCE

di·so·di·um phosphate \(ˌ)dī-ˌsōd-ē-əm-\ *n* **:** a sodium phosphate Na_2HPO_4

di·so·mic \(ˈ)dī-ˈsō-mik\ *adj* [*di-* + *-somic*] **:** having one or more chromosomes duplicated but not an entire genome duplicated

[1]dis·or·der \(ˈ)dis-ˈȯrd-ər, diz-\ *vt* **1 :** to disturb the order of **2 :** to disturb the regular or normal functions of

[2]disorder *n* **1 :** lack of order <clothes in ~> **2 :** breach of the peace or public order <troubled times marked by social ~*s*> **3 :** an abnormal physical or mental condition **:** AILMENT

dis·or·dered *adj* **1** *obs* **a :** morally reprehensible **b :** UNRULY **2 a :** marked by disorder **b :** not functioning in a normal orderly healthy way — **dis·or·dered·ly** *adv* — **dis·or·dered·ness** *n*

[1]dis·or·der·ly \-ˈȯrd-ər-lē\ *adv, archaic* **:** in a disorderly manner

[2]disorderly *adj* **1 :** characterized by disorder <a ~ pile of clothes> **2 :** engaged in conduct offensive to public order <charged with being drunk and ~> — **dis·or·der·li·ness** *n*

disorderly conduct *n* **:** a petty offense chiefly against public order and decency that falls short of an indictable misdemeanor

dis·or·ga·nize \(ˈ)dis-ˈȯr-gə-ˌnīz\ *vt* [F *désorganiser,* fr. *dés-* dis- + *organiser* to organize] **:** to destroy or interrupt the orderly structure or function of — **dis·or·ga·ni·za·tion** \(ˌ)dis-ˌȯrg-(ə-)nə-ˈzā-shən\ *n*

dis·or·ga·nized *adj* **:** lacking coherence, system, or central guiding agency <~ work habits>

dis·ori·ent \(ˈ)dis-ˈōr-ē-ˌent, -ˈȯr-\ *vt* [F *désorienter,* fr. *dés-* dis- + *orienter* to orient, fr. MF, fr. *orient,* n.] **1 a :** to cause to lose bearings **:** displace from normal position or relationship **b :** to cause to lose the sense of time, place, or identity **2 :** CONFUSE

dis·ori·en·tate \-ē-ən-ˌtāt, -ē-ˌen-\ *vt* **:** DISORIENT — **dis·ori·en·ta·tion** \(ˌ)dis-ˌōr-ē-ən-ˈtā-shən, -ˌȯr-, -ē-ˌen-\ *n*

dis·own \(ˈ)dis-ˈōn\ *vt* **1 :** to refuse to acknowledge as one's own **2 a :** to repudiate any connection or identification with **b :** to deny the validity or authority of — **dis·own·ment** \-mənt\ *n*

disp *abbr* dispensary

dis·par·age \dis-ˈpar-ij\ *vt* **-aged; -ag·ing** [ME *disparagen* to degrade by marriage below one's class, disparage, fr. MF *desparagier* to marry below one's class, fr. OF, fr. *des-* dis- + *parage* extraction, lineage, fr. *per* peer] **1 :** to lower in rank or reputation **:** DEGRADE **2 :** to depreciate by indirect means (as invidious comparison) **:** speak slightingly about ***syn*** see DECRY ***ant*** applaud — **dis·par·age·ment** \-ij-mənt\ *n* — **dis·par·ag·er** *n* — **dis·par·ag·ing** *adj* — **dis·par·ag·ing·ly** \-ij-iŋ-lē\ *adv*

dis·pa·rate \dis-ˈpar-ət, ˈdis-p(ə-)rət\ *adj* [L *disparatus,* pp. of *disparare* to separate, fr. *dis-* + *parare* to prepare — more at PARE] **1 :** markedly distinct in quality or character **2 :** containing or made up of fundamentally different and often incongruous elements ***syn*** see DIFFERENT ***ant*** comparable, analogous — **dis·pa·rate·ly** *adv* — **dis·pa·rate·ness** *n*

dis·par·i·ty \dis-ˈpar-ət-ē\ *n, pl* **-ties** [MF *desparité,* fr. LL *disparitat-, disparitas,* fr. L *dis-* + LL *paritat-, paritas* parity] **:** the state of being disparate **:** DIFFERENCE

dis·part \(ˈ)dis-ˈpärt\ *vb* [It & L; It *dispartire,* fr. L, fr. *dis-* + *partire* to divide — more at PART] *archaic* **:** SEPARATE, DIVIDE

dis·pas·sion \(ˈ)dis-ˈpash-ən\ *n* **:** absence of passion **:** COOLNESS

dis·pas·sion·ate \-(ə-)nət\ *adj* **:** not influenced by strong feeling; *esp* **:** not affected by personal or emotional involvement <a ~ critic> <a ~ approach to a problem> ***syn*** see FAIR — **dis·pas·sion·ate·ly** *adv* — **dis·pas·sion·ate·ness** *n*

[1]dis·patch \dis-ˈpach\ *vb* [Sp *despachar* or It *dispacciare,* fr. Prov *despachar* to get rid of, fr. MF *despeechier* to set free, fr. OF, fr. *des-* + *-peechier* (as in *empeechier* to hinder) — more at IMPEACH] *vt* **1 :** to send off or away with promptness or speed esp. on official business **2 a :** to kill with quick efficiency <~ an injured dog> **b** *obs* **:** DEPRIVE **3 :** to dispose of (as a task) rapidly or efficiently ~ *vi, archaic* **:** to make haste **:** HURRY ***syn*** see KILL — **dis·patch·er** *n*

[2]dispatch *n* **1 :** the act of dispatching: as **a** *obs* **:** DISMISSAL **b :** the act of killing **c** (1) **:** prompt settlement (as of an item of business) (2) **:** quick riddance **d :** a sending off **:** SHIPMENT **2 a :** a message sent with speed; *esp* **:** an important official message sent by a diplomatic, military, or naval officer <sent a ~ to the war department> <his military record brought him three mentions in ~*es* —*Current Biog.*> **b :** a news item sent in by a correspondent to a newspaper **3 :** promptness and efficiency in performance or transmission ***syn*** see HASTE

dispatch case *n* **:** a case for carrying papers

dis·pel \dis-ˈpel\ *vt* **dis·pelled; dis·pel·ling** [L *dispellere,* fr. *dis-* + *pellere* to drive, beat — more at FELT] **:** to drive away by scattering **:** DISSIPATE ***syn*** see SCATTER

dis·pens·able \dis-ˈpen(t)-sə-bəl\ *adj* **:** capable of being dispensed with **:** UNESSENTIAL — **dis·pens·abil·i·ty** \-ˌpen(t)-sə-ˈbil-ət-ē\ *n*

dis·pen·sa·ry \dis-ˈpen(t)s-(ə-)rē\ *n, pl* **-ries** **1 :** a place where medical or dental aid is dispensed **2 :** a store where liquor is sold under state regulations

dis·pen·sa·tion \ˌdis-pən-ˈsā-shən, -ˌpen-\ *n* **1 a :** a general state or ordering of things; *specif* **:** a system of revealed commands and promises regulating human affairs **b :** a particular arrangement or provision esp. of providence or nature **2 a :** an exemption from a law or from an impediment, vow, or oath **b :** a formal authorization **3 a :** the act of dispensing **b :** something dispensed or distributed — **dis·pen·sa·tion·al** \-shnəl, -shən-ᵊl\ *adj*

dis·pen·sa·to·ry \dis-ˈpen(t)-sə-ˌtōr-ē, -ˌtȯr-\ *n, pl* **-ries** **1 :** a medicinal formulary **2** *archaic* **:** a place for keeping medical supplies

dis·pense \dis-ˈpen(t)s\ *vb* **dis·pensed; dis·pens·ing** [ME *dispensen,* fr. ML & L; ML *dispensare* to grant dispensation, fr. L, to distribute, fr. *dispensus,* pp. of *dispendere* to weigh out, fr. *dis-* + *pendere* to weigh — more at SPAN] *vt* **1 a :** to deal out in portions **b :** ADMINISTER <~ justice> **2 :** to give dispensation to **:** EXEMPT **3 :** to prepare and distribute (medication) ~ *vi, archaic* **:** to grant dispensation ***syn*** see DISTRIBUTE — **dispense with** **1 :** to suspend the operation of <a people that has *dispensed with* its monarchy> **2 :** to do without <could *dispense with* his assistants>

dis·pens·er \-ˈpen(t)-sər\ *n* **:** one that dispenses: as **a :** a container that extrudes, sprays, or feeds out in convenient units **b :** a usu. mechanical device for vending merchandise

dis·peo·ple \(ˈ)dis-ˈpē-pəl\ *vt* **:** DEPOPULATE

dis·pers·al \dis-ˈpər-səl\ *n* **:** the act or result of dispersing; *specif* **:** the process or result of the spreading of organisms from one place to another

dis·per·sant \dis-ˈpər-sənt\ *n* **:** a dispersing agent; *esp* **:** a substance for promoting the formation and stabilization of a dispersion of one substance in another — **dispersant** *adj*

dis·perse \dis-ˈpərs\ *vb* **dis·persed; dis·pers·ing** [ME *dysparsen,* fr. MF *disperser,* fr. L *dispersus,* pp. of *dispergere* to scatter, fr. *dis-* + *spargere* to scatter — more at SPARK] *vt* **1 a :** to cause to break up <the meeting was *dispersed*> **b :** to cause to become spread widely **c :** to cause to evaporate or vanish <sunlight *dispersing* the vapor> **2 :** to spread or distribute from a fixed or constant source: as **a** *archaic* **:** DISSEMINATE **b :** to subject (as light) to dispersion **c :** to distribute (as fine particles) more or less evenly throughout a medium ~ *vi* **1 :** to break up in random fashion <the crowd *dispersed* at the policeman's request> **2 a :** to become dispersed **b :** DISSIPATE, VANISH <the fog *dispersed* toward morning> ***syn*** see SCATTER — **dis·persed·ly** \-ˈpər-səd-lē, -ˈpərst-lē\ *adv* — **dis·pers·er** *n* — **dis·pers·ible** \-ˈpər-sə-bəl\ *adj*

disperse system *n* **:** DISPERSION 5b

dis·per·sion \dis-ˈpər-zhən, -shən\ *n* **1** *cap* **:** DIASPORA 1a **2 :** the act or process of dispersing **:** the state of being dispersed **3 :** the scattering of the values of a frequency distribution from an average **4 :** the separation of light into colors by refraction or diffraction with formation of a spectrum; *also* **:** the separation of nonhomogeneous radiation into components in accordance with some characteristic (as energy) **5 a :** a dispersed substance **b :** a system consisting of a dispersed substance and the medium in which it is dispersed **:** COLLOID 1b

dis·per·sive \-ˈpər-siv, -ziv\ *adj* **1 :** of or relating to dispersion <a ~ medium> <the ~ power of a lens> **2 :** tending to disperse — **dis·per·sive·ly** *adv* — **dis·per·sive·ness** *n*

dis·per·soid \-ˈpər-ˌsȯid\ *n* **:** finely divided particles of one substance dispersed in another

dispir·it \(ˈ)dis-ˈpir-ət\ *vt* [*dis-* + *spirit*] **:** to deprive of morale or enthusiasm — **dispir·it·ed** *adj* — **dispir·it·ed·ly** *adv* — **dispir·it·ed·ness** *n*

dis·pit·eous \dis-ˈpit-ē-əs\ *adj* [alter. of *despiteous*] *archaic* **:** CRUEL

ə abut	ᵊ kitten	ər further	a back	ā bake	ä cot, cart
au̇ out	ch chin	e less	ē easy	g gift	i trip	ī life
j joke	ŋ sing	ō flow	ȯ flaw	ȯi coin	th thin	t͟h this
ü loot	u̇ foot	y yet	yü few	yu̇ furious	zh vision

dis·place \(ˈ)dis-ˈplās\ *vt* [prob. fr. MF *desplacer,* fr. *des-* dis- + *place*] **1 a :** to remove from the usual or proper place; *specif* **:** to expel or force to flee from home or homeland **b :** to remove from an office **c** *obs* **:** to drive out **:** BANISH **2 a :** to remove physically out of position <water *displaced* by a floating object> **b :** to take the place of (as in a chemical reaction) **:** SUPPLANT ***syn*** see REPLACE — **dis·place·able** \-ˈplā-sə-bəl\ *adj*

dis·place·ment \dis-ˈplā-smənt\ *n* **1 :** the act or process of displacing **:** the state of being displaced **2 a :** the volume or weight of a fluid (as water) displaced by a floating body (as a ship) of equal weight **b :** the difference between the initial position of a body and any later position **c :** the volume displaced by a piston (as in a pump or an engine) in a single stroke; *also* **:** the total volume so displaced by all the pistons in an internal-combustion engine (as in an automobile) **3 :** the substitution of another form of behavior for what is normal or expected esp. when the normal response is nonadaptive

dis·plant \dis-ˈplant\ *vt* [MF *desplanter,* fr. *des-* + *planter* to plant, fr. LL *plantare*] **1 :** DISPLACE, REMOVE **2 :** SUPPLANT

1**dis·play** \dis-ˈplā\ *vb* [ME *displayen,* fr. AF *despleier,* fr. L *displicare* to scatter, fr. *dis-* + *plicare* to fold — more at PLY] *vt* **1 a :** to put or spread before the view in display <~ the flag> **b :** to make evident <~*ed* great skill> **c** *obs* **:** to show off ostentatiously **2** *obs* **:** DESCRY ~ *vi* **1** *obs* **:** to show off **2 :** to make a breeding display <penguins ~*ed* and copulated>

2**display** *n, often attrib* **1 a** (1) **:** a setting or presentation of something in open view <a fireworks ~> (2) **:** a clear sign or evidence **:** EXHIBITION <a ~ of courage> **b :** ostentatious show **c :** type composition designed to catch the eye; *also* **:** printed matter so composed **d :** an eye-catching arrangement by which something is exhibited **e :** a device (as a cathode-ray tube) that gives information in visual form in communications <a computer ~> <a radar ~> **2 :** a pattern of behavior exhibited esp. by male birds in the breeding season

dis·please \(ˈ)dis-ˈplēz\ *vb* [ME *displesen,* fr. MF *desplaisir,* fr. (assumed) VL *displacēre,* fr. L *dis-* + *placēre* to please] *vt* **1 :** to incur the disapproval of esp. as accompanied by annoyance or dislike <fired any employee who *displeased* him> **2 :** to be offensive to <abstract art ~*s* him> ~ *vi* **:** to give displeasure <signs of inattention calculated to ~>

dis·plea·sure \(ˈ)dis-ˈplezh-ər, -ˈplāzh-\ *n* **1 :** the feeling of one that is displeased **:** DISFAVOR **2 :** DISCOMFORT, UNHAPPINESS **3** *archaic* **:** OFFENSE, INJURY

dis·plode \dis-ˈplōd\ *vb* **dis·plod·ed; dis·plod·ing** [L *displodere,* fr. *dis-* + *plaudere* to clap, applaud] *archaic* **:** EXPLODE — **dis·plo·sion** \-ˈplō-zhən\ *n*

1**dis·port** \dis-ˈpō(ə)rt, -ˈpȯ(ə)rt\ *n, archaic* **:** SPORT, PASTIME

2**disport** *vb* [ME *disporten,* fr. MF *desporter,* fr. *des-* + *porter* to carry] *vt* **1 :** DIVERT, AMUSE **2 :** DISPLAY ~ *vi* **:** to amuse oneself in light or lively fashion **:** FROLIC — **dis·port·ment** \-mənt\ *n*

1**dis·pos·able** \dis-ˈpō-zə-bəl\ *adj* **1 :** subject to or available for disposal; *specif* **:** remaining to an individual after deduction of taxes <~ income> **2 :** designed to be used once and then thrown away <~ towels> — **dis·pos·abil·i·ty** \-ˌpō-zə-ˈbil-ət-ē\ *n*

2**disposable** *n* **:** something (as a paper blanket) that is disposable

dis·pos·al \dis-ˈpō-zəl\ *n* **1 :** the act or process of disposing: as **a :** orderly placement or distribution **b :** REGULATION, ADMINISTRATION **c :** BESTOWAL **d :** systematic destruction; *esp* **:** destruction or transformation of garbage **2 :** the power or authority to dispose of <the car was at my ~> **3** [*garbage disposal unit*] **:** a device used to reduce waste matter (as by grinding)

1**dis·pose** \dis-ˈpōz\ *vb* **dis·posed; dis·pos·ing** [ME *disposen,* fr. MF *disposer,* fr. L *disponere* to arrange (perf. indic. *disposui*), fr. *dis-* + *ponere* to put — more at POSITION] *vt* **1 :** to give a tendency to **:** INCLINE <faulty diet ~*s* one to sickness> **2 a :** to put in place **:** set in readiness **:** ARRANGE <*disposing* troops for withdrawal> **b** *obs* **:** REGULATE **c :** BESTOW ~ *vi* **1 :** to settle a matter finally **2** *obs* **:** to come to terms ***syn*** see INCLINE — **dis·pos·er** *n* — **dispose of 1 :** to place, distribute, or arrange esp. in an orderly way **2 a :** to transfer to the control of another <*disposing of* his personal property> **b** (1) **:** to get rid of <waste that is hard to *dispose of*> (2) **:** to deal with conclusively <*disposed of* the matter efficiently>

2**dispose** *n* **1** *obs* **:** DISPOSAL **2** *obs* **a :** DISPOSITION **b :** DEMEANOR

dis·po·si·tion \ˌdis-pə-ˈzish-ən\ *n* [ME, fr. MF, fr. L *disposition-, dispositio,* fr. *dispositus,* pp. of *disponere*] **1 :** the act or the power of disposing or the state of being disposed: as **a :** ADMINISTRATION, CONTROL **b :** final arrangement **:** SETTLEMENT <the ~ of the case> **c** (1) **:** transfer to the care or possession of another (2) **:** the power of such transferal **d :** orderly arrangement **2 a :** prevailing tendency, mood, or inclination **b :** temperamental makeup **c :** the tendency of something to act in a certain manner under given circumstances

syn DISPOSITION, TEMPERAMENT, TEMPER, CHARACTER, PERSONALITY *shared meaning element* **:** the dominant quality or qualities distinguishing a person or group

dis·pos·i·tive \dis-ˈpäz-ət-iv\ *adj* **:** directed toward or effecting disposition (as of a case) <~ evidence>

dis·pos·sess \ˌdis-pə-ˈzes *also* -ˈses\ *vt* [MF *despossesser,* fr. *des-* dis- + *possesser* to possess]**:** to put out of possession or occupancy — **dis·pos·ses·sion** \-ˈzesh-ən *also* -ˈsesh-\ *n* — **dis·pos·ses·sor** \-ˈzes-ər *also* -ˈses-\ *n*

dis·pos·sessed *adj* **:** deprived of homes, possessions, and security <~ refugees living in camps>

dis·po·sure \dis-ˈpō-zhər\ *n, archaic* **:** DISPOSAL, DISPOSITION

1**dis·praise** \(ˈ)dis-ˈprāz\ *vt* [ME *dispraisen,* fr. OF *despreisier,* fr. *des-* dis- + *preisier* to praise]**:** to comment on with disapproval or censure — **dis·prais·er** *n* — **dis·prais·ing·ly** \-ˈprā-ziŋ-lē\ *adv*

2**dispraise** *n* **:** an expression of disapproval **:** DISPARAGEMENT

dispread \dis-ˈpred\ *vt* **:** to spread abroad or out

dis·prize \(ˈ)dis-ˈprīz\ *vt* [MF *despriser,* fr. OF *despreisier* to dispraise] *archaic* **:** UNDERVALUE, SCORN

dis·proof \(ˈ)dis-ˈprüf\ *n* **1 :** the action of disproving **2 :** evidence that disproves

1**dis·pro·por·tion** \ˌdis-prə-ˈpōr-shən, -ˈpȯr-\ *n* **:** lack of proportion, symmetry, or proper relation **:** DISPARITY; *also* **:** an instance of such disparity — **dis·pro·por·tion·al** \-shnəl, -shən-ᵊl\ *adj*

2**disproportion** *vt* **:** to make out of proportion **:** MISMATCH

dis·pro·por·tion·ate \-sh(ə-)nət\ *adj* **:** being out of proportion — **dis·pro·por·tion·ate·ly** *adv*

dis·pro·por·tion·ation \-ˌpōr-shə-ˈnā-shən, -ˌpȯr-\ *n* **:** the transformation of a substance into two or more dissimilar substances usu. by simultaneous oxidation and reduction — **dis·pro·por·tion·ate** \-ˈpōr-shə-ˌnāt, -ˈpȯr-\ *vi*

dis·prove \(ˈ)dis-ˈprüv\ *vt* [ME *disproven,* fr. MF *desprover,* fr. *des-* + *prover* to prove]**:** to prove to be false **:** REFUTE — **dis·prov·able** \-ˈprü-və-bəl\ *adj*

syn DISPROVE, REFUTE, CONFUTE, REBUT, CONTROVERT *shared meaning element* **:** to show or try to show by presenting evidence that something (as a claim, statement, or charge) is not true ***ant*** prove, demonstrate

dis·pu·tant \dis-ˈpyüt-ᵊnt, ˈdis-pyət-ənt\ *n* **:** one that is engaged in a dispute

dis·pu·ta·tion \ˌdis-pyə-ˈtā-shən\ *n* **1 :** the act of disputing **:** DEBATE **2 :** an academic exercise in oral defense of a thesis by formal logic

dis·pu·ta·tious \-shəs\ *adj* **1 :** inclined to dispute **2 :** provoking debate **:** CONTROVERSIAL — **dis·pu·ta·tious·ly** *adv* — **dis·pu·ta·tious·ness** *n*

1**dis·pute** \dis-ˈpyüt\ *vb* **dis·put·ed; dis·put·ing** [ME *disputen,* fr. OF *desputer,* fr. L *disputare* to discuss, fr. *dis-* + *putare* to think] *vi* **:** to engage in argument **:** DEBATE; *esp* **:** to argue irritably or with irritating persistence ~ *vt* **1 a :** to make the subject of disputation **b :** to call into question <the honesty of his intent was never *disputed*> **2 a :** to struggle against <*disputed* the advance of the invaders> **b :** to struggle over **:** CONTEST <the defending troops *disputed* every inch of ground> ***syn*** see DISCUSS — **dis·pu·ta·ble** \dis-ˈpyüt-ə-bəl, ˈdis-pyət-\ *adj* — **dis·pu·ta·bly** \-blē\ *adv* — **dis·put·er** *n*

2**dis·pute** \dis-ˈpyüt, ˈdis-ˌ\ *n* **1 a :** verbal controversy **:** DEBATE **b :** QUARREL **2** *obs* **:** physical combat

dis·qual·i·fi·ca·tion \(ˌ)dis-ˌkwäl-ə-fə-ˈkā-shən\ *n* **1 :** the act of disqualifying **:** the state of being disqualified <~ from office> **2 :** something that disqualifies or incapacitates

dis·qual·i·fy \(ˈ)dis-ˈkwäl-ə-ˌfī\ *vt* **1 :** to deprive of the required qualities, properties, or conditions **:** make unfit **2 :** to deprive of a power, right, or privilege **3 :** to make ineligible for a prize or for further competition because of violations of the rules

dis·quan·ti·ty \(ˈ)dis-ˈkwän(t)-ət-ē\ *vt, obs* **:** DIMINISH, LESSEN

1**dis·qui·et** \(ˈ)dis-ˈkwī-ət\ *vt* **:** to take away the peace or tranquillity of **:** DISTURB, ALARM ***syn*** see DISCOMPOSE ***ant*** tranquilize, soothe — **dis·qui·et·ing** *adj* — **dis·qui·et·ing·ly** \-iŋ-lē\ *adv*

2**disquiet** *n* **:** lack of peace or tranquillity **:** ANXIETY

3**disquiet** *adj, archaic* **:** UNEASY, DISQUIETED — **dis·qui·et·ly** *adv*

dis·qui·etude \(ˈ)dis-ˈkwī-ə-ˌt(y)üd\ *n* **:** AGITATION, ANXIETY

dis·qui·si·tion \ˌdis-kwə-ˈzish-ən\ *n* [L *disquisition-, disquisitio,* fr. *disquisitus,* pp. of *disquirere* to inquire diligently, fr. *dis-* + *quaerere* to seek — more at QUEST] **:** a formal inquiry into or discussion of a subject **:** DISCOURSE

dis·rate \(ˈ)dis-ˈrāt\ *vt* **:** to reduce in rank **:** DEMOTE ***syn*** see DEGRADE

1**dis·re·gard** \ˌdis-ri-ˈgärd\ *vt* **:** to pay no attention to **:** treat as unworthy of regard or notice ***syn*** see NEGLECT

2**disregard** *n* **:** the act of disregarding **:** the state of being disregarded **:** NEGLECT — **dis·re·gard·ful** \-fəl\ *adj*

dis·re·lat·ed \ˌdis-ri-ˈlāt-əd\ *adj* **:** not related

dis·re·la·tion \-ˈlā-shən\ *n* **:** lack of a fitting or proportionate connection or relationship

1**dis·rel·ish** \(ˈ)dis-ˈrel-ish\ *vt* **:** to find unpalatable or distasteful

2**disrelish** *n* **:** lack of relish **:** DISTASTE, DISLIKE

dis·re·mem·ber \ˌdis-ri-ˈmem-bər\ *vt* **:** FORGET <I ~ rightly what I did —Elizabeth C. Gaskell>

dis·re·pair \ˌdis-ri-ˈpa(ə)r, -ˈpe(ə)r\ *n* **:** the state of being in need of repair <a building fallen into ~>

dis·rep·u·ta·ble \(ˈ)dis-ˈrep-yət-ə-bəl\ *adj***:** not reputable — **dis·rep·u·ta·bil·i·ty** \(ˌ)dis-ˈrep-yət-ə-bil-ət-ē\ *n* — **dis·rep·u·ta·ble·ness** \(ˈ)dis-ˈrep-yət-ə-bəl-nəs\ *n* — **dis·rep·u·ta·bly** \-blē\ *adv*

dis·re·pute \ˌdis-ri-ˈpyüt\ *n* **:** lack or decline of good reputation **:** a state of being held in low esteem <the hotel fell into ~ after the bar was added> ***syn*** see DISGRACE ***ant*** repute

1**dis·re·spect** \ˌdis-ri-ˈspekt\ *vt* **:** to have disrespect for

2**disrespect** *n* **:** lack of respect or reverence — **dis·re·spect·ful** \-fəl\ *adj* — **dis·re·spect·ful·ly** \-fə-lē\ *adv* — **dis·re·spect·ful·ness** *n*

dis·re·spect·able \ˌdis-ri-ˈspek-tə-bəl\ *adj* **:** not respectable — **dis·re·spect·abil·i·ty** \-ˌspek-tə-ˈbil-ət-ē\ *n*

dis·robe \(ˈ)dis-ˈrōb\ *vb* [MF *desrober,* fr. *des-* dis- + *robe* garment — more at ROBE] *vt* **:** to strip of clothing or covering ~ *vi* **:** to take off one's clothing

dis·rupt \dis-ˈrəpt\ *vt* [L *disruptus,* pp. of *disrumpere,* fr. *dis-* + *rumpere* to break — more at RUPTURE] **1 a :** to break apart **:** RUPTURE **b :** to throw into disorder <agitators trying to ~ the meeting> **2 :** to cause to break down — **dis·rupt·er** *n* — **dis·rup·tion** \-ˈrəp-shən\ *n* — **dis·rup·tive** \-ˈrəp-tiv\ *adj* — **dis·rup·tive·ly** *adv* — **dis·rup·tive·ness** *n*

diss *abbr* dissertation

dis·sat·is·fac·tion \(ˌ)dis-ˌ(s)at-əs-ˈfak-shən\ *n* **:** the quality or state of being dissatisfied **:** DISCONTENT

dis·sat·is·fac·to·ry \-ˈfak-t(ə-)rē\ *adj* **:** causing dissatisfaction

dis·sat·is·fy \(ˈ)dis-ˈ(s)at-əs-ˌfī\ *vt* **:** to fail to satisfy **:** DISPLEASE

dis·save \(ˈ)dis-ˈ(s)āv\ *vi* **:** to use savings for current expenses

dis·seat \(ˈ)dis-ˈ(s)ēt\ *vt, archaic* **:** UNSEAT

dis·sect \dis-ˈekt; dī-ˈsekt, ˈdī-ˌ\ *vb* [L *dissectus,* pp. of *dissecare* to cut apart, fr. *dis-* + *secare* to cut — more at SAW] *vt* **1 :** to separate into pieces **:** expose the several parts of (as an animal) for scientific examination **2 :** to analyze and interpret minutely ~ *vi* **:** to make a dissection ***syn*** see ANALYZE — **dis·sec·tor** \-ər\ *n*

dis·sect·ed *adj* **1 :** cut deeply into fine lobes <a ~ leaf> **2 :** divided into hills and ridges (as by gorges) <a ~ plateau>

dis·sec·tion \dis-ˈek-shən; dī-ˈsek-, ˈdī-ˌ\ *n* **1 :** the act or process of dissecting **:** the state of being dissected **2 :** an anatomical specimen prepared by dissecting

dis·seise *or* **dis·seize** \(ˈ)dis-ˈ(s)ēz\ *vt* **dis·seised** *or* **dis·seized; dis·seis·ing** *or* **dis·seiz·ing** [ME *disseisen,* fr. ML *disseisiare* & AF *disseisir,* fr. OF *dessaisir,* fr. *des-* + *saisir* to put in possession of — more at SEIZE] **:** to deprive esp. wrongfully of seisin **:** DISPOSSESS

dis·sei·sin *or* **dis·sei·zin** \-ˈ(s)ēz-ᵊn\ *n* [ME *dysseysyne,* fr. AF *disseisine,* fr. OF *dessaisine,* fr. *des-* dis- + *saisine* seisin] **:** the act of disseising **:** the state of being disseised

dis·sem·ble \dis-ˈem-bəl\ *vb* **dis·sem·bled; dis·sem·bling** \-b(ə-)liŋ\ [alter. of obs. *dissimule,* fr. ME *dissimulen,* fr. MF *dissimuler,* fr. L *dissimulare* — more at DISSIMULATE] *vt* **1 :** to hide under a false appearance **2 :** to put on the appearance of **:** SIMULATE ~ *vi* **:** to put on a false appearance **:** conceal facts, intentions, or feelings under some pretense ***syn*** see DISGUISE — **dis·sem·bler** \-b(ə-)lər\ *n*

dis·sem·i·nate \dis-ˈem-ə-ˌnāt\ *vb* **-nat·ed; -nat·ing** [L *disseminatus,* pp. of *disseminare,* fr. *dis-* + *seminare* to sow, fr. *semin-, semen* seed — more at SEMEN] *vt* **1 :** to spread abroad as though sowing seed <~ ideas> **2 :** to disperse throughout ~ *vi* **:** to spread widely — **dis·sem·i·na·tion** \-ˌem-ə-ˈnā-shən\ *n* — **dis·sem·i·na·tor** \-ˈem-ə-ˌnāt-ər\ *n*

dis·sem·i·nule \dis-ˈem-ə-ˌn(y)ü(ə)l\ *n* **:** a part or organ (as a seed or spore) of a plant that ensures propagation

dis·sen·sion *also* **dis·sen·tion** \dis-ˈen-chən\ *n* [ME, fr. MF, fr. L *dissension-, dissensio,* fr. *dissensus,* pp. of *dissentire*] **:** DISAGREEMENT; *esp* **:** partisan and contentious quarreling ***syn*** see DISCORD ***ant*** accord, comity

[1]**dis·sent** \dis-ˈent\ *vi* [ME *dissenten,* fr. L *dissentire,* fr. *dis-* + *sentire* to feel — more at SENSE] **1 :** to withhold assent **2 :** to differ in opinion

[2]**dissent** *n* **:** difference of opinion: as **a :** religious nonconformity **b :** a justice's nonconcurrence with a decision of the majority — called also *dissenting opinion*

dis·sent·er \dis-ˈent-ər\ *n* **1 :** one that dissents **2** *cap* **:** an English Nonconformist

dis·sen·tient \dis-ˈen-ch(ē-)ənt\ *adj* [L *dissentient-, dissentiens,* prp. of *dissentire*] **:** expressing dissent — **dissentient** *n*

dis·sent·ing \dis-ˈent-iŋ\ *adj, often cap* **:** belonging to the party of English Nonconformists

dis·sep·i·ment \dis-ˈep-ə-mənt\ *n* [L *dissaepimentum* partition, fr. *dissaepire* to divide, fr. *dis-* + *saepire* to fence in — more at SEPTUM] **:** a dividing tissue **:** SEPTUM; *esp* **:** a partition between cells of a compound plant ovary

dis·sert \dis-ˈərt\ *vi* [L *dissertus,* pp. of *disserere,* fr. *dis-* + *serere* to join, arrange — more at SERIES] **:** DISCOURSE

dis·ser·tate \ˈdis-ər-ˌtāt\ *vi* **-tat·ed; -tat·ing** [L *dissertatus,* pp. of *dissertare,* fr. *dissertus*] **:** DISCOURSE — **dis·ser·ta·tor** \-ˌtāt-ər\ *n*

dis·ser·ta·tion \ˌdis-ər-ˈtā-shən\ *n* **:** an extended usu. written treatment of a subject; *specif* **:** one submitted for a doctorate

dis·serve \(ˈ)dis-ˈ(s)ərv\ *vt* **:** to serve badly or falsely **:** HARM <*disserving* the very democracy in which he ardently believes —*New Republic*>

dis·ser·vice \(ˈ)dis-ˈ(s)ər-vəs\ *n* **:** ill service **:** INJURY <they do a great ~ . . . to our society —Howard Kirschenbaum>

dis·sev·er \dis-ˈev-ər\ *vb* [ME *disseveren,* fr. OF *dessevrer,* fr. LL *disseparare,* fr. L *dis-* + *separare* to separate] *vt* **:** SEVER, SEPARATE ~ *vi* **:** to come apart **:** DISUNITE — **dis·sev·er·ance** \-ˈev-(ə-)rən(t)s\ *n* — **dis·sev·er·ment** \-ˈev-ər-mənt\ *n*

dis·si·dence \ˈdis-əd-ən(t)s\ *n* **:** DISSENT, DISAGREEMENT <arresting people for political ~ —Peggy Durdin>

dis·si·dent \-ənt\ *adj* [L *dissident-, dissidens,* prp. of *dissidēre* to sit apart, disagree, fr. *dis-* + *sedēre* to sit — more at SIT] **:** differing with an opinion or a group **:** DISAFFECTED — **dissident** *n*

dis·sim·i·lar \(ˈ)dis-ˈ(s)im-(ə-)lər\ *adj* **:** UNLIKE — **dis·sim·i·lar·i·ty** \(ˌ)dis-ˌ(s)im-ə-ˈlar-ət-ē\ *n* — **dis·sim·i·lar·ly** \(ˈ)dis-ˈ(s)im-(ə-)lər-lē\ *adv*

dis·sim·i·late \(ˈ)dis-ˈim-ə-ˌlāt\ *vb* **-lat·ed; -lat·ing** [*dis-* + *-similate* (as in *assimilate*)] *vt* **:** to make dissimilar ~ *vi* **:** to become dissimilar — **dis·sim·i·la·tive** \-ˌlāt-iv\ *adj* — **dis·sim·i·la·to·ry** \-(ə-)lə-ˌtōr-ē, -ˌtȯr-\ *adj*

dis·sim·i·la·tion \(ˌ)dis-ˌim-ə-ˈlā-shən\ *n* **:** the act of making or the process of becoming dissimilar: as **a :** CATABOLISM **b :** the development of dissimilarity between two identical or closely related sounds in a word

dis·si·mil·i·tude \ˌdis-(s)ə-ˈmil-ə-ˌt(y)üd\ *n* [L *dissimilitudo,* fr. *dissimilis* unlike, fr. *dis-* + *similis* like] **:** lack of resemblance

dis·sim·u·late \(ˈ)dis-ˈim-yə-ˌlāt\ *vb* **-lat·ed; -lat·ing** [L *dissimulatus,* pp. of *dissimulare,* fr. *dis-* + *simulare* to simulate] *vt* **:** to hide under a false appearance **:** DISSEMBLE ~ *vi* **:** to engage in dissembling — **dis·sim·u·la·tion** \(ˌ)dis-ˌim-yə-ˈlā-shən\ *n* — **dis·sim·u·la·tor** \(ˈ)dis-ˈim-yə-ˌlāt-ər\ *n*

dis·si·pate \ˈdis-ə-ˌpāt\ *vb* **-pat·ed; -pat·ing** [L *dissipatus,* pp. of *dissipare,* fr. *dis-* + *supare* to throw; akin to ON *svāf* spear, Skt *svapu* broom] *vt* **1 a :** to break up and drive off (as a crowd) **b :** to cause to spread out or spread thin to the point of vanishing **:** DISSOLVE **c :** to lose (as heat or electricity) irrecoverably **:** DISPEL **2 a :** to expend aimlessly or foolishly **b :** to use up esp. foolishly or heedlessly <soon *dissipated* his estate> ~ *vi* **1 :** to separate into parts and scatter or vanish **2 :** to be extravagant or dissolute in the pursuit of pleasure; *esp* **:** to drink to excess ***syn*** **1** see SCATTER **2** see WASTE ***ant*** accumulate, concentrate — **dis·si·pat·er** *n*

dis·si·pat·ed *adj* **:** given to or marked by dissipation **:** DISSOLUTE — **dis·si·pat·ed·ly** *adv* — **dis·si·pat·ed·ness** *n*

dis·si·pa·tion \ˌdis-ə-ˈpā-shən\ *n* **1 :** the act or process of dissipating **:** the state of being dissipated: **a :** DISPERSION, DIFFUSION **b** *archaic* **:** DISSOLUTION, DISINTEGRATION **c :** wasteful expenditure **d :** intemperate living; *esp* **:** excessive drinking **2 :** DIVERSION, AMUSEMENT

dis·si·pa·tive \ˈdis-ə-ˌpāt-iv\ *adj* **:** relating to dissipation esp. of heat

dis·so·cia·ble \(ˈ)dis-ˈō-sh(ē-)ə-bəl, -sē-ə-\ *adj* **:** SEPARABLE — **dis·so·cia·bil·i·ty** \(ˌ)dis-ˌō-sh(ē-)ə-ˈbil-ət-ē, -sē-ə-\ *n*

dis·so·cial \(ˈ)dis-ˈ(s)ō-shəl\ *adj* **:** UNSOCIAL, SELFISH

dis·so·ciant \dis-ˈō-s(h)ē-ənt, -ˈō-shənt\ *adj* **:** producing or resulting from dissociation; *specif* **:** MUTANT

dis·so·ci·ate \(ˈ)dis-ˈō-s(h)ē-ˌāt\ *vb* **-at·ed; -at·ing** [L *dissociatus,* pp. of *dissociare,* fr. *dis-* + *sociare* to join, fr. *socius* companion — more at SOCIAL] *vt* **1 :** to separate from association or union with another **:** DISCONNECT **2 :** DISUNITE; *specif* **:** to subject to chemical dissociation ~ *vi* **1 :** to undergo dissociation **2 :** to mutate esp. reversibly

dis·so·ci·a·tion \(ˌ)dis-ˌō-sē-ˈā-shən, -shē-\ *n* **1 :** the act or process of dissociating **:** the state of being dissociated: as **a :** the process by which a chemical combination breaks up into simpler constituents; *esp* **:** one that results from the action of energy (as heat) on a gas or of a solvent on a dissolved substance **b :** the separation of an idea or activity from the mainstream of consciousness or of behavior esp. as a mechanism of ego defense **2 :** the property inherent in some biological stocks (as of certain bacteria) of differentiating into two or more distinct and relatively permanent strains; *also* **:** such a strain — **dis·so·cia·tive** \(ˈ)dis-ˈō-s(h)ē-ˌāt-iv, -shət-iv\ *adj*

dis·sol·u·ble \dis-ˈäl-yə-bəl\ *adj* [L *dissolubilis,* fr. *dissolvere* to dissolve] **:** capable of being dissolved or disintegrated — **dis·sol·u·bil·i·ty** \-ˌäl-yə-ˈbil-ət-ē\ *n*

dis·so·lute \ˈdis-ə-ˌlüt, -lət\ *adj* [L *dissolutus,* fr. pp. of *dissolvere* to loosen, dissolve] **:** lacking restraint; *esp* **:** loose in morals — **dis·so·lute·ly** *adv* — **dis·so·lute·ness** *n*

dis·so·lu·tion \ˌdis-ə-ˈlü-shən\ *n* **1 :** the act or process of dissolving: as **a :** separation into component parts **b** (1) **:** DISINTEGRATION, DECAY (2) **:** DEATH <grew convinced of his friend's approaching ~ —Elinor Wylie> **c :** termination or destruction by breaking down, disrupting, or dispersing <the ~ of the republic> **d :** LIQUEFACTION **2** *obs* **:** PROFLIGACY

[1]**dis·solve** \diz-ˈälv, -ˈȯlv\ *vb* [ME *dissolven,* fr. L *dissolvere,* fr. *dis-* + *solvere* to loosen — more at SOLVE] *vt* **1 a :** to cause to disperse or disappear **:** DESTROY **b :** to separate into component parts **:** DISINTEGRATE **c :** to bring to an end **:** TERMINATE <~ parliament> **2 a :** to cause to pass into solution <~ sugar in water> **b :** MELT, LIQUEFY **c :** to cause to be emotionally moved **d :** to fade out (a motion-picture or television shot) in a dissolve **3** *archaic* **:** DETACH, LOOSEN **4 :** to clear up <~ the mystery> ~ *vi* **1 a :** to become dissipated or decomposed **b :** to break up **:** DISPERSE **c :** to fade away **2 a :** to become fluid **:** MELT **b :** to pass into solution **c :** to be overcome emotionally **d :** to resolve itself as if by dissolution ***syn*** see ADJOURN — **dis·solv·able** \-ˈäl-və-bəl, -ˈȯl-\ *adj* — **dis·solv·er** *n*

[2]**dissolve** *n* **:** a gradual superimposing of one motion-picture or television shot upon another on a screen

dis·sol·vent \diz-ˈäl-vənt, -ˈȯl-\ *adj* **:** SOLVENT 2 — **dissolvent** *n*

dis·so·nance \ˈdis-ə-nən(t)s\ *n* **1 :** a mingling of discordant sounds; *specif* **:** a clashing musical interval **2 :** lack of agreement; *specif* **:** inconsistency between the beliefs one holds or between one's actions and one's beliefs <cognitive ~> **:** DISCORD **3 :** an unresolved musical note or chord; *specif* **:** an interval not included in a major or minor triad or its inversions

dis·so·nant \-nənt\ *adj* [MF or L; MF, fr. L *dissonant-, dissonans,* prp. of *dissonare* to be discordant, fr. *dis-* + *sonare* to sound — more at SOUND] **1 :** marked by dissonance **:** DISCORDANT **2 :** INCONGRUOUS **3 :** harmonically unresolved — **dis·so·nant·ly** *adv*

dis·spir·it \(ˈ)dis-ˈ(s)pir-ət\ *var of* DISPIRIT

dis·suade \dis-ˈwād\ *vt* **dis·suad·ed; dis·suad·ing** [MF or L; MF *dissuader,* fr. L *dissuadēre,* fr. *dis-* + *suadēre* to urge — more at SUASION] **1 a** *archaic* **:** to advise against (an action) **b :** to advise (a person) against something **2 :** to turn from something by persuasion <~ a friend from joining the society> — **dis·suad·er** *n*

dis·sua·sion \dis-ˈwā-zhən\ *n* [MF or L; MF, fr. L *dissuasion-, dissuasio,* fr. *dissuasus,* pp. of *dissuadēre*] **:** the act of dissuading

dis·sua·sive \dis-ˈwā-siv, -ziv\ *adj* **:** tending to dissuade — **dis·sua·sive·ly** *adv* — **dis·sua·sive·ness** *n*

dis·syl·lab·ic \ˌdis-ə-ˈlab-ik, ˌdī-sə-\, **dis·syl·la·ble** \ˈdis-ˌil-ə-bəl, (ˈ)dis-ˈ(s)il-; ˈdī-ˌsil-, (ˈ)dī-ˈsil-\ *var of* DISYLLABIC, DISYLLABLE

dis·sym·me·try \(ˈ)dis-ˈ(s)im-ə-trē\ *n* **:** the absence of or the lack of symmetry — **dis·sym·met·ric** \ˌdis-(s)ə-ˈme-trik\ *adj*

1, distaff 1a

dist *abbr* **1** distance **2** district

[1]**dis·taff** \ˈdis-ˌtaf\ *n, pl* **distaffs** \-ˌtafs, -ˌtavz\ [ME *distaf,* fr. OE *distæf,* fr. *dis-* (akin to MLG *dise* bunch of flax) + *stæf* staff] **1 a :** a staff for holding the flax, tow, or wool in spinning **b :** woman's work or domain **2 :** the female branch or side of a family

2distaff *adj* : MATERNAL, FEMALE <the ~ side of the family> — compare SPEAR

dis·tain \dis-ˈtān\ *vt* [ME *disteynen,* fr. MF *desteindre* to take away the color of, fr. OF, fr. *des-* dis- + *teindre* to dye, fr. L *tingere* to wet, dye — more at TINGE] **1** *archaic* **:** STAIN **2** *archaic* **:** DISHONOR

dis·tal \ˈdis-tᵊl\ *adj* [*distant* + *-al*] **:** far from the point of attachment or origin — compare PROXIMAL — **dis·tal·ly** \-tᵊl-ē\ *adv*

distal convoluted tubule *n* : the convoluted portion of the vertebrate nephron that lies between the loop of Henle and the nonsecretory part of the nephron and that is concerned esp. with the concentration of urine

1dis·tance \ˈdis-tən(t)s\ *n* **1** *obs* : DISCORD **2 a :** separation in time **b :** the degree or amount of separation between two points, lines, surfaces, or objects measured along the shortest path joining them **c :** an extent of area or an advance along a route measured linearly **d :** an extent of advance away or along from a point considered primary or original **e :** EXPANSE **3 :** the quality or state of being distant: as **a :** spatial remoteness **b :** RESERVE, COLDNESS **c :** DIFFERENCE, DISPARITY **4 :** a distant point or region

2distance *vt* **dis·tanced; dis·tanc·ing 1 :** to place or keep at a distance **2 :** to leave far behind : OUTSTRIP

dis·tant \ˈdis-tənt\ *adj* [ME, fr. MF, fr. L *distant-, distans,* prp. of *distare* to stand apart, be distant, fr. *dis-* + *stare* to stand — more at STAND] **1 a :** separated in space : AWAY **b :** situated at a great distance : FAR-OFF **c :** separated by a great distance from each other : far apart **2 :** separated in a relationship other than spatial <a ~ relative> **3 :** different in kind **4 :** reserved or aloof in personal relationship : COLD <~ politeness> **5 a :** coming from or going to a distance <~ voyages> **b :** concerned with or directed toward things at a distance <~ thoughts> — **dis·tant·ly** *adv* — **dis·tant·ness** *n*

syn DISTANT, FAR, FAR-OFF, FARAWAY, REMOTE, REMOVED *shared meaning element* : not close in space, time, or relationship

1dis·taste \(ˈ)dis-ˈtāst\ *vt* **1** *archaic* : to feel aversion to **2** *archaic* : OFFEND, DISPLEASE ~ *vi, obs* : to have an offensive taste

2distaste *n* **1 a :** dislike of food or drink **b :** AVERSION, DISINCLINATION **2** *obs* : ANNOYANCE, DISCOMFORT

dis·taste·ful \(ˈ)dis-ˈtāst-fəl\ *adj* **1 a :** unpleasant to the taste : LOATHSOME **b :** objectionable because offensive to one's personal taste : DISAGREEABLE <boys who find study ~> **2 :** showing distaste or aversion <a ~ expression on her face> ***syn*** see REPUGNANT ***ant*** agreeable, palatable — **dis·taste·ful·ly** \-fə-lē\ *adv* — **dis·taste·ful·ness** *n*

1dis·tem·per \dis-ˈtem-pər\ *vt* [ME *distempren,* fr. LL *distemperare* to temper badly, fr. L *dis-* + *temperare* to temper] **1 :** to throw out of order **2** *archaic* : DERANGE, UNSETTLE

2distemper *n* **1 :** bad humor or temper **2 :** a disordered or abnormal bodily state esp. of quadruped mammals: as **a :** a highly contagious virus disease esp. of dogs marked by fever and by respiratory and sometimes nervous symptoms **b :** STRANGLES **c** : PANLEUCOPENIA **d :** a severe frequently fatal infectious nasopharyngeal inflammation of rabbits **3 :** political or social disorder <in the middle ages . . . resistance was an ordinary remedy for political ~*s* —T. B. Macaulay> — **dis·tem·per·ate** \-p(ə-)rət\ *adj*

3distemper *vt* [ME *distemperen,* fr. MF *destemprer,* fr. L *dis-* + *temperare*] **1** *obs* : to dilute with or soak, steep, or dissolve in a liquid **2 a :** to mix (ingredients) to produce distemper **b :** to paint in or with distemper

4distemper *n* **1 :** a process of painting in which the pigments are mixed with an emulsion of egg yolk, with size, or with white of egg as a vehicle and which is used for scene painting or mural decoration **2 a :** the paint or the prepared ground used in the distemper process **b :** a painting done in distemper **3 :** any of numerous paints using water as a vehicle

dis·tem·per·a·ture \dis-ˈtem-pə(r)-ˌchu̇(ə)r, -p(ə-)rə-, -chər, -ˌt(y)u̇(ə)r\ *n* : a disordered condition

dis·tem·per·oid \dis-ˈtem-pə-ˌrȯid\ *adj* : resembling distemper; *specif* : of, relating to, or being an attenuated canine distemper virus used to develop immunity to natural distemper infection

dis·tend \dis-ˈtend\ *vb* [ME *distenden,* fr. L *distendere,* fr. *dis-* + *tendere* to stretch — more at THIN] *vt* **1 :** EXTEND **2 :** to enlarge from internal pressure : SWELL ~ *vi* : to become expanded ***syn*** see EXPAND ***ant*** constrict

dis·ten·si·ble \-ˈten(t)-sə-bəl\ *adj* [LL *distensus,* pp. of L *distendere*] : capable of being distended — **dis·ten·si·bil·i·ty** \-ˌten(t)-sə-ˈbil-ət-ē\ *n*

dis·ten·sion *or* **dis·ten·tion** \dis-ˈten-chən\ [L *distention-, distentio,* fr. *distentus,* pp. of *distendere*] : the act of distending or the state of being distended esp. unduly or abnormally

dis·tent \dis-ˈtent\ *adj, obs* : spread out : DISTENDED

dis·tich \ˈdis-(ˌ)tik\ *n* [L *distichon,* fr. Gk, fr. neut. of *distichos* having two rows, fr. *di-* + *stichos* row, verse; akin to Gk *steichein* to go — more at STAIR] : a strophic unit of two lines

dis·ti·chous \ˈdis-ti-kəs\ *adj* [LL *distichus,* fr. Gk *distichos*] **1** : disposed in two vertical rows <~ leaves> **2 :** divided into two segments <~ antennae> — **dis·ti·chous·ly** *adv*

dis·till *also* **dis·til** \dis-ˈtil\ *vb* **dis·tilled; dis·till·ing** [ME *distillen,* fr. MF *distiller,* fr. LL *distillare,* alter. of L *destillare,* fr. *de-* + *stillare* to drip, fr. *stilla* drop; akin to OE *stān* stone — more at STONE] *vt* **1 :** to let fall, exude, or precipitate in drops or in a wet mist **2 a :** to subject to or transform by distillation **b :** to obtain by or as if by distillation **c :** to extract the essence of : CONCENTRATE ~ *vi* **1 a :** to fall or materialize in drops or in a fine moisture : DROP **b :** to appear slowly or in small quantities at a time **2 a :** to undergo distillation **b :** to condense or drop from a still after distillation

dis·til·late \ˈdis-tə-ˌlāt, -lət; dis-ˈtil-ət\ *n* **1 :** a liquid product condensed from vapor during distillation **2 :** something resembling a distillate in being a concentration, an abstract, or an essence <this book is a ~ of facts —*N. Y. Times Bk. Rev.*>

dis·til·la·tion \ˌdis-tə-ˈlā-shən\ *n* **1 :** a process that consists of driving gas or vapor from liquids or solids by heating and condensing to liquid products and that is used esp. for purification, fractionation, or the formation of new substances **2 :** DISTILLATE

dis·till·er \dis-ˈtil-ər\ *n* : one that distills esp. alcoholic liquors

dis·till·ery \dis-ˈtil-(ə-)rē\ *n, pl* **-er·ies :** the works where distilling (as of alcoholic liquors) is done

dis·tinct \dis-ˈtiŋ(k)t\ *adj* [ME, fr. MF, fr. L *distinctus,* fr. pp. of *distinguere*] **1 :** distinguishable to the eye or mind as discrete <things similar in effect but wholly ~ in motive —Hilaire Belloc> **2 :** readily perceptible to the senses or mind : presenting a clear unmistakable impression <a neat ~ handwriting> <the review gives a ~ idea of the book> **3** *archaic* : notably decorated **4 a** : NOTABLE <felt his sobriety a ~ achievement> **b :** DECIDED <there's a ~ possibility of snow> — **dis·tinct·ly** \-ˈtiŋ(k)-tlē, -ˈtiŋ-klē\ *adv* — **dis·tinct·ness** \-ˈtiŋt-nəs, -ˈtiŋk-nəs\ *n*

syn **1** DISTINCT, SEVERAL, SEPARATE, DISCRETE *shared meaning element* : not being each and every one the same
2 see EVIDENT ***ant*** indistinct, nebulous

dis·tinc·tion \dis-ˈtiŋ(k)-shən\ *n* **1 a** *archaic*: DIVISION **b :** CLASS **2 a :** the act of distinguishing a difference : DISCRIMINATION, DIFFERENTIATION **b :** the object or result of distinguishing : CONTRAST **3 :** a distinguishing mark **4 :** the quality or state of being distinguishable <there is no appreciable ~ between the twins> **5 a :** the quality or state of being distinguished <a man of some ~> **b :** special honor or recognition <graduated from college with ~> **c :** the quality or state of being worthy

dis·tinc·tive \dis-ˈtiŋ(k)-tiv\ *adj* **1 a :** serving to distinguish **b** : having or giving style or distinction **2 :** capable of making a segment of utterance different in meaning as well as in sound from an otherwise identical utterance ***syn*** see CHARACTERISTIC ***ant*** typical — **dis·tinc·tive·ly** *adv* — **dis·tinc·tive·ness** *n*

dis·tin·gué \ˌdēs-ˌtaŋ-ˈgā, (ˌ)dis-; di-ˈstaŋ-ˌ\ *adj* [F, fr. pp. of *distinguer*] : distinguished esp. in manner or bearing

dis·tin·guish \dis-ˈtiŋ-(g)wish\ *vb* [MF *distinguer,* fr. L *distinguere,* lit., to separate by pricking, fr. *dis-* + *-stinguere* (akin to L *instigare* to urge on) — more at STICK] *vt* **1 :** to perceive as being separate or different <~ the sound of a piano in an orchestra> **2 a :** to mark as separate or different **b :** to separate into kinds, classes, or categories **c :** to set above or apart from others **d :** CHARACTERIZE **3 a :** DISCERN <~*ed* a light in the distance> **b :** to single out ~ *vi* : to perceive a difference — **dis·tin·guish·abil·i·ty** \-ˌtiŋ-(g)wish-ə-ˈbil-ət-ē\ *n* — **dis·tin·guish·able** \-ˈtiŋ-(g)wish-ə-bəl\ *adj* — **dis·tin·guish·ably** \-blē\ *adv*

dis·tin·guished *adj* **1 :** marked by eminence, distinction, or excellence **2 :** befitting an eminent person ***syn*** see FAMOUS

Distinguished Conduct Medal *n* : a British military decoration awarded for distinguished conduct in the field

Distinguished Flying Cross *n* **1 :** a U.S. military decoration awarded for heroism or extraordinary achievement while participating in an aerial flight **2 :** a British military decoration awarded for acts of gallantry when flying in operations against an enemy

Distinguished Service Cross *n* **1 :** a U.S. Army decoration awarded for extraordinary heroism during operations against an armed enemy **2 :** a British military decoration awarded for distinguished service against the enemy

Distinguished Service Medal *n* **1 :** a U.S. military decoration awarded for exceptionally meritorious service to the government in a wartime duty of great responsibility **2 :** a British military decoration awarded for distinguished conduct in war

Distinguished Service Order *n* : a British military decoration awarded for special services in action

distn *abbr* distillation

di·stome \ˈdī-ˌstōm\ *n* [deriv. of Gk *di-* + *stomat-, stoma* mouth — more at STOMACH] : any of various trematode worms with both oral and ventral suckers

dis·tort \dis-ˈtȯ(ə)rt\ *vt* [L *distortus,* pp. of *distorquēre,* fr. *dis-* + *torquēre* to twist — more at TORTURE] **1 :** to twist out of the true meaning or proportion <~*ed* the news to make it sensational> **2** : to twist out of a natural, normal, or original shape or condition <a face ~*ed* by pain> **3 :** PERVERT ***syn*** see DEFORM — **dis·tort·er** *n*

dis·tor·tion \dis-ˈtȯr-shən\ *n* **1 :** the act of distorting **2 :** the quality or state of being distorted : a product of distortion: as **a** : a lack of proportionality in an image resulting from defects in the optical system **b :** falsified reproduction of an audio or video signal caused by change in the wave form of the original signal — **dis·tor·tion·al** \-shnəl, -shən-ᵊl\ *adj*

distr *abbr* distribute; distribution

1dis·tract \dis-ˈtrakt, ˈdis-ˌ\ *adj, archaic* : INSANE, MAD

2dis·tract \dis-ˈtrakt\ *vt* [ME *distracten,* fr. L *distractus,* pp. of *distrahere,* lit., to draw apart, fr. *dis-* + *trahere* to draw — more at DRAW] **1 a :** to turn aside : DIVERT **b :** to draw or direct (as one's attention) to a different object or in different directions at the same time **2 :** to stir up or confuse with conflicting emotions or motives : HARASS ***syn*** see PUZZLE ***ant*** collect (*as one's thoughts*) — **dis·tract·i·bil·i·ty** \-ˌtrak-tə-ˈbil-ət-ē\ *n* — **dis·tract·ible** \-ˈtrak-tə-bəl\ *adj* — **dis·tract·ing·ly** \-tiŋ-lē\ *adv*

dis·tract·ed·ly *adv* : in the manner of one that is distracted

dis·trac·tion \dis-ˈtrak-shən\ *n* **1 :** the act of distracting or the state of being distracted; *esp* : mental confusion **2 :** something that distracts; *esp* : AMUSEMENT — **dis·trac·tive** \-ˈtrak-tiv\ *adj*

dis·train \dis-ˈtrān\ *vb* [ME *distreynen,* fr. OF *destreindre,* fr. ML *distringere,* fr. L, to draw apart, detain, fr. *dis-* + *stringere* to bind tight — more at STRAIN] *vt* **1 :** to levy a distress upon **2 :** to seize by distress ~ *vi* : to levy a distress — **dis·train·able** \-ˈtrā-nə-bəl\ *adj* — **dis·train·er** \-ˈtrā-nər\ *or* **dis·train·or** \-ˈtrā-nər, -ˌtrā-ˈnȯ(ə)r\ *n*

dis·traint \dis-ˈtrānt\ *n* [*distrain* + *-t* (as in *constraint*)] : the act or action of distraining

dis·trait \di-ˈstrā\ *adj* [F, fr. L *distractus*] : ABSENTMINDED; *esp* : inattentive or distracted because of anxiety or apprehension

dis·traught \dis-ˈtrȯt\ *adj* [ME, fr. L *distractus*] **1 :** agitated with doubt or mental conflict **2 :** CRAZED — **dis·traught·ly** *adv*

1dis·tress \dis-ˈtres\ *n* [ME *destresse,* fr. OF, fr. (assumed) VL *districtia,* fr. L *districtus,* pp. of *distringere*] **1 a :** seizure and

detention of the goods of another as pledge or to obtain satisfaction of a claim by the sale of the goods seized; *broadly:* an act of distraining **b :** something that is distrained **2** *obs* **:** CONSTRAINT **3 a :** anguish of body or mind **:** TROUBLE **b :** a painful situation **:** MISFORTUNE **4 :** a state of danger or desperate need <a ship in ~>
syn DISTRESS, SUFFERING, MISERY, AGONY *shared meaning element* **:** the state of being in trouble or in mental or physical anguish

2distress *vt* **1 :** to subject to great strain or difficulties **2 :** to cause to worry or be troubled **:** UPSET **3** *archaic* **:** to force or overcome by inflicting pain **4 :** to mar (wood or furniture) deliberately to give an effect of age <~*ed* cherry> *syn* see TROUBLE — **dis·tress·ing·ly** \-iŋ-lē\ *adv*

3distress *adj* **1 :** offered for sale at a loss <~ merchandise> **2 :** involving distress goods <a ~ sale>

dis·tress·ful \dis-'tres-fəl\ *adj* **:** causing distress **:** full of distress — **dis·tress·ful·ly** \-fə-lē\ *adv* — **dis·tress·ful·ness** *n*

dis·trib·u·tary \dis-'trib-yə-ˌter-ē\ *n, pl* **-tar·ies :** a river branch flowing away from the main stream

dis·trib·ute \dis-'trib-yət, *Brit also* 'dis-trib-ˌyüt\ *vt* **-ut·ed; -ut·ing** [ME *distributen,* fr. L *distributus,* pp. of *distribuere,* fr. *dis-* + *tribuere* to allot — more at TRIBUTE] **1 :** to divide among several or many **:** APPORTION **2 a :** to spread out so as to cover something **:** SCATTER **b :** DELIVER <~ magazines to subscribers> **c :** to use (a term) so as to convey information about every member of the class named <the proposition "all men are mortal" ~*s* "man" but not "mortal"> **3 a :** to divide or separate esp. into kinds **b :** to return the units of (as typeset matter) to the proper storage places — **dis·trib·u·tee** \dis-ˌtrib-yə-'tē\ *n*
syn DISTRIBUTE, DISPENSE, DIVIDE, DEAL, DOLE *shared meaning element* **:** to give out, usu. in shares, to each member of a group *ant* collect (*as supplies*), amass (*as wealth*)

dis·trib·ut·ed *adj* **:** characterized by a statistical distribution of a particular kind <a normally ~ random variable>

dis·tri·bu·tion \ˌdis-trə-'byü-shən\ *n* **1 a :** the act or process of distributing **b :** the apportionment by a court of the personal property of an intestate **2 a :** the position, arrangement, or frequency of occurrence (as of the members of a group) over an area or throughout a space or unit of time **b :** the natural geographic range of an organism **3 a :** something distributed **b** (1) **:** FREQUENCY DISTRIBUTION (2) **:** PROBABILITY FUNCTION (3) **:** PROBABILITY DENSITY FUNCTION 2 **4 a :** a device by which something is distributed **b :** the pattern of branching and termination of a ramifying structure (as a nerve) **5 :** the marketing or merchandising of commodities — **dis·tri·bu·tion·al** \-shnəl, -shən-ᵊl\ *adj*

distribution function *n* **:** a function that gives the probability that a random variable is less than or equal to the independent variable of the function

dis·trib·u·tive \dis-'trib-yət-iv\ *adj* **1 :** of or relating to distribution: as **a :** dealing a proper share to each of a group **b :** diffusing more or less evenly **2** *of a word* **:** referring singly and without exception to the members of a group <*each, either,* and *none* are ~> **3 :** producing the same element when operating on a whole as when operating on each part and collecting the results <multiplication is ~ relative to addition since $a(b + c) = ab + ac$> — **dis·trib·u·tive·ly** *adv* — **dis·trib·u·tive·ness** *n* — **dis·trib·u·tiv·i·ty** \-ˌtrib-yə-'tiv-ət-ē\ *n*

distributive education *n, often cap D & E* **:** a vocational program set up between schools and employers in which the student receives both classroom instruction and on-the-job training

dis·trib·u·tor \dis-'trib-yət-ər\ *n* **1 :** one that distributes **2 :** one that markets a commodity; *esp* **:** WHOLESALER **3 :** an apparatus for directing the secondary current from the induction coil to the various spark plugs of an engine in their proper firing order

1dis·trict \'dis-(ˌ)trikt\ *n, often attrib* [F, fr. ML *districtus* jurisdiction, district, fr. *districtus,* pp. of *distringere* to distrain — more at DISTRAIN] **1 :** a territorial division (as for administrative or electoral purposes) **2 :** an area, region, or section with a distinguishing character

2district *vt* **:** to divide or organize into districts

district attorney *n* **:** the prosecuting officer of a judicial district

district court *n* **:** a trial court that has jurisdiction over certain cases within a specific judicial district

district superintendent *n* **:** a church official supervising a district

1dis·trust \(ˈ)dis-'trəst\ *vt* **:** to have no trust or confidence in

2distrust *n* **:** the lack or absence of trust **:** SUSPICION, WARINESS

dis·trust·ful \-'trəst-fəl\ *adj* **:** having or showing distrust — **dis·trust·ful·ly** \-fə-lē\ *adv* — **dis·trust·ful·ness** *n*

dis·turb \dis-'tərb\ *vb* [ME *disturben, destourben,* fr. OF & L; OF *destourber,* fr. L *disturbare,* fr. *dis-* + *turbare* to throw into disorder — more at TURBID] *vt* **1 a :** to interfere with **:** INTERRUPT **b :** to alter the position or arrangement of **c :** to break up or damage (as by shaking or jarring) **2 a :** to destroy the tranquillity or composure of **b :** to throw into disorder **c :** ALARM **d :** to put to inconvenience ~ *vi* **:** to cause disturbance *syn* see DISCOMPOSE — **dis·turb·er** *n* — **dis·turb·ing·ly** \-'tər-biŋ-lē\ *adv*

dis·tur·bance \dis-'tər-bən(t)s\ *n* **1 :** the act of disturbing **:** the state of being disturbed **2 :** a local variation from the average or normal wind conditions

dis·turbed *adj* **1 :** showing symptoms of emotional illness **2 :** designed for or occupied by disturbed patients <~ wards>

di·sub·sti·tut·ed \(ˈ)dī-'səb-stə-ˌt(y)üt-əd\ *adj* **:** having two substituent atoms or groups in a molecule

di·sul·fide \(ˈ)dī-'səl-ˌfīd\ *n* **1 :** a compound containing two atoms of sulfur combined with an element or radical **2 :** an organic compound containing the bivalent group SS composed of two sulfur atoms

di·sul·fi·ram \dī-'səl-fə-ˌram\ *n* [*disulf*ide + th*i*ourea + *am*yl] **:** a compound $C_{10}H_{20}N_2S_4$ that causes a severe physiological reaction to alcohol and is used in the treatment of alcoholism

di·sul·fo·ton \dī-'səl-fə-ˌtän\ *n* [*di*ethyl + *sulfo-* + *-ton* (prob. fr. *thi*o*nate*)] **:** an organophosphorus systemic insecticide $C_8H_{19}O_2PS_3$

dis·union \dish-'ü-nyən, (ˈ)dis(h)-'yü-\ *n* **1 :** the termination or destruction of union **:** SEPARATION **2 :** DISUNITY

dis·union·ist \-nyə-nəst\ *n* **:** one who favors disunion; *specif* **:** an American secessionist

dis·unite \ˌdish-ü-'nīt, ˌdis(h)-yü-\ *vt* **:** DIVIDE, SEPARATE

dis·uni·ty \dish-'ü-nət-ē, (ˈ)dis(h)-'yü-\ *n* **:** lack of unity; *esp* **:** DISSENSION

1dis·use \dish-'üz, (ˈ)dis(h)-'yüz\ *vt* **:** to discontinue the use or practice of

2dis·use \-'üs, -'yüs\ *n* **:** cessation of use or practice

dis·util·i·ty \ˌdish-ü-'til-ət-ē, ˌdis(h)-yü-\ *n* **:** ability to cause fatigue, inconvenience, discomfort, or pain <~ of labor>

1dis·val·ue \(ˈ)dis-'val-(ˌ)yü, -yə(-w)\ *vt* **1** *archaic* **:** UNDERVALUE, DEPRECIATE **2 :** to consider of little value

2disvalue *n* **1 :** DISREGARD, DISESTEEM **2 :** a negative value

di·syl·la·ble \'dī-ˌsil-ə-bəl, (ˈ)dī-'sil-; 'dis-ˌil-, (ˈ)dis-'(s)il-\ *n* [part trans. of MF *dissilabe,* fr. L *disyllabus* having two syllables, fr. Gk *disyllabos,* fr. *di-* + *syllabē* syllable] **:** a linguistic form consisting of two syllables — **di·syl·lab·ic** \ˌdī-sə-'lab-ik, ˌdis-(s)ə-\ *adj*

dit \'dit\ *n* [imit.] **:** a dot in radio or telegraphic code

1ditch \'dich\ *n* [ME *dich,* fr. OE *dīc* dike, ditch] **:** a long narrow excavation dug in the earth (as for defense, drainage, or irrigation)

2ditch *vt* **1 a :** to enclose with a ditch **b :** to dig a ditch in **2 a :** to cause (a train) to derail **b :** to drive (a car) into a ditch **c :** to make a forced landing of (an airplane) on water **3 :** to get rid of **:** DISCARD

ditch·dig·ger \-ˌdig-ər\ *n* **1 :** one that digs ditches **2 :** one employed at menial and usu. hard physical labor

ditch reed *n* **:** a tall No. American reed (*Phragmites communis*) with broad flat leaves

dite \'dīt\ *n* [alter. of *doit*] *dial* **:** MITE, BIT

1dith·er \'dit͟h-ər\ *vi* **dith·ered; dith·er·ing** \-(ə-)riŋ\ [ME *didderen*] **1 :** SHIVER, TREMBLE <the ~*ing* of grass —Wallace Stevens> **2 :** to act nervously or indecisively **:** VACILLATE — **dith·er·er** \-ər-ər\ *n*

2dither *n* **:** a highly nervous, excited, or agitated state **:** EXCITEMENT, CONFUSION — **dith·ery** \'dit͟h-ə-rē\ *adj*

dithi- *or* **dithio-** *comb form* [ISV *di-* + *thi-*] **:** containing two atoms of sulfur usu. in place of two oxygen atoms

di·thi·ol \(ˈ)dī-'thī-ˌōl, -ˌōl\ *adj* **:** containing two SH groups composed of sulfur and hydrogen

dith·y·ramb \'dith-i-ˌram(b)\ *n, pl* **-rambs** \-ˌramz\ [Gk *dithyrambos*] **1 :** a usu. short poem in an inspired wild irregular strain **2 :** a statement or writing in an exalted or enthusiastic vein — **dith·y·ram·bic** \ˌdith-i-'ram-bik\ *adj* — **dith·y·ram·bi·cal·ly** \-bi-k(ə-)lē\ *adv*

dit·ta·ny \'dit-ᵊn-ē\ *n, pl* **-nies** [ME *ditoyne,* fr. MF *ditayne,* fr. L *dictamnum,* fr. Gk *diktamnon*] **1 :** a pink-flowered herb (*Origanum dictamnus*) that is native to Crete **2 :** an American herb (*Conila origanoides*) of the mint family that has much-branched stems

1dit·to \'dit-(ˌ)ō\ *n, pl* **dittos** [It dial., pp. of It *dire* to say, fr. L *dicere* — more at DICTION] **1 :** a thing mentioned previously or above — used to avoid repeating a word; often symbolized by inverted commas or apostrophes **2 :** a ditto mark

2ditto *vt* **1 :** to repeat the action or statement of **2** [fr. *Ditto,* a trademark] **:** to copy (as printed matter) on a duplicator

3ditto *adv* **:** as before or aforesaid **:** in the same manner

4ditto *adj* **:** having the same characteristics **:** SIMILAR

dit·ty \'dit-ē\ *n, pl* **ditties** [ME *ditee,* fr. OF *ditié* poem, fr. pp. of *ditier* to compose, fr. L *dictare* to dictate, compose] **:** an esp. simple and unaffected song

dit·ty bag \'dit-ē-\ *n* **:** a bag used esp. by sailors to hold small articles of gear (as thread, needles, and tape)

ditty box *n* **:** a box used for the same purpose as a ditty bag

di·ure·sis \ˌdī-(y)ə-'rē-səs\ *n, pl* **di·ure·ses** \-ˌsēz\ [NL] **:** an increased excretion of urine

di·uret·ic \ˌdī-(y)ə-'ret-ik\ *adj* [ME, fr. MF or LL; MF *diuretique,* fr. LL *diureticus,* fr. Gk *diourētikos,* fr. *diourein* to urinate, fr. *dia-* + *ourein* to urinate — more at URINE] **:** tending to increase the flow of urine — **diuretic** *n* — **di·uret·i·cal·ly** \-i-k(ə-)lē\ *adv*

1di·ur·nal \dī-'ərn-ᵊl\ *adj* [ME, fr. L *diurnalis* — more at JOURNAL] **1 a :** recurring every day <~ task> **b :** having a daily cycle <~ tides> **2 a :** of, relating to, or occurring in the daytime <the city's ~ noises> **b :** opening during the day and closing at night <~ flowers> *syn* see DAILY — **di·ur·nal·ly** \-ᵊl-ē\ *adv*

2diurnal *n* **1** *archaic* **:** DAYBOOK, DIARY **2** *archaic* **:** JOURNAL

di·u·ron \'dī-(y)ə-ˌrän\ *n* [*di*chlor- + *urea* + *1-on*] **:** a persistent herbicide $C_9H_{10}Cl_2N_2O$ used esp. to control annual weeds

div *abbr* **1** divided **2** dividend **3** division **4** divorced

di·va \'dē-və\ *n, pl* **divas** *or* **di·ve** \-(ˌ)vā\ [It, lit., goddess, fr. L, fem. of *divus* divine, god — more at DEITY] **:** PRIMA DONNA 1

di·va·gate \'dī-və-ˌgāt, 'div-ə-\ *vi* **-gat·ed; -gat·ing** [LL *divagatus,* pp. of *divagari,* fr. L *dis-* + *vagari* to wander — more at VAGARY] **1 :** to wander about **2 :** DIVERGE — **di·va·ga·tion** \ˌdī-və-'gā-shən, ˌdiv-ə-\ *n*

di·va·lent \(ˈ)dī-'vā-lənt\ *adj* **:** BIVALENT

di·van \'dī-ˌvan, *esp in senses other than 3 also* di-'van, di-'vän, dī-'van\ *n* [Turk, fr. Per *dīwān* account book] **1 a :** the privy council of the Ottoman Empire **b :** COUNCIL **2 a :** a council chamber **b :** a smoking room **3 :** a large couch or sofa usu. without back or arms often designed for use as a bed **4 :** a collection of poems in Persian or Arabic usu. by one author

di·var·i·cate \dī-'var-ə-ˌkāt, də-\ *vi* **-cat·ed; -cat·ing** [L *divaricatus,* pp. of *divaricare,* fr. *dis-* + *varicare* to straddle — more at PREVARICATE] **:** to spread apart **:** branch off **:** DIVERGE

di·var·i·ca·tion \(ˌ)dī-ˌvar-ə-'kā-shən, də-\ *n* **1 :** the action, process, or fact of divaricating **2 :** a divergence of opinion

1dive \'dīv\ *vb* **dived** \'dīvd\ *or* **dove** \'dōv\; **dived; div·ing** [ME *diven, duven,* fr. OE *dȳfan* to dip & *dūfan* to dive; akin to OE *dyppan* to dip — more at DIP] *vi* **1 a :** to plunge into water headfirst; *specif* **:** to execute a dive **b :** SUBMERGE **2 a :** to descend or fall precipitously **b :** to plunge one's hand into something **c** *of an airplane* **:** to descend in a dive **3 a :** to plunge into some matter or activity **b :** LUNGE <*dived* for his legs> ~ *vt* **1 :** to thrust into something **2 :** to cause to descend ***syn*** see PLUNGE

2dive *n* **1 :** the act or an instance of diving: as **a** (1) **:** a plunge into water executed in a prescribed manner (2) **:** a submerging of a submarine (3) **:** a steep descent of an airplane at greater than the maximum horizontal speed **b :** a sharp decline **2 :** a disreputable bar **3 :** a faked knockout — usu. used in the phrase *take a dive* **4 :** an offensive play in football in which the ballcarrier plunges into the line for short yardage

dive–bomb \'dīv-ˌbäm\ *vt* **:** to bomb from an airplane by making a steep dive toward the target before releasing the bomb — **dive–bomb·er** *n*

div·er \'dī-vər\ *n* **1 :** one that dives **2 a :** a person who stays underwater for long periods by having air supplied from the surface or by carrying a supply of compressed air **b :** any of various diving birds; *esp* **:** LOON

di·verge \də-'vərj, dī-\ *vb* **di·verged; di·verg·ing** [ML *divergere,* fr. L *dis-* + *vergere* to incline — more at WRENCH] *vi* **1 a :** to move or extend in different directions from a common point **:** draw apart <*diverging* rays of light> **b :** to become or be different in character or form **:** differ in opinion **2 :** to turn aside from a path or course **:** DEVIATE **3 :** to be mathematically divergent ~ *vt* **:** DEFLECT ***syn*** see SWERVE

di·ver·gence \-'vər-jən(t)s\ *n* **1 a :** a drawing apart (as of lines extending from a common center) **b :** DIFFERENCE, DISAGREEMENT **c :** the acquisition of dissimilar characters by related organisms in unlike environments **2 :** a deviation from a course or standard **3 :** the state of being mathematically divergent

di·ver·gen·cy \-jən-sē\ *n, pl* **-cies :** DIVERGENCE

di·ver·gent \-jənt\ *adj* [L *divergent-, divergens,* prp. of *divergere*] **1 a :** diverging from each other **b :** differing from each other or from a standard **:** DEVIANT <the ~ interests of capital and labor> **2 :** of or relating to an infinite sequence that does not have a limit or to an infinite series whose partial sums do not have a limit **3 :** causing divergence of rays <a ~ lens> ***syn*** see DIFFERENT ***ant*** convergent — **di·ver·gent·ly** *adv*

di·vers \'dī-vərz\ *adj* [ME *divers, diverse*] **:** VARIOUS

di·verse \dī-'vərs, də-', 'dī-ˌ\ *adj* [ME *divers, diverse,* fr. OF & L; OF *divers,* fr. L *diversus,* fr. pp. of *divertere*] **1 :** differing from one another **:** UNLIKE **2 :** having various forms or qualities ***syn*** see DIFFERENT ***ant*** identical, selfsame — **di·verse·ly** *adv* — **di·verse·ness** *n*

di·ver·si·fy \də-'vər-sə-ˌfī, dī-\ *vb* **-fied; -fy·ing** *vt* **1 :** to make diverse **:** give variety to <~ a course of study> **2 :** to balance (as an investment portfolio) defensively by dividing funds among securities of different industries or of different classes (as common stocks and bonds) **3 :** to increase the variety of the products of ~ *vi* **1 :** to produce variety **2 :** to engage in varied operations — **di·ver·si·fi·ca·tion** \-ˌver-sə-fə-'kā-shən\ *n* — **di·ver·si·fi·er** \-'vər-sə-ˌfī(-ə)r\ *n*

di·ver·sion \də-'vər-zhən, dī-, -shən\ *n* **1 :** the act or an instance of diverting from a course, activity, or use **:** DEVIATION **2 :** something that diverts or amuses **:** PASTIME **3 :** an attack or feint that draws the attention and force of an enemy from the point of the principal operation — **di·ver·sion·ary** \-zhə-ˌner-ē, -shə-\ *adj*

di·ver·sion·ist \-zhə-nəst, -shə-\ *n* **1 :** one characterized by political deviation **2 :** one engaged in diversionary activities

di·ver·si·ty \də-'vər-sət-ē, dī-\ *n, pl* **-ties 1 :** the condition of being different or having differences **2 :** an instance or a point of difference

di·vert \də-'vərt, dī-\ *vb* [ME *diverten,* fr. MF & L; MF *divertir,* fr. L *divertere* to turn in opposite directions, fr. *dis-* + *vertere* to turn — more at WORTH] *vi* **:** to turn aside **:** DEVIATE <was trained as a doctor but ~*ed* to diplomacy> ~ *vt* **1 a :** to turn from one course or use to another **:** DEFLECT **b :** DISTRACT **2 :** to give pleasure to esp. by distracting the attention from what burdens or distresses ***syn*** see AMUSE

di·ver·tic·u·li·tis \ˌdī-vər-ˌtik-yə-'līt-əs\ *n* **:** inflammation of a diverticulum

di·ver·tic·u·lo·sis \-'lō-səs\ *n* **:** an intestinal disorder characterized by the presence of many diverticula

di·ver·tic·u·lum \ˌdī-vər-'tik-yə-ləm\ *n, pl* **-la** \-lə\ [NL, fr. L, bypath, prob. alter. of *deverticulum,* fr. *devertere* to turn aside, fr. *de-* + *vertere*] **1 :** a pocket or closed branch opening off a main passage **2 :** an abnormal pouch or sac opening from a hollow organ (as the intestine or bladder)

di·ver·ti·men·to \di-ˌvərt-ə-'ment-(ˌ)ō, -ˌvert-\ *n, pl* **-men·ti** \-'ment-(ˌ)ē\ *or* **-mentos** [It, lit., diversion, fr. *divertire* to divert, amuse, fr. F *divertir*] **1 :** an instrumental chamber work in several movements **2 :** DIVERTISSEMENT 1

di·ver·tisse·ment \di-'vərt-əs-mənt, -əz-, *F* dē-ver-tē-smäⁿ\ *n, pl* **divertissements** \-mən(t)s, -smäⁿ(z)\ [F, lit., diversion, fr. *divertiss-* (stem of *divertir*)] **1 :** a ballet suite used as an interlude **2 :** DIVERTIMENTO 1 **3 :** DIVERSION, ENTERTAINMENT

Di·ves \'dī-(ˌ)vēz\ *n* [ME, fr. L, rich, rich man; misunderstood as a proper name in Lk 16:19] **:** a rich man

di·vest \dī-'vest, də-\ *vt* [alter. of *devest*] **1 a :** to undress or strip esp. of clothing, ornament, or equipment **b :** to deprive or dispossess esp. of property, authority, or title **c :** RID, FREE **2 :** to take away from a person — **di·vest·ment** \-'ves(t)-mənt\ *n*

1di·vide \də-'vīd\ *vb* **di·vid·ed; di·vid·ing** [ME *dividen,* fr. L *dividere,* fr. *dis-* + *-videre* to separate — more at WIDOW] *vt* **1 a :** to separate into two or more parts, areas, or groups **b :** to separate into classes, categories, or divisions **c :** CLEAVE, PART **2 a :** to separate into portions and give out in shares **:** DISTRIBUTE **b :** to possess, enjoy, or make use of in common **c :** APPORTION **3 a :** to cause to be separate, distinct, or apart from one another **b :** to separate into opposing sides or parties **c :** to cause (a parliamentary body) to vote by division **4 a :** to mark divisions on **:** GRADUATE <~ a sextant> **b** (1) **:** to subject (a number or quantity) to the operation of finding how many times it contains another number or quantity <~ 42 by 14> (2) **:** to use as a divisor — used with *into* <~ 14 into 42> (3) **:** to locate one or more points on (a line or its extension) ~ *vi* **1 :** to perform mathematical division **2 a** (1) **:** to become separated into parts (2) **:** to branch out **b :** to become separated or disunited esp. in opinion or interest **c :** to vote by division ***syn* 1** see SEPARATE ***ant*** unite **2** see DISTRIBUTE — **di·vid·able** \-'vīd-ə-bəl\ *adj*

2divide *n* **1 :** an act of dividing **2 a :** a dividing ridge between drainage areas **:** WATERSHED **b :** a point or line of division

di·vid·ed *adj* **1 a :** separated into parts or pieces **b** *of a leaf* **:** cut into distinct parts by incisions extending to the base or to the midrib **c :** having the opposing streams of traffic separated (as by a median strip) <a ~ highway> **2 a :** disagreeing with each other **:** DISUNITED **b :** directed or moved toward conflicting interests, states, or objects **3 :** separated by distance <familiar objects from which she had never dreamed of being ~ —James Joyce>

div·i·dend \'div-ə-ˌdend, -əd-ənd\ *n* [ME *divident,* fr. L *dividendus,* gerundive of *dividere*] **1 :** an individual share of something distributed: as **a :** a share in a pro rata distribution (as of profits) to stockholders **b :** a share of surplus allocated to a policyholder in a participating insurance policy **2 :** BONUS **3 a :** a number to be divided **b :** a sum or fund to be divided and distributed

di·vid·er \də-'vīd-ər\ *n* **1 :** one that divides **2** *pl* **:** an instrument for measuring or marking (as in dividing lines and transferring dimensions) **3 :** something serving as a partition between separate spaces within a larger area

di·vi–di·vi \ˌdē-vē-'dē-vē, ˌdiv-ē-'div-ē\ *n* [Sp *dividivi* of Cariban origin; akin to Cumanagoto *diwidiwi* divi-divi] **:** a small leguminous tree (*Caesalpinia coriaria*) of tropical America with twisted astringent pods that contain a large proportion of tannin

div·i·na·tion \ˌdiv-ə-'nā-shən\ *n* [ME *divinacioun,* fr. L *divination-, divinatio,* fr. *divinatus,* pp. of *divinare*] **1 :** the art or practice that seeks to foresee or foretell future events or discover hidden knowledge usu. by the interpretation of omens or by the aid of supernatural powers **2 :** unusual insight **:** intuitive perception — **di·vi·na·to·ry** \də-'vin-ə-ˌtōr-ē, də-'vī-nə-, 'div-ə-nə-, -ˌtȯr-\ *adj*

1di·vine \də-'vīn\ *adj* **di·vin·er; -est** [ME *divin,* fr. MF, fr. L *divinus,* fr. *divus* god — more at DEITY] **1 a :** of, relating to, or proceeding directly from God or a god <the ~ right of kings> **b :** being a deity <the ~ Savior> **c :** directed to a deity <~ worship> **2 a :** supremely good **:** SUPERB <her pies were simply ~> **b :** HEAVENLY, GODLIKE — **di·vine·ly** *adv*

2divine *n* [ME, fr. ML *divinus,* fr. L, soothsayer, fr. *divinus,* adj.] **1 :** CLERGYMAN **2 :** THEOLOGIAN

3divine *vb* **di·vined; di·vin·ing** [ME *divinen,* fr. MF & L; MF *diviner,* fr. L *divinare,* fr. *divinus,* n.] *vt* **1 :** to discover intuitively **:** INFER **2 :** to discover or locate (as water) by means of a divining rod ~ *vi* **1 :** to practice divination **:** PROPHESY **2 :** to perceive intuitively ***syn*** see FORESEE

Divine Liturgy *n* **:** the Eastern Orthodox eucharistic rite

Divine Office *n* **:** the office for the canonical hours of prayer that priests and religious say daily

di·vin·er \də-'vī-nər\ *n* **1 :** one that practices divination **:** SOOTHSAYER **2 :** one that seeks to discover the location of water or minerals underground with the aid of a divining rod

divine right *n* **:** the right of a sovereign to rule as set forth by the theory of government that holds that a monarch receives his right to rule directly from God and not from the people

divine service *n* **:** a service of Christian worship; *specif* **:** such a service that is not sacramental in character

diving bell *n* **:** a diving apparatus consisting of a container open only at the bottom and supplied with compressed air by a hose

diving duck *n* **:** any of various ducks (as a bufflehead) that frequent deep waters and obtain their food by diving

diving suit *n* **:** a waterproof suit with a helmet that is supplied with air pumped through a tube

divining rod *n* **:** a forked rod believed to indicate the presence of water or minerals by dipping downward when held over a vein

di·vin·i·ty \də-'vin-ət-ē\ *n, pl* **-ties 1 :** the quality or state of being divine **2** *often cap* **:** a divine being: as **a :** GOD 1 **b** (1) **:** GOD 2 (2) **:** GODDESS **3 :** THEOLOGY **4 :** fudge made of whipped egg whites, sugar, and nuts

divinity school *n* **:** a professional school having a religious curriculum esp. for ministerial candidates

di·vis·i·bil·i·ty \də-ˌviz-ə-'bil-ət-ē\ *n* **:** the state of being divisible

di·vis·i·ble \də-'viz-ə-bəl\ *adj* **:** capable of being divided

di·vi·sion \də-'vizh-ən\ *n* [ME, fr. MF, fr. L *division-, divisio,* fr. *divisus,* pp. of *dividere* to divide] **1 a :** the act or process of dividing **:** the state of being divided **b :** the act, process, or an instance of distributing among a number **:** DISTRIBUTION **c** *obs* **:** a method of arranging or disposing (as troops) **2 :** one of the parts, sections, or groupings into which a whole is divided or is divisible **3 a :** a major military unit that contains the necessary tactical and administrative services to function as a self-contained unit capable of independent action **b :** a military unit made up normally of five battle groups **c** (1) **:** the basic unit of men for administration aboard ship and ashore (2) **:** a tactical subdivision of a squadron of ships **d :** a unit of the U. S. Air Force higher than a wing and lower than an air force **4 a :** a portion of a territorial unit marked off for a particular purpose (as administrative or judicial functions) **b :** an administrative or operating unit of a governmental, business, or educational organization **5 :** a group of organisms forming part of a larger group; *specif* **:** a primary category of the plant kingdom **6 :** competitive class or category (as in boxing or wrestling) **7 a :** something that divides, separates, or marks off **b :** the act, process, or an instance of separating or keeping apart **:** SEPARATION **8 :** the condition or an instance of being divided in opinion or interest **:** DISAGREEMENT, DISUNITY <exploited the ~*s* between the two countries> **9 :** the physical separation into different lobbies of the members of a

parliamentary body voting for and against a question **10 :** the mathematical operation of dividing **11 :** plant propagation by dividing parts and planting segments capable of producing roots and shoots ***syn*** see PART — **di·vi·sion·al** \-'vizh-nəl, -ən-ᵊl\ *adj*
di·vi·sion·ism \'vizh-ə-ˌniz-əm\ *n, often cap* : POINTILLISM — **di·vi·sion·ist** \-'vizh-(ə-)nəst\ *n or adj*
division of labor : the breakdown of labor into its components and their distribution among different persons, groups, or machines to increase productive efficiency
division sign *n* **1 :** the symbol ÷ used to indicate division **2 :** a diagonal / used to indicate a fraction
di·vi·sive \də-'vī-siv *also* -'vis-iv *or* -'viz-iv *or* -'vī-ziv\ *adj* : creating disunity or dissension — **di·vi·sive·ly** *adv* — **di·vi·sive·ness** *n*
di·vi·sor \də-'vī-zər\ *n* : the number by which a dividend is divided
[1]di·vorce \də-'vō(ə)rs, -'vȯ(ə)rs *also* dī-\ *n* [ME *divorse,* fr. MF, fr. L *divortium,* fr. *divertere, divortere* to divert, to leave one's husband] **1 :** a legal dissolution of a marriage **2 :** SEPARATION, SEVERANCE
[2]divorce *vt* **di·vorced; di·vorc·ing** **1 a :** to end marriage with (one's spouse) by divorce **b :** to dissolve the marriage contract between **2 :** to terminate an existing relationship or union : SEPARATE <~ church from state> ***syn*** see SEPARATE
di·vor·cée \də-ˌvōr-'sā, -ˌvȯr-, -'sē, -'vōr-ˌ, -'vȯr-ˌ\ *n* [F, fr. fem. of *divorcé,* pp. of *divorcer* to divorce, fr. MF *divorse*] : a divorced woman
di·vorce·ment \də-'vōr-smənt, -'vȯr- *also* dī-\ *n* : DIVORCE 2
div·ot \'div-ət\ *n* [origin unknown] **1** *Scot* : a square of turf or sod **2 :** a piece of turf dug from a golf fairway in making a shot
di·vulge \də-'vəlj, dī-\ *vt* **di·vulged; di·vulg·ing** [ME *divulgen,* fr. L *divulgare,* fr. *dis-* + *vulgare* to make known] **1** *archaic* : to make public : PROCLAIM **2 :** to make known (as a confidence or secret) ***syn*** see REVEAL — **di·vul·gence** \-'vəl-jən(t)s\ *n*
di·vul·sion \dī-'vəl-shən\ *n* [L *divulsion-, divulsio,* fr. *divulsus,* pp. of *divellere* to tear apart, fr. *dis-* + *vellere* to pluck — more at VULNERABLE] : a tearing apart
div·vy \'div-ē\ *vt* **div·vied; div·vy·ing** [by shortening & alter. fr. *divide*] : DIVIDE, SHARE — often used with *up* <*divvied* up the candy>
Dix·ie \'dik-sē\ *n* [name for the Southern states in the song *Dixie* (1859) by Daniel D. Emmett] : the Southern states of the U.S.
Dix·ie·crat \-ˌkrat\ *n* : a dissident southern Democrat; *specif* : a supporter of a 1948 presidential ticket opposing the civil rights stand of the Democrats — **Dix·ie·crat·ic** \ˌdik-sē-'krat-ik\ *adj*
dix·ie·land \-ˌland\ *n* [prob. fr. the *Original Dixieland Jazz Band*] : jazz music in duple time usu. played by a small band and characterized by ensemble and solo improvisation
di·zen \'dīz-ᵊn, 'diz-ᵊn\ *vt* [earlier *disen* to dress a distaff with flax, fr. MD] *archaic* : BEDIZEN
di·zy·got·ic \ˌdī-zī-'gät-ik\ *also* **di·zy·gous** \(ˈ)dī-'zī-gəs\ *adj* [*di-* + *zygotic, -zygous*] *of twins* : FRATERNAL
diz·zi·ness \'diz-ē-nəs\ *n* : the condition of being dizzy : VERTIGO
[1]diz·zy \'diz-ē\ *adj* **diz·zi·er; -est** [ME *disy,* fr. OE *dysig* stupid; akin to OHG *tusig* stupid, L *furere* to rage — more at DUST] **1 :** FOOLISH, SILLY **2 a :** having a whirling sensation in the head with a tendency to fall **b :** mentally confused **3 a :** causing giddiness or mental confusion **b :** caused by or marked by giddiness **c :** extremely rapid — **diz·zi·ly** \'diz-ə-lē\ *adv*
[2]dizzy *vt* **diz·zied; diz·zy·ing** **1 :** to make dizzy or giddy **2 :** BEWILDER <prospects so brilliant as to ~ the mind> — **diz·zy·ing·ly** \-ē-iŋ-lē\ *adv*
DJ *abbr* **1** disc jockey **2** district judge **3** doctor of jurisprudence **4** dust jacket
djel·la·ba *also* **djel·la·bah** \jə-'läb-ə\ *n* [F *djellaba,* fr. Ar *jallabah*] : a long loose garment with full sleeves and a hood
DJIA *abbr* Dow-Jones Industrial Average
djin *or* **djinn** \'jin\ *or* **djin·ni** *var of* JINN
dk *abbr* **1** dark **2** deck **3** dock
dkg *abbr* dekagram
dkl *abbr* dekaliter
dkm *abbr* dekameter
dks *abbr* dekastere
dl *abbr* deciliter
dl- \(ˈ)dē-'el, 'dē-ˌ\ *prefix* **1** *also* **d,l-** : consisting of equal amounts of the dextro and levo forms of a specified compound <*dl*-tartaric acid> **2 :** consisting of equal amounts of the D- and L- forms of a specified compound <DL-fructose>
D layer *n* : a layer that may exist within the D region of the ionosphere; *also* : D REGION
DLitt *or* **DLit** *abbr* [L *doctor litterarum*] doctor of letters; doctor of literature
DLO *abbr* **1** dead letter office **2** dispatch loading only
DLS *abbr* doctor of library science
dm *abbr* decimeter
DM *abbr* deutsche mark
DMD *abbr* [NL *dentariae medicinae doctor*] doctor of dental medicine
DML *abbr* doctor of modern languages
DMn *abbr* doctor of ministry
DMSO \ˌdē-ˌem-ˌes-'ō\ *n* : DIMETHYLSULFOXIDE
DMZ *abbr* demilitarized zone
dn *abbr* down
DNA \ˌdē-ˌen-'ā\ *n* [*d*eoxyribo*n*ucleic *a*cid] : any of various nucleic acids that are localized esp. in cell nuclei, are the molecular basis of heredity in many organisms, and are constructed of a double helix held together by hydrogen bonds between purine and pyrimidine bases which project inward from two chains containing alternate links of deoxyribose and phosphate
DN·ase \(ˈ)dē-'en-ˌās, -ˌāz\ *also* **DNA·ase** \(ˌ)dē-ˌen-'ā-ˌās, -ˌāz\ *n* : DEOXYRIBONUCLEASE
DNB *abbr* Dictionary of National Biography
[1]do \(ˈ)dü, də(-w)\ *vb* **did** \(ˈ)did, dəd\; **done** \'dən\; **do·ing** \'dü-iŋ\; **does** \(ˈ)dəz\ [ME *don,* fr. OE *dōn;* akin to OHG *tuon* to do, L *-dere* to put, *facere* to make, do, Gk *tithenai* to place, set] *vt* **1 :** to bring to pass : carry out **2 :** PUT — used chiefly in *do to death* **3 a :** PERFORM, EXECUTE <~ some work> <*did* his duty> **b :** COMMIT <crimes *done* deliberately> **4 a :** to bring about : EFFECT <sleep will ~ you good> **b :** to give freely : PAY <~ honor to his memory> **5 :** to bring to an end : FINISH — used in the past participle <the job is finally *done*> **6 :** to put forth : EXERT <*did* his best to win the race> **7 :** to wear out esp. by physical exertion : EXHAUST <at the end of the race the boys were pretty well *done*> **8 :** to bring into existence : PRODUCE <~ a biography on the general> **9 :** to play the part of <*did* the main character in several movies> **10 :** to treat unfairly; *esp* : CHEAT <*did* him out of his inheritance> **11 :** to treat or deal with in any way typically with the sense of preparation or with that of care or attention: **a (1) :** to put in order : CLEAN <was ~*ing* the kitchen when the phone rang> **(2) :** to make ready for use : WASH <*did* the dishes right after supper> **b :** COOK <likes his steak *done* rare> **c :** SET, ARRANGE <had her hair *done* in a style he didn't like> **d :** to apply cosmetics to <took half an hour to ~ her face> **e :** DECORATE, FURNISH <*did* the living room in Early American> **12 a :** to work at esp. as a vocation <what to ~ after college> **b :** to prepare or work out esp. by studying <~*ing* his homework> **13 a :** to pass over (as distance) : TRAVERSE **b :** to travel at a speed of <~*ing* 80 on the turnpike> **14 :** TOUR <~*ing* 12 countries in 12 days> **15 :** to serve out (as a term) in prison **16 :** to serve the needs of : SUIT <worms will ~ us for bait> **17 :** to approve esp. by custom, opinion, or propriety <you oughtn't to say a thing like that . . . it's not *done* —Dorothy Sayers> **18** — used as a substitute verb to avoid repetition <if you must make such a racket, ~ it somewhere else> ~ *vi* **1 :** ACT, BEHAVE <~ as I say> **2 a :** to get along : FARE <~ well in school> **b :** to carry on business or affairs : MANAGE <we can ~ without your help> **c :** to make good use <~ with a cup of coffee> **3 :** to take place : HAPPEN <what's ~*ing* across the street> **4 :** to come to or make an end : FINISH — used in the past participle **5 :** to be active or busy <let us then be up and ~*ing* —H. W. Longfellow> **6 :** to be adequate or sufficient : SERVE <half of that will ~> **7 :** to be fitting : conform to custom or propriety <won't ~ to be late> **8** — used as a substitute verb to avoid repetition <wanted to run and play as children ~> **9** — used in the imperative after an imperative to add emphasis <be quiet ~> ~ *verbal auxiliary* **1 a** — used with the infinitive without *to* to form present and past tenses in legal and parliamentary language <~ hereby bequeath> and in poetry <give what she *did* crave —Shak.> **b** — used with the infinitive without *to* to form present and past tenses in declarative sentences with inverted word order <fervently ~ we pray —Abraham Lincoln>, in interrogative sentences <*did* you hear that>, and in negative sentences <we *don't* know> <*don't* go> **2** — used with the infinitive without *to* to form present and past tenses expressing emphasis <I ~ say> <~ be careful> — **do away with 1 :** to put an end to : ABOLISH **2 :** to put to death : KILL — **do by :** to deal with : TREAT — **do for 1 :** to attend to the wants and needs of : take care of <*did for* her while she was sick> **2 :** to bring about the death or ruin of — **do one's thing :** to do what is personally satisfying — **do proud :** to give cause for pride or gratification — **to do :** necessary to be done <ten thousand times I've done my best and all's *to do* again —A. E. Housman>

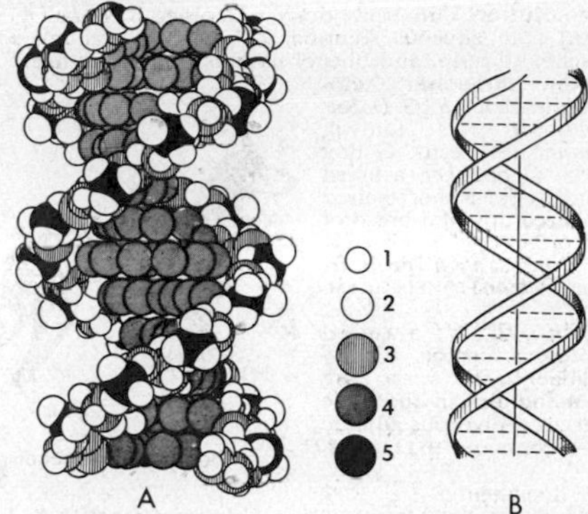

DNA: *A* molecular model, *1* hydrogen, *2* oxygen, *3* carbon in the helical phosphate ester chains, *4* carbon and nitrogen in the cross-linked purine and pyrimidine bases, *5* phosphorus; *B* double helix

[2]do \'dü\ *n, pl* **dos** *or* **do's** \'düz\ **1** *chiefly dial* : FUSS, ADO **2** *archaic* : DEED, DUTY **3** *chiefly Brit* **a :** a festive get-together : AFFAIR, PARTY **b :** BATTLE **4 :** a command or entreaty to do something <consider all the ~*s* and don'ts of the problem> **5** *Brit* : CHEAT, SWINDLE
[3]do \'dō\ *n* [It] : the 1st tone of the diatonic scale in solmization
[4]do *abbr* ditto
DO *abbr* **1** defense order **2** doctor of osteopathy
DOA *abbr* dead on arrival
do·able \'dü-ə-bəl\ *adj* : capable of being done : PRACTICABLE
DOB *abbr* date of birth
dob·bin \'däb-ən\ *n* [*Dobbin,* nickname for *Robert*] **1 :** a farm horse **2 :** a quiet plodding horse

Do·bell's solution \'dō-ˌbelz-, dō-ˌ\ *n* [Horace B. *Dobell* †1917 E physician] : an aqueous solution of borate of sodium, sodium bicarbonate, glycerin, and phenol used as a nose or throat spray

Do·ber·man pin·scher \ˌdō-bər-mən-'pin-chər\ *n* [G *Dobermann-pinscher,* fr. Ludwig *Dobermann,* 19th cent. G dog breeder + G *pinscher,* a breed of hunting dog] : a short-haired medium-sized dog of a breed of German origin

Doberman pinscher

dob·son \'däb-sən\ *n* [prob. fr. the name *Dobson*] : HELLGRAMMITE

dob·son·fly \-ˌflī\ *n* : a winged megalopterous insect (family Corydalidae) with very long slender mandibles in the male and a large carnivorous aquatic larva — compare HELLGRAMMITE

doc *abbr* document

do·cent \'dōs-ᵊnt, dō(t)-'sent\ *n* [obs. G (now *dozent*), fr. L *docent-, docens,* prp. of *docēre*] **1 :** a college or university teacher or lecturer **2 :** a person who conducts groups through a museum or art gallery

do·ce·tic \dō-'sēt-ik, -'set-\ *adj, often cap* [Gk *Dokētai* Docetists, fr. *dokein* to seem — more at DECENT] : of or relating to Docetism or the Docetists

Do·ce·tism \dō-'sēt-ˌiz-əm, 'dō-sə-ˌtiz-\ *n* : a belief opposed as heresy in early Christianity that Christ only seemed to have a human body and to suffer and die on the cross — **Do·ce·tist** \-'sēt-əst, -sət-əst\ *n*

doch–an–dor·rach \ˌdäk-ən-'dȯr-ək\ *or* **doch–an–dor·ris** \-'dȯr-əs\ *n* [ScGael & IrGael *deoch an doruis,* lit., drink of the door] *Scot & Irish* : a parting drink : STIRRUP CUP

doc·ile \'däs-əl *also* -ˌīl, *esp Brit* 'dō-ˌsīl\ *adj* [L *docilis,* fr. *docēre* to teach; akin to L *decēre* to be fitting — more at DECENT] **1 :** easily taught : TEACHABLE **2 :** easily led or managed : TRACTABLE ***syn*** see OBEDIENT ***ant*** indocile, unruly, ungovernable — **doc·ile·ly** \'däs-ə(l)-lē\ *adv* — **do·cil·i·ty** \dä-'sil-ət-ē, dō-\ *n*

[1]dock \'däk\ *n* [ME, fr. OE *docce;* akin to MD *docke* dock, ScGael *dogha* burdock] **1 :** any of a genus (*Rumex*) of the buckwheat family of coarse weedy plants that have long taproots and are used as potherbs and in folk medicine **2 :** any of several usu. broad-leaved weedy plants

[2]dock *n* [ME *dok,* fr. OE *-docca* (as in *fingirdocca* finger muscle); akin to OHG *tocka* doll, ON *dokka* bundle] **1 :** the solid part of an animal's tail as distinguished from the hair **2 :** the cropped tail of an animal after clipping the hair or cropping the end

[3]dock *vt* **1 a :** to cut off the end of a body part of; *specif* **:** to remove part of the tail of **b :** to cut (as ears or a tail) short **2 a :** to take away a part of : ABRIDGE **b :** to subject (as wages) to a deduction **3 :** to deprive of a benefit ordinarily due esp. as a penalty for a fault <~*ed* for tardiness>

[4]dock *n* [prob. fr. MD *docke* dock, ditch, fr. L *duction-, ductio* act of leading — more at DOUCHE] **1 :** a usu. artificial basin or enclosure for the reception of ships that is equipped with means for controlling the water height **2 :** the waterway extending between two piers for the reception of ships **3 :** a place (as a wharf or platform) for the loading or unloading of materials **4 :** scaffolding for the inspection and repair of aircraft; *broadly* : HANGAR

[5]dock *vt* **1 :** to haul or guide into a dock **2 :** to join (as two spacecraft) mechanically while in space ~ *vi* **1 :** to come into dock **2 :** to become docked

[6]dock *n* [Flem *docke* cage] : the place in a criminal court where a prisoner stands or sits during trial — **in the dock :** on trial <soon found himself *in the dock* for robbery>

dock·age \'däk-ij\ *n* **1 :** a charge for the use of a dock **2 :** docking facilities **3 :** the docking of ships

[1]dock·er \'däk-ər\ *n* : one that docks the tails of animals

[2]docker *n* : one connected with docks; *esp* : LONGSHOREMAN

[1]dock·et \'däk-ət\ *n* [ME *doggette*] **1 :** a brief written summary of a document : ABSTRACT **2 a** (1) **:** a formal abridged record of the proceedings in a legal action (2) **:** a register of such records **b** (1) **:** a list of legal causes to be tried (2) **:** a calendar of business matters to be acted on : AGENDA **3 :** an identifying statement about a document placed on its outer surface or cover

[2]docket *vt* **1 :** to inscribe (as a document) with an identifying statement **2 :** to make a brief abstract of (as a legal matter) and inscribe it in a list **3 :** to place on the docket for legal action

dock·hand \'däk-ˌhand\ *n* : LONGSHOREMAN

dock·land \-ˌland\ *n, Brit* : the part of a port occupied by docks; *also* : a residential section adjacent to docks

dock·side \-ˌsīd\ *n* : the shore or area adjacent to a dock

dock·work·er \-ˌwər-kər\ *n* : LONGSHOREMAN

dock·yard \-ˌyärd\ *n* **1 :** SHIPYARD **2** *Brit* : NAVY YARD

[1]doc·tor \'däk-tər\ *n* [ME *doctour* teacher, doctor, fr. MF & ML; MF, fr. ML *doctor,* fr. L, teacher, fr. *doctus,* pp. of *docēre* to teach — more at DOCILE] **1 a :** an eminent theologian declared a sound expounder of doctrine by the Roman Catholic Church — called also *doctor of the church* **b :** a learned or authoritative teacher **c :** a person who has earned one of the highest academic degrees (as a PhD) conferred by a university **d :** a person awarded an honorary doctorate (as an LLD or LittD) by a college or university **2 a :** one skilled or specializing in healing arts; *esp* : a physician, surgeon, dentist, or veterinarian licensed to practice his profession **b :** MEDICINE MAN **3 a :** material added (as to food) to produce a desired effect **b :** a blade (as of metal) for spreading a coating or scraping a surface **4 :** a usu. makeshift and emergency mechanical contrivance or attachment for remedying a difficulty **5 :** any of several brightly colored artificial flies — **doc·tor·al** \-t(ə-)rəl\ *adj* — **doc·tor·less** \-tər-ləs\ *adj* — **doc·tor·ship** \-ˌship\ *n*

[2]doctor *vb* **doc·tored; doc·tor·ing** \-t(ə-)riŋ\ *vt* **1 a :** to give medical treatment to **b :** to restore to good condition : REPAIR <~ an old clock> **2 a :** to adapt or modify for a desired end by alteration or special treatment <~*ed* the play to suit the audience> **b :** to alter deceptively <accused of ~*ing* the election returns> ~ *vi* **1 :** to practice medicine **2** *dial* : to take medicine

doc·tor·ate \'däk-t(ə-)rət\ *n* : the degree, title, or rank of a doctor

doctor book *n* : a book intended to supplement the knowledge of the individual in matters of home medication

[1]doc·tri·naire \ˌdäk-trə-'na(ə)r, -'ne(ə)r\ *n* [F, fr. *doctrine*] : one who attempts to put into effect an abstract doctrine or theory with little or no regard for practical difficulties

[2]doctrinaire *adj* : of, relating to, or characteristic of a doctrinaire : DOGMATIC ***syn*** see DICTATORIAL — **doc·tri·nair·ism** \-'na(ə)r-ˌiz-əm, -'ne(ə)r-\ *n*

doc·trin·al \'däk-trən-ᵊl, *esp Brit* däk-'trīn-\ *adj* : of, relating to, or preoccupied with doctrine — **doc·trin·al·ly** \-ᵊl-ē\ *adv*

doc·trine \'däk-trən\ *n* [ME, fr. MF & L; MF, fr. L *doctrina,* fr. *doctor*] **1** *archaic* : TEACHING, INSTRUCTION **2 a :** something that is taught **b :** a principle or position or the body of principles in a branch of knowledge or system of belief : DOGMA **c :** a principle of law established through past decisions **d :** a statement of fundamental government policy esp. in international relations

syn DOCTRINE, DOGMA, TENET *shared meaning element* : a principle accepted as valid and authoritative

doctrine of descent : a theory in biology: all animals and plants are direct descendants of previous animals or plants

[1]doc·u·ment \'däk-yə-mənt\ *n* [ME, fr. MF, fr. LL & L; LL *documentum* official paper, fr. L, lesson, proof, fr. *docēre* to teach — more at DOCILE] **1 a** *archaic* : PROOF, EVIDENCE **b :** an original or official paper relied on as the basis, proof, or support of something **2 a :** a writing conveying information **b :** a material substance (as a coin or stone) having on it a representation of the thoughts of men by means of some conventional mark or symbol **c :** DOCUMENTARY — **doc·u·men·tal** \ˌdäk-yə-'ment-ᵊl\ *adj*

[2]doc·u·ment \'däk-yə-ˌment\ *vt* **1 :** to furnish documentary evidence of **2 :** to furnish with documents **3 a :** to provide with factual or substantial support for statements made or a hypothesis proposed; *esp* : to equip with exact references to authoritative supporting information <the thesis was well ~*ed* with footnotes on every page> **b :** to construct or produce (as a movie or novel) with a high proportion of details closely reproducing authentic situations or events <his film ~*ed* the living conditions in the ghetto> **4 :** to furnish (a ship) with ship's papers as required by law for the manifesting of ownership and cargo — **doc·u·ment·able** \-ə-bəl, ˌdäk-yə-'\ *adj* — **doc·u·ment·er** \'däk-yə-ˌment-ər\ *n*

doc·u·men·tal·ist \ˌdäk-yə-'ment-ᵊl-əst\ *n* : a specialist in documentation

doc·u·men·tar·i·an \ˌdäk-yə-mən-'ter-ē-ən, -ˌmen-\ *n* [[2]*documentary*] : one who employs or advocates documentary presentation (as in photographic art or fiction)

doc·u·men·ta·rist \-'ment-ə-rəst\ *n* [[2]*documentary*] : DOCUMENTARIAN

[1]doc·u·men·ta·ry \ˌdäk-yə-'ment-ə-rē, -'men-trē\ *adj* **1 :** being or consisting of documents : contained or certified in writing <~ evidence> **2 :** of, relating to, or employing documentation in literature or art; *broadly* : FACTUAL, OBJECTIVE <a ~ film of the war> — **doc·u·men·tar·i·ly** \-mən-'ter-ə-lē, -ˌmen-\ *adv*

[2]documentary *n, pl* **-ries :** a documentary presentation (as a film or novel)

doc·u·men·ta·tion \ˌdäk-yə-mən-'tā-shən, -ˌmen-\ *n* **1 :** the act or an instance of furnishing or authenticating with documents **2 a :** the provision of documents in substantiation; *also* : documentary evidence **b** (1) **:** the use of historical documents (2) **:** conformity to historical or objective facts (3) **:** the provision of footnotes, appendices, or addenda referring to or containing documentary evidence **3 :** INFORMATION SCIENCE — **doc·u·men·ta·tion·al** \-shnəl, -shən-ᵊl\ *adj*

DOD *abbr* Department of Defense

[1]dod·der \'däd-ər\ *n* [ME *doder;* akin to OE *dydring* yolk, Norw *dudra* to tremble, L *fumus* smoke — more at FUME] : any of a genus (*Cuscuta*) of dicotyledonous leafless elongated wiry herbs that are deficient in chlorophyll and are parasitic on other plants

[2]dodder *vi* **dod·dered; dod·der·ing** \'däd-(ə-)riŋ\ [ME *dadiren*] **1 :** to tremble or shake from weakness or age **2 :** to progress feebly and unsteadily <an old man ~*ing* down the walk> — **dod·der·er** \-ər-ər\ *n*

dod·dered \'däd-ərd\ *adj* [prob. alter. of *dodded,* fr. pp. of E dial. *dod* to lop, fr. ME *dodden*] **1 :** deprived of branches through age or decay <a ~ oak> **2 :** INFIRM, ENFEEBLED

dod·der·ing \'däd-(ə-)riŋ\ *adj* : FOOLISH, SENILE <a ~ old man>

dod·dery \-(ə-)rē\ *adj* : DODDERED, DODDERING

dodeca- *or* **dodec-** *comb form* [L, fr. Gk *dōdeka-, dōdek-,* fr. *dōdeka, dyōdeka,* fr. *dyō, dyo* two + *deka* ten] : twelve <*dodecaphonic*>

do·deca·gon \dō-'dek-ə-ˌgän\ *n* [GK *dōdekagōnon,* fr. *dōdeka-* + *-gōnon* -gon] : a polygon of 12 angles and 12 sides

do·deca·he·dron \(ˌ)dō-ˌdek-ə-'hē-drən\ *n, pl* **-drons** *or* **-dra** \-drə\ [Gk *dōdekaedron,* fr. *dōdeka-* + *-edron* -hedron] : a solid having 12 plane faces — **do·deca·he·dral** \-drəl\ *adj*

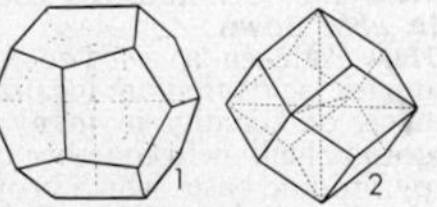

dodecahedrons: *1* pentagonal, *2* rhomboid

do·deca·phon·ic \(ˌ)dō-ˌdek-ə-'fän-ik\ *adj* [*dodeca-* + *phon-* + *-ic*] : TWELVE-TONE — **do·deca·phon·i·cal·ly** \-i-k(ə-)lē\ *adv* — **do·deca·pho·nist** \dō-'dek-ə-fə-nəst, -ˌfō-; ˌdōd-i-'kaf-ə-nəst\ *n* — **do·deca·pho·ny** \-nē\ *n*

[1]dodge \'däj\ *vb* **dodged; dodg·ing** [origin unknown] *vi* **1 :** to evade a responsibility or a duty esp. by trickery or deceit **2 a :** to move to and fro or from place to place usu. in an irregular course <*dodged* through the crowd> **b :** to make a sudden movement in a new direction (as to evade a blow) <*dodged* behind the door> ~ *vt* **1 :** to evade (as a duty) usu. indirectly and by trickery <*dodged* the draft by leaving the country> **2 a :** to evade by a sudden or repeated shift of position **b :** to avoid an encounter with **3 :** to reduce the intensity of (a portion of a photograph) by selectively shading during printing

²dodge *n* **1 :** an act of evading by sudden bodily movement **2 a :** an artful device to evade, deceive, or trick **b :** EXPEDIENT, SCHEME

dodge ball *n* **:** a game in which players stand in a circle and try to hit opponents within the circle with a large inflated ball

dodg·er \'däj-ər\ *n* **1 :** one that dodges; *esp* **:** one who uses tricky devices **2 :** a small leaflet **:** CIRCULAR **3 :** CORN DODGER

dodg·ery \'däj-(ə-)rē\ *n, pl* **-er·ies :** EVASION, TRICKERY

dodgy \'däj-ē\ *adj* **:** EVASIVE, TRICKY

do·do \'dōd-(ˌ)ō\ *n, pl* **dodoes** *or* **dodos** [Pg *doudo,* fr. *doudo* silly, stupid] **1 a :** an extinct heavy flightless bird (*Raphus cucullatus,* syn. *Didus ineptus*) related to the pigeons but larger than a turkey formerly present on the island of Mauritius **b :** an extinct bird of the island of Réunion that was similar to and apparently closely related to the dodo **2 a :** one hopelessly behind the times **b :** a stupid person

dodo 1a

doe \'dō\ *n, pl* **does** *or* **doe** [ME *do,* fr. OE *dā;* akin to G dial. *tē* doe] **:** the adult female fallow deer; *broadly* **:** the female esp. when adult of any of various mammals of which the male is called buck

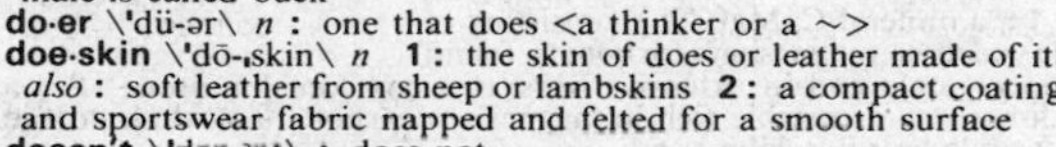

do·er \'dü-ər\ *n* **:** one that does <a thinker or a ~>

doe·skin \'dō-ˌskin\ *n* **1 :** the skin of does or leather made of it; *also* **:** soft leather from sheep or lambskins **2 :** a compact coating and sportswear fabric napped and felted for a smooth surface

doesn't \'dəz-ᵊnt\ **:** does not

do·est \'dü-əst\ *archaic pres 2d sing of* DO

do·eth \'dü-əth\ *archaic pres 3d sing of* DO

doff \'däf, 'dȯf\ *vt* [ME *doffen,* fr. *don* to do + *of* off] **1 :** to take off (one's clothes); *esp* **:** to take off or lift up (the hat) **2 :** to rid oneself of

¹dog \'dȯg\ *n, often attrib* [ME, fr. OE *docga*] **1 a :** a highly variable carnivorous domesticated mammal (*Canis familiaris*) prob. descended from the common wolf **b :** any of a family (Canidae, the dog family) of carnivores to which the dog belongs **c :** a male dog **2 a :** a worthless person **b :** FELLOW, CHAP <a lazy ~> **3 a :** any of various usu. simple mechanical devices for holding, gripping, or fastening that consist of a spike, rod, or bar **b :** ANDIRON **4 a :** SUN DOG **b :** FOGBOW **5 :** affected stylishness or dignity <liked to put on the ~> **6** *cap* **:** either of the constellations Canis Major or Canis Minor **7** *pl* **:** FEET **8 :** something inferior of its kind **9** *pl* **:** RUIN <go to the ~*s*> **10 a :** an investment (as a stock or bond) not worth its price **b :** a slow-moving or undesirable piece of merchandise **11 :** an unattractive woman or girl **12 :** a theatrical or musical flop **13 :** ¹HOT DOG — **dog·like** \'dȯ-ˌglīk\ *adj*

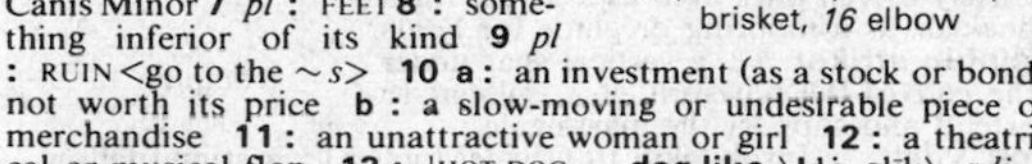

dog: *1* pastern, *2* chest, *3* flews, *4* muzzle, *5* stop, *6* occiput, *7* leather, *8* crest, *9* withers, *10* loin, *11* rump, *12* hock, *13* knee, *14* stifle, *15* brisket, *16* elbow

²dog *vt* **dogged; dog·ging 1 a :** to hunt or track like a hound **b :** to worry as if by dogs **:** HOUND **2 :** to fasten with a dog — **dog it :** to fail to do one's best **:** GOLDBRICK

³dog *adv* **:** EXTREMELY, UTTERLY <*dog*-tired>

⁴dog *adj* **1 :** CANINE **2 :** SPURIOUS; *esp* **:** unlike that used by native speakers or writers <~ Latin> <~ French>

dog·bane \'dȯg-ˌbān\ *n* **:** any of a genus (*Apocynum* of the family Apocynaceae, the dogbane family) comprising chiefly tropical and often poisonous plants with milky juice and usu. showy flowers

dog·ber·ry \-ˌber-ē\ *n* **:** any of several plants bearing unpalatable fruit: as **a :** a prickly wild gooseberry (*Ribes cynosbati*) **b :** a mountain ash (*Pyrus americana*) of the eastern U.S. and Canada

dog biscuit *n* **1 :** a hard dry cracker for dogs **2 :** a hard coarse cracker (as hardtack) for human consumption

dog·cart \'dȯg-ˌkärt\ *n* **1 :** a cart drawn by a dog **2 :** a light usu. one-horse two-wheeled carriage with two transverse seats set back to back

dog·catch·er \-ˌkach-ər, -ˌkech-\ *n* **:** a community official assigned to catch and dispose of stray dogs

dog collar *n* **1 :** a collar for a dog **2** *slang* **:** CLERICAL COLLAR **3 :** a wide flexible snug-fitting necklace

dog days *n pl* [fr. their being reckoned from the heliacal rising of the Dog Star (Sirius)] **1 :** the period between early July and early September when the hot sultry weather of summer usu. occurs in the northern hemisphere **2 :** a period of stagnation or inactivity

dog·dom \'dȯg-dəm\ *n* **:** the world of dogs or of dog fanciers <the elite of pure-bred ~ —W. R. Fletcher>

doge \'dōj\ *n* [It dial., fr. L *duc-, dux* leader — more at DUKE] **:** the chief magistrate in the republics of Venice and Genoa

dog–ear \'dȯ-ˌgi(ə)r\ *n* **:** the turned-down corner of a page esp. of a book — **dog–ear** *vt*

dog–eared \'dȯ-ˌgi(ə)rd\ *adj* **1 :** having dog-ears <a ~ book> **2 :** SHABBY, WORN

dog–eat–dog \ˌdȯ-ˌgēt-'dȯg\ *adj* **:** marked by ruthless self-interest <~ competition>

dog·face \'dȯg-ˌfās\ *n* **:** SOLDIER; *esp* **:** INFANTRYMAN

dog fennel *n* **1 :** a strong-scented European chamomile (*Anthemis cotula*) naturalized along roadsides in the U.S. **2 :** an annual composite weed (*Eupatorium capillifolium*) with dissected leaves and a lax inflorescence

dog·fight \'dȯg-ˌfīt\ *n* **1 :** a fight between dogs; *broadly* **:** a fiercely disputed contest **2 :** a fight between two or more fighter planes usu. at close quarters — **dogfight** *vi*

dog·fish \-ˌfish\ *n* **:** any of various small sharks (as of the families Squalidae, Carcharhinidae, and Scyliorhinidae) that often appear in schools near shore, are destructive to fish, and have livers valued for oil and flesh often made into fertilizer

dog·ged \'dȯ-gəd\ *adj* **:** stubbornly determined **:** TENACIOUS ***syn*** see OBSTINATE ***ant*** faltering — **dog·ged·ly** *adv* — **dog·ged·ness** *n*

¹dog·ger·el \'dȯg-(ə-)rəl, 'däg-\ *adj* [ME *dogerel*] **:** loosely styled and irregular in measure esp. for burlesque or comic effect; *also* **:** marked by triviality or inferior worth <~ lines of verse>

²doggerel *n* **1 :** doggerel verse **2 :** an example of doggerel verse

dog·gery \'dȯ-gə-rē\ *n, pl* **-ger·ies :** a cheap saloon **:** DIVE

dog·gie bag \'dȯ-gē-\ *n* [²*doggy;* fr. the presumption that such leftovers are intended for a pet dog] **:** a bag used for carrying home leftover food and esp. meat from a meal eaten at a restaurant

dog·gish \'dȯ-gish\ *adj* **1 :** CANINE **2 :** stylish in a showy way — **dog·gish·ly** *adv* — **dog·gish·ness** *n*

dog·go \'dȯ-(ˌ)gō\ *adv* [prob. fr. ¹*dog*] **:** in hiding — used chiefly in the phrase *to lie doggo*

¹dog·gone \'däg-'gän, 'dȯg-'gȯn\ *vb* **dog·goned; dog·gon·ing** [euphemism for *God damn*] **:** DAMN

²doggone *n* **:** DAMN

dog·goned *or* **dog·gone** \ˌdäg-ˌgän(d), ˌdȯg-ˌgȯn(d)\ *adj or adv* **:** DAMNED

¹dog·gy \'dȯ-gē\ *adj* **dog·gi·er; -est 1 :** resembling or suggestive of a dog <a ~ odor> **2 :** concerned with or fond of dogs <a book for ~ experts> **3 :** STYLISH, SHOWY

²dog·gy *or* **dog·gie** \'dȯ-gē\ *n, pl* **doggies 1 :** a small dog **2 —** used as a pet name or calling name for any dog

dog·house \'dȯg-ˌhau̇s\ *n* **:** a shelter for a dog — **in the doghouse :** in a state of disfavor

do·gie \'dō-gē\ *n* [origin unknown] *chiefly West* **:** a motherless calf in a range herd

dog in the manger [fr. the fable of the dog who prevented an ox from eating hay which he did not want himself] **:** a person who selfishly withholds from others something useless to himself

¹dog·leg \'dȯ-ˌgleg, -ˌgläg\ *n* **1 a :** something having an abrupt angle **b :** a sharp bend (as in a road) **2 :** a golf hole having an angled fairway

²dogleg *adj* **:** crooked or bent like a dog's hind leg

³dogleg *vi* **:** to proceed along a dogleg course <the single narrow street that ~*s* through town —Russ Leadabrand>

dog·ma \'dȯg-mə, 'däg-\ *n* [L *dogmat-, dogma,* fr. Gk, fr. *dokein* to seem — more at DECENT] **1 a :** something held as an established opinion; *esp* **:** a definite authoritative tenet **b :** a code of such tenets <pedagogical ~> **c :** a point of view or tenet put forth as authoritative without adequate grounds **2 :** a doctrine or body of doctrines concerning faith or morals formally stated and authoritatively proclaimed by a church ***syn*** see DOCTRINE

dog·mat·ic \dȯg-'mat-ik, däg-\ *adj* **1 :** characterized by or given to the use of dogmatism <a ~ critic> **2 :** of or relating to dogma ***syn*** see DICTATORIAL — **dog·mat·i·cal** \-i-kəl\ *adj* — **dog·mat·i·cal·ly** \-i-k(ə-)lē\ *adv* — **dog·mat·i·cal·ness** \-i-kəl-nəs\ *n*

dog·mat·ics \-iks\ *n pl but sing or pl in constr* **:** a branch of theology that seeks to interpret the dogmas of a religious faith

dogmatic theology *n* **:** DOGMATICS

dog·ma·tism \'dȯg-mə-ˌtiz-əm, 'däg-\ *n* **1 :** positiveness in assertion of opinion esp. when unwarranted or arrogant **2 :** a viewpoint or system of ideas based on insufficiently examined premises

dog·ma·tist \-mət-əst\ *n* **:** one who dogmatizes

dog·ma·tize \'dȯg-mə-ˌtīz, 'däg-\ *vb* **-tized; -tiz·ing** [F *dogmatiser,* fr. LL *dogmatizare,* fr. Gk *dogmatizein,* fr. *dogmat-, dogma*] *vi* **:** to speak or write dogmatically ~ *vt* **:** to state as a dogma or in a dogmatic manner — **dog·ma·ti·za·tion** \ˌdȯg-mət-ə-'zā-shən, ˌdäg-\ *n* — **dog·ma·tiz·er** *n*

dog·nap \'dȯg-ˌnap\ *vt* **-napped** *or* **-naped** \-ˌnapt\; **-nap·ping** *or* **-nap·ing** \-ˌnap-iŋ\ [¹*dog* + *-nap* (as in *kidnap*)] **:** to steal (a dog) often for the purpose of selling to a scientific laboratory — **dog·nap·per** *or* **dog·nap·er** *n*

do–good \'dü-ˌgu̇d\ *adj* **:** designed sometimes impracticably and too zealously toward bettering the conditions under which others live — **do–good·ism** \-ˌiz-əm\ *n*

do–good·er \-ər\ *n* **:** an earnest usu. impractical and often naive and ineffectual humanitarian or reformer

do–good·ing \-iŋ\ *n* **:** the activities of a do-gooder

dog paddle *n* **:** an elementary form of swimming in which the arms paddle in the water and the legs maintain a kicking motion — **dog–pad·dle** *vi*

dogs·body \'dȯgz-ˌbäd-ē\ *n* [Brit naval slang *dogsbody,* pudding made of peas, junior officer] *chiefly Brit* **:** one that performs menial tasks **:** DRUDGE

dog's chance *n* **:** a bare chance in one's favor <didn't have a *dog's chance*>

dog·sled \'dȯg-ˌsled\ *n* **:** a sled drawn by dogs

dog's life *n* **:** a miserable drab existence

Dog Star *n* **1 :** SIRIUS **2 :** PROCYON

dog tag *n* **1 :** a metal disk or plate on a dog collar bearing a license registration number **2 :** a military identification tag

dog·tooth \'dȯg-ˌtüth\ *n* **1 :** CANINE 1, EYETOOTH **2 :** an architectural ornament common in early English Gothic consisting usu. of four leaves radiating from a raised point at the center

dogtooth violet *n* **:** any of a genus (*Erythronium*) of small spring-flowering bulbous herbs of the lily family

1dog·trot \ˈdȯg-ˌträt\ *n* **1 :** a quick easy gait suggesting that of a dog **2** *South & Midland* **:** a roofed passage similar to a breezeway; *esp* **:** one connecting two parts of a cabin

2dogtrot *vi* **:** to move or progress at a dogtrot

dog·watch \ˈdȯ-ˌgwäch\ *n* **1 :** either of two watches of two hours on shipboard that extend from 4 to 6 and 6 to 8 p.m. **2 :** any of various night shifts; *esp* **:** the last shift

dog·wood \ˈdȯ-ˌgwu̇d\ *n* **:** any of a genus (*Cornus*)of trees and shrubs (family Cornaceae, the dogwood family) with heads of small flowers and often showy involucres

doi·ly \ˈdȯi-lē\ *n, pl* **doilies** [*Doily* or *Doyley fl* 1712 London draper] **1 :** a small napkin **2 :** a small often decorative mat

do in *vt* **1 a :** to bring about the defeat or destruction of **:** RUIN <the financial loss *did* him *in*> **b :** to bring about the death of **:** KILL <tried to *do* him *in* with a club> **c :** to wear out <walking all day nearly *did* us *in*> **2 :** CHEAT

do·ing \ˈdü-iŋ\ *n* **1 :** the act of performing or executing **:** ACTION <that will take a great deal of ~> **2** *pl* **a :** things that are done or that occur <everyday ~*s*> **b :** social activities

doit \ˈdȯit\ *n* [D *duit;* akin to ON *thveiti* small coin, *thveita* to hew] **1 :** an old Dutch coin equal to about ½ farthing **2 :** TRIFLE 1

do–it–yourself \ˌdü-ə-chər-ˈself\ *adj* **:** of, relating to, or designed for use by or as if by an amateur or hobbyist <~ tools> <~ car model kit> — **do–it–your·self·er** \-ˈsel-fər\ *n*

do·jo \ˈdō-(ˌ)jō\ *n, pl* **dojos** [Jap *dōjō,* fr. *dō* way, art + *-jō* ground] **:** a school for training in various arts of self-defense (as judo and karate)

dol *abbr* dollar

dol·ce \ˈdōl-(ˌ)chā\ *adj or adv* [It, lit., sweet, fr. L *dulcis* — more at DULCET] **:** SOFT, SMOOTH — used as a direction in music

dol·ce far nien·te \ˈdōl-chē-ˌfär-nē-ˈent-ē\ *n* [It, lit., sweet doing nothing] **:** pleasant relaxation in carefree idleness

dol·ce vi·ta \ˌdōl-chā-ˈvē-(ˌ)tä\ *n* [It, lit., sweet life] **:** a life of indolence and self-indulgence

dol·drums \ˈdōl-drəmz, ˈdäl-, ˈdȯl-\ *n pl* [prob. akin to OE *dol* foolish] **1 :** a spell of listlessness or despondency **:** BLUES **2 :** a part of the ocean near the equator abounding in calms, squalls, and light shifting winds **3 :** a state of inactivity, stagnation, or slump

1dole \ˈdōl\ *n* [ME, fr. OE *dāl* portion] **1** *archaic* **:** one's allotted share, portion, or destiny **2 a (1) :** a giving or distribution of food, money, or clothing to the needy **(2) :** a grant of government funds to the unemployed **b :** something distributed at intervals to the needy **c :** something portioned out and distributed usu. grudgingly or bit by bit ***syn*** see RATION

2dole *vt* **doled; dol·ing 1 :** to give or distribute as a charity **2 :** to give or deliver in small portions **:** PARCEL — used with *out* ***syn*** see DISTRIBUTE

3dole *n* [ME *dol,* fr. OF, fr. LL *dolus,* alter. of L *dolor*] *archaic* **:** GRIEF, SORROW

dole·ful \ˈdōl-fəl\ *adj* **1 :** causing grief or affliction <a ~ loss> **2 :** full of grief **:** CHEERLESS <a ~ face> **3 :** expressing grief **:** SAD <a ~ melody> — **dole·ful·ly** \-fə-lē\ *adv* — **dole·ful·ness** *n*

dol·er·ite \ˈdäl-ə-ˌrīt\ *n* [F *dolérite,* fr. Gk *doleros* deceitful, fr. *dolos* deceit; fr. its being easily mistaken for diorite — more at TALE] **1 :** any of various coarse basalts **2** *Brit* **:** DIABASE 3 **3 :** any of various dark igneous rocks whose constituents are not determinable megascopically — **dol·er·it·ic** \ˌdäl-ə-ˈrit-ik\ *adj*

dole·some \ˈdōl-səm\ *adj* **:** DOLEFUL

dolich- *or* **dolicho-** *comb form* [Gk, fr. *dolichos* — more at LONG] **:** long

dol·i·cho·ce·phal·ic \ˌdäl-i-kō-sə-ˈfal-ik\ *adj* [NL *dolichocephalus* dolichocephalic individual, fr. *dolich-* + *-cephalus* (fr. Gk *kephalē* head) — more at CEPHALIC] **:** having a relatively long head with cephalic index of less than 75 — **dol·i·cho·ceph·a·lism** \-ˈsef-ə-ˌliz-əm\ *n* — **dol·i·cho·ceph·a·ly** \-ˈsef-ə-lē\ *n*

dol·i·cho·cra·ni·al \-ˈkrā-nē-əl\ *also* **dol·i·cho·cra·nic** \-nik\ *adj* [ISV] **:** having a relatively long head with a cranial index of less than 75 — **dol·i·cho·cra·ny** \ˈdäl-i-kō-ˌkrā-nē\ *n*

doll \ˈdäl, ˈdȯl\ *n* [prob. fr. *Doll,* nickname for *Dorothy*] **1 :** a small-scale figure of a human being used esp. as a child's plaything **2 a (1) :** a pretty but often empty-headed young woman **(2) :** WOMAN **b :** DARLING, SWEETHEART **c :** an attractive person — **doll·ish** \-ish\ *adj* — **doll·ish·ly** *adv* — **doll·ish·ness** *n*

dol·lar \ˈdäl-ər\ *n, often attrib* [D or LG *daler,* fr. G *taler,* short for *joachimstaler,* fr. Sankt *Joachimsthal,* Bohemia, where talers were first made] **1 :** TALER **2 :** any of numerous coins patterned after the taler (as a Spanish peso) **3 a :** any of various basic monetary units (as in the U.S. and Canada) — see MONEY table **b :** a coin, note, or token representing one dollar

dollar averaging *n* **:** investment in a security at regular intervals of a uniform sum regardless of the price level in order to obtain an overall reduction in cost per unit — called also *dollar cost averaging*

dollar–a–year *adj* **:** compensated by a token salary usu. for government service <a ~ man>

dollar day *n* **:** a day on which a merchant makes special offerings of goods and services for one dollar; *broadly* **:** a day on which bargain prices in many lines are offered

dollar diplomacy *n* **1 :** diplomacy used by a country to promote its financial or commercial interests abroad **2 :** diplomacy that seeks to strengthen the power of a country or effect its purposes in foreign relations by the use of its financial resources

dollar gap *n* **:** the amount of additional dollar receipts required by a country to meet dollar obligations

dollar sign *n* **:** a mark $ placed before a number to indicate that it stands for dollars — called also *dollar mark*

doll·house \ˈdäl-ˌhau̇s, ˈdȯl-\ *n* **1 :** a child's small-scale toy house **2 :** a dwelling so small as to suggest resemblance to a house for dolls

dol·lop \ˈdäl-əp\ *n* [origin unknown] **1 a :** a lump or blob of a usu. semiliquid substance <a ~ of jelly> **b :** an unmeasured amount (as of hard liquor) **:** DASH <coffee laced with a ~ of brandy> **2 :** a small amount or admixture <prose without one ~ of sentimentality —Ann Currah>

doll up *vt* **1 :** to dress elegantly or extravagantly **2 :** to make more attractive (as by addition of decorative details)

1dol·ly \ˈdäl-ē, ˈdȯ-lē\ *n, pl* **dollies 1 :** DOLL **2 a :** a wooden-pronged instrument for beating and stirring clothes in the process of washing them in a tub **b :** a device turning on a vertical axis by a handle or winch for stirring ore to be washed **3 :** a heavy bar with a cupped head for holding against the head of a rivet while the other end is being headed **4 :** a compact narrow-gauge railroad locomotive for moving construction trains and for switching **5 a :** a platform on a roller or on wheels or casters for moving heavy objects **b :** a wheeled platform for a television or motion-picture camera

2dolly *vb* **dol·lied; dol·ly·ing** *vt* **1 :** to treat with a dolly **2 :** to move or convey on a dolly ~ *vi* **:** to move a motion-picture or television camera about on a dolly while shooting a scene

dol·man \ˈdōl-mən, ˈdȯl-, ˈdäl-\ *n, pl* **dolmans** [F *doliman,* fr. Turk *dolama,* a Turkish robe] **:** a woman's coat made with dolman sleeves

dolman sleeve *n* **:** a sleeve very wide at the armhole and tight at the wrist often cut in one piece with the bodice

dol·men \ˈdōl-mən, ˈdȯl-, ˈdäl-\ *n* [F, fr. Bret *tolmen,* fr. *tol* table + *men* stone] **:** a prehistoric monument of two or more upright stones supporting a horizontal stone slab found esp. in Britain and France and thought to be a tomb

dolmen

do·lo·mite \ˈdō-lə-ˌmīt, ˈdäl-ə-\ *n* [F, fr. Déodat de *Dolomieu* †1801 F geologist] **1 :** a mineral $CaMg(CO_3)_2$ consisting of a calcium magnesium carbonate found in crystals and in extensive beds as a compact limestone **2 :** a limestone or marble rich in magnesium carbonate — **do·lo·mit·ic** \ˌdō-lə-ˈmit-ik, ˌdäl-ə-\ *adj*

do·lo·mi·tize \ˈdō-lə-mə-ˌtīz, ˈdäl-ə-\ *vt* **-tized; -tiz·ing :** to convert into dolomite — **do·lo·mi·ti·za·tion** \ˌdō-lə-mət-ə-ˈzā-shən, ˌdäl-ə-, -ˌmīt-\ *n*

do·lor *or chiefly Brit* **do·lour** \ˈdō-lər, ˈdäl-ər\ *n* [ME *dolour,* fr. MF, fr. L *dolor* pain, grief, fr. *dolēre* to feel pain, grieve — more at CONDOLE] **:** mental suffering or anguish **:** SORROW

do·lor·ous \ˈdō-lə-rəs, ˈdäl-ə-\ *adj* **:** causing, marked by, or expressive of misery or grief — **do·lor·ous·ly** *adv* — **do·lor·ous·ness** *n*

dol·phin \ˈdäl-fən, ˈdȯl-\ *n* [ME, fr. MF *dophin, daufin,* fr. OF *dalfin,* fr. OProv, fr. ML *dalfinus,* alter. of L *delphinus,* fr. Gk *delphin-, delphis;* akin to Gk *delphys* womb, Skt *garbha*] **1 a :** any of various small toothed whales (family Delphinidae) with the snout more or less elongated into a beak and the neck vertebrae partially fused **b :** PORPOISE 1 **2 :** either of two active pelagic percoid food fishes (genus *Coryphaena*) of tropical and temperate seas **3** *cap* **:** DELPHINUS **4 :** a spar or buoy for mooring boats; *also* **:** a cluster of closely driven piles used as a fender for a dock or as a mooring or guide for boats

dolphin 1a

dolphin striker *n* **:** a vertical spar under the end of the bowsprit of a sailboat to extend and support the martingale

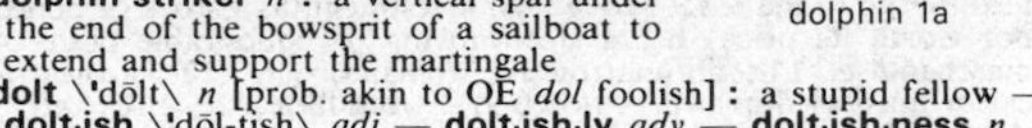

dolt \ˈdōlt\ *n* [prob. akin to OE *dol* foolish] **:** a stupid fellow — **dolt·ish** \ˈdōl-tish\ *adj* — **dolt·ish·ly** *adv* — **dolt·ish·ness** *n*

dom *abbr* **1** domestic **2** dominant **3** dominion

Dom [L *dominus* master] **1** \(ˌ)däm\ — used as a title for some monks and canons regular **2** \(ˌ)dōⁿ\ — used as a title prefixed to the Christian name of a Portuguese or Brazilian man of rank

DOM *abbr* [ML *Deo optimo maximo*] to God, the best and greatest

-dom \dəm\ *n suffix* [ME, fr. OE *-dōm;* akin to OHG *-tuom* -dom, OE *dōm* judgment — more at DOOM] **1 a :** dignity **:** office <duke*dom*> **b :** realm **:** jurisdiction <king*dom*> **c :** geographical area <Anglo-Saxon*dom*> **2 :** state or fact of being <free*dom*> **3 :** those having a (specified) office, occupation, interest, or character <official*dom*>

do·main \dō-ˈmān, də-\ *n* [MF *domaine, demaine,* fr. L *dominium,* fr. *dominus*] **1 a :** complete and absolute ownership of land — compare EMINENT DOMAIN **b :** land so owned **2 :** a territory over which dominion is exercised **3 :** a region distinctively marked by some physical feature <the ~ of rushing streams, tall trees, and lakes> **4 :** a sphere of influence or activity <the ~ of art> **5 :** the set of elements to which a mathematical or logical variable is limited; *specif* **:** the set on which a function is defined **6 :** any of the small randomly oriented regions of uniform magnetization in a ferromagnetic substance **7 :** INTEGRAL DOMAIN

1dome \ˈdōm\ *n* [F, It, & L; F *dôme* dome, cathedral, fr. It *duomo* cathedral, fr. ML *domus* church, fr. L, house — more at TIMBER] **1** *archaic* **:** a stately building **:** MANSION **2 :** a large hemispherical roof or ceiling **3 :** a natural formation or other structure that resembles the dome or cupola of a building **4 :** a form of crystal composed of planes parallel to a lateral axis that meet above in a horizontal edge like a roof — **dom·al** \ˈdō-məl\ *adj*

2dome *vb* **domed; dom·ing** *vt* **1 :** to cover with a dome **2 :** to form into a dome ~ *vi* **:** to swell upward or outward like a dome

Domes·day Book \ˈdümz-ˌdā-, ˈdōmz-\ *n* [ME, fr. *domesday* doomsday] **:** a record of a survey of English lands made by order of William the Conqueror about 1086

1do·mes·tic \də-ˈmes-tik\ *adj* [MF *domestique,* fr. L *domesticus,* fr. *domus*] **1 :** of or relating to the household or the family **2 :** of, relating to, or carried on within one and esp. one's own country <~ politics> <~ wines> **3 :** INDIGENOUS **4 a :** living near or about the habitations of man **b :** TAME, DOMESTICATED **5 :** devoted to home duties and pleasures — **do·mes·ti·cal·ly** \-ti-k(ə-)lē\ *adv*

²**domestic** *n* **1 :** a household servant **2 :** an article of domestic manufacture — usu. used in pl.
domestic animal *n* **:** any of various animals (as the horse or sheep) domesticated by man so as to live and breed in a tame condition
¹**do·mes·ti·cate** \də-ˈmes-ti-ˌkāt\ *vt* **-cat·ed; -cat·ing 1 :** to bring into domestic use **:** ADOPT **2 :** to fit for domestic life **3 :** to adapt (an animal or plant) to life in intimate association with and to the advantage of man **4 :** to bring to the level of ordinary people **:** FAMILIARIZE — **do·mes·ti·ca·tion** \-ˌmes-ti-ˈkā-shən\ *n*
²**do·mes·ti·cate** \-kət, -ˌkāt\ *n* **:** a domesticated animal or plant
domestic fowl *n* **1 :** POULTRY **2 :** a bird of one of the breeds developed from the jungle fowl (*Gallus gallus*) esp. for meat or egg production **:** CHICKEN
do·mes·tic·i·ty \ˌdō-ˌmes-ˈtis-ət-ē, -məs-; ˌdäm-əs-, -ˌes-; də-ˌmes-\ *n, pl* **-ties 1 :** the quality or state of being domestic or domesticated **2 :** domestic activities or life **3** *pl* **:** domestic affairs
domestic prelate *n* **:** a priest having permanent honorary membership in the papal household
domestic relations court *n* **:** COURT OF DOMESTIC RELATIONS
domestic science *n* **:** instruction and training in domestic management and the household arts (as cooking and sewing)
dom·i·cal \ˈdō-mi-kəl, ˈdäm-i-\ *adj* **:** relating to, shaped like, or having a dome
¹**do·mi·cile** \ˈdäm-ə-ˌsīl, ˈdō-mə-; ˈdäm-ə-səl\ *also* **dom·i·cil** \ˈdäm-ə-səl\ *n* [MF, fr. L *domicilium,* fr. *domus*] **1 :** a dwelling place **:** place of residence **:** HOME **2 a :** a person's fixed, permanent, and principal home for legal purposes **b :** RESIDENCE 2b
²**domicile** *vt* **-ciled; -cil·ing :** to establish in or provide with a domicile
do·mi·cil·i·ary \ˌdäm-ə-ˈsil-ē-ˌer-ē, ˌdō-mə-\ *adj* **:** of, relating to, or constituting a domicile: as **a :** provided or taking place in the home <~ meal service for elderly and housebound people> **b :** providing care and living space for persons (as veterans) so disabled as to be unable to live independently <the ~ section of the state hospital>
do·mi·cil·i·ate \ˌdäm-ə-ˈsil-ē-ˌāt, ˌdō-mə-\ *vb* **-at·ed; -at·ing** [L *domicilium*] *vt* **1 :** DOMICILE **2 :** DOMESTICATE 3, 4 ~ *vi* **:** RESIDE — **do·mi·cil·i·a·tion** \-ˌsil-ē-ˈā-shən\ *n*
dom·i·nance \ˈdäm-(ə-)nən(t)s\ *n* **:** the fact or state of being dominant: as **a :** dominant position in an order of forcefulness **:** ASCENDANCY; *specif* **:** the relative position of an individual in a social hierarchy **b :** the quality of one of a pair of alleles or traits that suppresses expression of the other in the heterozygous condition **c :** the influence or control over ecological communities exerted by a dominant **d :** functional asymmetry between a pair of bodily structures (as the right and left hands)
¹**dom·i·nant** \-nənt\ *adj* [MF or L; MF, fr. L *dominant-, dominans,* prp. of *dominari*] **1 :** commanding, controlling, or prevailing over all others **2 :** overlooking and commanding from a superior elevation **3 :** of, relating to, or exerting ecological dominance **4** *of paired bodily structures* **:** being the more effective or predominant one in action <~ eye> **5 :** of, relating to, or exerting genetic dominance — **dom·i·nant·ly** *adv*
syn DOMINANT, PREDOMINANT, PARAMOUNT, PREPONDERANT, SOVEREIGN *shared meaning element* **:** superior to all others in power, influence, or importance ***ant*** subordinate
²**dominant** *n* **1 a :** a dominant genetic character or factor **b :** any of one or more kinds of organism (as a species) in an ecological association that exerts a controlling influence on the environment and thereby largely determines what other kinds of organisms share in the association **c :** a dominant individual in a social hierarchy **2 :** the fifth note of a diatonic scale
dom·i·nate \ˈdäm-ə-ˌnāt\ *vb* **-nat·ed; -nat·ing** [L *dominatus,* pp. of *dominari,* fr. *dominus* master — more at DAME] *vt* **1 :** RULE, CONTROL **2 :** to exert the supreme determining or guiding influence on **3 :** to overlook from a superior elevation or command because of superior height **4 :** to have a commanding or preeminent place or position in <name brands ~ the market> ~ *vi* **1 :** to have or exert mastery, control, or preeminence **2 :** to occupy a more elevated or superior position — **dom·i·na·tive** \-ˌnāt-iv\ *adj* — **dom·i·na·tor** \-ˌnāt-ər\ *n*
dom·i·na·tion \ˌdäm-ə-ˈnā-shən\ *n* **1 :** supremacy or preeminence over another **2 :** exercise of mastery or preponderant influence **3** *pl* **:** DOMINION 3
dom·i·neer \ˌdäm-ə-ˈni(ə)r\ *vb* [D *domineren,* fr. F *dominer,* fr. L *dominari*] *vi* **:** to exercise arbitrary or overbearing control ~ *vt* **:** to tyrannize over
dom·i·neer·ing *adj* **:** inclined to domineer ***syn*** see MASTERFUL ***ant*** subservient — **dom·i·neer·ing·ly** \-iŋ-lē\ *adv* — **dom·i·neer·ing·ness** *n*
do·min·i·cal \də-ˈmin-i-kəl\ *adj* [LL *dominicalis,* fr. *dominicus* (*dies*) the Lord's day, fr. L *dominicus* of a lord, fr. *dominus* lord, master] **1 :** of or relating to Jesus Christ as Lord **2 :** of or relating to the Lord's day
dominical letter *n* **:** the letter designating Sundays in a given year (as for finding the date of Easter) when the first seven letters of the alphabet are applied consecutively to the days of the year beginning with *A* on Jan. 1 and skipping the intercalary day in leap year
Do·min·i·can \də-ˈmin-i-kən\ *n* [St. *Dominic*] **:** a member of a mendicant order of friars founded by St. Dominic in 1215 and dedicated esp. to preaching — **Dominican** *adj*
dom·i·nick \ˈdäm-ə-(ˌ)nik, -ˌnek\ *or* **dom·i·nick·er** \-ˌnek-ər, -ˌnik-\ *n, often cap* **:** DOMINIQUE
do·mi·nie *1 oftenest* ˈdäm-ə-nē, *2 oftenest* ˈdō-mə-\ *n* [L *domine,* voc. of *dominus*] **1 :** PEDAGOGUE **2 :** CLERGYMAN
do·min·ion \də-ˈmin-yən\ *n* [ME *dominioun,* fr. MF *dominion,* modif. of L *dominium,* fr. *dominus*] **1 :** supreme authority **:** SOVEREIGNTY **2 :** DOMAIN **3** *pl* **:** an order of angels — see CELESTIAL HIERARCHY **4** *often cap* **:** a self-governing nation of the British Commonwealth other than the United Kingdom that acknowledges the British monarch as chief of state **5 :** absolute ownership
Dominion Day *n* **:** July 1 observed as a legal holiday in Canada in commemoration of the proclamation of dominion status in 1867

dom·i·nique \ˈdäm-ə-(ˌ)nik, -ˌnək\ *n* [*Dominique* (Dominica), one of the Windward islands, West Indies] **:** any of an American breed of domestic fowl with a rose comb, yellow legs, and barred plumage; *broadly* **:** a barred fowl
dom·i·no \ˈdäm-ə-ˌnō\ *n, pl* **-noes** *or* **-nos** [F, prob. fr. L (in the ritual formula *benedicamus Domino* let us bless the Lord)] **1 a** (1) **:** a long loose hooded cloak usu. worn with a half mask as a masquerade costume (2) **:** a half mask worn with a masquerade costume **b :** a person wearing a domino **2** [F, fr. It] **a :** a flat rectangular block (as of wood or plastic) whose face is divided into two equal parts that are blank or bear from one to usu. six dots arranged as on dice faces **b** *pl but usu sing in constr* **:** any of several games played with a set of usu. 28 dominoes
domino theory *n* [fr. the fact that if a number of dominoes are stood on end one behind the other with slight intervening spaces, a slight push on the first will result in the toppling of all the others] **:** a theory that if one nation in Southeast Asia becomes Communist-controlled the neighboring nations will also become Communist-controlled
¹**don** \ˈdän\ *n* [Sp, fr. L *dominus* master — more at DAME] **1 :** a Spanish nobleman or gentleman — used as a title prefixed to the Christian name **2** *archaic* **:** a person of consequence **:** GRANDEE **3 :** a head, tutor, or fellow in a college of Oxford or Cambridge University; *broadly* **:** a college or university professor
²**don** \ˈdän\ *vt* **donned; don·ning** [*do* + *on*] **1 :** to put on (an article of wear) **2 :** to envelop oneself in **:** ASSUME
Don *abbr* Donegal
do·na \ˌdō-nə\ *n* [Pg, fr. L *domina*] **:** a Portuguese or Brazilian woman of rank — used as a title prefixed to the Christian name
do·ña \ˌdō-nyə\ *n* [Sp, fr. L *domina* lady] **:** a Spanish woman of rank — used as a title prefixed to the Christian name
do·nate \ˈdō-ˌnāt, dō-ˈ\ *vb* **do·nat·ed; do·nat·ing** [back-formation fr. *donation*] *vt* **1 :** to make a gift of; *esp* **:** to contribute to a public or charitable cause <~ a site for a park> **2 :** to give off or transfer (as electrons) ~ *vi* **:** to make a donation ***syn*** see GIVE
do·na·tion \dō-ˈnā-shən\ *n* [ME *donatyowne,* fr. L *donation-, donatio,* fr. *donatus,* pp. of *donare* to present, fr. *donum* gift; akin to L *dare* to give — more at DATE] **1 :** the action of making a gift esp. to a charity or public institution **2 :** a free contribution **:** GIFT
Do·na·tism \ˈdō-nə-ˌtiz-əm, ˈdän-ə-\ *n* [*Donatus,* 4th cent. bishop of Carthage] **:** the doctrines of a Christian sect arising in No. Africa in 311 and holding that sanctity is essential for the administration of sacraments and church membership — **Do·na·tist** \-təst\ *n*
¹**do·na·tive** \ˈdō-nət-iv, ˈdän-ət-\ *n* **:** a special gift or donation
²**do·na·tive** *same or* ˈdō-ˌnāt-, dō-ˈ\ *adj* [L *donativus,* fr. *donatus*] **:** characterized by, capable of, or subject to donation <a ~ trust>
do·na·tor \ˈdō-ˌnāt-ər, dō-ˈ\ *n* **:** DONOR
¹**done** \ˈdən\ *past part of* DO
²**done** *adj* **1 :** conformable to social convention **2 :** arrived at or brought to an end **:** THROUGH **3 :** physically exhausted **:** SPENT **4 :** gone by **:** OVER **5 :** doomed to failure, defeat, or death **6 :** cooked sufficiently
do·nee \dō-ˈnē\ *n* [*don*or] **:** a recipient of a gift
done for \ˈdən-ˌfȯ(ə)r\ *adj* **1 :** mortally stricken **:** DOOMED **2 :** left with no capacity or opportunity for recovery **:** RUINED **3 :** sunk in defeat **:** BEATEN
done·ness \ˈdən-nəs\ *n* **:** the condition of being cooked to the desired degree
¹**dong** \ˈdȯŋ, ˈdäŋ\ *n* [origin unknown] **:** PENIS — usu. considered vulgar
²**dong** *n* [Annamese] **1** — see MONEY table **2 :** a coin of South Vietnam worth one piaster
don·jon \ˈdän-jən, ˈdən-\ *n* [ME — more at DUNGEON] **:** a massive inner tower in a medieval castle
Don Juan \(ˈ)dän-ˈ(h)wän, dän-ˈjü-ən\ *n* [Sp] **1 :** a legendary Spaniard proverbial for his seduction of women **2 :** LIBERTINE, RAKE
don·key \ˈdäŋ-kē, ˈdəŋ-, ˈdȯŋ-\ *n, pl* **donkeys** [perh. fr. ¹*dun* + *-key* (as in *monkey*)] **1 :** the domestic ass (*Equus asinus*) **2 :** a stupid or obstinate person
donkey engine *n* **1 :** a small usu. portable auxiliary engine **2 :** a small locomotive used in switching
donkey's years *n pl* **:** a very long time <place where there'd been no fires for *donkey's years* —Malcolm Lowry>

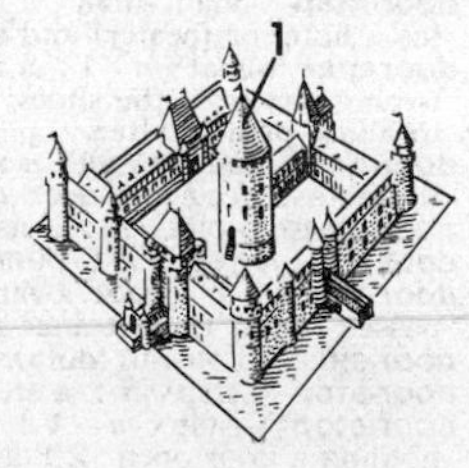

1 donjon

don·key·work \ˈdäŋ-kē-ˌwərk, ˈdəŋ-, ˈdȯŋ-\ *n* **:** monotonous and routine work **:** DRUDGERY
don·na \ˌdän-ə, ˌdȯn-\ *n, pl* **don·ne** \-(ˌ)ā\ [It, fr. L *domina*] **:** an Italian woman esp. of rank — used as a title prefixed to the Christian name
don·née \dȯ-ˈnā, (ˌ)də-\ *n, pl* **données** \-ˈnā(z)\ [F, fr. fem. of *donné,* pp. of *donner* to give, fr. L *donare* to donate] **:** the set of assumptions upon which a work of fiction or drama proceeds
don·nish \ˈdän-ish\ *adj* **:** of, relating to, or characteristic of a university don **:** PEDANTIC — **don·nish·ly** *adv* — **don·nish·ness** *n*
don·ny·brook \ˈdän-ē-ˌbrůk\ *n, often cap* [*Donnybrook* Fair, annual Irish event known for its brawls] **:** an uproarious brawl **:** FREE-FOR-ALL

do·nor \'dō-nər, -ˌnȯ(ə)r\ *n* [MF *doneur,* fr. L *donator,* fr. *donatus*] **1 :** one that gives, donates, or presents **2 :** one used as a source of biological material **3 a :** a compound capable of giving up a part (as an atom, radical, or elementary particle) for combination with an acceptor **b :** an impurity that is added to a semiconductor to increase the number of mobile electrons

1do–noth·ing \'dü-ˌnəth-iŋ\ *n* **:** a shiftless or habitually lazy person

2do–nothing *adj* **:** marked by inactivity; *specif* **:** marked by lack of initiative, disinclination to disturb the status quo, or failure to make positive progress — **do–noth·ing·ism** \-ˌiz-əm\ *n*

Don Qui·xote \ˌdän-kē-'(h)ōt-ē, ˌdäŋ-; dän-'kwik-sət\ *n* [Sp] **:** the idealistic and impractical hero of Cervantes' *Don Quixote*

don·sie *or* **don·sy** \'dän(t)-sē\ *adj* [perh. fr. ScGael *donas* evil, harm] **1** *dial Brit* **:** UNLUCKY **2** *Scot* **a :** RESTIVE **b :** SAUCY

1don't \(')dōnt\ **1 :** do not **2 :** does not — often used by educated speakers though the construction is sometimes objected to <there are simply certain things he ~ know —Ezra Pound>

2don't \'dōnt\ *n* **:** a command or entreaty not to do something **:** PROHIBITION <a long list of ~*s*>

donut *var of* DOUGHNUT

doo·dad \'dü-ˌdad\ *n* [origin unknown] **1 :** a small article whose common name is unknown or forgotten **:** GADGET **2 :** an ornamental attachment or decoration <a mantelpiece cluttered up with all kinds of ~*s*>

1doo·dle \'düd-ᵊl\ *vb* **doo·dled; doo·dling** \'düd-liŋ, -ᵊl-iŋ\ [perh. fr. *doodle* (to ridicule)] *vi* **1 :** to make a doodle **2 :** DAWDLE, TRIFLE ~ *vt* **:** to produce by doodling — **doo·dler** \'düd-lər, -ᵊl-ər\ *n*

2doodle *n* **:** an aimless scribble, design, or sketch

doo·dle·bug \'düd-ᵊl-ˌbəg\ *n* [prob. fr. *doodle* (fool) + *bug*] **1 :** the larva of an ant lion; *also* **:** any of several other insects **2 :** a device (as a divining rod) used in attempting to locate underground gas, water, oil, or ores **3 :** any of several small vehicles

doo·hick·ey \'dü-ˌhik-ē\ *n* [prob. fr. *doodad* + *hickey*] **:** DOODAD 1

1doom \'düm\ *n* [ME, fr. OE *dōm;* akin to OHG *tuom* condition, state, OE *dōn* to do] **1 :** a law or ordinance esp. in Anglo-Saxon England **2 a :** JUDGMENT, DECISION; *esp* **:** a judicial condemnation or sentence **b (1) :** JUDGMENT 3a **(2) :** JUDGMENT DAY 1 **3 a :** DESTINY; *esp* **:** unhappy destiny **b :** DEATH, RUIN ***syn*** see FATE

2doom *vt* **1 :** to give judgment against **:** CONDEMN **2 a :** to fix the fate of **:** DESTINE **b :** to make certain the failure or destruction of

doom·ful \'düm-fəl\ *adj* **:** presaging doom **:** OMINOUS — **doom·ful·ly** \-fə-lē\ *adv*

doom·say·er \'düm-ˌsā-ər\ *n* **:** one given to forebodings and predictions of impending calamity

dooms·day \'dümz-ˌdā\ *n* **:** JUDGMENT DAY

doom·ster \'düm(p)-stər\ *n* **1 :** JUDGE **2 :** DOOMSAYER

door \'dō(ə)r, 'dȯ(ə)r\ *n, often attrib* [ME *dure, dor,* fr. OE *duru* door & *dor* gate; akin to OHG *turi* door, L *fores,* Gk *thyra*] **1 :** a usu. swinging or sliding barrier by which an entry is closed and opened; *also* **:** a similar part of a piece of furniture **2 :** DOORWAY **3 :** a means of access <~ to success> — **door·less** \-ləs\ *adj* — **at one's door :** as a charge against one as being responsible <laid the blame *at our door*>

door·jamb \'dō(ə)r-ˌjam, 'dȯ(ə)r-\ *n* **:** an upright piece forming the side of a door opening

door·keep·er \-ˌkē-pər\ *n* **:** one that tends a door

door·knob \-ˌnäb\ *n* **:** a knob that when turned releases a door latch

door·man \-ˌman, -mən\ *n* **:** one that tends the door of a building (as a hotel or theater) and assists people (as in calling taxis)

door·mat \-ˌmat\ *n* **1 :** a mat placed before or inside a door for wiping dirt from the shoes **2 :** one that submits without protest to abuse or indignities

door·nail \-ˌnāl, -'nā(ə)l\ *n* **:** a large-headed nail — used chiefly in the phrase *dead as a doornail*

door·plate \-ˌplāt\ *n* **:** a nameplate on a door

door·post \-ˌpōst\ *n* **:** DOORJAMB

door prize *n* **:** a prize awarded to the holder of a winning ticket passed out at the entrance to an entertainment or function

door·sill \'dō(ə)r-ˌsil, 'dȯ(ə)r-\ *n* **:** SILL 1b

door·step \-ˌstep\ *n* **:** a step before an outer door

door·stop \-ˌstäp\ *n* **1 :** a device (as a wedge or weight) for holding a door open **2 :** a projection attached to a wall or floor and usu. having a rubber-tipped end for preventing damaging contact between an opened door and the wall

door–to–door \ˌdōrt-ə-'dō(ə)r, ˌdȯrt-ə-'dȯ(ə)r\ *adj* **1 :** being or making a usu. unsolicited call (as for selling or canvassing) at every residence in an area **2 :** providing delivery to a specified address <direct ~ service>

door·way \'dō(ə)r-ˌwā, 'dȯ(ə)r-\ *n* **1 :** the opening that a door closes; *esp* **:** an entrance into a building or room **2 :** a means of gaining access <exercise is a ~ to good health>

door·yard \-ˌyärd\ *n* **:** a yard about the door of a house

do·pa \'dō-pə, -(ˌ)pä\ *n* [*d*ihydr*o*xy*p*henyl*a*lanine]: an amino acid $C_9H_{11}NO_4$ that in the levorotatory form is found in the broad bean and is used in the treatment of Parkinson's disease

do·pa·mine \'dō-pə-ˌmēn\ *n* [*dopa* + *amine*] **:** a decarboxylated form of dopa found esp. in the adrenal glands; *also* **:** DOPA

dop·ant \'dō-pənt\ *n* [2*dope*] **:** an impurity added usu. in minute amounts to a pure substance to alter its properties

1dope \'dōp\ *n* [D *doop* sauce, fr. *dopen* to dip; akin to OE *dyppan* to dip — more at DIP] **1 a :** a thick liquid or pasty preparation **b :** a preparation for giving a desired quality to a substance or surface; *specif* **:** an antiknock added to gasoline **2 :** absorbent or adsorbent material used in various manufacturing processes (as the making of dynamite) **3 a (1) :** a narcotic preparation (as opium or heroin) **(2) :** a preparation given to a racehorse to stimulate it temporarily **b** *chiefly South* **:** a cola drink **c (1) :** a narcotic addict **(2) :** a stupid person **4 :** information esp. from a reliable source <inside ~ on the scandal>

2dope *vb* **doped; dop·ing** *vt* **1 :** to treat or affect with dope; *specif* **:** to give a narcotic to **2 :** to find a solution for ~ *vi* **:** to take dope — **dop·er** *n*

dope·ster \'dōp-stər\ *n* **:** a forecaster of the outcome of future events (as sports contests or elections)

dop·ey *or* **dopy** \'dō-pē\ *adj* **dop·i·er; -est 1 a :** dulled by alcohol or a narcotic **b :** SLUGGISH, STUPEFIED **2 :** DULL, STUPID — **dop·i·ness** *n*

dop·pel·gäng·er *or* **dop·pel·gang·er** \'dȯp-əl-ˌgeŋ-ər, ˌdəb-əl-'gaŋ-\ *n* [G *doppelgänger,* fr. *doppel-* double + *-gänger* goer] **:** a ghostly counterpart of a living person

Dopp·ler \'däp-lər\ *adj* **:** of, relating to, or utilizing a shift in frequency in accordance with the Doppler effect; *also* **:** of or relating to Doppler radar

Doppler effect *n* [Christian J. *Doppler*] **:** a change in the frequency with which waves (as sound, light, or radio waves) from a given source reach an observer when the source and the observer are in rapid motion with respect to each other so that the frequency increases or decreases according to the speed at which the distance is decreasing or increasing

Doppler radar *n* **:** a radar system that utilizes the Doppler effect for measuring velocity

dor·bee·tle \'dȯr-ˌbēt-ᵊl\ *n* [*dor* (buzzing insect)] **:** any of various beetles that fly with a buzzing sound; *specif* **:** a common European dung beetle (*Geotrupes stercorarius*)

Dor·cas \'dȯr-kəs\ *n* [Gk *Dorkas*] **:** a Christian woman of New Testament times who made clothing for the poor

dor·hawk \'dȯ(ə)r-ˌhȯk\ *n* [*dor* (buzzing insect); fr. its diet] **:** the common European nightjar (*Caprimulgus europaeus*)

Do·ri·an \'dōr-ē-ən, 'dȯr-\ *n* [L *dorius* of Doris, fr. Gk *dōrios,* fr. *Dōris,* region of ancient Greece] **:** one of an ancient Hellenic race that completed the overthrow of Mycenaean civilization and settled esp. in the Peloponnesus and Crete — **Dorian** *adj*

1Dor·ic \'dȯr-ik, 'där-\ *adj* **1 :** of, relating to, or constituting Doric **2 :** of, relating to, or characteristic of the Dorians **3 :** belonging to the oldest and simplest Greek architectural order

2Doric *n* **:** a dialect of ancient Greek spoken esp. in the Peloponnesus, Crete, Sicily, and southern Italy

dorm \'dȯ(ə)rm\ *n* **:** DORMITORY

dor·man·cy \'dȯr-mən-sē\ *n* **:** the quality or state of being dormant

dor·mant \'dȯr-mənt\ *adj* [ME, fixed, stationary, fr. MF, fr. prp. of *dormir* to sleep, fr. L *dormire;* akin to Skt *drāti* he sleeps] **1 :** represented on a coat of arms in a lying position with the head on the forepaws **2 :** marked by a suspension of activity: as **a :** temporarily devoid of external activity <a ~ volcano> **b :** temporarily in abeyance yet capable of being activated or resumed <a ~ judgment> **3 a :** ASLEEP, INACTIVE **b :** having the faculties suspended **:** SLUGGISH **c :** having biological activity suspended: as **(1) :** being in a state of suspended animation **(2) :** not actively growing but protected (as by bud scales) from the environment — used of plant parts **4 :** associated with, carried out, or applied during dormancy <~ grafting> ***syn*** see LATENT ***ant*** active

dor·mer \'dȯr-mər\ *n* [MF *dormeor* dormitory, fr. L *dormitorium*] **:** a window set vertically in a structure projecting through a sloping roof; *also* **:** the roofed structure containing such a window

dor·mie *or* **dor·my** \'dȯr-mē\ *adj* [origin unknown] **:** being ahead by as many holes in golf as remain to be played

dor·min \'dȯr-mən\ *n* [*dormancy* + *-in*] **:** ABSCISIC ACID

dor·mi·to·ry \'dȯr-mə-ˌtōr-ē, -ˌtȯr-\ *n, pl* **-ries** [L *dormitorium,* fr. *dormitus,* pp. of *dormire*] **1 :** a room for sleeping; *esp* **:** a large room containing numerous beds **2 :** a residence hall providing rooms for individuals or for groups usu. without private baths **3 :** a residential community from which the inhabitants commute to their places of employment

dor·mouse \'dȯ(ə)r-ˌmau̇s\ *n* [ME *dormowse,* perh. fr. MF *dormir* + ME *mous* mouse] **:** any of numerous small Old World rodents (family Gliridae) that resemble small squirrels

dormouse

dor·nick \'dȯr-nik, 'dän-ik\ *n* [prob. fr. IrGael *dornōg*] **:** a small stone or chunk of rock

do·ron·i·cum \də-'rän-i-kəm\ *n* [NL, genus name, fr. Ar *darūnaj,* a plant of this genus] **:** any of a genus (*Doronicum*) of Eurasian perennial composite herbs including several cultivated for their showy yellow flower heads

dorp \'dȯ(ə)rp\ *n* [D, fr. MD; akin to OHG *dorf* village — more at THORP] **:** VILLAGE

dor·per \'dȯr-pər\ *n* [*Dor*set Horn + Blackhead *Per*sian (a breed of sheep)] **:** any of a breed of mutton-producing sheep with white body and black face developed in southern Africa

Dors *abbr* Dorset

dors- *or* **dorsi-** *or* **dorso-** *comb form* [LL *dors-,* fr. L *dorsum*] **1 :** back <*dors*ad> **2 :** dorsal and <*dorso*lateral>

dor·sad \'dȯ(ə)r-ˌsad\ *adv* **:** toward the back **:** DORSALLY

1dor·sal \'dȯr-səl\ *adj* [LL *dorsalis,* fr. L *dorsum* back] **1 :** relating to or situated near or on the back esp. of an animal or of one of its parts **2 :** ABAXIAL — **dor·sal·ly** \-sə-lē\ *adv*

2dorsal *n* **:** a dorsally located part; *esp* **:** a thoracic vertebra

dorsal lip *n* **:** the margin of the fold of blastula wall that delineates the dorsal limit of the blastopore, constitutes the primary organizer, and forms the point of origin of chordamesoderm

dorsal root *n* **:** the one of the two roots of a spinal nerve that passes dorsally to the spinal cord and consists of sensory fibers

dor·set horn \'dȯr-sət-\ *n, often cap D&H* [*Dorset,* England] **:** any of an English breed of sheep that have very large horns

dor·si·ven·tral \ˌdȯr-si-ˈven-trəl\ *adj* **1 :** having distinct dorsal and ventral surfaces **2 :** DORSOVENTRAL 1 — **dor·si·ven·tral·i·ty** \-ven-ˈtral-ət-ē\ *n* — **dor·si·ven·tral·ly** \-ˈven-trə-lē\ *adv*

dor·so·lat·er·al \ˌdȯr-sō-ˈlat-ə-rəl, -ˈla-trəl\ *adj* **:** of, relating to, or involving both the back and the sides

dor·so·ven·tral \-ˈven-trəl\ *adj* [ISV] **1 :** extending from the dorsal toward the ventral side **2 :** DORSIVENTRAL 1 — **dor·so·ven·tral·i·ty** \-ven-ˈtral-ət-ē\ *n* — **dor·so·ven·tral·ly** \-trə-lē\ *adv*

dor·sum \ˈdȯr-səm\ *n, pl* **dor·sa** \-sə\ [L] **1 :** BACK: *esp* **:** the entire dorsal surface of an animal **2 :** the upper surface of an appendage or part

do·ry \ˈdōr-ē, ˈdȯr-\ *n, pl* **dories** [Miskito *dóri* dugout] **:** a flat-bottomed boat with high flaring sides, sharp bow, and deep V-shaped transom

dos·age \ˈdō-sij\ *n* **1 a :** the amount of a therapeutic dose **b** (1) **:** the giving of such a dose (2) **:** regulation or determination of doses **2 a :** the addition of an ingredient or the application of an agent in a measured dose **b :** the presence and relative representation or strength of a factor or agent **3 :** a dealing out of or an exposure to some experience in or as if in measured portions

¹dose \ˈdōs\ *n* [F, fr. LL *dosis*, fr. Gk, lit., act of giving, fr. *didonai* to give — more at DATE] **1 a :** the measured quantity of a therapeutic agent to be taken at one time **b :** the quantity of radiation administered or absorbed **2 :** a portion of a substance added during a process **3 :** a part of an experience to which one is exposed <a ~ of hard work> **4 :** a gonorrheal infection

²dose *vt* **dosed; dos·ing 1 :** to divide (as a medicine) into doses **2 :** to give a dose to; *esp* **:** to give medicine to **3 :** to treat with an application or agent

do–si–do \ˌdō-(ˌ)sē-ˈdō\ *n, pl* **do–si–dos** [F *dos-à-dos* back to back] **:** a square-dance figure: **a :** a figure in which the dancers pass each other right shoulder to right shoulder and circle each other back to back **b :** a figure in which the woman moves in a figure circling first her partner and then the man on her right

do·sim·e·ter \dō-ˈsim-ət-ər\ *n* [LL *dosis* + ISV *-meter*] **:** a device for measuring doses of X rays or of radioactivity — **do·si·met·ric** \ˌdō-sə-ˈme-trik\ *adj* — **do·sim·e·try** \dō-ˈsim-ə-trē\ *n*

¹doss \ˈdäs\ *n* [origin unknown] *chiefly Brit* **:** a crude or makeshift bed

²doss *vi, chiefly Brit* **:** to sleep or bed down in a convenient place

dos·sal \ˈdäs-əl\ *or* **dor·sal** \ˈdȯr-səl\ *or* **dos·sel** \ˈdäs-əl\ *n* [ML *dossale, dorsale*, fr. neut. of LL *dorsalis* dorsal] **:** an ornamental cloth hung behind and above an altar

dos·sier \ˈdȯs-ˌyā, ˈdȯs-ē-ˌā, ˈdäs-\ *n* [F, bundle of documents labeled on the back, dossier, fr. *dos* back, fr. L *dorsum*] **:** a file of papers containing a detailed report or detailed information

dost \(ˈ)dəst\ *archaic pres 2d sing of* DO

¹dot \ˈdät\ *n* [(assumed) ME, fr. OE *dott* head of a boil; akin to OHG *tutta* nipple] **1 :** a small spot **:** SPECK **2 a** (1) **:** a small point made with a pointed instrument <a ~ on the chart marked the ship's position> (2) **:** a small round mark used in orthography or punctuation <put a ~ over the *i*> **b :** a centered point used as a multiplication sign **c** (1) **:** a point after a note or rest in music indicating augmentation of the time value by one half (2) **:** a point over or under a note indicating that it is to be played staccato **3 :** a precise point esp. in time <arrived at six on the ~> **4 :** a short click or buzz forming a letter or part of a letter (as in the Morse code)

²dot *vb* **dot·ted; dot·ting** *vt* **1 :** to mark with a dot **2 :** to intersperse with dots or objects scattered at random <boats *dotting* the lake> ~ *vi* **:** to make a dot — **dot·ter** *n*

³dot \ˈdȯt\ *n* [F, fr. L *dot-, dos* dowry] **:** DOWRY 2a

dot·age \ˈdōt-ij\ *n* **:** a state or period of senile decay marked by decline of mental poise and alertness — called also *second childhood*

do·tal \ˈdōt-ᵊl\ *adj* [L *dotalis*, fr. *dot-, dos*] **:** of or relating to a woman's marriage dowry

dot·ard \ˈdōt-ərd\ *n* **:** a person in his dotage

dote \ˈdōt\ *vi* **dot·ed; dot·ing** [ME *doten*; akin to MLG *dotten* to be foolish] **1 :** to exhibit mental decline of or like that of old age **:** be in one's dotage **2 :** to show excessive or foolish affection or fondness — used esp. with *on* <*doted* on her only grandchild> — **dot·er** *n* — **dot·ing·ly** \ˈdōt-iŋ-lē\ *adv*

doth \(ˈ)dəth\ *archaic pres 3d sing of* DO

dot product *n* [¹*dot*; fr. its being commonly written *A·B*] **:** SCALAR PRODUCT

dotted swiss *n* **:** a sheer light muslin ornamented with evenly spaced raised dots

dot·ter·el \ˈdät-ə-rəl, ˈdä-trəl\ *n* [ME *dotrelle*, irreg. fr. *doten* to dote] **:** a Eurasian plover (*Charadrius morinellus*) formerly common in England; *also* **:** any of various congeners chiefly of eastern Asia, Australia, and So. America

dot·tle \ˈdät-ᵊl\ *n* [ME *dottel* plug, fr. (assumed) ME *dot*] **:** unburned and partially burned tobacco caked in the bowl of a pipe

¹dot·ty \ˈdät-ē\ *adj* **:** composed of or marked by dots

²dotty *adj* **dot·ti·er; -est** [alter. of Sc *dottle* fool, fr. ME *dotel*, fr. *doten*] **1 :** being obsessed or infatuated **2 a :** mentally unbalanced **:** CRAZY <thought the man was ~ for paying the boys so much money> **b :** amiably eccentric <an absentminded ~ old man> **3 :** amusingly absurd **:** RIDICULOUS <some sublimely ~ exchanges of letters> — **dot·ti·ly** \ˈdät-ᵊl-ē\ *adv* — **dot·ti·ness** \ˈdät-ē-nəs\ *n*

Dou·ay Version \dü-ˈā-\ *n* [*Douay*, France] **:** an English translation of the Vulgate used by Roman Catholics

¹dou·ble \ˈdəb-əl\ *adj* [ME, fr. OF, fr. L *duplus*, fr. *duo* two + *-plus* multiplied by; akin to Gk di*ploos* double, OE *fealdan* to fold — more at TWO, FOLD] **1 :** having a twofold relation or character **:** DUAL **2 :** consisting of two usu. combined members or parts <an egg with a ~ yolk> **3 a :** being twice as great or as many <~ the number of expected applicants> **b** *of a coin* **:** worth two of the specified amount <~ eagle> <~ crown> **4 :** marked by duplicity **:** DECEITFUL **5 :** folded in two **6 :** of extra size, strength, or value <a ~ martini> **7 :** having more than the normal number of floral leaves often at the expense of the sporophylls **8** *of rhyme* **:** involving correspondence of two syllables (as in *exciting* and *inviting*) — **dou·ble·ness** *n*

²double *n* **1 :** something twice the usual size, strength, speed, quantity, or value: as **a :** a double amount **b :** a base hit in baseball that enables the batter to reach second base **2 :** one that is the counterpart of another **:** DUPLICATE: as **a :** a living person that closely resembles another living person **b :** WRAITH **c** (1) **:** UNDERSTUDY (2) **:** one who resembles an actor and takes his place in scenes calling for special skills (3) **:** an actor who plays more than one role in a production **3 a :** a sharp turn (as in running) **:** REVERSAL **b :** an evasive shift **4 :** something consisting of two paired members: as **a :** FOLD **b :** a combined bet placed on two different contests **c :** two consecutive strikes in bowling **5** *pl* **:** a game between two pairs of players **6 :** an act of doubling in a card game

³double *adv* **1 :** to twice the extent or amount **2 :** two together

⁴double *vb* **dou·bled; dou·bling** \ˈdəb-(ə-)liŋ\ *vt* **1 :** to make twice as great or as many: as **a :** to increase by adding an equal amount **b :** to amount to twice the number of **c :** to make a call in bridge that increases the value of odd tricks or undertricks at (an opponent's bid) **2 a :** to make of two thicknesses **:** FOLD **b :** CLENCH <*doubled* his fist> **c :** to cause to stoop **3 :** to avoid by doubling **:** ELUDE **4 a :** to replace in a dramatic role **b :** to play (dramatic roles) by doubling **5 a** (1) **:** to advance or score (a base runner) by a double (2) **:** to bring about the scoring of (a run) by a double **b :** to put out (a base runner) in completing a double play ~ *vi* **1 a :** to become twice as much or as many **b :** to double a bid (as in bridge) **2 a :** to turn sharply and suddenly; *esp* **:** to turn back on one's course **b :** to follow a circuitous course **3 :** to become bent or folded usu. in the middle — usu. used with *up* <he *doubled* up in pain> **4 a :** to serve an additional purpose or perform an additional duty **b :** to play a dramatic role as a double **5 :** to make a double in baseball — **dou·bler** \-(ə-)lər\ *n*

double agent *n* **:** a spy pretending to serve one government while actually serving another

double bar *n* **:** two adjacent vertical lines or a heavy single line separating principal sections of a musical composition

dou·ble–bar·rel \ˌdəb-əl-ˈbar-əl\ *n* **:** a double-barreled gun

dou·ble–bar·reled \-əld\ *adj* **1** *of a firearm* **:** having two barrels mounted side by side **2 :** TWOFOLD: *esp* **:** having a double purpose <asked a ~ question>

double bars

double bass *n* **:** the largest instrument in the violin family tuned a fifth below the cello — **double bass·ist** \-ˈbā-səst\ *n*

double bassoon *n* **:** CONTRABASSOON

double bed *n* **:** a bed designed to sleep two persons

double bill *n* **:** a bill (as at a theater) offering two principal features

double bind *n* **:** a psychological dilemma in which a usu. dependent person (as a child) receives conflicting interpersonal communications from a single source or faces disparagement no matter what his response to a situation

dou·ble–blind \ˌdəb-əl-ˈblīnd\ *adj* **:** of, relating to, or being an experimental procedure in which neither the subjects nor the experimenters know the makeup of the test and control groups during the actual course of the experiments — compare SINGLE-BLIND

double boiler *n* **:** a cooking utensil consisting of two saucepans fitting into each other so that the contents of the upper can be cooked or heated by boiling water in the lower

double bond *n* **:** a chemical bond consisting of two covalent bonds between two atoms in a molecule

dou·ble–breast·ed \ˌdəb-əl-ˈbres-təd\ *adj* **1 :** having one half of the front lapped over the other and usu. a double row of buttons and a single row of buttonholes <a ~ coat> **2 :** having a double-breasted coat <a ~ suit>

double bass

double–check \ˌdəb-əl-ˈchek, ˈdəb-əl-ˌ\ *vt* **:** to subject to a double check <an article ~*ed* for accuracy> ~ *vi* **:** to make a double check

double check *n* **:** a careful checking to determine accuracy, condition, or progress esp. of something already checked

double counterpoint *n* **:** two-part counterpoint so constructed that either part may be played above or below the other

dou·ble–cov·er \ˌdəb-əl-ˈkəv-ər\ *vt* **:** DOUBLE-TEAM

dou·ble–cross \ˌdəb-əl-ˈkrȯs\ *vt* **:** to deceive by double-dealing **:** BETRAY — **dou·ble–cross·er** *n*

double cross *n* **1 a :** an act of winning or trying to win a fight or match after agreeing to lose it **b :** an act of betraying or cheating an associate **2 :** a cross between first-generation hybrids of four separate inbred lines (as in the production of hybrid seed corn)

double dagger *n* **:** the character ‡ used commonly as the third in the series of reference marks — called also *diesis*

double date *n* **:** a date participated in by two couples — **dou·ble–date** *vi*

dou·ble–deal·er \ˌdəb-əl-ˈdē-lər\ *n* **:** one who practices double-dealing

[1]**dou·ble–deal·ing** \-'dē-liŋ\ *n* : action contradictory to a professed attitude : DUPLICITY

[2]**double–dealing** *adj* : given to or marked by duplicity

dou·ble–deck \ˌdəb-əl-ˌdek\ *or* **dou·ble–decked** \-'dekt\ *adj* : having two decks, levels, or layers <a ~ bus> <a ~ sandwich>

dou·ble–deck·er \-'dek-ər\ *n* : something that is double-deck

double decomposition *n* : METATHESIS b

dou·ble–dome \'dəb-əl-ˌdōm\ *n* : EGGHEAD

double door *n* : an opening with two vertical doors that meet in the middle of the opening when closed — compare DUTCH DOOR

double dribble *n* : an illegal action in basketball made when a player dribbles the ball with two hands simultaneously or continues to dribble after allowing the ball to come to rest in one or both hands

dou·ble–edged \ˌdəb-ə-'lejd\ *adj* **1** : having two cutting edges **2 a** : having a dual purpose or effect <a spy with a ~ mission> **b** : capable of being understood or interpreted in two ways <a ~ slur>

dou·ble–end·ed \ˌdəb-ə-'len-dəd\ *adj* : similar at both ends <a ~ bolt>

dou·ble–end·er \-dər\ *n* : a ship with bow and stern of similar shape

dou·ble en·ten·dre \ˌdüb(-ə)-ˌlä^{n}(n)-'tä^{n}(n)drᵊ, ˌdəb-ə-, -'tä^{n}(n)d(-rə)\ *n, pl* **double entendres** \-'tä^{n}(n)drᵊ, -'tä^{n}(n)d-rəz, -'tä^{n}n(d)z\ [obs. F, lit., double meaning] **1** : ambiguity of meaning arising from language that lends itself to more than one interpretation **2** : a word or expression capable of two interpretations one of which often has a risqué connotation

double entry *n* : a method of bookkeeping that recognizes both the receiving and the giving sides of a business transaction by debiting the amount of the transaction to one account and crediting it to another account so that the total debits equal the total credits

dou·ble–faced \ˌdəb-əl-'fāst\ *adj* **1** : having two faces or sides designed for use <a ~ bookshelf> **2** : TWO-FACED, HYPOCRITICAL

dou·ble–fault \-ˈfȯlt\ *vi* : to lose a point in tennis by making two consecutive faults while serving

double feature *n* : a movie program consisting of two main films

double fertilization *n* : fertilization characteristic of seed plants in which one sperm nucleus fuses with the egg nucleus to form an embryo and another fuses with polar nuclei to form endosperm

dou·ble·head·er \ˌdəb-əl-'hed-ər\ *n* **1** : a train pulled by two locomotives **2** : two games, contests, or events held consecutively on the same program

double hyphen *n* : a punctuation mark ⸗ used in place of a hyphen at the end of a line to indicate that the word so divided is normally hyphenated

double indemnity *n* : a provision in a life-insurance or accident policy whereby the company agrees to pay twice the face of the contract in case of accidental death

double jeopardy *n* : the putting of a person on trial for an offense for which he has previously been put on trial under a valid charge : two adjudications for one offense

dou·ble–joint·ed \ˌdəb-əl-'jȯint-əd\ *adj* : having a joint that permits an exceptional degree of freedom of motion of the parts joined

double knit *n* : a knitted fabric (as wool) made with a double set of needles to produce a double thickness of fabric with each thickness joined by interlocking stitches

double negative *n* : a now substandard syntactic construction containing two negatives and having a negative meaning <"I didn't hear nothing" is a *double negative*>

dou·ble–park \ˌdəb-əl-'pärk\ *vi* : to double-park a vehicle ~ *vt* : to park (a vehicle) beside a row of automobiles already parked parallel to the curb

double play *n* : a play in baseball by which two players are put out

double precision *n* : the use of two computer words rather than one to represent a number

dou·ble–quick \'dəb-əl-ˌkwik\ *n* : DOUBLE TIME — **double–quick** *vi*

double reed *n* : two cane reeds bound and vibrating against each other and used as the mouthpiece of certain woodwind instruments

double refraction *n* : BIREFRINGENCE

dou·ble–ring \ˌdəb-əl-ˌriŋ\ *adj* : of or relating to a wedding ceremony in which each partner ceremonially gives the other a wedding ring while formally declaring wedded commitment

double salt *n* **1** : a salt (as an alum) yielding on hydrolysis two different cations or anions **2** : a salt regarded as a molecular combination of two distinct salts

dou·ble–space \ˌdəb-əl-'spās\ *vt* : to type (copy) leaving alternate lines blank ~ *vi* : to type on every other line

dou·ble·speak \'dəb-əl-ˌspēk\ *n* : DOUBLE-TALK 2

double standard *n* **1** : BIMETALLISM **2** : a set of principles that applies differently and usu. more rigorously to one group of people or circumstances than to another; *esp* : a code of morals that applies different and more severe standards of sexual behavior to women than to men

double star *n* **1** : BINARY STAR **2** : two stars in very nearly the same line of sight but seen as physically separate by means of a telescope

double sugar *n* : DISACCHARIDE

dou·blet \'dəb-lət\ *n* [ME, fr. MF, fr. *double*] **1** : a man's close-fitting jacket worn in Europe esp. during the Renaissance **2** : something consisting of two identical or similar parts: as **a** : a lens consisting of two components; *specif* : a small magnifying hand lens consisting of two single lenses in a metal cylinder **b** : a spectrum line having two close components **c** : a domino with the same number of spots on each end **3** : a set of two identical or similar things; *specif* : two thrown dice with the same number of spots on the upper face **4** : one of a pair; *specif* : one of two or more words (as *guard* and *ward*) in the same language derived by different routes of transmission from the same source

dou·ble take \'dəb-əl-ˌtāk\ *n* : a delayed reaction to a surprising or significant situation after an initial failure to notice anything unusual — usu. used in the phrase *do a double take*

dou·ble–talk \-ˌtȯk\ *n* **1** : language that appears to be earnest and meaningful but in fact is a mixture of sense and nonsense **2** : inflated, involved, and often deliberately ambiguous language — **double–talk** *vi* — **dou·ble–talk·er** *n*

dou·ble–team \-ˌtēm\ *vt* : to block or guard (an opponent) with two players at one time

Double Ten *n* [trans. of Chin (Pek) *shuang*[1] *shih*[2]; fr. its being the tenth day of the tenth month] : October 10 observed by Nationalist China in commemoration of the revolution of 1911

dou·ble·think \'dəb-əl-ˌthiŋk\ *n* : a simultaneous belief in two contradictory ideas

dou·ble–time \'dəb-əl-ˌtīm\ *vi* : to move at double time

double time *n* **1** : a marching cadence of 180 36-inch steps per minute **2** : payment of a worker at twice his regular wage rate

dou·ble–tongue \ˌdəb-əl-ˌtəŋ\ *vi* : to cause the tongue to alternate rapidly between the positions for *t* and *k* so as to produce a fast succession of detached notes on a wind instrument

dou·ble·tree \'dəb-əl-(ˌ)trē\ *n* : an equalizing bar for use with a two-horse team

double twill *n* : a twill weave with intersecting diagonal lines going in opposite directions

dou·ble–u *as at* w\ *n* : the letter *w*

double up *vi* : to share accommodations designed for one

double vision *n* : DIPLOPIA

dou·bloon \ˌdəb-'lün\ *n* [Sp *doblón*, aug. of *dobla*, an old Spanish coin, fr. L *dupla*, fem. of *duplus* double — more at DOUBLE] : an old gold coin of Spain and Spanish America

dou·bly \'dəb-(ə-)lē\ *adv* **1** : to twice the degree **2** : in a twofold manner

[1]**doubt** \'dau̇t\ *vb* [ME *douten*, fr. OF *douter* to doubt, fr. L *dubitare*; akin to L *dubius* dubious — more at DUBIOUS] *vt* **1** *archaic* : FEAR **2** : to be in doubt about <he ~*s* everyone's word> **3 a** : to lack confidence in : DISTRUST <find myself ~*ing* him even when I know that he is honest —H. L. Mencken> **b** : to consider unlikely <I ~ that it is authentic> ~ *vi* : to be uncertain — **doubt·able** \-ə-bəl\ *adj* — **doubt·er** *n* — **doubt·ing·ly** \-iŋ-lē\ *adv*

[2]**doubt** *n* **1 a** : uncertainty of belief or opinion that often interferes with decision-making **b** : a deliberate suspension of judgment **2** : a state of affairs giving rise to uncertainty, hesitation, or suspense **3 a** : a lack of confidence : DISTRUST **b** : an inclination not to believe or accept ***syn*** see UNCERTAINTY ***ant*** certitude, confidence — **no doubt** : [1]DOUBTLESS

doubt·ful \'dau̇t-fəl\ *adj* **1** : giving rise to doubt : open to question <it is ~ that they ever knew what happened> <a ~ proposition> **2 a** : lacking a definite opinion, conviction, or determination <they were ~ about the advantages of the new system> **b** : uncertain in outcome : UNDECIDED <a ~ progress> <the outcome of the election remains ~> **3** : marked by qualities that raise doubts about worth, honesty, or validity — **doubt·ful·ly** \-fə-lē\ *adv* — **doubt·ful·ness** *n*

syn DOUBTFUL, DUBIOUS, PROBLEMATIC, QUESTIONABLE *shared meaning element* : not affording assurance of the worth, soundness, success, or certainty of something or someone. *Doubtful* and *dubious* are sometimes used with little distinction <a *doubtful* (or *dubious*) reputation> <we are *doubtful* (or *dubious*) about their chances of success> but DOUBTFUL may positively impute worthlessness, unsoundness, failure, or uncertainty <their future prospects are very *doubtful*> <his title to the property is *doubtful*> while DUBIOUS can stress hesitation, mistrust, or suspicion (as in accepting or following); thus, a *doubtful* adherent to a party is one who cannot be counted on while a *dubious* adherent is less than wholeheartedly so because of uncertainties in his own mind; *doubtful* friends are probably not real friends while *dubious* friends give grounds for suspicion as to their worth or probity. PROBLEMATIC is applicable to any situation whose outcome is quite unpredictable <success in the control of inflation remains *problematic*> QUESTIONABLE may imply little more than the existence of doubt <the legality of his action is *questionable*> or it may stress doubt about propriety and imply strong or well-grounded suspicion <*questionable* behavior> <a man of *questionable* reputation> ***ant*** positive

doubting Thom·as \-'täm-əs\ *n* [*Thomas*, apostle of Jesus who doubted Jesus' resurrection until he had proof of it (Jn 20:24–29)] : a habitually doubtful person

[1]**doubt·less** \'dau̇t-ləs\ *adv* **1** : without doubt **2** : PROBABLY

[2]**doubtless** *adj* : free from doubt : CERTAIN — **doubt·less·ly** *adv* — **doubt·less·ness** *n*

douce \'düs\ *adj* [ME, sweet, pleasant, fr. MF, fr. fem. of *douz*, fr. L *dulcis*] *chiefly Scot* : SOBER, SEDATE <the ~ faces of the mourners —L. J. A. Bell> — **douce·ly** *adv, chiefly Scot*

dou·ceur \dü-'sər\ *n* [F, pleasantness, fr. LL *dulcor* sweetness, fr. L *dulcis* sweet] : a conciliatory gift

douche \'düsh\ *n* [F, fr. It *doccia*, fr. *docciare* to douche, fr. *doccia* water pipe, prob. back-formation fr. *doccione* conduit, fr. L *duction-, ductio* action of leading, fr. *ductus*, pp. of *ducere* to lead — more at TOW] **1 a** : a jet or current esp. of water directed against a part or into a cavity of the body **b** : an act of cleansing with a douche **2** : a device for giving douches — **douche** *vb*

dough \'dō\ *n* [ME *dogh*, fr. OE *dāg*; akin to OHG *teic* dough, L *fingere* to shape, Gk *teichos* wall] **1** : a mixture of flour and other ingredients stiff enough to knead or roll **2** : something resembling dough esp. in consistency **3** : MONEY **4** : DOUGHBOY — **dough·like** \-ˌlīk\ *adj*

dough·boy \-ˌbȯi\ *n* : an American infantryman esp. in World War I

dough·face \-ˌfās\ *n* : a northern congressman not opposed to slavery in the South before or during the Civil War; *also* : a northerner sympathetic to the South during the same period — **dough–faced** \-'fāst\ *adj*

dough·foot \-ˌfu̇t\ *n, pl* **dough·feet** \-ˌfēt\ *or* **doughfoots** : INFANTRYMAN

dough·nut \ˈdō-(ˌ)nət\ *n* **1 :** a small usu. ring-shaped cake fried in fat **2 :** something that resembles a doughnut esp. in shape; *specif* **:** TORUS 4

dough·ty \ˈdau̇t-ē\ *adj* **dough·ti·er; -est** [ME, fr. OE *dohtig;* akin to OHG *toug* is useful, Gk *teuchein* to make] **:** marked by fearless resolution **:** VALIANT — **dough·ti·ly** \ˈdau̇t-ᵊl-ē\ *adv* — **dough·ti·ness** \ˈdau̇t-ē-nəs\ *n*

doughy \ˈdō-ē\ *adj* **dough·i·er; -est :** resembling dough: as **a :** not thoroughly baked **b :** unhealthily pale **:** PASTY <a ~ complexion>

Doug·las fir \ˌdəg-ləs-\ *n* [David *Douglas* †1834 Sc botanist] **:** a tall evergreen timber tree (*Pseudotsuga taxifolia*) of the western U.S. having thick bark, pitchy wood, and pendulous cones — called also *Douglas spruce*

Dou·kho·bor \ˈdü-kə-ˌbȯ(ə)r\ *n* [Russ *dukhoborets,* fr. *dukh* spirit + *borets* wrestler] **:** a member of a Christian sect of 18th century Russian origin emphasizing the duty of obeying the inner light and rejecting church or civil authority

do up *vt* **1 a :** to clean and make ready for use or wear **:** LAUNDER <*do up* a shirt> **b :** to put in order <the maid will *do up* your room> **c :** REPAIR, RENOVATE <*do up* old furniture> **2 a :** to wrap up <*do up* a package> **b :** to put up **:** CAN **3 :** to deck out **:** CLOTHE **4 :** to wear out **:** EXHAUST

dour \ˈdau̇(ə)r, ˈdu̇(ə)r\ *adj* [ME, fr. L *durus* hard — more at DURING] **1 :** STERN, HARSH **2 :** OBSTINATE, UNYIELDING **3 :** GLOOMY, SULLEN — **dour·ly** *adv* — **dour·ness** *n*

[1]**douse** \ˈdüs, ˈdau̇s\ *n* [origin unknown] *Brit* **:** BLOW, STROKE

[2]**douse** \ˈdau̇s\ *vt* **doused; dous·ing 1 a :** to take in <~ a sail> **b :** SLACKEN <~ a rope> **2 :** DOFF <*doused* my cap on entering the porch —W. M. Thackeray>

[3]**douse** \ˈdau̇s *also* ˈdau̇z\ *vb* **doused; dous·ing** [prob. fr. obs. E *douse* (to smite), fr. [1]*douse*] *vt* **1 :** to plunge into water **2 a :** to throw a liquid on **:** DRENCH **b :** SLOSH **3 :** EXTINGUISH <~ the lights> ~ *vi* **:** to fall or become plunged into water — **dous·er** *n*

[4]**douse** \ˈdau̇s *also* ˈdau̇z\ *n* **:** a heavy drenching

[1]**dove** \ˈdəv\ *n* [ME, fr. (assumed) OE *dūfe;* akin to OHG *tūba* dove, and prob. to OE *dēaf* deaf] **1 :** any of numerous pigeons; *esp* **:** a small wild pigeon **2 :** a gentle woman or child **3 :** an individual who takes a conciliatory attitude (as in a dispute) and advocates negotiations and compromise; *esp* **:** an opponent of war — compare HAWK — **dov·ish** \ˈdəv-ish\ *adj* — **dov·ish·ness** *n*

[2]**dove** \ˈdōv\ *past of* DIVE

dove·cote \ˈdəv-ˌkōt, -ˌkät\ *or* **dove·cot** \-ˌkät\ *n* **1 :** a small compartmented raised house or box for domestic pigeons **2 :** a settled or harmonious group or organization <theological ~*s* throughout the world were set in an uproar —Cecil Roth>

dove·kie \ˈdəv-kē\ *n* [dim. of *dove*] **:** a small short-billed auk (*Plautus alle*) breeding on arctic coasts and ranging south in winter

doven *var of* DAVEN

Do·ver's powder \ˌdō-vərz-\ *n* [Thomas *Dover* †1742 E physician] **:** a powder of ipecac and opium compounded in the U.S. with lactose and in England with potassium sulfate and used as an anodyne and diaphoretic

[1]**dove·tail** \ˈdəv-ˌtāl\ *n* **:** something resembling a dove's tail; *esp* **:** a flaring tenon and a mortise into which it fits tightly making an interlocking joint between two pieces (as of wood)

[2]**dovetail** *vt* **1 a :** to join by means of dovetails **b :** to cut to a dovetail **2 a :** to fit skillfully to form a whole **b :** to fit together with ~ *vi* **:** to fit together into a whole

dovetail: *1* mortises, *2* tenons, *3* joint

dow \ˈdau̇\ *vi* **dought** \ˈdau̇t\ *or* **dowed** \ˈdau̇d\; **dow·ing** [ME *dow, deih* have worth, am able, fr. OE *dēah, dēag;* akin to OHG *toug* is worthy, is useful — more at DOUGHTY] *chiefly Scot* **:** to be able or capable

Dow \ˈdau̇\ *n* **:** DOW-JONES AVERAGE

dow·a·ger \ˈdau̇-i-jər\ *n* [MF *douagiere,* fr. *douage* dower, fr. *douer* to endow, fr. L *dotare,* fr. *dot-, dos* gift, dower — more at DOWRY] **1 :** a widow holding property or a title received from her deceased husband **2 :** a dignified elderly woman

[1]**dowdy** \ˈdau̇d-ē\ *n, pl* **dowd·ies 1** [dim. of *dowd* (dowdy), fr. ME *doude*] *archaic* **:** a dowdy woman **2 :** PANDOWDY

[2]**dowdy** *adj* **dowd·i·er; -est 1 :** not neat or becoming in appearance **:** SHABBY **2 a :** lacking smartness or taste **b :** OLD-FASHIONED — **dowd·i·ly** \ˈdau̇d-ᵊl-ē\ *adv* — **dowd·i·ness** \ˈdau̇d-ē-nəs\ *n* — **dowdy·ish** \-ish\ *adj*

[1]**dow·el** \ˈdau̇(-ə)l\ *n* [ME *dowle;* akin to OHG *tubili* plug, LGk *typhos* wedge] **1 :** a pin fitting into a hole in an abutting piece to prevent motion or slipping; *also* **:** a round rod or stick used esp. for cutting up into dowels **2 :** a piece of wood driven into a wall so that other pieces can be nailed to it

[2]**dowel** *vt* **-eled** *or* **-elled; -el·ing** *or* **-el·ling :** to fasten by or furnish with dowels

[1]**dow·er** \ˈdau̇(-ə)r\ *n* [ME *dowere,* fr. MF *douaire,* modif. of ML *dotarium* — more at DOWRY] **1 :** the part of or interest in the real estate of a deceased husband given by law to his widow during her life **2 :** DOWRY

[2]**dower** *vt* **:** to supply with a dower or dowry **:** ENDOW

dow·itch·er \ˈdau̇-i-chər\ *n, pl* **dowitchers** *also* **dowitcher** [of Iroquoian origin; akin to Mohawk *tawis* dowitcher] **:** a long-billed snipe (*Limnodromus griseus*) intermediate in characters between the typical snipes (genus *Capella*) and the sandpipers

Dow–Jones average \ˌdau̇-ˌjōnz-\ *n* [Charles H. *Dow* †1902 & Edward D. *Jones* †1920 Am financial statisticians] **:** an index of the relative price of securities based on the daily average price of selected lists of industrial, transportation, and utility common stocks

[1]**down** \ˈdau̇n\ *n* [ME *doun* hill, fr. OE *dūn;* akin to ON *dūnn* down of feathers] **1 :** an undulating usu. treeless upland with sparse soil — usu. used in pl. **2** *often cap* **:** a sheep of any breed originating in the downs of southern England

[2]**down** *adv* [ME *doun,* fr. OE *dūne,* short for *adūne, of dūne,* fr. *a-* (fr. *of*), *of* off, from + *dūne,* dat. of *dūn* hill] **1 a** (1) **:** toward or in a lower physical position (2) **:** to a lying or sitting position (3) **:** toward or to the ground, floor, or bottom **b :** on the spot **:** in cash <paid $10 ~> **c :** on paper <put ~ what he says> **2 :** in a direction that is the opposite of up: as **a :** SOUTHWARD **b :** to or toward a point away from the speaker or the speaker's point of reference **3** — often used as an intensive <cool ~ tensions and hostilities> <had the subject ~ pat> **4 :** to or toward a lower position in a series **5 :** to or in a lower or worse condition or status **6 :** from a past time **7 :** to or in a state of less activity or prominence **8 :** to a concentrated state <got his report ~ to three pages> <boiled the sap ~ into syrup> — **down to the ground :** PERFECTLY, COMPLETELY <that suits me *down to the ground*>

[3]**down** *adj* **1 a** (1) **:** occupying a low position; *specif* **:** lying on the ground <~ timber> (2) **:** directed or going downward **b :** lower in price **c :** not being in play in football because of wholly stopped progress or because the officials stop the play <marked the ball ~ on the 15-yard line> **d :** defeated or trailing an opponent (as in points scored) <~ two tricks> <~ by two touchdowns> **e** *baseball* **:** OUT **2 a :** being in a state of reduced or low activity **b** (1) **:** DEPRESSED, DEJECTED (2) **:** SICK <~ with flu> **3 :** FINISHED, DONE <eight ~ and two to go> — **down on :** having a low opinion of or dislike for <*down on* him>

[4]**down** \(ˈ)dau̇n\ *prep* **:** down along, around, through, toward, in, into, or on

[5]**down** \ˈdau̇n\ *n* **1 :** DESCENT, DEPRESSION **2 :** an instance of putting down **3 a :** a complete play to advance the ball in football **b :** one of a series of four attempts to advance a football 10 yards **4 :** DISLIKE, GRUDGE **5 :** DOWNER 1

[6]**down** *vt* **1 :** to cause to go or come down **2 :** to cause (a football) to be out of play **3 :** DEFEAT ~ *vi* **:** to go down

[7]**down** *n* [ME *doun,* fr. ON *dūnn*] **1 :** a covering of soft fluffy feathers **2 :** something soft and fluffy like down

down–and–out *adj* **1 :** physically weakened or incapacitated **2 :** DESTITUTE, IMPOVERISHED

[1]**down·beat** \ˈdau̇n-ˌbēt\ *n* **1 :** the downward stroke of a conductor indicating the principally accented note of a measure of music; *also* **:** the first beat of a measure **2 :** a decline in activity or prosperity

[2]**downbeat** *adj* **:** PESSIMISTIC, GLOOMY

down–bow \ˈdau̇n-ˌbō\ *n* **:** a stroke in playing a bowed instrument (as a violin) in which the bow is drawn across the strings from the heel to the tip

down·cast \ˈdau̇n-\ *adj* **1 :** low in spirit **:** DEJECTED **2 :** directed downward <with ~ eyes>

down·court \-ˈkō(ə)rt, -ˈkȯ(ə)rt\ *adv or adj* **:** in or into the opposite end of the court (as in basketball)

down east *adv or adj, often cap D & E* **:** in or into the northeast coastal section of the U.S. and parts of the Maritime Provinces of Canada; *specif* **:** in or into coastal Maine

down·er \ˈdau̇-nər\ *n* **1 :** a depressant drug; *esp* **:** BARBITURATE **2 :** a depressing experience or situation

down·fall \ˈdau̇n-ˌfȯl\ *n* **1 a :** a sudden fall (as from high rank or power) **b :** a fall (as of snow or rain) esp. when sudden or heavy **2 :** something that causes a downfall (as of a person) <drink was his ~> — **down·fall·en** \-ˌfȯ-lən\ *adj*

down·field \-ˈfē(ə)ld\ *adv or adj* **:** in or into the part of the field toward which the offensive team is headed

[1]**down·grade** \ˈdau̇n-ˌgrād\ *n* **1 :** a downward grade (as of a road) **2 :** a descent toward an inferior state — used esp. in the phrase *on the downgrade*

[2]**downgrade** *vt* **1 :** MINIMIZE, DEPRECIATE **2 :** to alter the status of (a job) so as to lower the rate of pay

down·haul \ˈdau̇n-ˌhȯl\ *n* **:** a rope or line for hauling down or holding down a sail or spar

down·heart·ed \-ˈhärt-əd\ *adj* **:** DOWNCAST, DEJECTED — **down·heart·ed·ly** *adv* — **down·heart·ed·ness** *n*

[1]**down·hill** \ˈdau̇n-ˌhil\ *n* **1 :** a descending gradient **2 :** a skiing race against time down a trail

[2]**down·hill** \-ˈhil\ *adv* **1 :** toward the bottom of a hill **2 :** toward a lower or inferior state or level — used esp. in the phrase *go downhill*

[3]**down·hill** \-ˌhil\ *adj* **1 :** sloping downhill **2 :** of or relating to skiing downhill **3 :** being the lower one or part esp. of a set; *specif* **:** being nearer the bottom of an incline <your ~ ski, knee, hip and shoulder are angled slightly lower —Perry Fairbank> **4 :** not difficult **:** EASY <had solved the biggest problems and the rest was ~>

down–home \ˌdau̇n-ˌhōm\ *adj* **:** of, relating to, or characteristic of the southern U.S. <a ~ drawl> <traveled widely through the South in rhythm-and-blues bands . . . and this ~ element has never left his music —A. B. Spellman>

down payment *n* **:** a part of the full price paid at the time of purchase or delivery with the balance to be paid later

down·play \ˈdau̇n-ˌplā\ *vt* **:** to play down **:** DE-EMPHASIZE

down·pour \-ˌpō(ə)r, -ˌpȯ(ə)r\ *n* **:** a pouring or streaming downward; *esp* **:** a heavy rain

down·range \-ˈrānj\ *adv* **:** away from a launching site and along the course of a test range <a missile landing 5000 miles ~> — **down·range** *adj*

ə abut	ᵊ kitten	ər further	a back	ā bake	ä cot, cart	
au̇ out	ch chin	e less	ē easy	g gift	i trip	ī life
j joke	ŋ sing	ō flow	ȯ flaw	ȯi coin	th thin	t͟h this
ü loot	u̇ foot	y yet	yü few	yu̇ furious	zh vision	

[1]**down·right** \-ˌrīt\ *adv* **1** *archaic* **:** straight down **2 :** THOROUGHLY, OUTRIGHT <~ mean> **3 :** with straightforward directness

[2]**downright** *adj* **1** *archaic* **:** directed vertically downward **2 :** ABSOLUTE, THOROUGH <a ~ lie> **3 :** PLAIN, BLUNT <a ~ man> — **down·right·ly** *adv* — **down·right·ness** *n*

down·riv·er \ˈdau̇n-ˈriv-ər\ *adv or adj* **:** toward or at a point nearer the mouth of a river

down·shift \-ˌshift\ *vi* **:** to shift an automotive vehicle into a lower gear — **downshift** *n*

Down's syndrome \ˈdau̇nz-\ *n* [J. L. H. *Down* †1896 E physician] **:** MONGOLISM

[1]**down·stage** \ˈdau̇n-ˈstāj\ *adv or adj* **1 :** toward or at the front of a theatrical stage **2 :** toward a motion-picture or television camera

[2]**down·stage** \-ˌstāj\ *n* **:** the part of a stage that is nearest the audience or camera

[1]**down·stairs** \ˈdau̇n-ˈsta(ə)rz, -ˈste(ə)rz\ *adv* **:** down the stairs **:** on or to a lower floor

[2]**downstairs** \ˌdau̇n-ˌsta(ə)rz, -ˌste(ə)rz\ *adj* **:** situated on the main, lower, or ground floor of a building

[3]**downstairs** \ˈdau̇n-ˈ, ˈdau̇n-ˌ\ *n pl but sing or pl in constr* **:** the lower floor of a building

down·state \-ˌstāt\ *n* **:** the chiefly southerly sections of a state of the U.S. as distinguished from a northerly part and esp. a metropolitan region often designated as *upstate* — **down·state** \-ˈstāt\ *adv or adj* — **down·stat·er** \-ˈstāt-ər\ *n*

down·stream \ˈdau̇n-ˈstrēm\ *adv or adj* **:** in the direction of the flow of a stream

down·stroke \-ˌstrōk\ *n* **:** a stroke made in a downward direction

down·swing \-ˌswiŋ\ *n* **1 :** a downward swing **2 :** a downward trend esp. in business activity

down–the–line *adj* **:** all the way **:** COMPLETE <a ~ union supporter>

down·time \ˈdau̇n-ˌtīm\ *n* **:** time during which a machine, department, or factory is inactive during normal operating hours

down–to–earth \ˌdau̇n-tə-ˈ(w)ərth\ *adj* **:** PRACTICAL, REALISTIC <a ~ appraisal of the situation> — **down–to–earth·ness** *n*

[1]**down·town** \ˈdau̇n-ˈtau̇n\ *adv* **:** to, toward, or in the lower part of a town or city; *esp* **:** to, toward, or in the main business district — **downtown** \ˌdau̇n-ˌtau̇n\ *adj*

[2]**downtown** \ˈdau̇n-ˌtau̇n\ *n* **:** the section of a town or city located downtown

down·trend \-ˌtrend\ *n* **:** a downturn esp. in business and economic activity

down·trod·den \ˈdau̇n-ˈträd-ᵊn\ *adj* **:** oppressed by superior power <the ~ peasants>

down·turn \-ˌtərn\ *n* **:** a downward turn esp. toward a decline in business activity

down under *adv* **:** into or in Australia or New Zealand

[1]**down·ward** \ˈdau̇n-wərd\ *or* **down·wards** \-wərdz\ *adv* **1 a :** from a higher to a lower place **b :** toward a direction that is the opposite of up **2 :** from a higher to a lower condition **3 a :** from an earlier time **b :** from an ancestor or predecessor

[2]**downward** *adj* **1 :** moving or extending downward **2 :** descending from a head, origin, or source — **down·ward·ly** *adv* — **down·ward·ness** *n*

down·wind \ˈdau̇n-ˈwind\ *adv or adj* **:** in the direction that the wind is blowing

downy \ˈdau̇-nē\ *adj* **down·i·er; -est 1 :** resembling a bird's down **2 :** covered with down **3 :** made of down **4 :** SOFT, SOOTHING <shake off this ~ sleep, death's counterfeit —Shak.>

downy mildew *n* **1 :** any of various parasitic lower fungi (family Peronosporaceae) that produce whitish masses of sporangiophores or conidiophores on the undersurface of the leaves of the host **2 :** a plant disease caused by a downy mildew

downy woodpecker *n* **:** a small black-and-white woodpecker (*Dendrocopos pubescens*) of No. America that has a white back and is smaller than the hairy woodpecker

dow·ry \ˈdau̇(ə)r-ē\ *n, pl* **dowries** [ME *dowarie,* fr. AF, irreg. fr. ML *dotarium,* fr. L *dot-, dos* gift, marriage portion; akin to L *dare* to give — more at DATE] **1** *archaic* **:** DOWER 1 **2 a :** the money, goods, or estate that a woman brings to her husband in marriage **b :** a sum of money or its equivalent required of postulants by some orders of cloistered nuns **3 :** a gift of money or property by a man to or for his bride **4 :** a natural gift **:** TALENT

dow·sa·bel \ˈdau̇-sə-ˌbel, -zə-\ *n* [*Dowsabel,* fem. name] *obs* **:** SWEETHEART

[1]**dowse** *var of* DOUSE

[2]**dowse** \ˈdau̇z\ *vb* **dowsed; dows·ing** [origin unknown] *vi* **:** to use a divining rod ~ *vt* **:** to find by dowsing

dows·er \ˈdau̇-zər\ *n* **:** DIVINING ROD; *also* **:** a person who uses it

Dow theory *n* **:** a system of stock-market forecasting based on the observed swings of the market itself

dox·ol·o·gy \däk-ˈsäl-ə-jē\ *n, pl* **-gies** [ML *doxologia,* fr. LGk, fr. Gk *doxa* opinion, glory (fr. *dokein* to seem, seem good) + *-logia* -logy — more at DECENT] **:** a usu. liturgical expression of praise to God

doxy \ˈdäk-sē\ *n, pl* **dox·ies** [perh. modif. of obs. D *docke* doll, fr. MD] **1 :** a woman of loose morals **:** PROSTITUTE **2 :** MISTRESS 5a

doy·en \dȯi-ˈen, -ˈ(y)en; ˈdwä-ˌyaⁿ(n)\ *n* [F, fr. LL *decanus* dean — more at DEAN] **1 a :** the senior man of a body or group **b :** a person uniquely skilled by long experience in some field of endeavor **2 :** the oldest example of a category <the ~ of the country's newspapers>

doy·enne \dȯi-ˈ(y)en, dwä-ˈyen\ *n* [F, fem. of *doyen*] **:** a female doyen

doy·ley *var of* DOILY

doz *abbr* dozen

[1]**doze** \ˈdōz\ *vb* **dozed; doz·ing** [prob. of Scand origin; akin to ON *dūsa* to doze] *vt* **:** to pass (as time) drowsily <*dozing* his life away> ~ *vi* **1 a :** to sleep lightly **b :** to fall into a light sleep — usu. used with *off* **2 :** to be in a dull or stupefied condition — **doze** *n* — **doz·er** *n*

[2]**doze** *vt* **dozed; doz·ing** [prob. back-formation fr. *dozer* (bulldozer)] **:** BULLDOZE 2 — **doz·er** *n*

doz·en \ˈdəz-ᵊn\ *n, pl* **dozens** *or* **dozen** [ME *dozeine,* fr. OF *dozaine,* fr. *doze* twelve, fr. L *duodecim,* fr. *duo* two + *decem* ten — more at TWO, TEN] **1 :** a group of 12 **2 :** an indefinitely large number <I've ~*s* of things to do> — **dozen** *adj* — **doz·enth** \-ᵊn(t)th\ *adj*

dozy \ˈdō-zē\ *adj* **doz·i·er; -est :** DROWSY, SLEEPY — **doz·i·ness** *n*

[1]**DP** \ˈdē-ˈpē\ *n, pl* **DP's** *or* **DPs :** DISPLACED PERSON

[2]**DP** *abbr* **1** data processing **2** degree of polymerization **3** dew point **4** doctor of podiatry **5** double play

DPE *abbr* doctor of physical education

DPh *abbr* doctor of philosophy

DPH *abbr* **1** department of public health **2** doctor of public health

DPN \ˌdē-ˌpē-ˈen\ *n* [*d*iphospho*p*yridine *n*ucleotide] **:** NAD

dpt *abbr* **1** department **2** deponent

dr *abbr* **1** debtor **2** drachma **3** dram **4** drive **5** drum

Dr *abbr* doctor

DR *abbr* **1** dead reckoning **2** dining room

[1]**drab** \ˈdrab\ *n* [perh. of Celt origin; akin to ScGael *drabag* dirty woman] **1 :** SLATTERN **2 :** HARLOT

[2]**drab** *vi* **drabbed; drab·bing :** to associate with prostitutes

[3]**drab** *n* [MF *drap* cloth, fr. LL *drappus*] **1 :** any of various cloths of a dull brown or gray color; *esp* **:** a thick woolen coating or a heavy cotton **2 a :** a light olive brown **b :** a dull, lifeless, or faded appearance or quality

[4]**drab** *adj* **drab·ber; drab·best 1 a :** of the dull brown color of drab **b :** of the color drab **2 :** characterized by dullness and monotony **:** CHEERLESS — **drab·ly** *adv* — **drab·ness** *n*

[5]**drab** *n* [prob. alter. of *drib*] **:** a small amount — usu. used in the phrase *dribs and drabs*

drab·bet \ˈdrab-ət\ *n* [[3]*drab* + *-et*] *dial Eng* **:** a coarse unbleached linen fabric

drab·ble \ˈdrab-əl\ *vb* **drab·bled; drab·bling** \-(ə-)liŋ\ [ME *drabelen*] *vt* **:** DRAGGLE ~ *vi* **:** to become wet and muddy

dra·cae·na \drə-ˈsē-nə\ *n* [NL, fr. LL, she-serpent, fr. Gk *drakaina,* fem. of *drakōn* serpent — more at DRAGON] **:** any of two genera (*Dracaena* and *Cordyline*) of Old World tropical shrubs or trees of the lily family with naked branches ending in tufts of sword-shaped leaves

drachm \ˈdram\ *n* [alter. of ME *dragme* — more at DRAM] **1 :** DRACHMA **2 :** DRAM

drach·ma \ˈdrak-mə\ *n, pl* **drach·mas** *or* **drach·mae** \-(ˌ)mē, -ˌmī\ *or* **drach·mai** \-ˌmī\ [L, fr. Gk *drachmē*— more at DRAM] **1 a :** any of various ancient Greek units of weight **b :** any of various modern units of weight; *esp* **:** DRAM 1 **2 a :** an ancient Greek silver coin equivalent to 6 obols **b** — see MONEY table

Dra·co \ˈdrā-(ˌ)kō\ *n* [L (gen. *Draconis*), lit., dragon — more at DRAGON] **:** a northern circumpolar constellation within which is the north pole of the ecliptic

dra·co·ni·an \drā-ˈkō-nē-ən, drə-\ *adj, often cap* [L *Dracon-, Draco*] **1 :** of, relating to, or characteristic of Draco or the severe code of laws held to have been framed by him **2 :** extremely harsh or cruel **:** RIGOROUS

[1]**dra·con·ic** \drə-ˈkän-ik\ *adj* [L *dracon-, draco*] **:** of or relating to a dragon

[2]**dra·con·ic** \drā-ˈkän-ik, drə-\ *adj* **:** DRACONIAN

[1]**draft** \ˈdraft, ˈdráft\ *n* [ME *draght;* akin to OE *dragan* to draw — more at DRAW] **1 :** the act of drawing a net; *also* **:** the quantity of fish taken at one drawing **2 a :** the act of moving loads by drawing or pulling **:** PULL **b :** a team of animals together with what they draw **3 a :** the force required to pull an implement **b :** load or load-pulling capacity **4 a :** the act or an instance of drinking or inhaling; *also* **:** the portion drunk or inhaled in one such act **b :** a portion poured out or mixed for drinking **:** DOSE **5 a :** DELINEATION, REPRESENTATION; *specif* **:** a construction plan <the ~ of a future building> **b :** SCHEME, DESIGN **c :** a preliminary sketch, outline, or version <the author's first ~> **6 :** the act, result, or plan of drawing out or stretching **7 a :** the act of drawing (as from a cask) **b :** a portion of liquid so drawn <a ~ of beer> **8 :** an allowance granted a buyer for loss in weight **9 :** the depth of water a ship draws esp. when loaded **10 a** (1) **:** a system or method for detaching or selecting individuals from a group (as for compulsory military service) (2) **:** an act or process of selecting an individual (as for political candidacy) without his expressed consent **b :** a group of individuals selected esp. by military draft **11 a :** an order for the payment of money drawn by one person or bank on another **b :** the act or an instance of drawing from or making demands upon something **:** DEMAND **12 a :** a current of air in a closed-in space **b :** a device for regulating the flow of air (as in a fireplace) **13 :** ANGLE, TAPER; *specif* **:** the taper given to a pattern or die so that the work can be easily withdrawn **14 :** a narrow border along the edge of a stone or across its face serving as a stonecutter's guide **15 :** a system whereby exclusive rights to selected new players are apportioned among professional teams — **on draft :** ready to be drawn from a receptacle <beer *on draft*>

[2]**draft** *adj* **1 :** used for drawing loads <~ animals> **2 :** constituting a preliminary or tentative version, sketch, or outline <a ~ treaty> **3 :** being on draft <~ beer>

[3]**draft** *vt* **1 :** to detach or select for some purpose: as **a :** to conscript for military service **b :** to select (a professional athlete) by draft **2 a :** to draw the preliminary sketch, version, or plan of **b :** COMPOSE, PREPARE **3 :** to draw off or away <water ~*ed* by pumps> **4 :** to mark (as a stone) with a draft in masonry ~ *vi* **1 :** to practice draftsmanship **2 :** to drive close behind another car while racing at high speed in order to take advantage of the reduced air pressure created by the leading car — **draft·able** \ˈdraf-tə-bəl, ˈdráf-\ *adj* — **draft·ee** \draf-ˈtē, dráf-\ *n* — **draft·er** \ˈdraf-tər, ˈdráf-\ *n*

draft board *n* **:** a civilian board that registers, classifies, and selects men for compulsory military service

draft horse *n* **:** a horse adapted for drawing heavy loads

drafts·man \'draf(t)-smən, 'dráf(t)-\ *n* **1 :** one who draws legal documents or other writings **2 :** one who draws plans and sketches (as of machinery or structures) **3 :** an artist who excels in drawing — **drafts·man·ship** \-,ship\ *n*

drafty \'draf-tē, 'dráf-\ *adj* **draft·i·er; -est :** of, relating to, or having a draft — **draft·i·ly** \-tə-lē\ *adv* — **draft·i·ness** \-tē-nəs\ *n*

¹drag \'drag\ *n* **1 :** something that is dragged, pulled, or drawn along or over a surface: as **a :** HARROW **b :** a sledge for conveying heavy bodies **c :** CONVEYANCE **2 :** something used to drag with; *esp* **:** a device for dragging under water to detect or obtain objects **3 a :** something that retards motion or action **b** (1) **:** the retarding force acting on a body (as an airplane) moving through a fluid (as air) parallel and opposite to the direction of motion (2) **:** friction between engine parts; *also* **:** retardation due to friction **c :** BURDEN, ENCUMBRANCE <the ~ of population growth on living standards> **4 a :** an object drawn over the ground to leave a scented trail **b :** a clog fastened to a trap to prevent the escape of a trapped animal **5 a :** the act or an instance of dragging or drawing: as (1) **:** a drawing along or over a surface with effort or pressure (2) **:** motion effected with slowness or difficulty; *also* **:** the condition of having or seeming to have such motion (3) **:** a draw on a pipe, cigarette, or cigar **:** PUFF; *also* **:** a draft of liquid **b :** a movement, inclination, or retardation caused by or as if by dragging **c** *slang* **:** influence securing special favor **6 :** STREET, ROAD <the main ~> **7** *slang* **:** a girl that one is escorting **8 :** woman's dress worn by a man — often used in the phrase *in drag* **9 :** DRAG RACE **10 :** one that is boring <school is a ~ for some youngsters>

²drag *vb* **dragged; drag·ging** [ME *draggen,* fr. ON *draga* or OE *dragan* — more at DRAW] *vt* **1 a** (1) **:** to draw slowly or heavily **:** HAUL (2) **:** to cause to move with painful or undue slowness or difficulty <*dragging* the musical tempo> (3) **:** to cause to trail along a surface <*dragged* his feet in the water> **b :** to bring by force or compulsion <had to ~ her husband to the opera> **c** (1) **:** to pass (time) in lingering pain, tedium, or unhappiness (2) **:** PROTRACT <~ a story out> **2 a :** to explore with a drag **b :** to catch with a dragnet or trawl **3 :** to hit (a bunt) by trailing the bat while moving toward first base ~ *vi* **1 :** to hang or lag behind **2 :** to fish or search with a drag **3 :** to trail along on the ground **4 :** to move on or proceed laboriously or tediously <the book ~*s*> **5 :** DRAW <~ on a cigarette> **6 :** to make a plucking or pulling movement **7 :** to participate in a drag race ***syn*** see PULL — **drag·ging·ly** \'draj-iŋ-lē\ *adv* — **drag one's feet** *or* **drag one's heels :** to act in a deliberately slow, dilatory, or ineffective manner

drag bunt *n* **:** a bunt in baseball made by a left-handed batter by trailing the bat while moving toward first base; *broadly* **:** a bunt made with the object of getting on base safely rather than sacrificing

dra·gée \dra-'zhā\ *n* [F, fr. MF *dragie* — more at DREDGE] **1 a :** a sugar-coated nut **b :** a silver-coated candy for decorating cakes **2 :** a sugar-coated medicated confection

drag·ger \'drag-ər\ *n* **:** one that drags; *specif* **:** a fishing boat operating a trawl or dragnet

drag·gle \'drag-əl\ *vb* **drag·gled; drag·gling** \-(ə-)liŋ\ [freq. of *drag*] *vt* **:** to make wet and dirty by dragging ~ *vi* **1 :** to trail on the ground **2 :** STRAGGLE

drag·gle–tail \'drag-əl-,tāl\ *n* **:** SLATTERN

drag·gy \'drag-ē\ *adj* **drag·gi·er; -est :** SLUGGISH, DULL

drag·line \'drag-,līn\ *n* **1 :** a line used in or for dragging **2 :** an excavating machine in which the bucket is attached by cables and operates by being drawn toward the machine

drag·net \'drag-,net\ *n* **1 a :** a net drawn along the bottom of a body of water **:** TRAWL **b :** a net used on the ground (as to capture small game) **2 :** a network of measures for apprehension (as of criminals)

drag·o·man \'drag-ə-mən\ *n, pl* **-mans,** *or* **-men** \-mən\ [ME *drogman,* fr. MF, fr. OIt *dragomanno,* fr. MGk *dragomanos,* fr. Ar *tarjumān,* fr. Aram *tūrgĕmānā*] **:** an interpreter chiefly of Arabic, Turkish, or Persian employed esp. in the Near East

drag·on \'drag-ən\ *n* [ME, fr. OF, fr. L *dracon-, draco* serpent, dragon, fr. Gk *drakōn* serpent; akin to OE *torht* bright, Gk *derkesthai* to see, look at] **1** *archaic* **:** a huge serpent **2 :** a fabulous animal usu. represented as a monstrous winged and scaly serpent or saurian with a crested head and enormous claws **3 :** a violent, combative, or very strict person **4 a :** a short musket formerly carried hooked to a soldier's belt; *also* **:** a soldier carrying such a musket **b :** an artillery tractor **5 :** any of numerous small brilliantly colored arboreal lizards (genus *Draco*) of the East Indies and southern Asia having the hind ribs on each side prolonged and covered with a web of skin **6** *cap* **:** DRACO **7 :** a formidable or baneful figure — **drag·on·ish** \-ə-nish\ *adj*

drag·on·et \,drag-ə-'net, 'drag-ə-nət\ *n* **1 :** a little dragon **2 :** any of various small often brightly colored scaleless marine fishes constituting a family (Callionymidae); *esp* **:** a European fish (*Callionymus lyra*) sometimes used as food

drag·on·fly \'drag-ən-,flī\ *n* **:** any of a suborder (Anisoptera) of odonate insects that are larger and stouter than damselflies, hold the wings horizontal in repose, and have rectal gills during the naiad stage; *broadly* **:** ODONATE

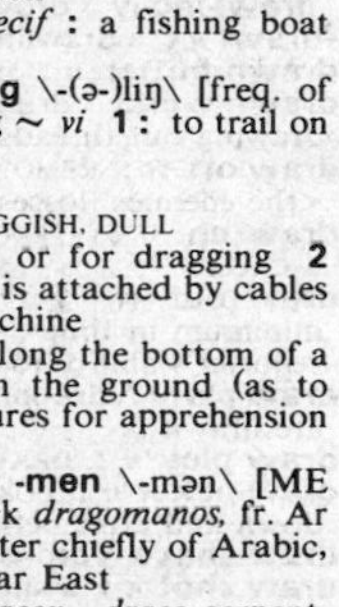

dragonfly

drag·on·head \-,hed\ *n* **:** any of several mints (genus *Dracocephalum*) often grown for their showy flower heads; *esp* **:** a No. American plant (*D. parviflorum*)

dragon lizard *n* **:** an Indonesian monitor lizard (*Varanus komodoensis*) that is the largest of all known lizards and reaches 11 feet in length

dragon's blood *n* **:** any of several resinous mostly dark-red plant products; *specif* **:** a resin from the fruit of a palm (genus *Daemonorops*) used for coloring varnish and in photoengraving

dragon's teeth *n pl* [fr. the dragon's teeth sown by Cadmus which sprang up as armed warriors who killed one another off] **1 :** seeds of strife **2 :** wedge-shaped concrete antitank barriers laid in multiple rows

¹dra·goon \drə-'gün, dra-\ *n* [F *dragon* dragon, dragoon, fr. MF] **:** a member of a European military unit formerly composed of heavily armed mounted troops

²dragoon *vt* **1 :** to reduce to subjection or persecute by harsh use of troops **2 :** to force or attempt to force into submission by violent measures **:** HARASS

drag race *n* **:** an acceleration contest between vehicles (as automobiles) — **drag racing** *n*

drag·rope \'drag-,rōp\ *n* **:** a rope that drags or is used for dragging

drag·ster \'drag-stər\ *n* **1 :** a vehicle (as an automobile) built or modified for use in a drag race **2 :** one who participates in a drag race

drag strip *n* **:** the site of a drag race; *specif* **:** a narrow strip of pavement with a racing area at least ¼ mile long

drail \'drā(ə)l\ *n* [obs. E *drail* to drag, trail] **:** a heavy fishhook used in trolling

¹drain \'drān\ *vb* [ME *draynen,* fr. OE *drēahnian*] *vt* **1** *obs* **:** FILTER **2 a :** to draw off (liquid) gradually or completely <~*ed* all the water out> **b :** to cause the gradual disappearance of **c :** to exhaust physically or emotionally **3 a :** to make gradually dry <~ a swamp> **b :** to carry away the surface water of <the river that ~*s* the valley> **c :** to deplete or empty by or as if by drawing off by degrees or in increments <war that ~*s* a nation of youth and wealth> **d :** to empty by drinking the contents of <~ a glass of beer> ~ *vi* **1 a :** to flow off gradually **b :** to disappear gradually **:** DWINDLE <money ~*ing* away in expenses> **2 :** to become emptied or freed of liquid by its flowing or dropping **3 :** to discharge surface or surplus water ***syn*** see DEPLETE — **drain·er** *n*

²drain *n* **1 :** a means (as a pipe) by which usu. liquid matter is drained **2 a :** the act of draining **b :** a gradual outflow or withdrawal **:** DEPLETION <a ruinous dollar ~> **3 :** something that causes depletion **:** BURDEN <a ~ on the national resources> — **down the drain :** being used wastefully or brought to nothing <years of work went *down the drain* in the fire>

drain·age \'drā-nij\ *n* **1 :** the act, process, or mode of draining; *also* **:** something drained off **2 :** a device for draining **:** DRAIN; *also* **:** a system of drains **3 :** an area or district drained

drain·pipe \'drān-,pīp\ *n* **:** a pipe for drainage

¹drake \'drāk\ *n* [ME, dragon, fr. OE *draca;* akin to ON *dreki* dragon; both fr. a prehistoric WGmc-NGmc word borrowed fr. L *draco* dragon — more at DRAGON] **1 :** a small piece of artillery of the 17th and 18th centuries **2 :** MAYFLY

²drake *n* [ME; akin to OHG *antrahho* drake] **:** a male duck

¹dram \'dram\ *n* [ME *dragme,* fr. MF & LL; MF, dram, drachma, fr. LL *dragma,* fr. L *drachma,* fr. Gk *drachmē,* lit., handful, fr. *drassesthai* to grasp] **1 a** — see WEIGHT table **b :** FLUIDRAM **2 a :** a small portion of something to drink **b :** a small amount

²dram *abbr* **1** dramatic **2** dramatist

dra·ma \'dräm-ə, 'dram-\ *n* [LL *dramat-, drama,* fr. Gk, deed, drama, fr. *dran* to do, act; prob. akin to Lith *daryti* to do] **1 :** a composition in verse or prose intended to portray life or character or to tell a story usu. involving conflicts and emotions through action and dialogue and typically designed for theatrical performance **:** PLAY — compare CLOSET DRAMA **2 :** dramatic art, literature, or affairs **3 a :** a state, situation, or series of events involving interesting or intense conflict of forces **b :** dramatic state, effect, or quality <the ~ of the courtroom proceedings>

dra·ma·logue \-,lóg, -,läg\ *n* [*drama* + mono*logue*] **:** a reading of a play to an audience

Dram·a·mine \'dram-ə-,mēn\ *trademark* — used for dimenhydrinate

dra·mat·ic \drə-'mat-ik\ *adj* **1 :** of or relating to the drama **2 a :** suitable to or characteristic of the drama **:** VIVID **b :** striking in appearance or effect **3** *of an opera singer* **:** having a powerful voice and a declamatory style — compare LYRIC — **dra·mat·i·cal·ly** \-i-k(ə-)lē\ *adv*

dramatic irony *n* **:** IRONY 3b

dramatic monologue *n* **:** a literary work in which a character reveals himself in a monologue usu. addressed to a second person

dra·mat·ics \drə-'mat-iks\ *n pl but sing or pl in constr* **1 :** the study or practice of theatrical arts (as acting and stagecraft) **2 :** dramatic behavior or expression

dramatic unities *n pl* **:** the unities of time, place, and action that are observed in classical drama

dra·ma·tis per·so·nae \,dram-ət-ə-spər-'sō-(,)nē, ,dräm-, -,nī\ *n pl* [NL] **1 :** the characters or actors in a drama **2** *sing in constr* **:** a list of the characters or actors in a drama

dra·ma·tist \'dram-ət-əst, 'dräm-\ *n* **:** PLAYWRIGHT

dra·ma·ti·za·tion \,dram-ət-ə-'zā-shən, ,dräm-\ *n* **1 :** the act or process of dramatizing **2 :** a dramatized version (as of a novel)

dra·ma·tize \'dram-ə-,tīz, 'dräm-\ *vb* **-tized; -tiz·ing** *vt* **1 :** to adapt (as a novel) for theatrical presentation **2 :** to present or represent in a dramatic manner ~ *vi* **1 :** to be suitable for dramatization **2 :** to behave dramatically **:** put on an act — **dra·ma·tiz·able** \-,tī-zə-bəl\ *adj*

dra·ma·turge \'dram-ə-,tərj, 'dräm-\ *n* **:** a specialist in dramaturgy

dra·ma·tur·gy \'dram-ə-,tər-jē, 'dräm-\ *n* [G *dramaturgie,* fr. Gk *dramatourgia* dramatic composition, fr. *dramatourgos* dramatist, fr. *dramat-, drama* + *-ourgos* worker, fr. *ergon* work — more at WORK] **:** the art or technique of dramatic composition and theatrical representation — **dra·ma·tur·gic** \,dram-ə-'tər-jik, ,dräm-\ *or*

ə abut ᵊ kitten ər further a back ā bake ä cot, cart
aů out ch chin e less ē easy g gift i trip ī life
j joke ŋ sing ō flow ȯ flaw ȯi coin th thin t͟h this
ü loot ů foot y yet yü few yů furious zh vision

dra·ma·tur·gi·cal \-ji-kəl\ *adj* — **dra·ma·tur·gi·cal·ly** \-ji-k(ə-)lē\ *adv*

dram·mock \'dram-ək\ *n* [ScGael *dramag* foul mixture] *chiefly Scot* : raw oatmeal mixed with cold water

dram·shop \'dram-ˌshäp\ *n* : BARROOM

drank *past of* DRINK

[1]**drape** \'drāp\ *vb* **draped; drap·ing** [ME *drapen* to weave, fr. MF *draper*, fr. *drap* cloth — more at DRAB] *vt* **1** : to cover or adorn with or as if with folds of cloth **2** : to cause to hang or stretch out loosely or carelessly <*draped* his legs over the chair> **3** : to arrange in flowing lines or folds <a cleverly *draped* suit> ~ *vi* : to become arranged in folds <this silk ~*s* beautifully> — **drap·able** *also* **drape·able** \'drā-pə-bəl\ *adj* — **drap·abil·i·ty** *also* **drape·abil·i·ty** \ˌdrā-pə-'bil-ət-ē\ *n*

[2]**drape** *n* **1 a** : a drapery esp. for a window : CURTAIN **b** : a sterile covering used in an operating room — usu. used in pl. **2** : arrangement in or of folds **3** : the cut or hang of clothing

drap·er \'drā-pər\ *n, chiefly Brit* : a dealer in cloth and sometimes also in clothing and dry goods

drap·ery \'drā-p(ə-)rē\ *n, pl* **-er·ies** **1** *Brit* : DRY GOODS **2 a** : a decorative piece of material usu. hung in loose folds and arranged in a graceful design **b** : hangings of heavy fabric for use as a curtain **3** : the draping or arranging of materials

dras·tic \'dras-tik\ *adj* [Gk *drastikos*, fr. *dran* to do] **1** : acting rapidly or violently <a ~ purgative> **2** : radical in effect or action : SEVERE <~ measures> — **dras·ti·cal·ly** \-ti-k(ə-)lē\ *adv*

drat \'drat\ *vb* **drat·ted; drat·ting** [prob. euphemistic alter. of *God rot*] : DAMN — used as a mild oath

draught \'draft\ *chiefly Brit var of* DRAFT

draughts \'draf(t)s\ *n pl but sing or pl in constr* [ME *draghtes*, fr. pl. of *draght* draft, move in chess] *Brit* : CHECKERS

draughts·man *chiefly Brit var of* DRAFTSMAN

Dra·vid·i·an \drə-'vid-ē-ən\ *n* [Skt *Draviḍa*] **1** : a member of an ancient Australoid race of southern India **2** : DRAVIDIAN LANGUAGES — **Dravidian** *adj*

Dravidian languages *n pl* : a language family of India, Ceylon, and West Pakistan that includes Tamil, Telugu, Gondi, and Malayalam

[1]**draw** \'drȯ\ *vb* **drew** \'drü\; **drawn** \'drȯn\; **draw·ing** [ME *drawen, dragen*, fr. OE *dragan*; akin to ON *draga* to draw, drag and perh. to L *trahere* to pull, draw] *vt* **1** : to cause to move continuously toward or after a force applied in advance : HAUL, DRAG **2** : to cause to go in a certain direction (as by leading) <*drew* him aside> **3 a** : to bring by inducement or allure : ATTRACT <honey ~*s* flies> **b** : to bring in or gather from a specified group or area <a college that ~*s* its students from many states> **c** : to bring on oneself : PROVOKE <*drew* enemy fire> **d** : to bring out by way of response : ELICIT <*drew* cheers from the audience> **4** : INHALE <*drew* a deep breath> **5 a** : to bring or pull out by effort <~ a knife> **b** : to extract the essence from <~ tea> **c** : EVISCERATE <plucking and ~*ing* a goose before cooking> **d** : to derive to one's benefit <*drew* inspiration from the old masters> **6** : to require (a specified depth) to float in <a ship that ~*s* 12 feet of water> **7 a** : ACCUMULATE, GAIN <~*ing* interest> **b** : to take (money) from a place of deposit **c** : to use in making a cash demand <~*ing* a check against his account> **d** : to receive regularly or in due course <~ a salary> **8 a** : to take (cards) from a stack or from the dealer **b** : to receive or take at random <*drew* a winning number> **9** : to bend (a bow) by pulling back the string **10** : to cause to shrink or tighten **11** : to strike (a ball) so as to impart a backward spin **12** : to leave (a contest) undecided : TIE **13 a** (1) : to produce a likeness of by making lines on a surface (2) : to give a portrayal of : DELINEATE <a writer who ~*s* his characters well> **b** : to write out in due form <~ a will> **c** : to design or describe in detail : FORMULATE <~ comparisons> **14** : to infer from evidence or premises <~ a conclusion> **15** : to spread or elongate (metal) by hammering or by pulling through dies; *also* : to shape (plastic) by stretching or by drawing through dies ~ *vi* **1** : to come or go steadily or gradually <night ~*s* near> **2 a** : to move something by pulling <~*ing* at the well> **b** : to exert an attractive force <the play is ~*ing* well> **3 a** : to pull back a bowstring **b** : to bring out a weapon <*drew*, aimed, and fired> **4 a** : to produce or allow a draft <the chimney ~*s* well> **b** : to swell out in a wind <all sails ~*ing*> **5 a** : to wrinkle or tighten up : SHRINK **b** : to change shape by pulling or stretching **6 a** : to cause blood or pus to localize at one point **b** : STEEP <give the tea time to ~> **7** : to create a likeness or a picture in outlines : SKETCH **8** : to come out even in a contest **9 a** : to make a written demand for payment of money or deposit **b** : to obtain resources (as of information) <~*ing* from a common fund of knowledge> *syn* see PULL — **draw·able** \-ə-bəl\ *adj* — **draw a bead on** : to take aim at — **draw a blank** : to fail to gain a desired object (as information sought) — **draw on** *or* **draw upon** : to use as a source of supply <*drawing on* the whole community for support> — **draw straws** : to decide an issue by lottery in which straws of unequal length are used — **draw the line** *or* **draw a line** **1** : to fix an arbitrary boundary between things that tend to intermingle <the difficulty of *drawing a line* between art and pornography> **2** : to fix a boundary excluding what one will not tolerate or engage in

[2]**draw** *n* **1** : the act or process of drawing: as **a** : a sucking pull on something held with the lips <take a ~ on his pipe> **b** : a removal of a handgun from its holster <the sheriff was quicker on the ~> **c** : backward spin given to a ball by striking it below center — compare FOLLOW **2** : something that is drawn: as **a** : a card drawn to replace a discard in poker **b** : a lot or chance drawn at random **c** : the movable part of a drawbridge **3** : a contest left undecided or deadlocked : TIE **4** : something that draws attention or patronage **5 a** : the distance from the string to the back of a drawn bow **b** : the force required to draw a bow fully **6** : a gully shallower than a ravine **7** : the deal in draw poker to improve the players' hands after discarding **8** : a football play in which the quarterback drops back as if to pass and then hands off to a back moving straight ahead — compare BOOTLEG 3

draw away *vi* : to move ahead (as of an opponent in a race)

draw·back \'drȯ-ˌbak\ *n* **1** : a refund of duties esp. on an imported product subsequently exported or used to produce a product for export **2** : an objectionable feature : HINDRANCE

draw back \drȯ-'bak\ *vi* : to avoid an issue or commitment : RETREAT

draw·bar \'drȯ-ˌbär\ *n* **1** : a railroad coupler **2** : a beam across the rear of a tractor to which implements are hitched

draw·bridge \-ˌbrij\ *n* : a bridge made to be raised up, let down, or drawn aside so as to permit or hinder passage

draw·down \-ˌdau̇n\ *n* **1** : a lowering of a water level (as in a reservoir) **2** : the process of depleting

draw down \(ˌ)drȯ-'dau̇n\ *vt* : to deplete by using or spending <an unfavorable trade balance *draws down* gold reserves>

draw·ee \drȯ-'ē\ *n* : the person on whom an order or bill of exchange is drawn

draw·er \'drȯ(-ə)r\ *n* **1** : one that draws: as **a** : a person who draws liquor **b** : DRAFTSMAN **c** : one who draws a bill of exchange or order for payment or makes a promissory note **2** : a sliding box or receptacle opened by pulling out and closed by pushing in **3** *pl* : an article of clothing (as underwear) for the lower body — **drawer·ful** \-ˌfu̇l\ *n*

draw in *vt* **1** : to cause or entice to enter or participate <heard the argument but would not be *drawn in*> **2** : to sketch roughly <*drawing in* the first outlines> ~ *vi* **1 a** : to draw to an end <the day *drew in*> **b** : to shorten seasonally <the evenings are already *drawing in*> **2** : to become more cautious or economical

draw·ing \'drȯ(-)iŋ\ *n* **1** : an act or instance of drawing; *specif* : the process of deciding something by drawing lots **2** : the art or technique of representing an object or outlining a figure, plan, or sketch by means of lines **3** : something drawn or subject to drawing: as **a** : an amount drawn from a fund **b** : a representation formed by drawing : SKETCH

drawing account *n* : an account showing payments made to an employee (as a salesman) in advance of actual earnings or for traveling expenses

drawing board *n* **1** : a board used as a base for drafting on paper **2** : a planning stage <a project still on the *drawing boards*>

drawing card *n* : something that attracts attention or patronage

drawing pin *n, Brit* : THUMBTACK

drawing room *n* [short for *withdrawing room*] **1 a** : a formal reception room **b** : a private room on a railroad passenger car with three berths and an enclosed toilet **2** : a formal reception

drawing table *n* : a table with a surface adjustable for elevation and angle of incline

draw·knife \'drȯ-ˌnīf\ *n* : a woodworker's tool having a blade with a handle at each end for use in shaving off surfaces — called also *drawshave*

drawknife

[1]**drawl** \'drȯl\ *vb* [prob. freq. of *draw*] *vi* : to speak slowly with vowels greatly prolonged ~ *vt* : to utter in a slow lengthened tone — **drawl·er** *n* — **drawl·ing·ly** \'drȯ-liŋ-lē\ *adv*

[2]**drawl** *n* : a drawling manner of speaking — **drawly** \'drȯ-lē\ *adj*

drawn butter *n* : melted butter often with seasoning

drawn·work \'drȯn-ˌwərk\ *n* : decoration on cloth made by drawing out threads according to a pattern

draw off *vt* : REMOVE, WITHDRAW ~ *vi* : to move apart : REGROUP <the enemies' losses forced them to *draw off*>

draw on *vi* : APPROACH <night *draws on*> ~ *vt* : to bring on : CAUSE

draw out *vt* **1** : REMOVE, EXTRACT **2** : to extend beyond a minimum in time : PROTRACT 2 **3** : to cause to speak freely <a reporter's ability to *draw* a person *out*>

draw·plate \'drȯ-ˌplāt\ *n* : a die with holes through which wires are drawn

draw play *n* : DRAW 8

draw poker *n* : poker in which each player is dealt five cards face down and after betting may discard cards and get replacements

draw·shave \'drȯ-ˌshāv\ *n* : DRAWKNIFE

draw shot *n* : a shot in billiards or pool made by striking the cue ball below its center to cause it to move back after striking the object ball

draw·string \'drȯ-ˌstriŋ\ *n* : a string, cord, or tape inserted into hems or casings or laced through eyelets for use in closing a bag or controlling fullness in garments or curtains

draw·tube \-ˌt(y)üb\ *n* : a telescoping tube (as for the eyepiece of a microscope)

draw up *vt* **1** : to bring (as troops) into array **2** : to draft in due form **3** : to straighten (oneself) to an erect posture esp. as an assertion of dignity or resentment **4** : to bring to a halt ~ *vi* : to come to a halt

[1]**dray** \'drā\ *n* [ME *draye*, a wheelless vehicle, fr. OE *dræge* dragnet; akin to OE *dragan* to pull — more at DRAW] : a vehicle used to haul goods; *specif* : a strong low cart or wagon without sides

[2]**dray** *vt* : to haul on a dray : CART

dray·age \'drā-ij\ *n* : the work or cost of hauling by dray

dray·man \'drā-mən\ *n* : one whose work is hauling by dray

[1]**dread** \'dred\ *vb* [ME *dreden*, fr. OE *drǣdan*] *vt* **1 a** : to fear greatly **b** *archaic* : to regard with awe **2** : to feel extreme reluctance to meet or face ~ *vi* : to be apprehensive or fearful

[2]**dread** *n* **1 a** : great fear esp. in the face of impending evil **b** : extreme uneasiness in the face of a disagreeable prospect <his ~ of paperwork> **c** *archaic* : AWE **2** : one causing fear or awe <fire was an omnipresent ~ —F. W. Saunders> *syn* see FEAR

[3]**dread** *adj* **1** : causing great fear or anxiety **2** : inspiring awe

[1]**dread·ful** \'dred-fəl\ *adj* **1 a** : inspiring dread : causing great and oppressive fear **b** : inspiring awe or reverence **2** : extremely distasteful, unpleasant, or shocking **3** : EXTREME <~ disorder> *syn* see FEARFUL — **dread·ful·ly** \-f(ə-)lē\ *adv* — **dread·ful·ness** \-fəl-nəs\ *n*

[2]**dreadful** *n* : a cheap and sensational story or periodical

dread·nought \'dred-ˌnȯt, -ˌnät\ *n* **1 :** a warm garment of thick cloth; *also* **:** the cloth **2** [*Dreadnought,* Brit. battleship] **:** a battleship whose main armament consists of big guns of the same caliber

1dream \'drēm\ *n, often attrib* [ME *dreem,* fr. OE *drēam* noise, joy] **1 :** a series of thoughts, images, or emotions occurring during sleep **2 :** an experience of waking life having the characteristics of a dream: as **a :** a visionary creation of the imagination **:** DAYDREAM **b :** a state of mind marked by abstraction or release from reality **:** REVERIE **c :** an object seen in a dreamlike state **:** VISION **3 :** something notable for its beauty, excellence, or enjoyable quality <the new car is a ~ to operate> **4 a :** a strongly desired goal or purpose <his ~ of becoming president> **b :** something that fully satisfies a wish **:** IDEAL <a meal that was a gourmet's ~> — **dream·ful** \-fəl\ *adj* — **dream·ful·ly** \-fə-lē\ *adv* — **dream·ful·ness** *n* — **dream·like** \'drēm-ˌlīk\ *adj*

2dream \'drēm\ *vb* **dreamed** \'drem(p)t, 'drēmd\ *or* **dreamt** \'drem(p)t\; **dream·ing** \'drē-miŋ\ *vi* **1 :** to have a dream **2 :** to indulge in daydreams or fantasies <~*ing* of a better future> **3 :** to appear tranquil or dreamy <houses ~*ing* in leafy shadows —Gladys Taber> ~ *vt* **1 :** to have a dream of **2 :** to consider as a possibility **:** IMAGINE **3 :** to pass (time) in reverie or inaction — usu. used with *away* <~*ing* the hours away> — **dream of :** to consider possible or fitting <wouldn't *dream of* disturbing you>

dream·er \'drē-mər\ *n* **1 :** one that dreams **2 a :** one who lives in a world of fancy and imagination **b :** one who has ideas or conceives projects regarded as impractical **:** VISIONARY

dream·land \'drēm-ˌland\ *n* **:** an unreal delightful country existing only in imagination or in dreams **:** NEVER-NEVER LAND

dream·less \-ləs\ *adj* **:** having or evidencing no dreams <a ~ sleep> — **dream·less·ly** *adv* — **dream·less·ness** *n*

dream up *vt* **:** DEVISE, CONCOCT

dream vision *n* **:** a usu. medieval poem having a framework in which the poet pictures himself as falling asleep and envisioning in his dream a series of allegorical people and events

dream·world \'drēm-ˌwərld\ *n* **:** a world of illusion or fantasy

dreamy \'drē-mē\ *adj* **dream·i·er; -est 1 a :** full of dreams <a ~ night's sleep> **b :** pleasantly abstracted from immediate reality **2 :** given to dreaming or fantasy <a ~ child> **3 a :** suggestive of a dream in vague or visionary quality <a ~ recollection of the incident> **b :** quiet and soothing **c :** DELIGHTFUL, PLEASING — **dream·i·ly** \-mə-lē\ *adv* — **dream·i·ness** \-mē-nəs\ *n*

drear \'dri(ə)r\ *adj* **:** DREARY

drea·ry \'dri(ə)r-ē\ *adj* **drea·ri·er; -est** [ME *drery,* fr. OE *drēorig* sad, bloody, fr. *drēor* gore; akin to OHG *trūrēn* to be sad, Goth *driusan* to fall, Gk *thrauein* to shatter] **1 :** SAD, DOLEFUL **2 :** causing feelings of cheerlessness **:** GLOOMY — **drea·ri·ly** \'drir-ə-lē\ *adv* — **drear·i·ness** \'drir-ē-nəs\ *n*

dreck \'drek\ *n* [Yiddish *drek* & G *dreck,* fr. MHG *drec;* akin to OE *threax* rubbish, L *stercus* excrement] **:** TRASH, RUBBISH

1dredge \'drej\ *n* [prob. fr. Sc *dreg-* (in *dregbot* dredge boat)] **1 :** an apparatus usu. in the form of an oblong iron frame with an attached bag net used esp. for gathering fish and shellfish **2 :** a machine for removing earth usu. by buckets on an endless chain or a suction tube **3 :** a barge used in dredging

2dredge *vb* **dredged; dredg·ing** *vt* **1 a :** to dig, gather, or pull out with a dredge **b :** to deepen (as a waterway) with a dredging machine — often used with *up* **2 :** to bring to light by deep searching <*dredging* up memories> ~ *vi* **1 :** to use a dredge **2 :** to search deeply — **dredg·er** *n*

3dredge *vt* **dredged; dredg·ing** [obs. *dredge,* n., sweetmeat, fr. ME *drage, drege,* fr. MF *dragie,* modif. of L *tragemata* sweetmeats, fr. Gk *tragēmata,* pl. of *tragēma* sweetmeat, fr. *trōgein* to gnaw — more at TERSE] **:** to coat (food) by sprinkling (as with flour) — **dredg·er** *n*

dree \'drē\ *vt* **dreed; dree·ing** [ME *dreen,* fr. OE *drēogan* — more at DRUDGE] *chiefly Scot* **:** ENDURE, SUFFER

dreg \'dreg\ *n* [ME, fr. ON *dregg;* akin to L *fraces* dregs of oil, Gk *thrassein* to trouble] **1 :** sediment contained in a liquid or precipitated from it **:** LEES — usu. used in pl. **2 :** the most undesirable part — usu. used in pl. <the ~*s* of society> **3 :** the last remaining part **:** VESTIGE

D region *n* **:** the lowest part of the ionosphere occurring between 25 and 40 miles above the surface of the earth

dreich \'drēk̲\ *adj* [ME, of Scand origin; akin to ON *drjūgr* lasting] *chiefly Scot* **:** DREARY

drei·del *also* **dreidl** \'drād-ᵊl\ *n* [Yiddish *dreidl,* fr. *dreien* to turn, fr. MHG *dræjen,* fr. OHG *drāen* — more at THROW] **1 :** a 4-sided toy marked with Hebrew letters and spun like a top in a game of chance **2 :** a children's game of chance played esp. at Hanukkah with a dreidel

1drench \'drench\ *n* **1 :** a poisonous or medicinal drink; *specif* **:** a large dose of medicine mixed with liquid and put down the throat of an animal **2 a :** something that drenches **b :** a quantity sufficient to drench or saturate

2drench *vt* [ME *drenchen,* fr. OE *drencan;* akin to OE *drincan* to drink] **1 a** *archaic* **:** to force to drink **b :** to administer a drench to (an animal) **2 :** to wet thoroughly (as by soaking or immersing in liquid) <desserts ~*ed* with brandy> **3 :** to soak or cover thoroughly with liquid that falls or is precipitated **4 :** to fill completely as if by soaking or precipitation **:** SATURATE <a mind ~*ed* with esoteric lore> ***syn*** see SOAK — **drench·er** *n*

1dress \'dres\ *vb* [ME *dressen,* fr. MF *dresser,* fr. (assumed) VL *directiare,* fr. L *directus* direct, pp. of *dirigere* to direct, fr. *dis-* + *regere* to lead straight — more at RIGHT] *vt* **1 a :** to make or set straight **b :** to arrange (as troops) in a straight line and at proper intervals **2** *archaic* **:** to dress down **3 a :** to put clothes on **b :** to provide with clothing **4 :** to add decorative details or accessories to **:** EMBELLISH **5 :** to prepare for use or service **6 a :** to apply dressings or medicaments to **b** (1) **:** to arrange (the hair) by combing, brushing, or curling (2) **:** to groom and curry (an animal) **c :** to kill and prepare for market **d :** CULTIVATE, TEND; *esp* **:** to apply manure or fertilizer to **e :** to put through a finishing process; *specif* **:** to make (as lumber or stone) trim and smooth ~ *vi* **1 a :** to put on clothing **b :** to put on or wear formal, elaborate, or fancy clothes <guests were expected to ~ for dinner> **2** *of a food animal* **:** to weigh after being dressed **3 :** to align oneself with the next soldier in a line to make the line straight — **dress ship :** to ornament a ship for a celebration by hoisting national ensigns at the mastheads and running a line of signal flags and pennants from bow to stern

2dress *n* **1 :** APPAREL, CLOTHING **2 :** an outer garment usu. for a woman or a girl **3 :** covering, adornment, or appearance appropriate or peculiar to a particular time **4 :** a particular form of presentation **:** GUISE

3dress *adj* **1 :** relating to or used for a dress **2 :** suitable for a formal occasion **3 :** requiring or permitting formal dress <a ~ affair>

dres·sage \drə-'säzh, dre-\ *n* **:** the execution by a horse of complex maneuvers in response to barely perceptible movements of a rider's hands, legs, and weight

dress circle *n* **:** the first or lowest curved tier of seats in a theater

dress down *vt* **:** to reprove severely

1dress·er \'dres-ər\ *n* **1** *obs* **:** a table or sideboard for preparing and serving food **2 :** a cupboard to hold dishes and cooking utensils **3 :** a chest of drawers or bureau with a mirror

2dresser *n* **:** one that dresses <a fashionable ~>

dresser set *n* **:** a set of toilet articles including hairbrush, comb, and mirror for use at a dresser or dressing table

dress·ing *n* **1 a :** the act or process of one who dresses **b :** an instance of such act or process **2 a :** a sauce for adding to a dish (as a salad) **b :** a seasoned mixture usu. used as a stuffing (as for poultry) **3 a :** material applied to cover a lesion **b :** fertilizing material (as manure or compost)

dressing glass *n* **:** a small mirror set to swing in a standing frame and used at a dresser or dressing table

dressing gown *n* **:** a robe (as of silk) worn esp. while dressing or resting

dressing room *n* **:** a room used chiefly for dressing; *esp* **:** a room in a theater for changing costumes and makeup

dressing station *n* **:** a station for giving first aid to the wounded

dressing table *n* **:** a table often fitted with drawers and a mirror in front of which one sits while dressing and grooming oneself

1dress·mak·er \'dres-ˌmā-kər\ *n* **:** one that does dressmaking

2dressmaker *adj, of women's clothes* **:** having softness, rounded lines, and intricate detailing <a ~ suit>

dress·mak·ing \-ˌmā-kiŋ\ *n* **:** the process or occupation of making dresses

dress rehearsal *n* **:** a full rehearsal of a play in costume and with stage properties shortly before the first performance

dress shirt *n* **:** a man's shirt esp. for wear with evening dress

dress suit *n* **:** a suit worn for full dress

dress uniform *n* **:** a uniform for formal wear

dress up *vt* **1 a :** to attire in best or formal clothes **b :** to attire in clothes suited to a particular role **2 :** to present or cause to appear in a certain light (as by distortion or exaggeration) <*dressed up* his story to make himself appear a hero> ~ *vi* **:** to get dressed up

dressy \'dres-ē\ *adj* **dress·i·er; -est 1 :** showy in dress **2 :** STYLISH, SMART — **dress·i·ness** *n*

drew *past of* DRAW

Drey·fu·sard \ˌdrī-f(y)ə-'sär(d), ˌdrā-, -'zär(d)\ *n* [F] **:** a defender or partisan of Alfred Dreyfus

drib \'drib\ *n* [prob. back-formation fr. *dribble* & *driblet*] **:** a small amount — usu. used in the phrase *dribs and drabs*

1drib·ble \'drib-əl\ *vb* **drib·bled; drib·bling** \-(ə-)liŋ\ [freq. of *drib* (to dribble)] *vi* **1 :** to fall or flow in drops or in a thin intermittent stream **:** TRICKLE **2 :** to let saliva trickle from a corner of the mouth **:** DROOL **3 :** to come or issue in piecemeal or desultory fashion **4 a :** to dribble a ball or puck **b :** to proceed by dribbling **c** *of a ball* **:** to move with short bounces ~ *vt* **1 :** to let or cause to fall in drops little by little **2 :** to issue sporadically and in small bits **3 a :** to propel by successive slight taps or bounces with hand, foot, or stick **b :** to hit (as a baseball) so as to cause a slow bouncing — **drib·bler** \-(ə-)lər\ *n*

2dribble *n* **1 a :** a small trickling stream or flow **b :** a drizzling shower **2 :** a tiny or insignificant bit or quantity **3 :** an act or instance of dribbling a ball or puck

drib·let \'drib-lət\ *n* **1 :** a trifling sum or part **2 :** a drop of liquid

dried–fruit beetle *n* **:** a small broad brown beetle (*Carpophilus hemipterus*) that is a cosmopolitan pest on stored products

dried–up \'drī-'dəp\ *adj* **:** being wizened and shrivelled

1drier *comparative of* DRY

2dri·er *also* **dry·er** \'drī(-ə)r\ *n* **1 :** something that extracts or absorbs moisture **2 :** a substance that accelerates drying (as of oils, paints, and printing inks) **3** *usu dryer* **:** a device for drying

driest *superlative of* DRY

1drift \'drift\ *n* [ME; akin to OE *drīfan* to drive — more at DRIVE] **1 a :** the act of driving something along **b :** the flow or the velocity of the current of a river or ocean stream **2 :** something driven, propelled, or urged along or drawn together in a clump by or as if by a natural agency: as **a :** wind-driven snow, rain, cloud, dust, or smoke usu. at or near the ground surface **b** (1) **:** a mass of matter (as sand) deposited together by or as if by wind or water (2) **:** a helter-skelter accumulation **c :** DROVE, FLOCK **d :** something (as driftwood) washed ashore **e :** rock debris deposited by natural agents; *specif* **:** a deposit of clay, sand, gravel, and boulders transported by a glacier or by running water from a glacier **3 a :** a general underlying design or tendency **b :** the underlying meaning, import, or purport of what is spoken or written **4** : something driven down upon or forced into a body: as **a** : a tool for ramming down or driving something **b** : a pin for stretching and aligning rivet holes **5** : the motion or action of drifting esp. spatially and usu. under external influence: as **a** : a ship's deviation from its course caused by currents **b** : one of the slower movements of oceanic circulation **c** : the lateral motion of an airplane due to air currents **d** : an easy moderate more or less steady flow or sweep along a spatial course **e** : a gradual shift in attitude, opinion, or position **f** : an aimless course; *esp* : a foregoing of any attempt at direction or control **g** : a deviation from a true reproduction, representation, or reading **6 a** : a nearly horizontal mine passageway driven on or parallel to the course of a vein or rock stratum **b** : a small crosscut in a mine connecting two larger tunnels **7 a** : an assumed trend toward a general change in the structure of a language over a period of time **b** : GENETIC DRIFT **c** : a gradual change in the zero reading of an instrument or in any quantitive characteristic that is supposed to remain constant ***syn*** see TENDENCY

[2]**drift** *vi* **1 a** : to become driven or carried along by a current of water, wind, or air **b** : to move or float smoothly and effortlessly **2 a** : to move along a line of least resistance **b** : to move in a random or casual way **c** : to become carried along subject to no guidance or control <the conversation ~*ed* from one topic to another> **3 a** : to accumulate in a mass or become piled up in heaps by wind or water **b** : to become covered with a drift **4** : to vary or deviate from a set adjustment ~ *vt* **1 a** : to cause to be driven in a current **b** *West* : to drive (livestock) slowly esp. to allow grazing **2 a** : to pile in heaps **b** : to cover with drifts <slopes that are heavily ~*ed* during the winter> — **drift·ing·ly** \'drif-tiŋ-lē\ *adv*

drift·age \'drif-tij\ *n* **1** : a drifting of some object esp. through the action of wind or water **2** : deviation from a set course due to drifting **3** : drifted material <seaweed and other ~>

drift·er \'drif-tər\ *n* : one that drifts; *esp* : one that travels or moves about aimlessly

drift fence *n* : a stretch of fence on range land esp. in the western U.S. for preventing cattle from drifting from their home range

drift·weed \'drif-ˌtwēd\ *n* : a seaweed (as of the genus *Laminaria*) that tends to break free and drift ashore

drift·wood \'drif-ˌtwu̇d\ *n* **1** : wood drifted or floated by water **2** : FLOTSAM 2

drifty \'drif-tē\ *adj* **drift·i·er; -est** : exhibiting or tending to form drifts

[1]**drill** \'dril\ *vb* [D *drillen;* akin to OHG *drāen* to turn — more at THROW] *vt* **1 a (1)** : to bore or drive a hole in **(2)** : to make by piercing action <~*ed* holes an inch apart> **b** : to hit with piercing effect <~*ed* a single to right field> **2 a** : to fix something in the mind or habit pattern of by repetitive instruction <~ pupils in spelling> **b** : to impart or communicate by repetition <impossible to ~ the simplest idea into some people> **c** : to train or exercise in military drill ~ *vi* **1** : to make a hole with a drill **2** : to engage in an exercise **3** : to act on with penetrating effect ***syn*** see PRACTICE — **drill·abil·i·ty** \ˌdril-ə-'bil-ət-ē\ *n* — **drill·able** \-ə-bəl\ *adj* — **drill·er** \'dril-ər\ *n*

[2]**drill** *n* **1** : an instrument with an edged or pointed end for making holes in hard substances by revolving or by a succession of blows; *also* : such an instrument with a machine for operating it **2** : the act or exercise of training soldiers in marching and the manual of arms **3 a** : a physical or mental exercise aimed at perfecting facility and skill esp. by regular practice **b** : a formal exercise by a team of marchers **c** *chiefly Brit* : the approved or correct procedure for accomplishing something efficiently **4 a** : a marine snail (*Urosalpinx cinerea*) destructive to oysters by boring through their shells and feeding on the soft parts **b** : any of several mollusks related to the drill **5** : a drilling sound

[3]**drill** *n* [prob. native name in West Africa] : a West African baboon (*Mandrillus leucophaeus*) closely related to the typical mandrills

[4]**drill** *n* [perh. fr. *drill* (rill)] **1 a** : a shallow furrow or trench into which seed is sown **b** : a row of seed sown in such a furrow **2** : a planting implement that makes holes or furrows, drops in the seed and sometimes fertilizer, and covers them with earth

[5]**drill** *vt* **1** : to sow (seeds) by dropping along a shallow furrow **2 a** : to sow with seed or set with seedlings inserted in drills **b** : to distribute seed or fertilizer in by means of a drill

[6]**drill** *n* [short for *drilling*] : a durable cotton fabric in twill weave

dril·ling \'dril-iŋ\ *n* [modif. of G *drillich,* fr. MHG *drilich* fabric woven with a threefold thread, fr. OHG *drilīh* made up of three threads, fr. L *trilic-, trilix,* fr. *tri-* + *licium* thread] : [6]DRILL

drill·mas·ter \'dril-ˌmas-tər\ *n* **1** : an instructor in military drill **2** : an instructor or director who maintains severe discipline and who often stresses the trivial and unimportant

drill press *n* : an upright drilling machine in which the drill is pressed to the work by a hand lever or by power

drill team *n* : an exhibition marching team that engages in precision drill

drily *var of* DRYLY

[1]**drink** \'driŋk\ *vb* **drank** \'draŋk\; **drunk** \'drəŋk\ *or* **drank; drink·ing** [ME *drinken,* fr. OE *drincan;* akin to OHG *trinkan* to drink] *vt* **1 a** : SWALLOW, IMBIBE **b** : to take in or suck up : ABSORB <~*ing* air into his lungs> **c** : to take in or receive avidly — usu. used with *in* <*drank* in every word of the lecture> **2** : to join in (a toast) **3** : to bring to a specified state by taking drink <*drank* himself into oblivion> <~*ing* his troubles away> ~ *vi* **1 a** : to take liquid into the mouth for swallowing **b** : to receive into one's consciousness **2** : to partake of alcoholic beverages **3** : to join in a toast

[2]**drink** *n* **1 a** : liquid suitable for swallowing **b** : alcoholic liquor **2** : a draft or portion of liquid **3** : excessive consumption of alcoholic beverages **4** : a sizable body of water — used with *the*

[1]**drink·able** \'driŋ-kə-bəl\ *adj* : suitable or safe for drinking — **drink·abil·i·ty** \ˌdriŋ-kə-'bil-ət-ē\ *n*

[2]**drinkable** *n* : a liquid suitable for drinking : BEVERAGE

drink·er \'driŋ-kər\ *n* **1 a** : one that drinks **b** : one that drinks alcoholic beverages esp. to excess **2** : a device that provides water for domestic animals or poultry

drinking fountain *n* : a fixture with nozzle that delivers a stream of water for drinking

drinking song *n* : a song on a convivial theme appropriate for a group engaged in social drinking

[1]**drip** \'drip\ *vb* **dripped; drip·ping** [ME *drippen,* fr. OE *dryppan;* akin to OE *dropa* drop] *vt* **1** : to let fall in drops **2** : to spill or let out copiously <her voice *dripping* sarcasm> ~ *vi* **1 a** : to let fall drops of moisture or liquid **b** : to overflow with or as if with moisture <a uniform *dripping* with gold braid> <a novel that ~*s* with sentimentality> **2** : to fall in or as if in drops **3** : to waft or pass gently — **drip·per** *n*

[2]**drip** *n* **1 a** : a falling in drops **b** : liquid that falls, overflows, or is extruded in drops **2** : the sound made by or as if by falling drops **3** : a part of a cornice or other member that projects to throw off rainwater; *also* : an overlapping metal strip serving the same purpose **4** : a device for the administration of a fluid at a slow rate esp. into a vein; *also* : a material so administered **5** *slang* : a dull or unattractive person

drip coffee *n* : coffee made by letting boiling water drip slowly through finely ground coffee

[1]**drip–dry** \'drip-'drī\ *vi* : to dry with few or no wrinkles when hung dripping wet

[2]**drip–dry** *adj* : made of a washable fabric that drip-dries

[3]**drip–dry** *n* : a drip-dry garment

drip·less \'drip-ləs\ *adj* : designed not to drip <~ candles>

drip pan *n* : a pan for catching drippings — called also *dripping pan*

[1]**drip·ping** \'drip-iŋ\ *n* : fat and juices drawn from meat during cooking — often used in pl.

[2]**dripping** *adv* : EXTREMELY — usu. used in the phrase *dripping wet*

drip pot *n* : a pot for making drip coffee

drip·py \'drip-ē\ *adj* **drip·pi·er; -est 1** : RAINY, DRIZZLY **2** : MAWKISH 2

drip·stone \'drip-ˌstōn\ *n* **1** : a stone drip (as over a window) **2** : calcium carbonate in the form of stalactites or stalagmites

[1]**drive** \'drīv\ *vb* **drove** \'drōv\; **driv·en** \'driv-ən\; **driv·ing** \'drī-viŋ\ [ME *driven,* fr. OE *drīfan;* akin to OHG *trīban* to drive] *vt* **1 a** : to impart a forward motion to by physical force <waves *drove* the boat against the shore> **b** : to repulse, remove, or cause to go by force, authority, or influence <~ the enemy back> **c** : to set or keep in motion or operation <~ machinery by electricity> **2 a** : to direct the motions and course of (a draft animal) **b** : to operate the mechanism and controls and direct the course of (as a vehicle) **c** : to convey in a vehicle **d** : to float (logs) down a stream **3** : to carry on or through energetically <*driving* a hard bargain> **4 a** : to exert inescapable or coercive pressure on : FORCE **b** : to compel to undergo or suffer a change (as in situation, awareness, or emotional state) <*drove* him crazy> **c** : to urge relentlessly to continuous exertion <the sergeant *drove* his recruits> **d** : to press or force into an activity, course, or direction <the expensive drug habit that ~*s* addicts to steal> **e** : to project, inject, or impress incisively <*drove* his point home> **5 a** : to cause (as game or cattle) to move in a desired direction **b** : to search (a district) for game **6** : to force (a passage) by pressing or digging **7 a** : to propel (an object of play) swiftly **b** : to hit (a golf ball) from the tee esp. with a driver **c** : to cause (a run or runner) to be scored in baseball — usu. used with *in* ~ *vi* **1 a** : to dash, plunge, or surge ahead rapidly or violently **b** : to rush along with force against an obstruction <rain *driving* against the windshield> **c** : to progress with strong momentum <the rain was *driving* hard> **2 a** : to operate a vehicle; *also* : HANDLE <an auto that ~*s* well> **b** : to have oneself carried in a vehicle **3** : to drive an object of play ***syn*** see MOVE — **driv·able** *also* **drive·able** \'drī-və-bəl\ *adj* — **drive at** : to have as an ultimate meaning or conclusion <did not understand what she was *driving at* —Eric Goldman>

[2]**drive** *n* **1** : an act of driving: **a** : a trip in a carriage or automobile **b** : a collection and driving together of animals; *also* : the animals gathered **c** : a driving of cattle or sheep overland **d** : a hunt or shoot in which the game is driven within the hunter's range **e** : the guiding of logs downstream to a mill; *also* : the floating logs amassed in a drive **f (1)** : the act or an instance of driving an object of play **(2)** : the flight of a ball **2 a** : a private road : DRIVEWAY 2 **b** : a public road for driving (as in a park) **3** : an offensive, aggressive, or expansionist move; *esp* : a strong military attack against enemy-held terrain **4** : the state of being hurried and under pressure **5 a** : a strong systematic group effort : CAMPAIGN **b** : a sustained offensive effort <the ~ that ended in a touchdown> **6 a** : an urgent, basic, or instinctual need : a motivating physiological condition of the organism <a sexual ~> **b** : an impelling culturally acquired concern, interest, or longing <enslaved by a ~ for perfection> **c** : dynamic quality **7 a** : the means for giving motion to a machine or machine part **b** : the means by which the propulsive power of an automobile is applied to the road <front wheel ~> **c** : the means by which the propulsion of an automotive vehicle is controlled and directed <a left-hand ~> **8** : a device including a transport and heads for reading or writing tape and esp. magnetic tape — **drive** *adj*

[1]**drive–in** \'drī-ˌvin\ *n* : a place of business (as a theater or restaurant) so laid out that patrons can be accommodated while remaining in their automobiles

[2]**drive–in** *adj* : laid out as a drive-in

[1]**driv·el** \'driv-əl\ *vb* **-eled** *or* **-elled; -el·ing** *or* **-el·ling** \-(ə-)liŋ\ [ME *drivelen,* fr. OE *dreflian;* akin to ON *draf* malt dregs, OE *deorc* dark] *vi* **1** : to let saliva dribble from the mouth : SLAVER **2** : to talk stupidly and carelessly ~ *vt* **1** : to utter in an infantile or imbecilic way **2** : to waste or fritter in a childish fashion — **driv·el·er** \-(ə-)lər\ *n*

[2]**drivel** *n* **1** *archaic* : saliva trickling from the mouth **2** : NONSENSE

drive·line \ˈdrīv-ˌlīn\ *n* **:** the parts including the universal joint and the drive shaft that connect the transmission with the driving axles of an automobile

driv·en *adj* **:** having a compulsive or urgent quality <a ~ sense of obligation> — **driv·en·ness** \ˈdriv-ən-nəs\ *n*

driv·er \ˈdrī-vər\ *n* **:** one that drives: as **a :** COACHMAN **b :** the operator of a motor vehicle **c :** an implement (as a hammer) for driving **d :** a mechanical piece for imparting motion to another piece **e :** a golf club with a wooden head and nearly straight face used in driving — **driv·er·less** \-ləs\ *adj*

driver ant *n* **:** ARMY ANT; *specif* **:** any of various African and Asian ants (*Dorylus* or related genera) that move in vast armies

driver's license *n* **:** a license issued under governmental authority that permits the holder to operate a motor vehicle

driver's seat *n* **:** the position of top authority or dominance

drive shaft *n* **:** a shaft that transmits mechanical power

drive·way \ˈdrīv-ˌwā\ *n* **1 :** a road or way along which animals are driven **2 :** a private road giving access from a public way to a building on abutting grounds

driv·ing *adj* **1 a :** communicating force <a ~ wheel> **b :** exerting pressure <a ~ influence> **2 a :** having great force <a ~ rain> **b :** acting with vigor **:** ENERGETIC <a hard-*driving* worker>

driving range *n* **:** an area equipped with distance markers, clubs, balls, and tees for practicing golf drives

[1]**driz·zle** \ˈdriz-əl\ *vb* **driz·zled; driz·zling** \-(ə-)liŋ\ [perh. alter. of ME *drysnen* to fall, fr. OE *-drysnian* to disappear; akin to Goth *driusan* to fall] *vi* **:** to rain in very small drops or very lightly **:** SPRINKLE ~ *vt* **1 :** to shed or let fall in minute drops or particles **2 :** to make wet with minute drops — **driz·zling·ly** \-(ə-)liŋ-lē\ *adv*

[2]**drizzle** *n* **:** a fine misty rain — **driz·zly** \ˈdriz-(ə-)lē\ *adj*

drogue \ˈdrōg\ *n* [prob. alter. of [1]*drag*] **1 :** SEA ANCHOR **2 a :** a cylindrical or funnel-shaped device towed as a target by an airplane **b :** a small parachute for stabilizing or decelerating something (as an astronaut's capsule) or for pulling a larger parachute out of stowage **3 :** a funnel-shaped device which is attached to the end of a long flexible hose suspended from a tanker airplane in flight and into which the probe of another airplane in flight is fitted so as to receive fuel from the tanker airplane

droit \ˈdrȯit, drə-ˈwä\ *n* [MF, fr. ML *directum*, fr. LL, neut. of *directus* just, fr. L, direct] **:** a legal right <~*s* of admiralty>

droit du sei·gneur \drwä-dü̅e-se-nʸœr\ *n* [F, right of the lord] **:** a supposed legal or customary right of a feudal lord to have sexual relations with a vassal's bride on her wedding night

[1]**droll** \ˈdrōl\ *adj* [F *drôle*, fr. *drôle* scamp, fr. MF *drolle*, fr. MD, imp] **:** having a humorous, whimsical, or odd quality ***syn*** see LAUGHABLE — **droll·ness** *n* — **drol·ly** \ˈdrō(l)-lē\ *adv*

[2]**droll** *n* **:** one that amuses or diverts **:** JESTER, COMEDIAN

[3]**droll** *vi, archaic* **:** to make fun **:** JEST, SPORT

droll·ery \ˈdrōl-(ə-)rē\ *n, pl* **-er·ies 1 :** something that is droll: as **a :** a comic picture or drawing **b :** a usu. brief comic show or entertainment **c :** an amusing story **:** JEST **2 :** the act or an instance of jesting or burlesquing **3 :** whimsical humor

-drome \ˌdrōm\ *n comb form* [*hippodrome*] **1 :** racecourse <motor-*drome*> **2 :** large specially prepared place <aero*drome*>

drom·e·dary \ˈdräm-ə-ˌder-ē *also* ˈdrəm-\ *n, pl* **-dar·ies** [ME *dromedarie*, fr. MF *dromedaire*, fr. LL *dromedarius*, fr. L *dromad-, dromas*, fr. Gk, running; akin to Gk *dramein* to run, *dromos* racecourse, OE *treppan* to tread] **1 :** a camel of unusual speed bred and trained esp. for riding **2 :** the one-humped camel (*Camelus dromedarius*) of western Asia and northern Africa

drom·ond \ˈdräm-ənd\ *n* [ME, fr. MF *dromont*, fr. LL *dromon-, dromo* light ship, fr. Gk *dromōn*, fr. *dramein* to run] **:** a large fast-sailing galley or cutter of medieval times

-d·ro·mous \d-rə-məs\ *adj comb form* [NL *-dromus*, fr. Gk *-dromos* (akin to Gk *dramein*)] **:** running <cata*dromous*>

[1]**drone** \ˈdrōn\ *n* [ME, fr. OE *drān*; akin to OHG *treno* drone] **1 :** the male of a bee (as the honeybee) that has no sting and gathers no honey — see HONEYBEE illustration **2 :** one that lives on the labors of others **:** PARASITE **3 :** a pilotless airplane, helicopter, or ship controlled by radio signals

[2]**drone** *vb* **droned; dron·ing** *vi* **1 a :** to make a sustained deep murmuring, humming, or buzzing sound **b :** to talk in a persistently dull or monotonous tone **2 :** to pass, proceed, or act in a dull, drowsy, or indifferent manner <the trial *droned* on for months> ~ *vt* **1 :** to utter or pronounce with a drone **2 :** to pass or spend in dull or monotonous activity or in idleness <*droned* away the precious years of youth> — **dron·er** *n* — **dron·ing·ly** \ˈdrō-niŋ-lē\ *adv*

[3]**drone** *n* **1 :** one of the usu. three pipes on a bagpipe that sound fixed continuous tones **2 :** a deep sustained or monotonous sound **:** HUM **3 :** an unvarying sustained bass note often serving as the tonic in a musical composition

[1]**drool** \ˈdrül\ *vb* [perh. alter. of *drivel*] *vi* **1 a :** to secrete saliva in anticipation of food **b :** DRIVEL 1 **2 :** to make an effusive show of pleasure **3 :** to talk nonsense ~ *vt* **:** to express sentimentally or effusively

[2]**drool** *n* **:** DRIVEL

[1]**droop** \ˈdrüp\ *vb* [ME *drupen*, fr. ON *drūpa*; akin to OE *dropa* drop — more at DROP] *vi* **1 :** to hang or incline downward **2 :** to sink gradually **3:** to become depressed or weakened **:** LANGUISH ~ *vt* **:** to let droop — **droop·ing·ly** \ˈdrü-piŋ-lē\ *adv*

[2]**droop** *n* **:** the condition or appearance of drooping

droopy \ˈdrü-pē\ *adj* **droop·i·er; -est 1 :** drooping or tending to droop **2 :** GLOOMY

[1]**drop** \ˈdräp\ *n, often attrib* [ME, fr. OE *dropa*; akin to Goth *driusan* to fall — more at DREARY] **1 a** (1) **:** the quantity of fluid that falls in one spherical mass (2) *pl* **:** a dose of medicine measured by drops; *specif* **:** a solution for dilating the pupil of the eye **b :** a minute quantity or degree of something nonmaterial or intangible **c :** a small quantity of drink **d :** the smallest practical unit of liquid measure **2 :** something that resembles a liquid drop: as **a :** a pendent ornament attached to a piece of jewelry; *also* **:** an earring with such a pendant **b :** a small globular cookie or candy **3** [[2]*drop*] **a :** the act or an instance of dropping **:** FALL **b :** a decline in quantity or quality **c :** a descent by parachute; *also* **:** the men or equipment dropped by parachute **d :** a central point or depository to which something (as mail) is brought for distribution or transmission **e :** a place used for the deposit and distribution of stolen or illegal goods **4 a :** the distance from a higher to a lower level or through which something drops **b :** a fall of electric potential **5 :** a slot into which something is to be dropped **6** [[2]*drop*] **:** something that drops, hangs, or falls: as **a :** a movable plate that covers the keyhole of a lock **b :** an unframed piece of cloth stage scenery; *also* **:** DROP CURTAIN **c :** a hinged platform on a gallows **d :** a fallen fruit **7 :** the advantage of having an opponent covered with a firearm; *broadly* **:** ADVANTAGE, SUPERIORITY — usu. used in the phrase *get the drop on*

[2]**drop** *vb* **dropped; drop·ping** *vi* **1 :** to fall in drops **2 a** (1) **:** to fall unexpectedly or suddenly (2) **:** to descend from one line or level to another **b :** to fall in a state of collapse or death **c** *of a card* **:** to become played by reason of the obligation to follow suit **d** *of a ball* **:** to roll into a hole or basket **3 :** to move with a favoring wind or current — usu. used with *down* **4 :** to enter as if without conscious effort of will into some state, condition, or activity <*dropped* into sleep> **5 a :** to cease to be of concern **:** LAPSE <let the matter ~> **b** to become less <production *dropped*> — often used with *off* ~ *vt* **1 :** to let fall **:** cause to fall **2 a :** to lower or cause to descend from one level or position to another **b :** to lower (wheels) in preparation for landing an airplane **c :** to cause to lessen or decrease **:** REDUCE <*dropped* his speed> **3 :** to set down from a ship or vehicle **:** UNLOAD; *also* **:** AIR-DROP **4 :** to cause (the voice) to be less loud **5 a :** to bring down with a shot or a blow **b :** to cause (a high card) to fall **c :** to toss or roll (a ball) into a hole or basket **6 a :** to give up (as an idea) **b :** to leave incomplete <*dropped* what he was doing> **c :** to break off an association or connection with **:** DISMISS <~ a failing student> **7 a :** to leave (a letter representing a speech sound) unsounded <~ the *g* in *running*> **b :** to leave out in writing **8 a :** to utter or mention in a casual way <~ a suggestion> **b :** WRITE <~ us a line soon> **9** *of an animal* **:** to give birth to **10 :** LOSE <*dropped* 3 games> <*dropped* $50 in a poker game> **11 :** to take (a drug) orally **:** SWALLOW <~ acid> — **drop back 1 :** to move toward the rear of an advancing line or column **2 :** to move straight back from the line of scrimmage — used of a back in football — **drop behind :** to fail to keep up — **drop by :** to pay a brief casual visit — **drop in :** to pay an unexpected visit

drop cloth *n* **:** a protective sheet (as of cloth or plastic) used esp. by painters to cover floors and furniture

drop curtain *n* **:** a stage curtain that can be lowered and raised

drop–forge \ˈdräp-ˈfō(ə)rj, -ˈfȯ(ə)rj\ *vt* **:** to forge between dies by a drop hammer or punch press — **drop forger** *n*

drop forging *n* **:** a forging made by the force of a dropped weight

drop front *n* **:** a hinged cover on the front of a desk that may be lowered to provide a surface for writing

drop hammer *n* **:** a power hammer raised and then released to drop (as on metal resting on an anvil or die)

drop·head \ˈdräp-ˌhed\ *n* **1 :** a device for a desk or table that enables an attached typewriter or sewing machine to be swung or dropped down to leave a flat table top **2** *Brit* **:** a convertible automobile

drop–in \ˈdräp-ˌin\ *n* **1 :** one who drops in **:** a casual visitor **2 :** an informal social gathering at which guests are invited to drop in

drop·kick \-ˌkik\ *n* **:** a kick made by dropping a football to the ground and kicking it at the moment it starts to rebound

drop–kick \-ˈkik\ *vi* **:** to make a dropkick ~ *vt* **:** to score (a goal) with a dropkick — **drop·kick·er** *n*

drop leaf *n* **:** a hinged leaf on the side or end of a table that can be folded down

drop·let \ˈdräp-lət\ *n* **:** a tiny drop (as of a liquid)

droplet infection *n* **:** infection transmitted by airborne droplets of sputum containing infectious organisms

drop letter *n* **:** a letter to be delivered from the office where mailed

drop·light \ˈdräp-ˌlīt\ *n* **:** an electric light suspended by a cord

drop–off \ˈdräp-ˌȯf\ *n* **1 :** a very steep or perpendicular descent **2 :** a marked dwindling or decline <a ~ in attendence>

drop off \dräp-ˈȯf\ *vi* **:** to fall asleep

drop·out \-ˌau̇t\ *n* **1 :** one who drops out of school **2 :** one who drops out of conventional society **3 :** a spot on a magnetic tape from which data has disappeared

drop out \dräp-ˈau̇t\ *vi* **:** to withdraw from participation or membership **:** QUIT; *esp* **:** to withdraw from conventional society because of disenchantment with its values and mores

drop·page \ˈdräp-ij\ *n* **:** the part of a fruit crop that falls from the tree before it is ready for picking

drop pass *n* **:** a pass in ice hockey in which the dribbler skates past the puck leaving it for a teammate following close behind

dropped egg *n* **:** a poached egg

drop·per \ˈdräp-ər\ *n* **1 :** one that drops **2 :** a short glass tube fitted with a rubber bulb and used to measure liquids by drops — called also *eyedropper, medicine dropper* — **drop·per·ful** \-ˌfu̇l\ *n*

drop·ping *n* **1 :** something dropped **2** *pl* **:** animal dung

drop seat *n* **1 :** a hinged seat (as in a taxi) that may be dropped down **2 :** a seat (as in an undergarment) that falls down when unbuttoned

drop·shot \ˈdräp-ˌshät\ *n* **:** a delicately hit ball or shuttlecock (as in tennis, badminton, or rackets) that drops quickly after crossing the net or dies after hitting a wall

drop·si·cal \ˈdräp-si-kəl\ *adj* **1 :** relating to or affected with dropsy **2 :** TURGID, SWOLLEN — **drop·si·cal·ly** \-k(ə-)lē\ *adv* — **drop·si·cal·ness** \-kəl-nəs\ *n*

drop·sonde \ˈdräp-ˌsänd\ *n* [*drop* + radio*sonde*] **:** a radiosonde dropped by parachute from a high-flying airplane

drop·sy \ˈdräp-sē\ *n* [ME *dropesie,* short for *ydropesie,* fr. OF, fr. L *hydropisis,* modif. of Gk *hydrōps,* fr. *hydōr* water — more at WATER] **:** EDEMA

drop zone *n* **:** the area in which troops, supplies, or equipment are to be air-dropped; *also* **:** the target on which a skydiver lands

dros·era \ˈdräs-ə-rə\ *n* [NL, genus name, fr. Gk, fem. of *droseros* dewy, fr. *drosos* dew] **:** SUNDEW

drosera

drosh·ky \ˈdräsh-kē\ *also* **dros·ky** \ˈdräs-kē\ *n, pl* **droshkies** *also* **droskies** [Russ *drozhki,* fr. *droga* pole of a wagon] **:** any of various 2- or 4-wheeled carriages used esp. in Russia

dro·soph·i·la \drō-ˈsäf-ə-lə\ *n* [NL, genus name, fr. Gk *drosos* + NL *-phila,* fem. of *-philus* -phil] **:** any of a genus (*Drosophila*) of small two-winged flies used in genetic research

dross \ˈdräs, ˈdrȯs\ *n* [ME *dros,* fr. OE *drōs* dregs] **1 :** the scum that forms on the surface of molten metal **2 :** waste or foreign matter **:** IMPURITY — **drossy** \-ē\ *adj*

drought *or* **drouth** \ˈdraüt(h)\ *n* [ME, fr. OE *drūgath,* fr. *drūgian* to dry up; akin to OE *drȳge* dry — more at DRY] **1 :** a prolonged period of dryness **2 :** a prolonged or chronic shortage or lack or something — **drought·i·ness** *n* — **droughty** \-ē\ *adj*

1**drove** \ˈdrōv\ *n* [ME, fr. OE *drāf,* fr. *drīfan* to drive — more at DRIVE] **1 :** a group of animals driven or moving in a body **2 a :** a crowd of people moving or acting together **b :** a large group of similar things **3 a :** a chisel used to form a grooved or roughly shaped surface on stone **b :** the grooved surface so formed

2**drove** *past of* DRIVE

drov·er \ˈdrō-vər\ *n* **:** one that drives cattle or sheep

drown \ˈdraün\ *or substand* **drownd** \ˈdraünd\ *vb* **drowned** \ˈdraünd\ *or substand* **drownd·ed** \ˈdraün-dəd\; **drown·ing** \ˈdraü-niŋ\ *or substand* **drownd·ing** \ˈdraün-diŋ\ [ME *drounen*] *vi***:** to become drowned ~ *vt* **1 a :** to suffocate by submersion esp. in water **b :** to submerge esp. by a rise in the water level **c :** to wet thoroughly <~*ed* the french fries with catsup> **2 :** to engage (oneself) deeply and strenuously <~*ed* himself in work> **3 :** to cause (a sound) not to be heard by making a loud noise <his speech was ~*ed* out by . . . boos —*New Yorker*> **4 :** to drive out (as a sensation or an idea) <~*ed* his sorrows in liquor>

1**drowse** \ˈdraüz\ *vb* **drowsed; drows·ing** [prob. akin to Goth *driusan* to fall — more at DREARY] *vi* **1 :** to fall into a light slumber **2 :** to be inactive ~ *vt* **1 :** to make drowsy or inactive **2 :** to pass (time) drowsily or in drowsing

2**drowse** *n* **:** the act or an instance of drowsing **:** DOZE

drowsy \ˈdraü-zē\ *adj* **drows·i·er; -est 1 a :** ready to fall asleep **b :** tending to induce drowsiness **c :** INDOLENT, LETHARGIC **2 :** giving the appearance of peaceful inactivity ***syn*** see SLEEPY — **drows·i·ly** \-zə-lē\ *adv* — **drows·i·ness** \-zē-nəs\ *n*

drub \ˈdrəb\ *vb* **drubbed; drub·bing** [perh. fr. Ar *ḍaraba*] *vt***:** to beat severely (as with a cudgel) **2 :** to abuse with words **:** BERATE <the book was *drubbed* by every critic> **3 :** to defeat decisively ~ *vi* **:** DRUM, STAMP — **drub·ber** *n*

1**drudge** \ˈdrəj\ *vb* **drudged; drudg·ing** [ME *druggen;* prob. akin to OE *drēogan* to work, endure, L *firmus* firm] *vi* **:** to do hard, menial, or monotonous work ~ *vt* **:** to force to do hard, menial, or monotonous work — **drudg·er** *n*

2**drudge** *n* **1 :** one who is obliged to do menial work **2 :** one whose work is routine and boring

drudg·ery \ˈdrəj-(ə-)rē\ *n, pl* **-er·ies :** dull, irksome, and distasteful work **:** uninspiring or menial labor ***syn*** see WORK

drudg·ing \ˈdrəj-iŋ\ *adj* **:** MONOTONOUS, TIRING — **drudg·ing·ly** \-iŋ-lē\ *adv*

1**drug** \ˈdrəg\ *n* [ME *drogge*] **1 a** *obs* **:** a substance used in dyeing or chemical operations **b :** a substance used as a medication or in the preparation of medication **c** *according to the Food, Drug, and Cosmetic Act* **(1) :** a substance recognized in an official pharmacopoeia or formulary **(2) :** a substance intended for use in the diagnosis, cure, mitigation, treatment, or prevention of disease **(3) :** a substance other than food intended to affect the structure or function of the body **(4) :** a substance intended for use as a component of a medicine but not a device or a component, part, or accessory of a device **2 :** a commodity that is not salable or for which there is no demand — used in the phrase *drug on the market* **3 :** a substance that causes addiction or habituation

2**drug** *vb* **drugged; drug·ging** *vt* **1 :** to affect with a drug; *esp* **:** to stupefy by a narcotic drug **2 :** to administer a drug to **3 :** to lull or stupefy as if with a drug ~ *vi* **:** to take drugs for narcotic effect

drug·get \ˈdrəg-ət\ *n* [MF *droguet,* dim. of *drogue* trash, drug] **1 :** a wool or partly wool fabric formerly used for clothing **2 :** a coarse durable cloth used chiefly as a floor covering **3 :** a rug having a cotton warp and a wool filling

drug·gist \ˈdrəg-əst\ *n* **:** one who sells or dispenses drugs and medicines: as **a :** PHARMACIST **b :** one who owns or manages a drugstore

drug·mak·er \ˈdrəg-ˌmā-kər\ *n* **:** one that manufactures pharmaceuticals

drug·store \-ˌstō(ə)r, -ˌstȯ(ə)r\ *n* **:** a retail store where medicines and miscellaneous articles (as food, cosmetics, and film) are sold **:** PHARMACY

drugstore cowboy *n* **1 :** one who wears cowboy clothes but has had no experience as a cowboy **2 :** one who loafs on street corners and in drugstores

dru·id \ˈdrü-əd\ *n, often cap* [L *druides, druidae,* pl. fr. Gaulish *druides;* akin to OE *trēow* tree] **:** one of an ancient Celtic priesthood appearing in Irish and Welsh sagas and Christian legends as magicians and wizards — **dru·id·ess** \-əs\ *n, often cap* — **dru·id·ic** \drü-ˈid-ik\ *or* **dru·id·i·cal** \-i-kəl\ *adj, often cap*

dru·id·ism \ˈdrü-ə-ˌdiz-əm\ *n, often cap* **:** the system of religion, philosophy, and instruction of the druids

1**drum** \ˈdrəm\ *n* [prob. fr. D *trom;* akin to MHG *trumme* drum] **1 :** a percussion instrument usu. consisting of a hollow cylinder with a drumhead stretched over each end that is beaten with a stick or a pair of sticks in playing; *broadly* **:** a nonmetallic hollow instrument or device beaten to produce a deep-toned rumbling or booming sound **2 :** TYMPANIC MEMBRANE **3 :** the sound of a drum; *also* **:** a sound similar to that of a drum **4 :** something resembling a drum in shape: as **a :** a cylindrical machine or mechanical device or part; *esp* **:** a metal cylinder coated with magnetic material on which data (as for a computer) may be recorded **b :** a cylindrical container; *specif* **:** a usu. metal container for liquids having a capacity between 12 and 110 gallons **c :** a disk-shaped magazine for an automatic weapon **5 :** any of various percoid fishes (family Sciaenidae) that make a drumming noise — **drum·like** \-ˌlīk\ *adj*

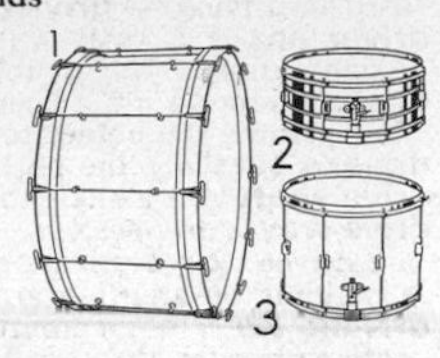

drums 1: *1* bass, *2* snare (for orchestra), *3* snare (for parades)

2**drum** *vb* **drummed; drum·ming** *vi* **1 :** to beat a drum **2 :** to make a succession of strokes or vibrations that produce sounds like drumbeats **3 :** to throb or sound rhythmically **4 :** to stir up interest **:** SOLICIT ~ *vt* **1 :** to summon or enlist by or as if by beating a drum <*drummed* into service> **2 :** to dismiss ignominiously **:** EXPEL — usu. used with *out* **3 :** to drive or force by steady effort or reiteration <*drummed* the speech into her head> **4 a :** to strike or tap repeatedly **b :** to produce (rhythmic sounds) by such action

3**drum** *n* [ScGael *druim* back, ridge, fr. OIr *druimm*] **1** *chiefly Scot* **:** a long narrow hill or ridge **2 :** DRUMLIN

drum·beat \ˈdrəm-ˌbēt\ *n* **1 :** a stroke on a drum or its sound **2 :** a cause advocated vociferously

drum·beat·er \-ər\ *n* **:** a vociferous supporter of a cause — **drum·beat·ing** \-iŋ\ *n*

drum·fire \ˈdrəm-ˌfī(ə)r\ *n* **1 :** artillery firing so continuous as to sound like a drumroll **2 :** something suggestive of drumfire in intensity <a ~ of publicity>

drum·head \-ˌhed\ *n* **1 :** the material (as skin or plastic) stretched over each end of a drum **2 :** the top of a capstan that is pierced with sockets for the levers used in turning it

drumhead court–martial *n* [fr. the use of a drumhead as a table] **:** a summary court-martial that tries offenses on the battlefield

drum·lin \ˈdrəm-lən\ *n* [IrGael *druim* back, ridge (fr. OIr *druimm*) + E *-lin* (alter. of *-ling*)] **:** an elongate or oval hill of glacial drift

drum major *n* **:** the marching leader of a band

drum ma·jor·ette \ˌdrəm-ˌmā-jə-ˈret\ *n* **1 :** a female drum major **2 :** a baton twirler who accompanies a marching band

drum·mer \ˈdrəm-ər\ *n* **1 :** one that plays a drum **2 :** TRAVELING SALESMAN

drum printer *n* **:** a line printer in which the printing element is a revolving drum

drum·roll \ˈdrəm-ˌrōl\ *n* **:** a roll on a drum or its sound

drum·stick \-ˌstik\ *n* **1 :** a stick for beating a drum **2 :** the segment of a fowl's leg between the thigh and tarsus

drum up *vt* **1 :** to bring about by persistent effort <*drum up* some business> **2 :** INVENT, ORIGINATE <*drum up* a new time-saving method>

1**drunk** *past part of* DRINK

2**drunk** \ˈdrəŋk\ *adj* [ME *drunke,* alter. of *drunken*] **1 :** having the faculties impaired by alcohol **2 :** dominated by an intense feeling <~ with power> **3 :** of, relating to, or caused by intoxication **:** DRUNKEN

3**drunk** *n* **:** a period of excessive drinking **2 :** DRUNKARD

drunk·ard \ˈdrəŋ-kərd\ *n* **:** one who is habitually drunk

drunk·en \ˈdrəŋ-kən\ *adj* [ME, fr. OE *druncen,* fr. pp. of *drincan* to drink] **1 :** DRUNK 1 **2** *obs* **:** saturated with liquid **3 a :** given to habitual excessive use of alcohol **b :** of, relating to, or characterized by intoxication <they come from . . . broken homes, ~ homes —P. B. Gilliam> **c :** resulting from or as if from intoxication <a ~ brawl> **4 :** unsteady or lurching as if from alcoholic intoxication — **drunk·en·ly** *adv* — **drunk·en·ness** \-kən-nəs\ *n*

drunk·o·me·ter \ˌdrəŋ-ˈkäm-ət-ər, ˈdrəŋ-kə-ˌmēt-\ *n* **:** a device for measuring alcohol content of the blood by chemical analysis of the breath

dru·pa·ceous \drü-ˈpā-shəs\ *adj* **1 :** of or relating to a drupe **2 :** bearing drupes

drupe \ˈdrüp\ *n* [NL *drupa,* fr. L overripe olive, fr. Gk *dryppa* olive] **:** a one-seeded indehiscent fruit having a hard bony endocarp, a fleshy mesocarp, and a thin exocarp that is flexible (as in the cherry) or dry and almost leathery (as in the almond)

drupe·let \ˈdrü-plət\ *n* **:** a small drupe; *specif* **:** one of the individual parts of an aggregate fruit (as the raspberry)

druth·ers \ˈdrəth-ərz\ *n pl* [*druther,* alter. of *would rather*] *dial* **:** free choice **:** PREFERENCE — used in the phrase *if one had one's druthers*

Druze *or* **Druse** \ˈdrüz\ *n* [Ar *Durūz,* pl., fr. Muḥammed ibn-Ismʿaīlal- *Daraziy* †1019 Muslim religious leader] **:** a member of a religious sect originating among Muslims and centered in the mountains of Lebanon and Syria

1**dry** \ˈdrī\ *adj* **dri·er** \ˈdrī(-ə-)r\; **dri·est** \ˈdrī-əst\ [ME, fr. OE *drȳge;* akin to OHG *truckan* dry] **1 a :** free or relatively free from

a liquid and esp. water **b :** not being in or under water <~ land> **c :** lacking precipitation or humidity <~ climate> **2 a :** characterized by exhaustion of a supply of water or liquid <a ~ well> <the fountain pen ran ~> **b :** devoid of running water <a ~ ravine> **c :** devoid of natural moisture <my throat was ~ after the long hike> **d :** no longer sticky or damp <the paint is ~> **e :** not giving milk <a ~ cow> **f :** lacking freshness : STALE **g :** ANHYDROUS **3 a :** marked by the absence or scantiness of secretions <a ~ cough> **b :** not shedding or accompanied by tears <a ~ sob> **4** *obs* : not accompanied by bloodshed or drowning **5 a :** marked by the absence of alcoholic beverages <a ~ party> **b :** prohibiting the manufacture or distribution of alcoholic beverages **6 :** served or eaten without butter <~ toast> **7 a :** lacking sweetness : SEC **b :** having all or most sugar fermented to alcohol <a ~ wine> **8 a :** solid as opposed to liquid <~ groceries> **b :** reduced to powder or flakes : DEHYDRATED <~ milk> **9 :** functioning without lubrication <a ~ clutch> **10** *of natural gas* : containing no recoverable hydrocarbon (as gasoline) **11 :** SLACK 6 **12 a :** built or constructed without a process which requires water: (1) : using no mortar <~ masonry> (2) : using prefabricated materials (as plasterboard) rather than a construction involving plaster or mortar <~ wall construction> **b :** requiring no liquid in preparation or operation <a ~ copy of the page> **13 a :** not showing or communicating warmth, enthusiam, or tender feeling : SEVERE <a ~ style of painting> **b :** WEARISOME, UNINTERESTING <~ passages of description> **c :** lacking embellishment : PLAIN <the ~ facts> **14 a :** not yielding what is expected or desired : UNPRODUCTIVE **b :** having no personal bias or emotional concern <the ~ light of reason> **c :** RESERVED, ALOOF **15 :** marked by matter-of-fact, ironic, or terse manner of expression <~ wit> **16 :** lacking smooth sound qualities <a ~ rasping voice> **17 :** being a dry run <a ~ rehearsal> — **dry·ly** *adv* — **dry·ness** *n*
syn DRY, ARID *shared meaning element* : lacking or deficient in moisture *ant* wet

[2]dry *vb* **dried; dry·ing** *vt* : to make dry ~ *vi* : to become dry — **dry·able** \'drī-ə-bəl\ *adj*

[3]dry *n, pl* **drys 1 :** the condition of being dry : DRYNESS **2 :** something dry; *esp* : a dry place **3 :** PROHIBITIONIST

dry·ad \'drī-əd, -ˌad\ *n* [L *dryad-, dryas,* fr. Gk, fr. *drys* tree — more at TREE] : WOOD NYMPH

dry·as·dust \'drī-əz-ˌdəst\ *adj* : PEDANTIC, UNINSPIRED — **dryasdust** *n*

dry cell *n* : a battery whose contents are not spillable

dry–clean \'drī-ˌklēn\ *vt* : to subject to dry cleaning ~ *vi* : to undergo dry cleaning — **dry–clean·able** \-'klē-nə-bəl\ *adj*

dry cleaner *n* : one that does dry cleaning

dry cleaning *n* **1 :** the cleansing of fabrics with substantially nonaqueous organic solvents **2 :** something that is dry-cleaned

dry–dock *vt* : to place in a dry dock

dry dock \'drī-ˌdäk\ *n* : a dock that can be kept dry for use during the construction or repairing of ships

dry·er *var of* DRIER

dry farm *n* : a nonirrigated farm on dry land operated on the basis of moisture-conserving tillage and drought-resistant crops — **dry–farm** *vt* — **dry farm·er** *n* — **dry farm·ing** *n*

dry fly *n* : an artificial angling fly designed to float upon the surface of the water

dry gangrene *n* : gangrene that develops in the presence of arterial obstruction, is sharply localized, and is characterized by dryness of the dead tissue which is sharply demarcated from adjacent tissue by a line of inflammation

dry goods \'drī-ˌgu̇dz\ *n pl* : textiles, ready-to-wear clothing, and notions as distinguished esp. from hardware and groceries

dry ice *n* : solidified carbon dioxide usu. in the form of blocks that at −78.5°C changes directly to a gas and that is used chiefly as a refrigerant

drying oil *n* : an oil (as linseed oil) that changes readily to a hard tough elastic substance when exposed in a thin film to air

dry kiln *n* : a heated chamber for drying and seasoning cut lumber

dry·lot \'drī-ˌlät\ *n* : an enclosure of limited size usu. bare of vegetation and used for fattening livestock

dry measure *n* : a series of units of capacity for dry commodities — see METRIC SYSTEM table, WEIGHT table

dry mop *n* : a long-handled mop for dusting floors — called also *dust mop*

dry–nurse *vt* **1 :** to act as dry nurse to **2 :** to give unnecessary supervision to

dry nurse *n* : a nurse who takes care of but does not breast-feed another woman's baby

dryo·pith·e·cine \ˌdrī-ō-ˌpith-ə-ˌsīn\ *n* [deriv. of Gk *drys* tree + *pithēkos* ape] : any of a subfamily (Dryopithecinae) of Miocene and Pliocene Old World anthropoid apes sometimes regarded as ancestors of both man and modern anthropoids — **dryopithecine** *adj*

dry out *vi* : to take a cure for alcoholism

dry pleurisy *n* : pleurisy in which exudation is mainly fibrinous

dry·point \'drī-ˌpȯint\ *n* : an engraving made with a steel or jeweled point instead of a burin directly into the metal plate without the use of acid as in etching; *also* : a print made from such an engraving

dry–rot *vt* : to affect with dry rot ~ *vi* : to become affected with dry rot

dry rot *n* **1 a :** a decay of seasoned timber caused by fungi that consume the cellulose of wood leaving a soft skeleton which is readily reduced to powder **b :** a fungous rot of plant tissue in which the affected areas are dry and often firmer than normal or more or less mummified **2 :** a fungus causing dry rot **3 :** decay from within caused esp. by resistance to new forces <art . . . infected by the *dry rot* of formalism —D. G. Mandelbaum>

dry run *n* **1 :** a practice firing without ammunition **2 :** a practice exercise : REHEARSAL, TRIAL

dry·salt·er \'drī-ˌsȯl-tər\ *n, Brit* : a dealer in crude dry chemicals and dyes — **dry·salt·ery** \-tə-rē\ *n, Brit*

dry–shod \'drī-'shäd\ *adj* : having dry shoes or feet

dry socket *n* : a tooth socket in which after extraction a blood clot fails to form or disintegrates without organizing

dry up *vi* **1 :** to disappear as if by evaporation, draining, or cutting off of a source of supply **2 :** to wither or die through gradual loss of vitality **3 :** to stop talking <wished his buddy would *dry up*>

dry wash *n* **1 :** laundry washed and dried but not ironed **2** *West* : WASH 3d

dry well *n* : a hole made in porous ground and filled with gravel or rubble to receive water (as drainage from a roof) and allow it to percolate away

ds *abbr* decistere

DS *abbr* **1** [It *dal segno*] from the sign **2** days after sight **3** detached service **4** document signed **5** drop siding

DSc *abbr* doctor of science

DSC *abbr* **1** distinguished service cross **2** doctor of surgical chiropody

DSM *abbr* Distinguished Service Medal

DSO *abbr* Distinguished Service Order

DSP *abbr* [L *decessit sine prole*] died without issue

DST *abbr* **1** daylight saving time **2** doctor of sacred theology

DT *abbr* **1** daylight time **2** delirium tremens **3** doctor of theology **4** double time

DTh *abbr* doctor of theology

d.t.'s \(ˈ)dē-'tēz\ *n pl, often cap D&T* : DELIRIUM TREMENS

Du *abbr* Dutch

du·ad \'d(y)ü-ˌad\ *n* [irreg. fr. Gk *dyad-, dyas* — more at DYAD] : PAIR

[1]du·al \'d(y)ü-əl\ *adj* [L *dualis,* fr. *duo* two — more at TWO] **1** *of grammatical number* : denoting reference to two **2 a :** consisting of two parts or elements or having two like parts : DOUBLE **b :** having a double character or nature — **du·al·ly** \-ə(l)-lē\ *adv*

[2]dual *n* **1 :** the dual number of a language **2 :** a linguistic form in the dual

dual citizenship *n* : the status of an individual who is a citizen of two or more nations

du·al·ism \'d(y)ü-ə-ˌliz-əm\ *n* **1 :** a theory that considers reality to consist of two irreducible elements or modes **2 :** the quality or state of being dual **3 a :** a doctrine that the universe is under the dominion of two opposing principles one of which is good and the other evil **b :** a view of man as constituted of two irreducible elements — **du·al·ist** \-ləst\ *n* — **du·al·is·tic** \ˌd(y)ü-ə-'lis-tik\ *adj* — **du·al·is·ti·cal·ly** \-ti-k(ə-)lē\ *adv*

du·al·i·ty \d(y)ü-'al-ət-ē\ *n, pl* **-ties** : DUALISM, DICHOTOMY

du·al·ize \'d(y)ü-ə-ˌlīz\ *vt* **-ized; -iz·ing** : to make dual

dual–purpose *adj* : intended for or serving two purposes <~ cattle bred for milk and meat>

dual–purpose fund *n* : a closed-end investment company with two classes of shares one of which is entitled to all dividend income and the other to all gains from capital appreciation

[1]dub \'dəb\ *vb* **dubbed; dub·bing** [ME *dubben,* fr. OE *dubbian;* akin to ON *dubba* to dub, OHG *tubili* plug] *vt* **1 a :** to confer knighthood on **b :** to dignify or give new character to **c :** to call by a descriptive name or epithet : NICKNAME **2 :** to trim or remove the comb and wattles of **3 a :** to hit (a golf ball) poorly **b :** to execute poorly ~ *vi* : THRUST, POKE — **dub·ber** *n*

[2]dub *n* : a clumsy person : DUFFER

[3]dub *n* [ME (Sc dial.) *dubbe*] *chiefly Scot* : POOL, PUDDLE

[4]dub *vt* **dubbed; dub·bing** [by shortening & alter. fr. *double*] **1 :** to provide (a motion-picture film) with a new sound track **2 :** to add (sound effects) to a film or to a radio or television production — usu. used with *in* **3 :** to transpose (sound already recorded) to a new record — **dub·ber** *n*

Dub *abbr* Dublin

dub·bin \'dəb-ən\ *also* **dub·bing** \-ən, -iŋ\ *n* [*dubbing,* gerund of *dub* (to dress leather)] : a dressing of oil and tallow for leather

du·bi·ety \d(y)u̇-'bī-ət-ē\ *n, pl* **-eties** [LL *dubietas,* fr. L *dubius*] **1 :** a usu. hesitant uncertainty or doubt that tends to cause vacillation **2 :** a matter of doubt *syn* see UNCERTAINTY *ant* decision

du·bi·os·i·ty \ˌd(y)ü-bē-'äs-ət-ē\ *n, pl* **-ties** : DOUBT

du·bi·ous \'d(y)ü-bē-əs\ *adj* [L *dubius,* fr. *dubare* to vacillate; akin to L *duo* two — more at TWO] **1 :** giving rise to doubt : EQUIVOCAL <they felt our scheme a little ~> **2 :** unsettled in opinion : UNDECIDED <they were a little ~ about our plan> **3 :** of doubtful promise or uncertain outcome <this seemed the most promising of all the ~ solutions proposed> **4 :** questionable as to value, quality, or origin <persons of ~ reliability and patriotism> *syn* see DOUBTFUL *ant* reliable, trustworthy — **du·bi·ous·ly** *adv* — **du·bi·ous·ness** *n*

du·bi·ta·ble \'d(y)ü-bət-ə-bəl\ *adj* [L *dubitabilis,* fr. *dubitare* to doubt — more at DOUBT] : open to doubt or question

du·bi·ta·tion \ˌd(y)ü-bə-'tā-shən\ *n, archaic* : DOUBT

Du·bon·net \ˌd(y)ü-bə-'nā\ *trademark* — used for an aperitif wine

du·cal \'d(y)ü-kəl\ *adj* [MF, fr. LL *ducalis* of a leader, fr. L *duc-, dux* leader — more at DUKE] : of or relating to a duke or dukedom — **du·cal·ly** \-kə-lē\ *adv*

duc·at \'dək-ət\ *n* [ME, fr. MF, fr. OIt *ducato* coin with the doge's portrait on it, fr. *duca* doge, fr. LGk *douk-, doux* leader, fr. L *duc-, dux*] : a usu. gold coin formerly used in various European countries

du·ce \'dü-(ˌ)chā\ *n* [It (*Il*) *Duce,* lit., the leader, title of Benito Mussolini, fr. L *duc-, dux*] : LEADER 2c(5)

duch·ess \'dəch-əs\ *n* [ME *duchesse,* fr. MF, fr. *duc* duke] **1 :** the wife or widow of a duke **2 :** a woman who holds a ducal title in her own right

---

ə abut   ᵊ kitten   ər further   a back   ā bake   ä cot, cart
au̇ out   ch chin   e less   ē easy   g gift   i trip   ī life
j joke   ŋ sing   ō flow   ȯ flaw   ȯi coin   th thin   t͟h this
ü loot   u̇ foot   y yet   yü few   yu̇ furious   zh vision

duchy \'dəch-ē\ *n, pl* **duch·ies** [ME *duche,* fr. MF *duché,* fr. *duc*] : the territory of a duke or duchess : DUKEDOM

¹duck \'dək\ *n, pl* **ducks** *often attrib* [ME *doke,* fr. OE *dūce*] **1** *or pl* **duck a :** any of various swimming birds (family Anatidae, the duck family) in which the neck and legs are short, the body more or less depressed, the bill often broad and flat, and the sexes almost always different from each other in plumage **b :** the flesh of any of these birds used as food **2 :** a female duck — compare DRAKE **3** *chiefly Brit* : DARLING — often used in pl. but sing. in constr. **4** : PERSON, CREATURE

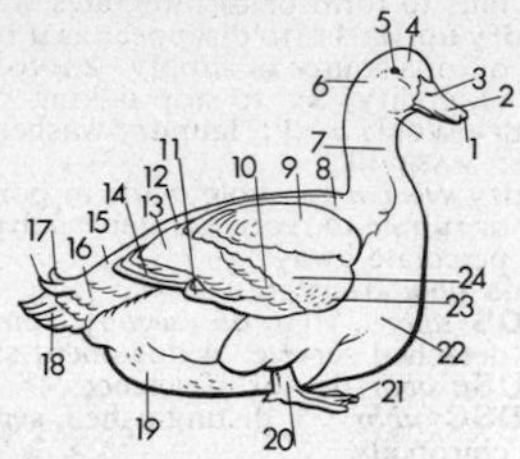

duck: *1* bean, *2* bill, *3* nostril, *4* head, *5* eye, *6* ear, *7* neck, *8* cape, *9* shoulder, *10* coverts, *11* flight coverts, *12* saddle, *13* secondaries, *14* primaries, *15* rump, *16* tail coverts, *17* drake feathers, *18* tail, *19* fluff, *20* shank, *21* web, *22* breast, *23* wing front, *24* wing bow

²duck *vb* [ME *douken;* akin to OHG *tūhhan* to dive, OE *dūce* duck] *vt* **1 :** to thrust under water **2 :** to lower (as the head) quickly : BOW **3** : AVOID, EVADE < ~ the issue> ~ *vi* **1 a :** to plunge under the surface of water **b :** to descend suddenly : DIP **2 a :** to move (as the head or body) suddenly : DODGE **b :** BOW, BOB **3 :** to evade a duty, question, or responsibility : back out — **duck·er** *n*

³duck *n* : an instance of ducking

⁴duck *n* [D *doek* cloth; akin to OHG *tuoh* cloth, and perh. to Skt *dhvaja* flag] **1 :** a durable closely woven usu. cotton fabric **2** *pl* : light clothes made of duck

⁵duck *n* [*DUKW,* its code designation] : an amphibious truck

duck·bill \'dək-,bil\ *n* **1 :** PLATYPUS **2 :** an edible paddlefish (*Polyodon spathula*) of the Mississippi river and its tributaries

duck·board \-,bō(ə)rd, -,bȯ(ə)rd\ *n* : a boardwalk or slatted flooring laid on a wet, muddy, or cold surface — usu. used in pl.

duck call *n* : a device for imitating the calls of ducks

duck·foot·ed \'dək-'fu̇t-əd\ *adv* : with feet pointed outward : FLAT-FOOTED

ducking stool *n* : a seat attached to a plank and formerly used to plunge culprits tied to it into water

duck·ling \'dək-liŋ\ *n* : a young duck

duck·pin \-,pin\ *n* **1 :** a small bowling pin shorter than a tenpin but proportionately wider at mid-diameter **2** *pl but sing in constr* : a bowling game using duckpins

ducks and drakes *or* **duck and drake** *n* : the pastime of skimming flat stones or shells along the surface of calm water — **play ducks and drakes with** *or* **make ducks and drakes of** : use recklessly : SQUANDER <*played ducks and drakes with* his money>

duck sickness *n* : a highly destructive botulism affecting esp. wild ducks in the western U.S.

duck soup *n* : something easy to do

duck·weed \'dək-,wēd\ *n* : a small floating aquatic monocotyledonous plant (family Lemnaceae, the duckweed family)

ducky \'dək-ē\ *adj* **duck·i·er; -est 1 :** SATISFACTORY, FINE <everything is just ~> **2 :** DARLING, CUTE <a ~ little tearoom>

¹duct \'dəkt\ *n* [NL *ductus,* fr. ML, aqueduct, fr. L, act of leading, fr. *ductus,* pp. of *ducere* to lead — more at TOW] **1 :** a bodily tube or vessel esp. when carrying the secretion of a gland **2 a :** a pipe, tube, or channel that conveys a substance **b :** a pipe or tubular runway for carrying an electric power line, telephone cables, or other conductors **3 a :** a continuous tube formed in plant tissue by a row of elongated cells that have lost their intervening end walls **b :** an elongated cavity (as a resin canal of a conifer) formed by disintegration or separation of cells **4 :** a layer (as in the atmosphere or the ocean) which occurs under usu. abnormal conditions and in which radio or sound waves are confined to a restricted path — **duct·less** \'dək-tləs\ *adj*

²duct *vt* : to convey (as a gas) through a duct; *also* : to propagate (as radio waves) through a duct

duc·tile \'dək-tᵊl, -,tīl\ *adj* [MF & L; MF, fr. L *ductilis,* fr. *ductus,* pp.] **1 :** capable of being fashioned into a new form **2 :** capable of being drawn out or hammered thin <~ metal> **3 :** easily led or influenced <the ~ masses> ***syn*** see PLASTIC — **duc·til·i·ty** \,dək-'til-ət-ē\ *n*

duct·ing \'dək-tiŋ\ *n* : a system of ducts; *also* : the material composing a duct

ductless gland *n* : ENDOCRINE GLAND

duct·ule \'dək-(,)t(y)ü(ə)l\ *n* : a small duct

duc·tus ar·te·ri·o·sus \'dək-təs-är-,tir-ē-'ō-səs\ *n* [NL, lit., arterial duct] : a short broad vessel in the fetus that connects the pulmonary artery with the aorta and conducts most of the blood directly from the right ventricle to the aorta bypassing the lungs

¹dud \'dəd\ *n* [ME *dudde*] **1** *pl* **a :** CLOTHES **b :** personal belongings **2 a :** FAILURE <the movie proved a box-office ~> **b** : MISFIT <he was reviled as a ~> **3 :** a bomb or missile that fails to explode

²dud *adj* : of little or no worth : VALUELESS <~ checks>

dud·die *or* **dud·dy** \'dəd-ē\ *adj, Scot* : RAGGED, TATTERED

dude \'d(y)üd\ *n* [origin unknown] **1 :** a man extremely fastidious in dress and manner : DANDY **2 :** a city man; *esp* : an Easterner in the West — **dud·ish** \'d(y)üd-ish\ *adj* — **dud·ish·ly** *adv*

du·deen \dü-'dēn\ *n* [IrGael *dúidín,* dim. of *dúd* pipe] : a short tobacco pipe made of clay

dude ranch *n* : a vacation resort offering activities (as horseback riding) typical of western ranches

¹dud·geon \'dəj-ən\ *n* [ME *dogeon,* fr. AF *digeon*] **1** *obs* : a wood used esp. for dagger hilts **2 a** *archaic* : a dagger with a handle of dudgeon **b** *obs* : a haft made of dudgeon

²dudgeon *n* [origin unknown] : a fit or state of angry indignation usu. provoked by opposition <she stalked out in a ~ when her plan was rejected> ***syn*** see OFFENSE

¹due \'d(y)ü\ *adj* [ME, fr. MF *deu,* pp. of *devoir* to owe, fr. L *debēre* — more at DEBT] **1 :** owed or owing as a debt **2 a :** owed or owing as a natural or moral right <everyone's right to dissent . . . is ~ the full protection of the Constitution —Nat Hentoff> **b :** according to accepted notions or procedures : APPROPRIATE **3 a :** satisfying or capable of satisfying a need, obligation, or duty : ADEQUATE **b :** REGULAR, LAWFUL <~ proof of loss> **4 :** capable of being attributed : ASCRIBABLE — used with *to* <this advance is partly ~ to a few men of genius —A. N. Whitehead> **5 :** having reached the date at which payment is required : PAYABLE **6 :** required or expected in the prescribed, normal, or logical course of events : SCHEDULED — **due·ness** *n*

²due *n* : something due or owed: as **a :** something that rightfully belongs to one <the artist has finally been accorded something of his ~> **b :** a payment or obligation required by law or custom : DEBT **c** *pl* : FEES, CHARGES

³due *adv* **1** *obs* : DULY **2 :** DIRECTLY, EXACTLY <~ north>

¹du·el \'d(y)ü-əl\ *n* [ML *duellum,* fr. OL, war] **1 :** a combat between two persons; *specif* : a formal combat with weapons fought between two persons in the presence of witnesses **2 :** a conflict between antagonistic persons, ideas, or forces

²duel *vb* **du·eled** *or* **du·elled; du·el·ing** *or* **du·el·ling** *vi* : to fight a duel ~ *vt* : to encounter (an opponent) in a duel — **du·el·er** *n* — **du·el·ist** \'d(y)ü-ə-ləst\ *n*

du·el·lo \d(y)ü-'el-(,)ō\ *n, pl* **-los** [It, fr. ML *duellum*] **1 :** the rules or practice of dueling **2 :** DUEL

du·en·de \dü-'en-(,)dā\ *n* [Sp dial., charm, fr. Sp, ghost, goblin, fr. *duen de casa,* prob. fr. *dueño de casa* owner of a house] : the power to attract through personal magnetism and charm

du·en·na \d(y)ü-'en-ə\ *n* [Sp *dueña,* fr. L *domina* mistress] **1** : an elderly woman serving as governess and companion to the younger ladies in a Spanish or a Portuguese family **2 :** CHAPERON — **du·en·na·ship** \-,ship\ *n*

due process *n* : a course of legal proceedings carried out regularly and in accordance with established rules and principles — called also *due process of law*

¹du·et \d(y)ü-'et\ *n* [It *duetto,* dim. of *duo*] : a composition for two performers

²duet *vi* **du·et·ted; du·et·ting :** to perform a duet

due to *prep* : because of

duff \'dəf\ *n* [E dial., alter. of *dough*] **1 :** a steamed pudding usu. containing raisins and currants **2 :** the partly decayed organic matter on the forest floor **3 :** fine coal : SLACK

duf·fel *or* **duf·fle** \'dəf-əl\ *n* [D *duffel,* fr. *Duffel,* Belgium] **1** : a coarse heavy woolen material with a thick nap **2 :** transportable personal belongings, equipment, and supplies **3 :** DUFFEL BAG

duffel bag *n* : a large cylindrical fabric bag for personal belongings

duf·fer \'dəf-ər\ *n* [origin unknown] **1 a :** a peddler esp. of cheap flashy articles **b :** something counterfeit or worthless **2 :** an incompetent, ineffectual, or clumsy person **3** *Austral* : a cattle rustler

¹dug *past of* DIG

²dug \'dəg\ *n* [perh. of Scand origin; akin to OSw *dæggia* to suckle; akin to OE *delu* nipple] : UDDER; *also* : TEAT — usu. used of a suckling animal but vulgar when used of a woman

du·gong \'dü-,gäŋ, -,gȯŋ\ *n* [NL, genus name, fr. Malay & Tag *duyong* sea cow] : an aquatic herbivorous mammal of a monotypic genus (*Dugong*) that has a bilobate tail and in the male upper incisors altered into tusks and that is related to the manatee — called also *sea cow*

dugong

dug·out \'dəg-,au̇t\ *n* **1 :** a boat made by hollowing out a large log **2 a :** a shelter dug in a hillside; *also* : a shelter dug in the ground and roofed with sod **b :** an area in the side of a trench for quarters, storage, or protection **3 :** either of two low shelters on either side of and facing a baseball diamond that contain the players' benches

dui·ker \'dī-kər\ *n* [Afrik, lit., diver, fr. *duik* to dive, fr. MD *dūken;* akin to OHG *tūhhan* to dive — more at DUCK] : any of several small African antelopes (*Cephalophus* or related genera)

duke \'d(y)ük\ *n* [ME, fr. OF *duc,* fr. L *duc-, dux,* fr. *ducere* to lead — more at TOW] **1 :** a sovereign ruler of a continental European duchy **2 :** a nobleman of the highest hereditary rank; *esp* : a member of the highest grade of the British peerage **3** *slang* : FIST, HAND — usu. used in pl. **4 :** any of several cultivated cherries between sweet cherries and sour cherries in character and prob. of hybrid origin — **duke·dom** \-dəm\ *n*

Du·kho·bor *var of* DOUKHOBOR

dul·cet \'dəl-sət\ *adj* [ME *doucet,* fr. MF, fr. *douz* sweet, fr. L *dulcis*] **1 :** sweet to the taste : LUSCIOUS **2 a :** sweet to the ear : MELODIOUS **b :** AGREEABLE, SOOTHING <could not . . . expect such ~ weather to last —Victoria Sackville-West> — **dul·cet·ly** *adv*

dul·ci·fy \'dəl-sə-,fī\ *vt* **-fied; -fy·ing** [LL *dulcificare,* fr. L *dulcis*] **1 :** to make sweet **2 :** to make agreeable : MOLLIFY

dul·ci·mer \'dəl-sə-mər\ *n* [ME *dowcemere,* fr. MF *doulcemer,* fr. OIt *dolcimelo*] : a stringed instrument of trapezoidal shape played with light hammers held in the hands

dul·ci·more \-,mō(ə)r, -,mȯ(ə)r\ *n* [alter. of *dulcimer*] : an American folk instrument resembling a violin and played like a Hawaiian guitar

dul·ci·nea \,dəl-sə-'nē-ə, -'sin-ē-ə\ *n* [Sp, fr. *Dulcinea* del Toboso, beloved of Don Quixote] : MISTRESS, SWEETHEART

¹dull \'dəl\ *adj* [ME *dul;* akin to OE *dol* foolish and prob. to L *fumus* smoke — more at FUME] **1 :** mentally slow : STUPID **2 a** : slow in perception or sensibility : INSENSIBLE **b :** lacking zest or

vivacity : LISTLESS **3 a :** slow in action : SLUGGISH **b :** marked by little business activity <a ~ season> **4 :** lacking sharpness of edge or point **5 :** lacking brilliance or luster **6 :** lacking in force or intensity: as **a :** not clear : INDISTINCT <the kerosine lamp gave a ~ light> **b :** not resonant or ringing <a ~ booming sound> **7** *of a color* **:** low in saturation and low in lightness **8 :** CLOUDY, OVERCAST **9 :** TEDIOUS, UNINTERESTING — **dull·ness** *or* **dul·ness** \'dəl-nəs\ *n* — **dul·ly** \'dəl-(l)ē\ *adv*
syn **1** see STUPID *ant* clever, bright
2 DULL, BLUNT, OBTUSE *shared meaning element* : not sharp, keen, or acute *ant* sharp (*as of an edge or point*), poignant (*as of sensations or emotions*), lively (*as of action or activity*)

[2]**dull** *vt* **:** to make dull <eyes and ears ~*ed* by age> ~ *vi* **:** to become dull

dull·ard \'dəl-ərd\ *n* **:** one that is stupid or insensitive

dull·ish \'dəl-ish\ *adj* **:** somewhat dull — **dull·ish·ly** *adv*

dulls·ville \'dəlz-ˌvil\ *n* [[1]*dull* + *-sville* (as in *Huntsville*)] *slang* **:** something that is dull or boring; *also* **:** BOREDOM

dulse \'dəls\ *n* [ScGael & IrGael *duileasg;* akin to W *delysg* dulse] **:** any of several coarse red seaweeds (esp. *Rhodymenia palmata*) found esp. in northern latitudes and used as a food condiment

du·ly \'d(y)ü-lē\ *adv* **:** in a due manner, time, or degree : PROPERLY

du·ma \'dü-mə, -(ˌ)mä\ *n* [Russ, of Gmc origin; akin to OE *dōm* judgment — more at DOOM] **:** a representative council in Russia; *specif* **:** the principal legislative assembly in czarist Russia

[1]**dumb** \'dəm\ *adj* [ME, fr. OE; akin to OHG *tumb* mute, OE *dēaf* deaf — more at DEAF] **1 :** devoid of the power of speech <deaf and ~ from birth> **2 :** naturally incapable of speech <~ animals> **3 :** not expressed in uttered words <~ grief> **4 a :** not willing to speak **b :** not having the usual accompaniment of speech or sound **5 :** lacking some usual attribute or accompaniment; *esp* **:** having no means of self-propulsion <~ barge> **6 :** markedly lacking in intelligence : exasperatingly obtuse *syn* see STUPID *ant* articulate — **dumb·ly** \'dəm-lē\ *adv* — **dumb·ness** *n*

[2]**dumb** *vt* **:** to make silent : DEADEN <would lie around, ~*ed* by the drugs —Norman Mailer>

Dumb *abbr* Dumbartonshire

dumb·bell \'dəm-ˌbel\ *n* **1 :** a short bar with two identical spheres or with adjustable weighted disks attached to each end and used usu. in pairs for calisthenic exercise **2 :** one that is dull and stupid : DUMMY

dumb·found *or* **dum·found** \ˌdəm-'fau̇nd\ *vt* [*dumb* + *-found* (as in *confound*)] **:** to confound briefly and usu. with astonishment *syn* see PUZZLE

dumb·foun·der *or* **dum·foun·der** \-'fau̇n-dər\ *vt* **:** DUMBFOUND

dumb show *n* **1 :** a part of a play presented in pantomime **2 :** signs and gestures without words : PANTOMIME

dumb·struck \'dəm-ˌstrək\ *adj* **:** made silent by astonishment

dumb·wait·er \'dəm-'wāt-ər\ *n* **1 :** a portable serving table or stand **2 :** a small elevator used for conveying food and dishes from one story of a building to another

dum·dum \'dəm-ˌdəm\ *n* [*Dum-Dum,* arsenal near Calcutta, India] **:** a bullet (as one with vertical cuts made in its point) that expands upon hitting an object

Dumf *abbr* Dumfriesshire

dum·ka \'du̇m-kə\ *n, pl* **dum·ky** \-kē\ [Czech, elegy, of Gmc origin; akin to Goth *dōms* judgment, OE *dōm* doom] **:** a Slavic folk ballad usu. melancholy but often alternately melancholy and gay

dumm·kopf \'du̇m-ˌkȯpf\ *n* [G, fr. *dumm* stupid + *kopf* head] **:** BLOCKHEAD

[1]**dum·my** \'dəm-ē\ *n, pl* **dummies** [[1]*dumb* + *-y*] **1 a :** one who is incapable of speaking **b :** one who is habitually silent **c :** one who is stupid **2 a :** the exposed hand in bridge played by the declarer in addition to his own hand **b :** a bridge player whose hand is a dummy **3 :** an imitation, copy, or likeness of something used as a substitute **4 :** one seeming to act for himself but in reality acting for or at the direction of another **5 :** something usu. mechanically operated that serves to replace or aid a human being's work **6 :** a pattern arrangement of matter to be reproduced esp. by printing

[2]**dummy** *adj* **1 a :** having the appearance of being real but lacking capacity to function : ARTIFICIAL **b :** existing in name only : FICTITIOUS <bank accounts held in ~ names> **2 :** apparently acting for oneself while really acting for or at the direction of another <a ~ director>

[3]**dummy** *vb* **dum·mied; dum·my·ing** *vt* **:** to make a dummy of <the book was *dummied* and ready to go to press> — often used with *up* <the editor *dummied* up the front page> ~ *vi, slang* **:** to refuse to talk — used with *up*

dummy variable *n* **:** an arbitrary mathematical symbol or variable that can be replaced by another without affecting the value of the expression in which it occurs <the variable of integration in a definite integral is a *dummy variable*>

du·mor·ti·er·ite \d(y)ü-'mȯrt-ē-ə-ˌrīt\ *n* [F *dumortiérite,* fr. Eugène *Dumortier* †1876 F paleontologist] **:** a bright blue or greenish blue mineral consisting of a silicate of aluminum and used esp. for jewelry

[1]**dump** \'dəmp\ *vb* [perh. fr. D *dompen* to immerse, topple; akin to OE *dyppan* to dip — more at DIP] *vt* **1 a :** to let fall in a heap or mass **b :** to get rid of unceremoniously or irresponsibly **c :** JETTISON <an airplane ~*ing* gasoline> **2** *slang* **:** to knock down : BEAT <the man rushed out and ~*ed* him —John Corry> **3 :** to sell in quantity at a very low price; *specif* **:** to sell abroad at less than the market price at home **4 :** to copy (data in a computer's internal storage) onto an external storage medium ~ *vi* **1 :** to fall abruptly : PLUNGE **2 :** to dump refuse — **dump·er** *n*

[2]**dump** *n* **1 a :** an accumulation of refuse or other discarded materials **b :** a place where such materials are dumped **2 a :** a quantity of reserve materials accumulated at one place **b :** a place where such materials are stored; *esp* **:** a place for the temporary storage of military supplies in the field <ammunition ~> **3 :** a disorderly, slovenly, or dilapidated place **4 :** an instance of dumping data stored in a computer

dump·ing *n* **:** the act of one that dumps; *esp* **:** the selling of goods in quantity at below market price (as to dispose of a surplus or to break down competition) esp. in international trade

dump·ish \'dəm-pish\ *adj* [*dumps*] **:** SAD, MELANCHOLY <remembrances . . . that . . . cheer and uplift the ~ heart of man —Douglas Jerrold>

dump·ling \'dəm-pliŋ\ *n* [perh. alter. of *lump*] **1 a :** a small mass of leavened dough cooked by boiling or steaming **b :** a dessert made by wrapping fruit in biscuit dough and baking **2 a :** one that is shaped like a dumpling **b :** a short fat person or animal

dumps \'dəm(p)s\ *n pl* [prob. fr. D *domp* haze, fr. MD *damp*] **:** a gloomy state of mind : DESPONDENCY <in the ~>

dump truck *n* **:** a motor or hand-propelled truck for transporting and dumping loose materials

dumpy \'dəm-pē\ *adj* **dump·i·er; -est** [E dial. *dump* (lump)] **:** being short and thick in build : SQUAT — **dump·i·ly** \-pə-lē\ *adv* — **dump·i·ness** \-pē-nəs\ *n*

dumpy level *n* **:** a surveyor's level with a short usu. inverting telescope rigidly fixed and rotating only in a horizontal plane

[1]**dun** \'dən\ *adj* [ME, fr. OE *dunn* — more at DUSK] **1 a :** having a dun color **b** *of a horse* **:** exhibiting reduced hair pigmentation **2 :** marked by dullness and drabness — **dun·ness** \'dən-nəs\ *n*

[2]**dun** *n* **1 :** a dun horse **2 :** a variable color averaging a nearly neutral slightly brownish dark gray **3 a :** a subadult mayfly; *also* **:** an artificial fly tied to imitate such an insect **b :** CADDIS FLY

[3]**dun** *vt* **dunned; dun·ning** [origin unknown] **1 :** to make persistent demands upon for payment **2 :** to plague or pester constantly

[4]**dun** *n* **1 :** one who duns **2 :** an urgent request; *esp* **:** a demand for payment

Dun·can Phyfe \ˌdəŋ-kən-'fīf\ *adj* **:** of, relating to, or constituting furniture designed and built by or in the style of Duncan Phyfe

dunce \'dən(t)s\ *n* [John *Duns* Scotus, whose once accepted writings were ridiculed in the 16th cent.] **:** one who is dull-witted or stupid

dunce cap *n* **:** a conical cap formerly used as a punishment for slow learners at school — called also *dunce's cap*

dun·der·head \'dən-dər-ˌhed\ *n* [perh. fr. D *donder* thunder + E *head;* akin to OHG *thonar* thunder — more at THUNDER] **:** DUNCE, BLOCKHEAD — **dun·der·head·ed** \ˌdən-dər-'hed-əd\ *adj*

dun·drea·ries \ˌdən-'dri(ə)r-ēz\ *n pl, often cap* [Lord *Dundreary,* character in the play *Our American Cousin* (1858), by Tom Taylor] **:** long flowing sideburns

dune \'d(y)ün\ *n* [F, fr. OF, fr. MD; akin to OE *dūn* down — more at DOWN] **:** a hill or ridge of sand piled up by the wind — **dune·like** \-ˌlīk\ *adj*

dune buggy *n* **:** BEACH BUGGY

dune·land \'d(y)ün-ˌland\ *n* **:** an area having many dunes

[1]**dung** \'dəŋ\ *n* [ME, fr. OE; akin to ON *dyngja* manure pile, Lith *dengti* to cover] **1 :** the excrement of an animal : MANURE **2 :** something repulsive — **dungy** \'dəŋ-ē\ *adj*

[2]**dung** *vt* **:** to fertilize or dress with manure

dun·ga·ree \ˌdəŋ-gə-'rē, 'dəŋ-gə-ˌ\ *n* [Hindi *dugrī*] **1 :** a heavy coarse durable cotton twill woven from colored yarns; *specif* **:** blue denim **2** *pl* **:** heavy cotton work clothes made usu. of blue dungaree

dung beetle *n* **:** a beetle (as a dorbeetle or tumblebug) that rolls balls of dung in which to lay eggs and on which the larvae feed

dun·geon \'dən-jən\ *n* [ME *donjon,* fr. MF, fr. (assumed) ML *dominion-, dominio,* fr. L *dominus* lord — more at DAME] **1 :** DONJON **2 :** a dark usu. underground prison or vault

dung·hill \'dəŋ-ˌhil\ *n* **1 :** a heap of dung **2 :** something (as a situation or condition) that is repulsive or degraded

du·nite \'dü-ˌnīt, 'dən-ˌīt\ *n* [Mt. *Dun,* New Zealand] **:** a granitoid igneous rock consisting chiefly of olivine — **du·nit·ic** \dü-'nit-ik, ˌdən-'it-\ *adj*

[1]**dunk** \'dəŋk\ *vb* [PaG *dunke,* fr. MHG *dunken,* fr. OHG *dunkōn*] *vt* **1 :** to dip (as a piece of bread) into liquid (as milk) while eating **2 :** to dip or submerge temporarily in liquid <~*ed* her in the swimming pool> **3 :** to throw (a basketball) into the basket from above the rim ~ *vi* **1 :** to submerge oneself in water **2 :** to make a dunk shot in basketball

[2]**dunk** *n* **:** the act or action of dunking; *esp* **:** DUNK SHOT

Dun·ker \'dəŋ-kər\ *or* **Dun·kard** \-kərd\ *n* [PaG *Dunker,* fr. *dunke*] **:** a member of the Church of the Brethren or any of several other orig. German Baptist denominations practicing trine immersion and love feasts and refusing to take oaths or to perform military service

dunk shot *n* **:** a shot in basketball made by jumping high into the air and throwing the ball down through the basket

dun·lin \'dən-lən\ *n, pl* **dunlins** *or* **dunlin** [[1]*dun* + *-lin* (alter. of *-ling*)] **:** a small widely distributed sandpiper (*Calidris alpina*) largely cinnamon to rusty brown above and white below

dun·nage \'dən-ij\ *n* [origin unknown] **1 :** loose materials used around a cargo to prevent damage; *also* **:** padding in a shipping container to protect contents against breakage **2 :** BAGGAGE

duo \'d(y)ü-(ˌ)ō\ *n, pl* **du·os** [It, fr. L, two — more at TWO] **1 :** DUET **2 :** PAIR

duo- *comb form* [L *duo*] **:** two

duo·de·cil·lion \ˌd(y)ü-ō-di-'sil-yən\ *n, often attrib* [L *duodecim* twelve + E *-illion* (as in *million*)] — see NUMBER table

duo·dec·i·mal \ˌd(y)ü-ə-'des-ə-məl\ *adj* [L *duodecim* — more at DOZEN] **:** of, relating to, or proceeding by twelve or the scale of twelves — **duodecimal** *n*

duo·dec·i·mo \-ˌmō\ *n, pl* **-mos** [L, abl. of *duodecimus* twelfth, fr. *duodecim*] **:** TWELVEMO

duoden- or **duodeno-** *comb form* [NL, fr. ML *duodenum*] : duodenum <*duodenitis*> <*duodenogram*>
du·o·de·num \ˌd(y)ü-ə-ˈdē-nəm, d(y)u̇-ˈäd-ᵊn-əm\ *n, pl* **-de·na** \-ˈdē-nə, ᵊn-ə\ *or* **-denums** [ME, fr. ML, fr. L *duodeni* twelve each, fr. *duodecim* twelve; fr. its length, about 12 fingers' breadth] : the first part of the small intestine extending from the pylorus to the jejunum — **du·o·de·nal** \-ˈdēn-ᵊl, -ᵊn-əl\ *adj*
duo·logue \ˈd(y)ü-ə-ˌlȯg, -ˌläg\ *n* : a dialogue between two persons
duo·mo \ˈdwō-(ˌ)mō\ *n, pl* **duomos** [It — more at DOME] : CATHEDRAL
du·op·o·ly \d(y)u̇-ˈäp-ə-lē\ *n, pl* **-lies** [*duo-* + *-poly* (as in *monopoly*)] **1** : an oligopoly limited to two sellers **2** : hegemony exercised by two great powers — **du·op·o·lis·tic** \-ˌäp-ə-ˈlis-tik\ *adj*
¹dup \ˈdəp\ *vt* [contr. of *do up*] *archaic* : OPEN
²dup *abbr* **1** duplex **2** duplicate
¹dupe \ˈd(y)üp\ *n* [F, fr. MF *duppe*, prob. alter. of *huppe* hoopoe] : one that is easily deceived or cheated : FOOL
²dupe *vt* **duped; dup·ing** : to make a dupe of : DECEIVE — **dup·er** *n*
syn DUPE, GULL, TRICK, HOAX *shared meaning element* : to delude by underhand methods or for one's own ends
³dupe *n or vb* : DUPLICATE
dup·ery \ˈd(y)ü-p(ə-)rē\ *n, pl* **-er·ies** **1** : the act or practice of duping **2** : the condition of being duped
du·ple \ˈd(y)ü-pəl\ *adj* [L *duplus* double — more at DOUBLE] **1** : having two elements **2 a** : marked by two or a multiple of two beats per measure of music <~ time> **b** *of rhythm* : consisting of a meter based on disyllabic feet
¹du·plex \ˈd(y)ü-ˌpleks\ *adj* [L, fr. *duo* two + *-plex* -fold — more at TWO, SIMPLE] **1** : DOUBLE, TWOFOLD; *specif* : having two parts that operate at the same time or in the same way <a ~ lathe> **2** : allowing telecommunication in opposite directions simultaneously
²duplex *n* : something duplex; *esp* : a two-family house
³duplex *vt* : to make duplex
duplex apartment *n* : an apartment having rooms on two floors
du·plex·er \ˈd(y)ü-ˌplek-sər\ *n* : a switching device that permits alternate transmission and reception with the same radio antenna
¹du·pli·cate \ˈd(y)ü-pli-kət\ *adj* [ME, fr. L *duplicatus*, pp. of *duplicare* to double, fr. *duplic-, duplex*] **1 a** : consisting of or existing in two corresponding or identical parts or examples <~ invoices> **b** : being the same as another **2** : being a card game in which players play identical hands in order to compare scores <~ bridge>
²duplicate *n* **1** : either of two things that exactly resemble or correspond to each other; *specif* : a legal instrument that is essentially identical with another and has equal validity as an original **2** : COPY, COUNTERPART **3** : two copies both alike — used with *in* <typed in ~>
³du·pli·cate \ˈd(y)ü-pli-ˌkāt\ *vb* **-cat·ed; -cat·ing** *vt* **1** : to make double or twofold <the walls should be *duplicated* . . . in order to have a second line of defense —J. A. Steers> **2 a** : to make an exact copy of <~ the document> **b** : to be a match for : EQUAL <a feat that can never be *duplicated*> ~ *vi* : to become duplicate : REPLICATE <DNA in chromosomes ~*s*> — **du·pli·ca·tive** \-ˌkāt-iv\ *adj*
du·pli·ca·tion \ˌd(y)ü-pli-ˈkā-shən\ *n* **1** : the act or process of duplicating : the quality or state of being duplicated **2** : DUPLICATE, COUNTERPART **3** : a chromosomal aberration in which a segment of genetic material is repeated
du·pli·ca·tor \ˈd(y)ü-pli-ˌkāt-ər\ *n* : one that duplicates; *specif* : a machine for making copies of typed, drawn, or printed matter
du·plic·i·tous \d(y)u̇-ˈplis-ət-əs\ *adj* : marked by duplicity — **du·plic·i·tous·ly** *adv*
du·plic·i·ty \d(y)u̇-ˈplis-ət-ē\ *n, pl* **-ties** **1** : contradictory doubleness of thought, speech, or action; *esp* : the belying of one's true intentions by deceptive words or action **2** : the quality or state of being double or twofold **3** : the technically incorrect use of two or more distinct items (as claims, charges, or defenses) in a single legal action
Dur *abbr* Durham
du·ra·ble \ˈd(y)u̇r-ə-bəl\ *adj* [ME, fr. MF, fr. L *durabilis*, fr. *durare* to last — more at DURING] : able to exist for a long time without significant deterioration; *also* : designed to be durable <~ goods> *syn* see LASTING — **du·ra·bil·i·ty** \ˌd(y)u̇r-ə-ˈbil-ət-ē\ *n* — **du·ra·ble·ness** \ˈd(y)u̇r-ə-bəl-nəs\ *n* — **du·ra·bly** \-blē\ *adv*
durable press *n* **1** : the process of treating a fabric with a chemical (as a resin) and heat for setting the shape and for aiding wrinkle resistance **2** : material treated by durable press **3** : the condition of material treated by durable press
du·ra·bles \ˈd(y)u̇r-ə-bəlz\ *n pl* : consumer goods (as vehicles and household appliances) that are typically used repeatedly over a period of years
du·ral·u·min \d(y)u̇-ˈral-yə-mən\ *n* [fr. *Duralumin*, a trademark] : an alloy of aluminum, copper, manganese, and magnesium comparable in strength and hardness to soft steel
du·ra ma·ter \ˈd(y)u̇r-ə-ˌmāt-ər, -ˌmät-\ *n* [ME, fr. ML, lit., hard mother] : the tough fibrous membrane that envelops the brain and spinal cord external to the arachnoid and pia mater
du·ra·men \d(y)u̇-ˈrā-mən\ *n* [NL, fr. L, hardness, fr. *durare* to harden — more at DURING] : HEARTWOOD
du·rance \ˈd(y)u̇r-ən(t)s\ *n* [MF, fr. *durer* to endure] **1** *archaic* : ENDURANCE **2** : IMPRISONMENT — often used in the phrase *durance vile* <after ~ vile of ten days he was released —J. E. Davies>
du·ra·tion \d(y)u̇-ˈrā-shən\ *n* **1** : continuance in time **2** : the time during which something exists or lasts <was in the army for the ~ of the war>
dur·bar \ˈdər-ˌbär, ˌdər-ˈ\ *n* [Hindi *darbār*, fr. Per, fr. *dar* door + *bār* admission, audience] **1** : court held by an Indian prince **2** : a formal reception marked by pledges of fealty given to an Indian or African prince by his subjects or to the British monarch by native princes
du·ress \d(y)u̇-ˈres\ *n* [ME *duresse*, fr. MF *duresce* hardness, severity, fr. L *duritia*, fr. *durus*] **1** : forcible restraint or restriction **2** : compulsion by threat; *specif* : unlawful constraint
Dur·ham \ˈdər-əm, ˈdə-rəm, ˈdu̇r-əm\ *n* [County *Durham*, England] : SHORTHORN
Durham Rule *n* [Monte *Durham*, 20th cent. Am litigant] : a legal hypothesis under which a person is not judged responsible for a criminal act that is attributed to a mental disease or defect
du·ri·an \ˈd(y)u̇r-ē-ən, -ē-ˌän\ *n* [Malay] **1** : a large oval tasty but foul-smelling fruit with a prickly rind **2** : an East Indian tree (*Durio zibethinus*) of the silk-cotton family that bears durians
dur·ing \ˌd(y)u̇r-iŋ\ *prep* [ME, fr. prp. of *duren* to last, fr. OF *durer*, fr. L *durare* to harden, endure, fr. *durus* hard; perh. akin to Skt *dāru* wood — more at TREE] **1** : throughout the duration of <swims every day ~ the summer> **2** : at a point in the course of : IN <takes his vacation ~ July>
dur·mast \ˈdər-ˌmast\ *n* [perh. alter. of *dun mast*, fr. ¹*dun* + *mast*] : a European oak (*Quercus sessiliflora* or *Q. petraea*) valued esp. for its dark heavy tough elastic wood
durn \ˈdərn\, **durned** \ˈdərn(d)\ *var of* DARN, DARNED
du·ro \ˈdu̇(ə)r-(ˌ)ō\ *n, pl* **duros** [Sp, short for *peso duro* hard peso] : a Spanish or Spanish American peso or silver dollar
du·roc \ˈd(y)u̇(ə)r-ˌäk\ *n* [*Duroc*, 19th cent. Am stallion] *often cap* : any of a breed of large vigorous red American hogs
du·rom·e·ter \d(y)u̇-ˈräm-ət-ər\ *n* [L *durus* hard] : an instrument for measuring hardness
dur·ra *also* **du·ra** \ˈdu̇r-ə\ *n* [Ar *dhurah*] : any of several grain sorghums widely grown in warm dry regions
du·rum wheat \ˌd(y)u̇r-əm-, ˌdər-əm-, ˌdə-rəm-\ *n* [NL *durum*, fr. L, neut. of *durus* hard] : a wheat (*Triticum durum*) that yields a glutenous flour used esp. in macaroni and spaghetti — called also *durum*
¹dusk \ˈdəsk\ *adj* [ME *dosk*, alter. of OE *dox*; akin to L *fuscus* dark brown, OE *dunn* dun, *dūst* dust] : DUSKY
²dusk *vi* : to become dark ~ *vt* : to make dark or gloomy <a gray light ~*ed* the room —William Sansom>
³dusk *n* **1** : the darker part of twilight esp. at night **2** : darkness or semidarkness caused by the shutting out of light
dusky \ˈdəs-kē\ *adj* **dusk·i·er; -est** **1** : somewhat dark in color; *specif* : having dark skin **2** : marked by slight or deficient light : SHADOWY — **dusk·i·ly** \-kə-lē\ *adv* — **dusk·i·ness** \-kē-nəs\ *n*
syn **1** see DARK
2 DUSKY, SWARTHY, TAWNY *shared meaning element* : tending toward darkness and dullness — used esp. in the description of human appearance ***ant*** light, bright
¹dust \ˈdəst\ *n* [ME, fr. OE *dūst*; akin to L *furere* to rage, Gk *thyein*] **1** : fine dry pulverized particles of matter and esp. earth **2** : the particles into which something disintegrates **3 a** : something worthless **b** : a state of humiliation **4 a** : the earth esp. as a place of burial **b** : the surface of the ground **5 a** : a cloud of dust <a thin ~ rising from the hooves —H. V. Morton> **b** : CONFUSION, DISTURBANCE **6** *archaic* : a single particle (as of earth) **7** *Brit* : refuse (as sweepings) ready for collection — **dust·less** \-ləs\ *adj* — **dust·like** \-ˌlīk\ *adj*
²dust *vt* **1** *archaic* : to make dusty **2 a** : to make free of dust **b** : to prepare to use again **3 a** : to sprinkle with fine particles **b** : to sprinkle in the form of dust ~ *vi* **1** *of a bird* : to work dust into the feathers **2** : to remove dust **3** : to give off dust
dust·bin \ˈdəs(t)-ˌbin\ *n, Brit* : a can for trash or garbage
dust bowl *n* : a region that suffers from prolonged droughts and dust storms
dust bowl·er \ˈdəs(t)-ˌbō-lər\ *n* : a resident of a dust bowl
dust·cov·er \-ˌkəv-ər\ *n* **1** : a cover (as of cloth or plastic) used to protect furniture or equipment from dust **2** : DUST JACKET
dust devil *n* : a small whirlwind containing sand or dust
dust·er \ˈdəs-tər\ *n* **1** : one that removes dust **2 a** : a lightweight overgarment to protect clothing from dust **b** : a dress-length housecoat **3** : one that scatters fine particles; *specif* : a device for applying insecticidal or fungicidal dusts to crops **4** : DUST STORM
dust·heap \ˈdəst-ˌ(h)ēp\ *n* **1** : a pile of refuse **2** : a category of forgotten items <the ~ of history —*New Republic*>
dust jacket *n* : a paper cover for a book
dust·man \ˈdəs(t)-mən\ *n, Brit* : a collector of trash or garbage
dust mop *n* : DRY MOP
dust·pan \ˈdəs(t)-ˌpan\ *n* : a shovel-shaped pan for sweepings
dust storm *n* **1** : a dust-laden whirlwind that moves across an arid region and is usu. associated with hot dry air and marked by high electrical tension **2** : strong winds bearing clouds of dust
dust·up \ˈdəs-ˌtəp\ *n* : QUARREL, ROW
dust wrapper *n* : DUST JACKET
dusty \ˈdəs-tē\ *adj* **dust·i·er; -est** **1** : covered or abounding with dust **2** : consisting of dust : POWDERY **3** : resembling dust **4** : lacking vitality : DRY <~ scholarship> — **dust·i·ly** \ˈdəs-tə-lē\ *adv* — **dust·i·ness** \-tē-nəs\ *n*
dusty miller *n* : any of several plants (as a mullein pink) having ashy-gray or white tomentose leaves
dutch \ˈdəch\ *adv, often cap* : with each person paying his own way
¹Dutch \ˈdəch\ *adj* [ME *Duch*, fr. MD *duutsch*; akin to OHG *diutisc* German, Goth *thiudisko* as a gentile, *thiuda* people, Oscan *touto* city] **1 a** *archaic* : of or relating to the Germanic peoples of Germany, Austria, Switzerland, and the Low Countries **b** : of or relating to the Netherlands or its inhabitants **c** : GERMAN **2 a** *archaic* : of, relating to, or in any of the Germanic languages of Germany, Austria, Switzerland, and the Low Countries **b** : of, relating to, or in the Dutch of the Netherlands **3** : of or relating to the Pennsylvania Dutch or their language — **Dutch·ly** *adv*
²Dutch *n* **1 a** *archaic* (1) : any of the Germanic languages of Germany, Austria, Switzerland, and the Low Countries (2) : GERMAN 2 **b** : the Germanic language of the Netherlands **2** **Dutch** *pl* **a** *archaic* : the Germanic peoples of Germany, Austria, Switzerland, and the Low Countries **b** *archaic* : people of Germanic descent **c** : the people of the Netherlands **3** : PENNSYL-

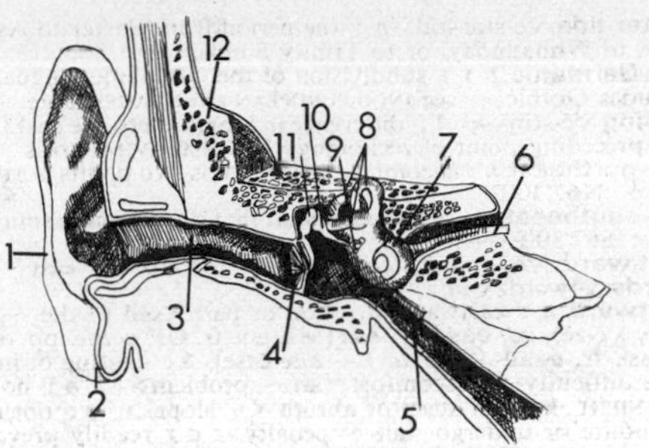

ear 1a: *1* pinna, *2* lobe, *3* auditory meatus, *4* tympanic membrane, *5* eustachian tube, *6* auditory nerve, *7* cochlea, *8* semicircular canals, *9* stapes, *10* incus, *11* malleus, *12* bones of skull

more at EDGE] : the fruiting spike of a cereal (as Indian corn) including both the seeds and protective structures

3ear *vi* : to form ears in the course of growing — often used with *up* <the rye should be ~*ing* up>

ear·ache \ˈi(ə)r-ˌāk\ *n* : an ache or pain in the ear

ear·drop \-ˌdräp\ *n* : EARRING; *esp* : one with a pendant

ear·drum \-ˌdrəm\ *n* : TYMPANIC MEMBRANE

eared \ˈi(ə)rd\ *adj* : having ears esp. of a specified kind or number <a big-*eared* man> <golden-*eared* corn>

eared seal *n* : any of a family (Otariidae) of seals including the sea lions and fur seals and having independent mobile hind limbs and small well-developed external ears

earflap *n* : a warm covering for the ears; *esp* : an extension on the lower edge of a cap that may be folded up or down

ear·ful \ˈi(ə)r-ˌfu̇l\ *n* **1** : an outpouring of news or gossip **2** : a sharp reprimand

ear·ing \ˈi(ə)r-iŋ\ *n* [perh. fr. 1*ear*] : a line used to fasten a corner of a sail to the yard or gaff or to haul a reef cringle to the yard

earl \ˈər(-ə)l\ *n* [ME *erl,* fr. OE *eorl* warrior, nobleman; akin to ON *jarl* warrior, nobleman] : a member of the British peerage ranking below a marquess and above a viscount — **earl·dom** \-dəm\ *n*

ear·less seal \ˌi(ə)r-ləs-\ *n* : any of a family (Phocidae, the earless-seal family) of seals including the hair seals and having the hind limbs reduced to swimming flippers and no external ears

earlier on *adv* : PREVIOUSLY <discussed the matter *earlier on*>

earl marshal *n* : an officer of state in England serving chiefly as a royal attendant on ceremonial occasions, as marshal of state processions, and as head of the College of Arms

ear·lobe \ˈi(ə)r-ˌlōb\ *n* : the pendent part of the ear of man or some fowls

ear·lock \-ˌläk\ *n* : a curl of hair hanging in front of the ear

1ear·ly \ˈər-lē\ *adv* **ear·li·er; -est** [ME *erly,* fr. OE *ǣrlice,* fr. *ǣr* early, soon — more at ERE] **1** : near the beginning of a period of time or of a process or series **2 a** : before the usual time **b** *archaic* : SOON **c** : sooner than related forms <these apples bear ~>

2early *adj* **ear·li·er; -est 1 a** : of, relating to, or occurring near the beginning of a period of time, a development, or a series **b** (1) : distant in past time (2) : PRIMITIVE **2 a** : occurring before the usual time **b** : occurring in the near future **c** : maturing or producing sooner than related forms <an ~ peach> — **ear·li·ness** *n*

Early American *n* : a style of furniture, architecture, or fabric originating in or characteristic of colonial America

early bird *n* [fr. the proverb, "the early bird catches the worm"] **1** : an early riser **2** : one that arrives early and esp. before possible competitors

early on *adv* : at or during an early point or stage <the reasons were obvious *early on* in the experiment>

ear·ly·wood \ˈər-lē-ˌwu̇d\ *n* : SPRINGWOOD

1ear·mark \ˈi(ə)r-ˌmärk\ *n* **1** : a mark of identification on the ear of an animal **2** : a distinguishing or identifying mark <all the ~*s* of poverty>

2earmark *vt* **1 a** : to mark (livestock) with an earmark **b** : to mark in a distinguishing manner <dissipation ~*s* a man> **2** : to designate (as funds) for a specific use or owner

ear·muff \ˈi(ə)r-ˌməf\ *n* : one of a pair of ear coverings connected by a flexible band and worn as protection against cold or noises

1earn \ˈərn\ *vt* [ME *ernen,* fr. OE *earnian*] **1** : to receive as return for effort and esp. for work done or services rendered **2 a** : to come to be duly worthy of or entitled or suited to <he had ~*ed* a promotion by his devotion to duty> **b** : to make worthy of or obtain for <his devotion to duty had ~*ed* him a promotion> ***syn*** see GET — **earn·er** *n*

2earn *vi* [prob. alter. of *yearn*] *obs* : GRIEVE

earned run average *n* : the average number of earned runs per game scored against a pitcher in baseball determined by dividing the total of earned runs scored against him by the total number of innings pitched and multiplying by nine

1ear·nest \ˈər-nəst\ *n* [ME *ernest,* fr. OE *eornost;* akin to OHG *ernust* earnest] : a serious and intent mental state <in ~>

2earnest *adj* **1** : characterized by or proceeding from an intense and serious state of mind **2** : GRAVE, IMPORTANT ***syn*** see SERIOUS ***ant*** frivolous — **ear·nest·ly** *adv* — **ear·nest·ness** \-nəs(t)-nəs\ *n*

3earnest *n* [ME *ernes, ernest,* fr. OF *erres,* pl. of *erre* earnest, fr. L *arra,* short for *arrabo,* fr. Gk *arrhabōn,* fr. Heb *ʽērābhōn*] **1** : something of value given by a buyer to a seller to bind a bargain **2** : a token of what is to come : PLEDGE

earn·ings \ˈər-niŋz\ *n pl* **1** : something earned **2** : the balance of revenue after deduction of costs and expenses

ear·phone \ˈi(ə)r-ˌfōn\ *n* : a device that converts electrical energy into sound waves and is worn over or inserted into the ear

ear pick *n* : a device often of precious metal for removing wax or foreign bodies from the ear

ear·piece \ˈi(ə)r-ˌpēs\ *n* **1** : a part of an instrument (as a stethoscope or hearing aid) to which the ear is applied; *esp* : EARPHONE **2** : one of the two sidepieces that support eyeglasses by passing over or behind the ears

ear·plug \-ˌpləg\ *n* : a device of pliable material for insertion into the outer opening of the ear (as for protection against water or to deaden sound)

ear·ring \ˈi(ə)r-(ˌ)iŋ, -ˌriŋ\ *n* : an ornament for the earlobe

ear rot *n* : a condition of Indian corn that is characterized by molding and decay of the ears and that is caused by fungi (genera *Diplodia, Fusarium,* or *Gibberella*)

ear shell *n* : ABALONE

ear·shot \ˈi(ə)r-ˌshät\ *n* : the range within which the unaided voice may be heard

ear·split·ting \-ˌsplit-iŋ\ *adj* : distressingly loud or shrill

1earth \ˈərth\ *n* [ME *erthe,* fr. OE *eorthe;* akin to OHG *erda* earth, Gk *eraze* to the ground] **1** : the fragmental material composing part of the surface of the globe; *esp* : cultivable soil **2** : the sphere of mortal life as distinguished from spheres of spirit life — compare HEAVEN, HELL **3 a** : areas of land as distinguished from sea and air **b** : the solid footing formed of soil : GROUND **4** *often cap* : the planet on which we live that is third in order from the sun — see PLANET table **5 a** : the people of the planet Earth **b** : the mortal body of man **c** : the pursuits and interests and pleasures of earthly life as distinguished from spiritual concerns **6** : the lair of a burrowing animal **7** : a difficultly reducible metallic oxide (as alumina) formerly classed as an element — **earth·like** \-ˌlīk\ *adj*

syn EARTH, WORLD, UNIVERSE *shared meaning element* : the entire area in which man thinks of himself as living and acting — **on earth** : among many possibilities — used as an intensive

2earth *vt* **1** : to drive to hiding in the earth **2** : to draw soil about (plants) **3** *chiefly Brit* : GROUND 3 ~ *vi, of a hunted animal* : to hide in the ground

earth·born \ˈərth-ˌbȯ(ə)rn\ *adj* **1** : born on this earth : MORTAL **2** : associated with earthly life <~ cares>

earth·bound \-ˌbau̇nd\ *adj* **1 a** : fast in or to the soil <~ roots> **b** : restricted to land or to the surface of the earth **2 a** : bound by earthly interests **b** : PEDESTRIAN, UNIMAGINATIVE

earth·en \ˈər-thən, -t͟hən\ *adj* **1** : made of earth **2** : EARTHLY

earth·en·ware \-ˌwa(ə)r, -ˌwe(ə)r\ *n* : ceramic ware made of slightly porous opaque clay fired at low heat

earth·i·ly \ˈər-thə-lē, -t͟hə-\ *adv* : in an earthy manner

earth·ling \ˈərth-liŋ\ *n* **1** : an inhabitant of the earth **2** : WORLDLING

earth·ly \ˈərth-lē\ *adj* **1 a** : characteristic of or belonging to this earth **b** : relating to man's actual life on this earth **2** : POSSIBLE <there is no ~ reason for such behavior> — **earth·li·ness** *n*

syn EARTHLY, TERRESTRIAL, MUNDANE, WORLDLY *shared meaning element* : belonging to or characteristic of the earth ***ant*** heavenly

earth mother *n, often cap E & M* **1** : the earth viewed (as in primitive theology) as the divine source of terrestrial life **2** : the female principle of fertility

earth·quake \ˈərth-ˌkwāk\ *n* : a shaking or trembling of the earth that is volcanic or tectonic in origin

earth science *n* : any of the sciences (as geology, meteorology, or oceanography) that deal with the earth or with one or more of its parts

earth·shak·er \ˈərth-ˌshā-kər\ *n* : something of fundamental importance

earth·shak·ing \-kiŋ\ *adj* : of fundamental importance — **earth·shak·ing·ly** \-kiŋ-lē\ *adv*

earth·shine \ˈərth-ˌshīn\ *n* : sunlight reflected by the earth that illuminates the dark part of the moon — called also *earthlight*

earth·star \-ˌstär\ *n* : a globose fungus (genus *Geastrum*) with a double wall whose outer layer splits into the shape of a star

earth·ward \-wərd\ *or* **earth·wards** \-wərdz\ *adv* : toward the earth

earth·work \ˈərth-ˌwərk\ *n* **1** : an embankment or other construction made of earth; *esp* : one used as a field fortification **2** : the operations connected with excavations and embankments of earth

earth·worm \-ˌwərm\ *n* : a terrestrial annelid worm (class Oligochaeta); *esp* : any of a family (Lumbricidae) of numerous widely distributed hermaphroditic worms that move through the soil by means of setae — see ANNELID illustration

earthy \ˈər-thē, -t͟hē\ *adj* **earth·i·er; -est 1** : consisting of, resembling, or suggesting earth <an ~ flavor> **2** *archaic* : EARTHLY, WORLDLY **3 a** : DOWN-TO-EARTH, PRACTICAL **b** : CRUDE, GROSS <~ humor> — **earth·i·ness** *n*

ear·wax \ˈi(ə)r-ˌwaks\ *n* : CERUMEN

1ear·wig \-ˌwig\ *n* [ME *erwigge,* fr. OE *ēarwicga,* fr. *ēare* ear + *wicga* insect — more at VETCH] : any of numerous insects (order Dermaptera) having slender many-jointed antennae and a pair of cerci resembling forceps at the end of the body

earwig

2earwig *vt* **ear·wigged; ear·wig·ging** : to annoy or attempt to influence by private talk

ear·wit·ness \ˈi(ə)r-ˈwit-nəs\ *n* : one who overhears something; *esp* : one who gives a report on what he has heard

ear·worm \-ˌwərm\ *n* : CORN EARWORM

1ease \ˈēz\ *n* [ME *ese,* fr. OF *aise* convenience, comfort, fr. L *adjacent-, adjacens* neighborhood, fr. neut. of prp. of *adjacēre* to lie near — more at ADJACENT] **1 :** the state of being comfortable: as **a :** freedom from pain or discomfort **b :** freedom from care **c :** freedom from labor or difficulty **d :** freedom from embarrassment or constraint : NATURALNESS **2 :** relief from discomfort or obligation **3 :** FACILITY, EFFORTLESSNESS **4 :** an act of easing or a state of being eased; *esp* **:** a lowering trend in prices — **ease·ful** \-fəl\ *adj* — **ease·ful·ly** \-fə-lē\ *adv* — **at ease 1 :** free from pain or discomfort **2 a :** free from restraint or formality **b :** standing silently (as in a military formation) with the feet apart, the right foot in place, and one or both hands behind the body — often used as a command

²ease *vb* **eased; eas·ing** *vt* **1 :** to free from something that pains, disquiets, or burdens **2 :** to make less painful : ALLEVIATE <~ his suffering> **3 a :** to lessen the pressure or tension of esp. by slackening, lifting, or shifting **b :** to moderate or reduce esp. in amount or intensity **4 :** to make less difficult <~ credit> **5 a :** to put the helm of (a ship) alee **b :** to let (a helm or rudder) come back a little after having been put hard over ~ *vi* **1 :** to give freedom or relief **2 :** to move or pass with freedom **3 :** MODERATE, SLACKEN

ea·sel \ˈē-zəl\ *n* [D *ezel* ass; akin to OE *esol* ass; both fr. a prehistoric EGmc-WGmc word borrowed fr. L *asinus* ass] **:** a frame for supporting something (as an artist's canvas)

ease·ment \ˈēz-mənt\ *n* **1 :** an act or means of easing or relieving (as from discomfort) **2 :** an interest in land owned by another that entitles its holder to a specific limited use or enjoyment

eas·i·ly \ˈēz-(ə-)lē\ *adv* **1 :** in an easy manner **2 :** by far

¹east \ˈēst\ *adv* [ME *est,* fr. OE *ēast;* akin to OHG *ōstar* to the east, L *aurora* dawn, Gk *ēōs, heōs*] **:** to, toward, or in the east

²east *adj* **1 :** situated toward or at the east <an ~ window> **2 :** coming from the east <an ~ wind>

³east *n* **1 a :** the general direction of sunrise : the direction toward the right of one facing north **b :** the place on the horizon where the sun rises when it is near one of the equinoxes **c :** the compass point directly opposite to west **2** *cap* **a :** regions lying to the east of a specified or implied point of orientation **b :** regions having a culture derived from ancient non-European esp. Asiatic areas **3 :** the altar end of a church **4** *often cap* **a :** the one of four positions at 90-degree intervals that lies to the east or to the right of South **b :** a person (as a bridge player) occupying this position in the course of a specified activity

east·bound \ˈēs(t)-ˌbau̇nd\ *adj* **:** traveling or heading east

east by north : a compass point that is one point north of due east : N78°45′E

east by south : a compass point that is one point south of due east : S78°45′E

east·er \ˈē-stər\ *n* **:** an easterly wind; *esp* **:** a storm coming from the east

Eas·ter \ˈē-stər\ *n* [ME *estre,* fr. OE *ēastre;* akin to OHG *ōstarun* (pl.) Easter; both fr. the prehistoric WGmc name of a pagan spring festival akin to OE *ēast* east] **:** a feast that commemorates Christ's resurrection and is observed with variations of date due to different calendars on the first Sunday after the full moon on or next after March 21 or one week later if the full moon falls on Sunday

EASTER DATES

YEAR	ASH WEDNESDAY	EASTER	YEAR	ASH WEDNESDAY	EASTER
1973	Mar 7	Apr 22	1983	Feb 16	Apr 3
1974	Feb 27	Apr 14	1984	Mar 7	Apr 22
1975	Feb 12	Mar 30	1985	Feb 20	Apr 7
1976	Mar 3	Apr 18	1986	Feb 12	Mar 30
1977	Feb 23	Apr 10	1987	Mar 4	Apr 19
1978	Feb 8	Mar 26	1988	Feb 17	Apr 3
1979	Feb 28	Apr 15	1989	Feb 8	Mar 26
1980	Feb 20	Apr 6	1990	Feb 28	Apr 15
1981	Mar 4	Apr 19	1991	Feb 13	Mar 31
1982	Feb 24	Apr 11	1992	Mar 4	Apr 19

Easter egg *n* **:** an egg that is dyed bright colors and that is associated with the celebration of Easter

Easter lily *n* **:** any of several white cultivated lilies (esp. *Lilium longiflorum*) that bloom in early spring

¹east·er·ly \ˈē-stər-lē\ *adj or adv* [obs. *easter* (eastern)] **1 :** situated toward or belonging to the east <the ~ shore of the lake> **2 :** coming from the east <an ~ storm>

²easterly *n, pl* **-lies :** a wind from the east

Easter Monday *n* **:** the Monday after Easter observed as a legal holiday in parts of the British Commonwealth and in No. Carolina

east·ern \ˈē-stərn\ *adj* [ME *estern,* fr. OE *ēasterne;* akin to OHG *ōstrōni* eastern, OE *ēast* east] **1** *cap* **:** of, relating to, or characteristic of a region conventionally designated East **2** *cap* **a :** of, relating to, or being the Christian churches originating in the church of the Eastern Roman Empire **b :** Eastern Orthodox **3 a :** lying toward the east **b :** coming from the east <an ~ wind> — **east·ern·most** \-ˌmōst\ *adj*

East·ern·er \ˈē-stə(r)-nər\ *n* **:** a native or inhabitant of the East; *esp* **:** a native or resident of the eastern part of the U.S.

eastern hemisphere *n* **:** the half of the earth to the east of the Atlantic ocean including Europe, Asia, and Africa

east·ern·ize \ˈē-stər-ˌnīz\ *vt* **-ized; -iz·ing 1 :** to imbue with qualities native to or associated with residents of the eastern U.S. **2 :** ORIENTALIZE

Eastern Orthodox *adj* **:** of or consisting of the Eastern churches that form a loose federation according primacy of honor to the patriarch of Constantinople and adhering to the decisions of the first seven ecumenical councils and to the Byzantine rite

eastern time *n, often cap E* **:** the time of the 5th time zone west of Greenwich that includes the eastern U.S. — see TIME ZONE illustration

eastern white pine *n* **:** WHITE PINE 1a

Eas·ter·tide \ˈē-stər-ˌtīd\ *n* **:** the period from Easter to Ascension Day, to Whitsunday, or to Trinity Sunday

East Germanic *n* **:** a subdivision of the Germanic languages that includes Gothic — see INDO-EUROPEAN LANGUAGES table

east·ing \ˈē-stiŋ\ *n* **1 :** difference in longitude to the east from the last preceding point of reckoning **2 :** easterly progress

east–northeast *n* **:** a compass point that is two points north of due east : N67°30′E

east–southeast *n* **:** a compass point that is two points south of due east : S67°30′E

¹east·ward \ˈēs-twərd\ *adv or adj* **:** toward the east — **east·wards** \-twərdz\ *adv*

²eastward *n* **:** eastward direction or part <sail to the ~>

¹easy \ˈē-zē\ *adj* **eas·i·er; -est** [ME *esy,* fr. OF *aaisié,* pp. of *aaisier* to ease, fr. *a-* ad- (fr. L *ad-*) + *aise* ease] **1 :** causing or involving little difficulty or discomfort <an ~ problem> **2 a :** not severe : LENIENT **b :** not steep or abrupt <~ slopes> **c :** not difficult to endure or undergo <an ~ penalty> **d :** readily prevailed on <~ prey> **e** (1) **:** plentiful in supply at low or declining interest rates <~ money> (2) **:** less in demand and usu. lower in price <bonds were *easier*> **3 a :** marked by peace and comfort <the ~ course of his life> **b :** not hurried or strenuous <~ pace> **4 a :** free from pain, annoyance, or anxiety <did all she could to make him *easier*> **b :** marked by social ease <~ manners> **c :** showing a disinclination to energetic individual action or resolute independent thought <an ~ disposition> **5 a :** giving ease, comfort, or relaxation <~ chairs> **b :** not burdensome or straitened <bought on ~ terms> <living in ~ circumstances> **c :** fitting comfortably <an ~ shoe> **d :** marked by ready facility <an ~ flowing style> **e :** felt or attained to readily, naturally, and spontaneously <~ emotions> ***syn*** see COMFORTABLE — **eas·i·ness** *n*

²easy *adv* **eas·i·er; -est 1 :** EASILY <promises come ~> **2 :** without undue speed or excitement : SLOWLY, CAUTIOUSLY <take it ~>

easy·go·ing \ˌē-zē-ˈgō-iŋ, -ˈgȯ(-)iŋ\ *adj* **1 :** taking life easy: as **a :** PLACID <an ~ man> **b :** indolent and careless <his inertia, his laziness, his ~ ways —*Times Lit. Supp.*> **c :** morally lax **2 :** UNHURRIED, COMFORTABLE <an ~ pace> — **easy·go·ing·ness** *n*

easy mark *n* **:** one easily imposed upon, duped, or overcome : PATSY

easy street *n* **:** a situation with no financial worries

easy virtue *n* **:** sexually promiscuous behavior or habits <a woman of *easy virtue*>

eat \ˈēt\ *vb* **ate** \ˈāt, *chiefly Brit or substand* ˈet\; **eat·en** \ˈēt-ᵊn\; **eat·ing** [ME *eten,* fr. OE *etan;* akin to OHG *ezzan* to eat, L *edere,* Gk *edmenai*] *vt* **1 :** to take in through the mouth as food : ingest, chew, and swallow in turn **2 :** to destroy, use up, or waste by or as if by eating : DEVOUR <locusts *ate* the country bare> **3 a :** to consume gradually : CORRODE **b :** to consume with vexation : BOTHER <what's ~*ing* her now> ~ *vi* **1 :** to take food or a meal **2 :** to affect something by gradual destruction or consumption — used with *into* — **eat·er** *n* — **eat crow :** to accept what one has fought against — **eat humble pie :** to apologize or retract under pressure — **eat one's heart out :** to grieve bitterly — **eat one's words :** to retract what one has said — **eat out of one's hand :** to accept the domination of another

¹eat·able \ˈēt-ə-bəl\ *adj* **:** fit to be eaten

²eatable *n* **1 :** something to eat **2** *pl* **:** FOOD

eat·ery \ˈēt-ə-rē\ *n, pl* **-er·ies :** LUNCHEONETTE, RESTAURANT

eath \ˈēth\ *adv or adj* [ME *ethe,* fr. OE *ēathe;* akin to OHG *ōdi* easy and perh. to L *avēre* to long for — more at AVID] *Scot* **:** EASY

eat·ing \ˈēt-iŋ\ *adj* **1 :** used for eating **2 :** fit to be eaten raw <makes a better cooking than ~ apple>

eat out *vi* **:** to eat away from home and esp. at a restaurant

eau de co·logne \ˌōd-ə-kə-ˈlōn\ *n, pl* **eaux de cologne** \ˌō(z)d-ə-\ [F, lit., Cologne water, fr. *Cologne,* Germany] **:** COLOGNE

eau–de–vie \ˌōd-ə-ˈvē\ *n, pl* **eaux–de–vie** \ˌō(z)d-ə-\ [F, lit., water of life, trans. of ML *aqua vitae*] **:** BRANDY

eaves \ˈēvz\ *n pl* [ME *eves* (sing.), fr. OE *efes;* akin to OHG *obasa* portico, OE *ūp* up — more at UP] **1 :** the lower border of a roof that overhangs the wall **2 :** a projecting edge (as of a hill)

eaves·drop \ˈēvz-ˌdräp\ *vi* [prob. back-formation fr. *eavesdropper,* lit., one standing under the drip from the eaves] **:** to listen secretly to what is said in private — **eaves·drop·per** *n*

EB *abbr* eastbound

¹ebb \ˈeb\ *n* [ME *ebbe,* fr OE *ebba;* akin to MD *ebbe* ebb, OE *of* from — more at OF] **1 :** the reflux of the tide toward the sea **2 :** a point or condition of decline <relations were at a low ~>

²ebb *vi* **1 :** to recede from the flood **2 :** to fall from a higher to a lower level or from a better to a worse state ***syn*** see ABATE ***ant*** flow (*as the tide*)

eb·bet \ˈeb-ət\ *n* [ME *evete,* fr. OE *efete*] **:** a common green newt (*Triturus viridescens*) of the eastern U.S.

ebb tide *n* **1 :** the tide while ebbing or at ebb **2 :** a period or state of decline

eb·on \ˈeb-ən\ *adj* **:** EBONY

eb·o·nite \ˈeb-ə-ˌnīt\ *n* **:** hard rubber esp. when black or unfilled

eb·o·nize \-ˌnīz\ *vt* **-nized; -niz·ing :** to stain black in imitation of ebony

¹eb·o·ny \ˈeb-ə-nē\ *n, pl* **-nies** [prob. fr. LL *hebeninus* of ebony, fr. Gk *ebeninos,* fr. *ebenos* ebony, fr. Egypt *hbnj*] **1 :** a hard heavy wood yielded by various Old World tropical dicotyledonous trees (genus *Diospyros*) of the ebony family (Ebonaceae) **2 a :** a tree yielding ebony **b :** any of several trees yielding wood resembling ebony

²ebony *adj* **1 :** made of or resembling ebony **2 :** BLACK, DARK

ebul·lience \i-ˈbu̇l-yən(t)s, -ˈbəl-\ *n* **:** the quality of lively or enthusiastic expression of thoughts or feelings : EXUBERANCE

ebul·lien·cy \-yən-sē\ *n* **:** EBULLIENCE

ebul·lient \-yənt\ *adj* [L *ebullient-, ebulliens,* prp. of *ebullire* to bubble out, fr. *e-* + *bullire* to bubble, boil — more at BOIL] **1 :** BOILING, AGITATED **2 :** characterized by ebullience — **ebul·lient·ly** *adv*

eb·ul·li·tion \ˌeb-ə-'lish-ən\ *n* **1 :** the act, process, or state of boiling or bubbling up **2 :** a sudden violent outburst or display

ec- *or* **eco-** *comb form* [LL *oeco-* household, fr. Gk *oik-*, *oiko-*, fr. *oikos* house — more at VICINITY] **1 :** habitat or environment <*eco*species> **2 :** ecology

[1]**ec·cen·tric** \ik-'sen-trik, ek-\ *adj* [ML *eccentricus*, fr. Gk *ekkentros*, fr. *ex* out of + *kentron* center] **1 :** not having the same center <~ spheres> **2 :** deviating from an established pattern or from accepted usage or conduct **3 a :** deviating from a circular path <an ~ orbit> **b :** located elsewhere than at the geometrical center; *also* **:** having the axis or support so located <an ~ wheel> — **ec·cen·tri·cal·ly** \-tri-k(ə-)lē\ *adv*

[2]**eccentric** *n* **1 :** a mechanical device consisting of a disk through which a shaft is keyed eccentrically and a circular strap which works freely round the rim of the disk for communicating its motion to one end of a rod whose other end is constrained to move in a straight line so as to produce reciprocating motion **2 :** an eccentric person

ec·cen·tric·i·ty \ˌek-ˌsen-'tris-ət-ē\ *n, pl* **-ties** **1 a :** the quality or state of being eccentric **b :** deviation from an established pattern, rule, or norm; *esp* **:** odd or whimsical behavior **2 :** a mathematical constant that for a given conic section is the ratio of the distances from any point of the conic section to a focus and the corresponding directrix
syn ECCENTRICITY, IDIOSYNCRASY *shared meaning element* **:** singularity of behavior or an instance of this

ec·chy·mo·sis \ˌek-i-'mō-səs\ *n, pl* **-mo·ses** \-ˌsēz\ [NL, fr. Gk *ekchymōsis*, fr. *ekchymousthai* to extravasate blood, fr. *ex-* + *chymos* juice — more at CHYME] **:** the escape of blood into the tissues from ruptured blood vessels — **ec·chy·mot·ic** \-'mät-ik\ *adj*

eccl *abbr* ecclesiastic; ecclesiastical

Eccles *abbr* Ecclesiastes

ecclesi- *or* **ecclesio-** *comb form* [ME *ecclesi-*, fr. LL *ecclesia*, fr. Gk *ekklēsia* assembly of citizens, church, fr. *ekkalein* to call forth, summon, fr. *ex-* + *kalein* to call] **:** church <*ecclesio*graphy>

ec·cle·si·al \ik-'lē-zē-əl, e-'klē-\ *adj* **:** of or relating to a church

Ec·cle·si·as·tes \ik-ˌlē-zē-'as-(ˌ)tēz, e-ˌklē-\ *n* [Gk *Ekklēsiastēs*, lit., preacher (trans. of Heb *Qōheleth*), fr. *ekklesiastēs* member of an assembly] **:** a book of wisdom literature in canonical Jewish and Christian Scripture — see BIBLE table

[1]**ec·cle·si·as·tic** \-'as-tik\ *adj* **:** ECCLESIASTICAL

[2]**ecclesiastic** *n* **:** CLERGYMAN

ec·cle·si·as·ti·cal \-ti-kəl\ *adj* [*ecclesiastical* fr. ME, fr. LL *ecclesiasticus*; *ecclesiastic* fr. MF *ecclesiastique*, fr. LL *ecclesiasticus*, fr. LGk *ekklēsiastikos*, fr. Gk, of an assembly of citizens, fr. *ekklēsiastēs* member of an assembly, fr. *ekklēsia*] **1 :** of or relating to a church esp. as a formal and established institution <~ law> **2 :** suitable for use in a church <~ vestments> — **ec·cle·si·as·ti·cal·ly** \-ti-k(ə-)lē\ *adv*

ec·cle·si·as·ti·cism \-tə-ˌsiz-əm\ *n* **:** excessive attachment to ecclesiastical forms and practices

Ec·cle·si·as·ti·cus \-ti-kəs\ *n* [LL, fr. *ecclesiasticus* ecclesiastic] **:** a didactic book included in the Roman Catholic canon of the Old Testament and in the Protestant Apocrypha — see BIBLE table

ec·cle·si·ol·o·gy \ik-ˌlē-zē-'äl-ə-jē, e-ˌklē-\ *n, pl* **-gies** **1 :** the study of church architecture and adornment **2 :** theological doctrine relating to the church — **ec·cle·si·o·log·i·cal** \-zē-ə-'läj-i-kəl\ *adj*

Ecclus *abbr* Ecclesiasticus

ec·crine \'ek-rən, -ˌrīn, -ˌrēn\ *adj* [ISV *ec-* (fr. Gk *ex* out) + Gk *krinein* to separate — more at CERTAIN] **:** producing a fluid secretion without removing cytoplasm from the secreting cells; *also* **:** produced by an eccrine gland

eccrine gland *n* **:** any of the rather small sweat glands that produce an eccrine secretion and that are restricted to the human skin — called also *eccrine sweat gland*

ec·dys·i·ast \ek-'diz-ē-ˌast, -ē-əst\ *n* **:** STRIPTEASER

ec·dy·sis \'ek-də-səs\ *n, pl* **ec·dy·ses** \-də-ˌsēz\ [NL, fr. Gk *ekdysis* act of getting out] **:** the act of molting or shedding an outer cuticular layer (as in insects and crustaceans)

ec·dy·sone \'ek-də-ˌsōn\ *also* **ec·dy·son** \-ˌsän\ *n* [ISV *ecdys*is + horm*one*] **:** any of several arthropod hormones that in insects are produced by the prothoracic gland and that trigger molting and metamorphosis

ece·sis \i-'sē-səs, -'kē-\ *n* [NL, fr. Gk *oikēsis* inhabitation] **:** the establishment of a plant or animal in a new habitat

ECG *abbr* electrocardiogram

ech *abbr* echelon

[1]**ech·e·lon** \'esh-ə-ˌlän\ *n* [F *échelon*, lit., rung of a ladder] **1 a** (1) **:** an arrangement of a body of troops with its units each somewhat to the left or right of the one in the rear like a series of steps (2) **:** a formation of units or individuals resembling such an echelon (3) **:** a flight formation in which each airplane flies at a certain elevation above or below and at a certain distance behind and to the right or left of the airplane ahead **b :** any of several military units in echelon formation **2 a :** one of a series of levels or grades (as of leadership or responsibility) in an organization or field of activity **b :** a group of individuals having a particular responsibility or occupying a particular level or grade

[2]**echelon** *vt* **:** to form or arrange in an echelon ~ *vi* **:** to take position in an echelon

ech·e·ve·ria \ˌech-ə-və-'rē-ə\ *n* [NL, genus name, fr. *Echeveria*, 19th cent. Mex botanical illustrator] **:** any of a large genus (*Echeveria*) of tropical American succulent plants of the orpine family that have showy rosettes of often plushy basal leaves and axillary clusters of flowers with erect petals spreading only at the tips and that are often grown in warm regions as ornamentals

echid·na \i-'kid-nə\ *n* [NL, fr. L, viper, fr. Gk] **:** an oviparous spiny-coated toothless burrowing nocturnal mammal (*Tachyglossus aculeatus*) of Australia, Tasmania, and New Guinea that has a long extensile tongue and long heavy claws and that feeds chiefly on ants — called also *spiny anteater*

echin- *or* **echino-** *comb form* [L, fr. Gk, fr. *echinos* sea urchin] **1 :** prickle <*Echino*dermata> **2 :** sea urchin <*echin*ite>

echidna

echi·no·coc·co·sis \i-ˌkī-nə-kä-'kō-səs\ *n, pl* **-co·ses** \-ˌsēz\ [NL] **:** infestation with or disease caused by a small tapeworm (*Echinococcus granulosus*)

echi·no·coc·cus \i-ˌkī-nə-'käk-əs\ *n, pl* **-coc·ci** \-'käk-ˌ(s)ī, -'käk-(ˌ)(s)ē\ [NL, genus name] **:** any of a genus (*Echinococcus*) of tapeworms that alternate a minute adult living as a commensal in the intestine of carnivores with a hydatid larva invading tissues esp. of the liver of cattle, sheep, swine, and man and acting as a dangerous pathogen

echi·no·derm \i-'kī-nə-ˌdərm\ *n* [NL *Echinodermata*, phylum name, fr. *echin-* + *-dermata* (fr. Gk *derma* skin)] **:** any of a phylum (Echinodermata) of radially symmetrical coelomate marine animals consisting of the starfishes, sea urchins, and related forms — **echi·no·der·ma·tous** \-ˌkī-nə-'dər-mət-əs\ *adj*

echi·noid \i-'kī-ˌnȯid, 'ek-ə-ˌnȯid\ *n* **:** SEA URCHIN

echi·nu·late \i-'kin-yə-lət, -'kīn-, -ˌlāt\ *adj* **:** set with small spines or prickles — **echi·nu·la·tion** \-ˌkin-yə-'lā-shən, -ˌkīn-\ *n*

echi·nus \i-'kī-nəs\ *n, pl* **-ni** \-ˌnī\ [ME, fr. L, fr. Gk *echinos* hedgehog, sea urchin, architectural echinus] **1 :** SEA URCHIN **2 a :** the rounded molding forming the bell of the capital in the Greek Doric order **b :** a similar member in other orders

echi·uroid \ˌek-i-'yu̇(ə)r-ˌȯid\ *n* [NL *Echiuroidea*, group name, deriv. of Gk *echis* viper + *oura* tail]**:** any of a group (Echiuroidea) of marine worms of uncertain taxonomic affinities that have a sensitive but nonretractile proboscis above the mouth

[1]**echo** \'ek-(ˌ)ō\ *n, pl* **ech·oes** [ME *ecco*, fr. MF & L; MF *echo*, fr. L, fr. Gk *ēchō*; akin to L *vagire* to wail, Gk *ēchē* sound] **1 a :** the repetition of a sound caused by reflection of sound waves **b :** the sound due to such reflection **2 a :** a repetition or imitation of another **:** REFLECTION **b :** REPERCUSSION, RESULT **c :** TRACE, VESTIGE **d :** RESPONSE **3 :** one who closely imitates or repeats another's words, ideas, or acts **4 :** a soft repetition of a musical phrase **5 a :** the repetition of a received radio signal due esp. to reflection of part of the wave from an ionized layer of the atmosphere **b** (1) **:** the reflection of transmitted radar signals by an object (2) **:** the visual indication of this reflection on a radarscope — **echo·ey** \'ek-ˌō-ē\ *adj*

[2]**echo** *vb* **ech·oed**; **echo·ing** \'ek-(ˌ)ō-iŋ, 'ek-ə-wiŋ\ *vi* **1 :** to resound with echoes **2 :** to produce an echo ~ *vt* **1 :** REPEAT, IMITATE **2 :** to send back or repeat (a sound) by the reflection of sound waves

[1]**Echo** *n* [Gk *Ēchō*]**:** a nymph in Greek legend who pined away for love of Narcissus until nothing was left of her but her voice

[2]**Echo** — a communications code word for the letter *e*

echo chamber *n* **:** a room with sound-reflecting walls used for producing hollow or echoing sound effects esp. in radio broadcasting

echo·en·ceph·a·log·ra·phy \ˌek-ō-in-ˌsef-ə-'läg-rə-fē\ *n* **:** the use of ultrasound in the examination and measurement of internal structures (as the ventricles) of the skull and in the diagnosis of abnormalities

echo·ic \i-'kō-ik, e-\ *adj* **1 :** of or relating to an echo **2 :** formed in imitation of some natural sound **:** ONOMATOPOEIC

echo·la·lia \ˌek-ō-'lā-lē-ə\ *n* [NL] **:** the often pathological repetition of what is said by other people as if echoing them — **echo·lal·ic** \-'lal-ik\ *adj*

echo·lo·ca·tion \ˌek-ō-lō-'kā-shən\ *n* **:** a process for locating distant or invisible objects (as prey) by means of sound waves reflected back to the emitter (as a bat or submarine) by the objects

echo sounder *n* **:** an instrument for determining the depth of a body of water or of an object below the surface by means of sound waves

echo·vi·rus \'ek-ō-ˌvī-rəs\ *n* [*e*nteric *c*ytopathogenic *h*uman *o*rphan + *virus*]**:** any of a group of picornaviruses that are found in the gastrointestinal tract, that cause cytopathic changes in cells in tissue culture, and that are sometimes associated with respiratory ailments and meningitis

éclair \ā-'kla(ə)r, i-, -'kle(ə)r, 'ā-ˌ, 'ē-ˌ\ *n* [F, lit., lightning]**:** a usu. chocolate-frosted oblong cream puff with whipped cream or custard filling

éclair·cis·se·ment \ā-kler-sēs-(ə-)mäⁿ\ *n, pl* **éclaircissements** \-smäⁿ(z)\ [F] **:** ENLIGHTENMENT, CLARIFICATION

eclamp·sia \i-'klam(p)-sē-ə\ *n* [NL, fr. Gk *eklampsis* sudden flashing, fr. *eklampein* to shine forth, fr. *ex* out + *lampein* to shine] **:** a convulsive state; *esp* **:** an attack of convulsions during pregnancy or parturition — **eclamp·tic** \-'klam(p)-tik\ *adj*

éclat \ā-'klä, 'ā-ˌ\ *n* [F, splinter, burst, éclat] **1 :** dazzling effect **:** BRILLIANCE **2 a :** ostentatious display **:** PUBLICITY **b** *archaic* **:** NOTORIETY **3 a :** brilliant or conspicuous success **b :** ACCLAIM, APPLAUSE

[1]**eclec·tic** \e-'klek-tik, i-\ *adj* [Gk *eklektikos*, fr. *eklegein* to select, fr. *ex* + *legein* to gather — more at LEGEND] **1 :** selecting what appears to be best in various doctrines, methods, or styles **2 :** composed of elements drawn from various sources — **eclec·ti·cal·ly** \-ti-k(ə-)lē\ *adv*

[2]**eclectic** *n* **:** one who uses an eclectic method or approach

eclec·ti·cism \-'klek-tə-ˌsiz-əm\ *n* **:** the theory or practice of an eclectic method

[1]**eclipse** \i-'klips\ *n* [ME, fr. OF, fr. L *eclipsis*, fr. Gk *ekleipsis*, fr. *ekleipein* to omit, fail, suffer eclipse, fr. *ex* + *leipein* to leave —

ə abut	ᵊ kitten	ər further	a back	ā bake	ä cot, cart
au̇ out	ch chin	e less	ē easy	g gift	i trip	ī life
j joke	ŋ sing	ō flow	ȯ flaw	ȯi coin	th thin	t̲h̲ this
ü loot	u̇ foot	y yet	yü few	yu̇ furious	zh vision

more at LOAN] **1 a :** the total or partial obscuring of one celestial body by another **b :** the passing into the shadow of a celestial body — compare OCCULTATION, TRANSIT **2 :** a falling into obscurity or decline : DISGRACE **3 :** the state of being in eclipse plumage

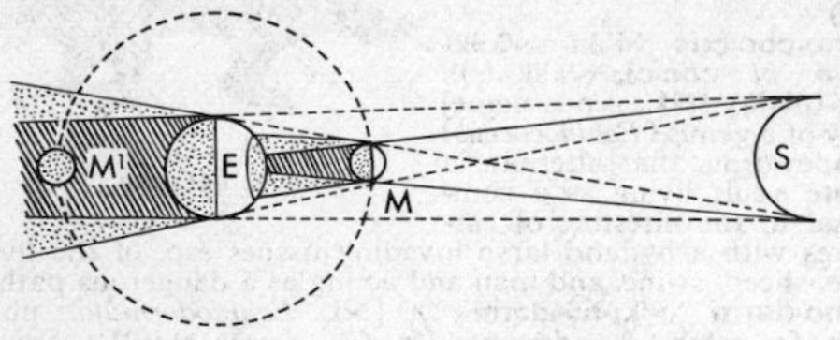

eclipse 1a: *S* sun; *E* earth; *M* moon in solar eclipse; *M'* moon in lunar eclipse

2eclipse *vt* **eclipsed; eclips·ing :** to cause an eclipse of: as **a :** OBSCURE, DARKEN **b :** to reduce in importance or repute : DISGRACE **c :** SURPASS

eclipse plumage *n* **:** comparatively dull plumage that is usu. of seasonal occurrence in birds which exhibit a distinct nuptial plumage

1eclip·tic \i-ˈklip-tik\ *n* [ME *ecliptik,* fr. LL *ecliptica linea,* lit., line of eclipses] **1 :** the great circle of the celestial sphere that is the apparent path of the sun among the stars or of the earth as seen from the sun : the plane of the earth's orbit extended to meet the celestial sphere **2 :** a great circle drawn on a terrestrial globe making an angle of about 23° 27′ with the equator and used for illustrating and solving astronomical problems

2ecliptic *adj* **:** of or relating to the ecliptic or an eclipse

ec·logue \ˈek-ˌlȯg, -ˌläg\ *n* [ME *eclog,* fr. L *Eclogae,* title of Vergil's pastorals, lit., selections, pl. of *ecloga,* fr. Gk *eklogē,* fr. *eklegein* to select] **:** a poem in which shepherds converse

eclo·sion \i-ˈklō-zhən\ *n* [F *éclosion*] *of an insect* **:** the act of emerging from the pupal case or hatching from the egg

ECM *abbr* European Common Market

eco- — see EC-

ecol *abbr* ecological; ecology

ecol·o·gy \i-ˈkäl-ə-jē, e-\ *n, pl* **-gies** [G *ökologie,* fr. *ök-* ec- + *-logie* -logy] **1 :** a branch of science concerned with the interrelationship of organisms and their environments **2 :** the totality or pattern of relations between organisms and their environment **3 :** HUMAN ECOLOGY — **eco·log·i·cal** \ˌē-kə-ˈläj-i-kəl, ˌek-ə-\ *also* **eco·log·ic** \-ik\ *adj* — **eco·log·i·cal·ly** \-i-k(ə-)lē\ *adv* — **ecol·o·gist** \i-ˈkäl-ə-jəst, e-\ *n*

econ *abbr* economics; economist; economy

econo·met·rics \i-ˌkän-ə-ˈme-triks\ *n pl but sing in constr* [blend of *economics* and *metric*] **:** the application of statistical methods to the study of economic data and problems — **econo·met·ric** \-trik\ *adj* — **econo·met·ri·cal·ly** \-tri-k(ə-)lē\ *adv* — **econo·me·tri·cian** \-mə-ˈtrish-ən\ *n* — **econo·met·rist** \-ˈme-trəst\ *n*

eco·nom·ic \ˌek-ə-ˈnäm-ik, ˌē-kə-\ *adj* **1** *archaic* **:** of or relating to a household or its management **2 :** ECONOMICAL 2 **3 a :** of or relating to economics **b :** of, relating to, or based on the production, distribution, and consumption of goods and services **c :** of or relating to an economy **4 :** having practical or industrial significance or uses : affecting material resources **5 :** PROFITABLE

eco·nom·i·cal \-ˈnäm-i-kəl\ *adj* **1** *archaic* **:** ECONOMIC 1 **2 :** marked by careful, efficient, and prudent use of resources : THRIFTY **3 :** operating with little waste or at a saving ***syn*** see SPARING ***ant*** extravagant — **eco·nom·i·cal·ly** \-i-k(ə-)lē\ *adv*

economic rent *n* **:** the return for the use of a factor in excess of the minimum required to bring forth its service

eco·nom·ics \ˌek-ə-ˈnäm-iks, ˌē-kə-\ *n pl but sing or pl in constr* **1 :** a social science concerned chiefly with description and analysis of the production, distribution, and consumption of goods and services **2 :** economic aspect or significance

econ·o·mist \i-ˈkän-ə-məst\ *n* **1** *archaic* **:** one who practices economy **2 :** a specialist in economics

econ·o·mize \-ˌmīz\ *vb* **-mized; -miz·ing** *vi* **:** to practice economy : be frugal ~ *vt* **:** to use more economically : SAVE — **econ·o·miz·er** *n*

1econ·o·my \i-ˈkän-ə-mē\ *n, pl* **-mies** [MF *yconomie,* fr. ML *oeconomia,* fr. Gk *oikonomia,* fr. *oikonomos* household manager, fr. *oikos* house + *nemein* to manage — more at VICINITY, NIMBLE] **1** *archaic* **:** the management of household or private affairs and esp. expenses **2 a :** thrifty and efficient use of material resources : frugality in expenditures; *also* **:** an instance or a means of economizing **b :** efficient and concise use of nonmaterial resources (as effort, language, or motion) for the end proposed **3 :** the arrangement or mode of operation of something : ORGANIZATION **4 :** the structure of economic life in a country, area, or period; *specif* **:** an economic system

2economy *adj* **:** designed to save money <~ cars> <~ measures>

eco·phys·i·ol·o·gy \ˌē-kō-ˌfiz-ē-ˈäl-ə-jē, ˌek-ō-\ *n* **:** the science of the interrelationships between the physiology of organisms and their environment — **eco·phys·i·o·log·i·cal** \-ē-ə-ˈläj-i-kəl\ *adj*

eco·spe·cies \ˈē-kō-ˌspē-(ˌ)shēz, ˌek-ō-, -(ˌ)sēz\ *n, pl* **ecospecies :** a subdivision of a cenospecies capable of free gene interchange between its members without impairment of fertility but less capable of fertile crosses with members of other subdivisions and typically more or less equivalent to the taxonomic species — **eco·spe·cif·ic** \ˌē-kō-spi-ˈsif-ik, ˌek-ō-\ *adj*

eco·sphere \ˈē-kō-ˌsfi(ə)r, ˈek-ō-\ *n* **:** the parts of the universe habitable by living organisms; *esp* **:** BIOSPHERE 1

eco·sys·tem \-ˌsis-təm\ *n* **:** the complex of a community and its environment functioning as an ecological unit in nature

eco·tone \ˈē-kə-ˌtōn, ˈek-ə-\ *n* [*ec-* + Gk *tonos* tension — more at TONE] **:** a transition area between two adjacent ecological communities usu. exhibiting competition between organisms common to both

eco·type \-ˌtīp\ *n* **:** a subdivision of an ecospecies that comprises individuals interfertile with each other and with members of other ecotypes of the same ecospecies but surviving as a distinct group through environmental selection and isolation and that is comparable with a taxonomic subspecies — **eco·typ·ic** \ˌē-kə-ˈtip-ik, ˌek-ə-\ *adj* — **eco·typ·i·cal·ly** \-i-k(ə-)lē\ *adv*

ecru \ˈek-(ˌ)rü, ˈā-(ˌ)krü\ *n* [F *écru* unbleached, fr. OF *escru,* fr. *es-* completely (fr. L *ex-*) + *cru* raw, fr. L *crudus* — more at RAW] **:** BEIGE 2

ec·sta·sy \ˈek-stə-sē\ *n, pl* **-sies** [ME *extasie,* fr. MF, fr. LL *ecstasis,* fr. Gk *ekstasis,* fr. *existanai* to derange, fr. *ex* out + *histanai* to cause to stand — more at EX-, STAND] **1 a :** a state of being beyond reason and self-control **b** *archaic* **:** SWOON **2 :** a state of overwhelming emotion; *esp* **:** rapturous delight **3 :** TRANCE; *esp* **:** a mystic or prophetic trance
syn ECSTASY, RAPTURE, TRANSPORT *shared meaning element* **:** intense exaltation of mind and feelings

1ec·stat·ic \ek-ˈstat-ik, ik-ˈstat-\ *adj* [ML *ecstaticus,* fr. Gk *ekstatikos,* fr. *existanai*] **:** of, relating to, or marked by ecstasy — **ec·stat·i·cal·ly** \-ˈstat-i-k(ə-)lē\ *adv*

2ecstatic *n* **:** one that is subject to ecstasies

ect- *or* **ecto-** *comb form* [NL, fr. Gk *ekto-,* fr. *ektos,* fr. *ex* out — more at EX-] **:** outside : external <*ecto*mere> — compare END-, EXO-

ec·to·blast \ˈek-tə-ˌblast\ *n* [ISV] **:** EPIBLAST — **ec·to·blas·tic** \ˌek-tə-ˈblas-tik\ *adj*

ec·to·com·men·sal \ˌek-tō-kə-ˈmen(t)-səl\ *n* **:** an organism that lives as a commensal on the body surface of another

ec·to·derm \ˈek-tə-ˌdərm\ *n* [ISV *ect-* + Gk *derma* skin — more at DERM-] **1 :** the outer cellular membrane of a diploblastic animal (as a jellyfish) **2 a :** the outermost of the three primary germ layers of an embryo **b :** a tissue (as neural tissue) derived from this germ layer — **ec·to·der·mal** \ˌek-tə-ˈdər-məl\ *or* **ec·to·der·mic** \-mik\ *adj*

ec·to·gen·ic \ˌek-tə-ˈjen-ik\ *adj* **:** ECTOGENOUS

ec·tog·e·nous \ek-ˈtäj-ə-nəs\ *adj* **:** capable of development apart from the host — used chiefly of pathogenic bacteria

ec·to·mere \ˈek-tə-ˌmi(ə)r\ *n* **:** a blastomere destined to form ectoderm — **ec·to·mer·ic** \ˌek-tə-ˈmer-ik, -ˈmi(ə)r-\ *adj*

ec·to·morph \ˈek-tə-ˌmȯrf\ *n* [*ecto*derm + *-morph*] **:** an ectomorphic individual

ec·to·mor·phic \ˌek-tə-ˈmȯr-fik\ *adj* [*ecto*derm + *-morphic;* fr. the predominance in such types of structures developed from the ectoderm] **1 :** of or relating to the component in W. H. Sheldon's classification of body types that measures the body's degree of slenderness, angularity, and fragility **2 :** having a light body build

-ec·to·my \ˈek-tə-mē\ *n comb form* [NL *-ectomia,* fr. Gk *ektemnein* to cut out, fr. *ex* out + *temnein* to cut — more at TOME] **:** surgical removal <gastr*ectomy*>

ec·to·par·a·site \ˌek-tō-ˈpar-ə-ˌsīt\ *n* [ISV] **:** a parasite that lives on the exterior of its host — **ec·to·par·a·sit·ic** \-ˌpar-ə-ˈsit-ik\ *adj*

ec·top·ic \ek-ˈtäp-ik\ *adj* [Gk *ektopos* out of place, fr. *ex-* out + *topos* place — more at TOPIC] **:** occurring in an abnormal position or in an unusual manner or form <~ lesions> <~ heartbeat>

ectopic pregnancy *n* **:** gestation elsewhere than in the uterus (as in a fallopian tube or in the peritoneal cavity)

ec·to·plasm \ˈek-tə-ˌplaz-əm\ *n* **1 :** the outer relatively rigid granule-free layer of the cytoplasm usu. held to be a reversible gel **2 :** a substance held to produce spirit materialization and telekinesis — **ec·to·plas·mic** \ˌek-tə-ˈplaz-mik\ *adj*

ec·to·therm \ˈek-tə-ˌthərm\ *n* **:** a cold-blooded animal : POIKILOTHERM — **ec·to·ther·mic** \ˌek-tə-ˈthər-mik\ *adj*

ec·to·tro·phic \ˌek-tə-ˈtrō-fik\ *also* **ec·to·tro·pic** \-ˈtrō-pik, -ˈträp-ik\ *adj, of a mycorrhiza* **:** growing in a close web on the surface of the associated root — compare ENDOTROPHIC

ecu \ˈā-ˌkyü, ā-ˈkü̅\ *n, pl* **ecus** \-ˌkyüz, -ˈkü̅z\ [MF, lit., shield, fr. OF *escu,* fr. L *scutum;* from the device of a shield on the coin — more at ESQUIRE] **:** any of various old French units of value; *also* **:** a coin representing this

Ecua *abbr* Ecuador

ec·u·men·i·cal \ˌek-yə-ˈmen-i-kəl\ *adj* [LL *oecumenicus,* fr. LGk *oikoumenikos,* fr. Gk *oikoumenē* the inhabited world, fr. fem. of *oikoumenos,* pres. pass. part. of *oikein* to inhabit, fr. *oikos* house — more at VICINITY] **1 :** worldwide or general in extent, influence, or application **2 a :** of, relating to, or representing the whole of a body of churches **b :** promoting or tending toward worldwide Christian unity or cooperation — **ec·u·men·i·cal·ly** \-k(ə-)lē\ *adv*

ec·u·men·i·cal·ism \-ˈmen-i-kə-ˌliz-əm\ *n* **:** ECUMENISM

ecumenical patriarch *n* **:** the patriarch of Constantinople as the dignitary given first honor in the Eastern Orthodox Church

ec·u·men·i·cism \ˌek-yə-ˈmen-ə-ˌsiz-əm\ *n* **:** ECUMENISM — **ec·u·men·i·cist** \-səst\ *n*

ec·u·me·nic·i·ty \ˌek-yə-mə-ˈnis-ət-ē, -me-\ *n* **:** the quality or state of being drawn close to others esp. through Christian ecumenical feeling or action

e·cu·men·ics \-ˈmen-iks\ *n pl but sing in constr* **:** the study of the nature, mission, problems, and strategy of the Christian church from the perspective of its ecumenical character

ecu·me·nism \e-ˈkyü-mə-ˌniz-əm, i- *also* ˈek-yə-mə-ˌniz- *or* ˌek-yə-ˈmen-ˌiz-\ *n* **:** ecumenical principles and practices esp. as exemplified among religious groups (as Christian denominations) — **ecu·me·nist** \e-ˈkyü-mə-nəst, i- *also* ˈek-yə-mə-nəst *or* ˌek-yə-ˈmen-əst\ *n*

ec·ze·ma \ig-ˈzē-mə, ˈeg-zə-mə, ˈek-sə-\ *n* [NL, fr. Gk *ekzema,* fr. *ekzein* to erupt, fr. *ex* out + *zein* to boil — more at EX-, YEAST] **:** an inflammatory condition of the skin characterized by redness, itching, and oozing vesicular lesions which become scaly, crusted, or hardened — **ec·zem·a·tous** \ig-ˈzem-ət-əs\ *adj*

ed *abbr* **1** edited; edition; editor **2** education

ED *abbr* extra duty

1-ed \d *after a vowel or* b, g, j, l, m, n, ŋ, r, th, v, z, zh; əd, id *after* d, t; t *after other sounds; exceptions are pronounced at their subentries* or entries\ *vb suffix or adj suffix* [ME, fr. OE *-ed, -od, -ad;* akin to OHG *-t,* pp. ending, L *-tus,* Gk *-tos,* suffix forming verbals] **1** — used to form the past participle of regular weak verbs <end*ed*> <fad*ed*> <tri*ed*> <patt*ed*> **2** — used to form adjectives of identical meaning from Latin-derived adjectives ending in *-ate* <crenulat*ed*> **3 a :** having : characterized by <cultur*ed*> <two-legg*ed*> **b :** having the characteristics of <bigot*ed*>

²-ed *vb suffix* [ME *-ede, -de,* fr. OE *-de, -ede, -ode, -ade;* akin to OHG *-ta,* past ending (1st sing.) and prob. to OHG *-t,* pp. ending] — used to form the past tense of regular weak verbs <judg*ed*> <deni*ed*> <dropp*ed*>

eda·cious \i-ˈdā-shəs\ *adj* [L *edac-, edax,* fr. *edere* to eat — more at EAT] **1** *archaic* **:** of or relating to eating **2 :** VORACIOUS — **edac·i·ty** \-ˈdas-ət-ē\ *n*

Edam \ˈēd-əm, ˈē-ˌdam\ *n* [*Edam,* Netherlands] **:** a yellow pressed cheese of Dutch origin usu. made in flattened balls and often coated with red wax

edaph·ic \i-ˈdaf-ik\ *adj* [Gk *edaphos* bottom, ground] **1 :** of or relating to the soil **2 a :** resulting from or influenced by the soil rather than the climate **b :** AUTOCHTHONOUS — **edaph·i·cal·ly** \-ˈdaf-i-k(ə-)lē\ *adv*

edaphic climax *n* **:** an ecological climax resulting from soil factors and commonly persisting through cycles of climactic and physiographic change — compare PHYSIOGRAPHIC CLIMAX

EDD *abbr* English Dialect Dictionary

Ed·dic \ˈed-ik\ *adj* [ON *Edda*] **:** of, relating to, or resembling the Old Norse *Edda* which is a 13th century collection of mythological, heroic, and aphoristic poems in alliterative verse

¹ed·dy \ˈed-ē\ *n, pl* **eddies** [ME (Sc dial.) *ydy,* prob. fr. ON *itha;* akin to OHG *ith-* again, L *et* and] **1 a :** a current of water or air running contrary to the main current; *esp* **:** a small whirlpool **b :** something moving similarly <little *eddies* of people were dancing with each other in the streets —L. C. Stevens> **2 :** a contrary or circular current (as of thought or policy)

²eddy *vb* **ed·died; ed·dy·ing** *vt* **:** to cause to move in an eddy ~ *vi* **:** to move in an eddy or in the manner of an eddy <the crowd frantically *eddied* in a half-moon shape —*Walker Report*>

eddy current *n* **:** an electric current induced by an alternating magnetic field

edel·weiss \ˈād-ᵊl-ˌwīs, -ˌvīs\ *n* [G, fr. *edel* noble + *weiss* white] **:** a small perennial composite herb (*Leontopodium alpinum*) having a dense woolly white pubescence and growing high in the Alps

ede·ma \i-ˈdē-mə\ *n* [NL, fr. Gk *oidēma* swelling, fr. *oidein* to swell; akin to OE *ātor* pus] **1 :** an abnormal excess accumulation of serous fluid in connective tissue or in a serous cavity **2 a :** watery swelling of plant organs or parts **b :** any of various plant diseases characterized by such swellings — **edem·a·tous** \-ˈdem-ət-əs\ *adj*

Eden \ˈēd-ᵊn\ *n* [LL, fr. Heb *ʿEdhen*] **1 :** the garden where according to the account in Genesis Adam and Eve first lived **2 :** PARADISE 2 — **Eden·ic** \i-ˈden-ik\ *adj*

¹eden·tate \(ˈ)ē-ˈden-ˌtāt\ *adj* [L *edentatus,* pp. of *edentare* to make toothless, fr. *-e* + *dent-, dens* tooth — more at TOOTH] **1 :** lacking teeth **2 :** being an edentate

²edentate *n* **:** any of an order (Edentata) of mammals having few or no teeth and including the sloths, armadillos, and New World anteaters and formerly also the pangolins and the aardvark

eden·tu·lous \(ˈ)ē-ˈden-chə-ləs\ *adj* [L *edentulus,* fr. *e-* + *dent-, dens*] **:** TOOTHLESS

Ed·gar \ˈed-gər\ *n* [*Edgar Allan Poe,* regarded as father of the detective story] **:** a statuette awarded annually by a professional organization for notable achievement in mystery-novel writing

¹edge \ˈej\ *n* [ME *egge,* fr. OE *ecg;* akin to L *acer* sharp, Gk *akmē* point] **1 a :** the cutting side of a blade **b :** the sharpness of a blade **c :** penetrating power **:** KEENNESS <an ~ of sarcasm in his voice> <took the ~ off the proposal> **2 a :** the line where an object or area begins or ends **:** BORDER <the town stands on the ~ of a plain> **b :** the narrow part adjacent to a border <walk on the ~ of the deck> **c :** a point near the beginning or the end <on the ~ of disaster> **d :** a favorable margin **:** ADVANTAGE <had the ~ on the competition> **3 :** a line or line segment that is the intersection of two plane faces (as of a pyramid) or of two planes *syn* see BORDER — **on edge :** ANXIOUS, NERVOUS

²edge *vb* **edged; edg·ing** *vt* **1 a :** to give an edge to **b :** to be on an edge of <grew up in a community still *edging* the wilderness —H. M. Kallen> **2 :** to move or force gradually <*edged* him off the road> **3 :** to incline (a ski) sideways so that one edge cuts into the snow **4 :** to defeat by a small margin — usu. used with *out* <*edged* out the opposing team by one point> ~ *vi* **:** to advance by short moves <the climbers *edged* along the cliff>

edged \ˈejd\ *adj* **1 :** having a specified kind of edge, boundary, or border or a specified number of edges <rough-*edged*> <two-*edged*> **2 :** SHARP, CUTTING <an ~ knife> <an ~ remark>

edge effect *n* **:** the result of the presence of two adjoining plant communities (as in an ecotone) on the numbers and kinds of animals present in the immediate vicinity

edge–grain \ˌej-ˌgrān\ *or* **edge–grained** \ˈej-ˈgrānd\ *adj* **:** QUARTERSAWED

edge in *vt* **:** to work in **:** INTERPOLATE <had difficulty *edging in* a word of his own>

edge·less \ˈej-ləs\ *adj* **:** lacking an edge **:** DULL

edg·er \ˈej-ər\ *n* **:** one that edges; *esp* **:** a tool used to trim the edge of a lawn along a sidewalk or curb

edge tool *n* **:** a tool with a sharp cutting edge

edge·ways \ˈej-ˌwāz\ *adv* **:** SIDEWAYS

edge·wise \-ˌwīz\ *adv* **:** EDGEWAYS

edg·ing *n* **:** something that forms an edge or border

edgy \ˈej-ē\ *adj* **edg·i·er; -est 1 :** having an edge **:** SHARP <often displayed a perceptive, ~ wit —*New Yorker*> **2 :** being on edge **:** TENSE, IRRITABLE — **edg·i·ly** \ˈej-ə-lē\ *adv* — **edg·i·ness** \ˈej-ē-nəs\ *n*

edh \ˈet͟h\ *n* [Icel *eth*] **:** a letter ð used in Old English and in Icelandic to represent an interdental fricative and in some phonetic alphabets to represent the voiced interdental fricative (as in *then*)

ed·i·ble \ˈed-ə-bəl\ *adj* [LL *edibilis,* fr. L *edere* to eat — more at EAT] **:** fit to be eaten **:** EATABLE — **ed·i·bil·i·ty** \ˌed-ə-ˈbil-ət-ē\ *n* — **edible** *n* — **ed·i·ble·ness** \ˈed-ə-bəl-nəs\ *n*

edict \ˈē-ˌdikt\ *n* [L *edictum,* fr. neut. of *edictus,* pp. of *edicere* to decree, fr. *e-* + *dicere* to say — more at DICTION] **1 :** an official public proclamation having the force of law **2 :** ORDER, COMMAND <we held firm to Grandmother's ~ —M. F. K. Fisher> — **edic·tal** \i-dik-tᵊl\ *adj*

ed·i·fi·ca·tion \ˌed-ə-fə-ˈkā-shən\ *n* **:** an act or process of edifying

edif·i·ca·to·ry \i-ˈdif-ə-kə-ˌtōr-ē, -ˌtȯr-\ *adj* **:** intended or suitable for edification

ed·i·fice \ˈed-ə-fəs\ *n* [ME, fr. MF, fr. L *aedificium,* fr. *aedificare*] **1 :** BUILDING; *esp* **:** a large or massive structure **2 :** a large abstract structure <the keystone which holds together the social ~ —R. H. Tawney>

ed·i·fy \ˈed-ə-ˌfī\ *vt* **-fied; -fy·ing** [ME *edifien,* fr. MF *edifier,* fr. LL & L; LL *aedificare* to instruct or improve spiritually, fr. L, to erect a house, fr. *aedes* temple, house; akin to OE *ād* funeral pyre, L *aestas* summer] **1** *archaic* **a :** BUILD **b :** ESTABLISH **2 :** to instruct and improve esp. in moral and religious knowledge **:** ENLIGHTEN

¹ed·it \ˈed-ət\ *vt* **1 a :** to prepare an edition of <~*ed* Poe's works> **b :** to assemble (as a moving picture or tape recording) by cutting and rearranging **c :** to alter, adapt, or refine esp. to bring about conformity to a standard or to suit a particular purpose <carefully ~*ed* his speech> **2 :** to direct the publication of <~*s* the daily newspaper> **3 :** DELETE — usu. used with *out* — **ed·it·able** \-ə-bəl\ *adj*

²edit *n* **:** an instance of editing

edi·tion \i-ˈdish-ən\ *n* [MF, fr. L *edition-, editio* publication, edition, fr. *editus,* pp. of *edere* to bring forth, publish, fr. *e-* + *-dere* to put or *-dere* (fr. *dare* to give) — more at DO, DATE] **1 a :** the form in which a text (as a printed book) is published **b (1) :** the whole number of copies published at one time **(2) :** the usu. special issue of a newspaper for a particular day <the Sunday ~> **(3) :** one of the several issues of a newspaper for a single day <the late afternoon ~> **2 a :** one of the forms in which something is presented <this year's ~ of the annual charity ball> **b :** the whole number of articles of one style put out at one time <a limited ~ of collectors' pieces> **3 :** COPY, VERSION

edi·tio prin·ceps \ā-ˌdit-ē-(ˌ)ō-ˈpriŋ-ˌkeps, i-ˌdish-ē-(ˌ)ō-ˈprin-ˌseps\ *n, pl* **edi·ti·o·nes prin·ci·pes** \ā-ˌdit-ē-ˈō-ˌnās-ˈpriŋ-kə-ˌpās, i-ˌdish-ē-ˈō-(ˌ)nēz-ˈprin(t)-sə-ˌpēz\ [NL, lit., first edition] **:** the first printed edition esp. of a work that circulated in manuscript before printing became common

ed·i·tor \ˈed-ət-ər\ *n* **1 :** one that edits esp. as an occupation **2 :** a person who writes editorials **3 :** a device used in editing motion-picture film or magnetic tape — **ed·i·tor·ship** \-ˌship\ *n*

¹ed·i·to·ri·al \ˌed-ə-ˈtōr-ē-əl, -ˈtȯr-\ *adj* **1 :** of or relating to an editor <an ~ office> **2 :** being or resembling an editorial <an ~ statement> — **ed·i·to·ri·al·ly** \-ē-ə-lē\ *adv*

²editorial *n* **:** a newspaper or magazine article that gives the opinions of the editors or publishers; *also* **:** an expression of opinion that resembles such an article <a television ~>

ed·i·to·ri·al·ist \-ē-ə-ləst\ *n* **:** a writer of editorials

ed·i·to·ri·al·ize \ˌed-ə-ˈtōr-ē-ə-ˌlīz, -ˈtȯr-\ *vi* **-ized; -iz·ing 1 :** to express an opinion in the form of an editorial **2 :** to introduce opinion into the reporting of facts **3 :** to express an opinion (as on a controversial issue) — **ed·i·to·ri·al·iza·tion** \-ˌtōr-ē-ə-lə-ˈzā-shən, -ˌtȯr-\ *n* — **ed·i·to·ri·al·iz·er** *n*

editor in chief *n* **:** an editor who is the head of an editorial staff (as of a publication)

ed·i·tress \ˈed-ə-trəs\ *n* **:** a female editor

EdM [NL *educationis magister*] *abbr* master of education

Edom·ite \ˈēd-ə-ˌmīt\ *n* [*Edom* (Esau), ancestor of the Edomites] **:** a member of a Semitic people living south of the Dead sea in biblical times

EDP *abbr* electronic data processing

EDT *abbr* eastern daylight time

EDTA \ˌē-ˌdē-ˌtē-ˈā\ *n* [*e*thylene*d*iamine*t*etra*a*cetic acid] **:** a white crystalline acid $C_{10}H_{16}N_2O_8$ used esp. as a chelating agent and in medicine as an anticoagulant and in the treatment of lead poisoning

educ *abbr* education; educational

¹ed·u·ca·ble \ˈej-ə-kə-bəl\ *adj* **:** capable of being educated; *specif* **:** capable of some degree of learning — **ed·u·ca·bil·i·ty** \ˌej-ə-kə-ˈbil-ət-ē\ *n*

²educable *n* **:** a mildly retarded person **:** MORON

ed·u·cate \ˈej-ə-ˌkāt\ *vb* **-cat·ed; -cat·ing** [ME *educaten* to rear, fr. L *educatus,* pp. of *educare* to rear, educate] *vt* **1 :** to provide schooling for **2 :** to develop mentally or morally esp. by instruction ~ *vi* **:** to educate a person or thing *syn* see TEACH

ed·u·cat·ed *adj* **1 :** having an education; *esp* **:** having an education beyond the average **2 a :** giving evidence of training or practice **:** SKILLED <Doc worked over him with his ~ fingers —Budd Schulberg> **b :** befitting one that is educated <~ conversation> **c :** based on some knowledge of fact <an ~ guess> — **ed·u·cat·ed·ly** *adv* — **ed·u·cat·ed·ness** *n*

ed·u·ca·tion \ˌej-ə-ˈkā-shən\ *n* **1 a :** the action or process of educating or of being educated; *also* **:** a stage of such a process **b :** the knowledge and development resulting from an educational process <a man of little ~> **2 :** the field of study that deals mainly with methods of teaching and learning in schools — **ed·u·ca·tion·al** \-shnəl, -shən-ᵊl\ *adj* — **ed·u·ca·tion·al·ly** \-ē\ *adv*

educational park *n* : a large centralized educational complex of elementary and secondary schools
educational psychology *n* : psychology concerned with human maturation, school learning, teaching methods, guidance, and evaluation of aptitude and progress by standardized tests — **educational psychologist** *n*
educational television *n* **1** : PUBLIC TELEVISION **2** : television that provides instruction esp. for students and sometimes by closed circuit
ed·u·ca·tion·ist \ˌej-ə-ˈkā-sh(ə-)nəst\ *also* **ed·u·ca·tion·al·ist** \-shnə-ləst, -shən-ᵊl-əst\ *n* **1** *chiefly Brit* : a professional educator **2** : an educational theorist
ed·u·ca·tive \ˈej-ə-ˌkāt-iv\ *adj* **1** : tending to educate : INSTRUCTIVE **2** : of or relating to education
ed·u·ca·tor \ˈej-ə-ˌkāt-ər\ *n* **1** : one skilled in teaching : TEACHER **2 a** : a student of the theory and practice of education : EDUCATIONIST 2 **b** : an administrator in education
educe \i-ˈd(y)üs\ *vt* **educed; educ·ing** [L *educere* to draw out, fr. *e-* + *ducere* to lead — more at TOW] **1** : to bring out (as something latent) **2** : DEDUCE — **educ·ible** \-ˈd(y)ü-sə-bəl\ *adj* — **educ·tion** \-ˈdək-shən\ *n*
syn EDUCE, EVOKE, ELICIT, EXTRACT, EXTORT *shared meaning element* : to draw out something hidden, latent, or reserved
educ·tor \i-ˈdək-tər\ *n* [LL, one that leads out, fr. L *eductus*, pp. of *educere*] **1** : one that educes; *specif* : EJECTOR 2 **2** : a device similar to an ejector for mixing two fluids
edul·co·rate \i-ˈdəl-kə-ˌrāt\ *vb* **-rat·ed; -rat·ing** [NL *edulcoratus*, pp. of *edulcorare*, fr. L *e-* + *dulcor* sweetness, fr. *dulcis* sweet] *vt* : to free from harshness (as of attitude) : make pleasant ~ *vi* : to make something more pleasant
Ed·war·di·an \e-ˈdwärd-ē-ən, -ˈdwȯrd-\ *adj* : of, relating to, or characteristic of Edward VII of England or his age: as **a** : characterized by opulence and a complacent sense of material security **b** *of clothing* : marked by the hourglass silhouette for women and long narrow fitted suits for men
EE *abbr* electrical engineer
[1]**-ee** \ˈē, ˌē, ē\ *n suffix* [ME *-e*, fr. MF *-é*, pp. ending, fr. L *-atus*] **1** : recipient or beneficiary of (a specified action) <appoint*ee*> <grant*ee*> **2** : person furnished with (a specified thing) <patent*ee*> **3** : person that performs (a specified action) <escap*ee*>
[2]**-ee** *n suffix* [prob. alter. of *-y*] **1** : one associated with <barg*ee*> **2** : a particular esp. small kind of <boot*ee*> **3** : one resembling or suggestive of <goat*ee*>
EEG *abbr* electroencephalogram; electroencephalograph
eel \ˈē(ə)l\ *n* [ME *ele*, fr. OE *ǣl*; akin to OHG *āl* eel] **1 a** : any of numerous voracious elongate snakelike teleost fishes (order Apodes) that have a smooth slimy skin, lack pelvic fins, and have the median fins confluent around the tail **b** : any of numerous other elongate fishes (as of the order Symbranchii) **2** : any of various nematodes — **eel·like** \ˈē(ə)l-ˌlīk\ *adj* — **eely** \ˈē-lē\ *adj*
eel·grass \ˈē(ə)l-ˌgras\ *n* **1** : a submerged marine plant (*Zostera marina*) that has very long narrow leaves, is abundant along the No. Atlantic coast, and with related forms constitutes a monocotyledonous family (Zosteraceae, the eelgrass family) **2** : TAPE GRASS
eel·pout \-ˌpau̇t\ *n* **1** : any of various marine fishes resembling blennies (family Zoarcidae) **2** : BURBOT
eel·worm \-ˌwərm\ *n* : a nematode worm; *esp* : any of various small free-living or plant-parasitic roundworms
-een \ˈēn\ *n suffix* [prob. fr. *ratteen*] : inferior fabric resembling (a specified fabric) : imitation <velvet*een*>
e'en \(ˈ)ēn\ *adv* : EVEN
EENT *abbr* eye, ear, nose, and throat
-eer \ˈi(ə)r\ *n suffix* [MF *-ier*, fr. L *-arius* — more at -ARY] **1** : one that is concerned with professionally, conducts, or produces <auction*eer*> <pamphlet*eer*> — often in words with derogatory meaning <profit*eer*> **2** : contemptible one <patriot*eer*>
e'er \(ˈ)e(ə)r, (ˈ)a(ə)r\ *adv* : EVER
ee·rie *also* **ee·ry** \ˈi(ə)r-ē\ *adj* **ee·ri·er; -est** [ME *eri*, fr. OE *earg* cowardly, wretched] **1** *chiefly Scot* : affected with fright : SCARED **2 a** : frightening because of strangeness or gloominess **b** : notably strange and mysterious : BAFFLING <the *eeriest* mystery in modern court records — a persistent riddle —*Life*> *syn* see WEIRD — **ee·ri·ly** \ˈir-ə-lē\ *adv* — **ee·ri·ness** \ˈir-ē-nəs\ *n*
ef \ˈef\ *n* : the letter *f*
eff *abbr* efficiency
ef·face \i-ˈfās, e-\ *vt* **ef·faced; ef·fac·ing** [MF *effacer*, fr. *ex-* + *face*] **1** : to eliminate or make indistinct by or as if by wearing away a surface <coins with dates *effaced* by wear> <regrowth has *effaced* the worst scars from the fire> **2** : to make (oneself) modestly or shyly inconspicuous *syn* see ERASE — **ef·face·able** \-ˈfā-sə-bəl\ *adj* — **ef·face·ment** \-ˈfā-smənt\ *n* — **ef·fac·er** *n*
[1]**ef·fect** \i-ˈfekt\ *n* [ME, fr. MF & L; MF, fr. L *effectus*, fr. *effectus*, pp. of *efficere* to bring about, fr. *ex-* + *facere* to make, do — more at DO] **1** : something that inevitably follows an antecedent (as a cause or agent) **2 a** : PURPORT, INTENT **b** : basic meaning : ESSENCE **3** : an outward sign : APPEARANCE **4** : ACCOMPLISHMENT, FULFILLMENT **5** : power to bring about a result : INFLUENCE **6** *pl* : movable property : GOODS <personal ~*s*> **7 a** : a distinctive impression <the color gives the ~ of being warm> **b** : the creation of a desired impression <her tears were purely for ~> **c** : something designed to produce a distinctive or desired impression <special lighting ~*s*> **8** : the quality or state of being operative : OPERATION <the law goes into ~ next week>
syn EFFECT, RESULT, CONSEQUENCE, EVENT, ISSUE, OUTCOME *shared meaning element* : a condition or occurrence traceable to a cause
ant cause
— **in effect** : in substance : VIRTUALLY <the . . . committee agreed to what was *in effect* a reduction in the hourly wage —*Current Biog.*> — **to the effect** : with the meaning <issued a statement *to the effect* that he would resign>
[2]**effect** *vt* **1** : to cause to come into being **2 a** : to bring about often by surmounting obstacles : ACCOMPLISH <~ a settlement of a dispute> **b** : to put into effect <the duty of the legislature to ~ the will of the citizens>
[1]**ef·fec·tive** \i-ˈfek-tiv\ *adj* **1 a** : producing a decided, decisive, or desired effect **b** : IMPRESSIVE, STRIKING <they did . . . develop sharply ~ criticisms of the monstrosities of social and economic inequality —R. L. Hoffman> **2** : ready for service or action <~ manpower> **3** : ACTUAL <the need to increase ~ demand for goods> **4** : being in effect : OPERATIVE <the tax becomes ~ next year> — **ef·fec·tive·ly** *adv* — **ef·fec·tive·ness** *n*
syn EFFECTIVE, EFFECTUAL, EFFICIENT, EFFICACIOUS *shared meaning element* : producing or capable of producing a result. EFFECTIVE emphasizes the actual production of or the power to produce an effect <*effective* thinking> <an *effective* rebuke> EFFECTUAL suggests the accomplishment of a desired result or the fulfillment of a purpose or intent esp. as viewed after the event <the remedy proved *effectual* and relieved her distress> EFFICIENT may apply to what is actually operative and producing a result <the *efficient* cause of an end result> or it may suggest an acting or a potential for action or use in such a way as to avoid loss or waste of energy in effecting, producing, or functioning <an *efficient* little car> <a very *efficient* worker> EFFICACIOUS implies possession of a special quality or virtue that gives effective power <quinine is still one of the most *efficacious* drugs for the control of malaria> *ant* ineffective, futile
[2]**effective** *n* : one that is effective; *esp* : a soldier equipped for duty
ef·fec·tiv·i·ty \ˌef-ˌek-ˈtiv-ət-ē, i-ˌfek-\ *n* : the quality or state of being effective : EFFECTIVENESS
ef·fec·tor \i-ˈfek-tər, -ˌtȯ(ə)r\ *n* **1** : a bodily organ (as a gland or muscle) that becomes active in response to stimulation **2** : a substance that induces protein synthesis by combining allosterically with a genetic repressor
ef·fec·tu·al \i-ˈfek-chə(-wə)l, -ˈfeksh-wəl\ *adj* : producing or able to produce a desired effect : ADEQUATE *syn* see EFFECTIVE *ant* ineffectual, fruitless — **ef·fec·tu·al·i·ty** \-ˌfek-chə-ˈwal-ət-ē\ *n* — **ef·fec·tu·al·ness** \-ˈfek-chə(-wə)l-nəs, -ˈfeksh-wəl-\ *n*
ef·fec·tu·al·ly \i-ˈfek-chə(-wə)-lē, -ˈfeksh-wə-\ *adv* **1** : in an effectual manner **2** : with great effect : COMPLETELY
ef·fec·tu·ate \i-ˈfek-chə-ˌwāt\ *vt* **-at·ed; -at·ing** : EFFECT 2 — **ef·fec·tu·a·tion** \-ˌfek-chə-ˈwā-shən\ *n*
ef·fem·i·na·cy \ə-ˈfem-ə-nə-sē\ *n* : the quality of being effeminate
[1]**ef·fem·i·nate** \-nət\ *adj* [ME, fr. L *effeminatus*, fr. pp. of *effeminare* to make effeminate, fr. *ex-* + *femina* woman — more at FEMININE] **1** : having feminine qualities (as weakness or softness) inappropriate to a man : not manly in appearance or manner **2** : marked by an unbecoming delicacy or overrefinement <~ art> <an ~ civilization>
[2]**effeminate** *n* : an effeminate person
ef·fen·di \e-ˈfen-dē, ə-\ *n* [Turk *efendi* master, fr. NGk *aphentēs*, alter. of Gk *authentēs* — more at AUTHENTIC] : a man of property, authority, or education in an eastern Mediterranean country
ef·fer·ent \ˈef-ə-rənt; ˈef-ˌer-ənt, ˈē-ˌfer-\ *adj* [F *efférent*, fr. L *efferent-*, *efferens*, prp. of *efferre* to carry outward, fr. *ex-* + *ferre* to carry — more at BEAR] : conducting outward from a part or organ; *specif* : conveying nervous impulses to an effector — compare AFFERENT — **efferent** *n* — **ef·fer·ent·ly** *adv*
ef·fer·vesce \ˌef-ər-ˈves\ *vi* **-vesced; -vesc·ing** [L *effervescere*, fr. *ex-* + *fervescere* to begin to boil, fr. *fervēre* to boil — more at BURN] **1** : to bubble, hiss, and foam as gas escapes **2** : to show liveliness or exhilaration — **ef·fer·ves·cence** \-ˈves-ᵊn(t)s\ *n* — **ef·fer·ves·cent** \-ᵊnt\ *adj* — **ef·fer·ves·cent·ly** *adv*
ef·fete \e-ˈfēt, i-\ *adj* [L *effetus*, fr. *ex-* + *fetus* fruitful — more at FEMININE] **1** : no longer fertile **2 a** : worn out with age : EXHAUSTED **b** : marked by weakness or decadence **c** : OUTMODED <an old but by no means ~ statute —Edward Jenks> **3** : EFFEMINATE <a good humored, ~ boy brought up by maiden aunts —Herman Wouk> — **ef·fete·ly** *adv* — **ef·fete·ness** *n*
ef·fi·ca·cious \ˌef-ə-ˈkā-shəs\ *adj* [L *efficac-*, *efficax*, fr. *efficere*] : having the power to produce a desired effect *syn* see EFFECTIVE *ant* inefficacious, powerless — **ef·fi·ca·cious·ly** *adv* — **ef·fi·ca·cious·ness** *n*
ef·fi·cac·i·ty \ˌef-ə-ˈkas-ət-ē\ *n* : EFFICACY
ef·fi·ca·cy \ˈef-i-kə-sē\ *n, pl* **-cies** : the power to produce an effect : EFFECTIVENESS
ef·fi·cien·cy \i-ˈfish-ən-sē\ *n, pl* **-cies** **1** : the quality or degree of being efficient **2 a** : efficient operation **b** (1) : effective operation as measured by a comparison of production with cost (as in energy, time, and money) (2) : the ratio of the useful energy delivered by a dynamic system to the energy supplied to it **3** : EFFICIENCY APARTMENT
efficiency apartment *n* : a small usu. furnished apartment with minimal kitchen and bath facilities
efficiency engineer *n* : one who analyzes methods, procedures, and jobs in order to secure maximum efficiency — called also *efficiency expert*
ef·fi·cient \i-ˈfish-ənt\ *adj* [ME, fr. MF or L; MF, fr. L *efficient-*, *efficiens*, fr. prp. of *efficere* to bring about] **1** : being or involving the immediate agent in producing an effect <the ~ action of heat in changing water to steam> **2** : productive of desired effects; *esp* : productive without waste *syn* see EFFECTIVE *ant* inefficient — **ef·fi·cient·ly** *adv*
ef·fi·gy \ˈef-ə-jē\ *n, pl* **-gies** [ME *effigie*, fr. L *effigies*, fr. *effingere* to form, fr. *ex-* + *fingere* to shape — more at DOUGH] : an image or representation esp. of a person; *specif* : a crude figure representing a hated person — **in effigy** : publicly in the form of an effigy <the football coach was burned *in effigy*>
ef·flo·resce \ˌef-lə-ˈres\ *vi* **-resced; -resc·ing** [L *efflorescere*, fr. *ex-* + *florescere* to begin to blossom — more at FLORESCENCE] **1** : to burst forth : BLOOM **2 a** : to change to a powder from loss of water of crystallization **b** : to form or become covered with a powdery crust <bricks may ~ owing to the deposition of soluble salts>
ef·flo·res·cence \-ˈres-ᵊn(t)s\ *n* **1** : the period or state of flowering **2 a** : the action or process of developing and unfolding as if

coming into flower : BLOSSOMING <periods of . . . intellectual and artistic ~ —Julian Huxley> **b** : an instance of such development **c** : fullness of manifestation : CULMINATION **3** : the process or product of efflorescing chemically **4** : a redness of the skin : ERUPTION — **ef·flo·res·cent** \-ᵊnt\ *adj*

ef·flu·ence \ˈef-ˌlü-ən(t)s; e-ˈflü-, ə-ˈ\ *n* **1** : something that flows out **2** : an action or process of flowing out

¹ef·flu·ent \-ənt\ *adj* [L *effluent-, effluens,* prp. of *effluere* to flow out, fr. *ex-* + *fluere* to flow — more at FLUID] : flowing out : EMANATING, OUTGOING <an ~ river>

²effluent *n* : something that flows out: as **a** : an outflowing branch of a main stream or lake **b** : waste material (as smoke, liquid industrial refuse, or sewage) discharged into the environment esp. when serving as a pollutant

ef·flu·vi·um \e-ˈflü-vē-əm\ *n, pl* **-via** \-vē-ə\ *often sing in constr or* **-vi·ums** [L *effluvium* act of flowing out, fr. *effluere*] **1** : an invisible emanation; *esp* : an offensive exhalation or smell **2** : a by-product esp. in the form of waste

ef·flux \ˈef-ˌləks\ *n* [L *effluxus,* pp. of *effluere*] **1** : EFFLUENCE **2** : a passing away : EXPIRATION — **ef·flux·ion** \e-ˈflək-shən\ *n*

ef·fort \ˈef-ərt, -ˌȯ(ə)rt\ *n* [MF, fr. OF *esfort,* fr. *esforcier* to force, fr. *ex-* + *forcier* to force] **1** : conscious exertion of power **2** : a serious attempt : TRY **3** : something produced by exertion or trying <the novel was his most ambitious ~> **4** : effective force as distinguished from the possible resistance called into action by such a force **5** : the total work done to achieve a particular end <the war ~>

syn EFFORT, EXERTION, PAINS, TROUBLE *shared meaning element* : the active use of energy in producing a result ***ant*** ease

ef·fort·ful \-ərt-fəl\ *adj* : showing or requiring effort — **ef·fort·ful·ly** \-fə-lē\ *adv*

ef·fort·less \-ərt-ləs\ *adj* : showing or requiring little or no effort — **ef·fort·less·ly** *adv* — **ef·fort·less·ness** *n*

ef·fron·tery \i-ˈfrənt-ə-rē, e-\ *n, pl* **-ter·ies** [F *effronterie,* deriv. of LL *effront-, effrons* shameless, fr. L *ex-* + *front-, frons* forehead — more at BRINK] : shameless boldness : INSOLENCE <the ~ to propound three such heresies —*Times Lit. Supp.*> *syn* see TEMERITY

ef·ful·gence \i-ˈfu̇l-jən(t)s, e-, -ˈfəl-\ *n* [LL *effulgentia,* fr. L *effulgent-, effulgens,* prp. of *effulgēre* to shine forth, fr. *ex-* + *fulgēre* to shine — more at FULGENT] : radiant splendor : BRILLIANCE — **ef·ful·gent** \-jənt\ *adj*

¹ef·fuse \i-ˈfyüz, e-\ *vb* **ef·fused; ef·fus·ing** [L *effusus,* pp. of *effundere,* fr. *ex-* + *fundere* to pour — more at FOUND] *vt* **1** : to pour out (a liquid) **2** : to give off : RADIATE ~ *vi* : to flow out : EMANATE

²ef·fuse \-ˈfyüs\ *adj* **1** : poured out freely : OVERFLOWING **2** : DIFFUSE; *specif* : spread out flat without definite form <~ lichens>

ef·fu·sion \i-ˈfyü-zhən, e-\ *n* **1** : an act of effusing **2** : unrestrained expression of words or feelings <greeted her with great ~ —Olive H. Prouty> **3 a** (1) : the escape of a fluid from anatomical vessels by rupture or exudation (2) : the flow of a gas through an aperture whose diameter is small as compared with the distance between the molecules of the gas **b** : the fluid that escapes

ef·fu·sive \i-ˈfyü-siv, e-, -ziv\ *adj* **1** *archaic* : pouring freely **2** : excessively demonstrative : GUSHING **3** : characterized or formed by a nonexplosive outpouring of lava <~ rocks> — **ef·fu·sive·ly** *adv* — **ef·fu·sive·ness** *n*

eft \ˈeft\ *n* [ME *evete, ewte,* fr. OE *efete*] : NEWT

eft·soons \eft-ˈsünz\ *adv* [ME *eftsones,* fr. *eft* after (fr. OE) + *sone* soon + *-s,* adv. suffix; akin to OE *æfter* after] *archaic* : soon after

e.g. \f(ə-)rig-ˈzam-pəl, (ˈ)ē-ˈjē\ *abbr* [L *exempli gratia*] for example

Eg *abbr* Egypt; Egyptian

egad \i-ˈgad\ *or* **egads** \-ˈgadz\ *interj* [prob. euphemism for *oh God*] — used as a mild oath

egal \ˈē-gəl\ *adj* [ME, fr. MF, fr. L *aequalis*] *obs* : EQUAL

egal·i·tar·i·an \i-ˌgal-ə-ˈter-ē-ən\ *adj* [F *égalitaire,* fr. *égalité* equality, fr. L *aequalitat-, aequalitas,* fr. *aequalis*] : asserting, promoting, or marked by egalitarianism — **egalitarian** *n*

egal·i·tar·i·an·ism \-ē-ə-ˌniz-əm\ *n* **1** : a belief in human equality esp. with respect to social, political, and economic rights and privileges **2** : a social philosophy advocating the removal of inequalities among men

éga·li·té \ā-gȧ-lē-tā\ *n* [F] : social or political equality

EGD *abbr* electrogasdynamics

eger *var of* EAGRE

Ege·ria \i-ˈjir-ē-ə\ *n* [L, a nymph who advised the legendary Roman king Numa Pompilius] : a woman adviser or companion

egest \i-ˈjest\ *vt* [L *egestus,* pp. of *egerere* to carry outside, discharge, fr. *e-* + *gerere* to carry — more at CAST] : DEFECATE; *broadly* : to rid the body of (waste material) — **eges·tion** \-ˈjes(h)-chən\ *n* — **eges·tive** \-ˈjes-tiv\ *adj*

eges·ta \i-ˈjes-tə\ *n pl* [NL, fr. L, neut. pl. of *egestus*] : something egested

¹egg \ˈeg, ˈāg\ *vt* [ME *eggen,* fr. ON *eggja;* akin to OE *ecg* edge — more at EDGE] : to incite to action — usu. used with *on* <~*ed* the mob on to riot>

²egg *n, often attrib* [ME *egge,* fr. ON *egg;* akin to OE *ǣg* egg, L *ovum,* Gk *ōion*] **1 a** : the hard-shelled reproductive body produced by a bird and esp. by domestic poultry **b** : an animal reproductive body consisting of an ovum together with its nutritive and protective envelopes and having the capacity to develop into a new individual capable of independent existence **c** : OVUM **2** : something resembling an egg **3** : FELLOW, GUY <he's a good ~>

³egg *vt* **1** : to cover with egg **2** : to pelt with eggs

egg and dart *n* : a carved ornamental design in relief consisting of an egg-shaped figure alternating with a figure somewhat like an elongated javelin or arrowhead

egg·beat·er \ˈeg-ˌbēt-ər, ˈāg-\ *n* **1** : a hand-operated kitchen utensil used for beating, stirring, or whipping; *esp* : a rotary device for these purposes **2** : HELICOPTER

egg case *n* : a protective case enclosing eggs : OOTHECA — called also *egg capsule*

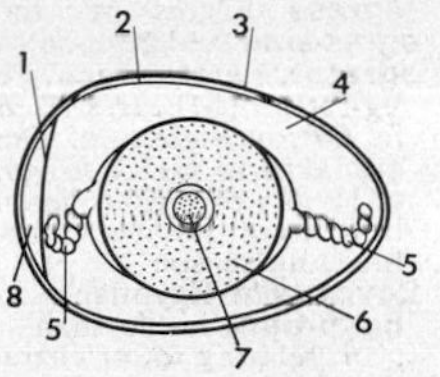

egg cell *n* : OVUM

egg·cup \ˈeg-ˌkəp, ˈāg-\ *n* : a cup for holding an egg that is to be eaten from the shell

egg·head \-ˌhed\ *n* : INTELLECTUAL, HIGHBROW <practical men who disdain the schemes and dreams of ~*s* —W. L. Miller>

egg·head·ed \-ˈhed-əd\ *adj* : having the characteristics of an egghead — **egg·head·ed·ness** *n*

egg·nog \-ˌnäg\ *n* : a drink consisting of eggs beaten up with sugar, milk or cream, and often alcoholic liquor

egg 1a: *1* inner shell membrane, *2* outer shell membrane, *3* shell, *4* albumen or white, *5* chalazae, *6* yolk, *7* blastodisc, *8* air space

egg·plant \-ˌplant\ *n* **1 a** : a widely cultivated perennial herb (*Solanum melongena*) yielding edible fruit **b** : the usu. smooth ovoid fruit of the eggplant **2** : a dark grayish or blackish purple

egg roll *n* : a thin egg-dough casing filled with minced vegetables and often bits of meat (as shrimp or chicken) and usu. fried in deep fat

eggs Ben·e·dict \-ˈben-ə-ˌdikt\ *n pl but sing or pl in constr* [prob. fr. the name *Benedict*] : poached eggs and broiled ham placed on toasted halves of English muffin and covered with hollandaise sauce

¹egg·shell \ˈeg-ˌshel, ˈāg-\ *n* **1** : the hard exterior covering of an egg **2** : something resembling an eggshell esp. in fragility

²eggshell *adj* **1** : thin and fragile **2** : slightly glossy

egg timer *n* : a small sandglass running about three minutes for timing the boiling of eggs

egg tooth *n* : a hard sharp prominence on the beak of an unhatched bird or the nose of an unhatched reptile that is used to break through the eggshell

egis \ˈē-jəs\ *var of* AEGIS

eg·lan·tine \ˈeg-lən-ˌtīn, -ˌtēn\ *n* [ME *eglentyn,* fr. MF *aiglent,* fr. (assumed) VL *aculentum,* fr. L *acus* needle; akin to L *acer* sharp — more at EDGE] : SWEETBRIER

ego \ˈē-(ˌ)gō *also* ˈeg-(ˌ)ō\ *n, pl* **egos** [NL, fr. L, I — more at I] **1** : the self esp. as contrasted with another self or the world **2 a** : EGOTISM **b** : SELF-ESTEEM 1 **3** : the one of the three divisions of the psyche in psychoanalytic theory that serves as the organized conscious mediator between the person and reality esp. by functioning both in the perception of and adaptation to reality — compare ¹ID, SUPEREGO

ego·cen·tric \ˌē-gō-ˈsen-trik *also* ˌeg-ō-\ *adj* **1** : concerned with the individual rather than society **2** : taking the ego as the starting point in philosophy **3 a** : limited in outlook or concern to one's own activities or needs **b** : SELF-CENTERED, SELFISH — **egocentric** *n* — **ego·cen·tri·cal·ly** \-tri-k(ə-)lē\ *adv* — **ego·cen·tric·i·ty** \-ˌsen-ˈtris-ət-ē\ *n* — **ego·cen·trism** \-ˈsen-ˌtriz-əm\ *n*

ego–defense \ˌē-(ˌ)gō-di-ˈfen(t)s *also* ˌeg-(ˌ)ō-\ *n* : a psychological mechanism designed consciously or unconsciously to protect one's self-image or self-esteem

ego ideal *n* : the positive standards, ideals, and ambitions that according to psychoanalytic theory are assimilated from the superego

ego–in·volve·ment \-in-ˈvälv-mənt, -ˈvȯlv-\ *n* : an involvement of one's self-esteem in the performance of a task or in an object

ego·ism \ˈē-gə-ˌwiz-əm *also* ˈeg-ə-\ *n* **1** : a doctrine that all the elements of knowledge are in the ego and its relations **2 a** : an ethical doctrine that individual self-interest is the actual motive of all conscious action **b** : an ethical doctrine that individual self-interest is the valid end of all actions **3** : EGOTISM

ego·ist \-wəst\ *n* **1** : a believer in egoism **2** : an egocentric or egotistic person — **ego·is·tic** \ˌē-gə-ˈwis-tik *also* ˌeg-ə-\ *also* **ego·is·ti·cal** \-ti-kəl\ *adj* — **ego·is·ti·cal·ly** \-ti-k(ə-)lē\ *adv*

egoistic hedonism *n* : the ethical theory that the valid aim of right conduct is one's own happiness

ego·ma·nia \ˌē-gō-ˈmā-nē-ə, -nyə\ *n* : the quality or state of being extremely egocentric

ego·ma·ni·ac \-nē-ˌak\ *n* : one characterized by egomania — **ego·ma·ni·a·cal** \-mə-ˈnī-ə-kəl\ *adj* — **ego·ma·ni·a·cal·ly** \-k(ə-)lē\ *adv*

ego·tism \ˈē-gə-ˌtiz-əm *also* ˈeg-ə-\ *n* [L *ego* + E *-tism* (as in *idiotism*)] **1 a** : excessive use of the first person singular personal pronoun **b** : the practice of talking about oneself too much **2** : an exaggerated sense of self-importance : CONCEIT

ego·tist \-təst\ *n* : one characterized by egotism — **ego·tis·tic** \ˌē-gə-ˈtis-tik *also* ˌeg-ə- *or* **ego·tis·ti·cal** \-ˈtis-ti-kəl\ *adj* — **ego·tis·ti·cal·ly** \-ˈtis-ti-k(ə-)lē\ *adv*

ego–trip \ˈē-gō-ˌtrip *also* ˈeg-ō-\ *vi* : to behave in a self-seeking manner <never overplayed, never *ego-tripped,* never grabbed the spotlight —Bob Palmer>

ego trip *n* : an act that enhances and satisfies one's ego

egre·gious \i-ˈgrē-jəs\ *adj* [L *egregius,* fr. *e-* + *greg-, grex* herd — more at GREGARIOUS] **1** *archaic* : DISTINGUISHED **2** : conspicuously bad : FLAGRANT <an ~ mistake> — **egre·gious·ly** *adv* — **egre·gious·ness** *n*

¹egress \ˈē-ˌgres\ *n* [L *egressus,* fr. *egressus,* pp. of *egredi* to go out, fr. *e-* + *gradi* to go — more at GRADE] **1** : the act or right of going or coming out; *specif* : the emergence of a celestial object from eclipse, occultation, or transit **2** : a place or means of going out : EXIT

2**egress** \ē-ˈgres\ *vi* : to go out : ISSUE

egres·sion \ē-ˈgresh-ən\ *n* : EGRESS, EMERGENCE

egret \ˈē-grət, i-ˈgret, ˈē-ˌgret, ˈeg-rət\ *n* [ME, fr. MF *aigrette,* fr. OProv *aigreta,* of Gmc origin; akin to OHG *heigaro* heron] : any of various herons that bear long plumes during the breeding season

egret

Egypt *abbr* Egyptian

1**Egyp·tian** \i-ˈjip-shən\ *adj* : of, relating to, or characteristic of Egypt or the Egyptians

2**Egyptian** *n* **1** : a native or inhabitant of Egypt **2** : the Afro-Asiatic language of the ancient Egyptians from earliest times to about the 3d century A.D. **3** *often not cap* : a typeface having little contrast between thick and thin strokes and squared serifs

EGYPTIAN

Egyptian clover *n* : BERSEEM

Egyptian cotton *n* : a fine long-staple often somewhat brownish cotton grown chiefly in Egypt

Egypto- *comb form* [prob. fr. F *Égypto-,* fr. Gk *Aigypto-,* fr. *Aigyptos*] : Egypt <*Egypto*logy>

Egyp·tol·o·gy \ˌē-(ˌ)jip-ˈtäl-ə-jē\ *n* : the study of Egyptian antiquities — **Egyp·tol·o·gist** \-jəst\ *n*

eh \ˈā, ˈe, ˈa(i), *also with* h *preceding and/or with nasalization*\ *interj* [ME *ey*] — used to ask for confirmation or to express inquiry

EHF *abbr* extremely high frequency

EHP *abbr* **1** effective horsepower **2** electric horsepower

EHV *abbr* extra high voltage

ei·der \ˈīd-ər\ *n* [D, G, or Sw, fr. Icel *æthur,* fr. ON *æthr*] **1** : any of several large northern sea ducks (*Somateria* or related genera) having fine soft down that is used by the female for lining the nest — called also *eider duck* **2** : EIDERDOWN 1

ei·der·down \-ˌdau̇n\ *n* [prob. fr. G *eiderdaune,* fr. Icel *æthardūnn,* fr. *æthur* + *dūnn* down] **1** : the down of the eider **2** : a comforter filled with eiderdown **3** : a soft lightweight clothing fabric knitted or woven and napped on one or both sides

ei·det·ic \ī-ˈdet-ik\ *adj* [Gk *eidētikos* of a form, fr. *eidos* form — more at WISE] : marked by or involving extraordinarily accurate and vivid recall esp. of visual images <an ~ memory> — **ei·det·i·cal·ly** \-i-k(ə-)lē\ *adv*

ei·do·lon \ī-ˈdō-lən\ *n, pl* **-lons** \-lənz\ *or* **-la** \-lə\ [Gk *eidōlon*] **1** : an unsubstantial image : PHANTOM **2** : IDEAL

ei·gen·val·ue \ˈī-gən-ˌval-(ˌ)yü, -yə(-w)\ *n* [part trans. of G *eigenwert,* fr. *eigen* own, peculiar, characteristic (fr. OHG *eigan*) + *wert* value — more at OWN] : CHARACTERISTIC ROOT

ei·gen·vec·tor \-ˌvek-tər\ *n* [ISV *eigen-* (fr. G *eigen*) + *vector*] : CHARACTERISTIC VECTOR

eight \ˈāt\ *n* [ME *eighte,* fr. *eighte,* adj., fr. OE *eahta;* akin to OHG *ahto* eight, L *octo,* Gk *oktō*] **1** — see NUMBER table **2** : the eighth in a set or series <sat in row ~> **3** : something having eight units or members: as **a** : an 8-oared racing boat or its crew **b** : an 8-cylinder engine or automobile — **eight** *adj or pron*

eight ball *n* **1** : a black pool ball numbered 8 **2** : MISFIT <tried to weed out the *eight balls*> — **behind the eight ball** : in a highly disadvantageous position or baffling situation

eigh·teen \(ˈ)ā(t)-ˈtēn\ *n* [ME *eightetene,* adj., fr. OE *eahtatīene;* akin to OE *tīen* ten] — see NUMBER table — **eighteen** *adj or pron* — **eigh·teenth** \-ˈtēn(t)th\ *adj or n*

eigh·teen·mo \ā(t)-ˈtēn-(ˌ)mō\ *n, pl* **-mos** : the size of a piece of paper cut 18 from a sheet; *also* : a book, a page, or paper of this size

eight·fold \ˈāt-ˌfōld, -ˈfōld\ *adj* **1** : having eight units or members **2** : being eight times as great or as many — **eight·fold** \-ˈfōld\ *adv*

eighth \ˈātth, *nonstand* ˈāth\ *n* **1** — see NUMBER table **2** : OCTAVE — **eighth** *adj or adv*

eighth note *n* : a musical note with the time value of ⅛ of a whole note — see NOTE illustration

eighth rest *n* : a musical rest corresponding in time value to an eighth note

eight·pen·ny nail \ˌāt-ˌpen-ē-\ *n* [eight + *-penny*] : a nail typically 2 ½ inches long

eighty \ˈāt-ē\ *n, pl* **eight·ies** [ME *eighty,* adj., fr. OE *eahtatig,* short for *hundeahtatig,* n., group of eighty, fr. *hund* hundred + *eahta* eight + *-tig* group of ten; akin to OE *tīen* ten] **1** — see NUMBER table **2** *pl* : the numbers 80 to 89; *specif* : the years 80 to 89 in a lifetime or century — **eight·i·eth** \ˈāt-ē-əth\ *adj or n* — **eighty** *adj or pron*

-ein *or* **-eine** *n suffix* [ISV, alter. of *-in, -ine*] : compound distinguished from a compound with a similar name ending in *-in* or *-ine* <phthal*ein*>

ein·korn \ˈīn-ˌkȯ(ə)rn\ *n* [G, fr. OHG, fr. *ein* one + *korn* grain — more at ONE, CORN] : a one-grained wheat (*Triticum monococum*) that is sometimes considered the most primitive wheat and is grown esp. in poor soils in central Europe — called also *einkorn wheat*

Ein·stein·ian \īn-ˈstī-nē-ən\ *adj* : of or relating to Albert Einstein or his theories

ein·stei·ni·um \-nē-əm\ *n* [NL, fr. Albert *Einstein* †1955 Am physicist & mathematician] : a radioactive element produced artificially — see ELEMENT table

ei·re·nic *var of* IRENIC

ei·ren·i·con \ī-ˈren-i-ˌkän\ *n* [LGk *eirēnikon,* fr. neut. of Gk *eirēnikos* irenic — more at IRENIC] : a statement that attempts to harmonize conflicting doctrines : RECONCILIATION

eis·ege·sis \ˌī-sə-ˈjē-səs\ *n, pl* **-ege·ses** \-ˌsēz\ [Gk *eis* into + E *exegesis;* akin to Gk *en* in — more at IN] : the interpretation of a text (as of the Bible) by reading into it one's own ideas — compare EXEGESIS

ei·stedd·fod \ī-ˈsteth-ˌvȯd, ā-\ *n* [W, lit., session, fr. *eistedd* to sit + *bod* being] : a Welsh competitive festival of the arts esp. in singing — **ei·stedd·fod·ic** \ˌī-ˌsteth-ˈvȯd-ik, ˌā-\ *adj*

1**ei·ther** \ˈē-thər *also* ˈī-\ *adj* [ME, fr. OE *ǣghwæther* both, each, fr. *ā* always + *ge-,* collective prefix + *hwæther* which of two, whether — more at AYE, CO-] **1** : being the one and the other of two : EACH <flowers blooming on ~ side of the walk> **2** : being the one or the other of two <take ~ road>

2**either** *pron* : the one or the other

3**either** *conj* — used as a function word before two or more coordinate words, phrases, or clauses joined usu. by *or* to indicate that what immediately follows is the first of two or more alternatives

4**either** *adv* **1** : LIKEWISE, MOREOVER — used for emphasis after a negative <not wise or handsome ~> **2** : for that matter — used for emphasis after an alternative following a question or conditional clause esp. where negation is implied <who answers for the Irish parliament? or army ~? —Robert Browning>

1**either–or** \ˌē-thə-ˈrō(ə)r *also* ˌī-\ *adj* : of or marked by either-or : BLACK-AND-WHITE

2**either–or** *n* : an unavoidable choice or exclusive division between only two alternatives : DICHOTOMY <never a matter of knowledge versus proficiency, never a simple ~ — H. J. Muller>

1**ejac·u·late** \i-ˈjak-yə-ˌlāt\ *vb* **-lat·ed; -lat·ing** [L *ejaculatus,* pp. of *ejaculari* to throw out, fr. *e-* + *jaculari* to throw, fr. *jaculum* dart, fr. *jacere* to throw — more at JET] *vt* **1** : to eject from a living body; *specif* : to eject (semen) in orgasm **2** : to utter suddenly and vehemently ~ *vi* : to eject a fluid

2**ejac·u·late** \-lət\ *n* : the semen released by one ejaculation

ejac·u·la·tion \i-ˌjak-yə-ˈlā-shən\ *n* **1** : an act of ejaculating; *specif* : a sudden discharging of a fluid from a duct **2** : something ejaculated; *esp* : a short sudden emotional utterance

ejac·u·la·to·ry \i-ˈjak-yə-lə-ˌtōr-ē, -ˌtȯr-\ *adj* **1** : casting or throwing out; *specif* : associated with or concerned in physiological ejaculation <~ vessels> **2** : marked by or given to vocal ejaculation

ejaculatory duct *n* : a duct through which semen is ejaculated; *specif* : either of the paired ducts in man that are formed by the junction of the duct from the seminal vesicle with the vas deferens, pass through the prostate, and open into or close to the prostatic utricle

eject \i-ˈjekt\ *vt* [ME *ejecten,* fr. L *ejectus,* pp. of *eicere,* fr. *e-* + *jacere*] **1 a** : to drive out esp. by physical force **b** : to evict from property **2** : to throw out or off from within <~*s* the empty cartridges> — **eject·able** \-ˈjek-tə-bəl\ *adj* — **ejec·tion** \-ˈjek-shən\ *n* — **ejec·tive** \-ˈjek-tiv\ *adj*

syn EJECT, EXPEL, OUST, EVICT, DISMISS *shared meaning element* : to drive or force out *ant* admit

ejec·ta \i-ˈjek-tə\ *n pl but sing or pl in constr* [NL, fr. L, neut. pl. of *ejectus*] : material thrown out (as from a volcano)

ejection seat *n* : an emergency escape seat for propelling an occupant out and away from an airplane by means of an explosive charge

eject·ment \i-ˈjek(t)-mənt\ *n* **1** : DISPOSSESSION **2** : an action for the recovery of possession of real property and damages and costs

ejec·tor \i-ˈjek-tər\ *n* **1** : one that ejects **2** : a jet pump for withdrawing a gas, fluid, or powdery substance from a space

eka- \ˌek-ə, ˌā-kə\ *comb form* [Skt *eka* one — more at ONE] : standing or assumed to stand next in order beyond (a specified element) in the same family of the periodic table — in names of chemical elements esp. when not yet discovered <*eka*cesium (now called francium)>

1**eke** \ˈēk\ *adv* [ME, fr. OE *ēac;* akin to OHG *ouh* also, L *aut* or, Gk *au* again] *archaic* : ALSO

2**eke** *vt* **eked; ek·ing** [ME *eken,* fr. OE *īecan, ēcan;* akin to OHG *ouhhōn* to add, L *augēre* to increase, Gk *auxein*] *archaic* : INCREASE, LENGTHEN

eke out *vt* **1 a** : to make up for the deficiencies of : SUPPLEMENT <*eked out* his income by getting a second job> **b** : to make (a supply) last by economy **2** : to make (as a living) by laborious or precarious means

EKG *abbr* [G *elektrokardiogramm*] electrocardiogram; electrocardiograph

ekis·tics \i-ˈkis-tiks\ *n pl but sing in constr* [NGk *oikistikē,* fr. fem. of *oikistikos* relating to settlement, fr. Gk, fr. *oikizein* to settle, colonize, fr. *oikos* house — more at VICINITY] : a science dealing with human settlements and drawing on the research and experience of professionals in various fields (as architecture, engineering, city planning, and sociology) — **ekis·tic** \-tik\ *adj*

Ek·man dredge \ˌek-mən-\ *n* [prob. fr. V. W. *Ekman* †1954 Sw oceanographer] : a dredge that has opposable jaws operated by a messenger traveling down a cable to release a spring catch and that is used in ecology for sampling the bottom of a body of water

ekt·ex·ine \(ˈ)ek-ˈtek-ˌsēn, -ˌsīn\ *n* [Gk *ekto-* outside + E *exine* — more at ECT-] : a structurally variable outer layer of the exine

1**el** \ˈel\ *n* : the letter *l*

2**el** *n, often cap* : ELEVATED RAILROAD

3**el** *abbr* elevation

1**elab·o·rate** \i-ˈlab-(ə-)rət\ *adj* [L *elaboratus,* fr. pp. of *elaborare* to work out, acquire by labor, fr. *e-* + *laborare* to work — more at LABORATORY] **1** : planned or carried out with great care : DETAILED <~ calculations> **2** : marked by complexity, fullness of detail, or ornateness : INTRICATE <a highly ~ coiffure> **3** : marked by painstaking diligence — **elab·o·rate·ly** *adv* — **elab·o·rate·ness** *n*

2**elab·o·rate** \i-ˈlab-ə-ˌrāt\ *vb* **-rat·ed; -rat·ing** *vt* **1** : to produce by labor **2** : to build up (complex organic compounds) from simple ingredients **3** : to work out in detail : DEVELOP ~ *vi* **1** : to become elaborate **2** : to expand something in detail <would you care to ~ on that statement> — **elab·o·ra·tion** \-ˌlab-ə-ˈrā-shən\ *n* — **elab·o·ra·tive** \-ˈlab-ə-ˌrāt-iv\ *adj*

Elaine \i-ˈlān\ *n* : any of several women in Arthurian legend; *esp* : one who dies for unrequited love of Lancelot

Elam·ite \ˈē-lə-ˌmīt\ *n* **:** a language of unknown affinities used in Elam approximately from the 25th to the 4th centuries B.C.

élan \ā-ˈläⁿ\ *n* [F, fr. MF *eslan* rush, fr. *(s')eslancer* to rush, fr. *ex-* + *lancer* to hurl — more at LANCE] **:** vigorous spirit or enthusiasm typically revealed by poise, verve, or liveliness of imagination

eland \ˈē-lənd, -ˌland\ *n* [Afrik, elk, fr. D, fr. obs. G *elend,* fr. Lith *elnis;* akin to OHG *elaho* elk — more at ELK] **:** either of two large African antelopes (*Taurotragus oryx* and *T. derbianus*) bovine in form with short spirally twisted horns in both sexes

eland

élan vi·tal \ā-ˈläⁿ-vē-ˈtäl\ *n* [F] **:** the vital force or impulse of life; *specif* **:** a creative principle held by Bergson to be immanent in all organisms and responsible for evolution

el·a·pid \ˈel-ə-pəd\ *n* [NL *Elap-, Elaps,* genus of snakes, fr. MGk, a fish, alter. of Gk *elops*] **:** any of a family (Elapidae) of venomous snakes with grooved fangs

[1]**elapse** \i-ˈlaps\ *vi* **elapsed; elaps·ing** [L *elapsus,* pp. of *elabi,* fr. *e-* + *labi* to slip — more at SLEEP] **:** to slip or glide away **:** PASS <four years *elapsed* before he returned>

[2]**elapse** *n* **:** PASSAGE <went back to college after an ~ of 15 years>

elapsed time *n* **:** the actual time taken (as by a boat or automobile) to travel over a specified course (as in racing)

elas·mo·branch \i-ˈlaz-mə-ˌbraŋk\ *n, pl* **-branchs** [deriv. of Gk *elasmos* metal plate (fr. *elaunein*) + L *branchia* gill] **:** any of a class (Chondrichthyes) of fishes with lamellate gills that comprise the sharks, rays, chimaeras, and various extinct related fishes — **elasmobranch** *adj*

elas·tase \i-ˈlas-ˌtās, -ˌtāz\ *n* **:** an enzyme esp. of pancreatic juice that digests elastin

[1]**elas·tic** \i-ˈlas-tik\ *adj* [NL *elasticus,* fr. LGk *elastos* ductile, beaten, fr. Gk *elaunein* to drive, beat out; akin to OIr *luid* he went] **1 a** *of a solid* **:** capable of recovering size and shape after deformation **b** *of a gas* **:** capable of indefinite expansion **2 :** capable of recovering quickly esp. from depression or disappointment **3 :** capable of being easily stretched or expanded and resuming former shape **:** FLEXIBLE **4 a :** capable of ready change or easy expansion or contraction **b :** receptive to new ideas **:** ADAPTABLE — **elas·ti·cal·ly** \-ti-k(ə-)lē\ *adv*

[2]**elastic** *n* **1 a :** an elastic fabric usu. made of yarns containing rubber **b :** something made from this fabric **2 a :** easily stretched rubber usu. prepared in cords, strings, or bands **b :** RUBBER BAND

elastic clause *n* **:** a clause in the U.S. Constitution that provides the Constitutional basis for the implied or potential powers of Congress

elastic collision *n* **:** a collision in which the total kinetic energy of the colliding particles remains unchanged

elas·tic·i·ty \i-ˌlas-ˈtis-ət-ē, ˌē-ˌlas-, -ˈtis-tē\ *n, pl* **-ties :** the quality or state of being elastic: as **a :** the capability of a strained body to recover its size and shape after deformation **:** SPRINGINESS **b :** RESILIENCE **c :** the quality of being adaptable

elas·ti·cized \i-ˈlas-tə-ˌsīzd\ *adj* **:** made with elastic thread or inserts

elastic scattering *n* **:** a scattering of particles as the result of elastic collision

elas·tin \i-ˈlas-tən\ *n* [ISV, fr. NL *elasticus*] **:** a protein that is similar to collagen and is the chief constituent of elastic fibers

elas·to·mer \-tə-mər\ *n* [*elastic* + *-o-* + Gk *meros* part — more at MERIT] **:** any of various elastic substances resembling rubber <polyvinyl ~*s*> — **elas·to·mer·ic** \i-ˌlas-tə-ˈmer-ik\ *adj*

[1]**elate** \i-ˈlāt\ *adj* **:** ELATED

[2]**elate** *vt* **elat·ed; elat·ing** [L *elatus* (pp. of *efferre* to carry out, elevate), fr. *e-* + *latus,* pp. of *ferre* to carry — more at TOLERATE, BEAR] **:** to fill with joy or pride

elat·ed *adj* **:** marked by high spirits **:** EXULTANT — **elat·ed·ly** *adv* — **elat·ed·ness** *n*

el·a·ter \ˈel-ət-ər\ *n* [NL, genus of beetles, fr. Gk *elatēr* driver, fr. *elaunein*] **1 :** CLICK BEETLE **2 :** a plant structure functioning in the distribution of spores: as **a :** one of the elongated filaments among the spores in the capsule of a liverwort **b :** one of the filamentous appendages of the spores in the scouring rushes

elat·er·ite \i-ˈlat-ə-ˌrīt\ *n* [G *elaterit,* fr. Gk *elatēr*] **:** a dark brown elastic mineral resin occurring in soft flexible masses

ela·tion \i-ˈlā-shən\ *n* **1 :** the quality or state of being elated **2 :** pathological euphoria

E layer *n* **:** a layer of the ionosphere occurring at about 60 miles above the earth's surface and capable of reflecting radio waves

[1]**el·bow** \ˈel-ˌbō\ *n* [ME *elbowe,* fr. OE *elboga;* akin to OHG *elinbogo* elbow; both fr. a prehistoric NGmc-WGmc compound whose constituents are akin to OE *eln* ell & OE *boga* bow — more at ELL, BOW] **1 a :** the joint of the arm **b :** a corresponding joint in the anterior limb of a lower vertebrate **2 :** something resembling an elbow; *specif* **:** an angular pipe fitting — **out at elbows 1 :** shabbily dressed **2 :** short of funds

elbows 2

[2]**elbow** *vt* **1 a :** to push with the elbow **:** JOSTLE **b :** to shove aside by pushing with the elbow **2 a :** to force (as one's way) by pushing with the elbow <~*ing* our way through the crowd> **b :** to force (as one's way) rudely or forwardly <~*s* her way into the best circles> ~ *vi* **1 :** to advance by pushing with the elbow **2 :** to make an angle **:** TURN <here the passage ~*s* and we are in another room>

elbow grease *n* **:** energy vigorously exerted esp. in physical labor <the first such expedition not powered solely by the *elbow grease* of oarsmen —*New Yorker*>

el·bow·room \ˈel-ˌbō-ˌrüm, -ˌrům\ *n* **1 a :** room for moving the elbows freely **b :** adequate space for work or operation <the large house gives plenty of ~> **2 :** free scope

eld \ˈeld\ *n* [ME, fr. OE *ieldo;* akin to OE *eald* old — more at OLD] **1** *archaic* **:** old age **2** *archaic* **:** old times **:** ANTIQUITY

[1]**el·der** \ˈel-dər\ *n* [ME *eldre,* fr. OE *ellærn;* prob. akin to OE *alor* alder — more at ALDER] **:** ELDERBERRY 2

[2]**elder** *adj* [ME, fr. OE *ieldra,* compar. of *eald* old] **1 :** of earlier birth or greater age <his ~ brother> **2 :** of or relating to earlier times **:** FORMER **3** *obs* **:** of or relating to a more advanced time of life **4 :** prior or superior in rank, office, or validity

[3]**elder** *n* **1 :** one living in an earlier period **2 a :** one who is older **:** SENIOR <the child trying to please his ~*s*> **b** *archaic* **:** an aged person **3 :** one having authority by virtue of age and experience <the village ~*s*> **4 :** any of various church officers: as **a :** PRESBYTER 1 **b :** a permanent officer elected by a Presbyterian congregation and ordained to serve on the session and assist the pastor at communion **c :** MINISTER 2a, 2b **d :** a Mormon ordained to the Melchizedek priesthood — **el·der·ship** \-ˌship\ *n*

el·der·ber·ry \ˈel-də(r)-ˌber-ē\ *n* **1 :** the edible black or red berrylike drupe of any of a genus (*Sambucus*) of shrubs or trees of the honeysuckle family bearing flat clusters of small white or pink flowers **2 :** a tree or shrub bearing elderberries

el·der·ly \ˈel-dər-lē\ *adj* **1 a :** rather old; *specif* **:** being past middle age **b :** OLD-FASHIONED **2 :** of, relating to, or characteristic of later life — **el·der·li·ness** *n*

elder statesman *n* **:** an eminent senior member of a group or organization; *esp* **:** a retired statesman who unofficially advises current leaders

el·dest \ˈel-dəst\ *adj* **:** of the greatest age or seniority **:** OLDEST

eldest hand *n* **:** the card player who first receives cards in the deal

El Do·ra·do \ˌel-də-ˈräd-(ˌ)ō, -ˈrād-\ *n* [Sp, lit., the gilded one] **1 :** a city or country of fabulous riches held by 16th century explorers to exist in So. America **2 :** a place of fabulous wealth, abundance, or opportunity

el·dritch \ˈel-drich\ *adj* [perh. fr. (assumed) ME *elfriche* fairyland, fr. ME *elf* + *riche* kingdom, fr. OE *rīce* — more at RICH] **:** WEIRD, EERIE

El·e·at·ic \ˌel-ē-ˈat-ik\ *adj* [L *Eleaticus,* fr. Gk *Eleatikos,* fr. *Elea* (Velia), ancient town in So. Italy] **:** of or relating to a school of Greek philosophers founded by Parmenides and developed by Zeno and marked by belief in the unity of being and the unreality of motion or change — **Eleatic** *n* — **El·e·at·i·cism** \-ˈat-ə-ˌsiz-əm\ *n*

elec *abbr* electric; electrical; electricity

ele·cam·pane \ˌel-i-ˌkam-ˈpān\ *n* [ME *elena campana,* fr. ML *enula campana,* lit., field elecampane, fr. *inula, enula* elecampane + *campana* of the field] **:** a large coarse European composite herb (*Inula helenium*) with yellow ray flowers naturalized in the U.S.

[1]**elect** \i-ˈlekt\ *adj* [ME, fr. L *electus* choice, fr. pp. of *eligere* to select, fr. *e-* + *legere* to choose — more at LEGEND] **1 :** carefully selected **:** CHOSEN **2 :** chosen for salvation through divine mercy **3 a :** chosen for office or position but not yet installed <the president-*elect*> **b :** chosen for marriage at some future time to a specific person <the bride-*elect*>

[2]**elect** *n, pl* **elect 1 :** one chosen or set apart (as by divine favor) **2** *pl* **:** a select or exclusive group of people

[3]**elect** *vt* **1 :** to select by vote for an office, position, or membership <~*ed* him class president> **2 :** to make a selection of <will ~ a heavy academic program> **3 :** to choose esp. by preference **:** decide on <might ~ to sell the business> ~ *vi* **:** to make a selection

elect·able \i-ˈlek-tə-bəl\ *adj* **:** capable of being elected; *specif* **:** eminently qualified to be elected to office — **elect·abil·i·ty** \-ˌlek-tə-ˈbil-ət-ē\ *n*

elec·tion \i-ˈlek-shən\ *n* **1 a :** an act or process of electing **b :** the fact of being elected **2 :** predestination to eternal life **3 :** the right, power, or privilege of making a choice ***syn*** see CHOICE

Election Day *n* **:** a day legally established for the election of public officials; *esp* **:** the first Tuesday after the first Monday in November in an even year designated for national elections in the U.S. and observed as a legal holiday in many states

elec·tion·eer \i-ˌlek-shə-ˈni(ə)r\ *vi* [*election* + *-eer* (as in *auctioneer,* v.)] **:** to take an active part in an election; *specif* **:** to work for the election of a candidate or party — **elec·tion·eer·er** *n*

[1]**elec·tive** \i-ˈlek-tiv\ *adj* **1 a :** chosen or filled by popular election <an ~ official> **b :** of or relating to election **c :** based on the right or principle of election <the presidency is an ~ office> **2 :** permitting a choice **:** OPTIONAL <an ~ course in school> **3 a :** tending to operate on one substance rather than another **b :** favorably inclined **:** SYMPATHETIC — **elec·tive·ly** *adv* — **elec·tive·ness** *n*

[2]**elective** *n* **:** an elective course or subject

elec·tor \i-ˈlek-tər, -ˌtȯ(ə)r\ *n* **1 :** one qualified to vote in an election **2 :** one entitled to participate in an election: as **a :** one of the German princes entitled to take part in choosing the Holy Roman Emperor **b :** a member of the electoral college in the U.S.

elec·tor·al \i-ˈlek-t(ə-)rəl\ *adj* **1 :** of or relating to an elector <the ~ vote> **2 :** of or relating to election <an ~ system>

electoral college *n* **:** a body of electors; *esp* **:** one that elects the president and vice-president of the U.S.

elec·tor·ate \i-ˈlek-t(ə-)rət\ *n* **1 :** the territory, jurisdiction, or dignity of a German elector **2 :** a body of people entitled to vote

electr- *or* **electro-** *comb form* [NL *electricus*] **1 a :** electricity <*electro*meter> **b :** electric <*electrode*> **:** electric and <*electro*chemical> **:** electrically <*electro*positive> **2 :** electrolytic <*electro*analysis> **3 :** electron <*electro*valence>

Elec·tra \i-'lek-trə\ *n* [L, fr. Gk *Elektra*] : a sister of Orestes who aids him in killing their mother Clytemnestra to avenge their murdered father Agamemnon
Electra complex *n* : the Oedipus complex when it occurs in a female
elec·tress \i-'lek-trəs\ *n* : the wife or widow of a German elector
elec·tret \i-'lek-trət, -,tret\ *n* [*electr*icity + mag*net*] : a dielectric body in which a permanent state of electric polarization has been set up
[1]**elec·tric** \i-'lek-trik\ *adj* [NL *electricus* produced from amber by friction, electric, fr. ML, of amber, fr. L *electrum* amber, electrum, fr. Gk *ēlektron;* akin to Gk *ēlektōr* beaming sun, Skt *ulkā* meteor] **1** : of, relating to, or operated by electricity **2** : producing an intensely stimulating effect : THRILLING <an ~ performance> **3 a** : ELECTRONIC 3a **b** : electronically amplifying sound — used of a musical instrument <an ~ guitar> — **elec·tri·cal** \-tri-kəl\ *adj* — **elec·tri·cal·ly** \-k(ə-)lē\ *adv* — **elec·tri·cal·ness** \-kəl-nəs\ *n*
[2]**electric** *n* **1** *archaic* : a nonconductor of electricity used to excite or accumulate electricity **2** : something (as a light, automobile, or train) operated by electricity
electrical storm *n* : THUNDERSTORM — called also *electric storm*
electrical transcription *n* **1** : a phonograph record or tape recording esp. designed for use in radiobroadcasting **2** : a radio program broadcast from an electrical transcription
electric chair *n* **1** : a chair used in legal electrocution **2** : the penalty of death by electrocution
electric eel *n* : a large eel-shaped fish (*Electrophorus electricus*) of the Orinoco and Amazon basins that is capable of giving a severe shock with its electric organs
electric eye *n* **1** : PHOTOELECTRIC CELL **2** : a miniature cathode-ray tube used to determine a condition (as of radio tuning)
elec·tri·cian \i-,lek-'trish-ən\ *n* **1** : a specialist in electricity **2** : one who installs, maintains, operates, or repairs electrical equipment
elec·tric·i·ty \i-,lek-'tris-ət-ē, -'tris-tē\ *n, pl* **-ties** **1 a** : a fundamental entity of nature consisting of negative and positive kinds composed respectively of electrons and protons or possibly of electrons and positrons, observable in the attractions and repulsions of bodies electrified by friction and in natural phenomena (as lightning or the aurora borealis), and usu. utilized in the form of electric currents **b** : electric current **2** : a science that deals with the phenomena and laws of electricity **3** : keen contagious excitement
electric organ *n* : a specialized tract of tissue (as in the electric eel) in which electricity is generated
electric ray *n* : any of various round-bodied short-tailed rays (family Torpedinidae) of warm seas with a pair of electric organs
elec·tri·fi·ca·tion \i-,lek-trə-fə-'kā-shən\ *n* **1** : an act or process of electrifying **2** : the state of being electrified
elec·tri·fy \i-'lek-trə-,fī\ *vt* **-fied; -fy·ing** **1 a** : to charge with electricity **b (1)** : to equip for use of electric power **(2)** : to supply with electric power **(3)** : to amplify (music) electronically **2** : to excite intensely or suddenly as if by an electric shock ***syn*** see THRILL
elec·tro·acous·tics \i-,lek-trō-ə-'kü-stiks\ *n pl but sing in constr* : a science that deals with the transformation of acoustic energy into electric energy or vice versa — **elec·tro·acous·tic** \-tik\ *adj* — **elec·tro·acous·ti·cal·ly** \-ti-k(ə-)lē\ *adv*
elec·tro·anal·y·sis \-ə-'nal-ə-səs\ *n* : chemical analysis by electrolytic methods — **elec·tro·an·a·lyt·ic** \-,an-ᵊl-'it-ik\ *or* **elec·tro·an·a·lyt·i·cal** \-'it-i-kəl\ *adj*
elec·tro·car·dio·gram \-'kärd-ē-ə-,gram\ *n* : the tracing made by an electrocardiograph
elec·tro·car·dio·graph \-,graf\ *n* : an instrument for recording the changes of electrical potential occurring during the heartbeat used esp. in diagnosing abnormalities of heart action — **elec·tro·car·dio·graph·ic** \-,kärd-ē-ə-'graf-ik\ *adj* — **elec·tro·car·dio·graph·i·cal·ly** \-i-k(ə-)lē\ *adv* — **elec·tro·car·di·og·ra·phy** \-ē-'äg-rə-fē\ *n*
elec·tro·chem·is·try \-'kem-ə-strē\ *n* : a science that deals with the relation of electricity to chemical changes and with the interconversion of chemical and electrical energy — **elec·tro·chem·i·cal** \-'kem-i-kəl\ *adj* — **elec·tro·chem·i·cal·ly** \-k(ə-)lē\ *adv*
elec·tro·con·vul·sive \i-,lek-trō-kən-'vəl-siv\ *adj* : of, relating to, or involving convulsive response to electroshock <impaired learning ability in rats due to ~ shocks>
electroconvulsive therapy *n* : ELECTROSHOCK THERAPY
elec·tro·cor·ti·co·gram \i-,lek-trō-'kȯrt-i-kə-,gram\ *n* [*electr-* + *cortico-* (fr. L *cortic- cortex* cortex) + *-gram*] : an electroencephalogram made with the electrodes in direct contact with the brain
elec·tro·cute \i-'lek-trə-,kyüt\ *vt* **-cut·ed; -cut·ing** [*electr-* + *-cute* (as in *execute*)] **1** : to execute (a criminal) by electricity **2** : to kill by electric shock — **elec·tro·cu·tion** \-,lek-trə-'kyü-shən\ *n*
elec·trode \i-'lek-,trōd\ *n* : a conductor used to establish electrical contact with a nonmetallic part of a circuit
[1]**elec·tro·de·pos·it** \i-,lek-trō-di-'päz-ət\ *n* : a deposit formed in or at an electrode by electrolysis
[2]**electrodeposit** *vt* : to deposit (as a metal or rubber) by electrolysis — **elec·tro·de·po·si·tion** \-,dep-ə-'zish-ən, -,dē-pə-\ *n*
elec·tro·di·al·y·sis \i-,lek-trō-dī-'al-ə-səs\ *n* : dialysis accelerated by an electromotive force applied to electrodes adjacent to the membranes — **elec·tro·di·a·lyt·ic** \-,dī-ə-'lit-ik\ *adj* — **elec·tro·di·a·lyze** \-'dī-ə-,līz\ *vt* — **elec·tro·di·a·lyz·er** *n*
elec·tro·dy·nam·ics \-dī-'nam-iks\ *n pl but sing in constr* : a branch of physics that deals with the effects arising from the interactions of electric currents with magnets, with other currents, or with themselves — **elec·tro·dy·nam·ic** \-ik\ *adj*
elec·tro·dy·na·mom·e·ter \-,dī-nə-'mäm-ət-ər\ *n* [ISV] : an instrument that measures current by indicating the strength of the forces between a current flowing in fixed coils and one flowing in movable coils
elec·tro·en·ceph·a·lo·gram \-in-'sef-ə-lə-,gram\ *n* [ISV] : the tracing of brain waves made by an electroencephalograph
elec·tro·en·ceph·a·lo·graph \-,graf\ *n* [ISV] : an apparatus for detecting and recording brain waves — **elec·tro·en·ceph·a·lo·graph·ic** \-,sef-ə-lə-'graf-ik\ *adj* — **elec·tro·en·ceph·a·log·ra·phy** \-'läg-rə-fē\ *n*
elec·tro·fish·ing \i-'lek-trō-,fish-iŋ\ *n* : the taking of fish by a system based on their tendency to respond positively to a source of direct electric current
elec·tro·form \i-'lek-trə-,fȯrm\ *vt* : to form (shaped articles) by electrodeposition on a mold
elec·tro·gen·e·sis \i-,lek-trə-'jen-ə-səs\ *n* : the production of electrical activity esp. in living tissue
elec·tro·gen·ic \-'jen-ik\ *adj* : of or relating to the production of electricity in living tissue <an ~ pump causing movement of sodium ions across a membrane>
elec·tro·gram \i-'lek-trə-,gram\ *n* : a tracing of the electrical potentials of a tissue (as the brain or heart) made by means of electrodes placed directly in the tissue instead of on the surface of the body
elec·tro·hy·drau·lic \i-,lek-trō-hī-'drō-lik\ *adj* **1** : of or relating to a combination of electric and hydraulic mechanisms **2** : involving or produced by the action of very brief but powerful pulse discharges of electricity under a liquid resulting in the generation of shock waves and highly reactive chemical species <an ~ effect> — **elec·tro·hy·drau·li·cal·ly** \-li-k(ə-)lē\ *adv*
elec·tro·jet \i-'lek-trə-,jet\ *n* : an overhead concentration of electric current found in the regions of strong auroral displays and along the magnetic equator
elec·tro·ki·net·ic \i-,lek-trō-kə-'net-ik, -kī-\ *adj* : of or relating to the motion of particles or liquids that results from or produces a difference of electric potential
elec·tro·ki·net·ics \-iks\ *n pl but sing in constr* : a branch of physics that deals with electrokinetic phenomena
elec·tro·less \i-'lek-,trō-ləs, -trə-\ *adj* : being or involving chemical deposition of metal instead of electrodeposition
elec·trol·o·gist \i-,lek-'träl-ə-jəst\ *n* [blend of *electrolysis* and *-logist* (fr. *-logy* + *-ist*)] : one that removes hair, warts, moles, and birthmarks by means of an electric current applied to the body with a needle-shaped electrode
elec·tro·lu·mi·nes·cence \i-,lek-trō-,lü-mə-'nes-ᵊn(t)s\ *n* : luminescence resulting from a high-frequency discharge through a gas or from application of an alternating current to a layer of phosphor — **elec·tro·lu·mi·nes·cent** \-ᵊnt\ *adj*
elec·trol·y·sis \i-,lek-'träl-ə-səs\ *n* **1 a** : the producing of chemical changes by passage of an electric current through an electrolyte **b** : subjection to this action **2** : the destruction of hair roots with an electric current
elec·tro·lyte \i-'lek-trə-,līt\ *n* **1** : a nonmetallic electric conductor in which current is carried by the movement of ions **2** : a substance that when dissolved in a suitable solvent or when fused becomes an ionic conductor
elec·tro·lyt·ic \i-,lek-trə-'lit-ik\ *adj* : of or relating to electrolysis or an electrolyte; *also* : involving or produced by electrolysis — **elec·tro·lyt·i·cal·ly** \-i-k(ə-)lē\ *adv*
elec·tro·lyze \i-'lek-trə-,līz\ *vt* **-lyzed; -lyz·ing** : to subject to electrolysis
elec·tro·mag·net \i-,lek-trō-'mag-nət\ *n* : a core of magnetic material surrounded by a coil of wire through which an electric current is passed to magnetize the core
elec·tro·mag·net·ic \-mag-'net-ik\ *adj* : of, relating to, or produced by electromagnetism — **elec·tro·mag·net·i·cal·ly** \-i-k(ə-)lē\ *adv*
electromagnetic radiation *n* : a series of electromagnetic waves
electromagnetic spectrum *n* : the entire range of wavelengths or frequencies of electromagnetic radiation extending from gamma rays to the longest radio waves and including visible light
electromagnetic unit *n* : any of a system of electrical units based primarily on the magnetic properties of electrical currents
electromagnetic wave *n* : one of the waves that are propagated by simultaneous periodic variations of electric and magnetic field intensity and that include radio waves, infrared, visible light, ultraviolet, X rays, and gamma rays
elec·tro·mag·ne·tism \i-,lek-trō-,mag-nə-,tiz-əm\ *n* **1** : magnetism developed by a current of electricity **2** : a branch of physical science that deals with the physical relations between electricity and magnetism
elec·tro·me·chan·i·cal \-mə-'kan-i-kəl\ *adj* : of or relating to a mechanical process or device actuated or controlled electrically; *specif* : being a transducer for converting mechanical energy to electrical energy or vice versa — **elec·tro·me·chan·i·cal·ly** \-k(ə-)lē\ *adv*
elec·tro·met·al·lur·gy \-'met-ᵊl-,ər-jē, *esp Brit* -mə-'tal-ər-\ *n* : a branch of metallurgy that deals with the application of electric current either for electrolytic deposition or as a source of heat
elec·trom·e·ter \i-,lek-'träm-ət-ər\ *n* : any of various instruments for detecting or measuring electric-potential differences or ionizing radiations by means of the forces of attraction or repulsion between charged bodies
elec·tro·mo·tive force \i-,lek-trə-,mōt-iv-\ *n* : something that moves or tends to move electricity : the amount of energy derived from an electrical source per unit quantity of electricity passing through the source (as a cell or generator)
elec·tro·myo·gram \i-'lek-trō-'mī-ə-,gram\ *n* : a tracing made with an electromyograph
elec·tro·myo·graph \-,graf\ *n* [*electr-* + *my-* + *-graph*] : an instrument for the simultaneous recording of a visual and sound record of electric waves associated with activity of skeletal muscle that is used in the diagnosis of neuromuscular disorders — **elec·tro·myo·graph·ic** \-,mī-ə-'graf-ik\ *also* **elec·tro·myo·graph·i·cal** \-i-kəl\ *adj* — **elec·tro·myo·graph·i·cal·ly** \-i-k(ə-)lē\ *adv* — **elec·tro·my·og·ra·phy** \-mī-'äg-rə-fē\ *n*
elec·tron \i-'lek-,trän\ *n* [*electr-* + *-on*] : an elementary particle consisting of a charge of negative electricity equal to about 1.602 x 10^{-19} coulomb and having a mass when at rest of about 9.107 x 10^{-28} gram or 1/1837 that of a proton

elec·tro·neg·a·tive \i-ˌlek-trō-ˈneg-ət-iv\ *adj* **1 :** charged with negative electricity **2 :** capable of acting as the negative electrode of a voltaic cell **3 :** having a tendency to attract electrons — **elec·tro·neg·a·tiv·i·ty** \-ˌneg-ə-ˈtiv-ət-ē\ *n*

electron gas *n* **:** a population of free electrons in a vacuum or in a metallic conductor

electron gun *n* **:** the electron-emitting cathode and its surrounding assembly in a cathode-ray tube for directing, controlling, and focusing the stream of electrons to a spot of desired size

1**elec·tron·ic** \i-ˌlek-ˈträn-ik\ *adj* **1 :** of or relating to electrons **2 :** of, relating to, or utilizing devices constructed or working by the methods or principles of electronics **3 a :** generating music by electronic means <an ~ organ> **b :** of, relating to, or being music that consists of sounds electronically generated or modified

2**electronic** *n* **:** an electronic circuit or device

elec·tron·ics \i-ˌlek-ˈträn-iks\ *n pl but sing in constr* **:** a branch of physics that deals with the emission, behavior, and effects of electrons (as in electron tubes and transistors) and with electronic devices

electron lens *n* **:** a device for converging or diverging a beam of electrons by means of an electric or a magnetic field

electron microscope *n* **:** an electron-optical instrument in which a beam of electrons focused by means of an electron lens is used to produce an enlarged image of a minute object on a fluorescent screen or photographic plate — **electron microscopist** *n* — **electron microscopy** *n*

electron multiplier *n* **:** a device utilizing secondary emission of electrons for amplifying a current of electrons

electron optics *n pl but sing in constr* **:** a branch of electronics that deals with those properties of beams of electrons that are analogous to the properties of rays of light

electron transport *n* **:** the sequential transfer of electrons esp. by cytochromes in cellular respiration from an oxidizable substrate to molecular oxygen by a series of oxidation-reduction reactions

electron tube *n* **:** an electronic device in which conduction by electrons takes place through a vacuum or a gaseous medium within a sealed glass or metal container and which has various common uses based on the controlled flow of electrons

electron volt *n* **:** a unit of energy equal to the energy gained by an electron in passing from a point of low potential to a point one volt higher in potential **:** $1.60\ 10^{-12}$ erg

elec·tro·oc·u·lo·gram \i-ˌlek-trō-ˈäk-yə-lə-ˌgram\ *n* [*electr-* + *ocul-* + *-gram*] **:** a record of the standing voltage between the front and back of the eye that is correlated with eyeball movement (as in sleep) and obtained by electrodes suitably placed on the skin near the eye

elec·tro–op·tics \-trō-ˈäp-tiks\ *n pl but sing in constr* **:** a branch of physics that deals with the effects of an electric field on light traversing it — **elec·tro–op·tic** \-tik\ *or* **elec·tro–op·ti·cal** \-ti-kəl\ *adj* — **elec·tro–op·ti·cal·ly** \-ti-k(ə-)lē\ *adv*

elec·tro·phil·ic \i-ˌlek-trə-ˈfil-ik\ *adj* **:** involving or having an affinity for electrons **:** electron-seeking <~ reagents> — **elec·tro·phi·lic·i·ty** \-trō-fil-ˈis-ət-ē\ *n*

elec·tro·pho·re·sis \-trə-fə-ˈrē-səs\ *n* [NL] **:** the movement of suspended particles through a fluid under the action of an electromotive force applied to electrodes in contact with the suspension — **elec·tro·pho·ret·ic** \-ˈret-ik\ *adj* — **elec·tro·pho·ret·i·cal·ly** \-i-k(ə-)lē\ *adv*

elec·tro·pho·reto·gram \-ˈret-ə-ˌgram\ *n* [*electrophoretic* + *-o-* + *-gram*] **:** a record that consists of the separated components of a mixture (as of proteins) produced by electrophoresis in a supporting medium (as filter paper)

elec·troph·o·rus \i-ˌlek-ˈträf-ə-rəs\ *n, pl* **-ri** \-ˌrī, -ˌrē\ [NL, fr. *electr-* + *-phorus* -phore (fr. Gk *-phoros*)] **:** an instrument for the production of electric charges by induction consisting of a disk that is negatively electrified by friction and a metal plate that becomes charged by induction when placed on the disk

elec·tro·pho·tog·ra·phy \i-ˌlek-trō-fə-ˈtäg-rə-fē\ *n* **:** photography in which images are produced by electrical means (as in xerography) — **elec·tro·pho·to·graph·ic** \-trə-ˌfōt-ə-ˈgraf-ik\ *adj*

elec·tro·phys·i·ol·o·gy \i-ˌlek-trō-ˌfiz-ē-ˈäl-ə-jē\ *n* **1 :** physiology that is concerned with the electrical aspects of physiological phenomena **2 :** electrical phenomena associated with a physiological process (as the function of a body or bodily part) <~ of the eye> — **elec·tro·phys·i·o·log·i·cal** \-ē-ə-ˈläj-i-kəl\ *also* **elec·tro·phys·i·o·log·ic** \-ik\ *adj* — **elec·tro·phys·i·o·log·i·cal·ly** \-i-k(ə-)lē\ *adv* — **elec·tro·phys·i·ol·o·gist** \-ē-ˈäl-ə-jəst\ *n*

elec·tro·plate \i-ˈlek-trə-ˌplāt\ *vt* **1 :** to plate with an adherent continuous coating by electrodeposition **2 :** ELECTROTYPE

elec·tro·pos·i·tive \i-ˌlek-trō-ˈpäz-ət-iv, -ˈpäz-tiv\ *adj* **1 a :** charged with positive electricity **b :** capable of acting as the positive electrode of a voltaic cell **2 :** having a tendency to release electrons

elec·tro·ret·i·no·gram \-ˈret-ᵊn-ə-ˌgram\ *n* **:** a graphic record of electrical activity of the retina used esp. in the diagnosis of retinal conditions

elec·tro·ret·i·no·graph \-ˌgraf\ *n* **:** an instrument for recording electrical activity in the retina — **elec·tro·ret·i·no·graph·ic** \-ˌret-ᵊn-ə-ˈgraf-ik\ *adj* — **elec·tro·ret·i·nog·ra·phy** \-ᵊn-ˈäg-rə-fē\ *n*

elec·tro·scope \i-ˈlek-trə-ˌskōp\ *n* [prob. fr. F *électroscope*] **:** any of various instruments for detecting the presence of an electric charge on a body, for determining whether the charge is positive or negative, or for indicating and measuring intensity of radiation

elec·tro·shock \-trō-ˌshäk\ *n* **1 :** 3SHOCK 5 **2 :** ELECTROSHOCK THERAPY

electroshock therapy *n* **:** the treatment of mental disorder by the induction of coma through the use of an electric current — called also *electroconvulsive therapy*

elec·tro·stat·ic \i-ˌlek-trə-ˈstat-ik\ *adj* [ISV] **1 :** of or relating to static electricity or electrostatics **2 :** of or relating to painting with a spray that utilizes electrically charged particles to ensure complete coating — **elec·tro·stat·i·cal·ly** \-ˈstat-i-k(ə-)lē\ *adv*

electrostatic generator *n* **:** an apparatus for the production of electrical discharges at high voltage commonly consisting of an insulated hollow conducting sphere that accumulates in its interior the charge continuously conveyed from a source of direct current by an endless belt of flexible nonconducting material

electrostatic printing *n* **:** a process (as xerography) for printing or copying in which electrostatic forces are used to form the image (as with powder or ink) directly on a surface

elec·tro·stat·ics \i-ˌlek-trə-ˈstat-iks\ *n pl but sing in constr* **:** physics that deals with phenomena due to attractions or repulsions of electric charges but not dependent upon their motion

electrostatic unit *n* **:** any of a system of electrical units based primarily on forces of interaction between electric charges — abbr. *esu*

elec·tro·sur·gery \i-ˌlek-trō-ˈsərj-(ə-)rē\ *n* **:** surgery by means of diathermy — **elec·tro·sur·gi·cal** \-ˈsər-ji-kəl\ *adj*

elec·tro·ther·a·py \-ˈther-ə-pē\ *n* **:** treatment of disease by means of electricity (as in diathermy)

elec·tro·ther·mal \-ˈthər-məl\ *or* **elec·tro·ther·mic** \-mik\ *adj* **:** relating to or combining electricity and heat; *specif* **:** relating to the generation of heat by electricity — **elec·tro·ther·mal·ly** \-mə-lē\ *adv*

elec·trot·o·nus \i-ˌlek-ˈträt-ᵊn-əs\ *n* [NL] **:** the altered sensitivity of a nerve when a constant current of electricity passes through any part of it — **elec·tro·ton·ic** \-trə-ˈtän-ik\ *adj*

1**elec·tro·type** \i-ˈlek-trə-ˌtīp\ *n* **1 :** a duplicate printing surface made by pressure molding in a plastic material the surface to be reproduced and electrodepositing on it a thin shell that is then backed up with lead **2 :** a copy of a coin made by an electroplating process

2**electrotype** *vt* **:** to make an electrotype from (a printing surface) ~ *vi* **:** to be reproducible by electrotyping — **elec·tro·typ·er** *n*

elec·tro·va·lence \i-ˌlek-trō-ˈvā-lən(t)s\ *n* **:** valence characterized by the transfer of electrons from one atom to another with the formation of ions; *also* **:** the number of charges acquired by an atom by the loss or gain of electrons — **elec·tro·va·lent** \-lənt\ *adj*

elec·tro·va·len·cy \-lən-sē\ *n* **:** ELECTROVALENCE

electrovalent bond *n* **:** a chemical bond formed between ions of opposite charge

elec·tro·win·ning \i-ˈlek-trō-ˌwin-iŋ\ *n* **:** the recovery esp. of metals from solutions by electrolysis

elec·trum \i-ˈlek-trəm\ *n* [ME, fr. L — more at ELECTRIC] **:** a natural pale yellow alloy of gold and silver

elec·tu·ary \i-ˈlek-chə-ˌwer-ē\ *n, pl* **-ar·ies** [ME *electuarie,* fr. L *electuarium,* prob. fr. Gk *ekleikton,* fr. *ekleichein* to lick up, fr. *ex-* + *leichein* to lick — more at LICK] **:** CONFECTION 2b

el·e·doi·sin \ˌel-ə-ˈdóis-ᵊn\ *n* [irreg. fr. NL *Eledone,* genus name] **:** a small protein $C_{54}H_{85}N_{13}O_{15}S$ from the salivary glands of several octopuses (genus *Eledone*) that is a powerful vasodilator and hypotensive agent

el·ee·mos·y·nary \ˌel-i-ˈmäs-ᵊn-ˌer-ē, -ˈmäz-\ *adj* [ML *eleemosynarius,* fr. LL *eleemosyna* alms — more at ALMS] **:** of, relating to, or supported by charity

el·e·gance \ˈel-i-gən(t)s\ *n* **1 a :** refined grace or dignified propriety **:** URBANITY **b :** tasteful richness of design or ornamentation <the sumptuous ~ of the furnishings> **c :** dignified gracefulness or restrained beauty of style **:** POLISH <the essay is marked by lucidity, wit, and ~> **d :** scientific precision, neatness, and simplicity <the ~ of a mathematical proof> **2 :** something that is elegant

el·e·gan·cy \-gən-sē\ *n, pl* **-cies :** ELEGANCE

el·e·gant \ˈel-i-gənt\ *adj* [MF or L; MF, fr. L *elegant-, elegans;* akin to L *eligere* to select — more at ELECT] **1 :** marked by elegance **2 :** of a high grade or quality **:** SPLENDID <~ gems priced at hundreds of thousands of dollars> *syn* see CHOICE — **el·e·gant·ly** *adv*

el·e·gi·ac \ˌel-ə-ˈjī-ək, -ˌak *also* i-ˈlē-jē-ˌak\ *also* **el·e·gi·a·cal** \ˌel-ə-ˈjī-ə-kəl\ *adj* [LL *elegiacus,* fr. Gk *elegeiakos,* fr. *elegeion*] **1 a :** of, relating to, or consisting of two dactylic hexameter lines the second of which lacks the arses in the third and sixth feet **b** (1) **:** written in or consisting of elegiac couplets (2) **:** noted for having written poetry in such couplets **c :** of or relating to the period in Greece about the seventh century B.C. when poetry written in such couplets flourished **2 :** of, relating to, or comprising elegy or an elegy; *esp* **:** expressing sorrow often for something now past <an ~ lament for departed youth> — **elegiac** *n* — **el·e·gi·a·cal·ly** \ˌel-ə-ˈjī-ə-k(ə-)lē\ *adv*

elegiac stanza *n* **:** a quatrain in iambic pentameter with a rhyme scheme of *abab*

ele·git \i-ˈlē-jət\ *n* [L, he has chosen, fr. *eligere*] **:** a judicial writ of execution by which a defendant's goods and if necessary his lands are delivered for debt to the plaintiff until the debt is paid

el·e·gize \ˈel-ə-ˌjīz\ *vb* **-gized; -giz·ing** *vi* **:** to lament or celebrate in an elegy ~ *vt* **:** to write an elegy on

el·e·gy \ˈel-ə-jē\ *n, pl* **-gies** [L *elegia* poem in elegiac couplets, fr. Gk *elegeia, elegeion,* fr. *elegos* song of mourning] **1 a :** a song or poem expressing sorrow or lamentation esp. for one who is dead **b :** something (as a speech) resembling such a song or poem **2 :** a poem in elegiac couplets **3 a :** a pensive or reflective poem that is usu. nostalgic or melancholy **b :** a short pensive musical composition

elem *abbr* elementary

el·e·ment \ˈel-ə-mənt\ *n* [ME, fr. OF & L; OF, fr. L *elementum*] **1 a :** one of the four substances air, water, fire, and earth formerly believed to compose the physical universe **b** *pl* **:** weather conditions caused by activities of the elements; *esp* **:** violent or severe weather **c :** the state or sphere natural or suited to a person or thing <at school she was in her ~> **2 :** a constituent part: as **a** *pl* **:** the simplest principles of a subject of study **:** RUDIMENTS **b**

(1) : a part of a geometric magnitude <an infinitesimal ~ of volume> (2) : a generator of a geometric figure (3) : a basic member of a mathematical class or set **c** : one of a number of distinct groups composing a human community <the criminal ~ in the city> **d** (1) : one of the necessary data or values on which calculations or conclusions are based (2) : one of the factors determining the outcome of a process **e** : any of more than 100 fundamental substances that consist of atoms of only one kind and that singly or in combination constitute all matter **f** : a distinct part of a composite device **g** : a subdivision of a military unit **h** : MEMBER 4d **3** *pl* : the bread and wine used in the Eucharist
syn ELEMENT, COMPONENT, CONSTITUENT, INGREDIENT, FACTOR *shared meaning element* : one of the parts, substances, or principles that make up a compound or complex whole ***ant*** compound, composite

CHEMICAL ELEMENTS

ELEMENT & SYMBOL	ATOMIC NUMBER	ATOMIC WEIGHT (C = 12)
actinium (Ac)	89	
aluminum (Al)	13	26.9815
americium (Am)	95	
antimony (Sb)	51	121.75
argon (Ar)	18	39.948
arsenic (As)	33	74.9216
astatine (At)	85	
barium (Ba)	56	137.34
berkelium (Bk)	97	
beryllium (Be)	4	9.01218
bismuth (Bi)	83	208.9806
boron (B)	5	10.81
bromine (Br)	35	79.904
cadmium (Cd)	48	112.40
calcium (Ca)	20	40.08
californium (Cf)	98	
carbon (C)	6	12.011
cerium (Ce)	58	140.12
cesium (Cs)	55	132.9055
chlorine (Cl)	17	35.453
chromium (Cr)	24	51.996
cobalt (Co)	27	58.9332
columbium (Cb)	(see niobium)	
copper (Cu)	29	63.546
curium (Cm)	96	
dysprosium (Dy)	66	162.50
einsteinium (Es)	99	
erbium (Er)	68	167.26
europium (Eu)	63	151.96
fermium (Fm)	100	
fluorine (F)	9	18.9984
francium (Fr)	87	
gadolinium (Gd)	64	157.25
gallium (Ga)	31	69.72
germanium (Ge)	32	72.59
gold (Au)	79	196.9665
hafnium (Hf)	72	178.49
helium (He)	2	4.00260
holmium (Ho)	67	164.9303
hydrogen (H)	1	1.0080
indium (In)	49	114.82
iodine (I)	53	126.9045
iridium (Ir)	77	192.22
iron (Fe)	26	55.847
krypton (Kr)	36	83.80
lanthanum (La)	57	138.9055
lawrencium (Lr)	103	
lead (Pb)	82	207.2
lithium (Li)	3	6.941
lutetium (Lu)	71	174.97
magnesium (Mg)	12	24.305
manganese (Mn)	25	54.9380
mendelevium (Md)	101	
mercury (Hg)	80	200.59
molybdenum (Mo)	42	95.94
neodymium (Nd)	60	144.24
neon (Ne)	10	20.179
neptunium (Np)	93	237.0482
nickel (Ni)	28	58.71
niobium (Nb)	41	92.9064
nitrogen (N)	7	14.0067
nobelium (No)	102	
osmium (Os)	76	190.2
oxygen (O)	8	15.9994
palladium (Pd)	46	106.4
phosphorus (P)	15	30.9738
platinum (Pt)	78	195.09
plutonium (Pu)	94	
polonium (Po)	84	
potassium (K)	19	39.102
praseodymium (Pr)	59	140.9077
promethium (Pm)	61	
protactinium (Pa)	91	231.0359
radium (Ra)	88	226.0254
radon (Rn)	86	
rhenium (Re)	75	186.2
rhodium (Rh)	45	102.9055
rubidium (Rb)	37	85.4678
ruthenium (Ru)	44	101.07
samarium (Sm)	62	150.4
scandium (Sc)	21	44.9559
selenium (Se)	34	78.96
silicon (Si)	14	28.086
silver (Ag)	47	107.868
sodium (Na)	11	22.9898
strontium (Sr)	38	87.62
sulfur (S)	16	32.06
tantalum (Ta)	73	180.9479
technetium (Tc)	43	98.9062
tellurium (Te)	52	127.60
terbium (Tb)	65	158.9254
thallium (Tl)	81	204.37
thorium (Th)	90	232.0381
thulium (Tm)	69	168.9342
tin (Sn)	50	118.69
titanium (Ti)	22	47.90
tungsten (W)	74	183.85
uranium (U)	92	238.029
vanadium (V)	23	50.9414
wolfram (W)	(see tungsten)	
xenon (Xe)	54	131.30
ytterbium (Yb)	70	173.04
yttrium (Y)	39	88.9059
zinc (Zn)	30	65.37
zirconium (Zr)	40	91.22

el·e·men·tal \ˌel-ə-'ment-ᵊl\ *adj* **1 a** : of, relating to, or being an element; *specif* : existing as an uncombined chemical element **b** : of, relating to, or being the basic or ultimate constituent of something : FUNDAMENTAL <certain ~ biological and social realities> **c** : of, relating to, or dealing with the rudiments of something : ELEMENTARY <taught ~ arts and crafts to the children> **d** : forming an integral part : INHERENT <an ~ sense of rhythm> **2** : of, relating to, or resembling a great force of nature <the rains come with ~ violence> <~ passions> — **elemental** *n* — **el·e·men·tal·ly** \-ᵊl-ē\ *adv*

el·e·men·ta·ry \ˌel-ə-'ment-ə-rē, -'men-trē\ *adj* **1 a** : of, relating to, or dealing with the simplest elements or principles of something <can't handle the most ~ decision-making> **b** : of or relating to an elementary school <an ~ curriculum> **2** : ELEMENTAL 1a, 1b **3** : ELEMENTAL 2 — **el·e·men·ta·ri·ly** \-ˌmen-'ter-ə-lē, -'men-trə-lē\ *adv* — **el·e·men·ta·ri·ness** \-'ment-ə-rē-nəs, -'men-trē-\ *n*

elementary body *n* : a distinguishable unit that makes up an inclusion body and probably is the infective particle of some viruses

elementary particle *n* **1** : any of the submicroscopic constituents of matter and energy (as the electron, proton, or photon) whose existence has not been attributed to the combination of other more fundamental entities **2** : OXYSOME

elementary school *n* : a school usu. including the first six or the first eight grades

el·e·mi \'el-ə-mē\ *n* [NL *elimi*] : any of various fragrant oleoresins obtained from tropical trees (family Burseraceae) and used chiefly in varnishes, lacquers, and printing inks

elen·chus \i-'leŋ-kəs\ *n, pl* **-chi** \-ˌkī, -(ˌ)kē\ [L, fr. Gk *elenchos*] : REFUTATION: *esp* : one in syllogistic form

el·e·phant \'el-ə-fənt\ *n, often attrib* [ME, fr. OF & L; OF *olifant*, fr. L *elephantus*, fr. Gk *elephant-, elephas*] : any of various thickset mostly very large nearly hairless four-footed mammals that constitute with related extinct forms a family (Elephantidae, the elephant family) and have the snout prolonged into a muscular trunk and two incisors in the upper jaw developed esp. in the male into long tusks which furnish ivory; *broadly* : a related animal or fossil

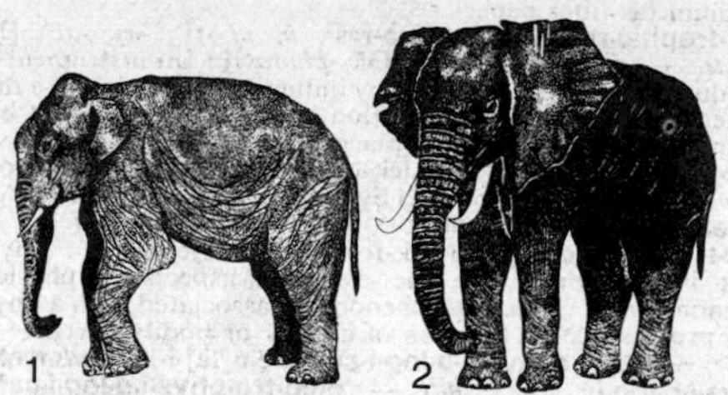

elephants: *1* Indian, *2* African

elephant grass *n* **1** : an Old World cattail (*Typha elephantina*) used esp. in making baskets **2** : NAPIER GRASS

el·e·phan·ti·a·sis \ˌel-ə-fən-'tī-ə-səs, -ˌfan-\ *n, pl* **-a·ses** \-ˌsēz\ [NL, fr. L, a kind of leprosy, fr. Gk, fr. *elephant-, elephas*] **1** : enlargement and thickening of tissues; *specif* : the enormous enlargement of a limb or the scrotum caused by obstruction of lymphatics by filarial worms **2** : an undesirable usu. enormous growth, enlargement, or overdevelopment <~ of intellect and atrophy of emotion —Michael Lerner>

el·e·phan·tine \ˌel-ə-'fan-ˌtēn, -ˌtīn, 'el-ə-fən-\ *adj* **1 a** : having enormous size or strength : MASSIVE **b** : CLUMSY, PONDEROUS **2** : of or relating to an elephant

elephant seal *n* : a nearly extinct large seal (*Mirounga angustirostris*) with a long inflatable proboscis that was formerly abundant along the coasts of California and Lower California; *also* : a related seal (*M. leonina*) formerly abundant on coasts of the southern hemisphere

El·eu·sin·i·an mysteries \ˌel-yü-ˌsin-ē-ən-\ *n pl* : religious mysteries celebrated at ancient Eleusis in worship of Demeter and Persephone

elev *abbr* elevation

[1]**el·e·vate** \'el-ə-ˌvāt, -vət\ *adj, archaic* : ELEVATED

[2]**el·e·vate** \-ˌvāt\ *vt* **-vat·ed; -vat·ing** [ME *elevaten*, fr. L *elevatus*, pp. of *elevare*, fr. *e-* + *levare* to raise — more at LEVER] **1** : to lift up : RAISE **2** : to raise in rank or status : EXALT **3** : to

improve morally, intellectually, or culturally **4 :** to raise the spirits of **:** ELATE ***syn*** see LIFT ***ant*** lower

el·e·vat·ed \ˈel-ə-ˌvāt-əd\ *adj* **1 :** raised esp. above the ground or other surface <an ~ highway> **2 a :** morally or intellectually on a high plane <an ~ mind> **b :** FORMAL, DIGNIFIED <~ diction> **3 :** exhilarated in mood or feeling

elevated railroad *n* **:** an urban or interurban railroad operating chiefly on an elevated structure — called also *elevated railway*

el·e·va·tion \ˌel-ə-ˈvā-shən\ *n* **1 :** the height to which something is elevated: as **a :** the angular distance of a celestial object above the horizon **b :** the degree to which a gun is aimed above the horizon **c :** the height above the level of the sea **:** ALTITUDE **2 :** a ballet dancer's or a skater's leap and seeming suspension in the air; *also* **:** the ability to achieve an elevation **3 :** an act or instance of elevating **4 :** something that is elevated: as **a :** an elevated place **b :** a swelling esp. on the skin **5 :** the quality or state of being elevated **6 :** a geometrical projection (as of a building) on a vertical plane ***syn*** see HEIGHT

el·e·va·tor \ˈel-ə-ˌvāt-ər\ *n* **1 :** one that raises or lifts something up: as **a :** an endless belt or chain conveyor with cleats, scoops, or buckets for raising material **b :** a cage or platform and its hoisting machinery for conveying something to different levels **c :** a building for elevating, storing, discharging, and sometimes processing grain **2 :** a movable auxiliary airfoil usu. attached to the tail plane of an airplane for producing motion up or down — see AIRPLANE illustration

elev·en \i-ˈlev-ən\ *n* [ME *enleven,* fr. *enleven,* adj., fr. OE *endleofan;* akin to OHG *einlif* eleven; both fr. a prehistoric Gmc compound whose first element is akin to OE *ān* one, and whose second element is prob. akin to OE *lēon* to lend] **1** — see NUMBER table **2 :** the 11th in a set or series **3 :** something having 11 units or members; *esp* **:** a football team — **eleven** *adj or pron* — **elev·enth** \-ən(t)th\ *adj or n*

elev·ens·es \-ən-zəz\ *n pl but sometimes sing in constr* [irreg. pl. of *eleven* (o'clock)] *Brit* **:** a light lunch or sometimes only coffee or tea taken around the middle of the morning

eleventh hour *n* **:** the latest possible time <won his reprieve at the *eleventh hour*>

el·e·von \ˈel-ə-ˌvän\ *n* [*elev*ator + ailer*on*] **:** an airplane control surface that combines the functions of elevator and aileron

elf \ˈelf\ *n, pl* **elves** \ˈelvz\ [ME, fr. OE *ælf;* akin to ON *alfr* elf] **1 :** a small often mischievous fairy **2 a :** a small creature; *esp* **:** a mischievous child **b :** a mischievous or malicious person — **elf·ish** \ˈel-fish\ *adj* — **elf·ish·ly** *adv*

ELF *abbr* extremely low frequency

elf·in \ˈel-fən\ *adj* [irreg. fr. *elf*] **1 a :** of, relating to, or produced by an elf **b :** resembling an elf **2 :** having an otherworldly or magical quality or charm

elf·lock \ˈel-ˌfläk\ *n* **:** hair matted as if by elves — usu. used in pl.

Eli \ˈē-ˌlī\ *n* [Heb *ʽĒlī*] **:** a judge and priest of Israel who according to the account in I Samuel was entrusted with the care of the boy Samuel

Eli·as \i-ˈlī-əs\ *n* [LL, fr. Gk *Elias,* fr. Heb *Ēlīyāh*] **:** ELIJAH

elic·it \i-ˈlis-ət\ *vt* [L *elicitus,* pp. of *elicere,* fr. *e-* + *lacere* to allure — more at DELIGHT] **1 a :** to draw forth or bring out (something latent or potential) **b :** to derive (as a truth) by logical processes **2 :** to call forth or draw out (a response or reaction) ***syn*** see EDUCE — **elic·i·ta·tion** \ i-ˌlis-ə-ˈtā-shən, ˌē-\ *n* — **elic·i·tor** \i-ˈlis-ət-ər\ *n*

elide \i-ˈlīd\ *vt* **elid·ed; elid·ing** [L *elidere* to strike out, fr. *e-* + *laedere* to injure by striking] **1 a :** to suppress or alter (as a vowel or syllable) by elision **b :** to strike out (as a written word or passage) **2 a :** to leave out of consideration **:** OMIT **b :** CURTAIL, ABRIDGE

el·i·gi·ble \ˈel-ə-jə-bəl\ *adj* [ME, fr. MF & LL; MF, fr. LL *eligibilis,* fr. L *eligere* to choose — more at ELECT] **1 a :** qualified to be chosen **:** ENTITLED <~ for sophomore standing> <~ to retire> **b :** permitted under football rules to catch a forward pass <an ~ receiver> **2 :** worthy of being chosen **:** DESIRABLE <an ~ young bachelor> — **el·i·gi·bil·i·ty** \ˌel-ə-jə-ˈbil-ət-ē\ *n* — **eligible** *n* — **el·i·gi·bly** \ˈel-ə-jə-blē\ *adv*

Eli·jah \i-ˈlī-jə\ *n* [Heb *Ēlīyāh*] **:** a Hebrew prophet of the 9th century B.C. who according to the account in I Kings championed the worship of Jehovah as against Baal

elim·i·nate \i-ˈlim-ə-ˌnāt\ *vt* **-nat·ed; -nat·ing** [L *eliminatus,* pp. of *eliminare,* fr. *e-* + *limin-, limen* threshold] **1 a :** to cast out or get rid of **:** REMOVE, ERADICATE <the need to ~ poverty> **b :** to set aside as unimportant **:** IGNORE **2 :** to expel (as waste) from the living body **3 :** to cause to disappear by combining two or more equations ***syn*** see EXCLUDE — **elim·i·na·tion** \-ˌlim-ə-ˈnā-shən\ *n* — **elim·i·na·tive** \-ˈlim-ə-ˌnāt-iv\ *adj* — **elim·i·na·tor** \-ˌnāt-ər\ *n*

Eli·sha \i-ˈlī-shə\ *n* [Heb *Ĕlīshāʽ*] **:** a Hebrew prophet and disciple and successor of Elijah

eli·sion \i-ˈlizh-ən\ *n* [LL *elision-, elisio,* fr. L *elisus,* pp. of *elidere*] **1 a :** the use of a speech form that lacks a final or initial sound which a variant speech form has <the use of *'s* instead of *is* in English *there's* is an example of ~> **b :** the omission of an unstressed vowel or syllable in a verse to achieve a uniform metrical pattern **2 :** the act or an instance of dropping out or omitting something **:** OMISSION

elite \ā-ˈlēt, i-\ *n* [F *élite,* fr. OF *eslite,* fr. fem. of *eslit,* pp. of *eslire* to choose, fr. L *eligere*] **1 a :** the choice part; *esp* **:** a socially superior group **b :** a powerful minority group <a power ~ inside the government> **2 :** a typewriter type providing 12 characters to the linear inch — **elite** *adj*

elit·ism \-ˈlēt-ˌiz-əm\ *n* **1 a :** leadership or rule by an elite **b :** belief in or advocacy of such elitism **2 :** consciousness of being or belonging to an elite — **elit·ist** \-ˈlēt-əst\ *n or adj*

elix·ir \i-ˈlik-sər\ *n* [ME, fr. ML, fr. Ar *al-iksīr* the elixir, fr. *al* the + *iksīr* elixir, prob. fr. Gk *xērion* desiccative powder, fr. *xēros* dry] **1 a :** a substance held capable of changing base metals into gold **:** PHILOSOPHERS' STONE **b** (1) **:** a substance held capable of prolonging life indefinitely (2) **:** CURE-ALL (3) **:** a sweetened liquid usu. containing alcohol that is used as a vehicle for medicinal agents **2 :** the essential principle

Eliz *abbr* Elizabethan

Eliz·a·be·than \i-ˌliz-ə-ˈbē-thən\ *adj* **:** of, relating to, or characteristic of Elizabeth I of England or her age — **Elizabethan** *n*

elk \ˈelk\ *n, pl* **elks** [ME, prob. fr. OE *eolh;* akin to OHG *elaho* elk, Gk *elaphos* deer] **1** *pl usu* **elk a :** the largest existing deer (*Alces alces*) of Europe and Asia resembling but not so large as the moose of No. America **b :** WAPITI **c :** any of various large Asiatic deer **2 :** soft tanned rugged leather **3** *cap* [Benevolent and Protective Order of *Elks*] **:** a member of a major benevolent and fraternal order

elk·hound \ˈelk-ˌhau̇nd, ˈel-ˌkau̇nd\ *n* **:** NORWEGIAN ELKHOUND

¹ell \ˈel\ *n* [ME *eln,* fr. OE] **1 :** a former English unit of length (as for cloth) equal to 45 inches **2 :** any of various units of length similar in use to the English ell

²ell *n* [alter. of ¹*el*] **1 :** an extension at right angles to the length of a building **2 :** an elbow in a pipe or conduit

el·lag·ic acid \ə-ˌlaj-ik-, e-\ *n* [F *ellagique,* fr. *ellag,* anagram of *galle* gall] **:** a crystalline phenolic compound $C_{14}H_6O_8$ with two lactone groupings that is obtained esp. from oak galls and some tannins

el·lipse \i-ˈlips, e-\ *n* [Gk *elleipsis*] **1 a :** OVAL **b :** a closed plane curve generated by a point moving in such a way that the sums of its distances from two fixed points is a constant: a plane section of a right circular cone that is a closed curve **2 :** ELLIPSIS

ellipse 1b: *F, F'* foci; *P, P', P"* any point on the curve; *FP + PF' = FP" + P" F' = FP' + P' F'*

el·lip·sis \i-ˈlip-səs, e-\ *n, pl* **el·lip·ses** \-ˌsēz\ [L, fr. Gk *elleipsis* ellipsis, ellipse, fr. *elleipein* to leave out, fall short, fr. *en* in + *leipein* to leave — more at IN, LOAN] **1 a :** the omission of one or more words that are obviously understood but that must be supplied to make a construction grammatically complete <"the man that he sees" may be changed by ~ to "the man he sees"> **b :** a leap or sudden passage without logical connectives from one topic to another **2 :** marks or a mark (as . . . or *** or —) indicating the omission esp. of letters or words

el·lip·soid \i-ˈlip-ˌsȯid, e-\ *n* **:** a surface all plane sections of which are ellipses or circles — **ellipsoid** *or* **el·lip·soi·dal** \i-ˌlip-ˈsȯid-ᵊl, (ˌ)e-\ *adj*

el·lip·tic \i-ˈlip-tik, e-\ *or* **el·lip·ti·cal** \-ti-kəl\ *adj* [Gk *elleiptikos* defective, marked by ellipsis, fr. *elleipein*] **1 a :** of, relating to, or shaped like an ellipse **b :** of, relating to, or being a space in which no line parallel to a given line passes through a point not on the line **2 a :** of, relating to, or marked by ellipsis or an ellipsis **b** (1) **:** of, relating to, or marked by extreme economy of speech or writing (2) **:** of or relating to studied obscurity of literary style — **el·lip·ti·cal·ly** \-ti-k(ə-)lē\ *adv*

el·lip·tic·i·ty \i-ˌlip-ˈtis-ət-ē, (ˌ)e-\ *n* **:** deviation of an ellipse or a spheroid from the form of a circle or a sphere

elm \ˈelm\ *n* [ME, fr. OE; akin to OHG *elme* elm, L *ulmus*] **1 :** any of a genus (*Ulmus* of the family Ulmaceae, the elm family) comprising large graceful trees with alternate stipulate leaves and small apetalous flowers **2 :** the wood of an elm

elm 1

elm bark beetle *n* **:** either of two beetles that are vectors for the fungus causing Dutch elm disease: **a :** a beetle (*Hylurgopinus rufipes*) native to eastern No. America **b :** a European beetle (*Scolytus multistriatus*) that is established in eastern No. America

elm blight *n* **:** DUTCH ELM DISEASE

elm leaf beetle *n* **:** a small orange-yellow black-striped Old World chrysomelid beetle (*Pyrrhalta luteola*) that is a leaf-eating pest of elms in eastern No. America as a larva and as an adult

el·o·cu·tion \ˌel-ə-ˈkyü-shən\ *n* [ME *elocucioun,* fr. L *elocution-, elocutio,* fr. *elocutus,* pp. of *eloqui*] **1 :** the art of effective public speaking **2 :** a style of speaking esp. in public — **el·o·cu·tion·ary** \-shə-ˌner-ē\ *adj* — **el·o·cu·tion·ist** \-sh(ə-)nəst\ *n*

elo·dea \i-ˈlōd-ē-ə\ *n* [NL, genus name, fr. Gk *helōdēs* marshy, fr. *helos* marsh; akin to Skt *saras* pond] **:** any of a small American genus (*Elodea*) of submerged aquatic monocotyledonous herbs

eloign \i-ˈlȯin\ *vt* [ME *eloynen,* fr. MF *esloigner,* fr. OF, fr. *es-* ex- (fr. L *ex-*) + *loing* (adv.) far, fr. L *longe,* fr. *longus* long] **1** *archaic* **:** to take (oneself) far away **2** *archaic* **:** to remove to a distant or unknown place **:** CONCEAL

¹elon·gate \i-ˈlȯŋ-ˌgāt\ *vb* **-gat·ed; -gat·ing** [LL *elongatus,* pp. of *elongare,* to withdraw, fr. L *e-* + *longus* long] *vt* **:** to extend the length of ~ *vi* **:** to grow in length ***syn*** see EXTEND ***ant*** abbreviate, shorten

²elongate *adj* **1 :** stretched out **:** LENGTHENED **2 :** long in proportion to width **:** SLENDER

elon·gat·ed *adj* **:** ELONGATE

elon·ga·tion \(ˌ)ē-ˌlȯŋ-ˈgā-shən\ *n* [LL *elongare* to withdraw] **1 a :** the angular distance of a celestial body from another around

ə abut	ᵊ kitten	ər further	a back	ā bake	ä cot, cart
au̇ out	ch chin	e less	ē easy	g gift	i trip	ī life
j joke	ŋ sing	ō flow	ȯ flaw	ȯi coin	th thin	th this
ü loot	u̇ foot	y yet	yü few	yu̇ furious	zh vision

which it revolves or from a particular point in the sky **b :** the daily extreme east or west position of a star with reference to the north celestial pole **2 a :** the state of being elongated or lengthened **b :** something that is elongated

elope \i-'lōp\ *vi* **eloped; elop·ing** [AF *aloper*] **1 a :** to run away from one's husband with a lover **b :** to run away secretly with the intention of getting married usu. without parental consent **2 :** to slip away : ESCAPE — **elope·ment** \-'lōp-mənt\ *n* — **elop·er** *n*

el·o·quence \'el-ə-kwən(t)s\ *n* **:** discourse marked by force and persuasiveness; *also* **:** the art or power of using such discourse

el·o·quent \-kwənt\ *adj* [ME, fr. MF, fr. L *eloquent-, eloquens,* fr. prp. of *eloqui* to speak out, fr. *e-* + *loqui* to speak] **1 :** marked by forceful and fluent expression <an ~ preacher> **2 :** vividly or movingly expressive or revealing <put his arm around her in an ~ gesture of reassurance> — **el·o·quent·ly** *adv*

[1]else \'els\ *adv* [ME *elles,* fr. OE; akin to L *alius* other, *alter* other of two, Gk *allos* other] **1 a :** in a different manner or place or at a different time <how ~ could he have acted> <here and nowhere ~> **b :** in an additional manner or place or at an additional time <where ~ is gold found> **2 :** if the facts are or were different **:** if not : OTHERWISE <do what you are told or ~ you'll be sorry> — used absolutely to express a threat <do what I tell you or ~>

[2]else *adj* **:** OTHER: **a :** being different in identity <it must have been somebody ~> **b :** being in addition <what ~ did he say>

else·where \-ˌ(h)we(ə)r, -ˌ(h)wa(ə)r\ *adv* **:** in or to another place <took his business ~>

ELSS *abbr* extravehicular life support system

el·u·ant *or* **el·u·ent** \'el-yə-wənt\ *n* [L *eluent-, eluens,* prp. of *eluere*] **:** a solvent used in eluting

el·u·ate \'el-yə-wət, -ˌwāt\ *n* [L *eluere* + E *-ate*] **:** the washings obtained by eluting

elu·ci·date \i-'lü-sə-ˌdāt\ *vb* **-dat·ed; -dat·ing** [LL *elucidatus,* pp. of *elucidare,* fr. L *e-* + *lucidus* lucid] *vt* **:** to make lucid esp. by explanation ~ *vi* **:** to give a clarifying explanation ***syn*** see EXPLAIN — **elu·ci·da·tion** \-ˌlü-sə-'dā-shən\ *n* — **elu·ci·da·tive** \-'lü-sə-ˌdāt-iv\ *adj* — **elu·ci·da·tor** \-ˌdāt-ər\ *n*

elu·cu·brate \i-'lü-k(y)ə-ˌbrāt\ *vt* **-brat·ed; -brat·ing** [L *elucubratus,* pp. of *elucubrare* to compose by lamplight, fr. *e-* + *lucubrare* to work by lamplight — more at LUCUBRATION] **:** to work out or express by studious effort — **elu·cu·bra·tion** \-ˌlü-k(y)ə-'brā-shən\ *n*

elude \ē-'lüd\ *vt* **elud·ed; elud·ing** [L *eludere,* fr. *e-* + *ludere* to play — more at LUDICROUS] **1 :** to avoid adroitly : EVADE **2 :** to escape the notice of ***syn*** see ESCAPE

Elul \e-'lül\ *n* [Heb *Ĕlūl*] **:** the 12th month of the civil year or the 6th month of the ecclesiastical year in the Jewish calendar — see MONTH table

elu·sion \ē-'lü-zhən\ *n* [ML *elusion-, elusio,* fr. LL, deception, fr. L *elusus,* pp. of *eludere*] **:** an act of eluding: as **a :** an adroit escape **b :** an evasion esp. of a problem or an order

elu·sive \ē-'lü-siv, -'lü-ziv\ *adj* **:** tending to elude: as **a :** tending to evade grasp or pursuit <an eligible though ~ bachelor> **b :** hard to comprehend or define <an ~ concept that means many things to many people> **c :** hard to isolate or identify <a haunting ~ aroma> — **elu·sive·ly** *adv* — **elu·sive·ness** *n*

elute \ē-'lüt\ *vt* **elut·ed; elut·ing** [L *elutus,* pp. of *eluere* to wash out, fr. *e-* + *lavere* to wash — more at LYE] **:** EXTRACT; *specif* **:** to remove (adsorbed material) from an adsorbent by means of a solvent — **elu·tion** \-'lü-shən\ *n*

elu·tri·ate \ē-'lü-trē-ˌāt\ *vt* **-at·ed; -at·ing** [L *elutriatus,* pp. of *elutriare,* irreg. fr. *elutus*] **:** to purify, separate, or remove by washing — **elu·tri·a·tor** \-ˌāt-ər\ *n*

elu·vi·al \ē-'lü-vē-əl\ *adj* **1 :** of, relating to, or composed of eluvium **2 :** of or relating to eluviation or to eluviated materials or areas

elu·vi·ate \-vē-ˌāt\ *vi* **-at·ed; -at·ing :** to undergo eluviation

elu·vi·a·tion \(ˌ)ē-ˌlü-vē-'ā-shən\ *n* **:** the transportation of dissolved or suspended material within the soil by the movement of water when rainfall exceeds evaporation

elu·vi·um \ē-'lü-vē-əm\ *n* [NL, fr. L *eluere* to wash out] **1 :** rock debris produced by the weathering and disintegration of rock in situ **2 :** fine soil or sand deposited by wind

el·ver \'el-vər\ *n* [alter. of *eelfare* (migration of eels)] **:** a young eel

elves *pl of* ELF

el·vish \'el-vish\ *adj* **1 :** of or relating to elves **2 :** MISCHIEVOUS

ely·sian \i-'lizh-ən\ *adj, often cap* **1 :** of or relating to Elysium **2 :** BLISSFUL, DELIGHTFUL

elysian fields *n pl, often cap E* **:** ELYSIUM

Ely·si·um \i-'liz(h)-ē-əm\ *n, pl* **-si·ums** *or* **-sia** \-ē-ə\ [L, fr. Gk *Elysion*] **1 :** the abode of the blessed after death in classical mythology **2 :** PARADISE 2

elytr- *or* **elytri-** *or* **elytro-** *comb form* [NL *elytron*] **:** elytron <*elytr*oid> <*elytri*ferous>

el·y·tron \'el-ə-ˌträn\ *also* **el·y·trum** \-trəm\ *n, pl* **-tra** \-trə\ [NL, fr. Gk *elytron* sheath, wing cover, fr. *eilyein* to roll, wrap — more at VOLUBLE] **:** one of the anterior wings in beetles and some other insects that serve to protect the posterior pair of functional wings

em \'em\ *n* **1 :** the letter *m* **2 :** the set dimension of an em quad used as a unit of measure **3 :** [1]PICA 2

EM *abbr* **1** electromagnetic **2** end matched **3** engineer of mines **4** enlisted man

em- — see EN-

ema·ci·ate \i-'mā-shē-ˌāt\ *vb* **-at·ed; at·ing** [L *emaciatus,* pp. of *emaciare,* fr. *e-* + *macies* leanness, fr. *macer* lean — more at MEAGER] *vt* **1 :** to cause to lose flesh so as to become very thin **2 :** to make feeble ~ *vi* **:** to waste away physically — **ema·ci·a·tion** \-ˌmā-s(h)ē-'ā-shən\ *n*

em·a·nate \'em-ə-ˌnāt\ *vb* **-nat·ed; -nat·ing** [L *emanatus,* pp. of *emanare,* fr. *e-* + *manare* to flow] *vi* **:** to come out from a source ~ *vt* **:** to give out : EMIT ***syn*** see SPRING

em·a·na·tion \ˌem-ə-'nā-shən\ *n* **1 a :** the action of emanating **b :** the origination of the world by a series of hierarchically descending radiations from the Godhead through intermediate stages to matter **2 a :** something that emanates or is produced by emanation : EFFLUENCE **b :** a heavy gaseous element produced by radioactive disintegration <radium ~> — **em·a·na·tion·al** \-shnəl, -shən-ᵊl\ *adj* — **em·a·na·tive** \'em-ə-ˌnāt-iv\ *adj*

eman·ci·pate \i-'man(t)-sə-ˌpāt\ *vt* **-pat·ed; -pat·ing** [L *emancipatus,* pp. of *emancipare,* fr. *e-* + *mancipare* to transfer ownership of, fr. *mancip-, manceps* purchaser, fr. *manus* hand + *capere* to take — more at MANUAL, HEAVE] **1 :** to release from paternal care and responsibility and make sui juris **2 :** to free from restraint, control, or the power of another; *esp* **:** to free from bondage ***syn*** see FREE — **eman·ci·pa·tor** \-ˌpāt-ər\ *n*

eman·ci·pa·tion \i-ˌman(t)-sə-'pā-shən\ *n* **:** the act or process of emancipating — **eman·ci·pa·tion·ist** \-sh(ə-)nəst\ *n*

emar·gin·ate \(ˈ)ē-'mär-jə-nət, -ˌnāt\ *adj* [L *emarginatus,* pp. of *emarginare* to deprive of a margin, fr. *e-* + *margin-, margo* margin] **:** having the margin notched — **emar·gi·na·tion** \(ˌ)ē-ˌmär-jə-'nā-shən\ *n*

emas·cu·late \i-'mas-kyə-ˌlāt\ *vt* **-lat·ed; -lat·ing** [L *emasculatus,* pp. of *emasculare,* fr. *e-* + *masculus* male — more at MALE] **1 :** to deprive of virile or procreative power : CASTRATE **2 :** to deprive of masculine vigor or spirit : WEAKEN **3 :** to remove the androecium of (a flower) in the process of artificial cross-pollination ***syn*** see UNNERVE — **emas·cu·late** \-lət\ *adj* — **emas·cu·la·tion** \-ˌmas-kyə-'lā-shən\ *n* — **emas·cu·la·tor** \-'mas-kyə-ˌlāt-ər\ *n*

em·balm \im-'bäm, -'bälm\ *vt* [ME *embaumen,* fr. MF *embaumer,* fr. OF *embasmer,* fr. *en-* + *basme* balm — more at BALM] **1 :** to treat (a dead body) so as to protect from decay **2 :** to fill with sweet odors : PERFUME **3 :** to protect from decay or oblivion **:** PRESERVE — **em·balm·er** *n* — **em·balm·ment** \-'bä(l)m-mənt\ *n*

em·bank \im-'baŋk\ *vt* **:** to enclose or confine by an embankment

em·bank·ment \-mənt\ *n* **1 :** the action of embanking **2 :** a raised structure to hold back water or to carry a roadway

em·bar·ca·de·ro \(ˌ)em-ˌbär-kə-'de(ə)r-(ˌ)ō\ *n, pl* **-ros** [Sp, fr. *embarcado,* pp. of *embarcar* to embark] *West* **:** a landing place esp. on an inland waterway

[1]em·bar·go \im-'bär-(ˌ)gō\ *n, pl* **-goes** [Sp, fr. *embargar* to bar, fr. (assumed) VL *imbarricare,* fr. L *in-* + (assumed) VL *barra* bar] **1 :** an order of a government prohibiting the departure of commercial ships from its ports **2 :** a legal prohibition on commerce <an ~ on arms shipments> **3 :** STOPPAGE, IMPEDIMENT; *esp* **:** PROHIBITION <I lay no ~ on anybody's words —Jane Austen> **4 :** a common carrier or public regulatory agency order prohibiting or restricting freight transportation

[2]embargo *vt* **-goed; -go·ing :** to place an embargo on (as ships or commerce)

em·bark \im-'bärk\ *vb* [MF *embarquer,* fr. OProv *embarcar,* fr. *em-* (fr. L *im-*) + *barca* bark] *vt* **1 :** to cause to go on board a boat or airplane **2 :** to engage, enlist, or invest in an enterprise ~ *vi* **1 :** to go on board a boat or airplane for transportation **2 :** to make a start : COMMENCE <~*ed* on a new career> — **em·bar·ka·tion** \ˌem-ˌbär-'kā-shən, -bər-\ *n* — **em·bark·ment** \im-'bärk-mənt\ *n*

em·bar·rass \im-'bar-əs\ *vt* [F *embarrasser,* fr. Sp *embarazar,* fr. Pg *embaraçar*] **1 a :** to hamper the movement of **b :** HINDER, IMPEDE **2 a :** to place in doubt, perplexity, or difficulties **b :** to involve in financial difficulties **c :** to cause to experience a state of self-conscious distress <bawdy stories ~*ed* her> **3 :** to make intricate : COMPLICATE **4 :** to impair the activity of (a bodily function) or the function of (a bodily part) <digestion ~*ed* by overeating> — **em·bar·rass·able** \-ə-bəl\ *adj*

syn EMBARRASS, DISCOMFIT, ABASH, DISCONCERT, RATTLE, FAZE *shared meaning element* **:** to distress by confusing or confounding

em·bar·rassed·ly \-əst-lē, -ə-səd-lē\ *adv* **:** with embarrassment <giggled ~>

em·bar·rass·ing·ly \-ə-siŋ-lē\ *adv* **:** to an embarrassing degree

em·bar·rass·ment \im-'bar-ə-smənt\ *n* **1 :** the state of being embarrassed; as **a :** confusion or disturbance of mind **b :** difficulty arising from the want of money to pay debts **c :** difficulty in functioning as a result of disease **2 a :** something that embarrasses : IMPEDIMENT **b :** an excessive quantity from which to select — used esp. in the phrase *embarrassment of riches*

em·bas·sage \'em-bə-sij\ *n* **1 :** the message or commission entrusted to an ambassador **2** *archaic* **:** EMBASSY

em·bas·sy \'em-bə-sē\ *n, pl* **-sies** [MF *ambassee,* of Gmc origin; akin to OHG *ambaht* service] **1 a :** the function or position of an ambassador **b :** a mission abroad undertaken officially esp. by an ambassador **2 :** EMBASSAGE 1 **3 :** a body of diplomatic representatives; *specif* **:** one headed by an ambassador **4 :** the official residence and offices of an ambassador

em·bat·tle \im-'bat-ᵊl\ *vt* **em·bat·tled; em·bat·tling** \-'bat-liŋ, -ᵊl-iŋ\ [ME *embatailen,* fr. MF *embatailler,* fr. *en-* + *batailler* to battle] **1 :** to arrange in order of battle : prepare for battle **2 :** FORTIFY

em·bat·tle·ment \-'bat-ᵊl-mənt\ *n* **:** BATTLEMENT

em·bay \im-'bā\ *vt* **:** to shut or shelter esp. in a bay <an ~*ed* fleet>

em·bay·ment \-'bā-mənt\ *n* **1 :** formation of a bay **2 :** a bay or a conformation resembling a bay

Emb·den \'em-dən\ *n* [*Emden,* Germany] **:** a breed of large white domestic geese with an orange bill and deep orange shanks and toes

em·bed \im-'bed\ *vb* **em·bed·ded; em·bed·ding** *vt* **1 a :** to enclose closely in or as if in a matrix **b :** to make something an integral part of **c :** to prepare (a microscopy specimen) for sectioning by infiltrating with and enclosing in a supporting substance **2 :** to place or fix firmly in surrounding matter <dirt *embedded* in a carpet> ~ *vi***:** to become embedded — **em·bed·ment** \-'bed-mənt\ *n*

em·bel·lish \im-'bel-ish\ *vt* [ME *embelisshen,* fr. MF *embeliss-,* stem of *embelir,* fr. *en-* + *bel* beautiful — more at BEAUTY] **1 :** to make beautiful with ornamentation : DECORATE **2 :** to heighten the attractiveness of by adding ornamental details **:** ENHANCE <events in his life, heavily ~*ed* by his biographers —Marvin Reznikoff> ***syn*** see ADORN — **em·bel·lish·er** *n*

em·bel·lish·ment \-ish-mənt\ *n* **1 :** the act or process of embellishing **2 :** something serving to embellish **3 :** ORNAMENT 5

em·ber \ˈem-bər\ *n* [ME *eymere,* fr. ON *eimyrja;* akin to OE *ǣmerge* ashes] **1 :** a glowing fragment (as of coal) from a fire; *esp* **:** one smoldering in ashes **2** *pl* **:** the smoldering remains of a fire **3** *pl* **:** slowly cooling emotions, memories, ideas, or responses still capable of being enlivened

ember day \ˈem-bər-\ *n* [ME, fr. OE *ymbrendæg,* fr. *ymbrene* circuit, anniversary + *dæg* day] **:** a Wednesday, Friday, or Saturday following the first Sunday in Lent, Whitsunday, September 14, or December 13 and set apart for fasting and prayer in Western churches

em·bez·zle \im-ˈbez-əl\ *vt* **em·bez·zled; em·bez·zling** \-(ə-)liŋ\ [ME *embesilen,* fr. AF *embeseiller,* fr. MF *en-* + *besillier* to destroy] **:** to appropriate (as property entrusted to one's care) fraudulently to one's own use — **em·bez·zle·ment** \-əl-mənt\ *n* — **em·bez·zler** \-(ə-)lər\ *n*

em·bit·ter \im-ˈbit-ər\ *vt* **1 :** to make bitter **2 :** to excite bitter feelings in — **em·bit·ter·ment** \-mənt\ *n*

1**em·blaze** \im-ˈblāz\ *vt* **em·blazed; em·blaz·ing** [*en-* + *blaze* (to blazon)] **1** *archaic* **:** EMBLAZON 1 **2 :** to adorn sumptuously <with gems and golden luster rich *emblazed* —John Milton>

2**emblaze** *vt* **em·blazed; em·blaz·ing 1 :** to illuminate esp. by a blaze **2 :** to set ablaze

em·bla·zon \im-ˈblāz-ᵊn\ *vt* **em·bla·zoned; em·bla·zon·ing** \-ˈblāz-niŋ, -ᵊn-iŋ\ **1 :** to inscribe or adorn with heraldic bearings or devices **2 a :** to deck in bright colors **b :** CELEBRATE, EXTOL <have his . . . deeds ~*ed* by a poet —Thomas Nash> — **em·bla·zon·er** \-ˈblāz-nər, -ᵊn-ər\ *n* — **em·bla·zon·ment** \-ˈblāz-ᵊn-mənt\ *n* — **em·bla·zon·ry** \-ᵊn-rē\ *n*

1**em·blem** \ˈem-bləm\ *n* [ME, fr. L *emblema* inlaid work, fr. Gk *emblēmat-, emblēma,* fr. *emballein* to insert, fr. *en-* + *ballein* to throw — more at DEVIL] **1 :** a picture with a motto or set of verses intended as a moral lesson **2 :** an object or the figure of an object symbolizing and suggesting another object or an idea **3 a :** a symbolic object used as a heraldic device **b :** a device, symbol, or figure adopted and used as an identifying mark

2**emblem** *vt* **:** EMBLEMATIZE

em·blem·at·ic \ˌem-blə-ˈmat-ik\ *also* **em·blem·at·i·cal** \-i-kəl\ *adj* **:** of, relating to, or constituting an emblem **:** SYMBOLIC — **em·blem·at·i·cal·ly** \-i-k(ə-)lē\ *adv*

em·blem·a·tize \em-ˈblem-ə-ˌtīz\ *vt* **-tized; -tiz·ing :** to represent by or as if by an emblem **:** SYMBOLIZE

em·ble·ments \ˈem-blə-mən(t)s\ *n pl* [ME *emblayment,* fr. MF *emblaement,* fr. *emblaer* to sow with grain, fr. *en-* + *blee* grain] **:** crops from annual cultivation legally belonging to the tenant

em·bodi·ment \im-ˈbäd-i-mənt\ *n* **1 :** the act of embodying **:** the state of being embodied **2 :** one that embodies something <the ~ of all our hopes>

em·body \im-ˈbäd-ē\ *vt* **em·bod·ied; em·body·ing 1 :** to give a body to (a spirit) **:** INCARNATE **2 a :** to deprive of spirituality **b :** to make concrete and perceptible **3 :** to cause to become a body or part of a body **:** INCORPORATE **4 :** to represent in human or animal form **:** PERSONIFY <men who greatly *embodied* the idealism of American life —A. M. Schlesinger *b*1917> — **em·bodi·er** *n*

embol- *or* **emboli-** *or* **embolo-** *comb form* [NL, fr. *embolus*] **:** embolus <*embol*ectomy>

em·bold·en \im-ˈbōl-dən\ *vt* **:** to instill with boldness or courage

em·bo·lec·to·my \ˌem-bə-ˈlek-tə-mē\ *n, pl* **-mies :** surgical removal of an embolus

em·bol·ic \em-ˈbäl-ik, im-\ *adj* **:** of or relating to an embolus or embolism

em·bo·lism \ˈem-bə-ˌliz-əm\ *n* [ME *embolisme,* fr. ML *embolismus,* fr. Gk *embol-* (fr. *emballein* to insert, intercalate) — more at EMBLEM] **1 :** the insertion of one or more days in a calendar **:** INTERCALATION **2 a :** the sudden obstruction of a blood vessel by an embolus **b :** EMBOLUS — **em·bo·lis·mic** \ˌem-bə-ˈliz-mik\ *adj*

em·bo·li·za·tion \ˌem-bə-lə-ˈzā-shən\ *n* **:** the process or state in which a blood vessel or organ is obstructed by the lodgment of a material mass (as an embolus)

em·bo·lus \ˈem-bə-ləs\ *n, pl* **-li** \-ˌlī\ [NL, fr. Gk *embolos* wedge-shaped object, stopper, fr. *emballein*] **:** an abnormal particle (as an air bubble) circulating in the blood — compare THROMBUS

em·bo·ly \ˈem-bə-lē\ *n* [Gk *embolē* insertion, fr. *emballein*] **:** gastrula formation by simple invagination of the blastula wall

em·bon·point \äⁿ-bōⁿ-pwaⁿ\ *n* [F, fr. MF, fr. *en bon point* in good condition] **:** plumpness of person **:** STOUTNESS

em·bo·som \im-ˈbu̇z-əm, -ˈbüz-\ *vt* **1** *archaic* **:** to take into or place in the bosom **2 :** to shelter closely **:** ENCLOSE <his house ~*ed* in the grove —Alexander Pope>

1**em·boss** \im-ˈbäs, -ˈbȯs\ *vt* [ME *embosen* to become exhausted fr. being hunted] *obs* **:** to drive (as a hunted animal) to bay

2**emboss** *vt* [ME *embosen,* fr. MF *embocer,* fr. *en-* + *boce* boss] **1 :** to raise the surface of into bosses; *esp* **:** to ornament with raised work **2 :** to raise in relief from a surface **3 :** ADORN, EMBELLISH — **em·boss·able** \-ə-bəl\ *adj* — **em·boss·er** \-ər\ *n* — **em·boss·ment** \-mənt\ *n*

em·bou·chure \ˌäm-bu̇-ˈshu̇(ə)r\ *n* [F, fr. (*s'*)*emboucher* to flow into, fr. *en-* + *bouche* mouth — more at DEBOUCH] **1 :** the position and use of the lips in producing a musical tone on a wind instrument **2 :** the mouthpiece of a musical instrument

em·bowed \im-ˈbōd\ *adj* **:** bent like a bow: as **a :** ARCHED, VAULTED <an ~ ceiling> **b :** curved outward to form a projecting recess

em·bow·el \im-ˈbau̇(-ə)l\ *vt* **-eled** *or* **-elled; -el·ing** *or* **-el·ling 1 :** DISEMBOWEL **2** *obs* **:** ENCLOSE

em·bow·er \im-ˈbau̇(-ə)r\ *vt* **:** to shelter or enclose in a bower <like a rose ~*ed* in its own green leaves —P. B. Shelley>

1**em·brace** \im-ˈbrās\ *vb* **em·braced; em·brac·ing** [ME *embracen,* fr. MF *embracer,* fr. OF *embracier,* fr. *en-* + *brace* two arms — more at BRACE] *vt* **1 a :** to clasp in the arms **:** HUG **b :** CHERISH, LOVE **2 :** ENCIRCLE, ENCLOSE **3 a :** to take up esp. readily or gladly <~ a cause> **b :** to avail oneself of **:** WELCOME <*embraced* the opportunity to study further> **4 a :** to take in or include as a part, item, or element of a more inclusive whole <charity ~*s* all acts that contribute to human welfare> **b :** to be equal or equivalent to <his assets *embraced* $10> ~ *vi* **:** to participate in an embrace ***syn* 1** see ADOPT ***ant*** spurn **2** see INCLUDE — **em·brace·able** \-ˈbrā-sə-bəl\ *adj* — **em·brace·ment** \-ˈbrā-smənt\ *n* — **em·brac·er** *n* — **em·brac·ing·ly** \-ˈbrā-siŋ-lē\ *adv*

2**embrace** *n* **1 :** a close encircling with the arms and pressure to the bosom esp. as a sign of affection **:** HUG **2 :** GRIP, ENCIRCLEMENT <helpless in the ~ of terror> **3 :** ACCEPTANCE <his ready ~ of new doctrines>

em·bra·ceor \im-ˈbrā-sər\ *n* [AF, fr. MF *embraseor* instigator, fr. *embraser* to set on fire, fr. *en-* + *brase, brese* live coals] **:** one guilty of embracery

em·brac·ery \im-ˈbrās-(ə-)rē\ *n, pl* **-er·ies** [ME, fr. AF *embraceor*] **:** an attempt to influence a jury corruptly (as by bribes or threats)

em·brac·ive \-ˈbrā-siv\ *adj* **1 :** disposed to embrace **2 :** INCLUSIVE, COMPREHENSIVE

em·branch·ment \im-ˈbranch-mənt\ *n* [F *embranchement,* fr. (*s'*)*embrancher* to branch out, fr. *en-* + *branche* branch] **1 :** a branching off or out (as of a valley) **2 :** BRANCH

em·bran·gle \im-ˈbraŋ-gəl\ *vt* **-gled; -gling** \-g(ə-)liŋ\ [*en-* + *brangle* (squabble)] **:** EMBROIL — **em·bran·gle·ment** \-gəl-mənt\ *n*

em·bra·sure \im-ˈbrā-zhər\ *n* [F, fr. obs. *embraser* to widen an opening] **1 :** a recess of a door or window **2 :** an opening with sides flaring outward in a wall or parapet of a fortification usu. for allowing the firing of cannon

em·brit·tle \im-ˈbrit-ᵊl\ *vb* **-brit·tled; -brit·tling** \-ˈbrit-liŋ, -ᵊl-iŋ\ *vt* **:** to make brittle ~ *vi* **:** to become brittle — **em·brit·tle·ment** \-ˈbrit-ᵊl-mənt\ *n*

em·bro·cate \ˈem-brə-ˌkāt\ *vt* **-cat·ed; -cat·ing** [LL *embrocatus,* pp. of *embrocare,* fr. Gk *embrochē* lotion, fr. *embrechein* to embrocate, fr. *en-* + *brechein* to wet] **:** to moisten and rub (a part of the body) with a lotion

em·bro·ca·tion \ˌem-brə-ˈkā-shən\ *n* **:** LINIMENT

embroglio *var of* IMBROGLIO

em·broi·der \im-ˈbrȯid-ər\ *vb* **em·broi·dered; em·broi·der·ing** \-(ə-)riŋ\ [ME *embroderen,* fr. MF *embroder,* fr. *en-* + *broder* to embroider, of Gmc origin; akin to OE *brord* point, *byrst* bristle] *vt* **1 a :** to ornament with needlework **b :** to form with needlework **2 :** to elaborate on **:** EMBELLISH ~ *vi* **1 :** to make embroidery **2 :** to provide embellishments **:** ELABORATE — **em·broi·der·er** \-ˈbrȯid-ər-ər\ *n*

em·broi·dery \im-ˈbrȯid-(ə-)rē\ *n, pl* **-der·ies 1 a :** the art or process of forming decorative designs with hand or machine needlework **b :** a design or decoration so formed **c :** an object decorated with embroidery **2 :** elaboration by use of decorative and often fictitious detail **3 :** something pleasing or desirable but unimportant <considered the humanities mere educational ~>

em·broil \im-ˈbrȯi(ə)l\ *vt* [F *embrouiller,* fr. MF, fr. *en-* + *brouiller* to broil] **1 :** to throw into disorder or confusion **2 :** to involve in conflict or difficulties — **em·broil·ment** \-mənt\ *n*

em·brown \im-ˈbrau̇n\ *vt* **1 :** DARKEN **2 :** to cause to turn brown

embrue *var of* IMBRUE

embry- *or* **embryo-** *comb form* [LL, fr. Gk, fr. *embryon*] **:** embryo <*embryo*geny>

em·bryo \ˈem-brē-ˌō\ *n, pl* **em·bry·os** [ML *embryon-, embryo,* fr. Gk *embryon,* fr. *en-* + *bryein* to swell; akin to Gk *bryon* moss] **1 a** *archaic* **:** a vertebrate at any stage of development prior to birth or hatching **b :** an animal in the early stages of growth and differentiation that are characterized by cleavage, the laying down of fundamental tissues, and the formation of primitive organs and organ systems; *esp* **:** the developing human individual from the time of implantation to the end of the eighth week after conception **2 :** the young sporophyte of a seed plant usu. comprising a rudimentary plant with plumule, radicle, and cotyledons **3 a :** something as yet undeveloped **b :** a beginning or undeveloped state of something <productions seen in ~ during their out-of-town tryout period —Henry Hewes>

em·bryo·gen·e·sis \ˌem-brē-ō-ˈjen-ə-səs\ *n* **:** the formation and development of the embryo — **em·bryo·ge·net·ic** \-jə-ˈnet-ik\ *adj*

em·bry·og·e·ny \ˌem-brē-ˈäj-ə-nē\ *n, pl* **-nies :** EMBRYOGENESIS — **em·bryo·gen·ic** \-brē-ō-ˈjen-ik\ *adj*

embryol *abbr* embryology

em·bry·ol·o·gy \ˌem-brē-ˈäl-ə-jē\ *n* [F *embryologie*] **1 :** a branch of biology dealing with embryos and their development **2 :** the features and phenomena exhibited in the formation and development of an embryo — **em·bry·o·log·ic** \-brē-ə-ˈläj-ik\ *or* **em·bry·o·log·i·cal** \-i-kəl\ *adj* **em·bry·o·log·i·cal·ly** \-i-k(ə-)lē\ *adv* — **em·bry·ol·o·gist** \-brē-ˈäl-ə-jəst\ *n*

embryon- *or* **embryoni-** *comb form* [ML *embryon-, embryo*] **:** embryo <*embryon*ic>

em·bry·o·nal \em-ˈbrī-ən-ᵊl\ *adj* **:** EMBRYONIC 1 — **em·bry·o·nal·ly** \-ˈbrī-ə-nə-lē\ *adv*

em·bry·o·nat·ed \ˈem-brē-ə-ˌnāt-əd\ *adj* **:** having an embryo

em·bry·on·ic \ˌem-brē-ˈän-ik\ *adj* **1 :** of or relating to an embryo **2 :** being in an early stage of development **:** INCIPIENT, RUDIMENTARY — **em·bry·on·i·cal·ly** \-i-k(ə-)lē\ *adv*

embryonic disk *n* **1 a :** BLASTODISC **b :** BLASTODERM **2 :** the part of the inner cell mass of a blastocyst from which the embryo of a placental mammal develops — called also *embryonic shield*

embryonic layer *n* **:** GERM LAYER

embryonic membrane *n* **:** a structure (as the amnion) that derives from the fertilized ovum but does not form a part of the embryo

em·bryo·phyte \'em-brē-ə-ˌfīt\ *n* : a plant (as a fern) producing an embryo and developing vascular tissues
embryo sac *n* : the female gametophyte of a seed plant consisting of a thin-walled sac within the nucellus that contains the egg nucleus and others which give rise to endosperm on fertilization
em·bry·ot·ic \ˌem-brē-'ät-ik\ *adj* [*embryo* + *-tic* (as in *patriotic*)] : EMBRYONIC 2
¹em·cee \'em-'sē\ *n* [*M. C.*] : MASTER OF CEREMONIES
²emcee *vb* **em·ceed; em·cee·ing** *vt* : to act as master of ceremonies of ~ *vi* : to act as master of ceremonies
Em·den *var of* EMBDEN
-eme \ˌēm\ *n suffix* [F *-ème* (fr. *phonème* speech sound, phoneme)] : significantly distinctive unit of language structure <tax*eme*>
emend \ē-'mend\ *vt* [ME *emenden,* fr. L *emendare* — more at AMEND] **1** *archaic* : to free from defects **2** : to correct usu. by textual alterations ***syn*** see CORRECT ***ant*** corrupt (*as a text*) — **emend·able** \-'men-də-bəl\ *adj* — **emend·er** *n*
emen·date \'ē-ˌmen-ˌdāt; 'em-ən-, -ˌen-\ *vt* **-dat·ed; -dat·ing** : EMEND 2 — **emen·da·tor** \-ˌdāt-ər\ *n* — **emen·da·to·ry** \ē-'men-də-ˌtōr-ē, -ˌtȯr-\ *adj*
emen·da·tion \ˌē-ˌmen-'dā-shən; ˌem-ən-, -ˌen-\ *n* **1** : the act of emending **2** : an alteration designed to correct or improve
emer *abbr* emeritus
¹em·er·ald \'em-(ə-)rəld\ *n* [ME *emerallde,* fr. MF *esmeralde,* fr. (assumed) VL *smaralda,* fr. L *smaragdus,* fr. Gk *smaragdos*] **1** : a rich green variety of beryl prized as a gemstone **2** : any of various green gemstones (as synthetic corundum or demantoid)
²emerald *adj* : brightly or richly green
emerald green *n* **1** : a clear bright green resembling that of the emerald **2** : any of various strong greens
emerge \i-'mərj\ *vi* **emerged; emerg·ing** [L *emergere,* fr. *e-* + *mergere* to plunge — more at MERGE] **1** : to rise from or as if from an enveloping fluid : come out into view **2** : to become manifest **3** : to rise from an obscure or inferior condition **4** : to come into being through evolution
emer·gence \i-'mər-jən(t)s\ *n* **1** : the act or an instance of emerging **2** : any of various superficial outgrowths of plant tissue usu. formed from both epidermis and immediately underlying tissues
emer·gen·cy \i-'mər-jən-sē\ *n, pl* **-cies 1** : an unforeseen combination of circumstances or the resulting state that calls for immediate action **2** : a pressing need ***syn*** see JUNCTURE
¹emer·gent \i-'mər-jənt\ *adj* [ME, fr. L *emergent-, emergens,* prp. of *emergere*] **1** : rising out of or as if out of a fluid **2 a** : arising unexpectedly **b** : calling for prompt action : URGENT **3** : arising as a natural or logical consequence **4** : newly formed <the ~ nations of Africa>
²emergent *n* **1** : something emergent **2 a** : a tree that rises above the surrounding forest **b** : a plant rooted in shallow water and having most of the vegetative growth above water
emergent evolution *n* : a biological and philosophical theory that new characters and qualities (as life and consciousness) appear in the evolutionary process at more complex organizational levels (as that of the molecule, the cell, and the organism) which cannot be predicted solely by studying less complex levels of organization but which are determined by a rearrangement of preexistent entities
emer·i·ta \i-'mer-ət-ə\ *adj* [L, fem. of *emeritus*] : EMERITUS — used of a woman <Professor *Emerita* Mary Smith>
¹emer·i·tus \i-'mer-ət-əs\ *adj* [L, pp. of *emereri* to serve out one's term, fr. *e-* + *mereri, merēre* to earn, deserve, serve — more at MERIT] **1** : holding after retirement an honorary title corresponding to that held last during active service **2** : retired from an office or position <professor ~> — converted to *emeriti* after a plural substantive <professors *emeriti*>
²emeritus *n, pl* **-i·ti** \-ə-ˌtī, -ˌtē\ : one retired from professional life but permitted to hold the rank of his last office as an honorary title
emersed \(ˈ)ē-'mərst\ *adj* : standing out of or rising above a surface (as of a fluid) <~ aquatic weeds>
emer·sion \(ˈ)ē-'mər-zhən, -shən\ *n* [L *emersus,* pp. of *emergere*] : an act of emerging : EMERGENCE
em·ery \'em-(ə-)rē\ *n, pl* **em·er·ies** *often attrib* [ME, fr. MF *emeri,* fr. OIt *smiriglio,* fr. ML *smiriglum,* fr. Gk *smyrid-, smyris*] : a dark granular mineral that consists essentially of corundum and is used for grinding and polishing; *also* : a hard abrasive powder
emery board *n* : a nail file made of cardboard covered with powdered emery
eme·sis \'em-ə-səs, i-'mē-\ *n, pl* **eme·ses** \-ˌsēz\ [NL, fr. Gk, fr. *emein*] : an act or instance of vomiting
emet·ic \i-'met-ik\ *n* [L *emetica,* fr. Gk *emetikē,* fr. fem. of *emetikos* causing vomiting, fr. *emein* to vomit — more at VOMIT] : an agent that induces vomiting — **emetic** *adj* — **emet·i·cal·ly** \-i-k(ə-)lē\ *adv*
em·e·tine \'em-ə-ˌtēn\ *n* : an amorphous alkaloid $C_{29}H_{40}N_2O_4$ extracted from ipecac root and used as an emetic and expectorant
émeute \ā-mœt\ *n, pl* **émeutes** *same*\ : an outbreak of disorder or violence; *esp* : a popular uprising
EMF *abbr* electromotive force
-emia *or* **-ae·mia** \'ē-mē-ə\ *also* **-he·mia** *or* **-hae·mia** \'hē-\ *n comb form* [NL *-emia, -aemia,* fr. Gk *-aimia,* fr. *haima* blood — more at HEM-] **1** : condition of having (such) blood <leuk*emia*> **2** : condition of having (a specified thing) in the blood <ur*emia*>
¹em·i·grant \'em-i-grənt\ *n* **1** : one who emigrates **2** : a migrant plant or animal
syn EMIGRANT, IMMIGRANT *shared meaning element* : one that leaves one place to settle in another
²emigrant *adj* : departing from a country to settle elsewhere
em·i·grate \'em-ə-ˌgrāt\ *vi* **-grat·ed; -grat·ing** [L *emigratus,* pp. of *emigrare,* fr. *e-* + *migrare* to migrate] : to leave one's place of abode or country for life or residence elsewhere — **em·i·gra·tion** \ˌem-ə-'grā-shən\ *n*
émi·gré *or* **emi·gré** \'em-i-ˌgrā, ˌem-i-'\ *n* [F *émigré,* fr. pp. of *émigrer* to emigrate, fr. L *emigrare*] : EMIGRANT; *esp* : a person forced to emigrate for political reasons
em·i·nence \'em-ə-nən(t)s\ *n* **1** : a position of prominence or superiority — used as a title for a cardinal **2** : something eminent, prominent, or lofty: as **a** : a person of high rank or attainments **b** : a natural elevation
émi·nence grise \ā-mē-nän-sə-grēz\ *n, pl* **éminences grises** *same*\ [F, lit., gray eminence, nickname of Père Joseph (François du Tremblay) †1638 F monk and diplomat, confidant of Cardinal Richelieu who was known as *Éminence Rouge* red eminence; fr. the colors of their respective habits] : a confidential agent; *esp* : one exercising unsuspected or unofficial power
em·i·nen·cy \'em-ə-nən-sē\ *n, pl* **-cies** : EMINENCE
em·i·nent \'em-ə-nənt\ *adj* [ME, fr. MF or L; MF, fr. L *eminent-, eminens,* prp. of *eminēre* to stand out, fr. *e-* + *-minēre* (akin to L *mont-, mons* mountain] **1** : standing out so as to be readily perceived or noted : CONSPICUOUS **2 a** : jutting out : PROJECTING **b** : LOFTY, TOWERING **3** : exhibiting eminence esp. in standing above others in some quality or position : PROMINENT ***syn*** see FAMOUS — **em·i·nent·ly** *adv*
eminent domain *n* : a right of a government to take private property for public use by virtue of the superior dominion of the sovereign power over all lands within its jurisdiction
emir \i-'mi(ə)r, ā-\ *n* [Ar *amīr* commander] : a native ruler in parts of Asia and Africa
emir·ate \i-'mir-ət, ā-, -'mi(ə)r-ˌāt\ *n* : the state or jurisdiction of an emir
em·is·sary \'em-ə-ˌser-ē\ *n, pl* **-sar·ies** [L *emissarius,* fr. *emissus,* pp. of *emittere*] **1** : one sent on a mission as the agent of another **2** : a secret agent
emis·sion \ē-'mish-ən\ *n* **1 a** : an act or instance of emitting : EMANATION **b** *archaic* : PUBLICATION **c** : a putting into circulation **2 a** : something sent forth by emitting: as (1) : electrons discharged from a surface (2) : electromagnetic waves radiated by an antenna or a celestial body (3) : substances discharged into the air (as by a smokestack or an automobile gasoline engine) **b** : EFFLUVIUM — **emis·sive** \-'mis-iv\ *adj*
emis·siv·i·ty \ˌem-ə-'siv-ət-ē, ˌē-ˌmis-'iv-\ *n, pl* **-ties** : the relative power of a surface to emit heat by radiation : the ratio of the radiant energy emitted by a surface to that emitted by a blackbody at the same temperature
emit \ē-'mit\ *vt* **emit·ted; emit·ting** [L *emittere* to send out, fr. *e-* + *mittere* to send — more at SMITE] **1 a** : to throw or give off or out (as light) **b** : to send out : EJECT **2 a** : to issue with authority; *esp* : to put (as money) into circulation **b** *obs* : PUBLISH **3** : to give utterance or voice to <*emitted* a groan> — **emit·ter** *n*
em·men·a·gogue \ə-'men-ə-ˌgäg, e-\ *n* [Gk *emmēna* menses (fr. neut. pl. of *emmēnos* monthly, fr. *en-* + *mēn* month) + E *-agogue* — more at MOON] : an agent that promotes the menstrual discharge
Em·men·ta·ler *or* **Em·men·tha·ler** \'em-ən-ˌtäl-ər\ *or* **Em·men·thal** \-ˌtäl\ *n* [G, fr. *Emmenthal,* Switzerland] : SWISS CHEESE
em·mer \'em-ər\ *n* [G, fr. OHG *amari*] : a hard red wheat (*Triticum dicoccum*) having spikelets with two kernels that remain in the glumes after threshing; *broadly* : a tetraploid wheat — called also *emmer wheat*
em·met \'em-ət\ *n* [ME *emete*] *chiefly dial* : ANT
Em·my \'em-ē\ *n, pl* **Emmys** [fr. alter. of *Immy,* nickname for *image orthicon* (a camera tube used in television)] : a statuette awarded annually by a professional organization for notable achievement in television
em·o·din \'em-ə-dən\ *n* [ISV *emodi-* (fr. NL *Rheum emodi,* species of rhubarb) + *-in*] : an orange crystalline phenolic compound $C_{15}H_{10}O_5$ that is obtained from plants (as rhubarb and cascara buckthorn) and is used as a laxative
¹emol·lient \i-'mäl-yənt\ *adj* [L *emollient-, emolliens,* prp. of *emollire* to soften, fr. *e-* + *mollis* soft — more at MELT] **1** : making soft or supple; *also* : soothing esp. to the skin or mucous membrane **2** : making less intense or harsh : MOLLIFYING <soothe us in our agonies with ~ words —H. L. Mencken>
²emollient *n* : something that softens or soothes
emol·u·ment \i-'mäl-yə-mənt\ *n* [ME, fr. L *emolumentum,* lit., miller's fee, fr. *emolere* to grind up, fr. *e-* + *molere* to grind — more at MEAL] **1** : the returns arising from office or employment usu. in the form of compensation or perquisites **2** *archaic* : ADVANTAGE ***syn*** see WAGE
emote \i-'mōt\ *vt* **emot·ed; emot·ing** [back-formation fr. *emotion*] : to give expression to emotion esp. in or as if in a play or movie
emo·tion \i-'mō-shən\ *n* [MF, fr. *emouvoir* to stir up, fr. L *exmovēre* to move away, disturb, fr. *ex-* + *movēre* to move] **1 a** *obs* : DISTURBANCE **b** : EXCITEMENT **2 a** : the affective aspect of consciousness : FEELING **b** : a state of feeling **c** : a psychic and physical reaction (as anger or fear) subjectively experienced as strong feeling and physiologically involving changes that prepare the body for immediate vigorous action ***syn*** see FEELING
emo·tion·al \-shnəl, -shən-ᵊl\ *adj* **1** : of or relating to emotion <an ~ disorder> **2** : dominated by or prone to emotion <an ~ person> **3** : appealing to or arousing emotion <an ~ sermon> **4** : markedly aroused or agitated in feeling or sensibilities <gets ~ at weddings> — **emo·tion·al·i·ty** \-ˌmō-shə-'nal-ət-ē\ *n* — **emo·tion·al·ly** \-ē\ *adv*
emo·tion·al·ism \i-'mō-shnə-ˌliz-əm, -shən-ᵊl-ˌiz-\ *n* **1** : undue indulgence in or display of emotion **2** : a tendency to regard things emotionally
emo·tion·al·ist \-shnə-ləst, -shən-ᵊl-əst\ *n* **1** : one who tends to rely on emotion as opposed to reason; *esp* : one who bases a theory or policy on an emotional conviction **2** : one given to emotionalism — **emo·tion·al·is·tic** \-ˌmō-shnə-'lis-tik, -shən-ᵊl-'is-\ *adj*
emo·tion·al·ize \i-'mō-shnə-ˌlīz, -shən-ᵊl-ˌīz\ *vt* **-ized; -iz·ing** : to give an emotional quality to
emo·tion·less \i-'mō-shən-ləs\ *adj* : showing or expressing no emotion <the colonel's words were short and ~ —*Infantry Jour.*> — **emo·tion·less·ness** *n*
emo·tive \i-'mōt-iv\ *adj* **1** : of or relating to the emotions **2** : appealing to or expressing emotion <the ~ use of language> — **emo·tive·ly** *adv* — **emo·tiv·i·ty** \i-ˌmō-'tiv-ət-ē, ˌē-ˌmō-\ *n*

emp *abbr* emperor; empress
empanel *var of* IMPANEL
em·pa·thet·ic \ˌem-pə-ˈthet-ik\ *adj* : EMPATHIC — **em·pa·thet·i·cal·ly** \-i-k(ə-)lē\ *adv*
em·path·ic \em-ˈpath-ik, im-\ *adj* : involving, characterized by, or based on empathy
em·pa·thize *vi* **-thized; -thiz·ing** : to experience empathy <adults unable to ~ with the frustrations of children>
em·pa·thy \ˈem-pə-thē\ *n* **1** : the imaginative projection of a subjective state into an object so that the object appears to be infused with it **2** : the capacity for participation in another's feelings or ideas ***syn*** see SYMPATHY
em·pen·nage \ˌäm-pə-ˈnäzh, ˌem-\ *n* [F, feathers of an arrow, empennage] : the tail assembly of an airplane
em·per·or \ˈem-pər-ər, -prər\ *n* [ME, fr. OF *empereor,* fr. L *imperator,* lit., commander, fr. *imperatus,* pp. of *imperare* to command, fr. *in-* + *parare* to prepare, order — more at PARE] : the sovereign or supreme monarch of an empire — **em·per·or·ship** \-ˌship\ *n*
em·pery \ˈem-p(ə-)rē\ *n, pl* **em·per·ies** [ME *emperie,* fr. OF, fr. *emperer* to command, fr. L *imperare*] : wide dominion : EMPIRE
em·pha·sis \ˈem(p)-fə-səs\ *n, pl* **em·pha·ses** \-ˌsēz\ [L, fr. Gk, exposition, emphasis, fr. *emphainein* to indicate, fr. *en-* + *phainein* to show — more at FANCY] **1 a** : force or intensity of expression that gives special impressiveness or importance to something <writing with ~ on the need for reform> **b** : a particular prominence given in reading or speaking to one or more words or syllables **2** : special consideration of or stress or insistence on something <the school's ~ on discipline>
em·pha·size \ˈem(p)-fə-ˌsīz\ *vt* **-sized; -siz·ing** : to give emphasis to : place emphasis on : STRESS <*emphasized* the need for reform>
em·phat·ic \im-ˈfat-ik, em-\ *adj* [Gk *emphatikos,* fr. *emphainein*] **1** : uttered with or marked by emphasis **2** : tending to express oneself in forceful speech or to take decisive action **3** : attracting special attention **4** : constituting or belonging to a set of tense forms in English consisting of the auxiliary *do* followed by an infinitive without *to* that are used to facilitate rhetorical inversion or to emphasize — **em·phat·i·cal·ly** \-ˈfat-i-k(ə-)lē\ *adv*
em·phy·se·ma \ˌem(p)-fə-ˈzē-mə, -ˈsē-\ *n* [NL, fr. Gk *emphysēma* bodily inflation] : a condition characterized by air-filled expansions of body tissues; *specif* : a condition of the lung marked by distension and frequently by impairment of heart action — **em·phy·se·ma·tous** \-ˈzem-ət-əs, -ˈsem-, -ˈzēm-, -ˈsēm-\ *adj*
em·pire \ˈem-ˌpī(ə)r\ *n* [ME, fr. OF *empire, empirie,* fr. L *imperium* absolute authority, empire, fr. *imperare* to command] **1 a (1)** : a major political unit having a territory of great extent or a number of territories or peoples under a single sovereign authority; *esp* : one having an emperor as chief of state **(2)** : the territory of such a political unit **b** : something held to resemble a political empire; *esp* : an extensive territory or enterprise under single domination or control <the beautiful heiress to a meat-packing ~ —*Punch*> **2** : imperial sovereignty, rule, or dominion
Em·pire \ˈäm-ˌpi(ə)r, ˈem-ˌpī(ə)r\ *adj* [F, fr. (*le premier*) *Empire* the first Empire of France] : of, relating to, or characteristic of a style (as of clothing or furniture) popular in early 19th century France
Em·pire Day \ˈem-ˌpī(ə)r-\ *n* : COMMONWEALTH DAY — used before the official adoption of *Commonwealth Day* in 1958
em·pir·ic \im-ˈpir-ik, em-\ *n* [L *empiricus,* fr. Gk *empeirikos* doctor relying on experience alone, fr. *empeiria* experience, fr. *en-* + *peiran* to attempt — more at FEAR] **1** *archaic* : CHARLATAN **2** : one who relies on practical experience
em·pir·i·cal \-i-kəl\ *also* **em·pir·ic** \-ik\ *adj* **1** : relying on experience or observation alone often without due regard for system and theory **2** : originating in or based on observation or experience <~ data> **3** : capable of being verified or disproved by observation or experiment <~ laws> — **em·pir·i·cal·ly** \-i-k(ə-)lē\ *adv*
empirical formula *n* : a chemical formula showing the simplest ratio of elements in a compound rather than the total number of atoms in the molecule <CH_2O is the *empirical formula* for glucose>
em·pir·i·cism \im-ˈpir-ə-ˌsiz-əm, em-\ *n* **1 a** : a former school of medical practice founded on experience without the aid of science or theory **b** : QUACKERY, CHARLATANRY **2 a** : the practice of relying on observation and experiment esp. in the natural sciences **b** : a tenet arrived at empirically **3 a** : a theory that all knowledge originates in experience **b** : LOGICAL POSITIVISM — **em·pir·i·cist** \-səst\ *n*
em·place \im-ˈplās\ *vt* [back-formation fr. *emplacement*] : to put into position <missiles *emplaced* around the city>
em·place·ment \-ˈplā-smənt\ *n* [F, fr. MF *emplacer* to emplace, fr. *en-* + *place*] **1** : the situation or location of something **2 a** : a prepared position for weapons or military equipment <radar ~*s*> **3** : a putting into position : PLACEMENT
em·plane \im-ˈplān\ *var of* ENPLANE
[1]**em·ploy** \im-ˈplȯi\ *vt* [ME *emploien,* fr. MF *emploier,* fr. L *implicare* to enfold, involve, implicate, fr. *in-* + *plicare* to fold — more at PLY] **1 a** : to make use of (someone or something inactive) <~ a fine pen to fill in the details> **b** : to occupy (as time) advantageously **c (1)** : to use or engage the services of **(2)** : to provide with a job that pays wages or a salary **2** : to devote to or direct toward a particular activity or person <~*ed* all her wiles to get him to propose> ***syn*** see USE — **em·ploy·er** *n*
[2]**employ** *n* **1** *archaic* **a** : USE **b** : OCCUPATION **2** : the state of being employed esp. for wages or a salary <in the government's ~>
[1]**em·ploy·able** \im-ˈplȯi-ə-bəl\ *adj* : capable of being employed — **em·ploy·abil·i·ty** \-ˌplȯi-ə-ˈbil-ət-ē\ *n*
[2]**employable** *n* : one who is employable
em·ploy·ee *or* **em·ploye** \im-ˌplȯ(i)-ˈē, (ˌ)em-; im-ˈplȯ(i)-ˌē, em-\ *n* : one employed by another usu. for wages or salary and in a position below the executive level
em·ploy·ment \im-ˈplȯi-mənt\ *n* **1** : USE, PURPOSE **2 a** : activity in which one engages or is employed <suitable ~ was hard to find> **b** : an instance of such activity **3** : the act of employing : the state of being employed
employment agency *n* : an agency whose business is to find jobs for people seeking them or to find people to fill jobs that are open
em·poi·son \im-ˈpȯiz-ᵊn\ *vt* [ME *empoysonen,* fr. MF *empoisoner,* fr. *en-* + *poison*] **1** *archaic* : POISON **2** : EMBITTER <a look of ~*ed* acceptance —Saul Bellow> — **em·poi·son·ment** \-mənt\ *n*
em·po·ri·um \im-ˈpōr-ē-əm, em-, -ˈpȯr-\ *n, pl* **-ri·ums** *also* **-ria** \-ē-ə\ [L, fr. Gk *emporion,* fr. *emporos* traveler, trader, fr. *en* in + *poros* passage, journey — more at IN, FARE] **1 a** : a place of trade; *esp* : a commercial center **b** : a usu. sizable place of business that serves customers **2** : a store carrying a diversity of merchandise
em·pow·er \im-ˈpau̇(-ə)r\ *vt* : to give official authority or legal power to ***syn*** see ENABLE — **em·pow·er·ment** \-mənt\ *n*
em·press \ˈem-prəs\ *n* [ME *emperesse,* fr. OF, fem. of *empereor* emperor] **1** : the wife or widow of an emperor **2** : a woman who holds an imperial title in her own right
em·presse·ment \äⁿ-pres-(ə-)mäⁿ\ *n* [F, fr. (*s'*)*empresser* to hurry, fr. *en-* + *presser* to press] : demonstrative warmth or cordiality
em·prise \em-ˈprīz\ *n* [ME, fr. MF, fr. OF, fr. *emprendre* to undertake, fr. (assumed) VL *imprehendere,* fr. L *in-* + *prehendere* to seize] : UNDERTAKING, ENTERPRISE; *esp* : an adventurous, daring, or chivalric enterprise
[1]**emp·ty** \ˈem(p)-tē\ *adj* [ME, fr. OE *ǣmettig* unoccupied, fr. *ǣmetta* leisure, fr. *ǣ-* without + *-metta* (fr. *mōtan* to have to) — more at MUST] **1 a** : containing nothing **b** : not occupied or inhabited **c** : UNFREQUENTED **d** : not pregnant <~ heifer> **e** : NULL 4a <the ~ set> **2 a** : lacking reality, substance, or value : HOLLOW <an ~ pleasure> **b** : destitute of effect or force **c** : devoid of sense : FOOLISH **3** : HUNGRY **4 a** : IDLE <~ hours> **b** : having no purpose or result : USELESS **5** : marked by the absence of human life, activity, or comfort — **emp·ti·ly** \-tə-lē\ *adv* — **emp·ti·ness** \-tē-nəs\ *n*
syn **1** EMPTY, VACANT, BLANK, VOID, VACUOUS *shared meaning element* : lacking contents which could or should be present. EMPTY implies a complete absence of contents, especially of usual or normal contents; VACANT, an absence of appropriate contents or occupants <an *empty* bucket> <his purse was *empty*> <a *vacant* apartment> <*vacant* professorships> BLANK stresses the absence of any significant, relieving, or intelligible features on a surface <the window faced a *blank* wall> Sometimes the word implies a vacancy intended to be filled; thus, a *blank* sheet of paper is one available for writing on. VOID implies absolute emptiness to the senses <the *void,* hollow, universal air —P. B. Shelley> VACUOUS suggests the emptiness of a vacuum and is often applied hyperbolically to what lacks intelligence or significance <there was nothing to be read in the *vacuous* face, blank as a school notice-board out of term —Graham Greene> ***ant*** full
2 see VAIN
[2]**empty** *vb* **emp·tied; emp·ty·ing** *vt* **1 a** : to make empty : remove the contents of **b** : DEPRIVE, DIVEST **c** : to discharge (itself) of contents **2** : to remove from what holds or encloses **3** : to transfer by emptying ~ *vi* **1** : to become empty **2** : to discharge its contents <the river *empties* into the ocean>
[3]**empty** *n, pl* **empties** : something that is empty: as **a** : an empty container **b** : an unoccupied vehicle
emp·ty-hand·ed \ˌem(p)-tē-ˈhan-dəd\ *adj* **1** : having or bringing nothing **2** : having acquired or gained nothing <came back ~>
emp·ty-head·ed \-ˈhed-əd\ *adj* : SCATTERBRAINED
em·pur·ple \im-ˈpər-pəl\ *vb* **em·pur·pled; em·pur·pling** \-ˈpər-p(ə-)liŋ\ *vt* : to tinge or color purple ~ *vi* : to become purple
em·py·ema \ˌem-ˌpī-ˈē-mə\ *n, pl* **-ema·ta** \-mət-ə\ *or* **-emas** [LL, fr. Gk *empyēma*] : the presence of pus in a bodily cavity — **em·py·emic** \-mik\ *adj*
em·py·re·al \ˌem-ˌpī-ˈrē-əl, -pə-; em-ˈpir-ē-əl, -ˈpī-rē-\ *adj* [LL *empyrius, empyreus,* fr. LGk *empyrios,* fr. Gk *en* in + *pyr* fire] **1** : of or relating to the empyrean : CELESTIAL **2** : SUBLIME
[1]**em·py·re·an** \-ən\ *adj* : EMPYREAL
[2]**empyrean** *n* **1 a** : the highest heaven or heavenly sphere in ancient and medieval cosmology usu. consisting of fire or light **b** : the true and ultimate heavenly paradise **2** : FIRMAMENT, HEAVENS
em quad *n* [fr. its use for the letter *m*] : a quad whose point dimension and set dimension are the same or very nearly the same : a quad with a square or almost square body
[1]**emu** \ˈē-(ˌ)myü\ *n* [modif. of Pg *ema* rhea] **1** : a swift-running Australian bird (*Dromiceius novae-hollandiae*) with undeveloped wings that is related to and smaller than the ostrich **2** : any of various tall flightless birds (as the rhea)

emu 1

[2]**emu** *abbr* electromagnetic unit
[1]**em·u·late** \ˈem-yə-ˌlāt\ *vt* **-lat·ed; -lat·ing** [L *aemulatus,* pp. of *aemulari,* fr. *aemulus* rivaling] **1 a** : to strive to equal or excel **b** : IMITATE; *specif* : to imitate by means of an emulator **2** : to equal or approach equality with ***syn*** see RIVAL
[2]**em·u·late** \-lət\ *adj, obs* : EMULOUS 1a <pricked on by a most ~ pride —Shak.>
em·u·la·tion \ˌem-yə-ˈlā-shən\ *n* **1** : ambition or endeavor to equal or excel others (as in achievement) **2 a** : IMITATION **b** : the use of or technique of using an emulator **3** *obs* : ambitious or envious rivalry — **em·u·la·tive** \ˈem-yə-ˌlāt-iv\ *adj* — **em·u·la·tive·ly** *adv*
em·u·la·tor \ˈem-yə-ˌlāt-ər\ *n* **1** : one that emulates **2** : a hardware device or a combination of hardware and software that

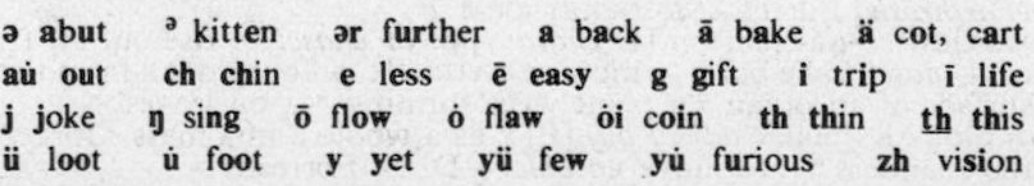

permits programs written for one computer to be run on another usu. newer computer

em·u·lous \'em-yə-ləs\ *adj* **1 a :** ambitious or eager to emulate **b :** inspired by or deriving from a desire to emulate **2** *obs* **:** JEALOUS — **em·u·lous·ly** *adv* — **em·u·lous·ness** *n*

emul·si·ble \i-'məl-sə-bəl\ *adj* [L, *emulsus,* pp. + E *-ible*] **:** capable of being emulsified

emul·si·fi·er \i-'məl-sə-ˌfī(-ə)r\ *n* **:** one that emulsifies; *esp* **:** a surface-active agent (as a soap) promoting the formation and stabilization of an emulsion

emul·si·fy \-ˌfī\ *vt* **-fied; -fy·ing :** to convert (as an oil) into an emulsion — **emul·si·fi·able** \-ˌfī-ə-bəl\ *adj* — **emul·si·fi·ca·tion** \i-ˌməl-sə-fə-'kā-shən\ *n*

emul·sion \i-'məl-shən\ *n* [NL *emulsion-, emulsio,* fr. L *emulsus,* pp. of *emulgēre* to milk out, fr. *e-* + *mulgēre* to milk; akin to OE *melcan* to milk, Gk *amelgein*] **1 a :** a system (as fat in milk) consisting of a liquid dispersed with or without an emulsifier in an immiscible liquid usu. in droplets of larger than colloidal size **b :** the state of such a system **2 :** SUSPENSION 2b(3); *esp* **:** a suspension of a sensitive silver salt or a mixture of silver halides in a viscous medium (as a gelatin solution) forming a coating on photographic plates, film, or paper — **emul·sive** \-'məl-siv\ *adj*

emul·soid \i-'məl-ˌsȯid\ *n* **1 :** a colloidal system consisting of a liquid dispersed in a liquid **2 :** a lyophilic sol (as a gelatin solution) — **emul·soi·dal** \-ˌməl-'sȯid-ᵊl\ *adj*

emunc·to·ry \i-'məŋ(k)-t(ə-)rē\ *n, pl* **-ries** [NL *emunctorium,* fr. L *emunctus,* pp. of *emungere* to clean the nose, fr. *e-* + *-mungere* (akin to *mucus*)] **:** an organ (as a kidney) or part of the body (as the skin) that carries off body wastes

en \'en\ *n* **1 :** the letter *n* **2 :** the set dimension of an en quad

[1]**en-** *also* **em-** \e *also occurs in these prefixes although only* i *may be shown as in "engage"*\ *prefix* [ME, fr. OF, fr. L *in-, im-,* fr. *in*] **1 :** put into or on to <*en*cradle> <*en*throne> **:** cover with <*en*verdure> **:** go into or on to <*em*bus> — in verbs formed from nouns **2 :** cause to be <*en*slave> — in verbs formed from adjectives or nouns **3 :** provide with <*em*power> — in verbs formed from nouns **4 :** so as to cover <*en*wrap> **:** thoroughly <*en*tangle> — in verbs formed from verbs; in all senses usu. *em-* before *b, m,* or *p*

[2]**en-** *also* **em-** *prefix* [ME, fr. L, fr. Gk, fr. *en* in — more at IN] **:** in **:** within <*en*zootic> — usu. *em-* before *b, m,* or *p* <*em*pathy>

[3]**en-** *comb form* [ISV, fr. *-ene*] **:** chemically unsaturated; *esp* **:** having one double bond <*en*amine>

[1]**-en** \ən, ᵊn\ *also* **-n** \n\ *adj suffix* [ME, fr. OE; akin to OHG *-īn* made of, L *-īnus* of or belonging to, Gk *-inos* made of, of or belonging to] **:** made of **:** consisting of <earth*en*> <silver*n*>

[2]**-en** *vb suffix* [ME *-nen,* fr. OE *-nian;* akin to OHG *-inōn* -en] **1 a :** cause to be <sharp*en*> **b :** cause to have <length*en*> **2 a :** come to be <steep*en*> **b :** come to have <length*en*>

en·able \in-'ā-bəl\ *vt* **en·abled; en·abling** \-b(ə-)liŋ\ **1 a :** to provide with the means or opportunity <training that ~*s* men to earn a living> **b :** to make possible, practical, or easy **2 :** to give legal power, capacity, or sanction to <legislation *enabling* the admission of a state>
syn ENABLE, EMPOWER *shared meaning element* **:** to make one able to do something

en·act \in-'akt\ *vt* **1 :** to establish by legal and authoritative act; *specif* **:** to make (as a bill) into law **2 :** to act out **:** REPRESENT <~ a role> — **en·ac·tor** \-'ak-tər\ *n*

en·act·ment \-'ak(t)-mənt\ *n* **1 :** the act of enacting **:** the state of being enacted **2 :** something (as a law) that has been enacted

[1]**enam·el** \in-'am-əl\ *vt* **-eled** *or* **-elled; -el·ing** *or* **-el·ling** \-(ə-)liŋ\ [ME *enamelen,* fr. MF *enamailler,* fr. *en-* + *esmail* enamel, of Gmc origin; akin to OHG *smelzan* to melt — more at SMELT] **1 :** to cover, inlay, or decorate with enamel **2 :** to beautify with a colorful surface **3 :** to form a glossy surface on (as paper, leather, or cloth) — **enam·el·er** \-(ə-)lər\ *n* — **enam·el·ist** \-ə-ləst\ *n*

[2]**enamel** *n* **1 :** a usu. opaque vitreous composition applied by fusion to the surface of metal, glass, or pottery **2 :** a surface or outer covering that resembles enamel **3 a :** something that is enameled **b :** ENAMELWARE **4 :** a cosmetic intended to give a smooth or glossy appearance **5 :** a calcareous substance that forms a thin layer capping the teeth **6 :** a paint that flows out to a smooth coat when applied and that dries with a glossy appearance

1

1, enamel 5

enam·el·ware \in-'am-əl-ˌwa(ə)r, -ˌwe(ə)r\ *n* **:** metalware (as kitchen utensils) coated with enamel

en·amine \'en-ə-ˌmēn\ *n* **:** an amine containing the double bond linkage C=C−N

en·am·or \in-'am-ər\ *vt* **en·am·ored; en·am·or·ing** \-(ə-)riŋ\ [ME *enamouren,* fr. OF *enamourer,* fr. *en-* + *amour* love — more at AMOUR] **:** to inflame with love **:** CHARM — usu. used in the passive with *of*

en·am·our *chiefly Brit var of* ENAMOR

en·an·tio·mer \in-'ant-ē-ə-mər\ *n* [Gk *enantios* + E *-mer*] **:** ENANTIOMORPH — **en·an·tio·mer·ic** \-ˌant-ē-ə-'mer-ik\ *adj*

en·an·tio·morph \in-'ant-ē-ə-ˌmȯrf\ *n* [Gk *enantios* opposite (fr. *enanti* facing, fr. *en* in + *anti* against) + ISV *-morph*] **:** either of a pair of chemical compounds or crystals whose molecular structures have a mirror-image relationship to each other — **en·an·tio·mor·phic** \-ˌant-ē-ə-'mȯr-fik\ *adj* — **en·an·tio·mor·phism** \-'mȯr-ˌfiz-əm\ *n* — **en·an·tio·mor·phous** \-'mȯr-fəs\ *adj*

en·ar·thro·sis \ˌen-ˌär-'thrō-səs\ *n, pl* **-thro·ses** \-ˌsēz\ [NL, fr. Gk *enarthrōsis*] **:** BALL-AND-SOCKET JOINT 2

ena·tion \i-'nā-shən\ *n* [L *enatus,* pp. of *enasci* to rise out of, fr. *e-* + *nasci* to be born — more at NATION] **:** an outgrowth from the surface of an organ <a plant virus forming ~*s* on leaves>

en bloc \äⁿ-'bläk\ *adv or adj* [F] **:** as a whole **:** in a mass <forced the islanders . . . to move *en bloc* —D. B. Forrester>

enc *or* **encl** *abbr* enclosure

En·cae·nia \en-'sē-nyə\ *n pl but sing or pl in constr* [NL, fr. L, dedication festival, fr. Gk *enkainia,* fr. *en* in + *kainos* new — more at IN, RECENT] **:** an annual university ceremony (as at Oxford) of commemoration with recital of poems and essays and conferring of degrees

en·cage \in-'kāj\ *vt* **:** CAGE 1

en·camp \in-'kamp\ *vt* **:** to place or establish in a camp ~ *vi* **:** to set up or occupy a camp

en·camp·ment \-mənt\ *n* **1 :** the act of encamping **:** the state of being encamped **2 a :** the place where a group (as a body of troops) is encamped **b :** the individuals that make up an encampment

en·cap·su·late \in-'kap-sə-ˌlāt\ *vb* **-lat·ed; -lat·ing** *vt* **1 :** to enclose in or as if in a capsule **2 :** EPITOMIZE, CONDENSE <~ a period of history> ~ *vi* **:** to become encapsulated — **en·cap·su·la·tion** \-ˌkap-sə-'lā-shən\ *n*

en·cap·su·lat·ed *adj* **:** surrounded by a gelatinous or membranous envelope <~ water bacteria>

en·cap·sule \in-'kap-səl, -(ˌ)sül\ *vt* **-suled; -sul·ing :** ENCAPSULATE

en·case \in-'kās\ *vt* **:** to enclose in or as if in a case

en·case·ment \in-'kā-smənt\ *n* **1 a :** the act or process of encasing **:** the state of being encased **b :** CASE, COVERING **2 :** the supposed enclosure in a living germ of the germs of all future generations that might develop from it

en·cash \in-'kash\ *vt, Brit* **:** CASH — **en·cash·ment** \-mənt\ *n, Brit*

en·caus·tic \in-'kȯ-stik\ *n* [*encaustic,* adj., fr. L *encausticus,* fr. Gk *enkaustikos,* fr. *enkaiein* to burn in, fr. *en-* + *kaiein* to burn — more at CAUSTIC] **1 :** a paint made from pigment mixed with melted beeswax and resin and after application fixed by heat **2 :** the method involving the use of encaustic; *also* **:** a work produced by this method — **encaustic** *adj*

-ence \ən(t)s, ᵊn(t)s\ *n suffix* [ME, fr. OF, fr. L *-entia,* fr. *-ent-, -ens,* prp. ending + *-ia* -y] **1 :** action or process <emerg*ence*> **:** instance of an action or process <refer*ence*> **2 :** quality or state <despond*ence*>

[1]**en·ceinte** \äⁿ(n)-'saⁿt\ *adj* [MF, fr. (assumed) VL *incienta,* alter. of L *incient-, inciens* being with young, fr. *in* + *-cient, -ciens* (akin to Gk *kyein* to be pregnant) — more at CAVE] **:** being with child **:** PREGNANT

[2]**enceinte** *n* [F, fr. OF, enclosing wall, fr. *enceindre* to surround, fr. L *incingere,* fr. *in-* + *cingere* to gird — more at CINCTURE] **:** a line of fortification enclosing a castle or town; *also* **:** the area or town so enclosed

encephal- *or* **encephalo-** *comb form* [F *encéphal-,* fr. Gk *enkephal-,* fr. *enkephalos*] **:** brain <*encephal*itis> <*encephalo*cele>

en·ce·phal·ic \ˌen(t)-sə-'fal-ik\ *adj* **:** of or relating to the brain; *also* **:** lying within the cranial cavity

en·ceph·a·li·tis \in-ˌsef-ə-'līt-əs\ *n, pl* **-lit·i·des** \-'lit-ə-ˌdēz\ **:** inflammation of the brain — **en·ceph·a·lit·ic** \-'lit-ik\ *adj*

en·ceph·a·li·to·gen·ic \-ˌlīt-ə-'jen-ik\ *adj* **:** tending to cause encephalitis <an ~ strain of a virus>

en·ceph·a·lo·gram \in-'sef-ə-lə-ˌgram\ *n* [ISV] **:** an X-ray picture of the brain made by encephalography

en·ceph·a·lo·graph \-ˌgraf\ *n* **1 :** ENCEPHALOGRAM **2 :** ELECTROENCEPHALOGRAPH

en·ceph·a·log·ra·phy \in-ˌsef-ə-'läg-rə-fē\ *n* [ISV] **:** roentgenography of the brain after the cerebrospinal fluid has been replaced by a gas (as air)

en·ceph·a·lo·my·eli·tis \in-ˌsef-ə-lō-ˌmī-ə-'līt-əs\ *n* [NL] **:** concurrent inflammation of the brain and spinal cord; *specif* **:** any of several virus diseases of horses

en·ceph·a·lo·myo·car·di·tis \-ˌmī-ə-kär-'dīt-əs\ *n* **:** an acute febrile virus disease characterized by degeneration and inflammation of skeletal and cardiac muscle and lesions of the central nervous system

en·ceph·a·lon \in-'sef-ə-ˌlän, -lən\ *n, pl* **-la** \-lə\ [NL, fr. Gk *enkephalos,* fr. *en* in + *kephalē* head — more at IN, CEPHALIC] **:** the vertebrate brain

en·ceph·a·lop·a·thy \in-ˌsef-ə-'läp-ə-thē\ *n* **:** a disease of the brain; *esp* **:** one involving alterations of brain structure — **en·ceph·a·lo·path·ic** \-lə-'path-ik\ *adj*

en·chain \in-'chān\ *vt* [ME *encheynen,* fr. MF *enchainer,* fr. OF, fr. *en-* + *chaeine* chain] **:** to bind or hold with or as if with chains — **en·chain·ment** \-mənt\ *n*

en·chant \in-'chant\ *vt* [ME *enchanten,* fr. MF *enchanter,* fr. L *incantare,* fr. *in-* + *cantare* to sing — more at CHANT] **1 :** to influence by charms and incantation **:** BEWITCH **2 :** to attract and move deeply **:** rouse to ecstatic admiration <the scene ~*ed* her to the point of tears —Elinor Wylie> *syn* see ATTRACT *ant* disenchant

en·chant·er *n* **:** one that enchants; *esp* **:** SORCERER

en·chant·ing *adj* **:** CHARMING — **en·chant·ing·ly** \-iŋ-lē\ *adv*

en·chant·ment \in-'chant-mənt\ *n* **1 a :** the act or art of enchanting **b :** the quality or state of being enchanted **2 :** something that enchants

en·chant·ress \in-'chan-trəs\ *n* **1 :** a woman who practices magic **:** SORCERESS **2 :** a fascinating woman

en·chase \in-'chās\ *vt* **en·chased; en·chas·ing** [ME *enchasen* to emboss, fr. MF *enchasser* to enshrine, set, fr. *en-* + *chasse* reliquary, fr. L *capsa* case — more at CASE] **1 :** SET <~ a gem> **2 :** ORNAMENT: as **a :** to cut or carve in relief **b :** INLAY

en·chi·la·da \ˌen-chə-'läd-ə\ *n* [AmerSp] **:** a tortilla on which meat filling is spread and which is rolled up and covered with chili-seasoned tomato sauce

en·chi·rid·i·on \ˌen-ˌkī-'rid-ē-ən\ *n, pl* **-rid·ia** \-ē-ə\ [LL, fr. Gk *encheiridion,* fr. *en* in + *cheir* hand — more at IN, CHIR-] **:** HANDBOOK, MANUAL

-en·chy·ma \'eŋ-kə-mə\ *n comb form, pl* **-en·chy·ma·ta** \ən-'kim-ət-ə, -'kī-mət-\ *or* **-enchymas** [NL, fr. *parenchyma*] **:** cellular tissue <coll*enchyma*>

en·ci·pher \in-'sī-fər, en-\ *vt* **:** to convert (a message) into cipher — **en·ci·pher·er** \-fər-ər\ *n* — **en·ci·pher·ment** \-fər-mənt\ *n*

en·cir·cle \in-'sər-kəl\ *vt* **1 :** to form a circle around : SURROUND **2 :** to pass completely around — **en·cir·cle·ment** \-mənt\ *n*
en·clasp \in-'klasp\ *vt* : to seize and hold : EMBRACE
en·clave \'en-ˌklāv; 'än-ˌklāv, 'äŋ-, -ˌkläv\ *n* [F, fr. MF, fr. *enclaver* to enclose, fr. (assumed) VL *inclavare* to lock up, fr. L *in-* + *clavis* key — more at CLAVICLE] **1 :** a territorial or culturally distinct unit enclosed within foreign territory <ethnic ~*s*> **2 :** a small often relict community of one kind of plant in an opening of a larger plant community
en·clit·ic \en-'klit-ik\ *adj* [LL *encliticus,* fr. Gk *enklitikos,* fr. *enklinesthai* to lean on, fr. *en-* + *klinein* to lean — more at LEAN] *of a word or particle* : being without independent accent and treated in pronunciation as forming a part of the preceding word <*thee* in *prithee* and *not* in *cannot* are ~> — **enclitic** *n*
en·close \in-'klōz\ *vt* [ME *enclosen,* prob. fr. *enclos* enclosed, fr. MF, pp. of *enclore* to enclose, fr. (assumed) VL *inclaudere,* alter. of L *includere* — more at INCLUDE] **1 a** (1) : to close in : SURROUND <~ a porch with glass> (2) : to fence off (common land) for individual use **b :** to hold in : CONFINE **2 :** to include along with something else in a parcel or envelope <a check is *enclosed* herewith>
en·clo·sure \in-'klō-zhər\ *n* **1 :** the act or action of enclosing : the quality or state of being enclosed **2 :** something that encloses **3 :** something enclosed <a letter with two ~*s*>
en·code \in-'kōd, en-\ *vt* : to convert (as a body of information) from one system of communication into another; *esp* : to convert (a message) into code — **en·cod·er** *n*
en·co·mi·ast \en-'kō-mē-ˌast, -mē-əst\ *n* [Gk *enkōmiastēs,* fr. *enkōmiazein* to praise, fr. *enkōmion*] : one that praises : EULOGIST — **en·co·mi·as·tic** \-ˌkō-mē-'as-tik\ *adj*
en·co·mi·um \en-'kō-mē-əm\ *n, pl* **-mi·ums** *or* **-mia** \-mē-ə\ [L, fr. Gk *enkōmion,* fr. *en* in + *kōmos* revel, celebration — more at IN, COMEDY] : glowing and warmly enthusiastic praise; *also* : an expression of this
syn ENCOMIUM, EULOGY, PANEGYRIC, TRIBUTE, CITATION *shared meaning element* : a formal expression of praise
en·com·pass \in-'kəm-pəs *also* -'käm-\ *vt* **1 a :** to form a circle about : ENCLOSE **b** *obs* : to go completely around **2 a :** ENVELOP **b :** INCLUDE <a plan that ~*es* a number of aims> **3 :** to bring about : ACCOMPLISH <~ a task> — **en·com·pass·ment** \-pə-smənt\ *n*
[1]**en·core** \'än-ˌkō(ə)r, -ˌkȯ(ə)r\ *n* [F, still, again] : a demand for repetition or reappearance made by an audience; *also* : a reappearance or additional performance in response to such a demand
[2]**encore** *vt* **en·cored; en·cor·ing :** to request an encore of or by
[1]**en·coun·ter** \in-'kaunt-ər\ *vb* **en·coun·tered; en·coun·ter·ing** \-'kaunt-ə-riŋ, -'kaun-triŋ\ [ME *encountren,* fr. OF *encontrer,* fr. ML *incontrare,* fr. LL *incontra* toward, fr. L *in-* + *contra* against — more at COUNTER] *vt* **1 a :** to meet as an adversary or enemy **b :** to engage in conflict with **2 :** to come upon face to face **3 :** to come upon unexpectedly ~ *vi* : to meet esp. by chance
[2]**encounter** *n* **1 a :** a meeting between hostile factions or persons **b :** a sudden often violent clash : COMBAT **2 a :** a chance meeting **b :** a direct often momentary meeting **3 :** a coming into the vicinity of a celestial body <the Martian ~ of a spacecraft>
encounter group *n* : a usu. leaderless and unstructured group that seeks to develop the capacity of the individual to openly express human feelings and to form close emotional ties by more or less unrestrained confrontation of individuals (as by physical contact, uninhibited verbalization, or nudity)
en·cour·age \in-'kər-ij, -'kə-rij\ *vt* **-aged; -ag·ing** [ME *encoragen,* fr. MF *encoragier,* fr. OF, fr. *en-* + *corage* courage] **1 :** to inspire with courage, spirit, or hope : HEARTEN **2 :** to spur on : STIMULATE **3 :** to give help or patronage to : FOSTER — **en·cour·ag·er** *n*
en·cour·age·ment \-ij-mənt, -rij-\ *n* **1 :** the act of encouraging : the state of being encouraged **2 :** something that encourages
en·cour·ag·ing *adj* : giving hope or promise : INSPIRITING — **en·cour·ag·ing·ly** \-iŋ-lē\ *adv*
en·crim·son \in-'krim-zən\ *vt* : to make or dye crimson
en·croach \in-'krōch\ *vi* [ME *encrochen* to get, seize, fr. MF *encrochier,* fr. OF, fr. *en-* + *croc, croche* hook — more at CROCHET] **1 :** to enter by gradual steps or by stealth into the possessions or rights of another **2 :** to advance beyond the usual or proper limits <the gradually ~*ing* sea> ***syn*** see TRESPASS — **en·croach·er** *n* — **en·croach·ment** \-'krōch-mənt\ *n*
en·crust \in-'krəst\ *vb* [prob. fr. L *incrustare,* fr. *in-* + *crusta* crust] *vt* : to cover, line, or overlay with a crust ~ *vi* : to form a crust
en·crus·ta·tion \(ˌ)in-ˌkrəs-'tā-shən, ˌen-\ *var of* INCRUSTATION
en·crypt \in-'kript, en-\ *vt* **1 :** ENCIPHER **2 :** ENCODE — **en·cryp·tion** \-'krip-shən\ *n*
en·cum·ber \in-'kəm-bər\ *vt* **en·cum·bered; en·cum·ber·ing** \-b(ə-)riŋ\ [ME *encombren,* fr. MF *encombrer,* fr. OF, fr. *en-* + (assumed) OF *combre* abatis] **1 :** to weigh down : BURDEN **2 :** to impede or hamper the function or activity of : HINDER **3 :** to burden with a legal claim (as a mortgage) <~ an estate>
en·cum·brance \in-'kəm-brən(t)s\ *n* : something that encumbers : IMPEDIMENT **2 :** a claim (as a mortgage) against property
en·cum·branc·er \-brən-sər\ *n* : one that holds an encumbrance
ency *or* **encyc** *abbr* encyclopedia
-en·cy \ən-sē, ᵊn-\ *n suffix* [ME *-encie,* fr. L *-entia* — more at -ENCE] : quality or state <despond*ency*>
[1]**en·cyc·li·cal** \in-'sik-li-kəl, en-\ *adj* [LL *encyclicus,* fr. Gk *enkyklios* circular, general, fr. *en* in + *kyklos* circle — more at IN, WHEEL] : addressed to all the individuals of a group : GENERAL
[2]**encyclical** *n* : an encyclical letter; *specif* : a papal letter to the bishops of the church as a whole or to those in one country
en·cy·clo·pe·dia *also* **en·cy·clo·pae·dia** \in-ˌsī-klə-'pēd-ē-ə\ *n* [ML *encyclopaedia* course of general education, fr. Gk *enkyklios paideia* general education] : a work that contains information on all branches of knowledge or treats comprehensively a particular branch of knowledge usu. in articles arranged alphabetically by subject
en·cy·clo·pe·dic *also* **en·cy·clo·pae·dic** \-'pēd-ik\ *adj* : of, relating to, or suggestive of an encyclopedia or its methods of treating or covering a subject : COMPREHENSIVE <an ~ mind> — **en·cy·clo·pe·di·cal·ly** \-i-k(ə-)lē\ *adv*
en·cy·clo·pe·dism \-'pē-ˌdiz-əm\ *n* : encyclopedic knowledge
en·cy·clo·pe·dist \-'pēd-əst\ *n* **1 :** one who compiles or writes for an encyclopedia **2** *often cap* : one of the writers of a French encyclopedia (1751-80) who were identified with the Enlightenment and advocated deism and scientific rationalism
en·cyst \in-'sist, en-\ *vt* : to enclose in or as if in a cyst ~ *vi* : to form or become enclosed in a cyst — **en·cyst·ment** \-'sis(t)-mənt\ *n*
en·cys·ta·tion \ˌen-ˌsis-'tā-shən\ *n* : the process of forming a cyst or becoming enclosed in a capsule
[1]**end** \'end\ *n* [ME *ende,* fr. OE; akin to OHG *enti* end, L *ante* before, Gk *anti* against] **1 a :** the part of an area that lies at the boundary **b** (1) : a point that marks the extent of something (2) : the point where something ceases to exist <world without ~> **c :** the extreme or last part lengthwise : TIP **d :** the terminal unit of something spatial that is marked off by units **e :** a player stationed at the extremity of a line (as in football) **2 a :** cessation of a course of action, pursuit, or activity **b :** DEATH, DESTRUCTION **c** (1) : the ultimate state (2) : RESULT, ISSUE **d :** the complex of events, parts, or sections that forms an extremity, termination, or finish **3 :** something incomplete, fragmentary, or undersized : REMNANT **4 a :** the goal toward which an agent acts or should act **b :** the object by virtue of or for the sake of which an event takes place **5 a :** a share in an undertaking <kept his ~ up> **b :** a particular phase of an undertaking or organization <the advertising ~ of a business> **6 :** something that is extreme : ULTIMATE — used with *the* **7 :** a period of action or activity in any of various sports events; *specif* : a turn for an individual or team — **end·ed** \'en-dəd\ *adj*
syn* 1** END, TERMINATION, ENDING, TERMINUS *shared meaning element* : the point or line beyond which something does not or cannot go ***ant beginning
2 see INTENTION
— **in the end :** after all : ULTIMATELY — **no end :** EXCEEDINGLY — **on end 1 :** with the end down : UPRIGHT <turn a box *on end*> **2 :** without a stop or letup <it rained for days *on end*>
[2]**end** *vt* **1 a :** to bring to an end **b :** DESTROY **2 :** to make up the end of ~ *vi* **1 a :** to come to an end **b :** to reach a specified ultimate rank or situation — often used with *up* <~*ed* up as a colonel> **2 :** DIE ***syn*** see CLOSE ***ant*** begin
[3]**end** *vt* [prob. alter. of E dial. *in* (to harvest)] *dial Eng* : to put (grain or hay) into a barn or stack
[4]**end** *adj* : FINAL, ULTIMATE <~ results> <~ markets > <~ user >
end- *or* **endo-** *comb form* [F, fr. Gk, fr. *endon* within, fr. *en* in + *-don* (akin to L *domus* house) — more at IN, TIMBER] **1 :** within : inside <*endo*skeleton> — compare ECT-, EXO- **2 :** taking in <*endo*thermal> **3** *endo-* : forming a bridge between two atoms in a cyclic system
en·dam·age \in-'dam-ij\ *vt* : to cause loss or damage to
end·amoe·ba \ˌen-də-'mē-bə\ *n* [NL, genus name] : any of a genus (*Endamoeba*) comprising amoebas parasitic in the intestines of insects and in some classifications various parasites of vertebrates including the amoeba (*E. histolytica*) that causes amebic dysentery in man — **end·amoe·bic** \-bik\ *adj*
en·dan·ger \in-'dān-jər\ *vt* **en·dan·gered; en·dan·ger·ing** \-'dānj-(ə-)riŋ\ : to bring into danger or peril — **en·dan·ger·ment** \-'dān-jər-mənt\ *n*
en·dan·gered *adj* : threatened with extinction <~ species>
en·darch \'en-ˌdärk\ *adj* : formed or taking place from the center outward <~ xylem> — **en·dar·chy** \-ˌdär-kē\ *n*
end around *n* : a football play in which an offensive end comes behind the line of scrimmage to take a handoff and attempts to carry the ball around the opposite flank
end·ar·ter·ec·to·my \ˌen-ˌdärt-ə-'rek-tə-mē\ *n* [NL *endarterium* intima of an artery (fr. *end-* + *arteria* artery) + E *-ectomy*] : surgical removal of the inner layer of an artery when thickened and atheromatous or occluded (as by intimal plaques)
end·brain \'en(d)-ˌbrān\ *n* : the anterior subdivision of the forebrain
end brush *n* : END PLATE
end bulb *n* : a bulbous termination of a sensory nerve fiber (as in the skin or in a mucous membrane)
en·dear \in-'di(ə)r\ *vt* **1** *obs* : to make higher in cost, value, or estimation **2 :** to cause to become beloved or admired — **en·dear·ing·ly** \-iŋ-lē\ *adv*
en·dear·ment \in-'di(ə)r-mənt\ *n* **1 :** the act or process of endearing **2 :** a word or an act (as a caress) expressing affection
[1]**en·deav·or** \in-'dev-ər\ *vb* **en·deav·ored; en·deav·or·ing** \-(ə-)riŋ\ [ME *endeveren* to exert oneself, fr. *en-* + *dever* duty — more at DEVOIR] *vt* **1** *archaic* : to strive to achieve or reach **2 :** to attempt (as the fulfillment of an obligation) by exertion of effort <~*ing* to control her disgust> ~ *vi* : to work with set purpose ***syn*** see ATTEMPT
[2]**endeavor** *n* : serious determined effort <fields of ~>; *also* : an instance of this
[1]**en·dem·ic** \en-'dem-ik, in-\ *adj* [F *endémique,* fr. *endémie* endemic disease, fr. Gk *endēmia* action of dwelling, fr. *endēmos* endemic, fr. *en* in + *dēmos* people, populace — more at DEMAGOGUE] **1 :** belonging or native to a particular people or country **2 :** restricted or peculiar to a locality or region <~ diseases><an ~ species> ***syn*** see NATIVE ***ant*** exotic, pandemic — **en·dem·i·cal·ly**

\-ˈdem-i-k(ə-)lē\ *adv* — **en·de·mic·i·ty** \ˌen-ˌdem-ˈis-ət-ē, -də-ˈmis-\ *n* — **en·de·mism** \ˈen-də-ˌmiz-əm\ *n*

²endemic *n* : NATIVE 2b

end·er·gon·ic \ˌen-ˌdər-ˈgän-ik\ *adj* [*end-* + Gk *ergon* work — more at WORK] : requiring expenditure of energy <~ biochemical reactions>

en·der·mic \en-ˈdər-mik\ *adj* : acting through the skin or by direct application to the skin — **en·der·mi·cal·ly** \-mi-k(ə-)lē\ *adv*

end·ex·ine \(ˈ)en-ˈdek-ˌsēn, -ˌsīn\ *n* : an inner membranous layer of the exine

end game *n* : the last stage in various games; *esp* : the stage of a chess game following serious reduction of forces

end·ing \ˈen-diŋ\ *n* : a thing that constitutes an end; *esp* : one or more letters or syllables added to a word base esp. in inflection ***syn*** see END ***ant*** beginning

endite *archaic var of* INDITE

en·dive \ˈen-ˌdīv\ *n* [ME, fr. MF, fr. LL *endivia,* fr. LGk *entubion,* fr. L *intubus*] **1** : an annual or biennial composite herb (*Cichorium endivia*) widely cultivated as a salad plant — called also *escarole* **2** : the developing crown of chicory when blanched for use as salad by growing in darkness or semidarkness

endive 1

end·leaf \ˈen-ˌdlēf\ *n* : ENDPAPER

end·less \ˈen-(d)ləs\ *adj* **1** : being or seeming to be without end **2** : extremely numerous **3** : joined at the ends <an ~ chain> — **end·less·ly** *adv* — **end·less·ness** *n*

end line *n* : a line marking an end or boundary esp. of a playing area: as **a** : a line at either end of a football field 10 yards beyond and parallel to the goal line **b** : a line at either end of a court (as in basketball or tennis) perpendicular to the sidelines

end·long \ˈen-ˌdlȯŋ\ *adv* [ME *endelong,* alter. of *andlong,* fr. OE *andlang* along, fr. *andlang,* prep. — more at ALONG] *archaic* : LENGTHWISE

end man *n* : a man at each end of the line of performers in a minstrel show who engages in comic repartee with the interlocutor

end·most \ˈen(d)-ˌmōst\ *adj* : situated at the very end : FARTHEST

en·do·bi·ot·ic \ˌen-dō-ˌbī-ˈät-ik, -bē-\ *adj* [ISV] : dwelling within the tissues of a host

en·do·blast \ˈen-də-ˌblast\ *n* [ISV] : HYPOBLAST — **en·do·blas·tic** \ˌen-də-ˈblas-tik\ *adj*

en·do·car·di·al \ˌen-dō-ˈkärd-ē-əl\ *adj* **1** : situated within the heart **2** : of or relating to the endocardium

en·do·car·di·tis \-ˌkär-ˈdīt-əs\ *n* : inflammation of the lining of the heart and its valves

en·do·car·di·um \-ˈkärd-ē-əm\ *n, pl* **-dia** [NL, fr. *end-* + Gk *kardia* heart] : a thin serous membrane lining the cavities of the heart

en·do·carp \ˈen-də-ˌkärp\ *n* [F *endocarpe*] : the inner layer of the pericarp of a fruit (as an apple or orange) when it consists of two or more layers of different texture or consistency — **en·do·car·pal** \ˌen-də-ˈkär-pəl\ *adj*

vertical section of a cherry, showing *1* exocarp, *2* mesocarp, *3* endocarp, *4* seed; *1, 2,* and *3* together form the pericarp

en·do·chon·dral \ˌen-də-ˈkän-drəl\ *adj* : occurring within the substance of cartilage <~ calcification>

en·do·cra·ni·al cast \ˌen-də-ˌkrā-nē-əl-\ *n* : a cast of the cranial cavity showing the approximate shape of the brain

¹en·do·crine \ˈen-də-krən, -ˌkrīn, -ˌkrēn\ *adj* [ISV *end-* + Gk *krinein* to separate — more at CERTAIN] **1 a** : secreting internally; *specif* : producing secretions that are distributed in the body by way of the bloodstream <an ~ system> **b** : of, relating to, or resembling that of an endocrine gland <~ tumors> **2** : HORMONAL

²endocrine *n* **1** : HORMONE **2** : ENDOCRINE GLAND

endocrine gland *n* : a gland (as the thyroid or the pituitary) that produces an endocrine secretion — called also *ductless gland*

en·do·cri·no·log·ic \ˌen-də-ˌkrin-ᵊl-ˈäj-ik, -ˌkrīn-, -ˌkrēn-\ *or* **en·do·cri·no·log·i·cal** \-i-kəl-\ *adj* : involving or relating to the endocrine glands or secretions or to endocrinology

en·do·cri·nol·o·gy \ˌen-də-kri-ˈnäl-ə-jē, -ˌkrī-\ *n* [ISV] : a science dealing with the endocrine glands — **en·do·cri·nol·o·gist** \-jəst\ *n*

en·do·cyt·ic \ˌen-də-ˈsit-ik\ *adj* : of or relating to endocytosis : ENDOCYTOTIC

en·do·cy·to·sis \-sī-ˈtō-səs\ *n* [NL, fr. *end-* + *-cytosis* (as in *phagocytosis*)] : incorporation of substances into a cell by phagocytosis or pinocytosis — **en·do·cy·tot·ic** \-ˈtät-ik\ *adj*

en·do·derm \ˈen-də-ˌdərm\ *n* [F *endoderme,* fr. *end-* + Gk *derma* skin — more at DERM-] : the innermost of the germ layers of an embryo that is the source of the epithelium of the digestive tract and its derivatives : HYPOBLAST; *also* : a tissue that is derived from this germ layer — **en·do·der·mal** \ˌen-də-ˈder-məl\ *adj*

en·do·der·mis \ˌen-də-ˈdər-məs\ *n* [NL] : the innermost tissue of the cortex in many roots and stems

end·odon·tia \ˌen-də-ˈdän-ch(ē-)ə\ *n* [NL, fr. *end-* + *-odontia*] : a branch of dentistry concerned with diseases of the pulp — **end·odon·tic** \-ˈdänt-ik\ *adj* — **end·odon·ti·cal·ly** \-ˈdänt-i-k(ə-)lē\ *adv* — **end·odon·tist** \-ˈdänt-əst\ *n*

end·odon·tics \-ˈdänt-iks\ *n pl but sing in constr* : ENDODONTIA

en·do·en·zyme \ˌen-dō-ˈen-ˌzīm\ *n* [ISV] : an enzyme that functions inside the cell

en·do·er·gic \ˌen-dō-ˈər-jik\ *adj* : absorbing energy : ENDOTHERMIC <~ nuclear reactions>

en·do·eryth·ro·cyt·ic \ˌen-dō-i-ˌrith-rə-ˈsit-ik\ *adj* : occurring within red blood cells — used chiefly of stages of malaria parasites

en·dog·a·my \en-ˈdäg-ə-mē\ *n* **1** : marriage within a specific group as required by custom or law **2** : sexual reproduction between near relatives; *esp* : pollination of a flower by pollen from another flower of the same plant — compare AUTOGAMY — **en·dog·a·mous** \-məs\ *or* **en·do·gam·ic** \ˌen-də-ˈgam-ik\ *adj*

en·do·gen \ˈen-də-jən\ *n* [F *endogène,* fr. *end-* + *-gène* -gen] : a plant that develops by endogenous growth

en·dog·e·nous \en-ˈdäj-ə-nəs\ *also* **en·do·gen·ic** \ˌen-də-ˈjen-ik\ *adj* **1 a** : growing from or on the inside : developing within the cell wall **b** : originating within the body **2** : constituting or relating to metabolism of the nitrogenous constituents of cells and tissues — **en·dog·e·nous·ly** *adv*

en·dog·e·ny \en-ˈdäj-ə-nē\ *n* : growth from within or from a deep layer

en·do·lymph \ˈen-də-ˌlim(p)f\ *n* [ISV] : the watery fluid in the membranous labyrinth of the ear — **en·do·lym·phat·ic** \ˌen-də-lim-ˈfat-ik\ *adj*

en·do·me·tri·osis \ˌen-dō-ˌmē-trē-ˈō-səs\ *n* : the presence of functioning endometrial tissue in places where it is not normally found

en·do·me·tri·um \-ˈmē-trē-əm\ *n, pl* **-tria** \-trē-ə\ [NL, fr. *end-* + Gk *mētra* uterus, fr. *mētr-, mētēr* mother — more at MOTHER] : the mucous membrane lining the uterus — **en·do·me·tri·al** \-trē-əl\ *adj*

en·do·mi·to·sis \-mī-ˈtō-səs\ *n* : division of chromosomes that is not followed by nuclear division and that results in an increased number of chromosomes in the cell

en·do·mix·is \-ˈmik-səs\ *n* [NL, fr. *end-* + Gk *mixis* act of mixing, fr. *mignynai* to mix — more at MIX] : a periodic nuclear reorganization in ciliated protozoans

en·do·morph \ˈen-də-ˌmȯrf\ *n* [ISV] **1** : a crystal of one species enclosed in one of another **2** [*endo*derm + *-morph*] : an endomorphic individual

en·do·mor·phic \ˌen-də-ˈmȯr-fik\ *adj* **1 a** : of or relating to an endomorph **b** : of, relating to, or produced by endomorphism **2** [*endo*derm + *-morphic;* fr. the predominance in such types of structures developed from the endoderm] **a** : of or relating to the component in W. H. Sheldon's classification of body types that measures the massiveness of the digestive viscera and the body's degree of roundedness and softness **b** : having a heavy rounded body build often with a marked tendency to become fat — **en·do·mor·phy** \ˈen-də-ˌmȯr-fē\ *n*

en·do·mor·phism \ˌen-də-ˈmȯr-ˌfiz-əm\ *n* **1** : a change produced in an intrusive rock by reaction with the wall rock **2** : a homomorphism that maps a mathematical set into itself — compare ISOMORPHISM

en·do·nu·cle·ase \ˌen-dō-ˈn(y)ü-klē-ˌās, -ˌāz\ *n* : an enzyme that breaks down a chain of nucleotides (as a nucleic acid) at points not adjacent to the end and thereby produces two or more shorter nucleotide chains — compare EXONUCLEASE

en·do·par·a·site \-ˈpar-ə-ˌsīt\ *n* [ISV] : a parasite that lives in the internal organs or tissues of its host — **en·do·par·a·sit·ism** \-ˌsīt-ˌiz-əm, -sə-ˌtiz-\ *n*

en·do·pep·ti·dase \-ˈpep-tə-ˌdās, -ˌdāz\ *n* : any of a group of enzymes that hydrolyze peptide bonds inside the long chains of protein molecules : PROTEINASE — compare EXOPEPTIDASE

en·doph·a·gous \en-ˈdäf-ə-gəs\ *adj* : feeding from within; *esp* : consuming vegetation or plant debris by burrowing in and disintegrating plant structures

en·do·phyte \ˈen-də-ˌfīt\ *n* [ISV] : a plant living within another plant — **en·do·phyt·ic** \ˌen-də-ˈfit-ik\ *adj*

en·do·plasm \ˈen-də-ˌplaz-əm\ *n* [ISV] : the inner relatively fluid part of the cytoplasm — **en·do·plas·mic** \ˌen-də-ˈplaz-mik\ *adj*

endoplasmic reticulum *n* : a system of interconnected vesicular and lamellar cytoplasmic membranes that functions esp. in the transport of materials within the cell and that is studded with ribosomes in some places

en·dop·o·dite \en-ˈdäp-ə-ˌdīt\ *n* [ISV] : the mesial or internal branch of a typical limb of a crustacean — **en·dop·o·dit·ic** \(ˌ)en-ˌdäp-ə-ˈdit-ik\ *adj*

en·do·poly·ploid \ˌen-dō-ˈpäl-i-ˌplȯid\ *adj* : of or relating to a polyploid state in which the chromosomes have divided repeatedly without subsequent division of the nucleus or cell — **en·do·poly·ploi·dy** \-ˌplȯid-ē\ *n*

en·do·ra·dio·sonde \-ˈrād-ē-ō-ˌsänd\ *n* : a microelectronic device introduced into the body to record physiological data not otherwise obtainable

end organ *n* : a structure forming the end of a neural path and consisting of an effector or a receptor with its associated nerve terminations

en·dorse \in-ˈdȯ(ə)rs\ *vt* **en·dorsed; en·dors·ing** [alter. of obs. *endoss,* fr. ME *endosen,* fr. MF *endosser,* fr. OF, to put on the back, fr. *en-* + *dos* back, fr. L *dorsum*] **1 a** : to write on the back of; *esp* : to sign one's name as payee on the back of (a check) in order to obtain the cash or credit represented on the face **b** : to inscribe (one's signature) on a check, bill, or note **c** : to inscribe (as an official document) with a title or memorandum **d** : to make over to another (the value represented in a check, bill, or note) by inscribing one's name on the document **e** : to acknowledge receipt of (a sum specified) by one's signature on a document **2** : to express approval of publicly and definitely <~ a mayoral candidate> ***syn*** see APPROVE — **en·dors·able** \-ˈdȯr-sə-bəl\ *adj* — **en·dors·ee** \in-ˌdȯr-ˈsē, ˌen-\ *n* — **en·dors·er** \in-ˈdȯr-sər\ *n*

en·dorse·ment \in-ˈdȯr-smənt\ *n* **1** : the act or process of endorsing **2 a** : something that is written in the process of endorsing **b** : a provision added to an insurance contract altering its scope or application **3** : SANCTION, APPROVAL

en·do·scope \ˈen-də-ˌskōp\ *n* [ISV] : an instrument for visualizing the interior of a hollow organ (as the rectum or urethra) — **en·dos·co·py** \en-ˈdäs-kə-pē\ *n*

en·do·scop·ic \ˌen-də-ˈskäp-ik\ *adj* : of, relating to, or performed by means of the endoscope or endoscopy — **en·do·scop·i·cal·ly** \-i-k(ə-)lē\ *adv*

en·do·skel·e·ton \ˌen-dō-ˈskel-ət-ᵊn\ *n* : an internal skeleton or supporting framework in an animal — **en·do·skel·e·tal** \-ət-ᵊl\ *adj*

end·os·mo·sis \ˌen-ˌdäs-ˈmō-səs, -ˌdäz-\ *n* [alter. of obs. *endosmose,* fr. F, fr. *end-* + Gk *ōsmos* act of pushing, fr. *ōthein* to push; akin to Skt *vadhati* he strikes] : passage (as of a surface-active sub-

stance) through a membrane from a region of lower to a region of higher concentration — **end·os·mot·ic** \-mät-ik\ *adj* — **end·os·mot·i·cal·ly** \-i-k(ə-)lē\ *adv*
en·do·sperm \'en-də-ˌspərm\ *n* [F *endosperme,* fr. *end-* + Gk *sperma* seed — more at SPERM] **:** a nutritive tissue in seed plants formed within the embryo sac — **en·do·sper·mic** \ˌen-də-'spər-mik\ *adj* — **en·do·sper·mous** \-məs\ *adj*
endosperm nucleus *n* **:** the triploid nucleus formed in the embryo sac of a seed plant by fusion of a sperm nucleus with two polar nuclei or with a nucleus formed by their prior fusion
en·do·spore \'en-də-ˌspō(ə)r, -ˌspȯ(ə)r\ *n* [ISV] **:** an asexual spore developed within the cell esp. in bacteria — **en·do·spor·ic** \ˌen-də-'spōr-ik, -'spȯr-\ *adj* — **en·do·spo·rous** \-əs; en-'däs-pə-rəs\ *adj*
end·os·te·al \en-'däs-tē-əl\ *adj* **1 :** of or relating to the endosteum **2 :** located within bone or cartilage — **end·os·te·al·ly** \-ə-lē\ *adv*
en·do·ster·nite \ˌen-dō-'stər-ˌnīt\ *n* [ISV *end-* + *sternum* + *-ite*] **:** a segment of the endoskeleton of an arthropod
end·os·te·um \en-'däs-tē-əm\ *n, pl* **-tea** \-tē-ə\ [NL, fr. *end-* + Gk *osteon* bone — more at OSSEOUS] **:** the layer of vascular connective tissue lining the medullary cavities of bone
en·do·style \'en-də-ˌstīl\ *n* [ISV *end-* + Gk *stylos* pillar — more at STEER] **:** a pair of parallel longitudinal folds projecting into the pharyngeal cavity and bounding a furrow lined with glandular ciliated cells in lower chordates (as the tunicates)
en·do·sul·fan \ˌen-də-'səl-fən, -ˌfan\ *n* [*endo-* + *sulf-* + *-an*] **:** a brownish crystalline insecticide $C_9H_6Cl_6O_3S$ that is used in the control of numerous crop insects and some mites
en·do·sym·bi·o·sis \ˌen-dō-ˌsim-bi-'ō-səs, -bē-\ *n* **:** symbiosis in which a symbiont dwells within the body of its symbiotic partner
en·do·the·ci·um \ˌen-dō-'thē-s(h)ē-əm\ *n, pl* **-cia** \-s(h)ē-ə\ [NL] **:** the inner lining of a mature anther
endotheli- *or* **endothelio-** *comb form* [ISV, fr. NL *endothelium*] **:** endothelium <*endothelio*ma>
en·do·the·li·um \ˌen-də-'thē-lē-əm\ *n, pl* **-lia** \-lē-ə\ [NL, fr. *end-* + epi*thelium*] **1 :** an epithelium of mesoblastic origin composed of a single layer of thin flattened cells that lines internal body cavities **2 :** the inner layer of the seed coat of some plants — **en·do·the·li·al** \-lē-əl\ *adj* — **en·do·the·loid** \-'thē-ˌlȯid\ *adj*
en·do·the·li·o·ma \-ˌthē-lē-'ō-mə\ *n, pl* **-o·mas** *or* **-o·ma·ta** \-mət-ə\ [NL] **:** a tumor developing from endothelial tissue
en·do·therm \'en-də-ˌthərm\ *n* **:** a warm-blooded animal
en·do·ther·mic \ˌen-də-'thər-mik\ *or* **en·do·ther·mal** \-məl\ *adj* [ISV] **1 :** characterized by or formed with absorption of heat **2 :** WARM-BLOODED
en·do·tox·in \ˌen-dō-'täk-sən\ *n* [ISV] **:** a toxin of internal origin; *specif* **:** a poisonous substance present in bacteria (as of typhoid fever) but separable from the cell body only on its disintegration — **en·do·tox·ic** \-sik\ *adj*
en·do·tra·che·al \'-trā-kē-əl\ *adj* **1 :** placed within the trachea <an ~ tube> **2 :** applied or effected through the trachea
en·do·tro·phic \ˌen-də-'trō-fik\ *also* **en·do·tro·pic** \-'trō-pik, -'träp-ik\ *adj, of a mycorrhiza* **:** penetrating into the associated root and ramifying between the cells — compare ECTOTROPHIC
en·dow \in-'dau̇\ *vt* [ME *endowen,* fr. AF *endouer,* fr. MF *en-* + *douer* to endow, fr. L *dotare,* fr. *dot-, dos* gift, dowry — more at DOWRY] **1 :** to furnish with a dower **2 :** to furnish with an income <~ a hospital> **3 a :** to provide or equip gratuitously **:** ENRICH **b :** CREDIT 5a
en·dow·ment \-mənt\ *n* **1 :** the act or process of endowing **2 :** something that is endowed; *specif* **:** the part of an institution's income derived from donations **3 :** natural capacity, power, or ability
en·do·zo·ic \ˌen-də-'zō-ik\ *adj* [ISV] **:** living within or involving passage through an animal <~ distribution of weeds>
end·pa·per \'en(d)-ˌpā-pər\ *n* **:** a once-folded sheet of paper having one leaf pasted flat against the inside of the front or back cover of a book and the other pasted at the base to the first or last page
end plate *n* **:** a flat plate or structure at the end of something; *specif* **:** a complex terminal arborization of a motor nerve fiber
end point *n* **1 :** a point marking the completion of a process or stage of a process **2** *usu* **end·point :** either of two points or values that mark the ends of a line segment or interval; *also* **:** a point that marks the end of a ray
end product *n* **:** the final product of a series of processes or activities
en·drin \'en-drən\ *n* [blend of *endo-* and *dieldrin*] **:** a chlorinated hydrocarbon insecticide $C_{12}H_8Cl_6O$ that is a stereoisomer of dieldrin and resembles dieldrin in toxicity
end run *n* **1 :** a football play in which the ballcarrier attempts to run wide around his own end **2 :** an evasive trick
end–stopped \'en(d)-ˌstäpt\ *adj* **:** marked by a logical or rhetorical pause at the end <an ~ line of verse> — compare RUN-ON
end table *n* **:** a small table that is usu. about the height of the arm of a chair and is used beside a larger piece of furniture (as a sofa)
en·due \in-'d(y)ü\ *vt* **en·dued; en·du·ing** [ME *enduen,* fr. MF *enduire* to bring in, introduce, fr. L *inducere* — more at INDUCE] **1 a :** PROVIDE, ENDOW **b :** IMBUE, TRANSFUSE **2** [ME *enduen,* fr. L *induere,* fr. *ind-* in (fr. OL *indu*) + *-uere* to put on — more at INDIGENOUS, EXUVIAE] **:** to put on **:** DON
en·dur·able \in-'d(y)u̇r-ə-bəl\ *adj* **:** capable of being endured **:** BEARABLE — **en·dur·ably** \-blē\ *adv*
en·dur·ance \in-'d(y)u̇r-ən(t)s\ *n* **1 :** PERMANENCE, DURATION **2 :** the ability to withstand hardship, adversity, or stress **3 :** SUFFERING, TRIAL
en·dure \in-'d(y)u̇(ə)r\ *vb* **en·dured; en·dur·ing** [ME *enduren,* fr. MF *endurer,* fr. (assumed) VL *indurare,* fr. L, to harden, fr. *in-* + *durare* to harden, endure — more at DURING] *vi* **1 :** to continue in the same state **:** LAST **2 :** to remain firm under suffering or misfortune without yielding ~ *vt* **1 :** to undergo (as a hardship) esp. without giving in **:** SUFFER **2 :** TOLERATE, PERMIT ***syn*** see BEAR, CONTINUE
en·dur·ing *adj* **:** LASTING, DURABLE — **en·dur·ing·ly** \-'d(y)u̇r-iŋ-lē\ *adv* — **en·dur·ing·ness** *n*
en·duro \in-'d(y)u̇(ə)r-(ˌ)ō\ *n, pl* **en·dur·os** [irreg. fr. *endurance*] **:** a long race (as for automobiles or motorcycles) stressing endurance rather than speed
end·ways \'en-ˌdwāz\ *adv or adj* **1 :** with the end forward (as toward the observer) **2 :** in or toward the direction of the ends **:** LENGTHWISE <~ pressure> **3 :** on end **:** UPRIGHT <boxes set ~>
end·wise \'en-ˌdwīz\ *adv or adj* **:** ENDWAYS
En·dym·i·on \en-'dim-ē-ən\ *n* [L, fr. Gk *Endymiōn*] **:** a beautiful youth loved by Selene
end zone *n* **:** the area at either end of a football field between the goal line and the end line
ENE *abbr* east-northeast
-ene \ˌēn\ *n suffix* [ISV, fr. Gk *-ēnē,* fem. of *-ēnos,* adj. suffix] **:** unsaturated carbon compound <benz*ene*>; *esp* **:** carbon compound with one double bond <ethyl*ene*>
en·e·ma \'en-ə-mə\ *n, pl* **enemas** *also* **ene·ma·ta** \ˌen-ə-'mät-ə, 'en-ə-mə-tə\ [LL, fr. Gk, fr. *enienai* to inject, fr. *en-* + *hienai* to send — more at JET] **1 :** the injection of liquid into the intestine by way of the anus **2 :** material for injection as an enema
en·e·my \'en-ə-mē\ *n, pl* **-mies** [ME *enemi,* fr. OF, fr. L *inimicus,* fr. *in-* ¹in- + *amicus* friend — more at AMIABLE] **1 :** one that is antagonistic to another; *esp* **:** one seeking to injure, overthrow, or confound an opponent **2 :** something harmful or deadly **3 a :** a military adversary **b :** a hostile unit or force
syn ENEMY, FOE *shared meaning element* **:** one who shows hostility or ill will
en·er·get·ic \ˌen-ər-'jet-ik\ *adj* [Gk *energētikos,* fr. *energein* to be active, fr. *energos*] **1 :** marked by energy **:** STRENUOUS **2 :** operating with vigor or effect **3 :** of or relating to energy <~ equation> — **en·er·get·i·cal·ly** \-i-k(ə-)lē\ *adv*
en·er·get·ics \-iks\ *n pl but sing in constr* **1 :** a branch of mechanics that deals primarily with energy and its transformations **2 :** the total energy relations and transformations of a system (as a chemical reaction or an ecological community) <~ of muscular contraction>
en·er·gid \'en-ər-jəd, -ˌjid\ *n* [ISV, fr. Gk *energos*] **:** a nucleus and the body of cytoplasm with which it interacts
en·er·gize \'en-ər-ˌjīz\ *vb* **-gized; -giz·ing** *vi* **:** to put forth energy **:** ACT ~ *vt* **1 :** to impart energy to **2 :** to make energetic or vigorous **3 :** to apply voltage to ***syn*** see VITALIZE
en·er·giz·er \-ˌjī-zər\ *n* **:** one that energizes; *esp* **:** ANTIDEPRESSANT
en·er·gy \'en-ər-jē\ *n, pl* **-gies** [LL *energia,* fr. Gk *energeia* activity, fr. *energos* active, fr. *en* in + *ergon* work — more at WORK] **1 :** the capacity of acting or being active <intellectual ~> **2 :** natural power vigorously exerted <work with ~> **3 :** the capacity for doing work
energy level *n* **:** one of the stable states of constant energy that may be assumed by a physical system — used esp. of the quantum states of electrons in atoms and of nuclei; called also *energy state*
1**ener·vate** \i-'nər-vət\ *adj* **:** lacking physical, mental, or moral vigor **:** ENERVATED
2**en·er·vate** \'en-ər-ˌvāt\ *vt* **-vat·ed; -vat·ing** [L *enervatus,* pp. of *enervare,* fr. *e-* + *nervus* sinew — more at NERVE] **1 :** to lessen the vitality or strength of **2 :** to reduce the mental or moral vigor of ***syn*** see UNNERVE — **en·er·va·tion** \ˌen-ər-'vā-shən\ *n* — **en·er·va·tive** \'en-ər-ˌvāt-iv\ *adj*
en·fant ter·ri·ble \äⁿ-fäⁿ-te-rēblᵊ\ *n, pl* **enfants terribles** *same*\ [F, lit., terrifying child] **:** one whose inopportune remarks or unconventional actions cause embarrassment
en·fee·ble \in-'fē-bəl\ *vt* **en·fee·bled; en·fee·bling** \-b(ə-)liŋ\ [ME *enfeblen,* fr. MF *enfeblir,* fr. OF, fr. *en-* + *feble* feeble] **:** to make feeble **:** deprive of strength ***syn*** see WEAKEN ***ant*** fortify — **en·fee·ble·ment** \-bəl-mənt\ *n*
en·feoff \in-'fef, -'fēf\ *vt* [ME *enfeoffen,* fr. AF *enfeoffer,* fr. OF *en-* + *fief*] **:** to invest with a fief, fee, or other possession — **en·feoff·ment** \-mənt\ *n*
en·fet·ter \in-'fet-ər\ *vt* **:** to bind in fetters **:** ENCHAIN
en·fe·ver \in-'fē-vər\ *vt* **:** FEVER
En·field rifle \ˌen-ˌfēld-\ *n* [*Enfield,* England] **:** a .30 caliber bolt-operated repeating rifle used by U.S. and British troops in World War I
1**en·fi·lade** \'en-fə-ˌlād, -ˌläd\ *n* [F, fr. *enfiler* to thread, enfilade, fr. OF, to thread, fr. *en-* + *fil* thread — more at FILE] **1 :** an arrangement (as of rooms) in opposite and parallel rows **2 :** gunfire directed along the length of an enemy battle line
2**enfilade** *vt* **-lad·ed; -lad·ing :** to rake or be in a position to rake with gunfire in a lengthwise direction
enflame *var of* INFLAME
en·fleu·rage \ˌäⁿ-ˌflər-'äzh\ *n* [F] **:** a process of extracting perfumes by exposing absorbents to the exhalations of flowers
en·fold \in-'fōld\ *vt* **1 a :** to cover with folds **:** ENVELOP **b :** to surround with a covering **:** CONTAIN **2 :** to clasp within the arms **:** EMBRACE
en·force \in-'fō(ə)rs, -'fȯ(ə)rs\ *vt* [ME *enforcen,* fr. MF *enforcier,* fr. OF, fr. *en-* + *force*] **1 :** to give force to **:** STRENGTHEN **2 :** to urge with energy **3 :** CONSTRAIN, COMPEL **4** *obs* **:** to effect or gain by force **5 :** to carry out effectively <~ laws> — **en·force·abil·i·ty** \-ˌfōr-sə-'bil-ət-ē, -ˌfȯr-\ *n* — **en·force·able** \-'fōr-sə-bəl, -'fȯr-\ *adj* — **en·force·ment** \-'fōr-smənt, -'fȯr-\ *n* — **en·forc·er** *n*
en·fran·chise \in-'fran-ˌchīz\ *vt* **-chised; -chis·ing** [ME *enfranchisen,* fr. MF *enfranchiss-,* stem of *enfranchir,* fr. OF, fr. *en-* + *franc* free — more at FRANK] **1 :** to set free (as from slavery) **2 :** to endow with a franchise: as **a :** to admit to the privileges of a citizen; *specif* **:** to admit to the right of suffrage **b :** to admit (a

ə abut	ᵊ kitten	ər further	a back	ā bake	ä cot, cart	
au̇ out	ch chin	e less	ē easy	g gift	i trip	ī life
j joke	ŋ sing	ō flow	ȯ flaw	ȯi coin	th thin	t͟h this
ü loot	u̇ foot	y yet	yü few	yu̇ furious	zh vision	

municipality) to political privileges or rights — **en·fran·chise·ment** \-ˌchīz-mənt, -chəz-\ *n*

eng *abbr* engine; engineer; engineering

Eng *abbr* England; English

en·gage \in-ˈgāj\ *vb* **en·gaged; en·gag·ing** [ME *engagen*, fr. MF *engagier*, fr. OF, fr. *en-* + *gage*] *vt* **1 :** to offer (as one's word) as security for a debt or cause **2 a** *obs* **:** to entangle or entrap in or as if in a snare or bog **b :** to attract and hold by influence or power **c :** to interlock with **:** MESH; *also* **:** to cause (mechanical parts) to mesh **3 :** to bind (as oneself) to do something; *esp* **:** to bind by a pledge to marry **4 a :** to provide occupation for **:** INVOLVE <~ him in a new project> **b :** to arrange to obtain the use or services of **:** HIRE **5 a :** to hold the attention of **:** ENGROSS <her work ~*s* her completely> **b :** to induce to participate <*engaged* the shy boy in conversation> **6 a :** to enter into contest with **b :** to bring together or interlock (weapons) ~ *vi* **1 a :** to pledge oneself **:** PROMISE **b :** GUARANTEE <he ~*s* for the honesty of his brother> **2 a :** to begin and carry on an enterprise <he *engaged* in trade for a number of years> **b :** to take part **:** PARTICIPATE <at college he *engaged* in gymnastics> **3 :** to enter into conflict **4 :** to be or become in gear

en·ga·gé \ˌäⁿ-ˌgäzh-ˈā\ *adj* [F, pp. of *engager* to engage, fr. MF *engagier*] **:** being actively involved in or committed esp. to political concerns

en·gaged \in-ˈgājd\ *adj* **1 :** involved in activity **:** OCCUPIED **2 :** pledged to be married **:** BETROTHED **3 :** greatly interested **:** COMMITTED **4 :** involved esp. in a hostile encounter **5 :** partly embedded in a wall <an ~ column> **6 :** being in gear **:** MESHED

en·gage·ment \in-ˈgāj-mənt\ *n* **1 a :** the act of engaging **:** the state of being engaged **b :** BETROTHAL **2 :** something that engages **:** PLEDGE **3 a :** a promise to be present at a specified time and place **b :** employment esp. for a stated time **4 :** the state of being in gear **5 :** a hostile encounter between military forces ***syn*** see BATTLE

en·gag·ing *adj* **:** tending to draw favorable attention **:** ATTRACTIVE ***syn*** see SWEET ***ant*** loathsome — **en·gag·ing·ly** \-ˈgā-jiŋ-lē\ *adv*

en·gar·land \in-ˈgär-lənd\ *vt* **:** to adorn with or as if with a garland

En·gel·mann spruce \ˌeŋ-gəl-mən-\ *n* [George *Engelmann* †1884 Am botanist] **:** a large spruce (*Picea engelmannii*) of the Rocky mountain region and British Columbia that yields a light-colored wood

en·gen·der \in-ˈjen-dər\ *vb* **en·gen·dered; en·gen·der·ing** \-d(ə-)riŋ\ [ME *engendren*, fr. MF *engendrer*, fr. L *ingenerare*, fr. *in-* + *generare* to generate] *vt* **1 :** BEGET, PROCREATE **2 :** to cause to exist or to develop **:** PRODUCE <angry words ~ strife> ~ *vi* **:** to assume form **:** ORIGINATE

en·gild \in-ˈgild\ *vt* **:** to make bright with or as if with light

1**en·gine** \ˈen-jən\ *n* [ME *engin*, fr. OF, fr. L *ingenium* natural disposition, talent, fr. *in-* + *gignere* to beget — more at KIN] **1** *obs* **a :** INGENUITY **b :** evil contrivance **:** WILE **2 :** something used to effect a purpose **:** AGENT, INSTRUMENT <mournful and terrible ~ of horror and of crime —E. A. Poe> **3 a :** a mechanical tool: as (1) **:** an instrument or machine of war (2) *obs* **:** a torture implement **b :** MACHINERY **c :** any of various mechanical appliances — compare FIRE ENGINE **4 :** a machine for converting any of various forms of energy into mechanical force and motion **5 :** a railroad locomotive

2**engine** *vt* **en·gined; en·gin·ing :** to equip with engines

-en·gined \ˈen-jənd\ *adj comb form* **:** having (such or so many) engines <front-*engined* cars> <four-*engined* planes>

1**en·gi·neer** \ˌen-jə-ˈni(ə)r\ *n* **1 :** a member of a military group devoted to engineering work **2** *obs* **:** a crafty schemer **:** PLOTTER **3 a :** a designer or builder of engines **b :** a person who is trained in or follows as a profession a branch of engineering **c :** a person who carries through an enterprise by skillful or artful contrivance **4 :** a person who runs or supervises an engine or an apparatus

2**engineer** *vt* **1 :** to lay out, construct, or manage as an engineer **2 a :** to contrive or plan out usu. with more or less subtle skill and craft **b :** to guide the course of ***syn*** see GUIDE

en·gi·neer·ing *n* **1 :** the art of managing engines **2 :** the application of science and mathematics by which the properties of matter and the sources of energy in nature are made useful to man in structures, machines, products, systems, and processes

en·gine·ry \ˈen-jən-rē\ *n* **1 :** instruments of war **2 :** machines and tools **:** MACHINERY

en·gird \in-ˈgərd\ *vt* **:** GIRD, ENCOMPASS

en·gir·dle \in-ˈgərd-ᵊl\ *vt* **:** to encircle with or as if with a girdle

en·gla·cial \en-ˈglā-shəl\ *adj* **:** embedded in a glacier

1**En·glish** \ˈiŋ-glish *also* ˈiŋ-lish\ *adj* [ME, fr. OE *englisc*, fr. *Engle* (pl.) Angles] **:** of, relating to, or characteristic of England, the English people, or the English language

2**English** *n* **1 a :** the language of the people of England and the U.S. and many areas now or formerly under British control **b :** a particular variety of English distinguished by peculiarities (as of pronunciation) **c :** English language, literature, or composition when a subject of study **2** *pl in constr* **:** the people of England **3 a :** an English translation **b :** idiomatic or intelligible English **4 :** spin around the vertical axis given to a ball by striking it to right or left of center (as in pool) or by the manner of releasing it (as in bowling) — compare DRAW, FOLLOW; BODY ENGLISH

3**English** *vt* **1 :** to translate into English **2 :** to adopt into English **:** ANGLICIZE

English breakfast tea *n* **:** CONGOU; *broadly* **:** any similar black tea

English cocker spaniel *n* **:** any of a breed of spaniels that have square muzzles, well-developed noses, and distinctive heads which are ideally half muzzle and half skull with the forehead and skull arched and slightly flattened

English daisy *n* **:** DAISY 1a

English foxhound *n* **:** any of a breed of foxhounds developed in England and characterized by a large heavily boned form, rather short ears, and lightly fringed tail

English horn *n* [trans. of It *corno inglese*] **:** a double-reed woodwind instrument resembling the oboe in design but having a longer tube and a range a fifth lower than that of the oboe

English horn

En·glish·man \ˈiŋ-glish-mən *also* ˈiŋ-lish-\ *n* **:** a native or inhabitant of England

English muffin *n* **:** bread dough rolled and cut into rounds, baked on a griddle, and split and toasted just before eating

En·glish·ness \ˈiŋ-glish-nəs *also* ˈiŋ-lish-\ *n* **:** the distinctive qualities or characteristics of the English people, their works, or their institutions

English rabbit *n* **:** any of a breed of white domestic rabbits having distinctive dark markings

English saddle *n* **:** a saddle with long side bars, steel cantle and pommel, no horn, and a leather seat supported by webbing stretched between the saddlebow and cantle

English setter *n* **:** any of a breed of bird dogs characterized by a moderately long flat silky coat of white or white with color and by feathering on the tail and legs

English shepherd *n* **:** any of a breed of vigorous medium-sized working dogs with a long and glossy black coat usu. with tan to brown markings that was developed in England for herding sheep and cattle

English sonnet *n* **:** a sonnet consisting of three quatrains and a couplet with a rhyme scheme of *abab cdcd efef gg* — called also *Shakespearean sonnet*

English sparrow *n* **:** a sparrow (*Passer domesticus*) native to most of Europe and parts of Asia that has been intentionally introduced into America, Australia, New Zealand and elsewhere to destroy insects although it feeds largely on grain seeds — called also *house sparrow*

English springer spaniel *n* **:** any of a breed of springer spaniels that may have originated in Spain and are characterized by deep-bodied muscular build and a moderately long straight or slightly wavy silky coat usu. of black and white hair — called also *English springer*

English toy spaniel *n* **:** any of a breed of small blocky spaniels with well-rounded upper skull projecting forward toward the short turned-up nose

English walnut *n* **:** a Eurasian walnut (*Juglans regia*) valued for its large edible nut and its hard richly figured wood; *also* **:** its nut

En·glish·wom·an \ˈiŋ-glish-ˌwu̇m-ən *also* ˈiŋ-lish-\ *n* **:** a woman of English birth, nationality, or origin

English yew *n* **:** YEW 1a

en·glut \in-ˈglət\ *vt* **en·glut·ted; en·glut·ting** [MF *engloutir*, fr. LL *inglutire*, fr. L *in-* + *gluttire* to swallow — more at GLUTTON] **:** to gulp down **:** SWALLOW

en·gorge \in-ˈgȯ(ə)rj\ *vb* [MF *engorgier*, fr. OF, to devour, fr. *en-* + *gorge* throat — more at GORGE] *vt* **:** GORGE, GLUT; *specif* **:** to fill with blood to the point of congestion ~ *vi* **:** to suck blood to the limit of body capacity — **en·gorge·ment** \-mənt\ *n*

engr *abbr* **1** engineer **2** engraved; engraver; engraving

en·graft \in-ˈgraft\ *vt* **1 :** GRAFT 1, 3 <~*ed* embryonic gill tissue into the back> **2 :** to join or fasten as if by grafting

en·grailed \in-ˈgrā(ə)ld\ *adj* [ME *engreled*, fr. MF *engreslé*, fr. *en-* + *gresle* slender, fr. L *gracilis*] **1 :** indented with small concave curves <an ~ heraldic bordure> **2 :** made of or bordered by a circle of raised dots <an ~ coin>

en·grain \in-ˈgrān\ *vt* **:** INGRAIN

en·gram *also* **en·gramme** \ˈen-ˌgram\ *n* [ISV] **:** MEMORY, TRACE; *specif* **:** a hypothetical change in neural tissue postulated in order to account for persistence of memory — **en·gram·mic** \en-ˈgram-ik\ *adj*

en·grave \in-ˈgrāv\ *vt* **en·graved; en·grav·ing** [MF *engraver*, fr. *en-* + *graver* to grave, of Gmc origin; akin to OE *grafan* to grave] **1 a :** to form by incision (as on wood or metal) **b :** to impress deeply as if with a graver <the incident was *engraved* in his memory> **2 a :** to cut figures, letters, or devices on for printing; *also* **:** to print from an engraved plate **b :** PHOTOENGRAVE — **en·grav·er** *n*

en·grav·ing *n* **1 :** the act or process of one that engraves **2 :** something that is engraved: as **a :** an engraved printing surface **b :** engraved work **3 :** an impression from an engraved printing surface

en·gross \in-ˈgrōs\ *vt* [ME *engrossen*, fr. AF *engrosser*, prob. fr. ML *ingrossare*, fr. L *in* + ML *grossa* large handwriting, fr. L, fem. of *grossus* thick] **1 a :** to copy or write in a large hand **b :** to prepare the usu. final handwritten or printed text of (an official document) **2** [ME *engrossen*, fr. MF *en gros* in large quantities] **a :** to purchase large quantities of (as for speculation) **b** *archaic* **:** AMASS, COLLECT **c :** to take or occupy the whole of <ideas that have ~*ed* the minds of scholars for generations> ***syn*** see MONOPOLIZE — **en·gross·er** *n*

en·grossed \-ˈgrōst\ *adj* **:** completely occupied or absorbed <a scholar ~ in his research> — **en·grossed·ly** \-ˈgrō-səd-lē, -ˈgrōst-lē\ *adv*

en·gross·ing \-ˈgrō-siŋ\ *adj* **:** taking up the attention completely **:** ABSORBING — **en·gross·ing·ly** \-siŋ-lē\ *adv*

en·gross·ment \in-ˈgrō-smənt\ *n* **1 :** the act of engrossing **2 :** the state of being absorbed or occupied **:** PREOCCUPATION

en·gulf \in-ˈgəlf\ *vt* **1 :** to flow over and enclose **:** OVERWHELM <the mounting seas threatened to ~ the island> **2 :** to take in (food) by or as if by flowing over and enclosing — **en·gulf·ment** \-mənt\ *n*

en·ha·lo \in-ˈhā-(ˌ)lō\ *vt* **:** to surround with or as if with a halo

en·hance \in-ˈhan(t)s\ *vt* **en·hanced; en·hanc·ing** [ME *enhauncen*, fr. AF *enhauncer*, alter. of OF *enhaucier*, fr. (assumed) VL *inaltiare*, fr. L *in* + *altus* high — more at OLD] **1** *obs* **:** RAISE **2 :** to make greater (as in value, desirability, or attractiveness) **:** HEIGHTEN <a hillside location *enhanced* by a broad vista> ***syn*** see INTENSIFY — **en·hance·ment** \-ˈhan(t)-smənt\ *n*

en·har·mon·ic \ˌen-(ˌ)här-ˈmän-ik\ *adj* [F *enharmonique*, fr. MF, of a scale employing quarter tones, fr. Gk *enarmonios*, fr. *en* in +

harmonia harmony, scale] **:** of, relating to, or being notes that are written differently (as A flat and G sharp) but sound the same — **en·har·mon·i·cal·ly** \-i-k(ə-)lē\ *adv*

enig·ma \i-ˈnig-mə\ *n* [L *aenigma*, fr. Gk *ainigmat-, ainigma*, fr. *ainissesthai* to speak in riddles, fr. *ainos* fable] **1 :** an obscure speech or writing **2 :** something hard to understand or explain **3 :** an inscrutable or mysterious person ***syn*** see MYSTERY

enig·mat·ic \ˌen-(ˌ)ig-ˈmat-ik *also* ˌē-(ˌ)nig-\ *adj* **:** of, relating to, or resembling an enigma **:** PUZZLING ***syn*** see OBSCURE ***ant*** explicit — **enig·mat·i·cal** \-i-kəl\ *adj* — **enig·mat·i·cal·ly** \-i-k(ə-)lē\ *adv*

en·isle \in-ˈī(ə)l\ *vt* **1 :** to place apart **:** ISOLATE **2 :** to make an island of

en·jamb·ment \in-ˈjam-mənt\ *or* **en·jambe·ment** *same, or* ä^{n}-zhä^{n}b(-ə)mä^{n}\ *n* [F *enjambement*, fr. MF, encroachment, fr. *enjamber* to straddle, encroach on, fr. *en-* + *jambe* leg — more at JAMB] **:** the running over of a sentence from one verse or couplet into another so that closely related words fall in different lines — compare RUN-ON

en·join \in-ˈjȯin\ *vt* [ME *enjoinen*, fr. OF *enjoindre*, fr. L *injungere*, fr. *in-* + *jungere* to join — more at YOKE] **1 :** to direct or impose by authoritative order or with urgent admonition **2 :** FORBID, PROHIBIT <was ~*ed* by conscience from telling a lie> ***syn*** see COMMAND

en·joy \in-ˈjȯi\ *vt* [MF *enjoir*, fr. OF, fr. *en-* + *joir* to enjoy, fr. L *gaudēre* to rejoice — more at JOY] **1 :** to take pleasure or satisfaction in **2 :** to have for one's use, benefit, or lot ***syn*** see HAVE — **en·joy·able** \-ə-bəl\ *adj* — **en·joy·able·ness** *n* — **en·joy·ably** \-blē\ *adv*

en·joy·ment \in-ˈjȯi-mənt\ *n* **1 a :** the action or state of enjoying **b :** possession and use <the ~ of civic rights> **2 :** something that gives keen satisfaction

en·kin·dle \in-ˈkin-dᵊl\ *vt* **1 :** to set (as fuel) on fire **2 :** to make bright and glowing ~ *vi* **:** to take fire **:** FLAME

enl *abbr* **1** enlarged **2** enlisted

en·lace \in-ˈlās\ *vt* [ME *enlacen*, fr. MF *enlacier*, fr. OF, fr. *en-* + *lacier* to lace] **1 :** ENCIRCLE, ENFOLD **2 :** ENTWINE, INTERLACE

en·lace·ment \in-ˈlā-smənt\ *n* **1 :** the process or result of interlacing **2 :** a pattern of interlacing elements

en·large \in-ˈlärj\ *vb* **en·larged; en·larg·ing** [ME *enlargen*, fr. MF *enlargier*, fr. OF, fr. *en-* + *large*] *vt* **1 :** to make larger **:** EXTEND **2 :** to give greater scope to **:** EXPAND **3 :** to set free (as a captive) ~ *vi* **1 :** to grow larger **2 :** to speak or write at length **:** ELABORATE <let me ~ upon that point> ***syn*** see INCREASE — **en·large·able** \-ˈlär-jə-bəl\ *adj* — **en·larg·er** *n*

en·large·ment \in-ˈlarj-mənt\ *n* **1 :** an act or instance of enlarging **:** the state of being enlarged **2 :** a photographic print that is larger than the negative and that is made by projecting through a lens an image of the negative upon a photographic printing surface

en·light·en \in-ˈlīt-ᵊn\ *vt* **en·light·ened; en·light·en·ing** \-ˈlīt-niŋ, -ᵊn-iŋ\ **1** *archaic* **:** ILLUMINATE **2 a :** to furnish knowledge to **:** INSTRUCT **b :** to give spiritual insight to

en·light·ened *adj* **1 :** freed from ignorance and misinformation <an ~ people> **2 :** based on full comprehension of the problems involved <issued an ~ ruling>

en·light·en·ment \in-ˈlīt-ᵊn-mənt\ *n* **1 :** the act or means of enlightening **:** the state of being enlightened **2** *cap* **:** a philosophic movement of the 18th century marked by questioning of traditional doctrines and values, a tendency toward individualism, and an emphasis on the idea of universal human progress, the empirical method in science, and the free use of reason — used with *the* **3** *Buddhism* **:** a final blessed state marked by the absence of desire or suffering

en·list \in-ˈlist\ *vt* **1 :** to engage (a person) for duty in the armed forces **2 a :** to secure the support and aid of **:** employ in advancing an interest <~ all the available resources> <~ the community in an experiment> **b :** to win over **:** ATTRACT <trying to ~ my sympathies> ~ *vi* **1 :** to enroll oneself in the armed forces **2 :** to participate heartily (as in a cause, drive, or crusade) — **en·list·ee** \-ˌlis-ˈtē\ *n* — **en·list·ment** \-ˈlis(t)-mənt\ *n*

en·list·ed \-ˈlis-təd\ *adj* **:** of, relating to, or constituting the part of a military or naval force below commissioned or warrant officers

enlisted man *n* **:** a man or woman in the armed forces ranking below a commissioned or warrant officer; *specif* **:** an enlisted man ranking below a noncommissioned officer or petty officer

en·liv·en \in-ˈlī-vən\ *vt* **:** to give life, action, or spirit to **:** ANIMATE ***syn*** see QUICKEN ***ant*** deaden, subdue

en masse \ä^{n}(n)-ˈmas\ *adv* [F] **:** in a body **:** as a whole

en·mesh \in-ˈmesh\ *vt* **:** to catch or entangle in or as if in meshes — **en·mesh·ment** \-mənt\ *n*

en·mi·ty \ˈen-mət-ē\ *n, pl* **-ties** [ME *enmite*, fr. MF *enemité*, fr. OF *enemistié*, irreg. fr. *enemi* enemy] **:** positive, active, and typically mutual hatred or ill will

syn ENMITY, HOSTILITY, ANTIPATHY, ANTAGONISM, RANCOR, ANIMOSITY, ANIMUS *shared meaning element* **:** deep-seated dislike or ill will or a manifestation of such feeling ***ant*** amity

en·ne·ad \ˈen-ē-ˌad\ *n* [Gk *ennead-, enneas*, fr. *ennea* nine — more at NINE] **:** a group of nine

en·no·ble \in-ˈō-bəl\ *vt* **en·no·bled; en·no·bling** \-b(ə-)liŋ\ [ME *ennobelen*, fr. MF *ennoblir*, fr. OF, fr. *en-* + *noble*] **1 :** to make noble **:** ELEVATE <believes that hard work ~*s* the human spirit> **2 :** to raise to the rank of nobility — **en·no·ble·ment** \-bəl-mənt\ *n* — **en·no·bler** \-b(ə-)lər\ *n*

en·nui \ˈän-ˈwē\ *n* [F, fr. OF *enui* annoyance, fr. *enuier* to annoy] **:** a feeling of weariness and dissatisfaction **:** BOREDOM

Enoch \ˈē-nək, -nik\ *n* [Gk *Enōch*, fr. Heb *Ḥanōkh*] **:** an Old Testament patriarch and father of Methuselah

enol \ˈē-ˌnȯl, -ˌnōl\ *n* [ISV *ene-* (fr. *-ene*) + *-ol*] **:** an organic compound that contains a hydroxyl group bonded to a carbon atom having a double bond and that is usu. characterized by the grouping C=C(OH) — **eno·lic** \ē-ˈnō-lik, -ˈnäl-ik\ *adj*

eno·lase \ˈē-nə-ˌlās, -ˌlāz\ *n* [ISV *enol* + *-ase*] **:** a crystalline enzyme that is found esp. in muscle and yeast and is important in the metabolism of carbohydrates

enol·o·gy \ē-ˈnäl-ə-jē\ *n* [Gk *oinos* wine + E *-logy* — more at WINE] **:** a science that deals with wine and wine making — **enol·o·gist** \-jəst\ *n*

enor·mi·ty \i-ˈnȯr-mət-ē\ *n, pl* **-ties** **1 :** the quality or state of being immoderate, monstrous, or outrageous; *esp* **:** great wickedness <the utter ~ of the crime> **2 :** a grave offense against order, right, or decency **3 :** the quality or state of being huge **:** IMMENSITY <the ~ of the task of teachers in slum schools — J. B. Conant>

enor·mous \i-ˈnȯr-məs\ *adj* [L *enormis*, fr. *e, ex* out of + *norma* rule] **1 a** *archaic* **:** ABNORMAL, INORDINATE **b :** exceedingly wicked **:** SHOCKING <an ~ sin> **2 :** marked by extraordinarily great size, number, or degree; *esp* **:** exceeding usual bounds or accepted notions ***syn*** see HUGE — **enor·mous·ly** *adv* — **enor·mous·ness** *n*

[1]**enough** \i-ˈnəf; *after* t, d, s, z *often* ᵊn-ˈəf\ *adj* [ME *ynough*, fr. OE *genōg;* akin to OHG *ginuog* enough; both fr. a prehistoric Gmc compound whose first constituent is represented by OE *ge-* (perfective prefix) and whose second constituent is akin to L *nancisci* to get, Gk *enenkein* to carry] **:** occurring in such quantity, quality, or scope as to fully satisfy demands or needs ***syn*** see SUFFICIENT

[2]**enough** *adv* **1 :** in or to a degree or quantity that satisfies or that is sufficient or necessary for satisfaction **:** SUFFICIENTLY **2 :** FULLY, QUITE **3 :** in a tolerable degree

[3]**enough** *pron* **:** a sufficient number, quantity, or amount <~ were present to constitute a quorum> <had ~ of their foolishness>

enounce \ē-ˈnaun(t)s\ *vt* **enounced; enounc·ing** [F *énoncer*, fr. L *enuntiare* to report — more at ENUNCIATE] **1 :** to set forth or state (as a proposition) **2 :** to pronounce distinctly **:** ARTICULATE

enow \i-ˈnau̇\ *adv or adj* [ME *inow*, fr. OE *genōg*] *archaic* **:** ENOUGH

en pas·sant \ˌä^{n}-ˌpä-ˈsä^{n}, -pə-\ *adv* [F] **:** in passing — used in chess of the capture of a pawn as it makes a first move of two squares by an enemy pawn in a position to threaten the first of these squares

en·phy·tot·ic \ˌen-fī-ˈtät-ik\ *adj* [[2]*en-* + *phyt-* + *-otic*] *of a plant disease* **:** occurring regularly in a district but only in moderate severity — **enphytotic** *n*

en·plane \in-ˈplān\ *vi* **:** to board an airplane

en prise \ä^{n}-ˈprēz\ *adj* [F] *of a chess piece* **:** exposed to capture

en·quire \in-ˈkwī(ə)r\, **en·qui·ry** \ˈin-ˌkwī(ə)r-ē, in-ˈ; ˈin-kwə-rē, ˈiŋ-\ *var of* INQUIRE, INQUIRY

en·rage \in-ˈrāj\ *vt* [MF *enrager* to become mad, fr. OF *enragier*, fr. *en-* + *rage*] **:** to fill with rage **:** ANGER

en rap·port \ˌä^{n}-rə-ˈpō(ə)r, -ˈpȯ(ə)r\ *adj* [F] **:** being in a state of mutual accord and harmony <we finished the drive in silence; spiritually we were not *en rapport* —W. A. Percy>

en·rapt \in-ˈrapt\ *adj* **:** wholly absorbed **:** RAPT; *also* **:** filled with delight

en·rap·ture \in-ˈrap-chər\ *vt* **en·rap·tured; en·rap·tur·ing** \-ˈrap-chə-riŋ, -ˈrap-shriŋ\ **:** to fill with delight ***syn*** see TRANSPORT

en·reg·is·ter \in-ˈrej-ə-stər\ *vt* [MF *enregistrer*, fr. OF, fr. *en-* + *registre* register] **:** to put on record

en·rich \in-ˈrich\ *vt* [ME *enrichen*, fr. MF *enrichir*, fr. OF, fr. *en-* + *riche* rich] **1 :** to make rich or richer <~*ing* himself in the stock market> <~*es* his cultural life by going to museums, concerts, and plays> **2 :** ADORN, ORNAMENT <~*ing* the ceiling with frescoes> **3 a :** to make richer in some quality <~ the gravy with a little flour browned in butter> **b :** to make (soil) more fertile **c :** to improve (a food) in nutritive value by adding nutrients (as vitamins or amino acids) and esp. by restoring part of the nutrients wasted in processing **d :** to increase the proportion of a valuable or desirable ingredient in <~ uranium in uranium 235>; *also* **:** to add a desirable substance to <~ natural gas> **4 :** to expand (a course of study) by increasing the variety of subjects and the depth of treatment <an ~*ed* curriculum for the brighter students> — **en·rich·er** *n* — **en·rich·ment** \-ˈrich-mənt\ *n*

en·robe \in-ˈrōb\ *vt* **:** to invest or adorn with or as if with a robe

en·roll *or* **en·rol** \in-ˈrōl\ *vb* **en·rolled; en·roll·ing** [ME *enrollen*, fr. MF *enroller*, fr. *en-* + *rolle* roll, register] *vt* **1 :** to insert, register, or enter in a list, catalog, or roll <the school ~*s* about 800 pupils> **2 :** to prepare a final perfect copy of (a bill passed by a legislature) in written or printed form **3 :** to roll or wrap up ~ *vi* **:** to enroll oneself or cause oneself to be enrolled <he ~*ed* in the history course> — **en·roll·ee** \-rō-ˈlē\ *n* — **en·roll·ment** \-ˈrōl-mənt\ *n*

en·root \in-ˈrüt, -ˈru̇t\ *vt* **:** to fix or implant by or as if by roots **:** ESTABLISH

en route \ä^{n}(n)-ˈrüt, en-, in-\ *adv or adj* [F] **:** on or along the way <likes to read *en route*> <in spite of various *en route* delays we arrived early>

ENS *abbr* ensign

en·sam·ple \in-ˈsam-pəl\ *n* [ME, fr. MF *ensample, example*] **:** EXAMPLE, INSTANCE

en·san·guine \in-ˈsaŋ-gwən\ *vt* **-guined; -guin·ing** **1 :** to make bloody **2 :** CRIMSON

en·sconce \in-ˈskän(t)s\ *vt* **en·sconced; en·sconc·ing** **1 :** SHELTER, CONCEAL **2 :** to settle comfortably or snugly <*ensconced* herself before the blazing hearth>

enscroll *var of* INSCROLL

en·sem·ble \ä^{n}(n)-ˈsäm-bəl\ *n* [F, fr. *ensemble* together, fr. L *insimul* at the same time, fr. *in-* + *simul* at the same time — more at SAME] **:** a group constituting an organic whole or producing together a single effect: as **a :** concerted music of two or more parts **b :** a complete costume of harmonizing or complementary pieces **c (1) :** the musicians engaged in the performance of a

musical ensemble (2) : a group of supporting players, singers, or dancers; *esp* : CORPS DE BALLET
ensemble acting *n* : a system of theatrical presentation in which balanced casting and careful integration of the whole performance replace the star system
en·serf \in-ˈsərf\ *vt* : to deprive of liberty and personal rights — **en·serf·ment** \-mənt\ *n*
en·sheathe \in-ˈshēth\ *vt* : to cover with or as if with a sheath
en·shrine \in-ˈshrīn, *esp South* -ˈsrīn\ *vt* **1** : to enclose in or as if in a shrine **2** : to preserve or cherish as sacred — **en·shrine·ment** \-mənt\ *n*
en·shroud \in-ˈshrau̇d, *esp South* -ˈsrau̇d\ *vt* : to cover or enclose with or as if with a shroud
en·si·form \ˈen(t)-sə-ˌfȯrm\ *adj* [F *ensiforme*, fr. L *ensis* sword + F *-forme* -form; akin to Skt *asi* sword] : having sharp edges and tapering to a slender point <~ leaves of the gladiolus>
en·sign \ˈen(t)-sən, *also* ˈen-ˌsīn *for 1, 2, & 3a*\ *n* [ME *ensigne*, fr. MF *enseigne*, fr. L *insignia* insignia, flags] **1** : a flag that is flown (as by a ship) as the symbol of nationality and that may also be flown with a distinctive badge added to its design (as by an organization having nautical associations) **2 a** : a badge of office, rank, or power **b** : EMBLEM, SIGN **3 a** *archaic* : STANDARD-BEARER **b** : a commissioned officer in the navy or coast guard ranking above a chief warrant officer and below a lieutenant junior grade
en·si·lage \ˈen(t)-s(ə-)lij, *for 1 also* in-ˈsī-lij\ *n* **1** : the process of preserving fodder by ensiling **2** : SILAGE
en·sile \en-ˈsī(ə)l, in-\ *vt* **en·siled; en·sil·ing** [F *ensiler*, fr. *en-* + *silo*, fr. Sp] : to prepare and store (fodder) for silage in a tight silo or pit
en·sky \in-ˈskī\ *vt* : to lift to or as if to the skies or heaven : EXALT
en·slave \in-ˈslāv\ *vt* : to reduce to or as if to slavery : SUBJUGATE — **en·slave·ment** \-mənt\ *n* — **en·slav·er** *n*
en·snare \in-ˈsna(ə)r, -ˈsne(ə)r\ *vt* : to take in or as if in a snare ***syn*** see CATCH
en·snarl \in-ˈsnär(ə)l\ *vt* : to involve in a snarl
en·soul \in-ˈsōl\ *vt* : to endow or imbue with a soul
en·sphere \in-ˈsfi(ə)r\ *vt* : to enclose in or as if in a sphere
en·sue \in-ˈsü\ *vb* **en·sued; en·su·ing** [ME *ensuen*, fr. MF *ensuivre*, fr. OF, fr. *en-* + *suivre* to follow — more at SUE] *vt* : to strive to attain : PURSUE <I wander, seeking peace, and *ensuing* it —Rupert Brooke> ~ *vi* : to take place afterward or as a result ***syn*** see FOLLOW
en suite \äⁿ-ˈswēt\ *adv or adj* [F] : in a succession, series, or set
en·sure \in-ˈshu̇(ə)r\ *vt* **en·sured; en·sur·ing** [ME *ensuren*, fr. AF *enseurer*, prob. alter. of OF *aseürer* — more at ASSURE] : to make sure, certain, or safe : GUARANTEE
syn ENSURE, INSURE, ASSURE, SECURE *shared meaning element* : to make an outcome sure
en·swathe \in-ˈswäth, -ˈswȯth, -ˈswāth\ *vt* : to enfold or enclose with or as if with a covering : SWATHE
ent- *or* **ento-** *comb form* [NL, fr. Gk *entos* within; akin to L *intus* within, Gk *en* in — more at IN] : inner : within <*ento*blast>
en·tab·la·ture \in-ˈtab-lə-ˌchu̇(ə)r, -chər, -ˌt(y)u̇(ə)r\ *n* [obs. F, modif. of It *intavolatura*, fr. *intavolare* to put on a board or table, fr. *in-* (fr. L) + *tavola* board, table, fr. L *tabula* — more at TABLE] : the upper section of a wall or story that is usu. supported on columns or pilasters and that in classical orders consists of architrave, frieze, and cornice; *also* : a similar part (as an elevated support for a machine part)

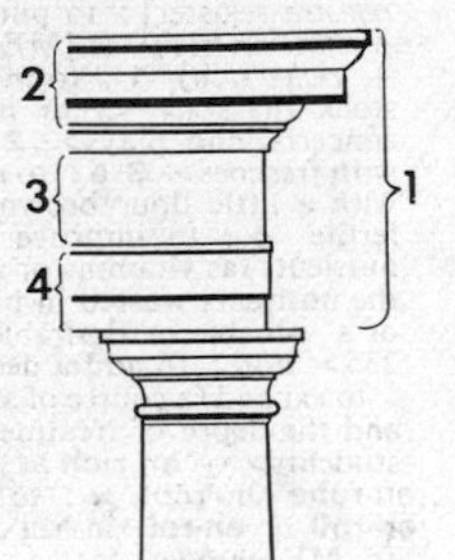

1 entablature, *2* cornice, *3* frieze, *4* architrave

en·ta·ble·ment \in-ˈtā-bəl-mənt, äⁿ-tä-blə-mäⁿ\ *n* [F, fr. OF, fr. *en-* + *table*] : a platform that supports a statue and that is placed above the dado
¹en·tail \in-ˈtā(ə)l\ *vt* **1** : to restrict (property) by limiting the inheritance to the owner's lineal descendants or to a particular class thereof (as his male children) **2 a** : to confer, assign, or transmit as if by entail : FASTEN <~*ed* on them indelible disgrace —Robert Browning> **b** : to fix (a person) permanently in some condition or status <~ him and his heirs unto the crown —Shak.> **3** : to impose, involve, or imply as a necessary accompaniment or result <the project will ~ considerable expense> — **en·tail·er** \-ˈtā-lər\ *n* — **en·tail·ment** \-ˈtā(ə)l-mənt\ *n*
²en·tail \ˈen-ˌtāl, in-ˈtā(ə)l\ *n* **1 a** : an entailing esp. of lands **b** : an entailed estate **c** : the rule fixing the descent **2** : something (as a quality) transmitted as if by entail
ent·amoe·ba \ˌent-ə-ˈmē-bə\ *n* : an endamoeba esp. of a vertebrate
en·tan·gle \in-ˈtaŋ-gəl\ *vt* **1** : to make tangled, complicated, or confused <his explanation only served to ~ the question further> **2** : to involve in a tangle <become *entangled* in a ruinous lawsuit> — **en·tan·gler** \-g(ə-)lər\ *n*
en·tan·gle·ment \in-ˈtaŋ-gəl-mənt\ *n* **1 a** : the action of entangling : the state of being entangled **b** : something that entangles, confuses, or ensnares **2** : the condition of being deeply involved
en·tel·e·chy \en-ˈtel-ə-kē, in-\ *n*, *pl* **-chies** [LL *entelechia*, fr. Gk *entelecheia*] **1** : the realization of form-giving cause as contrasted with potential existence **2** : a hypothetical agency that in some vitalist doctrines is considered inherent in living substances and regulates or directs the vital processes of an organism but is not discoverable by scientific investigation
en·tente \än-ˈtänt\ *n* [F, fr. OF, intent, understanding — more at INTENT] **1** : an international understanding providing for a common course of action **2** : a coalition of parties to an entente
en·ter \ˈent-ər\ *vb* **en·tered; en·ter·ing** \ˈent-ə-riŋ, ˈen-triŋ\ [ME *entren*, fr. OF *entrer*, fr. L *intrare*, fr. *intra* within; akin to L *inter* between — more at INTER-] *vi* **1** : to go or come in **2** : to come or gain admission into a group : JOIN **3 a** : to make a beginning <~*ing* upon a career> **b** : to begin to consider a subject **4** : to go upon land for the purpose of taking possession **5** : to play a part : be a factor <~ into a conversation> ~ *vt* **1** : to come or go into <~ a room> **2** : INSCRIBE, REGISTER <~ the names of qualified voters> **3** : to cause to be received or admitted <~ a boy at a school> **4** : to put in : INSERT **5 a** : to make a beginning in : take up <~ politics> **b** : to pass within the limits of (a particular period of time) <was famous by the time he ~*ed* his early thirties> **6** : to become a member of or an active participant in <~ the university> <~ a race> **7** : to make report of (a ship or her cargo) to customs authorities **8** : to place in proper form before a court of law or upon record <~ a writ> **9** : to go into or upon and take actual possession of (as land) **10** : to put formally on record <~*ing* a complaint against his business partner> — **en·ter·able** \ˈent-ə-rə-bəl, ˈen-trə-\ *adj*
syn ENTER, PENETRATE, PIERCE, PROBE *shared meaning element* : to make way into something ***ant*** issue (*from or out*)
— **enter into 1** : EXAMINE, CONSIDER <the book doesn't *enter into* the moral aspect of the issue> **2** : to make oneself a party to or in <*enter into* an important agreement> **3** : to form a constituent part of <tin *enters into* the composition of pewter> **4 a** : to participate or share in <cheerfully *entering into* the household tasks> **b** : to be in tune or sympathy with <couldn't *enter into* the festive spirit of the occasion>
enter- *or* **entero-** *comb form* [Gk, fr. *enteron*] : intestine <*enter*itis>
en·ter·al \ˈent-ə-rəl\ *adj* : ENTERIC — **en·ter·al·ly** \-rə-lē\ *adv*
en·ter·ic \en-ˈter-ik, in-\ *adj* **1** : of or relating to the intestines; *broadly* : ALIMENTARY **2** : of, relating to, or being a medicinal preparation treated to pass through the stomach unaltered and disintegrate in the intestines
en·ter·it·i·dis \ˌent-ə-ˈrit-əd-əs, -ˈrīt-\ *n* [NL (*Salmonella*) *enteritidis*, species of bacteria] : enteritis esp. in young animals
en·ter·i·tis \ˌent-ə-ˈrīt-əs\ *n* **1** : inflammation of the intestines and esp. of the human ileum **2** : a disease of domestic animals (as panleucopenia of cats) marked by enteritis and diarrhea
en·tero·bac·te·ri·um \ˌent-ə-rō-bak-ˈtir-ē-əm\ *n* : any of a family (Enterobacteriaceae) of gram-negative straight rod bacteria (as a salmonella or a colon bacillus) that ferment glucose and include saprophytes as well as some serious pathogens of man, lower animals, and plants — **en·tero·bac·te·ri·al** \-ē-əl\ *adj*
en·tero·bi·a·sis \-ˈbī-ə-səs\ *n*, *pl* **-a·ses** \-ˌsēz\ [NL, fr. *Enterobius*, genus name + *-iasis*] : infestation with or disease caused by pinworms (genus *Enterobius*) that occurs esp. in children
en·tero·chro·maf·fin \-ˈkrō-mə-fən\ *adj* [*enter-* + *chromaffin*] : of or relating to epithelial cells of the intestinal mucosa that stain esp. with chromium salts and usu. contain serotonin
en·tero·coc·cus \-ˈkäk-əs\ *n*, *pl* **-coc·ci** \-ˈkäk-ˌ(s)ī, -ˈkäk-(ˌ)(s)ē\ [NL, genus name] : STREPTOCOCCUS; *esp* : a streptococcus (as *Streptococcus faecalis*) normally present in the intestine — **en·tero·coc·cal** \-ˈkäk-əl\ *adj*
en·tero·coele *or* **en·tero·coel** \ˈent-ə-rō-ˌsēl\ *n* : a coelom originating by outgrowth from the archenteron — **en·tero·coe·lic** \ˌent-ə-rō-ˈsē-lik\ *adj* — **en·tero·coe·lous** \-ləs\ *adj*
en·tero·co·li·tis \ˌent-ə-rō-kə-ˈlīt-əs\ *n* [NL] : enteritis affecting both the large and small intestine
en·tero·gas·trone \-ˈgas-ˌtrōn\ *n* [*enter-* + *gastr-* + *hormone*] : a hormone that is produced by the duodenal mucosa and has an inhibitory action on gastric motility and secretion
en·tero·hep·a·ti·tis \-ˌhep-ə-ˈtīt-əs\ *n* [NL] : BLACKHEAD 2
en·tero·ki·nase \ˌent-ə-rō-ˈkī-ˌnās, -ˌnāz\ *n* [ISV] : an enzyme esp. of the upper intestinal mucosa that activates trypsinogen by converting it to trypsin
en·ter·on \ˈent-ə-ˌrän, -rən\ *n* [NL, fr. Gk, intestine — more at INTER-] : the alimentary canal or system — used esp. of the embryo
en·tero·patho·gen·ic \ˌent-ə-rō-ˌpath-ə-ˈjen-ik\ *adj* : tending to produce disease in the intestinal tract <~ bacteria>
en·ter·op·a·thy \ˌent-ə-ˈräp-ə-thē\ *n* : a disease of the intestinal tract
en·ter·os·to·my \ˌent-ə-ˈräs-tə-mē\ *n*, *pl* **-mies** [ISV] : a surgical formation of an opening into the intestine through the abdominal wall
en·tero·tox·in \ˌent-ə-rō-ˈtäk-sən\ *n* : a toxic substance that is produced by microorganisms (as some staphylococci) and is responsible for the gastrointestinal symptoms of some forms of food poisoning
en·tero·vi·rus \-ˈvī-rəs\ *n* [NL] : any of a group of picornaviruses (as a Coxsackie virus) that typically occur in the gastrointestinal tract but may be involved in respiratory ailments, meningitis, and neurological disorders — **en·tero·vi·ral** \-rəl\ *adj*
en·ter·prise \ˈent-ə(r)-ˌprīz\ *n* [ME *enterprise*, fr. MF *entreprise*, fr. *entreprendre* to undertake, fr. *entre-* inter- + *prendre* to take — more at PRIZE] **1** : a project or undertaking that is esp. difficult, complicated, or risky **2 a** : a unit of economic organization or activity; *esp* : a business organization **b** : a systematic purposeful activity <agriculture is the main economic ~ among these people> **3** : readiness to engage in daring action : INITIATIVE
en·ter·pris·er \-ˌprī-zər\ *n* : one who undertakes an enterprise; *specif* : ENTREPRENEUR
en·ter·pris·ing \-ˌprī-ziŋ\ *adj* : marked by an independent energetic spirit and by readiness to undertake or experiment
en·ter·tain \ˌent-ər-ˈtān\ *vb* [ME *entertinen*, fr. MF *entretenir*, fr. *entre-* inter- + *tenir* to hold — more at TENABLE] *vt* **1 a** *archaic* : MAINTAIN **b** *obs* : RECEIVE **2** : to show hospitality to **3 a** : to keep, hold, or maintain in the mind : HARBOR <I ~ grave doubts about her sincerity> **b (1)** : to receive and take into consideration <he refused to ~ her plea> **(2)** : TREAT, CONSIDER <~ a subject> **4** : to provide entertainment for **5** : to play against (an opposing team) on one's home field or court ~ *vi* : to provide entertainment esp. for guests ***syn*** see AMUSE — **en·ter·tain·er** *n*
en·ter·tain·ing *adj* : providing entertainment : DIVERTING — **en·ter·tain·ing·ly** \-ˈtā-niŋ-lē\ *adv*

en·ter·tain·ment \ˌent-ər-ˈtān-mənt\ *n* **1 :** the act of entertaining **2 a** *archaic* **:** MAINTENANCE, PROVISION **b** *obs* **:** EMPLOYMENT **3 :** something diverting or engaging: as **a :** a public performance **b :** a usu. light comic or adventure novel

en·thal·py \ˈen-ˌthal-pē, en-ˈ\ *n* [*en-* + Gk *thalpein* to heat] **:** the sum of the internal energy of a body and the product of its volume multiplied by the pressure

en·thrall *or* **en·thral** \in-ˈthrȯl\ *vt* **en·thralled; en·thrall·ing 1 :** to hold in or reduce to slavery **2 :** to hold spellbound **:** CHARM — **en·thrall·ment** *or* **en·thral·ment** \-ˈthrȯl-mənt\ *n*

en·throne \in-ˈthrōn\ *vt* **1 a :** to seat ceremonially on a throne **b :** to seat in a place associated with a position of authority or influence **2 :** to assign supreme virtue or value to **:** EXALT — **en·throne·ment** \-mənt\ *n*

en·thuse \in-ˈth(y)üz\ *vb* **en·thused; en·thus·ing** [back-formation fr. *enthusiasm*] *vt* **:** to make enthusiastic <proposals which . . . shocked the orthodox and *enthused* the rebellious *Times Lit. Supp.*> ~ *vi* **:** to show enthusiasm <tourists *enthusing* over a moribund culture —R. J. Clements> ***syn*** see THRILL

en·thu·si·asm \in-ˈth(y)ü-zē-ˌaz-əm\ *n* [Gk *enthousiasmos,* fr. *enthousiazein* to be inspired, fr. *entheos* inspired, fr. *en-* + *theos* god] **1 a :** belief in special revelations of the Holy Spirit **b :** religious fanaticism **2 a :** strong excitement of feeling **:** ARDOR **b :** something inspiring zeal or fervor ***syn*** see PASSION

en·thu·si·ast \-ˌast, -əst\ *n* **:** a person filled with enthusiasm: as **a :** one who is ardently attached to a cause, object, or pursuit <he's a sports car ~> **b :** one who tends to give himself completely to whatever engages his interest

en·thu·si·as·tic \in-ˌth(y)ü-zē-ˈas-tik\ *adj* **:** filled with or marked by enthusiasm — **en·thu·si·as·ti·cal·ly** \-ti-k(ə-)lē\ *adv*

en·thy·meme \ˈen(t)-thi-ˌmēm\ *n* [L *enthymema,* fr. Gk *enthymēma,* fr. *enthymeisthai* to keep in mind, fr. *en-* + *thymos* mind, soul — more at FUME] **:** a syllogism in which one of the premises is implicit

en·tice \in-ˈtīs\ *vt* **en·ticed; en·tic·ing** [ME *enticen,* fr. OF *enticier,* fr. (assumed) VL *intitiare,* fr. L *in-* + *titio* firebrand] **:** to draw on artfully or adroitly or by arousing hope or desire **:** TEMPT ***syn*** see LURE ***ant*** scare — **en·tice·ment** \-ˈtī-smənt\ *n*

[1]**en·tire** \in-ˈtī(ə)r, ˈen-ˌ\ *adj* [ME, fr. MF *entir,* fr. L *integer,* lit., untouched, fr. *in-* + *tangere* to touch — more at TANGENT] **1 :** having no element or part left out **:** WHOLE <was alone the ~ day> **2 :** complete in degree **:** TOTAL <his ~ devotion to his family> **3 a :** consisting of one piece **:** HOMOGENOUS <the book is ~ in mood> **b :** INTACT <strove to keep the collection ~> **4 :** not castrated **5 :** having the margin continuous or free from indentations <an ~ leaf> — **entire** *adv* — **en·tire·ness** *n*

[2]**entire** *n* **1** *archaic* **:** the whole **:** ENTIRETY **2 :** STALLION

en·tire·ly *adv* **1 :** in a whole, complete, or full manner <agreed with me ~> <you are ~ welcome> **2 :** in an exclusive manner **:** SOLELY <it is his fault ~>

en·tire·ty \in-ˈtī-rət-ē, -ˈtī-(ə)rt-ē\ *n, pl* **-ties 1 :** the state of being entire or complete **2 :** SUM TOTAL, WHOLE

en·ti·tle \in-ˈtīt-ᵊl\ *vt* **en·ti·tled; en·ti·tling** \-ˈtīt-liŋ, -ᵊl-iŋ\ [ME *entitlen,* fr. MF *entituler,* fr. LL *intitulare,* fr. L *in-* + *-titulus* title] **1 :** to give a title to **:** DESIGNATE **2 :** to furnish with proper grounds for seeking or claiming something <this ticket ~*s* the bearer to free admission> — **en·ti·tle·ment** \-ˈtīt-ᵊl-mənt\ *n*

en·ti·ty \ˈen(t)-ət-ē\ *n, pl* **-ties** [ML *entitas,* fr. L *ent-, ens* existing thing, fr. coined prp. of *esse* to be — more at IS] **1 a :** BEING, EXISTENCE; *esp* **:** independent, separate, or self-contained existence **b :** the existence of a thing as contrasted with its attributes **2 :** something that has separate and distinct existence and objective or conceptual reality

ento- — see ENT-

en·to·blast \ˈent-ə-ˌblast\ *n* **1 :** HYPOBLAST **2 :** a blastomere producing endoderm — **en·to·blas·tic** \ˌent-ə-ˈblas-tik\ *adj*

en·to·derm \ˈent-ə-ˌdərm\ *n* **:** ENDODERM — **en·to·der·mal** \ˌent-ə-ˈdər-məl\ *or* **en·to·der·mic** \-mik\ *adj*

en·toil \in-ˈtȯi(ə)l\ *vt* **:** ENTRAP, ENMESH

entom *or* **entomol** *abbr* entomological; entomology

entom- *or* **entomo-** *comb form* [F, fr. Gk *entomon*] **:** insect <*entomo*phagous>

en·tomb \in-ˈtüm\ *vt* [ME *entoumben,* fr. MF *entomber,* fr. *en-* + *tombe* tomb] **1 :** to deposit in a tomb **:** BURY **2 :** to serve as a tomb for — **en·tomb·ment** \-ˈtüm-mənt\ *n*

en·to·mo·fau·na \ˌent-ə-mō-ˈfȯn-ə, -ˈfän-\ *n* [NL] **:** a fauna of insects **:** the insects of an environment or region

en·to·mol·o·gy \ˌent-ə-ˈmäl-ə-jē\ *n* [F *entomologie,* fr. Gk *entomon* insect (fr. neut. of *entomos* cut up, fr. *en-* + *temnein* to cut) + F *-logie* -logy — more at TOME] **:** a branch of zoology that deals with insects — **en·to·mo·log·i·cal** \-mə-ˈläj-i-kəl\ *adj* — **en·to·mo·log·i·cal·ly** \-k(ə-)lē\ *adv* — **en·to·mol·o·gist** \ˌent-ə-ˈmäl-ə-jəst\ *n*

en·to·moph·a·gous \ˌent-ə-ˈmäf-ə-gəs\ *adj* **:** feeding on insects

en·to·moph·i·lous \ˌent-ə-ˈmäf-ə-ləs\ *adj* **:** being normally pollinated by insects — compare ZOOPHILOUS — **en·to·moph·i·ly** \-lē\ *n*

en·to·mos·tra·can \ˌent-ə-ˈmäs-tri-kən\ *n* [deriv. of *entom-* + Gk *ostrakon* shell — more at OYSTER] **:** any of numerous simple typically small crustaceans (as branchiopods, ostracods, copepods, and barnacles) sometimes placed in a subclass (Entomostraca) — **entomostracan** *or* **en·to·mos·tra·cous** \-kəs\ *adj*

en·to·proct \ˈent-ə-ˌpräkt\ *n* [deriv. of *ent-* + Gk *prōktos* anus] **:** any of a phylum (Entoprocta) of animals lacking a true coelom and having the anus adjacent to the mouth — **entoproct** *or* **en·to·proc·tous** \ˌent-ə-ˈpräk-təs\ *adj*

en·tou·rage \ˌän-tu̇-ˈräzh\ *n* [F, fr. MF, fr. *entourer* to surround, fr. *entour* around, fr. *en* in (fr. L *in*) + *tour* circuit — more at TURN] **1 :** one's attendants or associates **2 :** SURROUNDINGS

en·to·zoa \ˌent-ə-ˈzō-ə\ *n pl* [NL] **:** internal animal parasites; *esp* **:** the intestinal worms — **en·to·zo·an** \-ˈzō-ən\ *adj or n*

en·to·zo·ic \-ˈzō-ik\ *adj* **:** living within an animal <an ~ amoeba>

en·tr'acte \ˈäⁿ(n)-ˌtrakt, -ˌträkt, äⁿ(n)-ˈ\ *n* [F, fr. *entre-* inter- + *acte* act] **1 :** the interval between two acts of a play **2 :** a dance, piece of music, or interlude performed between two acts of a play

en·trails \ˈen-trəlz, -ˌtrālz\ *n pl* [ME *entrailles,* fr. MF, fr. ML *intralia,* alter. of L *interanea,* pl. of *interaneum* intestine, fr. neut. of *interaneus* interior] **:** GUTS, VISCERA; *broadly* **:** internal parts

[1]**en·train** \in-ˈtrān\ *vt* [MF *entrainer,* fr. *en-* + *trainer* to draw, drag — more at TRAIN] **1 :** to draw along with or after oneself **2 :** to draw in and transport (as solid particles or gas) by the flow of a fluid **3 :** to incorporate (air bubbles) into concrete **4 :** to determine or modify the phase or period of <circadian rhythms ~*ed* by a light cycle> — **en·train·er** *n* — **en·train·ment** \-ˈtrān-mənt\ *n*

[2]**entrain** *vt* **:** to put aboard a train ~ *vi* **:** to go aboard a train

[1]**en·trance** \ˈen-trən(t)s\ *n* **1 :** the act of entering **2 :** the means or place of entry **3 :** power or permission to enter **:** ADMISSION **4 :** the point at which a voice or instrument part begins in ensemble music **5 :** the first appearance of an actor in a scene

[2]**en·trance** \in-ˈtran(t)s\ *vt* **en·tranced; en·tranc·ing 1 :** to put into a trance **2 :** to carry away with delight, wonder, or rapture ***syn*** see TRANSPORT — **en·trance·ment** \-ˈtran(t)-smənt\ *n*

en·trant \ˈen-trənt\ *n* **:** one that enters; *esp* **:** one that enters a contest

en·trap \in-ˈtrap\ *vt* [MF *entraper,* fr. *en-* + *trape* trap] **1 :** to catch in or as if in a trap **2 :** to lure into a compromising statement or act ***syn*** see CATCH — **en·trap·ment** \-mənt\ *n*

en·treat \in-ˈtrēt\ *vb* [ME *entreten,* fr. MF *entraitier,* fr. *en-* + *traitier* to treat — more at TREAT] *vt* **1** *archaic* **:** to deal with **:** TREAT **2 :** to plead with esp. in order to persuade **:** ask urgently <~*ed* his boss for another chance> ~ *vi* **1** *obs* **a :** NEGOTIATE **b :** INTERCEDE **2 :** to make an earnest request **:** PLEAD ***syn*** see BEG — **en·treat·ing·ly** \-iŋ-lē\ *adv* — **en·treat·ment** \-mənt\ *n*

en·treaty \in-ˈtrēt-ē\ *n, pl* **-treat·ies :** an act of entreating **:** PLEA

en·tre·chat \ˌäⁿ(n)-trə-ˈshä\ *n* [F] **:** a leap in which a ballet dancer repeatedly crosses the legs and sometimes beats them together

en·trée *or* **en·tree** \ˈän-ˌtrā *also* än-ˈ\ *n* [F *entrée,* fr. OF] **1 a :** the act or manner of entering **:** ENTRANCE **b :** freedom of entry or access <had ~ into the best circles> **2 :** the principal dish of the meal in the U.S.

en·tre·mets *as sing,* ˌäⁿ(n)-trə-ˈmā, *as pl* -ˈmā(z)\ *n pl but sing or pl in constr* [F, fr. OF *entremes,* fr. L *intermissus,* pp. of *intermittere* to intermit] **:** dishes served in addition to the main course of a meal

en·trench \in-ˈtrench\ *vt* **1 a :** to place within or surround with a trench esp. for defense **b :** to place (oneself) in a strong defensive position **c :** to establish solidly **:** CONFIRM <pity only ~*es* him in his misery> **2 :** to cut into **:** FURROW; *specif* **:** to erode downward so as to form a trench ~ *vi* **1 :** to dig or occupy a trench for defensive purposes **2 :** to enter upon or take over something unfairly, improperly, or unlawfully **:** ENCROACH — used with *on* or *upon* ***syn*** see TRESPASS — **en·trench·ment** \-mənt\ *n*

en·tre·pôt \ˈäⁿ(n)-trə-ˌpō\ *n* [F] **:** an intermediary center of trade and transshipment

en·tre·pre·neur \ˌäⁿ-trə-p(r)ə-ˈnər, -ˈn(y)u̇(ə)r\ *n* [F, fr. OF, fr. *entreprendre* to undertake] **:** one who organizes, manages, and assumes the risks of a business or enterprise — **en·tre·pre·neur·ial** \-ˈn(y)u̇r-ē-əl, -ˈnər-\ *adj* — **en·tre·pre·neur·ship** \-ˈnər-ˌship, -ˈn(y)u̇(ə)r-\ *n*

en·tre·sol \ˈäⁿ(n)-trə-ˌsäl, -ˌsȯl\ *n* [F] **:** MEZZANINE

en·tro·py \ˈen-trə-pē\ *n, pl* **-pies** [G *entropie,* fr. Gk *en-* + *trepein* to turn, change — more at TROPE] **1 a :** a measure of the unavailable energy in a closed thermodynamic system so related to the state of the system that a change in the measure varies with change in the ratio of the increment of heat taken in to the absolute temperature at which it is absorbed **b :** a measure of the disorder of a closed thermodynamic system in terms of a constant multiple of the natural logarithm of the probability of the occurrence of a particular molecular arrangement of the system that by suitable choice of a constant reduces to the measure of unavailable energy **2 :** a measure of the amount of information in a message that is based on the logarithm of the number of possible equivalent messages **3 :** the degradation of the matter and energy in the universe to an ultimate state of inert uniformity

en·trust \in-ˈtrəst\ *vt* **1 :** to confer a trust on; *esp* **:** to deliver something in trust to **2 :** to commit to another with confidence ***syn*** see COMMIT — **en·trust·ment** \-ˈtrəs(t)-mənt\ *n*

en·try \ˈen-trē\ *n, pl* **entries** [ME *entre,* fr. OF *entree,* fr. fem. of *entré,* pp. of *entrer* to enter] **1 :** the act of entering **:** ENTRANCE **2 :** the right or privilege of entering **:** ENTRÉE **3 :** a place of entrance: as **a :** VESTIBULE, PASSAGE **b :** DOOR, GATE **4 a :** the act of making or entering a record **b :** something entered: as (1) **:** a record or notation of an occurrence, transaction, or proceeding (2) **:** a descriptive record (as in a card catalog or an index) (3) **:** HEADWORD (4) **:** a headword with its definition or identification (5) **:** VOCABULARY ENTRY **5 :** a person, thing, or group entered in a contest

en·try·way \-trē-ˌwā\ *n* **:** a passage for entrance

entry word *n* **:** HEADWORD

en·twine \in-ˈtwīn\ *vt* **:** to twine together or around ~ *vi* **:** to become twisted or twined

en·twist \in-ˈtwist\ *vt* **:** ENTWINE

enu·cle·ate \(ˈ)ē-ˈn(y)ü-klē-ˌāt\ *vt* **-at·ed; -at·ing** [L *enucleatus,* pp. of *enucleare,* lit., to remove the kernel from, fr. *e-* + *nucleus* kernel — more at NUCLEUS] **1** *archaic* **:** EXPLAIN **2 :** to deprive of a nucleus **3 :** to remove without cutting into <~ a tumor> — **enu·cle·ation** \(ˌ)ē-ˌn(y)ü-klē-ˈā-shən\ *n*

ə abut ᵊ kitten ər further a back ā bake ä cot, cart
au̇ out ch chin e less ē easy g gift i trip ī life
j joke ŋ sing ō flow ȯ flaw ȯi coin th thin t͟h this
ü loot u̇ foot y yet yü few yu̇ furious zh vision

enu·mer·a·ble \i-'n(y)üm-(ə-)rə-bəl\ *adj* : DENUMERABLE — **enu·mer·a·bil·i·ty** \-,n(y)üm-(ə-)rə-'bil-ət-ē\ *n*
enu·mer·ate \i-'n(y)ü-mə-,rāt\ *vt* **-at·ed; -at·ing** [L *enumeratus,* pp. of *enumerare,* fr. *e-* + *numerare* to count, fr. *numerus* number — more at NIMBLE] **1** : to ascertain the number of : COUNT **2** : to specify one after another : LIST — **enu·mer·a·tion** \-,n(y)ü-mə-'rā-shən\ *n* — **enu·mer·a·tive** \-'n(y)ü-mə-,rāt-iv, -'n(y)üm-(ə-)rət-\ *adj* — **enu·mer·a·tor** \-'n(y)ü-mə-,rāt-ər\ *n*
enun·ci·ate \ē-'nən(t)-sē-,āt\ *vb* **-at·ed; -at·ing** [L *enuntiatus,* pp. of *enuntiare* to report, declare, fr. *e-* + *nuntiare* to report — more at ANNOUNCE] *vt* **1 a** : to make a definite or systematic statement of : FORMULATE **b** : ANNOUNCE, PROCLAIM <*enunciated* the principles to be followed by the new administration> **2** : ARTICULATE, PRONOUNCE <~ your words clearly> ~ *vi* : to utter articulate sounds — **enun·cia·ble** \-'nən(t)-sē-ə-bəl, -'nən-ch(ē-)ə-\ *adj* — **enun·ci·a·tion** \-,nən(t)-sē-'ā-shən\ *n* — **enun·ci·a·tor** \-'nən(t)-sē-,āt-ər\ *n*
enure *var of* INURE
en·ure·sis \,en-yu̇-'rē-səs\ *n* [NL, fr. Gk *enourein* to urinate in, wet the bed, fr. *en-* + *ourein* to urinate] : an involuntary discharge of urine : incontinence of urine — **en·uret·ic** \-'ret-ik\ *adj or n*
env *abbr* envelope
en·vel·op \in-'vel-əp\ *vt* [ME *envolupen,* fr. MF *envoluper, envelopper,* fr. OF *envoloper,* fr. *en-* + *voloper* to wrap] **1** : to enclose or enfold completely with or as if with a covering **2** : to mount an attack on (an enemy's flank) — **en·vel·op·ment** \-mənt\ *n*
en·ve·lope \'en-və-,lōp, 'än-\ *n* **1** : something that envelops : WRAPPER <the ~ of air around the earth> **2** : a flat usu. paper container (as for a letter) **3 a** : the outer covering of an aerostat **b** : the bag containing the gas in a balloon or airship **4** : a natural enclosing covering (as a membrane, shell, or integument) **5 a** : a curve tangent to each of a family of curves **b** : a surface tangent to each of a family of surfaces
en·ven·om \in-'ven-əm\ *vt* [ME *envenimen,* fr. OF *envenimer,* fr. *en-* + *venim* venom] **1** : to make poisonous **2** : EMBITTER <jealousy ~*ing* his mind>
en·ven·om·iza·tion \in-,ven-ə-mə-'zā-shən\ *n* : a poisoning caused by a bite or sting
en·vi·able \'en-vē-ə-bəl\ *adj* : highly desirable — **en·vi·able·ness** *n* — **en·vi·ably** \-blē\ *adv*
en·vi·er \'en-vē-ər\ *n* : one that envies
en·vi·ous \'en-vē-əs\ *adj* **1** : feeling or showing envy <~ of her neighbor's success> <~ looks> **2** *archaic* **a** : EMULOUS **b** : ENVIABLE — **en·vi·ous·ly** *adv* — **en·vi·ous·ness** *n*
syn ENVIOUS, JEALOUS *shared meaning element* : begrudging another possession of something. In spite of their shared element of meaning, these words are not close synonyms and can rarely be interchanged without loss of precision or alteration of emphasis. ENVIOUS stresses a coveting of something (as riches or attainments) which belongs to another or of something (as success or good luck) which has come to another; it may imply an urgent, even malicious desire to see him dispossessed <some *envious* hand has sprinkled ashes just to spoil our slide —Eugene Field> or no more than a mild innocuous coveting <we are all *envious* of your new coat> JEALOUS is likely to stress intolerance of a rival for possession of what one regards as peculiarly one's own possession or due, or it may imply intensely zealous efforts to keep what one treasures. The term can be used without derogation <thou shalt have no other gods before me . . . for I the Lord thy God am a *jealous* God —Exod 20:3–5(AV)> but more often it carries a strong implication of distrust, suspicion, enviousness, or sometimes anger <stabbed by a *jealous* lover> <a *jealous* rage>
en·vi·ron \in-'vī-rən, -'vī(-ə)rn\ *vt* [ME *envirounen,* fr. MF *environner,* fr. *environ* around, fr. *en* in (fr. L *in*) + *viron* circle, fr. *virer* to turn, fr. (assumed) VL *virare*] : ENCIRCLE, SURROUND
en·vi·ron·ment \in-'vī-rən-mənt, -'vī(-ə)rn-\ *n* **1** : the circumstances, objects, or conditions by which one is surrounded **2 a** : the complex of climatic, edaphic, and biotic factors that act upon an organism or an ecological community and ultimately determine its form and survival **b** : the aggregate of social and cultural conditions that influence the life of an individual or community **3** : an artistic or theatrical work that involves or encompasses the spectator — **en·vi·ron·men·tal** \-,vī-rən-'ment-ᵊl, -,vī(-ə)rn-\ *adj* — **en·vi·ron·men·tal·ly** \-ᵊl-ē\ *adv*
en·vi·ron·men·tal·ism \-,vī-rən-'ment-ᵊl-,iz-əm, -,vī(-ə)rn-\ *n* : a theory that views environment rather than heredity as the important factor in the development and esp. the cultural and intellectual development of an individual or group
en·vi·ron·men·tal·ist \-ᵊl-əst\ *n* **1** : an advocate of environmentalism **2** : one concerned about the quality of the human environment; *specif* : a specialist in human ecology
en·vi·rons \in-'vī-rənz, -'vī(-ə)rnz\ *n pl* **1** : the districts around a city **2 a** : environing things : SURROUNDINGS **b** : an adjoining region or space : VICINITY
en·vis·age \in-'viz-ij\ *vt* **-aged; -ag·ing** [F *envisager,* fr. *en-* + *visage*] **1** : to view or regard in a certain way <~*s* himself as a sincere young man> **2** : to have a mental picture of esp. in advance of realization <~*s* an entirely new system of education> ***syn*** see THINK
en·vi·sion \in-'vizh-ən\ *vt* : to picture to oneself <~*s* a career dedicated to promoting peace> ***syn*** see THINK
en·voi *or* **en·voy** \'en-,vȯi, 'än-\ *n* [F *envoi,* lit., message, fr. OF *envei,* fr. *envoier* to send on one's way, fr. (assumed) VL *inviare,* fr. L *in-* + *via* way — more at VIA] : the usu. explanatory or commendatory concluding remarks to a poem, essay, or book; *specif* : a short fixed final stanza of a ballade serving as a summary or dedication
en·voy \'en-,vȯi, 'än-\ *n* [F *envoyé,* fr. pp. of *envoyer* to send, fr. OF *envoier*] **1 a** : a minister plenipotentiary accredited to a foreign government who ranks between an ambassador and a minister resident — called also *envoy extraordinary* **b** : a person delegated to represent one government in its dealings with another **2** : MESSENGER, REPRESENTATIVE

[1]**en·vy** \'en-vē\ *n, pl* **envies** [ME *envie,* fr. OF, fr. L *invidia,* fr. *invidus* envious, fr. *invidēre* to look askance at, envy, fr. *in-* + *vidēre* to see — more at WIT] **1** *obs* : MALICE **2** : painful or resentful awareness of an advantage enjoyed by another joined with a desire to possess the same advantage **3** : an object of envious notice or feeling <his beautiful wife made him the ~ of his friends>
[2]**envy** *vb* **en·vied; en·vy·ing** *vt* **1** : to feel envy toward or on account of **2** *obs* : BEGRUDGE ~ *vi, obs* : to feel or show envy — **en·vy·ing·ly** \-vē-iŋ-lē\ *adv*
en·wheel \in-'hwē(ə)l, -'wē(ə)l\ *vt, obs* : ENCIRCLE
en·wind \in-'wīnd\ *vt* **en·wound** \-'wau̇nd\; **en·wind·ing** : to wind in or about : ENFOLD
en·womb \in-'wüm\ *vt* : to shut up as if in a womb
en·wrap \in-'rap\ *vt* **1** : to wrap in a covering : ENFOLD **2 a** : ENVELOP **b** : to preoccupy or absorb mentally : ENGROSS
en·wreathe \in-'rēth\ *vt* : to encircle with or as if with a wreath : ENVELOP
en·zo·ot·ic \,en-zə-'wät-ik\ *adj* [*en-* + *zo-*] *of animal diseases* : peculiar to or constantly present in a locality — **enzootic** *n*
en·zy·got·ic \,en-zī-'gät-ik\ *adj* [*en-* + *zyg-*] *of twins* : IDENTICAL
en·zy·mat·ic \,en-zə-'mat-ik\ *also* **en·zy·mic** \en-'zī-mik\ *adj* : of, relating to, or produced by an enzyme — **en·zy·mat·i·cal·ly** \-'mat-i-k(ə-)lē\ *also* **en·zy·mi·cal·ly** \-'zī-mi-k(ə-)lē\ *adv*
en·zyme \'en-,zīm\ *n* [G *enzym,* fr. MGk *enzymos* leavened, fr. Gk *en-* + *zymē* leaven] : any of numerous complex proteins that are produced by living cells and catalyze specific biochemical reactions at body temperatures
en·zy·mol·o·gy \,en-zə-'mäl-ə-jē\ *n* [ISV] : a branch of science that deals with enzymes, their nature, activity, and significance — **en·zy·mol·o·gist** \-jəst\ *n*
EO *abbr* executive order
eo- *comb form* [Gk *ēō-* dawn, fr. *ēōs*] : earliest : oldest <*eolithic*>
Eo·cene \'ē-ə-,sēn\ *adj* : of, relating to, or being an epoch of the Tertiary between the Paleocene and the Oligocene or the corresponding system of rocks — **Eocene** *n*
eo·hip·pus \,ē-ō-'hip-əs\ *n* [NL, genus name, fr. *eo-* + Gk *hippos* horse — more at EQUINE] : any of a genus (*Eohippus*) of small primitive 4-toed horses from the Lower Eocene of the western U.S.

eohippus

eo·lian \ē-'ō-lē-ən, -'ōl-yən\ *adj* [L *Aeolus,* god of the winds] : borne, deposited, produced, or eroded by the wind
eo·lith \'ē-ə-,lith\ *n* : a very crudely chipped flint
Eo·lith·ic \,ē-ə-'lith-ik\ *adj* : of or relating to the early period of the Stone Age marked by the use of eoliths
EOM *abbr* end of month
eon \'ē-ən, 'ē-,än\ *var of* AEON
eo no·mi·ne \,ē-ō-'näm-ə-nē\ [L] : by or under that name
Eos \'ē-,äs\ *n* [Gk *Eōs*] : the Greek goddess of dawn — compare AURORA
eo·sin \'ē-ə-sən\ *or* **eo·sine** \-sən, -,sēn\ *n* [ISV, fr. Gk *ēōs* dawn] **1** : a red fluorescent dye $C_{20}H_8Br_4O_5$ obtained by the action of bromine on fluorescein and used esp. in cosmetics and as a toner; *also* : its red to brown sodium or potassium salt used esp. as a biological stain for cytoplasmic structures **2** : any of several dyes related to eosin
[1]**eo·sin·o·phil** \,ē-ə-'sin-ə-,fil\ *or* **eo·sin·o·phile** \-,fīl\ *n* : a leukocyte or other granulocyte with cytoplasmic inclusions readily stained by eosin
[2]**eosinophil** *or* **eosinophile** *adj* : EOSINOPHILIC 1
eo·sin·o·phil·ia \-'fil-ē-ə\ *n* : abnormal increase in the number of eosinophils in the blood that is characteristic of allergic states and various parasitic infections
eo·sin·o·phil·ic \,ē-ə-,sin-ə-'fil-ik\ *adj* **1** : staining readily with eosin **2** : of, relating to, or characterized by eosinophilia
Eo·zo·ic \,ē-ə-'zō-ik\ *adj or n* **1** : PRECAMBRIAN **2** : PROTEROZOIC
EP *abbr* **1** estimated position **2** European plan **3** extended play
epact \'ē-,pakt, 'ep-,akt\ *n* [MF *epacte,* fr. LL *epacta,* fr. Gk *epaktē,* fr. *epagein* to bring in, intercalate, fr. *epi-* + *agein* to drive — more at AGENT] : a period added to harmonize the lunar with the solar calendar
ep·ar·chy \'ep-,är-kē\ *n, pl* **-chies** [Gk *eparchia* province, fr. *eparchos* prefect, fr. *epi-* + *archos* ruler — more at ARCH-] : a diocese of an Eastern church
ep·au·let *also* **ep·au·lette** \,ep-ə-'let; 'ep-ə-,let, -lət\ *n* [F *épaulette,* dim. of *épaule* shoulder, fr. LL *spatula* shoulder blade, spoon, dim. of L *spatha* spoon, sword — more at SPADE] **1** : something that ornaments or protects the shoulder; *specif* : an ornamental fringed shoulder pad formerly worn as part of a military uniform **2** : a 5-sided step cut of a gem
épée \'ep-,ā, ā-'pā\ *n* [F, fr. L *spatha*] **1** : a fencing or dueling sword having a bowl-shaped guard and a rigid blade of triangular section with no cutting edge that tapers to a sharp point blunted for fencing — compare FOIL, SABER **2** : the art or sport of fencing with the épée

1, epaulets 1

épée·ist \-əst\ *n* : one who fences with an épée
ep·ei·rog·e·ny \,ep-,ī-'räj-ə-nē\ *n, pl* **-nies** [Gk *ēpeiros* mainland, continent + E *-geny*] : the deformation of the earth's crust by which the broader features of relief are produced — **epei·ro·gen·ic** \i-,pī-rə-'jen-ik\ *adj* — **epei·ro·gen·i·cal·ly** \-i-k(ə-)lē\ *adv*
epen·the·sis \i-'pen(t)-thə-səs, e-\ *n, pl* **-the·ses** \-,sēz\ [LL, fr. Gk, fr. *epentithenai* to insert a letter, fr. *epi-* + *entithenai* to put in, fr. *en-* + *tithenai* to put — more at DO] : the insertion or development of a sound or letter in the body of a word (as \ə\ in \'ath-ə-,lēt\ *athlete*) — **ep·en·thet·ic** \,ep-ən-'thet-ik\ *adj*

epergne \i-ˈpərn, ā-\ *n* [prob. fr. F *épargne* saving] **:** an often ornate tiered centerpiece consisting typically of a frame of wrought metal (as silver or gold) bearing dishes, vases, or candle holders or a combination of these

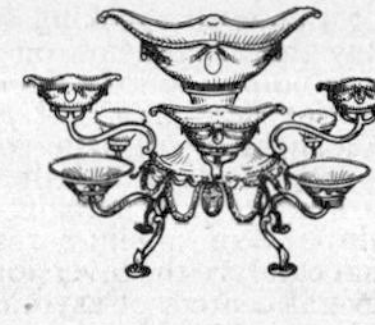
epergne

ep·ex·e·ge·sis \ˌep-ˌek-sə-ˈjē-səs\ *n, pl* **-ge·ses** \-ˌsēz\ [Gk *epexēgēsis,* fr. *epi-* + *exēgēsis*] **:** additional explanation or explanatory matter — **ep·ex·e·get·i·cal** \-ˈjet-i-kəl\ *or* **ep·ex·e·get·ic** \-ˈjet-ik\ *adj* — **ep·ex·e·get·i·cal·ly** \-ˈjet-i-k(ə-)lē\ *adv*

Eph *or* **Ephes** *abbr* Ephesians

ephah \ˈē-fə, ˈef-ə\ *n* [Heb *ēphāh,* fr. Egypt *ipt*] **:** an ancient Hebrew unit of dry measure equal to $^1/_{10}$ homer or a little over a bushel

ephebe \ˈef-ˌēb, i-ˈfēb\ *n* [L *ephebus*] **:** a young man; *esp* **:** EPHEBUS

ephe·bic \-bik\ *adj* **:** of or relating to the ephebi <~ education>

ephe·bus \i-ˈfē-bəs, e-\ *n, pl* **-bi** \-ˌbī\ [L, fr. Gk *ephēbos,* fr. *epi-* + *hēbē* youth, puberty] **:** a youth of ancient Greece; *esp* **:** an Athenian 18 or 19 years old in training for full citizenship

ephe·dra \i-ˈfed-rə, ˈef-ə-drə\ *n* [NL, genus name] **:** any of a large genus (*Ephedra* of the family Gnetaceae) of jointed nearly leafless desert shrubs with the leaves reduced to scales at the nodes

ephed·rine \i-ˈfed-rən\ *n* [NL *Ephedra,* genus of shrubs, fr. L, horsetail plant, fr. Gk, fr. *ephedros* sitting upon, fr. *epi-* + *hedra* seat — more at SIT] **:** a crystalline alkaloid $C_{10}H_{15}NO$ extracted from Chinese ephedras or synthesized and used in the form of a salt for relief of hay fever, asthma, and nasal congestion

1**ephem·er·al** \i-ˈfem-(ə-)rəl\ *adj* [Gk *ephēmeros* lasting a day, daily, fr. *epi-* + *hēmera* day] **1 :** lasting one day only <an ~ fever> **2 :** lasting a very short time <~ pleasures> *syn* see TRANSIENT — **ephem·er·al·ly** \-rə-lē\ *adv*

2**ephemeral** *n* **:** something ephemeral; *specif* **:** a plant that grows, flowers, and dies in a few days

ephem·er·al·i·ty \i-ˌfem-ə-ˈral-ət-ē\ *n, pl* **-ties 1 :** the quality or state of being ephemeral **2** *pl* **:** ephemeral things

ephem·er·id \i-ˈfem-ə-rəd\ *n* [deriv. of Gk *ephēmeron*] **:** MAYFLY — **ephemerid** *adj*

ephem·er·is \-ə-rəs\ *n, pl* **eph·e·mer·i·des** \ˌef-ə-ˈmer-ə-ˌdēz\ [L, diary, ephemeris, fr. Gk *ephēmeris,* fr. *ephēmeros*] **1 :** a tabular statement of the assigned places of a celestial body for regular intervals **2 :** EPHEMERAL

ephemeris time *n* **:** a uniform measure of time defined by the orbital motions of the planets

ephem·er·on \i-ˈfem-ə-ˌrän\ *n, pl* **ephem·era** \-ˈfem-(ə-)rə\ *also* **ephem·er·ons** \-ˈfem-ə-ˌränz\ [NL, fr. Gk *ephēmeron* mayfly, fr. neut. of *ephēmeros*] **1 :** EPHEMERID **2 :** EPHEMERAL

ephem·er·ous \i-ˈfem-(ə-)rəs\ *adj* **:** EPHEMERAL

Ephe·sians \i-ˈfē-zhənz\ *n pl but sing in constr* [short for *Epistle to the Ephesians*] **:** a letter addressed to early Christians and included as a book in the New Testament — see BIBLE table

eph·od \ˈef-ˌäd, ˈē-ˌfäd\ *n* [Heb *ēphōdh*] **1 :** a linen apron worn in ancient Hebrew rites; *esp* **:** a vestment for the high priest **2 :** an ancient Hebrew instrument of priestly divination

eph·or \ˈef-ˌȯr, -ō(ə)r\ *n* [L *ephorus,* fr. Gk *ephoros,* fr. *ephoran* to oversee, fr. *epi-* + *horan* to see — more at WARY] **1 :** one of five ancient Spartan magistrates having power over the king **2 :** a government official in modern Greece; *esp* **:** one who oversees public works — **eph·or·ate** \ˈef-ə-ˌrāt\ *n*

Ephra·im \ˈē-frē-əm\ *n* [Heb *Ephrayim*] **:** a son of Joseph and the traditional eponymous ancestor of one of the tribes of Israel

Ephra·im·ite \-ə-ˌmīt\ *n* **1 :** a member of the Hebrew tribe of Ephraim **2 :** a native or inhabitant of the biblical northern kingdom of Israel

epi- *or* **ep-** *prefix* [ME, fr. MF & L; MF, fr. L, fr. Gk, fr. *epi* on, at, besides, after; akin to OE *eofot* crime] **1 :** upon <*epi*phyte> **:** besides <*epi*phenomenon> **:** attached to <*epi*didymis> **:** over <*epi*center> **:** outer <*epi*blast> **:** after <*epi*genesis> **2 a :** chemical entity related to (such) another <*epi*cholesterol> **b :** chemical entity distinguished from (such) another by having a bridge connection <*epi*chlorohydrin>

epi·blast \ˈep-ə-ˌblast\ *n* **:** the outer layer of the blastoderm **:** ECTODERM — **epi·blas·tic** \ˌep-ə-ˈblas-tik\ *adj*

epib·o·ly \i-ˈpib-ə-lē\ *n, pl* **-lies** [Gk *epibolē* addition, fr. *epiballein* to throw on, fr. *epi-* + *ballein* to throw — more at DEVIL] **:** the growing of one part about another; *esp* **:** such growth of the dorsal lip area during gastrulation — **ep·i·bol·ic** \ˌep-ə-ˈbäl-ik\ *adj*

1**ep·ic** \ˈep-ik\ *adj* [L *epicus,* fr. Gk *epikos,* fr. *epos* word, speech, poem — more at VOICE] **1 :** of, relating to, or having the characteristics of an epic **2 a :** extending beyond the usual or ordinary esp. in size or scope <his genius was ~ —*Times Lit. Supp.*> **b :** HEROIC — **ep·i·cal** \-i-kəl\ *adj* — **ep·i·cal·ly** \-i-k(ə-)lē\ *adv*

2**epic** *n* **1 :** a long narrative poem in elevated style recounting the deeds of a legendary or historical hero <the *Iliad* and the *Odyssey* are ~*s*> **2 :** a work of art (as a novel or drama) that resembles or suggests an epic **3 :** a series of events or body of legend or tradition thought to form the proper subject of an epic <the winning of the West was a great American ~>

epi·ca·lyx \ˌep-i-ˈkā-liks *also* -ˈkal-iks\ *n* **:** an involucre resembling the calyx but consisting of a whorl of bracts that is exterior to the calyx or results from the union of the sepal appendages

epi·can·thic fold \ˌep-ə-ˌkan(t)-thik-\ *n* [NL *epicanthus* epicanthic fold, fr. *epi-* + *canthus*] **:** a prolongation of a fold of the skin of the upper eyelid over the inner angle or both angles of the eye — called also *Mongolian fold*

epi·car·di·al \ˌep-ə-ˈkärd-ē-əl\ *adj* **:** of or relating to the epicardium

epi·car·di·um \-ē-əm\ *n, pl* **-dia** \-ē-ə\ [NL, fr. *epi-* + Gk *kardia* heart] **:** the visceral part of the pericardium that closely invests the heart

epi·carp \ˈep-i-ˌkärp\ *n* [F *épicarpe,* fr. *épi-* epi- + *-carpe* -carp] **:** EXOCARP

epic drama *n* **:** twentieth century narrative drama that seeks to provoke critical thought about social problems by appealing to the viewer's reason rather than to his emotions

ep·i·cene \ˈep-ə-ˌsēn\ *adj* [ME, fr. L *epicoenus,* fr. Gk *epikoinos,* fr. *epi-* + *koinos* common — more at CO-] **1** *of a noun* **:** having but one form to indicate either sex **2 a :** having characteristics typical of the other sex **:** INTERSEXUAL **b :** EFFEMINATE **3 :** lacking characteristics of either sex — **epicene** *n* — **ep·i·cen·ism** \-ˌsē-ˌniz-əm, ˌep-ə-ˈ\ *n*

epi·cen·ter \ˈep-i-ˌsent-ər\ *n* [NL *epicentrum,* fr. *epi-* + L *centrum* center] **1 :** the part of the earth's surface directly above the focus of an earthquake **2 :** CENTER 2a, 2c — **epi·cen·tral** \ˌep-i-ˈsen-trəl\ *adj*

epi·chlo·ro·hy·drin \ˌep-i-ˌklōr-ə-ˈhī-drən, -ˌklȯr-\ *n* **:** a volatile liquid toxic epoxide C_3H_5ClO having a chloroform odor and used esp. in making epoxy resins and rubbers

epi·con·ti·nen·tal \ˌep-i-ˌkänt-ᵊn-ˈent-ᵊl\ *adj* **:** lying upon a continent or a continental shelf <~ seas>

epi·cot·yl \ˈep-i-ˌkät-ᵊl\ *n* [*epi-* + *cotyl*edon] **:** the portion of the axis of a plant embryo or seedling above the cotyledonary node

epi·cra·ni·al \ˌep-i-ˈkrā-nē-əl\ *adj* **:** situated on the cranium

ep·i·crit·ic \ˌep-ə-ˈkrit-ik\ *adj* [Gk *epikritikos* determinative, fr. *epikrinein* to decide, fr. *epi-* + *krinein* to judge — more at CERTAIN] **:** of, relating to, or being cutaneous sensory reception marked by accurate discrimination between small degrees of sensation

epic simile *n* **:** an extended simile that is used typically in epic poetry to intensify the heroic stature of the subject and to serve as decoration

epic theater *n* **:** theater that employs epic drama

ep·i·cure \ˈep-i-ˌkyu̇(ə)r\ *n* [*Epicurus*] **1** *archaic* **:** one devoted to sensual pleasure **:** SYBARITE **2 :** one with sensitive and discriminating tastes esp. in food or wine

syn EPICURE, BON VIVANT, GOURMET, GOURMAND, GLUTTON *shared meaning element* **:** one who takes pleasure in eating and drinking

ep·i·cu·re·an \ˌep-i-kyu̇-ˈrē-ən, -ˈkyu̇r-ē-\ *adj* **1** *cap* **:** of or relating to Epicurus or Epicureanism **2 :** of, relating to, or suited to an epicure

Epicurean *n* **1 :** a follower of Epicurus **2** *often not cap* **:** EPICURE 2

ep·i·cu·re·an·ism \-ə-ˌniz-əm\ *n* **1** *cap* **a :** the philosophy of Epicurus who subscribed to a hedonistic ethics that considered an imperturbable emotional calm the highest good, held intellectual pleasures superior to others, and advocated the renunciation of momentary in favor of more permanent pleasures **b :** a mode of life in consonance with Epicureanism **2 :** EPICURISM

ep·i·cur·ism \ˈep-i-ˌkyu̇(ə)r-ˌiz-əm, ˌep-i-ˈ\ *n* **:** the practices or tastes of an epicure or an epicurean

epi·cu·ti·cle \ˌep-i-ˈkyüt-i-kəl\ *n* **:** an outermost waxy layer of the insect exoskeleton — **epi·cu·tic·u·lar** \-kyu̇-ˈtik-yə-lər\ *adj*

epi·cy·cle \ˈep-ə-ˌsī-kəl\ *n* [ME *epicicle,* fr. LL *epicyclus,* fr. Gk *epikyklos,* fr. *epi-* + *kyklos* circle — more at WHEEL] **1** *in Ptolemaic astron* **:** a circle in which a planet moves and which has a center that is itself carried around at the same time on the circumference of a larger circle **2 :** a process going on within a larger one — **epi·cy·clic** \ˌep-ə-ˈsī-klik, -ˈsik-lik\ *adj*

epicyclic train *n* **:** a train (as of gear wheels) designed to have one or more parts travel around the circumference of another fixed or revolving part

epi·cy·cloid \ˌep-ə-ˈsī-ˌklȯid\ *n* **:** a curve traced by a point on a circle that rolls on the outside of a fixed circle

1**ep·i·dem·ic** \ˌep-ə-ˈdem-ik\ *adj* [F *épidémique,* fr. MF, fr. *epidemie,* n., epidemic, fr. LL *epidemia,* fr. Gk *epidēmia* visit, epidemic, fr. *epidēmos* visiting, epidemic, fr. *epi-* + *dēmos* people] **1 :** affecting or tending to affect many individuals within a population, community, or region at the same time <typhoid was ~> **2 a :** excessively prevalent **b :** CONTAGIOUS 4 <an ~ personality> **3 :** of, relating to, or constituting an epidemic <the practice had reached ~ proportions> — **ep·i·dem·i·cal** \-i-kəl\ *adj* — **ep·i·dem·i·cal·ly** \-i-k(ə-)lē\ *adv* — **ep·i·de·mic·i·ty** \-də-ˈmis-ət-ē\ *n*

2**epidemic** *n* **1 :** an outbreak of epidemic disease **2 :** an outbreak or product of sudden rapid spread, growth, or development; *specif* **:** a natural population suddenly and greatly enlarged

ep·i·de·mi·ol·o·gy \ˌep-ə-ˌdē-mē-ˈäl-ə-jē, -ˌdem-ē-\ *n* [LL *epidemia* + ISV *-logy*] **1 :** a branch of medical science that deals with the incidence, distribution, and control of disease in a population **2 :** the sum of the factors controlling the presence or absence of a disease or pathogen — **ep·i·de·mi·o·log·ic** \-ˌdē-mē-ə-ˈläj-ik, -ˌdem-ē-\ *or* **ep·i·de·mi·o·log·i·cal** \-i-kəl\ *adj* — **ep·i·de·mi·o·log·i·cal·ly** \-i-k(ə-)lē\ *adv* — **ep·i·de·mi·ol·o·gist** \-ˌdē-mē-ˈäl-ə-jəst, -ˌdem-ē-\ *n*

ep·i·den·drum \ˌep-ə-ˈden-drəm\ *or* **ep·i·den·dron** \-drən\ *n* [NL, genus name, fr. Gk *epi-* + *dendron* tree — more at DENDR-] **:** any of a large genus (*Epidendrum*) of chiefly epiphytic and tropical American orchids

epiderm- *or* **epidermo-** *comb form* [*epidermis*] **:** epidermis <*epi-derm*al>

epi·der·mal \ˌep-ə-ˈdər-məl\ *also* **epi·der·mic** \-mik\ *adj* **:** of, relating to, or arising from the epidermis

epi·der·mis \-məs\ *n* [LL, fr. Gk, fr. *epi-* + *derma* skin] **1 a :** the outer epithelial layer of the external integument of the animal body that is derived from the embryonic epiblast; *specif* **:** the outer nonsensitive and nonvascular layer of the skin of a vertebrate that overlies the dermis **b :** any of various animal integuments **2 :** a thin surface layer of tissue in higher plants formed by growth of a primary meristem

ə abut ᵊ kitten ər further a back ā bake ä cot, cart
au̇ out ch chin e less ē easy g gift i trip ī life
j joke ŋ sing ō flow ȯ flaw ȯi coin th thin t͟h this
ü loot u̇ foot y yet yü few yu̇ furious zh vision

epi·der·moid \-ˌmȯid\ *also* **epi·der·moi·dal** \-ˌdər-ˈmȯid-ᵊl\ *adj* : resembling epidermis or epidermal cells : made up of elements like those of epidermis <~ neoplasms>

epi·dia·scope \ˌep-ə-ˈdī-ə-ˌskōp\ *n* [ISV] **1** : a projector for images of opaque objects or for images or transparencies **2** : EPISCOPE

ep·i·did·y·mis \ˌep-ə-ˈdid-ə-məs\ *n, pl* **-mi·des** \-mə-ˌdēz\ [NL, fr. Gk, fr. *epi-* + *didymos* testicle — more at DIDYMOUS] : an elongated mass of convoluted efferent tubes at the back of the testis — **ep·i·did·y·mal** \-məl\ *adj*

ep·i·dote \ˈep-ə-ˌdōt\ *n* [F *épidote,* fr. Gk *epididonai* to give in addition, fr. *epi-* + *didonai* to give — more at DATE] : a yellowish green mineral $Ca_2(Al,Fe)_3Si_3O_{12}OH$ usu. occurring in grains or columnar masses and sometimes used as a gemstone

epi·du·ral \ˌep-i-ˈd(y)u̇r-əl\ *adj* : situated upon or administered outside the dura mater <~ anesthesia> <~ structures>

epi·fau·na \-ˈfȯn-ə, -ˈfän-\ *n* [NL] : benthic fauna living on the substrate and esp. on a hard sea floor — compare INFAUNA — **epi·fau·nal** \-ˈfȯn-ᵊl, -ˈfän-\ *adj*

epi·gas·tric \ˌep-i-ˈgas-trik\ *adj* **1** : lying upon or over the stomach **2** : of or relating to the anterior walls of the abdomen

epi·ge·al \ˌep-i-ˈjē-əl\ *or* **epi·ge·ous** \-ˈjē-əs\ *adj* [Gk *epigaios* upon the earth, fr. *epi-* + *gē* earth] **1** : growing above the surface of the ground **2 a** *of a cotyledon* : forced above ground by elongation of the hypocotyl **b** : marked by the production of epigeal cotyledons <~ germination>

epi·gen·e·sis \ˌep-ə-ˈjen-ə-səs\ *n* [NL] **1** : development of new characters (as of a whole new plant) in an initially undifferentiated entity (as a fertilized egg or spore) **2** : change in the mineral character of a rock owing to outside influences

epi·ge·net·ic \-jə-ˈnet-ik\ *adj* **1** : of, relating to, or produced by epigenesis <genetic versus ~ influences> **2** *or* **epi·gen·ic** \-ˈjen-ik\ *of deposit or structure* : formed after the laying down of the enclosing rock

epi·glot·tal \ˌep-ə-ˈglät-ᵊl\ *also* **epi·glot·tic** \-ˈglät-ik\ *adj* : of, relating to, or produced with the aid of the epiglottis

epi·glot·tis \-ˈglät-əs\ *n* [NL, fr. Gk *epiglōttis,* fr. *epi-* + *glōttis* glottis] : a thin plate of flexible cartilage in front of the glottis that folds back over and protects the glottis during swallowing — see LARYNX illustration

ep·i·gone \ˈep-ə-ˌgōn\ *n* [G, fr. L *epigonus* successor, fr. Gk *epigonos,* fr. *epigignesthai* to be born after, fr. *epi-* + *gignesthai* to be born — more at KIN] : an imitative follower; *esp* : an inferior imitator of a creative thinker or artist — **ep·i·gon·ic** \ˌep-ə-ˈgän-ik\ *or* **epig·o·nous** \i-ˈpig-ə-nəs, e-\ *adj* — **epig·o·nism** \-ˈpig-ə-ˌniz-əm\ *n*

epig·o·nus \i-ˈpig-ə-nəs, e-\ *n, pl* **-ni** \-ˌnī, -ˌnē\ [L] : EPIGONE

ep·i·gram \ˈep-ə-ˌgram\ *n* [ME *epigrame,* fr. L *epigrammat-, epigramma,* fr. Gk, fr. *epigraphein* to write on, inscribe, fr. *epi-* + *graphein* to write — more at CARVE] **1** : a concise poem dealing pointedly and often satirically with a single thought or event and often ending with an ingenious turn of thought **2** : a terse, sage, or witty and often paradoxical saying **3** : epigrammatic expression — **ep·i·gram·ma·tism** \ˌep-ə-ˈgram-ə-ˌtiz-əm\ *n* — **ep·i·gram·ma·tist** \-ˈgram-ət-əst\ *n*

ep·i·gram·mat·ic \ˌep-ə-grə-ˈmat-ik\ *adj* **1** : of, relating to, or resembling an epigram **2** : marked by or given to the use of epigrams — **ep·i·gram·mat·i·cal** \-i-kəl\ *adj* — **ep·i·gram·mat·i·cal·ly** \-i-k(ə-)lē\ *adv*

ep·i·gram·ma·tize \-ˈgram-ə-ˌtīz\ *vb* **-tized; -tiz·ing** *vt* **1** : to express in the form of an epigram **2** : to make an epigram about ~ *vi* : to make an epigram — **ep·i·gram·ma·tiz·er** *n*

ep·i·graph \ˈep-ə-ˌgraf\ *n* [Gk *epigraphē,* fr. *epigraphein*] **1** : an engraved inscription **2** : a quotation set at the beginning of a literary work or a division of it to suggest its theme

epig·ra·pher \i-ˈpig-rə-fər, e-\ *n* : EPIGRAPHIST

ep·i·graph·ic \ˌep-ə-ˈgraf-ik\ *also* **ep·i·graph·i·cal** \-i-kəl\ *adj* : of or relating to epigraphs or epigraphy — **ep·i·graph·i·cal·ly** \-i-k(ə-)lē\ *adv*

epig·ra·phist \i-ˈpig-rə-fəst, e-\ *n* : a specialist in epigraphy

epig·ra·phy \-fē\ *n* **1** : EPIGRAPHS, INSCRIPTIONS **2** : the study of inscriptions; *esp* : the deciphering of ancient inscriptions

epig·y·nous \i-ˈpij-ə-nəs, e-\ *adj* **1** *of a floral organ* : adnate to the surface of the ovary and appearing to grow from the top of it **2** : having epigynous floral organs — **epig·y·ny** \-nē\ *n*

epil *abbr* **1** epilepsy **2** epileptic

ep·i·la·tion \ˌep-ə-ˈlā-shən\ *n* [F *épilation,* fr. *épiler* to remove hair, fr. *é-* e- + L *pilus* hair — more at PILE] : the loss or removal of hair

ep·i·lep·sy \ˈep-ə-ˌlep-sē\ *n, pl* **-sies** [MF *epilepsie,* fr. LL *epilepsia,* fr. Gk *epilēpsia,* fr. *epilambanein* to seize, fr. *epi-* + *lambanein* to take, seize — more at LATCH] : any of various disorders marked by disturbed electrical rhythms of the central nervous system and typically manifested by convulsive attacks usu. with clouding of consciousness

epilept- *or* **epilepti-** *or* **epilepto-** *comb form* [Gk *epilēpt-,* fr. *epilēptos* seized by epilepsy, fr. *epilambanein*] : epilepsy <*epileptoid*>

ep·i·lep·tic \ˌep-ə-ˈlep-tik\ *adj* : relating to, affected with, or having the characteristics of epilepsy — **epileptic** *n* — **ep·i·lep·ti·cal·ly** \-ti-k(ə-)lē\ *adv*

ep·i·lep·ti·form \-ˈlep-tə-ˌfȯrm\ *adj* : resembling that of epilepsy <an ~ convulsion>

ep·i·lep·to·gen·ic \-ˌlep-tə-ˈjen-ik\ *adj* : inducing or tending to induce epilepsy

ep·i·lep·toid \-ˈlep-ˌtȯid\ *adj* **1** : EPILEPTIFORM **2** : exhibiting symptoms resembling those of epilepsy <the ~ person>

epi·lim·ni·on \ˌep-ə-ˈlim-nē-ˌän, -nē-ən\ *n* [NL, fr. *epi-* + Gk *limnion,* dim. of *limnē* marshy lake — more at LIMNETIC] : the water layer overlying the thermocline of a lake

ep·i·logue \ˈep-ə-ˌlȯg, -ˌläg\ *n* [ME *epiloge,* fr. MF *epilogue,* fr. L *epilogus,* fr. Gk *epilogos,* fr. *epilegein* to say in addition, fr. *epi-* + *legein* to say — more at LEGEND] **1** : a concluding section that rounds out the design of a literary work **2 a** : a speech often in verse addressed to the audience by an actor at the end of a play **b** : the actor speaking such an epilogue **c** : the final scene of a play that comments on or summarizes the main action **3** : the concluding section of a musical composition : CODA

epi·mer \ˈep-i-mər\ *n* [*epi-* + iso*mer*] : either of the stereoisomers of a sugar or sugar derivative that differ in the arrangement of the hydrogen atom and the hydroxyl group on the last asymmetric carbon atom of a chain — **epi·mer·ic** \ˌep-i-ˈmer-ik\ *adj*

epim·er·ase \i-ˈpim-ə-ˌrās, e-, -ˌrāz\ *n* : any of various isomerases that catalyze the inversion of asymmetric groups in a substrate with several centers of asymmetry

ep·i·mere \ˈep-ə-ˌmi(ə)r\ *n* [ISV] : the dorsal part of a mesodermal segment of a chordate embryo

epi·mor·pho·sis \ˌep-ə-ˈmȯr-fə-səs\ *n* [NL, fr. *epi-* + Gk *morphōsis* formation, fr. *morphoun* to form, fr. *morphē* form — more at FORM] : regeneration of a part or organism involving extensive cell proliferation followed by differentiation

epi·my·si·um \ˌep-ə-ˈmiz(h)-ē-əm\ *n, pl* **-sia** \-ē-ə\ [NL, fr. *epi-* + Gk *mys* mouse, muscle — more at MOUSE] : the external connective-tissue sheath of a muscle

epi·nas·ty \ˈep-ə-ˌnas-tē\ *n* : a nastic movement in which a plant part (as a flower petal) is bent outward and often downward

epi·neph·rine *also* **epi·neph·rin** \ˌep-ə-ˈnef-rən\ *n* [ISV *epi-* + Gk *nephros* kidney — more at NEPHRITIS] : a colorless crystalline feebly basic sympathomimetic adrenal hormone $C_9H_{13}NO_3$ used medicinally esp. as a heart stimulant, a vasoconstrictor, and a muscle relaxant — called also *adrenaline*

epi·neu·ri·um \ˌep-ə-ˈn(y)u̇r-ē-əm\ *n* [NL] : the external connective-tissue sheath of a nerve trunk

epi·pe·lag·ic \ˌep-i-pə-ˈlaj-ik\ *adj* : of, relating to, or constituting the part of the oceanic zone into which enough light penetrates for photosynthesis

ep·i·phan·ic \ˌep-ə-ˈfan-ik\ *adj* : of or having the character of an epiphany

epiph·a·nous \i-ˈpif-ə-nəs\ *adj* : EPIPHANIC

epiph·a·ny \i-ˈpif-ə-nē\ *n, pl* **-nies** [ME *epiphanie,* fr. MF, fr. LL *epiphania,* fr. LGk, pl., prob. alter. of Gk *epiphaneia* appearance, manifestation, fr. *epiphainein* to manifest, fr. *phainein* to show — more at FANCY] **1** *cap* : January 6 observed as a church festival in commemoration of the coming of the Magi as the first manifestation of Christ to the Gentiles or in the Eastern Church in commemoration of the baptism of Christ **2** : an appearance or manifestation esp. of a divine being **3 a** (1) : a usu. sudden manifestation or perception of the essential nature or meaning of something (2) : an intuitive grasp of reality through something (as an event) usu. simple and striking **b** : a literary representation of an epiphany

epi·phe·nom·e·nal \ˌep-i-fi-ˈnäm-ən-ᵊl\ *adj* : of or relating to an epiphenomenon : DERIVATIVE — **epi·phe·nom·e·nal·ly** \-ᵊl-ē\ *adv*

epi·phe·nom·e·nal·ism \-ᵊl-ˌiz-əm\ *n* : a doctrine that mental processes are epiphenomena of brain processes

epi·phe·nom·e·non \-ˈnäm-ə-ˌnän, -nən\ *n* : a secondary phenomenon accompanying another and caused by it

ep·i·phragm \ˈep-ə-ˌfram\ *n* [Gk *epiphragma* covering] : a closing membrane or septum (as of a snail shell or a moss capsule)

epiph·y·se·al \i-ˌpif-ə-ˈsē-əl\ *also* **ep·i·phys·i·al** \ˌep-ə-ˈfiz-ē-əl\ *adj* : of or relating to an epiphysis

epiph·y·sis \i-ˈpif-ə-səs\ *n, pl* **-y·ses** \-ˌsēz\ [NL, fr. Gk, growth, fr. *epiphyesthai* to grow on, fr. *epi-* + *phyesthai* to grow, pass. of *phyein* to bring forth — more at BE] **1** : a part or process of a bone that ossifies separately and later becomes ankylosed to the main part of the bone; *esp* : an end of a long bone **2** : PINEAL BODY

epi·phyte \ˈep-ə-ˌfīt\ *n* : a plant that derives its moisture and nutrients from the air and rain and grows usu. on another plant

epi·phyt·ic \ˌep-ə-ˈfit-ik\ *adj* **1** : of, relating to, or being an epiphyte **2** : living on the surface of plants — **epi·phyt·i·cal·ly** \-ˈfit-i-k(ə-)lē\ *adv*

ep·i·phy·tol·o·gy \ˌep-ə-ˌfī-ˈtäl-ə-jē\ *n* [*epiphyto*tic + *-logy*] **1** : a science that deals with character, ecology, and causes of outbreak of plant diseases **2** : the sum of the factors controlling the occurrence of a disease or pathogen of plants

ep·i·phy·tot·ic \-ˈtät-ik\ *adj* [*epi-* + Gk *phyton* plant] : of, relating to, or being a plant disease that tends to recur sporadically and to affect large numbers of susceptible plants — **epiphytotic** *n*

epi·ro·gen·ic, ep·i·rog·e·ny *var of* EPEIROGENIC, EPEIROGENY

Episc *abbr* Episcopal

epi·scia \i-ˈpish-(ē-)ə\ *n* [NL, genus name, fr. Gk *episkios* shaded, fr. *epi-* + *skia* shadow — more at SHINE] : any of a genus (*Episcia*) of tropical American herbs that have hairy foliage and are related to the African violet

epis·co·pa·cy \i-ˈpis-kə-pə-sē\ *n, pl* **-cies** **1** : government of the church by bishops or by a hierarchy **2** : EPISCOPATE

epis·co·pal \i-ˈpis-kə-pəl\ *adj* [ME, fr. LL *episcopalis,* fr. *episcopus* bishop — more at BISHOP] **1** : of or relating to a bishop **2** : of, having, or constituting government by bishops **3** *cap* : of or relating to the Protestant Episcopal Church representing the Anglican communion in the U.S. — **epis·co·pal·ly** \-p(ə-)lē\ *adv*

Episcopal *n* : EPISCOPALIAN

Epis·co·pa·lian \i-ˌpis-kə-ˈpāl-yən\ *n* **1** : an adherent of the episcopal form of church government **2** : a member of an episcopal church (as the Protestant Episcopal Church) — **Episcopalian** *adj* — **Epis·co·pa·lian·ism** \-yə-ˌniz-əm\ *n*

epis·co·pate \i-ˈpis-kə-pət, -ˌpāt\ *n* **1** : the rank, office, or term of bishop **2** : DIOCESE **3** : the body of bishops (as in a country)

epi·scope \ˈep-ə-ˌskōp\ *n* [ISV *epi-* + *-scope*] : a projector for images of opaque objects (as photographs)

epis·i·ot·o·my \i-ˌpiz-ē-ˈät-ə-mē\ *n* [NL *episio-* vulva, fr. Gk *epision* pubic region] : surgical enlargement of the vulval orifice for obstetrical purposes during parturition

ep·i·sode \ˈep-ə-ˌsōd *also* -ˌzōd\ *n* [Gk *epeisodion,* fr. neut. of *epeisodios* coming in besides, fr. *epi-* + *eisodios* coming in, fr. *eis* into (akin to Gk *en* in) + *hodos* road, journey — more at IN, CEDE] **1** : a usu. brief unit of action in a dramatic or literary work: as **a** : the part of an ancient Greek tragedy between two choric songs

b : a developed situation that is integral to but separable from a continuous narrative **:** INCIDENT **c :** one of a series of loosely connected stories or scenes **d :** the part of a serial presented at one performance **2 :** an event that is distinctive and separate although part of a larger series **3 :** a digressive subdivision in a musical composition ***syn*** see OCCURRENCE

ep·i·sod·ic \ˌep-ə-ˈsäd-ik *also* -ˈzäd-\ *also* **ep·i·sod·i·cal** \-i-kəl\ *adj* **1 :** made up of separate esp. loosely connected episodes **2 :** having the form of an episode **3 :** of or limited in duration or significance to a particular episode **:** TEMPORARY <may be able to establish whether the sea-floor spreading is continuous or ~ —A. I. Hammond> **4 :** occurring, appearing, or changing at usu. irregular intervals **:** OCCASIONAL, CAPRICIOUS <~ care of his patients> — **ep·i·sod·i·cal·ly** \-i-k(ə-)lē\ *adv*

epi·some \ˈep-ə-ˌsōm, -ˌzōm\ *n* **:** a genetic determinant (as the DNA of some bacteriophages) that can replicate autonomously in bacterial cytoplasm or as an integral part of the chromosomes — **epi·som·al** \ˌep-ə-ˈsō-məl, -ˈzō-\ *adj* — **epi·som·al·ly** \-mə-lē\ *adv*

epis·ta·sis \i-ˈpis-tə-səs\ *or* **epis·ta·sy** \-sē\ *n, pl* **-ta·ses** \-ˌsēz\ *or* **-ta·sies** \-sēz\ [NL *epistasis,* fr. Gk, act of stopping, fr. *ephistanai* to stop, fr. *epi-* + *histanai* to cause to stand — more at STAND] **:** suppression of the effect of a gene by a nonallelic gene — **ep·i·stat·ic** \ˌep-ə-ˈstat-ik\ *adj*

ep·i·stax·is \ˌep-ə-ˈstak-səs\ *n, pl* **-stax·es** \-ˌsēz\ [NL, fr. Gk, fr. *epistazein* to drip on, to bleed at the nose again, fr. *epi-* + *stazein* to drip — more at STAGNATE] **:** NOSEBLEED

ep·i·ste·mic \ˌep-ə-ˈstē-mik, -ˈstem-ik\ *adj* **:** of or relating to knowledge or knowing **:** COGNITIVE — **ep·i·ste·mi·cal·ly** \-(m)i-k(ə-)lē\ *adv*

epis·te·mol·o·gy \i-ˌpis-tə-ˈmäl-ə-jē\ *n* [Gk *epistēmē* knowledge, fr. *epistanai* to understand, know, fr. *epi-* + *histanai* to cause to stand — more at STAND] **:** the study or a theory of the nature and grounds of knowledge esp. with reference to its limits and validity — **epis·te·mo·log·i·cal** \-mə-ˈläj-i-kəl\ *adj* — **epis·te·mo·log·i·cal·ly** \-k(ə-)lē\ *adv* — **epis·te·mol·o·gist** \-ˈmäl-ə-jəst\ *n*

epi·ster·num \ˌep-i-ˈstər-nəm\ *n* [NL] **1 :** an anterior element of or associated with the sternum: as **a :** INTERCLAVICLE **b :** MANUBRIUM **2 :** a lateral division or piece of a somite of an arthropod

epis·tle \i-ˈpis-əl\ *n* [ME, letter, Epistle, fr. OF, fr. L *epistula, epistola* letter, fr. Gk *epistolē* message, letter, fr. *epistellein* to send to, fr. *epi-* + *stellein* to send — more at STALL] **1** *cap* **a :** one of the letters adopted as books of the New Testament **b :** a liturgical lection usu. from one of the New Testament Epistles **2 a :** LETTER; *esp* **:** a formal or elegant letter **b :** a composition in the form of a letter — **epis·tler** \-ˈpis-(ə-)lər\ *n*

epistle side *n, often cap E* [fr. the custom of reading the Epistle from this side] **:** the right side of an altar or chancel as one faces it

[1]**epis·to·lary** \i-ˈpis-tə-ˌler-ē\ *adj* **1 :** of, relating to, or suitable to a letter **2 :** contained in or carried on by letters <an endless sequence of . . . ~ love affairs —*Times Lit. Supp.*> **3 :** written in the form of a series of letters <~ novel>

[2]**epistolary** *n, pl* **-lar·ies :** a lectionary containing a body of liturgical epistles

epis·to·ler \i-ˈpis-tə-lər\ *n* **:** the reader of the liturgical Epistle esp. in Anglican churches

epis·tro·phe \i-ˈpis-trə-(ˌ)fē\ *n* [Gk *epistrophē,* lit., turning about, fr. *epi-* + *strophē* turning — more at STROPHE] **:** repetition of the same word or expression at the end of successive phrases, clauses, or sentences for rhetorical effect <Lincoln's "of the people, by the people, for the people" is an example of ~> — compare ANAPHORA

epi·style \ˈep-ə-ˌstīl\ *n* [L *epistylium,* fr. Gk *epistylion,* fr. *epi-* + Gk *stylos* pillar — more at STEER] **:** ARCHITRAVE 1

ep·i·taph \ˈep-ə-ˌtaf\ *n* [ME *epitaphe,* fr. MF, fr. ML *epitaphium,* fr. L, funeral oration, fr. Gk *epitaphion,* fr. *epi-* + *taphos* tomb, funeral; akin to Gk *thaptein* to bury, Arm *damban* grave] **1 :** an inscription on or at a tomb or a grave in memory of the one buried there **2 :** a brief statement commemorating or epitomizing a deceased person or something past — **ep·i·taph·ial** \ˌep-ə-ˈtaf-ē-əl\ *or* **ep·i·taph·ic** \-ˈtaf-ik\ *adj*

epit·a·sis \i-ˈpit-ə-səs\ *n, pl* **-a·ses** \-ˌsēz\ [Gk, increased intensity, fr. *epiteinein* to stretch tighter, fr. *epi-* + *teinein* to stretch — more at THIN] **:** the part of a play developing the main action and leading to the catastrophe

ep·i·taxy \ˈep-ə-ˌtak-sē\ *n* [*epi-* + *-taxy* (fr. Gk *-taxia* -taxis] **:** the growth on a crystalline substrate of a crystalline substance that mimics the orientation of the substrate — **ep·i·tax·i·al** \ˌep-ə-ˈtak-sē-əl\ *adj* — **ep·i·tax·i·al·ly** \-sē-ə-lē\ *adv*

ep·i·tha·la·mi·um \ˌep-ə-thə-ˈlā-mē-əm\ *or* **ep·i·tha·la·mi·on** \-mē-ən\ *n, pl* **-mi·ums** *or* **-mia** \-mē-ə\ [L & Gk; L *epithalamium,* fr. Gk *epithalamion,* fr. *epi-* + *thalamos* room, bridal chamber] **:** a song or poem in honor of a bride and bridegroom

epitheli- *or* **epithelio-** *comb form* [NL *epithelium*] **:** epithelium

ep·i·the·li·al \ˌep-ə-ˈthē-lē-əl\ *adj* **:** of or relating to epithelium

ep·i·the·li·oid \-lē-ˌȯid\ *adj* **:** resembling epithelium <~ cells>

ep·i·the·li·o·ma \-ˌthē-lē-ˈō-mə\ *n* **:** a benign or malignant tumor derived from epithelial tissue — **ep·i·the·li·o·ma·tous** \-mət-əs\ *adj*

ep·i·the·li·um \ˌep-ə-ˈthē-lē-əm\ *n, pl* **-lia** \-lē-ə\ [NL, fr. *epi-* + Gk *thēlē* nipple — more at FEMININE] **1 :** a membranous cellular tissue that covers a free surface or lines a tube or cavity of an animal body and serves esp. to enclose and protect the other parts of the body, to produce secretions and excretions, and to function in assimilation **2 :** a usu. thin layer of parenchyma that lines a cavity or tube of a plant

ep·i·the·lize \ˌep-ə-ˈthē-ˌlīz\ *also* **ep·i·the·li·al·ize** \-lē-ə-ˌlīz\ *vt* **-lized; -liz·ing :** to cover with or convert to epithelium <*epithelized* lesions>

ep·i·thet \ˈep-ə-ˌthet *also* -thət\ *n* [L *epitheton,* fr. Gk, fr. neut. of *epithetos* added, fr. *epitithenai* to put on, add, fr. *epi-* + *tithenai* to put — more at DO] **1 a :** a characterizing word or phrase accompanying or occurring in place of the name of a person or thing **b :** a disparaging or abusive word or phrase **c :** the part of a taxonomic name identifying a subordinate unit within a genus **2** *obs* **:** EXPRESSION — **ep·i·thet·ic** \ˌep-ə-ˈthet-ik\ *or* **ep·i·thet·i·cal** \-i-kəl\ *adj*

epit·o·me \i-ˈpit-ə-mē\ *n* [L, fr. Gk *epitomē,* fr. *epitemnein* to cut short, fr. *epi-* + *temnein* to cut — more at TOME] **1 a :** a summary of a written work **b :** a brief presentation or statement of something **2 :** a typical or ideal example **:** EMBODIMENT <the British monarchy itself is the ~ of tradition —Richard Joseph> **3 :** brief or miniature form — usu. used with *in* ***syn*** see ABRIDGMENT

epit·o·mize \-ˌmīz\ *vt* **-mized; -miz·ing 1 :** to make or give an epitome of **2 :** to serve as the typical or ideal example of

epi·zo·ic \ˌep-ə-ˈzō-ik\ *adj* **:** dwelling upon the body of an animal <an ~ plant> — **epi·zo·ism** \-ˌiz-əm\ *n* — **epi·zo·ite** \-ˌīt\ *n*

[1]**epi·zo·ot·ic** \ˌep-ə-zə-ˈwät-ik\ *adj* **:** of, relating to, or being a disease that affects many animals of one kind at the same time — **epi·zo·ot·i·cal·ly** \-i-k(ə-)lē\ *adv*

[2]**epizootic** *n* **:** an epizootic disease

epi·zo·ot·i·ol·o·gy \ˌep-ə-zə-ˌwät-ē-ˈäl-ə-jē\ *or* **epi·zo·otol·o·gy** \-ˌzō-ə-ˈtäl-ə-jē\ *or* **epi·zo·ol·o·gy** \-zə-ˈwäl-ə-jē\ *n* **1 :** a science that deals with the character, ecology, and causes of outbreaks of animal diseases **2 :** the sum of the factors controlling the occurrence of a disease or pathogen of animals — **epi·zo·oti·o·log·i·cal** \-zə-ˌwōt-ē-ə-ˈläj-i-kəl, -ˌwät-\ *also* **epi·zo·oti·o·log·ic** \-ik\ *adj* — **epi·zo·oti·o·log·i·cal·ly** \-i-k(ə-)lē\ *adv*

e plu·ri·bus unum \ˌē-ˌplu̇r-ə-bəs-ˈyü-nəm; ˌā-ˌplu̇r-, -bə-ˈsü-\ [L, one out of many] **:** one composed of many; *specif* **:** a national government formed by uniting many states — used on the seal of the U.S. and on several U.S. coins

ep·och \ˈep-ək, ˈep-ˌäk *also* ˈē-ˌpäk\ *n* [ML *epocha,* fr. Gk *epochē* cessation, fixed point, fr. *epechein* to pause, hold back, fr. *epi-* + *echein* to hold — more at SCHEME] **1 :** an instant of time or a date selected as a point of reference (as in astronomy) **2 a :** an event or a time marked by an event that begins a new period or development **b :** a memorable event or date **3 a :** an extended period of time usu. characterized by a distinctive development or by a memorable series of events **b :** a division of geologic time less than a period and greater than an age ***syn*** see PERIOD

ep·och·al \ˈep-ə-kəl, ˈep-ˌäk-əl\ *adj* **1 :** of or relating to an epoch **2 :** uniquely or highly significant **:** MOMENTOUS <his fights to advance . . . democracy during his three ~ years in the assembly —C. G. Bowers>; *also* **:** UNPARALLELED <the . . . delegates . . . have fallen for it out of their almost ~ dumbness —J. T. Flynn> — **ep·och·al·ly** \-ē\ *adv*

ep·ode \ˈep-ˌōd\ *n* [L *epodos,* fr. Gk *epōidos,* fr. *epōidos* sung or said after, fr. *epi-* + *aidein* to sing — more at ODE] **1 :** a lyric poem in which a long verse is followed by a shorter one **2 :** the third part of a triadically constructed Greek ode following the strophe and the antistrophe

ep·onym \ˈep-ə-ˌnim\ *n* [Gk *epōnymos,* fr. *epōnymos* eponymous, fr. *epi-* + *onyma* name — more at NAME] **1 :** the person for whom something is or is believed to be named **2 :** a name (as of a drug or a disease) based on or derived from an eponym — **ep·onym·ic** \ˌep-ə-ˈnim-ik\ *adj*

epon·y·mous \i-ˈpän-ə-məs, e-\ *adj* **:** of, relating to, or being the person for whom something is or is believed to be named

epon·y·my \-mē\ *n, pl* **-mies :** the explanation of a proper name (as of a town or tribe) by supposing a fictitious eponym

ep·o·pee \ˈep-ə-ˌpē\ *n* [F *épopée,* fr. Gk *epopoiia,* fr. *epos* + *poiein* to make — more at POET] **:** EPIC; *esp* **:** an epic poem

ep·os \ˈep-ˌäs\ *n* [Gk, word, epic poem] **1 :** a number of poems that treat an epic theme but are not formally united **2 :** EPIC

ep·ox·ide \(ˈ)ep-ˈäk-ˌsīd\ *n* **:** an epoxy compound

ep·ox·i·dize \-sə-ˌdīz\ *vt* **-dized; -diz·ing :** to convert into an epoxide <*epoxidized* oils>

[1]**ep·oxy** \ˈep-ˌäk-sē, ep-ˈ\ *adj* **1 :** containing oxygen attached to two different atoms already united in some other way; *specif* **:** containing a 3-membered ring consisting of one oxygen and two carbon atoms **2 :** of or relating to an epoxide

[2]**epoxy** *vt* **ep·ox·ied** *or* **ep·oxyed; ep·oxy·ing :** to glue with epoxy resin

epoxy resin *n* **:** a flexible usu. thermosetting resin made by polymerization of an epoxide and used chiefly in coatings and adhesives — called also *epoxy*

ep·si·lon \ˈep-sə-ˌlän, -lən\ *n* [Gk *e psilon,* lit., simple e] **1 :** the 5th letter of the Greek alphabet — see ALPHABET table **2 :** an arbitrarily small positive quantity in mathematical analysis

Ep·som salt \ˌep-səm-\ *n* **:** EPSOM SALTS

Epsom salts *n pl but sing in constr* [*Epsom,* England] **:** a bitter colorless or white crystalline salt $MgSO_4 \cdot 7H_2O$ that is a hydrated magnesium sulfate with cathartic properties

eq *abbr* **1** equal **2** equation

equa·ble \ˈek-wə-bəl, ˈē-kwə-\ *adj* [L *aequabilis,* fr. *aequare* to make level or equal, fr. *aequus*] **1 :** marked by lack of variation or change **:** UNIFORM **2 :** marked by lack of noticeable, unpleasant, or extreme variation or inequality ***syn*** see STEADY ***ant*** variable, changeable — **equa·bil·i·ty** \ˌek-wə-ˈbil-ət-ē, ˌē-kwə-\ *n* — **equa·ble·ness** \ˈek-wə-bəl-nəs, ˈē-kwə-\ *n* — **equa·bly** \-blē\ *adv*

[1]**equal** \ˈē-kwəl\ *adj* [ME, fr. L *aequalis,* fr. *aequus* level, equal] **1 a (1) :** of the same measure, quantity, amount, or number as another **(2) :** identical in mathematical value or logical denotation **:** EQUIVALENT **b :** like in quality, nature, or status **c :** like for each member of a group, class, or society <provide ~ employment opportunities> **2 :** regarding or affecting all objects in the same way **:** IMPARTIAL **3 :** free from extremes: as **a :** tranquil of mind or mood **b :** not showing variation in appearance, structure, or

ə abut ə kitten ər further a back ā bake ä cot, cart
au̇ out ch chin e less ē easy g gift i trip ī life
j joke ŋ sing ō flow ȯ flaw ȯi coin th thin t͟h this
ü loot u̇ foot y yet yü few yu̇ furious zh vision

proportion **4 a :** capable of meeting the requirements of a situation or a task **b :** SUITABLE <bored with work not ~ to his abilities> ***syn*** see SAME ***ant*** unequal

[2]**equal** *n* **1 :** one that is equal <insists that women can be absolute ~*s* with men —Anne Bernays> **2 :** an equal quantity

[3]**equal** *vt* **equaled** *or* **equalled; equal·ing** *or* **equal·ling 1** *archaic* **:** EQUALIZE **2 :** to be equal to; *esp* **:** to be identical in value to **3 :** to make or produce something equal to ***syn*** see MATCH

equal–area *adj, of a map projection* **:** maintaining constant ratio of size between quadrilaterals formed by the meridians and parallels and the quadrilaterals of the globe thereby preserving true areal extent of forms represented

equal·i·tar·i·an \i-ˌkwäl-ə-ˈter-ē-ən\ *adj or n* **:** EGALITARIAN — **equal·i·tar·i·an·ism** \-ē-ə-ˌniz-əm\ *n*

equal·i·ty \i-ˈkwäl-ət-ē\ *n, pl* **-ties 1 :** the quality or state of being equal **2 :** EQUATION 2a

equal·ize \ˈē-kwə-ˌlīz\ *vt* **-ized; -iz·ing 1 :** to make equal **2 a :** to compensate for **b :** to make uniform; *specif* **:** to distribute evenly or uniformly <~ the tax burden> **c :** to adjust or correct the frequency characteristics of (an electronic signal) by restoring to their original level high frequencies that have been attenuated — **equal·iza·tion** \ˌē-kwə-lə-ˈzā-shən\ *n*

equal·iz·er \-ˌlī-zər\ *n* **:** one that equalizes: as **a :** a device that provides for equal distribution (as of force) **b :** a score that ties a game

equal·ly \ˈē-kwə-lē\ *adv* **1 :** in an equal or uniform manner **:** EVENLY **2 :** to an equal degree **:** ALIKE <respected ~ by young and old>

equal opportunity employer *n* **:** an employer who agrees not to discriminate against any employee or job applicant because of race, color, religion, sex, or national origin

equal sign *n* **:** a sign = indicating mathematical or logical equivalence — called also *equality sign, equals sign*

equa·nim·i·ty \ˌē-kwə-ˈnim-ət-ē, ˌek-wə-\ *n, pl* **-ties** [L *aequanimitas,* fr. *aequo animo* with even mind] **1 :** evenness of mind esp. under stress **2 :** right disposition **:** BALANCE
syn EQUANIMITY, COMPOSURE, SANGFROID, PHLEGM *shared meaning element* **:** the characteristic quality of one who is self-possessed and not easily disturbed or perturbed

equate \i-ˈkwāt, ˈē-ˌ\ *vb* **equat·ed; equat·ing** [ME *equaten,* fr. L *aequatus,* pp. of *aequare*] *vt* **1 a :** to make equal **:** EQUALIZE **b :** to make such an allowance or correction in as will reduce to a common standard or obtain a correct result **2 :** to treat, represent, or regard as equal, equivalent, or comparable <~*s* disagreement with disloyalty> ~ *vi* **:** to correspond as equal

equa·tion \i-ˈkwā-zhən *also* -shən\ *n* **1 a :** the act or process of equating **b (1) :** an element affecting a process **:** FACTOR **(2) :** a complex of variable factors **c :** a state of being equated; *specif* **:** a state of association or identification of two or more things <bring governmental enterprises and payment for them into immediate ~ —R. G. Tugwell> **2 a :** a usu. formal statement of the equality or equivalence of mathematical or logical expressions **b :** an expression representing a chemical reaction quantitatively by means of chemical symbols

equa·tion·al \i-ˈkwāzh-nəl, -ən-ᵊl *also* -ˈkwāsh-\ *adj* **1 :** of, using, or involving equation or equations **2 :** dividing into two equal parts — used esp. of the mitotic cell division usu. following reduction in meiosis — **equa·tion·al·ly** \-ē\ *adv*

equation of time : the difference between mean time and apparent time usu. expressed as a correction which is to be added to apparent time to give local mean solar time

equa·tor \i-ˈkwāt-ər, ˈē-ˌ\ *n* [ME, fr. ML *aequator,* lit., equalizer, fr. L *aequatus;* fr. its containing the equinoxes] **1 :** the great circle of the celestial sphere whose plane is perpendicular to the axis of the earth **2 :** a great circle of the earth that is everywhere equally distant from the two poles and divides the earth's surface into the northern and southern hemispheres **3 :** a circle or circular band dividing the surface of a body into two usu. equal and symmetrical parts <the ~ of a dividing cell> **4 :** GREAT CIRCLE

[1]**equa·to·ri·al** \ˌē-kwə-ˈtōr-ē-əl, ˌek-wə-, -ˈtȯr-\ *adj* **1 a :** of, relating to, or located at the equator or an equator; *also* **:** being in the plane of the equator <an ~ orbit of a satellite> **b :** of, originating in, or suggesting the region around the geographic equator **2 a :** being or having a support that includes two axles at right angles to each other with one parallel to the earth's axis of rotation <an ~ telescope> **b :** extending in a direction essentially in the plane of a cyclic structure (as of cyclohexane) <~ hydrogens> — compare AXIAL

[2]**equatorial** *n* **:** an equatorial telescope

equatorial plane *n* **:** the plane perpendicular to the spindle of a dividing cell and midway between the poles

equatorial plate *n* **1 :** EQUATORIAL PLANE **2 :** METAPHASE PLATE

[1]**equa·tor·ward** \i-ˈkwāt-ər-wərd\ *adv* **:** toward the equator <currents flowing ~>

[2]**equatorward** *adj* **:** lying near or moving toward the equator <~ winds>

equer·ry \ˈek-wə-rē, i-ˈkwer-ē\ *n, pl* **-ries** [obs. *escuirie, equerry* stable, fr. MF *escuirie* office of a squire, stable, fr. *escuier* squire — more at ESQUIRE] **1 :** an officer of a prince or noble charged with the care of horses **2 :** one of the officers of the British royal household in personal attendance on the sovereign or another member of the royal family

[1]**eques·tri·an** \i-ˈkwes-trē-ən\ *adj* [L *equestr-, equester* of a horseman, fr. *eques* horseman, fr. *equus* horse — more at EQUINE] **1 a :** of, relating to, or featuring horseback riding **b** *archaic* **:** riding on horseback **:** MOUNTED **c :** representing a person on horseback <an ~ statue> **2 :** of, relating to, or composed of knights

[2]**equestrian** *n* **:** one who rides on horseback

eques·tri·enne \i-ˌkwes-trē-ˈen\ *n* [[2]*equestrian* + *-enne* (as in *tragedienne*)] **:** a female equestrian

equi- *comb form* [ME, fr. MF, fr. L *aequi-,* fr. *aequus* equal] **:** equal <*equi*poise> **:** equally <*equi*probable>

equi·an·gu·lar \ˌē-kwi-ˈaŋ-gyə-lər, ˌek-wi-\ *adj* **:** having all or corresponding angles equal <an ~ triangle> <~ polygons>

equi·ca·lor·ic \ˌē-kwə-kə-ˈlȯr-ik, ˌek-wə-, -ˈlär-\ *adj* **:** capable of yielding equal amounts of energy in the body <~ diets>

equi·dis·tance \-ˈdis-tən(t)s\ *n* **:** equal distance

equi·dis·tant \-tənt\ *adj* [MF or LL; MF, fr. LL *aequidistant-, aequidistans,* fr. L *aequi-* + *distant-, distans,* prp. of *distare* to stand apart] **1 :** equally distant **2 :** representing map distances true to scale in all directions — **equi·dis·tant·ly** *adv*

equi·lat·er·al \ˌē-kwə-ˈlat-ə-rəl, ˌek-wə-, -ˈla-trəl\ *adj* [LL *aequilateralis,* fr. L *aequi-* + *later-, latus* side — more at LATERAL] **1 a :** having all sides equal <~ triangle> **b :** having all the faces equal <~ polyhedron> **2 :** bilaterally symmetrical

equilateral hyperbola *n* **:** a hyperbola with its asymptotes at right angles

equil·i·brate \i-ˈkwil-ə-ˌbrāt\ *vb* **-brat·ed; -brat·ing** *vt* **:** to bring into or keep in equilibrium **:** BALANCE ~ *vi* **:** to bring about, come to, or be in equilibrium — **equil·i·bra·tion** \-ˌkwil-ə-ˈbrā-shən\ *n* — **equil·i·bra·tor** \-ˈkwil-ə-ˌbrāt-ər\ *n* — **equil·i·bra·to·ry** \-brə-ˌtōr-ē, -ˌtȯr-\ *adj*

equi·li·brist \ˌē-kwə-ˈlib-rəst, ˌek-wə-; i-ˈkwil-ə-brəst\ *n* **:** one who balances himself in unnatural positions and hazardous movements — **equil·i·bris·tic** \i-ˌkwil-ə-ˈbris-tik\ *adj*

equi·lib·ri·um \ˌē-kwə-ˈlib-rē-əm, ˌek-wə-\ *n, pl* **-ri·ums** *or* **-ria** \-rē-ə\ [L *aequilibrium,* fr. *aequilibris* being in equilibrium, fr. *aequi-* + *libra* weight, balance] **1 :** a state of balance between opposing forces or actions that is either static (as in a body acted on by forces whose resultant is zero) or dynamic (as in a reversible chemical reaction when the velocities in both directions are equal) **2 a :** a state of adjustment between opposing or divergent influences or elements **b :** a state of intellectual or emotional balance **:** POISE **3 :** the normal oriented state of the animal body in respect to its substrate that involves adjustment to changing gravitational and spatial relationships

equi·mol·al \-ˈmō-ləl\ *adj* **1 :** having equal molal concentration **2 :** EQUIMOLAR 1

equi·mo·lar \-ˈmō-lər\ *adj* **1 :** of or relating to an equal number of moles <an ~ mixture> **2 :** having equal molar concentration

equine \ˈē-ˌkwīn, ˈek-ˌwīn\ *adj* [L *equinus,* fr. *equus* horse; akin to OE *eoh* horse, Gk *hippos*] **:** of, relating to, or resembling a horse or the horse family — **equine** *n* — **equine·ly** *adv*

[1]**equi·noc·tial** \ˌē-kwə-ˈnäk-shəl, ˌek-wə-\ *adj* **1 :** relating to an equinox or to a state or the time of equal day and night **2 :** relating to the regions or climate of the equinoctial line or equator **3 :** relating to the time when the sun passes an equinoctial point

[2]**equinoctial** *n* **1 :** EQUATOR 1 **2 :** an equinoctial storm

equinoctial circle *n* **:** EQUATOR 1 — called also *equinoctial line*

equi·nox \ˈē-kwə-ˌnäks, ˈek-wə-\ *n* [ME, fr. MF or ML; MF *equinoxe,* fr. ML *equinoxium,* alter. of L *aequinoctium,* fr. *aequi-* equi- + *noct-, nox* night — more at NIGHT] **1 :** either of the two times each year when the sun crosses the equator and day and night are everywhere of equal length, being about March 21 and September 23 **2 :** either of the two points on the celestial sphere where the celestial equator intersects the ecliptic

[1]**equip** \i-ˈkwip\ *vt* **equipped; equip·ping** [MF *equiper,* of Gmc origin; akin to OE *scip* ship] **1 :** to furnish for service or action **:** make ready by appropriate provisioning **2 :** DRESS, ARRAY ***syn*** see FURNISH

[2]**equip** *abbr* equipment

eq·ui·page \ˈek-wə-pij\ *n* **1 a :** material or articles used in equipment **:** OUTFIT **b** *archaic* **(1) :** a set of small articles (as for table service) **(2) :** ETUI **c :** TRAPPINGS **2** *archaic* **:** RETINUE **3 :** a horse-drawn carriage with its servants; *also* **:** such a carriage alone

equip·ment \i-ˈkwip-mənt\ *n* **1 a :** the equipping of a person or thing **b :** the state of being equipped **2 a :** the set of articles or physical resources serving to equip a person or thing: as **(1) :** the implements used in an operation or activity **:** APPARATUS **(2) :** all the fixed assets other than land and buildings of a business enterprise **(3) :** the rolling stock of a railway **b :** a piece of such equipment **3 :** mental or emotional traits or resources **:** ENDOWMENT

[1]**equi·poise** \ˈek-wə-ˌpȯiz, ˈē-kwə-\ *n* **1 :** a state of equilibrium **2 :** COUNTERBALANCE

[2]**equipoise** *vt* **1 :** to serve as an equipoise to **2 :** to put or hold in equipoise

equi·pol·lence \ˌē-kwə-ˈpäl-ən(t)s, ˌek-wə-\ *n* **:** the quality of being equipollent

equi·pol·lent \-ənt\ *adj* [ME, fr. MF, fr. L *aequipollent-, aequipollens,* fr. *aequi-* equi- + *pollent-, pollens,* prp. of *pollēre* to be able] **1 :** equal in force, power, or validity **2 :** the same in effect or signification — **equipollent** *n* — **equi·pol·lent·ly** *adv*

equi·pon·der·ant \-ˈpän-d(ə-)rənt\ *adj* **:** evenly balanced

equi·pon·der·ate \-ˈpän-də-ˌrāt\ *vb* **-at·ed; -at·ing** [ML *aequiponderatus,* pp. of *equiponderare,* fr. L *aequi-* + *ponderare* to weigh, ponder] *vi* **:** to be equal in weight or force ~ *vt* **:** to equal or make equal in weight

equi·po·tent \ˌē-kwə-ˈpōt-ᵊnt, ˌek-wə-\ *adj* **:** having equal effects or capacities for development <~ genes> <~ regions of an egg>

equi·po·ten·tial \-pə-ˈten-chəl\ *adj* **:** having the same potential **:** of uniform potential throughout <~ points> <an ~ surface>

equi·prob·a·ble \-ˈpräb-(ə-)bəl\ *adj* **:** having the same degree of logical or mathematical probability <~ alternatives>

eq·ui·se·tum \ˌek-wə-ˈsēt-əm\ *n, pl* **-se·tums** *or* **-se·ta** \-ˈsēt-ə\ [NL, genus name, fr. L *equisaetum* horsetail (plant), fr. *equus* horse + *saeta* bristle] **:** any of a genus (*Equisetum*) of lower tracheophytes comprising perennial plants that spread by creeping rhizomes, are homosporous and asexual, and have leaves reduced to nodal sheaths on the hollow jointed grooved shoots — called also *scouring rush*

eq·ui·ta·ble \ˈek-wət-ə-bəl\ *adj* **1 :** having or exhibiting equity **:** dealing fairly and equally with all concerned **2 :** existing or valid in equity as distinguished from law ***syn*** see FAIR ***ant*** inequitable — **eq·ui·ta·bil·i·ty** \ˌek-wət-ə-ˈbil-ət-ē\ *n* — **eq·ui·ta·ble-**

ness \'ek-wət-ə-bəl-nəs\ *n* — **eq·ui·ta·bly** \-blē\ *adv*

eq·ui·tant \'ek-wət-ənt\ *adj* [L *equitant-, equitans,* prp. of *equitare* to ride on horseback, fr. *equit-, eques* horseman — more at EQUESTRIAN] *of leaves* : overlapping each other transversely at the base (as in an iris)

eq·ui·ta·tion \ˌek-wə-'tā-shən\ *n* : the act or art of riding on horseback

eq·ui·ty \'ek-wət-ē\ *n, pl* **-ties** [ME *equite,* fr. MF *equité,* fr. L *aequitat-, aequitas,* fr. *aequus* equal, fair] **1 a :** justice according to natural law or right; *specif* : freedom from bias or favoritism **b :** something that is equitable **2 a :** a system of law originating in the English chancery and comprising a settled and formal body of legal and procedural rules and doctrines that supplement, aid, or override common and statute law and are designed to protect rights and enforce duties fixed by substantive law **b :** trial or remedial justice under or by the rules and doctrines of equity **c :** a body of legal doctrines and rules developed to enlarge, supplement, or override a narrow rigid system of law **3 a :** a right, claim, or interest existing or valid in equity **b :** the money value of a property or of an interest in a property in excess of claims or liens against it **c :** a risk interest or ownership right in property

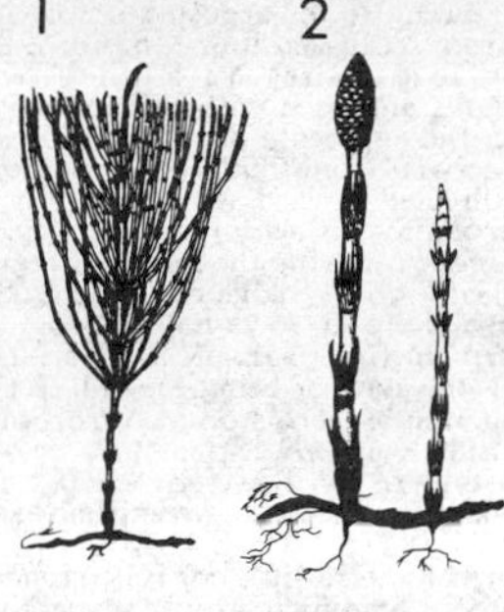

equisetum: *1* sterile stem, *2* fertile stem

equity capital *n* : VENTURE CAPITAL

equiv *abbr* equivalency; equivalent

equiv·a·lence \i-'kwiv(-ə)-lən(t)s\ *n* **1 a :** the state or property of being equivalent **b** (1) **:** the relation holding between two statements if they are either both true or both false (2) **:** the relation holding between two statements if to affirm one and to deny the other would result in a contradiction **2 :** a presentation of terms as equivalent **3 :** equality in metrical value of a regular foot and one in which there are substitutions

equivalence class *n* : a set for which an equivalence relation holds between every pair of elements

equivalence relation *n* : a relation (as equality) between elements of a set (as the real numbers) that is symmetric, reflexive, and transitive and for any two elements either holds or does not hold

equiv·a·len·cy \i-'kwiv(-ə)-lən-sē\ *n, pl* **-cies** : EQUIVALENCE

equiv·a·lent \-lənt\ *adj* [ME, fr. MF or LL; MF, fr. LL *aequivalent-, aequivalens,* prp. of *aequivalēre* to have equal power, fr. L *aequi-* + *valēre* to be strong — more at WIELD] **1 :** equal in force, amount, or value; *also* : equal in area or volume but not admitting of superposition <a square ~ to a triangle> **2 :** like in signification or import **3 :** corresponding or virtually identical esp. in effect or function **4** *obs* **:** equal in might or authority **5 :** having the same chemical combining capacity <~ quantities of two elements> **6 a :** having the same solution set <~ equations> **b :** capable of being placed in one-to-one correspondence <~ sets> **c :** related by an equivalence relation ***syn*** see SAME ***ant*** different — **equivalent** *n* — **equiv·a·lent·ly** *adv*

equivalent weight *n* : the weight of a substance esp. in grams that combines with or is chemically equivalent to eight grams of oxygen or one gram of hydrogen : the atomic or molecular weight divided by the valence

equiv·o·cal \i-'kwiv-ə-kəl\ *adj* [LL *aequivocus,* fr. *aequi-* equi- + *voc-, vox* voice — more at VOICE] **1 a :** subject to two or more interpretations and usu. used to mislead or confuse <he did not lie but his story of the party was certainly ~> **b :** uncertain as an indication or sign **2 a :** of uncertain nature or classification **b :** of uncertain disposition toward a person or thing : UNDECIDED **c :** of doubtful advantage, genuineness, or moral rectitude <~ behavior> ***syn*** see OBSCURE ***ant*** unequivocal — **equiv·o·cal·i·ty** \-ˌkwiv-ə-'kal-ət-ē\ *n* — **equiv·o·cal·ly** \-'kwiv-ə-k(ə-)lē\ *adv* — **equiv·o·cal·ness** \-kəl-nəs\ *n*

equiv·o·cate \i-'kwiv-ə-ˌkāt\ *vi* **-cat·ed; -cat·ing 1 :** to use equivocal language esp. with intent to deceive **2 :** to avoid committing oneself in what one says ***syn*** see LIE — **equiv·o·ca·tion** \-ˌkwiv-ə-'kā-shən\ *n* — **equiv·o·ca·tor** \-'kwiv-ə-ˌkāt-ər\ *n*

equi·voque *also* **equi·voke** \'ek-wə-ˌvōk, 'ē-kwə-\ *n* [F *équivoque,* fr. *équivoque* equivocal, fr. LL *aequivocus*] **1 :** an equivocal word or phrase; *specif* : PUN **2 a :** double meaning **b :** WORDPLAY

Er *symbol* erbium

ER *abbr* earned run

¹-er \ər; *after some vowels, often* r; *after* ŋ, *usu* gər\ *adj suffix or adv suffix* [ME *-er, -ere, -re,* fr. OE *-ra* (in adjectives), *-or* (in adverbs); akin to OHG *-iro,* adj. compar. suffix, L *-ior,* Gk *-iōn*] — used to form the comparative degree of adjectives and adverbs of one syllable <hott*er*> <dri*er*> and of some adjectives and adverbs of two syllables <complet*er*> and sometimes of longer ones <divineli*er*>

²-er \ər; *after some vowels, often* r\ *also* **-ier** \ē-ər, yər\ *or* **-yer** \yər\ *n suffix* [ME *-er, -ere, -ier, -iere;* partly fr. OE *-ere* (akin to OHG *-āri;* both fr. a prehistoric Gmc suffix borrowed fr. L *-arius*); partly fr. OF *-ier, -iere,* fr. L *-arius, -aria, -arium* -ary; partly fr. MF *-ere,* fr. L *-ator* -or — more at -ARY, -OR] **1 a :** person occupationally connected with <hatt*er*> <furr*ier*> <law*yer*> **b :** person or thing belonging to or associated with <head*er*> <old-tim*er*> **c :** native of : resident of <cottag*er*> <New York*er*> **d :** one that has <three-deck*er*> **e :** one that produces or yields <pork*er*> **2 a :** one that does or performs (a specified action) <report*er*> — sometimes added to both elements of a compound <build*er*-upp*er*> **b :** one that is a suitable object of (a specified action) <broil*er*> **3 :** one that is <foreign*er*> — *-yer* in a few words after *w, -ier* in a few words after other letters, otherwise *-er*

era \'ir-ə, 'er-ə, 'ē-rə\ *n* [LL *aera,* fr. L, counters, pl. of *aer-, aes* copper, money — more at ORE] **1 :** a system of chronological notation computed from a given date as basis **2 a :** a fixed point in time from which a series of years is reckoned **b :** a memorable or important date or event; *esp* : one that begins a new period in the history of a person or thing **3 a :** a period set off or typified by some prominent figure or characteristic feature **b :** a stage in the development of a person or thing; *esp* : one of the five major divisions of geologic time <Paleozoic ~> ***syn*** see PERIOD

ERA *abbr* earned run average

erad·i·cate \i-'rad-ə-ˌkāt\ *vt* **-cat·ed; -cat·ing** [L *eradicatus,* pp. of *eradicare,* fr. *e-* + *radic-, radix* root — more at ROOT] **1 :** to pull up by the roots **2 :** to do away with as if by pulling up by the roots <~ ignorance by better teaching> ***syn*** see EXTERMINATE — **erad·i·ca·ble** \-'rad-i-kə-bəl\ *adj* — **erad·i·ca·tion** \-ˌrad-ə-'kā-shən\ *n* — **erad·i·ca·tive** \-'rad-ə-ˌkāt-iv\ *adj* — **erad·i·ca·tor** \-ˌkāt-ər\ *n*

erase \i-'rās, *Brit* -'rāz\ *vb* **erased; eras·ing** [L *erasus,* pp. of *eradere,* fr. *e-* + *radere* to scratch, scrape — more at RAT] *vt* **1 a :** to rub or scrape out (as written, painted, or engraved letters) **b :** to remove (recorded matter) from a magnetic tape or wire **c :** to delete from a computer storage device **2 a :** to remove from existence or memory as if by erasing **b :** to nullify the effect or force of ~ *vi* : to yield to being erased — **eras·abil·i·ty** \-ˌrā-sə-'bil-ət-ē\ *n* — **eras·able** \-'rā-sə-bəl\ *adj*

syn ERASE, EXPUNGE, CANCEL, EFFACE, OBLITERATE, BLOT OUT, DELETE *shared meaning element* : to eradicate something so that it no longer has effect or existence

eras·er \i-'rā-sər\ *n* : one that erases; *specif* : a device (as a sharp instrument, a piece of rubber, or a felt pad) used to erase marks (as of ink or chalk)

Eras·tian \i-'ras-tē-ən, -'ras-chən\ *adj* [Thomas *Erastus* †1583 German-Swiss physician and Zwinglian theologian] : of, characterized by, or advocating the doctrine of state supremacy in ecclesiastical affairs — **Erastian** *n* — **Eras·tian·ism** \-ˌiz-əm\ *n*

era·sure \i-'rā-shər *also* -zhər\ *n* : an act or instance of erasing

Er·a·to \'er-ə-ˌtō\ *n* [Gk *Eratō*] : the Greek Muse of lyric and love poetry

er·bi·um \'ər-bē-əm\ *n* [NL, fr. *Ytterby,* Sweden] : a metallic element of the rare-earth group that occurs with yttrium — see ELEMENT table

¹ere \(ˌ)e(ə)r, (ˌ)a(ə)r\ *prep* [ME *er,* fr. OE *ǣr,* fr. *ǣr,* adv., early, soon; akin to OHG *ēr* earlier, Gk *ēri* early] : ²BEFORE 2 <contrived ~ the beginning of the world —Norman Douglas>

²ere *conj* : ³BEFORE <I will be thrown into Etna . . . ~ I will leave her —Shak.>

Er·e·bus \'er-ə-bəs\ *n* [L, fr. Gk *Erebos*] **1 :** a personification of darkness in Greek mythology **2 :** a place of darkness in the underworld on the way to Hades

¹erect \i-'rekt\ *adj* [ME, fr. L *erectus,* pp. of *erigere* to erect, fr. *e-* + *regere* to lead straight, guide — more at RIGHT] **1 a :** vertical in position; *specif* : not spread out or lying down **b :** standing up or out from the body <~ hairs> **c :** characterized by firm or rigid straightness in bodily posture <an ~ bearing> **2** *archaic* **:** directed upward **3** *obs* **:** ALERT, WATCHFUL **4 :** being in a state of physiological erection — **erect·ly** \-'rek-(t)lē\ *adv* — **erect·ness** \-'rek(t)-nəs\ *n*

²erect *vt* **1 a** (1) **:** to put up by the fitting together of materials or parts : BUILD (2) **:** to fix in an upright position (3) **:** to cause to stand up or out **b** *archaic* **:** to direct upward **c :** to change (an image) from an inverted to a normal position **2 :** to elevate in status **3 :** to set up : ESTABLISH **4** *obs* **:** ENCOURAGE, EMBOLDEN **5 :** to construct (as a perpendicular) upon a given base — **erect·able** \-'rek-tə-bəl\ *adj*

erec·tile \i-'rek-tᵊl, -ˌtīl\ *adj* : capable of being raised to an erect position; *esp* : CAVERNOUS 3 — **erec·til·i·ty** \-ˌrek-'til-ət-ē\ *n*

erec·tion \i-'rek-shən\ *n* **1 :** the act or process of erecting : CONSTRUCTION **2 a :** the state marked by firm turgid form and erect position of a previously flaccid bodily part containing cavernous tissue when that tissue becomes dilated with blood **b :** an occurrence of such a state in the penis or clitoris **3 :** something erected

erec·tor \i-'rek-tər\ *n* : one that erects; *esp* : a muscle that raises or keeps a part erect

E region *n* : the part of the ionosphere occurring between 40 and 90 miles above the surface of the earth and containing the daytime E layer and the sporadic E layer

ere·long \e(ə)r-'lȯŋ, a(ə)r-\ *adv* : before long : SOON

er·e·mite \'er-ə-ˌmīt\ *n* [ME — more at HERMIT] : HERMIT; *esp* : a religious recluse — **er·e·mit·ic** \ˌer-ə-'mit-ik\ *or* **er·e·mit·i·cal** \-i-kəl\ *adj* — **er·e·mit·ism** \'er-ə-ˌmīt-ˌiz-əm\ *n*

er·em·urus \ˌer-ə-'myu̇r-əs\ *n, pl* **-uri** \-'myu̇(ə)r-ˌī\ [NL, genus name, fr. Gk *erēmos* solitary + *oura* tail — more at RETINA, SQUIRREL] : FOXTAIL LILY

ere·now \e(ə)r-'nau̇, a(ə)r-\ *adv* : before now : HERETOFORE

erep·sin \i-'rep-sən\ *n* [ISV *er-* (prob. fr. L *eripere* to sweep away, fr. *e-* + *rapere* to sweep) + *pepsin* — more at RAPID] : a proteolytic fraction obtained esp. from the intestinal juice and known to be a mixture of exopeptidases

er·e·thism \'er-ə-ˌthiz-əm\ *n* [F *éréthisme,* fr. Gk *erethismos* irritation, fr. *erethizein* to irritate; akin to Gk *ornynai* to rouse — more at RISE] : abnormal irritability or responsiveness to stimulation — **er·e·this·mic** \ˌer-ə-'thiz-mik\ *adj*

ere·while \e(ə)r-'(h)wī(ə)l, a(ə)r-\ *also* **ere·whiles** \-'(h)wī(ə)lz\ *adv, archaic* : HERETOFORE

ə abut   ᵊ kitten   ər further   a back   ā bake   ä cot, cart
au̇ out   ch chin   e less   ē easy   g gift   i trip   ī life
j joke   ŋ sing   ō flow   ȯ flaw   ȯi coin   th thin   th this
ü loot   u̇ foot   y yet   yü few   yu̇ furious   zh vision

erg \'ərg\ *n* [Gk *ergon* work — more at WORK] : a cgs unit of work equal to the work done by a force of one dyne acting through a distance of one centimeter

erg- *or* **ergo-** *comb form* [Gk, fr. *ergon*] : work <*ergo*phobia>

er·gas·tic \(ˌ)ər-'gas-tik\ *adj* [Gk *ergastikos* able to work, fr. *ergazesthai* to work, fr. *ergon* work] : constituting the nonliving by-products of protoplasmic activity

er·gas·to·plasm \-tə-ˌplaz-əm\ *n* [ISV *ergastic* + *-o-* + *-plasm*] : ribosome-studded endoplasmic reticulum — **er·gas·to·plas·mic** \-ˌgas-tə-'plaz-mik\ *adj*

er·go \'e(ə)r-(ˌ)gō, 'ər-\ *adv* [L, fr. OL, because of, fr. (assumed) OL *e rogo* from the direction (of)] : THEREFORE, HENCE

ergo- *comb form* [F, fr. *ergot*] : ergot <*ergo*sterol>

er·go·dic \(ˌ)ər-'gōd-ik, -'gäd-\ *adj* [G *ergodenhypothese*, lit., hypothesis of the path of energy, fr. *erg-* + Gk *hodos* path, road] **1 :** of or relating to a process in which every sequence or sizable sample is equally representative of the whole (as in regard to a statistical parameter) **2 :** involving or relating to the probability that any state will recur; *esp* : having zero probability that any state will never recur — **er·go·dic·i·ty** \ˌər-gə-'dis-ət-ē\ *n*

er·go·graph \'ər-gə-ˌgraf\ *n* [ISV] : an apparatus for measuring the work capacity of a muscle

er·gom·e·ter \(ˌ)ər-'gäm-ət-ər\ *n* : an apparatus for measuring the work performed by a group of muscles — **er·go·met·ric** \ˌər-gə-'me-trik\ *adj*

er·go·nom·ic \ˌər-gə-'näm-ik\ *adj* [*erg-* + *economic*] : of or relating to biotechnology

er·go·nom·ics \-iks\ *n pl but sing or pl in constr* [*erg-* + *economics*] : BIOTECHNOLOGY

er·gon·o·mist \(ˌ)ər-'gän-ə-məst\ *n* : a specialist in biotechnology

er·go·no·vine \ˌər-gə-'nō-ˌvēn\ *n* [*ergo-* + L *novus* new — more at NEW] : an alkaloid $C_{19}H_{23}N_3O_2$ from ergot with similar pharmacological action but reduced toxicity

er·gos·ter·ol \(ˌ)ər-'gäs-tə-ˌrōl, -ˌrōl\ *n* [ISV] : a crystalline steroid alcohol $C_{28}H_{44}O$ that occurs esp. in yeast, molds, and ergot and is converted by ultraviolet irradiation ultimately into vitamin D_2

er·got \'ər-gət, -ˌgät\ *n* [F, lit., cock's spur] **1 :** the black or dark purple sclerotium of fungi (genus *Claviceps*) that occurs as a club-shaped body replacing the seed of a grass (as rye); *also* : a fungus bearing ergots **2 :** a disease of rye and other cereals caused by an ergot fungus **3 a :** the dried sclerotia of an ergot fungus grown on rye and containing several alkaloids (as ergonovine and ergotamine) **b :** any of such alkaloids used medicinally for their contractile effect on smooth muscle (as of peripheral arterioles) — **er·got·ic** \(ˌ)ər-'gät-ik\ *adj*

er·got·a·mine \(ˌ)ər-'gät-ə-ˌmēn\ *n* [ISV] : an alkaloid $C_{33}H_{35}N_5O_5$ from ergot that has the pharmacological action of ergot and is used esp. in treating migraine

er·got·ism \'ər-gət-ˌiz-əm\ *n* : a toxic condition produced by eating grain, grain products (as rye bread), or grasses infected with ergot fungus or by chronic excessive use of an ergot drug

er·got·ized \-ˌīzd\ *adj* : containing ergot <~ grain>

ERIC *abbr* educational resources information center

er·i·ca \'er-i-kə\ *n* [NL, genus name, fr. L *erice* heather, fr. Gk *ereikē*] : any of a large genus (*Erica*) of the heath family of low much-branched evergreen shrubs

er·i·ca·ceous \ˌer-ə-'kā-shəs\ *adj* : of, relating to, or being a heath or the heath family

er·i·coid \'er-ə-ˌkȯid\ *adj* : resembling heath

Erie \'i(ə)r-ē\ *n* **1 :** a member of an Amerindian people of the Lake Erie region **2 :** the language of the Erie people

erig·er·on \ə-'rij-ə-ˌrän\ *n* [NL, genus name, fr. L, groundsel, fr. Gk *ērigerōn*, fr. *ēri* early + *gerōn* old man; fr. the hoary down of some species — more at ERE, GERONT-] : any of a widely distributed genus (*Erigeron*) of composite herbs with flower heads that resemble asters but have fewer and narrower involucral bracts

Er·in \'er-ən\ *n* [OIr *Erinn*, dat. of *Eriu* Ireland] : Ireland

Eri·nys \i-'rin-əs, -'rī-nəs\ *n, pl* **Erin·y·es** \-'rin-ē-ˌēz\ [Gk] : FURY 2a

er·i·o·phy·id \ˌer-ē-'äf-ē-əd, -ē-ə-'fī-əd\ *n* [deriv. of Gk *erion* wool + *phyē* growth; akin to Gk *physis* growth — more at PHYSICS] : any of a large family (Eriophyidae) of minute plant-feeding mites that have two pairs of legs placed far anterior and lack a respiratory system — **eriophyid** *adj*

¹eris·tic \i-'ris-tik, e-\ *also* **eris·ti·cal** \-ti-kəl\ *adj* [Gk *eristikos* fond of wrangling, fr. *erizein* to wrangle, fr. *eris* strife] : characterized by disputatious and often subtle and specious reasoning — **eris·ti·cal·ly** \-ti-k(ə-)lē\ *adv*

²eristic *n* **1 :** a person devoted to logical disputation **2 :** the art or practice of disputation and polemics

Er·len·mey·er flask \ˌər-lən-ˌmī(-ə)r-, ˌer-lən-\ *n* [Emil *Erlenmeyer*] : a flat-bottomed conical laboratory flask

er·mine \'ər-mən\ *n, pl* **ermines** [ME, fr. OF, of Gmc origin; akin to OHG *harmo* weasel; akin to Lith *sarmuo* weasel] **1** *or pl* **ermine a :** any of several weasels that assume white winter pelage usu. with more or less black on the tail; *esp* : a large European weasel (*Mustela erminea*) **b :** the white fur of the ermine in winter pelage **2 :** a rank or office whose ceremonial or official robe is ornamented with ermine

er·mined \-mənd\ *adj* : clothed or adorned with ermine

erne *or* **ern** \'ərn, 'e(ə)rn\ *n* [ME, fr. OE *earn;* akin to OHG *arn* eagle, Gk *ornis* bird] : EAGLE; *esp* : WHITE-TAILED SEA EAGLE

erode \i-'rōd\ *vb* **erod·ed; erod·ing** [L *erodere* to eat away, fr. *e-* + *rodere* to gnaw — more at RAT] *vt* **1 :** to diminish or destroy by degrees: **a :** to eat into or away by slow destruction of substance : CORRODE **b :** to wear away by the action of water, wind, or glacial ice **c :** to cause to deteriorate or disappear as if by eating or wearing away <buying power is *eroded* with each inflationary year —R. H. McDonough> **2 :** to produce or form by eroding <glaciers ~ U-shaped valleys> ~ *vi* : to undergo erosion — **erod·ibil·i·ty** \-ˌrōd-ə-'bil-ət-ē\ *n* — **erod·ible** \-'rōd-ə-bəl\ *adj*

erog·e·nous \i-'räj-ə-nəs\ *also* **er·o·gen·ic** \ˌer-ə-'jen-ik\ *adj* [Gk *erōs* + E *-genous, -genic*] **1 :** producing sexual excitement or libidinal gratification when stimulated : sexually sensitive **2 :** of, relating to, or arousing sexual feelings

Eros \'e(ə)r-ˌäs, 'i(ə)r-\ *n* [Gk *Erōs*, fr. *erōs* love; akin to Gk *erasthai* to love, desire] **1 :** a son of Aphrodite who excites erotic love in gods and men with his arrows and torches — compare CUPID **2 :** the aggregate of pleasure-directed life instincts whose energy is derived from libido — compare THANATOS **3** *often not cap* : love directed toward self-realization

erose \i-'rōs\ *adj* [L *erosus*, pp. of *erodere*] : IRREGULAR, UNEVEN; *specif* : having the margin irregularly notched as if gnawed <an ~ leaf> <an ~ edge of a bacterial colony> — **erose·ly** *adv*

ero·si·ble \i-'rō-zə-bəl, -'rō-sə-\ *adj* : capable of being eroded

ero·sion \i-'rō-zhən\ *n* **1 a :** the action or process of eroding **b :** the state of being eroded **2 :** an instance or product of erosive action — **ero·sion·al** \-'rōzh-nəl, -'rō-zhən-ᵊl\ *adj* — **ero·sion·al·ly** \-ē\ *adv*

ero·sive \i-'rō-siv, -ziv\ *adj* : tending to erode or to induce or permit erosion — **ero·sive·ness** *n* — **ero·siv·i·ty** \i-ˌrō-'siv-ət-ē\ *n*

erot·ic \i-'rät-ik\ *adj* [Gk *erōtikos*, fr. *erōt-, erōs*] **1 :** of, devoted to, or tending to arouse sexual love or desire <~ art> **2 :** strongly affected by sexual desire — **erotic** *n* — **erot·i·cal** \-i-kəl\ *adj* — **erot·i·cal·ly** \-i-k(ə-)lē\ *adv*

erot·i·ca \i-'rät-i-kə\ *n pl but sing or pl in constr* [NL, fr. Gk *erōtika*, neut. pl. of *erōtikos*] : literary or artistic works having an erotic theme or quality

erot·i·cism \i-'rät-ə-ˌsiz-əm\ *n* **1 :** an erotic theme or quality **2 :** a state of sexual arousal **3 :** sexual impulse or desire esp. when abnormally insistent — **erot·i·cist** \-səst\ *n*

erot·i·cize \-ˌsīz\ *vt* **-cized; -ciz·ing :** to make erotic <a film version that ~s the original story> — **erot·i·ci·za·tion** \i-ˌrät-ə-sə-'zā-shən\ *n*

er·o·tism \'er-ə-ˌtiz-əm\ *n* [Gk *erōt-, erōs* + E *-ism*] : EROTICISM

ero·to·gen·ic \i-ˌrōt-ə-'jen-ik, -ˌrät-\ *adj* : EROGENOUS

err \'e(ə)r, 'ər\ *vi* [ME *erren*, fr. OF *errer*, fr. L *errare;* akin to OE *ierre* wandering, angry, ON *rās* race — more at RACE] **1** *archaic* : STRAY **2 a :** to make a mistake **b :** to violate an accepted standard of conduct

er·ran·cy \'er-ən-sē\ *n, pl* **-cies :** the state or an instance of erring

er·rand \'er-ənd\ *n* [ME *erend* message, business, fr. OE *ǣrend;* akin to OHG *ārunti* message] **1** *archaic* **a :** an oral message entrusted to a person **b :** EMBASSY, MISSION **2 a :** a short trip taken to attend to some business often for another <was on an ~ for his mother> **b :** the object or purpose of such a trip

er·rant \'er-ənt\ *adj* [ME *erraunt*, fr. MF *errant*, prp. of *errer* to err & *errer* to travel, fr. ML *iterare*, fr. L *iter* road, journey — more at ITINERANT] **1 :** traveling or given to traveling <an ~ knight> **2 a :** straying outside the proper path or bounds <an ~ calf> **b :** moving about aimlessly or irregularly <an ~ breeze> **c :** deviating from a standard (as of truth or propriety) <an ~ child> **3** *obs* : ARRANT — **errant** *n* — **er·rant·ly** *adv*

er·rant·ry \'er-ən-trē\ *n, pl* **-ries :** the quality, condition, or fact of wandering; *esp* : a roving in search of chivalrous adventure

er·ra·ta \e-'rät-ə, -'rāt-, -'rat-\ *n* [fr. pl. of *erratum*] : a list of corrigenda; *also* : a page bearing such a list

¹er·rat·ic \ir-'at-ik\ *adj* [ME, fr. MF or L; MF *erratique*, fr. L *erraticus*, fr. *erratus*, pp. of *errare*] **1 a :** having no fixed course : WANDERING <an ~ comet> **b** *archaic* : NOMADIC **2 :** transported from an original resting place esp. by a glacier <~ boulder> **3 a :** characterized by lack of consistency, regularity, or uniformity **b :** deviating from what is ordinary or standard : ECCENTRIC <an ~ genius> — **er·rat·i·cal** \-i-kəl\ *adj* — **er·rat·i·cal·ly** \-i-k(ə-)lē\ *adv* — **er·rat·i·cism** \-'at-ə-ˌsiz-əm\ *n*

²erratic *n* : one that is erratic; *esp* : an erratic boulder or block of rock

er·ra·tum \e-'rät-əm, -'rāt-, -rat-\ *n, pl* **-ta** \-ə\ [L, fr. neut. of *erratus*] : CORRIGENDUM

er·ro·ne·ous \ir-'ō-nē-əs, e-'rō-\ *adj* [ME, fr. L *erroneus*, fr. *erron-, erro* wanderer, fr. *errare*] **1** *archaic* : WANDERING **2 :** containing or characterized by error : MISTAKEN <~ assumptions> — **er·ro·ne·ous·ly** *adv* — **er·ro·ne·ous·ness** *n*

er·ror \'er-ər\ *n* [ME *errour*, fr. OF, fr. L *error*, fr. *errare*] **1 a :** an act or condition of ignorant or imprudent deviation from a code of behavior **b :** an act involving an unintentional deviation from truth or accuracy **c :** an act that through ignorance, deficiency, or accident departs from or fails to achieve what should be done: as (1) : a defensive misplay other than a wild pitch or passed ball made by a baseball player when normal play would have resulted in an out or prevented an advance by a base runner (2) : the failure of a player (as in tennis) to make a successful return of a ball during play **d :** a mistake in the proceedings of a court of record in matters of law or of fact **2 a :** the quality or state of erring **b** *Christian Science* : illusion about the nature of reality that is the cause of human suffering : the contradiction of truth **c :** an instance of false belief **3 :** something produced by mistake **4 a :** the difference between an observed or calculated value and a true value; *specif* : variation in measurements, calculations, or observations of a quantity due to mistakes or to uncontrollable factors **b :** the amount of deviation from a standard or specification — **er·ror·less** \'er-ər-ləs\ *adj*

syn ERROR, MISTAKE, SLIP, BLUNDER, LAPSE *shared meaning element* : a departure from what is true, right, or proper. ERROR suggests the existence of a standard or guide and a straying from the right course through failure to make effective use of this; thus, an *error* in addition involves some failure in following the rules of addition; an *error* in conduct is an infraction of an accepted code of morals or manners. MISTAKE implies misconception or inadvertence and usually expresses less severe criticism than *error* <willing to learn from his *mistakes*> BLUNDER regularly imputes stupidity or ignorance as a cause and connotes some degree of culpability <we usually call our *blunders* mistakes, and our friends style our mistakes *blunders* —H. B. Wheatley> SLIP stresses inadvertence or accident and applies especially to trivial but embarrassing mistakes <a social *slip* which makes us feel hot all over —L. P.

Smith> LAPSE, sometimes interchangeable with *slip*, is more likely to stress forgetfulness, weakness, or inattention as a cause <forever chiding him for his grammatical *lapses* —William Styron>
er·satz \'e(ə)r-,zäts, er-'\ *adj* [G *ersatz-*, fr. *ersatz*, n., substitute] : being a usu. artificial and inferior substitute <~ flour made from potatoes> **syn** see ARTIFICIAL — **ersatz** *n*
Erse \'ərs\ *n* [ME (Sc) *Erisch*, adj., Irish, alter. of *Irish*] **1** : SCOTTISH GAELIC **2** : IRISH GAELIC — **Erse** *adj*
erst \'ərst\ *adv* [ME *erest* earliest, formerly, fr. OE *ǣrest*, superl. of *ǣr* early — more at ERE] *archaic* : ERSTWHILE
¹erst·while \'ərst-,(h)wīl\ *adv* : in the past : FORMERLY <cultures, ~ unknown to each other — Robert Plank>
²erstwhile *adj* : FORMER, PREVIOUS <his ~ students>
eru·cic acid \i-,rü-sik-\ *n* [NL *Eruca*, genus of herbs, fr. L, caterpillar, garden rocket] : a crystalline fatty acid $C_{22}H_{42}O_2$ found in the form of glycerides esp. in rapeseed oil
eruct \i-'rəkt\ *vb* [L *eructare*, fr. *e-* + *ructare* to belch, fr. *-ructus*, pp. of *-rugere* to belch; akin to L *rugire* to roar] : BELCH
eruc·ta·tion \i-,rək-'tā-shən, ,ē-\ *n* : an act or instance of belching
er·u·dite \'er-(y)ə-,dīt\ *adj* [ME *erudit*, fr. L *eruditus*, fr. pp. of *erudire* to instruct, fr. *e-* + *rudis* rude, ignorant] : possessing or displaying erudition : LEARNED <an ~ scholar> — **er·u·dite·ly** *adv*
er·u·di·tion \,er-(y)ə-'dish-ən\ *n* : extensive knowledge acquired chiefly from books : profound, recondite, or bookish learning **syn** see KNOWLEDGE
erum·pent \i-'rəm-pənt\ *adj* [L *erumpent-*, *erumpens*, prp. of *erumpere*] : bursting forth <~ fungi>
erupt \i-'rəpt\ *vb* [L *eruptus*, pp. of *erumpere* to burst forth, fr. *e-* + *rumpere* to break — more at REAVE] *vi* **1 a** : to force out or release suddenly and often violently something (as lava or steam) that is pent up **b** (1) : to burst from limits or restraint (2) *of a tooth* : to emerge through the gum **c** : to become active or violent : EXPLODE <violence ~*ed* in the ghetto> **2** : to break out (as with a skin eruption) ~ *vt* : to force out or release usu. suddenly and violently — **erupt·ible** \-'rəp-tə-bəl\ *adj* — **erup·tive** \-tiv\ *adj* — **erup·tive·ly** *adv*
erup·tion \i-'rəp-shən\ *n* **1 a** : an act, process, or instance of erupting **b** : the breaking out of a rash on the skin or mucous membrane **2** : a product of erupting (as a skin rash)
-ery \(ə-)rē\ *n suffix* [ME *-erie*, fr. OF, fr. *-ier* -er + *-ie* -y] **1** : qualities collectively : character : -NESS <snobb*ery*> **2** : art : practice <quack*ery*> **3** : place of doing, keeping, producing, or selling (the thing specified) <fish*ery*> <bak*ery*> **4** : collection : aggregate <fin*ery*> **5** : state or condition <slav*ery*>
eryn·go \i-'riŋ-(,)gō\ *n, pl* **-goes** *or* **-gos** [modif. of L *eryngion* sea holly, fr. Gk *ēryngion*] **1** *obs* : candied sea-holly root made to be used as an aphrodisiac **2** : any of various plants (genus *Eryngium*) that have elongate spinulose-margined leaves and flowers in dense bracted heads
ery·sip·e·las \,er-ə-'sip-(ə-)ləs, ,ir-\ *n* [ME *erisipila*, fr. L *erysipelas*, fr. Gk, fr. *erysi-* (akin to Gk *erythros* red) + *-pelas* (akin to L *pellis* skin) — more at RED, FELL] : an acute febrile disease associated with intense edematous local inflammation of the skin and subcutaneous tissues caused by a hemolytic streptococcus
er·y·the·ma \,er-ə-'thē-mə\ *n* [NL, fr. Gk *erythēma*, fr. *erythainein* to redden, fr. *erythros*] : abnormal redness of the skin due to capillary congestion (as in inflammation) — **er·y·them·a·tous** \-'them-ət-əs\ *adj*
er·y·thor·bate \,er-ə-'thȯr-,bāt\ *n* : a salt of erythorbic acid that is used in foods as an antioxidant
er·y·thor·bic acid \-,thȯr-bik-\ *n* [*eryth*r- + asc*orbic acid*] : an optical isomer of ascorbic acid
erythr- *or* **erythro-** *comb form* [Gk, fr. *erythros* — more at RED] **1** : red <*erythro*cyte> **2** : erythrocyte <*erythr*oid>
er·y·thre·mia \,er-ə-'thrē-mē-ə\ *n* [NL] : POLYCYTHEMIA VERA
er·y·thrism \'er-ə-,thriz-əm\ *n* : a condition marked by exceptional prevalence of red pigmentation (as in skin or hair) — **er·y·thris·mal** \,er-ə-'thriz-məl\ *adj* — **er·y·thris·tic** \-'thris-tik\ *adj*
er·y·thrite \'er-ə-,thrīt\ *n* : a mineral $Co_3(AsO_4)_2.8H_2O$ consisting of a hydrous cobalt arsenate occurring esp. in monoclinic crystals
eryth·ro·blast \i-'rith-rə-,blast\ *n* [ISV] : a polychromatic nucleated cell of red marrow that is the first specifically identifiable stage in red blood cell formation; *broadly* : a cell ancestral to red blood cells — **eryth·ro·blas·tic** \-,rith-rə-'blas-tik\ *adj*
eryth·ro·blas·to·sis \i-,rith-rə-,blas-'tō-səs\ *n, pl* **-to·ses** \-,sēz\ [NL] : abnormal presence of erythroblasts in the circulating blood; *esp* : ERYTHROBLASTOSIS FETALIS
erythroblastosis fe·ta·lis \-fi-'tal-əs\ *n* [NL, fetal erythroblastosis] : a hemolytic disease of the fetus and newborn that is characterized by destruction of circulating erythrocytes, increase in circulating erythroblasts, and jaundice and that is usu. associated with Rh-factor incompatibility
eryth·ro·cyte \i-'rith-rə-,sīt\ *n* [ISV] : RED BLOOD CELL — **eryth·ro·cyt·ic** \-,rith-rə-'sit-ik\ *adj*
eryth·ro·cy·tom·e·ter \i-,rith-rə-sī-'täm-ət-ər\ *n* : HEMACYTOMETER
ery·throid \i-'rith-,rȯid, 'er-ə-,thrȯid\ *adj* : relating to erythrocytes or their precursors
eryth·ro·my·cin \i-,rith-rə-'mīs-ᵊn\ *n* : an antibiotic that is produced by an actinomycete (*Streptomyces erythreus*) and that is effective against amebiasis
er·y·thron \'er-ə-,thrän\ *n* [NL, fr. Gk, neut. of *erythros*] : the red blood cells and their precursors in the bone marrow
eryth·ro·poi·e·sis \i-,rith-rō-pȯi-'ē-səs\ *n* [NL, fr. *erythr-* + Gk *poiēsis* creation] : the production of red blood cells (as from the bone marrow) — **eryth·ro·poi·et·ic** \-'et-ik\ *adj*
eryth·ro·poi·e·tin \-'pȯi-ət-ᵊn\ *n* [*erythropoiet*ic + *-in*] : a hormonal substance that is prob. formed in the kidney and stimulates red blood cell formation
eryth·ro·sin \i-'rith-rə-sən\ *also* **eryth·ro·sine** \-sən, -,sēn\ *n* [ISV *erythr-* + *eosin*] : any of several dyes made by iodination of fluorescein that yield reddish shades
Es *symbol* einsteinium
¹-es \əz, iz *after* s, z, sh, ch; z *after* v *or a vowel*\ *n pl suffix* [ME *-es*, *-s* — more at ¹-s] **1** — used to form the plural of most nouns that end in *s* <glass*es*>, *z* <fuzz*es*>, *sh* <bush*es*>, *ch* <peach*es*>, or a final *y* that changes to *i* <ladi*es*> and of some nouns ending in *f* that changes to *v* <loav*es*>; compare ¹-s 1 **2** : ¹-s 2
²-es *vb suffix* [ME — more at ²-s] — used to form the third person singular present of most verbs that end in *s* <bless*es*>, *z* <fizz*es*>, *sh* <hush*es*>, *ch* <catch*es*>, or a final *y* that changes to *i* <defi*es*>; — compare ²-s
Esau \'ē-(,)sȯ\ *n* [L, fr. Gk *Esau*, fr. Heb *'Esāw*] : the elder son of Isaac and Rebekah who sold his birthright to his twin brother Jacob
es·ca·drille \'es-kə-,dril, -,drē\ *n* [F, flotilla, escadrille, fr. Sp *escuadrilla*, dim. of *escuadra* squadron, squad — more at SQUAD] : a unit of a European air command containing usu. six airplanes
es·ca·lade \'es-kə-,lād, -,läd\ *n* [F, fr. It *scalata*, fr. *scalare* to scale, fr. *scala* ladder, fr. LL — more at SCALE] : an act of scaling esp. the walls of a fortification — **escalade** *vt* — **es·ca·lad·er** *n*
es·ca·late \'es-kə-,lāt, *nonstand* -kyə-\ *vb* **-lat·ed; -lat·ing** [back-formation fr. *escalator*] *vi* : to increase in extent, volume, number, amount, intensity, or scope <a little war threatens to ~ into a huge ugly one —Arnold Abrams> ~ *vt* : EXPAND 1 — **es·ca·la·tion** \,es-kə-'lā-shən, *nonstand* -kyə-\ *n* — **es·ca·la·to·ry** \'es-kə-lə-,tōr-ē, -,tȯr-, *nonstand* -kyə-\ *adj*
¹es·ca·la·tor \'es-kə-,lāt-ər, *nonstand* -kyə-\ *n* [fr. *Escalator*, a trademark] **1 a** : a power-driven set of stairs arranged like an endless belt that ascend or descend continuously **b** : an upward course suggestive of an escalator <a never-stopping ~ of economic progress —D. W. Brogan> **2** : an escalator clause or provision
²escalator *adj* : providing for a periodic proportional upward or downward adjustment (as of prices or wages) <an ~ arrangement tying the base pay . . . to living costs —*N. Y. Times*>
es·cal·lop \is-'käl-əp, -'kal-\ *var of* SCALLOP
es·cap·able \is-'kā-pə-bəl\ *adj* : capable of being escaped : AVOIDABLE
es·ca·pade \'es-kə-,pād\ *n* [MF, fr. OIt *scappata*, fr. *scappare* to escape, fr. (assumed) VL *excappare*] : a usu. adventurous action that runs counter to approved or conventional conduct <childish ~*s*>
¹es·cape \is-'kāp\ *vb* **es·caped; es·cap·ing** [ME *escapen*, fr. ONF *escaper*, fr. (assumed) VL *excappare*, fr. L *ex-* + LL *cappa* head covering, cloak] *vi* **1 a** : to get away (as by flight) <*escaped* from prison> **b** : to issue from confinement <gas is *escaping*> **c** *of a plant* : to run wild from cultivation **2** : to avoid a threatening evil ~ *vt* **1** : to get or stay out of the way of : AVOID **2** : to fail to be noticed or recallable by <his name ~*s* me> **3 a** : to issue from **b** : to be uttered involuntarily by — **es·cap·er** *n*
syn ESCAPE, AVOID, EVADE, ELUDE, SHUN, ESCHEW *shared meaning element* : to get away or keep away from something one does not want to incur, endure, or encounter
²escape *n* **1** : an act or instance of escaping: as **a** : flight from confinement **b** : evasion of something undesirable **c** : leakage or outflow esp. of a fluid **d** : distraction or relief from routine or reality **2** : a means of escape **3** : a cultivated plant run wild
³escape *adj* **1** : providing a means of escape <an ~ hatch> <~ literature> **2** : providing a means of evading a regulation, claim, or commitment <an ~ clause in a contract>
escape artist *n* : one (as a showman or criminal) unusually adept at escaping from confinement
es·cap·ee \is-,kā-'pē, ,es-(,)kā-, ,es-kə-\ *n* : one that has escaped; *esp* : an escaped prisoner
escape mechanism *n* : a mode of behavior or thinking adopted to evade unpleasant facts or responsibilities
es·cape·ment \is-'kāp-mənt\ *n* **1 a** : a device in a timepiece which controls the motion of the train of wheelwork and through which the energy of the power source is delivered to the pendulum or balance by means of impulses that permit a tooth to escape from a pallet at regular intervals **b** : a ratchet device (as the spacing mechanism of a typewriter) that permits motion in one direction only in equal steps **2 a** : the act of escaping **b** : a way of escape : VENT

one form of escapement 1a

escape velocity *n* : the minimum velocity that a moving body (as a rocket) must have to escape from the gravitational field of the earth or of a celestial body and move outward into space
es·cap·ism \is-'kā-,piz-əm\ *n* : habitual diversion of the mind to purely imaginative activity or entertainment as an escape from reality or routine — **es·cap·ist** \-pəst\ *adj or n*
es·cap·ol·o·gy \is-,kā-'päl-ə-jē, ,es-(,)\ *n* : the art or practice of escaping — **es·cap·ol·o·gist** \-jəst\ *n*
es·car·got \,es-,kär-'gō\ *n, pl* **-gots** \-'gō(z)\ [F, fr. MF, fr. OProv *escaragol*] : a snail prepared for use as food
es·ca·role \'es-kə-,rōl\ *n* [F, fr. LL *escariola*, fr. L *escarius* of food, fr. *esca* food, fr. *edere* to eat — more at EAT] : ENDIVE 1
es·carp \is-'kärp\ *n or vt* [F *escarpe*, n., fr. It *scarpa*] : SCARP
es·carp·ment \-mənt\ *n* **1** : a steep slope in front of a fortification **2** : a long cliff or steep slope separating two comparatively level or more gently sloping surfaces and resulting from erosion or faulting
-es·cence \'es-ᵊn(t)s\ *n suffix* [MF, fr. L *-escentia*, fr. *-escent-*, *-escens* + *-ia* -y] : process of becoming <hyal*escence*>

-es·cent \'es-ᵊnt\ *adj suffix* [MF, fr. L *-escent-, -escens,* prp. suffix of incho. verbs in *-escere*] **1 :** beginning : beginning to be : slightly <alkal*escent*> **2 :** reflecting or emitting light (in a specified way) <fluor*escent*>

esch·a·lot \'esh-ə-ˌlät\ *n* [F *échalote*] **:** SHALLOT

¹es·char \'es-ˌkär\ *n* [ME *escare* — more at SCAR] **:** a scab formed esp. after a burn

²es·char \'es-kər\ *var of* ESKER

es·cha·rot·ic \ˌes-kə-'rät-ik\ *adj* [F or LL; F *escharotique,* fr. LL *escharoticus,* fr. Gk *escharōtikos,* fr. *escharoun* to form an eschar, fr. *eschara* eschar] **:** producing an eschar — **escharotic** *n*

es·cha·to·log·i·cal \(ˌ)es-ˌkat-ᵊl-'äj-i-kəl, ˌes-kət-\ *adj* **1 :** of or relating to eschatology or an eschatology **2 :** of or relating to the end of the world or the events associated with it in eschatology — **es·cha·to·log·i·cal·ly** \-i-k(ə-)lē\ *adv*

es·cha·tol·o·gy \ˌes-kə-'täl-ə-jē\ *n, pl* **-gies** [Gk *eschatos* last, farthest] **1 :** a branch of theology concerned with the final events in the history of the world or of mankind **2 :** a particular religious or mythological belief concerning the end of the world or of human history <Navaho ~>; *specif* **:** any of various Christian doctrines concerning the second coming of Christ, the resurrection of the dead, the Last Judgment, or the nature of human existence upon the completion of history

¹es·cheat \is(h)-'chēt\ *n* [ME *eschete,* fr. OF, reversion of property, fr. *escheoir* to fall, devolve, fr. (assumed) VL *excadēre,* fr. L *ex-* + (assumed) VL *cadēre* to fall, fr. L *cadere* — more at CHANCE] **1 :** escheated property **2 a :** the reversion of lands in English feudal law to the lord of the fee upon the failure of heirs capable of inheriting under the original grant **b :** the reversion of property to the crown in England or to the state in the U.S. by failure of persons legally entitled to hold the property

²escheat *vt* **:** to cause to revert by escheat ~ *vi* **:** to revert by escheat — **es·cheat·able** \-ə-bəl\ *adj*

es·chew \is(h)-'chü\ *vt* [ME *eschewen,* fr. MF *eschiuver,* of Gmc origin; akin to OHG *sciuhen* to frighten off — more at SHY] **:** to avoid habitually esp. on moral or practical grounds **:** SHUN ***syn*** see ESCAPE — **es·chew·al** \-əl\ *n*

es·co·lar \ˌes-kə-'lär\ *n, pl* **escolar** *or* **escolars** [Sp, lit., scholar, fr. ML *scholaris*] **:** a large widely distributed rough-scaled fish (*Ruvettus pretiosus*) that resembles a mackerel

¹es·cort \'es-ˌkȯ(ə)rt\ *n* [F *escorte,* fr. It *scorta,* fr. *scorgere* to guide, fr. (assumed) VL *excorrigere,* fr. L *ex-* + *corrigere* to make straight, correct — more at CORRECT] **1 a** (1) **:** a person or group of persons accompanying another to give protection or show courtesy (2) **:** the man who goes on a date with a woman **b :** a protective screen of warships or fighter planes or a single ship or plane used to fend off enemy attack from one or more vulnerable craft **2 :** accompaniment by a person or an armed protector (as a ship)

²es·cort \is-'kȯ(ə)rt, es-, 'es-ˌ\ *vt* **:** to accompany as an escort ***syn*** see ACCOMPANY

es·cot \is-'kät\ *vt* [MF *escoter,* fr. *escot* contribution, of Gmc origin; akin to ON *skot* contribution] *obs* **:** SUPPORT, MAINTAIN

es·cri·toire \'es-krə-ˌtwär\ *n* [obs. F, writing desk, scriptorium, fr. ML *scriptorium*] **:** a writing table or desk; *specif* **:** SECRETARY 4b

¹es·crow \'es-ˌkrō, es-'\ *n* [MF *escroue* scroll] **1 :** a deed, a bond, money, or a piece of property delivered to a third person to be delivered by him to the grantee only upon the fulfillment of a condition **2 :** a fund or deposit designed to serve as an escrow — **in escrow :** in trust as an escrow <have over $1000 *in escrow* to pay taxes>

²es·crow \es-'krō, 'es-ˌ\ *vt* **:** to place in escrow

es·cu·do \is-'küd-(ˌ)ō\ *n, pl* **-dos** [Sp & Pg, lit., shield, fr. L *scutum*] **1 :** any of various former gold or silver coins of Hispanic countries **2** — see MONEY table

es·cu·lent \'es-kyə-lənt\ *adj* [L *esculentus,* fr. *esca* food, fr. *edere* to eat — more at EAT] **:** EDIBLE — **esculent** *n*

es·cutch·eon \is-'kəch-ən\ *n* [ME *escochon,* fr. MF *escuchon,* fr. (assumed) VL *scution-, scutio,* fr. L *scutum* shield — more at ESQUIRE] **1 :** a defined area on which armorial bearings are displayed and which usu. consists of a shield **2 :** a protective or ornamental shield (as around a keyhole) **3 :** the part of a ship's stern on which the name is displayed

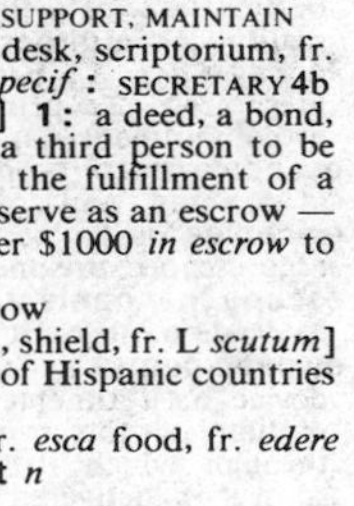

escutcheon 1: *A* dexter, *B* sinister, *1* dexter chief point, *2* middle chief point, *3* sinister chief point, *4* honor point, *5* fess point, *6* nombril, *7* middle base point, *8* dexter base point, *9* sinister base point

Esd *abbr* Esdras

Es·dras \'ez-drəs\ *n* [LL, fr. Gk, fr. Heb *'Ezrā*] **1 :** either of two books of the Roman Catholic canon of the Old Testament — see BIBLE table **2 :** either of two noncanonical books of Scripture included in the Protestant Apocrypha — see BIBLE table

ESE *abbr* east-southeast

¹-ese \'ēz, 'ēs\ *adj suffix* [Pg *-ês* & It *-ese,* fr. L *-ensis*] **:** of, relating to, or originating in (a certain place or country) <Japan*ese*>

²-ese *n suffix, pl* **-ese 1 :** native or resident of (a specified place or country) <Chin*ese*> **2 a :** language of (a particular place, country, or nationality) <Siam*ese*> **b :** speech, literary style, or diction peculiar to (a specified place, person, or group) — usu. in words applied in depreciation <journal*ese*>

es·em·plas·tic \ˌes-ˌem-'plas-tik, -əm-\ *adj* [Gk *es hen* into one + E *plastic*] **:** shaping or having the power to shape disparate things into a unified whole <the ~ power of the poetic imagination —W. H. Gardner>

es·er·ine \'es-ə-ˌrēn\ *n* [F *ésérine*] **:** PHYSOSTIGMINE

Esk *abbr* Eskimo

es·ker \'es-kər\ *n* [IrGael *eiscir* ridge] **:** a long narrow ridge or mound of sand, gravel, and boulders deposited by a stream flowing on, within, or beneath a stagnant glacier

Es·ki·mo \'es-kə-ˌmō\ *n* [Dan, of Algonquian origin; akin to Cree *askimowew* he eats it raw] **1** *pl* **Eskimo** *or* **Eskimos a :** a group of peoples of northern Canada, Greenland, Alaska, and eastern Siberia **b :** a member of such people **2 :** the language of the Eskimo people — **Es·ki·mo·an** \ˌes-kə-'mō-ən\ *adj*

Eskimo dog *n* **1 :** a broad-chested powerful dog of a breed native to Greenland and Labrador characterized by a long and shaggy outer coat and a soft dense woolly inner coat **2 :** a sled dog of American origin

ESL *abbr* English as a second language

esophag- *or* **esophago-** *comb form* **:** esophagus <*esophag*ectomy> **:** esophageal and <*esophago*gastric>

esoph·a·ge·al \i-ˌsäf-ə-'jē-əl\ *adj* **:** of or relating to the esophagus

esoph·a·gus \i-'säf-ə-gəs\ *n, pl* **-gi** \-ˌgī, -ˌjī\ [ME *ysophagus,* fr. Gk *oisophagos,* fr. *oisein* to be going to carry + *phagein* to eat — more at BAKSHEESH] **:** a muscular tube that leads from the pharynx to the stomach, passes down the neck between the trachea and the spinal column, and in man is about nine inches long — see LARYNX illustration

es·o·ter·ic \ˌes-ə-'ter-ik\ *adj* [LL *esotericus,* fr. Gk *esōterikos,* fr. *esōterō,* compar. of *eisō, esō* within, fr. *eis* into, fr. *en* in — more at IN] **1 a :** designed for or understood by the specially initiated alone <a body of ~ legal doctrine —B. N. Cardozo> **b :** of or relating to knowledge that is restricted to a small group **2 a :** limited to a small circle <~ pursuits> **b :** PRIVATE, CONFIDENTIAL <an ~ purpose> — **es·o·ter·i·cal·ly** \-i-k(ə-)lē\ *adv*

es·o·ter·i·ca \-i-kə\ *n pl* [NL, fr. Gk *esōterika,* neut. pl. of *esōterikos*] **:** esoteric items

es·o·ter·i·cism \-'ter-ə-ˌsiz-əm\ *n* **1 :** esoteric doctrines or practices **2 :** the quality or state of being esoteric

esp *abbr* especially

ESP \ˌē-ˌes-'pē\ *n* [*e*xtra*s*ensory *p*erception] **:** extrasensory perception

es·pa·drille \'es-pə-ˌdril\ *n* [F] **:** a flat sandal usu. having a fabric upper and a flexible sole

¹es·pal·ier \is-'pal-yər, -ˌyā\ *n* [F, deriv. of It *spalla* shoulder, fr. LL *spatula* shoulder blade — more at EPAULET] **1 :** a plant (as a fruit tree) trained to grow flat against a support (as a wall or trellis) **2 :** a railing or trellis on which fruit trees or shrubs are trained to grow flat

²espalier *vt* **1 :** to train as an espalier **2 :** to furnish with an espalier

es·par·to \is-'pärt-(ˌ)ō\ *n, pl* **-tos** [Sp, fr. L *spartum,* fr. Gk *sparton* — more at SPIRE] **:** either of two Spanish and Algerian grasses (*Stipa tenacissima* and *Lygeum spartum*) used esp. to make cordage, shoes, and paper

es·pe·cial \is-'pesh-əl\ *adj* [ME, fr. MF — more at SPECIAL] **:** being distinctive: as **a :** directed toward a particular individual, group, or end <sent ~ greetings to his son> <took ~ care to speak clearly> **b :** of special note or importance : unusually great or significant <a decision of ~ relevance> <illness puts an ~ burden on modest resources> **c :** highly distinctive or personal **:** PECULIAR <had an ~ dislike for music> **d :** CLOSE, INTIMATE <his ~ crony> **e :** capable of being specifically identified <had no ~ destination in mind> ***syn*** see SPECIAL — **es·pe·cial·ly** \-'pesh-(ə-)lē\ *adv* — **in especial :** in particular

es·per·ance \'es-p(ə-)rən(t)s\ *n* [ME *esperaunce,* fr. MF *esperance*] *obs* **:** HOPE, EXPECTATION

Es·pe·ran·to \ˌes-pə-'rant-(ˌ)ō, -'rän-(ˌ)tō\ *n* [Dr. *Esperanto,* pseudonym of L. L. Zamenhof †1917 Pol oculist, its inventor] **:** an artificial international language based as far as possible on words common to the chief European languages

es·pi·al \is-'pī(-ə)l\ *n* **1 :** OBSERVATION **2 :** an act of noticing **:** DISCOVERY

es·piè·gle \es-pyeglᵊ\ *adj* [F] **:** FROLICSOME, ROGUISH

es·piè·gle·rie \es-pyeg-lə-rē\ *n* [F, fr. *espiègle*] **:** the quality or state of being roguish or frolicsome

es·pi·o·nage \'es-pē-ə-ˌnäzh, -nij, -ˌnäj; is-'pē-ə-nij\ *n* [F *espionnage,* fr. MF, fr. *espionner* to spy, fr. *espion* spy, fr. OIt *spione,* fr. *spia,* of Gmc origin; akin to OHG *spehōn* to spy — more at SPY] **:** the practice of spying or the use of spies to obtain information about the plans and activities esp. of a foreign government or a competing company <industrial ~>

es·pla·nade \'es-plə-ˌnäd, -ˌnād\ *n* [F, fr. It *spianata,* fr. *spianare* to level, fr. L *explanare* — more at EXPLAIN] **:** a level open stretch of paved or grassy ground; *esp* **:** one designed for walking or driving along a shore

es·pous·al \is-'pau̇-zəl *also* -səl\ *n* **1 a :** BETROTHAL **b :** WEDDING **c :** MARRIAGE **2 :** a taking up or adopting of a cause or belief

es·pouse \is-'pau̇z *also* -'pau̇s\ *vt* **es·poused; es·pous·ing** [ME *espousen,* fr. MF *espouser,* fr. LL *sponsare* to betroth, fr. L *sponsus,* pp. of *spondēre* to promise, betroth — more at SPOUSE] **1 :** MARRY **2 :** to take up and support as a cause **:** become attached to <~ the problems of minority groups> ***syn*** see ADOPT — **es·pous·er** *n*

espres·so \e-'spres-(ˌ)ō\ *n, pl* **-sos** [It (*caffè*) *espresso,* lit., pressed out coffee] **:** coffee brewed by forcing steam through finely ground darkly roasted coffee beans

es·prit \is-'prē\ *n* [F, fr. L *spiritus* spirit] **1 :** vivacious cleverness or wit **2 :** ESPRIT DE CORPS

es·prit de corps \is-ˌprēd-ə-'kō(ə)r, -'kȯ(ə)r\ *n* [F] **:** the common spirit existing in the members of a group and inspiring enthusiasm, devotion, and strong regard for the honor of the group

es·py \is-'pī\ *vt* **es·pied; es·py·ing** [ME *espien,* fr. OF *espier* — more at SPY] **:** to catch sight of <among the several horses . . . she *espied* the white mustang —Zane Grey>

Esq *or* **Esqr** *abbr* esquire

-esque \'esk\ *adj suffix* [F, fr. It *-esco,* of Gmc origin; akin to OHG *-isc* -ish — more at -ISH] **:** in the manner or style of **:** like <statu*esque*>

Es·qui·mau \'es-kə-ˌmō\ *n, pl* **Esquimau** *or* **Es·qui·maux** \-ˌmō(z)\ [F, of Algonquian origin] **:** ESKIMO

es·quire \'es-ˌkwī(ə)r, is-'\ *n* [ME, fr. MF *esquier* squire, fr. LL *scutarius,* fr. L *scutum* shield; akin to OHG *sceida* sheath] **1 :** a member of the English gentry ranking below a knight **2 :** a candidate for knighthood serving as shield bearer and attendant to a knight **3** — used as a title of courtesy usu. placed in its

abbreviated form after the surname <John R. Smith, *Esq.*> **4** *archaic* : a landed proprietor
ess \'es\ *n* **1** : the letter *s* **2** : something resembling the letter *S* in shape; *esp* : an S-shaped curve in a road
-ess \əs, is *also* ,es\ *n suffix* [ME *-esse*, fr. OF, fr. LL *-issa*, fr. Gk] : female <giant*ess*>
[1]**es·say** \e-'sā, 'es-,ā\ *vt* **1 a** : to put to a test **b** : [2]ASSAY 2a **2** : to make an often tentative or experimental effort to perform ***syn*** see ATTEMPT — **es·say·er** *n*
[2]**es·say** *in sense 2* 'es-,ā, *in other senses also* e-'sā\ *n* [MF *essai*, fr. LL *exagium* act of weighing, fr. *ex-* + *agere* to drive — more at AGENT] **1 a** : EFFORT, ATTEMPT; *esp* : an initial tentative effort **b** : the result or product of an attempt **2 a** : an analytic or interpretative literary composition usu. dealing with its subject from a limited or personal point of view **b** : something resembling such a composition <a photographic ~> **3** : TRIAL, TEST **4** : a proof of an unaccepted design for a stamp or piece of paper money
es·say·ist \'es-,ā-əst\ *n* : a writer of essays
es·say·is·tic \,es-(,)ā-'is-tik\ *adj* **1** : of or relating to an essay or an essayist **2** : resembling an essay in quality or character
essay question *n* : an examination question that requires an answer in a sentence, paragraph, or short composition
essay test *n* : a test made up of essay questions — compare OBJECTIVE TEST
es·sence \'es-ᵊn(t)s\ *n* [ME, fr. MF & L; MF, fr. L *essentia*, fr. *esse* to be — more at IS] **1 a** : the permanent as contrasted with the accidental element of being **b** : the individual, real, or ultimate nature of a thing esp. as opposed to its existence **c** : the properties or attributes by means of which something can be placed in its proper class or identified as being what it is **2** : something that exists : ENTITY **3 a** (1) : a volatile substance or constituent (as of perfume) (2) : a constituent or derivative (as an extract or essential oil) possessing the special qualities (as of a plant or drug) in concentrated form; *also* : a preparation (as an alcoholic solution) of such an essence or a synthetic substitute **b** : ODOR, PERFUME **c** : something that resembles an extract in possessing a quality in concentrated form — **in essence** : in or by its very nature : ESSENTIALLY, BASICALLY <accusations which *in essence* are well-founded —*Times Lit. Supp.*> — **of the essence** : of the utmost importance : ESSENTIAL <time was *of the essence*>
Es·sene \is-'ēn, 'es-,ēn\ *n* [Gk *Essēnos*] : a member of a monastic brotherhood of Jews in Palestine from the 2d century B.C. to the 2d century A.D. — **Es·se·ni·an** \is-'ē-nē-ən, es-\ *or* **Es·se·nic** \-'en-ik, -'ē-nik\ *adj* — **Essenism** *n*
[1]**es·sen·tial** \i-'sen-chəl\ *adj* **1** : of, relating to, or constituting essence : INHERENT **2** : of the utmost importance : BASIC, INDISPENSABLE, NECESSARY <~ foods> <an ~ requirement for admission to college> **3** : IDIOPATHIC <~ disease> — **es·sen·ti·al·i·ty** \-,sen-chē-'al-ət-ē\ *n* — **es·sen·tial·ly** \-'sench-(ə-)lē\ *adv* — **es·sen·tial·ness** \-'sen-chəl-nəs\ *n*
syn ESSENTIAL, FUNDAMENTAL, VITAL, CARDINAL *shared meaning element* : so important as to be indispensable
[2]**essential** *n* **1** : something basic <the ~*s* of astronomy> **2** : something necessary, indispensable, or unavoidable
essential amino acid *n* : an amino acid (as lysine) that is required for normal health and growth, is manufactured in the body in insufficient quantities or not at all, and is usu. supplied by dietary protein
es·sen·tial·ism \i-'sen-chə-,liz-əm\ *n* **1** : an educational theory that ideas and skills basic to a culture should be taught to all alike by time-tested methods — compare PROGRESSIVISM **2 a** : REALISM **b** : a theory that gives priority to essence over existence — compare EXISTENTIALISM — **es·sen·tial·ist** \-ləst\ *adj or n*
es·sen·ti·al·i·ty \i-,sen-chē-'al-ət-ē\ *n, pl* **-ties** **1** : the quality or state of being essential <the ~ of freedom and justice —P. G. Hoffman> **2 a** : essential nature : ESSENCE **b** : an essential quality, property, or aspect
essential oil *n* : any of a class of volatile oils that impart the characteristic odors to plants and are used esp. in perfumes and flavorings — compare FIXED OIL
es·soin \is-'ȯin\ *n* [ME *essoine*, fr. MF, fr. ML *essonium*, fr. L *ex-* + LL *sonium* care, worry] **1** : an excuse for not appearing in an English law court at the appointed time **2** *obs* : EXCUSE, DELAY
es·so·nite \'es-ᵊn-,īt\ *n* [F, fr. Gk *hēsson* inferior; fr. its being less hard than true hyacinth] : a yellow to brown garnet
est *abbr* **1** established **2** estimate; estimated
EST *abbr* eastern standard time
[1]**-est** \əst, ist\ *adj suffix or adv suffix* [ME, fr. OE *-st, -est, -ost;* akin to OHG *-isto* (adj. superl. suffix), Gk *-istos*] — used to form the superlative degree of adjectives and adverbs of one syllable <fatt*est*> <lat*est*>, of some adjectives and adverbs of two syllables <lucki*est*> <often*est*>, and less often of longer ones <beggarli*est*>
[2]**-est** \əst, ist\ *or* **-st** \st\ *vb suffix* [ME, fr. OE *-est, -ast, -st;* akin to OHG *-ist, -ōst, -ēst,* 2d sing. ending] — used to form the archaic 2d person singular of English verbs (with *thou*) <gett*est*> <did*st*>
es·tab·lish \is-'tab-lish\ *vb* [ME *establissen*, fr. MF *establiss-*, stem of *establir*, fr. L *stabilire*, fr. *stabilis* stable] *vt* **1** : to make firm or stable **2** : to institute (as a law) permanently by enactment or agreement **3** *obs* : SETTLE 7 **4 a** : to bring into existence : FOUND <~*ed* a republic> **b** : to bring about : EFFECT <~*ed* friendly relations> **5 a** : to set on a firm basis <~ his son in business> **b** : to put into a favorable position **c** : to gain full recognition or acceptance of **6** : to make (a church) a national institution **7** : to put beyond doubt : PROVE <~*ed* his innocence> ~ *vi, of a plant* : to become naturalized <a grass that ~*es* on poor soil> ***syn*** see SET ***ant*** uproot (*as a plant or a practice*), abrogate (*as a privilege*) — **es·tab·lish·able** \-ə-bəl\ *adj* — **es·tab·lish·er** *n*
established church *n* : a church recognized by law as the official church of a nation and supported by civil authority
es·tab·lish·ment \is-'tab-lish-mənt\ *n* **1** : something established: as **a** : a settled arrangement; *esp* : a code of laws **b** : ESTABLISHED CHURCH **c** : a permanent civil or military organization **d** : a place of business or residence with its furnishings and staff **e** : a public or private institution **2** : an established order of society: as **a** *often cap* : a group of social, economic, and political leaders who form a ruling class (as of a nation) **b** *often cap* : a controlling group <the literary ~> **3 a** : the act of establishing **b** : the state of being established
es·tab·lish·men·tar·i·an \is-,tab-lish-mən-'ter-ē-ən, -,men-\ *adj* : of, relating to, or favoring the social or political establishment — **establishmentarian** *n* — **es·tab·lish·men·tar·i·an·ism** \-ē-ə-,niz-əm\ *n*
es·ta·mi·net \e-stá-mē-nā\ *n, pl* **-nets** \-nā(z)\ [F] : a small café : BISTRO
es·tate \is-'tāt\ *n* [ME *estat*, fr. MF — more at STATE] **1** : STATE, CONDITION **2** : social standing or rank esp. of a high order **3** : a social or political class; *specif* : one of the great classes (as the nobility, the clergy, and the commons) formerly vested with distinct political powers **4 a** : the degree, quality, nature, and extent of one's interest in land or other property **b** (1) : POSSESSIONS, PROPERTY; *esp* : a person's property in land and tenements <a man of small ~> (2) : the assets and liabilities left by a person at death **c** : a landed property usu. with a large house on it **5** *Brit* : ESTATE CAR
estate agent *n, Brit* : a real estate broker or manager
estate car *n, Brit* : STATION WAGON
estate tax *n* : an excise in the form of a percentage of the net estate that is levied on the privilege of an owner of property of transmitting his property to others after his death — compare INHERITANCE TAX 1
[1]**es·teem** \is-'tēm\ *n* **1** *archaic* : WORTH, VALUE **2** *archaic* : OPINION, JUDGMENT **3** : high regard <held in ~ by his colleagues>
[2]**esteem** *vt* [ME *estemen* to estimate, fr. MF *estimer*, fr. L *aestimare*] **1** *archaic* : APPRAISE **2 a** : to view as : CONSIDER <~ it a privilege> **b** : THINK, BELIEVE **3** : to set a high value on : regard highly and prize accordingly ***syn*** see REGARD ***ant*** abominate
es·ter \'es-tər\ *n* [G, fr. *essigäther* ethyl acetate, fr. *essig* vinegar + *äther* ether] : an often fragrant compound formed by the reaction between an acid and an alcohol usu. with elimination of water
es·ter·ase \'es-tə-,rās, -,rāz\ *n* : an enzyme that accelerates the hydrolysis or synthesis of esters
es·ter·i·fy \e-'ster-ə-,fī\ *vt* **-fied; -fy·ing** : to convert into an ester — **es·ter·i·fi·ca·tion** \-,ster-ə-fə-'kā-shən\ *n*
Esth *abbr* Esther
Es·ther \'es-tər\ *n* [L, fr. Heb *Estēr*] **1** : the Jewish heroine of the Old Testament book of Esther **2** : a narrative book of canonical Jewish and Christian Scripture — see BIBLE table
es·the·sia \es-'thē-zh(ē-)ə\ *n* [NL, back-formation fr. *anesthesia*] : capacity for sensation and feeling : SENSIBILITY
esthesio- *or* **aesthesio-** *comb form* [Gk *aisthēsis*] : sensation <*esthesio*logy>
es·the·si·om·e·ter \es-,thē-zē-'äm-ət-ər, -,thē-sē-\ *n* : an instrument for measuring sensory discrimination; *esp* : one for determining the distance by which two points pressed against the skin must be separated in order that they may be felt as separate
es·the·sis \es-'thē-səs\ *n* [NL, fr. Gk *aisthēsis*, fr. *aisthanesthai* to perceive — more at AUDIBLE] : SENSATION; *esp* : rudimentary sensation
esthete, esthetic, esthetics *var of* AESTHETE, AESTHETIC, AESTHETICS
es·ti·ma·ble \'es-tə-mə-bəl\ *adj* **1** *archaic* : VALUABLE **2** : worthy of esteem **3** : capable of being estimated — **es·ti·ma·ble·ness** *n*
[1]**es·ti·mate** \'es-tə-,māt\ *vt* **-mat·ed; -mat·ing** [L *aestimatus*, pp. of *aestimare* to value, estimate] **1** *archaic* **a** : ESTEEM **b** : APPRAISE **2 a** : to judge tentatively or approximately the value, worth, or significance of **b** : to determine roughly the size, extent, or nature of **c** : to produce a statement of the approximate cost of **3** : JUDGE, CONCLUDE — **es·ti·ma·tive** \-,māt-iv\ *adj*
syn ESTIMATE, APPRAISE, EVALUATE, VALUE, RATE, ASSESS *shared meaning element* : to judge something with respect to its worth or significance
[2]**es·ti·mate** \'es-tə-mət\ *n* **1** : the act of appraising or valuing : CALCULATION **2** : an opinion or judgment of the nature, character, or quality of a person or thing <an ~ of a man> **3 a** : a rough or approximate calculation **b** : a numerical value obtained from a statistical sample and assigned to a population parameter **4** : a statement of the cost of a job
es·ti·ma·tion \,es-tə-'mā-shən\ *n* **1** : JUDGMENT, OPINION **2 a** : the act of estimating **b** : the value, amount, or size arrived at in an estimate **3** : ESTEEM, HONOR
es·ti·ma·tor \'es-tə-,māt-ər\ *n* **1** : one that estimates **2** : ESTIMATE 3b; *also*: a statistical function whose value for a sample furnishes an estimate of a population parameter
estival, estivate, estivation *var of* AESTIVAL, AESTIVATE, AESTIVATION
Es·to·nian \e-'stō-nē-ən, -nyən\ *n* **1** : a member of a Finno-Ugric-speaking people of Estonia **2** : the Finno-Ugric language of the Estonian people — **Estonian** *adj*
es·top \e-'stäp\ *vt* **es·topped; es·top·ping** [ME *estoppen*, fr. MF *estouper*] **1** *archaic* : to stop up **2** : STOP, BAR; *specif* : to impede by estoppel
es·top·pel \e-'stäp-əl\ *n* [prob. fr. MF *estoupail* bung, fr. *estouper*] : a bar to alleging or denying a fact because of one's own previous actions or words to the contrary
estr- *or* **estro-** *or* **oestr-** *or* **oestro-** *comb form* : estrus <*estro*gen>

es·tra·di·ol \es-trə-ˈdī-ˌȯl, -ˌōl\ *n* [ISV *estra-* (fr. *estrin*) + *di-* + *-ol*] : an estrogenic hormone that is a phenolic steroid alcohol $C_{18}H_{24}O_2$ usu. made synthetically and that is often used combined as an ester esp. in treating menopausal symptoms

es·tral \ˈes-trəl\ *adj* : ESTROUS

estral cycle *n* : ESTROUS CYCLE

es·trange \is-ˈtrānj\ *vt* **es·tranged; es·trang·ing** [MF *estranger*, fr. ML *extraneare*, fr. L *extraneus* strange — more at STRANGE] **1** : to remove from customary environment or associations **2** : to arouse esp. mutual enmity or indifference in where there had formerly been love, affection, or friendliness : ALIENATE — **es·trange·ment** \-ˈtrānj-mənt\ *n* — **es·trang·er** *n*

syn ESTRANGE, ALIENATE, DISAFFECT, WEAN *shared meaning element* : to cause one to break a bond of affection or loyalty ***ant*** reconcile

[1]**es·tray** \is-ˈtrā\ *vi* [MF *estraier*] *archaic* : STRAY

[2]**estray** *n* : STRAY 1

es·trin \ˈes-trən\ *n* [NL *estrus*] : an estrogenic hormone; *esp* : ESTRONE

es·tri·ol \ˈes-ˌtrī-ˌȯl, e-ˈstrī-, -ˌōl\ *n* [*estrin* + *tri-* + *-ol*] : a crystalline estrogenic hormone that is a glycol $C_{18}H_{24}O_3$ usu. obtained from the urine of pregnant women

es·tro·gen \ˈes-trə-jən\ *n* [NL *estrus* + ISV *-o-* + *-gen*] : a substance (as a sex hormone) tending to promote estrus and stimulate the development of secondary sex characteristics in the female

es·tro·gen·ic \ˌes-trə-ˈjen-ik\ *adj* **1** : promoting estrus **2** : of, relating to, or caused by an estrogen — **es·tro·gen·i·cal·ly** \-i-k(ə-)lē\ *adv*

es·trone \ˈes-ˌtrōn\ *n* [ISV, fr. *estrin*] : an estrogenic hormone that is a ketone $C_{18}H_{22}O_2$, is usu. obtained from the urine of pregnant females, and is used similarly to estradiol

es·trous \ˈes-trəs\ *adj* **1** : of, relating to, or characteristic of estrus **2** : being in heat

estrous cycle *n* : the correlated phenomena of the endocrine and generative systems of a female mammal from the beginning of one period of estrus to the beginning of the next — called also *estral cycle*

es·tru·al \ˈes-trə-wəl\ *adj* : ESTROUS

es·trus \ˈes-trəs\ *or* **es·trum** \-trəm\ *n* [NL, fr. L *oestrus* gadfly, frenzy, fr. Gk *oistros* — more at IRE] **1 a** : a regularly recurrent state of sexual excitability during which the female of most mammals will accept the male and is capable of conceiving : HEAT **b** : a single occurrence of this state **2** : ESTROUS CYCLE

es·tu·ar·i·al \ˌes(h)-chə-ˈwer-ē-əl\ *adj* : ESTUARINE

es·tu·a·rine \ˈes(h)-chə-wə-ˌrīn, -ˌrēn\ *adj* : of, relating to, or formed in an estuary <~ currents> <~ animals> <~ environment>

es·tu·ary \ˈes(h)-chə-ˌwer-ē\ *n, pl* **-ar·ies** [L *aestuarium*, fr. *aestus* boiling, tide; akin to L *aestas* summer — more at AESTIVAL] : a water passage where the tide meets a river current; *esp* : an arm of the sea at the lower end of a river

ESU *abbr* electrostatic unit

esu·ri·ence \i-ˈsu̇r-ē-ən(t)s, -ˈzu̇r-\ *n* : the quality or state of being esurient

esu·ri·en·cy \-ən-sē\ *n* : ESURIENCE

esu·ri·ent \-ənt\ *adj* [L *esurient-, esuriens*, prp. of *esurire* to be hungry] : HUNGRY, GREEDY — **esu·ri·ent·ly** *adv*

ESV *abbr* earth satellite vehicle

et \ˈet\ *dial past of* EAT

Et *symbol* ethyl

ET *abbr* eastern time

-et \ˈet, ˌet, ət, it\ *n suffix* [ME, fr. OF *-et*, masc., & *-ete*, fem., fr. LL *-itus* & *-ita*] **1** : small one <baron*et*> <cellar*et*> **2** : group <oct*et*>

eta \ˈāt-ə, ˈēt-ə\ *n* [LL, fr. Gk *ēta*, of Sem origin; akin to Heb *ḥēth* heth] : the 7th letter of the Greek alphabet — see ALPHABET table

ETA *abbr* estimated time of arrival

éta·gère *or* **eta·gere** \ˌā-ˌtä-ˈzhe(ə)r, ˌāt-ə-\ *n* [F *étagère*] : an elaborate whatnot often with a large mirror at the back and sometimes with an enclosed cabinet as a base

etagere

et al \et-ˈal, -ˈȯl\ *abbr* [L *et alii* (masc.), *et aliae* (fem.), or *et alia* (neut.)] and others

eta·mine \ˈāt-ə-ˌmēn\ *n* [F *étamine*] : a light cotton or worsted fabric with an open mesh

etat·ism \ā-ˈtät-ˌiz-əm\ *n* [F *étatisme*, fr. *état* state, fr. OF *estat*] : STATE SOCIALISM — **etat·ist** \-ˈtät-əst\ *adj*

etc \ən-ˈsō-ˌfōrth, -ˌfȯrth; et-ˈset-ə-rə, -ˈse-trə\ *abbr* et cetera

et·cet·era *n* **1** : a number of unspecified additional persons or things **2** *pl* : unspecified additional items : ODDS AND ENDS

et cet·era \et-ˈset-ə-rə, -ˈse-trə\ [L] : and others esp. of the same kind : and so forth

[1]**etch** \ˈech\ *vb* [D *etsen*, fr. G *ätzen*, lit., to feed, fr. OHG *azzen*; akin to OHG *ezzan* to eat — more at EAT] *vt* **1 a** : to produce esp. on metal or glass by the corrosive action of an acid **b** : to subject to such etching **2** : to delineate or impress clearly <scenes that are indelibly ~*ed* in our minds> ~ *vi*: to practice etching — **etch·er** *n*

[2]**etch** *n* **1** : the action or effect of an etching acid on a surface **2** : a chemical agent used in etching

etch·ing *n* **1 a** : the act or process of etching **b** : the art of producing pictures or designs by printing from an etched metal plate **2 a** : an etched design **b** : an impression from an etched plate

ETD *abbr* estimated time of departure

[1]**eter·nal** \i-ˈtərn-ᵊl\ *adj* [ME, fr. MF, fr. LL *aeternalis*, fr. L *aeternus* eternal; akin to L *aevum* age, eternity — more at AYE] **1 a** : having infinite duration : EVERLASTING **b** : of or relating to eternity **c** : characterized by abiding fellowship with God <good teacher, what must I do to inherit ~ life? —Mk 10:17 (RSV)> **2 a** : continued without intermission : PERPETUAL **b** : seemingly endless **3** *archaic* : INFERNAL **4** : valid or existing at all times : TIMELESS <~ verities> — **eter·nal·ize** \-ᵊl-ˌīz\ *vt* — **eter·nal·ly** \-ᵊl-ē\ *adv* — **eter·nal·ness** *n*

[2]**eternal** *n* **1** *cap* : GOD 1 — used with *the* **2** : something eternal

eterne \i-ˈtərn\ *adj* [ME, fr. MF, fr. L *aeternus*] *archaic* : ETERNAL

eter·ni·ty \i-ˈtər-nət-ē\ *n, pl* **-ties** [ME *eternite*, fr. MF *eternité*, fr. L *aeternitat-, aeternitas*, fr. *aeternus*] **1** : the quality or state of being eternal **2** : infinite time **3** *pl* : AGES **4** : the state after death : IMMORTALITY **5** : a seemingly endless or immeasurable time <the posed motionless for a seeming ~ as the crowd roared with laughter and encouragement —J. W. Cross>

eter·nize \i-ˈtər-ˌnīz\ *vt* **-nized; -niz·ing** **1 a** : to make eternal **b** : to prolong indefinitely **2** : IMMORTALIZE — **eter·ni·za·tion** \-ˌtər-nə-ˈzā-shən\ *n*

ete·sian \i-ˈtē-zhən\ *adj, often cap* [L *etesius*, fr. Gk *etēsios*, fr. *etos* year — more at WETHER] : recurring annually — used of summer winds that blow over the Mediterranean — **etesian** *n, often cap*

eth \ˈet͟h\ *var of* EDH

eth- *or* **etho-** *comb form* [ISV] : ethyl <*eth*aldehyde> <*etho*chloride>

[1]**-eth** \əth, ith\ *or* **-th** \th\ *vb suffix* [ME, fr. OE *-eth, -ath, -th*; akin to OHG *-it, -ōt, -ēt*, 3d sing. ending, L *-t, -it*] — used to form the archaic third person singular present of verbs <go*eth*> <do*th*>

[2]**-eth** — see -TH

eth·a·cryn·ic acid \ˌeth-ə-ˌkrin-ik-\ *n* [perh. fr. *eth-* + *acetic* + buty*ryl* + phe*nol*] : a diuretic $C_{13}H_{12}Cl_2O_4$ used esp. in the treatment of edema

eth·am·bu·tol \eth-ˈam-byu̇-ˌtȯl, -ˌtōl\ *n* [*eth*ylene + *amine* + *butanol*] : a compound $C_{10}H_{24}N_2O_2$ used esp. in the treatment of tuberculosis

eth·ane \ˈeth-ˌān\ *n* [ISV, fr. *ethyl*] : a colorless odorless gaseous hydrocarbon C_2H_6 found in natural gas and used esp. as a fuel

eth·a·nol \ˈeth-ə-ˌnȯl, -ˌnōl\ *n* : ALCOHOL 1

eth·a·nol·amine \ˌeth-ə-ˈnäl-ə-ˌmēn, -ˈnōl-\ *n* : a colorless liquid amino alcohol C_2H_7NO used esp. as a solvent and in scrubbing gases

eth·ene \ˈeth-ˌēn\ *n* : ETHYLENE

ether \ˈē-thər\ *n* [ME, fr. L *aether*, fr. Gk *aithēr*, fr. *aithein* to ignite, blaze] **1 a** : the rarefied element formerly believed to fill the upper regions of space **b** : the upper regions of space : HEAVENS **2 a** : a medium that in the undulatory theory of light permeates all space and transmits transverse waves **b** : the medium that transmits radio waves **3 a** : a light volatile flammable liquid $C_4H_{10}O$ used chiefly as a solvent and anesthetic **b** : any of various organic compounds characterized by an oxygen atom attached to two carbon atoms — **ether·ish** \-thə-rish\ *adj* — **ether·like** \-thər-ˌlik\ *adj*

ethe·re·al \i-ˈthir-ē-əl\ *adj* **1 a** : of or relating to the regions beyond the earth **b** : CELESTIAL, HEAVENLY **c** : UNWORLDLY, SPIRITUAL **2 a** : lacking material substance : IMMATERIAL, INTANGIBLE **b** : marked by unusual delicacy and refinement <this smallest, most ~, and daintiest of birds —William Beebe> **3** : relating to, containing, or resembling a chemical ether — **ethe·re·al·i·ty** \-ˌthir-ē-ˈal-ət-ē\ *n* — **ethe·re·al·iza·tion** \-ē-ə-lə-ˈzā-shən\ *n* — **ethe·re·al·ize** \-ˈthir-ē-ə-ˌlīz\ *vt* — **ethe·re·al·ly** \-ē-ə-lē\ *adv* — **ethe·re·al·ness** *n*

ether extract *n* : the part of a complex organic material that is soluble in ether and consists chiefly of fats and fatty acids

ethe·ric \i-ˈther-ik, -ˈthir-\ *adj* : ETHEREAL

ether·ize \ˈē-thə-ˌrīz\ *vt* **-ized; -iz·ing** **1** : to treat or anesthetize with ether **2** : to make numb as if by anesthetizing — **ether·iza·tion** \ˌē-thə-rə-ˈzā-shən\ *n* — **ether·iz·er** *n*

eth·ic \ˈeth-ik\ *n* [ME *ethik*, fr. MF *ethique*, fr. L *ethice*, fr. Gk *ēthikē*, fr. *ēthikos*] **1** *pl but sing or pl in constr* : the discipline dealing with what is good and bad and with moral duty and obligation **2 a** : a set of moral principles or values **b** : a theory or system of moral values <the present-day materialistic ~> **c** *pl but sing or pl in constr* : the principles of conduct governing an individual or a group <professional ~*s*>

[1]**eth·i·cal** \ˈeth-i-kəl\ *also* **eth·ic** \-ik\ *adj* [ME *etik*, fr. L *ethicus*, fr. Gk *ēthikos*, fr. *ēthos* character] **1** : of or relating to ethics **2** : conforming to accepted professional standards of conduct **3** *of a drug* : restricted to sale only on a doctor's prescription ***syn*** see MORAL ***ant*** unethical — **eth·i·cal·i·ty** \ˌeth-ə-ˈkal-ət-ē\ *n* — **eth·i·cal·ly** \ˈeth-i-k(ə-)lē\ *adv* — **eth·i·cal·ness** \-kəl-nəs\ *n*

[2]**ethical** *n* : an ethical drug

ethi·cian \e-ˈthish-ən\ *n* : ETHICIST

eth·i·cist \ˈeth-ə-səst\ *n* : a specialist in ethics

eth·i·on \ˈeth-ē-ˌän\ *n* [blend of *eth-* and *thion-*] : an organophosphate $C_9H_{22}O_4P_2S_4$ used as a pesticide

eth·i·on·amide \ˌeth-ē-ˈän-ə-ˌmīd\ *n* [*eth-* + *thion-* + *amide*] : a compound $C_8H_{10}N_2S$ used against mycobacteria (as in tuberculosis and leprosy)

ethi·o·nine \e-ˈthī-ə-ˌnēn\ *n* [*eth-* + *thion-* + *-ine*] : an amino acid $C_6H_{13}NO_2S$ that is the ethyl homologue of methionine and is biologically antagonistic to methionine

Ethi·op \ˈē-thē-ˌäp\ *or* **Ethi·ope** \-ˌōp\ *n* [ME *Ethiope*, fr. L *Aethiops*, fr. Gk *Aithiops*] *archaic* : ETHIOPIAN

[1]**Ethi·o·pi·an** \ˌē-thē-ˈō-pē-ən\ *n* **1** : a member of any of the mythical or actual peoples usu. described by the ancient Greeks as dark-skinned and living far to the south **2** : NEGRO **3** : a native or inhabitant of Ethiopia

[2]**Ethiopian** *adj* **1** : of, relating to, or characteristic of the inhabitants or the country of Ethiopia **2** : of, relating to, or being the biogeographic region that includes Africa south of the Sahara, southern Arabia, and sometimes Madagascar and the adjacent islands

[1]**Ethi·o·pic** \-ˈäp-ik, -ˈō-pik\ *adj* **1** : ETHIOPIAN **2 a** : of, relating to, or constituting Ethiopic **b** : of, relating to, or constituting a group of related Semitic languages spoken in Ethiopia

[2]**Ethiopic** *n* **1 :** a Semitic language formerly spoken in Ethiopia and still used as the liturgical language of the Christian church in Ethiopia **2 :** the Ethiopic group of Semitic languages
eth·moid \'eth-ˌmȯid\ *or* **eth·moi·dal** \eth-'mȯid-ᵊl\ *adj* [F *ethoïde,* fr. Gk *ēthmoeidēs,* lit., like a strainer, fr. *ēthmos* strainer] **:** of, relating to, adjoining, or being one or more bones of the walls and septum of the nasal cavity — **ethmoid** *n*
[1]**eth·nic** \'eth-nik\ *adj* [ME, fr. LL *ethnicus,* fr. Gk *ethnikos* national, gentile, fr. *ethnos* nation, people] **1 :** neither Christian nor Jewish **:** HEATHEN **2 :** of or relating to races or large groups of people classed according to common traits and customs <~ minorities>
[2]**ethnic** *n* **:** a member of an ethnic group; *esp* **:** a member of a minority group who retains the customs, language, or social views of his group
eth·ni·cal \'eth-ni-kəl\ *adj* **1 :** ETHNIC **2 :** of or relating to ethnology **:** ETHNOLOGIC — **eth·ni·cal·ly** \-k(ə-)lē\ *adv*
eth·nic·i·ty \eth-'nis-ət-ē\ *n* **:** ethnic quality or affiliation
ethno- *comb form* [F, fr. Gk *ethno-, ethn-,* fr. *ethnos*] **:** race **:** people **:** cultural group <*ethno*centric>
eth·no·bi·ol·o·gy \ˌeth-nō-bī-'äl-ə-jē\ *n* **:** a branch of biology dealing with the relation between usu. primitive human societies and the plants and animals of their environment — **eth·no·bi·o·log·i·cal** \-ˌbī-ə-'läj-i-kəl\ *adj*
eth·no·cen·tric \ˌeth-nō-'sen-trik\ *adj* **1 :** having race as a central interest **2 :** characterized by or based on the attitude that one's own group is superior — **eth·no·cen·tri·cal·ly** \-tri-k(ə-)lē\ *adv* — **eth·no·cen·tric·i·ty** \-sen-'tris-ət-ē\ *n* — **eth·no·cen·trism** \-'sen-ˌtriz-əm\ *n*
eth·nog·ra·phy \eth-'näg-rə-fē\ *n* [F *ethnographie,* fr. *ethno-* + *-graphie* -graphy] **:** ETHNOLOGY; *specif* **:** descriptive anthropology — **eth·nog·ra·pher** \-fər\ *n* — **eth·no·graph·ic** \ˌeth-nə-'graf-ik\ *or* **eth·no·graph·i·cal** \-i-kəl\ *adj* — **eth·no·graph·i·cal·ly** \-i-k(ə-)lē\ *adv*
ethnol *abbr* ethnologist; ethnology
eth·nol·o·gy \eth-'näl-ə-jē\ *n* **1 :** a science that deals with the division of mankind into races and their origin, distribution, relations, and characteristics **2 :** anthropology dealing chiefly with the comparative and analytical study of cultures **:** CULTURAL ANTHROPOLOGY — **eth·no·log·ic** \ˌeth-nə-'läj-ik\ *or* **eth·no·log·i·cal** \-i-kəl\ *adj* — **eth·no·log·i·cal·ly** \-i-k(ə-)lē\ *adv* — **eth·nol·o·gist** \eth-'näl-ə-jəst\ *n*
eth·no·mu·si·col·o·gy \ˌeth-nō-ˌmyü-zi-'käl-ə-jē\ *n* **:** a study of the music of non-European cultures — **eth·no·mu·si·co·log·i·cal** \-kə-'läj-i-kəl\ *adj* — **eth·no·mu·si·col·o·gist** \-'käl-ə-jəst\ *n*
ethol·o·gy \ē-'thäl-ə-jē\ *n* **1 :** a branch of knowledge dealing with human ethos and with its formation and evolution **2 :** the scientific and objective study of animal behavior — **etho·log·i·cal** \ˌē-thə-'läj-i-kəl, ˌeth-ə-\ *adj* — **ethol·o·gist** \ē-'thäl-ə-jəst\ *n*
ethos \'ē-ˌthäs\ *n* [NL, fr. Gk *ēthos* custom, character] **:** the distinguishing character, sentiment, moral nature, or guiding beliefs of a person, group, or institution <the ~ of thrift, hard work, and wealth —N. P. Hurley>
eth·oxy \e-'thäk-sē\ *adj* **:** relating to or containing ethoxyl
eth·ox·yl \e-'thäk-səl\ *n* [ISV *eth-* + *ox-* + *-yl*] **:** the univalent radical C_2H_5O composed of ethyl united with oxygen
eth·yl \'eth-əl\ *n* [ISV *ether* + *-yl*] **:** a univalent hydrocarbon radical C_2H_5 — **eth·yl·ic** \e-'thil-ik\ *adj*
ethyl acetate *n* **:** a colorless fragrant volatile flammable liquid ester $C_4H_8O_2$ used esp. as a solvent
ethyl alcohol *n* **:** ALCOHOL 1
eth·yl·ate \'eth-ə-ˌlāt\ *vt* **-at·ed; -at·ing :** to introduce the ethyl group into (a compound) — **eth·yl·ation** \ˌeth-ə-'lā-shən\ *n*
ethyl cellulose *n* **:** any of various thermoplastic substances used esp. in plastics and lacquers
ethyl chloride *n* **:** a colorless pungent flammable gaseous or volatile liquid compound C_2H_5Cl used esp. as a local surface anesthetic
eth·yl·ene \'eth-ə-ˌlēn\ *n* **1 :** a colorless flammable gaseous unsaturated hydrocarbon C_2H_4 found in coal gas or obtained by pyrolysis of petroleum hydrocarbons **2 :** a bivalent hydrocarbon radical C_2H_4 derived from ethane — **eth·yl·enic** \ˌeth-ə-'lē-nik, -'len-ik\ *adj* — **eth·yl·eni·cal·ly** \-(n)i-k(ə-)lē\ *adv*
ethylene glycol *n* **:** a thick liquid alcohol $C_2H_6O_2$ used esp. as an antifreeze
ethylene oxide *n* **:** a colorless flammable toxic gaseous or liquid compound C_2H_4O used esp. in synthesis (as of ethylene glycol) and in sterilization and fumigation
ethyl ether *n* **:** ETHER 3a
ethy·nyl *or* **ethi·nyl** \e-'thīn-ᵊl, 'eth-ə-ˌnil\ *n* [*ethyne, ethine* (acetylene) (fr. *ethyl* + *-ine*) + *-yl*] **:** a univalent unsaturated radical $HC{\equiv}C$ derived from acetylene by removal of one hydrogen atom
-et·ic \'et-ik\ *adj suffix* [L & Gk; L *-eticus,* fr. Gk *-etikos, -ētikos,* fr. *-etos, -ētos,* ending of certain verbals] **:** -IC <limn*etic*> — often in adjectives corresponding to nouns ending in *-esis* <gen*etic*>
eti·o·late \'ēt-ē-ə-ˌlāt\ *vt* **-lat·ed; -lat·ing** [F *étioler*] **1 :** to bleach and alter the natural development of (a green plant) by excluding sunlight **2 a :** to make pale and sickly **b :** to take away the natural vigor or inhibit the potential for growth of (as by undue sheltering or pampering) — **eti·o·la·tion** \ˌēt-ē-ə-'lā-shən\ *n*
eti·o·log·ic \ˌēt-ē-ə-'läj-ik\ *or* **eti·o·log·i·cal** \-i-kəl\ *adj* **1 :** assigning or seeking to assign a cause **2:** of or relating to etiology — **eti·o·log·i·cal·ly** \-i-k(ə-)lē\ *adv*
eti·ol·o·gy \ˌēt-ē-'äl-ə-jē\ *n* [ML *aetiologia* statement of causes, fr. Gk *aitiologia,* fr. *aitia* cause; akin to L *aemulus* rivaling] **1 :** CAUSE, ORIGIN; *specif* **:** all of the causes of a disease or abnormal condition **2 :** a branch of knowledge dealing with causes
et·i·quette \'et-i-kət, -ˌket\ *n* [F *étiquette,* lit., ticket — more at TICKET] **:** the forms required by good breeding or prescribed by authority to be observed in social or official life
ETO *abbr* European theater of operations
Eton collar \ˌēt-ᵊn-\ *n* [*Eton* College, English public school] **:** a large stiff turnover collar
Eton jacket *n* **:** a short black jacket with long sleeves, wide lapels, and an open front
Etru·ri·an \i-'trůr-ē-ən\ *n* [*Etruria*] **:** ETRUSCAN — **Etrurian** *adj*
[1]**Etrus·can** \i-'trəs-kən\ *adj* [L *etruscus;* akin to L *Etruria,* ancient country] **:** of, relating to, or characteristic of Etruria, the Etruscans, or the Etruscan language
[2]**Etruscan** *n* **1 :** a native or inhabitant of ancient Etruria **2 :** the language of the Etruscans which is of unknown affiliation
ETS *abbr* Educational Testing Service
et seq *abbr* **1** [L *et sequens*] and the following one **2** [L *et sequentes* (masc. & fem. pl.), or *et sequentia* (neut. pl.)] and the following ones
-ette \'et, ˌet, ət, it\ *n suffix* [ME, fr. MF, fem. dim. suffix, fr. OF *-ete* — more at -ET] **1 :** little one <kitchen*ette*> **2 :** group <oct*ette*> **3 :** female <farmer*ette*> **4 :** imitation <beaver*ette*>
étude \'ā-ˌt(y)üd\ *n* [F, lit., study, fr. MF *estude, estudie*] **1 :** a piece of music for the practice of a point of technique **2 :** a composition built on a technical motive but played for its artistic value
etui \ā-'twē, 'ā-ˌ\ *n, pl* **etuis** [F *étui*] **:** a small ornamental case
ETV *abbr* educational television
et·y·mol·o·gist \ˌet-ə-'mäl-ə-jəst\ *n* **:** a specialist in etymology
et·y·mol·o·gize \-ˌjīz\ *vb* **-gized; -giz·ing** *vt* **:** to discover, formulate, or state an etymology for ~ *vi* **:** to study or formulate etymologies
et·y·mol·o·gy \-jē\ *n, pl* **-gies** [ME *ethimologie,* fr. L *etymologia,* fr. Gk, fr. *etymon* + *-logia* -logy] **1 :** the history of a linguistic form (as a word) shown by tracing its development since its earliest recorded occurrence in the language where it is found, by tracing its transmission from one language to another, by analyzing it into its component parts, by identifying its cognates in other languages, or by tracing it and its cognates to a common ancestral form in an ancestral language **2 :** a branch of linguistics concerned with etymologies — **et·y·mo·log·i·cal** \-mə-'läj-i-kəl\ *adj* — **et·y·mo·log·i·cal·ly** \-k(ə-)lē\ *adv*
et·y·mon \'et-ə-ˌmän\ *n, pl* **-ma** \-mə\ *also* **-mons** [L, fr. Gk, literal meaning of a word according to its origin, fr. *etymos* true; akin to Gk *eteos* true] **1 a :** an earlier form of a word in the same language or an ancestral language **b :** a word in a foreign language that is the source of a particular loanword **2 :** a word or morpheme from which words are formed by composition or derivation
Eu *symbol* europium
eu- *comb form* [ME, fr. L, fr. Gk, fr. *ey, eu,* fr. neut. of *eys* good; akin to Hitt *asus* good and perh. to L *esse* to be] **1 a :** well **:** easily <*eu*plastic> — compare DYS- **b :** good <*eu*daemon> — compare DYS- **2 a :** true <*eu*chromosome> <*eu*globulin> **b :** truly <*eu*coelomate>
eu·ca·lypt \'yü-kə-ˌlipt\ *n* **:** EUCALYPTUS
eu·ca·lyp·tole *or* **eu·ca·lyp·tol** \ˌyü-kə-'lip-ˌtȯl, -ˌtōl\ *n* **:** CINEOLE
eu·ca·lyp·tus \ˌyü-kə-'lip-təs\ *n, pl* **-ti** \-ˌtī, -ˌtē\ *or* **-tus·es** [NL, genus name, fr. *eu-* + Gk *kalyptos* covered, fr. *kalyptein* to conceal; fr. the conical covering of the buds — more at HELL] **:** any of a genus (*Eucalyptus*) of mostly Australian evergreen trees or rarely shrubs of the myrtle family that have rigid entire leaves and umbellate flowers and are widely cultivated for their gums, resins, oils, and useful woods
eu·cary·ote *or* **eu·kary·ote** \(')yü-'kar-ē-ˌōt, -ē-ət\ *n* [*eu-* + Gk *karyōtos* provided with nuts, fr. *karyon* nut — more at CAREEN] **:** an organism composed of one or more cells with visibly evident nuclei — compare PROCARYOTE — **eu·cary·ot·ic** \(ˌ)yü-ˌkar-ē-'ät-ik\ *adj*
Eu·cha·rist \'yü-k(ə-)rəst\ *n* [ME *eukarist,* fr. MF *euchariste,* fr. LL *eucharistia,* fr. Gk, Eucharist, gratitude, fr. *eucharistos* grateful, fr. *eu-* + *charizesthai* to show favor, fr. *charis* favor, grace, gratitude; akin to Gk *chairein* to rejoice — more at YEARN] **1 :** COMMUNION 2a **2** *Christian Science* **:** spiritual communion with God — **eu·cha·ris·tic** \ˌyü-kə-'ris-tik\ *adj, often cap*
[1]**eu·chre** \'yü-kər\ *n* [origin unknown] **1 :** a card game in which each player is dealt five cards and the player making trump must take three tricks to win a hand **2 :** the action of euchring an opponent
[2]**euchre** *vt* **eu·chred; eu·chring** \-k(ə-)riŋ\ **1 :** to prevent from winning three tricks in euchre **2 :** CHEAT, TRICK <*euchred* out of their life savings —Pete Martin>
eu·chro·ma·tin \(')yü-'krō-mət-ən\ *n* [G, fr. *eu-* + *chromatin*] **:** the genetically active portion of chromatin that is largely composed of genes — **eu·chro·mat·ic** \ˌyü-krō-'mat-ik\ *adj*
eu·cil·i·ate \yü-'sil-ē-ət\ *n* [deriv. of NL *eu-* + *cilium*] **:** any of a subclass (Euciliata) of ciliated protozoans with a trophic macronucleus and a reproductive micronucleus — **euciliate** *adj*
eu·clase \'yü-ˌklās, -ˌklāz\ *n* [F, fr. *eu-* (fr. L) + Gk *klasis* breaking, fr. *klan* to break — more at HALT] **:** a mineral $BeAlSiO_4(OH)$ that consists of a brittle silicate of beryllium and aluminum in pale-yellow, green, or blue prismatic crystals and is used esp. as a gemstone
eu·clid·e·an *also* **eu·clid·i·an** \yů-'klid-ē-ən\ *adj, often cap* **:** of or relating to the geometry of Euclid or a geometry based on similar axioms
euclidean algorithm *n, often cap E* **:** a method of finding the greatest common divisor of two numbers by dividing the first by the second, the second by the remainder, the first remainder by the second remainder, and so on until exact division is obtained whence the greatest common divisor is the exact divisor
euclidean geometry *n, often cap E* **1 :** geometry based on Euclid's axioms **2 :** the geometry of a euclidean space

euclidean space *n, often cap E* : a space in which Euclid's axioms and definitions (as of straight and parallel lines and angles of plane triangles) apply

eu·clid's algorithm \ˌyü-klədz-\ *n, often cap E* : EUCLIDEAN ALGORITHM

eu·crite \ˈyü-ˌkrīt\ *n* [G *eukrit,* fr. Gk *eukritos* easily discerned] **1** : a meteorite composed essentially of anorthite and augite **2** : a rock consisting of a very basic gabbro — **eu·crit·ic** \yü-ˈkrit-ik\ *adj*

eu·dae·mo·nism \yu̇-ˈdē-mə-ˌniz-əm\ *or* **eu·dai·mo·nism** \-ˈdī-\ *n* [Gk *eudaimonia* happiness, fr. *eudaimōn* having a good attendant spirit, happy, fr. *eu-* + *daimōn* spirit] : a theory that defines moral obligation by reference to personal well-being through a life governed by reason — **eu·dae·mo·nist** \-nəst\ *n* — **eu·dae·mo·nis·tic** \-ˌdē-mə-ˈnis-tik\ *adj*

eu·di·om·e·ter \ˌyüd-ē-ˈäm-ət-ər\ *n* [It *eudiometro,* fr. Gk *eudia* fair weather (fr. *eu-* + *-dia* weather — akin to L *dies* day) + It *-metro* -meter, fr. Gk *metron* measure] : an instrument for the volumetric measurement and analysis of gases — **eu·dio·met·ric** \ˌyüd-ē-ə-ˈme-trik\ *adj* — **eu·dio·met·ri·cal·ly** \-tri-k(ə-)lē\ *adv*

eu·gen·ic \yu̇-ˈjen-ik\ *adj* [Gk *eugenēs* wellborn, fr. *eu-* + *-genēs* born — more at -GEN] **1** : relating to or fitted for the production of good offspring **2** : of or relating to eugenics — **eu·gen·i·cal·ly** \-i-k(ə-)lē\ *adv*

eu·gen·i·cist \-ˈjen-ə-səst\ *n* : a student or advocate of eugenics

eu·gen·ics \yu̇-ˈjen-iks\ *n pl but sing or pl in constr* : a science that deals with the improvement (as by control of human mating) of hereditary qualities of a race or breed

eu·ge·nol \ˈyü-jə-ˌnȯl, -ˌnōl\ *n* [F *eugénol,* fr. NL *Eugenia,* genus of tropical trees] : a colorless aromatic liquid phenol $C_{10}H_{12}O_2$ found esp. in clove oil and used chiefly in flavors and perfumes

eu·geo·syn·cline \(ˌ)yü-ˌjē-ō-ˈsin-ˌklīn\ *n* : a narrow rapidly subsiding geosyncline usu. with volcanic materials mingled with clastic sediments — **eu·geo·syn·cli·nal** \-(ˌ)sin-ˈklīn-ᵊl\ *adj*

eu·gle·na \yu̇-ˈglē-nə\ *n* [NL, genus name, fr. *eu-* + Gk *glēnē* eyeball, socket of a joint; prob. akin to Gk *glainoi* ornaments — more at CLEAN] : any of a genus (*Euglena*) of green freshwater flagellates often classed as algae

eu·gle·noid \-ˌnȯid\ *n* : any of a taxon (Euglenoidina or Euglenophyta) of varied flagellates (as a euglena) that are typically green or colorless stigma-bearing solitary organisms with one or two flagella emerging from a well-defined gullet — **euglenoid** *adj*

euglenoid movement *n* : writhing usu. nonprogressive protoplasmic movement of plastic-bodied euglenoid flagellates

euglena

eu·glob·u·lin \yü-ˈgläb-yə-lən\ *n* [ISV *eu-* + *globulin*] : a simple protein that does not dissolve in pure water

eu·he·mer·ism \yu̇-ˈhē-mə-ˌriz-əm, -ˈhem-ə-\ *n* [*Euhemerus,* 4th cent. B.C. Gk mythographer] : interpretation of myths as traditional accounts of historical persons and events — **eu·he·mer·ist** \-rəst\ *n* — **eu·he·mer·is·tic** \-ˌhē-mə-ˈris-tik, -ˌhem-ə-\ *adj* — **eu·he·mer·is·ti·cal·ly** \-ti-k(ə-)lē\ *adv* — **eu·he·mer·ize** \-ˈhē-mə-ˌrīz, -ˈhem-ə-\ *vt*

eu·la·chon \ˈyü-lə-ˌkän, -li-kən\ *n, pl* **eulachon** *or* **eulachons** [Chinook Jargon *ulâkân*] : a marine food fish (*Thaleichthys pacificus*) of the north Pacific coast related to the smelt — called also *candlefish*

eu·la·mel·li·branch \ˌyü-lə-ˈmel-ə-ˌbraŋk\ *n, pl* **-branchs** [NL *Eulamellibranchia,* order name, fr. *eu-* + *Lamellibranchia,* class of mollusks — more at LAMELLIBRANCH] : any of an order (Eulamellibranchia) of lamellibranchiate bivalve mollusks with filamentous gills forming two continuous flattened layers on each side of the body — **eu·la·mel·li·bran·chi·ate** \-ˌmel-ə-ˈbraŋ-kē-ət\ *adj or n*

eu·lo·gist \ˈyü-lə-jəst\ *n* : one who eulogizes

eu·lo·gi·um \yu̇-ˈlō-jē-əm\ *n, pl* **-gia** \-jē-ə\ *or* **-gi·ums** [ML] : EULOGY

eu·lo·gize \ˈyü-lə-ˌjīz\ *vt* **-gized; -giz·ing** : to speak or write in high praise of : EXTOL — **eu·lo·giz·er** *n*

eu·lo·gy \ˈyü-lə-jē\ *n, pl* **-gies** [ME *euloge,* fr. ML *eulogium,* fr. Gk *eulogia* praise, fr. *eu-* + *-logia* -logy] **1** : a commendatory formal statement or set oration **2** : high praise ***syn*** see ENCOMIUM ***ant*** calumny, tirade — **eu·lo·gis·tic** \ˌyü-lə-ˈjis-tik\ *adj* — **eu·lo·gis·ti·cal·ly** \-ti-k(ə-)lē\ *adv*

Eu·men·i·des \yu̇-ˈmen-ə-ˌdēz\ *n pl* [L, fr. Gk] : the Furies in Greek mythology

eu·mor·phic \(ˈ)yü-ˈmȯr-fik\ *adj* : MESOMORPHIC, ATHLETIC 3

eu·nuch \ˈyü-nək, -nik\ *n* [ME *eunuk,* fr. L *eunuchus,* fr. Gk *eunouchos,* fr. *eunē* bed + *echein* to have, have charge of — more at SCHEME] **1** : a castrated man placed in charge of a harem or employed as a chamberlain in a palace **2** : a man or boy deprived of the testes or external genitals — **eu·nuch·ism** \-ˌiz-əm\ *n*

eu·nuch·oid \-ˌȯid\ *n* : a sexually deficient individual; *esp* : one lacking in sexual differentiation and tending toward the intersex state — **eunuchoid** *adj*

eu·on·y·mus \yu̇-ˈän-ə-məs\ *n* [NL, genus name, fr. L *euonymos* spindle tree, fr. Gk *euōnymos,* fr. *euōnymos* having an auspicious name, fr. *eu-* + *onyma* name — more at NAME] : any of a genus (*Euonymus*) of often evergreen shrubs, small trees, or vines of the staff tree family — called also *spindle tree*

eu·pa·trid \yu̇-ˈpa-trəd, ˈyü-pə-\ *n, pl* **eu·pat·ri·dae** \yu̇-ˈpa-trə-ˌdē\ *often cap* [Gk *eupatridēs,* fr. *eu-* + *patr-, patēr* father — more at FATHER] : one of the hereditary aristocrats of ancient Athens

eu·pep·sia \yu̇-ˈpep-shə, -sē-ə\ *n* [NL, fr. *eu-* + *-pepsia* (as in *dyspepsia*)] : good digestion

eu·pep·tic \-ˈpep-tik\ *adj* **1** : of, relating to, or having good digestion **2** : CHEERFUL, OPTIMISTIC — **eu·pep·ti·cal·ly** \-ti-k(ə-)lē\ *adv*

eu·phau·si·id \yu̇-ˈfȯ-zē-əd\ *n* [NL *Euphausia,* genus of crustaceans] : any of an order (Euphausiacea) of small usu. luminescent malacostracan crustaceans that resemble shrimps and in some areas form an important element in marine plankton — **euphausiid** *adj*

eu·phe·mism \ˈyü-fə-ˌmiz-əm\ *n* [Gk *euphēmismos,* fr. *euphēmos* auspicious, sounding good, fr. *eu-* + *phēmē* speech, fr. *phanai* to speak — more at BAN] : the substitution of an agreeable or inoffensive expression for one that may offend or suggest something unpleasant; *also* : the expression so substituted <that vandalism which goes under the ~ of souvenir hunting —*Saturday Rev.*> — **eu·phe·mis·tic** \ˌyü-fə-ˈmis-tik\ *adj* — **eu·phe·mis·ti·cal·ly** \-ti-k(ə-)lē\ *adv*

eu·phe·mize \ˈyü-fə-ˌmīz\ *vb* **-mized; -miz·ing** *vt* : to express by a euphemism <the uneasy effort in America to ~ death —W. J. Fisher> ~ *vi* : to make use of euphemistic expressions — **eu·phe·miz·er** *n*

eu·phen·ics \yu̇-ˈfen-iks\ *n pl but sing in constr* [*eu-* + *phen-* (fr. *phenotype*) + *-ics*; after E *genotype: eugenics*] : a science that deals with the biological improvement of human beings after birth — **euphen·ic** \-ik\ *adj*

eu·pho·ni·ous \yu̇-ˈfō-nē-əs\ *adj* : pleasing to the ear — **eu·pho·ni·ous·ly** *adv* — **eu·pho·ni·ous·ness** *n* — **eu·pho·nize** \ˈyü-fə-ˌnīz\ *vt*

eu·pho·ni·um \yu̇-ˈfō-nē-əm\ *n* [Gk *euphōnos* + E *-ium* (as in *harmonium*)] : a brass instrument having a conical bore, a cup-shaped mouthpiece, and a range from B flat below the bass staff upward for three octaves

eu·pho·ny \ˈyü-fə-nē\ *n, pl* **-nies** [F *euphonie,* fr. LL *euphonia,* fr. Gk *euphōnia,* fr. *euphōnos* sweet-voiced, musical, fr. *eu-* + *phōnē* voice — more at BAN] **1** : pleasing or sweet sound; *esp* : the acoustic effect produced by words so formed or combined as to please the ear **2** : a harmonious succession of words having a pleasing sound — **eu·phon·ic** \yu̇-ˈfän-ik\ *adj* — **eu·phon·i·cal·ly** \-i-k(ə-)lē\ *adv*

eu·phor·bia \yu̇-ˈfȯr-bē-ə\ *n* [NL, genus name, alter. of L *euphorbea* euphorbia, fr. *Euphorbus,* 1st cent. A.D. physician] : any of a large genus (*Euphorbia* of the family Euphorbiaceae) of plants that have a milky juice and flowers lacking a calyx and included in an involucre which surrounds a group of several staminate flowers and a central pistillate flower with 3-lobed pistils; *broadly* : SPURGE

euphonium

eu·pho·ria \yu̇-ˈfȯr-ē-ə, -ˈfȯr-\ *n* [NL, fr. Gk, fr. *euphoros* healthy, fr. *eu-* + *pherein* to bear — more at BEAR] : a feeling of well-being or elation — **eu·phor·ic** \-ˈfȯr-ik, -ˈfär-\ *adj* — **eu·phor·i·cal·ly** \-i-k(ə-)lē\ *adv*

eu·pho·tic \yü-ˈfōt-ik\ *adj* [ISV] : of, relating to, or constituting the upper layers of a body of water into which sufficient light penetrates to permit growth of green plants

Eu·phros·y·ne \yu̇-ˈfräs-ᵊn-(ˌ)ē\ *n* [L, fr. Gk *Euphrosynē*] : one of the three Graces

eu·phu·ism \ˈyü-fyə-ˌwiz-əm\ *n* [*Euphues,* character in prose romances by John Lyly] **1** : an elegant Elizabethan literary style marked by excessive use of balance, antithesis, and alliteration and by frequent use of similes drawn from mythology and nature **2** : artificial elegance of language — **eu·phu·ist** \-wəst\ *n* — **eu·phu·is·tic** \ˌyü-fyə-ˈwis-tik\ *adj* — **eu·phu·is·ti·cal·ly** \-ti-k(ə-)lē\ *adv*

eu·plas·tic \yu̇-ˈplas-tik\ *adj* : adapted to the formation of tissue : BLASTEMATIC

eu·ploid \ˈyü-ˌplȯid\ *adj* [ISV] : having a chromosome number that is an exact multiple of the monoploid number — compare ANEUPLOID — **euploid** *n* — **eu·ploi·dy** \-ˌplȯid-ē\ *n*

eup·nea *also* **eup·noea** \ˈyüp-nē-ə\ *n* [NL, fr. Gk *eupnoia,* fr. *eupnous* breathing freely, fr. *eu-* + *pnein* to breathe — more at SNEEZE] : normal respiration — **eup·ne·ic** \-nē-ik\ *adj*

Eur *abbr* Europe; European

Eur- *or* **Euro-** *comb form* [*Europe*] : European and <*Eur*american>

Eur·amer·i·can \ˌyu̇r-ə-ˈmer-ə-kən\ *or* **Eu·ro–Amer·i·can** \ˌyu̇r-ō-ə-ˈmer-\ *adj* : common to Europe and America <culture patterns that are variants of our common ~ culture —W. H. Wickwar>

Eur·asian \yu̇-ˈrā-zhən, -shən\ *adj* **1** : of or relating to Europe and Asia **2** : of a mixed European and Asiatic origin — **Eurasian** *n*

eu·re·ka \yu̇-ˈrē-kə\ *interj* [Gk *heurēka* I have found, fr. *heuriskein* to find; fr. the exclamation attributed to Archimedes on discovering a method for determining the purity of gold — more at HEURISTIC] — used to express triumph on a discovery

eu·ro \ˈyu̇(ə)r-(ˌ)ō\ *n, pl* **euros** [native name in Australia] : a large reddish gray kangaroo (*Macrobus robustus*)

Eu·ro·bond \ˈyu̇r-ō-ˌbänd\ *n* [*Europe* + *bond*] : a bond of a U.S. corporation that is sold outside the U.S. and that is denominated and paid for in dollars and yields interest in dollars

Eu·ro·crat \ˈyu̇r-ə-ˌkrat\ *n* [*Euro*pean Common Market + *-crat* (as in *bureaucrat*)] : a staff member of the administrative commission of the European Common Market

Eu·ro·dol·lar \ˈyu̇r-ō-ˌdäl-ər\ *n* [*Europe* + *dollar*] : a U.S. dollar held (as by a bank) outside the U.S. and esp. in Europe

Eu·ro·pa \yu̇-ˈrō-pə\ *n* [L, fr. Gk *Europē*] : a Phoenician princess carried off by Zeus in the form of a white bull and by him mother of Minos, Rhadamanthus, and Sarpedon

Eu·ro·pe·an \ˌyu̇r-ə-ˈpē-ən\ *n* **1** : a native or inhabitant of Europe **2** : a person of European descent — **European** *adj* — **Eu·ro·pe·an·iza·tion** \-ˌpē-ə-nə-ˈzā-shən\ *n* — **Eu·ro·pe·an·ize** \-ˈpē-ə-ˌnīz\ *vt*

European chafer *n* : an Old World beetle (*Amphimallon majalis*) now established in parts of eastern No. America where its larva is a destructive pest on the roots of turf grasses

European corn borer *n* : an Old World moth (*Ostrinia nubilalis*) that is widespread in eastern No. America where its larva is a major pest esp. in the stems and crowns of Indian corn, dahlias, and potatoes

European plan *n* **:** a hotel plan whereby the daily rates cover only the cost of the room — compare AMERICAN PLAN

European red mite *n* **:** a small bright or brownish red oval mite (*Panonychus ulmi*) that is a destructive orchard pest

eu·ro·pi·um \yu̇-ˈrō-pē-əm\ *n* [NL, fr. *Europa* Europe] **:** a bivalent and trivalent metallic element of the rare-earth group found in monazite sand — see ELEMENT table

Eu·ro·po·cen·tric \yu̇-ˌrō-pə-ˈsen-trik\ *adj* [*Europe* + E *-o-* + *-centric*] **:** centered on Europe and the Europeans <world history texts . . . showed a markedly ~ orientation —J. W. Hall> — **Eu·ro·po·cen·trism** \-ˌtriz-əm\ *n*

eury- *comb form* [NL, fr. Gk, fr. *eurys*; akin to Skt *uru* broad, wide] **:** broad **:** wide <*eury*haline>

eu·ry·bath·ic \ˌyu̇r-i-ˈbath-ik\ *adj* [*eury-* + Gk *bathos* depth] **:** capable of living on the bottom in both deep and shallow water <~ gastropods>

Eu·ryd·i·ce \yu̇-ˈrid-ə-(ˌ)sē\ *n* [L, fr. Gk *Eurydikē*] **:** the wife of Orpheus whom according to Greek myth he nearly succeeds in bringing back from Hades to the land of the living

eu·ry·ha·line \ˌyu̇r-i-ˈhā-ˌlīn, -ˈhal-ˌīn\ *adj* [ISV *eury-* + Gk *halinos* of salt, fr. *hals* salt — more at SALT] **:** able to live in waters of a wide range of salinity

eu·ryp·ter·id \yu̇-ˈrip-tə-rəd\ *n* [deriv. of Gk *eury-* + *pteron* wing — more at FEATHER] **:** any of an order (Eurypterida) of usu. large aquatic Paleozoic arthropods related to the king crabs — **eurypterid** *adj*

eu·ry·therm \ˈyu̇r-i-ˌthərm\ *n* [prob. fr. G *eurytherm* eurythermal, fr. *eury-* + Gk *thermē* heat] **:** an organism that tolerates a wide range of temperature — **eu·ry·ther·mal** \ˌyu̇r-i-ˈthər-məl\ *or* **eu·ry·ther·mic** \-mik\ *or* **eu·ry·ther·mous** \-məs\ *adj*

eu·ryth·mic *or* **eu·rhyth·mic** \yu̇-ˈrith-mik\ *adj* **1 :** HARMONIOUS **2 :** of or relating to eurythmy or eurythmics

eu·ryth·mics *or* **eu·rhyth·mics** \-miks\ *n pl but sing or pl in constr* **:** the art of harmonious bodily movement esp. through expressive timed movements in response to improvised music

eu·ryth·my *or* **eu·rhyth·my** \-mē\ *n* [G *eurhythmie*, fr. L *eurythmia* rhythmical movement, fr. Gk, fr. *eurythmos* rhythmical, fr. *eu-* + *rhythmos* rhythm] **:** a system of harmonious body movement to the rhythm of spoken words

eu·ry·top·ic \ˌyu̇r-i-ˈtäp-ik\ *adj* [prob. fr. G *eurytop*, fr. *eury-* + Gk *topos* place] **:** tolerant of wide variation in one or more physical factors of the environment — **eu·ry·to·pic·i·ty** \-tō-ˈpis-ət-ē, -tä-\ *n*

eu·sta·chian tube \yu̇-ˌstā-sh(ē-)ən- *also* -ˌstā-kē-ən-\ *n, often cap E* [Bartolommeo *Eustachio*] **:** a bony and cartilaginous tube connecting the middle ear with the nasopharynx and equalizing air pressure on both sides of the tympanic membrane — see EAR illustration

eu·stat·ic \yu̇-ˈstat-ik\ *adj* [ISV] **:** relating to or characterized by worldwide change of sea level

eu·stele \ˈyü-ˌstēl, yu̇-ˈstē-lē\ *n* **:** a stele in which the vascular cylinder is broken at leaf emergences and by interfascicular areas

eu·tec·tic \yu̇-ˈtek-tik\ *adj* [Gk *eutēktos* easily melted, fr. *eu-* + *tēktos* melted, fr. *tēkein* to melt — more at THAW] **1** *of an alloy or solution* **:** having the lowest melting point possible **2 :** of or relating to a eutectic alloy or solution or its melting or freezing point — **eutectic** *n* — **eu·tec·toid** \-ˌtȯid\ *adj or n*

Eu·ter·pe \yu̇-ˈtər-pē\ *n* [L, fr. Gk *Euterpē*] **:** the Greek Muse of music

eu·tha·na·sia \ˌyü-thə-ˈnā-zh(ē-)ə\ *n* [Gk, easy death, fr. *eu-* + *thanatos* death — more at THANATOS] **:** the act or practice of killing individuals (as persons or domestic animals) that are hopelessly sick or injured for reasons of mercy — **eu·tha·na·sic** \-zik, -sik\ *adj*

eu·then·ics \yu̇-ˈthen-iks\ *n pl but sing or pl in constr* [Gk *euthenein* to thrive, fr. *eu-* + *-thenein* (akin to Skt *āhanas* swelling)] **:** a science that deals with development of human well-being by improvement of living conditions — **eu·the·nist** \yu̇-ˈthen-əst, ˈyü-thə-nəst\ *n*

eu·the·ri·an \yu̇-ˈthir-ē-ən\ *adj* [deriv. of NL *eu-* + Gk *thērion* beast — more at TREACLE] **:** of or relating to a major division (Eutheria) of mammals comprising the placental mammals — **eutherian** *n*

eu·thy·roid \(ˈ)yü-ˈthī-ˌrȯid\ *adj* **:** characterized by normal thyroid function

eu·tro·phic \yu̇-ˈtrō-fik\ *adj* [prob. fr. G *eutroph* eutrophic, fr. Gk *eutrophos* well nourished, nourishing, fr. *eu-* + *trephein* to nourish — more at ATROPHY] *of a body of water* **:** rich in dissolved nutrients (as phosphates) but often shallow and seasonally deficient in oxygen — compare MESOTROPHIC, OLIGOTROPHIC — **eu·tro·phi·ca·tion** \-ˌtrō-fə-ˈkā-shən\ *n* — **eu·tro·phy** \ˈyü-trə-fē\ *n*

EV *abbr* electron volt

EVA *abbr* extravehicular activity

evac·u·ate \i-ˈvak-yə-ˌwāt\ *vb* **-at·ed; -at·ing** [L *evacuatus*, pp. of *evacuare*, fr. *e-* + *vacuus* empty — more at VACUUM] *vt* **1 :** to remove the contents of **:** EMPTY **2 :** to discharge from the body as waste **:** VOID **3 :** to remove something (as gas or water) from esp. by pumping **4 a :** to remove esp. from a military zone or dangerous area **b :** to withdraw from military occupation of **c :** VACATE <were ordered to ~ the building> ~ *vi* **1 :** to withdraw from a place in an organized way esp. for protection **2 :** to pass urine or feces from the body — **evac·u·a·tive** \-ˌwāt-iv\ *adj*

evac·u·a·tion \i-ˌvak-yə-ˈwā-shən\ *n* **1 :** the act or process of evacuating **2 :** something evacuated or discharged

evac·u·ee \i-ˌvak-yə-ˈwē\ *n* **:** an evacuated person

evade \i-ˈvād\ *vb* **evad·ed; evad·ing** [MF & L; MF *evader*, fr. L *evadere*, fr. *e-* + *vadere* to go, walk — more at WADE] *vi* **1 :** to slip away **2 :** to take refuge in evasion ~ *vt* **1 :** to elude by dexterity or stratagem **2 a :** to avoid facing up to <*evaded* the real issues> **b :** to avoid the performance of **:** DODGE, CIRCUMVENT; *esp* **:** to fail to pay (taxes) **c :** to avoid answering directly **:** turn aside **3 :** to be elusive to **:** BAFFLE <the simple, personal meaning *evaded* them —C. D. Lewis> ***syn*** see ESCAPE — **evad·able** \-ˈvād-ə-bəl\ *adj* — **evad·er** *n*

evag·i·na·tion \i-ˌvaj-ə-ˈnā-shən\ *n* [LL *evagination-*, *evaginatio*, act of unsheathing, fr. L *evaginare* to unsheathe, fr. *e-* + *vagina* sheath] **1 :** an act or instance of everting **2 :** a product of eversion **:** OUTGROWTH

eval·u·ate \i-ˈval-yə-ˌwāt\ *vt* **-at·ed; -at·ing** [back-formation fr. *evaluation*] **1 :** to determine or fix the value of **2 :** to determine the significance or worth of usu. by careful appraisal and study <~ a new antibiotic> ***syn*** see ESTIMATE — **eval·u·a·tion** \-ˌval-yə-ˈwā-shən\ *n* — **eval·u·a·tive** \-ˈval-yə-ˌwāt-iv\ *adj* — **eval·u·a·tor** \-ˌwāt-ər\ *n*

ev·a·nesce \ˌev-ə-ˈnes\ *vi* **-nesced; -nesc·ing** [L *evanescere* — more at VANISH] **:** to dissipate like vapor

ev·a·nes·cence \ˌev-ə-ˈnes-ᵊn(t)s\ *n* **1 :** the process or fact of evanescing **2 :** evanescent quality

ev·a·nes·cent \-ᵊnt\ *adj* [L *evanescent-*, *evanescens*, prp. of *evanescere*] **:** tending to vanish like vapor ***syn*** see TRANSIENT

[1]**evan·gel** \i-ˈvan-jəl\ *n* [ME *evangile*, fr. MF, fr. LL *evangelium*, fr. Gk *euangelion* good news, gospel, fr. *euangelos* bringing good news, fr. *eu-* + *angelos* messenger] **:** GOSPEL

[2]**evangel** *n* **:** EVANGELIST

evan·gel·i·cal \ˌē-ˌvan-ˈjel-i-kəl, ˌev-ən-\ *also* **evan·gel·ic** \-ik\ *adj* **1 :** of, relating to, or being in agreement with the Christian gospel esp. as it is presented in the four Gospels **2 :** PROTESTANT **3 :** emphasizing salvation by faith in the atoning death of Jesus Christ through personal conversion, the authority of Scripture, and the importance of preaching as contrasted with ritual **4 a** *cap* **:** of or relating to the Evangelical Church in Germany **b** *often cap* **:** of, adhering to, or marked by fundamentalism **:** FUNDAMENTALIST **c** *often cap* **:** Low Church **5 :** marked by militant or crusading zeal **:** EVANGELISTIC, ZEALOUS <the ~ ardor of the movement's leaders —Amos Vogel> — **Evan·gel·i·cal·ism** \-i-kə-ˌliz-əm\ *n* — **evan·gel·i·cal·ly** \-i-k(ə-)lē\ *adv*

Evangelical *n* **:** one holding evangelical principles or belonging to an evangelical party or church

evan·ge·lism \i-ˈvan-jə-ˌliz-əm\ *n* **1 :** the winning or revival of personal commitments to Christ **2 :** militant or crusading zeal — **evan·ge·lis·tic** \-ˌvan-jə-ˈlis-tik\ *adj* — **evan·ge·lis·ti·cal·ly** \-ti-k(ə-)lē\ *adv*

evan·ge·list \i-ˈvan-jə-ləst\ *n* **1** *often cap* **:** a writer of any of the four Gospels **2 :** one who evangelizes; *specif* **:** a Protestant minister or layman who preaches at special services

evan·ge·lize \i-ˈvan-jə-ˌlīz\ *vb* **-lized; -liz·ing** *vt* **1 :** to preach the gospel to **2 :** to convert to Christianity ~ *vi* **:** to preach the gospel — **evan·ge·li·za·tion** \-ˌvan-jə-lə-ˈzā-shən\ *n*

evan·ish \i-ˈvan-ish\ *vi* [ME *evanisshen*, fr. MF *evaniss-*, stem of *evanir*] **:** VANISH — **evan·ish·ment** \-mənt\ *n*

evap *abbr* evaporate

evap·o·rate \i-ˈvap-ə-ˌrāt\ *vb* **-rat·ed; -rat·ing** [ME *evaporaten*, fr. L *evaporatus*, pp. of *evaporare*, fr. *e-* + *vapor* steam, vapor] *vi* **1 a :** to pass off in vapor or in invisible minute particles **b (1) :** to pass off or away **:** DISAPPEAR <my despair *evaporated* —J. F. Wharton> **(2) :** to diminish quickly **2 :** to give forth vapor ~ *vt* **1 a :** to convert into vapor; *also* **:** to dissipate or draw off in vapor or fumes **b :** to deposit (as a metal) in the form of a film by sublimation **2 a :** to expel moisture from **b :** EXPEL <~ electrons from a hot wire> — **evap·o·ra·tion** \-ˌvap-ə-ˈrā-shən\ *n* — **evap·o·ra·tive** \-ˈvap-ə-ˌrāt-iv\ *adj* — **evap·o·ra·tive·ly** *adv* — **evap·o·ra·tiv·i·ty** \-ˌvap-ə-rə-ˈtiv-ət-ē\ *n* — **evap·o·ra·tor** \-ˈvap-ə-ˌrāt-ər\ *n*

evaporated milk *n* **:** milk concentrated by evaporation without the addition of sugar to one half or less of its bulk and usu. to a specified amount of milk fat and milk solids

evap·o·rite \i-ˈvap-ə-ˌrīt\ *n* [*evaporation* + *-ite*] **:** a sedimentary rock (as gypsum) that originates by evaporation of sea water in an enclosed basin — **evap·o·rit·ic** \-ˌvap-ə-ˈrit-ik\ *adj*

evapo·trans·pi·ra·tion \i-ˈvap-ō-ˌtran(t)-spə-ˈrā-shən\ *n* [*evaporation* + *transpiration*] **:** loss of water from the soil both by evaporation and by transpiration from the plants growing thereon

eva·sion \i-ˈvā-zhən\ *n* [ME, fr. MF or LL; MF, fr. LL *evasion-*, *evasio*, fr. L *evasus*, pp. of *evadere* to evade] **1 :** the act or an instance of evading **:** ESCAPE <suspected of tax ~> **2 :** a means of evading **:** DODGE

eva·sive \i-ˈvā-siv, -ziv\ *adj* **:** tending or intended to evade **:** EQUIVOCAL <~ answers> — **eva·sive·ly** *adv* — **eva·sive·ness** *n*

eve \ˈēv\ *n* [ME *eve, even*] **1 :** EVENING **2 :** the evening or the day before a special day **3 :** the period immediately preceding

Eve \ˈēv\ *n* [OE *Efe*, fr. LL *Eva*, fr. Heb *Ḥawwāh*] **:** the first woman and wife of Adam

evec·tion \i-ˈvek-shən\ *n* [L *evection-*, *evectio* rising, fr. *evectus*, pp. of *evehere* to carry out, raise up, fr. *e-* + *vehere* to carry — more at WAY] **:** perturbation of the moon's orbital motion due to the attraction of the sun

[1]**even** \ˈē-vən\ *n* [ME, *even, eve*, fr. OE *ǣfen*] *archaic* **:** EVENING

[2]**even** *adj* [ME, fr. OE *efen*; akin to OHG *eban* even] **1 a :** having a horizontal surface **:** FLAT <~ ground> **b :** being without break, indentation, roughness, or other irregularity **:** SMOOTH **c :** being in the same plane or line **2 a :** free from irregularity or variation **:** UNIFORM <his disposition was ~> **b :** LEVEL 4 **3 a** *obs* **:** CANDID **b :** EQUAL, FAIR <an ~ exchange> **c (1) :** leaving nothing due on either side **:** SQUARE <we will not be ~ until you repay my visit> **(2) :** fully revenged **d :** being in equilibrium **:** BALANCED; *specif* **:** showing neither profit nor loss **4 a :** being one of the sequence of natural numbers beginning with two and

counting by twos that are exactly divisible by two **b :** marked by an even number **5 :** EXACT, PRECISE <an ~ dollar> **6 :** as likely as not : FIFTY-FIFTY <he stands an ~ chance of winning> ***syn* 1** see LEVEL ***ant*** uneven **2** see STEADY ***ant*** uneven — **even·ly** *adv* — **even·ness** \-vən-nəs\ *n*

[3]**even** *adv* [ME, fr. OE *efne,* fr. *efen,* adj.] **1 a :** EXACTLY, PRECISELY **b :** to a degree that extends : FULLY, QUITE <faithful ~ unto death> **c :** at the very time **2 a** — used as an intensive to emphasize the identity or character of something <he looked content, ~ happy> **b** — used as an intensive to indicate something unexpected <refused ~ to look at her> **c** — used as an intensive to stress the comparative degree <he did ~ better>

[4]**even** *vb* **evened; even·ing** \'ēv-(ə-)niŋ\ *vt* **:** to make even ~ *vi* **:** to become even — **even·er** \-(ə-)nər\ *n*

even·fall \'ē-vən-ˌfȯl\ *n* **:** the beginning of evening : DUSK

even function *n* **:** a function that remains unchanged by reversing the sign of its argument such that $f(x)=f(-x)$

even·hand·ed \ˌē-vən-'han-dəd\ *adj* **:** FAIR, IMPARTIAL — **even·hand·ed·ly** *adv* — **even·hand·ed·ness** *n*

eve·ning \'ēv-niŋ\ *n, often attrib* [ME, fr. OE *ǣfnung,* fr. *ǣfnian* to grow toward evening, fr. *ǣfen* evening; akin to OHG *āband* evening and perh. to Gk *epi* on] **1 a :** the latter part and close of the day and early part of the night **b** *chiefly South & Midland* **:** AFTERNOON **c :** the period from sunset or the evening meal to bedtime **2 :** the latter portion **3 :** the period of an evening's entertainment

evening dress *n* **:** dress for evening social occasions

evening prayer *n, often cap E & P* **:** the daily evening office of the Anglican liturgy

evening primrose *n* **:** any of several dicotyledonous plants of a family (Onagraceae, the evening-primrose family) and esp. of the type genus (*Oenothera*); *esp* **:** a coarse biennial herb (*O. biennis*) with yellow flowers that open in the evening

eve·nings \'ēv-niŋz\ *adv* **:** in the evening repeatedly : on any evening <goes bowling ~>

evening star *n* **1 :** a bright planet (as Venus) seen esp. in the western sky at or after sunset **2 :** a planet that rises before midnight

even permutation *n* **:** a permutation that is produced by the successive application of an even number of interchanges of pairs of elements

even·song \'ē-vən-ˌsȯŋ\ *n, often cap* [ME, fr. OE *ǣfensang,* fr. *ǣfen* even + *sang* song] **1 :** VESPERS 1 **2 :** EVENING PRAYER

event \i-'vent\ *n* [MF or L; MF, fr. L *eventus,* fr. *eventus,* pp. of *evenire* to happen, fr. *e-* + *venire* to come — more at COME] **1 a :** something that happens : OCCURRENCE **b :** a noteworthy happening **c :** a social occasion or activity **2 a** *archaic* **:** OUTCOME **b :** the issue of a legal action as finally determined **c :** an outcome, condition, or event that is postulated <in the ~ that I am not there, call the house> **3 :** any of the contests in a program of sports **4 :** the fundamental entity of observed physical reality represented by a point designated by three coordinates of place and one of time in the space-time continuum postulated by the theory of relativity **5 :** a subset of the possible outcomes of an experiment <7 is an ~ in the throwing of two dice> ***syn*** see EFFECT, OCCURRENCE — **event·less** \-ləs\ *adj* — **at all events :** in any case — **in any event :** in any case — **in the event** *Brit* **:** as it turns out

event·ful \i-'vent-fəl\ *adj* **1 :** full of or rich in events **2 :** MOMENTOUS — **event·ful·ly** \-fə-lē\ *adv* — **event·ful·ness** *n*

even·tide \'ē-vən-ˌtīd\ *n* **:** the time of evening : EVENING

even·tu·al \i-'vench-(ə-)wəl, -'ven-chəl\ *adj* **1** *archaic* **:** CONTINGENT, CONDITIONAL **2 :** taking place at an unspecified later time : ultimately resulting <they counted on his ~ success> ***syn*** see LAST — **even·tu·al·ly** \-ē\ *adv*

even·tu·al·i·ty \i-ˌven-chə-'wal-ət-ē\ *n, pl* **-ties :** a possible event or outcome : POSSIBILITY

even·tu·ate \i-'ven-chə-ˌwāt\ *vi* **-at·ed; -at·ing :** to come out finally : RESULT <emotional growth . . . ~*s* in balance and control —*Encyc. Americana*>

ev·er \'ev-ər\ *adv* [ME, fr. OE *ǣfre*] **1 :** ALWAYS <~ striving to improve> <the *ever*-increasing population> **2 a :** at any time <more than ~ before> **b :** in any way <how can I ~ thank you> **3** — used as an intensive esp. with *so* <looks ~ so angry>

ev·er·bloom·ing \ˌev-ər-'blü-miŋ\ *adj* **:** blooming more or less continuously throughout the growing season

ev·er·glade \'ev-ər-ˌglād\ *n* [the *Everglades,* Fla.] **:** a swampy grassland esp. in southern Florida usu. containing sawgrass and at least seasonally covered by slowly moving water — usu. used in pl.

[1]**ev·er·green** \'ev-ər-ˌgrēn\ *adj* **1 :** having foliage that remains green and functional through more than one growing season — compare DECIDUOUS **2 :** ever retaining its freshness, interest, or popularity : PERENNIAL, ENDURING <the ~ hope of discovering the consummate woman —A. L. Burt>

[2]**evergreen** *n* **1 :** an evergreen plant; *also* **:** CONIFER **2** *pl* **:** twigs and branches of evergreen plants used for decoration **3 :** something that retains its freshness, interest, or popularity

evergreen oak *n* **:** any of various oaks (as a holm oak or tan oak) with foliage that persists for two years so that the plant is more or less continuously green

[1]**ev·er·last·ing** \ˌev-ər-'las-tiŋ\ *adj* **1 :** lasting or enduring through all time : ETERNAL **2 a** (1) **:** continuing long or indefinitely : PERPETUAL (2) *of a plant* **:** retaining its form or color for a long time when dried **b :** tediously persistent <the ~ sympathy-seeker who demands attention —H. A. Overstreet> **3 :** wearing indefinitely : DURABLE — **ev·er·last·ing·ly** \-tiŋ-lē\ *adv* — **ev·er·last·ing·ness** *n*

[2]**everlasting** *n* **1** *cap* **:** GOD 1 — used with *the* **2 :** ETERNITY <from ~ > **3 a :** any of several chiefly composite plants (as cudweed) with flowers that can be dried without loss of form or color **b :** the flower of an everlasting

ev·er·more \ˌev-ər-'mō(ə)r, -'mȯ(ə)r\ *adv* **1 :** ALWAYS, FOREVER **2 :** in the future

evert \i-'vərt\ *vt* [L *evertere,* fr. *e-* + *vertere* to turn — more at WORTH] **1 :** OVERTHROW, UPSET **2 :** to turn outward or inside out — **ever·si·ble** \-'vər-sə-bəl\ *adj* — **ever·sion** \-zhən, -shən\ *n*

ev·ery \'ev-rē\ *adj* [ME *everich, every,* fr. OE *ǣfre ǣlc,* fr. *ǣfre* ever + *ǣlc* each] **1 :** being each individual or part of a group without exception **2** *obs* **:** being all taken severally **3 :** being each within a range of possibilities <was given ~ chance> **4 :** COMPLETE, ENTIRE — **every now and then** *or* **every now and again** *or* **every so often :** at intervals : OCCASIONALLY

ev·ery·body \'ev-ri-ˌbäd-ē, -bəd-\ *pron* **:** every person : EVERYONE

ev·ery·day \ˌev-rē-ˌdā\ *adj* **:** encountered or used routinely or typically : ORDINARY <clothes for ~ wear> — **ev·ery·day·ness** \-dā-nəs\ *n*

ev·ery·man \'ev-rē-ˌman\ *n* [*Everyman,* allegorical character in *The Summoning of Everyman,* 15th cent. E morality play] *often cap* **:** the typical or ordinary man <an *Everyman,* always tempted, always guileless, always rueful —Walter Terry>

ev·ery·one \-(ˌ)wən\ *pron* **:** EVERYBODY

ev·ery·place \-ˌplās\ *adv* **:** EVERYWHERE

ev·ery·thing \'ev-rē-ˌthiŋ\ *pron* **1 a :** all that exists **b :** all that relates to the subject **2 :** something that is most important or excellent : all that counts <he meant ~ to her>

ev·ery·where \'ev-rē-ˌ(h)we(ə)r, -ˌ(h)wa(ə)r\ *adv* **:** in every place or part

every which way \ˌev-rē-'hwich-ˌwā, -'wich-\ *adv* [prob. by folk etymology fr. ME *everich way* every way] **1 :** in every direction **2 :** in a disorderly manner : IRREGULARLY <toys scattered about *every which way*>

evg *abbr* evening

evict \i-'vikt\ *vt* [ME *evicten,* fr. LL *evictus,* pp. of *evincere,* fr. L, to vanquish, win a point — more at EVINCE] **1 a :** to recover (property) from a person by legal process **b :** to put (a tenant) out by legal process **2 :** to force out : EXPEL ***syn*** see EJECT — **evic·tion** \-'vik-shən\ *n* — **evic·tor** \-'vik-tər\ *n*

evict·ee \i-ˌvik-'tē\ *n* **:** an evicted person

[1]**ev·i·dence** \'ev-əd-ən(t)s, -ə-ˌden(t)s\ *n* **1 a :** an outward sign : INDICATION **b :** something that furnishes proof : TESTIMONY; *specif* **:** something legally submitted to a tribunal to ascertain the truth of a matter **2 :** one who bears witness; *esp* **:** one who voluntarily confesses a crime and testifies for the prosecution against his accomplices — **in evidence 1 :** to be seen : CONSPICUOUS <trim lawns . . . are everywhere *in evidence* —*Amer. Guide Series: N.C.*> **2 :** as evidence

[2]**evidence** *vt* **-denced; -denc·ing :** to offer evidence of : PROVE, EVINCE ***syn*** see SHOW

ev·i·dent \'ev-əd-ənt, -ə-ˌdent\ *adj* [ME, fr. MF, fr. L *evident-, evidens,* fr. *e-* + *vident-, videns,* prp. of *vidēre* to see — more at WIT] **:** clear to the vision or understanding

syn EVIDENT, MANIFEST, PATENT, DISTINCT, OBVIOUS, APPARENT, PLAIN, CLEAR *shared meaning element* **:** readily perceived or apprehended. EVIDENT implies the presence of signs that point unmistakably to a conclusion <her enjoyment of the music was *evident*> MANIFEST implies signs so evident that little or no inference is needed <the verdict is against the *manifest* weight of the evidence —L. B. Howard> PATENT applies to a cause, effect, or significant feature that is clear and unmistakable once attention is drawn to it <*patent* defects are those readily perceptible on inspection> <a *patent* lie> DISTINCT implies such sharpness of outline or definition as makes discernment or identification easy <a neat *distinct* handwriting> OBVIOUS implies such ease in discovering or accounting for as may suggest conspicuity in the thing or little need of perspicuity in the observer <his guilt was *obvious* to all> APPARENT may add to *evident* the notion of recognition through more or less elaborate reasoning <it is *apparent* from comparison of their stories that one of them is lying> *Plain* and *clear* both apply to something that is immediately apprehended or unmistakably understood, but PLAIN implies lack of complexity or elaboration and CLEAR, an absence of anything that confuses or obscures <told the *plain* truth> <gave a *clear* account of the accident>

ev·i·den·tial \ˌev-ə-'den-chəl\ *adj* **:** being, relating to, or affording evidence <photographs of ~ value> — **ev·i·den·tial·ly** \-'dench-(ə-)lē\ *adv*

ev·i·den·tia·ry \ˌev-ə-'den-chə-rē, -chē-ˌer-ē\ *adj* **1 :** EVIDENTIAL **2 :** conducted so that evidence may be presented <an ~ hearing>

ev·i·dent·ly \'ev-əd-ənt-lē, -ə-ˌdent-, *esp for 2 often* ˌev-ə-'dent-\ *adv* **1 :** in an evident manner : CLEARLY, OBVIOUSLY <any style that is . . . so ~ bad or second-rate —T. S. Eliot> **2 :** on the basis of available evidence <he was born . . . ~ in Texas —Robert Coughlan>

[1]**evil** \'ē-vəl\ *adj* **evil·er** *or* **evil·ler; evil·est** *or* **evil·lest** [ME, fr. OE *yfel;* akin to OHG *ubil* evil] **1 a :** morally reprehensible : SINFUL, WICKED <an ~ impulse> **b :** arising from actual or imputed bad character or conduct <a man of ~ reputation> **2 a** *archaic* **:** INFERIOR **b :** causing discomfort or repulsion : OFFENSIVE <an ~ odor> **c :** DISAGREEABLE <woke late and in an ~ temper> **3 a :** causing harm : PERNICIOUS <the ~ institution of slavery> **b :** marked by misfortune : UNLUCKY ***syn*** see BAD ***ant*** exemplary, salutary — **evil** *adv, archaic* — **evil·ly** \-və(l)-lē\ *adv* — **evil·ness** \-vəl-nəs\ *n*

[2]**evil** *n* **1 :** something that brings sorrow, distress, or calamity **2 a :** the fact of suffering, misfortune, and wrongdoing **b :** a cosmic evil force

evil·do·er \ˌē-vəl-'dü-ər\ *n* **:** one who does evil

evil·do·ing \-'dü-iŋ\ *n* **:** the act or action of doing evil

evil eye *n* **:** an eye or glance held capable of inflicting harm; *also* **:** a person believed to have such an eye or glance

evil–mind·ed \ˌē-vəl-'mīn-dəd\ *adj* **:** having an evil disposition or evil thoughts — **evil–mind·ed·ly** *adv* — **evil–mind·ed·ness** *n*

evince \i-'vin(t)s\ *vt* **evinced; evinc·ing** [L *evincere* to vanquish, win a point, fr. *e-* + *vincere* to conquer — more at VICTOR] **1 :** to constitute outward evidence of **2 :** to display clearly : REVEAL ***syn*** see SHOW — **evinc·ible** \-'vin(t)-sə-bəl\ *adj*

evis·cer·ate \i-ˈvis-ə-ˌrāt\ *vb* **-at·ed; -at·ing** [L *evisceratus*, pp. of *eviscerare*, fr. *e-* + *viscera*] *vt* **1 a :** to take out the entrails of : DISEMBOWEL **b :** to deprive of vital content or force **2 :** to remove an organ from (a patient) or the contents of (an organ) ~ *vi* **:** to protrude through a surgical incision or suffer protrusion of a part through an incision — **evis·cer·a·tion** \-ˌvis-ə-ˈrā-shən\ *n*

ev·i·ta·ble \ˈev-ət-ə-bəl\ *adj* [L *evitabilis*, fr. *evitare* to avoid, fr. *e-* + *vitare* to shun] **:** capable of being avoided

evo·ca·ble \ˈev-ə-kə-bəl, i-ˈvō-kə-\ *adj* **:** capable of being evoked

evo·ca·tion \ˌē-vō-ˈkā-shən, ˌev-ə-\ *n* [L *evocation-*, *evocatio*, fr. *evocatus*, pp. of *evocare*] **1 :** the act or fact of evoking : SUMMONING: as **a :** the summoning of a spirit **b :** imaginative recreation <a contemporary film rather than an ~ of the past —R. M. Coles> **2 :** INDUCTION 4e; *specif* **:** initiation of development of a primary embryonic axis — **evo·ca·tor** \ˈē-vō-ˌkāt-ər, ˈev-ə-\ *n*

evoc·a·tive \i-ˈväk-ət-iv\ *adj* **:** tending or serving to evoke <settings . . . so ~ that they bring tears to the eyes —Eric Malpass> — **evoc·a·tive·ly** *adv* — **evoc·a·tive·ness** *n*

evoke \i-ˈvōk\ *vt* **evoked; evok·ing** [F *évoquer*, fr. L *evocare*, fr. *e-* + *vocare* to call — more at VOCATION] **1 :** to call forth or up: as **a :** CONJURE 2a <~ evil spirits> **b :** to cite esp. with approval or for support : INVOKE **c :** to bring to mind or recollection <this place ~*s* memories of happier years> **2 :** to re-create imaginatively *syn* see EDUCE

evo·lute \ˈev-ə-ˌlüt *also* ˈē-və-\ *n* **:** the locus of the center of curvature or the envelope of the normals of a curve

evo·lu·tion \ˌev-ə-ˈlü-shən *also* ˌē-və-\ *n* [L *evolution-*, *evolutio* unrolling, fr. *evolutus*, pp. of *evolvere*] **1 a :** a process of change in a certain direction : UNFOLDING **b :** the action or an instance of forming and giving something off : EMISSION **c (1) :** a process of continuous change from a lower, simpler, or worse to a higher, more complex, or better state : GROWTH **(2) :** a process of gradual and relatively peaceful social, political, and economic advance **d :** something evolved **2 :** one of a set of prescribed movements **3 :** the process of working out or developing **4 :** the extraction of a mathematical root **5 a :** the historical development of a biological group (as a race or species) : PHYLOGENY **b :** a theory that the various types of animals and plants have their origin in other preexisting types and that the distinguishable differences are due to modifications in successive generations **6 :** a process in which the whole universe is a progression of interrelated phenomena — **evo·lu·tion·ari·ly** \-shə-ˌner-ə-lē\ *adv* — **evo·lu·tion·ary** \-shə-ˌner-ē\ *adj* — **evo·lu·tion·ism** \-shə-ˌniz-əm\ *n* — **evo·lu·tion·ist** \-sh(ə-)nəst\ *n or adj*

evolve \i-ˈvälv, -ˈvȯlv\ *vb* **evolved; evolv·ing** [L *evolvere* to unroll, fr. *e-* + *volvere* to roll — more at VOLUBLE] *vt* **1 :** to give off : EMIT **2 a :** DERIVE, EDUCE **b :** to work out : DEVELOP <~ social, political, and literary philosophies —L. W. Doob> **c :** to produce by natural evolutionary processes ~ *vi* **:** to undergo evolutionary change — **evolv·able** \-ˈväl-və-bəl, -ˈvȯl-\ *adj* — **evolve·ment** \-ˈvälv-mənt, -ˈvȯlv-\ *n*

evon·y·mus \i-ˈvän-ə-məs, e-\ *n* **:** EUONYMUS

EVR *abbr* electronic video recorder, electronic video recording

evul·sion \i-ˈvəl-shən\ *n* [L *evulsion-*, *evulsio*, fr. *evulsus*, pp. of *evellere* to pluck out, fr. *e-* + *vellere* to pluck — more at VULNERABLE] **:** EXTRACTION

ev·zone \ˈev-ˌzōn\ *n* [NGk *euzōnos*, fr. Gk, active, lit., well girt, fr. *eu-* + *zōnē* girdle — more at ZONE] **:** a member of a select Greek infantry unit

EW *abbr* enlisted woman

ewe \ˈyü, ˈyō\ *n* [ME, fr. OE *ēowu*] **:** the female of the sheep esp. when mature; *also* **:** the female of various related animals

Ewe \ˈā-ˌwā, ˈā-ˌvā\ *n* **:** a Kwa language of Ghana and Togo

ewe–neck \-ˈnek\ *n* **:** a thin neck having an insufficient, faulty, or concave arch and occurring as a defect in dogs and horses — **ewe–necked** \-ˈnekt\ *adj*

ew·er \ˈyü-ər, ˈyu̇(-ə)r\ *n* [ME, fr. AF, fr. OF *evier*, fr. (assumed) VL *aquarium*, fr. L, neut. of *aquarius* of water, fr. *aqua* water — more at ISLAND] **:** a vase-shaped pitcher or jug

ewer

[1]ex \ˈeks\ *n* [[1]*ex-*] **:** one that formerly held a specified position or place; *esp* **:** a former spouse

[2]ex \(ˌ)eks\ *prep* [L] **1 :** out of : FROM: as **a :** from a specified place or source **b :** from a specified dam <a promising calf by Eric XVI ~ Heatherbell> **2 :** free from : WITHOUT: as **a :** without an indicated value or right — used esp. of securities **b :** free of charges precedent to removal from the specified place with purchaser to provide means of subsequent transportation <~ dock>

[3]ex \ˈeks\ *n* **:** the letter *x*

[4]ex *abbr* **1** example **2** exchange **3** executive **4** express **5** extra

Ex *abbr* Exodus

[1]ex- \e *also occurs in this prefix where only* i *is shown below (as in "express") and* ks *sometimes occurs where only* gz *is shown (as in "exact")*\ *prefix* [ME, fr. OF & L; OF, fr. L (also, intensive prefix), fr. *ex* out of, from; akin to Gk *ex*, *ex-* out of, from, OSlav *iz*] **1 :** out of : outside <*ex*clave> **2 :** not <*ex*stipulate> **3** \(ˌ)eks, ˈeks\ [ME, fr. LL, fr. L] **:** former <*ex*-president> <*ex*-child actor>

[2]ex- — see EXO-

ex·ac·er·bate \ig-ˈzas-ər-ˌbāt\ *vt* **-bat·ed; -bat·ing** [L *exacerbatus*, pp. of *exacerbare*, fr. *ex-* + *acerbus* harsh, bitter, fr. *acer* sharp — more at EDGE] **:** to make more violent, bitter, or severe <the proposed shutdown . . . would ~ unemployment problems —*Science*> — **ex·ac·er·ba·tion** \-ˌzas-ər-ˈbā-shən\ *n*

[1]ex·act \ig-ˈzakt\ *vt* [ME *exacten*, fr. L *exactus*, pp. of *exigere* to drive out, demand, measure, fr. *ex-* + *agere* to drive — more at AGENT] **1 :** to call for forcibly or urgently and obtain : press for <from them has been ~*ed* the ultimate sacrifice —D. D. Eisenhower> **2 :** to call for as necessary, appropriate, or desirable *syn* see DEMAND — **ex·act·able** \-ˈzak-tə-bəl\ *adj* — **ex·ac·tor** *also* **ex·act·er** \-ˈzak-tər\ *n*

[2]exact *adj* [L *exactus*, fr. pp. of *exigere*] **1 :** exhibiting or marked by strict, particular, and complete accordance with fact **2 :** marked by thorough consideration or minute measurement of small factual details *syn* see CORRECT *ant* inexact — **exact·ness** \-ˈzak(t)-nəs\ *n*

ex·ac·ta \ig-ˈzak-tə\ *n* [AmerSp *quiniela exacta* exact quiniela] **:** PERFECTA

exact differential *n* **:** a differential expression of the form $X_1dx_1 + \ldots + X_ndx_n$ where the *X's* are the partial derivatives of a function $f(x_1, \ldots, x_n)$ with respect to $x_1, \ldots, x_n$ respectively

ex·act·ing \ig-ˈzak-tiŋ\ *adj* **1 :** tryingly or unremittingly severe in making demands **2 :** requiring careful attention and precise accuracy *syn* see ONEROUS — **ex·act·ing·ly** \-tiŋ-lē\ *adv* — **ex·act·ing·ness** *n*

ex·ac·tion \ig-ˈzak-shən\ *n* **1 a :** the act or process of exacting **b :** EXTORTION **2 :** something exacted; *esp* **:** a fee, reward, or contribution demanded or levied with severity or injustice

ex·ac·ti·tude \ig-ˈzak-tə-ˌt(y)üd\ *n* **:** the quality or an instance of being exact : EXACTNESS

ex·act·ly \ig-ˈzak-(t)lē\ *adv* **1 a :** in an exact manner : PRECISELY **b :** ALTOGETHER, ENTIRELY <not ~ what I had in mind> **2 :** quite so — used to express agreement

ex·ag·ger·ate \ig-ˈzaj-ə-ˌrāt\ *vb* **-at·ed; -at·ing** [L *exaggeratus*, pp. of *exaggerare*, lit., to heap up, fr. *ex-* + *agger* heap, fr. *aggerere* to carry toward, fr. *ad-* + *gerere* to carry — more at CAST] *vt* **1 :** to enlarge beyond bounds or the truth : OVERSTATE <a friend ~*s* a man's virtues —Joseph Addison> **2 :** to enlarge or increase esp. beyond the normal : OVEREMPHASIZE ~ *vi* **:** to make an overstatement — **ex·ag·ger·at·ed·ly** *adv* — **ex·ag·ger·at·ed·ness** *n* — **ex·ag·ger·a·tion** \-ˌzaj-ə-ˈrā-shən\ *n* — **ex·ag·ger·a·tive** \-ˈzaj-ə-ˌrāt-iv, -ˈzaj-(ə-)rət-\ *adj* — **ex·ag·ger·a·tor** \-ˈzaj-ə-ˌrāt-ər\ *n* — **ex·ag·ger·a·to·ry** \-ˈzaj-(ə-)rə-ˌtōr-ē, -ˌtȯr-\ *adj*

ex·alt \ig-ˈzȯlt\ *vb* [ME *exalten*, fr. MF & L; MF *exalter*, fr. L *exaltare*, fr. *ex-* + *altus* high — more at OLD] *vt* **1 :** to raise high : ELEVATE **2 :** to raise in rank, power, or character **3 :** to elevate by praise or in estimation : GLORIFY **4** *obs* **:** ELATE **5 :** to enhance the activity of : INTENSIFY <rousing and ~*ing* the imagination —George Eliot> ~ *vi* **:** to induce exaltation — **ex·alt·ed·ly** *adv* — **ex·alt·er** *n*

ex·al·ta·tion \ˌeg-ˌzȯl-ˈtā-shən, ˌek-ˌsȯl-\ *n* **1 :** an act of exalting **:** the state of being exalted **2 :** an excessively intensified sense of well-being, power, or importance <pursued ~ through drink and sex —Howard Kaye> **3 :** an increase in degree or intensity <~ of virulence of a virus>

ex·am \ig-ˈzam\ *n* **:** EXAMINATION

ex·a·men \ig-ˈzā-mən\ *n* [L, tongue of a balance, examination, fr. *exigere* — more at EXACT] **1 :** EXAMINATION **2 :** a critical study

ex·am·i·nant \-ˈzam-ə-nənt\ *n* **1 :** one who examines : EXAMINER **2 :** EXAMINEE

ex·am·i·na·tion \ig-ˌzam-ə-ˈnā-shən\ *n* **1 :** the act or process of examining : the state of being examined **2 :** an exercise designed to examine progress or test qualification or knowledge **3 :** a formal interrogation — **ex·am·i·na·tion·al** \-shnəl, -shən-ᵊl\ *adj*

ex·am·i·na·to·ri·al \-nə-ˈtōr-ē-əl, -ˈtȯr-\ *adj* **:** of or relating to an examiner or examination

ex·am·ine \ig-ˈzam-ən\ *vt* **ex·am·ined; ex·am·in·ing** \-(ə-)niŋ\ [ME *examinen*, fr. MF *examiner*, fr. L *examinare*, fr. *examen*] **1 a :** to inspect closely **b :** to test the condition of **c :** to inquire into carefully : INVESTIGATE **2 a :** to interrogate closely <~ a prisoner> **b :** to test by questioning in order to determine progress, fitness, or knowledge *syn* see SCRUTINIZE — **ex·am·in·able** \-ˈzam-ə-nə-bəl\ *adj* — **ex·am·in·er** \-ˈzam-(ə-)nər\ *n*

ex·am·in·ee \ig-ˌzam-ə-ˈnē\ *n* **:** a person who is examined

[1]ex·am·ple \ig-ˈzam-pəl\ *n* [ME, fr. MF, fr. L *exemplum*, fr. *eximere* to take out, fr. *ex-* + *emere* to take — more at REDEEM] **1 :** a particular single item, fact, incident, or aspect that is representative of all of a group or type **2 :** one that serves as a pattern to be imitated or not to be imitated <a good ~ > <a bad ~> **3 :** a parallel or closely similar case esp. when serving as a precedent or model **4 :** a punishment inflicted on someone as a warning to others; *also* **:** an individual so punished **5 :** an instance (as a problem to be solved) serving to illustrate a rule or precept or to act as an exercise in the application of a rule *syn* see INSTANCE, MODEL — **for example** \fər-ig-ˈzam-pəl, frig-\ **:** as an example <there are many sources of air pollution; exhaust fumes, *for example*>

[2]example *vt* **ex·am·pled; ex·am·pling** \-p(ə-)liŋ\ **1 :** to serve or use as an example of **2** *archaic* **:** to be or set an example to

ex·an·i·mate \eg-ˈzan-ə-mət\ *adj* [L *exanimatus*, pp. of *exanimare* to deprive of life or spirit, fr. *ex-* + *anima* breath, soul — more at ANIMATE] **1 :** lacking animation : SPIRITLESS **2 :** lifeless or appearing lifeless

ex·an·them \eg-ˈzan(t)-thəm, ˈek-ˌsan-ˌthem\ *also* **ex·an·the·ma** \ˌeg-ˌzan-ˈthē-mə\ *n, pl* **exanthems** *also* **ex·an·them·a·ta** \ˌeg-ˌzan-ˈthem-ət-ə\ *or* **exanthemas** [LL *exanthema*, fr. Gk *exanthēma*, fr. *exanthein* to bloom, break out, fr. *ex-* + *anthos* flower — more at ANTHOLOGY] **:** an eruptive disease (as measles) or its symptomatic eruption — **ex·an·them·a·tous** \ˌeg-ˌzan-ˈthem-ət-əs\ *adj*

[1]ex·arch \ˈek-ˌsärk\ *n* [LL *exarchus*, fr. LGk *exarchos*, fr. Gk, leader, fr. *exarchein* to begin, take the lead, fr. *ex-* + *archein* to rule, begin — more at ARCH-] **1 :** a Byzantine viceroy **2 :** an Eastern bishop ranking below a patriarch and above a metropolitan; *specif* **:** the head of an independent church — **ex·ar·chal**

\ek-ˈsär-kəl\ *adj* — **ex·arch·ate** \ˈek-ˌsär-kət\ *n* — **ex·ar·chy** \ˈek-ˌsär-kē\ *n*

[2]**exarch** *adj* [*exo-* + *-arch*] **:** formed or taking place from the periphery toward the center <~ xylem>

[1]**ex·as·per·ate** \ig-ˈzas-pə-ˌrāt\ *vt* **-at·ed; -at·ing** [L *exasperatus,* pp. of *exasperare,* fr. *ex-* + *asper* rough] **1 a :** to excite or inflame the anger of **:** ENRAGE **b :** to cause irritation or annoyance to **2** *obs* **:** to make grievous or more grievous or malignant ***syn*** see IRRITATE — **ex·as·per·at·ed·ly** *adv* — **ex·as·per·at·ing·ly** \-ˌrāt-iŋ-lē\ *adv*

[2]**ex·as·per·ate** \-p(ə-)rət\ *adj* **1 :** irritated or annoyed esp. to the point of injudicious action **:** EXASPERATED **2 :** roughened with irregular prickles or elevations <~ seed coats>

ex·as·per·a·tion \ig-ˌzas-pə-ˈrā-shən\ *n* **1 :** the state of being exasperated **2 :** the act or an instance of exasperating

exc *abbr* **1** excellent **2** except

Ex·cal·i·bur \ek-ˈskal-ə-bər\ *n* [OF *Escalibor,* fr. ML *Caliburnus*] **:** the legendary sword of King Arthur

ex·car·di·na·tion \(ˌ)ek-ˌskärd-ᵊn-ˈā-shən\ *n* [[1]*ex-* + *-cardination* (as in *incardination*)] **:** the transfer of a clergyman from one diocese to another

ex ca·the·dra \ˌek-skə-ˈthē-drə\ *adv or adj* [NL, lit., from the chair] **:** by virtue of or in the exercise of one's office <*ex cathedra* pronouncements>

ex·ca·vate \ˈek-skə-ˌvāt\ *vb* **-vat·ed; -vat·ing** [L *excavatus,* pp. of *excavare,* fr. *ex-* + *cavare* to make hollow — more at CAVATINA] *vt* **1 :** to form a cavity or hole in **2 :** to form by hollowing **3 :** to dig out and remove **4 :** to expose to view by digging away a covering ~ *vi* **:** to make excavations

ex·ca·va·tion \ˌek-skə-ˈvā-shən\ *n* **1 :** the action or process of excavating **2 :** a cavity formed by cutting, digging, or scooping — **ex·ca·va·tion·al** \-shnəl, -shən-ᵊl\ *adj*

ex·ca·va·tor \ˈek-skə-ˌvāt-ər\ *n* **:** one that excavates; *esp* **:** a power-operated shovel

ex·ceed \ik-ˈsēd\ *vb* [ME *exceden,* fr. MF *exceder,* fr. L *excedere,* fr. *ex-* + *cedere* to go — more at CEDE] *vt* **1 :** to extend outside of <the river will ~ its banks> **2 :** to be greater than or superior to **3 :** to go beyond a limit set by <~*ed* his authority> ~ *vi* **1** *obs* **:** OVERDO **2 :** PREDOMINATE

syn EXCEED, SURPASS, TRANSCEND, EXCEL, OUTDO, OUTSTRIP *shared meaning element* **:** to go or be beyond a stated or implied limit, measure, or degree

ex·ceed·ing *adj* **:** exceptional in amount, quality, or degree <the ~ darkness which surrounds man's existence —L. H. Harshbarger>

ex·ceed·ing·ly \-iŋ-lē\ *or* **ex·ceed·ing** *adv* **:** to an extreme degree **:** EXTREMELY

ex·cel \ik-ˈsel\ *vb* **ex·celled; ex·cel·ling** [ME *excellen,* fr. L *excellere,* fr. *ex-* + *-cellere* to rise, project; akin to L *collis* hill — more at HILL] *vt* **:** to be superior to **:** surpass in accomplishment or achievement ~ *vi* **:** to be distinguishable by superiority **:** surpass others <~ in mathematics> ***syn*** see EXCEED

ex·cel·lence \ˈek-s(ə-)lən(t)s\ *n* **1 :** the quality of being excellent **2 :** an excellent or valuable quality **:** VIRTUE **3 :** EXCELLENCY 2

ex·cel·len·cy \-s(ə-)lən-sē\ *n, pl* **-cies 1 :** EXCELLENCE; *esp* **:** outstanding or valuable quality — usu. used in pl. <so crammed, as he thinks, with *excellencies* —Shak.> **2** — used as a title for certain high dignitaries of state (as a governor or an ambassador) and church (as a Roman Catholic archbishop or bishop)

ex·cel·lent \ˈek-s(ə-)lənt\ *adj* [ME, fr. MF, fr. L *excellent-, excellens,* fr. prp. of *excellere*] **1** *archaic* **:** SUPERIOR **2 :** very good of its kind **:** eminently good **:** FIRST-CLASS — **ex·cel·lent·ly** *adv*

ex·cel·si·or \ik-ˈsel-sē-ər\ *n* [trade name, fr. L, higher, compar. of *excelsus* high, fr. pp. of *excellere*] **:** fine curled wood shavings used esp. for packing fragile items

[1]**ex·cept** \ik-ˈsept\ *vb* [ME *excepten,* fr. MF *excepter,* fr. L *exceptare,* fr. *exceptus,* pp. of *excipere* to take out, except, fr. *ex-* + *capere* to take — more at HEAVE] *vt* **:** to take or leave out from a number or a whole **:** EXCLUDE ~ *vi* **:** to take exception **:** OBJECT

[2]**except** *also* **ex·cept·ing** *prep* **:** with the exclusion or exception of <daily ~ Sundays>

[3]**except** *also* **excepting** *conj* **1 :** on any other condition than that **:** UNLESS <~ you repent> **2 :** ONLY <I would go ~ it's too far>

except for *prep* **:** but for <*except for* you I would be dead>

ex·cep·tion \ik-ˈsep-shən\ *n* **1 :** the act of excepting **:** EXCLUSION **2 :** one that is excepted; *esp* **:** a case to which a rule does not apply **3 :** QUESTION, OBJECTION <witnesses whose authority is beyond ~ —T. B. Macaulay> **4 :** an oral or written legal objection (as to a court's ruling)

ex·cep·tion·able \ik-ˈsep-sh(ə-)nə-bəl\ *adj* **:** being likely to cause objection **:** OBJECTIONABLE <visitors even drink the ~ beer —W. D. Howells> — **ex·cep·tion·abil·i·ty** \-ˌsep-sh(ə-)nə-ˈbil-ət-ē\ *n* — **ex·cep·tion·ably** \-ˈsep-sh(ə-)nə-blē\ *adv*

ex·cep·tion·al \ik-ˈsep-shnəl, -shən-ᵊl\ *adj* **1 :** forming an exception **:** RARE <an ~ number of rainy days> **2 :** better than average **:** SUPERIOR **3 :** deviating from the norm; *esp* **:** below average <schools for ~ children> — **ex·cep·tion·al·i·ty** \-ˌsep-shə-ˈnal-ət-ē\ *n* — **ex·cep·tion·al·ly** \-ˈsep-shnə-lē, -shən-ᵊl-ē\ *adv* — **ex· cep·tion·al·ness** *n*

ex·cep·tive \ik-ˈsep-tiv\ *adj* **1 :** relating to, containing, or constituting exception **2** *archaic* **:** CAPTIOUS

[1]**ex·cerpt** \ek-ˈsərpt, eg-ˈzərpt, ˈek-ˌ, ˈeg-ˌ\ *vt* [L *excerptus,* pp. of *excerpere,* fr. *ex-* + *carpere* to gather, pluck — more at HARVEST] **1 :** to select (a passage) for quoting **:** EXTRACT **2 :** to take extracts from (as a book) — **ex·cerpt·er** *also* **ex·cerp·tor** *n* — **ex·cerp·tion** \ek-ˈsərp-shən, eg-ˈzərp-\ *n*

[2]**ex·cerpt** \ˈek-ˌsərpt, ˈeg-ˌzərpt\ *n* **:** a passage (as from a book or musical composition) selected, performed, or copied **:** EXTRACT

[1]**ex·cess** \ik-ˈses, ˈek-ˌ\ *n* [ME, fr. MF or LL; MF *exces,* fr. LL *excessus,* fr. L, departure, projection, fr. *excessus,* pp. of *excedere* to exceed] **1 a :** the state or an instance of surpassing usual, proper, or specified limits **:** SUPERFLUITY **b :** the amount or degree by which one thing or quantity exceeds another <an ~ of ten bushels> **2 :** undue or immoderate indulgence **:** INTEMPERANCE <prevent ~*es* and abuses by newly created local powers —Albert Shanker> — **in excess of :** to an amount or degree beyond **:** OVER

[2]**excess** *adj* **:** more than the usual, proper, or specified amount <charges for ~ baggage>

ex·ces·sive \ik-ˈses-iv\ *adj* **:** exceeding the usual, proper, or normal — **ex·ces·sive·ly** *adv* — **ex·ces·sive·ness** *n*

syn EXCESSIVE, IMMODERATE, INORDINATE, EXTRAVAGANT, EXORBITANT, EXTREME *shared meaning element* **:** going beyond a normal or acceptable limit ***ant*** deficient

exch *abbr* exchange; exchanged

[1]**ex·change** \iks-ˈchānj, ˈeks-ˌ\ *n, often attrib* [ME *exchaunge,* fr. MF *eschange,* fr. *eschangier* to exchange, fr. (assumed) VL *excambiare,* fr. L *ex-* + *cambiare* to exchange — more at CHANGE] **1 :** the act of giving or taking one thing in return for another **:** TRADE <an ~ of prisoners> **2 a :** the act of substituting one thing for another **b :** reciprocal giving and receiving **3 :** something offered, given, or received in an exchange; *also***:** an item or article reprinted from a newspaper **4 a :** funds payable currently at a distant point either in a foreign currency or in domestic currency **b (1) :** interchange or conversion of the money of two countries or of current and uncurrent money with allowance for difference in value **(2) :** EXCHANGE RATE **(3) :** the amount of the difference in value between two currencies or between values of a particular currency at two places **c :** instruments (as checks or bills of exchange) presented in a clearinghouse for settlement **5 :** a place where things or services are exchanged: as **a :** an organized market or center for trading in securities or commodities **b :** a store or shop specializing in merchandise usu. of a particular type **c :** a cooperative store or society **d :** a central office in which telephone lines are connected to permit communication

[2]**exchange** *vb* **ex·changed; ex·chang·ing** *vt* **1 a :** to part with, give, or transfer in consideration of something received as an equivalent **b :** to have replaced by other merchandise <*exchanged* the shirt for one in a larger size> **2 :** to part with for a substitute <*exchanging* future security for immediate pleasure> **3 :** BARTER, SWAP ~ *vi* **1 :** to pass or become received in exchange **2 :** to engage in an exchange — **ex·change·abil·i·ty** \iks-ˌchān-jə-ˈbil-ət-ē\ *n* — **ex·change·able** \iks-ˈchān-jə-bəl\ *adj* — **ex·chang·er** \iks-ˈchān-jər, eks-ˌ\ *n*

ex·chang·ee \iks-ˌchān-ˈjē, ˌeks-\ *n* **:** a participant (as a student or teacher) in an exchange program

exchange rate *n* **:** the ratio at which the principal unit of two currencies may be traded

exchange student *n* **:** a student from one country received into an institution in another country in exchange for one sent to an institution in the home country of the first

Ex·chang·ite \iks-ˈchān-ˌjīt\ *n* [(*National*) *Exchange* (*club*)] **:** a member of a major national service club

ex·che·quer \ˈeks-ˌchek-ər, iks-ˈ\ *n* [ME *escheker,* fr. AF, fr. OF *eschequier* chessboard, counting table — more at CHECKER] **1** *cap* **:** a department or office of state in medieval England charged with the collection and management of the royal revenue and judicial determination of all revenue causes **2** *cap* **:** a former superior court having jurisdiction in England and Wales primarily over revenue matters and now merged with King's Bench **3** *often cap* **a :** the department or office of state in Great Britain and Northern Ireland charged with the receipt and care of the national revenue **b :** the national banking account of this realm **4 :** TREASURY; *esp* **:** a national or royal treasury **5 :** pecuniary resources **:** FUNDS

ex·cide \ek-ˈsīd\ *vt* **ex·cid·ed; ex·cid·ing** [L *excidere*] **:** to cut out **:** EXCISE

ex·cip·i·ent \ik-ˈsip-ē-ənt\ *n* [L *excipient-, excipiens,* prp. of *excipere* to take out, take up — more at EXCEPT] **:** an inert substance (as gum arabic or starch) that forms a vehicle (as for a drug)

ex·ci·ple \ˈek-sə-pəl\ *n* [NL *excipulum,* fr. L, receptacle, fr. *excipere*] **:** a saucer-shaped rim around the hymenium of various lichens

ex·cis·able \ˈek-ˌsī-zə-bəl, -ˌsī-sə-, ek-ˈ\ *adj* **:** subject to excise

[1]**ex·cise** \ˈek-ˌsīz, -ˌsīs\ *n* [obs. D *excijs* (now *accijus*), fr. MD, prob. modif. of OF *assise* session, assessment — more at ASSIZE] **1 :** an internal tax levied on the manufacture, sale, or consumption of a commodity within a country **2 :** any of various taxes on privileges often assessed in the form of a license or other fee

[2]**excise** *vt* **ex·cised; ex·cis·ing :** to impose an excise on

[3]**ex·cise** \ik-ˈsīz\ *vt* **ex·cised; ex·cis·ing** [L *excisus,* pp. of *excidere,* fr. *ex-* + *caedere* to cut — more at CONCISE] **:** to remove by or as if by cutting out — **ex·ci·sion** \-ˈsizh-ən\ *n*

ex·cise·man \ˈek-ˌsīz-mən, -ˌsīs-, -ˌman, ek-ˈ\ *n* **:** an officer who inspects and rates articles liable to excise under British law

ex·cit·able \ik-ˈsīt-ə-bəl\ *adj* **:** capable of being readily roused into action or a state of excitement or irritability; *specif* **:** capable of being activated by and reacting to stimuli — **ex·cit·abil·i·ty** \-ˌsīt-ə-ˈbil-ət-ē\ *n* — **ex·cit·able·ness** \-ˈsīt-ə-bəl-nəs\ *n*

ex·ci·tant \ik-ˈsīt-ᵊnt, ˈek-sət-ənt\ *adj* **:** tending to excite or augment <~ drugs> — **excitant** *n*

ex·ci·ta·tion \ˌek-ˌsī-ˈtā-shən, ˌek-sə-\ *n* **:** EXCITEMENT; *esp* **:** the disturbed or altered condition resulting from stimulation of an individual, organ, tissue, or cell

ex·cit·ative \ik-ˈsīt-ət-iv\ *adj* **:** tending or able to excite

ex·cit·ato·ry \ik-ˈsīt-ə-ˌtōr-ē, -ˌtȯr-\ *adj* **1 :** EXCITATIVE **2 :** exhibiting or marked by excitement or excitation

ex·cite \ik-ˈsīt\ *vt* **ex·cit·ed; ex·cit·ing** [ME *exciten,* fr. MF *exciter,* fr. L *excitare,* fr. *ex-* + *citare* to rouse — more at CITE] **1 a :** to call to activity **b :** to rouse to feeling usu. by a profound moving <scenes to ~ the hardest man to pity and help> **c :** to arouse (as an emotional response) by appropriate stimuli <~ enthusiasm for the new regime —Arthur Knight> **2 a :** ENERGIZE <~ an electromagnet> **b :** to produce a magnetic field in <~ a dynamo> **3 :** to increase the activity of (as a living organism) **:** STIMULATE **4 :** to raise (as an atomic nucleus, an atom, or a molecule) to a higher energy level ***syn*** see PROVOKE ***ant*** soothe, quiet (*as persons*), allay (*as fears*)

ex·cit·ed *adj* **:** having or showing strong feelings — **ex·cit·ed·ly** *adv*
excited state *n* **:** a state of a physical system (as an atomic nucleus, an atom, or a molecule) that is higher in energy than the ground state
ex·cite·ment \ik-'sīt-mənt\ *n* **1 :** the action of exciting **:** the state of being excited **2 :** something that excites or rouses
ex·cit·er \ik-'sīt-ər\ *n* **1 :** one that excites **2 a :** a dynamo or battery that supplies the electric current used to produce the magnetic field in another dynamo or motor **b :** an electrical oscillator that generates the carrier frequency (as for a radio transmitter)
ex·cit·ing \ik-'sīt-iŋ\ *adj* **:** producing excitement — **ex·cit·ing·ly** \-iŋ-lē\ *adv*
ex·ci·ton \'ek-sə-ˌtän, -ˌsī-\ *n* [ISV *excitation* + *-on*] **:** a mobile combination of an electron and a hole in an excited crystal (as of a semiconductor) — **ex·ci·ton·ic** \ˌek-sə-'tän-ik, -ˌsī-\ *adj*
ex·ci·tor \ik-'sīt-ər\ *n, archaic* **:** EXCITER
ex·claim \iks-'klām\ *vb* [MF *exclamer,* fr. L *exclamare,* fr. *ex-* + *clamare* to cry out — more at CLAIM] *vi* **1 :** to cry out or speak in strong or sudden emotion <~*ed* in delight> **2 :** to speak loudly or vehemently <~*ed* against immorality> ~ *vt* **:** to utter sharply, passionately, or vehemently **:** PROCLAIM — **ex·claim·er** *n*
ex·cla·ma·tion \ˌeks-klə-'mā-shən\ *n* **1 :** a sharp or sudden utterance **2 :** vehement expression of protest or complaint
exclamation point *n* **:** a mark ! used esp. after an interjection or exclamation to indicate forceful utterance or strong feeling
ex·clam·a·to·ry \iks-'klam-ə-ˌtōr-ē, -ˌtȯr-\ *adj* **:** containing, expressing, using, or relating to exclamation <an ~ phrase>
ex·clave \'eks-ˌklāv, -ˌkläv\ *n* [*ex-* + *-clave* (as in *enclave*)] **:** a portion of a country separated from the main part and constituting an enclave in respect to the surrounding territory
ex·clo·sure \eks-'klō-zhər\ *n* [*ex-* + *-closure* (as in *enclosure*)] **:** an area from which intruders (as animals) are excluded esp. by fencing
ex·clud·able *or* **ex·clud·ible** \iks-'klüd-ə-bəl\ *adj* **:** subject to exclusion <~ income> — **ex·clud·abil·i·ty** \-ˌklüd-ə-'bil-ət-ē\ *n*
ex·clude \iks-'klüd\ *vt* **ex·clud·ed; ex·clud·ing** [ME *excluden,* fr. L *excludere,* fr. *ex-* + *claudere* to close — more at CLOSE] **1 a :** to shut out **b :** to bar from participation, consideration, or inclusion **2 :** to expel esp. from a place or position previously occupied — **ex·clud·er** *n*
syn EXCLUDE, DEBAR, ELIMINATE, SUSPEND *shared meaning element* **:** to shut or put out ***ant*** admit (*persons*), include (*things*)
ex·clu·sion \iks-'klü-zhən\ *n* [L *exclusion-, exclusio,* fr. *exclusus,* pp. of *excludere*] **1 :** the act or an instance of excluding **2 :** the state of being excluded — **ex·clu·sion·ary** \-zhə-ˌner-ē\ *adj*
ex·clu·sion·ist \iks-'klüzh-(ə-)nəst\ *n* **:** one who would exclude another from some right or privilege — **exclusionist** *adj*
exclusion principle *n* **:** a principle in physics: no two electrons in an atom or molecule will be exactly equivalent
[1]**ex·clu·sive** \iks-'klü-siv, -ziv\ *adj* **1 a :** excluding or having power to exclude **b :** limiting or limited to possession, control, or use by a single individual or group **2 a :** excluding others from participation **b :** snobbishly aloof **3 a :** accepting or soliciting only a socially restricted patronage (as of the upper class) **b :** STYLISH, FASHIONABLE **c :** restricted in distribution, use, or appeal because of expense **4 a :** SINGLE, SOLE <~ jurisdiction> **b :** WHOLE, UNDIVIDED <his ~ attention> — **ex·clu·sive·ly** *adv* — **ex·clu·sive·ness** *n*
[2]**exclusive** *n* **:** something exclusive: as **a :** a newspaper story at first released to or printed by only one newspaper **b :** an exclusive right (as to sell a particular product in a certain area)
exclusive disjunction *n* **:** a statement of a logical proposition expressing alternatives usu. taking the form *p* + *q* meaning *p* or *q* but not both — see TRUTH TABLE table
exclusive of *prep* **:** not taking into account <there were four of us *exclusive of* the guide>
ex·clu·siv·i·ty \ˌeks-ˌklü-'siv-ət-ē, iks-, -'ziv-\ *n, pl* **-ties 1 :** the quality or state of being exclusive **2 :** exclusive rights or services
ex·cog·i·tate \ek-'skäj-ə-ˌtāt\ *vt* [L *excogitatus,* pp. of *excogitare,* fr. *ex-* + *cogitare* to cogitate] **:** to think out **:** DEVISE — **ex·cog·i·ta·tion** \(ˌ)ek-ˌskäj-ə-'tā-shən\ *n* — **ex·cog·i·ta·tive** \ek-'skäj-ə-ˌtāt-iv\ *adj*
[1]**ex·com·mu·ni·cate** \ˌek-skə-'myü-nə-ˌkāt\ *vt* [ME *excommunicaten,* fr. LL *excommunicatus,* pp. of *excommunicare,* fr. L *ex-* + LL *communicare* to communicate] **:** to subject to excommunication — **ex·com·mu·ni·ca·tor** \-ˌkāt-ər\ *n*
[2]**ex·com·mu·ni·cate** \-ni-kət\ *adj* **:** interdicted from the rites of the church **:** EXCOMMUNICATED — **excommunicate** *n*
ex·com·mu·ni·ca·tion \-ˌmyü-nə-'kā-shən\ *n* **1 :** an ecclesiastical censure depriving a person of the rights of church membership **2 :** exclusion from fellowship in a group or community — **ex·com·mu·ni·ca·tive** \-'myü-nə-ˌkāt-iv, -ni-kət-\ *adj*
ex·co·ri·ate \ek-'skōr-ē-ˌāt, -'skȯr-\ *vt* **-at·ed; -at·ing** [ME *excoriaten,* fr. LL *excoriatus,* pp. of *excoriare,* fr. L *ex-* + *corium* skin, hide — more at CUIRASS] **1 :** to wear off the skin of **:** ABRADE **2 :** to censure scathingly <we ~ and scorn the public servant who takes a bribe —Estes Kefauver> — **ex·co·ri·a·tion** \(ˌ)ek-ˌskōr-ē-'ā-shən, -ˌskȯr-\ *n*
ex·cre·ment \'ek-skrə-mənt\ *n* [L *excrementum,* fr. *excernere*] **:** waste matter discharged from the body; *esp* **:** waste discharged from the alimentary canal — **ex·cre·men·tal** \ˌek-skrə-'ment-ᵊl\ *adj* — **ex·cre·men·ti·tious** \-ˌmen-'tish-əs, -mən-\ *adj*
ex·cres·cence \ik-'skres-ᵊn(t)s\ *n* **:** an often excessive or abnormal outgrowth or enlargement
ex·cres·cen·cy \-ᵊn-sē\ *n, pl* **-cies :** EXCRESCENCE
ex·cres·cent \-ᵊnt\ *adj* [L *excrescent-, excrescens,* prp. of *excrescere* to grow out, fr. *ex-* + *crescere* to grow — more at CRESCENT] **1 :** forming an abnormal, excessive, or useless outgrowth **2 :** of, relating to, or constituting epenthesis — **ex·cres·cent·ly** *adv*
ex·cre·ta \ik-'skrēt-ə\ *n pl* [NL, fr. L, neut. pl. of *excretus*] **:** waste matter eliminated or separated from an organism; *esp* **:** EXCRETIONS — **ex·cre·tal** \-'skrēt-ᵊl\ *adj*
ex·crete \ik-'skrēt\ *vt* **ex·cret·ed; ex·cret·ing** [L *excretus,* pp. of *excernere* to sift out, discharge, fr. *ex-* + *cernere* to sift — more at CERTAIN] **:** to separate and eliminate or discharge (waste) from the blood or tissues or from the active protoplasm — **ex·cret·er** *n*
ex·cre·tion \ik-'skrē-shən\ *n* **1 :** the act or process of excreting **2 :** something excreted; *esp* **:** useless, superfluous, or harmful material (as urea) that is eliminated from the body and that differs from a secretion in not being produced to perform a useful function
ex·cre·to·ry \'ek-skrə-ˌtōr-ē, -ˌtȯr-\ *adj* **:** of, relating to, or functioning in excretion <~ ducts>
ex·cru·ci·ate \ik-'skrü-shē-ˌāt\ *vt* **-at·ed; -at·ing** [L *excruciatus,* pp. of *excruciare,* fr. *ex-* + *cruciare* to crucify, fr. *cruc-, crux* cross — more at RIDGE] **1 :** to inflict intense pain on **:** TORTURE **2 :** to subject to intense mental distress
ex·cru·ci·at·ing *adj* **1 :** causing great pain or anguish **:** AGONIZING <the nation's most ~ dilemma —W. H. Ferry> **2 :** very intense **:** EXTREME <~ pain> <the characters are paired off with an ~ regard for balance —Douglas Watt> — **ex·cru·ci·at·ing·ly** \-ˌāt-iŋ-lē\ *adv*
ex·cru·ci·a·tion \ik-ˌskrü-s(h)ē-'ā-shən\ *n* **:** the act of excruciating **:** the state or an instance of being excruciated
ex·cul·pate \'ek-(ˌ)skəl-ˌpāt, (')ek-'\ *vt* **-pat·ed; -pat·ing** [(assumed) ML *exculpatus,* pp. of *exculpare,* fr. L *ex* + *culpa* blame] **:** to clear from alleged fault or guilt — **ex·cul·pa·tion** \ˌek-(ˌ)skəl-'pā-shən\ *n*
ex·cul·pa·to·ry \ek-'skəl-pə-ˌtōr-ē, -ˌtȯr-\ *adj* **:** tending or serving to exculpate
ex·cur·rent \(')ek-'skər-ənt, -'skə-rənt\ *adj* [L *excurrent-, excurrens,* prp. of *excurrere* to run out, extend, fr. *ex-* + *currere* to run — more at CAR] **:** running or flowing out: as **a (1) :** having the axis prolonged to form an undivided main stem or trunk (as in conifers) **(2) :** projecting beyond the apex — used esp. of the midrib of a mucronate leaf **b :** characterized by a current that flows outward <~ canals of a sponge>
ex·cur·sion \ik-'skər-zhən\ *n* [L *excursion-, excursio,* fr. *excursus,* pp. of *excurrere*] **1 a :** a going out or forth **:** EXPEDITION **b (1) :** a usu. brief pleasure trip **(2) :** a trip at special reduced rates **2 :** deviation from a direct, definite, or proper course; *esp* **:** DIGRESSION <needless ~*s* into abstruse theory> **3 a :** a movement outward and back or from a mean position or axis; *also* **:** the distance traversed **:** AMPLITUDE <the ~ of a piston> **b :** one complete movement of expansion and contraction of the lungs and their membranes (as in breathing)
ex·cur·sion·ist \-'skərzh-(ə-)nəst\ *n* **:** a person who goes on an excursion
ex·cur·sive \-'skər-siv\ *adj* **:** constituting a digression **:** characterized by digression — **ex·cur·sive·ly** *adv* — **ex·cur·sive·ness** *n*
ex·cur·sus \ik-'skər-səs\ *n, pl* **ex·cur·sus·es** *also* **ex·cur·sus** \-səs, -ˌsüs\ [L, digression, fr. *excursus,* pp.] **:** an appendix or digression that contains further exposition of some point or topic
ex·cu·sa·to·ry \-zə-ˌtōr-ē, -ˌtȯr-\ *adj* **:** making or containing excuse
[1]**ex·cuse** \ik-'skyüz, *imperatively often without* ik-\ *vt* **ex·cused; ex·cus·ing** [ME *excusen,* fr. OF *excuser,* fr. L *excusare,* fr. *ex-* + *causa* cause, explanation] **1 a :** to make apology for <quietly *excused* his clumsiness> **b :** to try to remove blame from <*excused* himself for being so careless> **2 :** to forgive entirely or overlook as of trivial import **:** regard as excusable <she graciously *excused* his thoughtlessness> **3 :** to grant exemption or release to <the class was *excused*> **4 :** to serve as excuse for **:** JUSTIFY <nothing can ~ such heedlessness> — **ex·cus·able** \ik-'skyü-zə-bəl\ *adj* — **ex·cus·able·ness** *n* — **ex·cus·ably** \-blē\ *adv* — **ex·cus·er** *n*
syn EXCUSE, CONDONE, PARDON, FORGIVE *shared meaning element* **:** to exact neither punishment nor redress for (an offense) or from (an offender). Both *excuse* and *condone* imply a passing over without censure or meet punishment. Distinctively, one may EXCUSE specific acts especially in social or conventional situations or the person responsible for these <*excuse* an interruption> <always ready to *excuse* her children for little faults> Often the term implies extenuating circumstances <injustice *excuses* strong responses> or in some contexts self-justification <always ready to *excuse* himself from any responsibility for the results of his behavior> One more often CONDONES a kind of behavior (as dishonesty, folly, or violence) and especially one that constitutes a grave breach (as of a moral or legal code) or a person or institution responsible for such behavior <a culture that *condones* drink but not drugs> *Pardon* and *forgive* are often interchangeable, but their implications can be distinct. One PARDONS when one remits a penalty rightfully due for an admitted or established offense <*pardon* a criminal> <*pardon* the noisy enthusiasm of a child> One FORGIVES when one gives up all claim to requital and to resentment or vengeful feelings <to err is human, to *forgive* divine —Alexander Pope> ***ant*** punish
[2]**excuse** \ik-'skyüs\ *n* **1 :** the act of excusing **2 a :** something offered as justification or as grounds for being excused **b** *pl* **:** an expression of regret for failure to do something **c :** a note of explanation of an absence **3 :** JUSTIFICATION, REASON ***syn*** see APOLOGY
ex–di·rec·to·ry \ˌeks-də-'rek-t(ə-)rē, -dī-\ *adj* [L *ex* out of — more at EX-] *Brit* **:** not listed in a telephone directory **:** UNLISTED
[1]**ex·ec** \ig-'zek\ *n* **:** EXECUTIVE OFFICER
[2]**exec** *abbr* executive
ex·e·cra·ble \'ek-si-krə-bəl\ *adj* **1 :** deserving to be execrated **:** DETESTABLE <~ crimes> **2 :** very bad **:** WRETCHED <~ hotel food> — **ex·e·cra·ble·ness** *n* — **ex·e·cra·bly** \-blē\ *adv*

ex·e·crate \'ek-sə-ˌkrāt\ *vt* **-crat·ed; -crat·ing** [L *exsecratus,* pp. of *exsecrari* to put under a curse, fr. *ex* + *sacr-, sacer* sacred] **1** : to declare to be evil or detestable : DENOUNCE **2** : to detest utterly — **ex·e·cra·tive** \-ˌkrāt-iv\ *adj* — **ex·e·cra·tor** \-ˌkrāt-ər\ *n*

syn EXECRATE, CURSE, DAMN, ANATHEMATIZE *shared meaning element* : to denounce violently

ex·e·cra·tion \ˌek-sə-'krā-shən\ *n* **1** : the act of cursing or denouncing; *also* : the curse so uttered **2** : an object of curses : something detested

ex·ec·u·tant \ig-'zek-(y)ət-ənt\ *n* : one who executes or performs; *esp* : one skilled in the technique of an art : PERFORMER

ex·e·cute \'ek-si-ˌkyüt\ *vt* **-cut·ed; -cut·ing** [ME *executen,* fr. MF *executer,* back-formation fr. *execution*] **1** : to carry out fully : put completely into effect <is a soldier morally responsible for a command that he ~*s*> **2** : to do what is provided or required by <~ a decree> **3** : to put to death esp. in compliance with a legal sentence **4** : to make or produce (as a work of art) esp. by carrying out a design **5** : to perform what is required to give validity to <~ a deed> **6** : PLAY <~ a piece of music> — **ex·e·cut·able** \-ˌkyüt-ə-bəl\ *adj*

syn **1** see PERFORM

2 EXECUTE, ADMINISTER *shared meaning element* : to carry out the declared intent of another

3 see KILL

ex·e·cu·tion \ˌek-si-'kyü-shən\ *n* [ME, fr. MF, fr. L *exsecution-, exsecutio,* fr. *exsecutus,* pp. of *exsequi* to execute, fr. *ex-* + *sequi* to follow — more at SUE] **1** : the act or process of executing : PERFORMANCE **2** : a putting to death esp. as a legal penalty **3** : a judicial writ empowering an officer to carry out a judgment **4** : the act or mode or result of performance **5** : effective or destructive action <his brandished steel, which smoked with bloody ~ —Shak.> — usu. used with *do* <as soon as day came, we went out to see what ~ we had done —Daniel Defoe>

ex·e·cu·tion·er \-sh(ə-)nər\ *n* : one who executes; *esp* : one who puts to death

[1]**ex·ec·u·tive** \ig-'zek-(y)ət-iv\ *adj* **1** : designed for or relating to execution or carrying into effect <~ board> **2 a** : of or relating to the execution of the laws and the conduct of public and national affairs **b** : belonging to the branch of government that is charged with such powers as diplomatic representation, superintendence of the execution of the laws, and appointment of officials and that usu. has some power over legislation (as through veto) — compare JUDICIAL, LEGISLATIVE **3** : of or relating to an executive <the ~ offices>

[2]**executive** *n* **1** : the executive branch of a government; *also* : the persons who constitute the executive magistracy of a state **2** : an individual or group constituting the agency that controls or directs an organization **3** : one who holds a position of administrative or managerial responsibility

executive agreement *n* : an agreement between the U.S. and a foreign government made by the executive branch of the government alone and dealing usu. with routine matters

executive council *n* **1** : a council constituted to advise or share in the functions of a political executive **2** : a council that exercises supreme executive power

executive officer *n* : the officer second in command of a military or naval organization

executive order *n* : REGULATION 2b

executive secretary *n* : a secretary having administrative duties; *specif* : a paid full-time official who is responsible for organizing and administering the activities and business affairs of an organization or association

executive session *n* : a usu. closed session (as of a legislative body) that functions as an executive council (as of the U.S. Senate when considering appointments or the ratification of treaties)

ex·ec·u·tor \ig-'zek-(y)ət-ər *or in sense 1* 'ek-sə-ˌkyüt-\ *n* [ME, fr. OF, fr. L *exsecutor,* fr. *exsecutus*] **1 a** : one who executes something **b** *obs* : EXECUTIONER **2** : the person appointed by a testator to execute his will — **ex·ec·u·to·ri·al** \ig-ˌzek-(y)ə-'tōr-ē-əl, -'tȯr-\ *adj*

ex·ec·u·to·ry \ig-'zek-(y)ə-ˌtōr-ē, -ˌtȯr-\ *adj* **1** : relating to administration **2** : designed or of such a nature as to be executed in time to come or to take effect on a future contingency <an agreement to sell is an ~ contract>

ex·ec·u·trix \ig-'zek-(y)ə-(ˌ)triks\ *n, pl* **ex·ec·u·tri·ces** \-ˌzek-(y)ə-'trī-(ˌ)sēz\ *or* **ex·ec·u·trix·es** \-'zek-(y)ə-ˌtrik-səz\ : a female executor

ex·e·dra \'ek-sə-drə\ *n, pl* **-drae** \-ˌdrē, -ˌdrī\ [L, fr. Gk, fr. *ex-* + *hedra* seat — more at SIT] **1** *in ancient Greece and Rome* : a room for conversation formed by an open or columned recess often semicircular in shape and furnished with seats **2** : a large outdoor nearly semicircular seat with a solid back

ex·e·ge·sis \ˌek-sə-'jē-səs\ *n, pl* **-ge·ses** \-'jē-(ˌ)sēz\ [NL, fr. Gk *exēgēsis,* fr. *exēgeisthai* to explain, interpret, fr. *ex-* + *hēgeisthai* to lead — more at SEEK] : EXPOSITION, EXPLANATION; *esp* : an explanation or critical interpretation of a text

ex·e·gete \'ek-sə-ˌjēt\ *n* [Gk *exēgētēs,* fr. *exēgeisthai*] : one who practices exegesis

ex·e·get·i·cal \ˌek-sə-'jet-i-kəl\ *or* **ex·e·get·ic** \-ik\ *adj* [Gk *exēgētikos,* fr. *exēgeisthai*] : of or relating to exegesis : EXPLANATORY — **ex·e·get·i·cal·ly** \-i-k(ə-)lē\ *adv*

ex·e·get·ist \-'jet-əst\ *n* : EXEGETE

ex·em·plar \ig-'zem-ˌplär, -plər\ *n* [ME, fr. L, fr. *exemplum* example] : something that serves as a model or example: as **a** : an ideal model **b** : a typical or standard specimen **c** : a copy of a book or writing **d** : IDEA 1a *syn* see MODEL

ex·em·pla·ry \ig-'zem-plə-rē\ *adj* **1 a** : serving as a pattern **b** : deserving imitation : COMMENDABLE <his courage was ~> **2** : serving as a warning : MONITORY **3** : serving as an example, instance, or illustration — **ex·em·plar·i·ly** \ˌeg-ˌzem-'pler-ə-lē\ *adv* — **ex·em·pla·ri·ness** \ig-'zem-plə-rē-nəs\ *n* — **ex·em·plar·i·ty** \ˌeg-ˌzem-'plar-ət-ē\ *n*

ex·em·pli·fi·ca·tion \ig-ˌzem-plə-fə-'kā-shən\ *n* **1** : an exemplified copy of a document **2 a** : the act or process of exemplifying **b** : a case in point : EXAMPLE

ex·em·pli·fy \ig-'zem-plə-ˌfī\ *vt* **-fied; -fy·ing** [ME *exemplifien,* fr. MF *exemplifier,* fr. ML *exemplificare,* fr. L *exemplum*] **1** : to show or illustrate by example **2** : to make an attested copy or transcript of (a document) under seal **3 a** : to be an instance of or serve as an example : EMBODY **b** : to be typical of

ex·em·pli gra·tia \ig-ˌzem-(ˌ)plē-'grät-ē-ˌä\ *adv* [L] : for example

ex·em·plum \ig-'zem-pləm\ *n, pl* **-pla** \-plə\ [L] **1** : EXAMPLE, MODEL **2** : an anecdote or short narrative used to point a moral or sustain an argument

[1]**ex·empt** \ig-'zem(p)t\ *adj* [ME, fr. L *exemptus,* pp. of *eximere* to take out — more at EXAMPLE] **1** *obs* : set apart **2** : free or released from some liability or requirement to which others are subject <was ~ from jury duty>

[2]**exempt** *n* : one exempted or freed from duty

[3]**exempt** *vt* **1** *obs* : to set apart **2** : to release or deliver from some liability or requirement to which others are subject : EXCUSE <a man ~*ed* from military service>

ex·emp·tion \ig-'zem(p)-shən\ *n* **1** : the act of exempting or state of being exempt : IMMUNITY **2** : one that exempts or is exempted; *esp* : a source or amount of income exempted from taxation

ex·en·ter·ate \ig-ˌzent-ə-ˌrāt\ *vt* **-at·ed; -at·ing** [L *exenteratus,* pp. of *exenterare* to disembowel, modif. of Gk *exenterizein,* fr. *ex-* + *enteron* intestine — more at INTER-] : to remove the contents of (as the orbit or pelvis) — **ex·en·ter·a·tion** \-ˌzent-ə-'rā-shən\ *n*

[1]**ex·er·cise** \'ek-sər-ˌsīz\ *n* [ME, fr. MF *exercice,* fr. L *exercitium,* fr. *exercitus,* pp. of *exercēre* to drive on, keep busy, fr. *ex-* + *arcēre* to enclose, hold off — more at ARK] **1 a** : the act of bringing into play or realizing in action : USE **b** : the discharge of an official function or professional occupation **2 a** : regular or repeated use of a faculty or bodily organ **b** : bodily exertion for the sake of developing and maintaining physical fitness **3** : something performed or practiced in order to develop, improve, or display a specific power or skill <arithmetic ~*s*> **4** : a performance having a strongly marked secondary or ulterior aspect <party politics has always been an ~ in compromise —H.S. Ashmore> **5 a** : a maneuver, operation, or drill carried out for training and discipline **b** *pl* : a program including speeches, announcements of awards and honors, and various traditional practices of secular or religious character <commencement ~*s*>

[2]**exercise** *vb* **-cised; -cis·ing** *vt* **1 a** : to make effective in action : USE <didn't ~ good judgment> **b** : to bring to bear : EXERT <~ influence> **2 a** : to use repeatedly in order to strengthen or develop **b** : to train (as troops) by drills and maneuvers **c** : to put through exercises <~ the horses> **3 a** : to engage the attention and effort of **b** : to cause anxiety, alarm, or indignation in <citizens *exercised* about pollution> ~ *vi* : to take exercise *syn* see PRACTICE — **ex·er·cis·able** \-ˌsī-zə-bəl\ *adj* — **ex·er·cis·er** *n*

ex·er·ci·ta·tion \ig-ˌzər-sə-'tā-shən\ *n* [ME *exercitacioun,* fr. L *exercitation-, exercitatio,* fr. *exercitatus,* pp. of *exercitare* to exercise diligently, fr. *exercitus,* pp. of *exercēre*] : EXERCISE

ex·er·gon·ic \ˌek-(ˌ)sər-'gän-ik\ *adj* [*exo-* + Gk *ergon* work — more at WORK] : liberating energy <an ~ biochemical reaction>

ex·ergue \'ek-ˌsərg, 'eg-ˌzərg\ *n* [F, fr. NL *exergum,* fr. Gk *ex* out of + *ergon* work] : a space on a coin, token, or medal usu. on the reverse below the central part of the design

ex·ert \ig-'zərt\ *vt* [L *exsertus,* pp. of *exserere* to thrust out, fr. *ex-* + *serere* to join — more at SERIES] **1 a** : to put forth (as strength) **b** : to put (oneself) into action or to tiring effort **2** : to bring to bear esp. with sustained effort or lasting effect **3** : EMPLOY, WIELD <~*ed* his leadership abilities intelligently>

ex·er·tion \ig-'zər-shən\ *n* : the act or an instance of exerting; *esp* : a laborious or perceptible effort *syn* see EFFORT

ex·e·unt \'ek-sē-(ˌ)ənt, -ˌu̇nt\ [L, they go out, fr. *exire* to go out — more at EXIT] — used as a stage direction to specify that all or certain named characters leave the stage

ex·fo·li·ate \(ˈ)eks-'fō-lē-ˌāt\ *vb* **-at·ed; -at·ing** [LL *exfoliatus,* pp. of *exfoliare* to strip of leaves, fr. L *ex-* + *folium* leaf — more at BLADE] *vt* **1** : to cast off in scales, laminae, or splinters **2** : to remove the surface of in scales or laminae **3** : to spread or extend by or as if by opening out leaves ~ *vi* **1** : to split into or give off scales, laminae, or body cells **2** : to come off in a thin piece **3** : to grow by or as if by producing or unfolding leaves — **ex·fo·li·a·tion** \(ˌ)eks-ˌfō-lē-'ā-shən\ *n* — **ex·fo·li·a·tive** \eks-'fō-lē-ˌāt-iv\ *adj*

ex gra·tia \(ˈ)eks-'grā-sh(ē-)ə\ *adj or adv* [NL] : as a favor : not compelled by legal right <*ex gratia* pension payments>

ex·hal·ant *or* **ex·hal·ent** \eks-'(h)ā-lənt\ *adj* : bearing out or outward : EMISSIVE <an ~ siphon of a clam>

ex·ha·la·tion \ˌeks-(h)ə-'lā-shən\ *n* **1** : an act of exhaling **2** : something exhaled or given off : EMANATION

ex·hale \eks-'(h)ā(ə)l\ *vb* **ex·haled; ex·hal·ing** [ME *exalen,* fr. L *exhalare,* fr. *ex-* + *halare* to breathe; akin to L *anima* breath — more at ANIMATE] *vt* **1 a** : to breathe out **b** : to give forth (gaseous matter) : EMIT **2** *archaic* : to cause to be emitted in vapor ~ *vi* **1** : to rise or be given off as vapor **2** : to emit breath or vapor

[1]**ex·haust** \ig-'zȯst\ *vb* [L *exhaustus,* pp. of *exhaurire,* fr. *ex-* + *haurire* to draw; akin to MHG *œsen* to empty, Gk *auein* to take] *vt* **1 a** : to draw off or let out completely **b** : to empty by drawing off the contents; *specif* : to create a vacuum in **2 a** : to use up : consume entirely <~*ed* our funds in a week> **b** : to tire extremely or completely <~*ed* by overwork> **c** : to deprive of a valuable quality or constituent <~ a photographic developer> <~ a soil of fertility> **3 a** : to develop (a subject) completely **b** : to try out the whole number of <~*ed* all the possibilities> ~ *vi* : DISCHARGE, EMPTY <the engine ~*s* through the muffler> *syn* see DEPLETE, TIRE — **ex·haust·er** *n* — **ex·haust·ibil·i·ty** \-ˌzȯ-stə-'bil-ət-ē\ *n* — **ex·haust·ible** \-'zȯ-stə-bəl\ *adj*

[2]**exhaust** *n* **1 a** : the escape of used gas or vapor from an engine **b** : the gas or vapor thus escaping **2 a** : the conduit through

which used gases escape **b :** an arrangement for withdrawing fumes, dusts, or odors from an enclosure **3 :** EXHAUSTION

ex·haus·tion \ig-ˈzȯs-chən\ *n* **:** the act or process of exhausting **:** the state of being exhausted

ex·haus·tive \ig-ˈzȯ-stiv\ *adj* **1 :** serving or tending to exhaust **2 :** testing all possibilities or considering all elements **:** THOROUGH <conducted an ~ investigation> — **ex·haus·tive·ly** *adv* — **ex·haus·tive·ness** *n* — **ex·haus·tiv·i·ty** \-ˌzȯ-ˈstiv-ət-ē\ *n*

ex·haust·less \ig-ˈzȯst-ləs\ *adj* **:** not to be exhausted **:** INEXHAUSTIBLE — **ex·haust·less·ly** *adv* — **ex·haust·less·ness** *n*

exhbn *abbr* exhibition

[1]**ex·hib·it** \ig-ˈzib-ət\ *vb* [ME *exhibiten,* fr. L *exhibitus,* pp. of *exhibēre,* fr. *ex-* + *habēre* to have, hold — more at GIVE] *vt* **1 :** to present to view: as **a :** to show or display outwardly esp. by visible signs or actions <~*ed* no fear> **b :** to have as a readily discernible quality or feature <in all cultures we know, men ~ an aesthetic sense —H. J. Muller> **c :** to show publicly esp. for purposes of competition or demonstration **2 :** to submit (as a document) to a court or officer in course of proceedings; *also* **:** to present or offer officially or in legal form **3 :** to administer for medical purposes <the patient should fast . . . before chloroform is ~*ed* —A. B. Garrod> ~ *vi* **:** to display something for public inspection — **ex·hib·i·tive** \-ət-iv\ *adj* — **ex·hib·i·tor** \-ət-ər\ *n* — **ex·hib·i·to·ry** \-ə-ˌtōr-ē, -ˌtȯr-\ *adj*

[2]**exhibit** *n* **1 :** an act or instance of exhibiting **2 :** something exhibited **3 :** a document or material object produced and identified in court or before an examiner for use as evidence

ex·hi·bi·tion \ˌek-sə-ˈbish-ən\ *n* **1 :** an act or instance of exhibiting **2** *Brit* **:** a grant drawn from the funds of a school or university to help maintain a student **3 :** a public showing (as of works of art, objects of manufacture, or athletic skill)

ex·hi·bi·tion·er \-ˈbish-(ə-)nər\ *n, Brit* **:** one who holds a grant from a school or university

ex·hi·bi·tion·ism \-ˈbish-ə-ˌniz-əm\ *n* **1 a :** a perversion marked by a tendency to indecent exposure **b :** an act of such exposure **2 :** the act or practice of behaving so as to attract attention to oneself — **ex·hi·bi·tion·ist** \-ˈbish-(ə-)nəst\ *n or adj* — **ex·hi·bi·tion·is·tic** \-ˌbish-ə-ˈnis-tik\ *adj*

ex·hil·a·rant \ig-ˈzil-ə-rənt\ *adj* **:** EXHILARATING

ex·hil·a·rate \ig-ˈzil-ə-ˌrāt\ *vt* **-rat·ed; -rat·ing** [L *exhilaratus,* pp. of *exhilarare,* fr. *ex-* + *hilarare* to gladden, fr. *hilarus* cheerful — more at HILARIOUS] **1 a :** to make cheerful **b :** ENLIVEN, EXCITE **2 :** REFRESH, STIMULATE — **ex·hil·a·ra·tive** \-ˌrāt-iv\ *adj*

ex·hil·a·rat·ing \-ˌrāt-iŋ\ *adj* **:** that exhilarates <~ effect of mountain air> — **ex·hil·a·rat·ing·ly** \-iŋ-lē\ *adv*

ex·hil·a·ra·tion \ig-ˌzil-ə-ˈrā-shən\ *n* **1 :** the action of exhilarating **2 :** the feeling or the state of being exhilarated

ex·hort \ig-ˈzȯ(ə)rt\ *vb* [ME *exhorten,* fr. MF *exhorter,* fr. L *exhortari,* fr. *ex-* + *hortari* to incite — more at YEARN] *vt* **:** to incite by argument or advice **:** urge strongly ~ *vi* **:** to give warnings or advice **:** make urgent appeals — **ex·hort·er** *n*

ex·hor·ta·tion \ˌek-ˌsȯr-ˈtā-shən, ˌegz-, -ər-\ *n* **1 :** an act or instance of exhorting **2 :** language intended to incite and encourage

ex·hor·ta·tive \ig-ˈzȯrt-ət-iv\ *adj* **:** serving to exhort

ex·hor·ta·to·ry \-ə-ˌtōr-ē, -ˌtȯr-\ *adj* **:** using exhortation **:** EXHORTATIVE

ex·hume \igz-ˈ(y)üm, iks-ˈ(h)yüm\ *vt* **ex·humed; ex·hum·ing** [F or ML; F *exhumer,* fr. ML *exhumare,* fr. L *ex* out of + *humus* earth — more at EX-, HUMBLE] **1 :** DISINTER **2 :** to bring back from neglect or obscurity — **ex·hu·ma·tion** \ˌeks-(h)yü-ˈmā-shən, ˌegz-(y)ü-\ *n* — **ex·hum·er** \igz-ˈ(y)ü-mər, iks-ˈ(h)yü-\ *n*

ex·i·gence \ˈek-sə-jən(t)s\ *n* **:** EXIGENCY

ex·i·gen·cy \ˈek-sə-jən-sē, ig-ˈzij-ən-\ *n, pl* **-cies 1 a :** the quality or state of being exigent **b :** a state of affairs that makes urgent demands <the president must be free to act in any sudden ~> **2 :** such need or necessity as belongs to the occasion **:** that which is required in a particular situation — usu. used in pl. ***syn*** see JUNCTURE, NEED

ex·i·gent \ˈek-sə-jənt\ *adj* [L *exigent-, exigens,* prp. of *exigere* to demand — more at EXACT] **1 :** requiring immediate aid or action **2 :** requiring or calling for much **:** DEMANDING — **ex·i·gent·ly** *adv*

ex·i·gu·i·ty \ˌeg-zi-ˈgyü-ət-ē\ *n, pl* **-ities :** the quality or state of being exiguous **:** SCANTINESS

ex·ig·u·ous \ig-ˈzig-yə-wəs\ *adj* [L *exiguus,* fr. *exigere*] **:** excessively scanty **:** INADEQUATE <attempting to build up their ~ navy> ***syn*** see MEAGER ***ant*** capacious, ample — **ex·ig·u·ous·ly** *adv* — **ex·ig·u·ous·ness** *n*

[1]**ex·ile** \ˈeg-ˌzīl, ˈek-ˌsīl\ *n* [ME *exil,* fr. MF, fr. L *exilium*] **1 a :** forced removal from one's country or home **b :** voluntary absence from one's country or home **2 a :** a person expelled from his country or home by authority **b :** one who separates himself from his home

[2]**exile** *vt* **ex·iled; ex·il·ing :** to banish or expel from one's own country or home ***syn*** see BANISH

ex·il·ic \eg-ˈzil-ik\ *adj* **:** of or relating to exile (as that of the Jews in Babylon)

ex·im·i·ous \eg-ˈzim-ē-əs\ *adj* [L *eximius,* fr. *eximere* to take out — more at EXAMPLE] *archaic* **:** CHOICE, EXCELLENT

ex·ine \ˈek-ˌsēn, -ˌsīn\ *n* [prob. fr. G, fr. *ex-* + NL *in-* fibrous tissue, fr. Gk *in-, is* tendon] **:** the outer of the two major layers forming the walls of some spores and esp. pollen grains

ex·ist \ig-ˈzist\ *vi* [L *exsistere* to come into being, exist, fr. *ex-* + *sistere* to stand; akin to L *stare* to stand — more at STAND] **1 a :** to have real being whether material or spiritual <do unicorns ~> **b :** to have being in space and time <the greatest poet who ever ~*ed*> **c :** to have being in a specified place or with respect to understood limitations or conditions <strange ideas ~*ed* in his mind> **2 :** to continue to be <racism still ~*s* to varying degrees> **3 a :** to have life or the functions of vitality <man cannot ~ without oxygen> **b :** to live at an inferior level or under adverse circumstances <starving people ~*ing* from one day to the next> **4** *in existentialism* **:** to have contingent but free and responsible being

ex·is·tence \ig-ˈzis-tən(t)s\ *n* **1 a** *obs* **:** reality as opposed to appearance **b :** reality as presented in experience **c (1) :** the totality of existent things **(2) :** a particular being <all the fair ~*s* of heaven —John Keats> **d :** sentient or living being **:** LIFE **2 a :** the state or fact of having being esp. independently of human consciousness and as contrasted with nonexistence **b :** the manner of being that is common to every mode of being **c :** being with respect to a limiting condition or under a particular aspect **3 :** continued or repeated manifestation **4** *in existentialism* **:** the condition of a person aware of his radically contingent yet free and responsible nature

ex·is·tent \-tənt\ *adj* [L *exsistent-, exsistens,* prp. of *exsistere*] **1 :** having being **:** EXISTING **2 :** existing now **:** PRESENT — **existent** *n*

ex·is·ten·tial \ˌeg-(ˌ)zis-ˈten-chəl, ˌek-(ˌ)sis-\ *adj* **1 :** of, relating to, or affirming existence <~ propositions> **2 a :** grounded in existence or the experience of existence **:** EMPIRICAL **b :** having being in time and space **3** [trans. of Dan *eksistentiel* & G *existential*] **a :** concerned with or involving an individual as radically free and responsible **b :** EXISTENTIALIST — **ex·is·ten·tial·ly** \-ˈtench-(ə-)lē\ *adv*

ex·is·ten·tial·ism \-ˈten-chə-ˌliz-əm\ *n* **:** a chiefly 20th century philosophy that is centered upon the analysis of existence and of the way man finds himself existing in the world, that regards human existence as not exhaustively describable or understandable in scientific terms, and that stresses the freedom and responsibility of the individual, the irreducible uniqueness of an ethical or religious situation, and usu. the isolation and subjective experiences (as of anxiety, guilt, dread, anguish) of an individual therein

[1]**ex·is·ten·tial·ist** \-ləst\ *n* **:** an adherent of existentialism

[2]**existentialist** *adj* **1 :** of or relating to existentialism or existentialists **2 :** EXISTENTIAL 3a — **ex·is·ten·tial·is·tic** \-ˌten-chə-ˈlis-tik\ *adj* — **ex·is·ten·tial·is·ti·cal·ly** \-ti-k(ə-)lē\ *adv*

existential quantifier *n* **:** a quantifier that asserts that there exists at least one value of a variable — called also *existential operator*

[1]**ex·it** \ˈeg-zət, ˈek-sət\ [L, he goes out, fr. *exire* to go out, fr. *ex-* + *ire* to go — more at ISSUE] — used as a stage direction to specify who goes off stage

[2]**exit** *n* [L *exitus,* fr. *exitus,* pp. of *exire*] **1** [[1]*exit*] **:** a departure from a stage **2 a :** the act of going out or going away **b :** DEATH **3 :** a way out of an enclosed place or space — **exit** *vi*

ex li·bris \eks-ˈlē-brəs, -ˌbrēs\ *n, pl* **ex libris** [NL, from the books; used before the owner's name on bookplates] **:** BOOKPLATE

Ex·moor \ˈek-ˌsmu̇(ə)r, -ˌsmō(ə)r, -ˌsmȯ(ə)r\ *n* [*Exmoor,* England] **1 :** any of a breed of horned sheep of Devonshire in England valued esp. for mutton **2 :** any of a breed of hardy heavy-maned ponies native to the Exmoor district

ex ni·hi·lo \(ˈ)eks-ˈnē-(h)ə-ˌlō, -ˈni-, -ˈnī-\ *adv or adj* [L] **:** from or out of nothing <creation *ex nihilo*>

exo- *or* **ex-** *comb form* [Gk *exō* out, outside, fr. *ex* out of — more at EX-] **1 :** outside <*exo*gamy> **:** outer <*exo*skeleton> — compare ECT-, END- **2 :** turning out <*exo*ergic>

exo·bi·ol·o·gy \ˌek-sō-bī-ˈäl-ə-jē\ *n* **:** extraterrestrial biology — **exo·bi·o·log·i·cal** \-ˌbī-ə-ˈläj-i-kəl\ *adj* — **exo·bi·ol·o·gist** \-bī-ˈäl-ə-jəst\ *n*

exo·carp \ˈek-sō-ˌkärp\ *n* [ISV] **:** the outermost layer of the pericarp of a fruit — see ENDOCARP illustration

exo·crine \ˈek-sə-krən, -ˌkrīn, -ˌkrēn\ *adj* [ISV *exo-* + Gk *krinein* to separate — more at CERTAIN] **:** secreting externally <~ pancreatic cells>

exocrine gland *n* **:** a gland (as a sweat gland or a kidney) that releases a secretion external to or at the surface of an organ by means of a canal or duct

exo·cy·clic \ˌek-sō-ˈsī-klik, -ˈsik-lik\ *adj* **:** situated outside of a ring in a chemical structure

Exod *abbr* Exodus

exo·der·mis \ˌek-sō-ˈdər-məs\ *n* [NL] **:** a layer of the outer living cortical cells that takes over the functions of the epidermis in roots lacking secondary thickening

ex·odon·tia \ˌek-sə-ˈdän-ch(ē-)ə\ *n* [NL, fr. *ex-* + *-odontia*] **:** a branch of dentistry that deals with the extraction of teeth — **ex·odon·tist** \-ˈdänt-əst\ *n*

ex·o·dus \ˈek-səd-əs, ˈeg-zəd-\ *n* [L, fr. Gk *Exodos,* lit., road out, fr. *ex-* + *hodos* road — more at CEDE] **1** *cap* **:** the mainly narrative second book of canonical Jewish and Christian Scripture — see BIBLE table **2 :** a mass departure **:** EMIGRATION

exo·en·zyme \ˌek-sō-ˈen-ˌzīm\ *n* [ISV] **:** an extracellular enzyme

exo·er·gic \ˌek-sō-ˈər-jik\ *adj* **:** releasing energy **:** EXOTHERMIC <~ nuclear reaction>

exo·eryth·ro·cyt·ic \ˌek-sō-i-ˌrith-rə-ˈsit-ik\ *adj* **:** occurring outside the red blood cells — used of stages of malaria parasites

ex of·fi·cio \ˌek-sə-ˈfish-ē-ˌō\ *adv or adj* [LL] **:** by virtue or because of an office <the Vice President serves *ex officio* as president of the Senate>

ex·og·a·my \ek-ˈsäg-ə-mē\ *n, pl* **-mies 1 :** marriage outside of a specific group esp. as required by custom or law **2 :** sexual reproduction between organisms that are not closely related — **ex·og·a·mous** \ek-ˈsäg-ə-məs\ *or* **exo·gam·ic** \ˌek-sə-ˈgam-ik\ *adj*

ex·og·e·nous \ek-ˈsäj-ə-nəs\ *adj* [F *exogène* exogenous, fr. *exo-* + *-gène* (fr. Gk *-genēs* born) — more at -GEN] **:** originating from or due to external causes: as **a :** growing from or on the outside <~ spores> **b (1) :** caused by a factor (as food) or an agent from outside the organism <~ obesity> <~ infection> **(2) :** introduced from or produced outside the organism <~ supply of a vitamin> **c :** of, relating to, or produced by the metabolism of nitrogenous substances obtained from food — **ex·og·e·nous·ly** *adv*

ə abut	ə kitten	ər further	a back	ā bake	ä cot, cart
au̇ out	ch chin	e less	ē easy	g gift	i trip	ī life
j joke	ŋ sing	ō flow	ȯ flaw	ȯi coin	th thin	t͟h this
ü loot	u̇ foot	y yet	yü few	yu̇ furious	zh vision

ex·on·er·ate \ig-'zän-ə-ˌrāt\ *vt* **-at·ed; -at·ing** [ME *exoneraten,* fr. L *exoneratus,* pp. of *exonerare* to unburden, fr. *ex-* + *oner-, onus* load] **1 :** to relieve of a responsibility, obligation, or hardship **2 :** to clear from accusation or blame — **ex·on·er·a·tion** \-ˌzän-ə-'rā-shən\ *n* — **ex·on·er·a·tive** \-'zän-ə-ˌrāt-iv\ *adj*

exo·nu·cle·ase \ˌek-sō-'n(y)ü-klē-ˌās, -ˌāz\ *n* [*exo-* + *nucle-* + *-ase*] **:** an enzyme that breaks down a nucleic acid by removing nucleotides one by one from the end of a chain — compare ENDONUCLEASE

exo·pep·ti·dase \-'pep-tə-ˌdās, -ˌdāz\ *n* [*exo-* + *peptide* + *-ase*] **:** any of a group of enzymes that hydrolyze peptide bonds formed by the terminal amino acids of peptide chains **:** PEPTIDASE — compare ENDOPEPTIDASE

ex·oph·thal·mos *also* **ex·oph·thal·mus** \ˌek-säf-'thal-məs, -səf-, -säp-\ *n* [NL, fr. Gk *exophthalmos* having prominent eyes, fr. *ex* out + *ophthalmos* eye] **:** abnormal protrusion of the eyeball — **ex·oph·thal·mic** \-mik\ *adj*

exor *abbr* executor

ex·or·bi·tance \ig-'zȯr-bət-ən(t)s\ *n* **1 :** an exorbitant action or procedure; *esp* **:** excessive or gross deviation from rule, right, or propriety **2 :** the tendency or disposition to be exorbitant

ex·or·bi·tant \-ənt\ *adj* [ME, fr. MF, fr. LL *exorbitant-, exorbitans,* prp. of *exorbitare* to deviate, fr. L *ex-* + *orbita* track, rut — more at ORB] **1 :** not coming within the orbit or scope of the law **2 :** exceeding in intensity, quality, or size the customary or appropriate limits ***syn*** see EXCESSIVE ***ant*** just (*price, charge*) — **ex·or·bi·tant·ly** *adv*

ex·or·cise \'ek-ˌsȯr-ˌsīz, -sər-\ *vt* **-cised; -cis·ing** [ME *exorcisen,* fr. MF *exorciser,* fr. LL *exorcizare,* fr. Gk *exorkizein,* fr. *ex-* + *horkizein* to bind by oath, adjure, fr. *horkos* oath; akin to Gk *herkos* fence, L *sarcire* to mend] **1 a :** to expel (an evil spirit) by adjuration **b :** to get rid of (something troublesome, menacing, or oppressive) **2 :** to free of an evil spirit — **ex·or·cis·er** *n*

ex·or·cism \-ˌsiz-əm\ *n* **1 :** the act or practice of exorcising **2 :** a spell or formula used in exorcising — **ex·or·cist** \-ˌsist, -səst\ *n* — **ex·or·cis·ti·cal** \ˌek-ˌsȯr-'sis-ti-kəl, -sər-\ *or* **ex·or·cis·tic** \-tik\ *adj*

ex·or·di·um \eg-'zȯrd-ē-əm\ *n, pl* **-diums** *or* **-dia** \-ē-ə\ [L, fr. *exordiri* to begin, fr. *ex-* + *ordiri* to begin — more at ORDER] **:** a beginning or introduction esp. to a discourse or composition — **ex·or·di·al** \-ē-əl\ *adj*

exo·skel·e·ton \ˌek-sō-'skel-ət-ᵊn\ *n* **1 :** an external supportive covering of an animal **2 :** bony or horny parts of a vertebrate produced from epidermal tissues — **exo·skel·e·tal** \-ət-ᵊl\ *adj*

ex·os·mo·sis \ˌek-(ˌ)säs-'mō-səs, -(ˌ)säz-\ *n* [alter. of obs. *exosmose,* fr. F, fr. *ex-* + Gk *ōsmos* act of pushing — more at ENDOSMOSIS] **:** passage of material through a membrane from a region of higher to a region of lower concentration — **ex·os·mot·ic** \-'mät-ik\ *adj*

exo·sphere \'ek-sō-ˌsfi(ə)r\ *n* [ISV] **:** the outer fringe region of the atmosphere of the earth or a planet — **exo·spher·ic** \ˌek-sō-'sfi(ə)r-ik, -'sfer-\ *adj*

exo·spore \'ek-sə-ˌspō(ə)r, -ˌspȯ(ə)r\ *n* [ISV] **:** an asexual spore formed by abstriction from a parent cell

ex·os·to·sis \ˌek-(ˌ)säs-'tō-səs\ *n, pl* **-to·ses** \-ˌsēz\ [NL, fr. Gk *exostōsis,* fr. *ex* out of + *osteon* bone — more at EX-, OSSEOUS] **:** a spur or bony outgrowth from a bone or the root of a tooth

ex·o·ter·ic \ˌek-sə-'ter-ik\ *adj* [L & Gk; L *exotericus,* fr. Gk *exōterikos,* lit., external, fr. *exōterō* more outside, compar. of *exō* outside — more at EXO-] **1 a :** suitable to be imparted to the public <the ~ doctrine> — compare ESOTERIC **b :** belonging to the outer or less initiate circle **2 :** relating to the outside **:** EXTERNAL — **ex·o·ter·i·cal·ly** \-i-k(ə-)lē\ *adv*

exo·ther·mic \ˌek-sō-'thər-mik\ *or* **exo·ther·mal** \-məl\ *adj* [ISV] **:** characterized by or formed with evolution of heat — **exo·ther·mi·cal·ly** \-mi-k(ə-)lē\ *adv*

ex·ot·ic \ig-'zät-ik\ *adj* [L *exoticus,* fr. Gk *exōtikos,* fr. *exō*] **1 :** introduced from another country **:** not native to the place where found **2** *archaic* **:** OUTLANDISH, ALIEN **3 :** strikingly or excitingly different or unusual **4 :** of or relating to striptease <~ dancing> — **ex·ot·i·cal·ly** \-i-k(ə-)lē\ *adv* — **ex·ot·ic·ness** \-ik-nəs\ *n*

ex·ot·i·ca \ig-'zät-i-kə\ *n pl* [NL, fr. L, neut. pl. of *exoticus*] **:** things excitingly different or unusual; *esp* **:** literary or artistic items having an exotic theme or nature

ex·ot·i·cism \ig-'zät-ə-ˌsiz-əm\ *also* **ex·o·tism** \'eg-zə-ˌtiz-əm, 'ek-sə-\ *n* **1 :** the quality or state of being exotic **2 :** EXOTIC

exo·tox·in \ˌek-sō-'täk-sən\ *n* [ISV] **:** a soluble poisonous substance given off during growth of a microorganism

exp *abbr* **1** expense **2** experiment; experimental **3** export **4** express

ex·pand \ik-'spand\ *vb* [ME *expaunden,* fr. L *expandere,* fr. *ex-* + *pandere* to spread — more at FATHOM] *vt* **1 :** to increase the extent, number, volume, or scope of **:** ENLARGE **2 a :** to express fully or in detail **b :** to write out in full **c :** to state in enlarged form **:** develop in a mathematical series ~ *vi* **1 :** to open out **2 :** to increase in extent, number, volume, or scope **3 :** to speak or write fully or in detail <intend to ~ on this theme tomorrow> **4 :** to feel generous or optimistic — **ex·pand·able** \-'span-də-bəl\ *adj*

syn EXPAND, AMPLIFY, SWELL, DISTEND, INFLATE, DILATE *shared meaning element* **:** to increase in size or volume ***ant*** contract, abridge

expanded metal *n* **:** sheet metal cut and expanded into a lattice and used esp. as lath

expanded plastic *n* **:** lightweight cellular plastic used esp. as insulation and protective packing material — called also *foamed plastic, plastic foam*

ex·pan·der \ik-'span-dər\ *n* **:** one that expands; *specif* **:** any of several colloidal substances of high molecular weight used as a blood or plasma substitute for increasing the blood volume

ex·panse \ik-'span(t)s\ *n* [NL *expansum,* fr. L, neut. of *expansus,* pp. of *expandere*] **:** something spread out typically over a wide area: as **a :** FIRMAMENT **b :** an extensive stretch of land or sea <the vast ~ of the ocean>

ex·pan·si·ble \ik-'span(t)-sə-bəl\ *adj* **:** capable of being expanded — **ex·pan·si·bil·i·ty** \-ˌspan(t)-sə-'bil-ət-ē\ *n*

ex·pan·sile \ik-'span(t)-səl, -'span-ˌsīl\ *adj* **:** of, relating to, or capable of expansion

ex·pan·sion \ik-'span-chən\ *n* **1 :** the act or process of expanding <territorial ~> **2 :** the quality or state of being expanded **3 :** EXPANSE **4 :** the increase in volume of working fluid (as steam) in an engine cylinder after cutoff or in an internal-combustion engine after explosion **5 a :** an expanded part **b :** something that results from an act of expanding <the book is an ~ of a lecture series> **6 :** the result of carrying out an indicated mathematical operation **:** the expression of a function in the form of a series — **ex·pan·sion·al** \-'panch-nəl, -ən-ᵊl\ *adj*

ex·pan·sion·ary \ik-'span-chə-ˌner-ē\ *adj* **:** tending toward expansion <an ~ economy>

ex·pan·sion·ism \ik-'span-chə-ˌniz-əm\ *n* **:** a policy or practice of usu. territorial expansion by a nation — **ex·pan·sion·ist** \-'spanch-(ə-)nəst\ *n* — **expansionist** *or* **ex·pan·sion·is·tic** \-ˌspan-chə-'nis-tik\ *adj*

ex·pan·sive \ik-'span(t)-siv\ *adj* **1 :** having a capacity or a tendency to expand **2 :** causing or tending to cause expansion **3 a :** characterized by high spirits or benevolent inclinations <he grew ~ after dinner> **b :** marked by or indicative of exaggerated euphoria and delusions of self-importance **4 :** having considerable extent **5 :** characterized by largeness or magnificence of scale <~ living> — **ex·pan·sive·ly** *adv* — **ex·pan·sive·ness** *n*

ex·pan·siv·i·ty \ˌek-ˌspan-'siv-ət-ē, ik-\ *n* **:** the quality or state of being expansive; *esp* **:** the capacity to expand

ex par·te \(')ek-'spärt-ē\ *adv or adj* [ML] **1 :** on or from one side only — used of legal proceedings **2 :** from a one-sided or partisan point of view

ex·pa·ti·ate \ek-'spā-shē-ˌāt\ *vi* **-at·ed; -at·ing** [L *exspatiatus,* pp. of *exspatiari* to wander, digress, fr. *ex-* + *spatium* space, course — more at SPEED] **1 :** to move about freely or at will **:** WANDER **2 :** to speak or write at length or in detail <was *expatiating* upon the value of the fabric —Thomas Hardy> — **ex·pa·ti·a·tion** \(ˌ)ek-ˌspā-shē-'ā-shən\ *n*

¹ex·pa·tri·ate \ek-'spā-trē-ˌāt\ *vb* **-at·ed; -at·ing** [ML *expatriatus,* pp. of *expatriare* to leave one's own country, fr. L *ex-* + *patria* native country, fr. fem. of *patrius* of a father, fr. *patr-, pater* father — more at FATHER] *vt* **1 :** to drive into exile **:** BANISH **2 :** to withdraw (oneself) from residence in or allegiance to one's native country ~ *vi* **:** to leave one's native country; *specif* **:** to renounce allegiance to one's native country — **ex·pa·tri·a·tion** \(ˌ)ek-ˌspā-trē-'ā-shən\ *n*

²ex·pa·tri·ate \ek-'spā-trē-ˌāt, -trē-ət\ *adj* **:** living in a foreign country **:** EXPATRIATED

³ex·pa·tri·ate \-ˌāt, -ət\ *n* **:** one who lives in a foreign country; *specif* **:** one who has renounced his native country

ex·pect \ik-'spekt\ *vb* [L *exspectare* to look forward to, fr. *ex-* + *spectare* to look at, fr. *spectus,* pp. of *specere* to look — more at SPY] *vi* **1** *archaic* **:** WAIT, STAY **2 :** to look forward **3 :** to be pregnant ~ *vt* **1** *archaic* **:** to wait for **2 :** SUPPOSE, THINK **3 :** to anticipate or look forward to the coming or occurrence of <~*ed* a telephone call> **4 a :** to consider probable or certain <~ to be forgiven> **b :** to consider reasonable, due, or necessary <he ~*ed* respect from his students> **c :** to consider bound in duty or obligated <they ~*ed* him to pay his dues> — **ex·pect·able** \-'spek-tə-bəl\ *adj* — **ex·pect·ably** \-blē\ *adv* — **ex·pect·ed·ly** *adv* — **ex·pect·ed·ness** *n*

syn EXPECT, LOOK, HOPE, AWAIT *shared meaning element* **:** to anticipate in the mind some occurrence or outcome ***ant*** despair (*of*)

ex·pec·tance \ik-'spek-tən(t)s\ *n* **:** EXPECTANCY

ex·pec·tan·cy \-tən-sē\ *n, pl* **-cies** **1 a :** the act, action, or state of expecting **b :** the state of being expected **2 a :** something expected **b :** the expected amount (as of the number of years of life) based on statistical probability

¹ex·pec·tant \-tənt\ *adj* **1 :** characterized by expectation **2 :** expecting the birth of a child — **ex·pec·tant·ly** *adv*

²expectant *n* **:** one who is expectant; *esp* **:** a candidate for a position

ex·pec·ta·tion \ˌek-ˌspek-'tā-shən, ik-\ *n* **1 :** the act or state of expecting **:** ANTICIPATION <had given rise to a general ~ of their marriage —Jane Austen> **2 a :** something expected **b :** prospects of inheritance — usu. used in pl. **3 :** the state of being expected **4 a :** EXPECTANCY 2b **b :** EXPECTED VALUE

ex·pec·ta·tive \ik-'spek-tət-iv\ *adj* **:** of, relating to, or constituting an object of expectation

expected value *n* **:** the mean value of a random variable

ex·pec·to·rant \ik-'spek-t(ə-)rənt\ *adj* **:** tending to promote discharge of mucus from the respiratory tract — **expectorant** *n*

ex·pec·to·rate \-tə-ˌrāt\ *vb* **-rat·ed; -rat·ing** [prob. fr. (assumed) NL *expectoratus,* pp. of *expectorare,* fr. L, to cast out of the mind, fr. *ex-* + *pector-, pectus* breast, soul — more at PECTORAL] *vt* **1 :** to eject from the throat or lungs by coughing or hawking and spitting **2 :** SPIT ~ *vi* **1 :** to discharge matter from the throat or lungs by coughing or hawking and spitting **2 :** SPIT — **ex·pec·to·ra·tion** \-ˌspek-tə-'rā-shən\ *n*

ex·pe·di·ence \ik-'spēd-ē-ən(t)s\ *n* **:** EXPEDIENCY

ex·pe·di·en·cy \-ən-sē\ *n, pl* **-cies** **1** *obs* **:** HASTE, DISPATCH **2 :** the quality or state of being suited to the end in view **:** SUITABILITY, FITNESS **3 :** cultivation of or adherence to expedient means and methods <put more emphasis on ~ than on principle —W. H. Jones> **4 :** a means of achieving a particular end **:** EXPEDIENT — **ex·pe·di·en·tial** \-ˌspēd-ē-'en-chəl\ *adj*

¹ex·pe·di·ent \ik-'spēd-ē-ənt\ *adj* [ME, fr. MF or L; MF, fr. L *expedient-, expediens* prp. of *expedire* to extricate, arrange, be advantageous, fr. *ex-* + *ped-, pes* foot — more at FOOT] **1 :** suitable for achieving a particular end **2 :** characterized by concern with what is opportune; *specif* **:** governed by self-interest — **ex·pe·di·ent·ly** *adv*

syn EXPEDIENT, POLITIC, ADVISABLE *shared meaning element* **:** dictated by practical or prudential motives ***ant*** inexpedient

[2]expedient *n* **1 :** something expedient : a means to an end **2 :** a means devised or used in an exigency : MAKESHIFT *syn* see RESOURCE

ex·pe·dite \ˈek-spə-ˌdīt\ *vt* **-dit·ed; -dit·ing** [L *expeditus,* pp. of *expedire*] **1 :** to execute promptly **2 :** to accelerate the process or progress of : FACILITATE <the new representatives should ~ the passage of the bill> **3 :** to send out : DISPATCH

ex·pe·dit·er *also* **ex·pe·di·tor** \-ˌdīt-ər\ *n* : one that expedites; *specif* : one employed to ensure adequate supplies of raw materials and equipment or to coordinate the flow of materials, tools, parts, and processed goods within a plant

ex·pe·di·tion \ˌek-spə-ˈdish-ən\ *n* **1 a :** a journey or excursion undertaken for a specific purpose **b :** the group of persons making such a journey **2 :** efficient promptness : SPEED **3 :** a sending or setting forth *syn* see HASTE *ant* procrastination

ex·pe·di·tion·ary \-ˈdish-ə-ˌner-ē\ *adj* : of, relating to, or constituting an expedition; *also* : sent on military service abroad <an ~ force>

ex·pe·di·tious \ˌek-spə-ˈdish-əs\ *adj* : characterized by or acting with promptness and efficiency : SPEEDY *syn* see FAST *ant* sluggish — **ex·pe·di·tious·ly** *adv* — **ex·pe·di·tious·ness** *n*

ex·pel \ik-ˈspel\ *vt* **ex·pelled; ex·pel·ling** [ME *expellen,* fr. L *expellere,* fr. *ex-* + *pellere* to drive — more at FELT] **1 :** to force out from or as if from a receptacle <the well *expelled* great quantities of gas> **2 :** to drive away; *esp* : DEPORT **3 :** to cut off from membership <*expelled* from college> *syn* see EJECT *ant* admit — **ex·pel·la·ble** \-ˈspel-ə-bəl\ *adj* — **ex·pel·ler** *n*

ex·pel·lee \ˌek-ˌspel-ˈē, ik-\ *n* : one who is expelled; *specif* : one transferred from the country of residence for resettlement in the country with which he is ethnically associated

ex·pend \ik-ˈspend\ *vt* [ME *expenden,* fr. L *expendere* to weigh out, expend, fr. *ex-* + *pendere* to weigh — more at SPAN] **1 :** to pay out : SPEND <the social services upon which public revenue is ~*ed* — J. A. Hobson> **2 :** to consume by use : use up <projects on which he ~*ed* great energy> — **ex·pend·er** *n*

[1]ex·pend·able \ik-ˈspen-də-bəl\ *adj* : that may be expended: as **a :** normally used up or consumed in service <~ supplies like pencils and paper> **b :** more economically replaced than rescued, salvaged, or protected — **ex·pend·abil·i·ty** \-ˌspen-də-ˈbil-ət-ē\ *n*

[2]expendable *n* : one that is expendable — usu. used in pl.

ex·pen·di·ture \ik-ˈspen-di-chər, -də-ˌchu̇(ə)r, -də-ˌt(y)u̇(ə)r\ *n* [irreg. fr. *expend*] **1 :** the act or process of expending <renovations required an ~ of several thousand dollars> **2 :** something expended : DISBURSEMENT, EXPENSE

[1]ex·pense \ik-ˈspen(t)s\ *n* [ME, fr. AF or LL; AF, fr. LL *expensa,* fr. L, fem. of *expensus,* pp. of *expendere*] **1 a** *archaic* : the act or practice of expending money : SPENDING **b (1)** *archaic* : the act or process of using up : CONSUMPTION **(2)** *obs* : LOSS **2 a :** something expended to secure a benefit or bring about a result **b :** financial burden or outlay : COST <he built the monument at his own ~> **c :** the charges incurred by an employee in connection with the performance of his duties — usu. used in pl. **d :** an item of business outlay chargeable against revenue for a specific period **3 :** a cause or occasion of expenditure <an estate is a great ~> **4 :** SACRIFICE — usu. used in the phrase *at the expense of* <develop a boy's physique at the ~ of his intelligence —Bertrand Russell>

[2]expense *vt* **ex·pensed; ex·pens·ing** **1 :** to charge with expenses **2 a :** to charge to an expense account **b :** to write off as an expense

expense account *n* : an account of expenses reimbursable to an employee

ex·pen·sive \ik-ˈspen(t)-siv\ *adj* **1 :** involving expense <an ~ hobby> **2 :** commanding a high price and esp. one that is not based on intrinsic worth or is beyond a prospective buyer's means *syn* see COSTLY *ant* inexpensive — **ex·pen·sive·ly** *adv* — **ex·pen·sive·ness** *n*

[1]ex·pe·ri·ence \ik-ˈspir-ē-ən(t)s\ *n* [ME, fr. MF, fr. L *experientia* act of trying, fr. *experient-, experiens,* prp. of *experiri* to try, fr. *ex-* + *-periri* (akin to *periculum* attempt) — more at FEAR] **1 a :** the usu. conscious perception or apprehension of reality or of an external, bodily, or psychic event **b :** facts or events or the totality of facts or events observed **2 a :** direct participation in events **b :** the state or result of being engaged in an activity or in affairs <business ~> **c :** knowledge, skill, or practice derived from direct observation of or participation in events **3 a :** the conscious events that make up an individual life **b :** the events that make up the conscious past of a community or nation or mankind generally **4 :** something personally encountered, undergone, or lived through

[2]experience *vt* **-enced; -enc·ing** **1 :** to have experience of : UNDERGO <*experienced* severe hardships as a child> **2 :** to learn by experience <I have *experienced* that a landscape and the sky unfold the deepest beauty —Nathaniel Hawthorne> — **experience religion :** to undergo religious conversion

ex·pe·ri·enced \-ən(t)st\ *adj* : made skillful or wise through observation of or participation in a particular activity or in affairs generally : PRACTICED <an ~ driver>

ex·pe·ri·en·tial \ik-ˌspir-ē-ˈen-chəl\ *adj* : derived from, based on, or relating to experience : EMPIRICAL — **ex·pe·ri·en·tial·ly** \-ˈench-(ə-)lē\ *adv*

[1]ex·per·i·ment \ik-ˈsper-ə-mənt *also* -ˈspir-\ *n* [ME, fr. MF, fr. L *experimentum,* fr. *experiri*] **1 a :** TEST, TRIAL <make another ~ of his suspicion —Shak.> **b :** a tentative procedure or policy **c :** an operation carried out under controlled conditions in order to discover an unknown effect or law, to test or establish a hypothesis, or to illustrate a known law **2** *obs* : EXPERIENCE **3 :** the process of testing : EXPERIMENTATION

[2]ex·per·i·ment \-ˌment\ *vi* : to carry out experiments — **ex·per·i·men·ta·tion** \ik-ˌsper-ə-mən-ˈtā-shən, -ˌmen- *also* -ˌspir-\ *n* — **ex·per·i·ment·er** \-ˈsper-ə-ˌment-ər *also* -ˈspir-\ *n*

ex·per·i·men·tal \ik-ˌsper-ə-ˈment-ᵊl *also* -ˌspir-\ *adj* **1 :** of, relating to, or based on experience : EMPIRICAL **2 :** founded on or derived from experiment <the heart of the ~ method is the direct control of the thing studied —B. F. Skinner> **3 a :** serving the ends of or used as a means of experimentation <an ~ school> **b :** relating to or having the characteristics of experiment : TENTATIVE <still in the ~ stage> — **ex·per·i·men·tal·ly** \-ᵊl-ē\ *adv*

ex·per·i·men·tal·ism \-ᵊl-ˌiz-əm\ *n* : reliance on or advocacy of experimental or empirical principles and procedures; *specif* : INSTRUMENTALISM

ex·per·i·men·tal·ist \-ᵊl-əst\ *n* : one who experiments; *specif* : a person conducting scientific experiments

experiment station *n* : an establishment for scientific research (as in agriculture) where experiments are carried out, studies of practical application are made, and information is disseminated

[1]ex·pert \ˈek-ˌspərt, ik-ˈ\ *adj* [ME, fr. MF & L; MF, fr. L *expertus,* fr. pp. of *experiri*] **1** *obs* : EXPERIENCED **2 :** having, involving, or displaying special skill or knowledge derived from training or experience *syn* see PROFICIENT *ant* amateurish — **ex·pert·ly** *adv* — **ex·pert·ness** *n*

[2]ex·pert \ˈek-ˌspərt\ *n* [F, fr. *expert,* adj.] : one who has acquired special skill in or knowledge of a particular subject : AUTHORITY

[3]ex·pert \ˈek-ˌspərt\ *vt* : to serve as an expert for ~ *vi* : to serve as an expert

ex·per·tise \ˌek-(ˌ)spər-ˈtēz *also* -ˈtēs\ *n* [F, fr. MF, expertness, fr. *expert*] **1 :** expert opinion or commentary **2 :** skill in a particular field : KNOW-HOW <technical ~>

ex·pert·ism \ˈek-ˌspərt-ˌiz-əm\ *n* : EXPERTISE 2

ex·pert·ize \ˈek-spər-ˌtīz\ *vb* **-ized; -iz·ing** *vi* : to give a professional opinion usu. after careful study ~ *vt* : to examine and give expert judgment on

ex·pi·a·ble \ˈek-spē-ə-bəl\ *adj* : capable of being expiated

ex·pi·ate \ˈek-spē-ˌāt\ *vb* **-at·ed; -at·ing** [L *expiatus,* pp. of *expiare* to atone for, fr. *ex-* + *piare* to atone for, appease — more at PIOUS] *vt* **1** *obs* : to put an end to **2 a :** to extinguish the guilt incurred by **b :** to pay the penalty for **c :** to make amends for <permission to ~ their offences by their assiduous labours —Francis Bacon> ~ *vi* : to make expiation — **ex·pi·a·tor** \-ˌāt-ər\ *n*

ex·pi·a·tion \ˌek-spē-ˈā-shən\ *n* **1 :** the act of making atonement **2 :** the means by which atonement is made

ex·pi·a·to·ry \ˈek-spē-ə-ˌtōr-ē, -ˌtȯr-\ *adj* : serving to expiate

ex·pi·ra·tion \ˌek-spə-ˈrā-shən\ *n* **1 a :** the act or process of releasing air from the lungs through the nose or mouth **b** *archaic* : the last emission of breath : DEATH **2 :** the fact of coming to an end : TERMINATION **3 :** something produced by breathing out

ex·pi·ra·to·ry \ik-ˈspī-rə-ˌtōr-ē, ek-ˈ, -ˌtȯr-; ˈek-sp(ə-)rə-\ *adj* : of, relating to, or employed in the expiration of air from the lungs

ex·pire \ik-ˈspī(ə)r, *oftenest for vi 3 and vt 2* ek-\ *vb* **ex·pired; ex·pir·ing** [ME *expiren,* fr. MF or L; MF *expirer,* fr. L *exspirare,* fr. *ex-* + *spirare* to breathe — more at SPIRIT] *vi* **1 :** to breathe one's last breath : DIE **2 :** to come to an end <his term of office ~*s* this year> **3 :** to emit the breath ~ *vt* **1** *obs* : CONCLUDE **2 :** to breathe out from or as if from the lungs **3** *archaic* : to give off

ex·pi·ry \ik-ˈspī(ə)r-ē, ˈek-spə-rē\ *n, pl* **-ries** **1 a :** exhalation of breath **b :** DEATH **2 :** TERMINATION; *esp* : the termination of a time or period fixed by law, contract, or agreement

ex·plain \ik-ˈsplān\ *vb* [ME *explanen,* fr. L *explanare,* lit., to make level, fr. *ex-* + *planus* level, flat — more at FLOOR] *vt* **1 :** to make plain or understandable <a commentary that ~*s* the more difficult passages of the poem> **2 :** to give the reason for or cause of <unable to ~ his conduct> **3 :** to show the logical development or relationships of ~ *vi* : to make something plain or understandable — **ex·plain·able** \-ˈsplā-nə-bəl\ *adj* — **ex·plain·er** *n*

syn EXPLAIN, EXPOUND, EXPLICATE, ELUCIDATE, INTERPRET *shared meaning element* : to make something clear or understandable — **explain oneself :** to clarify one's statements or the reasons for one's conduct

explain away *vt* **1 :** to get rid of by or as if by explanation **2 :** to minimize the significance of by or as if by explanation <evidence which it was hard to *explain away* —A. G. N. Flew>

ex·pla·na·tion \ˌek-splə-ˈnā-shən\ *n* **1 :** the act or process of explaining **2 :** something that explains <the ~*s* offered for mistakes followed a set pattern —V. G. Heiser> **3 :** a mutual discussion designed to correct a misunderstanding or reconcile differences

ex·plan·a·tive \ik-ˈsplan-ət-iv\ *adj* : EXPLANATORY — **ex·plan·a·tive·ly** *adv*

ex·plan·a·to·ry \ik-ˈsplan-ə-ˌtōr-ē, -ˌtȯr-\ *adj* : serving or disposed to explain <~ notes> — **ex·plan·a·to·ri·ly** \-ˌsplan-ə-ˈtōr-ə-lē, -ˈtȯr-\ *adv*

[1]ex·plant \(ˈ)ek-ˈsplant\ *vt* [*ex-* + *-plant* (as in *implant*)] : to remove (living tissue) esp. to a medium for tissue culture — **ex·plan·ta·tion** \ˌek-ˌsplan-ˈtā-shən\ *n*

[2]ex·plant \ˈek-ˌsplant\ *n* : living tissue removed from an organism and placed in a medium for tissue culture

[1]ex·ple·tive \ˈek-splət-iv\ *adj* [LL *expletivus,* fr. L *expletus,* pp. of *explēre* to fill out, fr. *ex-* + *plēre* to fill — more at FULL] **1 :** serving to fill up <~ phrases> **2 :** marked by the use of expletives

[2]expletive *n* **1 a :** a syllable, word, or phrase inserted to fill a vacancy (as in a sentence or a metrical line) without adding to the sense; *esp* : a word (as *it* in "make it clear which you prefer") that occupies the position of the subject or object of a verb in normal English word order and anticipates a subsequent word or phrase that supplies the needed meaningful content **b :** an exclamatory word or phrase; *esp* : one that is obscene or profane **2 :** one that serves as a filler

ex·ple·to·ry \ˈek-splə-ˌtōr-ē, -ˌtȯr-\ *adj* : EXPLETIVE

ex·pli·ca·ble \ek-ˈsplik-ə-bəl, ˈek-(ˌ)splik-\ *adj* : capable of being explained — **ex·pli·ca·bly** \-blē\ *adv*

ə abut	ᵊ kitten	ər further	a back	ā bake	ä cot, cart
au̇ out	ch chin	e less	ē easy	g gift	i trip	ī life
j joke	ŋ sing	ō flow	ȯ flaw	ȯi coin	th thin	th this
ü loot	u̇ foot	y yet	yü few	yu̇ furious	zh vision

ex·pli·cate \ˈek-splə-ˌkāt\ *vt* **-cat·ed; -cat·ing** [L *explicatus,* pp. of *explicare,* lit., to unfold, fr. *ex-* + *plicare* to fold — more at PLY] **1 :** to give a detailed explanation of **2 :** to develop the implications of : analyze logically ***syn*** see EXPLAIN — **ex·pli·ca·tion** \ˌek-splə-ˈkā-shən\ *n* — **ex·pli·ca·tor** \ˈek-splə-ˌkāt-ər\ *n*

ex·pli·ca·tion de texte \ek-splē-kä-syōⁿ-də-tekst\ *n, pl* **explications de texte** *same*\ [F, lit., explanation of text] **:** a method of literary criticism involving a detailed analysis of each part of a work

1**ex·pli·ca·tive** \ek-ˈsplik-ət-iv, ˈek-splə-ˌkāt-\ *adj* **:** serving to explicate **:** EXPLANATORY; *specif* **:** serving to explain logically what is contained in the subject <an ~ proposition> — **ex·pli·ca·tive·ly** *adv*

2**explicative** *n* **:** an explicative expression

ex·pli·ca·to·ry \ek-ˈsplik-ə-ˌtōr-ē, ˈek-(ˌ)splik-, -ˌtȯr-\ *adj* **:** EXPLICATIVE

ex·plic·it \ik-ˈsplis-ət\ *adj* [F or ML; F *explicite,* fr. ML *explicitus,* fr. L, pp. of *explicare*] **1 a :** free from all vagueness and ambiguity <an ~ statement of the problem> **b :** fully developed or formulated <an ~ statement of his objectives> **2 :** unreserved and unambiguous in expression **3 :** externally visible **4 :** involving direct payment <~ costs> — **ex·plic·it·ly** *adv* — **ex·plic·it·ness** *n*

syn EXPLICIT, EXPRESS, SPECIFIC, DEFINITE *shared meaning element* **:** perfectly clear and unambiguous ***ant*** ambiguous

explicit function *n* **:** a mathematical function defined by an expression containing only independent variables — compare IMPLICIT FUNCTION

ex·plode \ik-ˈsplōd\ *vb* **ex·plod·ed; ex·plod·ing** [L *explodere* to drive off the stage by clapping, fr. *ex-* + *plaudere* to clap] *vt* **1** *archaic* **:** to drive from the stage by noisy disapproval **2 :** to bring into disrepute or discredit <~ a rumor> **3 :** to cause to explode or burst noisily <~ dynamite> <~ a bomb> ~ *vi* **1 :** to burst forth with sudden violence or noise <~ with anger> **2 a :** to undergo a rapid chemical or nuclear reaction with the production of noise, heat, and violent expansion of gases <dynamite ~*s*> <an atomic bomb ~*s*> **b :** to burst violently as a result of pressure from within — **ex·plod·er** *n*

ex·plod·ed *adj* **:** showing the parts separated but in correct relationship to each other <an ~ view of a carburetor>

ex·plod·ent \ik-ˈsplōd-ᵊnt\ *n* [L *explodent-, explodens,* prp. of *explodere*] **:** EXPLOSIVE

1**ex·ploit** \ˈek-ˌsplȯit, ik-ˈ\ *n* [ME, outcome, success, fr. OF, fr. L *explicitum,* neut. of *explicitus,* pp.] **:** DEED, ACT; *esp* **:** a notable or heroic act ***syn*** see FEAT

2**ex·ploit** \ik-ˈsplȯit, ˈek-ˌ\ *vt* **1 a :** to turn to economic account <~ a mine> **b :** to take advantage of **:** UTILIZE <~*ing* the qualities of the material> **2 :** to make use of meanly or unjustly for one's own advantage <~*s* his friends> — **ex·ploit·able** \-ə-bəl\ *adj* — **ex·ploit·er** *n*

ex·ploi·ta·tion \ˌek-ˌsplȯi-ˈtā-shən\ *n* **1 :** an act of exploiting: as **a :** utilization or working of a natural resource **b :** an unjust or improper use of another person for one's own profit or advantage **c :** coaction between organisms in which one is benefited at the expense of the other **2 :** PUBLICITY, ADVERTISING — **ex·ploit·ative** \ik-ˈsplȯit-ət-iv\ *adj* — **ex·ploit·ative·ly** *adv*

ex·ploit·ive \ik-ˈsplȯit-iv\ *adj* **:** of or relating to exploitation

ex·plo·ra·tion \ˌek-splə-ˈrā-shən, -ˌsplō-\ *n* **:** the act or an instance of exploring — **ex·plo·ra·tion·al** \-shnəl, -shən-ᵊl\ *adj*

ex·plor·ative \ik-ˈsplōr-ət-iv, -ˈsplȯr-\ *adj* **:** EXPLORATORY — **ex·plor·ative·ly** *adv*

ex·plor·ato·ry \-ə-ˌtōr-ē, -ˌtȯr-\ *adj* **:** of or relating to exploration <~ surgery>

ex·plore \ik-ˈsplō(ə)r, -ˈsplȯ(ə)r\ *vb* **ex·plored; ex·plor·ing** [L *explorare,* fr. *ex-* + *plorare* to cry out; prob. fr. the outcry of hunters on sighting game] *vt* **1** *obs* **:** to seek for or after **2 a :** to search through or into <~ the possibilities of reaching an agreement> **b :** to examine minutely esp. for diagnostic purposes **c :** to penetrate into or range over for purposes of geographical discovery ~ *vi* **:** to make or conduct a systematic search <~ for oil>

ex·plor·er \ik-ˈsplōr-ər, -ˈsplȯr-\ *n* **:** one that explores; *esp* **:** a person who travels in search of geographical or scientific information

ex·plo·si·ble \ik-ˈsplō-zə-bəl, -ˈsplō-sə-\ *adj* **:** capable of being exploded — **ex·plo·si·bil·i·ty** \-ˌsplō-zə-ˈbil-ət-ē, -sə-\ *n*

ex·plo·sion \ik-ˈsplō-zhən\ *n* [L *explosion-, explosio* act of driving off by clapping, fr. *explosus,* pp. of *explodere*] **1 :** the act or an instance of exploding: as **a :** a large-scale, rapid, and spectacular expansion, outbreak, or upheaval <the population ~> **b :** a violent outburst of feeling **2 :** the release of occluded breath that occurs in one kind of articulation of stop consonants

1**ex·plo·sive** \ik-ˈsplō-siv, -ziv\ *adj* **1 :** relating to, characterized by, or operated by explosion <an ~ engine> **2 :** tending to explode <an ~ person> — **ex·plo·sive·ly** *adv* — **ex·plo·sive·ness** *n*

2**explosive** *n* **1 :** an explosive substance **2 :** a consonant characterized by explosion in its articulation when it occurs in certain environments **:** STOP

ex·po \ˈek-(ˌ)spō\ *n, pl* **expos :** EXPOSITION 3b

ex·po·nent \ik-ˈspō-nənt, ˈek-ˌ\ *n* [L *exponent-, exponens,* prp. of *exponere*] **1 :** a symbol written above and to the right of a mathematical expression to indicate the operation of raising to a power <in the expression a^3, the ~ *3* indicates that *a* is to be multiplied by itself twice> **2 a :** one that expounds or interprets **b :** one that champions, advocates, or exemplifies

ex·po·nen·tial \ˌek-spə-ˈnen-chəl\ *adj* **1 :** of or relating to an exponent **2 :** involving a variable in an exponent <10^x is an ~ expression> **3 :** expressible or approximately expressible by an exponential equation <an ~ growth rate> — **ex·po·nen·tial·ly** \-ˈnench-(ə-)lē\ *adv*

exponential equation *n* **:** an equation involving an exponential function of a variable

exponential function *n* **:** a mathematical function in which an independent variable appears in one of the exponents — called also *exponential*

ex·po·nen·ti·a·tion \ˌek-spə-ˌnen-chē-ˈā-shən\ *n* [*exponent* + *-iation* (as in *differentiation*)] **:** INVOLUTION 2

1**ex·port** \ek-ˈspō(ə)rt, -ˈspȯ(ə)rt, ˈek-ˌ\ *vb* [L *exportare,* fr. *ex-* + *portare* to carry — more at FARE] *vt* **1 :** to carry away **:** REMOVE **2 :** to carry or send (as a commodity) to some other place (as another country) ~ *vi* **:** to export something abroad — **ex·port·abil·i·ty** \(ˌ)ek-ˌspōrt-ə-ˈbil-ət-ē, -ˌspȯrt-\ *n* — **ex·port·able** \ek-ˈspōrt-ə-bəl, -ˈspȯrt-, ˈek-ˌ\ *adj*

2**ex·port** \ˈek-ˌspō(ə)rt, -ˌspȯ(ə)rt\ *n* **1 :** something exported; *specif* **:** a commodity conveyed from one country or region to another for purposes of trade **2 :** an act of exporting **:** EXPORTATION <the ~ of wheat>

3**export** \ˈek-ˌ\ *adj* **:** of or relating to exportation or exports <~ duties>

ex·por·ta·tion \ˌek-ˌspōr-ˈtā-shən, -ˌspȯr-, -spər-\ *n* **:** an act of exporting; *also* **:** a commodity exported

ex·port·er \ek-ˈspōrt-ər, -ˈspȯrt-, ˈek-ˌ\ *n* **:** one that exports; *specif* **:** a wholesaler who sells to merchants or industrial consumers in foreign countries

ex·pose \ik-ˈspōz\ *vt* **ex·posed; ex·pos·ing** [ME *exposen,* fr. MF *exposer,* fr. L *exponere* to set forth, explain (perf. indic. *exposui*), fr. *ex-* + *ponere* to put, place — more at POSITION] **1 a :** to deprive of shelter, protection, or care <~ troops needlessly> **b :** to submit or subject to an action or influence; *specif* **:** to subject (a sensitive photographic film, plate, or paper) to the action of radiant energy **c :** to abandon (an infant) esp. by leaving in the open **:** DESERT **2 :** to lay open to view: as **a :** to offer publicly for sale **b :** to exhibit for public veneration **c :** to reveal the face of (a playing card) **3 a :** to bring to light (as something shameful) **:** UNMASK **b :** to disclose the faults or crimes of <~ a murderer> — **ex·pos·er** *n*

ex·po·sé *or* **ex·po·se** \ˌek-spō-ˈzā, -spə-\ *n* [F *exposé,* fr. pp. of *exposer*] **1 :** a formal recital or exposition of facts **:** STATEMENT **2 :** an exposure of something discreditable <a newspaper ~ of crime conditions>

ex·posed \ik-ˈspōzd\ *adj* **1 :** open to view <an ~ card> **2 :** not shielded or protected <an ~ electric wire>

ex·pos·it \ik-ˈspäz-ət\ *vt* [L *expositus,* pp. of *exponere*] **:** EXPOUND

ex·po·si·tion \ˌek-spə-ˈzish-ən\ *n* **1 :** a setting forth of the meaning or purpose (as of a writing) **2 a :** discourse or an example of it designed to convey information or explain what is difficult to understand **b (1) :** the first part of a musical composition in sonata form in which the thematic material of the movement is presented **(2) :** the opening section of a fugue **3 :** an act or an instance of exposing: as **a :** abandonment of an infant **b :** a public exhibition or show — **ex·po·si·tion·al** \-ˈzish-nəl, -ən-ᵊl\ *adj*

ex·pos·i·tive \ik-ˈspäz-ət-iv\ *adj* **:** DESCRIPTIVE, EXPOSITORY

ex·pos·i·tor \-ət-ər\ *n* [ME *expositour,* fr. MF *expositeur,* fr. LL *expositor,* fr. L *expositus*] **:** one who expounds or explains **:** COMMENTATOR

ex·pos·i·to·ry \-ə-ˌtōr-ē, -ˌtȯr-\ *adj* **:** of, relating to, or containing exposition <~ writing>

1**ex post fac·to** \ˌek-ˌspōst-ˈfak-(ˌ)tō\ *adj* [LL, from a thing done afterward] **1 :** done, made, or formulated after the fact <*ex post facto* approval> **2 :** disregarding or altering the previous status or setting of the event or thing concerning which a conclusion is reached or at which action is directed <*ex post facto* laws>

2**ex post facto** *adv* **:** after the fact **:** RETROACTIVELY

ex·pos·tu·late \ik-ˈspäs-chə-ˌlāt\ *vb* [L *expostulatus,* pp. of *expostulare* to demand, dispute, fr. *ex-* + *postulare* to ask for — more at POSTULATE] *vt, obs* **:** DISCUSS, EXAMINE ~ *vi* **:** to reason earnestly with a person for purposes of dissuasion or remonstrance ***syn*** see OBJECT

ex·pos·tu·la·tion \-ˌspäs-chə-ˈlā-shən\ *n* **:** an act or an instance of expostulating **:** REMONSTRANCE <all his ~*s* proved futile> — **ex·pos·tu·la·to·ry** \-ˈspäs-chə-lə-ˌtōr-ē, -ˌtȯr-\ *adj*

ex·po·sure \ik-ˈspō-zhər\ *n* **1 :** the act or an instance of exposing: as **a :** disclosure to view <skillful ~ of goods in a store window> **b (1) :** a disclosure esp. of a weakness or something shameful or criminal **:** UNMASKING <continued his ~ of electoral frauds> **(2) :** PRESENTATION, EXPOSITION **c :** an act of abandoning esp. in the open **d (1) :** the act of exposing a sensitized photographic material **(2) :** a section of a film for an individual picture **(3) :** the total amount of light or other radiant energy received per unit area on the sensitized material usu. expressed for cameras in terms of the time and the lens *f*-number **2 a :** a condition or an instance of being exposed; *specif* **:** the condition of being exposed to the elements **b :** a position with respect to the points of the compass or to climatic or weather influences <a house with a western ~>

exposure meter *n* **:** a device for indicating correct photographic exposure under varying conditions of illumination

ex·pound \ik-ˈspau̇nd\ *vb* [ME *expounden,* fr. MF *expondre,* fr. L *exponere* to explain — more at EXPOSE] *vt* **1 a :** to set forth **:** STATE **b :** to defend with argument **2 :** to explain by setting forth in careful and often elaborate detail <~ a law> ~ *vi* **:** to make a statement ***syn*** see EXPLAIN — **ex·pound·er** *n*

1**ex·press** \ik-ˈspres\ *adj* [ME, fr. MF *expres,* fr. L *expressus,* pp. of *exprimere* to press out, express, fr. *ex-* + *premere* to press — more at PRESS] **1 a :** directly, firmly, and explicitly stated <he disobeyed my ~ orders> **b :** EXACT, PRECISE **2 a :** designed for or adapted to its purpose **b :** of a particular sort **:** SPECIFIC <he came for that ~ purpose> **3 a :** traveling at high speed; *specif* **:** traveling with few or no stops along the way <~ train> **b :** adapted or suitable for travel at high speed <an ~ highway> **c** *Brit* **:** designated to be delivered without delay by special messenger <~ mail> ***syn*** see EXPLICIT

2**express** *adv* **1** *obs* **:** EXPRESSLY **2 :** by express <send a package ~>

3**express** *n* **1 a** *Brit* **:** a messenger sent on a special errand **b** *Brit* **:** a dispatch conveyed by a special messenger **c (1) :** a system for the prompt and safe transportation of parcels, money, or goods at rates higher than standard freight charges (2) : a company operating such a merchandise freight service (3) : the goods or shipments so transported **d** *Brit* : SPECIAL DELIVERY **2** : an express vehicle

[4]**express** *vt* [ME *expressen,* fr. MF & L; MF *expresser,* fr. OF, fr. *expres,* adj., fr. L *expressus,* pp.] **1 a** : DELINEATE, DEPICT **b** : to represent in words : STATE **c** : to give or convey a true impression of : SHOW, REFLECT **d** : to make known the opinions or feelings of (oneself) <~ *ed* himself very strongly on that subject> **e** : to give expression to the artistic or creative impulses or abilities of (oneself) **f** : to represent by a sign or symbol : SYMBOLIZE **2 a** : to force out (as the juice of a fruit) by pressure **b** : to subject to pressure so as to extract something **3** : to send by express — **ex·press·er** *n* — **ex·press·ible** \-ə-bəl\ *adj*
syn EXPRESS, VENT, UTTER, VOICE, BROACH, AIR *shared meaning element* : to let out what one thinks or feels *ant* imply

ex·press·age \ik-ˈspres-ij\ *n* : a carrying of parcels by express; *also* : a charge for such carrying

ex·pres·sion \ik-ˈspresh-ən\ *n* **1 a** : an act, process, or instance of representing in a medium (as words) : UTTERANCE <freedom of ~> **b** (1) : something that manifests, embodies, or symbolizes something else <this gift is an ~ of my admiration for you> (2) : a significant word or phrase (3) : a mathematical or logical symbol or a meaningful combination of symbols (4) : the detectable effect of a gene; *also* : EXPRESSIVITY **2 a** : a mode, means, or use of significant representation or symbolism; *esp* : felicitous or vivid indication or depiction of mood or sentiment <read the poem with ~> **b** (1) : the quality or fact of being expressive (2) : facial aspect or vocal intonation as indicative of feeling **3** : an act or product of pressing out — **ex·pres·sion·al** \-ˈspresh-nəl, -ən-ᵊl\ *adj*

ex·pres·sion·ism \ik-ˈspresh-ə-ˌniz-əm\ *n* : a theory or practice in art of seeking to depict not objective reality but the subjective emotions and responses that objects and events arouse in the artist — **ex·pres·sion·ist** \-ˈspresh-(ə-)nəst\ *n or adj* — **ex·pres·sion·is·tic** \-ˌspresh-ə-ˈnis-tik\ *adj* — **ex·pres·sion·is·ti·cal·ly** \-ti-k(ə-)lē\ *adv*

ex·pres·sion·less \ik-ˈspresh-ən-ləs\ *adj* : lacking expression <an ~ face> — **ex·pres·sion·less·ly** *adv* — **ex·pres·sion·less·ness** *n*

ex·pres·sive \ik-ˈspres-iv\ *adj* **1** : of or relating to expression <the ~ function of language> **2** : serving to express, utter, or represent <he used foul and novel terms ~ of rage —H. G. Wells> **3** : full of expression : SIGNIFICANT <an ~ silence> — **ex·pres·sive·ly** *adv* — **ex·pres·sive·ness** *n*

ex·pres·siv·i·ty \ˌek-ˌspres-ˈiv-ət-ē\ *n, pl* **-ties** **1** : the relative capacity of a gene to affect the phenotype of the organism of which it is a part **2** : the quality of being expressive

ex·press·ly \ik-ˈspres-lē\ *adv* **1** : in an express manner : EXPLICITLY <he ~ rejected socialism> **2** : for the express purpose : PARTICULARLY <needed a clinic ~ for the treatment of addicts>

ex·press·man \ik-ˈspres-ˌman, -mən\ *n* : a person employed in the express business

ex·press·way \ik-ˈspres-ˌwā\ *n* : a high-speed divided highway for through traffic with access partially or fully controlled and grade separations at important intersections with other roads

ex·pro·pri·ate \ek-ˈsprō-prē-ˌāt\ *vt* **-at·ed; -at·ing** [ML *expropriatus,* pp. of *expropriare,* fr. L *ex-* + *proprius* own] **1** : to deprive of possession or proprietary rights **2** : to transfer (the property of another) to one's own possession <*expropriated* all the land within a 10 mile radius> — **ex·pro·pri·a·tor** \-ˌāt-ər\ *n*

ex·pro·pri·a·tion \(ˌ)ek-ˌsprō-prē-ˈā-shən\ *n* : the act of expropriating or the state of being expropriated; *specif* : the action of the state in taking or modifying the property rights of an individual in the exercise of its sovereignty

expt *abbr* experiment

exptl *abbr* experimental

ex·pulse \ik-ˈspəls\ *vt* **ex·pulsed; ex·puls·ing** : EXPEL

ex·pul·sion \ik-ˈspəl-shən\ *n* [ME, fr. L *expulsion-, expulsio,* fr. *expulsus,* pp. of *expellere* to expel] : the act of expelling : the state of being expelled — **ex·pul·sive** \-ˈpəl-siv\ *adj*

ex·punc·tion \ik-ˈspəŋ(k)-shən\ *n* [L *expunctus,* pp. of *expungere*] : the act of expunging : the state of being expunged : ERASURE

ex·punge \ik-ˈspənj\ *vt* **ex·punged; ex·pung·ing** [L *expungere* to mark for deletion by dots, fr. *ex-* + *pungere* to prick — more at PUNGENT] **1** : to strike out, obliterate, or mark for deletion **2** : to efface completely : DESTROY *syn* see ERASE — **ex·pung·er** *n*

ex·pur·gate \ˈek-spər-ˌgāt\ *vt* **-gat·ed; -gat·ing** [L *expurgatus,* pp. of *expurgare,* fr. *ex-* + *purgare* to purge] : to cleanse of something morally harmful, offensive, or erroneous; *esp* : to expunge objectionable parts from before publication or presentation <~ a book> — **ex·pur·ga·tion** \ˌek-spər-ˈgā-shən\ *n* — **ex·pur·ga·tor** \ˈek-spər-ˌgāt-ər\ *n*

ex·pur·ga·to·ri·al \(ˌ)ek-ˌspər-gə-ˈtōr-ē-əl, -ˈtȯr-\ *adj* : relating to expurgation or an expurgator : EXPURGATORY

ex·pur·ga·to·ry \ek-ˈspər-gə-ˌtōr-ē, -ˌtȯr-\ *adj* : serving to purify from something morally harmful, offensive, or erroneous

expy *abbr* expressway

[1]**ex·qui·site** \ek-ˈskwiz-ət, ˈek-(ˌ)\ *adj* [ME *exquisit,* fr. L *exquisitus,* fr. pp. of *exquirere* to search out, fr. *ex-* + *quaerere* to seek] **1** : carefully selected : CHOICE **2** *archaic* : ACCURATE **3 a** : marked by flawless craftsmanship or by beautiful, ingenious, delicate, or elaborate execution **b** : keenly appreciative : DISCRIMINATING <~ taste> **c** : ACCOMPLISHED, PERFECTED <an ~ gentleman> **4 a** : pleasing through beauty, fitness, or perfection <an ~ white blossom> **b** : ACUTE, INTENSE <~ pain> **c** : having uncommon or esoteric appeal *syn* see CHOICE — **ex·qui·site·ly** *adv* — **ex·qui·site·ness** *n*

[2]**exquisite** *n* : one who is overly fastidious in dress or ornament

exrx *abbr* executrix

ex·san·gui·nate \ek(s)-ˈsaŋ-gwə-ˌnāt\ *vt* **-nat·ed; -nat·ing** [L *exsanguinatus* bloodless, fr. *ex-* + *sanguin-, sanguis* blood] : to drain of blood — **ex·san·gui·na·tion** \(ˌ)ek(s)-ˌsaŋ-gwə-ˈnā-shən\ *n*

ex·scind \ek-ˈsind\ *vt* [L *exscindere,* fr. *ex-* + *scindere* to cut, tear — more at SHED] : to cut off or out : EXCISE

ex·sert \ek-ˈsərt\ *vt* [L *exsertus,* pp. of *exserere* — more at EXERT] : to thrust out — **ex·ser·tile** \-ˈsərt-ᵊl, -ˈsər-ˌtīl\ *adj* — **ex·ser·tion** \-ˈsər-shən\ *n*

ex·sert·ed *adj* : projecting beyond an enclosing organ or part

ex·sic·cate \ˈek-si-ˌkāt\ *vt* **-cat·ed; -cat·ing** [L *exsiccatus,* pp. of *exsiccare,* fr. *ex-* + *siccare* to dry, fr. *siccus* dry — more at SACK] : to remove moisture from : DRY — **ex·sic·ca·tion** \ˌek-si-ˈkā-shən\ *n*

ex·stip·u·late \(ˈ)ek(s)-ˈstip-yə-lət\ *adj* : having no stipules

ext *abbr* **1** extension **2** exterior **3** external **4** externally **5** extra **6** extract

ex·tant \ˈek-stənt; ek-ˈstant, ˈek-ˌ\ *adj* [L *exstant-, exstans,* prp. of *exstare* to stand out, be in existence, fr. *ex-* + *stare* to stand — more at STAND] **1** *archaic* : standing out or above **2 a** : currently or actually existing <~ and projected programs> <the most charming writer ~ —G. W. Johnson> **b** : not destroyed or lost <~ manuscripts>

ex·tem·po·ral \ek-ˈstem-p(ə-)rəl\ *adj* [L *extemporalis,* fr. *ex tempore*] *archaic* : EXTEMPORANEOUS — **ex·tem·po·ral·ly** \-ē\ *adv*

ex·tem·po·ra·ne·ity \(ˌ)ek-ˌstem-pə-rə-ˈnē-ət-ē, -ˈnā-\ *n* : the quality or state of being extemporaneous

ex·tem·po·ra·ne·ous \(ˌ)ek-ˌstem-pə-ˈrā-nē-əs\ *adj* [LL *extemporaneus,* fr. L *ex tempore*] **1 a** (1) : composed, performed, or uttered on the spur of the moment : IMPROMPTU (2) : carefully prepared but delivered without notes or text **b** : skilled at or given to extemporaneous utterance **c** : happening suddenly and often unexpectedly and usu. without clearly known causes or relationships <a great deal of criminal and delinquent behavior is . . . ~ —W. C. Reckless> **2** : provided, made, or put to use as an expedient : MAKESHIFT — **ex·tem·po·ra·ne·ous·ly** *adv* — **ex·tem·po·ra·ne·ous·ness** *n*

ex·tem·po·rary \ik-ˈstem-pə-ˌrer-ē\ *adj* : EXTEMPORANEOUS — **ex·tem·po·rar·i·ly** \-ˌstem-pə-ˈrer-ə-lē\ *adv*

ex·tem·po·re \ik-ˈstem-pə-(ˌ)rē\ *adv* [L *ex tempore,* fr. *ex* + *tempore,* abl. of *tempus* time] : in an extemporaneous manner <speaking ~>

ex·tem·po·ri·za·tion \ik-ˌstem-pə-rə-ˈzā-shən\ *n* **1** : the act of extemporizing : IMPROVISATION **2** : something extemporized

ex·tem·po·rize \ik-ˈstem-pə-ˌrīz\ *vb* **-rized; -riz·ing** *vi* **1** : to do something extemporaneously : IMPROVISE; *esp* : to speak extemporaneously **2** : to get along in a makeshift manner ~ *vt* : to compose, perform, or utter extemporaneously : IMPROVISE — **ex·tem·po·riz·er** *n*

ex·tend \ik-ˈstend\ *vb* [ME *extenden,* fr. MF or L; MF *estendre,* fr. L *extendere,* fr. *ex-* + *tendere* to stretch — more at THIN] *vt* **1** [ME *extenden,* fr. ML *extendere* (fr. L) or AF *estendre,* fr. OF] **a** *Brit* : to take possession of (as lands) by a writ of extent **b** *obs* : to take by force **2** : to spread or stretch forth : UNBEND <~ *ed* both her arms> **3 a** : to stretch out to fullest length **b** : to cause (as a horse) to move at full stride **c** : to exert (oneself) to full capacity <could work long and hard without seeming to ~ himself> **d** (1) : to increase the bulk of (as by the addition of a cheaper substance or a modifier) (2) : ADULTERATE **4 a** : to make the offer of : PROFFER <~ *ing* aid to the needy> **b** : to make available <~ *ing* credit to customers> **5 a** : to cause to reach (as in distance or scope) <national authority was ~ *ed* over new territories> **b** : to cause to be longer : prolong in time <~ *ed* their visit another day>; *esp* : to prolong the time of payment of **c** : ADVANCE, FURTHER <~ *ing* his potential through job training> **6 a** : to cause to be of greater area or volume : ENLARGE **b** : to increase the scope, meaning, or application of : BROADEN <beauty, I suppose, opens the heart, ~*s* the consciousness —Algernon Blackwood> **c** *archaic* : EXAGGERATE ~ *vi* **1** : to stretch out in distance, space, or time : REACH <his jurisdiction ~ *ed* over the whole area> **2** : to reach in scope or application <his concern ~*s* beyond mere business to real service to his customers> — **ex·tend·able** *or* **ex·tend·ible** \-ˈsten-də-bəl\ *adj*
syn EXTEND, LENGTHEN, ELONGATE, PROLONG, PROTRACT *shared meaning element* : to draw out or add to so as to increase in length *ant* abridge, shorten

ex·tend·ed *adj* **1** : INTENSIVE <~ efforts> **2** : having spatial magnitude : being larger than a point <an ~ source of light> **3** : EXTENSIVE <made available ~ information —Ruth G. Strickland> **4** : DERIVATIVE 1, SECONDARY 2a <an ~ sense of a word> — **ex·tend·ed·ly** *adv* — **ex·tend·ed·ness** *n*

extended family *n* : a family that includes in one household near relatives in addition to a nuclear family

extended play *n* : a 45-rpm phonograph record with a playing time of about 6 to 8 minutes

ex·tend·er \ik-ˈsten-dər\ *n* : one that extends; *esp* : a substance added to a product esp. in the capacity of a diluent, adulterant, or modifier

ex·ten·si·ble \ik-ˈsten(t)-sə-bəl\ *adj* : capable of being extended — **ex·ten·si·bil·i·ty** \-ˌsten(t)-sə-ˈbil-ət-ē\ *n*

ex·ten·sile \ik-ˈsten(t)-səl, -ˈsten-ˌsīl\ *adj* : EXTENSIBLE

ex·ten·sion \ik-ˈsten-chən\ *n* [ME, fr. MF or LL; MF, fr. LL *extension-, extensio,* fr. L *extensus,* pp. of *extendere*] **1 a** : the action of extending : state of being extended **b** : an enlargement in scope or operation <tools are ~*s* of human hands> **2 a** : the total range over which something extends : COMPASS **b** : DENOTATION 2 **3 a** : the stretching of a fractured or luxated limb so as to restore it to its natural position **b** : the unbending of a joint between the bones of a limb by which the angle between the bones is increased — compare FLEXION **4** : a property whereby something occupies space **5 :** an increase in length of time; *specif* **:** an increase in time allowed under agreement or concession <was granted an ~> **6 :** a program that geographically extends the educational resources of an institution by special arrangements (as correspondence courses) to persons otherwise unable to take advantage of such resources **7 a :** a part constituting an addition **b :** a section forming an additional length **c :** an extra telephone connected to the principal line **8 :** a mathematical set (as a field or group) that includes a given and similar set as a subset

ex·ten·sion·al \ik-ˈstench-nəl, -ˈsten-chən-ᵊl\ *adj* **1 :** of, relating to, or marked by extension; *specif* **:** DENOTATIVE **2 :** concerned with objective reality — **ex·ten·sion·al·i·ty** \-ˌsten-chə-ˈnal-ət-ē\ *n* — **ex·ten·sion·al·ly** \-ˈstench-nə-lē, -ˈsten-chən-ᵊl-ē\ *adv*

extension cord *n* **:** CORD 3b

ex·ten·si·ty \ik-ˈsten(t)-sət-ē\ *n, pl* **-ties 1 a :** the quality of having extension **b :** degree of extension **:** RANGE **2 :** an attribute of sensation whereby space or size is perceived

ex·ten·sive \ik-ˈsten(t)-siv\ *adj* **1 :** EXTENSIONAL **2 :** having wide or considerable extent <~ reading> **3 :** of, relating to, or constituting farming in which large areas of land are utilized with minimum outlay and labor — **ex·ten·sive·ly** *adv* — **ex·ten·sive·ness** *n*

ex·ten·som·e·ter \ˌek-ˌsten-ˈsäm-ət-ər\ *n* [*extension* + *-o-* + *-meter*] **:** an instrument for measuring minute deformations of test specimens caused by tension, compression, bending, or twisting

ex·ten·sor \ik-ˈsten(t)-sər\ *n* **:** a muscle serving to extend a bodily part (as a limb)

ex·tent \ik-ˈstent\ *n* [ME, fr. AF & MF; AF *extente* land valuation, fr. MF, area, surveying of land, fr. *extendre* to extend] **1** *archaic* **:** valuation (as of land) in Great Britain esp. for taxation **2 a :** seizure (as of land) in execution of a writ of extent in Great Britain **:** the condition of being so seized **b :** a writ giving to a creditor temporary possession of his debtor's property **3 a :** the range over which something extends **:** SCOPE <the ~ of his authority> **b :** the point, degree, or limit to which something extends <using talents to the greatest ~> **c :** the amount of space or surface that something occupies or the distance over which it extends **:** MAGNITUDE <the ~ of the forest>

ex·ten·u·ate \ik-ˈsten-yə-ˌwāt\ *vt* **-at·ed; -at·ing** [L *extenuatus,* pp. of *extenuare,* fr. *ex-* + *tenuis* thin — more at THIN] **1 a** *archaic* **:** to make light of **b :** to lessen or to try to lessen the seriousness or extent of by making partial excuses **:** MITIGATE **c** *obs* **:** DISPARAGE **2 a** *archaic* **:** to make thin or emaciated **b :** to lessen the strength or effect of — **ex·ten·u·a·tor** \-ˌwāt-ər\ *n* — **ex·ten·u·a·to·ry** \-wə-ˌtōr-ē, -ˌtȯr-\ *adj*

ex·ten·u·a·tion \ik-ˌsten-yə-ˈwā-shən\ *n* **1 :** the act of extenuating or state of being extenuated; *esp* **:** partial justification **2 :** something extenuating; *esp* **:** a partial excuse

1**ex·te·ri·or** \ek-ˈstir-ē-ər\ *adj* [L, compar. of *exter, exterus* being on the outside, foreign, fr. *ex*] **1 :** being on an outside surface **:** situated on the outside **2 :** observable by outward signs <his ~ quietness is belied by an occasional nervous twitch —*Current Biog.*> **3 :** suitable for use on outside surfaces — **ex·te·ri·or·ly** *adv*

2**exterior** *n* **1 a :** an exterior part or surface **:** OUTSIDE **b :** outward manner or appearance **2 :** a representation of an outdoor scene

exterior angle *n* **1 :** the angle between a side of a polygon and an extended adjacent side **2 :** an angle between a line crossing two parallel lines and either of the latter on the outside

ex·te·ri·or·i·ty \(ˌ)ek-ˌstir-ē-ˈȯr-ət-ē, -ˈär-\ *n* **:** the quality or state of being exterior or exteriorized **:** EXTERNALITY

ex·te·ri·or·ize \ek-ˈstir-ē-ə-ˌrīz\ *vt* **-ized; -iz·ing 1 :** EXTERNALIZE **2 :** to bring out of the abdomen (as for surgery) — **ex·te·ri·or·iza·tion** \-ˌstir-ē-ə-rə-ˈzā-shən\ *n*

ex·ter·mi·nate \ik-ˈstər-mə-ˌnāt\ *vt* **-nat·ed; -nat·ing** [L *exterminatus,* pp. of *exterminare,* fr. *ex-* + *terminus* boundary — more at TERM] **:** to get rid of completely usu. by killing off <~ crabgrass from a lawn> — **ex·ter·mi·na·tion** \-ˌstər-mə-ˈnā-shən\ *n* — **ex·ter·mi·na·tor** \-ˈstər-mə-ˌnāt-ər\ *n*

syn EXTERMINATE, EXTIRPATE, ERADICATE, UPROOT *shared meaning element* **:** to effect the destruction or abolition of

ex·ter·mi·na·to·ry \ik-ˈstərm-(ə-)nə-ˌtōr-ē, -ˌtȯr-\ *adj* **:** of, relating to, or marked by extermination

ex·ter·mine \ik-ˈstər-mən\ *vt* **-mined; -min·ing** *obs* **:** EXTERMINATE

1**ex·tern** \ek-ˈstərn, ˈek-ˌ\ *adj* [MF or L; MF *externe,* fr. L *externus*] *archaic* **:** EXTERNAL

2**ex·tern** *also* **ex·terne** \ˈek-ˌstərn\ *n* **:** a person connected with an institution but not living or boarding in it; *specif* **:** a nonresident doctor or medical student at a hospital — **ex·tern·ship** \-ˌship\ *n*

1**ex·ter·nal** \ek-ˈstərn-ᵊl\ *adj* [ME, fr L *externus* external, fr. *exter*] **1 a :** capable of being perceived outwardly <~ signs of a disease> <~ reality> **b (1) :** having merely the outward appearance of something **:** SUPERFICIAL **(2) :** not intrinsic or essential <~ circumstances> **2 a :** of, relating to, or connected with the outside or an outer part **b :** applied or applicable to the outside **3 a (1) :** situated outside, apart, or beyond; *specif* **:** situated away from the mesial plane **(2) :** arising or acting from outside <~ force> **b :** of or relating to dealings or relationships with foreign countries **c :** having existence independent of the mind <~ reality> — **ex·ter·nal·ly** \-ᵊl-ē\ *adv*

2**external** *n* **:** something that is external: as **a** *archaic* **:** an outer part **b :** an external feature or aspect — usu. used in pl. <the ~*s* of religion>

external–combustion engine *n* **:** a heat engine (as a steam engine) that derives its heat from fuel consumed outside the engine cylinder

ex·ter·nal·ism \ek-ˈstərn-ᵊl-ˌiz-əm\ *n* **1 :** EXTERNALITY 1 **2 :** attention to externals; *esp*: excessive preoccupation with externals

ex·ter·nal·i·ty \ˌek-ˌstər-ˈnal-ət-ē\ *n, pl* **-ties 1 :** the quality or state of being external or externalized **2 :** something that is external

ex·ter·nal·iza·tion \ek-ˌstərn-ᵊl-ə-ˈzā-shən\ *n* **1 a :** the action or process of externalizing **b :** the quality or state of being externalized **2 :** something externalized **:** EMBODIMENT

ex·ter·nal·ize \ek-ˈstərn-ᵊl-ˌīz\ *vt* **-ized; iz·ing 1 :** to make external or externally manifest **:** EMBODY **2 :** to attribute to causes outside the self **:** RATIONALIZE <~ his failure>

external respiration *n* **:** exchange of gases between the external environment and a distributing system of the animal body (as the lungs of higher vertebrates or the tracheal tubes of insects) or between the alveoli of the lungs and the blood

ex·tero·cep·tive \ˌek-stə-rō-ˈsep-tiv\ *adj* [L *exter* + E *-o-* + *-ceptive* (as in *receptive*)] **:** activated by, relating to, or being stimuli received by an organism from outside

ex·tero·cep·tor \-tər\ *n* [NL, fr. L *exter* + NL *-o-* + *-ceptor* (as in *receptor*)] **:** a sense organ excited by exteroceptive stimuli

ex·ter·ri·to·ri·al \ˌek-ˌster-ə-ˈtōr-ē-əl, -ˈtȯr-\ *adj* **:** EXTRATERRITORIAL — **ex·ter·ri·to·ri·al·i·ty** \-ˌtōr-ē-ˈal-ət-ē, -ˌtȯr-\ *n*

extg *abbr* extracting

1**ex·tinct** \ik-ˈstiŋ(k)t, ˈek-ˌ\ *adj* [ME, fr. L *exstinctus,* pp. of *exstinguere*] **1 a :** no longer burning **b :** no longer active <an ~ volcano> **2 :** no longer existing <an ~ animal> **3 a :** gone out of use **:** SUPERSEDED **b :** having no qualified claimant <an ~ title>

2**extinct** *vt, archaic* **:** EXTINGUISH

ex·tinc·tion \ik-ˈstiŋ(k)-shən\ *n* **1 :** the act of making extinct or causing to be extinguished **2 :** the condition or fact of being extinct or extinguished **3 :** the process of eliminating or reducing a conditioned response by not reinforcing it

ex·tinc·tive \ik-ˈstiŋ(k)-tiv\ *adj* **:** tending or serving to extinguish or make extinct

ex·tin·guish \ik-ˈstiŋ-(g)wish\ *vt* [L *exstinguere* (fr. *ex-* + *stinguere* to extinguish) + E *-ish* (as in *abolish*); akin to L in*stigare* to incite — more at STICK] **1 a :** to cause to cease burning **:** QUENCH **b (1) :** to bring to an end **:** make an end of <hope for their safety was slowly ~*ed*> **(2) :** to reduce to silence or ineffectiveness **c :** to cause extinction of (a conditioned response) **d :** to dim the brightness of **:** ECLIPSE **2 a :** to cause to be void **:** NULLIFY <~ a claim> **b :** to get rid of usu. by payment <~ a debt> ***syn* 1** see CRUSH ***ant*** inflame **2** see ABOLISH — **ex·tin·guish·able** \-ə-bəl\ *adj* — **ex·tin·guish·er** \-ər\ *n* — **ex·tin·guish·ment** \-mənt\ *n*

ex·tir·pate \ˈek-stər-ˌpāt\ *vt* **-pat·ed; -pat·ing** [L *exstirpatus,* pp. *exstirpare,* fr. *ex-* + *stirp-, stirps* trunk, root — more at TORPID] **1 a :** to pull up by the root **b :** to destroy completely **:** wipe out **2 :** to cut out by surgery ***syn*** see EXTERMINATE — **ex·tir·pa·tion** \ˌek-stər-ˈpā-shən\ *n* — **ex·tir·pa·tive** \ˈek-stər-ˌpāt-iv, ek-ˈstər-pət-\ *adj* — **ex·tir·pa·tor** \ˈek-stər-ˌpāt-ər\ *n*

ex·tol *also* **ex·toll** \ik-ˈstōl\ *vt* **ex·tolled; ex·tol·ling** [ME *extollen,* fr. L *extollere,* fr. *ex-* + *tollere* to lift up — more at TOLERATE] **:** to praise highly **:** GLORIFY — **ex·tol·ler** *n* — **ex·tol·ment** \-ˈstōl-mənt\ *n*

ex·tor·sion \ek-ˈstȯr-shən, ˈek-ˌ\ *n* **:** outward rotation (as of a body part) about an axis or fixed point

ex·tort \ik-ˈstȯ(ə)rt\ *vt* [L *extortus,* pp. of *extorquēre* to wrench out, extort, fr. *ex-* + *torquēre* to twist — more at TORTURE] **:** to obtain from a person by force or undue or illegal power or ingenuity **:** WRING ***syn*** see EDUCE — **ex·tort·er** *n* — **ex·tor·tive** \-ˈstȯrt-iv\ *adj*

ex·tor·tion \ik-ˈstȯr-shən\ *n* **1 :** the act or practice of extorting esp. money or other property; *specif* **:** the offense committed by an official engaging in such practice **2 :** something extorted; *esp* **:** a gross overcharge — **ex·tor·tion·er** \-sh(ə-)nər\ *n* — **ex·tor·tion·ist** \-sh(ə-)nəst\ *n*

ex·tor·tion·ary \-shə-ˌner-ē\ *adj, archaic* **:** EXTORTIONATE 1

ex·tor·tion·ate \ik-ˈstȯr-sh(ə-)nət\ *adj* **1 :** characterized by extortion **2 :** EXCESSIVE, EXORBITANT — **ex·tor·tion·ate·ly** *adv*

1**ex·tra** \ˈek-strə\ *adj* [prob. short for *extraordinary*] **1 a :** more than is due, usual, or necessary **:** ADDITIONAL <~ work> **b :** subject to an additional charge <room service is ~> **2 :** SUPERIOR <~ quality>

2**extra** *n* **1 :** something extra or additional: as **a :** an added charge **b :** a special edition of a newspaper **c :** an additional worker; *specif* **:** one hired to act in a group scene in a motion picture or stage production **2 :** something of superior quality or grade

3**extra** *adv* **:** beyond the usual size, extent, or degree <~ large>

extra- *prefix* [ME, fr. L, fr. *extra,* adv. & prep., outside, except, beyond, fr. *exter* being on the outside — more at EXTERIOR] **:** outside **:** beyond <*extra*judicial>

extra–base hit *n* **:** a hit in baseball good for more than one base

ex·tra·cel·lu·lar \ˌek-strə-ˈsel-yə-lər\ *adj* **:** situated or occurring outside a cell or the cells of the body <~ digestion> <~ enzymes> — **ex·tra·cel·lu·lar·ly** *adv*

ex·tra·chro·mo·som·al \-ˌkrō-mə-ˈsō-məl, -ˈzō-\ *adj* **:** situated or controlled by factors outside the chromosome <~ inheritance>

ex·tra·cor·po·re·al \-kȯr-ˈpōr-ē-əl, -ˈpȯr-\ *adj* **:** occurring or based outside the living body <heart surgery employing ~ circulation> — **ex·tra·cor·po·re·al·ly** \-ē-ə-lē\ *adv*

ex·tra·cra·ni·al \-ˈkrā-nē-əl\ *adj* **:** situated or occurring outside the cranium

1**ex·tract** \ik-ˈstrakt, *oftenest in sense* 5 ˈek-ˌ\ *vt* [ME *extracten,* fr. L *extractus,* pp. of *extrahere,* fr. *ex-* + *trahere* to draw — more at DRAW] **1 a :** to draw forth (as by research) <~ data> **b :** to pull or take out forcibly <~*ed* a wisdom tooth> **c :** to obtain by much effort from someone unwilling <~*ed* a confession> **2 :** to withdraw (as a juice or fraction) by physical or chemical process; *also* **:** to treat with a solvent so as to remove a soluble substance **3 :** to separate (a metal) from an ore **4 :** to determine (a mathematical root) by calculation **5 :** to select (excerpts) and copy out or cite ***syn*** see EDUCE — **ex·tract·abil·i·ty** \ik-ˌstrak-tə-ˈbil-ət-ē, (ˌ)ek-\ *n* — **ex·tract·able** *or* **ex·tract·ible** \ik-ˈstrak-tə-bəl, ˈek-ˌ\ *adj* — **ex·trac·tor** \ik-ˈstrak-tər, ˈek-ˌ\ *n*

2**ex·tract** \ˈek-ˌstrakt\ *n* **1 :** a selection from a writing or discourse **:** EXCERPT **2 :** a product (as an essence or concentrate) prepared by extracting; *esp* **:** a solution (as in alcohol) of essential constituents of a complex material (as meat or an aromatic plant) <beef ~> <lemon ~>

ex·trac·tion \ik-ˈstrak-shən\ *n* **1 :** the act or process of extracting **2 :** ORIGIN, LINEAGE **3 :** something extracted

¹ex·trac·tive \ik-ˈstrak-tiv, ˈek-ˌ\ *adj* **1 a :** of, relating to, or involving extraction <~ processes> **b :** tending toward or resulting in withdrawal of natural resources by extraction with no provision for replenishment <~ agriculture> **2 :** capable of being extracted — **ex·trac·tive·ly** *adv*

²extractive *n* **:** something extracted or extractable **:** EXTRACT

ex·tra·cur·ric·u·lar \ˌek-strə-kə-ˈrik-yə-lər\ *adj* **1 :** not falling within the scope of a regular curriculum; *specif* **:** of or relating to officially or semiofficially approved and usu. organized student activities (as athletics) connected with school and usu. carrying no academic credit **2 :** lying outside one's regular duties or routine <worked extra hours on ~ tasks>

ex·tra·dit·able \ˈek-strə-ˌdīt-ə-bəl\ *adj* **1 :** subject or liable to extradition **2 :** making liable to extradition <an ~ offense>

ex·tra·dite \ˈek-strə-ˌdīt\ *vt* **-dit·ed; -dit·ing** [back-formation fr. *extradition*] **1 :** to deliver up to extradition **2 :** to obtain the extradition of

ex·tra·di·tion \ˌek-strə-ˈdish-ən\ *n* [F, fr. *ex-* + L *tradition-, traditio* act of handing over — more at TRADITION] **:** the surrender of an alleged criminal usu. under the provisions of a treaty or statute by one state or other authority to another having jurisdiction to try the charge

ex·tra·dos \ˈek-strə-ˌdäs, -ˌdō; ek-ˈstrā-ˌdäs\ *n, pl* **ex·tra·dos** \-ˌdōz, -däs\ *or* **ex·tra·dos·es** \-ˌdäs-əz\ [F, fr. L *extra* + F *dos* back — more at DOSSIER] **:** the exterior curve of an arch

1 extrados

ex·tra·ga·lac·tic \ˌek-strə-gə-ˈlak-tik\ *adj* [ISV] **:** lying or coming from outside the Milky Way

ex·tra·he·pat·ic \-hi-ˈpat-ik\ *adj* **:** situated or originating outside the liver

ex·tra·ju·di·cial \-jü-ˈdish-əl\ *adj* **1 a :** not forming a valid part of regular legal proceedings <an ~ investigation> **b :** delivered without legal authority **:** PRIVATE 2a(2) <the judge's ~ statements> **2 :** done in contravention of due process of law <an ~ execution> — **ex·tra·ju·di·cial·ly** \-ˈdish-(ə-)lē\ *adv*

ex·tra·le·gal \ˌek-strə-ˈlē-gəl\ *adj* **:** not regulated or sanctioned by law — **ex·tra·le·gal·ly** \-gə-lē\ *adv*

ex·tra·lim·it·al \-ˈlim-ət-ᵊl\ *adj* **:** not present in a given area — used of kinds of organisms (as species)

ex·tra·lin·guis·tic \-liŋ-ˈgwis-tik\ *adj* **:** lying outside the province of linguistics — **ex·tra·lin·guis·ti·cal·ly** \-ti-k(ə-)lē\ *adv*

ex·tral·i·ty \ek-ˈstral-ət-ē\ *n* [by contr.] **:** EXTRATERRITORIALITY

ex·tra·mar·i·tal \ˌek-strə-ˈmar-ət-ᵊl\ *adj* **:** of or relating to a married person's sexual intercourse with other than his or her spouse **:** ADULTEROUS

ex·tra·mun·dane \ˌek-strə-ˌmən-ˈdān, -ˈmən-ˌ\ *adj* [LL *extramundanus*, fr. L *extra* + *mundus* the world] **:** situated in or relating to a region beyond the material world

ex·tra·mu·ral \-ˈmyu̇r-əl\ *adj* **1 :** existing or functioning outside or beyond the walls, boundaries, or precincts of an organized unit <~ medical care provided by hospital personnel> **2** *chiefly Brit* **:** of, relating to, or taking part in extension courses or facilities — **ex·tra·mu·ral·ly** \-ə-lē\ *adv*

ex·tra·mu·si·cal \-ˈmyü-zi-kəl\ *adj* **:** lying outside the province of music

ex·tra·ne·ous \ek-ˈstrā-nē-əs\ *adj* [L *extraneus* — more at STRANGE] **1 :** existing on or coming from the outside **2 a :** not forming an essential or vital part <an ~ scene that added nothing to the play> **b :** having no relevance <~ points that do not serve his argument> **3 :** being a number obtained in solving an equation that is not a solution of the equation <~ roots> ***syn*** see EXTRINSIC ***ant*** relevant — **ex·tra·ne·ous·ly** *adv* — **ex·tra·ne·ous·ness** *n*

ex·tra·nu·cle·ar \ˌek-strə-ˈn(y)ü-klē-ər\ *adj* **1 :** situated in or affecting the parts of a cell external to the nucleus **:** CYTOPLASMIC **2 :** situated outside the nucleus of an atom

extraocular muscle \ˌek-strə-ˈäk-yə-lər-\ *n* **:** any of six small voluntary muscles that pass between the eyeball and the orbit and control the movement of the eyeball in relation to the orbit

ex·traor·di·nary \ik-ˈstrȯrd-ᵊn-ˌer-ē, ˌek-strə-ˈȯrd-\ *adj* [ME *extraordinarie*, fr. L *extraordinarius*, fr. *extra ordinem* out of course, fr. *extra* + *ordinem*, acc. of *ordin-, ordo* order] **1 a :** going beyond what is usual, regular, or customary <~ powers> **b :** exceptional to a very marked extent **:** REMARKABLE <~ beauty> **2 :** employed for or sent on a special function or service <an ambassador ~> — **ex·traor·di·nari·ly** \ik-ˌstrȯrd-ᵊn-ˈer-ə-lē, ˌek-strə-ˌȯrd-\ *adv* — **ex·traor·di·nari·ness** \ik-ˈstrȯrd-ᵊn-ˌer-ē-nəs, ˌek-strə-ˈȯrd-\ *n*

extra point *n* **:** a point gained on a conversion in football

ex·trap·o·late \ik-ˈstrap-ə-ˌlāt\ *vb* **-lat·ed; -lat·ing** [L *extra* outside + E *-polate* (as in *interpolate*) — more at EXTRA-] *vt* **1 :** to infer (values of a variable in an unobserved interval) from values within an already observed interval **2 a :** to project, extend, or expand (known data or experience) into an area not known or experienced so as to arrive at a usu. conjectural knowledge of the unknown area <~s present trends to construct an image of the future> **b :** to predict by projecting past experience or known data <~ public sentiment on one issue from known public reaction on others> ~ *vi* **:** to perform the act or process of extrapolating — **ex·trap·o·la·tion** \-ˌstrap-ə-ˈlā-shən\ *n* — **ex·trap·o·la·tive** \-ˈstrap-ə-ˌlāt-iv\ *adj* — **ex·trap·o·la·tor** \-ˌlāt-ər\ *n*

ex·tra·sen·so·ry \ˌek-strə-ˈsen(t)s-(ə-)rē\ *adj* **:** residing beyond or outside the ordinary senses <instances of ~ perception>

ex·tra·sys·to·le \-ˈsis-tə-(ˌ)lē\ *n* [NL] **:** a premature beat of one of the chambers of the heart that leads to momentary arrhythmia — **ex·tra·sys·tol·ic** \-sis-ˈtäl-ik\ *adj*

¹ex·tra·ter·res·tri·al \-tə-ˈres-trē-əl, -ˈres(h)-chəl\ *adj* **:** originating or existing outside the earth or its atmosphere <~ life>; *also* **:** of or relating to extraterrestrial space <~ exploration>

²extraterrestrial *n* **:** an extraterrestrial being

ex·tra·ter·ri·to·ri·al \-ˌter-ə-ˈtōr-ē-əl, -ˈtȯr-\ *adj* **:** existing or taking place outside the territorial limits of a jurisdiction

ex·tra·ter·ri·to·ri·al·i·ty \-ˌtōr-ē-ˈal-ət-ē, -ˌtȯr-\ *n* **:** exemption from the application or jurisdiction of local law or tribunals

ex·tra·trop·i·cal cyclone \ˌek-strə-ˌträp-i-kəl-\ *n* **:** a cyclone in the middle latitudes often being 1500 miles in diameter and usu. containing a cold front that extends toward the equator for hundreds of miles

ex·tra·uter·ine \ˌek-strə-ˈyüt-ə-rən, -ˌrīn\ *adj* [ISV] **:** situated or occurring outside the uterus <~ pregnancy>

ex·trav·a·gance \ik-ˈstrav-i-gən(t)s\ *n* **1 a :** an instance of excess or prodigality; *specif* **:** an excessive outlay of money **b :** something extravagant **2 :** the quality or fact of being extravagant

ex·trav·a·gan·cy \-gən-sē\ *n, pl* **-cies :** EXTRAVAGANCE

ex·trav·a·gant \ik-ˈstrav-i-gənt\ *adj* [ME, fr. MF, fr. ML *extravagant-, extravagans*, fr. L *extra-* + *vagant-, vagans*, prp. of *vagari* to wander about — more at VAGARY] **1 a** *archaic* **:** WANDERING **b** *obs* **:** STRANGE, CURIOUS **2 a :** exceeding the limits of reason or necessity <~ claims> **b :** lacking in moderation, balance, and restraint <~ praise> **c :** extremely or excessively elaborate **3 a :** spending much more than necessary **b :** PROFUSE **4 :** unreasonably high in price ***syn*** see EXCESSIVE ***ant*** restrained — **ex·trav·a·gant·ly** *adv*

ex·trav·a·gan·za \ik-ˌstrav-ə-ˈgan-zə\ *n* [It *estravaganza*, lit., extravagance, fr. *estravagante* extravagant, fr. ML *extravagant-, extravagans*] **1 :** a literary or musical work marked by extreme freedom of style and structure and usu. by elements of burlesque or parody **2 :** a lavish or spectacular show or event

ex·trav·a·gate \ik-ˈstrav-ə-ˌgāt\ *vi* **-gat·ed; -gat·ing** *archaic* **:** to go beyond proper limits

¹ex·trav·a·sate \ik-ˈstrav-ə-ˌsāt, -ˌzāt\ *vb* **-sat·ed; -sat·ing** [L *extra* + *vas* vessel — more at VASE] *vt* **:** to force out or cause to escape from a proper vessel or channel ~ *vi* **1 :** to pass by infiltration or effusion from a proper vessel or channel (as a blood vessel) into surrounding tissue **2 :** to erupt in liquid form from a vent — **ex·trav·a·sa·tion** \-ˌstrav-ə-ˈsā-shən, -ˈzā-\ *n*

²extravasate *n* **:** an extravasated fluid (as blood)

ex·tra·vas·cu·lar \ˌek-strə-ˈvas-kyə-lər\ *adj* **:** destitute of or not contained in body vessels <~ plant fibers> <~ tissue fluids>

ex·tra·ve·hic·u·lar \-vē-ˈhik-yə-lər\ *adj* **:** taking place outside a vehicle (as a spacecraft) <~ activity>

ex·tra·ver·sion *or* **ex·tro·ver·sion** \ˌek-strə-ˈvər-zhən, -shən\ *n* [G, fr. *extra-* or *extro-* + L *versus*, pp. of *vertere* to turn] **:** the act, state, or habit of directing attention toward and obtaining gratification from what is outside the self — **ex·tra·ver·sive** \-siv, -ziv\ *adj*

¹ex·tra·vert *or* **ex·tro·vert** \ˈek-strə-ˌvərt\ *adj* [modif. of G *extravertiert, extrovertiert*, fr. *extra-* or *extro-* + L *vertere*] **:** EXTRAVERTED

²extravert *or* **extrovert** *n* **:** one whose attention and interests are directed wholly or predominantly toward what is outside the self

ex·tra·vert·ed *or* **ex·tro·vert·ed** \-ˌvərt-əd\ *adj* **:** marked by extraversion

¹ex·treme \ik-ˈstrēm\ *adj* [ME, fr. MF, fr. L *extremus*, superl. of *exter, exterus* being on the outside — more at EXTERIOR] **1 a :** existing in a very high degree <~ poverty> **b :** going to great or exaggerated lengths <went on an ~ diet> **c :** exceeding the ordinary, usual, or expected **2** *archaic* **:** LAST **3 :** situated at the farthest possible point from a center <the country's ~ north> **4 a :** most advanced or thoroughgoing <the ~ political left> **b :** MAXIMUM ***syn*** see EXCESSIVE — **ex·treme·ness** *n*

²extreme *n* **1 a :** something situated at or marking one end or the other of a range <~s of heat and cold> **b :** the first term or the last term of a mathematical proportion **c :** the major term or minor term of a syllogism **2 a :** a very pronounced or excessive degree <his enthusiasm was carried to an ~> **b :** highest degree **:** MAXIMUM **3 :** an extreme measure or expedient <going to ~s> — **in the extreme :** to the greatest possible extent <find the task wearisome *in the extreme* —L. R. McColvin>

ex·treme·ly *adv* **1 :** in an extreme manner **2 :** to an extreme extent

extremely high frequency *n* **:** a radio frequency in the highest range of the radio spectrum — see RADIO FREQUENCY table

extremely low frequency *n* **:** a radio frequency in the lowest range of the radio spectrum — see RADIO FREQUENCY table

extreme unction \ik-ˌstrē-ˈməŋ(k)-shən, ˌek-(ˌ)strē-\ *n* **:** a sacrament in which a priest anoints a critically ill or injured person and prays for his recovery and salvation

ex·trem·ism \ik-ˈstrē-ˌmiz-əm\ *n* **:** the quality or state of being extreme; *esp* **:** advocacy of extreme political measures **:** RADICALISM — **ex·trem·ist** \-məst\ *n or adj*

ex·trem·i·ty \ik-ˈstrem-ət-ē\ *n, pl* **-ties 1 a :** the farthest or most remote part, section, or point **b :** a limb of the body; *esp* **:** a human hand or foot **2 a :** extreme danger or critical need **b :** a moment marked by imminent destruction or death **3 a :** an intense degree <the ~ of his participation — *Saturday Rev.*> **b :** the utmost degree (as of emotion or pain) **4 :** a drastic or desperate act or measure <driven to *extremities*>

ex·tre·mum \ik-ˈstrē-məm\ *n, pl* **-ma** \-mə\ [NL, fr. L, neut. of *extremus*] **:** a maximum or a minimum of a mathematical function

ex·tri·cate \ˈek-strə-ˌkāt\ *vt* **-cat·ed; -cat·ing** [L *extricatus*, pp. of *extricare*, fr. *ex-* + *tricae* trifles, perplexities] **1 a** *archaic* **:** UNRAVEL **b :** to distinguish from a related thing **2 :** to free or

ə abut	ᵊ kitten	ər further	a back	ā bake	ä cot, cart	
au̇ out	ch chin	e less	ē easy	g gift	i trip	ī life
j joke	ŋ sing	ō flow	ȯ flaw	ȯi coin	th thin	t͟h this
ü loot	u̇ foot	y yet	yü few	yu̇ furious	zh vision	

remove from an entanglement or difficulty — **ex·tri·ca·ble** \ik-'strik-ə-bəl, ek-'; 'ek-(,)\ *adj* — **ex·tri·ca·tion** \,ek-strə-'kā-shən\ *n*
syn EXTRICATE, DISENTANGLE, UNTANGLE, DISENCUMBER, DISEMBARRASS *shared meaning element* : to free from what binds or holds back

ex·trin·sic \ek-'strin-zik, -'strin(t)-sik\ *adj* [F & LL; F *extrinsèque,* fr. LL *extrinsecus,* fr. L, adv., from without; akin to L *exter* outward and to L *sequi* to follow — more at EXTERIOR, SUE] **1 a** : not forming part of or belonging to a thing : EXTRANEOUS **b** : originating from or on the outside; *esp* : originating outside a part and acting upon the part as a whole **2** : EXTERNAL — **ex·trin·si·cal·ly** \-zi-k(ə-)lē, -si-\ *adv*
syn EXTRINSIC, EXTRANEOUS, FOREIGN, ALIEN *shared meaning element* : external to a thing, its essential nature, or original character *ant* intrinsic

extrinsic factor *n* : VITAMIN B_{12}

extro- *prefix* [alter. of L *extra-*] : outward <*extro*vert> — compare INTRO-

ex·trorse \'ek-,strȯ(ə)rs\ *adj* [prob. fr. (assumed) NL *extrorsus,* fr. LL, adv., outward, fr. L *extra-* + *-orsus* (as in *introrsus*) — more at INTRORSE] : turned away from the axis of growth <an ~ anther> — **ex·trorse·ly** *adv*

extroversion, extrovert *var of* EXTRAVERSION, EXTRAVERT

ex·trude \ik-'strüd\ *vb* **ex·trud·ed; ex·trud·ing** [L *extrudere,* fr. *ex-* + *trudere* to thrust] *vt* **1** : to force, press, or push out **2** : to shape (as metal or plastic) by forcing through a die ~ *vi* : to become extruded — **ex·trud·abil·i·ty** \-,strüd-ə-'bil-ət-ē\ *n* — **ex·trud·able** \-'strüd-ə-bəl\ *adj* — **ex·trud·er** \-'strüd-ər\ *n*

ex·tru·sion \ik-'strü-zhən\ *n* [ML *extrusion-, extrusio,* fr. L *extrusus,* pp. of *extrudere*] : the act or process of extruding; *also* : a form or product produced by this process

ex·tru·sive \ik-'strü-siv, -ziv\ *adj* : formed by crystallization of lava poured out at the earth's surface <~ rock>

ex·u·ber·ance \ig-'zü-b(ə-)rən(t)s\ *n* **1** : the quality or state of being exuberant **2** : an exuberant act or expression

ex·u·ber·ant \-b(ə-)rənt\ *adj* [ME, fr. MF, fr. L *exuberant-, exuberans,* prp. of *exuberare* to be abundant, fr. *ex-* + *uber* fruitful, fr. *uber* udder — more at UDDER] **1 a** : joyously unrestrained and enthusiastic **b** : lacking compactness and discipline : flamboyantly overdone <writing spoiled by ~ overdrawn metaphors> **2** : extreme or excessive in degree, size, or extent **3** : produced in extreme abundance : PLENTIFUL *syn* see PROFUSE *ant* austere, sterile — **ex·u·ber·ant·ly** *adv*

ex·u·ber·ate \-bə-,rāt\ *vi* **-at·ed; -at·ing** **1** *archaic* : to have something in abundance : OVERFLOW **2** : to become exuberant : show exuberance <*exuberated* over his victory>

ex·u·date \'ek-s(y)ü-,dāt, -shü-\ *n* : exuded matter

ex·u·da·tion \,ek-s(y)ü-'dā-shən, -shü-\ *n* **1** : the process of exuding **2** : EXUDATE — **ex·u·da·tive** \ig-'züd-ət-iv; 'ek-s(y)ü-,dāt-iv, -shü-\ *adj*

ex·ude \ig-'züd\ *vb* **ex·ud·ed; ex·ud·ing** [L *exsudare,* fr. *ex-* + *sudare* to sweat — more at SWEAT] *vi* **1** : to ooze out **2** : to undergo diffusion ~ *vt* **1** : to cause to ooze or spread out in all directions **2** : to display conspicuously or abundantly <~*s* charm>

ex·ult \ig-'zəlt\ *vi* [MF *exulter,* fr. L *exsultare,* lit., to leap up, fr. *ex-* + *saltare* to leap — more at SALTATION] **1** *obs* : to leap for joy **2** : to be extremely joyful : REJOICE — **ex·ult·ing·ly** \-'zəl-tiŋ-lē\ *adv*

ex·ul·tance \ig-'zəlt-ᵊn(t)s\ *n* : EXULTATION

ex·ul·tan·cy \-'zəlt-ᵊn-sē\ *n* : EXULTATION

ex·ul·tant \ig-'zəlt-ᵊnt\ *adj* : filled with or expressing great joy or triumph : JUBILANT — **ex·ul·tant·ly** *adv*

ex·ul·ta·tion \,ek-(,)səl-'tā-shən, ,eg-(,)zəl-\ *n* : the act of exulting : the state of being exultant

ex·urb \'ek-,sərb, 'eg-,zərb\ *n* [*ex-* + *-urb* (as in *suburb*)] : a region or district that lies outside a city and usu. beyond its suburbs and that is inhabited chiefly by well-to-do families — **ex·ur·ban** \ek-'sər-bən; eg-'zər-, ig-\ *adj*

ex·ur·ban·ite \ek-'sər-bə-,nīt; eg-'zər-, ig-\ *n* : one who lives in an exurb

ex·ur·bia \-bē-ə\ *n* : the generalized region of exurbs

ex·u·vi·ae \ig-'zü-vē-,ē, -vē-,ī\ *n pl* [L, fr. *exuere* to take off, fr. *ex-* + *-uere* to put on; akin to ORuss *izuti* to take off footwear] : the natural coverings of animals (as the skins of snakes) after they have been sloughed off — **ex·u·vi·al** \-vē-əl\ *adj*

ex·u·vi·a·tion \-,zü-vē-'ā-shən\ *n* : the process of molting

¹ex-vo·to \(')eks-'vōt-(,)ō\ *n, pl* **ex-votos** [L *ex voto* according to a vow] : a votive offering

²ex-voto *adj* : VOTIVE

-ey — see -Y

ey·as \'ī-əs\ *n* [ME, alter. (by incorrect division of *a neias*) of *neias,* fr. MF *niais* fresh from the nest, fr. (assumed) VL *nidax* nestling, fr. L *nidus* nest — more at NEST] : an unfledged bird; *specif* : a nestling hawk

¹eye \'ī\ *n* [ME, fr. OE *ēage;* akin to OHG *ouga* eye, L *oculus,* Gk *ōps* eye, face] **1 a** : an organ of sight; *esp* : a nearly spherical hollow organ that is lined with a sensitive retina, is lodged in a bony orbit in the skull, is the vertebrate organ of sight, and is normally paired **b** : all the visible structures within and surrounding the orbit and including eyelids, eyelashes, and eyebrows **c** (1) : the faculty of seeing with eyes (2) : the faculty of intellectual or aesthetic perception or appreciation <an ~ for beauty> **d** : LOOK, GLANCE <caught his ~> **e** : an attentive look <kept an ~ on his valuables> **f** : POINT OF VIEW, JUDGMENT <beauty is in the ~ of the beholder> — often used in pl. <an offender in the ~*s* of the law> **2** : something having an appearance suggestive of an eye: as **a** : the hole through the head of a needle **b** : a usu. circular marking (as on a peacock's tail) **c** : LOOP; *esp* : a loop or other catch to receive a hook **d** : an undeveloped bud (as on a potato) **e** : an area like a hole in the center of a tropical cyclone marked by only light winds or complete calm with no precipitation **f** : the center of a flower esp. when differently colored or marked; *specif* : the disk of a composite **g** (1) : a triangular piece of beef cut from between the top and bottom of a round (2) : the chief muscle of a chop (3) : a compact mass of muscular tissue usu. embedded in fat in a rib or loin cut of meat **h** : a device (as a photoelectric cell) that functions in a manner analogous to human vision **3** : something central : CENTER <the ~ of the problem —Norman Mailer> **4** : the direction from which the wind is blowing — **eye·less** \'ī-ləs\ *adj* — **eye·like** \-,līk\ *adj* — **my eye** — used to express mild disagreement or sometimes surprise <a diamond, *my eye!* That's glass> — **with an eye to** : with a view to

1 2 3 4 5 6 7 8 9 10 11 12 13 14 15

eye 1a: *1* optic nerve, *2* blind spot, *3* fovea, *4* sclera, *5* choroid, *6* retina, *7* ciliary body, *8* posterior chamber, *9* anterior chamber, *10* cornea, *11* lens, *12* iris, *13* suspensory ligament, *14* conjunctiva, *15* vitreous humor

²eye *vb* **eyed; eye·ing** *or* **ey·ing** *vt* **1 a** : to fix the eyes on **b** : to watch sharply **2** : to furnish with an eye ~ *vi, obs* : SEEM, LOOK — **ey·er** \'ī(-ə)r\ *n*

¹eye·ball \'ī-,bȯl\ *n* : the more or less globular capsule of the vertebrate eye formed by the sclera and cornea together with their contained structures

²eyeball *vt* : to look at intently

eyeball–to–eyeball *adj* : FACE-TO-FACE

eye bank *n* : a storage place for human corneas from the newly dead for transplanting to the eyes of those blind through corneal defects

eye·bolt \'ī-'bōlt\ *n* : a bolt with a looped head

eye·bright \'ī-,brīt\ *n* : any of several herbs (genus *Euphrasia*) of the figwort family with opposite toothed or cut leaves

eye·brow \'ī-,brau̇\ *n* : the ridge over the eye or hair growing on it

eyebrow pencil *n* : a cosmetic pencil for the eyebrows

eye–catch·er \'ī-,kach-ər, -,kech-\ *n* : something strongly attracting the eye — **eye–catch·ing** \-iŋ\ *adj*

eye·cup \'ī-,kəp\ *n* : a small oval cup with a rim curved to fit the orbit of the eye used for applying liquid remedies to the eyes

eyed \'īd\ *adj* : having an eye or eyes esp. of a specified kind or number — often used in combination <an almond-*eyed* girl>

eye dialect *n* : the use of pronunciation-based spellings (as *sez* for *says*) in the representation of speech esp. to convey an impression of illiteracy

eyed·ness \'īd-nəs\ *n* [*-eyed* (as in *right-eyed, left-eyed*)] : preference (as in using a monocular microscope) for the use of one eye instead of the other

eye·drop·per \'ī-,dräp-ər\ *n* : DROPPER 2 — **eye·drop·per·ful** \-,fu̇l\ *n*

eye·ful \'ī-,fu̇l\ *n* **1** : a full or completely satisfying view **2** : one that is visually attractive; *esp* : a strikingly beautiful woman

eye·glass \'ī-,glas\ *n* **1 a** : EYEPIECE **b** : a lens worn to aid vision; *specif* : MONOCLE **c** *pl* : GLASSES, SPECTACLES **2** : EYECUP

eye·hole \'ī-,hōl\ *n* **1** : ORBIT 1 **2** : PEEPHOLE

eye·lash \'ī-,lash\ *n* : the fringe of hair edging the eyelid; *esp* : a single hair of this fringe

eye lens *n* : the lens nearest the eye in an eyepiece

eye·let \'ī-lət\ *n* [ME *oilet,* fr. MF *oillet,* dim. of *oil* eye, fr. L *oculus*] **1 a** : a small hole designed to receive a cord or used for decoration (as in embroidery) **b** : a small typically metal ring to reinforce an eyelet : GROMMET **2** : an aperture for observing : PEEPHOLE, LOOPHOLE

eye·lid \'ī-,lid\ *n* : one of the movable lids of skin and muscle that can be closed over the eyeball

eye·lin·er \'ī-,lī-nər\ *n* : makeup used to emphasize the contour of the eyes

ey·en \'ī(-ə)n\ *archaic pl of* EYE

eye–open·er \'ī-,ōp(-ə)-nər\ *n* **1** : a drink intended to wake one up **2** : something startling or surprising — **eye–open·ing** \-niŋ\ *adj*

eye·piece \'ī-,pēs\ *n* : the lens or combination of lenses at the eye end of an optical instrument

eye·point \'ī-,pȯint\ *n* : the point at which the eye is placed in using an optical instrument (as a microscope)

eye·pop·per \'ī-,päp-ər\ *n* : something that excites or astonishes — **eye–pop·ping** \-,päp-iŋ\ *adj*

eye rhyme *n* : an imperfect rhyme that appears to have identical vowel sounds from similarity of spelling (as *move* and *love*)

eye·shade \'ī-,shād\ *n* : a visor that shields the eyes from strong light and is fastened on with a headband

eye shadow *n* : a cosmetic cream or powder in one of various colors that is applied to the eyelids to accent the eyes

eye·shot \'ī-,shät\ *n* : the range of the eye : VIEW

eye·sight \'ī-,sīt\ *n* **1** : SIGHT 4a **2** *archaic* : OBSERVATION 1

eye·sore \'ī-,sō(ə)r, -,sȯ(ə)r\ *n* : something offensive to the sight

eye·spot \'ī-,spät\ *n* **1 a** : a simple visual organ of pigment or pigmented cells covering a sensory termination : OCELLUS **b** : a small pigmented body of various unicellular algae **2** : a spot of color

eye·stalk \'ī-,stȯk\ *n* : one of the movable peduncles bearing an eye at the tip in a decapod crustacean

eye·strain \'ī-,strān\ *n* : weariness or a strained state of the eye

eye·strings \'ī-,striŋz\ *n pl, obs* : organic eye attachments formerly believed to break at death or blindness

eye·tooth \'ī-'tüth\ *n* : a canine tooth of the upper jaw

eye·wash \'ī-,wȯsh, -,wäsh\ *n* **1** : an eye lotion **2** : misleading or deceptive statements, actions, or procedures

eye·wink \'ī-,wiŋk\ *n* **1** : a wink of the eye **2** *obs* : LOOK, GLANCE

eye·wit·ness \'ī-'wit-nəs\ *n* : one who sees an occurrence or an object; *esp* : one who gives a report on what he has seen

eyre \'a(ə)r, 'e(ə)r\ *n* [ME *eire,* fr. AF, fr. OF *erre* trip, fr. *errer* to travel — more at ERRANT] **1** : periodic circuit <medieval English

justices in ~> **2 :** a medieval English court held by itinerant royal justices

ey·rie \ˈī(ə)r-ē, *or like* AERIE\ *var of* AERIE

ey·rir \ˈā-ˌri(ə)r\ *n, pl* **au·rar** \ˈaů-ˌrär, ˈœl-\ [Icel, fr. ON, money (in pl.)] — see *krona* at MONEY table

Ez *or* **Ezr** *abbr* Ezra

Ezech *abbr* Ezechiel

Eze·chiel \i-ˈzē-kyəl, -kē-əl\ *n* [LL] **:** EZEKIEL

Ezek *abbr* Ezekiel

Eze·kiel \i-ˈzē-kyəl, -kē-əl\ *n* [LL *Ezechiel,* fr. Heb *Yĕḥezqēl*] **1 :** a Hebrew priest and prophet of the 6th century B.C. **2 :** a prophetic book of canonical Jewish and Christian Scripture written by Ezekiel — see BIBLE table

Ez·ra \ˈez-rə\ *n* [LL, fr. Heb *ʻEzrā*] **1 :** a Hebrew priest, scribe, and reformer of Judaism of the 5th century B.C. in Babylon and Jerusalem **2 :** a narrative book of canonical Jewish and Christian Scripture — see BIBLE table

1f \ˈef\ *n, pl* **f's** *or* **fs** \ˈefs\ *often cap, often attrib* **1 a :** the 6th letter of the English alphabet **b :** a graphic representation of this letter **c :** a speech counterpart of orthographic *f* **2 :** the 4th tone of a C-major scale **3 :** a graphic device for reproducing the letter *f* **4 :** one designated *f* esp. as the 6th in order or class **5 a :** a grade rating a student's work as failing **b :** one graded or rated with an F **6 :** something shaped like the letter F

2f *abbr, often cap* **1** Fahrenheit **2** failure **3** false **4** family **5** farad **6** feast **7** female **8** feminine **9** femto- **10** fermi **11** fine **12** finish **13** fluid; fluidness **14** force **15** forte **16** fragile **17** French **18** frequency **19** from **20** full

3f *symbol* **1** faraday **2** focal length **3** the relative aperture of a photographic lens — often written *f/* **4** function <*y* = *f*(*x*)>

F *symbol* fluorine

fa \ˈfä\ *n* [ME, fr. ML, fr. the syllable sung to this note in a medieval hymn to St. John the Baptist] **:** the 4th tone of the diatonic scale in solmization

FA *abbr* **1** field artillery **2** fielding average **3** football association

FAA *abbr* **1** Federal Aviation Agency **2** free of all average

fa·ba·ceous \fə-ˈbā-shəs\ *adj* [NL *Fabaceae,* family of legumes, fr. *Faba,* type genus, fr. L, bean] **1 :** of or relating to the legume family **:** LEGUMINOUS **2 :** relating to, resembling, or being a bean

Fa·bi·an \ˈfā-bē-ən\ *adj* **1 a :** of, relating to, or in the manner of the Roman general Quintus Fabius Maximus known for his defeat of Hannibal in the Second Punic War by the avoidance of decisive contests **b :** CAUTIOUS, DILATORY **2** [the *Fabian* Society; fr. the members' belief in slow rather than revolutionary change in government] **:** of, relating to, or being a society of socialists organized in England in 1884 to spread socialist principles gradually — **Fabian** *n* — **Fa·bi·an·ism** \-ə-ˌniz-əm\ *n*

1fa·ble \ˈfā-bəl\ *n* [ME, fr. MF, fr. L *fabula* conversation, story, play, fr. *fari* to speak — more at BAN] **:** a fictitious narrative or statement: as **a :** a legendary story of supernatural happenings **b :** a narration intended to enforce a useful truth; *esp* **:** one in which animals speak and act like human beings **c :** FALSEHOOD, LIE

2fable *vb* **fa·bled; fa·bling** \-b(ə-)liŋ\ *vi, archaic* **:** to tell fables ~ *vt* **:** to talk or write about as if true — **fa·bler** \-b(ə-)lər\ *n*

fa·bled \ˈfā-bəld\ *adj* **1 :** FICTITIOUS **2 :** told or celebrated in fables

fab·li·au \ˈfab-lē-ˌō\ *n, pl* **-aux** \-ˌō(z)\ [F, fr. OF, dim. of *fable*] **:** a short usu. comic, frankly coarse, and often cynical tale in verse popular in the 12th and 13th centuries

fab·ric \ˈfab-rik\ *n* [MF *fabrique,* fr. L *fabrica* workshop, structure — more at FORGE] **1 a :** STRUCTURE, BUILDING **b :** underlying structure **:** FRAMEWORK <the ~ of society> **2 :** an act of constructing **:** ERECTION; *specif* **:** the construction and maintenance of a church building **3 a :** structural plan or style of construction **b :** TEXTURE, QUALITY — used chiefly of textiles **c :** the arrangement of physical components (as of soil) in relation to each other **4 a :** CLOTH 1a **b :** a material that resembles cloth **5 :** the appearance or pattern produced by the shapes and arrangement of the crystal grains in a rock

fab·ri·cant \ˈfab-ri-kənt\ *n* **:** MANUFACTURER

fab·ri·cate \ˈfab-ri-ˌkāt\ *vt* **-cat·ed; -cat·ing** [ME *fabricaten,* fr. L *fabricatus,* pp. of *fabricari,* fr. *fabrica*] **1 :** CONSTRUCT, MANUFACTURE; *specif* **:** to construct from diverse and usu. standardized parts **2 :** INVENT, CREATE **3 :** to make up for the purpose of deception ***syn*** see MAKE — **fab·ri·ca·tion** \ˌfab-ri-ˈkā-shən\ *n* — **fab·ri·ca·tor** \ˈfab-ri-ˌkāt-ər\ *n*

fab·u·lar \ˈfab-yə-lər\ *adj* **:** of, relating to, or having the form of a fable

fab·u·list \ˈfab-yə-ləst\ *n* **1 :** a creator or writer of fables **2 :** LIAR

fab·u·lous \ˈfab-yə-ləs\ *adj* [L *fabulosus,* fr. *fabula*] **1 :** resembling a fable esp. in incredible, marvelous, or exaggerated quality **2 :** told in or based on fable ***syn*** see FICTITIOUS — **fab·u·lous·ly** *adv* — **fab·u·lous·ness** *n*

fac *abbr* **1** facsimile **2** faculty

fa·cade *also* **fa·çade** \fə-ˈsäd\ *n* [F *façade,* fr. It *facciata,* fr. *faccia* face, fr. (assumed) VL *facia*] **1 :** the front of a building; *also* **:** any other face (as on a street or court) of a building given special architectural treatment **2 :** a false, superficial, or artificial appearance or effect **:** FACE

facade 1

1face \ˈfās\ *n, often attrib* [ME, fr. OF, fr. (assumed) VL *facia,* fr. L *facies* make, form, face, fr. *facere* to make, do — more at DO] **1 :** the front part of the human head including the chin, mouth, nose, cheeks, eyes, and usu. the forehead **2** *archaic* **:** PRESENCE, SIGHT **3 a :** facial expression **b :** GRIMACE **c :** MAKEUP 3a **4 a :** outward appearance <suspicious on the ~ of it> **b :** DISGUISE, PRETENSE **c (1) :** ASSURANCE, CONFIDENCE <maintaining a firm ~ in spite of adversity> **(2) :** EFFRONTERY <how anyone could have the ~ to ask that question> **d :** DIGNITY, PRESTIGE <afraid to lose ~> **5 :** SURFACE: **a (1) :** a front, upper, or outer surface **(2) :** the front of something having two or four sides **(3) :** FACADE **(4) :** an exposed surface of rock **(5) :** any of the plane surfaces that bound a geometric solid **b :** a surface specially prepared: as **(1) :** the principal dressed surface (as of a disk) **(2) :** the right side (as of cloth or leather) **(3) :** an inscribed, printed, or marked side **c (1) :** the surface (as of type) that receives the ink and transfers it to the paper — see TYPE illustration **(2) :** a style of type **6 :** the end or wall of a mine tunnel, drift, or excavation at which work is progressing — **face·less** \-ləs\ *adj* — **face·less·ness** *n* — **face to face 1 :** within each other's sight or presence **:** in person <we met *face to face* for the first time> **2 :** under the necessity of having to make a decision or to take action <finally came *face to face* with the problem> — **in the face of** *or* **in face of :** in opposition to **:** DESPITE <succeed *in the face of* great difficulties> — **to one's face :** in one's presence or so that one is fully aware of what is going on **:** FRANKLY

2face *vb* **faced; fac·ing** *vt* **1 :** to confront impudently **2 a :** to line near the edge esp. with a different material **b :** to cover the front or surface of <*faced* the building with marble> **3 :** to bring face-to-face **4 a :** to stand or sit with the face toward **b :** to front on <a house *facing* the park> **5 a :** to meet firmly and without evasion <~ the facts> **b :** to master by confronting with determination — used with *down* <*faced* down the critics of his policy> **6 :** to turn (as a playing card) face-up **7 :** to make the surface of (as a stone) flat or smooth **8 :** to cause (troops) to face in a particular direction on command ~ *vi* **1 :** to have the face or front turned in a specified direction **2 :** to turn the face in a specified direction — **face the music :** to meet an unpleasant situation, a danger, or the consequences of one's actions

face angle *n* **:** an angle formed by two edges of a polyhedral angle

face card *n* **:** a king, queen, or jack in a deck of cards

face·cloth \ˈfās-ˌklȯth\ **:** WASHCLOTH

-faced \ˈfāst\ *adj comb form* **:** having (such) a face or (so many) faces <*two-faced*> <*rosy-faced*>

face·down \ˈfās-ˈdaůn\ *adv* **:** with the face down <sliding ~>

ə abut	ᵊ kitten	ər further	a back	ā bake	ä cot, cart
aů out	ch chin	e less	ē easy	g gift	i trip	ī life
j joke	ŋ sing	ō flow	ȯ flaw	ȯi coin	th thin	th this
ü loot	ů foot	y yet	yü few	yů furious	zh vision

face fly *n* **:** a European fly (*Musca autumnalis*) that is similar to the house fly, is widely established in No. America, and causes great distress in livestock by clustering about the face

face–hard·en \'fās-ˌhärd-ᵊn\ *vt* **:** to harden the surface of (as steel)

face–lift·ing \'fā-ˌslif-tiŋ\ *n* **1 :** a plastic operation for removal of facial defects (as wrinkles) typical of aging **2 :** an alteration or restyling intended to modernize

face–off \'fā-ˌsȯf\ *n* **1 :** a method of putting a puck in play in ice hockey by dropping it between two opposing players each of whom attempts to gain control of the puck or hit it to a teammate **2 :** CONFRONTATION

face·plate \'fā-ˌsplāt\ *n* **1 :** a disk fixed with its face at right angles to the live spindle of a lathe for the attachment of the work **2 :** a protective cover for the human face (as of a diver) **3 :** the glass front of a kinescope on which the image is seen

fac·er \'fā-sər\ *n* **1 :** a stunning check or defeat **2 :** one that faces; *specif* **:** a cutter for facing a surface

face–sav·er \'fās-ˌsā-vər\ *n* **:** something (as a compromise) that saves face

face–sav·ing \-ˌsā-viŋ\ *n* **:** the act or an instance of preserving one's prestige or dignity

fac·et \'fas-ət\ *n* [F *facette,* dim. of *face*] **1 :** a small plane surface (as on a cut gem) — see BRILLIANT illustration **2 :** any of the definable aspects that make up a subject (as of contemplation) or an object (as of consideration) **3 :** the external corneal surface of an ommatidium **4 :** a smooth flat circumscribed anatomical surface **5 :** a fillet between the flutes of a column ***syn*** see PHASE — **fac·et·ed** *or* **fac·et·ted** \'fas-ət-əd\ *adj*

fa·cete \fə-'sēt\ *adj* [L *facetus*] *archaic* **:** FACETIOUS, WITTY

fa·ce·ti·ae \fə-'sē-shē-ˌē\ *n pl* [L, fr. pl. of *facetia* jest, fr. *facetus*] **:** witty or humorous writings or sayings

fa·ce·tious \fə-'sē-shəs\ *adj* [MF *facetieux,* fr. *facetie* jest, fr. L *facetia*] **1 :** jocular in an often clumsy or inappropriate manner **2 :** characterized by pleasantry or levity **:** JOCOSE <a ~ remark> ***syn*** see WITTY ***ant*** lugubrious — **fa·ce·tious·ly** *adv* — **fa·ce·tious·ness** *n*

face–to–face *adj* **:** being within each other's sight or presence <a ~ interview>

face·up \'fā-'səp\ *adv* **:** with the face up

face up *vi* **:** to meet without shrinking — usu. used with *to* <*faced up* to the situation>

face value *n* **1 :** the value indicated on the face (as of a postage stamp or a stock certificate) **2 :** the apparent value or significance <if their results may be taken at *face value*>

fa·cia \'fāsh-(ē-)ə\ *var of* FASCIA

[1]**fa·cial** \'fā-shəl\ *adj* **1 :** of or relating to the face **2 :** concerned with or used in improving the appearance of the face — **fa·cial·ly** \-shə-lē\ *adv*

[2]**facial** *n* **:** a facial treatment

facial index *n* **:** the ratio of the breadth of the face to its length multiplied by 100

facial nerve *n* **:** either of the seventh pair of cranial nerves that supply motor fibers esp. to the muscles of the face and jaw and send a separate mixed branch to the tongue

-fa·cient \'fā-shənt\ *adj comb form* [L *-facient-, -faciens* (as in *calefacient-, calefaciens* making warm, prp. of *calefacere* to warm) — more at CHAFE] **:** making **:** causing <somni*facient*>

fa·cies \'fā-sh(ē-)ˌēz\ *n, pl* **facies** [NL, fr. L, face] **1 :** an appearance and expression of the face characteristic of a particular condition **2 a :** general appearance <a plant species with a particularly distinct ~> **b :** a particular local aspect or modification of an ecological community **3 :** a rock or group of rocks that differs from comparable rocks (as in composition, age, or fossil content)

fac·ile \'fas-əl\ *adj* [MF, fr. L *facilis,* fr. *facere* to do — more at DO] **1 a (1) :** easily accomplished or attained <a ~ victory> **(2) :** SPECIOUS, SUPERFICIAL <I am not concerned . . . with offering any ~ solution for so complex a problem —T. S. Eliot> **b :** used or comprehended with ease **c :** readily manifested and often lacking sincerity or depth <~ tears> **2 :** mild or pleasing in manner or disposition **3 a :** READY, FLUENT <~ prose> **b :** ASSURED, POISED — **fac·ile·ly** \-ə(l)-lē\ *adv* — **fac·ile·ness** \-əl-nəs\ *n*

fa·cil·i·tate \fə-'sil-ə-ˌtāt\ *vt* **-tat·ed; -tat·ing :** to make easier — **fa·cil·i·ta·tive** \-ˌtāt-iv\ *adj* — **fa·cil·i·ta·tor** \-ˌtāt-ər\ *n*

fa·cil·i·ta·tion \fə-ˌsil-ə-'tā-shən\ *n* **1 :** the act of facilitating **:** the state of being facilitated **2 :** the lowering of the threshold for reflex conduction along a particular neural pathway esp. from repeated use of that pathway

fa·cil·i·ty \fə-'sil-ət-ē\ *n, pl* **-ties 1 :** the quality of being easily performed **2 :** ease in performance **:** APTITUDE **3 :** readiness of compliance **4 a :** something that promotes the ease of an action, operation, or course of conduct — usu. used in pl. <provide books and other *facilities* for independent study> **b :** something (as a hospital) that is built, installed, or established to serve a particular purpose

fac·ing \'fā-siŋ\ *n* **1 a :** a lining at the edge esp. of a garment **b** *pl* **:** the collar, cuffs, and trimmings of a uniform coat **2 :** an ornamental or protective layer **3 :** material for facing

fac·sim·i·le \fak-'sim-ə-lē\ *n* [L *fac simile* make similar] **1 :** an exact copy **2 :** the transmission of graphic matter (as printing or still pictures) by wire or radio and its reproduction — **facsimile** *vt*

fact \'fakt\ *n* [L *factum,* fr. neut. of *factus,* pp. of *facere*] **1 :** a thing done: as **a :** CRIME <accessory after the ~> **b** *obs* **:** FEAT **c** *archaic* **:** ACTION **2** *archaic* **:** PERFORMANCE, DOING **3 :** the quality of being actual **:** ACTUALITY <a question of ~ brings on actual evidence> **4 a :** something that has actual existence <space travel is now a ~> **b :** an actual occurrence **:** EVENT <the ~ of his presence is proven by witnesses> **5 :** a piece of information presented as having objective reality — **fac·tic·i·ty** \fak-'tis-ət-ē\ *n* — **in fact :** in truth **:** ACTUALLY

fact finder *n* **:** one that tries to determine the realities of a case, situation, or relationship; *esp* **:** an impartial examiner designated by a government agency to appraise the facts underlying a particular matter (as a labor dispute) — **fact–find·ing** *n*

fac·tion \'fak-shən\ *n* [MF & L; MF, fr. L *faction-, factio* act of making, faction — more at FASHION] **1 :** a party or group (as within a government that is often contentious or self-seeking **:** CLIQUE **2 :** party spirit esp. when marked by dissension — **fac·tion·al** \-shnəl, -shən-ᵊl\ *adj* — **fac·tion·al·ism** \-shnə-ˌliz-əm, -shən-ᵊl-ˌiz-\ *n* — **fac·tion·al·ly** \-ē\ *adv*

-fac·tion \'fak-shən\ *n comb form* [ME *-faccioun,* fr. MF & L; MF *-faction,* fr. L *-faction-, -factio* (as in *satisfaction-, satisfactio* satisfaction)] **:** making **:** -FICATION <petri*faction*>

fac·tious \'fak-shəs\ *adj* [MF or L; MF *factieux,* fr. L *factiosus,* fr. *factio*] **:** of or relating to faction: as **a :** caused by faction <~ disputes> **b :** inclined to faction or the formation of factions **c :** SEDITIOUS — **fac·tious·ly** *adv* — **fac·tious·ness** *n*

fac·ti·tious \fak-'tish-əs\ *adj* [L *facticius,* fr. *factus,* pp. of *facere* to make, do — more at DO] **1 :** produced by man rather than by natural forces **2 a :** formed by or adapted to an artificial or conventional standard **b :** produced by special effort **:** SHAM <created a ~ demand by spreading rumors of shortage> ***syn*** see ARTIFICIAL ***ant*** bona fide, veritable — **fac·ti·tious·ly** *adv* — **fac·ti·tious·ness** *n*

fac·ti·tive \'fak-tət-iv\ *adj* [NL *factitivus,* irreg. fr. L *factus*] **:** of or relating to a transitive verb that in some constructions requires an objective complement as well as an object — **fac·ti·tive·ly** *adv*

-fac·tive \'fak-tiv\ *adj comb form* [MF *-factif,* fr. *-faction*] **:** making **:** causing <petri*factive*>

fact of life 1 facts of life *pl* **:** the fundamental physiological processes and behavior involved in sex and reproduction **2 :** something that exists and must be taken into consideration

[1]**fac·tor** \'fak-tər\ *n* [ME, fr. MF *facteur,* fr. L *factor* doer, fr. *factus*] **1 :** one who acts or transacts business for another: as **a :** COMMISSION MERCHANT **b :** one that lends money to producers and dealers (as on the security of accounts receivable) **2 a :** something that actively contributes to the production of a result **:** INGREDIENT **b :** a good or service used in the process of production **3 :** GENE **4 a :** any of the numbers or symbols in mathematics that when multiplied together form a product; *also* **:** a number or symbol that divides another number or symbol **b :** a quantity by which a given quantity is multiplied or divided in order to indicate a difference in measurement **c :** the number by which a given time is multiplied in photography to give the complete time for exposure or development ***syn*** see ELEMENT — **fac·tor·ship** \-ˌship\ *n*

[2]**factor** *vb* **fac·tored; fac·tor·ing** \-t(ə-)riŋ\ *vt* **:** to resolve into factors ~ *vi* **:** to work as a factor — **fac·tor·able** \-t(ə-)rə-bəl\ *adj*

fac·tor·age \-t(ə-)rij\ *n* **1 :** the charges made by a factor for his services **2 :** the business of a factor

factor analysis *n* **:** the transformation of statistical data (as measurements) into linear combinations of variables that are usu. not correlated — **factor analytic** *adj*

[1]**fac·to·ri·al** \fak-'tōr-ē-əl, -'tȯr-\ *n* **1 :** the product of all the positive integers from one to *n* — symbol *n!* **2 :** the quantity *0!* arbitrarily defined as equal to 1

[2]**factorial** *adj* **:** of or relating to a factor or a factorial

fac·tor·ize \'fak-tə-ˌrīz\ *vt* **-ized; -iz·ing :** FACTOR — **fac·tor·iza·tion** \ˌfak-tə-rə-'zā-shən\ *n*

fac·to·ry \'fak-t(ə-)rē\ *n, pl* **-ries 1 :** a station where resident factors trade **2 a :** a building or set of buildings with facilities for manufacturing **b :** the seat of some kind of production <the vice *factories* of the slums>

fac·to·tum \fak-'tōt-əm\ *n* [NL, lit., do everything, fr. L *fac* do + *totum* everything] **1 :** a person having many diverse activities or responsibilities **2 :** a general servant

fac·tu·al \'fak-chə(-wə)l, 'faksh-wəl\ *adj* **1 :** of or relating to facts **2 :** restricted to or based on fact — **fac·tu·al·i·ty** \ˌfak-chə-'wal-ət-ē\ *n* — **fac·tu·al·ly** \'fak-chə(-wə)-lē, 'faksh-wə-\ *adv* — **fac·tu·al·ness** *n*

fac·tu·al·ism \'fak-chə(-wə)-ˌliz-əm, 'faksh-wə-\ *n* **:** adherence or dedication to facts — **fac·tu·al·ist** \-ləst\ *n*

fac·ture \'fak-chər\ *n* [ME, fr. MF, fr. L *factura* action of making, fr. *factus*] **:** the manner in which something (as an artistic work) is made **:** EXECUTION <his modelling of faces . . . his delicate yet firm ~ —J. C. Vandyke>

fac·u·la \'fak-yə-lə\ *n, pl* **-lae** \-ˌlē, -ˌlī\ [NL, fr. L, dim. of *fac-, fax* torch] **:** any of the bright regions of the sun's photosphere seen most easily near the sun's edge

fac·ul·ta·tive \'fak-əl-ˌtāt-iv\ *adj* **1 a :** of or relating to the grant of permission, authority, or privilege <~ legislation> **b :** OPTIONAL **2 :** of or relating to mental faculty **3 a :** taking place under some conditions but not under others <~ diapause> <~ parasitism> **b :** showing the typical life style under some environmental conditions but not under others <~ anaerobes> <~ homosexuals> — **fac·ul·ta·tive·ly** *adv*

fac·ul·ty \'fak-əl-tē\ *n, pl* **-ties** [ME *faculte,* fr. MF *faculté,* fr. ML & L; ML *facultat-, facultas* branch of learning or teaching, fr. L, ability, abundance, fr. *facilis* facile] **1 :** ABILITY, POWER: as **a :** innate or acquired ability to act or do **b :** an inherent capability, power, or function <the ~ of hearing> **c :** one of the powers of the mind formerly held by psychologists to form a basis for the explanation of all mental phenomena **d :** natural aptitude <he has a ~ for saying the right things> **2 a :** a branch of teaching or learning in an educational institution **b** *archaic* **:** something in which one is trained or qualified **3 a :** the members of a profession **b :** the teaching and administrative staff and those members of the administration having academic rank in an educational institution **4 :** power, authority, or prerogative given or conferred ***syn*** see POWER, GIFT

fad \'fad\ *n* [origin unknown] **:** a practice or interest followed for a time with exaggerated zeal **:** CRAZE ***syn*** see FASHION — **fad·dish** \'fad-ish\ *adj* — **fad·dish·ness** *n* — **fad·dism** \'fad-ˌiz-əm\ *n* — **fad·dist** \'fad-əst\ *n*

FAD \ˌef-ˌā-'dē\ *n* **:** FLAVIN ADENINE DINUCLEOTIDE

[1]**fade** \ˈfād\ *vb* **fad·ed; fad·ing** [ME *faden,* fr. MF *fader,* fr. *fade* feeble, insipid, fr. (assumed) VL *fatidus,* alter. of L *fatuus* fatuous, insipid] *vi* **1 :** to lose freshness or vitality : WITHER **2** *of an automobile brake* : to lose braking power gradually **3 :** to lose freshness or brilliance of color **4 :** to sink away : VANISH **5 :** to change gradually in loudness, strength, or visibility — used of a motion-picture image or of an electronics signal and usu. with *in* or *out* **6 :** to move back from the line of scrimmage — used of a quarterback ~ *vt* : to cause to fade

[2]**fade** *n* **1 :** a gradual changing of one picture to another in a motion-picture or television sequence **2 :** a fading of an automobile brake

[3]**fade** \ˈfäd\ *adj* [F, fr. MF] : INSIPID, COMMONPLACE

fade·away \ˈfād-ə-ˌwā\ *n* **1 :** an act or instance of fading away **2 a :** SCREWBALL 1 **b :** a slide in which a base runner throws his body sideways to avoid the tag

fad·ed·ly \ˈfād-əd-lē\ *adv* : in the manner of one that has faded <a ~ handsome woman>

fade·less \ˈfād-ləs\ *adj* : not susceptible to fading — **fade·less·ly** *adv*

FADM *abbr* fleet admiral

fa·do \ˈfäth-(ˌ)ü, ˈfath-\ *n, pl* **fados** [Pg, lit., fate, fr. L *fatum*] : a plaintive Portuguese folk song

fae·cal, fae·ces *var of* FECAL, FECES

fa·e·na \fä-ˈā-(ˌ)nä\ *n* [Sp, lit., task, fr. obs. Catal, fr. L *facienda* things to be done, fr. *facere* to do — more at DO] : a series of final passes leading to the kill made by the matador in a bullfight

fa·er·ie *also* **fa·ery** \ˈfā-(ə-)rē, ˈfa(ə)r-ē, ˈfe(ə)r-ē\ *n, pl* **fa·er·ies** [MF *faerie* — more at FAIRY] **1 :** the realm of fairies **2 :** FAIRY — **faery** *adj*

Faero·ese \ˌfar-ə-ˈwēz, ˌfer-, -ˈwēs\ *n, pl* **Faeroese** **1 :** a member of the Germanic people inhabiting the Faeroes **2 :** the Germanic language of the Faeroese people — **Faeroese** *adj*

Faf·nir \ˈfäv-nər, -ˌni(ə)r\ *n* [ON *Fāfnir*] : a dragon of Norse myth that guards the Nibelungs' gold hoard until slain by Sigurd

[1]**fag** \ˈfag\ *vb* **fagged; fag·ging** [obs. *fag* to droop, perh. fr. *fag* (fag end)] *vi* **1 :** to work hard : TOIL **2 :** to act as a fag esp. in an English public school <*fagging* for older boys during his first year> ~ *vt* : to tire by strenuous activity : EXHAUST *syn* see TIRE

[2]**fag** *n* **1** *chiefly Brit* : TOIL, DRUDGERY **2 a :** an English public-school boy who acts as servant to an older schoolmate **b :** DRUDGE

[3]**fag** *n* [*fag end*] : CIGARETTE

[4]**fag** *n* [prob. short for *faggot*] : HOMOSEXUAL

fag end *n* [earlier *fag,* fr. ME *fagge* flap] **1 a :** the last part or coarser end of a web of cloth **b :** the untwisted end of a rope **2 a :** a poor or worn-out end : REMNANT **b :** the extreme end <not quite too late for the *fag end* of lunch —Earle Birney>

fag·got \ˈfag-ət\ *n* [origin unknown] : HOMOSEXUAL

fa·gin \ˈfā-gən\ *n* [*Fagin,* character in Charles Dickens' *Oliver Twist* (1839)] : an adult who instructs others (as children) in crime

FAGO *abbr* Fellow of the American Guild of Organists

[1]**fag·ot** *or* **fag·got** \ˈfag-ət\ *n* [ME *fagot,* fr. MF] : BUNDLE; *as* **a :** a bundle of sticks **b :** a bundle of pieces of wrought iron to be shaped by rolling or hammering at high temperature

[2]**fagot** *or* **faggot** *vt* : to make a fagot of : bind together into a bundle <~*ed* sticks>

fag·ot·ing *or* **fag·got·ing** *n* **1 :** an embroidery produced by pulling out horizontal threads from a fabric and tying the remaining cross threads into groups of an hourglass shape **2 :** an openwork stitch joining hemmed edges

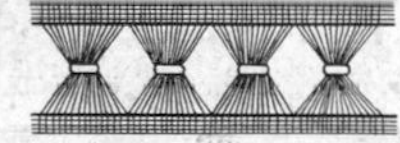

fagoting 1

Fah *or* **Fahr** *abbr* Fahrenheit

Fahr·en·heit \ˈfar-ən-ˌhīt\ *adj* [Gabriel D. *Fahrenheit*] : relating or conforming to a thermometric scale on which under standard atmospheric pressure the boiling point of water is at 212 degrees above the zero of the scale, the freezing point is at 32 degrees above zero, and the zero point approximates the temperature produced by mixing equal quantities by weight of snow and common salt — abbr. *F*

fa·ience *or* **fa·ïence** \fā-ˈän(t)s, fī-, -ˈä^{n}s\ *n* [F, fr. *Faenza,* Italy] : earthenware decorated with opaque colored glazes

[1]**fail** \ˈfā(ə)l\ *vb* [ME *failen,* fr. OF *faillir,* fr. (assumed) VL *fallire,* alter. of L *fallere* to deceive, disappoint; prob. akin to Gk *phēlos* deceitful] *vi* **1 a :** to lose strength : WEAKEN <her health was ~*ing*> **b :** to fade or die away <until our family line ~*s*> **c :** to stop functioning <the patient's heart ~*ed*> **2 a :** to fall short <~*ed* in his duty> **b :** to be or become absent or inadequate <the water supply ~*ed*> **c :** to be unsuccessful (as in passing an examination) **d :** to become bankrupt or insolvent ~ *vt* **1 a :** to disappoint the expectations or trust of <his friends ~*ed* him> **b :** to miss performing an expected service or function for <for once his wit ~*ed* him> **2 :** to be deficient in : LACK <our youth . . . never ~*ed* an invincible courage —Douglas MacArthur> **3 :** to leave undone : NEGLECT **4 a :** to be unsuccessful in passing (as a test) **b :** to grade (as a student) as not passing — **fail·ing·ly** \ˈfā-liŋ-lē\ *adv*

[2]**fail** *n* **1 :** FAILURE — usu. used in the phrase *without fail* **2 :** a failure (as by a security dealer) to deliver or receive securities within a prescribed period after purchase or sale

[1]**fail·ing** \ˈfā-liŋ\ *n* : a slight or insignificant defect in character or conduct *syn* see FAULT *ant* perfection

[2]**failing** *prep* : in absence or default of <~ specific instructions, use your own judgment>

faille \ˈfī(ə)l\ *n* [F] : a somewhat shiny closely woven silk, rayon, or cotton fabric characterized by slight ribs in the weft

fail–safe \ˈfā(ə)l-ˌsāf\ *adj* **1 :** incorporating some feature for automatically counteracting the effect of an anticipated possible source of failure **2 :** being or relating to a safeguard that prevents continuing on a bombing mission according to a preconceived plan

fail·ure \ˈfā(ə)l-yər\ *n* [alter. of earlier *failer,* fr. AF, fr. OF *faillir* to fail] **1 a :** omission of occurrence or performance; *specif* : a failing to perform a duty or expected action **b :** a state of inability to perform a normal function <heart ~> **2 a :** lack of success **b :** a failing in business : BANKRUPTCY **3 a :** a falling short : DEFICIENCY <a crop ~> **b :** DETERIORATION, DECAY **4 :** one that has failed

[1]**fain** \ˈfān\ *adj* [ME *fagen, fayn,* fr. OE *fægen;* akin to ON *fegiun* happy, OE *fæger* fair] **1** *archaic* : HAPPY, PLEASED **2** *archaic* : INCLINED, DESIROUS **3** *archaic* : WILLING **b :** being obliged or constrained : COMPELLED

[2]**fain** *adv* **1** *archaic* : with pleasure **2** *archaic* : RATHER

[1]**fai·né·ant** \fā-nā-ä^{n}\ *n, pl* **fainéants** \-ä^{n}(z)\ [F, fr. MF *fait-nient,* lit., does nothing, by folk etymology fr. *faignant,* fr. prp. of *faindre, feindre* to feign] : an irresponsible idler

[2]**fainéant** \fā-nā-ä^{n}\ *or* **fai·ne·ant** \ˈfā-nē-ənt\ *adj* : idle and ineffectual : INDOLENT

[1]**faint** \ˈfānt\ *adj* [ME *faint, feint,* fr. OF, fr. pp. of *faindre, feindre* to feign, shirk — more at FEIGN] **1 :** lacking courage and spirit : COWARDLY **2 :** weak, dizzy, and likely to faint **3 :** lacking strength or vigor : performed, offered, or accomplished weakly or languidly **4 :** producing a sensation of faintness : OPPRESSIVE <the ~ atmosphere of a tropical port> **5 :** lacking distinctness : DIM — **faint·ish** \-ish\ *adj* — **faint·ish·ness** *n* — **faint·ly** *adv* — **faint·ness** *n*

[2]**faint** *vi* **1** *archaic* : to lose courage or spirit **2** *archaic* : to become weak **3 :** to lose consciousness because of a temporary decrease in the blood supply to the brain **4 :** to lose brightness

[3]**faint** *n* : an act or condition of fainting : SYNCOPE

faint·heart·ed \ˈfānt-ˈhärt-əd\ *adj* : lacking courage or resolution : TIMID — **faint·heart·ed·ly** *adv* — **faint·heart·ed·ness** *n*

[1]**fair** \ˈfa(ə)r, ˈfe(ə)r\ *adj* [ME *fager, fair* fr. OE *fæger;* akin to OHG *fagar* beautiful and perh. to Lith *puosti* to decorate] **1 :** pleasing to the eye or mind esp. because of fresh, charming, or flawless quality **2 :** superficially pleasing : SPECIOUS <she trusted his ~ promises> **3 a :** CLEAN, PURE <~ sparkling water> <a man of ~ fame> **b :** CLEAR, LEGIBLE **4 :** not stormy or foul : FINE <a ~ sky> <~ weather> **5 :** AMPLE <a ~ estate> **6 a :** marked by impartiality and honesty : free from self-interest, prejudice, or favoritism <a very ~ man to do business with > **b :** conforming with the established rules : ALLOWED **c :** open to legitimate pursuit or attack <~ game> **7 a :** PROMISING, LIKELY <he was in a ~ way to win> **b :** favorable to a ship's course <a ~ wind> **8** *archaic* : free of obstacles **9 :** not dark : BLOND **10 :** sufficient but not ample : ADEQUATE <a ~ understanding of the work> **11 :** being such to the utmost : UTTER <a ~ treat to watch him —*New Republic*> — **fair·ness** *n*

syn **1** see BEAUTIFUL ***ant*** foul, ill-favored

2 FAIR, JUST, EQUITABLE, IMPARTIAL, UNBIASED, DISPASSIONATE, OBJECTIVE *shared meaning element* : free from favor toward either or any side. FAIR implies an elimination of personal feelings, interests, or prejudices so as to achieve a proper balance of conflicting needs, rights, or demands <a *fair* distribution of a treat> <the judge's decision was absolutely *fair*> JUST implies a precise following of a standard of what is right and proper <it is easier to be kind than *just*> EQUITABLE implies a less rigorous standard than *just* and usually a fair and equal treatment of all concerned <a form of society which will provide for an *equitable* distribution of . . . riches —J. W. Krutch> IMPARTIAL stresses absence of favor and prejudice <law shall be uniform and *impartial* —B. N. Cardozo> UNBIASED reinforces the notion of freedom from favoritism and prejudice with that of a firm interest to be fair to all <furnish the cabinet with *unbiased* and helpful advice —R. M. Dawson> DISPASSIONATE stresses freedom from emotional involvement and tends to imply cool detachment in judging <a *dispassionate* appraisal of a health program> OBJECTIVE stresses a tendency to view events or phenomena as apart from oneself and therefore to be judged dispassionately and without reference to personal feelings or interests <we shall be like ice when relating passions and adventures . . . we shall be . . . *objective* and impersonal —William Troy> ***ant*** unfair

[2]**fair** *n* **1** *obs* : BEAUTY, FAIRNESS **2 :** something that is fair or fortunate **3** *archaic* : WOMAN; *esp* : SWEETHEART — **for fair :** to the greatest extent or degree : FULLY <the rush was on *for fair* —R. L. Neuberger> — **no fair :** something that is not according to the rules <that's *no fair*>

[3]**fair** *adv* : FAIRLY

[4]**fair** *vi, of the weather* : CLEAR ~ *vt* : to join so that the external surfaces blend smoothly

[5]**fair** *n* [ME *feire,* fr. OF, fr. ML *feria* weekday, fair, fr. LL, festal day, fr. L *feriae* (pl.) holidays — more at FEAST] **1 :** a gathering of buyers and sellers at a particular place and time for trade **2 a :** a competitive exhibition (as of farm products) usu. with accompanying entertainment and amusements **b :** an exhibition designed to acquaint prospective buyers or the general public with a product **3 :** a sale of a collection of articles usu. for a charitable purpose

fair ball *n* : a batted baseball that lands within the foul lines or that is within the foul lines when bounding to the outfield past first or third base or when going beyond the outfield for a home run

fair catch *n* : a catch of a kicked football by a player who gives a prescribed signal, may not advance the ball, and may not be tackled

fair copy *n* : a neat and exact copy esp. of a corrected draft

fair·ground \ˈfa(ə)r-ˌgraund, ˈfe(ə)r-\ *n* : an area where outdoor fairs, circuses, or exhibitions are held — often used in pl. with sing. constr. <what a spot for a ~*s* —W. L. Gresham>

[1]**fair·ing** \ˈfa(ə)r-iŋ, ˈfe(ə)r-\ *n* **1** *Brit* **a :** a present bought or given at a fair **b :** GIFT **2** *Brit* : [3]DESERT 2

ə abut	ə kitten	ər further	a back	ā bake	ä cot, cart
aù out	ch chin	e less	ē easy	g gift	i trip
ī life	j joke	ŋ sing	ō flow	ȯ flaw	ȯi coin
th thin	th this	ü loot	ù foot	y yet	yü few
yù furious	zh vision				

[2]**fairing** *n* : a member or structure whose primary function is to produce a smooth outline and to reduce drag or air resistance (as on an airplane)
fair·ish \'fa(ə)r-ish, 'fe(ə)r-\ *adj* : fairly good <a ~ wage for those days> — **fair·ish·ly** *adv*
fair·lead \'fa(ə)r-ˌlēd, 'fe(ə)r-\ *n* **1** *also* **fair·lead·er** \-ər\ : a block, ring, or strip of plank with holes that serves as a guide for the running rigging or any ship's rope and keeps it from chafing **2** : a course of running ship's rope that avoids all chafing
fair·ly \'fa(ə)r-lē, 'fe(ə)r-\ *adv* **1** : in a handsome manner <a table ~ set> **2** *obs* **a** : in a gentle manner : QUIETLY **b** : in a courteous manner **3** : in a manner of speaking : QUITE <~ bursting with pride> **4 a** : in a proper or legal manner <~ priced stocks> **b** : without bias or distortion : IMPARTIALLY <a story told ~ and objectively> **5** : to a full degree or extent : PLAINLY, DISTINCTLY <had ~ caught sight of him> **6** : for the most part : RATHER <a ~ easy job>
fair–mind·ed \'fa(ə)r-'mīn-dəd, 'fe(ə)r-\ *adj* : JUST, UNPREJUDICED — **fair–mind·ed·ness** *n*
fair play *n* : equitable or impartial treatment : JUSTICE
fair shake *n* : a fair chance <give the negative side a *fair shake* —S. L. Payne>
fair–spok·en \'fa(ə)r-'spō-kən, 'fe(ə)r-\ *adj* : pleasant and courteous in speech <a ~ youth>
fair–trade \'fa(ə)r-'trād, 'fe(ə)r-\ *vt* : to market (a commodity) in compliance with the provisions of a fair-trade agreement — **fair trader** *n*
fair trade *n* : trade in conformity with a fair-trade agreement
fair–trade agreement *n* : an agreement between a producer and a seller that commodities bearing a trademark, label, or brand name belonging to the producer be sold at or above a specified price
fair·way \'fa(ə)r-ˌwā, 'fe(ə)r-\ *n* **1 a** : a navigable part of a river, bay, or harbor **b** : an open path or space **2** : the mowed part of a golf course between a tee and a green
fair–weather *adj* **1** : suitable for, done during, or made in fair weather <a ~ sail> **2** : loyal only during a time of success <a ~ friend>
fairy \'fa(ə)r-ē, 'fe(ə)r-\ *n, pl* **fairies** [ME *fairie* fairyland, fairy people, fr. OF *faerie,* fr. *feie, fee* fairy, fr. L *Fata,* goddess of fate, fr. *fatum* fate] **1** : a mythical being of folklore and romance usu. having diminutive human form and magic powers **2** : a male homosexual — **fairy** *adj* — **fairy·like** \-ˌlīk\ *adj*
fairy·ism \-ˌiz-əm\ *n, archaic* : the power to enchant
fairy·land \-ˌland\ *n* **1** : the land of fairies **2** : a place of delicate beauty or magical charm
fairy ring *n* [fr. the folk belief that such rings were dancing places of the fairies] **1** : a ring of mushrooms produced at the periphery of a body of mycelium which has grown centrifugally from an initial growth point; *also* : a ring of luxuriant vegetation associated with these mushrooms **2** : a mushroom (esp. *Marasmius oreades*) that commonly grows in fairy rings
fairy shrimp *n* : any of several delicate transparent freshwater branchiopod crustaceans (order Anostraca)
fairy–tale *adj* : characteristic of or suitable to a fairy tale; *esp* : marked by unusual grace or beauty
fairy tale *n* **1** : a narrative of adventures involving fantastic forces and beings (as fairies, wizards, and goblins) — called also *fairy story* **2** : a made-up story usu. designed to mislead
fait ac·com·pli \'fāt-ˌak-ˌōⁿ(m)-'plē, ˌfe-ˌtak-\ *n, pl* **faits accomplis** *same, or* -'plēz\ [F, accomplished fact] : a thing accomplished and presumably irreversible
[1]**faith** \'fāth\ *n, pl* **faiths** \'fāths, 'fāthz\ [ME *feith,* fr. OF *feid, foi,* fr. L *fides;* akin to L *fidere* to trust — more at BIDE] **1 a** : allegiance to duty or a person : LOYALTY **b** : fidelity to one's promises **2 a (1)** : belief and trust in and loyalty to God **(2)** : belief in the traditional doctrines of a religion **b (1)** : firm belief in something for which there is no proof **(2)** : complete confidence **3** : something that is believed esp. with strong conviction; *esp* : a system of religious beliefs ***syn*** see BELIEF ***ant*** doubt — **in faith** : without doubt or question : VERILY
[2]**faith** *vt, archaic* : BELIEVE, TRUST
[1]**faith·ful** \'fāth-fəl\ *adj* **1** *obs* : full of faith **2** : steadfast in affection or allegiance : LOYAL **3** : firm in adherence to promises or in observance of duty : CONSCIENTIOUS **4** : given with strong assurance : BINDING <~ promise> **5** : true to the facts or to an original <the portrait is a ~ likeness> — **faith·ful·ly** \-fə-lē\ *adv* — **faith·ful·ness** *n*

syn FAITHFUL, LOYAL, CONSTANT, STAUNCH, STEADFAST, RESOLUTE *shared meaning element* : firm in adherence to whatever one owes allegiance ***ant*** faithless

[2]**faithful** *n, pl* **faithful** *or* **faithfuls** : one that is faithful: as **a** : church members in full communion and good standing — used with *the* **b** : the body of adherents of the Muslim religion — used with *the* **c** : a loyal follower or member <party ~*s*>
faith healing *n* : a method of treating diseases by prayer and exercise of faith in God — **faith healer** *n*
faith·less \'fāth-ləs\ *adj* **1** : not true to allegiance or duty : TREACHEROUS, DISLOYAL <a ~ servant> **2** : not to be relied on : UNTRUSTWORTHY <a ~ tool> — **faith·less·ly** *adv* — **faith·less·ness** *n*

syn FAITHLESS, FALSE, DISLOYAL, TRAITOROUS, TREACHEROUS, PERFIDIOUS *shared meaning element* : untrue to what has a right to one's fidelity or allegiance ***ant*** faithful

fai·tour \'fāt-ər\ *n* [ME, fr. AF, fr. OF *faitor* perpetrator, fr. L *factor* doer — more at FACTOR] *archaic* : CHEAT, IMPOSTOR
[1]**fake** \'fāk\ *vt* **faked; fak·ing** [ME *faken*] : to coil (as a fire hose) in fakes
[2]**fake** *n* : one loop of a coil (as of ship's rope) coiled free for running
[3]**fake** *vb* **faked; fak·ing** [origin unknown] *vt* **1** : to alter, manipulate, or treat so as to impart a false character or appearance to **2** : COUNTERFEIT, SIMULATE **3 a** : to deceive (an opponent) in a sports contest by simulated movement **b** : to give a fake to (an opponent) **4** : IMPROVISE, AD-LIB <whistle a few bars . . . and I'll ~ the rest —Robert Sylvester> ~ *vi* **1** : to engage in faking something : PRETEND **2** : to give a fake to an opponent — **fak·er** *n* — **fak·ery** \'fā-k(ə-)rē\ *n*
[4]**fake** *n* : one that is not what it purports to be: as **a** : a worthless imitation passed off as genuine **b** : IMPOSTOR, CHARLATAN **c** : a simulated movement in a sports contest (as a pretended kick, pass, or jump or a quick movement in one direction before going in another) designed to deceive an opponent **d** : a device or apparatus used by a magician to achieve the illusion of magic in a trick ***syn*** see IMPOSTURE
[5]**fake** *adj* : COUNTERFEIT, SHAM
fa·kir *n* [Ar *faqīr,* lit., poor man] **1** \fə-'ki(ə)r, fä-, fa-\ **a** : a Muslim mendicant : DERVISH **b** : an itinerant Hindu ascetic or wonder-worker **2** \'fā-kər\ : IMPOSTOR; *esp* : SWINDLER
fa la \fä-'lä\ *n* [*fa-la,* meaningless syllables often occurring in its refrain] : a 16th and 17th century part-song
Fa·lan·gist \fə-'lan-jəst, 'fā-ˌ\ *n* [Sp *Falangista,* fr. *Falange española* Spanish Phalanx, a fascist organization] : a member of the fascist political party governing Spain after the civil war of 1936–39
fal·cate \'fal-ˌkāt, 'fȯl-\ *also* **fal·cat·ed** \-ˌkāt-əd\ *adj* [L *falcatus,* fr. *falc-, falx* sickle, scythe] : hooked or curved like a sickle
fal·chion \'fȯl-chən\ *n* [ME *fauchoun,* fr. OF *fauchon,* fr. *fauchier* to mow, fr. (assumed) VL *falcare,* fr. L *falc-, falx*] **1** : a broad-bladed slightly curved sword of medieval times **2** *archaic* : SWORD
fal·ci·form \'fal-sə-ˌfȯrm, 'fȯl-\ *adj* [L *falc-, falx* + E *-iform*] : having the shape of a scythe or sickle
fal·con \'fal-kən *also* 'fȯl- *sometimes* 'fȯ-kən\ *n* [ME, fr. OF, fr. LL *falcon-, falco,* prob. of Gmc origin; akin to OHG *falcho* falcon] **1 a** : any of various hawks trained for use in falconry; *esp* : PEREGRINE — used technically only of a female; compare TIERCEL **b** : any of various hawks (family Falconidae) distinguished by long wings and a notch and tooth on the edge of the upper mandible **c** : HAWK 1 **2** : a light cannon used from the 15th to the 17th centuries
fal·con·er \-kə-nər\ *n* **1** : one who hunts with hawks **2** : a breeder or trainer of hawks for hunting
fal·con·et \ˌfal-kə-'net, ˌfȯ(l)-\ *n* **1** : a very small cannon used in the 16th and 17th centuries **2** : any of several very small Asiatic falcons constituting a genus (*Microhierax*)
fal·con–gen·tle \-kən-'jent-ᵊl\ *n* [ME *faucon gentil* peregrine falcon, fr. MF, lit., noble falcon] : the female peregrine falcon
fal·con·ry \'fal-kən-rē *also* 'fȯl- *sometimes* 'fȯ-kən-\ *n* **1** : the art of training falcons to pursue game **2** : the sport of hunting with falcons
fal·de·ral \'fäl-də-ˌräl\ *var of* FOLDEROL
fald·stool \'fȯl(d)-ˌstül\ *n* [ML *faldistolium,* of Gmc origin; akin to OHG *faltistuol* folding chair, fr. a prehistoric WGmc compound whose first constituent is akin to OHG *faldan* to fold and whose second constituent is represented by OHG *stuol* chair — more at FOLD, STOOL] **1** : a folding stool or chair; *specif* : one used by a bishop **2** : a folding stool or small desk at which one kneels during devotions; *esp* : one used by the sovereign of England at his coronation **3** : the desk from which the litany is read in Anglican churches

faldstool 1

[1]**fall** \'fȯl\ *vb* **fell** \'fel\; **fall·en** \'fȯ-lən\; **fall·ing** [ME *fallen,* fr. OE *feallan;* akin to OHG *fallan* to fall and perh. to Lith *pulti*] *vi* **1 a** : to descend freely by the force of gravity **b** : to hang freely <her hair ~*s* over her shoulders> **c** : to drop oneself to a lower position <*fell* to his knees> **d** : to come as if by descending <darkness ~*s* early in the winter> **2** : to become born — usu. used of lambs **3 a** : to become lower in degree or level <the temperature *fell* 10°> **b** : to drop in pitch or volume <their voices *fell* to a whisper> **c** : ISSUE <wisdom that *fell* from his lips> **d** : to become lowered <her eyes *fell*> **4 a** : to leave an erect position suddenly and involuntarily <slipped and *fell* on the ice> **b** : to enter as if unawares : STUMBLE, STRAY <*fell* into error> **c** : to drop down wounded or dead; *esp* : to die in battle **d** : to suffer military capture <after a long siege the city *fell*> **e** : to lose office <the party *fell* from power> **f** : to suffer ruin, defeat, or failure <we must stand or ~ together> <the deal *fell* through> **5** : to commit an immoral act; *esp* : to lose one's chastity **6 a** : to move or extend in a downward direction <the land ~*s* away to the east> **b** : SUBSIDE, ABATE <the wind is ~*ing*> **c** : to decline in quality, activity, or quantity <production *fell* off because of the strike> **d** : to lose weight — used with *off* or *away* **e** : to assume a look of shame, disappointment, or dejection <his face *fell*> **f** : to decline in financial value or price <stocks *fell* sharply after the President's speech> **7 a** : to occur at a certain time **b** : to come by chance <it *fell* into my mind to write you> <*fell* in with a fast crowd> **c** : to come or pass by lot, assignment, or inheritance : DEVOLVE <it *fell* to him to break the news> **d** : to have the proper place or station <the accent ~*s* on the second syllable> **8** : to come within the limits, scope, or jurisdiction of something <this word ~*s* into the class of verbs> **9** : to pass suddenly and passively into a state of body or mind or a new state or condition <~ asleep> <~ in love> <the book *fell* apart> **10** : to set about heartily or actively <*fell* to work> **11** : STRIKE, IMPINGE <music ~*ing* on the ear> ~ *vt* : FELL 1 — **fall behind 1** : to lag behind **2** : to be in arrears — **fall flat** : to produce no response or result <the joke *fell flat*> — **fall for 1** : to fall in love with **2** : to become a victim of <he *fell for* the trick> — **fall foul 1** : to have a collision — used chiefly of ships **2** : to have a quarrel : CLASH — often used with *of* — **fall from grace 1** : to lapse morally : SIN **2** : BACKSLIDE — **fall home** : to curve inward — used of the timbers or upper parts of a ship's side — **fall into line** : to comply with a certain course of action — **fall on** *or* **fall upon** : to meet with <he *fell on* hard times> — **fall over oneself** *or* **fall over backward** : to display excessive eagerness — **fall short 1** : to be deficient **2** : to fail to attain something (as a goal or target)

[2]fall *n* **1 :** the act of falling by the force of gravity **2 a :** a falling out, off, or away : DROPPING <the ~ of leaves> <a ~ of snow> **b :** the season when leaves fall from trees : AUTUMN **c :** a thing or quantity that falls or has fallen <a ~ of rock at the base of the cliff>; *specif* : one or more meteorites or their fragments that have fallen together **d** (1) : BIRTH (2) : the quantity born — usu. used of lambs **3 a :** a costume decoration of lace or thin fabric arranged to hang loosely and gracefully **b :** a very wide turned-down collar worn in the 17th century **c :** the part of a turned-over collar from the crease to the outer edge **d :** a wide front flap on trousers (as those worn by sailors) **e :** the freely hanging lower edge of the skirt of a coat **f :** one of the three outer and often drooping segments of the flower of an iris **g :** long hair overhanging the face of certain terriers **h :** a usu. long straight portion of hair that is attached to a person's own hair **4 :** a hoisting-tackle rope or chain; *esp* : the part of it to which the power is applied **5 a :** loss of greatness : COLLAPSE <the ~ of the Roman Empire> **b :** the surrender or capture of a besieged place <the ~ of Troy> **c :** lapse or departure from innocence or goodness **d :** loss of a woman's chastity **6 a :** the downward slope (as of a hill) : DECLIVITY **b :** a precipitous descent of water : WATERFALL — usu. used in pl. but sing. or pl. in constr. **c :** a musical cadence **d :** a falling-pitch intonation in speech **7 :** a decrease in size, quantity, or degree; *specif* : a decrease in price or value **8 a :** the distance which something falls **b :** INCLINATION, PITCH **9 a :** the act of felling **b :** the quantity of trees cut down **c** (1) : an act of forcing a wrestler's shoulders to the mat for a specified time (as three seconds) (2) : a bout of wrestling **10** *Scot* : FORTUNE, LOT

[3]fall *adj* : of or relating to autumn <a new ~ coat>

fal·la·cious \fə-ˈlā-shəs\ *adj* **1 :** embodying a fallacy **2 :** tending to deceive or mislead : DELUSIVE — **fal·la·cious·ly** *adv* — **fal·la·cious·ness** *n*

fal·la·cy \ˈfal-ə-sē\ *n, pl* **-cies** [L *fallacia,* fr. *fallac-, fallax* deceitful, fr. *fallere* to deceive — more at FAIL] **1 a** *obs* : GUILE, TRICKERY **b :** deceptive appearance : DECEPTION **2 a :** a false idea <the popular ~ that poets are impractical> **b :** erroneous or fallacious character : ERRONEOUSNESS **3 :** an argument failing to satisfy the conditions of valid or correct inference

fal–lal \fa-ˈlal, ˈfal-ˌ(l)al\ *n* [perh. alter. of *falbala* (furbelow)] : a fancy ornament esp. in dress — **fal·lal·ery** \fa-ˈlal-ə-rē\ *n*

fall armyworm *n* : a migratory American moth (*Spodoptera frugiperda*) that is esp. destructive to small grains and grasses as a larva

fall away *vi* **1 a :** to withdraw friendship or support **b :** to renounce one's faith **2 a :** to diminish gradually in size **b :** to drift off a course

fall·back \ˈfȯl-ˌbak\ *n* **1 :** something on which one can fall back : RESERVE **2 :** a falling back : RETREAT **3 :** something that falls back <the ~ from an explosion>

fall back \-ˈbak\ *vi* : RETREAT, RECEDE — **fall back on** *or* **fall back upon :** to have recourse to <when facts were scarce he *fell back on* his imagination>

fall down *vi* : to fail to meet expectations or requirements <he *fell down* on the job>

fall·er \ˈfȯ-lər\ *n* **1 :** a logger who fells trees **2 :** a machine part that acts by falling

fall·fish \ˈfȯl-ˌfish\ *n* : a common cyprinid fish (*Semotilus corporalis*) of the streams of northeastern No. America — compare CHUB

fall guy *n* **1 :** one that is easily duped **2 :** SCAPEGOAT

fal·li·bil·i·ty \ˌfal-ə-ˈbil-ət-ē\ *n* : liability to err

fal·li·ble \ˈfal-ə-bəl\ *adj* [ME, fr. ML *fallibilis,* fr. L *fallere*] **1 :** liable to be erroneous <a ~ generalization> **2 :** capable of making a mistake <all men are ~> — **fal·li·bly** \-blē\ *adv*

fall in *vi* **1 :** to sink inward <the roof *fell in*> **2 :** to take one's proper place in a military formation — **fall in with 1 :** to concur with <had to *fall in with* her wishes> **2 :** to harmonize with <it *falls in* exactly *with* my views>

falling diphthong *n* : a diphthong with less stress on the second element than on the first (as \ȯi\ in \ˈnȯiz\ *noise*)

fall·ing–out \ˌfȯ-liŋ-ˈau̇t\ *n, pl* **fallings–out** *or* **falling–outs :** an instance of falling out : QUARREL

falling rhythm *n* : rhythm with stress occurring regularly on the first syllable of each foot — compare RISING RHYTHM

falling star *n* : METEOR 2a

fall line *n* **1 :** a line joining the waterfalls on numerous rivers that marks the point where each river descends from the upland to the lowland and the limit of the navigability of each river **2 :** the natural downhill course (as for skiing) between two points on a slope

fall·off \ˈfȯ-ˌlȯf\ *n* : a decline esp. in quantity or quality <a ~ in exports> <a ~ of light intensity>

fall off \(ˈ)fȯ-ˈlȯf\ *vi* **1 :** TREND 1b **2** *of a ship* : to deviate to leeward of the point to which the bow was directed

fal·lo·pi·an tube \fə-ˌlō-pē-ən-\ *n, often cap F* [Gabriel *Fallopius* †1562 It anatomist] : either of the pair of tubes conducting the egg from the ovary to the uterus

fall·out \ˈfȯ-ˌlau̇t\ *n* **1 a :** the often radioactive particles stirred up by or resulting from a nuclear explosion and descending through the atmosphere; *also* : other polluting particles (as volcanic ash) descending likewise **b :** descent (as of fallout) through the atmosphere **2 :** an incidental result or product <the war . . . produced its own literary ~ —a profusion of books —*Newsweek*>

fall out \(ˈ)fȯ-ˈlau̇t\ *vi* **1 :** to turn out : HAPPEN <as it *fell out* we couldn't have made it on time> **2 :** QUARREL <friends who have *fallen out*> **3 a :** to leave one's place in the ranks **b :** to leave a building in order to take one's place in a military formation

[1]fal·low \ˈfal-(ˌ)ō, -ə(-w)\ *adj* [ME *falow,* fr. OE *fealu;* akin to OHG *falo* pale, fallow, L *pallēre* to be pale, Gk *polios* gray] : of a light yellowish brown color

[2]fallow *n* [ME *falwe, falow,* fr. OE *fealg* — more at FELLY] **1** *obs* : plowed land **2 :** usu. cultivated land that is allowed to lie idle during the growing season **3 :** the state or period of being fallow **4 :** the tilling of land without sowing it for a season

[3]fallow *vt* : to plow, harrow, and break up (land) without seeding to destroy weeds and conserve soil moisture

[4]fallow *adj* **1 :** left untilled or unsown after plowing **2 :** DORMANT, INACTIVE — used esp. in the phrase *to lie fallow* <at this very moment there are probably important inventions lying ~ —*Harper's*> — **fal·low·ness** *n*

fallow deer *n* : a small European deer (*Dama dama*) with broad antlers and a pale yellow coat spotted with white in the summer

fallow deer

fall to \ˈfȯl-ˈtü\ *vi* : to begin doing something (as working or eating) esp. vigorously — often used in invitation or command

[1]false \ˈfȯls\ *adj* **fals·er; fals·est** [ME *fals,* fr. OF & L; OF, fr. L *falsus,* fr. pp. of *fallere* to deceive] **1 :** not genuine <~ documents> <~ teeth> **2 a :** intentionally untrue <~ testimony> **b :** adjusted or made so as to deceive <~ scales> <a trunk with a ~ bottom> **c :** tending to mislead <a ~ promise> **3 :** not true <~ concepts> **4 a :** not faithful or loyal : TREACHEROUS **b** *obs* : not solid **5 a :** not essential or permanent — used of parts of a structure that are temporary or supplemental **b :** fitting over a main part to strengthen it, to protect it, or to disguise its appearance <a ~ ceiling> **c :** appearing forced or artificial : UNCONVINCING <a ~ scene in a movie> **6 :** of a kind related to or resembling another kind that is usu. designated by the unqualified vernacular <~ oats> **7 :** inaccurate in pitch <a ~ note> **8 a :** based on mistaken ideas <~ pride> **b :** inconsistent with the true facts <a ~ position> <a ~ sense of security> **9 :** IMPRUDENT, UNWISE <don't make a ~ move> — **false·ly** *adv* — **false·ness** *n*

syn* 1** FALSE, WRONG *shared meaning element* : neither true nor right ***ant true
2 see FAITHLESS ***ant*** true

[2]false *adv* : in a false or faithless manner : TREACHEROUSLY <his wife played him ~>

false alarm *n* **1 :** an alarm (as a fire or burglar alarm) that is set off needlessly **2 :** one that raises but fails to meet expectations

false arrest *n* : an arrest not justifiable under law

false·hood \ˈfȯls-ˌhu̇d\ *n* **1 :** an untrue statement : LIE **2 :** absence of truth or accuracy : FALSITY **3 :** the practice of lying : MENDACITY

false horizon *n* : HORIZON 1c

false imprisonment *n* : imprisonment of a person contrary to law

false miterwort *n* : FOAMFLOWER

false pregnancy *n* : PSEUDOCYESIS, PSEUDOPREGNANCY

false rib *n* : a rib whose cartilages unite indirectly or not at all with the sternum — compare FLOATING RIB

false Solomon's–seal *n* : any of a genus (*Smilacina*) of herbs of the lily family that differ from Solomon's seal in having flowers in a terminal raceme or panicle

[1]fal·set·to \fȯl-ˈset-(ˌ)ō\ *n, pl* **-tos** [It, fr. dim. of *falso* false, fr. L *falsus*] **1 :** an artificially high voice; *specif* : an artificially produced singing voice that overlaps and extends above the range of the full voice esp. of a tenor **2 :** a singer who uses falsetto

[2]falsetto *adv* : in falsetto

fals·ie \ˈfȯl-sē\ *n* : a breast-shaped usu. fabric or rubber cup used to pad a brassiere — usu. used in pl.

fal·si·fy \ˈfȯl-sə-ˌfī\ *vb* **-fied; -fy·ing** [ME *falsifien,* fr. MF *falsifier,* fr. ML *falsificare,* fr. L *falsus*] *vt* **1 :** to prove or declare false **2 :** to make false: as **a :** to make false by mutilation or addition <his accounts were *falsified* to conceal a theft> **b :** to represent falsely : MISREPRESENT **3 :** to prove unsound by experience ~ *vi* : to tell lies : LIE ***syn*** see MISREPRESENT — **fal·si·fi·ca·tion** \ˌfȯl-sə-fə-ˈkā-shən\ *n* — **fal·si·fi·er** \ˈfȯl-sə-ˌfī(-ə)r\ *n*

fal·si·ty \ˈfȯl-sət-ē\ *n, pl* **-ties 1 :** something false : LIE **2 :** the quality or state of being false

Fal·staff \ˈfȯl-ˌstaf\ *n* : a convivial roguish character in Shakespeare's *Merry Wives of Windsor* and *Henry IV* — **Fal·staff·ian** \fȯl-ˈstaf-ē-ən\ *adj*

falt·boat \ˈfält-ˌbōt, ˈfōlt-\ *n* [part trans. of G *faltboot* folding boat, fr. *falten* to fold (fr. OHG *faldan*) + *boot* boat] : FOLDBOAT

[1]fal·ter \ˈfȯl-tər\ *vb* **fal·tered; fal·ter·ing** \-t(ə-)riŋ\ [ME *falteren*] *vi* **1 a :** to walk unsteadily : STUMBLE **b :** to give way : TOTTER <could feel his legs ~*ing*> **c :** to move waveringly or hesitatingly <forced to bail out of ~*ing* airplanes —*Nat'l Geographic*> **2 :** to speak brokenly or weakly : STAMMER **3 a :** to hesitate in purpose or action : WAVER **b :** to lose drive or effectiveness : FAIL, WEAKEN <the business was ~*ing*> ~ *vt* : to utter hesitatingly or brokenly ***syn*** see HESITATE — **fal·ter·er** \-tər-ər\ *n* — **fal·ter·ing·ly** \-t(ə-)riŋ-lē\ *adv*

[2]falter *n* : an act or instance of faltering

fam *abbr* **1** familiar **2** family

[1]fame \ˈfām\ *n* [ME, fr. OF, fr. L *fama* report, fame; akin to L *fari* to speak — more at BAN] **1 a :** public estimation : REPUTATION **b :** popular acclaim : RENOWN **2** *archaic* : RUMOR

[2]fame *vt* **famed; fam·ing 1 :** REPORT, REPUTE **2 :** to make famous

famed \ˈfāmd\ *adj* : known widely and well : FAMOUS <a ~ university>

fa·mil·ial \fə-ˈmil-yəl\ *adj* [F, fr. L *familia*] **1 :** of, relating to, or characteristic of a family **2 :** tending to occur in more members of a family than expected by chance alone <a ~ disorder>

---

[1]**fa·mil·iar** \fə-ˈmil-yər\ *n* **1 :** an intimate associate : COMPANION **2 :** a member of the household of a high official **3 :** a spirit often embodied in an animal and held to attend and serve or guard a person **4 a :** one who is well acquainted with something **b :** one who frequents a place

[2]**familiar** *adj* [ME *familier,* fr. OF, fr. L *familiaris,* fr. *familia*] **1 :** closely acquainted : INTIMATE <a ~ family friend> **2** *obs* **:** AFFABLE, SOCIABLE **3 a :** of or relating to a family <remembering past ~ celebrations> **b :** frequented by families <a ~ resort> **4 a :** being free and easy <the ~ association of old friends> **b :** marked by informality <a ~ essay> **c :** overly free and unrestrained : PRESUMPTUOUS <grossly ~ behavior> **d :** moderately tame <~ animals> **5 a :** frequently seen or experienced **b :** of everyday occurrence ***syn*** see COMMON — **fa·mil·iar·ly** *adv* — **fa·mil·iar·ness** *n*

fa·mil·iar·i·ty \fə-ˌmil-ˈyar-ət-ē, -ˌmil-ē-ˈ(y)ar-\ *n, pl* **-ties** **1 a :** the quality or state of being familiar **b :** a state of close relationship : INTIMACY **2 a :** absence of ceremony : INFORMALITY **b :** an unduly informal act or expression : IMPROPRIETY **c :** a sexual liberty **3 :** close acquaintance with something <his ~ with American history>

fa·mil·iar·ize \fə-ˈmil-yə-ˌrīz\ *vt* **-ized; -iz·ing** **1 :** to make known or familiar <Shakespeare . . . ~*s* the wonderful —Samuel Johnson> **2 :** to make well acquainted <~ students with good literature> — **fa·mil·iar·iza·tion** \-ˌmil-yə-rə-ˈzā-shən\ *n*

familiar spirit *n* **1 :** a spirit or demon that serves or prompts an individual **2 :** the spirit of a dead person invoked by a medium to advise or prophesy

[1]**fam·i·ly** \ˈfam-(ə-)lē\ *n, pl* **-lies** [ME *familie,* fr. L *familia* household (including servants as well as kin of the householder), fr. *famulus* servant; perh. akin to Skt *dhāman* dwelling place] **1 a :** a group of people united by certain convictions (as of religion or philosophy) : FELLOWSHIP **b :** the staff of a high official (as the President) **2 a :** a group of persons of common ancestry : CLAN **b :** a people or group of peoples regarded as deriving from a common stock : RACE **3 :** a group of individuals living under one roof and usu. under one head : HOUSEHOLD **4 a :** a group of things related by common characteristics or properties **b :** a closely related series of elements or chemical compounds **c :** a group of soils that have similar profiles and include one or more series **d :** a group of related languages descended from a single ancestral language **5 :** the basic unit in society having as its nucleus two or more adults living together and cooperating in the care and rearing of their own or adopted children **6 a :** a group of related plants or animals forming a category ranking above a genus and below an order and usu. comprising several to many genera **b** *in livestock breeding* **(1) :** the descendants or line of a particular individual esp. of some outstanding female **(2) :** an identifiable strain within a breed **c :** an ecological community consisting of a single kind of organism and usu. being of limited extent and representing an early stage of a succession **7 :** a set of curves or surfaces whose equations differ only in parameters

[2]**family** *adj* **:** of or relating to a family

family Bible *n* **:** a large Bible usu. having special pages for recording births, marriages, and deaths

family circle *n* **:** a gallery in a theater or opera house usu. located above or behind a gallery containing more expensive seats

family court *n* **:** COURT OF DOMESTIC RELATIONS

family doctor *n* **:** a doctor regularly called by a family in time of illness — called also *family physician*

family man *n* **1 :** a man with a wife and children dependent on him **2 :** a responsible man of domestic habits

family name *n* **:** SURNAME 2

family planning *n* **:** a system of controlling family size and approximate birth dates of children by appropriate use of contraceptive techniques

family room *n* **:** a large room designed as a recreation center for members of a family

family style *adv or adj* **:** with the food placed on the table in serving dishes from which those eating may help themselves <meals are served *family style*>

family tree *n* **1 :** GENEALOGY **2 :** a genealogical diagram

fam·ine \ˈfam-ən\ *n* [ME, fr. MF, fr. (assumed) VL *famina,* fr. L *fames* hunger] **1 :** an extreme scarcity of food **2** *archaic* **:** STARVATION **3** *archaic* **:** a ravenous appetite **4 :** a great shortage

fam·ish \ˈfam-ish\ *vb* [ME *famishen,* prob. alter. of *famen,* fr. MF *afamer,* fr. (assumed) VL *affamare,* fr. L *ad-* + *fames*] *vt* **1 :** to cause to suffer severely from hunger **2** *archaic* **:** to cause to starve to death ~ *vi* **1** *archaic* **:** STARVE **2 :** to suffer for lack of something necessary <this invention of language, at a moment when French poetry in particular was ~*ing* for such invention —T. S. Eliot> — **fam·ish·ment** \-mənt\ *n*

fa·mous \ˈfā-məs\ *adj* [ME, fr. MF *fameux,* fr. L *famosus,* fr. *fama* fame] **1 a :** widely known **b :** honored for achievement **2 :** EXCELLENT, FIRST-RATE <~ weather for a walk> — **fa·mous·ly** *adv* — **fa·mous·ness** *n*

syn FAMOUS, RENOWNED, CELEBRATED, NOTED, DISTINGUISHED, EMINENT, ILLUSTRIOUS *shared meaning element* **:** known far and wide ***ant*** obscure

fam·u·lus \ˈfam-yə-ləs\ *n, pl* **-li** \-ˌlī, -ˌlē\ [G, assistant to a professor, fr. L, servant] **:** a private secretary or attendant

[1]**fan** \ˈfan\ *n* [ME, fr. OE *fann,* fr. L *vannus* — more at WINNOW] **1 :** any of various devices for winnowing grain **2 :** an instrument for producing a current of air: as **a :** a device for cooling the person that is usu. shaped like a segment of a circle and is composed of material (as feathers or paper) mounted on thin rods or slats moving about a pivot so that the device may be closed compactly when not in use **b :** a device for producing a current of air that consists of a series of vanes radiating from a hub rotated on its axle by a motor **c** *slang* **:** an airplane propeller **3 :** something resembling an open fan — **fan·like** \-ˌlīk\ *adj*

[2]**fan** *vb* **fanned; fan·ning** *vt* **1 a :** to drive away the chaff of (grain) by means of a current of air **b :** to eliminate (as chaff) by winnowing **2 :** to move or impel (air) with a fan **3 :** to blow or breathe upon <the breeze *fanning* her hair> **4 a :** to direct a current of air upon with a fan **b :** to stir up to activity as if by fanning : STIMULATE <he was *fanning* her antagonism with insults> **5** *archaic* **:** WAVE **6** *slang* **:** SPANK **7 :** to spread like a fan <the peacock *fanned* his tail> **8 :** to strike (a batter) out in baseball **9 :** to fire a series of shots from (a revolver) by holding the trigger back and successively striking the hammer to the rear with the free hand ~ *vi* **1 :** to move like a fan : FLUTTER **2 :** to spread like a fan — often used with *out* <deputies *fanning* out on the hunt> **3** *of a baseball batter* **:** to strike out

[3]**fan** *n* [prob. short for *fanatic*] **1 :** an enthusiastic devotee (as of a sport or a performing art) usu. as a spectator **2 :** an ardent admirer or enthusiast (as of a celebrity or a pursuit) <science-fiction ~*s*>

fa·nat·ic \fə-ˈnat-ik\ *or* **fa·nat·i·cal** \-i-kəl\ *adj* [L *fanaticus* inspired by a deity, frenzied, fr. *fanum* temple — more at FEAST] **:** marked by excessive enthusiasm and often intense uncritical devotion <he's ~ about politics> — **fanatic** *n* — **fa·nat·i·cal·ly** \fə-ˈnat-i-k(ə-)lē\ *adv* — **fa·nat·i·cal·ness** \-kəl-nəs\ *n*

fa·nat·i·cism \fə-ˈnat-ə-ˌsiz-əm\ *n* **:** fanatic outlook or behavior

fa·nat·i·cize \-ˌsīz\ *vt* **-cized; -ciz·ing :** to cause to become fanatic

fan·ci·er \ˈfan(t)-sē-ər\ *n* **:** one that has a special liking or interest; *esp* **:** a person who breeds or grows a particular animal or plant for points of excellence <a pigeon ~>

fan·ci·ful \ˈfan(t)-si-fəl\ *adj* **1 :** marked by fancy or unrestrained imagination rather than by reason and experience **2 :** existing in fancy only **3 :** marked by or as if by fancy or whim <gave ~ names to her children> ***syn*** see IMAGINARY ***ant*** realistic — **fan·ci·ful·ly** \-f(ə-)lē\ *adv* — **fan·ci·ful·ness** \-fəl-nəs\ *n*

fan·ci·ly \ˈfan(t)-sə-lē\ *adv* **1 :** with fancy or imagination esp. when studied or affected **2 :** in an elaborate or ornate manner <~ dressed>

fan·ci·ness \-sē-nəs\ *n* **:** fancy quality or form

[1]**fan·cy** \ˈfan(t)-sē\ *n, pl* **fancies** [ME *fantasie, fantsy* fantasy, fancy, fr. MF *fantasie,* fr. L *phantasia,* fr. Gk, appearance, imagination, fr. *phantazein* to present to the mind (middle voice, to imagine), fr. *phainein* to show; akin to OE ge*bōn*ed polished, Gk *phōs* light] **1 a :** a liking formed by caprice rather than reason : INCLINATION <took a ~ to the strange little animal> **b :** amorous fondness : LOVE **2 a :** NOTION, WHIM **b :** an image or representation of something formed in the mind **3** *archaic* **:** fantastic quality or state **4 a :** imagination esp. of a capricious or delusive sort **b :** the power of conception and representation used in artistic expression (as by a poet) **5 :** TASTE, JUDGMENT **6 a :** devotees of some particular art, practice, or amusement **b :** the object of interest of such a fancy; *esp* **:** PUGILISM ***syn*** see IMAGINATION

[2]**fancy** *vt* **fan·cied; fan·cy·ing** **1 :** to have a fancy for : LIKE **2 :** to form a conception of : IMAGINE <~ our embarrassment> **3 :** to form an idea about on the basis of inadequate evidence or in the absence of evidence <she *fancied* she had met him before> ***syn*** see THINK

[3]**fancy** *adj* **fan·ci·er; -est** **1 :** dependent or based on fancy : WHIMSICAL **2 a :** not plain : ORNAMENTAL <a ~ hairdo> **b :** of particular excellence or highest grade <~ tuna> **c** *of an animal or plant* **:** bred esp. for bizarre or ornamental qualities that lack practical utility **3 :** based on conceptions of the fancy <~ sketches> **4 a :** dealing in fancy goods **b :** above real value or the usual market price; *esp* **:** EXTRAVAGANT <paying ~ prices for inferior goods> **5 :** executed with technical skill and superior grace <~ diving> **6 :** PARTI-COLORED <~ carnations>

fancy dress *n* **:** a costume (as for a masquerade) chosen to suit the wearer's fancy

fan·cy–free \ˈfan(t)-sē-ˌfrē\ *adj* **1 :** free to imagine or fancy **2 :** free from amorous attachment or engagement

fancy man *n* **:** a woman's paramour; *also* **:** PIMP

fancy up *vt* **:** to add superficial adornment to <*fancy up* an old dress with ruffles>

fancy woman *n* **:** a woman of questionable morals; *specif* **:** PROSTITUTE

fan·cy·work \ˈfan(t)-sē-ˌwərk\ *n* **:** decorative needlework

F and A *abbr* fore and aft

fan·dan·go \fan-ˈdaŋ-(ˌ)gō\ *n, pl* **-gos** [Sp] **1 :** a lively Spanish or Spanish-American dance in triple time that is usu. performed by a man and a woman to the accompaniment of guitar and castanets; *also* **:** music for this dance **2 :** TOMFOOLERY

fan·dom \ˈfan-dəm\ *n* **:** all the fans (as of a sport)

fane \ˈfān\ *n* [ME, fr. L *fanum* — more at FEAST] **1 :** TEMPLE **2 :** CHURCH

fan·fare \ˈfan-ˌfa(ə)r, -ˌfe(ə)r\ *n* [F] **1 :** a flourish of trumpets **2 :** a showy outward display

fan·far·o·nade \ˌfan-ˌfar-ə-ˈnād, -ˈnäd\ *n* [F *fanfaronnade,* fr. Sp *fanfarronada,* fr. *fanfarrón* braggart] **:** empty boasting : BLUSTER

fan·fold \ˈfan-ˌfōld\ *n* **:** a business form made from a web of paper folded like a fan both lengthwise and crosswise

fang \ˈfaŋ\ *n* [ME, fr. OE; akin to OHG *fang* seizure, OE *fōn* to seize — more at PACT] **1 a :** a long sharp tooth: as **(1) :** one by which an animal's prey is seized and held or torn **(2) :** one of the long hollow or grooved and often erectile teeth of a venomous snake **b :** one of the chelicerae of a spider at the tip of which a poison gland opens **2 :** the root of a tooth or one of the processes or prongs into which a root divides **3 :** a projecting tooth or prong — **fanged** \ˈfaŋd\ *adj*

fan·ion \ˈfan-yən\ *n* [F, fr. *fanon* maniple, pennon, of Gmc origin; akin to OHG *fano* cloth — more at VANE] **:** a small flag used by soldiers and surveyors to mark positions

fan–jet \ˈfan-ˌjet\ *n* **1 :** a jet engine having a fan that operates in a duct and draws in extra air whose compression and expulsion provide extra thrust **2 :** an airplane powered by a fan-jet engine

fan letter *n* **:** a letter sent to a public figure (as in sports or the movies) by an admirer

fan·light \ˈfan-ˌlīt\ *n* **:** a semicircular window with radiating sash bars like the ribs of a fan that is placed over a door or window

fan mail *n* : FAN LETTERS

fan·ner \'fan-ər\ *n* : one that fans

fan·ny \'fan-ē\ *n, pl* **fannies** [fr. *Fanny,* nickname of *Frances*] : BUTTOCKS

fan·tail \'fan-ˌtāl\ *n* **1** : a fan-shaped tail or end **2** : a domestic pigeon having a broad rounded tail often with 30 or 40 feathers **3** : an architectural part resembling a fan **4** : a counter or after overhang of a ship shaped like a duck's bill

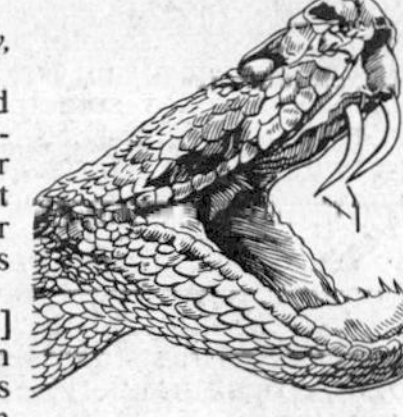

1 fangs of a rattlesnake

fan–tan \'fan-ˌtan\ *n* [Chin *fan¹-t'an¹*] **1** : a Chinese gambling game in which the banker divides a pile of objects (as beans) into fours and players bet on what number will be left at the end of the count **2** : a card game in which players must build in sequence upon sevens and attempt to be the first one out of cards

fan·ta·sia \fan-'tā-zhə, -z(h)ē-ə; ˌfant-ə-'zē-ə\ *also* **fan·ta·sie** \ˌfant-ə-'zē, ˌfänt-\ *n* [It *fantasia* & G *fantasie,* lit., fancy, fr. L *phantasia* — more at FANCY] **1 a** : a free instrumental composition not in strict form **b** : a potpourri of operatic arias or familiar airs **2 a** : a work (as a poem or play) in which the author's fancy roves unrestricted **b** : something possessing grotesque, bizarre, or unreal qualities

fan·ta·sied \'fant-ə-sēd, -zēd\ *adj* **1** : existing only in the imagination : FANCIED **2** *obs* : full of fancies or strange whims

fan·ta·sist \-səst, -zəst\ *n* : one who creates fantasias or fantasies

fan·ta·size \-ˌsīz\ *vb* **-sized; -siz·ing** *vt* : FANTASY <likes to ~ herself as very wealthy> ~ *vi* : to indulge in reverie : create or develop imaginative and often fantastic views or ideas <doing things I'd *fantasized* about in my sheltered childhood —Diane Arbus>

fantasm *var of* PHANTASM

fan·tast \'fan-ˌtast\ *n* [G, fr. ML *fantasta,* prob. back-formation fr. LL *phantasticus*] **1** : VISIONARY **2** : a fantastic or eccentric person **3** : FANTASIST

¹fan·tas·tic \fan-'tas-tik, fən-\ *adj* [ME *fantastic, fantastical,* fr. MF & LL; MF *fantastique,* fr. LL *phantasticus,* fr. Gk *phantastikos* producing mental images, fr. *phantazein* to present to the mind] **1 a** : based on fantasy : not real **b** : conceived or seemingly conceived by unrestrained fancy **c** : so extreme as to challenge belief : UNBELIEVABLE; *broadly* : excessively large or great **2** : marked by extravagant fantasy or extreme individuality : ECCENTRIC — **fan·tas·ti·cal** \-ti-kəl\ *adj* — **fan·tas·ti·cal·i·ty** \(ˌ)fan-ˌtas-tə-'kal-ət-ē, fən-\ *n* — **fan·tas·ti·cal·ly** \fan-'tas-ti-k(ə-)lē, fən-\ *adv* — **fan·tas·ti·cal·ness** \-kəl-nəs\ *n*

syn **1** see IMAGINARY

2 FANTASTIC, BIZARRE, GROTESQUE *shared meaning element* : conceived or made or carried out without evident reference to reality, truth, or common sense

²fantastic *n* : ECCENTRIC 2

fan·tas·ti·cate \fan-'tas-tə-ˌkāt, fən-\ *vt* **-cat·ed; -cat·ing** : to make fantastic — **fan·tas·ti·ca·tion** \(ˌ)fan-ˌtas-tə-'kā-shən, fən-\ *n*

fan·tas·ti·co \fan-'tas-ti-ˌkō, fən-\ *n, pl* **-coes** [It, fantastic (adj.), fr. LL *phantasticus*] : a ridiculously fantastic individual

¹fan·ta·sy \'fant-ə-sē, -zē\ *n, pl* **-sies** [ME *fantasie* — more at FANCY] **1** *obs* : HALLUCINATION **2** : FANCY; *esp* : the free play of creative imagination **3** : a creation of the imaginative faculty whether expressed or merely conceived: as **a** : a fanciful design or invention **b** : a chimerical or fantastic notion **c** : FANTASIA 1 **d** : imaginative fiction featuring esp. strange settings and grotesque characters — called also *fantasy fiction* **4** : CAPRICE **5** : the power or process of creating esp. unrealistic or improbable mental images in response to psychological need <an object of ~>; *also* : a mental image so created : DAYDREAM <sexual *fantasies* of adolescence> **6** : a coin usu. not intended for circulation as currency and often issued by a dubious authority (as a government-in-exile) *syn* see IMAGINATION

²fantasy *vb* **-sied; -sy·ing** *vt* : to portray in the mind : FANCY ~ *vi* : to indulge in reverie : DAYDREAM

fan·toc·ci·ni \ˌfänt-ə-'chē-nē, ˌfant-\ *n pl* [It, pl. of *fantoccino,* dim. of *fantoccio* doll, aug. of *fante* child, fr. L *infant-, infans* infant] **1** : puppets operated by strings or mechanical devices **2** : a puppet show using fantoccini

fan·tod \'fan-ˌtäd\ *n* [perh. alter. of E dial. *fantique, fanteeg*] **1** *pl* **a** : a state of irritability and tension **b** : FIDGETS **2** : an emotional outburst : FIT

fantom *var of* PHANTOM

fan tracery *n* : decorative tracery on vaulting in which the ribs diverge like the rays of a fan

fan·wise \'fan-ˌwīz\ *adv or adj* : in the manner or position of the slats of an open fan <boats anchored ~ at the pier>

FAO *abbr* Food and Agriculture Organization of the United Nations

FAQ *abbr* fair average quality

¹far \'fär\ *adv* **far·ther** \-t͟hər\ *or* **fur·ther** \'fər-\; **far·thest** *or* **fur·thest** \-t͟həst\ [ME *fer,* fr. OE *feorr;* akin to OHG *ferro* far, OE *faran* to go — more at FARE] **1** : at or to a considerable distance in space <wandered ~ from home> **2 a** : by a broad interval : WIDELY <the ~ distant future> **b** : of a distinctly different quality — usu. used with *from* <the trip was ~ from a failure> **3** : to or at a definite distance, point, or degree <as ~ as I know> **4 a** : to an advanced point or extent <a bright student will go ~> <worked ~ into the night> **b** : to a great extent : MUCH <~ better methods> **5** : at a considerable distance in time <not ~ from the year 1870> — **by far** : far and away <is *by far* the best runner> — **far and away** : by a considerable margin <was *far and away* the superior team> — **how far** : to what extent, degree, or distance <didn't know *how far* to trust him> — **so far** : to a certain extent, degree, or distance <when the water rose *so far,* the villagers sought higher ground> **2** : up to the present <has written just one novel *so far*> — **thus far** : so far <*thus far* our findings have been negative>

²far *adj* **farther** *or* **further; farthest** *or* **furthest** **1 a** : remote in space **b** : distinctly different in quality or relationship **c** : remote in time **2 a** : LONG <a ~ journey> **b** : of notable extent : COMPREHENSIVE <a man of ~ vision> **3** : the more distant of two **4** *of a political position* : EXTREME <the ~ left> <a ~ right organization> *syn* see DISTANT *ant* near, nigh, nearby

³far *abbr* farthing

far·ad \'fa(ə)r-ˌad, 'far-əd\ *n* [Michael *Faraday*] : the unit of capacitance equal to the capacitance of a capacitor between whose plates there appears a potential of one volt when it is charged by one coulomb of electricity

far·a·day \'far-ə-ˌdā, -əd-ē\ *n* [Michael *Faraday*] : the quantity of electricity transferred in electrolysis per equivalent weight of an element or ion equal to about 96,500 coulombs

fa·rad·ic \fə-'rad-ik, far-'ad-\ *also* **far·a·da·ic** \ˌfar-ə-'dā-ik\ *adj* : of or relating to an asymmetric alternating current of electricity produced by an induction coil

far·a·dism \'far-ə-ˌdiz-əm\ *n* : the application of a faradic current of electricity (as for therapeutic purposes)

far·an·dole \'far-ən-ˌdōl\ *n* [F *farandole,* fr. Prov *farandoulo*] **1** : a lively Provençal dance in which men and women hold hands, form a chain, and follow a leader through a serpentine course **2** : music in sextuple time for a farandole

far and wide *adv* : in every direction : EVERYWHERE <advertised the event *far and wide*>

far·away \ˌfär-ə-ˌwā\ *adj* **1** : lying at a great distance : REMOTE **2** : DREAMY, ABSTRACTED <a ~ look in her eyes> *syn* see DISTANT *ant* near, nigh, nearby

¹farce \'färs\ *vt* **farced; farc·ing** [ME *farsen,* fr. MF *farcir,* fr. L *farcire;* akin to Gk *phrassein* to enclose] **1** : STUFF **2** : to make more acceptable (as a literary work) by padding or spicing

²farce *n* [ME *farse,* fr. MF *farce,* fr. (assumed) VL *farsa,* fr. L, fem. of *farsus,* pp. of *farcire*] **1** : a savory stuffing : FORCEMEAT **2** : a light dramatic composition marked by broadly satirical comedy and improbable plot **3** : the broad humor characteristic of farce or pretense **4 a** : ridiculous or empty show **b** : MOCKERY <the upholding of this law became a ~>

far·ceur \fär-'sər\ *n* [F, fr. MF, fr. *farcer* to joke, fr. OF, fr. *farce*] **1** : JOKER, WAG **2** : a writer or actor of farce

far·ci *or* **far·cie** \fär-'sē\ *adj* [F, fr. pp. of *farcir*] : stuffed esp. with forcemeat <oysters ~>

far·ci·cal \'fär-si-kəl\ *adj* **1** : of, relating to, or resembling farce : LUDICROUS **2** : laughably inept : ABSURD — **far·ci·cal·i·ty** \ˌfär-sə-'kal-ət-ē\ *n* — **far·ci·cal·ly** \'fär-si-k(ə-)lē\ *adv*

far·cy \'fär-sē\ *n* [ME *farsin, farsi,* fr. MF *farcin,* fr. LL *farcimen,* fr. L, sausage, fr. *farcire*] **1** : GLANDERS; *esp* : cutaneous glanders **2** : a chronic ultimately fatal actinomycosis of cattle

¹fard \'färd\ *vt* [ME *farden,* fr. MF *farder;* akin to OHG *faro* colored — more at PERCH] **1** : to paint (the face) with cosmetics **2** *archaic* : to gloss over

²fard *n, archaic* : paint used on the face

far·del \'färd-ᵊl\ *n* [ME, fr. MF, prob. fr. Ar *fardah*] **1** : BUNDLE **2** : BURDEN

¹fare \'fa(ə)r, 'fe(ə)r\ *vi* **fared; far·ing** [ME *faren,* fr. OE *faran;* akin to OHG *faran* to go, L *portare* to carry, Gk *poros* passage, journey] **1** : GO, TRAVEL **2** : to get along : SUCCEED <how did you ~ on your exam?> **3** : EAT, DINE

²fare *n* [ME, journey, passage, supply of food, fr. OE *faru, fær;* akin to OE *faran* to go] **1 a** : the price charged to transport a person **b** : a paying passenger on a public conveyance **2 a** : range of food : DIET **b** : material provided for use, consumption, or enjoyment

fare–thee–well \'fa(ə)r-(ˌ)t͟hē-ˌwel, 'fe(ə)r-\ *or* **fare–you–well** \-yə-, -yü-, -yē-\ *n* **1** : a state of perfection <imitated the speaker's pompous manner to a ~> **2** : the utmost degree <drubbed the burglar to a ~>

¹fare·well \fa(ə)r-'wel, fe(ə)r-\ *vb imper* : get along well — used interjectionally to or by one departing

²farewell *n* **1** : a wish of well-being at parting : GOOD-BYE **2 a** : an act of departure : LEAVE-TAKING **b** : a formal occasion honoring a person about to leave or retire

³fare·well \ˌfa(ə)r-ˌwel, ˌfe(ə)r-\ *adj* : of or relating to leave-taking : FINAL <a ~ appearance>

⁴fare·well \fa(ə)r-'wel, fe(ə)r-\ *vt* : to bid farewell

far·fel *or* **far·fal** \'fär-fəl\ *n* [Yiddish *farfl* (pl.), fr. MHG *varveln*] : noodles in the form of small pellets or granules

far·fetched \'fär-'fecht\ *adj* **1** : brought from a remote time or place **2** : not easily or naturally deduced or introduced : IMPROBABLE — **far·fetched·ness** \-'fech(t)-nəs, -'fech-əd-nəs\ *n*

far–flung \-'fləŋ\ *adj* **1** : widely spread or distributed <~ trading operations> **2** : REMOTE <~ sections of the city>

far–gone \'fär-'gȯn *also* -'gän\ *adj* : nearing an end <a nightmare vision of the . . . mother, ~ in pregnancy, clawing with her hands —R. E. Long>

fa·ri·na \fə-'rē-nə\ *n* [L, meal, flour, fr. *far* spelt — more at BARLEY] **1** : a fine meal of vegetable matter (as cereal grains) used chiefly for puddings or as a breakfast cereal **2** : any of various powdery or mealy substances

far·i·na·ceous \ˌfar-ə-'nā-shəs\ *adj* **1** : containing or rich in starch **2** : having a mealy texture or surface — **far·i·na·ceous·ly** *adv*

fa·ri·nha \fə-'rēn-yə\ *n* [Pg, flour, cassava meal, fr. L *farina*] : cassava meal

far·kle·ber·ry \'fär-kəl-ˌber-ē\ *n* [prob. alter. of *whortleberry*] : a shrub or small tree (*Vaccinium arboreum*) of the heath family of the southeastern U.S. having a black berry with stony seeds

farl *or* **farle** \'fär(ə)l\ *n* [contr. of Sc *fardel*, lit., fourth part, fr. ME (Sc), fr. *ferde del*; fr. *ferde* fourth + *del* part] *Scot* : a small scone

[1]**farm** \'färm\ *n* [ME *ferme* rent, lease, fr. OF, lease, fr. *fermer* to fix, make a contract, fr. L *firmare* to make firm, fr. *firmus* firm] **1** *obs* : a sum or due fixed in amount and payable at fixed intervals **2** : a letting out of revenues or taxes for a fixed sum to one authorized to collect and retain them **3** : a district or division of a country leased out for the collection of government revenues **4** : a tract of land devoted to agricultural purposes **5 a** : a plot of land devoted to the raising of animals and esp. domestic livestock **b** : a tract of water reserved for the artificial cultivation of some aquatic life form **6** : a minor-league baseball club associated with a major-league club as a subsidiary to which recruits are assigned until needed or for further training

[2]**farm** *vt* **1** *obs* : RENT **2** : to collect and take the fees or profits of (an occupation or business) on payment of a fixed sum **3** : to give up (as an estate or a business) to another on condition of receiving in return a fixed sum **4 a** : to devote to agriculture **b** : to manage and cultivate as a farm ~ *vi* : to engage in raising crops or livestock

farm·er \'fär-mər\ *n* **1** : a person who pays a fixed sum for some privilege or source of income **2** : a person who cultivates land or crops or raises livestock **3** : YOKEL, BUMPKIN

farmer cheese *n* : a pressed unripened cheese similar to but drier and firmer than cottage cheese — called also *farm cheese*

farm·er·ette \ˌfär-mə-'ret\ *n* : a female farmer or farmhand

farm·hand \'färm-ˌhand\ *n* : a farm laborer; *esp* : a hired laborer on a farm

farm·house \-ˌhau̇s\ *n* : a dwelling on a farm

farm·ing *n* : the practice of agriculture

farm·land \'färm-ˌland\ *n* : land used or suitable for farming

farm out *vt* **1** : to turn over for performance (as a job) or use usu. on contract **2 a** : to put (as children or prisoners) into the hands of a private individual for care in return for a fee **b** : to send (a baseball player) to a farm team **3** : to exhaust (land) by farming esp. by continuously raising one crop

farm·stead \'färm-ˌsted\ *also* **farm·stead·ing** \-iŋ\ *n* : the buildings and adjacent service areas of a farm

farm·yard \-ˌyärd\ *n* : space around or enclosed by farm buildings; *esp* : BARNYARD

faro \'fa(ə)r-(ˌ)ō, 'fe(ə)r-\ *n, pl* **faros** [prob. alter. of earlier *pharaoh*, trans. of F *pharaon*] : a gambling game in which players bet on cards drawn from a dealing box

Faro·ese *var of* FAEROESE

far–off \'fär-'ȯf\ *adj* : remote in time or space ***syn*** see DISTANT ***ant*** near, nigh, nearby

fa·rouche \fə-'rüsh\ *adj* [F, wild, shy, fr. LL *forasticus* belonging outside, fr. L *foras* outdoors; akin to L *fores* door — more at DOOR] : marked by shyness and lack of polish; *also* : WILD

far–out \'fär-'au̇t\ *adj* : marked by a considerable departure from the conventional or traditional : EXTREME <~ clothes> — **far–out·ness** *n*

far point *n* : the point farthest from the eye at which an object is accurately focused on the retina at full accommodation

far·rag·i·nous \fə-'raj-ə-nəs\ *adj* : formed of various materials

far·ra·go \fə-'räg-(ˌ)ō, -'rā-(ˌ)gō\ *n, pl* **-goes** [L *farragin-*, *farrago* mixed fodder, mixture, fr. *far* spelt — more at BARLEY] : a confused collection : MIXTURE

far–reach·ing \'fär-'rē-chiŋ\ *adj* : having a wide range or effect

far–red \-'red\ *adj* **1** : lying in the part of the infrared spectrum farthest from the red — used of radiations with wavelengths between 30 and about 1000 microns **2** : lying in the part of the infrared spectrum nearest to the red — used of radiations with wavelengths starting at about .8 micron

far·ri·er \'far-ē-ər\ *n* [alter. of ME *ferrour*, fr. MF *ferrour* blacksmith, fr. OF *ferreor*, fr. *ferrer* to fit with iron, fr. (assumed) VL *ferrare*, fr. L *ferrum* iron] : one that attends to or shoes horses

[1]**far·row** \'far-(ˌ)ō, -ə(-w)\ *vb* [ME *farwen*, fr. (assumed) OE *feargian*, fr. OE *fearh* young pig; akin to OHG *farah* young pig, L *porcus* pig] *vt* : to give birth to (a farrow) ~ *vi, of swine* : to bring forth young — often used with *down*

[2]**farrow** *n* **1** : a litter of pigs **2** : an act of farrowing

[3]**farrow** *adj* [ME (Sc) *ferow*; prob. akin to OE *fearr* bull, ox — more at PARE] *of a cow* : not in calf : not settled

far·see·ing \'fär-'sē-iŋ\ *adj* : FARSIGHTED 1

far side *n* : the farther side — **on the far side of** : BEYOND <just *on the far side of* 40>

far·sight·ed \'fär-'sīt-əd\ *adj* **1 a** : seeing or able to see to a great distance **b** : having foresight or good judgment : SAGACIOUS **2** : affected with hyperopia — **far·sight·ed·ly** *adv*

far·sight·ed·ness *n* **1** : the quality or state of being farsighted **2** : HYPEROPIA

[1]**fart** \'färt\ *vi* [ME *ferten, farten*; akin to OHG *ferzan* to break wind, ON *freta*, Gk *perdesthai*, Skt *pardate* he breaks wind] : to expel intestinal gas from the anus — usu. considered vulgar

[2]**fart** *n* [ME *fert, fart*, fr. *ferten, farten*; v.] : an expulsion of intestinal gas — usu. considered vulgar

[1]**far·ther** \'fär-thər\ *adv* [ME *ferther*, alter. of *further*] **1** : at or to a greater distance or more advanced point <~ down the corridor> **2** : to a greater degree or extent <we do not extend the one-man idea any ~ than we have to —G. F. Eliot>

[2]**farther** *adj* **1** : more distant : REMOTER **2** : [2]FURTHER 2 <clearing his throat preparatory to ~ revelations —Edith Wharton>

far·ther·most \-ˌmōst\ *adj* : most distant : FARTHEST

[1]**far·thest** \'fär-thəst\ *adj* : most distant in space or time

[2]**farthest** *adv* **1** : to or at the greatest distance in space or time <who can jump the ~> **2** : to the most advanced point <goes ~ toward answering the question> **3** : by the greatest degree or extent : MOST <the essay ~ removed from this reviewer's comprehension —*Saturday Rev.*>

far·thing \'fär-thiŋ\ *n* [ME *ferthing*, fr. OE *fēorthung*; akin to MHG *vierdunc* fourth part, OE *fēortha* fourth] **1 a** : a former British monetary unit equal to ¼ of a penny **b** : a coin representing this unit **2** : something of small value : MITE

far·thin·gale \'fär-thən-ˌgāl, -thiŋ-\ *n* [modif. of MF *verdugale*, fr. OSp *verdugado*, fr. *verdugo* young shoot of a tree, fr. *verde* green, fr. L *viridis* — more at VERDANT] : a support (as of hoops) worn esp. in the 16th century beneath a skirt to expand it at the hip line

Queen Elizabeth in a farthingale

FAS *abbr* **1** firsts and seconds **2** Foreign Agricultural Service **3** free alongside ship

fasc *abbr* fascicle

fas·ces \'fas-ˌēz\ *n pl but sing or pl in constr* [L, fr. pl. of *fascis* bundle; akin to L *fascia*] : a bundle of rods and among them an ax with projecting blade borne before ancient Roman magistrates as a badge of authority

fas·cia \ *1b, 1c, & 4 are usu* 'fāsh-(ē-)ə, *other senses are usu* 'fash-\ *n, pl* **-ci·ae** \-ē-ˌē\ *or* **-cias** [It, fr. L, band, bandage; akin to MIr *basc* necklace] **1** : a flat horizontal member of an order or building having the form of a flat band or broad fillet: as **a** : one of the three bands making up the architrave in the Ionic order **b** *or* **fascia board** : a horizontal piece (as a board) covering the joint between the top of a wall and the projecting eaves **c** : a nameplate over the front of a shop **2** : a broad and well-defined band of color **3** : a sheet of connective tissue covering or binding together body structures; *also* : tissue of this character **4** *Brit* : the dashboard of an automobile — **fas·cial** \'fash-(ē-)əl\ *adj*

fas·ci·at·ed \'fash-ē-ˌāt-əd\ *adj* **1** : arranged in fascicles **2** : exhibiting fasciation

fas·ci·a·tion \ˌfas(h)-ē-'ā-shən\ *n* : a malformation of plant stems commonly manifested as enlargement and flattening as if several were fused

fas·ci·cle \'fas-i-kəl\ *n* [L *fasciculus*, dim. of *fascis*] **1** : a small bundle: as **a** : an inflorescence consisting of a compacted cyme less capitate than a glomerule **b** : FASCICULUS 1 **2** : one of the divisions of a book published in parts — **fas·ci·cled** \-kəld\ *adj*

fas·cic·u·lar \fə-'sik-yə-lər, fa-\ *adj* : of, relating to, or consisting of fascicles — **fas·cic·u·lar·ly** *adv*

fas·cic·u·late \-lət\ *adj* : FASCICULAR

fas·cic·u·la·tion \fə-ˌsik-yə-'lā-shən, fa-\ *n* [NL *fasciculus* + E *-ation* (as in *fibrillation*)] : muscular twitching involving contiguous groups of muscle fibers

fas·ci·cule \'fas-i-ˌkyü(ə)l\ *n* [F, fr. L *fasciculus*] : FASCICLE 2

fas·cic·u·lus \fə-'sik-yə-ləs, fa-\ *n, pl* **-li** \-ˌlī\ [NL, fr. L] **1** : a slender bundle of anatomical fibers **2** : FASCICLE 2

fas·ci·nate \'fas-ᵊn-ˌāt\ *vb* **-nat·ed; -nat·ing** [L *fascinatus*, pp. of *fascinare*, fr. *fascinum* witchcraft] *vt* **1** *obs* : BEWITCH **2 a** : to transfix and hold spellbound by an irresistible power <believed that the serpent could ~ its prey> **b** : to command the interest of : ALLURE <was *fascinated* by her personality> ~ *vi* : to be irresistibly attractive ***syn*** see ATTRACT

fas·ci·nat·ing *adj* : extremely interesting or charming : CAPTIVATING — **fas·ci·nat·ing·ly** \-ˌnāt-iŋ-lē\ *adv*

fas·ci·na·tion \ˌfas-ᵊn-'ā-shən\ *n* **1** : the quality or power of fascinating **2** : the state of being fascinated

fas·ci·na·tor \'fas-ᵊn-ˌāt-ər\ *n* **1** : one that fascinates **2** : a woman's lightweight head scarf usu. of crochet or lace

fas·cine \fa-'sēn, fə-\ *n* [F, fr. L *fascina*, fr. *fascis*] : a long bundle of sticks of wood bound together and used for such purposes as filling ditches and making revetments for river banks

fa·sci·o·li·a·sis \fə-ˌsē-ə-'lī-ə-səs, -ˌsī-\ *n, pl* **-a·ses** \-ˌsēz\ [NL, fr. *Fasciola*, genus of flukes + *-iasis*] : infestation with or disease caused by liver flukes (genus *Fasciola*)

fas·cism \'fash-ˌiz-əm *also* 'fas-ˌiz-\ *n* [It *fascismo*, fr. *fascio* bundle, fasces, group, fr. L *fascis* bundle & *fasces* fasces] **1** : a political philosophy, movement, or regime (as that of the Fascisti) that exalts nation and race above the individual and that stands for a centralized autocratic government headed by a dictatorial leader, severe economic and social regimentation, and forcible suppression of opposition **2** : a tendency toward or actual exercise of strong autocratic or dictatorial control <early instances of army ~ and brutality —J. W. Aldridge> — **fas·cist** \-əst\ *n or adj, often cap* — **fas·cis·tic** \fa-'shis-tik *also* -'sis-\ *adj, often cap* — **fas·cis·ti·cal·ly** \-ti-k(ə-)lē\ *adv, often cap*

Fa·sci·sta \fä-'shē-(ˌ)stä\ *n, pl* **-sti** \-(ˌ)stē\ [It, fr. *fascio*] : a member of an Italian political organization under Mussolini governing Italy 1922–1943 according to the principles of fascism

fas·cist·ize \'fash-ə-ˌstīz *also* 'fas-ə-\ *vt* **-ized; -iz·ing** : to make over or transform into a Fascista : convert to the principles of fascism — **fas·cist·iza·tion** \ˌfash-ə-stə-'zā-shən *also* ˌfas-ə-\ *n*

fash \'fash\ *vb* [MF *fascher*, fr. (assumed) VL *fastidiare* to disgust, fr. L *fastidium* disgust — more at FASTIDIOUS] *chiefly Scot* : VEX — **fash** *n, chiefly Scot*

[1]**fash·ion** \'fash-ən\ *n* [ME *facioun, fasoun* shape, manner, fr. OF *façon*, fr. L *faction-*, *factio* act of making, faction, fr. *factus*, pp. of *facere* to make — more at DO] **1 a** : the make or form of something **b** *archaic* : KIND, SORT **2 a** : an often personal manner or way <he will, after his sour ~, tell you —Shak.> **b** : mode of action or operation <the people assembled in an orderly ~> **3 a** : a prevailing custom, usage, or style **b** (1) : the prevailing style (as in dress) during a particular time (2) : a garment in such a style <always wears the latest ~*s*> **c** : social standing or prominence esp. as signalized by dress or conduct
syn **1** see METHOD

2 FASHION, STYLE, MODE, VOGUE, FAD, RAGE, CRAZE *shared meaning element* : the choice or usage (as in dressing, decorating, or living) generally accepted by those who regard themselves as up-to-date and sophisticated
— **after a fashion** : in an approximate or rough way <became an artist *after a fashion*>

²**fashion** *vt* **fash·ioned; fash·ion·ing** \ˈfash-(ə-)niŋ\ **1 a** : to give shape or form to : MOLD **b** : ALTER, TRANSFORM **c** : to mold into a particular character by influencing or training **d** : to make or construct usu. with the use of imagination and ingenuity <~ a lamp from an old churn> **2** : FIT, ADAPT **3** *obs* : CONTRIVE ***syn*** see MAKE — **fash·ion·er** \-(ə-)nər\ *n*

¹**fash·ion·able** \ˈfash-(ə-)nə-bəl\ *adj* **1** : conforming to the custom, fashion, or established mode **2** : of or relating to the world of fashion — **fash·ion·abil·i·ty** \ˌfash-(ə-)nə-ˈbil-ət-ē\ *n* — **fash·ion·able·ness** \ˈfash-(ə-)nə-bəl-nəs\ *n* — **fash·ion·ably** \-blē\ *adv*

²**fashionable** *n* : a fashionable person

fash·ion·mon·ger \ˈfash-ən-ˌməŋ-gər, -ˌmäŋ-\ *n* : one that studies, imitates, or sets the fashion

fashion plate *n* **1** : an illustration of a clothing style **2** : a person who dresses in the newest fashion

¹**fast** \ˈfast\ *adj* [ME, fr. OE *fæst;* akin to OHG *festi* firm, ON *fastr,* Arm *hast*] **1 a** : firmly fixed <roots that are ~ in the ground> **b** : tightly shut <all the drawers were ~> **c** : adhering firmly <the glued sheets became ~> **d** : not easily freed : STUCK <a shell ~ in the chamber of a gun> **e** : STABLE <movable items were made ~ to the deck> **2** : firmly loyal <became ~ friends over the years> **3 a** : characterized by quick motion, operation, or effect: **(1)** : moving or able to move rapidly : SWIFT **(2)** : taking a comparatively short time **(3)** : imparting quickness of motion <a ~ bowler> **(4)** : accomplished quickly **(5)** : agile of mind; *esp* : quick to learn <a special class for ~ students> **b** : conducive to rapidity of play or action <a ~ track> **c (1)** *of a timepiece or weighing device* : indicating in advance of what is correct **(2)** : according to daylight saving time **d** : contributing to a shortening of exposure time <~ lens> **e** : acquired with unusually little effort and often by shady or dishonest methods <made some ~ money on the numbers> **4 a** : securely attached <a rope ~ to the wharf> **b** : TENACIOUS <kept a ~ hold on her purse> **5 a** *archaic* : sound asleep **b** *of sleep* : not easily disturbed **6** : permanently dyed **7 a** : WILD <runs around with a pretty ~ bunch> **b** : daringly unconventional esp. in sexual matters <a ~ woman> **8** : resistant to change (as from destructive action or fading) — often used in combination < sun*fast*> <acid-*fast* bacteria>
syn FAST, RAPID, SWIFT, FLEET, QUICK, SPEEDY, HASTY, EXPEDITIOUS *shared meaning element* : moving, proceeding, or acting with celerity ***ant*** slow

²**fast** *adv* **1** : in a firm or fixed manner **2** : in a sound manner : DEEPLY <fell ~ asleep> **3 a** : in a rapid manner : QUICKLY **b** : in quick succession <kaleidoscopic impressions that come so thick and ~ —M. B. Tucker> **4** : in a reckless manner : DISSIPATEDLY **5** : ahead of a correct time or posted schedule **6** *archaic* : CLOSE, NEAR

³**fast** *vi* [ME *fasten,* fr. OE *fæstan*] **1** : to abstain from food **2** : to eat sparingly or abstain from some foods

⁴**fast** *n* **1** : the practice of fasting **2** : a time of fasting

⁵**fast** *n* [alter. of ME *fest,* fr. ON *festr* rope, mooring cable, fr. *fastr* firm] : something that fastens or holds a fastening

fast and loose *adv* **1** : in a craftily deceitful way <manipulated evidence . . . and played *fast and loose* with the truth —C. V. Woodward> **2** : in a reckless or irresponsible manner <playing *fast and loose* with his wife's money>

fast·back \ˈfas(t)-ˌbak\ *n* : an automobile roof with a long curving downward slope to the rear; *also* : an automobile with such a roof

fast·ball \ˈfas(t)-ˌbȯl\ *n* : a baseball pitch thrown at full speed and often rising slightly as it nears the plate — compare CURVEBALL, SLIDER, KNUCKLE BALL, CHANGE-UP, SCREWBALL

fast break *n* : a quick offensive drive toward a goal (as in basketball) in an attempt to score before the opponent's defense is set up — **fast–break** *vi*

fas·ten \ˈfas-ᵊn\ *vb* **fas·tened; fas·ten·ing** \ˈfas-niŋ, -ᵊn-iŋ\ [ME *fastnen,* fr. OE *fæstnian* to make fast; akin to OHG *festinōn* to make fast, OE *fæst* fast] *vt* **1 a** : to attach esp. by pinning, tying, or nailing **b** : to make fast and secure **c** : to fix firmly or securely **d** : to secure against opening **2** : to fix or set steadily <~*ed* his attention on the main problem> **3** : to take a firm grip with <the dog ~*ed* his teeth in the old shoe> **4 a** : to attach (oneself) persistently and usu. objectionably **b** : IMPOSE <~*ed* the blame on the wrong man> ~ *vi* **1** : to become fast or fixed **2 a** : to take a firm grip or hold **b** : to focus attention — **fas·ten·er** \ˈfas-nər, -ᵊn-ər\ *n*
syn FASTEN, FIX, ATTACH, AFFIX *shared meaning element* : to make something stay firmly in place ***ant*** unfasten, loosen, loose

fas·ten·ing *n* : something that fastens : FASTENER

fast–food \ˌfas(t)-ˌfüd\ *adj* : specializing in the rapid preparation and service of food (as hamburgers or fried chicken) <a ~ restaurant chain>

fas·tid·i·ous \fa-ˈstid-ē-əs, fə-\ *adj* [ME, fr. L *fastidiosus,* fr. *fastidium* disgust, prob. fr. *fastus* arrogance + *taedium* irksomeness; akin to L *fastigium* top] **1** *archaic* : SCORNFUL **2 a** : having high and often capricious standards : difficult to satisfy or please <must surely give pleasure to the most ~ reader, for her art is scrupulous —Richard Church> **b** : showing or demanding excessive delicacy or care <highbrow critics . . . so ~ that they can talk only to a small circle of initiates —Granville Hicks> **c** : reflecting a meticulous, sensitive, or demanding attitude <~ workmanship> **3** : having complex nutritional requirements <~ microorganisms> ***syn*** see NICE — **fas·tid·i·ous·ly** *adv* — **fas·tid·i·ous·ness** *n*

fas·tig·i·ate \fa-ˈstij-ē-ət\ *adj* [prob. fr. (assumed) NL *fastigiatus,* fr. L *fastigium*] : narrowing toward the top; *esp* : having upright usu. clustered branches — **fas·tig·i·ate·ly** *adv*

fas·tig·i·um \-ē-əm\ *n* [NL, fr. L, top, gable end] : the period of greatest intensity (as of a disease)

fast·ness \ˈfas(t)-nəs\ *n* **1** : the quality or state of being fast: as **a** : the quality or state of being fixed **b** : the quality or state of being swift **c** : colorfast quality **d** : resistance (as of an organism) to the action of a usu. toxic substance **2 a** : a fortified or secure place **b** : a remote and secluded place <spent the weekend in his mountain ~>

Fast of Esther : a Jewish fast day observed the day before Purim in commemoration of a fast proclaimed by Queen Esther

fast–talk \ˈfas(t)-ˈtȯk\ *vt* : to influence or persuade by fluent, facile, and usu. deceptive or tricky talk <~*ed* tribal chieftains . . . out of a parcel of rain-drenched, tropical real estate —*Newsweek*>

fas·tu·ous \ˈfas-chə-wəs\ *adj* [L *fastuosus,* fr. *fastus* arrogance — more at FASTIDIOUS] **1** : HAUGHTY, ARROGANT <a ~ air of finality —Carl Van Vechten> **2** : OSTENTATIOUS, SHOWY <a period when ~ living was very much the order of the day —*Times Lit. Supp.*>

¹**fat** \ˈfat\ *adj* **fat·ter; fat·test** [ME, fr. OE *fætt,* pp. of *fǣtan* to cram; akin to OHG *feizit* fat, L *opimus* fat, copious] **1** : notable for having an unusual amount of fat: **a** : PLUMP **b** : OBESE **c** *of a meat animal* : fattened for market **d** *of food* : OILY, GREASY **2 a** : well filled out : THICK, BIG <a ~ volume of verse> **b** : FULL, RICH <a gorgeous ~ bass voice —*Irish Digest*> **c** : well stocked <a ~ refrigerator> **d** : PROSPEROUS, WEALTHY <grew ~ on the war —*Time*> **e** : being substantial and impressive <a ~ bank account> **3 a** : richly rewarding or profitable <a ~ part in a new play> <accepted a ~ contract> **b** : practically nonexistent <a ~ chance> **4** : PRODUCTIVE, FERTILE <a ~ year for crops> **5 a** *of soil* : containing minerals that cause a greasy feel **b** *of wood* : having a high resin content **6** : STUPID, FOOLISH **7** : SWOLLEN <got a ~ lip from the fight> — **fat·ness** *n*

²**fat** *n* **1** : animal tissue consisting chiefly of cells distended with greasy or oily matter **2 a** : oily or greasy matter making up the bulk of adipose tissue and often abundant in seeds **b** : any of numerous compounds of carbon, hydrogen, and oxygen that are glycerides of fatty acids, the chief constituents of plant and animal fat, and a major class of energy-rich food, that are soluble in organic solvents (as ether) but not in water, and that are widely used industrially **c** : a solid or semisolid fat as distinguished from an oil **3** : the best or richest part **4** : the condition of fatness : OBESITY **5** : something in excess : SUPERFLUITY

³**fat** *vt* **fat·ted; fat·ting** : to make fat : FATTEN

⁴**fat** *var of* PHAT

fa·tal \ˈfāt-ᵊl\ *adj* [ME, fr. MF & L; MF, fr. L *fatalis,* fr. *fatum*] **1** *obs* : FATED **2** : FATEFUL <a ~ hour> **3 a** : of or relating to fate **b** : resembling fate in foretelling destiny : PROPHETIC **c** : resembling fate in proceeding according to a fixed sequence **d** : determining one's fate **4 a** : causing death **b** : bringing ruin ***syn*** see DEADLY

fa·tal·ism \-ˌiz-əm\ *n* : a doctrine that events are fixed in advance for all time in such a manner that human beings are powerless to change them; *also* : a belief in or attitude determined by this doctrine — **fa·tal·ist** \-əst\ *n* — **fa·tal·is·tic** \ˌfāt-ᵊl-ˈis-tik\ *adj* — **fa·tal·is·ti·cal·ly** \-ti-k(ə-)lē\ *adv*

fa·tal·i·ty \fā-ˈtal-ət-ē, fə-\ *n, pl* **-ties** **1** : something established by fate **2 a** : the quality or state of causing death or destruction : DEADLINESS **b** : the quality or condition of being destined for disaster **3 a** : FATE 1 **b** : FATALISM **4** : the agent or agency of fate **5 a** : death resulting from a disaster **b** : one that experiences or is subject to a fatal outcome <one of the *fatalities* was a small child>

fa·tal·ly \ˈfāt-ᵊl-ē\ *adv* **1** : in a way determined by fate **2** : in a manner suggesting fate or an act of fate: as **a** : in a manner resulting in death : MORTALLY <~ wounded> **b** : beyond repair : IRREVOCABLY **c** : in a manner resulting in ruin or evil <it is ~ easy to pass off our prejudices as our opinions —W. F. Hambly> **d** : IRRESISTIBLY <thinks she is ~ attractive —J. W. Krutch>

fa·ta mor·ga·na \ˌfät-ə-ˌmȯr-ˈgän-ə, -ˈgan-\ *n* [It, lit., Morgan the fay, sorceress of Arthurian legend] : MIRAGE

fat·back \ˈfat-ˌbak\ *n* : the strip of fat from the back of a hog carcass usu. cured by drying and salting — see PORK illustration

fat body *n* : an insect fatty tissue esp. of nearly mature larvae that serves as a food reserve

fat cat *n* **1 a** : a wealthy contributor to a political campaign fund **b** : a wealthy and privileged person **c** : BIG SHOT **2** : a lethargic, complacent person

¹**fate** \ˈfāt\ *n* [ME, fr. MF or L; MF, fr. L *fatum,* lit., what has been spoken, fr. neut. of *fatus,* pp. of *fari* to speak — more at BAN] **1** : the principle or determining cause or will by which things in general are believed to come to be as they are or events to happen as they do : DESTINY **2 a** : an inevitable and often adverse outcome, condition, or end **b** : DISASTER; *esp* : DEATH **3 a** : final outcome **b** : the expected result of normal development <prospective ~ of embryonic cells> **4** *pl, cap* : the three goddesses of classical mythology who determine the course of human life
syn FATE, DESTINY, LOT, PORTION, DOOM *shared meaning element* : a predetermined state or end

²**fate** *vt* **fat·ed; fat·ing** : DESTINE; *also* : DOOM <the deep antipathy . . . seeming to ~ them to antagonism —Les Savage>

fat·ed *adj* : decreed, controlled, or marked by fate

fate·ful \ˈfāt-fəl\ *adj* **1** : having a quality of ominous prophecy <a ~ remark> **2 a** : involving momentous consequences : DECISIVE <made his ~ decision to declare war —W. L. Shirer> **b** : DEADLY, CATASTROPHIC **3** : controlled by fate : FOREORDAINED ***syn*** see OMINOUS — **fate·ful·ly** \-fə-lē\ *adv* — **fate·ful·ness** *n*

fath *abbr* fathom

ə abut	ᵊ kitten	ər further	a back	ā bake	ä cot, cart
aů out	ch chin	e less	ē easy	g gift	i trip ī life
j joke	ŋ sing	ō flow	ȯ flaw	ȯi coin	th thin t͟h this
ü loot	ů foot	y yet	yü few	yů furious	zh vision

fat·head \ˈfat-ˌhed\ *n* : a slow-witted or stupid person : FOOL — **fat·head·ed** \-ˈhed-əd\ *adj* — **fat·head·ed·ly** *adv* — **fat·head·ed·ness** *n*

1**fa·ther** \ˈfäth-ər\ *n* [ME *fader,* fr. OE *fæder;* akin to OHG *fater* father, L *pater,* Gk *patēr*] **1 a :** a man who has begotten a child; *also* : SIRE 3 **b** *cap* (1) : GOD 1 (2) : the first person of the Trinity **2 :** FOREFATHER **3 a :** one related to another in a way suggesting that of father to child **b :** an old man — used as a respectful form of address **4** *often cap* **:** a pre-Scholastic Christian writer accepted by the church as an authoritative witness to its teaching and practice — called also *church father* **5 a :** one that originates or institutes <the ~ of modern science> **b :** SOURCE <the sun, the ~ of warmth and light —Lena M. Whitney> **c :** PROTOTYPE **6 :** a priest of the regular clergy; *broadly* : PRIEST — used esp. as a title **7 :** one of the leading men (as of a city) — usu. used in pl. — **fa·ther·hood** \-ˌhu̇d\ *n* — **fa·ther·less** \-ləs\ *adj*

2**father** *vb* **fa·thered; fa·ther·ing** \ˈfäth-(ə-)riŋ\ *vt* **1 a :** BEGET **b :** to make oneself the founder, producer, or author of <~*ed* a plan for improving the city's schools> **c :** to accept responsibility for **2 :** to fix the paternity or origin of **3 :** FOIST, IMPOSE ~ *vi* **:** to care for or look after someone as a father might

Father Christmas *n, Brit* : SANTA CLAUS

father figure *n* : one often of particular power or influence who serves as an emotional substitute for a father

father image *n* : an idealization of one's father often projected onto someone to whom one looks for guidance and protection

father–in–law \ˈfäth-(ə-)rən-ˌlȯ, -ərn-ˌlȯ\ *n, pl* **fa·thers–in–law** \-ər-zən-\ **1 :** the father of one's spouse **2 :** STEPFATHER

fa·ther·land \ˈfäth-ər-ˌland\ *n* **1 :** one's native land or country **2 :** the native land or country of one's father or ancestors

fa·ther·like \-ˌlīk\ *adj or adv* : FATHERLY

fa·ther·li·ness \-lē-nəs\ *n* : paternal quality

fa·ther·ly \ˈfäth-ər-lē\ *adj* **1 :** of, relating to, or befitting a father <~ responsibilities> **2 :** resembling a father (as in affection or care) <a ~ old man> — **fatherly** *adv*

Father's Day *n* : the third Sunday in June appointed for the honoring of fathers

1**fath·om** \ˈfath-əm\ *n* [ME *fadme,* fr. OE *fæthm* outstretched arms, length of the outstretched arms; akin to ON *fathmr* fathom, L *patēre* to be open, *pandere* to spread out, Gk *petannynai*] **1 :** a unit of length equal to 6 feet used esp. for measuring the depth of water **2 :** COMPREHENSION

2**fathom** *vt* **1 :** to measure by a sounding line **2 :** to penetrate and come to understand <couldn't ~ the problem> ~ *vi* **1 :** to take soundings **2 :** PROBE — **fath·om·able** \ˈfath-ə-mə-bəl\ *adj*

Fa·thom·e·ter \fa-ˈthäm-ət-ər, ˈfath-ə(m)-ˌmēt-\ *trademark* — used for a sonic depth finder

fath·om·less \ˈfath-əm-ləs\ *adj* : incapable of being fathomed — **fath·om·less·ly** *adv* — **fath·om·less·ness** *n*

fa·tid·ic \fā-ˈtid-ik, fə-\ *or* **fa·tid·i·cal** \-i-kəl\ *adj* [L *fatidicus,* fr. *fatum* fate + *dicere* to say — more at DICTION] : of or relating to prophecy

fa·ti·ga·bil·i·ty \fə-ˌtē-gə-ˈbil-ət-ē, ˌfat-i-gə-\ *n* : susceptibility to fatigue

fa·ti·ga·ble \fə-ˈtē-gə-bəl, ˈfat-i-gə-\ *adj* : susceptible to fatigue

1**fa·tigue** \fə-ˈtēg\ *n* [F, fr. MF, fr. *fatiguer* to fatigue, fr. L *fatigare;* akin to L af*fatim* sufficiently and prob. to L *fames* hunger] **1 a** (1) : weariness from labor or exertion (2) : nervous exhaustion **b :** the temporary loss of power to respond induced in a sensory receptor or motor end organ by continued stimulation **2 a :** LABOR **b :** manual or menial work performed by military personnel **c** *pl* : the uniform or work clothing worn on fatigue and in the field **3 :** the tendency of a material to break under repeated stress

2**fatigue** *vb* **fa·tigued; fa·tigu·ing** *vt* **1 :** to weary with labor or exertion **2 :** to induce a condition of fatigue in ~ *vi* : to suffer fatigue ***syn*** see TIRE — **fa·tigu·ing·ly** \-ˈtē-giŋ-lē\ *adv*

3**fatigue** *adj* **1 :** consisting of, done, or used in fatigue <~ detail> **2 :** belonging to fatigues <a ~ cap>

fat·ling \ˈfat-liŋ\ *n* : a young animal fattened for slaughter

fat·ly *adv* **1 :** RICHLY **2 :** in the manner of one that is fat **3 :** in a smug manner : COMPLACENTLY <snickered ~ at his wife's mistake>

fats·hed·era \fats-ˈ(h)ed-ə-rə\ *n* [NL *Fatsia,* genus of shrubs + *Hedera,* genus of vines, fr. L, ivy] : a vigorous upright hybrid ornamental foliage plant (*Hedera helix* x *Aralia elata*) with glossy deeply lobed palmate leaves

fat·so \ˈfat-(ˌ)sō\ *n, pl* **fatsoes** [prob. fr. *Fats,* nickname for a fat person + *-o*] : a fat person — often used as a disparaging form of address

fat–sol·u·ble \ˈfat-ˌsäl-yə-bəl\ *adj* : soluble in fats or fat solvents

fat·stock \-ˌstäk\ *n* : livestock that is fat and ready for market

fat–tailed sheep \ˌfat-ˌtāld-\ *n* : a coarse-wooled mutton sheep that has great quantities of fat on each side of the tail bones

fat·ten \ˈfat-ᵊn\ *vb* **fat·tened; fat·ten·ing** \ˈfat-niŋ, -ᵊn-iŋ\ *vt* **1 a :** to make fat, fleshy, or plump; *esp* : to feed (as a stock animal) for slaughter **b :** to make more substantial **2 :** to make fertile ~ *vi* : to become fat — **fat·ten·er** \ˈfat-nər, -ᵊn-ər\ *n*

fat·tish \ˈfat-ish\ *adj* : somewhat fat

1**fat·ty** \ˈfat-ē\ *adj* **fat·ti·er; -est** **1 :** containing fat esp. in unusual amounts; *also* : unduly stout : CORPULENT **2 :** GREASY **3 :** derived from or chemically related to fat — **fat·ti·ness** *n*

2**fatty** *n, pl* **fatties** : one that is fat

fatty acid *n* **1 :** any of numerous saturated aliphatic monocarboxylic acids $C_nH_{2n+1}COOH$ (as acetic acid) including many that occur naturally usu. in the form of esters in fats, waxes, and essential oils **2 :** any of the saturated or unsaturated monocarboxylic acids (as palmitic acid) usu. with an even number of carbon atoms that occur naturally in the form of glycerides in fats and fatty oils

fa·tu·ity \fə-ˈt(y)ü-ət-ē, fa-\ *n, pl* **-ities** [MF *fatuité* foolishness, fr. L *fatuitat-, fatuitas,* fr. *fatuus*] **1 a :** something foolish or stupid **b :** STUPIDITY, FOOLISHNESS **2** *archaic* : IMBECILITY, DEMENTIA

fat·u·ous \ˈfach-(ə-)wəs\ *adj* [L *fatuus* foolish — more at BATTLE] : complacently or inanely foolish : SILLY ***syn*** see SIMPLE ***ant*** sensible — **fat·u·ous·ly** *adv* — **fat·u·ous·ness** *n*

fat–wit·ted \ˈfat-ˈwit-əd\ *adj* : STUPID, IDIOTIC

fau·bourg \fō-ˈbu̇(ə)r\ *n* [ME *fabour,* fr. MF *fauxbourg,* alter. of *forsbourg,* fr. OF *forsborc,* fr. *fors* outside + *borc* town] **1 :** SUBURB; *esp* : a suburb of a French city **2 :** a city quarter

fau·ces \ˈfȯ-ˌsēz\ *n pl but sing or pl in constr* [L, pl., throat, fauces] : the narrow passage from the mouth to the pharynx situated between the soft palate and the base of the tongue — **fau·cial** \ˈfȯ-shəl\ *adj*

fau·cet \ˈfȯs-ət, ˈfäs-\ *n* [ME, bung, faucet, fr. MF *fausset* bung, fr. *fausser* to damage, fr. LL *falsare* to falsify, fr. L *falsus* false] : a fixture for drawing a liquid from a pipe, cask, or other vessel

faugh *a strong* p-*sound or lip trill; often read as* ˈfȯ\ *interj* — used to express contempt, disgust, or abhorrence

1**fault** \ˈfȯlt\ *n* [ME *faute,* fr. OF, fr. (assumed) VL *fallita,* fr. fem. of *fallitus,* pp. of L *fallere* to deceive, disappoint — more at FAIL] **1** *obs* : LACK **2 a :** WEAKNESS, FAILING; *esp* : a moral weakness less serious than a vice **b :** a physical or intellectual imperfection or impairment **c :** an error in a racket game (as tennis) **3 a :** MISDEMEANOR **b :** MISTAKE **4 :** responsibility for wrongdoing or failure <the accident was the driver's ~> **5 :** a fracture in the earth's crust accompanied by a displacement of one side of the fracture with respect to the other and in a direction parallel to the fracture

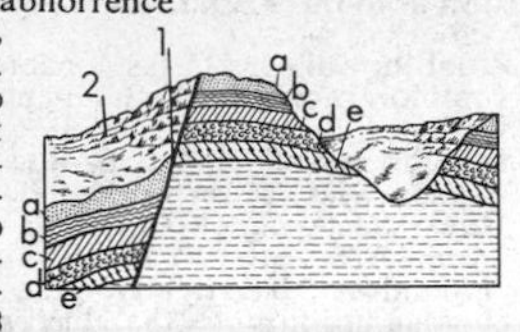

fault 5: *1* fault with strata a,b,c,d,e; parts with the same letter are of the same stratum; *2* scarp

syn FAULT, FAILING, FRAILTY, FOIBLE, VICE *shared meaning element* : an imperfection or weakness of character ***ant*** merit

— **at fault 1 :** unable to find the scent and continue chase : PUZZLED **2 :** open to blame : RESPONSIBLE <couldn't determine who was really *at fault*> — **to a fault :** to an excessive degree <particular *to a fault*>

2**fault** *vi* **1 :** to commit a fault : ERR **2 :** to fracture so as to produce a geologic fault ~ *vt* **1 :** to find a fault in <equally easy to praise this book and to ~ it —H. G. Roepke> **2 :** to produce a geologic fault in **3 :** BLAME, CENSURE <one cannot ~ him for publishing as much as he did —R. M. Elman>

fault·find·er \ˈfȯlt-ˌfīn-dər\ *n* : one given to faultfinding

1**fault·find·ing** \-diŋ\ *n* : CRITICISM; *esp* : petty, nagging, or unreasonable censure

2**faultfinding** *adj* : disposed to find fault : captiously critical ***syn*** see CRITICAL

fault·less \ˈfȯlt-ləs\ *adj* : having no fault : IRREPROACHABLE <~ workmanship> — **fault·less·ly** *adv* — **fault·less·ness** *n*

faulty \ˈfȯl-tē\ *adj* **fault·i·er; -est** : marked by fault, blemish, or defect : IMPERFECT — **fault·i·ly** \-tə-lē\ *adv* — **fault·i·ness** \-tē-nəs\ *n*

faun \ˈfȯn, ˈfän\ *n* [ME, fr. L *faunus,* fr. *Faunus*] : a figure of Roman mythology similar to the satyr

fau·na \ˈfȯn-ə, ˈfän-\ *n, pl* **faunas** *also* **fau·nae** \-ˌē, -ˌī\ [NL, fr. LL *Fauna,* sister of Faunus] : animals or animal life: as **a :** the animals or animal life of a region, period, or geological stratum — compare FLORA **b :** the animals or animal life developed or adapted for living in a specified environment — **fau·nal** \-ᵊl\ *adj* — **fau·nal·ly** \-ᵊl-ē\ *adv*

fau·nis·tic \fȯ-ˈnis-tik, fä-\ *adj* : of or relating to zoogeography : FAUNAL — **fau·nis·ti·cal·ly** \-ti-k(ə-)lē\ *adv*

Fau·nus \ˈfȯn-əs, ˈfän-\ *n* [L] : the Roman god of animals

Faust \ˈfau̇st\ *or* **Fau·stus** \ˈfau̇-stəs, ˈfȯ-\ *n* [G] : a magician of German legend who enters into a compact with the devil

Faust·ian \ˈfau̇-stē-ən, ˈfȯ-\ *adj* : of, belonging to, resembling, or befitting Faust or Faustus: as **a :** sacrificing spiritual values for material gains **b :** striving insatiably for knowledge and mastery **c :** constantly troubled and tormented by spiritual dissatisfaction or spiritual striving

faute de mieux \ˌfōt-də-ˈmyə(r), -ˈmyœ̄\ *adv* [F] : for lack of something better or more desirable <sherry made him dopey but he drank it *faute de mieux* —F. T. Marsh>

fau·vism \ˈfō-ˌviz-əm\ *n, often cap* [F *fauvisme,* fr. *fauve* wild animal, fr. *fauve* tawny, wild, of Gmc origin; akin to OHG *falo* fallow — more at FALLOW] : a movement in painting typified by the work of Matisse and characterized by vivid colors, free treatment of form, and a resulting vibrant and decorative effect — **fau·vist** \-vəst\ *n, often cap*

faux pas \ˈfō-ˈpä\ *n, pl* **faux pas** \-ˈpä(z)\ [F, lit., false step] : BLUNDER; *esp* : a social blunder

fa·va bean \ˌfäv-ə-\ *n* [It *fava,* fr. L *faba* bean] : BROAD BEAN

fa·vo·ni·an \fə-ˈvō-nē-ən\ *adj* [L *favonianus,* fr. *Favonius,* the west wind] : of or relating to the west wind : MILD

1**fa·vor** \ˈfā-vər\ *n* [ME, friendly regard, attractiveness, fr. OF *favor* friendly regard, fr. L, fr. *favēre* to be favorable; akin to OHG *gouma* attention, OSlav *gověti* to revere] **1** *archaic* **a :** APPEARANCE **b** (1) : FACE (2) : a facial feature **2 a** (1) : friendly regard shown toward another esp. by a superior (2) : approving consideration or attention : APPROBATION **b :** PARTIALITY **c** *archaic* : LENIENCY **d** *archaic* : PERMISSION **e :** POPULARITY **3 a :** gracious kindness; *also* : an act of such kindness **b** *archaic* : HELP, ASSISTANCE **c** *pl* : effort in one's behalf or interest : ATTENTION **4 a :** a token of love (as a ribbon) usu. worn conspicuously **b :** a small gift or decorative item given out at a party **c :** BADGE **5 a :** a special privilege or right granted or conceded **b :** sexual privileges — usu. used in pl. **6** *archaic* : LETTER **7 :** BEHALF, INTEREST

syn FAVOR, GOODWILL, COUNTENANCE *shared meaning element* : approving interest ***ant*** disfavor, animus

— **in favor of 1 a :** in accord or sympathy with **b :** for the acquittal of <returned a verdict *in favor of* the accused> **c :** in support of **2 :** to the order of **3 :** in order to choose : out of preference for <was offered athletic scholarships . . . but he turned them down *in favor of* a career in professional baseball —*Current Biog.*> — **in one's favor 1 :** in one's good graces <doing extra work to get back *in the teacher's favor*> **2 :** to one's advantage <the odds were *in his favor*> — **out of favor :** UNPOPULAR, DISLIKED <was *out of favor* with his neighbors>

[2]**favor** *vt* **fa·vored; fa·vor·ing** \ˈfāv-(ə-)riŋ\ **1 a :** to regard or treat with favor **b** (1) **:** to do a kindness for : OBLIGE (2) **:** ENDOW **c :** to treat gently or carefully : SPARE <~*ed* his injured leg> **2 :** to show partiality toward : PREFER **3 a :** to give support or confirmation to : SUSTAIN **b :** to afford advantages for success to : FACILITATE <good weather ~*ed* the outing> **4 :** to bear a resemblance to <he ~*s* his father> ***syn*** see OBLIGE — **fa·vor·er** \ˈfā-vər-ər\ *n*

fa·vor·able \ˈfāv-(ə-)rə-bəl, ˈfā-vər-bəl\ *adj* **1 a :** disposed to favor : PARTIAL **b :** expressing approval : COMMENDATORY **c :** giving a result that is in one's favor <a ~ comparison> **d :** AFFIRMATIVE **2 :** winning approval : PLEASING **3 a :** tending to promote or facilitate : ADVANTAGEOUS <~ wind> **b :** marked by success — **fa·vor·able·ness** *n* — **fa·vor·ably** \-blē\ *adv*

syn FAVORABLE, AUSPICIOUS, PROPITIOUS *shared meaning element* : pointing towards a felicitous outcome ***ant*** unfavorable, antagonistic

fa·vored \ˈfā-vərd\ *adj* **1 :** endowed with special advantages or gifts **2 :** having an appearance or features of a particular kind <hard-*favored*> **3 :** providing preferential treatment

[1]**fa·vor·ite** \ˈfāv-(ə-)rət\ *n* [It *favorito,* pp. of *favorire* to favor, fr. *favore* favor, fr. L *favor*] **1 :** one that is treated or regarded with special favor or liking; *specif* **:** one unusually loved, trusted, or provided with favors by a person of high rank or authority **2 :** a competitor (as a horse in a race) judged most likely to win

[2]**favorite** *adj* **:** constituting a favorite; *specif* **:** markedly popular

favorite son *n* **:** one favored by the delegates of his state as presidential candidate at a national political convention

fa·vor·it·ism \ˈfāv-(ə-)rət-ˌiz-əm\ *n* **1 :** the showing of special favor : PARTIALITY **2 :** the state or fact of being a favorite

fa·vour *chiefly Brit var of* FAVOR

fa·vus \ˈfā-vəs\ *n* [NL, fr. L, honeycomb] **:** a contagious skin disease caused by a fungus (as *Achorion schoenleinii*) occurring in man and many domestic animals and fowls

[1]**fawn** \ˈfȯn, ˈfän\ *vi* [ME *faunen,* fr. OE *fagnian* to rejoice, fr. *fægen, fagan* glad — more at FAIN] **1 :** to show affection — used esp. of a dog **2 :** to court favor by a cringing or flattering manner : GROVEL — **fawn·er** *n* — **fawn·ing·ly** \-iŋ-lē\ *adv*

syn FAWN, TOADY, TRUCKLE, CRINGE, COWER *shared meaning element* : to act or behave with abjectness ***ant*** domineer

[2]**fawn** *n* [ME *foun,* fr. MF *feon, faon* young of an animal, fr. (assumed) VL *feton-, feto,* fr. L *fetus* offspring — more at FETUS] **1 :** a young deer; *esp* **:** one still unweaned or retaining a distinctive baby coat **2 :** KID 1 **3 :** a variable color averaging a light grayish brown

fawn lily *n* **:** DOGTOOTH VIOLET

fawny \ˈfȯn-ē, ˈfän-\ *adj* **:** of a color approximating fawn

[1]**fay** \ˈfā\ *vb* [ME *feien,* fr. OE *fēgan;* akin to OHG *fuogen* to fit, L *pangere* to fasten — more at PACT] **:** to fit or join closely or tightly

[2]**fay** *n* [ME *fai, fei,* fr. OF *feid, fei* — more at FAITH] *obs* **:** FAITH

[3]**fay** *n* [ME *faie,* fr. MF *feie, fee* — more at FAIRY] **:** FAIRY, ELF

[4]**fay** *adj* **:** resembling an elf

[5]**fay** *n* **:** OFAY

faze \ˈfāz\ *vt* **fazed; faz·ing** [alter. of *feeze* (to drive away, frighten), fr. ME *fesen,* fr. OE *fēsian* to drive away] **:** to disturb the composure of : DISCONCERT, DAUNT ***syn*** see EMBARRASS

FB *abbr* **1** foreign body **2** freight bill

FBA *abbr* Fellow of the British Academy

FBI *abbr* Federal Bureau of Investigation

FBOA *abbr* Fellow of the British Optical Association

FC *abbr* **1** fire control; fire controlman **2** follow copy **3** food control **4** footcandle

FCA *abbr* **1** Farm Credit Administration **2** Fellow of the Chartered Accountants

FCC *abbr* Federal Communications Commission

FCIS *abbr* Fellow of the Chartered Institute of Secretaries

F clef *n* **:** BASS CLEF

fcp *abbr* foolscap

FCS *abbr* Fellow of the Chemical Society

fcy *abbr* fancy

FD *abbr* **1** fire department **2** free dock

FDA *abbr* Food and Drug Administration

FDIC *abbr* Federal Deposit Insurance Corporation

F distribution *n* [Sir Ronald *F*isher †1962 E geneticist and statistician] **:** a probability density function that is used esp. in analysis of variance and is a function of the ratio of two independent random variables (as the variances of two random samples) each of which has a chi-square distribution and is divided by its number of degrees of freedom

Fe *symbol* [L *ferrum*] iron

fe·al·ty \ˈfē(-ə)l-tē\ *n, pl* **-ties** [alter. of ME *feute,* fr. OF *feelté, fealté,* fr. L *fidelitat-, fidelitas* — more at FIDELITY] **1 a :** the fidelity of a vassal or feudal tenant to his lord **b :** the obligation of such fidelity **2 :** intense and compelling fidelity ***syn*** see FIDELITY ***ant*** perfidy

[1]**fear** \ˈfi(ə)r\ *n* [ME *fer,* fr. OE *fǣr* sudden danger; akin to L *periculum* attempt, peril, Gk *peiran* to attempt, OE *faran* to go — more at FARE] **1 a :** an unpleasant often strong emotion caused by anticipation or awareness of danger **b** (1) **:** an instance of this emotion (2) **:** a state marked by this emotion **2 :** anxious concern : SOLICITUDE **3 :** profound reverence and awe esp. toward God **4 :** reason for alarm : DANGER

syn* 1** FEAR, DREAD, FRIGHT, ALARM, PANIC, TREPIDATION *shared meaning element* : painful agitation in the presence or anticipation of danger ***ant fearlessness

2 see REVERENCE

[2]**fear** *vt* **1** *archaic* **:** FRIGHTEN **2** *archaic* **:** to feel fear in (oneself) **3 :** to have a reverential awe of <~ God> **4 :** to be afraid of **:** consider or expect with alarm ~ *vi* **:** to be afraid or apprehensive — **fear·er** *n*

fear·ful \ˈfi(ə)r-fəl\ *adj* **1 :** causing or likely to cause fear, fright, or alarm esp. because of dangerous quality <a ~ storm> **2 a :** full of fear **b :** indicating or arising from fear <a ~ glance> **c :** inclined to fear : TIMOROUS **3 :** being extreme (as in badness, intensity, or size) <a ~ waste> <~ slum conditions> — **fear·ful·ly** \-f(ə-)lē\ *adv* — **fear·ful·ness** \-fəl-nəs\ *n*

syn* 1** FEARFUL, APPREHENSIVE, AFRAID *shared meaning element* : disturbed by fear ***ant fearless, intrepid

2 FEARFUL, AWFUL, DREADFUL, FRIGHTFUL, TERRIBLE, TERRIFIC, APPALLING *shared meaning element* : of a kind to cause grave distress of mind. Additionally, all these words and their corresponding adverbs have a lighter, chiefly conversational value in which they are used as intensives and mean little more than *extreme* (or *extremely*). Basically, FEARFUL applies to what produces fear, agitation, or loss of courage <our *fearful* trip is done, the ship has weathered every rack —Walt Whitman> AWFUL implies striking with an awareness of transcendent overpowering force, might, or significance <the *awful* arithmetic of the atomic bomb —D. D. Eisenhower> DREADFUL applies to what fills one with dread and suggests a blending of fear and aversion <shuddering at the *dreadful* loss of life> FRIGHTFUL implies a startling or outrageous quality that induces utter consternation or a paralysis of fear <a *frightful* spectacle of poverty, barbarity, and ignorance —T. B. Macaulay> TERRIBLE suggests painfulness too great to be endured or a capacity to induce and prolong intense fear <those five *terrible* days of war —*New Yorker*> TERRIFIC applies to what is intended or fitted to inspire fear <the storm was *terrific* beyond imagining> APPALLING describes something that strikes with dismay as well as fear or horror <taken aback when he grasped the *appalling* risk involved>

fear·less \ˈfi(ə)r-ləs\ *adj* **:** free from fear : BRAVE — **fear·less·ly** *adv* — **fear·less·ness** *n*

fear·some \ˈfi(ə)r-səm\ *adj* **1 :** causing fear **2 :** TIMID, TIMOROUS — **fear·some·ly** *adv* — **fear·some·ness** *n*

fea·si·ble \ˈfē-zə-bəl\ *adj* [ME *faisible,* fr. MF, fr. *fais-,* stem of *faire* to make, do, fr. L *facere*] **1 :** capable of being done or carried out <a ~ plan> **2 :** capable of being used or dealt with successfully : SUITABLE **3 :** REASONABLE, LIKELY ***syn*** see POSSIBLE ***ant*** unfeasible, infeasible, chimerical (*as a scheme or project*) — **fea·si·bil·i·ty** \ˌfē-zə-ˈbil-ət-ē\ *n* — **fea·si·ble·ness** \ˈfē-zə-bəl-nəs\ *n* — **fea·si·bly** \-blē\ *adv*

[1]**feast** \ˈfēst\ *n* [ME *feste* festival, feast, fr. OF, festival, fr. L *festa,* pl. of *festum* festival, fr. neut. of *festus* solemn, festal; akin to L *feriae* holidays, *fanum* temple, Arm *dikʻ* gods] **1 a :** an elaborate meal often accompanied by a ceremony or entertainment : BANQUET **b :** something that gives unusual or abundant pleasure **2 :** a periodic religious observance commemorating an event or honoring a deity, person, or thing

[2]**feast** *vi* **:** to take part in a feast ~ *vt* **1 :** to give a feast for **2 :** DELIGHT, GRATIFY — **feast·er** *n*

Feast of Tabernacles : SUKKOTH

[1]**feat** \ˈfēt\ *adj* [ME *fete, fayt,* fr. MF *fait,* pp. of *faire*] **1** *archaic* **:** BECOMING, NEAT **2** *archaic* **:** SMART, DEXTEROUS

[2]**feat** *n* [ME *fait,* fr. MF, fr. L *factum,* fr. neut. of *factus,* pp. of *facere* to make, do — more at DO] **1 :** ACT, DEED **2 a :** a deed notable esp. for courage **b :** an act or product of skill, endurance, or ingenuity

syn FEAT, EXPLOIT, ACHIEVEMENT *shared meaning element* : a remarkable deed

[1]**feath·er** \ˈfeth-ər\ *n* [ME *fether,* fr. OE; akin to OHG *federa* wing, L *petere* to go to, seek, Gk *petesthai* to fly, *piptein* to fall, *pteron* wing] **1 a :** one of the light horny epidermal outgrowths that form the external covering of the body of birds and that consist of a shaft bearing on each side a series of barbs which bear barbules which in turn bear barbicels commonly ending in hooked hamuli and interlocking with the barbules of an adjacent barb to link the barbs into a continuous vane **b :** PLUME **c :** the vane of an arrow **2 a :** PLUMAGE **b :** KIND, NATURE <birds of a ~ flock together> **c :** ATTIRE, DRESS **d :** CONDITION, MOOD **3 :** FEATHERING 2 **4 :** a projecting strip, rib, fin, or flange **5 :** a feathery flaw in the eye or in a precious stone **6 :** the act of feathering an oar — **feath·ered** \-ərd\ *adj* — **a feather in one's cap :** a mark of distinction : HONOR

[2]**feather** *vb* **feath·ered; feath·er·ing** \-(ə-)riŋ\ *vt* **1 a :** to furnish (as an arrow) with a feather **b :** to cover, clothe, or adorn with feathers **2 a :** to turn (an oar blade) almost horizontal when lifting from the water at the end of a stroke to reduce air resistance **b** (1) **:** to change the angle of (airplane propeller blades) so that the chords become approximately parallel to the line of flight; *also* **:** to change the angle of airplane propeller blades of (an engine) in such a manner (2) **:** to change the angle of (a rotor blade of a rotary-wing aircraft) periodically in forward flight **3 :** to reduce the edge of to a featheredge **4 :** to cut (as air) with or as if with a wing **5 :** to join by a tongue and groove ~ *vi* **1 :** to grow or form feathers **2 :** to have or take on the appearance of a feather or something feathered **3 :** to soak in and spread : BLUR — used of ink or a printed impression **4 :** to feather an oar or an airplane propeller blade — **feather one's nest :** to provide for oneself esp. while in a position of trust

[1]**feath·er·bed** \ˈfeth-ər-ˌbed\ *adj* **:** calling for, sanctioning, or resulting from featherbedding

[2]**featherbed** *vi* **1 a :** to require more workmen than are needed **b :** to limit production under a featherbed rule **2 :** to do featherbed work or put in time under a featherbed rule ~ *vt* **1 :** to bring under a featherbed rule **2 :** to assist (as an industry) by government aid

feather bed *n* **1 :** a feather mattress **2 :** a bed having a feather mattress

feath·er·bed·ding *n* **:** the requiring of an employer usu. under a union rule or safety statute to hire more employees than are needed or to limit production

feath·er·brain \-ˌbrān\ *n* **:** a foolish scatterbrained person — **feath·er·brained** \ˌfeth-ər-ˈbrānd\ *adj*

feath·er·edge \ˈfeth-ə-ˌrej, ˌfeth-ə-ˈ\ *n* **:** a very thin sharp edge; *esp* **:** one that is easily broken or bent over — **featheredge** *vt*

feath·er·head \ˈfeth-ər-ˌhed\ *n* **:** FEATHERBRAIN — **feath·er·head·ed** \ˌfeth-ər-ˈhed-əd\ *adj*

feath·er·ing \ˈfeth-(ə-)riŋ\ *n* **1 a :** a covering of feathers **:** PLUMAGE **b :** a style in which feathers are attached to arrows; *also* **:** the feathers of an arrow **2 :** a fringe of hair (as on the legs of a dog)

feath·er·less \ˈfeth-ər-ləs\ *adj* **:** having no feathers

feather star *n* **:** COMATULID

feath·er·stitch \ˈfeth-ər-ˌstich\ *n* **:** an embroidery stitch consisting of a line of diagonal blanket stitches worked alternately to the left and right — **featherstitch** *vb*

feath·er·weight \-ˌwāt\ *n* **1 :** one that is very light in weight; *specif* **:** a boxer who weighs more than 118 but not more than 126 pounds **2 :** a person of limited intelligence or effectiveness

feath·ery \ˈfeth-(ə-)rē\ *adj* **:** resembling, suggesting, or covered with feathers

[1]**feat·ly** \ˈfēt-lē\ *adv* [ME *fetly*, fr. *fete* feat (adj.)] **1 :** SUITABLY, PROPERLY **2 :** in a graceful manner **:** NIMBLY **3 :** with skill and ingenuity

[2]**featly** *adj* **:** GRACEFUL, NEAT

[1]**fea·ture** \ˈfē-chər\ *n* [ME *feture*, fr. MF, fr. L *factura* act of making, fr. *factus*, pp. of *facere* to make — more at DO] **1 a :** the structure, form, or appearance esp. of a person **b** *obs* **:** physical beauty **2 a :** the makeup or appearance of the face or its parts **b :** a part of the face **:** LINEAMENT **3 :** a prominent part or characteristic **4 :** a special attraction: as **a :** the principal motion picture shown on a program with other pictures **b :** a distinctive article, story, or special department in a newspaper or magazine **c :** something offered to the public or advertised as particularly attractive

[2]**feature** *vb* **fea·tured; fea·tur·ing** \ˈfēch-(ə-)riŋ\ *vt* **1** *chiefly dial* **:** to resemble in features **2 :** to picture or portray in the mind **:** IMAGINE **3 a :** to give special prominence to **b :** to have as a characteristic or feature ~ *vi* **:** to play an important part

fea·tured \ˈfē-chərd\ *adj* **1 :** having facial features of a particular kind — used in combination <a heavy-*featured* man> <a grim-*featured* shrew> **2 :** displayed, advertised, or presented as a special attraction

fea·ture·less \ˈfē-chər-ləs\ *adj* **:** having no distinctive features

feaze \ˈfēz, ˈfāz\ *var of* FAZE

Feb *abbr* February

febri- *comb form* [LL, fr. L *febris*] **:** fever <*febri*fic>

fe·brif·ic \fi-ˈbrif-ik\ *adj, archaic* **:** FEVERISH

feb·ri·fuge \ˈfeb-rə-ˌfyüj\ *n* [F *fébrifuge*, prob. fr. (assumed) NL *febrifuga*, fr. LL *febrifuga, febrifugia* centaury, fr. *febri-* + *-fuga* -fuge] **:** ANTIPYRETIC — **febrifuge** *adj*

fe·brile \ˈfeb-ˌrīl *also* ˈfēb-\ *adj* [ML *febrilis*, fr. L *febris* fever — more at FEVER] **:** of or relating to fever **:** FEVERISH

Feb·ru·ary \ˈfeb-(y)ə-ˌwer-ē, ˈfeb-rə-\ *n* [ME *Februarie*, fr. L *Februarius*, fr. *Februa*, pl., feast of purification; perh. akin to L *fumus* smoke] **:** the 2d month of the Gregorian calendar

fec *abbr* [L *fecit*] he made it

fe·cal \ˈfē-kəl\ *adj* **:** of, relating to, or constituting feces

fe·ces \ˈfē-(ˌ)sēz\ *n pl* [ME, fr. L *faec-, faex* (sing.) dregs] **:** bodily waste discharged through the anus **:** EXCREMENT

feck·less \ˈfek-ləs\ *adj* [Sc, fr. *feck* effect, majority, fr. ME (Sc) *fek*, alter. of ME *effect*] **1 :** INEFFECTUAL, WEAK **2 :** WORTHLESS, IRRESPONSIBLE — **feck·less·ly** *adv* — **feck·less·ness** *n*

feck·ly \ˈfek-lē\ *adv* [Sc, fr. *feck* + *-ly*] *chiefly Scot* **:** ALMOST, NEARLY

fec·u·lent \ˈfek-yə-lənt\ *adj* [ME, fr. L *faeculentus*, fr. *faec-, faex*] **:** foul with impurities **:** FECAL — **fe·cu·lence** \-lən(t)s\ *n*

fe·cund \ˈfek-ənd, ˈfēk-\ *adj* [ME, fr. MF *fecond*, fr. L *fecundus* — more at FEMININE] **1 :** fruitful in offspring or vegetation **:** PROLIFIC **2 :** intellectually productive or inventive to a marked degree ***syn*** see FERTILE ***ant*** barren — **fe·cun·di·ty** \fi-ˈkən-dət-ē, fe-\ *n*

fe·cun·date \ˈfek-ən-ˌdāt, ˈfē-kən-\ *vt* **-dated; -dat·ing** [L *fecundatus*, pp. of *fecundare*, fr. *fecundus*] **1 :** to make fecund **2 :** to make fertile **:** IMPREGNATE — **fe·cun·da·tion** \ˌfek-ən-ˈdā-shən, ˌfē-kən-\ *n*

[1]**fed** \ˈfed\ *n, often cap* **:** FEDERAL 2

[2]**fed** *abbr* federal; federation

fe·da·yee \fi-ˌda-ˈ(y)ē, -ˌdä-\ *n, pl* **fe·da·yeen** \-ˈ(y)ēn\ [Ar *fidā'ī*, lit., one who sacrifices himself] **:** a member of an Arab commando group operating esp. against Israel

fed·er·al \ˈfed(-ə)-rəl\ *adj* [L *foeder-, foedus* compact, league; akin to L *fidere* to trust — more at BIDE] **1** *archaic* **:** of or relating to a compact or treaty **2 a :** formed by a compact between political units that surrender their individual sovereignty to a central authority but retain limited residuary powers of government **b :** of or constituting a form of government in which power is distributed between a central authority and a number of constituent territorial units **c :** of or relating to the central government of a federation as distinguished from the governments of the constituent units **3** *cap* **:** advocating or friendly to the principle of a federal government with strong centralized powers; *esp* **:** of or relating to the American Federalists **4** *often cap* **:** of, relating to, or loyal to the federal government or the Union armies of the U.S. in the American Civil War — **fed·er·al·ly** \-rə-lē\ *adv*

Federal *n* **1 :** a supporter of the government of the U.S. in the Civil War; *specif* **:** a soldier in the federal armies **2 :** a federal agent or officer

federal court *n* **:** a court established by authority of a federal government; *esp* **:** one established under the constitution and laws of the U.S.

federal district *n* **:** a district set apart as the seat of the central government of a federation

federal district court *n* **:** a district trial court of law and equity that hears cases under federal jurisdiction

fed·er·al·ism \ˈfed(-ə)-rə-ˌliz-əm\ *n* **1 a** *often cap* **:** the federal principle of organization **b :** support or advocacy of this principle **2** *cap* **:** the principles of the Federalists

fed·er·al·ist \-ləst\ *n* **1 :** an advocate of federalism: as **a** *often cap* **:** an advocate of a federal union between the American colonies after the Revolution and of the adoption of the U.S. Constitution **b** *often cap* **:** WORLD FEDERALIST **2** *cap* **:** a member of a major political party in the early years of the U.S. favoring a strong centralized national government — **federalist** *adj, often cap*

fed·er·al·iza·tion \ˌfed(-ə)-rə-lə-ˈzā-shən\ *n* **1 :** the act of federalizing **2 :** the state of being federalized

fed·er·al·ize \ˈfed(-ə)-rə-ˌlīz\ *vt* **-ized; -iz·ing 1 :** to unite in or under a federal system **2 :** to bring under the jurisdiction of a federal government

Federal Reserve bank *n* **:** one of 12 banks set up under the Federal Reserve system to hold reserves and discount commercial paper for affiliated banks in their respective districts

[1]**fed·er·ate** \ˈfed(-ə)-rət\ *adj* [L *foederatus*, fr. *foeder-, foedus*] **:** united in an alliance or federation **:** FEDERATED

[2]**fed·er·ate** \ˈfed-ə-ˌrāt\ *vt* **-at·ed; -at·ing :** to join in a federation

federated church *n* **:** a local church uniting two or more congregations that maintain different denominational ties

fed·er·a·tion \ˌfed-ə-ˈrā-shən\ *n* **1 :** the act of federating; *esp* **:** the formation of a federal union **2 :** something formed by federation: as **a :** a federal government **b :** a union of organizations

fed·er·a·tive \ˈfed-ə-ˌrāt-iv, ˈfed(-ə)-rət-\ *adj*: FEDERAL — **fed·er·a·tive·ly** *adv*

fedn *abbr* federation

fe·do·ra \fi-ˈdōr-ə, -ˈdȯr-\ *n* [*Fédora*, drama by V. Sardou] **:** a low soft felt hat with the crown creased lengthwise

fed up *adj* **:** tired, sated, or disgusted beyond endurance <*fed up* with things as they are>

[1]**fee** \ˈfē\ *n* [ME, fr. OF *fé, fief*, of Gmc origin; akin to OE *feoh* cattle, property, OHG *fihu* cattle; akin to L *pecus* cattle, *pecunia* money, *pectere* to comb] **1 a (1) :** an estate in land held in feudal law from a lord on condition of homage and service **(2) :** a piece of land so held **b :** an inherited or heritable estate in land **2 a (1) :** a fixed charge **(2) :** a charge for a professional service **b :** TIP ***syn*** see WAGE — **in fee :** in absolute and legal possession

[2]**fee** *vt* **feed; fee·ing 1** *chiefly Scot* **:** HIRE **2 :** TIP

fee·ble \ˈfē-bəl\ *adj* **fee·bler** \-b(ə-)lər\; **fee·blest** \-b(ə-)ləst\ [ME *feble*, fr. OF, fr. L *flebilis* lamentable, wretched, fr. *flēre* to weep — more at BLEAT] **1 a :** markedly lacking in strength **b :** indicating weakness **2 a :** deficient in qualities or resources that indicate vigor, authority, force, or efficiency **b :** INADEQUATE, INFERIOR ***syn*** see WEAK ***ant*** robust — **fee·ble·ness** \-bəl-nəs\ *n* — **fee·bly** \-blē\ *adv*

fee·ble·mind·ed \ˌfē-bəl-ˈmīn-dəd\ *adj* **1** *obs* **:** IRRESOLUTE, VACILLATING **2 :** mentally deficient **3 :** FOOLISH, STUPID — **fee·ble·mind·ed·ly** *adv* — **fee·ble·mind·ed·ness** *n*

fee·blish \ˈfē-b(ə-)lish\ *adj* **:** somewhat feeble

[1]**feed** \ˈfēd\ *vb* **fed** \ˈfed\; **feed·ing** [ME *feden*, fr. OE *fēdan*; akin to OE *fōda* food — more at FOOD] *vt* **1 a :** to give food to **b :** to give as food **2 :** to furnish something essential to the growth, sustenance, maintenance, or operation of **3 :** to produce or provide food for **4 a :** SATISFY, GRATIFY **b :** SUPPORT, ENCOURAGE **5 a :** to supply for use or consumption **b (1) :** to supply (a signal) to an electronic circuit **(2) :** to send by wire to a transmitting station for broadcast **6 :** to supply with cues and situations that make a role more effective **7 :** to pass or throw a ball or puck to (a teammate) esp. for a shot at the goal ~ *vi* **1 a :** to consume food **:** EAT **b :** PREY — used with *on, upon,* or *off* **2 :** to become nourished or satisfied as if by food **3 :** to move into a machine or opening in order to be used or processed

[2]**feed** *n* **1 a :** an act of eating **b :** MEAL; *esp* **:** a large meal **2 a :** food for livestock; *specif* **:** a mixture or preparation for feeding livestock **b :** the amount given at each feeding **3 a :** material supplied (as to a furnace or machine) **b :** a mechanism by which the action of feeding is effected **c :** the motion or process of carrying forward the material to be operated upon (as in a machine) **4 :** ASSIST 2

feed·back \ˈfēd-ˌbak\ *n* **1 :** the return to the input of a part of the output of a machine, system, or process (as for producing changes in an electronic circuit that improve performance or in an automatic control device that provide self-corrective action) **2 a :** the partial reversion of the effects of a process to its source or to a preceding stage **b :** the return to a point of origin of evaluative or corrective information about an action or process <student ~ was solicited to help revise the curriculum> <we welcome . . . ~ from our readers — brickbats as well as bouquets —*Johns Hopkins Mag.*>; *also* **:** the information so transmitted

feedback inhibition *n* **:** inhibition of an enzyme controlling an early stage of a series of biochemical reactions by the end product when it reaches a critical concentration

feed·er \ˈfēd-ər\ *n* **:** one that feeds: as **a :** a device or apparatus for supplying food **b (1) :** TRIBUTARY **(2) :** a source of supply **(3) :** a heavy wire conductor supplying electricity at some point of an electric distribution system (as from a substation) **(4) :** a transmission line running from a radio transmitter to an antenna **(5) :** a branch transportation line **c :** an animal being fattened or suitable for fattening **d :** an actor or role that serves as a foil for another

feed·lot \ˈfēd-ˌlät\ *n* **:** a plot of land on which livestock are fattened for market

feed·stock \-ˌstäk\ *n* : raw material supplied to a machine or processing plant

feed·stuff \-ˌstəf\ *n* : FEED 2a; *also* : any of the constituent nutrients of an animal ration

[1]feel \ˈfē(ə)l\ *vb* **felt** \ˈfelt\; **feel·ing** [ME *felen,* fr. OE *fēlan;* akin to OHG *fuolen* to feel, L *palpare* to caress, and perh. to Gk *pallein* to brandish — more at POLEMIC] *vt* **1 a :** to handle or touch in order to examine, test, or explore some quality <*felt* the coat to see if it was wet> **b :** to perceive by a physical sensation coming from discrete end organs (as of the skin or muscles) **2 a :** to undergo passive experience of **b :** to have one's sensibilities markedly affected by **3 :** to ascertain by cautious trial — often used with *out* **4 a :** to be aware of by instinct or inference **b :** BELIEVE, THINK ~ *vi* **1 a :** to receive or be able to receive a tactile sensation **b :** to search for something by using the sense of touch **2 :** to be conscious of an inward impression, state of mind, or physical condition **3 :** to seem esp. to the sense of touch **4 :** to have sympathy or pity ***syn*** see TOUCH

[2]feel *n* **1 :** the sense of touch **2 :** SENSATION, FEELING **3 a :** the quality of a thing as imparted through or as if through touch **b :** typical or peculiar quality or atmosphere **4 :** intuitive knowledge or ability

feel·er \ˈfē-lər\ *n* : one that feels: as **a :** a tactile process (as a tentacle) of an animal **b :** something (as a proposal) ventured to ascertain the views of others

[1]feel·ing \ˈfē-liŋ\ *n* **1 a** (1) **:** the one of the basic physical senses of which the skin contains the chief end organs and of which the sensations of touch and temperature are characteristic : TOUCH (2) **:** a sensation experienced through this sense **b :** generalized bodily consciousness or sensation **c :** appreciative or responsive awareness or recognition <experienced a ~ of safety> **2 a :** an emotional state or reaction <had a kindly ~ toward the child> **b** *pl* **:** susceptibility to impression : SENSITIVITY <the remark hurt her ~*s*> **3 a :** the undifferentiated background of one's awareness considered apart from any identifiable sensation, perception, or thought **b :** the overall quality of one's awareness **c :** conscious recognition : SENSE **4 a :** often unreasoned opinion or belief : SENTIMENT **b :** PRESENTIMENT **5 :** capacity to respond emotionally esp. with the higher emotions <a man of noble ~> **6 :** the character ascribed to something as a result of one's impression or emotional state : ATMOSPHERE **7 a :** the quality of a work of art that embodies and conveys the emotion of the artist **b :** sympathetic aesthetic response **8 :** FEEL 4 <lacks a ~ for words>
***syn* 1** see SENSATION
2 FEELING, AFFECTION, EMOTION, SENTIMENT, PASSION *shared meaning element* : subjective response or reaction (as to a person or situation) or an instance of this

[2]feeling *adj* **1 a :** SENTIENT, SENSITIVE **b :** easily moved emotionally **2** *obs* **:** deeply felt **3 :** expressing emotion or sensitivity — **feel·ing·ly** \-liŋ-lē\ *adv* — **feel·ing·ness** *n*

fee simple *n, pl* **fees simple :** a fee without limitation to any class of heirs or restrictions on transfer of ownership

fee splitting *n* **:** payment by a specialist (as a doctor or a lawyer) of a part of his fee to the person who made the referral

feet *pl of* FOOT

fee tail *n, pl* **fees tail :** a fee limited to a particular class of heirs

feet·first \ˈfēt-ˈfərst\ *adv* **:** with the feet foremost <jumped into the water ~>

feet of clay [fr. the feet of the idol in Dan 2:33] **:** a generally concealed or unobserved but marked weakness or frailty <a towering figure, posthumously judged to have *feet of clay* —*Times Lit. Supp.*>

feeze \ˈfēz, ˈfāz\ *n* [ME *veze,* fr. *fesen, vesen* to drive away — more at FAZE] **1** *chiefly dial* **:** RUSH **2** *dial* **:** a state of alarm or excitement

Feh·ling's solution \ˈfā-liŋz-\ *n* [Hermann *Fehling* †1885 G chemist] **:** a blue solution of Rochelle salt and copper sulfate used as an oxidizing agent in testing for sugars and aldehydes

feign \ˈfān\ *vb* [ME *feignen,* fr. OF *feign-,* stem of *feindre,* fr. L *fingere* to shape, feign — more at DOUGH] *vt* **1 a :** to give a false appearance of **:** induce as a false impression <~ death> <he ~*ed* that he believed her story> **b :** to assert as if true **:** PRETEND **2** *archaic* **a :** INVENT, IMAGINE **b :** to give fictional representation to **3** *obs* **:** DISGUISE, CONCEAL ~ *vi* **:** PRETEND, DISSEMBLE ***syn*** see ASSUME — **feign·er** *n*

feigned *adj* **1 :** FICTITIOUS **2 :** not genuine or real

[1]feint \ˈfānt\ *n* [F *feinte,* fr. OF, fr. *feint,* pp. of *feindre*] **:** something feigned; *specif* **:** a mock blow or attack on or toward one part in order to distract attention from the point one really intends to attack ***syn*** see TRICK

[2]feint *vi* **:** to make a feint ~ *vt* **1 :** to lure or deceive with a feint **2 :** to make a pretense of

fei·rie \ˈfē-rē\ *adj* [ME (Sc) *fery,* fr. ME *fere* strong, fr. OE *fēre* able to go; akin to OE *faran* to travel, fare] *Scot* **:** NIMBLE, STRONG

feist \ˈfīst\ *n* [obs. *fisting hound,* fr. obs. *fist* (to break wind)] *chiefly dial* **:** a small dog

feisty \ˈfī-stē\ *adj* **feist·i·er; -est :** being in a state of excitement or agitation: as **a :** full of nervous energy **:** FIDGETY **b :** being touchy and quarrelsome <found us irritated, upset, ~ —E. E. Rebstock> **c :** being frisky and exuberant

feld·spar \ˈfel(d)-ˌspär\ *n* [modif. of obs. G *feldspath* (now *feldspat*), fr. G *feld* field + obs. G *spath* (now *spat*) spar] **:** any of a group of crystalline minerals that consist of aluminum silicates with either potassium, sodium, calcium, or barium and that are an essential constituent of nearly all crystalline rocks (hardness 6–6.5, sp. gr. 2.5–2.9)

feld·spath·ic \fel(d)-ˈspath-ik\ *adj* [*feldspath* (var. of *feldspar*), fr. obs. G] **:** relating to or containing feldspar — used esp. of a porcelain glaze

fe·li·cif·ic \ˌfē-lə-ˈsif-ik\ *adj* [L *felic-, felix*] **:** causing or intended to cause happiness

felicific calculus *n* **:** a method of determining the rightness of an action by balancing the probable pleasures and pains that it would produce

[1]fe·lic·i·tate \fi-ˈlis-ə-ˌtāt\ *adj* [LL *felicitatus,* pp. of *felicitare* to make happy, fr. L *felicitas*] *obs* **:** made happy

[2]felicitate *vt* **-tat·ed; -tat·ing 1** *archaic* **:** to make happy **2 a :** to consider happy or fortunate **b :** to offer congratulations to — **fe·lic·i·ta·tion** \-ˌlis-ə-ˈtā-shən\ *n* — **fe·lic·i·ta·tor** \-ˈlis-ə-ˌtāt-ər\ *n*

fe·lic·i·tous \fi-ˈlis-ət-əs\ *adj* **1 :** very well suited or expressed **:** APT <a ~ remark> **2 :** PLEASANT, DELIGHTFUL ***syn*** see FIT ***ant*** infelicitous — **fe·lic·i·tous·ly** *adv* — **fe·lic·i·tous·ness** *n*

fe·lic·i·ty \fi-ˈlis-ət-ē\ *n, pl* **-ties** [ME *felicite,* fr. MF *felicité,* fr. L *felicitat-, felicitas,* fr. *felic-, felix* fruitful, happy — more at FEMININE] **1 a :** the quality or state of being happy; *esp* **:** great happiness **b :** an instance of happiness **2 :** something that causes happiness **3 :** a pleasing faculty esp. in art or language **:** APTNESS **4 :** an apt expression

fe·lid \ˈfē-ləd\ *n* [NL *Felidae,* family name, fr. *Felis,* genus of cats, fr. L, cat] **:** CAT 1b — **felid** *adj*

fe·line \ˈfē-ˌlīn\ *adj* [L *felinus,* fr. *felis*] **1 :** of or relating to cats or the cat family **2 :** resembling a cat: as **a :** sleekly graceful **b :** SLY, TREACHEROUS **c :** STEALTHY — **feline** *n* — **fe·line·ly** *adv* — **fe·lin·i·ty** \fē-ˈlin-ət-ē\ *n*

feline distemper *n* **1 :** PANLEUCOPENIA **2 :** a gastrointestinal disease of cats closely related to panleucopenia

[1]fell \ˈfel\ *n* [ME, fr. OE; akin to OHG *fel* skin, L *pellis*] **:** SKIN, HIDE, PELT

[2]fell *vt* [ME *fellen,* fr. OE *fellan;* akin to OE *feallan* to fall — more at FALL] **1 a :** to cut, beat, or knock down **b :** KILL **2 :** to sew (a seam) by folding one raw edge under the other and sewing flat on the wrong side — **fell·able** \ˈfel-ə-bəl\ *adj* — **fell·er** *n*

[3]fell *past of* FALL

[4]fell *adj* [ME *fel,* fr. OF — more at FELON] **1 a :** FIERCE, CRUEL, TERRIBLE **b :** very destructive or painful **:** DEADLY **2** *Scot* **:** SHARP, PUNGENT — **fell·ness** *n* — **fel·ly** \ˈfel-lē\ *adv* — **at one fell swoop :** all at once; *also* **:** with a single concentrated effort

fel·lah \ˈfel-ə, fə-ˈlä\ *n, pl* **fel·la·hin** *or* **fel·la·heen** \ˌfel-ə-ˈhēn, fə-ˌlä-ˈhēn\ [Ar *fallāh*] **:** a peasant or agricultural laborer in an Arab country (as Egypt)

fel·la·tio \fə-ˈlā-shē-ˌō, fe-, -ˈlät-ē-\ *also* **fel·la·tion** \-ˈlā-shən\ *n* [NL *fellation-, fellatio,* fr. L *fellatus,* pp. of *felare, fellare,* lit., to suck — more at FEMININE] **:** oral stimulation of the penis

fell·mon·ger \ˈfel-ˌməŋ-gər, -ˌmäŋ-\ *n, Brit* **:** one who removes hair or wool from hides in preparation for leather making — **fell·mon·gered** \-gərd\ *adj, Brit* — **fell·mon·ger·ing** \-g(ə-)riŋ\ *or* **fell·mon·gery** \-g(ə-)rē\ *n, Brit*

fel·low \ˈfel-(ˌ)ō, -ə(-w)\ *n* [ME *felawe,* fr. OE *fēolaga,* fr. ON *fēlagi,* fr. *fēlag* partnership, fr. *fē* cattle, money + *lag* act of laying] **1 :** COMRADE, ASSOCIATE **2 a :** an equal in rank, power, or character **:** PEER **b :** one of a pair **:** MATE **3 :** a member of a group having common characteristics; *specif* **:** a member of an incorporated literary or scientific society **4 a** *obs* **:** a person of one of the lower social classes **b :** a worthless man or boy **c :** MAN, BOY **d :** BOYFRIEND, BEAU **5 :** an incorporated member of a college or collegiate foundation esp. in a British university **6 :** a person appointed to a position granting a stipend and allowing for advanced study or research

fellow feeling *n* **:** a feeling of community of interest or of mutual understanding <*fellow feeling* . . . in the face of the impersonality of urban life —Richard Poirier>

fel·low·ly \-ō-lē, -ə-lē\ *adj* **:** SOCIABLE — **fellowly** *adv*

fel·low·man \ˌfel-ō-ˈman, -ə-\ *n* **:** a kindred human being

fellow servant *n* **:** an employee working with another employee under such circumstances that each one if negligent may expose the other to harm which the employer cannot reasonably be expected to guard against or be held legally liable for

[1]fel·low·ship \ˈfel-ō-ˌship, -ə-\ *n* **1 :** COMPANIONSHIP, COMPANY **2 a :** community of interest, activity, feeling, or experience **b :** the state of being a fellow or associate **3 :** a company of equals or friends **:** ASSOCIATION **4 :** the quality or state of being comradely **5** *obs* **:** MEMBERSHIP, PARTNERSHIP **6 a :** the position of a fellow (as of a university) **b :** the stipend of a fellow **c :** a foundation for the providing of such a stipend

[2]fellowship *vb* **-shipped** *also* **-shiped** \-ˌshipt\; **-ship·ping** *also* **-ship·ing** \-ˌship-iŋ\ *vi* **:** to join in fellowship esp. with a church member ~ *vt* **:** to admit to fellowship (as in a church)

fellow traveler *n* [trans. of Russ *poputchik*] **:** one that sympathizes with and often furthers the ideals and program of an organized group (as the Communist party) without membership in the group or regular participation in its activities — **fel·low-trav·el·ing** *adj*

fel·ly \ˈfel-ē\ *or* **fel·loe** \-(ˌ)ō\ *n, pl* **fellies** *or* **felloes** [ME *fely, felive,* fr. OE *felg;* akin to OHG *felga* felly, OE *fealg* piece of plowed land] **:** the exterior rim or a segment of the rim of a wheel supported by the spokes

felo-de-se \ˌfel-ōd-ə-ˈsā, -ˈsē\ *n, pl* **fe·lo·nes-de-se** \fə-ˌlō-(ˌ)nēz-də-\ *or* **felos-de-se** \ˌfel-ōz-də-\ [ML *felo de se, fello de se,* lit., evildoer upon himself] **1 :** one who deliberately kills himself or who dies from the effects of his commission of an unlawful malicious act **2 :** an act of deliberate self-destruction **:** SUICIDE

[1]fel·on \ˈfel-ən\ *adj* [ME, fr. OF *felon, fel,* fr. ML *fellon-, fello* evildoer, villain] **1** *archaic* **a :** CRUEL **b :** EVIL **2** *archaic* **:** WILD

[2]felon *n* **1 :** one who has committed a felony **2** *archaic* **:** VILLAIN **3 :** a deep usu. suppurative inflammation of the finger or toe esp. near the end or around the nail

---

ə abut ᵊ kitten ər further a back ā bake ä cot, cart
aù out ch chin e less ē easy g gift i trip ī life
j joke ŋ sing ō flow ò flaw òi coin th thin th this
ü loot ù foot y yet yü few yù furious zh vision

fe·lo·ni·ous \fə-ˈlō-nē-əs\ *adj* **1** *archaic* **:** very evil **:** VILLAINOUS **2 :** of, relating to, or having the quality of a felony — **fe·lo·ni·ous·ly** *adv* — **fe·lo·ni·ous·ness** *n*

fel·on·ry \ˈfel-ən-rē\ *n* **:** FELONS; *specif* **:** the convict population of a penal colony

fel·o·ny \ˈfel-ə-nē\ *n, pl* **-nies** **1 :** an act on the part of a feudal vassal involving the forfeiture of his fee **2 a :** a grave crime formerly differing from a misdemeanor under English common law by involving forfeiture in addition to any other punishment **b :** a grave crime declared to be a felony by the common law or by statute regardless of the punishment actually imposed **c :** a crime declared a felony by statute because of the punishment imposed **d :** a crime for which the punishment in federal law may be death or imprisonment for more than one year

fel·site \ˈfel-ˌsīt\ *n* [*felspar*] **:** a dense igneous rock that consists almost entirely of feldspar and quartz — **fel·sit·ic** \fel-ˈsit-ik\ *adj*

fel·spar *var of* FELDSPAR

1**felt** \ˈfelt\ *n* [ME, fr. OE; akin to OHG *filz* felt, L *pellere* to drive, beat, Gk *pelas* near] **1 a :** a cloth made of wool and fur often mixed with natural or synthetic fibers through the action of heat, moisture, chemicals, and pressure **b :** a firm woven cloth of wool or cotton heavily napped and shrunk **2 :** an article made of felt **3 :** a material resembling felt: as **a :** a heavy paper of organic or asbestos fibers impregnated with asphalt and used in building construction **b :** semirigid pressed fiber insulation used in building

2**felt** *vt* **1 :** to make into felt or a similar substance **2 :** to cause to adhere and mat together **3 :** to cover with felt

3**felt** *past of* FEEL

felt·ing \ˈfel-tiŋ\ *n* **1 :** the process by which felt is made **2 :** FELT

fe·luc·ca \fə-ˈlü-kə, -ˈlək-ə\ *n* [It *feluca*] **:** a narrow fast lateen-rigged sailing ship chiefly of the Mediterranean area

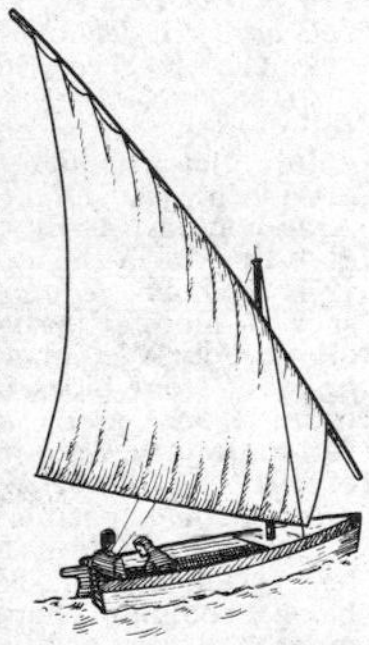

felucca

fem *abbr* **1** female **2** feminine

1**fe·male** \ˈfē-ˌmāl\ *n* [ME, alter. of *femel, femelle,* fr. MF & ML; MF *femelle,* fr. ML *femella,* fr. L, girl, dim. of *femina*] **1 :** an individual that bears young or produces eggs as distinguished from one that begets young; *esp* **:** a woman or girl as distinguished from a man or boy **2 :** a pistillate plant

2**female** *adj* **1 a :** of, relating to, or being the sex that bears young or produces eggs **b :** PISTILLATE **2 :** having some quality (as gentleness or delicacy) associated with the female sex **3 :** designed with a hollow into which a corresponding male part fits <~ coupling of a hose> — **fe·male·ness** *n*

1**fem·i·nine** \ˈfem-ə-nən\ *adj* [ME, fr. MF *feminin,* fr. L *femininus,* fr. *femina* woman; akin to OE *delu* nipple, L *filius* son, *felix, fetus, & fecundus* fruitful, *felare* to suck, Gk *thēlē* nipple] **1 :** FEMALE 1a **2 :** characteristic of or appropriate or peculiar to women **3 :** of, relating to, or constituting the gender that ordinarily includes most words or grammatical forms referring to females <a ~ noun> **4 a :** having an unstressed and usu. hypermetric final syllable <~ ending> **b** *of rhyme* **:** having an unstressed final syllable **c :** having the final chord occurring on a weak beat <music in ~ cadences> — **fem·i·nine·ly** *adv* — **fem·i·nine·ness** \-nə(n)-nəs\ *n*

2**feminine** *n* **1 :** the female principle <eternal ~> **2 a :** a noun, pronoun, adjective, or inflectional form or class of the feminine gender **b :** the feminine gender

fem·i·nin·i·ty \ˌfem-ə-ˈnin-ət-ē\ *n* **1 :** the quality or nature of the female sex **2 :** EFFEMINACY **3 :** WOMEN, WOMANKIND

fem·i·nism \ˈfem-ə-ˌniz-əm\ *n* **1 :** the theory of the political, economic, and social equality of the sexes **2 :** organized activity on behalf of women's rights and interests — **fem·i·nist** \-nəst\ *n or adj* — **fem·i·nis·tic** \ˌfem-ə-ˈnis-tik\ *adj*

fe·min·i·ty \fe-ˈmin-ət-ē, fə-\ *n* **:** FEMININITY

fem·i·nize \ˈfem-ə-ˌnīz\ *vt* **-nized; -niz·ing** **1 :** to give a feminine quality to **2 :** to cause (a male or castrate) to take on feminine characters (as by implantation of ovaries or administration of estrogenic substances) — **fem·i·ni·za·tion** \ˌfem-ə-nə-ˈzā-shən\ *n*

femme fa·tale \ˌfem-fə-ˈtal, ˌfam-, -ˈtäl\ *n, pl* **femmes fa·tales** \-ˈtal(z), -ˈtäl(z)\ [F, lit., disastrous woman] **1 :** a seductive woman who lures men into dangerous or compromising situations **:** SIREN **2 :** a woman who attracts men by an aura of charm and mystery

fem·o·ral \ˈfem-(ə-)rəl\ *adj* **:** of or relating to the femur or thigh

femoral artery *n* **:** the chief artery of the thigh lying in its anterior inner part

fem·to- \ˌfem(p)-tō\ *comb form* [ISV, fr. Dan or Norw *femten* fifteen, fr. ON *fimmtān;* akin to OE *fiftēne* fifteen] **:** one quadrillionth (10^{-15}) part of <*femto*ampere>

fe·mur \ˈfē-mər\ *n, pl* **fe·murs** *or* **fem·o·ra** \ˈfem-(ə-)rə\ [NL *femor-, femur,* fr. L, thigh] **1 :** the proximal bone of the hind or lower limb — called also *thighbone* **2 :** the segment of an insect's leg that is third from the body

1**fen** \ˈfen\ *n* [ME, fr. OE *fenn;* akin to OHG *fenna* fen, Skt *paṅka* mud] **:** low land covered wholly or partly with water unless artificially drained

2**fen** \ˈfən\ *n, pl* **fen** [Chin (Pek) *fên*1] — see *yuan* at MONEY table

1**fence** \ˈfen(t)s\ *n, often attrib* [ME *fens,* short for *defens* defense] **1** *archaic* **:** a means of protection **:** DEFENSE **2 :** a barrier intended to prevent escape or intrusion or to mark a boundary; *esp* **:** such a barrier made of posts and wire or boards **3 :** FENCING 1 **4 a :** a receiver of stolen goods **b :** a place where stolen goods are bought — **fence·less** \-ləs\ *adj* — **fence·less·ness** *n* — **on the fence :** in a position of neutrality or indecision

2**fence** *vb* **fenced; fenc·ing** *vt* **1 a :** to enclose with a fence **b** (1) **:** to keep in or out with a fence (2) **:** to ward off **2 :** to provide a defense for ~ *vi* **1 a :** to practice fencing **b** (1) **:** to use tactics of attack and defense resembling those of fencing (2) **:** to parry arguments by shifting ground **2** *archaic* **:** to provide protection — **fenc·er** *n*

fence–sit·ting \ˈfen(t)s-ˌsit-iŋ\ *n* **:** a state of indecision or neutrality with respect to conflicting positions — **fence sitter** *n*

fenc·ing *n* **1 :** the art or practice of attack and defense with the foil, épee, or saber **2 a** (1) **:** FENCE 2 (2) **:** the fences of a property or region **b :** material used for building fences

1**fend** \ˈfend\ *vb* [ME *fenden,* short for *defenden*] *vt* **1 :** DEFEND **2 :** to keep or ward off **:** REPEL — often used with *off* **3** *dial Brit* **:** to provide for **:** SUPPORT ~ *vi* **1** *dial Brit* **:** to make an effort **:** STRUGGLE **2 a :** to try to get along without help **:** SHIFT **b :** to provide a livelihood

2**fend** *n, chiefly Scot* **:** an effort or attempt esp. for oneself

fend·er \ˈfen-dər\ *n* **:** a device that protects: as **a :** a cushion (as foam rubber, a bundle of rope, or a wood float) between a boat and a dock or between two boats that lessens shock and prevents chafing **b :** RAILING **c :** a device in front of locomotives and streetcars to lessen injury to animals or pedestrians in case of collision **d :** a guard over the wheel of a motor vehicle **e :** a low metal frame or a screen before an open fireplace **f :** an oblong or triangular shield of leather attached to the stirrup leather of a saddle to protect a rider's legs

fe·nes·tra \fə-ˈnes-trə\ *n, pl* **-trae** \-ˌtrē, -ˌtrī\ [NL, fr. L, window] **1 :** a small opening: as **a :** an oval opening between the middle ear and the vestibule having the base of the stapes or columella attached to its membrane — called also *fenestra ovalis, fenestra vestibuli* **b :** a round opening between the middle ear and the cochlea — called also *fenestra cochleae, fenestra rotunda* **2 :** an opening cut in bone **3 :** a transparent spot (as in the wings of a moth) — **fe·nes·tral** \-trəl\ *adj*

fe·nes·trate \fə-ˈnes-ˌtrāt, ˈfen-ə-ˌstrāt\ *adj* [L *fenestratus,* fr. *fenestra*] **:** FENESTRATED 2

fen·es·trat·ed \ˈfen-ə-ˌstrāt-əd\ *adj* **1 :** provided with or characterized by windows **2 :** having one or more openings or pores <~ blood capillaries>

fen·es·tra·tion \ˌfen-ə-ˈstrā-shən\ *n* **1 :** the arrangement, proportioning, and design of windows and doors in a building **2 :** an opening in a surface (as a wall or membrane) **3 :** the operation of cutting an opening in the bony labyrinth between the inner ear and tympanum to replace natural fenestrae that are not functional

Fe·ni·an \ˈfē-nē-ən\ *n* [IrGael *Fēinne,* pl. of *Fiann,* legendary band of Irish warriors] **1 :** one of a legendary band of warriors defending Ireland in the 2d and 3d centuries A.D. **2 :** a member of a secret 19th century Irish and Irish-American organization dedicated to the overthrow of British rule in Ireland — **Fenian** *adj* — **Fe·ni·an·ism** \-ə-ˌniz-əm\ *n*

fen·nec \ˈfen-ik\ *n* [Ar *fanak*] **:** a small pale-fawn African fox (*Fennecus zerda*) with large ears

fennec

fen·nel \ˈfen-ᵊl\ *n* [ME *fenel,* fr. OE *finugl,* fr. (assumed) VL *fenuculum,* fr. L *feniculum* fennel, dim. of *fenum* hay; perh. akin to L *fetus* fruitful — more at FEMININE] **:** a perennial European herb (*Foeniculum vulgare*) of the carrot family adventive in No. America and cultivated for its aromatic seeds and its foliage

fen·ny \ˈfen-ē\ *adj* [ME, fr. OE *fennig,* fr. *fenn* fen] **1 :** having the characteristics of a fen **:** BOGGY **2 :** peculiar to or found in a fen

fenu·greek \ˈfen-yə-ˌgrēk\ *n* [ME *fenugrek,* fr. MF *fenugrec,* fr. L *fenum Graecum,* lit., Greek hay] **:** a leguminous annual Asiatic herb (*Trigonella foenumgraecum*) with aromatic seeds

feoff·ee \fe-ˈfē, fē-ˈfē\ *n* **:** the person to whom a feoffment is made

feoff·ment \ˈfef-mənt, ˈfēf-\ *n* [ME *feoffement,* fr. AF, fr. *feoffer* to invest with a fee, fr. OF *fief* fee] **:** the granting of a fee

feof·for \ˈfef-ər, ˈfēf-; fe-ˈfȯ(ə)r, fē-\ *or* **feoff·er** \ˈfef-ər, ˈfēf-\ *n* **:** one who makes a feoffment

FEPA *abbr* Fair Employment Practices Act

FEPC *abbr* Fair Employment Practices Commission

-fer \fər\ *n comb form* [F & L; F *-fère,* fr. L *-fer* bearing, one that bears, fr. *ferre* to carry — more at BEAR] **:** one that bears <aqui*fer*>

FERA *abbr* Federal Emergency Relief Administration

fe·rae na·tu·rae \ˈfer-ˌī-nə-ˈtu̇(ə)r-ˌī\ *adj* [L, of a wild nature] **:** wild by nature and not usu. tamed

fe·ral \ˈfir-əl, ˈfer-\ *adj* [ML *feralis,* fr. L *fera* wild animal, fr. fem. of *ferus* wild — more at FIERCE] **1 :** of, relating to, or suggestive of a wild beast **:** SAVAGE **2 a :** not domesticated or cultivated **:** WILD 1a **b :** having escaped from domestication and become wild

fer·bam \ˈfər-ˌbam\ *n* [*fer*ric dimethyl-dithiocar*bam*ate] **:** an agricultural fungicide $FeC_9H_{18}N_3S_6$ used esp. on fruit trees

fer–de–lance \ˈferd-ᵊl-ˈan(t)s, -ˈän(t)s\ *n, pl* **fer–de–lance** [F, lit., lance iron, spearhead] **:** a large extremely venomous pit viper (*Bothrops atrox*) of Central and So. America

fere \ˈfi(ə)r\ *n* [ME, fr. OE *gefēra;* akin to OE *faran* to go, travel — more at FARE] **1** *archaic* **:** COMPANION, COMRADE **2** *archaic* **:** SPOUSE

1**fe·ria** \ˈfir-ē-ə, ˈfer-\ *n* [ML — more at FAIR] **:** a weekday of a church calendar on which no feast is celebrated — **fe·ri·al** \-ē-əl\ *adj*

2**fe·ria** \ˈfer-ē-ə, -ē-ˌä\ *n* [Sp, fair, market, fr. ML — more at FAIR] **:** an Hispanic market festival often in observance of a religious holiday

fe·rine \ˈfi(ə)r-ˌīn\ *adj* [L *ferinus,* fr. *fera*] **:** FERAL

fer·i·ty \ˈfer-ət-ē\ *n* [L *feritas,* fr. *ferus*] **:** the quality or state of being feral

fer·lie *also* **fer·ly** \'fer-lē\ *n, pl* **ferlies** [ME, fr. *ferly* strange, fr. OE *fǣrlīc* unexpected, fr. *fǣr* sudden danger — more at FEAR] *Scot* : WONDER
Ferm *abbr* Fermanagh
fer·ma·ta \fər-'mät-ə\ *n* [It, lit., stop, fr. *fermare* to stop, fr. L *firmare* to make firm] : a prolongation at the discretion of the performer of a musical note, chord, or rest beyond its given time value; *also* : the sign denoting such a prolongation

fermata

¹fer·ment \(,)fər-'ment\ *vi* **1** : to undergo fermentation **2** : to be in a state of agitation or intense activity ~ *vt* **1** : to cause to undergo fermentation **2** : to work up (as into a state of agitation) : FOMENT — **fer·ment·able** \-ə-bəl\ *adj* — **fer·ment·er** *n*
²fer·ment \'fər-,ment *also* (,)fər-'\ *n* [ME, fr. L *fermentum* yeast — more at BARM] **1** : an agent (as an enzyme or an organism) capable of bringing about fermentation **2 a** : FERMENTATION 1 **b** (1) : a state of unrest : AGITATION (2) : a process of active often disorderly development <the great period of creative ~ in literature —William Barrett>
fer·men·ta·tion \,fər-mən-'tā-shən, -,men-\ *n* **1 a** : a chemical change with effervescence **b** : an enzymatically controlled anaerobic breakdown of an energy-rich compound (as a carbohydrate to carbon dioxide and alcohol or to an organic acid); *broadly* : an enzymatically controlled transformation of an organic compound **2** : FERMENT 2b
fer·men·ta·tive \(,)fər-'ment-ət-iv\ *adj* **1** : causing fermentation **2** : of, relating to, or produced by fermentation **3** : capable of undergoing fermentation
fer·mi \'fe(ə)r-(,)mē, 'fər-\ *n* [Enrico *Fermi*] : a unit of length equal to 10^{-13} centimeter
fer·mi·on \'fer-mē-,än, 'fər-\ *n* [Enrico *Fermi* + E ²*-on*] : a particle (as an electron, proton, or neutron) having a half-odd-integer number of units of spin (as $\frac{1}{2}$, $\frac{3}{2}$, $\frac{5}{2}$)
fer·mi·um \'fer-mē-əm, 'fər-\ *n* [Enrico *Fermi*] : a radioactive metallic element artificially produced (as by bombardment of plutonium with neutrons) — see ELEMENT table
fern \'fərn\ *n* [ME, fr. OE *fearn;* akin to OHG *farn* fern, Skt *parṇa* wing, leaf] : any of numerous flowerless seedless plants constituting a class (Filicineae) of lower vascular plants; *esp* : any of an order (Filicales) resembling seed plants in being differentiated into root, stem, and leaflike fronds and in having vascular tissue but differing in reproducing by spores — **fern·like** \-,līk\ *adj* — **ferny** \'fər-nē\ *adj*

ferns: *1* Christmas fern, *2* walking leaf

fern·ery \'fərn-(ə-)rē\ *n, pl* **-er·ies** **1** : a place or stand where ferns grow **2** : a collection of growing ferns
fern seed *n* : the dustlike asexual spores of ferns formerly taken for seeds and thought to make the possessor invisible
fe·ro·cious \fə-'rō-shəs\ *adj* [L *feroc-, ferox,* lit., fierce looking, fr. *ferus* + *-oc-, -ox* (akin to Gk *ōps* eye) — more at EYE] **1** : exhibiting or given to extreme fierceness and unrestrained violence and brutality **2** : unbearably intense : EXTREME <~ heat> ***syn*** see FIERCE — **fe·ro·cious·ly** *adv* — **fe·ro·cious·ness** *n*
fe·roc·i·ty \fə-'räs-ət-ē\ *n* : the quality or state of being ferocious
-f·er·ous \f-(ə-)rəs\ *adj comb form* [ME, fr. L *-fer* & MF *-fere* (fr. L *-fer*)] : bearing : producing <carboni*ferous*>
fer·rate \'fe(ə)r-,āt\ *n* [ISV, fr. L *ferrum* iron] : a compound containing iron and oxygen in the anion; *esp* : a red salt analogous to the chromates and sulfates
fer·re·dox·in \,fer-ə-'däk-sən\ *n* [L *fe*rrum iron + E *redox* + *-in*] : an iron-containing plant protein that functions as an electron carrier in photosynthetic organisms and in some anaerobic bacteria
¹fer·ret \'fer-ət\ *n* [ME *furet, ferret,* fr. MF *furet,* fr. (assumed) VL *furittus,* lit., little thief, dim. of L *fur* thief] **1** : a partially domesticated usu. albino European polecat that is sometimes classed as a separate species (*Mustela furo*) and is used esp. for hunting rodents **2** : an active and persistent searcher — **fer·rety** \-ət-ē\ *adj*

ferret 1

²ferret *vi* **1** : to hunt with ferrets **2** : to search about ~ *vt* **1 a** (1) : to hunt (as rabbits) with ferrets (2) : to drive esp. from covert **b** : to find and bring to light by searching — usu. used with *out* <~ out the answers> **2** : HARRY, WORRY — **fer·ret·er** *n*
³ferret *n* [prob. modif. of It *fioretti* floss silk, fr. pl. of *fioretto,* dim. of *fiore* flower, fr. L *flor-, flos* — more at BLOW] : a narrow cotton, silk, or wool tape — called also *ferreting*
ferri- *comb form* [L, fr. *ferrum*] **1** : iron <*ferri*ferous> **2** : ferric iron <*ferri*cyanic>
fer·ri·age \'fer-ē-ij\ *n* **1** : the fare paid for a ferry passage **2** : the act or business of transporting by ferry
fer·ric \'fer-ik\ *adj* **1** : of, relating to, or containing iron **2** : being or containing iron usu. with a valence of three
ferric ammonium citrate *n* : a complex salt containing varying amounts of iron and used esp. for making blueprints
ferric chloride *n* : a deliquescent dark salt $FeCl_3$ that readily hydrates to the yellow-orange form and that is used in sewage treatment and as an astringent
ferric hydroxide *n* : a hydrate $Fe_2O_3 \cdot nH_2O$ of ferric oxide that is capable of acting both as a base and as a weak acid
ferric oxide *n* : the red or black oxide of iron Fe_2O_3 found in nature as hematite and as rust and also obtained synthetically and used as a pigment and for polishing
fer·ri·cy·a·nide \,fer-,ī-'sī-ə-,nīd, ,fer-i-\ *n* [ISV] : a complex iron salt containing the trivalent radical $Fe(CN)_6$ and used in making blue pigments
fer·rif·er·ous \fə-'rif-(ə-)rəs, fe-\ *adj* : containing or yielding iron
fer·ri·mag·net·ic \'fer-,ī-mag-'net-ik, ,fer-i-\ *adj* : of or relating to a substance (as ferrite) characterized by magnetization in which one group of magnetic ions is polarized in a direction opposite to the other — **fer·ri·mag·net** \'fer-,ī-,mag-nət, 'fer-i-\ *n* — **fer·ri·mag·net·i·cal·ly** \'fer-,ī-mag-'net-i-k(ə-)lē, ,fer-i-\ *adv* — **fer·ri·mag·ne·tism** \-'mag-nə-,tiz-əm\ *n*
Fer·ris wheel \'fer-əs-\ *n* [G. W. G. *Ferris* †1896 Am engineer] : an amusement device consisting of a large upright power-driven wheel carrying seats that remain horizontal around its rim
fer·rite \'fe(ə)r-,īt\ *n* **1** : any of several magnetic substances that consist essentially of an iron oxide combined with one or more metals (as manganese, nickel, or zinc), have high magnetic permeability and high electrical resistivity, and are used esp. in computer memories **2** : a solid solution in which alpha iron is the solvent — **fer·rit·ic** \fə-'rit-ik, fe-\ *adj*
fer·ri·tin \'fer-ət-ᵊn\ *n* [*ferrite* + *-in*] : a crystalline iron-containing protein that functions in the storage of iron and is found esp. in the liver and spleen
ferro- *comb form* [ML, fr. L *ferrum*] **1** : iron <*ferro*concrete> **2** : iron and <*ferro*nickel> — chiefly in names of alloys **3** : ferrous iron <*ferro*cyanic>
fer·ro·cene \'fer-ō-,sēn\ *n* [*ferro-* + cyclopentadi*ene*] : a crystalline stable organometallic coordination compound $(C_5H_5)_2Fe$; *also* : an analogous compound with a heavy metal (as chromium)
fer·ro·con·crete \,fer-ō-'kän-,krēt, -kän-'\ *n* : REINFORCED CONCRETE
fer·ro·cy·a·nide \-'sī-ə-,nīd\ *n* : a complex iron salt containing the tetravalent radical $Fe(CN)_6$ and used in making blue pigments (as Prussian blue)
fer·ro·elec·tric \,fer-ō-i-'lek-trik\ *adj* : of or relating to crystalline substances having spontaneous electric polarization reversible by an electric field — **ferroelectric** *n* — **fer·ro·elec·tric·i·ty** \-,lek-'tris-ət-ē, -'tris-tē\ *n*
fer·ro·mag·ne·sian \-mag-'nē-zhən, -shən\ *adj* : containing iron and magnesium <~ minerals>
fer·ro·mag·net·ic \-'net-ik\ *adj* : of or relating to substances with an abnormally high magnetic permeability, a definite saturation point, and appreciable residual magnetism and hysteresis — **ferromagnetic** *n* — **fer·ro·mag·ne·tism** \-'mag-nə-,tiz-əm\ *n*
¹fer·ro·type \'fer-ə-,tīp\ *n* **1** : a positive photograph made by a collodion process on a thin iron plate having a darkened surface **2** : the process by which a ferrotype is made
²ferrotype *vt* : to give a gloss to (a photographic print) by squeegeeing facedown while wet on a ferrotype plate and allowing to dry
fer·rous \'fer-əs\ *adj* [NL *ferrosus,* fr. L *ferrum*] **1** : of, relating to, or containing iron **2** : being or containing iron with a valence of two
ferrous oxide *n* : a black easily oxidizable powder FeO that is the monoxide of iron
ferrous sulfate *n* : a salt $FeSO_4$; *esp* : COPPERAS
fer·ru·gi·nous \fə-'rü-jə-nəs, fe-\ *or* **fer·ru·gin·e·ous** \,fer-(y)ü-'jin-ē-əs\ *adj* [L *ferrugineus, ferruginus,* fr. *ferrugin-, ferrugo* iron rust, fr. *ferrum*] **1** : of, relating to, or containing iron <a ~ soil> **2** : resembling iron rust in color
¹fer·rule \'fer-əl\ *n* [alter. of ME *virole,* fr. MF, fr. L *viriola,* dim. of *viria* bracelet, of Celtic origin; akin to OIr *fiar* oblique — more at VEER] **1** : a ring or cap usu. of metal put around a slender shaft (as a cane or a tool handle) to strengthen it or prevent splitting **2** : a short tube or bushing for making a tight joint (as between pipes)
²ferrule *vt* **fer·ruled; fer·rul·ing** : to supply with a ferrule
¹fer·ry \'fer-ē\ *vb* **fer·ried; fer·ry·ing** [ME *ferien,* fr. OE *ferian* to carry, convey; akin to OE *faran* to go — more at FARE] *vt* **1 a** : to carry by boat over a body of water **b** : to cross by a ferry **2 a** : to convey (as by aircraft or motor vehicle) from one place to another : TRANSPORT **b** : to fly (an airplane) from the factory or other shipping point to a designated delivery point or from one base to another ~ *vi* : to cross water in a boat
²ferry *n, pl* **ferries** **1** : a place where persons or things are carried across a body of water (as a river) in a boat **2** : FERRYBOAT **3** : a franchise or right to operate a ferry service across a body of water **4** : an organized service and route for flying airplanes esp. across a sea or continent for delivery to the user
fer·ry·boat \'fer-ē-,bōt\ *n* : a boat used to ferry passengers, vehicles, or goods
fer·ry·man \-mən\ *n* : a person who operates a ferry
fer·tile \'fərt-ᵊl\ *adj* [ME, fr. MF & L; MF, fr. L *fertilis,* fr. *ferre* to carry, bear — more at BEAR] **1 a** : producing or bearing fruit in great quantities : PRODUCTIVE **b** : characterized by great resourcefulness of thought or imagination : INVENTIVE <a ~ mind> **c** *obs* : PLENTIFUL **2 a** (1) : capable of sustaining abundant plant growth <~ soil> (2) : affording abundant possibilities for development <a ~ area for research> **b** : capable of growing or developing <~ egg> **c** (1) : capable of producing fruit (2) *of an anther* : containing pollen (3) : developing spores or spore-bearing organs **d** : capable of breeding or reproducing **3** : capable of being converted into fissionable material <~ uranium 238> — **fer·tile·ly** \-ᵊl-(l)ē\ *adv* — **fer·tile·ness** \-ᵊl-nəs\ *n*
syn FERTILE, FECUND, FRUITFUL, PROLIFIC *shared meaning element* : producing or having the power to produce offspring or fruit ***ant*** infertile, sterile

fer·til·i·ty \(ˌ)fər-ˈtil-ət-ē\ *n* **1 :** the quality or state of being fertile **2 :** the birthrate of a population

fer·til·iza·tion \ˌfərt-ᵊl-ə-ˈzā-shən\ *n* **:** an act or process of making fertile: as **a :** the application of fertilizer **b** (1) **:** an act or process of fecundation, insemination, impregnation, or pollination (2) **:** the process of union of two germ cells whereby the somatic chromosome number is restored and the development of a new individual is initiated — **fer·til·iza·tion·al** \-shnəl, -shən-ᵊl\ *adj*

fer·til·ize \ˈfərt-ᵊl-ˌīz\ *vt* **-ized; -iz·ing :** to make fertile: as **a :** to cause the fertilization of **b :** to apply a fertilizer to <~ land> — **fer·til·iz·able** \-ˌī-zə-bəl\ *adj*

fer·til·iz·er \-ˌī-zər\ *n* **:** one that fertilizes; *specif* **:** a substance (as manure or a chemical mixture) used to make soil more fertile

fer·u·la \ˈfer-(y)ə-lə\ *n* [NL, genus name, fr. L, giant fennel]: any of a genus (*Ferula*) of Old World plants of the carrot family yielding various gum resins (as galbanum and asafetida)

fer·ule \ˈfer-əl\ *also* **fer·u·la** \ˈfer-(y)ə-lə\ *n* [L *ferula* giant fennel, ferule] **1 :** an instrument (as a flat piece of wood) used to punish children **2 :** school discipline

fe·ru·lic acid \fə-ˌrü-lik-\ *n* [*ferula*] **:** a white crystalline acid that is structurally related to vanillin and is obtained esp. from plant sources (as aspen bark)

fer·ven·cy \ˈfər-vən-sē\ *n, pl* **-cies :** FERVOR

fer·vent \ˈfər-vənt\ *adj* [ME, fr. MF & L; MF, fr. L *fervent-, fervens,* prp. of *fervēre* to boil, glow — more at BURN] **1 :** very hot **:** GLOWING **2 :** marked by great warmth of feeling **:** exhibiting deep sincere emotion <~ prayers> ***syn*** see IMPASSIONED — **fer·vent·ly** *adv*

fer·vid \ˈfər-vəd\ *adj* [L *fervidus,* fr. *fervēre*] **1 :** very hot **:** BURNING **2 :** marked by warm spontaneity or sometimes febrile urgency <his ~ manner of lovemaking offended her —Arnold Bennett> ***syn*** see IMPASSIONED — **fer·vid·ly** *adv* — **fer·vid·ness** *n*

fer·vor \ˈfər-vər\ *n* [ME *fervour,* fr. MF & L; MF *ferveur,* fr. L *fervor,* fr. *fervēre*] **1 :** intense heat **2 :** warm steady intensity of feeling or expression ***syn*** see PASSION

fer·vour *chiefly Brit var of* FERVOR

fes·cen·nine \ˈfes-ᵊn-ˌīn, -ˌēn\ *adj* [L *fescennini* (*versus*), ribald songs sung at rustic weddings, prob. fr. *fescinninus* of Fescennium, fr. *Fescennium,* town in Etruria] **:** SCURRILOUS, OBSCENE

fes·cue \ˈfes-(ˌ)kyü\ *n* [ME *festu* stalk, straw, fr. MF, fr. LL *festucum,* fr. L *festuca*] **1 :** a small pointer (as a stick) used to point out letters to children learning to read **2 :** any of a genus (*Festuca*) of tufted perennial grasses with panicled spikelets

fescue foot *n* **:** a disease of the feet of cattle resembling ergotism that is associated with feeding on fescue grasses

[1]**fess** *also* **fesse** \ˈfes\ *n* [ME *fesse,* fr. MF *faisse,* fr. L *fascia* band] **1 :** a broad horizontal bar across the middle of a heraldic field **2 :** the center point of an armorial escutcheon

[2]**fess** \ˈfes\ *vi* [short for *confess*] **:** to own up **:** CONFESS — usu. used with *up*

-fest \ˌfest\ *n comb form* [G, fr. *fest* celebration, fr. L *festum*] **:** meeting or occasion marked by (such) activity <song*fest*>

fes·tal \ˈfest-ᵊl\ *adj* [L *festum* festival — more at FEAST] **:** of or relating to a feast or festival **:** FESTIVE — **fes·tal·ly** \-ᵊl-ē\ *adv*

[1]**fes·ter** \ˈfes-tər\ *n* [ME, fr. MF *festre,* fr. L *fistula* pipe, fistulous ulcer] **:** a suppurating sore **:** PUSTULE

[2]**fester** *vb* **fes·tered; fes·ter·ing** \-t(ə-)riŋ\ *vi* **1 :** to generate pus **2 :** PUTREFY, ROT **3 a :** to cause increasing poisoning or irritation **:** RANKLE **b :** to undergo or exist in a state of progressive deterioration ~ *vt* **:** to make inflamed or corrupt

[1]**fes·ti·nate** \ˈfes-tə-nət, -ˌnāt\ *adj* [L *festinatus,* pp. of *festinare* to hasten — more at BORZOI] **:** HASTY — **fes·ti·nate·ly** *adv*

[2]**fes·ti·nate** \-ˌnāt\ *vb* **-nat·ed; -nat·ing :** HASTEN

[1]**fes·ti·val** \ˈfes-tə-vəl\ *adj* [ME, fr. MF, fr. L *festivus* festive] **:** of, relating to, appropriate to, or set apart as a festival

[2]**festival** *n* **1 a :** a time of celebration marked by special observances **b :** FEAST 2 **2 :** a periodic season or program of cultural events or entertainment **3 :** GAIETY, CONVIVIALITY

fes·ti·val·go·er \-ˌgō(-ə)r\ *n* **:** one who attends a festival

fes·tive \ˈfes-tiv\ *adj* [L *festivus,* fr. *festum*] **1 :** of, relating to, or suitable for a feast or festival **2 :** JOYOUS, GAY — **fes·tive·ly** *adv* — **fes·tive·ness** *n*

fes·tiv·i·ty \fes-ˈtiv-ət-ē, fəs-\ *n, pl* **-ties 1 :** FESTIVAL 1 **2 :** the quality or state of being festive **:** GAIETY **3 :** festive activity

[1]**fes·toon** \fes-ˈtün\ *n* [F *feston,* fr. It *festone,* fr. *festa* festival, fr. L — more at FEAST] **1 :** a decorative chain or strip hanging between two points **2 :** a carved, molded, or painted ornament representing a decorative chain **3 :** one of the somewhat quadrangular segments bordering the body of some ticks

[2]**festoon** *vt* **1 :** to hang or form festoons on **2 :** to shape into festoons

fes·toon·ery \fes-ˈtü-nə-rē\ *n* **:** an arrangement of festoons

fest·schrift \ˈfest-ˌshrift\ *n, pl* **fest·schrif·ten** \-ˌshrif-tən\ *or* **festschrifts** *often cap* [G, fr. *fest* festival, celebration + *schrift* writing] **:** a volume of writings by different authors presented as a tribute or memorial esp. to a scholar

fe·ta \ˈfet-ə, ˈfe-ˌtä\ *n* [NGk (*tyri*) *pheta,* fr. *tyri* cheese + *pheta* slice, fr. It *fetta*] **:** a firm white Greek cheese made of sheep's or goat's milk and cured in brine

fe·tal \ˈfēt-ᵊl\ *adj* **:** of, relating to, or being a fetus

fetal hemoglobin *n* **:** a hemoglobin variant that predominates in the blood of a newborn and persists in increased proportions in some forms of anemia (as thalassemia)

fetal position *n* **:** a resting position in which the body is curved, the legs and arms are bent and drawn toward the chest, and the head is bowed forward and which is assumed in some forms of psychic regression

fe·ta·tion \fē-ˈtā-shən\ *n* **:** the formation of a fetus **:** PREGNANCY

[1]**fetch** \ˈfech\ *vb* [ME *fecchen,* fr. OE *fetian, feccan;* akin to OE *fōt* foot — more at FOOT] *vt* **1 a :** to go or come after and bring or take back **b :** DERIVE, DEDUCE **2 a :** to cause to come **b :** to bring in (as a price) **:** REALIZE **c :** INTEREST, ATTRACT **3 a :** to give (a blow) by striking **:** DEAL **b** *chiefly dial* **:** to bring about **:** ACCOMPLISH **c** (1) **:** to take in (as a breath) **:** DRAW (2) **:** to bring forth (as a sound) **:** HEAVE <~ a sigh> **4 a :** to reach by sailing esp. against the wind or tide **b :** to arrive at **:** REACH ~ *vi* **1 :** to get and bring something; *specif* **:** to retrieve killed game **2 :** to take a roundabout way **:** CIRCLE **3 a :** to hold a course on a body of water **b :** VEER — **fetch·er** *n*

[2]**fetch** *n* **1 :** an act or instance of fetching **2 :** TRICK, STRATAGEM **3 a :** the distance along open water or land over which the wind blows **b :** the distance traversed by waves without obstruction

[3]**fetch** *n* [origin unknown] **1 :** DOPPELGÄNGER **2 :** GHOST

fetch·ing *adj* **:** ATTRACTIVE, PLEASING — **fetch·ing·ly** \-iŋ-lē\ *adv*

fetch up *vt* **1 :** to bring up or out **:** PRODUCE **2 :** to make up (as leeway) **3 :** to bring to a stop ~ *vi* **:** to come to a standstill, stopping place, or result **:** ARRIVE

[1]**fete** *or* **fête** \ˈfāt, ˈfet\ *n* [F *fête,* fr. OF *feste* — more at FEAST] **1 :** FESTIVAL **2 a :** a lavish often outdoor entertainment **b :** a large elaborate party

[2]**fete** *or* **fête** *vt* **fet·ed** *or* **fêt·ed; fet·ing** *or* **fêt·ing 1 :** to honor or commemorate with a fete **2 :** to pay high honor to

fête cham·pê·tre \ˌfāt-ˌshäⁿ(m)-ˈpetrᵊ, ˌfet-\ *n, pl* **fêtes champêtres** *same*\ [F, lit., rural festival] **:** an outdoor entertainment

fet·er·i·ta \ˌfet-ə-ˈrēt-ə\ *n* [Sudanese Ar] **:** any of various grain sorghums with compact oval heads of large soft white seeds

fe·ti·cide \ˈfēt-ə-ˌsīd\ *n* **:** the act of killing a fetus

fet·id \ˈfet-əd, *esp Brit* ˈfē-tid\ *adj* [ME, fr. L *foetidus,* fr. *foetēre* to stink; akin to L *fumus* smoke — more at FUME] **:** having a heavy offensive smell ***syn*** see MALODOROUS — **fet·id·ly** *adv* — **fet·id·ness** *n*

fe·tish *also* **fe·tich** \ˈfet-ish *also* ˈfēt-\ *n* [F & Pg; F *fétiche,* fr. Pg *feitiço,* fr. *feitiço* artificial, false, fr. L *facticius* factitious] **1 a :** an object believed among a primitive people to have magical power to protect or aid its owner; *broadly* **:** a material object regarded with superstitious or extravagant trust or reverence **b :** an object of irrational reverence or obsessive devotion **:** PREPOSSESSION **c :** an object or bodily part whose real or fantasied presence is psychologically necessary for sexual gratification and that is an object of fixation to the extent that it may interfere with complete sexual expression **2 :** a rite or cult of fetish worshipers **3 :** FIXATION

syn FETISH, TALISMAN, CHARM, AMULET *shared meaning element* **:** an object believed useful in averting evil or attracting good

fe·tish·ism *also* **fe·tich·ism** \-ish-ˌiz-əm\ *n* **1 :** belief in magical fetishes **2 :** extravagant irrational devotion **3 :** the pathological displacement of erotic interest and satisfaction to a fetish — **fe·tish·ist** \-ish-əst\ *n* — **fe·tish·is·tic** \ˌfet-ish-ˈis-tik *also* ˈfēt-\ *adj*

fet·lock \ˈfet-ˌläk\ *n* [ME *fitlok, fetlak;* akin to OE *fōt* foot] **1 a :** a projection bearing a tuft of hair on the back of the leg above the hoof of a horse or similar animal — see HORSE illustration **b :** the tuft of hair itself **2 :** the joint of the limb at the fetlock

feto- *or* **feti-** *also* **foeto-** *or* **foeti-** *comb form* [NL *fetus*] **:** fetus <*feti*cide> **:** fetal and <*feto*placental>

fe·tol·o·gy \fē-ˈtäl-ə-jē\ *n* **:** a branch of medical science concerned with the study and treatment of the fetus in the uterus — **fe·tol·o·gist** \-jəst\ *n*

fe·tor \ˈfēt-ər, ˈfē-ˌtȯ(ə)r\ *n* [ME *fetoure,* fr. L *foetor,* fr. *foetēre*] **:** a strong offensive smell **:** STENCH

[1]**fet·ter** \ˈfet-ər\ *n* [ME *feter,* fr. OE; akin to OE *fōt* foot] **1 :** a chain or shackle for the feet **2 :** something that confines **:** RESTRAINT

[2]**fetter** *vt* **1 :** to put fetters on **:** SHACKLE **2 :** to restrain from motion or action ***syn*** see HAMPER

[1]**fet·tle** \ˈfet-ᵊl\ *vt* **fet·tled; fet·tling** \ˈfet-liŋ, -ᵊl-iŋ\ [ME *fetlen* to shape, prepare; prob. akin to OE *fæt* vessel — more at VAT] **:** to cover or line the hearth of (as a reverberatory furnace) with fettling

[2]**fettle** *n* **1 a :** a state of physical fitness or order **:** CONDITION **b :** state of mind **:** SPIRITS <the good news put him in fine ~> **2 :** FETTLING

fet·tling \ˈfet-liŋ, -ᵊl-iŋ\ *n* **:** loose material (as ore or sand) thrown on the hearth of a furnace to protect it

fet·tuc·ci·ne *or* **fet·tu·ci·ne** \ˌfet-ə-ˈchē-nē\ *n pl but sing or pl in constr* [It, pl. of *fettuccina,* dim. of *fettuccia* small slice, ribbon, dim. of *fetta* slice] **:** pasta in the form of narrow ribbons; *also* **:** a dish of which fettuccine forms the base

fe·tus \ˈfēt-əs\ *n* [NL, fr. L, act of bearing young, offspring; akin to L *fetus* newly delivered, fruitful — more at FEMININE] **:** an unborn or unhatched vertebrate esp. after attaining the basic structural plan of its kind; *specif* **:** a developing human from usu. three months after conception to birth

[1]**feud** \ˈfyüd\ *n* [alter. of ME *feide,* fr. MF, of Gmc origin; akin to OHG *fēhida* hostility, feud, OE *fāh* hostile — more at FOE] **:** a mutual enmity or quarrel that is often prolonged or inveterate; *esp* **:** a lasting state of hostilities between families or clans marked by violent attacks for revenge — **feud** *vi*

[2]**feud** *n* [ML *feodum, feudum,* of Gmc origin; akin to OE *feoh* cattle, property — more at FEE] **:** FEE 1a

feu·dal \ˈfyüd-ᵊl\ *adj* **1 :** of, relating to, or having the characteristics of a medieval fee **2 :** of, relating to, or suggestive of feudalism <~ law> — **feu·dal·ly** \-ᵊl-ē\ *adv*

feu·dal·ism \ˈfyüd-ᵊl-ˌiz-əm\ *n* **1 :** the system of political organization prevailing in Europe from the 9th to about the 15th centuries having as its basis the relation of lord to vassal with all land held in fee and as chief characteristics homage, the service of tenants under arms and in court, wardship, and forfeiture **2 :** any of various political or social systems similar to medieval feudalism — **feu·dal·ist** \-ᵊl-əst\ *n* — **feu·dal·is·tic** \ˌfyüd-ᵊl-ˈis-tik\ *adj*

feu·dal·i·ty \fyü-ˈdal-ət-ē\ *n, pl* **-ties 1 :** the quality or state of being feudal **2 :** a feudal holding, domain, or concentration of power

feu·dal·ize \ˈfyüd-ᵊl-ˌīz\ *vt* **-ized; -iz·ing :** to make feudal — **feu·dal·iza·tion** \ˌfyüd-ᵊl-ə-ˈzā-shən\ *n*

[1]**feu·da·to·ry** \ˈfyüd-ə-ˌtōr-ē, -ˌtȯr-\ *adj* [ML *feudatorius,* fr. *feudatus,* pp. of *feudare* to enfeoff, fr. *feudum*] **1 :** owing feudal allegiance **2 :** being under the overlordship of a foreign state

[2]**feudatory** *n, pl* **-ries 1 :** one holding lands by feudal tenure **2 :** a dependent lordship **:** FEE

1**feud·ist** \ˈfyüd-əst\ *n* : a specialist in feudal law
2**feudist** *n* : one who feuds
feuil·le·ton \ˌfə(r)-yə-ˈtōⁿ, ˌfœ-yə-\ *n* [F, fr. *feuillet* sheet of paper, fr. OF *foillet,* dim. of *foille* leaf — more at FOIL] **1** : a part of a European newspaper or magazine devoted to material designed to entertain the general reader **2** : something (as an installment of a novel) printed in a feuilleton **3 a** : a novel printed in installments **b** : a work of fiction catering to popular taste **4** : a short literary composition often having a familiar tone and reminiscent content — **feuil·le·ton·ism** \-ˈtō(ⁿ)-ˌniz-əm\ *n* — **feuil·le·ton·ist** \-nəst\ *n*
Feul·gen \ˈfȯil-gən\ *adj* : of, relating to, utilizing, or staining by the Feulgen reaction <positive ~ mitochondria>
Feulgen reaction *n* [Robert *Feulgen b*1884 G physiologist] : the development of a brilliant purple color by DNA in a microscopic preparation stained with a modified Schiff reagent
1**fe·ver** \ˈfē-vər\ *n* [ME, fr. OE *fēfer,* fr. L *febris;* akin to L *fovēre* to warm] **1 a** : a rise of body temperature above the normal **b** : any of various diseases of which fever is a prominent symptom **2 a** : a state of heightened or intense emotion or activity **b** : a contagious usu. transient enthusiasm : CRAZE
2**fever** *vb* **fe·vered; fe·ver·ing** \ˈfēv-(ə-)riŋ\ *vt* : to throw into a fever : AGITATE ~ *vi* : to contract or be in a fever : be or become feverish
fever blister *n* : COLD SORE
fe·ver·few \ˈfē-vər-ˌfyü\ *n* [ME, fr. (assumed) AF *fevrefue,* fr. LL *febrifugia* centaury — more at FEBRIFUGE] : a perennial European composite herb (*Chrysanthemum parthenium*)
fe·ver·ish \ˈfēv-(ə-)rish\ *adj* **1 a** : having the symptoms of a fever **b** : indicating or relating to fever **c** : tending to cause fever **2** : marked by intense emotion, activity, or instability — **fe·ver·ish·ly** *adv* — **fe·ver·ish·ness** *n*
fe·ver·ous \ˈfēv-(ə-)rəs\ *adj* : FEVERISH — **fe·ver·ous·ly** *adv*
fever pitch *n* : a state of intense excitement and agitation
fe·ver·root \ˈfē-və(r)-ˌrüt, -ˌrůt\ *n* : FEVERWORT
fever thermometer *n* : CLINICAL THERMOMETER
fever tree *n* : any of several shrubs or trees that are thought to indicate regions free from fever or that yield remedies for fever: as **a** : a blue gum (*Eucalyptus globulus*) **b** : an ornamental tree (*Pinckneya pubens*) of the southeastern U.S.
fe·ver·wort \ˈfē-vər-ˌwərt, -ˌwȯ(ə)rt\ *n* : a coarse American herb (*Triosteum perfoliatum*) of the honeysuckle family — called also *feverroot, horse gentian*
1**few** \ˈfyü\ *pron, pl in constr* [ME *fewe,* pron. & adj., fr. OE *fēawa;* akin to OHG *fō* little, L *paucus* little, *pauper* poor, Gk *paid-, pais* child, Skt *putra* son] : not many persons or things <~ were present> <~ of his stories are true>
2**few** *adj* **1** : consisting of or amounting to only a small number <one of his ~ pleasures> **2** : at least some but indeterminately small in number — used with *a* <caught a ~ fish> — **few·ness** *n*
3**few** *n, pl in constr* **1** : a small number of units or individuals <a ~ of them> **2** : a special limited number <the discriminating ~>
1**few·er** *pron, pl in constr* : a smaller number of persons or things
2**fewer** *adj, comparative of* FEW ***syn*** see LESS
few·trils \ˈfyü-trəlz\ *n pl* [origin unknown] *dial Eng* : things of little value : TRIFLES
fey \ˈfā\ *adj* [ME *feye,* fr. OE *fǣge;* akin to OHG *feigi* fey and perh. to OE *fāh* hostile, outlawed — more at FOE] **1 a** *chiefly Scot* : fated to die : DOOMED **b** : marked by a foreboding of death or calamity **2 a** : able to see into the future : VISIONARY **b** : marked by an otherworldly air or attitude **c** : CRAZY, TOUCHED — **fey·ness** *n*
fez \ˈfez\ *n, pl* **fez·zes** *also* **fez·es** [F, fr. *Fez,* Morocco] : a brimless cone-shaped flat-crowned hat that usu. has a tassel, is usu. made of red felt, and is worn esp. by men in eastern Mediterranean countries
ff *abbr* **1** folios **2** following **3** fortissimo
FG *abbr* fine grain
FHA *abbr* Federal Housing Administration
FHWA *abbr* Federal Highway Administration
fia·cre \fē-ˈäkrᵊ\ *n, pl* **fia·cres** *same, or* -ˈäk-rəz\ [F, fr. the Hotel St. *Fiacre,* Paris] : a small hackney coach
fi·an·cé \ˌfē-ˌän-ˈsā, fē-ˈän-ˌ\ *n* [F, fr. MF, fr. pp. of *fiancer* to promise, betroth, fr. OF *fiancier,* fr. *fiance* promise, trust, fr. *fier* to trust, fr. (assumed) VL *fidare,* alter. of L *fidere* — more at BIDE] : a man engaged to be married

fez

fi·an·cée \ˌfē-ˌän-ˈsā, fē-ˈän-ˌ\ *n* [F, fem. of *fiancé*] : a woman engaged to be married
fi·an·chet·to \ˌfē-ən-ˈket-(ˌ)ō, -ˈchet-\ *vb* [*fianchetto* (an opening in chess), fr. It, dim. of *fianco* side, flank, fr. OF *flanc*] *vt* : to develop (a bishop) in a chess game to the second square on the adjacent knight's file ~ *vi* : to fianchetto a bishop in a chess game
fi·as·co *n, pl* **-coes** [It, of Gmc origin; akin to OHG *flaska* bottle] **1** \fē-ˈäs-(ˌ)kō\ *pl also* **fi·as·chi** \-(ˌ)kē\ : BOTTLE, FLASK; *esp* : a long-necked straw-covered bottle for wine **2** \-ˈas- *also* -ˈäs-\ [F, fr. It] : a complete failure
fi·at \ˈfē-ət, -ˌat, -ˌät; ˈfī-ət, -ˌat\ *n* [L, let it be done, 3d sing. pres. subj. of *fieri* to become, be done — more at BE] **1** : a command or act of will that creates something without or as if without further effort **2** : an authoritative decision of consciousness <a ~ of conscience> **3** : an authoritative or arbitrary order : DECREE <government by ~>
fiat money *n* : money (as paper currency) not convertible into coin or specie of equivalent value
1**fib** \ˈfib\ *n* [perh. by shortening & alter. fr. *fable*] : a trivial or childish lie
2**fib** *vi* **fibbed; fib·bing** : to tell a fib ***syn*** see LIE — **fib·ber** *n*
3**fib** *vb* **fibbed; fib·bing** [origin unknown] *Brit* : BEAT, PUMMEL

fi·ber *or* **fi·bre** \ˈfī-bər\ *n* [F *fibre,* fr. L *fibra*] **1** : a thread or a structure or object resembling a thread: as **a** (1) : a slender root (as of a grass) (2) : an elongated tapering thick-walled plant cell void at maturity that imparts elasticity, flexibility, and tensile strength **b** (1) : a strand of nerve tissue : AXON, DENDRITE (2) : one of the filaments composing most of the intercellular matrix of connective tissue (3) : one of the elongated contractile cells of muscle tissue **c** : a slender and greatly elongated natural or synthetic filament (as of wool, cotton, asbestos, gold, glass, or rayon) typically capable of being spun into yarn **2** : material made of fibers; *specif* : VULCANIZED FIBER **3 a** : an element that gives texture or substance **b** : basic toughness : STRENGTH, FORTITUDE **c** : essential structure or character <the very ~ of a person's being> — **fi·bered** \-bərd\ *adj*
fi·ber·board \-ˌbō(ə)rd, -ˌbȯ(ə)rd\ *n* : a material made by compressing fibers (as of wood) into stiff sheets
fi·ber·glass \-ˌglas\ *n* : glass in fibrous form used in making various products (as glass wool, yarns, textiles, and structures) <a ~ boat> <~ insulation>
fi·ber·ize \ˈfī-bə-ˌrīz\ *vt* **-ized; -iz·ing** : to break into fibers — **fi·ber·iza·tion** \ˌfī-b(ə-)rə-ˈzā-shən\ *n*
fiber optic *n* : a very thin transparent homogeneous fiber of glass or plastic that is enclosed by material of lower index of refraction and transmits light throughout its length by internal reflections; *also* : a bundle of such fibers used in an instrument for bending light or seeing around corners
fiber optics *n pl but sing in constr* : the technique of the use of fiber optics
fi·ber·scope \ˈfī-bər-ˌskōp\ *n* : a flexible instrument utilizing fiber optics and used esp. in medicine for examination of inaccessible areas (as the stomach)
Fi·bo·nac·ci number \ˌfē-bə-ˌnäch-ē-\ *n* [Leonardo *Fibonacci* †*ab* 1250 It mathematician] : a number in the infinite series 0, 1, 1, 2, 3, 5, 8, 13, . . . of which the first two terms are 0 and 1 and each succeeding term is the sum of the two immediately preceding
fibr- *or* **fibro-** *comb form* [L *fibra*] : fiber : fibrous tissue <*fibroid*> : fibrous and <*fibrovascular*>
fi·bril \ˈfīb-rəl, ˈfib-\ *n* [NL *fibrilla,* dim. of L *fibra*] : a small filament or fiber: as **a** : ROOT HAIR **b** (1) : one of the fine threads into which a striated muscle fiber can be longitudinally split (2) : NEUROFIBRIL — **fi·bril·lar** \ˈfib-rə-lər, ˈfīb-\ *adj* — **fi·bril·li·form** \fī-ˈbril-ə-ˌfȯrm, fə-\ *adj* — **fi·bril·lose** \ˈfib-rə-ˌlōs, ˈfīb-\ *adj*
fi·bril·late \ˈfib-rə-ˌlāt, ˈfīb-\ *vb* **-lat·ed; -lat·ing** *vi* : to undergo or exhibit fibrillation ~ *vt* : to cause to undergo fibrillation <~ plastic film into fibrils>
fi·bril·la·tion \ˌfib-rə-ˈlā-shən, ˌfīb-\ *n* **1** : an act or process of forming fibers or fibrils **2 a** : a muscular twitching involving individual muscle fibers acting without coordination **b** : very rapid irregular contractions of the muscle fibers of the heart resulting in a lack of synchronism between heartbeat and pulse
fi·brin \ˈfī-brən\ *n* : a white insoluble fibrous protein formed from fibrinogen by the action of thrombin esp. in the clotting of blood
fi·brin·o·gen \fī-ˈbrin-ə-jən\ *n* [ISV] : a globulin that is produced in the liver, that is present esp. in the blood plasma, and that is converted into fibrin during clotting of blood
fi·bri·noid \ˈfīb-rə-ˌnȯid, ˈfib-\ *n* : a homogeneous acidophilic refractile material that somewhat resembles fibrin and is formed in the walls of blood vessels and in connective tissue in some pathological conditions and normally in the placenta
fi·bri·no·ly·sin \ˌfī-brən-ᵊl-ˈīs-ᵊn\ *n* [ISV] **1** : PLASMIN **2** : STREPTOKINASE
fi·bri·no·ly·sis \-ˈī-səs, -brə-ˈnäl-ə-səs\ *n* [NL] : the usu. enzymatic breakdown of fibrin — **fi·bri·no·lyt·ic** \-brən-ᵊl-ˈit-ik\ *adj*
fi·bri·nous \ˈfīb-rə-nəs, ˈfib-\ *adj* : marked by the presence of fibrin
fi·bro·blast \ˈfīb-rə-ˌblast, ˈfib-\ *n* [ISV] : a mesenchyme cell giving rise to connective tissue — **fi·bro·blas·tic** \ˌfīb-rə-ˈblas-tik, ˌfib-\ *adj*
fi·bro·cyte \ˈfīb-rə-ˌsīt, ˈfib-\ *n* [ISV] : a spindle-shaped cell of fibrous tissue — **fi·bro·cyt·ic** \ˌfīb-rə-ˈsit-ik, ˌfib-\ *adj*
1**fi·broid** \ˈfīb-ˌrȯid, ˈfib-\ *adj* : resembling, forming, or consisting of fibrous tissue
2**fibroid** *n* : a benign tumor made up of fibrous and muscular tissue that occurs esp. in the uterine wall
fi·bro·in \ˈfīb-rə-wən, ˈfib-\ *n* [F *fibroïne,* fr. *fibr-* + *-ine* -in] : an insoluble protein comprising the filaments of the raw silk fiber
fi·bro·ma \fī-ˈbrō-mə\ *n, pl* **-mas** *also* **-ma·ta** \-mət-ə\ : a benign tumor consisting mainly of fibrous tissue — **fi·bro·ma·tous** \-mət-əs\ *adj*
fi·bro·sar·co·ma \ˌfīb-rə-sär-ˈkō-mə, ˌfib-\ *n* : a sarcoma of relatively low malignancy made up chiefly of spindle-shaped cells that tend to form collagenous fibrils
fi·bro·sis \fī-ˈbrō-səs\ *n* : a condition marked by increase of interstitial fibrous tissue — **fi·brot·ic** \-ˈbrät-ik\ *adj*
fi·bro·si·tis \ˌfīb-rə-ˈsīt-əs, ˌfib-\ *n* [NL, fr. *fibrosus* fibrous, fr. ISV *fibrous*] : a rheumatic disorder of fibrous tissue
fi·brous \ˈfī-brəs\ *adj* [F *fibreux,* fr. *fibre* fiber, fr. L *fibra*] **1 a** : containing, consisting of, or resembling fibers **b** : characterized by fibrosis **c** : capable of being separated into fibers <a ~ mineral> **2** : TOUGH, SINEWY <~ texture> — **fi·brous·ly** *adv* — **fi·brous·ness** *n*
fibrous root *n* : a root (as in most grasses) that has no prominent central axis and that branches in all directions
fi·bro·vas·cu·lar \ˌfīb-rō-ˈvas-kyə-lər, ˌfib-\ *adj* : having or consisting of fibers and conducting cells <~ bundles in leaves>
fibrovascular bundle *n* : VASCULAR BUNDLE

fib·u·la \'fib-yə-lə\ *n, pl* **-lae** \-lē, -lī\ *or* **-las** [L] **1 :** a clasp resembling a safety pin used by the ancient Greeks and Romans **2 :** the outer and usu. the smaller of the two bones of the hind limb below the knee — **fib·u·lar** \-lər\ *adj*

fibulae 1

-fic \fik\ *adj suffix* [MF & L; MF *-fique,* fr. L *-ficus,* fr. *facere* to make — more at DO] **:** making **:** causing <felici*fic*>

FICA *abbr* Federal Insurance Contributions Act

-fi·ca·tion \fə-'kā-shən\ *n comb form* [ME *-ficacioun,* fr. MF & L; MF *-fication,* fr. L *-fication-, -ficatio,* fr. *-ficatus,* pp. ending of verbs ending in *-ficare* to make, fr. *-ficus*] **:** making **:** production <rei*fication*>

fice \'fīs\ *var of* FEIST

fiche \'fēsh *also* 'fish\ *n, pl* **fiche** *also* **fiches :** MICROFICHE

fi·chu \'fish-(,)ü, 'fēsh-\ *n* [F, fr. pp. of *ficher* to stick in, throw on, fr. (assumed) VL *figicare,* fr. L *figere* to fasten, pierce — more at DIKE] **:** a woman's light triangular scarf that is draped over the shoulders and fastened in front or worn to fill in a low neckline

fi·cin \'fīs-ᵊn\ *n* [L *ficus* fig] **:** a proteinase that is obtained from the latex of fig trees and is used as an anthelmintic and protein digestive

fick·le \'fik-əl\ *adj* [ME *fikel* deceitful, inconstant, fr. OE *ficol* deceitful; akin to OE *befician* to deceive, L *pigēre* to irk and prob. to OE *fāh* hostile — more at FOE] **:** marked by lack of steadfastness, constancy, or stability **:** given to erratic and even perverse changeableness ***syn*** see INCONSTANT ***ant*** constant, true — **fick·le·ness** *n*

fi·co \'fē-(,)kō\ *n, pl* **ficoes** [obs. *fico,* obscene gesture of contempt, modif. of It *fica* fig, vulva, gesture of contempt, fr. (assumed) VL *fica* fig — more at FIG] **:** FIG 2

fict *abbr* **1** fiction **2** fictitious

fic·tile \'fik-tᵊl, -,tīl\ *adj* [L *fictilis* molded of clay, fr. *fictus*] **1 :** molded or moldable of earth, clay, or other soft material **2 :** of or relating to pottery

fic·tion \'fik-shən\ *n* [ME *ficcioun,* fr. MF *fiction,* fr. L *fiction-, fictio* act of fashioning, fiction, fr. *fictus,* pp. of *fingere* to shape, fashion, feign — more at DOUGH] **1 a :** something invented by the imagination or feigned; *specif* **:** an invented story <distinguish fact from ~> **b :** fictitious literature (as novels or short stories) <a writer of ~> **2 :** an assumption of a possibility as a fact irrespective of the question of its truth <a legal ~> **3 :** the action of feigning or of creating with the imagination — **fic·tion·al** \-shnəl, -shən-ᵊl\ *adj* — **fic·tion·al·ly** \-ē\ *adv*

fic·tion·al·iza·tion \,fik-shnə-lə-'zā-shən, -shən-ᵊl-ə-'zā-\ *n* **:** an act, process, or product of fictionalizing

fic·tion·al·ize \'fik-shnə-,līz, -shən-ᵊl-,īz\ *vt* **-ized; -iz·ing :** to make into or treat in the manner of fiction <~ the diary he kept in prison>

fic·tion·eer \,fik-shə-'ni(ə)r\ *n* **:** one who writes fiction esp. in quantity and without high standards — **fic·tion·eer·ing** *n*

fic·tion·ist \'fik-sh(ə-)nəst\ *n* **:** a writer of fiction; *esp* **:** NOVELIST

fic·tion·ize \'fik-shə-,nīz\ *vt* **-ized; -iz·ing :** FICTIONALIZE — **fic·tion·iza·tion** \,fik-shə-nə-'zā-shən\ *n*

fic·ti·tious \fik-'tish-əs\ *adj* [L *ficticius* artificial, feigned, fr. *fictus*] **1 :** of, relating to, or characteristic of fiction **:** IMAGINARY **2 a :** conventionally or hypothetically assumed or accepted <a ~ concept> **b** *of a name* **:** FALSE, ASSUMED **3 :** not genuinely felt **:** FEIGNED, SIMULATED — **fic·ti·tious·ly** *adv* — **fic·ti·tious·ness** *n*
syn FICTITIOUS, FABULOUS, LEGENDARY, MYTHICAL, APOCRYPHAL *shared meaning element* **:** being the product of imagination or mental invention ***ant*** historical

fic·tive \'fik-tiv\ *adj* **1 :** not genuine **:** FEIGNED **2 :** of, relating to, or capable of imaginative creation — **fic·tive·ly** *adv*

fid \'fid\ *n* [origin unknown] **1 :** a square bar of wood or iron used to support a topmast **2 :** a pin usu. of hard wood that tapers to a point and is used in opening the strands of a rope

-fid \fəd, ,fid\ *adj comb form* [L *-fidus,* fr. *findere* to split — more at BITE] **:** divided into (so many) parts <sexi*fid*> or (such) parts <pinnati*fid*>

¹fid·dle \'fid-ᵊl\ *n* [ME *fidel,* fr. OE *fithele,* prob. fr. ML *vitula*] **1 :** VIOLIN **2 :** a device (as a slat, rack, or light railing of cords) to keep dishes from sliding off a table aboard ship **3 :** FIDDLESTICKS — used as an interjection **4** *Brit* **:** SWINDLE

²fiddle *vb* **fid·dled; fid·dling** \'fid-liŋ, -ᵊl-iŋ\ *vi* **1 :** to play on a fiddle **2 a :** to move the hands or fingers restlessly **b :** to spend time in aimless or fruitless activity **:** PUTTER <*fiddled* around with the engine for hours> **c :** MEDDLE, TAMPER ~ *vt* **:** to play (as a tune) on a fiddle — **fid·dler** \'fid-lər, -ᵊl-ər\ *n*

fiddle away *vt* **:** to fritter away <*fiddled away* his time>

fid·dle·back \'fid-ᵊl-,bak\ *n* **:** something resembling a fiddle

fid·dle–fad·dle \'fid-ᵊl-,fad-ᵊl\ *n* [redupl. of *fiddle* (fiddlesticks)] **:** NONSENSE — often used as an interjection

fid·dle–foot·ed \,fid-ᵊl-'fu̇t-əd\ *adj* **1 :** SKITTISH, JUMPY <a ~ horse> **2 :** prone to wander <the nameless ~ drifters, the shifty riders who traveled the back trails —Luke Short>

fid·dle·head \'fid-ᵊl-,hed\ *n* **1 :** an ornament on a ship's bow curved like the scroll at the head of a violin **2 :** one of the young unfurling fronds of some ferns that are often eaten as greens

fiddler crab *n* **:** a burrowing crab (genus *Uca*) that has one claw much enlarged in the male

fid·dle·stick \'fid-ᵊl-,stik\ *n* **1 a** *archaic* **:** a violin bow **b** *South* **:** a small stick or switch used to strike the strings of a fiddle in time to the music while the fiddler plays with a bow — usu. used in pl. **2 a :** something of little value **:** TRIFLE <didn't care a ~ for that> **b** *pl* **:** NONSENSE — used as an interjection

fid·dling \'fid-liŋ, -lən\ *adj* **:** TRIFLING, PETTY <made some ~ excuse>

fi·de·ism \'fēd-(,)ā-,iz-əm\ *n* [prob. fr. F *fidéisme,* fr. L *fides* faith] **:** reliance on faith rather than reason esp. in metaphysics — **fi·de·ist** \-ā-əst\ *n* — **fi·de·is·tic** \,fēd-(,)ā-'is-tik\ *adj*

fi·del·i·ty \fə-'del-ət-ē, fī-\ *n, pl* **-ties** [ME *fidelite,* fr. MF *fidelité,* fr. L *fidelitat-, fidelitas,* fr. *fidelis* faithful, fr. *fides* faith — more at BIDE] **1 a :** the quality or state of being faithful **b :** accuracy in details **:** EXACTNESS **2 :** the degree to which an electronic device (as a record player, radio, or television) accurately reproduces its effect (as sound or picture)
syn FIDELITY, ALLEGIANCE, FEALTY, LOYALTY, DEVOTION, PIETY *shared meaning element* **:** faithfulness to something to which one is bound by a pledge, by duty, or by a sense of what is right or appropriate ***ant*** faithlessness, perfidy

fidge \'fij\ *vi* **fidged; fidg·ing** [prob. alter. of E dial. *fitch,* fr. ME *fichen*] *chiefly Scot* **:** FIDGET

¹fid·get \'fij-ət\ *n* [irreg. fr. *fidge*] **1 :** uneasiness or restlessness as shown by nervous movements — usu. used in pl. **2** [²*fidget*] **:** one that fidgets

²fidget *vi* **:** to move or act restlessly or nervously ~ *vt* **:** to cause to move or act nervously

fid·gety \'fij-ət-ē\ *adj* **1 :** inclined to fidget **2 :** making unnecessary fuss **:** FUSSY — **fid·get·i·ness** *n*

fi·do \'fīd-(,)ō\ *n, pl* **fidos** [*f*reaks + *i*rregulars + *d*efects + *o*ddities] **:** a coin having a minting error

fi·du·cial \fə-'d(y)ü-shəl, fī-\ *adj* **1 :** taken as standard of reference <a ~ mark> **2 :** founded on faith or trust **3 :** having the nature of a trust **:** FIDUCIARY — **fi·du·cial·ly** \-,d(y)üsh-(ə-)lē\ *adv*

¹fi·du·cia·ry \-'d(y)ü-shē-,er-ē, -shə-rē\ *n, pl* **-ries :** one that holds a fiduciary relation or acts in a fiduciary capacity

²fiduciary *adj* [L *fiduciarius,* fr. *fiducia* confidence, trust, fr. *fidere*] **:** of, relating to, or involving a confidence or trust: as **a :** held or founded in trust or confidence **b :** holding in trust **c :** depending on public confidence for value or currency <~ fiat money>

fie \'fī\ *interj* [ME *fi,* fr. OF] — used to express disgust or shock

fief \'fēf\ *n* [F — more at FEE] **1 :** a feudal estate **:** FEE **2 :** something over which one has rights or exercises control <a politician's ~>

fief·dom \'fēf-dəm, -təm\ *n* **:** FIEF

¹field \'fē(ə)ld\ *n* [ME, fr. OE *feld;* akin to OHG *feld* field, OE *flōr* floor] **1 a :** an open land area free of woods and buildings **b** (1) **:** an area of cleared enclosed land used for cultivation or pasture <a ~ of wheat> (2) **:** land containing a natural resource <coal ~> **c :** the place where a battle is fought; *also* **:** BATTLE **d :** a large unbroken expanse (as of ice) **2 a :** an area or division of an activity <a lawyer eminent in his ~> **b :** the sphere of practical operation outside a laboratory, office, or factory <geologists working in the ~> **c :** an area for military exercises or maneuvers **d** (1) **:** an area constructed, equipped, or marked for sports (2) **:** the portion of an indoor or outdoor sports area enclosed by the running track and on which are conducted field events (3) **:** either of the three sections of a baseball outfield <hits to all ~*s*> **3 :** a space on which something is drawn or projected: as **a :** the space on the surface of a coin, medal, or seal that does not contain the design **b :** the ground of each division in a flag **c :** the whole surface of an escutcheon **4 :** the individuals that make up all or part of the participants in a sports activity; *esp* **:** all participants with the exception of the favorite or the winner in a contest where more than two are entered **5 :** a complex of forces that serve as causative agents in human behavior **6 a :** a set of mathematical elements that is subject to two binary operations the second of which is distributive relative to the first and both of which yield an element and that constitutes a commutative group under the first operation and also under the second if the zero or unit element under the first is omitted **b :** a region or space in which a given effect (as magnetism) exists **7 :** the area visible through the lens of an optical instrument **8 :** a series of drain tiles and an absorption area **9 :** a particular area (as a column or set of columns on a punch card) in which the same type of information is regularly recorded

²field *vt* **1 a :** to catch or pick up (a batted ball) and usu. throw to a teammate **b :** to give an impromptu answer or solution to <the senator ~*ed* the reporters' questions> **2 :** to put into the field <~ an army> <~ a team>; *also* **:** to enter in competition ~ *vi* **:** to play as a fielder

³field *adj* **:** of or relating to a field: as **a :** growing in or inhabiting the fields or open country **b :** made, conducted, or used in the field <~ operations> **c :** operating or active in the field <a ~ agent>

field artillery *n* **:** artillery other than antiaircraft artillery used with armies in the field

field corn *n* **:** an Indian corn (as dent corn or flint corn) with starchy kernels grown for feeding stock or for market grain

field crop *n* **:** an agricultural crop (as hay, grain, or cotton) grown on large areas

field day *n* **1 a :** a day for military exercises or maneuvers **b :** an outdoor meeting or social gathering **c :** a day of sports and athletic competition **2 :** a time of unusual pleasure or unexpected success <the newspaper had a *field day* with the scandal>

field·er \'fēl-dər\ *n* **:** one that fields; *esp* **:** a defensive player stationed in the field (as in baseball)

fielder's choice *n* **:** a situation in baseball in which a batter reaches base safely because the fielder attempts to put out another base runner on the play

field event *n* **:** an event (as weight-throwing or jumping) in a track-and-field meet other than a race

field·fare \'fē(ə)l(d)-,fa(ə)r, -,fe(ə)r\ *n* [ME *feldefare,* fr. OE *feldeware,* fr. *feld* + *-ware* dweller] **:** a medium-sized Eurasian thrush (*Turdus pilaris*) with ash-colored head and chestnut wings

field glass *n* **:** a hand-held optical instrument for use outdoors usu. consisting of two telescopes on a single frame with a focusing device — usu. used in pl.

field goal *n* **1 :** a score in football made by drop-kicking or place-kicking the ball over the crossbar from ordinary play **2 :** a goal in basketball made while the ball is in play

field grade *n* **:** the rank of a field officer

field hand *n* **:** an outdoor farm laborer

field hockey *n* **:** a game played on a turfed field between two teams of 11 players each whose object is to direct a ball into the opponent's goal with a hockey stick

field house *n* **1 :** a building at an athletic field for housing equipment or providing dressing facilities **2 :** a building enclosing a large area suitable for various forms of athletics and usu. providing seats for spectators
fielding average *n* **:** the average (as of a baseball fielder) determined by dividing the number of putouts and assists by the number of chances — compare BATTING AVERAGE
field judge *n* **:** a football official whose duties include covering action on kicks and forward passes and timing intermission periods and time outs
field lens *n* **:** the lens in a compound eyepiece that is nearer the objective
field magnet *n* **:** a magnet for producing and maintaining a magnetic field esp. in a generator or electric motor
field marshal *n* **:** the highest ranking military officer (as in the British army)
field mouse *n* **:** any of various mice that inhabit fields; *esp* **:** VOLE
field officer *n* **:** a commissioned officer in the army, air force, or marine corps of the rank of colonel, lieutenant colonel, or major — called also *field grade officer;* compare COMPANY OFFICER, GENERAL OFFICER
field of force : FIELD 6b
field of honor 1 : a place where a duel is fought **2 :** BATTLEFIELD
field of view : FIELD 7
field of vision : VISUAL FIELD
field pea *n* **:** a small-seeded pea (*Pisum sativum* var. *arvense*) widely grown for forage and food
field·piece \ˈfē(ə)l(d)-ˌpēs\ *n* **:** a gun or howitzer for use in the field
field spaniel *n* **:** any of a breed of large usu. black hunting and retrieving spaniels that have a dense flat or slightly waved coat
field·stone \ˈfē(ə)l(d)-ˌstōn\ *n* **:** stone used as taken from the field (as in building)
field·strip \-ˌstrip\ *vt* **:** to take apart (a weapon) to the extent authorized for routine cleaning, lubrication, and minor repairs
field–test \-ˌtest\ *vt* **:** to test (as a procedure or product) in a natural environment for various things (as utility and acceptability by intended users) — **field test** *n*
field theory *n* **:** a detailed mathematical description of the assumed physical properties of a region under some influence (as gravitation)
field trial *n* **:** a trial of sporting dogs in actual performance
field trip *n* **:** a visit made by students and usu. a teacher for purposes of firsthand observation (as to a factory, farm, or museum)
field winding *n* **:** the winding of the field magnet of a dynamo or motor
field·work \ˈfē(ə)l-ˌdwərk\ *n* **1 :** a temporary fortification thrown up by an army in the field **2 :** work done in the field (as by students) to gain practical experience through firsthand observation **3 :** the gathering of anthropological or sociological data through the interviewing of subjects in the field — **field–work·er** *n*
fiend \ˈfēnd\ *n* [ME, fr. OE *fiend;* akin to OHG *fīant* enemy, Skt *pīyati* he scorns] **1 a :** DEVIL 1 **b :** DEMON **c :** a person of great wickedness or maliciousness **2 :** a person excessively devoted to a pursuit or study **:** FANATIC <a golf ~> **3 :** a person who uses immoderate quantities of something **:** ADDICT <a dope ~> **4 :** a person remarkably clever at something **:** WIZARD 3 <a ~ at mathematics>
fiend·ish \ˈfēn-dish\ *adj* **1 :** perversely diabolical <took a ~ pleasure in hurting people> **2 :** extremely cruel or wicked <a ~ old man> **3 :** excessively bad, unpleasant, or difficult <~ weather> — **fiend·ish·ly** *adv* — **fiend·ish·ness** *n*
fierce \ˈfi(ə)rs\ *adj* **fierc·er; fierc·est** [ME *fiers,* fr. OF, fr. L *ferus* wild, savage; akin to Gk *thēr* wild animal] **1 a :** violently hostile or aggressive in temperament **b :** given to fighting or killing **:** PUGNACIOUS **2 a :** marked by unrestrained zeal or vehemence <a ~ argument> **b :** extremely vexatious, disappointing, or intense <~ pain> **3 :** furiously active or determined <make a ~ effort> **4 :** wild or menacing in appearance — **fierce·ly** *adv* — **fierce·ness** *n*
syn FIERCE, FEROCIOUS, BARBAROUS, SAVAGE, CRUEL *shared meaning element* **:** showing fury or malignity in looks or actions ***ant*** tame, mild
fi·eri fa·cias \ˌfī-(ə-)rē-ˈfā-sh(ē-)əs\ *n* [L, cause (it) to be done] **:** a writ authorizing the sheriff to obtain satisfaction of a judgment in debt or damages from the goods and chattels of the defendant
fi·ery \ˈfī(-ə)-rē\ *adj* **fi·er·i·er; -est** [ME, fr. *fire, fier* fire] **1 a :** consisting of fire **b :** BURNING, BLAZING <the ~ interior of a furnace> **c :** using or carried out with fire <~ experiments of the alchemists> **d :** liable to catch fire or explode **:** FLAMMABLE <a ~ vapor> **2 a :** hot like a fire **b (1) :** being in an inflamed state or condition <a ~ boil> **(2) :** feverish and flushed <a ~ forehead> **3 a :** of the color of fire **:** RED <a ~ sunset> **b :** intensely or unnaturally red <~ lips and fingernails> **4 a :** full of or exuding emotion or spirit <a ~ sermon> **b :** easily provoked **:** IRRITABLE — **fi·eri·ly** \-rə-lē\ *adv* — **fi·eri·ness** \-rē-nəs\ *n* — **fiery** *adv*
fi·es·ta \fē-ˈes-tə\ *n* [Sp, fr. L *festa* — more at FEAST] **:** FESTIVAL; *specif* **:** a saint's day celebrated in Spain and Latin America with processions and dances
fi fa \ˈfī-ˈfā\ *abbr* fieri facias
fife \ˈfīf\ *n* [G *pfeife* pipe, fife, fr. OHG *pfīfa* — more at PIPE] **:** a small flute with six to eight finger holes and no keys that is used chiefly to accompany the drum
fife rail *n* **:** a rail about the mast near the deck to which running rigging is belayed
FIFO *abbr* first in, first out
fif·teen \fif-ˈtēn\ *n* [ME *fiftene,* adj., fr. OE *fīftēne;* akin to OE *tīen* ten] **1 —** see NUMBER table **2 :** the first point scored by a side in a game of tennis — called also *five* — **fifteen** *adj or pron* — **fif·teenth** \-ˈtēn(t)th\ *adj or n*
fifth \ˈfif(t)th\ *n* **1 —** see NUMBER table **2 a :** the musical interval embracing five diatonic degrees **b :** a tone at this interval; *specif* **:** DOMINANT 2 **c :** the harmonic combination of two tones at this interval **3 :** a unit of measure for liquor equal to one fifth of a U.S. gallon **4** *cap* **:** the Fifth Amendment of the U.S. Constitution — **fifth** *adj or adv* — **fifth·ly** *adv*
fifth column *n* [name applied to rebel sympathizers in Madrid in 1936 when four rebel columns were advancing on the city] **:** a group of secret sympathizers or supporters of an enemy that engage in espionage or sabotage within defense lines or national borders — **fifth col·um·nism** \-ˈkäl-əm-ˌ(n)iz-əm\ *n* — **fifth col·um·nist** \-(n)əst\ *n*
fifth wheel *n* **1 a :** a horizontal wheel or segment of a wheel that consists of two parts rotating on each other above the fore axle of a carriage and that forms support to prevent tipping **b :** a similar coupling between tractor and trailer of a semitrailer **2 :** a spare wheel **3 :** one that is superfluous, unnecessary, or burdensome
fif·ty \ˈfif-tē\ *n, pl* **fifties** [ME, fr. *fifty,* adj., fr. OE *fīftig,* fr. *fīftig,* n., group of 50, fr. *fīf* five + *-tig* group of ten — more at EIGHTY] **1 —** see NUMBER table **2** *pl* **:** the numbers 50 to 59; *specif* **:** the years 50 to 59 in a lifetime or century **3 :** a 50-dollar bill — **fif·ti·eth** \-tē-əth\ *adj or n* — **fifty** *adj or pron*
fif·ty–fif·ty \ˌfif-tē-ˈfif-tē\ *adj* **1 :** shared, assumed, or borne equally <a ~ proposition> **2 :** half favorable and half unfavorable <a ~ chance> — **fifty–fifty** *adv*
[1]**fig** \ˈfig\ *n* [ME *fige,* fr. OF, fr. OProv *figa,* fr. (assumed) VL *fica,* fr. L *ficus* fig tree, fig] **1 a :** an oblong or pear-shaped fruit that is a syconium **b :** any of a genus (*Ficus*) of trees of the mulberry family bearing fruits that are syconia; *esp* **:** a widely cultivated tree (F. *carica*) that produces edible figs **2 :** a contemptibly worthless trifle <not worth a ~>

fig: leaves and fruit

[2]**fig** *n* [*fig* (to adorn)] **:** DRESS, ARRAY <a young woman in dazzling royal full ~ —Mollie Panter-Downes>
[3]**fig** *abbr* **1** figurative; figuratively **2** figure
[1]**fight** \ˈfīt\ *vb* **fought** \ˈfȯt\; **fight·ing** [ME *fighten,* fr. OE *feohtan;* akin to OHG *fehtan* to fight, L *pectere* to comb — more at FEE] *vi* **1 a :** to contend in battle or physical combat; *esp* **:** to strive to overcome a person by blows or weapons **b :** to engage in boxing **2 :** to put forth a determined effort ~ *vt* **1 a (1) :** to contend against in or as if in battle or physical combat **(2) :** to box against in the ring **b (1) :** to attempt to prevent the success or effectiveness of <the company *fought* the strike for months> **(2) :** to oppose the passage or development of <~ a bad habit> **2 a :** to carry on **:** WAGE **b :** to take part in (as a boxing match) **3 :** to struggle to endure or surmount <~ out a storm at sea> **4 a :** to gain by struggle <~*s* his way through> **b :** to resolve by struggle <*fought* out their differences in court> **5 a :** to manage (a ship) in a battle or storm **b :** to cause to struggle or contend **c :** to manage in an unnecessarily rough or awkward manner — **fight shy of :** to avoid facing or meeting
[2]**fight** *n* **1 a :** a hostile encounter **:** BATTLE, COMBAT **b :** a boxing match **c :** a verbal disagreement **:** ARGUMENT **2 :** a struggle for a goal or an objective <a ~ for justice> **3 :** strength or disposition for fighting **:** PUGNACITY <still full of ~>
fight·er *n* **:** one that fights: as **a (1) :** WARRIOR, SOLDIER **(2) :** a pugnacious or game individual **(3) :** BOXER **b :** an airplane of high speed and maneuverability with armament designed to destroy enemy aircraft
fighting chair *n* **:** a chair from which a salt-water angler plays a hooked fish
fighting chance *n* **:** a chance that may be realized by a struggle <the patient had a *fighting chance* to live>
fig leaf *n* **1 :** the leaf of a fig tree **2** [fr. the use by Adam and Eve of fig leaves to cover their nakedness after eating the forbidden fruit (Gen. 3:7)] **:** something that conceals or camouflages usu. inadequately or dishonestly
fig marigold *n* **:** any of several carpetweeds (genus *Mesembryanthemum*) with showy white or pink flowers
fig·ment \ˈfig-mənt\ *n* [ME, fr. L *figmentum,* fr. *fingere* to shape — more at DOUGH] **:** something made up, fabricated, or contrived <a ~ of the author's imagination>
fig·ur·al \ˈfig-(y)ə-rəl\ *adj* **:** of, relating to, or consisting of human or animal figures <a ~ composition>
fig·u·ra·tion \ˌfig-(y)ə-ˈrā-shən\ *n* **1 :** the act or process of creating or providing a figure <Dante's unique ~ of the underworld> **2 :** FORM, OUTLINE **3 :** an act or instance of representation in figures and shapes <cubism was explained as a synthesis of colored ~*s* of objects —Janet Flanner> **4 :** ornamentation of a musical passage by using decorative and usu. repetitive figures
fig·u·ra·tive \ˈfig-(y)ə-rət-iv\ *adj* **1 a :** representing by a figure or resemblance **:** EMBLEMATIC **b :** of or relating to representation of form or figure in art <~ sculpture> **2 a :** expressing one thing in terms normally denoting another with which it may be regarded as analogous **:** METAPHORICAL <~ language> **b :** characterized by figures of speech <a ~ description> — **fig·u·ra·tive·ly** *adv* — **fig·u·ra·tive·ness** *n*
[1]**fig·ure** \ˈfig-yər, *esp Brit* ˈfig-ər\ *n* [ME, fr. OF, fr. L *figura,* fr. *fingere*] **1 a :** a number symbol **:** NUMERAL, DIGIT <a salary running into six ~*s*> **b** *pl* **:** arithmetical calculations <good at ~*s*> **c :** a written or printed character **d :** value esp. as expressed in numbers **:** PRICE <the house sold at a low ~> **2 a :** bodily shape or form esp. of a person <a slender ~> **b :** an object noticeable only as a shape or form <~*s* moving in the dusk>

ə abut	ᵊ kitten	ər further	a back	ā bake	ä cot, cart
au̇ out	ch chin	e less	ē easy	g gift	i trip	ī life
j joke	ŋ sing	ō flow	ȯ flaw	ȯi coin	th thin	t͟h this
ü loot	u̇ foot	y yet	yü few	yu̇ furious	zh vision

3 a : the graphic representation of a form esp. of a person **b :** a diagram or pictorial illustration of textual matter **c :** a geometric diagram **4 :** a person, thing, or action representative of another **5 :** an intentional deviation from the ordinary form or syntactical relation of words **6 :** the form of a syllogism with respect to the relative position of the middle term **7 :** an often repetitive pattern or design in a manufactured article (as cloth) or natural product (as wood) <a polka-dot ~> **8 :** appearance made : impression produced <the couple cut quite a ~> **9 a :** a series of movements in a dance **b :** an outline representation of a form traced by a series of evolutions (as with skates on an ice surface or by an airplane in the air) **10 :** a prominent personality : PERSONAGE <great ~*s* of history> **11 :** a short coherent group of tones or chords that may grow into a phrase, theme, or composition ***syn*** see FORM

[2]**figure** *vb* **fig·ured; fig·ur·ing** \ˈfig-yə-riŋ, ˈfig(-ə)-\ *vt* **1 :** to represent by or as if by a figure or outline : PORTRAY **2 :** to decorate with a pattern; *specif* **:** to write figures over or under (the bass) in order to indicate the accompanying chords **3 :** to indicate or represent by numerals **4 a :** CALCULATE **b :** CONCLUDE, DECIDE <he *figured* there was no use in further effort> **c :** REGARD, CONSIDER <backed him because they *figured* him an upright man> ~ *vi* **1 a :** to be or appear important or conspicuous <the vice-president really *figured* in the company> **b :** to be a part of : be implicated in <persons who *figured* in a robbery> **2 :** to perform a figure in dancing **3 :** COMPUTE, CALCULATE **4 :** to seem rational, normal, or expected <that ~*s*> — **fig·ur·er** \-(y)ər-ər\ *n* — **figure on 1 :** to take into consideration (as in planning) <*figuring on* $50 a month extra income> **2 :** to rely on **3 :** PLAN <I *figure on* going into town>

fig·ured \-(y)ərd\ *adj* **1 :** being represented : PORTRAYED **2 :** adorned with, formed into, or marked with a figure <~ muslin> <~ wood> **3 :** indicated by figures

figured bass *n* **:** CONTINUO

figure eight *n* **:** something resembling the Arabic numeral eight in form or shape: as **a :** a small knot — see KNOT illustration **b :** an embroidery stitch **c :** a dance pattern **d :** a skater's figure

fig·ure·head \ˈfig-(y)ər-ˌhed\ *n* **1 :** the figure on a ship's bow **2 :** a head or chief in name only

figure in *vt* **:** to include esp. in a reckoning <forgetting to *figure in* occasional expenses>

figure of speech : a form of expression (as a simile or metaphor) used to convey meaning or heighten effect often by comparing or identifying one thing with another that has a meaning or connotation familiar to the reader or listener

figure out *vt* **1 :** DISCOVER, DETERMINE <try to *figure out* a way to solve the problem> **2 :** SOLVE, FATHOM <*figure out* a problem> <I just can't *figure* him *out*>

figurehead 1

figure skating *n* **:** skating in which the skater describes or outlines prescribed figures

fig·u·rine \ˌfig-(y)ə-ˈrēn\ *n* **:** a small carved or molded figure : STATUETTE

fig wasp *n* **:** a minute wasp (*Blastophaga psenes* of the family Agaontidae) that breeds in the caprifig and is the agent of caprification; *broadly* **:** a wasp of the same family

fig·wort \ˈfig-ˌwərt, -ˌwȯ(ə)rt\ *n* **:** any of a genus (*Scrophularia* of the family Scrophulariaceae, the figwort family) of chiefly herbaceous plants with leaves having no stipules, an irregular bilabiate corolla, and a 2-celled ovary

Fi·ji·an \ˈfē-(ˌ)jē-ən, fi-ˈ\ *n* **1 :** a member of a Melanesian people of the Fiji islands **2 :** the Austronesian language of the Fijians — **Fijian** *adj*

fila *pl of* FILUM

fil·a·ment \ˈfil-ə-mənt\ *n* [MF, fr. ML *filamentum,* fr. LL *filare* to spin — more at FILE] **:** a single thread or a thin flexible threadlike object, process, or appendage: as **a :** a tenuous conductor (as of carbon or metal) made incandescent by the passage of an electric current; *specif* **:** a cathode in the form of a metal wire in an electron tube **b** (1) **:** a thin and fine elongated constituent part of a gill (2) **:** an elongated thin series of cells attached one to another or a very long thin cylindrical single cell (as of some algae, fungi, or bacteria) **c :** the anther-bearing stalk of a stamen — see FLOWER illustration — **fil·a·men·ta·ry** \ˌfil-ə-ˈment-ə-rē, -ˈmen-trē\ *adj* — **fil·a·men·tous** \-ˈment-əs\ *adj*

fi·lar \ˈfī-lər\ *adj* [L *filum* thread] **:** of or relating to a thread or line; *esp* **:** having threads across the field of view <a ~ eyepiece>

fi·lar·ia \fə-ˈlar-ē-ə, -ˈler-\ *n, pl* **-i·ae** \-ē-ˌē, -ē-ˌī\ [NL, fr. L *filum*] **:** any of numerous slender filamentous nematodes (of *Filaria* and related genera) that as adults are parasites in the blood or tissues of mammals and as larvae usu. develop in biting insects — **fi·lar·i·al** \-ē-əl\ *adj* — **fi·lar·i·id** \-ē-əd\ *adj or n*

fil·a·ri·a·sis \ˌfil-ə-ˈrī-ə-səs\ *n, pl* **-a·ses** \-ˌsēz\ **:** infestation with or disease caused by filariae

fil·a·ture \ˈfil-ə-ˌchu̇(ə)r, -chər, -ˌt(y)u̇(ə)r\ *n* [F, fr. LL *filatus,* pp. of *filare*] **1 :** the reeling of silk from cocoons **2 :** a reel for drawing off silk from cocoons **3 :** a factory where silk is reeled

fil·bert \ˈfil-bərt\ *n* [ME, fr. AF *philber,* fr. St. *Philibert* † 684 Frankish abbot whose feast day falls in the nutting season] **1 :** either of two European hazels (*Corylus avellana pontica* and *C. maxima*); *also* **:** the sweet thick-shelled nut of the filbert **2 :** HAZELNUT

filch \ˈfilch\ *vt* [ME *filchen*] **:** to appropriate furtively or casually <~ a doughnut from the platter> ***syn*** see STEAL

[1]**file** \ˈfī(ə)l\ *n* [ME, fr. OE *fēol;* akin to OHG *fīla* file] **1 :** a tool usu. of hardened steel with cutting ridges for forming or smoothing surfaces esp. of metal **2 :** a shrewd or crafty person

[2]**file** *vt* **filed; fil·ing :** to rub, smooth, or cut away with or as if with a file

[3]**file** *vt* **filed; fil·ing** [ME *filen,* fr. OE *fȳlan,* fr. *fūl* foul] *chiefly dial* **:** DEFILE, CORRUPT

[4]**file** *vb* **filed; fil·ing** [ME *filen,* fr. MF *filer* to string documents on a string or wire, fr. *fil* thread, fr. L *filum;* akin to Arm *jil* sinew] *vt* **1 :** to arrange in order for preservation and reference <~ letters> **2 a :** to place among official records as prescribed by law <~ a mortgage> **b :** to send (copy) to a newspaper <*filed* a good story> **c :** to return to the office of the clerk of a court without action on the merits **3 :** to perform the first act of (as a lawsuit) <threatened to ~ charges against him> ~ *vi* **1 :** to register as a candidate esp. in a primary election <~ for county attorney> **2 :** to place items (as letters) in a file

[5]**file** *n* **1 :** a device (as a folder, case, or cabinet) by means of which papers are kept in order **2 a** *archaic* **:** ROLL, LIST **b :** a collection of papers or publications usu. arranged or classified <a ~ of back issues of a newspaper>

[6]**file** *n* [MF, fr. *filer* to spin, fr. LL *filare,* fr. L *filum*] **1 :** a row of persons, animals, or things arranged one behind the other **2 :** any of the rows of squares that extend across a chessboard from white's side to black's side

[7]**file** *vi* **filed; fil·ing :** to march or proceed in file

file clerk *n* **:** a clerk who works on files

file·fish \ˈfī(ə)l-ˌfish\ *n* **:** any of various plectognath fishes (esp. genera *Aluterus, Cantherhines,* and *Monacanthus* of the family Balistidae) with rough granular leathery skins

fi·let \fi-ˈlā\ *n* [F, lit., net] **:** a lace with a square mesh and geometric designs

fi·let mi·gnon \ˌfil-(ˌ)ā-mēn-ˈyōⁿ, fi-ˌlā-\ *n, pl* **filets mignons** \-(ˌ)ā-mēn-ˈyōⁿz, -ˌlā-\ [F, lit., dainty fillet] **:** a fillet of beef cut from the thick end of a beef tenderloin

fili- *or* **filo-** *comb form* [L *filum*] **:** thread <*fili*form>

fil·ial \ˈfil-ē-əl, ˈfil-yəl\ *adj* [ME, fr. LL *filialis,* fr. L *filius* son — more at FEMININE] **1 :** of, relating to, or befitting a son or daughter <~ obedience> **2 :** having or assuming the relation of a child or offspring — **fil·ial·ly** \-ē-ə-lē, -yə-lē\ *adv*

filial generation *n* **:** a generation in a breeding experiment that is successive to a parental generation — symbol F_1 for the first, F_2 for the second, etc.

fil·i·a·tion \ˌfil-ē-ˈā-shən\ *n* **1 a :** filial relationship esp. of a son to his father **b :** the adjudication of paternity : AFFILIATION **2 :** an offshoot or branch of a culture or language **3 a :** descent or derivation esp. from a culture or language **b :** the act or process of determining such relationship

[1]**fil·i·bus·ter** \ˈfil-ə-ˌbəs-tər\ *n* [Sp *filibustero,* lit., freebooter] **1 :** an irregular military adventurer; *specif* **:** an American engaged in fomenting insurrections in Latin America in the mid-19th century **2** [[2]*filibuster*] **a :** the use of extreme dilatory tactics in an attempt to delay or prevent action esp. in a legislative assembly **b :** an instance of this practice

[2]**filibuster** *vb* **fil·i·bus·tered; fil·i·bus·ter·ing** \-t(ə-)riŋ\ *vi* **1 :** to carry out insurrectionist or revolutionary activities in a foreign country **2 :** to engage in a filibuster ~ *vt* **:** to subject to a filibuster — **fil·i·bus·ter·er** \-tər-ər\ *n*

fil·i·form \ˈfil-ə-ˌfȯrm, ˈfī-lə-\ *adj* **:** shaped like a filament

[1]**fil·i·gree** \ˈfil-ə-ˌgrē\ *n* [F *filigrane,* fr. It *filigrana,* fr. L *filum* + *granum* grain] **1 :** ornamental work esp. of fine wire of gold, silver, or copper applied chiefly to gold and silver surfaces **2 a :** ornamental openwork of delicate or intricate design **b :** a pattern or design resembling such openwork <a ~ of frost on a window>

[2]**filigree** *vt* **fil·i·greed; fil·i·gree·ing :** to adorn with or as if with filigree

fil·ing \ˈfī-liŋ\ *n* **1 :** an act or instance of using a file **2 :** a fragment rubbed off in filing <iron ~*s*>

fil·io·pi·etis·tic \ˈfil-ē-ō-ˌpī-ə-ˈtis-tik\ *adj* [*fil*ial + *-o-* + *piety* + *-istic*] **:** of or relating to an often excessive veneration of ancestors or tradition

Fil·i·pi·no \ˌfil-ə-ˈpē-(ˌ)nō\ *n, pl* **Filipinos** [Sp] **1 :** a native of the Philippine islands; *specif* **:** a member of Christianized Philippine people **2 :** a citizen of the Republic of the Philippines — **Filipino** *adj*

[1]**fill** \ˈfil\ *vb* [ME *fillen,* fr. OE *fyllan;* akin to OE *full*] *vt* **1 a :** to put into as much as can be held or conveniently contained <~ a cup with water> **b :** to supply with a full complement <the class is already ~*ed*> **c** (1) **:** to cause to swell or billow <wind ~*ed* the sails> (2) **:** to trim (a sail) to catch the wind **d :** to raise the level of with fill <~*ed* land> **e :** to repair the cavities of (teeth) **f :** to stop up : OBSTRUCT, PLUG <wreckage ~*ed* the channel> <~ the chink> **g :** to stop up the interstices, crevices, or pores of (as cloth, wood, or leather) with a foreign substance **2 a :** FEED, SATIATE **b :** SATISFY, FULFILL <~*s* all requirements> **c :** to make out : COMPLETE — often used with *out* or *in* <~ out a form> <~ in the blanks> **3 a :** to occupy the whole of <smoke ~*ed* the room> **b :** to spread through **c :** to make full (as the mind or spirit) <a mind ~*ed* with fantasies> **4 a :** to possess and perform the duties of : HOLD <~ an office> **b :** to place a person in <~ a vacancy> **5 :** to supply as directed <~ a prescription> **6 :** to cover the surface of with a layer of precious metal ~ *vi* **:** to become full <the stadium ~*ed* and overflowed> — **fill one's shoes :** to take over one's job, position, or responsibilities — **fill the bill :** to answer a need : serve the purpose satisfactorily

[2]**fill** *n* **1 :** a full supply; *esp* **:** a quantity that satisfies or satiates <eat your ~> **2 :** material used to fill a receptacle, cavity, passage, or low place

fill away *vi* **1 :** to trim a sail to catch the wind **2 :** to proceed on the course esp. after being brought up in the wind

filled milk *n* **:** skim milk with fat content increased by the addition of vegetable oils

[1]**fill·er** \ˈfil-ər\ *n* **:** one that fills: as **a :** a substance added to a product (as to increase bulk, weight, viscosity, opacity, or strength) **b :** a composition used to fill the pores and grain of a wood or

other surface before painting or varnishing **c :** a plate or other piece used to cover or fill in a space between two parts of a structure **d :** tobacco used to form the core of a cigar **e :** material (as a brief item of fact) used to fill extra space in a column or page of a newspaper or magazine **f :** a pack of paper used esp. in a loose-leaf notebook

²fil·ler \ˈfil-ˌe(ə)r\ *n, pl* **fillers** *or* **filler** [Hung *fillér*] — see *forint* at MONEY table

¹fil·let \ˈfil-ət, *in sense 2b also* fi-ˈlā, ˈfil-(ˌ)ā\ *also* **fi·let** \fi-ˈlā, ˈfil-(ˌ)ā\ *n* [ME *filet*, fr. MF, dim. of *fil* thread — more at FILE] **1 :** a ribbon or narrow strip of material used esp. as a headband **2 :** a thin narrow strip of material: as **a :** a band of anatomical fibers; *specif* **:** LEMNISCUS **b :** a piece or slice of boneless meat or fish; *specif* **:** the tenderloin of beef **3 a :** a concave junction formed where two surfaces meet **b :** a curved strip forming such a junction **4 :** a narrow flat architectural member: **a :** a flat molding separating others **b :** the space between two flutings in a shaft **5 :** a design impressed on a book cover

1, fillet 1

²fil·let \ˈfil-ət, *in sense 2 also* fi-ˈlā, ˈfil-(ˌ)ā\ *vt* **1 :** to bind, furnish, or adorn with or as if with a fillet **2 :** to cut into fillets

fill–in \ˈfil-ˌin\ *n* **:** someone or something that fills in

fill in \(ˈ)fil-ˈin\ *vt* **1 :** to give (a person) necessary or recently acquired information <friends *filled* him *in* on the latest gossip> **2 :** to enrich (as a design) with detail ~ *vi* **:** to fill a vacancy usu. temporarily **:** SUBSTITUTE <he often *filled in* in emergencies>

fill·ing \ˈfil-iŋ\ *n* **1 :** an act or instance of filling **2 :** something used to fill a cavity, container, or depression <a ~ for a tooth> **3 :** something that completes: as **a :** the yarn interlacing the warp in a fabric; *also* **:** yarn for the shuttle **b :** a food mixture used to fill pastry or sandwiches

filling station *n* **:** SERVICE STATION 1

¹fil·lip \ˈfil-əp\ *n* [prob. of imit. origin] **1 a :** a blow or gesture made by the sudden forcible straightening of a finger curled up against the thumb **b :** a short sharp blow **:** BUFFET **2 :** something tending to arouse or excite

²fillip *vt* **1 a :** to strike or tap with a fillip <~*ed* him on the nose> **b :** to make a filliping motion with <~*ed* his fingers toward them> **2 :** to project quickly by or as if by a fillip <~*ed* crumbs off the table> **3 :** STIMULATE <with this to ~ his spirits —Robert Westerby>

fill out *vi* **:** to put on flesh

fil·ly \ˈfil-ē\ *n, pl* **fillies** [ME *fyly*, fr. ON *fylja*; akin to OE *fola* foal] **1 :** a young female horse usu. of less than four years **2 :** a young woman **:** GIRL

¹film \ˈfilm\ *n, often attrib* [ME *filme*, fr. OE *filmen*; akin to Gk *pelma* sole of the foot, OE *fell* skin — more at FELL] **1 a :** a thin skin or membranous covering **:** PELLICLE **b :** an abnormal growth on or in the eye **2 :** a thin covering or coating <a ~ of ice on the pond> **3 a :** an exceedingly thin layer **:** LAMINA **b (1) :** a thin flexible transparent sheet (as of plastic) used as a wrapping **(2) :** such a sheet of cellulose acetate or cellulose nitrate coated with a light-sensitive emulsion for taking photographs **4 :** MOTION PICTURE

²film *vt* **1 :** to cover with or as if with a film **2 :** to make a motion picture of or from <~ a scene> <~ a novel> ~ *vi* **1 :** to become covered or obscured with or as if with a film **2 a :** to be suitable for photographing <a scene that would ~ well> **b :** to make a motion picture <~*ing* on location>

film badge *n* **:** a small pack of sensitive photographic film worn as a badge for indicating exposure to radiation

film·card \ˈfilm-ˌkärd\ *n* **:** MICROFICHE

film·dom \ˈfilm-dəm\ *n* **1 :** the motion-picture industry **2 :** the personnel of the motion-picture industry

film·ic \ˈfil-mik\ *adj* **:** of, relating to, or resembling motion pictures — **film·i·cal·ly** \-mi-k(ə-)lē\ *adv*

film·mak·er \ˈfilm-ˌmā-kər\ *n* **:** MOVIEMAKER

film·mak·ing \-ˌmā-kiŋ\ *n* **:** the making of movies

film·og·ra·phy \fil-ˈmäg-rə-fē\ *n, pl* **-phies** [*film* + *-ography* (as in *bibliography*)] **:** a list of motion pictures featuring the work of a prominent film figure (as an actor) or relating to a particular topic

film·set·ting \ˈfilm-ˌset-iŋ\ *n* **:** PHOTOCOMPOSITION — **film·set** *adj* — **filmset** *vt* — **film·set·ter** *n*

film·strip \ˈfilm-ˌstrip\ *n* **:** a strip of usu. 35 millimeter film bearing photographs, diagrams, or graphic matter for still projection

filmy \ˈfil-mē\ *adj* **film·i·er; -est 1 :** of, resembling, or composed of film **:** GAUZY <~ draperies> **2 :** covered with a haze or film — **film·i·ly** \-mə-lē\ *adv* — **film·i·ness** \-mē-nəs\ *n*

filo- — see FILI-

fils \ˈfils\ *n, pl* **fils** [Ar] — see *dinar* at MONEY table

¹fil·ter \ˈfil-tər\ *n* [ME *filtre*, fr. ML *filtrum*, piece of felt used as a filter, of Gmc origin; akin to OHG *filz* felt — more at FELT] **1 :** a porous article or mass (as of paper or sand) through which a gas or liquid is passed to separate out matter in suspension **2 :** an apparatus containing a filter medium **3 a :** a device or material for suppressing or minimizing waves or oscillations of certain frequencies (as of electricity, light, or sound) **b :** a transparent material (as colored glass) that absorbs light of certain wavelengths or colors selectively and is used for modifying light that reaches a sensitized photographic material — called also *color filter*

²filter *vb* **fil·tered; fil·ter·ing** \-t(ə-)riŋ\ *vt* **1 :** to subject to the action of a filter **2 :** to remove by means of a filter ~ *vi* **1 :** to pass or move through or as if through a filter **2 :** to enter or cross over in small units over a period of time <people began ~*ing* into the hall>

fil·ter·able *also* **fil·tra·ble** \ˈfil-t(ə-)rə-bəl\ *adj* **:** capable of being filtered or of passing through a filter — **fil·ter·abil·i·ty** \ˌfil-t(ə-)rə-ˈbil-ət-ē\ *n*

filterable virus *n* **:** a virus so small that a fluid containing it remains virulent after passing through a filter

filter bed *n* **:** a bed of sand or gravel for filtering water or sewage

filter feeder *n* **:** an animal that obtains its food by filtering organic matter or minute organisms from a current of water that passes through some part of its system

filter paper *n* **:** porous unsized paper used esp. for filtering

filter tip *n* **:** a cigar or cigarette tip designed to filter the smoke before it enters the smoker's mouth; *also* **:** a cigar or cigarette provided with such a tip — **fil·ter–tipped** \ˌfil-tər-ˈtipt\ *adj*

filth \ˈfilth\ *n* [ME, fr. OE *fӯlth*, fr. *fūl* foul] **1 :** foul or putrid matter; *esp* **:** loathsome dirt or refuse **2 a :** moral corruption or defilement **b :** something that tends to corrupt or defile **:** OBSCENITY

filthy \ˈfil-thē\ *adj* **filth·i·er; -est 1 :** covered with or containing filth **:** offensively dirty **2 a :** UNDERHAND, VILE **b :** OBSCENE ***syn*** see DIRTY — **filth·i·ly** \-thə-lē\ *adv* — **filth·i·ness** \-thē-nəs\ *n*

¹fil·trate \ˈfil-ˌtrāt\ *vb* **fil·trat·ed; fil·trat·ing** [ML *filtratus*, pp. of *filtrare*, fr. *filtrum*] **:** FILTER

²filtrate *n* **:** material that has passed through a filter

fil·tra·tion \fil-ˈtrā-shən\ *n* **1 :** the process of filtering **2 :** the process of passing through or as if through a filter; *also* **:** DIFFUSION <the kidney produces urine by ~>

fi·lum \ˈfī-ləm\ *n, pl* **fi·la** \-lə\ [NL, fr. L — more at FILE] **:** filamentous structure **:** FILAMENT

fim·bria \ˈfim-brē-ə\ *n, pl* **-bri·ae** \-brē-ˌē, -ˌī\ [NL, fr. L, fringe] **:** a bordering fringe esp. at the entrance of the fallopian tubes — **fim·bri·al** \-brē-əl\ *adj*

fim·bri·ate \-ˌāt\ *or* **fim·bri·at·ed** \-ˌāt-əd\ *adj* **:** having the edge or extremity bordered by slender processes **:** FRINGED — **fim·bri·a·tion** \ˌfim-brē-ˈā-shən\ *n*

¹fin \ˈfin\ *n* [ME *finn*, fr. OE; akin to L *spina* thorn, spine] **1 :** an external membranous process of an aquatic animal (as a fish) used in propelling or guiding the body — see FISH illustration **2 :** something resembling a fin esp. in appearance or function: **a :** HAND, ARM **b (1) :** an appendage of a boat (as a submarine) **(2) :** an airfoil attached to an airplane for directional stability **c :** FLIPPER 1b **d :** any of the projecting ribs on a radiator or an engine cylinder — **fin·like** \-ˌlīk\ *adj* — **finned** \ˈfind\ *adj*

²fin *vb* **finned; fin·ning** *vi* **:** to show the fins above the water ~ *vt* **:** to equip with fins

³fin *n* [Yiddish *finf* five, fr. OHG] *slang* **:** a 5-dollar bill

⁴fin *abbr* **1** finance; financial **2** finish

fi·na·gle \fə-ˈnā-gəl\ *vb* **fi·na·gled; fi·na·gling** \-g(ə-)liŋ\ [perh. alter. of *fainaigue* (to renege)] *vt* **1 :** to obtain by indirect or involved means **2 :** to obtain by trickery **:** SWINDLE ~ *vi* **:** to use devious and often dishonest methods to achieve one's ends — **fi·na·gler** \-g(ə-)lər\ *n*

¹fi·nal \ˈfīn-ᵊl\ *adj* [ME, fr. MF, fr. L *finalis*, fr. *finis* boundary, end] **1 a :** not to be altered or undone **:** CONCLUSIVE **b :** of or relating to a concluding court action or proceeding <~ decree> **2 :** being the last **:** constituting the closing element in a series, process, or progress <the ~ chapter of a book> **3 :** of or relating to the ultimate purpose or result of a process <the ~ goal of life> **4 :** relating to or occurring at the end or conclusion ***syn*** see LAST — **fi·nal·ly** \ˈfīn-ᵊl-ē, ˈfīn-lē\ *adv*

²final *n* **:** something that is final: as **a :** a deciding match, game, heat, or trial **b :** the last examination in a course

fi·na·le \fə-ˈnal-ē, fi-ˈnäl-\ *n* [It, fr. *finale*, adj., final, fr. L *finalis*] **1 :** the close or termination of something: as **a :** the last section of an instrumental musical composition **b :** the closing part, scene, or number in a public performance **c :** the last and often climactic event or item in a sequence

fi·nal·ist \ˈfīn-ᵊl-əst\ *n* **:** a contestant in the finals of a competition

fi·nal·i·ty \fī-ˈnal-ət-ē, fə-\ *n, pl* **-ties 1 a :** the character or condition of being final, settled, irrevocable, or complete **b :** the condition of being at an ultimate point esp. of development or authority **2 :** something final; *esp* **:** a fundamental fact, action, or belief

fi·nal·ize \ˈfīn-ᵊl-ˌīz\ *vt* **-ized; -iz·ing 1 :** to put in final or finished form <soon my conclusion will be *finalized* —D. D. Eisenhower> **2 :** to give final approval to <ties up the day's loose ends, *finalizing* the papers prepared and presented by his staff —*Newsweek*> — **fi·nal·iza·tion** \ˌfīn-ᵊl-ə-ˈzā-shən\ *n*

¹fi·nance \fə-ˈnan(t)s, ˈfī-ˌ, fī-ˈ\ *n* [ME, payment, ransom, fr. MF, fr. *finer* to end, pay, fr. *fin* end — more at FINE] **1** *pl* **:** money or other liquid resources of a government, business, group, or individual **2 :** the system that includes the circulation of money, the granting of credit, the making of investments, and the provision of banking facilities **3 :** the science or study of the management of funds **4 :** the obtaining of funds or capital **:** FINANCING

²finance *vt* **fi·nanced; fi·nanc·ing 1 a :** to raise or provide funds or capital for <~ a new house> **b :** to furnish with necessary funds <~ a son through college> **2 :** to sell something to on credit **:** provide with credit <auto producers unable to ~ their dealers>

fi·nan·cial \fə-ˈnan-chəl, fī-\ *adj* **:** relating to finance or financiers — **fi·nan·cial·ly** \-ˈnanch-(ə-)lē\ *adv*

syn FINANCIAL, MONETARY, PECUNIARY, FISCAL *shared meaning element* **:** of or relating to money and its use and distribution

¹fi·nan·cier \ˌfin-ən-ˈsi(ə)r; fə-ˌnan-, ˌfī-\ *n* **1 :** one who specializes in raising and expending public moneys **2 :** one who deals with finance and investment on a large scale

²financier *vi* **:** to conduct financial operations often by sharp or reprehensible practices

fi·nanc·ing *n* **:** the act or process or an instance of raising or providing funds; *also* **:** the funds thus raised or provided

---

ə abut ᵊ kitten ər further a back ā bake ä cot, cart
au̇ out ch chin e less ē easy g gift i trip ī life
j joke ŋ sing ō flow ȯ flaw ȯi coin th thin th this
ü loot u̇ foot y yet yü few yu̇ furious zh vision

fin·back \ˈfin-ˌbak\ *n* **:** a common whalebone whale (*Balaenoptera physalus*) of the Atlantic coast of the U.S. that attains a length of over 60 feet; *broadly* **:** RORQUAL

finch \ˈfinch\ *n* [ME, fr. OE *finc;* akin to OHG *fincho* finch, Gk *spiza* chaffinch] **:** any of numerous songbirds (as the sparrows, grosbeaks, crossbills, goldfinches, linnets, and buntings of the family Fringillidae) having a short stout conical bill adapted for crushing seeds

[1]**find** \ˈfīnd\ *vb* **found** \ˈfau̇nd\; **find·ing** [ME *finden,* fr. OE *findan;* akin to OHG *findan* to find, L *pont-, pons* bridge, Gk *pontos* sea, Skt *patha* way, course] *vt* **1 a :** to come upon often accidentally **:** ENCOUNTER **b :** to meet with (a particular reception) <hoped to ~ favor> **2 a :** to come upon by searching or effort <the committee must ~ a suitable person for the job> **b :** to discover by study or experiment <~ an answer to a problem> **c :** to obtain by effort or management <~ the time to study> **d :** ATTAIN, REACH <the bullet *found* its mark> **e :** to discover by sounding <~ bottom in a lake> **3 a :** EXPERIENCE, DETECT <~ much pleasure in his company> **b :** to perceive (oneself) to be in a certain place or condition <*found* himself in a dilemma> **c :** to gain or regain the use or power of <trying to ~ his tongue> **d :** to bring (oneself) to a realization of one's powers or of one's proper sphere of activity <must help the student to ~ himself as an individual —N. M. Pusey> **4 a :** PROVIDE, SUPPLY **b :** to furnish (room and board) esp. as a condition of employment **5 :** to settle upon and make a statement about (as a conclusion) <~ a verdict> ~ *vi* **:** to determine a case judicially by a verdict <~ for the defendant> — **find fault :** to criticize unfavorably

[2]**find** *n* **1 :** an act or instance of finding **2 :** something found: as **a :** a valuable item <an archaeological ~> **b :** a person whose ability proves to be unexpectedly great <the young actress was the theatrical ~ of the year>

find·er \ˈfīn-dər\ *n* **1 :** one that finds **2 :** a small astronomical telescope of low power and wide field attached to a larger telescope for finding an object **3 :** a device on a camera for showing the area of the subject to be included in the picture

fin de siè·cle \ˌfaⁿ-də-sē-ˈeklᵊ\ *adj* [F, end of the century] **:** of, relating to, or characteristic of the close of the 19th century and esp. its literary and artistic climate of sophistication, world-weariness, and fashionable despair

find·ing \ˈfīn-diŋ\ *n* **1 a :** the act of one that finds **b :** FIND 2 **2** *pl* **:** small tools and supplies used by an artisan (as a dressmaker, jeweler, or shoemaker) **3 a :** the result of a judicial examination or inquiry **b :** the results of an investigation — usu. used in pl. <basic research ~*s*>

find out *vt* **1 :** to learn by study, observation, or search **:** DISCOVER **2 a :** to catch in an offense (as a crime) <the culprits were soon *found out*> **b :** to ascertain the true character or identity of **:** UNMASK <if you pretend, you may be *found out*> ~ *vi* **:** to discover, learn, or verify something <I don't know, but I'll *find out* for you>

[1]**fine** \ˈfīn\ *n* [ME, fr. OF *fin,* fr. L *finis* boundary, end] **1** *obs* **:** END, CONCLUSION **2 :** a compromise of a fictitious suit used as a form of conveyance of lands **3 a :** a sum imposed as punishment for an offense **b :** a forfeiture or penalty paid to an injured party in a civil action — **in fine :** in short

[2]**fine** *vt* **fined; fin·ing :** to impose a fine on **:** punish by a fine

[3]**fine** *adj* **fin·er; fin·est** [ME *fin,* fr. OF, fr. L *finis,* n., end, limit] **1 a :** free from impurity **b** *of a metal* **:** having a stated proportion of pure metal in the composition **2 a** (1) **:** very thin in gauge or texture <~ thread> (2) **:** not coarse <~ sand> (3) **:** very small <~ print> (4) **:** KEEN <a knife with a ~ edge> **b :** physically trained or hardened close to the limit of efficiency — used of an athlete or animal **3 a** (1) **:** having a delicate or subtle quality <a wine of ~ bouquet> (2) **:** subtle or sensitive in perception or discrimination <a ~ distinction> **b :** performed with extreme care and accuracy <a ~ adjustment> **4 :** superior in quality, conception, or appearance **:** EXCELLENT <a ~ musician> <a ~ view> **5 :** marked by or affecting elegance or refinement <~ manners> **6 :** very well <feel ~> **7 :** AWFUL — used as an intensive <the leader, in a ~ frenzy, beheaded one of his wives —Brian Crozier> — **fine·ness** \ˈfīn-nəs\ *n*

[4]**fine** *adv* **:** FINELY

[5]**fine** *vb* **fined; fin·ing** *vt* **1 :** PURIFY, CLARIFY <~ and filter wine> **2 :** to make finer in quality or size ~ *vi* **1 :** to become pure or clear <the ale will ~> **2 :** to become smaller in lines or proportions **:** DIMINISH

[6]**fi·ne** \ˈfē-(ˌ)nā\ *n* [It, fr. L *finis* end] **:** END — used as a direction in music to mark the closing point after a repeat

fine art *n* **1 a :** art (as painting, sculpture, or music) concerned primarily with the creation of beautiful objects — usu. used in pl. **b :** objects of fine art **2 :** an activity requiring a fine skill <the *fine art* of making friends>

fine·ly \ˈfīn-lē\ *adv* **:** in a fine manner: as **a :** extremely well **:** EXCELLENTLY <you did ~> **b :** with close discrimination **:** PRECISELY **c :** with delicacy or subtlety **:** SENSITIVELY <a leader ~ attuned to the needs of his people> **d :** MINUTELY <~ ground meal>

fine print *n* **:** something thoroughly and often deliberately obscure; *esp* **:** a part of an agreement (as a contract) spelling out restrictions and limitations often in small type or obscure language

fin·ery \ˈfīn-(ə-)rē\ *n, pl* **-er·ies :** ORNAMENT, DECORATION; *esp* **:** dressy or showy clothing and jewels

fines \ˈfīnz\ *n pl* [[3]*fine*] **:** finely crushed or powdered material (as ore or coal); *also* **:** very small particles in a mixture of various sizes

fines herbes \fēn-ˈze(ə)rb, fē-ˈne(ə)rb\ *n pl* [F, lit., fine herbs] **:** a mixture of herbs (as parsley, chives, and tarragon) used as a seasoning or garnish

fine·spun \ˈfīn-ˈspən\ *adj* **:** developed with extreme care or delicacy; *also* **:** developed in excessively fine or subtle detail

[1]**fi·nesse** \fə-ˈnes\ *n* [ME, fr. MF, fr. *fin*] **1 :** refinement or delicacy of workmanship, structure, or texture **2 :** skillful handling of a situation **:** adroit maneuvering <accomplish by ~ what could not have been accomplished by force> **3 :** the withholding of one's highest card or trump in the hope that a lower card will take the trick because the only opposing higher card is in the hand of an opponent who has already played

[2]**finesse** *vb* **fi·nessed; fi·ness·ing** *vi* **:** to make a finesse in playing cards — sometimes used with *for* or *against* <~ for the jack> <~ against the queen> ~ *vt* **1 :** to play (a card) in a finesse **2 a :** to bring about or manage by adroit maneuvering <~ his way through tight places —Marquis James> **b :** EVADE, TRICK <trying to ~ an eagle-eyed editor —J. C. G. Conniff>

fin·est \ˈfī-nəst\ *n, pl in constr* [superl. of [3]*fine*] **:** POLICEMEN — usu. used with the possessive form of a city or area <the city's ~>

fine structure *n* **:** microscopic structure of a biological entity or one of its parts esp. as studied in preparations for the electron microscope — **fine structural** *adj*

fine–tooth comb \ˌfīn-ˌtüth-\ *n* **1 :** a comb with close-set teeth used esp. for clearing parasites or foreign matter from the hair **2 :** an attitude or system of thorough searching or scrutinizing <went over the report with a *fine-tooth comb* without finding any discrepancies>

fin·fish \ˈfin-ˌfish\ *n* **:** a true fish — compare SHELLFISH

[1]**fin·ger** \ˈfiŋ-gər\ *n* [ME, fr. OE; akin to OHG *fingar* finger] **1 :** one of the five terminating members of the hand **:** a digit of the forelimb; *esp* **:** one other than the thumb **2 a :** something that resembles a finger <a narrow ~ of land extending into the sea> **b :** a part of a glove into which a finger is inserted **c :** a projecting piece (as a pawl for a ratchet) brought into contact with an object to affect its motion **3 :** the breadth of a finger **4 :** INTEREST, SHARE — often used in the phrase *to have a finger in the pie* — **fin·ger·like** \-ˌlīk\ *adj*

[2]**finger** *vb* **fin·gered; fin·ger·ing** \-g(ə-)riŋ\ *vt* **1 a :** to play (a musical instrument) with the fingers **b :** to play (as notes or chords) with a specific fingering **c :** to mark the notes of (a music score) as a guide in playing **2 :** to touch or feel with the fingers **:** HANDLE **3 :** to point out **:** IDENTIFY **4 :** to extend into or penetrate in the shape of a finger ~ *vi* **1 :** to touch or handle something <~*s* through the cards> **2 a :** to use the fingers in playing a musical instrument **b :** to have a certain fingering — used of a musical instrument <~*s* like a clarinet> **3 :** to extend in the shape or manner of a finger

fin·ger·board \ˈfiŋ-gər-ˌbō(ə)rd, -ˌbȯ(ə)rd\ *n* **:** the part of a stringed instrument against which the fingers press the strings to vary the pitch — see VIOLIN illustration

finger bowl *n* **:** a small water bowl for rinsing the fingers at the table

fin·gered \ˈfiŋ-gərd\ *adj* **1 :** having fingers esp. of a specified kind or number — used in combination <stubby-*fingered*> <five-*fingered*> **2 :** having projections or processes like fingers <a ~ cranberry scoop>

finger hole *n* **1 :** any of several holes in the side of a wind instrument (as a recorder) which may be covered or left open by the fingers to change the pitch of the tone **2 :** a hole (as in a telephone dial or a bowling ball) into which the finger is placed to provide a grip

fin·ger·ing \ˈfiŋ-g(ə-)riŋ\ *n* **1 :** the act or process of handling or touching with the fingers **2 a :** the act or method of using the fingers in playing an instrument **b :** the marking (as by figures on a musical score) of the method of fingering

fin·ger·ling \ˈfiŋ-gər-liŋ\ *n* **:** a small fish esp. up to one year of age

fin·ger·nail \ˈfiŋ-gər-ˌnāl, ˌfiŋ-gər-ˈnā(ə)l\ *n* **:** the nail of a finger

finger painting *n* **1 :** a technique of spreading pigment on wet paper chiefly with the fingers **2 :** a picture produced by finger painting

fin·ger·post \ˈfiŋ-gər-ˌpōst\ *n* **1 :** a post bearing one or more signs often terminating in a pointing finger **2 :** something serving as a guide to understanding or knowledge

fin·ger·print \-ˌprint\ *n* **1 :** the impression of a fingertip on any surface; *esp* **:** an ink impression of the lines upon the fingertip taken for purpose of identification **2 :** the chromatogram or electrophoretogram obtained by cleaving a protein by enzymatic action and subjecting the resulting collection of peptides to two-dimensional chromatography or electrophoresis — **fingerprint** *vt* — **fin·ger·print·ing** *n*

fingerprints 1: *1* arch, *2* loop, *3* whorl, *4* composite

[1]**fin·ger·tip** \-ˌtip\ *n* **1 :** the tip of a finger **2 :** a protective covering for the end of a finger — **at one's fingertips :** instantly or readily available

[2]**fingertip** *adj* **1 :** extending from head or shoulders to mid-thigh — used of clothing **2 :** readily accessible **:** being in close proximity <~ information> <~ controls>

finger wave *n* **:** a method of setting hair by dampening with water or wave solution and forming waves or curls with the fingers and a comb

fin·i·al \ˈfin-ē-əl\ *n* [ME, fr. *final, finial* final] **1 :** a usu. foliated ornament forming an upper extremity esp. in Gothic architecture **2 :** a crowning ornament or detail (as a decorative knob)

fin·i·cal \ˈfin-i-kəl\ *adj* [prob. fr. [3]*fine*] **:** FINICKY ***syn*** see NICE — **fin·i·cal·ly** \-k(ə-)lē\ *adv* — **fin·i·cal·ness** \-kəl-nəs\ *n*

fin·ick·ing \-kiŋ, -kən\ *adj* [alter. of *finical*] **:** FINICKY

fin·icky \ˈfin-i-kē\ *adj* [alter. of *finicking*] **:** excessively nice, exacting, or meticulous in taste or standards ***syn*** see NICE — **fin·icki·ness** *n*

fi·nis \ˈfin-əs, ˈfī-nəs\ *n* [ME, fr. L] **:** END, CONCLUSION

[1]**fin·ish** \ˈfin-ish\ *vb* [ME *finisshen,* fr. MF *finiss-,* stem of *finir,* fr. L *finire,* fr. *finis*] *vt* **1 a :** to bring to an end **:** TERMINATE <~*ed* his speech and sat down> **b :** to use or dispose of entirely <her sandwich ~*ed* the loaf> **2 a :** to bring to completion or issue **:** PERFECT <hope to ~ their new home before winter> **b :** to

provide with a finish; *esp* : to put a final coat or surface on <~ a table with varnish> **3 a** : to bring to an end the significance or effectiveness of <the scandal ~*ed* his career> **b** : to bring about the death of ~ *vi* **1** : to come to an end : TERMINATE **2** : to come to the end of a course, task, or undertaking **3** : to end a competition in a specified manner or position <~*ed* third in the race> ***syn*** see CLOSE — **fin·ish·er** *n*

finial 2

²**finish** *n* **1 a** : the final stage : END **b** : the cause of one's ruin **2** : something that completes or perfects: as **a** : the fine or decorative work required for a building or one of its parts **b** : a finishing material used in painting **c** : the final treatment or coating of a surface **3** : the result or product of a finishing process **4** : the quality or state of being perfected

fin·ished *adj* : marked by the highest quality : CONSUMMATE

finishing school *n* : a private school for girls that emphasizes cultural studies and prepares students esp. for social activities

finish line *n* : a line marking the end of a racecourse

fi·nite \'fī-ˌnīt\ *adj* [ME *finit*, fr. L *finitus*, pp. of *finire*] **1 a** : having definite or definable limits <~ number of possibilities> <a ~ community> **b** : having a limited nature of existence <~ beings> **2** : completely determinable in theory or in fact by counting, measurement, or thought : neither infinite nor infinitesimal <a ~ distance> <the ~ velocity of light> **3 a** : less than an arbitrary positive integer and greater than the negative of that integer **b** : having a finite number of elements <a ~ set> **4** : showing distinction of grammatical person and number in a verb or verb form — **finite** *n* — **fi·nite·ly** *adv* — **fi·nite·ness** *n*

fi·ni·tude \'fī-nə-ˌt(y)üd, 'fin-ə-\ *n* : finite quality or state

fink \'fiŋk\ *n* [origin unknown] **1** : INFORMER 2 **2** : STRIKEBREAKER **3** : one who is disapproved of or is held in contempt

fink out *vi* **1** : to fail miserably **2** : to back out : cop out

¹**Finn** \'fin\ *n* [Sw *Finne*] **1** : a member of a people speaking Finnish or a Finnic language **2 a** : a native or inhabitant of Finland **b** : one who is of Finnish descent

²**Finn** *abbr* Finnish

fin·nan had·die \ˌfin-ən-'had-ē\ *n* [*finnan* alter. of *findon*, fr. *Findon*, Scotland] : smoked haddock — called also *finnan haddock*

Fin·nic \'fin-ik\ *adj* **1** : of or relating to the Finns **2** : of, relating to, or constituting the branch of the Finno-Ugric subfamily of the Uralic family of languages that includes Finnish, Estonian, and Lapp

¹**Finn·ish** \'fin-ish\ *adj* : of, relating to, or characteristic of Finland, the Finns, or Finnish

²**Finnish** *n* : a Finno-Ugric language spoken in Finland, Karelia, and small areas of Sweden and Norway

Fin·no–Ugric \ˌfin-ō-'(y)ü-grik\ *adj* **1** : of or relating to any of various peoples of northern and eastern Europe and northwestern Siberia speaking related languages and including the Finnish, Hungarian, and Bulgarian peoples and the Lapps and Estonians **2** : of, relating to, or constituting a subfamily of the Uralic family of languages comprising various languages spoken in Hungary, Lapland, Finland, Estonia, and northwestern U.S.S.R. — **Finno–Ugric** *n*

fin·ny \'fin-ē\ *adj* **1** : provided with or characterized by fins **2** : relating to or being fish

fin sec *abbr* financial secretary

FIO *abbr* free in and out

fiord *var of* FJORD

fio·ri·tu·ra \fē-ˌor-ə-'tùr-ə\ *n, pl* **-tu·re** \-'tùr-ē\ [It, lit., flowering, fr. *fiorito*, pp. of *fiorire* to flower, fr. (assumed) VL *florire* — more at FLOURISH] : ORNAMENT 5

fip·ple flute \ˌfip-əl-\ *n* [origin unknown] : a tubular wind instrument (as a flageolet, pipe, or recorder) characterized mainly by a whistle mouthpiece and finger holes

¹**fir** \'fər\ *n* [ME, fr. OE *fyrh*; akin to OHG *forha* fir, L *quercus* oak] **1** : any of a genus (*Abies*) of north temperate evergreen trees of the pine family that have flattish leaves, smooth circular leaf scars, and erect cones and are valued for their wood; *also* : any of various conifers (as the Douglas fir) of other genera **2** : the wood of a fir

²**fir** *abbr* firkin

¹**fire** \'fī(ə)r\ *n, often attrib* [ME, fr. OE *fȳr*; akin to OHG *fiur* fire, Gk *pyr*] **1 a** (1) : the phenomenon of combustion manifested in light, flame, and heat (2) : one of the four elements of the alchemists **b** (1) : burning passion : ARDOR (2) : liveliness of imagination : INSPIRATION **2** : fuel in a state of combustion (as on a hearth) **3 a** : a destructive burning (as of a building) **b** (1) : death or torture by fire (2) : severe trial or ordeal **4** : BRILLIANCY, LUMINOSITY <the ~ of a gem> **5 a** : the discharge of firearms **b** : intense verbal attack **c** : a rapidly delivered series (as of remarks) — **fire·less** \-ləs\ *adj* — **on fire** : EAGER, BURNING — **under fire** **1** : exposed to the firing of an enemy's weapons **2** : under attack

²**fire** *vb* **fired; fir·ing** *vt* **1 a** : to set on fire : KINDLE; *also* : IGNITE <~ a rocket engine> **b** (1) : to give life or spirit to : INSPIRE (2) : to fill with passion : INFLAME **c** : to light up as if by fire **2 a** : to drive out or away by or as if by fire **b** : to dismiss from a position **3 a** (1) : to cause to explode : DETONATE (2) : to propel from or as if from a gun : DISCHARGE, LAUNCH <~ a rocket> (3) : to score (a number) in a game or contest **b** : to throw with speed : HURL **c** : to utter with force and rapidity **4** : to apply fire or fuel to: as **a** : to process by applying heat **b** : to feed or serve the fire of ~ *vi* **1 a** : to take fire : KINDLE, IGNITE **b** *of an internal-combustion engine* : to have the explosive charge ignite at the proper time **2 a** : to become irritated or angry — often used with *up* **b** : to become filled with excitement or enthusiasm **3 a** : to discharge a firearm **b** : to emit or let fly an object **4** : to tend a fire ***syn*** see LIGHT — **fir·er** *n*

fire ant *n* : any of a genus (*Solenopsis*) of fiercely stinging omnivorous ants; *esp* : IMPORTED FIRE ANT

fire·arm \'fī(ə)r-ˌärm\ *n* : a weapon from which a shot is discharged by gunpowder — usu. used only of small arms

fire·ball \'fī(ə)r-ˌbȯl\ *n* **1** : a ball of fire; *also* : something resembling such a ball <the primordial ~ associated with the beginning of the universe —*Scientific American*> **2** : a brilliant meteor that may trail bright sparks **3** : the highly luminous cloud of vapor and dust created by a nuclear explosion **4** : a highly energetic person : HUSTLER

fire·bird \-ˌbərd\ *n* : any of several small birds (as the Baltimore oriole or the scarlet tanager) having brilliant orange or red plumage

fire blight *n* : a destructive highly infectious disease of apples, pears, and related fruits caused by a bacterium (*Erwinia amylovora*)

fire·boat \'fī(ə)r-ˌbōt\ *n* : a ship equipped with fire-fighting apparatus

fire·bomb \-ˌbäm\ *n* : an incendiary bomb — **firebomb** *vt*

fire·box \-ˌbäks\ *n* **1** : a chamber (as of a furnace or steam boiler) that contains a fire **2** : a box containing an apparatus for transmitting an alarm to a fire station

fire·brand \-ˌbrand\ *n* **1** : a piece of burning wood **2** : one that creates unrest or strife : AGITATOR

fire·break \-ˌbrāk\ *n* : a barrier of cleared or plowed land intended to check a forest or grass fire

fire·brick \-ˌbrik\ *n* : a refractory brick capable of sustaining high temperature that is used esp. for lining furnaces or fireplaces

fire brigade *n* : a body of fire fighters: as **a** : a private, institutional, or temporary fire-fighting organization **b** *Brit* : FIRE DEPARTMENT

fire·bug \'fī(ə)r-ˌbəg\ *n* : INCENDIARY, PYROMANIAC

fire·clay \-ˌklā\ *n* : clay capable of withstanding high temperatures that is used esp. for firebrick and crucibles

fire control *n* **1** : the planning, preparation, and delivery of gunfire on targets **2** : the control or extinction of fires

fire·crack·er \'fī(ə)r-ˌkrak-ər\ *n* : a usu. paper cylinder containing an explosive and a fuse and usu. discharged to make a noise

fire–cured \-'kyù(ə)rd\ *adj* : cured over open fires in direct contact with the smoke <~ tobacco> — compare FLUE-CURED

fire·damp \-ˌdamp\ *n* : a combustible mine gas that consists chiefly of methane; *also* : the explosive mixture of this gas with air

fire department *n* **1** : an organization for preventing or extinguishing fires; *esp* : a government division (as in a municipality) having these duties **2** : the members of a fire department

fire·drake \'fī(ə)r-ˌdrāk\ *n* [ME *firdrake*, fr. OE *fȳrdraca*, fr. *fȳr* + *draca* dragon — more at DRAKE] : a fire-breathing dragon esp. in Teutonic mythology

fire drill *n* : a practice drill in extinguishing fires or in the conduct and manner of exit in case of fire

fire–eat·er \'fī(ə)r-ˌēt-ər\ *n* **1** : a performer who pretends to eat fire **2 a** : a violent or pugnacious person **b** : one who displays very militant or aggressive partisanship (as on political questions)

fire–eat·ing \-ˌēt-iŋ\ *adj* : violent or highly militant in disposition, bearing, or policy <a ~ radical>

fire engine *n* : a usu. mobile apparatus for directing an extinguishing agent upon fires

fire escape *n* : a device for escape from a burning building; *esp* : a metal stairway attached to the outside of a building

fire extinguisher *n* : a portable or wheeled apparatus for putting out small fires by ejecting fire-extinguishing chemicals

fire·fight \'fī(ə)r-ˌfīt\ *n* : an often spontaneous exchange of fire between opposing military units

fire fighter *n* : one who fights fires : FIREMAN 1 — **fire fighting** *n*

fire·fly \'fī(ə)r-ˌflī\ *n* : any of various winged nocturnal beetles (esp. family Lampyridae) that produce a bright soft intermittent light by oxidation of luciferin esp. for courtship purposes

fire·guard \-ˌgärd\ *n* **1** : FIRE SCREEN **2** : FIREBREAK **3** : one who watches for the outbreak of fire; *also* : one whose duty is to extinguish fires

fire hall *n* : FIRE STATION

fire·house \'fī(ə)r-ˌhaùs\ *n* : FIRE STATION

fire irons *n pl* : utensils (as tongs) for tending a fire esp. in a fireplace

fire·light \'fī(ə)r-ˌlīt\ *n* : the light of a fire (as in a fireplace)

fire·lock \-ˌläk\ *n* **1** : a gunlock employing a slow match to ignite the powder charge; *also* : a gun having such a lock **2 a** : FLINTLOCK **b** : WHEEL LOCK

fire·man \-mən\ *n* **1** : a member of a company organized to fight fires : FIRE FIGHTER **2** : one who tends or feeds fires : STOKER **3** : an enlisted man in the navy who works with engineering machinery **4** : a relief pitcher in baseball

fire opal *n* : GIRASOL 2

fire·place \'fī(ə)r-ˌplās\ *n* **1** : a framed opening made in a chimney to hold an open fire : HEARTH; *also* : a metal container with a smoke pipe used for the same purpose **2** : an outdoor structure of brick, stone, or metal for an open fire

fire·plug \-ˌpləg\ *n* : HYDRANT

fire·pow·er \-ˌpaù(-ə)r\ *n* **1** : the capacity (as of a military unit) to deliver effective fire on a target **2** : the aggregate of effective missiles that can be placed upon a target **3** : the scoring action or potential of a team

¹**fire·proof** \-'prüf\ *adj* : proof against or resistant to fire

²**fireproof** *vt* : to make fireproof

fire·room \'fī(ə)r-ˌrüm, -ˌrùm\ *n* : STOKEHOLD 2

fire sale *n* : a sale of merchandise damaged in a fire

fire screen *n* : a protective and often ornamental screen before a fireplace

fire ship *n* **:** a ship carrying combustibles or explosives sent among the enemy's ships or works to set them on fire
1**fire·side** \ˈfī(ə)r-ˌsīd\ *n* **1 :** a place near the fire or hearth **2 :** HOME
2**fireside** *adj* **:** having an informal or intimate quality <a report written in ~ language> <a ~ chat>
fire station *n* **:** a building housing fire apparatus and usu. firemen
fire·stone \ˈfī(ə)r-ˌstōn\ *n* **1 :** pyrite formerly used for striking fire; *also* **:** FLINT **2 :** a stone that will endure high heat
fire–stop \-ˌstäp\ *n* **:** material used to close open parts of a structure (as a building) for preventing the spread of fire — **fire–stop** *vt*
fire tower *n* **:** a tower (as in a forest) from which a watch for fires is maintained
fire·trap \ˈfī(ə)r-ˌtrap\ *n* **:** a place (as a building) apt to catch on fire or difficult to escape from in case of fire
fire truck *n* **:** an automotive vehicle equipped with fire-fighting apparatus
fire wall *n* **:** a wall constructed to prevent the spread of fire
fire·wa·ter \ˈfī(ə)r-ˌwȯt-ər, -ˌwät-\ *n* **:** strong alcoholic beverage
fire·weed \-ˌwēd\ *n* **:** any of several plants that grow esp. in clearings or burned districts: as **a :** a weedy composite (*Erechtites hieracifolia*) that has clusters of brush-shaped flower heads with no ray flowers **b :** a tall perennial (*Epilobium angustifolium*) of the evening-primrose family that has long spikes of pinkish purple flowers and is an important honey plant in some areas — called also *willow herb*
fire·wood \-ˌwu̇d\ *n* **:** wood cut for fuel
fire·work \-ˌwərk\ *n* **1 :** a device for producing a striking display (as of light, noise, or smoke) by the combustion of explosive or flammable compositions **2** *pl* **:** a display of fireworks **3** *pl* **a :** a display of temper or intense conflict **b :** a spectacular display (as of artistic brilliance) <~*s* of virtuosity>
fir·ing \ˈfī(ə)r-iŋ\ *n* **1 :** the act or process of one that fires **2 :** the process of maturing ceramic products by the application of heat **3 :** FIREWOOD, FUEL **4 :** the scorching of plants esp. by unfavorable soil conditions
firing line *n* **1 :** a line from which fire is delivered against a target **2 :** the forefront of an activity — used esp. in the phrase *on the firing line*
firing pin *n* **:** the pin that strikes the cartridge primer in the breech mechanism of a firearm
firing squad *n* **1 :** a detachment detailed to fire volleys over the grave of one buried with military honors **2 :** a detachment detailed to carry out a sentence of death by shooting
fir·kin \ˈfər-kən\ *n* [ME, deriv. of MD *veerdel* fourth] **1 :** a small wooden vessel or cask **2 :** any of various British units of capacity usu. equal to ¼ barrel
1**firm** \ˈfərm\ *adj* [ME *ferm,* fr. MF, fr. L *firmus;* akin to Gk *thronos* chair, throne] **1 a :** securely or solidly fixed in place **b :** not weak or uncertain **:** VIGOROUS **c :** having a solid or compact structure that resists stress or pressure **2 a** (1) **:** not subject to change or revision **:** SET, DEFINITE <they gave us a ~ price> (2) **:** not subject to price weakness **:** STEADY **b :** not easily moved or disturbed **:** STEADFAST **c :** WELL-FOUNDED **3 :** indicating firmness or resolution <a ~ mouth> — **firm·ly** *adv* — **firm·ness** *n*
syn FIRM, HARD, SOLID *shared meaning element* **:** having a texture or consistency that resists deformation. FIRM implies such compactness and coherence and often elasticity of substance as provides resistance to pulling, distorting, cutting, or displacement <a *firm* close-woven cloth> <*firm* healthy flesh> <the ground was *firm* enough to walk on> HARD implies inpenetrability or strong resistance to pressure or tension but not elasticity <diamond is one of the *hardest* of substances> SOLID implies such density and coherence as enable a thing to maintain a fixed form in spite of external deforming forces <ice is a *solid* form of water> In extended use FIRM stresses stability, fixedness, or resolution <a *firm* disciplinarian> <his purpose is *firm*> HARD implies obduracy or lack of normal responsiveness <a *hard* man to do business with> SOLID typically implies substantiality or genuineness <demand *solid* facts> <lived in *solid* comfort> or it may imply complete reliability <one of the most *solid* citizens of the community> or sometimes unbroken continuity (as in time, feeling, or opinion) <there had been a *solid* week of rain> ***ant*** loose, flabby
2**firm** *vt* **1 a :** to make secure or fast **:** TIGHTEN <~*ing* his grip on the racquet> — often used with *up* **b :** to make solid or compact <~ the soil> **2 :** to put into final form **:** SETTLE <~ a contract> — often used with *up* **3 :** to give additional support to **:** STRENGTHEN — usu. used with *up* <help ~ up the French franc —Herbert Harris> ~ *vi* **1 :** to become firm **:** HARDEN <his face ~*ed* and he spoke with restrained anger> — often used with *up* <his opinions have not yet ~*ed* up> **2 :** to recover from a decline **:** IMPROVE <the market ~*ed* slightly> — often used with *up*
3**firm** *n* [G *firma,* fr. It, signature, deriv. of L *firmare* to make firm, confirm, fr. *firmus*] **1 :** the name or title under which a company transacts business **2 :** a partnership of two or more persons not recognized as a legal person distinct from the members composing it **3 :** a business unit or enterprise
fir·ma·ment \ˈfər-mə-mənt\ *n* [ME, fr. LL & L; LL *firmamentum,* fr. L, support, fr. *firmare*] **1 :** the vault or arch of the sky **:** HEAVENS **2** *obs* **:** BASIS — **fir·ma·men·tal** \ˌfər-mə-ˈment-ᵊl\ *adj*
fir·mer chisel \ˈfər-mər-\ *n* [F *fermoir* chisel, alter. of MF *formoir,* fr. *former* to form] **:** a woodworking chisel with a thin flat blade — see CHISEL illustration
firn \ˈfi(ə)rn\ *n* [G] **:** NÉVÉ
1**first** \ˈfərst\ *adj* [ME, fr. OE *fyrst;* akin to OHG *furist* first, OE *faran* to go — more at FARE] **:** preceding all others in time, order, or importance: as **a :** EARLIEST **b :** being the lowest forward gear or speed of a motor vehicle **c :** relating to or having the highest or most prominent part among a group of similar voices or instruments in concerted or ensemble music <~ tenor> <~ violins>
2**first** *adv* **1 a :** before another in time, space, or importance <~ we had cocktails> — often used with *off* <~ off he thanked us for the invitation> **b :** for the first time **2 :** in preference to something else **:** SOONER
3**first** *n* **1** — see NUMBER table **2 :** something that is first: as **a :** the first occurrence or item of a kind **b :** the first forward gear or speed of a motor vehicle **c :** the highest or chief voice or instrument of a group **d :** an article of commerce of the finest grade **e :** the winning or highest place in a competition, examination, or contest **3 :** FIRST BASE — **at first :** at the beginning **:** INITIALLY
first aid *n* **:** emergency care or treatment given to an ill or injured person before regular medical aid can be obtained
first base *n* **1 :** the base that must be touched first by a base runner in baseball **2 :** the player position for defending the area around first base **3 :** the first step or stage in a course of action <his plan never got to *first base*> — **first baseman** *n*
first·born \ˈfərs(t)-ˈbȯ(ə)rn\ *adj* **:** first brought forth **:** ELDEST — **firstborn** *n*
first cause *n* **:** the self-created source of all causality
first class *n* **:** the first or highest group in a classification: as **a :** the highest of usu. three classes of travel accommodations **b :** a class of mail that comprises letters, postcards, or matter sealed against inspection — **first–class** *adj or adv*
first class·man \ˈfərs(t)-ˈklas-mən\ *n* **:** a fourth-year student in a military school (as West Point)
first consonant shift *n* **:** CONSONANT SHIFT a
first day cover *n* **:** a philatelic cover franked with a newly issued postage stamp and postmarked on the first day of issue at a city officially chosen for first day sale
first–degree burn *n* **:** a mild burn characterized by heat, pain, and reddening of the burned surface but not exhibiting blistering or charring of tissues
first down *n* **1 :** the first of a series of four downs in which a football team must net a 10-yard gain to retain possession of the ball **2 :** a gain of a total of 10 or more yards within four downs giving the team the right to start a new series of downs
first edition *n* **1 a :** the copies of a literary work first printed from the same type and issued at the same time **b :** the first pressrun of a newspaper for a given date **2 :** a single copy from a first edition
first estate *n, often cap F&E* **:** the first of the traditional political estates; *specif* **:** CLERGY
first floor *n* **1 :** GROUND FLOOR **2** *Brit* **:** the floor next above the ground floor
first·fruits \ˈfərs(t)-ˈfrüts\ *n pl* **1 :** the earliest gathered fruits offered to the Deity in acknowledgment of the gift of fruitfulness **2 :** the earliest products or results of an endeavor
first·hand \ˈfərst-ˈhand\ *adj* **:** coming directly from the original source — **firsthand** *adv*
first lady *n, often cap F&L* **1 :** the wife or hostess of the chief executive of a country or jurisdiction **2 :** the leading woman of an art or profession
first lieutenant *n* **1 :** a commissioned officer in the army, air force, or marine corps ranking above a second lieutenant and below a captain **2 :** a naval officer responsible for a ship's upkeep
first·ling \ˈfərst-liŋ\ *n* **1 :** the first of a class or kind **2 :** the first produce or result of something
first·ly \-lē\ *adv* **:** in the first place **:** FIRST
first mortgage *n* **:** a mortgage that has priority as a lien over all mortgages and liens except those imposed by law
first name *n* **:** the name that stands first in one's full name
first night *n* **1 :** the night on which a theatrical production is first performed at a given place **2 :** the performance given on a first night
first–night·er \ˈfərs(t)-ˈnīt-ər\ *n* **:** a spectator at a first-night performance
first offender *n* **:** one legally convicted of an offense for the first time
first papers *n pl* **:** papers declaring intention filed by an applicant for citizenship as the first step in the naturalization process
first person *n* **1 a :** a set of linguistic forms (as verb forms, pronouns, and inflectional affixes) referring to the speaker or writer of the utterance in which they occur **b :** a linguistic form belonging to such a set **c :** reference of a linguistic form to the speaker or writer of the utterance in which it occurs **2 :** a style of discourse marked by general use of verbs and pronouns of the first person <a novel narrated in the *first person*>
1**first–rate** \ˈfər-ˈstrāt\ *adj* **:** of the first order of size, importance, or quality — **first–rate·ness** *n* — **first–rat·er** \-ˈstrāt-ər\ *n*
2**first–rate** *adv* **:** very well
First Reader *n* **:** a Christian Scientist chosen to conduct meetings for a specified time and specif. to read aloud from the writings of Mary Baker Eddy
first reading *n* **:** the first submitting of a bill before a quorum of a legislative assembly usu. by title or number only
first sergeant *n* **1 :** a noncommissioned officer serving as the chief assistant to the commander of a military unit (as a company or squadron) **2 :** the rank of a first sergeant; *specif* **:** a rank in the army above a platoon sergeant and below a command sergeant major and in the marine corps above a gunnery sergeant and below a sergeant major
first–string \ˈfərs(t)-ˈstriŋ\ *adj* **1 :** being a regular as distinguished from a substitute (as on a football team) **2 :** FIRST-RATE
first water *n* **1 :** the purest luster — used of gems **2 :** the highest grade, degree, or quality <this is choral music of the *first water* —P. H. Lang>
firth \ˈfərth\ *n* [ME, fr. ON *fjörthr* — more at FORD] **:** ESTUARY
fisc \ˈfisk\ *n* [L *fiscus*] **:** a state or royal treasury
1**fis·cal** \ˈfis-kəl\ *adj* [L *fiscalis,* fr. *fiscus* basket, treasury; akin to Gk *pithos* wine jar] **1 :** of or relating to taxation, public revenues, or public debt <~ policy> **2 :** of or relating to financial matters <~ agent> ***syn*** see FINANCIAL — **fis·cal·ly** \-kə-lē\ *adv*
2**fiscal** *n* **:** REVENUE STAMP
fiscal year *n* **:** an accounting period of 12 months

[1]**fish** \ˈfish\ *n, pl* **fish** *or* **fish·es** *often attrib* [ME, fr. OE *fisc;* akin to OHG *fisc* fish, L *piscis*] **1 a :** an aquatic animal — usu. used in combination <star*fish*> <cuttle*fish*> **b :** any of numerous cold-blooded strictly aquatic craniate vertebrates that have typically an elongated somewhat spindle-shaped body terminating in a broad caudal fin, limbs in the form of fins when present at all, and a 2-chambered heart by which blood is sent through thoracic gills to be oxygenated **c** *fishes pl, cap* **:** PISCES **2 :** the flesh of fish used as food **3 :** FELLOW, CHAP <a queer ~> **4 :** something that resembles a fish: as **a :** a purchase used to fish the anchor **b :** a piece of wood or iron fastened alongside another member to strengthen it — **fish·less** \ˈfish-ləs\ *adj* — **fish·like** \-ˌlīk\ *adj* — **fish out of water :** a person who is out of his proper sphere or element — **neither fish nor fowl :** one that does not belong to a particular class or category

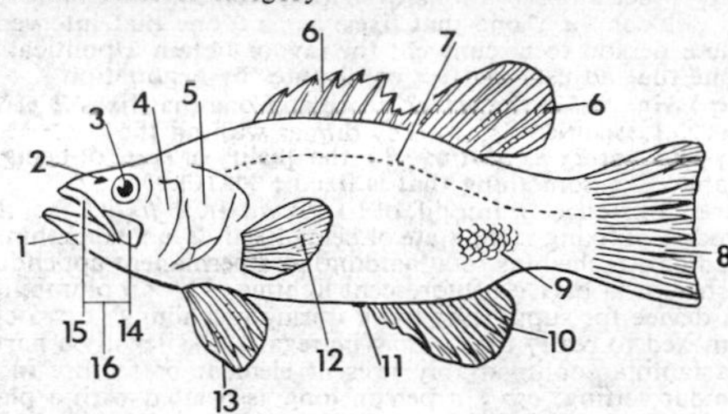

fish 1b: *1* mandible, *2* external naris, *3* eye, *4* cheek, *5* operculum, *6* dorsal fins, *7* lateral line, *8* caudal fin, *9* scales, *10* anal fin, *11* anus, *12* pectoral fin, *13* pelvic fin, *14* maxilla, *15* premaxilla, *16* upper jaw

[2]**fish** *vi* **1 :** to attempt to catch fish **2 :** to seek something by round-about means <~*ing* for praise> **3 a :** to search for something underwater (as with a dredge) <~ for pearls> **b :** to engage in a search by groping or feeling <~*ing* around in her purse for her keys> ~ *vt* **1 a :** to try to catch fish in <~ the stream> **b :** to fish with **:** use (as a boat, net, or bait) in fishing **2 a :** to catch or try to catch **b :** to draw forth as if fishing <~*ed* the ball from under the car> — **fish or cut bait :** to make a choice between alternatives

fish·able \ˈfish-ə-bəl\ *adj* **:** suitable, promising, or legally open for fishing — **fish·abil·i·ty** \ˌfish-ə-ˈbil-ət-ē\ *n*

fish–and–chips \ˌfish-ən-ˈchips\ *n pl* **:** fried fish and french fried potatoes

fish·bone \ˈfish-ˌbōn\ *n* **:** a bone of a fish

fish·bowl \-ˌbōl\ *n* **1 :** a bowl for the keeping of live fish **2 :** a place or condition that affords no privacy

fish cake *n* **:** a round fried cake made of shredded fish and mashed potato

fish duck *n* **:** MERGANSER

fish·er \ˈfish-ər\ *n* **1 :** one that fishes **2 a :** a large dark brown No. American arboreal carnivorous mammal (*Martes pennanti*) related to the weasels **b :** the fur or pelt of this animal

fish·er·man \-mən\ *n* **1 :** one who engages in fishing as an occupation or for pleasure **2 :** a ship used in commercial fishing

fisherman's bend *n* **:** a knot made by passing the end twice round a spar or through a ring and then back under both turns — see KNOT illustration

fish·ery \ˈfish-(ə-)rē\ *n, pl* **-er·ies 1 :** the act, process, occupation, or season of taking fish or other sea animals (as sponges or seals) **:** FISHING **2 :** a place for catching fish or taking other sea animals (as sponges or seals) **3 :** a fishing establishment; *also* **:** its fishermen **4 :** the legal right to take fish at a particular place or in particular waters **5 :** the technology of fishery — usu. used in pl.

fisher 2a

fish–eye \ˈfish-ˌī\ *adj* **:** being, having, or produced by a wide-angle photographic lens that has a highly curved protruding front, that covers an angle of about 180 degrees, and that gives a circular image <a ~ lens>

fish fry *n* **1 :** a meal (as a picnic) featuring fried fish **2 :** fried fish

fish hawk *n* **:** OSPREY 1

fish·hook \ˈfish-ˌhu̇k\ *n* **:** a usu. barbed hook for catching fish

fish·ing *n* **1 :** the sport or business of catching fish **2 :** a place for catching fish

fishing expedition *n* **1 :** a legal interrogation or examination to discover information for a later proceeding **2 :** an investigation that does not stick to a stated objective and that uses questionable methods (as the irrelevant questioning of witnesses) in hope of uncovering incriminating or newsworthy evidence

fish joint *n* **:** a butt joint of timbers or rails in which the two abutting members are held in alignment by one or more fishplates

fish ladder *n* **:** a series of pools arranged like steps by which fishes can pass over a dam in going upstream

fish meal *n* **:** ground dried fish and fish waste used as fertilizer and animal food

fish·mong·er \ˈfish-ˌməŋ-gər, -ˌmäŋ-\ *n, chiefly Brit* **:** a fish dealer

fish·net \-ˌnet\ *n* **1 :** netting fitted with floats and weights or a supporting frame for catching fish **2 :** a coarse open-mesh fabric

fish out *vt* **:** to exhaust the supply of fish in by fishing <this lake has been *fished out*>

fish·plate \-ˌplāt\ *n* **:** a steel plate used to lap a butt joint

fish protein concentrate *n* **:** a protein-rich food additive obtained as a nearly colorless and tasteless powder from ground whole fish — abbr. *FPC*

fish stick *n* **:** a small elongated breaded fillet of fish

fish story *n* [fr. the traditional exaggeration by fishermen of the size of fish almost caught] **:** an extravagant or incredible story

fish·tail \ˈfish-ˌtāl\ *vi* **1 :** to swing the tail of an airplane from side to side to reduce speed esp. when landing **2 :** to have the rear end slide from side to side out of control while moving forward <the car ~*ed* on the icy curve>

fish·way \-ˌwā\ *n* **:** a contrivance for enabling fish to pass around a fall or dam in a stream; *specif* **:** FISH LADDER

fish·wife \-ˌwīf\ *n* **1 :** a woman who sells fish **2 :** a vulgar abusive woman

fishy \ˈfish-ē\ *adj* **fish·i·er; -est 1 :** of or resembling fish esp. in taste or odor **2 :** creating doubt or suspicion **:** QUESTIONABLE

fishy·back \-ˌbak\ *n* [*fish* + *-y* + *-back* (as in *piggyback*)] **:** the movement of truck trailers or freight containers by barge or ship — compare BIRDYBACK, PIGGYBACK

fis·sile \ˈfis-əl, ˈfis-ˌīl\ *adj* **1 :** capable of being split or divided in the direction of the grain or along natural planes of cleavage <~ wood> <~ crystals> **2 :** FISSIONABLE — **fis·sil·i·ty** \fis-ˈil-ət-ē\ *n*

[1]**fis·sion** \ˈfish-ən *also* ˈfizh-\ *n* [L *fission-, fissio,* fr. *fissus,* pp. of *findere* to split — more at BITE] **1 :** a splitting or breaking up into parts **2 :** reproduction by spontaneous division of the body into two or more parts each of which grows into a complete organism **3 a :** the splitting of a molecule into simpler molecules **b :** the splitting of an atomic nucleus resulting in the release of large amounts of energy — **fis·sion·al** \-ᵊl\ *adj*

[2]**fission** *vb* **fis·sioned; fis·sion·ing** \ˈfish-(ə-)niŋ, ˈfizh-\ *vt* **:** to cause to undergo fission ~ *vi* **:** to undergo fission

fis·sion·able \ˈfish-(ə-)nə-bəl, ˈfizh-\ *adj* **:** capable of undergoing fission — **fis·sion·abil·i·ty** \ˌfish-(ə-)nə-ˈbil-ət-ē, ˌfizh-\ *n* — **fissionable** *n*

fission bomb *n* **:** ATOM BOMB 1

fis·sip·a·rous \fis-ˈip-ə-rəs\ *adj* [L *fissus* + E *-parous*] **1 :** producing new biological units or individuals by fission **2 :** tending to break up into parts **:** DIVISIVE <he knows how to reconcile ~ elements in his party —W. H. Stevenson> — **fis·sip·a·rous·ly** *adv* — **fis·sip·a·rous·ness** *n*

fis·si·ped \ˈfis-ə-ˌped\ *adj* [LL *fissiped-, fissipes,* fr. L *fissus* + *ped-, pes* foot — more at FOOT] **:** of or relating to a suborder (Fissipeda) of carnivores (as cats, dogs, and bears) — **fissiped** *n*

[1]**fis·sure** \ˈfish-ər\ *n* **1 :** a narrow opening or crack of considerable length and depth usu. occurring from some breaking or parting **2 :** a separation or disagreement in thought or viewpoint **:** SCHISM <~*s* in a political party> **3 a :** a natural cleft between body parts or in the substance of an organ **b :** a break or lesion in tissue usu. at the junction of skin and mucous membrane

[2]**fissure** *vb* **fis·sured; fis·sur·ing** *vt* **:** to break into fissures **:** CLEAVE ~ *vi* **:** CRACK, DIVIDE

[1]**fist** \ˈfist\ *n* [ME, fr. OE *fȳst;* akin to OHG *fūst* fist, OSlav *pęstĭ*] **1 :** the hand clenched with the fingers doubled into the palm and the thumb doubled inward across the fingers **2 :** the hand closed as in grasping **:** CLUTCH **3 :** INDEX 5

[2]**fist** *vt* **1 :** to clench into a fist **2 :** to grip with the fist **:** HANDLE

-fist·ed \ˈfis-təd\ *comb form* **:** having (such or so many) fists <two-*fisted*> <tight*fisted*>

fist·fight \ˈfist-ˌfīt\ *n* **:** a usu. spontaneous fight with bare fists

fist·ful \-ˌfu̇l\ *n* **1 :** HANDFUL <a ~ of coins> **2 :** a considerable number <a whole ~ of musicians —Thomas Lask>

fist·ic \ˈfis-tik\ *adj* **:** of or relating to boxing or to fighting with the fists

fist·i·cuffs \ˈfis-ti-ˌkəfs\ *n pl* [alter. of *fisty cuff,* fr. *fisty* (fistic) + *cuff*] **:** a fight with the fists

fist·note \ˈfis(t)-ˌnōt\ *n* **:** matter in a text to which attention is directed by means of an index mark ☞

fis·tu·la \ˈfis(h)-chə-lə\ *n, pl* **-las** *or* **-lae** \-ˌlē, -ˌlī\ [ME, fr. L, pipe, fistula] **:** an abnormal passage leading from an abscess or hollow organ to the body surface or from one hollow organ to another

fis·tu·lous \-ləs\ *adj* **1 :** of, relating to, or having the form or nature of a fistula **2 :** hollow like a pipe or reed

fistulous withers *n pl but sing or pl in constr* **:** a deep-seated chronic inflammation of the withers of the horse in which bloody fluid is discharged

[1]**fit** \ˈfit\ *n* [ME, fr. OE *fitt;* akin to OS *fittea* division of a poem, OHG *fizza* skein] *archaic* **:** a division of a poem or song

[2]**fit** *n* [ME, fr. OE *fitt* strife] **1 a :** a sudden violent attack of a disease (as epilepsy) esp. when marked by convulsions or unconsciousness **:** PAROXYSM **b :** a sudden but transient attack of a physical disturbance **2 :** a sudden burst or flurry (as of activity) <in a ~ of efficiency he answered all his mail in an hour> **3 :** an emotional outburst <a ~ of anger> — **by fits** *or* **by fits and starts :** in an impulsive and irregular manner

[3]**fit** *adj* **fit·ter; fit·test** [ME; akin to ME *fitten*] **1 a (1) :** adapted to an end or design **:** suitable by nature or by art **(2) :** adapted to the environment so as to be capable of surviving **b :** acceptable from a particular viewpoint (as of competence or morality) <not ~ to be a father> **2 a :** put into a suitable state **:** made ready <get the house ~ for company> **b :** being in such a state as to be ready to do or suffer something <fair ~ to cry I was —Bryan MacMahon> **3 :** COMPETENT, QUALIFIED **4 :** sound physically and mentally **:** HEALTHY — **fit·ly** *adv* — **fit·ness** *n*

syn FIT, SUITABLE, MEET, PROPER, APPROPRIATE, FITTING, APT, HAPPY, FELICITOUS *shared meaning element* : right with respect to some end, need, use, or circumstance *ant* unfit
— **fit to be tied** : extremely angry or irritated

4**fit** *vb* **fit·ted** *also* **fit; fit·ting** [ME *fitten,* fr. or akin to MD *vitten* to be suitable; akin to OHG *fizza* skein] *vt* **1 a :** to be suitable for or to : harmonize with **b** *archaic* : to be seemly or proper for <it ~*s* us then to be as provident as fear may teach us —Shak.> **2 a :** to be correctly adjusted to or shaped for **b :** to insert or adjust until correctly in place **c :** to make a place or room for : ACCOMMODATE **3 :** to be in agreement or accord with <the theory ~*s* all the facts> **4 a :** to put into a condition of readiness **b :** to bring to a required form and size : ADJUST **c :** to cause to conform to or suit something **5 :** SUPPLY, EQUIP <*fitted* the ship with new engines> — often used with *out* **6 :** to adjust (a smooth curve of a specified type) to a given set of points ~ *vi* **1** *archaic* : to be seemly, proper, or suitable **2 :** to conform to a particular shape or size **3 :** to be in harmony or accord : BELONG *syn* see PREPARE — **fit·ter** *n*

5**fit** *n* **1 :** the quality, state, or manner of being fitted or adapted **2 :** the manner in which clothing fits the wearer **3 :** the degree of closeness with which surfaces are brought together in an assembly of parts **4 :** the conformity between an experimental result and theoretical expectation or between data and an approximating curve <a statistical test of goodness of ~>

6**fit** *dial past of* FIGHT

fitch \'fich\ *or* **fitch·ew** \'fich-(,)ü\ *n* [ME *fiche, ficheux,* fr. MF or MD; MF *fichau,* fr. MD *vitsau*] **1 :** POLECAT 1 **2 :** the fur or pelt of the polecat

fitch·et \'fich-ət\ *n* : POLECAT 1

fit·ful \'fit-fəl\ *adj* **1** *obs* : characterized by fits or paroxysms **2 :** having a spasmodic or intermittent character : IRREGULAR <~ sleep> — **fit·ful·ly** \-fə-lē\ *adv* — **fit·ful·ness** *n*
syn FITFUL, SPASMODIC, CONVULSIVE *shared meaning element* : lacking steadiness or regularity (as in course, movement, or activity) *ant* constant

fit·ment \'fit-mənt\ *n* [4*fit*] **1 :** EQUIPMENT **2** *pl* : FITTINGS

1**fit·ting** \'fit-iŋ\ *adj* : of a kind appropriate to the situation <made a ~ answer> *syn* see FIT *ant* unfitting — **fit·ting·ly** \-iŋ-lē\ *adv* — **fit·ting·ness** *n*

2**fitting** *n* **1 :** an action or act of one that fits; *specif* : a trying on of clothes which are in the process of being made or altered **2 :** a small often standardized accessory part <a plumbing ~> <an electrical ~>

five \'fīv\ *n* [ME, fr. *five,* adj., fr. OE *fīf;* akin to OHG *finf* five, L *quinque,* Gk *pente*] **1** — see NUMBER table **2 :** the fifth in a set or series <the ~ of clubs> **3 :** something having five units or members; *esp* : a basketball team **4 :** a 5-dollar bill **5 :** FIFTEEN 2 — **five** *adj or pron*

five-and-ten \,fī-vən-'ten\ *also* **five-and-dime** \-'dīm\ *n* [fr. the fact that all articles in such stores were formerly priced at either 5 or 10 cents] : a variety store that carries chiefly inexpensive items

five-fin·ger \'fīv-,fiŋ-gər\ *n* : CINQUEFOIL 1

five·fold \'fīv-,fōld, -'fōld\ *adj* **1 :** having five units or members **2 :** being five times as great or as many — **five·fold** \-'fōld\ *adv*

five of a kind : four cards of the same rank plus a wild card in one hand — see POKER illustration

fiv·er \'fī-vər\ *n* **1** *slang* : a 5-dollar bill **2** *slang* : a 5-pound note

five-star \,fīv-'stär\ *adj* : of first class or quality <there are not enough ~ works of art to go around —J. T. Soby>

1**fix** \'fiks\ *vb* [ME *fixen,* fr. L *fixus,* pp. of *figere* to fasten — more at DIKE] *vt* **1 a :** to make firm, stable, or stationary **b :** to give a permanent or final form to: as **(1) :** to change into a stable compound or available form <bacteria that ~ nitrogen> **(2) :** to kill, harden, and preserve for microscopic study **(3) :** to make the image of (a photographic film) permanent by removing unused salts **c :** AFFIX, ATTACH **2 :** to hold or direct steadily <~*es* his eyes on the horizon> **3 a :** to set or place definitely : ESTABLISH **b :** ASSIGN <~ the blame> **4 :** to set in order : ADJUST **5 :** to get ready : PREPARE <~ lunch> **6 a :** REPAIR, MEND <~ the clock> **b :** RESTORE, CURE <the doctor ~*ed* him up> **c :** SPAY, CASTRATE **7 a :** to get even with **b :** to influence the actions, outcome, or effect of by improper or illegal methods <the jury had been ~*ed*> ~ *vi* **1 :** to become firm, stable, or fixed **2 :** to get set : be about to <we're ~*ing* to leave soon> *syn* **1** see SET *ant* alter, abrogate (*as a rule*) **2** see FASTEN — **fix·able** \'fik-sə-bəl\ *adj*

2**fix** *n* **1 :** a position of difficulty or embarrassment : a trying predicament **2 a :** the position (as of a ship) determined by bearings, observations, or radio **b :** a determination of one's position **3 :** an act of obtaining special privilege or immunity from the law by bribery or collusion; *also* : the money paid to obtain such privilege **4 :** a shot of a narcotic **5 :** FIXATION

fix·ate \'fik-,sāt\ *vb* **fix·at·ed; fix·at·ing** *vt* **1 :** to make fixed, stationary, or unchanging **2 :** to focus one's gaze on **3 :** to direct (the libido) toward an infantile form of gratification ~ *vi* **1 :** to focus or concentrate one's gaze or attention **2 :** to undergo arrestment at a stage of development

fix·a·tion \fik-'sā-shən\ *n* : the act, process, or result of fixing or fixating: as **a :** stereotyped behavior (as in response to frustration) **b :** an obsessive or unhealthy preoccupation or attachment **c :** a persistent concentration of libidinal energies upon pregenital objects

fix·a·tive \'fik-sət-iv\ *n* : something that fixes or sets: as **a :** a substance added to a perfume esp. to prevent too rapid evaporation **b :** a varnish used esp. for the protection of crayon drawings **c :** a substance used to fix living tissue — **fixative** *adj*

fixed \'fikst\ *adj* **1 a :** securely placed or fastened : STATIONARY **b (1) :** NONVOLATILE **(2) :** formed into a chemical compound **c (1) :** not subject to change or fluctuation : SETTLED <a ~ income> **(2) :** firmly set in the mind <a ~ idea> **(3) :** having a final or crystallized form or character **(4) :** recurring on the same date from year to year <~ holidays> **d :** IMMOBILE, CONCENTRATED <a ~ stare> **2 :** supplied with something (as money) needed or desirable <comfortably ~ by the standards of his class —Frederick Lane> — **fixed·ly** \'fik-səd-lē, 'fiks-tlē\ *adv* — **fixed·ness** \'fik-səd-nəs, 'fiks(t)-nəs\ *n*

fixed charge *n* **1 :** a regularly recurring expense (as rent, taxes, or interest) that must be met when due **2 :** FIXED COST

fixed cost *n* : an indirect cost (as maintenance) that continues with little variation irrespective of the level of production

fixed oil *n* : a nonvolatile oil; *esp* : a fatty oil — compare ESSENTIAL OIL

fixed-point *adj* : involving or being a mathematical notation (as in a decimal system) in which the point separating whole numbers and fractions is fixed — compare FLOATING-POINT

fixed star *n* : a star so distant that its motion can be measured only by very precise observations over long periods

fix·er \'fik-sər\ *n* : one that fixes: as **a :** one that intervenes to enable a person to circumvent the law or obtain a political favor **b :** one that adjusts matters or disputes by negotiation

fix·ing \-siŋ\ *n* **1 :** the act or process of one that fixes **2** *pl* *often* -sənz\ : TRIMMINGS <a turkey dinner with all the ~*s*>

fix·i·ty \'fik-sət-ē\ *n, pl* **-ties 1 :** the quality or state of being fixed or stable **2 :** something that is fixed : FIXTURE

fix·ture \'fiks-chər\ *n* [modif. of LL *fixura,* fr. L *fixus*] **1 :** the act or process of fixing : the state of being fixed **2 a :** something that is fixed or attached (as to a building) as a permanent appendage or as a structural part <a fluorescent lighting ~> <a plumbing ~> **b :** a device for supporting work during machining **c :** a chattel so annexed to realty that it may be regarded as legally a part of it **3 :** a familiar or invariably present element or feature in some particular setting; *esp* : a person long associated with a place or activity **4 :** a settled date or time esp. for a sporting or festive event; *also* : such an event esp. as a regularly scheduled affair

1**fizz** \'fiz\ *vi* [prob. of imit. origin] **1 :** to make a hissing or sputtering sound : EFFERVESCE **2 :** to exhibit excitement or exhilaration

2**fizz** *n* **1 a :** a hissing sound **b :** SPIRIT, LIVELINESS **2 :** an effervescent beverage — **fizzy** \-ē\ *adj*

1**fiz·zle** \'fiz-əl\ *vi* **fiz·zled; fiz·zling** \-(ə-)liŋ\ [prob. alter. of *fist* (to break wind)] **1 :** FIZZ **2 :** to fail or end feebly esp. after a promising start — often used with *out*

2**fizzle** *n* : an abortive effort : FAILURE

fjeld \fē-'el\ *n* [Dan] : a barren plateau of the Scandinavian upland

fjord \fē-'ó(ə)rd\ *n* [Norw *fjord,* fr. ON *fjörthr* — more at FORD] : a narrow inlet of the sea between cliffs or steep slopes

FJP *abbr* Federation of Jewish Philanthropies of New York

fl *abbr* **1** floor **2** florin **3** [L *floruit*] flourished **4** fluid

FL *abbr* **1** Florida **2** focal length **3** foreign language

Fla *abbr* Florida

flab \'flab\ *n* [back-formation fr. *flabby*] : soft flabby body tissue

flab·ber·gast \'flab-ər-,gast\ *vt* [origin unknown] : to overwhelm with shock, surprise, or wonder : DUMBFOUND *syn* see SURPRISE — **flab·ber·gast·ing·ly** \-,gas-tiŋ-lē\ *adv*

flab·by \'flab-ē\ *adj* **flab·bi·er; -est** [alter. of *flappy*] **1 :** lacking resilience or firmness : FLACCID **2 :** weak and ineffective : FEEBLE *syn* see LIMP *ant* firm — **flab·bi·ly** \'flab-ə-lē\ *adv* — **flab·bi·ness** \'flab-ē-nəs\ *n*

fla·bel·late \flə-'bel-ət, 'flab-ə-,lāt\ *adj* : shaped like a fan

flabelli- *comb form* [L, fr. *flabellum*] : fan <*flabelli*form>

fla·bel·li·form \flə-'bel-ə-,fórm\ *adj* : FLABELLATE

fla·bel·lum \flə-'bel-əm\ *n, pl* **-la** \-ə\ [NL, fr. L, fan] : a body organ or part resembling a fan

flac·cid \'flak-səd, 'flas-əd\ *adj* [L *flaccidus,* fr. *flaccus* flabby] **1 a :** lacking normal or youthful firmness : FLABBY <~ muscles> **b** *of a plant part* : deficient in turgor **2 :** lacking vigor or force <~ leadership> *syn* see LIMP *ant* resilient — **flac·cid·i·ty** \fla(k)-'sid-ət-ē\ *n* — **flac·cid·ly** \'flak-səd-lē, 'flas-əd-\ *adv*

1**flack** \'flak\ *n* [origin unknown] : one who provides publicity; *esp* : PRESS AGENT

2**flack** *var of* FLAK

fla·con \'flak-ən, -,än; fla-'kōⁿ\ *n* [F, fr. MF, bottle — more at FLAGON] : a small usu. ornamental bottle with a tight cap

1**flag** \'flag\ *n* [ME *flagge* reed, rush] : any of various monocotyledonous plants with long ensiform leaves: as **a :** IRIS; *esp* : a wild iris **b :** SWEET FLAG **c :** CATTAIL

2**flag** *n* [ME *flagge,* fr. ON *flaga* slab; akin to OE *flēan* to flay — more at FLAY] : a hard evenly stratified stone that splits into flat pieces suitable for paving; *also* : a piece of such stone

3**flag** *vt* **flagged; flag·ging :** to lay (as a pavement) with flags

4**flag** *n, often attrib* [perh. fr. 1*flag*] **1 :** a usu. rectangular piece of fabric of distinctive design that is used as a symbol (as of a nation) or as a signaling device **2 a :** something used like a flag to signal or attract attention **b :** one of the cross strokes of a musical note less than a quarter note in value **c :** MASTHEAD 2b **3 a :** FLAGSHIP **b :** an admiral functioning in his office of command **c :** NATIONALITY; *esp* : the nationality of registration of a ship or aircraft

5**flag** *vt* **flagged; flag·ging 1 :** to put a flag on (as for identification) <*flagged* the important pages by clipping red tabs to the margin> **2 :** to signal with or as if with a flag; *esp* : to signal to stop <*flagged* the train>

6**flag** *vi* **flagged; flag·ging** [origin unknown] **1 a :** to hang loose without stiffness **b** *of a plant* : to droop esp. from lack of water **2 a :** to become unsteady, feeble, or spiritless : DROOP <his interest *flagged*> **b :** to decline in interest or attraction <when everyone had had a say the topic *flagged*>

flag day *n* **1** *cap F&D* : June 14 observed in various states in commemoration of the adoption in 1777 of the official U.S. flag **2** *Brit* : a day on which charitable contributions are solicited in exchange for small flags

fla·gel·lant \'flaj-ə-lənt, flə-'jel-ənt\ *n* : one that whips: as **a :** a person who scourges himself as a public penance **b :** a person who responds sexually to being beaten by or to beating another person — **flagellant** *adj* — **fla·gel·lant·ism** \-,iz-əm\ *n*

fla·gel·lar \flə-ˈjel-ər, ˈflaj-ə-lər\ *adj* : of or relating to a flagellum

[1]**flag·el·late** \ˈflaj-ə-ˌlāt\ *vt* **-lat·ed; -lat·ing** [L *flagellatus*, pp. of *flagellare*, fr. *flagellum*, dim. of *flagrum* whip; akin to ON *blaka* to wave] **1** : WHIP, SCOURGE **2** : to drive or punish as if by whipping

[2]**fla·gel·late** \ˈflaj-ə-lət, -ˌlāt; flə-ˈjel-ət\ *adj* [NL *flagellatus*, fr. *flagellum*] **1 a** *or* **flag·el·lat·ed** \ˈflaj-ə-ˌlāt-əd\ : having flagella **b** : shaped like a flagellum **2** [[1]*flagellate*] : of, relating to, or caused by flagellates <~ diarrhea>

[3]**flagellate** *like*[2]\ *n* [NL *Flagellata*, class of unicellular organisms, fr. neut. pl. of *flagellatus*] : a flagellate protozoan or alga

[1]**flag·el·la·tion** \ˌflaj-ə-ˈlā-shən\ *n* : the act or practice of flagellating; *esp* : the practice of a flagellant

[2]**flagellation** *n* : the formation or arrangement of flagella

fla·gel·lum \flə-ˈjel-əm\ *n, pl* **-la** \-ə\ *also* **-lums** [NL, fr. L, whip, shoot of a plant] : any of various elongated filiform appendages of plants or animals: as **a** : the slender distal part of an antenna **b** : a long tapering process that projects singly or in groups from a cell and is the primary organ of motion of many microorganisms **c** : a long slender shoot

fla·geo·let \ˌflaj-ə-ˈlet, -ˈlā\ *n* [F, fr. OF *flajolet*, fr. *flajol* flute, fr. (assumed) VL *flabeolum*, fr. L *flare* to blow — more at BLOW] : a small fipple flute resembling the treble recorder

flag football *n* : a variation of football in which a player must remove a flag attached to the ballcarrier's clothing to stop the play

[1]**flag·ging** \ˈflag-iŋ\ *adj* **1** : LANGUID, WEAK **2** : becoming progressively less : DWINDLING — **flag·ging·ly** \-iŋ-lē\ *adv*

[2]**flagging** *n* : a pavement or walk of flagstones

fla·gi·tious \flə-ˈjish-əs\ *adj* [ME *flagicious*, fr. L *flagitiosus*, fr. *flagitium* shameful thing; akin to L *flagrum* whip] : marked by outrageous or scandalous crime or vice : VILLAINOUS ***syn*** see VICIOUS — **fla·gi·tious·ly** *adv* — **fla·gi·tious·ness** *n*

flag·man \ˈflag-mən\ *n* : one who signals with or as if with a flag

flag officer *n* [fr. his being entitled to display a flag with one or more stars indicating his rank] : any of the officers in the navy or coast guard above captain — compare GENERAL OFFICER

flag of truce : a white flag carried or displayed to an enemy as an invitation to conference or parley

flag·on \ˈflag-ən\ *n* [ME, fr. MF *flascon*, *flacon* bottle, fr. LL *flascon-*, *flasco* — more at FLASK] **1 a** : a large usu. metal or pottery vessel with handle and spout and often a lid **b** : a large bulging short-necked bottle **2** : the contents of a flagon

flagon 1a

flag·pole \ˈflag-ˌpōl\ *n* : a pole on which to raise a flag

fla·grance \ˈflā-grən(t)s *also* ˈflag-rən(t)s\ *n* : FLAGRANCY

fla·gran·cy \ˈflā-grən-sē *also* ˈflag-rən-\ *n* : the quality or state of being flagrant

flag rank *n* : the rank of a flag officer

fla·grant \ˈflā-grənt *also* ˈflag-rənt\ *adj* [L *flagrant-*, *flagrans*, prp. of *flagrare* to burn — more at BLACK] **1** *archaic* : FLAMING, GLOWING **2** : extremely or purposefully conspicuous usu. because of uncommon objectionableness or evil — **fla·grant·ly** *adv*

syn FLAGRANT, GLARING, GROSS, RANK *shared meaning element* : conspicuously bad or objectionable. FLAGRANT applies usually to offenses or errors so bad that they can neither escape notice nor be condoned <open and *flagrant* mutiny> <*flagrant* abuse of his office> GLARING implies painful or damaging obtrusiveness of something that is conspicuously wrong, faulty, or improper <this evil is so *glaring*, so inexcusable — G. B. Shaw> <a *glaring* inconsistency in his argument> GROSS, more likely to apply to attitudes, qualities, or faults than to specific evil acts or offenses, attributes an unbounded and inexcusable badness to what it describes <*gross* carelessness> <*gross* stupidity> RANK applies to what is openly and extremely objectionable and utterly condemned <O, my offense is *rank*, it smells to heaven — Shak.>

fla·gran·te de·lic·to \flə-ˌgrant-ē-di-ˈlik-(ˌ)tō\ *adv* [ML, lit., while the crime is blazing] : in the very act of committing a misdeed : RED-HANDED

flag·ship \ˈflag-ˌship\ *n* **1** : the ship that carries the commander of a fleet or subdivision thereof and flies his flag **2** : the finest, largest, or most important one esp. in a fleet of ships, a radio network, or a chain of newspapers <the editorial tone of the fiercely conservative chain is set by the ~ paper — J. C. Goulden>

flag·staff \-ˌstaf\ *n* : a staff on which a flag is hoisted

flag·stick \-ˌstik\ *n* : a stick for a flag marking the location of a golf cup

flag·stone \-ˌstōn\ *n* : [2]FLAG

flag stop *n* : a point at which a vehicle in public transportation stops only on prearrangement or signal

flag-wav·ing \ˈflag-ˌwā-viŋ\ *n* : passionate appeal to patriotic or partisan sentiment : CHAUVINISM

[1]**flail** \ˈflā(ə)l\ *n* [ME *fleil*, *flail*, partly fr. (assumed) OE *flegel* (akin to OHG *flegil* flail; both fr. a prehistoric WGmc word borrowed fr. LL *flagellum* flail, fr. L, whip) & partly fr. MF *flaiel*, fr. LL *flagellum* — more at FLAGELLATE] : a hand threshing implement consisting of a wooden handle at the end of which a stouter and shorter stick is so hung as to swing freely

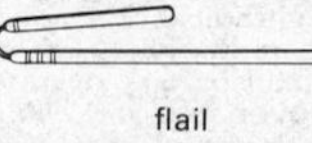

flail

[2]**flail** *vt* **1 a** : to strike with or as if with a flail <his arms ~*ing* the water> **b** : to move, swing, or beat as though wielding a flail <~*ing* his club to drive away the insects> **2** : to thresh (grain) with a flail ~ *vi* : to engage in flailing : THRASH <~*ed* away at each other>

flair \ˈfla(ə)r, ˈfle(ə)r\ *n* [F, lit., sense of smell, fr. OF, odor, fr. *flairier* to give off an odor, fr. LL *flagrare*, fr. L *fragrare* — more at FRAGRANT] **1** : instinctive attraction to and keen discernment about something <a woman with a ~ for style> **2** : natural aptitude : BENT **3** : a uniquely attractive quality (as elegance, smartness, or sophistication) <fashionable dresses with a ~ all their own> ***syn*** see LEANING

flak \ˈflak\ *n, pl* **flak** [G, fr. *flieger**a**bwehr**k**anonen*, fr. *flieger* flyer + *abwehr* defense + *kanonen* cannons] **1** : antiaircraft guns **2** : the bursting shells fired from flak **3** : agitated discussion, opposition, or accusation : DISSENSION <this modest proposal ran into ~ — Charles MacDonald>

[1]**flake** \ˈflāk\ *n* [ME, hurdle, fr. ON *flaki*; akin to OHG *flah* smooth, Gk *pelagos* sea, L *placēre* to please — more at PLEASE] : a stage, platform, or tray for drying fish or produce

[2]**flake** *n* [ME, of Scand origin; akin to Norw *flak* disk] **1** : a small loose mass or bit **2** : a thin flattened piece or layer : CHIP

[3]**flake** *vb* **flaked; flak·ing** *vi* : to separate into flakes ~ *vt* **1** : to form into flakes : CHIP **2** : to cover with or as if with flakes — **flak·er** *n*

flak jacket *n* : a jacket of heavy fabric containing metal plates for protection against flak — called also *flak vest*

flaky \ˈflā-kē\ *adj* **flak·i·er; -est** **1** : consisting of flakes <~ snow> **2** : tending to flake <a ~ piecrust> **3** *slang* : slightly eccentric : SCREWY <the rock writer's ~, half-literate idiom — Benjamin DeMott> — **flak·i·ness** *n*

[1]**flam** \ˈflam\ *n* [prob. short for *flimflam*] **1** : FALSEHOOD, TRICK **2** : HUMBUG, NONSENSE

[2]**flam** *n* [prob. imit.] : a drumbeat of two strokes of which the first is a very quick grace note

[1]**flam·bé** \fläm-ˈbā, flän-\ *adj* [F *flambé*, fr. pp. of *flamber* to flame, singe, fr. OF, fr. *flambe* flame] : dressed or served covered with flaming liquor — usu. used postpositively <chicken ~> <crepe suzettes ~>

[2]**flambé** *vt* **flam·béed; flam·bé·ing** : to douse with a liquer and ignite <pineapple *flambéed* with kirsch>

flam·beau \ˈflam-ˌbō\ *n, pl* **flam·beaux** \-ˌbōz\ *or* **flambeaus** [F, fr. MF, fr. *flambe* flame] : a flaming torch; *broadly* : TORCH

flam·boy·ance \flam-ˈbȯi-ən(t)s\ *n* : the quality or state of being flamboyant

flam·boy·an·cy \-ən-sē\ *n* : FLAMBOYANCE

[1]**flam·boy·ant** \-ənt\ *adj* [F, fr. prp. of *flamboyer* to flame, fr. OF, fr. *flambe*] **1** *often cap* : characterized by waving curves suggesting flames <windows ornamented with ~ tracery> **2** : FLORID, ORNATE; *also* : RESPLENDENT **3** : given to dashing display : SHOWY — **flam·boy·ant·ly** *adv*

[2]**flamboyant** *n* : ROYAL POINCIANA

[1]**flame** \ˈflām\ *n* [ME *flaume*, *flaumbe*, fr. MF *flamme* (fr. L *flamma*) & *flambe*, fr. OF, fr. *flamble*, fr. L *flammula*, dim. of *flamma* flame; akin to L *flagrare* to burn — more at BLACK] **1** : the glowing gaseous part of a fire **2 a** : a state of blazing combustion <the car burst into ~> **b** : a condition or appearance suggesting a flame **c** : BRILLIANCE, BRIGHTNESS **3** : burning zeal or passion **4** : SWEETHEART ***syn*** see BLAZE

[2]**flame** *vb* **flamed; flam·ing** *vi* **1** : to burn with a flame : BLAZE **2** : to burst or break out violently or passionately <*flaming* with indignation> **3** : to shine brightly : GLOW <color *flaming* up in her cheeks> ~ *vt* **1** : to send or convey by means of flame <~ a message by signal fires> **2** : to treat or affect with flame: as **a** : to cleanse, sterilize, or destroy by fire **b** : to dress food with flaming liquor <~ pork chops at the table> — **flam·er** *n*

flame cell *n* : a hollow cell that has a tuft of vibratile cilia and is part of the excretory system of various lower invertebrates (as a flatworm)

flame cultivator *n* : a flamethrower for destroying small weeds

fla·men \ˈflā-mən\ *n, pl* **flamens** *or* **flam·i·nes** \ˈflam-ə-ˌnēz\ [ME *flamin*, fr. L *flamin-*, *flamen*] : PRIEST; *esp* : a priest of a Roman god

fla·men·co \flə-ˈmeŋ-(ˌ)kō\ *n, pl* **-cos** [Sp, Flemish, like a gypsy, fr. MD *Vlaminc* Fleming] **1** : a vigorous rhythmic dance style of the Andalusian gypsies; *also* : a dance in flamenco style **2** : music or song suitable to accompany a flamenco dance

flame·out \ˈflā-ˌmau̇t\ *n* : the unintentional cessation of operation of a jet airplane engine

flame photometer *n* : a spectrophotometer in which a spray of metallic salts in solution is vaporized in a very hot flame and subjected to quantitative analysis by measuring the intensities of the spectrum lines of the metals present — **flame photometric** *adj* — **flame photometry** *n*

flame·proof \ˈflām-ˈprüf\ *adj* **1** : resistant to the action of flame **2** : not burning on contact with flame — **flameproof** *vt* — **flame·proof·er** *n*

flame·throw·er \-ˌthrō(-ə)r\ *n* : a device that expels from a nozzle a burning stream of liquid or semiliquid fuel under pressure

flamingo

flame tree *n* : any of several trees or shrubs with showy scarlet or yellow flowers: as **a** : a tree (*Brachychiton acerifolium*) of southern Australia with panicles of brilliant scarlet flowers **b** : ROYAL POINCIANA

flam·ing \ˈflā-miŋ\ *adj* **1** : being on fire : BLAZING **2** : resembling or suggesting a flame in color, brilliance, or wavy outline <the ~ sunset sky> <~ red hair> **3** : ARDENT, PASSIONATE <~ youth> — **flam·ing·ly** \-miŋ-lē\ *adv*

fla·min·go \flə-ˈmiŋ-(ˌ)gō\ *n, pl* **-gos** *also* **-goes** [obs. Sp *flamengo*

ə abut	ᵊ kitten	ər further	a back	ā bake	ä cot, cart	
au̇ out	ch chin	e less	ē easy	g gift	i trip	ī life
j joke	ŋ sing	ō flow	ȯ flaw	ȯi coin	th thin	th this
ü loot	u̇ foot	y yet	yü few	yu̇ furious	zh vision	

(now *flamenco*), fr. MD *Vlaminc* Fleming]: any of several aquatic birds (family Phoenicopteridae) with long legs and neck, webbed feet, a broad lamellate bill resembling that of a duck but abruptly bent downward, and usu. rosy-white plumage with scarlet wing coverts and black wing quills

flam·ma·bil·i·ty \ˌflam-ə-ˈbil-ət-ē\ *n* **:** ability to support combustion; *esp* **:** a high capacity for combustion

flam·ma·ble \ˈflam-ə-bəl\ *adj* [L *flammare* to flame, set on fire, fr. *flamma*] **:** capable of being easily ignited and of burning with extreme rapidity — **flammable** *n*

flan \ˈflan, ˈflän(n)\ *n* [F, fr. OF *flaon*, fr. LL *fladon-, flado* flat cake] **1 :** a large usu. straight-sided open pie filled with custard, cheese, jam, or fruit and often glazed with a fruit syrup **2 :** the metal disk of a coin, token, or medal as distinguished from the design and lettering stamped on it

flâ·ne·rie \ˌflän-(ə-)ˈrē\ *n* [F]**:** the state of being aimless **:** IDLENESS

flâ·neur \flä-ˈnər\ *n* [F *flâneur* idler] **:** an aimless person: as **a :** MAN-ABOUT-TOWN **b :** an intellectual trifler

[1]flange \ˈflanj\ *n* [perh. alter. of *flanch* (a curving charge on a heraldic shield)] **:** a rib or rim for strength, for guiding, or for attachment to another object <a ~ on a pipe> <a ~ on a wheel> <the ~ of an I beam>

[2]flange *vt* **flanged; flang·ing :** to furnish with a flange — **flang·er** *n*

[1]flank \ˈflaŋk\ *n* [ME, fr. OF *flanc*, of Gmc origin; akin to OHG *hlanca* loin, flank — more at LANK] **1 a :** the fleshy part of the side between the ribs and the hip; *broadly* **:** the side of a quadruped **b :** a cut of meat from this part of an animal — see BEEF illustration **2 a :** SIDE **b :** the right or left of a formation <attacked the enemy on both ~*s*> **3 :** the area along either side of a heraldic shield

[2]flank *vt* **1 :** to protect a flank of **2 a :** to attack or threaten the flank of (as a body of troops) **b :** to turn the flank of **3 a :** to be situated at the side of **:** BORDER <a road ~*ed* with linden trees> **b :** to place something on each side of

flank·er *n* **:** a football player stationed wide of the formation; *esp* **:** an offensive halfback who lines up on the flank slightly behind the line of scrimmage and serves chiefly as a pass receiver — called also *flanker back*

flank steak *n* **:** a pear-shaped muscle of the beef flank; *also* **:** a steak cut from this muscle — see BEEF illustration

flan·nel \ˈflan-ᵊl\ *n* [ME *flaunneol* woolen cloth or garment] **1 a :** a soft twilled wool or worsted fabric with a loose texture and a slightly napped surface **b :** a stout cotton fabric usu. napped on one side **2** *pl* **a :** flannel underwear **b :** outer garments of flannel; *esp* **:** men's trousers — **flannel** *adj* — **flan·nel·ly** \-ᵊl-ē\ *adj*

flan·nel·ette \ˌflan-ᵊl-ˈet\ *n* **:** a napped cotton flannel

[1]flap \ˈflap\ *n* [ME *flappe*] **1 :** a stroke with something broad **:** SLAP **2** *obs* **:** something broad and flat used for striking **3 :** something that is broad, limber, or flat and usu. thin and that hangs loose or projects freely: as **a :** a piece on a garment that hangs free **b :** a piece of tissue partly severed from its place of origin for use in surgical grafting **c :** an extended part forming the closure (as of an envelope or carton) **d :** a movable auxiliary airfoil usu. attached to an airplane wing's trailing edge to increase lift or drag — see AIRPLANE illustration **4 :** the motion of something broad and limber (as a sail or wing) **5 a :** a state of excitement or panicky confusion **:** UPROAR **b :** CRISIS

[2]flap *vb* **flapped; flap·ping** *vt* **1 :** to beat with or as if with a flap **2 :** to toss sharply **:** FLING **3 :** to move or cause to move in flaps ~ *vi* **1 :** to sway loosely usu. with a noise of striking and esp. when moved by wind <curtains *flapping* in the breeze> **2 a :** to beat or pulsate wings or something suggesting wings **b :** to progress by flapping **c :** to flutter ineffectively **3 :** to talk foolishly and persistently <always *flapping* about his own importance>

flap·doo·dle \ˈflap-ˌdüd-ᵊl\ *n* [origin unknown] **:** NONSENSE

flap·jack \-ˌjak\ *n* **:** PANCAKE

flap·per \ˈflap-ər\ *n* **1 a :** one that flaps **b :** something (as a flyswatter) used in flapping or striking **c :** FLIPPER 1 **2 :** a young woman; *specif* **:** a young woman of the period of World War I and the decade thereafter who showed bold freedom from conventions in conduct and dress

flap·py \ˈflap-ē\ *adj* **:** flapping or tending to flap

[1]flare \ˈfla(ə)r, ˈfle(ə)r\ *vb* **flared; flar·ing** [origin unknown] *vi* **1 a :** to stream in the wind **b :** to burn with an unsteady flame **2 a :** to shine with a sudden light <a match ~*s* in the darkness> **b (1) :** to become suddenly excited or angry — usu. used with *up* <she ~*s* up at the slightest thing> **(2) :** to break out or intensify usu. suddenly or violently — often used with *up* <ground fighting *flared* up after a two-week lull> **c :** to express strong emotion (as anger) <*flaring* out at such abuses> **3 :** to open or spread outward <the pants ~ gently at the bottom> ~ *vt* **1 :** to display conspicuously <*flaring* her scarf to attract attention> **2 :** to cause to flare <the breeze ~*s* the candle> **3 :** to signal with a flare or by flaring

[2]flare *n* **1 :** an unsteady glaring light **2 a :** a fire or blaze of light used to signal, illuminate, or attract attention; *also* **:** a device or composition used to produce such a flare **b :** a temporary outburst of energy from a small area of the sun's surface; *also* **:** a sudden increase and decrease in the brightness of a star often amounting to several magnitudes **3 :** a sudden outburst (as of sound, excitement, or anger) **4 a :** a spreading outward; *also* **:** a place or part that spreads <the ~ of a fireplace> **b :** an area of skin flush **5 :** light resulting from reflection (as between lens surfaces) or an effect of this light (as a fogged or dense area in a photographic negative) **6 :** a short pass in football thrown to a back who is running toward the sideline ***syn*** see BLAZE

flare·back \ˈfla(ə)r-ˌbak, ˈfle(ə)r-\ *n* **:** a burst of flame back or out (as from a furnace) in a direction opposite to that of normal operation

flare–up \-ˌəp\ *n* **1 :** a sudden bursting (as of a smoldering fire) into flame or light **2 :** a sudden outburst or intensification <a new ~ of border disputes>

flar·ing \ˈfla(ə)r-iŋ, ˈfle(ə)r-\ *adj* **1 a :** flaming brightly or unsteadily **b :** GAUDY <a ~ resort hotel> **2 :** opening or spreading outward <~ nostrils> — **flar·ing·ly** \-iŋ-lē\ *adv*

[1]flash \ˈflash\ *vb* [ME *flaschen*, of imit. origin] *vi* **1 :** RUSH, DASH — used of flowing water **2 :** to break forth in or like a sudden flame or flare <lightning ~*ing* in the sky> **3 a :** to appear suddenly <an idea ~*es* into her mind> **b :** to move with great speed <the days ~ by> **4 a :** to break forth or out so as to make a sudden display <the sun ~*ed* from behind a cloud> **b :** to act or speak vehemently and suddenly esp. in anger **5 a :** to give off light suddenly or in transient bursts **b :** to glow or gleam esp. with animation or passion <his eyes ~*ed* in a sinister fashion> **6 :** to change suddenly or violently into vapor <hot water ~*ing* to steam under reduced pressure> ~ *vt* **1 a** *archaic* **:** SPLASH **b :** to fill by a sudden inflow of water **2 a :** to cause the sudden appearance of (light) **b :** to cause to burst violently into flame; *also* **:** to burn for determining character of residue **c (1) :** to cause (light) to reflect **(2) :** to cause (as a mirror) to reflect light **(3) :** to cause (a lamp) to flash **d :** to convey by means of flashes of light **3 a :** to make known or cause to appear with great speed <~ a message on the screen> **b :** to display obtrusively and ostentatiously <always ~*es* his fat wallet in public> **c :** to expose to view suddenly and briefly <~*ing* a shy smile> **4 :** to cover with or form into a thin layer: as **a :** to protect against rain by covering with sheet metal or a substitute **b :** to coat (as glass) with a thin layer (as of metal or a differently colored glass) **5 :** to subject (an exposed photographic negative or positive) to a supplementary uniform exposure to light before development in order to modify detail or tone

syn FLASH, GLEAM, GLANCE, GLINT, SPARKLE, GLITTER, GLISTEN, GLIMMER, CORUSCATE, SHIMMER *shared meaning element* **:** to send forth light

[2]flash *n* **1 a :** a sudden burst of light **b :** a movement of a flag in signaling **2 :** a sudden and often brilliant burst <a ~ of wit> <had a ~ of intuition> **3 :** a brief time <I'll be back in a ~> **4 a :** SHOW, DISPLAY; *esp* **:** a vulgar ostentatious display **b** *archaic* **:** a showy ostentatious person **c :** one that attracts notice; *esp* **:** an outstanding athlete **5** *obs* **:** thieves' slang **6 :** a rush of water released to permit passage of a boat **7 :** something flashed: as **a :** GLIMPSE, LOOK **b :** SMILE **c :** a first brief news report **d :** FLASHLIGHT 2,3 **e :** a quick-spreading flame or momentary intense outburst of radiant heat **8 :** an immediate intensely pleasurable feeling resulting from an intravenous injection (as of heroin or amphetamines) **9 :** the rapid conversion of a liquid into vapor

[3]flash *adj* **1 a :** FLASHY, SHOWY **b :** of, relating to, or characteristic of flashy people or things <~ behavior> **c :** of, relating to, or characteristic of persons considered social outcasts <~ language> **2 :** of sudden origin and short duration <a ~ fire>

flash·back \ˈflash-ˌbak\ *n* **1 :** interruption of chronological sequence in a literary or theatrical work by interjection of events of earlier occurrence **2 :** a recession of flame to an unwanted position (as into a blowpipe)

flash·board \-ˌbō(ə)rd, -ˌbȯ(ə)rd\ *n* **:** one or more boards projecting above the top of a dam to increase the depth of the water

flash·bulb \-ˌbəlb\ *n* **:** an electric flash lamp in which metal foil or wire is burned

flash card *n* **:** a card bearing words, numbers, or pictures that someone briefly displays to another usu. as a learning aid

flash·cube \ˈflash-ˌkyüb\ *n* **:** a cubical device that incorporates four flashbulbs, is usu. attached to a camera, and can be turned for taking four pictures in rapid succession

flash·er \ˈflash-ər\ *n* **:** one that flashes: as **a :** a light (as a traffic signal or automobile light) that catches the attention by flashing **b :** a device for automatically flashing a light

flash flood *n* **:** a local flood of great volume and short duration generally resulting from heavy rainfall in the immediate vicinity — **flash flood** *vt*

flash–for·ward \ˈflash-ˈfȯr-wərd\ *n* **:** a literary or theatrical technique that involves interruption of the chronological sequence of events by interjection of events or scenes of future occurrence

flash·gun \-ˌgən\ *n* **1 :** a device for holding and igniting flashlight powder **2 :** a device for holding and operating a flashbulb or a flashtube

flash·ing \ˈflash-iŋ\ *n* **:** sheet metal used in waterproofing roof valleys or hips or the angle between a chimney and a roof

flash in the pan [fr. the firing of the priming in the pan of a flintlock musket without discharging the piece] **1 :** a sudden spasmodic effort that accomplishes nothing **2 :** one that appears promising but turns out to be disappointing or worthless

flash lamp *n* **:** a lamp for producing a brief but intense flash of light for taking photographs

flash·light \ˈflash-ˌlīt\ *n* **1 :** a flash of light or a light that flashes; *esp* **:** a scintillating light or a light of regularly varying brightness in a lighthouse **2 a :** a sudden bright artificial light used in taking photographic pictures **b :** a photograph taken by such a light **3 :** a small battery-operated portable electric light

flash·over \-ˌō-vər\ *n* **1 :** an abnormal electrical discharge (as through the air to the ground from a high potential source or between two conducting portions of a structure) **2 :** the sudden spread of flame over an area when it becomes heated to the flash point

flash point *n* **1 :** the lowest temperature at which vapors above a volatile combustible substance ignite in air when exposed to flame **2 :** a point at which someone or something bursts suddenly into action or being

flash·tube \ˈflash-ˌt(y)üb\ *n* **:** a gas discharge tube that produces very brief intense flashes of light and is used esp. in photography

flashy \ˈflash-ē\ *adj* **flash·i·er; -est 1** *chiefly dial* **:** lacking in substance or flavor **:** INSIPID **2 :** momentarily dazzling **3 a :** superficially attractive **:** BRIGHT **b :** ostentatious or showy beyond the bounds of good taste; *esp* : marked by gaudy brightness ***syn*** see GAUDY — **flash·i·ly** \ˈflash-ə-lē\ *adv* — **flash·i·ness** \ˈflash-ē-nəs\ *n*

flask \ˈflask\ *n* [MF *flasque* powder flask, deriv. of LL *flascon-, flasco* bottle, prob. of Gmc origin; akin to OHG *flaska* bottle] **1** : a container often somewhat narrowed toward the outlet and often fitted with a closure; *esp* : a broad flattened necked vessel used esp. to carry alcoholic beverages on the person **2** : a frame that holds molding sand used in a foundry

¹flat \ˈflat\ *adj* **flat·ter; flat·test** [ME, fr. ON *flatr;* akin to OHG *flaz* flat, Gk *platys* — more at PLACE] **1** : having a continuous horizontal surface **2 a** : lying at full length or spread out upon the ground : PROSTRATE **b** : resting with a surface against something **3** : having a relatively smooth or even surface **4** : arranged or laid out so as to be level or even **5** : having the major surfaces essentially parallel and distinctly greater than the minor surfaces <a ~ piece of wood> **6 a** : clearly unmistakable : DOWNRIGHT <gave a ~ denial> **b** (1) : ABSOLUTE, FIXED <charged a ~ rate> (2) : having no fraction either lacking or in excess : EXACT <ran the race in four minutes ~> **7 a** : lacking in animation, zest, or vigor : DULL <how weary, stale, ~ and unprofitable, seem to me all the uses of this world — Shak.> **b** : lacking flavor : TASTELESS **c** : lacking effervescence or sparkle <~ ginger ale> **d** : lacking air : DEFLATED — used of tires **8 a** (1) *of a tone* : lowered a half step in pitch (2) : lower than the proper pitch **b** *of the vowel a* : pronounced as in *bad* or *bat* **9 a** : having a low trajectory **b** *of a tennis ball* : hit squarely without being spun by the racket **10** *of a sail* : TAUT **11 a** : uniform in hue or shade **b** *of a painting* : having little or no illusion of depth **c** *of a photograph or negative* : lacking contrast **d** *of a photographic lighting arrangement* : not emphasizing shadows or contours **e** : free from gloss ***syn*** see LEVEL, INSIPID — **flat·ly** *adv* — **flat·ness** *n*

²flat *n* **1** : a level surface of land with little or no relief : PLAIN — often used in pl. <sagebrush ~*s*> **2** : a flat part or surface <the ~ of one's hand> **3 a** : a musical note or tone one half step lower than a specified note or tone **b** : a character on a line or space of the musical staff indicating a half step drop in pitch **4** : something flat: as **a** : a shallow box in which seedlings are started **b** : a flat-bottomed boat **c** : a flat piece of theatrical scenery **d** : a shoe or slipper having a flat heel or no heel **5** : a deflated tire **6** : the area to either side of an offensive football formation

flat 3b

³flat *adv* **1** : in a flat manner : DIRECTLY, POSITIVELY **2 a** : on or against a flat surface <lying ~ on his back> **b** : at full length <fell ~ on his face> **3** : in a complete manner : WHOLLY <~ broke> **4** : below the proper musical pitch **5** : without interest charge; *esp* : without allowance or charge for accrued interest <bonds sold ~>

⁴flat *vb* **flat·ted; flat·ting** *vt* **1** : FLATTEN **2** : to lower in pitch esp. by a half step ~ *vi* : to sing or play below the true pitch

⁵flat *n* **1** : a floor or story in a building **2** : an apartment on one floor

¹flat·bed \ˌflat-ˌbed\ *adj* : having a horizontal bed on which a horizontal printing surface rests <a ~ printing press>

²flat·bed \ˈflat-ˌbed\ *n* : a motortruck or trailer with a body in the form of a platform or shallow box

flat·boat \-ˌbōt\ *n* : a boat with a flat bottom and square ends used for transportation of bulky freight esp. in shallow waters

flat·cap \-ˌkap\ *n* **1** : a round low-crowned cap worn in 16th and 17th century London **2** : a wearer of a flatcap; *esp* : a Londoner

flat·car \-ˌkär\ *n* : a railroad freight car without permanent raised sides, ends, or covering

flat–coat·ed retriever \ˌflat-ˌkōt-əd-\ *n* : any of an English breed of active medium-sized sporting dogs that have a close dense smooth black or liver colored coat and a rather long head

flat·fish \ˈflat-ˌfish\ *n* : any of an order (Heterosomata) of marine teleost fishes (as the halibuts, flounders, turbots, and soles) that as adults swim on one side of the laterally compressed body and have both eyes on the upper side

flat·foot \-ˌfu̇t (*always so in sense 3*), -ˈfu̇t\ *n, pl* **flat·feet** \-ˌfēt, -ˈfēt\ **1** : a condition in which the arch of the instep is flattened so that the entire sole rests upon the ground **2** : a foot affected with flatfoot **3 a** *or pl* **flatfoots** *slang* : POLICEMAN; *esp* : a patrolman walking a regular beat **b** *slang* : SAILOR

¹flat–foot·ed \-ˈfu̇t-əd\ *adj* **1** : affected with flatfoot; *broadly* : walking with a dragging or shambling gait **2 a** : firm and well balanced on the feet **b** : free from reservation : FORTHRIGHT <had an honest ~ way of saying a thing> **3** : found unprepared : UNREADY — used chiefly in the phrase *catch one flat-footed* — **flat–foot·ed·ly** *adv* — **flat–foot·ed·ness** *n*

²flat–footed *adv* : in an open and determined manner : FLATLY

flat–hat \ˈflat-ˌhat\ *vi* [fr. an alleged incident in which a pedestrian's hat was crushed by a low-flying plane] : to fly low in an airplane in a reckless manner : HEDGEHOP — **flat–hat·ter** *n*

Flat·head \-ˌhed\ *n, pl* **Flatheads** *or* **Flathead 1** : a member of any of several No. American Indian peoples that practiced head-flattening **2** : an Amerindian people of Montana **3** *not cap* : any of various fishes with more or less flat heads; *esp* : any of a family (Percophididae) of chiefly Indo-Pacific marine food fishes that resemble sculpins

flat·iron \ˈflat-ˌī(-ə)rn\ *n* : IRON 2d

flat knot *n* : REEF KNOT

flat·land \ˈflat-ˌland\ *n* **1** : land that lacks significant variation in elevation **2** : a region in which the land is predominantly flat — usu. used in pl. — **flat·land·er** \-ˌlan-dər\ *n*

flat·let \ˈflat-lət\ *n, Brit* : EFFICIENCY APARTMENT

flat·ling \ˈflat-liŋ\ *or* **flat·lings** \-liŋz\ *adv, dial Brit* : with a flat side or edge

flat–out \ˈflat-ˌau̇t\ *adj* **1** : ALL-OUT, DOWNRIGHT <it was a ~ lie> **2** *chiefly Brit* : being or going at maximum effort or speed

flat out \-ˈau̇t\ *adv* **1** *chiefly dial* : in a blunt and direct manner : OPENLY <called *flat out* for revolution —*Nat'l Review*> **2** : at top speed or peak performance <the car does 180 m.p.h. *flat out*>

flat race *n* : a race (as for horses) on a level course without obstacles (as hurdles) — compare STEEPLECHASE

flat silver *n* : eating or serving utensils (as knives, forks, and spoons) made of or plated with silver

flat·ten \ˈflat-ᵊn\ *vb* **flat·tened; flat·ten·ing** \ˈflat-niŋ, -ᵊn-iŋ\ *vt* **1** : to make flat: as **a** : to make level or smooth **b** : to lay low : RUIN **2** : to make (as paint) lusterless ~ *vi* **1** : to become flat or flatter: as **a** : to become dull or spiritless **b** : to extend in or into a flat position or form <hills ~*ing* into coastal plains> **c** : to become uniform or stabilized often at a new lower level — usu. used with *out* <performance tended to ~ out after an initial period of improvement> **2 a** : to manipulate an airplane so as to bring its longitudinal axis parallel with the ground — used with *out* **b** *of an airplane* : to assume such a position — **flat·ten·er** \ˈflat-nər, -ᵊn-ər\ *n*

¹flat·ter \ˈflat-ər\ *vb* [ME *flateren,* fr. OF *flater* to lick, flatter, of Gmc origin; akin to OHG *flaz* flat] *vt* **1** : to praise excessively esp. from motives of self-interest **2 a** *archaic* : SOOTHE, BEGUILE **b** : to raise the hope of or gratify esp. by false or specious representations <~ him by asking his advice> **3 a** : to portray too favorably <that picture ~*s* her — she's not that pretty> **b** : to display to advantage <candlelight often ~*s* the face> ~ *vi* : to use flattery — **flat·ter·er** \-ər-ər\ *n* — **flat·ter·ing·ly** \-ə-riŋ-lē\ *adv*

²flatter *n* : one that flattens: as **a** : a drawplate with a narrow rectangular orifice for drawing flat strips **b** : a flat-faced swage used in smithing

flat·tery \ˈflat-ə-rē\ *n, pl* **-ter·ies 1 a** : the act or practice of flattering **b** (1) : something that flatters (2) : insincere or excessive praise **2** *obs* : a pleasing self-deception

flat·tish \ˈflat-ish\ *adj* : somewhat flat

flat·top \ˈflat-ˌtäp\ *n* : something with a flat or flattened upper surface: as **a** : AIRCRAFT CARRIER **b** : CREW CUT

flat·u·lence \ˈflach-ə-lən(t)s\ *n* : the quality or state of being flatulent

flat·u·len·cy \-lən-sē\ *n* : FLATULENCE

flat·u·lent \-lənt\ *adj* [MF, fr. L *flatus* act of blowing, wind, fr. *flatus,* pp. of *flare* to blow — more at BLOW] **1 a** : marked by or affected with gases generated in the intestine or stomach **b** : likely to cause digestive flatulence **2** : pretentious without real worth or substance : TURGID — **flat·u·lent·ly** *adv*

fla·tus \ˈflāt-əs\ *n* [L, act of blowing, act of breaking wind] : gas generated in the stomach or bowels

flat·ware \ˈflat-ˌwa(ə)r, -ˌwe(ə)r\ *n* : tableware more or less flat and usu. formed or cast in a single piece; *esp* : eating and serving utensils (as knives, forks, and spoons) — compare HOLLOWWARE

flat·ways \-ˌwāz\ *adv* : FLATWISE

flat·wise \-ˌwīz\ *adv* : with the flat surface presented in some expressed or implied position

flat·work \-ˌwərk\ *n* : laundry that can be finished mechanically and doesn't require hand ironing

flat·worm \-ˌwərm\ *n* : PLATYHELMINTH; *esp* : TURBELLARIAN

flaunt \ˈflȯnt, ˈflänt\ *vb* [prob. of Scand origin; akin to ON *flana* to rush around — more at PLANET] *vi* **1** : to wave or flutter showily <the flag ~*s* in the breeze> **2** : to display or obtrude oneself to public notice ~ *vt* **1** : to display ostentatiously or impudently : PARADE <~*ing* his superiority> **2** : to treat contemptuously <~*ed* the rules —Louis Untermeyer> — **flaunt** *n* — **flaunt·ing·ly** \-iŋ-lē\ *adv* — **flaunty** \-ē\ *adj*

flau·tist \ˈflȯt-əst, ˈflau̇t-\ *n* [It *flautista,* fr. *flauto* flute, fr. OProv *flaut*] : FLUTIST

fla·va·none \ˈflā-və-ˌnōn\ *n* [L *flavus* + ISV *-ane* + *-one*] : a colorless crystalline ketone $C_{15}H_{12}O_2$; *also* : any of the derivatives of this ketone many of which occur in plants often in the form of glycosides

fla·vin \ˈflā-vən\ *n* [ISV, fr. L *flavus* yellow — more at BLUE] : a yellow water-soluble nitrogenous pigment derived from isoalloxazine and occurring in the form of nucleotides as coenzymes of flavoproteins; *esp* : RIBOFLAVIN

flavin adenine dinucleotide *n* : a coenzyme $C_{27}H_{33}N_9O_{15}P_2$ of some flavoproteins

fla·vine \ˈflā-ˌvēn\ *n* [ISV, fr. L *flavus*] : a yellow acridine dye (as acriflavine) often used medicinally for its antiseptic properties

flavin mononucleotide *n* : FMN

fla·vone \ˈflā-ˌvōn\ *n* [ISV, fr. L *flavus*] : a colorless crystalline ketone $C_{15}H_{10}O_2$ found in the leaves, stems, and seed capsules of many primroses; *also* : any of the derivatives of this ketone many of which occur as yellow plant pigments in the form of glycosides and are used as dyestuffs

fla·vo·nol \ˈflā-və-ˌnȯl, -ˌnōl\ *n* : any of various hydroxy derivatives of flavone

fla·vo·pro·tein \ˌflā-vō-ˈprō-ˌtēn, -ˈprōt-ē-ən\ *n* [ISV *flavin* + *-o-* + *protein*] : a dehydrogenase that contains a flavin and often a metal and plays a major role in biological oxidations

¹fla·vor \ˈflā-vər\ *n* [ME, fr. MF *flaor, flavor,* fr. (assumed) VL *flator,* fr. L *flare* to blow — more at BLOW] **1 a** *archaic* : ODOR, FRAGRANCE **b** : the quality of something that affects the sense of taste : SAVOR <condiments give ~ to food> **c** : the blend of taste and smell sensations evoked by a substance in the mouth <the ~ of ripe fruit> **2** : a substance that flavors <hard candy with artificial ~> **3** : characteristic or predominant quality <the newspaper retains a community ~> — **fla·vored** \-vərd\ *adj* — **fla·vor·less** \-vər-ləs\ *adj*

2flavor *vt* **fla·vored; fla·vor·ing** \ˈflāv-(ə-)riŋ\ **:** to give or add flavor to
fla·vor·ful \ˈflā-vər-fəl\ *adj* **:** full of flavor **:** SAVORY — **fla·vor·ful·ly** \-fə-lē\ *adv*
fla·vor·ing *n* **:** FLAVOR 2
fla·vor·some \ˈflā-vər-səm\ *adj* **:** FLAVORFUL
fla·vour *chiefly Brit var of* FLAVOR
1flaw \ˈflȯ\ *n* [ME, prob. of Scand origin; akin to Sw *flaga* flake, flaw; akin to OE *flēan* to flay] **1** *obs* **:** FRAGMENT **2 :** an often hidden defect that may cause failure under stress: as **a :** a faulty part (as a crack or break) <the axle broke at a ~> **b :** a weakness in something immaterial <vanity was the great ~ in his character> **c :** a fault in a legal paper that may nullify it ***syn*** see BLEMISH — **flaw·less** \-ləs\ *adj* — **flaw·less·ly** *adv* — **flaw·less·ness** *n*
2flaw *vt* **:** to make flaws in ~ *vi* **:** to become defective
3flaw *n* [of Scand origin; akin to Norw *flaga* gust; akin to L *plangere* to beat — more at PLAINT] **1 :** a sudden brief burst of wind; *also* **:** a spell of stormy weather **2** *obs* **:** an outburst esp. of passion
flax \ˈflaks\ *n, often attrib* [ME, fr. OE *fleax;* akin to OHG *flahs* flax, L *plectere* to braid — more at PLY] **1 :** any of a genus (*Linum* of the family Linaceae, the flax family) of herbs; *esp* **:** a slender erect annual (*L. usitatissimum*) with blue flowers commonly cultivated for its bast fiber and seed **2 :** the fiber of the flax plant esp. when prepared for spinning **3 :** any of several plants resembling flax
flax·en \ˈflak-sən\ *adj* **1 :** made of flax **2 :** resembling flax esp. in pale soft strawy color <~ hair>
flax·seed \ˈflak(s)-ˌsēd\ *n* **:** the seed of flax used as a source of oil and medicinally as a demulcent and emollient
flaxy \ˈflak-sē\ *adj* **flax·i·er; -est :** resembling flax esp. in texture **:** FLAXEN
flay \ˈflā\ *vt* [ME *flen,* fr. OE *flēan;* akin to ON *flā* to flay, Lith *plėsti* to tear] **1 :** to strip off the skin or surface of **:** SKIN **2 a :** to strip of possessions **:** FLEECE **b :** to criticize harshly **:** EXCORIATE
F layer *n* **1 :** the highest and most densely ionized regular layer of the ionosphere occurring at night within the F region **2 :** the forest soil zone marked by abundant plant remains undergoing decay
fl dr *abbr* fluidram
flea \ˈflē\ *n* [ME *fle,* fr. OE *flēa;* akin to OHG *flōh* flea, OE *flēon* to flee] **1 :** any of an order (Siphonaptera) of wingless bloodsucking insects that have a hard laterally compressed body and legs adapted to leaping and that feed on warm-blooded animals **2 :** FLEA BEETLE — **flea in one's ear :** an irritating hint or warning **:** REBUKE

dog flea

flea·bag \ˈflē-ˌbag\ *n* **:** an inferior hotel or rooming house
flea·bane \-ˌbān\ *n* **:** any of various composite plants (as of the genus *Erigeron*) that were once supposed to drive away fleas
flea beetle *n* **:** any of various small chrysomelid beetles (as of the genera *Altica* and *Epitrix*) with legs adapted for leaping that feed on foliage and sometimes serve as vectors of virus diseases of plants
flea·bite \ˈflē-ˌbīt\ *n* **1 :** the bite of a flea; *also* **:** the red spot caused by such a bite **2 :** a trifling pain or annoyance
flea–bit·ten \-ˌbit-ᵊn\ *adj* **1 :** bitten by or infested with fleas **2** *of a horse* **:** having a white or gray coat flecked with bay or sorrel
flea·hop·per \-ˌhäp-ər\ *n* **:** any of various small jumping bugs that feed on cultivated plants
flea market *n* [trans. of F *Marché aux Puces,* a market in Paris] **:** a usu. open-air market for secondhand articles and antiques
flea weevil *n* **:** any of various small broad weevils with legs adapted for leaping and with larvae that are leaf miners
flea·wort \ˈflē-ˌwərt, -ˌwȯ(ə)rt\ *n* **:** an Old World plantain (*Plantago psyllium*) whose seeds swell and become gelatinous when moist and are sometimes used as a mild laxative
flèche \ˈflāsh, ˈflesh\ *n* [F, lit., arrow] **:** SPIRE; *esp* **:** a slender spire above the intersection of the nave and transepts of a church
flé·chette \flā-ˈshet, fle-\ *n* [F, fr. dim. of *flèche* arrow] **:** a small dart-shaped projectile that is clustered in an explosive warhead, dropped as a missile from an airplane, or fired from a hand-held gun
1fleck \ˈflek\ *vt* [back-formation fr. *flecked* spotted, fr. ME, prob. fr. ON *flekkōttr,* fr. *flekkr* spot] **:** STREAK, SPOT <whitecaps ~*ed* the blue sea>
2fleck *n* **1 :** SPOT, MARK <a brown tweed with ~*s* of yellow> **2 :** FLAKE, PARTICLE <~*s* of snow drifted down>
flec·tion *var of* FLEXION
fledge \ˈflej\ *vb* **fledged; fledg·ing** [*fledge* (capable of flying), fr. ME *flegge,* fr. OE *-flycge;* akin to OHG *flucki* capable of flying, OE *flēogan* to fly — more at FLY] *vi* **1** *of a bird* **:** to acquire the feathers necessary for flight **2** *of an insect* **:** to attain the winged adult stage ~ *vt* **1 :** to rear until ready for flight or independent activity **2 :** to cover with or as if with feathers or down **3 :** to furnish (as an arrow) with feathers
fledg·ling \ˈflej-liŋ\ *n* **1 :** a young bird just fledged **2 :** an immature or inexperienced person
flee \ˈflē\ *vb* **fled** \ˈfled\; **flee·ing** [ME *flen,* fr. OE *flēon;* akin to OHG *fliohan* to flee] *vi* **1 :** to run away from danger or evil **:** FLY **2 :** to pass away swiftly **:** VANISH <mists ~*ing* before the rising sun> ~ *vt* **:** to run away from **:** SHUN
1fleece \ˈflēs\ *n* [ME *flees,* fr. OE *flēos;* akin to MHG *vlius* fleece, L *pluma* feather, down] **1 a :** the coat of wool covering a wool-bearing animal (as a sheep) **b :** the wool obtained from a sheep at one shearing **2 a :** any of various soft or woolly coverings **b :** a soft bulky deep-piled knitted or woven fabric used chiefly for clothing
2fleece *vt* **fleeced; fleec·ing 1 :** to remove the fleece from **:** SHEAR **2 a :** to strip of money or property by fraud or extortion **b :** to charge excessively for goods or services <nightclubs where the customer knew he would be *fleeced*> **3 :** to dot or cover with fleecy masses
fleeced \ˈflēst\ *adj* **1 :** covered with or as if with a fleece **2** *of a textile* **:** having a soft nap
fleech \ˈflēch\ *vb* [ME (Sc) *flechen*] *dial* **:** COAX, WHEEDLE
fleecy \ˈflē-sē\ *adj* **fleec·i·er; -est :** covered with, made of, or resembling fleece <a ~ winter coat>
1fleer \ˈfli(ə)r\ *vi* [ME *fleryen,* of Scand origin; akin to Norw *flire* to giggle — more at FLIMFLAM] **:** to laugh or grimace in a coarse derisive manner **:** SNEER ***syn*** see SCOFF — **fleer·ing·ly** \-iŋ-lē\ *adv*
2fleer *n* **:** a word or look of derision or mockery
1fleet \ˈflēt\ *vb* [ME *fleten,* fr. OE *flēotan;* akin to OHG *fliozzan* to float, OE *flōwan* to flow] *vi* **1** *obs* **:** DRIFT **2 a** *archaic* **:** FLOW **b :** to fade away **:** VANISH **3 :** to fly swiftly ~ *vt* **1 :** to cause (time) to pass usu. quickly or imperceptibly **2** [alter. of *flit*] **:** to move or change in position <~ a hawser> ***syn*** see WHILE
2fleet *n* [ME *flete,* fr. OE *flēot* ship, fr. *flēotan*] **1 :** a number of warships under a single command; *specif* **:** an organization of ships and aircraft under the command of a flag officer and suitable to undertake major naval operations **2 :** a group (as of ships, planes, or trucks) operated under unified control
3fleet *adj* [prob. fr. *1fleet*] **1 :** swift in motion **:** NIMBLE **2 :** EVANESCENT, FLEETING ***syn*** see FAST — **fleet·ly** *adv* — **fleet·ness** *n*
fleet admiral *n* **:** an admiral of the highest rank in the navy whose insignia is five stars
fleet·ing *adj* **:** passing swiftly **:** TRANSITORY ***syn*** see TRANSIENT ***ant*** lasting — **fleet·ing·ly** \-iŋ-lē\ *adv* — **fleet·ing·ness** *n*
Fleet Street \ˈflēt-\ *n* [*Fleet Street,* London, England, center of the London newspaper district] **:** the London press
flei·shig \ˈflā-shik\ *adj* [Yiddish, fr. MHG *vleischic* meaty, fr. *vleisch* flesh, meat, fr. OHG *fleisk* — more at FLESH] **:** made of, prepared with, or used for meat or meat products
Flem *abbr* Flemish
Flem·ing \ˈflem-iŋ\ *n* [ME, fr. MD *Vlaminc,* fr. *Vlam-* (as in *Vlamland* Flanders)] **:** a member of the Germanic people inhabiting northern Belgium and a small section of northern France
1Flem·ish \ˈflem-ish\ *adj* **:** of, relating to, or characteristic of Flanders or the Flemings or their language
2Flemish *n* **1 :** the Germanic language of the Flemings **2** *pl in constr* **:** FLEMINGS
Flemish giant *n* **:** a rabbit of a breed prob. of Belgian origin that is characterized by large size, vigor, and solid coat color in black, white, or gray
flense \ˈflen(t)s\ *vt* **flensed; flens·ing** [D *flensen* or Dan & Norw *flense*] **:** to strip (as a whale) of blubber or skin
1flesh \ˈflesh\ *n* [ME, fr. OE *flǣsc;* akin to OHG *fleisk* flesh] **1 a :** the soft parts of the body of an animal and esp. of a vertebrate; *esp* **:** the parts composed chiefly of skeletal muscle as distinguished from visceral structures, bone, and integuments **b :** sleek well-fatted condition of body **c :** SKIN **2 a :** edible parts of an animal **b :** flesh of a mammal or bird that is an article of diet <abstain from ~ during religious fasts> **3 a :** the physical being of man <the spirit indeed is willing, but the ~ is weak —Mt 26:41 (AV)> **b :** human nature **4 a :** human beings **:** MANKIND **b :** living beings **c :** STOCK, KINDRED **5 :** a fleshy plant part used as food; *also* **:** the fleshy part of a fruit **6** *Christian Science* **:** an illusion that matter has sensation — **in the flesh :** in person and alive
2flesh *vt* **1 a :** to feed (as a hawk) with flesh from the kill to encourage interest in the chase **b :** to initiate or habituate esp. by giving a foretaste **2** *archaic* **:** GRATIFY **3 :** to clothe or cover with or as if with flesh; *broadly* **:** to give substance to <~*ed* out his argument with solid fact> **4 :** to free from flesh ~ *vi* **:** to become fleshy — often used with *up* or *out*
flesh and blood *n* **1 :** corporeal nature as composed of flesh and of blood <such neglect was more than *flesh and blood* could stand> **2 :** near kindred — used chiefly in the phrase *one's own flesh and blood* **3 :** SUBSTANCE, REALITY <attempting to give *flesh and blood* to nebulous ideas>
fleshed \ˈflesht\ *adj* **:** having flesh esp. of a specified kind — often used in combination <pink-*fleshed*> <thick-*fleshed*>
flesh fly *n* **:** a two-winged fly whose maggots feed on flesh; *esp* **:** one of a family (Sarcophagidae) of flies some of which cause myiasis
flesh·i·ness \ˈflesh-ē-nəs\ *n* **:** the state of being fleshy **:** CORPULENCE
flesh·ing \ˈflesh-iŋ\ *n* **1** *pl* **:** close-fitting usu. flesh-colored tights **2** *pl* **:** material removed in fleshing a hide or skin **3 a :** the distribution of the lean and fat on an animal **b :** the capacity of an animal to put on fat
flesh·ly \ˈflesh-lē\ *adj* **1 a :** CORPOREAL, BODILY **b :** of, relating to, or characterized by indulgence of bodily appetites; *esp* **:** LASCIVIOUS <~ desires> **c :** not spiritual **:** WORLDLY **2 :** FLESHY, PLUMP **3 :** having a sensuous quality <~ art> ***syn*** see CARNAL
flesh·ment \ˈflesh-mənt\ *n* [*2flesh*] *obs* **:** excitement associated with a successful beginning
flesh·pot \ˈflesh-ˌpät\ *n* **1** *pl* **:** bodily comfort **:** LUXURY **2 :** a place of luxurious entertainment — usu. used in pl. <a tour of the city's ~*s*>
flesh wound *n* **:** an injury involving penetration of the body musculature without damage to skeletal or visceral structures
fleshy \ˈflesh-ē\ *adj* **flesh·i·er; -est 1 a :** marked by, consisting of, or resembling flesh **b :** marked by abundant flesh; *esp* **:** CORPULENT **2 a :** SUCCULENT, PULPY <the rich ~ texture of a perfectly ripe melon> **b :** not thin, dry, or membranaceous <~ fungi>
fleshy fruit *n* **:** a fruit (as a berry, drupe, or pome) consisting largely of soft succulent tissue
fletch \ˈflech\ *vt* [back-formation fr. *fletcher*] **:** FEATHER <~ an arrow>
fletch·er \ˈflech-ər\ *n* [ME *fleccher,* fr. OF *flechier,* fr. *fleche* arrow] **:** a maker of arrows
fleur de coin \ˌflərd-ə-ˈkwaⁿ\ *adj* [F *à fleur de coin,* lit., with the bloom of the die] **:** being in the preserved mint condition

fleur–de–lis *or* **fleur–de–lys** \ˌflərd-ᵊl-ˈē, ˌflu̇rd-\ *n, pl* **fleurs–de–lis** *or* **fleur–de–lis** *or* **fleurs–de–lys** *or* **fleur–de–lys** \ˌflərd-ᵊl-ˈē(z), ˌflu̇rd-\ [ME *flourdelis,* fr. MF *flor de lis,* lit., lily flower] **1** : IRIS 3 **2** : a conventionalized iris in art and heraldry

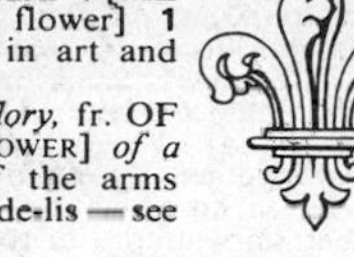
fleur-de-lis 2

fleu·ry \ˈflu̇(ə)r-ē\ *adj* [alter. of ME *flory,* fr. OF *floré,* fr. *flor* flower — more at FLOWER] *of a heraldic cross* : having the ends of the arms broadening out into the heads of fleurs-de-lis — see CROSS illustration

flew *past of* FLY

flews \ˈflüz\ *n pl* [origin unknown] : the pendulous lateral parts of a dog's upper lip — see DOG illustration

[1]**flex** \ˈfleks\ *vb* [L *flexus,* pp. of *flectere*] *vt* **1** : to bend esp. repeatedly <sat ~*ing* the strap as he talked> **2 a** : to move muscles so as to cause flexion of (a joint) <stretching and ~*ing* his knees> **b** : to move (a muscle or muscles) so as to flex a joint <~*ed* their biceps and went to work> ~ *vi* : BEND

[2]**flex** *n* **1** : an act or instance of flexing **2** [short for *flexible cord*] *chiefly Brit* : electric cord

flex·i·ble \ˈflek-sə-bəl\ *adj* **1** : capable of being flexed : PLIANT **2** : yielding to influence : TRACTABLE **3** : capable of responding or conforming to changing or new situations <a highly ~ curriculum> <a ~ personality> — **flex·i·bil·i·ty** \ˌflek-sə-ˈbil-ət-ē\ *n* — **flex·i·bly** \ˈflek-sə-blē\ *adv*

flex·ile \ˈflek-səl, -ˌsīl\ *adj* : FLEXIBLE

flex·ion \ˈflek-shən\ *n* [L *flexion-, flexio,* fr. *flexus,* pp. of *flectere*] **1** : the act of flexing or bending **2** : a part bent : BEND **3** : INFLECTION 3 **4 a** : a bending of a joint between the bones of a limb that diminishes the angle between the bones — compare EXTENSION 3b **b** : a forward raising of the arm or leg by a movement at the shoulder or hip joint

flex·og·ra·phy \flek-ˈsäg-rə-fē\ *n* [*flex*ible + *-o-* + *-graphy*] : a process of rotary letterpress printing utilizing flexible rubber plates and rapid-drying inks — **flexo·graph·ic** \ˌflek-sə-ˈgraf-ik\ *adj* — **flexo·graph·i·cal·ly** \-i-k(ə-)lē\ *adv*

flex·or \ˈflek-sər, -ˌsȯ(ə)r\ *n* : a muscle that produces flexion

flex·u·ous \ˈfleksh-(ə-)wəs\ *adj* [L *flexuosus,* fr. *flexus* bend, fr. *flexus,* pp.] **1** : having turns or windings **2** : lacking rigidity in structure or action <its ~ and elastic body> — **flex·u·ous·ly** *adv*

flex·ur·al \ˈflek-sh(ə-)rəl\ *adj* **1** : of, relating to, or resulting from flexure **2** : characterized by flexure

flex·ure \ˈflek-shər\ *n* **1** : the quality or state of being flexed : FLEXION **2** : TURN, FOLD

fley \ˈflā\ *vt* [ME *flayen,* fr. OE *āflēgan,* fr. *ā-,* perfective prefix + *-flēgan* to put to flight] *Scot* : FRIGHTEN

flib·ber·ti·gib·bet \ˌflib-ərt-ē-ˈjib-ət\ *n* [ME *flepergebet*] : a silly flighty person — **flib·ber·ti·gib·bety** \-ət-ē\ *adj*

flic \ˈflēk\ *n* [F] : a Parisian policeman

[1]**flick** \ˈflik\ *n* [imit.] **1** : a light sharp jerky stroke or movement **2** : a sound produced by a flick **3** : DAUB, SPLOTCH

[2]**flick** *vt* **1 a** : to strike lightly with a quick sharp motion <~*ed* the old horse with a whip> **b** : to remove with light blows <~*ed* the dust off his boots with a handkerchief> **2** : to cause to move with a flick <~*ed* his cigarette against the ashtray> ~ *vi* **1** : FLUTTER **2** : to direct flicks at something

[3]**flick** *n* [short for [2]*flicker*] : MOVIE

[1]**flick·er** \ˈflik-ər\ *vb* **flick·ered; flick·er·ing** \-(ə-)riŋ\ [ME *flikeren,* fr. OE *flicorian*] *vi* **1** : to move irregularly or unsteadily : FLUTTER <her eyes ~*ed* over the group> **2** : to burn fitfully or with a fluctuating light **3** : to appear in a tremulous incomplete form ~ *vt* **1** : to cause to flicker **2** : to produce by flickering <~ a signal with a mirror> — **flick·er·ing·ly** \-(ə-)riŋ-lē\ *adv*

[2]**flicker** *n* **1 a** : an act of flickering **b** : a sudden brief movement **c** : a momentary quickening <a ~ of anger> **2** : a wavering light **3** : MOVIE — often used in pl. — **flick·ery** \ˈflik-(ə-)rē\ *adj*

[3]**flicker** *n* [prob. fr. [2]*flick*] : a common large brightly marked woodpecker (*Colaptes auratus*) of eastern No. America; *also* : any of several related birds of the southern and western U.S.

flick·er·tail \ˈflik-ər-ˌtāl\ *n* : a ground squirrel (*Citellus richardsoni*) chiefly of the north-central U.S. and adjacent Canada

flied *past of* FLY

fli·er \ˈflī(-ə)r\ *n* **1** : one that flies; *specif* : AIRMAN **2** : a reckless or speculative venture <took a ~ in politics soon after getting his degree> **3** : an advertising circular for mass distribution **4** : a step in a straight flight of steps

[1]**flight** \ˈflīt\ *n* [ME, fr. OE *flyht;* akin to MD *vlucht* flight, OE *flēogan* to fly] **1 a** : an act or instance of passing through the air by the use of wings <the ~ of a bee> **b** : the ability to fly <~ is natural to birds> **2 a** : a passing through the air or through space outside the earth's atmosphere <~ of an arrow> <~ of a rocket to the moon> **b** : the distance covered in such a flight **c** : swift movement **3 a** : a trip made by or in an airplane or spacecraft <a rough ~ through storm clouds> **b** : a scheduled airplane flight <a ~ delayed because of poor weather conditions> **4** : a group of similar beings or objects flying through the air together **5** : a brilliant, imaginative, or unrestrained exercise or display <a ~ of fancy> **6 a** : a continuous series of stairs from one landing or floor to another **b** : a series (as of terraces or conveyors) resembling a flight of stairs **7** : a unit of the U.S. Air Force below a squadron — **flight·less** \-ləs\ *adj*

[2]**flight** *vi* : to rise, settle, or fly in a flock <geese ~*ing* on the marsh> ~ *vt* : [1]FLUSH

[3]**flight** *n* [ME *fluht, fliht;* akin to OHG *fluht* flight, OE *flēon* to flee] : an act or instance of running away

flight bag *n* [[1]*flight*] **1** : a lightweight traveling bag with zippered outside pockets **2** : a small canvas satchel

flight control *n* **1** : the control from a ground station of an airplane or spacecraft esp. by radio **2** : the system of control devices of an airplane

flight deck *n* **1** : the uppermost complete deck of an aircraft carrier **2** : the forward compartment in some airplanes

flight engineer *n* : a flight crewman responsible for mechanical operation

flight feather *n* : one of the quills of a bird's wing or tail that support it in flight — compare CONTOUR FEATHER

flight lieutenant *n* : a commissioned officer in the British air force who ranks with a captain in the army

flight line *n* **1** : a parking and servicing area for airplanes **2** : the line in air or space along which something (as an airplane or missile) travels or is intended to travel

flight path *n* : the path in the air or space made or followed by something (as a particle, an airplane, or a spacecraft) in flight

flight pay *n* : an additional allowance paid to military personnel on flight status

flight plan *n* : a usu. written statement (as by a pilot) of the details of an intended flight (as of an airplane or spacecraft) usu. filed with an authority

flight status *n* : the status of a person in the military participating in regular authorized aircraft flights

flight strip *n* : an emergency landing field beside a highway

flight surgeon *n* : an air force medical officer trained in aeromedicine

flight–test \ˈflīt-ˌtest\ *vt* : to test (as an airplane or spacecraft) in flight

flighty \ˈflīt-ē\ *adj* **flight·i·er; -est** **1** : SWIFT **2** : lacking stability or steadiness: **a** : easily upset : VOLATILE <a ~ temper> **b** : easily excited : SKITTISH <a ~ horse> **c** : IRRESPONSIBLE, SILLY <a ~ young girl> — **flight·i·ly** \ˈflīt-ᵊl-ē\ *adv* — **flight·i·ness** \ˈflīt-ē-nəs\ *n*

[1]**flim·flam** \ˈflim-ˌflam\ *n* [prob. of Scand origin; akin to ON *flim* mockery] **1** : DECEPTION, FRAUD **2** : HANKY-PANKY

[2]**flimflam** *vt* **flim·flammed; flim·flam·ming** : to subject to a flimflam — **flim·flam·mer** *n*

[1]**flim·sy** \ˈflim-zē\ *adj* **flim·si·er; -est** [perh. alter. of [1]*film* + *-sy* (as in *tricksy*)] **1 a** : lacking in physical strength or substance <~ silks> **b** : of inferior materials and workmanship **2** : having little worth or plausibility <a ~ excuse> ***syn*** see LIMP — **flim·si·ly** \-zə-lē\ *adv* — **flim·si·ness** \-zē-nəs\ *n*

[2]**flimsy** *n, pl* **flimsies** **1** : a lightweight paper used esp. for multiple copies **2** : a document printed on flimsy

flinch \ˈflinch\ *vi* [MF *flenchir* to bend] : to shrink from or as if from physical pain : WINCE; *esp* : to tense the muscles involuntarily in fear ***syn*** see RECOIL — **flinch** *n* — **flinch·er** *n*

flin·ders \ˈflin-dərz\ *n pl* [ME *flendris*] : SPLINTERS, FRAGMENTS

[1]**fling** \ˈfliŋ\ *vb* **flung** \ˈfləŋ\; **fling·ing** \ˈfliŋ-iŋ\ [ME *flingen,* of Scand origin; akin to ON *flengja* to whip, *flā* to flay — more at FLAY] *vi* **1** : to move in a brusque or headlong manner <~*ing* out of the room in a rage> **2** : to kick or plunge vigorously **3** *Scot* : CAPER ~ *vt* **1 a** : to throw with force or recklessness <*flung* his books on the table> **b** : to cast aside : DISCARD <*flung* off all restraint> **2** : to place or send suddenly and unceremoniously <the attack *flung* the enemy force into confusion> **3** : SPREAD, DIFFUSE **4** : to give unrestrainedly ***syn*** see THROW — **fling·er** \ˈfliŋ-ər\ *n*

[2]**fling** *n* **1** : an act or instance of flinging **2** : a casual try <willing to take a ~ at almost anything> **3** : a period devoted to self-indulgence <determined to have one last ~ before settling down>

flint \ˈflint\ *n* [ME, fr. OE; akin to OHG *flins* pebble, hard stone] **1** : a massive hard quartz that produces a spark when struck by steel **2** : an implement of flint used by primitive man **3** : a material used for producing a spark; *esp* : an alloy (as of iron and cerium) used in lighters **4** : something resembling flint in hardness — **flint·like** \-ˌlīk\ *adj*

Flint *or* **Flints** *abbr* Flintshire

flint corn *n* : an Indian corn (*Zea mays indurata*) having hard horny usu. rounded kernels with the soft endosperm enclosed by a hard outer layer

flint glass *n* : heavy brilliant glass that contains lead oxide, has a relatively high index of refraction, and is used for optical structures

flint·lock \ˈflint-ˌläk\ *n* **1** : a lock for a gun or pistol of the 17th and 18th centuries having a flint in the hammer for striking a spark to ignite the charge **2** : a firearm fitted with a flintlock

flinty \ˈflint-ē\ *adj* **flint·i·er; -est** **1** : composed of or covered with flint **2** : UNYIELDING, STERN — **flint·i·ly** \ˈflint-ᵊl-ē\ *adv* — **flint·i·ness** \ˈflint-ē-nəs\ *n*

[1]**flip** \ˈflip\ *vb* **flipped; flip·ping** [prob. imit.] *vt* **1 a** : to toss with a sharp movement so as to cause to turn over in the air <~ a coin> **b** : THROW <the shortstop *flipped* the ball to second base> **2** : FLICK 1 **3** : to turn over <*flipped* the record and played the other side> ~ *vi* **1 a** : to make a twitching or flicking movement **b** : to strike at something with such a movement **2** : to move jerkily **3** : LEAF 2 <*flipped* through the pages> **4** *slang* **a** : to lose one's mind, composure, or self-control — often used with *out* **b** : to become extremely enthusiastic : go wild <I just *flipped* over that vest>

[2]**flip** *n* **1** : an act or instance of flipping **2** : the motion used in flipping **3** : a somersault esp. when performed in the air **4** : a short quick football pass **5** : a mixed drink usu. consisting of a sweetened spiced liquor (as beer, wine, or rum) to which beaten eggs have been added

[3]**flip** *adj* : FLIPPANT, IMPERTINENT

flip–flop \ˈflip-ˌfläp\ *n* **1** : the sound or motion of something flapping loosely **2 a** : a backward handspring **b** : a sudden reversal of direction or point of view **3** : a usu. electronic device or a circuit (as in a computer) capable of assuming either of two stable states — **flip–flop** *vi*

flip·pan·cy \ˈflip-ən-sē\ *n, pl* **-cies :** unbecoming levity or pertness esp. in respect to grave or sacred matters ***syn*** see LIGHTNESS ***ant*** seriousness

flip·pant \ˈflip-ənt\ *adj* [prob. fr. [1]*flip*] **1** *archaic* **:** GLIB, TALKATIVE **2 :** lacking proper respect or seriousness <a ~ answer to a serious question> — **flip·pant·ly** *adv*

flip·per \ˈflip-ər\ *n* **1 a :** a broad flat limb (as of a seal) adapted for swimming **b :** a flat rubber shoe with the front expanded into a paddle used in skin diving **2 :** one that flips

flip side *n* [[1]*flip*] **:** the reverse and usu. less popular side of a phonograph record

[1]**flirt** \ˈflərt\ *vb* [origin unknown] *vt* **1 :** FLICK **2 :** to move in a jerky manner ~ *vi* **1 :** to move erratically **:** FLIT **2 a :** to behave amorously without serious intent **b :** to show superficial or casual interest or liking <~*ed* with the idea of getting a job> ***syn*** see TRIFLE — **flir·ta·tion** \ˌflər-ˈtā-shən\ *n* — **flirt·er** *n* — **flirty** \ˈflərt-ē\ *adj*

[2]**flirt** *n* **1 :** an act or instance of flirting **2 :** a person who flirts

flir·ta·tious \ˌflər-ˈtā-shəs\ *adj* **:** inclined to flirt **:** COQUETTISH — **flir·ta·tious·ly** *adv* — **flir·ta·tious·ness** *n*

flit \ˈflit\ *vi* **flit·ted; flit·ting** [ME *flitten*, of Scand origin; akin to ON *flytjask* to move, OE *flēotan* to float] **1 :** to pass quickly or abruptly from one place or condition to another <her imagination *flitted* back to her childhood> **2** *archaic* **:** ALTER, SHIFT **3 :** to move in an erratic fluttering manner — **flit** *n*

flitch \ˈflich\ *n* [ME *flicche*, fr. OE *flicce*] **1 :** a side of pork cured and smoked as bacon **2 a :** a longitudinal section of a log **b :** a bundle of sheets of veneer laid together in sequence **3 :** one of the parts secured together to make a girder or beam

[1]**flit·ter** \ˈflit-ər\ *vi* [freq. of *flit*] **:** FLUTTER, FLICKER

[2]**flitter** *n* **:** one that flits

fliv·ver \ˈfliv-ər\ *n* [origin unknown] **:** a small cheap usu. old automobile

[1]**float** \ˈflōt\ *n* [ME *flote* boat, float, fr. OE *flota* ship; akin to OHG *flōz* raft, stream, OE *flēotan* to float — more at FLEET] **1 :** an act or instance of floating **2 :** something that floats in or on the surface of a fluid: as **a :** a device (as a cork) buoying up the baited end of a fishing line **b :** a floating platform anchored near a shoreline for use by swimmers or boats **c :** a hollow ball that floats at the end of a lever in a cistern, tank, or boiler and regulates the liquid level **d :** a sac containing air or gas and buoying up the body of a plant or animal **:** PNEUMATOPHORE **e :** a watertight structure giving an airplane buoyancy on water **3 :** a tool or apparatus for smoothing a surface **4 :** a government grant of a fixed amount of land not yet located by survey out of a larger specific tract **5 a :** a vehicle with a platform used to carry an exhibit in a parade **b :** the vehicle and exhibit together **6 :** an amount of money represented by checks outstanding and in process of collection **7 :** a drink consisting of ice cream floating in a beverage — **floaty** \ˈflōt-ē\ *adj*

[2]**float** *vi* **1 :** to rest on the surface of or be suspended in a fluid **2 a :** to drift on or through or as if on or through a liquid <yellow leaves ~*ed* down> **b :** WANDER **3 :** to lack firmness of purpose **:** VACILLATE **4** *of a currency* **:** to find a level in the international exchange market in response to the law of supply and demand and without any restrictive effect of artificial support or control <proposed that the mark be allowed to ~> ~ *vt* **1 :** to cause to float in or on the surface of a liquid **2 :** to support (a structure) on a mat or raft foundation when the ground gives poor support **3 :** FLOOD <~ a cranberry bog> **4 :** to smooth (as plaster or cement) with a float **5 a :** to gain support for **b :** to place (an issue of securities) on the market **c :** to obtain money for the establishment or development of (an enterprise) by issuing and selling securities **d :** NEGOTIATE <~ a loan>

float·age *var of* FLOTAGE

floa·ta·tion *var of* FLOTATION

float·er \ˈflōt-ər\ *n* **1 a :** one that floats **b :** a person who floats something **2 a :** a person who votes illegally in various polling places **b :** a person who represents an irregular constituency **3 a :** a person without a permanent residence or regular employment **:** VAGRANT **b :** an employee without a specific job **4 :** a slow baseball pitch with little or no spin

float·ing *adj* **1 :** buoyed on or in a fluid **2 :** located out of the normal position <a ~ kidney> **3 a :** continually drifting or changing position <the ~ population> **b :** not presently committed or invested <~ capital> **c :** short-term and usu. not funded <~ debt> **4 :** connected or constructed so as to operate and adjust smoothly <a ~ axle>

floating dock *n* **:** a dock that floats on the water and can be partly submerged to permit entry of a ship and raised to keep the ship high and dry — called also *floating drydock*

floating island *n* **:** a dessert consisting of custard with floating masses of whipped white of egg

floating–point *adj* **:** involving or being a mathematical notation in which a quantity is denoted by one number multiplied by a power of the number base <the fixed-point value 99.9 could be expressed in a ~ system as .999 x 10^2> —compare FIXED-POINT

floating rib *n* **:** a rib (as one of either of the last two pairs in man) that has no attachment to the sternum — compare FALSE RIB

float·plane \ˈflōt-ˌplān\ *n* **:** a seaplane supported on the water by one or more floats

[1]**floc** \ˈfläk\ *n* [short for *floccule*] **1 :** a flocculent mass formed by the aggregation of a number of fine suspended particles **2 :** [3]FLOCK 1,2,3

[2]**floc** *vb* **flocced** \ˈfläkt\; **floc·cing** \ˈfläk-iŋ\ *vi* **:** to aggregate into flocs ~ *vt* **:** to cause to floc

[1]**floc·cu·late** \ˈfläk-yə-ˌlāt\ *vb* **-lat·ed; -lat·ing** *vt* **:** to cause to aggregate into a flocculent mass <~ clay> ~ *vi* **:** to become flocculated — **floc·cu·lant** \-lənt\ *n* — **floc·cu·la·tion** \ˌfläk-yə-ˈlā-shən\ *n* — **floc·cu·la·tor** \ˈfläk-yə-ˌlāt-ər\ *n*

[2]**floc·cu·late** \-lət, -ˌlāt\ *n* **:** something that has flocculated

floc·cule \ˈfläk-(ˌ)yü(ə)l\ *n* [LL *flocculus*] **:** a small loosely aggregated bit of material suspended in or precipitated from a liquid

floc·cu·lence \ˈfläk-yə-lən(t)s\ *n* **:** a flocculent quality or state

floc·cu·lent \-lənt\ *adj* [L *floccus* + E *-ulent*] **1 :** resembling wool esp. in loose fluffy organization **2 :** made up of flocs or floccules <a ~ precipitate>

floc·cu·lus \-ləs\ *n, pl* **-li** \-ˌlī, -ˌlē\ [LL, dim. of L *floccus* flock of wool; akin to OHG *blaha* coarse linen] **1 :** a small loosely aggregated mass **2 :** a bright or dark patch on the sun

[1]**flock** \ˈfläk\ *n* [ME, fr. OE *flocc* crowd, band; akin to ON *flokkr* crowd, band] **1 :** a group of birds or mammals assembled or herded together **2 :** a group under the guidance of a leader; *specif* **:** a church congregation in relation to the pastor **3 :** a large number <a whole ~ of tourists>

[2]**flock** *vi* **:** to gather or move in a crowd <they ~*ed* to the beach>

[3]**flock** *n* [ME] **1 :** a tuft of wool or cotton fiber **2 :** woolen or cotton refuse used for stuffing furniture and mattresses **3 :** very short or pulverized fiber used esp. to form a velvety pattern on cloth or paper or a protective covering on metal **4 :** FLOC

[4]**flock** *vt* **1 :** to fill with flock **2 :** to decorate with flock

flock·ing \ˈfläk-iŋ\ *n* **:** a design in flock

floe \ˈflō\ *n* [prob. fr. Norw *flo* flat layer] **1 :** floating ice formed in a large sheet on the surface of a body of water **2 :** ICE FLOE

flog \ˈfläg\ *vt* **flogged; flog·ging** [perh. modif. of L *flagellare* to whip — more at FLAGELLATE] **1 :** to beat with a rod or whip **:** LASH **2 :** to criticize harshly <newspapers *flogging* the government over tax inequities> **3 :** to force into action **:** DRIVE <*flogging* his keen retentive memory —Nevil Shute> **4** *chiefly Brit* **:** SELL; *esp* **:** to sell stolen goods — **flog·ger** *n* — **flog a dead horse :** to attempt to revive interest in a worn-out or forgotten subject

[1]**flood** \ˈfləd\ *n* [ME, fr. OE *flōd;* akin to OHG *fluot* flood, OE *flōwan* to flow] **1 :** a rising and overflowing of a body of water esp. onto normally dry land <a covenant never to destroy the earth again by ~ —John Milton> **2 :** the flowing in of the tide **3 :** an overwhelming quantity or volume <a ~ of mail at Christmas time> **4 :** FLOODLIGHT

[2]**flood** *vt* **1 :** to cover with a flood **:** INUNDATE **2 a :** to fill abundantly or excessively <strawberries ~*ed* the market and prices dropped> **b :** to supply to (the carburetor of an internal-combustion engine) an excess of fuel so that engine operation is hampered **3 :** to send more than one pass receiver into (the same defensive area in football) ~ *vi* **1 :** to pour forth in a flood **2 :** to become filled with a flood — **flood·er** *n*

flood·gate \ˈfləd-ˌgāt\ *n* **1 :** a gate for shutting out, admitting, or releasing a body of water **:** SLUICE **2 :** something serving to restrain an outburst

[1]**flood·light** \-ˌlīt\ *n* **1 a :** artificial illumination in a broad beam **b :** a source of such illumination **2 :** a lighting unit for projecting a beam of light

[2]**floodlight** *vt* **:** to illuminate by means of one or more floodlights

flood·plain \ˈfləd-ˌplān\ *n* **1 :** level land that may be submerged by floodwaters **2 :** a plain built up by stream deposition

flood tide *n* **1 :** a rising tide **2 a :** an overwhelming quantity **b :** a high point **:** PEAK

flood·wall \ˈfləd-ˌwȯl\ *n* **:** a wall (as a levee) built to prevent inundation by high water

flood·wa·ter \-ˌwȯt-ər, -ˌwät-\ *n* **:** the water of a flood

flood·way \-ˌwā\ *n* **:** a channel for diverting floodwaters

floo·ey \ˈflü-ē\ *adj* [origin unknown] **:** AWRY, ASKEW

[1]**floor** \ˈflō(ə)r, ˈflȯ(ə)r\ *n* [ME *flor*, fr. OE *flōr;* akin to OHG *fluor* meadow, L *planus* level, Gk *planasthai* to wander] **1 :** the level base of a room **2 a :** the lower inside surface of a hollow structure (as a cave or bodily part) **b :** a ground surface <the ocean ~> **3 a :** a structure dividing a building into stories; *also* **:** STORY **b :** the occupants of such a floor <the whole third ~ is furious> **4 :** the surface of a structure on which one travels <the ~ of a bridge> **5 a :** a main level space (as in a legislative chamber) distinguished from a platform or gallery **b :** the members of an assembly <concluded by calling for questions from the ~> **c :** the right to address an assembly <the senator from Utah has the ~> **6 :** a lower limit **:** BASE <a ~ under prices or wages> — **floor** *adj*

[2]**floor** *vt* **1 :** to cover with a floor or flooring **2 a :** to knock to the floor **b :** SHOCK, OVERWHELM **c :** to reduce to silence or defeat **3 :** to press (the accelerator of a vehicle) to the floorboard — **floor·er** *n*

floor·age \ˈflōr-ij, ˈflȯr-\ *n* **:** floor space

floor·board \ˈflō(ə)r-ˌbō(ə)rd, ˈflȯ(ə)r-ˌbȯ(ə)rd\ *n* **1 :** a board in a floor **2 :** the floor of an automobile

floor exercise *n* **:** an event in gymnastics competition consisting of various ballet and tumbling movements (as jumps, somersaults, and handstands) performed without apparatus

floor furnace *n* **:** a small furnace located close below the floor

floor·ing \ˈflōr-iŋ, ˈflȯr-\ *n* **1 :** FLOOR, BASE **2 :** material for floors <the disadvantages of softwood ~>

floor lamp *n* **:** a tall lamp that stands on the floor

floor leader *n* **:** a member of a legislative body chosen by his party to have charge of its organization and strategy on the floor

floor–length *adj* **:** reaching to the floor <a ~ gown>

floor manager *n* **1 :** FLOORWALKER **2 :** a person who directs something (as the activities in support of a candidate at a nominating convention) from the floor

floor sample *n* **:** an article offered for sale at a reduced price because it has been used for display or demonstration

floor show *n* **:** a series of acts presented in a nightclub

floor·walk·er \ˈflōr-ˌwȯ-kər, ˈflȯr-\ *n* **:** a person employed in a retail store to oversee the salespeople and aid customers

floo·zy *or* **floo·zie** \ˈflü-zē\ *n, pl* **floozies** [origin unknown] **:** a tawdry or immoral woman; *specif* **:** PROSTITUTE

[1]**flop** \ˈfläp\ *vb* **flopped; flop·ping** [alter. of [2]*flap*] *vi* **1 :** to swing or bounce loosely **2 :** to throw or move oneself in a heavy, clumsy, or relaxed manner <*flopped* into the chair with a sigh of relief> **3 :** to change suddenly **4 :** to go to bed <so tired I had to ~> **5 :** to fail completely <in spite of good reviews the play *flopped*> ~ *vt* **:** to move or drop heavily and noisily <*flopped* the bundles down with a thud> — **flop·per** *n*

²flop *n* **1** : an act or sound of flopping **2** : a complete failure : DUD
³flop *adv* : RIGHT, SQUARELY <fell ~ on his face>
flop·house \'fläp-,haùs\ *n* : a cheap rooming house or hotel
flop·over \-,ō-vər\ *n* : a defect in television reception in which a succession of frames appears to traverse the screen vertically
flop·py \'fläp-ē\ *adj* **flop·pi·er; -est** : tending to flop; *esp* : being both soft and flexible ***syn*** see LIMP — **flop·pi·ly** \'fläp-ə-lē\ *adv* — **flop·pi·ness** \'fläp-ē-nəs\ *n*
flo·ra \'flōr-ə, 'flòr-\ *n, pl* **floras** *also* **flo·rae** \'flō(ə)r-,ē, 'flò(ə)r-, -,ī\ [NL, fr. L *Flora,* Roman goddess of flowers] **1** : a treatise on or list of the plants of an area or period **2** : plant life; *esp* : the plant life characteristic of a region, period, or special environment — compare FAUNA
flo·ral \'flōr-əl, 'flòr-\ *adj* [L *flor-, flos* flower — more at BLOW] : of or relating to flowers or a flora — **flo·ral·ly** \-ə-lē\ *adv*
floral envelope *n* : PERIANTH
floral leaf *n* **1** : a modified leaf (as a sepal or petal) of the perianth of a flower **2** : BRACT
Flor·ence flask \,flòr-ən(t)s-, ,flär-\ *n* [*Florence,* Italy; fr. the use of flasks of this shape for certain Italian wines] : a round usu. flat-bottomed laboratory vessel with a long neck
flo·res·cence \flō-'res-ᵊn(t)s, flə-\ *n* [NL *florescentia,* fr. L *florescent-, florescens,* prp. of *florescere,* incho. of *florēre* to blossom, flourish — more at FLOURISH] : a state or period of flourishing — **flo·res·cent** \-ᵊnt\ *adj*
flo·ret \'flōr-ət, 'flòr-\ *n* [ME *flourette,* fr. MF *flouret,* dim. of *flour* flower] : a small flower; *esp* : one of the small flowers forming the head of a composite plant
flori- *comb form* [L, fr. *flor-, flos*] : flower or flowers <*flori*culture>
flo·ri·at·ed \'flōr-ē-,āt-əd, 'flòr-\ *adj* : having floral ornaments or a floral form <a ~ border on a book cover> — **flo·ri·a·tion** \,flōr-ē-'ā-shən, ,flòr-\ *n*
flo·ri·bun·da \,flōr-ə-'bən-də, ,flòr-\ *n* [NL, fem. of *floribundus* flowering freely] : any of various bush roses with large flowers in open clusters that derive from crosses of polyantha and tea roses
flo·ri·cul·ture \'flōr-ə-,kəl-chər, 'flòr-\ *n* : the cultivation and management of ornamental and flowering plants — **flo·ri·cul·tur·al** \,flōr-ə-'kəlch(-ə)-rəl, ,flòr-\ *adj* — **flo·ri·cul·tur·al·ly** \-rə-lē\ *adv* — **flo·ri·cul·tur·ist** \-rəst\ *n*
flor·id \'flòr-əd, 'flär-\ *adj* [L *floridus* blooming, flowery, fr. *florēre*] **1 a** *obs* : covered with flowers **b** : excessively flowery in style : ORNATE **2** : tinged with red : RUDDY <a ~ complexion> **3** *archaic* : HEALTHY **4** : fully developed : manifesting a complete and typical clinical syndrome <the ~ stage of a disease> — **flo·rid·i·ty** \flə-'rid-ət-ē, flō-\ *n* — **flor·id·ly** \'flòr-əd-lē, 'flär-\ *adv* — **flor·id·ness** *n*
flo·rif·er·ous \flō-'rif-(ə-)rəs\ *adj* [L *florifer,* fr. *flori-*] : bearing flowers; *esp* : blooming freely — **flo·rif·er·ous·ly** *adv* — **flo·rif·er·ous·ness** *n*
flo·ri·gen \'flōr-ə-jən, 'flòr-\ *n* [ISV] : a hormone or hormonal agent that promotes flowering — **flo·ri·gen·ic** \,flōr-ə-'jen-ik, ,flòr-\ *adj*
flo·ri·le·gium \,flōr-ə-'lē-j(ē-)əm, ,flòr-\ *n, pl* **-gia** \-j(ē-)ə\ [NL, fr. L *florilegus* culling flowers, fr. *flori-* + *legere* to gather — more at LEGEND] : a volume of writings : ANTHOLOGY
flo·rin \'flòr-ən, 'flär-, 'flōr-\ *n* [ME, fr. MF, fr. OIt *fiorino,* fr. *fiore* flower, fr. L *flor-, flos;* fr. the lily on the coins] **1 a** : an old gold coin first struck at Florence in 1252 **b** : any of various gold coins of European countries patterned after the Florentine florin **2 a** : a British silver coin worth two shillings **b** : any of several similar coins issued in British Commonwealth countries **3** : GULDEN **4** : FORINT
flo·rist \'flōr-əst, 'flòr-\ *n* : one who sells or grows for sale flowers and ornamental plants — **flo·rist·ry** \-ə-strē\ *n*
flo·ris·tic \flō-'ris-tik\ *adj* : of or relating to flowers, a flora, or floristics — **flo·ris·ti·cal·ly** \-ti-k(ə-)lē\ *adv*
flo·ris·tics \-tiks\ *n pl but sing in constr* : a branch of phytogeography that deals numerically with plants and plant groups
-flo·rous \'flōr-əs, 'flòr-\ *adj comb form* [LL *-florus,* fr. L *flor-, flos*] : having or bearing (such or so many) flowers <uni*florous*>
flo·ru·it \'flòr-(y)ə-wət, 'flär-\ *n* [L, he flourished, fr. *florēre* to flourish] : a period of flourishing (as of a person, movement, or school)
floss \'fläs, 'flòs\ *n* [fr. or akin to D *vlos;* akin to MHG *vlus, vlius* fleece — more at FLEECE] **1** : waste or short silk fibers that cannot be reeled **2 a** : soft thread of silk or mercerized cotton for embroidery **b** : a lightweight wool knitting yarn **3** : fluffy fibrous material; *esp* : SILK COTTON
floss·flow·er \-,flaù(-ə)r\ *n* : AGERATUM
flossy \'fläs-ē, 'flòs-\ *adj* **floss·i·er; -est** **1 a** : of, relating to, or having the characteristics of floss **b** : DOWNY **2** : stylish or glamorous esp. at first impression <slick ~ writing>
flo·ta \'flōt-ə\ *n* [Sp] : a fleet of Spanish ships
flo·tage \'flōt-ij\ *n* [²*float*] **1** : FLOTATION 1 **2** : material that floats : FLOTSAM **3** *usu* **floatage** : the charge for transferring railroad cars on a barge
flo·ta·tion \flō-'tā-shən\ *n* [²*float*] **1** : the act, process, or state of floating **2** : an act or instance of financing (as an issue of stock) **3** : the separation of the particles of a mass of pulverized ore according to their relative capacity for floating on a given liquid; *also* : any of various similar processes involving the relative capacity of materials for floating **4** : the ability (as of a tire) to stay on the surface of soft ground or snow
flo·til·la \flō-'til-ə\ *n* [Sp, dim. of *flota* fleet, fr. OF *flote,* fr. ON *floti;* akin to OE *flota* ship, fleet — more at FLOAT] **1** : a fleet of ships; *specif* : a navy organizational unit consisting of two or more squadrons of small warships **2** : a large force of moving things <cleared by a ~ of bulldozers —R.L. Neuberger>
flot·sam \'flät-səm\ *n* [AF *floteson,* fr. OF *floter* to float, of Gmc origin; akin to OE *flotian* to float, *flota* ship] **1** : floating wreckage of a ship or its cargo; *broadly* : floating debris **2 a** : vagrant impoverished people **b** : unimportant miscellaneous material
¹flounce \'flaùn(t)s\ *vi* **flounced; flounc·ing** [perh. of Scand origin; akin to Norw *flunsa* to hurry] **1 a** : to move with exaggerated jerky motions <little girls *flouncing* about in their mothers' clothes> **b** : to go with sudden determination <she *flounced* out of the room in a huff> **2** : FLOUNDER, STRUGGLE
²flounce *n* : an act or instance of flouncing — **flouncy** \'flaùn(t)-sē\ *adj*
³flounce *n* [alter. of earlier *frounce,* fr. ME *frouncen* to curl] : a strip of fabric attached by one edge; *also* : a wide ruffle — **flouncy** \'flaùn(t)-sē\ *adj*
⁴flounce *vt* **flounced; flounc·ing** : to trim with flounces
flounc·ing \'flaùn(t)-siŋ\ *n* : material used for flounces
¹floun·der \'flaùn-dər\ *n, pl* **flounder** *or* **flounders** [ME, of Scand origin; akin to ON *flythra* flounder, *flatr* flat] : FLATFISH; *esp* : one of either of two families (Pleuronectidae and Bothidae) that include important marine food fishes

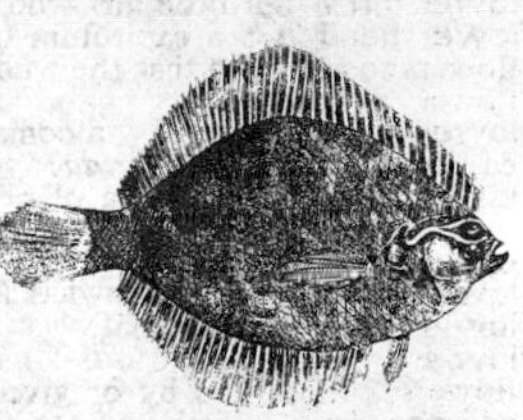
flounder

²flounder *vi* **floun·dered; floun·der·ing** \-d(ə-)riŋ\ [prob. alter. of *founder*] **1** : to struggle to move or obtain footing **2** : to proceed or act clumsily or ineffectually <a bright student ~*ing* because of poor study habits>
¹flour \'flaù(ə)r\ *n* [ME — more at FLOWER] **1** : finely ground meal of wheat usu. largely freed from bran; *also* : a similar meal of another material (as a cereal grain, an edible seed, or dried processed fish) **2** : a fine soft powder — **floury** \-ē\ *adj*
²flour *vt* : to coat with or as if with flour ~ *vi* : to break up into particles
¹flour·ish \'flər-ish, 'flə-rish\ *vb* [ME *florisshen,* fr. MF *floriss-,* stem of *florir,* fr. (assumed) VL *florire,* alter. of L *florēre,* fr. *flor-, flos* flower] *vi* **1** : to grow luxuriantly : THRIVE **2 a** : to achieve success : PROSPER **b** : to be in a state of activity or production <~*ed* around 1850> **c** : to reach a height of development or influence **3** : to make bold and sweeping gestures ~ *vt* : to wield with dramatic gestures : BRANDISH ***syn*** **1** see SUCCEED ***ant*** languish **2** see SWING — **flour·ish·er** *n* — **flour·ish·ing·ly** \-iŋ-lē\ *adv*
²flourish *n* **1** : a period of thriving **2 a** : an extraneous florid embellishment or passage **b** : an act or instance of brandishing : WAVE **c** : a studied or ostentatious action
¹flout \'flaùt\ *vb* [prob. fr. ME *flouten* to play the flute, fr. *floute* flute] *vt* : to treat with contemptuous disregard : SCORN <~*ing* the rules> ~ *vi* : to indulge in scornful behavior ***syn*** see SCOFF — **flout·er** *n*
²flout *n* **1** : INSULT **2** : MOCKERY
¹flow \'flō\ *vb* [ME *flowen,* fr. OE *flōwan;* akin to OHG *flouwen* to rinse, wash, L *pluere* to rain, Gk *plein* to sail, float] *vi* **1 a** (1) : to issue or move in a stream (2) : CIRCULATE **b** : to move with a continual change of place among the constituent particles <the molasses ~*ed* slowly> **2** : RISE <the tide ebbs and ~*s*> **3** : ABOUND **4 a** : to proceed smoothly and readily <conversation ~*ed* easily> **b** : to have a smooth uninterrupted continuity <the ~*ing* lines of the car> **5** : to hang loose and billowing **6** : to derive from a source : COME <the wealth that ~*s* from our industries> **7** : to deform under stress without cracking or rupturing — used esp. of minerals and rocks **8** : MENSTRUATE ~ *vt* **1 a** : to cause to flow **b** : to cover with water : FLOOD **2** : to discharge in a flow ***syn*** see SPRING — **flow·ing·ly** \-iŋ-lē\ *adv*
²flow *n* **1** : an act of flowing **2** : FLOOD 1, 2 **3 a** : a smooth uninterrupted movement **b** : STREAM **c** : the direction of movement or apparent movement (as of a play in football) **4** : the quantity that flows in a certain time **5 a** : MENSTRUATION **b** : YIELD, PRODUCTION **6 a** : the motion characteristic of fluids **b** : a continuous transfer of energy
flow·age \'flō-ij\ *n* **1 a** : an overflowing onto adjacent land **b** : a body of water formed by overflowing or damming **c** : floodwater esp. of a stream **2** : gradual deformation of a body of plastic solid (as rock) by intermolecular shear

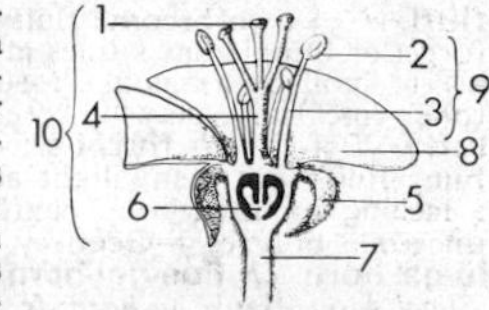

a flower in section: *1* stigma, *2* anther, *3* filament, *4* style, *5* sepal, *6* ovary, *7* pedicel, *8* petal, *9* stamen, *10* pistil

flow·chart \-,chärt\ *n* : a diagram consisting of a set of symbols (as rectangles or diamonds) and connecting lines that shows step-by-step progression through a usu. complicated procedure or system
flow diagram *n* : FLOWCHART
¹flow·er \'flaù(-ə)r\ *n* [ME *flour* flower, best of anything, flour, fr. OF *flor, flour,* fr. L *flor-, flos* — more at BLOW] **1 a** : BLOSSOM, INFLORESCENCE **b** : a shoot of the sporophyte of a higher plant that is modified for reproduction and consists of a shortened axis bearing modified leaves **c** : a plant cultivated for its blossoms **2 a** : the best part or example <the ~ of a nation's youth sent off to war> **b** : the finest most vigorous period **c** : a state of blooming or flourishing **3** *pl* : a finely divided powder produced esp. by condensation or sublimation <~*s* of sulfur> — **flow·ered** \'flaù(-ə)rd\ *adj* — **flow·er·less** \'flaù(-ə)r-ləs\ *adj* — **flow·er·like** \-,līk\ *adj*

[2]**flower** *vi* **1 :** to produce flowers : BLOSSOM **2 a :** DEVELOP <~*ed* into young womanhood> **b :** FLOURISH ~ *vt* **1 :** to cause to bear flowers **2 :** to decorate with floral designs — **flow·er·er** \ˈflaů(-ə)r-ər\ *n*
flow·er·age \ˈflaů(-ə)r-ij\ *n* **:** a flowering state
flower bud *n* **:** a plant bud that produces only a flower
flower bug *n* **:** any of various small mostly black-and-white predaceous bugs (family Anthocoridae) that frequent flowers and feed on pest insects (as aphids and thrips)
flower child *n* [fr. his displaying of flowers as a symbol of his sentiments] **:** a hippie who advocates love, beauty, and peace
flow·er·et \ˈflaů(-ə)r-ət\ *n* **:** FLORET
flower girl *n* **:** a little girl who carries flowers at a wedding
flower head *n* **:** a capitulum (as of a composite) having sessile flowers so arranged that the whole inflorescence looks like a single flower
flowering dogwood *n* **:** a common spring-flowering white-bracted dogwood (*Cornus florida*)
flowering plant *n* **1 :** a plant that produces flowers, fruit, and seed : ANGIOSPERM **2 :** a plant notable for or cultivated for its ornamental flowers
flower people *n pl* **:** FLOWER CHILDREN
flow·er·pot \ˈflaů(-ə)r-ˌpät\ *n* **:** a pot in which to grow plants
flow·ery \ˈflaů(-ə)r-ē\ *adj* **1 :** of, relating to, or resembling flowers **2 :** marked by or given to rhetorical elegance — **flow·er·i·ness** *n*
[1]**flown** \ˈflōn\ *past part of* FLY
[2]**flown** *adj* [archaic pp. of [1]*flow*] **:** filled to excess
flow sheet *n* **:** FLOWCHART
flow·stone \ˈflō-ˌstōn\ *n* **:** travertine found where water flowing in a very thin sheet over rocks has deposited mineral matter
fl oz *abbr* fluidounce
FLS *abbr* Fellow of the Linnean Society
FLSA *abbr* Fair Labor Standards Act
flu \ˈflü\ *n* **1 :** INFLUENZA **2 :** any of several virus diseases marked esp. by respiratory symptoms
[1]**flub** \ˈfləb\ *vb* **flubbed; flub·bing** [origin unknown] *vt* **:** to make a mess of : BOTCH ~ *vi* **:** BLUNDER
[2]**flub** *n* **:** an act or instance of flubbing
flub·dub \ˈfləb-ˌdəb\ *n* [origin unknown] **:** CLAPTRAP, BUNKUM
fluc·tu·ant \ˈflək-chə-wənt\ *adj* **1 :** moving in waves **2 :** VARIABLE, UNSTABLE **3 :** being movable and compressible <a ~ abscess>
fluc·tu·ate \ˈflək-chə-ˌwāt\ *vb* **-at·ed; -at·ing** [L *fluctuatus*, pp. of *fluctuare*, fr. *fluctus* flow, wave, fr. *fluctus*, pp. of *fluere*] *vi* **1 :** to ebb and flow in waves **2 :** to shift back and forth uncertainly ~ *vt* **:** to cause to fluctuate ***syn*** see SWING — **fluc·tu·a·tion** \ˌflək-chə-ˈwā-shən\ *n*
flue \ˈflü\ *n* [origin unknown] **:** an enclosed passageway for directing a current: as **a :** a channel in a chimney for conveying flame and smoke to the outer air **b :** a pipe for conveying flame and hot gases around or through water in a steam boiler **c :** an air channel leading to the lip of a wind instrument
flue–cured \-ˌkyů(ə)rd\ *adj* **:** cured with heat transmitted through a flue without exposure to smoke or fumes <~ tobacco> — compare FIRE-CURED
flu·en·cy \ˈflü-ən-sē\ *n* **:** the quality or state of being fluent
flu·ent \ˈflü-ənt\ *adj* [L *fluent-, fluens*, prp. of *fluere*] **1 :** capable of flowing : FLUID **2 a :** ready or facile in speech <~ in Spanish> **b :** effortlessly smooth and rapid : POLISHED <a ~ performance> — **flu·ent·ly** *adv*
flue pipe *n* **:** an organ pipe whose tone is produced by an air current striking the lip and causing the air within to vibrate — compare REED PIPE
flu·er·ic \flü-ˈer-ik\ *adj* **:** FLUIDIC — **flu·er·ics** \-iks\ *n pl but sing in constr*
flue stop *n* **:** an organ stop made up of flue pipes
[1]**fluff** \ˈfləf\ *n* [prob. alter. of *flue* (fluff)] **1 :** NAP, DOWN **2 :** something fluffy **3 :** something inconsequential **4 :** BLUNDER; *esp* **:** an actor's lapse of memory
[2]**fluff** *vi* **1 :** to become fluffy **2 :** to make a mistake; *esp* **:** to forget or bungle one's lines in a play ~ *vt* **1 :** to make fluffy **2 a :** to spoil by a mistake : BOTCH **b :** to deliver badly or forget (one's lines) in a play
fluffy \ˈfləf-ē\ *adj* **fluff·i·er; -est** **1 a :** covered with or resembling fluff **b :** being light and soft or airy <a ~ omelet> **2 :** lacking in intellectual content or decisive quality <vague, ~, uncertain policies —Geoffrey Crowther> — **fluff·i·ness** *n*
flü·gel·horn *or* **flue·gel·horn** \ˈflü-gəl-ˌhȯ(ə)rn, ˈflue-\ *n* [G, fr. *flügel* wing, flank + *horn*; fr. its use to signal the flanking drivers in a battue] **:** a valved brass instrument resembling a cornet but having a larger bore
[1]**flu·id** \ˈflü-əd\ *adj* [F or L; F *fluide*, fr. L *fluidus*, fr. *fluere* to flow; akin to Gk *phlyzein* to boil over, L *flare* to blow — more at BLOW] **1 a :** having particles that easily move and change their relative position without a separation of the mass and that easily yield to pressure : capable of flowing **b :** likely or tending to change or move **2 :** characterized by or employing a smooth easy style <the ballerina's ~ movements> **3 a :** available for a different use **b :** easily converted into cash <~ assets> — **flu·id·ly** *adv* — **flu·id·ness** *n*
[2]**fluid** *n* **:** a substance (as a liquid or gas) tending to flow or conform to the outline of its container — **flu·id·al** \-əd-ᵊl\ *adj* — **flu·id·al·ly** \-ᵊl-ē\ *adv*
fluid drive *n* **:** an automotive power coupling that operates on a hydraulic turbine principle with the flywheel having a set of turbine blades connected directly to it and driving them in oil thereby turning another set of turbine blades attached to the transmission gears
flu·id·ex·tract \ˌflü-ə-ˈdek-ˌstrakt\ *n* **:** an alcohol preparation of a vegetable drug containing the active constituents of one gram of the dry drug in each milliliter
flu·id·ic \flü-ˈid-ik\ *adj* **:** of, relating to, or being a device (as an amplifier or control) that depends for operation on the pressures and flows of a fluid in precisely shaped channels — **fluidic** *n* — **flu·id·ics** \-iks\ *n pl but sing in constr*
flu·id·i·ty \flü-ˈid-ət-ē\ *n* **1 :** the quality or state of being fluid **2 :** the physical property of a substance that enables it to flow
flu·id·ize \ˈflü-ə-ˌdīz\ *vt* **-ized; -iz·ing** **1 :** to cause to flow like a fluid **2 :** to suspend (as solid particles) in a rapidly moving stream of gas or vapor to induce flowing motion of the whole; *esp* **:** to fluidize the particles of (a loose bed of material) in an upward flow (as of a gas) for enhancing a chemical or physical reaction —**flu·id·iza·tion** \ˌflü-əd-ə-ˈzā-shən\ *n* — **flu·id·iz·er** \ˈflü-ə-ˌdī-zər\ *n*
fluid mechanics *n pl but sing or pl in constr* **:** a branch of mechanics dealing with the properties of liquids and gases
flu·id·ounce \ˌflü-ə-ˈdaůn(t)s\ *n* **1 :** a U.S. unit of liquid capacity equal to $\frac{1}{16}$ pint — see WEIGHT table **2 :** a British unit of liquid capacity equal to $\frac{1}{20}$ pint — see WEIGHT table
flu·idram \ˌflü-ə(d)-ˈdram\ *n* [blend of [1]*fluid* and *dram*] **:** a unit of liquid capacity equal to $\frac{1}{8}$ fluidounce — see WEIGHT table
[1]**fluke** \ˈflük\ *n* [ME, fr. OE *flōc*; akin to OHG *flah* smooth — more at FLAKE] **1 :** FLATFISH **2 :** a flattened digenetic trematode worm; *broadly* **:** TREMATODE
[2]**fluke** *n* [perh. fr. [1]*fluke*] **1 :** the part of an anchor that fastens in the ground — see ANCHOR illustration **2 :** a barbed head (as of a harpoon) **3 :** one of the lobes of a whale's tail
[3]**fluke** *n* [origin unknown] **1 :** an accidentally successful stroke at billiards or pool **2 :** a stroke of luck <the discovery was a ~>
fluky *also* **fluk·ey** \ˈflü-kē\ *adj* **fluk·i·er; -est** **1 :** happening by or depending on chance **2 :** being unsteady or uncertain : CHANGEABLE <a ~ wind>
flume \ˈflüm\ *n* [prob. fr. ME *flum* river, fr. OF, fr. L *flumen*, fr. *fluere*] **1 :** a ravine or gorge with a stream running through it **2 :** an inclined channel for conveying water (as for power)
flum·mery \ˈfləm-(ə-)rē\ *n, pl* **-mer·ies** [W *llymru*] **1 a :** a soft jelly or porridge made with flour or meal **b :** any of several sweet desserts **2 :** MUMMERY, MUMBO JUMBO
flum·mox \ˈfləm-əks, -iks\ *vt* [origin unknown] **:** CONFUSE
[1]**flump** \ˈfləmp\ *n* [imit.] **:** a dull heavy sound (as of a fall)
[2]**flump** *vi* **:** to move or fall suddenly and heavily <~*ed* down into his chair with a sigh> ~ *vt* **:** to place or drop with a flump
flung *past of* FLING
[1]**flunk** \ˈfləŋk\ *vb* [perh. blend of *flinch* and *funk*] *vi* **:** to fail esp. in an examination or course ~ *vt* **1 :** to give a failing grade to **2 :** to get a failing grade in — **flunk·er** *n*
[2]**flunk** *n* **:** an act or instance of flunking
flunk out *vi* **:** to be dismissed from a school or college for failure ~ *vt* **:** to dismiss from a school or college for failure
flun·ky *or* **flun·key** \ˈfləŋ-kē\ *n, pl* **flunkies** *or* **flunkeys** [Sc, of unknown origin] **1 a :** a liveried servant **b :** one performing menial duties <worked as a ~ in a lumber camp> **2 :** YES-MAN
flu·o·cin·o·lone ac·e·to·nide \ˌflü-ə-ˈsin-ᵊl-ˌōn-ˌas-ə-ˈtō-ˌnīd\ *n* [*fluor-* + *cin-* (of unknown origin) + *-ol* + cortis*one* + *acetone* + *-ide*] **:** a steroid $C_{24}H_{30}F_2O_6$ used esp. as an anti-inflammatory agent in the treatment of skin diseases
flu·or \ˈflü-ˌȯ(ə)r, ˈflü-ər\ *n* [NL, mineral belonging to a group used as fluxes and including fluorite, fr. L, flow, fr. *fluere* — more at FLUID] **:** FLUORITE
fluor- *or* **fluoro-** *comb form* [F, fr. *fluorine*] **1 :** fluorine <*fluo*ride> **2** *also* **fluori-** **:** fluorescence <*fluoro*scope> <*fluori*meter>
flu·o·resce \ˌflů(-ə)r-ˈes, flōr-, flȯr-\ *vi* **-resced; -resc·ing** [back-formation fr. *fluorescence*] **:** to produce, undergo, or exhibit fluorescence — **flu·o·resc·er** *n*
flu·o·res·ce·in \-ˈes-ē-ən\ *n* **:** a yellow or red crystalline dye $C_{20}H_{12}O_5$ with a bright yellow-green fluorescence in alkaline solution
flu·o·res·cence \-ˈes-ᵊn(t)s\ *n* **:** emission of or the property of emitting electromagnetic radiation usu. as visible light resulting from and occurring only during the absorption of radiation from some other source; *also* **:** the radiation emitted
flu·o·res·cent \-ˈes-ᵊnt\ *adj* **1 :** having or relating to fluorescence **2 :** bright and glowing as a result of fluorescence <a ~ pink>
fluorescent lamp *n* **:** a tubular electric lamp having a coating of fluorescent material on its inner surface and containing mercury vapor whose bombardment by electrons from the cathode provides ultraviolet light which causes the material to emit visible light
flu·o·ri·date \ˈflůr-ə-ˌdāt, ˈflōr-, ˈflȯr-\ *vt* **-dat·ed; -dat·ing** **:** to add a fluoride to (as drinking water) — **flu·o·ri·da·tion** \ˌflůr-ə-ˈdā-shən, ˌflōr-, ˌflȯr-\ *n*
flu·o·ride \ˈflů(-ə)r-ˌīd\ *n* **:** a compound of fluorine usu. with another element or a radical
flu·o·ri·nate \ˈflůr-ə-ˌnāt, ˈflōr-, ˈflȯr-\ *vt* **-nat·ed; -nat·ing** **:** to treat or cause to combine with fluorine or a compound of fluorine — **flu·o·ri·na·tion** \ˌflůr-ə-ˈnā-shən, ˌflōr-, ˌflȯr-\ *n*
flu·o·rine \ˈflů(-ə)r-ˌēn, -ən\ *n* [F, fr. NL *fluor*] **:** a nonmetallic univalent halogen element that is normally a pale yellowish flammable irritating toxic gas — see ELEMENT table
flu·o·rite \ˈflů(-ə)r-ˌīt\ *n* [It] **:** a transparent or translucent mineral CaF_2 of different colors that consists of calcium fluoride and is used as a flux and in the making of opalescent and opaque glasses
flu·o·ro·car·bon \ˌflů(-ə)r-ō-ˈkär-bən\ *n* **:** any of various chemically inert compounds containing carbon and fluorine used chiefly as lubricants and refrigerants and in making resins and plastics
flu·o·ro·chrome \ˈflů(-ə)r-ə-ˌkrōm\ *n* **:** any of various fluorescent substances used in biological staining to produce fluorescence in a specimen
flu·o·rog·ra·phy \ˌflů(-ə)r-ˈäg-rə-fē\ *n* **:** PHOTOFLUOROGRAPHY — **flu·o·ro·graph·ic** \ˌflů(-ə)r-ə-ˈgraf-ik\ *adj*
flu·o·rom·e·ter \ˌflů(-ə)r-ˈäm-ət-ər\ *or* **flu·o·rim·e·ter** \-ˈim-\ *n* **:** an instrument for measuring fluorescence and related phenomena (as intensity of radiation) — **flu·o·ro·met·ric** *or* **flu·o·ri·met·ric** \ˌflů(-ə)r-ə-ˈme-trik\ *adj* — **flu·o·rom·e·try** \ˌflů(-ə)r-ˈäm-ə-trē\ *or* **flu·o·rim·e·try** \-ˈim-\ *n*
[1]**flu·o·ro·scope** \ˈflůr-ə-ˌskōp\ *n* [ISV] **:** an instrument used for observing the internal structure of an opaque object (as the living body) by means of X rays — **flu·o·ro·scop·ic** \ˌflůr-ə-ˈskäp-ik\ *adj*

— **flu·o·ro·scop·i·cal·ly** \-i-k(ə-)lē\ *adv* — **flu·o·ros·co·pist** \ˌflu̇(-ə)r-ˈäs-kə-pəst\ *n* — **flu·o·ros·co·py** \-pē\ *n*

2fluoroscope *vt* **-scoped; -scop·ing** : to examine by fluoroscopy

flu·o·ro·sis \ˌflu̇(-ə)r-ˈō-səs\ *n* : an abnormal condition (as of the teeth) caused by fluorine or its compounds — **flu·o·rot·ic** \-ˈät-ik\ *adj*

flu·o·ro·ura·cil \ˌflu̇(-ə)r-ō-ˈyu̇r-ə-ˌsil, -ˌsəl\ *n* [*fluor-* + *uracil*] : a fluorine-containing pyrimidine base $C_4H_3FN_2O_2$ used to treat some kinds of cancer

flu·or·spar \ˈflu̇(-ə)r-ˌspär\ *n* : FLUORITE

flu·phen·azine \flü-ˈfen-ə-ˌzēn\ *n* [*fluor-* + *phenazine*] : a tranquilizing compound $C_{22}H_{26}F_3N_3OS$ used esp. combined as a salt

1flur·ry \ˈflər-ē, ˈflə-rē\ *n, pl* **flurries** [prob. fr. *flurr* (to throw scatteringly)] **1 a** : a gust of wind **b** : a brief light snowfall **2** : a state of nervous upset or scurrying bustle **3** : a brief advance or decline in prices : a short-lived outburst of trading activity ***syn*** see STIR

2flurry *vb* **flur·ried; flur·ry·ing** *vt* : to cause to become agitated and confused ~ *vi* : to become flurried ***syn*** see DISCOMPOSE

1flush \ˈfləsh\ *vb* [ME *flusshen*] *vi* : to take wing suddenly ~ *vt* **1** : to cause (a bird) to flush **2** : to expose or chase from a place of concealment <~*ed* the boys from their hiding place>

2flush *n* [perh. modif. of L *fluxus* — more at FLUX] **1** : a sudden flow (as of water); *also* : a rinsing or cleansing with or as if with a flush of water **2 a** : a sudden increase or expansion; *esp* : sudden and usu. abundant new plant growth **b** : a surge of emotion <felt a ~ of anger at the insult> **3 a** : a tinge of red : BLUSH **b** : a fresh and vigorous state <in the first ~ of womanhood> **4** : a transitory sensation of extreme heat

3flush *vi* **1** : to flow and spread suddenly and freely **2 a** : to glow brightly **b** : BLUSH <~*ed* when she saw the picture> **3** : to produce new growth <the plants ~*ed* twice during the year> ~ *vt* **1 a** : to cause to flow **b** : to pour liquid over or through; *esp* : to cleanse or wash out with or as if with a rush of liquid <~ the toilet> <~ the lungs with air> **2** : INFLAME, EXCITE — usu. used passively <~*ed* with victory> **3** : to cause to blush **4** : to prepare (sheep) for breeding by special feeding

4flush *adj* **1 a** : filled to overflowing **b** : AFFLUENT **2 a** : full of life and vigor : LUSTY **b** : of a ruddy healthy color **3** : readily available : ABUNDANT **4 a** : having or forming a continuous plane or unbroken surface <~ paneling> **b** : directly abutting or immediately adjacent: as **(1)** : set even with an edge of a type page or column : having no indention **(2)** : arranged edge to edge so as to fit snugly — **flush·ness** *n*

5flush *adv* **1** : in a flush manner **2** : SQUARELY <hit him ~ on the chin>

6flush *vt* : to make flush <~ the headings on a page>

7flush *n* [MF *flus, fluz,* fr. L *fluxus* flow] **1** : a hand of playing cards all of the same suit; *specif* : a poker hand containing five cards of the same suit but not in sequence — see POKER illustration **2** : a series of three or more slalom gates set vertically on a slope

1flus·ter \ˈfləs-tər\ *vb* **flus·tered; flus·ter·ing** \-t(ə-)riŋ\ [prob. of Scand origin; akin to Icel *flaustur* hurry] *vt* **1** : to make tipsy **2** : to put into a state of agitated confusion : UPSET ~ *vi* : to move or behave in an agitated or confused manner ***syn*** see DISCOMPOSE

2fluster *n* : a state of agitated confusion

1flute \ˈflüt\ *n* [ME *floute,* fr. MF *flahute,* fr. OProv *flaut*] **1 a** : RECORDER 3 **b** : a keyed woodwind instrument consisting of a cylindrical tube which is stopped at one end and which has a side hole over which air is blown to produce the tone and having a range from middle C upward for three octaves **2 a** : a grooved pleat (as on a hat brim) **b** : a rounded groove; *specif* : one of the vertical parallel grooves on a classical architectural column — **flute·like** \-ˌlīk\ *adj*

flute 1b

2flute *vb* **flut·ed; flut·ing** *vi* **1** : to play a flute **2** : to produce a flutelike sound ~ *vt* **1** : to utter with a flutelike sound **2** : to form flutes in — **flut·er** *n*

flut·ing \ˈflüt-iŋ\ *n* **1** : a series of flutes : FLUTE <the ~ of a column> **2** : fluted material

flut·ist \ˈflüt-əst\ *n* : one who plays a flute

1flut·ter \ˈflət-ər\ *vb* [ME *floteren* to float, flutter, fr. OE *floterian,* freq. of *flotian* to float; akin to OE *flēotan* to float — more at FLEET] *vi* **1** : to flap the wings rapidly **2 a** : to move with quick wavering or flapping motions <flags ~*ing* in the wind> **b** : to vibrate in irregular spasms **3** : to move about or behave in an agitated aimless manner ~ *vt* : to cause to flutter — **flut·ter·er** \-ər-ər\ *n* — **flut·tery** \-ə-rē\ *adj*

2flutter *n* **1** : an act of fluttering **2 a** : a state of nervous confusion or excitement **b** : FLURRY, COMMOTION **c** : abnormal spasmodic fluttering of a body part <treatment of atrial ~> **3 a** : a distortion in reproduced sound similar to but of a higher pitch than wow **b** : fluctuation in the brightness of a television image **4** : an unwanted oscillation (as of an aileron or a bridge) set up by natural forces **5** *chiefly Brit* : a small speculative venture or gamble <took a ~ on the ponies>

flut·ter·board \ˈflət-ər-ˌbō(ə)rd, -ˌbo̊(ə)rd\ *n* : a rectangular board used by swimmers in practicing leg strokes

flutter kick *n* : an alternating whipping motion of the legs used in various swimming styles (as the crawl)

flu·vi·al \ˈflü-vē-əl\ *adj* [L *fluvialis,* fr. *fluvius* river, fr. *fluere*] **1** : of, relating to, or living in a stream or river **2** : produced by stream action

flu·vi·a·tile \ˈflü-vē-ə-ˌtīl\ *adj* [MF, fr. L *fluviatilis,* irreg. fr. *fluvius*] : FLUVIAL

1flux \ˈfləks\ *n* [ME, fr. MF & ML; MF, fr. ML *fluxus,* fr. L, flow, fr. *fluxus,* pp. of *fluere* to flow — more at FLUID] **1** : a flowing of fluid from the body; *esp* : an excessive abnormal discharge from the bowels **2** : a continuous moving on or passing by (as of a stream) **3** : a continued flow : FLOOD **4 a** : INFLUX **b** : CHANGE, FLUCTUATION <the program was in a state of ~> **5 a** : a substance used to promote fusion esp. of metals or minerals **b** : a substance (as rosin) applied to surfaces to be joined by soldering, brazing, or welding to clean and free them from oxide and promote their union **6** : the rate of transfer of fluid, particles, or energy across a given surface

2flux *vt* **1** : to cause to become fluid **2** : to treat with a flux ~ *vi* : to become fluid : FUSE

flux gate *n* : a device used to indicate the direction of the terrestrial magnetic field — called also *flux valve*

flux·ion \ˈflək-shən\ *n* **1** : constant change **2** *pl, archaic* : CALCULUS 3b — **flux·ion·al** \-shnəl, -shən-ᵊl\ *adj*

1fly \ˈflī\ *vb* **flew** \ˈflü\; **flown** \ˈflōn\; **fly·ing** [ME *flien,* fr. OE *flēogan;* akin to OHG *fliogan* to fly, OE *flōwan* to flow] *vi* **1 a** : to move in or pass through the air with wings **b** : to move through the air or before the wind <clouds ~*ing* across the sky>; *also* : to move through outer space **c** : to float, wave, or soar in the air <flags ~*ing* at half-mast> **2 a** : to take flight : FLEE **b** : to fade and disappear : VANISH **3 a** : to move or pass swiftly **b** : to be moved with violence <*flew* into a rage> **c** : to seem to pass quickly <our vacation simply *flew*> **4** : to become expended or dissipated rapidly **5** : to pursue or attack in flight **6** : to operate or travel in an airplane or spacecraft ~ *vt* **1 a** : to cause to fly or float in the air <was ~*ing* his kite> **b** : to operate (as a balloon, aircraft, rocket, or spacecraft) in flight **c** : to journey over by flying **2 a** : to flee or escape from **b** : AVOID, SHUN **3** : to transport by airplane — **fly at** : to assail suddenly and violently — **fly blind** : to fly an airplane solely by instruments — **fly contact** : to fly an airplane with the aid of visible landmarks or reference points — **fly high** : to be elated — **fly in the face of** *or* **fly in the teeth of** : to act forthrightly or brazenly in defiance or disobedience of

2fly *n, pl* **flies** **1** : the action or process of flying : FLIGHT **2 a** : a device consisting of two or more radial vanes capable of rotating on a spindle to act as a fan or to govern the speed of clockwork or very light machinery **b** : FLYWHEEL **3 a** : a horse-drawn public coach or delivery wagon **b** *chiefly Brit* : a light covered carriage or cab **4** *pl* : the space over a theater stage where scenery and equipment can be hung **5** : something attached by one edge: as **a** : a garment closing concealed by a fold of cloth extending over the fastener **b** : the outer canvas of a tent with double top **c (1)** : the length of an extended flag from its staff or support **(2)** : the outer or loose end of a flag **6** : a baseball hit high into the air **7** : FLYLEAF **8** : a football pass pattern in which the receiver runs straight downfield — **on the fly** **1** : continuously active : very busy **2** : while still in the air : without the ball bouncing <the ball carried 400 feet *on the fly*>

3fly *vi* **flied; fly·ing** : to hit a fly in baseball

4fly *n, pl* **flies** [ME *flie,* fr. OE *flēoge;* akin to OHG *flioga* fly, OE *flēogan* to fly] **1** : a winged insect **2** : TWO-WINGED FLY; *esp* : one that is large and stout-bodied **3** : a fishhook dressed (as with feathers or tinsel) to suggest an insect — **fly in the ointment** : a detracting factor or element

5fly *adj* [prob. fr. *1fly*] *chiefly Brit* : KEEN, ARTFUL

fly·able \ˈflī-ə-bəl\ *adj* : suitable for flying or for being flown

fly agaric *n* : a poisonous mushroom (*Amanita muscaria*) with a usu. bright red cap

fly ash *n* : fine solid particles of noncombustible ash carried out of a bed of solid fuel by the draft

fly·away \ˈflī-ə-ˌwā\ *adj* **1** : lacking in order and practical sense : FLIGHTY <a pretty, careless, ~ sort of woman> **2** : made loose and flowing esp. because of unconfined fullness at the back <a ~ jacket> **3 a** : ready to fly <~ aircraft> **b** : of or relating to an airplane that is ready to fly <~ price>

fly ball *n* : 2FLY 6

fly·belt \ˈflī-ˌbelt\ *n* : an area infested with tsetse fly

1fly·blow \-ˌblō\ *n* [*3fly* + *blow* (deposit of insect eggs)] **1** : an egg or young larva deposited by a flesh fly or blowfly **2** : FLY-STRIKE

2flyblow *vt* **-blew; -blown** **1** : to deposit flyblows in **2** : TAINT, CONTAMINATE

fly·blown \ˈflī-ˌblōn\ *adj* **1 a** : infested with flyblows **b** : covered with flyspecks **2 a** : not pure : TAINTED <a world ~ with the vices of irresponsible power —V. L. Parrington> **b** : not bright and new : SEEDY, MOTH-EATEN **c** : TRITE, HACKNEYED <a long list of ~ metaphors —*Horizon*>

fly·boat \-ˌbōt\ *n* [modif. of D *vlieboot,* fr. *Vlie,* channel between North sea & Zuider Zee + *boot* boat] : any of various fast boats

fly book *n* : a case usu. in the form of a book for storing fishing flies

fly-boy \ˈflī-ˌbo̊i\ *n* : a member of the air force

fly bridge *n* : an open deck on a cabin cruiser located above the bridge on the cabin roof and usu. having a duplicate set of navigating equipment

fly·by \ˈflī-ˌbī\ *n, pl* **flybys** **1** : a usu. low-altitude flight past a predesignated place by one or more airplanes **2 a** : a flight of a spacecraft past a celestial body (as Mars) close enough to obtain scientific data; *also* : a suborbital flight around the moon **b** : a spacecraft that makes a flyby

1fly-by-night \ˈflī-bə-ˌnīt\ *n* **1** : one that seeks to evade responsibilities and esp. creditors by flight **2** : one without established reputation or standing; *esp* : a shaky business enterprise

2fly-by-night *adj* **1** : given to making a quick profit usu. by shady or irresponsible acts <~ promoters trying to cash in —Tom McSloy> **2** : TRANSITORY, PASSING <~ fashions>

fly-by-night·er \ˌflī-bə-ˈnīt-ər\ *n* : FLY-BY-NIGHT
fly casting *n* : the casting of artificial flies in fly-fishing or as a competitive sport
fly·catch·er \ˈflī-ˌkach-ər, -ˌkech-\ *n* : a bird (order Passeriformes) that feeds on insects taken on the wing
fly dope *n* **1** : a dressing that makes fishing flies water-resistant so that they will float **2** : an insect repellent
fly·er *var of* FLIER
fly-fish·ing \ˈflī-ˌfish-iŋ\ *n* : a method of fishing in which an artificial fly is cast by use of a long flexible rod, a reel, and a relatively heavy oiled or treated line
fly front *n* : a concealed closing on the front of coats, skirts, shirts, or dresses — compare ²FLY 5a
fly gallery *n* : a narrow raised platform at the side of a theater stage from which flying scenery lines are operated
¹**fly·ing** \ˈflī-iŋ\ *adj* **1 a** : moving or capable of moving in the air **b** : rapidly moving <~ feet> **c** : very brief **2** : intended for ready movement or action <a ~ squad car> **3** : having stylized wings — used esp. of livestock brand marks **4** : of or relating to the operation of aircraft <belongs to a ~ club> **5** : traversed or to be traversed (as in speed-record trials) after a running start <~ kilometer> <~ mile> — **with flying colors** : with complete or eminent success <passed the exam *with flying colors*>
²**flying** *n* **1** : travel by air **2** : the operation of an aircraft or spacecraft
flying boat *n* : a seaplane with a hull adapted for floating
flying bomb *n* : ROBOT BOMB
flying bridge *n* **1** : the highest navigational bridge on a ship **2** : FLY BRIDGE
flying buttress *n* : a masonry structure that typically consists of a straight inclined bar carried on an arch and a solid pier or buttress against which it abuts and that receives the thrust of a roof or vault
flying column *n* : a strong military detachment that operates at a distance from the main force
Flying Dutchman *n* **1** : a legendary Dutch mariner condemned to sail the seas until Judgment Day **2** : a spectral ship that according to legend haunts the seas near the Cape of Good Hope in stormy weather
flying field *n* : a field with a graded area for airplane landings and takeoffs
flying fish *n* : any of numerous fishes (family Exocoetidae) chiefly of tropical and warm seas that have long pectoral fins suggesting wings and are able to move some distance through the air
flying fox *n* : FRUIT BAT
flying gurnard *n* : any of several marine fishes (family Dactylopteridae) that resemble gurnards and have large pectoral fins allowing them to glide above the water for short distances

1 flying buttresses

flying jib *n* : a sail outside the jib on an extension of the jibboom — see SAIL illustration
flying jibboom *n* : an extension of a jibboom
flying lemur *n* : an East Indian or a Philippine arboreal nocturnal mammal (genus *Cynocephalus*) that is about the size of a cat with a broad fold of skin from the neck to the tail on each side that embraces the limbs and forms a parachute used in making long sailing leaps and that is usu. isolated in a distinct order (Dermoptera)
flying machine *n* : an apparatus for navigating the air
flying mare *n* : a wrestling maneuver in which the aggressor seizes his opponent's wrist, turns about, and jerks him over his back
flying officer *n* : a commissioned officer in the British air force who ranks with a first lieutenant in the army
flying saucer *n* : any of various unidentified moving objects repeatedly reported as seen in the air and usu. described as being saucer-shaped or disk-shaped — called also *flying disk*
flying spot *n* : a spot of light that is moved over a surface (as one bearing printing or an image) so that light reflected from or transmitted by different parts of the surface is translated into electrical signals for transmission (as in television or computers)
flying squad *n* : a usu. small standby group of people ready to move or act swiftly; *esp* : a police unit formed to respond quickly in an emergency
flying squirrel *n* : a small large-eyed nocturnal No. American squirrel (*Glaucomys volans*) with folds of skin connecting the forelegs and hind legs that enable it to make long gliding leaps; *also* : any of several similar squirrels
flying start *n* : a start in racing in which the participants are already moving when they cross the starting line or receive the starting signal
flying wedge *n* : a moving formation (as of guards or police) resembling a wedge

flying squirrel

fly·leaf \ˈflī-ˌlēf\ *n* : one of the free endpapers of a book
fly·man \-mən, -ˌman\ *n* : a worker in the flies of a theater who manipulates curtains and scenery
fly net *n* : a net to exclude or keep off insects (as from a harness horse)
fly·over \ˈflī-ˌō-vər\ *n* **1** : a low-altitude flight over a public gathering or place by one or more airplanes **2** *Brit* : OVERPASS
fly·pa·per \-ˌpā-pər\ *n* : paper coated with a sticky often poisonous substance for killing flies
fly·past \-ˌpast\ *n, Brit* : FLYBY
fly rod *n* : a light springy fishing rod used in fly casting
flysch \ˈflish\ *n* [G dial.] : a thick and extensive deposit largely of sandstone that is formed in a geosyncline adjacent to a rising mountain belt and is esp. common in the Alpine region of Europe
fly sheet *n* **1** : a small loose advertising sheet : HANDBILL **2** : a sheet of a folder, booklet, or catalog giving directions for the use of or information about the material that follows
fly·speck \ˈflī-ˌspek\ *n* **1** : a speck made by fly excrement **2** : something small and insignificant — **flyspeck** *vt*
fly-strike \-ˌstrīk\ *n* : infestation with fly maggots
fly·swat·ter \-ˌswät-ər\ *n* : a device for killing insects that consists of a flat piece of perforated rubber or plastic or fine-mesh wire netting attached to a handle
fly·ti·er \ˈflī-ˌtī(-ə)r\ *n* [*fly* + *tier* (one that ties)] : a maker of flies for fishing
flyt·ing \ˈflīt-iŋ\ *n* [gerund of E dial. *flyte* to quarrel] : a dispute or exchange of personal abuse in verse form (as in an epic)
fly·way \ˈflī-ˌwā\ *n* : an established air route of migratory birds
fly·weight \-ˌwāt\ *n* : a boxer weighing 112 pounds or less
flywheel \-ˌhwēl, -ˌwēl\ *n* : a heavy wheel for opposing and moderating by its inertia any fluctuation of speed in the machinery with which it revolves
fly whisk *n* : a whisk for brushing away flies
fm *abbr* fathom
Fm *symbol* fermium
FM *abbr* **1** field manual **2** frequency modulation
FMB *abbr* Federal Maritime Board
FMCS *abbr* Federal Mediation and Conciliation Service
FMN \ˌef-ˌem-ˈen\ *n* [*f*lavin *mono*nucleotide] : a yellow crystalline phosphoric ester $C_{17}H_{21}N_4O_9P$ of riboflavin that is a coenzyme of several flavoprotein enzymes — called also *flavin mononucleotide*
fn *abbr* footnote
FNMA *sometimes* ˌfan-ē-ˈmā\ *abbr* Federal National Mortgage Association
f-num·ber \ˈef-ˌnəm-bər\ *n* [*f*ocal length] **1** : the ratio of the focal length to the aperture in an optical system **2** : a number following the symbol f/ that expresses the effectiveness of the aperture of a camera lens in relation to brightness of image so that the smaller the number the brighter the image and therefore the shorter the exposure required
fo *or* **fol** *abbr* folio
FO *abbr* **1** field officer **2** field order **3** finance officer **4** flight officer **5** foreign office **6** forward observer
¹**foal** \ˈfōl\ *n* [ME *fole*, fr. OE *fola*; akin to L *pullus* young of an animal, Gk *pais* child — more at FEW] : the young of an animal of the horse family; *esp* : one under one year
²**foal** *vi* : to give birth to a foal
¹**foam** \ˈfōm\ *n* [ME *fome*, fr. OE *fām*; akin to OHG *feim* foam, L *spuma* foam, *pumex* pumice] **1** : a light frothy mass of fine bubbles formed in or on the surface of a liquid: as **a** : a frothy mass formed in salivating or sweating **b** : a stabilized froth produced chemically or mechanically and used esp. in fighting oil fires **c** : a material in a lightweight cellular form resulting from introduction of gas bubbles during manufacture **2** : SEA **3** : something resembling foam — **foam·less** \-ləs\ *adj*
²**foam** *vi* **1 a** : to produce or form foam **b** : to froth at the mouth esp. in anger; *broadly* : to be angry **2** : to gush out in foam **3** : to become covered with or as if with foam <streets . . . ~*ing* with life —Thomas Wolfe> ~ *vt* **1** : to cause to foam; *specif* : to cause air bubbles to form in **2** : to convert (as a plastic) into a foam — **foam·er** *n*
foamed plastic *n* : EXPANDED PLASTIC
foam·flow·er \ˈfōm-ˌflau̇(-ə)r\ *n* : an American woodland spring-flowering herb (*Tiarella cordifolia*) that has white flowers with very long stamens and no stem leaves — called also *false miterwort*
foam rubber *n* : spongy rubber of fine texture made from latex by foaming (as by whipping) before vulcanization
foamy \ˈfō-mē\ *adj* **foam·i·er; -est** **1** : covered with foam : FROTHY **2** : full of, consisting of, or resembling foam — **foam·i·ly** \-mə-lē\ *adv* — **foam·i·ness** \-mē-nəs\ *n*
¹**fob** \ˈfäb\ *vt* **fobbed; fob·bing** [ME *fobben*] *archaic* : DECEIVE, CHEAT
²**fob** *n* [perh. akin to G dial. *fuppe* pocket] **1** : WATCH POCKET **2** : a short strap, ribbon, or chain attached to a watch carried in a watch pocket or a vest pocket **3** : an ornament attached to a fob chain
FOB *abbr* free on board
fob off *vt* **1** : to put off with a trick or excuse **2** : to pass or offer (something spurious) as genuine **3** : to put aside <now *fob off* what once they would have welcomed eagerly —Walter Lippmann>
FOC *abbr* free of charge
fo·cal \ˈfō-kəl\ *adj* : of, relating to, or having a focus — **fo·cal·ly** \-kə-lē\ *adv*
focal infection *n* : a persistent bacterial infection of some organ or region; *esp* : one causing symptoms elsewhere in the body
fo·cal·ize \ˈfō-kə-ˌlīz\ *vb* **-ized; -iz·ing** *vt* **1** : to bring to a focus **2** : to adjust the focus of **3** : LOCALIZE ~ *vi* : to become focalized — **fo·cal·iza·tion** \ˌfō-kə-lə-ˈzā-shən\ *n*
focal length *n* : the distance of a focus from the surface of a lens or concave mirror
focal plane *n* : a plane that is perpendicular to the axis of a lens or mirror and passes through the focus
focal point *n* : FOCUS 5 <the fireplace was the *focal point* of the room>
focal ratio *n* : F-NUMBER 1
fo'·c'sle *var of* FORECASTLE
¹**fo·cus** \ˈfō-kəs\ *n, pl* **fo·cus·es** *or* **fo·ci** \-ˌsī\ [NL, fr. L, hearth] **1** : a point at which rays (as of light, heat, or sound) converge or from which they diverge or appear to diverge; *specif* : the point where the geometrical lines or their prolongations conforming to the rays diverging from or converging toward another point intersect and give rise to an image after reflection by a mirror or refraction by a lens or optical system **2 a** : FOCAL LENGTH **b** : adjustment for distinct vision; *also* : the area that may be seen

distinctly or resolved into a clear image **c :** a position in which something must be placed for clarity of perception <tried to bring the issues into ~> **3 :** one of the fixed points that with the corresponding directrix defines a conic section **4 :** a localized area of disease or the chief site of a generalized disease or infection **5 :** a center of activity, attraction, or attention <the ~ of the meeting was on drug abuse> **6 :** the place of origin of an earthquake — **fo·cus·less** \-ləs\ *adj* — **in focus :** having or giving the proper sharpness of outline due to good focusing — **out of focus :** not in focus

focus 1: *A* convex lens: light rays *a* converge to form principal focus *b*; *B* concave lens: light rays *c* refracted as at *d* form virtual focus *e*

[2]focus *vb* **fo·cused** *also* **fo·cussed; fo·cus·ing** *also* **fo·cus·sing** *vt* **1 :** to bring to a focus : CONCENTRATE **2 :** to cause to be concentrated <~*ed* their attention on the most urgent problems> **3 a :** to adjust the focus of **b :** to bring into focus ~ *vi* **1 :** to come to a focus : CONVERGE **2 :** to adjust one's eye or a camera to a particular range — **fo·cus·able** \-kəs-ə-bəl\ *adj* — **fo·cus·er** *n*

fod·der \ˈfäd-ər\ *n* [ME, fr. OE *fōdor;* akin to OHG *fuotar* food — more at FOOD] **1 :** something fed to domestic animals; *esp* **:** coarse food for cattle, horses, or sheep **2 :** something that is used to supply a constant demand <collected data which became computer ~> — **fodder** *vt*

fod·gel \ˈfäj-əl\ *adj* [origin unknown] *Scot* : BUXOM

foe \ˈfō\ *n* [ME *fo,* fr. OE *fāh,* fr. *fāh* hostile; akin to OHG *gifēh* hostile] **1 :** one who has personal enmity for another **2 :** an enemy in war : ADVERSARY **3 :** one who opposes on principle <a ~ of needless expenditures> **4 :** something prejudicial or injurious *syn* see ENEMY *ant* friend

FOE *abbr* Fraternal Order of Eagles

foehn *or* **föhn** \ˈfə(r)n, ˈfœn, ˈfān\ *n* [G *föhn*] **:** a warm dry wind blowing down the side of a mountain

foe·man \ˈfō-mən\ *n* **:** an enemy in war : FOE

foe·tal, foe·tus *var of* FETAL, FETUS

foe·tid *var of* FETID

foeto- *or* **foeti-** — see FETO-

[1]fog \ˈfȯg, ˈfäg\ *n* [ME, rank grass] **1** *dial* **a :** dead or decaying grass in the winter **b :** a second growth of grass **2** *dial* : MOSS

[2]fog *n* [prob. of Scand origin; akin to Dan *fog* spray, shower; akin to L *pustula* blister, pimple, Gk *physan* to blow] **1 a :** vapor condensed to fine particles of water suspended in the lower atmosphere that differs from cloud only in being near the ground **b :** a fine spray or a foam for fire fighting **2 :** a murky condition of the atmosphere or a substance causing it **3 a :** a state of confusion or bewilderment **b :** something that confuses or obscures <hid behind a ~ of rhetoric> **4 :** cloudiness or partial opacity in a developed photographic image caused by chemical action or stray radiation *syn* see HAZE — **fog·less** \-ləs\ *adj*

[3]fog *vb* **fogged; fog·ging** *vt* **1 :** to cover, envelop, or suffuse with or as if with fog <~ the barns with pesticide> **2 :** to make obscure or confusing <accusations which *fogged* the real issues> **3 :** to make confused **4 :** to produce fog on (as a photographic film) during development ~ *vi* **1 :** to become covered or thick with fog **2 a :** to become blurred by a covering of fog or mist **b :** to become indistinct through exposure to light or radiation

fog·bound \ˈfȯg-ˌbau̇nd, ˈfäg-\ *adj* **1 :** covered with or surrounded by fog <~ coast> **2 :** unable to move because of fog <~ ship>

fog·bow \-ˌbō\ *n* **:** a nebulous arc or circle of white or yellowish light sometimes seen in fog

fog·dog \-ˌdȯg\ *n* : FOGBOW

fog·gage \ˈfȯg-ij, ˈfäg-\ *n, chiefly Scot* : [1]FOG, MOSS

fog·ger \-ər\ *n* **:** one that fogs; *esp* **:** an apparatus for spreading a fog of pesticide

fog·gy \ˈfȯg-ē, ˈfäg-\ *adj* **fog·gi·er; -est 1 a :** filled or abounding with fog **b :** covered or made opaque by moisture or grime **2 :** blurred or obscured as if by fog <hadn't the *foggiest* notion what they were voting for> — **fog·gi·ly** \ˈfȯg-ə-lē, ˈfäg-\ *adv* — **fog·gi·ness** \ˈfȯg-ē-nəs, ˈfäg-\ *n*

Foggy Bottom *n* [*Foggy Bottom,* district in Washington, D.C., on the Potomac river where the State Department building is located] **:** the U.S. Department of State

fog·horn \ˈfȯg-ˌhȯ(ə)rn, ˈfäg-\ *n* **1 :** a horn (as on a ship) sounded in a fog to give warning **2 :** a loud hoarse voice

fo·gy *also* **fo·gey** \ˈfō-gē\ *n, pl* **fogies** *also* **fogeys** [origin unknown] **:** a person with old-fashioned ideas — usu. used with *old* — **fo·gy·ish** \-gē-ish\ *adj* — **fo·gy·ism** \-ˌiz-əm\ *n*

foi·ble \ˈfȯi-bəl\ *n* [obs. F (now *faible*), fr. obs. *foible* weak, fr. OF *feble* feeble] **1 :** the part of a sword or foil blade between the middle and point **2 :** a minor flaw or shortcoming in personal character or behavior : WEAKNESS *syn* see FAULT

foie gras \ˈfwä-ˈgrä\ *n* [F] **:** liver esp. of a goose usu. in the form of a pâté

[1]foil \ˈfȯi(ə)l\ *vt* [ME *foilen* to trample, full cloth, fr. MF *fouler* — more at FULL] **1** *obs* : TRAMPLE **2 a :** to prevent from attaining an end : DEFEAT **b :** to bring to naught *syn* see FRUSTRATE

[2]foil *n* **1** *archaic* : DEFEAT **2** *archaic* **:** the track or trail of an animal **3 a :** a light fencing sword having a usu. circular guard and a flexible blade of rectangular section tapering to a blunted point — compare ÉPÉE, SABER **b :** the art or sport of fencing with the foil — often used in pl.

[3]foil *n* [ME, leaf, fr. MF *foille* (fr. L *folia,* pl. of *folium*) & *foil,* fr. L *folium* — more at BLADE] **1 a :** an indentation between cusps in Gothic tracery **b :** one of several arcs that enclose a complex figure **2 a :** very thin sheet metal **b :** a thin coat of tin or silver laid on the back of a mirror **3 :** a thin piece of material (as metal) put under an inferior or paste stone to add color or brilliance **4 :** one that serves as a contrast to another <acted as a ~ for a comedian> **5 :** HYDROFOIL 1

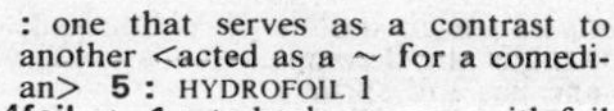

foils 1a

[4]foil *vt* **1 :** to back or cover with foil **2 :** to enhance by contrast

foiled \ˈfȯi(ə)ld\ *adj* **:** ornamented with foils <a ~ arch>

foils·man \ˈfȯi(ə)lz-mən\ *n* **:** one who fences with a foil

[1]foin \ˈfȯin\ *vi* [ME *foinen,* fr. *foin* fork for spearing fish, fr. MF *foisne*] *archaic* **:** to thrust with a pointed weapon : LUNGE

[2]foin *n, archaic* **:** a pass in fencing : LUNGE

foi·son \ˈfȯiz-ᵊn\ *n* [ME *foisoun,* fr. MF *foison*] **1** *archaic* **:** rich harvest **2** *chiefly Scot* **:** physical energy or strength **3** *pl, obs* : RESOURCES

foist \ˈfȯist\ *vt* [prob. fr. obs. D *vuisten* to take into one's hand, fr. MD *vuysten,* fr. *vuyst* fist; akin to OE *fȳst* fist] **1 a :** to introduce or insert surreptitiously or without warrant **b :** to force another to accept esp. by stealth or deceit **2 :** to pass off as genuine or worthy <~ costly and valueless products on the public —Jonathan Spivak>

fo·la·cin \ˈfō-lə-sən\ *n* [*folic acid* + *-in*] : FOLIC ACID

fo·late \ˈfō-ˌlāt\ *n* : FOLIC ACID

[1]fold \ˈfōld\ *n* [ME, fr. OE *falod;* akin to MLG *vālt* enclosure] **1 :** an enclosure for sheep **2 a :** a flock of sheep **b :** a group of people adhering to a common faith, belief, or enthusiasm

[2]fold *vt* **:** to pen up or confine (as sheep) in a fold

[3]fold *vb* [ME *folden,* fr. OE *fealdan;* akin to OHG *faldan* to fold, Gk di*plasios* twofold] *vt* **1 :** to lay one part over another part of <~ a letter> **2 :** to reduce the length or bulk of by doubling over <~ his legs> **3 :** to clasp together : ENTWINE <~ his hands> **4 :** to clasp or enwrap closely : EMBRACE **5 :** to bend (as a layer of rock) into folds **6 :** to incorporate (a food ingredient) into a mixture by repeated gentle overturnings without stirring or beating **7 :** to bring to an end ~ *vi* **1 :** to become doubled or pleated **2 :** to fail completely : COLLAPSE; *esp* **:** to stop production or operation for lack of business <the new restaurant ~*ed* in less than a year> — often used with *up* — **fold·able** \ˈfōl-də-bəl\ *adj*

[4]fold *n* **1 :** a doubling or folding over **2 :** a part doubled or laid over another part : PLEAT **3 :** something that is folded together or that enfolds **4 a :** a bend or flexure produced in rock by forces operative after the depositing or consolidation of the rock **b** *chiefly Brit* **:** an undulation in the landscape **5 :** a margin apparently formed by the doubling upon itself of a membrane or other flat anatomical structure

-fold \ˌfōld, ˈfōld\ *suffix* [ME, fr. OE *-feald;* akin to OHG *-falt* -fold, OE *fealdan*] **1 :** multiplied by (a specified number) : times — in adjectives <a twelve*fold* increase> and adverbs <repay you ten*fold*> **2 :** having (so many) parts <three*fold* aspect of the problem>

fold·away \ˌfōl-də-ˌwā\ *adj* **:** designed to fold out of the way or out of sight <~ doors> <~ bed>

foldboat \ˈfōl(d)-ˌbōt\ *n* **:** a small collapsible canoe made of rubberized sailcloth stretched over a framework

fold·boat·ing \-iŋ\ *n* **:** the sport of shooting rapids and cruising on swift water in a foldboat — **fold·boat·er** \-ər\ *n*

fold·er \ˈfōl-dər\ *n* **1 :** one that folds **2 :** a printed circular folded usu. so that the printed matter does not cross the fold **3 :** a folded cover or large envelope for holding or filing loose papers

fol·de·rol \ˈfäl-də-ˌräl\ *n* [*fol-de-rol,* a refrain in some old songs] **1 :** a useless ornament or accessory : TRIFLE **2 :** NONSENSE

folding door *n* **:** a door with jointed sections that can be folded together like an accordion

folding money *n* : PAPER MONEY

fold·out \ˈfōl-ˌdau̇t\ *n* **:** a folded insert (as a map) in a publication (as a book) larger in some dimension than the page

fo·li·a·ceous \ˌfō-lē-ˈā-shəs\ *adj* **1 :** of, relating to, or resembling a foliage leaf **2 :** consisting of thin laminae <~ spar>

fo·liage \ˈfō-l(ē-)ij, -lyij\ *n* [MF *fuellage,* fr. *foille* leaf — more at FOIL] **1 :** the aggregate of leaves of one or more plants produced in nature **2 :** a cluster of leaves, flowers, and branches **3 :** a representation of leaves, flowers, and branches for architectural ornamentation — **fo·liaged** \-l(ē-)ijd, -lyijd\ *adj*

foliage leaf *n* **:** an ordinary green leaf as distinguished from a floral leaf, scale, or bract

foliage plant *n* **:** a plant grown primarily for its decorative foliage

fo·li·ar \ˈfō-lē-ər\ *adj* **:** of, relating to, or applied to leaves <~ sprays>

[1]fo·li·ate \ˈfō-lē-ət, -ˌāt\ *adj* [L *foliatus* leafy fr. *folium* leaf — more at BLADE] **1 :** shaped like a leaf <a ~ sponge> **2 :** FOLIATED

[2]fo·li·ate \-ˌāt\ *vb* **-at·ed; -at·ing** *vt* **1 :** to beat into a leaf or thin foil **2 :** to spread over with a thin coat of tin amalgam **3 :** to number the leaves of (as a manuscript) **4 a :** to form (as an arch) into foils **b :** to ornament (as a pedestal) with foliage ~ *vi* **:** to divide into laminae or leaves

-fo·li·ate \-ət, -ˌāt\ *adj comb form* **:** having (such or so many) leaves or leaflets <tri*foliate*>

fo·li·at·ed \-ˌāt-əd\ *adj* **1 :** composed of laminae **2 :** separable into layers <a ~ rock>

fo·li·a·tion \ˌfō-lē-ˈā-shən\ *n* **1 a :** the process of forming into a leaf **b :** the state of being in leaf **c :** VERNATION **2 :** the act of numbering the leaves of a book; *also* **:** the total count of leaves so numbered **3 a :** ornamentation with foliage **b :** a decoration resembling a leaf **4 :** the enrichment of an opening by foils **5 :** the act of beating a metal into a thin plate or foil **6 :** foliated texture

ə abut	ᵊ kitten	ər further	a back	ā bake	ä cot, cart
au̇ out	ch chin	e less	ē easy	g gift	i trip	ī life
j joke	ŋ sing	ō flow	ȯ flaw	ȯi coin	th thin	t͟h this
ü loot	u̇ foot	y yet	yü few	yu̇ furious	zh vision

fo·lic acid \ˌfō-lik-\ *n* [L *folium*] **:** a crystalline pteroylglutamic acid $C_{19}H_{19}N_7O_6$ that is a vitamin of the B complex and is used in the treatment of nutritional anemias and sprue

fo·lie à deux \fȯ-lē-ä-dœ̄, ˌfäl-ē-ˌäd-ˈə(r)\ *n* [F, lit., double madness] **:** the presence of the same or similar delusional ideas in two persons closely associated with one another

fo·li·ic·o·lous \ˌfō-lē-ˈik-ə-ləs\ *adj* [L *folium* + ISV *-colous*] **:** growing or parasitic on leaves <the ~ ascomycetes>

[1]fo·lio \ˈfō-lē-ˌō\ *n, pl* **fo·li·os** [ME, fr. L, abl. of *folium*] **1 a :** a leaf esp. of a manuscript or book **b :** a leaf number **c :** a page number **d :** an identifying reference in accounting used in posting **2 a :** a sheet of paper folded once **b :** a case or folder for loose papers **3 a :** the size of a piece of paper cut two from a sheet; *also* **:** paper or a page of this size **b :** a book printed on folio pages **c :** a book of the largest size **4 :** a certain number of words taken as a unit or division in a document for purposes of measurement or reference

[2]folio *vt* **:** to put a serial number on each leaf or page of

-fo·li·o·late \ˈfō-lē-ə-ˌlāt\ *adj comb form* [LL *foliolum* leaflet, dim. of *folium*] **:** having (such or so many) leaflets <tri*foliolate*>

fo·li·ose \ˈfō-lē-ˌōs\ *adj* [L *foliosus* leafy] **:** having a flat, thin, and usu. lobed thallus attached to the substratum <~ lichens> — compare CRUSTOSE, FRUTICOSE

fo·li·um \ˈfō-lē-əm\ *n, pl* **fo·lia** \-lē-ə\ [NL, fr. L, leaf] **:** a thin layer occurring esp. in metamorphic rocks

[1]folk \ˈfōk\ *n, pl* **folk** *or* **folks** [ME, fr. OE *folc;* akin to OHG *folc* people] **1** *archaic* **:** a group of kindred tribes forming a nation **:** PEOPLE **2 :** the great proportion of the members of a people that determines the group character and that tends to preserve its characteristic form of civilization and its customs, arts and crafts, legends, traditions, and superstitions from generation to generation **3** *pl* **:** a certain kind or class of people <old ~*s*> <just plain ~> **4** *folks pl* **:** people generally **5** *folks pl* **:** the persons of one's own family **:** RELATIVES

[2]folk *adj* **1 a :** originating or traditional with the common people of a country or region and typically reflecting their life-style **b :** being a form of contemporary music written in imitation of and having qualities of traditional folk music such as stanzaic form, refrain, and simplicity of melody **2 :** of or relating to the common people or to the study of the common people <~ sociology>

folk etymology *n* **:** the transformation of words so as to give them an apparent relationship to other better-known or better-understood words (as in the change of Spanish *cucaracha* to English *cockroach*)

folk·ish \ˈfō-kish\ *adj* **:** FOLKLIKE — **folk·ish·ness** *n*

folk·like \ˈfō-ˌklīk\ *adj* **:** having a folk character

folk·lore \ˈfō-ˌklō(ə)r, -ˌklȯ(ə)r\ *n* **1 :** traditional customs, tales, or sayings preserved orally among a people **2 :** a comparative science that investigates the life and spirit of a people as revealed in their folklore **3 :** a widely held unsupported specious notion or body of notions — **folk·lor·ic** \-ˌklōr-ik, -ˌklȯr-\ *adj* — **folk·lor·ish** \-ish\ *adj* — **folk·lor·ist** \-əst\ *n* — **folk·lor·is·tic** \ˌfō-ˌklōr-ˈis-tik, -ˌklȯr-\ *adj*

folk mass *n* **:** a mass in which traditional liturgical music is replaced by folk music

folk medicine *n* **:** traditional medicine as practiced nonprofessionally by people isolated from modern medical services and involving esp. the use of vegetable remedies on an empirical basis

folk·moot \ˈfōk-ˌmüt\ *or* **folk·mote** \-ˌmōt\ *n* **:** a general assembly of the people (as of a shire) in early England

folk·sing·er \-ˌsiŋ-ər\ *n* **:** one who sings folk songs or sings in a style associated with folk songs — **folk·sing·ing** \-ˌsiŋ-iŋ\ *n*

folksy \ˈfōk-sē\ *adj* **folks·i·er; -est** [*folks* + *-y*] **1 :** SOCIABLE, FRIENDLY **2 :** informal, casual, or familiar in manner or style <gave us a ~ little talk —O. J. Magee> — **folks·i·ly** \-sə-lē\ *adv* — **folks·i·ness** \-sē-nəs\ *n*

folk·tale \ˈfōk-ˌtāl\ *n* **:** a characteristically anonymous, timeless, and placeless tale circulated orally among a people

folk·way \ˈfō-ˌkwā\ *n* **:** a mode of thinking, feeling, or acting common to a people or to a social group; *esp* **:** a traditional social custom

fol·li·cle \ˈfäl-i-kəl\ *n* [NL *folliculus*, fr. L, dim. of *follis* bag — more at FOOL] **1 a :** a small anatomical cavity or deep narrow-mouthed depression **b :** a small lymph node **c :** GRAAFIAN FOLLICLE **2 :** a dry dehiscent one-celled many-seeded fruit that has a single carpel and opens along only one suture — **fol·lic·u·lar** \fə-ˈlik-yə-lər, fä-\ *adj* — **fol·lic·u·late** \-lət\ *also* **fol·lic·u·lat·ed** \-ˌlāt-əd\ *adj*

follicle mite *n* **:** any of several minute mites (genus *Demodex*) parasitic in hair follicles

follicle-stimulating hormone *n* **:** a hormone from an anterior lobe of the pituitary body that stimulates the growth of Graafian follicles and activates sperm-forming cells

fol·lic·u·lin \fə-ˈlik-yə-lən, fä-\ *n* **:** ESTROGEN; *esp* **:** ESTRONE

[1]fol·low \ˈfäl-(ˌ)ō, -ə(-w)\ *vb* [ME *folwen*, fr. OE *folgian;* akin to OHG *folgēn* to follow] *vt* **1 :** to go, proceed, or come after <~*ed* the guide> **2 a :** to pursue in an effort to overtake **b :** to seek to attain <~ knowledge> **3 :** to accept as authority **:** OBEY <~*ed* his conscience> **4 :** to copy after **:** IMITATE **5 a :** to walk or proceed along <~ a path> **b :** to engage in as a calling or way of life **:** PURSUE <wheat-growing is generally ~*ed* here> **6 a :** to come or take place after in time, sequence, or order **b :** to cause to be followed <~*ed* dinner with a liqueur> **7 :** to come into existence or take place as a result or consequence of <disaster ~*ed* the blunder> **8 a :** to watch steadily <~*ed* the ball over the fence> **b :** to keep the mind on <~ a speech> **c :** to attend closely to **:** keep abreast of <she ~*ed* his career with interest> **d :** to understand the logic of (as a line of thought) <I don't quite ~ you> ~ *vi* **1 :** to go or come after a person or thing in place, time, or sequence **2 :** to result or occur as a consequence, effect, or inference

syn **1** FOLLOW, SUCCEED, ENSUE, SUPERVENE *shared meaning element* **:** to come after something or someone ***ant*** precede (*in order*), forsake (*as a leader*)

2 FOLLOW, CHASE, PURSUE, TRAIL *shared meaning element* **:** to go after or on the track of someone or something ***ant*** precede

— **follow one's nose 1 :** to go in a straight or obvious course **2 :** to proceed without plan or reflection **:** obey one's instincts — **follow suit 1 :** to play a card of the same suit as the card led **2 :** to follow an example set

[2]follow *n* **1 :** the act or process of following **2 :** forward spin given to a ball by striking it above center — compare DRAW

fol·low·er \ˈfäl-ə-wər\ *n* **1 a :** one in the service of another **:** RETAINER **b :** one that follows the opinions or teachings of another **c :** one that imitates another **2** *archaic* **:** one that chases **3 :** a sheet added to the first sheet of an indenture or other deed **4 :** a machine part that receives motion from another part

syn FOLLOWER, ADHERENT, DISCIPLE, PARTISAN, SATELLITE *shared meaning element* **:** one who attaches himself to another ***ant*** leader

fol·low·er·ship \-ˌship\ *n* **1 :** FOLLOWING **2 :** the capacity or willingness to follow a leader

[1]fol·low·ing \ˈfäl-ə-wiŋ\ *adj* **1 :** next after **:** SUCCEEDING <the ~ day> **2 :** that immediately follows <trains will leave at the ~ times>

[2]following *n* **:** a group of followers, adherents, or partisans

[3]following *prep* **:** subsequent to <~ the lecture tea was served>

follow out *vt* **1 :** to follow to the end or to a conclusion **2 :** to carry out **:** EXECUTE <*followed out* his orders>

follow shot *n* **1 :** a shot in billiards or pool made by striking the cue ball above its center to cause it to continue forward after striking the object ball **2 :** a camera shot in which the camera follows the movement of the subject

fol·low–through \ˈfäl-ō-ˌthrü, ˌfäl-ō-ˈ, -ə-\ *n* **1 :** the act or an instance of following through **2 :** the part of the stroke following the striking of a ball

follow through *vi* **1 :** to continue a stroke or motion to the end of its arc **2 :** to press on in an activity or process esp. to a conclusion

[1]fol·low–up \ˌfäl-ə-ˌwəp\ *adj* **1 :** of, relating to, or being something that follows up <~ action by the police —Frank Faulkner> **2 :** done, conducted, or administered in the course of following up persons esp. after institutionalization <~ care for discharged hospital patients —*N.Y. Times Mag.*>

[2]follow–up \ˈfäl-ə-ˌwəp\ *n* **1 a :** the act or an instance of following up **b :** something that follows up **2 :** maintenance of contact with or reexamination of a person (as a patient) at usu. prescribed intervals following diagnosis or treatment **3 :** a news story presenting new information on a story published earlier

follow up \ˌfäl-ə-ˈwəp\ *vt* **1 :** to follow with something similar, related, or supplementary <*following up* his convictions with action —G. P. Merrill> **2 :** to maintain contact with (a person) in order to evaluate a diagnosis or to determine the effectiveness of treatment received <patients who are *followed up* after their discharge> ~ *vi* **:** to take appropriate action <*follow up* on . . . complaints, and customer suggestions — *Marketing*>

fol·ly \ˈfäl-ē\ *n, pl* **follies** [ME *folie*, fr. OF, fr. *fol* fool] **1 :** lack of good sense or normal prudence and foresight **2 :** a foolish act or idea **3 a** *obs* **:** EVIL, WICKEDNESS; *esp* **:** lewd behavior **b :** criminally or tragically foolish actions or conduct **4 :** an excessively costly or unprofitable undertaking

Fol·som \ˈfōl-səm\ *adj* [*Folsom*, N.M.] **:** of or relating to a prehistoric culture of No. America on the east side of the Rocky mountains that is characterized by flint projectile points having a concave base with side projections and a longitudinal groove on each face

fo·ment \fō-ˈment\ *vt* [ME *fomenten*, fr. LL *fomentare*, fr. L *fomentum* fomentation, fr. *fovēre* to warm, fondle, foment] **1 :** to treat with moist heat (as for easing pain) **2 :** to promote the growth or development of **:** ROUSE, INCITE <~ a rebellion> ***syn*** see INCITE ***ant*** quell — **fo·ment·er** *n*

fo·men·ta·tion \ˌfō-mən-ˈtā-shən, -ˌmen-\ *n* **1 a :** the application of hot moist substances to the body to ease pain **b :** the material so applied **2 :** the act of fomenting **:** INSTIGATION

[1]fond \ˈfänd\ *adj* [ME, fr. *fonne* fool] **1 :** FOOLISH, SILLY <~ pride> **2 a :** prizing highly **:** DESIROUS <~ of praise> **b :** having an affection or liking — used with *of* <he has always been ~ of music> **3 a :** foolishly tender **:** INDULGENT <spoiled by a ~ mother> **b :** AFFECTIONATE, LOVING <a ~ wife> <absence makes the heart grow ~*er*> **4 :** cherished with great affection **:** doted on <his ~*est* hopes>

[2]fond *vi, obs* **:** to be foolish **:** DOTE

[3]fond \ˈfōⁿ\ *n, pl* **fonds** \ˈfōⁿ(z)\ [F — more at FUND] **1 :** BACKGROUND, BASIS **2** *obs* **:** FUND

fon·dant \ˈfän-dənt\ *n* [F, fr. prp. of *fondre* to melt — more at FOUND] **1 :** a soft creamy preparation of sugar, water, and flavorings that is used as a basis for candies or icings **2 :** a candy consisting chiefly of fondant

fon·dle \ˈfän-dᵊl\ *vb* **fon·dled; fon·dling** \-(d)liŋ, -dᵊl-iŋ\ [freq. of obs. *fond*] *vt* **1** *obs* **:** PAMPER **2 :** to handle tenderly, lovingly, or lingeringly ~ *vi* **:** to show affection or desire by caressing ***syn*** see CARESS — **fon·dler** \-(d)lər, -dᵊl-ər\ *n*

fond·ling \ˈfän-(d)liŋ\ *n* [obs. *fond* (to fondle)] **:** one that is fondled or caressed

fond·ly \ˈfän-(d)lē\ *adv* **1** *archaic* **:** in a foolish manner **:** FOOLISHLY **2 :** in a fond manner **:** AFFECTIONATELY **3 :** in a willingly credulous manner <~ imagine that human beings today think faster —Warwick Braithwaite>

fond·ness \ˈfän(d)-nəs\ *n* **1** *obs* **:** FOOLISHNESS, FOLLY **2 :** tender affection **3 :** APPETITE, RELISH <had a ~ for argument>

fon·due *also* **fon·du** \fän-ˈd(y)ü, ˈfän-ˌ\ *n* [F *fondue*, fr. fem. of *fondu*, pp. of *fondre*] **1 a (1) :** a preparation of melted cheese (as Swiss cheese and Gruyère) usu. flavored with white wine and kirsch **(2) :** a dish that consists of small pieces of food (as meat or fruit) cooked in or dipped into a hot liquid <beef ~> <chocolate ~> **b :** a chafing dish in which fondue is made **2 :** a soufflé made with bread crumbs

F₁ layer \'ef-'wən-\ *n* : the lower of the two layers into which the F region of the ionosphere splits in the daytime occurring at varying heights from about 90 to 150 miles above the earth's surface

¹font \'fänt\ *n* [ME, fr. OE, fr. LL *font-, fons,* fr. L, fountain] **1 a** : a receptacle for baptismal water **b** : a receptacle for holy water **c** : a receptacle for various liquids **2** : FOUNTAIN, SOURCE <a ~ of information> — **font·al** \'fänt-ᵊl\ *adj*

²font *n* [MF *fonte* act of founding, fr. (assumed) VL *fundita,* fem. of *funditus,* pp. of L *fundere* to found, pour — more at FOUND] : an assortment of type all of one size and style

fon·ta·nel *also* **fon·ta·nelle** \ˌfänt-ᵊn-'el, 'fänt-ᵊn-ˌ\ *n* [ME *fontinelle,* a bodily hollow or pit, fr. MF *fontenele,* dim. of *fontaine* fountain] : a membrane-covered opening in bone or between bones; *specif* : one of the intervals closed by membranous structures between the uncompleted angles of the parietal bones and the neighboring bones of a fetal or young skull

fon·ti·na \fän-'tē-nə\ *n, often cap* [It] : a semisoft to hard ripened mild to medium sharp cheese of Italian origin

food \'füd\ *n, often attrib* [ME *fode,* fr. OE *fōda;* akin to OHG *fuotar* food, fodder, L *panis* bread, *pascere* to feed] **1 a** : material consisting essentially of protein, carbohydrate, and fat used in the body of an organism to sustain growth, repair, and vital processes and to furnish energy; *also* : such food together with supplementary substances (as minerals, vitamins, and condiments) **b** : inorganic substances absorbed by plants in gaseous form or in water solution **2** : nutriment in solid form **3** : something that nourishes, sustains, or supplies <~ for thought> — **food·less** \-ləs\ *adj* — **food·less·ness** *n*

food chain *n* : an arrangement of the organisms of an ecological community according to the order of predation in which each uses the next usu. lower member as a food source

food cycle *n* : a group of food chains constituting all or most of the food relations that enable an ecological community to survive

food poisoning *n* : an acute gastrointestinal disorder caused by bacteria or their toxic products or by chemical residues in food

food pyramid *n* : an ecological hierarchy of food relationships esp. when expressed quantitatively (as in mass, numbers, or energy) in which a chief predator is at the top, each level preys on the next lower level, and usu. green plants are at the bottom

food stamp *n* : a government-issued stamp that is sold or given to low-income persons and is redeemable for food

food·stuff \'füd-ˌstəf\ *n* : a substance with food value; *specif* : the raw material of food before or after processing

food vacuole *n* : a vacuole (as in an amoeba) in which ingested food is digested

food web *n* : the totality of interacting food chains in an ecological community

foo·fa·raw \'fü-fə-ˌrȯ\ *n* [origin unknown] **1** : frills and flashy finery **2** : a disturbance or to-do over a trifle : FUSS

¹fool \'fül\ *n* [ME, fr. OF *fol,* fr. LL *follis,* fr. L, bellows, bag; akin to L *flare* to blow — more at BLOW] **1** : a person lacking in judgment or prudence **2 a** : a retainer formerly kept in great households to provide casual entertainment and commonly dressed in motley with cap, bells, and bauble **b** : one who is victimized or made to appear foolish : DUPE **3 a** : a harmlessly deranged person or one lacking in common powers of understanding **b** : one with a marked propensity or talent for a certain activity <a letter-writing ~> **4 a** : mashed fruit and cream **b** : a dessert made of pulped fruit covered with a custard and cream <blueberry ~>

syn FOOL, IDIOT, IMBECILE, MORON, SIMPLETON, NATURAL *shared meaning element* : one who is mentally defective

²fool *vi* **1 a** : to spend time idly or aimlessly <just ~*ing* around all day> **b** : to meddle or tamper thoughtlessly or ignorantly <don't ~ with that gun> **2 a** : to play or improvise a comic role **b** : to speak in jest : JOKE <I was only ~*ing*> **3** : to contend or fight without serious intent or with less than full strength : TOY <a dangerous man to ~ with> ~ *vt* **1** : to make a fool of : DECEIVE **2** *obs* : INFATUATE **3** : to spend on trifles or without advantage : FRITTER — used with *away*

³fool *adj* : FOOLISH, SILLY <barking his ~ head off>

fool·ery \'fül-(ə-)rē\ *n, pl* **-er·ies** **1** : foolish behavior **2** : a foolish act, utterance, or belief

fool·har·dy \'fül-ˌhärd-ē\ *adj* : foolishly adventurous and bold : RASH *syn* see ADVENTUROUS — **fool·har·di·ly** \-ˌhärd-ᵊl-ē\ *adv* — **fool·har·di·ness** \-ˌhärd-ē-nəs\ *n*

fool·ish \'fü-lish\ *adj* **1** : marked by or proceeding from folly **2 a** : ABSURD, RIDICULOUS **b** : marked by a loss of composure : NONPLUSSED, ABASHED **3** : INSIGNIFICANT, TRIFLING, HUMBLE *syn* see SIMPLE — **fool·ish·ly** *adv*

fool·ish·ness *n* **1** : foolish behavior : FOLLY **2** : a foolish act or idea

fool·proof \'fül-'prüf\ *adj* : so simple, plain, or reliable as to leave no opportunity for error, misuse, or failure <a ~ plan>

fools·cap *or* **fool's cap** \'fül-ˌskap\ *n* **1** : a cap or hood usu. with bells worn by jesters **2** : a conical cap for slow or lazy students **3** [fr. the watermark of a fool's cap formerly applied to such paper] *usu foolscap* : a size of paper that is typically 16 x 13 inches

fool's gold *n* **1** : PYRITE **2** : CHALCOPYRITE

fool's paradise *n* : a state of delusory happiness

fool's parsley *n* : a poisonous European weed (*Aethusa cynapium*) of the carrot family resembling parsley

¹foot \'fu̇t\ *n, pl* **feet** \'fēt\ *also* **foot** [ME *fot,* fr. OE *fōt;* akin to L *ped-, pes* foot, Gk *pod-, pous*] **1** : the terminal part of the vertebrate leg upon which an individual stands **2** : an invertebrate organ of locomotion or attachment; *esp* : a ventral muscular surface or process of a mollusk **3** : any of various units of length based on the length of the human foot; *esp* : a unit equal to ⅓ yard and comprising 12 inches <a 10-*foot* pole> <6 *feet* tall> — see WEIGHT table **4** : the basic unit of verse meter consisting of any of various fixed combinations or groups of stressed and unstressed or long and short syllables **5 a** : motion or power of walking or running : STEP <fleet of ~> **b** : SPEED, SWIFTNESS **6** : something resembling a foot in position or use: as **a** : the lower end of the leg of a chair or table **b** : one of the areas of the base of a piece of printing type — see TYPE illustration **c** (1) : the basal portion of the sporogonium in mosses (2) : a specialized outgrowth by which the embryonic sporophyte of many ferns and related plants and some seed plants absorbs nourishment from the gametophyte **d** : a piece on a sewing machine that presses the cloth against the feed **7** *foot pl, chiefly Brit* : INFANTRY **8** : the lower edge (as of a sail) **9** : the lowest part : BOTTOM <the ~ of the hill> **10 a** : the end that is lower or opposite the head <the ~ of the bed> **b** : the part (as of a stocking) that covers the foot **11 foots** *pl but sing or pl in constr* : material deposited esp. in aging or refining : DREGS **12 foots** *pl* : FOOTLIGHTS — **foot·like** \'fu̇t-ˌlīk\ *adj* — **at one's feet** : under one's spell or influence — **off one's feet** : in a sitting or lying position — **on foot** : by walking or running <tour the campus *on foot*> — **on one's feet** **1** : in a standing position **2** : in an established position or state **3** : in a recovered condition (as from illness) **4** : in an extemporaneous manner <good debaters can think *on their feet*>

²foot *vi* **1** : DANCE **2** : to go on foot **3** *of a sailboat* : to make speed : MOVE ~ *vt* **1 a** : to perform the movements of (a dance) **b** : to walk, run, or dance on, over, or through **2** *archaic* **a** : KICK **b** : REJECT **3** *archaic* : ESTABLISH **4 a** : to add up **b** : to pay or stand credit for <agreed to ~ the bill> **5** : to make or renew the foot of (as a stocking)

foot·age \'fu̇t-ij\ *n* : length or quantity expressed in feet: as **a** : BOARD FEET **b** : the total number of running feet of motion-picture film used (as for a scene or subject)

foot-and-mouth disease *n* : an acute contagious febrile virus disease esp. of cloven-footed animals marked by ulcerating vesicles in the mouth, about the hoofs, and on the udder and teats — called also *foot-and-mouth, hoof-and-mouth disease*

foot·ball \'fu̇t-ˌbȯl\ *n* **1** : any of several games played between two teams on a rectangular field having two goalposts at each end and whose object is to get the ball over a goal line or between goalposts by running, passing, or kicking: as **a** *Brit* : SOCCER **b** *Brit* : RUGBY **c** : an American game played between two teams of 11 players each in which the ball is in possession of one side at a time and is advanced by running or passing **d** *Austral* : AUSTRALIAN RULES FOOTBALL **e** *Canad* : CANADIAN FOOTBALL **2 a** : an inflated oval ball used in the game of football **b** *Brit* : a soccer ball **3** : something tossed or kicked about : PLAYTHING <the bill became a political ~ in Congress>

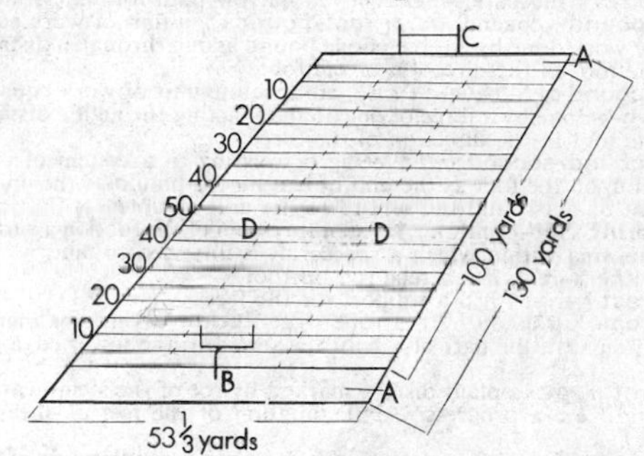

football field: *A* end zones, *B* goalposts (professional) at goal line, *C* goalposts (college) at end line, *D* inbounds lines

foot·ball·er \-ˌbȯ-lər\ *n* : one who plays football or soccer

foot·bath \'fu̇t-ˌbath, -ˌbath\ *n* : a bath (as at the entrance to an indoor swimming pool) for cleansing, warming, or disinfecting the feet

foot·board \'fu̇t-ˌbō(ə)rd, -ˌbȯ(ə)rd\ *n* **1** : a narrow platform on which to stand or brace the feet **2** : a board forming the foot of a bed

foot·boy \-ˌbȯi\ *n* : a serving boy : PAGE, ATTENDANT

foot·bridge \'fu̇t-ˌbrij\ *n* : a bridge for pedestrians

foot·can·dle \-'kan-dᵊl\ *n* : a unit of illuminance on a surface that is everywhere one foot from a uniform point source of light of one candle and equal to one lumen per square foot

foot·cloth \-ˌklȯth\ *n* **1** *archaic* : an ornamental cloth draped over the back of a horse to reach the ground on each side **2** : CARPET

foot–drag·ging \-ˌdrag-iŋ\ *n* : failure to act with the necessary promptness or vigor

foot·ed \'fu̇t-əd\ *adj* : having a foot or feet esp. of a specified kind or number — often used in combination <a four-*footed* animal>

foot·er \'fu̇t-ər\ *n, archaic* : PEDESTRIAN

-foot·er \'fu̇t-ər\ *comb form* : one that is a specified number of feet in height, length, or breadth <a six-*footer*>

foot·fall \'fu̇t-ˌfȯl\ *n* : the sound of a footstep

foot fault *n* : a fault that occurs (as in tennis) when a server fails to keep both feet behind the baseline until the ball is served

foot·gear \'fu̇t-ˌgi(ə)r\ *n* : FOOTWEAR

foot·hill \-ˌhil\ *n* : a hill at the foot of higher hills

foot·hold \-ˌhōld\ *n* **1 :** a hold for the feet : FOOTING **2 :** a position usable as a base for further advance <secured a ~ in the plastics market>

foot·ing \'fu̇t-iŋ\ *n* **1 :** a stable position or placing of the feet **2 :** a surface or its condition with respect to one walking or running on it; *specif* **:** the condition of a racetrack **3 :** the act of moving on foot : STEP, TREAD **4 a :** a place or space for standing : FOOTHOLD **b :** established position : STATUS; *esp* **:** position or rank in relation to others <they all started off on an equal ~> **5 :** BASIS **6 :** an enlargement at the lower end of a foundation wall, pier, or column to distribute the load **7 :** the sum of a column of figures

foo·tle \'füt-ᵊl\ *vi* **foo·tled; foo·tling** \'füt-liŋ, -ᵊl-iŋ\ [alter. of *footer* (to footle)] **1 :** to waste time : TRIFLE, FOOL **2 :** to talk or act foolishly — **footle** *n* — **foo·tler** \'füt-lər, -ᵊl-ər\ *n*

foot·less \'fu̇t-ləs\ *adj* **1 a :** having no feet **b :** lacking foundation : UNSUBSTANTIAL **2 :** STUPID, INEPT <dawdling and ~ conferences —Howard Lindsay> — **foot·less·ly** *adv* — **foot·less·ness** *n*

foot·lights \-ˌlīts\ *n pl* **1 :** a row of lights set across the front of a stage floor **2 :** the stage as a profession

foo·tling \'füt-liŋ, -ᵊl-iŋ\ *adj* [*footle*] **1 :** lacking judgment or ability : INEPT <~ amateurs who understand nothing —E. R. Bentley> **2 :** lacking use or value : TRIVIAL

foot·lock·er \'fu̇t-ˌläk-ər\ *n* **:** a small trunk designed to be placed at the foot of a bed (as in a barracks)

foot·loose \-ˌlüs\ *adj* **:** having no ties : free to move about

foot·man \-mən\ *n* **1 a** *archaic* **:** a traveler on foot : PEDESTRIAN **b :** INFANTRYMAN **2 a :** a servant in livery formerly attending a rider or required to run in front of his master's carriage **b :** a servant who serves at table, tends the door, and runs errands

foot·mark \-ˌmärk\ *n* **:** FOOTPRINT

1**foot·note** \-ˌnōt\ *n* **1 :** a note of reference, explanation, or comment usu. placed below the text on a printed page **2 :** something that is subordinately related to a larger event or work <that biography is an illuminating ~ to the history of our times>

2**footnote** *vt* **:** to furnish with a footnote : ANNOTATE

foot·pace \'fu̇t-ˌpās\ *n* **1 :** a walking pace **2 :** PLATFORM, DAIS

1**foot·pad** \-ˌpad\ *n* [*foot* + *pad* (highwayman)] **:** one who robs a pedestrian

2**footpad** *n* [*foot* + 1*pad*] **:** a flattish foot on the leg of a spacecraft for distributing weight to minimize sinking into a surface

foot·path \'fu̇t-ˌpath, -ˌpȧth\ *n* **:** a narrow path for pedestrians

foot–pound \-'pau̇nd\ *n, pl* **foot–pounds :** a unit of work equal to the work done by a force of one pound acting through a distance of one foot in the direction of the force

foot–pound·al \-'pau̇n-dᵊl\ *n* **:** an absolute unit of work equal to the work done by a force of one poundal acting through a distance of one foot in the direction of the force

foot–pound–second *adj* **:** being or relating to a system of units based upon the foot as the unit of length, the pound as the unit of weight or mass, and the second as the unit of time

foot·print \'fu̇t-ˌprint\ *n* **1 :** an impression of the foot on a surface **2 :** an area within which a spacecraft is intended to land

foot·race \-ˌrās\ *n* **:** a race run on foot

foot·rest \-ˌrest\ *n* **:** a support for the feet

foot·rope \-ˌrōp\ *n* **1 :** a rope rigged below a yard for men to stand on **2 :** the part of a boltrope sewed to the lower edge of a sail

foot rot *n* **1 :** a plant disease marked by rot of the stem near the ground **2 :** a progressive inflammation of the feet of sheep or cattle

foot·slog \'fu̇t-ˌsläg\ *vi* **:** to march or tramp through mud — **foot·slog·ger** *n*

foot soldier *n* **:** INFANTRYMAN

foot·sore \'fu̇t-ˌsō(ə)r, -ˌsȯ(ə)r\ *adj* **:** having sore or tender feet (as from much walking) — **foot·sore·ness** *n*

foot·stall \-ˌstȯl\ *n* **:** the plinth, base, or pedestal of a pillar

foot·step \-ˌstep\ *n* **1 a :** TREAD **b :** distance covered by a step : PACE **2 :** the mark of the foot : TRACK **3 :** a step on which to ascend or descend **4 :** a way of life, conduct, or action <followed in his father's ~*s*>

foot·stone \-ˌstōn\ *n* **:** a stone placed at the foot of a grave

foot·stool \-ˌstül\ *n* **:** a low stool used to support the feet

foot·wall \-ˌwȯl\ *n* **1 :** the lower underlying wall of a vein, ore deposit, or coal seam in a mine **2 :** the lower wall of an inclined fault

foot·way \-ˌwā\ *n* **:** a narrow way or path for pedestrians

foot·wear \-ˌwa(ə)r, -ˌwe(ə)r\ *n* **:** wearing apparel (as shoes or boots) for the feet

foot·work \-ˌwərk\ *n* **1 :** the management of the feet (as in boxing); *also* **:** the work done with them **2 :** the activity of moving from place to place <the investigation entailed a lot of ~>

foo·ty \'fu̇t-ē\ *adj* [F *foutu*] **1** *chiefly dial* **:** INSIGNIFICANT, PALTRY **2** *chiefly dial* **:** poorly kept : SHABBY

1**foo·zle** \'fü-zəl\ *vt* **foo·zled; foo·zling** \'füz-(ə-)liŋ\ [perh. fr. G dial. *fuseln* to work carelessly] **:** to manage or play awkwardly : BUNGLE

2**foozle** *n* **:** an act of foozling; *esp* **:** a bungling golf stroke

1**fop** \'fäp\ *n* [ME; akin to ME *fobben* to deceive, MHG *voppen*] **1** *obs* **:** a foolish or silly person **2 :** a man who is devoted to or vain about his appearance or dress : COXCOMB, DANDY

2**fop** *vt* **fopped; fop·ping** *obs* **:** FOOL, DUPE

fop·pery \'fäp-(ə-)rē\ *n, pl* **-per·ies 1 :** foolish character or action : FOLLY **2 :** the behavior or dress of a fop

fop·pish \'fäp-ish\ *adj* **1** *obs* **:** FOOLISH, SILLY **2 a :** characteristic of a fop <a ~ embroidered nightshirt —A. Conan Doyle> **b :** behaving or dressing in the manner of a fop — **fop·pish·ly** *adv* — **fop·pish·ness** *n*

1**for** \fər, (')fō(ə)r, *South also* (')fär\ *prep* [ME, fr. OE; akin to L *per* through, *prae* before, *pro* before, for, ahead, Gk *pro*, OE *faran* to go — more at FARE] **1 a** — used as a function word to indicate purpose <a grant ~ studying medicine> **b** — used as a function word to indicate an intended goal <left ~ home> <acted ~ the best> **c** — used as a function word to indicate the object or recipient of a perception, desire, or activity <now ~ a good rest> <run ~ your life> <an eye ~ a bargain> <called ~ hands to take in the sail> **2 a :** as being or constituting <take him ~ a fool> <eggs ~ breakfast> **b** — used as a function word to indicate an actual or implied enumeration or selection <~ one thing, the price is too high> **3 :** because of <cried ~ joy> **4** — used as a function word to indicate suitability or fitness <it is not ~ the president to make that decision> <ready ~ action> **5 a :** in place of **b :** on behalf of : REPRESENTING **6 :** in spite of — usu. used with *all* <~ all his large size, he moves gracefully> **7 :** with respect to : CONCERNING <a stickler ~ detail> **8** — used as a function word to indicate equivalence in exchange <$10 ~ a hat>, equality in number or quantity <point ~ point>, or correspondence or correlation <~ one good one, you'll find five that don't work> **9** — used as a function word to indicate duration of time or extent of space **10 :** in honor of : AFTER

2**for** *conj* **:** for this reason or on this ground

3**for** *abbr* **1** foreign **2** forestry

FOR *abbr* free on rail

for- *prefix* [ME, fr. OE; akin to OHG *fur-* for-, OE *for*] **1 :** so as to involve prohibition, exclusion, omission, failure, neglect, or refusal <*for*say> **2 :** destructively or detrimentally <*for*do> **3 :** completely : excessively : to exhaustion : to pieces <*for*spent>

fora *pl of* FORUM

1**for·age** \'fȯr-ij, 'fär-\ *n* [ME, fr. MF, fr. OF, fr. *forre* fodder, of Gmc origin; akin to OHG *fuotar* food, fodder — more at FOOD] **1 :** food for animals esp. when taken by browsing or grazing **2** [2*forage*] **:** the act of foraging : search for provisions

2**forage** *vb* **for·aged; for·ag·ing** *vt* **1 :** to strip of provisions : collect forage from **2 :** to secure by foraging <*foraged* a chicken for the feast> ~ *vi* **1 :** to wander in search of forage or food **2 :** to secure forage (as for horses) by stripping the country **3 :** RAVAGE, RAID **4 :** to make a search : RUMMAGE — **for·ag·er** *n*

forage acre *n* **:** a unit of grazing value equivalent to one acre of land entirely covered with herbage that can be completely utilized by grazing animals

fo·ram \'fōr-əm, 'fȯr-\ *n* **:** FORAMINIFER

fo·ra·men \fə-'rā-mən\ *n, pl* **fo·ram·i·na** \-'ram-ə-nə\ *or* **fo·ra·mens** \-'rā-mənz\ [L *foramin-*, *foramen*, fr. *forare* to bore — more at BORE] **:** a small opening, perforation, or orifice : FENESTRA — **fo·ram·i·nal** \fə-'ram-ən-ᵊl\ *or* **fo·ram·i·nous** \-ə-nəs\ *adj*

fo·ra·men mag·num \fə-ˌrā-mən-'mag-nəm\ *n* [NL, lit., great opening] **:** the opening in the skull through which the spinal cord passes to become the medulla oblongata

foramen ova·le \-ō-'val-ē, -'väl-, -'vāl-\ *n* [NL, lit., oval opening] **:** an opening in the septum between the two atria of the heart that is normally present only in the fetus

for·a·min·i·fer \ˌfȯr-ə-'min-ə-fər, ˌfär-\ *n* **:** any of an order (Foraminifera) of large chiefly marine rhizopods usu. having calcareous shells that often are perforated with minute holes for protrusion of slender pseudopodia and form the bulk of chalk and nummulitic limestone — **fo·ra·mi·nif·er·al** \fə-ˌram-ə-'nif-(ə-)rəl; ˌfȯr-ə-mə-'nif-, ˌfär-\ *or* **fo·ra·mi·nif·er·ous** \-(ə-)rəs\ *adj*

fo·ra·mi·nif·era \fə-ˌram-ə-'nif-(ə-)rə; ˌfȯr-ə-mə-'nif-, ˌfär-\ *n pl* [NL, fr. L *foramin-*, *foramen* + *-fera*, neut. pl. of *-fer* -fer] **:** organisms that are foraminifers

fo·ra·mi·nif·er·an \-(ə-)rən\ *n* **:** FORAMINIFER

for and *conj, obs* **:** and also

for·as·much as \'fȯr-əz-ˌməch-əz\ *conj* **:** in view of the fact that : SINCE

1**for·ay** \'fȯr-ˌā, 'fōr-, 'fär- *also* fō-'rā *or* fə-'\ *vb* [ME *forrayen*, fr. MF *forrer*, fr. *forre* fodder — more at FORAGE] *vt, archaic* **:** to ravage in search of spoils : PILLAGE ~ *vi* **:** to make a raid or brief invasion <~*ed* into enemy territory> — **for·ay·er** *n*

2**foray** *n* **1 :** a sudden or irregular invasion or attack for war or spoils : RAID **2 :** a brief excursion or attempt esp. outside one's accustomed sphere <the housewife's ~ into politics>

forb \'fō(ə)rb\ *n* [Gk *phorbē* fodder, food, fr. *pherbein* to graze; akin to OE *beorgan* to taste] **:** an herb other than grass

1**for·bear** \fȯr-'ba(ə)r, fər-, -'be(ə)r\ *vb* **-bore** \-'bō(ə)r, -'bȯ(ə)r\; **-borne** \-'bō(ə)rn, -'bȯ(ə)rn\; **-bear·ing** [ME *forberen*, fr. OE *forberan* to endure, do without, fr. *for-* + *beran* to bear] *vt* **1** *obs* **:** to leave alone : SHUN <~ his presence —Shak.> **2** *obs* **:** to do without **3 :** to hold oneself back from esp. with an effort of self-restraint ~ *vi* **1 :** to hold back : ABSTAIN **2 :** to control oneself when provoked : be patient ***syn*** see REFRAIN — **for·bear·er** *n*

2**forbear** *var of* FOREBEAR

for·bear·ance \fȯr-'bar-ən(t)s, fər-, -'ber-\ *n* **1 :** a refraining from the enforcement of something (as a debt, right, or obligation) that is due **2 :** the act of forbearing : PATIENCE **3 :** the quality of being forbearing : LENIENCY

1**for·bid** \fər-'bid, fȯr-\ *vt* **-bade** \-'bad, -'bād\ *or* **-bad** \-'bad\; **-bid·den** \-'bid-ᵊn\; **-bid·ding** [ME *forbidden*, fr. OE *forbēodan*, fr. *for-* + *bēodan* to bid — more at BID] **1 :** to proscribe from or as if from the position of one in authority : command against <the law ~*s* stores to sell liquor to minors> <her mother ~*s* her to go> <he ~*s* her the car> **2 :** to hinder or prevent as if by an effectual command <space ~*s* further treatment of the subject here> — **for·bid·der** *n*

syn FORBID, PROHIBIT, INTERDICT, INHIBIT, BAN *shared meaning element* **:** to debar one from using, doing, or entering or to order that something not be used, done, or entered ***ant*** permit, bid

2**forbid** *adj, archaic* **:** ACCURSED <he shall live a man ~ —Shak.>

for·bid·dance \fər-'bid-ᵊn(t)s, fȯr-\ *n* **:** the act of forbidding

for·bid·den \-'bid-ᵊn\ *adj* **:** not conforming to the usual selection principles — used of quantum phenomena <~ transition> <~ radiation> <~ spectral line>

for·bid·ding *adj* **1 :** such as to make approach or passage difficult or impossible <~ walls> **2 :** DISAGREEABLE, REPELLENT <his father was a stern ~ figure> — **for·bid·ding·ly** \-'bid-iŋ-lē\ *adv* — **for·bid·ding·ness** *n*

forbode *var of* FOREBODE

[1]**for·by** *or* **for·bye** \fȯr-ˈbī\ *prep* [ME *forby,* prep. & adv., fr. *fore-* + *by*] **1** *archaic* **a :** PAST **b :** NEAR **2** *chiefly Scot* **:** BESIDES
[2]**forby** *or* **forbye** *adv, chiefly Scot* **:** in addition **:** BESIDES
[1]**force** \ˈfō(ə)rs, ˈfȯ(ə)rs\ *n* [ME, fr. MF, fr. (assumed) VL *fortia,* fr. L *fortis* strong] **1 a :** strength or energy exerted or brought to bear **:** cause of motion or change **:** active power <the ~*s* of nature> <the love of justice has been a powerful motivating ~ in his life> **b :** moral or mental strength **c :** capacity to persuade or convince <couldn't resist the ~ of his argument> **2 a :** military strength **b (1) :** a body (as of troops or ships) assigned to a military purpose **(2)** *pl* **:** the whole military strength (as of a nation) **c :** a body of persons or things available for a particular end <a labor ~> <the missile ~> **d :** an individual or group having the power of effective action <police and citizens must join ~*s* to prevent violence> <he was a ~ behind the passing of that bill> **3 :** violence, compulsion, or constraint exerted upon or against a person or thing **4 :** an agency or influence that if applied to a free body results chiefly in an acceleration of the body and sometimes in elastic deformation and other effects **5 :** the quality of conveying impressions intensely in writing or speech — **force·less** \-ləs\ *adj* — **in force 1 :** in great numbers <police were summoned *in force*> **2 :** VALID, OPERATIVE <his suspension from school must remain *in force*>
[2]**force** *vt* **forced; forc·ing 1 :** to do violence to; *esp* **:** RAPE **2 :** to compel by physical, moral, or intellectual means **3 :** to make or cause through natural or logical necessity <*forced* to admit he was right> **4 a :** to press, drive, attain to, or effect against resistance or inertia <~ a bill through the legislature> **b :** to impose or thrust urgently, importunately, or inexorably <~ unwanted attentions on a woman> **5 :** to achieve or win by strength in struggle or violence: **a :** to win one's way into <~ a castle> <*forced* the mountain passes> **b :** to break open or through <~ a lock> **6 a :** to raise or accelerate to the utmost <*forcing* the pace> **b :** to produce only with unnatural or unwilling effort <she *forced* a smile in spite of her distress> **c :** to wrench, strain, or use (language) with marked unnaturalness and lack of ease **7 a :** to hasten the rate of progress or growth of **b :** to bring (as plants) to maturity out of the normal season <*forcing* lilies for the Easter trade> **8 :** to induce (as a particular bid or play by another player) in a card game by some conventional act, play, bid, or response **9 a :** to cause (a runner in baseball) to be put out on a force play **b :** to cause (a run) to be scored in baseball by giving a base on balls when the bases are full — **forc·er** *n*

syn FORCE, COMPEL, COERCE, CONSTRAIN, OBLIGE *shared meaning element* **:** to make someone or something yield. FORCE, the general term, implies an overcoming of resistance by the exertion of strength, weight, power, stress, or duress <*forced* his way through the crowd> <*forced* to submit to questioning> <used threats to *force* agreement to their terms> COMPEL usually implies an exertion of authority or the working of an irresistible force <*compelled* by necessity to seek help> COERCE suggests the overcoming of resistance by severe methods (as violence or duress) or by threat and intimidation <no one can claim that he was *coerced* by bribery. This is reserved for threats and direct pleas —W. D. Falk> CONSTRAIN suggests a forcing by what does or seems to constrict, press, confine, or bind <*constrained* by sickness from a normal life> <he was *constrained* to confess by the evidence against him> OBLIGE implies the constraint of necessity, sometimes physical but often moral or intellectual <ill health *obliged* him to retire> <he was *obliged* to admit he had been wrong>
— **force one's hand :** to cause one to act precipitously **:** force one to reveal his purpose or intention

forced \ˈfō(ə)rst, ˈfȯ(ə)rst\ *adj* **1 :** compelled by force **:** INVOLUNTARY <a ~ landing> **2 :** done or produced with effort, exertion, or pressure <a ~ laugh> — **forced·ly** \ˈfōr-səd-lē, ˈfȯr-\ *adv*
force–feed *vt* **1 :** to feed (as an animal) by forcible administration of food **2 :** to force to take in <~ students a literary education>
force·ful \ˈfōrs-fəl, ˈfȯrs-\ *adj* **:** possessing or filled with force **:** EFFECTIVE — **force·ful·ly** \-fə-lē\ *adv* — **force·ful·ness** *n*
force ma·jeure \ˌfōr-smä-ˈzhər, ˌfȯr-, -smə-\ *n* [F, superior force] **:** an event or effect that cannot be reasonably anticipated or controlled — compare ACT OF GOD
force·meat \ˈfōr-ˌsmēt, ˈfȯr-\ *n* [*force* (alter. of *farce*) + *meat*] **:** finely chopped and highly seasoned meat or fish that is either served alone or used as a stuffing — called also *farce*
force of habit : behavior made involuntary or automatic by repeated practice
force–out \ˈfōr-ˌsau̇t, ˈfȯr-\ *n* **:** FORCE PLAY
force play *n* **:** a play in baseball in which a runner is put out when he is forced to advance to the next base but fails to do so safely
for·ceps \ˈfȯr-səps\ *n, pl* **forceps** [L, fr. *formus* warm + *capere* to take — more at WARM, HEAVE] **:** an instrument for grasping, holding firmly, or exerting traction upon objects esp. for delicate operations (as by jewelers or surgeons) — **for·ceps·like** \-ˌlīk\ *adj*

forceps

force pump *n* **:** a pump with a solid piston for drawing and forcing through valves a liquid (as water) to a considerable height above the pump or under a considerable pressure
forc·ible \ˈfōr-sə-bəl, ˈfȯr-\ *adj* **1 :** effected by force used against opposition or resistance **2 :** characterized by force, efficiency, or energy **:** POWERFUL — **forc·i·ble·ness** *n* — **forc·i·bly** \-blē\ *adv*
[1]**ford** \ˈfō(ə)rd, ˈfȯ(ə)rd\ *n* [ME, fr. OE; akin to ON *fjǫrthr* fiord, L *portus* port, OE *faran* to go — more at FARE] **:** a shallow part of a body of water that may be crossed by wading
[2]**ford** *vt* **:** to cross (a body of water) by wading — **ford·able** \ˈfōrd-ə-bəl, ˈfȯrd-\ *adj*
for·do *or* **fore·do** \fȯr-ˈdü, fōr-\ *vt* **-did** \-ˈdid\; **-done** \-ˈdən\; **-do·ing** \-ˈdü-iŋ\ [ME *fordon,* fr. OE *fordōn,* fr. *for-* + *dōn* to do] **1** *archaic* **:** to do away with **:** DESTROY **2 :** to overcome with fatigue **:** EXHAUST — used only as past participle <quite *fordone* with the heat>
[1]**fore** \ˈfō(ə)r, ˈfȯ(ə)r\ *adv* [ME, fr. OE; akin to OE *for*] **1** *obs* **:** at an earlier time or period **2 :** in, toward, or adjacent to the front **:** FORWARD
[2]**fore** *also* **ˈfore** *prep* **1** *chiefly dial* **:** BEFORE **2 :** in the presence of
[3]**fore** *adj* [*fore-*] **1 :** prior in order of occurrence **:** FORMER **2 :** situated in front of something else **:** FORWARD
[4]**fore** *n* **:** something that occupies a front position — **to the fore :** in or into a position of prominence **:** FORWARD <a younger generation of idealists is coming *to the fore*>
[5]**fore** *interj* [prob. short for *before*] — used by a golfer to warn anyone within range of the probable line of flight of his ball
fore- *comb form* [ME *for-, fore-,* fr. OE *fore-,* fr. *fore,* adv.] **1 a :** earlier **:** beforehand <*fore*see> **b :** occurring earlier **:** occurring beforehand <*fore*payment> **2 a :** situated at the front **:** in front <*fore*leg> **b :** front part of (something specified) <*fore*arm>
fore–and–aft \ˌfōr-ə-ˈnaft, ˌfȯr-\ *adj* **1 :** lying, running, or acting in the general line of the length of a construction (as a ship or a house) **:** LONGITUDINAL **2 :** having no square sails
fore and aft *adv* **1 :** lengthwise of a ship **:** from stem to stern **2 :** in, at, or toward both the bow and stern
fore–and–aft·er \-ˈnaf-tər\ *n* **:** a ship with a fore-and-aft rig; *esp* **:** SCHOONER
fore–and–aft rig *n* **:** a sailing-ship rig in which most or all of the sails are not attached to yards but are bent to gaffs or set on the masts or on stays in a fore-and-aft line
[1]**fore·arm** \(ˈ)fōr-ˈärm, (ˈ)fȯr-\ *vt* **:** to arm in advance **:** PREPARE
[2]**fore·arm** \ˈfōr-ˌärm, ˈfȯr-\ *n* **:** the part of the arm between the elbow and the wrist; *also* **:** the corresponding part in other vertebrates
fore·bay \ˈfō(ə)r-ˌbā, ˈfȯ(ə)r-\ *n* **:** a reservoir or canal from which water is taken to run equipment (as a waterwheel or turbine)
fore·bear *or* **for·bear** \-ˌba(ə)r, -ˌbe(ə)r\ *n* [ME (Sc) *forebear,* fr. *fore-* + *-bear* (fr. *been* to be)] **:** ANCESTOR, FOREFATHER — usu. used in pl.
fore·bode *also* **for·bode** \fōr-ˈbōd, fȯr-\ *vt* **1 :** FORETELL, PORTEND <such heavy air ~*s* storm> **2 :** to have an inward conviction of (as coming ill or misfortune) ~ *vi* **:** AUGUR, PREDICT — **fore·bod·er** *n*
[1]**fore·bod·ing** \-ˈbōd-iŋ\ *n* **:** the act of one who forebodes; *also* **:** an omen, prediction, or presentiment esp. of coming evil **:** PORTENT
[2]**foreboding** *adj* **:** indicative of or marked by foreboding — **fore·bod·ing·ly** \-iŋ-lē\ *adv* — **fore·bod·ing·ness** *n*
fore·brain \ˈfō(ə)r-ˌbrān, ˈfȯ(ə)r-\ *n* **1 :** the anterior of the three primary divisions of the developing vertebrate brain **2 a :** the part of the brain of the adult that develops from the embryonic forebrain and includes the telencephalon and diencephalon **b :** TELENCEPHALON
fore·cad·die \-ˌkad-ē\ *n* **:** a golf caddie who is stationed in the fairway and who indicates the position of balls on the course
[1]**fore·cast** \-ˌkast; fōr-ˈkast, fȯr-ˈ\ *vb* **forecast** *or* **fore·cast·ed; fore·cast·ing** *vt* **1 a :** to calculate or predict (some future event or condition) usu. as a result of rational study and analysis of available pertinent data; *esp* **:** to predict (weather conditions) on the basis of correlated meteorological observations **b :** to indicate as likely to occur **2 :** to serve as a forecast of **:** PRESAGE <such events may ~ peace> ~ *vi* **:** to calculate the future ***syn*** see FORETELL — **fore·cast·er** *n*
[2]**fore·cast** \ˈfō(ə)r-ˌkast, ˈfȯ(ə)r-\ *n* **1** *archaic* **:** foresight of consequences and provision against them **:** FORETHOUGHT **2 :** a prophecy, estimate, or prediction of a future happening or condition
fore·cas·tle \ˈfōk-səl; ˈfōr-ˌkas-əl, ˈfȯr-\ *n* **1 :** the part of the upper deck of a ship forward of the foremast or of the fore channels **2 :** the forward part of a merchantman where the crew is housed
fore–check \ˈfō(ə)r-ˌchek, ˈfȯ(ə)r-\ *vi* **:** to guard an opponent in ice hockey in his own defensive zone
fore·close \fōr-ˈklōz, fȯr-\ *vb* [ME *forclosen,* fr. OF *forclos,* pp. of *forclore,* fr. *fors* outside (fr. L *foris*) + *clore* to close — more at FORUM] *vt* **1 :** to shut out **:** DEBAR **2 :** to hold exclusively **3 :** to deal with or close in advance **4 :** to subject to foreclosure proceedings ~ *vi* **:** to foreclose a mortgage
fore·clo·sure \-ˈklō-zhər\ *n* **:** an act or instance of foreclosing; *specif* **:** a legal proceeding that bars or extinguishes a mortgagor's right of redeeming a mortgaged estate
fore·deck \ˈfō(ə)r-ˌdek, ˈfȯ(ə)r-\ *n* **:** the forepart of a ship's main deck
foredo *var of* FORDO
fore·doom \fōr-ˈdüm, fȯr-\ *vt* **:** to doom beforehand
fore·face \ˈfō(ə)r-ˌfās, ˈfȯ(ə)r-\ *n* **:** the part of the head of a quadruped that is in front of the eyes
fore·fa·ther \-ˌfät͟h-ər\ *n* **1 :** ANCESTOR 1a **2 :** a person of an earlier period and common heritage
fore·feel \fōr-ˈfē(ə)l, fȯr-\ *vt* **-felt** \-ˈfelt\; **-feel·ing :** to have a presentiment of
forefend *var of* FORFEND
fore·fin·ger \ˈfō(ə)r-ˌfiŋ-gər, ˈfȯ(ə)r-\ *n* **:** the finger next to the thumb — called also *index finger*
fore·foot \-ˌfu̇t\ *n* **1 :** one of the anterior feet of a quadruped or multiped **2 :** the forward part of a ship where the stem and keel meet
fore·front \-ˌfrənt\ *n* **:** the foremost part or place **:** VANGUARD <was in the ~ of the progressive movement>

ə abut	ᵊ kitten	ər further	a back	ā bake	ä cot, cart
au̇ out	ch chin	e less	ē easy	g gift	i trip	ī life
j joke	ŋ sing	ō flow	ȯ flaw	ȯi coin	th thin	t͟h this
ü loot	u̇ foot	y yet	yü few	yu̇ furious	zh vision

fore·gath·er *var of* FORGATHER

1fore·go \fōr-ˈgō, fȯr-\ *vt* **-went** \-ˈwent\; **-gone** \-ˈgȯn *also* -ˈgän\; **-go·ing** \-ˈgō-iŋ, -ˈgȯ(-)iŋ\ : to go before : PRECEDE — **fore·go·er** \-ˈgō(-ə)r\ *n*

2forego *var of* FORGO

fore·go·ing \-ˈgō-iŋ, -ˈgȯ(-)iŋ\ *adj* : going before <the ~ statement is open to challenge> ***syn*** see PRECEDING ***ant*** following

fore·gone \ˌfōr-ˌgȯn, ˌfȯr- *also* -ˌgän\ *adj* : PREVIOUS, PAST

foregone conclusion *n* **1** : a conclusion that has preceded argument or examination **2** : an inevitable result : CERTAINTY <the victory was a *foregone conclusion*>

fore·ground \ˈfō(ə)r-ˌgrau̇nd, ˈfȯ(ə)r-\ *n* **1** : the part of a scene or representation that is nearest to and in front of the spectator **2** : a position of prominence : FOREFRONT

fore·gut \-ˌgət\ *n* : the anterior part of the alimentary canal of a vertebrate embryo that develops into the pharynx, esophagus, stomach, and extreme anterior part of the intestine

1fore·hand \-ˌhand\ *n* **1** *archaic* : superior position : ADVANTAGE **2** : the part of a horse that is before the rider **3** : a forehand stroke (as in tennis or racquets); *also* : the side on which such strokes are made

2forehand *adv* : with a forehand stroke

3forehand *adj* **1** *obs* : done or given in advance : PRIOR **2** : made with the palm of the hand turned in the direction in which the hand is moving <a ~ tennis stroke>

forehand 3

fore·hand·ed \(ˈ)fōr-ˈhan-dəd, (ˈ)fȯr-\ *adj* **1 a** : mindful of the future : PRUDENT **b** : WELL-TO-DO **2** : FOREHAND 2 — **fore·hand·ed·ly** *adv* — **fore·hand·ed·ness** *n*

fore·head \ˈfȯr-əd, ˈfär-; ˈfō(ə)r-ˌhed, ˈfȯ(ə)r-\ *n* **1** : the part of the face above the eyes **2** : the front or forepart of something <flames in the ~ of the morning sky —John Milton>

fore·hoof \ˈfō(ə)r-ˌhu̇f, ˈfȯ(ə)r-, -ˌhüf\ *n* : the hoof of a forefoot

for·eign \ˈfȯr-ən, ˈfär-\ *adj* [ME *forein*, fr. OF, fr. LL *foranus* on the outside, fr. L *foris* outside — more at FORUM] **1** : situated outside a place or country; *esp* : situated outside one's own country **2** : born in, belonging to, or characteristic of some place or country other than the one under consideration **3** : of, relating to, or proceeding from some other person or material thing than the one under consideration **4** : alien in character : not connected or pertinent **5** : related to or dealing with other nations **6** : occurring in an abnormal situation in the living body and commonly introduced from without **7** : not being within the jurisdiction of a political unit (as a state) ***syn*** see EXTRINSIC ***ant*** germane — **for·eign·ness** \-ən-nəs\ *n*

foreign affairs *n pl* : matters having to do with international relations and with the interests of the home country in foreign countries

foreign aid *n* : assistance (as economic aid) provided by one nation to another esp. as a tool in molding opinion in the recipient nation

foreign bill *n* : a bill of exchange that is not both drawn and payable within a particular jurisdiction

for·eign–born \ˌfȯr-ən-ˈbȯ(ə)rn, ˌfär-\ *adj* : foreign by birth

foreign correspondent *n* : a correspondent employed to send from a foreign country news or comment for publication (as in a newspaper)

for·eign·er \ˈfȯr-ə-nər, ˈfär-\ *n* **1** : a person belonging to or owing allegiance to a foreign country : ALIEN **2** *chiefly dial* : STRANGER 1c

foreign exchange *n* **1** : a process of settling accounts or debts between persons residing in different countries **2** : foreign currency or current short-term credit instruments payable in such currency

for·eign·ism \ˈfȯr-ə-ˌniz-əm, ˈfär-\ *n* : something peculiar to a foreign language or people; *specif* : a foreign idiom or custom

foreign minister *n* : a governmental minister for foreign affairs

foreign policy *n* : the policy of a sovereign state in its interaction with other sovereign states

foreign service *n* : the field force of a foreign office comprising diplomatic and consular personnel

1fore·judge *or* **for·judge** \fər-ˈjəj, fōr-, fȯr-\ *vt* [ME *forjuggen*, fr. MF *forjugier*, fr. *fors* outside (fr. L *foris*) + *jugier* to judge] : to expel, oust, or put out by judgment of a court

2fore·judge \(ˈ)fōr-ˈjəj, (ˈ)fȯr-\ *vt* : PREJUDGE

fore·know \(ˈ)fōr-ˈnō, (ˈ)fȯr-\ *vt* **-knew** \-ˈn(y)ü\; **-known** \-ˈnōn\; **-know·ing** : to have previous knowledge of : know beforehand esp. by paranormal means or by revelation ***syn*** see FORESEE — **fore·knowl·edge** \-ˈnäl-ij\ *n*

fore·la·dy \ˈfō(ə)r-ˌlād-ē, ˈfȯ(ə)r-\ *n* : a woman who acts as a foreman

fore·land \ˈfōr-lənd, ˈfȯr-\ *n* : PROMONTORY, HEADLAND

fore·leg \ˈfō(ə)r-ˌleg, ˈfȯ(ə)r-, -ˌlāg\ *n* : a front leg

fore·limb \-ˌlim\ *n* : an arm, fin, wing, or leg that is or is homologous to a foreleg <the ~ of a bat>

fore·lock \-ˌläk\ *n* : a lock of hair growing from the front of the head

fore·man \ˈfōr-mən, ˈfȯr-\ *n* : a first or chief man: as **a** : a member of a jury who acts as chairman and spokesman **b** (1) : a chief and often specially trained workman who works with and commonly leads a gang or crew (2) : a person in authority over a group of workers, a particular operation, or a section of a plant — **fore·man·ship** \-ˌship\ *n*

fore·mast \ˈfō(ə)r-ˌmast, ˈfȯ(ə)r-, -məst\ *n* : the mast nearest the bow of a ship

fore·milk \-ˌmilk\ *n* **1** : first-drawn milk **2** : COLOSTRUM

1fore·most \-ˌmōst\ *adj* [ME *formest*, fr. OE, superl. of *forma* first; akin to OHG *fruma* advantage, OE *fore* fore] **1** : first in a series or progression **2** : of first rank or position : PREEMINENT

2foremost *adv* **1** : in the first place **2** : most importantly <first and ~>

fore·moth·er \ˈfō(ə)r-ˌmət͟h-ər, ˈfȯ(ə)r-\ *n* : a female ancestor

fore·name \-ˌnām\ *n* : a name that precedes one's surname

fore·named \-ˌnāmd\ *adj* : named previously : AFORESAID

fore·noon \ˈfō(ə)r-ˌnün, ˈfȯ(ə)r-, fōr-ˈ, fȯr-ˈ\ *n* : the early part of the day ending with noon : MORNING

1fo·ren·sic \fə-ˈren(t)-sik, -ˈren-zik\ *adj* [L *forensis* public, forensic, fr. *forum*] **1** : belonging to, used in, or suitable to courts of judicature or to public discussion and debate **2** : ARGUMENTATIVE, RHETORICAL — **fo·ren·si·cal·ly** \-si-k(ə-)lē, -zi-\ *adv*

2forensic *n* **1** : an argumentative exercise **2** *pl but sing or pl in constr* : the art or study of argumentative discourse

forensic medicine *n* : a science that deals with the relation and application of medical facts to legal problems

fore·or·dain \ˌfōr-ȯr-ˈdān, ˌfȯr-\ *vt* : to dispose or appoint in advance : PREDESTINE — **fore·or·di·na·tion** \-ˌȯrd-ᵊn-ˈā-shən\ *n*

fore·part \ˈfō(ə)r-ˌpärt, ˈfȯ(ə)r-\ *n* **1** : the anterior part of something **2** : the earlier part of a period of time

fore·passed *or* **fore·past** \-ˌpast\ *adj* : BYGONE

fore·paw \-ˌpȯ\ *n* : the paw of a foreleg

fore·peak \-ˌpēk\ *n* : the extreme forward lower compartment or tank used for trimming or storage in a ship

fore·play \-ˌplā\ *n* : erotic stimulation preceding sexual intercourse

fore·quar·ter \-ˌkwȯ(r)t-ər\ *n* : the front half of a lateral half of the body or carcass of a quadruped <a ~ of beef>

fore·reach \fōr-ˈrēch, fȯr-\ *vi, of a ship* : to gain ground in tacking ~ *vt* : to gain on or overhaul and go ahead of (a ship) when close-hauled

fore·run \-ˈrən\ *vt* **-ran** \-ˈran\; **-run; -run·ning** **1** : to run before **2** : to come before as a token of something to follow **3** : FORESTALL, ANTICIPATE

fore·run·ner \ˈfō(ə)r-ˌrən-ər, ˈfȯ(ə)r-\ *n* **1** : one going or sent before to give notice of the approach of others: as **a** : a premonitory sign or symptom **b** : a skier who runs the course before the start of a race **2** : PREDECESSOR, FOREBEAR

syn FORERUNNER, PRECURSOR, HARBINGER, HERALD *shared meaning element* : one who goes before or announces the coming of another

fore·sad·dle \-ˌsad-ᵊl\ *n* : a wholesale cut of mutton, lamb, or veal that consists of the undivided forequarters of a carcass

fore·said \-ˌsed\ *adj, archaic* : AFORESAID

fore·sail \ˈfō(ə)r-ˌsāl, ˈfȯ(ə)r-, -səl\ *n* **1** : a sail carried on the foreyard of a square-rigged ship that is the lowest sail on the foremast **2** : the lower sail set abaft a schooner's foremast — see SAIL illustration **3** : FORESTAYSAIL

fore·see \fōr-ˈsē, fȯr-\ *vt* **-saw** \-ˈsȯ\; **-seen** \-ˈsēn\; **-see·ing** : to see (as a development) beforehand — **fore·see·able** \-ˈsē-ə-bəl, fər-\ *adj* — **fore·se·er** \fōr-ˈsē-ər, fȯr-, -ˈsi(-ə)r\ *n*

syn FORESEE, FOREKNOW, DIVINE, APPREHEND, ANTICIPATE *shared meaning element* : to know beforehand

fore·shad·ow \-ˈshad-(ˌ)ō, -ə(-w)\ *vt* : to represent or typify beforehand : PREFIGURE <present trends ~ future events> — **fore·shad·ow·er** \-ə-wər\ *n*

fore·shank \ˈfō(ə)r-ˌshaŋk, ˈfȯ(ə)r-\ *n* : a beef shin

fore·sheet \-ˌshēt\ *n* **1** : one of the sheets of a foresail **2** *pl* : the forward part of an open boat

fore·shore \-ˌshō(ə)r, -ˌshȯ(ə)r\ *n* **1** : a strip of land margining a body of water **2** : the part of a seashore between high-water and low-water marks

fore·short·en \fōr-ˈshȯrt-ᵊn, fȯr-\ *vt* **1** : to shorten by proportionately contracting in the direction of depth so that an illusion of projection or extension in space is obtained **2** : to make more compact

fore·show \-ˈshō\ *vt* **-showed; -shown** \-ˈshōn\ *or* **-showed; -show·ing** **1** : FORETELL **2** : to show beforehand

fore·side \ˈfō(ə)r-ˌsīd, ˈfȯ(ə)r-\ *n* : the front side or part : FRONT

fore·sight \ˈfō(ə)r-ˌsīt, ˈfȯ(ə)r-\ *n* **1** : an act or the power of foreseeing : PRESCIENCE **2** : an act of looking forward; *also* : a view forward **3** : provident care : PRUDENCE <had the ~ to invest his money wisely> — **fore·sight·ed** \-əd\ *adj* — **fore·sight·ed·ly** *adv* — **fore·sight·ed·ness** *n* — **fore·sight·ful** \-ˌsīt-fəl\ *adj*

fore·skin \-ˌskin\ *n* : a fold of skin that covers the glans of the penis — called also *prepuce*

fore·speak \fōr-ˈspēk, fȯr-\ *vt* **-spoke** \-ˈspōk\; **-spo·ken** \-ˈspō-kən\; **-speak·ing** **1** : FORETELL, PREDICT **2** : to arrange for in advance

1for·est \ˈfȯr-əst, ˈfär-\ *n, often attrib* [ME, fr. OF, fr. ML *forestis*, fr. L *foris* outside — more at FORUM] **1** : a tract of wooded land in England formerly owned by the sovereign and used for game **2** : a dense growth of trees and underbrush covering a large tract **3** : something resembling a forest esp. in profusion <a ~ of TV antennas> — **for·est·al** \-əs-tᵊl\ *or* **fo·res·tial** \fə-ˈres-tē-əl, fō-, -ˈres(h)-chəl\ *adj* — **for·est·ed** \ˈfȯr-ə-stəd, ˈfär-\ *adj*

2forest *vt* : to cover with trees or forest — **for·es·ta·tion** \ˌfȯr-ə-ˈstā-shən, ˌfär-\ *n*

fore·stage \ˈfō(ə)r-ˌstāj, ˈfȯ(ə)r-\ *n* : APRON 2g

fore·stall \fōr-ˈstȯl, fȯr-\ *vt* [ME *forstallen*, fr. *forstall* act of waylaying, fr. OE *foresteall*, fr. *fore-* + *steall* position, stall] **1** *archaic* : INTERCEPT **2** : to exclude, hinder, or prevent by prior occupation or measures **3** : to get ahead of : ANTICIPATE **4** *obs* : OBSTRUCT, BESET **5** : to prevent the normal trading in by buying or diverting goods or by persuading persons to raise prices — **fore·stall·er** *n* — **fore·stall·ment** \-ˈstȯl-mənt\ *n*

fore·stay \ˈfō(ə)r-ˌstā, ˈfȯ(ə)r-\ *n* : a stay from the foremast head to the deck of a ship

fore·stay·sail \-ˌsāl, -səl\ *n* : the triangular aftermost headsail of a schooner, ketch, or yawl set on hanks on the forestay — see SAIL illustration

for·est·er \ˈfȯr-ə-stər, ˈfär-\ *n* **1** : a person trained in forestry **2** : an inhabitant of a forest **3** : any of various woodland moths (family Agaristidae) **4** *cap* : a member of a major benevolent and fraternal order

forest floor *n* : the richly organic layer of soil and debris characteristic of forested land

forest green *n* : a dark yellowish or moderate olive green

for·est·land \'fȯr-əst-ˌland, 'fär-\ *n* **:** land covered with forest or reserved for the growth of forests

forest ranger *n* **:** an officer charged with the patrolling and guarding of a forest; *esp* **:** one in charge of the management and protection of a portion of a public forest

for·est·ry \'fȯr-ə-strē, 'fär-\ *n* **1 :** forest land **2 a :** the science of developing, caring for, or cultivating forests **b :** the management of growing timber

forest tent caterpillar *n* **:** a moth (*Malacosoma disstria*) whose orange-marked larva is a tent caterpillar and a serious defoliator of deciduous trees

foreswear, foresworn *var of* FORSWEAR, FORSWORN

[1]**fore·taste** \'fō(ə)r-ˌtāst, 'fȯ(ə)r-\ *n* **1 :** an advance indication or warning **2 :** a small anticipatory sample ***syn*** see PROSPECT

[2]**fore·taste** \fōr-'tāst, fȯr-', 'fō(ə)r-ˌ, 'fȯ(ə)r-ˌ\ *vt* **:** to taste beforehand **:** ANTICIPATE

fore·tell \fōr-'tel, fȯr-\ *vt* **-told** \-'tōld\; **-tell·ing :** to tell beforehand **:** PREDICT — **fore·tell·er** *n*

syn FORETELL, PREDICT, FORECAST, PROPHESY, PROGNOSTICATE *shared meaning element* **:** to tell beforehand

[1]**fore·thought** \'fō(ə)r-ˌthȯt, 'fȯ(ə)r-\ *n* **1 :** a thinking or planning out in advance **:** PREMEDITATION **2 :** consideration for the future

[2]**forethought** *adj* **:** thought of or planned beforehand **:** DELIBERATE

fore·thought·ful \-fəl\ *adj* **:** full of or having forethought — **fore·thought·ful·ly** \-fə-lē\ *adv* — **fore·thought·ful·ness** *n*

fore·time \'fō(ə)r-ˌtīm, 'fȯ(ə)r-\ *n* **:** former or past time **:** the time before the present

[1]**fore·to·ken** \'fō(ə)r-ˌtō-kən, 'fȯ(ə)r-\ *n* **:** a premonitory sign

[2]**fore·to·ken** \fōr-'tō-kən, fȯr-\ *vt* **fore·to·kened; fore·to·ken·ing** \-'tōk-(ə-)niŋ\ **:** to indicate or warn of in advance

fore·top \'fō(ə)r-ˌtäp, 'fȯ(ə)r-, *in sense 2 often* 'fōrt-əp *or* 'fȯrt-\ *n* **1 :** hair on the forepart of the head; *esp* **:** the forelock of a horse **2 :** the platform at the head of a ship's foremast

fore–top·gal·lant \ˌfōr-ˌtäp-ˌgal-ənt, ˌfȯr-; ˌfōrt-ə-ˌgal-, ˌfȯrt-\ *adj* **:** being the part next above the fore-topmast

fore·top·man \'fōr-ˌtäp-mən, 'fȯr-; 'fōrt-əp-, 'fȯrt-\ *n* **:** a sailor on duty on the foremast and above

fore–top·mast \'fōr-ˌtäp-məst, 'fȯr-; 'fōrt-əp-ˌmast, 'fȯrt-\ *n* **:** a mast next above the foremast

fore–top·sail \'fōr-ˌtäp-səl, 'fȯr-; 'fōrt-əp-, 'fȯrt-\ *n* **:** the sail above the foresail

[1]**for·ev·er** \fə-'rev-ər, fō-\ *adv* **1 :** for a limitless time <wants to live ~> **2 :** at all times <is ~ jingling the change in his pocket>

[2]**forever** *n* **:** an unspecified length of time <it took her ~ to find the answer>

for·ev·er·more \-ˌrev-ə(r)-'mō(ə)r, -'mȯ(ə)r\ *adv* **:** FOREVER

for·ev·er·ness \-'rev-ər-nəs\ *n* **:** ETERNITY

fore·warn \fōr-'wȯ(ə)rn, fȯr-\ *vt* **:** to warn in advance ***syn*** see WARN

fore wing *n* **:** either of the anterior wings of a 4-winged insect

fore·wom·an \'fō(ə)r-ˌwu̇m-ən, 'fȯ(ə)r-\ *n* **:** FORELADY

fore·word \'fōr-(ˌ)wərd, 'fȯr-\ *n* **:** PREFACE

foreworn *var of* FORWORN

fore·yard \'fō(ə)r-ˌyärd, 'fȯ(ə)r-\ *n* **:** the lowest yard on a foremast

[1]**for·feit** \'fȯr-fət\ *n* [ME *forfait,* fr. MF, fr. pp. of *forfaire* to commit a crime, forfeit, prob. fr. *fors* outside (fr. L *foris*) + *faire* to do, fr. L *facere* — more at FORUM, DO] **1 :** something forfeited or subject to being forfeited (as for a crime, offense, or neglect of duty) **:** PENALTY **2 :** forfeiture esp. of civil rights **3 a :** something deposited (as for making a mistake in a game) and then redeemed on payment of a fine **b** *pl* **:** a game in which forfeits are exacted

[2]**forfeit** *vt* **1 :** to lose or lose the right to by some error, offense, or crime **2 :** to subject to confiscation as a forfeit — **for·feit·able** \-ə-bəl\ *adj* — **for·feit·er** *n*

[3]**forfeit** *adj* **:** forfeited or subject to forfeiture

for·fei·ture \'fȯr-fə-ˌchu̇(ə)r, -chər, -ˌt(y)u̇(ə)r\ *n* **1 :** the act of forfeiting **:** the loss of property or money because of a breach of a legal obligation **2 :** something (as money or property) that is forfeited **:** PENALTY

for·fend *also* **fore·fend** \fȯr-'fend, fōr-\ *vt* **1 a** *archaic* **:** FORBID **b :** to ward off **:** PREVENT **2 :** PROTECT, PRESERVE

for·gath·er *or* **fore·gath·er** \fȯr-'gat͟h-ər, fōr-, -'get͟h-\ *vi* **1 :** to come together **:** ASSEMBLE **2 :** to meet someone usu. by chance

[1]**forge** \'fō(ə)rj, 'fȯ(ə)rj\ *n* [ME, fr. OF, fr. L *fabrica,* fr. *fabr-, faber* smith — more at DAFT] **1 :** a furnace or a shop with its furnace where metal is heated and wrought **:** SMITHY **2 :** a workshop where wrought iron is produced or where iron is made malleable

[2]**forge** *vb* **forged; forg·ing** *vt* **1 a :** to form (as metal) by heating and hammering **b :** to form (metal) by a mechanical or hydraulic press with or without heat **2 :** to form or bring into being esp. by an expenditure of effort <made every effort to ~ party unity> **3 :** to make or imitate falsely esp. with intent to defraud **:** COUNTERFEIT ~ *vi* **1 :** to work at a forge **2 :** to commit forgery — **forge·abil·i·ty** \ˌfōr-jə-'bil-ət-ē, ˌfȯr-\ *n* — **forge·able** \'fōr-jə-bəl, 'fȯr-\ *adj*

[3]**forge** *vi* **forged; forg·ing** [origin unknown] **1 :** to move forward slowly and steadily <the great ship *forged* ahead through the waves> **2 :** to move with a sudden increase of speed and power <the horse *forged* into the lead in the homestretch>

forg·er \'fōr-jər, 'fȯr-\ *n* **1 a :** one that falsifies; *specif* **:** a creator of false tales **b :** a person guilty of forgery **2 :** one that forges metals

forg·ery \'fōrj-(ə-)rē, 'fȯrj-\ *n, pl* **-er·ies 1** *archaic* **:** INVENTION **2 :** an act of forging; *esp* **:** the crime of falsely and fraudulently making or altering a document (as a check) **3 :** something forged

for·get \fər-'get, fȯr-\ *vb* **-got** \-'gät\; **-got·ten** \-'gät-ᵊn\ *or* **-got; -get·ting** [ME *forgeten,* fr. OE *forgietan,* fr. *for-* + *-gietan* (akin to ON *geta* to get)] *vt* **1 a :** to lose the remembrance of <I ~ his name> **b** *obs* **:** to cease from doing **2 :** to treat with inattention or disregard <*forgot* his old friends> **3 :** to disregard intentionally **:** OVERLOOK — usu. used in the imperative <~ it> ~ *vi* **1 :** to cease remembering or noticing <he forgives and ~*s*> **2 :** to fail to become mindful at the proper time <~ about paying the bill> ***syn*** see NEGLECT ***ant*** remember — **for·get·ter** *n* — **forget oneself :** to lose one's dignity, temper, or self-control

for·get·ful \-'get-fəl\ *adj* **1 :** likely to forget **2 :** characterized by negligent failure to remember **:** NEGLECTFUL **3 :** inducing oblivion <~ sleep> — **for·get·ful·ly** \-fə-lē\ *adv* — **for·get·ful·ness** *n*

syn FORGETFUL, OBLIVIOUS, UNMINDFUL *shared meaning element* **:** losing from one's mind something once known or learned

for·ge·tive \'fōr-jət-iv, 'fȯr-\ *adj* [prob. fr. [2]*forge* + *-tive* (as in *inventive*)] *archaic* **:** INVENTIVE, IMAGINATIVE

for·get–me–not \fər-'get-mē-ˌnät, fȯr-\ *n* **:** any of a genus (*Myosotis*) of small herbs of the borage family having bright-blue or white flowers usu. arranged in a curving spike

for·get·ta·ble \fər-'get-ə-bəl, fȯr-\ *adj* **:** fit or likely to be forgotten

forg·ing \'fōr-jiŋ, 'fȯr-\ *n* **1 :** the art or process of forging **2 :** a piece of forged work **3 :** FORGERY 2

for·give \fər-'giv, fȯr-\ *vb* **-gave** \-'gāv\; **-giv·en** \-'giv-ən\; **-giv·ing** [ME *forgiven,* fr. OE *forgifan,* fr. *for-* + *gifan* to give] *vt* **1 :** to cease to feel resentment against (an offender) **:** PARDON <~ one's enemies> **2 a :** to give up resentment of or claim to requital for <~ an insult> **b :** to grant relief from payment of <~ a debt> ~ *vi* **:** to grant forgiveness ***syn*** see EXCUSE — **for·giv·able** \-'giv-ə-bəl\ *adj* — **for·giv·ably** \-blē\ *adv* — **for·giv·er** *n*

for·give·ness \-'giv-nəs\ *n* **:** the act of forgiving **:** PARDON

for·giv·ing *adj* **:** willing or able to forgive — **for·giv·ing·ly** \-'giv-iŋ-lē\ *adv* — **for·giv·ing·ness** *n*

for·go *or* **fore·go** \fȯr-'gō, fōr-\ *vt* **-went** \-'went\; **-gone** \-'gȯn *also* -'gän\; **-go·ing** \-'gō-iŋ, -'gȯ(-)iŋ\ [ME *forgon,* fr. OE *forgān* to pass by, forgo, fr. *for-* + *gān* to go] **1** *archaic* **:** FORSAKE **2 :** to abstain from **:** RENOUNCE <~ immediate gratification for the sake of future gains> — **for·go·er** \-'gō(-ə)r\ *n*

for·got·ten man \fər-ˌgät-ᵊn-, fȯr-\ *n* **:** a person or category of persons that receives less attention than is merited

fo·rint \'fō(ə)r-ˌint\ *n* [Hung] — see MONEY table

forjudge *var of* FOREJUDGE

[1]**fork** \'fȯ(ə)rk\ *n* [ME *forke,* fr. OE & ONF; OE *forca* & ONF *forque,* fr. L *furca*] **1 :** an implement with two or more prongs used esp. for taking up (as in eating), pitching, or digging **2 :** a forked part, tool, or piece of equipment **3 a :** a division into branches or the place where something divides into branches **b :** CONFLUENCE **4 a :** one of the branches into which something forks **b :** ALTERNATIVE, CHOICE **5 :** an attack by one chess piece (as a knight) on two pieces simultaneously — **fork·ful** \-ˌfu̇l\ *n*

[2]**fork** *vi* **1 :** to divide into two or more branches <where the road ~*s*> **2 a :** to use or work with a fork **b :** to make a turn into or travel a fork ~ *vt* **1 :** to give the form of a fork to <~*ing* her fingers> **2 :** to raise, pitch, dig, or work with a fork <~ hay> **3 :** to attack (two chessmen) simultaneously **4 :** PAY, CONTRIBUTE <had to ~ out $5000 to keep the matter quiet> — **fork·er** *n*

forked \'fȯ(ə)rkt, 'fȯr-kəd\ *adj* **1 :** resembling a fork esp. in having one end divided into two or more branches or points <~ lightning> **2 :** shaped like a fork or having a forked part <a ~ road>

fork·lift \'fȯr-ˌklift\ *n* **:** a self-propelled machine for hoisting and transporting heavy objects by means of steel fingers inserted under the load

forky \'fȯr-kē\ *adj* **fork·i·er; -est :** FORKED <a ~ beard>

for·lorn \fər-'lȯ(ə)rn\ *adj* [ME *forloren,* fr. OE, pp. of *forlēosan* to lose, fr. *for-* + *lēosan* to lose] **1 a :** BEREFT, FORSAKEN <left quite ~ of hope> **b :** sad and lonely because of isolation or desertion **:** DESOLATE **2 :** being in poor condition **:** MISERABLE, WRETCHED <~ tumbledown buildings> **3 :** nearly hopeless <a ~ attempt> ***syn*** see ALONE — **for·lorn·ly** *adv* — **for·lorn·ness** \-'lȯ(ə)rn-nəs\ *n*

forlorn hope *n* [by folk etymology fr. D *verloren hoop,* lit., lost band] **1 :** a body of men selected to perform a perilous service **2 :** a desperate or extremely difficult enterprise

[1]**form** \'fȯ(ə)rm\ *n* [ME *forme,* fr. OF, fr. L *forma*] **1 a :** the shape and structure of something as distinguished from its material **b :** a body (as of a person) esp. in its external appearance or as distinguished from the face **:** FIGURE **c** *archaic* **:** BEAUTY **2 :** the essential nature of a thing as distinguished from its matter: as **a :** IDEA 1a **b :** the component of a thing that determines its kind **3 a :** established method of expression or proceeding **:** procedure according to rule or rote **b :** a prescribed and set order of words **:** FORMULA <the ~ of the marriage service> **4 :** a printed or typed document with blank spaces for insertion of required or requested information <tax ~*s*> **5 a (1) :** conduct regulated by extraneous controls (as of custom or etiquette) **:** CEREMONY **(2) :** show without substance **b :** manner or conduct as tested by a prescribed or accepted standard <rudeness is simply bad ~> **c :** manner or style of performing or accomplishing according to recognized standards of technique <a strong swimmer but weak on ~> **6 a :** the resting place of a hare **b :** a long seat **:** BENCH **7 a :** a supporting frame model of the human figure or part (as the torso) of the human figure usu. used for displaying apparel **b :** a proportioned and often adjustable model for fitting clothes **c :** a mold in which concrete is placed to set **8 :** the printing type or other matter arranged and secured in a chase ready for printing **9 a :** one of the different modes of existence, action, or manifestation of a particular thing or substance **:** KIND <one ~ of respiratory disorder> <a ~ of art> **b :** a distinguishable group of organisms **10 a (1) :** orderly method of arrangement (as in the presentation of ideas) **:** manner of coordinating elements (as of an artistic production or course of reasoning) **(2) :** a particular kind

or instance of such arrangement <the sonnet is a poetical ~> **b** : PATTERN, SCHEMA <arguments of the same logical ~> **c** : the structural element, plan, or design of a work of art — compare CONTENT 2c **d** : a visible and measurable unit defined by a contour : a bounded surface or volume **11** : a grade in a British secondary school or in some American private schools **12 a** (1) : the past performance of a race horse (2) : a table giving details (as handicaps and odds) of a horse's past performance which are used by bettors in making selections **b** : known ability to perform <a singer at the top of his ~> **c** : condition suitable for performing (as in athletic competition) **13 a** : LINGUISTIC FORM **b** : one of the different aspects a word may take as a result of inflection or change of spelling or pronunciation <verbal ~*s*> **14** : a mathematical expression of a particular type <an equation in parametric ~>

syn FORM, FIGURE, SHAPE, CONFORMATION, CONFIGURATION *shared meaning element* : outward appearance

²**form** *vt* **1** : to give form or shape to : FASHION **2 a** : to give a particular shape to : shape or mold into a certain state or after a particular model : ARRANGE <~*ed* the dough into various shapes> <a state ~*ed* along the lines of the Roman Republic> **b** : to arrange themselves in <the women ~*ed* a line> **c** : to model by instruction and discipline <a mind ~*ed* by classical education> **3** : DEVELOP, ACQUIRE <~ a habit> **4** : to serve to make up or constitute : be a usu. essential or basic element of **5 a** : to assume an inflection so as to produce (as a tense) <~*s* the past in *-ed*> **b** : to combine to make (a compound word) **c** : to make up : CONSTITUTE <~ a clause> **6** : to arrange in order : draw up ~ *vi* **1** : to become formed or shaped **2** : to take form : come into existence : ARISE **3** : to take on a definite form, shape, or arrangement ***syn*** see MAKE — **form·abil·i·ty** \ˌfȯr-mə-ˈbil-ət-ē\ *n* — **form·able** \ˈfȯr-mə-bəl\ *adj* — **form on** : to take up a formation next to

form- *or* **formo-** *comb form* [*formic*] : formic acid <*form*ate>

-form \ˌfȯrm\ *adj comb form* [MF & L; MF *-forme*, fr. L *-formis*, fr. *forma*] : in the form or shape of : resembling <ovi*form*>

¹**for·mal** \ˈfȯr-məl\ *adj* **1 a** : belonging to or being the essential constitution or structure <~ cause> **b** : relating to, concerned with, or constituting the outward form of something as distinguished from its content **2 a** : following or according with established form, custom, or rule : CONVENTIONAL <lacked ~ qualifications for the job> **b** : done in due or lawful form <a ~ contract> **3 a** : based on conventional forms and rules **b** : characterized by punctilious respect for form : METHODICAL <very ~ in all his dealings> **c** : rigidly ceremonious : PRIM **4** : having the appearance without the substance <~ Christians who go to church only at Easter> ***syn*** see CEREMONIAL ***ant*** informal — **for·mal·ly** \-mə-lē\ *adv* — **for·mal·ness** *n*

²**formal** *n* : something (as a dance or a dress) formal in character

³**formal** *adj* [*form*ula + *-al*] : ³MOLAR 2

form·al·de·hyde \fȯr-ˈmal-də-ˌhīd, fər-\ *n* [ISV *form-* + *aldehyde*] : a colorless pungent irritating gas CH_2O used chiefly as a disinfectant and preservative and in synthesizing other compounds and resins

for·ma·lin \ˈfȯr-mə-lən, -ˌlēn\ *n* [fr. *Formalin*, a trademark] : a clear aqueous solution of formaldehyde containing a small amount of methanol

for·mal·ism \ˈfȯr-mə-ˌliz-əm\ *n* : the practice or the doctrine of strict adherence to prescribed or external forms (as in religion or art); *also* : an instance of this — **for·mal·ist** \-ləst\ *n or adj* — **for·mal·is·tic** \ˌfȯr-mə-ˈlis-tik\ *adj* — **for·mal·is·ti·cal·ly** \-ti-k(ə-)lē\ *adv*

for·mal·i·ty \fȯr-ˈmal-ət-ē\ *n, pl* **-ties** **1** : the quality or state of being formal **2** : compliance with formal or conventional rules : CEREMONY **3** : an established form that is required or conventional

for·mal·ize \ˈfȯr-mə-ˌlīz\ *vt* **-ized; -iz·ing** **1** : to give a certain or definite form to : SHAPE **2 a** : to make formal **b** : to give formal status or approval to — **for·mal·iz·able** \-ˌlī-zə-bəl\ *adj* — **for·mal·iza·tion** \ˌfȯr-mə-lə-ˈzā-shən\ *n* — **for·mal·iz·er** \ˈfȯr-mə-ˌlī-zər\ *n*

formal logic *n* : a system of logic (as Aristotelian logic or symbolic logic) that abstracts the forms of thought from its content to establish abstract criteria of consistency

for·mant \ˈfȯr-mənt, -ˌmant\ *n* : a characteristic component of the quality of a speech sound; *specif* : any of several resonance bands held to determine the phonetic quality of a vowel

¹**for·mat** \ˈfȯ(ə)r-ˌmat\ *n* [F or G; F, fr. G, fr. L *formatus*, pp. of *formare* to form, fr. *forma*] **1** : the shape, size, and general makeup (as of something printed) **2** : general plan of organization or arrangement (as of a television show)

²**format** *vt* **for·mat·ted; for·mat·ting** : to produce in a specified form or style <*formatted* output of a computer>

for·mate \ˈfȯ(ə)r-ˌmāt\ *n* : a salt or ester of formic acid

for·ma·tion \fȯr-ˈmā-shən\ *n* **1** : an act of giving form or shape to something or of taking form : DEVELOPMENT **2** : something that is formed <new word ~*s*> **3** : the manner in which a thing is formed : STRUCTURE <the peculiar ~ of the heart> **4** : the largest unit in an ecological community comprising two or more associations and their precursors **5 a** : any igneous, sedimentary, or metamorphic rock represented as a unit **b** : any sedimentary bed or consecutive series of beds sufficiently homogeneous or distinctive to be a unit **6** : an arrangement of a body or group of persons or things in some prescribed manner or for a particular purpose — **for·ma·tion·al** \-shnəl, -shən-ᵊl\ *adj*

¹**for·ma·tive** \ˈfȯr-mət-iv\ *adj* **1 a** : giving or capable of giving form : CONSTRUCTIVE <a ~ influence> **b** : used in word formation or inflection **2** : capable of alteration by growth and development; *also* : producing new cells and tissues **3** : of, relating to, or characterized by formative effects or formation <~ years> — **for·ma·tive·ly** *adv* — **for·ma·tive·ness** *n*

²**formative** *n* **1** : the element in a word that serves to give the word appropriate form and is not part of the base **2** : the minimal syntactically functioning element in a transformational grammar

form class *n* : a class of linguistic forms that can be used in the same position in a construction and that have one or more morphological or syntactical features in common

form critical *adj* : based on or applying form criticism

form criticism *n* : a method of criticism for determining the sources and historicity of esp. biblical writings through analysis of the writings in terms of traditional literary forms (as love poems, parables, and sayings) — **form critic** *n*

formed \ˈfȯrmd\ *adj* : organized in a way characteristic of living matter <mitochondria are ~ bodies of the cell> <red blood cells are ~ elements of the blood>

for·mée \ˈfȯr-ˌmā, fȯr-ˈ\ *adj* [ME *forme*, fr. MF *formé*] *of a heraldic cross* : having the arms narrow at the center and expanding toward the ends — see CROSS illustration

¹**for·mer** \ˈfȯr-mər\ *adj* [ME, fr. *forme* first, fr. OE *forma* — more at FOREMOST] **1 a** : coming before in time **b** : of, relating to, or occurring in the past <~ correspondence> **2** : preceding in place or arrangement : FOREGOING <~ part of the chapter> **3** : first mentioned or in order of two things mentioned or understood <of these two evils the ~ is the lesser> ***syn*** see PRECEDING ***ant*** latter

²**form·er** \ˈfȯr-mər\ *n* **1** : one that forms **2** *chiefly Brit* : a member of a school form — usu. used in combination <sixth ~>

for·mer·ly \ˈfȯr-mə(r)-lē\ *adv* **1** *obs* : just before **2** : at an earlier time : PREVIOUSLY

form·fit·ting \ˈfȯrm-ˌfit-iŋ\ *adj* : conforming to the outline of the body : fitting snugly <a ~ sweater>

form·ful \ˈfȯrm-fəl\ *adj* : exhibiting or notable for form (as in a sport)

form genus *n* : an artificial taxonomic category established for organisms (as imperfect fungi) of obscure true relationships

for·mic \ˈfȯr-mik\ *adj* [L *formica* ant — more at PISMIRE] : derived from formic acid

For·mi·ca \fȯr-ˈmī-kə, fər-\ *trademark* — used for any of various laminated plastic products used esp. for surface finish

formic acid *n* : a colorless pungent fuming vesicant liquid acid CH_2O_2 found esp. in ants and in many plants and used chiefly in dyeing and finishing textiles

for·mi·cary \ˈfȯr-mə-ˌker-ē\ *n, pl* **-car·ies** [ML *formicarium*, fr. L *formica*] : an ant nest

for·mi·da·ble \ˈfȯr-məd-ə-bəl *also* fȯr-ˈmid- *or* fər-ˈmid-\ *adj* [ME, fr. L *formidabilis*, fr. *formidare* to fear, fr. *formido* fear; akin to Gk *mormō* she-monster] **1** : causing fear, dread, or apprehension <a ~ prospect> **2** : having qualities that discourage approach or attack **3** : tending to inspire awe or wonder — **for·mi·da·bil·i·ty** \ˌfȯr-məd-ə-ˈbil-ət-ē; fȯr-ˌmid-, fər-ˌ\ *n* — **for·mi·da·ble·ness** \ˈfȯr-məd-ə-bəl-nəs; fȯr-ˈmid-, fər-ˈ\ *n* — **for·mi·da·bly** \-blē\ *adv*

form·less \ˈfȯrm-ləs\ *adj* **1** : having no regular form or shape **2** : lacking order or arrangement **3** : having no physical existence — **form·less·ly** *adv* — **form·less·ness** *n*

form letter *n* **1** : a letter on a subject of frequent recurrence that can be sent to different people without essential change except in the address **2** : a letter that is printed in many copies, has a very general salutation (as *Dear Friend*), and is sent to a usu. large number of people

formo- — see FORM-

¹**for·mu·la** \ˈfȯr-myə-lə\ *n, pl* **-las** *or* **-lae** \-ˌlē, -ˌlī\ [L, dim. of *forma* form] **1 a** : a set form of words for use in a ceremony or ritual **b** : a conventionalized statement intended to express some fundamental truth or principle esp. as a basis for negotiation or action **2 a** (1) : RECIPE (2) : PRESCRIPTION **b** : a milk mixture or substitute for feeding an infant **3 a** : a general fact, rule, or principle expressed in symbols **b** : a symbolic expression of the chemical composition or constitution of a substance **c** : a group of numerical symbols associated to express briefly a single concept **d** : a combination of signs in a logical calculus **4** : a prescribed or set form or method (as of writing) : an established rule or custom — often used derogatorily <television programs that were unimaginative ~ works> — **for·mu·la·ic** \ˌfȯr-myə-ˈlā-ik\ *adj* — **for·mu·la·ical·ly** \-ˈlā-ə-k(ə-)lē\ *adv*

²**formula** *adj, of a racing car* : conforming to prescribed specifications as to size, weight, and engine displacement and usu. having a long narrow body, open wheels, a single-seat open cockpit, and the engine in the rear

for·mu·la·ri·za·tion \ˌfȯr-myə-lə-rə-ˈzā-shən\ *n* : an act or a product of formularizing

for·mu·la·rize \ˈfȯr-myə-lə-ˌrīz\ *vt* **-rized; -riz·ing** : to state in or reduce to a formula : FORMULATE — **for·mu·la·riz·er** *n*

for·mu·lary \ˈfȯr-myə-ˌler-ē\ *n, pl* **-lar·ies** **1** : a book or other collection of stated and prescribed forms (as oaths or prayers) **2** : a prescribed form or model : FORMULA **3** : a book containing a list of medicinal substances and formulas — **formulary** *adj*

for·mu·late \ˈfȯr-myə-ˌlāt\ *vt* **-lat·ed; -lat·ing** **1 a** : to reduce to or express in a formula **b** : to put into a systematized statement or expression **c** : DEVISE <~ policy> **2 a** : to develop a formula for the preparation of (as a soap or plastic) **b** : to prepare according to a formula — **for·mu·la·tor** \-ˌlāt-ər\ *n*

for·mu·la·tion \ˌfȯr-myə-ˈlā-shən\ *n* : an act or the product of formulating

formula weight *n* : MOLECULAR WEIGHT — used esp. of ionic compounds

for·mu·li·za·tion \ˌfȯr-myə-lə-ˈzā-shən\ *n* : FORMULATION

for·mu·lize \ˈfȯr-myə-ˌlīz\ *vt* **-lized; -liz·ing** : FORMULATE 1

form word *n* : FUNCTION WORD

for·myl \ˈfȯr-ˌmil\ *n* [ISV] : the radical HCO of formic acid that is also characteristic of aldehydes

for·ni·cate \ˈfȯr-nə-ˌkāt\ *vb* **-cat·ed; -cat·ing** [LL *fornicatus*, pp. of *fornicare*, fr. L *fornic-*, *fornix* arch, vault, brothel] *vi* : to commit fornication ~ *vt* : to commit fornication with — **for·ni·ca·tor** \-ˌkāt-ər\ *n*

for·ni·ca·tion \ˌfȯr-nə-ˈkā-shən\ *n* **1** : human sexual intercourse other than between a man and his wife : sexual intercourse between a spouse and an unmarried person : sexual intercourse between unmarried people **2** : sexual intercourse on the part of an

unmarried person accomplished with consent and not deemed adultery
for·nix \'fȯr-niks\ *n, pl* **for·ni·ces** \-nə-ˌsēz\ [NL, fr. L] **:** an anatomical arch or fold
for·rad·er *also* **for·rard·er** \'fär-əd-ər\ *adv* [E dial., compar. of E *forward*] *chiefly Brit* **:** further ahead
for·sake \fər-'sāk, fȯr-\ *vt* **for·sook** \-'su̇k\; **for·sak·en** \-'sā-kən\; **for·sak·ing** [ME *forsaken*, fr. OE *forsacan*, fr. *for-* + *sacan* to dispute; akin to OE *sacu* action at law — more at SAKE] **1 :** to renounce (as something once cherished) without intent to recover or resume <~ a bad habit> **2 :** to quit or leave entirely **:** withdraw from <*forsook* the theater for politics> ***syn*** see ABANDON ***ant*** return (*to*), revert (*to*)
for·sooth \fər-'süth\ *adv* [ME *for soth*, fr. OE *forsōth*, fr. *for* + *sōth* sooth] **:** in truth **:** INDEED — often used to imply contempt or doubt
for·spent \fər-'spent, fȯr-\ *adj, archaic* **:** worn out **:** EXHAUSTED
for·swear *or* **fore·swear** \fȯr-'swa(ə)r, fōr-, -'swe(ə)r\ *vb* **-swore** \-'swō(ə)r, -'swȯ(ə)r\; **-sworn** \-'swō(ə)rn, -'swȯ(ə)rn\; **-swear·ing** *vt* **1 a :** to reject or renounce under oath **b :** to renounce earnestly **2 :** to deny under oath **3 :** to make a liar of (oneself) under or as if under oath <~ himself> ~ *vi* **:** to swear falsely ***syn*** see ABJURE
for·sworn *or* **fore·sworn** \-'swō(ə)rn, -'swȯ(ə)rn\ *adj* **:** guilty of perjury **:** marked by perjury
for·syth·ia \fər-'sith-ē-ə\ *n* [NL, genus name, fr. William *Forsyth* †1804 Brit botanist] **:** any of a genus (*Forsythia*) of ornamental shrubs of the olive family with opposite leaves and yellow bell-shaped flowers appearing before the leaves in early spring
fort \'fō(ə)rt, 'fȯ(ə)rt\ *n* [ME *forte*, fr. MF *fort*, fr. *fort* strong, fr. L *fortis*] **1 :** a strong or fortified place; *esp* **:** a fortified place occupied only by troops and surrounded with such works as a ditch, rampart, and parapet **:** FORTIFICATION **2 :** a permanent army post — often used in place names
for·ta·lice \'fȯrt-ᵊl-əs\ *n* [ME, fr. ML *fortalitia* — more at FORTRESS] **1** *archaic* **:** FORTRESS **2** *archaic* **:** a small fort
1**forte** \'fō(ə)rt, 'fȯ(ə)rt; 'fȯr-ˌtā *and* 'fȯrt-ē *are frequent for 1*\ *n* [MF *fort*, fr. *fort* strong] **1 :** one's strong point **2 :** the part of a sword or foil blade between the middle and the hilt; *also* **:** the strongest part of the blade
2**for·te** \'fȯr-ˌtā, 'fȯrt-ē\ *adv or adj* [It, fr. *forte* strong, fr. L *fortis*] **:** in a loud and often forceful manner — used as a direction in music
3**for·te** \'fȯr-ˌtā, 'fȯrt-ē\ *n* **:** a tone or passage played forte
for·te–pi·a·no \ˌfȯr-ˌtā-pē-'än-(ˌ)ō, ˌfȯrt-ē-\ *adv or adj* **:** loud then immediately soft — used as a direction in music
1**forth** \'fō(ə)rth, 'fȯ(ə)rth\ *adv* [ME, fr. OE; akin to OE *for*] **1 :** onward in time, place, or order **:** FORWARD <from that day ~> **2 :** out into notice or view <put ~ leaves> **3** *obs* **:** AWAY, ABROAD
2**forth** *prep, archaic* **:** forth from **:** out of
forth·com·ing \(')fōrth-'kəm-iŋ, (')fȯrth-\ *adj* [obs. *forthcome* (to come forth)] **1 :** being about to appear **:** APPROACHING <the ~ holidays> **2 a :** readily available <new funds will be ~ next year> **b :** SOCIABLE, AFFABLE <a ~, accessible, and courteous man>
forth of *prep* **:** out of **:** out from
1**forth·right** \'fōr-ˌthrīt, 'fȯr-\ *adv* **1 a :** directly forth or ahead **b :** without hesitation **:** FRANKLY **2** *archaic* **:** at once
2**forthright** *adj* **1** *archaic* **:** proceeding straight on **2 :** going straight to the point without ambiguity or hesitation <a ~ critic> <a ~ appraisal of a problem> ***syn*** see STRAIGHTFORWARD ***ant*** furtive — **forth·right·ly** *adv* — **forth·right·ness** *n*
3**forthright** *n, archaic* **:** a straight path
forth·with \(')fōrth-'with, (')fȯrth-, -'with\ *adv* **:** IMMEDIATELY
for·ti·fi·ca·tion \ˌfȯrt-ə-fə-'kā-shən\ *n* **1 :** an act or process of fortifying **2 :** something that fortifies, defends, or strengthens; *esp* **:** works erected to defend a place or position
fortified wine *n* **:** a wine (as most dessert wines) to which alcohol usu. in the form of grape brandy has been added during or after fermentation
for·ti·fi·er \'fȯrt-ə-ˌfī(-ə)r\ *n* **:** one that fortifies
for·ti·fy \-ˌfī\ *vb* **-fied; -fy·ing** [ME *fortifien*, fr. MF *fortifier*, fr. LL *fortificare*, fr. L *fortis* strong] *vt* **:** to make strong: as **a :** to strengthen and secure (as a town) by forts or batteries **b :** to give physical strength, courage, or endurance to **:** INVIGORATE <*fortified* himself with a glass of wine> **c :** to add mental or moral strength to **:** ENCOURAGE <*fortified* by prayer> **d :** to add material to for strengthening or enriching ~ *vi* **:** to erect fortifications
for·tis \'fȯrt-əs\ *adj* [NL, fr. L, strong] **:** produced with relatively great articulatory tenseness and strong expiration <\t\ in *toe* is ~, \d\ in *doe* is lenis>
1**for·tis·si·mo** \fȯr-'tis-ə-ˌmō\ *adv or adj* [It, superl. of *forte*] **:** very loud — used as a direction in music
2**fortissimo** *n, pl* **-mos** *or* **-mi** \-ˌmē\ **:** a very loud passage, sound, or tone
for·ti·tude \'fȯrt-ə-ˌt(y)üd\ *n* [ME, fr. L *fortitudin-*, *fortitudo*, fr. *fortis*] **1** *obs* **:** STRENGTH **2 :** strength of mind that enables a person to encounter danger or bear pain or adversity with courage ***syn*** FORTITUDE, GRIT, BACKBONE, PLUCK, GUTS, SAND *shared meaning element* **:** courage and staying power ***ant*** pusillanimity
fort·night \'fȯrt-ˌnīt, 'fȯrt-\ *n* [ME *fourtenight*, alter. of *fourtene night*, fr. OE *fēowertȳne niht* fourteen nights] **:** two weeks
1**fort·night·ly** \-lē\ *adj* **:** occurring or appearing once in a fortnight
2**fortnightly** *adv* **:** once in a fortnight **:** every fortnight
3**fortnightly** *n, pl* **-lies :** a publication issued fortnightly
FOR·TRAN *or* **For·tran** \'fȯ(ə)r-ˌtran\ *n* [*for*mula *tran*slation] **:** an algebraic and logical language for programming a computer
for·tress \'fȯr-trəs\ *n* [ME *forteresse*, fr. MF *forteresce*, fr. ML *fortalitia*, fr. L *fortis* strong] **:** a fortified place **:** STRONGHOLD; *esp* **:** a large and permanent fortification sometimes including a town
for·tu·itous \fȯr-'t(y)ü-ət-əs, fər-\ *adj* [L *fortuitus*; akin to L *fort-*, *fors*] **1 :** occurring by chance **2 :** FORTUNATE, LUCKY ***syn*** see ACCIDENTAL — **for·tu·itous·ly** *adv* — **for·tu·itous·ness** *n*
for·tu·ity \-ət-ē\ *n, pl* **-ities** [irreg. fr. *fortuitous*] **1 :** the quality or state of being fortuitous **2 :** a chance event or occurrence
for·tu·nate \'fȯrch-(ə-)nət\ *adj* **1 :** bringing some good thing not foreseen as certain **:** AUSPICIOUS **2 :** receiving some unexpected good ***syn*** see LUCKY ***ant*** unfortunate, disastrous — **for·tu·nate·ly** *adv* — **for·tu·nate·ness** *n*
1**for·tune** \'fȯr-chən\ *n* [ME, fr. MF, fr. L *fortuna*; akin to L *fort-*, *fors* chance, luck, *ferre* to carry — more at BEAR] **1** *often cap* **:** a hypothetical force or personified power that unpredictably determines events and issues favorably or unfavorably **2** *obs* **:** ACCIDENT, INCIDENT **3 a :** prosperity attained partly through luck **:** SUCCESS **b :** LUCK 1 **4 :** DESTINY, FATE <tell his ~ with cards>; *also* **:** a prediction of fortune <get your weight and ~ for a penny> **5 a :** possession of material goods **:** WEALTH <a man of ~> **b :** a store of material possessions <the family ~> **c :** a very large sum of money <won a ~ playing the races>
2**fortune** *vb* **for·tuned; for·tun·ing** *vt* **1** *obs* **:** to give good or bad fortune to **2** *archaic* **:** to endow with a fortune ~ *vi, archaic* **:** HAPPEN, CHANCE
fortune cookie *n* **:** a thin folded cookie containing a slip of paper on which is printed a fortune, proverb, or humorous statement
fortune hunter *n* **:** a person who seeks wealth esp. by marriage
for·tune–tell·er \-ˌtel-ər\ *n* **:** one that professes to foretell future events — **for·tune–tell·ing** \-iŋ\ *n or adj*
for·ty \'fȯrt-ē\ *n, pl* **forties** [ME *fourty*, adj., fr. OE *fēowertig*, fr. *fēowertig* group of 40, fr. *fēower* four + *-tig* group of 10 — more at EIGHTY] **1** — see NUMBER table **2** *pl* **:** the numbers 40 to 49; *specif* **:** the years 40 to 49 in a lifetime or century **3 :** the third point scored by a side in a game of tennis — **for·ti·eth** \'fȯrt-ē-əth\ *adj or n* — **forty** *adj or pron*
for·ty–eight·mo \ˌfȯrt-ē-'āt-(ˌ)mō\ *n, pl* **-mos :** the size of a piece of paper cut 48 from a sheet; *also* **:** a book, a page, or paper of this size
for·ty–five \ˌfȯrt-ē-'fīv\ *n* **1** — see NUMBER table **2 :** a .45 caliber pistol — usu. written .45 **3 :** a microgroove phonograph record designed to be played at 45 revolutions per minute — usu. written 45 — **forty–five** *adj or pron*
Forty Hours *n pl but sing or pl in constr* **:** a Roman Catholic devotion in which the churches of a diocese in two-day turns have the Blessed Sacrament exposed on the altar for continuous daytime veneration
for·ty–nin·er \ˌfȯrt-ē-'nī-nər\ *n* **:** one taking part in the rush to California for gold in 1849
forty winks *n pl but sing or pl in constr* **:** a short sleep **:** NAP
fo·rum \'fōr-əm, 'fȯr-\ *n, pl* **forums** *also* **fo·ra** \-ə\ [L; akin to L *foris* outside, *fores* door — more at DOOR] **1 a :** the marketplace or public place of an ancient Roman city forming the center of judicial and public business **b :** a public meeting place for open discussion **c :** a medium (as a newspaper) of open discussion **2 :** a judicial body or assembly **:** COURT **3 a :** a public meeting or lecture involving audience discussion **b :** a program (as on radio or television) involving discussion of a problem usu. by several authorities
1**for·ward** \'fȯr-wərd, *South also* 'fär-\ *adj* [ME, fr. OE *foreweard* fr. *fore-* + *-weard* -ward] **1 a :** near, being at, or belonging to the forepart **b :** situated in advance **2 a :** strongly inclined **:** READY **b :** lacking modesty or reserve **:** BRASH **3 :** notably advanced or developed **:** PRECOCIOUS **4 :** moving, tending, or leading toward a position in front; *also* **:** moving toward an opponent's goal **5 a :** advocating an advanced policy in the direction of what is considered progress **b :** EXTREME, RADICAL <on the ~ fringe of liberalism> **6 :** of, relating to, or getting ready for the future <~ buying of produce> — **for·ward·ly** *adv* — **for·ward·ness** *n*
2**forward** *adv* **:** to or toward what is ahead or in front <from that time ~> <moved slowly ~ through the mud>
3**forward** *n* **:** a mainly offensive player in any of several games stationed at or near the front of his side or team (as in hockey or soccer) or in the corner (as in basketball)
4**forward** *vt* **1 :** to help onward **:** PROMOTE <~*ed* his friend's career> **2 a :** to send forward **:** TRANSMIT <will ~ the goods on receipt of his check> **b :** to send or ship onward from an intermediate post or station in transit <~ mail to the new address> ***syn*** see ADVANCE ***ant*** hinder, balk
for·ward·er \-wərd-ər\ *n* **:** one that forwards; *esp* **:** an agent who performs services (as receiving, transshipping, or delivering) designed to assure and facilitate the passage of goods of his principal to their destination
for·ward·ing \-wərd-iŋ\ *n* **:** the act of one that forwards; *esp* **:** the business of a forwarder of goods
for·ward–look·ing \'fȯr-wərd-ˌlu̇k-iŋ\ *adj* **:** concerned with or planning for the future
forward pass *n* **:** a pass in football thrown in the direction of the opponents' goal
for·wards \'fȯr-wərdz\ *adv* **:** FORWARD
for·worn \fər-'wō(ə)rn, -'wȯ(ə)rn\ *adj, archaic* **:** worn out
forz *abbr* forzando
for·zan·do \fȯrt-'sän-(ˌ)dō\ *adj or adv* [It] **:** SFORZANDO
FOS *abbr* free on steamer
fos·sa \'fäs-ə\ *n, pl* **fos·sae** \-ˌē, -ˌī\ [NL, fr. L, ditch] **:** an anatomical pit or depression — **fos·sate** \-ˌāt\ *adj*
fosse *or* **foss** \'fäs\ *n* [ME *fosse*, fr. OF, fr. L *fossa*, fr. fem. of *fossus*] **:** DITCH, MOAT
fos·sick \'fäs-ik\ *vb* [E dial. *fussick*, *fussock* to potter, irreg. fr. E *fuss*] *vi* **1** *Austral* **:** to search for gold typically by picking over abandoned workings **2** *chiefly Austral* **:** to search about **:** RUMMAGE ~ *vt, chiefly Austral* **:** to search for, by, or as if by rummaging **:** ferret out — **fos·sick·er** *n, chiefly Austral*

[1]**fos·sil** \'fäs-əl\ *n* [L *fossilis* dug up, fr. *fossus,* pp. of *fodere* to dig — more at BED] **1 :** a remnant, impression, or trace of an animal or plant of past geological ages that has been preserved in the earth's crust **2 a :** one whose views are outmoded **:** FOGY **b :** something (as a theory) that has become rigidly fixed **3 :** an old word or word element preserved only by idiom (as *fro* in *to and fro*)

[2]**fossil** *adj* **1 :** having the characteristics of a fossil: as **a :** ultimately derived from living things <coal, oil, and natural gas are ~ fuels> <amber is a ~ resin> **b :** preserved in a mineralized or petrified form from a geological age <~ imprint of a raindrop> <a ~ beach> <a ~ nuclear track in mica> **c :** being water that accumulated in an underground reservoir in a past geologic age **2 :** being or resembling a fossil

fos·sil·if·er·ous \ˌfäs-ə-'lif-(ə-)rəs\ *adj* **:** containing fossils <~ limestone>

fos·sil·ize \'fäs-ə-ˌlīz\ *vb* **-ized; -iz·ing** *vt* **1 :** to convert into a fossil **2 :** to make outmoded, rigid, or fixed ~ *vi* **:** to become changed into a fossil — **fos·sil·iza·tion** \'fäs-ə-lə-'zā-shən\ *n*

fos·so·ri·al \fä-'sōr-ē-əl, -'sȯr-\ *adj* [ML *fossorius,* fr. L *fossus,* pp.] **:** adapted to digging <a ~ foot>

[1]**fos·ter** \'fȯs-tər, 'fäs-\ *adj* [ME, fr. OE *fōstor-,* fr. *fōstor* food, feeding; akin to OE *fōda* food] **:** affording, receiving, or sharing nurture or parental care though not related by blood or legal ties

[2]**foster** *vt* **fos·tered; fos·ter·ing** \-t(ə-)riŋ\ **1 :** to give parental care to **:** NURTURE **2 :** to promote the growth or development of **:** ENCOURAGE — **fos·ter·er** \-tər-ər\ *n*

fos·ter·age \-tə-rij\ *n* **1 :** the act of fostering **2 :** a custom once prevalent in Ireland, Wales, and Scotland of entrusting one's child to foster parents to be brought up

fos·ter·ling \-tər-liŋ\ *n* **:** a foster child

FOT *abbr* free on truck

fou \'fü\ *adj* [ME (Sc) *fow* full, fr. ME *full*] *Scot* **:** DRUNK

fou·droy·ant \fü-'drȯi-ənt, fü-drwä-yä^{n}\ *adj* [F] **:** sudden and overwhelming in effect **:** DAZZLING

fought *past of* FIGHT

[1]**foul** \'faů(ə)l\ *adj* [ME, fr. OE *fūl;* akin to OHG *fūl* rotten, L *pus* pus, *putēre* to stink, Gk *pyon* pus] **1 a :** offensive to the senses **:** LOATHSOME **b :** filled or covered with offensive matter **2 :** full of dirt or mud **3 a :** morally or spiritually odious **:** DETESTABLE <a ~ crime> **b :** notably unpleasant or distressing **:** WRETCHED, HORRID <if my day has been ~, I can turn on my . . . radio and everything's mellow — Adrian Dove> **4 :** OBSCENE, ABUSIVE <~ language> **5 a :** being wet and stormy **b :** obstructive to navigation <a ~ tide> **6** *dial Brit* **:** HOMELY, UGLY <~ of face> **7 a :** TREACHEROUS, DISHONORABLE <fair means or ~> **b :** constituting an infringement of rules in a game or sport <a ~ blow in boxing> **8 a :** marked up or defaced by changes <~ manuscript> **b** *of a proof* **:** pulled before the latest alterations in type **9 :** encrusted, clogged or choked with a foreign substance <the chimney was ~ and smoked badly> **10 :** being odorous and impure **:** POLLUTED <~ air> **11 :** placed in a situation that impedes physical movement **:** ENTANGLED **12 :** being outside the foul lines in baseball <~ grounder> ***syn*** see DIRTY — **foul·ness** *n*

[2]**foul** *n* **1** *archaic* **:** bad luck **2 :** an entanglement or collision esp. in angling or sailing **3 a :** an infringement of the rules in a game or sport **b :** FREE THROW **4 :** FOUL BALL

[3]**foul** *adv* **:** FOULLY

[4]**foul** *vi* **1 :** to become or be foul: as **a :** DECOMPOSE, ROT **b :** to become encrusted, clogged, or choked with a foreign substance **c :** to become entangled or come into collision **2 :** to commit a violation of the rules in a sport or game **3 :** to hit a foul ball ~ *vt* **1 :** to make foul: as **a :** to make dirty **:** POLLUTE **b :** to become entangled or come into collision with **c :** to encrust with a foreign substance <a ship's bottom ~*ed* with barnacles> **d :** OBSTRUCT, BLOCK **2 :** DISHONOR, DISCREDIT **3 :** to commit a foul against **4 :** to hit (a baseball) foul

fou·lard \fü-'lärd\ *n* [F] **1 a :** a lightweight plain-woven or twilled silk usu. decorated with a printed pattern **b :** an imitation of this fabric **2 :** an article of clothing (as a scarf) made of foulard

foul ball *n* **:** a baseball batted into foul territory

foul·brood \'faůl-ˌbrüd\ *n* **:** a destructive bacterial disease of the larvae of the honeybee

foul·ing *n* **:** DEPOSIT, INCRUSTATION <~ on a ship's bottom>

foul line *n* **1 :** either of two straight lines extending from the rear corner of home plate through the outer corners of first and third base respectively and prolonged to the boundary of a baseball field **2 :** a line across a bowling alley that a player must not step over when delivering the ball **3 :** either of two lines on a basketball court parallel to and 15 feet from the backboards behind which a player must stand while shooting a free throw

foul·ly \'faů(l)-lē\ *adv* **:** in a foul manner

foul·mouthed \'faůl-'maůthd, -'maůtht\ *adj* **:** given to the use of obscene, profane, or abusive language

foul out *vi* **:** to be put out of a basketball game for exceeding the number of fouls permitted

foul play *n* **:** VIOLENCE; *esp* **:** MURDER

foul tip *n* [*foul* + *tip* (tap)] **:** a pitched ball in baseball that is slightly deflected by the bat; *specif* **:** a tipped pitch legally caught by the catcher and counting as a full strike with the ball remaining in play

foul–up \'faů-ˌləp\ *n* **1 :** a state of confusion caused by ineptitude, carelessness, or mismanagement <~*s* in transportation> **2 :** a mechanical difficulty <a ~ in the steering mechanism — *Springfield (Mass.) Union*>

foul up \(')faů-'ləp\ *vt* **1 :** to make dirty **:** CONTAMINATE **2 :** to spoil by making mistakes or using poor judgment **:** CONFUSE **3 :** ENTANGLE, BLOCK <*fouled up* communications> ~ *vi* **:** to become confused **:** get into difficulty **:** BUNGLE <it was his fault. He had *fouled up* — Pat Frank>

[1]**found** \'faůnd\ *past of* FIND

[2]**found** *adj* **1 :** having all usual, standard, or reasonably expected equipment <the boat comes fully ~, ready to go — *Holiday*> **2 :** presented as or incorporated into an artistic work essentially as found <sculpture of fabric, wood, and other ~ materials — Hilton Kramer>

[3]**found** *n* **:** free food and lodging in addition to wages <they're paid $175 a month and ~ — *New Yorker*>

[4]**found** *vt* [ME *founden,* fr. OF *fonder,* fr. L *fundare,* fr. *fundus* bottom — more at BOTTOM] **1 :** to take the first steps in building **2 :** to set or ground on something solid **:** BASE **3 :** to establish (as an institution) often with provision for future maintenance

[5]**found** *vt* [MF *fondre* to pour, melt, fr. L *fundere;* akin to OE *gēotan* to pour, Gk *chein*] **:** to melt (metal) and pour into a mold

foun·da·tion \faůn-'dā-shən\ *n* **1 :** the act of founding **2 :** the basis upon which something stands or is supported **3 a :** funds given for the permanent support of an institution **:** ENDOWMENT **b :** an organization or institution established by endowment with provision for future maintenance **4 :** an underlying natural or prepared base or support; *esp* **:** the whole masonry substructure of a building **5 a :** a body or ground upon which something is built up or overlaid **b :** a woman's supporting undergarment **:** CORSET ***syn*** see BASE ***ant*** superstructure — **foun·da·tion·al** \-shnəl, -shən-^{ə}l\ *adj* — **foun·da·tion·al·ly** \-ē\ *adv* — **foun·da·tion·less** \-shən-ləs\ *adj*

foundation stone *n* **1 :** a stone in the foundation of a building; *esp* **:** such a stone laid with public ceremony — compare CORNERSTONE **2 :** BASIS, GROUNDWORK

[1]**found·er** \'faůn-dər\ *n* **:** one that founds or establishes — **found·ress** \-drəs\ *n*

[2]**foun·der** \'faůn-dər\ *vb* **foun·dered; foun·der·ing** \-d(ə-)riŋ\ [ME *foundren* to send to the bottom, collapse, fr. MF *fondrer,* deriv. of L *fundus*] *vi* **1 :** to become disabled; *esp* **:** to go lame **2 :** to give way **:** COLLAPSE **3 :** to sink below the surface of the water **4 :** to come to grief **:** FAIL ~ *vt* **:** to disable (an animal) esp. by excessive feeding

[3]**foun·der** *n* [[2]*founder*] **:** the condition of a foundered horse

[4]**found·er** *n* **:** one that founds metal; *specif* **:** TYPEFOUNDER

foun·der·ous *or* **foun·drous** \'faůn-d(ə-)rəs\ *adj* **:** likely to cause one to founder **:** MIRY

founding father *n* **1 :** an originator of an institution or movement **:** FOUNDER **2** *cap both Fs* **:** a member of the American Constitutional Convention of 1787

found·ling \'faůn-(d)liŋ\ *n* **:** an infant found after its unknown parents have abandoned it

found object *n* **:** OBJET TROUVÉ

found·ry \'faůn-drē\ *n, pl* **foundries** **1 :** the act, process, or art of casting metals; *also* **:** CASTINGS **2 :** an establishment where founding is carried on

foundry proof *n* **:** a proof taken from a form that has been locked up and made ready for plating

[1]**fount** \'faůnt\ *n* [MF *font,* fr. L *font-, fons*] **:** FOUNTAIN, SOURCE

[2]**fount** \'fänt, 'faůnt\ *n* [F *fonte*] *Brit* **:** a type font

[1]**foun·tain** \'faůnt-^{ə}n\ *n* [ME, fr. MF *fontaine,* fr. LL *fontana,* fr. L, fem. of *fontanus* of a spring, fr. *font-, fons*] **1 :** a spring of water issuing from the earth **2 :** SOURCE **3 :** an artificially produced jet of water; *also* **:** the structure from which it rises **4 :** a reservoir containing a liquid that can be drawn off as needed

[2]**fountain** *vi* **:** to flow or spout like a fountain ~ *vt* **:** to cause to flow like a fountain

foun·tain·head \-ˌhed\ *n* **1 :** a spring that is the source of a stream **2 :** principal source **:** ORIGIN

fountain pen *n* **:** a pen containing a reservoir that automatically feeds the writing point with ink

four \'fō(ə)r, 'fȯ(ə)r\ *n* [ME, fr. *four* adj., fr. OE *fēower;* akin to OHG *fior* four, L *quattuor,* Gk *tessares, tettares*] **1** — see NUMBER table **2 :** the fourth in a set or series <the ~ of hearts> **3 :** something having four units or members: as **a :** a 4-oared racing shell or its crew **b :** a 4-cylinder engine or automobile — **four** *adj or pron*

four–bag·ger \-'bag-ər\ *n* **:** HOME RUN

four–ball \-ˌbȯl\ *adj* **:** relating to or being a golf match in which the best individual score of one partnership is matched against the best individual score of another partnership for each hole

four·chée \fů(ə)r-'shā\ *adj* [F] *of a heraldic cross* **:** having the end of each arm forked — see CROSS illustration

four–dimensional *adj* **:** relating to or having four dimensions <~ space-time continuum>; *esp* **:** consisting of or relating to elements requiring four coordinates to determine them

four·dri·nier \ˌfōr-drə-'ni(ə)r, ˌfȯr-; fůr-'drin-ē-ər, fōr-, fȯr-\ *n* [Henry *Fourdrinier* & Sealy *Fourdrinier*] **:** a machine for making paper in an endless web

four–flush *vi* **:** to bluff in poker holding a four flush; *broadly* **:** to make a false claim **:** BLUFF — **four–flush·er** *n*

four flush *n* **:** four cards of the same suit in a five-card poker hand

four·fold \'fō(ə)r-ˌfōld, 'fȯ(ə)r-, -'fōld\ *adj* **1 :** having four units or members **2 :** being four times as great or as many — **four·fold** \-'fōld\ *adv*

four–foot·ed \-'fůt-əd\ *adj* **:** having four feet **:** QUADRUPED

four·gon \fů(ə)r-'gō^{n}\ *n, pl* **fourgons** \-'gō^{n}(z)\ [F] **:** a wagon for carrying baggage

4–H \(')fō(ə)r-'āch, (')fȯ(ə)r-\ *adj* [fr. the fourfold aim of improving the head, heart, hands, and health] **:** of or relating to a program set up by the U.S. Department of Agriculture to instruct rural young people in modern farm practices and in good citizenship <~ club> — **4–H'·er** \-ər\ *n*

four–hand \'fō(ə)r-ˌhand, 'fȯ(ə)r-\ *adj* **:** FOUR-HANDED

four–hand·ed \-'han-dəd\ *adj* **1 :** designed for four hands <a ~ musical composition> **2 :** engaged in by four persons <a ~ card game>

Four Horsemen *n pl* [fr. the apocalyptic vision in Rev 6:2–8] **:** war, famine, pestilence, and death personified as the four major plagues of mankind

Four Hundred *or* **400** *n* **:** the exclusive social set of a community — used with *the*

Fou·ri·er analysis \ˌfůr-ē-ˌā-\ *n* **:** the fitting of terms of a Fourier series to periodic data

Fou·ri·er·ism \'fu̇r-ē-ə-ˌriz-əm, -ē-ˌā-ˌiz-\ *n* [F *fouriérisme,* fr. F.M.C. *Fourier*] : a system for reorganizing society into cooperative communities of small groups living in common — **Fou·ri·er·ist** \-ē-ə-rəst, -ē-ˌā-əst\ *n*

Fou·ri·er series \ˌfu̇r-ē-ˌā-\ *n* [Baron J.B.J. *Fourier* †1830 F geometrician & physicist] : an infinite series in which the terms are constants multiplied by sine or cosine functions of integer multiples of the variable and which is used in the analysis of periodic functions

Fourier's theorem *n* [J. B. J. *Fourier*] : a theorem in mathematics : any periodic function can be resolved under suitable conditions into sine and cosine terms involving known constants

Fourier transform *n* : a function (as $F(u)$) that under suitable conditions can be obtained from a given function (as $f(x)$) by multiplying by e^{iux} and integrating over all values of x

four–in–hand \'fōr-ən-ˌhand, 'fȯr-\ *n* **1 a** : a team of four horses driven by one person **b** : a vehicle drawn by such a team **2** : a necktie tied in a slipknot with long ends overlapping vertically in front

four–letter word *n* : any of a group of vulgar or obscene words typically made up of four letters

four–line octave *n* [fr. the four accent marks appended to the letters representing its notes] : the musical octave that begins on the third C above middle C — see PITCH illustration

four–o'clock \'fōr-ə-ˌkläk, 'fȯr-\ *n* : any of a genus (*Mirabilis*) of chiefly American annual or perennial herbs (family Nyctaginaceae, the four-o'clock family) having apetalous flowers with a showy involucre simulating a calyx; *esp* : a garden plant (*M. jalapa*) with fragrant yellow, red, or white flowers opening late in the afternoon

four of a kind : four cards of the same rank in one hand — see POKER illustration

four·pen·ny nail \ˌfōr-ˌpen-ē-, ˌfȯr-\ *n* : a nail 1 ³⁄₈ inches long

four–post·er \(')fōr-'pō-stər, (')fȯr-\ *n* : a bed with tall often carved corner posts orig. designed to support curtains or a canopy

four-poster

four·ra·gère \ˌfu̇r-ə-'zhe(ə)r\ *n* [F] : a braided cord worn usu. around the left shoulder; *esp* : such a cord awarded to a military unit

four·score \'fōr-'skō(ə)r, 'fȯr-'skȯ(ə)r\ *adj* : being four times twenty : EIGHTY

four·some \'fōr-səm, 'fȯr-\ *n* **1 a** : a group of four persons or things : QUARTET **b** : two couples **2** : a golf match between two pairs of partners

four–square \-'skwa(ə)r, -'skwe(ə)r\ *adj* **1** : SQUARE **2** : marked by boldness and conviction : FORTHRIGHT — **four-square** *adv*

four–star \-'stär\ *adj* [fr. the number of asterisks used to denote relative excellence in guidebooks] : of a superior degree of excellence <a ~ French restaurant>

four·teen \(')fōr(t)-'tēn, (')fȯr(t)-\ *n* [ME *fourtene,* fr. OE *fēowertēne,* fr. *fēowertēne,* adj.; akin to OE *tīen* ten] — see NUMBER table — **fourteen** *adj or pron* — **four·teenth** \-'tēn(t)th\ *adj or n*

four·teen·er \-'tē-nər\ *n* : a verse consisting of 14 syllables or esp. of 7 iambic feet

fourth \'fō(ə)rth, 'fȯ(ə)rth\ *n* **1** — see NUMBER table **2 a** : the musical interval embracing four diatonic degrees **b** : a tone at this interval; *specif* : SUBDOMINANT **a c** : the harmonic combination of two tones a fourth apart **3** : the 4th forward gear or speed of a motor vehicle **4** *cap* : INDEPENDENCE DAY — **fourth** *adj or adv* — **fourth·ly** *adv*

fourth class *n* **1** : a class or group ranking fourth in a series **2** : a class of mail in the U.S. that comprises merchandise and non-second-class printed matter and is not sealed against inspection

fourth dimension *n* **1** : a dimension in addition to length, breadth, and depth; *specif* : a coordinate in addition to three rectangular coordinates esp. when interpreted as the time coordinate in a space-time continuum **2** : something outside the range of ordinary experience <a *fourth dimension* of meaning that transcends . . . the issue of clarity versus obscurity — Peter Viereck> — **fourth–dimensional** *adj*

fourth estate *n, often cap F&E* : the public press

Fourth of July : INDEPENDENCE DAY

four–way \'fōr-'wā, 'fȯr-\ *adj* **1** : allowing passage in any of four directions **2** : including four participants

four–wheel \ˌfōr-ˌhwēl, ˌfȯr-, -ˌwēl\ *or* **four–wheeled** \'fōr-'hwē(ə)ld, 'fȯr-, -'wē(ə)ld\ *adj* **1** : having four wheels **2** : acting on or by means of four wheels of an automotive vehicle <~ drive>

four–wheel·er \-'hwē-lər, -'wē-\ *n* : a vehicle with four wheels

fo·vea \'fō-vē-ə\ *n, pl* **fo·ve·ae** \-vē-ˌē, -vē-ˌī\ [NL, fr. L, pit] : a small fossa; *esp* : a rodless area of the retina affording acute vision — see EYE illustration — **fo·ve·al** \-vē-əl\ *adj* — **fo·ve·ate** \-vē-ˌāt, -ət\ *adj* — **fo·ve·iform** \-vē-ə-ˌfȯrm\ *adj*

fovea cen·tra·lis \-sen-'tral-əs, -'träl-, -'trāl-\ *n* [NL, central fovea] : FOVEA

fow *abbr* first open water

¹fowl \'fau̇(ə)l\ *n, pl* **fowl** *or* **fowls** [ME *foul,* fr. OE *fugel;* akin to OHG *fogal* bird] **1** : a bird of any kind **2 a** : a domestic cock or hen; *esp* : an adult hen **b** : any of several domesticated or wild gallinaceous birds **3** : the meat of fowls used as food

²fowl *vi* : to seek, catch, or kill wildfowl — **fowl·er** *n*

fowling piece *n* : a light gun for shooting birds or small quadrupeds

¹fox \'fäks\ *n, pl* **fox·es** *or* **fox** *often attrib* [ME, fr. OE; akin to OHG *fuhs* fox, Skt *puccha* tail] **1 a** : any of various alert carnivorous mammals (esp. genus *Vulpes*) of the dog family related to but smaller than wolves with shorter legs, more pointed muzzle, large erect ears, and long bushy tail **b** : the fur of a fox **2** : a clever crafty person **3** *archaic* : SWORD **4** *cap* : a member of an Indian people formerly living in Wisconsin **5** : rope yarns twisted and tarred to make small cordage used for lashings or for weaving mats

²fox *vt* **1 a** : to trick by ingenuity or cunning : OUTWIT **b** : BAFFLE **2** *obs* : INTOXICATE **3 a** : to repair (a shoe) by renewing the upper **b** : to add a strip to; *esp* : to trim (a shoe) with a strip of material (as leather)

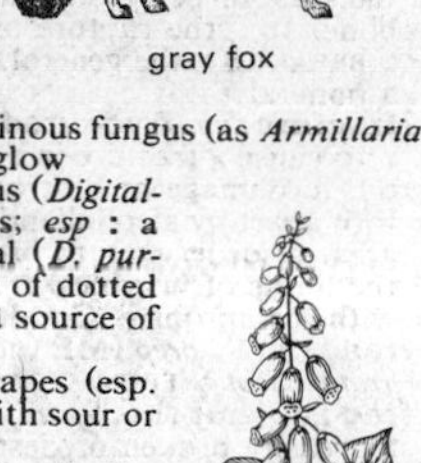
gray fox

foxed \'fäkst\ *adj* : discolored with yellowish brown stains <~ leaves of old books>

fox fire *n* : an eerie phosphorescent light (as of decaying wood); *also* : a luminous fungus (as *Armillaria mellea*) that causes decaying wood to glow

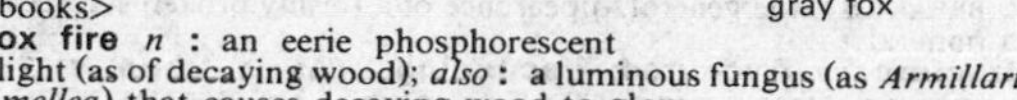

fox·glove \'fäks-ˌgləv\ *n* : any of a genus (*Digitalis*) of the figwort family of erect herbs; *esp* : a common European biennial or perennial (*D. purpurea*) cultivated for its showy racemes of dotted white or purple tubular flowers and as a source of digitalis

foxglove

fox grape *n* : any of several native grapes (esp. *Vitis labrusca*) of eastern No. America with sour or musky fruit

fox·hole \'fäks-ˌhōl\ *n* : a pit dug usu. hastily for individual cover against enemy fire

fox·hound \-ˌhau̇nd\ *n* : any of various large swift powerful hounds of great endurance used in hunting foxes and developed to form several breeds and many distinctive strains — compare AMERICAN FOXHOUND, ENGLISH FOXHOUND

fox·tail \'fäk-ˌstāl\ *n* **1 a** : the tail of a fox **b** : something resembling the tail of a fox **2** : any of several grasses (esp. genera *Alopecurus, Hordeum,* and *Setaria*) with spikes resembling brushes

foxtail lily *n* : any of a genus (*Eremurus*) of the lily family of perennial herbs with tall racemes of showy blooms

foxtail millet *n* : a coarse drought-resistant but frost-sensitive annual grass (*Setaria italica*) grown for grain, hay, and forage

fox terrier *n* : a small lively terrier formerly used to dig out foxes and known in smooth-haired and wirehaired varieties

¹fox–trot \'fäk-ˌsträt\ *n* **1** : a short broken slow trotting gait in which the hind foot of the horse hits the ground a trifle before the diagonally opposite forefoot **2** : a ballroom dance in duple time that includes slow walking steps, quick running steps, and two-steps

²fox–trot *vi* : to dance the fox-trot

Foxtrot — a communications code word for the letter *f*

foxy \'fäk-sē\ *adj* **fox·i·er; -est** **1** : resembling or suggestive of a fox <a narrow ~ face>: as **a** : cunningly shrewd in conniving and contriving : warily guileful **b** : of a warm reddish brown color <~ eyebrows> **2** : defective in some way (as from age or decay) and esp. so as to be discolored or spotted : FOXED **3** : having a sharp brisk flavor <~ grapes> <~ wine> **4** : physically attractive <now there's a ~ girl> ***syn*** see SLY — **fox·i·ly** \'fäk-sə-lē\ *adv* — **fox·i·ness** \-sē-nəs\ *n*

foy \'fȯi\ *n* [D dial. *fooi* feast at end of the harvest] *chiefly Scot* : a farewell feast or gift

foy·er \'fȯi(-ə)r, 'fȯi-ˌ(y)ā *also* 'fwä-ˌyā\ *n* [F, lit., fireplace, fr. ML *focarius,* fr. L *focus* hearth] : an anteroom or lobby esp. of a theater; *also* : an entrance hallway : VESTIBULE

fp *abbr* freezing point

FPA *abbr* **1** Foreign Press Association **2** free of particular average

FPC *abbr* **1** Federal Power Commission **2** fish protein concentrate **3** Friends Peace Committee

FPM *abbr* feet per minute

FPO *abbr* fleet post office

FPS *abbr* **1** feet per second **2** foot-pound-second

fr *abbr* **1** father **2** franc **3** friar **4** from

¹Fr *abbr* French

²Fr *symbol* francium

Fra \(ˌ)frä\ *n* [It, short for *frate,* fr. L *frater* — more at BROTHER] : BROTHER — used as a title preceding the name of an Italian monk or friar

fra·cas \'frāk-əs, 'frak-, *Brit* 'frak-ˌä\ *n, pl* **fra·cas·es** \-ə-səz\ *or Brit* **fra·cas** \-ˌäz\ [F, din, row, fr. It *fracasso,* fr. *fracassare* to shatter] : a noisy quarrel : BRAWL

fract·ed \'frak-təd\ *adj* [L *fractus*] *obs* : BROKEN

frac·tion \'frak-shən\ *n* [ME *fraccioun,* fr. LL *fraction-, fractio* act of breaking, fr. L *fractus,* pp. of *frangere* to break — more at BREAK] **1 a** : a numerical representation (as ¼, ⁵⁄₈, 3.234) of two numbers whose quotient is to be determined **b (1)** : a piece broken off : FRAGMENT **(2)** : a discrete unit : PORTION **2** : BIT, LITTLE <a ~ closer> **3** : one of several portions (as of a distillate) separable by fractionation

frac·tion·al \-shnəl, -shən-ᵊl\ *adj* **1** : of, relating to, or being a fraction **2** : relatively small : INCONSIDERABLE **3** : of, relating to, or being fractional currency **4** : of, relating to, or involving a process for separating components of a mixture through differences in physical or chemical properties <~ distillation> — **frac·tion·al·ly** \-ē\ *adv*

fractional currency *n* **1** : paper money in denominations of less than one dollar issued by the U.S. 1863–76 **2** : currency in denominations less than the basic monetary unit

frac·tion·al·ize \'frak-shnə-ˌlīz, -shən-ᵊl-ˌīz\ *vt* **-ized; -iz·ing** : to break up into parts or sections <control of the river is *fractionalized* among four countries —Ted Shoemaker> — **frac·tion·al·iza·tion** \ˌfrak-shnə-lə-'zā-shən, -shən-ᵊl-ə-'zā-\ *n*

frac·tion·ate \ˈfrak-shə-ˌnāt\ *vt* **-at·ed; -at·ing** **1 :** to separate (as a mixture) into different portions **2 :** to divide or break up — **frac·tion·ation** \ˌfrak-shə-ˈnā-shən\ *n* — **frac·tion·ator** \ˈfrak-shə-ˌnāt-ər\ *n*

frac·tious \ˈfrak-shəs\ *adj* [*fraction* (discord) + *-ous*] **1 :** tending to be troublesome : UNRULY **2 :** QUARRELSOME, IRRITABLE — **frac·tious·ly** *adv* — **frac·tious·ness** *n*

[1]**frac·ture** \ˈfrak-chər\ *n* **1 a :** the act or process of breaking or the state of being broken; *specif* : the breaking of hard tissue (as bone) **b :** the rupture of soft tissue **2 :** the result of fracturing : BREAK **3 :** the general appearance of a freshly broken surface of a mineral

[2]**fracture** *vb* **frac·tured; frac·tur·ing** \-chə-riŋ, -shriŋ\ *vt* **1 a :** to cause a fracture in : BREAK <~ a rib> **b :** RUPTURE, TEAR **2 a :** to damage or destroy as if by rupturing <a *fractured* family torn apart by alcohol and insanity —R. A. Sokolov> **b :** to cause great disorder **c :** to break up : FRACTIONATE **d :** to go beyond the limits of (as rules) : VIOLATE <*fractured* the English language with malaprops —Goodman Ace> ~ *vi* : to undergo fracture

frae \(ˈ)frā\ *prep* [ME (northern) *fra, frae,* fr. ON *frā;* akin to OE *from*] *Scot* : FROM

frag·ile \ˈfraj-əl, -ˌīl\ *adj* [MF, fr. L *fragilis* — more at FRAIL] **1 a :** easily broken or destroyed : FRAIL **b :** constitutionally delicate : lacking in physical vigor **2 :** TENUOUS, SLIGHT — **fra·gil·i·ty** \frə-ˈjil-ət-ē\ *n*
syn **1** FRAGILE, FRANGIBLE, BRITTLE, CRISP, FRIABLE *shared meaning element* : easily broken ***ant*** durable
2 see WEAK ***ant*** durable

[1]**frag·ment** \ˈfrag-mənt\ *n* [ME, fr. L *fragmentum,* fr. *frangere* to break — more at BREAK] : a part broken off, detached, or incomplete ***syn*** see PART

[2]**frag·ment** \-ˌment\ *vb* : FRAGMENTIZE

frag·men·tal \frag-ˈment-ᵊl\ *adj* : FRAGMENTARY — **frag·men·tal·ly** \-ᵊl-ē\ *adv*

frag·men·tary \ˈfrag-mən-ˌter-ē\ *adj* : consisting of fragments : INCOMPLETE — **frag·men·tari·ly** \ˌfrag-mən-ˈter-ə-lē\ *adv* — **frag·men·tari·ness** \-ˌter-ē-nəs\ *n*

frag·men·tate \ˈfrag-mən-ˌtāt\ *vb* **-tat·ed; -tat·ing** : FRAGMENTIZE — **frag·men·ta·tion** \ˌfrag-mən-ˈtā-shən, -ˌmen-\ *n*

fragmentation bomb *n* : a bomb or shell whose relatively thick casing is splintered upon explosion and thrown in fragments in all directions

frag·men·tize \ˈfrag-mən-ˌtīz\ *vb* **-tized; -tiz·ing** *vt* : to break up or apart into fragments ~ *vi* : to fall to pieces — **frag·men·tiz·er** *n*

fra·grance \ˈfrā-grən(t)s\ *n* **1 :** the quality or state of having a sweet odor **2 a :** a sweet or delicate odor (as of fresh flowers) **b :** the odor of perfume, cologne, or toilet water
syn FRAGRANCE, PERFUME, SCENT, INCENSE, BOUQUET *shared meaning element* : a sweet or pleasing odor ***ant*** stench, stink

fra·gran·cy \-grən-sē\ *n, archaic* : FRAGRANCE

fra·grant \ˈfrā-grənt\ *adj* [ME, fr. L *fragrant-, fragrans,* fr. prp. of *fragrare* to be fragrant; akin to MHG *bræhen* to smell] : marked by fragrance — **fra·grant·ly** *adv*

frail \ˈfrā(ə)l\ *adj* [ME, fr. MF *fraile,* fr. L *fragilis* fragile, fr. *frangere*] **1 :** easily led into evil <~ humanity> **2 :** easily broken or destroyed : FRAGILE **3 a :** physically weak **b :** SLIGHT, UNSUBSTANTIAL ***syn*** see WEAK ***ant*** robust — **frail·ly** \ˈfrā(ə)l-lē\ *adv* — **frail·ness** *n*

frail·ty \ˈfrā(-ə)l-tē\ *n, pl* **frailties** **1 :** the quality or state of being frail **2 :** a fault due to weakness esp. of moral character ***syn*** see FAULT

fraise \ˈfrāz\ *n* [F] : an obstacle of pointed stakes driven into the ramparts of a fortification in a horizontal or inclined position

Frak·tur \fräk-ˈtu̇(ə)r\ *n* [G, fr. L *fractura* fracture] : a German style of black-letter text type

Fraktur

fram·able *or* **frame·able** \ˈfrā-mə-bəl\ *adj* : capable of being framed

fram·be·sia \fram-ˈbē-zh(ē-)ə\ *n* [NL, fr. F *framboise* raspberry; fr. the appearance of the lesions] : YAWS

[1]**frame** \ˈfrām\ *vb* **framed; fram·ing** [ME *framen* to benefit, construct, fr. OE *framian* to benefit, make progress; akin to ON *fram* forward, OE *from* from] *vi* **1** *archaic* : PROCEED, GO **2** *obs* : MANAGE ~ *vt* **1 a :** PLAN, CONTRIVE <*framed* a new method of achieving their purpose> **b :** to give expression to : FORMULATE **c :** SHAPE, CONSTRUCT **d :** to draw up (as a document) **2 :** to fit or adjust esp. to something or for an end : ARRANGE **3** *obs* : PRODUCE **4 :** to construct by fitting and uniting the parts of the skeleton of (a structure) **5 :** to enclose in a frame; *also* : to enclose as if in a frame **6 a :** to devise falsely (as a criminal charge) **b :** to contrive the evidence against (an innocent man) so that a verdict of guilty is assured **c :** to prearrange (as a contest) so that a particular outcome is assured — **fram·er** *n*

[2]**frame** *n* **1 a :** something composed of parts fitted together and united **b :** the physical makeup of an animal and esp. a human body : PHYSIQUE, FIGURE **2 a :** the constructional system that gives shape or strength (as to a building); *also* : a frame dwelling **b :** such a skeleton not filled in or covered **3 a :** an open case or structure made for admitting, enclosing, or supporting something <a window ~> **b :** a machine built upon or within a framework <a spinning ~> **c :** a structural unit in an automobile chassis supported on the axles and supporting the rest of the chassis and the body **d** (1) **:** a part of a pair of glasses that holds one of the lenses (2) *pl* : that part of a pair of glasses other than the lenses **4** *obs* : the act or manner of framing **5 :** a particular state or disposition (as of the mind) : MOOD **6 a :** an enclosing border **b :** the matter or area enclosed in such a border: as (1) **:** one of the squares in which scores for each round are recorded (as in bowling); *also* : a round in bowling (2) **:** boxed matter in a newspaper; *esp* : a box of a comic strip (3) **:** one picture of the series on a length of motion-picture or other film (4) **:** a complete image being transmitted by television **c :** an inning in baseball **d :** a limiting, typical, or esp. appropriate set of circumstances <studies made within the ~ of our society and culture> **e :** an event that forms the background for the action of a novel or play **7 :** FRAME-UP **8 :** a minimal unit of instruction or stimulus in a programmed instruction routine : a unit of programmed instruction calling for a response by the student

[3]**frame** *adj* : having a wood frame <~ houses>

frame of reference **1 :** an arbitrary set of axes with reference to which the position or motion of something is described or physical laws are formulated **2 :** a set or system (as of facts or ideas) serving to orient or give particular meaning : VIEWPOINT, THEORY

frame·shift \ˈfrām-ˌshift\ *n* : the addition or deletion of a pair of purine or pyrimidine bases from a gene so that the codon sequence is read incorrectly in the formation of messenger RNA — called also *frameshift mutation*

frame–up \ˈfrā-ˌməp\ *n* **1 :** an act or series of actions in which someone is framed **2 :** an action that is framed

[1]**frame·work** \ˈfrām-ˌwərk\ *n* **1 a :** a skeletal, openwork, or structural frame **b :** a basic structure (as of ideas) **2 :** FRAME OF REFERENCE **3 :** the larger branches of a tree that determine its shape

[2]**framework** *vt* : to graft scions of another variety on the framework of (a tree)

fram·ing \ˈfrā-miŋ\ *n* : FRAME, FRAMEWORK

franc \ˈfraŋk\ *n* [F] **1** — see MONEY table **2** — see *dirham* at MONEY table

[1]**fran·chise** \ˈfran-ˌchīz\ *n* [ME, fr. OF, fr. *franchir* to free, fr. *franc* free] **1 :** freedom or immunity from some burden or restriction vested in a person or group **2 a :** a special privilege granted to an individual or group; *esp* : the right to be and exercise the powers of a corporation **b :** a constitutional or statutory right or privilege; *esp* : the right to vote **c** (1) **:** the right or license granted to an individual or group to market a company's goods or services in a particular territory (2) **:** the territory involved in such a right

[2]**franchise** *vt* **fran·chised; fran·chis·ing** **1** *archaic* : FREE **2 :** to grant a franchise to

fran·chi·see \ˌfran-ˌchī-ˈzē, -chə-\ *n* : one that is granted a franchise

fran·chis·er \ˈfran-ˌchī-zər\ *n* [in sense 1, fr. [1]*franchise;* in sense 2, fr. [2]*franchise*] **1 :** FRANCHISEE **2 :** FRANCHISOR

fran·chi·sor \ˌfran-ˌchī-ˈzȯ(ə)r, -chə-\ *n* [[2]*franchise* + *-or*] : one that grants a franchise

Fran·cis·can \fran-ˈsis-kən\ *n* [ML *Franciscus* Francis] : a member of the Order of Friars Minor founded by St. Francis of Assisi in 1209 and dedicated esp. to preaching, missions, and charities — **Franciscan** *adj*

fran·ci·um \ˈfran(t)-sē-əm\ *n* [NL, fr. *France*] : a radioactive element of the alkali-metal group discovered as a disintegration product of actinium and obtained artificially by the bombardment of thorium with protons — see ELEMENT table

Franco- *comb form* [ML, fr. *Francus* Frenchman, fr. LL, Frank] : French and <*Franco*-German> : French <*Franco*phile>

Fran·co–Amer·i·can \ˌfraŋ-kō-ə-ˈmer-ə-kən\ *n* : an American of French or esp. French-Canadian descent — **Franco–American** *adj*

fran·co·lin \ˈfraŋ-k(ə-)lən\ *n* [F, fr. It *francolino*] : any of numerous partridges (*Francolinus* and related genera) of southern Asia and Africa

Fran·co·phile \ˈfraŋ-kə-ˌfīl\ *or* **Fran·co·phil** \-ˌfil\ *adj* : markedly friendly to France or French culture — **Francophile** *n*

Fran·co·phobe \-ˌfōb\ *adj* : marked by a fear or strong dislike of France or French culture or customs — **Francophobe** *n*

fran·co·phone \-ˌfōn\ *adj, often cap* : consisting of or belonging to a French-speaking population — **Francophone** *n*

franc–ti·reur \ˌfräⁿ-(ˌ)tē-ˈrər\ *n* [F, fr. *franc* free + *tireur* shooter] : a civilian fighter or sniper

fran·gi·ble \ˈfran-jə-bəl\ *adj* [ME, fr. MF & ML; MF, fr. ML *frangibilis,* fr. L *frangere* to break — more at BREAK] : readily or easily broken ***syn*** see FRAGILE — **fran·gi·bil·i·ty** \ˌfran-jə-ˈbil-ət-ē\ *n*

fran·gi·pane \ˈfran-jə-ˌpān, fräⁿ-zhē-pȧn\ *n* [F, frangipani (perfume), frangipane, fr. It, fr. Marquis Muzio *Frangipane,* 16th cent. It nobleman] : a custard usu. flavored with almonds

fran·gi·pa·ni *also* **fran·gi·pan·ni** \ˌfran-jə-ˈpan-ē, -ˈpän-\ *n, pl* **-pani** *or* **-panis** [modif. of It *frangipane*] **1 :** a perfume derived from or imitating the odor of the flower of the red jasmine **2 :** a tropical American shrub or small tree (genus *Plumeria*) of the dogbane family (as red jasmine)

Fran·glais \fräⁿ-ˈglā\ *n* [F, blend of *français* French and *anglais* English] : French marked by a considerable number of borrowings from English

[1]**frank** \ˈfraŋk\ *adj* [ME, free, fr. OF *franc,* fr. ML *francus,* fr. LL *Francus* Frank] **1 :** marked by free, forthright, and sincere expression <a ~ reply> **2 :** clinically evident : UNMISTAKABLE <~ pus> — **frank·ness** *n*
syn FRANK, CANDID, OPEN, PLAIN *shared meaning element* : showing willingness to say what one thinks or feels ***ant*** reticent

[2]**frank** *vt* **1 a :** to mark (a piece of mail) with an official signature or sign indicating the right of the sender to free mailing **b :** to mail free **c :** to affix to (mail) a stamp or a marking indicating the payment of postage **2 :** to enable to pass or go freely or easily — **frank·er** *n*

[3]**frank** *n* **1 a :** the signature of the sender on a piece of franked mail serving in place of a postage stamp **b :** a mark or stamp on a piece of mail indicating postage paid **c :** a franked envelope **2 :** the privilege of sending mail free of charge

[4]**frank** *n* : FRANKFURTER

Frank \ˈfraŋk\ *n* [ME, partly fr. OE *Franca;* partly fr. OF *Franc,* fr. LL *Francus,* of Gmc origin; akin to OHG *Franko* Frank, OE *Franca*] : a member of a West Germanic people that entered the Roman provinces in A.D. 253, occupied the Netherlands and most of Gaul, and established themselves along the Rhine

Fran·ken·stein \ˈfraŋ-kən-ˌstīn, -ˌstēn\ *n* **1 :** a student of physiology in Mary W. Shelley's novel *Frankenstein* whose life is ruined

by a monster he creates **2 :** a work or agency that ruins its originator **3 :** a monster in the shape of a man

frank·furt·er *or* **frank·fort·er** \ˈfraŋk-fə(r)t-ər, -ˌfərt-\ *or* **frank·furt** *or* **frank·fort** \-fərt\ *n* [G *frankfurter* of Frankfurt, fr. *Frankfurt am Main,* Germany] **:** a cured cooked sausage (as of beef or beef and pork) that may be skinless or stuffed in a casing

frank·in·cense \ˈfraŋ-kən-ˌsen(t)s\ *n* **:** a fragrant gum resin from chiefly East African or Arabian trees (genus *Boswellia* of the family Burseraceae) that is an important incense resin

1Frank·ish \ˈfraŋ-kish\ *adj* **:** of or relating to the Franks

2Frankish *n* **:** the Germanic language of the Franks

frank·lin \ˈfraŋ-klən\ *n* [ME *frankeleyn,* fr. AF *fraunclein,* fr. OF *franc*] **:** a medieval English landowner of free but not noble birth

frank·lin·ite \-klə-ˌnīt\ *n* [*Franklin,* N.J.] **:** a black slightly magnetic mineral $ZnFe_2O_4$ consisting of an oxide of iron and zinc

Frank·lin stove \ˌfraŋ-klən-\ *n* [Benjamin *Franklin,* its inventor] **:** a metal heating stove resembling an open fireplace but designed to be set out in a room

Franklin stove

frank·ly \ˈfraŋ-klē\ *adv* **1 :** in a frank manner **2 :** in truth **:** INDEED

frank·pledge \ˈfraŋk-ˌplej\ *n* **:** an Anglo-Saxon system under which each adult male member of a tithing was responsible for the good conduct of the others; *also* **:** the member himself or the tithing

fran·se·ria \fran-ˈsir-ē-ə\ *n* [NL, genus name, fr. Antonio *Franseri,* 18th cent. Sp botanist] **:** any of a genus (*Franseria*) of annual or perennial composite herbs or shrubs

fran·tic \ˈfrant-ik\ *adj* [ME *frenetik, frantik* — more at FRENETIC] **1 a** *archaic* **:** mentally deranged **b :** emotionally out of control <~ with anger and frustration> **2 :** marked by fast and nervous, disordered, or anxiety-driven activity <made a ~ search for the lost child> — **fran·ti·cal·ly** \-i-k(ə-)lē\ *adv* — **fran·tic·ly** \-i-klē\ *adv* — **fran·tic·ness** \-ik-nəs\ *n*

frap \ˈfrap\ *vt* **frapped; frap·ping** [ME *frapen* to strike, beat, fr. MF *fraper*] **:** to draw tight (as with ropes or cables)

1frap·pé *or* **frap·pe** \fra-ˈpā\ *adj* [F *frappé,* fr. pp. of *frapper* to strike, chill, fr. MF *fraper* to strike] *of a beverage* **:** chilled or partly frozen

2frap·pé \fra-ˈpā\ *or* **frappe** \ˈfrap, fra-ˈpā\ *n* **1 a :** a partly frozen drink (as of fruit juice) **b :** a liqueur served over shaved ice **2 :** a thick milk shake

frat \ˈfrat\ *n* **:** FRATERNITY

fra·ter·nal \frə-ˈtərn-ᵊl\ *adj* [ME, fr. ML *fraternalis,* fr. L *fraternus,* fr. *frater* brother — more at BROTHER] **1 a :** of, relating to, or involving brothers **b :** of, relating to, or being a fraternity or society **2 :** derived from two ova **:** DIZYGOTIC <~ twins> **3 :** FRIENDLY, BROTHERLY — **fra·ter·nal·ism** \-ᵊl-ˌiz-əm\ *n* — **fra·ter·nal·ly** \-ᵊl-ē\ *adv*

fra·ter·ni·ty \frə-ˈtər-nət-ē\ *n, pl* **-ties** **1 :** a group of people associated or formally organized for a common purpose, interest, or pleasure: as **a :** a fraternal order **b :** GUILD **c :** a men's student organization formed chiefly for social purposes having secret rites and a name consisting of Greek letters **d :** a student organization for scholastic, professional, or extracurricular activities <a debating ~> **2 :** the quality or state of being brothers **:** BROTHERLINESS **3 :** men of the same class, profession, character, or tastes <the racetrack ~> **4 a :** the entire progeny of a single mating **b :** a group of siblings

frat·er·nize \ˈfrat-ər-ˌnīz\ *vi* **-nized; -niz·ing** **1 :** to associate or mingle as brothers or on fraternal terms **2 a :** to associate on close terms with members of a hostile group esp. when contrary to military orders <*fraternizing* with the enemy> **b :** to be friendly or amiable — **frat·er·ni·za·tion** \ˌfrat-ər-nə-ˈzā-shən\ *n* — **frat·er·niz·er** \ˈfrat-ər-ˌnī-zər\ *n*

frat·ri·cide \ˈfra-trə-ˌsīd\ *n* [in sense 1, fr. ME, fr. MF or L; MF, fr. L *fratricida,* fr. *fratr-, frater* brother + *-cida* -cide; in sense 2, fr. MF or L; MF, fr. L *fratricidium,* fr. *fratr-, frater* + *-cidium* -cide] **1 :** one that murders or kills his own brother or sister **2 :** the act of a fratricide — **frat·ri·cid·al** \ˌfra-trə-ˈsīd-ᵊl\ *adj*

Frau \ˈfrau̇\ *n, pl* **Frau·en** \ˈfrau̇(-ə)n [G, woman, wife, fr. OHG *frouwa* mistress, lady; akin to OE *frēa* lord] **:** a German married woman **:** WIFE — used as a title equivalent to *Mrs.*

fraud \ˈfrȯd\ *n* [ME *fraude,* fr. MF, fr. L *fraud-, fraus;* akin to Skt *dhvarati* he bends, injures] **1 a :** DECEIT, TRICKERY; *specif* **:** intentional perversion of truth in order to induce another to part with something of value or to surrender a legal right **b :** an act of deceiving or misrepresenting **:** TRICK **2 a :** one who is not what he pretends to be **:** IMPOSTOR; *also* **:** one who defrauds **:** CHEAT **b :** one that is not what it seems or is represented to be ***syn*** see IMPOSTURE

fraud·u·lence \ˈfrȯ-jə-lən(t)s\ *n* **:** the quality or state of being fraudulent

fraud·u·lent \-lənt\ *adj* **:** characterized by, based on, or done by fraud **:** DECEITFUL — **fraud·u·lent·ly** *adv* — **fraud·u·lent·ness** *n*

1fraught \ˈfrȯkt\ *n* [ME, freight, load, fr. MD or MLG *vracht, vrecht*] *chiefly Scot* **:** LOAD, CARGO

2fraught *vt* **fraught·ed** *or* **fraught; fraught·ing** [ME *fraughten,* fr. [1]*fraught*] *chiefly Scot* **:** LOAD, FREIGHT

3fraught \ˈfrȯt\ *adj* [ME, fr. pp. of *fraughten*] **1** *archaic* **a :** LADEN **b :** well supplied or provided **2 :** full of or accompanied by something specified **:** CHARGED — used with *with* <the situation . . . is ~ with a very high violence potential —Harvey Wheeler>

fräu·lein \ˈfrȯi-ˌlīn\ *n* [G] **1** *cap* **:** an unmarried German woman — used as a title equivalent to *Miss* **2 :** a German governess

frax·i·nel·la \ˌfrak-sə-ˈnel-ə\ *n* [NL, dim. of L *fraxinus* ash tree — more at BIRCH] **:** a Eurasian perennial herb (*Dictamnus albus*) of the rue family with flowers that exhale a flammable vapor in hot weather — called also *gas plant*

1fray \ˈfrā\ *vt* [ME *fraien,* short for *affraien* to affray] *archaic* **:** SCARE; *also* **:** to frighten away

2fray *n* **:** BRAWL, FIGHT; *also* **:** DISPUTE, DEBATE

3fray *vb* [MF *froyer, frayer* to rub, fr. L *fricare* — more at FRICTION] *vt* **1 a :** to wear (as an edge of cloth) by rubbing **:** FRET **b :** to separate the threads at the edge of **2 :** STRAIN, IRRITATE <his temper became a bit ~*ed*> ~ *vi* **:** to wear out or into shreds

4fray *n* **:** a raveled place or worn spot (as on fabric)

fray·ing *n* **:** something rubbed or worn off by fraying

1fraz·zle \ˈfraz-əl\ *vb* **fraz·zled; fraz·zling** \ˈfraz-(ə-)liŋ\ [alter. of E dial. *fazle* (to tangle, fray)] *vt* **1 :** [3]FRAY **2 a :** to put in a state of extreme physical or nervous fatigue **b :** UPSET ~ *vi* **:** to become frazzled

2frazzle *n* **1 :** the state of being frazzled **2 :** a condition of fatigue or nervous exhaustion <worn to a ~>

FRCM *abbr* Fellow of the Royal College of Music

FRCO *abbr* Fellow of the Royal College of Organists

FRCP *abbr* Fellow of the Royal College of Physicians

FRCS *abbr* Fellow of the Royal College of Surgeons

1freak \ˈfrēk\ *n* [origin unknown] **1 a :** a sudden and odd or seemingly pointless idea or turn of the mind **b :** a seemingly capricious action or event **2** *archaic* **:** a whimsical quality or disposition **3 :** one that is markedly unusual or abnormal <by some ~ of the storm one car in the line was completely buried>: as **a :** a person or animal with a physical oddity who appears in a circus sideshow **b** *slang* **(1) :** a sexual deviate **(2) :** a person who uses an illicit drug **c** *slang* **:** a highly individualistic critic or rebel **d :** an ardent enthusiast <something from which the casual moviegoer as well as the dedicated film ~ can learn —Richard Schickel> **e :** an atypical postage stamp usu. caused by a unique defect in paper (as a crease) or a unique event in the manufacturing process (as a speck of dirt on the plate) that does not produce a constant or systematic effect ***syn*** see CAPRICE

2freak *adj* **:** having the character of a freak <a ~ accident>

3freak *vt* **:** to streak esp. with color <silver and mother-of-pearl ~*ing* the intense azure —Robert Bridges †1930>

freak·ish \ˈfrē-kish\ *adj* **1 :** WHIMSICAL, CAPRICIOUS **2 :** being or befitting a freak — **freak·ish·ly** *adv* — **freak·ish·ness** *n*

freak of nature : FREAK 3a

freak–out \ˈfrē-ˌkau̇t\ *n* **1 :** a withdrawal from reality esp. by means of drugs **2 a :** a drug-induced state of mind characterized by nightmarish hallucinations **:** a bad trip **b :** an irrational act **3 :** a gathering of hippies **4 :** one who freaks out

freak out \ˈfrē-ˈkau̇t\ *vi* **1 :** to withdraw from reality esp. by taking drugs **2 :** to experience nightmarish hallucinations as a result of taking drugs **:** have a bad trip **3 :** to behave irrationally or unconventionally under or as if under the influence of drugs ~ *vt* **1 :** to put under the influence of a psychedelic drug **2 :** to put into a state of intense excitement

freak show *n* **:** an exhibition (as a sideshow) featuring freaks of nature

freaky \ˈfrē-kē\ *adj* **freak·i·er; -est :** FREAKISH

1freck·le \ˈfrek-əl\ *n* [ME *freken, frekel,* of Scand origin; akin to ON *freknōttr* freckled; akin to OE *spearca* spark] **:** one of the small brownish spots in the skin that are usu. due to precipitation of pigment and that increase in number and intensity on exposure to sunlight — **freck·ly** \ˈfrek-(ə-)lē\ *adv*

2freckle *vb* **freck·led; freck·ling** \ˈfrek-(ə-)liŋ\ *vt* **:** to sprinkle or mark with freckles or small spots ~ *vi* **:** to become marked with freckles

1free \ˈfrē\ *adj* **fre·er; fre·est** [ME, fr. OE *frēo;* akin to OHG *frī* free, Gk *prays* gentle] **1 a :** having the legal and political rights of a citizen **b :** enjoying civil and political liberty <~ citizens> **c :** enjoying political independence or freedom from outside domination **d :** enjoying personal freedom **:** not subject to the control or domination of another **2 a :** not determined by anything beyond its own nature or being **:** choosing or capable of choosing for itself **b :** determined by the choice of the actor or by his wishes <~ actions> **c :** made, done, or given voluntarily or spontaneously **:** SPONTANEOUS **3 a :** exempt, relieved, or released esp. from a burdensome, noxious, or deplorable condition or obligation <~ from pain> **b :** not bound, confined, or detained by force <prisoner was now ~> **4 a :** having no trade restrictions **b :** not subject to government regulation **c** *of foreign exchange* **:** not subject to restriction or official control **5 a :** having no obligations (as to work) or commitments (as to duty or custom) <I'll be ~ this evening> **b :** not taken up with commitments or obligations <a ~ evening> **6 :** having a scope not restricted by qualification <a ~ variable> **7 a (1) :** not obstructed or impeded **:** CLEAR <a ~ and open highway> **(2) :** not being used or occupied <waved with his ~ hand> **b :** not hampered or restricted in its normal operation **:** LOOSE **8 a :** not fastened <the ~ end of the rope> **b :** not confined to a particular position or place; *also* **:** not having a specific opponent to cover in football <a ~ safety> **c :** capable of moving or turning in any direction <a ~ particle> **d :** performed without apparatus <~ tumbling> **9 a :** not parsimonious <~ spending> **b :** OUTSPOKEN **c :** availing oneself of something without stint **d :** FRANK, OPEN **e :** overly familiar or forward in action or attitude **f :** LICENTIOUS **10 :** not costing or charging anything **11 a (1) :** not united with, attached to, or combined with something else **:** SEPARATE <~ ores> <a ~ surface of a bodily part> **(2) :** FREESTANDING <a ~ column> **b :** chemically uncombined <~ oxygen> <~ acids> **c :** not permanently attached but able to move about <a ~ electron in a metal> **d :** capable of being used alone as a meaningful linguistic form <the word *hats* is a ~ form> — compare [4]BOUND 7 **12 a :** not literal or exact <~ translation>

ə abut	ᵊ kitten	ər further	a back	ā bake	ä cot, cart
au̇ out	ch chin	e less	ē easy	g gift	i trip ī life
j joke	ŋ sing	ō flow	ȯ flaw	ȯi coin	th thin th this
ü loot	u̇ foot	y yet	yü few	yu̇ furious	zh vision

b : not restricted by or conforming to conventional forms <~ skating> **13 :** FAVORABLE — used of a wind blowing from a direction more than six points from straight ahead **14 :** not allowing slavery **15 :** open to all comers — **free·ly** *adv*
syn FREE, INDEPENDENT, AUTONOMOUS, SOVEREIGN *shared meaning element* **:** not subject to the rule or control of another

[2]**free** *adv* **1 :** in a free manner **2 :** without charge <admitted ~> **3 :** with the wind more than six points from dead ahead <sailing ~>

[3]**free** *vt* **freed; free·ing 1 a :** to cause to be free **b :** to relieve or rid of what restrains, confines, restricts, or embarrasses <~ a man from debt> **c :** DISENTANGLE, CLEAR **2** *obs* **:** BANISH — **fre·er** *n*
syn FREE, RELEASE, LIBERATE, EMANCIPATE, MANUMIT, DISCHARGE *shared meaning element* **:** to loose from constraint or restraint

free agent *n* **:** a professional athlete (as a football player) who is not under contract to any team

free alongside ship *adv or adj* **:** with delivery at the side of the ship free of charges and the buyer's liability then beginning

free alongside vessel *adv or adj* **:** free alongside ship

free and easy *adj* **1 :** marked by informality and lack of constraint <the *free and easy,* open-air life of the plains —Allan Murray> **2 :** not observant of strict demands <his *free and easy* literary judgments> — **free and easy** *adv*

free association *n* **1 a :** the verbal or written expression of all the content of consciousness without censorship or control as an aid in gaining access to unconscious processes esp. in psychoanalysis **b :** the reporting of the first thought that comes to mind in response to a given stimulus (as a word) **2 :** an idea or image elicited by free association **3 :** a method using free association

free·bie *or* **free·bee** \ˈfrē-bē\ *n* [by alter. fr. obs. slang *freeby* gratis, fr. *free* + *-by,* of unknown origin]**:** something (as a theater ticket) given or received without charge

free·board \ˈfrē-ˌbō(ə)rd, -ˌbȯ(ə)rd\ *n* **1 :** the distance between the waterline and the freeboard deck of a ship or between the level of the water and the upper edge of the side of a small boat **2 :** the height above the recorded high-water mark of a structure (as a dam) associated with the water **3 :** the space between the surface of the ground and the undercarriage of an automobile

freeboard deck *n* **:** the deck below which all bulkheads are made watertight

free·boot \ˈfrē-ˌbüt\ *vi* [back-formation fr. *freebooter*]**:** to act as a freebooter **:** PLUNDER

free·boo·ter \-ər\ *n* [D *vrijbuiter,* fr. *vrijbuit* plunder, fr. *vrij* free + *buit* booty]**:** PIRATE, PLUNDERER

free·born \ˈfrē-ˈbȯ(ə)rn\ *adj* **1 :** not born in vassalage or slavery **2 :** of, relating to, or befitting one that is freeborn

free diver *n* **:** one who engages in skin diving — **free diving** *n*

freed·man \ˈfrēd-mən, -ˌman\ *n* **:** a man freed from slavery

free·dom \ˈfrēd-əm\ *n* **1 :** the quality or state of being free: as **a :** the absence of necessity, coercion, or constraint in choice or action **b :** liberation from slavery or restraint or from the power of another **:** INDEPENDENCE **c :** the quality or state of being exempt or released usu. from something onerous <~ from care> **d :** EASE, FACILITY <spoke the language with ~> **e :** the quality of being frank, open, or outspoken <answered the questions with ~> **f :** improper familiarity **g :** boldness of conception or execution **h :** unrestricted use <gave him the ~ of their home> **2 a :** a political right **b :** FRANCHISE, PRIVILEGE
syn FREEDOM, LIBERTY, LICENSE *shared meaning element* **:** the power or condition of acting without compulsion. FREEDOM may imply total or moderate absence of restraint or merely an unawareness of being unduly hampered or frustrated <*Freedom* . . . in the medieval sense, when there was no abstract *freedom* but only countable *Freedoms,* each bestowed . . . all subject to forfeiture —Martin Joos> <enjoyed the *freedom* of her isolated life> LIBERTY may carry more clearly an implication of the power to choose or one of deliverance from constraint or compulsion <in totalitarian states there is no *liberty* of expression for writers —Aldous Huxley> <restore a prisoner's *liberty*> LICENSE can imply unusual freedom (as from rules or restraints) tolerated because of special circumstances <poetic *license*> but more often it implies an abuse of liberty (as by disregard of propriety or the rights of others) <enjoying their victory in the *license* which is miscalled liberty —J. A. Froude>

freedom of the seas : the right of a merchant ship to travel any waters except territorial waters either in peace or war

freedom ride *n, often cap F&R* **:** a ride made by civil rights workers through states of the southern U.S. to ascertain whether public facilities (as bus terminals) are desegregated — **freedom rider** *n*

freed·wom·an \ˈfrēd-ˌwu̇m-ən\ *n* **:** a woman freed from slavery

free enterprise *n* **:** freedom of private business to organize and operate for profit in a competitive system without interference by government beyond regulation necessary to protect public interest and keep the national economy in balance

free–fall \ˈfrē-ˈfȯl\ *n* **1 :** the condition of unrestrained motion in a gravitational field; *also* **:** such motion **2 :** the part of a parachute jump before the parachute opens

free–float·ing \-ˈflōt-iŋ\ *adj* **1 :** relatively uncommitted (as to a particular purpose) <was not sure how the ~ intellectuals would vote> **2 :** felt as an emotion without apparent cause <~ anxiety>

free–for–all \ˈfrē-fə-ˌrȯl\ *n* **:** a competition, dispute, or fight open to all comers and usu. with no rules **:** BRAWL — **free–for–all** *adj*

free·hand \ˈfrē-ˌhand\ *adj* **:** done without mechanical aids or devices **:** FREE <~ drawing> — **freehand** *adv*

free hand \-ˈhand\ *n* **:** freedom of action or decision

free·hand·ed \ˈfrē-ˈhan-dəd\ *adj* **:** OPENHANDED, GENEROUS — **free·hand·ed·ly** *adv*

free·heart·ed \-ˈhärt-əd\ *adj* **1 :** FRANK, UNRESERVED **2 :** GENEROUS — **free·heart·ed·ly** *adv*

free·hold \ˈfrē-ˌhōld\ *n* **1 :** a tenure of real property by which an estate of inheritance in fee simple or fee tail or for life is held; *also* **:** an estate held by such tenure — compare FEE 1 **2 :** a tenure of an office or dignity similar to a freehold — **free·hold·er** \-ˌhōl-dər\ *n*

free kick *n* **:** a kick (as in football, soccer, or rugby) with which an opponent may not interfere; *specif* **:** an unhindered kick (as in soccer) in any direction awarded because of an infraction of the rules by an opponent

[1]**free–lance** *adj* **:** of, relating to, or befitting a free lance **:** INDEPENDENT

[2]**free–lance** *vi* **:** to act as a free lance ~ *vt* **:** to offer or contract for the purchase of in the manner of a free lance — **free–lanc·er** *n*

free lance *n* **1 a :** a knight or roving soldier available for hire by a state or commander **b :** one who acts independently without regard to party lines or deference to authority **2 :** one who pursues a profession without long-term contractual commitments to any one employer

free–liv·ing \ˈfrē-ˈliv-iŋ\ *adj* **1 :** marked by more than usual freedom in the gratification of appetites **2 :** neither parasitic nor symbiotic

free·load \-ˈlōd\ *vi* **:** to impose upon another's generosity or hospitality without sharing in the cost or responsibility involved **:** SPONGE — **free·load·er** *n*

free love *n* **:** the practice of living openly with one of the opposite sex without marriage

free·man \ˈfrē-mən, -ˌman\ *n* **1 :** one enjoying civil or political liberty **2 :** one having the full rights of a citizen

free market *n* **:** an economic market operating by free competition

free·mar·tin \ˈfrē-ˌmärt-ᵊn\ *n* [origin unknown]**:** a sexually imperfect usu. sterile female calf twinborn with a male

Free·ma·son \-ˈmās-ᵊn\ *n* **:** a member of a major secret fraternal society called Free and Accepted Masons

free·ma·son·ry \-rē\ *n* **1** *cap* **:** the principles, institutions, or practices of Freemasons — called also *Masonry* **2 :** natural or instinctive fellowship or sympathy

free·ness *n* **:** FREEDOM

free on board *adv or adj* **:** without charge for delivery to and placing on board a carrier at a specified point

free port *n* **:** an enclosed port or section of a port where goods are received and shipped free of customs duty

free radical *n* **:** an atom or a group of atoms having at least one unpaired electron and participating in various reactions

free reed *n* **:** a reed in a musical instrument (as a harmonium) that vibrates in an air opening just large enough to allow the reed to move freely — compare BEATING REED

free rein *n* **:** unrestricted liberty of action or decision

free ride *n* **:** something (as entertainment, acclaim, or a profit) obtained without the usual cost or effort — **free ride** *vi* — **free rider** *n*

free·sia \ˈfrē-zh(ē-)ə, -zē-ə\ *n* [NL, genus name, fr. F. H. T. *Freese* †1876 G physician]**:** any of a genus (*Freesia*) of the iris family of sweet-scented African herbs with red, white, or yellow flowers

free–soil *adj* **1:** characterized by free soil <~ states> **2** *cap F&S* **:** opposing the extension of slavery into U.S. territories and the admission of slave states into the Union prior to the Civil War; *specif* **:** of, relating to, or constituting a minor U.S. political party having these aims — **Free–Soil·er** \-ˈsȯi-lər\ *n*

free soil *n* **:** U.S. territory where prior to the Civil War slavery was prohibited

free–spo·ken \ˈfrē-ˈspō-kən\ *adj* **:** speaking freely **:** OUTSPOKEN

freest *superlative of* FREE

free·stand·ing \ˈfrē-ˈstan-diŋ\ *adj* **:** standing alone or on its own foundation free of architectural or supporting frame or attachment <a ~ wall>

free·stone \ˈfrē-ˌstōn\ *n* **1 :** a stone that may be cut freely without splitting **2 a :** a fruit stone to which the flesh does not cling **b :** a fruit having such a stone

free·style \ˈfrē-ˌstīl\ *n, often attrib* **:** a competition in which a contestant uses a style (as of swimming) of his choice instead of a specified style

free–swim·ming \-ˈswim-iŋ\ *adj* **:** able to swim about **:** not attached <the ~ larva of the barnacle>

free–swing·ing \-ˈswiŋ-iŋ\ *adj* **:** bold, forthright, and heedless of personal consequences <a ~ soldier of fortune —Will Herberg>

free·think·er \-ˈthiŋ-kər\ *n* **:** one that forms opinions on the basis of reason independently of authority; *esp* **:** one who doubts or denies religious dogma *syn* see ATHEIST — **free·think·ing** \-kiŋ\ *n or adj*

free thought *n* **:** free thinking or unorthodox thought; *specif* **:** 18th century deism

free throw *n* **:** an unhindered shot in basketball made from behind a set line and awarded because of a foul by an opponent

free throw lane *n* **:** a 12 or 16 foot wide lane on a basketball court that extends from underneath the goal to a line 15 feet in front of the backboard and from which players are excluded during a free throw

free trade *n* **:** trade based upon the unrestricted international exchange of goods with tariffs used only as a source of revenue

free trader *n* **:** one that practices, supports, or advocates free trade

free university *n* **:** an unaccredited autonomous free institution established within a university by students to present and discuss subjects not usu. dealt with in the academic curriculum

free verse *n* **:** verse whose meter is irregular in some respect or whose rhythm is not metrical

free·way \ˈfrē-ˌwā\ *n* **1 :** an expressway with fully controlled access **2 :** a toll-free highway

[1]**free·wheel** \-ˈ(h)wē(ə)l\ *n* **1 :** a power-transmission system in a motor vehicle with a device that permits the propeller shaft to run freely when its speed is greater than that of the engine shaft **2 :** a clutch fitted in the rear hub of a bicycle that permits the rear wheel to run on free from the rear sprocket when the pedals are stopped

[2]**freewheel** *vi* **:** to move, live, or drift along freely or irresponsibly — **free·wheel·er** *n*

free·wheel·ing *adj* : relatively heedless of formalities, rules, responsibilities, or consequences — **free·wheel·ing·ness** *n*
free·will \ˌfrē-ˌwil\ *adj* : VOLUNTARY, SPONTANEOUS
free will *n* **1** : the power asserted of moral beings of choosing within limitations or with respect to some matters without restraint of physical or divine necessity or causal law **2** : the ability to choose between alternatives so that the choice and action are to an extent creatively determined by the conscious subject
Freewill Baptist *n* : a member of a Baptist group holding to Arminian doctrine and practicing open communion
free world *n* : the part of the world where democracy and capitalism or moderate socialism rather than totalitarian or Communist political and economic systems prevail
[1]**freeze** \ˈfrēz\ *vb* **froze** \ˈfrōz\; **fro·zen** \ˈfrōz-ᵊn\; **freez·ing** [ME *fresen*, fr. OE *frēosan*; akin to OHG *friosan* to freeze, L *pruina* hoarfrost] *vi* **1 a** : to become congealed into ice by cold **b** : to solidify as a result of abstraction of heat **2 a** : to become chilled with cold <almost *froze* to death> **b** : to become coldly formal in manner **3** : to adhere solidly by or as if by freezing <pressure caused the metals to ~> **4** : to become clogged with ice <the water pipes *froze*> **5** : to become fixed or motionless; *esp* : to become incapable of acting or speaking ~ *vt* **1 a** : to harden into ice **b** : to convert from a liquid to a solid by cold **2 a** : to make extremely cold : CHILL **b** : to act toward in a stiff and formal way **3 a** : to act on usu. destructively by frost **b** : to anesthetize by cold **4** : to cause to grip tightly or remain in immovable contact **5 a** : to cause to become fixed, immovable, or unalterable **b** : to forbid further manufacture, use, or sale of (a raw material) **c** : to immobilize by governmental regulation the expenditure, withdrawal, or exchange of (foreign-owned bank balances) **6** : to attempt to retain continuous possession of (a ball or puck) without an attempt to score usu. in order to protect a small lead
[2]**freeze** *n* **1** : a state of weather marked by low temperature esp. when below the freezing point **2 a** : an act or instance of freezing **b** : the state of being frozen
freeze–dry \ˈfrēz-ˈdrī\ *vt* : to dry (as food) in a frozen state under high vacuum esp. for preservation — **freeze–dried** *adj*
freeze–etch·ing \ˈfrē-ˈzech-iŋ\ *n* : preparation of a replica for electron microscopic examination of the exposed surface of quick-frozen material (as a tissue) after fracture along natural structural lines
freez·er \ˈfrē-zər\ *n* : one that freezes or keeps cool; *esp* : an insulated cabinet, compartment, or room for keeping food at a subfreezing temperature or for freezing perishable food rapidly
freezing point *n* : the temperature at which a liquid solidifies <the *freezing point* of water is 0° C or 32° F>
free zone *n* : an area within which goods may be received and stored without payment of duty
F region *n* : the highest region of the ionosphere occurring from 90 to more than 250 miles above the earth
[1]**freight** \ˈfrāt\ *n, often attrib* [ME, fr. MD or MLG *vracht, vrecht*] **1** : the compensation paid for the transportation of goods **2 a** : something that is loaded for transportation : CARGO **b** : LOAD, BURDEN **3 a** : the ordinary transportation of goods afforded by a common carrier and distinguished from express **b** : a train designed or used for such transportation
[2]**freight** *vt* **1 a** : to load with goods for transportation **b** : BURDEN, CHARGE **2** : to transport or ship by freight
freight·age \ˈfrāt-ij\ *n* : FREIGHT
freight·er \-ər\ *n* **1** : one that loads or charters and loads a ship **2** : SHIPPER **3** : a ship or airplane used chiefly to carry freight
freight ton *n* : TON 2c
frem·i·tus \ˈfrem-ət-əs\ *n* [NL, fr. L, murmur, fr. *fremitus*, pp. of *fremere* to murmur; akin to OE *bremman* to roar] : a sensation felt by a hand placed on a part of the body (as the chest) that vibrates during speech
french \ˈfrench\ *vt, often cap* [*French bean*] : to cut (snap beans) in thin lengthwise strips before cooking
[1]**French** \ˈfrench\ *adj* [ME, fr. OE *frencisc*, fr. *Franca* Frank] : of, relating to, or characteristic of France, its people, or their language — **French·ness** *n*
[2]**French** *n* **1** : a Romance language that developed out of the Vulgar Latin of Transalpine Gaul and became the literary and official language of France **2** *pl in constr* : the French people
French bean *n* **1** *chiefly Brit* : a bean (as a green bean) of which the whole young pod is eaten : SNAP BEAN **2** *chiefly Brit* : KIDNEY BEAN 2
French bulldog *n* : any of a breed of small compact heavy-boned bat-eared dogs developed in France supposedly by crossing small bulldogs with native dogs
French Canadian *n* : one of the descendants of French settlers in Lower Canada
French chalk *n* : a soft white granular variety of steatite used esp. for drawing lines on cloth and for removing grease in dry cleaning
French chop *n* : a rib chop with the meat trimmed from the end of the rib
French cuff *n* : a soft double cuff that is made by turning back part of a wide cuff band and that fastens by cuff links
French door *n* : a light door with rectangular glass panels extending the full length; *also* : one of a pair of such doors in a single frame
French dressing *n* **1** : a salad dressing made with oil and vinegar or lemon juice, salt and pepper, and often condiments (as mustard and herbs) **2** : a commercial salad dressing that is creamy and typically orange-red in color
French endive *n* : ENDIVE 2
[1]**french fry** *vt, often cap 1st F* [back-formation fr. *French fried* (*potatoes*)] : to fry (as strips of potato) in deep fat until brown
[2]**french fry** *n, often cap 1st F* : a strip of potato fried in deep fat — usu. used in pl.
French heel *n* : a woman's shoe heel that is usu. high, pitched well forward, and markedly curved
French horn *n* : a circular valved brass instrument having a conical bore, a funnel-shaped mouthpiece, and a usual range from B below the bass staff upward for more than three octaves
french·ify \ˈfren-chə-ˌfī\ *vt* **-ified; -ify·ing** *often cap* : to make French in qualities, traits, or typical practices — **french·ifi·ca·tion** \ˌfren-chə-fə-ˈkā-shən\ *n, often cap*

French horn

French kiss *n* : an open-mouth kiss usu. involving tongue-to-tongue contact — **French–kiss** *vb*
French leave *n* [fr. an 18th cent. French custom of leaving a reception without taking leave of the host or hostess] : an informal, hasty, or secret departure
French·man \ˈfrench-mən\ *n* **1** : a native or inhabitant of France **2** : one who is of French descent
French pastry *n* : fancy pastry made usu. of puff paste baked in individual portions and filled esp. with custard or fruit
French provincial *n, often cap P* : a style of furniture, architecture, or fabric originating in or characteristic of the 17th and 18th century French provinces
French telephone *n* : HANDSET
French toast *n* : bread dipped in a mixture of egg and milk and sautéed
French window *n* **1** : a French door placed in an exterior wall **2** : a casement window
French·wom·an \ˈfrench-ˌwu̇m-ən\ *n* **1** : a female native or inhabitant of France **2** : a woman of French descent
fre·net·ic \fri-ˈnet-ik\ *adj* [ME *frenetik* insane, fr. MF *frenetique*, fr. L *phreneticus*, modif. of Gk *phrenitikos*, fr. *phrenitis* inflammation of the brain, fr. *phren-*, *phrēn* diaphragm, mind] : FRENZIED, FRANTIC — **fre·net·i·cal·ly** \-i-k(ə-)lē\ *adv*
fren·u·lum \ˈfren-yə-ləm\ *n, pl* **-la** \-lə\ [NL, dim. of L *frenum*] **1** : a connecting fold of membrane serving to support or restrain a part (as the tongue) **2** : a bristle or group of bristles on the front edge of the posterior wings of some lepidoptera that unites the wings by interlocking with a process on the front wings
fre·num \ˈfrē-nəm\ *n, pl* **frenums** *or* **fre·na** \-nə\ [L, lit., bridle; akin to L *firmus* firm] : FRENULUM 1
fren·zied \ˈfren-zēd\ *adj* : marked by frenzy — **fren·zied·ly** *adv*
[1]**fren·zy** \ˈfren-zē\ *n, pl* **frenzies** [ME *frenesie*, fr. MF, fr. ML *phrenesia*, alter. of L *phrenesis*, fr. *phreneticus*] **1 a** : a temporary madness **b** : a violent mental or emotional agitation **2** : intense usu. wild and often disorderly compulsive or agitated activity
[2]**frenzy** *vt* **fren·zied; fren·zy·ing** : to affect with frenzy
Fre·on \ˈfrē-ˌän\ *trademark* — used for any of various nonflammable gaseous and liquid fluorinated hydrocarbons used as refrigerants and as propellants for aerosols
freq *abbr* frequency; frequent; frequentative; frequently
fre·quence \ˈfrē-kwən(t)s\ *n* : FREQUENCY
fre·quen·cy \ˈfrē-kwən-sē\ *n, pl* **-cies** **1** : the fact or condition of occurring frequently **2 a** : the number of times that a periodic function repeats the same sequence of values during a unit variation of the independent variable **b** : the number of individuals in a single class when objects are classified according to variations in a set of one or more specified attributes **3** : the number of repetitions of a periodic process in a unit of time: as **a** : the number of complete alternations per second of an alternating current **b** : the number of sound waves per second produced by a sounding body **c** : the number of complete oscillations per second of an electromagnetic wave
frequency distribution *n* : an arrangement of statistical data that exhibits the frequency of the occurrence of the values of a variable
frequency modulation *n* : modulation of the frequency of the carrier wave in accordance with speech or a signal; *also* : a broadcasting system using such modulation
frequency response *n* : the ability of a device (as an audio amplifier) to handle the frequencies applied to it; *also* : a graph representing this ability
[1]**fre·quent** \ˈfrē-kwənt\ *adj* [ME, fr. MF or L; MF, fr. L *frequent-*, *frequens*] **1** *obs* : FULL, THRONGED **2 a** : COMMON, USUAL **b** : happening at short intervals **3** : HABITUAL, PERSISTENT **4** *archaic* : INTIMATE, FAMILIAR — **fre·quent·ness** *n*
[2]**fre·quent** \frē-ˈkwent, ˈfrē-kwənt\ *vt* **1** : to associate with, be in, or resort to often or habitually **2** *archaic* : to read systematically or habitually — **fre·quen·ta·tion** \ˌfrē-ˌkwen-ˈtā-shən, -kwən-\ *n* — **fre·quent·er** *n*
[1]**fre·quen·ta·tive** \frē-ˈkwent-ət-iv\ *adj* : denoting repeated or recurrent action or state — used of a verb aspect, verb form, or meaning
[2]**frequentative** *n* : a frequentative verb or verb form
fre·quent·ly \ˈfrē-kwənt-lē\ *adv* : at frequent or short intervals
fres·co \ˈfres-(ˌ)kō\ *n, pl* **frescoes** *or* **frescos** [It, fr. *fresco* fresh, of Gmc origin; akin to OHG *frisc* fresh] **1** : the art of painting on freshly spread moist lime plaster with pigments suspended in a water vehicle **2** : a painting executed in fresco — **fresco** *vt*
[1]**fresh** \ˈfresh\ *adj* [ME, fr. OF *freis*, of Gmc origin; akin to OHG *frisc* fresh; akin to OE *fersc* fresh] **1 a** : not salt <~ water> **b** (1) : free from taint : PURE <~ air> (2) *of wind* : STRONG **2 a** : not altered by processing <~ vegetables> **b** : having its original qualities unimpaired: as (1) : full of or renewed in vigor or readiness for action : REFRESHED <rose ~ from a good night's sleep> (2) : not stale, sour, or decayed <~ bread> (3) : not faded (4) : not worn or rumpled : SPRUCE <a ~ white shirt> **3 a** (1) : experienced, made, or received newly or anew <form ~ friendships> (2) : ADDITIONAL, ANOTHER <make a ~ start> **b**

: ORIGINAL, VIVID **c** : lacking experience : RAW **d** : newly or just come or arrived <~ from school> **e** : having the milk flow recently established <a ~ cow> **4** [prob. by folk etymology fr. G *frech*] : disposed to take liberties : IMPUDENT ***syn*** see NEW ***ant*** stale — **fresh·ly** *adv* — **fresh·ness** *n*

2fresh *adv* : just recently : NEWLY <a ~ laid egg>

3fresh *n* **1** : an increased flow or rush (as of water) : FRESHET **2** : a stream of fresh water running into salt water

fresh breeze *n* : wind having a speed of 19 to 24 miles per hour

fresh·en \'fresh-ən\ *vb* **fresh·ened; fresh·en·ing** \-(ə-)niŋ\ *vi* **1** : to grow or become fresh: as **a** *of wind* : to increase in strength **b** : to become fresh in appearance or vitality — usu. used with *up* <~ up with a shower> **c** *of water* : to lose saltiness **2** *of a milch animal* : to come into milk ~ *vt* : to make fresh; *also* : REFRESH, REVIVE

fresh·et \'fresh-ət\ *n* **1** *archaic* : STREAM 1 **2 a** : a great rise or overflowing of a stream caused by heavy rains or melted snow **b** : something resembling or suggesting a freshet esp. in being in sudden large supply <~*s* of applause —Douglas Watt>

fresh gale *n* : wind having a speed of 39 to 46 miles per hour

fresh·man \'fresh-mən\ *n, often attrib* **1** : NOVICE, NEWCOMER **2** : a student in his first year or having chiefly first-year standing

fresh·wa·ter \ˌfresh-ˌwȯt-ər, -ˌwät-\ *adj* **1** : of, relating to, or living in fresh water **2** : accustomed to navigating only in fresh waters <a ~ sailor>; *also* : UNSKILLED **3** : inland and usu. provincial <a ~ college>

Fres·nel lens \ˌfrez-nəl-, frā-ˌnel-\ *n* [Augustin J. *Fresnel*] : a lens that has a surface consisting of a concentric series of simple lens sections so that a thin lens with a short focal length and large diameter is possible and that is used esp. for spotlights

1fret \'fret\ *vb* **fret·ted; fret·ting** [ME *freten* to devour, fret, fr. OE *fretan* to devour; akin to OHG *frezzan* to devour, *ezzan* to eat — more at EAT] *vt* **1** : to cause to suffer emotional strain : VEX **2 a** : to eat or gnaw into : CORRODE; *also* : FRAY **b** : RUB, CHAFE **c** : to make by wearing away a substance <the stream *fretted* a channel> **3** : to pass (as time) in fretting **4** : AGITATE, RIPPLE ~ *vi* **1 a** : to eat into something **b** : to affect something as if by gnawing or biting : GRATE **2 a** : WEAR, CORRODE **b** : CHAFE **c** : FRAY **3 a** : to become vexed or worried **b** *of running water* : to become agitated

2fret *n* **1 a** : the action of wearing away : EROSION **b** : a worn or eroded spot **2** : an agitation of mind : IRRITATION

3fret *vt* **fret·ted; fret·ting** [ME *fretten*, fr. MF *freter* to bind with a ferrule, fret, fr. OF, fr. *frete* ferrule] **1 a** : to decorate with interlaced designs **b** : to form a pattern upon **2** : to enrich with embossed or pierced carved patterns

4fret *n* **1** : an ornamental network; *esp* : a medieval metallic or jeweled net for a woman's headdress **2** : an ornament or ornamental work often in relief consisting of small straight bars intersecting one another in right or oblique angles

frets 2

5fret *n* [prob. fr. MF *frete* ferrule] : one of a series of ridges fixed across the fingerboard of a stringed musical instrument (as a guitar)

6fret *vt* **fret·ted; fret·ting** : to furnish (a stringed instrument) with frets

fret·ful \'fret-fəl\ *adj* **1** : disposed to fret : IRRITABLE **2 a** *of water* : showing agitation **b** *of wind* : GUSTY — **fret·ful·ly** \-fə-lē\ *adv* — **fret·ful·ness** *n*

fret·saw \'fret-ˌsȯ\ *n* : a narrow-bladed fine-toothed saw held under tension in a frame and used for cutting curved outlines

fret·work \-ˌwərk\ *n* **1** : decoration consisting of work adorned with frets **2** : ornamental openwork or work in relief

Freud·ian \'frȯid-ē-ən\ *adj* : of, relating to, or according with the psychoanalytic theories or practices of Freud — **Freudian** *n* — **Freud·ian·ism** \-ə-ˌniz-əm\ *n*

Freudian slip *n* : a slip of the tongue that is motivated by and reveals some unconscious aspect of the mind

Freund's adjuvant \'frȯin(d)z-, 'frȯin(t)s-\ *n* [Jules T. *Freund* †1960 Am immunologist] : any of various substances (as killed tubercle bacilli) added to an antigen to increase its antigenicity

Frey \'frā\ *n* [ON *Freyr*] : the Norse god of fertility, crops, peace, and prosperity

Freya \'frā-ə\ *n* [ON *Freyja*] : the Norse goddess of love and beauty

FRGS *abbr* Fellow of the Royal Geographical Society

Fri *abbr* Friday

fri·a·ble \'frī-ə-bəl\ *adj* [MF or L; MF, fr. L *friabilis*, fr. *friare* to crumble] : easily crumbled or pulverized <~ soil> ***syn*** see FRAGILE — **fri·a·bil·i·ty** \ˌfrī-ə-'bil-ət-ē\ *n* — **fri·a·ble·ness** *n*

fri·ar \'frī(-ə)r\ *n* [ME *frere, fryer*, fr. OF *frere*, lit., brother, fr. L *fratr-, frater* — more at BROTHER] : a member of a mendicant order

fri·ar·ly \-lē\ *adj* : resembling a friar : relating to friars

friar's lantern *n* : IGNIS FATUUS

fri·ary \'frī(-ə)r-ē\ *n, pl* **-ar·ies** : a monastery of friars

1frib·ble \'frib-əl\ *vb* **frib·bled; frib·bling** \-(ə-)liŋ\ [origin unknown] *vi* : TRIFLE, DODDER ~ *vt* : to trifle or fool away

2fribble *n* : a frivolous person, thing, or idea : TRIFLER — **fribble** *adj*

fric·an·deau \'frik-ən-ˌdō\ *n* [F] : larded veal roasted and glazed in its own juices

1fric·as·see \'frik-ə-ˌsē, ˌfrik-ə-'\ *n* [MF, fr. fem. of *fricassé*, pp. of *fricasser* to fricassee] : a dish made of cut-up pieces of meat (as chicken or veal) stewed in a gravy

2fricassee *vt* **-seed; -see·ing** : to cook as a fricassee

fric·a·tive \'frik-ət-iv\ *n* [L *fricatus*, pp. of *fricare*] : a consonant characterized by frictional passage of the expired breath through a narrowing at some point in the vocal tract <\f v th t͟h s z sh zh h\ are ~*s*> — **fricative** *adj*

fric·tion \'frik-shən\ *n* [MF or L; MF, fr. L *friction-, frictio*, fr. *frictus*, pp. of *fricare* to rub; akin to L *friare* to crumble, Skt *bhriṇanti* they injure] **1 a** : the rubbing of one body against another **b** : resistance to relative motion between two bodies in contact **2** : the clashing between two persons or parties of opposed views : DISAGREEMENT — **fric·tion·less** \-ləs\ *adj* — **fric·tion·less·ly** *adv*

fric·tion·al \'frik-shnəl, -shən-ᵊl\ *adj* **1** : of or relating to friction **2** : moved or produced by friction — **fric·tion·al·ly** \-ē\ *adv*

friction clutch *n* : a clutch in which connection is made through sliding friction

friction drive *n* : an automobile power-transmission system that transmits motion by surface friction instead of teeth and provides a full range of variation in desired speed ratios

friction match *n* : 3MATCH 2

friction tape *n* : a usu. cloth tape impregnated with water-resistant insulating material and an adhesive and used esp. to protect, insulate, and support electrical conductors

Fri·day \'frīd-ē\ *n* [ME, fr. OE *frīgedæg*; akin to OHG *frīatag*; both fr. a prehistoric WGmc compound whose components are akin to OHG *Frīa*, goddess of love and to OE *dæg* day] : the sixth day of the week — **Fri·days** \-ēz\ *adv*

fridge *also* **frig** \'frij\ *n* [by shortening & alter.] *chiefly Brit* : REFRIGERATOR

fried·cake \'frīd-ˌkāk\ *n* : DOUGHNUT, CRULLER

1friend \'frend\ *n* [ME *frend*, fr. OE *frēond*; akin to OHG *friunt* friend; both fr. the prp. of a prehistoric Gmc verb represented by OE *frēon* to love; akin to OE *frēo* free] **1 a** : one attached to another by affection or esteem **b** : ACQUAINTANCE **2 a** : one that is not hostile **b** : one that is of the same nation, party, or group **3** : one that favors or promotes something (as a charity) **4** *obs* : PARAMOUR **5** *cap* : a member of a Christian sect that stresses Inner Light, rejects sacraments and an ordained ministry, and opposes war — called also *Quaker* — **friend·less** \'fren-(d)ləs\ *adj* — **friend·less·ness** *n*

2friend *vt* : to act as the friend of : BEFRIEND

friend·li·ly \'fren-(d)lə-lē\ *adv* : in a friendly manner

1friend·ly \'fren-(d)lē\ *adj* **friend·li·er; -est** : of, relating to, or befitting a friend: as **a** : showing kindly interest and goodwill **b** : not hostile **c** : inclined to favor **d** : CHEERFUL, COMFORTING ***syn*** see AMICABLE ***ant*** unfriendly, belligerent — **friend·li·ness** *n*

2friendly *adv* : in a friendly manner : AMICABLY

3friendly *n, pl* **friendlies** : one that is friendly; *esp* : a native who is friendly to settlers or invaders

friendship \'fren(d)-ˌship\ *n* **1** : the state of being friends **2** : the quality or state of being friendly : FRIENDLINESS **3** *obs* : AID

fri·er *var of* FRYER

Frie·sian \'frē-zhən\ *n, chiefly Brit* : HOLSTEIN

1frieze \'frēz *or (compare* FRISÉ*)* frē-'zā\ *n* [ME *frise*, fr. MF, fr. MD *vriese*] **1** : a heavy durable coarse wool and shoddy fabric with a rough surface **2** : a pile surface of uncut loops or of patterned cut and uncut loops

2frieze \'frēz\ *n* [MF, perh. fr. ML *phrygium, frisium* embroidered cloth, fr. L *phrygium*, fr. neut. of *Phrygius* Phrygian, fr. *Phrygia*] **1** : the part of an entablature between the architrave and the cornice — see ENTABLATURE illustration **2** : a sculptured or richly ornamented band (as on a building) **3** : a band, line, or series suggesting a frieze <a constant ~ of visitors wound its way around the . . . ruins —Mollie Panter-Downes>

frieze 2

frig \'frig\ *vi* **frigged; frig·ging** [prob. fr. E dial. *frig* to rub] : COPULATE — usu. considered vulgar

frig·ate \'frig-ət\ *n* [MF, fr. OIt *fregata*] **1** : a light boat propelled orig. by oars but later by sails **2** : a square-rigged war vessel intermediate between a corvette and a ship of the line **3** : a British or Canadian escort ship between a corvette and a destroyer in size **4** : a U.S. warship of 5000 to 7000 tons that is smaller than a cruiser and larger than a destroyer

frigate bird *n* : any of several strong-winged seabirds (family Fregatidae) noted for their rapacious habits

Frig·ga \'frig-ə\ *n* [ON *Frigg*] : the Norse goddess of married love and of the hearth who shares dominion of the heavens with her husband Odin

1fright \'frīt\ *n* [ME, fr. OE *fyrhto, fryhto*; akin to OHG *forhta* fear] **1** : fear excited by sudden danger : ALARM **2** : something strange, ugly, or shocking <his beard was a ~> ***syn*** see FEAR

2fright *vt* : to alarm suddenly : FRIGHTEN

fright·en \'frīt-ᵊn\ *vb* **fright·ened; fright·en·ing** \'frīt-niŋ, -ᵊn-iŋ\ *vt* **1** : to make afraid : TERRIFY **2** : to drive or force by frightening <~*ed* the boy into confessing> ~ *vi* : to become frightened — **fright·en·ing·ly** \-niŋ-lē, -ᵊn-iŋ-\ *adv*

fright·ful \'frīt-fəl\ *adj* **1** : causing intense fear or alarm : TERRIFYING **2** : causing shock or horror : STARTLING **3** : EXTREME <~ thirst> ***syn*** see FEARFUL — **fright·ful·ly** \-fə-lē\ *adv* — **fright·ful·ness** *n*

fright wig *n* : a wig with hair that stands out from the head

frig·id \'frij-əd\ *adj* [L *frigidus*, fr. *frigēre* to be cold; akin to L *frigus* frost, cold, Gk *rhigos*] **1 a** : intensely cold **b** : lacking warmth or ardor : INDIFFERENT **2** : lacking imaginative qualities : INSIPID **3** : abnormally averse to sexual intercourse — used esp. of women — **frig·id·ly** *adv* — **frig·id·ness** *n*

Frig·i·daire \ˌfrij-ə-'da(ə)r, -'de(ə)r\ *trademark* — used for a mechanical refrigerator

fri·gid·i·ty \frij-'id-ət-ē\ *n* : the quality or state of being frigid; *specif* : marked or abnormal sexual indifference esp. in a woman

frigid zone *n* : the area or region between the arctic circle and the north pole or between the antarctic circle and the south pole

frig·o·rif·ic \ˌfrig-ə-'rif-ik\ *adj* [L *frigorificus*, fr. *frigor-, frigus* frost] : causing cold : CHILLING

fri·jol \frē-'hōl, 'frē-ˌ\ *also* **fri·jo·le** \frē-'hō-lē\ *n, pl* **fri·jo·les** \frē-'hō-lēz, 'frē-ˌ\ [AmerSp *frijol*] *chiefly Southwest* : BEAN 1b

1frill \'fril\ *vt* : to provide or decorate with a frill

[2]frill *n* [perh. fr. Flem *frul*] **1 a :** a gathered, pleated, or bias-cut fabric edging used on clothing **b :** a strip of paper curled at one end and rolled to be slipped over the bone end (as of a chop) in serving **2 :** a ruff of hair or feathers about the neck of an animal **3 a :** AFFECTATION, AIR — usu. used in pl. <an honest . . . man who had no ~*s*, . . . no nonsense about him —W. A. White> **b :** something decorative but not essential : LUXURY — **frilly** \ˈfril-ē\ *adj*

[1]fringe \ˈfrinj\ *n, often attrib* [ME *frenge*, fr. MF, fr. (assumed) VL *frimbia*, fr. L *fimbriae* (pl.)] **1 :** an ornamental border consisting of short straight or twisted threads or strips hanging from cut or raveled edges or from a separate band **2 a :** something resembling a fringe : BORDER **b :** one of various light or dark bands produced by the interference or diffraction of light **3 a :** something that is marginal, additional, or secondary to some activity, process, or subject matter **b :** a group with marginal or extremist views **c :** FRINGE BENEFIT

[2]fringe *vt* **fringed; fring·ing** \ˈfrin-jiŋ\ **1 :** to furnish or adorn with a fringe **2 :** to serve as a fringe for : BORDER

fringe area *n* **:** a region in which reception from a given broadcasting station is weak or subject to serious distortion

fringe benefit *n* **:** an employment benefit (as a pension, a paid holiday, or health insurance) granted by an employer that involves a money cost without affecting basic wage rates

fringe tree *n* **:** a small tree (*Chionanthus virginica*) of the olive family that has clusters of white flowers and occurs in the southern U.S. but is widely planted elsewhere

fringy \ˈfrin-jē\ *adj* **fring·i·er; -est :** adorned with or resembling fringes

[1]frip·pery \ˈfrip-(ə-)rē\ *n, pl* **-per·ies** [MF *friperie*, deriv. of ML *faluppa* piece of straw] **1** *obs* **a :** cast-off clothes **b :** a place where old clothes are sold **2 a :** FINERY; *esp* **:** something showy, tawdry, or nonessential **b :** affected elegance : OSTENTATION

[2]frippery *adj* **:** TRIFLING, TAWDRY

Fris·bee \ˈfriz-bē\ *trademark* — used for a plastic disk several inches in diameter sailed between players by a flip of the wrist

fri·sé \frē-ˈzā\ *n* [F, fr. pp. of *friser* to curl] **:** FRIEZE

Frise aileron \ˈfrēz-\ *n* [Leslie George *Frise* b1897 E engineer] **:** an aileron having a nose portion projecting ahead of the hinge axis and a lower surface in line with the lower surface of the wing

fri·sette \frē-ˈzet\ *n* [F] *archaic* **:** a fringe of hair or curls worn on the forehead by women

fri·seur \frē-ˈzər\ *n* [F] **:** HAIRDRESSER

[1]Fri·sian \ˈfrizh-ən, ˈfrē-zhən\ *adj* [L *Frisii* Frisians] **:** of, relating to, or characteristic of Friesland, the Frisians, or Frisian

[2]Frisian *n* **1 :** a member of a people that inhabit principally the Netherlands province of Friesland and the Frisian islands in the North sea **2 :** the Germanic language of the Frisian people

[1]frisk \ˈfrisk\ *vb* [obs. *frisk* (lively)] *vi* **:** to leap, skip, or dance in a lively or playful way : GAMBOL ~ *vt* **:** to search (a person) for something (as a concealed weapon) by running the hand rapidly over the clothing and through the pockets — **frisk·er** *n*

[2]frisk *n* **1 a** *archaic* **:** CARACOLE, CAPER **b :** GAMBOL, ROMP **c :** DIVERSION **2 :** an act of frisking

frisk·i·ly \ˈfris-kə-lē\ *adv* **:** in a frisky manner

frisky \ˈfris-kē\ *adj* **frisk·i·er; -est :** inclined to frisk : FROLICSOME — **frisk·i·ness** *n*

fris·son \frē-ˈsōⁿ\ *n, pl* **frissons** \-ˈsōⁿ(z)\ [F] **:** SHUDDER, THRILL

[1]frit \ˈfrit\ *n* [It *fritta*] **1 :** the calcined or partly fused materials of which glass is made **2 :** any of various chemically complex glasses used ground esp. to introduce soluble or unstable ingredients into glazes or enamels

[2]frit *vt* **frit·ted; frit·ting 1 :** to prepare (materials for glass) by heat : FUSE **2 :** to convert into a frit

frith \ˈfrith\ *n* **:** FIRTH

frit·il·lar·ia \ˌfrit-ᵊl-ˈer-ē-ə, -ˈar-\ *n* [NL, fr. L *fritillus* dice cup; fr. the markings of the petals] **:** any of a genus (*Fritillaria*) of bulbous herbs of the lily family with mottled or checkered flowers

frit·il·lary \ˈfrit-ᵊl-ˌer-ē\ *n, pl* **-lar·ies** [NL *fritillaria*] **1 :** FRITILLARIA **2 :** any of numerous nymphalid butterflies (esp. genera *Argynnis* and *Speyeria*) that usu. are orange with black spots on the upper side of both wings and silver spotted on the underside of the hind wing

[1]frit·ter \ˈfrit-ər\ *n* [ME *fritour*, fr. MF *friture*, fr. (assumed) VL *frictura*, fr. *frictus*, pp. of *frigere* to fry — more at FRY] **:** a small quantity of fried or sautéed batter often containing fruit or meat

[2]fritter *vb* [*fritter*, n. (fragment, shred)] *vt* **1 :** to spend or waste bit by bit, on trifles, or without commensurate return <~*ing* away our natural resources> **2 :** to break into small fragments ~ *vi* **:** DISSIPATE, DWINDLE ***syn*** see WASTE — **frit·ter·er** \-ər-ər\ *n*

friv·ol \ˈfriv-əl\ *vi* **-oled** *or* **-olled; -ol·ing** *or* **-ol·ling** \-(ə-)liŋ\ [back-formation fr. *frivolous*] **:** to act frivolously : TRIFLE — **friv·ol·er** *or* **friv·ol·ler** \-(ə-)lər\ *n*

fri·vol·i·ty \friv-ˈäl-ət-ē\ *n, pl* **-ties 1 :** the quality or state of being frivolous **2 :** a frivolous act or thing ***syn*** see LIGHTNESS ***ant*** staidness

friv·o·lous \ˈfriv-(ə-)ləs\ *adj* [ME, fr. L *frivolus*] **1 :** of little weight or importance **2 a :** lacking in seriousness : irresponsibly self-indulgent **b :** marked by unbecoming levity — **friv·o·lous·ly** *adv* — **friv·o·lous·ness** *n*

[1]frizz \ˈfriz\ *vb* [F *friser*] *vt* **:** to form into small tight curls ~ *vi, of hair* **:** to form a mass of tight curls

[2]frizz *n* **1 :** a tight curl **2 :** hair that is tightly curled

[3]frizz *vb* [alter. of [1]FRY] *vt* **:** to fry or sear with a sizzling noise ~ *vi* **:** SIZZLE

friz·i·ly \ˈfriz-ə-lē\ *adv* **:** in a frizzy manner

[1]friz·zle \ˈfriz-əl\ *vb* **friz·zled; friz·zling** \-(ə-)liŋ\ [prob. akin to OE *frīs* curly, OFris *frisle* curl] **:** FRIZZ, CURL

[2]frizzle *n* **:** a crisp curl

[3]frizzle *vb* **friz·zled; friz·zling** [[1]*fry* + *sizzle*] *vt* **1 :** to fry until crisp and curled **2 :** BURN, SCORCH ~ *vi* **:** to cook with a sizzling noise

friz·zly \ˈfriz-(ə-)lē\ *adj* **friz·zli·er; -est :** FRIZZY

frizzy *adj* **frizz·i·er; -est :** tightly curled — **frizz·i·ness** *n*

[1]fro \frə, (ˈ)frō\ *prep* [ME, fr. ON *frā*; akin to OE *from*] *dial Brit* **:** FROM

[2]fro \ˈfrō\ *adv* **:** BACK, AWAY — used in the phrase *to and fro*

[1]frock \ˈfräk\ *n* [ME *frok*, fr. MF *froc*, of Gmc origin; akin to OHG *hroch* mantle, coat] **1 :** an outer garment worn by monks and friars : HABIT **2 :** an outer garment worn chiefly by men: **a :** a long loose mantle **b :** a workman's outer shirt; *esp* **:** SMOCK FROCK **c :** a woolen jersey worn esp. by sailors **3 :** a woman's dress

[2]frock *vt* **1 :** to clothe in a frock **2 :** to make a cleric of

frock coat *n* **:** a man's usu. double-breasted coat having knee-length skirts front and back

froe \ˈfrō\ *n* [perh. alter. of obs. *froward* turned away, fr. ME; fr. the position of the handle] **:** a cleaving tool for splitting cask staves and shingles from the block

frog \ˈfrȯg, ˈfräg\ *n* [ME *frogge*, fr. OE *frogga*; akin to OHG *frosk* frog, Skt *pravate* he jumps up] **1 :** any of various smooth-skinned web-footed largely aquatic tailless agile leaping amphibians (as of the suborder Diplasiocoela) — compare TOAD **2 :** a condition in the throat that produces hoarseness <had a ~ in his throat> **3 :** the triangular elastic horny pad in the middle of the sole of the foot of a horse — see HOOF illustration **4 a :** a loop attached to a belt to hold a weapon or tool **b :** an ornamental braiding for fastening the front of a garment that consists of a button and a loop through which it passes **5 :** a device permitting the wheels on one rail of a track to cross an intersecting rail **6 :** the nut of a violin bow — see BOW illustration **7 :** a small holder (as of metal, glass, or plastic) with perforations or spikes for holding flowers in place in a bowl or vase

frog 4b

frog·eye \-ˌī\ *n* **:** any of numerous leaf diseases characterized by concentric rings about the diseased spots

frog·hop·per \-ˌhäp-ər\ *n* **:** SPITTLEBUG

frog kick *n* **:** a breaststroke kick that is executed with the knees pointed outward

frog·man \ˈfrȯg-ˌman, ˈfräg-, -mən\ *n* **:** a person equipped (as with face mask, flippers, and air supply) for extended periods of underwater swimming; *esp* **:** a person so equipped for military reconnaissance and demolition

frog spit *n* **1 :** CUCKOO SPIT 1 **2 :** an alga that forms slimy masses on quiet water

[1]frol·ic \ˈfräl-ik\ *adj* [D *vroolijk*, fr. MD *vrolijc*, fr. *vro* happy; akin to OHG *frō* happy, OE *frogga* frog] **:** full of fun : MERRY

[2]frolic *vi* **frol·icked; frol·ick·ing 1 :** to make merry **2 :** to play and run about happily : ROMP

[3]frolic *n* **1 :** a playful mischievous action **2 a :** FUN, MERRIMENT **b :** PARTY

frol·ic·some \ˈfräl-ik-səm\ *adj* **:** full of gaiety : SPORTIVE

from \(ˈ)frəm, ˈfräm *also* fəm\ *prep* [ME, fr. OE; akin to OHG *fram*, adv., forth, away, OE *faran* to go — more at FARE] **1** — used as a function word to indicate a starting point: as (1) a place where a physical movement begins <came here ~ the city> (2) a starting point in measuring or reckoning or in a statement of limits <a week ~ today> <cost ~ $5 to $10> **2** — used as a function word to indicate separation: as (1) physical separation (2) an act or condition of removal, abstention, exclusion, release, or differentiation <protection ~ the sun> <relief ~ anxiety> **3** — used as a function word to indicate the source, cause, agent, or basis <a call ~ my lawyer> <inherited a love of music ~ his father> <read ~ his new book of poems> <worked hard ~ necessity>

frond \ˈfränd\ *n* [L *frond-, frons* foliage] **1 :** LEAF; *esp* **:** the leaf of a palm **2 a :** a thallus or thalloid shoot resembling a leaf **b :** the leaf of a fern — **frond·ed** \ˈfrän-dəd\ *adj*

fron·deur \frōⁿ-ˈdər\ *n* [F, slinger, participant in a 17th cent. revolt in which the rebels were compared to schoolboys using slings only when the teacher was not looking] **:** REBEL, MALCONTENT

fron·dose \ˈfrän-ˌdōs\ *adj* **:** bearing or resembling fronds — **fron·dose·ly** *adv*

[1]front \ˈfrənt\ *n* [ME, fr. OF, fr. L *front-, frons* — more at BRINK] **1 a :** FOREHEAD; *also* **:** the whole face **b** (1) **:** demeanor or bearing esp. in the face of danger or other trial (2) **:** external and often feigned appearance (3) **:** an artificial or self-important manner **2 a** (1) **:** VANGUARD (2) **:** a line of battle (3) *often cap* **:** a zone of conflict between armies (4) **:** lateral space occupied by a military unit **b** (1) **:** a stand in reference to some issue : POLICY — usu. used with *change* (2) **:** a sphere of activity <progress on the educational ~> (3) **:** a movement linking divergent elements to achieve certain common objectives; *esp* **:** a political coalition <and to create a popular democratic ~ —*Collier's Yr. Bk.*> **3 :** a side of a building; *esp* **:** the side that contains the principal entrance **4 a :** the forward part or surface **b** (1) **:** FRONTAGE (2) **:** a beach promenade at a seaside resort **c :** DICKEY 1a **d :** the boundary between two dissimilar air masses **5** *archaic* **:** BEGINNING **6 a** (1) **:** a position ahead of a person or of the foremost part of a thing (2) — used as a call by a hotel desk clerk in summoning a bellboy **b :** a position of leadership or superiority **7 a :** a person, group, or thing used to mask the identity or true character or activity of the actual controlling agent **b :** a person who serves as the nominal head or spokesman of an enterprise or group to lend it prestige — **in front of :** directly before or ahead of <watching the road *in front of* him> — **out front :** in the audience — **up front :** in the frontcourt; *specif* **:** in the position of forward or center

ə abut ᵊ kitten ər further a back ā bake ä cot, cart
aù out ch chin e less ē easy g gift i trip ī life
j joke ŋ sing ō flow ȯ flaw ȯi coin th thin t͟h this
ü loot ù foot y yet yü few yù furious zh vision

2front *vi* **1 :** FACE <the house ~*s* toward the east> — often used with *on* <a ten-acre plot ~*ing* on a lake —*Current Biog.*> **2 :** to serve as a front <~*ing* for special interests> ~ *vt* **1 a :** CONFRONT <went to the woods because I wished . . . to ~ only the essential facts of life —H. D. Thoreau> **b :** to appear before <daily ~*ed* him in some fresh splendor —Alfred Tennyson> **2 :** to be in front of <lawn ~*ing* the house> **3 :** to supply a front to <~*ed* the building with bricks> **4 :** to face toward <the house ~*s* the street> **5 :** to articulate (a sound) with the tongue farther forward

3front *adj* **1 :** of, relating to, or situated at the front **2 :** articulated at or toward the front of the oral passage <~ vowels> **3 :** constituting the first nine holes of an 18-hole golf course — **front** *adv*

4front *abbr* frontispiece

front·age \'frənt-ij\ *n* **1 a :** a piece of land that fronts **b :** the land between the front of a building and the street **2 :** the front side of a building **3 :** the act or fact of facing a given way

frontage road *n* **:** a local street or road that generally parallels an expressway or through street and that provides access to property isolated from the expressway through access controls — called also *service road*

1fron·tal \'frənt-ᵊl\ *n* **1** [ME *frontel*, fr. ML *frontellum*, dim. of L *front-, frons*] **:** a cloth hanging over the front of an altar **2 :** FACADE

2frontal *adj* [NL *frontalis*, fr. L *front-, frons*] **1 :** of, relating to, or adjacent to the forehead or the frontal bone **2 a :** of, relating to, or situated at the front **b :** directed against the front or at the main point or issue **:** DIRECT <~ assault> **3 :** parallel to the main axis of the body and at right angles to the sagittal plane **4 :** of or relating to a meteorological front — **fron·tal·ly** \-ᵊl-ē\ *adv*

frontal bone *n* **:** either of a pair of membrane bones forming the forehead

fron·tal·i·ty \ˌfrən-'tal-ət-ē\ *n* **1** *sculpture* **:** a schematic composition of the front view that is complete without lateral movement **2** *painting* **:** the depiction of an object, figure, or scene in a plane parallel to the plane of the picture surface

frontal lobe *n* **:** the anterior division of each cerebral hemisphere

front·court \'frənt-'kō(ə)rt, -'kȯ(ə)rt\ *n* **:** a basketball team's offensive half of the court; *also* **:** the positions of forward and center on a basketball team

front dive *n* **:** a dive from a position facing the water

front–end load *n* **:** the part of the total load taken out of early payments under a contract plan for the periodic purchase of investment-company shares

fron·te·nis \ˌfrən-'ten-əs, frän-\ *n* [AmerSp, blend of *frontón* pelota court and *tenis* tennis] **:** a game of Mexican origin played with rackets and a rubber ball on a 3-walled court

fron·tier \ˌfrən-'ti(ə)r, 'frən-ˌ, frän-', 'frän-ˌ\ *n* [ME *fronter*, fr. MF *frontiere*, fr. *front*] **1 a :** a border between two countries **b** *obs* **:** a stronghold on a frontier **2 a :** a region that forms the margin of settled or developed territory **b :** the farthermost limits of knowledge or achievement with respect to a particular subject **c :** a new field that offers scope for exploitative or developmental activity — **frontier** *adj*

fron·tiers·man \ˌfrən-'ti(ə)rz-mən, frän-\ *n* **:** a man living on the frontier

fron·tis·piece \'frənt-ə-ˌspēs\ *n* [MF *frontispice*, fr. LL *frontispicium*, lit., view of the front, fr. L *front-, frons* + *-i-* + *specere* to look at — more at SPY] **1 a :** the principal front of a building **b :** a decorated pediment over a portico or window **2 :** an illustration preceding and usu. facing the title page of a book or magazine

front·less \'frənt-ləs\ *adj, archaic* **:** SHAMELESS

front·let \-lət\ *n* [ME *frontlette*, fr. MF *frontelet*, dim. of *frontel*, fr. L *frontale*, fr. *front-, frons*] **1 :** a band or phylactery worn on the forehead **2 :** FOREHEAD; *esp* **:** the forehead of a bird when distinctively marked

front–line *adj* **1 :** situated or suitable for use at a military front <~ ambulances> **2 a :** of or relating to the most advanced or significant activity or procedure in a field or enterprise **b :** relating to or being proficient or competent in a field <~ teachers>; *also* **:** FIRST-STRING <~ catchers>

front line *n* **1 :** a military line formed by the most advanced tactical combat units; *also* **:** FRONT **2 :** the most advanced, responsible, or significant position in a field or activity

front man *n* **:** a person serving as a front or figurehead

front matter *n* **:** matter preceding the main text of a book

fronto- *comb form* [ISV, fr. L *front-, frons*] **1 :** frontal and <*fronto*parietal> **2** [1*front*] **:** boundary of an air mass <*fronto*genesis>

front office *n* **:** the policy-making officials of an organization

front·o·gen·e·sis \ˌfrənt-ō-'jen-ə-səs\ *n* [NL] **:** the coming together into a distinct front of two dissimilar air masses that commonly react upon each other to induce cloud and precipitation

front·ol·y·sis \ˌfrənt-'äl-ə-səs\ *n* [NL] **:** a process tending to destroy a meteorological front

fron·ton \'frän-ˌtän\ *n* [Sp *frontón* gable, wall of a pelota court, fronton, fr. dim. of *frenta* forehead, fr. L *front-, frons*] **:** a jai alai arena

1front–page \'frənt-'pāj\ *adj* **:** very newsworthy

2front–page *vt* **:** to print or report on the front page of a newspaper

front room *n* **:** LIVING ROOM, PARLOR

front–run·ner \'frənt-'rən-ər\ *n* **1 :** a contestant who runs best when in the lead **2 :** a leading contestant in a rivalry or competition

frore \'frō(ə)r, 'frȯ(ə)r\ *adj* [ME *froren*, fr. OE, pp. of *frēosan* to freeze] **:** FROSTY, FROZEN

frosh \'fräsh\ *n, pl* **frosh** [by shortening & alter.] **:** FRESHMAN

1frost \'frȯst\ *n* [ME, fr. OE; akin to OHG *frost*, OE *frēosan* to freeze] **1 a :** the process of freezing **b :** the temperature that causes freezing **c :** a covering of minute ice crystals on a cold surface **2 a :** coldness of deportment or temperament **:** an indifferent, reserved, or unfriendly manner **b :** FAILURE <he may be a ~ as a man, but he has his ear to the ground as a newspaper pro —James Purdy>

2frost *vt* **1 a :** to cover with or as if with frost; *esp* **:** to put icing on (cake) **b :** to produce a fine-grained slightly roughened surface on (as metal or glass) **2 :** to injure or kill (as plants) by frost ~ *vi* **:** to become frosted **:** FREEZE

1frost·bite \'frȯs(t)-ˌbīt\ *vt* **-bit** \-ˌbit\; **-bit·ten** \-ˌbit-ᵊn\; **-bit·ing** \-ˌbīt-iŋ\ **:** to blight or nip with frost

2frostbite *n* **:** the freezing or the local effect of a partial freezing of some part of the body

3frostbite *adj* **:** done in cold weather <~ sailing>; *also* **:** of or relating to cold-weather sailing <~ sailors>

frost·bit·ing \-ˌbīt-iŋ\ *n* **:** the sport of sailing in cold weather

frost·ed \'frȯ-stəd\ *adj* **:** QUICK-FROZEN <~ vegetables>

frost heave *n* **:** an upthrust of ground or pavement caused by freezing of moist soil — called also *frost heaving*

frost·ing \'frȯ-stiŋ\ *n* **1 a :** ICING **b :** TRIMMING, ORNAMENTATION **2 :** lusterless finish of metal or glass **:** MAT; *also* **:** a white finish produced on glass (as by etching) **3 :** the lightening (as by chemicals) of small strands of hair throughout the entire head to produce a two-tone effect — compare STREAKING

frost·work \'frȯs-ˌtwərk\ *n* **1 :** the figures that moisture sometimes forms in freezing (as on a windowpane) **2 :** ornamentation (as on silver, glass, or paper) imitative of the figures of frostwork

frosty \'frȯ-stē\ *adj* **frost·i·er; -est 1 :** attended with or producing frost **:** FREEZING **2 :** covered or appearing as if covered with frost **:** HOARY **3 :** marked by coolness or extreme reserve in manner <his smile was distinctly ~ —Erle Stanley Gardner> — **frost·i·ly** \-stə-lē\ *adv* — **frost·i·ness** \-stē-nəs\ *n*

1froth \'frȯth\ *n, pl* **froths** \'frȯths, 'frȯt͟hz\ [ME, fr. ON *frotha*; akin to OE *āfrēothan* to froth, Gk *prēthein* to blow up] **1 a :** bubbles formed in or on a liquid **:** FOAM **b :** a foamy slaver sometimes accompanying disease or exhaustion **2 :** something unsubstantial or of little value <swayed by popular fads and ~ —Gay Talese>

2froth \'frȯth, 'frȯt͟h\ *vt* **1 :** to cause to foam **2 :** VENT, VOICE **3 :** to cover with froth ~ *vi* **1 :** to foam at the mouth **2 :** to throw froth out or up

frothy \'frȯ-thē, -t͟hē\ *adj* **froth·i·er; -est 1 :** full of or consisting of froth <~ surf> **2 a :** gaily frivolous or light in content or treatment <~ poetry> **b :** made of light thin material <~ garments> — **froth·i·ly** \-thə-lē, -t͟hə-\ *adv* — **froth·i·ness** \-thē-nəs, -t͟hē-\ *n*

frot·tage \frȯ-'täzh\ *n* [F, fr. *frotter* to rub] **:** the technique of creating a design by rubbing (as with a pencil) over an object placed underneath the paper; *also* **:** a composition so made

frou·frou \'frü-(ˌ)frü\ *n* [F, of imit. origin] **1 :** a rustling esp. of a woman's skirts **2 :** frilly ornamentation esp. in women's clothing

frow \'frō\ *var of* FROE

fro·ward \'frō-(w)ərd\ *adj* [ME, turned away, froward, fr. *fro* + *-ward*] **1 :** habitually disposed to disobedience and opposition **2** *archaic* **:** ADVERSE ***syn*** see CONTRARY ***ant*** compliant — **fro·ward·ly** *adv* — **fro·ward·ness** *n*

1frown \'fraun\ *vb* [ME *frounen*, fr. MF *froigner* to snort, frown, of Celt origin; akin to W *ffroen* nostril] *vi* **1 :** to contract the brow in displeasure or concentration **2 :** to give evidence of displeasure or disapproval by or as if by facial expression ~ *vt* **:** to show displeasure with or disapproval of esp. by facial expression — **frown·er** *n* — **frown·ing·ly** \'frau-niŋ-lē\ *adv*

syn FROWN, SCOWL, GLOWER, LOWER *shared meaning element* **:** to put on a dark or malignant countenance or aspect ***ant*** smile

2frown *n* **1 :** a wrinkling of the brow in displeasure or concentration **2 :** an expression of displeasure

frows·ty \'frau-stē\ *adj* **frowst·i·er; -est** [alter. of *frowsy*] *chiefly Brit* **:** MUSTY

frow·sy *also* **frow·zy** \'frau-zē\ *adj* **frow·si·er** *also* **frow·zi·er; -est** [origin unknown] **1 :** having a slovenly or uncared-for appearance **2 :** MUSTY, STALE

froze *past of* FREEZE

fro·zen \'frōz-ᵊn\ *adj* **1 a :** treated, affected, or crusted over by freezing **b :** subject to long and severe cold <~ north> **2 a** (1) **:** drained or incapable of emotion (2) **:** expressing or characterized by cold unfriendliness **b :** incapable of being changed, moved, or undone; *specif* **:** debarred by official action from movement or from change in status <wages were ~> **c :** not available for present use <~ capital> — **fro·zen·ly** *adv* — **fro·zen·ness** \-ᵊn-(n)əs\ *n*

frozen daiquiri *n* **:** a daiquiri beaten with shaved ice to a slushy consistency

frozen food *n* **:** food that has been subjected to rapid freezing and is kept frozen until used

FRS *abbr* **1** Federal Reserve System **2** Fellow of the Royal Society

frt *abbr* freight

fruc·ti·fi·ca·tion \ˌfrək-tə-fə-'kā-shən, ˌfrük-\ *n* **1 :** the forming or producing of fruit **2 a :** FRUIT 1d **b :** SPOROPHORE

fruc·ti·fy \'frək-tə-ˌfī, 'frük-\ *vb* **-fied; -fy·ing** [ME *fructifien*, fr. MF *fructifier*, fr. L *fructificare*, fr. *fructus* fruit] *vi* **:** to bear fruit <its seeds shall ~ —Amy Lowell> <no partnership can ~ without candor on both sides —D. M. Ogilvy> ~ *vt* **:** to make fruitful or productive <social philosophy *fructified* the political thinking of liberals at the end of the century —*Times Lit. Supp.*>

fruc·tose \'frək-ˌtōs, 'frük-, 'frük-, -ˌtōz\ *n* **1 :** a sugar $C_6H_{12}O_6$ known in three forms that are optically different with respect to polarized light **2 :** the very sweet soluble levorotatory D-form of fructose that occurs esp. in fruit juices and honey — called also *levulose*

fruc·tu·ous \'frək-chə-wəs, 'frük-\ *adj* **:** FRUITFUL <a ~ land>

fru·gal \'frü-gəl\ *adj* [MF or L; MF, fr. L *frugalis* virtuous, frugal, alter. of *frugi*, fr. dat. of *frug-, frux* fruit, value; akin to L *frui* to enjoy] **:** characterized by or reflecting economy in the expenditure of resources ***syn*** see SPARING ***ant*** wasteful — **fru·gal·i·ty** \frü-'gal-ət-ē\ *n* — **fru·gal·ly** \'frü-gə-lē\ *adv*

fru·giv·o·rous \frü-'jiv-ə-rəs\ *adj* [L *frug-, frux* + E *-vorous*]

: feeding on fruit

1fruit \ˈfrüt\ *n, often attrib* [ME, fr. OF, fr. L *fructus* fruit, use, fr. *fructus*, pp. of *frui* to enjoy, have the use of — more at BROOK] **1 a :** a product of plant growth (as grain, vegetables, or cotton) <the ~*s* of the field> **b** (1) **:** the usu. edible reproductive body of a seed plant; *esp* **:** one having a sweet pulp associated with the seed <the ~ of the tree> (2) **:** a succulent plant part used chiefly in a dessert or sweet course **c :** a dish, quantity, or diet of fruits <please pass the ~> **d :** a product of fertilization in a plant with its modified envelopes or appendages; *specif* **:** the ripened ovary of a seed plant and its contents **2 :** OFFSPRING, PROGENY **3 a :** the state of bearing fruit <a tree in ~> **b :** the effect or consequence of an action or operation **:** PRODUCT, RESULT <the ~*s* of his labor> <his work bore ~> — **fruit·ed** \-əd\ *adj*

2fruit *vi* **:** to bear fruit ~ *vt* **:** to cause to bear fruit

fruit·age \ˈfrüt-ij\ *n* **1 a :** the condition or process of bearing fruit **b :** FRUIT **2 :** the product or result of an action

fruit bat *n* **:** any of a suborder (Megachiroptera) of large Old World fruit-eating bats of warm regions — called also *flying fox*

fruit·cake \ˈfrüt-ˌkāk\ *n* **:** a rich cake containing nuts, dried or candied fruits, and spices

fruit·er·er \ˈfrüt-ər-ər\ *n* [ME, modif. of MF *fruitier*, fr. *fruit*] **:** one that deals in fruit

fruit fly *n* **:** any of various small two-winged flies whose larvae feed on fruit or decaying vegetable matter

fruit·ful \ˈfrüt-fəl\ *adj* **1 a :** yielding or producing fruit **b :** conducive to an abundant yield **2 :** abundantly productive ***syn*** see FERTILE ***ant*** unfruitful, fruitless — **fruit·ful·ly** \-fə-lē\ *adv* — **fruit·ful·ness** *n*

fruiting body *n* **:** a plant organ specialized for producing spores

fru·ition \frü-ˈish-ən\ *n* [ME *fruicioun*, fr. MF or LL; MF *fruition*, fr. LL *fruition-*, *fruitio*, fr. L *fruitus*, alter. of *fructus*, pp.] **1 :** pleasurable use or possession **:** ENJOYMENT **2 a :** the state of bearing fruit **b :** REALIZATION, ACCOMPLISHMENT

fruit·less \ˈfrüt-ləs\ *adj* **1 :** lacking or not bearing fruit **2 :** productive of no good effect **:** UNSUCCESSFUL ***syn*** see FUTILE ***ant*** fruitful — **fruit·less·ly** *adv* — **fruit·less·ness** *n*

fruit·let \-lət\ *n* **1 :** a fruit of small size **2 :** a unit of a collective fruit

fruit sugar *n* **:** FRUCTOSE 2

fruity \ˈfrüt-ē\ *adj* **fruit·i·er; -est 1 a :** relating to or resembling a fruit **b :** having the flavor of the unfermented fruit <~ wine> **2 a :** extremely effective, interesting, or enjoyable **b :** sweet or sentimental esp. to excess **3** *slang* **:** CRAZY, NUTTY, SILLY

fru·men·ty \ˈfrü-mən-tē\ *n, pl* **-ties** [ME, fr. MF *frumentee*, fr. *frument* grain, fr. L *frumentum*, fr. *frui*] **:** a dish of wheat boiled in milk and usu. flavored with sugar, spice, and raisins

frump \ˈfrəmp\ *n* [prob. fr. *frumple* (to wrinkle)] **1 :** a dowdy unattractive girl or woman **2 :** a staid, drab, old-fashioned person — **frump·ish** \ˈfrəm-pish\ *adj*

frumpy \ˈfrəm-pē\ *adj* **frump·i·er; -est :** generally uninteresting and unattractive **:** DRAB, DOWDY

1frus·trate \ˈfrəs-ˌtrāt\ *vt* **frus·trat·ed; frus·trat·ing** [ME *frustraten*, fr. L *frustratus*, pp. of *frustrare* to deceive, frustrate, fr. *frustra* in error, in vain; akin to L *fraus* fraud — more at FRAUD] **1 a :** to balk or defeat in an endeavor **b :** to induce feelings of discouragement in **2 a :** to make ineffectual **:** bring to nothing <nagging daily cares that ~ a man's aspirations> **b :** to make invalid or of no effect **:** NULLIFY

syn FRUSTRATE, THWART, FOIL, BAFFLE, BALK, CIRCUMVENT, OUTWIT *shared meaning element* **:** to come between a person and his aim or desire or to defeat another's plan ***ant*** fulfill

2frustrate *adj* **:** FRUSTRATED

frus·trat·ed *adj* **1 :** balked or discouraged in some endeavor or purpose **:** DISAPPOINTED <looked upon the critics as merely ~ writers> **2 :** filled with a sense of frustration **:** feeling deep insecurity, discouragement, or dissatisfaction <learned not to resort to aggressiveness when ~ —Ashley Montagu>

frus·trat·ing \-ˌtrāt-iŋ\ *adj* **:** tending to produce or characterized by frustration <the bungling attempt for fourteen ~ years . . . to make democracy work —W. L. Shirer> — **frus·trat·ing·ly** \-iŋ-lē\ *adv*

frus·tra·tion \(ˌ)frəs-ˈtrā-shən\ *n* **1 :** the act of frustrating **2 a :** the state or an instance of being frustrated **:** DISAPPOINTMENT **b :** a deep chronic sense or state of insecurity and dissatisfaction arising from unresolved problems or unfulfilled needs **3 :** something that frustrates

frus·tule \ˈfrəs-(ˌ)chü(ə)l, -(ˌ)t(y)ü(ə)l\ *n* [F, fr. L *frustulum*, dim. of *frustum*] **:** the 2-valved siliceous shell of a diatom

frus·tum \ˈfrəs-təm\ *n, pl* **frustums** *or* **frus·ta** \-tə\ [NL, fr. L, piece, bit — more at BRUISE] **:** the part of a cone-shaped solid next to the base that is formed by cutting off the top by a plane parallel to the base; *also* **:** the part of a solid intersected between two usu. parallel planes

frustums

fru·tes·cent \frü-ˈtes-ᵊnt\ *adj* [L *frutex* shrub + E *-escent*] **:** having or approaching the habit or appearance of a shrub **:** SHRUBBY

fru·ti·cose \ˈfrüt-i-ˌkōs\ *adj* [L *fruticosus*, fr. *frutic-*, *frutex* shrub; akin to OHG *broz* bud, OIr *broth* whisker] **:** having a shrubby bushy thallus with flattened or cylindrical branches <~ lichens> — compare CRUSTOSE, FOLIOSE

frwy *abbr* freeway

1fry \ˈfrī\ *vb* **fried; fry·ing** [ME *frien*, fr. OF *frire*, fr. L *frigere*; akin to Gk *phrygein* to roast, fry, Skt *bhrjjati* he roasts] *vt* **:** to cook in a pan or on a griddle over a fire esp. with the use of fat ~ *vi* **:** to undergo frying

2fry *n, pl* **fries 1 :** a dish of something fried **2 :** a social gathering or picnic where food is fried and eaten <a fish ~>

3fry *n, pl* **fry** [ME, prob. fr. ONF *fri*, fr. OF *frier*, *froyer* to rub, spawn — more at FRAY] **1 a :** recently hatched fishes **b :** the young of other animals **2 :** very small adult fishes **3 :** members of a group or class **:** INDIVIDUALS <small ~> <a great part of the earth is peopled with these ~ —Katherine Mansfield>

fry·er \ˈfrī(-ə)r\ *n* **:** something intended for or used in frying: as **a :** a young chicken **b :** a deep utensil for frying foods

frying pan *n* **:** a metal pan with a handle that is used for frying foods — called also *fry pan* — **out of the frying pan into the fire :** clear of one difficulty only to fall into a greater one

FS *abbr* **1** filmstrip **2** Foreign Service

FSA *abbr* **1** Fellow of the Society of Actuaries **2** Fellow of the Society of Antiquaries

FSH *abbr* follicle-stimulating hormone

FSLIC *abbr* Federal Savings and Loan Insurance Corporation

FSP *abbr* Food Stamp Program

f–stop \ˈef-ˌstäp\ *n* **:** a camera lens aperture setting indicated by an f-number

ft *abbr* **1** feet; foot **2** fort

FT *abbr* free throw

FTC *abbr* Federal Trade Commission

fth *abbr* fathom

ft lb *abbr* foot-pound

F_2 layer \ˈef-ˈtü-\ *n* **:** the upper of the two layers into which the F region of the ionosphere splits in the daytime at varying heights from about 150 to 250 miles above the earth

fubsy \ˈfəb-zē\ *adj* [obs. E *fubs* (chubby person)] **:** being chubby and somewhat squat

fuch·sia \ˈfyü-shə\ *n* [NL, genus name, fr. Leonhard *Fuchs* †1566 G botanist] **1 :** any of a genus (*Fuchsia*) of decorative shrubs of the evening-primrose family having showy nodding flowers usu. in deep pinks, reds, and purples **2 :** a vivid reddish purple

fuch·sine *or* **fuch·sin** \ˈfyük-sən, -ˌsēn\ *n* [F *fuchsine*, prob. fr. NL *Fuchsia*; fr. its color] **:** a dye that is produced by oxidation of a mixture of aniline and toluidines and yields a brilliant bluish red

1fuck \ˈfək\ *vb* [perh. of Scand origin; akin to Norw dial. *fukka* to copulate, Sw dial. *focka* to copulate, strike, push, *fock* penis; perh. akin to L *pugnus* fist, *pungere* to prick, sting, Gk *pygmē* fist] *vi* **:** COPULATE — usu. considered obscene; sometimes used in the present participle as a meaningless intensive ~ *vt* **:** to engage in coitus with — usu. considered obscene

2fuck *n* **:** an act of copulation — usu. considered obscene

1fu·coid \ˈfyü-ˌkȯid\ *adj* **:** relating to or resembling the rockweeds

2fucoid *n* **:** a fucoid seaweed or fossil

fu·cose \ˈfyü-ˌkōs, -ˌkōz\ *n* [ISV *fuc-* (fr. L *fucus*) + *-ose*] **:** an aldose sugar that occurs in bound form in the dextrorotatory D-form in various glycosides and in the levorotatory L-form in some brown algae and in mammalian polysaccharides typical of some blood groups

fu·co·xan·thine \ˌfyü-kō-ˈzan-ˌthēn\ *n* **:** a brown carotenoid pigment $C_{40}H_{60}O_6$ occurring esp. in the ova of brown algae

fu·cus \ˈfyü-kəs\ *n* [L, archil, rouge, fr. Gk *phykos* seaweed, archil, rouge, of Sem origin; akin to Heb *pūkh* antimony used as a cosmetic] **1** *obs* **:** a face paint **2** [NL, genus name, fr. L] **:** any of a genus (*Fucus*) of cartilaginous brown algae used in the kelp industry; *broadly* **:** any of various brown algae

fud \ˈfəd\ *n* **:** FUDDY-DUDDY

fud·dle \ˈfəd-ᵊl\ *vb* **fud·dled; fud·dling** \ˈfəd-liŋ, -ᵊl-iŋ\ [origin unknown] *vi* **:** to take part in a drinking bout **:** TIPPLE ~ *vt* **1 :** to make drunk **:** INTOXICATE **2 :** to make confused **:** MUDDLE

fud·dy–dud·dy \ˈfəd-ē-ˌdəd-ē\ *n, pl* **-dies** [perh. redupl. of Sc *fuddy* short-tailed animal, tail, fr. *fud* tail] **:** one who is old-fashioned, pompous, unimaginative, or concerned about trifles — **fuddy–duddy** *adj*

1fudge \ˈfəj\ *vb* **fudged; fudg·ing** [origin unknown] *vi* **1 :** to exceed the proper bounds or limits of something <feel that the author has *fudged* a little on the . . . rules for crime fiction —*Newsweek*>; *also* **:** CHEAT <*fudging* on an exam> **2 :** to fail to live up to something **:** fail to perform as expected **3 :** to avoid commitment **:** HEDGE <the government's tendency to ~ on delicate matters of policy —Claire Sterling> ~ *vt* **1 a :** to devise as a substitute or without adequate basis **:** FAKE <any chap . . . who could ~ up a yarn like that —Thomas Wood †1950> **b :** EXAGGERATE, FALSIFY <*fudged* the figures> **2 :** to fail to come to grips with <has too often blessed war, condoned injustice, *fudged* the racial issue —M. A. Kapp>

2fudge *n* **1 :** foolish nonsense — often used interjectionally to express annoyance, disappointment, or disbelief **2 :** a soft creamy candy made typically of sugar, milk, butter, and flavoring

Fue·gian \f(y)ü-ˈā-gē-ən, -ˈā-j(ē-)ən\ *n* **:** a member of an American Indian people of Tierra del Fuego

1fu·el \ˈfyü-əl\ *n, often attrib* [ME *fewel*, fr. OF *fouaille*, fr. *feu* fire, fr. LL *focus*, fr. L, hearth — more at FOCUS] **1 a :** a material used to produce heat or power by burning **b :** nutritive material **c :** a material from which atomic energy can be liberated esp. in a reactor **2 :** a source of sustenance or incentive

2fuel *vb* **-eled** *or* **-elled; -el·ing** *or* **-el·ling** *vt* **1 :** to provide with fuel **2 :** SUPPORT, STIMULATE <this movement is ~*ed* by massive grants-in-aid —Allen Schick> ~ *vi* **:** to take in fuel — often used with *up*

fuel cell *n* **:** a cell that continuously changes the chemical energy of a fuel and oxidant to electrical energy

fu·el·er \ˈfyü-ə-lər\ *n* **:** a dragster that uses specially blended fuel rather than gasoline

fuel oil *n* **:** an oil that is used for fuel and that usu. has a higher flash point than kerosine

1fug \ˈfəg\ *n* [prob. alter. of 2*fog*] **:** an odorous emanation; *esp* **:** the stuffy atmosphere of a poorly ventilated space — **fug·gy** \ˈfəg-ē\ *adj*

ə abut ᵊ kitten ər further a back ā bake ä cot, cart
au̇ out ch chin e less ē easy g gift i trip ī life
j joke ŋ sing ō flow ȯ flaw ȯi coin th thin th this
ü loot u̇ foot y yet yü few yu̇ furious zh vision

²fug *vb* **fugged; fug·ging** *vi* : to loll indoors in a stuffy atmosphere ~ *vt* : to make stuffy and odorous
fu·ga·cious \fyü-'gā-shəs\ *adj* [L *fugac-, fugax,* fr. *fugere*] **1** : lasting a short time : EVANESCENT **2** : disappearing before the usual time — used chiefly of plant parts (as stipules) other than floral organs — **fu·gac·i·ty** \-'gas-ət-ē\ *n*
fu·gal \'fyü-gəl\ *adj* : of, relating to, or being in the style of a musical fugue — **fu·gal·ly** \-gə-lē\ *adv*
-fuge \ˌfyüj\ *n comb form* [F, fr. LL *-fuga,* fr. L *fugare* to put to flight, fr. *fuga*] : one that drives away <insecti*fuge*>
¹fu·gi·tive \'fyü-jət-iv\ *adj* [ME, fr. MF & L; MF *fugitif,* fr. L *fugitivus,* fr. *fugitus,* pp. of *fugere* to flee; akin to Gk *pheugein* to flee and prob. to OHG *biogan* to bend — more at BOW] **1** : running away or intending flight <~ slave> <~ debtor> **2** : moving from place to place : WANDERING **3 a** : being of short duration **b** : difficult to grasp or retain : ELUSIVE **c** : likely to evaporate, deteriorate, change, fade, or disappear **4** : being of transient interest ***syn*** see TRANSIENT — **fu·gi·tive·ly** *adv* — **fu·gi·tive·ness** *n*
²fugitive *n* **1** : one who flees or tries to escape; *specif* : REFUGEE **2** : something elusive or hard to find
fu·gle \'fyü-gəl\ *vi* [back-formation fr. *fugleman*] *archaic* : to act as fugleman
fu·gle·man \'fyü-gəl-mən\ *n* [modif. of G *flügelmann,* fr. *flügel* wing + *mann* man] **1** : a trained soldier formerly posted in front of a line of men at drill to serve as a model in their exercises **2** : one who heads a group; *specif* : a political manager
fugue \'fyüg\ *n* [prob. fr. It *fuga* flight, fugue, fr. L, flight, fr. *fugere*] **1** : a polyphonic musical composition in which one or two themes are repeated or imitated by successively entering voices and contrapuntally developed in a continuous interweaving of the voice parts **2** : a disturbed state of consciousness in which the one affected performs acts of which he appears to be conscious but of which on recovery he has no recollection — **fugue** *vb* — **fugu·ist** \'fyü-gəst\ *n*
füh·rer *or* **fueh·rer** \'fyu̇r-ər, 'fir-\ *n* [G *führer* leader, guide, fr. MHG *vüerer* bearer, fr. *vüeren* to lead, bear, fr. OHG *fuoren* to lead; akin to OE *faran* to go — more at FARE] **1 a** : LEADER 2c(5) — used chiefly of the leader of the German Nazis **b** : a lesser Nazi party official **2** : a leader exercising tyrannical authority
fu·ji \'f(y)ü-(ˌ)jē\ *n* [*Fuji* mountain, Japan] : a spun silk clothing fabric in plain weave orig. made in Japan
¹-ful \fəl\ *adj suffix, sometimes* **-ful·ler;** *sometimes* **-ful·lest** [ME, fr. OE, fr. *full,* adj] **1** : full of <event*ful*> **2** : characterized by <peace*ful*> **3** : having the qualities of <master*ful*> **4** : -ABLE <mourn*ful*>
²-ful \ˌfu̇l\ *n suffix* : number or quantity that fills or would fill <room*ful*>
Fu·la *or* **Fu·lah** \'fü-lə\ *n, pl* **Fula** *or* **Fulas** *or* **Fulah** *or* **Fulahs** **1** : a Sudanese people of African Negroid stock and Mediterranean Caucasoid admixture **2** : a member of the Fula people
Fu·la·ni \'fü-ˌlän-ē, fü-'\ *n, pl* **Fulani** *or* **Fulanis** **1 a** : FULA 1; *esp* : the Fula of northern Nigeria and adjacent areas **b** : a member of the Fulani people **2** : the language of the Fula people
ful·crum \'fu̇l-krəm, 'fəl-\ *n, pl* **fulcrums** *or* **ful·cra** \-krə\ [LL, fr. L, bedpost, fr. *fulcire* to prop — more at BALK] **1 a** : PROP; *specif* : the support about which a lever turns **b** : one that supplies capability for action **2** : a part of an animal that serves as a hinge or support
ful·fill *or* **ful·fil** \fu̇l-'fil\ *vt* **ful·filled; ful·fill·ing** [ME *fulfillen,* fr. OE *fullfyllan,* fr. *full* + *fyllan* to fill] **1** *archaic* : to make full : FILL <her subtle, warm, and golden breath . . . ~*s* him with beatitude —Alfred Tennyson> **2 a** : to put into effect **b** : to bring to an end **c** : to measure up to : SATISFY **3 a** : to convert into reality **b** : to develop the full potentialities of ***syn*** see PERFORM, SATISFY — **ful·fill·er** *n* — **ful·fill·ment** \-mənt\ *n*
ful·gent \'fu̇l-jənt, 'fəl-\ *adj* [ME, fr. L *fulgent-, fulgens,* prp. of *fulgēre* to shine; akin to L *flagrare* to burn — more at BLACK] : dazzlingly bright — **ful·gent·ly** *adv*
ful·gu·rant \'fu̇l-g(y)ə-rənt, 'fu̇l-jə-, 'fəl-\ *adj* : flashing like lightning : DAZZLING
ful·gu·rate \-ˌrāt\ *vt* **-rat·ed; -rat·ing** [L *fulguratus,* pp. of *fulgurare* to flash with lightning, fr. *fulgur* lightning, fr. *fulgēre*] : to emit flashes of <blue eyes that *fulgurated* . . . terror, love, or hate —*New Yorker*> — **ful·gu·ra·tion** \ˌfu̇l-g(y)ə-'rā-shən, ˌfu̇l-jə-, ˌfəl-\ *n*
ful·gu·rite \'fu̇l-g(y)ə-ˌrīt, 'fu̇l-jə-, 'fəl-\ *n* [ISV, fr. L *fulgur*] : an often tubular vitrified crust produced by the fusion of sand or rock by lightning
ful·gu·rous \-rəs\ *adj* [L *fulgur*] : emitting flashes of or like lightning
ful·ham \'fu̇l-əm\ *n* [alter. of earlier *fullan,* perh. fr. *full* + *one*] *archaic* : a loaded die
fu·lig·i·nous \fyü-'lij-ə-nəs\ *adj* [LL *fuliginosus,* fr. L *fuligin-, fuligo* soot; akin to L *fumus* smoke — more at FUME] **1 a** : SOOTY **b** : OBSCURE, MURKY **2** : having a dark or dusky color — **fu·lig·i·nous·ly** *adv*
¹full \'fu̇l\ *adj* [ME, fr. OE; akin to OHG *fol* full, L *plenus* full, *plēre* to fill, Gk *plērēs* full, *plēthein* to be full] **1** : containing as much or as many as is possible or normal <a bin ~ of corn> **2 a** : complete esp. in detail, number, or duration <a ~ report> <his ~ share> <gone a ~ hour> **b** : lacking restraint, check, or qualification <~ retreat> <~ support> **c** : having all distinguishing characteristics : enjoying all authorized rights and privileges <~ member> <~ professor> **d** : not lacking in any essential : PERFECT <in ~ control of his senses> **3 a** : being at the highest or greatest degree : MAXIMUM <~ strength> <~ speed> **b** : being at the height of development <~ bloom> **4** : convexly rounded in outline <a ~ figure> **5 a** : possessing or containing a great number or amount — used with *of* <a room ~ of pictures> **b** : having an abundance of material esp. in the form of gathered, pleated, or flared parts <a ~ skirt> **c** : rich in experience <a ~ life> **6 a** : satisfied esp. with food or drink **b** : large enough to satisfy <a ~ meal> **7** *archaic* : completely weary <I am ~ of the burnt offerings of rams . . . and I delight not in the blood of bullocks, or of lambs —Isa 1:11 (AV)> **8** : having both parents in common <~ sisters> **9** : having volume or depth of sound <~ tones> **10** : completely occupied esp. with a thought or plan <~ of his own concerns> **11** : posessing a rich or pronounced quality <a food of ~ flavor> **12** — used as an intensive <wound up winning by a ~ four strokes — William Johnson> — **full·ness** *also* **ful·ness** \'fu̇l-nəs\ *n*
syn FULL, COMPLETE, PLENARY, REPLETE *shared meaning element* : containing all that is wanted or needed or possible ***ant*** empty
²full *adv* **1 a** : VERY, EXTREMELY <knew ~ well he had lied to me> **b** : ENTIRELY <swung ~ around —Morley Callaghan> **2 a** : EXACTLY <~ in the center of the sacred wood —Joseph Addison> **b** : STRAIGHT, SQUARELY <hit him ~ in the face>
³full *n* **1 a** : the utmost extent <enjoy to the ~> **b** : the highest or fullest state or degree <the ~ of the moon> **2** : the requisite or complete amount <paid in ~>
⁴full *vi, of the moon* : to become full ~ *vt* : to make full in sewing
⁵full *vt* [ME *fullen,* fr. MF *fouler,* fr. (assumed) VL *fullare,* fr. L *fullo* fuller] : to shrink and thicken (woolen cloth) by moistening, heating, and pressing
full·back \'fu̇l-ˌbak\ *n* **1** : an offensive football back used primarily for line plunges and blocking **2** : a primarily defensive player usu. stationed nearest the defended goal (as in soccer, field hockey, or rugby)
full blood *n* **1** \'fu̇l-'bləd\ : descent from parents both of one pure breed **2** \-ˌbləd\ : an individual of full blood
full–blood·ed \'fu̇l-'bləd-əd\ *adj* **1** : of unmixed ancestry : PUREBRED **2** : FLORID, RUDDY <of ~ face> **3** : FORCEFUL <~ prose style> **4 a** : lacking no particulars : GENUINE **b** : containing fullness of substance : RICH — **full–blood·ed·ness** *n*
full–blown \-'blōn\ *adj* **1 a** : being at the height of bloom **b** : fully mature **2** : possessing all the usual or necessary features <now at least a general philosophy, if not a ~ idealogy, is emerging —W. H. Jones>
full–bod·ied \-'bäd-ēd\ *adj* **1** : having a large body **2** : marked by richness and fullness esp. of flavor <a ~ wine> **3** : having importance, significance, or meaningfulness <~ study of literature>
full circle *adv* : through a series of developments that lead back to the original source, position, or situation or to a complete reversal of the original position — usu. used in the phrase *come full circle*
full–dress *adj* **1** : complete down to the last formal detail <a ~ rehearsal> **2** : carried out by all possible means
full dress *n* : the style of dress prescribed for ceremonial or formal social occasions
¹full·er \'fu̇l-ər\ *n* : one that fulls cloth
²ful·ler \'fu̇l-ər\ *n* [*fuller* (to form a groove in)] : a blacksmithing hammer for grooving and spreading iron
fuller's earth *n* : an earthy substance that consists chiefly of clay mineral but lacks plasticity and that is used in fulling cloth, as a filter medium, and as a catalyst
ful·ler's teasel *n* : TEASEL 1a
full–fash·ioned \'fu̇l-'fash-ənd\ *adj* : employing or produced by a knitting process for shaping to conform to body lines <~ hosiery>
full–fledged \-'flejd\ *adj* **1** : fully developed : TOTAL, COMPLETE <a ~ debate> **2** : having full plumage **3** : having attained complete status <~ lawyer>
full house *n* : a poker hand containing three of a kind and a pair — see POKER illustration
full–length \'fu̇l-'leŋ(k)th\ *adj* **1** : showing or adapted to the entire length esp. of the human figure <a ~ mirror> <a ~ dress> **2** : having a length as great as that which is normal or standard for an object of its kind <a ~ play>
full marks *n pl, Brit* : due credit or commendation
full moon *n* : the moon with its whole apparent disk illuminated
full·mouthed \'fu̇l-'mau̇thd, -'mau̇tht\ *adj* **1** : having a full mouth; *esp* : having a full complement of teeth **2** : uttered with full power or sound : LOUD
full nelson *n* : a wrestling hold in which both arms are thrust under the corresponding arms of an opponent and the hands clasped behind the opponent's head — compare HALF NELSON
full–scale \-'skā(ə)l\ *adj* **1** : identical to an original in proportion and size <~ drawing> **2 a** : involving full use of available resources <a ~ biography> **b** : TOTAL, COMPLETE <a ~ musical renaissance —*Current Biog.*>
full–size \-'sīz\ *adj* **1** : having the usual or normal size of its kind **2** : having the dimensions 54 inches by 75 inches — used of a bed; compare KING-SIZE, QUEEN-SIZE, TWIN-SIZE
full stop *n* : PERIOD 4a
full tilt *adv* [²*tilt*] : at high speed
full–time *adj* : employed for or involving full time <~ employees>
full time *n* : the amount of time considered the normal or standard amount for working during a given period
ful·ly \'fu̇l-(l)ē\ *adv* **1** : in a full manner or degree : COMPLETELY **2** : at least <~ nine tenths of us>
ful·mar \'fu̇l-mər, -ˌmär\ *n* [of Scand origin; akin to ON *fūlmār* fulmar, fr. *fūll* foul + *mār* gull] : an arctic seabird (*Fulmarus glacialis*) closely related to the petrels; *also* : any of several related birds of southern seas
ful·mi·nant \'fu̇l-mə-nənt, 'fəl-\ *adj* : FULMINATING 3
¹ful·mi·nate \-ˌnāt\ *vb* **-nat·ed; -nat·ing** [ME *fulminaten,* fr. ML *fulminatus,* pp. of *fulminare,* fr. L, to flash with lightning, strike with lightning, fr. *fulmin-, fulmen* lightning; akin to L *flagrare* to burn — more at BLACK] *vt* **1** : to utter or send out with denunciation **2** : to cause to explode ~ *vi* **1** : to send forth censures or invectives **2** : to make a sudden loud noise : EXPLODE — **ful·mi·na·tion** \ˌfu̇l-mə-'nā-shən, ˌfəl-\ *n* — **ful·mi·na·tor** \'fu̇l-mə-ˌnāt-ər, 'fəl-\ *n*
²fulminate *n* [*fulminic acid*] : an often explosive salt (as mercury fulminate) containing the radical CNO
ful·mi·nat·ing *adj* **1** : exploding with a vivid flash **2** : hurling denunciations or menaces **3** : coming on suddenly with great severity <~ infection>

ful·mine \ˈfu̇l-mən, ˈfəl-\ *vb, archaic* : FULMINATE

ful·some \ˈfu̇l-səm\ *adj* [ME *fulsom* copious, cloying, fr. *full* + *-som* -some] **1** : characterized by abundance : COPIOUS <describes in ~ detail —G. N. Shuster> **2** : offensive to the senses or to moral or aesthetic sensibility : DISGUSTING **3 a** : excessively complimentary or flattering : LAVISH <an admiration whose extent I did not express, lest I be thought ~ —A. J. Liebling> **b** : OBSEQUIOUS **4** : exceeding the bounds of good taste : OVERDONE <the ~ chromium glitter of the escalators dominating the central hall approaches the motorcar designer's concept of heaven —Lewis Mumford> — **ful·some·ly** *adv* — **ful·some·ness** *n*

ful·vous \ˈfu̇l-vəs, ˈfəl-\ *adj* [L *fulvus;* perh. akin to L *flavus* yellow — more at BLUE] : of a dull brownish yellow : TAWNY

Fu Man·chu mustache \ˌfü-(ˌ)man-ˈchü-\ *n* [*Fu Manchu,* Chinese villain in stories by "Sax Rohmer" (A. S. Ward †1955)] : a heavy mustache with ends that turn down to the chin

fu·ma·rase \ˈfyü-mə-ˌrās, -ˌrāz\ *n* : an enzyme that catalyzes the interconversion (as in the Krebs cycle) of fumaric acid and malic acid or their salts

fu·ma·rate \-ˌrāt\ *n* : a salt or ester of fumaric acid

fu·mar·ic acid \fyu̇-ˌmar-ik-\ *n* [ISV, fr. NL *Fumaria,* genus of herbs, fr. LL, fumitory, fr. L *fumus*] : a crystalline acid $C_4H_4O_4$ found in various plants or made synthetically and used esp. in making resins

fu·ma·role \ˈfyü-mə-ˌrōl\ *n* [It *fumarola,* modif. of LL *fumariolum,* fr. L *fumarium* smoke chamber for aging wine, fr. *fumus* fume] : a hole in a volcanic region from which hot gases and vapors issue — **fu·ma·rol·ic** \ˌfyü-mə-ˈrō-lik\ *adj*

[1]**fum·ble** \ˈfəm-bəl\ *vb* **fum·bled; fum·bling** \-b(ə-)liŋ\ [prob. of Scand origin; akin to Sw *fumla* to fumble] *vi* **1 a** : to grope for or handle something clumsily or aimlessly **b** : to make awkward attempts to do or find something <*fumbled* in his pocket for a coin> **c** : to search by trial and error **d** : BLUNDER **2** : to feel one's way or move awkwardly **3 a** : to drop or juggle or fail to play cleanly a grounder **b** : to lose hold of a football while handling or running with it ~ *vt* **1** : to bring about by clumsy manipulation **2 a** : to feel or handle clumsily **b** : to deal with in a blundering way : BUNGLE **3** : to make (one's way) in a clumsy manner **4 a** : MISPLAY <~ a grounder> **b** : to lose hold of (a football) while handling or running — **fum·bler** \-b(ə-)lər\ *n* — **fum·bling·ly** \-b(ə-)liŋ-lē\ *adv*

[2]**fumble** *n* **1** : an act or instance of fumbling **2** : a fumbled ball

[1]**fume** \ˈfyüm\ *n* [ME, fr. MF *fum,* fr. L *fumus;* akin to OHG *toumen* to be fragrant, Gk *thymos* mind, spirit] **1 a** : a smoke, vapor, or gas esp. when irritating or offensive <engine exhaust ~*s*> **b** : an often noxious suspension of particles in a gas (as air) **2** : something (as an emotion) that impairs one's reasoning <sometimes his head gets a little hot with the ~*s* of patriotism —Matthew Arnold> **3** : a state of excited irritation or anger — usu. used in the phrase *in a fume* — **fumy** \ˈfyü-mē\ *adj*

[2]**fume** *vb* **fumed; fum·ing** *vt* **1** : to expose to or treat with fumes **2** : to give off in fumes <*fuming* thick black smoke> ~ *vi* **1 a** : to emit fumes **b** : to be in a state of excited irritation or anger <he fretted and *fumed* over the delay> **2** : to rise in or as if in fumes

fu·mi·gant \ˈfyü-mi-gənt\ *n* : a substance used in fumigating

fu·mi·gate \ˈfyü-mə-ˌgāt\ *vt* **-gat·ed; -gat·ing** [L *fumigatus,* pp. of *fumigare,* fr. *fumus* + *-igare* (akin to L *agere* to drive) — more at AGENT] : to apply smoke, vapor, or gas to esp. for the purpose of disinfecting or of destroying pests — **fu·mi·ga·tion** \ˌfyü-mə-ˈgā-shən\ *n* — **fu·mi·ga·tor** \ˈfyü-mə-ˌgāt-ər\ *n*

fu·mi·to·ry \ˈfyü-mə-ˌtōr-ē, -ˌtȯr-\ *n* [ME *fumeterre,* fr. MF, fr. ML *fumus terrae,* lit., smoke of the earth, fr. L *fumus* + *terrae,* gen. of *terra* earth — more at TERRACE] : any of a genus (*Fumaria* of the family Fumariaceae, the fumitory family) of erect or climbing herbs; *esp* : a common European herb (*F. officinalis*)

[1]**fun** \ˈfən\ *n* [E dial. *fun* to hoax, perh. alter. of ME *fonnen,* fr. *fonne* dupe] **1** : what provides amusement or enjoyment; *specif* : playful often boisterous action or speech <a lively person full of ~> **2** : a mood for finding or making amusement <the teasing was all in ~> **3 a** : AMUSEMENT, ENJOYMENT <sickness takes all the ~ out of life> **b** : derisive jest : SPORT, RIDICULE <made him a figure of ~> **4** : violent or excited activity or argument <let a snake loose in the classroom; then the ~ began>

syn FUN, JEST, SPORT, GAME, PLAY *shared meaning element* : action or speech that provides amusement or arouses laughter

[2]**fun** *vi* **funned; fun·ning** : to indulge in banter or play : JOKE

[3]**fun** *adj* : providing entertainment, amusement, or enjoyment <a ~ party> <a ~ person to be with>

fu·nam·bu·lism \fyu̇-ˈnam-byə-ˌliz-əm\ *n* [L *funambulus* ropewalker, fr. *funis* rope + *ambulare* to walk] **1** : tightrope walking **2** : a show esp. of mental agility — **fu·nam·bu·list** \-ləst\ *n*

fun and games *n pl but sing or pl in constr* : light amusement : DIVERSION

[1]**func·tion** \ˈfəŋ(k)-shən\ *n* [L *function-, functio* performance, fr. *functus,* pp. of *fungi* to perform; prob. akin to Skt *bhuṅkte* he enjoys] **1** : professional or official position : OCCUPATION **2** : the action for which a person or thing is specially fitted or used or for which a thing exists **3** : one of a group of related actions contributing to a larger action; *esp* : the normal and specific contribution of a bodily part to the economy of a living organism **4** : an impressive, elaborate, or formal ceremony or social gathering **5 a** : a mathematical entity that assigns to each element of one set at least one element of the same or another set **b** : a quality, trait, or fact dependent on and varying with another **c** : SENTENTIAL FUNCTION — **func·tion·less** \-ləs\ *adj*

syn **1** FUNCTION, OFFICE, DUTY, PROVINCE *shared meaning element* : the acts or operations expected of a person or thing. FUNCTION, referable to anything living, material, or constructed, implies a definite end or purpose that the one in question serves or a particular kind of work it is intended to perform <the *function* of language is two-fold: to communicate emotion and to give information —Aldous Huxley> <the *function* of a plumbing system basically is to provide and carry away water> OFFICE is typically applied to the function or service expected of a person by reason of his trade or profession or his special relationship to others <it is the proper *office* of a parent to guide and correct his children> DUTY applies to a task or responsibility imposed by one's occupation, rank, status, or calling <the new cook performed her *duties* well> <it is the judicial *duty* of the court, to examine the whole case —R. B. Taney> PROVINCE applies to a function, office, or duty that naturally or logically falls to one <nursing does not belong to a man; it is not his *province* —Jane Austen> **2** see POWER

[2]**function** *vi* **func·tioned; func·tion·ing** \-sh(ə-)niŋ\ **1** : to have a function : SERVE <an attributive noun ~*s* as an adjective> **2** : to be in action : OPERATE <a government ~*s* through numerous divisions>

func·tion·al \ˈfəŋ(k)-shnəl, -shən-ᵊl\ *adj* **1 a** : of, connected with, or being a function **b** : affecting physiological or psychological functions but not organic structure <~ heart disease> **2** : used to contribute to the development or maintenance of a larger whole <~ and practical school courses>; *also* : designed or developed chiefly from the point of view of use <~ clothing> **3** : performing or able to perform a regular function **4** : placing related functions (as in an industry) under the direction of a specialist — **func·tion·al·ly** \-ē\ *adv*

functional calculus *n* : PREDICATE CALCULUS

functional group *n* : a characteristic reactive unit of a chemical compound

functional illiterate *n* : a person having had some schooling but not meeting a minimum standard of literacy

func·tion·al·ism \ˈfəŋ(k)-shnə-ˌliz-əm, -shən-ᵊl-ˌiz-\ *n* **1** : a philosophy of design (as in architecture) holding that form should be adapted to use, material, and structure **2** : a theory that stresses the interdependence of the patterns and institutions of a society and their interaction in maintaining cultural and social unity **3** : a doctrine or practice that emphasizes practical utility or functional relations — **func·tion·al·ist** \-shnə-ləst, -shən-ᵊl-əst\ *n* — **functionalist** *or* **func·tion·al·is·tic** \ˌfən(k)-shnə-ˈlis-tik, -shən-ᵊl-ˈis-\ *adj*

functional shift *n* : the process by which a word or form comes to be used in a second or third grammatical function <the *functional shift* of "go" from verb to adjective as in "all systems are go">

func·tion·ary \ˈfəŋ(k)-shə-ˌner-ē\ *n, pl* **-ar·ies** **1** : one who serves in a certain function **2** : one holding office in a government or political party

function word *n* : a word (as a preposition, auxiliary verb, or conjunction) expressing primarily grammatical relationship

func·tor \ˈfəŋ(k)-tər\ *n* **1** : something that performs a function or an operation **2** : a sign for a nonpropositional function

[1]**fund** \ˈfənd\ *n* [L *fundus* bottom, piece of landed property — more at BOTTOM] **1** : an available quantity of material or intangible resources : SUPPLY **2 a** : a sum of money or other resources whose principal or interest is set apart for a specific objective **b** : money on deposit on which checks or drafts can be drawn — usu. used in pl. **c** : CAPITAL **d** *pl* : the stock of the British national debt — usu. used with *the* **3** *pl* : available pecuniary resources **4** : an organization administering a special fund

[2]**fund** *vt* **1 a** : to make provision of resources for discharging the interest or principal of **b** : to provide funds for <a science program federally ~*ed*> **2** : to place in a fund : ACCUMULATE **3** : to convert into a debt that is payable either at a distant date or at no definite date and that bears a fixed interest <~ a floating debt>

[3]**fund** *abbr* fundamental

fun·da·ment \ˈfən-də-mənt\ *n* [ME, fr. OF *fondement,* fr. L *fundamentum,* fr. *fundare* to found, fr. *fundus*] **1 a** : the base on which a structure is erected **b** : an underlying ground, theory, or principle **2 a** : BUTTOCKS **b** : ANUS **3** : the part of a land surface that has not been altered by human activities

[1]**fun·da·men·tal** \ˌfən-də-ˈment-ᵊl\ *adj* **1 a** : serving as an original or generating source : PRIMARY <a discovery ~ to scientific progress> **b** : serving as a basis supporting existence or determining essential structure or function : BASIC **2 a** : of or relating to essential structure, function, or facts : RADICAL <~ change>; *specif* : of or dealing with general principles rather than practical application <~ science> **b** : adhering to fundamentalism **3 a** *of a musical chord or its position* : having the root in the bass **b** : of, relating to, or produced by the lowest component of a complex vibration **4** : of central importance : PRINCIPAL <~ purpose> **5** : belonging to one's innate or ingrained characteristics : DEEP-ROOTED <hard to spoil his ~ good humor> *syn* see ESSENTIAL — **fun·da·men·tal·ly** \-ᵊl-ē\ *adv*

[2]**fundamental** *n* **1** : something fundamental; *esp* : one of the minimum constituents without which a thing or a system would not be what it is **2 a** : the prime tone of a harmonic series **b** : the root of a chord **3** : the harmonic component of a complex wave that has the lowest frequency and commonly the greatest amplitude

fun·da·men·tal·ism \-ᵊl-ˌiz-əm\ *n* **1 a** *often cap* : a movement in 20th century Protestantism emphasizing the literally interpreted Bible as fundamental to Christian life and teaching **b** : the beliefs of this movement **c** : adherence to such beliefs **2** : a movement or attitude stressing strict and literal adherence to a set of basic principles

fun·da·men·tal·ist \-ᵊl-əst\ *n* : an adherent of fundamentalism — **fundamentalist** *adj* — **fun·da·men·tal·is·tic** \-ˌment-ᵊl-ˈis-tik\ *adj*

fundamental law *n* : the organic or basic law of a political unit as distinguished from legislative acts; *specif* : CONSTITUTION

fundamental particle *n* : ELEMENTARY PARTICLE
fundamental tissue *n* : plant tissue other than dermal and vascular tissues that consists typically of relatively undifferentiated parenchymatous and supportive cells
fun·dic \ˈfən-dik\ *adj* : of or relating to a fundus
fun·dus \ˈfən-dəs\ *n, pl* **fun·di** \-ˌdī, -ˌdē\ [NL, fr. L, bottom] : the bottom of or part opposite the aperture of the internal surface of a hollow organ: as **a** : the greater curvature of the stomach **b** : the lower back part of the bladder **c** : the large upper end of the uterus **d** : the part of the eye opposite the pupil
1**fu·ner·al** \ˈfyün-(ə-)rəl\ *adj* [ME, fr. LL *funeralis,* fr. L *funer-, funus* funeral (n.); perh. akin to ON *deyja* to die — more at DIE] **1** : of, relating to, or constituting a funeral **2** : FUNEREAL 2
2**funeral** *n* **1** : the observances held for a dead person usu. before burial or cremation **2** *chiefly dial* : a funeral sermon **3** : a funeral party in transit **4** : an end of something's existence **5** : a matter of concern to one : RESPONSIBILITY <if you get lost in the desert, that's your ~>
funeral director *n* : one whose profession is the management of funerals and who is usu. an embalmer
funeral home *n* : an establishment with facilities for the preparation of the dead for burial or cremation, for the viewing of the body, and for funerals — called also *funeral parlor*
fu·ner·ary \ˈfyü-nə-ˌrer-ē\ *adj* : of, used for, or associated with burial <a pharaoh's ~ chamber>
fu·ne·re·al \fyu̇-ˈnir-ē-əl\ *adj* [L *funereus,* fr. *funer-, funus*] **1** : of or relating to a funeral **2** : befitting or suggesting a funeral (as in solemnity) — **fu·ne·re·al·ly** \-ə-lē\ *adv*
fun·fair \ˈfən-ˌfa(ə)r, -ˌfe(ə)r\ *n, chiefly Brit* : AMUSEMENT PARK
fun·gal \ˈfəŋ-gəl\ *adj* : FUNGOUS
fungi- *comb form* [L *fungus*] : fungus <*fungi*form>
1**fun·gi·ble** \ˈfən-jə-bəl\ *n* : something that is fungible — usu. used in pl.
2**fungible** *adj* [NL *fungibilis,* fr. L *fungi* to perform — more at FUNCTION] **1** : of such a kind or nature that one specimen or part may be used in place of another specimen or equal part in the satisfaction of an obligation **2** : INTERCHANGEABLE — **fun·gi·bil·i·ty** \ˌfən-jə-ˈbil-ət-ē\ *n*
fun·gi·cid·al \ˌfən-jə-ˈsīd-ᵊl, ˌfəŋ-gə-\ *adj* : destroying fungi; *broadly* : inhibiting the growth of fungi — **fun·gi·cid·al·ly** \-ᵊl-ē\ *adv*
fun·gi·cide \ˈfən-jə-ˌsīd, ˈfəŋ-gə-\ *n* [ISV] : an agent that destroys fungi or inhibits their growth
fun·gi·form \ˈfən-jə-ˌfȯrm, ˈfəŋ-gə-\ *adj* : shaped like a mushroom
fun·go \ˈfəŋ-(ˌ)gō\ *n, pl* **fungoes** [origin unknown] : a fly ball hit esp. for practice fielding by a player who tosses a ball in the air and hits it as it comes down
fun·goid \ˈfəŋ-ˌgȯid\ *adj* : resembling, characteristic of, or being a fungus — **fungoid** *n*
fun·gous \ˈfəŋ-gəs\ *adj* **1** : of, relating to, or having the characteristics of fungi **2** : caused by a fungus
fun·gus \ˈfəŋ-gəs\ *n, pl* **fun·gi** \ˈfən-ˌjī, ˈfəŋ-ˌgī\ *also* **fun·gus·es** \ˈfəŋ-gə-səz\ *often attrib* [L] **1** : any of a major group (Fungi) of saprophytic and parasitic lower plants that lack chlorophyll and include molds, rusts, mildews, smuts, mushrooms, and usu. bacteria **2** : infection with a fungus

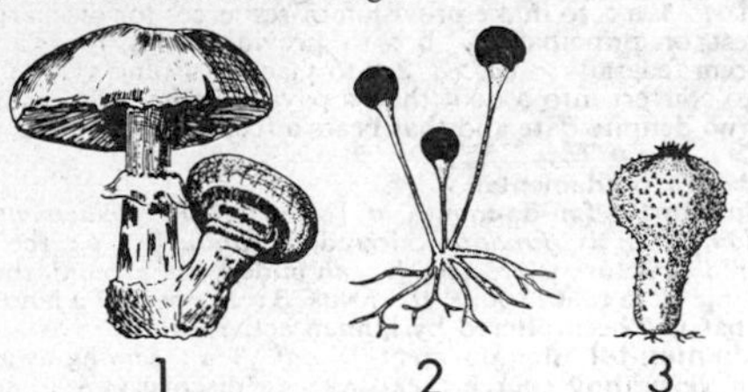

fungi 1: *1* meadow mushroom, *2* rhizopus, *3* puffball

fun house *n* : a building in an amusement park that contains various devices designed to startle or amuse
1**fu·nic·u·lar** \fyu̇-ˈnik-yə-lər, fə-\ *adj* [L *funiculus* small rope] **1** : dependent on the tension of a cord or cable **2** : having the form of or associated with a cord **3** [NL *funiculus*] : of, relating to, or being a funiculus
2**funicular** *n* : a cable railway ascending a mountain; *esp* : one in which an ascending car counterbalances a descending car
fu·nic·u·lus \-ləs\ *n, pl* **-li** \-ˌlī, -ˌlē\ [NL, fr. L, dim. of *funis* rope] **1** : a bodily structure suggesting a cord: as **a** : UMBILICAL CORD **b** : a bundle of nerve fibers **c** : SPERMATIC CORD **2** : the stalk of a plant ovule
1**funk** \ˈfəŋk\ *n* [prob. fr. obs. Flem *fonck*] **1 a** : a state of paralyzing fear **b** : a depressed state of mind **2** [3*funk*] : one that funks : COWARD <must be a bit of a ~ . . . to be afraid of a poor old lady —L. P. Hartley>
2**funk** *n* [back-formation fr. 2*funky*] : funky music
3**funk** *vi* : to become frightened and shrink back ~ *vt* **1** : to be afraid of : DREAD **2** : to shrink from undertaking or facing
funk hole *n* **1** : DUGOUT 2 **2** : a place of safe retreat
fun·kia \ˈfəŋ-kē-ə, ˈfu̇ŋ-\ *n* [NL, genus name fr. C. H. *Funck* †1839 G botanist] : PLANTAIN LILY
1**funky** \ˈfəŋ-kē\ *adj* : being in a state of funk : PANICKY
2**funky** *adj* **funk·i·er; -est** [*funk* (offensive odor)] **1** : having an offensive odor : FOUL **2** : having an earthy, unsophisticated style and feeling; *esp* : having the style and feeling of blues <~ piano playing> **3** : having an earthily sexual quality — **funk·i·ness** *n*
1**fun·nel** \ˈfən-ᵊl\ *n* [ME *fonel,* fr. OProv *fonilh,* fr. ML *fundibulum,* short for L *infundibulum,* fr. *infundere* to pour in, fr. *in-* + *fundere* to pour — more at FOUND] **1 a** : a utensil that is usu. a hollow cone with a tube extending from the smaller end and that is designed to catch and direct a downward flow **b** : something shaped like a funnel **2** : a stack or flue for the escape of smoke or for ventilation
2**funnel** *vb* **-neled** *also* **-nelled; -nel·ing** *also* **-nel·ling** *vi* **1** : to have or take the shape of a funnel **2** : to pass through or as if through a funnel ~ *vt* **1** : to form in the shape of a funnel <~*ed* his hands and shouted through them> **2** : to move to a focal point or into a central channel <contributions were ~*ed* into one account>
fun·nel·form \ˈfən-ᵊl-ˌfȯrm\ *adj* : INFUNDIBULIFORM <~ flowers>
1**fun·ny** \ˈfən-ē\ *adj* **fun·ni·er; -est** **1 a** : affording light mirth and laughter : AMUSING **b** : seeking or intended to amuse : FACETIOUS **2** : differing from the ordinary in a suspicious way : QUEER **3** : involving trickery or deception <told his prisoner not to try anything ~> ***syn*** see LAUGHABLE — **fun·ni·ly** \ˈfən-ᵊl-ē\ *adv* — **fun·ni·ness** \ˈfən-ē-nəs\ *n* — **funny** *adv*
2**funny** *n, pl* **funnies** : a comic strip or comic section of a periodical — usu. used in pl.
funny bone *n* [fr. the tingling felt when it is struck] **1** : the place at the back of the elbow where the ulnar nerve rests against a prominence of the humerus **2** : a sense of humor <tickled his *funny bone*>
funny book *n* : COMIC BOOK
funny car *n* : a specialized dragster that has a one-piece molded body resembling the body of a mass-produced car
fun·ny·man \ˈfən-ē-ˌman\ *n* : one noted for humor : COMEDIAN 2
funny paper *n* : a comic section of a newspaper
1**fur** \ˈfər\ *vb* **furred; fur·ring** [ME *furren,* fr. MF *fourrer,* fr. OF *forrer,* fr. *fuerre* sheath, of Gmc origin; akin to OHG *fuotar* sheath; akin to Gk *pōy* herd, Skt *pāti* he protects] *vt* **1** : to cover, line, trim, or clothe with fur **2** : to coat or clog as if with fur **3** : to apply furring to ~ *vi* : to become coated or clogged as if with fur
2**fur** *n, often attrib* **1** : a piece of the dressed pelt of an animal used to make, trim, or line wearing apparel **2** : an article of clothing made of or with fur **3** : the hairy coat of a mammal esp. when fine, soft, and thick; *also* : such a coat with the skin **4** : a coating resembling fur: as **a** : a coat of epithelial debris on the tongue **b** : the thick pile of a fabric (as chenille) — **fur·less** \ˈfər-ləs\ *adj*
3**fur** *abbr* furlong
fu·ran \ˈfyu̇(ə)r-ˌan, fyu̇-ˈran\ *also* **fu·rane** \ˈfyu̇(ə)r-ˌān, fyu̇-ˈrān\ *n* [ISV, fr. *furfural*] : a flammable liquid C_4H_4O that is obtained from wood oils of pines or made synthetically and is used esp. in the manufacture of nylon
fu·ra·nose \ˈfyu̇r-ə-ˌnōs, -ˌnōz\ *n* [*furan* + *-ose*] : a sugar having an oxygen-containing ring of five atoms
fu·ran·o·side \fyu̇-ˈran-ə-ˌsīd\ *n* : a glycoside containing the ring characteristic of furanose
fu·ra·zol·i·done \ˌfyu̇r-ə-ˈzäl-ə-ˌdōn\ *n* [*fur*fural + *azole* + *ide* + *-one*] : a compound $C_8H_7N_3O_5$ used esp. against parasitic infections
fur·bear·er \ˈfər-ˌbar-ər, -ˌber-\ *n* : an animal that bears fur esp. of a commercially desired quality
fur·be·low \ˈfər-bə-ˌlō\ *n* [by folk etymology fr. F dial. *farbella*] **1** : a pleated or gathered piece of material; *specif* : a flounce on women's clothing **2** : something that suggests a furbelow esp. in being showy or superfluous — **furbelow** *vt*
fur·bish \ˈfər-bish\ *vt* [ME *furbisshen,* fr. MF *fourbiss-,* stem of *fourbir,* of Gmc origin; akin to OHG *furben* to polish] **1** : to make lustrous : POLISH **2** : to give a new look to : RENOVATE — often used with *up* — **fur·bish·er** *n*
fur·cate \ˈfər-ˌkāt\ *adj* [LL *furcatus,* fr. L *furca* fork] : branching like a fork : FORKED — **fur·cate·ly** *adv*
fur·ca·tion \ˌfər-ˈkā-shən\ *n* [ML *furcation-, furcatio,* fr. *furcatus,* pp. of *furcare* to branch, fr. L *furca*] **1** : something that is branched : FORK **2** : the act or process of branching
fur·cu·la \ˈfər-kyə-lə\ *n, pl* **-lae** \-ˌlē, -ˌlī\ [NL, fr. L, forked prop, dim. of *furca*] : a forked process or part: as **a** : WISHBONE **b** : the forked leaping appendage arising from the fourth abdominal segment of a collembolan — **fur·cu·lar** \-lər\ *adj*
fur·fu·ra·ceous \ˌfər-f(y)ə-ˈrā-shəs\ *adj* [LL *furfuraceus,* fr. L *furfur* bran] : consisting of or covered with flaky particles <~ eczema>
fur·fu·ral \ˈfər-f(y)ə-ˌral\ *n* [L *furfur* + ISV *-al*] : a liquid aldehyde $C_5H_4O_2$ of penetrating odor that is usu. made from plant materials and used esp. in making furan or phenolic resins and as a solvent
fur·fur·al·de·hyde \ˌfər-f(y)ə-ˈral-də-ˌhīd\ *n* [L *furfur* + ISV *aldehyde* — more at GRIT] : FURFURAL
fur·fu·ran \ˈfər-f(y)ə-ˌran\ *n* : FURAN
fu·ri·o·so \ˌfyu̇r-ē-ˈō-(ˌ)sō, -(ˌ)zō\ *adj or adv* [It, lit., furious] : with great force or vigor — used as a direction in music
fu·ri·ous \ˈfyu̇r-ē-əs\ *adj* **1 a** : exhibiting or goaded by anger **b** : giving a stormy or turbulent appearance <~ bursts of flame from the windswept fire> **c** : marked by noise, excitement, or activity **2** : INTENSE 1a <the ~ growth of tropical vegetation> — **fu·ri·ous·ly** *adv*
1**furl** \ˈfər(-ə)l\ *vb* [MF *ferler,* fr. ONF *ferlier* to tie tightly, fr. OF *fer, ferm* tight (fr. L *firmus* firm) + *lier* to tie, fr. L *ligare* — more at LIGATURE] *vt* : to wrap or roll (as a sail or a flag) close to or around something ~ *vi* : to curl or fold as in being furled
2**furl** *n* **1** : the act of furling **2** : a furled coil
fur·long \ˈfər-ˌlȯŋ\ *n* [ME, fr. OE *furlang,* fr. *furh* furrow + *lang* long] : a unit of distance equal to 220 yards
1**fur·lough** \ˈfər-(ˌ)lō\ *n* [D *verlof,* lit., permission, fr. MD, fr. *ver-* for- + *lof* permission; akin to OE *for-* and to MHG *loube* permission — more at FOR-, LEAVE] : a leave of absence from duty granted esp. to a soldier; *also* : a document authorizing such a leave of absence
2**furlough** *vt* **1** : to grant a furlough to **2** : to lay off from work
fur·mi·ty \ˈfər-mət-ē\ *var of* FRUMENTY
fur·nace \ˈfər-nəs\ *n* [ME *furnas,* fr. OF *fornaise,* fr. L *fornac-, fornax;* akin to L *formus* warm — more at WARM] : an enclosed structure in which heat is produced (as for heating a house or for reducing ore)

fur·nish \ˈfər-nish\ *vt* [ME *furnisshen,* fr. MF *fourniss-,* stem of *fournir* to complete, equip, of Gmc origin; akin to OHG *frummen* to further, *fruma* advantage — more at FOREMOST] **1 :** to provide with what is needed; *esp* **:** to equip with furniture **2 :** SUPPLY, GIVE <~*ed* food and shelter for the refugees> — **fur·nish·er** *n*
syn FURNISH, EQUIP, OUTFIT, APPOINT, ACCOUTER, ARM *shared meaning element* **:** to supply one with what is needed (as for daily living or a particular activity)

fur·nish·ing *n* **1 :** an article or accessory of dress — usu. used in pl. **2 :** an object that tends to increase comfort or utility; *specif* **:** an article of furniture for the interior of a building — usu. used in pl.

fur·ni·ture \ˈfər-ni-chər\ *n* [MF *fourniture,* fr. *fournir*] **1 :** equipment that is necessary, useful, or desirable: as **a** *archaic* **:** the trappings of a horse **b :** movable articles used in readying an area (as a room or patio) for occupancy or use **2 :** pieces of wood or metal less than type high placed in printing forms to fill in blank spaces

fu·ror \ˈfyu̇(ə)r-ˌȯ(ə)r, -ˌō(ə)r\ *n* [MF & L; MF, fr. L, fr. *furere* to rage — more at DUST] **1 :** an angry or maniacal fit **:** RAGE **2 :** FURY 4 **3 :** a fashionable craze **:** VOGUE **4 a :** furious or hectic activity **b :** an outburst of public excitement or indignation **:** UPROAR

fu·rore \ˈfyu̇(ə)r-ˌō(ə)r, -ˌȯ(ə)r, *esp Brit* fyu̇-ˈrō-ri\ *n* [It, fr. L *furor*] **1 :** FUROR 3 **2 :** FUROR 4b

fu·ro·se·mide \fyu̇-ˈrō-sə-ˌmīd\ *n* [*fur*fural + *-osemide,* of unknown origin] **:** a powerful diuretic $C_{12}H_{11}ClN_2O_5S$ used esp. to treat edema — called also *fursemide*

furred \ˈfərd\ *adj* **1 :** lined, trimmed, or faced with fur **2 :** coated as if with fur; *specif* **:** having a coating consisting chiefly of mucus and dead epithelial cells <a ~ tongue> **3 :** bearing or wearing fur **4 :** provided with furring <~ wall>

fur·ri·er \ˈfər-ē-ər, ˈfə-rē-\ *n* **1 :** a fur dealer **2 a :** one that dresses furs **b :** one that makes, repairs, alters, or cleans fur garments

fur·ri·ery \-ə-rē\ *n* **1 :** the fur business **2 :** fur craftsmanship

fur·rin·er \ˈfər-ə-nər\ *n* [alter. of *foreigner*] *chiefly dial* **:** one not native to a community <that was a ~ come from outside —Muriel E. Sheppard>

fur·ring \ˈfər-iŋ\ *n* **1 :** a fur trimming or lining **2 a :** the application of thin wood, brick, or metal to joists, studs, or walls to form a level surface (as for attaching wallboard) or an air space **b :** the material used in this process

[1]**fur·row** \ˈfər-(ˌ)ō, -ə(-w); ˈfə-(ˌ)rō, -rə(-w)\ *n* [ME *furgh, forow,* fr. OE *furh;* akin to OHG *furuh* furrow, L *porca*] **1 a :** a trench in the earth made by a plow **b :** rural land **:** FIELD **2 :** something that resembles the track of a plow: as **a :** a marked narrow depression **:** GROOVE **b :** a deep wrinkle <~*s* in his brow>

[2]**furrow** *vt* **:** to make furrows, grooves, wrinkles, or lines in ~ *vi* **:** to make or form furrows, grooves, wrinkles, or lines

fur·ry \ˈfər-ē\ *adj* **fur·ri·er; -est 1 :** consisting of or resembling fur <animals with ~ coats> **2 :** covered with fur **3 :** thick in quality <spoke with a ~ voice>

fur seal *n* **:** any of various eared seals that have a double coat with a dense soft underfur used esp. for clothing and trimmings

fur·se·mide \ˈfər-sə-ˌmīd\ *n* **:** FUROSEMIDE

[1]**fur·ther** \ˈfər-t͟hər\ *adv* [ME, fr. OE *furthor;* akin to OHG *furthar* further; both compars. fr. the root of OE *forth*] **1 :** [1]FARTHER 1 <my ponies are tired, and I have ~ to go —Thomas Hardy> **2 :** in addition **:** MOREOVER **3 :** to a greater degree or extent <~ annoyed by a second intrusion>

[2]**further** *adj* **1 :** [2]FARTHER 1 <rode . . . across the valley and up the ~ slopes —T. E. Lawrence> **2 :** going or extending beyond **:** ADDITIONAL <~ volumes> <~ education>

[3]**further** *vt* **fur·thered; fur·ther·ing** \ˈfərt͟h-(ə-)riŋ\ **:** to help forward **:** PROMOTE <~*ed* his education in graduate school> ***syn*** see ADVANCE — **fur·ther·er** \ˈfər-t͟hər-ər\ *n*

fur·ther·ance \ˈfərt͟h-(ə-)rən(t)s\ *n* **:** the act of furthering **:** ADVANCEMENT

further education *n, Brit* **:** ADULT EDUCATION

fur·ther·more \ˈfər-t͟hə(r)-ˌmō(ə)r, -ˌmȯ(ə)r\ *adv* **:** in addition to what precedes **:** BESIDES

fur·ther·most \-ər-ˌmōst\ *adj* **:** most distant **:** FARTHEST

fur·thest \ˈfər-t͟həst\ *adv or adj* **:** FARTHEST

fur·tive \ˈfərt-iv\ *adj* [F or L; F *furtif,* fr. L *furtivus,* fr. *furtum* theft, fr. *fur* thief; akin to Gk *phōr* thief, L *ferre* to carry — more at BEAR] **1 a :** done by stealth **:** SURREPTITIOUS **b :** expressive of stealth **:** SLY <had the ~ look of one with something to hide> **2 :** obtained underhandedly **:** STOLEN ***syn*** see SECRET ***ant*** forthright, brazen — **fur·tive·ly** *adv* — **fur·tive·ness** *n*

fu·run·cle \ˈfyu̇(ə)r-ˌəŋ-kəl\ *n* [L *furunculus* petty thief, sucker, furuncle, dim. of *furon-, furo* ferret, thief, fr. *fur*] **:** a localized inflammatory swelling of the skin and underlying tissues that is caused by infection by a bacterium in a hair follicle or skin gland and that discharges pus and a central core of dead tissue **:** BOIL — **fu·run·cu·lar** \fyu̇-ˈrəŋ-kyə-lər\ *adj* — **fu·run·cu·lous** \-ləs\ *adj*

fu·run·cu·lo·sis \fyu̇-ˌrəŋ-kyə-ˈlō-səs\ *n, pl* **-lo·ses** \-ˌsēz\ **1 :** the condition of having or tending to develop multiple furuncles **2 :** a highly infectious disease of various salmonoid fishes (as trout) that is caused by a bacterium (*Bacterium salmonicida*) and is esp. virulent in dense fish populations (as in hatcheries)

fu·ry \ˈfyu̇(ə)r-ē\ *n, pl* **furies** [ME *furie,* fr. MF & L; MF, fr. L *furia,* fr. *furere* to rage — more at DUST] **1 :** intense, disordered, and often destructive rage **2 a** *cap* **:** one of the avenging deities who according to Greek mythology tormented criminals and inflicted plagues **b :** an avenging spirit **c :** one who resembles an avenging spirit; *esp* **:** a spiteful woman **3 :** extreme fierceness or violence **4 :** a state of inspired exaltation **:** FRENZY ***syn*** see ANGER

furze \ˈfərz\ *n* [ME *firse,* fr. OE *fyrs*] **:** a spiny yellow-flowered evergreen leguminous European shrub (*Ulex europaeus*); *broadly* **:** any of several related plants (genera *Ulex* and *Genista*) — **furzy** \ˈfər-zē\ *adj*

fus·cous \ˈfəs-kəs\ *adj* [L *fuscus* —more at DUSK] **:** of any of several colors averaging a brownish gray

[1]**fuse** \ˈfyüz\ *n* [It *fuso* spindle, fr. L *fusus,* of unknown origin] **1 :** a continuous train of a combustible substance enclosed in a cord or cable for setting off an explosive charge by transmitting fire to it **2** *usu* **fuze :** a mechanical or electrical detonating device for setting off the bursting charge of a projectile, bomb, or torpedo

[2]**fuse** *or* **fuze** \ˈfyüz\ *vt* **fused** *or* **fuzed; fus·ing** *or* **fuz·ing :** to equip with a fuse

[3]**fuse** *vb* **fused; fus·ing** [L *fusus,* pp. of *fundere* to pour, melt — more at FOUND] *vt* **1 :** to reduce to a liquid or plastic state by heat **2 :** to blend thoroughly by or as if by melting together **:** make indissolubly one **3 :** to stitch by applying heat and pressure with or without the use of an adhesive ~ *vi* **1 :** to become fluid with heat; *also* **:** to fail because of the blowing of a fuse **2 :** to become blended by or as if by melting together ***syn*** see MIX

[4]**fuse** *n* **:** an electrical safety device consisting of or including a wire or strip of fusible metal that melts and interrupts the circuit when the current exceeds a particular amperage

fused quartz *n* **:** QUARTZ GLASS — called also *fused silica*

fu·see \fyu̇-ˈzē\ *n* [F *fusée,* lit., spindleful of yarn, fr. OF, fr. *fus* spindle, fr. L *fusus*] **1 :** a conical spirally grooved pulley in a timepiece from which a cord or chain unwinds onto a barrel containing the spring and which by its increasing diameter compensates for the lessening power of the spring **2 :** [1]FUSE 1 **3 :** a friction match with a bulbous head not easily blown out **4 :** a red signal flare used esp. for protecting stalled trains and trucks

fu·se·lage \ˈfyü-sə-ˌläzh, -zə-\ *n* [F, fr. *fuselé* spindle-shaped, fr. MF, fr. *fusel,* dim. of *fus*] **:** the central body portion of an airplane designed to accommodate the crew and the passengers or cargo

fu·sel oil \ˈfyü-zəl-\ *n* [G *fusel* bad liquor] **:** an acrid oily liquid occurring in insufficiently distilled alcoholic liquors, consisting chiefly of amyl alcohol, and used esp. as a source of alcohols and as a solvent

fusi- *comb form* [L *fusus*] **:** spindle <*fusi*form>

fus·ible \ˈfyü-zə-bəl\ *adj* **:** capable of being fused and esp. liquefied by heat — **fus·i·bil·i·ty** \ˌfyü-zə-ˈbil-ət-ē\ *n*

fu·si·form \ˈfyü-zə-ˌfȯrm\ *adj* **:** tapering toward each end <~ bacteria>

[1]**fu·sil** \ˈfyü-zəl\ *or* **fu·sile** \ˈfyü-zəl, -ˌzīl\ *adj* [ME, fr. L *fusilis,* fr. *fusus,* pp.] **1** *archaic* **a :** made by melting and pouring into forms **:** CAST **b :** liquefied by heat **2** *archaic* **:** FUSIBLE

[2]**fusil** *n* [F, lit., steel for striking fire, fr. OF *foisil,* fr. (assumed) VL *focilis,* fr. LL *focus* fire — more at FUEL] **:** a light flintlock musket

fu·sil·ier *or* **fu·sil·eer** \ˌfyü-zə-ˈli(ə)r\ *n* [F *fusilier,* fr. *fusil*] **1 :** a soldier armed with a fusil **2 :** a member of a British regiment formerly armed with fusils

[1]**fu·sil·lade** \ˈfyü-sə-ˌläd, -ˌlād, ˌfyü-sə-ˈ, -zə-\ *n* [F, fr. *fusiller* to shoot, fr. *fusil*] **1 :** a number of shots fired simultaneously or in rapid succession **2 :** a spirited outburst esp. of criticism

[2]**fusillade** *vt* **-lad·ed; -lad·ing :** to attack or shoot down by a fusillade

fu·sion \ˈfyü-zhən\ *n, often attrib* [L *fusion-, fusio,* fr. *fusus,* pp.] **1 a :** the act or process of liquefying or rendering plastic by heat **b :** the liquid or plastic state induced by heat **2 :** a union by or as if by melting: as **a :** a merging of diverse elements into a unified whole **b :** a political partnership **:** COALITION <a ~ of the major parties> **c :** the union of atomic nuclei to form heavier nuclei resulting in the release of enormous quantities of energy when certain light elements unite

fusion bomb *n* **:** a bomb in which nuclei of a light chemical element unite to form nuclei of heavier elements with a release of energy; *esp* **:** HYDROGEN BOMB

fu·sion·ist \ˈfyüzh-(ə-)nəst\ *n* **:** one who promotes or takes part in a coalition esp. of political parties

[1]**fuss** \ˈfəs\ *n* [perh. of imit. origin] **1 a :** needless bustle or excitement **:** COMMOTION **b :** a show of flattering attention <made a big ~ over his favorite niece> **2 a :** a state of agitation esp. over a trivial matter **b :** OBJECTION, PROTEST **c :** an often petty controversy or quarrel <ended up having a pretty good ~ with my wife —Mac Hyman> ***syn*** see STIR

[2]**fuss** *vi* **1 a :** to create or be in a state of restless activity; *specif* **:** to shower flattering attentions <doting grandparents ~*ing* over the grandchildren> **b :** to pay close or undue attention to small details <~*ed* with her hair> **2 a :** to become upset **:** WORRY **b :** to express annoyance or pique **:** COMPLAIN <a mother who has to cope with ~*ing* children> ~ *vt* **:** AGITATE, UPSET — **fuss·er** *n*

fuss·bud·get \ˈfəs-ˌbəj-ət\ *n* **:** one who fusses about trifles — **fuss·bud·gety** \-ət-ē\ *adj*

fuss·pot \ˈfəs-ˌpät\ *n* **:** FUSSBUDGET

fussy \ˈfəs-ē\ *adj* **fuss·i·er; -est 1 :** easily upset **:** IRRITABLE **2 a :** requiring or giving close attention to details <~ bookkeeping procedures> **b :** revealing a concern for niceties **:** FASTIDIOUS <not ~ about food> ***syn*** see NICE — **fuss·i·ly** \ˈfəs-ə-lē\ *adv* — **fuss·i·ness** \ˈfəs-ē-nəs\ *n*

fus·tian \ˈfəs-chən\ *n* [ME, fr. OF *fustaine,* fr. ML *fustaneum,* prob. fr. *fustis* tree trunk, fr. L, club] **1 a :** a strong cotton and linen fabric **b :** a class of cotton fabrics usu. having a pile face and twill weave **2 :** pretentious and banal writing or speech ***syn*** see BOMBAST — **fustian** *adj*

fus·tic \ˈfəs-tik\ *n* [ME *fustik,* fr. MF *fustoc,* fr. Ar *fustuq,* fr. Gk *pistakē* pistachio tree — more at PISTACHIO] **1 :** the wood of a tropical American tree (*Chlorophora tinctoria*) of the mulberry family that yields a yellow dye; *also* **:** any of several similar dyewoods **2 :** a tree yielding fustic

fus·ti·gate \ˈfəs-tə-ˌgāt\ *vt* **-gat·ed; -gat·ing** [LL *fustigatus,* pp. of *fustigare,* fr. L *fustis* + *-igare* (akin to *agere* to drive) — more at

AGENT] **1 :** CUDGEL **2 :** to criticize severely — **fus·ti·ga·tion** \ˌfəs-tə-ˈgā-shən\ *n*

fus·ty \ˈfəs-tē\ *adj* [ME, fr. *fust* wine cask, fr. MF, club, cask, fr. L *fustis*] **1** *Brit* **:** impaired by age or dampness **:** MOLDY **2 :** saturated with dust and stale odors **:** MUSTY **3 :** rigidly old-fashioned or reactionary ***syn*** see MALODOROUS — **fus·ti·ly** \-tə-lē\ *adv* — **fus·ti·ness** \-tē-nəs\ *n*

fut *abbr* future

fu·thark \ˈfü-ˌthärk\ *also* **fu·thorc** *or* **fu·thork** \-ˌthȯ(ə)rk\ *n* [fr. the first six letters, *f, u,* þ (*th*), *o* (or *a*), *r, c* (=k)] **:** the runic alphabet

fu·tile \ˈfyüt-ᵊl, ˈfyü-ˌtīl\ *adj* [MF or L; MF, fr. L *futilis* that pours out easily, useless, fr. *fut-* (akin to *fundere* to pour) — more at FOUND] **1 :** serving no useful purpose **:** completely ineffective <efforts to convince him were ~> **2 :** occupied with trifles **:** FRIVOLOUS — **fu·tile·ly** \-ᵊl-(l)ē, -ˌtīl-lē\ *adv* — **fu·tile·ness** \-ᵊl-nəs, -ˌtīl-nəs\ *n*

syn FUTILE, VAIN, FRUITLESS *shared meaning element* **:** barren of results

fu·til·i·tar·i·an \fyu̇-ˌtil-ə-ˈter-ē-ən, ˌfyü-\ *n* [blend of *futile* and *utilitarian*] **:** one who believes that human striving is futile — **futilitarian** *adj* — **fu·til·i·tar·i·an·ism** \-ē-ə-ˌniz-əm\ *n*

fu·til·i·ty \fyu̇-ˈtil-ət-ē\ *n, pl* **-ties 1 :** the quality or state of being futile **:** USELESSNESS **2 :** a useless act or gesture <the *futilities* of debate for its own sake —W. A. White>

fut·tock \ˈfət-ək\ *n* [prob. alter. of *foothook* (futtock)] **:** one of the curved timbers scarfed together to form the lower part of the compound rib of a ship

futtock shroud *n* **:** a short iron rod connecting the topmast rigging with the lower mast

[1]**fu·ture** \ˈfyü-chər\ *adj* [ME, fr. OF & L; OF *futur,* fr. L *futurus* about to be — more at BE] **1 :** that is to be; *specif* **:** existing after death **2 :** of, relating to, or constituting a verb tense expressive of time yet to come

[2]**future** *n* **1 a :** time that is to come **b :** what is going to happen **2 :** an expectation of advancement or progressive development **3 :** something (as a bulk commodity) bought for future acceptance or sold for future delivery — usu. used in pl. <the use of grain ~*s* as a hedge against price changes> **4 a :** the future tense of a language **b :** a verb form in the future tense

fu·ture·less \ˈfyü-chər-ləs\ *adj* **:** having no prospect of future success

future perfect *adj* **:** of, relating to, or constituting a verb tense that is traditionally formed in English with *will have* and *shall have* and that expresses completion of an action by a specified time that is yet to come — **future perfect** *n*

fu·tur·ism \ˈfyü-chə-ˌriz-əm\ *n* **1 :** a movement in art, music, and literature begun in Italy about 1910 and marked esp. by an effort to give formal expression to the dynamic energy and movement of mechanical processes **2 :** a point of view that finds meaning or fulfillment in the future rather than in the past or present — **fu·tur·ist** \ˈfyüch-(ə-)rəst\ *n*

fu·tur·is·tic \ˌfyü-chə-ˈris-tik\ *adj* **1 :** of or relating to the future **2 :** of or relating to futurism — **fu·tur·is·ti·cal·ly** \-ti-k(ə-)lē\ *adv*

fu·tu·ri·ty \fyu̇-ˈt(y)u̇r-ət-ē, -ˈchu̇r-\ *n, pl* **-ties 1 :** time to come **:** FUTURE **2 :** the quality or state of being future **3** *pl* **:** future events or prospects **4 a :** a horse race usu. for two-year-olds in which the competitors are nominated at birth or before **b :** a race or competition for which entries are made well in advance of the event

fuze, fu·zee *var of* FUSE, FUSEE

[1]**fuzz** \ˈfəz\ *n* [prob. back-formation fr. *fuzzy*] **:** fine light particles or fibers (as of down or fluff)

[2]**fuzz** *vi* **:** to fly off in or become covered with fluffy particles ~ *vt* **1 :** to make fuzzy **2 :** to envelop in a haze **:** BLUR

[3]**fuzz** *n* [origin unknown] **:** POLICE; *also* **:** a police officer

fuzzy \ˈfəz-ē\ *adj* **fuzz·i·er; -est** [perh. fr. LG *fussig* loose, spongy; akin to OHG *fūl* rotten — more at FOUL] **1 :** marked by or giving a suggestion of fuzz <a ~ covering of felt> **2 :** not clear **:** INDISTINCT <moving the camera causes ~ photos> — **fuzz·i·ly** \ˈfəz-ə-lē\ *adv* — **fuzz·i·ness** \ˈfəz-ē-nəs\ *n*

FV *abbr* [L *folio verso* the page being turned] on the back of the page

fwd *abbr* **1** foreword **2** forward

FWD *abbr* front-wheel drive

FWPCA *abbr* Federal Water Pollution Control Administration

FX *abbr* foreign exchange

FY *abbr* fiscal year

-fy \ˌfī\ *vb suffix* [ME *-fien,* fr. OF *-fier,* fr. L *-ficare,* fr. *-ficus* -fic] **1 :** make **:** form into <dandi*fy*> **2 :** invest with the attributes of **:** make similar to <citi*fy*>

fyce \ˈfīs\ *var of* FEIST

FYI *abbr* for your information

fyke \ˈfīk\ *n* [D *fuik*] **:** a long bag net kept open by hoops

fyl·fot \ˈfil-ˌfät\ *n* [ME, device used to fill the lower part of a painted glass window, fr. *fillen* to fill + *fot* foot] **:** SWASTIKA

fz *abbr* [It *forzando, forzato*] accented

FZS *abbr* Fellow of the Zoological Society

G

[1]**g** \ˈjē\ *n, pl* **g's** *or* **gs** \ˈjēz\ *often cap, often attrib* **1 a :** the 7th letter of the English alphabet **b :** a graphic representation of this letter **c :** a speech counterpart of orthographic *g* **2 :** the 5th tone of a C-major scale **3 :** a graphic device for reproducing the letter *g* **4 :** one designated *g* esp. as the 7th in order or class **5** [*gravity*] **:** a unit of force equal to the force exerted by gravity on a body at rest and used to indicate the force to which a body is subjected when accelerated **6** [grand] *slang* **:** a sum of $1000 **7 :** something shaped like the letter G

[2]**g** *abbr, often cap* **1** game **2** gauge **3** gender **4** German **5** giga- **6** good **7** gram **8** grand **9** gravity **10** gulf

[1]**G** *adj* [general] *of a motion picture* **:** of such a nature that all ages may be allowed admission — compare PG, R, X

[2]**G** *symbol* **1** conductance **2** weight

ga *abbr* gauge

[1]**Ga** *abbr* Georgia

[2]**Ga** *symbol* gallium

GA *abbr* **1** general agent **2** general assembly **3** general average **4** general of the army **5** Georgia

[1]**gab** \ˈgab\ *vi* **gabbed; gab·bing** [prob. short for *gabble*] **:** to talk in a rapid or thoughtless manner **:** CHATTER

[2]**gab** *n* **:** TALK; *esp* **:** idle talk

gab·ar·dine \ˈgab-ər-ˌdēn\ *n* [MF *gaverdine*] **1 :** GABERDINE **2 a :** a firm hard-finish durable fabric (as of wool or rayon) twilled with diagonal ribs on the right side **b :** a garment of gabardine

gab·ber \ˈgab-ər\ *n* **:** one that talks much, habitually, and usu. idly

gab·ble \ˈgab-əl\ *vb* **gab·bled; gab·bling** \-(ə-)liŋ\ [prob. of imit. origin] *vi* **1 :** to talk fast or foolishly **:** JABBER **2 :** to utter inarticulate or animal sounds <a skein of duck . . . *gabbling* softly to themselves —Naomi Mitchison> ~ *vt* **:** to say with incoherent rapidity **:** BABBLE — **gabble** *n* — **gab·bler** \-(ə-)lər\ *n*

gab·bro \ˈgab-(ˌ)rō\ *n, pl* **gabbros** [It] **:** a granular igneous rock composed essentially of calcic plagioclase, a ferromagnesian mineral, and accessory minerals — **gab·bro·ic** \ga-ˈbrō-ik\ *adj*

gab·broid \ˈgab-ˌrȯid\ *adj* **:** resembling gabbro

gab·by \ˈgab-ē\ *adj* **gab·bi·er; -est :** TALKATIVE, GARRULOUS

ga·belle \gə-ˈbel\ *n* [ME, fr. MF, fr. OIt *gabella* tax, fr. Ar *qabālah*] **:** a tax on salt levied in France prior to 1790

gab·er·dine \ˈgab-ər-ˌdēn\ *n* [MF *gaverdine*] **1 a :** a coarse long coat or smock worn chiefly by Jews in medieval times **b :** an English laborer's smock **c :** GARMENT **2 :** GABARDINE

gab·fest \ˈgab-ˌfest\ *n* **1 :** an informal gathering for general talk <political ~*s*> **2 :** an extended conversation

ga·bi·on \ˈgā-bē-ən, ˈgab-ē-\ *n* [MF, fr. OIt *gabbione,* lit., large cage, aug. of *gabbia* cage, fr. L *cavea* — more at CAGE] **:** a hollow wickerwork or iron cylinder filled with earth and used esp. in building fieldworks or in mining

ga·ble \ˈgā-bəl\ *n* [ME, fr. MF, of Gmc origin; akin to ON *gafl* gable — more at CEPHALIC] **1 a :** the vertical triangular end of a building from cornice or eaves to ridge **b :** the similar end of a gambrel roof **c :** the end wall of a building **2 :** a triangular furniture or building part

1, gables 1a

ga·bled \-bəld\ *adj* **:** built with a gable

gable roof *n* **:** a double-sloping roof that forms a gable at each end

gab·oon \gä-ˈbün, gə-\ *n* [alter. of [1]*gob* + *-oon* (as in *spittoon*)] *dial* **:** CUSPIDOR, SPITTOON

Ga·bri·el \ˈgā-brē-əl\ *n* [Heb *Gabhrīʼēl*] **:** one of the four archangels named in Hebrew tradition

ga·by \ˈgā-bē\ *n, pl* **gabies** [perh. of Scand origin; akin to ON *gapa* to gape — more at GAPE] *dial chiefly Eng* **:** SIMPLETON

[1]gad \'gad\ *n* [ME, spike, fr. ON *gaddr;* akin to OE *geard* rod — more at YARD] **1 :** a chisel or pointed iron or steel bar for loosening ore or rock **2** *chiefly dial* **:** ROD, STICK

[2]gad *vi* **gad·ded; gad·ding** [ME *gadden*] **:** to be on the go to little purpose <too busy *gadding* about to get any work done> — **gad·der** *n*

[3]gad *interj* [euphemism for *God*] — used as a mild oath

Gad \'gad\ *n* [Heb *Gādh*] **:** a son of Jacob and the traditional eponymous ancestor of one of the tribes of Israel — **Gad·ite** \-,īt\ *n*

gad·about \'gad-ə-,baůt\ *n* **:** a person who flits about in social activity — **gadabout** *adj*

gad·a·rene \'gad-ə-,rēn\ *adj, often cap* [fr. the demon-possessed *Gadarene* swine (Mt 8:28) that rushed into the sea] **:** HEADLONG, PRECIPITATE <a ~ rush to the cities>

gad·fly \'gad-,flī\ *n* [[1]*gad*] **1 :** any of various flies (as a horsefly, botfly, or warble fly) that bite or annoy livestock **2 :** a usu. intentionally annoying person who stimulates or provokes others esp. by persistent irritating criticism

gad·get \'gaj-ət\ *n* [origin unknown] **:** an often small mechanical or electronic device esp. on a piece of machinery **:** CONTRIVANCE — **gad·ge·teer** \,gaj-ə-'ti(ə)r\ *n* — **gad·get·ry** \'gaj-ə-trē\ *n* — **gad·gety** \-ət-ē\ *adj*

ga·doid \'gād-,ȯid, 'gad-\ *adj* [NL *Gadus,* genus of fishes, fr. Gk *gados,* a fish] **:** resembling or related to the cods — **gadoid** *n*

gad·o·lin·ite \'gad-ᵊl-ə-,nīt\ *n* [G *gadolinit,* fr. Johann *Gadolin* †1852 Finn chemist] **:** a black or brown mineral $Be_2FeY_4Si_2O_{10}$ that is a source of rare earths and consists of silicate of iron, beryllium, yttrium, cerium, and erbium

gad·o·lin·i·um \,gad-ᵊl-'in-ē-əm\ *n* [NL, fr. J. *Gadolin*] **:** a magnetic metallic element of the rare-earth group occurring in combination in gadolinite and several other minerals — see ELEMENT table

ga·droon \gə-'drün\ *n* [F *godron* round plait, gadroon] **1 :** the ornamental notching or carving of a rounded molding **2 :** a short often oval fluting or reeding used in decoration — **ga·droon·ing** *n*

1, gadroon 2

gad·wall \'gad-,wȯl\ *n, pl* **gad·walls** *or* **gadwall** [origin unknown] **:** a grayish brown dabbling duck (*Anas strepera*) about the size of the mallard

gad·zooks *interj, often cap, archaic* — used as a mild oath

Gaea \'jē-ə\ *n* [Gk *Gaia*] **:** the Greek earth goddess and mother of the Titans

Gael \'gā(ə)l\ *n* [ScGael *Gàidheal* & IrGael *Gaedheal*] **1 :** a Scottish Highlander **2 :** a Celtic esp. Gaelic-speaking inhabitant of Ireland, Scotland, or the Isle of Man

Gael·ic \'gāl-ik, 'gal-, 'gäl-\ *adj* **1 :** of or relating to the Gaels and esp. the Celtic Highlanders of Scotland **2 :** of, relating to, or constituting the Goidelic speech of the Celts in Ireland, the Isle of Man, and the Scottish Highlands — **Gaelic** *n*

[1]gaff \'gaf\ *n* [F *gaffe,* fr. Prov *gaf*] **1 a :** a spear or spearhead for taking fish or turtles **b :** a handled hook for holding or lifting heavy fish **c :** a metal spur for a gamecock **d :** a butcher's hook **e :** a climbing iron or its steel point used by a telephone lineman **2 :** the spar upon which the head of a fore-and-aft sail is extended **3 a :** HOAX, FRAUD **b :** GIMMICK, TRICK **4 a :** something painful or difficult to bear **:** ORDEAL; *esp* **:** persistent raillery or criticism **b :** rough treatment **:** ABUSE **5 :** GAFFE

[2]gaff *vt* **1 a :** to strike or secure with a gaff **b :** to fit (a gamecock) with a gaff **2 :** DECEIVE, TRICK; *also* **:** FLEECE **3 :** to fix for the purpose of cheating **:** GIMMICK <~ the dice>

[3]gaff *n* [origin unknown] *Brit* **:** a cheap theater or music hall

gaffe \'gaf\ *n* [F, gaff, gaffe] **:** a social blunder **:** FAUX PAS

gaf·fer \'gaf-ər\ *n* [prob. alter. of *godfather*] **1 :** an old man — compare GAMMER **2** *Brit* **a :** EMPLOYER **b :** FOREMAN, OVERSEER **3 :** a head glassblower **4 :** a lighting electrician on a motion-picture or television set

gaff–top·sail \'gaf-'täp-,sāl, -səl\ *n* **:** a usu. triangular topsail with its foot extended upon the gaff and its luff upon the topmast — see SAIL illustration

[1]gag \'gag\ *vb* **gagged; gag·ging** [ME *gaggen* to strangle, of imit. origin] *vt* **1 a :** to stop the mouth of with something inserted **b :** to pry or hold open with a gag **c :** to prevent from free speech or expression **2 :** to cause to retch **3 :** OBSTRUCT, CHOKE <~ a valve> **4 :** to provide with quips or pranks <~ a show> ~ *vi* **1 :** HEAVE, RETCH **2 :** to be unable to endure something **:** BALK **3 :** to make quips

[2]gag *n* **1 :** something thrust into the mouth to keep it open **2 a :** something thrust into the mouth to prevent speech or outcry **b :** CLOTURE **c :** a check to free speech **3 :** a laugh-provoking remark or act **4 :** HOAX, TRICK ***syn*** see JEST

ga·ga \'gä-(,)gä\ *adj* [F, fr. *gaga* fool, of imit. origin] **1 :** CRAZY, FOOLISH **2 :** marked by wild enthusiasm **:** INFATUATED

[1]gage \'gāj\ *n* [ME, fr. MF, of Gmc origin; akin to OHG *wetti* pledge — more at WED] **1 :** a token of defiance; *specif* **:** a glove or cap cast on the ground to be taken up by an opponent as a pledge of combat **2 :** something deposited as a pledge of performance

[2]gage *vt* **1** *archaic* **:** PLEDGE **2** *archaic* **:** STAKE, RISK

[3]gage *var of* GAUGE

[4]gage *n* **:** GREENGAGE

gag·ger \'gag-ər\ *n* **1 :** one that gags **2 :** JOKER, GAGMAN

gag·gle \'gag-əl\ *n* [ME *gagyll,* fr. *gagelen* to cackle] **1 :** FLOCK; *esp* **:** a flock of geese when not in flight — compare SKEIN **2 :** AGGREGATION, CLUSTER <a ~ of reporters and photographers>

gag·man \'gag-,man\ *n* **1 :** a gag writer **2 :** a comedian who uses gags

gag rule *n* **:** a rule restricting freedom of debate or expression esp. in a legislative body

gag·ster \'gag-stər\ *n* **:** GAGMAN; *also* **:** one who plays practical jokes

gahn·ite \'gän-,īt\ *n* [G *gahnit,* fr. J. G. *Gahn* †1818 Sw chemist] **:** a usu. dark green mineral $ZnAl_2O_4$ consisting of an oxide of zinc and aluminum

gai·ety \'gā-ət-ē\ *n, pl* **-eties** **1 :** MERRYMAKING; *also* **:** festive activity — often used in pl. **2 :** gay spirits or manner **3 :** FINERY, SHOW <a ~ of dress better suited to one half her age>

gail·lar·dia \gə-'lärd-(ē-)ə\ *n* [NL, genus name, fr. *Gaillard* de Marentonneau, 18th cent. F botanist] **:** any of a genus (*Gaillardia*) of chiefly western American composite herbs with showy flower heads

gai·ly \'gā-lē\ *adv* **:** in a gay manner

[1]gain \'gān\ *n* [ME *gayne,* fr. MF *gaigne, gain,* fr. OF *gaaigne, gaaing,* fr. *gaaignier* to till, earn, gain, of Gmc origin; akin to OHG *weidanōn* to hunt for food, L *vis* power — more at VIM] **1 :** resources or advantage acquired or increased **:** PROFIT <made substantial ~*s* last year> **2 :** the obtaining of profit or possessions **3 a :** an increase in amount, magnitude, or degree <a ~ in efficiency> **b :** the ratio of increase of output over input in an amplifier **c :** the effectiveness of a directional antenna expressed as the ratio in decibels of standard antenna input power to the directional antenna input power that will produce the same field strength in the desired direction

[2]gain *vt* **1 a :** to get possession of usu. by industry, merit, or craft <~ an advantage> <he stood to ~ a fortune> **b :** to win in competition or conflict <the attackers ~*ed* the day> **c :** to get by a natural development or process <~ strength> **d :** MAKE, ACQUIRE <~ a friend> **e** (1) **:** to arrive at <~*ed* the river that night> (2) **:** TRAVERSE, COVER <~*ed* 10 yards on the play> **2 :** to win to one's side **:** PERSUADE <~ adherents to a cause> **3 :** to cause to be obtained or given **:** ATTRACT <~ attention> **4 :** to increase in <~ momentum> **5** *of a timepiece* **:** to run fast by the amount of <the clock ~*s* a minute a day> ~ *vi* **1 :** to get advantage **:** PROFIT <hoped to ~ from his crime> **2 a :** INCREASE <the day was ~*ing* in warmth> **b :** to increase in weight **c :** to improve in health **3** *of a timepiece* **:** to run fast ***syn*** **1** see GET ***ant*** forfeit, lose **2** see REACH ***ant*** forfeit, lose — **gain ground :** to make progress

[3]gain *n* [origin unknown] **1 :** a beveled shoulder above a tenon **2 :** a notch or mortise for insertion of a girder or joist

gain·er \'gā-nər\ *n* **1 :** one that gains **2 :** a fancy dive in which the diver from a forward position executes a backward somersault and enters the water feetfirst and facing away from the board

gain·ful \'gān-fəl\ *adj* **:** productive of gain **:** PROFITABLE <~ employment> — **gain·ful·ly** \-fə-lē\ *adv* — **gain·ful·ness** *n*

gain·giv·ing \'gān-,giv-iŋ, (')gān-'\ *n* [*gain-* (against) + *giving*] *archaic* **:** MISGIVING

gain·less \'gān-ləs\ *adj* **:** producing no gain **:** PROFITLESS — **gain·less·ness** *n*

gain·ly \'gān-lē\ *adj* [*gain* (handy)] **:** graceful and generally pleasing <a ~ boy with charming manners>

gain·say \gān-'sā\ *vt* **-said** \-'sād, -'sed\; **-say·ing** \-'sā-iŋ\; **-says** \-'sāz, -'sez\ [ME *gainsayen,* fr. *gain-* against (fr. OE *gēan-*) + *sayen* to say — more at AGAIN] **1 :** DENY, DISPUTE <couldn't ~ the statistics> **2 :** to stand in opposition to esp. by disputing the truth of something put forward **:** CONTRADICT, OPPOSE ***syn*** see DENY ***ant*** admit — **gain·say·er** *n*

[1]gait \'gāt\ *n* [ME *gait, gate* gate, way] **1 :** a manner of walking or moving on foot **2 :** a sequence of foot movements (as a walk, trot, pace, or canter) by which a horse moves forward **3 :** a manner or rate of movement or progress <the leisurely ~ of a summer in the country>

[2]gait *vt* **1 :** to train (a horse) to use a particular gait or set of gaits **2 :** to lead (a show dog) before a judge to display carriage and movement

[3]gait *n* [prob. alter. of [1]*gate*] **1 :** the distance between two adjoining carriages of a lace-making frame **2** *Brit* **:** a full repeat of a pattern in harness weaving of woolens

gait·ed \'gāt-əd\ *adj* **:** having a particular gait <slow-*gaited*>

gai·ter \'gāt-ər\ *n* [F *guêtre*] **1 :** a cloth or leather leg covering reaching from the instep to ankle, mid-calf, or knee **2 a :** an ankle-high shoe with elastic gores in the sides **b :** an overshoe with fabric upper

[1]gal \'gal\ *n* [by alter.] **:** GIRL

[2]gal *n* [*Galileo* †1642 It astronomer] **:** a unit of acceleration equivalent to one centimeter per second per second — used esp. for values of gravity

[3]gal *abbr* **1** gallery **2** gallon

Gal *abbr* Galatians

ga·la \'gā-lə, 'gal-ə, 'gäl-ə\ *n* [It, fr. MF *gale* festivity, pleasure — more at GALLANT] **:** a gay celebration **:** FESTIVITY — **gala** *adj*

galact- *or* **galacto-** *comb form* [L *galact-,* fr. Gk *galakt-, galakto-,* fr. *galakt-, gala*] **1 :** milk <*galacto*poiesis> **2 :** related to galactose <*galacto*mannan>

ga·lac·tic \gə-'lak-tik\ *adj* **1 :** of or relating to a galaxy and esp. the Milky Way galaxy **2 :** HUGE <a ~ sum of money>

galactic noise *n* **:** radio-frequency radiation from the Milky Way

ga·lac·to·poi·e·sis \gə-,lak-tə-pȯi-'ē-səs\ *n* [NL] **:** formation and secretion of milk — **ga·lac·to·poi·et·ic** \-'et-ik\ *adj or n*

ga·lac·tos·amine \gə-,lak-'tō-sə-,mēn, -zə-\ *n* **:** an amino derivative $C_6H_{13}O_5N$ of galactose that occurs in cartilage

ga·lac·tose \gə-'lak-,tōs, -,tōz\ *n* [F, fr. *galact-*] **:** a sugar $C_6H_{12}O_6$ less soluble and less sweet than glucose

ga·lac·tos·emia \gə-,lak-tə-'sē-mē-ə\ *n* **:** an inherited metabolic disorder in which galactose accumulates in the blood due to deficiency of an enzyme catalyzing its conversion to glucose — **ga·lac·tos·emic** \-mik\ *adj*

ə abut ᵊ kitten ər further a back ā bake ä cot, cart
aů out ch chin e less ē easy g gift i trip ī life
j joke ŋ sing ō flow ȯ flaw ȯi coin th thin t͟h this
ü loot ů foot y yet yü few yů furious zh vision

ga·lac·to·si·dase \gə-ˌlak-ˈtō-sə-ˌdās, -zə-ˌdāz\ *n* **:** an enzyme (as lactase) that hydrolyzes a galactoside

ga·lac·to·side \gə-ˈlak-tə-ˌsīd\ *n* **:** a glycoside that yields galactose on hydrolysis

ga·lac·to·syl \gə-ˈlak-tə-ˌsil\ *n* **:** a glycosyl radical $C_6H_{11}O_5$ that is derived from galactose

ga·lact·uron·ic acid \gə-ˌlak-t(y)ü-ˌrän-ik-\ *n* [ISV *galact-* + *-uronic*] **:** a crystalline aldehyde-acid $C_6H_{10}O_7$ that occurs esp. in polymerized form in pectin

ga·la·go \gə-ˈlā-(ˌ)gō, -ˈläg-(ˌ)ō\ *n, pl* **-gos** [NL, genus name, perh. fr. Wolof *golokh* monkey] **:** any of two genera (*Galago* and *Euoticus*) of small active nocturnal arboreal African primates with long ears, a long tail, and elongated hind limbs that enable them to leap with great agility — called also *bush baby*

ga·lah \gə-ˈlä\ *n* [native name in Australia] **:** a showy Australian cockatoo (*Kakatoë roseicapilla*) that is a destructive pest in wheat-growing areas and is often kept as a cage bird

Gal·a·had \ˈgal-ə-ˌhad\ *n* **:** the knight of the Round Table who successfully seeks the Holy Grail

gal·an·tine \ˈgal-ən-ˌtēn\ *n* [F] **:** a cold dish consisting of boned meat or fish that has been stuffed, poached, and covered with aspic

ga·lan·ty show \gə-ˈlant-ē-\ *n* [perh. fr. It *galante* gallant, fr. MF *galant*] **:** SHADOW PLAY

Gal·a·tea \ˌgal-ə-ˈtē-ə\ *n* [L, fr. Gk *Galateia*] **1 :** a nymph killed by the jealous Cyclops Polyphemus while in the arms of her lover Acis **2 :** a female figure sculpted by Pygmalion and given life by Aphrodite in fulfillment of his prayer

Ga·la·tians \gə-ˈlā-shənz\ *n pl but sing in constr* **:** an argumentative letter of St. Paul written to the Christians of Galatia and included as a book in the New Testament — see BIBLE table

gal·a·vant *var of* GALLIVANT

ga·lax \ˈgā-ˌlaks\ *n* [NL, genus name] **:** any of a genus (*Galax*) of evergreen herbs related to the true heaths with leaves widely used for decorations

gal·axy \ˈgal-ək-sē\ *n, pl* **-ax·ies** [ME *galaxie, galaxias,* fr. LL *galaxias,* fr. Gk, fr. *galakt-, gala* milk; akin to L *lac* milk] **1 a** *often cap* **:** MILKY WAY GALAXY **b :** one of billions of systems each including stars, nebulae, star clusters, globular clusters, and interstellar matter that make up the universe **2 :** an assemblage of brilliant or notable persons or things

gal·ba·num \ˈgal-bə-nəm, ˈgȯl-\ *n* [ME, fr. L, fr. Gk *chalbanē,* fr. Heb *ḥelbĕnāh*] **:** a yellowish to green or brown aromatic bitter gum resin derived from several Asiatic plants (as *Ferula galbaniflua*) and used for medicinal purposes and in incense

¹gale \ˈgā(ə)l\ *n* [origin unknown] **1 a :** a strong current of air: (1) **:** a wind from 32 to 63 miles per hour (2) **:** FRESH GALE — see BEAUFORT SCALE table **b** *archaic* **:** BREEZE **2 :** an emotional outburst **:** GUST

²gale *n* [prob. alter. of ¹*gavel*] *Brit* **:** a periodic payment of rent

ga·lea \ˈgā-lē-ə\ *n* [NL, fr. L, helmet] **:** an anatomical part suggesting a helmet: as **a :** the upper lip of the corolla of a mint **b :** the outer or lateral lobe of the maxilla in mandibulate insects — **ga·le·ate** \-lē-ˌāt\ *also* **ga·le·at·ed** \-ˌāt-əd\ *adj* — **ga·le·iform** \gə-ˈlē-ə-ˌfȯrm, ˈgā-lē-\ *adj*

ga·le·na \gə-ˈlē-nə\ *n* [L, lead ore] **:** a bluish gray mineral PbS with metallic luster consisting of lead sulfide, showing highly perfect cubic cleavage, and constituting the principal ore of lead

Ga·len·ic \gā-ˈlen-ik\ *adj* **:** of or relating to Galen or his medical principles or method — **Ga·len·i·cal** \-i-kəl\ *adj*

galenical *n* **:** a medicine prepared by extracting one or more active constituents of a plant

Ga·len·ism \ˈgā-lə-ˌniz-əm\ *n* **:** the Galenic system of medical practice

ga·lère \ga-ˈle(ə)r\ *n* [F, lit., galley, fr. MF, fr. Catal *galera,* fr. MGk *galea*] **:** a group of people having a marked common quality or relationship

gal Friday *n* **:** GIRL FRIDAY

Ga·li·bi \gə-ˈlē-bē, ˈgal-ə-bē\ *n, pl* **Galibi** *or* **Galibis 1 :** a member of a Carib people of French Guiana **2 :** the language of the Galibi people

Gal·i·le·an \ˌgal-ə-ˈlē-ən, -ˈlā-\ *adj* **:** of or relating to Galileo Galilei, founder of experimental physics and astronomy

gal·i·lee \ˈgal-ə-ˌlē\ *n* [AF, fr. ML *galilaea*] **:** a chapel or porch at the entrance of an English church

gal·i·ma·ti·as \ˌgal-ə-ˈmā-shē-əs, -mə-ˈtyä\ *n* [F] **:** a confused and often pretentious mixture esp. of words **:** GOBBLEDYGOOK

gal·in·gale \ˈgal-ən-ˌgāl, -iŋ-\ *n* [ME, a kind of ginger, fr. MF *galingal,* fr. Ar *khalanjān*] **:** an Old World sedge (*Cyperus longus*) with an aromatic root; *broadly* **:** any of various plants related to galingale

gal·i·ot *var of* GALLIOT

gal·i·pot \ˈgal-ə-ˌpät, -ˌpō\ *n* [F] **:** the crude turpentine oleoresin exuded from a southern European pine (*Pinus pinaster*)

¹gall \ˈgȯl\ *n* [ME, fr. OE *gealla;* akin to Gk *cholē, cholos* gall, wrath, OE *geolu* yellow — more at YELLOW] **1 a :** BILE; *esp* **:** bile obtained from an animal and used in the arts or medicine **b :** something bitter to endure **c :** bitterness of spirit **:** RANCOR **2 :** brazen boldness coupled with impudent assurance and insolence ***syn*** see TEMERITY

²gall *n* [ME *galle,* fr. OE *gealla,* fr. L *galla* gallnut] **1 a :** a skin sore caused by chronic irritation **b :** a cause or state of exasperation **2** *archaic* **:** FLAW

³gall *vt* **1 a :** to fret and wear away by friction **:** CHAFE <the loose saddle ~*ed* the horse's back> <the ~*ing* of a metal bearing> **b :** IRRITATE, VEX <sarcasm ~*s* her> **2 :** HARASS <~*ed* by enemy fire> ~ *vi* **1 :** to become sore or worn by rubbing **2 :** SEIZE 2

⁴gall *n* [ME *galle,* fr. MF, fr. L *galla*] **:** a swelling of plant tissue usu. due to fungi or insect parasites and sometimes forming an important source of tannin

Gal·la \ˈgal-ə\ *n, pl* **Galla** *or* **Gallas 1 :** a member of any of several groups of Cushitic-speaking peoples of British East Africa and southern Ethiopia **2 :** the Cushitic language of the Galla

gal·la·mine tri·eth·io·dide \ˈgal-ə-ˌmēn-ˌtrī-ˌeth-ˈī-ə-ˌdīd\ *n* [pyro*gall*ol + *amine* + *triethyl* + *iodide*] **:** a substituted ammonium salt $C_{30}H_{60}I_3N_3O_3$ that is used to produce muscle relaxation esp. during anesthesia — called also *gallamine*

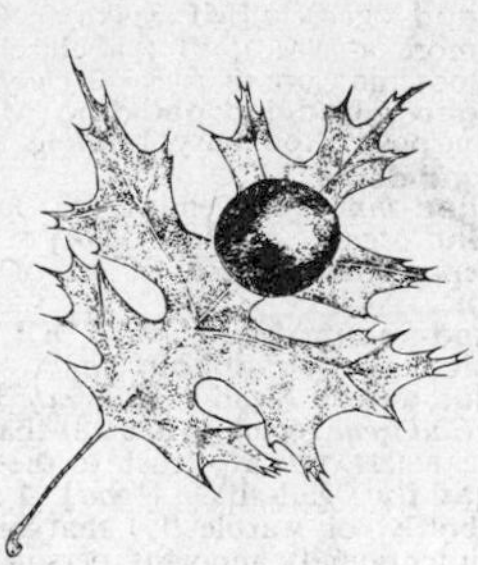

gall on an oak leaf

¹gal·lant \gə-ˈlant, gə-ˈlänt, ˈgal-ənt\ *n* **1 :** a young man of fashion **2 a :** LADIES' MAN **b :** SUITOR **c :** PARAMOUR

²gal·lant \ˈgal-ənt (*usu in sense 2*); gə-ˈlant, gə-ˈlänt (*usu in sense 3*)\ *adj* [ME *galaunt,* fr. MF *galant,* fr. prp. of *galer* to have a good time, fr. *gale* pleasure, of Gmc origin; akin to OE *wela* weal — more at WEAL] **1 :** showy in dress or bearing **:** SMART **2 a :** SPLENDID, STATELY <a ~ ship> **b :** SPIRITED, BRAVE <~ efforts against the enemy> **c :** nobly chivalrous and often self-sacrificing **3 a :** courteously and elaborately attentive esp. to ladies **b :** given to amorous intrigue ***syn*** see CIVIL ***ant*** ungallant — **gal·lant·ly** *adv*

³gal·lant \gə-ˈlant, -ˈlänt\ *vt* **1 :** to pay court to (a lady) **:** ATTEND **2** *obs* **:** to manipulate (a fan) in a modish manner ~ *vi* **:** to pay court to ladies

gal·lant·ry \ˈgal-ən-trē\ *n, pl* **-ries 1** *archaic* **:** gallant appearance **2 a :** an act of marked courtesy **b :** courteous attention to a lady **c :** amorous attention or pursuit **3 :** spirited and conspicuous bravery ***syn*** see HEROISM ***ant*** dastardliness

gal·late \ˈgal-ˌāt, ˈgȯl-\ *n* **:** a salt or ester of gallic acid

gall·blad·der \ˈgȯl-ˌblad-ər\ *n* **:** a membranous muscular sac in which bile from the liver is stored

gal·le·ass \ˈgal-ē-əs\ *n* [MF *galeasse*] **:** a large fast war galley of southern Europe in the 16th and 17th centuries

gal·lein \ˈgal-ē-ən, ˈgal-ˌēn\ *n* [*gall*ic acid + phthal*ein*] **:** a metallic-green crystalline phthalein dye $C_{20}H_{12}O_7$ used esp. in dyeing textiles violet and as an indicator

gal·le·on \ˈgal-ē-ən\ *n* [OSp *galeón,* fr. MF *galion,* fr. OF *galie* galley] **:** a heavy square-rigged sailing ship of the 15th to early 18th centuries used for war or commerce esp. by the Spanish

gal·lery \ˈgal(-ə)-rē\ *n, pl* **-ler·ies** [ME *galerie,* fr. ML *galeria*] **1 a :** a roofed promenade **:** COLONNADE **b :** CORRIDOR **2 a :** an outdoor balcony **b** *South & Midland* **:** PORCH, VERANDA **c** (1) **:** a platform at the quarters or stern of a ship (2) **:** a gun platform or emplacement on a ship **d :** a railed walk around the upper part of an engine to facilitate oiling or inspection **3 a :** a long and narrow passage, apartment, or corridor **b :** a subterranean passageway in a cave or military mining system; *also* **:** a working drift or level in mining **c :** an underground passage made by a mole or ant or a passage made in wood by an insect **4 a :** a room or building devoted to the exhibition of works of art **b :** an institution or business exhibiting or dealing in works of art **c :** COLLECTION, AGGREGATION <the rich ~ of characters in this novel —H. S. Canby> **5 a :** a structure projecting from one or more interior walls of an auditorium to accommodate additional people; *esp* **:** the highest balcony in a theater commonly having the cheapest seats **b :** the part of a theater audience seated in the top gallery **c :** the undiscriminating general public **d :** the spectators at a tennis or golf match **6 :** a photographer's studio — **gal·ler·ied** \-rēd\ *adj*

gallery forest *n* **:** a forest growing along a watercourse in a region otherwise devoid of trees

gal·lery·go·er \ˈgal(-ə)-rē-ˌgō(-ə)r\ *n* **:** one who frequently goes to art galleries

ga·lle·ta \gə-ˈyet-ə, gī-ˈet-ə\ *n* [Sp, hardtack] **:** either of two perennial forage grasses (*Hilaria rigida* and *H. jamesii*) used for hay in the southwestern U.S. and in Mexico

gal·ley \ˈgal-ē\ *n, pl* **galleys** [ME *galeie,* fr. OF *galie,* deriv. of MGk *galea*] **1 :** a large low medieval ship propelled by sails and oars and used in the Mediterranean for war and trading **2 :** a seagoing ship of classical antiquity propelled chiefly by oars **3 :** a large open rowing boat formerly used in England **4 :** the kitchen and cooking apparatus esp. of a ship or airplane **5 a :** an oblong tray commonly of pressed steel with upright sides to hold set type **b :** a proof from type on a galley before it is made up in pages

galley slave *n* **1 :** a slave or criminal acting as a rower on a galley **2 :** DRUDGE 1

gal·ley–west \ˌgal-ē-ˈwest\ *adv* [prob. alter. of E dial. *collywest* (badly askew)] **:** into destruction or confusion <was knocked ~>

gall·fly \ˈgȯl-ˌflī\ *n* **:** an insect (as a gall wasp) that deposits its eggs in plants and causes galls in which the larvae feed

¹gal·liard \ˈgal-yərd\ *adj* [ME *gaillard,* fr. MF] *archaic* **:** GAY, LIVELY

²galliard *n* **:** a gay dance with five steps to a phrase popular in the 16th and 17th centuries

Gal·lic \ˈgal-ik\ *adj* [L *Gallicus,* fr. *Gallia* Gaul] **:** of or relating to Gaul or France

gal·lic acid \ˌgal-ik-, ˌgȯ-lik-\ *n* [F *gallique,* fr. *galle* gall] **:** a white crystalline acid $C_7H_6O_5$ found widely in plants or combined in tannins and used esp. in dyes and writing ink and as a photographic developer

Gal·li·can \ˈgal-i-kən\ *adj* **1 :** GALLIC **2** *often not cap* **:** of or relating to Gallicanism — **Gallican** *n*

Gal·li·can·ism \-kə-ˌniz-əm\ *n* **:** a movement originating in France and advocating administrative independence from papal control for the Roman Catholic Church in each nation

gal·li·cism \ˈgal-ə-ˌsiz-əm\ *n, often cap* **1 :** a characteristic French idiom or expression appearing in another language **2 :** a French trait

gal·li·cize \-ˌsīz\ *vt* **-cized; -ciz·ing :** to cause to conform to a French mode or idiom — **gal·li·ci·za·tion** \ˌgal-ə-sə-ˈzā-shən\ *n*

gal·li·gas·kins \ˌgal-i-ˈgas-kənz\ *n pl* [prob. modif. of MF *garguesques,* fr. OSp *greguescos,* fr. *griego* Greek, fr. L *Graecus*] **1 a** : loose wide hose or breeches worn in the 16th and 17th centuries **b** : very loose trousers **2** *chiefly dial* : LEGGINGS
gal·li·mau·fry \ˌgal-ə-ˈmȯ-frē\ *n, pl* **-fries** [MF *galimafree* hash] : MEDLEY, JUMBLE
gal·li·na·ceous \ˌgal-ə-ˈnā-shəs\ *adj* [L *gallinaceus* of domestic fowl, fr. *gallina* hen, fr. *gallus* cock] : of or relating to an order (Galliformes) of heavy-bodied largely terrestrial birds including the pheasants, turkeys, grouse, and the common domestic fowl
gall·ing \ˈgȯ-liŋ\ *adj* : markedly irritating : VEXING <suffered a ~ defeat> — **gall·ing·ly** \-liŋ-lē\ *adv*
gal·li·nip·per \ˈgal-ə-ˌnip-ər\ *n* [origin unknown] : a very large American mosquito (*Psorophora ciliata*); *also* : an insect that bites or is thought to bite
gal·li·nule \ˈgal-ə-ˌn(y)ü(ə)l\ *n* [NL *Gallinula,* genus of birds, fr. L, pullet, dim. of *gallina*] : any of several aquatic birds of the rail family with unlobed feet and a frontal shield on the head
gal·li·ot \ˈgal-ē-ət\ *n* [ME *galiote,* fr. MF, fr. ML *galeota,* dim. of *galea* galley, fr. MGk] **1** : a small swift galley formerly used in the Mediterranean **2** [D *galjoot,* fr. MF *galiote*] : a long narrow light-draft Dutch merchant sailing ship
gal·li·pot \ˈgal-i-ˌpät\ *n* [ME *galy pott*] **1** : a small usu. ceramic vessel **2** *archaic* : DRUGGIST
gal·li·um \ˈgal-ē-əm\ *n* [NL, fr. L *gallus* (intended as trans. of Paul *Lecoq* de Boisbaudran †1912 F chemist] : a rare bluish white metallic element that is hard and brittle at low temperatures but melts just above room temperature and expands on freezing — see ELEMENT table
gal·li·vant \ˈgal-ə-ˌvant\ *vi* [perh. alter. of [3]*gallant*] **1** : to go about usu. ostentatiously or indiscreetly with members of the opposite sex **2** : to travel or roam about for pleasure
gall midge *n* : any of numerous minute two-winged flies (family Cecidomyiidae) most of which cause gall formation in plants
gall mite *n* : any of various minute 4-legged mites (family Eriophyidae) that form galls on plants
gall·nut \ˈgȯl-ˌnət\ *n* [[4]*gall*] : a gall resembling a nut
Gal·lo·ma·nia \ˌgal-ō-ˈmā-nē-ə, -nyə\ *n* [NL, fr. L *Gallus* Gaul] : a strong prejudice in favor of what is French
gal·lon \ˈgal-ən\ *n* [ME *galon,* a liquid measure, fr. ONF, fr. ML *galeta* pail, a liquid measure] : a unit of liquid capacity equal to 231 cubic inches or four quarts — see WEIGHT table
gal·lon·age \ˈgal-ə-nij\ *n* : amount in gallons
gal·loon \gə-ˈlün\ *n* [F *galon*] : a narrow trimming esp. of lace, embroidery, or braid with metallic threads — **gal·looned** \-ˈlünd\ *adj*
[1]**gal·lop** \ˈgal-əp\ *n* [MF *galop*] **1** : a springing gait of a quadruped; *specif* : a fast natural 3-beat gait of the horse — compare [3]CANTER, RUN **2** : a ride or run at a gallop **3** : a rapid or hasty progression <rushed through the reports at a ~>
[2]**gallop** *vi* **1** : to progress or ride at a gallop **2** : to run fast ~ *vt* **1** : to cause to gallop **2** : to transport at a gallop — **gal·lop·er** *n*
gal·lo·pade \ˌgal-ə-ˈpād, -ˈpäd\ *n* : GALOP
Gal·lo·phile \ˈgal-ə-ˌfīl\ *n* [L *Gallus* Gaul + E *-phile*] : FRANCOPHILE — **Gallophile** *adj*
gal·lop·ing *adj* : progressing or increasing rapidly <~ inflation> <a ~ disease> <~ corruption in government — *Atlantic*>
Gal·lo·way \ˈgal-ə-ˌwā\ *n* [*Galloway,* Scotland] : any of a breed of hardy medium-sized hornless chiefly black beef cattle native to southwestern Scotland
gal·low·glass \ˈgal-ō-ˌglas\ *n* [IrGael *gallōglach,* fr. *gall* foreigner + *ōglach* soldier] **1** : a mercenary or retainer of an Irish chief **2** : an armed Irish foot soldier
[1]**gal·lows** \ˈgal-(ˌ)ōz, -əz, *in sense 3 also* -əs\ *n, pl* **gallows** *or* **gal·lows·es** [ME *galwes,* pl. of *galwe,* fr. OE *gealga;* akin to OHG *galgo* gallows, Arm *jatk* twig] **1 a** : a frame usu. of two upright posts and a crossbeam from which criminals are hanged — called also *gallows tree* **b** : the punishment of hanging <got the ~ for murder> **2** : a structure consisting of an upright frame with a crosspiece **3** *chiefly dial* : SUSPENDER 2a
[2]**gallows** *adj* : deserving the gallows
gallows bird *n* : a person who deserves hanging
gallows humor *n* [trans. of G *galgenhumor*] : humor that makes fun of a very serious or terrifying situation
gall·stone \ˈgȯl-ˌstōn\ *n* : a calculus formed in the gallbladder or biliary passages
Gal·lup poll \ˌgal-əp-\ *n* [George H. *Gallup* b1901 Am public opinion statistician] : a sampling of public opinion taken by questioning a representative cross section <we can . . . find out who are the supporters only by organizing inquiries and *Gallup polls* — Barbara & Robert North>
gal·lus \ˈgal-əs\ *n* [alter. of [1]*gallows*] *chiefly dial* : SUSPENDER 2a — usu. used in pl.
gal·lused \ˈgal-əst\ *adj, chiefly dial* : wearing galluses
gall wasp *n* : a hymenopterous gallfly (family Cynipidae)
gal·ly \ˈgal-ē\ *vt* **gal·lied; gal·ly·ing** [origin unknown] *chiefly dial* : FRIGHTEN, TERRIFY
Ga·lois theory \ˈgal-ˌwä-\ *n* [Évariste *Galois* †1832 F mathematician] : a part of the theory of mathematical groups concerned esp. with the conditions under which a solution to a polynomial equation with coefficients in a given mathematical field can be obtained in the field by the repetition of operations and the extraction of nth roots
ga·loot \gə-ˈlüt\ *n* [origin unknown] *slang* : FELLOW; *esp* : one that is strange or foolish
ga·lop \ˈgal-əp, ga-ˈlō\ *n* [F] : a lively dance in duple measure; *also* : the music of a galop
ga·lore \gə-ˈlō(ə)r, -ˈlȯ(ə)r\ *adj* [IrGael *go leor* enough] : ABUNDANT, PLENTIFUL — used postpositively <bargains ~>
ga·losh \gə-ˈläsh\ *n* [ME *galoche,* fr. MF] **1** *obs* : a shoe with a heavy sole **2** : a high overshoe worn esp. in snow and slush — **ga·loshed** \-ˈläsht\ *adj*

ga·lumph \gə-ˈləm(p)f\ *vi* [prob. alter. of [1]*gallop*] : to move with a clumsy heavy tread
galv *abbr* galvanized
gal·van·ic \gal-ˈvan-ik\ *adj* **1** : of, relating to, or producing a direct current of electricity <a ~ cell> **2 a** : having an electric effect : STIMULATING <a ~ personality> **b** : produced as if by an electric shock : JERKY, NERVOUS <a ~ response> — **gal·van·i·cal·ly** \-i-k(ə-)lē\ *adv*
galvanic couple *n* : a pair of dissimilar substances (as metals) capable of acting together as an electric source when brought in contact with an electrolyte
gal·va·nism \ˈgal-və-ˌniz-əm\ *n* [F or It; F *galvanisme,* fr. It *galvanismo,* fr. Luigi *Galvani*] **1** : a direct current of electricity esp. when produced by chemical action **2** : the therapeutic use of direct electric current **3** : vital or forceful activity
gal·va·nize \ˈgal-və-ˌnīz\ *vt* **-nized; -niz·ing 1 a** : to subject to the action of an electric current esp. for the purpose of stimulating physiologically <~ a muscle> **b** : to stimulate or excite as if by an electric shock <the candidate *galvanized* his followers into action> **2** : to coat (iron or steel) with zinc — **gal·va·ni·za·tion** \ˌgal-və-nə-ˈzā-shən\ *n* — **gal·va·niz·er** \ˈgal-və-ˌnī-zər\ *n*
galvano- *comb form* [*galvanic*] : galvanic current <*galvano*meter>
gal·va·nom·e·ter \ˌgal-və-ˈnäm-ət-ər\ *n* : an instrument for detecting or measuring a small electric current by movements of a magnetic needle or of a coil in a magnetic field — **gal·va·no·met·ric** \-nō-ˈme-trik\ *adj*
gal·va·no·scope \gal-ˈvan-ə-ˌskōp, ˈgal-və-nə-\ *n* : an instrument for detecting the presence and direction of an electric current by the deflection of a magnetic needle
gal·yak \ˈgal-ˌyak\ *n* [native name in Uzbekistan, U.S.S.R.] : a short-haired flat or slightly moiré fur derived from the pelt of a stillborn lamb or kid
[1]**gam** \ˈgam\ *n* [prob. fr. F dial. *gambe,* fr. ONF, fr. LL *gamba*] *slang* : LEG
[2]**gam** *n* [perh. short for obs. *gammon* (talk)] **1** : a visit or friendly conversation at sea or ashore esp. between whalers **2** : a school of whales
[3]**gam** *vb* **gammed; gam·ming** *vi* : to engage in a gam ~ *vt* **1** : to have a gam with **2** : to spend or pass (as time) talking
gam- *or* **gamo-** *comb form* [NL, fr. Gk, marriage, fr. *gamos* — more at BIGAMY] **1** : united : joined <*gamo*sepalous> **2** : sexual : sexuality <*gam*ic> <*gamo*genesis>
gama grass \ˈgam-ə-\ *n* [prob. alter. of *grama*] : a tall coarse American grass (*Tripsacum dactyloides*) valuable for forage — called also *gama*
gamba *n* : VIOLA DA GAMBA
[1]**gam·ba·do** \gam-ˈbād-(ˌ)ō\ *n, pl* **-does** *also* **-dos** [perh. modif. of It *gambale,* fr. *gamba* leg] : a horseman's legging
[2]**gambado** *n, pl* **-does** *also* **-dos** [modif. of F *gambade* — more at GAMBOL] **1** : a spring of a horse **2** : CAPER, GAMBOL
gam·bier *also* **gam·bir** \ˈgam-ˌbi(ə)r\ *n* [Malay *gambir*] : a yellowish catechu that is obtained from a Malayan woody vine and is used for chewing with the betel nut and for tanning and dyeing
gam·bit \ˈgam-bət\ *n* [It *gambetto,* lit., act of tripping someone, fr. *gamba* leg, fr. LL *gamba, camba,* modif. of Gk *kampē* bend — more at CAMP] **1** : a chess opening in which a player risks one or more minor pieces to gain an advantage in position **2 a** (1) : a remark intended to start a conversation or make a telling point (2) : TOPIC **b** : a calculated move : STRATAGEM
[1]**gam·ble** \ˈgam-bəl\ *vb* **gam·bled; gam·bling** \-b(ə-)liŋ\ [prob. back-formation fr. *gambler,* prob. alter. of obs. *gamner,* fr. obs. *gamen* (to play)] *vi* **1 a** : to play a game for (as money or property) **b** : to bet on an uncertain outcome **2** : to stake something on a contingency : SPECULATE ~ *vt* **1** : to risk by gambling : WAGER **2** : VENTURE, HAZARD — **gam·bler** \-blər\ *n*
[2]**gamble** *n* **1** : the playing of a game of chance for stakes **2 a** : an act having an element of risk **b** : something chancy
gam·boge \gam-ˈbōj, -ˈbüzh\ *n* [NL *gambogium,* alter. of *cambugium,* irreg. fr. *Cambodia*] **1** : an orange to brown gum resin from southeast Asian trees (genus *Garcinia,* family Guttiferae) that is used as a yellow pigment and cathartic **2** : a strong yellow
[1]**gam·bol** \ˈgam-bəl\ *n* [modif. of MF *gambade* spring of a horse, gambol, prob. fr. OProv *camba* leg, fr. LL] : a skipping or leaping about in play
[2]**gambol** *vi* **-boled** *or* **-bolled; -bol·ing** *or* **-bol·ling** \-bə-liŋ *also* -bliŋ\ : to skip about in play : FRISK
gam·brel \ˈgam-brəl\ *n* [ONF *gamberel,* fr. *gambe* leg, fr. LL *gamba*] **1** : a stick or iron for suspending slaughtered animals **2** : the hock of an animal
gambrel roof *n* : a curb roof of the same section in all parts with a lower steeper slope and an upper flatter one

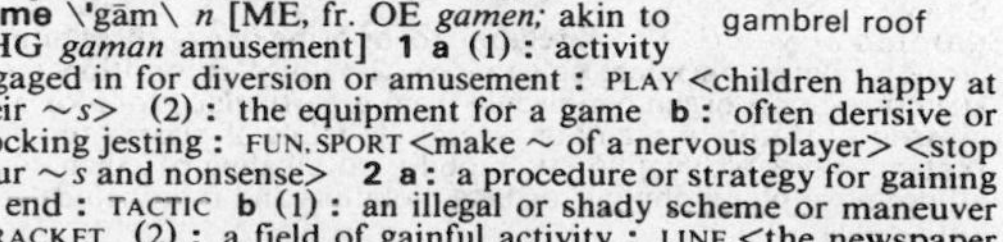
gambrel roof

gam·bu·sia \gam-ˈb(y)ü-zh(ē-)ə\ *n* [NL, genus name, modif. of AmerSp *gambusino* gambusia] : any of a genus (*Gambusia*) of topminnows introduced as valuable exterminators of mosquito larvae in warm fresh waters
[1]**game** \ˈgām\ *n* [ME, fr. OE *gamen;* akin to OHG *gaman* amusement] **1 a** (1) : activity engaged in for diversion or amusement : PLAY <children happy at their ~*s*> (2) : the equipment for a game **b** : often derisive or mocking jesting : FUN, SPORT <make ~ of a nervous player> <stop your ~*s* and nonsense> **2 a** : a procedure or strategy for gaining an end : TACTIC **b** (1) : an illegal or shady scheme or maneuver : RACKET (2) : a field of gainful activity : LINE <the newspaper ~> (3) : a specified type of activity or mode of behavior <the

dating ~> <the ~ of politics> **3 a** (1) **:** a physical or mental competition conducted according to rules with the participants in direct opposition to each other (2) **:** a division of a larger contest (3) **:** the number of points necessary to win (4) **:** points scored in certain card games (as in all fours) by a player whose cards count up the highest (5) **:** the manner of playing in a contest (6) **:** the set of rules governing a game **b** *pl* **:** organized athletics **c :** a situation that involves contest, rivalry, or struggle <got into aviation early in the ~>; *esp* **:** one in which opposing interests given specific information are allowed a choice of moves with the object of maximizing their wins and minimizing their losses **4 a** (1) **:** animals under pursuit or taken in hunting; *esp* **:** wild animals hunted for sport or food (2) **:** the flesh of game animals **b** *archaic* **:** PLUCK **c :** an object of ridicule or attack — often used in the phrase *fair game* ***syn*** see FUN

[2]**game** *vb* **gamed; gam·ing** *vi* **:** to play for a stake ~ *vt, archaic* **:** to lose or squander by gambling

[3]**game** *adj* **1 :** having a resolute unyielding spirit <~ to the end> **2 :** of or relating to game <~ laws>

[4]**game** *adj* [perh. fr. [3]*game*] **:** LAME <a ~ leg>

game·cock \'gām-ˌkäk\ *n* **:** a male game fowl

game fish *n* **1 :** a fish of a family (Salmonidae) including salmons, trouts, chars, and whitefishes **2 :** SPORT FISH; *esp* **:** a fish made a legal catch by law

game fowl *n* **:** a domestic fowl of a strain developed for the production of fighting cocks

game·keep·er \'gām-ˌkē-pər\ *n* **:** one that has charge of the breeding and protection of game animals or birds on a private preserve

gam·elan \'gam-ə-ˌlan\ *n* [Jav] **1 :** a Javanese instrument resembling the xylophone **2 :** a flute, string, and percussion orchestra of southeast Asia

game·ly \'gām-lē\ *adv* **:** in a plucky manner

game·ness \'gām-nəs\ *n* **:** ENDURANCE, PLUCK

game of chance : a game (as a dice game) in which chance rather than skill determines the outcome

game of skill : a game (as chess) in which skill rather than chance determines the outcome

game plan *n* **:** a strategy for achieving an objective

game point *n* **:** a situation (as in tennis) in which one player will win the game by winning the next point; *also* **:** the point won

games·man·ship \'gāmz-mən-ˌship\ *n* **:** the art or practice of winning games by questionable expedients without actually violating the rules

game·some \'gām-səm\ *adj* **:** MERRY, FROLICSOME — **game·some·ly** *adv* — **game·some·ness** *n*

game·ster \'gām-stər\ *n* **:** a person who plays games; *esp* **:** GAMBLER

gamet- *or* **gameto-** *comb form* [NL, fr. *gameta*] **:** gamete <*gameto*phore>

gam·etan·gi·um \ˌgam-ə-'tan-jē-əm\ *n, pl* **-gia** \-jē-ə\ [NL, fr. *gamet-* + Gk *angeion* vessel — more at ANGI-] **:** a cell or organ in which gametes are developed

ga·mete \gə-'mēt, 'gam-ˌēt\ *n* [NL *gameta,* fr. Gk *gametēs* husband, fr. *gamein* to marry, fr. *gamos* marriage — more at BIGAMY] **:** a mature germ cell possessing a haploid chromosome set and capable of initiating formation of a new individual by fusion with another gamete — **ga·met·ic** \gə-'met-ik\ *adj* — **ga·met·i·cal·ly** \-i-k(ə-)lē\ *adv*

game theory *n* **:** THEORY OF GAMES

ga·me·to·cyte \gə-'mēt-ə-ˌsīt\ *n* [ISV] **:** a cell that divides to produce gametes

ga·me·to·gen·e·sis \gə-ˌmēt-ə-'jen-ə-səs\ *n* [NL] **:** the production of gametes — **ga·me·to·gen·ic** \-'jen-ik\ *or* **gam·etog·e·nous** \ˌgam-ə-'täj-ə-nəs\ *adj* — **gam·etog·e·ny** \-nē\ *n*

ga·me·to·phore \gə-'mēt-ə-ˌfō(ə)r, -ˌfȯ(ə)r\ *n* **:** a modified branch bearing gametangia — **ga·me·to·phor·ic** \-ˌmēt-ə-'fȯr-ik, -'fär-\ *adj*

ga·me·to·phyte \gə-'mēt-ə-ˌfīt\ *n* [ISV] **:** the individual or generation of a plant exhibiting alternation of generations that bears sex organs — compare SPOROPHYTE — **ga·me·to·phyt·ic** \-ˌmēt-ə-'fit-ik\ *adj*

gam·ic \'gam-ik\ *adj* **:** requiring fertilization **:** SEXUAL

-gam·ic \'gam-ik\ *adj comb form* [ISV, fr. Gk *-gamos* -gamous] **:** having (such) reproductive organs <cleisto*gamic*>

gam·in \'gam-ən\ *n* [F] **1 :** a boy who hangs out on the streets **:** URCHIN **2 :** GAMINE 2

ga·mine \ga-'mēn\ *n* [F, fem. of *gamin*] **1 :** a girl who hangs out on the streets **:** TOMBOY **2 :** a girl of elfin appeal

gam·ing \'gā-miŋ\ *n* **1 :** the practice of gambling **2 :** the playing of games that simulate actual conditions (as of business or war) esp. for training or testing purposes

[1]**gam·ma** \'gam-ə\ *n* [ME, fr. LL, fr. Gk, of Sem origin; akin to Heb *gīmel* gimel] **1 :** the 3d letter of the Greek alphabet — see ALPHABET table **2 :** the degree of contrast of a developed photographic image or of a television image **3 :** a unit of magnetic intensity equal to 0.00001 oersted **4 :** GAMMA RAY **5 :** MICROGRAM

[2]**gamma** *or* γ- *adj* **1 :** of, relating to, or being one of three or more closely related chemical substances **2 :** third in position in the structure of an organic molecule from a particular group or atom

gamma globulin *n* **:** any of several globulins of plasma or serum that have less electrophoretic mobility at alkaline pH than serum albumins, alpha globulins, or beta globulins and that include most antibodies

gamma ray *n* **1 :** a photon or radiation quantum emitted spontaneously by a radioactive substance; *also* **:** a high-energy photon **2 :** a continuous stream of gamma rays — called also *gamma radiation*

gam·mer \'gam-ər\ *n* [prob. alter. of *godmother*] **:** an old woman — compare GAFFER

[1]**gam·mon** \'gam-ən\ *n* [ONF *gambon* ham, aug. of *gambe* leg — more at GAM] **1** *chiefly Brit* **:** HAM 2 **2** *chiefly Brit* **a :** a side of bacon **b :** the lower end of a side of bacon

[2]**gammon** *n* [perh. alter. of ME *gamen* game] **1** *archaic* **:** BACKGAMMON **2 :** the winning of a backgammon game before the loser removes any men from the board

[3]**gammon** *vt* **:** to beat by scoring a gammon

[4]**gammon** *n* [obs. *gammon* (talk)] **:** talk intended to deceive **:** HUMBUG

[5]**gammon** *vi* **1 :** to talk gammon **2 :** PRETEND, FEIGN ~ *vt* **:** DECEIVE, FOOL

gamo- — see GAM-

gamo·deme \'gam-ə-ˌdēm\ *n* **:** a more or less isolated breeding community of organisms

gamo·gen·e·sis \ˌgam-ə-'jen-ə-səs\ *n* [NL] **:** sexual reproduction — **gamo·ge·net·ic** \-jə-'net-ik\ *adj* — **gamo·ge·net·i·cal·ly** \-i-k(ə-)lē\ *adv*

gamo·pet·al·ous \-'pet-ᵊl-əs\ *adj* **:** having the corolla composed of united petals <the morning glory is ~>

gamo·phyl·lous \-'fil-əs\ *adj* **:** having united leaves or leaflike parts

gamo·sep·al·ous \-'sep-ə-ləs\ *adj* **:** having the sepals united

-g·a·mous \g-ə-məs\ *adj comb form* [Gk *-gamos,* fr. *gamos* marriage — more at BIGAMY] **1 :** characterized by having or practicing (such) a marriage or (such or so many) marriages <exo*gamous*> **2 :** -GAMIC <hetero*gamous*>

gamp \'gamp\ *n* [Sarah *Gamp,* nurse with a large umbrella in *Martin Chuzzlewit* by Charles Dickens] *Brit* **:** a large umbrella

gam·ut \'gam-ət\ *n* [ML *gamma,* lowest note of Guido's scale (fr. LL, 3d letter of the Greek alphabet) + *ut*] **1 :** the whole series of recognized musical notes **2 :** an entire range or series <the letters she received ran the ~ from praise to contempt>

gamy *or* **gam·ey** \'gā-mē\ *adj* **gam·i·er; -est 1 :** BRAVE, PLUCKY — used esp. of animals **2 a :** having the flavor of game; *esp* **:** having the flavor of game near tainting **b :** SMELLY **3 a :** SCANDALOUS, SPICY <gave her all the ~ details> **b :** CORRUPT, DISREPUTABLE <a ~ character> — **gam·i·ly** \-mə-lē\ *adv* — **gam·i·ness** \-mē-nəs\ *n*

-g·a·my \g-ə-mē\ *n comb form* [ME *-gamie,* fr. LL *-gamia,* fr. Gk — more at BIGAMY] **1 :** marriage <exo*gamy*> **2 :** union for propagation or reproduction <allo*gamy*> **3 :** possession of (such) reproductive organs or (such) a mode of fertilization <cleisto*gamy*>

gan *past of* GIN

Gan·da \'gan-də\ *n, pl* **Ganda** *or* **Gandas 1 :** a member of a Bantu-speaking people of Uganda **2 :** the Bantu language of the Ganda people used as the official language of Uganda

[1]**gan·der** \'gan-dər\ *n* [ME, fr. OE *gandra;* akin to OE *gōs* goose] **1 :** the adult male goose **2 :** SIMPLETON

[2]**gander** *vi, dial* **:** WANDER, RAMBLE

[3]**gander** *n* [prob. fr. [1]*gander;* fr. the outstretched neck of a person craning to look at something] *slang* **:** LOOK, GLANCE <talking and taking ~*s* at the girls — *Life*>

Gan·dhi·an \'gän-dē-ən, 'gan-\ *adj* **:** of or relating to the Indian political and spiritual leader Mohandas K. Gandhi or his principle of nonviolence

gan·dy dancer \'gan-dē-\ *n* [perh. fr. the *Gandy* Manufacturing Company, Chicago, Illinois, toolmakers] **1 :** a laborer in a railroad section gang **2 :** an itinerant or seasonal laborer

ga·nef \'gän-əf\ *n* [Yiddish, fr. Heb *gannābh* thief] *slang* **:** THIEF, RASCAL

Ga·ne·lon \ˌgan-ᵊl-'ōⁿ\ *n* [F] **:** the traitor in the Charlemagne romances who schemes for the defeat of Charlemagne's rear guard at Roncesvalles

[1]**gang** \'gaŋ\ *n* [ME, fr. OE; akin to OHG *gang* act of going, Skt *jaṅghā* shank] **1** *dial Brit* **:** JOURNEY, WAY **2 a** (1) **:** a set of articles **:** OUTFIT <a ~ of oars> (2) **:** a combination of similar implements or devices arranged for convenience to act together <a ~ of saws> **b :** GROUP: as (1) **:** a group of persons working together (2) **:** a group of persons working to unlawful or antisocial ends; *esp* **:** a band of antisocial adolescents **3 :** a group of persons having informal and usu. close social relations <have the ~ over for a party>

[2]**gang** *vt* **1 :** to attack in a gang **2 a :** to assemble or operate simultaneously as a group **b :** to arrange in or produce as a gang (as type pages) ~ *vi* **:** to move or act as a gang <everyone ~*ed* toward the door>

[3]**gang** *vi* [ME *gangen,* fr. OE *gangan;* akin to OE *gang*] *Scot* **:** GO

gang·er \'gaŋ-ər\ *n, Brit* **:** the foreman of a gang of workmen

gang hook *n* **:** two or three fishhooks with their shanks joined together

gang·land \'gaŋ-ˌland\ *n* **:** the world of organized crime

gangli- *or* **ganglio-** *comb form* [NL, fr. Gk *ganglion*] **:** ganglion <*gangli*ectomy> <*ganglio*plexus>

gan·gling \'gaŋ-gliŋ, -glən\ *adj* [perh. irreg. fr. Sc *gangrel* vagrant, lanky person] **:** being loosely and awkwardly built **:** LANKY <a ~ gawky child>

gan·gli·on \'gaŋ-glē-ən\ *n, pl* **-glia** \-glē-ə\ *also* **-gli·ons** [LL, fr. Gk] **1 a :** a small cystic tumor connected either with a joint membrane or tendon sheath **b :** a mass of nerve tissue containing nerve cells external to the brain or spinal cord; *also* **:** NUCLEUS 2b **2 :** a focus of strength or energy — **gan·gli·on·at·ed** \'gaŋ-glē-ə-ˌnāt-əd\ *adj* — **gan·gli·on·ic** \ˌgaŋ-glē-'än-ik\ *adj*

gan·gli·o·side \'gaŋ-glē-ə-ˌsīd\ *n* [ISV *ganglion* + [2]*-ose* + *-ide*] **:** any of a group of lipids that yield a hexose sugar on hydrolysis and are found esp. in ganglion cells

gan·gly \'gaŋ-glē\ *adj* **gan·gli·er; -est :** GANGLING

gang·plank \'gaŋ-ˌplaŋk\ *n* **:** a movable bridge used in boarding or leaving a ship at a pier

gang·plow \-ˌplau̇\ *n* **:** a plow designed to turn two or more furrows at one time

gang·rel \'gaŋ-(ə-)rəl\ *n* [ME, irreg. fr. *gangen* to go, fr. OE *gangan;* akin to OE *gang*] *Scot* **:** VAGRANT

[1]**gan·grene** \'gaŋ-ˌgrēn, gaŋ-', 'gan-ˌ, gan-'\ *n* [L *gangraena,* fr. Gk *gangraina;* akin to Gk *gran* to gnaw] **1 :** local death of soft tissues

due to loss of blood supply **2 :** a pervasive mortal evil — **gan·gre·nous** \'gaŋ-grə-nəs\ *adj*

[2]gangrene *vb* **gan·grened; gan·gren·ing** *vt* **:** to make gangrenous ~ *vi* **:** to become gangrenous

gang·ster \'gaŋ-stər\ *n* **:** a member of a gang of criminals **:** RACKETEER — **gang·ster·ism** \-stə-ˌriz-əm\ *n*

gangue \'gaŋ\ *n* [F, fr. G *gang* vein of metal, fr. OHG, act of going] **:** the worthless rock or vein matter in which valuable metals or minerals occur

gang up *vi* **1 :** to combine for a specific purpose <*ganged up* to raise prices> **2 :** to make a joint assault <*ganged up* on him and beat him up> **3 :** to exert group pressure <the class *ganged up* against the teacher>

gang·way \'gaŋ-ˌwā\ *n* **1 :** PASSAGEWAY; *esp* **:** a temporary way of planks **2 a :** either of the sides of the upper deck of a ship **b :** the opening by which a ship is boarded **c :** GANGPLANK **3** *Brit* **:** AISLE **4 :** a main level or haulageway in a mine **5 a :** a cross aisle dividing the front benches from the back benches in the British House of Commons **b :** an aisle in the British House of Commons that separates government and opposition benches **6 :** a clear passage through a crowd — often used as an interjection

gan·is·ter *or* **gan·nis·ter** \'gan-ə-stər\ *n* [origin unknown] **1 :** a fine-grained quartzite used in the manufacture of refractory brick **2 :** a mixture of ground quartz and fireclay used for lining metallurgical furnaces

gan·ja \'gän-jə, 'gan-\ *n* [Hindi *gā̃jā,* fr. Skt *gañjā*] **:** a potent and selected preparation of cannabis used esp. for smoking

gan·net \'gan-ət\ *n, pl* **gannets** *also* **gannet** [ME *ganet,* fr. OE *ganot;* akin to OE *gōs* goose] **:** any of several large fish-eating seabirds (family Sulidae) that breed in large colonies chiefly on offshore islands

gan·oid \'gan-ˌȯid\ *adj* [deriv. of Gk *ganos* brightness; akin to Gk *gēthein* to rejoice — more at JOY] **:** of or relating to a subclass (Ganoidei) of living and extinct teleost fishes (as the sturgeons) with usu. hard rhombic enameled scales — **ganoid** *n*

gante·lope *or* **gant·lope** \'gant-ˌlōp\ *n* [modif. of Sw *gatlopp,* fr. OSw *gatulop,* fr. *gata* road + *lop* course] *archaic* **:** [2]GAUNTLET

[1]gant·let \'gȯnt-lət, 'gänt-\ *var of* GAUNTLET

[2]gantlet *n* [[2]*gauntlet*] **:** a stretch of railroad track where two lines of track overlap so that one rail of each track is within the rails of the other in order to obviate switching

gant·line \'gant-ˌlīn, -lən\ *n* [perh. alter. of *girtline* (gantline)] **:** a line rove through a block aloft on a ship and used for hoisting

gan·try \'gan-trē\ *n, pl* **gantries** [perh. modif. of ONF *gantier,* fr. L *cantherius* trellis] **1 :** a frame for supporting barrels **2 :** a frame structure raised on side supports so as to span over or around something: as **a :** a platform made to carry a traveling crane and supported by towers or side frames running on parallel tracks; *also* **:** a movable structure with platforms at different levels used for erecting and servicing rockets before launching **b :** a structure spanning several railroad tracks and displaying signals for each

gantry 2b

Gan·y·mede \'gan-i-ˌmēd\ *n* [L *Ganymedes,* fr. Gk *Ganymēdēs*] **1 :** a beautiful youth in classical mythology carried off to Olympus to be the cupbearer of the gods **2 :** a youth who serves liquors **:** CUPBEARER **3 :** the 4th satellite of Jupiter

GAO *abbr* General Accounting Office

gaol \'jā(ə)l\ *chiefly Brit var of* JAIL

[1]gap \'gap\ *n* [ME, fr. ON, chasm, hole; akin to ON *gapa*] **1 a :** a break in a barrier (as a wall, hedge, or line of military defense) **b :** an assailable position **2 a :** a mountain pass **b :** RAVINE **3 :** SPARK GAP **4 :** a separation in space **5 :** a break in continuity **:** HIATUS <there were unexplained ~*s* in his story> **6 :** a break in the vascular cylinder of a plant where a vascular trace departs from the central cylinder **7 :** lack of balance **:** DISPARITY <the ~ between imports and exports> **8 :** a wide difference in character or attitude <the generation ~> — **gap·py** \-ē\ *adj*

[2]gap *vb* **gapped; gap·ping** *vt* **:** to make an opening in ~ *vi* **:** to fall or stand open

GAPA *abbr* ground-to-air pilotless aircraft

[1]gape \'gāp *also* 'gap\ *vi* **gaped; gap·ing** [ME *gapen,* fr. ON *gapa;* akin to L *hiare* to gape, yawn — more at YAWN] **1 a :** to open the mouth wide **b :** to open or part widely <holes *gaped* in the pavement> **2 :** to gaze stupidly or in openmouthed surprise or wonder **3 :** YAWN ***syn*** see GAZE — **gap·ing·ly** \'gā-piŋ-lē, 'gap-iŋ-\ *adj*

[2]gape *n* **1 :** an act of gaping: **a :** YAWN **b :** an openmouthed stare **2 :** an unfilled space or extent **3 a :** the median margin-to-margin length of the open mouth **b :** the line along which the mandibles of a bird close **c :** the width of an opening **4** *pl but sing in constr* **a :** a disease of young birds in which gapeworms invade and irritate the trachea **b :** a fit of yawning

gap·er \'gā-pər, 'gap-ər\ *n* **1 :** one that gapes **2 :** any of several large sluggish burrowing clams (family Myacidae) including several used for food

gape·worm \-ˌwərm\ *n* **:** a nematode worm (*Syngamus trachea*) that causes gapes of birds

gapped scale *n* **:** a musical scale derived from a larger system of tones by omitting certain tones

[1]gar \'gär\ *interj* [euphemism for *God*] — used as a mild oath

[2]gar *n* [short for *garfish*] **:** any of various fishes that have an elongate body resembling that of a pike and long and narrow jaws: as **a :** NEEDLEFISH **b :** any of several predaceous No. American freshwater ganoid fishes with rank tough flesh

[3]gar *abbr* garage

GAR *abbr* Grand Army of the Republic

[1]ga·rage \gə-'räzh, -'räj\ *n* [F, act of docking, garage, fr. *garer* to dock, of Gmc origin; akin to OHG bi*warōn* to protect — more at WARE] **:** a shelter or repair shop for automotive vehicles

[2]garage *vt* **ga·raged; ga·rag·ing :** to keep or put in a garage

ga·rage·man \-ˌman\ *n* **:** a garage worker

garage sale *n* **:** a sale of used household or personal articles (as furniture, tools, or clothing) held on the seller's own premises

Ga·rand rifle \gə-'rand-, ˌgar-ənd-\ *n* [John C. *Garand*] **:** M1 RIFLE

garb \'gärb\ *n* [MF or OIt; MF *garbe* graceful contour, grace, fr. OIt *garbo* grace] **1** *obs* **:** FASHION, MANNER **2 a :** style of apparel **b :** outward form **:** APPEARANCE <give . . . their madness the outward ~ of sanity —Lewis Mumford> — **garb** *vt*

gar·bage \'gär-bij\ *n* [ME, animal entrails] **1 a :** food waste **:** REFUSE **b :** unwanted or useless material **2 :** worthless writing or speech **:** TRASH

gar·ban·zo \gär-'ban-(ˌ)zō\ *n, pl* **-zos** [Sp] **:** CHICK-PEA — called also *garbanzo bean*

[1]gar·ble \'gär-bəl\ *vt* **gar·bled; gar·bling** \-b(ə-)liŋ\ [ME *garbelen,* fr. OIt *garbellare* to sift, fr. Ar *ghirbāl* sieve, fr. LL *cribellum;* akin to L *cernere* to sift — more at CERTAIN] **1** *archaic* **:** CULL **2 :** to sift impurities from **3 a :** to so alter or distort as to create a wrong impression or change the meaning <~ a story in repeating it> **b :** to introduce textual error into (a message) by inaccurate encipherment, transmission, or decipherment ***syn*** see MISREPRESENT — **gar·bler** \-b(ə-)lər\ *n*

[2]garble *n* **1 :** the impurities removed from spices in sifting **2 :** an act or an instance of garbling

gar·board \'gär-ˌbō(ə)rd, -ˌbȯ(ə)rd\ *n* [obs. D *gaarboord*] **:** the strake next to a ship's keel

gar·boil \-ˌbȯil\ *n* [MF *garbouil*] *archaic* **:** a confused disordered state **:** TURMOIL

gar·çon \gär-'sō^{n}\ *n, pl* **garçons** \-'sō^{n}(z)\ [F, boy, servant] **:** WAITER

garde–man·ger \ˌgärd-(ə-)ˌmä^{n}-'zhā\ *n, pl* **garde–mangers** \-'zhā(z)\ [F] **:** the cold meat department of a large kitchen; *also* **:** the chef in charge of it

[1]gar·den \'gärd-^{ə}n\ *n* [ME *gardin,* fr. ONF, of Gmc origin; akin to OHG *gart* enclosure — more at YARD] **1 a :** a plot of ground where herbs, fruits, flowers, or vegetables are cultivated **b :** a rich well-cultivated region **c :** a container (as a window box) planted with usu. a variety of small plants <herb ~*s*> <a dish ~> **2 a :** a public recreation area or park <a botanical ~> **b :** an open-air eating or drinking place — **gar·den·ful** \-ˌfu̇l\ *n*

[2]garden *vb* **gar·dened; gar·den·ing** \'gärd-niŋ, -^{ə}n-iŋ\ *vi* **:** to lay out or work in a garden ~ *vt* **1 :** to make into a garden **2 :** to ornament with gardens — **gar·den·er** \'gärd-nər, -^{ə}n-ər\ *n*

[3]garden *adj* **1 :** of, relating to, or frequenting a garden **2 a :** of a kind grown in the open as distinguished from one more delicate <~ plant> **b :** ORDINARY, COMMONPLACE <he was merely a common or ~ blackmailer —Dorothy Sayers>

garden apartment *n* **:** a multiple-unit dwelling having considerable lawn or garden space

garden city *n* **:** a planned residential community with park and planted areas

garden cress *n* **:** an Asiatic annual herb (*Lepidium sativum*) of the mustard family sometimes cultivated for its pungent basal leaves

garden heliotrope *n* **1 :** a tall rhizomatous Old World valerian (*Valeriana officinalis*) widely cultivated for its fragrant tiny flowers and for its roots which yield the drug valerian **2 :** a shrubby Peruvian heliotrope (*Heliotropium arborescens*) with fragrant usu. lilac or violet flowers

gar·de·nia \gär-'dē-nyə\ *n* [NL, genus name, fr. Alexander *Garden* †1791 Sc naturalist] **:** any of a large genus (*Gardenia*) of Old World tropical trees and shrubs of the madder family with showy fragrant white or yellow flowers

garden–variety *adj* **:** GARDEN 2b

garde·robe \'gär-ˌdrōb\ *n* [ME, fr. MF; akin to ONF *warderobe* wardrobe] **1 :** a wardrobe or its contents **2 :** a private room **:** BEDROOM **3 :** PRIVY

gar·dy·loo \ˌgärd-ē-'lü\ *interj* [perh. fr. F *garde à l'eau!* look out for the water!] — used in Edinburgh as a warning cry when it was customary to throw slops from the windows into the streets

Gar·eth \'gar-əth\ *n* **:** a knight of the Round Table and nephew of King Arthur

gar·fish \'gär-ˌfish\ *n* [ME *garfysshe*] **:** GAR

Gar·gan·tua \gär-'ganch(-ə)-wə\ *n* [F] **:** a gigantic king in Rabelais' *Gargantua* having a great capacity for food and drink

gar·gan·tuan \-wən\ *adj, often cap* [*Gargantua*] **:** of tremendous size or volume **:** GIGANTIC, COLOSSAL <entire cities fleeing before ~ walls of water —William Cleary>

gar·get \'gär-gət\ *n* [prob. fr. ME, throat, fr. MF *gargate;* akin to MF *gargouiller*] **:** mastitis of domestic animals; *esp* **:** chronic bovine mastitis with gross changes in the form and texture of the udder — **gar·gety** \-gət-ē\ *adj*

gargoyle 1a

[1]gar·gle \'gär-gəl\ *vb* **gar·gled; gar·gling** \-g(ə-)liŋ\ [MF *gargouiller* to gargle, of imit. origin] *vt* **1 a :** to hold (a liquid) in the mouth or throat and agitate with air from the lungs **b :** to cleanse or disinfect (the oral cavity) in this manner **2 :** to utter with a gargling sound ~ *vi* **1 :** to use a gargle **2 :** to speak or sing as if gargling

[2]gargle *n* **1 :** a liquid used in gargling **2 :** a gargling sound

gar·goyle \'gär-ˌgȯil\ *n* [ME *gargoyl,* fr. MF *gargouille;* akin to MF *gargouiller*] **1 a :** a spout in the form of a grotesque human or animal figure projecting from a roof gutter to throw rainwater clear of a building **b :** a grotesquely carved figure **2 :** a person with an ugly face — **gar·goyled** \-ˌgȯild\ *adj*

gar·i·bal·di \ˌgar-ə-ˈbȯl-dē\ *n* **:** a woman's blouse copied from the red shirt worn by the Italian patriot Garibaldi

gar·ish \ˈga(ə)r-ish, ˈge(ə)r-\ *adj* [origin unknown] **1 :** clothed in vivid colors **2 a :** excessively vivid **:** FLASHY **b :** offensively or distressingly bright **:** GLARING **3 :** tastelessly showy ***syn*** see GAUDY ***ant*** somber — **gar·ish·ly** *adv* — **gar·ish·ness** *n*

[1]**gar·land** \ˈgär-lənd\ *n* [ME, fr. MF *garlande*] **1 :** WREATH, CHAPLET **2 :** a grommet or ring of rope used aboard ship in hoisting or to prevent chafing **3 :** ANTHOLOGY, COLLECTION

[2]**garland** *vt* **:** to form into or deck with a garland

gar·lic \ˈgär-lik\ *n* [ME *garlek*, fr. OE *gārlēac*, fr. *gār* spear + *lēac* leek — more at GORE]**:** a European bulbous herb (*Allium sativum*) of the lily family widely cultivated for its pungent compound bulbs much used in cookery; *also* **:** one of the bulbs — **gar·licky** \-li-kē\ *adj*

garlic salt *n* **:** a seasoning of ground dried garlic and salt

[1]**gar·ment** \ˈgär-mənt\ *n* [ME, fr. MF *garnement*, fr. OF, fr. *garnir* to equip — more at GARNISH]**:** an article of clothing

[2]**garment** *vt* **:** to clothe with or as if with a garment

[1]**gar·ner** \ˈgär-nər\ *n* [ME, fr. OF *grenier*, fr. L *granarium*, fr. *granum* grain] **1 a :** GRANARY **b :** a grain bin **2 :** something that is collected **:** ACCUMULATION

[2]**garner** *vt* **gar·nered; gar·ner·ing** \ˈgärn-(ə-)riŋ\ **1 a :** to gather into storage **b :** to deposit as if in a granary <volumes in which he has ~*ed* the fruits of his lifetime labors —Reinhold Niebuhr> **2 a :** to acquire by effort **:** EARN **b :** ACCUMULATE, COLLECT

gar·net \ˈgär-nət\ *n* [ME *grenat*, fr. MF, fr. *grenat*, adj., red like a pomegranate, fr. (*pomme*) *grenate* pomegranate] **1 :** a brittle and more or less transparent usu. red silicate mineral that has a vitreous luster, occurs mainly in crystals but also massive and in grains, is found commonly in gneiss and mica schist, and is used as a semiprecious stone and as an abrasive (hardness 6.5–7.5, sp. gr. 3.15–4.3) **2 :** a variable color averaging a dark red

gar·net·if·er·ous \ˌgär-nət-ˈif-(ə-)rəs\ *adj* **:** containing garnets

garnet paper *n* **:** an abrasive paper with crushed garnet as the abrasive

gar·ni·er·ite \ˈgär-nē-ə-ˌrīt\ *n* [Jules *Garnier* †1904 F geologist] **:** a soft mineral prob. $(Mg, Ni)_3Si_2O_5(OH)_4$ consisting of hydrous nickel magnesium silicate and constituting an important ore of nickel

[1]**gar·nish** \ˈgär-nish\ *vt* [ME *garnishen*, fr. MF *garniss-*, stem of *garnir* to warn, equip, garnish, of Gmc origin; akin to OHG *warnōn* to take heed — more at WARN] **1 a :** DECORATE, EMBELLISH **b :** to add decorative or savory touches to (food) **2 :** to equip with accessories **:** FURNISH **3 :** GARNISHEE ***syn*** see ADORN

[2]**garnish** *n* **1 :** EMBELLISHMENT, ORNAMENT **2 :** a savory or decorative condiment (as watercress or parsley) **3 a :** an unauthorized fee formerly extorted from a new inmate of an English jail **b :** a similar payment required of a new workman

[1]**gar·nish·ee** \ˌgär-nə-ˈshē\ *n* **:** one who is served with a garnishment

[2]**garnishee** *vt* **-eed; -ee·ing 1 :** to serve with a garnishment **2 :** to take (as a debtor's wages) by legal authority

gar·nish·ment \ˈgär-nish-mənt\ *n* **1 :** GARNISH **2 :** a legal summons or warning concerning the attachment of property to satisfy a debt **3 :** a stoppage of a specified sum from wages to satisfy a creditor

gar·ni·ture \ˈgär-ni-chər, -nə-ˌchu̇(ə)r\ *n* [MF, equipment, alter. of OF *garnesture*, fr. *garnir*] **:** EMBELLISHMENT, TRIMMING

gar·pike \ˈgär-ˌpīk\ *n* **:** GAR b

gar·ret \ˈgar-ət\ *n* [ME *garette* watchtower, fr. MF *garite*, perh. fr. OProv *garida*, fr. *garir* to protect, of Gmc origin; akin to OHG *werien*]**:** a room or unfinished part of a house just under the roof

[1]**gar·ri·son** \ˈgar-ə-sən\ *n* [ME *garisoun* protection, fr. OF *garison*, fr. *garir* to protect, of Gmc origin; akin to OHG *werien* to defend — more at WEIR] **1 :** a military post; *esp* **:** a permanent military installation **2 :** the troops stationed at a garrison

[2]**garrison** *vt* **gar·ri·soned; gar·ri·son·ing** \ˈgar-ə-s(ə-)niŋ\ **1 :** to station troops in **2 a :** to assign as a garrison **b :** to occupy with troops

garrison cap *n* **:** a visorless folding cap worn as part of a military uniform — compare SERVICE CAP

Gar·ri·son finish \ˌgar-ə-sən-\ *n* [prob. fr. Snapper *Garrison*, 19th cent. Am jockey]**:** a finish in which the winner comes from behind at the end

garrison house *n* **1 :** a house fortified against Indian attack **2 :** BLOCKHOUSE **3 :** a house having the second story overhanging the first in the front

garrison state *n* **:** a state organized on a primarily military basis; *esp* **:** one whose military preparations threaten to convert it into a totalitarian state

gar·ron \ˈgar-ən, gə-ˈrōn\ *n* [IrGael *gearrān* & ScGael *gearran*, gelding] *Scot & Irish* **:** a small sturdy work horse

[1]**gar·rote** *or* **ga·rotte** \gə-ˈrät, -ˈrōt\ *n* [Sp *garrote*] **1 a :** a method of execution by strangling with an iron collar **b :** the iron collar used **2 a :** strangulation esp. with robbery as the motive **b :** an implement for this purpose

[2]**garrote** *or* **garotte** *vt* **gar·rot·ed** *or* **ga·rott·ed; gar·rot·ing** *or* **ga·rott·ing 1 :** to execute with or as if with a garrote **2 :** to strangle and rob — **gar·rot·er** *n*

gar·ru·li·ty \gə-ˈrü-lət-ē, ga-\ *n* **:** the quality or state of being talkative

gar·ru·lous \ˈgar-ə-ləs *also* ˈgar-yə-\ *adj* [L *garrulus*, fr. *garrire* to chatter — more at CARE]**:** given to prosy, rambling, or tedious loquacity **:** pointlessly or annoyingly talkative ***syn*** see TALKATIVE ***ant*** taciturn — **gar·ru·lous·ly** *adv* — **gar·ru·lous·ness** *n*

[1]**gar·ter** \ˈgärt-ər\ *n* [ME, fr. ONF *gartier*, fr. *garet* bend of the knee, of Celt origin; akin to OIr *gairri* calves of the legs] **1 a :** a band worn to hold up a stocking or sock **b :** a strap hanging from a girdle or corset to support a stocking **c :** a band worn to hold up a shirt sleeve **2** *cap* **a :** the British Order of the Garter **b :** the blue velvet garter that is its badge **c :** membership in the order

[2]**garter** *vt* **:** to support with or as if with a garter

garter snake *n* **:** any of numerous harmless viviparous American snakes (genus *Thamnophis*) with longitudinal stripes on the back

garth \ˈgärth\ *n* [ME, fr. ON *garthr* yard; akin to OHG *gart* enclosure — more at YARD] *archaic* **:** a small yard or enclosure **:** CLOSE

gar·vey \ˈgär-vē\ *n*, *pl* **garveys** [prob. fr. the name *Garvey*] **:** a small scow of the New Jersey coast

[1]**gas** \ˈgas\ *n*, *pl* **gas·es** *also* **gas·ses** [NL, alter. of L *chaos* space, chaos] **1 :** a fluid (as air) that has neither independent shape nor volume but tends to expand indefinitely **2 a :** a gas or gaseous mixture with the exception of atmospheric air: as (1) **:** a gas or gaseous mixture used to produce anesthesia (2) **:** a combustible gaseous mixture (as for fuel) **b :** a substance that can be used to produce a poisonous, asphyxiating, or irritant atmosphere **3** *slang* **:** empty talk **:** BOMBAST **4 :** GASOLINE **5** *slang* **:** one that has unusual appeal <if you dig skinny-dipping with kindred souls, it is a ~ —*Berkeley Barb*>

[2]**gas** *vb* **gassed; gas·sing** *vt* **1 a :** to treat chemically with gas **b :** to poison or otherwise affect adversely with gas **2 :** to supply with gas or esp. gasoline <~ up the automobile> ~ *vi* **1 :** to give off gas **2** *slang* **:** to talk idly **3 :** to fill the tank (as of an automobile) with gasoline — often used with *up*

gas·bag \ˈgas-ˌbag\ *n* **1 :** a bag for holding gas **2 :** an idle talker

gas chamber *n* **:** a chamber in which prisoners are executed by poison gas

gas·con \ˈgas-kən\ *n* **1** *cap* **:** a native of Gascony **2 :** a boastful swaggering person — **Gascon** *adj*

gas·con·ade \ˌgas-kə-ˈnād\ *n* [F *gasconnade*, fr. *gasconner* to boast, fr. *gascon* gascon, boaster]**:** BRAVADO, BOASTING — **gasconade** *vi* — **gas·con·ad·er** *n*

gas·eous \ˈgas-ē-əs, ˈgash-əs\ *adj* **1 a :** having the form of or being gas; *also* **:** of or relating to gases **b :** heated so as to remain free from suspended liquid droplets — used of a vapor not in contact with its own liquid **2 :** lacking substance or solidity **:** TENUOUS — **gas·eous·ness** *n*

gas fitter *n* **:** a workman who installs or repairs gas pipes and appliances

gas gangrene *n* **:** progressive gangrene marked by impregnation of the dead and dying tissue with gas and caused by one or more toxin-producing clostridia

[1]**gash** \ˈgash\ *vb* [ME *garsen*, fr. ONF *garser*, fr. (assumed) VL *charissare*, fr. Gk *charassein* to scratch, engrave — more at CHARACTER] *vt* **:** to make a gash in ~ *vi* **:** to make a gash **:** CUT

[2]**gash** *n* **1 :** a deep long cut esp. in flesh **2 :** a deep narrow depression in land whether natural or man-made

[3]**gash** *adj* [origin unknown] **1** *chiefly Scot* **:** KNOWING, WITTY **2** *chiefly Scot* **:** well dressed **:** TRIM

gas·hold·er \ˈgas-ˌhōl-dər\ *n* **:** a container for gas; *esp* **:** a large cylindrical tank for storing fuel gas under pressure commonly having two parts one of which telescopes into the other

gas·house \-ˌhau̇s\ *n* **:** GASWORKS

gas·ify \ˈgas-ə-ˌfī\ *vb* **-ified; -ify·ing** *vt* **:** to convert into gas <~ coal> ~ *vi* **:** to become gaseous — **gas·i·fi·ca·tion** \ˌgas-ə-fə-ˈkā-shən\ *n* — **gas·i·fi·er** \ˈgas-ə-ˌfī(-ə)r\ *n*

gas·ket \ˈgas-kət\ *n* [prob. alter. of F *garcette*] **1 :** a line or band used to lash a furled sail **2 a :** plaited hemp or tallowed rope for packing pistons or making pipe or other joints fluid-tight **b :** packing for the same purpose made of other material (as rubber, asbestos, or metal)

gas·kin \ˈgas-kən\ *n* [prob. short for *galligaskins*] **1** *pl*, *obs* **:** HOSE, BREECHES **2 :** a part of the hind leg of a quadruped between the stifle and the hock — see HORSE illustration

gas·light \ˈgas-ˌlīt, -ˈlīt\ *n* **1 :** light made by burning illuminating gas **2 :** a gas flame or gas lighting fixture

gas·lit \-ˌlit, -ˈlit\ *adj* **:** illuminated by gaslight

gas log *n* **:** a hollow perforated imitation log used as a gas burner in a fireplace

gas mask *n* **:** a mask connected to a chemical air filter and used to protect the face and lungs against poison gases; *broadly* **:** RESPIRATOR 1

gas mask

gas·ogene \ˈgas-ə-ˌjēn\ *n* [F *gazogène*, fr. *gaz* gas (fr. NL *gas*) + *-o-* + *-gène* -gen] **1 :** a portable apparatus for carbonating liquids **2 :** an apparatus carried by a vehicle to produce gas for fuel by partial burning of charcoal or wood

gas oil *n* **:** a hydrocarbon oil used as a fuel oil; *esp* **:** a petroleum distillate intermediate in boiling range and viscosity between kerosine and lubricating oil

gas·olier \ˌgas-ə-ˈli(ə)r\ *n* [alter. of *gaselier*, fr. *gas* + *-elier* (as in *chandelier*)] **:** a gaslight chandelier

gas·o·line *or* **gas·o·lene** \ˈgas-ə-ˌlēn, ˌgas-ə-ˈ\ *n* [[1]*gas* + *-ol* + *-ine* or *-ene*] **:** a volatile flammable liquid hydrocarbon mixture used as a fuel esp. for internal-combustion engines and blended from several products of natural gas and petroleum — **gas·o·lin·ic** \ˌgas-ə-ˈlē-nik, -ˈlin-ik\ *adj*

gas·om·e·ter \ga-ˈsäm-ət-ər\ *n* [F *gazomètre*, fr. *gaz* + *-o-* + *-mètre* -meter] **1 :** a laboratory apparatus for holding and measuring gases **2 :** GASHOLDER

gas–operated *adj*, *of a firearm* **:** utilizing part of the powder gases to operate the action

gasp \ˈgasp\ *vi* [ME *gaspen*; akin to ON *geispa* to yawn] **1 :** to catch the breath convulsively and audibly (as with shock) **2 :** to breathe laboriously **:** PANT — **gasp** *n*

gasp·er \ˈgäs-pə(r)\ *n*, *slang Brit* **:** CIGARETTE

gas plant *n* : FRAXINELLA

gas·ser \'gas-ər\ *n* **1 :** an oil well that yields gas **2** *slang* **:** a talkative person **3** *slang* **:** something outstanding

gas station *n* : SERVICE STATION 1

gas·sy \'gas-ē\ *adj* **gas·si·er; -est 1 :** full of or containing gas **2 :** having the characteristics of gas **3 :** full of boastful or insincere talk — **gas·si·ness** *n*

gast \'gast\ *vt* [ME *gasten,* fr. *gast, gost* ghost] *obs* : SCARE

gaster- *or* **gastero-** *comb form* [NL, fr. Gk *gastero-* belly, fr. *gastr-, gaster-, gastēr*] : ventral area <*Gastero*poda>

gas·tight \'gas-'tīt\ *adj* : impervious to gas — **gas·tight·ness** *n*

gast·ness \'gas(t)-nəs\ *n, obs* : FRIGHT, TERROR

gastr- *or* **gastro-** *also* **gastri-** *comb form* [Gk, fr. *gastr-, gastēr*] **1 :** belly <*Gastro*poda> : stomach <*gastr*itis> **2 :** gastric and <*gastro*intestinal>

gas·traea *also* **gas·trea** \ga-'strē-ə\ *n* [NL, fr. Gk *gastr-, gastēr*] : a hypothetical metazoan ancestral form corresponding in organization to a simple invaginated gastrula — **gas·trae·al** \-əl\ *adj*

gas·tral \'gas-trəl\ *adj* : of or relating to the stomach or digestive tract

gas·trec·to·my \ga-'strek-tə-mē\ *n, pl* **-mies** [ISV] : surgical removal of all or part of the stomach

gas·tric \'gas-trik\ *adj* [Gk *gastr-, gastēr,* alter. of (assumed) Gk *grastēr,* fr. Gk *gran* to gnaw, eat] : of or relating to the stomach

gastric juice *n* : a thin watery acid digestive fluid secreted by glands in the mucous membrane of the stomach

gastric ulcer *n* : a peptic ulcer situated in the stomach

gas·trin \'gas-trən\ *n* : a polypeptide hormone that is secreted by the gastric mucosa and induces secretion of gastric juice

gas·tri·tis \ga-'strīt-əs\ *n* : inflammation esp. of the mucous membrane of the stomach

gas·troc·ne·mi·us \gas-(,)träk-'nē-mē-əs, -trək-\ *n, pl* **-mii** \-mē-,ī\ [NL, fr. Gk *gastroknēmē* calf of the leg, fr. *gastr-* + *knēmē* shank] : the largest and most superficial muscle of the calf of the leg arising by two heads from the condyles of the femur and having its tendon of insertion incorporated as part of the Achilles tendon

gas·tro·coel *also* **gas·tro·coele** \'gas-trə-,sēl\ *n* [F *gastrocèle,* fr. *gastr-* + *-cèle* -coele] : ARCHENTERON

gas·tro·du·o·de·nal \'gas-trō-,d(y)ü-ə-'dēn-ᵊl, -d(y)ù-'äd-ᵊn-əl\ *adj* : of, relating to, or involving both the stomach and the duodenum

gas·tro·en·ter·i·tis \,gas-trō-,ent-ə-'rīt-əs\ *n* : inflammation of the lining membrane of the stomach and the intestines

gas·tro·en·ter·ol·o·gy \-,ent-ə-'räl-ə-jē\ *n* [ISV] : the study of the diseases and pathology of the stomach and intestines — **gas·tro·en·ter·o·log·i·cal** \-rə-'läj-i-kəl\ *adj* — **gas·tro·en·ter·ol·o·gist** \-,ent-ə-'räl-ə-jəst\ *n*

gas·tro·esoph·a·ge·al \'gas-trō-i-,säf-ə-'jē-əl\ *adj* : of, relating to, or involving the stomach and esophagus

gas·tro·gen·ic \,gas-trə-'jen-ik\ *or* **gas·trog·e·nous** \ga-'sträj-ə-nəs\ *adj* : of gastric origin <~ anemia>

gas·tro·in·tes·ti·nal \,gas-trō-in-'tes-tən-ᵊl, -'tes(t)-nəl\ *adj* : of or relating to both stomach and intestine

gas·tro·nome \'gas-trə-,nōm\ *n* [F, back-formation fr. *gastronomie*] : EPICURE, GOURMET

gas·tro·nom·ic \,gas-trə-'näm-ik\ *also* **gas·tro·nom·i·cal** \-i-kəl\ *adj* : of or relating to gastronomy — **gas·tro·nom·i·cal·ly** \-i-k(ə-)lē\ *adv*

gas·tron·o·mist \ga-'strän-ə-məst\ *n* : GASTRONOME

gas·tron·o·my \-mē\ *n* [F *gastronomie,* fr. Gk *Gastronomia,* title of a 4th cent. B.C. poem, fr. *gastro-* belly + *-nomia* -nomy] **1 :** good eating or its lore **2 :** culinary customs or style

gas·tro·pod \'gas-trə-,päd\ *n* [NL *Gastropoda,* class name] : any of a large class (Gastropoda) of mollusks (as snails) with a univalve shell or none and usu. with a distinct head bearing sensory organs — **gastropod** *also* **gas·trop·o·dan** \ga-'sträp-əd-ən\ *or* **gas·trop·o·dous** \-əd-əs\ *adj*

gas·tro·scope \'gas-trə-,skōp\ *n* [ISV] : an instrument for viewing the interior of the stomach — **gas·tro·scop·ic** \,gas-trə-'skäp-ik\ *adj* — **gas·tros·co·pist** \ga-'sträs-kə-pəst\ *n* — **gas·tros·co·py** \-pē\ *n*

gas·tro·trich \'gas-trə-,trik\ *n* [deriv. of Gk *gastr-* + *trich-, thrix* hair — more at TRICH-] : any of a small group (Gastrotricha) of minute freshwater multicellular animals superficially resembling infusorians — **gas·trot·ri·chan** \ga-'strä-tri-kən\ *adj or n*

gas·tro·vas·cu·lar \,gas-trō-'vas-kyə-lər\ *adj* [ISV] : functioning in both digestion and circulation <the ~ cavity of a coelenterate>

gas·tru·la \'gas-trə-lə\ *n, pl* **-las** *or* **-lae** \-,lē, -,lī\ [NL, fr. *gastr-*] : an early metazoan embryo consisting of a hollow 2-layered cellular cup made up of an outer epiblast and an inner hypoblast that meet along the marginal line of a blastopore and jointly enclose the archenteron — **gas·tru·lar** \-lər\ *adj*

gas·tru·late \-,lāt\ *vi* **-lat·ed; -lat·ing :** to become or form a gastrula — **gas·tru·la·tion** \,gas-trə-'lā-shən\ *n*

gas turbine *n* : an internal-combustion engine in which turbine blades are driven by hot gases whose pressure and velocity are intensified by compressed air introduced into the combustion chamber

gas·works \'gas-,wərks\ *n pl but sing in constr* : a plant for manufacturing gas and esp. illuminating gas

¹gat \(')gat\ *archaic past of* GET

²gat \'gat\ *n* [prob. fr. D, lit., hole; akin to OE *geat*] : a natural or artificial channel or passage

³gat \'gat\ *n* [short for *Gatling gun*] *slang* : PISTOL

¹gate \'gāt\ *n* [ME, fr. OE *geat;* akin to ON *gat* opening, Gk *chezein* to defecate] **1 :** an opening in a wall or fence **2 :** a city or castle entrance often with defensive structures (as towers) **3 :** the frame or door that closes a gate **4 a :** a means of entrance or exit **b :** a pass or defile in mountains **c :** a space between two markers through which a skier must pass in the course of a slalom race **d :** a mechanically operated barrier used as a starting device for a race (as in skiing) **5 a :** a door, valve, or other device for controlling the passage esp. of fluid **b :** a signal that makes an electronic circuit operative for a short period **c :** a device (as in a computer) that outputs a signal when specified input conditions are met <logic ~> **6 :** a channel in a foundry mold through which the molten metal flows into the cavity made by the pattern **7 :** the total admission receipts or the number of spectators at a sports event **8** *slang* : DISMISSAL <gave him the ~>

²gate *vt* **gat·ed; gat·ing 1 :** to supply with a gate **2** *Brit* **:** to punish by confinement to a campus or dormitory **3 :** to control by means of a gate

³gate *n* [ME, fr. ON *gata* road; akin to OHG *gazza* road] **1** *archaic* : WAY, PATH **2** *dial* : METHOD, STYLE

gate–crash·er \'gāt-,krash-ər\ *n* : one who enters, attends, or participates without ticket or invitation — **gate–crash** *vb*

gate·fold \-,fōld\ *n* : FOLDOUT

gate·keep·er \-,kē-pər\ *n* : one that tends or guards a gate

gate·leg table \,gāt-,leg-, -,lāg-\ *n* : a table with drop leaves supported by movable paired legs

gateleg table

gate·post \'gāt-,pōst\ *n* : the post to which a gate is hung or the one against which it closes

gate·way \-,wā\ *n* **1 :** an opening for a gate **2 :** GATE 4a

¹gath·er \'gath-ər, 'geth-\ *vb* **gath·ered; gath·er·ing** \-(ə-)riŋ\ [ME *gaderen,* fr. OE *gaderian;* akin to Skt *gadh* to hold fast — more at GOOD] *vt* **1 :** to bring together : COLLECT **2 a :** PICK, HARVEST **b :** to pick up little by little **c :** to accumulate and place in readiness <~*ed* up his tools> **d :** to assemble (volume signatures) in sequence for binding **3 :** to serve as a center of attraction for **4 :** to effect the collection of (as tax) **5 a :** to summon up <~*ed* his courage> **b :** to gain by gradual increase : ACCUMULATE <~ speed> **c :** to prepare (as oneself) by mustering strength **6 a :** to bring together the parts of **b :** to draw about or close to something <~*ing* his cloak about him> **c :** to pull (fabric) along a line of stitching so as to draw into puckers **d :** to haul in **7 :** to reach a conclusion often intuitively from hints or through inferences <I ~ that you are ready to leave> ~ *vi* **1 a :** to come together in a body **b :** to cluster around a focus of attraction **2 a :** to swell and fill with pus **b :** GROW, INCREASE — **gath·er·er** \-ər-ər\ *n*

syn **1** GATHER, COLLECT, ASSEMBLE, CONGREGATE *shared meaning element* : to come or bring together into a group, mass, or unit **2** see INFER

²gather *n* **1 :** something gathered; *esp* **:** a puckering in cloth made by gathering **2 :** an act or instance of gathering

gath·er·ing *n* **1 :** ASSEMBLY, MEETING **2 :** a suppurating swelling : ABSCESS **3 :** the collecting of food and raw materials from the wild **4 :** COLLECTION, COMPILATION **5 :** a gather in cloth

Gat·ling gun \,gat-liŋ-\ *n* [Richard J. *Gatling* †1903 Am inventor] : an early machine gun with a crank-operated revolving cluster of barrels fired once each per revolution

GATT *abbr* General Agreement on Tariffs and Trade

gauche \'gōsh\ *adj* [F, lit., left] **1 :** lacking social experience or grace : CRUDE **2 :** not planar <~ conformation of molecules> *syn* see AWKWARD — **gauche·ly** *adv* — **gauche·ness** *n*

gau·che·rie \,gōsh-(ə-)'rē\ *n* : a tactless or awkward act

gau·cho \'gaù-(,)chō\ *n, pl* **gauchos** [AmerSp] : a cowboy of the So. American pampas

gaud \'gòd, 'gäd\ *n* [ME *gaude*] : ORNAMENT, TRINKET

gaud·ery \-ə-rē\ *n* : showy ornamentation; *esp* : personal finery

¹gaudy \'gòd-ē, 'gäd-\ *adj* **gaud·i·er; -est :** ostentatiously or tastelessly ornamented — **gaud·i·ly** \'gòd-ᵊl-ē, 'gäd-\ *adv* — **gaud·i·ness** \'gòd-ē-nəs, 'gäd-\ *n*

syn GAUDY, TAWDRY, GARISH, FLASHY, MERETRICIOUS *shared meaning element* : vulgarly or cheaply showy. GAUDY implies a tasteless use of overly bright, often clashing colors or excessive ornamentation <false eloquence, like the prismatic glass, its *gaudy* colors spreads on every place —Alexander Pope> TAWDRY applies to what is at once gaudy and cheap and sleazy <the woman . . . big, bovine in a motley of cheap and *tawdry* clothes —William Styron> GARISH describes what is distressingly or offensively bright <hide me from day's *garish* eye —John Milton> FLASHY implies an effect of brilliance quickly and easily seen to be shallow or vulgar <two painted *flashy* women with fine legs —Graham Greene> MERETRICIOUS stresses falsity and may describe a tawdry show that beckons with a false allure or promise <soldiers . . . circled displays of colored postcards, and picked up *meretricious* mementos —James Baldwin> *ant* quiet (*in taste or color*)

²gau·dy \'gòd-ē, 'gäd-\ *n, pl* **gaudies** [prob. fr. L *gaudium* joy — more at JOY] : a feast or entertainment esp. in the form of an annual college dinner in a British university

gauf·fer \'gäf-ər, 'gòf-, 'gōf-\ *var of* GOFFER

¹gauge \'gāj\ *n* [ME *gauge,* fr. ONF] **1 a :** measurement according to some standard or system **b :** DIMENSIONS, SIZE **2 :** an instrument for or a means of measuring or testing: as **a :** an instrument for measuring a dimension or for testing mechanical accuracy **b :** an instrument with a graduated scale or dial for measuring or indicating quantity **3 :** relative position of a ship with reference to another ship and the wind **4 a :** the distance between the rails of a railroad **b :** the distance between a pair of wheels on an axle **5 :** the quantity of plaster of paris used with mortar to accelerate its setting **6 :** the size of a shotgun expressed as the number of lead balls each just fitting the interior diameter of the barrel required to make a pound <a 12-*gauge* shotgun> **7 a :** the thickness of a thin material (as sheet metal or plastic film) **b :** the diameter of a slender object (as wire, a hypodermic needle, or a screw) **c :** the fineness of a knitted fabric expressed by the number of loops per 1½ inch so that the higher the number the finer the texture ***syn*** see STANDARD

gauges 2a: *1* feeler, *2* wire or sheet metal, *3* depth, *4* marking, *5* go no-go, *6* thread

2gauge *vt* **gauged; gaug·ing** **1 a :** to measure the size, dimensions, or other measurable quantity of exactly **b :** to determine the capacity or contents of **c :** ESTIMATE, JUDGE **2 a :** to check for conformity to specifications or limits **b :** to measure off or set out **3 :** to mix (plaster) in definite proportions **4 :** to dress (as bricks) to size by rubbing or chipping — **gauge·able** \ˈgā-jə-bəl\ *adj* — **gauge·ably** \-blē\ *adv*

gaug·er \ˈgā-jər\ *n* **1 :** one that gauges **2** *chiefly Brit* **:** an exciseman who inspects dutiable bulk goods

Gaul \ˈgȯl\ *n* **1 :** a Celt of ancient Gaul **2 :** FRENCHMAN

1Gaul·ish \ˈgȯ-lish\ *adj* **:** of or relating to the Gauls or their language or land

2Gaulish *n* **:** the Celtic language of the ancient Gauls — see INDO-EUROPEAN LANGUAGES table

Gaull·ism \ˈgō-ˌliz-əm, ˈgȯ-\ *n* **1 :** a French political movement during World War II led by Charles de Gaulle in opposition to the Vichy regime **2 :** a postwar French political movement led by Charles de Gaulle — **Gaull·ist** \-ləst\ *adj or n*

gault \ˈgȯlt\ *n* [prob. of Scand origin; akin to ON *gald* hard-packed snow] **:** a heavy thick clay soil

gaum \ˈgȯm, ˈgäm\ *vt* [perh. alter. of 4*gum*] *dial* **:** SMUDGE, SMEAR

gaunt \ˈgȯnt, ˈgänt\ *adj* [ME] **1 :** excessively thin and angular often as a result of suffering **2 :** BARREN, DESOLATE ***syn*** see LEAN — **gaunt·ly** *adv* — **gaunt·ness** *n*

1gaunt·let \ˈgȯnt-lət, ˈgänt-\ *n* [ME, fr. MF *gantelet*, dim. of *gant* glove, of Gmc origin; akin to MD *want* mitten, ON *vöttr* gloves] **1 :** a glove to protect the hand worn with medieval armor **2 :** any of various protective gloves used esp. in industry **3 :** a challenge to combat **4 :** a dress glove extending above the wrist — **gaunt·let·ed** \-lət-əd\ *adj*

gauntlet 1

2gauntlet *n* [by folk etymology fr. *gantelope*] **1 :** a double file of men facing each other and armed with clubs or other weapons with which to strike at an individual who is made to run between them **2 :** a cross fire of any kind; *also* **:** ORDEAL <ran the ~ of criticism and censure>

gaur \ˈgau̇(ə)r\ *n* [Hindi, fr. Skt *gaura;* akin to Skt *go* bull, cow — more at COW] **:** a large East Indian wild ox (*Bibos gaurus*) with a broad forehead and short thick conical horns

gauss \ˈgau̇s\ *n, pl* **gauss** *also* **gauss·es** [Karl F. *Gauss*] **:** the cgs unit of magnetic induction equal to the magnetic flux density that will induce an electromotive force of one one-hundred millionth of a volt in each linear centimeter of a wire moving laterally with a speed of one centimeter per second at right angles to a magnetic flux

Gauss·ian distribution \ˌgau̇-sē-ən-\ *n* [Karl F. *Gauss*] **:** NORMAL DISTRIBUTION

gauze \ˈgȯz\ *n* [MF *gaze*] **1 a :** a thin often transparent fabric used chiefly for clothing or draperies **b :** a loosely woven cotton surgical dressing **c :** a firm woven fabric of metal or plastic filaments **2 :** HAZE, MIST — **gauze·like** \-ˌlīk\ *adj* — **gauz·i·ly** \ˈgȯ-zə-lē\ *adv* — **gauz·i·ness** \-zē-nəs\ *n* — **gauzy** \-zē\ *adj*

ga·vage \gə-ˈväzh, gä-\ *n* [F] **:** introduction of material into the stomach by a tube

gave *past of* GIVE

1gav·el \ˈgav-əl\ *n* [ME, fr. OE *gafol;* akin to OE *giefan* to give] **:** rent or tribute in medieval England

2gavel *n* [origin unknown] **1 :** a mason's setting maul **2 :** a mallet used (as by a presiding officer or auctioneer) for commanding attention or confirming an action (as a vote or sale)

3gavel *vt* **-eled** *or* **-elled; -el·ing** *or* **-el·ling** \ˈgav-(ə-)liŋ\ **:** to bring or force by use of a gavel

gav·el·kind \ˈgav-əl-ˌkīnd\ *n* [ME *gavelkynde*, fr. 1*gavel* + *kinde* kind] **:** a tenure of land existing chiefly in Kent from Anglo-Saxon times until 1925 and providing for division of an intestate's estate equally among the sons or other heirs

gave·lock \ˈgav-lək\ *n* [ME *gavelok*, fr. OE *gafeluc*, of Celt origin; akin to W *gaflach* javelin] *dial Brit* **:** an iron crowbar

ga·votte \gə-ˈvät\ *n* [F, fr. MF, fr. OProv *gavato*] **1 :** a dance of French peasant origin marked by the raising rather than sliding of the feet **2 :** a tune for the gavotte in moderately quick 4/4 time — **gavotte** *vi*

GAW *abbr* guaranteed annual wage

Ga·wain \gə-ˈwān, ˈgä-ˌwän, ˈgau̇-ən\ *n* **:** a nephew of King Arthur and a knight of the Round Table

1gawk \ˈgȯk\ *vi* [perh. alter. of obs. *gaw* (to stare)] **:** to gape or stare stupidly — **gawk·er** *n*

2gawk *n* [prob. fr. E dial. *gawk* (left-handed)] **:** a clumsy stupid person **:** LOUT

gawk·ish \ˈgȯ-kish\ *adj* **:** AWKWARD, DULL — **gawk·ish·ly** *adv* — **gawk·ish·ness** *n*

gawky \ˈgȯ-kē\ *adj* **gawk·i·er; -est :** AWKWARD, CLUMSY <a ~ child with long arms and legs> — **gawk·i·ly** \-kə-lē\ *adv* — **gawky** *n*

gaw·sie *or* **gaw·sy** \ˈgȯ-sē\ *adj* [origin unknown] *chiefly Scot* **:** prosperous and jolly looking

gay \ˈgā\ *adj* [ME, fr. MF *gai*] **1 a :** happily excited **:** MERRY **b :** keenly alive and exuberant **:** having or inducing high spirits <he turned from a sober traditional style to one more timely and ~> **2 a :** BRIGHT, LIVELY <~ sunny meadows> **b :** brilliant in color **3 :** given to social pleasures; *also* **:** LICENTIOUS **4 a :** HOMOSEXUAL **b :** being a socially integrated group oriented toward and concerned with the welfare of the homosexual ***syn*** see LIVELY ***ant*** grave, sober — **gay** *adv* — **gay·ness** *n*

gay·ety *var of* GAIETY

gayly *var of* GAILY

gaz *abbr* gazette

1gaze \ˈgāz\ *vi* **gazed; gaz·ing** [ME *gazen*] **:** to fix the eyes in a steady and intent look and often with eagerness or studious attention — **gaz·er** *n*

syn GAZE, GAPE, STARE, GLARE, PEER, GLOAT *shared meaning element* **:** to look at long and attentively

2gaze *n* **:** a fixed intent look

ga·ze·bo \gə-ˈzā-(ˌ)bō, -ˈzē-\ *n, pl* **-bos** [perh. fr. 1*gaze* + L *-ebo* (as in *videbo* I shall see)] **1 :** BELVEDERE **2 :** a freestanding roofed structure usu. open on the sides

gaze·hound \ˈgāz-ˌhau̇nd\ *n* **:** a dog that hunts by sight rather than by scent; *esp* **:** GREYHOUND

ga·zelle \gə-ˈzel\ *n, pl* **gazelles** *also* **gazelle** [F, fr. MF, fr. Ar *ghazāl*] **:** any of numerous small, graceful, and swift African and Asiatic antelopes (of *Gazella* and related genera) noted for their soft lustrous eyes

1ga·zette \gə-ˈzet\ *n* [F, fr. It *gazetta*] **1 :** NEWSPAPER **2 :** an official journal **3** *Brit* **:** an announcement in an official gazette

2gazette *vt* **ga·zett·ed; ga·zett·ing** **1** *chiefly Brit* **:** to announce or publish in a gazette **2** *Brit* **:** to announce the appointment or status of in an official gazette

gaz·et·teer \ˌgaz-ə-ˈti(ə)r\ *n* **1** *archaic* **:** JOURNALIST, PUBLICIST **2** [*The Gazetteer's: or, Newsman's Interpreter*, a geographical index edited by Laurence Echard] **:** a geographical dictionary; *also* **:** a book in which something (as wines or restaurants) is treated esp. in regard to geographical distribution and regional specialization

gaz·o·gene \ˈgaz-ə-ˌjēn\ *var of* GASOGENE

gaz·pa·cho \gəz-ˈpäch-(ˌ)ō, gəs-\ *n, pl* **-chos** [Sp] **:** a cold soup whose ingredients include tomatoes, olive oil, garlic, spices, and bread crumbs

1GB \(ˈ)jē-ˈbē\ *n* [code name] **:** SARIN

2GB *abbr* Great Britain

GBF *abbr* Great Books Foundation

GC *abbr* gigacycle

GCA *abbr* ground-controlled approach

GCB *abbr* Knight Grand Cross of the Bath

GCD *abbr* greatest common divisor

GCF *abbr* greatest common factor

G clef *n* **:** TREBLE CLEF

GCT *abbr* Greenwich civil time

gd *abbr* good

Gd *symbol* gadolinium

Ge *symbol* germanium

GE *abbr* gilt edges

ge- *or* **geo-** *comb form* [ME *geo-*, fr. MF & L; MF, fr. L, fr. Gk *gē-*, *geō-*, fr. *gē*] **1 :** earth **:** ground **:** soil <*ge*anticline> <*geo*phyte> **2 :** geographical **:** geography and <*geo*politics>

ge·an·ti·cline \jē-ˈant-i-ˌklīn\ *also* **ge·an·ti·cli·nal** \(ˌ)jē-ˌant-i-ˈklīn-ᵊl\ *n* **:** a great upward flexure of the earth's crust — compare GEOSYNCLINE

1gear \ˈgi(ə)r\ *n* [ME *gere*, fr. OE *gearwe;* akin to OHG *garuwi* equipment, clothing, OE *gearu* ready — more at YARE] **1 a :** CLOTHING, GARMENTS **b :** movable property **:** GOODS **2 :** EQUIPMENT, PARAPHERNALIA <fishing ~> **3 a :** the rigging of a ship or boat **b :** the harness esp. of horses **4** *dial chiefly Brit* **:** absurd talk **:** NONSENSE **5** *dial chiefly Brit* **:** DOINGS **6 a** (1) **:** a mechanism that performs a specific function in a complete machine <steering ~> (2) **:** a toothed wheel (3) **:** working relation, position, or adjustment <in ~> **b :** one of two or more adjustments of a transmission (as of a bicycle or motor vehicle) that determine mechanical advantage, relative speed, and direction of travel — **gear·less** \-ləs\ *adj*

2gear *vt* **1 a :** to provide (as machinery) with gearing **b :** to connect by gearing **c :** to put into gear **2 a :** to make ready for effective operation **b :** to adjust so as to match, blend with, or satisfy something <an institution ~*ed* to the needs of the blind> ~ *vi* **1** *of machinery* **:** to be in or come into gear **2 :** to become adjusted so as to match, blend, or harmonize

gear·box \ˈgi(ə)r-ˌbäks\ *n* **1 :** TRANSMISSION 3 **2 :** GEARING 2

gear·ing \ˈgi(ə)r-iŋ\ *n* **1 :** the act or process of providing or fitting with gears **2 :** the parts by which motion is transmitted from one portion of machinery to another; *esp* **:** a train of gear wheels

gear·shift \ˈgi(ə)r-ˌshift\ *n* **:** a mechanism by which the transmission gears in a power-transmission system are engaged and disengaged

gear wheel *n* **:** a toothed wheel that gears with another piece of a mechanism; *specif* **:** COGWHEEL

Geat \ˈgēt, ˈyaət\ *n* [OE *Gēat*] **:** a member of a Scandinavian people of southern Sweden subjugated by the Swedes in the 6th century — **Geat·ish** \-ish\ *adj*

gecko \ˈgek-(ˌ)ō\ *n, pl* **geck·os** *or* **geck·oes** [Malay *ge'kok*, of imit. origin] **:** any of numerous small harmless chiefly tropical and nocturnal insectivorous lizards (family Gekkonidae)

1gee \ˈjē\ *vb imper* [origin unknown] — used as a direction to turn to the right or move ahead; compare 5HAW ~ *vi* **geed; gee·ing :** to turn to the right side

2gee *n* **1 :** the letter *g* **2** [*grand*] *slang* **:** a thousand dollars

3gee *interj* [euphemism for *Jesus*] — used as an introductory expletive or to express surprise or enthusiasm

gee·gaw \ˈjē-(ˌ)gȯ, ˈgē-\ *var of* GEWGAW

geek \ˈgēk\ *n* [prob. fr. E dial. *geek, geck* fool, fr. LG *geck*, fr. MLG] **:** a carnival performer often billed as a wild man whose act usu. includes biting the head off a live chicken or snake

geese *pl of* GOOSE

geest \ˈgāst, ˈgēst\ *n* [G] **1 :** alluvial matter not of recent origin on the surface of land **2 :** loose material (as earth or soil) formed by decay of rocks in a place

gee–whiz \(ˈ)jē-ˈ(h)wiz\ *adj* **1 :** designed to arouse wonder or excitement or to amplify the merits or significance of something esp. by the use of clever or sensational language <a welcome antidote to the . . . play-by-play specialists who wallow in ~ banality — Jack Gould> **2 :** marked by spectacular or astonishing qualities or achievement <some people still look upon atom power as in the ~ stage —*Kiplinger Washington Letter*> **3 :** characterized by wide-eyed enthusiasm, excitement, and wonder <he never was a ~ guy by nature — A. J. Daley>

gee whiz *interj* : [3]GEE

Ge·ez \gē-'ez\ *n* [Ethiopic *ge'ez*] : ETHIOPIC 1

gee·zer \'gē-zər\ *n* [prob. alter. of Sc *gulser* (one in disguise)] : a queer, odd, or eccentric man

ge·fil·te fish \gə-'fil-tə-\ *n* [Yiddish, lit., filled fish] : a dish of stewed or baked fish stuffed with a mixture of the fish flesh, bread crumbs, eggs, and seasoning or prepared as balls or oval cakes boiled in a fish stock

ge·gen·schein \'gā-gən-ˌshīn\ *n, often cap* [G, fr. *gegen* against, counter- + *schein* shine] : a faint light about 20° across on the celestial sphere opposite the sun probably associated in origin with the zodiacal light

Ge·hen·na \gi-'hen-ə\ *n* [LL, fr. Gk *Geenna*, fr. Heb *Gê' Hinnōm*, lit., valley of Hinnom] **1** : HELL 1a(2) **2** : a place or state of misery

Gei·ger counter \ˌgī-gər-\ *or* **Gei·ger–Mül·ler counter** \-'myül-ər-, -'mil-, -'məl-\ *n* [Hans *Geiger* †1945 G physicist & W. *Müller*, 20th cent. G physicist] : an instrument for detecting the presence and intensity of radiations (as cosmic rays or particles from a radioactive substance) by means of the ionizing effect on an enclosed gas which results in a pulse that is amplified and fed to a device giving a visible or audible indication

gei·sha \'gā-shə, 'gē-\ *n, pl* **geisha** *or* **geishas** [Jap, fr. *gei* art + *-sha* person] : a Japanese girl who is trained to provide entertaining and lighthearted company esp. for a man or a group of men

[1]gel \'jel\ *n* [*gelatin*] **1** : a colloid in a more solid form than a sol **2** : JELLY 2

[2]gel *vi* **gelled; gel·ling** : to change into or take on the form of a gel — **gel·able** \'jel-ə-bəl\ *adj*

ge·län·de·läu·fer \gə-'len-də-ˌlȯi-fər\ *n* [G, fr. *gelände* open fields + *läufer* runner] : a skier making a cross-country run : LANGLÄUFER

ge·län·de·sprung \-ˌs(h)prüŋ\ *n* [G, fr. *gelände* open fields + *sprung* jump] : a jump in skiing made from a low crouching position with the aid of both ski poles and usu. over an obstacle

gel·ate \'jel-ˌāt\ *vi* **gel·at·ed; gel·at·ing** : GEL

gel·a·tin *also* **gel·a·tine** \'jel-ət-ᵊn\ *n* [F *gélatine* edible jelly, gelatin, fr. It *gelatina*, fr. *gelato*, pp. of *gelare* to freeze, fr. L — more at COLD] **1** : glutinous material obtained from animal tissues by boiling; *esp* : a colloidal protein used as a food, in photography, and in medicine **2 a** : any of various substances (as agar) resembling gelatin **b** : an edible jelly made with gelatin **c** : a thin colored transparent sheet used over a stage light to color it

ge·la·ti·nize \jə-'lat-ᵊn-ˌīz, 'jel-ət-ᵊn-\ *vb* **-nized; -niz·ing** *vt* **1** : to convert into a gelatinous form or into a jelly **2** : to coat or treat with gelatin ~ *vi* : to become gelatinous or change into a jelly — **ge·la·ti·ni·za·tion** \jə-ˌlat-ᵊn-ə-'zā-shən, ˌjel-ət-ᵊn-\ *n*

ge·lat·i·nous \jə-'lat-nəs, -ᵊn-əs\ *adj* **1** : resembling gelatin or jelly : VISCOUS <a ~ precipitate> **2** : of, relating to, or containing gelatin — **ge·lat·i·nous·ly** *adv* — **ge·lat·i·nous·ness** *n*

[1]ge·la·tion \ji-'lā-shən\ *n* [L *gelation-*, *gelatio*, fr. *gelatus*, pp. of *gelare*] : the action or process of freezing

[2]gel·ation \je-'lā-shən\ *n* [[1]*gel* + *-ation*] : the formation of a gel from a sol

[1]geld \'geld\ *vt* [ME *gelden*, fr. ON *gelda*; akin to OE *gelte* young sow, Gk *gallos* eunuch, priest of Cybele] **1** : CASTRATE; *also* : SPAY **2** : to deprive of a natural or essential part <sick of workingmen being ~*ed* of their natural expression . . . A workingman bereft of his profanity is a silent man — *Atlantic*>

[2]geld *n* [OE *gield*, *geld* service, tribute; akin to OE *gieldan* to pay, yield — more at YIELD] : the crown tax paid under Anglo-Saxon and Norman kings

geld·ing \'gel-diŋ\ *n* [ME, fr. ON *geldingr*, fr. *gelda*] **1** : a castrated animal; *specif* : a castrated male horse **2** : EUNUCH

ge·lée \zhə-'lā\ *n* [F, jelly, fr. MF — more at JELLY] : a cosmetic gel

gel·id \'jel-əd\ *adj* [L *gelidus*, fr. *gelu* frost, cold — more at COLD] : extremely cold : ICY <the ~ waters of the North Atlantic> <a man of ~ reserve — *New Yorker*> — **ge·lid·i·ty** \jə-'lid-ət-ē, je-\ *n* — **gel·id·ly** \'jel-əd-lē\ *adv*

gel·ig·nite \'jel-ig-ˌnīt\ *n* [*gel*atin + L *ign*is fire + E *-ite* — more at IGNITE] : a dynamite in which the adsorbent base is largely potassium nitrate or a similar nitrate usu. with some wood pulp

gel·lant *also* **gel·ant** \'jel-ənt\ *n* : a substance used to produce gelling

gelt \'gelt\ *n* [D & G *geld* & Yiddish *gelt*; all akin to OE *geld* service, tribute] *slang* : MONEY

[1]gem \'jem\ *n* [ME *gemme*, fr. MF, fr. L *gemma* bud, gem] **1 a** : JEWEL **b** : a precious or sometimes semiprecious stone cut and polished for ornament **2 a** : something prized esp. for great beauty or perfection **b** : a highly prized or well-beloved person **3** : MUFFIN

[2]gem *vt* **gemmed; gem·ming** : to adorn with or as if with gems

GEM *abbr* ground-effect machine

gem- \(ˈ)jem\ *comb form* : geminal <*gem*dichloride>

Ge·ma·ra \gə-'mär-ə, -'mȯr-\ *n* [Aram *gĕmārā* completion] : a commentary on the Mishnah forming the second part of the Talmud — **Ge·ma·ric** \-ik\ *adj* — **Ge·ma·rist** \-əst\ *n*

ge·mein·schaft \gə-'mīn-ˌshäft\ *n* : a spontaneously arising organic social relationship characterized by strong reciprocal bonds of sentiment and kinship within a common tradition; *also* : a community or society characterized by this relationship — compare GESELLSCHAFT

gem·i·nal \'jem-ən-ᵊl\ *adj* [L *geminus* twin] : relating to or characterized by two usu. similar substituents on the same atom — **gem·i·nal·ly** \-ᵊl-ē\ *adv*

[1]gem·i·nate \'jem-ə-nət, -ˌnāt\ *adj* [L *geminatus*, pp. of *geminare* to double, fr. *geminus* twin] : arranged in pairs : DUPLICATE — **gem·i·nate·ly** *adv*

[2]gem·i·nate \-ˌnāt\ *vb* **-nat·ed; -nat·ing** *vt* : DOUBLE ~ *vi* : to become double or paired — **gem·i·na·tion** \ˌjem-ə-'nā-shən\ *n*

Gem·i·ni \'jem-ə(ˌ)nē, -ˌnī; 'gem-ə-ˌnē\ *n pl but sing in constr* [L (gen. *Geminorum*), lit., the twins (Castor and Pollux)] **1** : the 3d zodiacal constellation pictorially represented as the twins Castor and Pollux sitting together and located on the opposite side of the Milky Way from Taurus and Orion **2 a** : the 3d sign of the zodiac in astrology — see ZODIAC table **b** : one born under this sign

gem·ma \'jem-ə\ *n, pl* **gem·mae** \-ˌē\ [L] : BUD; *broadly* : an asexual reproductive body that becomes detached from a parent plant — **gem·ma·ceous** \je-'mā-shəs\ *adj* — **gem·ma·tion** \-shən\ *n*

gem·mate \'jem-ˌāt\ *adj* **1** : having gemmae **2** : reproducing by a bud

gem·mip·a·rous \je-'mip-ə-rəs\ *adj* : producing or reproducing by buds — **gem·mip·a·rous·ly** *adv*

gem·mu·la·tion \ˌjem-yə-'lā-shən\ *n* : formation of or reproduction by gemmules

gem·mule \'jem-(ˌ)yü(ə)l\ *n* [F, fr. L *gemmula*, dim. of *gemma* bud] : a small bud: **a** : a minute particle that in the theory of pangenesis mediates the production in a new individual of cells like that in which it originated **b** : an internal resistant reproductive bud (as of a sponge) — **gem·mu·lif·er·ous** \ˌjem-yü-'lif-(ə-)rəs\ *adj*

gem·my \'jem-ē\ *adj* **1** : having the characteristics desired in a gemstone **2** : BRIGHT, GLITTERING

gem·ol·o·gist *or* **gem·mol·o·gist** \je-'mäl-ə-jəst, jə-\ *n* : a specialist in gems; *specif* : one who appraises gems

gem·ol·o·gy *or* **gem·mol·o·gy** \-jē\ *n* [L *gemma* gem] : the science of gems — **gem·olog·i·cal** *or* **gem·mo·log·i·cal** \ˌjem-ə-'läj-i-kəl\ *adj*

ge·mot *or* **ge·mote** \gə-'mōt\ *n* [OE *gemōt*, fr. *ge-* (perfective prefix) + *mōt* assembly — more at CO-, MOOT] : a judicial or legislative assembly in Anglo-Saxon England

gems·bok \'gemz-ˌbäk\ *n* [Afrik, lit., male chamois, fr. G *gemsbock*, fr. *gems* chamois + *bock* male goat] : a large and strikingly marked oryx (*Oryx gazella*) formerly abundant in southern Africa

gem·stone \'jem-ˌstōn\ *n* : a mineral or petrified material that when cut and polished can be used in jewelry

ge·müt·lich·keit \gə-'mu̇et-lik-ˌkīt\ *n* [G, fr. *gemütlich* good-natured, comfortable, fr. *gemüt* spirit, heart] : CORDIALITY, FRIENDLINESS

gen *abbr* **1** general **2** genitive **3** genus

Gen *abbr* Genesis

[1]gen- *or* **geno-** *comb form* [Gk *genos* birth, race, kind — more at KIN] **1** : race <*geno*cide> **2** : genus : kind <*geno*type>

[2]gen- *or* **geno-** *comb form* : gene <*geno*cline>

-gen \jən *also esp when two unstressed syllables precede* ˌjen\ *also* **-gene** \ˌjēn\ *n comb form* [F *-gène*, fr. Gk *-genēs* born; akin to Gk *genos* birth] **1** : producer <andro*gen*> **2** : one that is (so) produced <culti*gen*> <phos*gene*>

Gen AF *abbr* general of the air force

gen·darme \'zhän-ˌdärm *also* 'jän-\ *n* [F, fr. MF, back-formation fr. *gensdarmes*, pl. of *gent d'armes*, lit., armed people] **1** : one of a body of soldiers esp. in France serving as an armed police force for the maintenance of public order **2** : POLICEMAN

gen·dar·mer·ie *or* **gen·dar·mery** \jän-'därm-ə-rē, zhän-\ *n, pl* **-mer·ies** [MF *gendarmerie*, fr. *gendarme*] : a body of gendarmes

[1]gen·der \'jen-dər\ *n* [ME, *gendre*, fr. MF *genre*, *gendre*, fr. L *gener-*, *genus* birth, race, kind, gender — more at KIN] **1** : SEX <black divinities of the feminine ~ —Charles Dickens> **2 a** : a subclass within a grammatical class (as noun, pronoun, adjective, or verb) of a language that is partly arbitrary but also partly based on distinguishable characteristics (as shape, social rank, manner of existence, or sex) and that determines agreement with and selection of other words or grammatical forms **b** : membership of a word or a grammatical form in such a subclass **c** : an inflectional form showing membership in such a subclass

[2]gender *vb* **gen·dered; gen·der·ing** \-d(ə-)riŋ\ [ME *gendren*, fr. MF *gendrer*, fr. L *generare* — more at GENERATE] : ENGENDER

gene \'jēn\ *n* [G *gen*, short for *pangen*, fr. *pan-* + *-gen*] : an element of the germ plasm that controls transmission of a hereditary character by specifying the structure of a particular protein or by controlling the function of other genetic material and that consists of a specific sequence of purine and pyrimidine bases usu. in DNA

ge·ne·al·o·gist \ˌjē-nē-'äl-ə-jəst, ˌjen-ē-, -'al-\ *n* : a person who traces or studies the descent of persons or families

ge·ne·al·o·gy \-jē\ *n, pl* **-gies** [ME *genealogie*, fr. MF, fr. LL *genealogia*, fr. Gk, fr. *genea* race, family + *-logia* -logy; akin to Gk *genos* race] **1** : an account of the descent of a person, family, or group from an ancestor or from older forms **2** : regular descent of a person, family, or group of organisms from a progenitor or older form : PEDIGREE **3** : the study of family pedigrees — **ge·ne·a·log·i·cal** \ˌjē-nē-ə-'läj-i-kəl, ˌjen-ē-\ *adj* — **ge·ne·a·log·i·cal·ly** \-k(ə-)lē\ *adv*

gene flow *n* : the passage and establishment of genes typical of one breeding population into the gene pool of another by hybridization and backcrossing

gene frequency *n* : the frequency of occurrence of a specified gene in a population compared to its alleles

gene mutation *n* : mutation due to fundamental intramolecular reorganization of a gene

gene pool *n* : the whole body of genes in an interbreeding population that includes each gene at a certain frequency in relation to its alleles

genera *pl of* GENUS

gen·er·a·ble \'jen-(ə-)rə-bəl\ *adj* : capable of being generated

[1]**gen·er·al** \ˈjen-(ə-)rəl\ *adj* [ME, fr. MF, fr. L *generalis,* fr. *gener-, genus* kind, class — more at KIN] **1 :** involving or applicable to the whole **2 :** involving, relating to, or applicable to every member of a class, kind, or group **3 a :** applicable to or characteristic of the majority of individuals involved : PREVALENT **b :** concerned or dealing with universal rather than particular aspects **4 :** relating to, determined by, or concerned with main elements rather than limited details <bearing a ~ resemblance to the original> **5 :** not confined by specialization or careful limitation **6 :** belonging to the common nature of a group of like individuals : GENERIC **7 :** holding superior rank or taking precedence over others similarly titled <the ~ manager> <~ secretary> ***syn*** see UNIVERSAL

[2]**general** *n* **1 :** something (as a concept, principle, or statement) that involves or is applicable to the whole **2** *archaic* **:** the general public : PEOPLE **3 :** SUPERIOR GENERAL **4 a :** GENERAL OFFICER **b :** a commissioned officer in the army, air force, or marine corps who ranks above a lieutenant general and whose insignia is four stars — compare ADMIRAL — **in general :** for the most part : GENERALLY

general admission *n* **:** a fee paid for admission to a usu. unreserved seating area (as in an auditorium or stadium)

general agent *n* **1 :** one employed to transact generally all legal business entrusted to him by his principal **2 :** an insurance company agent who administers the company's business within a specified area

general assembly *n* **1 :** the highest governing body in a religious denomination (as the United Presbyterian Church) **2 :** a legislative assembly; *esp* **:** a U.S. state legislature **3** *cap G&A* **:** the supreme deliberative body of the United Nations

General Court *n* **:** a legislative assembly; *specif* **:** the state legislature in Massachusetts and New Hampshire

general delivery *n* **:** a department of a post office that handles the delivery of mail at a post office window to persons who call for it

general election *n* **:** an election usu. held at regular intervals in which candidates are elected in all or most constituencies of a nation or state

gen·er·a·lis·si·mo \ˌjen-(ə-)rə-ˈlis-ə-ˌmō\ *n, pl* **-mos** [It, fr. *generale* general] **:** the chief commander of an army : COMMANDER IN CHIEF

gen·er·al·ist \ˈjen-(ə-)rə-ləst\ *n* **:** one whose skills or interests extend to several different fields

gen·er·al·i·ty \ˌjen-ə-ˈral-ət-ē\ *n, pl* **-ties** **1 :** the quality or state of being general : total applicability **2 a :** GENERALIZATION 2 **b :** a vague or inadequate statement **3 :** the greatest part : BULK

gen·er·al·iza·tion \ˌjen-(ə-)rə-lə-ˈzā-shən\ *n* **1 :** the act or process of generalizing **2 :** a general statement, law, principle, or proposition **3 :** the act or process whereby a response is made to a stimulus similar to but not identical with a reference stimulus

gen·er·al·ize \ˈjen-(ə-)rə-ˌlīz\ *vb* **-ized; -iz·ing** *vt* **1 :** to give a general form to **2 a :** to derive or induce (a general conception or principle) from particulars **b :** to draw a general conclusion from **3 :** to give general applicability to <~ a law>; *also* **:** to make indefinite ~ *vi* **1 :** to form generalizations; *also* **:** to make vague or indefinite statements **2 :** to extend throughout the body — **gen·er·al·iz·able** \-ˌlī-zə-bəl\ *adj* — **gen·er·al·iz·er** *n*

gen·er·al·ized *adj* **:** made general; *esp* **:** not highly differentiated biologically nor strictly adapted to a particular environment

gen·er·al·ly \ˈjen-(ə-)rə-lē, ˈjen-ər-lē\ *adv* **:** in a general manner: as **a :** in disregard of specific instances and with regard to an overall picture <~ speaking> **b :** as a rule : USUALLY

general officer *n* **:** any of the officers in the army, air force, or marine corps above colonel — compare COMPANY OFFICER, FIELD OFFICER

general of the air force : a general of the highest rank in the air force whose insignia is five stars

general of the army : a general of the highest rank in the army whose insignia is five stars

general paresis *n* **:** insanity caused by syphilitic alteration of the brain that leads to dementia and paralysis

general practitioner *n* **:** a physician or veterinarian who does not limit his practice to a specialty; *broadly* **:** GENERALIST

general–purpose *adj* **:** suitable to be used for two or more basic purposes

general semantics *n pl but sing or pl in constr* **:** a doctrine and educational discipline intended to improve habits of response of human beings to their environment and one another esp. by training in the more critical use of words and other symbols

gen·er·al·ship \ˈjen-(ə-)rəl-ˌship\ *n* **1 :** office or tenure of office of a general **2 :** military skill in a high commander **3 :** LEADERSHIP

general store *n* **:** a retail store located usu. in a small or rural community that carries a wide variety of goods including groceries but is not divided into departments

general theory of relativity : RELATIVITY 3b

general will *n* **:** the collective will of a community that is the embodiment or expression of its common interest

gen·er·ate \ˈjen-ə-ˌrāt\ *vt* **-at·ed; -at·ing** [L *generatus,* pp. of *generare,* fr. *gener-, genus* birth — more at KIN] **1 :** to bring into existence: as **a :** PROCREATE, BEGET **b :** to originate by a vital or chemical process : PRODUCE <~ electricity> **2 :** to define (as a mathematical or linguistic set or structure) by the application of one or more rules or operations to given quantities; *esp* **:** to trace out (as a curve) by a moving point or trace out (as a surface) by a moving curve **3 :** to be the cause of (a situation, action, or state of mind) <these stories . . . ~ a good deal of psychological suspense —*Atlantic*>

gen·er·a·tion \ˌjen-ə-ˈrā-shən\ *n* **1 a :** a body of living beings constituting a single step in the line of descent from an ancestor **b :** a group of individuals born and living contemporaneously **c :** a group of individuals having contemporaneously a status (as that of students in a school) which each one holds only for a limited period **d :** a type or class of objects usu. developed from an earlier type <first of the . . . new ~ of powerful supersonic fighters — Kenneth Koyen> **2 :** the average span of time between the birth of parents and that of their offspring **3 a :** the action or process of producing offspring : PROCREATION **b :** origination by a mathematical, chemical, or other process : PRODUCTION; *specif* **:** formation of a geometrical figure by motion of another **c :** the process of coming or bringing into being <~ of income> — **gen·er·a·tion·al** \-shnəl, -shən-ᵊl\ *adj*

gen·er·a·tive \ˈjen-ə-ˌrāt-iv, -(ə-)rət-\ *adj* **:** having the power or function of generating, originating, producing, or reproducing

generative cell *n* **:** a sexual reproductive cell : GAMETE

generative grammar *n* **1 :** a description in the form of an ordered set of rules for producing the grammatical sentences of a language **2 :** TRANSFORMATIONAL GRAMMAR

generative nucleus *n* **:** the one of the two nuclei resulting from the first division in the pollen grain of a seed plant that gives rise to sperm nuclei — compare TUBE NUCLEUS

gen·er·a·tor \ˈjen-ə-ˌrāt-ər\ *n* **1 :** one that generates **2 :** an apparatus in which vapor or gas is formed **3 :** a machine by which mechanical energy is changed into electrical energy **4 :** a mathematical entity that when subjected to one or more operations yields another mathematical entity or its elements; *specif* **:** GENERATRIX

gen·er·a·trix \ˌjen-ə-ˈrā-triks\ *n, pl* **-er·a·tri·ces** \-trə-ˌsēz, -ə-rə-ˈtrī-(ˌ)sēz\ **:** a point, line, or surface whose motion generates a line, surface, or solid

[1]**ge·ner·ic** \jə-ˈner-ik\ *adj* [F *générique,* fr. L *gener-, genus* birth, kind, class] **1 a :** relating to or characteristic of a whole group or class : GENERAL **b :** not protected by trademark registration **2 :** relating to or having the rank of a biological genus ***syn*** see UNIVERSAL — **ge·ner·i·cal·ly** \-i-k(ə-)lē\ *adv* — **ge·ner·ic·ness** *n*

[2]**generic** *n* **:** a generic drug

gen·er·os·i·ty \ˌjen-ə-ˈräs-ət-ē, -ˈräs-tē\ *n, pl* **-ties** **1 a :** liberality in spirit or act; *esp* **:** liberality in giving **b :** a generous act **2 :** ABUNDANCE

gen·er·ous \ˈjen-(ə-)rəs\ *adj* [MF or L; MF *genereus,* fr. L *generosus,* fr. *gener-, genus* birth, family] **1** *archaic* **:** HIGHBORN **2 a :** characterized by a noble or forbearing spirit : MAGNANIMOUS, KINDLY **b :** liberal in giving : OPENHANDED **c :** marked by abundance or ample proportions : COPIOUS **d :** full flavored <~ wine> ***syn*** see LIBERAL ***ant*** stingy — **gen·er·ous·ly** *adv* — **gen·er·ous·ness** *n*

gen·e·sis \ˈjen-ə-səs\ *n, pl* **-e·ses** \-ˌsēz\ [L, fr. Gk, fr. *gignesthai* to be born — more at KIN] **:** the origin or coming into being of something

Genesis *n* [Gk] **:** the mainly narrative first book of canonical Jewish and Christian Scriptures — see BIBLE table

gen·et \ˈjen-ət\ *n* [ME *genete,* fr. MF, fr. Ar *jarnayt*] **:** any of several small Old World carnivorous mammals (genus *Genetta*) related to the civets but with scent glands less developed and claws fully retractile

ge·net·ic \jə-ˈnet-ik\ *also* **ge·net·i·cal** \-i-kəl\ *adj* [*genesis*] **1 :** relating to or determined by the origin, development, or causal antecedents of something **2 a :** of, relating to, or involving genetics **b :** GENIC — **ge·net·i·cal·ly** \-i-k(ə-)lē\ *adv*

-ge·net·ic \jə-ˈnet-ik\ *adj comb form* **:** -GENIC 1, 2 <psycho*genetic*> <spermato*genetic*>

genetic code *n* **:** the biochemical basis of heredity consisting of codons that determine the specific amino acid sequence in proteins and that are uniform for the forms of life studied so far

genetic drift *n* **:** changes of gene frequency in small populations due to chance preservation or extinction of particular genes

genetic map *n* **:** MAP 3

genetic marker *n* **:** a usu. dominant gene or trait that serves esp. to identify genes or traits linked with it

ge·net·ics \jə-ˈnet-iks\ *n pl but sing in constr* **1 a :** a branch of biology that deals with the heredity and variation of organisms **b :** a treatise or textbook on genetics **2 :** the genetic makeup and phenomena of an organism, type, group, or condition **3 :** GENESIS — **ge·net·i·cist** \-ˈnet-ə-səst\ *n*

ge·ne·va \jə-ˈnē-və\ *n* [modif. of obs. D *genever* (now *jenever*), lit., juniper, deriv. of L *juniperus*] **:** a strongly alcoholic liquor flavored with juniper berries and made in the Netherlands

Ge·ne·va bands \jə-ˌnē-və-\ *n pl* [*Geneva,* Switzerland; fr. their use by the Calvinist clergy of Geneva] **:** two strips of white cloth suspended from the front of a clerical collar and sometimes used by Protestant clergymen — called also *Geneva tabs*

Geneva bands

Geneva convention *n* **:** one of a series of agreements concerning the treatment of prisoners of war and of the sick, wounded, and dead in battle first made at Geneva, Switzerland, in 1864 and subsequently accepted in later revisions by most nations

Geneva cross *n* [fr. its adoption by the Geneva convention] **:** RED CROSS

Geneva gown *n* [fr. its use by the Calvinist clergy of Geneva] **:** a loose large-sleeved black academic gown widely used as a vestment by Protestant clergymen

Ge·ne·van \jə-ˈnē-vən\ *adj* **1 :** of or relating to Geneva, Switzerland **2 :** of or relating to Geneva about the time of the beginning of the Reformation; *specif* **:** of or relating to Calvinism — **Genevan** *n*

[1]**ge·nial** \ˈjē-nyəl\ *adj* [L *genialis,* fr. *genius*] **1** *obs* **:** of or relating to marriage or generation <the ~ bed —John Milton> **2 a :** favorable to growth or comfort : MILD <~ sunshine> **b :** marked by or diffusing sympathy or friendliness : KINDLY **3** *obs* **:** NATIVE, INBORN **4 :** displaying or marked by genius ***syn*** see GRACIOUS ***ant*** saturnine (*as manner or aspect*), caustic (*as remarks*) — **ge·nial·i·ty** \ˌjē-nē-ˈal-ət-ē, jēn-ˈyal-\ *n* — **ge·nial·ly** \ˈjē-nyə-lē\ *adv* — **ge·nial·ness** *n*

[2]**ge·ni·al** \ji-ˈnī(-ə)l\ *adj* [Gk *geneion* chin, fr. *genys* jaw — more at CHIN] **:** of or relating to the chin

gen·ic \ˈjēn-ik, ˈjen-\ *adj* **:** of, relating to, or being a gene — **gen·i·cal·ly** \-i-k(ə-)lē\ *adv*

-gen·ic \ˈjen-ik *sometimes* ˈjē-nik\ *adj comb form* [ISV *-gen* & *-geny* + *-ic*] **1 :** producing **:** forming <ero*genic*> **2 :** produced by **:** formed from <phyto*genic*> **3** [*photogenic*] **:** suitable for production or reproduction by (such) a medium <tele*genic*>

ge·nic·u·late \jə-ˈnik-yə-lət\ *or* **ge·nic·u·lat·ed** \-ˌlāt-əd\ *adj* [L *geniculatus*, fr. *geniculum*, dim. of *genu* knee — more at KNEE] **:** bent abruptly at an angle like a bent knee — **ge·nic·u·late·ly** *adv*

ge·nie \ˈjē-nē *also* ˈjen-ē\ *n, pl* **ge·nies** *also* **ge·nii** \ˈjē-nē-ˌī\ [F *génie*, fr. Ar *jinnīy*] **:** JINN

gen·i·tal \ˈjen-ə-tᵊl\ *adj* [ME, fr. L *genitalis*, fr. *genitus*, pp. of *gignere* to beget — more at KIN] **1 :** GENERATIVE **2 :** of, relating to, or being a sexual organ **3 :** of, relating to, or characterized by the stage of psychosexual development in which oral and anal impulses are subordinated to adaptive interpersonal mechanisms — **gen·i·tal·ly** \-tə-lē\ *adv*

gen·i·ta·lia \ˌjen-ə-ˈtāl-yə\ *n pl* [L, fr. neut. pl. of *genitalis*] **:** the organs of the reproductive system; *esp* **:** the external genital organs — **gen·i·ta·lic** \-ˈtal-ik, -ˈtāl-\ *adj*

gen·i·tals \ˈjen-ə-tᵊlz\ *n pl* **:** GENITALIA

gen·i·ti·val \ˌjen-ə-ˈtī-vəl\ *adj* **:** of, relating to, or formed with or from the genitive case — **gen·i·ti·val·ly** \-və-lē\ *adv*

gen·i·tive \ˈjen-ət-iv\ *adj* [ME, fr. L *genetivus*, *genitivus*, lit., of generation (erroneous translation of Gk *genikos* genitive), fr. *genitus*] **1 :** of, relating to, or constituting a grammatical case marking typically a relationship of possessor or source — compare POSSESSIVE **2 :** not characterized by case inflection but nevertheless expressing a relationship that in some inflected languages is often marked by a genitive case — used esp. of English prepositional phrases introduced by *of* — **genitive** *n*

genito- *comb form* [*genital*] **:** genital and <*genito*urinary>

gen·i·to·uri·nary \ˌjen-ə-tō-ˈyu̇r-ə-ˌner-ē\ *adj* **:** of or relating to the genital and urinary organs or functions

gen·i·ture \ˈjen-ə-ˌchu̇(ə)r, -chər, -ˌt(y)u̇(ə)r\ *n* **:** NATIVITY, BIRTH

ge·nius \ˈjē-nyəs, -nē-əs\ *n, pl* **ge·nius·es** *or* **ge·nii** \-nē-ˌī\ [L, tutelary spirit, fondness for social enjoyment, fr. *gignere* to beget] **1 a** *pl genii* **:** an attendant spirit of a person or place **b** *pl usu genii* **:** a person who influences another for good or bad **2 :** a strong leaning or inclination **:** PENCHANT <fate did not allow him to indulge his ~ till those last few years — Norman Douglas> **3 a :** a peculiar, distinctive, or identifying character or spirit **b :** the associations and traditions of a place **c :** a personification or embodiment esp. of a quality or condition **4** *pl usu genii* **:** SPIRIT, JINN **5** *pl usu geniuses* **a :** a single strongly marked capacity or aptitude <had a ~ for getting along with boys — Mary Ross> **b :** extraordinary intellectual power esp. as manifested in creative activity **c :** a person endowed with transcendent mental superiority; *specif* **:** a person with a very high intelligence quotient ***syn*** see GIFT

genius lo·ci \-ˈlō-ˌsī, -ˌkē\ *n* [L] **1 :** a tutelary deity of a place **2 :** the pervading spirit of a place

genl *abbr* general

geno- — see GEN-

geno·cide \ˈjen-ə-ˌsīd\ *n* **:** the deliberate and systematic destruction of a racial, political, or cultural group — **geno·cid·al** \ˌjen-ə-ˈsīd-ᵊl\ *adj*

ge·nome \ˈjē-ˌnōm\ *or* **ge·nom** \-ˌnäm\ *n* [G *genom*, fr. *gen-* [2]gen- + chromos*om* chromosome] **:** one haploid set of chromosomes with the genes they contain — **ge·no·mic** \ji-ˈnō-mik, -ˈnäm-ik\ *adj*

ge·no·spe·cies \ˌjē-nō-ˈspē-(ˌ)shēz, -(ˌ)sēz\ *n* **:** the sum of the genotypes of a taxonomic species

ge·no·type \ˈjē-nə-ˌtīp, ˈjen-ə-\ *n* **1** [[1]*gen-*] **:** TYPE SPECIES **2** [[2]*gen-*] **a :** the genetic constitution of an individual or group **b :** a class or group of individuals sharing a specified genetic makeup — compare PHENOTYPE — **ge·no·typ·ic** \ˌjē-nə-ˈtip-ik, ˌjen-ə-\ *also* **ge·no·typ·i·cal** \-i-kəl\ *adj* — **ge·no·typ·i·cal·ly** \-i-k(ə-)lē\ *adv* — **ge·no·ty·pic·i·ty** \-tī-ˈpis-ət-ē\ *n*

-g·e·nous \j-ə-nəs\ *adj comb form* [*-gen* + *-ous*] **1 :** producing **:** yielding <pyro*genous*> **2 :** having (such) an origin <hypo*genous*>

genre \ˈzhän-rə, ˈzhä^{n}-, ˈzhäŋ-; ˈzhä^{n}(-ə)r\ *n* [F, fr. MF *genre* kind, gender — more at GENDER] **1 :** KIND, SORT **2 :** a category of artistic, musical, or literary composition characterized by a particular style, form, or content <the movie won international acclaim as a masterpiece of the suspense ~ — *Current Biog.*>; *esp* **:** painting that depicts scenes or events from everyday life usu. realistically

gen·ro \ˈgen-ˈrō\ *n pl, often cap* [Jap *genrō*] **:** the elder statesmen of Japan who formerly advised the emperor

gens \ˈjenz, ˈgen(t)s\ *n, pl* **gen·tes** \ˈjen-ˌtēz, ˈgen-ˌtās\ [L *gent-*, *gens* — more at GENTLE] **1 :** a Roman clan embracing the families of the same stock in the male line with the members having a common name and being united in worship of their common ancestor **2 :** CLAN; *esp* **:** a patrilineal clan **3 :** a distinguishable group of related organisms

[1]gent \ˈjent\ *adj* [ME, noble, graceful, fr. OF, fr. L *genitus*, pp. of *gignere* to beget — more at KIN] *archaic* **:** PRETTY, GRACEFUL

[2]gent *n* [short for *gentlemen*] **:** MAN, FELLOW

gen·ta·mi·cin \ˌjent-ə-ˈmīs-ᵊn\ *n* [alter. of earlier *gentamycin*, fr. *genta-* (prob. irreg. fr. *gentian violet*; fr. the color of the organism from which it is produced) + *-mycin*] **:** a broad-spectrum antibiotic that is derived from an actinomycete (*Micromonospora purpurea* or *M. echinospora*)

gen·teel \jen-ˈtē(ə)l\ *adj* [MF *gentil* gentle] **1 a :** having an aristocratic quality or flavor **:** STYLISH **b :** of or relating to the gentry or upper class **c :** elegant or graceful in manner, appearance, or shape **d :** free from vulgarity or rudeness **:** POLITE **2 a :** maintaining or striving to maintain the appearance of superior or middle-class social status or respectability **b (1) :** marked by false delicacy, prudery, or affectation **(2) :** conventionally or insipidly pretty <timid and ~ artistic style> — **gen·teel·ly** \-ˈtē(ə)l-lē\ *adv* — **gen·teel·ness** *n*

gen·teel·ism \-ˈtē(ə)l-ˌiz-əm\ *n* **:** a word believed by its user to be genteel (as *stomach* for *belly*)

gen·tian \ˈjen-chən\ *n* [ME *gencian*, fr. MF *gentiane*, fr. L *gentiana*] **1 :** any of two genera (*Gentiana* and *Dasystephana*) of herbs of a family (Gentianaceae, the gentian family) with opposite smooth leaves and showy usu. blue flowers **2 :** the rhizome and roots of a yellow-flowered gentian (*Gentiana lutea*) of southern Europe that is used as a tonic and stomachic

gen·tia·nel·la \ˌjen-ch(ē-)ə-ˈnel-ə\ *n* [NL, dim. of L *gentiana*] **:** any of several gentians; *esp* **:** an often cultivated blue-flowered alpine gentian (*Gentiana acaulis*)

gentian violet *n, often cap G&V* **:** a dye consisting of one or more methyl derivatives of pararosaniline used as a biological stain, as a bactericide, fungicide, and anthelmintic, and in the treatment of burns

[1]gen·tile \ˈjen-ˌtīl\ *n* [ME, fr. LL *gentilis*, fr. L *gent-*, *gens* nation] **1** *often cap* **:** a person of a non-Jewish nation or of non-Jewish faith; *esp* **:** a Christian as distinguished from a Jew **2 :** HEATHEN, PAGAN **3** *often cap* **:** a non-Mormon

[2]gentile *adj* **1** *often cap* **a :** of or relating to the nations at large as distinguished from the Jews; *also* **:** of or relating to Christians as distinguished from the Jews **b :** of or relating to non-Mormons **2 :** PAGAN, HEATHEN **3** [L *gentilis*] **:** relating to a tribe or clan

gen·ti·lesse \ˌjent-ᵊl-ˈes\ *n* [ME, fr. MF, fr. *gentil*] *archaic* **:** decorum of conduct befitting a member of the gentry

gen·til·i·ty \jen-ˈtil-ət-ē\ *n, pl* **-ties 1 a :** the condition of belonging to the gentry **b :** the members of the upper class **:** GENTRY **2 a (1) :** decorum of conduct **:** COURTESY **(2) :** attitudes or activity marked by false delicacy, prudery, or affectation **b (1) :** superior social status or prestige evidenced by manners, possessions, or mode of life **(2) :** the maintenance of the appearance of superior or middle-class social status esp. in the face of decayed prosperity

gen·tis·ic acid \jen-ˌtis-ik-, -ˌtiz-\ *n* [ISV fr. *gentisin* (a pigment obtained from gentian root)] **:** a crystalline acid $C_7H_6O_4$ used medicinally as an analgesic and diaphoretic

[1]gen·tle \ˈjent-ᵊl\ *adj* **gen·tler** \ˈjent-lər, -ᵊl-ər\; **gen·tlest** \ˈjent-ləst, -ᵊl-əst\ [ME *gentil*, fr. OF, fr. L *gentilis* of a clan, of the same clan, fr. *gent-*, *gens* clan, nation; akin to L *gignere* to beget — more at KIN] **1 a :** belonging to a family of high social station **b** *archaic* **:** CHIVALROUS **c :** HONORABLE, DISTINGUISHED; *specif* **:** of or relating to a gentleman **d :** KIND, AMIABLE — used esp. in address as a complimentary epithet <~ reader> **e :** suited to a person of high social station **2 a :** TRACTABLE, DOCILE **b :** free from harshness, sternness, or violence <a ~ zephyr> <O sleep, O ~ sleep, Nature's soft nurse —Shak.> **3 :** SOFT, DELICATE <heard a ~ knock on the door> **4 :** MODERATE ***syn*** see SOFT ***ant*** rough, harsh — **gent·ly** \ˈjent-lē\ *adv*

[2]gentle *n* **:** a person of gentle birth or status

[3]gentle *vt* **gen·tled; gen·tling** \ˈjent-liŋ, -ᵊl-iŋ\ **1 :** to raise from the commonalty **:** ENNOBLE **2 a :** to make mild, docile, soft, or moderate **b :** MOLLIFY, PLACATE **c :** to stroke soothingly **:** PET

gentle breeze *n* **:** wind having a speed of 8 to 12 miles per hour

gen·tle·folk \ˈjent-ᵊl-ˌfōk\ *also* **gen·tle·folks** \-ˌfōks\ *n pl* **:** persons of gentle or good family and breeding

gen·tle·man \ˈjent-ᵊl-mən\ *n, often attrib* **1 a :** a man of noble or gentle birth **b :** a man belonging to the landed gentry **c (1) :** a man who combines gentle birth or rank with chivalrous qualities **(2) :** a man whose conduct conforms to a high standard of propriety or correct behavior **d (1) :** a man of independent means who does not engage in any occupation or profession for gain **(2) :** a man who does not engage in a menial occupation or in manual labor for gain **2 :** VALET — often used in the phrase *gentleman's gentleman* **3 :** a man of any social class or condition — often used in a courteous reference <show this ~ to a seat> or usu. in the pl. in address <ladies and *gentlemen*> — **gen·tle·man·like** \-mən-ˌlīk\ *adj* — **gen·tle·man·like·ness** *n*

gentleman-at-arms *n, pl* **gentlemen-at-arms :** one of a military corps of 40 gentlemen who attend the British sovereign on state occasions

gentleman-commoner *n, pl* **gentlemen-commoners :** one of a privileged class of commoners formerly required to pay higher fees than ordinary commoners at the universities of Oxford and Cambridge

gentleman farmer *n, pl* **gentlemen farmers :** a man of superior social position and wealth who farms mainly for pleasure rather than for profit

gen·tle·man·ly \-lē\ *adj* **:** characteristic of or having the character of a gentleman — **gen·tle·man·li·ness** *n*

gentleman of fortune : ADVENTURER

gentleman's agreement *or* **gentlemen's agreement** *n* **:** an agreement secured only by the honor of the participants

gen·tle·ness \ˈjent-ᵊl-nəs\ *n* **:** the quality or state of being gentle; *esp* **:** mildness of manners or disposition

gentle sex *n* **:** the female sex **:** women in general

gen·tle·wom·an \ˈjent-ᵊl-ˌwu̇m-ən\ *n* **1 a :** a woman of noble or gentle birth **b :** a woman attendant upon a lady of rank **2 :** a woman of refined manners or good breeding **:** LADY

Gen·too \ˈjen-(ˌ)tü\ *n, pl* **Gentoos** [Pg *gentio*, lit., gentile, fr. LL *gentilis*] *archaic* **:** HINDU

gen·trice \ˈjen-trəs\ *n* [ME *gentrise*, fr. OF *genterise*, alter. of *gentelise*, fr. *gentil* gentle] *archaic* **:** gentility of birth **:** RANK

gen·try \ˈjen-trē\ *n, pl* **gentries** [ME *gentrie*, alter. of *gentrise*] **1 a** *obs* **:** the qualities appropriate to a person of gentle birth; *esp* **:** COURTESY **b :** the condition or rank of a gentleman **2 a :** upper or ruling class **:** ARISTOCRACY **b :** a class whose members are entitled to bear a coat of arms though not of noble rank; *esp* **:** the landed proprietors having such status **3 :** people of a

ə abut	ᵊ kitten	ər further	a back	ā bake	ä cot, cart
au̇ out	ch chin	e less	ē easy	g gift	i trip ī life
j joke	ŋ sing	ō flow	ȯ flaw	ȯi coin	th thin th this
ü loot	u̇ foot	y yet	yü few	yu̇ furious	zh vision

specified class or kind : FOLKS <no real heroes or heroines among the academic ~ — R. G. Hanvey>
gen·u·flect \'jen-yə-ˌflekt\ *vi* [LL *genuflectere,* fr. L *genu* knee + *flectere* to bend — more at KNEE] **1 a :** to bend the knee **b :** to touch the knee to the floor or ground esp. in worship **2 :** to be servilely obedient or respectful : KOWTOW — **gen·u·flec·tion** \ˌjen-yə-'flek-shən\ *n*
gen·u·ine \'jen-yə-wən\ *adj* [L *genuinus* native, genuine; akin to L *gignere* to beget — more at KIN] **1 a :** actually having the reputed or apparent qualities or character <~ vintage wines> **b :** actually produced by or proceeding from the alleged source or author <the signature is ~> **c :** sincerely and honestly felt or experienced <a deep and ~ love> **2 :** free from hypocrisy or pretense : SINCERE ***syn*** see AUTHENTIC ***ant*** counterfeit, fraudulent — **gen·u·ine·ly** *adv* — **gen·u·ine·ness** \-wən-(n)əs\ *n*
ge·nus \'jē-nəs\ *n, pl* **gen·era** \'jen-ə-rə\ [L *gener-, genus* birth, race, kind — more at KIN] **1 :** a class, kind, or group marked by common characteristics or by one common characteristic; *specif* **:** a category of biological classification ranking between the family and the species, comprising structurally or phylogenetically related species or an isolated species exhibiting unusual differentiation, and being designated by a Latin or latinized capitalized singular noun **2 :** a class of objects divided into several subordinate species
-g·e·ny \j-ə-nē\ *n comb form* [Gk *-geneia* act of being born, fr. *-genēs* born — more at -GEN] **:** generation : production <bio*geny*>
geo- — see GE-
geo·bot·a·ny \ˌjē-ō-'bät-ᵊn-ē, -'bät-nē\ *n* : PHYTOGEOGRAPHY — **geo·bo·tan·i·cal** \-bə-'tan-i-kəl\ *also* **geo·bo·tan·ic** \-ik\ *adj* — **geo·bo·tan·i·cal·ly** \-i-k(ə-)lē\ *adv* — **geo·bot·a·nist** \-'bät-ᵊn-əst, -'bät-nəst\ *n*
geo·cen·tric \ˌjē-ō-'sen-trik\ *adj* **1 a :** relating to, measured from, or as if observed from the earth's center — compare TOPOCENTRIC **b :** having or relating to the earth as center — compare HELIOCENTRIC **2 :** taking or based on the earth as the center of perspective and valuation — **geo·cen·tri·cal·ly** \-tri-k(ə-)lē\ *adv*
geo·chem·is·try \ˌjē-ō-'kem-ə-strē\ *n* **1 :** a science that deals with the chemical composition of and chemical changes in the crust of the earth **2 :** the related chemical and geological properties of a substance — **geo·chem·i·cal** \-'kem-i-kəl\ *adj* — **geo·chem·i·cal·ly** \-k(ə-)lē\ *adv* — **geo·chem·ist** \-'kem-əst\ *n*
geo·chro·nol·o·gy \-krə-'näl-ə-jē\ *n* **:** the chronology of the past as indicated by geologic data — **geo·chro·no·log·ic** \-ˌkrän-ᵊl-'äj-ik, -ˌkrōn-\ *or* **geo·chro·no·log·i·cal** \-i-kəl\ *adj* — **geo·chro·no·log·i·cal·ly** \-i-k(ə-)lē\ *adv* — **geo·chro·nol·o·gist** \-krə-'näl-ə-jəst\ *n*
geo·chro·nom·e·try \-krə-'näm-ə-trē\ *n* **:** the measurement of past time by geochronological methods — **geo·chro·no·met·ric** \-ˌkrän-ə-'me-trik, -ˌkrōn-\ *adj*
ge·ode \'jē-ˌōd\ *n* [L *geodes,* a gem, fr. Gk *geōdēs* earthlike, fr. *gē* earth] **1 :** a nodule of stone having a cavity lined with crystals or mineral matter **2 :** the cavity in a geode
[1]**geo·de·sic** \ˌjē-ə-'des-ik, -'dēs-, -'dez-, -'dēz-\ *adj* **1 :** GEODETIC **2 :** made of light straight structural elements mostly in tension <a ~ dome>
[2]**geodesic** *n* **:** the shortest line between two points that lies in a given surface
ge·od·e·sy \jē-'äd-ə-sē\ *n* [Gk *geōdaisia,* fr. *geō-* ge- + *daiesthai* to divide — more at TIDE] **:** a branch of applied mathematics that determines the exact positions of points and the figures and areas of large portions of the earth's surface, the shape and size of the earth, and the variations of terrestrial gravity and magnetism — **ge·od·e·sist** \-səst\ *n*
geo·det·ic \ˌjē-ə-'det-ik\ *adj* [*geodesy;* after such pairs as *heresy: heretic*] **1 :** of, relating to, or determined by geodesy **2 :** relating to the geometry of geodetic lines — **geo·det·i·cal** \-i-kəl\ *adj* — **geo·det·i·cal·ly** \-i-k(ə-)lē\ *adv*
geodetic line *n* **:** a geodesic on the earth's surface
geodetic survey *n* **:** a survey of a large land area in which corrections are made for the curvature of the earth's surface
Geo·dim·e·ter \ˌjē-ə-'dim-ət-ər\ *trademark* — used for an electronic-optical device that measures distance on the basis of the velocity of light
geo·duck \'gü-ē-ˌdək\ *n* [Chinook Jargon *go-duck*] **:** an edible clam (*Panope generosa*) of the Pacific coast that weighs as much as five pounds
geo–eco·nom·ic \'jē-ō-ˌek-ə-'näm-ik, -ˌē-kə-\ *adj* **:** of, relating to, or characterized by economic conditions or policies that are influenced by geographic factors and are international in scope
geog *abbr* geographic; geographical; geography
ge·og·ra·pher \jē-'äg-rə-fər\ *n* **:** a specialist in geography
geo·graph·ic \ˌjē-ə-'graf-ik\ *or* **geo·graph·i·cal** \-i-kəl\ *adj* **1 :** of or relating to geography **2 :** belonging to or characteristic of a particular region — **geo·graph·i·cal·ly** \-i-k(ə-)lē\ *adv*
geographical mile *n* : NAUTICAL MILE
ge·og·ra·phy \jē-'äg-rə-fē\ *n, pl* **-phies** [L *geographia,* fr. Gk *geōgraphia,* fr. *geōgraphein* to describe the earth's surface, fr. *geō-* + *graphein* to write — more at CARVE] **1 :** a science that deals with the earth and its life; *esp* **:** the description of land, sea, air, and the distribution of plant and animal life including man and his industries **2 :** the geographic features of an area **3 :** a treatise on geography **4 :** a delineation or systematic arrangement of constituent elements : CONFIGURATION <the philosphers . . . have tried to construct *geographies* of human reason —*Times Lit. Supp.*>
geo·hy·drol·o·gy \ˌjē-ō-hī-'dräl-ə-jē\ *n* **:** a science that deals with the character, source, and mode of occurrence of underground water — **geo·hy·dro·log·ic** \-ˌhī-drə-'läj-ik\ *adj*
ge·oid \'jē-ˌȯid\ *n* [G, fr. Gk *geoeidēs* earthlike, fr. *gē*] **:** the surface within or around the earth that is everywhere normal to the direction of gravity and coincides with mean sea level in the oceans — **ge·oi·dal** \jē-'ȯid-ᵊl\ *adj*
geol *abbr* geologic; geological; geology
geo·log·ic \ˌjē-ə-'läj-ik\ *or* **geo·log·i·cal** \-i-kəl\ *adj* **:** of, relating to, or based on geology — **geo·log·i·cal·ly** \-i-k(ə-)lē\ *adv*
geologic time *n* **:** the long period of time occupied by the earth's geologic history
ge·ol·o·gize \jē-'äl-ə-ˌjīz\ *vi* **-gized; -giz·ing :** to study geology or make geologic investigations
ge·ol·o·gy \jē-'äl-ə-jē\ *n, pl* **-gies** [NL *geologia,* fr. *ge-* + *-logia* -logy] **1 a :** a science that deals with the history of the earth and its life esp. as recorded in rocks **b :** a study of the solid matter of a celestial body (as the moon) **2 :** geologic features **3 :** a treatise on geology — **ge·ol·o·gist** \-jəst\ *n*
geom *abbr* geometric; geometrical; geometry
geo·mag·net·ic \ˌjē-ō-mag-'net-ik\ *adj* **:** of or relating to terrestrial magnetism — **geo·mag·net·i·cal·ly** \-i-k(ə-)lē\ *adv* — **geo·mag·ne·tism** \-'mag-nə-ˌtiz-əm\ *n*
geomagnetic storm *n* : MAGNETIC STORM
geo·man·cer \'jē-ə-ˌman(t)-sər\ *n* **:** one that practices geomancy
geo·man·cy \-sē\ *n* [ME *geomancie,* fr. MF, fr. ML *geomantia,* fr. LGk *geōmanteia,* fr. Gk *geō-* + *-manteia* -mancy] **:** divination by means of figures or lines or geographical features — **geo·man·tic** \ˌjē-ə-'mant-ik\ *adj*
ge·om·e·ter \jē-'äm-ət-ər\ *n* **1 :** a specialist in geometry **2 :** GEOMETRID
geo·met·ric \ˌjē-ə-'me-trik\ *or* **geo·met·ri·cal** \-'me-tri-kəl\ *adj* **1 a :** of, relating to, or according to the methods or principles of geometry **b :** increasing in a geometric progression <~ population growth> **2** *cap* **:** of or relating to a style of ancient Greek pottery characterized by geometric decorative motifs **3 a :** utilizing rectilinear or simple curvilinear motifs or outlines in design **b :** of or relating to art based on simple geometric shapes (as straight lines, circles, or squares) <~ abstractions> — **geo·met·ri·cal·ly** \-tri-k(ə-)lē\ *adv*
geo·me·tri·cian \(ˌ)jē-ˌäm-ə-'trish-ən, ˌjē-ə-mə-\ *n* : GEOMETER 1
geometric mean *n* **:** the nth root of the product of *n* numbers; *specif* **:** a number that is the second term of three consecutive terms of a geometric progression <the *geometric mean* of 9 and 4 is 6>
geometric progression *n* **:** a sequence (as 1, ½, ¼) in which the ratio of a term to its predecessor is always the same — called also *geometric sequence*
geometric series *n* **:** a series (as $1 + x + x^2 + x^3 + \ldots$) whose terms form a geometric progression
geo·me·trid \jē-'äm-ə-trəd, ˌjē-ə-'me-trəd\ *n* [deriv. of Gk *geōmetrēs* geometer, fr. *geōmetrein*] **:** any of a family (Geometridae) of medium-sized moths with large wings and larvae that are loopers — **geometrid** *adj*
ge·om·e·trize \jē-'äm-ə-ˌtrīz\ *vb* **-trized; -triz·ing** *vi* **:** to work by or as if by geometric methods or laws ~ *vt* **1 :** to represent geometrically **2 :** to make conform to geometric principles and laws
ge·om·e·try \jē-'äm-ə-trē\ *n, pl* **-tries** [ME *geometrie,* fr. MF, fr. L *geometria,* fr. Gk *geōmetria,* fr. *geōmetrein* to measure the earth, fr. *geō-* ge- + *metron* measure — more at MEASURE] **1 a :** a branch of mathematics that deals with the measurement, properties, and relationships of points, lines, angles, surfaces, and solids; *broadly* **:** the study of properties of given elements that remain invariant under specified transformations **b :** a particular type or system of geometry **c :** a treatise on geometry **2 a :** CONFIGURATION **b :** surface shape **3 :** an arrangement of objects or parts that suggests geometrical figures
geo·mor·phic \ˌjē-ə-'mȯr-fik\ *adj* **:** of or relating to the form of the earth or a celestial body (as the moon) or its solid surface features
geo·mor·phol·o·gy \-mȯr-'fäl-ə-jē\ *n* [ISV] **1 :** a science that deals with the land and submarine relief features of the earth's surface or the comparable relief features of a celestial body (as the moon) and seeks a genetic interpretation of them **2 a :** the features dealt with in geomorphology **b :** a treatise on geomorphology — **geo·mor·pho·log·ic** \-ˌmȯr-fə-'läj-ik\ *or* **geo·mor·pho·log·i·cal** \-i-kəl\ *adj* — **geo·mor·pho·log·i·cal·ly** \-i-k(ə-)lē\ *adv* — **geo·mor·phol·o·gist** \-mȯr-'fäl-ə-jəst\ *n*
ge·oph·a·gy \jē-'äf-ə-jē\ *n* [ISV] **:** a practice of eating earthy substances (as clay) widespread among primitive or depressed peoples on a scanty or unbalanced diet
geo·phone \'jē-ə-ˌfōn\ *n* **:** an instrument for detecting vibrations passing through rocks, soil, or ice
geo·phys·ics \ˌjē-ə-'fiz-iks\ *n pl but sing or pl in constr* [ISV] **:** the physics of the earth including the fields of meteorology, hydrology, oceanography, seismology, volcanology, magnetism, radioactivity, and geodesy — **geo·phys·i·cal** \-i-kəl\ *adj* — **geo·phys·i·cal·ly** \-i-k(ə-)lē\ *adv* — **geo·phys·i·cist** \-'fiz-(ə-)səst\ *n*
geo·phyte \'jē-ə-ˌfīt\ *n* **:** a perennial plant that bears its overwintering buds below the surface of the soil
geo·po·lit·i·cal \ˌjē-ō-pə-'lit-i-kəl\ *adj* **:** of, relating to, or based on geopolitics — **geo·po·lit·i·cal·ly** \-k(ə-)lē\ *adv*
geo·pol·i·ti·cian \-ˌpäl-ə-'tish-ən\ *n* **:** a specialist in geopolitics
geo·pol·i·tics \-'päl-ə-ˌtiks\ *n pl but sing in constr* **1 :** a study of the influence of such factors as geography, economics, and demography on the politics and esp. the foreign policy of a state **2 :** a governmental policy guided by geopolitics **3 :** the combination of political and geographic factors characterizing a particular state or region
geo·pon·ic \ˌjē-ə-'pän-ik\ *adj* [Gk *geōponikos,* fr. *geōponein* to plow, fr. *geō-* + *ponein* to toil, fr. *ponos* labor] : AGRICULTURAL
geo·pon·ics \-iks\ *n pl but sing or pl in constr* **:** the art or science of cultivating the earth : HUSBANDRY
George \'jȯ(ə)rj\ *n* [St. *George,* patron saint of England] **1 :** either of two of the insignia of the British Order of the Garter **2 :** a British coin bearing the image of St. George
geor·gette \jȯr-'jet\ *n* [fr. *Georgette,* a trademark] **:** a thin strong clothing crepe of fibers woven from hard twisted yarns to produce a dull pebbly surface
[1]**Geor·gian** \'jȯr-jən\ *n* **1 :** a native or inhabitant of Georgia in the Caucasus **2 :** the language of the Georgian people
[2]**Georgian** *adj* **:** of, relating to, or constituting Georgia in the Caucasus, the Georgians, or Georgian
[3]**Georgian** *n* **:** a native or resident of the state of Georgia

GEOLOGIC TIME AND FORMATIONS

ERAS	PERIODS AND SYSTEMS	EPOCHS AND SERIES	APPROXIMATE NO. OF YEARS AGO	EARLIEST RECORD OF ANIMALS	EARLIEST RECORD OF PLANTS
	Quaternary	Holocene (Recent) Pleistocene (Glacial)			
Cenozoic				mankind	
	Tertiary	Pliocene Miocene Oligocene Eocene Paleocene	70,000,000		
				placental mammals	
	Cretaceous	Upper			
		Lower			grasses and cereals
Mesozoic				birds	
	Jurassic		160,000,000	mammals	flowering plants
	Triassic				ginkgoes
	Permian		230,000,000		cycads and conifers
	Pennsylvanian			insects	primitive gymnosperms
	Mississippian			reptiles	
				amphibians	
Paleozoic	Devonian		390,000,000		vascular plants: lycopodiums equisetums, ferns, etc.
	Silurian			fishes	
	Ordovician		500,000,000		mosses
	Cambrian		620,000,000		
Proterozoic	not divided into periods		1,420,000,000	invertebrates	spores of uncertain relationship marine algae
Archeozoic			2,300,000,000		

4**Georgian** *adj* : of, relating to, or characteristic of the state of Georgia or its people

5**Georgian** *adj* **1** : of, relating to, or characteristic of the reigns of the first four Georges of Great Britain **2** : of, relating to, or characteristic of the reign of George V of Great Britain

6**Georgian** *n* **1** : one belonging to either of the Georgian periods **2** : Georgian taste or style

Geor·gia pine \ˌjȯr-jə-\ *n* : LONGLEAF PINE

1**geor·gic** \ˈjȯr-jik\ *n* [the *Georgics,* poem by Vergil] : a poem dealing with agriculture

2**georgic** *adj* [L *georgicus,* fr. Gk *geōrgikos,* fr. *geōrgos* farmer, fr. *geō-* ge- + *ergon* work — more at WORK] : of or relating to agriculture

geo·sci·ence \ˌjē-ō-ˈsī-ən(t)s\ *n* **1** : the sciences (as geology, geophysics, and geochemistry) dealing with the earth **2** : any of the geosciences — **geo·sci·en·tist** \-ənt-əst\ *n*

geo·sta·tion·ary \-ˈstā-shə-ˌner-ē\ *adj* : of, relating to, or being an artificial satellite that travels above the equator and at the same speed as the earth rotates so that the satellite seems to remain in the same place

geo·strat·e·gy \-ˈstrat-ə-jē\ *n* **1** : a branch of geopolitics that deals with strategy **2** : the combination of geopolitical and strategic factors characterizing a particular geographic region **3** : the use by a government of strategy based on geopolitics — **geo·stra·te·gic** \-strə-ˈtē-jik\ *adj* — **geo·strat·e·gist** \-ˈstrat-ə-jəst\ *n*

geo·stroph·ic \ˌjē-ə-ˈsträf-ik\ *adj* [*ge-* + Gk *strophikos* turned, fr. *strophē* turning — more at STROPHE] : of or relating to deflective force due to the rotation of the earth — **geo·stroph·i·cal·ly** \-i-k(ə-)lē\ *adv*

geo·syn·chro·nous \ˌjē-ō-ˈsiŋ-krə-nəs, -ˈsin-\ *adj* : GEOSTATIONARY

geo·syn·cline \-ˈsin-ˌklīn\ *or* **geo·syn·cli·nal** \-sin-ˈklīn-ᵊl\ *n* : a great downward flexure of the earth's crust — compare GEANTICLINE — **geosynclinal** *adj*

geo·tac·tic \ˌjē-ō-ˈtak-tik\ *adj* : of or relating to geotaxis — **geo·tac·ti·cal·ly** \-ti-k(ə-)lē\ *adv*

geo·tax·is \-ˈtak-səs\ *n* [NL] : a taxis in which the force of gravity is the directive factor

geo·tec·ton·ic \-tek-ˈtän-ik\ *adj* : of or relating to the form, arrangement, and structure of rock masses of the earth's crust resulting from folding or faulting — **geo·tec·ton·i·cal·ly** \-i-k(ə-)lē\ *adv*

geo·ther·mal \-ˈthər-məl\ *or* **geo·ther·mic** \-mik\ *adj* [ISV] : of or relating to the heat of the earth's interior; *also* : produced by such heat <~ steam> — **geo·ther·mal·ly** \-mə-lē\ *adv*

geo·tro·pic \ˌjē-ə-ˈtrō-pik, -ˈträp-ik\ *adj* : of or relating to geotropism — **geo·tro·pi·cal·ly** \-ˈtrō-pi-k(ə-)lē, -ˈträp-i-\ *adv*

ge·ot·ro·pism \jē-ˈä-trə-ˌpiz-əm\ *n* [ISV] **1** : tropism in which gravity is the orienting factor **2** : tropism in which turning or movement is toward rather than away from the earth

ger *abbr* gerund

Ger *abbr* German; Germany

ge·rah \ˈgir-ə\ *n* [Heb *gērāh,* lit., grain] : an ancient Hebrew unit of weight equal to 1/20 shekel

ge·ra·ni·ol \jə-ˈrā-nē-ˌȯl, -ˌōl\ *n* [ISV, fr. NL *Geranium*] : a fragrant liquid unsaturated alcohol $C_{10}H_{18}O$ used chiefly in perfumes and soap

ge·ra·ni·um \jə-ˈrā-nē-əm, -nyəm\ *n* [NL, genus name, fr. L, geranium, fr. Gk *geranion,* fr. dim. of *geranos* crane — more at CRANE] **1** : any of a widely distributed genus (*Geranium* of the family Geraniaceae, the geranium family) of plants having regular flowers without spurs and with glands that alternate with the petals **2** : PELARGONIUM **3** : a vivid or strong red

ge·rar·dia \jə-ˈrärd-ē-ə\ *n* [NL, genus name, fr. John *Gerard* †1612 E botanist] : any of a genus (*Gerardia*) of often root-parasitic herbs of the figwort family having showy pink, purple, or yellow flowers

ger·bera \ˈgər-bə-rə, ˈjər-\ *n* [NL, genus name, fr. Traugott *Gerber* †1743 G naturalist] : any of a genus (*Gerbera*) of Old World composite herbs having basal tufted leaves and showy heads of yellow, pink, or orange flowers with prominent rays

ger·bil *also* **ger·bille** \ˈjər-bəl\ *n* [F *gerbille,* fr. NL *Gerbillus,* genus name, dim. of *jerboa*] : any of numerous Old World burrowing desert rodents (of *Gerbillus* and related genera) with long hind legs adapted for leaping

ge·rent \ˈjir-ənt\ *n* [L *gerent-, gerens* prp. of *gerere* to bear, carry on — more at CAST] : one that rules or manages

gerfalcon *var of* GYRFALCON

ge·ri·at·ric \ˌjer-ē-ˈa-trik, ˌjir-\ *adj* [Gk *gēras* old age + E *-iatric*] : of or relating to geriatrics, the aged, or the process of aging

ger·i·a·tri·cian \ˌjer-ē-ə-ˈtrish-ən, ˌjir-\ *n* : a specialist in geriatrics

ge·ri·at·rics \-triks\ *n pl but sing in constr* : a branch of medicine that deals with the problems and diseases of old age and aging people — compare GERONTOLOGY

ge·ri·a·trist \ˌjer-ē-ˈa-trəst, ˌjir-; jə-ˈrī-ə-\ *n* : GERIATRICIAN

germ \ˈjərm\ *n* [F *germe,* fr. L *germin-, germen,* fr. *gignere* to beget — more at KIN] **1 a** : a small mass of living substance capable of developing into an organism or one of its parts **b** : the embryo with the scutellum of a cereal grain that is usu. separated from the starchy endosperm during milling **2** : something that serves as an origin : RUDIMENT **3** : MICROORGANISM; *esp* : a microorganism causing disease

1**ger·man** \ˈjər-mən\ *adj* [ME *germain,* fr. MF, fr. L *germanus* having the same parents, irreg. fr. *germen*] : having the same parents or the same grandparents on either the maternal or paternal side — usu. used after the noun which it modifies and joined to it by a hyphen <brother-*german*> <cousin-*german*>

2**german** *n, obs* : a near relative

1**Ger·man** \ˈjər-mən\ *n* [ML *Germanus,* fr. L, any member of the Germanic peoples] **1 a** : a native or inhabitant of Germany **b** : a person of German descent **c** : one who speaks German outside Germany (as a Swiss German) **2 a** : the Germanic language spoken mainly in Germany, Austria, and parts of Switzerland **b** : the literary and official language of Germany **3** *often not cap* **a** : a dance consisting of intricate figures that are improvised and intermingled with waltzes **b** *chiefly Midland* : a dancing party; *specif* : one at which the german is danced

2**German** *adj* : of, relating to, or characteristic of Germany, the Germans, or German

German cockroach *n* : a small active winged cockroach (*Blatella germanica*) prob. of African origin but now common in many urban buildings in the U.S. — called also *Croton bug*

ger·man·der \(ˌ)jər-ˈman-dər\ *n* [deriv. of Gk *chamaidrys,* fr. *chamai* on the ground + *drys* tree — more at HUMBLE, TREE] **1** : any of a genus (*Teucrium*) of plants of the mint family with flowers having four exserted stamens, a short corolla tube, and a prominent lower lip **2** : any of several speedwells

ger·mane \(ˌ)jər-ˈmān\ *adj* [ME *germain,* lit., having the same parents, fr. MF] **1** *obs* : closely akin **2** : being at once relevant and appropriate : FITTING ***syn*** see RELEVANT ***ant*** foreign — **ger·mane·ly** *adv*

1**Ger·man·ic** \(ˌ)jər-ˈman-ik\ *adj* **1** : GERMAN **2** : of, relating to, or characteristic of the Germanic-speaking peoples **3** : of, relating to, or constituting Germanic

2**Germanic** *n* : a branch of the Indo-European language family containing English, German, Dutch, Afrikaans, Flemish, Frisian, the Scandinavian languages, and Gothic — see INDO-EUROPEAN LANGUAGES table

Ger·man·ism \ˈjər-mə-ˌniz-əm\ *n* **1** : a characteristic feature of German occurring in another language **2** : partiality for Germany or German customs **3** : the practices or objectives characteristic of the Germans

Ger·man·ist \-nəst\ *n* : a specialist in German or Germanic language, literature, or culture

ger·ma·ni·um \(ˌ)jər-ˈmā-nē-əm\ *n* [NL, fr. ML *Germania* Germany] : a grayish white hard brittle metalloid element that resembles silicon and is used as a semiconductor — see ELEMENT table

ger·man·iza·tion \ˌjər-mə-nə-ˈzā-shən\ *n, often cap* : the act or process of germanizing : the state of being germanized

ger·man·ize \ˈjər-mə-ˌnīz\ *vb* **-ized; -iz·ing** *often cap, vt* **1** *archaic* : to translate into German **2** : to cause to acquire German characteristics ~ *vi* : to have or acquire German customs or predilections

German measles *n pl but sing or pl in constr* : an acute contagious virus disease that is milder than typical measles but is damaging to the fetus when occurring early in pregnancy

Ger·mano- \(ˌ)jər-ˈman-ō-\ *comb form* : German <*Germano*phile> : German and <*Germano*-Russian>

1**Ger·mano·phile** \(ˌ)jər-ˈman-ə-ˌfīl\ *adj* : approving or favoring the German people and their institutions and customs

2**Germanophile** *n* : one that is Germanophile

German shepherd *n* : a working dog of a breed originating in northern Europe that is intelligent and responsive and is often used in police work and as a guide dog for the blind

German shorthaired pointer *n* : any of a German breed of liver or liver and white hunting dogs that were developed by hybridizing several types of pointer with the bloodhound

German silver *n* : NICKEL SILVER

German wirehaired pointer *n* : any of a German breed of liver or liver and white hunting dogs that have a flat-lying wiry coat composed of hairs one and one-half to two inches in length

germ cell *n* : an egg or sperm cell or one of their antecedent cells

ger·men \ˈjər-mən\ *n* [L] *archaic* : GERM 1a, 2

germ·free \ˈjərm-ˌfrē\ *adj* : free of microorganisms : AXENIC

ger·mi·cid·al \ˌjər-mə-ˈsīd-ᵊl\ *adj* : of or relating to a germicide; *also* : destroying germs

ger·mi·cide \ˈjər-mə-ˌsīd\ *n* : an agent that destroys germs

ger·mi·na·bil·i·ty \ˌjər-mə-nə-ˈbil-ət-ē\ *n* : the capacity to germinate

ger·mi·nal \ˈjərm-nəl, -ən-ᵊl\ *adj* [F, fr. L *germin-, germen* — more at GERM] **1 a** : being in the earliest stage of development **b** : CREATIVE, PRODUCTIVE **2** : of, relating to, or having the characteristics of a germ cell or early embryo — **ger·mi·nal·ly** \-ē\ *adv*

germinal area *n* : the part of the blastoderm that forms the embryo proper of an amniote vertebrate

germinal disc *n* **1** : BLASTODISC **2** : GERMINAL AREA

germinal vesicle *n* : the enlarged nucleus of the egg before completion of the reduction divisions

ger·mi·nate \ˈjər-mə-ˌnāt\ *vb* **-nat·ed; -nat·ing** [L *germinatus,* pp. of *germinare* to sprout, fr. *germin-, germen* bud, germ] *vt* : to cause to sprout or develop ~ *vi* **1** : to begin to grow : SPROUT **2** : to come into being : EVOLVE <before Western civilization began to ~ —A. L. Kroeber> — **ger·mi·na·tion** \ˌjər-mə-ˈnā-shən\ *n* — **ger·mi·na·tive** \ˈjər-mə-ˌnāt-iv\ *adj*

germ layer *n* : any of the three primary layers of cells differentiated in most embryos during and immediately following gastrulation

germ plasm *n* **1** : germ cells and their precursors serving as the bearers of heredity and being fundamentally independent of other cells **2** : the hereditary material of the germ cells : GENES

germ·proof \ˈjərm-ˈprüf\ *adj* : impervious to the penetration or action of germs

germ theory *n* : a theory in medicine: infections, contagious diseases, and various other conditions result from the action of microorganisms

germ warfare *n* : the use of harmful bacteria as weapons in war

germy \ˈjər-mē\ *adj* **germ·i·er; -est** : full of germs <~ river water>

geront- *or* **geronto-** *comb form* [F *géront-, géronto-,* fr. Gk *geront-, geronto-,* fr. *geront-, gerōn* old man; akin to Gk *gēras* old age — more at CORN] : aged one : old age <*geronto*logy>

ge·ron·tic \jə-ˈrän-tic\ *adj* : of or relating to decadence or old age

ger·on·toc·ra·cy \ˌjer-ən-ˈtäk-rə-sē\ *n, pl* **-cies** [F *gérontocratie,* fr. *géront-* geront- + *-cratie* -cracy] : rule by elders; *specif* : a form of social organization in which a group of old men or a council of elders dominates or exercises control — **ge·ron·to·crat** \jə-ˈränt-ə-ˌkrat\ *n* — **ge·ron·to·crat·ic** \-ˌränt-ə-ˈkrat-ik\ *adj*

ger·on·tol·o·gy \ˌjer-ən-ˈtäl-ə-jē\ *n* [ISV] : a branch of knowledge dealing with aging and the problems of the aged — compare GERIATRICS — **ge·ron·to·log·i·cal** \jə-ˌränt-ᵊl-ˈäj-i-kəl\ *or* **ge·ron·to·log·ic** \-ik\ *adj* — **ger·on·tol·o·gist** \ˌjer-ən-ˈtäl-ə-jəst\ *n*

ge·ron·to·mor·pho·sis \jə-ˌränt-ə-ˈmȯr-fə-səs\ *n* [NL] : phylogenetic change involving specialization of the adult with decreased capacity for further change indicative of racial senescence

-g·er·ous \j-(ə-)rəs\ *adj comb form* [L *-ger*, fr. *gerere* to bear — more at CAST] : bearing : producing <denti*gerous*>

¹ger·ry·man·der \ˌjer-ē-ˈman-dər, ˈjer-ē-ˌ, *also* ˌger-, ˈger-\ *n* [Elbridge *Gerry* + sala*mander*; fr. the shape of an election district formed during Gerry's governorship of Massachusetts] **1 :** the act or method of gerrymandering **2 :** a district or pattern of districts varying greatly in size or population as a result of gerrymandering

gerrymander 2

²gerrymander *vt* **ger·ry·man·dered; ger·ry·man·der·ing** \-d(ə-)riŋ\ **1 :** to divide (a territorial unit) into election districts to give one political party an electoral majority in a large number of districts while concentrating the voting strength of the opposition in as few districts as possible **2 :** to divide (an area) into political units to give special advantages to one group <~ a school district>

ger·und \ˈjer-ənd\ *n* [LL *gerundium*, fr. L *gerundus*, gerundive of *gerere* to bear, carry on — more at CAST] **1 :** a verbal noun in Latin that expresses generalized or uncompleted action **2 :** any of several linguistic forms analogous to the Latin gerund in languages other than Latin; *esp* **:** the English verbal noun in *-ing* that has the function of a substantive and at the same time shows the verbal features of tense, voice, and capacity to take adverbial qualifiers and to govern objects

ge·run·dive \jə-ˈrən-div\ *n* **1 :** the Latin future passive participle that functions as the verbal adjective, that expresses the fitness or necessity of the action to be performed, and that has the same suffix as the gerund **2 :** a verbal adjective in a language other than Latin analogous to the gerundive

ge·sell·schaft \gə-ˈzel-ˌshäft\ *n* [G, companionship, society, fr. *gesell* companion + *-schaft* -ship] : a rationally developed mechanistic type of social relationship characterized by impersonally contracted associations between persons; *also* **:** a community or society characterized by this relationship — compare GEMEINSCHAFT

ges·so \ˈjes-(ˌ)ō\ *n, pl* **gessoes** [It, lit., gypsum, fr. L *gypsum*] **1 :** plaster of paris or gypsum prepared with glue for use in painting or making bas-reliefs **2 :** a paste prepared by mixing whiting with size or glue and spread upon a surface to fit it for painting or gilding

gest *or* **geste** \ˈjest\ *n* [ME *geste* — more at JEST] **1 :** ADVENTURE, EXPLOIT **2 :** a tale of adventures; *esp* **:** a romance in verse

ge·stalt \gə-ˈs(h)tält, -ˈs(h)tȯlt\ *n, pl* **ge·stalt·en** \-ᵊn\ *or* **gestalts** [G, lit., shape, form] : a structure, configuration, or pattern of physical, biological, or psychological phenomena so integrated as to constitute a functional unit with properties not derivable from its parts in summation

Gestalt psychology *n* **:** the study of perception and behavior from the standpoint of an organism's response to configurational wholes with stress on the identity of psychological and physiological events and rejection of atomistic or elemental analysis of stimulus, percept, and response

ge·sta·po \gə-ˈstäp-(ˌ)ō\ *n, pl* **-pos** [G, fr. *Ge*heime *Sta*ats *po*lizei, lit., secret state police] : a secret-police organization operating esp. against persons suspected of treason or sedition and often employing underhanded and terrorist methods

ges·tate \ˈjes-ˌtāt\ *vb* **ges·tat·ed; ges·tat·ing** [back-formation fr. *gestation*] *vt* **1 :** to carry in the uterus during pregnancy **2 :** to conceive and gradually develop in the mind ~ *vi* **:** to be in the process of gestation

ges·ta·tion \je-ˈstā-shən\ *n* [L *gestation-*, *gestatio*, fr. *gestatus*, pp. of *gestare* to bear, fr. *gestus*, pp. of *gerere* to bear — more at CAST] **1 :** the carrying of young in the uterus : PREGNANCY **2 :** conception and development esp. in the mind — **ges·ta·tion·al** \-shnəl, -shən-ᵊl\ *adj*

geste *also* **gest** \ˈjest\ *n* [MF *geste*, fr. L *gestus*, fr. *gestus*, pp. of *gerere*] **1** *archaic* **:** DEPORTMENT **2** *archaic* **:** GESTURE

ges·tic \ˈjes-tik\ *adj* **:** relating to or consisting of bodily movements or gestures

ges·tic·u·lant \je-ˈstik-yə-lənt\ *adj* **:** making gesticulations

ges·tic·u·late \je-ˈstik-yə-ˌlāt\ *vi* **-lat·ed; -lat·ing** [L *gesticulatus*, pp. of *gesticulari*, fr. (assumed) L *gesticulus*, dim. of L *gestus*] **:** to make gestures esp. when speaking <talking excitedly and *gesticulating* with her hands —Louis Auchincloss> — **ges·tic·u·la·tor** \-ˌlāt-ər\ *n* — **ges·tic·u·la·to·ry** \-lə-ˌtōr-ē, -ˌtȯr-\ *adj*

ges·tic·u·la·tion \je-ˌstik-yə-ˈlā-shən\ *n* **1 :** the act of making gestures **2 :** GESTURE; *esp* **:** an expressive gesture made in showing strong feeling or in enforcing an argument

ges·tic·u·la·tive \je-ˈstik-yə-ˌlāt-iv\ *adj* **:** inclined to or marked by gesticulation

¹ges·ture \ˈjes(h)-chər\ *n* [ML *gestura* mode of action, fr. L *gestus*, pp.] **1** *archaic* **:** CARRIAGE, BEARING **2 :** the use of motions of the limbs or body as a means of expression **3 :** a movement usu. of the body or limbs that expresses or emphasizes an idea, sentiment, or attitude **4 :** something said or done by way of formality or courtesy, as a symbol or token, or for its effect on the attitudes of others <a political ~ to draw popular support —V. L. Parrington> — **ges·tur·al** \-chə-rəl\ *adj*

²gesture *vb* **ges·tured; ges·tur·ing** *vi* **:** to make a gesture ~ *vt* **:** to express or direct by a gesture

gesture language *n* **:** communication by gestures; *esp* **:** SIGN LANGUAGE

ge·sund·heit \gə-ˈzu̇nt-ˌhīt\ *interj* [G, lit., health] — used to wish good health esp. to one who has just sneezed

¹get \(ˈ)get; *often* git, *without stress, when a heavily stressed syllable follows, as in* "get up"\ *vb* **got** \(ˈ)gät\; **got** *or* **got·ten** \ˈgät-ᵊn\; **get·ting** [ME *geten*, fr. ON *geta* to get, beget; akin to OE bi*gietan* to beget, L pre*hendere* to seize, grasp, Gk *chandanein* to hold, contain] *vt* **1 a :** to gain possession of **b :** to receive as a return : EARN <he *got* a bad reputation for carelessness> **2 a :** to obtain or receive by way of benefit or advantage <he *got* little for his trouble> <~ the better of an enemy> **b :** to achieve as a result of military activity **3 a :** to obtain by concession or entreaty <~ your mother's permission to go> **b :** to become affected by : CATCH <*got* measles from his sister> **4 a :** to seek out and obtain <hoped to ~ dinner at the inn> **b :** to obtain and bring where wanted or needed <~ a pencil from the desk> **5 :** BEGET **6 a :** to cause to come or go <quickly *got* his luggage through customs> **b :** to cause to move <~ him out of the house> **c :** to cause to be in a certain position or condition <*got* his feet wet> **d :** to make ready : PREPARE **7 a :** SEIZE **b :** OVERCOME **c :** to have an emotional effect on <the sight of her tears *got* him> **d :** PUZZLE **e :** IRRITATE **f :** to take vengeance on; *specif* **:** KILL **g :** HIT **8 a :** to be subjected to <*got* a bad fall> **b :** to receive by way of punishment **c :** to suffer a specified injury to **9 a :** MEMORIZE <*got* the verse by heart> **b :** to find out by calculation <~ the answer to a problem> **c :** HEAR **d :** UNDERSTAND **10 :** to prevail on : CAUSE <finally *got* the boy to start his homework> **11 a :** HAVE — used in the present perfect tense form with present meaning <I've *got* no money> **b :** to have as an obligation or necessity — used in the present perfect tense form with present meaning <he has *got* to come> **12 :** to establish communication with **13 :** to put out in baseball ~ *vi* **1 a :** to succeed in coming or going <~ to the city> **b :** to reach or enter into a certain condition <*got* to sleep after midnight> <they *got* married last week> **2 :** to acquire wealth **3 :** to be able : CONTRIVE **4 a :** to succeed in becoming <how to ~ clear of all the debts I owe —Shak.> **b :** to become involved <people who ~ into trouble with the law> **5 :** to leave immediately <told them to ~> — **get after :** to pursue with exhortation, reprimand, or attack — **get ahead :** to achieve success <determined to *get ahead* in life> — **get around 1 :** to get the better of : CIRCUMVENT **2 :** EVADE — **get at 1 :** to reach effectively **2 :** to influence corruptly : BRIBE **3 :** to turn one's attention to **4 :** to try to prove or make clear <what is he *getting at*> — **get away with 1 :** to do (as a reprehensible act) without criticism or penalty **2 :** to take as food or drink : CONSUME <the crew *got away with* over ten cases of beer that afternoon> — **get cracking :** to make a start : get going <ought to *get cracking* on that assignment> — **get even :** to get revenge — **get even with :** to repay in kind — **get it :** to receive a scolding or punishment — **get on :** to produce an unfortunate effect on : UPSET <the noise *got on* my nerves> — **get one's goat :** to make one angry or annoyed — **get over 1 a :** OVERCOME, SURMOUNT **b :** to recover from **2 :** to move or travel across — **get somewhere :** to be successful — **get there :** to be successful — **get through 1 :** to reach the end of : COMPLETE **2 :** to while away <hardly knew how to *get through* his days> — **get to 1 a :** BEGIN <she *gets to* worrying over nothing at all> **b :** to be ready to begin or deal with <I'll *get to* the accounts as soon as I can> **2 :** to have an effect on : INFLUENCE — **get together 1 :** to bring together : ACCUMULATE **2 :** to come together : ASSEMBLE **3 :** to reach agreement — **get wind of :** to become aware of — **get with it :** to become alert or aware : show sophisticated consciousness

syn **1** GET, OBTAIN, PROCURE, SECURE, ACQUIRE, GAIN, WIN, EARN *shared meaning element* **:** to come into possession of. GET is both general in meaning and simple and familiar in use. Thus, one may *get* something by fetching <*get* a book from the shelf> by extracting <*get* gold from ore> by receiving <*get* a present> or by earning <*get* good wages> OBTAIN is more likely to suggest attainment of something sought, often after expenditure of time and effort <*obtain* a graduate degree> PROCURE stresses effort employed in obtaining <pursued with unflagging energy his program of building up the armed services and *procuring* arms for them —W. L. Shirer> SECURE may suggest safe lasting possession or control <safety against infection could be *secured* by the simple precaution of using safe, potable water —V. G. Heiser> or the obtaining of what is hard to come by <*secure* bookings for a new singer> ACQUIRE often suggests addition to what is already possessed <*acquire* a taste for olives> GAIN adds to *obtain* the notion of struggle or competition and often imputes material worth to the thing obtained <worked hard to *gain* an education> WIN may differ from *gain* in suggesting the influence of favoring factors or circumstances <her excellent performance *won* her an award> EARN implies a correspondence between one's effort and what one gains thereby <his behavior *earned* him general condemnation> **2** see INDUCE

²get \ˈget\ *n* **1 a :** something begotten: (1) **:** OFFSPRING (2) **:** the entire progeny of a male animal **b :** LINEAGE **2 :** a successful return of a difficult shot in a game (as tennis)

get about *vi* **1 :** to be up and about : begin to walk <has recovered from his injuries and is able to *get about* again> **2 :** to become current : CIRCULATE

get across *vi* **:** to become clear or convincing ~ *vt* **:** to make clear or convincing <she can't *get* her point *across*>

get along *vi* **1 a :** to proceed toward a destination : PROGRESS **b :** to approach an advanced stage; *esp* **:** to approach old age **2 :** to meet one's needs : MANAGE **3 :** to be or remain on congenial terms

get·at·able \get-ˈat-ə-bəl\ *adj* : ACCESSIBLE, APPROACHABLE

get·away \ˈget-ə-ˌwā\ *n* : an act or instance of getting away: as **a** : START **b** : ESCAPE

get back *vi* **1** : to come or go again to a person, place, or condition : RETURN, REVERT <*getting back* to the main topic of the lecture> **2** : to gain revenge : RETALIATE — used with *at*

get by *vi* **1** : to make ends meet : SURVIVE **2** : to succeed with the least possible effort or accomplishment **3** : to proceed without being discovered, criticized, or punished

get down *vi* **1** : to alight esp. from a vehicle : DESCEND **2** : to give one's attention or consideration — used with *to* <*get down* to business> ~ *vt* **1** : to cause to be physically, mentally, or emotionally exhausted : DEPRESS <the weather was *getting* her *down*> **2** : to bring oneself to eat : SWALLOW **3** : to commit to writing : DESCRIBE

Geth·sem·a·ne \geth-ˈsem-ə-nē\ *n* [Gk *Gethsēmanē*] **1** : the garden outside Jerusalem mentioned in Mk 14 as the scene of the agony and arrest of Jesus **2** : a place or occasion of great mental or spiritual suffering

get off *vi* **1** : START, LEAVE <intended to *get off* on his trip early in the morning> **2** : to escape from a dangerous situation or from punishment <expected to *get off* with a light prison term —S. L. A. Marshall> **3** : to leave work with permission <*got off* early and went to the ball game> ~ *vt* **1** : to secure the release of or procure a modified penalty for <his lawyers *got* him *off* with little difficulty> **2 a** : UTTER <*get off* a joke> **b** : to write and send : DISPATCH

get on *vi* **1** : to get along **2** : to gain knowledge or understanding <*got on* to the racket>

get out *vi* **1** : EMERGE, ESCAPE <doubted that he would *get out* alive> **2** : to become known : leak out <their secret *got out*> ~ *vt* **1** : to cause to emerge or escape <how can I *get* myself *out* of this muddle —C. W. H. Johnson> **2** : to bring before the public; *esp* : PUBLISH

get round *vi* : to get around

get·ter \ˈget-ər\ *n* **1** : one that gets **2** : a substance introduced into a vacuum tube or electric lamp to remove traces of gas

get–to·geth·er \ˈget-tə-ˌgeth-ər\ *n* : MEETING; *esp* : an informal social gathering

get·up \ˈget-ˌəp\ *n* **1** : general composition or structure **2** : OUTFIT, COSTUME

get up \get-ˈəp, git-\ *vi* **1 a** : to arise from bed **b** : to rise to one's feet **c** : CLIMB, ASCEND **2** : to go ahead or faster — used in the imperative as a command esp. to driven animals ~ *vt* **1** : to make preparations for : ORGANIZE <*got up* a party for the newcomers> **2** : to arrange as to external appearance : DRESS **3** : to acquire a knowledge of **4** : to create in oneself <cannot *get up* an atom of sympathy for them>

ge·um \ˈjē-əm\ *n* [L] : AVENS

GeV *abbr* giga-electron-volt

gew·gaw \ˈg(y)ü-(ˌ)gȯ\ *n* [origin unknown] : a showy trifle : BAUBLE, TRINKET

gey \(ˈ)gā\ *adv* [alter. of *gay*, adv.] *chiefly Scot* : VERY, QUITE

gey·ser \ˈgī-zər, *Brit sometimes* ˈgā- *or* ˈgē- *for 1 & usu* ˈgē- *for 2*\ *n* [Icel *geysir* gusher, fr. *geysa* to rush forth, fr. ON; akin to OE *gēotan* to pour — more at FOUND] **1** : a spring that throws forth intermittent jets of heated water and steam **2** *Brit* : an apparatus for heating water rapidly with a gas flame (as for a bath)

gey·ser·ite \-zə-ˌrīt\ *n* [F *geysérite*, fr. *geyser*, fr. Icel *geysir*] : a hydrous silica that constitutes one variety of opal and is deposited around some hot springs and geysers in white or grayish concretionary masses

GFE *abbr* government-furnished equipment

GFWC *abbr* General Federation of Women's Clubs

GGPA *abbr* graduate grade-point average

ghar·ry \ˈgar-ē, ˈgär-\ *n, pl* **gharries** [Hindi *gāṛī*] : a horse-drawn cab used esp. in India and Egypt

ghast \ˈgast\ *adj, archaic* : GHASTLY

ghast·ful \-fəl\ *adj, archaic* : FRIGHTFUL — **ghast·ful·ly** *adv, archaic*

ghast·ly \ˈgast-lē\ *adj* **ghast·li·er; -est** [ME *gastly*, fr. *gasten* to terrify] **1 a** : terrifyingly horrible to the senses : FRIGHTENING <a ~ crime> **b** : intensely unpleasant, disagreeable, or objectionable <such a life seems ~ in its emptiness and sterility —Aldous Huxley> **2** : resembling a ghost **3** *obs* : filled with fear : TERRIFIED **4** : very great <~ mistake> — **ghast·li·ness** *n* — **ghastly** *adv*

ghat \ˈgȯt, ˈgät\ *n* [Hindi *ghāṭ*] : a broad flight of steps that is situated on an Indian riverbank and that provides access to the water esp. for bathing

ghee *or* **ghi** \ˈgē\ *n* [Hindi, *ghī*, fr. Skt *ghṛta*; akin to MIr *gert* milk] : a semifluid clarified butter made esp. in India

gher·kin \ˈgər-kən\ *n* [D *gurken*, pl. of *gurk* cucumber, deriv. of Pol *ogurek*, fr. MGk *agouros*] **1** : a small prickly fruit used for pickling; *also* : the slender annual vine (*Cucumis anguria*) of the gourd family that bears it **2** : the immature fruit of the cucumber

[1]ghet·to \ˈget-(ˌ)ō\ *n, pl* **ghettos** *or* **ghettoes** [It] **1** : a quarter of a city in which Jews were formerly required to live **2** : a quarter of a city in which members of a minority group live esp. because of social, legal, or economic pressure

[2]ghetto *vt* : GHETTOIZE

ghet·to·ize \ˈget-ō-ˌīz\ *vt* **-ized; -iz·ing** : to isolate in or as if in a ghetto — **ghet·to·iza·tion** \ˌget-ō-ə-ˈzā-shən\ *n*

Ghib·el·line \ˈgib-ə-ˌlēn, -ˌlīn, -lən\ *n* [It *Ghibellino*] : a member of an aristocratic political party in medieval Italy supporting the authority of the German emperors — compare GUELF

ghib·li \ˈgib-lē\ *n* [Ar *giblīy* south wind] : a hot desert wind of northern Africa

ghillie *var of* GILLIE

[1]ghost \ˈgōst\ *n* [ME *gost*, *gast*, fr. OE *gāst*; akin to OHG *geist* spirit, Skt *heḍa* anger] **1** : the seat of life or intelligence : SOUL <give up the ~> **2** : a disembodied soul; *esp* : the soul of a dead person believed to be an inhabitant of the unseen world or to appear to the living in bodily likeness **3** : SPIRIT, DEMON **4 a** : a faint shadowy trace <a ~ of a smile> **b** : the least bit : IOTA <didn't have a ~ of a chance> **5** : a false image in a photographic negative or on a television screen caused esp. by reflection **6** : one who ghostwrites **7** : a red blood cell that has lost its hemoglobin — **ghost·like** \-ˌlīk\ *adj* — **ghosty** \ˈgō-stē\ *adj*

[2]ghost *vt* **1** : to haunt like a ghost **2** : GHOSTWRITE ~ *vi* **1** : to move silently like a ghost **2** : GHOSTWRITE

ghost dance *n* : a group dance for communication with the spirits of the dead characteristic of an Amerindian messianic cult

ghost·ly \ˈgōst-lē\ *adj* **ghost·li·er; -est** **1** : of or relating to the soul : SPIRITUAL **2** : of, relating to, or having the characteristics of a ghost : SPECTRAL **3** : of or relating to a ghost-writer — **ghost·li·ness** *n* — **ghostly** *adv*

ghost story *n* **1** : a story about ghosts **2** : a tale based on imagination rather than fact

ghost town *n* : a once-flourishing town wholly or nearly deserted usu. as a result of the exhaustion of some natural resource (as gold)

ghost word *n* : a word form never in established usage; *esp* : one arising from an editorial or typographical error or a mistaken pronunciation

ghost·write \ˈgō-ˌstrīt\ *vb* **-wrote** \-ˌstrōt\; **-writ·ten** \-ˌstrit-ᵊn\ [back-formation fr. *ghost-writer*] *vi* : to write for and in the name of another ~ *vt* : to write (as a speech) for another who is the presumed author — **ghost-writ·er** *n*

ghoul \ˈgül\ *n* [Ar *ghūl*] **1** : a legendary evil being that robs graves and feeds on corpses **2** : one suggestive of a ghoul — **ghoul·ish** \ˈgü-lish\ *adj* — **ghoul·ish·ly** *adv* — **ghoul·ish·ness** *n*

GHQ *abbr* general headquarters

GHz *abbr* gigahertz

gi *abbr* gill

[1]GI \(ˈ)jē-ˈī\ *adj* [galvanized *i*ron; fr. abbr. used in listing such articles as garbage cans, but taken as abbr. for *government issue*] **1** : provided by an official U.S. military supply department <~ shoes> **2** : of, relating to, or characteristic of U.S. military personnel **3** : conforming to military regulations or customs <a ~ haircut>

[2]GI *n, pl* **GI's** *or* **GIs** \-ˈīz\ : a member or former member of the U.S. armed forces; *esp* : a man enlisted in the army

[3]GI *vt* **GI'd** \-ˈīd\; **GI'·ing** \-ˈī-iŋ\ : to clean thoroughly (as floors) in preparation for or as if for a military inspection

[4]GI *adv* : in strict conformity with military regulations or customs

[5]GI *abbr* **1** galvanized iron **2** gastrointestinal **3** general issue **4** government issue

[1]gi·ant \ˈjī-ənt\ *n* [ME *giaunt*, fr. MF *geant*, fr. L *gigant-*, *gigas*, fr. Gk] **1** : a legendary being of great stature and strength and of more than mortal but less than godlike power **2 a** : a living being of great size **b** : a person of extraordinary powers <a literary ~> **3** : something unusually large or powerful — **gi·ant·ess** \-əs\ *n* — **gi·ant·like** \-ˌlīk\ *adj*

[2]giant *adj* : characterized by extremely large size, proportion, or power

gi·ant·ism \ˈjī-ənt-ˌiz-əm\ *n* **1** : the quality or state of being a giant <~ in industry> **2** : GIGANTISM 2

giant panda *n* : PANDA 2

giant reed *n* : a tall European grass (*Arundo donax*) with woody stems used in making organ reeds

giant schnauzer *n* : any of a breed of robust, sinewy, heavyset schnauzers that attain a height of 21 1/2 to 25 1/2 inches

giant sequoia *n* : BIG TREE

giant star *n* : a star of great intrinsic luminosity and of large mass

giaour \ˈjau̇(ə)r\ *n* [Turk *gâvur*] : one outside the Muslim faith : INFIDEL 2a

[1]gib \ˈgib\ *n* [ME, fr. *Gib*, nickname for *Gilbert*] : a male cat; *specif* : a castrated male cat

[2]gib *n* [origin unknown] : a plate of metal or other material machined to hold other parts in place, to afford a bearing surface, or to provide means for taking up wear

[3]gib *vt* **gibbed; gib·bing** : to fasten with a gib

Gib *abbr* Gibraltar

gib·ber \ˈjib-ər\ *vi* **gib·bered; gib·ber·ing** \-(ə-)riŋ\ [imit.] : to speak rapidly, inarticulately, and often foolishly : CHATTER — **gibber** *n*

gib·ber·el·lic acid \ˌjib-ə-ˌrel-ik-\ *n* : a crystalline acid $C_{19}H_{22}O_6$ associated with and similar in effect to the gibberellins

gib·ber·el·lin \-ˈrel-ən\ *n* [NL *Gibberella fujikoroi*, fungus from which it was first isolated] : any of several plant-growth regulators that in low concentrations promote shoot growth

gib·ber·ish \ˈjib-(ə-)rish, ˈgib-\ *n* [prob. fr. *gibber*] : unintelligible or meaningless language: **a** : a technical or esoteric language **b** : pretentious or needlessly obscure language

[1]gib·bet \ˈjib-ət\ *n* [ME *gibet*, fr. OF] **1** : GALLOWS **2** : an upright post with a projecting arm for hanging the bodies of executed criminals as a warning

[2]gibbet *vt* **1 a** : to hang on a gibbet **b** : to expose to infamy or public scorn **2** : to execute by hanging on a gibbet

gib·bon \ˈgib-ən\ *n* [F] : any of several tailless apes (genera *Hylobates* and *Symphalangus*) of southeastern Asia and the East Indies that are the smallest and most arboreal anthropoid apes

gib·bos·i·ty \jib-ˈäs-ət-ē, gib-\ *n, pl* **-ties** : PROTUBERANCE, SWELLING

gib·bous \ˈjib-əs, ˈgib-\ *adj* [ME, fr. MF *gibbeux*, fr. LL *gibbosus* humpbacked, fr. L *gibbus* hump] **1 a** : marked by convexity : PROTUBERANT **b** *of the moon or a planet* : seen with more than half but not all of the apparent disk illuminated **c** : swollen on one side **2** : having a hump : HUMPBACKED — **gib·bous·ly** *adv* — **gib·bous·ness** *n*

gibe \ˈjīb\ *vb* **gibed; gib·ing** [perh. fr. MF *giber* to shake, handle roughly] *vi* : to utter taunting words ~ *vt* : to deride or tease with taunting words ***syn*** see SCOFF — **gibe** *n* — **gib·er** *n*

giblets \ˈjib-ləts *also* ˈgib-\ *n pl* [ME *gibelet* entrails, garbage, fr. MF, stew of wildfowl] : the edible viscera of a fowl

Gibr *abbr* Gibraltar

Gi·bral·tar \jə-ˈbrȯl-tər\ *n* [*Gibraltar*, fortress in the Brit. colony of Gibraltar] : an impregnable stronghold

Gib·son \ˈgib-sən\ *n* [fr. the name *Gibson*] **:** a cocktail made of gin or vodka and dry vermouth and garnished with onions

gid \ˈgid\ *n* [back-formation fr. *giddy*] **:** a disease esp. of sheep caused by the larva of a tapeworm (*Multiceps multiceps*) in the brain

gid·dap \gid-ˈap; ˌgid-ē-ˈap, -ˈəp\ *vb imper* [alter. of *get up*] — a command to a horse to go ahead or go faster

¹**gid·dy** \ˈgid-ē\ *adj* **gid·di·er; -est** [ME *gidy* mad, foolish, fr. OE *gydig* possessed, mad; akin to OE *god*] **1 :** lightheartedly silly **:** FRIVOLOUS **2 a :** DIZZY <~ from the unaccustomed exercise> **b :** causing dizziness <a ~ height> **c :** whirling rapidly — **gid·di·ly** \ˈgid-ᵊl-ē\ *adv* — **gid·di·ness** \ˈgid-ē-nəs\ *n*

²**giddy** *vb* **gid·died; gid·dy·ing** *vt* **:** to make giddy ~ *vi* **:** to become giddy

Gid·e·on \ˈgid-ē-ən\ *n* [Heb *Gidh'ōn*] **1 :** an early Hebrew hero noted for his defeat of the Midianites **2 :** a member of an interdenominational organization whose activities include the placing of Bibles in hotel rooms

gie \ˈgē\ *chiefly Scot var of* GIVE

¹**gift** \ˈgift\ *n* [ME, fr. ON, something given, talent; akin to OE *giefan* to give] **1 :** a notable capacity or talent **2 :** something voluntarily transferred by one person to another without compensation **3 :** the act, right, or power of giving

syn GIFT, FACULTY, APTITUDE, BENT, TALENT, GENIUS, KNACK *shared meaning element* **:** a special ability or an unusual capacity for doing or achieving something

²**gift** *vt* **1 :** to endow with some power, quality, or attribute **2 :** PRESENT <generously ~*ed* us with a copy —*Saturday Rev.*>

gift certificate *n* **:** a certified statement entitling the recipient to select merchandise in the establishment of the issuer to the amount stated thereon

gift·ed \ˈgif-təd\ *adj* **1 :** having great natural ability **:** TALENTED <~ children> **2 :** revealing a special gift <~ voices> — **gift·ed·ly** *adv* — **gift·ed·ness** *n*

gift of gab : the ability to talk glibly and persuasively

gift wrap *vt* **:** to wrap (merchandise intended as a gift) decoratively

¹**gig** \ˈgig\ *n* [ME *gigg* top, perh. of Scand origin; akin to ON *geiga* to turn aside; akin to OE *geonian* to yawn — more at YAWN] **1 :** something that whirls or is whirled: as **a** *obs* **:** TOP, WHIRLIGIG **b :** a 3-digit selection in a numbers game **2 :** a person of odd or grotesque appearance **3 a :** a long light ship's boat propelled by oars, sail, or motor **b :** a rowboat designed for speed rather than for work **4 :** a light two-wheeled one-horse carriage

gig 4

²**gig** *vi* **gigged; gig·ging :** to travel in a gig

³**gig** *n* [short for earlier *fizgig, fishgig,* of unknown origin] **1 :** a pronged spear for catching fish **2 :** an arrangement of hooks to be drawn through a school of fish when they will not bite in order to hook them in the bodies

⁴**gig** *vb* **gigged; gig·ging** *vt* **1 :** to spear with a gig **2 a** *chiefly West* **:** SPUR, JAB **b :** GOAD, PROVOKE ~ *vi* **:** to fish with a gig

⁵**gig** *n* [origin unknown] **:** a military demerit

⁶**gig** *vt* **gigged; gig·ging :** to give a military gig to

⁷**gig** *n* [origin unknown] **:** JOB; *esp* **:** a musician's engagement for a specified time

giga- \ˈjig-ə, ˈgig-ə\ *comb form* [ISV, fr. Gk *gigas* giant] **:** billion <*giga*ton> <*giga*volt>

giga·bit \-ˌbit\ *n* **:** a unit of information equal to one billion bits

giga·cy·cle \-ˌsī-kəl\ *n* **:** GIGAHERTZ

giga·hertz \-ˌhərts, -ˌhe(ə)rts\ *n* **:** a unit of frequency equal to one billion hertz

gigant- *or* **giganto-** *comb form* [Gk, fr. *gigant-, gigas*] **:** giant <*gigant*ism>

gi·gan·tesque \ˌjī-ˌgan-ˈtesk, -gən-\ *adj* **:** of enormous or grotesquely large proportions

gi·gan·tic \jī-ˈgant-ik, jə-\ *adj* **:** exceeding the usual or expected (as in size, force, or prominence) <a man of ~ stature> <made a last ~ effort> <the growth of ~ industrial combines> *syn* see HUGE — **gi·gan·ti·cal·ly** \-i-k(ə-)lē\ *adv*

gi·gan·tism \jī-ˈgan-ˌtiz-əm, jə-; ˈjī-gən-\ *n* **1 :** GIANTISM 1 **2 :** development to abnormally large size **3 :** excessive vegetative growth often accompanied by the inhibiting of reproduction

gi·gas \ˈjī-gəs\ *adj* [NL, fr. L, giant, fr. Gk] *of a polyploid plant* **:** having thicker stem, taller growth, darker thicker leaves, and larger flowers and seeds than a corresponding diploid

giga·watt \ˈjig-ə-ˌwät, ˈgig-\ *n* **:** a unit of power equal to one billion watts

gig·gle \ˈgig-əl\ *vb* **gig·gled; gig·gling** \-(ə-)liŋ\ [imit.] *vi* **:** to laugh with repeated short catches of the breath **:** laugh in a silly manner ~ *vt* **:** to utter with a giggle — **giggle** *n* — **gig·gler** \-(ə-)lər\ *n* — **gig·gling·ly** \-(ə-)liŋ-lē\ *adv* — **gig·gly** \-(ə-)lē\ *adj*

gig·o·lo \ˈjig-ə-ˌlō, ˈzhig-\ *n, pl* **-los** [F] **1 :** a man living on the earnings of or supported by a woman **2 :** a professional dancing partner or male escort

gi·got \ˈjig-ət, zhē-ˈgō\ *n, pl* **gi·gots** \-əts, -ˈgō(z)\ [MF, dim. of *gigue* fiddle; fr. its shape — more at JIG] **1 :** a leg of meat (as lamb) esp. when cooked **2 :** a leg-of-mutton sleeve

gigue \ˈzhēg\ *n* [F — more at JIG] **:** a lively dance movement (as of a suite) having compound triple rhythm and consisting of two sections each of which is repeated

Gi·la monster \ˌhē-lə-\ *n* [*Gila* river, Arizona] **:** a large orange and black venomous lizard (*Heloderma suspectum*) of the southwestern U.S.; *also* **:** a related lizard (*H. horridum*) of Mexico

gil·bert \ˈgil-bərt\ *n* [William *Gilbert* †1603 E physicist] **:** the cgs unit of magnetomotive force equivalent to $10 \div 4\pi$ ampere-turn

¹**gild** \ˈgild\ *vt* **gild·ed** \ˈgil-dəd\ *or* **gilt** \ˈgilt\; **gild·ing** [ME *gilden,* fr. OE *gyldan;* akin to OE *gold*] **1 :** to overlay with or as if with a thin covering of gold **2 a :** to give money to **b :** to give an attractive but often deceptive appearance to **c** *archaic* **:** to make bloody — **gild·er** *n* — **gild·ing** *n* — **gild the lily :** to add unnecessary ornamentation to something beautiful in its own right

Gila monster

²**gild** *var of* GUILD

Gil·ga·mesh \ˈgil-gə-ˌmesh\ [Sumerian *Gil-ga-mes*] **:** the King of Uruk and hero of the Babylonian Epic of Gilgamesh to whom is related according to the epic an account of the Flood that covers the earth

¹**gill** \ˈjil\ *n* [ME *gille*] — see WEIGHT table

²**gill** \ˈgil\ *n* [ME *gile, gille*] **1 :** an organ (as of a fish) for obtaining oxygen from water **2 a :** WATTLE 2a **b :** the flesh under or about the chin or jaws — usu. used in pl. **c :** one of the radiating plates forming the undersurface of the cap of a mushroom fungus — **gilled** \ˈgild\ *adj*

³**gill** \ˈgil\ *vt* **:** GILLNET ~ *vi, of fish* **:** to become entangled in a gill net — **gill·er** *n*

⁴**gill** \ˈgil\ *n* [ME *gille,* fr. ON *gil*] **1** *Brit* **:** RAVINE **2** *Brit* **:** a narrow stream or rivulet

⁵**gill** \ˈjil\ *n, often cap* [ME, fr. *Gill,* nickname for *Gillian*] **:** GIRL, SWEETHEART

gill arch *n* **1 :** one of the bony or cartilaginous arches or curved bars extending dorsoventrally and placed one behind the other on each side of the pharynx and supporting the gills of fishes and amphibians **2 :** one of the rudimentary ridges in the embryos of all higher vertebrates that correspond to the gill arches

gill cleft *n* **:** GILL SLIT 1, 2

gill fungus *n* **:** a basidiomycete (as an agaric) having gills

¹**gil·lie** *or* **gil·ly** *or* **ghil·lie** \ˈgil-ē\ *n, pl* **gillies** *or* **ghillies** [ScGael *gille* & IrGael *giolla* boy] **1 :** a male attendant on a Scottish Highland chief **2** *Scot & Irish* **:** a fishing and hunting guide **3** *usu ghillie* **:** a low-cut shoe with decorative lacing

²**gillie** *vi* **gil·lied; gil·ly·ing :** to serve as a gillie

gill·net \ˈgil-ˌnet\ *vt* **:** to catch (fish) with a gill net — **gill–net·ter** *n*

gill net *n* **:** a flat net suspended vertically in the water with meshes that allow the head of a fish to pass but entangle it as it seeks to withdraw

gill raker *n* **:** one of the bony processes on a gill arch that divert solid substances from the gills

gill slit *n* **1 :** one of the openings or clefts between the gill arches in vertebrates that breathe by gills through which water taken in at the mouth passes to the exterior and so bathes the gills **2 :** one of the rudimentary grooves in the neck region of the embryos of air-breathing vertebrates that correspond to the gill slits **3 :** the external opening to the cavity containing the gills when a protective covering of the gills is present

gil·ly·flow·er \ˈjil-ē-ˌflau̇(-ə)r\ *n* [by folk etymology fr. ME *gilofre* clove, fr. MF *girofle, gilofre,* fr. L *caryophyllum,* fr. Gk *karyophyllon,* fr. *karyon* nut + *phyllon* leaf — more at CAREEN, BLADE] **1 :** an Old World pink (*Dianthus caryophyllus*) widely cultivated for its clove-scented flowers — called also *clove pink* **2 :** any of several plants (genus *Dianthus*) related to the gillyflower

Gil·son·ite \ˈgil-sə-ˌnit\ *trademark* — used for uintaite

¹**gilt** \ˈgilt\ *adj* [ME, fr. pp. of *gilden* to gild] **:** covered with gold or gilt **:** of the color of gold

²**gilt** *n* **1 :** gold or something that resembles gold laid on a surface **2** *slang* **:** MONEY **3 :** superficial brilliance

³**gilt** *n* [ME *gylte,* fr. ON *gyltr;* akin to OE *gelte* young sow — more at GELD] **:** a young female swine

gilt–edged \ˈgil-ˈtejd\ *or* **gilt–edge** \-ˈtej\ *adj* **1 :** having a gilt edge **2 :** of the best quality <~ securities>

gilt·head \ˈgilt-ˌhed\ *n* **:** any of several marine fishes: as **a :** a percoid food fish (*Sparus auratus*) of the Mediterranean **b :** a cunner (*Crenilabrus melops*) of the British coasts

¹**gim·bal** \ˈgim-bəl, ˈjim-\ *n* [alter. of obs. *gemel* (double ring)] **:** a device that permits a body to incline freely in any direction or suspends it so that it will remain level when its support is tipped — usu. used in pl.; called also *gimbal ring*

²**gimbal** *vt* **-balled** *or* **-baled; -bal·ling** *or* **-bal·ing :** to provide with or support on gimbals

gim·crack \ˈjim-ˌkrak\ *n* [origin unknown] **:** a showy object of little use or value **:** GEWGAW — **gimcrack** *adj* — **gim·crack·ery** \-(ə-)rē\ *n*

gim·el \ˈgim-əl\ *n* [Heb *gīmel*] **:** the 3d letter of the Hebrew alphabet — see ALPHABET table

¹**gim·let** \ˈgim-lət\ *n* [ME, fr. MF *guimbelet*] **:** a small tool with a screw point, grooved shank, and cross handle for boring holes

gimlet

²**gimlet** *adj* **:** having a piercing or penetrating quality

³**gimlet** *vt* **:** to pierce with or as if with a gimlet

⁴**gimlet** *n* [prob. fr. ¹*gimlet*] **:** a drink consisting of sweetened lime juice, gin, or vodka and carbonated or plain water

gim·mal \ˈgim-əl, ˈjim-\ *n* [alter. of obs. *gemel* (double ring)] **1** *pl* **:** joined work (as in a clock) whose parts move within each other **2 :** a pair or series of interlocked rings

¹**gim·mick** \ˈgim-ik\ *n* [origin unknown] **1 a :** a mechanical device for secretly and dishonestly controlling gambling apparatus **b :** an ingenious or novel mechanical device **:** GADGET **2 a :** an important feature that is not immediately apparent **:** CATCH <what's the ~ ... what's in it for you —Maxwell Griffith> **b :** a new and ingenious scheme or angle — **gim·micky** \-i-kē\ *adj*

[2]**gimmick** *vt* **1 :** to alter or influence by means of a gimmick **2 :** to provide with a gimmick (as an attention-getting device, a novel twist, or a gadget)
gim·mick·ry \'gim-i-krē\ *n, pl* **-ries :** an array or profusion of gimmicks
[1]**gimp** \'gimp\ *n* [perh. fr. D] **:** an ornamental flat braid or round cord used as a trimming
[2]**gimp** *n* [origin unknown] **:** SPIRIT, VIM
[3]**gimp** *n* [origin unknown] **1 :** CRIPPLE **2 :** LIMP <walks with a ~ —Damon Runyon> — **gimpy** \'gim-pē\ *adj*
[4]**gimp** *vi* **:** LIMP, HOBBLE <came ~*ing* across the floor on three legs —Nelson Algren>
[1]**gin** \'gin\ *vb* **gan** \'gan\; **gin·ning** [ME *ginnen,* short for *beginnen*] *archaic* **:** BEGIN
[2]**gin** \'jin\ *n* [ME *gin,* modif. of OF *engin* — more at ENGINE] **:** any of various tools or mechanical devices: as **a :** a snare or trap for game **b :** a machine for raising or moving heavy weights **c :** COTTON GIN
[3]**gin** \'jin\ *vt* **ginned; gin·ning 1 :** SNARE **2 :** to separate (cotton fiber) from seeds and waste material — **gin·ner** *n* — **gin·ning** *n*
[4]**gin** \(,)gin\ *conj* [perh. alter. of Sc & E dial. *gif,* fr. ME *yif, if*] *dial* **:** IF
[5]**gin** \'jin\ *n* [by shortening & alter. fr. *geneva*] **1 a :** an alcoholic liquor made by distilling a mash of grain with juniper berries **b :** a liquor similar to gin made from plain spirit flavored with an aromatic **2 a :** GIN RUMMY **b :** the act of laying down a full hand of matched cards in gin rummy — **gin·ny** \'jin-ē\ *adj*
gin and tonic *n* **:** a drink that consists of gin and quinine water garnished with a wedge of lime or lemon
[1]**gin·ger** \'jin-jər\ *n* [ME, fr. OE *gingifer,* fr. ML *gingiber,* alter. of L *zingiber,* fr. Gk *zingiberi*] **1 a** (1) **:** a thickened pungent aromatic rhizome that is used as a spice and sometimes in medicine (2) **:** the spice usu. prepared by drying and grinding ginger **b :** any of a genus (*Zingiber* of the family Zingiberaceae, the ginger family) of herbs with pungent aromatic rhizomes; *esp* **:** a widely cultivated tropical herb (*Z. officinale*) that supplies most of the ginger of commerce **2 :** high spirit **:** PEP <the ~ to care hard and work hard —Willa Cather> **3 :** a strong brown — **gin·gery** \'jinj-(ə-)rē\ *adj*
[2]**ginger** *vt* **gin·gered; gin·ger·ing** \'jinj-(ə-)riŋ\ **:** to make lively **:** pep up <~ up the tourist trade —*N.Y. Times*>
ginger ale *n* **:** a sweetened carbonated nonalcoholic beverage flavored mainly with ginger extract
ginger beer *n* **:** a sweetened carbonated nonalcoholic beverage heavily flavored with ginger or capsicum or both
gin·ger·bread \'jin-jər-,bred\ *n* **1 :** a cake whose ingredients include molasses and ginger **2** [fr. the fancy shapes and gilding formerly often applied to gingerbread] **:** lavish or superfluous ornament esp. in architecture — **gin·ger·bready** \-ē\ *adj*
gin·ger·ly \'jin-jər-lē\ *adj* [perh. fr. [1]*ginger*] **:** very cautious or careful — **gin·ger·li·ness** *n* — **gingerly** *adv*
gin·ger·snap \-,snap\ *n* **:** a thin brittle cookie sweetened with molasses and flavored with ginger
ging·ham \'giŋ-əm\ *n* [modif. of Malay *genggang* checkered cloth] **:** a clothing fabric usu. of yarn-dyed cotton in plain weave
gingiv- *or* **gingivo-** *comb form* [L *gingiva*] **:** gum **:** gums <*gingivitis*>
gin·gi·va \'jin-jə-və, jin-'jī-\ *n, pl* **-vae** \-,vē\ [L — more at CONGER EEL] **:** [1]GUM — **gin·gi·val** \'jin-jə-vəl\ *adj*
gin·gi·vi·tis \,jin-jə-'vīt-əs\ *n* **:** inflammation of the gums
gink \'giŋk\ *n* [origin unknown] *slang* **:** PERSON, GUY
gink·go *also* **ging·ko** \'giŋ-(,)kō *also* 'giŋk-(,)gō\ *n, pl* **ginkgoes** [NL *Ginkgo,* genus name, fr. Jap *ginkyo*] **:** a showy gymnospermous tree (*Ginkgo biloba*) of eastern China with fan-shaped leaves and yellow fruit often grown as a shade tree
gin mill *n* **:** BAR, SALOON
gin rummy *n* [[5]*gin*] **:** a rummy game for two players in which each player is dealt 10 cards and in which a player may win a hand by matching all his cards or may end play when his unmatched cards count up to less than 10

ginkgo

gin·seng \'jin-,saŋ, -,seŋ, -(,)siŋ\ *n* [Chin (Pek) *jen²-shen¹*] **1 a :** a Chinese perennial herb (*Panax schinseng* of the family Araliaceae, the ginseng family) having 5-foliolate leaves, scarlet berries, and an aromatic root valued locally as a medicine **b :** any of several plants related to ginseng; *esp* **:** a No. American herb (*P. quinquefolius*) **2 :** the root of a ginseng
Gipsy *var of* GYPSY
gi·raffe \jə-'raf\ *n, pl* **giraffes** [It *giraffa,* fr. Ar *zirāfah*] **1** *or pl* **giraffe :** a large fleet African ruminant mammal (*Giraffa camelopardalis*) that is the tallest of living quadrupeds and has a very long neck and a black-blotched fawn or cream coat **2** *cap* **:** CAMELOPARDALIS — **gi·raff·ish** \-'raf-ish\ *adj*
gir·an·dole \'jir-ən-,dōl\ *n* [F & It; F, fr. It *girandola,* fr. *girare* to turn, fr. LL *gyrare,* fr. L *gyrus* gyre] **1 :** a radiating and showy composition (as a cluster of skyrockets fired together) **2 :** an ornamental branched candle holder
gir·a·sol *or* **gir·a·sole** \'jir-ə-,sól, -,sōl, -,säl\ *n* [It *girasole,* fr. *girare* + *sole* sun, fr. L *sol* — more at SOLAR] **1 :** JERUSALEM ARTICHOKE **2 :** an opal of varying color that gives out fiery reflections in bright light
[1]**gird** \'gərd\ *vb* **gird·ed** \'gərd-əd\ *or* **girt** \'gərt\; **gird·ing** [ME *girden,* fr. OE *gyrdan;* akin to OE *geard* yard — more at YARD] *vt* **1 a :** to encircle or bind with a flexible band (as a belt) **b :** to make fast (as a sword by a belt or clothing with a cord) **c :** SURROUND **2 :** PROVIDE, EQUIP; *esp* **:** to invest with the sword of knighthood **3 :** to prepare (oneself) for action ~ *vi* **:** to prepare for action — **gird one's loins :** to prepare for action **:** muster up one's resources
[2]**gird** *vb* [ME *girden* to strike, thrust] *vt* **:** to sneer at **:** MOCK ~ *vi* **:** GIBE, RAIL
[3]**gird** *n* **:** a sarcastic remark

girandole 2

gird·er \'gərd-ər\ *n* [[1]*gird*] **:** a horizontal main structural member (as in a building or bridge) that supports vertical loads and that consists of a single piece or of more than one piece bound together
[1]**gir·dle** \'gərd-ᵊl\ *n* [ME *girdel,* fr. OE *gyrdel;* akin to OHG *gurtil* girdle, OE *gyrdan* to gird] **1 :** something that encircles or confines: as **a :** an article of dress encircling the body usu. at the waist **b :** a woman's close-fitting undergarment often boned and usu. elasticized that extends from the waist to below the hips **c :** either of two more or less complete bony rings at the anterior and posterior ends of the vertebrate trunk supporting the arms and legs respectively **d :** a ring made by the removal of the bark and cambium around a plant stem **2 :** the edge of a brilliant that is grasped by the setting — see BRILLIANT illustration
[2]**girdle** *vt* **gir·dled; gir·dling** \'gərd-liŋ, -ᵊl-iŋ\ **1 :** to encircle with a girdle **2 :** to move around **:** CIRCLE <*girdled* the world> **3 :** to cut a girdle around (a plant) usu. to kill by interrupting the circulation of water and nutrients
gir·dler \'gərd-lər, -ᵊl-ər\ *n* **1 :** a maker of girdles **2 :** one that girdles; *esp* **:** an insect that feeds on bark and gnaws grooves about stems and twigs
girl \'gər(-ə)l\ *n* [ME *gurle, girle* young person of either sex] **1 a :** a female child **b :** a young unmarried woman **c :** a single or married woman of any age **2 a :** a female servant or employee **b :** SWEETHEART **c :** DAUGHTER — **girl·hood** \-,hu̇d\ *n*
girl Friday *n* [*girl* + *Friday* as in *man Friday*] **:** a female assistant (as in an office) entrusted with a wide variety of tasks
girl friend *n* **1 :** a female friend **2 :** a frequent or regular female companion of a boy or man **3 :** MISTRESS 5a
girl guide *n* **:** a member of the British Girl Guides
girl·ie *or* **girly** \'gər-lē\ *adj* **:** featuring scantily clothed girls <~ magazines> <~ show>
girl·ish \'gər-lish\ *adj* **:** of, relating to, or having the characteristics of a girl or girlhood <~ laughter> — **girl·ish·ly** *adv* — **girl·ish·ness** *n*
girl scout *n* **:** a member of the Girl Scouts of the United States of America
girn \'gi(ə)rn\ *vi* [ME *girnen,* alter. of *grinnen* to grin, snarl] *chiefly Scot* **:** SNARL — **girn** *n, chiefly Scot*
gi·ro \'zhi(ə)r-(,)ō, 'ji(ə)r-\ *n* [G, fr. It, turn, transfer, fr. L *gyrus* gyre] **:** a highly computerized low-cost system of money transfer comparable to a checking account that is one of the national post office services in many European countries
giron *var of* GYRON
Gi·rond·ist \jə-'rän-dəst, zhi-\ *n* [F *girondiste,* fr. *Gironde,* a political party, fr. *Gironde,* department of France represented by its leaders] **:** a member of the moderate republican party in the French legislative assembly in 1791
girt \'gərt\ *vb* [ME *girten,* alter. of *girden*] *vt* **1 :** GIRD **2 :** to fasten by means of a girth ~ *vi* **:** to measure in girth
[1]**girth** \'gərth\ *n* [ME, fr. ON *gjǫrth;* akin to OE *gyrdan* to gird] **1 :** a band or strap that encircles the body of an animal to fasten something (as a saddle) upon its back **2 a :** a measure around a body <for the man of more than average ~ —Agnes M. Miall> **b :** SIZE, DIMENSIONS <the river was twice its usual ~>
[2]**girth** *vt* **1 :** ENCIRCLE **2 :** to bind or fasten with a girth **3 :** to measure the girth of
gi·sarme \giz-'ärm\ *n* [ME, fr. OF] **:** a medieval weapon consisting of a sharpened blade mounted on a long staff and carried by foot soldiers
gist \'jist\ *n* [AF, it lies, fr. MF, fr. *gesir* to lie, fr. L *jacēre* — more at ADJACENT] **1 :** the ground of a legal action **2 :** the main point of a matter **:** ESSENCE <the ~ of an argument>
git·tern \'git-ərn\ *n* [ME *giterne,* fr. MF *guiterne,* modif. of OSp *guitarra* guitar] **:** a medieval guitar
[1]**give** \'giv\ *vb* **gave** \'gāv\; **giv·en** \'giv-ən\; **giv·ing** [ME *given,* of Scand origin; akin to OSw *giva* to give; akin to OE *giefan, gifan* to give, L *habēre* to have, hold] *vt* **1 :** to make a present of <~ a doll to a child> **2 a :** to grant or bestow by formal action <the law ~*s* citizens the right to vote> **b :** to accord or yield to another <*gave* him her confidence> **3 a :** to put into the possession of another for his use **b** (1) **:** to administer as a sacrament (2) **:** to administer as a medicine **c :** to commit to another as a trust or responsibility and usu. for an expressed reason <*gave* her his coat to hold> **d :** to transfer from one's authority or custody <the sheriff *gave* the prisoner to the warden> **e :** to execute and deliver <all employees must ~ bond> **f :** to convey to another <~ my regards to your family> **4 a :** to offer to the action of another **:** PROFFER <*gave* his hand to the visitor> **b :** to yield to a man in sexual intercourse **5 a :** to present in public performance <~ a concert> **b :** to present to view or observation <*gave* the signal to start> **6 :** to provide by way of entertainment <~ a party> **7 :** to propose as a toast **8 a :** to designate as a share or portion **:** ALLOT <all the earth to thee and to thy race I ~ —John Milton> **b :** to make assignment of (a name) **c :** to set forth as an actual or hypothetical datum <~ the dimensions of the room> **d :** to attribute in thought or utterance **:** ASCRIBE <*gave* all the glory to God> **9 a :** to yield as a product, consequence, or effect **:** PRODUCE <cows ~ milk> <84 divided by 12 ~*s* 7> **b :** to bring forth **:** BEAR **10 a :** to yield possession of by way of exchange **:** PAY **b :** to dispose of for a price **:** SELL **11 a :** to deliver by some bodily action <*gave* him a push> **b :** to carry out (as a bodily movement) <*gave* a cynical smile> **c :** to inflict as punishment <*gave* the boy a whipping> **d :** to award by formal verdict <judgment was *given* against the

plaintiff> **12 :** to offer for consideration, acceptance, or use <~*s* no reason for his absence> **13 a :** to suffer the loss of : SACRIFICE **b :** to offer as appropriate or due esp. to something higher or more worthy <*gave* his spirit to God> <~ one's time to the service of others> **c :** to apply freely or fully <children *giving* themselves to their play> **d :** to offer as a pledge <I ~ you my word> **14 a :** to cause one to have or receive <mountains always *gave* him pleasure> **b :** to cause a person to catch by contagion, infection, or exposure **15 :** to allow one to have or take <~ me time to consider your plan> **16 :** to care to the extent of <didn't ~ a hang> ~ *vi* **1 :** to make gifts or presents **2 a :** to yield to physical force or strain **b :** to collapse from the application of force or pressure **3 a** *of weather* **:** to become mild **b** *of frozen ground* **:** THAW **4 :** to afford a view or passage : OPEN **5** *slang* **:** to take place : go on <he demanded to know what *gave*>
syn GIVE, PRESENT, DONATE, BESTOW, CONFER, AFFORD *shared meaning element* **:** to convey to another as his possession. GIVE, the general term, is applicable to any passing over of anything by any means <*give* alms> <*give* a boy a ride on a pony> <*give* my love to your mother and sisters —John Keats> PRESENT carries a note of formality and ceremony <*present* an award> <pray, *present* my respects to Lady Scott —Lord Byron> DONATE is likely to imply a publicized giving (as to charity) <*donate* a piano to the orphanage> BESTOW implies the conveying of something as a gift and may suggest condescension on the part of the giver <*bestow* unwanted advice> <large gifts have I *bestowed* on learned clerks —Shak.> CONFER implies a gracious giving (as of a favor or honor) <the Queen *confers* her titles and degrees —Alexander Pope> AFFORD implies a giving or bestowing usually as a natural or legitimate consequence of the character of the giver <do the laws of his country *afford* him a remedy? —John Marshall> <the trees *afforded* us a welcome shade>
— **give a good account of :** to acquit (oneself) well — **give ground :** to withdraw before superior force : RETREAT — **give the gun :** to open the throttle of : speed up — **give tongue** *of hounds* **:** to begin barking on the scent — **give way 1a :** RETREAT **b :** to yield the right of way **2 :** to yield oneself without restraint or control **3a :** to yield to or as if to physical stress <the wind caused the roof to *give way*> **b :** to yield to entreaty or insistence **4 :** to yield place **5 :** to begin to row

[2]**give** *n* **1 :** capacity or tendency to yield to force or strain **2 :** the quality or state of being springy

give–and–take \ˌgiv-ən-ˈtāk\ *n* **1 :** the practice of making mutual concessions : COMPROMISE **2 :** good-natured exchange of ideas

give·away \ˈgiv-ə-ˌwā\ *n* **1 :** an unintentional revelation or betrayal **2 :** something given away free; *specif* **:** PREMIUM **3 :** a radio or television program on which prizes are given away

give away *vt* **1 :** to make a present of **2 :** to deliver (a bride) to the bridegroom at a wedding **3 a :** BETRAY **b :** DISCLOSE, REVEAL **4 :** to give (as weight) by way of a handicap

give back *vi* **:** RETIRE, RETREAT ~ *vt* **:** to send in return or reply : RESTORE, RETURN

give in *vt* **:** DELIVER, SUBMIT <*gave in* his resignation> ~ *vi* **:** to yield under insistence or entreaty : SURRENDER

giv·en \ˈgiv-ən\ *adj* **1 :** presented as a gift : bestowed without compensation **2 :** PRONE, DISPOSED < ~ to swearing> **3** *of an official document* **:** having been executed : DATED **4 a :** FIXED, SPECIFIED <at a ~ time> **b :** assumed as actual or hypothetical : GRANTED <~ that all men are equal before the law> **5 :** immediately present in experience — **given** *n*

given name *n* **:** CHRISTIAN NAME 1

give off *vt* **1 :** to send out as a branch **2 :** EMIT <*gave off* an unpleasant smell> ~ *vi* **:** to branch off

give out *vt* **1 a :** DECLARE, PUBLISH <*giving out* that the doctor . . . required a few days of complete rest —Charles Dickens> **b :** to read aloud the words of (a hymn or psalm) for congregational singing **2 :** EMIT <*gave out* a constant hum> **3 :** ISSUE <*gave out* new uniforms> ~ *vi* **1 :** to become exhausted : COLLAPSE **2 :** to break down : FAIL

give over *vt* **1 :** CEASE **2 a :** to yield without restraint or control : ABANDON <she *gave* herself *over* to laughter before she could go on —H. D. Skidmore> **b :** to set apart for a particular purpose or use : DEVOTE **3** *archaic* **:** to pronounce incurable **4 :** ENTRUST ~ *vi* **:** to bring an activity to an end : STOP <told him to *give over* and let me alone —Brendan Behan>

giv·er \ˈgiv-ər\ *n* **:** one that gives : DONOR

give up *vt* **1 :** SURRENDER <*gave up* his job> **2 :** to desist from <refused to *give up* his efforts> **3 a :** to abandon (oneself) to a particular feeling, influence, or activity <*gave* himself *up* to despair> **b :** to devote to a particular purpose or use **4 :** to declare incurable or insoluble **5 :** to despair of seeing <we'd *given* you *up*> **6 :** to allow (a hit or run in baseball) while pitching ~ *vi* **:** to withdraw from an activity or course of action

giz·mo *or* **gis·mo** \ˈgiz-(ˌ)mō\ *n, pl* **gizmos** *or* **gismos** [origin unknown] **:** GADGET

giz·zard \ˈgiz-ərd\ *n* [alter. of ME *giser,* fr. ONF *guisier,* fr. L *gigeria* (pl.) giblets] **1 a :** the muscular enlargement of the alimentary canal of birds that immediately follows the crop and has usu. thick muscular walls and a tough horny lining for grinding the food **b :** a thickened part of the alimentary canal in some animals (as an insect or an earthworm) that is similar in function to the crop of a bird **2 :** INNARDS

gjet·ost \ˈyāt-ˌōst\ *n* [Norw, fr. *gjet* goat + *ost* cheese] **:** a Norwegian whey cheese similar to mysost

Gk *abbr* Greek

gla·bel·la \glə-ˈbel-ə\ *n, pl* **-bel·lae** \-ˈbel-(ˌ)ē, -ˌī\ [NL, fr. L, fem. of *glabellus* hairless, dim. of *glaber*] **:** the smooth prominence between the eyebrows — **gla·bel·lar** \-ˈbel-ər\ *adj*

gla·bres·cent \glā-ˈbres-ᵊnt\ *adj* **1 :** somewhat glabrous **2 :** tending to become glabrous

gla·brous \ˈglā-brəs\ *adj* [L *glabr-, glaber* smooth, bald — more at GLAD] **:** SMOOTH; *esp* **:** having a surface without hairs or projections <~ skin> — **gla·brous·ness** *n*

gla·cé \gla-ˈsā\ *adj* [F, fr. pp. of *glacer* to freeze, ice, glaze, fr. L *glaciare,* fr. *glacies*] **1 :** made or finished so as to have a smooth glossy surface <~ silk> **2 :** coated with a glaze : CANDIED <~ cherries>

gla·cial \ˈglā-shəl\ *adj* [L *glacialis,* fr. *glacies*] **1 a :** extremely cold : FRIGID <a ~ wind> **b :** devoid of warmth and cordiality <a ~ handshake> **c :** coldly imperturbable <maintained a ~ calm> **2 a :** of, relating to, or produced by glaciers **b :** suggestive of the very slow movement of glaciers <progress on the bill has been ~> **c (1) :** of, relating to, or being any of those parts of geologic time from Precambrian onward when a much larger portion of the earth was covered by glaciers than at present **(2)** *cap* **:** PLEISTOCENE **3 :** resembling ice in appearance <~ acetic acid> — **gla·cial·ly** \-shə-lē\ *adv*

gla·ci·ate \ˈglā-shē-ˌāt\ *vt* **-at·ed; -at·ing 1 :** FREEZE **2 a :** to cover with a glacier **b :** to subject to glacial action; *also* **:** to produce glacial effects in or on — **gla·ci·a·tion** \ˌglā-s(h)ē-ˈā-shən\ *n*

gla·cier \ˈglā-shər *also* -zhər, *esp Brit* ˈglas-ē-ər *or* ˈglās-ē-\ *n* [F dial., fr. MF dial., fr. MF *glace* ice, fr. L *glacies;* akin to L *gelu* frost — more at COLD] **:** a large body of ice moving slowly down a slope or valley or spreading outward on a land surface

glacio- *comb form* **1 :** glacier <*glacio*logy> **2** \ˌglā-sh(ē-)ō, -sē-ō\ **:** glacial and <*glacio*fluvial>

gla·ci·ol·o·gy \ˌglā-s(h)ē-ˈäl-ə-jē\ *n* [ISV *glacier* + *-o-* + *-logy*] **1 :** any of the branches of science dealing with snow or ice accumulation, glaciation, or glacial epochs **2 :** the glacial features of a region — **gla·ci·o·log·ic** \-ə-ˈläj-ik\ *or* **gla·ci·o·log·i·cal** \-i-kəl\ *adj* — **gla·ci·ol·o·gist** \-ˈäl-ə-jəst\ *n*

gla·cis \gla-ˈsē, ˈglas-ē\ *n, pl* **glacis** \-ˈsēz, -ēz\ [F, fr. *glacer* to freeze, slide] **1 a :** a gentle slope : INCLINE **b :** a slope that runs downward from a fortification **2 :** BUFFER STATE; *also* **:** BUFFER ZONE

[1]**glad** \ˈglad\ *adj* **glad·der; glad·dest** [ME, shining, glad, fr. OE *glæd;* akin to OHG *glat* shining, smooth, L *glaber* smooth, bald] **1** *archaic* **:** having a cheerful or happy disposition by nature **2 a :** experiencing pleasure, joy, or delight : made happy **b :** marked by a feeling of pleased or satisfied gratification **c :** very willing : <~ to do it> **3 a :** marked by, expressive of, or caused by happiness and joy <a ~ shout> **b :** causing happiness and joy : PLEASANT <~ tidings> **4 :** full of brightness and cheerfulness <a ~ spring morning> — **glad·ly** *adv* — **glad·ness** *n*
syn GLAD, HAPPY, CHEERFUL, LIGHTHEARTED, JOYFUL, JOYOUS *shared meaning element* **:** characterized by or expressing the mood of one who is pleased or delighted ***ant*** sad

[2]**glad** *vb* **glad·ded; glad·ding** *archaic* **:** GLADDEN

[3]**glad** *n* **:** GLADIOLUS 1

glad·den \ˈglad-ᵊn\ *vb* **glad·dened; glad·den·ing** \ˈglad-niŋ, -ᵊn-iŋ\ *vt* **:** to make glad ~ *vi, archaic* **:** to be glad

glade \ˈglād\ *n* [perh. fr. [1]*glad*] **:** an open space surrounded by woods — **glady** \ˈglād-ē\ *adj*

glad–hand \ˈglad-ˌhand\ *vt* **:** to extend a glad hand to <candidates ~*ing* everyone they meet> ~ *vi* **:** to extend a glad hand <~*ing* as if he were running for mayor> — **glad–hand·er** \ˈglad-ˈhan-dər\ *n*

glad hand *n* **:** a warm welcome or greeting often prompted by ulterior reasons

glad·i·a·tor \ˈglad-ē-ˌāt-ər\ *n* [L, fr. *gladius* sword, of Celt origin; akin to W *cleddyf* sword; akin to L *clades* destruction, Gk *klados* sprout, branch — more at HALT] **1 :** a person engaged in a fight to the death as public entertainment for ancient Romans **2 :** a person engaging in a public fight or controversy **3 :** a trained fighter; *specif* **:** PRIZEFIGHTER — **glad·i·a·to·ri·al** \ˌglad-ē-ə-ˈtōr-ē-əl, -ˈtȯr-\ *adj*

glad·i·o·la \ˌglad-ē-ˈō-lə\ *n* [back-formation fr. *gladiolus,* taken as a pl.] **:** GLADIOLUS 1

glad·i·o·lus \ˌglad-ē-ˈō-ləs\ *n, pl* **-li** \-(ˌ)lē, -ˌlī\ [NL, genus name, fr. L, gladiolus, fr. dim. of *gladius*] **1** *or pl* **gladiolus** *or* **gla·di·o·lus·es :** any of a genus (*Gladiolus*) of chiefly African plants of the iris family with erect sword-shaped leaves and spikes of brilliantly colored irregular flowers arising from flattened corms **2 :** the large middle portion of the sternum

glad rags *n pl* **:** dressy clothes

glad·some \ˈglad-səm\ *adj* **:** giving or showing joy : CHEERFUL — **glad·some·ly** *adv* — **glad·some·ness** *n*

glad·stone \ˈglad-ˌstōn, *chiefly Brit* -stən\ *n, often cap* [W. E. Gladstone] **:** a traveling bag with flexible sides on a rigid frame that opens flat into two equal compartments

glai·kit *or* **glai·ket** \ˈglā-kət\ *adj* [ME (Sc) *glaikit*] *chiefly Scot* **:** FOOLISH, GIDDY

glair *or* **glaire** \ˈgla(ə)r, ˈgle(ə)r\ *n* [ME *gleyre* egg white, fr. MF *glaire,* modif. of (assumed) VL *claria,* fr. L *clarus* clear — more at CLEAR] **1 :** a sizing liquid made from egg white **2 :** a viscid substance suggestive of an egg white

glairy \-ē\ *adj* **glair·i·er; -est :** having the characteristics of or overlaid with glair

glaive \ˈglāv\ *n* [ME, fr. MF, javelin, sword, modif. of L *gladius* sword] *archaic* **:** SWORD; *esp* **:** BROADSWORD

Glam *abbr* Glamorganshire

glam·or·ize *also* **glam·our·ize** \ˈglam-ə-ˌrīz\ *vt* **-ized; -iz·ing 1 :** to make glamorous <~ the living room> **2 :** to look upon as glamorous : ROMANTICIZE <the novel ~*s* war> — **glam·or·iza·tion** \ˌglam-ə-rə-ˈzā-shən\ *n* — **glam·or·iz·er** \ˈglam-ə-ˌrī-zər\ *n*

glam·or·ous *also* **glam·our·ous** \ˈglam-(ə-)rəs\ *adj* **:** full of glamour — **glam·or·ous·ly** *adv* — **glam·or·ous·ness** *n*

glam·our or **glam·or** \'glam-ər\ *n* [Sc *glamour,* alter. of E *grammar;* fr. the popular association of erudition with occult practices] **1 :** a magic spell <the girls appeared to be under a ~—Llewelyn Powys> **2 :** a romantic, exciting, and often illusory attractiveness; *esp* **:** alluring or fascinating personal attraction — **glamour** *vt* — **glam·our·less** \-ləs\ *adj*

glamour boy *n* **:** a man (as an actor) who is considered to have glamour or to lead a glamorous life

glamour girl *n* **:** a woman (as an actress) who is considered to have glamour or to lead a glamorous life

glamour puss *n* **:** one that has a glamorously attractive face

[1]**glance** \'glan(t)s\ *vb* **glanced; glanc·ing** [ME *glencen, glenchen*] *vi* **1 :** to strike a surface obliquely so as to go off at an angle <the bullet *glanced* off the wall> **2 a :** to flash or gleam with quick intermittent rays of light <brooks *glancing* in the sun> **b :** to make sudden quick movements <dragonflies *glancing* over the pond> **3 :** to touch on a subject or refer to it briefly or indirectly <the work ~*s* at the customs of ancient cultures> **4 a** *of the eyes* **:** to move swiftly from one thing to another **b :** to take a quick look at something <*glanced* at his watch> ~ *vt* **1** *archaic* **a :** to take a quick look at **b :** to catch a glimpse of **2 :** to give an oblique path of direction to: **a :** to throw or shoot so that the object glances from a surface **b** *archaic* **:** to aim (as an innuendo) indirectly **:** INSINUATE ***syn*** see FLASH

[2]**glance** *n* **1 a :** a quick intermittent flash or gleam **b** *archaic* **:** a sudden quick movement **2 a** *archaic* **:** a rapid oblique movement **b :** a deflected impact or blow **3 a :** a swift movement of the eyes **b :** a quick or cursory look **4** *archaic* **a :** GIBE **b :** ALLUSION — **at first glance :** on first consideration <*at first glance* the subject seems harmless enough>

[3]**glance** *n* [G *glanz* luster, glance; akin to OHG *glanz* bright — more at GLINT]**:** any of several mineral sulfides that are usu. dark colored and have a metallic luster

glanc·ing \'glan(t)-siŋ\ *adj* **1 :** having a slanting direction <a ~ blow> **2 :** INCIDENTAL, INDIRECT <made ~ allusions to her past> — **glanc·ing·ly** \-siŋ-lē\ *adv*

[1]**gland** \'gland\ *n* [F *glande,* fr. OF, glandular swelling on the neck, gland, modif. of L *gland-, glans* acorn; akin to Gk *balanos* acorn] **1 a :** a cell or group of cells that selectively removes materials from the blood, concentrates or alters them, and secretes them for further use in the body or for elimination from the body **b :** any of various animal structures suggestive of glands though not secretory in function <lymph ~> **2 :** any of various secreting organs (as a nectary) of plants — **gland·less** \'glan-dləs\ *adj*

[2]**gland** *n* [origin unknown] **1 :** a device for preventing leakage of fluid past a joint in machinery **2 :** the movable part of a stuffing box by which the packing is compressed

glan·dered \'glan-dərd\ *adj* **:** affected with glanders

glan·ders \-dərz\ *n pl but sing or pl in constr* [MF *glandre* glandular swelling on the neck, fr. L *glandulae,* fr. pl. of *glandula,* dim. of *gland-, glans*]**:** a contagious and destructive disease esp. of horses caused by a bacterium (*Actinobacillus mallei*) and characterized by caseating nodular lesions that tend to break down and form ulcers

gland of Bartholin : BARTHOLIN'S GLAND

gland of external secretion : EXOCRINE GLAND

gland of internal secretion : ENDOCRINE GLAND

glan·du·lar \'glan-jə-lər\ *adj* **1 a :** of, relating to, or involving glands, gland cells, or their products **b :** having the characteristics or function of a gland **2 a :** INNATE, INHERENT <the almost ~ . . . instinct for adventure and romance —*Newsweek*> **b :** PHYSICAL, SEXUAL — **glan·du·lar·ly** *adv*

glans \'glanz\ *n, pl* **glan·des** \'glan-ˌdēz\ [L *gland-, glans,* lit., acorn] **1 a :** a conical vascular body forming the extremity of the penis — called also *glans penis* **b :** a similar body of the clitoris — called also *glans clitoris* **2 :** a nut enclosed by an involucre

[1]**glare** \'gla(ə)r, 'gle(ə)r\ *vb* **glared; glar·ing** [ME *glaren;* akin to OE *glæs* glass] *vi* **1 a :** to shine with a harsh uncomfortably brilliant light <light *glaring* from the unshaded bulb> **b** *archaic* **:** to stand out offensively **:** OBTRUDE **2 :** to stare angrily or fiercely ~ *vt* **1 :** to express (as hostility) by staring angrily **2** *archaic* **:** to cause to be sharply reflected ***syn*** see GAZE

[2]**glare** *n* **1 a :** a harsh uncomfortably bright light; *specif* **:** painfully bright sunlight **b :** cheap showy brilliance **:** GARISHNESS **2 :** an angry or fierce stare ***syn*** see BLAZE

[3]**glare** *n* [prob. fr. [2]*glare*]**:** a surface or sheet of ice with a smooth slippery surface

glar·ing \'gla(ə)r-iŋ, 'gle(ə)r-\ *adj* **1 :** having a fixed look of hostility, fierceness, or anger **2 a :** shining with or reflecting an uncomfortably bright light **b (1) :** GARISH **(2) :** vulgarly ostentatious **3 :** painfully and obtrusively obvious <a ~ error> ***syn*** see FLAGRANT — **glar·ing·ly** \-iŋ-lē\ *adv* — **glar·ing·ness** *n*

glary \'gla(ə)r-ē, 'gle(ə)r-\ *adj* **glar·i·er; -est :** having a dazzling brightness **:** GLARING

[1]**glass** \'glas\ *n, often attrib* [ME *glas,* fr. OE *glæs;* akin to OE *geolu* yellow — more at YELLOW] **1 a :** an amorphous inorganic usu. transparent or translucent substance consisting of a mixture of silicates or sometimes borates or phosphates formed by fusion of silica or of oxides of boron or phosphorus with a flux and a stabilizer into a mass that cools to a rigid condition without crystallization **b :** a substance resembling glass esp. in hardness and transparency <organic ~*es* made from plastics> **c :** a substance (as pumice) produced by the quick cooling of an igneous magma **2 a :** something made of glass: as **(1) :** TUMBLER **(2) :** MIRROR **(3) :** BAROMETER **b (1) :** an optical instrument or device that has one or more lenses and is designed to aid in the viewing of objects not readily seen **(2)** *pl* **:** a device used to correct defects of vision or to protect the eyes that consists typically of a pair of glass lenses and the frame by which they are held in place — called also *eyeglasses, spectacles* **3 :** the quantity held by a glass container **4 :** GLASSWARE — **glass·ful** \'glas-ˌfu̇l\ *n* — **glass·less** \-ləs\ *adj*

[2]**glass** *vt* **1 a :** to provide with glass **:** GLAZE 1 **b :** to enclose, case, or wall with glass <the sun porch was ~*ed* in> **c :** to put in a glass container **2 :** to make glassy **3 a :** REFLECT **b :** to see mirrored **4 :** to scan (as for game or forest fires) with an optical instrument ~ *vi* **1 :** to become glassy **2 :** to look for game through an optical instrument

glass·blow·er \'glas-ˌblō(-ə)r\ *n* **:** one skilled in glassblowing

glass·blow·ing \-ˌblō-iŋ\ *n* **:** the art of shaping a mass of glass that has been softened by heat by blowing air into it through a tube

glass eye *n* **1 :** an artificial eye made of glass **2 :** an eye having a pale, whitish, or colorless iris — **glass–eyed** \-'īd\ *adj*

glass·house \'glas-ˌhau̇s\ *n* **1 :** GLASSWORKS **2** *chiefly Brit* **:** GREENHOUSE

glass·ie \'glas-ē\ or **glassy** *n, pl* **glass·ies :** a playing marble made of glass

glass·ine \gla-'sēn\ *n* **:** a thin dense transparent or semitransparent paper highly resistant to the passage of air and grease

glass jaw *n* **:** vulnerability (as of a boxer) to knockout punches

glass·mak·er \'glas-ˌmā-kər\ *n* **:** one that makes glass

glass·mak·ing \-kiŋ\ *n* **:** the art or process of manufacturing glass

glass snake *n* **:** a limbless snakelike lizard (*Ophisaurus ventralis*) of the southern U.S. with a fragile tail that readily breaks into pieces; *also* **:** any of several similar Old World lizards

glass sponge *n* **:** a siliceous sponge (class Hyalospongiae) with 6-rayed spicules and a skeleton often resembling glass when dried

glass·ware \'glas-ˌwa(ə)r, -ˌwe(ə)r\ *n* **:** articles made of glass

glass wool *n* **:** glass fibers in a mass resembling wool and being used esp. for thermal insulation and air filters

glass·work \'glas-ˌwərk\ *n* **1 a :** the manufacture of glass or glassware; *also* **:** glaziers' work **b** *pl* **:** a place where glass is made **2 :** GLASSWARE — **glass·work·er** \-ˌwər-kər\ *n*

glass·wort \-ˌwərt, -ˌwȯ(ə)rt\ *n* [fr. its former use in the manufacture of glass] **:** any of a genus (*Salicornia*) of woody jointed succulent herbs of the goosefoot family with leaves reduced to fleshy sheaths

glassy \'glas-ē\ *adj* **glass·i·er; -est 1 :** resembling glass **2 :** having little animation **:** DULL, LIFELESS <~ eyes> — **glass·i·ly** \'glas-ə-lē\ *adv* — **glass·i·ness** \'glas-ē-nəs\ *n*

Glau·ber salt \ˌglau̇-bər-\ *n* **:** GLAUBER'S SALT

Glau·ber's salt \ˌglau̇-bər(z)-\ *n* [Johann R. *Glauber* †1668 G chemist]**:** a colorless crystalline sulfate of sodium $Na_2SO_4.10H_2O$ used esp. in dyeing and as a cathartic — sometimes used in pl.

glau·co·ma \glau̇-'kō-mə, glȯ-\ *n* [L, cataract, fr. Gk *glaukōma,* fr. *glaukos*]**:** a disease of the eye marked by increased pressure within the eyeball, damage to the optic disk, and gradual loss of vision

glau·co·nite \'glȯ-kə-ˌnīt\ *n* [G *glaukonit,* irreg. fr. Gk *glaukos*] **:** a mineral consisting of a dull green earthy iron potassium silicate occurring abundantly in greensand — **glau·co·nit·ic** \ˌglȯ-kə-'nit-ik\ *adj*

glau·cous \'glȯ-kəs\ *adj* [L *glaucus* gleaming, gray, fr. Gk *glaukos*] **1 a :** of a pale yellow green color **b :** of a light bluish gray or bluish white color **2 :** having a powdery or waxy coating that gives a frosted appearance and tends to rub off <~ fruits> — **glau·cous·ness** *n*

[1]**glaze** \'glāz\ *vb* **glazed; glaz·ing** [ME *glasen,* fr. *glas* glass] *vt* **1 :** to furnish or fit with glass **2 a :** to coat with or as if with a glaze <the storm *glazed* trees with ice> **b :** to apply a glaze to <~ doughnuts> **3 :** to give a smooth glossy surface to ~ *vi* **1 :** to become glazed or glassy <his eyes *glazed* over> **2 :** to form a glaze — **glaz·er** *n*

[2]**glaze** *n* **1 :** a smooth slippery coating of thin ice **2 a (1) :** a liquid preparation applied to food on which it hardens and forms a firm glossy coating **(2) :** a mixture predominantly of oxides (as silica and alumina) applied to the surface of ceramic wares to form a moisture-impervious and often lustrous or ornamental coating **b :** a transparent or translucent color applied to modify the effect of a painted surface **c :** a smooth glossy or lustrous surface or finish **3 :** a glassy film

[3]**glaze** *vi* **glazed; glaz·ing** [prob. blend of *glare* and *gaze*] *archaic* **:** STARE

glazed \'glāzd\ *adj* **1 :** covered with or as if with a glassy film <~ eyes> **2 :** marked by rigidity of expression **:** grimly set <the ~ faces of the survivors>

gla·zier \'glā-zhər, -zē-ər\ *n* **:** one who sets glass — **gla·ziery** \'glāzh(-ə)-rē, 'glā-zē-ə-\ *n*

glaz·ing \'glā-ziŋ\ *n* **1 :** the action, process, or trade of using or applying glaze **2 a :** GLASSWORK **b :** GLAZE

[1]**gleam** \'glēm\ *n* [ME *gleem,* fr. OE *glǣm;* akin to OE *geolu* yellow — more at YELLOW] **1 a :** a transient appearance of subdued or partly obscured light <the ~ of dawn in the east> **b (1) :** a small bright light <the ~ of a match> **(2) :** GLINT <a ~ of anticipation in his eyes> **2 :** a brief or faint appearance or occurrence **:** TRACE <a ~ of hope> — **gleamy** \'glē-mē\ *adj*

[2]**gleam** *vi* **1 :** to shine with subdued steady light or moderate brightness **2 :** to appear briefly or faintly <a light ~*ed* in the darkness> ~ *vt* **:** to cause to gleam ***syn*** see FLASH

glean \'glēn\ *vb* [ME *glenen,* fr. MF *glener,* fr. LL *glennare;* akin to MIr di*gliunn* I glean, OHG *glanz* bright — more at GLINT] *vi* **1 :** to gather grain or other produce left by reapers **2 :** to gather information or other material bit by bit ~ *vt* **1 a :** to pick up after a reaper **b :** to strip (as a field) of the leavings of reapers **2 a :** to gather (as information) bit by bit **b :** to pick over in search of relevant material <~*ing* old letters for information on the founding of the town> **3 :** to find out **:** LEARN, ASCERTAIN — **glean·able** \'glē-nə-bəl\ *adj* — **glean·er** *n*

glean·ings \'glē-niŋz\ *n pl* **:** things acquired by gleaning

glebe \'glēb\ *n* [L *gleba* clod, land — more at CLIP] **1** *archaic* **:** LAND; *specif* **:** a plot of cultivated land **2 :** land belonging or yielding revenue to a parish church or ecclesiastical benefice

glede \'glēd\ *n* [ME, fr. OE *glida;* akin to OE *glīdan* to glide] **:** any of several birds of prey (as the European kite)

glee \'glē\ *n* [ME, fr. OE *glēo* entertainment, music; akin to ON *glȳ* joy, Gk *chleuē* joke] **1 :** exultant high-spirited joy **:** MERRIMENT **2 :** an unaccompanied song for three or more usu. male solo voices ***syn*** see MIRTH

glee club *n* **:** a chorus organized for singing usu. short choral pieces

gleed \ˈglēd\ *n* [ME, fr. OE *glēd;* akin to OE *glōwan* to glow] *archaic* **:** a glowing coal

glee·ful \ˈglē-fəl\ *adj* **:** full of glee **:** MERRY — **glee·ful·ly** \-fə-lē\ *adv* — **glee·ful·ness** *n*

gleek \ˈglēk\ *vi* [origin unknown] *archaic* **:** to make a gibe or jest

glee·man \ˈglē-mən\ *n* **:** MINSTREL

glee·some \ˈglē-səm\ *adj, archaic* **:** GLEEFUL

gleet \ˈglēt\ *n* [ME *glet* slimy or mucous matter, fr. MF *glete,* fr. L *glittus* viscous; akin to LL *glut-, glus* glue — more at CLAY] **:** a chronic inflammation of a bodily orifice usu. accompanied by an abnormal discharge; *also* **:** the discharge itself (as from the urethra in gonorrhea) — **gleety** \-ē\ *adj*

gleg \ˈgleg\ *adj* [ME, fr. ON *glöggr* clear-sighted] *Scot* **:** QUICK, SHARP

glei·za·tion \glā-ˈzā-shən\ *n* **:** development of or conversion into gley

glen \ˈglen\ *n* [ME (Sc), valley, fr. (assumed) ScGael *glenn;* akin to MIr *glend* valley] **:** a secluded narrow valley

glen·gar·ry \glen-ˈgar-ē\ *n, pl* **-ries** *often cap* [*Glengarry,* valley in Scotland] **:** a woolen cap of Scottish origin

glengarry

glen plaid \ˈglen-\ *n* [short for *glenurquhart plaid,* fr. *Glen Urquhart,* prob. alter. of *Clan Urquhart,* Scottish clan] **:** a twill pattern of broken checks; *also* **:** a fabric woven in this pattern — called also *glen check*

gley \ˈglā\ *n* [Russ *gleĭ* clay; akin to OE *clǣg* clay — more at CLAY] **:** a sticky clay layer formed under the surface of some waterlogged soils

gli·a·din \ˈglī-əd-ən\ *n* [It *gliadina,* fr. MGk *glia* glue — more at CLAY] **:** PROLAMIN; *esp* **:** one obtained by alcoholic extraction of gluten from wheat and rye

gli·al \ˈglē-əl, ˈglī-əl\ *adj* [NL *glia* neuroglia, fr. MGk, glue] **:** of or relating to neuroglia

glib \ˈglib\ *adj* **glib·ber; glib·best** [prob. modif. of LG *glibberig* slippery] **1** *archaic* **:** SMOOTH, SLIPPERY **2 a :** marked by ease and informality **:** NONCHALANT **b :** showing little forethought or preparation **:** lacking depth and substance **:** SUPERFICIAL, SLICK <mouthing ~ solutions to knotty problems> **3 :** marked by ease and fluency in speaking or writing often to the point of being superficial or tricky <a ~ politician> — **glib·ly** *adv* — **glib·ness** *n*

¹glide \ˈglīd\ *vb* **glid·ed; glid·ing** [ME *gliden,* fr. OE *glīdan;* akin to OHG *glītan* to glide] *vi* **1 a :** to move smoothly, continuously, and effortlessly <swans *gliding* over the lake> **b :** to move stealthily **:** CREEP <*gliding* along the wall until they were out of sight> **2 :** to pass gradually and imperceptibly **3** *of an airplane* **:** to descend at a normal angle without engine power sufficient for level flight **4 :** to change the tongue position in the articulation of a glide ~ *vt* **:** to cause to glide

²glide *n* **1 :** the act or action of gliding **2 :** a calm stretch of shallow water flowing smoothly **3 a :** PORTAMENTO **b :** a nonsignificant sound produced by the passing of the vocal organs to or from the articulatory position of a speech sound **4 :** a device for facilitating movement of something; *esp* **:** a circular usu. metal button attached to the bottom of furniture legs to provide a smooth surface

glide path *n* **:** the path of descent of an airplane as marked out by a radio beam that guides a pilot in landing; *also* **:** the radio beam

glid·er \ˈglīd-ər\ *n* **1 :** one that glides: as **a :** an aircraft similar to an airplane but without an engine **b :** a porch seat suspended from an upright framework by short chains or straps **2 :** something that aids gliding; *specif* **:** GLIDE 4

glide slope *n* **:** GLIDE PATH

glim \ˈglim\ *n* [perh. short for *²glimmer*] **1 :** GLIMMER **2 :** something (as a lamp, candle, or flashlight) that furnishes light; *also* **:** illumination esp. from a particular source of light

¹glim·mer \ˈglim-ər\ *vi* **glim·mered; glim·mer·ing** \-(ə-)riŋ\ [ME *glimeren;* akin to OE *glǣm* gleam] **1 a :** to shine faintly or unsteadily **b :** to shimmer softly **2 :** to appear indistinctly with a faintly luminous quality ***syn*** see FLASH

²glimmer *n* **1 a :** a feeble or intermittent light **b :** a soft shimmer **2 a :** a dim perception or faint idea **:** INKLING <I had only the vaguest ~ of why I was there> **b :** a small amount **:** BIT <a ~ of intelligence>

glim·mer·ing *n* **:** GLIMMER

¹glimpse \ˈglim(p)s\ *vb* **glimpsed; glimps·ing** [ME *glimsen;* akin to MHG *glimsen* to glimmer, OE *glǣm* gleam] *vi* **1** *archaic* **:** GLIMMER **2 :** to take a brief look ~ *vt* **:** to get a brief look at — **glimps·er** *n*

²glimpse *n* **1** *archaic* **:** GLIMMER **2 :** a brief fleeting view or look

¹glint \ˈglint\ *vb* [ME *glinten* to dart obliquely, glint, alter. of *glenten,* of Scand origin; akin to Sw dial. *glänta* to clear up; akin to OHG *glanz* bright, OE *geolu* yellow — more at YELLOW] *vi* **1 a** *archaic* **:** to glance off an object **b** *of rays of light* **:** to strike a reflecting surface obliquely and dart out at an angle **2 :** to shine by reflection: **a :** to shine with tiny bright flashes **:** SPARKLE **b :** GLITTER **c :** GLEAM **3 :** to look quickly or briefly **:** GLANCE **4 :** to appear briefly or faintly ~ *vt* **:** to cause to glint ***syn*** see FLASH

²glint *n* **1 :** a tiny bright flash of light **:** SPARKLE **2 :** a brief or faint manifestation <detected a ~ of recognition in her expression>

gli·o·ma \glē-ˈō-mə, glī-\ *n, pl* **-mas** *or* **-ma·ta** \-mət-ə\ [NL, fr. *glia* neuroglia] **:** a tumor arising from neuroglia

¹glis·sade \glis-ˈäd, -ˈād\ *vi* **glis·sad·ed; glis·sad·ing** [F, n., slide, glissade, fr. *glisser* to slide, fr. OF *glicier,* alter. of *glier,* of Gmc origin; akin to OHG *glītan* to glide] **1 :** to slide in a standing or squatting position down a snow-covered slope without the aid of skis **2 :** to perform a ballet glissade — **glis·sad·er** *n*

²glissade *n* **1 :** the action of glissading **2 :** a gliding step in ballet

glis·san·do \gli-ˈsän-(ˌ)dō\ *n, pl* **-di** \-(ˌ)dē\ *or* **-dos** [prob. modif. of F *glissade*] **:** a rapid sliding up or down the musical scale

¹glis·ten \ˈglis-ᵊn\ *vi* **glis·tened; glis·ten·ing** \ˈglis-niŋ, -ᵊn-iŋ\ [ME *glistnen,* fr. OE *glisnian;* akin to OE *glisian* to glitter, *geolu* yellow — more at YELLOW] **:** to shine by reflection with a sparkling radiance or with the mild luster of a wet or oiled surface ***syn*** see FLASH

²glisten *n* **:** GLITTER, SPARKLE

glis·ter \ˈglis-tər\ *vi* **glis·tered; glis·ter·ing** \-t(ə-)riŋ\ [ME *glistren;* akin to OE *glisian*] **:** GLISTEN — **glister** *n*

glitch \ˈglich\ *n* [prob. fr. G *glitschen* to slide, slip; akin to OHG *glītan* to glide — more at GLIDE] **1 a :** an unwanted brief surge of electric power **b :** a false or spurious electronic signal **2 :** MALFUNCTION <a ~ in a spacecraft's fuel cell> **3 :** MISHAP; *also* **:** a minor technical problem

¹glit·ter \ˈglit-ər\ *vi* [ME *gliteren,* fr. ON *glitra;* akin to OE *geolu* yellow] **1 a :** to shine by reflection with brilliant or metallic luster <~*ing* sequins> **b :** SPARKLE **c :** to shine with a hard cold glassy brilliance <his little eyes ~*ed* cruelly> **2 :** to be brilliantly attractive in a superficial or misleading way <the chance of success ~*ed* before them> <the ~*ing* generalities of propaganda> ***syn*** see FLASH — **glit·ter·ing·ly** \-ə-riŋ-lē\ *adv*

²glitter *n* **1 :** sparkling brilliance, showiness, or attractiveness **2 :** small glittering objects used for ornamentation — **glit·tery** \ˈglit-ə-rē\ *adj*

gloam \ˈglōm\ *n* [Sc *gloam* to become twilight, back-formation fr. *gloaming*] *archaic* **:** TWILIGHT

gloam·ing \ˈglō-miŋ\ *n* [ME (Sc) *gloming,* fr. OE *glōming,* fr. *glōm* twilight; akin to OE *glōwan* to glow] **:** TWILIGHT, DUSK

¹gloat \ˈglōt\ *vi* [prob. of Scand origin; akin to ON *glotta* to grin scornfully; akin to OE *geolu* yellow] **1** *obs* **:** to look or glance admiringly or amorously **2 :** to observe or think about something with great and often greedy or malicious satisfaction, gratification, or delight <~ over an enemy's misfortune> ***syn*** see GAZE — **gloat·er** *n*

²gloat *n* **1 :** the act of gloating **2 :** a feeling of triumphant or malicious satisfaction

glob \ˈgläb\ *n* [perh. blend of *globe* and *blob*] **1 :** a small drop **:** BLOB <little ~*s* of ink> **2 :** a usu. large and rounded lump <a dessert with great ~*s* of whipped cream>

glob·al \ˈglō-bəl\ *adj* **1 :** SPHERICAL **2 :** of, relating to, or involving the entire world **:** WORLDWIDE <~ warfare> <a ~ system of communication> **3 :** of, relating to, or embracing all or virtually all considerations **:** GENERAL, COMPREHENSIVE <away from a ~ view of readiness toward one of greater specificity —Jeanne S. Chall> — **glob·al·ly** \ˈglō-bə-lē\ *adv*

glob·al·ism \ˈglō-bə-ˌliz-əm\ *n* **1 :** GLOBALIZATION **2 :** a policy or system favoring or promoting globalization — **glob·al·ist** \-ləst\ *n*

glob·al·iza·tion \ˌglō-bə-lə-ˈzā-shən\ *n* **:** the act of globalizing **:** the state of being globalized

glob·al·ize \ˈglō-bə-ˌlīz\ *vt* **-ized; -iz·ing :** to make global; *esp* **:** to make worldwide in scope or application

¹globe \ˈglōb\ *n* [MF, fr. L *globus* — more at CLIP] **:** something spherical or rounded: as **a :** a spherical representation of the earth, a heavenly body, or the heavens **b :** EARTH **c :** ORB 5

²globe *vt* **globed; glob·ing** *archaic* **:** to form into a globe

globe·fish \ˈglōb-ˌfish\ *n* **:** any of a family (Tetraodontidae) of chiefly tropical marine spiny-finned fishes which can distend themselves to a globular form and most of which are highly poisonous

globe·flow·er \-ˌflau̇(-ə)r\ *n* **:** any of a genus (*Trollius*) of plants of the buttercup family with globose yellow flowers

globe–trot·ter \-ˌträt-ər\ *n* **:** one that travels widely — **globe–trot·ting** \-ˌträt-iŋ\ *n or adj*

glo·bin \ˈglō-bən\ *n* [ISV, back-formation fr. *hemoglobin*] **:** a colorless protein obtained by removal of heme from a conjugated protein and esp. hemoglobin

glo·boid \ˈglō-ˌbȯid\ *n* **:** SPHEROID — **globoid** *adj*

glo·bose \ˈglō-ˌbōs\ *adj* **:** GLOBULAR 1a — **glo·bose·ly** *adv* — **glo·bos·i·ty** \glō-ˈbäs-ət-ē\ *n*

glob·u·lar \ˈgläb-yə-lər\ *adj* [partly fr. L *globus* + E *-ular;* partly fr. L *globulus* + E *-ar*] **1 a :** having the shape of a globe or globule <~ proteins> **b :** WORLDWIDE **2 :** having or consisting of globules — **glob·u·lar·ly** *adv* — **glob·u·lar·ness** *n*

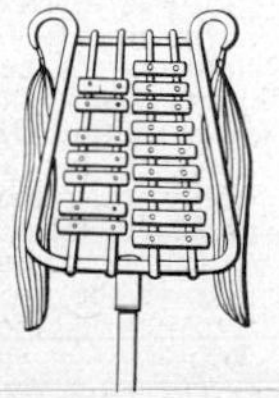
glockenspiel

glob·ule \ˈgläb-(ˌ)yü(ə)l\ *n* [F, fr. L *globulus,* dim. of *globus*] **:** a tiny globe or ball <~*s* of mercury>

glob·u·lin \ˈgläb-yə-lən\ *n* **:** any of a class of simple proteins (as myosin) that are insoluble in pure water but are soluble in dilute salt solutions and that occur widely in plant and animal tissues

glo·chid·i·ate \glō-ˈkid-ē-ət\ *adj* **1 :** having glochidia **2 :** having barbed tips <~ leaves>

glo·chid·i·um \-ē-əm\ *n, pl* **-ia** \-ē-ə\ [NL, fr. Gk *glōchis* projecting point + NL *-idium*] **1 :** a barbed hair or spine (as on a cactus) **2 :** a larval freshwater mussel (family Unionidae) that develops as an external parasite on fish

glock·en·spiel \ˈgläk-ən-ˌs(h)pēl\ *n* [G, fr. *glocke* bell + *spiel* play] **:** a percussion instrument consisting of a series of graduated metal bars tuned to the chromatic scale and played with two hammers

glom \ˈgläm\ *vt* **glommed; glom·ming** [prob. alter. of E dial. *glaum* to grab] **1** *slang* **:** TAKE, STEAL **2** *slang* **:** SEIZE, CATCH — **glom on to** *slang* **:** to take possession of

glo·mer·u·lar \glə-ˈmer-(y)ə-lər, glō-\ *adj* **:** of, relating to, or produced by a glomerulus <~ nephritis> <~ capillaries>

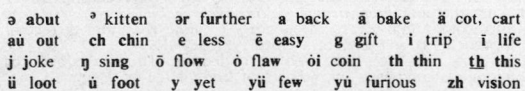

glo·mer·u·late \glə-ˈmer-(y)ə-lət, glō-\ *adj* **:** arranged in small compact clusters

glom·er·ule \ˈgläm-ə-ˌrül, -ər-ˌyü(ə)l\ *n* [NL *glomerulus*] **:** a compacted cyme like the flower head of a composite

glo·mer·u·lo·ne·phri·tis \-ˌmer-(y)ə-lō-ni-ˈfrīt-əs\ *n, pl* **-phrit·i·des** \-ˈfrit-ə-ˌdēz\ **:** nephritis marked by inflammation of the capillaries of the renal glomeruli

glo·mer·u·lus \glə-ˈmer-(y)ə-ləs, glō-\ *n, pl* **-li** \-ˌlī, -ˌlē\ [NL, glomerulus, glomerule, dim. of L *glomer-, glomus* ball] **:** a small convoluted or intertwined mass; *esp* **:** a tuft of capillaries at the point of origin of each vertebrate nephron

glo·mus \ˈglō-məs\ *n, pl* **glo·mera** \ˈgläm-ə-rə, ˈglōm-\ [NL, fr. L *glomer-, glomus* ball] **:** a small arteriovenous anastomosis together with its supporting structures

[1]**gloom** \ˈglüm\ *vb* [ME *gloumen;* akin to OE *geolu* yellow — more at YELLOW] *vi* **1 :** to look, feel, or act sullen or despondent **2 :** to be or become overcast **3 :** to loom up dimly or somberly <the castle ~*ed* before them> ~ *vt* **1** *archaic* **:** SADDEN **2 :** to make dark, murky, or somber

[2]**gloom** *n* **1 a :** partial or total darkness **b :** a dark or shadowy place <in the green ~*s* of the forest> **2 a :** lowness of spirits **:** DEJECTION **b :** an atmosphere of despondency <a ~ fell over the household>

gloomy \ˈglü-mē\ *adj* **gloom·i·er; -est 1 a :** partially or totally dark; *esp* **:** dismally and depressingly dark <~ weather> **b :** having a frowning or scowling appearance **:** FORBIDDING <a ~ countenance> **c :** low in spirits **:** MELANCHOLY <felt ~ after the play> **2 a :** causing gloom **:** DEPRESSING <a ~ story> <a bleak ~ landscape> **b :** marked by little or no hopefulness **:** PESSIMISTIC <~ prophecies> ***syn*** see DARK ***ant*** brilliant (*of light or illumination*) — **gloom·i·ly** \-mə-lē\ *adv* — **gloom·i·ness** \-mē-nəs\ *n*

glop \ˈgläp\ *n* [prob. imit.] *slang* **:** a jumbled or messy mass or mixture <clotting its rhetoric with gooey slabs of prose ~ —Pete Hamill>

Glo·ria \ˈglōr-ē-ə, ˈglȯr-\ *n* [L, glory] **1 :** GLORIA IN EXCELSIS **2 :** GLORIA PATRI

Gloria in Ex·cel·sis \-ˌin-eks-ˈchel-səs, -ek-ˈshel-\ [LL, glory (be to God) on high] **:** a Christian liturgical hymn having the verse form of the Psalms

Gloria Pa·tri \-ˈpä-(ˌ)trē\ *n* [LL, glory (be) to the Father] **:** a 2-verse doxology to the Trinity

glo·ri·fy \ˈglōr-ə-ˌfī, ˈglȯr-\ *vt* **-fied; -fy·ing 1 a :** to make glorious by bestowing honor, praise, or admiration **b :** to elevate to celestial glory **2 :** to shed radiance or splendor on <a large chandelier *glorifies* the whole room> **3 a :** to cause to have great beauty, charm, or appeal <romantic love is *glorified* in song and literature> **b :** to cause to be or seem to be better than the actual condition <a recipe for ~*ing* pancakes> <his new position is just a *glorified* version of his old stockroom job> **4 :** to give glory to (as in worship) — **glo·ri·fi·ca·tion** \ˌglōr-ə-fə-ˈkā-shən, ˌglȯr-\ *n* — **glo·ri·fi·er** \ˈglōr-ə-ˌfī(-ə)r, ˈglȯr-\ *n*

glo·ri·ous \ˈglōr-ē-əs, ˈglȯr-\ *adj* **1 a :** possessing or deserving glory **:** ILLUSTRIOUS **b :** conferring glory <a ~ victory> **2 :** marked by great beauty or splendor **:** MAGNIFICENT **3 :** DELIGHTFUL, WONDERFUL <had a ~ weekend> ***syn*** see SPLENDID ***ant*** inglorious — **glo·ri·ous·ly** *adv* — **glo·ri·ous·ness** *n*

[1]**glo·ry** \ˈglōr-ē, ˈglȯr-\ *n, pl* **glories** [ME *glorie,* fr. MF & L; MF, fr. L *gloria*] **1 a :** praise, honor, or distinction extended by common consent **:** RENOWN **b :** worshipful praise, honor, and thanksgiving <giving ~ to God> **2 a :** something that secures praise or renown <the ~ of a brilliant career> **b :** a highly commendable asset <he was a ~ to his profession> **3 a (1) :** RESPLENDENCE, MAGNIFICENCE <the ~ that was Greece and the grandeur that was Rome —E. A. Poe> **(2) :** something marked by beauty or resplendence <a perfect ~ of a day> **b :** the splendor and beatific happiness of heaven; *broadly* **:** ETERNITY **4 a :** a state of great gratification or exaltation <when she's acting she's in her ~> **b :** a height of prosperity or achievement **5 :** a ring or spot of light: as **a :** AUREOLE **b :** CORONA 2a, 2b

[2]**glory** *vi* **glo·ried; glo·ry·ing :** to rejoice proudly **:** EXULT <*glories* in his great physical strength>

Glos *abbr* Gloucestershire

[1]**gloss** \ˈgläs, ˈglȯs\ *n* [prob. of Scand origin; akin to Icel *glossa* to glow; akin to OE *geolu* yellow] **1 :** a surface luster or brightness **:** POLISH **2 :** a deceptively attractive appearance **:** SEMBLANCE <selfishness that had a ~ of humanitarianism about it>

[2]**gloss** *vt* **1 a :** to make appear right and acceptable **:** WHITEWASH — usu. used with *over* <there is no use in attempting to ignore or ~ over the profundity of this conflict — Dean Acheson> **b :** to veil or hide by treating rapidly or superficially — usu. used with *over* <~*ing* over humiliations, gilding small moments of glory —*Times Lit. Supp.*>

[3]**gloss** *n* [ME *glose,* fr. OF, fr. L *glossa* unusual word requiring explanation, fr. Gk *glōssa, glōtta* tongue, language, unusual word; akin to Gk *glōchis* projecting point] **1 a :** a brief explanation (as in the margin or between the lines of a text) of a difficult or obscure word or expression **b :** a false and often willfully misleading interpretation (as of a text) **2 a :** GLOSSARY **b :** an interlinear translation **c :** a continuous commentary accompanying a text

[4]**gloss** *vt* **1 :** to furnish glosses for **2 :** to dispose of (as a difficult problem) by false or perverse interpretation <trying to ~ away the irrationalities of the universe —Irwin Edman>

gloss- *or* **glosso-** *comb form* [L, fr. Gk *glōss-, glōsso-,* fr. *glōssa*] **1 :** tongue <*gloss*algia> **2 :** language <*glosso*logy>

glos·sa \ˈgläs-ə, ˈglȯs-\ *n, pl* **glos·sae** \-ˌē, -ˌī\ *also* **glossas** [NL, fr. Gk *glōssa*] **:** a tongue or lingual structure esp. in an insect; *esp* **:** the median distal lobe of the labium of an insect

glos·sal \-əl\ *adj* **:** of or relating to the tongue

glos·sar·i·al \glä-ˈsar-ē-əl, glȯ-, -ˈser-\ *adj* **:** of, relating to, or having the characteristics of a glossary

glos·sa·rist \ˈgläs-ə-rəst, ˈglȯs-\ *n* **1 :** one that makes textual glosses **2 :** a compiler of a glossary

glos·sa·ry \-(ə-)rē\ *n, pl* **-ries :** a collection of textual glosses or of terms limited to a special area of knowledge or usage

glos·sa·tor \ˈgläs-ˌāt-ər, ˈglȯs-\ *n* **:** GLOSSARIST

glos·si·na \glä-ˈsī-nə, glȯ-, -ˈsē-\ *n* [NL, genus name, fr. Gk *glōssa* tongue; fr. its long proboscis] **:** TSETSE

glos·sog·ra·pher \glä-ˈsäg-rə-fər, glȯ-\ *n* [Gk *glōssographos,* fr. *glōssa* + *graphein* to write — more at CARVE] **:** GLOSSARIST

glos·so·la·lia \ˌgläs-ə-ˈlā-lē-ə, ˌglȯs-\ *n* [NL, fr. Gk *gloss-* + *lalia* chatter, fr. *lalein* to chatter, talk] **:** TONGUE 4c(1)

glos·so·pha·ryn·geal \ˌgläs-ō-ˌfar-ən-ˈjē-əl, ˌglȯs-, -fə-ˈrin-j(ē-)əl\ *adj* **:** of or relating to both tongue and pharynx

glossopharyngeal nerve *n* **:** either of the 9th pair of cranial nerves that are mixed nerves and supply chiefly the pharynx, posterior tongue, and parotid gland

[1]**glossy** \ˈgläs-ē, ˈglȯs-\ *adj* **gloss·i·er; -est 1 :** having a surface luster or brightness <rich ~ leather> <~ paper> **2 :** attractive in an artificially opulent, sophisticated, or smoothly captivating manner **:** SHOWY <a ~ musical> <lots of ~ and phony chatter> — **gloss·i·ly** \-ə-lē\ *adv* — **gloss·i·ness** \-ē-nəs\ *n*

[2]**glossy** *n, pl* **gloss·ies 1 :** SLICK 3 **2 :** a photograph printed on smooth shiny paper

glossy magazine *n, chiefly Brit* **:** SLICK 3

glott- *or* **glotto-** *comb form* [Gk *glōtt-, glōtto-* tongue, fr. *glōssa, glōtta*] **:** language <*glotto*logy>

glot·tal \ˈglät-ᵊl\ *adj* **:** of, relating to, or produced in or by the glottis <~ constriction>

glottal stop *n* **:** a speech sound produced by interruption of the breath stream by closure of the glottis

glot·tis \ˈglät-əs\ *n, pl* **glot·tis·es** *or* **glot·ti·des** \-ə-ˌdēz\ [Gk *glōttid-, glōttis,* fr. *glōtta* tongue — more at GLOSS] **:** the elongated space between the vocal cords; *also* **:** the structures that surround this space — compare EPIGLOTTIS

glot·to·chro·nol·o·gy \ˌglät-ō-krə-ˈnäl-ə-jē\ *n* **:** a linguistic method that makes use of the rate of vocabulary replacement in order to estimate the date of divergence for distinct but genetically related languages — **glot·to·chro·no·log·i·cal** \-ˌkrän-ᵊl-ˈäj-i-kəl, -ˌkrōn-\ *adj*

glout \ˈglüt, ˈglau̇t\ *vi* [ME *glouten,* prob. of Scand origin; akin to ON *glotta* to grin scornfully — more at GLOAT] *archaic* **:** FROWN, SCOWL

[1]**glove** \ˈgləv\ *n* [ME, fr. OE *glōf;* akin to ON *glōfi* glove] **1 a :** a covering for the hand having separate sections for each of the fingers and the thumb and often extending part way up the arm **b :** [1]GAUNTLET 1, 3 **2 a (1) :** a padded leather covering for the hand used in baseball when catching a thrown or batted ball; *specif* **:** one having individual thumb and finger sections usu. connected with a lacing or webbing — compare MITT **(2) :** fielding ability <he's got a good ~ at three positions and can pinch-hit —Casey Stengel> **b :** BOXING GLOVE

[2]**glove** *vt* **gloved; glov·ing 1 a :** to cover with or as if with a glove **b :** to furnish with gloves **2 :** to catch (a baseball) in one's gloved hand

glove box *n* **1** *chiefly Brit* **:** GLOVE COMPARTMENT **2 :** a sealed protectively lined compartment having holes to which are attached gloves for use in handling dangerous materials inside the compartment

glove compartment *n* **:** a small storage cabinet in the dashboard of an automobile

glov·er \ˈgləv-ər\ *n* **:** one that makes or sells gloves

[1]**glow** \ˈglō\ *vi* [ME *glowen,* fr. OE *glōwan;* akin to OE *geolu* yellow — more at YELLOW] **1 a :** to shine with or as if with an intense heat <the fire ~*ing* in the darkness> **b (1) :** to have a rich warm typically ruddy color <cheeks ~*ing* with health> **(2) :** FLUSH, BLUSH <the children ~*ed* with excitement> **2 a :** to experience a sensation of or as if of heat <~*ing* with rage> **b :** to show exuberance or elation <~ with pride> — **glow·ing·ly** \-iŋ-lē\ *adv*

[2]**glow** *n* **1 :** brightness or warmth of color; *esp* **:** REDNESS <the ~ of his cheeks> **2 a :** warmth of feeling or emotion **b :** a sensation of warmth <the drug produces a sustained ~> **3 a :** the state of glowing with heat and light **b :** light such as is emitted by a solid body heated to luminosity **:** INCANDESCENCE ***syn*** see BLAZE

[1]**glow·er** \ˈglau̇(-ə)r\ *vi* [ME (Sc) *glowren;* perh. of Scand origin; akin to Norw dial. *glyra* to look askance; Icel *glossa* to glow — more at GLOW] **:** to look or stare with sullen annoyance or anger ***syn*** see FROWN

[2]**glower** *n* **:** a sullen brooding look indicative of annoyance or anger

glow lamp *n* **:** a gas-discharge electric lamp in which most of the light proceeds from the glow of the gas near the cathode

glow·worm \ˈglō-ˌwərm\ *n* **:** any of various luminous insect larvae or adults with wings rudimentary or lacking; *esp* **:** a larva or wingless female of a beetle (family Lampyridae) that emits light from the abdomen

glox·in·ia \gläk-ˈsin-ē-ə\ *n* [NL, genus name, fr. B. P. *Gloxin* 18th cent. G botanist] **:** any of a genus (*Shinningia*) of Brazilian tuberous herbs of a family (Gesneriaceae, the gloxinia family); *esp* **:** a plant (*S. speciosa*) widely cultivated for its showy bell-shaped flowers

[1]**gloze** \ˈglōz\ *vt* **glozed; gloz·ing** [ME *glosen* to gloss, flatter, fr. *glose* gloss] *archaic* **:** [4]GLOSS 1

[2]**gloze** *vt* **glozed; gloz·ing :** [2]GLOSS 1 — often used with *over*

gluc- *or* **gluco-** *comb form* [ISV] **1 a :** glucose **b :** related to or containing glucose **2 :** GLYC-

glu·ca·gon \ˈglü-kə-ˌgän\ *n* [*gluc-* + *-agon* (perh. fr. Gk *agōn,* prp. of *agein* to lead, drive) — more at AGENT] **:** a protein hormone that is obtained esp. from the islets of Langerhans and that increases the content of sugar in the blood by increasing the rate of breakdown of glycogen in the liver

glu·co·cor·ti·coid \ˌglü-kō-ˈkȯrt-i-ˌkȯid\ *n* **:** a corticoid (as cortisol) that tends to increase liver glycogen and blood sugar by increasing gluconeogenesis

glu·co·ki·nase \-ˈkī-ˌnās, -ˌnāz\ *n* **:** a hexokinase that catalyzes the phosphorylation of glucose

glu·co·nate \ˈglü-kə-ˌnāt\ *n* **:** a salt of gluconic acid

glu·co·neo·gen·e·sis \ˌglü-kə-ˌnē-ə-ˈjen-ə-səs\ *n* [NL] **:** formation of glucose within the animal body esp. by the liver from substances (as fats and proteins) other than carbohydrates

glu·con·ic acid \(ˌ)glü-ˌkän-ik-\ *n* [ISV, irreg. fr. *glucose* + *-ic*] **:** a crystalline acid $C_6H_{12}O_7$ obtained by oxidation of glucose and used chiefly in cleaning metals

glu·cos·amine \glü-ˈkō-sə-ˌmēn, -zə-\ *n* **:** an amino derivative $C_6H_{13}NO_5$ of glucose that occurs esp. as a constituent of polysaccharides (as chitin) in animal supporting structures and some plant cell walls

glu·cose \ˈglü-ˌkōs, -ˌkōz\ *n* [F, modif. of Gk *gleukos* must, sweet wine; akin to Gk *glykys* sweet] **1 :** a sugar $C_6H_{12}O_6$ known in dextrorotatory, levorotatory, and racemic forms; *esp* **:** the sweet colorless soluble dextrorotatory form that occurs widely in nature and is the usual form in which carbohydrate is assimilated by animals **2 :** a light-colored syrup made from cornstarch

glucose-1-phosphate *n* [fr. the position at which the phosphate radical is attached] **:** an ester $C_6H_{13}O_9P$ that reacts in the presence of a phosphorylase with aldoses and ketoses to yield disaccharides or with itself in liver and muscle to yield glycogen and phosphoric acid

glucose phosphate *n* **:** a phosphate ester of glucose: as **a :** GLUCOSE-1-PHOSPHATE **b :** GLUCOSE-6-PHOSPHATE

glucose-6-phosphate *n* [fr. the position at which the phosphate radical is attached] **:** an ester $C_6H_{13}O_9P$ that is formed from glucose and ATP in the presence of a glucokinase and that is an essential early stage in glucose metabolism

glu·co·si·dase \glü-ˈkō-sə-ˌdās, -zə-ˌdāz\ *n* **:** an enzyme (as maltase) that hydrolyzes a glucoside

glu·co·side \ˈglü-kə-ˌsīd\ *n* **:** GLYCOSIDE; *esp* **:** a glycoside that yields glucose on hydrolysis — **glu·co·sid·ic** \ˌglü-kə-ˈsid-ik\ *adj* — **glu·co·sid·i·cal·ly** \-i-k(ə-)lē\ *adv*

gluc·uron·ic acid \ˌglü-kyə-ˌrän-ik-\ *n* [*gluc-* + *-uronic*] **:** a compound $C_6H_{10}O_7$ that occurs esp. as a constituent of mucopolysaccharides (as hyaluronic acid) and combined as a glucuronide

gluc·uron·i·dase \-ˈrän-ə-ˌdās, -ˌdāz\ *n* **:** an enzyme that hydrolyzes a glucuronide; *esp* **:** one that occurs widely (as in liver and spleen) and hydrolyzes the beta form of a glucuronide

gluc·uro·nide \glü-ˈkyůr-ə-ˌnīd\ *n* **:** any of various derivatives of glucuronic acid that are formed esp. as combinations with often toxic aromatic hydroxyl compounds (as phenols) and are excreted in the urine

¹glue \ˈglü\ *n* [ME *glu*, fr. MF, fr. LL *glut-, glus* —more at CLAY] **1 :** any of various strong adhesive substances; *esp* **:** a hard protein chiefly gelatinous substance that absorbs water to form a viscous solution with strong adhesive properties and that is obtained by cooking down collagenous materials (as hides or bones) **2 :** a solution of glue used for sticking things together — **glu·ey** \ˈglü-ē\ *adj* — **glu·i·ly** \ˈglü-ə-lē\ *adv*

²glue *vt* **glued; glu·ing** *also* **glue·ing 1 :** to cause to stick tightly with glue <*gluing* the wings onto the model airplane> **2 :** to fix (as the eyes) on an object steadily or with deep concentration <kept his eyes *glued* to the TV screen>

glum \ˈgləm\ *adj* **glum·mer; glum·mest** [prob. akin to ME *gloumen* to gloom] **1 :** broodingly morose <became ~ when they heard the news> **2 :** DREARY, GLOOMY <a ~ countenance> ***syn*** see SULLEN ***ant*** cheerful — **glum·ly** *adv* — **glum·ness** *n*

glu·ma·ceous \glü-ˈmā-shəs\ *adj* **:** consisting or having the character of glumes <~ flowers>

glume \ˈglüm\ *n* [NL *gluma*, fr. L, hull, husk; akin to L *glubere* to peel — more at CLEAVE] **:** a chaffy bract; *specif* **:** either of two empty bracts at the base of the spikelet in grasses

¹glut \ˈglət\ *vb* **glut·ted; glut·ting** [ME *glouten*] *vt* **1 :** to fill esp. with food to satiety **:** SATIATE **2 :** to flood (the market) with goods so that supply exceeds demand ~ *vi* **:** to eat gluttonously ***syn*** see SATIATE

²glut *n* **1** *archaic* **:** the act or process of glutting **2 :** an excessive quantity **:** OVERSUPPLY

³glut *vt* **glut·ted; glut·ting** [prob. fr. obs. *glut*, n. (swallow)] *archaic* **:** to swallow greedily

glu·ta·mate \ˈglüt-ə-ˌmāt\ *n* **:** a salt or ester of glutamic acid; *esp* **:** MONOSODIUM GLUTAMATE

glu·tam·ic acid \(ˌ)glü-ˌtam-ik-\ *n* [ISV *gluten* + *amino* + *-ic*] **:** a crystalline amino acid $C_5H_9NO_4$ widely distributed in plant and animal proteins and used in the form of a sodium salt as a seasoning

glu·ta·min·ase \ˈglüt-ə-mə-ˌnās, glü-ˈtam-ə-, -ˌnāz\ *n* **:** an enzyme that hydrolyzes glutamine to glutamic acid and ammonia

glu·ta·mine \ˈglüt-ə-ˌmēn\ *n* [ISV *gluten* + *amine*] **:** a crystalline amino acid $C_5H_{10}N_2O_3$ that is found both free and in proteins in plants and animals and that yields glutamic acid and ammonia on hydrolysis

glu·tar·al·de·hyde \ˌglüt-ə-ˈral-də-ˌhīd\ *n* [*glutaric* acid + *aldehyde*] **:** a compound $C_5H_8O_2$ that contains two aldehyde groups and is used esp. in leather tanning, disinfection, and fixation of biological tissues

glu·tar·ic acid \glü-ˌtar-ik-\ *n* [prob. fr. *gluten* + *-aric* (as in *tartaric acid*)] **:** a crystalline acid $C_5H_8O_4$ used esp. in organic synthesis

glu·ta·thi·one \ˌglüt-ə-ˈthī-ˌōn\ *n* [ISV *gluta-* (fr. *glutamic acid*) + *thi-* + *-one*] **:** a peptide $C_{10}H_{17}N_3O_6S$ that contains one amino-acid residue each of glutamic acid, cysteine, and glycine, that occurs widely in plant and animal tissues, and that plays an important role in biological oxidation-reduction processes and the activation of some enzymes

glu·te·al \ˈglüt-ē-əl, glü-ˈtē-\ *adj* **:** of or relating to the gluteus muscles

glu·ten \ˈglüt-ᵊn\ *n* [L *glutin-, gluten* glue; akin to LL *glut-, glus* glue — more at CLAY] **:** a tenacious elastic protein substance esp. of wheat flour that gives cohesiveness to dough — **glu·ten·ous** \ˈglüt-nəs, -ᵊn-əs\ *adj*

glu·te·us \ˈglüt-ē-əs, glü-ˈtē-\ *n, pl* **glu·tei** \ˈglüt-ē-ˌī, -ē-ˌē; glü-ˈtē-ˌī\ [NL *glutaeus, gluteus*, fr. Gk *gloutos* buttock — more at CLOUD] **:** any of the large muscles of the buttocks

glu·ti·nous \ˈglüt-nəs, -ᵊn-əs\ *adj* [MF or L; MF *glutineux*, fr. L *glutinosus*, fr. *glutin-, gluten*] **:** having the quality of glue **:** GUMMY — **glu·ti·nous·ly** *adv* — **glu·ti·nous·ness** *n*

glut·ton \ˈglət-ᵊn\ *n* [ME *glotoun*, fr. OF *gloton*, fr. L *glutton-, glutto*; akin to L *gluttire* to swallow, *gula* throat, OE *ceole*] **1 a :** one given habitually to greedy and voracious eating and drinking **b :** one that has a great capacity for accepting or enduring something <he's a ~ for punishment> **2 a :** a shaggy thickset carnivorous mammal (*Gulo gulo* of the weasel family) of northern Europe and Asia related to the marten and the sable **b :** WOLVERINE 1 ***syn*** see EPICURE

glut·ton·ous \ˈglət-nəs, -ᵊn-əs\ *adj* **:** marked by or given to gluttony — **glut·ton·ous·ly** *adv* — **glut·ton·ous·ness** *n*

glut·tony \ˈglət-nē, -ᵊn-ē\ *n, pl* **-ton·ies :** excess in eating or drinking

glyc- *or* **glyco-** *comb form* [ISV, fr. Gk *glyk-* sweet, fr. *glykys*] **1 :** sugar <*glyco*protein> **2 :** glycine <*glyc*yl>

gly·can \ˈglī-ˌkan\ *n* **:** POLYSACCHARIDE

glycer- *or* **glycero-** *comb form* [ISV, fr. *glycerin*] **1 :** glycerol <*glycer*yl> **2 :** related to glycerol or glyceric acid <*glycer*aldehyde>

glyc·er·al·de·hyde \ˌglis-ə-ˈral-də-ˌhīd\ *n* **:** a sweet crystalline compound $C_3H_6O_3$ that is formed as an intermediate in carbohydrate metabolism by the breakdown of sugars and that yields glycerol on reduction

gly·cer·ic acid \glis-ˌer-ik-\ *n* [ISV, fr. *glycerin*] **:** a syrupy acid $C_3H_6O_4$ obtainable by oxidation of glycerol or glyceraldehyde

glyc·er·ide \ˈglis-ə-ˌrīd\ *n* **:** an ester of glycerol esp. with fatty acids — **glyc·er·id·ic** \ˌglis-ə-ˈrid-ik\ *adj*

glyc·er·in *or* **glyc·er·ine** \ˈglis-(ə-)rən\ *n* [F *glycérine*, fr. Gk *glykeros* sweet; akin to Gk *glykys*] **:** GLYCEROL

glyc·er·in·ate \ˈglis-(ə-)rə-ˌnāt\ *vt* **-at·ed; -at·ing :** to treat with or preserve in glycerin — **glyc·er·in·ation** \ˌglis-(ə-)rə-ˈnā-shən\ *n*

glyc·er·ol \ˈglis-ə-ˌrōl, -ˌrȯl\ *n* [*glycerin* + *-ol*] **:** a sweet syrupy hygroscopic trihydroxy alcohol $C_3H_8O_3$ usu. obtained by the saponification of fats and used esp. as a solvent and plasticizer

glyc·er·yl \ˈglis-(ə-)rəl\ *n* **:** a radical derived from glycerol by removal of hydroxide; *esp* **:** a trivalent radical CH_2CHCH_2

gly·cine \ˈglī-ˌsēn, ˈglis-ᵊn\ *n* **:** a sweet crystalline amino acid $C_2H_5NO_2$ obtained esp. by hydrolysis of proteins

gly·co·gen \ˈglī-kə-jən\ *n* **:** a white amorphous tasteless polysaccharide $(C_6H_{10}O_5)x$ that is the chief storage carbohydrate of animals

gly·co·gen·e·sis \ˌglī-kə-ˈjen-ə-səs\ *n* [NL] **1 :** formation of sugar from glycogen **2 :** formation of glycogen — **gly·co·ge·net·ic** \-jə-ˈnet-ik\ *adj*

gly·col \ˈglī-ˌkȯl, -ˌkōl\ *n* [ISV *glyc-* + *-ol*] **:** ETHYLENE GLYCOL; *broadly* **:** a related alcohol containing two hydroxyl groups

gly·co·late *also* **gly·col·late** \ˈglī-kə-ˌlāt\ *n* [ISV *glycol* + *-ate*] **:** a salt or ester of glycolic acid

gly·col·ic acid *also* **gly·col·lic acid** \(ˌ)glī-ˌkäl-ik-\ *n* [ISV *glycol* + *-ic*] **:** a translucent crystalline compound $C_2H_4O_3$ found esp. in unripe grapes and sugar beets and used esp. in textile and leather processing

gly·co·lip·id \ˌglī-kō-ˈlip-əd\ *n* **:** a lipid (as a ganglioside or a cerebroside) that contains a carbohydrate radical

gly·col·y·sis \glī-ˈkäl-ə-səs\ *n* [NL] **:** the enzymatic breakdown of a carbohydrate (as glucose or glycogen) by way of phosphate derivatives — **gly·co·lyt·ic** \ˌglī-kə-ˈlit-ik\ *adj* — **gly·co·lyt·i·cal·ly** \-i-k(ə-)lē\ *adv*

gly·co·pep·tide \ˌglī-kō-ˈpep-ˌtīd\ *n* **:** GLYCOPROTEIN

gly·co·pro·tein \-ˈprō-ˌtēn, -ˈprōt-ē-ən\ *n* **:** a conjugated protein in which the nonprotein group is a carbohydrate

gly·co·si·dase \glī-ˈkō-sə-ˌdās, -zə-ˌdāz\ *n* **:** an enzyme that catalyzes the hydrolysis of a bond joining a sugar of a glycoside to an alcohol or another sugar unit

gly·co·side \ˈglī-kə-ˌsīd\ *n* **:** any of numerous sugar derivatives that contain a nonsugar group attached through an oxygen or nitrogen bond and that on hydrolysis yield a sugar (as glucose) — **gly·co·sid·ic** \ˌglī-kə-ˈsid-ik\ *adj* — **gly·co·sid·i·cal·ly** \-i-k(ə-)lē\ *adv*

gly·cos·uria \ˌglī-kō-ˈshůr-ē-ə, -kəs-ˈyůr-\ *n* [NL] **:** the presence in the urine of abnormal amounts of sugar — **gly·cos·uric** \-ˈshů(ə)r-ik, -ˈyů(ə)r-\ *adj*

gly·co·syl \ˈglī-kə-ˌsil\ *n* **:** a univalent radical derived from a cyclic form of glucose by removal of the hemiacetal hydroxyl group

gly·cyl \ˈglī-səl\ *n* **:** the univalent acyl radical C_2H_4NO of glycine

glyph \ˈglif\ *n* [Gk *glyphē* carved work, fr. *glyphein* to carve — more at CLEAVE] **1 :** an ornamental vertical groove esp. in a Doric frieze **2 :** a symbolic figure or a character usu. incised or carved in relief **3 :** a symbol (as a curved arrow on a road sign) that conveys information nonverbally — **glyph·ic** \-ik\ *adj*

Glyp·tal \ˈglip-tᵊl\ *trademark* — used for an alkyd

glyp·tic \ˈglip-tik\ *n* [prob. fr. F *glyptique*, fr. Gk *glyptikē*, fr. *glyphein*] **:** the art or process of carving or engraving esp. on gems

gm *abbr* gram

GM *abbr* **1** general manager **2** grand master **3** guided missile

G-man \ˈjē-ˌman\ *n* [prob. fr. *government man*] **:** a special agent of the Federal Bureau of Investigation

GMT *abbr* Greenwich mean time

GMW *abbr* gram-molecular weight

gn *abbr* guinea

gnar *or* **gnarr** \ˈnär\ *vi* **gnarred; gnar·ring** [imit.] **:** SNARL, GROWL

¹gnarl \ˈnär(ə)l\ *vi* [prob. freq. of *gnar*] **:** SNARL, GROWL

²gnarl *vt* [back-formation fr. *gnarled*] **:** to twist into a state of deformity

ə abut	ᵊ kitten	ər further	a back	ā bake	ä cot, cart
au̇ out	ch chin	e less	ē easy	g gift	i trip
ī life	j joke	ŋ sing	ō flow	ȯ flaw	ȯi coin
th thin	t͟h this	ü loot	ů foot	y yet	yü few
yů furious	zh vision				

[3]gnarl *n* : a hard protuberance with twisted grain on a tree
gnarled \ˈnär(ə)ld\ *adj* [prob. alter. of *knurled*] **1 :** full of knots or gnarls : KNOTTY <~ cypresses> **2 :** crabbed in disposition, aspect, or character
gnarly \ˈnär-lē\ *adj* : GNARLED
gnash \ˈnash\ *vt* [alter. of ME *gnasten*] : to strike or grind (as the teeth) together — **gnash** *n*
gnat \ˈnat\ *n* [ME, fr. OE *gnætt;* akin to OE *gnagan* to gnaw] : any of various small usu. biting two-winged flies — **gnat·ty** \-ē\ *adj*

gnat

gnat·catch·er \ˈnat-ˌkach-ər, -ˌkech-\ *n* : any of a genus (*Polioptila* of the family Sylviidae) of several very small No. and So. American insectivorous warblers
gnath- *or* **gnatho-** *comb form* [NL, fr. Gk *gnath-*, fr. *gnathos;* akin to Gk *genys* jaw — more at CHIN] : jaw <*gnatho*plasty>
gnath·ic \ˈnath-ik\ *or* **gna·thal** \ˈnā-thəl, ˈnath-əl\ *adj* : of or relating to the jaw
gna·thite \ˈnā-ˌthīt, ˈna-\ *n* : a mouth appendage of an arthropod
-gna·thous *adj comb form* [NL *-gnathus,* fr. Gk *gnathos*] : having (such) a jaw <opistho*gnathous*>
gnaw \ˈnȯ\ *vb* [ME *gnawen,* fr. OE *gnagan;* akin to OHG *gnagan* to gnaw] *vt* **1 a :** to bite or chew on with the teeth; *esp* : to wear away by persistent biting or nibbling <a dog ~*ing* a bone> **b :** to make by gnawing <rats ~*ed* a hole> **2 a :** to be a source of vexation to : PLAGUE <anxiety always ~*ing* him> **b :** to affect like gnawing <hunger ~*ing* his vitals> **3 :** ERODE, CORRODE ~ *vi* **1 :** to bite or nibble persistently <~*ing* at her under lip> **2 :** to destroy or reduce by or as if by gnawing <waves ~*ing* away at the cliffs> — **gnaw·er** \ˈnȯ(-ə)r\ *n*
gneiss \ˈnīs\ *n* [G *gneis*] : a foliated metamorphic rock corresponding in composition to granite or some other feldspathic plutonic rock — **gneiss·ic** \ˈnī-sik\ *adj* — **gneiss·oid** \-ˌsȯid\ *adj* — **gneiss·ose** \-ˌsōs\ *adj*
GNI *abbr* gross national income
[1]gnome \ˈnōm\ *n* [Gk *gnōmē,* fr. *gignōskein* to know — more at KNOW] : MAXIM, APHORISM
[2]gnome *n* [F, fr. NL *gnomus*] **1 :** an ageless and often deformed dwarf of folklore who lives in the earth and usu. guards precious ores or treasure **2 :** an elemental being in the theory of Paracelsus that inhabits earth — **gnom·ish** \ˈnō-mish\ *adj*
gno·mic \ˈnō-mik\ *adj* **1 :** characterized by aphorism <~ poetry> **2 :** given to the composition of gnomic poetry <a ~ poet>
gno·mon \ˈnō-ˌmän, -mən\ *n* [L, fr. Gk *gnōmōn* interpreter, pointer on a sundial, fr. *gignōskein*] **1 :** an object that by the position or length of its shadow serves as an indicator esp. of the hour of the day: as **a :** the style of an ordinary sundial **b :** a column or shaft erected perpendicular to the horizon **2 :** the remainder of a parallelogram after the removal of a similar parallelogram containing one of its corners

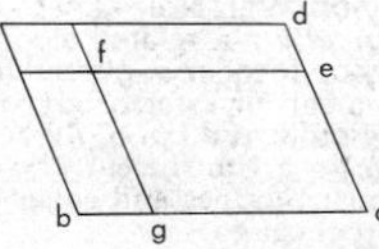

bcdefg gnomon 2

gno·mon·ic \nō-ˈmän-ik\ *adj* : of or relating to the gnomon or its use in telling time
gno·sis \ˈnō-səs\ *n* [Gk *gnōsis,* lit., knowledge, fr. *gignōskein*] : esoteric knowledge of spiritual truth held by the ancient Gnostics to be essential to salvation
-gno·sis \(g-)ˈnō-səs\ *n comb form, pl* **-gno·ses** \-ˌsēz\ [L, fr. Gk *gnōsis*] : knowledge : recognition <psycho*gnosis*>
Gnos·tic \ˈnäs-tik\ *n* [LL *gnosticus,* fr. Gk *gnōstikos* of knowledge, fr. *gignōskein*] : an adherent of gnosticism — **Gnostic** *adj*
gnos·ti·cism \ˈnäs-tə-ˌsiz-əm\ *n, often cap* : the thought and practice esp. of various cults of late pre-Christian and early Christian centuries distinguished by the conviction that matter is evil and that emancipation comes through gnosis
gno·to·bi·ot·ic \ˌnōt-ō-bī-ˈät-ik, -bē-\ *adj* [Gk *gnōtos* known (fr. *gignōskein* to know) + *biotē* life, way of life — more at KNOW, BIOTA] : of, relating to, living in, or being a controlled environment containing one or a few kinds of organisms; *also* : AXENIC — **gno·to·bi·ot·i·cal·ly** \-i-k(ə-)lē\ *adv*
GNP *abbr* gross national product
gnu \ˈn(y)ü\ *n, pl* **gnu** *or* **gnus** [modif. of Bushman *nqu*] : any of several large African antelopes (genera *Connochaetes* and *Gorgon*) with a head like that of an ox, short mane, long tail, and horns in both sexes that curve downward and outward

gnu

[1]go \ˈgō\ *vb* **went** \ˈwent\; **gone** \ˈgȯn *also* ˈgän\; **go·ing** \ˈgō-iŋ, ˈgȯ(-)iŋ; "*going to*" *indicating intent is often* ˈgō-nə *or* ˈgȯ-nə\; **goes** \ˈgōz\ [ME *gon,* fr. OE *gān;* akin to OHG *gān* to go, Gk *kichanein* to reach, attain] *vi* **1 :** to move on a course : PROCEED — compare STOP <~ slow> <*went* by train> **2 :** to move out of or away from a place expressed or implied : LEAVE, DEPART <they *went* from school to the party> <she is *going* away for the summer> **3 a :** to take a certain course or follow a certain procedure <reports ~ through channels to the president> **b :** to pass by means of a process like journeying <the message *went* by wire> **c :** to proceed without delay and often in a thoughtless or reckless manner — used esp. to intensify a complementary verb <why did he have to ~ and spoil everything> **d** (1) **:** to extend from point to point or in a certain direction : RUN <his land ~*es* almost to the river> (2) **:** to give access : LEAD <that door ~*es* to the cellar> **4** *obs* : WALK **5 :** to be habitually in a certain state or condition <~ bareheaded> <~ armed after dark> **6 a :** to become lost, consumed, or spent <the time allotted me was *gone*> **b :** DIE **c :** to slip away : ELAPSE <the evening *went* pleasantly enough> **d :** to come to be given up or discarded <these slums have to ~> **e :** to pass by sale <*went* for a good price> **f :** to become impaired or weakened <his hearing started to ~> **g :** to give way esp. under great force or pressure : BREAK **7 a :** to take place : HAPPEN <what's ~*ing* on> **b :** to have course or issue : FARE <everything was ~*ing* well> **c :** to be in general or on an average <cheap, as yachts ~> **d :** to be or become esp. as the result of a contest <decision *went* against him> **e :** to turn out well : SUCCEED <worked hard to make the party ~> **8 a :** to apply oneself <*went* to fighting among themselves> **b :** to put or subject oneself <*went* to unnecessary expense> **c** *chiefly South & Midland* : INTEND <I didn't ~ to do it> **9 :** to have recourse to another for corroboration, vindication, or decision : RESORT <~ to court to recover damages> **10 a :** to begin an action or motion <here ~*es*> **b :** to maintain or perform a certain action or motion <drums had been ~*ing* strong> **c :** to function in the proper or expected manner <trying to get the motor to ~> **11 a :** to have currency <now ~*es* by another name> **b :** to pass from person to person : CIRCULATE <the story ~*es* that the expedition was a failure> **12 a :** to act in accordance or harmony <a good rule to ~ by> **b :** to come to be determined <dreams ~ by contraries> **c :** to come to be applied or appropriated <part of the budget ~*es* for military purposes> **d :** to pass by award, assignment, or lot <the prize *went* to a sophomore> **e :** to contribute to an end or result <qualities that ~ to make a hero> **13 :** to be about, intending, or expecting something <is ~*ing* to leave town> **14 a :** EXTEND <his knowledge fails to ~ very deep> **b :** to come or arrive at a certain state or condition <~ to sleep> **c :** to come to be <the tire *went* flat> **15 a :** to be in phrasing or expression : READ <as the phrase ~*es*> **b :** to be capable of being sung or played <the tune ~*es* like this> **16 :** to be compatible, suitable, or becoming : HARMONIZE <claret ~*es* with beef> **17 a :** to be capable of passing, extending, or being contained or inserted <will these clothes ~ in your suitcase> **b :** to have a usual or proper place or position : BELONG <these books ~ on the top shelf> **18 :** to have a tendency : CONDUCE <it ~*es* to show he can be trusted> **19 a** (1) **:** to carry authority <what she said *went*> (2) **:** to be acceptable, satisfactory, or adequate <anything ~*es* here> **b :** to hold true : be valid **20 :** to empty the bladder or bowels ~ *vt* **1 :** to proceed along or according to : FOLLOW <if I were ~*ing* his way> **2 :** to pass through : TRAVERSE **3 a :** to make a wager of : BET <~ a dollar on the outcome> **b :** to make an offer of : BID <willing to ~ $50 for the clock> **4 a :** to assume the function or obligation of <promised to ~ bail for his friend> **b :** to participate to the extent of <decided to ~ halves if either of them found the treasure> **5 :** YIELD, WEIGH <striped bass that would ~ a hundred pounds> **6 a :** to put up with : TOLERATE — usu. used negatively <left because he couldn't ~ the noise> **b :** AFFORD <can't ~ the price> **c :** ENJOY <I could ~ a soda> — **go·er** \ˈgō(-ə)r\ *n*

syn GO, LEAVE, DEPART, QUIT, WITHDRAW, RETIRE *shared meaning element* : to move out of or away from the place where one is — **go about :** to set about : UNDERTAKE — **go after :** SEEK, PURSUE — **go all the way 1 :** to enter into complete agreement **2 :** to engage in sexual intercourse — **go ape 1 :** to become extremely angry or upset : lose control **2 :** to become highly excited or enthusiastic — **go at 1 a :** to make an attack on **b :** to make an approach to **2 :** UNDERTAKE — **go back on 1 :** ABANDON **2 :** BETRAY **3 :** FAIL — **go begging :** to be in little demand — **go by the board 1 :** to be carried over a ship's side **2 :** to be discarded — **go down the drain :** to become outmoded, discarded, or lost — **go down the line :** to give wholehearted support — **go fly a kite :** to stop being an annoyance or disturbance <got mad and told him to *go fly a kite*> — **go for 1 :** to pass for or serve as **2 :** to try to secure <he *went for* the last penny> **3 a :** FAVOR, ACCEPT <cannot *go for* your idea> **b :** to have an interest in or liking for <she *went for* him in a big way —Chandler Brossard> **4 :** ATTACK, ASSAIL <*went for* him when his back was turned> — **go for broke :** to put forth all one's strength or resources — **go great guns :** to achieve great success — **go hang :** to cease to be of interest or concern — **go into :** to be contained in <5 *goes into* 60 12 times> — **go it 1 :** to behave in a reckless, excited, or impromptu manner **2 :** to proceed in a rapid or furious manner **3 :** to conduct one's affairs : ACT <insists on *going it* alone> — **go one better :** OUTDO, SURPASS — **go over 1 :** EXAMINE **2 a :** REPEAT **b :** STUDY, REVIEW — **go places :** to be on the way to success — **go public** *of a close corporation* : to offer shares for sale to the general public — **go steady :** to date one person exclusively and frequently — **go the distance :** to complete a course of action : finish a contest in a specified capacity <the pitcher *went the distance* allowing only three runs on nine hits> — **go the vole :** to risk all for great gains — **go through 1 :** to subject to thorough examination, consideration, or study **2 :** EXPERIENCE, UNDERGO **3 :** to carry out : PERFORM <*went through* his work in a daze> — **go to bat for :** to give active support or assistance to : DEFEND, CHAMPION — **go to one's head 1 :** to cause one to become confused, excited, or dizzy **2 :** to cause one to become conceited or overconfident — **go to pieces :** to become shattered (as in nerves or health) — **go to town 1 :** to work or act rapidly or efficiently **2 :** to be markedly successful **3 :** to indulge oneself excessively — **go with :** DATE — **go without saying :** to be self-evident
[2]go \ˈgō\ *n, pl* **goes 1 :** the act or manner of going **2 :** the height of fashion : RAGE <elegant shawls labeled . . . "quite the ~" —R. S. Surtees> **3 :** an often unexpected turn of affairs : OCCURRENCE **4 :** the quantity used or furnished at one time <you can obtain a ~ of brandy for sixpence —C. B. Fairbanks> **5 :** ENERGY, VIGOR **6 a :** a turn in an activity (as a game) <told his opponent that it was his ~> **b :** ATTEMPT, TRY <have a ~ at painting> **7 :** a spell of activity <finished the job at one ~> **8 :** SUCCESS <made a ~ of the business> **9 :** permission to proceed : GO-AHEAD <gave the

astronauts a ~ for another orbit> — **no go :** to no avail : USELESS — **on the go :** constantly or restlessly active

[3]**go** *adj* : functioning properly : being in good and ready condition <declared all systems ~>

[4]**go** *n* [Jap] : an Oriental game played between two players who alternately place black and white stones on a board checkered by 19 vertical lines and 19 horizontal lines in an attempt to enclose the larger area on the board

GO *abbr* general order

[1]**goad** \'gōd\ *n* [ME *gode,* fr. OE *gād* spear, goad; akin to Langobardic *gaida* spear, Skt *hinoti* he urges on] **1 :** a pointed rod used to urge on an animal **2 a :** something that pricks like a goad : THORN **b :** something that urges or stimulates into action : SPUR ***syn*** see MOTIVE

[2]**goad** *vt* **1 :** to drive (as cattle) with a goad **2 :** to incite or rouse as if with a goad

[1]**go–ahead** \'gō-ə-ˌhed\ *adj* **1 :** marked by energy and enterprise : PROGRESSIVE <a vigorous ~ company> **2 :** indicating that one may proceed <~ signal>

[2]**go–ahead** *n* **1 a :** ENERGY, SPIRIT <had a great deal of courage and ~> **b :** one possessing go-ahead **2 :** a sign, signal, or authority to proceed : GREEN LIGHT

goal \'gōl, *chiefly in uncultivated or children's speech* 'gül\ *n* [ME *gol* boundary, limit] **1 :** the terminal point of a race **2 :** the end toward which effort is directed : AIM **3 a :** an area or object toward which players in various games attempt to advance a ball or puck and usu. through or into which it must go in order to score points **b :** the act or action of causing a ball or puck to go through or into such a goal **c :** the score resulting from such an act ***syn*** see INTENTION — **goal** *vi*

goal·ie \'gō-lē\ *n* : GOALKEEPER

goal·keep·er \'gōl-ˌkē-pər\ *n* : a player who defends the goal in any of various games (as hockey, lacrosse, or soccer)

goal kick *n* : a free kick in soccer awarded to a defensive player when the ball is driven out of bounds over the end line by an opposing player

goal line *n* : a line at either end and usu. running the width of a playing area on which a goal or goal post is situated

goal·mouth \'gōl-ˌmau̇th\ *n* : the area directly in front of the goal (as in soccer or hockey)

go along *vi* **1 :** to move along : PROCEED **2 :** to go or travel as a companion **3 :** to act in cooperation

goal·post \'gōl-ˌpōst\ *n* : one of usu. two vertical posts that with or without a crossbar constitute the goal in various games

goal·tend·er \'gōl-ˌten-dər\ *n* : GOALKEEPER

goal·tend·ing \-diŋ\ *n* **1 :** the act of guarding a goal (as in hockey) **2 :** the act of touching or deflecting a basketball that is on its downward path toward the basket or that is within the rim of the basket

Goa powder \ˌgō-ə-\ *n* [*Goa,* India] : a bitter powder found in the wood of a Brazilian leguminous tree (*Vataireopsis araroba*) and valued as the chief source of the drug chrysarobin

go–around \'gō-ə-ˌrau̇nd\ *n* **1 a :** ROUND <reached an apparent agreement during the first ~> **b :** a heated argument or struggle <had a real ~ with her about it> **2 :** RUNAROUND <he's been giving me the ~> **3 :** an act or instance of going around (as in an air traffic pattern)

go around \ˌgō-ə-'rau̇nd\ *vi* **1 a :** to pass from place to place : go here and there **b :** to have currency : CIRCULATE <an amusing story is *going around*> **2 :** to satisfy demand : fill the need <not enough jobs to *go around*>

goat \'gōt\ *n, pl* **goats** [ME *gote,* fr. OE *gāt;* akin to OHG *geiz* goat, L *haedus* kid] **1 a** *or pl* **goat :** any of various hollow-horned ruminant mammals (esp. of the genus *Capra*) related to the sheep but of lighter build and with backwardly arching horns, a short tail, and usu. straight hair **b** *cap* : CAPRICORN **2 :** a licentious man : LECHER **3 :** SCAPEGOAT — **goat·ish** \'gōt-ish\ *adj* — **goat·like** \-ˌlīk\ *adj*

goa·tee \gō-'tē\ *n* [fr. its resemblance to the beard of a he-goat] : a small pointed or tufted beard on a man's chin

goat·fish \'gōt-ˌfish\ *n* : MULLET 2

goat·herd \-ˌhərd\ *n* : one who tends goats

goat·skin \-ˌskin\ *n* **1 :** the skin of a goat **2 :** leather made from goatskin

goat·suck·er \-ˌsək-ər\ *n* : any of a family (Caprimulgidae) of medium-sized long-winged crepuscular or nocturnal birds (as the whippoorwills and nighthawks) having a short wide bill, short legs, and soft mottled plumage and feeding on insects which they catch on the wing

[1]**gob** \'gäb\ *n* [ME *gobbe,* fr. MF *gobe* large piece of food, back-formation fr. *gobet*] **1 :** LUMP **2 :** a large amount — usu. used in pl. <~*s* of money>

[2]**gob** *n* [origin unknown] : SAILOR

gob·bet \'gäb-ət\ *n* [ME *gobet,* fr. MF, mouthful, piece] **1 :** a piece or portion (as of meat) **2 :** LUMP, MASS **3 :** a small quantity of liquid : DROP

[1]**gob·ble** \'gäb-əl\ *vt* **gob·bled; gob·bling** \-(ə-)liŋ\ [prob. irreg. fr. [1]*gob*] **1 :** to swallow or eat greedily **2 :** to take eagerly : GRAB — often used with *up* **3 :** to read rapidly or greedily — often used with *up*

[2]**gobble** *vi* **gob·bled; gob·bling** \-(ə-)liŋ\ [imit.] **1 :** to make the natural guttural noise of a male turkey **2 :** to make a sound resembling the gobble of a turkey — **gobble** *n*

gob·ble·dy·gook *or* **gob·ble·de·gook** \ˌgäb-əl-dē-'gu̇k, -'gük\ *n* [irreg. fr. *gobble,* n.] : wordy and generally unintelligible jargon

gob·bler \'gäb-lər\ *n* : a male turkey

Go·be·lin \'gō-bə-lən, 'gäb-ə-\ *adj* [*Gobelin* dyehouse and tapestry works, Paris, France] : of, relating to, or characteristic of tapestry produced at the Gobelin works in Paris — **Gobelin** *n*

go–be·tween \'gō-bə-ˌtwēn\ *n* : an intermediate agent : BROKER

gob·let \'gäb-lət\ *n* [ME *gobelet,* fr. MF] **1** *archaic* : a bowl-shaped drinking vessel without handles **2 :** a drinking vessel (as of glass) with a foot and stem — compare TUMBLER

goblet cell *n* [fr. its shape] : a mucus-secreting epithelial cell (as of intestinal columnar epithelium) that is distended at the free end

gob·lin \'gäb-lən\ *n* [ME *gobelin,* fr. MF, fr. ML *gobelinus,* deriv. of Gk *kobalos* rogue] : an ugly or grotesque sprite that is michievous and sometimes evil and malicious

go·bo \'gō-(ˌ)bō\ *n, pl* **gobos** *also* **goboes** [origin unknown] **1 :** a dark strip (as of wallboard) to shield a motion-picture or television camera from light **2 :** a device to shield a microphone from sound

go·by \'gō-bē\ *n, pl* **gobies** *also* **goby** [L *gobius* gudgeon, fr. Gk *kōbios*] : any of numerous spiny-finned fishes (family Gobiidae) with the pelvic fins thoracic and often united to form a sucking disk

go by *vi* **1 :** PASS <as time *goes by*> **2 :** to make a brief visit : CALL <all the family was at home when we *went by* yesterday>

go–cart \'gō-ˌkärt\ *n* **1 a :** WALKER **b :** STROLLER **2 :** HANDCART **3 :** a light open carriage

[1]**god** \'gäd *also* 'gȯd\ *n* [ME, fr. OE; akin to OHG *got* god] **1** *cap* : the supreme or ultimate reality: as **a :** the Being perfect in power, wisdom, and goodness whom men worship as creator and ruler of the universe **b** *Christian Science* : the incorporeal divine Principle ruling over all as eternal Spirit : infinite Mind **2 :** a being or object believed to have more than natural attributes and powers and to require man's worship; *specif* : one controlling a particular aspect or part of reality **3 :** a person or thing of supreme value **4 :** a powerful ruler

[2]**god** *vt* **god·ded; god·ding :** to treat as a god : IDOLIZE, DEIFY

god–aw·ful \gäd-'ō-fəl\ *adj* [*god*damned + *awful*] : extremely unpleasant or disagreeable : ABOMINABLE <~ explosions of violence —*Playboy*>

god·child \'gäd-ˌchīld *also* 'gȯd-\ *n* : a person for whom another person becomes sponsor at baptism

[1]**god·damn** *or* **god·dam** \'gäd-'dam\ *n, often cap* : DAMN <they were in no mood to give a good ~ about anything —Robert Lowry>

[2]**goddamn** *or* **goddam** *vb, often cap, vt* : DAMN <I'll be ~*ed*> ~ *vi* : DAMN <you feel like swearing and ~*ing* worse and worse —Ernest Hemingway>

[1]**god·damned** \ˌgäd-ˌdam(d)\ *or* **god·damn** *or* **god·dam** \-ˌdam\ *adj* : DAMNED

[2]**goddamned** *or* **goddamn** *or* **goddam** *adv* : DAMNED

god·daugh·ter \'gäd-ˌdȯt-ər *also* 'gȯd-\ *n* : a female godchild

god·dess \'gäd-əs\ *n* **1 :** a female god **2 :** a woman whose great charm or beauty arouses adoration

go–dev·il \'gō-ˌdev-əl\ *n* : any of various devices: as **a :** a weight formerly dropped in a bored hole (as of an oil well) to explode a cartridge previously lowered **b :** a cleaning scraper rotated and propelled through a pipeline by the force of the flowing fluid **c :** a handcar or small gasoline car used on a railroad for transporting laborers and supplies

[1]**god·fa·ther** \'gäd-ˌfa̱th-ər *also* 'gȯd-\ *n* **1 :** a man who sponsors a person at baptism **2 :** one having a relation to someone or something analogous to that of a male sponsor to his godchild <made him the ~ of a whole generation of rebels —*Times Lit. Supp.*>

[2]**godfather** *vt* : to act as godfather to

God–fear·ing \-ˌfi(ə)r-iŋ\ *adj* : having a reverent feeling toward God : DEVOUT

god·for·sak·en \-fər-ˌsā-kən\ *adj* **1 :** situated in a remote or desolate place <a ~ deserted road> **2 :** neglected in appearance : DISMAL <the toughest, dreariest, most ~ looking country —Richard Bissell> **3 :** pitiable in circumstances : MISERABLE <poor ~ orphans>

god·head \-ˌhed\ *n* [ME *godhed,* fr. *god* + *-hed* -hood; akin to ME *-hod* -hood] **1 :** divine nature or essence : DIVINITY **2** *cap* **a :** GOD 1 **b :** the nature of God esp. as existing in three persons — used with *the*

god·hood \-ˌhu̇d\ *n* : DIVINITY

Go·di·va \gə-'dī-və\ *n* : an English earl's wife who in legend rode naked through Coventry to save the citizens from a tax

god·less \'gäd-ləs *also* 'gȯd-\ *adj* : not acknowledging a deity or divine law — **god·less·ness** *n*

god·like \-ˌlīk\ *adj* : resembling or having the qualities of God or a god : DIVINE — **god·like·ness** *n*

god·ling \-liŋ\ *n* : an inferior or local god

god·ly \-lē\ *adj* **god·li·er; -est 1 :** DIVINE **2 :** PIOUS, DEVOUT — **god·li·ness** *n* — **godly** *adv*

god·moth·er \-ˌmə̱th-ər\ *n* : a woman who sponsors a person at baptism

go·down \'gō-ˌdau̇n\ *n* [Malay *gudang*] : a warehouse in an oriental country

go down *vi* **1 a :** to fall to or as if to the ground <the plane *went down* in flames> **b :** to go below the horizon : SET <the sun *went down*> **c :** to become submerged : SINK <the ship *went down* with all hands> **2 :** to admit of being swallowed <the medicine *went down* easily> **3 :** to undergo defeat **4 a :** to find acceptance <will the plan *go down* with the farmers> **b :** to come to be remembered esp. in posterity <he will *go down* in history as a great president> **5 :** to undergo a decline or decrease <the fever *went down*> <the market is *going down*> **6** *Brit* : to leave a university — **go down on :** to perform fellatio or cunnilingus on

god·par·ent \'gäd-ˌpar-ənt, -ˌper- *also* 'gȯd-\ *n* : a sponsor at baptism

God's acre *n* : CHURCHYARD

god·send \'gäd-ˌsend *also* 'gȯd-\ *n* [back-formation fr. *god-sent*] : a desirable or needed thing or event that comes unexpectedly

god·son \-ˌsən\ *n* : a male godchild

ə abut	ᵊ kitten	ər further	a back	ā bake	ä cot, cart	
au̇ out	ch chin	e less	ē easy	g gift	i trip	ī life
j joke	ŋ sing	ō flow	ȯ flaw	ȯi coin	th thin	th this
ü loot	u̇ foot	y yet	yü few	yu̇ furious	zh vision	

God·speed \-ˈspēd\ *n* [ME *god speid,* fr. the phrase *God spede you* God prosper you] : a prosperous journey : SUCCESS <bade him ~>

god·wit \ˈgäd-ˌwit\ *n* [origin unknown] : any of a genus (*Limosa*) of long-billed wading birds related to the snipes but similar to curlews

goe·thite \ˈgə(r)-ˌtīt\ *n* [G *göthit,* fr. J. W. von *Goethe*] : a mineral $HFeO_2$ that consists of an iron hydrogen oxide and is the commonest constituent of many forms of natural rust

gof·fer \ˈgäf-ər, ˈgȯf-\ *vt* [F *gaufrer*] : to crimp, plait, or flute (as linen or lace) esp. with a heated iron — **goffer** *n*

go–get·ter \ˈgō-ˌget-ər\ *n* : an aggressively enterprising person : HUSTLER — **go–get·ting** \-ˌget-iŋ\ *adj or n*

1gog·gle \ˈgäg-əl\ *vi* **gog·gled; gog·gling** \-(ə-)liŋ\ [ME *gogelen* to squint] : to stare with wide or protuberant eyes — **gog·gler** \-(ə-)lər\ *n*

2goggle *adj* : PROTUBERANT, STARING <~ eyes> — **gog·gly** \ˈgäg-(ə-)lē\ *adj*

gog·gle–eye \ˈgäg-ə-ˌlī\ *n* **1** : ROCK BASS 1 **2** : WARMOUTH

gog·gle–eyed \ˌgäg-ə-ˈlīd\ *adj* : having bulging or rolling eyes

gog·gles \ˈgäg-əlz\ *n pl* : protective glasses set in a flexible frame (as of rubber or plastic) that fits snugly against the face

go–go \ˈgō-(ˌ)gō\ *adj* [*a-go-go*] **1 a** : of, relating to, or being a discotheque or the music or dances performed there **b** : employed to entertain in a discotheque <~ dancers> **2 a** : not conservative : UNRESTRAINED <~ baseball> **b** : very up-to-date : HIP **c** : using such tools of speculation as leverage and short selling : SPECULATIVE <a ~ mutual fund>

1Goi·del·ic \gȯi-ˈdel-ik\ *adj* [MIr *Gōidel* Gael] **1** : of, relating to, or characteristic of the Gaels **2** : of, relating to, or constituting Goidelic

2Goidelic *n* : the branch of the Celtic languages that includes Irish Gaelic, Scottish Gaelic, and Manx — see INDO-EUROPEAN LANGUAGES table

go in *vi* **1 a** : ENTER **b** : to make an approach (as in attacking) **2 a** : to take part in a game or contest **b** : to call the opening bet in poker : STAY **3** *of a celestial body* : to become obscured by a cloud **4** : to form a union or alliance : JOIN — often used with *with* <asked the rest of us to *go in* with them> — **go in for** **1** : to give support to : ADVOCATE **2** : to have or show an interest in or a liking for **3** : to engage in : take part in

1go·ing \ˈgō-iŋ, ˈgȯ(-)iŋ\ *n* **1** : an act or instance of going **2** *pl* : BEHAVIOR, ACTIONS <for his eyes are upon the ways of man, and he seeth all hi: ~*s* —Job 34:21 (AV)> **3** : the condition of the ground (as f(r walking) **4** : advance toward an objective : PROGRESS <fo nd the ~ too slow and gave up the job>

2going *adj* **1 a** : that goes — often used in combination <easy*going*> <out*going*> **b** : WORKING, MOVING <everything was in ~ order> **2** : LIVING, EXISTING <the best novelist ~> **3** : CURRENT, PREVAILING <~ price> **4** : conducting business with the expectation of indefinite continuance <~ concern> — **going on** : drawing near to : APPROACHING

go·ing–over \ˌgō-iŋ-ˈō-vər, ˌgȯ(-)iŋ-\ *n, pl* **go·ings–over** **1** : a thorough examination or investigation **2 a** : a severe scolding **b** : BEATING

go·ings–on \ˌgō-iŋ-ˈzȯn, (ˌ)gȯ(-)iŋ-, -ˈzän\ *n pl* **1** : ACTIONS, EVENTS <studying the ~ in the . . . world around her —Jean C. Jones> **2** : irregular or reprehensible happenings or conduct <titillating stories about the ~ of the carefree millionaires —Eleanor Early>

goi·ter *also* **goi·tre** \ˈgȯit-ər\ *n* [F *goitre,* fr. MF, back-formation fr. *goitron* throat, fr. (assumed) VL *guttrion-, guttrio,* fr. L *guttur* — more at COT] : an enlargement of the thyroid gland visible as a swelling of the front of the neck — compare HYPERTHYROIDISM, HYPOTHYROIDISM — **goi·trous** \ˈgȯi-trəs, ˈgȯit-ə-rəs\ *adj*

goi·tro·gen \ˈgȯi-trə-jən\ *n* : a substance (as thiourea or thiouracil) that induces goiter formation

goi·tro·gen·ic \ˌgȯi-trə-ˈjen-ik\ *also* **goi·ter·o·gen·ic** \ˌgȯit-ə-rō-ˈjen-\ *adj* : producing or tending to produce goiter — **goi·tro·ge·nic·i·ty** \ˌgȯi-trə-jə-ˈnis-ət-ē\ *n*

Gol·con·da \gäl-ˈkän-də\ *n* [*Golconda,* India, famous for its diamonds] : a rich mine; *broadly* : a source of great wealth

gold \ˈgōld\ *n, often attrib* [ME, fr. OE; akin to OE *geolu* yellow — more at YELLOW] **1** : a malleable ductile yellow metallic element that occurs chiefly free or in a few minerals and is used esp. in coins, jewelry, and dentures — see ELEMENT table **2 a** (1) : gold coins (2) : a gold piece **b** : MONEY **c** : GOLD STANDARD **3** : a variable color averaging deep yellow **4** : something resembling gold; *esp* : something valued as the finest of its kind <a heart of ~>

gold·beat·er \ˈgōl(d)-ˌbēt-ər\ *n* : one that beats gold into gold leaf — **gold·beat·ing** \-ˌbēt-iŋ\ *n*

1gold·brick \-ˌbrik\ *n* **1 a** : a worthless brick that appears to be of gold **b** : something that appears to be valuable but is actually worthless **2** : a person (as a soldier) who shirks assigned work

2goldbrick *vt* : SWINDLE ~ *vi* : to shirk duty or responsibility : goof off

gold·bug \-ˌbəg\ *n* : a supporter of the gold standard

Gold Democrat *n* : a member of the Democratic party favoring the gold standard; *esp* : one supporting an independent ticket in the presidential election of 1896

gold digger *n* : a woman who uses feminine charm to extract money or gifts from men

gold·en \ˈgōl-dən\ *adj* **1** : consisting of, relating to, or containing gold **2 a** : having the color of gold **b** : BLOND 1a **3** : LUSTROUS, SHINING **4** : of a high degree of excellence : SUPERB **5** : PROSPEROUS, FLOURISHING <~ days> **6 a** : radiantly youthful and vigorous **b** : possessing talents that promise worldly success — often used with *boy* **c** : highly favored : POPULAR **7** : FAVORABLE, ADVANTAGEOUS <a ~ opportunity> **8** : of, relating to, or marking a 50th anniversary **9** : MELLOW, RESONANT <a smooth ~ tenor> — **gold·en·ly** *adv* — **gold·en·ness** \-dən-(n)əs\ *n*

golden age *n* : a period of great happiness, prosperity, and achievement

gold·en·ag·er \ˈgōl-də-ˌnā-jər\ *n* : an elderly and often retired person usu. engaging in club activities

golden al·ex·an·ders \-ˌal-ig-ˈzan-dərz, -ˌel-\ *n pl but sing or pl in constr, often cap A* [ML *alexandrum*] : a showy No. American yellow-flowered perennial herb (*Zizia aurea*) of the carrot family that occurs in moist woods and meadows; *also* : any of several related herbs

golden club *n* : an American aquatic plant (*Orontium aquaticum*) of the arum family with a spadix of minute yellow flowers

golden eagle *n* : a large eagle (*Aquila chrysaëtos*) of the northern hemisphere with brownish yellow tips on the head and neck feathers

gold·en·eye \ˈgōl-də-ˌnī\ *n* **1 a** : a large-headed swift-flying Holarctic diving duck (*Bucephala clangula*) having the male strikingly marked in black and white **b** : a closely related duck **2** : a lacewing (family Chrysopidae) with yellow eyes

Golden Fleece *n* : a fleece of gold placed by the king of Colchis in a dragon-guarded grove and recovered by the Argonauts

golden glow *n* : a tall branching composite herb (*Rudbeckia laciniata hortensia*) with showy yellow much-doubled flower heads

golden hamster *n* : a small tawny hamster (*Mesocricetus auratus*) native to Asia Minor but kept as a pet in many parts of the world

Golden Horde *n* [fr. the golden tent of the Mongol ruler] : a body of Mongol Tatars that overran eastern Europe in the 13th century and dominated Russia until 1486

golden mean *n* : the medium between extremes : MODERATION

golden nematode *n* : a small yellowish Old World nematode worm (*Heterodera rostochiensis*) established locally as a pest of potatoes in eastern No. America

gold·en·rain tree \ˌgōl-dən-ˈrān-\ *n* : a round-headed tree (*Koelreuteria paniculata* of the family Sapindaceae) that has very long showy clusters of yellow flowers

golden retriever *n* : a medium-sized golden-coated retriever developed by interbreeding Russian shepherd dogs with bloodhounds

gold·en·rod \ˈgōl-dən-ˌräd\ *n* : any of numerous chiefly No. American composite biennial or perennial plants (esp. of the genus *Solidago*) with stems resembling wands and heads of small yellow or sometimes white flowers often clustered in panicles — compare RAYLESS GOLDENROD

golden rule *n* **1** : a rule of ethical conduct referring to Mt 7:12 and Lk 6:31 and stating that one should do to others as he would have others do to him **2** : a guiding principle

gold·en·seal \ˈgōl-dən-ˌsēl\ *n* : a perennial American herb (*Hydrastis canadensis*) of the crowfoot family with large rounded leaves and a thick knotted yellow rootstock sometimes used in pharmacy — compare HYDRASTIS

golden section *n* : division of a line or the proportion of a geometrical figure such that the smaller dimension is to the greater as the greater is to the whole

golden shiner *n* : a common cyprinid fish (*Notemigonus crysoleucas*) of eastern No. America having silvery sides with bright golden reflections

golden yellow *n* **1** : a vivid or light yellow **2** : a moderate to strong orange yellow

gold·field \ˈgōl(d)-ˌfēld\ *n* : a gold-mining district

gold–filled \-ˈfild\ *adj* : covered with a layer of gold so as to constitute filled gold <~ bracelet>

gold·finch \-ˌfinch\ *n* **1** : a small largely red, black, and yellow European finch (*Carduelis carduelis*) often kept as a cage bird **2** : any of several small American finches (genus *Spinus*) typically having the male in summer plumage variably yellow with black wings, tail, and crown

1gold·fish \-ˌfish\ *n* : a small usu. golden yellow or orange cyprinid fish (*Carassius auratus*) much used as an aquarium and pond fish

2goldfish *adj* [fr. the keeping of goldfish in transparent bowls] : exposed to public view <had patiently endured this ~ life —*Time*>

gold leaf *n* : a sheet of gold ordinarily varying from four to five millionths of an inch in thickness that is used esp. for gilding

gold mine *n* : a rich source of something desired (as information)

gold of pleasure : an annual herb (*Camelina sativa*) of the mustard family formerly grown for its oil-rich seeds

gold rush *n* **1** : a rush to newly discovered goldfields in pursuit of riches **2** : the headlong pursuit of sudden wealth in a new or lucrative field

gold·smith \ˈgōl(d)-ˌsmith\ *n* : one who makes or deals in articles of gold

gold standard *n* : a monetary standard under which the basic unit of currency is defined by a stated quantity of gold and which is usu. characterized by the coinage and circulation of gold, unrestricted convertibility of other money into gold, and the free export and import of gold for the settlement of international obligations

gold·stone \ˈgōl(d)-ˌstōn\ *n* : aventurine glass spangled close and fine with particles of gold-colored material

go·lem \ˈgō-ləm, ˈgȯi-, ˈgā-\ *n* [Yiddish *goylem,* fr. Heb *gōlem* shapeless mass] **1** : an artificial human being of Hebrew folklore endowed with life **2** : something resembling a golem: as **a** : AUTOMATON **b** : BLOCKHEAD

golf \ˈgälf, ˈgȯlf, ˈgäf, ˈgȯf\ *n, often attrib* [ME (Sc)] : a game in which a player using special clubs attempts to sink a ball into each of the 9 or 18 successive holes on a course with as few strokes as possible — **golf** *vi*

Golf — a communications code word for the letter *g*

golf bag *n* : a usu. tubular bag with outside pockets that is designed to carry golf equipment (as clubs, balls, and clothing)

golf cart *n* **1** : a small cart for wheeling a golf bag around a golf course **2** : a motorized cart for carrying a golfer and his equipment over a golf course — called also *golf car*

golf course *n* : an area of land laid out for the game of golf with a series of 9 or 18 holes each including tee, fairway, and putting green and often one or more natural or artificial hazards — called also *golf links*

golf·er *n* : one who plays golf

golf·ing *n* : the sport or practice of playing golf

golf widow *n* : a woman whose husband spends much time on the golf course

Gol·gi \ˈgȯl-(ˌ)jē\ *adj* : of or relating to the Golgi apparatus, Golgi bodies, or a method of staining for them <~ vesicles>

Golgi apparatus *n* [Camillo *Golgi*] : a cytoplasmic component that prob. plays a part in elaboration and secretion of cell products and appears in electron microscopy as a series of parallel sometimes vesicular membranes without ribosomes — called also *Golgi complex*

Golgi body *n* : a discrete particle of the Golgi apparatus as observed in a stained preparation

go·liard \ˈgōl-yərd, -ˌyärd\ *n* [F] : a wandering student of the 12th or 13th century given to the writing of satiric Latin verse and to convivial living and minstrelsy — **go·liar·dic** \gōl-ˈyärd-ik\ *adj*

Go·li·ath \gə-ˈlī-əth\ *n* [Heb *Golyath*] **1** : a Philistine champion who in I Samuel 17 is killed by David in single combat **2** : GIANT <slug it out with business ~*s* —Warner Olivier>

gol·li·wog *or* **gol·li·wogg** \ˈgäl-ē-ˌwäg\ *n* [*Golliwogg*, an animated doll in children's fiction by Bertha Upton] **1** : a grotesque black doll **2** : a grotesque person

gom·er·al *or* **gom·er·il** \ˈgäm-(ə-)rəl\ *n* [origin unknown] *Scot* : SIMPLETON, FOOL

gom·pho·sis \gäm-ˈfō-səs\ *n, pl* **-pho·ses** [NL, fr. Gk *gomphōsis*, lit., a bolting together] : an immovable articulation in which a hard part is received into a bone cavity (as the teeth into the jaws)

gon- *or* **gono-** *comb form* [Gk, fr. *gonos* procreation, seed, fr. *gignesthai* to be born — more at KIN] : sexual : generative : semen : seed <*gono*duct>

-gon \ˌgän *also* -gən\ *n comb form* [NL *-gonum*, fr. Gk *-gōnon*, fr. *gōnia* angle; akin to Gk *gony* knee — more at KNEE] : figure having (so many) angles <deca*gon*>

go·nad \ˈgō-ˌnad\ *n* [NL *gonad-*, *gonas*, fr. Gk *gonos*] : one of the primary sex glands that include the ovaries and testes — **go·nad·al** \gō-ˈnad-ᵊl\ *adj*

go·nad·ec·to·my \ˌgō-nə-ˈdek-tə-mē\ *n, pl* **-mies** : surgical removal of an ovary or testis — **go·nad·ec·to·mized** \-ˌmīzd\ *adj*

go·nad·o·tro·phic \gō-ˌnad-ə-ˈtrō-fik, -ˈträf-ik\ *or* **go·nad·o·trop·ic** \-ˈträp-ik\ *adj* [ISV] : acting on or stimulating the gonads

go·nad·o·tro·phin \-ˈtrō-fən\ *or* **go·nad·o·tro·pin** \-pən\ *n* : a gonadotrophic hormone (as follicle-stimulating hormone)

Gond \ˈgänd\ *n* : a member of a Dravidian or pre-Dravidian people of central India

Gondi \ˈgän-dē\ *n* : the Dravidian language of the Gonds

gon·do·la \ˈgän-də-lə (*usual for sense 1*), gän-ˈdō-\ *n* [It, fr. ML *gondula*, dim. of (assumed) VL *condua*] **1** : a long narrow flat-bottomed boat with a high prow and stern used on the canals of Venice **2** : a heavy flat-bottomed boat used on New England rivers and on the Ohio and Mississippi rivers **3** : a railroad car with no top, a flat bottom, and fixed sides that is used chiefly for hauling heavy bulk commodities **4 a** : an elongated car attached to the underside of an airship **b** : an often spherical airtight enclosure suspended from a balloon for carrying passengers or instruments **c** : an enclosed car suspended from a cable and used for transporting passengers; *esp* : one used as a ski lift **5** : an upholstered chair whose back curves forward at both sides to form the arms **6** : a fixture approachable from all sides used in self-service retail stores to display merchandise **7** : a motortruck or trailer having a large hopper-shaped container for transporting mixed concrete

gondola 1

gon·do·lier \ˌgän-də-ˈli(ə)r\ *n* : the boatman who propels a gondola

Gon·dwa·ni·an \gän-ˈdwän-ē-ən\ *adj* : of or relating to the hypothetical prehistoric landmass Gondwana

gone \ˈgȯn *also* ˈgän\ *adj* [fr. pp. of *go*] **1** : PAST <memories of ~ summers —John Cheever> **2 a** : INVOLVED, ABSORBED <far ~ in hysteria> **b** : possessed with a strong attachment or a foolish or unreasoning love or desire : INFATUATED — often used with *on* <was real ~ on that man —Pete Martin> **c** : PREGNANT <she's six months ~> **3 a** : DEAD **b** : LOST, RUINED <unless you're prepared to scuffle . . . you're a ~ goose —Warren Burnett> **c** : characterized by sinking or dropping <the empty or ~ feeling in the abdomen so common in elevators —H. G. Armstrong> **4** *slang* : GREAT <a real ~ fashion reporter —Inez Robb>

gon·er \ˈgȯn-ər *also* ˈgän-ər\ *n* : one whose case is hopeless <if you fall behind . . . you're ~*s* —Kenneth Roberts>

gon·fa·lon \ˈgän-fə-ˌlän, -lən\ *n* [It *gonfalone*] **1** : the ensign of certain princes or states (as the medieval republics of Italy) **2** : a flag that hangs from a crosspiece or frame

gon·fa·lon·ier \ˌgän-fə-ˌlä-ˈni(ə)r, -lə-\ *n* : one who bears a gonfalon

gong \ˈgäŋ, ˈgȯŋ\ *n* [Malay & Jav, of imit. origin] **1** : a disk-shaped percussion instrument that produces a resounding tone when struck with a usu. padded hammer **2 a** : a flat saucer-shaped bell **b** : a wire rod wound in a flat spiral for sounding the time or chime or alarm (as in a clock) — **gong** *vi*

Gon·go·rism \ˈgäŋ-gə-ˌriz-əm\ *n* [Sp *gongorismo*, fr. Luis de *Góngora* y Argote †1627 Sp poet] : a literary style characterized by studied obscurity and by the use of various ornate devices — **gon·go·ris·tic** \ˌgäŋ-gə-ˈris-tik\ *adj*

goni- *or* **gonio-** *comb form* [Gk *gōnia*] : corner : angle <*gonio*meter>

go·nid·i·al \gō-ˈnid-ē-əl\ *adj* : of or relating to a gonidium

go·nid·i·um \-ē-əm\ *n, pl* **-ia** \-ē-ə\ [NL, fr. *gon-* + *-idium*] **1** : an asexual reproductive cell or group of cells in or on a gametophyte **2** : a green chlorophyll-bearing cell within the thallus of a lichen

go·ni·om·e·ter \ˌgō-nē-ˈäm-ət-ər\ *n* **1** : an instrument for measuring angles **2** : DIRECTION FINDER — **go·nio·met·ric** \-nē-ə-ˈme-trik\ *adj* — **go·ni·om·e·try** \-nē-ˈäm-ə-trē\ *n*

gono·coc·cus \ˌgän-ə-ˈkäk-əs\ *n, pl* **-coc·ci** \-ˈkäk-ˌ(s)ī, -ˈkäk-(ˌ)(s)ē\ [NL] : a pus-producing bacterium (*Neisseria gonorrhoeae*) that causes gonorrhea — **gono·coc·cal** \-ˈkäk-əl\ *or* **gono·coc·cic** \-ˈkäk-(s)ik\ *adj*

gono·cyte \ˈgän-ə-ˌsīt\ *n* [ISV] : a cell that produces gametes; *esp* : GAMETOCYTE

gono·gen·e·sis \ˌgän-ə-ˈjen-ə-səs\ *n* [NL] : maturation of germ cells that includes oogenesis and spermatogenesis

gon·oph \ˈgän-əf\ *var of* GANEF

gono·phore \ˈgän-ə-ˌfō(ə)r, -ˌfȯ(ə)r\ *n* [ISV] **1** : a sporophyll-bearing prolongation of a plant axis **2** : an attached reproductive zooid of a hydroid colony — **gono·phor·ic** \ˌgän-ə-ˈfȯr-ik, -ˈfōr-\ *adj* — **go·noph·o·rous** \gə-ˈnäf-ə-rəs, gä-\ *adj*

gono·pore \ˈgän-ə-ˌpō(ə)r, -ˌpȯ(ə)r\ *n* : a genital pore

gon·or·rhea \ˌgän-ə-ˈrē-ə\ *n* [NL, fr. LL, morbid loss of semen, fr. Gk *gonorrhoia*, fr. *gon-* + *-rrhoia* -rrhea] : a contagious inflammation of the genital mucous membrane caused by the gonococcus — called also *clap* — **gon·or·rhe·al** \-ˈrē-əl\ *adj*

-g·o·ny \g-ə-nē\ *n comb form* [L *-gonia*, fr. Gk, fr. *gonos*] : generation : reproduction : manner of coming into being <sporo*gony*>

goo \ˈgü\ *n* [perh. alter. of *glue*] **1** : a viscid or sticky substance **2** : cloying sentimentality — **goo·ey** \-ē\ *adj*

goo·ber \ˈgü-bər, ˈgu̇b-ər\ *n* [of African origin; akin to Kongo *nguba* peanut] *South & Midland* : PEANUT

[1]**good** \ˈgu̇d\ *adj* **bet·ter** \ˈbet-ər\; **best** \ˈbest\ [ME, fr. OE *gōd*; akin to OHG *guot* good, Skt *gadh* to hold fast] **1 a** (1) : of a favorable character or tendency <~ news> (2) : BOUNTIFUL, FERTILE <~ land> (3) : HANDSOME, ATTRACTIVE <~ looks> **b** (1) : SUITABLE, FIT <~ to eat> (2) : free from injury or disease : WHOLE <one ~ arm> (3) : not depreciated <bad money drives out ~> (4) : commercially sound <a ~ risk> (5) : certain to last or live <~ for another year> (6) : certain to pay or contribute <~ for a hundred dollars> (7) : certain to elicit a specified result <always ~ for a laugh> (8) : PROFITABLE, ADVANTAGEOUS <made a very ~ deal> **c** (1) : AGREEABLE, PLEASANT (2) : SALUTARY, WHOLESOME <~ for a cold> (3) : AMUSING, CLEVER <a ~ joke> **d** (1) : CONSIDERABLE, AMPLE <a ~ margin> (2) : FULL <weighs a ~ 200 pounds —*Current Biog.*> **e** (1) : WELL-FOUNDED, COGENT <~ reasons> (2) : TRUE <holds ~ for society at large> (3) : REAL, ACTUALIZED <made ~ his promises> (4) : deserving of respect : HONORABLE <in ~ standing> (5) : legally valid or effectual <~ title> **f** (1) : ADEQUATE, SATISFACTORY <~ care> (2) : conforming to a standard <~ English> (3) : CHOICE, DISCRIMINATING <~ taste> (4) : containing less fat and being less tender than higher grades — used of meat and esp. of beef **2 a** (1) : VIRTUOUS, JUST, COMMENDABLE <a ~ man> (2) : RIGHT <~ conduct> (3) : KIND, BENEVOLENT <~ intentions> **b** : UPPER-CLASS <a ~ family> **c** : COMPETENT, SKILLFUL <a ~ doctor> **d** : LOYAL <a ~ party man> <a ~ Catholic> — **good·ish** \ˈgu̇d-ish\ *adj* — **as good as** : in effect : VIRTUALLY <*as good as* dead> — **as good as gold 1** : of the highest worth or reliability <his promise is *as good as gold*> **2** : well-behaved <the child was *as good as gold*> — **good and** \ˌgu̇d-ᵊn\ : VERY, ENTIRELY <was *good and* mad>

[2]**good** *n* **1 a** : something that is good **b** (1) : something conforming to the moral order of the universe (2) : praiseworthy character : GOODNESS **c** : a good element or portion **2** : PROSPERITY, BENEFIT <for the ~ of the community> **3 a** : something that has economic utility or satisfies an economic want **b** *pl* : personal property having intrinsic value but usu. excluding money, securities, and negotiable instruments **c** *pl* : CLOTH **d** *pl* : WARES, COMMODITIES, MERCHANDISE <canned ~*s*> **4** : good persons — used with *the* <the ~ die young> **5** *pl* : proof of wrongdoing <didn't have the ~*s* on him —T. G. Cooke> — **for good** : FOREVER, PERMANENTLY — **in good with** : in a favored or preferred position with — **to the good 1** : for the best : BENEFICIAL <the government's efforts to restrict credit were all *to the good* — *Time*> **2** : in a position of net gain or profit <he wound up the game $10 *to the good*>

[3]**good** *adv* : WELL <he showed me how ~ I was doing —Herbert Gold>

good book *n, often cap G&B* : BIBLE

good–bye *or* **good–by** \gu̇d-ˈbī, gə(d)-\ *n* [alter. of *God be with you*] : a concluding remark or gesture at parting

good fellow *n* : an affable companionable person — **good–fel·low·ship** \ˈgu̇d-ˈfel-ō-ˌship, -ˈfel-ə-\ *n*

[1]**good–for–noth·ing** \ˈgu̇d-fər-ˌnəth-iŋ\ *adj* : of no value : USELESS, WORTHLESS <he was fat, lazy, ~ —C. G. Norris>

[2]**good–for–nothing** *n* : an idle worthless person

Good Friday *n* [fr. its special sanctity] : the Friday before Easter observed in churches as the anniversary of the crucifixion of Christ and in some states of the U.S. as a legal holiday

good–heart·ed \ˈgu̇d-ˈhärt-əd\ *adj* : having a kindly generous disposition — **good–heart·ed·ly** *adv* — **good–heart·ed·ness** *n*

good–hu·mored \-ˈ(h)yü-mərd\ *adj* : GOOD-NATURED, CHEERFUL — **good–hu·mored·ly** *adv* — **good–hu·mored·ness** *n*

good life *n* **1** : a virtuous life **2** : a life marked by a high standard of living

good–look·ing \ˈgu̇d-ˈlu̇k-iŋ\ *adj* : having a pleasing or attractive appearance — **good–look·er** \-ˈlu̇k-ər\ *n*

good·ly \ˈgu̇d-lē\ *adj* **good·li·er; -est 1** : pleasantly attractive : HANDSOME **2** : significantly large : CONSIDERABLE <a ~ number>

good·man \ˈgu̇d-mən\ *n* **1** *archaic* : the master of a household **2** *archaic* : MR.

ə abut	ᵊ kitten	ər further	a back	ā bake	ä cot, cart
au̇ out	ch chin	e less	ē easy	g gift	i trip	ī life
j joke	ŋ sing	ō flow	ȯ flaw	ȯi coin	th thin	th this
ü loot	u̇ foot	y yet	yü few	yu̇ furious	zh vision

good–na·tured \-ˈnā-chərd\ *adj* **:** of a pleasant cheerful cooperative disposition ***syn*** see AMIABLE ***ant*** contrary — **good–na·tured·ly** *adv* — **good–na·tured·ness** *n*

good–neighbor *adj* **:** marked by principles of friendship, cooperation, and noninterference in the internal affairs of another country <ambassadors of goodwill in advancing the ~ policy —Norman Cousins>

good·ness \ˈgu̇d-nəs\ *n* **1 :** the quality or state of being good **2 :** the nutritious, flavorful, or beneficial portion or element of something <boil all the ~ out of the coffee>

Good Sa·mar·i·tan \-sə-ˈmar-ət-ᵊn, -ˈmer-\ *n* **:** SAMARITAN 2

good–tem·pered \ˈgu̇d-ˈtem-pərd\ *adj* **:** having an even temper **:** not easily vexed — **good–tem·pered·ly** *adv* — **good–tem·pered·ness** *n*

good·wife \ˈgu̇d-ˌwīf\ *n* **1** *archaic* **:** the mistress of a household **2** *archaic* **:** MRS.

good·will \ˈgu̇d-ˈwil\ *n* **1 a :** a kindly feeling of approval and support **:** benevolent interest or concern **b :** the favor or prestige that a business has acquired beyond the mere value of what it sells **2 a :** cheerful consent **b :** willing effort ***syn*** see FAVOR — **good·willed** \-ˈwild\ *adj*

[1]**goody** \ˈgu̇d-ē\ *n* [alter. of *goodwife*] *archaic* **:** a usu. married woman of lowly station — used as a title preceding a surname

[2]**goody** *n, pl* **good·ies :** something that is particularly attractive, pleasurable, good, or desirable <such *goodies* as model trains, cameras, microscopes, and college educations —*Time*>

[1]**goody–goody** \ˌgu̇d-ē-ˈgu̇d-ē\ *adj* **:** affectedly or ingratiatingly good or proper

[2]**goody–goody** *n* **:** a goody-goody person

[1]**goof** \ˈgüf\ *n* [prob. alter. of E dial. *goff* (simpleton)] **1 :** a ridiculous stupid person **2 :** BLUNDER

[2]**goof** *vi* **1 :** to make a usu. foolish or careless mistake **:** BLUNDER **2** *slang* **:** to spend time idly or foolishly — often used with *off* <somebody is ~*ing* off on the job —*Springfield (Mass.) Daily News*> ~ *vt* **:** to make a mess of **:** BUNGLE — often used with *up*

goof·ball \ˈgüf-ˌbȯl\ *n* **1** *slang* **:** a barbiturate sleeping pill **2** *slang* **:** a mentally abnormal person

go off *vi* **1 :** EXPLODE **2 :** to burst forth or break out in a sudden or noisy manner **3 :** to go forth or away **:** DEPART, LEAVE **4 :** to undergo decline or deterioration **5 :** to follow the expected or desired course **:** PROCEED <the party *went off* well> **6 :** to make a characteristic noise **:** SOUND — **go off the deep end 1 :** to enter recklessly on a course **2 :** to become very much excited or perturbed

goof–off \ˈgü-ˌfȯf\ *n* **:** one who evades work or responsibility

goofy \ˈgü-fē\ *adj* **goof·i·er; -est :** CRAZY, SILLY — **goof·i·ly** \-fə-lē\ *adv* — **goof·i·ness** \-fē-nəs\ *n*

goo·gol \ˈgü-ˌgȯl\ *n* [coined by a child] **:** the figure 1 followed by 100 zeroes equal to 10^{100}

goo·gol·plex \-ˌpleks\ *n* [*googol* + *-plex* (as in *duplex*)] **:** the figure 1 followed by a googol of zeroes equal to

$$10^{10^{100}}$$

[1]**goo–goo** \ˈgü-(ˌ)gü\ *adj* [prob. alter. of [2]*goggle*] **:** LOVING, ENTICING — used chiefly in the phrase *goo-goo eyes* <make ~ eyes at each other —*New Republic*>

[2]**goo–goo** \ˈgü-(ˌ)gü\ *n, pl* **goo–goos** [fr. *good government*] **:** a member or advocate of a political reform movement <this group was contemptuously dismissed by machine politicians as ~*s* —*Fortune*>

[1]**gook** \ˈgu̇k\ *n* [origin unknown] **:** a native belonging usu. to a brown or yellow race — usu. used disparagingly

[2]**gook** \ˈgu̇k, ˈgük\ *n* [perh. alter. of *goo*] **:** GOO — **gooky** \-ē\ *adj*

goon \ˈgün\ *n* [partly short for E dial. *gooney* (simpleton), partly fr. Alice the *Goon*, subhuman comic-strip creature by E. C. Segar] **1 :** a man hired to terrorize or eliminate opponents **2** *slang* **:** DOPE, SAP — **goony** \-ē\ *adj*

go on *vi* **1 a :** to continue with or as if with a journey **b :** to continue in or as if in a course of action **2 a :** to proceed by or as if by a logical step **b** *of time* **:** PASS **3 :** to take place **:** HAPPEN **4 :** to be capable of being put on <her gloves wouldn't *go on*> **5 :** to talk esp. in an effusive manner <the way people *go on* about their ancestors —Hamilton Basso> **6 a :** to come into operation, action, or production <the lights *went on* at sunset> **b :** to appear on the stage <an actor waiting to *go on*>

goo·ney *also* **goo·ny** *or* **goo·nie** \ˈgü-nē\ *n, pl* **gooneys** *or* **goonies** [prob. fr. E dial. *gooney* (simpleton)] **:** BLACK-FOOTED ALBATROSS

gooney bird *n* **:** BLACK-FOOTED ALBATROSS

goo·san·der \gü-ˈsan-dər\ *n* [origin unknown] **:** the common merganser (*Mergus merganser*) of the northern hemisphere

[1]**goose** \ˈgüs\ *n, pl* **geese** \ˈgēs\ [ME *gos*, fr. OE *gōs*; akin to OHG *gans* goose, L *anser*] **1 a :** any of numerous large waterfowl (family Anatidae) that are intermediate between the swans and ducks and have long necks, feathered lores, and reticulate tarsi **b :** a female goose as distinguished from a gander **2 :** SIMPLETON, DOLT **3** *pl* **goos·es :** a tailor's smoothing iron with a gooseneck handle **4** *pl* **goos·es :** a poke between the buttocks — **goos·ey** \ˈgü-sē\ *adj*

[2]**goose** *vt* **goosed; goos·ing :** to poke between the buttocks with an upward thrust

goose·ber·ry \ˈgüs-ˌber-ē, ˈgüz-, -b(ə-)rē, *chiefly Brit* ˈgu̇z-\ *n* **1 a :** the acid usu. prickly fruit of any of several shrubs (genus *Ribes*) of the rose family **b :** a shrub bearing gooseberries **2 :** CURRANT 2

goose bumps *n pl* **:** GOOSEFLESH

goose egg *n* **:** ZERO, NOTHING; *esp* **:** a score of zero in a game or contest

goose·flesh \ˈgüs-ˌflesh\ *n* **:** a roughness of the skin produced by erection of its papillae usu. from cold or fear

goose·foot \-ˌfu̇t\ *n, pl* **goose·foots :** any of a genus (*Chenopodium*) or family (Chenopodiaceae, the goosefoot family) of glabrous herbs with utricular fruit

goose grass *n* **1 :** CLEAVERS 1 **2 :** YARD GRASS

goose·neck \ˈgü-ˌsnek\ *n, often attrib* **:** something (as a flexible jointed metal pipe) curved like the neck of a goose or U-shaped — **goose·necked** \-ˌsnekt\ *adj*

goose pimples *n pl* **:** GOOSEFLESH

goose step *n* **:** a straight-legged stiff-kneed step used by troops of some armies when passing in review — **goose–step·per** \ˈgüs-ˌstep-ər\ *n*

go out *vi* **1 a :** to go forth, abroad, or outdoors; *specif* **:** to leave one's house **b (1) :** to take the field as a soldier **(2) :** to participate as a principal in a duel **c :** to travel as or as if a colonist or immigrant **d :** to work away from home **2 a :** to come to an end **b :** to become extinguished <the hall light *went out*> **c :** to give up office **:** RESIGN **d:** to become obsolete or unfashionable **e (1) :** to play the last card of one's hand **(2) :** to reach or exceed the total number of points required for game in cards **3 :** to go on strike **4 :** BREAK, COLLAPSE **5 :** to become a candidate <*went out* for the football team>

go over *vi* **1 :** to go on a journey **2 :** to become converted **3 :** to receive approval **:** SUCCEED <my stand should *go over* well with the . . . women's groups —M. J. Rosenberg>

GOP *abbr* Grand Old Party (Republican)

go·pher \ˈgō-fər\ *n* [origin unknown] **1 :** a burrowing edible land tortoise (*Gopherus polyphemus*) of the southern U.S.; *broadly* **:** any of several related land tortoises **2 a :** any of several burrowing rodents (family Geomyidae) of western No. America, Central America, and the southern U.S. that are the size of a large rat and have large cheek pouches opening beside the mouth **b :** any of numerous small ground squirrels (genus *Citellus*) of the prairie region of No. America closely related to the chipmunks **3 :** GOPHER BALL

gopher 2a

gopher ball *n* **:** a pitched baseball hit for a home run

gopher snake *n* **1 :** INDIGO SNAKE **2 :** BULL SNAKE

Gor·di·an knot \ˌgȯrd-ē-ən-\ *n* **1 :** a knot tied by Gordius, king of Phrygia, held to be capable of being untied only by the future ruler of Asia, and cut by Alexander the Great with his sword **2 :** an intricate problem; *esp* **:** a problem insoluble in its own terms

Gor·don setter \ˌgȯrd-ᵊn-\ *n* [Alexander, 4th Duke of *Gordon* †1827 Sc sportsman] **:** any of a breed of large long-haired bird dogs that are deep black with tan, chestnut, or mahogany markings

[1]**gore** \ˈgō(ə)r, ˈgȯ(ə)r\ *n* [ME, filth, fr. OE *gor*; akin to OE *wearm* warm] **:** BLOOD; *esp* **:** clotted blood

[2]**gore** *n* [ME, fr. OE *gāra*; akin to OE *gār* spear, Gk *chaios* shepherd's staff] **1 :** a small usu. triangular piece of land **2 :** a tapering or triangular piece (as of cloth in a skirt)

[3]**gore** *vt* **gored; gor·ing 1 :** to cut into a tapering triangular form **2 :** to provide with a gore

[4]**gore** *vt* **gored; gor·ing** [ME *goren*] **:** to pierce or wound with a horn or tusk

[1]**gorge** \ˈgȯ(ə)rj\ *n* [ME, fr. MF, fr. LL *gurga*, alter. of L *gurges* throat, whirlpool — more at VORACIOUS] **1 :** THROAT **2 a :** a hawk's crop **b :** STOMACH, BELLY **3 :** the entrance into an outwork (as a bastion) of a fort **4 :** a narrow passage through land; *esp* **:** a narrow steep-walled canyon or part of a canyon **5 :** a primitive device used instead of a fishhook that consists of an object (as a piece of bone attached in the middle of a line) easy to swallow but difficult to eject **6 :** a mass choking a passage <a river dammed by an ice ~>

[2]**gorge** *vb* **gorged; gorg·ing** *vi* **:** to eat greedily or to repletion ~ *vt* **1 a :** to stuff to capacity **:** GLUT **b :** to fill completely or to the point of distension <veins *gorged* with blood> **2 :** to swallow greedily ***syn*** see SATIATE — **gorg·er** *n*

gor·geous \ˈgȯr-jəs\ *adj* [ME *gorgayse*, fr. MF *gorgias* elegant, fr. *gorgias* neckerchief, fr. *gorge*] **:** splendidly or showily brilliant or magnificent ***syn*** see SPLENDID — **gor·geous·ly** *adv* — **gor·geous·ness** *n*

gor·get \ˈgȯr-jət\ *n* [ME, fr. MF, fr. *gorge*] **1 :** a piece of armor protecting the throat — see ARMOR illustration **2 a :** an ornamental collar **b :** a part of a wimple covering the throat and shoulders

gor·gon \ˈgȯr-gən\ *n* [L *Gorgon-*, *Gorgo*, fr. Gk *Gorgōn*] **1** *cap* **:** any of three snaky-haired sisters in Greek mythology whose glance turns the beholder to stone **2 :** an ugly or repulsive woman — **Gor·go·ni·an** \gȯr-ˈgō-nē-ən\ *adj*

gor·go·ni·an \gȯr-ˈgō-nē-ən\ *n* [deriv. of L *gorgonia* coral, fr. *Gorgon-*, *Gorgo*] **:** any of an order (Gorgonacea) of colonial anthozoans with a usu. horny and branching axial skeleton — **gorgonian** *adj*

gor·gon·ize \ˈgȯr-gə-ˌnīz\ *vt* **-ized; -iz·ing :** to have a paralyzing or mesmerizing effect on **:** STUPEFY, PETRIFY

Gor·gon·zo·la \ˌgȯr-gən-ˈzō-lə\ *n* [It, fr. *Gorgonzola*, Italy] **:** a blue cheese of Italian origin usu. made of cow's milk

go·ril·la \gə-ˈril-ə\ *n* [deriv. of Gk *Gorillai*, an African tribe of hairy women] **1 :** an anthropoid ape (*Gorilla gorilla*) of western equatorial Africa related to the chimpanzee but less erect and much larger **2 a :** an ugly or brutal man **b :** THUG, GOON

gor·man·dize \ˈgȯr-mən-ˌdīz\ *vb* **-dized; -diz·ing** [*gormand*, alter. of *gourmand*] *vi* **:** to eat gluttonously or ravenously ~ *vt* **:** to eat greedily **:** DEVOUR — **gor·man·diz·er** *n*

go–round \ˈgō-ˌrau̇nd\ *n* **:** GO-AROUND

gorse \ˈgȯ(ə)rs\ *n* [ME *gorst*, fr. OE — more at HORROR] **1 :** FURZE **2 :** JUNIPER — **gorsy** \ˈgȯr-sē\ *adj*

gory \ˈgō(ə)r-ē, ˈgȯ(ə)r-\ *adj* **gor·i·er; -est 1 :** covered with gore **:** BLOODSTAINED **2 :** BLOODCURDLING, SENSATIONAL

gos·hawk \ˈgäs-ˌhȯk\ *n* [ME *goshawke*, fr. OE *gōshafoc*, fr. *gōs* goose + *hafoc* hawk] **:** any of several long-tailed accipitrine hawks with short rounded wings; *esp* **:** a hawk (*Accipiter gentilis*) of the northern parts of both the Old and the New World that is larger than a crow and has a conspicuous white stripe above and behind the eye

gos·ling \'gäz-liŋ, 'gȯz-, -lən\ *n* [ME, fr. *gos* goose] **1 :** a young goose **2 :** a foolish or callow person

¹gos·pel \'gäs-pəl\ *n* [ME, fr. OE *gōdspel, fr. gōd* good + *spell* tale — more at SPELL] **1 a** *often cap* **:** the message concerning Christ, the kingdom of God, and salvation **b** *cap* **:** one of the first four New Testament books telling of the life, death, and resurrection of Jesus Christ; *also* **:** a similar apocryphal book **c :** an interpretation of the Christian message <the social ~> **2** *cap* **:** a lection from one of the New Testament Gospels **3 :** the message or teachings of a religious teacher **4 :** something accepted as infallible truth or as a guiding principle <the ~ of conservation —R. M. Hodesh>

gorilla 1

²gospel *adj* **1 a :** having a basis in or being in accordance with the gospel **:** EVANGELICAL <ordained to the ~ ministry —*Christian Century*> **b :** marked by special or fervid emphasis on the gospel <a ~ meeting> **2 :** of, relating to, or being religious songs of American origin associated with evangelism and popular devotion and marked by simple melody and harmony and elements of folk songs, spirituals, and occas. jazz <a ~ singer>

gos·pel·er *or* **gos·pel·ler** \'gäs-pə-lər\ *n* **1 :** one who preaches or propounds a gospel **2 :** one who reads or sings the liturgical Gospel

gospel side *n, often cap G* [fr. the custom of reading the Gospel from this side] **:** the left side of an altar or chancel as one faces it

Gos·plan \'gäs-,plan, 'gȯs-,plän\ *n* [Russ *Gos*udarstvennaya *Plan*ovaya (Komissiya) State Planning Commission] **:** a Soviet agency that makes long-term economic and social plans and generally supervises their execution

gos·port \'gäs-,pō(ə)rt, -,pȯ(ə)rt\ *n* [*Gosport,* England] **:** a flexible one-way speaking tube for communication between separate cockpits of an airplane

gos·sa·mer \'gäs-ə-mər *also* 'gäz(-ə)-mər\ *n* [ME *gossomer,* fr. *gos* goose + *somer* summer] **1 :** a film of cobwebs floating in air in calm clear weather **2 :** something light, delicate, insubstantial, or tenuous <the ~ of youth's dreams —Andrea Parke> — **gossamer** *adj* — **gos·sa·mery** \-mə-rē\ *adj*

gos·san \'gäs-ᵊn\ *n* [Corn *gossen*] **:** decomposed rock or vein material of reddish or rusty color that results from oxidized pyrites

¹gos·sip \'gäs-əp\ *n* [ME *gossib,* fr. OE *godsibb,* fr. *god* + *sibb* kinsman, fr. *sibb* related] **1 a** *dial Brit* **:** GODPARENT **b :** COMPANION, CRONY **c :** a person who habitually reveals personal or sensational facts **2 a :** rumor or report of an intimate nature **b :** a chatty talk **c :** the subject matter of gossip <his infidelities were common ~> ***syn*** see REPORT — **gos·sip·ry** \-ə-prē\ *n*

²gossip *vi* **:** to relate gossip — **gos·sip·er** *n*

gos·sipy \'gäs-ə-pē\ *adj* **:** full of or given to gossip <a ~ letter> <~ neighbors>

gos·sy·pol \'gäs-ə-,pȯl, -,pōl\ *n* [ISV, deriv. of L *gossypion* cotton] **:** a toxic phenolic pigment $C_{30}H_{30}O_8$ in cottonseed

got *past of* GET

¹Goth \'gäth\ *n* [LL *Gothi,* pl.] **:** a member of a Germanic people that overran the Roman Empire in the early centuries of the Christian era

²Goth *abbr* Gothic

¹Goth·ic \'gäth-ik\ *adj* **1 a :** of, relating to, or resembling the Goths, their civilization, or their language **b :** TEUTONIC, GERMANIC **c (1) :** MEDIEVAL **(2) :** UNCOUTH, BARBAROUS **2 a :** of, relating to, or having the characteristics of a style of architecture developed in northern France and spreading through western Europe from the middle of the 12th century to the early 16th century that is characterized by the converging of weights and strains at isolated points upon slender vertical piers and counterbalancing buttresses and by pointed arches and vaulting **b :** of or relating to an architectural style reflecting the influence of the medieval Gothic **3** *often not cap* **:** of or relating to a style of fiction characterized by the use of desolate or remote settings and macabre, mysterious, or violent incidents — **goth·i·cal·ly** \-i-k(ə-)lē\ *adv* — **Goth·ic·ness** \-ik-nəs\ *n*

²Gothic *n* **1 :** the East Germanic language of the Goths — see INDO-EUROPEAN LANGUAGES table **2 :** Gothic art style or decoration; *specif* **:** the Gothic architectural style **3 a :** BLACK LETTER **b :** SANS SERIF **4 :** a work of fiction in the gothic style

Gothic arch *n* **:** a pointed arch; *esp* **:** one with a joint instead of a keystone at its apex

Goth·i·cism \'gäth-ə-,siz-əm\ *n* **1 :** barbarous lack of taste or elegance **2 :** conformity to or practice of Gothic style — **Goth·i·cist** \-səst\ *n*

goth·i·cize \-,sīz\ *vt* **-cized; -ciz·ing** *often cap* **:** to make Gothic

gö·thite *var of* GOETHITE

go through *vi* **1 :** to continue firmly or obstinately to the end <I was *going through* with it if it killed me —A. W. Long> **2 a :** to receive approval or sanction **:** PASS **b :** to come to a desired or satisfactory conclusion

gotten *past part of* GET

gouache \'gwäsh\ *n* [F, deriv. of L *aquatio* act of fetching water, fr. *aquatus,* pp. of *aquari* to fetch water, fr. *aqua* water — more at ISLAND] **1 :** a method of painting with opaque watercolors **2 a :** a picture painted by gouache **b :** the pigment used in gouache

Gou·da \'gaüd-ə, 'güd-\ *n* [*Gouda,* Netherlands] **:** a mild pressed cheese of Dutch origin that is similar to Edam but contains more fat

¹gouge \'gaüj\ *n* [ME *gowge,* fr. MF *gouge,* fr. LL *gulbia,* of Celt origin; akin to OIr *gulban* sting] **1 :** a chisel with a concavo-convex cross section **2 a :** the act of gouging **b :** a groove or cavity scooped out **3 :** an excessive or improper exaction **:** EXTORTION

²gouge *vt* **gouged; goug·ing** **1 :** to scoop out with or as if with a gouge **2 a :** to force out (an eye) with the thumb **b :** to thrust the thumb into the eye of **3 :** to subject to extortion or undue exaction **:** OVERCHARGE — **goug·er** *n*

gou·lash \'gü-,läsh, -,lash\ *n* [Hung *gulyás* herdsman's stew] **1 :** a beef stew made with assorted vegetables and paprika **2 :** a round in bridge played with hands produced by a redistribution of previously dealt cards **3 :** a mixture of heterogeneous elements **:** JUMBLE

go under *vi* **:** to be overwhelmed, destroyed, or defeated **:** FAIL

gourd \'gō(ə)rd, 'gȯ(ə)rd, 'gu̇(ə)rd\ *n* [ME *gourde,* fr. MF, fr. L *cucurbita*] **1 :** any of a family (Cucurbitaceae, the gourd family) of chiefly herbaceous tendril-bearing vines including the cucumber, melon, squash, and pumpkin **2 :** the fruit of a gourd **:** PEPO; *esp* **:** any of various hard-rinded inedible fruits of plants of two genera (*Lagenaria* and *Cucurbita*) often used for ornament or for vessels and utensils

gourde \'gu̇(ə)rd\ *n* [AmerF] — see MONEY table

gour·mand \'gu̇(ə)r-,mänd, -mənd\ *n* [MF *gourmant*] **1 :** one who is excessively fond of eating and drinking **2 :** one who is heartily interested in good food and drink ***syn*** see EPICURE — **gour·mand·ism** \'gu̇(ə)r-,män-,diz-əm, -mən-\ *n*

gour·met \'gu̇(ə)r-,mā, gu̇r-'\ *n* [F, fr. MF, alter. of *gromet* boy servant, vintner's assistant, fr. ME *grom* groom] **:** a connoisseur of food and drink ***syn*** see EPICURE — **gourmet** *adj*

gout \'gaüt\ *n* [ME *goute,* fr. OF, gout, drop, fr. L *gutta* drop] **1 :** a metabolic disease marked by a painful inflammation of the joints, deposits of urates in and around the joints, and usu. an excessive amount of uric acid in the blood **2 :** a mass or aggregate of something fluid or sticky <~*s* of lava> — **gouty** \-ē\ *adj*

gov *abbr* **1** government **2** governor

gov·ern \'gəv-ərn\ *vb* [ME *governen,* fr. OF *governer,* fr. L *gubernare* to steer, govern, fr. Gk *kybernan*] *vt* **1 a :** to exercise continuous sovereign authority over; *esp* **:** to control and direct the making and administration of policy in **b :** to rule without sovereign power and usu. without having the authority to determine basic policy **2 a** *archaic* **:** MANIPULATE **b :** to control the speed of (as a machine) esp. by automatic means **3 a :** to control, direct, or strongly influence the actions and conduct of **b :** to exert a determining or guiding influence in or over <income must ~ expenditure> <availability often ~*s* choice> **c :** to hold in check **:** RESTRAIN **4 :** to require (a word) to be in a certain case <in English a transitive verb ~*s* a noun in the common case> **5 :** to serve as a precedent or deciding principle for <habits and customs that ~ human decisions> ~ *vi* **1 :** to prevail or have decisive influence **:** CONTROL **2 :** to exercise authority — **gov·ern·able** \-ər-nə-bəl\ *adj*

syn GOVERN, RULE *shared meaning element* **:** to exercise power and authority in controlling. GOVERN implies a keeping in a straight course, under proper control, or in smooth operation for the good of the individual or the whole <you must learn to *govern* your temper> <the rules that *govern* creative writing> <to *govern* is to organize the common activities of a society . . . power rests on organization; where there is no organization there is no government —*Times Lit. Supp.*> RULE is likely to stress power to lay down laws which determine the action of others or to issue commands which must be obeyed, and it may suggest arbitrary or capricious exercise of power <resolved to ruin or to *rule* the state —John Dryden> < [testified] that . . . police stood idly by while white toughs *ruled* with bricks and clubs —*Springfield (Mass.) Union*>

gov·er·nance \'gəv-ər-nən(t)s\ *n* **:** GOVERNMENT

gov·ern·ess \'gəv-ər-nəs\ *n* **1 :** a woman who governs **2 :** a woman entrusted with the care and supervision of a child esp. in a private household **3 :** the wife of a governor

gov·ern·essy \-nə-sē\ *adj* **:** having the characteristics of or suggesting a governess

gov·ern·ment \'gəv-ər(n)-mənt, 'gəv-ᵊm-ənt\ *n, often attrib* **1** *obs* **:** moral conduct or behavior **:** DISCRETION **2 :** the act or process of governing; *specif* **:** authoritative direction or control **3 a :** the office, authority, or function of governing **b** *obs* **:** the term during which a governing official holds office **4 a :** the continuous exercise of authority over and the performance of functions for a political unit **:** RULE **b :** the political function of policy making as distinguished from the administration of policy decisions **5 a :** the organization, machinery, or agency through which a political unit exercises authority and performs functions and which is usu. classified according to the distribution of power within it **b :** the complex of political institutions, laws, and customs through which the function of governing is carried out in a specific political unit **6 :** the body of persons that constitutes the governing authority of a political unit or organization: as **a :** the officials comprising the governing body of a political unit and constituting the organization as an active agency **b** *cap* **:** the executive branch of the U.S. federal government including the political officials and usu. the permanent civil service employees **c** *cap* **:** a small group of persons holding simultaneously the principal political executive offices of a nation or other political unit and being responsible for the direction and supervision of public affairs: **(1) :** such a group in a parliamentary system constituted by the cabinet or by the ministry **(2) :** ADMINISTRATION 4b **7 :** POLITICAL SCIENCE — **gov·ern·men·tal** \,gəv-ər(n)-'ment-ᵊl\ *adj* — **gov·ern·men·tal·ly** \-ᵊl-ē\ *adv*

gov·ern·men·tal·ism \ˌgəv-ər(n)-ˈment-ᵊl-ˌiz-əm\ *n* **1 :** a theory advocating extension of the sphere and degree of government activity **2 :** the tendency toward extension of the role of government — **gov·ern·men·tal·ist** \-ᵊl-əst\ *n*

gov·ern·men·tal·ize \-ᵊl-ˌīz\ *vt* **-ized; -iz·ing :** to subject to the regulation or control of a government

government note *n* **:** a currency note issued by a government

gov·er·nor \ˈgəv(-ə)-nər *also* ˈgəv-ər-nər\ *n* **1 :** one that governs: as **a :** one that exercises authority esp. over an area or group **b :** an official elected or appointed to act as ruler, chief executive, or nominal head of a political unit **c :** COMMANDANT **d :** the managing director and usu. the principal officer of an institution or organization **e :** a member of a group that directs or controls an institution or society **2 :** TUTOR **3 a** *slang* **:** one (as a father, guardian, or employer) looked upon as governing **b :** MISTER, SIR — usu. used as a term of address **4 a :** an attachment to a machine (as a gasoline engine) for automatic control or limitation of speed **b :** a device giving automatic control (as of pressure or temperature) — **gov·er·nor·ate** \-ət, -ˌāt\ *n*

governor-general *n, pl* **governors-general** *or* **governor-generals :** a governor of high rank; *esp* **:** one who governs a large territory or has deputy governors under him — **governor-generalship** *n*

governor's council *n* **:** an executive or legislative council chosen to advise or assist a governor

gov·er·nor·ship \ˈgəv(-ə)-nər-ˌship *also* ˈgəv-ər-\ *n* **1 :** the office of governor **2 :** the period of incumbency of a governor

govt *abbr* government

gow·an \ˈgau̇-ən\ *n* [prob. alter. of ME *gollan*] *chiefly Scot* **:** DAISY 1; *broadly* **:** a white or yellow field flower

gow·any \-ə-nē\ *adj, chiefly Scot* **:** abounding in gowans <sweeter than ~ glens —Allan Ramsay †1758>

gown \ˈgau̇n\ *n* [ME, fr. MF *goune,* fr. LL *gunna,* a fur or leather garment] **1 a :** a loose flowing outer garment formerly worn by men **b :** a distinctive robe worn by a professional or academic person **c :** a woman's dress **d (1) :** DRESSING GOWN **(2) :** NIGHTGOWN **e :** a coverall worn in an operating room **2 a :** an office or profession symbolized by a distinctive robe **b :** the body of students and faculty of a college or university <powerful rivalry in . . . society between town and ~ —Robertson Davies>

gowns·man \ˈgau̇nz-mən\ *n* **:** a professional or academic person

gox \ˈgäks\ *n* [*g*aseous *ox*ygen] **:** gaseous oxygen

goy \ˈgȯi\ *n, pl* **goy·im** \ˈgȯi-əm\ *or* **goys** [Yiddish, fr. Heb *gōy* people, nation] **:** GENTILE 1 — **goy·ish** \ˈgȯi-ish\ *adj*

gp *abbr* group

GP *abbr* **1** general practice; general practitioner **2** geometric progression

GPA *abbr* grade-point average

GPD *abbr* gallons per day

GPM *abbr* gallons per minute

GPO *abbr* **1** general post office **2** Government Printing Office

GPS *abbr* gallons per second

GQ *abbr* general quarters

gr *abbr* **1** grade **2** grain **3** gram **4** gravity **5** gross

Gr *abbr* Greece; Greek

Graaf·ian follicle \ˌgräf-ē-ən-, ˌgraf-\ *n* [Regnier de *Graaf* †1673 D anatomist] **:** a vesicle in a mammal ovary enclosing a developing egg

¹grab \ˈgrab\ *vb* **grabbed; grab·bing** [obs. D or LG *grabben;* akin to ME *graspen* to grasp, Skt *gṛbhṇāti* he seizes] *vt* **1 :** to take or seize by a sudden motion or grasp **2 :** to obtain unscrupulously **3 :** to take hastily **4 :** to forcefully engage the attention of <the technique of *grabbing* an audience —Pauline Kael> ~ *vi* **1 :** to make a grab **:** SNATCH **2** *of a horse* **:** OVERREACH ***syn*** see TAKE — **grab·ber** *n*

²grab *n* **1 a :** a sudden snatch **b :** an unlawful or unscrupulous seizure **c :** something grabbed **2 a :** a device for clutching an object **b :** CLAMSHELL — **up for grabs :** available for anyone to take or win

³grab *adj* **1 :** intended to be grabbed <a ~ rail> **2 :** taken at random <~ samples of rocks>

⁴grab *n* [Ar *ghurāb,* lit., raven] **:** an oriental coasting ship of light draft and broad beam having lateen sails and usu. two masts

grab bag *n* **1 :** a receptacle (as a bag) containing small articles which are to be drawn (as at a party or fair) without being seen **2 :** something resembling a grab bag (as in providing an assortment of items)

grab·ble \ˈgrab-əl\ *vi* **grab·bled; grab·bling** \-(ə-)liŋ\ [D *grabbelen,* fr. MD, freq. of *grabben*] **1 :** to search with the hand **:** GROPE **2 :** to lie or fall prone **:** SPRAWL — **grab·bler** \-(ə-)lər\ *n*

grab·by \ˈgrab-ē\ *adj* **grab·bi·er; -est :** tending to grab **:** GRASPING, GREEDY

gra·ben \ˈgräb-ən\ *n* [G, ditch] **:** a depressed segment of the earth's crust bounded on at least two sides by faults

¹grace \ˈgrās\ *n* [ME, fr. OF, fr. L *gratia* favor, charm, thanks, fr. *gratus* pleasing, grateful; akin to OHG *queran* to sigh, Skt *gṛṇāti* he praises] **1 a :** unmerited divine assistance given man for his regeneration or sanctification **b :** a state of sanctification enjoyed through divine grace **c :** a virtue coming from God **2 :** a short prayer at a meal asking a blessing or giving thanks **3 a :** disposition to or an act or instance of kindness or clemency **b** *archaic* **:** MERCY, PARDON **c :** a special favor **:** PRIVILEGE <each in his place, by right, not ~, shall rule his heritage —Rudyard Kipling> **d :** a temporary exemption **:** REPRIEVE **e :** APPROVAL, FAVOR <stayed in his good ~*s*> **4 a :** a charming trait or accomplishment **b :** a pleasingly graceful appearance or effect **:** CHARM **c :** ease and suppleness of movement or bearing **5 :** a musical trill, turn, or appoggiatura **6 —** used as a title of address or reference for a duke, a duchess, or an archbishop **7 a :** sense of propriety or right **b :** the quality or state of being considerate or thoughtful **8** *pl, cap* **:** three sister goddesses in Greek mythology who are the givers of charm and beauty ***syn*** see MERCY

²grace *vt* **graced; grac·ing 1 :** to confer dignity or honor on **2 :** ADORN, EMBELLISH

grace cup *n* **:** a cup used in drinking a final health after the grace at the end of a meal; *also* **:** a health drunk from it

grace·ful \ˈgrās-fəl\ *adj* **:** displaying grace in form or action **:** pleasing or attractive in line, proportion, or movement — **grace·ful·ly** \-fə-lē\ *adv* — **grace·ful·ness** *n*

grace·less \ˈgrā-sləs\ *adj* **1 :** lacking in divine grace **:** IMMORAL, UNREGENERATE **2 a :** lacking a sense of propriety **b :** devoid of attractive qualities **3 :** artistically inept or unbeautiful — **grace·less·ly** *adv* — **grace·less·ness** *n*

grace note *n* **:** a musical note added as an ornament; *esp* **:** APPOGGIATURA

grac·ile \ˈgras-əl, -ˌīl\ *adj* [L *gracilis*] **1 :** SLENDER, SLIGHT **2 :** GRACEFUL — **grac·ile·ness** *n* — **gra·cil·i·ty** \gra-ˈsil-ət-ē\ *n*

gra·ci·o·so \ˌgräs-ē-ˈō-(ˌ)sō, -(ˌ)zō\ *n, pl* **-sos** [Sp, fr. *gracioso,* adj., agreeable, amusing, fr. L *gratiosus*] **:** a buffoon in Spanish comedy

gra·cious \ˈgrā-shəs\ *adj* [ME, fr. MF *gracieus,* fr. L *gratiosus* enjoying favor, agreeable, fr. *gratia*] **1 a** *obs* **:** GODLY **b** *archaic* **:** PLEASING, ACCEPTABLE **2 a :** marked by kindness and courtesy **b :** GRACEFUL **c :** marked by tact and delicacy **:** URBANE **d :** characterized by charm, good taste, and generosity of spirit **3 :** MERCIFUL, COMPASSIONATE — used conventionally of royalty and high nobility — **gra·cious·ly** *adv* — **gra·cious·ness** *n*

syn GRACIOUS, CORDIAL, AFFABLE, GENIAL, SOCIABLE *shared meaning element* **:** markedly pleasant and easy in social contacts ***ant*** ungracious

grack·le \ˈgrak-əl\ *n* [deriv. of L *graculus* jackdaw] **1 :** any of various Old World starlings (as the hill mynas) **2 :** any of several rather large American blackbirds (family Icteridae) having glossy iridescent black plumage

grad *abbr* graduate; graduated

gra·date \ˈgrā-ˌdāt\ *vb* **gra·dat·ed; gra·dat·ing** [back-formation fr. *gradation*] *vi* **:** to shade into the next color, note, or stage ~ *vt* **:** to arrange in a progression, scale, or series

gra·da·tion \grā-ˈdā-shən, grə-\ *n* **1 a :** a series forming successive stages **b :** a step or place in an ordered scale **2 :** an advance by regular degrees **3 :** the act or process of grading **4 :** a gradual passing from one tint or shade to another (as in a painting) **5 :** ABLAUT — **gra·da·tion·al** \-shnəl, -shən-ᵊl\ *adj* — **gra·da·tion·al·ly** \-ē\ *adv*

¹grade \ˈgrād\ *n* [F, fr. L *gradus* step, degree; akin to L *gradi* to step, go, Lith *gridyti* to go, wander] **1 a (1) :** a stage in a process **(2) :** a position in a scale of ranks or qualities **b :** a class organized for the work of a particular year of a school course **c :** a military or naval rank **d :** a degree of severity in illness <~ III carcinoma> **2 a :** a class of things of the same stage or degree **b :** a mark indicating a degree of accomplishment in school **c :** a standard of food quality <the government has established ~*s* for meat> **3 a :** the degree of inclination of a road or slope; *also* **:** a sloping road **b :** a datum or reference level; *esp* **:** ground level **c :** ELEVATION 1c **4 :** a domestic animal with one parent purebred and the other of inferior breeding **5** *pl* **:** the elementary school system <taught in the ~*s* for 19 years> — **grade·less** \-ləs\ *adj*

²grade *vb* **grad·ed; grad·ing** *vt* **1 a :** to arrange in grades **:** SORT **b :** to arrange in a scale or series **c :** to assign to a grade or assign a grade to **2 :** to level off to a smooth horizontal or sloping surface **3 :** to improve by breeding females to purebred males ~ *vi* **1 a :** to form a series **b :** BLEND **2 :** to be of a particular grade — **grad·able** \ˈgrād-ə-bəl\ *adj*

-grade \ˌgrād\ *adj comb form* [F, fr. L *-gradus,* fr. *gradi*] **:** walking <planti*grade*>

grade crossing *n* **:** a crossing of highways, railroad tracks, or pedestrian walks or combinations of these on the same level

grade point *n* **:** QUALITY POINT

grade point average *n* **:** QUALITY POINT AVERAGE

grad·er \ˈgrād-ər\ *n* **1 :** one that grades **2 :** a machine for leveling earth **3 :** a pupil in an elementary or secondary school grade <a fifth ~>

grade school *n* **:** ELEMENTARY SCHOOL

grade separation *n* **:** a highway or railroad crossing using an underpass or overpass

gra·di·ent \ˈgrād-ē-ənt\ *n* [L *gradient-, gradiens,* prp. of *gradi*] **1 a :** the rate of regular or graded ascent or descent **:** INCLINATION **b :** a part sloping upward or downward **2 :** change in the value of a quantity with change in a given variable and esp. per unit distance in a specified direction <vertical temperature ~> **3 :** the vector sum of the partial derivatives with respect to the three coordinate variables *x, y,* and *z* of a scalar quantity whose value varies from point to point **4 :** a graded difference in physiological activity along an axis (as of the body or an embryonic field) **5 :** change in response with distance from the stimulus

gra·din \ˈgrād-ᵊn\ *or* **gra·dine** \ˈgrā-ˌdēn, grə-ˈ\ *n* [F *gradin*] **:** one of a series of tiered steps or seats

gra·di·om·e·ter \ˌgrād-ē-ˈäm-ət-ər\ *n* [*gradi*ent + *-o-* + *-meter*] **:** an instrument for measuring the gradient of a physical quantity (as the earth's magnetic field)

¹grad·u·al \ˈgraj-(ə-)wəl, ˈgraj-əl\ *n, often cap* [ME *graduale,* fr. *gradus* step, fr. its being sung on the steps of the altar] **1 :** a pair of verses (as from the Psalms) proper after the Epistle in the Mass **2 :** a book containing the choral parts of the Mass

²gradual *adj* [ML *gradualis,* fr. *gradus*] **1 :** proceeding by steps or degrees **2 :** moving, changing, or developing by fine, slight, or often imperceptible degrees — **grad·u·al·ly** *adv* — **grad·u·al·ness** *n*

grad·u·al·ism \-ˌiz-əm\ *n* **:** the policy of approaching a desired end by gradual stages — **grad·u·al·ist** \-əst\ *n or adj*

grad·u·and \ˌgraj-ə-ˈwand\ *n* [ML *graduandus,* gerundive of *graduare*] *Brit* **:** one about to graduate **:** a candidate for a degree

¹grad·u·ate \ˈgraj-(ə-)wət, -ə-ˌwāt\ *n* **1 :** a holder of an academic degree or diploma **2 :** a graduated cup, cylinder, or flask for measuring

²graduate *adj* **1 :** holding an academic degree or diploma **2 :** of, relating to, or engaged in studies beyond the first or bachelor's degree <~ school> <a ~ student>
³grad·u·ate \ˈgraj-ə-ˌwāt\ *vb* **-at·ed; -at·ing** [ML *graduare,* fr. L *gradus* step, degree] *vt* **1 :** to grant an academic degree or diploma to **2 :** to admit to a particular standing or grade **3 a :** to mark with degrees of measurement **b :** to divide into grades or intervals ~ *vi* **1 :** to receive an academic degree or diploma **2 :** to pass from one stage of experience, proficiency, or prestige to a usu. higher one **3 :** to change gradually — **grad·u·a·tor** \-ˌwāt-ər\ *n*
grad·u·a·tion \ˌgraj-ə-ˈwā-shən\ *n* **1 :** a mark on an instrument or vessel indicating degrees or quantity; *also* **:** these marks **2 a :** the award or acceptance of an academic degree or diploma **b :** COMMENCEMENT **3 :** arrangement in degrees or ranks
Graeco- — see GRECO-
graf·fi·to \grə-ˈfēt-(ˌ)ō, grə-, grä-\ *n, pl* **-ti** \-(ˌ)ē\ [It] **:** an inscription or drawing made on a rock or wall
¹graft \ˈgraft\ *vb* [ME *graften,* alter. of *graffen,* fr. *graffe* graft, fr. MF *grafe,* fr. ML *graphium,* fr. L, stylus, fr. Gk *grapheion,* fr. *graphein* to write — more at CARVE] *vt* **1 a :** to cause (a scion) to unite with a stock; *also* **:** to unite (plants or scion and stock) to form a graft **b :** to propagate (a plant) by grafting **2 a :** to unite closely **b :** to attach (a chemical unit) to a main molecular chain **3 :** to implant (living tissue) surgically **4 :** to get (illicit gain) by graft ~ *vi* **1 :** to become grafted **2 :** to perform grafting **3 :** to practice graft — **graft·er** *n*
²graft *n* **1 a :** a grafted plant **b :** SCION 1 **c :** the point of insertion of a scion upon a stock **2 a :** the act of grafting **b :** something grafted; *specif* **:** living tissue used in grafting **3 :** the acquisition of gain (as money) in dishonest or questionable ways; *also* **:** illegal or unfair gain

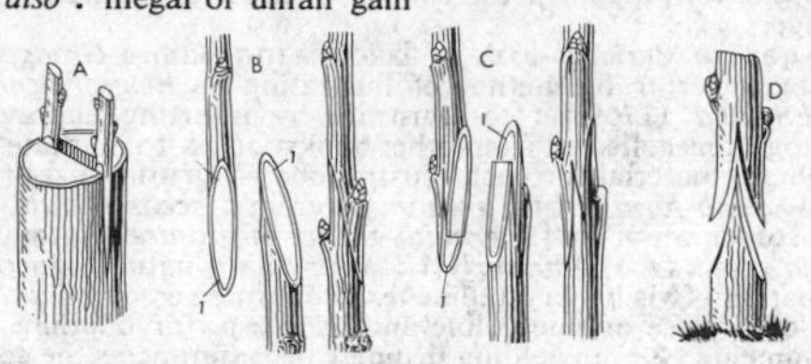

graft 1c: *A* cleft, *B* splice, *C* whip, *D* saddle, *1* cambium

graft·age \ˈgraf-tij\ *n* **:** the principles and practice of grafting
gra·ham cracker \ˌgrā-əm-, ˌgra(-ə)m-\ *n* [*graham flour*] **:** a slightly sweet cracker made of whole wheat flour
graham flour *n* [Sylvester *Graham* †1851 Am dietary reformer] **:** whole wheat flour
grail \ˈgrā(ə)l\ *n* [ME *graal,* fr. MF, bowl, grail, fr. ML *gradalis*] **1** *cap* **:** the cup or platter used according to medieval legend by Christ at the Last Supper and thereafter the object of knightly quests — called also *Holy Grail* **2 :** the object of an extended or difficult quest <the twin ~*s* of American life, Money and Success —Richard Pollak>
¹grain \ˈgrān\ *n* [ME, partly fr. MF *grain* cereal grain, fr. L *granum;* partly fr. MF *graine* seed, kermes, fr. L *grana,* pl. of *granum* — more at CORN] **1 a (1)** *obs* **:** a single small hard seed **(2) :** a seed or fruit of a cereal grass **:** CARYOPSIS **b :** the seeds or fruits of various food plants including the cereal grasses and in commercial and statutory usage other plants (as the soybean) **c :** plants producing grain **2 a :** a small hard particle or crystal (as of sand or salt) **b :** a minute portion or particle **c :** the least amount possible <not a ~ of truth in what he said> **d :** fine crystallization (as of sugar) **3 a :** kermes or a scarlet dye made from it **b :** cochineal or a brilliant scarlet dye made from it **c :** a fast dye **d** *archaic* **:** COLOR, TINT **4 a :** a granulated surface or appearance **b :** the outer or hair side of a skin or hide **5 :** a unit of weight based on the weight of a grain of wheat taken as an average of the weight of grains from the middle of the ear — see WEIGHT table **6 a :** the stratification of the wood fibers in a piece of wood **b :** a texture due to constituent particles or fibers <the ~ of a rock> **7 :** tactile quality **8 a :** natural disposition **:** TEMPER **b :** a basic or characteristic quality <anti-intellectual... doctrines are very much in the American ~ —R. W. Noland> — **grained** \ˈgrānd\ *adj* — **against the grain :** counter to one's inclination, disposition, or feeling — **with a grain of salt :** with a skeptical attitude <take his predictions *with a grain of salt*>
²grain *vt* **1 :** INGRAIN **2 :** to form into grains **:** GRANULATE **3 :** to paint in imitation of the grain of wood or stone ~ *vi* **:** to become granular **:** GRANULATE — **grain·er** *n*
grain alcohol *n* **:** ALCOHOL 1
grain elevator *n* **:** ELEVATOR 1c
grain·field \ˈgrān-ˌfēld\ *n* **:** a field where grain is grown
grain rust *n* **:** a rust that attacks a cereal grass
grains of paradise : the pungent seeds of a West African plant (*Aframomum melegueta* of the family Zingiberaceae) that are used as a spice
grain sorghum *n* **:** any of several sorghums cultivated primarily for grain — compare SORGO
grainy \ˈgrā-nē\ *adj* **grain·i·er; -est 1 :** consisting of or resembling grains **:** GRANULAR **2 :** having or resembling the grain of wood — **grain·i·ness** *n*
¹gram \ˈgram\ *n* [obs. Pg (now *grão*), grain, fr. L *granum*] **:** any of several leguminous plants (as a chick-pea) grown esp. for their seed
²gram *or* **gramme** \ˈgram\ *n* [F *gramme,* fr. LL *gramma,* a small weight, fr. Gk *grammat-, gramma* letter, writing, a small weight, fr. *graphein* to write — more at CARVE] **:** a metric unit of mass and weight equal to $^{1}/_{1000}$ kilogram and nearly equal to one cubic centimeter of water at its maximum density — see METRIC SYSTEM table
³gram *n* [by shortening & alter.] **:** GRANDMOTHER
⁴gram *abbr* grammar; grammatical
-gram \ˌgram\ *n comb form* [L *-gramma,* fr. Gk, fr. *gramma*] **:** drawing **:** writing **:** record <chrono*gram*> <tele*gram*>
grama \ˈgram-ə\ *n* [Sp] **:** a pasture grass (genus *Bouteloua*) of the western U.S. — called also *grama grass*
gram·a·rye \ˈgram-ə-rē\ *n* [ME, fr. MF *gramaire* grammar, grammar book, book of sorcery] **:** MAGIC
gram atom *n* **:** the atomic weight of an element in grams — called also *gram-atomic weight*
gram calorie *n* **:** CALORIE 1a
gram equivalent *n* **:** the quantity of an element, radical, or compound that has a weight in grams equal to the equivalent weight
gra·mer·cy \grə-ˈmər-sē\ *interj* [ME *grand mercy,* fr. MF *grand merci* great thanks] *archaic* — used to express gratitude or astonishment
gram·i·ci·din \ˌgram-ə-ˈsīd-ᵊn\ *n* [*gram*-positive + *-i-* + *-cide* + *-in*] **:** a toxic crystalline polypeptide antibiotic produced by a soil bacterium (*Bacillus brevis*) and used against gram-positive bacteria in local infections
gra·min·e·ous \grə-ˈmin-ē-əs\ *adj* [L *gramineus,* fr. *gramin-, gramen* grass] **:** of or relating to a grass — **gra·min·e·ous·ness** *n*
gram·i·niv·o·rous \ˌgram-ə-ˈniv-(ə-)rəs\ *adj* [L *gramin-, gramen*] **:** feeding on grass
gram·mar \ˈgram-ər\ *n* [ME *gramere,* fr. MF *gramaire,* modif. of L *grammatica,* fr. Gk *grammatikē,* fr. fem. of *grammatikos* of letters, fr. *grammat-, gramma*] **1 a :** the study of the classes of words, their inflections, and their functions and relations in the sentence **b :** a study of what is to be preferred and what avoided in inflection and syntax **2 :** the characteristic system of inflections and syntax of a language **3 a :** a grammar textbook **b :** speech or writing evaluated according to its conformity to grammatical rules **4 :** the principles or rules of an art, science, or technique <a ~ of the theater> — **gram·mar·i·an** \grə-ˈmer-ē-ən, -ˈmar-\ *n*
grammar school *n* **1 a :** a secondary school emphasizing Latin and Greek in preparation for college **b :** a British college preparatory school **2 :** a school intermediate between primary school and high school **3 :** ELEMENTARY SCHOOL
gram·mat·i·cal \grə-ˈmat-i-kəl\ *adj* **1 :** of or relating to grammar **2 :** conforming to the rules of grammar — **gram·mat·i·cal·i·ty** \-ˌmat-ə-ˈkal-ət-ē\ *n* — **gram·mat·i·cal·ly** \-ˈmat-i-k(ə-)lē\ *adv* — **gram·mat·i·cal·ness** \-kəl-nəs\ *n*
grammatical meaning *n* **:** the part of meaning that varies from one inflectional form to another (as from *plays* to *played* to *playing*) — compare LEXICAL MEANING
gram molecule *n* **:** the quantity of a compound or element that has a weight in grams numerically equal to the molecular weight — called also *gram-molecular weight*
Gram·my \ˈgram-ē\ *n, pl* **Grammys** [*Gram*ophone + *-my* (as in *Emmy*)] **:** a statuette presented annually by a professional organization for notable achievement in the recording industry
gram–neg·a·tive \ˈgram-ˈneg-ət-iv\ *adj* **:** not holding the purple dye when stained by Gram's method — used chiefly of bacteria
gram·o·phone \ˈgram-ə-ˌfōn\ *n* [fr. *Gramophone,* a trademark] **:** PHONOGRAPH
gramp \ˈgramp\ *or* **gramps** \ˈgram(p)s\ *n, pl* **gramps** [by shortening & alter.] **:** GRANDFATHER
gram–pos·i·tive \ˈgram-ˈpäz-ət-iv, -ˈpäz-tiv\ *adj* **:** holding the purple dye when stained by Gram's method — used chiefly of bacteria
gram·pus \ˈgram-pəs\ *n* [alter. of ME *graspey, grapay,* fr. MF *graspeis,* fr. *gras* fat (fr. L *crassus*) + *peis* fish, fr. L *piscis* — more at FISH] **1 :** a cetacean (*Grampus griseus*) related to the blackfish; *broadly* **:** any of various small cetaceans (as the blackfish or killer whale) **2 :** the giant whip scorpion (*Mastigoproctus giganteus*) of the southern U.S.
Gram's method \ˈgramz-\ *n* [Hans C. J. *Gram* †1938 Dan physician] **:** a method for the differential staining of bacteria by which some species remain colored and some are decolorized by treatment with Gram's solution after staining with gentian violet
Gram's solution *n* **:** a watery solution of iodine and the iodide of potassium used in staining bacteria by Gram's method
gram–vari·able \ˈgram-ˈver-ē-ə-bəl, -ˈvar-\ *adj* **:** staining irregularly or inconsistently by Gram's method
grana *pl of* GRANUM
gran·a·dil·la \ˌgran-ə-ˈdil-ə, -ˈdē-(y)ə\ *n* [Sp] **:** the oblong fruit of various passionflowers (esp. *Passiflora quadrangularis* of tropical America) widely used as a dessert
gra·na·ry \ˈgrān-(ə-)rē, ˈgran-\ *n, pl* **-ries** [L *granarium,* fr. *granum* grain] **1 a :** a storehouse for threshed grain **b :** a region producing grain in abundance **2 :** a chief source or storehouse
¹grand \ˈgrand\ *adj* [MF, large, great, grand, fr. L *grandis*] **1 a :** having more importance than others **:** FOREMOST **b :** having higher rank than others bearing the same general designation <the ~ champion> **2 a :** INCLUSIVE, COMPREHENSIVE <the ~ total of all money paid out> **b :** DEFINITIVE, INCONTROVERTIBLE <~ example> **3 :** MAIN, PRINCIPAL **4 :** large and striking in size, scope, extent, or conception **5 a :** LAVISH, SUMPTUOUS <a ~ celebration> **b :** marked by a regal form and dignity **c :** fine or imposing in appearance or impression **d :** LOFTY, SUBLIME <writing in the ~ style> **6 a :** pretending to social superiority **:** SUPERCILIOUS **b :** intended to impress <a man of ~ gestures and pretentious statements> **7 :** very good **:** WONDERFUL <a ~ time> <a ~ old

man> — **grand·ly** \'gran-(d)lē\ *adv* — **grand·ness** \'gran(d)-nəs\ *n*

syn GRAND, MAGNIFICENT, IMPOSING, STATELY, MAJESTIC, GRANDIOSE *shared meaning element* : large and impressive

2**grand** *n, slang* : a thousand dollars

gran·dam \'gran-ˌdam, -dəm\ *or* **gran·dame** \-ˌdām, -dəm\ *n* [ME *graundam,* fr. AF *graund dame,* lit., great lady] **1** : GRANDMOTHER **2** : an old woman

grand·aunt \'gran-'dant, -'dänt\ *n* : the aunt of one's father or mother — called also *great-aunt*

grand·ba·by \'gran(d)-ˌbā-bē\ *n* : an infant grandchild

grand·child \-ˌchīld\ *n* : the child of one's son or daughter

grand·dad *or* **gran·dad** \'gran-ˌdad\ *n* : GRANDFATHER

grand·dad·dy \-ˌdad-ē\ *also* **gran·dad·dy** *n* **1** : GRANDFATHER **2** : one that is the first, earliest, most ancient, or most venerable of its kind <the ~ of . . . modern technical analysis —J. W. Schulz>

grand·daugh·ter \-ˌdȯt ər\ *n* : the daughter of one's son or daughter

grand duchess *n* **1** : the wife or widow of a grand duke **2** : a woman who rules a grand duchy in her own right

grand duchy *n* : the territory or dominion of a grand duke or grand duchess

grand duke *n* **1** : the sovereign duke of any of various European states **2** : a son or male descendant of a Russian czar in the male line

grande dame \grän-'däm, gräⁿd-däm\ *n* [F, lit., great lady] : a usu. elderly woman of great prestige or ability

gran·dee \gran-'dē\ *n* [Sp *grande,* fr. *grande,* adj., large, great, fr. L *grandis*] : a man of elevated rank or station; *esp* : a Spanish or Portuguese nobleman of the first rank

gran·deur \'gran-jər, -ˌju̇(ə)r, -ˌd(y)u̇(ə)r, -d(y)ər\ *n* [ME, fr. MF, fr. *grand*] **1** : the quality or state of being grand : MAGNIFICENCE <the glory that was Greece and the ~ that was Rome —E. A. Poe> **2** : an instance or example of grandeur

grand·fa·ther \'gran(d)-ˌfäth-ər\ *n* : the father of one's father or mother; *also* : ANCESTOR 1a — **grand·fa·ther·ly** \-lē\ *adj*

grandfather clause *n* : a clause creating an exemption based on circumstances previously existing; *esp* : a provision in several southern state constitutions designed to enfranchise poor whites and disfranchise Negroes by waiving high voting requirements for descendants of men voting before 1867

grandfather clock *n* [fr. the song *My Grandfather's Clock* (1876) by Henry C. Work] : a tall pendulum clock standing directly on the floor — called also *grandfather's clock*

grandfather clock

grand fir *n* : a lofty tree (*Abies grandis*) of the northwestern Pacific coastal region of No. America with cylindrical greenish cones and soft wood

Grand Gui·gnol \ˌgräⁿ-gēn-'yȯl, -'yōl\ *n* [*Le Grand Guignol,* small theater in Montmartre, Paris, specializing in such performances] : dramatic entertainment featuring the gruesome or horrible — **Grand Guignol** *adj*

gran·di·flo·ra \ˌgran-də-'flōr-ə, -'flȯr-\ *n* [NL, fr. L *grandis* great + *flor-, flos* flower — more at BLOW] : a bush rose derived from crosses of floribunda and hybrid tea roses and characterized by production of blooms both singly and in clusters on the same plant

gran·dil·o·quence \gran-'dil-ə-kwən(t)s\ *n* [prob. fr. MF, fr. L *grandiloquus* using lofty language, fr. *grandis* + *loqui* to speak] : lofty or pompous eloquence : BOMBAST — **gran·dil·o·quent** \-kwənt\ *adj* — **gran·dil·o·quent·ly** *adv*

gran·di·ose \'gran-dē-ˌōs, ˌgran-dē-'\ *adj* [F, fr. It *grandioso,* fr. *grande* great, fr. L *grandis*] **1** : impressive because of uncommon largeness, scope, effect, or grandeur **2** : characterized by affectation of grandeur or splendor or by absurd exaggeration *syn* see GRAND — **gran·di·ose·ly** *adv* — **gran·di·ose·ness** *n* — **gran·di·os·i·ty** \ˌgran-dē-'äs-ət-ē\ *n*

gran·di·o·so \ˌgrän-dē-'ō-(ˌ)sō, ˌgran-, -(ˌ)zō\ *adv or adj* [It] : in a broad and noble style — used as a direction in music

grand jury *n* : a jury that examines accusations against persons charged with crime and if the evidence warrants makes formal charges on which the accused persons are later tried

Grand Lama *n* : DALAI LAMA

grand larceny *n* : larceny of property of a value greater than that fixed as constituting petit larceny

grand·ma \'gran(d)-ˌmä, -ˌmȯ; 'gram-ˌä, -ˌȯ\ *n* : GRANDMOTHER

grand mal \'grän(d)-ˌmäl, 'gräⁿ-ˌmäl, -ˌmal; 'gran(d)-ˌmal\ *n* [F, lit., great illness] : severe epilepsy

grand march *n* : an opening ceremony at a ball that consists of a march participated in by all the guests

grand master *n* : an expert player (as of chess) who has consistently scored high in international competition

grand·moth·er \'gran(d)-ˌməth-ər\ *n* : the mother of one's father or mother; *also* : a female ancestor — **grand·moth·er·ly** \-lē\ *adj*

grandmother clock *n* : a pendulum clock that is about two thirds the size of a grandfather clock

grand·neph·ew \'gran(d)-'nef-(ˌ)yü, *chiefly Brit* -'nev-\ *n* : a grandson of one's brother or sister

grand·niece \-'nēs\ *n* : a granddaughter of one's brother or sister

grand opera *n* : opera in which the plot is elaborated as in serious drama and the entire text set to music

grand·pa \'gran(d)-ˌpä, -ˌpȯ; 'gram-ˌpä, -ˌpȯ\ *n* : GRANDFATHER

grand·par·ent \'gran(d)-ˌpar-ənt, -ˌper-\ *n* : a parent of one's father or mother — **grand·pa·ren·tal** \ˌgran(d)-pə-'rent-ᵊl\ *adj* — **grand·par·ent·hood** \'gran(d)-'par-ent-ˌhu̇d, -'per-\ *n*

Grand Penitentiary *n* : PENITENTIARY 1b

grand piano *n* : a piano with horizontal frame and strings — compare UPRIGHT PIANO

grand prix \'gräⁿ-'prē\ *n, pl* **grand prix** \-'prē(z)\ *often cap G&P* [F *Grand Prix de Paris,* an international horse race established 1863, lit., grand prize of Paris] : a long-distance auto race usu. over a road course; *specif* : one of a series of international formula car races

grand·sire \'gran(d)-ˌsī(ə)r\ *or* **grand·sir** \'gran(t)-sər\ *n* **1** *dial* : GRANDFATHER **2** *archaic* : FOREFATHER **3** *archaic* : an aged man

grand–slam *adj* : being a home run made with the bases loaded

grand slam *n* **1** : the winning of all the tricks in one hand of a card game (as bridge) **2** : a clean sweep or total success; *specif* : the winning of all the major or specified tournaments on a tour <he twice won the tennis *grand slam*>

grand·son \'gran(d)-ˌsən\ *n* : the son of one's son or daughter

1**grand·stand** \-ˌstand\ *n* **1** : a usu. roofed stand for spectators at a racecourse or stadium **2** : AUDIENCE

2**grandstand** *vi* : to play or act so as to impress onlookers — **grand·stand·er** *n*

grand tour *n* **1** : an extended tour of the Continent that was formerly a usual part of the education of young British gentlemen **2** : an extensive and usu. educational tour <making the *grand tour* of the markets, quais, and parks —E. G. Robinson *b*1933>

grand touring car *n* : a usu. 2-passenger coupe — called also *grand tourer*

grand·un·cle \'gran-'dəŋ-kəl\ *n* : an uncle of one's father or mother

grange \'grānj\ *n* [ME, fr. MF, fr. ML *granica,* fr. L *granum* grain] **1** *archaic* : GRANARY, BARN **2** : FARM; *esp* : a farmhouse with outbuildings **3** *cap* : one of the lodges of a national fraternal association of farmers; *also* : the association itself

grang·er \'grān-jər\ *n* **1** *cap* : a member of a Grange **2** *chiefly West* : FARMER, HOMESTEADER

1**gran·ger·ism** \'grān-jə-ˌriz-əm\ *n* : the practice of grangerizing

2**grang·er·ism** \'grān-jə-ˌriz-əm\ *n* : the policy or methods of the grangers

gran·ger·ize \'grān-jə-ˌrīz\ *vt* **-ized; -iz·ing** [James *Granger* †1776 E biographer; fr. his method of illustrating his *Biographical History of England* (1769)] : to illustrate by inserting engravings or photographs collected from other books; *also* : to mutilate (books) to obtain material for such illustrations — **gran·ger·iz·er** *n*

grani- *comb form* [L, fr. *granum*] : grain : seeds <*grani*vorous>

gran·ite \'gran-ət\ *n* [It *granito,* fr. pp. of *granire* to granulate, fr. *grano* grain, fr. L *granum*] **1** : a very hard natural igneous rock formation of visibly crystalline texture formed essentially of quartz and orthoclase or microcline and used esp. for building and for monuments **2** : unyielding firmness or endurance <the cold ~ of Puritan formalism —V. L. Parrington> — **gran·ite·like** \-ət-ˌlīk\ *adj* — **gra·nit·ic** \gra-'nit-ik\ *adj* — **gran·it·oid** \'gran-ət-ˌȯid\ *adj*

granite paper *n* : a paper containing a small proportion of deeply colored mottling fibers

gran·ite·ware \'gran-ət-ˌwa(ə)r, -ˌwe(ə)r\ *n* : ironware with mottled enamel usu. in two tones of gray

gra·niv·o·rous \grə-'niv-(ə-)rəs, grā-\ *adj* : feeding on seeds or grain

gran·ny *or* **gran·nie** \'gran-ē\ *n, pl* **grannies** [by shortening & alter.] **1 a** : GRANDMOTHER **b** : a fussy person **2** *South & Midland* : MIDWIFE

granny knot *n* : an insecure knot often made instead of a square knot — see KNOT illustration

grano- *comb form* [G, fr. *granit,* fr. It *granito*] : granite : granitic <*grano*gabbro>

grano·di·o·rite \ˌgran-ō-'dī-ə-ˌrīt\ *n* : a granular intrusive quartzose igneous rock intermediate between granite and quartz diorite with plagioclase predominant over orthoclase — **grano·di·o·rit·ic** \-ˌdī-ə-'rit-ik\ *adj*

grano·lith \'gran-ə-ˌlith\ *n* : an artificial stone of crushed granite and cement — **grano·lith·ic** \ˌgran-ə-'lith-ik\ *adj*

grano·phyre \'gran-ə-ˌfī(ə)r\ *n* [ISV] : a porphyritic igneous rock chiefly of feldspar and quartz with granular groundmass — **grano·phyr·ic** \ˌgran-ə-'fir-ik\ *adj*

1**grant** \'grant\ *vt* [ME *granten,* fr. OF *creanter, graanter,* fr. (assumed) VL *credentare,* fr. L *credent-, credens,* prp. of *credere* to believe — more at CREED] **1 a** : to consent to carry out for a person : allow fulfillment of <~ a child his wish> <~ a request> **b** : to permit as a right, privilege, or favor <luggage allowances ~*ed* to passengers> **2** : to bestow or transfer formally <~ a scholarship to a student> ; *specif* : to give the possession or title of by a deed **3 a** : to be willing to concede **b** : to assume to be true <~*ing* that you are correct, you may find it hard to prove your point> — **grant·able** \-ə-bəl\ *adj* — **grant·er** \-ər\ *n* — **grant·or** \'grant-ər, -ˌȯ(ə)r; grant-'ȯ(ə)r\ *n*

syn GRANT, CONCEDE, VOUCHSAFE, ACCORD, AWARD *shared meaning element* : to give as a favor or a right. One GRANTS, usually to a claimant or petitioner and often a subordinate, something sought that could be withheld <acceding to her pleas, he *granted* her another period of six months in which to make good —*Current Biog.*> One CONCEDES something when one yields it reluctantly in response to a rightful or compelling claim <even his harshest critics *concede* him a rocklike integrity —*Time*> One VOUCHSAFES something as a courtesy or an act of gracious condescension <occasionally a true poet is *vouchsafed* to the world —Rumer Godden> As often used in supplications, the word implies humility in the suppliant <*vouchsafe,* O Lord: to keep us this day without sin —*Bk. of Com. Prayer*> One ACCORDS to another what is due or proper <children easily appreciate justice, and will readily *accord* to others what others *accord* to them —Bertrand Russell> One AWARDS what is deserved or merited; typically the word implies careful weighing of pertinent factors <*award* a contract to build a new school> <*award* a prize for the best essay>

2**grant** *n* **1** : the act of granting **2** : something granted; *esp* : a gift for a particular purpose **3 a** : a transfer of property by deed or writing **b** : the instrument by which such a transfer is made; *also* : the property so transferred **4** : a minor territorial division of Maine, New Hampshire, or Vermont orig. granted by the state to an individual or institution

grant·ee \grant-'ē\ *n* : one to whom a grant is made

grant-in-aid \ˌgrant-ᵊn-ˈād\ *n, pl* **grants-in-aid** \ˌgran(t)-sə-ˈnād\ **1 :** a grant or subsidy for public funds paid by a central to a local government in aid of a public undertaking **2 :** a grant or subsidy to a school or individual for an educational or artistic project

grants·man \ˈgran(t)-smən\ *n* **:** a specialist in grantsmanship

grants·man·ship \-ˌship\ *n* [*grants* + *-manship*] **:** the art of obtaining grants (as for research)

granul- *or* **granuli-** *or* **granulo-** *comb form* [LL *granulum*] **:** granule <*granulose*>

gran·u·lar \ˈgran-yə-lər\ *adj* **:** consisting of or appearing to consist of granules **:** having a grainy texture — **gran·u·lar·i·ty** \ˌgran-yə-ˈlar-ət-ē\ *n* — **gran·u·lar·ly** \ˈgran-yə-lər-lē\ *adv*

gran·u·late \ˈgran-yə-ˌlāt\ *vb* **-lat·ed; -lat·ing** *vt* **:** to form or crystallize into grains or granules ~ *vi* **1 :** to collect into grains or granules **2 :** to form granulations <an open *granulating* wound> — **gran·u·la·tive** \-ˌlāt-iv\ *adj* — **gran·u·la·tor** \-ˌlāt-ər\ *n*

gran·u·la·tion \ˌgran-yə-ˈlā-shən\ *n* **1 :** the act or process of granulating **:** the condition of being granulated **2 :** one of the minute red granules of new capillaries formed on the surface of a wound in healing **3 :** GRANULE 2

granulation tissue *n* **:** tissue made up of granulations that temporarily replaces lost tissue in a wound

gran·ule \ˈgran-(ˌ)yü(ə)l\ *n* [LL *granulum*, dim. of L *granum* grain] **1 :** a small particle; *esp* **:** one of numerous particles forming a larger unit **2 :** one of the small short-lived brilliant spots on the sun's seething photosphere

gran·u·lite \ˈgran-yə-ˌlīt\ *n* **:** a banded or laminated whitish granular rock consisting of feldspar, quartz, and small red garnets and occurring with crystalline schists — **gran·u·lit·ic** \ˌgran-yə-ˈlit-ik\ *adj*

gran·u·lo·cyte \ˈgran-yə-lō-ˌsīt\ *n* [ISV] **:** a cell with granule-containing cytoplasm — **gran·u·lo·cyt·ic** \ˌgran-yə-lō-ˈsit-ik\ *adj*

gran·u·lo·cy·to·poi·e·sis \ˈgran-yə-lō-ˌsīt-ə-pȯi-ˈē-səs\ *n* [NL] **:** the formation of blood granulocytes typically in the bone marrow

gran·u·lo·ma \ˌgran-yə-ˈlō-mə\ *n, pl* **-mas** *or* **-ma·ta** \-mət-ə\ **:** a mass or nodule of chronically inflamed tissue with granulations that is usu. associated with an infective process — **gran·u·lo·ma·tous** \-mət-əs\ *adj*

granuloma in·gui·na·le \-ˌiŋ-gwə-ˈnal-ē, -ˈnäl-, -ˈnāl-\ *n* [NL, lit., inguinal granuloma] **:** a venereal disease characterized by ulceration and formation of granulations beginning in the groin and spreading to the buttocks and genitals and caused by a bacterium (*Donovania granulomatis*)

granuloma ve·ne·re·um \-və-ˈnir-ē-əm\ *n* **:** GRANULOMA INGUINALE

gran·u·lose \ˈgran-yə-ˌlōs\ *adj* **:** GRANULAR; *esp* **:** having the surface roughened with granules

gran·u·lo·sis \ˌgran-yə-ˈlō-səs\ *n, pl* **-lo·ses** \-ˌsēz\ [NL] **:** a virus disease of insect larvae distinguished by the presence of minute granular inclusions in infected cells

gra·num \ˈgrā-nəm\ *n, pl* **gra·na** \-nə\ [NL, fr. L, grain] **:** one of the lamellar stacks of chlorophyll-containing material in plant chloroplasts

grape \ˈgrāp\ *n, often attrib* [ME, fr. OF *crape, grape* hook, grape stalk, bunch of grapes, grape, of Gmc origin; akin to OHG *krāpfo* hook — more at CRAVE] **1 :** a smooth-skinned juicy greenish white to deep red or purple berry eaten dried or fresh as a fruit or fermented to produce wine **2 :** any of numerous woody vines (genus *Vitis* of the family Vitaceae, the grape family) that usu. climb by tendrils, produce clustered fruits that are grapes, and are nearly cosmopolitan in cultivation **3 :** GRAPESHOT

grape·fruit \ˈgrāp-ˌfrüt\ *n* **1 :** a large citrus fruit with a bitter yellow rind and inner skin and a highly flavored somewhat acid juicy pulp **2 :** a small roundheaded tree (*Citrus paradisi*) that produces grapefruit and is prob. derived from the shaddock

grape hyacinth *n* **:** any of several small bulbous spring-flowering herbs (genus *Muscari*) of the lily family with racemes of usu. blue flowers

grape·shot \ˈgrāp-ˌshät\ *n* **:** a cluster of small iron balls used as a cannon charge

grape sugar *n* **:** DEXTROSE

grape·vine \ˈgrāp-ˌvīn\ *n* **1 :** GRAPE 2 **2 a :** an informal person-to-person means of circulating information or gossip <heard about the meeting through the ~> **b :** a secret source of information

[1]**graph** \ˈgraf\ *n* [short for *graphic formula*] **1 :** a diagram (as a series of points, a line, a curve, or an area) that represents the variation of a variable in comparison with that of one or more other variables **2 :** the collection of all points whose coordinates satisfy a given functional relation

[2]**graph** *vt* **1 :** to represent by a graph **2 :** to plot on a graph

[3]**graph** *n* [prob. fr. *-graph*] **1 :** a spelling of a word **2 :** a single occurrence of a letter of an alphabet in any of its various shapes (as D, d) **3 :** a letter or combination of letters taken as a minimum unit in determining the phonemes of a language from written records — compare GRAPHEME

-graph \ˌgraf\ *n comb form* [MF *-graphe*, fr. L *-graphum*, fr. Gk *-graphon*, fr. neut. of *-graphos* written, fr. *graphein* to write] **1 :** something written <mono*graph*> **2** [F *-graphe*, fr. LL *-graphus*] **:** instrument for making or transmitting records <chrono*graph*>

graph·eme \ˈgraf-ˌēm\ *n* **1 :** a unit (as a letter) of a writing system **2 :** the set of units of a writing system (as letters and letter combinations) that represent a phoneme <the *f* of *fin*, the *ph* of *phantom*, and the *gh* of *laugh* are members of one ~> — **gra·phe·mic** \gra-ˈfē-mik\ *adj* — **gra·phe·mi·cal·ly** \-mi-k(ə-)lē\ *adv*

gra·phe·mics \gra-ˈfē-miks\ *n pl but sing or pl in constr* **:** the study and analysis of a writing system in terms of graphemes

-g·ra·pher \g-rə-fər\ *n comb form* [LL *-graphus*, fr. Gk *-graphos*, fr. *graphein*] **:** one that writes about (specified) material or in a (specified) way <cranio*grapher*>

[1]**graph·ic** \ˈgraf-ik\ *also* **graph·i·cal** \-i-kəl\ *adj* [L *graphicus*, fr. Gk *graphikos*, fr. *graphein*] **1 :** formed by writing, drawing, or engraving **2 a :** marked by or capable of clear and lively description or striking imaginative power **b :** sharply outlined or delineated **3 a :** of or relating to the pictorial arts **b :** of, relating to, or involving such reproductive methods as those of engraving, etching, lithography, photography, serigraphy, and woodcut **c :** of or relating to the art of printing **d :** relating or according to graphics **4 :** having mineral crystals resembling written or printed characters **5 :** of, relating to, or represented by a graph **6 :** of or relating to the written or printed word or the symbols or devices used in writing or printing to represent sound or convey meaning — **graph·i·cal·ly** \-i-k(ə-)lē\ *adv* — **graph·ic·ness** \-ik-nəs\ *n* ***syn*** GRAPHIC, VIVID, PICTURESQUE, PICTORIAL *shared meaning element* **:** giving a clear visual impression esp. in words

[2]**graphic** *n* **1 a :** a product of graphic art **b** *pl* **:** the graphic media **2 :** a picture, map, or graph used for illustration or demonstration **3 :** a graphic representation displayed by a computer (as on a CRT)

-graph·ic \ˈgraf-ik\ *or* **-graph·i·cal** \-i-kəl\ *adj comb form* [LL *-graphicus*, fr. Gk *-graphikos*, fr. *graphikos*] **1 :** written or transmitted in a (specified) way <stylo*graphic*> **2 :** of or relating to writing in a (specified) field or on a (specified) subject <oro*graphic*>

graphic arts *n pl* **:** the fine and applied arts of representation, decoration, and writing or printing on flat surfaces together with the techniques and crafts associated with them

graph·ics \ˈgraf-iks\ *n pl but sing or pl in constr* **1 :** the art or science of drawing a representation of an object on a two-dimensional surface according to mathematical rules of projection **2 :** the process whereby a computer displays graphics on a CRT and an operator can manipulate them (as with a light pen)

graph·ite \ˈgraf-ˌīt\ *n* [G *graphit*, fr. Gk *graphein* to write] **:** a soft black lustrous carbon that conducts electricity and is used in lead pencils, crucibles, electrolytic anodes, as a lubricant, and as a moderator in atomic-energy plants — **gra·phit·ic** \gra-ˈfit-ik\ *adj*

graph·i·tize \ˈgraf-ə-ˌtīz, -ˌīt-īz\ *vt* **-tized; -tiz·ing 1 :** to convert into graphite **2 :** to impregnate or coat with graphite — **graph·i·tiz·able** \-ˌtī-zə-bəl, -īz-\ *adj* — **graph·i·ti·za·tion** ˌgraf-ət-ə-ˈzā-shən, -ˌīt-\ *n*

grapho- *comb form* [F, fr. MF, fr. Gk, fr. *graphē*, fr. *graphein* to write] **:** writing

gra·phol·o·gist \gra-ˈfäl-ə-jəst\ *n* **:** a specialist in graphology

gra·phol·o·gy \-jē\ *n* [F *graphologie*, fr. *grapho-* + *-logie* -logy] **:** the study of handwriting esp. for the purpose of character analysis — **graph·o·log·i·cal** \ˌgraf-ə-ˈläj-i-kəl\ *adj*

graph·o·phone \ˈgraf-ə-ˌfōn\ *n* [fr. *Graphophone*, a trademark] **:** a phonograph using wax records

graph paper *n* **:** paper ruled for drawing graphs

-g·ra·phy \g-rə-fē\ *n comb form* [L *-graphia*, fr. Gk, fr. *graphein*] **1 :** writing or representation in a (specified) manner or by a (specified) means or of a (specified) object <phono*graphy*> <photo*graphy*> <steno*graphy*> **2 :** writing on a (specified) subject or in a (specified) field <oceano*graphy*>

grap·nel \ˈgrap-nᵊl\ *n* [ME *grapenel*, fr. (assumed) MF *grapinel*, dim. of *grapin*, dim. of *grape* hook — more at GRAPE] **:** a small anchor with four or five flukes or claws used in dragging or grappling operations and for anchoring a dory or skiff

grap·pa \ˈgräp-ə\ *n* [It] **:** a dry colorless brandy distilled from fermented grape pomace

[1]**grap·ple** \ˈgrap-əl\ *n* [MF *grappelle*, dim. of *grape* hook — more at GRAPE] **1 a :** an instrument with iron claws used to fasten an enemy ship alongside before boarding **b :** GRAPNEL **2 a :** the act or an instance of grappling **b :** a hand-to-hand struggle **c :** a contest for superiority or mastery **3 :** a bucket similar to a clamshell but usu. having more jaws

[2]**grapple** *vb* **grap·pled; grap·pling** \ˈgrap-(ə-)liŋ\ *vt* **1 :** to seize with or as if with a grapple **2 :** to come to grips with **:** WRESTLE **3 :** to bind closely ~ *vi* **1 :** to make a ship fast with a grapple **2 :** to come to grips **:** WRESTLE **3 :** to use a grapple — **grap·pler** \-(ə-)lər\ *n*

grap·pling *n* **1 :** GRAPPLE 1a **2 :** GRAPNEL

grappling iron *n* **:** a hooked iron for anchoring a boat, grappling ships to each other, or recovering sunken objects — called also *grappling hook*

grap·to·lite \ˈgrap-tə-ˌlīt\ *n* [Gk *graptos* painted (fr. *graphein* to write, paint) + E *-lite*] **:** any of numerous extinct fossil colonial Paleozoic animals (group Graptolitoidea) with zooids in cups along a chitinous support

grapy \ˈgrā-pē\ *adj* **grap·i·er; -est 1 :** of or relating to grapes or the vine **2 :** having a grape taste as well as a wine taste — used of wines

GRAS *abbr* generally recognized as safe

[1]**grasp** \ˈgrasp\ *vb* [ME *graspen* — more at GRAB] *vi* **:** to make the motion of seizing **:** CLUTCH ~ *vt* **1 :** to take or seize eagerly **2 :** to clasp or embrace with or as if with the fingers or arms **3 :** to lay hold of with the mind **:** COMPREHEND ***syn*** see TAKE — **grasp·able** \ˈgras-pə-bəl\ *adj* — **grasp·er** *n*

[2]**grasp** *n* **1 a :** HANDLE **b :** the fluke of an anchor **c :** EMBRACE **2 :** HOLD, CONTROL **3 a :** the reach of the arms **b :** the power of seizing and holding or attaining <perfection always will elude our ~ —A. J. Celebrezze> **4 :** COMPREHENSION <showed a firm ~ of her subject>

grasp·ing *adj* **:** desiring material possessions urgently and excessively and often to the point of ruthlessness ***syn*** see COVETOUS — **grasp·ing·ly** \ˈgras-piŋ-lē\ *adv* — **grasp·ing·ness** *n*

[1]**grass** \ˈgras\ *n, often attrib* [ME *gras*, fr. OE *græs*; akin to OHG *gras* grass, OE *grōwan* to grow] **1 :** herbage suitable or used for grazing animals **2 :** any of a large family (Gramineae) of

monocotyledonous mostly herbaceous plants with jointed stems, slender sheathing leaves, and flowers borne in spikelets of bracts **3 :** land on which grass is grown <keep off the ~> **4** *pl* **:** a leaf or plant of grass **5 :** a state or place of retirement <an old horse put out to ~> **6 :** electronic noise on a radarscope that takes the form of vertical lines resembling lawn grass **7 :** MARIJUANA — **grass·like** \-ˌlīk\ *adj*

[2]**grass** *vt* **1 :** to feed (livestock) on grass sometimes without grain or other concentrates **2 :** to cover with grass; *esp* **:** to seed to grass ~ *vi* **:** to produce grass

grass carp *n* **:** an herbivorous fish (*Ctenopharyngodon idella*) of Russia and mainland China that has been introduced elsewhere to control aquatic weeds

grass court *n* **:** a tennis court with a grass surface

grass green *n* **1 :** a moderate to strong yellowish green **2 :** a moderate yellow green

grass·hop·per \ˈgras-ˌhäp-ər\ *n* **1 :** any of numerous plant-eating orthopterous insects (suborder Saltatoria) having the hind legs adapted for leaping and sometimes engaging in migratory flights in which whole regions may be stripped of vegetation **2 :** a light unarmed scouting and liaison airplane **3 :** a cocktail made with crème de menthe, crème de cacao, and light cream

grass·land \-ˌland\ *n* **1 :** farmland occupied chiefly by forage plants and esp. grasses **2 a :** land on which the natural dominant plant forms are grasses and forbs **b :** an ecological community in which the characteristic plants are grasses

grass roots *n pl but sing or pl in constr* **1 :** soil at or near the surface **2 :** society at the local level esp. in rural areas as distinguished from the centers of political leadership <cultural changes occurring at the *grass roots* —C. A. Buss> **3 :** the very foundation or source

grass tree *n* **1 :** any of a genus (*Xanthorrhoea*) of Australian plants of the lily family with a thick woody trunk bearing a cluster of stiff linear leaves and a terminal spike of small flowers **2 :** any of several Australasian trees (as a ti) with grasslike foliage

grass widow *n* **1** *chiefly dial* **a :** a discarded mistress **b :** a woman who has had an illegitimate child **2 a :** a woman divorced or separated from her husband **b :** a woman whose husband is temporarily away from her

grass widower *n* **1 :** a man divorced or separated from his wife **2 :** a man whose wife is temporarily away from him

grassy \ˈgras-ē\ *adj* **grass·i·er; -est 1 a :** covered or abounding with grass <~ lawns> **b :** consisting of or having a flavor or odor of grass <~ butter> **2 :** resembling grass esp. in color

grat *past of* GREET

[1]**grate** \ˈgrāt\ *n* [ME, fr. ML *crata, grata* hurdle, modif. of L *cratis* — more at HURDLE] **1** *obs* **:** CAGE, PRISON **2 :** a frame of parallel bars or a lattice of crossed ones blocking a passage **3 a :** a frame or bed of iron bars to hold a stove or furnace fire **b :** FIREPLACE **c :** a barred frame for cooking over a fire **4 :** a screen or sieve for grading ore

[2]**grate** *vt* **grat·ed; grat·ing :** to furnish with a grate

[3]**grate** *vb* **grat·ed; grat·ing** [ME *graten,* fr. MF *grater* to scratch, of Gmc origin; akin to OHG *krazzōn* to scratch] *vt* **1** *archaic* **:** ABRADE **2 :** to pulverize by rubbing with something rough <~ cheese> **3 :** FRET, IRRITATE **4 a :** to gnash or grind noisily **b :** to cause to make a rasping sound **c :** to utter in a harsh voice ~ *vi* **1 :** to rub or rasp noisily **2 :** to cause irritation **:** JAR <dry, cerebral talk that tends to ~ on the nerves —Hollis Alpert> — **grat·er** *n*

grate·ful \ˈgrāt-fəl\ *adj* [obs. *grate* pleasing, thankful, fr. L *gratus* — more at GRACE] **1 a :** appreciative of benefits received **b :** expressing gratitude **2 a :** affording pleasure or contentment **:** PLEASING **b :** pleasing by reason of comfort supplied or discomfort alleviated — **grate·ful·ly** \-fə-lē\ *adv* — **grate·ful·ness** *n*
syn* 1** GRATEFUL, THANKFUL *shared meaning element* **:** feeling or expressing gratitude ***ant ungrateful
2 see PLEASANT ***ant*** obnoxious

grat·i·cule \ˈgrat-ə-ˌkyü(ə)l\ *n* [F, fr. L *craticula* fine latticework, dim. of *cratis*] **1 :** a scale on transparent material in the focal plane of an optical instrument for the location and measurement of objects **2 :** the network of lines of latitude and longitude upon which a map is drawn

grat·i·fi·ca·tion \ˌgrat-ə-fə-ˈkā-shən\ *n* **1 :** the act of gratifying **:** the state of being gratified **2** *archaic* **:** REWARD, RECOMPENSE; *esp* **:** GRATUITY **3 :** a source of satisfaction or pleasure

grat·i·fy \ˈgrat-ə-ˌfī\ *vt* **-fied; -fy·ing** [MF *gratifier,* fr. L *gratificari,* lit., to make oneself pleasing, fr. *gratus* + *-ificari,* pass. of *-ificare* -ify] **1** *archaic* **:** REMUNERATE **2 :** to be a source of or give pleasure or satisfaction to <it *gratified* him to have his wife wear jewels —Willa Cather> **3 :** to give in to **:** INDULGE, SATISFY <~ a whim>

grat·i·fy·ing *adj* **:** giving pleasure esp. through satisfying hope, desire, conscience, or vanity ***syn*** see PLEASANT — **grat·i·fy·ing·ly** \-iŋ-lē\ *adv*

gra·tin \ˈgrat-ᵊn, ˈgrät-\ *n* [F, fr. MF, fr. *grater* to scratch] **:** a brown crust formed on food that has been cooked with a topping of buttered crumbs or grated cheese

grat·ing \ˈgrāt-iŋ\ *n* **1 :** a partition, covering, or frame of parallel bars or crossbars **:** GRATE **2 :** a wooden or metal lattice used to close or floor any of various openings **3 :** a system of close equidistant and parallel lines or bars ruled on a polished surface to produce spectra by diffraction

gra·tis \ˈgrat-əs, ˈgrāt-\ *adv or adj* [ME, fr. L *gratiis, gratis,* fr. abl. pl. of *gratia* favor — more at GRACE] **:** without charge or recompense **:** FREE

grat·i·tude \ˈgrat-ə-ˌt(y)üd\ *n* [ME, fr. MF or ML; MF, fr. ML *gratitudo,* fr. L *gratus* grateful] **:** the state of being grateful **:** THANKFULNESS

gra·tu·itous \grə-ˈt(y)ü-ət-əs\ *adj* [L *gratuitus,* fr. *gratus*] **1 a :** given unearned or without recompense **b :** costing nothing **:** FREE **c :** not involving a return benefit, compensation, or consideration **2 :** not called for by the circumstances **:** UNWARRANTED <~ insolence> <a ~ assumption> ***syn*** see SUPEREROGATORY — **gra·tu·itous·ly** *adv* — **gra·tu·itous·ness** *n*

gra·tu·ity \grə-ˈt(y)ü-ət-ē\ *n, pl* **-ities :** something given voluntarily or beyond obligation usu. in return for or in anticipation of some service; *esp* **:** TIP

grat·u·late \ˈgrach-ə-ˌlāt\ *vt* [L *gratulatus,* pp. of *gratulari* — more at CONGRATULATE] *archaic* **:** CONGRATULATE — **grat·u·la·tion** \ˌgrach-ə-ˈlā-shen\ *n* — **grat·u·la·to·ry** \ˈgrach-ə-lə-ˌtōr-ē, -ˌtȯr-\ *adj*

grau·pel \ˈgrau̇-pəl\ *n* [G] **:** granular snow pellets — called also *soft hail*

Grau·stark \ˈgrau̇-ˌstärk, ˈgrȯ-\ *n* [*Graustark,* imaginary country in the novel *Graustark* (1901) by George B. McCutcheon] **:** an imaginary land of high romance; *also* **:** a highly romantic piece of writing — **Grau·stark·ian** \grau̇-ˈstär-kē-ən, grȯ-\ *adj*

gra·va·men \grə-ˈvā-mən\ *n, pl* **-va·mens** *or* **-vam·i·na** \-ˈvam-ə-nə\ [LL, burden, fr. L *gravare* to burden, fr. *gravis*] **:** the material or significant part of a grievance or complaint

[1]**grave** \ˈgrāv\ *vt* **graved; grav·en** \ˈgrā-vən\ *or* **graved; grav·ing** [ME *graven,* fr. OE *grafan;* akin to OHG *graban* to dig, OSlav po*greti* to bury] **1** *archaic* **:** DIG, EXCAVATE **2 a :** to carve or shape with a chisel **:** SCULPTURE **b :** to carve or cut (as letters or figures) into a hard surface **:** ENGRAVE **3 :** to impress or fix (as a thought) deeply

[2]**grave** *n* [ME, fr. OE *græf;* akin to OHG *grab* grave, OE *grafan* to dig] **:** an excavation for burial of a body; *broadly* **:** TOMB

[3]**grave** *vt* **graved; grav·ing** [ME *graven*] **:** to clean and pay with pitch (as a ship's bottom)

[4]**grave** \ˈgrāv, *in sense 5 also* ˈgräv\ *adj* [MF, fr. L *gravis* heavy, grave — more at GRIEVE] **1 a** *obs* **:** AUTHORITATIVE, WEIGHTY **b :** meriting serious consideration **:** IMPORTANT <~ problems> **c :** likely to produce great harm or danger <a ~ mistake> **2 :** having a serious and dignified quality or demeanor <a ~ man little given to laughter> <his manner was ~ and calm> **3 :** drab in color **:** SOMBER **4 :** low-pitched in sound **5 a :** having the form ` **b :** marked with a grave accent **c :** of the variety indicated by a grave accent ***syn*** see SERIOUS ***ant*** gay — **grave·ly** *adv* — **grave·ness** *n*

[5]**grave** \ˈgrāv, ˈgräv\ *n* **:** a grave accent ` used to show that a vowel is pronounced with a fall of pitch (as in ancient Greek), that a vowel has a certain quality (as *e* in French), that a final *e* is stressed and close and that a final *o* is stressed and open (as in Italian), that a syllable has a degree of stress between maximum and minimum (as in phonetic transcription), or that the *e* of the English ending *-ed* is to be pronounced (as in "this cursed day")

[6]**gra·ve** \ˈgräv-(ˌ)ā\ *adv or adj* [It, lit., grave, fr. L *gravis*] **:** slowly and solemnly — used as a direction in music

[1]**grav·el** \ˈgrav-əl\ *n* [ME, fr. MF *gravele,* fr. OF, dim. of *grave, greve* pebbly ground, beach] **1** *obs* **:** SAND **2 a :** loose rounded fragments of rock **b :** a stratum or deposit of gravel; *also* **:** a surface covered with gravel <a ~ road> **3 :** a deposit of small calculous concretions in the kidneys and urinary bladder

[2]**gravel** *adj* **:** GRAVELLY 2 — used of the human voice

[3]**gravel** *vt* **-eled** *or* **-elled; -el·ing** *or* **-el·ling** \ˈgrav-(ə-)liŋ\ **1 :** to cover or spread with gravel **2 a :** PERPLEX, CONFOUND **b :** IRRITATE, NETTLE

grav·el–blind \ˈgrav-əl-ˌblīnd\ *adj* [suggested by *sand-blind*] **:** having very weak vision

grave·less \ˈgrāv-ləs\ *adj* **1 :** UNBURIED <these ~ bones> **2 :** not requiring graves **:** DEATHLESS <the ~ home of the blessed>

grav·el·ly \ˈgrav-(ə-)lē\ *adj* **1 :** of, containing, or covered with gravel **2 :** having a harsh grating sound <a ~ voice>

graven image *n* **:** an object of worship carved usu. from wood or stone **:** IDOL

grav·er \ˈgrā-vər\ *n* **1 :** SCULPTOR, ENGRAVER **2 :** any of various cutting or shaving tools used in graving or in hand metal-turning

Graves' disease \ˈgrāvz(-əz)-\ *n* [Robert J. *Graves* †1853 Ir physician] **:** HYPERTHYROIDISM; *specif* **:** exophthalmic goiter

grave·stone \ˈgrāv-ˌstōn\ *n* **:** a burial monument

grave·yard \-ˌyärd\ *n* **1 :** CEMETERY **2 :** a storage place for disused, obsolete, or worn-out things <go down to an auto ~ and build a makeshift car out of parts —*Harper's*>

graveyard shift *n* **:** a work shift beginning late at night (as 11 o'clock); *also* **:** the workers on such a shift

gravi- *comb form* [MF, fr. L, fr. *gravis*] **:** heavy

grav·id \ˈgrav-əd\ *adj* [L *gravidus,* fr. *gravis* heavy] **:** PREGNANT — **gra·vid·i·ty** \gra-ˈvid-ət-ē\ *n* — **grav·id·ly** \ˈgrav-əd-lē\ *adv* — **grav·id·ness** *n*

grav·i·da \ˈgrav-əd-ə\ *n, pl* **-i·das** *or* **-i·dae** \-ə-ˌdē\ [L, fr. fem. of *gravidus*] **:** a pregnant woman — often used in combination with a number or figure to indicate the number of pregnancies a woman has had <a 4-*gravida*>

gra·vi·me·ter \gra-ˈvim-ət-ər, ˈgrav-ə-ˌmēt-\ *n* [F *gravimètre,* fr. *gravi-* + *-mètre* -meter] **1 :** a device similar to a hydrometer for determining specific gravity **2 :** a sensitive weighing instrument for measuring variations in the gravitational field of the earth or moon

gravi·met·ric \ˌgrav-ə-ˈme-trik\ *adj* **1 :** of or relating to measurement by weight **2 :** of or relating to variations in the gravitational field determined by means of a gravimeter — **gravi·met·ri·cal·ly** \-tri-k(ə-)lē\ *adv*

gra·vim·e·try \gra-ˈvim-ə-trē\ *n* **:** the measurement of weight, a gravitational field, or density

graving dock *n* **:** DRY DOCK

grav·i·tate \ˈgrav-ə-ˌtāt\ *vb* **-tat·ed; -tat·ing** *vi* **1 :** to move under the influence of gravitation **2 a :** to move toward something **b :** to become attracted <youngsters . . . ~ toward a strong leader —Rose Friedman> ~ *vt* **:** to move by gravitation

grav·i·ta·tion \ˌgrav-ə-ˈtā-shən\ *n* **1 a :** a force manifested by acceleration toward each other of two free material particles or bodies or of radiant-energy quanta **b :** the action or process of gravitating **2 :** an attraction to something — **grav·i·ta·tion·al** \-shnəl, -shən-ᵊl\ *adj* — **grav·i·ta·tion·al·ly** \-ē\ *adv* — **grav·i·ta·tive** \ˈgrav-ə-ˌtāt-iv\ *adj*

gravitational wave *n* : a hypothetical wave which travels at the speed of light and by means of which gravitational attraction effect is propagated — called also *gravity wave*

grav·i·ton \'grav-ə-ˌtän\ *n* [ISV *gravity* + [2]*-on*] : a hypothetical particle with zero charge and rest mass that is held to be the quantum of the gravitational field

grav·i·ty \'grav-ət-ē\ *n, pl* **-ties** [MF or L; MF *gravité,* fr. L *gravitat-, gravitas,* fr. *gravis*] **1 a** : dignity or sobriety of bearing **b** : IMPORTANCE, SIGNIFICANCE; *esp* : SERIOUSNESS **c** : a serious situation or problem **2** : the quality of having weight **3** : WEIGHT — used chiefly in the phrase *center of gravity* **4 a** : the gravitational attraction of the mass of the earth, the moon, or a planet for bodies at or near its surface; *broadly* : GRAVITATION **b** : ACCELERATION OF GRAVITY **c** : SPECIFIC GRAVITY — **gravity** *adj*

gra·vure \grə-'vyu̇(ə)r, grā-\ *n* [F, fr. *graver* to grave, of Gmc origin; akin to OHG *graban* to dig, engrave — more at GRAVE] **1** : the process of printing from an intaglio plate **2** : PHOTOGRAVURE

gra·vy \'grā-vē\ *n, pl* **gravies** [ME *gravey,* fr. MF *gravé*] **1** : a sauce made from the thickened and seasoned juices of cooked meat **2 a** : something pleasing or valuable that occurs or is acquired over and above what would ordinarily be expected <with expenses now paid, future money is pure ~ —K. Crossen> **b** : unearned or illicit gain : GRAFT

gravy train *n* : a much exploited source of easy money <has him a *gravy train* out there, with these cost-plus contracts and all —*Harper's*>; *also* : GRAVY 2a

[1]**gray** \'grā\ *adj* [ME, fr. OE *grǣg;* akin to OHG *grāo* gray, OSlav *zirĕti* to see] **1 a** : of the color gray **b** : tending toward gray <blue-*gray* eyes> **c** : dull in color **2** : having the hair gray : HOARY **3** : clothed in gray **4** : lacking cheer or brightness in mood, outlook, style, or flavor; *also* : DISMAL, GLOOMY <a ~ day> **5** : intermediate in position, condition, or character <a large but indeterminate ~ zone . . . containing books that are relatively respectable but not wholly so —R. D. Altick> **6** *slang* : of or relating to the Caucasian race — **gray·ly** *adv* — **gray·ness** *n*

[2]**gray** *n* **1** : something (as a horse, garment, cloth, or spot) of a gray color **2** : any of a series of neutral colors ranging between black and white **3** : one who wears a gray uniform: as **a** : a soldier in the Confederate army during the American Civil War **b** : the Confederate army **4** *slang* : a member of the Caucasian race

[3]**gray** *vt* : to make gray ~ *vi* : to become gray

gray·beard \'grā-ˌbi(ə)rd\ *n* : an old man

gray birch *n* **1** : a small coarse No. American birch (*Betula populifolia*) that has many lateral branches, grayish white bark, triangular leaves, and soft wood which is worthless as timber and that occurs esp. as a colonizer of old fields which are reverting to woodland **2** : YELLOW BIRCH

gray eminence *n* [trans. of F *Éminence Grise,* nickname of Pére Joseph (François Joseph du Tremblay) †1638 F monk and diplomat who was confidant of Cardinal Richelieu, styled *Éminence Rouge* (red eminence); fr. the colors of their respective habits] : a person who exercises power behind the scenes

gray·fish \'grā-ˌfish\ *n* : DOGFISH

gray·ish \'grā-ish\ *adj* **1** : somewhat gray **2** *of a color* : low in saturation

gray·ling \'grā-liŋ\ *n, pl* **grayling** *also* **graylings** : any of several freshwater salmonoid fishes (genus *Thymallus*) valued as food and sport fishes

gray matter *n* **1** : neural tissue esp. of the brain and spinal cord that contains nerve-cell bodies as well as nerve fibers and has a brownish gray color **2** : BRAINS, INTELLECT

gray mullet *n* : MULLET 1

gray squirrel *n* : a common light gray to black squirrel (*Sciurus carolinensis*) that is native to eastern No. America and has been introduced into England

gray trout *n* : WEAKFISH 1

gray·wacke \'grā-ˌwak(-ə)\ *n* [[1]*gray* + *wacke* (graywacke), fr. G] : a coarse usu. dark gray sandstone or fine-grained conglomerate composed of firmly cemented rounded fragments (as of quartz and feldspars)

gray whale *n* : a rather large whalebone whale (*Rhachianectes glaucus*) of the northern Pacific

[1]**graze** \'grāz\ *vb* **grazed; graz·ing** [ME *grasen,* fr. OE *grasian,* fr. *graes* grass] *vi* : to feed on growing herbage, attached algae, or phytoplankton ~ *vt* **1 a** : to crop and eat in the field **b** : to feed on the herbage of **2 a** : to put to graze <*grazed* his cows on the meadow> **b** : to put cattle to graze on **3** : to supply herbage for the grazing of — **graze·able** *or* **graz·able** \'grā-zə-bəl\ *adj* — **graz·er** *n*

[2]**graze** *n* **1** : an act of grazing **2** : herbage for grazing

[3]**graze** *vb* **grazed; graz·ing** [perh. fr. [1]*graze*] *vt* **1** : to touch lightly in passing **2** : ABRADE, SCRATCH <*grazed* her knee when she fell> ~ *vi* : to touch or rub against something in passing <our fenders just *grazed*>

[4]**graze** *n* : a scraping along a surface or an abrasion made by it; *esp* : a superficial abrasion of the skin

gra·zier \'grā-zhər\ *n* **1** : a person who grazes cattle; *broadly* : RANCHER **2** *Austral* : a sheep raiser

GRE *abbr* graduate record examination

[1]**grease** \'grēs\ *n* [ME *grese,* fr. OF *craisse, graisse,* fr. (assumed) VL *crassia,* fr. L *crassus* fat] **1 a** : rendered animal fat **b** : oily matter **c** : a thick lubricant **2** : wool as it comes from the sheep retaining the natural oils or fats — **grease·less** \'grē-sləs\ *adj* — **grease·proof** \'grē-'sprüf\ *adj* — **in the grease** *of wool or fur* : in the natural uncleaned condition

[2]**grease** \'grēs, 'grēz\ *vt* **greased; greas·ing** **1** : to smear or daub with grease **2** : to lubricate with grease **3** : to soil with grease **4** : to hasten the process or progress of : ACCELERATE <this ~*s* the decline in department store sales —*Wall Street Jour.*> — **greas·er** *n* — **grease the hand** *or* **grease the palm** : BRIBE

grease monkey *n* **1** : one that greases machinery **2** : an airplane mechanic

grease·paint \'grē-ˌspānt\ *n* **1** : a melted tallow or grease used in theater makeup **2** : theater makeup

greas·er \'grē-zər, -sər\ *n* [[1]*grease*] : a native or inhabitant of Latin America; *esp* : MEXICAN — usu. taken to be offensive

grease·wood \'grē-ˌswu̇d\ *n* : a low stiff shrub (*Sarcobatus vermiculatus*) of the goosefoot family common in alkaline soils in the western U.S.; *also* : any of various related or similar shrubs

greasy \'grē-sē, -zē\ *adj* **greas·i·er; -est** **1 a** : smeared or soiled with grease <~ clothes> **b** : oily in appearance, texture, or manner <his ~ smile —Jack London> **c** : SLIPPERY **2** : containing an unusual amount of grease <~ food> —**greas·i·ly** \-sə-lē, -zə-\ *adv* — **greas·i·ness** \-sē-nəs, -zē-\ *n*

greasy spoon *n, slang* : a small cheap usu. unsanitary restaurant

[1]**great** \'grāt, *South also* 'gre(ə)t\ *adj* [ME *grete,* fr. OE *grēat;* akin to OHG *grōz* large] **1 a** : notably large in size : HUGE **b** : of a kind characterized by relative largeness — used in plant and animal names **c** : ELABORATE, AMPLE <~ detail> **2 a** : large in number : NUMEROUS <~ multitudes> **b** : PREDOMINANT <the ~ majority> **3** : remarkable in magnitude, degree, or effectiveness <~ bloodshed> **4** : full of emotion <~ with anger> **5 a** : EMINENT, DISTINGUISHED <a ~ poet> **b** : ARISTOCRATIC, GRAND <~ ladies> **6** : long continued <~ while> **7** : MAIN, PRINCIPAL <a reception in the ~ hall> **8** : more remote in a family relationship by a single generation than a specified relative <*great*-grandfather> **9** : markedly superior in character or quality; *esp* : NOBLE <~ of soul> **10 a** : remarkably skilled <~ at tennis> **b** : enthusiastic about <~ on science fiction> **11** — used as a generalized term of approval <had a ~ time> <it was just ~> ***syn*** see LARGE ***ant*** little — **great** *adv* — **great·ly** *adv* — **great·ness** *n*

[2]**great** *n, pl* **great** *or* **greats** : one that is great

great ape *n* : any of the recent anthropoid apes

great auk *n* : an extinct large flightless auk (*Pinguinus impennis*) formerly abundant along No. Atlantic coasts

great-aunt *n* : GRANDAUNT

Great Bear *n* : the constellation Ursa Major

great blue heron *n* : a large slaty-blue American heron (*Ardea herodias*) with a crested head

great circle *n* : a circle formed on the surface of a sphere by the intersection of a plane that passes through the center of the sphere; *specif* : such a circle on the surface of the earth an arc of which connecting two terrestrial points constitutes the shortest distance on the earth's surface between them

great·coat \'grāt-ˌkōt\ *n* : a heavy overcoat

Great Dane *n* : any of a breed of tall massive powerful smooth-coated dogs

great divide *n* [the *Great Divide,* No. American watershed] **1** : a watershed between major drainage systems **2** : a significant point of division; *esp* : DEATH <he crossed the *great divide* bravely>

great·en \'grāt-ᵊn\ *vb* **great·ened; great·en·ing** \'grāt-niŋ, -ᵊn-iŋ\ *vt* : to make greater ~ *vi* : to become greater

great·er *adj, often cap* [compar. of GREAT] : consisting of a central city together with adjacent areas that are naturally or administratively connected with it <*Greater* London>

greater yellowlegs *n pl but sing or pl in constr* : a common No. American marsh and shore bird (*Tringa melanoleuca*) that is largely gray above and white below with black or dark gray flecks and yellow legs — compare LESSER YELLOWLEGS

greatest common divisor *n* : the largest integer or the polynomial of highest degree that is an exact divisor of each of two or more integers or polynomials — called also *greatest common factor*

great·heart·ed \'grāt-'härt-əd\ *adj* **1** : characterized by bravery : COURAGEOUS **2** : GENEROUS, MAGNANIMOUS — **great·heart·ed·ly** *adv* — **great·heart·ed·ness** *n*

great horned owl *n* : a large No. American owl (*Bubo virginianus*) with conspicuous ear tufts

great laurel *n* : a large-leaved evergreen rhododendron (*Rhododendron maxima*) of eastern No. America that has rosy bell-shaped flowers more or less speckled with green

great-nephew *n* : GRANDNEPHEW

great-niece *n* : GRANDNIECE

great octave *n* : the musical octave that begins on the second C below middle C — see PITCH illustration

great power *n, often cap G&P* : one of the nations that figure most decisively in international affairs

Great Pyr·e·nees \-'pir-ə-ˌnēz\ *n* : any of a breed of large heavy-coated white dogs that resemble the Newfoundland

Great Russian *n* : a member of the Russian-speaking people of the central and northeastern U.S.S.R. — **Great Russian** *adj*

great seal *n* : a large seal that constitutes an emblem of sovereignty and is used esp. for the authentication of important documents

great skua *n* : a large stocky jaeger (*Catharacta skua*) that has dusky plumage and broad rounded wings, breeds chiefly along arctic and antarctic shores, and forages over most cold and temperate seas

great soil group *n* : a group of soils that is characterized by common characteristics usu. developed under the influence of environmental factors (as vegetation and climate) active over a considerable geographic range and that comprises one or more families of soil — called also *great group*

great-uncle *n* : GRANDUNCLE

great white shark *n* : WHITE SHARK

great year *n* : the period of about 25,800 years of one complete cycle of precession of the equinoxes

greave \'grēv\ *n* [ME *greve,* fr. MF] : armor for the leg below the knee — usu. used in pl.

grebe \'grēb\ *n* [F *grèbe*] : any of a family (Podicipitidae or Podicipedidae) of swimming and diving birds closely related to the loons but having lobate toes — compare DABCHICK

grebe

Gre·cian \'grē-shən\ *adj* [L *Graecia* Greece] : GREEK — **Grecian** *n* — **gre·cian·ize** \-shə-ˌnīz\ *vt, often cap*

Gre·cism \'grē-ˌsiz-əm\ *n* **1 :** a Greek idiom **2 :** a quality or style imitative of Greek art or culture

gre·cize \-ˌsīz\ *vt* **gre·cized; gre·ciz·ing** *often cap* : to make Greek or Hellenistic in character

Gre·co- *or* **Grae·co-** \'grek-ō, 'grē-kō\ *comb form* [L *Graeco-*, fr. *Graecus*] **1 :** Greece : Greeks <*Greco*phile> <*Greco*mania> **2 :** Greek and <*Graeco*-Roman>

¹gree \'grē\ *n* [ME, fr. MF *gré* step, degree, fr. L *gradus* — more at GRADE] *Scot* : MASTERY, SUPERIORITY

²gree *vb* **greed; gree·ing** [ME *green*, short for *agreen*] *dial* : AGREE

greed \'grēd\ *n* [back-formation fr. *greedy*] : excessive or reprehensible acquisitiveness : AVARICE

greedy \'grēd-ē\ *adj* **greed·i·er; -est** [ME *gredy*, fr. OE *grǣdig*; akin to OHG *grātag* greedy] **1 :** having a strong desire for food or drink **2 :** marked by greed **3 :** EAGER, KEEN <elated and ~ for the future — Frances G. Patton> ***syn*** see COVETOUS — **greed·i·ly** \'grēd-ᵊl-ē\ *adv* — **greed·i·ness** \'grēd-ē-nəs\ *n*

¹Greek \'grēk\ *n* [ME *Greke*, fr. OE *Grēca*, fr. L *Graecus*, fr. Gk *Graikos*] **1 a :** a native or inhabitant of ancient or modern Greece **b :** a person of Greek descent **2 a :** the language used by the Greeks from prehistoric times to the present constituting a branch of Indo-European — see INDO-EUROPEAN LANGUAGES table **b :** ancient Greek as used from the time of the earliest records to the end of the 2d century A.D. — see INDO-EUROPEAN LANGUAGES table **c** *not cap* [trans. of L *Graecum* (in the medieval phrase *Graecum est; non potest legi* It is Greek; it cannot be read)] : something unintelligible **3 :** a member of a Greek-letter fraternity or sorority

²Greek *adj* **1 :** of, relating to, or characteristic of Greece, the Greeks, or Greek <~ architecture> **2 a :** Eastern Orthodox **b :** of or relating to an Eastern church using the Byzantine rite in Greek **c :** of or relating to the established Orthodox church of Greece

Greek Catholic *n* **1 :** a member of an Eastern church **2 :** a member of an Eastern rite of the Roman Catholic Church

Greek cross *n* : a cross having an upright and a transverse shaft equal in length and intersecting at their middles —see CROSS illustration

Greek fire *n* : an incendiary composition used in warfare by the Byzantine Greeks and said to have burst into flame on wetting

Greek Orthodox *adj* : Eastern Orthodox; *specif* : GREEK 2c

¹green \'grēn\ *adj* [ME *grene*, fr. OE *grēne*; akin to OE *grōwan* to grow] **1 :** of the color green **2 a :** covered by green growth or foliage <~ fields> **b** *of winter* : MILD, CLEMENT **c :** consisting of green plants and usu. edible herbage <a ~ salad> **3 :** pleasantly alluring **4 :** YOUTHFUL, VIGOROUS **5 :** not ripened or matured : IMMATURE <~ apples> <tender ~ grasses> **6 :** FRESH, NEW **7 a :** marked by a pale, sickly, or nauseated appearance <he looks a little ~ around the gills> **b :** affected by intense emotion — used esp. in the phrase *green with envy* **8 a :** not fully processed or treated: as (1) : not aged <~ liquor> (2) : not dressed or tanned <~ hides> (3) : freshly sawed : UNSEASONED **b :** not in condition for a particular use **c** (1) *of a female fish* : not ready to spawn (2) : not quite ready to shed <~ crab> **9 a :** deficient in training, knowledge, or experience **b :** deficient in sophistication and savoir faire : NAIVE **c :** not fully qualified for or experienced in a particular function <~ horse> **10 :** indicating that everything is in order and to proceed according to plan <all systems are ~> ***syn*** see RUDE ***ant*** experienced — **green·ly** *adv* — **green·ness** \'grēn-nəs\ *n*

²green *vi* : to become green

³green *n* **1 :** a color whose hue is somewhat less yellow than that of growing fresh grass or of the emerald or is that of the part of the spectrum lying between blue and yellow **2 :** something of a green color **3 :** green vegetation: as **a** *pl* : leafy parts of plants for use as decoration **b** *pl* (1) : leafy herbs (as spinach, dandelions, Swiss chard) that are boiled or steamed as a vegetable : POTHERB (2) : GREEN VEGETABLE **4 :** a grassy plain or plot: as **a :** a common or park in the center of a town or village **b :** PUTTING GREEN — **greeny** \'grē-nē\ *adj*

green alga *n* : an alga in which the chlorophyll is not masked by other pigments; *specif* : such an alga of a division (Chlorophyta)

green·back \'grēn-ˌbak\ *n* : a legal-tender note issued by the U.S. government

green·back·er \-ər\ *n* **1** *cap* : a member of a post-Civil War American political party opposing reduction in the amount of paper money in circulation **2 :** one who advocates a paper currency backed only by the U.S. government — **green·back·ism** \-ˌiz-əm\ *n*

green bean *n* : a kidney bean that is used as a snap bean when the pods are colored green

green·belt \'grēn-ˌbelt\ *n* : a belt of parkways, parks, or farmlands that encircles a community

green·bri·er \-ˌbrī(-ə)r\ *n* : any of a genus (*Smilax*) of plants of the lily family; *esp* : a prickly vine (*S. rotundifolia*) of the eastern U.S. with umbels of small greenish flowers

green·bug \-ˌbəg\ *n* : a green aphid (*Schizaphis graminum*) very destructive to small grains

green corn *n* : the young tender ears of Indian corn suitable for cooking

green dragon *n* : an American arum (*Arisaema dracontium*) with digitate leaves, slender greenish yellow spathe, and elongated spadix

green·ery \'grēn-(ə-)rē\ *n, pl* **-er·ies** **1 :** green foliage or plants **2 :** GREEN 3a

green–eyed \'grē-'nīd\ *adj* : JEALOUS <the ~ locals who had spied on him —E. O. Schlunke>

green–eyed monster *n* : JEALOUSY

green·finch \'grēn-ˌfinch\ *n* : a very common European finch (*Chloris chloris*) having olive-green and yellow plumage

green fingers *n pl* : GREEN THUMB

green·fly \'grēn-ˌflī\ *n, Brit* : APHID; *esp* : GREEN PEACH APHID

green·gage \-ˌgāj\ *n* [*green* + Sir William *Gage* †1820 E botanist] : any of several rather small rounded greenish or greenish yellow cultivated plums

green gland *n* : one of a pair of large green glands in some crustaceans (as crayfishes) that have an excretory function and open at the bases of the larger antennae

green·gro·cer \'grēn-ˌgrō-sər\ *n, chiefly Brit* : a retailer of fresh vegetables and fruit — **green·gro·cery** \-ˌgrōs-(ə-)rē\ *n*

green·heart \-ˌhärt\ *n* : tropical So. American evergreen tree (*Nectandra rodioei*) with a hard somewhat greenish wood; *also* : its wood

green·horn \-ˌhȯ(ə)rn\ *n* [obs. *greenhorn* (animal with young horns)] **1 :** an inexperienced or unsophisticated person **2 :** a newcomer (as to a country) unacquainted with local manners and customs

green·house \-ˌhau̇s\ *n* **1 :** a glassed enclosure used for the cultivation or protection of tender plants **2 :** a clear plastic shell covering a section of an airplane

greenhouse effect *n* : warming of the lower layers of the atmosphere that tends to increase with increasing atmospheric carbon dioxide and that is caused by conversion of solar radiation into heat in a process involving selective transmission of short wave solar radiation by the atmosphere, its absorption by the earth's surface, and reradiation as infrared which is absorbed by carbon dioxide and water vapor in the air

green·ing \'grē-niŋ\ *n* : any of several green-skinned apples

green·ish \'grē-nish\ *adj* : somewhat green — **green·ish·ness** *n*

green·let \'grēn-lət\ *n* : VIREO

green light *n* [fr. the green traffic light which signals permission to proceed] : authority or permission to undertake a project

green·ling \'grēn-liŋ\ *n* **1 :** any of several food fishes (family Hexagrammidae) of the rocky coasts of the northern Pacific; *esp* : a common food and sport fish (*Hexagrammos decagrammus*) **2 :** LINGCOD

green–manure *vt* : to fertilize with green manure

green manure *n* : an herbaceous crop (as clover) plowed under while green to enrich the soil

green mold *n* : a green or green-spored mold (as of the genera *Penicillium* or *Aspergillus*)

green monkey *n* : a long-tailed monkey (*Cercopithecus sabaeus*) of West Africa that has greenish-appearing hair and is often used in medical research

gree·nock·ite \'grē-nə-ˌkit\ *n* [Charles M. Cathcart, Lord *Greenock* †1859 E soldier] : a mineral CdS consisting of native cadmium sulfide occurring in yellow translucent hexagonal crystals or as an earthy incrustation

green onion *n* : a young onion pulled before the bulb has enlarged and used esp. in salads

green peach aphid *n* : a nearly cosmopolitan yellowish green aphid (*Myzus persicae*) that is frequently a vector of plant virus diseases and is destructive esp. to peaches — called also *greenfly*

green pepper *n* : SWEET PEPPER

green·room \'grēn-ˌrüm, -ˌru̇m\ *n* : a room in a theater or concert hall where actors or musicians relax before, between, or after appearances

green·sand \-ˌsand\ *n* : a sedimentary deposit that consists largely of dark greenish grains of glauconite often mingled with clay or sand

greens fee \'grēnz-\ *n* : a fee paid for the privilege of playing on a golf course — called also *green fee*

green·shank \'grēn-ˌshaŋk\ *n* : an Old World sandpiper (*Tringa nebularia*) related to the yellowlegs of America

green·sick \-ˌsik\ *adj* [back-formation fr. *greensickness*] : affected with chlorosis

green·sick·ness *n* : CHLOROSIS

green snake *n* : either of two bright green harmless largely insectivorous No. American colubrid snakes (*Liopeltis vernalis* and *Ophiodrys aestivus*)

green soap *n* : a soft soap made from vegetable oils and used esp. in the treatment of skin diseases

green·stick fracture \'grēn-ˌstik-\ *n* : a bone fracture in a young individual in which the bone is partly broken and partly bent

green·stone \'grēn-ˌstōn\ *n* **1 :** any of numerous usu. altered dark green compact rocks (as diorite) **2 :** NEPHRITE

green·stuff \-ˌstəf\ *n* : green vegetation used as foodstuff

green·sward \-ˌswȯ(ə)rd\ *n* : turf that is green with growing grass

green tea *n* : tea that is light in color from incomplete fermentation of the leaf before firing

green thumb *n* : an unusual ability to make plants grow — **green–thumbed** \'grēn-'thəmd\ *adj*

green turtle *n* : a large sea turtle (*Chelonia mydas*) with a smooth greenish or olive-colored shell, highly nutritious eggs, and flesh used for food

green vegetable *n* : a vegetable whose foliage or foliage-bearing stalks are the chief edible part

Green·wich time \'grin-ij-, 'gren-, -ich-\ *n* [*Greenwich*, England] : the mean solar time of the meridian of Greenwich used as the prime basis of standard time throughout the world — called also *Greenwich mean time*

green·wing \'grēn-ˌwiŋ\ *n* : GREEN-WINGED TEAL

green–winged teal \ˌgrēn-ˌwiŋ(d)-\ *n* : a small river duck (*Anas carolinensis*) the male of which has a chestnut head with a green eye patch and a metallic green area on the wing speculum

green·wood \'grēn-ˌwu̇d\ *n* : a forest green with foliage

1greet \'grēt\ *vt* [ME *greten,* fr. OE *grētan;* akin to OE *grǣtan* to weep] **1 :** to address with expression of kind wishes : HAIL **2 :** to meet or react to in a specified manner <the candidate was ~*ed* with catcalls> **3 :** to be perceived by <a surprising sight ~*ed* her eyes> — **greet·er** *n*

2greet *vi* **grat** \'grat\; **grut·ten** \'grət-ᵊn\ [ME *greten,* fr. OE *grǣtan;* akin to ON *grāta* to weep] *Scot* : WEEP, LAMENT

greet·ing *n* **1 :** a salutation at meeting **2 :** an expression of good wishes : REGARDS — usu. used in plural <holiday ~*s*>

greeting card *n* **:** a card that bears a message of goodwill and is usu. sent or given on special occasions (as a birthday or a holiday)

greg·a·rine \'greg-ə-ˌrīn\ *n* [deriv. of L *gregarius*] **:** any of a large order (Gregarinida) of parasitic vermiform sporozoan protozoans that usu. occur in insects and other invertebrates — **gregarine** *or* **greg·a·rin·i·an** \ˌgreg-ə-'rin-ē-ən\ *adj*

gre·gar·i·ous \gri-'gar-ē-əs, -'ger-\ *adj* [L *gregarius* of a flock or herd, fr. *greg-, grex* flock, herd; akin to Gk *ageirein* to collect, *agora* assembly] **1 a :** tending to associate with others of one's kind : SOCIAL **b :** marked by or indicating a liking for companionship : SOCIABLE **c :** of or relating to a social group **2 a** *of a plant* **:** growing in a cluster or a colony **b :** living in contiguous nests but not forming a true colony — used esp. of wasps and bees — **gre·gar·i·ous·ly** *adv* — **gre·gar·i·ous·ness** *n*

1Gre·go·ri·an \gri-'gōr-ē-ən, -'gȯr-\ *adj* **:** of or relating to Pope Gregory XIII or the Gregorian calendar

2Gregorian *adj* **1 :** of or relating to Pope Gregory I **2 :** of, relating to, or having the characteristics of Gregorian chant

3Gregorian *adj* [St. *Gregory* the Illuminator †332, apostle of Armenia] **:** of or relating to the Armenian national church

Gregorian calendar *n* **:** a calendar in general use introduced in 1582 by Pope Gregory XIII as a revision of the Julian calendar, adopted in Great Britain and the American colonies in 1752, and marked by the suppression of 10 days or after 1700 11 days and the restriction that only those centesimal years divisible by 400 should be leap years — see MONTH table

Gregorian chant *n* **:** a monodic and rhythmically free liturgical chant of the Roman Catholic Church

greige \'grā(zh)\ *adj* [F *grège* raw (of silk), fr. It *greggio*] **:** being in an unbleached undyed state as taken from a loom — used of textiles

grei·sen \'grīz-ᵊn\ *n* [G] **:** a crystalline rock consisting of quartz and mica that is common in Cornwall and Saxony

grem·lin \'grem-lən\ *n* [perh. modif. of IrGael *gruaimín* ill-humored little fellow] **:** a small gnome held to be responsible for malfunction of equipment esp. in an airplane

grem·mie *also* **grem·my** \'grem-ē\ *n, pl* **gremmies** [*grem*lin + *-ie*] **:** a young or inexperienced surfer; *esp* **:** one whose behavior is objectionable — called also *gremlin*

gre·nade \grə-'nād\ *n* [MF, pomegranate, fr. LL *granata,* fr. L, fem. of *granatus* seedy, fr. *granum* grain — more at CORN] **1 :** a small missile that contains an explosive or a chemical agent (as tear gas, a flame producer, or a smoke producer) and that is thrown by hand or projected (as by a rifle or special launcher) **2 :** a glass bottle or globe that contains volatile chemicals and can be burst by throwing (as for extinguishing a fire)

gren·a·dier \ˌgren-ə-'di(ə)r\ *n* **1 a :** a soldier who carries and throws grenades **b :** a member of a special regiment or corps formerly armed with grenades **2 :** any of various deep-sea fishes (family Macruridae) that are related to the cods and have an elongate tapering body and compressed pointed tail — called also *rattail*

gren·a·dine \ˌgren-ə-'dēn, 'gren-ə-ˌ\ *n* [F, fr. *grenade*] **1 :** a plain or figured open-weave fabric of various fibers **2 :** a moderate reddish orange **3 :** a syrup flavored with pomegranates and used in mixed drinks

Gren·del \'gren-dᵊl\ *n* [OE] **:** a monstrous man-eating descendant of Cain slain by Beowulf in the Old English poem *Beowulf*

Gresh·am's law \ˌgresh-əmz-\ *n* [Sir Thomas *Gresham*] **:** an observation in economics: when two coins are equal in debt-paying value but unequal in intrinsic value, the one having the lesser intrinsic value tends to remain in circulation and the other to be hoarded or exported as bullion

Gret·na Green \ˌgret-nə-'grēn\ *n* [*Gretna Green,* Scotland] **:** a place where many eloping couples are married

grew *past of* GROW

grew·some *var of* GRUESOME

grey *var of* GRAY

grey friar *n, often cap G&F* **:** a Franciscan friar

grey·hound \'grā-ˌhau̇nd\ *n* [ME *grehound,* fr. OE *grīghund,* fr. *grīg-* (akin to ON *grey* bitch) + *hund* hound] **:** a tall slender graceful smooth-coated dog of a breed characterized by swiftness and keen sight and used for coursing game and racing; *also* **:** any of several related dogs

greyhound

grey·lag \-ˌlag\ *n* **:** the common gray wild goose (*Anser anser* syn. *A. cinereus*) of Europe — called also *greylag goose*

grib·ble \'grib-əl\ *n* [prob. dim. of 2*grub*] **:** a small marine isopod crustacean (*Limnoria lignorum* or *L. terebrans*) that destroys submerged timber

grid \'grid\ *n* [back-formation fr. *gridiron*] **1 :** GRATING **2 a** (1) **:** a perforated or ridged metal plate used as a conductor in a storage battery (2) **:** an electrode consisting of a mesh or a spiral of fine wire in an electron tube (3) **:** a network of conductors for distribution of electric power; *also* **:** a network of radio or television stations **b :** a network of uniformly spaced horizontal and perpendicular lines (as for locating points on a map); *also* **:** something resembling such a network <a road ~> **c :** GRIDIRON 2; *broadly* **:** FOOTBALL **3 :** the starting positions of cars on a racecourse **4 :** a device (as of glass) in a photocomposer on which are located the characters to be exposed on the film as the text is composed

grid·dle \'grid-ᵊl\ *n* [ME *gredil* gridiron, fr. ONF, fr. L *craticulum,* dim. of *cratis* wickerwork — more at HURDLE] **:** a flat metal surface or pan on which food is cooked by dry heat

griddle cake *n* **:** PANCAKE

grid·iron \'grid-ˌī(-ə)rn\ *n* [ME *gredire*] **1 :** a grate for broiling food **2 :** something consisting of or covered with a network; *esp* **:** a football field

grief \'grēf\ *n* [ME *gref,* fr. OF, heavy, grave, fr. (assumed) VL *grevis,* alter. of L *gravis*] **1** *obs* **:** GRIEVANCE 3 **2 a :** deep and poignant distress caused by or as if by bereavement **b :** a cause of such suffering **3 a :** MISHAP, MISADVENTURE **b :** TROUBLE, ANNOYANCE <enough ~ for one day> **c :** an unfortunate outcome : DISASTER — used chiefly in the phrase *come to grief* ***syn*** see SORROW — **grief·less** \-ləs\ *adj*

griev·ance \'grē-vən(t)s\ *n* **1** *obs* **:** SUFFERING, DISTRESS **2 :** a cause of distress (as an unsatisfactory working condition) felt to afford reason for complaint or resistance **3 :** the formal expression of a grievance : COMPLAINT ***syn*** see INJUSTICE

grievance committee *n* **:** a committee formed by a labor union or by employer and employees jointly to discuss and where possible to eliminate grievances

griev·ant \-vənt\ *n* **:** one who submits a grievance for arbitration

grieve \'grēv\ *vb* **grieved; griev·ing** [ME *greven,* fr. OF *grever,* fr. L *gravare* to burden, fr. *gravis* heavy, grave; akin to Goth *kaurjos,* pl., heavy, Gk *barys,* Skt *guru*] *vt* **:** to cause to suffer : DISTRESS ~ *vi* **:** to feel grief : SORROW — **griev·er** *n*

syn GRIEVE, MOURN, SORROW ***shared meaning element*** **:** to feel or express deep distress ***ant*** rejoice

griev·ous \'grē-vəs\ *adj* **1 :** OPPRESSIVE, ONEROUS <~ costs of war> **2 :** causing or characterized by severe pain, suffering, or sorrow <a ~ wound> <a ~ loss> **3 :** SERIOUS, GRAVE <~ fault> — **griev·ous·ly** *adv* — **griev·ous·ness** *n*

grif·fin *or* **grif·fon** \'grif-ən\ *n* [ME *griffon,* fr. MF *grifon,* fr. *grif,* fr. L *gryphus,* fr. Gk *gryp-, gryps,* fr. *grypos* curved; akin to OE *cradol* cradle] **:** a fabulous animal typically having head, forepart, and wings like those of an eagle and body, hind legs, and tail like those of a lion

griffin

grif·fon \'grif-ən\ *n* [F, lit., griffin] **1 :** BRUSSELS GRIFFON **2 :** WIREHAIRED POINTING GRIFFON

grift \'grift\ *vt* [*grift,* n., perh. alter. of *graft*] *slang* **:** to obtain (money) illicitly (as in a confidence game) — **grift** *n, slang* — **grift·er** *n, slang*

grig \'grig\ *n* [ME *grege*] **:** a gay lively usu. small or young person

gri·gri *var of* GRIS-GRIS

1grill \'gril\ *vt* **1 :** to broil on a grill; *also* **:** to fry or toast on a griddle **2 a :** to torment as if by broiling <the intense sun slowly ~*ed* them> **b :** to question intensely <the police ~*ed* the suspect> — **grill·er** *n*

2grill *n* [F *gril,* fr. L *craticulum* — more at GRIDDLE] **1 :** a cooking utensil of parallel bars on which food is exposed to heat (as from charcoal or electricity) **2 :** food that is broiled usu. on a grill — compare MIXED GRILL **3 :** a usu. informal restaurant or dining room esp. in a hotel

gril·lage \'gril-ij\ *n* **1 :** a framework of timber or steel for support in marshy or treacherous soil **2 :** a framework for supporting a load (as a column)

grille *or* **grill** \'gril\ *n* [F *grille,* alter. of OF *greille,* fr. L *craticula,* dim. of *cratis* wickerwork — more at HURDLE] **1 :** a grating forming a barrier or screen; *specif* **:** an ornamental metal one at the front end of an automobile **2 :** an opening covered with a grille

grill·room \'gril-ˌrüm, -ˌru̇m\ *n* **:** GRILL 3

grill·work \'gril-ˌwərk\ *n* **:** work constituting or resembling a grille

grilse \'grils\ *n, pl* **grilse** [ME *grills*] **:** a young mature Atlantic salmon returning from the sea to spawn for the first time; *broadly* **:** any of various salmon at such a stage of development

grim \'grim\ *adj* **grim·mer; grim·mest** [ME, fr. OE *grimm;* akin to OHG *grimm* fierce, Gk *chromados* action of gnashing] **1 :** fierce in disposition or action : SAVAGE **2 :** stern or forbidding in action or appearance <a ~ overcast winter day> **3 :** UNFLINCHING, UNYIELDING <~ determination> **4 :** ghastly, repellent, or sinister in character <a ~ tale> — **grim·ly** *adv* — **grim·ness** *n*

gri·mace \'grim-əs, grim-'ās\ *n* [F, fr. MF, alter. of *grimache,* of Gmc origin; akin to OE *grīma* mask] **:** a facial expression usu. of disgust or disapproval — **grimace** *vi* — **gri·mac·er** *n*

gri·mal·kin \grim-'ȯ(l)-kən, -'al-\ *n* [*gray* + *malkin*] **:** CAT 1a; *esp* **:** an old female cat

grime \'grīm\ *n* [Flem *grijm,* fr. MD *grime* soot, mask; akin to OE *grīma* mask, Gk *chriein* to anoint — more at CHRISM] **:** soot, smut, or dirt adhering to or embedded in a surface; *broadly* **:** accumulated dirtiness and disorder <the ~ of the slums> — **grime** *vt*

Grimm's law \'grimz-\ *n* [Jacob *Grimm* †1863 G philologist] **:** a statement in historical linguistics: Proto-Indo-European voiceless stops became Proto-Germanic voiceless fricatives (as in Greek *pyr, treis, kardia* compared with English *fire, three, heart*), Proto-Indo-European voiced stops became Proto-Germanic voice-

---

ə abut ᵊ kitten ər further a back ā bake ä cot, cart
au̇ out ch chin e less ē easy g gift i trip ī life
j joke ŋ sing ō flow ȯ flaw ȯi coin th thin th this
ü loot u̇ foot y yet yü few yu̇ furious zh vision

less stops (as in Latin *duo, genus* compared with English *two, kin*), and Proto-Indo-European voiced aspirated stops became Proto-Germanic voiced fricatives (as in Sanskrit *nābhi, madhya* "mid" compared with English *navel,* Old Norse *mithr* "mid")

grimy \'grī-mē\ *adj* **grim·i·er; -est** : full of or covered with grime : DIRTY — **grim·i·ness**

grin \'grin\ *vi* **grinned; grin·ning** [ME *grennen,* fr. OE *grennian;* akin to OHG *grennen* to snarl] : to draw back the lips so as to show the teeth (as in amusement or laughter) — **grin** *n* — **grin·ner** *n* — **grin·ning·ly** \'grin-iŋ-lē\ *adv*

1**grind** \'grīnd\ *vb* **ground** \'graund\; **grind·ing** [ME *grinden,* fr. OE *grindan;* akin to L *frendere* to crush, grind, Gk *chondros* grain, OE *grēot* grit] *vt* **1** : to reduce to powder or small fragments by friction (as in a mill or with the teeth) **2** : to wear down, polish, or sharpen by friction : WHET <~ an ax> **3 a** : to rub or press harshly <*ground* the cigarette out with his heel> **b** : to press together with a rotating motion <~ the teeth> **4** : OPPRESS, HARASS <the nobility *ground* down the peasants with a variety of exactions> **5 a** : to operate or produce by turning a crank <~ a hand organ> **b** : to produce in a mechanical way <~ out best-sellers> ~ *vi* **1** : to perform the operation of grinding **2** : to become pulverized, polished, or sharpened by friction **3** : to move with difficulty or friction esp. so as to make a grating noise <~*ing* gears> **4** : DRUDGE; *esp* : to study hard <~ for an exam> **5** : to rotate the hips in an erotic manner (as in a burlesque striptease) — **grind·ing·ly** \'grīn-diŋ-lē\ *adv*

2**grind** *n* **1 a** : an act of grinding **b** : the sound of grinding **2 a** : dreary monotonous labor or routine; *esp* : intensive study **b** : a student who studies excessively **3** : the result of grinding; *esp* : material obtained by grinding to a particular degree of fineness <a percolator ~ of coffee> **4** : the act of rotating the hips in an erotic manner **syn** see WORK

grind·er \'grīn-dər\ *n* **1 a** : MOLAR **b** *pl* : TEETH **2** : one that grinds **3** : a machine or device for grinding **4** : SUBMARINE 2

grind·stone \'grīn-,stōn\ *n* **1** : MILLSTONE 1 **2** : a flat circular stone of natural sandstone that revolves on an axle and is used for grinding, shaping, or smoothing

grindstone 2

grin·go \'griŋ-(,)gō\ *n, pl* **gringos** [Sp, alter. of *griego* Greek, stranger, fr. L *Graecus* Greek] : a foreigner in Spain or Latin America esp. when of English or American origin — often used disparagingly

1**grip** \'grip\ *vt* **gripped; grip·ping** [ME *grippen,* fr. OE *grippan;* akin to OE *gripan*] **1** : to seize or hold firmly **2** : to hold strongly the interest of <a story that ~*s* the reader> — **grip·per** *n* — **grip·ping·ly** \'grip-iŋ-lē\ *adv*

2**grip** *n* **1 a** : a strong or tenacious grasp **b** : strength in gripping **c** : manner or style of gripping **2 a** : a firm tenacious hold typically giving control, mastery, or understanding <could not free himself from the ~ of these new ideas> **b** : mental grasp : APPREHENSION **3** : a part or device for gripping **4** : a part by which something is grasped; *esp* : HANDLE **5** : TRAVELING BAG **6** : STAGEHAND **syn** see HOLD

1**gripe** \'grīp\ *vb* **griped; grip·ing** [ME *gripen,* fr. OE *grīpan;* akin to OHG *grīfan* to grasp, Lith *griebti*] *vt* **1** : SEIZE, GRASP **2 a** : AFFLICT, DISTRESS **b** : IRRITATE, VEX <*griped* by new income-tax provisions> **3** : to cause pinching and spasmodic pain in the bowels of ~ *vi* **1** : to experience griping **2** : to complain with sustained grumbling — **grip·er** *n*

2**gripe** *n* **1** : CLUTCH, GRASP; *broadly* : CONTROL, MASTERY **2** : GRIEVANCE, COMPLAINT **3** : a pinching spasmodic intestinal pain — usu. used in pl. **4** : HANDLE, GRIP **5** : a device (as a brake) for grasping or holding

grippe \'grip\ *n* [F, lit., seizure] : an acute febrile contagious virus disease identical with or resembling influenza — **grippy** \'grip-ē\ *adj*

grip·sack \'grip-,sak\ *n* : TRAVELING BAG

gri·saille \gri-'zī, -'zā(ə)l\ *n* [F] : decoration in tones of a single color and esp. gray designed to produce a three-dimensional effect

Gri·sel·da \griz-'el-də\ *n* [It] : a woman of humble origins in medieval legend who endures tests of wifely patience laid on her by her wellborn husband

gris·eo·ful·vin \,griz-ē-ō-'fu̇l-vən, ,gris-, -'fəl-\ *n* [NL *griseofulvum,* specific epithet of *Penicillium griseofulvum,* mold from which it is obtained] : an antibiotic $C_{17}H_{17}ClO_6$ used esp. against fungi

gris·eous \'griz-ē-əs, 'gris-\ *adj* [ML *griseus,* of Gmc origin; akin to OHG *grīs* gray] : of a light color or white mottled with black or brown : GRIZZLED

gri·sette \gri-'zet\ *n* [F] **1** : a young French working-class woman **2** : a young woman combining part-time prostitution with some other occupation

gris–gris \'grē-(,)grē\ *n, pl* **gris–gris** \-(,)grēz\ [of African origin; akin to Balante *grigri* amulet] : an amulet or incantation used chiefly by people of African Negro ancestry

gris·ly \'griz-lē\ *adj* **gris·li·er; -est** [ME, fr. OE *grislic,* fr. *gris-* (akin to OE *āgrīsan* to fear); akin to OHG *grīsenlīh* terrible] **1** : inspiring horror or intense fear : FORBIDDING <houses that were dark and ~ under the blank, cold sky —D. H. Lawrence> **2** : inspiring disgust or distaste <a ~ account of the fire> — **gris·li·ness** *n*

grist \'grist\ *n* [ME, fr. OE *grīst;* akin to OE *grindan* to grind] **1 a** : grain or a batch of grain for grinding **b** : the product obtained from a grist of grain including the flour or meal and the grain offals **2** : a required or usual amount **3** : matter of interest or value forming the basis of a story or analysis **4** : something turned to advantage — used esp. in the phrase *grist for one's mill*

gris·tle \'gris-əl\ *n* [ME *gristil,* fr. OE *gristle;* akin to MLG *gristel* gristle] : CARTILAGE; *broadly* : tough cartilaginous, tendinous, or fibrous matter esp. in table meats

gris·tly \'gris-(ə-)lē\ *adj* **gris·tli·er; -est** : consisting of or containing gristle <~ steak> — **gris·tli·ness** *n*

grist·mill \'grist-,mil\ *n* : a mill for grinding grain

1**grit** \'grit\ *n* [ME *grete,* fr. OE *grēot;* akin to OHG *grioz* sand, L *furfur* bran, Gk *chrōs* skin] **1 a** *obs* : SAND, GRAVEL **b** : a hard sharp granule (as of sand); *also* : material (as many abrasives) composed of such granules **2** : any of several sandstones **3** : the structure of a stone that adapts it to grinding **4** : firmness of mind or spirit : unyielding courage in the face of hardship or danger **syn** see FORTITUDE **ant** faintheartedness

2**grit** *vb* **grit·ted; grit·ting** *vi* : to give forth a grating sound ~ *vt* **1** : to cover or spread with grit; *esp* : to smooth (as marble) by means of a coarse abrasive **2** : to cause (as one's teeth) to grind or grate

grith \'grith\ *n* [ME, fr. OE, fr. ON, security] : peace, security, or sanctuary imposed or guaranteed in early medieval England under various special conditions

grits \'grits\ *n pl but sing or pl in constr* [ME *gryt,* fr. OE *grytt;* akin to OE *grēot*] : coarsely ground hulled grain; *specif* : HOMINY GRITS

grit·ty \'grit-ē\ *adj* **grit·ti·er; -est** **1** : containing or resembling grit **2** : courageously persistent : PLUCKY — **grit·ti·ly** \'grit-ᵊl-ē\ *adv* — **grit·ti·ness** \'grit-ē-nəs\ *n*

1**griz·zle** \'griz-əl\ *n* [ME *grisel,* adj., gray, fr. MF, fr. *gris,* of Gmc origin; akin to OHG *grīs* gray] **1** *archaic* : gray hair **2 a** : a roan coat pattern or color **b** : a gray or roan animal

2**grizzle** *vb* **griz·zled; griz·zling** \'griz-(ə-)liŋ\ *vt* : to make grayish ~ *vi* : to become grayish

griz·zled \'griz-əld\ *adj* : sprinkled or streaked with gray : GRAYING <a ~ beard>

1**griz·zly** \'griz-lē\ *adj* **griz·zli·er; -est** : somewhat gray : GRIZZLED

2**grizzly** *var of* GRISLY

grizzly bear *n* : a very large powerful typically brownish yellow bear (*Ursus horribilis*) of the uplands of western No. America — called also *grizzly*

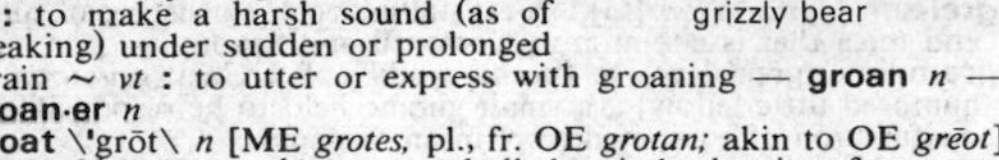
grizzly bear

gro *abbr* gross

groan \'grōn\ *vb* [ME *gronen,* fr. OE *grānian;* akin to OHG *grīnan* to growl] *vi* **1** : to utter a deep moan indicative of pain, grief, or annoyance **2** : to make a harsh sound (as of creaking) under sudden or prolonged strain ~ *vt* : to utter or express with groaning — **groan** *n* — **groan·er** *n*

1**groat** \'grōt\ *n* [ME *grotes,* pl., fr. OE *grotan;* akin to OE *grēot*] **1** *usu pl but sing or pl in constr* : hulled grain broken into fragments larger than grits **2** : a grain (as of oats) exclusive of the hull

2**groat** *n* [ME *groot,* fr. MD] : an old British coin worth four pennies

gro·cer \'grō-sər\ *n* [ME, fr. MF *grossier* wholesaler, fr. *gros* coarse, wholesale — more at GROSS] : a dealer in staple foodstuffs, household supplies, and usu. meats, produce, and dairy products

grocer's itch *n* : an itching dermatitis that results from prolonged contact with some mites (esp. family Acaridae), their products, or materials (as feeds) infested with them

gro·cery \'grōs-(ə-)rē\ *n, pl* **-cer·ies** **1** *pl* : commodities sold by a grocer — usu. sing. in Brit. usage **2** : a grocer's store

grog \'gräg\ *n* [*Old Grog,* nickname of Edward Vernon †1757 E admiral responsible for diluting the sailors' rum] **1** : alcoholic liquor; *specif* : liquor (as rum) cut with water and now often served hot with lemon juice and sugar sometimes added **2** : refractory materials (as crushed pottery and firebricks) used in the manufacture of refractory products (as crucibles) to reduce shrinkage in drying and firing

grog·gy \'gräg-ē\ *adj* **grog·gi·er; -est** [*grog*] : weak and unsteady on the feet or in action — **grog·gi·ly** \'gräg-ə-lē\ *adv* — **grog·gi·ness** \'gräg-ē-nəs\ *n*

gro·gram \'gräg-rəm, 'grōg-\ *n* [MF *gros grain* coarse texture] : a coarse loosely woven fabric of silk, silk and mohair, or silk and wool — compare GROSGRAIN

grog·shop \'gräg-,shäp\ *n, chiefly Brit* : a usu. low-class barroom

1**groin** \'grȯin\ *n* [alter. of ME *grynde,* fr. OE, abyss; akin to OE *grund* ground] **1** : the fold or depression marking the juncture of the lower abdomen and the inner part of the thigh; *also* : the region of this line **2 a** : the projecting curved line along which two intersecting vaults meet **b** : a rib that covers this edge **3** : a rigid structure built out from a shore to protect the shore from erosion, to trap sand, or to direct a current for scouring a channel

groin 2a

2**groin** *vt* : to build or equip with groins

grom·met \'gräm-ət, 'grəm-\ *n* [perh. fr. obs. F *gormette* curb of a bridle] **1** : a flexible loop that serves as a fastening, support, or reinforcement **2** : an eyelet of firm material to strengthen or protect an opening or to insulate or protect something passed through it

grom·well \'gräm-,wel, -wəl\ *n* [ME *gromil,* fr. MF] : any of a genus (*Lithospermum*) of plants of the borage family having polished white stony nutlets

1**groom** \'grüm, 'gru̇m\ *n* [ME *grom*] **1** *archaic* : MAN, FELLOW **2 a** (1) *archaic* : MANSERVANT (2) : one of several officers of the English royal household **b** : a man or boy in charge of the feeding, conditioning, and stabling of horses **3** : BRIDEGROOM

2**groom** *vt* **1** : to clean and care for (as a horse) **2** : to make neat or attractive <an impeccably ~*ed* woman> **3** : to get into readiness for a specific objective : PREPARE <was being ~*ed* as a presidential candidate> ~ *vi* : to groom oneself

groom·er \'grü-mər\ *n* : one who grooms (as dogs)

grooms·man \'grümz-mən, 'gru̇mz-\ *n* **:** a male friend who attends a bridegroom at his wedding

[1]**groove** \'grüv\ *n* [ME *groof;* akin to OE *grafan* to dig — more at GRAVE] **1 :** a long narrow channel or depression **2 a :** a fixed routine **:** RUT **b :** a situation suited to one's abilities or interests **:** NICHE **3 :** top form <a great talker when he is in the ~> **4 :** the line or course to follow for best results <his every pitch was right in the ~> **5 :** an enjoyable, pleasurable, or exciting experience

[2]**groove** *vb* **grooved; groov·ing** *vt* **1 a :** to make a groove in **b :** to join by a groove **2 a :** to enjoy appreciatively <~*s* exciting experiences> **b :** to excite pleasurably <*grooving* their minds with cannabis —Stephen Nemo> ~ *vi* **1 :** to become joined or fitted by a groove **2 :** to form a groove **3 :** to enjoy oneself intensely **:** experience keen pleasure **4 :** to interact harmoniously <contemporary minds and rock ~ together — Benjamin DeMott> — **groov·er** *n*

groovy \'grü-vē\ *adj* **groov·i·er; -est :** MARVELOUS, WONDERFUL, EXCELLENT <felt that this poetry was interesting, enjoyable, not to mention ~ —R. M. Muccigrosso>

grope \'grōp\ *vb* **groped; grop·ing** [ME *gropen,* fr. OE *grāpian;* akin to OE *grīpan* to seize] *vi* **1 :** to feel about blindly or uncertainly in search <*groped* for the light switch> **2 :** to look for something blindly or uncertainly <*groping* for the right words> **3 :** to feel one's way ~ *vt* **1 :** to pass the hands over (the person of another) for the sake of sexual pleasure **2 :** to find (as one's way) by groping — **grope** *n* — **grop·er** *n*

gros·beak \'grōs-ˌbēk\ *n* [part trans. of F *grosbec,* fr. *gros* thick + *bec* beak] **:** any of several finches of Europe or America having large stout conical bills

gro·schen \'grō-shən, 'grȯ-\ *n, pl* **groschen** [G] — see *schilling* at MONEY table

gros·grain \'grō-ˌgrān\ *n* [F *gros grain* coarse texture] **:** a strong close-woven corded fabric usu. of silk or rayon and often with cotton filler — compare GROGRAM

[1]**gross** \'grōs\ *adj* [ME, fr. MF *gros* thick, coarse, fr. L *grossus*] **1 a** *archaic* **:** immediately obvious **b (1) :** glaringly noticeable usu. because of inexcusable badness or objectionableness <~ error> **(2) :** OUT-AND-OUT, UTTER <~ injustice> **c :** visible without the aid of a microscope **2 a :** BIG, BULKY; *esp* **:** excessively fat **b :** growing or spreading with excessive luxuriance **3 a :** of, relating to, or dealing with general aspects or broad distinctions **b :** consisting of an overall total exclusive of deductions <~ income> — compare NET **4 :** made up of material or perceptible elements **:** CORPORAL <the ~*er* part of human nature> **5** *archaic* **:** not fastidious in taste **:** UNDISCRIMINATING **6 :** deficient in knowledge **:** IGNORANT, UNTUTORED **7 a :** coarse in nature or behavior **:** UNREFINED **b :** gravely deficient in civility or decency **:** crudely vulgar <merely ~, a scatological rather than a pornographic impropriety —Aldous Huxley> ***syn* 1** see COARSE ***ant*** delicate, dainty, ethereal **2** see FLAGRANT — **gross·ly** *adv* — **gross·ness** *n*

[2]**gross** *n* **1** *obs* **:** AMOUNT, SUM **2 :** an overall total exclusive of deductions

[3]**gross** *vt* **:** to earn or bring in (an overall total) exclusive of deductions (as for taxes or expenses) — **gross·er** *n*

[4]**gross** *n, pl* **gross** [ME *groce,* fr. MF *grosse,* fr. fem. of *gros*] **:** an aggregate of 12 dozen things <~ of pencils>

gross anatomy *n* **:** a branch of anatomy that deals with the macroscopic structure of tissues and organs

gross national product *n* **:** the total value of the goods and services produced in a nation during a specified period (as a year)

gros·su·lar \'gräs(h)-ə-lər, 'gräs-yə-\ *n* [NL *Grossularia,* genus name of the gooseberry] **:** GROSSULARITE

gros·su·la·rite \-lə-ˌrīt\ *n* [G *grossularit,* fr. NL *Grossularia*] **:** a colorless or green, yellow, brown, or red garnet $Ca_3Al_2(SiO_4)_3$

grosz \'grȯsh\ *n, pl* **gro·szy** \'grȯ-shē\ [Pol] — see *zloty* at MONEY table

grot \'grät\ *n* [MF *grotte,* fr. It *grotta*] **:** GROTTO

[1]**gro·tesque** \grō-'tesk\ *n* [MF & OIt; MF, fr. OIt (*pittura*) *grottesca,* lit., cave painting, fem. of *grottesco* of a cave, fr. *grotta*] **1 a :** a style of decorative art characterized by fanciful or fantastic human and animal forms often interwoven with foliage or similar figures that may distort the natural into absurdity, ugliness, or caricature **b :** a piece of work in this style **2 :** one that is grotesque **3 :** SANS SERIF

[2]**grotesque** *adj* **:** of, relating to, or having the characteristics of the grotesque: as **a :** FANCIFUL, BIZARRE **b :** absurdly incongruous **c :** departing markedly from the natural, the expected, or the typical ***syn*** see FANTASTIC — **gro·tesque·ly** *adv* — **gro·tesque·ness** *n*

gro·tes·que·rie *also* **gro·tes·que·ry** \grō-'tes-kə-rē\ *n, pl* **-ries** [*grotesque* + *-erie* -ery] **1 :** something that is grotesque **2 :** the quality or state of being grotesque **:** GROTESQUENESS

grot·to \'grät-(ˌ)ō\ *n, pl* **grottoes** *also* **grottos** [It *grotta, grotto,* fr. L *crypta* cavern, crypt] **1 :** CAVE **2 :** an artificial recess or structure made to resemble a natural cave

grouch \'grau̇ch\ *n* [prob. alter. of *grutch* (grudge)] **1 a :** a fit of bad temper **b :** GRUDGE, COMPLAINT <never nursed a ~ five minutes —W. A. White> **2 :** an habitually irritable or complaining person **:** GRUMBLER — **grouch** *vi*

grouchy \'grau̇-chē\ *adj* **grouch·i·er; -est :** given to grumbling **:** PEEVISH — **grouch·i·ly** \-chə-lē\ *adv* — **grouch·i·ness** \-chē-nəs\ *n*

[1]**ground** \'grau̇nd\ *n* [ME, fr. OE *grund;* akin to OHG *grunt* ground, Gk *chrainein* to touch slightly] **1 a :** the bottom of a body of water **b** *pl* **(1) :** SEDIMENT 1 **(2) :** ground coffee beans after brewing **2 a :** a basis for belief, action, or argument <~ for complaint> — often used in pl. **b (1) :** a fundamental logical condition **(2) :** a basic metaphysical cause **3 a :** a surrounding area **:** BACKGROUND **b :** material that serves as a substratum **4 a :** the surface of the earth **b :** an area used for a particular purpose <parade ~> <fishing ~*s*> **c** *pl* **:** the area around and belonging to a house or other building **d :** an area to be won or defended in or as if in battle **e :** an area of knowledge or special interest <covered a lot of ~ in his lecture> **5 a :** SOIL, EARTH **b :** a special soil **c :** rock or formation through which mine workings are driven **6 a :** an object that makes an electrical connection with the earth **b :** a large conducting body (as the earth) used as a common return for an electric circuit and as an arbitrary zero of potential **c :** electric connection with a ground **7 :** a football offense utilizing primarily running plays ***syn*** see BASE — **from the ground up 1 :** entirely new or afresh **2 :** from top to bottom **:** THOROUGHLY — **into the ground :** beyond what is necessary or tolerable **:** to exhaustion <labored an issue *into the ground* —*Newsweek*> — **off the ground :** in or as if in flight **:** under way <the program never got *off the ground*>

[2]**ground** *vt* **1 :** to bring to or place on the ground **2 a :** to provide a reason or justification for <our fears about technological change may be well ~*ed* —L. K. Williams> **b :** to instruct in fundamentals **3 :** to connect electrically with a ground **4 :** to restrict to the ground <~ a pilot> **5 :** to throw (a football) intentionally to the ground to avoid being tackled for a loss ~ *vi* **1 :** to have a ground or basis **:** RELY **2 :** to run aground **3 :** to hit a grounder

[3]**ground** *past of* GRIND

ground ball *n* **:** a batted baseball that bounds or rolls along the ground

ground bass *n* **:** a short bass passage continually repeated below constantly changing melody and harmony

ground–cher·ry \'grau̇n(d)-'cher-ē\ *n* **:** a plant (genus *Physalis*) of the nightshade family with pulpy fruits in papery husks; *also* **:** the fruit of this plant

ground cloth *n* **:** a waterproof sheet placed on the ground for protection (as of a sleeping bag) against soil moisture

ground cover *n* **1 :** the small plants in a forest except young trees **2 a :** a planting of low plants (as ivy) that covers the ground in place of turf **b :** a plant adapted for use as ground cover

ground crew *n* **:** the mechanics and technicians who maintain and service an airplane

ground–effect machine *n* [fr. the support provided by the cushion of air as if the vehicle rode on the ground] **:** a vehicle for traveling short distances that is supported above the surface of land or water by a cushion of air produced by downwardly directed fans

ground·er \'grau̇n-dər\ *n* **:** GROUND BALL

ground fir *n* **:** a club moss (as *Lycopodium sabaenifolium* or *L. alpinum*) having a stiff erect habit

ground floor *n* **:** the floor of a house most nearly on a level with the ground — compare FIRST FLOOR

ground glass *n* **:** glass with a light-diffusing surface produced by etching or abrading

ground·hog \'grau̇nd-ˌhȯg, -ˌhäg\ *n* **:** WOODCHUCK

Groundhog Day *n* [fr. the legend that the groundhog comes out and is frightened back into hibernation if he sees his shadow] **:** February 2 that traditionally indicates six more weeks of winter if sunny or an early spring if cloudy

ground·ing \'grau̇n-diŋ\ *n* **:** training or instruction in the fundamentals of a field of knowledge

ground itch *n* **:** an itching inflammation of the skin marking the point of entrance into the body of larval hookworms

ground ivy *n* **:** a trailing mint (*Nepeta hederacea*) with rounded leaves and blue-purple flowers

ground·less \'grau̇n-(d)ləs\ *adj* **:** having no ground or foundation <~ fears> — **ground·less·ly** *adv* — **ground·less·ness** *n*

ground·ling \'grau̇n-(d)liŋ\ *n* **1 a :** a spectator who stood in the pit of an Elizabethan theater **b :** a person of unsophisticated taste **2 :** one that lives or works on or near the ground

ground loop *n* **:** a sharp uncontrollable turn made by an airplane on the ground in landing, taking off, or taxiing

ground·mass \'grau̇n(d)-ˌmas\ *n* **:** the fine-grained or glassy base of a porphyry in which the larger distinct crystals are embedded

ground meristem *n* **:** the part of a primary apical meristem remaining after differentiation of dermatogen and procambium

ground·nut \'grau̇n(d)-ˌnət\ *n* **1 a :** any of several plants having edible tuberous roots; *esp* **:** a No. American leguminous vine (*Apios tuberosa*) with pinnate leaves and clusters of brownish purple fragrant flowers **b :** the root of a groundnut **2** *chiefly Brit* **:** PEANUT

ground·out \'grau̇n-ˌdau̇t\ *n* [*grounder*] **:** a play in baseball in which a batter is put out after hitting a grounder to an infielder

ground pine *n* **1 :** a European bugle (*Ajuga chamaepitys*) with a resinous odor **2 :** any of several club mosses (esp. *Lycopodium clavatum* and *L. complanatum*) with long creeping stems and erect branches **:** GROUND FIR

ground plan *n* **1 :** a plan of a floor of a building as distinguished from an elevation **2 :** a first or basic plan

ground rent *n* **:** the rent paid by a lessee for the use of land esp. for building

ground rule *n* **1 :** a sports rule adopted to modify play on a particular field, court, or course **2 :** a rule of procedure <*ground rules* for selecting a superintendent —*Amer. School Board Jour.*>

[1]**ground·sel** \'grau̇n(d)-səl\ *n* [ME *groundeswele,* fr. OE *grundeswelge,* fr. *grund* ground + *swelgan* to swallow — more at SWALLOW] **:** any of a large genus (*Senecio*) of composite plants with mostly yellow flower heads

[2]**groundsel** *n* [ME *ground sille,* fr. *ground* + *sille* sill] **:** a foundation timber

ground·sheet \'grau̇n(d)-ˌshēt\ *n* **:** GROUND CLOTH

ground speed *n* **:** the speed (as of an airplane) with relation to the ground — compare AIR SPEED

ground squirrel *n* **:** any of various burrowing rodents (as of the genus *Citellus*) that are related to the squirrels and that live in colonies esp. in open areas, often damage crops, and include vectors of plague — called also *spermophile*

ground state *n* **:** the energy level (as of a system of interacting elementary particles, an atomic nucleus, or an atom) having the least energy of all its possible states — called also *ground level*

ground stroke *n* **:** a stroke made (as in tennis) by hitting a ball that has rebounded from the ground — compare VOLLEY

ground substance *n* **:** a more or less homogeneous matrix that forms the background in which the specific differentiated elements of a system are suspended: **a :** the intercellular substance of tissues **b :** HYALOPLASM

ground swell *n* **1 :** a broad deep undulation of the ocean caused by an often distant gale or seismic disturbance **2 :** a rapid spontaneous growth (as of political opinion) <public *ground swell* of support for broad and far-reaching change —A. H. Quie>

ground·wa·ter \'grau̇n-ˌdwȯt-ər, -ˌdwät-\ *n* **:** water within the earth that supplies wells and springs; *specif* **:** water in the part of the ground that is wholly saturated

ground wave *n* **:** a radio wave that is propagated along the surface of the earth

ground·work \'grau̇n-ˌdwərk\ *n* **:** FOUNDATION, BASIS <a plan that provides the ~ for a bold new program>

[1]**group** \'grüp\ *n, often attrib* [F *groupe,* fr. It *gruppo,* of Gmc origin; akin to OHG *kropf* craw — more at CROP] **1 :** two or more figures forming a complete unit in a composition **2 a :** a number of individuals assembled together or having some unifying relationship **b :** an assemblage of objects regarded as a unit **c** (1) **:** a military unit consisting of a headquarters and attached battalions (2) **:** a unit of the U.S. Air Force higher than a squadron and lower than a wing **3 a :** an assemblage of related organisms — often used to avoid taxonomic connotations when the kind or degree of relationship is not clearly defined **b** (1) **:** an assemblage of atoms forming part of a molecule **:** RADICAL <a methyl ~> (2) **:** an assemblage of elements forming one of the vertical columns of the periodic table **c :** a stratigraphic division comprising rocks deposited during an era **4 :** a mathematical set that is closed under a binary associative operation and has an identity element and an inverse for every element
syn GROUP, CLUSTER, BUNCH, PARCEL, LOT *shared meaning element* **:** a collection or assemblage of separate units

[2]**group** *vt* **1 :** to combine in a group **2 :** to assign to a group **:** CLASSIFY ~ *vi* **1 :** to form a group **2 :** to belong to a group **3 :** to make well-defined groups of hits on a target <the gun ~*ed* beautifully —R. C. Ruark> — **group·able** \'grü-pə-bəl\ *adj*

group captain *n* **:** a commissioned officer in the British air force who ranks with a colonel in the army

group dynamics *n pl but sing or pl in constr* **:** the interacting forces within a small human group; *also* **:** the sociological study of these forces

grou·per \'grü-pər\ *n, pl* **groupers** *also* **grouper** [Pg *garoupa*] **1 :** any of numerous fishes (family Serranidae and esp. genera *Epinephelus* and *Mycteroperea*) that are typically large solitary bottom fishes of warm seas **2 :** any of several rockfishes (family Scorpaenidae)

group·ie \'grü-pē\ *n* **:** a female fan of a rock group who usu. follows the group around on concert tours

group·ing \'grü-piŋ\ *n* **1 :** the act or process of combining in groups **2 :** a set of objects combined in a group <a furniture ~>

group practice *n* **:** medicine practiced by a group of associated physicians (as specialists in different fields) working as partners or as partners and employees

group therapy *n* **:** therapy in the presence of a therapist in which several patients discuss and share their personal problems — called also *group psychotherapy* — **group therapist** *n*

group·think \'grüp-ˌthiŋk\ *n* [[1]*group* + *-think* (as in *doublethink*)] **:** conformity to group values and ethics

[1]**grouse** \'grau̇s\ *n, pl* **grouse** [origin unknown] **:** any of numerous birds (family Tetraonidae) that have a plump body, strong feathered legs, and plumage less brilliant than that of pheasants usu. with reddish brown or other protective color and that include many important game birds

[2]**grouse** *vi* **groused; grous·ing** [origin unknown] **:** COMPLAIN, GRUMBLE — **grous·er** *n*

[3]**grouse** *n* **:** COMPLAINT <his main ~ . . . is over the inadequacy of the pay —*Times Lit. Supp.*>

[1]**grout** \'grau̇t\ *n* [OE *grūt* coarse meal; akin to OE *grytt* grit] **1 :** LEES **2 a :** thin mortar used for filling spaces (as the joints in masonry); *also* **:** any of various other materials (as a mixture of cement and water or chemicals that solidify) used for a similar purpose **b :** PLASTER

[2]**grout** *vt* **1 :** to fill up or finish with grout **2 :** to fix in place by means of grout <~ a bolt into a wall> — **grout·er** *n*

grove \'grōv\ *n* [ME, fr. OE *grāf*] **1 :** a small wood without underbrush <a picnic ~> **2 :** a planting of fruit or nut trees

grov·el \'gräv-əl, 'grəv-\ *vi* **-eled** *or* **-elled; -el·ing** *or* **-el·ling** \-(ə-)liŋ\ [back-formation fr. *groveling* prone, fr. *groveling,* adv., fr. ME, fr. *gruf,* adv., on the face (fr. ON *ā grūfu*) + *-ling;* akin to OE *crēopan* to creep] **1 :** to creep with the body prostrate in token of subservience or abasement **b :** to abase oneself **3 :** to give oneself over to what is base or unworthy **:** WALLOW <~*ing* in sentimentality —James Stern> — **grov·el·er** \-(ə-)lər\ *n* — **grov·el·ing·ly** \-(ə-)liŋ-lē\ *adv*

groves of academe [*the olive grove of Academe,* phrase applied to Plato's Academy in Milton's *Paradise Regained*] **:** the academic world

grow \'grō\ *vb* **grew** \'grü\; **grown** \'grōn\; **grow·ing** [ME *growen,* fr. OE *grōwan;* akin to OHG *gruowan* to grow] *vi* **1 a :** to spring up and develop to maturity **b :** to be able to grow in some place or situation <trees that ~ only in the tropics> **c :** to assume some relation through or as if through a process of natural growth <a tree with limbs *grown* together> <ferns ~*ing* from the rocks> **2 a :** to increase in size by addition of material either by assimilation into the living organism or by accretion in a nonbiological process (as crystallization) **b :** INCREASE, EXPAND <~*s* in wisdom> **3 :** to develop from a parent source <the book *grew* out of a series of lectures> **4 a :** to pass into a condition **:** BECOME <*grew* pale> **b :** to have an increasing influence <habit ~*s* on a man> **c :** to become increasingly acceptable or attractive <didn't like it at first, but it *grew* on him> ~ *vt* **1 :** to cause to grow **:** PRODUCE <~ wheat> **2 :** DEVELOP 5 — **grow·er** \'grō(-ə)r\ *n* — **grow·ing·ly** \'grō-iŋ-lē\ *adv*

growing pains *n pl* **1 :** pains in the legs of growing children having no demonstrable relation to growth **2 :** the stresses and strains attending a new project or development

growing point *n* **:** the undifferentiated end of a plant shoot from which additional shoot tissues differentiate

[1]**growl** \'grau̇(ə)l\ *vb* [prob. imit.] *vi* **1 a :** RUMBLE <his stomach ~*ed*> **b :** to utter a growl <the dog ~*ed* at the stranger> **2 :** to complain angrily ~ *vt* **:** to utter with a growl

[2]**growl** *n* **:** a deep guttural inarticulate sound

growl·er \'grau̇-lər\ *n* **1 :** one that growls **2 :** a container (as a can or pitcher) for beer bought by the measure **3 :** a small iceberg **4 :** an electromagnetic device with two adjustable pole pieces used for finding short-circuited coils and for magnetizing and demagnetizing

growl·ing \'grau̇-liŋ\ *adj* **:** marked by a growl <a low ~ voice> <listened to the ~ thunder> — **growl·ing·ly** \-liŋ-lē\ *adv*

growly \'grau̇-lē\ *adj* **growl·i·er; -est :** resembling a growl <a ~ voice> — **growl·i·ness** *n*

grown \'grōn\ *adj* **1 :** fully grown **:** MATURE <~ men> **2 :** covered or surrounded with vegetation <land well ~ with trees> **3 a :** cultivated or produced in a specified way or locality — used in combination <shade-*grown* tobacco> **b :** overgrown with — used in combination <a weed-*grown* patio>

[1]**grown–up** \'grō-ˌnəp\ *adj* **:** not childish or immature **:** ADULT <men and women incapable of ~ behavior> ***syn*** see MATURE ***ant*** childish, callow

[2]**grown–up** *n* **:** ADULT

growth \'grōth\ *n* **1 a** (1) **:** a stage in the process of growing **:** SIZE (2) **:** full growth **b :** the process of growing **c :** progressive development **:** EVOLUTION **d :** INCREASE, EXPANSION <the ~ of the oil industry> **2 a :** something that grows or has grown **b :** an abnormal proliferation of tissue (as a tumor) **c :** OUTGROWTH **d :** the result of growth **:** PRODUCT **3 :** a producing esp. by growing <fruits of his own ~>

growth company *n* **:** a company that grows at a greater rate than the economy as a whole and that usu. directs a relatively high proportion of income back into the business

growth factor *n* **:** a substance (as a vitamin) that promotes the growth of an organism

growth hormone *n* **1 :** a vertebrate hormone that is secreted by the anterior lobe of the pituitary gland and regulates growth **2 :** any of various plant substances (as an auxin or gibberellin) that regulate growth

growth ring *n* **:** a layer of wood (as an annual ring) produced during a single period of growth

grow up *vi* **:** to grow toward or arrive at full stature or physical or mental maturity <*growing up* intellectually, socially, and physically>

groyne \'grȯin\ *n* [by alter.] **:** GROIN 3

GR–S \ˌjē-ˌär-'es\ *n* [government *r*ubber + *s*tyrene] **:** a synthetic rubber made by copolymerizing emulsions of butadiene and styrene and used esp. in tires

[1]**grub** \'grəb\ *vb* **grubbed; grub·bing** [ME *grubben;* akin to OE *grafan* to dig — more at GRAVE] *vt* **1 :** to clear by digging up roots and stumps **2 :** to dig up by or as if by the roots ~ *vi* **1 a :** to dig in the ground esp. for something that is difficult to find or extract **b :** to search about **:** RUMMAGE <*grubbed* in the countryside for food and fuel —*Lamp*> **2 :** TOIL, DRUDGE <folks who ~ for money —James Street> — **grub·ber** *n*

[2]**grub** *n* [ME *grubbe,* fr. *grubben*] **1 :** a soft thick wormlike larva of an insect **2 a :** one who does menial work **:** DRUDGE **b :** a slovenly person **3 :** FOOD

grub·by \'grəb-ē\ *adj* **grub·bi·er; -est 1 :** infested with fly maggots **2 a :** DIRTY, GRIMY <~ hands> **b :** SLOVENLY, SLOPPY **3 :** worthy of contempt **:** BASE <~ political motives> — **grub·bi·ly** \'grəb-ə-lē\ *adv* — **grub·bi·ness** \'grəb-ē-nəs\ *n*

[1]**grub·stake** \'grəb-ˌstāk\ *n* **1 :** supplies or funds furnished a mining prospector on promise of a share in his discoveries **2 :** material assistance (as a loan) provided for launching an enterprise or for a person in difficult circumstances

[2]**grubstake** *vt* **:** to provide with a grubstake — **grub·stak·er** *n*

Grub Street \'grəb-\ *n* [*Grub Street,* London, formerly inhabited by literary hacks] **:** the world or category of needy literary hacks

[1]**grudge** \'grəj\ *vt* **grudged; grudg·ing** [ME *grucchen, grudgen* to grumble, complain, fr. OF *groucier,* of Gmc origin; akin to MHG *grogezen* to howl] **:** to be unwilling to give or admit **:** give or allow with reluctance or resentment **:** BEGRUDGE <*grudged* the money to pay taxes> — **grudg·er** *n*

[2]**grudge** *n* **:** a feeling of deep-seated resentment or ill will ***syn*** see MALICE

grudg·ing \'grəj-iŋ\ *adj* **1 :** UNWILLING, RELUCTANT **2 :** given or allowed unwillingly or reluctantly <~ compliance with the physical and mental demands —Caryl Chessman> — **grudg·ing·ly** \-iŋ-lē\ *adv*

gru·el \'grü-əl\ *n* [ME *grewel,* fr. MF *gruel,* of Gmc origin; akin to OE *grūt* grout] **1 :** a thin porridge **2** *chiefly Brit* **:** PUNISHMENT

gru·el·ing *or* **gru·el·ling** \'grü-ə-liŋ\ *adj* [fr. prp. of obs. *gruel* (to exhaust)] **:** trying or taxing to the point of exhaustion **:** PUNISHING <a ~ race> — **gru·el·ing·ly** \-liŋ-lē\ *adv*

grue·some \'grü-səm\ *adj* [alter. of earlier *growsome,* fr. E dial. *grow, grue* to shiver, fr. ME *gruen,* prob. fr. MD *grūwen;* akin to OHG in*grūēn* to shiver] **:** inspiring horror or repulsion **:** GRISLY <~ scenes of battle and death —E. J. Fitzgerald> — **grue·some·ly** *adv* — **grue·some·ness** *n*

¹gruff \'grəf\ *adj* [D *grof;* akin to OHG *grob* coarse, *hruf* scurf — more at DANDRUFF] **1 :** rough, brusque, or stern in manner, speech, or aspect <a ~ reply> **2 :** being deep and harsh : HOARSE <a ~ voice> ***syn*** see BLUFF — **gruff·ly** *adv* — **gruff·ness** *n*
²gruff *vt* **:** to utter in a gruff voice or manner
grum \'grəm\ *adj* **grum·mer; grum·mest** [prob. blend of *grim* and *glum*] **:** MOROSE, GLUM
grum·ble \'grəm-bəl\ *vb* **grum·bled; grum·bling** \-b(ə-)liŋ\ [prob. fr. MF *grommeler* deriv. of MD *grommen;* akin to OHG *grimm* grim] *vi* **1 :** to mutter in discontent **2 :** GROWL, RUMBLE ~ *vt* **:** to express with grumbling — **grumble** *n* — **grum·bler** \-b(ə-)lər\ *n* — **grum·bling·ly** \-b(ə-)liŋ-lē\ *adv* — **grum·bly** \-b(ə-)lē\ *adj*
grum·met \'grəm-ət\ *var of* GROMMET
¹grump \'grəmp\ *n* [obs. E *grumps* (snubs, slights)] **1** *pl* **:** a fit of ill humor or sulkiness **2 :** a person given to complaining
²grump *vi* **1 :** SULK **2 :** GRUMBLE, COMPLAIN ~ *vt* **:** to utter in a grumpy manner
grumpy \'grəm-pē\ *adj* **grump·i·er; -est :** moodily cross **:** SURLY — **grump·i·ly** \-pə-lē\ *adv* — **grump·i·ness** \-pē-nəs\ *n*
grun·ion \'grən-yən\ *n* [prob. fr. Sp. *gruñón* grunter] **:** a silversides (*Leuresthes tenuis*) of the California coast notable for the regularity with which it comes inshore to spawn at nearly full moon
¹grunt \'grənt\ *vb* [ME *grunten,* fr. OE *grunnettan,* freq. of *grunian,* of imit. origin] *vi* **:** to utter a grunt ~ *vt* **:** to utter with a grunt — **grunt·er** *n*
²grunt *n* **1 a :** the deep short sound characteristic of a hog **b :** a similar sound **2** [fr. the noise it makes when taken from the water] **:** any of numerous chiefly tropical marine percoid fishes (family Pomadasidae) related to the snappers **3 :** a U.S. army or marine foot soldier esp. in the Vietnam war
grun·tle \'grənt-ᵊl\ *vt* **grun·tled; grun·tling** \'grənt-liŋ, -ᵊl-iŋ\ [back-formation fr. *disgruntle*] **:** to put in a good humor <were *gruntled* with a good meal and good conversation —W. P. Webb>
grutch \'grəch\ *vt* [ME *grucchen*] *obs* **:** BEGRUDGE
grutten *past part of* GREET
Gru·yère \grü-'ye(ə)r, grē-'(y)e(ə)r\ *n* [*Gruyère,* district in Switzerland] **1 :** a pale yellow pressed cheese with smaller holes and somewhat sharper flavor than Swiss cheese **2 :** a process cheese made from natural Gruyère
gr wt *abbr* gross weight
gryph·on *var of* GRIFFIN
GS *abbr* **1** general staff **2** ground speed
GSA *abbr* **1** General Services Administration **2** Girl Scouts of America
GSC *abbr* general staff corps
GSO *abbr* general staff officer
GST *abbr* Greenwich sidereal time
G–string \'jē-ˌstriŋ\ *n* [origin unknown] **:** a strip of cloth passed between the legs and supported by a waist cord that is worn esp. by striptease dancers
G suit *n* [*g*ravity *suit*] **:** a suit designed to counteract the physiological effects of acceleration on an aviator or astronaut
GSV *abbr* guided space vehicle
gt *abbr* **1** gilt top **2** great **3** [L *gutta*] drop
GT *abbr* gross ton
Gt Brit *abbr* Great Britain
GTC *abbr* good till canceled
gtd *abbr* guaranteed
gtt *abbr* [L *guttae*] drops
GU *abbr* **1** genitourinary **2** Guam
gua·ca·mo·le \ˌgwäk-ə-'mō-lē\ *n* [AmerSp, fr. Nahuatl *ahuacamolle*] **:** sieved or mashed avocado seasoned with condiments
gua·cha·ro \'gwäch-ə-ˌrō\ *n, pl* **-ros** *or* **-roes** [Sp *guácharo*] **:** OILBIRD
guai·ac \'g(w)ī-ˌak\ *n* [NL *Guaiacum*] **:** GUAIACUM 2
guai·a·cum \'g(w)ī-ə-kəm\ *n* [NL, genus name, fr. Sp *guayaco,* fr. Taino *guayacan*] **1 :** any of a genus (*Guaiacum* of the family Zygophyllaceae) of tropical American trees and shrubs having pinnate leaves, mostly blue flowers, and capsular fruit **2 a :** the hard greenish brown wood of a guaiacum (esp. *Guaiacum officinale*) **b :** a resin with a faint balsamic odor obtained from the trunk of two guaiacums (*G. officinale* and *G. sanctum*)
guan \'gwän\ *n* [AmerSp] **:** any of various large tropical American lowland-forest birds (family Cracidae) that somewhat resemble turkeys
gua·na·co \gwə-'näk-(ˌ)ō\ *n, pl* **-cos** *also* **-co** [Sp, fr. Quechua *huanacu*] **:** a So. American mammal (*Lama guanicoe*) with a soft thick fawn-colored coat that is related to the camel but lacks a dorsal hump
gua·neth·i·dine \gwä-'neth-ə-ˌdēn\ *n* [blend of *guanidine* and *eth-*] **:** a drug $C_{10}H_{22}N_4$ used esp. in treating severe high blood pressure
gua·ni·dine \'gwän-ə-ˌdēn\ *n* [ISV, fr. *guanine*] **:** a strong deliquescent crystalline base CH_5N_3 found esp. in young tissues and used in organic synthesis and medicine
gua·nine \'gwän-ˌēn\ *n* [*guano* + *-ine;* fr. its being found esp. in guano] **:** a purine base $C_5H_5N_5O$ that codes genetic information in the polynucleotide chain of DNA or RNA — compare ADENINE, CYTOSINE, THYMINE, URACIL
gua·no \'gwän-(ˌ)ō\ *n* [Sp, fr. Quechua *huanu* dung] **1 :** a substance composed chiefly of the excrement of seafowl and used as a fertilizer **2 :** a product similar to guano <a ~ of fish-cannery refuse>
gua·no·sine \'gwän-ə-ˌsēn\ *n* [blend of *guanine* and *ribose*] **:** a nucleoside $C_{10}H_{13}N_5O_5$ that consists of guanine combined with ribose
guar \'gwär\ *n* [Hindi *guār*] **:** a drought-tolerant legume (*Cyanopsis psoralioides*) grown for forage and for its seeds which produce a gum used as a thickening agent and as a sizing material for paper and textiles
gua·ra·ni \ˌgwär-ə-'nē\ *n* [Sp *guaraní*] **1** *cap* **a** *pl* **guarani** *or* **guaranis :** a member of a Tupi-Guaranian people of Bolivia, Paraguay, and southern Brazil **b :** the language of this people **2** *pl* **guaranis** *or* **guaranies** — see MONEY table
¹guar·an·tee \ˌgar-ən-'tē, ˌgär-\ *n* [prob. alter. of ¹*guaranty*] **1 :** GUARANTOR **2 :** GUARANTY 1 **3 :** an assurance for the fulfillment of a condition: as **a :** an agreement by which one person undertakes to secure another in the possession or enjoyment of something **b :** an assurance of the quality of or of the length of use to be expected from a product offered for sale often with a promise of reimbursement **4 :** GUARANTY 3
²guarantee *vt* **-teed; -tee·ing 1 :** to undertake to answer for the debt, default, or miscarriage of **2 :** to engage for the existence, permanence, or nature of **:** undertake to do or secure (something) <~ the winning of three tricks> **3 :** to give security to
guar·an·tor \ˌgar-ən-'tó(ə)r, 'gar-ən-tər, ˌgär-, 'gär-\ *n* [*guaranty* + ¹*-or*] **1 :** one that guarantees **2 :** one that makes or gives a guaranty
¹guar·an·ty \'gar-ən-tē, 'gär-\ *n, pl* **-ties** [MF *garantie,* fr. OF, fr. *garantir* to guarantee, fr. *garant* warrant, of Gmc origin; akin to OHG *werēnto* guarantor — more at WARRANT] **1 :** an undertaking to answer for the payment of a debt or the performance of a duty of another in case of the other's default or miscarriage **2 :** GUARANTEE 3 **3 :** something given as security **:** PLEDGE **4 :** GUARANTOR **5 :** the protection of a right afforded by legal provision (as in a constitution)
²guaranty *vt* **-tied; -ty·ing :** GUARANTEE
¹guard \'gärd\ *n* [ME *garde,* fr. MF, fr. OF, fr. *garder* to guard, defend, of Gmc origin; akin to OHG *wartēn* to watch, take care — more at WARD] **1 :** a defensive position (as in boxing) **2 a :** the act or duty of protecting or defending **b :** the state of being protected **:** PROTECTION **3** *archaic* **:** PRECAUTION **4 a :** a person or a body of men on sentinel duty **b** *pl* **:** troops attached to the person of the sovereign **c (1) :** BRAKEMAN **(2)** *Brit* **:** CONDUCTOR **5 a :** a position or player next to the center in a football line **b :** a player stationed in the backcourt in basketball **6 :** a protective or safety device; *specif* **:** a device for protecting a machine part or the operator of a machine
²guard *vt* **1 :** to protect an edge of with an ornamental border **2 a :** to protect from danger esp. by watchful attention **:** make secure <policemen *~ing* our cities> <a room *~ed* by locked doors> **b :** to stand at the entrance of as if on guard or as a barrier **c :** to protect (a card or man) in a game by safeguards or support <the separated pawns could not both be *~ed*> **3** *archaic* **:** ESCORT **4 a :** to watch over so as to prevent escape, disclosure, or indiscretion **b :** to attempt to prevent (an opponent) from playing effectively or scoring ~ *vi* **:** to watch by way of caution or defense **:** stand guard ***syn*** see DEFEND — **guard·er** *n*
¹guar·dant \'gärd-ᵊnt\ *adj* [MF *gardant,* prp. of *garder* to guard, look at] **:** having the head turned toward the spectator — used of a heraldic animal whose body is seen from the side <a lion passant ~>
²guardant *n, obs* **:** GUARDIAN
guard cell *n* **:** one of the two crescent-shaped epidermal cells that border and open and close a plant stoma

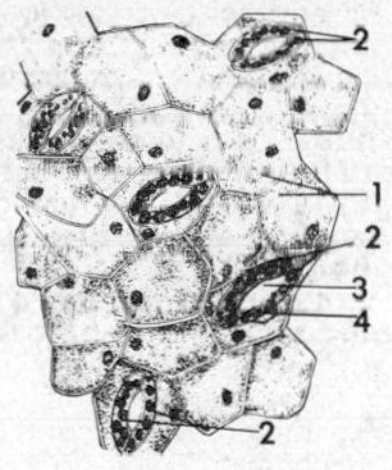

guard cell: *1* epithelial cells, *2* guard cells *3* stoma, *4* chloroplasts

guard·ed \'gärd-əd\ *adj* **:** CAUTIOUS, CIRCUMSPECT — **guard·ed·ly** *adv* — **guard·ed·ness** *n*
guard hair *n* **:** one of the long coarse hairs forming a protective coating over the underfur of a mammal
guard·house \'gärd-ˌhaùs\ *n* **1 :** a building occupied by a guard or used as a headquarters by soldiers on guard duty **2 :** a military jail
guard·ian \'gärd-ē-ən\ *n* **1 :** one that guards **:** CUSTODIAN **2 :** a superior of a Franciscan monastery **3 :** one who has the care of the person or property of another — **guard·ian·ship** \-ˌship\ *n*
guard of honor : HONOR GUARD
guard·rail \'gär-ˌdrāl\ *n* **:** a railing for guarding against danger or trespass; *esp* **:** a barrier (as of steel cables) placed along the edge of a highway at dangerous points
guard·room \'gär-ˌdrüm\ *n* **1 :** a room occupied by a military guard during its term of duty **2 :** a room where military prisoners are confined
guards·man \'gärdz-mən\ *n* **:** a member of a military body called *guard* or *guards*
guar gum *n* **:** a gum that consists of the ground endosperm of guar seeds and is used esp. as a thickening agent and as a sizing material
Guar·ne·ri·us \gwär-'nir-ē-əs, -'ner-\ *n* [NL, fr. It *Guarneri*] **:** a violin made by one of the Italian Guarneri family in the 17th and 18th centuries
gua·va \'gwäv-ə\ *n* [modif. of Sp *guayaba,* of Arawakan origin; akin to Tupi *guayava* guava] **1 :** any of several tropical American shrubs or small trees (genus *Psidium*) of the myrtle family; *esp* **:** a shrubby tree (*P. guajava*) widely cultivated for its sweet acid yellow fruit **2 :** the fruit of a guava
gua·yu·le \(g)wī-'ü-lē\ *n* [AmerSp, fr. Nahuatl *cuauhuli*] **:** a much-branched composite subshrub (*Parthenium argentatum*) of Mexico and the southwestern U.S. that has been cultivated as a source of rubber
gu·ber·na·to·ri·al \ˌgüb-ə(r)-nə-'tōr-ē-əl, ˌgyüb-, ˌgùb-, -'tòr-\ *adj* [L *gubernator* governor, fr. *gubernatus,* pp. of *gubernare* to govern — more at GOVERN] **:** of or relating to a governor
guck \'gək\ *n* [perh. fr. goo + *muck*] **:** oozy sloppy dirt or debris **:** GOO, GUNK

[1]**gud·geon** \ˈgəj-ən\ *n* [ME *gudyon,* fr. MF *goujon*] **1 :** PIVOT, JOURNAL **2 :** a socket for a rudder pintle

[2]**gudgeon** *n* [ME *gojune,* fr. MF *gouvion, gougon,* fr. L *gobion-, gobio,* alter. of *gobius* — more at GOBY] **1 :** a small European freshwater fish (*Gobio gobio*) related to the carps and often used for food or bait **2 :** any of several Australian fishes (family Eleotridae)

gudgeon pin *n* **:** WRIST PIN

Gud·run \ˈgu̇d-ˌrün\ *n* [ON *Guthrūn*] **:** the wife of Sigurd and later of Atli in Norse mythology

guel·der rose \ˌgel-də(r)-\ *n* [*Guelderland, Gelderland,* Netherlands] **:** a bush of a cultivated variety of the cranberry bush with large globose heads of sterile flowers

Guelf *or* **Guelph** \ˈgwelf\ *n* [It *Guelfo*] **:** a member of a papal and popular political party in medieval Italy that opposed the authority of the German emperors in Italy — compare GHIBELLINE

gue·non \gə-nōⁿ\ *n* [F]**:** any of various long-tailed chiefly arboreal African monkeys (*Cercopithecus* and related genera)

guer·don \ˈgərd-ᵊn\ *n* [ME, fr. MF, modif. of OHG *widarlōn,* fr. *widar* back + *lōn* reward — more at WITH, LUCRE] **:** REWARD, RECOMPENSE — **guerdon** *vt*

guern·sey \ˈgərn-zē\ *n, pl* **guernseys** *often cap* [*Guernsey,* Channel islands] **:** any of a breed of fawn and white dairy cattle that are larger than the jersey and produce rich yellowish milk

guer·ril·la *or* **gue·ril·la** \gə-ˈril-ə, ge-; g(y)ir-ˈil-\ *n* [Sp *guerrilla,* fr. dim. of *guerra* war, of Gmc origin; akin to OHG *werra* strife — more at WAR] **1** *archaic* **:** irregular warfare by independent bands **2 :** one who engages in irregular warfare esp. as a member of an independent unit carrying out harassment and sabotage

guerrilla theater *n* **:** drama dealing with controversial social and political issues that is usu. performed outdoors (as on streets or in parks) — called also *street theater*

[1]**guess** \ˈges\ *vb* [ME *gessen,* prob. of Scand origin; akin to ON *geta* to get, guess — more at GET] *vt* **1 :** to form an opinion of from little or no evidence **2 :** to arrive at a correct conclusion about by conjecture, chance, or intuition <~ the answer> **3 :** BELIEVE, SUPPOSE <I ~ you're right> ~ *vi* **:** to make a guess *syn* see CONJECTURE — **guess·er** *n*

[2]**guess** *n* **:** CONJECTURE, SURMISE

guess·ti·mate \ˈges-tə-mət\ *n, slang* [blend of *guess* and *estimate*] **:** an estimate made without adequate information — **guess·ti·mate** \-ˌmāt\ *vt, slang*

guess·work \ˈges-ˌwərk\ *n* **:** work performed or results obtained by guess **:** CONJECTURE

[1]**guest** \ˈgest\ *n* [ME *gest,* fr. ON *gestr;* akin to OE *gæst* guest, stranger, L *hostis* stranger, enemy] **1 a :** a person entertained in one's house **b :** a person to whom hospitality is extended **c :** a person who pays for the services of an establishment (as a hotel or restaurant) **2 :** an organism (as an insect) sharing the dwelling of another; *esp* **:** INQUILINE **3 :** a mineral or rock in a host mineral or rock; *also* **:** a substance that is incorporated in a host substance **4 :** a person not a regular member of a cast who appears on a program

[2]**guest** *vt* **:** to receive as a guest ~ *vi* **:** to appear as a guest

guff \ˈgəf\ *n* [prob. imit.] **:** HUMBUG, NONSENSE

guf·faw \(ˌ)gə-ˈfȯ, ˈgəf-ˌȯ\ *n* [imit.] **:** a loud or boisterous burst of laughter — **guf·faw** \(ˌ)gə-ˈfȯ\ *vi*

gug·gle \ˈgəg-əl\ *vi* **gug·gled; gug·gling** \-(ə-)liŋ\ [imit.] **:** GURGLE — **guggle** *n*

guid·able \ˈgīd-ə-bəl\ *adj* **:** capable of being guided

guid·ance \ˈgīd-ᵊn(t)s\ *n* **1 :** the act or process of guiding **2 :** advice on vocational or educational problems given to students **3 :** the process of controlling the course of a projectile by a built-in mechanism

[1]**guide** \ˈgīd\ *n* [ME, fr. MF, fr. OProv *guida,* of Gmc origin; akin to OE *witan* to look after, *witan* to know — more at WIT] **1 a :** one who leads or directs another in his way **b :** one who exhibits and explains points of interest **c :** something that provides a person with guiding information **d :** SIGNPOST **e :** one who directs a person in his conduct or course of life **2 a :** a device for steadying or directing the motion of something **b :** a ring or loop for holding the line of a fishing rod in position **c :** a sheet or a card with projecting tab for labeling inserted in a card index to facilitate reference **3 :** a member of a unit upon whom the movements or alignments of a military command are regulated — used esp. in commands <~ right>

[2]**guide** *vb* **guid·ed; guid·ing** *vt* **1 :** to act as a guide to **:** direct in a way or course **2 a :** to direct or supervise usu. to a particular end **b :** to superintend the training or instruction of ~ *vi* **:** to act or work as a guide — **guid·er** *n*

syn GUIDE, LEAD, STEER, PILOT, ENGINEER *shared meaning element* **:** to direct in a course or show the way to be followed. GUIDE implies intimate knowledge of the way and of its dangers and difficulties <some heavenly power *guide* us out of this fearful country — Shak.> LEAD implies a keeping in advance to show the way and often exertion of a controlling influence <*lead* a horse to pasture> <the law has to *lead* the people sometimes — Burke Marshall> STEER implies ability to keep to a course and may stress a capacity for correct and effective maneuvering <secure in the faith that his reasoned intelligence will *steer* him correctly at all times — H. N. Maclean> PILOT emphasizes special skill or knowledge used in guiding and imputes difficulty to the course <*pilot* a ship through a narrow channel> <*pilot* a bill through the legislature> ENGINEER, often pejorative in tone, implies facility in evading or overcoming obstacles often by dubious means <*engineer* an elaborate fraud> ***ant*** misguide

guide·book \ˈgīd-ˌbu̇k\ *n* **:** HANDBOOK 1; *esp* **:** a book of information for travelers

guided missile *n* **:** a missile whose course may be altered during flight (as by a target-seeking radar device)

guide·line \ˈgīd-ˌlīn\ *n* **:** a line by which one is guided: as **a :** a cord or rope to aid a passer over a difficult point or to permit retracing a course **b :** an indication or outline (as by a government) of policy or conduct

guide·post \-ˌpōst\ *n* **1 :** INDICATION, SIGN **2 :** GUIDELINE b

guide·way \-ˌwā\ *n* **:** a channel or track for controlling the line of motion of something

guide word *n* **:** either of the terms to left and right of the head of a page of an alphabetical reference work (as a dictionary) indicating the alphabetically first and last words on the page

gui·don \ˈgīd-ˌän, -ᵊn\ *n* [MF] **1 :** a small flag; *esp* **:** one borne by a military unit as a unit marker **2 :** one who carries a guidon

guid·will·ie \gœ̄d-ˈwil-ē, gid-\ *adj* [Sc *guidwill* goodwill] *Scot* **:** CORDIAL, CHEERING

guild \ˈgild\ *n* [ME *gilde,* fr. ON *gildi* payment, guild; akin to OE *gield* tribute, guild — more at GELD] **:** an association of men with similar interests or pursuits; *esp* **:** a medieval association of merchants or craftsmen — **guild·ship** \ˈgil(d)-ˌship\ *n*

guil·der \ˈgil-dər\ *n* [modif. of D *gulden*] **:** GULDEN

guild·hall \ˈgild-ˌhȯl\ *n* **:** a hall where a guild or corporation usu. assembles **:** TOWN HALL

guilds·man \ˈgil(d)z-mən\ *n* **1 :** a guild member **2 :** an advocate of guild socialism

guild socialism *n* **:** an early 20th century English socialistic theory advocating state ownership of industry with control and management by guilds of workers

guile \ˈgī(ə)l\ *n* [ME, fr. OF] **1 :** deceitful cunning **:** DUPLICITY **2** *obs* **:** STRATAGEM, TRICK — **guile·ful** \-fəl\ *adj* — **guile·ful·ly** \-fə-lē\ *adv* — **guile·ful·ness** *n*

guile·less \ˈgī(ə)l-ləs\ *adj* **:** INNOCENT, NAIVE — **guile·less·ly** *adv* — **guile·less·ness** *n*

guil·le·mot \ˈgil-ə-ˌmät\ *n* [F, fr. MF, dim. of *Guillaume* William] **:** any of several narrow-billed auks of northern seas constituting two genera (*Uria* and *Cepphus*)

guil·loche \gil-ˈōsh, gē-ˈ(y)ōsh\ *n* [F *guillochis*] **:** an architectural ornament formed of two or more interlaced bands with openings containing round devices

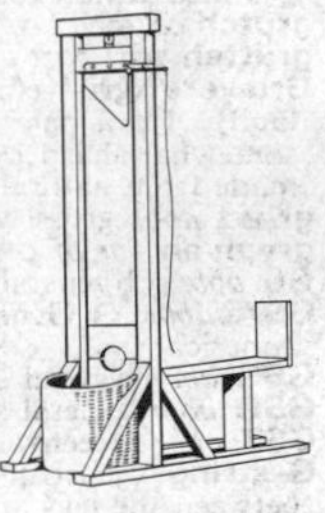
guillotine 1

guil·lo·tine \ˈgil-ə-ˌtēn; ˌgē-(y)ə-ˈ, ˈgē-(y)ə-ˌ\ *n* [F, fr. Joseph *Guillotin* †1814 F physician] **1 :** a machine for beheading by means of a heavy blade that slides down in vertical guides **2 :** a shearing machine or instrument (as a paper cutter) that in action resembles a guillotine **3 :** closure by the imposition of a predetermined time limit on the consideration of specific sections of a bill or portions of other legislative business — **guillotine** *vt*

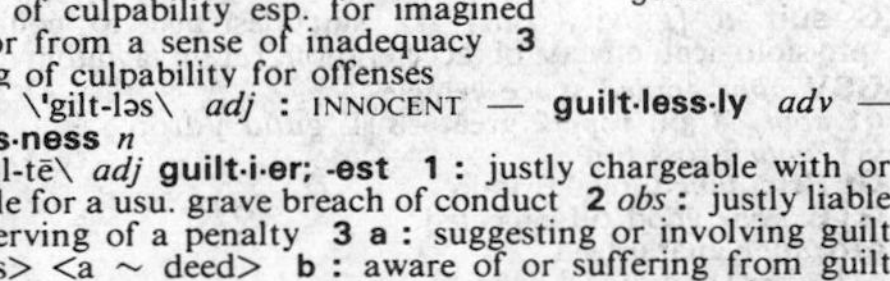

guilt \ˈgilt\ *n* [ME, delinquency, guilt, fr. OE *gylt* delinquency] **1 :** the fact of having committed a breach of conduct esp. violating law and involving a penalty; *broadly* **:** guilty conduct **2 a :** the state of one who has committed an offense esp. consciously **b :** feelings of culpability esp. for imagined offenses or from a sense of inadequacy **3 :** a feeling of culpability for offenses

guilt·less \ˈgilt-ləs\ *adj* **:** INNOCENT — **guilt·less·ly** *adv* — **guilt·less·ness** *n*

guilty \ˈgil-tē\ *adj* **guilt·i·er; -est** **1 :** justly chargeable with or responsible for a usu. grave breach of conduct **2** *obs* **:** justly liable to or deserving of a penalty **3 a :** suggesting or involving guilt <~ looks> <a ~ deed> **b :** aware of or suffering from guilt <their ~ consciences> ***syn*** see BLAMEWORTHY ***ant*** innocent, guiltless — **guilt·i·ly** \-tə-lē\ *adv* — **guilt·i·ness** \-tē-nəs\ *n*

guimpe \ˈgamp, ˈgimp\ *n* [F, fr. OF *guimple,* of Gmc origin; akin to OE *wimpel* wimple] **1 :** a blouse worn under a jumper or pinafore **2 :** a wide cloth used to cover the neck and shoulders by some nuns **3** [by alter.] **:** [1]GIMP

guin·ea \ˈgin-ē\ *n* [*Guinea,* Africa, supposed source of the gold from which it was made] **1 :** an English gold coin issued from 1663 to 1813 and fixed in 1717 at 21 shillings **2 :** a unit of value equal to one pound and one shilling

guinea fowl *n* **:** a West African bird (*Numida meleagris*) related to the pheasants, raised for food in most parts of the world, and marked by a bare neck and head and slaty plumage speckled with white; *broadly* **:** any of several related birds of continental Africa and Madagascar

guinea grass *n* **:** a tall African forage grass (*Panicum maximum*) introduced into tropical America and the southern U.S.

guinea hen *n* **:** a female guinea fowl; *broadly* **:** GUINEA FOWL

guinea pepper *n* **:** GRAINS OF PARADISE

guinea pig *n* **1 :** a small stout-bodied short-eared nearly tailless domesticated rodent (*Cavia cobaya*) often kept as a pet and widely used in biological research — called also *cavy* **2 :** a subject of scientific research, experimentation, or testing

guinea worm *n* **:** a slender nematode worm (*Dracunculus medinensis*) attaining a length of several feet and occurring as an adult in the subcutaneous tissues of various mammals including man in warm countries

Guin·e·vere \ˈgwin-ə-ˌvi(ə)r\ *n* **:** the wife of King Arthur and mistress of Lancelot according to Arthurian legend

gui·pure \gi-ˈp(y)u̇(ə)r\ *n* [F]**:** a heavy large-patterned decorative lace

gui·ro \ˈ(g)wi(ə)r-(ˌ)ō\ *n* [AmerSp *güiro,* calabash, guiro] **:** a percussion instrument of Latin-American origin made of a serrated gourd and played by scraping a stick along its surface

gui·sard \ˈgī-zərd\ *n* [obs. Sc *gyze* to disguise, fr. ME *gyzen* to dress, fr. *guise, gyze* guise] **:** MASKER, MUMMER

guise \ˈgīz\ *n* [ME, fr. OF, of Gmc origin; akin to OHG *wīsa* manner — more at WISE] **1 :** a form or style of dress **:** COSTUME **2 a** *obs* **:** MANNER, FASHION **b** *archaic* **:** a customary way of speaking or behaving **3 :** external appearance **:** SEMBLANCE

gui·tar \gə-ˈtär, gi-\ *n* [F *guitare,* fr. Sp *guitarra,* fr. Ar *qītār,* fr. Gk *kithara* cithara] **:** a flat-bodied stringed instrument with a long fretted neck and usu. six strings plucked with a pick or with the fingers — **gui·tar·ist** \-əst\ *n*

guitar

gui·tar·fish \-ˌfish\ *n* : any of several viviparous rays (family Rhinobatidae) somewhat resembling a guitar in outline when viewed from above

Gu·ja·ra·ti \ˌgü-jə-ˈrät-ē, ˌgu̇j-ə-\ *n, pl* **Gujarati** [Hindi *gujarātī*, fr. *Gujarāt* Gujarat] **1** *or* **Gujerati** : the language of Gujarat and neighboring regions in northwestern India **2** *or* **Guj·ra·ti** \gu̇j-ˈrät-, gu̇j-ˈrät-\ : a member of a people chiefly of Gujarat speaking the Gujarati language

gul \ˈgül\ *n* [Per] : ROSE

gu·lar \ˈg(y)ü-lər\ *adj* [L *gula* throat — more at GLUTTON] : of, relating to, or situated on the throat

gulch \ˈgəlch\ *n* [perh. fr. E dial. *gulch* to gulp, fr. ME *gulchen*] : a deep or precipitous cleft : RAVINE; *esp* : one occupied by a torrent

gul·den \ˈgül-dən, ˈgu̇l-\ *n, pl* **guldens** *or* **gulden** [ME (Sc), fr. MD *gulden florijn* golden florin] — see MONEY table

gules \ˈgyü(ə)lz\ *n, pl* **gules** [ME *goules*, fr. MF] : the heraldic color red

¹gulf \ˈgəlf\ *n* [ME *goulf*, fr. MF *golfe*, fr. It *golfo*, fr. LL *colpus*, fr. Gk *kolpos* bosom, gulf; akin to OE *hwealf* vault, OHG *walbo*] **1** : a part of an ocean or sea extending into the land **2** : a deep chasm : ABYSS **3** : WHIRLPOOL **4** : an unbridgeable gap <the ~ between theory and practice>

²gulf *vt* : ENGULF

gulf·weed \ˈgəlf-ˌwēd\ *n* [*Gulf* of Mexico] : any of several sargassums; *esp* : a branching olive-brown seaweed (*Sargassum bacciferum*) of tropical American seas with numerous berrylike air vesicles

¹gull \ˈgəl\ *n* [ME, of Celt origin; akin to W *gwylan* gull] : any of numerous long-winged web-footed aquatic birds (family Laridae); *esp* : a largely white bird (as of the genus *Larus*) that differs from a tern in usu. larger size, stouter build, thicker bill somewhat hooked at the tip, less pointed wings, and short unforked tail

²gull *vt* [obs. *gull* gullet, fr. ME *golle*, fr. MF *goule*] : to take advantage of (one who is foolish or unwary) : DUPE

³gull *n* : a person who is easily deceived or cheated : DUPE

gull·able \ˈgəl-ə-bəl\ *adj* : GULLIBLE

Gul·lah \ˈgəl-ə\ *n* **1** : a member of a group of Negroes inhabiting the sea islands and coastal districts of So. Carolina, Georgia, and northeastern Florida **2** : the English dialect of the Gullahs that is marked by an admixture of vocabulary and grammatical elements from various African languages

gul·let \ˈgəl-ət\ *n* [ME *golet*, fr. MF *goulet*, dim. of *goule* throat, fr. L *gula* — more at GLUTTON] **1** : ESOPHAGUS; *broadly* : THROAT **2** : an invagination of the protoplasm in various protozoans (as a paramecium) that sometimes functions in the intake of food **3** : the space between the tips of adjacent saw teeth

gull·ible \ˈgəl-ə-bəl\ *adj* : easily deceived, cheated, or duped — **gull·ibil·i·ty** \ˌgəl-ə-ˈbil-ət-ē\ *n* — **gull·ibly** \ˈgəl-ə-blē\ *adv*

Gul·li·ver \ˈgəl-ə-vər\ *n* : an Englishman in Jonathan Swift's satire *Gulliver's Travels* who makes voyages to the imaginary lands of the Lilliputians, Brobdingnagians, Laputans, and Houyhnhnms

¹gul·ly \ˈgül-ē, ˈgəl-\ *n, pl* **gullies** [short for E dial. *gully knife*] *dial Brit* : a large knife

²gul·ly \ˈgəl-ē\ *n, pl* **gullies** [obs. E *gully* (gullet)] : a trench worn in the earth by running water after rains

³gul·ly \ˈgəl-ē\ *vb* **gul·lied; gul·ly·ing** *vt* : to make gullies in ~ *vi* : to undergo erosion : form gullies

gully erosion *n* : soil erosion produced by running water

gu·los·i·ty \g(y)ü-ˈläs-ət-ē\ *n* [ME *gulosite*, fr. LL *gulositas*, fr. L *gulosus* gluttonous, fr. *gula* gullet] : excessive appetite : GREEDINESS

gulp \ˈgəlp\ *vb* [ME *gulpen*, fr. a MD or MLG word akin to D & Fris *gulpen* to bubble forth, drink deep; akin to OE *gielpan* to boast — more at YELP] *vt* **1** : to swallow hurriedly or greedily or in one swallow **2** : to keep back as if by swallowing <~ down a sob> ~ *vi* : to catch the breath as if in taking a long drink — **gulp** *n* — **gulp·er** *n*

¹gum \ˈgəm\ *n* [ME *gome*, fr. OE *gōma* palate; akin to OHG *guomo* palate, Gk *chaos* abyss] : the tissue that surrounds the necks of teeth and covers the alveolar parts of the jaws; *broadly* : the alveolar portion of a jaw with its enveloping soft tissues

²gum *vt* **gummed; gum·ming** **1** : to enlarge gullets of (a saw) **2** : to chew with the gums

³gum *n* [ME *gomme*, fr. OF, fr. L *cummi*, *gummi*, fr. Gk *kommi*, fr. Egypt *qmy.t*] **1 a** : any of numerous colloidal polysaccharide substances of plant origin that are gelatinous when moist but harden on drying and are salts of complex organic acids — compare MUCILAGE 1 **b** : any of various plant exudates (as a mucilage, oleoresin, or gum resin) **2** : a substance or deposit resembling a plant gum (as in sticky or adhesive quality) **3 a** : a tree (as a sour gum or sapodilla) that yields gum **b** *Austral* : EUCALYPTUS **4** : the wood or lumber of a gum; *esp* : that of the sweet gum **5** : CHEWING GUM

⁴gum *vb* **gummed; gum·ming** *vt* : to smear, seal, or clog with or as if with gum <~ up the works> ~ *vi* **1** : to exude or form gum **2** : to become gummy — **gum·mer** *n*

gum ammoniac *n* : AMMONIAC

gum arabic *n* : a water-soluble gum obtained from several acacias (esp. *Acacia senegal* and *A. arabica*) and used esp. in the manufacture of adhesives, in confectionery, and in pharmacy

gum·bo \ˈgəm-(ˌ)bō\ *n* [AmerF *gombo*, of Bantu origin; akin to Umbundu *ochinggômbo* okra] **1** : OKRA 1 **2** : a soup thickened with okra pods and usu. containing vegetables with meat or seafoods **3 a** : any of various fine-grained silty soils esp. of the central U.S. that when wet become impervious and soapy or waxy and very sticky **b** : a heavy sticky mud **4** *often cap* [AmerF *gombo*, perh. fr. Kongo *nkômbô* runaway slave] : a patois used by Negroes and Creoles esp. in Louisiana **5** : MIXTURE, MÉLANGE — **gumbo** *adj*

gum·boil \ˈgəm-ˌbȯil\ *n* : an abscess in the gum

gum·bo–lim·bo \ˌgəm-bō-ˈlim-(ˌ)bō\ *n* [perh. fr. *gumbo* + *limbo*, of Bantu origin; akin to Kongo *edimbu* birdlime] : a tree (*Bursera simaruba*) of southern Florida and the American tropics that has a smooth coppery bark and supplies a reddish resin used locally in cements and varnishes

gum·drop \ˈgəm-ˌdräp\ *n* : a sugar-coated candy made usu. from corn syrup with gelatin or gum arabic

gum·ma \ˈgəm-ə\ *n, pl* **gummas** *also* **gum·ma·ta** \ˈgəm-ət-ə\ [NL *gummat-*, *gumma*, fr. LL, gum, alter. of L *gummi*] : a tumor of gummy or rubbery consistency that is characteristic of the tertiary stage of syphilis — **gum·ma·tous** \-ət-əs\ *adj*

gum·mite \ˈgəm-ˌīt\ *n* : a yellow to reddish brown mixture of hydrous oxides of uranium, thorium, and lead consisting perhaps largely of curite

gum·mo·sis \ˌgə-ˈmō-səs\ *n* : a pathological production of gummy exudate in a plant; *also* : a plant disease marked by gummosis

gum·mous \ˈgəm-əs\ *adj* : resembling or composed of gum : GUMMY

gum·my \ˈgəm-ē\ *adj* **gum·mi·er; -est** **1 a** : consisting of or containing gum **b** : covered with gum **2** : VISCOUS, STICKY — **gum·mi·ness** *n*

gump·tion \ˈgəm(p)-shən\ *n* [origin unknown] **1** : shrewd practical common sense esp. as actively applied to the problems of life **2** : ENTERPRISE, INITIATIVE ***syn*** see SENSE

gum resin *n* : a product consisting essentially of a mixture of gum and resin usu. obtained by making an incision in a plant and allowing the juice which exudes to solidify

¹gum·shoe \ˈgəm-ˌshü\ *n* : DETECTIVE

²gumshoe *vi* : to engage in detective work

gum tragacanth *n* : TRAGACANTH

gum tree *n* : ³GUM 3

gum turpentine *n* : TURPENTINE 2a

gum·wood \ˈgəm-ˌwu̇d\ *n* : ³GUM 4

¹gun \ˈgən\ *n* [ME *gonne*, *gunne*] **1 a** : a piece of ordnance usu. with high muzzle velocity and comparatively flat trajectory **b** : a portable firearm (as a rifle or pistol) **c** : a device that throws a projectile **2 a** : a discharge of a gun in a salute or as a signal **b** : a signal marking a beginning or ending **3 a** : HUNTER **b** : one who is skilled with a gun **4** : something suggesting a gun in shape or function **5** : THROTTLE — **gunned** \ˈgənd\ *adj*

²gun *vb* **gunned; gun·ning** *vi* : to hunt with a gun ~ *vt* **1 a** : to fire on **b** : SHOOT **2** : to open up the throttle of so as to increase speed <~ the engine> — **gun for** : to aim at usu. with determination or effort

gun·boat \ˈgən-ˌbōt\ *n* : an armed ship of shallow draft

gun·cot·ton \-ˌkät-ᵊn\ *n* : CELLULOSE NITRATE; *esp* : an explosive highly nitrated product used chiefly in smokeless powder

gun·dog \-ˌdȯg\ *n* : a dog trained to accompany sportsmen when they hunt with guns

gun·fight \-ˌfīt\ *n* : a duel with guns — **gun·fight·er** \-ər\ *n*

gun·fire \-ˌfī(ə)r\ *n* : the firing of guns

gun·flint \-ˌflint\ *n* : a small sharp flint to ignite the priming in a flintlock

gung ho \ˈgəŋ-ˈhō\ *adj* [*Gung ho!*, motto (interpreted as meaning "work together") of certain U.S. marine raiders in World War II, fr. Chin (Pek) *kung¹-ho²*, short for *chung¹-kuo² kung¹-yeh⁴ ho²-tso⁴ she⁴* Chinese Industrial Cooperatives Society] : extremely or overly zealous or enthusiastic

gunk \ˈgəŋk\ *n* [prob. imit.] : filthy, sticky, or greasy matter

gun·lock \ˈgən-ˌläk\ *n* : a mechanism attached to or integral with a firearm by which the charge is ignited

gun·man \-mən\ *n* **1** : a man armed with a gun; *esp* : a professional killer **2** : a man noted for speed or skill in handling a gun

gun·met·al \ˈgən-ˌmet-ᵊl\ *n* **1** : a metal used for guns; *specif* : a bronze formerly much used as a material for cannon **2** : an alloy or metal treated to imitate nearly black tarnished copper-alloy gunmetal

gun moll \-ˌmäl\ *n, slang* : the girl friend of a gangster

Gun·nar \ˈgu̇n-ˌär, ˈgün-, -ər\ *n* [ON *Gunnarr*] : the king of the Nibelungs and husband of Brynhild in the *Volsunga Saga*

gun·nel \ˈgən-ᵊl\ *n* [origin unknown] : a small slimy elongate north Atlantic blenny (*Pholis gunnellus*); *also* : a fish of the family (Pholidae) to which the gunnel belongs

gun·ner \ˈgən-ər\ *n* **1** : a soldier or airman who operates or aims a gun **2** : one who hunts with a gun **3** : a warrant officer who supervises ordnance and ordnance stores

gun·nery \ˈgən-(ə-)rē\ *n* : the use of guns; *specif* : the science of the flight of projectiles and of the effective use of guns

gunnery sergeant *n* : a noncommissioned officer in the marine corps ranking above a staff sergeant and below a master sergeant or first sergeant

gun·ny \ˈgən-ē\ *n* [Hindi *ganī*] **1** : coarse jute sacking **2** : BURLAP

gun·ny·sack \-ˌsak\ *n* : a sack made of gunny

gun·play \ˈgən-ˌplā\ *n* : the shooting of small arms with intent to scare or kill

gun·point \-ˌpȯint\ *n* : the point of a gun — **at gunpoint** : under a threat of death by being shot

gun·pow·der \-ˌpau̇d-ər\ *n* **:** an explosive mixture of potassium nitrate, charcoal, and sulfur used in gunnery and blasting; *broadly* **:** any of various powders used in guns as propelling charges
gun room *n* **:** quarters on a British warship orig. used by the gunner and his mates but now by midshipmen and junior officers
gun·run·ner \ˈgən-ˌrən-ər\ *n* **:** one that traffics in contraband arms and ammunition — **gun·run·ning** \-ˌrən-iŋ\ *n*
gun·sel \ˈgən(t)-səl\ *n* [slang *gunsel* (stupid person, traitor)] *slang* **:** GUNMAN
gun·ship \ˈgən-ˌship\ *n* **:** an armed helicopter used esp. for protecting troop transport helicopters against ground fire
gun·shot \ˈgən-ˌshät\ *n* **1 :** shot or a projectile fired from a gun **2 :** the range of a gun **3 :** the firing of a gun
gun–shy \-ˌshī\ *adj* **1 :** afraid of loud noise (as that of a gun) **2 :** markedly distrustful
gun·sling·er \-ˌsliŋ-ər\ *n* **:** GUNMAN
gun·sling·ing \-ˌsliŋ-iŋ\ *n* **:** the shooting of a gun esp. in a gunfight
gun·smith \-ˌsmith\ *n* **:** one whose occupation is the designing, making, or repairing of small firearms
Gun·ter's chain \ˌgənt-ərz-\ *n* [Edmund *Gunter* †1626 E mathematician] **:** a chain 66 feet long that is the unit of length for surveys of U.S. public lands
Gun·ther \ˈgu̇nt-ər\ *n* [G] **:** a Burgundian king and husband of Brunhild in Germanic legend
gun·wale *or* **gun·nel** \ˈgən-ᵊl\ *n* [ME *gonnewale,* fr. *gonne* gun + *wale;* fr. its former use as a support for guns] **:** the upper edge of a ship's or boat's side
gup·py \ˈgəp-ē\ *n, pl* **guppies** [R.J.L. *Guppy* †1916 Trinidadian naturalist] **:** a small topminnow (*Lebistes reticulatus* or *Poecilia reticulata*) of the Barbados, Trinidad, and Venezuela frequently kept as an aquarium fish
gur·gle \ˈgər-gəl\ *vi* **gur·gled; gur·gling** \-g(ə-)liŋ\ [prob. imit.] **1 :** to flow in a broken irregular current <the brook *gurgling* over the rocks> **2 :** to make a sound like that of a gurgling liquid <the baby *gurgling* in his crib> — **gurgle** *n*
Gur·kha \ˈgu̇(ə)r-kə, ˈgər-\ *n* [*Ghurka,* member of race dominant in Nepal] **:** a soldier from Nepal in the British or Indian army
gur·nard \ˈgər-nərd\ *n, pl* **gurnard** *or* **gurnards** [ME, fr. MF *gornart,* irreg. fr. *grognier* to grunt, fr. L *grunnire,* of imit. origin] **:** SEA ROBIN
gur·ney \ˈgər-nē\ *n, pl* **gurneys** [prob. fr. the name *Gurney*] *West* **:** a wheeled cot or stretcher
gur·ry \ˈgər-ē,ˈgə-rē\ *n* [origin unknown] **:** fishing offal
gu·ru \gə-ˈrü, ˈgü(ə)r-(ˌ)ü\ *n, pl* **gurus** [Hindi *gurū,* fr. Skt *guru,* fr. *guru,* adj., heavy, venerable — more at GRIEVE] **1 :** a personal religious teacher and spiritual guide in Hinduism **2 a :** a teacher and esp. intellectual guide in matters of fundamental concern **b :** one who is an acknowledged leader or chief proponent (as of a cult, movement, or idea) <one of the New Left's most revered ~*s* — A. H. Raskin> <the ~ of modern jazz — Nat Hentoff>
[1]**gush** \ˈgəsh\ *vb* [ME *guschen*] *vi* **1 :** to issue copiously or violently **2 :** to emit a sudden copious flow **3 :** to make an effusive display of affection or enthusiasm <women ~*ing* over the baby> ~ *vt* **:** to emit in a copious free flow ***syn*** see POUR
[2]**gush** *n* **1 a :** a sudden outpouring **b :** something emitted in a gushing forth **2 :** an effusive display of sentiment or enthusiasm
gush·er \ˈgəsh-ər\ *n* **:** one that gushes; *specif* **:** an oil well with a copious natural flow
gushy \ˈgəsh-ē\ *adj* **gush·i·er; -est :** marked by effusive sentimentality — **gush·i·ly** \ˈgəsh-ə-lē\ *adv* — **gush·i·ness** \ˈgəsh-ē-nəs\ *n*
gus·set \ˈgəs-ət\ *n* [ME, piece of armor covering the joints in a suit of armor, fr. MF *gouchet*] **1 :** a usu. diamond-shaped or triangular insert in a seam (as of a sleeve, pocketbook, or shoe upper) to provide expansion or reinforcement **2 :** a plate or bracket for strengthening an angle in framework (as in a building or bridge) — **gusset** *vt*
gus·sy up \ˌgəs-ē-\ *vt* [origin unknown] **:** to dress up <most of the items are *gussied up* with gold plating — *Newsweek*>
[1]**gust** \ˈgəst\ *n* [ME *guste,* fr. L *gustus;* akin to L *gustare* to taste — more at CHOOSE] **1** *obs* **a :** the sensation of taste **b :** INCLINATION, LIKING **2 :** keen delight
[2]**gust** *n* [prob. fr. ON *gustr;* akin to OHG *gussa* flood, OE *gēotan* to pour — more at FOUND] **1 :** a sudden brief rush of wind **2 :** a sudden outburst **:** SURGE <a ~ of emotion> — **gust·i·ly** \ˈgəs-tə-lē\ *adv* — **gust·i·ness** \-tē-nəs\ *n* — **gusty** \-tē\ *adj*
[3]**gust** *vi* **:** to blow in gusts <winds ~*ing* up to 40 mph>
gus·ta·tion \ˌgəs-ˈtā-shən\ *n* [L *gustation-, gustatio,* fr. *gustatus,* pp. of *gustare*] **:** the act or sensation of tasting
gus·ta·tive \ˈgəs-tət-iv\ *adj* **:** GUSTATORY — **gus·ta·tive·ness** *n*
gus·ta·to·ri·al \ˌgəs-tə-ˈtōr-ē-əl, -ˈtȯr-\ *adj* **:** GUSTATORY — **gus·ta·to·ri·al·ly** \-ē-ə-lē\ *adv*
gus·ta·to·ry \ˈgəs-tə-ˌtōr-ē, -ˌtȯr-\ *adj* **:** relating to, associated with, or being the sense of taste — **gus·ta·to·ri·ly** \ˌgəs-tə-ˈtōr-ə-lē, -ˈtȯr-\ *adv*
gus·to \ˈgəs-(ˌ)tō\ *n, pl* **gustoes** [Sp, fr. L *gustus*] **1 a :** an individual or special taste <we must make allowance for different ~*es*> **b :** enthusiastic and vigorous enjoyment or appreciation **c :** vitality marked by an overabundance of vigor and enthusiasm **2** *archaic* **:** artistic style ***syn*** see TASTE
[1]**gut** \ˈgət\ *n* [ME, fr. OE *guttas,* pl.; akin to OE *gēotan* to pour] **1 a** (1) **:** BOWELS, ENTRAILS — usu. used in pl. (2) **:** the basic visceral or emotional part of a person <wishes to appeal to the ~ rather than the mind — Clive Barnes> **b :** the alimentary canal or part of it (as the intestine or stomach) **c :** BELLY, ABDOMEN **d :** CATGUT **2** *pl* **:** the inner essential parts <the ~*s* of a car> **3 :** a narrow passage; *also* **:** a narrow waterway or small creek **4 :** the sac of silk taken from a silkworm ready to spin its cocoon and drawn out into a thread for use as a snell **5** *pl* **:** fortitude and stamina in coping with what alarms, repels, or discourages **:** COURAGE ***syn*** see FORTITUDE
[2]**gut** *vt* **gut·ted; gut·ting 1 :** EVISCERATE **2 a :** to destroy the inside of <fire *gutted* the building> **b :** to destroy the essential power or effectiveness of <inflation *gutting* the economy of a country>
[3]**gut** *adj* **1 :** arising from one's inmost self **:** VISCERAL <a ~ reaction to the misery he has seen — J. A. Lukas> **2 :** having strong impact or immediate relevance <~ issues>
gut·buck·et \ˈgət-ˌbək-ət\ *n* **1 :** BARRELHOUSE 2 **2 :** a homemade bass fiddle consisting of a stick attached to an inverted washtub and having a single usu. catgut string
gut course *n* [origin unknown] **:** a course (as in college) that is easily passed
gut·less \ˈgət-ləs\ *adj* **1 :** lacking courage **:** COWARDLY **2 :** lacking significance or vitality — **gut·less·ness** *n*
gutsy *adj* **guts·i·er; -est 1 :** COURAGEOUS <a ~ little fighter> **2 :** expressing or appealing strongly to the physical passions **:** LUSTY <belting out ~ rock> — **guts·i·ness** *n*
gut·ta \ˈgət-ə, ˈgu̇t-ə\ *n, pl* **gut·tae** \ˈgə-ˌtē, ˈgu̇-, -ˌtī\ [L, lit., drop — more at GOUT] **:** one of a series of ornaments in the Doric entablature that is usu. in the form of a frustum of a cone
gut·ta–per·cha \ˌgət-ə-ˈpər-chə\ *n* [Malay *gĕtah-pĕrcha,* fr. *gĕtah* sap, latex + *pĕrcha,* tree producing gutta-percha] **:** a tough plastic substance from the latex of several Malaysian trees (genera *Payena* and *Palaquium*) of the sapodilla family that resembles rubber but contains more resin and is used esp. as insulation and in dentistry
gut·tate \ˈgə-ˌtāt\ *adj* [L *guttatus,* fr. *gutta*] **:** having small usu. colored spots or drops <~ skin lesions>
gut·ta·tion \ˌgə-ˈtā-shən\ *n* [L *gutta* drop] **:** the exudation of liquid water from the uninjured surface of a plant

1 guttas

[1]**gut·ter** \ˈgət-ər\ *n* [ME *goter,* fr. OF *goutiere,* fr. *goute* drop, fr. L *gutta*] **1 a :** a trough along the eaves to catch and carry off rainwater **b :** a low area (as at the edge of a street) to carry off surface water (as to a sewer) **c :** a trough or groove to catch and direct something <the ~*s* of a bowling alley> **2 :** a white space formed by the adjoining inside margins of two facing pages (as of a book) **3 :** the lowest or most vulgar level or condition of human life
[2]**gutter** *vt* **1 :** to cut or wear gutters in **2 :** to provide with a gutter ~ *vi* **1 a :** to flow in rivulets **b** *of a candle* **:** to melt away through a channel out of the side of the cup hollowed out by the burning wick **2 :** to incline downward in a draft <the candle flame ~*ing* in the breeze>
[3]**gutter** *adj* **:** of, relating to, or characteristic of the gutter; *esp* **:** marked by extreme vulgarity, cheapness, or indecency <~ journalism> <~ politics>
gutter out *vi* **1 :** to become gradually weaker and then go out <the candle *guttered out*> **2 :** to end feebly or undramatically <his screen career had slowly *guttered out*>
gut·ter·snipe \ˈgət-ər-ˌsnīp\ *n* **1 :** STREET ARAB **2 :** a person of the lowest moral or economic station — **gut·ter·snip·ish** \-ˌsnī-pish\ *adj*
gut·tur·al \ˈgət-ə-rəl, ˈgə-trəl\ *adj* [MF, prob. fr. ML *gutturalis,* fr. L *guttur* throat — more at COT] **1 :** of or relating to the throat **2 a :** articulated in the throat <~ sounds> **b :** VELAR **c :** being or marked by utterance that is strange, unpleasant, or disagreeable — **guttural** *n* — **gut·tur·al·ism** \ˈgət-ə-rə-ˌliz-əm, ˈgə-trə-\ *n* — **gut·tur·al·i·ty** \ˌgət-ə-ˈral-ət-ē\ *n* — **gut·tur·al·ly** \ˈgət-ə-rə-lē, ˈgə-trə-lē\ *adv* — **gut·tur·al·ness** *n*
gut·tur·al·iza·tion \ˌgət-ə-rə-lə-ˈzā-shən, ˌgə-trə-lə-\ *n* **:** the act or process of gutturalizing **:** the state of being gutturalized
gut·tur·al·ize \ˈgət-ə-rə-ˌlīz, ˈgə-trə-\ *vt* **-ized; -iz·ing 1 :** to pronounce in a guttural manner **2 :** VELARIZE
gut·ty \ˈgət-ē\ *adj* **gut·ti·er; -est 1 :** marked by courage or fortitude <a ~ quarterback> **2 :** having a vigorous challenging quality <~ realism>
[1]**guy** \ˈgī\ *n* [prob. fr. D *gei* brail] **:** a rope, chain, or rod attached to something as a brace or guide
[2]**guy** *vt* **:** to steady or reinforce with a guy
[3]**guy** *n* [*Guy* Fawkes] **1** *often cap* **:** a grotesque effigy of Guy Fawkes paraded and burned in England on Guy Fawkes Day **2** *chiefly Brit* **:** a person of grotesque appearance **3 :** MAN, FELLOW
[4]**guy** *vt* **:** to make fun of **:** RIDICULE
Guy Fawkes Day \ˈgī-ˈfȯks-\ *n* **:** November 5 observed in England in commemoration of the seizure of Guy Fawkes in 1605 for an attempt to blow up the houses of parliament
guy·ot \ˈgē-(ˌ)ō\ *n* [Arnold H. *Guyot* †1884 Am geographer & geologist] **:** a flat-topped seamount
guz·zle \ˈgəz-əl\ *vb* **guz·zled; guz·zling** \-(ə-)liŋ\ [origin unknown] *vi* **:** to drink esp. liquor greedily, continually, or habitually ~ *vt* **:** to drink greedily or habitually <~ beer> — **guz·zler** \-(ə-)lər\ *n*
gwe·duc \ˈgü-ē-ˌdək\ *var of* GEODUCK
gybe \ˈjīb\ *var of* JIBE
gym \ˈjim\ *n* **1 :** GYMNASIUM **2 :** PHYSICAL EDUCATION **3 :** a metal frame supporting an assortment of outdoor play equipment (as a swing, seesaw, and rings)
gym·kha·na \jim-ˈkän-ə, -ˈkan-\ *n* [prob. modif. of Hindi *gend-khāna* racket court] **:** a meet featuring sports contests or athletic skills; *specif* **:** a timed contest for automobiles featuring a series of events (as obstacle runs) designed to test driving skill
gymn- *or* **gymno-** *comb form* [NL, fr. Gk, fr. *gymnos* — more at NAKED] **:** naked **:** bare <*gymno*gynous>
gym·na·si·um *in sense 1* jim-ˈnā-zē-əm *also* -zhəm, *in sense 2* gim-ˈnä-zē-əm\ *n, pl* **-na·si·ums** *or* **-na·sia** \-ˈnā-zē-ə *also* -ˈnā-zhə; -ˈnä-zē-ə\ [L, exercise ground, school, fr. Gk *gymnasion,* fr. *gymnazein* to exercise naked, fr. *gymnos*] **1 a :** a large room used for various indoor sports (as basketball, boxing, or volleyball) and usu. equipped with gymnastic apparatus **b :** a building (as on a

college campus) containing space and equipment for various indoor sports activities and usu. including spectator accommodations, locker and shower rooms, offices, classrooms, and a swimming pool **2** [G, fr. L, school] **:** a German secondary school that prepares students for the university

gym·nast \ˈjim-ˌnast, -nəst\ *n* [MF *gymnaste,* fr. Gk *gymnastēs* trainer, fr. *gymnazein*] **:** one trained in gymnastics

¹gym·nas·tic \jim-ˈnas-tik\ *adj* **:** of or relating to gymnastics **:** ATHLETIC — **gym·nas·ti·cal·ly** \-ti-k(ə-)lē\ *adv*

²gymnastic *n* **1** *pl but sing in constr* **a :** physical exercises designed to develop strength and coordination **b :** a competitive sport in which individuals perform optional and prescribed acrobatic feats mostly on special apparatus in order to demonstrate strength, balance, and body control **2 :** an exercise in intellectual or artistic dexterity <my earlier philosophic study had been an intellectual ~ —John Dewey> <mental ~*s*> **3 :** a physical feat or contortion <the ~*s* necessary for the killer to have swung from the fire escape —E. D. Radin>

gym·nos·o·phist \jim-ˈnäs-ə-fəst\ *n* [L *gymnosophista,* fr. Gk *gymnosophistēs,* fr. *gymn-* + *sophistēs* wise man, sophist] **:** one of a sect of naked ascetics of ancient India

gym·no·sperm \ˈjim-nə-ˌspərm\ *n* [deriv. of NL *gymn-* + Gk *sperma* seed — more at SPERM] **:** any of a class or subdivision (Gymnospermae) of woody vascular seed plants (as conifers) that produce naked seeds not enclosed in an ovary and that in some instances have motile spermatozoids — **gym·no·sper·mous** \ˌjim-nə-ˈspər-məs\ *adj* — **gym·no·sper·my** \ˈjim-nə-ˌspər-mē\ *n*

gyn *or* **gynecol** *abbr* gynecology

gyn- *or* **gyno-** *comb form* [Gk *gyn-,* fr. *gynē*— more at QUEEN] **1 :** woman <*gyn*iatrics> <*gyno*cracy> **2 :** female reproductive organ **:** ovary <*gyno*phore> **:** pistil <*gyno*dioecious>

gyn·an·dro·morph \(ˈ)gīn-ˈan-drə-ˌmȯrf, (ˈ)jin-\ *n* [ISV] **:** an abnormal individual exhibiting characters of both sexes in various parts of the body **:** a sexual mosaic — **gyn·an·dro·mor·phic** \(ˌ)gīn-ˌan-drə-ˈmȯr-fik, (ˌ)jin-\ *adj* — **gyn·an·dro·mor·phism** \-ˌfiz-əm\ *n* — **gyn·an·dro·mor·phous** \-fəs\ *adj* — **gyn·an·dro·mor·phy** \(ˈ)gīn-ˈan-drə-ˌmȯr-fē, (ˈ)jin-\ *n*

gyn·an·drous \(ˈ)gīn-ˈan-drəs, (ˈ)jin-\ *adj* [Gk *gynandros* of doubtful sex, fr. *gynē* woman + *andr-, anēr* man — more at ANDR-] **:** having the androecium and gynoecium united in a column

-gyne \ˌjīn, -ˌgīn\ *n comb form* [Gk *gynē*] **1 :** woman **:** female <pseudo*gyne*> **2 :** female reproductive organ <tricho*gyne*>

gynec- *or* **gyneco-** *also* **gynaec-** *or* **gynaeco-** *comb form* [Gk *gynaik-, gynaiko-,* fr. *gynaik-, gynē* woman — more at QUEEN] **:** woman <*gyne*coid>

gy·ne·coc·ra·cy \ˌgīn-i-ˈkäk-rə-sē, ˌjin-\ *n, pl* **-cies** [Gk *gynaikokratia,* fr. *gynaik-* + *-kratia* -cracy] **:** political supremacy of women — **gy·ne·co·crat** \ˈgīn-i-kō-ˌkrat, ˈjin-\ *n* — **gy·ne·co·crat·ic** \ˌgīn-i-kō-ˈkrat-ik, ˌjin-\ *adj*

gy·ne·coid \ˈgīn-i-ˌkȯid, ˈjin-\ *adj* **:** having female characteristics; *also* **:** typical of a woman

gy·ne·col·o·gy \ˌgīn-ə-ˈkäl-ə-jē, ˌjin-\ *n* [ISV] **:** a branch of medicine that deals with the diseases and hygiene of women — **gy·ne·co·log·ic** \ˌgīn-i-kə-ˈläj-ik, ˌjin-\ *or* **gy·ne·co·log·i·cal** \-i-kəl\ *adj* — **gy·ne·col·o·gist** \ˌgīn-ə-ˈkäl-ə-jəst, ˌjin-\ *n*

gy·noe·ci·um \jin-ˈē-s(h)ē-əm, gīn-\ *n, pl* **-cia** \-s(h)ē-ə\ [NL, alter. of L *gynaeceum* women's apartments, fr. Gk *gynaikeion,* fr. *gynaik-, gynē*] **:** the aggregate of carpels in a flower **:** PISTILS

gy·no·gen·e·sis \ˌgīn-ə-ˈjen-ə-səs\ *n* [NL] **:** development in which the embryo contains only maternal chromosomes due to activation of an egg by a sperm that degenerates without fusing with the egg nucleus — **gy·no·ge·net·ic** \-jə-ˈnet-ik\ *adj*

gy·no·phore \ˈgīn-ə-ˌfō(ə)r, ˈjin-, -ˌfȯ(ə)r\ *n* **:** a prolongation of the receptacle (as in a caper flower) that bears the gynoecium at its apex — **gy·no·phor·ic** \ˌgīn-ə-ˈfȯr-ik, ˌjin-, -ˈfär-\ *adj*

-g·y·nous \j-ə-nəs\ *adj comb form* [NL *-gynus,* fr. Gk *-gynos,* fr. *gynē* woman — more at QUEEN] **:** of, relating to, or having (such or so many) females <hetero*gynous*> **2 a :** having (such or so many) styles or pistils <tetra*gynous*> **b :** situated (in a specified place) in relation to a female organ of a plant <hypo*gynous*>

-g·y·ny \j-ə-nē\ *n comb form* **1 :** existence of or condition of having (such or so many) females <poly*gyny*> **2 :** the condition of being situated (in a specified place) in relation to a female organ of a plant <epi*gyny*>

¹gyp \ˈjip\ *n* [prob. short for *gypsy*] **1** *Brit* **:** a college servant **2 a :** CHEAT, SWINDLER **b :** FRAUD, SWINDLE

²gyp *vb* **gypped; gyp·ping :** CHEAT

gyp·se·ous \ˈjip-sē-əs\ *adj* **:** resembling, containing, or consisting of gypsum <~ clay loam>

gyp·sif·er·ous \jip-ˈsif-(ə-)rəs\ *adj* **:** bearing gypsum

gyp·soph·i·la \jip-ˈsäf-ə-lə\ *n* [NL, genus name, fr. L *gypsum* + *-phila* -phil] **:** any of a large genus (*Gypsophila*) of Old World herbs of the pink family having small delicate paniculate flowers

gyp·sum \ˈjip-səm\ *n* [L, fr. Gk *gypsos,* of Sem origin; akin to Ar *jibs* plaster] **1 :** a widely distributed mineral $CaSO_4.2H_2O$ consisting of hydrous calcium sulfate that is used esp. as a soil amendment and in making plaster of paris **2 :** PLASTERBOARD

gypsy *vi* **gyp·sied; gyp·sy·ing :** to live or roam like a Gypsy

Gyp·sy \ˈjip-sē\ *n, pl* **Gypsies** [by shortening & alter. fr. *Egyptian*] **1 :** one of a dark Caucasoid people coming orig. from India to Europe in the 14th or 15th century and living and maintaining a migratory way of life chiefly in Europe and the U.S. **2 :** ROMANY 2 **3** *not cap* **:** one that resembles a Gypsy (as in appearance or mode of life); *esp* **:** WANDERER

gypsy moth *n* **:** an Old World tussock moth (*Porthetria dispar*) that was introduced about 1869 into the U.S. and has a grayish brown mottled hairy caterpillar which is a destructive defoliator of many trees

gyr- *or* **gyro-** *comb form* [prob. fr. MF, fr. L, fr. Gk, fr. *gyros*] **1 :** ring **:** circle **:** spiral <*gyro*magnetic> **2 :** gyroscope <*gyro*compass>

¹gy·rate \ˈjī-ˌrāt\ *adj* **:** winding or coiled around **:** CONVOLUTED <~ branches of a tree>

²gyrate *vi* **gy·rat·ed; gy·rat·ing 1 :** to revolve around a point or axis **2 :** to oscillate with or as if with a circular or spiral motion — **gy·ra·tor** \-ˌrāt-ər\ *n* — **gy·ra·to·ry** \ˈjī-rə-ˌtōr-ē, -ˌtȯr-\ *adj*

gy·ra·tion \jī-ˈrā-shən\ *n* **1 :** an act or instance of gyrating **2 :** something (as a coil of a shell) that is gyrate — **gy·ra·tion·al** \-shnəl, -shən-ᵊl\ *adj*

¹gyre \ˈjī(ə)r\ *vi* **gyred; gyr·ing** [ME *giren* fr. LL *gyrare,* fr. *gyrus*] **:** to move in a circle or spiral

²gyre *n* [L *gyrus,* fr. Gk *gyros* — more at COWER] **:** a circular or spiral motion or form — **gy·ral** \ˈjī-rəl\ *adj*

gy·rene \ji-ˈrēn\ *n* [prob. alter. of *marine*] *slang* **:** a U.S. marine

gyr·fal·con \ˈjər-ˌfal-kən *also* -ˌfȯl- *sometimes* -ˌfō-kən\ *n* [ME *gerfaucun,* fr. MF *girfaucon*] **:** an arctic falcon (*Falco rusticolus*) that occurs in several forms, is the largest of all falcons, and is more powerful though less active than the peregrine falcon

gyrfalcon

gy·ro \ˈjī-(ˌ)rō\ *n, pl* **gyros 1 :** GYROSCOPE **2 :** GYROCOMPASS

Gy·ro \ˈjī-(ˌ)rō\ *n, pl* **Gyros** [*Gyro* International (association)] **:** a member of a major international service club

gy·ro·com·pass \ˈjī-rō-ˌkəm-pəs *also* -ˌkäm-\ *n* **:** a compass consisting of a continuously driven gyroscope whose spinning axis is confined to a horizontal plane so that the earth's rotation causes it to assume a position parallel to the earth's axis and thus point to the true north

gy·ro·fre·quen·cy \-ˌfrē-kwən-sē\ *n* **:** the frequency with which a charged particle (as an electron) executes spiral gyrations in moving obliquely across a magnetic field

gyro horizon *n* **:** ARTIFICIAL HORIZON 2

gy·ro·mag·net·ic \ˌjī-rō-mag-ˈnet-ik\ *adj* **:** of or relating to the magnetic properties of a rotating electrical particle

gyromagnetic ratio *n* **:** the ratio of the magnetic moment of a spinning charged particle to its angular momentum

gy·ron \ˈjī-rən\ *n* [MF *giron* gore, of Gmc origin; akin to OHG *gēra* wedge-shaped object, OE *gāra* gore] **:** a heraldic charge of triangular form having one side at the edge of the field and the opposite angle usu. at the fess point

gy·ro·plane \ˈjī-rə-ˌplān\ *n* [ISV] **:** an airplane balanced and supported by the aerodynamic forces acting on rapidly rotating horizontal or slightly inclined airfoils

gy·ro·scope \ˈjī-rə-ˌskōp\ *n* [F, fr. *gyr-* + *-scope;* fr. its original use to illustrate the rotation of the earth] **:** a wheel or disk mounted to spin rapidly about an axis and also free to rotate about one or both of two axes perpendicular to each other and to the axis of spin so that a rotation of one of the two mutually perpendicular axes results from application of torque to the other when the wheel is spinning and so that the entire apparatus offers considerable opposition depending on the angular momentum to any torque that would change the direction of the axis of spin — **gy·ro·scop·ic** \ˌjī-rə-ˈskäp-ik\ *adj* — **gy·ro·scop·i·cal·ly** \-i-k(ə-)lē\ *adv*

gy·ro·sta·bi·liz·er \ˌjī-rō-ˈstā-bə-ˌlī-zər\ *n* **:** a stabilizing device (as for a ship or airplane) that consists of a continuously driven gyro spinning about a vertical axis and pivoted so that its axis of spin may be tipped fore-and-aft in the vertical plane and that serves to oppose sideways motion

gy·ro·stat \ˈjī-rə-ˌstat\ *n* **:** GYROSTABILIZER

gy·rus \ˈjī-rəs\ *n, pl* **gy·ri** \ˈjī-ˌrī\ [NL, fr. L, circle — more at GYRE] **:** a convoluted ridge between anatomical grooves

Gy Sgt *abbr* gunnery sergeant

gyve \ˈjīv, ˈgīv\ *n* [ME] **:** FETTER, SHACKLE — **gyve** *vt*

[1]**h** \'āch\ *n, pl* **h's** *or* **hs** \'ā-chəz\ *often cap, often attrib* **1 a :** the 8th letter of the English alphabet **b :** a graphic representation of this letter **c :** a speech counterpart of orthographic *h* **2 :** a graphic device for reproducing the letter *h* **3 :** one designated *h* esp. as the 8th in order or class **4 :** something shaped like the letter H

[2]**h** *abbr, often cap* **1** half **2** harbor **3** hard; hardness **4** height **5** heroin **6** high **7** hit **8** humidity **9** hundred **10** Hungary **11** husband

[3]**h** *symbol* Planck's constant

H *symbol* **1** enthalpy **2** Hamiltonian **3** hydrogen

[1]**ha** \'hä\ *interj* [ME] — used esp. to express surprise or joy

[2]**ha** *abbr* **1** hectare **2** [L *hoc anno*] in this year

HA *abbr* hour angle

Hab *abbr* Habakkuk

Ha·ba·cuc \'hab-ə-ˌkək, hə-'bak-ək\ *n* [LL, fr. Heb *Ḥabhaqqūq*] **:** HABAKKUK

Ha·bak·kuk \'hab-ə-ˌkək, hə-'bak-ək\ *n* [Heb *Ḥăbhaqqūq*] **1 :** a Hebrew prophet of 7th century Judah who prophesied an imminent Chaldean invasion **2 :** a prophetic book of canonical Jewish and Christian Scripture — see BIBLE table

ha·ba·ne·ra \ˌ(h)äb-ə-'ner-ə\ *n* [Sp *(danza) habanera,* lit., Havanan dance] **1 :** a Cuban dance in slow duple time **2 :** the music for the habanera

hab corp *abbr* habeas corpus

hab·da·lah \ˌhäv-də-'lä, häv-'dō-lə\ *n, often cap* [Heb *habhdālāh* separation] **:** a Jewish ceremony marking the close of a Sabbath or holy day

ha·be·as cor·pus \ˌhā-bē-ə-'skȯr-pəs\ *n* [ME, fr. ML, lit., you should have the body (the opening words of the writ)] **1 :** any of several common-law writs issued to bring a party before a court or judge; *esp* **:** HABEAS CORPUS AD SUBJICIENDUM **2 :** the right of a citizen to obtain a writ of habeas corpus as a protection against illegal imprisonment

habeas corpus ad sub·ji·ci·en·dum \-pə-ˌsad-səb-ˌyik-ē-'en-dəm\ *n* [NL, lit., you should have the body for submitting] **:** a writ for inquiring into the lawfulness of the restraint of a person who is imprisoned or detained in another's custody

hab·er·dash·er \'hab-ə(r)-ˌdash-ər\ *n* [ME *haberdassher,* fr. modif. of AF *hapertas* petty merchandise] **1** *Brit* **:** a dealer in small wares or notions **2 :** a dealer in men's furnishings

hab·er·dash·ery \-ˌdash-(ə-)rē\ *n, pl* **-er·ies** **1 :** goods sold by a haberdasher **2 :** a haberdasher's shop

hab·er·geon \'hab-ər-jən, hə-'bər-j(ē-)ən\ *n* [ME *haubergeoun,* fr. MF *haubergeon,* dim. of *hauberc* hauberk] **1 :** a medieval jacket of mail shorter than a hauberk **2 :** HAUBERK

hab·ile \'hab-əl, -ˌīl\ *adj* [F, fr. L *habilis* — more at ABLE] **:** having general skill **:** ABLE, SKILLFUL

ha·bil·i·ment \hə-'bil-ə-mənt\ *n* [MF *habillement,* fr. *habiller* to dress a log, dress, fr. *bille* log — more at BILLET] **1** *pl* **:** characteristic apparatus **:** FITTINGS <the ~*s* of civilization —W. P. Webb> **2 a :** the dress characteristic of an occupation or occasion — usu. used in pl. **b :** CLOTHES — usu. used in pl.

ha·bil·i·tate \hə-'bil-ə-ˌtāt\ *vb* **-tat·ed; -tat·ing** [LL *habilitatus,* pp. of *habilitare,* fr. L *habilitas* ability — more at ABILITY] *vt* **1** *archaic* **:** to make capable **:** QUALIFY **2 :** CLOTHE, DRESS ~ *vi* **:** to qualify oneself <*habilitated* as a privatdocent in the theological faculty —Jack Finegan> — **ha·bil·i·ta·tion** \-ˌbil-ə-'tā-shən\ *n*

[1]**hab·it** \'hab-ət\ *n* [ME, fr. OF, fr. L *habitus* condition, character, fr. *habitus,* pp. of *habēre* to have, hold — more at GIVE] **1** *archaic* **:** CLOTHING **2 a :** a costume characteristic of a calling, rank, or function **b :** a costume worn for horseback riding **3 :** manner of conducting oneself **:** BEARING **4 :** bodily appearance or makeup esp. as indicative of one's capacities and condition <a man of fleshy ~> **5 :** the prevailing disposition or character of a person's thoughts and feelings **:** mental makeup **6 :** a settled tendency or usual manner of behavior **7 a :** a behavior pattern acquired by frequent repetition or physiologic exposure that shows itself in regularity or increased facility of performance **b :** an acquired mode of behavior that has become nearly or completely involuntary **c :** ADDICTION **8 :** characteristic mode of growth or occurrence **9** *of a crystal* **:** characteristic assemblage of forms at crystallization leading to a usual appearance

syn **1** HABIT, HABITUDE, PRACTICE, USAGE, CUSTOM, USE, WONT *shared meaning element* **:** a way of acting fixed through repetition. HABIT implies a doing unconsciously and often compulsively <trying to break a bad *habit*> HABITUDE suggests a fixed attitude or usual state of mind <the sense of fitness and proportion that comes from years of *habitude* in the practice of an art —B. N. Cardozo> PRACTICE describes a method followed regularly and usually through choice <it was his *practice* to take a stroll each morning> USAGE suggests a customary course so generally followed that it has become a social norm <difficult . . . to earn a living in a business community without yielding to its *usages* —W. H. Hamilton> CUSTOM implies such firm fixation in the behavior pattern of an individual or group as to have the force of unwritten law <the universal tendency to resist change in long-established *custom*> <the icy chains of *custom* —P. B. Shelley> USE stresses the fact of customary usage <more haste than is his *use* —Shak.> and often attributes a distinctive quality <conform to the *uses* of polite society> WONT, close to *use,* is often coupled with the latter as a term of equivalent content <this nice balance between sovereignty and liberty is maintained by use and *wont* —V. L. Parrington>
2 see PHYSIQUE

[2]**habit** *vt* **:** CLOTHE, DRESS

hab·it·able \'hab-ət-ə-bəl\ *adj* **:** capable of being lived in **:** suitable for habitation — **hab·it·abil·i·ty** \ˌhab-ət-ə-'bil-ət-ē\ *n* — **hab·it·able·ness** \'hab-ət-ə-bəl-nes\ *n* — **hab·it·ably** \-blē\ *adv*

ha·bi·tant *n* **1** \'hab-ət-ənt\ **:** INHABITANT, RESIDENT **2** \ˌ(h)ab-i-'tä"\ *or* **ha·bi·tan** \-'tä"\ **:** a settler or descendant of a settler of French origin belonging to the farming class in Canada

hab·i·tat \'hab-ə-ˌtat\ *n* [L, it inhabits, fr. *habitare*] **1 a :** the place or type of site where a plant or animal naturally or normally lives and grows **b :** the typical place of residence of a person or a group **c :** a housing for a controlled physical environment in which people can live under surrounding inhospitable conditions (as under the sea) **2 :** the place where something is commonly found

habitat group *n* **:** a museum exhibit showing plant and animal specimens in such attitudes and with their natural surroundings so reproduced as to picture their habits and habitat

hab·i·ta·tion \ˌhab-ə-'tā-shən\ *n* [ME *habitacioun,* fr. MF *habitation,* fr. L *habitation-, habitatio,* fr. *habitatus,* pp. of *habitare* to inhabit, fr. *habitus,* pp.] **1 :** the act of inhabiting **:** OCCUPANCY **2 :** a dwelling place **:** RESIDENCE **3 :** SETTLEMENT, COLONY

hab·it–form·ing \'hab-ət-ˌfȯr-miŋ\ *adj* **:** inducing the formation of an addiction

ha·bit·u·al \hə-ˌbich-(ə-)wəl, ha-, -'bich-əl\ *adj* **1 :** having the nature of a habit **:** being in accordance with habit **:** CUSTOMARY <~ smoking> **2 :** doing, practicing, or acting in some manner by force of habit <~ drunkard> **3 :** resorted to on a regular basis <his ~ diet> **4 :** inherent in an individual <~ grace> ***syn*** see USUAL ***ant*** occasional — **ha·bit·u·al·ly** \-ē\ *adv* — **ha·bit·u·al·ness** *n*

ha·bit·u·ate \hə-'bich-ə-ˌwāt, ha-\ *vb* **-at·ed; -at·ing** *vt* **1 :** to make used to **:** ACCUSTOM **2** *archaic* **:** FREQUENT ~ *vi* **:** to cause habituation <marijuana may be *habituating*>

ha·bit·u·a·tion \-ˌbich-ə-'wā-shən\ *n* **1 :** the act or process of making habitual or accustomed **2 a :** tolerance to the effects of a drug acquired through continued use **b :** psychologic dependence on a drug after a period of use — compare ADDICTION

hab·i·tude \'hab-ə-ˌt(y)üd\ *n* **1** *archaic* **:** native or essential character **2** *obs* **:** habitual association **3 a :** habitual disposition or mode of behavior or procedure **b :** CUSTOM ***syn*** see HABIT

ha·bi·tué \hə-'bich-ə-ˌwā, ha-\ *n* [F, fr. pp. of *habituer* to frequent, fr. LL *habituare* to habituate, fr. L *habitus*] **:** one who frequents a place or numerous places of the same category <~*s* of Paris> <~*s* of the theater>

hab·i·tus \'hab-ət-əs\ *n, pl* **habitus** \-ət-əs, -ə-ˌtüs\ [NL, fr. L] **:** HABIT; *specif* **:** body build and constitution esp. as related to predisposition to disease

Habs·burg \'haps-, 'häps-\ *var of* HAPSBURG

ha·ček \'häch-ˌek\ *n* [Czech *háček,* lit., little hook] **:** a diacritic ˅ placed over a letter (as in *č*) to modify it **:** an inverted circumflex

ha·cen·da·do \ˌ(h)äs-ᵊn-'däd-(ˌ)ō\ *also* **ha·ci·en·da·do** \ˌhäs-ē-en-\ *n, pl* **-dos** [Sp *hacendado,* fr. *hacienda*] **:** the owner or proprietor of a hacienda

[1]**ha·chure** \ha-'shu̇(ə)r\ *n* [F] **:** a short line used for shading and denoting surfaces in relief (as in map drawing) and drawn in the direction of slope

[2]**hachure** *vt* **ha·chured; ha·chur·ing :** to shade with or show by hachures

ha·ci·en·da \ˌ(h)äs-ē-'en-də\ *n* [Sp] **1 :** a large estate esp. in a Spanish-speaking country **:** PLANTATION **2 :** the main dwelling of a hacienda

[1]**hack** \'hak\ *vb* [ME *hakken,* fr. OE *-haccian;* akin to OHG *hacchōn* to hack, OE *hōc* hook] *vt* **1 a :** to cut with repeated irregular or unskillful blows **b :** to sever with repeated blows **2 :** to clear by cutting away vegetation <~*ed* his way through the brush> **3 :** to manage successfully <he tried sales work, but he just couldn't ~ it> ~ *vi* **1 :** to make cutting blows or rough cuts **:** CHOP **2 :** to cough in a short dry manner — **hack·er** *n*

[2]**hack** *n* **1 :** an implement for hacking **2 :** NICK, NOTCH; *esp* **:** a blaze cut in a tree **3 :** a short dry cough **4 :** a hacking blow **5 :** restriction to quarters as punishment for naval officers — usu. used in the phrase *under hack*

[3]**hack** *n* [short for *hackney*] **1 a (1) :** a horse let out for common hire **(2) :** a horse used in all kinds of work **b :** a horse worn out in service **:** JADE **c :** a light easy saddle horse; *esp* **:** a three-gaited saddle horse **2 a :** HACKNEY **b (1) :** TAXICAB **(2) :** CABDRIVER **3 :** one who forfeits individual freedom of action or professional integrity in exchange for wages or other assured reward; *esp* **:** a writer who works mainly for hire

[4]**hack** *adj* **1 :** working for hire esp. with loose or easy professional standards **2 :** performed by, suited to, or characteristic of a hack <~ writing> **3 :** HACKNEYED, TRITE

[5]**hack** *vt* **1 :** to make trite and commonplace by frequent and indiscriminate use **2 :** to use as a hack ~ *vi* **1 :** to ride or drive at an ordinary pace or over the roads as distinguished from racing or riding across country **2 :** to operate a taxicab — **hack·er** *n*

hack·a·more \'hak-ə-ˌmō(ə)r, -ˌmȯ(ə)r\ *n* [by folk etymology fr. Sp *jáquima*] **:** a bridle with a loop capable of being tightened about the nose in place of a bit or with a slip noose passed over the lower jaw

hack·ber·ry \'hak-ˌber-ē\ *n* [alter. of *hagberry* (a cherry resembling the chokecherry)] **:** any of a genus (*Celtis*) of trees and shrubs of the elm family with small often edible berries; *also* **:** its wood

hack·but \'hak-(ˌ)bət\ *or* **hag·but** \'hag-\ *n* [MF *haguebute*] **:** HARQUEBUS — **hack·but·eer** \ˌhak-bə-'ti(ə)r\ *or* **hack·but·ter** \'hak-(ˌ)bət-ər\ *n*

hack·ie \'hak-ē\ *n* **:** CABDRIVER

[1]**hack·le** \'hak-əl\ *n* [ME *hakell;* akin to OHG *hāko* hook — more at HOOK] **1 :** a comb or board with long metal teeth for dressing flax, hemp, or jute **2 a :** one of the long narrow feathers on the neck or saddle of a bird — see COCK illustration **b :** the neck plumage of the male domestic fowl **3** *pl* **a :** erectile hairs along the neck and back esp. of a dog **b :** TEMPER, DANDER **4 a :** an artificial fishing fly made chiefly of the filaments of a cock's neck feathers **b :** filaments of cock feather projecting downward from the head of an artificial fly

2hackle *vt* **hack·led; hack·ling** \ˈhak-(ə-)liŋ\ **1 :** to comb out with a hackle **2 :** to furnish with a hackle — **hack·ler** \-(ə-)lər\ *n*
3hackle *vt* **hack·led; hack·ling** [freq. of 1*hack*] **:** to cut or chop up **:** chop off roughly **:** HACK
4hackle *n* **:** a fracture resulting in hackly edges
hack·ly \ˈhak-(ə-)lē\ *adj* **:** having the appearance of something hacked **:** JAGGED
hack·man \ˈhak-mən\ *n* **:** CABDRIVER
hack·ma·tack \ˈhak-mə-ˌtak\ *n* [of Algonquian origin; akin to Abnaki *akemantak* snowshoe wood] **1 :** TAMARACK **2 :** BALSAM POPLAR
1hack·ney \ˈhak-nē\ *n, pl* **hack·neys** [ME *hakeney*] **1 a :** a horse suitable for ordinary riding or driving **b :** a trotting horse used chiefly for driving **c :** any of a breed of rather compact usu. chestnut, bay, or brown English horses with a conspicuously high knee and hock flexion in stepping **2** *obs* **:** one that works for hire **:** DRUDGE **3 :** a carriage or automobile kept for hire

hackney 1c

2hackney *adj* **1 :** kept for public hire **2 :** HACKNEYED **3** *archaic* **:** done or suitable for doing by a drudge
3hackney *vt* **hack·neyed; hack·ney·ing** **1 a :** to make common or frequent use of **b :** to make trite, vulgar, or commonplace **2** *archaic* **:** to make sophisticated or jaded
hackney coach *n* **:** a coach kept for hire; *esp* **:** a four-wheeled carriage drawn by two horses and having seats for six persons
hack·neyed \ˈhak-nēd\ *adj* **:** lacking in freshness or originality
hack·saw \ˈhak-ˌsȯ\ *n* **:** a fine-tooth saw that has a blade under tension in a frame for cutting hard materials (as metal)
hack·work \-ˌwərk\ *n* **:** literary, artistic, or professional work done on order usu. according to formula and in conformity with commercial standards
had *past of* HAVE
ha·dal \ˈhād-ᵊl\ *adj* [F, fr. *Hadès* Hades] **:** of, relating to, or being the parts of the ocean below 6000 meters
had·dock \ˈhad-ək\ *n, pl* **haddock** *also* **haddocks** [ME *haddok*] **:** an important food fish (*Melanogrammus aeglefinus*) that is usu. smaller than the related common cod and that occurs on both sides of the Atlantic
hade \ˈhād\ *n* [*hade* (to incline from the vertical), of unknown origin] **:** the angle made by a rock fault plane or a vein with the vertical
Ha·des \ˈhad-(ˌ)ēz\ *n* [Gk *Haidēs*] **1 :** PLUTO **2 :** the underground abode of the dead in Greek mythology **3 :** SHEOL **4** *often not cap* **:** HELL
hadj, hadji *var of* HAJJ, HAJJI
hadn't \ˈhad-ᵊnt\ **:** had not
had·ron \ˈhad-ˌrän\ *n* [ISV *hadr-* thick, heavy (fr. Gk. *hadros*) + 2*-on*] **:** any of a class of elementary particles consisting of the pion and all heavier particles that takes part in the strong interactions — **ha·dron·ic** \ha-ˈdrän-ik\ *adj*
hadst \(ˈ)hadst, hədst, *or* t *for* d\ *archaic past 2d sing of* HAVE
hae \(ˈ)hā\ *chiefly Scot var of* HAVE
haem *var of* HEME
haem- *or* **haemo-** — see HEM-
haema- — see HEMA-
haemat- *or* **haemato-** — see HEMAT-
hae·ma·tox·y·lon \ˌhē-mə-ˈtäk-sə-ˌlän\ *n* [NL, fr. *hemat-* + Gk *xylon* wood] **:** the wood or dye of logwood
-haemia — see -EMIA
haemoglobin *var of* HEMOGLOBIN
haet \ˈhāt\ *n* [contr. of Sc *hae it* (as in *Deil hae it!* Devil take it!)] *chiefly Scot* **:** a small quantity **:** WHIT, BIT
haf·fet *or* **haf·fit** \ˈhaf-ət\ *n* [ME (Sc) *halfheid,* fr. ME *half* + *hed* head] *Scot* **:** CHEEK, TEMPLE
haf·ni·um \ˈhaf-nē-əm\ *n* [NL, fr. *Hafnia* (Copenhagen), Denmark] **:** a metallic element resembling zirconium chemically, occurring in zirconium minerals, and being useful because of its ready emission of electrons — see ELEMENT table
1haft \ˈhaft\ *n* [ME, fr. OE *hæft;* akin to OE *hebban* to lift — more at HEAVE] **:** the handle of a weapon or tool
2haft *vt* **:** to set in or furnish with a haft
haf·ta·rah *or* **haf·to·rah** \ˌhäf-tə-ˈrä, häf-ˈtō-rə\ *n* [Heb *haphṭārāh* conclusion] **:** one of the biblical selections from the Books of the Prophets read after the parashah at the conclusion of the Jewish synagogue service
1hag \ˈhag\ *n* [ME *hagge*] **1** *archaic* **a :** a female demon **b :** an evil or frightening spirit **:** HOBGOBLIN **2 :** WITCH **3 :** an ugly, slatternly, or evil-looking old woman — **hag·gish** \ˈhag-ish\ *adj*
2hag *n* [E dial., felled timber, of Scand origin; akin to ON *högg* stroke, blow; akin to OE *hēawan* to hew] **1** *Brit* **:** QUAGMIRE, BOG **2** *Brit* **:** a firm spot in a bog
Hag *abbr* Haggai
Ha·gar \ˈhā-ˌgär, -gər\ *n* [Heb *Hāghār*] **:** a concubine of Abraham driven into the desert with her son Ishmael because of Sarah's jealousy according to the account in Genesis
hag·fish \ˈhag-ˌfish\ *n* **:** any of several marine cyclostomes (order Hyperotreta) that are related to the lampreys and in general resemble eels but have a round mouth surrounded by eight tentacles and that feed upon fishes by boring into their bodies
Hag·ga·dah \hə-ˈgäd-ə, hä-, -ˈgȯd-\ *n, pl* **Hag·ga·doth** \-ˈgäd-ˌōt(h), -ˈgȯd-\ [Heb *haggādhāh*] **1 :** ancient Jewish lore forming esp. the nonlegal part of the Talmud **2 :** the Jewish ritual for the seder — **hag·ga·dic** \-ˈgad-ik, -ˈgäd-, -ˈgȯd-\ *adj, often cap*
hag·ga·dist \-ˈgäd-əst, -ˈgȯd-\ *n, often cap* **1 :** a haggadic writer **2 :** a student of the Haggadah — **hag·ga·dis·tic** \ˌhag-ə-ˈdis-tik, ˌhäg-\ *adj, often cap*
Hag·gai \ˈhag-ē-ˌī, ˈhag-ˌī\ *n* [Heb *Haggai*] **1 :** a Hebrew prophet who flourished about 500 B.C. and who advocated that the Temple in Jerusalem be rebuilt **2 :** a prophetic book of canonical Jewish and Christian Scriptures — see BIBLE table
1hag·gard \ˈhag-ərd\ *adj* [MF *hagard*] **1** *of a hawk* **:** not tamed **2 a :** wild in appearance **b :** having a worn or emaciated appearance **:** GAUNT — **hag·gard·ly** *adv* — **hag·gard·ness** *n*
2haggard *n* **1 :** an adult hawk caught wild **2** *obs* **:** an intractable person
hag·gis \ˈhag-əs\ *n* [ME *hagese*] **:** a pudding popular esp. in Scotland that is made of the heart, liver, and lungs of a sheep or a calf minced with suet, onions, oatmeal, and seasonings and boiled in the stomach of the animal
1hag·gle \ˈhag-əl\ *vb* **hag·gled; hag·gling** \-(ə-)liŋ\ [freq. of *hag* (to hew)] *vt* **1 :** to cut roughly or clumsily **:** HACK **2** *archaic* **:** to annoy or exhaust with wrangling ~ *vi* **:** BARGAIN, WRANGLE — **hag·gler** \-(ə-)lər\ *n*
2haggle *n* **:** an act or instance of haggling
hagi- *or* **hagio-** *comb form* [LL, fr. Gk, fr. *hagios*] **1 :** holy <*hagio*scope> **2 :** saints <*hagio*graphy>
Ha·gi·og·ra·pha \ˌhag-ē-ˈäg-rə-fə, ˌhā-jē-\ *n pl but sing or pl in constr* [LL, fr. LGk, fr. *hagio-* + *graphein* to write — more at CARVE] **:** the third part of the Jewish scriptures — see BIBLE table
ha·gi·og·ra·pher \-fər\ *n* **:** a writer of hagiography
ha·gio·graph·ic \ˌhag-ē-ə-ˈgraf-ik, ˈhā-jē-\ *also* **ha·gio·graph·i·cal** \-i-kəl\ *adj* **1 :** of or relating to the Hagiographa **2 :** of or relating to hagiography
ha·gi·og·ra·phy \ˌhag-ē-ˈäg-rə-fē, ˌhā-jē-\ *n* **1 :** biography of saints or venerated persons **2 :** idealizing or idolizing biography
ha·gi·ol·o·gy \-ˈäl-ə-jē\ *n* **1 :** literature dealing with venerated persons or writings **2 :** a list of venerated figures — **ha·gi·o·log·ic** \-ə-ˈläj-ik\ *or* **ha·gi·o·log·i·cal** \-i-kəl\ *adj* — **ha·gi·o·log·i·cal·ly** \-i-k(ə-)lē\ *adv*
ha·gio·scope \ˈhag-ē-ə-ˌskōp, ˈhā-jē-\ *n* **:** an opening in the interior walls of a cruciform church so placed as to afford a view of the altar to those in the transept — **ha·gio·scop·ic** \ˌhag-ē-ə-ˈskäp-ik, ˌhā-jē-\ *adj*
hag·ride \ˈhag-ˌrīd\ *vt* **-rode** \-ˌrōd\; **-rid·den** \-ˌrid-ᵊn\ **:** HARASS, TORMENT
hah *var of* HA
1ha–ha \(ˈ)hä-ˈhä\ *interj* [ME, fr. OE *ha ha*] — used to express amusement or derision
2ha–ha \ˈhä-ˌhä\ *n* [F *haha*] **:** SUNK FENCE
haik \ˈhīk\ *n* [Ar *ḥā'ik*] **:** a voluminous piece of usu. white cloth worn as an outer garment in northern Africa
hai·ku \ˈhī-(ˌ)kü\ *n, pl* **haiku** [Jap] **:** an unrhymed Japanese verse form of three lines containing 5, 7, and 5 syllables respectively; *also* **:** a poem in this form — compare TANKA
1hail \ˈhā(ə)l\ *n* [ME, fr. OE *hægl;* akin to OHG *hagal* hail, Gk *kachlēx* pebble] **1 :** precipitation in the form of small balls or lumps usu. consisting of concentric layers of clear ice and compact snow **2 :** something that gives the effect of falling hail <met a ~ of rifle fire from the ridge>
2hail *vi* **1 :** to precipitate hail <it was ~*ing* hard> **2 :** to pour down or strike like hail
3hail *interj* [ME, fr. ON *heill,* fr. *heill* healthy — more at WHOLE] **1** — used to express acclamation <~ to the chief —Sir Walter Scott> **2** *archaic* — used as a salutation
4hail *vt* **1 a :** SALUTE, GREET **b :** to greet with enthusiastic approval **:** ACCLAIM **2 :** to greet or summon by calling <~ a taxi> ~ *vi* **:** to call out; *esp* **:** to call a greeting to a passing ship — **hail from :** to be or have been a native or resident of
5hail *n* **1 :** an exclamation of greeting or acclamation **2 :** a calling to attract attention **3 :** hearing distance <stayed within ~>
hail·er \ˈhā-lər\ *n* **1 :** one that hails **2 :** BULLHORN 1
hail–fel·low \ˈhāl-ˌfel-(ˌ)ō, -ə(-w)\ *adj* **:** HAIL-FELLOW-WELL-MET — **hail–fel·low** *n*
hail–fel·low–well–met \-ō-ˌwel-ˈmet, -ə-ˌwel-\ *adj* [fr. the archaic salutation "Hail, fellow! Well met!"] **:** heartily informal **:** COMRADELY — **hail–fel·low–well–met** *n*
Hail Mary *n* [trans. of ML *Ave, Maria*] **:** a Roman Catholic prayer to the Virgin Mary that consists of salutations and a plea for her intercession
hail·stone \ˈhā(ə)l-ˌstōn\ *n* **:** a pellet of hail
hail·storm \-ˌstȯ(ə)rm\ *n* **:** a storm accompanied by hail

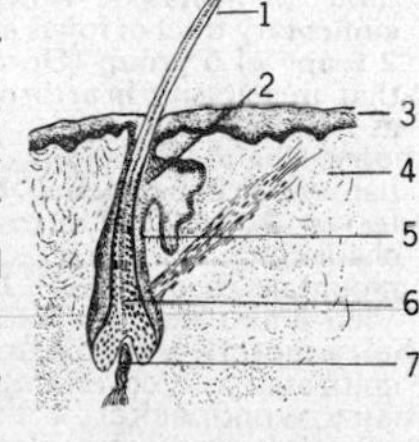

hair 1a: *1* shaft, *2* sebaceous gland, *3* epidermis, *4* dermis, *5* hair follicle, *6* bulb, *7* papilla

hair \ˈha(ə)r, ˈhe(ə)r\ *n* [ME, fr. OE *hǣr;* akin to OHG *hār* hair] **1 a :** a slender threadlike outgrowth of the epidermis of an animal; *esp* **:** one of the usu. pigmented filaments that form the characteristic coat of a mammal **b :** the hairy covering of an animal or a body part; *esp* **:** the coating of hairs on a human head **2 :** HAIRCLOTH **3 a :** a minute distance or amount **:** TRIFLE <won by a ~> **b :** a precise degree **:** NICETY <aligned to a ~> **4** *obs*

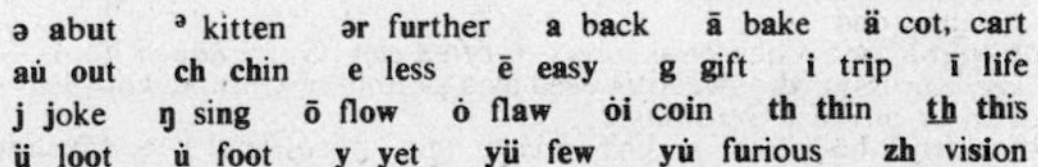
ə abut ᵊ kitten ər further a back ā bake ä cot, cart
au̇ out ch chin e less ē easy g gift i trip ī life
j joke ŋ sing ō flow ȯ flaw ȯi coin th thin t͟h this
ü loot u̇ foot y yet yü few yu̇ furious zh vision

: NATURE, CHARACTER **5** : a filamentous structure that resembles hair <leaf ~> — **hair·like** \-ˌlīk\ *adj*

hair ball *n* : a compact mass of hair formed in the stomach esp. of a shedding animal (as a cat) that cleanses its coat by licking

¹hair·breadth \ˈha(ə)r-ˌbredth, ˈhe(ə)r-, -ˌbretth\ *or* **hairs·breadth** \ˈha(ə)rz-, ˈhe(ə)rz-\ *n* : a very small distance or margin

²hairbreadth *adj* : very narrow : CLOSE <a ~ escape>

hair·brush \ˈha(ə)r-ˌbrəsh, ˈhe(ə)r-\ *n* : a brush for the hair

hair cell *n* : a cell with hairlike processes; *esp* : one of the sensory cells in the auditory epithelium of the organ of Corti

hair·cloth \ˈha(ə)r-ˌklȯth, ˈhe(ə)r-\ *n* : any of various stiff wiry fabrics esp. of horsehair or camel's hair used for upholstery or for stiffening in garments

hair·cut \-ˌkət\ *n* : the act, process, or result of cutting and shaping the hair — **hair·cut·ter** \-ˌkət-ər\ *n* — **hair·cut·ting** \-ˌkət-iŋ\ *n*

hair·do \-ˌdü\ *n, pl* **hairdos** : a way of dressing a woman's hair : COIFFURE

hair·dress·er \-ˌdres-ər\ *n* **1** : one whose occupation is the dressing or cutting of hair **2** *Brit* : BARBER

hair·dress·ing \-ˌdres-iŋ\ *n* **1 a** : the action or process of washing, cutting, curling, or arranging the hair **b** : the occupation of a hairdresser **2** : a preparation (as a liquid or cream) used in grooming and styling the hair

haired \ˈha(ə)rd, ˈhe(ə)rd\ *adj* : having hair esp. of a specified kind — usu. used in combination <fair-*haired*>

hair follicle *n* : the tubular epithelial sheath that surrounds the lower part of the hair shaft and encloses at the bottom a vascular papilla supplying the growing basal part of the hair with nourishment

hair·less \ˈha(ə)r-ləs, ˈhe(ə)r-\ *adj* : lacking hair — **hair·less·ness** *n*

hair·line \-ˈlīn\ *n* **1** : a very slender line: as **a** : a tiny line or crack on a surface **b** : a fine line connecting thicker strokes in a printed letter **2 a** : a textile design consisting of lengthwise or crosswise lines usu. one thread wide **b** : a fabric with such a design **3 a** : the line at which the hair meets the scalp **b** : the way the hair frames the face — **hairline** *adj*

hair·piece \-ˌpēs\ *n* **1** : TOUPEE 2 **2** : supplementary hair (as a switch) used in some feminine coiffures

¹hair·pin \-ˌpin\ *n* **1** : a pin to hold the hair in place; *specif* : a two-pronged U-shaped pin **2** : something shaped like a hairpin; *specif* : a sharp turn in a road

²hairpin *adj* : having the shape of a hairpin <a ~ turn>; *also* : having hairpin turns <a steep ~ road>

hair–rais·er \ˈha(ə)r-ˌrā-zər, ˈhe(ə)r-\ *n* : THRILLER

hair–rais·ing \-ˌrā-ziŋ\ *adj* : causing terror, excitement, or astonishment — **hair–rais·ing·ly** \-ziŋ-lē\ *adv*

hair seal *n* **1** : EARLESS SEAL **2** : the fur of a hair seal

hair shirt *n* : a shirt made of rough animal hair worn next to the skin as a penance

hair space *n* : a very thin space used in printing

hair·split·ter \ˈha(ə)r-ˌsplit-ər, ˈhe(ə)r-\ *n* : one that makes excessively fine distinctions in reasoning : QUIBBLER — **hair·split·ting** \-ˌsplit-iŋ\ *adj or n*

hair·spring \-ˌspriŋ\ *n* : a slender spiraled recoil spring that regulates the motion of the balance wheel of a timepiece

hair·streak \-ˌstrēk\ *n* : any of various small butterflies (*Strymon* or a related genus) usu. having striped markings on the underside of the wings and thin filamentous projections from the hind wings

hair stroke *n* : a delicate stroke in writing or printing

hair·style \ˈha(ə)r-ˌstīl, ˈhe(ə)r-\ *n* : a way of wearing the hair : COIFFURE

hair·styl·ing \-ˌstī-liŋ\ *n* : the work of a hairstylist

hair·styl·ist \-ˌstī-ləst\ *n* : HAIRDRESSER; *esp* : one who does creative styling of coiffures

hair–trigger *adj* **1** : immediately responsive to the slightest stimulus <a ~ temper> **2** : delicately adjusted or easily disrupted <a ~ balance>

hair trigger *n* : a gun trigger so adjusted as to permit the firearm to be fired by a very slight pressure

hair·worm \ˈha(ə)r-ˌwərm, ˈhe(ə)r-\ *n* **1** : any of a genus (*Capillaria*) of nematode worms that include serious parasites of the alimentary tract of fowls and tissue and organ parasites of mammals **2** : any of a group (Gordiacea) of very slender elongated worms that are parasitic in arthropods as larvae and are free-living in water as adults

hairy \ˈha(ə)r-ē, ˈhe(ə)r-\ *adj* **hair·i·er; -est** **1 a** : covered with hair or hairlike material **b** : having a downy fuzz on the stems and leaves **2** : made of or resembling hair **3** : presenting high risk or challenge : RUGGED 6b <a ~ . . . scramble up a steep or tortuous mountain road —R. F. Jones> <a ~ adventure> — **hair·i·ness** \ˈhar-ē-nəs, ˈher-\ *n*

hairy vetch *n* : a European vetch (*Vicia villosa*) extensively cultivated as a cover and early forage crop

hairy woodpecker *n* : a common No. American woodpecker (*Dendrocopos villosus*) closely resembling but larger than the downy woodpecker

Hai·tian \ˈhā-shən *also* ˈhāt-ē-ən\ *n* **1** : a native or inhabitant of Haiti **2** : HAITIAN CREOLE — **Haitian** *adj*

Haitian Creole *n* : the language that is spoken by the great majority of Haitian inhabitants and that is based on French and various West African languages

hajj \ˈhaj\ *n* [Ar *ḥajj*] : the pilgrimage to Mecca prescribed as a religious duty for Muslims

hajji \ˈhaj-ē\ *n* [Ar *ḥajjī*, fr. *ḥajj*] : one who has made a pilgrimage to Mecca — often used as a title

hake \ˈhāk\ *n* [ME] : any of several marine food fishes (as of the genera *Merluccius* and *Urophycis*) that are related to the common Atlantic cod

ha·ken·kreuz \ˈhäk-ən-ˌkrȯits\ *n, often cap* [G, fr. *haken* hook + *kreuz* cross] : the swastika used as a symbol of German anti-Semitism or of Nazi Germany

¹ha·kim \hə-ˈkēm\ *n* [Ar *ḥakīm*, lit., wise one] : a Muslim physician

²ha·kim \ˈhäk-əm\ *n* [Ar *ḥākim*] : a Muslim ruler, governor, or judge

hal- *or* **halo-** *comb form* [F, fr. Gk, fr. *hals* — more at SALT] **1** : salt <*halo*phyte> **2** [ISV, fr. *halogen*] : halogen <*hal*ide>

ha·la·kah \hä-ˈläk-ə, ˌhä-lə-ˈkä\ *n, often cap* [Heb *halākhāh*, lit., way] : the body of Jewish law supplementing the scriptural law and forming esp. the legal part of the Talmud — **ha·lak·ic** \hə-ˈlak-ik, hä-ˈläk-\ *adj, often cap*

ha·la·la *also* **ha·la·lah** \hə-ˈläl-ə\ *n, pl* **halala** *or* **halalas** [Ar] — see *riyal* at MONEY table

ha·la·tion \hā-ˈlā-shən\ *n* [*halo* + *-ation*] **1** : the spreading of light beyond its proper boundaries in a developed photographic image **2** : a bright ring that sometimes surrounds a bright object on a television screen

hal·berd \ˈhal-bərd, ˈhȯl-\ *or* **hal·bert** \-bərt\ *n* [ME *halberd*, fr. MF *hallebarde*] : a weapon esp. of the 15th and 16th centuries consisting typically of a battle-ax and pike mounted on a handle about six feet long — **hal·berd·ier** \ˌhal-bər-ˈdi(ə)r, ˌhȯl-\ *n*

¹hal·cy·on \ˈhal-sē-ən\ *n* [ME *alceon*, fr. L *halcyon*, fr. Gk *alkyōn*, *halkyōn*] **1** : a bird identified with the kingfisher and held in ancient legend to nest at sea about the time of the winter solstice and to calm the waves during incubation **2** : KINGFISHER

²halcyon *adj* **1** : of or relating to the halcyon or its nesting period **2 a** : CALM, PEACEFUL **b** : HAPPY, GOLDEN **c** : PROSPEROUS, AFFLUENT

halberd heads

Hal·cy·o·ne \hal-ˈsī-ə-(ˌ)nē\ *n* [L, modif. of Gk *Alkyonē*] : a daughter of Aeolus who drowns herself on learning of her husband's death and is with him turned into one of a pair of birds having power to calm the sea

¹hale \ˈhā(ə)l\ *adj* [partly fr. ME (northern) *hale*, fr. OE *hāl*; partly fr. ME *hail*, fr. ON *heill* — more at WHOLE] : free from defect, disease, or infirmity : SOUND; *also* : retaining exceptional health and vigor <a ~ and hearty old man> ***syn*** see HEALTHY ***ant*** infirm

²hale *vt* **haled; hal·ing** [ME *halen*, fr. MF *haler* — more at HAUL] **1** : HAUL, PULL **2** : to compel to go

ha·ler \ˈhäl-ər, -ˌe(ə)r\ *n, pl* **halers** *or* **ha·le·ru** \ˈhäl-ə-ˌrü\ [Czech] — see *koruna* at MONEY table

¹half \ˈhaf, ˈhȧf\ *n, pl* **halves** \ˈhavz, ˈhȧvz\ [ME, fr. OE *healf*; akin to L *scalpere* to cut, OE *sciell* shell] **1 a** : one of two equal parts into which a thing is divisible; *also* : a part of a thing approximately equal to the remainder **b** : half an hour — used in designation of time **2** : one of a pair: as **a** : PARTNER **b** : SEMESTER, TERM **3** : HALF-DOLLAR **4** : HALFBACK — **by half** : by a great deal — **by halves** : in part : HALF-HEARTEDLY — **half as much again** : one-and-a-half times as much — **in half** : into two equal or nearly equal parts

²half *adj* **1 a** : being one of two equal parts <a ~ share> <a ~ sheet of paper> **b** (1) : amounting to approximately half <a ~ mile> <a ~ million> (2) : falling short of the full or complete thing : PARTIAL <~ measures> <a ~ smile> **2** : extending over or covering only half <a ~ window> <a ~ mask> — **half·ness** *n*

³half *adv* **1 a** : in an equal part or degree <the crowd was ~ jeering, ~ respectful> **b** : only partially : not completely <~ persuaded> <*half*-remembered legends from her childhood> **2** — used with a negative to imply the opposite of what is expressed <her singing isn't ~ bad>

half–and–half \ˌhaf-ən-ˈhaf, ˌhȧf-ən-ˈhȧf\ *n* : something that is approximately half one thing and half another: as **a** : a mixture of two malt beverages (as beer and stout) **b** : a mixture of cream and whole milk — **half–and–half** *adj* — **half–and–half** *adv*

half·back \ˈhaf-ˌbak, ˈhȧf-\ *n* **1** : one of the backs stationed near either flank in football **2** : a player stationed immediately behind the forward line (as in field hockey, soccer, or rugby)

half–baked \-ˈbākt\ *adj* **1** : imperfectly baked : UNDERDONE **2 a** : not well planned <a ~ scheme for getting rich quick> **b** : lacking judgment, intelligence, or common sense <a ~ film critic>

half blood *n* **1 a** : the relation between persons having only one parent in common **b** : a person so related to another **2** : HALF-BREED **3** : GRADE 4

half–blood·ed \ˈhaf-ˈbləd-əd, ˈhȧf-\ *adj* : having half blood or being a half blood

half boot *n* : a boot with a top reaching above the ankle and ending below the knee

half–bound \ˈhaf-ˈbau̇nd, ˈhȧf-\ *adj, of a book* : bound in material of two qualities with the material of better quality on the spine and corners — **half binding** *n*

half–bred \-ˌbred\ *adj* : having one purebred parent — **half–bred** *n*

half–breed \-ˌbrēd\ *n* : the offspring of parents of different races; *esp* : the offspring of an American Indian and a Caucasian — **half–breed** *adj*

half brother *n* : a brother related through one parent only

half–caste \ˈhaf-ˌkast, ˈhȧf-\ *n* : one of mixed racial descent : HALF-BREED — **half–caste** *adj*

half cock *n* **1** : the position of the hammer of a firearm when about half retracted and held by the sear so that it cannot be operated by a pull on the trigger **2** : a state of inadequate preparation or mental confusion

half–cocked \ˈhaf-ˈkäkt, ˈhȧf-\ *adj* **1** : being at half cock **2** : lacking adequate preparation or forethought

half crown *n* : a British coin worth two shillings and sixpence

half dime *n* : a silver 5-cent coin struck by the U.S. mint in 1792 and from 1794 to 1873

half disme *n* : a half dime struck in 1792

half–dol·lar \ˈhaf-ˈdäl-ər, ˈhȧf-\ *n* **1** : a coin representing one half of a dollar **2** : the sum of 50 cents

half eagle *n* : a 5-dollar gold piece issued by the U.S. 1795–1916 and in 1929

half-evergreen *adj* **1 :** having functional and persistent foliage during part of the winter or dry season **2 :** tending to be evergreen in a mild climate but deciduous in a rigorous climate
half gainer *n* **:** a gainer in which the diver executes a half-backward somersault and enters the water headfirst and facing the board
half-hardy *adj, of a plant* **:** able to withstand a moderately low temperature but injured by severe freezing and surviving the winter in cold climates only if carefully protected
half-heart·ed \ˈhaf-ˈhärt-əd, ˈháf-\ *adj* **:** lacking heart, spirit, or interest <~ attempts to start a conversation> — **half-heart·ed·ly** *adv* — **half-heart·ed·ness** *n*
half hitch *n* **:** a simple knot so made as to be easily unfastened — see KNOT illustration
half hour *n* **1 :** thirty minutes **2 :** the middle point of an hour — **half-hour·ly** \ˈhaf-ˈaù(ə)r-lē, ˈháf-\ *adv or adj*
half-knot \ˈhaf-ˌnät, ˈháf-\ *n* **:** a knot joining the ends of two cords and used in tying other knots
half-length \ˈhaf-ˈleŋ(k)th, ˈháf-\ *n* **:** something (as a portrait) that is or represents only half the complete length
half-life \-ˌlīf\ *n* **:** the time required for half of something to undergo a process: as **a :** the time required for half of the atoms of a radioactive substance present to become disintegrated **b :** the time required for half the amount of a substance (as a drug or radioactive tracer) in or introduced into a living system to be eliminated by natural processes
half-light \-ˌlīt\ *n* **:** grayish light (as of a dim interior or evening)
half line *n* **:** a straight line extending from a point in one direction only
half-long \ˈhaf-ˈlȯŋ, ˈháf-\ *adj* **:** intermediate in duration between long and short
[1]half-mast \-ˈmast\ *n* **:** a point some distance but not necessarily halfway down below the top of a mast or staff or the peak of a gaff
[2]half-mast *vt* **:** to cause to hang at half-mast <~ a flag>
half-moon \ˈhaf-ˌmün, ˈháf-\ *n* **1 :** the moon when half its disk appears illuminated **2 :** something shaped like a crescent **3 :** LUNULE
half nelson *n* **:** a wrestling hold in which one arm is thrust under the corresponding arm of an opponent and the hand placed on the back of the opponent's neck — compare FULL NELSON
half note *n* **:** a musical note with the time value of ½ of a whole note — see NOTE illustration
half·pen·ny \ˈhāp-(ə-)nē, *US also* ˈhaf-ˌpen-ē, ˈháf-\ *n* **1** *pl* **half·pence** \ˈhā-pən(t)s, *US also* ˈhaf-ˌpen(t)s, ˈháf-\ *or* **halfpennies :** a British coin representing one half of a penny **2 :** the sum of half a penny **3 :** a small amount — **halfpenny** *adj*
[1]half-pint \ˈhaf-ˌpīnt, ˈháf-\ *n* **1 :** half a pint **2 :** a short, small, or inconsequential person
[2]half-pint *adj* **:** of less than average size **:** DIMINUTIVE
half plane *n* **:** the part of a plane on one side of an indefinitely extended straight line drawn in the plane
half rest *n* **:** a musical rest corresponding in time value to a half note
half sister *n* **:** a sister related through one parent only
half-slip \ˈhaf-ˌslip, ˈháf-\ *n* **:** a topless slip with an elasticized waistband
half-sole *vt* **:** to put half soles on
half sole *n* **:** a shoe sole extending from the shank forward
half sovereign *n* **:** a British gold coin worth 10 shillings
half-staff \ˈhaf-ˈstaf, ˈháf-\ *n* **:** HALF-MAST
half step *n* **1 :** a walking step of 15 inches or in double time of 18 inches **2 :** the musical interval (as E–F or B–C) equivalent to the interval between any two adjacent keys on a keyboard instrument — called also *semitone*
half-timber *or* **half-tim·bered** \ˈhaf-ˈtim-bərd, ˈháf-\ *adj, of a building* **:** constructed of wood framing with spaces filled with masonry — **half-tim·ber·ing** \-b(ə-)riŋ\ *n*
halftime \-ˌtīm\ *n* **:** an intermission marking the completion of half of a game or contest (as in football or basketball)
half title *n* **:** the title of a book standing alone on a right-hand page immediately preceding the title page
half·tone \ˈhaf-ˌtōn, ˈháf-\ *n* **1 :** HALF STEP 2 **2 a :** any of the shades of gray between the darkest and the lightest parts of a photographic image **b :** a photoengraving made from an image photographed through a screen and then etched so that the details of the image are reproduced in dots — **halftone** *adj*
half-track \-ˌtrak\ *n* **1 :** an endless chain-track drive system that propels a vehicle supported in front by a pair of wheels **2 :** a motor vehicle propelled by half-tracks; *specif* **:** one lightly armored for military use — **half-track** *or* **half-tracked** \-ˌtrakt\ *adj*
half-truth \-ˌtrüth\ *n* **1 :** a statement that is only partially true **2 :** a statement that mingles truth and falsehood with deliberate intent to deceive
half volley *n* **:** a stroke of a ball at the instant it rebounds from the ground — **half-volley** *vb*
half·way \ˈhaf-ˈwā, ˈháf-\ *adj* **1 :** midway between two points **2 :** PARTIAL — **halfway** *adv*
halfway house *n* **1 a :** a place to stop midway on a journey **b :** a halfway place in a progression **2 :** a center for formerly institutionalized individuals (as mental patients or drug addicts) that is designed to facilitate their readjustment to private life
half-wit \ˈhaf-ˌwit, ˈháf-\ *n* **:** a foolish or imbecilic person — **half-wit·ted** \-ˈwit-əd\ *adj* — **half-wit·ted·ness** *n*
half-world \-ˌwərld\ *n* **:** DEMIMONDE
hal·i·but \ˈhal-ə-bət, ˈhäl-\ *n, pl* **halibut** *also* **halibuts** [ME *halybutte,* fr. *haly, holy* holy + *butte* flatfish, fr. MD or MLG *but;* fr. its being eaten on holy days] **:** a marine food fish that is the largest flatfish and one of the largest teleost fishes, attains a weight of several hundred pounds in the female, and is now usu. classified as an Atlantic species (*Hippoglossus hippoglossus*) and a Pacific one (*H. stenolepis*)
ha·lide \ˈhal-ˌīd, ˈhā-ˌlīd\ *n* **:** a binary compound of a halogen with a more electropositive element or radical
hal·i·dom \ˈhal-əd-əm\ *or* **hal·i·dome** \-ə-ˌdōm\ *n* [ME, fr. OE *hāligdōm,* fr. *hālig* holy] *archaic* **:** something held sacred
ha·lite \ˈhal-ˌīt, ˈhā-ˌlīt\ *n* **:** native salt **:** ROCK SALT
hal·i·to·sis \ˌhal-ə-ˈtō-səs\ *n* [NL, fr. L *halitus* breath, fr. *halare* to breathe — more at EXHALE] **:** a condition of having fetid breath
hall \ˈhȯl\ *n* [ME *halle,* fr. OE *heall;* akin to L *cella* small room, *celare* to conceal — more at HELL] **1 a :** the castle or house of a medieval king or noble **b :** the chief living room in such a structure **2 :** the manor house of a landed proprietor **3 :** a large usu. imposing building for public or semipublic purposes **4 a** (1) **:** a building used by a college or university for some special purpose (2) **:** DORMITORY **b :** a college or a division of a college at some universities **c** (1) **:** the common dining room of an English college (2) **:** a meal served there **5 a :** the entrance room of a building **:** LOBBY **b :** a corridor or passage in a building **6 :** a large room for assembly **:** AUDITORIUM **7 :** a place used for public entertainment
Hal·lel \hä-ˈlā(ə)l\ *n* [Heb *hallēl* praise] **:** a selection comprising Psalms 113–118 chanted during Jewish feasts (as the Passover)
[1]hal·le·lu·jah \ˌhal-ə-ˈlü-yə\ *interj* [Heb *halalūyāh* praise (ye) the Lord] — used to express praise, joy, or thanks
[2]hallelujah *n* **:** a shout or song of praise or thanksgiving
hal·liard *var of* HALYARD
[1]hall·mark \ˈhȯl-ˌmärk\ *n* [Goldsmiths' *Hall,* London, England, where gold and silver articles were assayed and stamped] **1 a :** an official mark stamped on gold and silver articles in England to attest their purity **b :** a mark or device placed or stamped on an article of trade to indicate origin, purity, or genuineness **2 :** a distinguishing characteristic, trait, or feature <the dramatic flourishes which are the ~ of the trial lawyer —Marion K. Sanders>
[2]hallmark *vt* **:** to stamp with a hallmark
hal·lo \hə-ˈlō, ha-\ *or* **hal·loo** \-ˈlü\ *var of* HOLLO
Hall of Fame 1 : a structure housing memorials to famous or illustrious individuals usu. chosen by a group of electors **2 :** a group of individuals in a particular category (as a sport) who have been selected as particularly illustrious —**Hall of Famer**
hal·low \ˈhal-(ˌ)ō, -ə(-w)\ *vt* [ME *halowen,* fr. OE *hālgian,* fr. *hālig* holy — more at HOLY] **1 :** to make holy or set apart for holy use **2 :** to respect greatly **:** VENERATE ***syn*** see DEVOTE
hal·lowed \ˈhal-(ˌ)ōd, ˈhal-əd, *in the Lord's Prayer also* ˈhal-ə-wəd\ *adj* **1 :** HOLY, CONSECRATED **2 :** SACRED, REVERED <the ~ traditions from the past>
Hal·low·een \ˌhal-ə-ˈwēn, ˌhäl-\ *n* [short for *All Hallow Even*] **:** October 31 observed with festivity and the playing of pranks by children during the evening
Hal·low·mas \ˈhal-ō-ˌmas, ˈhal-ə-, -məs\ *n* [short for ME *Alholowmesse,* fr. OE *ealra halgena mæsse,* lit., all saints' mass] **:** ALL SAINTS' DAY
halls of ivy [fr. the traditional training of ivy on the walls of older college buildings] **:** an institution of higher education **:** UNIVERSITY, COLLEGE
Hall·statt *or* **Hall·stadt** \ˈhȯl-ˌstat, ˈhäl-ˌs(h)tät\ *adj* [*Hallstatt,* Austria] **:** of or relating to the earlier period of the Iron Age in Europe
hal·lu·ci·nate \hə-ˈlüs-ᵊn-ˌāt\ *vb* **-nat·ed; -nat·ing** [L *hallucinatus,* pp. of *hallucinari* to prate, dream] *vt* **1 :** to affect with visions or imaginary perceptions **2 :** to perceive or experience as an hallucination ~ *vi* **:** to have hallucinations
hal·lu·ci·na·tion \hə-ˌlüs-ᵊn-ˈā-shən\ *n* **1 a :** perception of objects with no reality usu. arising from disorder of the nervous system or in response to drugs (as LSD) **b :** the object of an hallucinatory perception **2 :** a completely unfounded or mistaken impression or notion **:** DELUSION ***syn*** see DELUSION — **hal·lu·ci·na·tion·al** \-shnəl, -shən-ᵊl\ *adj* — **hal·lu·ci·na·tive** \-ˈlüs-ᵊn-ˌāt-iv\ *adj*
hal·lu·ci·na·to·ry \hə-ˈlüs-ᵊn-ə-ˌtōr-ē, -ˈlüs-nə-, -ˌtȯr-\ *adj* **1 :** tending to produce hallucination <~ drugs> **2 :** resembling or being an hallucination <~ dreams> <an ~ figure> <an ~ painting>
hal·lu·ci·no·gen \hə-ˈlüs-ᵊn-ə-jən\ *n* [*hallucin*ation + *-o-* + *-gen*] **:** a substance that induces hallucinations — **hal·lu·ci·no·gen·ic** \-ˌlüs-ᵊn-ə-ˈjen-ik\ *adj*
hal·lu·ci·no·sis \hə-ˌlüs-ᵊn-ˈō-səs\ *n* **:** a pathological mental state characterized by hallucinations
hal·lux \ˈhal-əks\ *n, pl* **hal·lu·ces** \ˈhal-(y)ə-ˌsēz\ [NL, fr. L *hallus, hallux*] **:** the first or preaxial digit of the hind limb
hall·way \ˈhȯl-ˌwā\ *n* **1 :** an entrance hall **2 :** CORRIDOR
[1]ha·lo \ˈhā-(ˌ)lō\ *n, pl* **halos** *or* **haloes** [L *halos,* fr. Gk *halōs* threshing floor, disk, halo] **1 :** a circle of light appearing to surround the sun or moon and resulting from refraction or reflection of light by ice particles in the atmosphere **2 :** something resembling a halo: as **a :** NIMBUS **b :** a differentiated zone surrounding a central object **3 :** the aura of glory, veneration, or sentiment surrounding an idealized person or thing
[2]halo *vt* **:** to form into or surround with a halo <rainbows ~*ed* the waterfalls —Michael Crawford>
halo- — see HAL-
halo·bi·ont \ˌhal-ō-ˈbī-ˌänt\ *n* [*hal-* + Gk *biount-, biōn,* prp. of *bioun* to live, fr. *bios* life — more at QUICK] **:** HALOPHILE
halo·car·bon \-ˈkär-bən\ *n* **:** any of various compounds (as fluorocarbon) of carbon and one or more halogens
halo·cline \ˈhal-ə-ˌklīn\ *n* **:** a usu. vertical gradient in salinity
halo effect *n* **:** generalization from the perception of one outstanding personality trait to an overly favorable evaluation of the whole personality
halo·gen \ˈhal-ə-jən\ *n* [Sw] **:** any of the five elements fluorine, chlorine, bromine, iodine, and astatine that form part of group VII

A of the periodic table and exist in the free state normally as diatomic molecules — **ha·log·e·nous** \ha-'läj-ə-nəs\ *adj*

ha·lo·ge·nate \'hal-ə-jə-,nāt, ha-'läj-ə-\ *vt* **-nat·ed; -nat·ing** : to treat or cause to combine with a halogen — **ha·lo·ge·na·tion** \,hal-ə-jə-'nā-shən, ha-,läj-ə-\ *n*

hal·o·ge·ton \,hal-ə-'jē-,tän\ *n* [NL, genus name, fr. *hal-* + Gk *geitōn* neighbor] : a coarse annual herb (*Halogeton glomeratus*) of the goosefoot family that is a noxious weed in western American ranges

halo·mor·phic \,hal-ə-'mȯr-fik\ *adj, of a soil* : developed in the presence of neutral or alkali salts or both — **halo·mor·phism** \-,fiz-əm\ *n*

hal·o·per·i·dol \,hal-ō-'per-ə-,dȯl, -,dōl\ *n* [*hal-* + pi*peridine* + *-ol*] : a depressant $C_{21}H_{23}ClFNO_2$ of the central nervous system used esp. as a tranquilizer

halo·phile \'hal-ə-,fīl\ *n* [ISV] : an organism that flourishes in a salty environment — **halo·phil·ic** \,hal-ə-'fil-ik\ *or* **ha·loph·i·lous** \ha-'läf-ə-ləs\ *adj*

halo·phyte \'hal-ə-,fīt\ *n* [ISV] : a plant (as saltbush or sea lavender) that grows in salty soil and usu. has a physiological resemblance to a true xerophyte — **halo·phyt·ic** \,hal-ə-'fit-ik\ *adj*

hal·o·thane \'hal-ə-,thān\ *n* [*halo-* + *ethane*] : a nonexplosive inhalational anesthetic $C_2HBrClF_3$

[1]**halt** \'hȯlt\ *adj* [ME, fr. OE *healt;* akin to OHG *halz* lame, L *clades* destruction, Gk *klan* to break] : LAME

[2]**halt** *vi* **1** : to walk or proceed lamely : LIMP **2** : to stand in perplexity or doubt between alternate courses : WAVER **3** : to display weakness or imperfection : FALTER

[3]**halt** *n* [G, fr. MHG, *halt*, imper. of *halten* to hold, fr. OHG *haltan* — more at HOLD] : STOP

[4]**halt** *vi* **1** : to cease marching or journeying **2** : DISCONTINUE, TERMINATE <the project ~*ed* for lack of funds> ~ *vt* **1** : to bring to a stop <the labor conflict has ~*ed* subways and buses> **2** : to cause the discontinuance of : END

[1]**hal·ter** \'hȯl-tər\ *n* [ME, fr. OE *hælftre;* akin to OHG *halftra* halter, OE *hielfe* helve] **1 a** : a rope or strap for leading or tying an animal **b** : a headstall usu. with noseband and throatlatch to which a lead may be attached **2** : a rope for hanging criminals : NOOSE; *also* : death by hanging **3** : a woman's blouse that leaves the back, arms, and midriff bare and that is typically held in place by straps around the neck and across the back

[2]**halter** *vt* **hal·tered; hal·ter·ing** \-t(ə-)riŋ\ **1 a** : to catch with or as if with a halter; *also* : to put a halter on **b** : HANG **2** : to put restraint upon : HAMPER

hal·ter·break \'hȯl-tər-,brāk\ *vt* **-broke** \-,brōk\; **-bro·ken** \-,brō-kən\; **-break·ing** : to break (as a colt) to a halter

hal·tere \'hȯl-,ti(ə)r, 'hal-\ *also* **hal·ter** \-tər\ *n, pl* **hal·teres** \'hȯl-,ti(ə)rz, 'hal-; hȯl-'ti(ə)r-ēz, hal-\ [NL *halter*, fr. L, jumping weight, fr. Gk *haltēr*, fr. *hallesthai* to leap — more at SALLY] : one of a pair of club-shaped organs in a dipterous insect that are the modified second pair of wings and function as sensory flight instruments

halt·ing \'hȯl-tiŋ\ *adj* : marked by a lack of sureness or effectiveness <the witness spoke in a ~ manner> — **halt·ing·ly** \-tiŋ-lē\ *adv*

hal·vah *or* **hal·va** \häl-'vä; 'häl-(,)vä, -və\ *n* [Yiddish *halva*, fr. Rum, fr. Turk *helva*, fr. Ar *ḥalwā* sweetmeat] : a flaky confection of crushed sesame seeds in a base of syrup (as of honey)

halve \'hav, 'häv\ *vt* **halved; halv·ing** [ME *halven*, fr. *half*] **1 a** : to divide into two equal parts **b** : to reduce to one half <*halving* the present cost> **c** : to share equally **2** : to play (as a hole in golf) in the same number of strokes as one's opponent

halv·ers \'hav-ərz, 'häv-\ *n pl* : half shares : HALVES

halves *pl of* HALF

hal·yard \'hal-yərd\ *n* [ME *halier*, fr. *halen* to pull — more at HALE] : a rope or tackle for hoisting and lowering

[1]**ham** \'ham\ *n* [ME *hamme*, fr. OE *hamm;* akin to OHG *hamma* ham, Gk *knēmē* shinbone] **1 a** : the hollow of the knee **b** : a buttock with its associated thigh — usu. used in pl. **2** : a cut of meat consisting of a thigh; *esp* : one from a hog — see PORK illustration **3** [short for *hamfatter*, fr. "The *Ham-fat* Man," Negro minstrel song] **a** : a showy performer; *esp* : an actor performing in an exaggerated theatrical style **b** : a licensed operator of an amateur radio station — **ham** *adj*

[2]**ham** *vb* **hammed; ham·ming** *vt* : to execute with exaggerated speech or gestures : OVERACT ~ *vi* : to overplay a part

Ham \'ham\ *n* : a son of Noah and progenitor of the Egyptians, Nubians, and Canaanites

hama·dry·ad \,ham-ə-'drī-əd, -,ad\ *n* [L *hamadryad-, hamadryas*, fr. Gk, fr. *hama* together with + *dryad-, dryas* dryad — more at SAME] **1** : WOOD NYMPH **2 a** : KING COBRA **b** : a baboon (*Papio hamadryas*) venerated by the ancient Egyptians — called also *sacred baboon*

ha·mal *also* **ham·mal** \hə-'mäl\ *n* [Ar *ḥammāl* porter] : a porter in eastern countries (as Turkey)

Ha·man \'hā-mən\ *n* [Heb *Hāmān*] : an enemy of the Jews hanged according to the book of Esther for plotting their destruction

ha·mar·tia \,häm-,är-'tē-ə\ *n* [Gk, fr. *hamartanein* to miss the mark, err] : TRAGIC FLAW

[1]**ha·mate** \'hā-,māt\ *adj* [L *hamatus*, fr. *hamus* hook] : shaped like a hook

[2]**hamate** *n* : a bone on the inner side of the second row of the carpus in mammals — called also *unciform*

Ham·burg \'ham-,bərg\ *n* [*Hamburg*, Germany] : any of a European breed of rather small domestic fowls with rose combs and lead-blue legs

ham·burg·er \'ham-,bər-gər\ *or* **ham·burg** \-,bərg\ *n* [G *Hamburger* of Hamburg] **1 a** : ground beef **b** : a patty of ground beef **2** : a sandwich consisting of a patty of hamburger in a split round bun

[1]**hame** \'hām\ *n* [ME] : one of two curved projections which are attached to the collar of a draft horse and to which the traces are fastened

[2]**hame** *Scot var of* HOME

ham-fist·ed \'ham-'fis-təd\ *adj, chiefly Brit* : HAM-HANDED

ham-hand·ed \-'han-dəd\ *adj* : lacking dexterity or grace : HEAVY-HANDED

[1]**Ham·il·to·ni·an** \,ham-əl-'tō-nē-ən\ *adj* : of or relating to Alexander Hamilton or to Hamiltonianism

[2]**Hamiltonian** *n* : a follower or advocate of the doctrines of Alexander Hamilton

[3]**Hamiltonian** *n* [Sir William *Hamilton* †1865 Brit mathematician] : a function that is used to describe a dynamic system (as the motion of a particle) in terms of components of momentum and coordinates of space and time and that is equal to the total energy of the system when time is not explicitly part of the function — compare LAGRANGIAN

Ham·il·to·ni·an·ism \-,iz-əm\ *n* : the political principles and ideas held by or associated with Alexander Hamilton that center around a belief in a strong unitary central government, broad interpretation of the federal constitution, encouragement of an industrial and commercial economy, and a general distrust of the political capacity or wisdom of the common man

Ham·ite \'ham-,īt\ *n* [*Ham*] : a member of a group of chiefly northern African peoples that are mostly Muslims and are highly variable in appearance but mainly Caucasoid

[1]**Ham·it·ic** \ha-'mit-ik, hə-\ *adj* : of, relating to, or characteristic of the Hamites or one of the Hamitic languages

[2]**Hamitic** *n* : HAMITIC LANGUAGES

Hamitic languages *n pl* : the Berber, Cushitic, and sometimes Egyptian branches of the Afro-Asiatic languages

Ham·i·to-Se·mit·ic \,ham-ə-(,)tō-sə-'mit-ik\ *adj* : of, relating to, or constituting the Afro-Asiatic languages — **Hamito-Semitic** *n*

Hamito-Semitic languages *n pl* : AFRO-ASIATIC LANGUAGES

ham·let \'ham-lət\ *n* [ME, fr. MF *hamelet*, dim. of *ham* village, of Gmc origin; akin to OE *hām* village, home] : a small village

Ham·let \'ham-lət\ *n* : a legendary Danish prince and hero of Shakespeare's play *Hamlet*

[1]**ham·mer** \'ham-ər\ *n* [ME *hamer*, fr. OE *hamor;* akin to OHG *hamar* hammer, Gk *akmē* point, edge — more at EDGE] **1 a** : a hand tool consisting of a solid head set crosswise on a handle and used for pounding **b** : a power tool that often substitutes a metal block or a drill for the hammerhead **2** : something that resembles a hammer in form or action: as **a** : a lever with a striking head for ringing a bell or striking a gong **b** (1) : an arm that strikes the cap in a percussion lock to ignite the propelling charge (2) : a part of the action of a modern gun that strikes the primer of the cartridge in firing or that strikes the firing pin to ignite the cartridge **c** : MALLEUS **d** : GAVEL **e** (1) : a padded mallet in a piano action for striking a string (2) : a hand mallet for playing on various percussion instruments (as a xylophone) **3** : a metal sphere that usu. weighs 16 pounds and that is thrown for distance in the hammer throw — **under the hammer** : for sale at auction

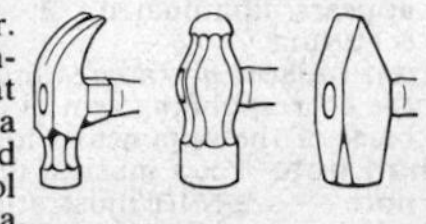
hammers 1a

[2]**hammer** *vb* **ham·mered; ham·mer·ing** \'ham-(ə-)riŋ\ *vi* **1** : to strike blows esp. repeatedly with or as if with a hammer : POUND **2** : to make repeated efforts; *esp* : to reiterate an opinion or attitude <the lectures all ~*ed* away at the same points> ~ *vt* **1 a** : to beat, drive, or shape with repeated blows of a hammer **b** : to fasten or build with a hammer **2** : to strike or drive as if with a hammer <~*ed* in three home runs in one game> <wanted to ~ him into submission> **3** : to produce or bring about as if by repeated blows <~ out a policy> — **ham·mer·er** \'ham-ər-ər\ *n*

hammer and sickle *n* : an emblem consisting of a crossed hammer and sickle used chiefly as a symbol of Communism in the Soviet Union

hammer-and-tongs *adj* : characterized by great force, vigor, or violence <has gone at his job in a ~ way that has annoyed . . . businessmen —*Newsweek*>

hammer and tongs *adv* : with great force, vigor, or violence <went at each other *hammer and tongs*>

ham·mered *adj* : having surface indentations produced or appearing to have been produced by hammering <~ copper>

ham·mer·head \'ham-ər-,hed\ *n* **1** : the striking part of a hammer **2** : BLOCKHEAD **3** : any of various active voracious medium-sized sharks that have the eyes at the ends of lateral extensions of the flattened head and that with the shovelheads constitute a family (Sphyrnidae)

ham·mer·less \-ləs\ *adj* : having the hammer concealed <a ~ gun>

ham·mer·lock \-,läk\ *n* : a wrestling hold in which an opponent's arm is held bent behind his back

hammer throw *n* : a field event in which a metal sphere attached to a flexible handle is thrown for distance

ham·mer·toe \,ham-ər-'tō\ *n* : a toe and usu. the second that is deformed by permanent angular flexion

[1]**ham·mock** \'ham-ək\ *n* [Sp *hamaca*, fr. Taino] : a swinging couch or bed usu. made of netting or canvas and slung by cords from supports at each end

[2]**hammock** *n* [origin unknown] **1** : HUMMOCK **2** : a fertile area in the southern U.S. and esp. Florida that is usu. higher than its surroundings and that is characterized by hardwood vegetation and deep humus-rich soil

ham·my \'ham-ē\ *adj* **ham·mi·er; -est** : marked by exaggerated and usu. self-conscious theatricality — **ham·mi·ly** \'ham-ə-lē\ *adv* — **ham·mi·ness** \'ham-ē-nəs\ *n*

[1]**ham·per** \'ham-pər\ *vt* **ham·pered; ham·per·ing** \-p(ə-)riŋ\ [ME *hamperen*] **1 a** : to restrict the movement of by bonds or obstacles : IMPEDE **b** : to interfere with the operation of : DISRUPT **2 a** : CURB, RESTRAIN **b** : to interfere with : ENCUMBER ***syn*** HAMPER, TRAMMEL, CLOG, FETTER, SHACKLE, MANACLE *shared meaning element* : to hinder or impede in moving, progressing, or acting ***ant*** assist (*as a person*), expedite (*as work*)

²hamper *n* **1 :** something that impedes : OBSTRUCTION **2 :** TOP-HAMPER 1

³hamper *n* [ME *hampere,* alter. of *hanaper,* lit., case to hold goblets, fr. MF *hanapier,* fr. *hanap* goblet, of Gmc origin; akin to OE *hnæpp* bowl] : a large basket usu. with a cover for packing, storing, or transporting articles (as food or laundry)

Hamp·shire \'ham(p)-ˌshi(ə)r, -shər\ *n* [*Hampshire,* England] **1 :** any of an American breed of black white-belted swine with white forelegs, rather long head, and straight face **2 :** any of a British breed of medium-wooled mutton-producing sheep that are large, thick-fleshed, and hornless — called also *Hampshire Down*

ham·ster \'ham(p)-stər\ *n* [G, fr. OHG *hamustro,* of Slavic origin; akin to OSlav *chomĕstorŭ* hamster] : any of numerous Old World rodents (*Cricetus* or a related genus) having very large cheek pouches

hamster

¹ham·string \'ham-ˌstriŋ\ *n* **1 a :** either of two groups of tendons at the back of the human knee **b :** HAMSTRING MUSCLE **2 :** a large tendon above and behind the hock of a quadruped

²hamstring *vt* **-strung** \-ˌstrəŋ\; **-string·ing** \-ˌstriŋ-iŋ\ **1 :** to cripple by cutting the leg tendons **2 :** to make ineffective or powerless : CRIPPLE <teachers . . . *hamstrung* by excessive teaching schedules —N. M. Pusey>

hamstring muscle *n* : any of three muscles at the back of the thigh that function to extend the thigh when the leg is flexed

ham·u·lus \'ham-yə-ləs\ *n, pl* **-u·li** \-ˌlī, -ˌlē\ [NL, fr. L, dim. of *hamus* hook] : a hook or hooked process

ham·za *or* **ham·zah** \'ham-zə\ *n* [Ar *hamzah,* lit., compression] : the sign for a glottal stop in Arabic orthography usu. represented in English by an apostrophe

Han \'hän\ *n* **1 :** a Chinese dynasty dated 207B.C.–A.D.220 and marked by centralized control through an appointive bureaucracy, a revival of learning, and the penetration of Buddhism **2 :** the Chinese peoples esp. as distinguished from Mongol, Manchu, or other non-Chinese elements in the population : the Chinese race

¹hand \'hand\ *n, often attrib* [ME, fr. OE; akin to OHG *hant* hand] **1 a (1) :** the terminal part of the vertebrate forelimb when modified (as in man) as a grasping organ **(2) :** the segment of the forelimb of a vertebrate above the fishes that corresponds to the hand (as the pinion of a bird) irrespective of its form or functional specialization **b :** a part serving the function of or resembling a hand: as **(1) :** the hind foot of an ape **(2) :** the chela of a crustacean **c :** something resembling a hand: as **(1) :** an indicator or pointer on a dial **(2) :** a stylized figure of a hand with forefinger extended to point a direction or call attention to something; *specif* : INDEX 5 **(3) :** a cluster of bananas developed from a single flower group **(4) :** a branched rootstock of ginger **(5) :** a bunch of large leaves tied together usu. with another leaf **2 a :** personal possession — usu. used in pl. <the documents fell into the ~*s* of the enemy> **b :** CONTROL, SUPERVISION — usu. used in pl. <the reception was in the ~*s* of the caterer> **3 a :** SIDE, DIRECTION <men fighting on either ~> **b :** one of two sides or aspects of an issue or argument <on the one ~ we can appeal for peace, or on the other declare war> **4 :** a pledge esp. of betrothal or bestowal in marriage **5 a :** style of penmanship : HANDWRITING **b :** SIGNATURE **6 a :** SKILL, ABILITY <tried her ~ at sailing> **b :** an instrumental part <had a ~ in the crime> **7 :** a unit of measure equal to 4 inches used esp. for the height of horses **8 a :** assistance or aid esp. involving physical effort <lend a ~> **b :** PARTICIPATION, INTEREST **c :** a round of applause **9 a (1) :** a player in a card game or board game **(2) :** the cards or pieces held by a player **b :** a single round in a game **c :** the force or solidity of one's position (as in negotiations) **10 a :** one who performs or executes a particular work <two portraits by the same ~> **b (1) :** one employed at manual labor or general tasks <a ranch ~> **(2) :** WORKER, EMPLOYEE <employed over a hundred ~*s*> **c :** a member of a ship's crew <all ~*s* on deck> **d :** one skilled in a particular action or pursuit **e :** a specialist in a usu. designated activity or region <an old China ~> **11 a :** HANDIWORK **b :** style of execution : WORKMANSHIP <the ~ of a master> **c :** the feel of or tactile reaction to something (as silk or leather) — **at hand :** near in time or place — **at the hands of** *or* **at the hand of :** by the act or instrumentality of — **by hand :** with the hands — **in hand 1 a :** in one's possession or control **b :** at one's disposal **2 :** in preparation — **off one's hands :** out of one's care or charge — **on all hands** *or* **on every hand :** EVERYWHERE — **on hand 1 :** in present possession **2 :** about to appear : PENDING **3 :** in attendance : PRESENT — **on one's hands :** in one's possession, care, or management — **out of hand 1 :** without delay : FORTHWITH **2 :** done with : FINISHED **3 :** out of control — **to hand 1 :** into possession **2 :** within reach **3 :** into control or subjection — **with a heavy hand 1 :** with little mercy : STERNLY **2 :** without grace : CLUMSILY

²hand *vt* **1 a** *obs* **:** to touch or manage with the hands; *also* : to deal with **b :** FURL **2 :** to lead, guide, or assist with the hand <~ a lady into a bus> **3 a :** to give, pass, or transmit with the hand <~ a letter to her> **b :** PRESENT, PROVIDE <~*ed* him a surprise> — **hand it to :** to give credit to : concede the excellence of

hand and foot *adv* : TOTALLY, ASSIDUOUSLY

hand ax *n* **1 :** a prehistoric stone tool having one end pointed for cutting and the other end rounded for holding in the hand **2 :** a short-handled ax intended for use with one hand

hand·bag \'han(d)-ˌbag\ *n* **1 :** TRAVELING BAG **2 :** a woman's bag held in the hand or hung from a shoulder strap and used for carrying small personal articles and money

hand·ball \-ˌbȯl\ *n* **1 :** a small rubber ball used in the game of handball **2 :** a game played in a walled court or against a single wall or board by two or four players who use their hands to strike the ball

hand·bar·row \-ˌbar-(ˌ)ō, -ə(-w)\ *n* : a flat rectangular frame with handles at both ends that is carried by two persons

hand·bill \-ˌbil\ *n* : a small printed sheet to be distributed (as for advertising) by hand

hand·book \-ˌbu̇k\ *n* **1 a :** a book capable of being conveniently carried as a ready reference : MANUAL **b :** a concise reference book covering a particular subject **2 a :** a bookmaker's book of bets **b :** a place where bookmaking is carried on

hand·breadth \-ˌbredth, -ˌbretth\ *n* : any of various units of length varying from about 2½ to 4 inches based on the breadth of a hand

hand·car \'han(d)-ˌkär\ *n* : a small four-wheeled railroad car propelled by a hand-operated mechanism or by a small motor

hand·cart \-ˌkärt\ *n* : a cart drawn or pushed by hand

hand cheese *n* : a soft cheese that was orig. molded by hand and that has a sharp pungent odor and flavor

hand·clasp \'han(d)-ˌklasp\ *n* : HANDSHAKE

¹hand·craft \-ˌkraft\ *n* : HANDICRAFT

²handcraft *vt* : to fashion by handicraft

hand·craft·man \-ˌkraf(t)-mən\ *or* **hand·crafts·man** \-ˌkraf(t)-smən\ *n* : one who is skilled in handicraft

¹hand·cuff \-ˌkəf\ *vt* **1 :** to apply handcuffs to : MANACLE **2 :** to hold in check : make ineffective or powerless

²handcuff *n* : a metal fastening that can be locked around a wrist and is usu. connected by a chain or bar with another such fastening

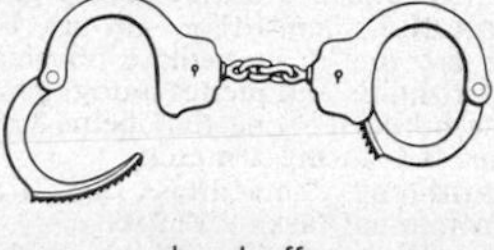
handcuffs

hand down *vt* **1 :** to transmit in succession (as from father to son) **2 :** to make official formulation of and express (the opinion of a court)

hand·ed \'han-dəd\ *adj* **1 :** having a hand or hands esp. of a specified kind or number — usu. used in combination <a large-*handed* man> **2 :** using a specified hand or number of hands — used in combination <right-*handed*> <a one-*handed* catch>

hand·ed·ness \-nəs\ *n* : a tendency to use one hand rather than the other

hand·fast \'han(d)-ˌfast\ *n, archaic* : a contract or covenant esp. of betrothal or marriage

hand–feed \'han(d)-'fēd\ *vt* **-fed** \-'fed\; **-feed·ing :** to provide and apportion rations to (animals) at regular intervals in quantities sufficient for a single feeding — compare SELF-FEED

hand·ful \'han(d)-ˌfu̇l\ *n, pl* **handfuls** \-ˌfu̇lz\ *also* **hands·ful** \'han(d)z-ˌfu̇l\ **1 :** as much or as many as the hand will grasp **2 :** a small quantity or number **3 :** as much as one can manage

hand glass *n* : a small mirror with a handle

hand·grip \'han(d)-ˌgrip\ *n* **1 :** a grasping with the hand **2 :** HANDLE **3** *pl* **:** hand-to-hand combat

hand·gun \-ˌgən\ *n* : a firearm held and fired with one hand

hand·hold \'hand-ˌhōld\ *n* **1 :** HOLD, GRIP **2 :** something to hold on to (as in mountain climbing)

¹hand·i·cap \'han-di-ˌkap\ *n* [obs. E *handicap* (a game in which forfeits were held in a cap), fr. *hand in cap*] **1 a :** a race or contest in which an artificial advantage is given or disadvantage imposed on a contestant to equalize chances of winning **b :** an advantage given or disadvantage imposed usu. in the form of points, strokes, weight to be carried, or distance from the target or goal **2 :** a disadvantage that makes achievement unusually difficult; *esp* : a physical disability

²handicap *vt* **-capped; -cap·ping 1 a :** to give a handicap to **b :** to assign handicaps to **2 :** to put at a disadvantage

hand·i·cap·per \-ˌkap-ər\ *n* **1 :** one who assigns handicaps **2 :** one who predicts the winners in a horse race usu. for publication **3 :** one who competes with a (specified) handicap — usu. used in combination <a 5-*handicapper*>

hand·i·craft \'han-di-ˌkraft\ *n* [ME *handi-crafte,* alter. of *handcraft*] **1 a :** manual skill **b :** an occupation requiring skill with the hands **2 :** the articles fashioned by those engaged in handicraft — **hand·i·craft·er** \-ˌkraf-tər\ *n*

hand·i·crafts·man \-ˌkraf(t)-smən\ *n* : one who engages in a handicraft : ARTISAN

Hand·ie–Talk·ie \ˌhan-dē-'tȯ-kē\ *trademark* — used for a small portable radio transmitter-receiver

hand·i·ly \'han-də-lē\ *adv* **1 :** in a dexterous manner **2 :** EASILY <defeated the other candidate ~> **3 :** conveniently nearby <kept the eraser ~ by him while he wrote>

hand in glove *or* **hand and glove** *adv* : in extremely close relationship or agreement <were found to be working *hand in glove* with the racketeers>

hand in hand *adv* **1 :** with hands clasped (as in intimacy or affection) **2 :** in close association

hand·i·work \'han-di-ˌwərk\ *n* [ME *handiwerk,* fr. OE *handgeweorc,* fr. *hand* + *geweorc,* fr. *ge-* (collective prefix) + *weorc* work] **1 a :** work done by the hands **b :** work done personally **2 :** the product of handiwork

hand·ker·chief \'haŋ-kər-chəf, -(ˌ)chif, -ˌchēf\ *n, pl* **-chiefs** *also* **-chieves** \-chəfs, -(ˌ)chifs, -ˌchēvz (*used by many who have sing.* -chəf *or* -(ˌ)chif), -ˌchēfs, -chəvz, -(ˌ)chivz\ **1 :** a small usu. square piece of cloth used for various usu. personal purposes (as blowing the nose or wiping the eyes) or as an accessory on one's attire **2 :** KERCHIEF 1

¹han·dle \'han-dᵊl\ *n* [ME *handel,* fr. OE *handle;* akin to OE *hand*] **1 :** a part that is designed esp. to be grasped by the hand **2 :** something that resembles a handle **3 :** NAME, TITLE **4 :** the feel of a textile **5 :** the total amount of money bet on a race, game, or event — **han·dled** \-dᵊld\ *adj* — **han·dle·less** \-dᵊl-(l)əs\ *adj* — **off the handle :** into a state of sudden and violent anger

2**handle** *vb* **han·dled; han·dling** \'han-(d)liŋ, -dᵊl-iŋ\ *vt* **1 a :** to try or examine (as by touching, feeling or moving) with the hand <~ silk to judge its weight> **b :** to manage with the hands <~ a horse> **2 a :** to deal with in writing or speaking or in the plastic arts **b :** MANAGE, DIRECT <a lawyer ~*s* all my affairs> **c :** to train and act as second for (a prizefighter) **3 :** to deal with, act on, or dispose of <~ the day's mail> **4 :** to engage in the buying, selling, or distributing of (a commodity) ~ *vi* **:** to act, behave, or feel in a certain way when handled or directed <car that ~*s* well> — **han·dle·able** \-dᵊl-ə-bəl\ *adj*
syn **1** HANDLE, MANIPULATE, WIELD *shared meaning element* **:** to manage dexterously or efficiently
2 see TREAT
3 see TOUCH

handlebar mustache *n* **:** a heavy mustache with long sections that curve upward at each end

han·dle·bars \'han-dᵊl-ˌbärz\ *n pl* **:** a straight or bent bar with a handle at each end; *specif* **:** one used to steer a bicycle or similar vehicle

hand lens *n* **:** a magnifying glass to be held in the hand

han·dler \'han-(d)lər, -dᵊl-ər\ *n* **1 :** one that handles something **2 a :** one in immediate physical charge of an animal; *esp* **:** one that holds and incites a dog, gamecock, or other animal in a match or hunt **b :** one that helps to train a prizefighter or acts as his second during a match

hand·less \'han-(d)ləs\ *adj* **1 :** having no hands **2 :** inefficient in manual tasks **:** CLUMSY

han·dling \-(d)liŋ, -dᵊl-iŋ\ *n* **1 a :** the action of one that handles something **b :** a process by which something is handled in a commercial transaction; *esp* **:** the packaging and shipping of an object or material (as to a consumer) **2 :** the manner in which something is treated (as in a musical, literary, or art work)

hand·list \'han-ˌ(d)list\ *n* **:** a list (as of books) for purposes of reference or checking

hand·made \'han(d)-'mād\ *adj* **:** made by hand or a hand process

hand·maid·en \-ˌmād-ᵊn\ *or* **hand·maid** \-ˌmād\ *n* **1 :** a personal maid or female servant **2 :** something whose essential function is to serve or assist <good sense which . . . is the indispensable ~ of the critical art —Carlos Baker>

hand–me–down \'han(d)-mē-ˌdau̇n\ *adj* **1 :** ready-made and usu. cheap and shoddy **2 :** put in use by one person or group after being used, discarded, or handed down by another <~ clothes> — **hand–me–down** *n*

hand mower *n* **:** a motorless lawn mower designed to be pushed by hand

hand off \(ˈ)han-'dȯf\ *vt* **:** to hand (a football) to a nearby teammate on a play ~ *vi* **:** to hand off a football — **hand·off** \'han-ˌdȯf\ *n*

hand on *vt* **:** to hand down <the father *handed on* his good reputation to his son>

hand organ *n* **:** a barrel organ operated by a hand crank

hand·out \'han-ˌdau̇t\ *n* **1 :** a portion of food, clothing, or money given to or as if to a beggar **2 :** a folder or circular of information for free distribution **3 a :** a release by a news service **b :** a prepared statement released to the news media

hand out \(ˈ)han-'dau̇t\ *vt* **1 a :** to give without charge **b :** to give freely **2 :** ADMINISTER <*handed out* a severe punishment>

hand over *vt* **:** to yield control of

hand over fist *adv* **:** quickly and in large amounts

hand·pick \'han(d)-'pik\ *vt* **1 :** to pick by hand as opposed to a machine process **2 :** to select personally or for personal ends

hand·press \-ˌpres\ *n* **:** a hand-operated press

hand·print \-ˌprint\ *n* **:** an impression of a hand on a surface

hand puppet *n* **:** PUPPET 1a

hand·rail \'han-ˌdrāl\ *n* **:** a narrow rail for grasping with the hand as a support

hand–ride \-ˌdrīd\ *vb* **-rode** \-ˌdrōd\; **-rid·den** \-ˌdrid-ᵊn\; **-rid·ing** \-ˌdrīd-iŋ\ *vt* **:** to ride (a horse) without using a whip or spurs during a race ~ *vi* **:** to hand-ride a racehorse

hand running *adv* **:** in unbroken succession **:** CONSECUTIVELY

hand·saw \'han(d)-ˌsȯ\ *n* **:** a saw usu. operated with one hand

hands·breadth \'han(d)z-ˌbredth, -ˌbretth\ *var of* HANDBREADTH

hands–down \ˌhan(d)z-ˌdau̇n\ *adj* **1 :** achieved without much effort **2 :** being unquestionable

hands down \'han(d)z-'dau̇n\ *adv* **1 :** without much effort **:** EASILY **2 :** without question

1**hand·sel** \'han(t)-səl\ *n* [ME *hansell*] **1 :** a gift made as a token of good wishes or luck esp. at the beginning of a new year **2 :** something received first (as in a day of trading) and taken to be a token of good luck **3 a :** a first installment **:** earnest money **b :** EARNEST, FORETASTE

2**handsel** *vt* **-seled** *or* **-selled; -sel·ing** *or* **-sel·ling** \-s(ə-)liŋ\ **1 :** to give a handsel to **2 :** to inaugurate with a token or gesture of luck or pleasure **3 :** to use or do for the first time

hand·set \'han(d)-ˌset\ *n* **:** a combined telephone transmitter and receiver mounted on a handle

hand·shake \-ˌshāk\ *n* **:** a clasping of right hands by two people (as in greeting or farewell)

hands–off \'han(d)-'zȯf\ *adj* **:** characterized by noninterference <a ~ policy toward the internal affairs of other nations>

hand·some \'han(t)-səm\ *adj* [ME *handsom* easy to manipulate] **1** *chiefly dial* **:** APPROPRIATE, SUITABLE **2 :** moderately large **:** SIZABLE <a painting that commanded a ~ price> **3 :** marked by skill or cleverness **:** ADROIT **4 :** marked by graciousness or generosity **:** LIBERAL <~ contributions to charity> **5 :** having a pleasing and usu. impressive or dignified appearance *syn* see BEAUTIFUL — **hand·some·ly** *adv* — **hand·some·ness** *n*

hand·spike \'han(d)-ˌspīk\ *n* [by folk etymology fr. D *handspaak,* fr. *hand* + *spaak* pole] **:** a bar used as a lever

hand·spring \-ˌspriŋ\ *n* **:** an acrobatic feat in which the body turns forward or backward in a full circle from a standing position and lands first on the hands and then on the feet

hand·stand \-ˌstand\ *n* **:** an act of supporting the body on the hands with the trunk and legs balanced in the air

hand–to–hand \ˌhan-tə-ˌhand, -də-\ *adj* **:** involving physical contact

hand to hand \-'hand\ *adv* **:** in a manner involving physical contact

hand–to–mouth \-ˌmau̇th\ *adj* **:** having or providing nothing to spare **:** PRECARIOUS <a ~ existence>

hand truck *n* **:** a small hand-propelled truck; *esp* **:** TRUCK 3b

hand·wheel \'han(d)-ˌhwēl, 'han-ˌdwēl\ *n* **:** a wheel worked by hand

hand·work \'han-ˌdwərk\ *n* **:** work done with the hands and not by machines **:** HANDIWORK — **hand·work·er** \-ˌdwər-kər\ *n*

hand·wo·ven \-'dwō-vən\ *adj* **1 :** produced on a hand-operated loom **2 :** woven by hand <~ baskets>

hand·write \-ˌdrīt\ *vt* **-wrote** \-ˌdrōt\; **-writ·ten** \-ˌdrit-ᵊn\; **-writ·ing** \-ˌdrīt-iŋ\ [back-formation fr. *handwriting*] **:** to write by hand

hand·writ·ing \'han-ˌdrīt-iŋ\ *n* **1 :** writing done by hand; *esp* **:** the form of writing peculiar to a particular person **2 :** something written by hand **:** MANUSCRIPT — **handwriting on the wall :** an omen of one's unpleasant fate

hand·wrought \'han-'drȯt\ *adj* **:** fashioned by hand or chiefly by hand processes <~ silver>

handy \'han-dē\ *adj* **hand·i·er; -est** **1 a :** conveniently near **b :** convenient for use **c** *of a ship* **:** easily handled **2 :** clever in using the hands esp. in a variety of useful ways <a woman ~ with a gun as well as a needle> — **hand·i·ness** *n*

handy·man \-dē-ˌman\ *n* **1 :** one who does odd jobs **2 :** one competent in a variety of small skills or inventive or ingenious in repair or maintenance work

1**hang** \'haŋ\ *vb* **hung** \'həŋ\ *also* **hanged** \'haŋd\; **hang·ing** \'haŋ-iŋ\ [partly fr. ME *hon,* fr. OE *hōn,* v.t.; partly fr. ME *hangen,* fr. OE *hangian,* v.i. & v.t.; both akin to OHG *hāhan,* v.t., to hang, *hangēn,* v.i.] *vt* **1 a :** to fasten to some elevated point without support from below **:** SUSPEND **b :** to suspend by the neck until dead — sometimes *hanged* in the past; often used as a mild oath <I'll be ~*ed*> **c :** to fasten so as to allow free motion within given limits upon a point of suspension <~ a door> **d :** to fit or fix in position or at a proper angle <~ an ax to its helve> **e :** to adjust the hem of (a skirt) so as to hang evenly and at a proper height **2 :** to decorate or furnish by hanging (as flags or bunting) **3 :** to hold or bear in a suspended or inclined manner <*hung* his head in shame> **4 :** to fasten (as with paste) to a wall <~ wallpaper> **5 :** to display (pictures) in a gallery **6 :** to throw (as a curve) in such a way as to fail to break ~ *vi* **1 a :** to remain suspended or fastened to some point above without support from below **:** DANGLE **b :** to die by hanging — sometimes *hanged* in the past <he ~*ed* for his crimes> **2 :** to remain poised or stationary in the air <clouds ~*ing* low overhead> **3 :** to stay with persistence **4 :** to be imminent **:** IMPEND <doom *hung* over the nation> **5 :** to fall or droop from a usu. tense or taut position **6 :** DEPEND <election ~*s* on one vote> **7 a** (1) **:** to take hold for support **:** CLING <she *hung* on his arm> (2) **:** to keep persistent contact <dogs *hung* to the trail> **b :** to be burdensome or oppressive <time ~*s* on his hands> **8 :** to be uncertain or in suspense <the decision is still ~*ing*> **9 :** to lean, incline, or jut over or downward **10 :** to be in a state of rapt attention <*hung* on his every word> **11 :** to fit or fall from the figure in easy lines <the coat ~*s* loosely> **12** *of a thrown ball* **:** to fail to break or drop as intended — **hang·able** \'haŋ-ə-bəl\ *adj* — **hang fire** **1 :** to be slow in the explosion of a charge after its primer has been discharged **2 :** DELAY, HESITATE — **hang five :** to ride a surfboard with the weight of the body forward and the toes of one foot turned over the front edge of the board — **hang one on** **1 :** to inflict a blow on **2** *slang* **:** to get very drunk — **hang ten :** to ride a surfboard with the weight of the body forward and the toes of both feet turned over the edge of the board

2**hang** *n* **1 :** the manner in which a thing hangs **2 :** DECLIVITY, SLOPE; *also* **:** DROOP **3 a :** the peculiar and significant order or meaning **b :** the special method of doing, using, or dealing with something **:** KNACK **4 :** a hesitation or slackening in motion or in a course — **give a hang** *or* **care a hang :** to be concerned or worried

1**han·gar** \'haŋ-ər, 'haŋ-gər\ *n* [F] **:** SHELTER, SHED; *esp* **:** a covered and usu. enclosed area for housing and repairing aircraft

2**hangar** *vt* **:** to place or store in a hangar

hang around *vi* **1 :** to pass time or stay aimlessly **:** loiter idly **2 :** to spend one's time in company

hang back *vi* **1 :** to drag behind others **2 :** to be reluctant **:** HESITATE, FALTER

1**hang·dog** \'haŋ-ˌdȯg\ *adj* **1 :** ASHAMED, GUILTY **2 :** ABJECT, COWED

2**hangdog** *n* **:** a despicable or miserable person

hang·er \'haŋ-ər\ *n* **1 :** one that hangs or causes to be hung or hanged **2 :** something that hangs, overhangs, or is suspended: as **a :** a decorative strip of cloth **b :** a small sword formerly used by seamen **c** *chiefly Brit* **:** a small wood on steeply sloping land **3 :** a device by which or to which something is hung or hangs: as **a :** a strap on a sword belt by which a sword or dagger can be suspended **b :** a loop by which a garment is hung up **c :** a device that fits inside or around a garment for hanging from a hook or rod

hang·er–on \'haŋ-ə-ˌrȯn, -ˌrän\ *n, pl* **hangers–on** [*hang on* + *-er*] **:** one that hangs around a person, place, or institution esp. for personal gain

hang in *vi* **:** to refuse to be discouraged or intimidated **:** show pluck **:** PERSIST

1**hang·ing** \'haŋ-iŋ\ *n* **1 :** an execution by strangling or breaking the neck by a suspended noose **2 :** something hung: as **a :** CURTAIN **b :** a covering (as a tapestry) for a wall **3 :** a downward slope **:** DECLIVITY

[2]**hanging** *adj* **1 :** situated or lying on steeply sloping ground **2 a :** jutting out : OVERHANGING <a ~ rock> **b :** supported only by the wall on one side <a ~ staircase> **3** *archaic* **:** downcast in appearance **4 :** adapted for sustaining a hanging object **5 :** deserving, likely to cause, or prone to inflict death by hanging <a ~ judge>

hanging indention *n* **:** indention of all the lines of a paragraph except the first

hang·man \ˈhaŋ-mən\ *n* **:** one who hangs a condemned person; *also* **:** a public executioner

hang·nail \-ˌnāl\ *n* [by folk etymology fr. *agnail*] **:** a bit of skin hanging loose at the side or root of a fingernail

hang off *vi* **:** to hang back

hang on *vi* **1 :** to keep hold : hold onto something **2 :** to persist tenaciously <a cold that *hung on* all spring> **3 :** to keep a telephone connection open <*hang on* a second while I look it up> — **hang on to :** to hold, grip, or keep tenaciously <learned to *hang on to* his money>

hang·out \ˈhaŋ-ˌau̇t\ *n* **:** a favorite or usual place of resort

hang out \(ˈ)haŋ-ˈau̇t\ *vi* **1 :** to protrude in a downward direction **2 a** *slang* **:** LIVE, RESIDE **b :** to spend one's time idly or in loitering around ~ *vt* **:** to display outside as an announcement to the public

hang·over \ˈhaŋ-ˌō-vər\ *n* **1 :** something (as a surviving custom) that remains from what is past **2 a :** disagreeable physical effects following heavy consumption of alcohol **b :** disagreeable aftereffects from the use of drugs **c :** a letdown following great excitement or excess

hang·tag \ˈhaŋ-ˌtag\ *n* **:** a tag attached to an article of merchandise giving information about the quality of its material and about its proper care

hang together *vi* **1 :** to remain united : stand by one another **2 :** to form a consistent or coherent whole

hang–up \ˈhaŋ-ˌəp\ *n* **:** a source of mental or emotional difficulty

hang up \(ˈ)haŋ-ˈəp\ *vt* **1 a :** to place on a hook or hanger designed for the purpose <told the child to *hang up* his coat> **b :** to replace (a telephone receiver) on the cradle so that the connection is broken **2 :** to keep delayed, suspended, or held up <the negotiations were *hung up* for a week> **3 :** to cause (a record) to be set : ACHIEVE <*hung up* a new record for the 50-yard dash> **4 :** to cause to stick or snag immovably <the ship was *hung up* on a sandbar> ~ *vi* **1 :** to terminate a telephone conversation **2 :** to become stuck or snagged so as to be immovable

hank \ˈhaŋk\ *n* [ME, of Scand origin; akin to ON *hönk* hank; akin to OE *hangian* to hang] **1 :** COIL, LOOP; *specif* **:** a coiled or looped bundle (as of yarn, rope, or wire) usu. containing a definite yardage **2 :** a ring attached to the edge of a jib or staysail and running on a stay

han·ker \ˈhaŋ-kər\ *vi* **han·kered; han·ker·ing** \-k(ə-)riŋ\ [prob. fr. Flem *hankeren,* freq. of *hangen* to hang; akin to OE *hangian*] **:** to desire strongly or persistently *syn* see LONG — **han·ker·er** \-kər-ər\ *n*

han·ker·ing *n* **:** a strong or persistent desire

han·kie *or* **han·ky** \ˈhaŋ-kē\ *n, pl* **hankies** [*hand*k*erchief* + *-ie*] **:** HANDKERCHIEF

han·ky–pan·ky \ˌhaŋ-kē-ˈpaŋ-kē\ *n* [alter. of *hocus-pocus*] **:** questionable or underhand activity : TRICKERY

[1]**Han·o·ver·i·an** \ˌhan-ə-ˈvir-ē-ən, -ˈver-\ *adj* [*Hanover,* Germany] **1 :** of, relating to, or supporting the German ducal house of Hanover **2 :** of, relating to, or supporting the British royal house that reigned from 1714 to 1901

[2]**Hanoverian** *n* **1 :** a member or supporter of the ducal or of the British royal Hanoverian house **2 :** any of a breed of horses developed by crossing heavy German horses with Thoroughbreds

Han·sa \ˈhan(t)-sə, ˈhän-(ˌ)zä\ *or* **Hanse** \ˈhan(t)s, ˈhän-zə\ *n* [*Hansa* fr. ML, fr. MLG *hanse; Hanse* fr. ME, fr. MF, fr. MLG] **1 :** a medieval merchant guild or trading association **2 :** a league orig. constituted of merchants of various free German cities dealing abroad in the medieval period and later of the cities themselves and organized to secure greater safety and privileges in trading — **Han·se·at·ic** \ˌhan(t)-sē-ˈat-ik\ *n or adj*

Han·sard \ˈhan(t)-sərd, ˈhan-ˌsärd\ *n* [Luke *Hansard* †1828 E printer] **:** the official published verbatim report of proceedings in the British parliament

han·sel *var of* HANDSEL

Han·sen's disease \ˈhan(t)-sənz-\ *n* [Armauer *Hansen* †1912 Norw physician] **:** LEPROSY

han·som \ˈhan(t)-səm\ *n* [Joseph A. *Hansom* †1882 E architect] **:** a light 2-wheeled covered carriage with the driver's seat elevated behind — called also *hansom cab*

hansom

hant \ˈhant\ *dial var of* HAUNT

Ha·nuk·kah \ˈkän-ə-kə, ˈhän-\ *n* [Heb *ḥanukkāh* dedication] **:** an 8-day Jewish holiday beginning on the 25th of Kislev and commemorating the rededication of the Temple of Jerusalem after its defilement by Antiochus of Syria

hao·le \ˈhau̇-lē, -(ˌ)lā\ *n* [Hawaiian] **:** one who is not a member of the native race of Hawaii; *esp* **:** WHITE

[1]**hap** \ˈhap\ *n* [ME, fr. ON *happ* good luck; akin to OE *gehæp* suitable, OSlav *kobĭ* augury] **1 :** HAPPENING 1 **2 :** CHANCE, FORTUNE

[2]**hap** *vi* **happed; hap·ping :** HAPPEN

[3]**hap** *vt* **happed; hap·ping** [ME *happen*] *dial* **:** CLOTHE, COVER

[4]**hap** *n, dial* **:** something (as a bed quilt or cloak) that serves as a covering or wrap

ha·pa hao·le \ˌhäp-ə-ˈhau̇-lē, -(ˌ)lā\ *adj* [Hawaiian, fr. *hapa* half (fr. E *half*) + *haole*] **:** of part-white ancestry or origin; *esp* **:** Hawaiian-Caucasian

ha·pax le·go·me·non \ˌhap-ˌak-sli-ˈgäm-ə-ˌnän, -nən\ *n, pl* **hapax le·go·me·na** \-nə\ [Gk, something said only once] **:** a word or form evidenced by a single occurrence

hap·chance \ˈhap-ˌchan(t)s\ *n* **:** a fortuitous or chance event or circumstance

ha'·pen·ny *n* **:** HALFPENNY

[1]**hap·haz·ard** \(ˈ)hap-ˈhaz-ərd\ *n* [[1]*hap* + *hazard*] **:** CHANCE

[2]**haphazard** *adj* **:** marked by lack of plan, order, or direction : AIMLESS *syn* see RANDOM — **haphazard** *adv* — **hap·haz·ard·ly** *adv* — **hap·haz·ard·ness** *n*

hap·haz·ard·ry \-ər-drē\ *n* **:** haphazard character or order : FORTUITY

hapl- *or* **haplo-** *comb form* [NL, fr. Gk, fr. *haploos,* fr. *ha-* one + *-ploos* multiplied by; akin to Gk *homos* same — more at SAME, DOUBLE] **1 :** single : simple **2** [*haploid*] **:** of or relating to the haploid generation or condition <*haplo*sis>

hap·less \ˈhap-ləs\ *adj* **:** having no luck : UNFORTUNATE — **hap·less·ly** *adv* — **hap·less·ness** *n*

hap·lo·bi·ont \ˌhap-lō-ˈbī-ˌänt\ *n* **:** a plant producing only sexual haploid individuals — **hap·lo·bi·on·tic** \-bī-ˈänt-ik\ *adj*

hap·loid \ˈhap-ˌlȯid\ *adj* [ISV, fr. Gk *haploeidēs* single, fr. *haploos*] **:** having the gametic number of chromosomes or half the number characteristic of somatic cells : MONOPLOID — **haploid** *n* — **hap·loi·dy** \-ˌlȯid-ē\ *n*

hap·lont \ˈhap-ˌlänt\ *n* [ISV] **:** an organism with somatic cells having the haploid chromosome number and only the zygote diploid — compare DIPLONT — **hap·lon·tic** \ha-ˈplänt-ik\ *adj*

hap·ly \ˈhap-lē\ *adv* **:** by chance, luck, or accident

hap·pen \ˈhap-ən, -ᵊm\ *vi* **hap·pened; hap·pen·ing** \ˈhap-(ə-)niŋ\ [ME *happenen,* fr. *hap*] **1 :** to occur by chance — often used with *it* <it so ~*s* I'm going your way> **2 a :** to come into being **b :** to take place : OCCUR **3 :** to have the luck or fortune : do, encounter, or attain something by or as if by chance <he ~*ed* to overhear the plotters> **4 a :** to meet something by chance <~*ed* upon a system that worked —Richard Corbin> **b :** to come or go casually : make a chance appearance <he ~*ed* into the room just as we were leaving> **5 :** to come esp. by way of injury or harm <I promise nothing will ~ to you>

syn HAPPEN, CHANCE, OCCUR, TRANSPIRE *shared meaning element* **:** to come about

hap·pen·chance \ˈhap-ən-ˌchan(t)s, ˈhap-ᵊm-\ *n* **:** HAPPENSTANCE

hap·pen·ing *n* **1 :** something that happens : OCCURRENCE **2 :** an event or series of events designed to evoke a spontaneous reaction to sensory, emotional, or spiritual stimuli *syn* see OCCURRENCE

hap·pen·stance \ˈhap-ən-ˌstan(t)s, ˈhap-ᵊm-\ *n* [*happen* + *circumstance*] **:** a circumstance regarded as due to chance

hap·pi·ly \ˈhap-ə-lē\ *adv* **1 :** in a fortunate manner : LUCKILY **2** *archaic* **:** by chance **3 :** in a happy manner or state <lived ~ ever after> **4 :** in an adequate or fitting manner : SUCCESSFULLY

hap·pi·ness \ˈhap-i-nəs\ *n* **1** *obs* **:** good fortune : PROSPERITY **2 a :** a state of well-being and contentment : JOY **b :** a pleasurable satisfaction **3 :** FELICITY, APTNESS

hap·py \ˈhap-ē\ *adj* **hap·pi·er; -est** [ME, fr. *hap*] **1 :** favored by luck or fortune : FORTUNATE **2 :** notably well adapted or fitting : FELICITOUS <a ~ choice> **3 a :** enjoying well-being and contentment : JOYOUS **b :** expressing or suggestive of happiness : PLEASANT **c :** GLAD, PLEASED **4 a :** characterized by a dazed irresponsible state <a punch-*happy* prizefighter> **b :** impulsively or obsessively quick to use something <trigger-*happy*> **c :** enthusiastic to the point of obsession : OBSESSED <a nation . . . education-conscious and statistic-*happy* —Helen Rowen> **d :** having or marked by an atmosphere of good fellowship : FRIENDLY *syn* **1** see LUCKY *ant* unhappy **2** see FIT *ant* unhappy **3** see GLAD *ant* unhappy, disconsolate

hap·py–go–lucky \ˌhap-ē-gō-ˈlək-ē\ *adj* **:** blithely unconcerned : CAREFREE

happy hunting ground *n* **1 :** the Amerindian paradise to which the souls of warriors and hunters pass after death to spend a happy hereafter in hunting and feasting **2 :** a choice or profitable area of operation or exploitation <junkyards . . . have become *happy hunting grounds* for the man in search of spare parts —G. H. Waltz>

[1]**Haps·burg** \ˈhaps-ˌbərg, ˈhäps-ˌbu̇(ə)rg\ *adj* [*Habsburg,* Aargau, Switzerland] **:** of or relating to a princely German family that reigned in Austria from 1278 to 1918 and in Spain from 1516 to 1700

[2]**Hapsburg** *n* **:** a member of the Hapsburg family; *esp* **:** a Hapsburg monarch

hap·ten \ˈhap-ˌten\ *also* **hap·tene** \-ˌtēn\ *n* [G *hapten*] **:** a substance that does not stimulate antibody formation but reacts selectively in vitro with an antibody; *also* **:** one that in combination with a carrier antigen confers specificity or antigenicity or both — **hap·ten·ic** \hap-ˈten-ik\ *adj*

hap·tic \ˈhap-tik\ *or* **hap·ti·cal** \-ti-kəl\ *adj* [ISV, fr. Gk *haptesthai* to touch] **1 :** relating to or based on the sense of touch **2 :** characterized by a predilection for the sense of touch <a ~ person>

hap·to·glo·bin \ˈhap-tə-ˌglō-bən\ *n* [Gk *haptein* to fasten, bind + E *-o-* + hemo*globin*] **:** a carbohydrate-containing serum alpha globulin that can combine with and may have a protective action toward hemoglobin

hara–kiri \ˌhar-i-ˈkir-ē, -ˈkar-ē\ *n* [Jap *harakiri*] **:** suicide by disembowelment practiced by the Japanese samurai or formerly decreed by a court in lieu of the death penalty

[1]**ha·rangue** \hə-'raŋ\ *n* [ME *arang,* fr. MF *arenge,* fr. OIt *aringa*] **1 :** a speech addressed to a public assembly **2 :** a bombastic ranting speech or writing **3 :** LECTURE

[2]**harangue** *vb* **ha·rangued; ha·rangu·ing** *vi* **:** to make a harangue **:** DECLAIM ~ *vt* **:** to address in a harangue <that lady was still *haranguing* the girl —F. M. Ford> — **ha·rangu·er** *n*

ha·rass \hə-'ras, 'har-əs\ *vt* [F *harasser,* fr. MF, fr. *harer* to set a dog on, fr. OF *hare,* interj. used to incite dogs, of Gmc origin; akin to OHG *hier* here — more at HERE] **1 :** to worry and impede by repeated raids <~*ed* the enemy> **2 a :** EXHAUST, FATIGUE **b :** to annoy persistently ***syn*** see WORRY — **ha·rass·er** *n* — **ha·rass·ment** \-mənt\ *n*

[1]**har·bin·ger** \'här-bən-jər\ *n* [ME *herbergere,* fr. OF, host, fr. *herberge* hostelry, of Gmc origin; akin to OHG *heriberga*] **1** *archaic* **:** a person sent ahead to provide lodgings **2 a :** one that pioneers in or initiates a major change **:** PRECURSOR **b :** something that presages or foreshadows what is to come ***syn*** see FORERUNNER

[2]**harbinger** *vt* **:** to be a harbinger of **:** PRESAGE

[1]**har·bor** \'här-bər\ *n* [ME *herberge;* akin to OHG *heriberga* army encampment, hostelry; both fr. a prehistoric WGmc-NGmc compound whose components are akin respectively to OHG *heri* army and to OHG *bergan* to shelter — more at HARRY, BURY] **1 :** a place of security and comfort **:** REFUGE **2 :** a part of a body of water protected and deep enough to furnish anchorage; *esp* **:** one with port facilities — **har·bor·ful** \-,fu̇l\ *n* — **har·bor·less** \-ləs\ *adj*

[2]**harbor** *vb* **har·bored; har·bor·ing** \-b(ə-)riŋ\ *vt* **1 a (1) :** to give shelter or refuge to **(2) :** to have (an animal) in one's keeping **b :** to be the home or habitat of **:** CONTAIN <the ledges still ~ rattlesnakes> **2 :** to hold a thought or feeling of <~*ed* a grudge> ~ *vi* **1 :** to take shelter in or as if in a harbor **2 a** *of an animal* **:** to rest or hide away esp. habitually **b :** LIVE — **har·bor·er** \-bər-ər\ *n*

har·bor·age \-bə-rij\ *n* **:** SHELTER, HARBOR

harbor master *n* **:** an officer who executes the regulations respecting the use of a harbor

harbor seal *n* **:** a small seal (*Phoca vitulina*) that occurs along north Atlantic coasts and often ascends rivers; *also* **:** a similar seal (*P. richardii*) of the north Pacific coasts

har·bour *chiefly Brit var of* HARBOR

[1]**hard** \'härd\ *adj* [ME, fr. OE *heard;* akin to OHG *hart* hard, Gk *kratos* strength] **1 a :** not easily penetrated **:** not easily yielding to pressure **b** *of cheese* **:** not capable of being spread **:** very firm **2 a** *of liquor* **(1) :** having a harsh or acid taste **(2) :** strongly alcoholic; *specif* **:** having an alcoholic content of more than 22.5 percent **b :** characterized by the presence of salts (as of calcium or magnesium) that prevent lathering with soap <~ water> **3 a :** of or relating to radiation of relatively high penetrating power <~ X rays> **b :** having or producing relatively great photographic contrast <a ~ negative> **4 a :** metallic as distinct from paper <~ money> **b** *of currency* **:** convertible into gold **:** stable in value **c :** being high and firm <~ prices> **5 a :** firmly and closely twisted <~ yarns> **b :** having a smooth close napless finish <a ~ worsted> **6 a :** physically fit <in good ~ condition> **b :** resistant to stress (as disease) **c :** free of weakness or defects **7 a (1) :** FIRM, DEFINITE <reached a ~ agreement> **(2) :** not speculative or conjectural **:** FACTUAL <~ evidence> **b :** CLOSE, SEARCHING <gave a ~ look> **c :** free from sentimentality or illusion **:** REALISTIC <good ~ sense> **d :** lacking in responsiveness **:** OBDURATE, UNFEELING <a ~ heart> **8 a (1) :** difficult to bear or endure <~ luck> <~ times> **(2) :** OPPRESSIVE, INEQUITABLE <sales taxes are ~ on the poor> <a ~ restriction> **b (1) :** lacking consideration, compassion, or gentleness **:** CALLOUS <a ~ greedy landlord> **(2) :** INCORRIGIBLE, TOUGH <a ~ gang> **c (1) :** harsh, severe, or offensive in tendency or effect <said some ~ things> **(2) :** RESENTFUL <~ feelings> **(3) :** STRICT, UNRELENTING <drives a ~ bargain> **d :** INCLEMENT <~ winter> **e (1) :** intense in force, manner, or degree <~ blows> **(2) :** demanding the exertion of energy **:** calling for stamina and endurance <~ work> **(3) :** performing or carrying on with great energy, intensity, or persistence <a ~ worker> **9 a :** characterized by sharp or harsh outline, rigid execution, and stiff drawing **b :** sharply defined **:** STARK <~ shadows> **c :** lacking in shading, delicacy, or resonance <~ singing tones> **d :** sounding as in *arcing* and *geese* respectively — used of *c* and *g* **10 a (1) :** difficult to accomplish or resolve **:** TROUBLESOME <~ problems> **(2) :** difficult to comprehend or explain <a ~ concept> **b :** having difficulty in doing something <~ of hearing> **c :** difficult to magnetize or demagnetize **11 :** being at once addictive and gravely detrimental to health <such ~ drugs as heroin> **12 :** resistant to biodegradation <~ detergents> <~ pesticides like DDT>
syn **1** see FIRM ***ant*** soft
2 HARD, DIFFICULT, ARDUOUS *shared meaning element* **:** demanding toil and effort ***ant*** easy
— **hard up 1 :** short of money **2 :** poorly provided <he was *hard up* for friends>

[2]**hard** *adv* **1 a :** with great or utmost effort or energy **:** STRENUOUSLY <were ~ at work> **b :** in a violent manner **:** FIERCELY **c :** to the full extent — used in nautical directions <steer ~ aport> **d :** in a searching, close, or concentrated manner <stared ~ at him> **2 a :** in such a manner as to cause hardship, difficulty, or pain **:** SEVERELY **b :** with rancor, bitterness, or grief <took his defeat ~> **3 :** in a firm manner **:** TIGHTLY **4 :** to the point of hardness <the water froze ~> **5 :** close in time or space <the house stood ~ by the river>

hard–and–fast \,härd-ᵊn-'fast\ *adj* **:** not to be modified or evaded **:** STRICT <a ~ rule>

hard·back \'härd-,bak\ *n* **:** a book bound in hard covers

hard·ball \-,bȯl\ *n* **:** BASEBALL

hard–bill \-,bil\ *n* **:** any of numerous birds (as a finch) with a hard strong bill adapted to cracking seeds and nuts — compare SOFT-BILL

hard–bit·ten \-'bit-ᵊn\ *adj* **1 :** inclined to bite hard **2 :** seasoned or steeled by difficult experience **:** TOUGH

hard·board \'härd-,bō(ə)rd, -,bȯ(ə)rd\ *n* **:** composition board made by compressing shredded wood chips often with a binder at high temperatures

hard–boil \-'bȯi(ə)l\ *vt* [back-formation fr. *hard-boiled*] **:** to cook (an egg) in the shell until both white and yolk have solidified

hard–boiled \-'bȯi(ə)ld\ *adj* **1 :** devoid of sentimentality **:** TOUGH <a ~ drill sergeant> **2 :** HARDHEADED, PRACTICAL <handle aid programs on a friendly but ~ business basis —*N.Y. Times*>

hard·boot \-,büt\ *n* **:** HORSEMAN <Kentucky ~*s* . . . had picked the right horse —*Time*>

hard·bound \-,bau̇nd\ *adj* **:** having rigid boards on the sides covered in cloth or paper <a ~ book> — **hardbound** *n*

hard candy *n* **:** a candy made of sugar and corn syrup boiled without crystallizing and usu. fruit-flavored

hard·case \'härd-'kās\ *adj* **:** HARD-BITTEN, TOUGH <the keen, eye-puckered, ~ seamen, silent, lean —John Masefield>

hard case \-,kās\ *n* **:** a tough or hardened person

hard cider *n* **:** fermented apple juice containing usu. less than 10 percent alcohol

hard clam *n* **:** a clam with a thick hard shell; *specif* **:** QUAHOG

hard coal *n* **:** ANTHRACITE

hard–coat·ed \'härd-'kōt-əd\ *adj, of a dog* **:** having a crisp harsh-textured coat

hard copy *n* **:** copy (as produced in connection with a computer or produced from microfilm) that is readable without the use of a special device

hard–core \-'kō(ə)r\ *adj* **1 :** of, relating to, or being persons whose economic position and educational background are substandard and who experience chronic unemployment <the ~ unemployed> **2** *of pornography* **:** being extremely graphic in presentation

hard·cov·er \'härd-'kəv-ər\ *adj* **:** HARDBOUND

hard–edge \'härd-'ej\ *adj* **:** of or relating to abstract painting characterized by geometric forms with clearly defined boundaries

hard·en \'härd-ᵊn\ *vb* **hard·ened; hard·en·ing** \'härd-niŋ, -ᵊn-iŋ\ *vt* **1 :** to make hard or harder **:** INDURATE **2 :** to confirm in disposition, feelings, or action; *esp* **:** to make callous <~*ed* his heart> **3 a :** INURE, TOUGHEN <~ troops> **b :** to inure to cold or other unfavorable environmental conditions — often used with *off* <*harden* off half-hardy annual plants> **4 :** to protect from possible danger from blast or heat with concrete or earth or by situating underground <~ a missile emplacement> ~ *vi* **1 :** to become hard or harder **2 a :** to become confirmed or strengthened <opposition began to ~> **b :** to assume an appearance of harshness or severity <her face ~*ed* at the word> **3 :** to become higher or less subject to fluctuations downward <prices ~*ed* quickly>

hard·en·er \'härd-nər, -ᵊn-ər\ *n* **:** one that hardens; *esp* **:** a substance added (as to a paint or varnish) to harden the film

hard·en·ing *n* **1 :** something that hardens **2 :** SCLEROSIS <~ of the arteries>

hard·fist·ed \'härd-'fis-təd\ *adj* **1 :** HARDHANDED **2 :** STINGY, CLOSEFISTED

hard goods *n pl* **:** DURABLES

hard·hack \'härd-,hak\ *n* **:** a shrubby American spirea (*Spiraea tomentosa*) with rusty hairy leaves and dense terminal panicles of pink or occas. white flowers

hard·hand·ed \-'han-dəd\ *adj* **1 :** having hands made hard by labor **2 :** STRICT, OPPRESSIVE — **hard·hand·ed·ness** *n*

hard hat *usu* -'hat *for 1 and* -,hat *for 2 & 3*\ *n* **1 :** a protective hat made of rigid material (as metal or fiberglass) and worn esp. by construction workers **2 :** a construction worker **3 :** SUPERPATRIOT

hard·head \'härd-,hed\ *n* **1 a :** a hardheaded person **b :** BLOCKHEAD **2 a :** any of several fishes esp. with a spiny or bony head; *esp* **:** ATLANTIC CROAKER **b :** any of several ducks **3 :** any of several knapweeds (esp. *Centaurea nigra*) — usu. used in pl. but sing. or pl. in constr.

hard·head·ed \-'hed-əd\ *adj* **1 :** STUBBORN, WILLFUL **2 :** SOBER, REALISTIC <~ common sense> — **hard·head·ed·ly** *adv* — **hard·head·ed·ness** *n*

hardhead sponge *n* **:** any of several commercial sponges of the West Indies and Central America with a harsh but elastic fiber

hard·heart·ed \'härd-'härt-əd\ *adj* **:** lacking in sympathetic understanding **:** UNFEELING, PITILESS — **hard·heart·ed·ly** *adv* — **hard·heart·ed·ness** *n*

hard–hit·ting \-'hit-iŋ\ *adj* **:** VIGOROUS, EFFECTIVE <a ~ series of articles>

har·di·hood \'härd-ē-,hu̇d\ *n* **1 a :** resolute courage and fortitude **b :** resolute and self-assured audacity often carried to the point of impudent insolence **2 :** VIGOR, ROBUSTNESS ***syn*** see TEMERITY

har·di·ment \-mənt\ *n* [ME, fr. MF, fr. OF, fr. *hardi* bold, hardy] **1** *archaic* **:** HARDIHOOD **2** *obs* **:** a bold deed

har·ding·grass \'härd-iŋ-,gras\ *n, often cap* [prob. fr. the name *Harding*] **:** a perennial grass (*Phalaris tuberosa stenoptera*) of Australia and southern Africa introduced into No. America as a forage grass

hard labor *n* **:** compulsory labor of imprisoned criminals as a part of the prison discipline

hard–line \'härd-'līn\ *adj* **:** advocating or involving a persistently firm course of action **:** UNYIELDING <a ~ policy toward polluters> — **hard–lin·er** \-'lī-nər\ *n*

hard lines *n pl, chiefly Brit* **:** hard luck

hard·ly \'härd-lē\ *adv* **1 :** with force **:** VIGOROUSLY **2 :** in a severe manner **:** HARSHLY **3 :** with difficulty **:** PAINFULLY **4 :** only just **:** BARELY <I ~ knew her> **5 :** certainly not <that news is ~ surprising>

hardly ever *adv* **:** almost never **:** very seldom <we *hardly ever* see them anymore>

hard maple *n* **:** SUGAR MAPLE

hard·mouthed \'härd-'mau̇thd, -'mau̇tht\ *adj* **1** *of an animal* **:** not responding satisfactorily to pressure (as of a bit) on the mouth **2 :** OBSTINATE, STUBBORN <~ women who laid down the law —John Galsworthy>

hard·ness *n* **1 :** the quality or state of being hard **2 :** the cohesion of the particles on the surface of a mineral as determined by its capacity to scratch another or be itself scratched — compare MOHS' SCALE

hard–nosed \ˈhärd-ˈnōzd\ *adj* **1 :** HARD-BITTEN, STUBBORN **2 :** HARDHEADED 2 <~ budgeting>

hard–of–hear·ing \ˌhärd-ə(v)-ˈhi(ə)r-iŋ\ *adj* **:** of or relating to a defective but functional sense of hearing

hard–on \ˈhärd-ˌȯn, -ˌän\ *n, pl* **hard–ons :** an erection of the penis — usu. considered vulgar

hard palate *n* **:** the bony anterior part of the palate forming the roof of the mouth

hard·pan \ˈhärd-ˌpan\ *n* **1 :** a cemented or compacted and often clayey layer in soil that is impenetrable by roots **2 :** a fundamental part **:** BEDROCK

hard pine *n* **:** a pine (as longleaf pine or pitch pine) that has hard wood and leaves usu. in groups of two or three; *also* **:** the wood of a hard pine

hard put *adj* **:** barely able **:** faced with difficulty or perplexity <was *hard put* to find an explanation>

hard rock *n* **:** basic rock music played in its original style

hard rubber *n* **:** a firm rubber or rubber product; *esp* **:** a normally black horny substance made by vulcanizing natural rubber with high percentages of sulfur

hard sauce *n* **:** a creamed mixture of butter and powdered sugar often with added cream and flavoring (as vanilla or rum)

hard·scrab·ble \ˈhärd-ˌskrab-əl\ *adj* **:** yielding or gaining a meager living by great labor <~ farms>

hard sell *n* **:** aggressive high-pressure salesmanship — compare SOFT SELL

hard–set \ˈhärd-ˈset\ *adj* **:** RIGID, FIXED

hard–shell \-ˌshel\ *adj* **:** UNCOMPROMISING, CONFIRMED <a ~ conservative>

hard–shell clam \ˌhärd-ˌshel-\ *n* **:** QUAHOG —called also *hard-shelled clam*

hard–shell crab *n* **:** a crab that has not recently shed its shell — called also *hard-shelled crab*

hard·ship \ˈhärd-ˌship\ *n* **1 :** SUFFERING, PRIVATION **2 :** something that causes or entails suffering or privation ***syn*** see DIFFICULTY

hard·stand \-ˌstand\ *n* **:** a hard-surfaced area for parking an airplane

hard·stand·ing \-ˌstan-diŋ\ *n* **:** HARDSTAND

hard–sur·face \-ˈsər-fəs\ *vt* **:** to provide with a paved surface

hard·tack \-ˌtak\ *n* **1 :** a saltless hard biscuit or bread made of flour and water **2 :** any of several mountain mahoganies

hard·top \-ˌtäp\ *n* **:** an automobile styled to resemble a convertible in lacking a center post between front and rear windows but having a permanent rigid top

hard·ware \ˈhär-ˌdwa(ə)r, -ˌdwe(ə)r\ *n* **1 :** ware (as fittings, cutlery, tools, utensils, or parts of machines) made of metal **2 :** major items of military or police equipment or their components **3 :** the physical components (as electronic and electrical devices) of a vehicle (as a spacecraft) or an apparatus (as a computer) **4 :** devices (as tape recorders, phonographs, or closed-circuit television) used as instructional equipment <educational ~>

hard wheat *n* **:** a wheat with hard flinty kernels that are high in gluten and that yield a strong flour esp. suitable for bread and macaroni

¹hard·wood \ˈhär-ˌdwu̇d\ *n* **1 :** the wood of an angiospermous tree as distinguished from that of a coniferous tree **2 :** a tree that yields hardwood

²hardwood *adj* **1 :** having or made of hardwood <~ floors> **2 :** consisting of mature woody tissue <~ cuttings>

hard–wood·ed \ˈhär-ˈdwu̇d-əd\ *adj* **1 :** having hard wood that is difficult to work or finish **2 :** HARDWOOD 1

hard·work·ing \ˈhär-ˈdwər-kiŋ\ *adj* **:** INDUSTRIOUS

har·dy \ˈhärd-ē\ *adj* **har·di·er; -est** [ME *hardi,* fr. OF, fr. (assumed) OF *hardir* to make hard, of Gmc origin; akin to OE *heard* hard] **1 :** BOLD, BRAVE **2 :** AUDACIOUS, BRAZEN **3 a :** inured to fatigue or hardships **:** ROBUST **b :** capable of living outdoors over winter without artificial protection or of withstanding other adverse conditions <~ plants> <~ cattle> — **har·di·ly** \ˈhärd-ᵊl-ē\ *adv* — **har·di·ness** \ˈhärd-ē-nəs\ *n*

Har·dy–Wein·berg law \ˌhärd-ē-ˈwīn-ˌbərg-\ *n* [G. H. *Hardy* †1947 E mathematician and W. *Weinberg,* 20th cent. G scientist] **:** a fundamental principle of population genetics: population gene frequencies remain constant from generation to generation if mating is random and if mutation, selection, immigration, and emigration do not occur — called also *Hardy-Weinberg principle*

¹hare \ˈha(ə)r, ˈhe(ə)r\ *n, pl* **hare** *or* **hares** [ME, fr. OE *hara;* akin to OHG *haso* hare, L *canus* hoary, gray] **:** any of various swift timid long-eared mammals (order Lagomorpha and esp. genus *Lepus*) having a divided upper lip, long hind legs, a short cocked tail, and the young open-eyed and furred at birth

²hare *vi* **hared; har·ing :** RUN

hare and hounds *n* **:** a game in which some of the players scatter bits of paper for a trail and others try to find and catch them

hare·bell \ˈha(ə)r-ˌbel, ˈhe(ə)r-\ *n* **1 :** a slender blue-flowered herb (*Campanula rotundifolia*) with linear leaves on the stem **2 :** WOOD HYACINTH

hare·brained \-ˈbrānd\ *adj* **:** FLIGHTY, FOOLISH

hare·lip \-ˈlip\ *n* **:** a congenital deformity in which the upper lip is split like that of a hare — **hare·lipped** \-ˈlipt\ *adj*

har·em \ˈhar-əm, ˈher-\ *n* [Ar *ḥarīm,* lit., something forbidden & *ḥaram,* lit., sanctuary] **1 a :** a usu. secluded house or part of a house allotted to women in a Muslim household **b :** the wives, concubines, female relatives, and servants occupying a harem **2 :** a group of women associated with one man **3 :** a group of females associated with one male — used of polygamous animals

ha·ri·a·na \ˌhar-ē-ˈan-ə, ˌhär-ē-ˈän-ə\ *n, often cap* [*Hariana,* India] **:** any of an Indian breed of large rugged milk and draft cattle included among the Brahmans in American studbooks

har·i·cot \ˈ(h)ar-i-ˌkō\ *n* [F]**:** the ripe seed or the unripe pod of any of several beans (genus *Phaseolus* and esp. *P. vulgaris*)

ha·ri·jan \ˌhär-i-ˈjän\ *n, often cap* [Skt *harijana* one belonging to the god Vishnu, fr. *Hari* Vishnu + *jana* person] **:** a member of the outcaste group in India **:** UNTOUCHABLE

hari–kari \ˌhar-i-ˈkar-ē, -ˈkir-\ *var of* HARA-KIRI

hark \ˈhärk\ *vi* [ME *herken;* akin to OHG *hōrechen* to listen] **:** to pay close attention **:** LISTEN

hark back *vi* **:** to turn back to an earlier topic or circumstance

harken *var of* HEARKEN

har·le·quin \ˈhär-li-k(w)ən\ *n* [It *arlecchino,* fr. MF *Helquin,* a demon] **1 a** *cap* **:** a character in comedy and pantomime with a shaved head, masked face, variegated tights, and wooden sword **b :** BUFFOON **2 a :** a variegated pattern (as of a textile) **b :** a combination of colors in patches on a solid ground (as in the coats of some dogs)

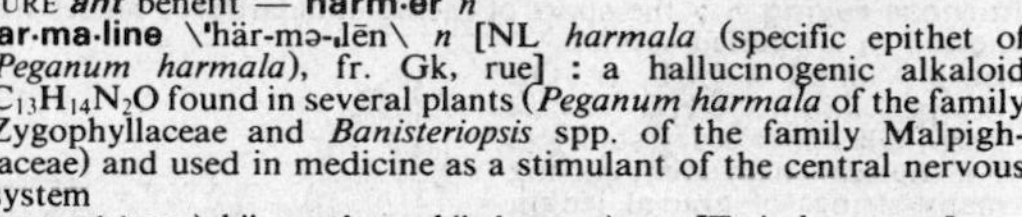

Harlequin

har·le·quin·ade \ˌhär-li-k(w)ə-ˈnād\ *n* **:** a play or pantomime in which Harlequin has a leading role

har·lot \ˈhär-lət\ *n* [ME, fr. OF *herlot* rogue] **:** PROSTITUTE

har·lot·ry \-lə-trē\ *n, pl* **-ries 1 :** sexual profligacy **:** PROSTITUTION **2 :** an unprincipled or immoral woman <he sups tonight with a ~ —Shak.>

¹harm \ˈhärm\ *n* [ME, fr. OE *hearm;* akin to OHG *harm* injury, OSlav *sramŭ* shame] **1 :** physical or mental damage **:** INJURY **2 :** MISCHIEF, HURT

²harm *vt* **:** to cause harm to ***syn*** see INJURE ***ant*** benefit — **harm·er** *n*

har·ma·line \ˈhär-mə-ˌlēn\ *n* [NL *harmala* (specific epithet of *Peganum harmala*), fr. Gk, rue] **:** a hallucinogenic alkaloid $C_{13}H_{14}N_2O$ found in several plants (*Peganum harmala* of the family Zygophyllaceae and *Banisteriopsis* spp. of the family Malpighiaceae) and used in medicine as a stimulant of the central nervous system

har·mat·tan \ˌhär-mə-ˈtan, här-ˈmat-ᵊn\ *n* [Twi *haramata*] **:** a dust-laden wind on the Atlantic coast of Africa in some seasons

harm·ful \ˈhärm-fəl\ *adj* **:** of a kind likely to be damaging **:** INJURIOUS — **harm·ful·ly** \-fə-lē\ *adv* — **harm·ful·ness** *n*

har·mine \ˈhär-ˌmēn\ *n* [NL *harmala* + E *-ine*] **:** a hallucinogenic alkaloid $C_{13}H_{12}N_2O$ whose distribution in plants and use in medicine is similar to harmaline

harm·less \ˈhärm-ləs\ *adj* **1 :** free from harm, liability, or loss **2 :** lacking capacity or intent to injure **:** INNOCUOUS— **harm·less·ly** *adv* — **harm·less·ness** *n*

¹har·mon·ic \här-ˈmän-ik\ *adj* **1 :** MUSICAL **2 :** of or relating to musical harmony, a harmonic, or harmonics **3 :** pleasing to the ear **:** HARMONIOUS **4 :** expressible in terms of sine or cosine functions <~ function> **5 :** of an integrated nature **:** CONGRUOUS — **har·mon·i·cal** \-i-kəl\ *adj* — **har·mon·i·cal·ly** \-i-k(ə-)lē\ *adv* — **har·mon·i·cal·ness** \-i-kəl-nəs\ *n*

²harmonic *n* **1 a :** OVERTONE; *esp* **:** one whose vibration frequency is an integral multiple of that of the fundamental **b :** a flutelike tone produced on a stringed instrument by touching a vibrating string at a nodal point **2 :** a component frequency of a harmonic motion (as of an electromagnetic wave) that is an integral multiple of the fundamental frequency

har·mon·i·ca \här-ˈmän-i-kə\ *n* [It *armonica,* fem. of *armonico* harmonious] **1 :** a musical instrument consisting of a series of hemispherical glasses played by touching the edges with a dampened finger **2 :** a small rectangular wind instrument with free reeds recessed in air slots from which tones are sounded by exhaling and inhaling

harmonic analysis *n* **:** the expression of a periodic function as a sum of sines and cosines and specif. by means of a Fourier series

harmonic mean *n* **:** the reciprocal of the arithmetic mean of the reciprocals of a finite set of numbers

harmonic motion *n* **:** a periodic motion (as of a sounding violin string or swinging pendulum) that has a single frequency or amplitude or a periodic motion that is composed of two or more such simple periodic motions

harmonic progression *n* **:** a progression the reciprocals of whose terms form an arithmetic progression

har·mon·ics \här-ˈmän-iks\ *n* **:** the study of the physical characteristics of musical sounds

harmonic series *n* **:** a series of the form $1 + \frac{1}{2^\alpha} + \frac{1}{3^\alpha} + \frac{1}{4^\alpha} \ldots$ which diverges for $0 \leq \alpha \leq 1$ and converges for $\alpha > 1$

har·mo·ni·ous \här-ˈmō-nē-əs\ *adj* **1 :** musically concordant **2 :** having the parts agreeably related **:** CONGRUOUS <the flowers blended into a ~ whole> **3 :** marked by accord in sentiment or action — **har·mo·ni·ous·ly** *adv* — **har·mo·ni·ous·ness** *n*

har·mo·nist \ˈhär-mə-nəst\ *n* **:** one who harmonizes or is skilled in musical harmony; *esp* **:** one who composes or performs music — **har·mo·nis·tic** \ˌhär-mə-ˈnis-tik\ *adj* — **har·mo·nis·ti·cal·ly** \-ti-k(ə-)lē\ *adv*

har·mo·ni·um \här-ˈmō-nē-əm\ *n* [F, fr. MF *harmonie, armonie*] **:** REED ORGAN

har·mo·nize \ˈhär-mə-ˌnīz\ *vb* **-nized; -niz·ing** *vi* **1 :** to play or sing in harmony **2 :** to be in harmony ~ *vt* **1 :** to bring into

ə abut	ᵊ kitten	ər further	a back	ā bake	ä cot, cart
au̇ out	ch chin	e less	ē easy	g gift	i trip	ī life
j joke	ŋ sing	ō flow	ȯ flaw	ȯi coin	th thin	t͟h this
ü loot	u̇ foot	y yet	yü few	yu̇ furious	zh vision

consonance or accord **2 :** to provide or accompany with harmony *syn* see AGREE *ant* clash, conflict — **har·mo·ni·za·tion** \ˌhär-mə-nə-ˈzā-shən\ *n* — **har·mo·niz·er** \ˈhär-mə-ˌnī-zər\ *n*

har·mo·ny \ˈhär-mə-nē\ *n, pl* **-nies** [ME *armony,* fr. MF *armonie,* fr. L *harmonia,* fr. Gk, joint, harmony, fr. *harmos* joint — more at ARM] **1** *archaic* **:** tuneful sound **:** MELODY **2 a :** the combination of simultaneous musical notes in a chord **b :** the structure of music with respect to the composition and progression of chords **c :** the science of the structure, relation, and progression of chords **3 a :** pleasing or congruent arrangement of parts <a painting exhibiting ~ of color and line> **b :** CORRESPONDENCE, ACCORD <lives in ~ with her neighbors> **c :** internal calm **:** TRANQUILLITY **4 a :** an interweaving of different accounts into a single narrative **b :** a systematic arrangement of parallel literary passages (as of the Gospels) for the purpose of showing agreement or harmony

har·mo·tome \ˈhär-mə-ˌtōm\ *n* [F, fr. Gk *harmos* + *tomē* section, fr. *temnein* to cut — more at TOME] **:** a mineral $(Ba,K)(Al,Si)_2Si_6O_{16}.6H_2O$ consisting of a hydrous silicate of aluminum, barium, and potassium

[1]**har·ness** \ˈhär-nəs\ *n* [ME *herneis* baggage, gear, fr. OF] **1 a :** the gear other than a yoke of a draft animal **b :** GEAR, EQUIPMENT; *esp* **:** military equipment for a horse or man **2 a :** occupational surroundings or routine <get back into ~ after a vacation> **b :** close association <ability to work in ~ with others —R. P. Brooks> **3 a :** something that resembles a harness (as in holding or fastening something) <a parachute ~> <an automobile rider's shoulder ~> **b :** prefabricated wiring with insulation and terminals ready to be attached **4 :** a part of a loom which holds and controls the heddles

[2]**harness** *vt* **1 a :** to put a harness on **b :** to attach by means of a harness **2 :** to tie together **:** YOKE **3 :** UTILIZE <~ nuclear energy>

harness horse *n* **:** a horse for racing or working in harness

harness racing *n* **:** the sport of racing standardbred horses harnessed to 2-wheeled sulkies

[1]**harp** \ˈhärp\ *n* [ME, fr. OE *hearpe;* akin to OHG *harpha* harp, Gk *karphos* dry stalk] **1 :** a musical instrument having many strings of graded length stretched across an open triangular frame with a curving top and played by plucking with the fingers **2 :** something that resembles a harp **3 :** HARMONICA 2 — **harp·ist** \ˈhär-pəst\ *n*

harps: *1* modern orchestra harp, *2* medieval harp

[2]**harp** *vi* **1 :** to play on a harp **2 :** to dwell on or recur to a subject tiresomely or monotonously

harp·er \ˈhär-pər\ *n* **1 :** a harp player **2 :** one that harps

har·poon \här-ˈpün\ *n* [prob. fr. D *harpoen,* fr. OF *harpon* brooch, fr. *harper* to grapple] **:** a barbed spear or javelin used esp. in hunting large fish or whales — **harpoon** *vt* — **har·poon·er** *n*

harp·si·chord \ˈhärp-si-ˌkȯ(ə)rd\ *n* [modif. of It *arpicordo,* fr. *arpa* harp + *corda* string] **:** a stringed instrument resembling a grand piano but usu. having two keyboards and two or more strings for each note and producing tones by the plucking of strings with quills or leather points — **harp·si·chord·ist** \-ˌkȯrd-əst\ *n*

har·py \ˈhär-pē\ *n, pl* **harpies** [L *Harpyia,* fr. Gk] **1** *cap* **:** a foul malign creature of Greek mythology that is part woman and part bird **2 a :** a predatory person **:** LEECH **b :** a shrewish woman

har·que·bus \ˈhär-kwi-(ˌ)bəs, -kə-bəs\ *n* [MF *harquebuse, arquebuse*]**:** a matchlock gun invented in the 15th century which was portable but heavy and was usu. fired from a support — **har·que·bus·ier** \ˌhär-kwi-(ˌ)bə-ˈsi(ə)r, -kə-bə-\ *n*

har·ri·dan \ˈhar-əd-ᵊn\ *n* [perh. modif. of F *haridelle* old horse, gaunt woman] **:** SHREW 2

har·ried \ˈhar-ēd\ *adj* **:** beset by disturbing problems **:** HARASSED <a . . . ~ journalist trying to produce a maximum of copy —Edmund Wilson>

[1]**har·ri·er** \ˈhar-ē-ər\ *n* [irreg. fr. [1]*hare*] **1 :** a hunting dog that resembles a small foxhound and is used esp. for hunting rabbits **2 :** a runner on a cross-country team

[2]**harrier** *n* **1 :** one that harries **2** [alter. of *harrower,* fr. [1]*harrow*] **:** any of various slender hawks (genus *Circus*) with long angled wings and long legs that feed chiefly on small mammals, reptiles, and insects

[1]**har·row** \ˈhar-(ˌ)ō, -ə(-w)\ *vt* [ME *harwen,* fr. OE *hergian*] *archaic* **:** PILLAGE, PLUNDER

[2]**harrow** *n* [ME *harwe*] **:** a cultivating implement set with spikes, spring teeth, or disks and used primarily for pulverizing and smoothing the soil

[3]**harrow** *vt* **1 :** to cultivate with a harrow **2 :** TORMENT, VEX — **har·row·er** \ˈhar-ə-wər\ *n*

har·ry \ˈhar-ē\ *vt* **har·ried; har·ry·ing** [ME *harien,* fr. OE *hergian;* akin to OHG *heriōn* to lay waste, *heri* army, Gk *koiranos* commander] **1 :** to make a pillaging or destructive raid on **:** ASSAULT **2 :** to force (a person) to move along <saga of migratory laborers *harried* across the continent —J. D. Hart> **3 :** to torment by or as if by constant attack *syn* see WORRY

harsh \ˈhärsh\ *adj* [ME *harsk,* of Scand origin; akin to Norw *harsk* harsh] **1 :** having a coarse uneven surface that is rough to the touch **2 :** causing a disagreeable or painful sensory reaction **:** IRRITATING **3 :** unduly exacting **:** SEVERE **4 :** lacking in aesthetic appeal or refinement **:** CRUDE *syn* see ROUGH — **harsh·ly** *adv* — **harsh·ness** *n*

harsh·en \ˈhär-shən\ *vb* **harsh·ened; harsh·en·ing** \-sh(ə-)niŋ\ *vt* **:** to make (as a voice) harsh ~ *vi* **:** to become harsh <saw the grain of his skin ~*ing* over face bones —Elizabeth Bowen>

hart \ˈhärt\ *n* [ME *hert,* fr. OE *heort;* akin to L *cervus* hart, Gk *keras* horn — more at HORN] *chiefly Brit* **:** the male of the red deer esp. when over five years old **:** STAG — compare HIND

harte·beest \ˈhärt-(ə-)ˌbēst\ *n* [obs. Afrik (now *hartbees*), fr. D, fr. *hart* deer + *beest* beast] **:** a large African antelope (*Alcelaphus caama*) with annulate divergent horns

hartebeest

harts·horn \ˈhärts-ˌhȯ(ə)rn\ *n* [fr. the earlier use of hart's horns as the chief source of ammonia] **:** a preparation of ammonia used as smelling salts

har·um–scar·um \ˌhar-əm-ˈskar-əm, ˌher-əm-ˈsker-\ *adj* [perh. alter. of *helter-skelter*] **:** RECKLESS, IRRESPONSIBLE — **harum–scarum** *adv*

ha·rus·pex \hə-ˈrəs-ˌpeks, ˈhar-əs-\ *n, pl* **ha·rus·pi·ces** \hə-ˈrəs-pə-ˌsēz\ [L] **:** a diviner in ancient Rome basing his predictions on inspection of the entrails of sacrificial animals

[1]**har·vest** \ˈhär-vəst\ *n, often attrib* [ME *hervest,* fr. OE *hærfest;* akin to L *carpere* to pluck, gather, Gk *karpos* fruit, *keirein* to cut — more at SHEAR] **1 :** the season for gathering in agricultural crops **2 :** the act or process of gathering in a crop **3 a :** a mature crop (as of grain or fruit) **:** YIELD **b :** the quantity of a natural product gathered in a single season **4 :** the product or reward of exertion

[2]**harvest** *vt* **1 a :** to gather in (a crop) **:** REAP **b :** to gather (a natural product) as if by harvesting **2 :** to win by achievement <the team ~*ed* several awards> ~ *vi* **:** to gather in a food crop — **har·vest·able** \-və-stə-bəl\ *adj* — **har·vest·er** *n*

harvest fly *n* **:** CICADA

harvest home *n* **1 :** the gathering or the time of harvest **2 :** a feast at the close of harvest **3 :** a song sung by the reapers at the close of the harvest

har·vest·man \ˈhär-vəs(t)-mən\ *n* **:** an arachnid (order Phalangida) that superficially resembles a true spider but has a small rounded body and very long slender legs — called also *daddy longlegs*

harvest mite *n* **:** CHIGGER 2

harvest moon *n* **:** the full moon nearest the time of the September equinox

har·vest·time \ˈhär-vəs(t)-ˌtīm\ *n* **:** the time during which an annual crop (as wheat) is harvested

has *pres 3d sing of* HAVE

has–been \ˈhaz-ˌbin, *chiefly Brit* -ˌbēn\ *n* **:** one that has passed the peak of effectiveness or popularity <a seedy ~ of an actor traveling a comeback trail —Gordon Allison>

ha·sen·pfef·fer \ˈhäz-ᵊn-ˌ(p)fef-ər\ *n* [G, fr. *hase* hare + *pfeffer* pepper] **:** a highly seasoned stew made of marinated rabbit meat

[1]**hash** \ˈhash\ *vt* [F *hacher,* fr. OF *hachier,* fr. *hache* battle-ax, of Gmc origin; akin to OHG *hāppa* sickle; akin to Gk *koptein* to cut — more at CAPON] **1 a :** to chop (as meat and potatoes) into small pieces **b :** CONFUSE, MUDDLE **2 :** to talk about **:** REVIEW

[2]**hash** *n* **1 :** chopped food; *specif* **:** chopped meat mixed with potatoes and browned **2 :** a restatement of something that is already known **3 :** HODGEPODGE, JUMBLE

[3]**hash** *n* **:** HASHISH

Hash·im·ite *or* **Hash·em·ite** \ˈhash-ə-ˌmīt\ *n* [*Hashim,* great-grandfather of Muhammad] **:** a member of an Arab family having common ancestry with Muhammad and founding dynasties in countries of the eastern Mediterranean

hash·ish \ˈhash-ˌēsh, -(ˌ)ish\ *n* [Ar *hashīsh*] **:** the unadulterated resin from the flowering tops of the female hemp plant (*Cannabis sativa*) that is smoked, chewed, or drunk for its intoxicating effect — called also *charas;* compare BHANG, MARIJUANA

hash mark *n* **1 :** SERVICE STRIPE **2 :** INBOUNDS LINE

Ha·sid \ˈhas-əd, ˈkäs-\ *n, pl* **Ha·si·dim** \ˈhas-əd-əm, k̲ä-ˈsēd-\ [Heb *hāsīdh* pious] **1 :** a member of a Jewish sect of the second century B.C. opposed to Hellenism and devoted to the strict observance of the ritual law **2** *also* **Has·sid :** a member of a Jewish mystical sect founded in Poland about 1750 in opposition to rationalism and ritual laxity — **Ha·sid·ic** \ha-ˈsid-ik, hä-, k̲ä-\ *adj*

Ha·si·dism \ˈhas-ə-ˌdiz-əm, ˈhäs-, ˈkäs-\ *n* **1 :** the practices and beliefs of the Hasidim **2 :** the Hasidic movement

Has·mo·nae·an *or* **Has·mo·ne·an** \ˌhaz-mə-ˈnē-ən\ *n* [LL *Asmonaeus* Hasmon, ancestor of the Maccabees, fr. Gk *Asamōnaios*] **:** a member of the Maccabees — **Hasmonaean** *or* **Hasmonean** *adj*

hasn't \ˈhaz-ᵊnt\ **:** has not

hasp \ˈhasp\ *n* [ME, fr. OE *hæsp;* akin to MHG *haspe* hasp] **:** any of several devices for fastening; *esp* **:** a fastener esp. for a door or lid consisting of a hinged metal strap that fits over a staple and is secured by a pin or padlock — **hasp** *vt*

hasp

[1]**has·sle** \ˈhas-əl\ *n* [perh. fr. [2]*haggle* + [2]*tussle*] **1 :** a heated often protracted argument **:** WRANGLE **2 :** a violent skirmish **:** FIGHT **3 a :** a state of confusion **:** TURMOIL **b :** a strenuous effort **:** STRUGGLE

[2]**hassle** *vb* **has·sled; has·sling** \-(ə-)liŋ\ *vi* **:** ARGUE, FIGHT <*hassled* with the umpire> ~ *vt* **:** BOTHER, CHALLENGE <he gets *hassled* in the street because he dresses funny —William Kloman>

has·sock \ˈhas-ək\ *n* [ME, sedge, fr. OE *hassuc*] **1 :** TUSSOCK **2 a :** a cushion for kneeling <a church ~> **b :** a padded cushion or low stool that serves as a seat or leg rest

hast \(ˈ)hast, (h)əst\ *archaic pres 2d sing of* HAVE

has·tate \ˈhas-ˌtāt\ *adj* [NL *hastatus,* fr. L *hasta* spear — more at YARD] **1 :** triangular with sharp basal lobes spreading away from the base of the petiole <~ leaves> **2 :** shaped like a spear or the head of a spear <a ~ spot of a bird> — **has·tate·ly** *adv*

[1]**haste** \ˈhāst\ *n* [ME, fr. OF, of Gmc origin; akin to OE *hǣst* violence] **1 :** rapidity of motion : SWIFTNESS **2 :** rash or headlong action : PRECIPITATENESS <the beauty of speed uncontaminated by ~ —*Harper's*> **3 :** undue eagerness to act

syn HASTE, HURRY, SPEED, EXPEDITION, DISPATCH *shared meaning element* : quickness in movement or action. HASTE implies urgency or precipitancy in persons <out of breath from *haste* —Jane Austen> and may suggest rashness or carelessness <*haste* makes waste> HURRY, often interchangeable with *haste*, can carry a stronger implication of agitated bustle or confusion <in the *hurry* of departure she forgot her toothbrush> SPEED suggests swift efficiency in movement or action <the more haste, the less *speed* —*Old Proverb*> *Expedition* and *dispatch* are close to speed especially in application to business or affairs, but EXPEDITION is likely to stress efficiency in performance, and DISPATCH promptness in bringing matters to a conclusion <put her things on with remarkable *expedition* —Arnold Bennett> <there was no task in all the household . . . which her mistress could not do far better and with more *dispatch* than she —Thomas Wolfe> *ant* deliberation

[2]**haste** *vb* **hast·ed; hast·ing** *vt, archaic* : to urge on : HASTEN ~ *vi* : to move or act swiftly

has·ten \ˈhās-ᵊn\ *vb* **has·tened; has·ten·ing** \ˈhās-niŋ, -ᵊn-iŋ\ *vt* **1 :** to urge on <~*ed* her to the door —A. J. Cronin> **2 :** ACCELERATE <~ the coming of a new order —D. W. Brogan> ~ *vi* : to move or act quickly — **has·ten·er** \ˈhās-nər, -ᵊn-ər\ *n*

hast·i·ly \ˈhā-stə-lē\ *adv* : in haste : HURRIEDLY

hasty \ˈhā-stē\ *adj* **hast·i·er; -est** **1 a** *archaic* : rapid in action or movement : SPEEDY **b :** done or made in a hurry **c :** fast and typically superficial <made a ~ examination of the wound> **2 :** EAGER, IMPATIENT **3 :** PRECIPITATE, RASH **4 :** prone to anger : IRRITABLE *syn* see FAST — **hast·i·ness** *n*

hasty pudding *n* **1** *Brit* : a porridge of oatmeal or flour boiled in water **2** *NewEng* : cornmeal mush

[1]**hat** \ˈhat\ *n* [ME, fr. OE *hæt*; akin to OHG *huot* head covering — more at HOOD] **1 :** a covering for the head usu. having a shaped crown and brim **2 a :** a distinctive head covering worn as a symbol of office **b :** OFFICE, POSITION — **hat·less** \-ləs\ *adj*

[2]**hat** *vb* **hat·ted; hat·ting** *vt* : to furnish or provide with a hat ~ *vi* : to make or supply hats

hat·band \ˈhat-ˌband\ *n* : a band (as of fabric, leather, or cord) around the crown of a hat just above the brim

hat·box \-ˌbäks\ *n* **1 :** a box for holding or storing a hat **2 :** a usu. round piece of luggage designed esp. for carrying hats

[1]**hatch** \ˈhach\ *n* [ME *hache*, fr. OE *hæc*; akin to MD *hecke* trapdoor] **1 :** a small door or opening (as in an airplane) <an escape ~> **2 a :** an opening in the deck of a ship or in the floor or roof of a building **b :** the covering for such an opening **c :** HATCHWAY **d :** COMPARTMENT **3 :** FLOODGATE

[2]**hatch** *vb* [ME *hacchen*; akin to MHG *hecken* to mate] *vi* **1 :** to produce young by incubation **2 :** to emerge from an egg or pupa **3 :** to incubate eggs : BROOD ~ *vt* **1 :** to produce (young) from an egg by applying natural or artificial heat : INCUBATE **2 :** to bring into being : ORIGINATE; *esp* : to concoct in secret — **hatch·abil·i·ty** \ˌhach-ə-ˈbil-ət-ē\ *n* — **hatch·able** \ˈhach-ə-bəl\ *adj* — **hatch·er** *n*

[3]**hatch** *n* **1 :** an act or instance of hatching **2 :** a brood of hatched young

[4]**hatch** *vt* [ME *hachen*, fr. MF *hacher* to inlay, chop up] **1 :** to inlay with narrow bands of distinguishable material <a silver handle ~*ed* with gold> **2 :** to mark (as a drawing or engraving) with fine closely spaced lines

[5]**hatch** *n* : LINE; *esp* : one used to give the effect of shading

hatch·back \ˈhach-ˌbak\ *n* **1 :** a back on a closed passenger automobile (as a coupe) having an upward-opening hatch **2 :** an automobile having a hatchback

hat·check \ˈhat-ˌchek\ *adj* **1 :** being one that checks hats and other articles of outdoor clothing <a ~ girl> **2 :** used in the checking of hats <a ~ stand>

hatch·ery \ˈhach-(ə-)rē\ *n, pl* **-er·ies** **1 :** a place for hatching eggs **2 :** a place for the large-scale production of weanling feeder pigs

hatch·et \ˈhach-ət\ *n* [ME *hachet*, fr. MF *hachette*, dim. of *hache* battle-ax — more at HASH] **1 :** a short-handled ax with a hammerhead to be used with one hand **2 :** TOMAHAWK

hatchet face *n* : a thin sharp face — **hatch·et–faced** \ˌhach-ət-ˈfāst\ *adj*

hatchet man *n* **1 :** one hired for murder, coercion, or attack **2 :** a writer specializing in invective without regard to personal scruples and often on orders from an employer

hatch·ing *n* : the engraving or drawing of fine lines in close proximity chiefly to give an effect of shading; *also* : the pattern so created

hatch·ling \ˈhach-liŋ\ *n* : a recently hatched animal

hatch·ment \ˈhach-mənt\ *n* [perh. alter. of *achievement*] : a panel on which a coat of arms of a deceased person is temporarily displayed

hatch·way \ˈhach-ˌwā\ *n* : a passage giving access usu. by a ladder or stairs to an enclosed space (as a cellar); *also* : HATCH 2a

[1]**hate** \ˈhāt\ *n* [ME, fr. OE *hete*; akin to OHG *haz* hate, Gk *kēdos* grief] **1 a :** intense hostility and aversion usu. deriving from fear, anger, or sense of injury **b :** extreme dislike or antipathy : LOATHING <had a great ~ of hard work> **2 :** an object of hatred <a generation whose finest ~ had been big business —F. L. Paxson>

[2]**hate** *vb* **hat·ed; hat·ing** *vt* **1 :** to feel extreme enmity toward <~*s* his country's enemies> **2 :** to have a strong aversion to <*hated* to have to meet strangers> <~ hypocrisy> ~ *vi* : to express or feel extreme enmity or active hostility — **hat·er** *n*

syn HATE, DETEST, ABHOR, ABOMINATE, LOATHE *shared meaning element* : to feel strong aversion or intense dislike for *ant* love

— **hate one's guts :** to hate someone with great intensity

hate·ful \ˈhāt-fəl\ *adj* **1 :** full of hate : MALICIOUS **2 :** deserving of or arousing hate — **hate·ful·ly** \-fə-lē\ *adv* — **hate·ful·ness** *n*

hath \(ˈ)hath, (h)əth\ *archaic pres 3d sing of* HAVE

hat in hand *adv* : in an attitude of respectful humility <have to apologize *hat in hand*>

hat·mak·er \ˈhat-ˌmā-kər\ *n* : one who makes hats

ha·tred \ˈhā-trəd\ *n* [ME, fr. *hate* + OE *rǣden* condition — more at KINDRED] **1 :** HATE **2 :** prejudiced hostility or animosity <old racial prejudices and national ~*s* —Peter Thomson>

hat·ter \ˈhat-ər\ *n* : one that makes, sells, or cleans and repairs hats

hat trick *n* [prob. fr. the former practice of rewarding the feat with the gift of a hat] **1 :** the retiring of three batsmen with three consecutive balls by a bowler in cricket **2 :** the scoring of three goals in one game (as of hockey or soccer) by a single player

hau·berk \ˈhȯ-(ˌ)bərk\ *n* [ME, fr. OF *hauberc*, of Gmc origin; akin to OE *healsbeorg* neck armor] : a tunic of chain mail worn as defensive armor from the 12th to the 14th century

1 hauberk

haugh \ˈhȯ(k)\ *n* [ME (Sc) *holch*, fr. OE *heolh* corner of land; akin to OE *holh* hole] *Scot* : a low-lying meadow by the side of a river

haugh·ty \ˈhȯt-ē, ˈhät-\ *adj* **haugh·ti·er; -est** [obs. *haught*, fr. ME *haute*, fr. MF *haut*, lit., high, fr. L *altus* — more at OLD] : blatantly and disdainfully proud *syn* see PROUD *ant* lowly — **haugh·ti·ly** \ˈhȯt-ᵊl-ē, ˈhät-\ *adv* — **haugh·ti·ness** \ˈhȯt-ē-nəs, ˈhät-\ *n*

[1]**haul** \ˈhȯl\ *vb* [ME *halen* to pull, fr. OF *haler*, of Gmc origin; akin to MD *halen* to pull; akin to OE *geholian* to obtain] *vt* **1 :** to change the course of (a ship) esp. so as to sail closer to the wind **2 a :** to exert traction on : DRAW <~ a wagon> **b :** to obtain or move by or as if by hauling <was ~*ed* to parties night after night by his wife> **c :** to transport in a vehicle : CART **3 :** to bring before an authority for interrogation or judgment : HALE <~ traffic violators into court> ~ *vi* **1 :** to exert traction : PULL **2 :** to furnish transportation **3** *of the wind* : SHIFT *syn* see PULL

[2]**haul** *n* **1 a :** the act or process of hauling : PULL **b :** a device for hauling **2 a :** the result of an effort to collect : TAKE <the burglar's ~> **b :** the fish taken in a single draft of a net **3 a :** transportation by hauling **b :** the distance or route over which a load is transported <a long ~> **c :** a quantity transported : LOAD

haul·age \ˈhȯ-lij\ *n* **1 :** the act or process of hauling **2 :** a charge made for hauling

haul·age·way \-ˌwā\ *n* : a passage in a coal mine along which coal is transported

haul·er \ˈhȯ-lər\ *n* : one that hauls; *esp* : a commercial establishment whose business is hauling or one of its automotive vehicles

haul·ier \ˈhȯl-yər\ *Brit var of* HAULER

haulm \ˈhȯm\ *n* [ME *halm*, fr. OE *healm*; akin to OHG *halm* stem, L *culmus* stalk, Gk *kalamos* reed] **1 :** the stems or tops of cultivated plants (as peas, beans, or potatoes) esp. after the crop has been gathered **2 :** a plant stem (as the culm of a grass)

haunch \ˈhȯnch, ˈhänch\ *n* [ME *haunche*, fr. OF *hanche*, of Gmc origin; akin to MD *hanke* haunch] **1 a :** HIP 1a **b :** HINDQUARTER 2 — usu. used in pl. **2 :** HINDQUARTER 1 **3 :** either side of an arch between the springing and the crown — **on one's haunches** : in a squatting position

[1]**haunt** \ˈhȯnt, ˈhänt\ *vb* [ME *haunten*, fr. OF *hanter*] *vt* **1 a :** to visit often : FREQUENT **b :** to continually seek the company of (a person) **2 a :** to recur constantly and spontaneously to <the tune ~*ed* her all day> **b :** to reappear continually in <a sense of tension that ~*s* his writing> **3 :** to visit or inhabit as a ghost ~ *vi* **1 :** to stay around or persist : LINGER **2 :** to appear habitually as a ghost — **haunt·er** *n* — **haunt·ing·ly** \-iŋ-lē\ *adv*

[2]**haunt** \ˈhȯnt, ˈhänt, *2 is usu* ˈhant\ *n* **1 :** a place habitually frequented **2** *chiefly dial* : GHOST

Hau·sa \ˈhau̇-sə, -zə\ *n, pl* **Hausa** *or* **Hausas** **1 :** a member of a Negroid people of the Sudan between Lake Chad and the Niger **2 :** the language of the Hausa people widely used in west Africa as a trade language

haus·frau \ˈhau̇s-ˌfrau̇\ *n* [G, fr. *haus* house + *frau* woman, wife] : HOUSEWIFE

haus·tel·late \hȯ-ˈstel-ət, ˈhȯ-stə-ˌlāt\ *adj* : having a haustellum

haus·tel·lum \hȯ-ˈstel-əm\ *n, pl* **-la** \-ə\ [NL, fr. L *haustus*, pp. of *haurire* to drink, draw — more at EXHAUST] : a proboscis (as of an insect) adapted to suck blood or juices of plants

haus·to·ri·al \hȯ-ˈstōr-ē-əl, -ˈstȯr-\ *adj* : having a haustorium

haus·to·ri·um \-ē-əm\ *n, pl* **-ria** \-ē-ə\ [NL, fr. L *haustus*] : a food-absorbing outgrowth of a hypha, stem, or other plant organ

haut·bois *or* **haut·boy** \ˈ(h)ō-ˌbȯi\ *n, pl* **hautbois** \-ˌbȯiz\ *or* **hautboys** [ME *hautbois*, fr. *haut* high + *bois* wood] : OBOE

haute cou·ture \ˌōt-kü-ˈtu̇(ə)r\ *n* [F, lit., high sewing] : the houses or designers that create exclusive and often trend-setting fashions for women; *also* : the fashions created

haute cui·sine \-kwi-ˈzēn\ *n* [F, lit., high cooking] : artful or elaborate cuisine

haute école \-ā-ˈkȯl, -ˈkəl\ *n* [F, lit., high school] : a highly stylized form of classical riding : advanced dressage

hau·teur \hȯ-ˈtər, (h)ō-\ *n* [F, fr. *haut* high — more at HAUGHTY] : ARROGANCE, HAUGHTINESS

haut monde \ō-ˈmänd, ō-mōⁿd\ *n* [F] : high society

Ha·vana \hə-ˈvan-ə\ *n* [prob. fr. Sp *habano*, fr. *habano* of Havana, fr. La *Habana* (Havana), Cuba] **1 :** a cigar made from Cuban tobacco **2 :** tobacco raised in Cuba

havdalah *var of* HABDALAH

1have \(ˈ)hav, (h)əv, v; *in sense 2 before "to" usu* ˈhaf\ *vb* **had** \(ˈ)had, (h)əd, d\; **hav·ing** \ˈhav-iŋ\; **has** \(ˈ)haz, (h)əz, z, s; *in sense 2 before "to" usu* ˈhas\ [ME *haven,* fr. OE *habban;* akin to OHG *habēn* to have, *hevan* to lift — more at HEAVE] *vt* **1 a** : to hold in possession as property **b** : to hold in one's use, service, or affection or at one's disposal <~ your cake and eat it too> **c** : to consist of : CONTAIN **2** : to feel obligation or necessity in regard to <~ to go> <learn to get along better, as people ~ to in . . . society —H. J. Muller> **3** : to stand in relationship to <~ enemies> **4 a** : to acquire or get possession of : OBTAIN <these shoes are the best to be *had*> **b** : RECEIVE <*had* news> **c** : ACCEPT; *specif* : to accept in marriage **d** : to copulate with **5 a** : to be marked or characterized by <~ red hair> **b** : EXHIBIT, SHOW <*had* the gall to refuse> **c** : USE, EXERCISE <~ mercy on us> **6 a** : to experience esp. by submitting to, undergoing, or suffering <~ a cold> **b** : to carry on : PERFORM, TAKE <~ a look at that cut> <~ a fight> **c** : to entertain in the mind <~ an opinion> **7 a** : to cause to by persuasive or forceful means — used with the infinitive without *to* <~ the children stay> **b** : to cause to be <*has* people around at all times> **8** : ALLOW <we'll ~ no more of that> **9** : to be competent in <*has* only a little French> **10 a** : to hold in a position of disadvantage or certain defeat <we ~ him now> **b** : to take advantage of : TRICK, FOOL <been *had* by a partner> **11** : to be able to exercise : be entitled to <I ~ my rights> **12** : BEGET, BEAR <~ a baby> **13** : to partake of <~ dinner> **14** : BRIBE, SUBORN <can be *had* for a price> ~ *verbal auxiliary* — used with the past participle to form the present perfect, past perfect, or future perfect <*has* gone home> <*had* already eaten> <will ~ finished dinner by then>
  syn HAVE, HOLD, OWN, POSSESS, ENJOY *shared meaning element* : to keep, control, retain, or experience as one's own
— **have at** \ha-ˈvat\ : to go at or deal with : ATTACK — **have coming** : to deserve or merit what one gets, benefits by, or suffers <he *had* that *coming*> — **have done** : FINISH, STOP — **have done with** : to bring to an end : have no further concern with <let us *have done with* name-calling> — **have had it 1** : to have had or have done all one is going to be allowed to **2** : to have experienced, endured, or suffered all one can — **have it in for** \ˌhav-ət-ˈin-fər, -ˌfȯ(ə)r\ : to intend to do harm to — **have it out** : to settle a matter of contention by discussion or a fight — **have one's eye on 1 a** : to look at **b** : to watch constantly and attentively **2** : to have as an objective — **have to do with 1** : to deal with **2** : to have in the way of connection or relation with or effect on <the lawyer would *have* nothing *to do with* the case>

2have \ˈhav\ *n* : one that is well-endowed esp. in material wealth <the ~*s* and the have-nots>

have·lock \ˈhav-ˌläk, -lək\ *n* [Sir Henry *Havelock*] : a covering attached to a cap to protect the neck from the sun or bad weather

ha·ven \ˈhā-vən\ *n* [ME, fr. OE *hæfen;* akin to MHG *habene* harbor, OE *hebban* to lift — more at HEAVE] **1** : HARBOR, PORT **2** : a place of safety : ASYLUM — **haven** *vt*

have–not \ˈhav-ˌnät, -ˈnät\ *n* : one that is poor esp. in material wealth

haven't \ˈhav-ənt\ : have not

have on *vt* **1** : WEAR <*has on* a new suit> **2** : to plan to take part in : have (something) planned <*have* a dance *on* for that night>

ha·ver \ˈhā-vər\ *vi* [origin unknown] *chiefly Brit* : to hem and haw : stall for time (as by useless talk)

ha·vers \ˈhā-vərz\ *n pl* [*haver*] *chiefly Scot* : NONSENSE, POPPYCOCK

hav·er·sack \ˈhav-ər-ˌsak\ *n* [F *havresac,* fr. G *habersack* bag for oats, fr. *haber* oats + *sack* bag] : a bag similar to a knapsack but worn over one shoulder

ha·ver·sian canal \hə-ˌvər-zhən-\ *n, often cap H* [Clopton *Havers* †1702 E physician & anatomist] : any of the small canals through which the blood vessels ramify in bone

haversian system *n, often cap H* : a haversian canal with the concentrically arranged laminae of bone that surround it

1hav·oc \ˈhav-ək, -ik\ *n* [ME *havok,* fr. AF, modif. of OF *havot* plunder] **1** : wide and general destruction : DEVASTATION **2** : great confusion and disorder <several small children can create ~ in a house> *syn* see RUIN

2havoc *vt* **hav·ocked; hav·ock·ing** : to lay waste : DESTROY, DEVASTATE

1haw \ˈhȯ\ *n* [ME *hawe,* fr. OE *haga* — more at HEDGE] **1** : a hawthorn berry **2** : HAWTHORN

2haw *n* [origin unknown] : NICTITATING MEMBRANE; *esp* : an inflamed nictitating membrane of a domesticated mammal

3haw *vi* [imit.] **1** : to utter the sound represented by *haw* <hemmed and ~*ed* before answering> **2** : EQUIVOCATE <the administration hemmed and ~*ed* at the students' demands>

4haw *interj* — often used to indicate a vocalized pause in speaking

5haw \ˈhȯ\ *vb imper* [origin unknown] — used as a direction to turn to the left; compare GEE ~ *vi* : to turn to the near or left side

Ha·wai·ian \hə-ˈwä-yən, -ˈwī-(y)ən, -ˈwȯ-yən\ *n* **1** : a native or resident of Hawaii; *esp* : one of Polynesian ancestry **2** : the Polynesian language of the Hawaiians — **Hawaiian** *adj*

Hawaiian guitar *n* : a usu. electric stringed instrument consisting of a long soundboard and six to eight steel strings that are plucked while being pressed with a movable steel bar

Hawaii time *n* : the time of the 10th time zone west of Greenwich that includes the Hawaiian islands

haw·finch \ˈhȯ-ˌfinch\ *n* [*1haw*] : a Eurasian finch (*Coccothraustes coccothraustes*) with a large heavy bill and short thick neck and the male marked with black, white, and brown

1hawk \ˈhȯk\ *n* [ME *hauk,* fr. OE *hafoc;* akin to OHG *habuh* hawk, Russ *kobets,* a falcon] **1** : any of numerous diurnal birds of prey belonging to a suborder (Falcones of the order Falconiformes) and including all the smaller members of this group; *esp* : ACCIPITER — compare OWL **2** : a small board or metal sheet with a handle on the underside used to hold mortar **3** : an individual who takes a militant attitude (as in a dispute) and advocates immediate vigorous action; *esp* : a supporter of a war or warlike policy — compare DOVE — **hawk·ish** \ˈhȯ-kish\ *adj* — **hawk·ish·ly** *adv* — **hawk·ish·ness** *n*

2hawk *vi* **1** : to hunt birds by means of a trained hawk **2** : to soar and strike like a hawk ~ *vt* : to hunt on the wing like a hawk

3hawk *vt* [back-formation fr. *2hawker*] : to offer for sale by calling out in the street <~*ing* newspapers>

4hawk *vb* [imit.] *vi* : to utter a harsh guttural sound in or as if in trying to clear the throat ~ *vt* : to raise by hawking <~ up phlegm>

5hawk *n* : an audible effort to force up phlegm from the throat

1hawk·er \ˈhȯ-kər\ *n* : FALCONER

2hawker *n* [by folk etymology fr. LG *hōker,* fr. MLG *hōker,* fr. *hōken* to peddle, squat; akin to OE *hēah* high] : one that hawks wares

Hawk·eye \ˈhȯ-ˌkī\ *n* : a native or resident of Iowa — used as a nickname

hawk·moth \ˈhȯk-ˌmȯth\ *n* : any of numerous rather large stout-bodied moths (family Sphingidae) with a long proboscis which at rest is kept coiled, long strong narrow fore wings more or less pointed at the ends, and small hind wings — called also *sphinx*

hawks·bill \ˈhȯks-ˌbil\ *n* : a carnivorous sea turtle (*Eretmochelys imbricata*) whose shell yields a valuable tortoiseshell

hawk·weed \ˈhȯ-ˌkwēd\ *n* : any of several composite plants (as of the genera *Hieracium, Picris,* and *Erechtites*) usu. having flower heads with red or orange rays

hawse \ˈhȯz\ *n* [ME *halse,* fr. ON *hals* neck, hawse — more at COLLAR] **1 a** : HAWSEHOLE **b** : the part of a ship's bow that contains the hawseholes **2** : the arrangement of the anchor cables of a ship when both a port and starboard anchor are used **3** : the distance between a ship's bow and her anchor

hawse·hole \-ˌhōl\ *n* : a hole in the bow of a ship through which a cable passes

haw·ser \ˈhȯ-zər\ *n* [ME, fr. AF *hauceour,* fr. MF *haucier* to hoist, fr. (assumed) VL *altiare,* fr. L *altus* high — more at OLD] : a large rope for towing, mooring, or securing a ship

hawser bend *n* : a method of joining the ends of two heavy ropes by means of seizings

haw·ser–laid \ˌhȯ-zər-ˈlād\ *adj* : CABLE-LAID

haw·thorn \ˈhȯ-ˌthȯ(ə)rn\ *n* [ME *hawethorn,* fr. OE *hagathorn,* fr. *haga* hawthorn + *thorn* — more at HEDGE] : any of a genus (*Crataegus*) of spring-flowering spiny shrubs (as the European *C. oxyacantha* and the American *C. coccinea*) of the rose family with glossy and often lobed leaves, white or pink fragrant flowers, and small red fruits

1hay \ˈhā\ *n* [ME *hey,* fr. OE *hīeg;* akin to OHG *hewi* hay, OE *hēawan* to hew] **1** : herbage and esp. grass mowed and cured for fodder **2** : REWARD <got some political ~ out of his association with underworld characters> **3** *slang* : BED **4** : a small sum of money

2hay *vi* : to cut, cure, and store for hay ~ *vt* : to feed with hay

hay·cock \ˈhā-ˌkäk\ *n* : a conical pile of hay

hay·er \ˈhā-ər, ˈhe(-ə)r\ *n* : one that hays

hay fever *n* : an acute allergic nasal catarrh and conjunctivitis; *esp* : POLLINOSIS

hay·fork \ˈhā-ˌfȯ(ə)rk\ *n* : a fork that is mechanically operated or held in the hand and that is used for loading or unloading hay

hay·lage \ˈhā-lij\ *n* [*hay* + *silage*] : a stored forage that is essentially a grass silage wilted to 35 to 50 percent moisture

hay·loft \ˈhā-ˌlȯft\ *n* : a loft esp. for storing hay

hay·mak·er \-ˌmā-kər\ *n* **1** : HAYER **2** : a powerful blow <a ~ to the jaw>

hay·mow \-ˌmau̇\ *n* : a mow esp. of or for hay

hay·rack \-ˌrak\ *n* **1** : a frame mounted on the running gear of a wagon and used esp. in hauling hay or straw; *also* : a wagon equipped with a hayrack **2** : a feeding rack that holds hay for livestock

hay·rick \-ˌrik\ *n* : a relatively large sometimes thatched outdoor pile of hay : HAYSTACK

hay·ride \-ˌrīd\ *n* : a pleasure ride usu. at night by a group in a wagon, sleigh, or open truck partly filled with straw or hay

hay·seed \ˈhā-ˌsēd\ *n, pl* **hayseed** *or* **hayseeds 1 a** : seed shattered from hay **b** : clinging bits of straw or chaff from hay **2** *pl* **hayseeds** : BUMPKIN, YOKEL

hay·stack \-ˌstak\ *n* : a stack of hay

hay·wire \-ˌwī(ə)r\ *adj* [fr. the use of baling wire for makeshift repairs] **1** : hastily or shoddily made **2** : being out of order — often used with *go* <the radio went ~> **3** : emotionally or mentally upset : CRAZY — often used with *go* <went completely ~ after the accident>

ha·zan \k̲ə-ˈzän, ˈkäz-ᵊn\ *n, pl* **ha·za·nim** \k̲ə-ˈzän-əm\ [LHeb *ḥazzān*] **1** : an official of a Jewish synagogue or community of the talmudic period **2** : CANTOR 2

1haz·ard \ˈhaz-ərd\ *n* [ME, fr. MF *hasard,* fr. Ar *az-zahr* the die] **1** : a game of chance like craps played with two dice **2** : a source of danger **3 a** : CHANCE **b** : a chance event : ACCIDENT **4** *obs* : STAKE 3a **5** : a golf-course obstacle — **at hazard** : at stake

2hazard *vt* : VENTURE, RISK <~ a guess>

haz·ard·ous \ˈhaz-ərd-əs\ *adj* **1** : depending on hazard or chance **2** : involving or exposing one to risk (as of loss or harm) <a ~ occupation> <handling ~ materials> *syn* see DANGEROUS — **haz·ard·ous·ly** *adv* — **haz·ard·ous·ness** *n*

1haze \ˈhāz\ *vb* **hazed; haz·ing** [prob. back-formation fr. *hazy*] *vi* : to become hazy or cloudy ~ *vt* : to make hazy, dull, or cloudy

2haze *n* [prob. back-formation fr. *hazy*] **1 a** : fine dust, smoke, or light vapor causing lack of transparency of the air **b** : a cloudy appearance in a transparent liquid or solid; *also* : a dullness of finish (as on furniture) **2** : vagueness of mind or mental perception
  syn HAZE, FOG, MIST, SMOG *shared meaning element* : an atmospheric condition that deprives the air of its transparency

3haze *vt* **hazed; haz·ing** [origin unknown] **1 a** : to harass by exacting unnecessary or disagreeable work **b** : to harass by banter, ridicule, or criticism **2** : to haze by way of initiation <~ the fraternity pledges> **3** *West* **:** to drive (as cattle or horses) from horseback — **haz·er** *n* — **haz·ing** *n*

[1]**ha·zel** \ˈhā-zəl\ *n* [ME *hasel,* fr. OE *hæsel;* akin to OHG *hasal* hazel, L *corulus*] **1 :** any of a genus (*Corylus*) of shrubs or small trees of the birch family (esp. the American *C. americana* and the European *C. cornuta*) bearing nuts enclosed in a leafy involucre **2 :** a light brown to strong yellowish brown

[2]**hazel** *adj* **1 :** consisting of hazels or of the wood of the hazel **2 :** of the color hazel

hazel hen *n* **:** a European woodland grouse (*Tetrastes bonasia*) related to the American ruffed grouse

ha·zel·nut \ˈhā-zəl-ˌnət\ *n* **:** the nut of a hazel

hazy \ˈhā-zē\ *adj* **haz·i·er; -est** [origin unknown] **1 :** obscured or made dim or cloudy by or as if by haze <a ~ view of the mountains> <a mirror ~ with steam> **2 :** VAGUE, INDEFINITE <had only a ~ recollection of what happened> — **haz·i·ly** \-zə-lē\ *adv* — **haz·i·ness** \-zē-nəs\ *n*

Hb *symbol* hemoglobin

HBM *abbr* Her Britannic Majesty; His Britannic Majesty

H–bomb \ˈāch-ˌbäm\ *n* **:** HYDROGEN BOMB

h.c. [L *honoris causa*] for the sake of honor

HC *abbr* **1** Holy Communion **2** House of Commons

HCF *abbr* highest common factor

HCL *abbr* high cost of living

hd *abbr* head

HD *abbr* heavy-duty

hdbk *abbr* handbook

hdkf *abbr* handkerchief

hdwe *abbr* hardware

[1]**he** \(ˈ)hē, ē\ *pron* [ME, fr. OE *hē;* akin to OE *hēo* she, *hit* it, OHG *hē* he, L *cis, citra* on this side, Gk *ekeinos* that person] **1 :** that male one who is neither speaker nor hearer <~ is my father> — compare HIM, HIS, IT, SHE, THEY **2** — used in a generic sense or when the sex of the person is unspecified <~ that hath ears to hear, let him hear —Mt 11:15 (AV)> <one should do the best ~ can>

[2]**he** \ˈhē\ *n* **1 :** a male person or animal **2 :** one that is strongly masculine or virile — usu. used in combination <a real *he*-man>

[3]**he** \ˈhā\ *n* [Heb *hē*ʼ] **:** the 5th letter of the Hebrew alphabet — see ALPHABET table

He *symbol* helium

HE *abbr* **1** high explosive **2** his eminence **3** his excellency

[1]**head** \ˈhed\ *n* [ME *hed,* fr. OE *hēafod;* akin to OHG *houbit* head, L *caput*] **1 :** the upper or anterior division of the body (as of a man or an insect) that contains the brain, the chief sense organs, and the mouth **2 a :** the seat of the intellect **:** MIND <two ~*s* are better than one> **b :** natural aptitude or talent <a good ~ for figures> **c :** mental or emotional control **:** POISE <a level ~> **d :** HEADACHE **3 :** the obverse of a coin — usu. used in pl. <~*s,* I win> **4 a :** PERSON, INDIVIDUAL <count ~*s*> **b** *pl* **head :** one of a number (as of domestic animals) **5 a :** the end that is upper or higher or opposite the foot <the ~ of the table> **b :** the source of a stream **c :** either end of something (as a drum) whose two ends need not be distinguished **d :** a horizontal passage in a coal mine **6 :** DIRECTOR, LEADER: as **a :** HEADMASTER **b :** one in charge of a division or department in an office or institution <the ~ of the English department> **7 a :** CAPITULUM 2 **b :** the foliaged part of a plant esp. when consisting of a compact mass of leaves or close fructification **8 a :** the leading element of a military column or a procession **b :** HEADWAY **9 a :** the uppermost extremity or projecting part of an object **:** TOP **b :** the striking part of a weapon, tool, or implement **c :** the oval part of a printed musical note **10 a :** a body of water kept in reserve at a height; *also* **:** the containing bank, dam, or wall **b :** a mass of water in motion **11 a :** the difference in elevation between two points in a body of fluid **b :** the resulting pressure of the fluid at the lower point expressible as this height; *broadly* **:** pressure of a fluid **12 a :** the bow and adjacent parts of a ship **b :** a ship's toilet; *broadly* **:** TOILET **13 :** the approximate length of the head of a horse <won by a ~> **14 :** the place of leadership, honor, or command <at the ~ of his class> **15 a (1) :** a word often in larger letters placed above a passage in order to introduce or categorize **(2) :** a separate part or topic **b :** a portion of a page or sheet that is above the first line of printing **16 a :** the topmost edge of a book **b :** the upper edge of a sail **17 :** the foam or scum that rises on a fermenting or effervescing liquid (as beer) **18 a :** the part of a boil, pimple, or abscess at which it is likely to break **b :** culminating point of action **:** CRISIS <events came to a ~> **19 a :** a part or attachment of a machine or machine tool containing a device (as a cutter or drill); *also* **:** the part of an apparatus that performs the chief function or a particular function **b :** MAGNETIC HEAD **20 :** an immediate constituent of a construction that has the same grammatical function as the whole (as *man* in "an old man", "a very old man", or "the man in the street") **21 :** one who uses a drug (as LSD or marijuana) — **by the head :** drawing the greater depth of water forward — **off one's head :** CRAZY, DISTRACTED — **out of one's head :** DELIRIOUS — **over one's head 1 :** beyond one's comprehension <liked pictures but art criticism was *over his head*> **2 :** so as to pass over one's superior standing or authority <went *over his* supervisor's *head* to complain>

[2]**head** *adj* **1 :** of, relating to, or intended for the head **2 :** PRINCIPAL, CHIEF <~ cook> **3 :** situated at the head **4 :** coming from in front <~ sea>

[3]**head** *vt* **1 :** BEHEAD **2 a :** to cut back the upper or terminal growth of (a plant or plant part) — often used with *back* **b :** to harvest (a cereal grass) by cutting off the heads **3 a :** to put a head on **:** fit a head to <~ an arrow> **b :** to form the head or top of <tower ~*ed* by a spire> **4 :** to put oneself at the head of **:** act as leader to <~ a revolt> **5 a :** to face or oppose head on <~ the waves> **b :** to get in front of so as to hinder, stop, or turn back **c :** to take a lead over (as in a race) **:** SURPASS **d :** to pass (a stream) by going round above the source **6 a :** to put something at the head of (as a list) **b :** to stand as the first or leading member of <~*s* the list of heroes> **7 :** to set the course of <~ a ship northward> **8 :** to drive (as a soccer ball) with the head ~ *vi* **1 :** to form a head <this cabbage ~*s* early> **2 :** to point or proceed in a certain direction <the fleet was ~*ing* out> **3 :** to have a source **:** ORIGINATE

head·ache \ˈhed-ˌāk\ *n* **1 :** pain in the head **2 :** a vexatious or baffling situation or problem — **head·achy** \-ˌā-kē\ *adj*

head and shoulders *adv* **:** beyond comparison **:** by far <stood *head and shoulders* above the rest in character and ability>

head·band \ˈhed-ˌband\ *n* **1 :** a band worn on or around the head **2 :** a plain or decorative band printed or engraved at the head of a page or a chapter **3 :** a narrow strip of cloth sewn or glued by hand to a book at the extreme ends of the backbone

head·board \-ˌbō(ə)rd, -ˌbȯ(ə)rd\ *n* **:** a board forming the head (as of a bed)

head·cheese \-ˌchēz\ *n* **:** a jellied loaf or sausage made from edible parts of the head, feet, and sometimes the tongue and heart esp. of a pig

head cold *n* **:** a common cold centered in the nasal passages and adjacent mucous tissues

head·dress \ˈhed-ˌdres\ *n* **:** an often elaborate covering for the head

head·ed \ˈhed-əd\ *adj* **1 :** having a head or a heading **2 :** having a head or heads of a specified kind or number — used in combination <a cool-*headed* businessman> <a round*headed* screw>

head·er \ˈhed-ər\ *n* **1 :** one that removes heads; *esp* **:** a grain-harvesting machine that cuts off the grain heads and elevates them to a wagon **2 a :** a brick or stone laid in a wall with its end toward the face of the wall **b :** a beam fitted at one side of an opening to support free ends of floor joists, studs, or rafters **c :** a horizontal structural or finish piece over an opening **:** LINTEL **d :** a conduit (as the exhaust manifold of a many-cylindered engine) into which smaller conduits open **e :** a mounting plate through which electrical terminals pass from a sealed device (as a transistor) **3 :** a fall or dive head foremost **4 :** a shot or pass in soccer made by heading the ball

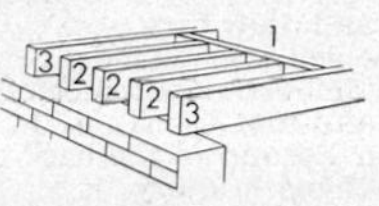

header 2b: *1* header, *2* tail beams, *3* trimmers

head·first \ˈhed-ˈfərst\ *adv* **:** with the head foremost **:** HEADLONG <dove ~ into the waves> — **headfirst** *adj*

head·fore·most \-ˈfō(ə)r-ˌmōst, -ˈfȯ(ə)r-\ *adv* **:** HEADFIRST, HEADLONG

head·gate \ˈhed-ˌgāt\ *n* **:** a gate for controlling the water flowing into a channel (as an irrigation ditch)

head·gear \-ˌgi(ə)r\ *n* **1 :** a covering or protective device for the head **2 :** a harness for a horse's head

head·hunt·er \-ˌhənt-ər\ *n* **1 :** one that engages in head-hunting **2 :** a recruiter of personnel esp. at the executive level

head–hunt·ing \-ˌhənt-iŋ\ *n* **1 :** the act or custom of seeking out, decapitating, and preserving the heads of enemies as trophies **2 :** a seeking to deprive usu. political enemies of position or influence

head·ing \ˈhed-iŋ\ *n* **1 :** the compass direction in which the longitudinal axis of a ship or aircraft points; *broadly* **:** DIRECTION **2 a :** something that forms or serves as a head; *esp* **:** an inscription, headline, or title standing at the top or beginning (as of a letter or chapter) **b :** the address and date at the beginning of a letter showing its place and time of origin **3 :** DRIFT 6

head·lamp \-ˌlamp\ *n* **:** HEADLIGHT

head·land \ˈhed-lənd, -ˌland\ *n* **1 :** unplowed land at the ends of furrows or near a fence **2 :** a point of usu. high land jutting out into a body of water **:** PROMONTORY

head·less \-ləs\ *adj* **1 a :** having no head **b :** having the head cut off **:** BEHEADED **2 :** having no chief **3 :** lacking good sense or prudence **:** FOOLISH — **head·less·ness** *n*

head·light \-ˌlīt\ *n* **1 :** a light with a reflector and special lens mounted on the front of an automotive vehicle; *also* **:** the beam cast by a headlight **2 :** a light worn on the forehead (as of a miner or physician)

[1]**head·line** \-ˌlīn\ *n* **1 :** a head of a newspaper story or article usu. printed in large type and devised to summarize the story or article that follows **2 :** words set at the head of a passage or page to introduce or categorize

[2]**headline** *vt* **1 :** to provide with a headline **2 :** to publicize highly **3 :** to be engaged as a leading performer in (a show)

head·lin·er \ˈhed-ˌlī-nər\ *n* **:** a performer whose name is given prominent billing **:** STAR

head linesman *n* **:** a football linesman

head·lock \ˈhed-ˌläk\ *n* **:** a wrestling hold in which one encircles his opponent's head with one arm

[1]**head·long** \-ˈlȯŋ\ *adv* [ME *hedlong,* alter. of *hedling,* fr. *hed* head] **1 :** HEADFIRST **2 :** without deliberation **:** RECKLESSLY **3 :** without pause or delay

[2]**head·long** \-ˌlȯŋ\ *adj* **1 :** lacking in calmness or restraint **:** PRECIPITATE <releasing the ~ torrent of her emotion in tears> **2 :** plunging headforemost **3** *archaic* **:** STEEP, PRECIPITOUS ***syn*** see PRECIPITATE

head louse *n* **:** one of a variety (*Pediculus humanus capitis*) of the common louse that lives on the scalp of man

head·man *n* **1 a** \ˈhed-ˈman\ **:** OVERSEER, FOREMAN **b** \-ˈman, -ˌman\ **:** a lesser chief of a primitive community **2** \-mən\ **:** HEADSMAN

head·mas·ter \ˈhed-ˌmas-tər, -ˈmas-\ *n* **:** a man heading the staff of a private school **:** PRINCIPAL — **head·mas·ter·ship** \-ˌship\ *n*

head·mis·tress \-ˌmis-trəs, -ˈmis-\ *n* **:** a woman heading the staff of a private school

head·most \ˈhed-ˌmōst\ *adj* : most advanced : LEADING
head·note \-ˌnōt\ *n* **1** : a prefixed note of comment or explanation **2** : a note prefixed to the report of a decided legal case
head off *vt* : to turn back or turn aside : BLOCK, PREVENT <*head* them *off* at the pass> <attempts to *head off* the imminent crisis>
1**head–on** \ˈhed-ˈȯn, -ˈän\ *adv* **1** : with the head or front making the initial contact <the cars collided ~> **2** : in direct opposition or contradiction <what happens to the savage when he meets civilization ~ —J. F. McComas>
2**head–on** *adj* **1** : having the front facing in the direction of initial contact or line of sight <a ~ collision> <a ~ view of a building> **2** : FRONTAL
head over heels *adv* **1 a** : in or as if in a somersault : HELTER-SKELTER **b** : upside down **2** : very much : HOPELESSLY, DEEPLY <*head over heels* in love>
head·phone \ˈhed-ˌfōn\ *n* : an earphone held over the ear by a band worn on the head
head·piece \-ˌpēs\ *n* **1** : a protective or defensive covering for the head **2** : BRAINS, INTELLIGENCE **3** : an ornament esp. at the beginning of a chapter
head·pin \-ˌpin\ *n* : a bowling pin that stands foremost in the arrangement of pins
head·quar·ter \ˈhed-ˌkwȯ(r)t-ər, (ˈ)hed-ˈ\ *vi* : to make one's headquarters ~ *vt* : to place in headquarters
head·quar·ters \-ərz\ *n pl but sing or pl in constr* **1** : a place from which a commander performs the functions of command **2** : the administrative center of an enterprise
head·rest \-ˌrest\ *n* **1** : a support for the head **2** : a resilient pad at the top of the back of an automobile seat esp. for preventing whiplash injury
head rhyme *n* : BEGINNING RHYME
head·room \ˈhed-ˌrüm, -ˌru̇m\ *n* : vertical space in which to stand or move
head·sail \-ˌsāl, -səl\ *n* : a sail set forward of the foremast
head·set \-ˌset\ *n* **1** : an attachment for holding an earphone and transmitter at one's head **2** : a pair of headphones
head·ship \-ˌship\ *n* : the position, office, or dignity of a head
head·shrink·er \-ˌshriŋ-kər, *esp South* -ˌsriŋ-\ *n, slang* : PSYCHIATRIST
heads·man \ˈhedz-mən\ *n* : one that beheads : EXECUTIONER
head·spring \ˈhed-ˌspriŋ\ *n* : FOUNTAINHEAD, SOURCE
head·stall \-ˌstȯl\ *n* : a part of a bridle or halter that encircles the head
head start *n* **1** : an advantage granted or achieved at the beginning of a race, a chase, or a competition <a 10-minute *head start*> **2** : a favorable or promising beginning
head·stock \ˈhed-ˌstäk\ *n* : a bearing or pedestal for a revolving or moving part; *specif* : a part of a lathe that holds the revolving spindle and its attachments
head·stone \-ˌstōn\ *n* : a memorial stone placed at the head of a grave
head·stream \-ˌstrēm\ *n* : a stream that is the source of a river
head·strong \-ˌstrȯŋ\ *adj* **1** : not easily restrained : impatient of control, advice, or suggestions **2** : directed by ungovernable will <violent ~ actions> ***syn*** see UNRULY
heads–up \ˌhed-ˌzəp\ *adj* : ALERT, RESOURCEFUL <fast, aggressive, ~ football>
heads up \(ˈ)hed-ˈzəp\ *interj* — used as a warning to look out for danger overhead or to clear a passageway
head·wait·er \ˈhed-ˈwāt-ər\ *n* : the head of the dining-room staff of a restaurant or hotel
head·wa·ter \-ˌwȯt-ər, -ˌwät-\ *n* : the source of a stream — usu. used in pl.
head·way \-ˌwā\ *n* **1 a** : motion or rate of motion in a forward direction **b** : ADVANCE, PROGRESS **2** : headroom (as under an arch) sufficient to allow passage **3** : the time interval between two vehicles traveling in the same direction on the same route
head wind *n* : a wind blowing in a direction opposite to a course esp. of a ship or aircraft
head·word \ˈhed-ˌwərd\ *n* **1** : a word or term placed at the beginning (as of a chapter or an entry in an encyclopedia) **2** : HEAD 20
head·work \-ˌwərk\ *n* : mental labor; *esp* : clever thinking
heady \ˈhed-ē\ *adj* **head·i·er; -est** **1 a** : WILLFUL, RASH <~ opinions> **b** : VIOLENT, IMPETUOUS **2 a** : tending to make giddy : INTOXICATING <~ wine> <a ~ triumph> **b** : GIDDY, EXHILARATED <~ with his success> **3** : SHREWD — **head·i·ly** \ˈhed-ᵊl-ē\ *adv* — **head·i·ness** \ˈhed-ē-nəs\ *n*
heal \ˈhē(ə)l\ *vb* [ME *helen,* fr. OE *hǣlan;* akin to OHG *heilen* to heal, OE *hāl* whole — more at WHOLE] *vt* **1 a** : to make sound or whole <~ a wound> **b** : to restore to health **2 a** : to cause (an undesirable condition) to be overcome : MEND <the troubles . . . had not been forgotten, but they had been ~*ed* — William Power> **b** : to patch up (a breach or division) <~ a breach between friends> **3** : to restore to original purity or integrity <~*ed* of sin> ~ *vi* : to return to a sound state ***syn*** see CURE
heal·er \ˈhē-lər\ *n* **1** : one that heals **2** : a Christian Science practitioner
health \ˈhelth\ *n, often attrib* [ME *helthe,* fr. OE *hǣlth,* fr. *hāl*] **1 a** : the condition of being sound in body, mind, or spirit; *esp* : freedom from physical disease or pain **b** : the general condition of the body <in poor ~> <enjoys good ~> **2** : flourishing condition : WELL-BEING <the economic ~ of a country> **3** : a toast to someone's health or prosperity
health·ful \ˈhelth-fəl\ *adj* **1** : beneficial to health of body or mind **2** : HEALTHY <a mind . . . ~ and so well-proportioned — T. B. Macaulay>
health insurance *n* : insurance against loss through illness of the insured
health officer *n* : an officer charged with the enforcement of health and sanitation laws
healthy \ˈhel-thē\ *adj* **health·i·er; -est** **1** : enjoying health and vigor of body, mind, or spirit : WELL **2** : evincing health <a ~ complexion> **3** : conducive to health <walk three miles every day . . . a beastly bore, but ~ — G. S. Patton> **4 a** : PROSPEROUS, FLOURISHING **b** : not small or feeble : CONSIDERABLE — **health·i·ly** \-thə-lē\ *adv* — **health·i·ness** \-thē-nəs\ *n*
syn HEALTHY, SOUND, WHOLESOME, ROBUST, HALE, WELL *shared meaning element* : enjoying or indicative of good health ***ant*** unhealthy
1**heap** \ˈhēp\ *n* [ME *heep,* fr. OE *hēap;* akin to OE *hēah* high] **1** : a collection of things thrown one on another : PILE **2** : a great number or large quantity : LOT
2**heap** *vt* **1 a** : to throw or lay in a heap : pile or collect in great quantity <his sole object was to ~ up riches> **b** : to form or round into a heap <~*ed* the dirt into a mound> **2** : to accord or bestow lavishly or in large quantities <~*ed* the plates with food> <~*ed* honors upon him>
hear \ˈhi(ə)r\ *vb* **heard** \ˈhərd\; **hear·ing** \ˈhi(ə)r-iŋ\ [ME *heren,* fr. OE *hieran;* akin to OHG *hōren* to hear, L *cavēre* to be on guard, Gk *akouein* to hear] *vt* **1** : to perceive or apprehend by the ear **2** : to gain knowledge of by hearing **3 a** : to listen to with attention : HEED **b** : ATTEND <~ mass> **4 a** : to give a legal hearing to **b** : to take testimony from <~ witnesses> ~ *vi* **1** : to have the capacity of apprehending sound **2** : to gain information : LEARN **3** : to entertain the idea — used in the negative <wouldn't ~ of it> — **hear·er** \ˈhir-ər\ *n*
hear·ing *n* **1 a** : the process, function, or power of perceiving sound; *specif* : the special sense by which noises and tones are received as stimuli **b** : EARSHOT **2 a** : opportunity to be heard, to present one's side of a case, or to be generally known or appreciated **b (1)** : a listening to arguments **(2)** : a preliminary examination in criminal procedure **c** : a session (as of a legislative committee) in which witnesses are heard and testimony is taken **3** *chiefly dial* : a piece of news : RUMOR
hearing aid *n* : an electronic device usu. worn by a person for amplifying sound before it reaches the receptor organs
hear·ken \ˈhär-kən\ *vb* **hear·kened; hear·ken·ing** \ˈhärk-(ə-)niŋ\ [ME *herknen,* fr. OE *heorcnian;* akin to OHG *hōrechen* to listen — more at HARK] *vi* **1** : LISTEN **2** : to give respectful attention ~ *vt, archaic* : to give heed to : HEAR
hear·say \ˈhi(ə)r-ˌsā\ *n* : something heard from another : RUMOR ***syn*** see REPORT
hearsay evidence *n* : evidence based not on a witness's personal knowledge but on matters told him by another
1**hearse** \ˈhərs\ *n* [ME *herse,* fr. MF *herce* harrow, frame for holding candles, fr. L *hirpic-, hirpex* harrow] **1 a** : a triangular candelabrum for 15 candles used esp. at Tenebrae **b** : an elaborate framework erected over a coffin or tomb to which memorial verses or epitaphs are attached **2 a** *archaic* : COFFIN **b** *obs* : BIER 2 **3** : a vehicle for conveying the dead to the grave
2**hearse** *vt* **hearsed; hears·ing** **1 a** *archaic* : to place on or in a hearse **b** : to convey in a hearse **2** : BURY
1**heart** \ˈhärt\ *n* [ME *hert,* fr. OE *heorte;* akin to OHG *herza* heart, L *cord-, cor,* Gk *kardia*] **1 a** : a hollow muscular organ of vertebrate animals that by its rhythmic contraction acts as a force pump maintaining the circulation of the blood **b** : a structure in an invertebrate animal functionally analogous to the vertebrate heart **c** : BREAST, BOSOM **d** : something resembling a heart in shape; *specif* : a conventionalized representation of a heart **2 a** : a playing card marked with a conventionalized figure of a heart **b** *pl* : the suit comprising cards so marked **c** *pl but sing in constr* : a game in which the object is to avoid taking tricks containing hearts **3 a** : the whole personality including intellectual as well as emotional functions or traits **b** *obs* : INTELLECT **4** : the emotional or moral as distinguished from the intellectual nature: as **a** : generous disposition : COMPASSION **b** : LOVE, AFFECTIONS **c** : COURAGE, ARDOR **5** : one's innermost character, feelings, or inclinations <a man after my own ~> **6 a** : the central or innermost part : CENTER **b** : the essential or most vital part of something — **by heart** : by rote or from memory — **to heart** : with deep concern

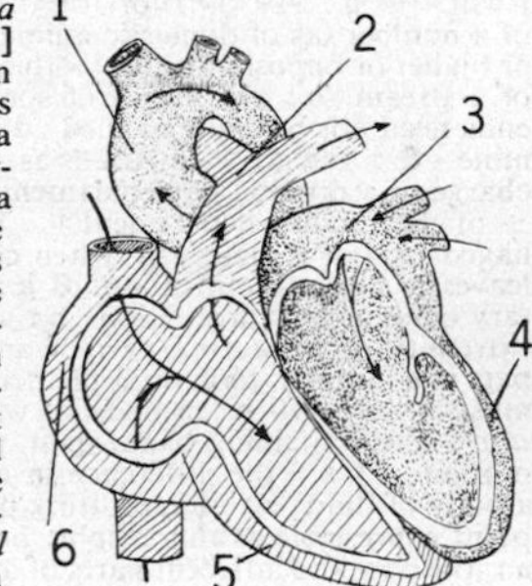

heart 1a: *1* aorta, *2* pulmonary artery, *3* left auricle, *4* left ventricle, *5* right ventricle, *6* right auricle

2**heart** *vt* **1** *archaic* : HEARTEN **2** *archaic* : to fix or seat in the heart
heart·ache \ˈhärt-ˌāk\ *n* : anguish of mind : SORROW
heart attack *n* : an acute episode of heart disease; *esp* : CORONARY THROMBOSIS
heart·beat \ˈhärt-ˌbēt\ *n* **1** : one complete pulsation of the heart **2** : the vital center or driving impulse
heart block *n* : incoordination of the heartbeat in which the auricles and ventricles beat independently and which is marked by decreased cardiac output
heart·break \ˈhärt-ˌbrāk\ *n* : crushing grief
heart·break·ing \-ˌbrā-kiŋ\ *adj* **1 a** : causing intense sorrow or distress <the ~ waste of heightened human consciousness — Richard Poirier> **b** : extremely trying or difficult <a ~ climb to the top of the mountain> **2** : producing an intense emotional reaction or response <~ beauty> — **heart·break·ing·ly** \-kiŋ-lē\ *adv*
heart·bro·ken \-ˌbrō-kən\ *adj* : overcome by sorrow : BROKENHEARTED
heart·burn \-ˌbərn\ *n* : a burning discomfort behind the lower part of the sternum usu. related to spasm of the lower end of the esophagus or of the upper part of the stomach
heart·burn·ing \-ˌbər-niŋ\ *n* : intense or rancorous jealousy or resentment

heart disease *n* **:** an abnormal organic condition of the heart or of the heart and circulation

heart·ed \ˈhärt-əd\ *adj* **1 :** having a heart esp. of a specified kind — usu. used in combination <a faint*hearted* leader> <a light*hearted* wanderer> **2 :** seated in the heart

heart·en \ˈhärt-ᵊn\ *vt* **heart·ened; heart·en·ing** \ˈhärt-niŋ, -ᵊn-iŋ\ **:** to give heart to **:** ENCOURAGE — **heart·en·ing·ly** \-niŋ-lē, -ᵊn-iŋ-\ *adv*

heart failure *n* **1 :** a condition in which the heart is unable to pump blood at an adequate rate or in adequate volume **2 :** cessation of heartbeat **:** DEATH

heart·felt \ˈhärt-ˌfelt\ *adj* **:** deeply felt **:** EARNEST ***syn*** see SINCERE

heart-free \ˈhärt -ˌfrē\ *adj* **:** not in love

hearth \ˈhärth\ *n* [ME *herth,* fr. OE *heorth;* akin to OHG *herd* hearth, Skt *kūḍayati* he singes] **1 a :** a brick, stone, or cement area in front of a fireplace **b :** the floor of a fireplace **c (1) :** the lowest section of a blast furnace **(2) :** the bottom of a refinery, reverberatory, or open-hearth furnace on which the ore or metal is exposed to the flame **(3) :** the inside bottom of a foundry cupola **2 :** HOME **3 :** a vital or creative center <the central ~ of occidental civilization —A. L. Kroeber>

hearth·stone \-ˌstōn\ *n* **1 a :** stone forming a hearth **b :** HOME **2 :** a soft stone or composition of powdered stone and pipe clay used to whiten or scour hearths and doorsteps

heart·i·ly \ˈhärt-ᵊl-ē\ *adv* **1 :** in a hearty manner **2 a :** with all sincerity **:** WHOLEHEARTEDLY **b :** with zest or gusto **3 :** QUITE, THOROUGHLY <~ sick of all this talk>

heart·land \ˈhärt-ˌland\ *n* **:** a central and vital area; *esp* **:** a central land area (as northern Eurasia) held by geopoliticians to have strategic advantages for mastery of the world

heart·less \-ləs\ *adj* **1** *archaic* **:** SPIRITLESS **2 :** lacking feeling **:** CRUEL — **heart·less·ly** *adv* — **heart·less·ness** *n*

heart-lung machine *n* **:** a mechanical pump that shunts the body's blood away from the heart and maintains the circulation during heart surgery

heart·rend·ing \ˈhärt-ˌren-diŋ\ *adj* **:** HEARTBREAKING 1a — **heart·rend·ing·ly** \-diŋ-lē\ *adv*

hearts·ease \ˈhärt-ˌsēz\ *n* **1 :** peace of mind **:** TRANQUILLITY **2 :** any of various violas; *esp* **:** WILD PANSY

heart·sick \ˈhärt-ˌsik\ *adj* **:** very despondent **:** DEPRESSED — **heart·sick·ness** *n*

heart·some \ˈhert-səm\ *adj, chiefly Scot* **:** giving spirit or vigor **:** ANIMATING, ENLIVENING — **heart·some·ly** *adv, chiefly Scot*

heart·sore \ˈhärt-ˌsō(ə)r, -ˌsȯ(ə)r\ *adj* **:** HEARTSICK

heart·string \-ˌstriŋ\ *n* **1** *obs* **:** a nerve once believed to sustain the heart **2 :** the deepest emotions or affections <pulled at his ~*s*>

heart·throb \-ˌthräb\ *n* **1 :** the throb of a heart **2 a :** sentimental emotion **:** PASSION **b :** SWEETHEART

heart-to-heart \ˌhärt-tə-ˌhärt\ *adj* **:** SINCERE, FRANK <a ~ talk>

heart·warm·ing \ˈhärt-ˌwȯr-miŋ\ *adj* **:** inspiring sympathetic feeling **:** CHEERING

heart-whole \-ˌhōl\ *adj* **1 :** HEART-FREE **2 :** SINCERE, GENUINE

heart·wood \-ˌwu̇d\ *n* **:** the older harder nonliving central portion of wood that is usu. darker, denser, less permeable, and more durable than the surrounding sapwood — called also *duramen*

[1]**hearty** \ˈhärt-ē\ *adj* **heart·i·er; -est** **1 a :** giving unqualified support **:** THOROUGHGOING **b :** enthusiastically or exuberantly cordial **:** JOVIAL **c :** expressed unrestrainedly **2 a :** exhibiting vigorous good health **b :** ABUNDANT <a ~ meal> **c :** NOURISHING <a ~ beef stew> **3 :** VIGOROUS, VEHEMENT ***syn*** see SINCERE ***ant*** hollow — **heart·i·ness** *n*

[2]**hearty** *n, pl* **heart·ies :** a bold brave fellow **:** COMRADE; *also* **:** SAILOR

[1]**heat** \ˈhēt\ *vb* [ME *heten,* fr. OE *hǣtan;* akin to OE *hāt* hot] *vi* **1 :** to become warm or hot **2 :** to become hot and start to spoil ~ *vt* **1 :** to make warm or hot **2 :** EXCITE — **heat·able** \-ə-bəl\ *adj* — **heat·ed·ly** *adv*

[2]**heat** *n* **1 a (1) :** a condition of being hot **:** WARMTH **(2) :** a marked or notable degree of hotness **b :** pathological excessive bodily temperature **c :** a hot place or situation **d (1) :** a period of heat **(2) :** a single complete operation of heating; *also* **:** the quantity of material so heated **e (1) :** added energy that causes substances to rise in temperature, fuse, evaporate, expand, or undergo any of various other related changes, that flows to a body by contact with or radiation from bodies at higher temperatures, and that can be produced in a body (as by compression) **(2) :** the energy associated with the random motions of the molecules, atoms, or smaller structural units of which matter is composed **f :** appearance, condition, or color of a body as indicating its temperature **g :** one of a series of intensities of heating **2 a :** intensity of feeling or reaction **b :** the height or stress of an action or condition <in the ~ of battle> **c :** sexual excitement esp. in a female mammal; *specif* **:** ESTRUS **3 :** pungency of flavor **4 :** a single continuous effort: as **a :** a single round of a contest (as a race) having two or more rounds for each contestant **b :** one of several preliminary contests held to eliminate less competent contenders **5 a (1)** *slang* **:** the intensification of law-enforcement activity or investigation **(2)** *slang* **:** POLICE **b :** PRESSURE, COERCION — **heat·less** \ˈhēt-ləs\ *adj*

heat cramps *n pl* **:** a condition that is marked by sudden development of cramps in skeletal muscles and that results from prolonged work in high temperatures accompanied by profuse perspiration with loss of sodium chloride from the body

heat·ed \ˈhēt-əd\ *adj* **:** marked by anger <a ~ argument>

heat engine *n* **:** a mechanism (as an internal-combustion engine) for converting heat energy into mechanical energy

heat·er \ˈhēt-ər\ *n* **1 :** a device that imparts heat or holds something to be heated **2 :** one whose work is to heat something

heat exhaustion *n* **:** a condition marked by weakness, nausea, dizziness, and profuse sweating that results from physical exertion in a hot environment — called also *heat prostration;* compare HEATSTROKE

heath \ˈhēth\ *n* [ME *heth,* fr. OE *hǣth;* akin to OHG *heida* heather, OW *coit* forest] **1 a :** any of a family (Ericaceae, the heath family) of shrubby dicotyledonous and often evergreen plants that thrive on open barren usu. acid and ill-drained soil; *esp* **:** an evergreen subshrub of either of two genera (*Erica* and *Calluna*) with whorls of needlelike leaves and clusters of small flowers **b :** any of various plants that resemble true heaths **2 a :** a tract of wasteland **b :** an extensive area of rather level open uncultivated land usu. with poor coarse soil, inferior drainage, and a surface rich in peat or peaty humus — **heath·less** \-ləs\ *adj* — **heath·like** \-ˌlīk\ *adj* — **heathy** \ˈhē-thē\ *adj*

[1]**hea·then** \ˈhē-t͟hən\ *adj* [ME *hethen,* fr. OE *hǣthen;* akin to OHG *heidan* heathen] **1 :** of or relating to heathens, their religions, or their customs **2 :** STRANGE, UNCIVILIZED

[2]**heathen** *n, pl* **heathens** *or* **heathen 1 :** an unconverted member of a people or nation that does not acknowledge the God of the Bible **2 :** an uncivilized or irreligious person — **hea·then·dom** \-dəm\ *n* — **hea·then·ism** \-t͟hə-ˌniz-əm\ *n* — **hea·then·ize** \-t͟hə-ˌnīz\ *vt*

hea·then·ish \ˈhē-t͟hə-nish\ *adj* **:** resembling or characteristic of heathens **:** BARBAROUS — **hea·then·ish·ly** *adv*

[1]**heath·er** \ˈhet͟h-ər\ *n* [ME (northern) *hather*] **:** HEATH 1a; *esp* **:** a common heath (*Calluna vulgaris*) of northern and alpine regions that has small crowded sessile leaves and racemes of tiny usu. purplish pink flowers

[2]**heather** *adj* **:** HEATHERY

heath·ery \ˈhet͟h-(ə-)rē\ *adj* **1 :** of, relating to, or resembling heather **2 :** having flecks of various colors <a soft ~ tweed>

heath hen *n* **:** a now extinct grouse (*Tympanuchus cupido cupido*) of the northeastern U.S. — compare PRAIRIE CHICKEN

heat lightning *n* **:** vivid and extensive flashes of electric light without thunder seen near the horizon esp. at the close of a hot day and ascribed to far-off lightning reflected by high clouds

heat prostration *n* **:** HEAT EXHAUSTION

heat pump *n* **:** an apparatus for heating or cooling a building by transferring heat by mechanical means from or to a reservoir (as the ground, water, or air) outside the building

heat rash *n* **:** PRICKLY HEAT

heat sink *n* **:** a substance or device for the absorption or dissipation of unwanted heat (as from a process or an electronic device)

heat·stroke \ˈhēt-ˌstrōk\ *n* **:** a condition marked esp. by cessation of sweating, extremely high body temperature, and collapse that results from prolonged exposure to high temperature — compare HEAT EXHAUSTION

heat-treat \ˈhēt-ˌtrēt\ *vt* **:** to subject to heat; *esp* **:** to treat (as metals) by heating and cooling in a way that will produce desired properties — **heat treater** *n* — **heat treatment** *n*

heat wave *n* **:** a period of unusually hot weather

[1]**heave** \ˈhēv\ *vb* **heaved** *or* **hove** \ˈhōv\; **heav·ing** [ME *heven,* fr. OE *hebban;* akin to OHG *hevan* to lift, L *capere* to take] *vt* **1** *obs* **:** ELEVATE **2 :** to cause to be lifted upward or onward **3 :** THROW, CAST **4 :** to utter with obvious effort **5 a :** to cause to swell or rise **b :** to displace (as a rock stratum) esp. by a fault **6 :** HAUL, DRAW ~ *vi* **1 :** to rise or become thrown or raised up **2 :** to strain to do something **:** LABOR **3 a :** to rise and fall rhythmically **b :** PANT **4 :** RETCH **5 a :** PULL, PUSH **b :** to move a ship in a specified direction or manner **c** *of a ship* **:** to move in an indicated way ***syn*** see LIFT — **heav·er** *n*

[2]**heave** *n* **1 a :** an effort to heave or raise **b :** HURL, CAST **2 :** an upward motion **:** RISING; *esp* **:** a rhythmical rising **3 :** the horizontal displacement by the faulting of a rock **4** *pl but sing or pl in constr* **:** chronic pulmonary emphysema of the horse resulting in difficult expiration, heaving of the flanks, and a persistent cough

heav·en \ˈhev-ən\ *n* [ME *heven,* fr. OE *heofon;* akin to OHG *himil* heaven] **1 :** the expanse of space that seems to be over the earth like a dome **:** FIRMAMENT — usu. used in pl. **2 a** *often cap* **:** the dwelling place of the Deity and the joyful abode of the blessed dead **b :** a spiritual state of everlasting communion with God **3** *cap* **:** GOD 1 **4 :** a place or condition of utmost happiness **5** *Christian Science* **:** a state of immortality in which sin is absent and all manifestations of Mind are harmoniously ordered under the divine Principle

heav·en·ly \-lē\ *adj* **1 :** of or relating to heaven or the heavens **:** CELESTIAL <the ~ choirs> **2 a :** suggesting the blessed state of heaven **:** BEATIFIC <~ peace> **b :** DELIGHTFUL — **heav·en·li·ness** *n*

heav·en-sent \-ˌsent\ *adj* **:** PROVIDENTIAL

heav·en·ward \-wərd\ *adv or adj* **:** toward heaven

heav·en·wards \-wərdz\ *adv* **:** HEAVENWARD

heavier-than-air *adj* **:** having greater weight than displacement

heavi·ly \ˈhev-ə-lē\ *adv* **1 :** in a heavy manner **2 :** slowly and laboriously **:** DULLY **3** *archaic* **:** with sorrow **:** GRIEVOUSLY **4 :** to a great degree **:** SEVERELY

Heav·i·side layer \ˌhev-i-ˌsīd-\ *n* [Oliver *Heaviside*] **:** IONOSPHERE

[1]**heavy** \ˈhev-ē\ *adj* **heavi·er; -est** [ME *hevy,* fr. OE *hefig;* akin to OHG *hebīc* heavy, OE *hebban* to lift — more at HEAVE] **1 a :** having great weight **b :** having a high specific gravity **:** having great weight in proportion to bulk **c (1)** *of an isotope* **:** having or being atoms of greater than normal mass **(2)** *of a compound* **:** containing heavy isotopes **2 :** hard to bear; *specif* **:** GRIEVOUS, AFFLICTIVE <a ~ sorrow> **3 :** of weighty import **:** SERIOUS **4 :** DEEP, PROFOUND **5 a :** borne down by something oppressive **:** BURDENED **b :** PREGNANT; *esp* **:** approaching parturition **6 a :** slow or dull from loss of vitality or resiliency **:** SLUGGISH **b :** lacking sparkle or vivacity **:** DRAB **c :** lacking mirth or gaiety **:** DOLEFUL **d :** characterized by declining prices **7 :** dulled with

weariness : DROWSY **8** : greater in quantity or quality than the average of its kind or class: as **a** : unusually large <~ traffic> **b** : of great force <~ seas> **c** : OVERCAST **d** (1) : impeding motion (2) : full of clay and inclined to hold water **e** : coming as if from a depth : LOUD **f** : THICK, COARSE **g** : OPPRESSIVE <~ odor> **h** : STEEP, ACUTE **i** : LABORIOUS, DIFFICULT **j** : of large capacity or output **9 a** : digested with difficulty because of excessive richness or seasoning <~ fruitcake> **b** : not properly raised or leavened <~ bread> **10** : producing goods (as coal, steel, or chemicals) used in the production of other goods <~ industry> **11 a** : armed with guns of large caliber **b** : heavily armored **12 a** : having stress <~ rhythm> — used esp. of syllables in accentual verse **b** : being the strongest degree of stress in speech **13** : relating to theatrical parts of a grave or somber nature — **heavi·ness** *n*
syn HEAVY, WEIGHTY, PONDEROUS, CUMBROUS, CUMBERSOME *shared meaning element* : having great weight ***ant*** light

[2]**heavy** *adv* : in a heavy manner : HEAVILY

[3]**heavy** *n, pl* **heav·ies** **1** *pl* : heavy cavalry **2** : HEAVYWEIGHT 2 **3 a** : a theatrical role of a dignified or somber character; *also* : an actor playing such a role **b** : VILLAIN 4 **c** : a person of importance or significance

heavy chain *n* : either of the two larger of the four polypeptide chains comprising antibodies — compare LIGHT CHAIN

heavy–du·ty \ˌhev-ē-ˈd(y)üt-ē\ *adj* : able or designed to withstand unusual strain

heavy–foot·ed \-ˈfüt-əd\ *adj* : heavy and slow in movement : DULL <~ literary style>

heavy–hand·ed \-ˈhan-dəd\ *adj* **1** : CLUMSY, UNGRACEFUL **2** : OPPRESSIVE, HARSH — **heavy–hand·ed·ly** *adv* — **heavy–hand·ed·ness** *n*

heavy·heart·ed \-ˈhärt-əd\ *adj* : DESPONDENT, SADDENED — **heavy·heart·ed·ly** *adv* — **heavy·heart·ed·ness** *n*

heavy hydrogen *n* : an isotope of hydrogen having a mass number greater than 1; *esp* : DEUTERIUM

heavy·set \ˌhev-ē-ˈset\ *adj* : stocky and compact and sometimes tending to stoutness in build

heavy spar *n* : BARITE

heavy water *n* : water containing more than the usual proportion of heavy isotopes; *esp* : water enriched in deuterium

heavy·weight \ˈhev-ē-ˌwāt\ *n* **1** : one that is above average in weight **2** : one in the usu. heaviest class of contestants: as **a** : a boxer weighing over 175 pounds **b** : a wrestler weighing over 175 pounds or 191 pounds **c** : a weight lifter weighing over 181 pounds

Heb *abbr* **1** Hebrew **2** Hebrews

heb·do·mad \ˈheb-də-ˌmad\ *n* [L *hebdomad-, hebdomas,* fr. Gk, fr. *hebdomos* seventh, fr. *hepta* seven — more at SEVEN] **1** : a group of seven **2** : a period of seven days : WEEK

heb·dom·a·dal \heb-ˈdäm-əd-ᵊl\ *adj* : WEEKLY — **heb·dom·a·dal·ly** \-ᵊl-ē\ *adv*

He·be \ˈhē-bē\ *n* [L, fr. Gk *Hēbē*] : the Greek goddess of youth and a cupbearer to the gods

he·be·phre·nia \ˌhē-bə-ˈfrē-nē-ə, -ˈfren-ē-\ *n* [NL, fr. Gk *hēbē* youth; fr. the childish behavior which is often found with it] : a schizophrenic reaction characterized by silliness, delusions, hallucinations, and regression — **he·be·phre·nic** \-ˈfren-ik, -ˈfrē-nik\ *adj*

heb·e·tate \ˈheb-ə-ˌtāt\ *vt* **-tat·ed; -tat·ing** [L *hebetatus,* pp. of *hebetare,* fr. *hebet-, hebes* dull] : to make dull or obtuse — **heb·e·ta·tion** \ˌheb-ə-ˈtā-shən\ *n*

heb·e·tude \ˈheb-ə-ˌt(y)üd\ *n* : LETHARGY, DULLNESS — **heb·e·tu·di·nous** \ˌheb-ə-ˈt(y)üd-nəs, -ᵊn-əs\ *adj*

He·bra·ic \hi-ˈbrā-ik\ *adj* [ME *Ebrayke,* fr. LL *Hebraicus,* fr. Gk *Hebraikos,* fr. *Hebraios*] : of, relating to, or characteristic of the Hebrews or their language or culture — **He·bra·i·cal·ly** \-ˈbrā-ə-k(ə-)lē\ *adv*

He·bra·ism \ˈhē-(ˌ)brā-ˌiz-əm\ *n* **1** : a characteristic feature of Hebrew occurring in another language **2** : the thought, spirit, or practice characteristic of the Hebrews **3** : a moral theory or emphasis attributed to the Hebrews

He·bra·ist \-ˌbrā-əst\ *n* : a specialist in Hebrew and Hebraic studies

He·bra·is·tic \ˌhē-brā-ˈis-tik\ *adj* **1** : HEBRAIC **2** : marked by Hebraisms

he·bra·ize \ˈhē-brā-ˌīz\ *vb* **-ized; -iz·ing** *often cap, vi* : to use Hebraisms ~ *vt* : to make Hebraic in character or form — **he·bra·iza·tion** \ˌhē-ˌbrā-ə-ˈzā-shən\ *n, often cap*

He·brew \ˈhē-(ˌ)brü\ *n* [ME *Ebreu,* fr. OF, fr. LL *Hebraeus,* fr. L, adj., fr. Gk *Hebraios,* fr. Aram *ʻEbrai*] **1** : a member of or descendant from one of a group of northern Semitic peoples including the Israelites; *esp* : ISRAELITE **2 a** : the Semitic language of the ancient Hebrews **b** : any of various later forms of this language — **Hebrew** *adj*

He·brews \-(ˌ)brüz\ *n pl but sing in constr* : a theological treatise addressed to early Christians and included as a book in the New Testament — see BIBLE table

Hec·ate \ˈhek-ət-ē, *archaic* -ət\ *n* [L, fr. Gk *Hekatē*] : a Greek goddess associated esp. with the underworld, night, and witchcraft

hec·a·tomb \ˈhek-ə-ˌtōm\ *n* [L *hecatombe,* fr. Gk *hekatombē,* fr. *hekaton* hundred + *bous* cow — more at HUNDRED, COW] **1** : an ancient Greek and Roman sacrifice of 100 oxen or cattle **2** : the sacrifice or slaughter of many victims

heck \ˈhek\ *n* [euphemism] : HELL 2a <a ~ of a lot of money>

heck·le \ˈhek-əl\ *vt* **heck·led; heck·ling** \-(ə-)liŋ\ [ME *hekelen,* fr. *heckele* hackle; akin to OHG *hāko* hook — more at HOOK] : to harass and try to disconcert with questions, challenges, or gibes : BADGER ***syn*** see BAIT — **heck·ler** \-(ə-)lər\ *n*

hect- *or* **hecto-** *comb form* [F, irreg. fr. Gk *hekaton*] : hundred <*hecto*graph>

hect·are \ˈhek-ˌta(ə)r, -ˌte(ə)r, -ˌtär\ *n* [F, fr. *hect-* + *are*] — see METRIC SYSTEM table

hec·tic \ˈhek-tik\ *adj* [ME *etyk,* fr. MF *etique,* fr. LL *hecticus,* fr. Gk *hektikos* habitual, consumptive, fr. *echein* to have — more at SCHEME] **1** : of, relating to, or being a fluctuating but persistent fever (as in tuberculosis) **2** : having a hectic fever **3** : RED, FLUSHED **4** : filled with excitement or confusion <the ~ days before Christmas> — **hec·ti·cal·ly** \-ti-k(ə-)lē\ *adv*

hec·to·gram \ˈhek-tə-ˌgram\ *n* [F *hectogramme,* fr. *hect-* + *gramme* gram] — see METRIC SYSTEM table

hec·to·graph \-ˌgraf\ *n* [G *hektograph,* fr. *hekto-* hect- + *-graph*] : a machine for making copies of a writing or drawing produced on a gelatin surface — **hectograph** *vt* — **hec·to·graph·ic** \ˌhek-tə-ˈgraf-ik\ *adj*

hec·to·li·ter \ˈhek-tə-ˌlēt-ər\ *n* [F *hectolitre,* fr. *hect-* + *litre* liter] — see METRIC SYSTEM table

hec·to·me·ter \ˈhek-tə-ˌmēt-ər, hek-ˈtäm-ət-ər\ *n* [F *hectomètre,* fr. *hect-* + *mètre* meter] — see METRIC SYSTEM table

[1]**hec·tor** \ˈhek-tər\ *n* [L, fr. Gk *Hektōr*] **1** *cap* : a son of Priam, husband of Andromache, and Trojan champion slain by Achilles **2** : BULLY, BRAGGART

[2]**hector** *vb* **hec·tored; hec·tor·ing** \-t(ə-)riŋ\ *vi* : to play the bully : SWAGGER ~ *vt* : to intimidate by bluster or personal pressure ***syn*** see BAIT — **hec·tor·ing·ly** \-t(ə-)riŋ-lē\ *adv*

Hec·u·ba \ˈhek-yə-bə\ *n* [L, fr. Gk *Hekabē*] : the wife of Priam in Homer's *Iliad*

he'd \(ˌ)hēd, ēd\ : he had : he would

hed·dle \ˈhed-ᵊl\ *n* [prob. alter. of ME *helde,* fr. OE *hefeld;* akin to ON *hafald* heddle, OE *hebban* to lift — more at HEAVE] : one of the sets of parallel cords or wires that with their mounting compose the harness used to guide warp threads in a loom

he·der \ˈkād-ər, ˈked-\ *n* [Yiddish *kheyder,* fr. Heb *ḥedher* room] : an elementary Jewish school in which children are taught to read the Pentateuch, the Prayer Book, and other books in Hebrew

[1]**hedge** \ˈhej\ *n* [ME *hegge,* fr. OE *hecg;* akin to OE *haga* hedge, hawthorn, L *colum* sieve] **1 a** : a fence or boundary formed by a dense row of shrubs or low trees **b** : BARRIER, LIMIT **2** : a means of protection or defense (as against financial loss) **3** : a calculatedly noncommittal or evasive statement

[2]**hedge** *vb* **hedged; hedg·ing** *vt* **1** : to enclose or protect with or as if with a hedge : ENCIRCLE **2** : to hem in or obstruct with or as if with a barrier : HINDER <*hedged* about by special regulations and statutes —Sandi Rosenbloom> **3** : to protect oneself from losing by a counterbalancing transaction <~ a bet> ~ *vi* **1** : to plant, form, or trim a hedge **2** : to evade the risk of commitment esp. by leaving open a way of retreat : TRIM **3** : to protect oneself financially: as **a** : to buy or sell commodity futures as a protection against loss due to price fluctuation **b** : to minimize the risk of a bet — **hedg·er** *n* — **hedg·ing·ly** \ˈhej-iŋ-lē\ *adv*

[3]**hedge** *adj* **1** : of, relating to, or designed for a hedge **2** : born, living, or made near or as if near hedges : ROADSIDE **3** : INFERIOR

hedge fund *n* : an investing group usu. in the form of a limited partnership that employs speculative techniques in the hope of obtaining large capital gains

hedge·hog \ˈhej-ˌhòg, -ˌhäg\ *n* **1 a** : any of a genus (*Erinaceus*) of Old World nocturnal insectivorous mammals having both hair and spines that they present outwardly by rolling themselves up **b** : any of several spiny mammals (as a porcupine) **2 a** : a military defensive obstacle (as of barbed wire) **b** : a well-fortified military stronghold

hedgehog 1a

hedge·hop \-ˌhäp\ *vi* [back-formation fr. *hedgehopper*] : to fly an airplane close to the ground and rise over obstacles as they appear — **hedge·hop·per** *n*

hedge·pig \-ˈpig\ *n* : HEDGEHOG

hedge·row \-ˌrō\ *n* : a row of shrubs or trees enclosing or separating fields

he·don·ic \hi-ˈdän-ik\ *adj* **1** : of, relating to, or characterized by pleasure **2** : HEDONISTIC — **he·don·i·cal·ly** \-i-k(ə-)lē\ *adv*

hedonic calculus *n* : FELICIFIC CALCULUS

he·do·nism \ˈhēd-ᵊn-ˌiz-əm\ *n* [Gk *hēdonē* pleasure; akin to Gk *hēdys* sweet — more at SWEET] **1** : the doctrine that pleasure or happiness is the sole or chief good in life — compare PSYCHOLOGICAL HEDONISM **2** : a way of life based on or suggesting the principles of hedonism — **he·do·nist** \-ᵊn-əst\ *n* — **he·do·nis·tic** \ˌhēd-ᵊn-ˈis-tik\ *adj* — **he·do·nis·ti·cal·ly** \-ti-k(ə-)lē\ *adv*

-he·dral \ˈhē-drəl\ *adj comb form* [NL *-hedron*] : having (such) a surface or (such or so many) surfaces <di*hedral*>

-he·dron \ˈhē-drən\ *n comb form, pl* **-hedrons** *or* **-he·dra** \-drə\ [NL, fr. Gk *-edron,* fr. *hedra* seat — more at SIT] : crystal or geometrical figure having a (specified) form or number of surfaces <penta*hedron*> <trapezo*hedron*>

hee·bie–jee·bies \ˌhē-bē-ˈjē-bēz\ *n pl* [coined by Billy DeBeck †1942 Am cartoonist] : JITTERS, WILLIES

[1]**heed** \ˈhēd\ *vb* [ME *heeden,* fr. OE *hēdan;* akin to OHG *huota* guard] *vi* : to pay attention ~ *vt* : to take notice of : pay attention to <the individual's right to ~ his conscience —Mary J. White>

[2]**heed** *n* : ATTENTION, NOTICE

heed·ful \ˈhēd-fəl\ *adj* : taking heed : ATTENTIVE <~ of what they were doing> — **heed·ful·ly** \-fə-lē\ *adv* — **heed·ful·ness** *n*

heed·less \-ləs\ *adj* : not taking heed : INCONSIDERATE, THOUGHTLESS <~ follies of unbridled youth —John DeBruyn> — **heed·less·ly** *adv* — **heed·less·ness** *n*

hee–haw \ˈhē-ˌhò, -ˈhò\ *n* [imit.] **1** : the bray of a donkey **2** : a loud rude laugh : GUFFAW — **hee–haw** *vi*

[1]**heel** \ˈhē(ə)l\ *n* [ME, fr. OE *hēla;* akin to ON *hæll* heel, OE *hōh* — more at HOCK] **1 a** : the back of the human foot below the ankle and behind the arch **b** : the back of the hind limb of other vertebrates homologous with the human heel **2** : an anatomical structure suggestive of the human heel **3 a** : one of the crusty ends of a loaf of bread **b** : one of the rind ends of a cheese **4 a**

: the part (as of a shoe) that covers the human heel **b** : a solid attachment of a shoe or boot forming the back of the sole under the heel of the foot **5** : a rear, low, or bottom part: as **a** : the after end of a ship's keel or the lower end of a mast **b** : the base of a tuber or cutting of a plant used for propagation **c** : the base of a ladder **6** : a contemptible person — **heeled** \ˈhē(ə)ld\ *adj* — **heel·less** \ˈhē(ə)l-ləs\ *adj* — **by the heels** : in a tight grip — **down at heel** *or* **down at the heel** : in or into a run-down or shabby condition — **on the heels of** : immediately following — **to heel 1** : close behind **2** : into agreement or line <a vast world brought *to heel* at man's command —R. C. Buck> — **under heel** : under control or subjection

²heel *vt* **1 a** : to furnish with a heel **b** : to supply esp. with money **2** : to exert pressure on, propel, or strike with the heel <~*ed* her horse> ~ *vi* : to move along at the heels of someone <a dog that ~*s* well>

³heel *vb* [alter. of ME *heelden,* fr. OE *hieldan;* akin to OHG *hald* inclined, Lith *šalis* side, region] *vi* : to tilt to one side : TIP, LIST ~ *vt* : to cause (a boat) to list

⁴heel *n* : a tilt (as of a boat) to one side : LIST; *also* : the extent of a list

heel-and-toe \ˌhē-lən-ˈtō\ *adj* : marked by a stride in which the heel of one foot touches the ground before the toe of the other foot leaves it <~ walking>

heel·ball \ˈhē(ə)l-ˌbȯl\ *n* : a composition of wax and lampblack used by shoemakers for polishing and by antiquarians for making rubbings of inscriptions

heel·er \ˈhē-lər\ *n* **1** : one that heels **2 a** : a henchman of a local political boss **b** : a worker for a local party organization; *esp* : WARD HEELER

heel fly *n* : any of several warble flies (genus *Hypoderma*) that attack cattle; *esp* : COMMON CATTLE GRUB

heel·piece \ˈhē(ə)l-ˌpēs\ *n* : a piece designed for or forming the heel (as of a shoe)

heel·tap \-ˌtap\ *n* : a small quantity of liquor remaining (as in a glass after drinking)

HEFA *abbr* Higher Education Facilities Act

¹heft \ˈheft\ *n* [irreg. fr. *heave*] **1 a** : WEIGHT, HEAVINESS **b** : IMPORTANCE, INFLUENCE **2** *archaic* : the greater part of something : BULK

²heft *vt* **1** : to heave up : HOIST **2** : to test the weight of by lifting <~*ing* the rod . . . to get the feel of it —*Consumer Reports*>

hefty \ˈhef-tē\ *adj* **heft·i·er; -est 1** : quite heavy **2 a** : marked by bigness, bulk, and usu. strength <a ~ football player> **b** : POWERFUL, MIGHTY **c** : impressively large <~ servings of steaks —*Boston Spectator*> — **heft·i·ly** \-tə-lē\ *adv* — **heft·i·ness** \-tē-nəs\ *n*

he·gari \hi-ˈga(ə)r-ē, -ˈga(ə)r-ə, -ˈge(ə)r-; ˈhi-ˌgi(ə)r\ *n* [Ar (Sudan) *hegiri*] : any of several Sudanese grain sorghums having chalky white seeds including one grown in the southwestern U.S.

¹He·ge·li·an \hā-ˈgā-lē-ən, hig-ˈā-\ *adj* : of, relating to, or characteristic of Hegel, his philosophy, or his dialectic method

²Hegelian *n* : a follower of Hegel : an adherent of Hegelianism

He·ge·li·an·ism \-lē-ə-ˌniz-əm\ *n* : the philosophy of Hegel that equates the rational and the real and that uses dialectic to comprehend an absolute idea of which phenomena are partial representations

he·gem·o·ny \hi-ˈjem-ə-nē, -ˈgem-; ˈhej-ə-ˌmō-nē\ *n* [Gk *hēgemonia,* fr. *hēgemōn* leader, fr. *hēgeisthai* to lead — more at SEEK] : preponderant influence or authority esp. of one nation over others — **heg·e·mon·ic** \ˌhej-ə-ˈmän-ik, ˌheg-\ *adj*

he·gi·ra *also* **he·ji·ra** \hi-ˈjī-rə, ˈhej-(ə-)rə\ *n* [the *Hegira,* flight of Muhammad from Mecca in A.D. 622, fr. ML, fr. Ar *hijrah,* lit., flight] : a journey esp. when undertaken to escape from a dangerous or undesirable situation : EXODUS

Hei·del·berg man \ˌhīd-ᵊl-ˌbərg-, -ˌbe(ə)rg-\ *n* [*Heidelberg,* Germany] : an early Pleistocene man known from a massive fossilized jaw with distinctly human dentition

heif·er \ˈhef-ər\ *n* [ME *hayfare,* fr. OE *hēahfore*] : a young cow; *esp* : one that has not had a calf

heigh-ho \ˈhī-ˈhō, ˈhā-\ *interj* — used typically to express boredom, weariness, or sadness or sometimes as a cry of encouragement

height \ˈhīt, ˈhītth\ *n* [ME *heighthe,* fr. OE *hiehthu;* akin to OHG *hōhida* height, OE *hēah* high] **1 a** : the highest part : SUMMIT **b** : the highest or most advanced point : ZENITH <at the ~ of his powers> **2 a** : the distance from the bottom to the top of something standing upright **b** : the extent of elevation above a level **3** : the condition of being tall or high **4 a** : an extent of land rising to a considerable degree above the surrounding country **b** : a high point or position **5** *obs* : an advanced social rank **6** : degree of geographical latitude

syn HEIGHT, ALTITUDE, ELEVATION *shared meaning element* : vertical distance either between the top and bottom of something or between a base and something above it

height·en \ˈhīt-ᵊn\ *vb* **height·ened; height·en·ing** \ˈhīt-niŋ, -ᵊn-iŋ\ *vt* **1 a** : to increase the amount or degree of : AUGMENT **b** : to make brighter or more intense : DEEPEN **c** : to bring out more strongly : point up **d** : to make more acute : SHARPEN **2 a** : to raise high or higher : ELEVATE **b** : to raise above the ordinary or trite **3** *obs* : ELATE ~ *vi* **1** *archaic* : GROW, RISE **2 a** : to become great or greater in amount, degree, or extent **b** : to become brighter or more intense *syn* see INTENSIFY

height to paper : the height of printing type measured from foot to face and standardized at 0.9186 inch in English-speaking countries

hei·nous \ˈhā-nəs\ *adj* [ME, fr. MF *haineus,* fr. *haine* hate, fr. *hair* to hate, of Gmc origin; akin to OHG *haz* hate — more at HATE] : hatefully or shockingly evil : ABOMINABLE *syn* see OUTRAGEOUS — **hei·nous·ly** *adv* — **hei·nous·ness** *n*

¹heir \ˈa(ə)r, ˈe(ə)r\ *n* [ME, fr. OF, fr. L *hered-, heres;* akin to Gk *chēros* bereaved, OE *gān* to go] **1** : one who inherits or is entitled to inherit property: as **a** : HEIR AT LAW **b** : one who receives the property of a deceased person esp. by operation of law or by virtue of a will **2** : one who inherits or is entitled to succeed to a hereditary rank, title, or office **3** : one who receives or is entitled to receive some endowment or quality from a parent or predecessor — **heir·less** \-ləs\ *adj* — **heir·ship** \-ˌship\ *n*

²heir *vt, chiefly dial* : INHERIT <the loveliest maid . . . that ever ~*ed* a crown —Sir Walter Scott>

heir apparent *n, pl* **heirs apparent 1** : an heir whose right to an inheritance is indefeasible in law if he survives the legal ancestor **2** : HEIR PRESUMPTIVE **3** : one whose succession esp. to a position or role appears certain under existing circumstances

heir at law : an heir in whom an intestate's real property is vested by operation of law

heir·ess \ˈar-əs, ˈer-\ *n* : a female heir; *esp* : a female heir to great wealth

heir·loom \ˈa(ə)r-ˌlüm, ˈe(ə)r-\ *n* [ME *heirlome,* fr. *heir* + *lome* implement — more at LOOM] **1** : a piece of property that descends to the heir as an inseparable part of an inheritance **2** : something of special value handed on from one generation to another

heir presumptive *n, pl* **heirs presumptive** : an heir whose legal right to an inheritance may be defeated (as by the birth of a nearer relative)

¹heist \ˈhīst\ *vt* [alter. of ¹*hoist*] **1** *chiefly dial* : HOIST **2** *slang* **a** : to commit armed robbery on **b** : to take unlawfully and usu. with violence : STEAL

²heist *n, slang* : armed robbery : HOLDUP; *also* : THEFT

Hel \ˈhel\ *n* [ON] : the Norse goddess of the dead and queen of the underworld

held *past of* HOLD

hel·den·te·nor \ˈhel-dən-tā-ˌnȯ(ə)r, -ˌnō(ə)r, -ˌten-ər\ *n, often cap* [G, fr. *held* hero + *tenor*] : a tenor with a dramatic voice well suited to heroic (as Wagnerian) roles

Helen of Troy \ˌhel-ə-nəv-ˈtrȯi\ : the wife of Menelaus whose abduction by Paris brought about the Trojan War

heli- *or* **helio-** *comb form* [L, fr. Gk *hēli-, hēlio-,* fr. *hēlios* — more at SOLAR] : sun <*helio*centric>

he·li·a·cal \hi-ˈlī-ə-kəl\ *adj* [LL *heliacus,* fr. Gk *hēliakos,* fr. *hēlios*] : relating to or near the sun — used esp. of the last setting of a star before and its first rising after invisibility due to conjunction with the sun — **he·li·a·cal·ly** \-k(ə-)lē\ *adv*

helic- *or* **helico-** *comb form* [Gk *helik-, heliko-,* fr. *helik-, helix* spiral — more at HELIX] : helix : spiral <*helic*al>

he·li·cal \ˈhel-i-kəl, ˈhē-li-\ *adj* : of, relating to, or having the form of a helix; *broadly* : SPIRAL 1a — **he·li·cal·ly** \-k(ə-)lē\ *adv*

he·li·coid \ˈhel-ə-ˌkȯid, ˈhē-lə-\ *or* **he·li·coi·dal** \ˌhel-ə-ˈkȯid-ᵊl, ˌhē-lə-\ *adj* **1** : forming or arranged in a spiral **2** : having the form of a flat coil or flattened spiral <~ snail shell>

hel·i·con \ˈhel-ə-ˌkän, -i-kən\ *n* [prob. fr. Gk *helik-, helix* + E *-on* (as in *bombardon*); from its tube's forming a spiral encircling the player's body] : a large circular tuba similar to a sousaphone but lacking an adjustable bell

he·li·copt \ˈhel-ə-ˌkäpt, ˈhē-lə-\ *vb* [back-formation fr. ¹*helicopter*] : HELICOPTER

¹he·li·cop·ter \ˈhel-ə-ˌkäp-tər, ˈhē-lə-\ *n* [F *hélicoptère,* fr. Gk *heliko-* + *pteron* wing — more at FEATHER] : an aircraft whose support in the air is derived chiefly from the aerodynamic forces acting on one or more rotors turning about substantially vertical axes

²helicopter *vi* : to travel by helicopter ~ *vt* : to transport by helicopter

he·lio·cen·tric \ˌhē-lē-ō-ˈsen-trik\ *adj* **1** : referred to or measured from the sun's center or appearing as if seen from it **2** : having or relating to the sun as a center — compare GEOCENTRIC

he·lio·chrome \ˈhē-lē-ə-ˌkrōm\ *n* : a photograph in natural colors

he·lio·gram \-ˌgram\ *n* : a message transmitted by a heliograph

¹he·lio·graph \-ˌgraf\ *n* [ISV] **1 a** : PHOTOENGRAVING 2b **b** : PHOTOHELIOGRAPH **2** : an apparatus for telegraphing by means of the sun's rays thrown from a mirror

²heliograph *vt* : to signal by means of a heliograph — **he·li·og·ra·pher** \ˌhē-lē-ˈäg-rə-fər, ˈhē-lē-ə-ˌgraf-ər\ *n*

he·lio·graph·ic \ˌhē-lē-ə-ˈgraf-ik\ *adj* **1** : of or relating to heliography or a heliograph **2** : SOLAR 1 <~ latitude>

he·li·og·ra·phy \ˌhē-lē-ˈäg-rə-fē, ˈhē-lē-ə-ˌgraf-ē\ *n* **1** : an early photographic process producing a photoengraving on a metal plate; *broadly* : PHOTOGRAPHY **2** : the system or practice of signaling with a heliograph

heliograph 2

he·lio·gra·vure \ˌhē-lē-ō-grə-ˈvyu̇(ə)r\ *n* [F *héliogravure,* fr. *hélio-* heli- + *gravure*] : PHOTOGRAVURE

he·li·ol·a·try \ˌhē-lē-ˈäl-ə-trē\ *n* : sun worship — **he·li·ol·a·trous** \-trəs\ *adj*

he·li·om·e·ter \ˌhē-lē-ˈäm-ət-ər\ *n* [F *héliomètre,* fr. *hélio-* heli- + *-mètre* -meter] : a visual telescope that has a divided objective designed for measuring the apparent diameter of the sun but later used for measuring angles between celestial bodies or between points on the moon — **he·lio·met·ric** \ˌhē-lē-ō-ˈme-trik\ *adj* — **he·lio·met·ri·cal·ly** \-tri-k(ə-)lē\ *adv*

he·lio·phyte \ˈhē-lē-ə-ˌfīt\ *n* : a plant thriving in or tolerating full sunlight

he·lio·stat \ˈhē-lē-ə-ˌstat\ *n* [NL *heliostata,* fr. *heli-* + Gk *-statēs* -stat] : an instrument consisting of a mirror mounted on an axis moved by clockwork by which a sunbeam is steadily reflected in one direction

he·lio·tax·is \ˌhē-lē-ō-ˈtak-səs\ *n* [NL] **:** phototaxis in which sunlight is the stimulus

he·lio·trope \ˈhēl-yə-ˌtrōp, *Brit usu* ˈhel-\ *n* [L *heliotropium*, fr. Gk *hēliotropion*, fr. *hēlio-* heli- + *tropos* turn; fr. its flowers' turning toward the sun — more at TROPE] **1 :** any of a genus (*Heliotropium*) of herbs or shrubs of the borage family — compare GARDEN HELIOTROPE **2 :** BLOODSTONE **3 a :** a variable color averaging a moderate purple **b :** a moderate reddish purple

he·li·ot·ro·pism \ˌhē-lē-ˈä-trə-ˌpiz-əm\ *n* **:** phototropism in which sunlight is the orienting stimulus — **he·lio·tro·pic** \-lē-ə-ˈtrōp-ik, -ˈträp-\ *adj* — **he·lio·tro·pi·cal·ly** \-i-k(ə-)lē\ *adv*

he·lio·zo·an \ˌhē-lē-ə-ˈzō-ən\ *n* [NL *Heliozoa*, order name, fr. *heli-* + *-zoa*] **:** any of an order (Heliozoa) of free-living holozoic usu. freshwater rhizopod protozoans that reproduce by binary fission or budding — **heliozoan** *adj* — **he·lio·zo·ic** \-ˈzō-ik\ *adj*

he·li·pad \ˈhel-ə-ˌpad, ˈhē-lə-\ *n* **:** HELIPORT

he·li·port \-ˌpō(ə)rt, -ˌpȯ(ə)rt\ *n* [*helicopter* + *port*] **:** a landing and takeoff place for a helicopter

he·li·stop \-ˌstäp\ *n* **:** HELIPORT

he·li·um \ˈhē-lē-əm\ *n* [NL, fr. Gk *hēlios*] **:** a light colorless nonflammable gaseous element found esp. in natural gases and used chiefly for inflating airships and balloons, for filling incandescent lamps, and for cryogenic research

he·lix \ˈhē-liks\ *n, pl* **he·li·ces** \ˈhel-ə-ˌsēz, ˈhē-lə-\ *also* **he·lix·es** \ˈhē-lik-səz\ [L, fr. Gk; akin to Gk *eilyein* to roll, wrap — more at VOLUBLE] **1 :** something spiral in form: as **a :** an ornamental volute **b :** a coil formed by winding wire around a uniform tube **2 :** the incurved rim of the external ear **3 :** a curve traced on a cylinder by the rotation of a point crossing its right sections at a constant oblique angle; *broadly* **:** SPIRAL 1b

hell \ˈhel\ *n* [ME, fr. OE; akin to OHG *helan* to conceal, L *celare*, Gk *kalyptein*] **1 a** (1) **:** a nether world in which the dead continue to exist **:** HADES (2) **:** the nether realm of the devil and the demons in which the damned suffer everlasting punishment **b** *Christian Science* **:** ERROR 2b, SIN **2 a :** a place or state of torment or wickedness — often used as an interjection, an intensive, or a generalized term of abuse <war is ~ —W. T. Sherman> <a ~ of a nice guy> <go to ~> **b :** a place or state of turmoil or destruction <all ~ broke loose> **c :** a severe scolding <got ~ for coming in late> **d :** unrestrained fun or sportiveness <the kids were full of ~ and tore the house apart> **3 a** *archaic* **:** a tailor's receptacle **b :** HELLBOX — **hell or high water :** difficulties of whatever kind or size <will stand by his convictions come *hell or high water*> — **hell to pay :** serious trouble <if he's late there'll be *hell to pay*>

he'll \(ˌ)hē(ə)l, hil, ēl, il\ **:** he will **:** he shall

hell·ben·der \ˈhel-ˌben-dər\ *n* **:** a large voracious aquatic salamander (*Cryptobranchus alleganiensis*) of the Ohio valley

hell–bent \-ˌbent\ *adj* **1 :** stubbornly and often recklessly determined <~ to cut taxes again before election —*New Republic*> **2 :** moving at full speed **:** RECKLESS <drivers . . . on a ~ mission of self-destruction —Jerome Beatty, Jr.>

hell·box \-ˌbäks\ *n* **:** a receptacle into which a printer throws damaged or discarded type

hell·broth \-ˌbrȯth\ *n* **:** a brew for working black magic

hell·cat \-ˌkat\ *n* **1 :** WITCH 2 **2 :** one given to tormenting others; *esp* **:** SHREW

hel·le·bore \ˈhel-ə-ˌbō(ə)r, -ˌbȯ(ə)r\ *n* [L *helleborus*, fr. Gk *helleboros*] **1 :** any of a genus (*Helleborus*) of herbs of the buttercup family having showy flowers with petaloid sepals; *also* **:** the dried rhizome or an extract or powder of this formerly used in medicine **2 :** a poisonous herb (genus *Veratrum*) of the lily family; *also* **:** the dried rhizome of a hellebore (*Veratrum album* or *V. viride*) or a powder or extract of this containing alkaloids used as a cardiac and respiratory depressant and as an insecticide

Hel·lene \ˈhel-ˌēn\ *n* [Gk *Hellēn*] **:** GREEK

1**Hel·len·ic** \he-ˈlen-ik, hə-\ *adj* **:** of or relating to Greece, its people, or its language

2**Hellenic** *n* **:** GREEK 2a

Hel·le·nism \ˈhel-ə-ˌniz-əm\ *n* **1 :** GRECISM 1 **2 :** devotion to or imitation of ancient Greek thought, customs, or styles **3 :** Greek civilization esp. as modified in the Hellenistic period by oriental influences **4 :** a body of humanistic and classical ideals associated with ancient Greece and including reason, the pursuit of knowledge and the arts, moderation, civic responsibility, and bodily development

Hel·le·nist \-nəst\ *n* **1 :** a person living in Hellenistic times who was Greek in language, outlook, and way of life but was not Greek in ancestry; *esp* **:** a hellenized Jew **2 :** a specialist in the language or culture of ancient Greece

Hel·le·nis·tic \ˌhel-ə-ˈnis-tik\ *adj* **1 :** of or relating to Greek history, culture, or art after Alexander the Great **2 :** of or relating to the Hellenists — **Hel·le·nis·ti·cal·ly** \-ti-k(ə-)lē\ *adv*

hel·le·nize \ˈhel-ə-ˌnīz\ *vb* **-nized; -niz·ing** *often cap, vi* **:** to become Greek or Hellenistic ~ *vt* **:** to make Greek or Hellenistic in form or culture — **hel·le·ni·za·tion** \ˌhel-ə-nə-ˈzā-shən\ *n, often cap*

hell·er \ˈhel-ər\ *n* **:** HELLION

hel·leri \ˈhel-ə-ˌrī, -(ˌ)rē\ *n* [NL (specific epithet of *Xiphophorus helleri*), fr. C. *Heller*, 20th cent. tropical fish collector] **1 :** SWORDTAIL **2 :** any of various brightly colored topminnows developed by hybridization of swordtails and platys

1**hell–for–leather** *adv* **:** in a hell-for-leather manner **:** at full speed <rode ~ down the trail>

2**hell–for–leather** *adj* **:** marked by determined recklessness or great speed or force <a cocky, ~ fighting man —H. H. Martin>

hell·gram·mite \ˈhel-grə-ˌmīt\ *n* [origin unknown] **:** a carnivorous aquatic No. American insect larva that is the young form of a dobsonfly (esp. *Corydalis cornutus*) and is used for fish bait

hell·hole \ˈhel-ˌhōl\ *n* **1 :** the pit of hell **2 :** a place of extreme discomfort or squalor

hell·hound \-ˌhau̇nd\ *n* **1 :** a dog represented in mythology as a guardian of the underworld **2 :** a fiendish person

hel·lion \ˈhel-yən\ *n* [prob. alter. of *hallion* (scamp)] **:** a troublesome or mischievous person

hell·ish \ˈhel-ish\ *adj* **:** of, resembling, or befitting hell **:** DEVILISH <nothing more ~ than warfare within the soul —Frank Yerby> — **hell·ish·ly** *adv* — **hell·ish·ness** *n*

hel·lo \hə-ˈlō, he-\ *n, pl* **hellos** [alter. of *hollo*] **:** an expression or gesture of greeting — used interjectionally in greeting, in answering the telephone, or to express surprise

1**helm** \ˈhelm\ *n* [ME, fr. OE] **:** HELMET 1

2**helm** *vt* **:** to cover or furnish with a helmet

3**helm** *n* [ME *helme*, fr. OE *helma*; akin to OHG *helmo* tiller] **1 a :** a lever or wheel controlling the rudder of a ship for steering; *broadly* **:** the entire apparatus for steering a ship **b :** deviation of the position of the helm from the amidships position **2 :** a position of control **:** HEAD <a new dean is at the ~ of the medical school>

4**helm** *vt* **:** to direct with or as if with a helm **:** STEER

hel·met \ˈhel-mət\ *n* [MF, dim. of *helme* helmet, of Gmc origin; akin to OE *helm* helmet, OHG *helan* to conceal — more at HELL] **1 :** a covering or enclosing headpiece of ancient or medieval armor **2 :** any of various protective head coverings usu. made of a hard material to resist impact **3 :** something resembling a helmet; *specif* **:** a hood-shaped upper sepal or petal of some flowers — **hel·met·ed** \-mət-əd\ *adj* — **hel·met·like** \-mət-ˌlīk\ *adj*

hel·minth \ˈhel-ˌmin(t)th\ *n* [Gk *helminth-*, *helmis*; akin to Gk *eilyein* to roll — more at VOLUBLE] **:** WORM; *esp* **:** an intestinal worm — used esp. by parasitologists — **hel·min·thic** \hel-ˈmin(t)-thik\ *adj*

helminth- *or* **helmintho-** *comb form* [NL, fr. Gk *helminth-*, *helmis*] **:** helminth <*helminth*iasis> <*helmintho*logy>

hel·min·thi·a·sis \ˌhel-mən-ˈthī-ə-səs\ *n* [NL] **:** infestation with or disease caused by parasitic worms

hel·min·thol·o·gy \-ˈthäl-ə-jē\ *n* **:** a branch of zoology concerned with helminths; *esp* **:** the study of parasitic worms

helms·man \ˈhelmz-mən\ *n* **:** the person at the helm **:** STEERSMAN — **helms·man·ship** \-ˌship\ *n*

hel·ot \ˈhel-ət\ *n* [L *Helotes*, pl., fr. Gk *Heilōtes*] **1** *cap* **:** a member of a class of serfs in ancient Sparta **2 :** SERF, SLAVE — **hel·ot·ry** \ˈhel-ə-trē\ *n*

hel·ot·ism \ˈhel-ət-ˌiz-əm\ *n* **1 :** SERFDOM **2 :** a symbiotic relation (as in a lichen) in which one member (as an alga) functions as the slave of the other (as a fungus)

1**help** \ˈhelp, *South also* ˈhep\ *vb* [ME *helpen*, fr. OE *helpan*; akin to OHG *helfan* to help, Lith *selpti*] *vt* **1 :** to give assistance or support to <~ a child to understand his lesson> **2 a :** to make more pleasant or bearable **:** RELIEVE <bright curtains will ~ the room> <took an aspirin to ~ her headache> **b** *archaic* **:** RESCUE, SAVE **c :** to get (oneself) out of a difficulty **3 a :** to be of use to **:** BENEFIT **b :** to further the advancement of **:** PROMOTE **4 a :** to change for the better **b :** to refrain from <couldn't ~ laughing> **c :** to keep from occurring **:** PREVENT <they couldn't ~ the accident> **5 :** to serve with food or drink esp. at a meal **6 :** to appropriate for the use of (oneself) ~ *vi* **:** to be of use or benefit

syn* 1** HELP, AID, ASSIST *shared meaning element* **:** to supply what is needed to accomplish an end. HELP carries a strong implication of advance toward an objective <every little bit *helps*> <how games can *help* children to learn —*Johns Hopkins Mag.*> AID strongly suggests the need of help or relief and often imputes weakness to the one aided <the fund was *aided* by a series of sales> <saints will *aid* if men will call —S. T. Coleridge> ASSIST distinctively imputes a secondary role to the assistant or a secondary character to the assistance; thus, a deputy *assists* rather than *aids* his superior; a good light *assists* (not *aids*) the eyes in reading ***ant hinder
2 see IMPROVE

— **cannot help but :** cannot but <*could not help but* smile at the answer> — **so help me :** on my word **:** believe it or not

2**help** *n* **1 :** AID, ASSISTANCE **2 :** a source of aid <printed ~*s* to the memory —C. S. Braden> **3 :** REMEDY, RELIEF **4 a :** one who is in the service of or who assists another **:** HELPER **b :** the services of a paid worker <~ wanted> **5 :** HELPING

help·er *n* **:** one that helps; *esp* **:** a relatively unskilled worker who assists a skilled worker usu. by manual labor

help·ful \ˈhelp-fəl\ *adj* **:** of service or assistance **:** USEFUL — **help·ful·ly** \-fə-lē\ *adv* — **help·ful·ness** *n*

help·ing *n* **:** a serving of food

help·less \ˈhel-pləs\ *adj* **1 :** lacking protection or support **:** DEFENSELESS **2 :** lacking strength or effectiveness **:** POWERLESS <the fever . . . laid him low, prostrate and ~ —William Styron> — **help·less·ly** *adv* — **help·less·ness** *n*

help·mate \ˈhelp-ˌmāt\ *n* [by folk etymology fr. *helpmeet*] **:** one who is a companion and helper; *esp* **:** WIFE

help·meet \-ˌmēt\ *n* [2*help* + *meet*, adj.] **:** HELPMATE

1**hel·ter–skel·ter** \ˌhel-tər-ˈskel-tər\ *adv* [imit.] **1 :** in headlong disorder **:** PELL-MELL <ran ~, getting in each other's way —F. V. W. Mason> **2 :** in random order **:** HAPHAZARDLY

2**helter–skelter** *n* **:** a disorderly confusion **:** TURMOIL

3**helter–skelter** *adj* **1 :** confusedly hurried **:** PRECIPITATE **2 :** HAPHAZARD, HIT-OR-MISS <the ~ arrangement of the papers, all mussed and frayed —Jean Stafford>

helve \ˈhelv\ *n* [ME, fr. OE *hielfe*; akin to OE *healf* half] **:** a handle of a tool or weapon **:** HAFT

Hel·ve·tian \hel-ˈvē-shən\ *adj* **:** of or relating to the Helvetii or Helvetia **:** SWISS — **Helvetian** *n*

Hel·ve·tii \-shē-ˌī\ *n pl* [L] **:** an early Celtic people of western Switzerland in the time of Julius Caesar

1**hem** \ˈhem\ *n* [ME, fr. OE; akin to MHG *hemmen* to hem in, Arm *kamel* to press] **1 a :** a border of a cloth article doubled back and stitched down **b :** a similar border on an article of sheet metal, plastic, rubber, or leather **2 :** RIM, MARGIN <bright green ~ of reeds about the ponds —R. M. Lockley>

2**hem** *vb* **hemmed; hem·ming** *vt* **1 a :** to finish with a hem **b :** BORDER, EDGE **2 :** to surround in a restrictive manner **:** CONFINE — usu. used with *in* <*hemmed* in by enemy troops> ~ *vi* **:** to make a hem in sewing — **hem·mer** *n*

[3]**hem** *usually read as* ˈhem\ *interj* [imit.] — often used to indicate a vocalized pause in speaking

[4]**hem** \ˈhem\ *vi* **hemmed; hem·ming** **1 :** to utter the sound represented by *hem* <*hemmed* and hawed before answering> **2 :** EQUIVOCATE <the administration *hemmed* and hawed over the students' demands>

hem- *or* **hemo-** *or* **haem-** *or* **haemo-** *comb form* [MF *hemo-*, fr. L *haem-, haemo-*, fr. Gk *haim-, haimo-*, fr. *haima*]: blood <*hem*al> <*hemo*flagellate>

hema- *or* **haema-** *comb form* [NL, fr. Gk *haima*] **:** HEM- <*hema*cytometer>

he·ma·cy·tom·e·ter \ˌhē-mə-sī-ˈtäm-ət-ər\ *n* **:** an instrument for counting blood cells

hem·ag·glu·ti·nate \ˌhē-mə-ˈglüt-ᵊn-ˌāt\ *vt* **:** to cause agglutination of red blood cells — **hem·ag·glu·ti·na·tion** \-glüt-ᵊn-ˈā-shən\ *n*

hem·ag·glu·ti·nin \-ˈglüt-ᵊn-ən\ *n* [ISV]**:** an agglutinin that causes hemagglutination

he·mal \ˈhē-məl\ *adj* **1 :** of or relating to the blood or blood vessels **2 :** relating to or situated on the side of the spinal cord where the heart and chief blood vessels are placed

he–man \ˈhē-ˈman\ *n* **:** a strong virile man

hem·an·gi·o·ma \ˌhē-ˌman-jē-ˈō-mə\ *n* [NL, fr. *hem-* + *angioma*] **:** a usu. benign tumor made up of blood vessels that typically occurs as a purplish or reddish slightly elevated area of skin

hemat- *or* **hemato-** *or* **haemat-** *or* **haemato-** *comb form* [L *haemat-, haemato-*, fr. Gk *haimat-, haimato-*, fr. *haimat-, haima*] **:** HEM- <*hemat*oid> <*hemato*genous>

he·ma·tein \ˌhē-mə-ˈtē-ən, ˈhē-mə-ˌtēn\ *n* **:** a reddish brown crystalline compound $C_{16}H_{12}O_6$ constituting the essential dye in logwood extracts

he·mat·ic \hi-ˈmat-ik\ *adj* **1 :** of, relating to, or containing blood **2 :** affecting the blood

he·ma·tin \ˈhē-mə-tən\ *n* **1 :** HEMATEIN **2 a :** a brownish black or bluish black derivative $C_{34}H_{33}N_4O_5Fe$ of oxidized heme; *also* **:** any of several similar compounds **b :** HEME

he·ma·tin·ic \ˌhē-mə-ˈtin-ik\ *n* **:** an agent that tends to stimulate blood cell formation or to increase the hemoglobin in the blood — **hematinic** *adj*

he·ma·tite \ˈhē-mə-ˌtīt\ *n* **:** a mineral Fe_2O_3 constituting an important iron ore and occurring in crystals or in a red earthy form — **he·ma·ti·tic** \ˌhē-mə-ˈtit-ik\ *adj*

he·ma·to·blast \ˈhē-mət-ə-ˌblast, hi-ˈmat-ə-\ *n* [ISV] **1 :** BLOOD PLATELET **2 :** an immature blood cell — **he·ma·to·blas·tic** \ˌhē-mət-ə-ˈblas-tik, hi-ˌmat-ə-\ *adj*

he·mat·o·crit \hi-ˈmat-ə-krət, -ˌkrit\ *n* [ISV *hemat-* + Gk *kritēs* judge, fr. *krinein* to judge — more at CERTAIN] **1 :** an instrument for determining usu. by centrifugation the relative amounts of plasma and corpuscles in blood **2 :** a ratio of volume of packed red blood cells to volume of whole blood determined by a hematocrit

he·ma·tog·e·nous \ˌhē-mə-ˈtäj-ə-nəs\ *adj* **1 :** producing blood **2 :** spread by or arising in the blood <~ tuberculosis>

he·ma·to·log·ic \ˌhē-mət-ᵊl-ˈäj-ik\ *or* **he·ma·to·log·i·cal** \-i-kəl\ *adj* **:** of or relating to blood or to hematology

he·ma·tol·o·gy \ˌhē-mə-ˈtäl-ə-jē\ *n* **:** a branch of biology that deals with the blood and blood-forming organs — **he·ma·tol·o·gist** \-jəst\ *n*

he·ma·to·ma \-ˈtō-mə\ *n, pl* **-mas** *or* **-ma·ta** \-mət-ə\ **:** a tumor or swelling containing blood

he·ma·toph·a·gous \-ˈtäf-ə-gəs\ *adj* [ISV] **:** feeding on blood

he·ma·to·poi·e·sis \hi-ˌmat-ə-pȯi-ˈē-səs, ˌhē-mət-ō-\ *n* [NL] **:** the formation of blood or of blood cells in the living body — **he·ma·to·poi·et·ic** \-ˈet-ik\ *adj* — **he·ma·to·poi·et·i·cal·ly** \-i-k(ə-)lē\ *adv*

he·ma·tox·y·lin \ˌhē-mə-ˈtäk-sə-lən\ *n* [ISV, fr. NL *Haematoxylon*, genus of plants]**:** a crystalline phenolic compound $C_{16}H_{14}O_6$ found in logwood and used chiefly as a biological stain

he·ma·tu·ria \-ˈt(y)u̇r-ē-ə\ *n* [NL]**:** the presence of blood or blood cells in the urine

heme \ˈhēm\ *n* [ISV, fr. *hematin*] **:** the deep red iron-containing prosthetic group $C_{34}H_{32}N_4O_4Fe$ of hemoglobin

hem·el·y·tron \he-ˈmel-ə-ˌträn\ *n, pl* **-tra** \-trə\ [NL, fr. *hemi-* + *elytron*] **:** one of the basally thickened anterior wings of various insects (as true bugs)

hem·er·a·lo·pia \ˌhem-ə-rə-ˈlō-pē-ə\ *n* [NL, fr. Gk *hēmeralōps*, fr. *hēmera* day + *alaos* blind + *ōps* eye — more at EPHEMERAL, EYE] **1 :** a defect of vision characterized by reduced visual capacity in bright lights **2 :** NIGHT BLINDNESS — **hem·er·a·lo·pic** \-ˈlō-pik\ *adj*

hem·ero·cal·lis \ˌhem-ə-rō-ˈkal-əs\ *n* [NL, fr. Gk *hēmerokalles*, fr. *hēmera* + *kallos* beauty — more at CALLIGRAPHY] **:** DAY LILY 1

hem·er·y·thrin \hē-ˈmer-ə-thrən\ *n* [*hem-* + *erythr-* + *-in*] **:** an iron-containing respiratory pigment in the blood of various invertebrates (as some annelids)

hemi- *prefix* [ME, fr. L, fr. Gk *hēmi-* — more at SEMI-] **:** half <*hemi*hedral>

-hemia — see -EMIA

hemi·ac·e·tal \ˌhem-ē-ˈas-ə-ˌtal\ *n* **:** any of a class of compounds characterized by the grouping C(OH)(OR) where R is an alkyl group and usu. formed as intermediates in the preparation of acetals from aldehydes or ketones

he·mic \ˈhē-mik\ *adj* **:** of or relating to blood

hemi·cel·lu·lose \ˌhem-i-ˈsel-yə-ˌlōs, -ˌlōz\ *n* [ISV]**:** any of various plant polysaccharides less complex than cellulose and easily hydrolyzable to simple sugars and other products

hemi·chor·date \-ˈkȯrd-ət, -ˈkō(ə)r-ˌdāt\ *n* [NL *Hemichordata*, group name, fr. *hemi-* + *Chordata* chordates] **:** any of a division (Hemichordata) of chordates comprising vermiform marine animals (as an acorn worm) that have in the proboscis an outgrowth of the pharyngeal wall which suggests and is probably homologous with the notochord of higher chordates

hemi·cy·cle \ˈhem-i-ˌsī-kəl\ *n* [F *hémicycle*, fr. L *hemicyclium*, fr. Gk *hēmikyklion*, fr. *hēmi-* + *kyklos* circle — more at CYCLE] **:** a curved or semicircular structure or arrangement

hemi·demi·semi·qua·ver \ˌhem-i-ˌdem-i-ˈsem-i-ˌkwā-vər\ *n* **:** SIXTY-FOURTH NOTE

hemi·he·dral \ˌhem-i-ˈhē-drəl\ *adj* [*hemi-* + *-hedron*] *of a crystal* **:** having half the faces required by complete symmetry — compare HOLOHEDRAL, TETARTOHEDRAL — **hemi·he·dral·ly** \-drə-lē\ *adv*

hemi·hy·drate \-ˈhī-ˌdrāt\ *n* **:** a hydrate (as plaster of paris) containing half a molecule of water to one molecule of the compound forming the hydrate — **hemi·hy·drat·ed** \-ˌdrāt-əd\ *adj*

hemi·me·tab·o·lism \-mə-ˈtab-ə-ˌliz-əm\ *n* **:** incomplete metamorphosis esp. in various insects with aquatic larvae that do not resemble the adult — **hemi·me·tab·o·lous** \-ləs\ *also* **hemi·met·a·bol·ic** \-ˌmet-ə-ˈbäl-ik\ *adj*

hemi·mor·phic \ˌhem-i-ˈmȯr-fik\ *adj* [ISV] **:** unsymmetrical in form as regards the two ends of an axis — **hemi·mor·phism** \-ˌfiz-əm\ *n*

hemi·mor·phite \-ˌfīt\ *n* **:** a mineral $Zn_4Si_2O_7OH.H_2O$ that is a basic zinc silicate in usu. colorless transparent orthorhombic crystals

he·min \ˈhē-mən\ *n* [ISV] **:** a red-brown to blue-black crystalline salt $C_{34}H_{32}N_4O_4FeCl$ derived from oxidized heme but usu. obtained in a characteristic crystalline form from hemoglobin

hemi·o·la \ˌhem-ē-ˈō-lə\ *n* [LL *hemiolia*, fr. Gk *hēmiolia* ratio of one and a half to one, fr. *hēmi-* + *holos* whole — more at SAFE] **:** a musical rhythmic alteration consisting of three beats in place of two or two beats in place of three

hemi·par·a·site \ˌhem-i-ˈpar-ə-ˌsīt\ *n* [ISV] **1 :** a facultative parasite **2 :** a parasitic plant (as the mistletoe) that contains some chlorophyll and is capable of photosynthesis — **hemi·par·a·sit·ic** \-ˌpar-ə-ˈsit-ik\ *adj*

hemi·ple·gia \ˌhem-i-ˈplē-j(ē-)ə\ *n* [NL, fr. MGk *hēmiplēgia* paralysis, fr. Gk *hēmi-* + *-plēgia* -plegia]**:** paralysis of one lateral half of the body or part of it resulting from injury to the motor centers of the brain — **hemi·ple·gic** \-jik\ *adj or n*

he·mip·ter·an \hi-ˈmip-tə-rən\ *n* [deriv. of Gk *hēmi-* + *pteron* wing — more at FEATHER] **:** any of a large order (Hemiptera) of insects (as the true bugs) that have mouthparts adapted to piercing and sucking and usu. two pairs of wings, undergo an incomplete metamorphosis, and include many important pests — **he·mip·ter·oid** \-ˌrȯid\ *adj* — **he·mip·ter·on** \-ˌrän\ *n* — **he·mip·ter·ous** \-rəs\ *adj*

hemi·sphere \ˈhem-ə-ˌsfi(ə)r\ *n* [ME *hemispere*, fr. L *hemisphaerium*, fr. Gk *hēmisphairion*, fr. *hēmi-* + *sphairion*, dim. of *sphaira* sphere] **1 a :** a half of the celestial sphere divided into two halves by the horizon, the celestial equator, or the ecliptic **b :** the northern or southern half of the earth divided by the equator or the eastern or western half divided by a meridian **c :** the inhabitants of a terrestrial hemisphere **2 :** REALM, PROVINCE **3 :** one of two half spheres formed by a plane through the sphere's center **4 :** a map or projection of a celestial or terrestrial hemisphere **5 :** CEREBRAL HEMISPHERE — **hemi·spher·ic** \ˌhem-ə-ˈsfi(ə)r-ik, -ˈsfer-\ *or* **hemi·spher·i·cal** \-ˈsfir-i-kəl, -ˈsfer-\ *adj*

hemi·stich \ˈhem-i-ˌstik\ *n* [L *hemistichium*, fr. Gk *hēmistichion*, fr. *hēmi-* + *stichos* line, verse; akin to Gk *steichein* to go — more at STAIR] **:** half a poetic line of verse usu. divided by a caesura

hemi·ter·pene \ˌhem-i-ˈtər-ˌpēn\ *n* [ISV] **:** a compound C_5H_8 whose formula represents half that of a terpene; *esp* **:** ISOPRENE

hemi·zy·gous \-ˈzī-gəs\ *adj* **:** having or characterized by one or more genes (as in a genetic deficiency or in an X chromosome paired with a Y chromosome) that have no allelic counterparts

hem·line \ˈhem-ˌlīn\ *n* **:** the line formed by the lower edge of a dress, skirt, or coat

hem·lock \ˈhem-ˌläk\ *n* [ME *hemlok*, fr. OE *hemlic*] **1 a :** any of several poisonous herbs (as a poison hemlock or a water hemlock) of the carrot family having finely cut leaves and small white flowers **b :** a poisonous drink made from the fruit of the hemlock — compare CONIINE **2 :** any of a genus (*Tsuga*) of evergreen coniferous trees of the pine family; *also* **:** the soft light splintery wood of a hemlock

hemo- — see HEM-

he·mo·blast \ˈhē-mə-ˌblast\ *n* [ISV] **:** HEMATOBLAST

he·mo·chro·ma·to·sis \ˌhē-mə-ˌkrō-mə-ˈtō-səs\ *n* [NL, fr. *hem-* + *chromat-* + *osis*]**:** a disorder of iron metabolism that occurs usu. in males and that is characterized by bronzing of the skin due to deposition of iron-containing pigments in the tissues and frequently by diabetic symptoms

he·mo·coel *also* **he·mo·coele** \ˈhē-mə-ˌsēl\ *n* **:** a body cavity (as in arthropods or some mollusks) that normally contains blood and functions as part of the circulatory system

he·mo·cy·a·nin \ˌhē-mō-ˈsī-ə-nən\ *n* [ISV] **:** a colorless copper-containing respiratory pigment in solution in the blood plasma of various arthropods and mollusks

he·mo·cyte \ˈhē-mə-ˌsīt\ *n* [ISV]**:** a blood cell esp. of an invertebrate animal

he·mo·cy·tom·e·ter \ˌhē-mə-sī-ˈtäm-ət-ər\ *n* [ISV]**:** HEMACYTOMETER

he·mo·di·al·y·sis \ˌhē-mō-dī-ˈal-ə-səs\ *n* **:** purification of the blood (as in a kidney patient) by dialysis

he·mo·di·lu·tion \-dī-ˈlü-shən, -də-\ *n* **:** decreased concentration (as after hemorrhage) of cells and solids in the blood resulting from gain of fluid from the tissues

he·mo·dy·nam·ic \-dī-ˈnam-ik, -də-\ *adj* **1 :** of, relating to, or involving hemodynamics **2 :** concerned with or functioning in the mechanics of blood circulation — **he·mo·dy·nam·i·cal·ly** \-i-k(ə-)lē\ *adv*

ə abut	ᵊ kitten	ər further	a back	ā bake	ä cot, cart
au̇ out	ch chin	e less	ē easy	g gift	i trip ī life
j joke	ŋ sing	ō flow	ȯ flaw	ȯi coin	th thin t͟h this
ü loot	u̇ foot	y yet	yü few	yu̇ furious	zh vision

he·mo·dy·nam·ics \-iks\ *n pl but sing or pl in constr* **1 :** a branch of physiology that deals with the circulation of the blood **2 :** the forces or mechanisms involved in circulation (as of a particular body part)

he·mo·fla·gel·late \ˌhē-mō-ˈflaj-ə-lət, -ˌlāt; -flə-ˈjel-ət\ *n* **:** a flagellate (as a trypanosome) that is a blood parasite

he·mo·glo·bin \ˈhē-mə-ˌglō-bən\ *n* [ISV, short for earlier *hematoglobulin*] **1 a :** an iron-containing conjugated protein respiratory pigment occurring in the red blood cells of vertebrates **b :** a dark purplish crystallizable form of hemoglobin found chiefly in the venous blood of vertebrates that is a conjugated protein composed of heme and globin **2 :** any of numerous iron-containing respiratory pigments of invertebrates and some plants (as yeasts) — **he·mo·glo·bin·ic** \ˌhē-mə-glō-ˈbin-ik\ *adj* — **he·mo·glo·bin·ous** \-ˈglō-bə-nəs\ *adj*

he·mo·glo·bin·op·a·thy \ˌhē-mə-ˌglō-bə-ˈnäp-ə-thē\ *n, pl* **-thies :** a blood disorder (as sickle-cell anemia) caused by a genetically determined change in the molecular structure of hemoglobin

hemoglobin S *n* **:** a hemoglobin that occurs in the red blood cells in sickle-cell anemia and sickle-cell trait

he·mo·glo·bin·uria \ˌhē-mə-ˌglō-bə-ˈn(y)u̇r-ē-ə\ *n* [NL] **:** the presence of free hemoglobin in the urine — **he·mo·glo·bin·uric** \-ˈn(y)u̇(ə)r-ik\ *adj*

he·mo·lymph \ˈhē-mə-ˌlim(p)f\ *n* **:** the circulatory fluid of various invertebrate animals that is functionally comparable to the blood and lymph of vertebrates

he·mo·ly·sin \ˌhē-mə-ˈlīs-ᵊn\ *n* [ISV] **:** a substance that causes the dissolution of red blood cells

he·mo·ly·sis \hi-ˈmäl-ə-səs, ˌhē-mə-ˈlī-səs\ *n* [NL] **:** lysis of red blood cells with liberation of hemoglobin — **he·mo·lyt·ic** \ˌhē-mə-ˈlit-ik\ *adj*

hemolytic anemia *n* **:** anemia caused by excessive destruction (as in chemical poisoning, infection, or sickle-cell anemia) of red blood cells

hemolytic disease of the newborn : ERYTHROBLASTOSIS FETALIS

he·mo·lyze \ˈhē-mə-ˌlīz\ *vb* **-lyzed; -lyz·ing** [irreg. fr. *hemolysis*] *vt* **:** to cause hemolysis of ~ *vi* **:** to undergo hemolysis

he·mo·phil·ia \ˌhē-mə-ˈfil-ē-ə\ *n* [NL] **:** a sex-linked hereditary blood defect of males characterized by delayed clotting of the blood and consequent difficulty in controlling hemorrhage even after minor injuries

1**he·mo·phil·i·ac** \-ē-ˌak\ *n* **:** one affected with hemophilia — called also *bleeder*

2**hemophiliac** *adj* **:** HEMOPHILIC 1

he·mo·phil·ic \-ˈfil-ik\ *adj* **1 :** of, resembling, or affected with hemophilia **2 :** tending to thrive in blood <~ bacteria>

he·mo·poi·e·sis \ˌhē-mə-pȯi-ˈē-səs\ *n* [NL] **:** HEMATOPOIESIS — **he·mo·poi·et·ic** \-ˈet-ik\ *adj*

he·mo·pro·tein \-ˈprō-ˌtēn, -ˈprōt-ē-ən\ *n* **:** a conjugated protein (as hemoglobin or cytochrome) whose prosthetic group is a porphyrin combined with iron

he·mop·ty·sis \hi-ˈmäp-tə-səs\ *n* [NL, fr. *hem-* + Gk *ptysis* act of spitting, fr. *ptyein* to spit — more at SPEW] **:** expectoration of blood from some part of the respiratory tract

1**hem·or·rhage** \ˈhem-(ə-)rij\ *n* [F & L; F *hémorrhagie*, fr. L *haemorrhagia*, fr. Gk *haimorrhagia*, fr. *haimo-* hem- + *-rrhagia*] **:** a copious discharge of blood from the blood vessels — **hem·or·rhag·ic** \ˌhem-ə-ˈraj-ik\ *adj*

2**hemorrhage** *vi* **-rhaged; -rhag·ing :** to undergo heavy or uncontrollable bleeding

hem·or·rhoid \ˈhem-(ə-)ˌrȯid\ *n* [MF *hemorrhoides*, pl., fr. L *haemorrhoidae*, fr. Gk *haimorrhoides*, fr. *haimorrhoos* flowing with blood, fr. *haimo-* hem- + *rhein* to flow — more at STREAM] **:** a mass of dilated veins in swollen tissue situated near the anal sphincter — usu. used in pl.; called also *piles*

1**hem·or·rhoid·al** \ˌhem-ə-ˈrȯid-ᵊl\ *adj* **1 :** of, relating to, or involving hemorrhoids **2 :** RECTAL

2**hemorrhoidal** *n* **:** a hemorrhoidal part (as an artery or vein)

he·mo·sid·er·in \ˌhē-mō-ˈsid-ə-rən\ *n* [ISV] **:** a yellowish brown granular pigment formed by breakdown of hemoglobin and composed essentially of colloidal ferric oxide

he·mo·sta·sis \ˌhē-mə-ˈstā-səs\ *n* [NL, fr. Gk *haimostasis* styptic, fr. *haimo-* hem- + *-stasis*] **:** arrest of bleeding

he·mo·stat \ˈhē-mə-ˌstat\ *n* **:** HEMOSTATIC; *esp* **:** an instrument for compressing a bleeding vessel

1**he·mo·stat·ic** \ˌhē-mə-ˈstat-ik\ *n* **:** an agent that checks bleeding

2**hemostatic** *adj* **1 :** of or caused by hemostasis **2 :** serving to check bleeding

hemp \ˈhemp\ *n* [ME, fr. OE *hænep;* akin to OHG *hanaf* hemp; both prob. fr. the source of Gk *kannabis* hemp] **1 a :** a tall widely cultivated Asiatic herb (*Cannabis sativa*) of the mulberry family with tough bast fiber used esp. for cordage **b :** the fiber of hemp **c :** a psychoactive drug (as marijuana or hashish) from hemp **2 :** a fiber (as jute) from a plant other than the true hemp; *also* **:** a plant yielding such fiber

hemp 1a

hemp·en \ˈhem-pən\ *adj* **:** of, relating to, or resembling hemp

hemp nettle *n* **:** any of a genus (*Galeopsis*) of coarse Old World herbs of the mint family; *esp* **:** a bristly Eurasian herb (*G. tetrahit*) common in the U.S. as a weed

1**hem·stitch** \ˈhem-ˌstich\ *vt* **:** to decorate (as a border) with hemstitch — **hem·stitch·er** *n*

2**hemstitch** *n* **1 :** decorative needlework similar to drawnwork that is used esp. on or next to the stitching line of hems **2 :** a stitch used in hemstitching

hen \ˈhen\ *n* [ME, fr. OE *henn;* akin to OE *hana* rooster — more at CHANT] **1 a :** a female domestic fowl esp. over a year old; *broadly* **:** a female bird **b :** the female of various mostly aquatic animals (as lobsters or fish) **2 :** WOMAN; *specif* **:** a fussy middle-aged woman

hemstitch

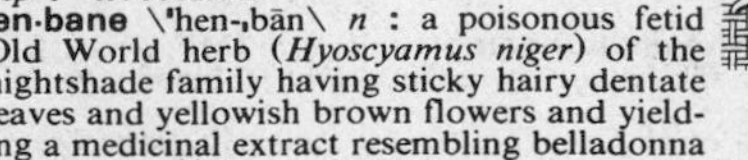

hen and chickens *n* **:** any of several plants having offsets, runners, or proliferous flowers; *esp* **:** HOUSELEEK

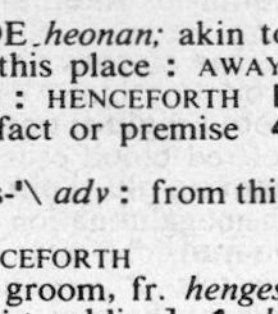

hen·bane \ˈhen-ˌbān\ *n* **:** a poisonous fetid Old World herb (*Hyoscyamus niger*) of the nightshade family having sticky hairy dentate leaves and yellowish brown flowers and yielding a medicinal extract resembling belladonna

hence \ˈhen(t)s\ *adv* [ME *hennes, henne,* fr. OE *heonan;* akin to OHG *hinnan* away, OE *hēr* here] **1 :** from this place **:** AWAY; *specif* **:** from this world or life **2 a** *archaic* **:** HENCEFORTH **b :** from this time **3 :** because of a preceding fact or premise **4 :** from this source or origin

hence·forth \ˈhen(t)s-ˌfō(ə)rth, -ˌfȯ(ə)rth, hen(t)s-ˈ\ *adv* **:** from this point on

hence·for·ward \hen(t)s-ˈfȯr-wərd\ *adv* **:** HENCEFORTH

hench·man \ˈhench-mən\ *n* [ME *hengestman* groom, fr. *hengest* stallion (fr. OE) + *man;* akin to OHG *hengist* gelding] **1** *obs* **:** a squire or page to a person of high rank **2 a :** a trusted follower **:** a right-hand man **b :** a political follower whose support is chiefly for personal advantage **c :** an unscrupulous often violent member of a gang

hen·deca·syl·lab·ic \(ˌ)hen-ˌdek-ə-sə-ˈlab-ik\ *adj* [L *hendecasyllabus*, fr. Gk *hendeka* eleven (fr. *hen-, heis* one + *deka* ten) + *syllabē* syllable — more at SAME, TEN] **:** consisting of 11 syllables or composed of verses of 11 syllables — **hendecasyllabic** *n* — **hen·deca·syl·la·ble** \hen-ˈdek-ə-ˌsil-ə-bəl, (ˌ)hen-ˌdek-ə-ˈ\ *n*

hen·di·a·dys \hen-ˈdī-əd-əs\ *n* **:** the expression of an idea by the use of usu. two independent words connected by *and* (as *nice and warm*) instead of the usual combination of independent word and its modifier (as *nicely warm*)

hen·e·quen \ˈhen-i-kən, ˌhen-i-ˈken\ *n* [Sp *henequén*] **:** a strong yellowish or reddish hard fiber obtained from the leaves of a tropical American agave chiefly in Yucatan and used esp. for binder twine; *also* **:** a plant (*Agave fourcroydes*) that yields henequen

Hen·le's loop \ˌhen-lēz-\ *n* **:** LOOP OF HENLE

1**hen·na** \ˈhen-ə\ *n* [Ar *hinnā'*] **1 :** an Old World tropical shrub or small tree (*Lawsonia inermis*) of the loosestrife family with small opposite leaves and axillary panicles of fragrant white flowers **2 :** a reddish brown dye obtained from leaves of the henna plant and used esp. on hair

2**henna** *vt* **:** to dye (as hair) with henna

hen·nery \ˈhen-ə-rē\ *n, pl* **-ner·ies :** a poultry farm; *also* **:** an enclosure for poultry

heno·the·ism \ˈhen-ə-(ˌ)thē-ˌiz-əm\ *n* [G *henotheismus*, fr. Gk *hen-, heis* one + *theos* god — more at SAME] **:** the worship of one god without denying the existence of other gods — **heno·the·ist** \-ˌthē-əst\ *n* — **heno·the·is·tic** \ˌhen-ə-thē-ˈis-tik\ *adj*

hen party *n* **:** a party for women only

hen·peck \ˈhen-ˌpek\ *vt* **:** to subject (one's husband) to persistent nagging and domination

hen·ry \ˈhen-rē\ *n, pl* **henrys** *or* **henries** [Joseph *Henry*] **:** the practical mks unit of inductance equal to the self-inductance of a circuit or the mutual inductance of two circuits in which the variation of one ampere per second results in an induced electromotive force of one volt

hent \ˈhent\ *vt* [ME *henten*, fr. OE *hentan* — more at HUNT] *archaic* **:** SEIZE

hen track *n* **:** an illegible or scarcely legible mark intended as handwriting — called also *hen scratch*

1**hep** \ˈhep, ˈhəp, ˈhət\ *interj* [origin unknown] — used to mark a marching cadence

2**hep** \ˈhep\ *var of* HIP

hep·a·rin \ˈhep-ə-rən\ *n* [ISV, fr. Gk *hēpar* liver] **:** a polysaccharide sulfuric acid ester that is found esp. in liver, that prolongs the clotting time of blood, and that is used medically

hep·a·rin·ize \-rə-ˌnīz\ *vt* **-ized; -iz·ing :** to treat with heparin

hepat- *or* **hepato-** *comb form* [L, fr. Gk *hēpat-, hēpato-,* fr. *hēpat-, hēpar*] **1 :** liver <*hepat*ectomy> <*hepato*toxic> **2 :** hepatic and <*hepato*biliary>

hep·a·tec·to·my \ˌhep-ə-ˈtek-tə-mē\ *n, pl* **-mies :** excision of the liver or of part of the liver — **hep·a·tec·to·mize** \-ˌmīz\ *vt*

1**he·pat·ic** \hi-ˈpat-ik\ *adj* [L *hepaticus*, fr. Gk *hēpatikos*, fr. *hēpat-, hēpar;* akin to L *jecur* liver] **:** of, relating to, or resembling the liver

2**hepatic** *n* **:** LIVERWORT

he·pat·i·ca \hi-ˈpat-i-kə\ *n* [NL, genus name, fr. ML, liverwort, fr. L, fem. of *hepaticus*] **:** a plant of a genus (*Hepatica*) of herbs of the buttercup family with lobed leaves and delicate flowers

hep·a·ti·tis \ˌhep-ə-ˈtīt-əs\ *n, pl* **-tit·i·des** \-ˈtit-ə-ˌdēz\ **:** inflammation of the liver; *also* **:** a condition marked by such inflammation

he·pa·to·cel·lu·lar \ˌhep-ət-ō-ˈsel-yə-lər, hi-ˌpat-ə-ˈsel-\ *adj* **:** of or involving hepatocytes <~ jaundice>

he·pa·to·cyte \hi-ˈpat-ə-ˌsīt, ˈhep-ət-ə-\ *n* **:** an epithelial parenchymatous cell of the liver

hep·a·to·ma \ˌhep-ə-ˈtō-mə\ *n* [NL] **:** a usu. malignant tumor of the liver

he·pa·to·pan·cre·as \ˌhep-ət-ō-ˈpaŋ-krē-əs, hi-ˌpat-ə-ˈpaŋ-, -ˈpan-\ *n* **:** a glandular structure (as of a crustacean) that combines the digestive functions of the vertebrate liver and pancreas

hep·a·top·a·thy \ˌhep-ə-ˈtäp-ə-thē\ *n, pl* **-thies :** an abnormal or diseased state of the liver

hep·a·to·tox·ic \ˌhep-ət-ō-ˈtäk-sik, hi-ˌpat-ə-ˈtäk-\ *adj* **:** capable of causing injury to the liver <~ drugs>

hep·a·to·tox·ic·i·ty \-täk-ˈsis-ət-ē\ *n* **1 :** a state of toxic damage to the liver **2 :** a tendency or capacity to cause hepatotoxicity

hep·cat \ˈhep-ˌkat\ *n* **:** HIPSTER

He·phaes·tus \hi-ˈfes-təs, -ˈfēs-\ *n* [L, fr. Gk *Hēphaistos*] **:** the Greek god of fire and metalworking — compare VULCAN

hepped up \ˈhep-ˈtəp\ *adj* **:** ENTHUSIASTIC

Hep·ple·white \ˈhep-əl-ˌhwīt, -ˌwīt\ *adj* [George *Hepplewhite*] **:** of, relating to, or imitating a style of furniture originating in late 18th century England

hepta- *or* **hept-** *comb form* [Gk, fr. *hepta* — more at SEVEN] **1** : seven <*hepta*meter> **2** : containing seven atoms, groups, or equivalents <*hept*ane>

hep·ta·chlor \ˈhep-tə-ˌklō(ə)r, -ˌklȯ(ə)r\ *n* [*hepta-* + *chlor*ine] : a persistent cyclodiene chlorinated hydrocarbon pesticide $C_{10}H_5Cl_7$

hep·tad \ˈhep-ˌtad\ *n* [Gk *heptad-, heptas,* fr. *hepta*] : a group of seven

hep·ta·gon \ˈhep-tə-ˌgän\ *n* [Gk *heptagōnos* heptagonal, fr. *hepta* + *gōnia* angle — more at -GON] : a polygon of seven angles and seven sides — **hep·tag·o·nal** \hep-ˈtag-ən-ᵊl\ *adj*

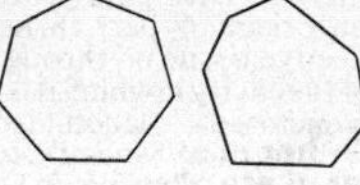
heptagons

hep·tam·e·ter \hep-ˈtam-ət-ər\ *n* : a line of verse consisting of seven metrical feet

hep·tane \ˈhep-ˌtān\ *n* : any of several isomeric hydrocarbons C_7H_{16} of the methane series; *esp* : the liquid normal isomer occurring in petroleum and used esp. as a solvent and in determining octane numbers

hep·tar·chy \ˈhep-ˌtär-kē\ *n* : a hypothetical confederacy of seven Anglo-Saxon kingdoms of the 7th and 8th centuries

Hep·ta·teuch \ˈhep-tə-ˌt(y)ük\ *n* [LL *heptateuchos,* fr. Gk, fr. *hepta* + *teuchos* book — more at PENTATEUCH] : the first seven books of the canonical Jewish and Christian Scriptures

hep·tose \ˈhep-ˌtōs, -ˌtōz\ *n* : a monosaccharide $C_7H_{14}O_7$ containing seven carbon atoms in the molecule

¹her \(h)ər, ˌhər\ *adj* [ME *hire,* fr. OE *hiere,* gen. of *hēo* she — more at HE] : of or relating to her or herself esp. as possessor, agent, or object of an action <~ house> <~ research> <~ rescue> — compare ¹SHE

²her \ər, (ˈ)hər\ *pron, objective case of* SHE

³her *abbr* heraldry

He·ra \ˈhir-ə, ˈhē-rə\ *n* [Gk *Hēra, Hērē*] : the sister and consort of Zeus — compare JUNO

Her·a·cles \ˈher-ə-ˌklēz\ *n* [Gk *Hēraklēs*] : HERCULES

¹her·ald \ˈher-əld\ *n* [ME, fr. MF *hiraut,* fr. an (assumed) Gmc compound whose first component is akin to OHG *heri* army, and whose second is akin to OHG *waltan* to rule — more at HARRY, WIELD] **1 a** : an official at a tournament of arms with duties including the making of announcements and the marshaling of combatants **b** : an officer with the status of ambassador acting as official messenger between leaders esp. in war **c (1)** : OFFICER OF ARMS **(2)** : an officer of arms ranking above a pursuivant and below a king of arms **2** : an official crier or messenger **3 a** : HARBINGER **b** : one that conveys news or proclaims : ANNOUNCER <it was the lark, the ~ of the morn —Shak.> **c** : one that supports or advocates : SPOKESMAN ***syn*** see FORERUNNER

²herald *vt* **1** : to give notice of : ANNOUNCE **2** : to greet esp. with enthusiasm : HAIL

he·ral·dic \he-ˈral-dik, hə-\ *adj* : of or relating to heralds or heraldry — **he·ral·di·cal·ly** \-di-k(ə-)lē\ *adv*

her·ald·ry \ˈher-əl-drē\ *n, pl* **-ries** **1** : the practice of devising, blazoning, and granting armorial insignia and of tracing and recording genealogies **2** : an armorial ensign; *broadly* : INSIGNIA **3** : PAGEANTRY

herb \ˈ(h)ərb\ *n, often attrib* [ME *herbe,* fr. OF, fr. L *herba*] **1** : a seed-producing annual, biennial, or perennial that does not develop persistent woody tissue but dies down at the end of a growing season **2** : a plant or plant part valued for its medicinal, savory, or aromatic qualities — **herb·like** \ˈ(h)ər-ˌblīk\ *adj* — **herby** \ˈ(h)ər-bē\ *adj*

her·ba·ceous \ˌ(h)ər-ˈbā-shəs\ *adj* **1 a** : of, relating to, or having the characteristics of an herb **b** *of a stem* : having little or no woody tissue and persisting usu. for a single growing season **2** : having the texture, color, or appearance of a leaf

herb·age \ˈ(h)ər-bij\ *n* **1** : herbaceous vegetation (as grass) esp. when used for grazing **2** : the succulent parts of herbaceous plants

¹herb·al \ˈ(h)ər-bəl\ *n* **1** : a book about plants esp. with reference to their medical properties **2** *archaic* : HERBARIUM 1

²herbal *adj* : of, relating to, or made of herbs

herb·al·ist \(ˈ)(h)ər-bə-ləst\ *n* **1** : one that collects or grows herbs **2** : HERB DOCTOR

her·bar·i·um \ˌ(h)ər-ˈbar-ē-əm, -ˈber-\ *n, pl* **-ia** \-ē-ə\ **1** : a collection of dried plant specimens usu. mounted and systematically arranged for reference **2** : a place that houses an herbarium

herb doctor *n* : one who practices healing by the use of herbs

her·bi·cide \ˈ(h)ər-bə-ˌsīd\ *n* [L *herba* + ISV *-cide*] : an agent used to destroy or inhibit plant growth — **her·bi·cid·al** \ˌ(h)ər-bə-ˈsīd-ᵊl\ *adj* — **her·bi·cid·al·ly** \-ᵊl-ē\ *adv*

her·bi·vore \ˈ(h)ər-bə-ˌvō(ə)r, -ˌvȯ(ə)r\ *n* [NL *Herbivora,* group of mammals, fr. neut. pl. of *herbivorus*] : a plant-eating animal; *esp* : UNGULATE

her·biv·o·rous \ˌ(h)ər-ˈbiv-ə-rəs\ *adj* [NL *herbivorus,* fr. L *herba* grass + *-vorus* -vorous] **1** : feeding on plants **2** : having a stout body and a long small intestine : ENDOMORPHIC — **her·biv·o·rous·ly** *adv*

herb Rob·ert \ˌ(h)ərb-ˈräb-ərt\ *n* [prob. fr. *Robertus* (St. Robert) †1067 F ecclesiastic] : a sticky low geranium (*Geranium robertianum*) with small reddish purple flowers

Her·cu·le·an \ˌhər-kyə-ˈlē-ən, ˌhər-ˈkyü-lē-\ *adj* **1** : of, relating to, or characteristic of Hercules **2** *often not cap* : of extraordinary power, size, or difficulty

Her·cu·les \ˈhər-kyə-ˌlēz\ *n* [L, fr. Gk *Hēraklēs*] **1** : a mythical Greek hero fabled for his great strength and esp. for performing 12 labors imposed on him by Hera **2** [L (gen. *Herculis*)] : a northern constellation between Corona Borealis and Lyra

Her·cu·les'–club \ˌhər-kyə-ˌlēz-ˈkləb\ *n* **1** : a small prickly eastern U.S. tree (*Aralia spinosa*) of the ginseng family — called also *angelica tree* **2** : a prickly shrub or tree (genus *Zanthoxylum,* esp. *Z. clava-herculis*) of the rue family

¹herd \ˈhərd\ *n* [ME, fr. OE *heord;* akin to OHG *herta* herd, Gk *korthys* heap] **1 a** : a number of animals of one kind kept together under human control **b** : a congregation of gregarious wild animals **2 a** : a group of people usu. having a common bond <entered the troop with the midwinter ~ of tenderfeet —MacKinlay Kantor> **b** : the undistinguished masses : CROWD <isolate the individual prophets from the ~ —Norman Cousins> — **herd·like** \-ˌlīk\ *adj*

²herd *vi* **1** : to assemble or move in a herd **2** : to place oneself in a group : ASSOCIATE ~ *vt* **1 a** : to keep or move (animals) together **b** : to gather, lead, or drive as if in a herd <seventy-five boys and girls were ~*ed* by six or eight teachers —W. A. White> **2** : to place in a group

herd·er \ˈhərd-ər\ *n* : one that herds; *specif* : HERDSMAN

her·dic \ˈhərd-ik\ *n* [Peter *Herdic* †1888 Am inventor] : a small 19th century American horse-drawn cab having side seats and an entrance at the back

herds·man \ˈhərdz-mən\ *n* **1** : a manager, breeder, or tender of livestock **2** *cap* : BOÖTES

¹here \ˈhi(ə)r\ *adv* [ME, fr. OE *hēr;* akin to OHG *hier* here, OE *hē* he] **1 a** : in or at this place <turn ~> — often used interjectionally esp. in answering a roll call **b** : NOW <~ it's morning already> **2** : at or in this point or particular <~ we agree> **3** : in the present life or state **4** : HITHER <come ~> **5** — used interjectionally in rebuke or encouragement — **here goes** —used interjectionally to express resolution or resignation esp. at the beginning of a difficult or unpleasant undertaking — **neither here nor there** : having no interest or relevance : of no consequence <matters of comfort are *neither here nor there* to a real sailing fan>

²here *adj* **1** — used for emphasis esp. after a demonstrative pronoun or after a noun modified by a demonstrative adjective <this book ~> **2** *substand* — used for emphasis after a demonstrative adjective but before the noun modified <this ~ book>

³here *n* : this place

here·abouts \ˈhi(ə)r-ə-ˌbau̇ts\ *or* **here·about** \-ˌbau̇t\ *adv* : in this vicinity

¹here·af·ter \hi(ə)r-ˈaf-tər\ *adv* **1** : after this in sequence or in time **2** : in some future time or state

²hereafter *n, often cap* **1** : FUTURE **2** : an existence beyond earthly life

³hereafter *adj, archaic* : FUTURE

here and now *n* : the present time — used with *the* <man's obligation is in the *here and now* —W. H. Whyte>

here and there *adv* **1** : in one place and another **2** : from time to time

here·away \ˈhi(ə)r-ə-ˌwā\ *or* **here·aways** \-ˌwāz\ *adv, dial* : HEREABOUTS

here·by \hi(ə)r-ˈbī, ˈhi(ə)r-ˌ\ *adv* : by this means

her·e·dit·a·ment \ˌher-ə-ˈdit-ə-mənt\ *n* [ML *hereditamentum,* fr. LL *hereditare,* fr. L *hered-, heres*] : heritable property

he·red·i·tar·i·an \hə-ˌred-ə-ˈter-ē-ən\ *n* : an advocate of hereditarianism — **hereditarian** *adj*

he·red·i·tar·i·an·ism \-ē-ə-ˌniz-əm\ *n* : the theory that individual differences in human beings can be accounted for primarily on the basis of genetics

he·red·i·tary \hə-ˈred-ə-ˌter-ē\ *adj* **1 a** : genetically transmitted or transmittable from parent to offspring **b** : characteristic of or fostered by one's predecessors **2 a** : received or passing by inheritance or required to pass by inheritance or by reason of birth **b** : having title or possession through inheritance or by reason of birth **3** : of a kind established by tradition <~ enemy> **4** : of or relating to inheritance or heredity ***syn*** see INNATE — **he·red·i·tar·i·ly** \-ˌred-ə-ˈter-ə-lē\ *adv*

he·red·i·ty \hə-ˈred-ət-ē\ *n* [MF *heredité,* fr. L *hereditat-, hereditas,* fr. *hered-, heres* heir — more at HEIR] **1 a** : INHERITANCE **b** : TRADITION **2 a** : the sum of the qualities and potentialities genetically derived from one's ancestors **b** : the transmission of qualities from ancestor to descendant through a mechanism lying primarily in the chromosomes of the germ cells

Heref *abbr* Herefordshire

Her·e·ford \ˈhər-fərd *sometimes* ˈher-ə-\ *n* [*Hereford* co., England] : any of an English breed of hardy red beef cattle with white faces and markings now extensively raised in the western U.S.

here·in \hi(ə)r-ˈin\ *adv* : in this

here·in·above \(ˌ)hi(ə)r-ˌin-ə-ˈbəv\ *adv* : at a prior point in this writing or document

here·in·af·ter \ˌhi(ə)r-ə-ˈnaf-tər\ *adv* : in the following part of this writing or document

here·in·be·fore \(ˌ)hi(ə)r-ˌin-bi-ˈfō(ə)r, -ˈfȯ(ə)r\ *adv* : in the preceding part of this writing or document

here·in·be·low \-bi-ˈlō\ *adv* : at a subsequent point in this writing or document

here·of \hi(ə)r-ˈəv, -ˈäv\ *adv* : of this

here·on \-ˈȯn, -ˈän\ *adv* : on this

He·re·ro \hə-ˈre(ə)r-(ˌ)ō, ˈher-ə-ˌrō\ *n, pl* **Herero** *or* **Hereros** : a member of a Bantu people of the central part of southwest Africa

he·re·si·arch \hə-ˈrē-zē-ˌärk, ˈher-ə-sē-\ *n* [LL *haeresiarcha,* fr. LGk *hairesiarchēs,* fr. *hairesis* + Gk *-archēs* -arch] : an originator or chief advocate of a heresy

her·e·sy \ˈher-ə-sē\ *n, pl* **-sies** [ME *heresie,* fr. OF, fr. LL *haeresis,* fr. LGk *hairesis,* fr. Gk, action of taking, choice, sect, fr. *hairein* to take] **1 a** : adherence to a religious opinion contrary to church dogma **b** : denial of a revealed truth by a baptized member of the Roman Catholic Church **c** : an opinion or doctrine contrary to church dogma **2 a** : dissent from a dominant theory or opinion **b** : an opinion or doctrine contrary to the truth or to generally accepted beliefs

her·e·tic \'her-ə-,tik\ *n* **1 :** a dissenter from established church dogma; *esp* **:** a baptized member of the Roman Catholic Church who disavows a revealed truth **2 :** one who dissents from an accepted belief or doctrine **:** NONCONFORMIST

he·ret·i·cal \hə-'ret-i-kəl\ *also* **he·re·tic** \'her-ə-,tik, hə-'ret-ik\ *adj* **1 :** of, relating to, or characterized by heresy **2 :** of, relating to, or characterized by departure from accepted beliefs or standards **:** UNORTHODOX — **he·ret·i·cal·ly** \hə-'ret-i-k(ə-)lē\ *adv* — **he·ret·i·cal·ness** \-kəl-nəs\ *n*

here·to \hi(ə)r-'tü\ *adv* **:** to this writing or document

here·to·fore \'hi(ə)rt-ə-,fō(ə)r, -,fȯ(ə)r, ,hirt-ə-'\ *adv* **:** up to this time **:** HITHERTO

here·un·der \hi(ə)r-'ən-dər\ *adv* **:** under or in accordance with this writing or document

here·un·to \hi(ə)r-'ən-(,)tü, ,hi(ə)r-(,)ən-'tü\ *adv* **:** to this

here·upon \'hi(ə)r-ə-,pȯn, -,pän, ,hir-ə-'\ *adv* **:** on this **:** immediately after this

here·with \hi(ə)r-'with, -'with\ *adv* **1 :** with this **:** enclosed in this **2 :** HEREBY

her·i·ot \'her-ē-ət\ *n* [ME, fr. OE *heregeatwe,* pl., military equipment, fr. *here* army + *geatwe* equipment; akin to OHG *heri* army — more at HARRY] **:** a feudal duty or tribute due under English law to a lord on the death of a tenant

her·i·ta·ble \'her-ət-ə-bəl\ *adj* **1 :** capable of being inherited or of passing by inheritance **2 :** HEREDITARY — **her·i·ta·bil·i·ty** \,her-ət-ə-'bil-ət-ē\ *n*

her·i·tage \'her-ət-ij\ *n* [ME, fr. MF, fr. *heriter* to inherit, fr. LL *hereditare,* fr. L *hered-, heres* heir — more at HEIR] **1 :** property that descends to an heir **2 :** something transmitted by or acquired from a predecessor **:** LEGACY **3 :** something possessed as a result of one's natural situation or birth **:** BIRTHRIGHT <the nation's ~ of tolerance>
syn HERITAGE, INHERITANCE, PATRIMONY, BIRTHRIGHT *shared meaning element* **:** something received from a parent or predecessor

her·i·tor \'her-ət-ər\ *n* **:** INHERITOR

herm \'hərm\ *n* [L *hermes,* fr. Gk *hermēs* statue of Hermes, herm, fr. *Hermēs*] **:** a statue in the form of a square stone pillar surmounted by a bust or head esp. of Hermes — called also *herma*

her·ma \'hər-mə\ *n* **:** HERM

her·maph·ro·dite \(,)hər-'maf-rə-,dīt\ *n* [ME *hermofrodite,* fr. L *hermaphroditus,* fr. Gk *hermaphroditos,* fr. *Hermaphroditos*] **1 a :** an animal or plant having both male and female reproductive organs **b :** HOMOSEXUAL **2 :** something that is a combination of diverse elements — **hermaphrodite** *adj* — **her·maph·ro·dit·ic** \(,)hər-,maf-rə-'dit-ik\ *adj* — **her·maph·ro·dit·i·cal·ly** \-i-k(ə-)lē\ *adv* — **her·maph·ro·dit·ism** \-'maf-rə-,dīt-,iz-əm\ *n*

hermaphrodite brig *n* **:** a 2-masted vessel square-rigged forward and schooner-rigged aft

Her·maph·ro·di·tus \(,)hər-,maf-rə-'dīt-əs\ *n* [L, fr. Gk *Hermaphroditos,* fr. *Hermēs* + *Aphroditē* Aphrodite] **:** a son of Hermes and Aphrodite whose body coalesces with that of a nymph who is in love with him

hermaphrodite brig

her·ma·typ·ic \,hər-mə-'tip-ik\ *adj* [Gk *herma* prop, reef + *typtein* to strike, coin + E *-ic* — more at TYPE] **:** building reefs <~ corals>

her·me·neu·ti·cal \,hər-mə-'n(y)üt-i-kəl\ *or* **her·me·neu·tic** \-ik\ *adj* [Gk *hermēneutikos,* fr. *hermēneuein* to interpret, fr. *hermēneus* interpreter] **:** of or relating to hermeneutics **:** INTERPRETATIVE — **her·me·neu·ti·cal·ly** \-i-k(ə-)lē\ *adv*

her·me·neu·tics \-iks\ *n pl but sing or pl in constr* **:** the study of the methodological principles of interpretation (as of the Bible)

Her·mes \'hər-(,)mēz\ *n* [L, fr. Gk *Hermēs*] **:** a Greek god who serves as herald and messenger of the other gods — compare MERCURY

Hermes Tris·me·gis·tus \-,tris-mə-'jis-təs\ *n* [Gk *Hermēs trismegistos,* lit., Hermes thrice greatest] **:** a legendary author of works embodying magical, astrological, and alchemical doctrines

her·met·ic \(,)hər-'met-ik\ *also* **her·met·i·cal** \-i-kəl\ *adj* [NL *hermeticus,* fr. *Hermet-, Hermes Trismegistus*] **1** *often cap* **a :** of or relating to the Gnostic writings or teachings arising in the first three centuries A.D. and attributed to Hermes Trismegistus **b :** relating to or characterized by occultism or abstruseness **:** RECONDITE **2** [fr. the belief that Hermes Trismegistus invented a magic seal to keep vessels airtight] **a :** AIRTIGHT <~ seal> **b :** impervious to external influence <trapped inside the ~ military machine —Jack Newfield> — **her·met·i·cal·ly** \-i-k(ə-)lē\ *adv*

her·met·i·cism \-'met-ə-,siz-əm\ *n, often cap* **:** HERMETISM

her·me·tic·i·ty \,hər-mə-'tis-ət-ē\ *n* **:** the state or condition of being airtight **:** AIRTIGHTNESS <~ of a pipeline>

her·me·tism \'hər-mə-,tiz-əm\ *n, often cap* **1 :** a system of ideas based on hermetic teachings **2 :** adherence to hermetic doctrine — **her·me·tist** \-mət-əst\ *n*

her·mit \'hər-mət\ *n* [ME *eremite,* fr. OF, fr. LL *eremita,* fr. LGk *erēmitēs,* fr. Gk, adj., living in the desert, fr. *erēmia* desert, fr. *erēmos* lonely — more at RETINA] **1 a :** one that retires from society and lives in solitude esp. for religious reasons **:** RECLUSE **b** *obs* **:** BEADSMAN **2 :** a spiced molasses cookie — **her·mit·ism** \-,iz-əm\ *n*

her·mit·age \'hər-mət-ij\ *n* **1 a :** the habitation of a hermit **b :** a secluded residence or private retreat **:** HIDEAWAY **c :** MONASTERY **2 :** the life or condition of a hermit

Her·mi·tage \,(h)er-mi-'täzh\ *n* [Tain-l'*Ermitage,* commune in France] **:** a chiefly red Rhone valley wine; *also* **:** a similar wine made elsewhere

hermit crab *n* **:** any of numerous chiefly marine decapod crustaceans (families Paguridae and Parapaguridae) having soft asymmetrical abdomens and occupying the empty shells of gastropods

her·mi·tian matrix \er-,mē-shən-, ,hər-,mish-ən-\ *n* [Charles *Hermite* †1901 F mathematician] **:** a square matrix having the property that each pair of elements in the *i*th row and *j*th column and in the *j*th row and *i*th column are conjugate complex numbers

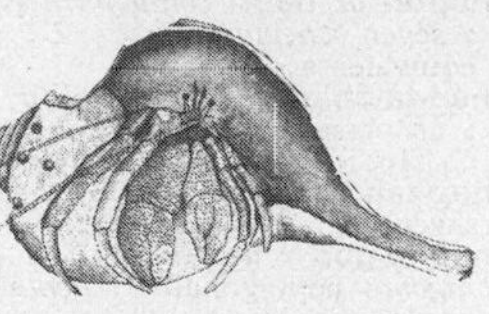

hermit crab

hern \'he(ə)rn, 'hərn\ *dial var of* HERON

her·nia \'hər-nē-ə\ *n, pl* **-ni·as** *or* **-ni·ae** \-nē-,ē, -nē-,ī\ [L — more at YARN] **:** a protrusion of an organ or part through connective tissue or through a wall of the cavity in which it is normally enclosed — called also *rupture* — **her·ni·al** \-nē-əl\ *adj*

her·ni·ate \'hər-nē-,āt\ *vi* **-at·ed; -at·ing :** to protrude through an abnormal body opening — **her·ni·a·tion** \,hər-nē-'ā-shən\ *n*

he·ro \'hē-(,)rō, 'hi(ə)r-(,)ō\ *n, pl* **heroes** [L *heros,* fr. Gk *hērōs*] **1 a :** a mythological or legendary figure often of divine descent endowed with great strength or ability **b :** an illustrious warrior **c :** a man admired for his achievements and qualities **d :** one that shows great courage **2 a :** the principal male character in a literary or dramatic work **b :** the central figure in an event or period **3** *pl usu* **heros :** SUBMARINE 2

Hero *n* [L, fr. Gk *Hērō*] **:** a legendary priestess of Aphrodite loved by Leander

[1]he·ro·ic \hi-'rō-ik\ *also* **he·ro·ical** \-i-kəl\ *adj* **1 :** of, relating to, or resembling heroes esp. of antiquity **2 a :** exhibiting or marked by courage and daring **b :** GRAND, NOBLE **3 :** of impressive size, power, or effect **:** LARGE, POWERFUL, POTENT <~ doses> **4 :** of, relating to, or constituting drama written during the Restoration in heroic couplets and concerned with a conflict between love and honor — **he·ro·ical·ly** \-i-k(ə-)lē\ *adv*

[2]heroic *n* **1 :** a heroic verse or poem **2** *pl* **a :** heroic behavior **b :** showy behavior

heroic couplet *n* **:** a rhyming couplet in iambic pentameter

he·roi·com·ic \hi-,rō-i-'käm-ik\ *or* **he·roi·com·i·cal** \-'käm-i-kəl\ *adj* [F *héroïcomique,* fr. *héroïque* heroic + *comique* comic] **:** comic by being ludicrously noble, bold, or elevated

heroic poem *n* **:** an epic or a poem in epic style

heroic stanza *n* **:** a rhymed quatrain in heroic verse with a rhyme scheme of *abab* — called also *heroic quatrain*

heroic verse *n* **1 :** dactylic hexameter esp. of epic verse of classical times — called also *heroic meter* **2 :** the iambic pentameter used esp. in English epic poetry during the 17th and 18th centuries — called also *heroic line, heroic meter*

her·o·in \'her-ə-wən\ *n* [fr. *Heroin,* a trademark] **:** a strongly physiologically addictive narcotic $C_{21}H_{23}NO_5$ made from but more potent than morphine — **her·o·in·ism** \-wə-,niz-əm\ *n*

her·o·ine \'her-ə-wən\ *n* [L *heroina,* fr. Gk *hērōinē,* fem. of *hērōs*] **1 a :** a mythological or legendary woman having the qualities of a hero **b :** a woman admired and emulated for her achievements and qualities **2 a :** the principal female character in a literary or dramatic work **b :** the central female figure in an event or period

her·o·ism \'her-ə-,wiz-əm\ *n* **1 :** extreme self-sacrificing courage esp. in fulfilling a high purpose or attaining a noble end **2 :** the qualities of a hero
syn HEROISM, VALOR, PROWESS, GALLANTRY *shared meaning element* **:** conspicuous courage

he·ro·ize \'hē-(,)rō-,īz, 'hir-(,)ō-; 'her-ə-,wīz\ *vt* **-ized; -iz·ing :** to make heroic

her·on \'her-ən\ *n, pl* **herons** *also* **heron** [ME *heiroun,* fr. MF *hairon,* of Gmc origin; akin to OHG *heigaro* heron, Gk *krizein* to creak, OHG *scrian* to scream] **:** any of various long-necked wading birds (family Ardeidae) with a long tapering bill, large wings, and soft plumage

her·on·ry \-ən-rē\ *n, pl* **-ries :** a heron rookery

hero–worship *vt* **:** to feel or express hero worship for — **hero–worshiper** *n*

hero worship *n* **1 :** veneration of a hero **2 :** foolish or excessive adulation for an individual

her·pes \'hər-(,)pēz\ *n* [L, fr. Gk *herpēs,* fr. *herpein* to creep — more at SERPENT] **:** any of several inflammatory virus diseases of the skin characterized by clusters of vesicles; *esp* **:** HERPES SIMPLEX — **her·pet·ic** \(,)hər-'pet-ik\ *adj*

herpes sim·plex \,hər-(,)pēz-'sim-,pleks\ *n* [NL, lit., simple herpes] **:** a virus disease marked by groups of watery blisters on the skin or mucous membranes (as of the mouth, lips, or genitals)

her·pes·vi·rus \-'vī-rəs\ *n* **:** any of a group of DNA-containing viruses that replicate in cell nuclei and produce herpes

herpes zos·ter \,hər-(,)pē(z)-'zōs-tər, -'zäs-\ *n* [NL, lit., girdle herpes] **:** an acute viral inflammation of the sensory ganglia of spinal and cranial nerves associated with a vesicular eruption and neuralgic pains — called also *shingles*

herpet- *or* **herpeto-** *comb form* [Gk *herpeton,* fr. neut. of *herpetos* creeping, fr. *herpein*] **1 :** reptile or reptiles <*herpeto*fauna> <*herpeto*logy> **2** [L *herpet-, herpes*] **:** herpes <*herpeti*form>

her·pe·tol·o·gy \,hər-pə-'täl-ə-jē\ *n* **:** a branch of zoology dealing with reptiles and amphibians — **her·pe·to·log·ic** \-pət-ᵊl-'äj-ik\ *or* **her·pe·to·log·i·cal** \-i-kəl\ *adj* — **her·pe·to·log·i·cal·ly** \-i-k(ə-)lē\ *adv* — **her·pe·tol·o·gist** \,hər-pə-'täl-ə-jəst\ *n*

Herr \(,)he(ə)r\ *n, pl* **Her·ren** \,her-ən, (,)he(ə)rn\ [G] — used among German-speaking people as a title equivalent to *Mr.*

her·ren·volk \'her-ən-,fōk, -,fōlk\ *n, often cap* [G] **:** MASTER RACE

her·ring \'her-iŋ\ *n, pl* **herring** *or* **herrings** [ME *hering,* fr. OE *hǣring;* akin to OHG *hārinc* herring] **:** a valuable clupeid food fish (*Clupea harengus*) that is abundant in the temperate and colder parts of the north Atlantic and that is preserved in the adult state by smoking or salting and in the young state is extensively canned and sold as sardines; *broadly* **:** a fish of the same family (Clupeidae)

[1]her·ring·bone \'her-iŋ-,bōn\ *n* **1 :** a pattern made up of rows of parallel lines which in any two adjacent rows slope in opposite directions **2 a :** a twilled fabric with a herringbone pattern; *also* **:** a suit made of this fabric **b :** a herringbone arrangement (as of materials or parts) **3 :** a method in skiing of ascending a slope by herringboning

2**herringbone** *vt* **1 :** to produce a herringbone pattern on **2 :** to arrange in a herringbone pattern ~ *vi* **1 :** to produce a herringbone pattern **2 :** to ascend a slope by toeing out on skis and placing the weight on the inner side

herringbone 1

herring gull *n* **:** a common large gull (*Larus argentatus*) of the northern hemisphere that as an adult is largely white with blue-gray mantle and dark wing tips and pink feet

hers \ˈhərz\ *pron, sing or pl in constr* **:** that which belongs to her — used without a following noun as a pronoun equivalent in meaning to the adjective *her*

her·self \(h)ər-ˈself\ *pron* **1 :** that identical female one — compare 1SHE; used reflexively, for emphasis, or in absolute constructions <she considers ~ lucky> <she ~ did it> <~ an orphan, she understood the situation> **2 :** her normal, healthy, or sane condition or self **3** *Irish & Scot* **:** a woman of consequence; *esp* **:** the mistress of the house

Herts *abbr* Hertfordshire

hertz \ˈhe(ə)rts, ˈhərts\ *n, pl* **hertz** [Heinrich R. *Hertz*] **:** a unit of frequency equal to one cycle per second — abbr. *Hz*

hertz·ian wave \ˌhert-sē-ən-, ˌhərt-\ *n* [Heinrich R. *Hertz*] **:** an electromagnetic wave produced by the oscillation of electricity in a conductor (as a radio antenna) and of a length ranging from less than a millimeter to many kilometers

he's \(ˌ)hēz, ēz\ **:** he is **:** he has

Hesh·van \ˈkesh-vən\ *n* [Heb *Ḥeshwān*] **:** the 2d month of the civil year or the 8th month of the ecclesiastical year in the Jewish calendar — see MONTH table

hes·i·tance \ˈhez-ə-tən(t)s\ *n* **:** HESITANCY

hes·i·tan·cy \-tən-sē\ *n, pl* **-cies** **1 :** the quality or state of being hesitant: as **a :** INDECISION <people . . . who didn't understand the *hesitancies,* the ambiguities of choice —Daniel Stern> **b :** RELUCTANCE <we are putting our judgment ahead of yours . . . which we do only with the greatest ~ —Gay Talese> **2 :** an act or instance of hesitating

hes·i·tant \ˈhez-ə-tənt\ *adj* **:** tending to hesitate ***syn*** see DISINCLINED — **hes·i·tant·ly** *adv*

hes·i·tate \ˈhez-ə-ˌtāt\ *vi* **-tat·ed; -tat·ing** [L *haesitatus,* pp. of *haesitare* to stick fast, hesitate, fr. *haesus,* pp. of *haerēre* to stick; akin to Lith *gaišti* to loiter] **1 :** to hold back in doubt or indecision **2 :** to delay momentarily **:** PAUSE **3 :** STAMMER — **hes·i·tat·er** *n* — **hes·i·tat·ing·ly** \-ˌtāt-iŋ-lē\ *adv*

syn HESITATE, WAVER, VACILLATE, FALTER *shared meaning element* **:** to show irresolution or uncertainty

hes·i·ta·tion \ˌhez-ə-ˈtā-shən\ *n* **1 :** an act or instance of hesitating **2 :** a pausing or faltering in speech

Hes·pe·ri·an \he-ˈspir-ē-ən\ *adj* [L *Hesperia,* the west, fr. Gk, fr. fem. of *hesperios* of the evening, western, fr. *hesperos* evening — more at WEST] **:** WESTERN, OCCIDENTAL

Hes·per·i·des \he-ˈsper-ə-ˌdēz\ *n pl* [L, fr. Gk] **1 :** the nymphs in classical mythology who guard with the aid of a dragon a garden in which golden apples grow **2 :** a legendary garden at the western extremity of the world producing golden apples

hes·per·i·din \he-ˈsper-əd-ᵊn\ *n* [NL *hesperidium,* orange, fr. L *Hesperides*] **:** a crystalline glycoside $C_{28}H_{34}O_{15}$ found in most citrus fruits and esp. in orange peel

hes·per·id·i·um \ˌhes-pə-ˈrid-ē-əm\ *n, pl* **-id·ia** \-ē-ə\ [NL, orange] **:** a berry (as an orange or lime) having a leathery rind

Hes·per·us \ˈhes-p(ə-)rəs\ *n* [L, fr. Gk *Hesperos*] **:** EVENING STAR 1

hes·sian \ˈhesh-ən\ *n* **1** *cap* **a :** a native of Hesse **b :** a German mercenary serving in the British forces during the American Revolution; *broadly* **:** a mercenary soldier **2 :** BURLAP

Hessian boot *n* **:** a high boot that extends to just below the knee and is commonly ornamented with a tassle and that was introduced into England by the Hessians early in the 19th century

Hessian fly *n* **:** a small two-winged fly (*Mayetiola destructor*) that is destructive to wheat in America

hess·ite \ˈhes-ˌīt\ *n* [G *hessit,* fr. Henry *Hess* †1850 Swiss chemist] **:** a mineral Ag_2Te consisting of a lead-gray sectile silver telluride

hes·so·nite \ˈhes-\ *var of* ESSONITE

hest \ˈhest\ *n* [ME *hest, hes,* fr. OE *hǣs;* akin to OE *hātan* to command — more at HIGHT] *archaic* **:** COMMAND, PRECEPT

Hes·tia \ˈhes-tē-ə, ˈhes(h)-chə\ *n* [Gk] **:** the Greek goddess of the hearth and chief goddess of domestic activity — compare VESTA

he·tae·ra \hi-ˈtir-ə\ *or* **he·tai·ra** \-ˈtī-rə\ *n, pl* **he·tae·rae** \-ˈti(ə)r-(ˌ)ē\ *or* **hetaeras** *or* **hetairas** *or* **he·tai·rai** \-ˈti(ə)r-ˌī\ [Gk *hetaira,* lit., companion, fem. of *hetairos*] **1 :** one of a class of highly cultivated courtesans in ancient Greece **2 :** DEMIMONDAINE

heter- *or* **hetero-** *comb form* [MF or LL; MF, fr. LL, fr. Gk, fr. *heteros;* akin to Gk *heis* one — more at SAME] **1 :** other than usual **:** other **:** different <*hetero*phyllous> **2 :** containing atoms of different kinds <*hetero*cyclic>

het·ero \ˈhet-ə-ˌrō\ *n, pl* **-er·os** **:** HETEROSEXUAL

het·ero·at·om \ˈhet-ə-rō-ˌat-əm\ *n* **:** an atom other than carbon in the ring of a heterocyclic compound

het·ero·au·to·tro·phic \ˈhet-ə-(ˌ)rō-ˌȯt-ə-ˈtrō-fik\ *adj* **:** requiring a simple organic source of carbon but utilizing inorganic nitrogen for metabolism

het·ero·aux·in \ˌhet-ə-rō-ˈȯk-sən\ *n* **:** INDOLEACETIC ACID

het·ero·cer·cal \-ˈsər-kəl\ *adj* **1 :** having the upper lobe larger than the lower with the end of the vertebral column prolonged and somewhat upturned in the upper lobe **2 :** having or relating to a heterocercal tail fin

het·ero·chro·mat·ic \-krə-ˈmat-ik\ *adj* **1 :** of, relating to, or having different colors **2 :** made up of various wavelengths or frequencies **3** [*heterochromatin*] **:** of or relating to heterochromatin — **het·ero·chro·ma·tism** \-ˈkrō-mə-ˌtiz-əm\ *n*

het·ero·chro·ma·tin \-ˈkrō-mət-ən\ *n* [G] **:** densely staining chromatin that appears as nodules in or along chromosomes and contains relatively few genes

het·ero·chro·mo·some \-ˈkrō-mə-ˌsōm, -ˌzōm\ *n* [ISV] **:** SEX CHROMOSOME

1**het·ero·clite** \ˈhet-ə-rə-ˌklīt\ *n* **1 :** a word irregular in inflection; *esp* **:** a noun irregular in declension **2 :** one that deviates from common rules or forms

2**heteroclite** *adj* [MF or LL; MF, fr. LL *heteroclitus,* fr. Gk *heteroklitos,* fr. *heter-* + *klinein* to lean, inflect — more at LEAN] **:** deviating from common forms or rules

het·ero·crine \ˈhet-ə-rə-ˌkrin, -ˌkrīn, -ˌkrēn\ *adj* [*heter-* + *-crine* (as in *endocrine*)] **:** having both an endocrine and an exocrine secretion

het·ero·cy·clic \ˌhet-ə-rō-ˈsī-klik, -ˈsik-lik\ *adj* [ISV] **:** relating to, characterized by, or being a ring composed of atoms of more than one kind — **het·ero·cy·cle** \ˈhet-ə-rō-ˌsī-kəl\ *n* — **heterocyclic** *n*

het·ero·cyst \ˈhet-ə-rō-ˌsist\ *n* **:** a large transparent thick-walled cell that resembles a spore and occurs at intervals along the filament in some blue-green algae

het·ero·dox \ˈhet-ə-rə-ˌdäks, ˈhe-trə-\ *adj* [LL *heterodoxus,* fr. Gk *heterodoxos,* fr. *heter-* + *doxa* opinion — more at DOXOLOGY] **1 :** contrary to or different from an acknowledged standard <a ~ sermon> **2 :** holding unorthodox opinions or doctrines <the societies representing the orthodox practice of medicine have generally succeeded in keeping . . . ~ practitioners out —D. D. McKean>

het·ero·doxy \-ˌdäk-sē\ *n, pl* **-dox·ies** **1 :** the quality or state of being heterodox **2 :** a heterodox opinion or doctrine

1**het·ero·dyne** \ˈhet-ə-rə-ˌdīn, ˈhe-trə-\ *adj* **:** of or relating to the production of an electrical beat between two radio frequencies of which one usu. is that of a received signal-carrying current and the other that of an uninterrupted current introduced into the apparatus; *also* **:** of or relating to the production of a beat between two optical frequencies

2**heterodyne** *vt* **-dyned; dyn·ing :** to combine (as a radio frequency) with a different frequency so that a beat is produced

het·er·oe·cious *or* **het·er·ecious** \ˌhet-ə-ˈrē-shəs\ *adj* [*heter-* + Gk *oikia* house — more at VICINITY] **:** passing through the different stages in the life cycle on alternate and often unrelated hosts <~ insects> — **het·er·oe·cism** \-ˈrē-ˌsiz-əm\ *n*

het·ero·ga·mete \ˌhet-ə-rō-gə-ˈmēt, -ˈgam-ˌēt\ *n* [ISV] **:** either of a pair of gametes that differ in form, size, or behavior and occur typically as large nonmotile oogametes and small motile sperms

het·ero·ga·met·ic \-gə-ˈmet-ik\ *adj* **:** forming two kinds of germ cells of which one produces male offspring and the other female offspring <the human male is ~ >

het·er·og·a·mous \ˌhet-ə-ˈräg-ə-məs\ *adj* **1 :** bearing flowers of two kinds (as perfect and pistillate) — used esp. of sedges and composites **2 :** having or characterized by fusion of unlike gametes — compare ANISOGAMOUS, ISOGAMOUS

het·er·og·a·my \-mē\ *n* **1 :** sexual reproduction involving fusion of unlike gametes often differing in size, structure, and physiology **2 :** the condition of reproducing by heterogamy

het·er·o·ge·ne·ity \ˌhet-ə-rō-jə-ˈnē-ət-ē, ˌhe-trō-\ *n* **:** the quality or state of being heterogeneous

het·er·o·ge·neous \ˌhet-ə-rə-ˈjē-nē-əs, ˌhe-trə-, -nyəs\ *adj* [ML *heterogeneus, heterogenus,* fr. Gk *heterogenēs,* fr. *heter-* + *genos* kind — more at KIN] **:** consisting of dissimilar ingredients or constituents **:** MIXED — **het·er·o·ge·neous·ly** *adv* — **het·er·o·ge·ne·ous·ness** *n*

het·ero·gen·e·sis \ˌhet-ə-rō-ˈjen-ə-səs\ *n* [NL] **1 :** ABIOGENESIS **2 :** ALTERNATION OF GENERATIONS — **het·ero·ge·net·ic** \-jə-ˈnet-ik\ *adj*

het·er·og·e·nous \ˌhet-ə-ˈräj-ə-nəs\ *adj* **1 :** originating in an outside source; *esp* **:** derived from another species <~ bone graft> **2 :** HETEROGENEOUS

het·er·og·e·ny \-nē\ *n* **:** a heterogenous collection or group

het·ero·gon·ic \ˌhet-ə-rə-ˈgän-ik\ *adj* **1 :** ALLOMETRIC **2 :** being that course of development in which a generation of parasites is succeeded by a free-living generation — used of some nematode worms

het·er·og·o·ny \ˌhet-ə-ˈräg-ə-nē\ *n* **1 :** ALTERNATION OF GENERATIONS; *esp* **:** alternation of a dioecious generation with a parthenogenetic one **2 :** ALLOMETRY

het·ero·graft \ˈhet-ə-rō-ˌgraft\ *n* **:** a graft of tissue taken from a donor of one species and grafted into a recipient of another species — compare HOMOGRAFT

het·ero·kary·on \ˌhet-ə-rō-ˈkar-ē-ˌän, -ən\ *also* **het·ero·cary·on** *n* [NL, fr. *heter-* + *karyon, caryon* nucleus, fr. Gk *karyon* nut, kernel — more at CAREEN] **:** a cell in the mycelium of a fungus that contains two or more genetically unlike nuclei

het·ero·kary·o·sis \ˈhet-ə-rō-ˌkar-ē-ˈō-səs\ *also* **het·ero·cary·o·sis** *n* [NL] **:** the condition of having cells that are heterokaryons

het·ero·kary·ot·ic *also* **het·ero·cary·ot·ic** \-ē-ˈät-ik\ *adj* **:** of, relating to, or consisting of heterokaryons

het·er·ol·o·gous \-ˈräl-ə-gəs\ *adj* **1 :** characterized by heterology **2 :** derived from a different species <~ DNAs> <~ transplants> — **het·er·ol·o·gous·ly** *adv*

het·er·ol·o·gy \ˌhet-ə-ˈräl-ə-jē\ *n* [ISV *heter-* + *-logy* (as in *analogy*)] **:** a lack of correspondence of apparently similar bodily parts due to differences in fundamental makeup or origin

het·ero·ly·sis \ˌhet-ə-ˈräl-ə-səs, -ə-rə-ˈlī-səs\ *n* [NL] **:** decomposition of a compound into two oppositely charged particles or ions — **het·ero·lyt·ic** \-ə-rə-ˈlit-ik\ *adj*

het·ero·mor·phic \ˌhet-ə-rə-ˈmȯr-fik\ *or* **het·ero·mor·phous** \-fəs\ *adj* [ISV] **1 :** deviating from the usual form **2 :** exhibit-

ə abut ᵊ kitten ər further a back ā bake ä cot, cart
aù out ch chin e less ē easy g gift i trip ī life
j joke ŋ sing ō flow ȯ flaw ȯi coin th thin t͟h this
ü loot u̇ foot y yet yü few yu̇ furious zh vision

ing diversity of form or forms <~ pairs of chromosomes> <~ alternation of generations> — **het·ero·mor·phism** \-ˌfiz-əm\ *n*

het·er·on·o·mous \ˌhet-ə-ˈrän-ə-məs\ *adj* [*heter-* + *-nomous* (as in *autonomous*)] **1 :** specialized along different lines of growth or under different controlling forces **2 :** subject to external controls and impositions — **het·er·on·o·mous·ly** *adv*

het·er·on·o·my \-mē\ *n* [*heter-* + *-nomy* (as in *autonomy*)] **:** subjection to something else; *esp* **:** a lack of moral freedom or self-determination <a life of alienation, a life of ~ rather than autonomy —Mary Aloysius>

het·ero·phile \ˈhet-ə-rə-ˌfīl\ *or* **het·ero·phil** \-ˌfil\ *adj* **:** reacting serologically with an antigen of another species

het·er·oph·o·ny \ˌhet-ə-ˈräf-ə-nē\ *n, pl* **-nies** [Gk *heterophōnia* diversity of note, fr. *heter-* + *-phōnia* -phony] **:** the performance of a single melody by two or more individuals who add their own individual rhythmic or melodic modifications

het·ero·phyl·lous \ˌhet-ə-rō-ˈfil-əs\ *adj* **:** having the foliage leaves of more than one form on the same plant or stem — **het·ero·phyl·ly** \ˈhet-ə-rō-ˌfil-ē\ *n*

het·ero·phyte \ˈhet-ə-rə-ˌfīt\ *n* **:** a plant (as a parasite or saprophyte) that is dependent for food materials upon other organisms or their products — **het·ero·phyt·ic** \ˌhet-ə-rə-ˈfit-ik\ *adj*

het·ero·ploid \ˈhet-ə-rə-ˌplȯid\ *adj* [ISV] **:** having a chromosome number that is not a simple multiple of the haploid chromosome number — **heteroploid** *n* — **het·ero·ploi·dy** \-ˌplȯid-ē\ *n*

het·ero·po·lar \ˌhet-ə-rə-ˈpō-lər\ *adj* [ISV] **:** POLAR 5, IONIC — **het·ero·po·lar·i·ty** \-rō-pə-ˈlar-ət-ē\ *n*

het·er·op·ter·ous \ˌhet-ə-ˈräp-tə-rəs\ *adj* [deriv. of Gk *heter-* + *pteron* wing — more at FEATHER] **:** of or relating to an insect order or suborder (Heteroptera) comprising the true bugs

[1]**het·ero·sex·u·al** \ˌhet-ə-rō-ˈseksh-(ə-)wəl, -ˈsek-shəl\ *adj* [ISV] **1 :** of, relating to, or marked by heterosexuality **2 :** of or relating to different sexes — **het·ero·sex·u·al·ly** \-ē\ *adv*

[2]**heterosexual** *n* **:** a heterosexual individual

het·ero·sex·u·al·i·ty \-ˌsek-shə-ˈwal-ət-ē\ *n* **:** the manifestation of sexual desire for one or more members of the opposite sex

het·er·o·sis \ˌhet-ə-ˈrō-səs\ *n* [NL] **:** a marked vigor or capacity for growth often shown by crossbred animals or plants — **het·er·ot·ic** \-ˈrät-ik\ *adj*

het·ero·spo·rous \ˌhet-ə-rə-ˈspōr-əs, -ˈspȯr-; -ˈräs-pə-rəs\ *adj* **:** characterized by heterospory

het·ero·spo·ry \ˈhet-ə-rə-ˌspōr-ē, -ˌspȯr-; ˌhet-ə-ˈräs-pə-rē\ *n* **1 :** the production of asexual spores of more than one kind **2 :** the production of microspores and megaspores (as in ferns and seed plants)

het·ero·thal·lic \ˌhet-ə-rō-ˈthal-ik\ *adj* [*heter-* + *thall-* + *-ic*] **1 :** having two or more genetically incompatible but morphologically similar haploid phases that function as separate sexes or strains — used esp. of some algae or fungi or of the unisexual spores producing them **2 :** DIOECIOUS — **het·ero·thal·lism** \-ˈthal-ˌiz-əm\ *n*

het·ero·top·ic \-rə-ˈtäp-ik\ *adj* [*heter-* + Gk *topos* place — more at TOPIC] **:** occurring in an abnormal place <~ bone formation> <~ liver transplantation>

het·ero·troph \ˈhet-ə-rə-ˌtrōf, -ˌträf\ *n* **:** a heterotrophic individual

het·ero·tro·phic \ˌhet-ə-rə-ˈtrō-fik\ *adj* **:** requiring complex organic compounds of nitrogen and carbon for metabolic synthesis — **het·ero·tro·phi·cal·ly** \-fi-k(ə-)lē\ *adv*

het·ero·typ·ic \ˌhet-ə-rō-ˈtip-ik\ *also* **het·ero·typ·i·cal** \-i-kəl\ *adj* **1 :** of or being the reduction division of meiosis as contrasted with typical mitotic division **2 :** different in kind, arrangement, or form

het·ero·zy·go·sis \ˌhet-ə-rō-(ˌ)zī-ˈgō-səs\ *n* [NL] **1 :** a union of genetically dissimilar gametes forming a heterozygote **2 :** HETEROZYGOSITY

het·ero·zy·gos·i·ty \-ˈgäs-ət-ē\ *n* **:** the state of being a heterozygote

het·ero·zy·gote \-ˈzī-ˌgōt\ *n* **:** an animal or plant in which the two genes of at least one genetic locus are different alleles — **het·ero·zy·gous** \-gəs\ *adj*

heth \ˈkät(h), ˈket(h)\ *n* [Heb *ḥēth*] **:** the 8th letter of the Hebrew alphabet — see ALPHABET table

het·man \ˈhet-mən\ *n, pl* **hetmans** [Pol, commander in chief] **:** a cossack leader

het up \ˈhet-ˈəp\ *adj* [*het,* dial. past of *heat*] **:** highly excited **:** UPSET

heu·land·ite \ˈhyü-lən-ˌdīt\ *n* [Henry *Heuland,* 19th cent. E mineral collector] **:** a zeolite consisting of a hydrous aluminosilicate of sodium and calcium

[1]**heu·ris·tic** \hyu̇-ˈris-tik\ *adj* [G *heuristisch,* fr. NL *heuristicus,* fr. Gk *heuriskein* to discover; akin to OIr *fúar* I have found] **:** providing aid or direction in the solution of a problem but otherwise unjustified or incapable of justification <~ techniques> <a ~ assumption>; *specif* **:** of or relating to exploratory problem-solving techniques that utilize self-educating techniques (as the evaluation of feedback) to improve performance <a ~ computer program>

[2]**heuristic** *n* **1 :** the study or practice of heuristic procedure **2 :** heuristic argument **3 :** a heuristic method or procedure

hew \ˈhyü\ *vb* **hewed; hewed** *or* **hewn** \ˈhyün\; **hew·ing** [ME *hewen,* fr. OE *hēawan;* akin to OHG *houwan* to hew, L *cudere* to beat] *vt* **1 :** to cut with blows of a heavy cutting instrument **2 :** to fell by blows of an ax <~ a tree> **3 :** to give form or shape to with or as if with heavy cutting blows ~ *vi* **1 :** to make cutting blows **2 :** to conform strictly **:** ADHERE — often used in the phrase *hew to the line* <there is no pressure . . . on newspapers to ~ to the official line —*N.Y. Times Mag.*> — **hew·er** *n*

HEW *abbr* Department of Health, Education, and Welfare

[1]**hex** \ˈheks\ *vb* [PaG *hexe,* fr. G *hexen,* fr. *hexe* witch] *vi* **:** to practice witchcraft ~ *vt* **1 :** to put a hex on **2 :** to affect as if by an evil spell **:** JINX <giving in to an unscientific fear of ~*ing* the whole project —Daniel Lang> — **hex·er** *n*

[2]**hex** *n* **1 :** SPELL, JINX **2 :** a person who practices witchcraft **:** WITCH

[3]**hex** *adj* **:** HEXAGONAL <a bolt with a ~ head>

[4]**hex** *abbr* hexagon; hexagonal

hexa- *or* **hex-** *comb form* [Gk, fr. *hex* six — more at SIX] **1 :** six <*hexa*merous> **2 :** containing six atoms, groups, or equivalents <*hex*ane>

hexa·bi·ose *or* **hexo·bi·ose** \ˌhek-sə-ˈbī-ˌōs, -ˌōz\ *n* **:** a disaccharide (as maltose) yielding two hexose molecules on hydrolysis

hexa·chlo·ride \ˌhek-sə-ˈklō(ə)r-ˌīd, -ˈklȯ(ə)r-\ *n* **:** a chloride containing six atoms of chlorine in a molecule

hexa·chlo·ro·eth·ane \-ˌklōr-ə-ˈweth-ˌān, -ˌklȯr-\ *or* **hexa·chlor·eth·ane** \-ˌklōr-ˈeth-, -ˌklȯr-\ *n* [ISV] **:** a toxic crystalline compound C_2Cl_6 used esp. in smoke bombs and in the control of liver flukes in ruminants

hexa·chlo·ro·phene \-ˈklōr-ə-ˌfēn, -ˈklȯr-\ *n* [*hexa-* + *chlor-* + *phenol*] **:** a crystalline phenolic bacteria-inhibiting agent $C_{13}Cl_6H_6O_2$ used esp. in soap

hexa·chord \ˈhek-sə-ˌkȯ(ə)rd\ *n* [*hexa-* + Gk *chordē* string — more at YARN] **:** a diatonic series of six tones having a semitone between the third and fourth tones

hex·ad \ˈhek-ˌsad\ *or* **hex·ade** \-ˌsād\ *n* [LL *hexad-, hexas,* fr. Gk, fr. *hex*] **:** a group or series of six — **hex·ad·ic** \hek-ˈsad-ik\ *adj*

hexa·dec·i·mal \ˌhek-sə-ˈdes-(ə-)məl\ *adj* **:** of, relating to, or being a number system with a base of 16

hexa·gon \ˈhek-sə-ˌgän\ *n* [Gk *hexagōnon,* neut. of *hexagōnos* hexagonal, fr. *hexa-* + *gōnia* angle — more at -GON] **:** a polygon of six angles and six sides

hex·ag·o·nal \hek-ˈsag-ən-ᵊl\ *adj* **1 :** having six angles and six sides **2 :** having a hexagon as section or base **3 :** relating to or being a crystal system characterized by three equal lateral axes intersecting at angles of 60 degrees and a vertical axis of variable length at right angles — **hex·ag·o·nal·ly** \-ᵊl-ē\ *adv*

hexa·gram \ˈhek-sə-ˌgram\ *n* [ISV] **:** a figure formed by completing externally an equilateral triangle on each side of a regular hexagon

hexagram

hexa·he·dron \ˌhek-sə-ˈhē-drən\ *n, pl* **-drons** *also* **-dra** \-drə\ [LL, fr. Gk *hexaedron,* fr. neut. of *hexaedros* of six surfaces, fr. *hexa-* + *hedra* seat — more at SIT] **:** a polyhedron of six faces

hexa·hy·drate \-ˈhī-ˌdrāt\ *n* **:** a chemical compound with six molecules of water — **hexa·hy·drat·ed** \-ˌdrāt-əd\ *adj*

hex·am·e·ter \hek-ˈsam-ət-ər\ *n* [L, fr. Gk *hexametron,* fr. neut. of *hexametros* having six measures, fr. *hexa-* + *metron* measure — more at MEASURE] **:** a line of verse consisting of six metrical feet

hexa·me·tho·ni·um \ˌhek-sə-mə-ˈthō-nē-əm\ *n* [*hexa-* + *meth-* + *-onium*] **:** either of two compounds $C_{12}H_{30}Br_2N_2$ or $C_{12}H_{30}Cl_2N_2$ used as ganglionic blocking agents in the treatment of hypertension

hexa·meth·y·lene·tet·ra·mine \ˌhek-sə-ˈmeth-ə-ˌlēn-ˈte-trə-ˌmēn\ *n* [ISV] **:** a crystalline compound $C_6H_{12}N_4$ used esp. as an accelerator in vulcanizing rubber, as an absorbent for phosgene, and as a diuretic

hex·ane \ˈhek-ˌsān\ *n* [ISV] **:** any of several isomeric volatile liquid paraffin hydrocarbons C_6H_{14} found in petroleum

hex·a·no·ic acid \ˌhek-sə-ˌnō-ik-\ *n* [ISV *hexane* + *-oic*] **:** CAPROIC ACID

hexa·ploid \ˈhek-sə-ˌplȯid\ *adj* [ISV] **:** having or being six times the monoploid chromosome number — **hexaploid** *n* — **hexa·ploi·dy** \-ˌplȯid-ē\ *n*

[1]**hexa·pod** \ˈhek-sə-ˌpäd\ *n* [Gk *hexapod-, hexapous* having six feet, fr. *hexa-* + *pod-, pous* foot — more at FOOT] **:** INSECT 1b

[2]**hexapod** *adj* **1 :** six-footed **2 :** of or relating to insects

Hexa·teuch \ˈhek-sə-ˌt(y)ük\ *n* [*hexa-* + Gk *teuchos* book — more at PENTATEUCH] **:** the first six books of the Old Testament

hex·en·be·sen \ˈhek-sən-ˌbāz-ᵊn\ *n* [G, fr. *hexen* (pl. of *hexe* witch) + *besen* broom, fr. OHG *besmo* — more at BESOM] **:** WITCHES'-BROOM

hex·e·rei \ˌhek-sə-ˈrī\ *n* [PaG, fr. G] **:** WITCHCRAFT

hexo·bar·bi·tal \ˌhek-sə-ˈbär-bə-ˌtȯl\ *n* [*hexo-* (fr. *hexa-*) + *barbital*] **:** a barbiturate $C_{12}H_{16}N_2O_3$ used as a sedative and hypnotic and in the form of its soluble sodium salt as an intravenous anesthetic of short duration

hexo·ki·nase \ˌhek-sə-ˈkī-ˌnās, -ˌnāz\ *n* [*hexose* + *kinase*] **:** any of a group of enzymes that accelerate the phosphorylation of hexoses (as in the formation of glucose-6-phosphate from glucose and ATP) in carbohydrate metabolism

hex·o·san \ˈhek-sə-ˌsan\ *n* **:** a polysaccharide yielding only hexoses on hydrolysis

hex·ose \ˈhek-ˌsōs, -ˌsōz\ *n* [ISV] **:** a monosaccharide (as glucose) containing six carbon atoms in the molecule

hex·yl \ˈhek-səl\ *n* [ISV] **:** an alkyl radical C_6H_{13} derived from a hexane

hex·yl·res·or·cin·ol \ˌhek-səl-rə-ˈzȯrs-ᵊn-ˌȯl, -ˌōl\ *n* **:** a crystalline phenol $C_{12}H_{18}O_2$ used as an antiseptic and anthelmintic

hey \ˈhā\ *interj* [ME] — used esp. to call attention or to express interrogation, surprise, or exultation

[1]**hey·day** \ˈhā-ˌdā\ *interj* [irreg. fr. *hey*] *archaic* — used to express elation or wonder

[2]**heyday** *n* **1** *archaic* **:** high spirits **2 :** the period of one's greatest strength, vigor, or prosperity

Hez·e·ki·ah \ˌhez-ə-ˈkī-ə\ *n* [Heb *Ḥizqīyāh*] **:** a king of Judah under whom the kingdom underwent a ruinous Assyrian invasion at the end of the 8th century B.C.

hf *abbr* half

Hf *symbol* hafnium

HF *abbr* **1** height finding **2** high frequency **3** home forces

hg *abbr* **1** hectogram **2** heliogram **3** hemoglobin

Hg *symbol* [NL *hydrargyrum,* lit., water silver] mercury

HGH *abbr* human growth hormone

hgt *abbr* height

hgwy *abbr* highway

HH *abbr* **1** Her Highness; His Highness **2** His Holiness

HHD *abbr* [NL *Humanitatum Doctor*] doctor of humanities

HHFA *abbr* Housing and Home Finance Agency

hi \ˈhī(-ē)\ *interj* [ME *hy*] — used esp. as a greeting

HI *abbr* **1** Hawaii **2** high intensity **3** humidity index

HIA *abbr* Horological Institute of America
HIAA *abbr* Health Insurance Association of America
hi·a·tal \hī-ˈāt-ᵊl\ *adj* : HIATUS <~ hernia>
1**hi·a·tus** \hī-ˈāt-əs\ *n* [L, fr. *hiatus,* pp. of *hiare* to yawn — more at YAWN] **1 a :** a break in or as if in a material object : GAP <the ~ between the theory and the practice of the party —J. G. Colton> **b :** a gap or passage in an anatomical part or organ **2 a :** a lapse in continuity **b :** the occurrence of two vowel sounds without pause or intervening consonantal sound
2**hiatus** *adj* **1 :** involving a hiatus **2** *of a hernia* **:** having a part that herniates through the esophageal hiatus of the diaphragm
Hi·a·wa·tha \ˌhī-ə-ˈwȯ-thə, ˌhē-ə-, -ˈwäth-ə\ *n* : the Indian hero of Longfellow's poem *The Song of Hiawatha*
hi·ba·chi \hi-ˈbäch-ē\ *n* [Jap] : a charcoal brazier
hi·ber·nac·u·lum \ˌhī-bər-ˈnak-yə-ləm\ *n, pl* **-la** \-lə\ [NL, fr. L, winter residence, fr. *hibernare*] : a shelter occupied during the winter by a dormant animal (as an insect)
hi·ber·nal \hī-ˈbərn-ᵊl\ *adj* : of, relating to, or occurring in winter : WINTRY
hi·ber·nate \ˈhī-bər-ˌnāt\ *vi* **-nat·ed; -nat·ing** [L *hibernatus,* pp. of *hibernare* to pass the winter, fr. *hibernus* of winter; akin to L *hiems* winter, Gk *cheimōn*] **1 :** to pass the winter in a torpid or resting state **2 :** to be or become inactive or dormant — **hi·ber·na·tion** \ˌhī-bər-ˈnā-shən\ *n* — **hi·ber·na·tor** \ˈhī-bər-ˌnāt-ər\ *n*
1**Hi·ber·ni·an** \hī-ˈbər-nē-ən\ *adj* [L *Hibernia* Ireland] : of, relating to, or characteristic of Ireland or the Irish
2**Hibernian** *n* **:** a native or inhabitant of Ireland
hi·bis·cus \hī-ˈbis-kəs, hə-\ *n* [NL, genus name, fr. L, marshmallow] : any of a large genus (*Hibiscus*) of herbs, shrubs, or small trees of the mallow family with dentate leaves and large showy flowers
HIC *abbr* Health Insurance Council
1**hic·cup** *also* **hic·cough** \ˈhik-(ˌ)əp\ *n* [imit.] **1 :** a spasmodic inhalation with closure of the glottis accompanied by a peculiar sound **2 :** an attack of hiccuping — usu. used in pl. but sing or pl. in constr.
2**hiccup** *also* **hiccough** *vi* **hic·cuped** *also* **hic·cupped; hic·cup·ing** *also* **hic·cup·ping :** to make a hiccup; *also* **:** to be affected with hiccups
hic ja·cet \(ˈ)hik-ˈjā-sət, (ˈ)hēk-ˈyäk-ət\ *n* [L, here lies] : EPITAPH
1**hick** \ˈhik\ *n* [*Hick,* nickname for *Richard*] : an unsophisticated provincial person
2**hick** *adj* : UNSOPHISTICATED, PROVINCIAL <a ~ town>
1**hick·ey** \ˈhik-ē\ *n, pl* **hickeys** [origin unknown] **1 a :** a threaded coupling between an electrical fixture and an outlet box **b :** a device for bending pipe and conduit **2 :** DEVICE, GADGET
2**hickey** *n, pl* **hickeys** [origin unknown] **1 :** PIMPLE **2 :** a temporary red mark produced in lovemaking by biting and sucking the skin
hick·o·ry \ˈhik-(ə-)rē\ *n, pl* **-ries** [short for obs. *pokahickory,* fr. *pawcohiccora* food prepared from pounded nuts (in some Algonquian language of Virginia)] **1 a :** any of a genus (*Carya*) of No. American hardwood trees of the walnut family that often have sweet edible nuts **b :** the usu. tough pale wood of a hickory **2 :** a switch or cane (as of hickory wood) used esp. for punishing a child — **hickory** *adj*
hid \ˈhid\ *adj* : HIDDEN
HID *abbr* headache, insomnia, depression
hi·dal·go \hid-ˈal-(ˌ)gō, ē-ˈthäl-\ *n, pl* **-gos** *often cap* [Sp] : a member of the lower nobility of Spain
hid·den \ˈhid-ᵊn\ *adj* **1 :** being out of sight : CONCEALED **2 :** OBSCURE, UNEXPLAINED
hid·den·ite \ˈhid-ᵊn-ˌīt\ *n* [William E. *Hidden* †1918 Am mineralogist] : a transparent yellow to green spodumene valued as a gem
hidden tax *n* : INDIRECT TAX
1**hide** \ˈhīd\ *n* [ME, fr. OE *hīgid*] : any of various old English units of land area; *esp* **:** a unit of 120 acres
2**hide** *vb* **hid** \ˈhid\; **hid·den** \ˈhid-ᵊn\ *or* **hid; hid·ing** \ˈhīd-iŋ\ [ME *hiden,* fr. OE *hȳdan;* akin to Gk *keuthein* to conceal, OE *hȳd* hide, skin] *vt* **1 a :** to put out of sight : SECRETE **b :** to conceal for shelter or protection; SHIELD **2 :** to keep secret **3 :** to screen from view **4 :** to turn (the eyes or face) away in shame or anger ~ *vi* **1 :** to remain out of sight **2 :** to seek protection or evade responsibility <heads of companies who are not . . . gift-minded ~ behind their boards of directors —*Saturday Rev.*> — **hid·er** \ˈhīd-ər\ *n*

syn HIDE, CONCEAL, SCREEN, SECRETE, BURY *shared meaning element* **:** to withhold or withdraw from sight
3**hide** *n* [ME, fr. OE *hȳd;* akin to OHG *hūt* hide, L *cutis* skin, Gk *kytos* hollow vessel] : the skin of an animal whether raw or dressed — used esp. of large heavy skins — **hide or hair** *or* **hide nor hair :** a vestige or trace of someone or something <a wife he hadn't seen *hide or hair* of in over 20 years —H. L. Davis>
4**hide** *vt* **hid·ed; hid·ing :** to give a beating to : FLOG
hide·away \ˈhīd-ə-ˌwā\ *n* : RETREAT, HIDEOUT
hide·bound \-ˌbau̇nd\ *adj* **1 a** *of a domestic animal* **:** having a dry skin lacking in pliancy and adhering closely to the underlying flesh **b** *of a tree* **:** having the bark so close and constricting that it impedes growth **2 :** having an inflexible character
hid·eous \ˈhid-ē-əs\ *adj* [alter. of ME *hidous,* fr. OF, fr. *hisde, hide* terror] **1 :** offensive to the senses and esp. to sight : exceedingly ugly **2 :** morally offensive : SHOCKING **syn** see UGLY **ant** fair — **hid·eous·ly** *adv* — **hid·eous·ness** *n*
hide·out \ˈhī-ˌdau̇t\ *n* : a place of refuge or concealment
hid·ey–hole *or* **hidy–hole** \ˈhīd-ē-ˌhōl\ *n* [alter. of earlier *hiding-hole*] : HIDEAWAY
hi·dro·sis \hid-ˈrō-səs, hī-ˈdrō-\ *n* [NL, fr. Gk *hidrōsis, fr. hidroun* to sweat, fr. *hidrōs* sweat — more at SWEAT] : excretion of sweat : PERSPIRATION — **hi·drot·ic** \-ˈrät-ik, -ˈdrät-\ *adj*
hie \ˈhī\ *vb* **hied; hy·ing** *or* **hie·ing** [ME *hien,* fr. OE *hīgian* to strive, hasten; akin to OSw *hikka* to pant, Skt *sighra* quick] : HASTEN
hi·emal \ˈhī-ə-məl\ *adj* [L *hiemalis,* fr. *hiems* winter — more at HIBERNATE] : HIBERNAL
hier- *or* **hiero-** *comb form* [LL, fr. Gk, fr. *hieros* — more at IRE] : sacred : holy <*hiero*logy>
hi·er·arch \ˈhī-(ə-)ˌrärk\ *n* [MF or ML; MF *hierarche,* fr. ML *hierarcha,* fr. Gk *hierarchēs,* fr. *hier-* + *-archēs* -arch] **1 :** a religious leader in a position of authority **2 :** a person high in a hierarchy — **hi·er·ar·chal** \ˌhī-(ə-)ˈrär-kəl\ *adj*
hi·er·ar·chi·cal \ˌhī-(ə-)ˈrär-ki-kəl\ *or* **hi·er·ar·chic** \-kik\ *adj* : of, relating to, or arranged in a hierarchy — **hi·er·ar·chi·cal·ly** \-ki-k(ə-)lē\ *adv*
hi·er·ar·chy \ˈhī-(ə-)ˌrär-kē\ *n, pl* **-chies** **1 :** a division of angels **2 a :** a ruling body of clergy organized into orders or ranks each subordinate to the one above it; *specif* **:** the bishops of a province or nation **b :** church government by a hierarchy **3 :** a body of persons in authority **4 :** a graded or ranked series <Christian ~ of values> <a machine's ~ of responses>
hi·er·at·ic \ˌhī-(ə-)ˈrat-ik\ *adj* [L *hieraticus* sacerdotal, fr. Gk *hieratikos,* deriv. of *hieros*] **1 :** constituting or belonging to a cursive form of ancient Egyptian writing simpler than the hieroglyphic **2 :** SACERDOTAL — **hi·er·at·i·cal·ly** \-i-k(ə-)lē\ *adv*
hi·ero·dule \ˈhī-(ə-)rō-ˌd(y)ü(ə)l, hī-ˈer-ə-\ *n* [LL *hierodulus,* fr. Gk *hierodoulos,* fr. *hier-* + *doulos* slave] : a slave in the service of a temple — **hi·ero·du·lic** \ˌhī-(ə-)rō-ˈd(y)ü-lik, (ˌ)hī-ˌer-ə-\ *adj*
hi·ero·glyph \ˈhī-(ə-)rə-ˌglif\ *n* [F *hiéroglyphe,* fr. MF, back-formation fr. *hieroglyphique*] **1 :** a character used in a system of hieroglyphic writing **2 :** something that resembles a hieroglyph in form or symbolism
1**hi·ero·glyph·ic** \ˌhī-(ə-)rə-ˈglif-ik\ *or* **hi·ero·glyph·i·cal** \-i-kəl\ *adj* [MF *hieroglyphique,* fr. LL *hieroglyphicus,* fr. Gk *hieroglyphikos,* fr. *hier-* + *glyphein* to carve — more at CLEAVE] **1 :** written in, constituting, or belonging to a system of writing mainly in pictorial characters **2 :** inscribed with hieroglyphic **3 :** resembling hieroglyphic in difficulty of decipherment — **hi·ero·glyph·i·cal·ly** \-i-k(ə-)lē\ *adv*
2**hieroglyphic** *n* **1 :** HIEROGLYPH **2 :** a system of hieroglyphic writing; *specif* **:** the picture script of the ancient Egyptian priesthood — often used in pl. but sing. or pl. in constr. **3 :** something that resembles a hieroglyphic esp. in difficulty of decipherment

Egyptian hieroglyphics

hi·ero·phant \ˈhī-(ə-)rə-ˌfant, hī-ˈer-ə-fənt\ *n* [LL *hierophanta,* fr. Gk *hierophantēs,* fr. *hier-* + *phainein* to show] **1 :** a priest in ancient Greece; *specif* **:** the chief priest of the Eleusinian mysteries **2 a :** EXPOSITOR **b :** ADVOCATE — **hi·ero·phan·tic** \ˌhī-(ə-)rə-ˈfant-ik, (ˌ)hī-ˌer-ə-\ *adj*
HIF *abbr* Health Information Foundation
hi–fi \ˈhī-ˈfī\ *n* **1 :** HIGH FIDELITY **2 :** equipment for reproduction of sound with high fidelity
hig·gle \ˈhig-əl\ *vi* **hig·gled; hig·gling** \-(ə-)liŋ\ [prob. alter. of *haggle*] : HAGGLE — **hig·gler** \-(ə-)lər\ *n*
hig·gle·dy–pig·gle·dy \ˌhig-əl-dē-ˈpig-əl-dē\ *adv* [origin unknown] : in confusion : TOPSY-TURVY <tiny hovels piled ~ against each other —Edward Behr> — **higgledy–piggledy** *adj*
1**high** \ˈhī\ *adj* [ME, fr. OE *hēah;* akin to OHG *hōh* high, L *cacumen* point, top] **1 a :** having large extension upward : taller than average, usual, or expected <a ~ hill> <rooms with ~ ceilings> **b :** having a specified elevation : TALL <six feet ~> — often used in combinations <sky-*high*> <waist-*high*> **2 a** (1) **:** advanced toward the acme or culmination <~ summer> (2) **:** advanced toward the most active or culminating period <a vacation on the Riviera during ~ season> (3) **:** constituting the late, most fully developed, or most creative stage or period <~ Gothic> **b :** verging on lateness — usu. used in the phrase *high time* **c :** long past : REMOTE <~ antiquity> **3 :** elevated in pitch <a ~ note> **4 :** relatively far from the equator <~ latitude> **5 :** slightly tainted <~ game>; *also* **:** MALODOROUS **6 :** exalted in character : NOBLE <set out with ~ purposes> **7 :** of greater degree, amount, cost, value, or content than average, usual, or expected <~ prices> <food ~ in iron> <submitted a ~ bid> **8 :** of relatively great importance: as **a :** foremost in rank, dignity, or standing <~ officials> **b :** SERIOUS, GRAVE <~ crimes> **c :** CRITICAL, CLIMACTIC <the ~ point of the novel is the escape> **d :** marked by sublime, heroic, or stirring events or subject matter <~ tragedy> <~ adventure> **9 :** FORCIBLE, STRONG <~ winds> **10 a :** showing elation or excitement <~ spirits> **b :** INTOXICATED; *also* **:** excited or stupefied by a drug (as marijuana or heroin) **11 :** advanced in complexity, development, or elaboration <~*er* nerve centers> <~*er* mathematics> **12 :** articulated with some part of the tongue close to the palate <\ē\ is a ~ vowel> — **high·ly** *adv*

syn HIGH, TALL, LOFTY *shared meaning element* **:** above the average in height **ant** low
2**high** *adv* **1 :** at or to a high place, altitude, or degree <climbed ~*er* on the ladder> <the bids went too ~> **2 :** WELL, LUXURIOUSLY — often used in the phrases *high off the hog* and *high on the hog*
3**high** *n* **1 :** an elevated place or region: as **a :** HILL, KNOLL **b :** the space overhead : SKY — usu. used with *on* **c :** HEAVEN — usu. used with *on* **2 :** a region of high barometric pressure — called also *anticyclone* **3 a :** a high point or level : HEIGHT <sales have reached a new ~> **b :** the transmission gear of an automotive vehicle giving the highest ratio of propeller-shaft to engine-shaft speed and consequently the highest speed of travel **4 :** an excited or stupefied state produced by a drug
high altar *n* **:** the principal altar in a church

high analysis *adj, of a fertilizer* **:** containing more than 20 percent of total plant nutrients
high and dry *adv* **1 :** out of reach of the current or tide **:** out of water **2 :** in a helpless or abandoned position **:** without recourse
high and low *adv* **:** EVERYWHERE
high–and–mighty *adj* **:** characterized by arrogance **:** IMPERIOUS
¹high·ball \ˈhī-ˌbȯl\ *n* **1 a :** a railroad signal for a train to proceed at full speed **b :** a fast train **2 :** a drink of alcohol (as whiskey) and water or a carbonated beverage
²highball *vi* **:** to go at full or high speed <a ~*ing* express train>
high beam *n* **:** the long-range focus of a vehicle headlight
high·bind·er \ˈhī-ˌbīn-dər\ *n* [the *Highbinders,* gang of vagabonds in New York City *ab*1806] **1 :** a professional killer operating in the Chinese quarter of an American city **2 :** a corrupt or scheming politician
high blood pressure *n* **:** HYPERTENSION
high·born \ˈhī-ˈbȯ(ə)rn\ *adj* **:** of noble birth
high·boy \-ˌbȯi\ *n* **:** a tall chest of drawers with a legged base
high·bred \-ˈbred\ *adj* **:** coming from superior stock
high·brow \-ˌbrau̇\ *n* **:** a person who possesses or has pretensions to superior learning or culture — **highbrow** *adj* — **high·browed** \-ˌbrau̇d\ *adj* — **high·brow·ism** \-ˌbrau̇-ˌiz-əm\ *n*
high·bush \-ˈbu̇sh\ *adj* **:** forming a notably tall or erect bush; *also* **:** borne on a highbush plant
highbush blueberry *n* **:** a variable moisture-loving No. American shrub (*Vaccinium corymbosum*) that is the source of most cultivated blueberries; *also* **:** its fruit
high chair *n* **:** a child's chair with long legs, a footrest, and usu. a feeding tray
High Church *adj* **:** tending esp. in Anglican worship to stress the sacerdotal, liturgical, ceremonial, traditional, and Catholic elements in worship — **High Churchman** *n*

highboy

high–class \ˈhī-ˈklas\ *adj* **:** SUPERIOR, FIRST-CLASS
high comedy *n* **:** comedy employing subtle characterizations and witty dialogue — compare LOW COMEDY
high command *n* **1 :** the supreme headquarters of a military force **2 :** the highest leaders in an organization
high commissioner *n* **:** a principal or a high-ranking commissioner; *esp* **:** an ambassadorial representative of the government of one country stationed in another
high–count \ˈhī-ˈkau̇nt\ *adj* **:** having a large number of warp and weft yarns to the square inch <~ percale sheeting>
high court *n* **:** SUPREME COURT
high–energy *adj* **1 a :** having such speed and kinetic energy as to exhibit relativistic departure from classical laws of motion — used esp. of elementary particles whose velocity has been imparted by an accelerator **b :** of or relating to high-energy particles <a ~ reaction> **2 :** yielding a relatively large amount of energy when undergoing hydrolysis <~ phosphate bonds in ATP>
high–energy physics *n* **:** a branch of physics dealing with the constitution, properties, and interactions of elementary particles esp. as revealed in experiments with particle accelerators
higher criticism *n* **:** study of biblical writings to determine their literary history and the purpose and meaning of the authors — compare LOWER CRITICISM — **higher critic** *n*
higher education *n* **:** education beyond the secondary level; *esp* **:** education provided by a college or university
higher fungus *n* **:** a fungus with hyphae well-developed and septate
higher law *n* **:** a principle of divine or moral law that is considered to be superior to constitutions and enacted legislation
higher learning *n* **:** education, learning, or scholarship on the collegiate or university level
high·er–up \ˌhī-ə-ˈrəp, ˈhī-ə-ˌ\ *n* **:** a superior officer or official
high explosive *n* **:** an explosive (as TNT) that generates gas with extreme rapidity and has a shattering effect
high·fa·lu·tin \ˌhī-fə-ˈlüt-ᵊn\ *adj* [perh. fr. ²*high* + alter. of *fluting,* prp. of *flute*] **1 :** PRETENTIOUS **2 :** expressed in or marked by the use of high-flown bombastic language **:** POMPOUS
high fashion *n* **1 :** HIGH STYLE **2 :** HAUTE COUTURE
high fidelity *n* **:** the reproduction of sound with a high degree of faithfulness to the original
high finance *n* **:** large and complex financial operations; *also* **:** the major financial institutions that engage in them
high–flown \ˈhī-ˈflōn\ *adj* **1 :** exceedingly or excessively high or favorable **2 :** having an excessively embellished or inflated character **:** PRETENTIOUS <inflated rhetoric and ~ vocabulary —James Yaffe>
high–fly·ing \-ˈflī-iŋ\ *adj* **1 :** rising to considerable height **2 :** marked by extravagance, pretension, or excessive ambition
high frequency *n* **:** a radio frequency between very high frequency and medium frequency — see RADIO FREQUENCY table
high gear *n* **1 :** HIGH 3b **2 :** a state of intense or maximum activity
High German *n* **1 :** German as natively used in southern and central Germany **2 :** GERMAN 2b
high–grade *adj* **1 :** of superior grade or quality <~ bonds> **2 :** being near the upper or most favorable extreme of a specified range <a ~ moron approaches normality>
high grade *n* **:** a grade animal that in conformation and economic qualities approximates the breed to which its known purebred ancestors belong
high–grown \ˈhī-ˈgrōn\ *adj, of coffee* **:** grown at a high altitude
high–hand·ed \-ˈhan-dəd\ *adj* **:** ARBITRARY, OVERBEARING — **high–hand·ed·ly** *adv* — **high–hand·ed·ness** *n*
high–hat \ˈhī-ˈhat\ *adj* **:** SUPERCILIOUS, SNOBBISH — **high–hat** *vt*
high hat *n* **:** BEAVER 2
High Holiday *n* **:** either of two important Jewish holidays: **a :** ROSH HASHANAH **b :** YOM KIPPUR
high horse *n* **:** an arrogant and unyielding mood or attitude <wanted to get on her *high horse* and treat him as if he were nothing — William Heuman>
high jump *n* **:** a jump for height in a track-and-field contest
¹high·land \ˈhī-lənd\ *n* **:** elevated or mountainous land
²highland *adj* **1 :** of or relating to a highland **2** *cap* **:** of or relating to the Highlands of Scotland
high·land·er \-lən-dər\ *n* **1 :** an inhabitant of a highland **2** *cap* **:** an inhabitant of the Highlands of Scotland
Highland fling *n* **:** a lively Scottish folk dance
high–lev·el \ˈhī-ˈlev-əl\ *adj* **1 :** occurring, done, or placed at a high level **2 :** being of high importance or rank <~ diplomats>
¹high·light \ˈhī-ˌlīt\ *n* **1 :** the lightest spot or area (as in a painting) **:** any of several spots in a modeled drawing or painting that receives the greatest amount of illumination **2 :** an event or detail of major significance or special interest
²highlight *vt* **1 :** to throw a strong light upon **2 a :** to center attention upon **:** EMPHASIZE **b :** to constitute a highlight of
high–low–jack \ˌhī-ˌlō-ˈjak\ *n* **:** a card game in which scores are made by winning the highest trump, the lowest trump, the jack of trumps, and either the ten of trumps or the most points
high mass *n, often cap H&M* **:** a mass marked by the singing of prescribed parts by the celebrant and the choir or congregation
high–mind·ed \ˈhī-ˈmīn-dəd\ *adj* **:** marked by elevated principles and feelings — **high–mind·ed·ly** *adv* — **high–mind·ed·ness** *n*
high–muck–a–muck \ˌhī-ˌmək-i-ˈmək\ *or* **high–muck·e·ty–muck** \ˌhī-ˌmək-ət-ē-ˈmək\ *n* [by folk etymology fr. Chinook Jargon *hiu muckamuck* plenty to eat] **:** an important and often arrogant person
high·ness \ˈhī-nəs\ *n* **1 :** the quality or state of being high **2 —** used as a title for a person of exalted rank (as a king or prince)
high noon *n* **1 :** precisely noon **2 :** the most advanced, flourishing, or creative stage or period <the *high noon* of his genius —John Pfeiffer>
high–octane *adj* **1 :** having a high octane number and hence good antiknock properties <~ gasoline> **2 :** HIGH-POWERED
high–pitched \ˈhī-ˈpicht\ *adj* **1 :** having a high pitch <a ~ voice> **2 :** marked by or exhibiting strong feeling **:** AGITATED <a ~, almost frantic campaign —Geoffrey Rice>
high place *n* **:** a temple or altar used by the ancient Semites and built usu. on a hill or elevation
high polymer *n* **:** a substance (as polystyrene) consisting of molecules that are large multiples of units of low molecular weight
high–pow·ered \ˈhī-ˈpau̇(-ə)rd\ *also* **high–pow·er** \-ˈpau̇(-ə)r\ *adj* **:** having great drive, energy, or capacity **:** DYNAMIC
¹high–pressure *adj* **1 a :** having or involving a high or comparatively high pressure esp. greatly exceeding that of the atmosphere **b :** having a high barometric pressure **2 a :** using or involving aggressive and insistent sales techniques **b :** imposing or involving severe strain or tension <~ occupations>
²high–pressure *vt* **:** to sell or influence by high-pressure tactics
high priest *n* **1 :** a chief priest esp. of the ancient Jewish Levitical priesthood traditionally traced from Aaron **2 :** a priest of the Melchizedek priesthood in the Mormon Church **3 :** the head of a movement or chief expounder of a doctrine or an art — **high priestess** *n* — **high priesthood** *n*
high relief *n* **:** sculptural relief in which at least half of the circumference of the modeled form projects
high–rise \ˈhī-ˈrīz\ *adj* **1 :** being multistory and equipped with elevators <~ apartments> **2 :** of, relating to, or characterized by high-rise buildings **3 :** of, relating to, or being extra-long bicycle handlebars or a bicycle equipped with them — **high rise** *n*
high·road \ˈhī-ˌrōd\ *n* **1** *chiefly Brit* **:** HIGHWAY **2 :** the easiest course
high roller *n* **1 :** one who spends freely in fast or luxurious living **2 :** one who gambles recklessly or for high stakes
¹high school *n* **:** a school usu. including grades 9–12 or 10–12 — **high school·er** \-ˈskü-lər\ *n*
²high school *n* **:** a system of advanced exercises in horsemanship
high sea *n* **:** the open part of a sea or ocean esp. outside territorial waters — usu. used in pl.
high–sound·ing \ˈhī-ˈsau̇n-diŋ\ *adj* **:** POMPOUS, IMPOSING
high–speed \ˈhī-ˈspēd\ *adj* **1 :** operated or adapted for operation at high speed **2 :** relating to the production of short-exposure photographs of rapidly moving objects or events of short duration
high–spir·it·ed \-ˈspir-ət-əd\ *adj* **:** characterized by a bold or energetic spirit — **high–spir·it·ed·ly** *adv* — **high–spir·it·ed·ness** *n*
high–stick·ing \-ˈstik-iŋ\ *n* **:** the act of carrying the blade of the stick at an illegal height in ice hockey
high street *n, Brit* **:** a main or principal street
high–strung \ˈhī-ˈstrəŋ\ *adj* **:** having an extremely nervous or sensitive temperament
high style *n* **:** the newest in fashion or design and usu. adopted by a limited number of people
hight \ˈhīt\ *adj* [ME, irreg. pp. of *hoten* to command, call, be called, fr. OE *hātan;* akin to OHG *heizzan* to command, call, and prob. to L *ciēre* to move, Gk *kinein*] *archaic* **:** being called **:** NAMED
high table *n* **:** an elevated table in the dining room of a British college for use by the master and fellows of the college and distinguished guests
high·tail \ˈhī-ˌtāl\ *vi* **:** to move at full speed esp. in making a retreat — often used with *it*
high tea *n, Brit* **:** a fairly substantial late afternoon or early evening meal
high–tension *adj* **:** having a high voltage; *also* **:** relating to apparatus to be used at high voltage
high–test *adj* **:** passing a difficult test; *specif* **:** having a high volatility <~ gasoline>
high tide *n* **1 :** the tide when the water is at its greatest elevation **2 :** culminating point **:** CLIMAX

high–toned \ˈhī-ˈtōnd\ *adj* **1 :** high in social, moral, or intellectual quality <discreet, decorous, and ~ establishments —Eugene Burr> **2 :** PRETENTIOUS, POMPOUS

high treason *n* **:** TREASON 2

high–water *adj* **:** unusually short <~ pants>

high water *n* **:** a high stage of the water in a river or lake; *also* **:** HIGH TIDE

high·way \ˈhī-ˌwā\ *n* **:** a public way; *esp* **:** a main direct road

high·way·man \-mən\ *n* **:** a person who robs travelers on a road

highway robbery *n* **1 :** robbery committed on or near a public highway usu. against travelers **2 :** excessive profit or advantage derived from a business transaction

high–wrought \ˈhī-ˈrȯt\ *adj* **:** extremely agitated

high yal·ler \-ˈyal-ər\ *n* [*yaller,* alter. of *yellow*] **:** a mulatto or Negro of light-brown color — called also *high yellow*

HII *abbr* Health Insurance Institute

hi·jack *or* **high–jack** \ˈhī-ˌjak\ *vt* [origin unknown] **1 a :** to steal by stopping a vehicle on the highway **b :** to commandeer a flying airplane (as by coercing the pilot at gunpoint) **c :** to stop and steal from (a vehicle in transit) **2 a :** to steal or rob as if by hijacking **b :** to subject to extortion or swindling — **hijack** *n* — **hi·jack·er** *n*

[1]**hike** \ˈhīk\ *vb* **hiked; hik·ing** [perh. akin to [1]*hitch*] *vt* **1 a :** to move, pull, or raise with a sudden motion <*hiked* himself onto the top bunk> **b :** SNAP 6b **c :** to raise in amount sharply or suddenly <~ rents> **2 :** to take on a hike ~ *vi* **1 a :** to go on a hike **b :** to travel by any means **2 :** to rise up; *esp* **:** to work upward out of place <skirt had *hiked* up in back> — **hik·er** *n*

[2]**hike** *n* **1 :** a long walk esp. for pleasure or exercise **2 :** an increase or rise (as of a quantity or amount) <a new wage ~> **3 :** SNAP 11

hi·lar \ˈhī-lər\ *adj* **:** of, relating to, or located near a hilum

hi·lar·i·ous \hil-ˈar-ē-əs, -ˈer-; hī-ˈlar-, -ˈler-\ *adj* [irreg. fr. L *hilarus, hilaris* cheerful, fr. Gk *hilaros*] **:** marked by or affording hilarity — **hi·lar·i·ous·ly** *adv* — **hi·lar·i·ous·ness** *n*

hi·lar·i·ty \-ət-ē\ *n* **:** exhilaration of spirits that may be carried to the point of boisterous conviviality or merriment ***syn*** see MIRTH

Hil·bert space \ˌhil-bərt-\ *n* [David *Hilbert* †1943 G mathematician] **:** a vector space for which a scalar product is defined and which has the property that if a sequence of elements is such that any two members are arbitrarily close together if the members are chosen far enough along in the sequence, the sequence converges to a limit belonging to the vector space

hil·ding \ˈhil-diŋ\ *n* [*hilding,* adj. (base)] *archaic* **:** a base contemptible person

[1]**hill** \ˈhil\ *n* [ME, fr. OE *hyll;* akin to L *collis* hill, *culmen* top] **1 :** a usu. rounded natural elevation of land lower than a mountain **2 :** an artificial heap or mound (as of earth) **3 :** several seeds or plants planted in a group rather than a row — **over the hill 1 :** past one's prime **2 :** advanced in age

[2]**hill** *vt* **1 :** to form into a heap **2 :** to draw earth around the roots or base of — **hill·er** *n*

hill·bil·ly \ˈhil-ˌbil-ē\ *n, pl* **-lies** [[1]*hill* + *Billy,* nickname for *William*] **:** a person from a backwoods area

hillbilly music *n* **:** COUNTRY MUSIC

hill climb *n* **:** a road race for automobiles or motorcycles in which competitors are individually timed up a hill

hill·crest \ˈhil-ˌkrest\ *n* **:** the top line of a hill

hill myna *n* **:** a largely black Asiatic starling (*Gracula religiosa*) often tamed and taught to pronounce words

hill·ock \ˈhil-ək\ *n* **:** a small hill — **hill·ocky** \-ə-kē\ *adj*

Hill reaction \ˌhil-\ *n* [Robin *Hill,* 20th cent. Brit biochemist] **:** the light dependent transfer of electrons by chloroplasts in photosynthesis that results in the cleavage of water molecules and liberation of oxygen

hill·side \-ˌsīd\ *n* **:** a part of a hill between the summit and the foot

hill·top \ˈhil-ˌtäp\ *n* **:** the highest part of a hill

hilly \ˈhil-ē\ *adj* **hill·i·er; -est 1 :** abounding in hills **2 :** STEEP

hilt \ˈhilt\ *n* [ME, fr. OE; akin to OE *healt* lame — more at HALT] **:** a handle esp. of a sword or dagger — **to the hilt :** to the very limit **:** COMPLETELY

hi·lum \ˈhī-ləm\ *n, pl* **hi·la** \-lə\ [NL, fr. L, trifle] **1 a :** a scar on a seed (as a bean) marking the point of attachment of the ovule **b :** the nucleus of a starch grain **2 :** a notch in or opening from a bodily part suggesting the hilum of a bean

1, hilum 1a on a bean seed

him \im, (ˈ)him\ *pron, objective case of* HE

Hi·ma·la·yan \ˌhim-ə-ˈlā-ən, him-ˈäl-(ə-)yən\ *n* [*Himalaya* mountains] **:** any of a breed of small white domesticated rabbits with black nose, feet, tail, and ear tips

hi·mat·ion \him-ˈat-ē-ˌän, -ən\ *n* [Gk, fr. *hennynai* to clothe — more at WEAR] **:** a rectangular cloth draped over the left shoulder and about the body and worn as a garment in ancient Greece

him·self \(h)im-ˈself\ *pron* **1 a :** that identical male one — compare [1]HE; used reflexively, for emphasis, or in absolute constructions <considers ~ lucky> <he ~ did it> <~ unhappy, he understood the situation> **b —** used reflexively when the sex of the antecedent is unspecified <everyone must fend for ~> **2 :** his normal, healthy, or sane condition **3** *Irish & Scot* **:** a man of consequence; *esp* **:** the master of the house

[1]**Him·yar·ite** \ˈhim-yə-ˌrīt\ *n* [*Himyar,* legendary king in Yemen] **1 :** a member of an ancient people of southern Arabia **2 :** an Arab of a group of related ancient peoples of southern Arabia

[2]**Himyarite** *or* **Him·yar·it·ic** \ˌhim-yə-ˈrit-ik\ *adj* **:** of or relating to the ancient Himyarites or their language

hin \ˈhin\ *n* [Heb *hīn,* fr. Egypt *hnw*] **:** an ancient Hebrew unit of liquid measure equal to about a gallon and a half

Hi·na·ya·na \ˌhē-nə-ˈyän-ə\ *n* [Skt *hīnayāna,* lit., lesser vehicle] **:** THERAVADA — **Hi·na·ya·nist** \-ˈyän-əst\ *n* — **Hi·na·ya·nis·tic** \-yä-ˈnis-tik\ *adj*

[1]**hind** \ˈhīnd\ *n, pl* **hinds** *also* **hind** [ME, fr. OE; akin to OHG *hinta* hind, Gk *kemas* young deer] **1 :** a female of the red deer — compare HART **2 :** any of various spotted groupers (esp. genus *Epinephelus*)

[2]**hind** *n* [ME *hine* servant, farmhand, fr. OE *hīna,* gen. of *hīwan,* pl., members of a household; akin to OE *hām* home — more at HOME] **1 :** a British farm assistant **2** *archaic* **:** RUSTIC

[3]**hind** *adj* [ME, prob. back-formation fr. OE *hinder,* adv., behind; akin to OHG *hintar,* prep., behind] **:** of or forming the part that follows or is behind **:** REAR

Hind *abbr* **1** Hindi **2** Hindustani

hind·brain \ˈhīn(d)-ˌbrān\ *n* **1 a :** the posterior of the three primary divisions of the vertebrate brain or the parts developed from it including the cerebellum, pons, and medulla oblongata **b :** METENCEPHALON **c :** MYELENCEPHALON **2 :** the posterior segment of the brain of an invertebrate

[1]**hin·der** \ˈhin-dər\ *vb* **hin·dered; hin·der·ing** \-d(ə-)riŋ\ [ME *hindren,* fr. OE *hindrian;* akin to OE *hinder* behind] *vt* **1 :** to make slow or difficult the progress of **:** HAMPER **2 :** to hold back **:** CHECK ~ *vi* **:** to delay, impede, or prevent action — **hin·der·er** \-dər-ər\ *n*

syn HINDER, IMPEDE, OBSTRUCT, BLOCK *shared meaning element* **:** to interfere with the activity or progress of ***ant*** further

[2]**hind·er** \ˈhīn-dər\ *adj* [ME, fr. OE *hinder,* adv.] **:** situated behind or in the rear **:** POSTERIOR

hind·gut \ˈhīn(d)-ˌgət\ *n* **:** the posterior part of the alimentary canal

Hin·di \ˈhin-(ˌ)dē\ *n* [Hindi *hindī,* fr. *Hind,* India, fr. Per] **1 :** a literary and official language of northern India **2 :** a complex of Indic dialects of northern India for which Hindi is the usual literary language — **Hindi** *adj*

hind·most \ˈhīn(d)-ˌmōst\ *adj* **:** farthest to the rear **:** LAST

hind·quar·ter \-ˌkwȯ(r)t-ər\ *n* **1 :** the back half of a side of beef, veal, mutton, or lamb including a leg and usu. one or more ribs **2** *pl* **:** the hind pair of legs of a quadruped; *broadly* **:** all the structures of a quadruped that lie posterior to the attachment of the hind legs to the trunk

hin·drance \ˈhin-drən(t)s\ *n* **1 :** the state of being hindered **2 :** the action of hindering **3 :** IMPEDIMENT

hind·sight \ˈhīn(d)-ˌsīt\ *n* **1 :** a rear sight of a firearm **2 :** perception of the nature and demands of an event after it has happened

[1]**Hin·du** *also* **Hin·doo** \ˈhin-(ˌ)dü\ *n* [Per *Hindū* inhabitant of India, fr. *Hind* India] **1 :** an adherent of Hinduism **2 :** a native or inhabitant of India

[2]**Hindu** *also* **Hindoo** *adj* **:** of, relating to, or characteristic of the Hindus or Hinduism

Hindu calendar *n* **:** a lunar calendar usu. dating from 3101 B.C. and used esp. in India — see MONTH table

Hin·du·ism \ˈhin-(ˌ)dü-ˌiz-əm\ *n* **:** the dominant cultic religion of India emphasizing dharma with its resulting ritual and social observances and often mystical contemplation and ascetic practices

[1]**Hin·du·stani** *also* **Hin·do·stani** \ˌhin-dü-ˈstan-ē, -ˈstän-ē\ *n* [Hindi *Hindūstānī,* fr. Per *Hindūstān* India] **1 :** a group of Indic dialects of northern India of which literary Hindi and Urdu are considered diverse written forms **2 :** a form of speech allied to Urdu but less divergent from Hindi used in some urban areas

[2]**Hindustani** *also* **Hindostani** *adj* **:** of or relating to Hindustan or its people or Hindustani

hind wing *n* **:** either of the posterior wings of a 4-winged insect

[1]**hinge** \ˈhinj\ *n* [ME *heng;* akin to MD *henge* hook, OE *hangian* to hang] **1 a :** a jointed or flexible device on which a door, lid, or other swinging part turns **b :** a flexible ligamentous joint **c :** a small piece of thin gummed paper used in fastening a postage stamp in an album **2 :** a determining factor **:** TURNING POINT

[2]**hinge** *vb* **hinged; hing·ing** *vt* **:** to attach by or furnish with hinges ~ *vi* **:** to be contingent on a single consideration or point — used with *on* or *upon*

hinge joint *n* **:** a joint between bones (as at the elbow) that permits motion in only one plane

hin·ny \ˈhin-ē\ *n, pl* **hinnies** [L *hinnus*] **:** a hybrid between a stallion and a she-ass — compare MULE

[1]**hint** \ˈhint\ *n* [prob. alter. of obs. *hent* act of seizing, fr. *hent* vb.] **1** *archaic* **:** OPPORTUNITY, TURN **2 a :** an indirect or summary suggestion <helpful ~*s*> **b :** a statement conveying by implication what it is preferred not to say explicitly **3 :** a slight indication of the existence or nature of something **:** CLUE

[2]**hint** *vt* **:** to convey indirectly and by allusion rather than explicitly <a suspicion that she scarcely dared to ~> ~ *vi* **:** to give a hint <~ for an invitation> ***syn*** see SUGGEST — **hint·er** *n*

hin·ter·land \ˈhint-ər-ˌland, -lənd\ *n* [G, fr. *hinter* hinder + *land*] **1 :** a region lying inland from a coast **2 a :** a region remote from urban areas **b :** a region lying beyond major metropolitan or cultural centers

[1]**hip** \ˈhip\ *n* [ME *hipe,* fr. OE *hēope;* akin to OHG *hiafo* hip] **:** the ripened accessory fruit of a rose that consists of a fleshy receptacle enclosing numerous achenes

[2]**hip** *n* [ME, fr. OE *hype;* akin to OHG *huf* hip, L *cubitum* elbow, *cubare* to lie, Gk *kybos* cube, die, OE *hēah* high — more at HIGH] **1 a :** the laterally projecting region of each side of the lower or posterior part of the mammalian trunk formed by the lateral parts of the pelvis and upper part of the femur together with the fleshy parts covering them **b :** HIP JOINT **2 :** the external angle formed by the meeting of two sloping sides of a roof that have their wall plates running in different directions

[3]**hip** *vt* **hipped; hip·ping :** to make (as a roof) with a hip

ə abut	ᵊ kitten	ər further	a back	ā bake	ä cot, cart	
au̇ out	ch chin	e less	ē easy	g gift	i trip	ī life
j joke	ŋ sing	ō flow	ȯ flaw	ȯi coin	th thin	th this
ü loot	u̇ foot	y yet	yü few	yu̇ furious	zh vision	

4hip *interj* [origin unknown] — usu. used to begin a cheer <~ ~ hooray>

5hip *also* **hep** *adj* **hip·per; hip·pest** [*hip,* alter. of *hep,* of unknown origin] **:** characterized by a keen informed awareness of or interest in the newest developments

6hip *n* **:** HIPNESS

hip and thigh *adv* **:** in an overwhelming manner **:** UNSPARINGLY

hip·bone \'hip-'bōn, -,bōn\ *n* **:** INNOMINATE BONE

hip boot *n* **:** a boot reaching to the hips that is worn esp. by fishermen

hip joint *n* **:** the articulation between the femur and the innominate bone

hip·ness \'hip-nəs\ *n* **:** the quality or state of being hip

hipp- *or* **hippo-** *comb form* [L, fr. Gk, fr. *hippos* — more at EQUINE] **:** horse <*hippo*phagous>

1hipped \'hipt\ *adj* **:** having hips esp. of a specified kind — often used in combination <broad-*hipped*>

2hipped *adj* [*hip* (hypochondria)] **1 :** DEPRESSED **2 :** absorbed or interested to an extreme degree <~ on astrology>

hip·pie *or* **hip·py** \'hip-ē\ *n, pl* **hippies** [5*hip* + *-ie*] **:** a usu. young person who rejects the mores of established society (as by dressing unconventionally or favoring communal living), advocates a nonviolent ethic, and often uses psychedelic drugs or marijuana; *broadly* **:** a long-haired unconventionally dressed young person — **hip·pie·dom** \-ēd-əm\ *n* — **hip·pie·hood** \-ē-,hu̇d\ *n*

hip·po \'hip-(,)ō\ *n, pl* **hippos :** HIPPOPOTAMUS

hip·po·cam·pal \,hip-ə-'kam-pəl\ *adj* **:** of or relating to the hippocampus

hip·po·cam·pus \-pəs\ *n, pl* **-pi** \-,pī, -(,)pē\ [NL, fr. Gk *hippokampos* sea horse, fr. *hipp-* + *kampos* sea monster] **:** a curved elongated ridge that extends over the floor of the descending horn of each lateral ventricle of the brain and consists of gray matter covered on the ventricular surface with white matter

hip·po·cras \'hip-ə-,kras\ *n* [ME *ypocras,* fr. *Ypocras* Hippocrates, its legendary inventor] **:** a highly spiced wine of medieval Europe

Hip·po·crat·ic \,hip-ə-'krat-ik\ *adj* **:** of or relating to Hippocrates or to the school of medicine that took his name

Hippocratic oath *n* **:** an oath embodying a code of medical ethics usu. taken by those about to begin medical practice

Hip·po·crene \'hip-ə-,krēn, ,hip-ə-'krē-nē\ *n* [L, fr. Gk *Hippokrēnē*] **:** a fountain on Mount Helicon sacred to the Muses and believed to be a source of poetic inspiration

hip·po·drome \'hip-ə-,drōm\ *n* [MF, fr. L *hippodromos,* fr. Gk, fr. *hipp-* + *dromos* racecourse — more at DROMEDARY] **1 :** an oval stadium for horse and chariot races in ancient Greece **2 :** an arena for equestrian performances

hip·po·griff \-,grif\ *n* [F *hippogriffe,* fr. It *ippogrifo,* fr. *ippo-* hipp- (fr. L *hipp-*) + *grifo* griffin, fr. L *gryphus*] **:** a legendary animal having the foreparts of a griffin and the body and hindquarters of a horse

Hip·pol·y·ta \hip-'äl-ət-ə\ *n* [L, fr. Gk *Hippolytē*] **:** a queen of the Amazons given in marriage to Theseus by Hercules

Hip·pol·y·tus \-ət-əs\ *n* [L, fr. Gk *Hippolytos*] **:** a son of Theseus and Hippolyta falsely accused of amorous advances by his stepmother Phaedra and killed by his father through the agency of Poseidon

Hip·pom·e·nes \hip-'äm-ə-,nēz\ *n* [L, fr. Gk *Hippomenēs*] **:** the successful suitor of Atalanta according to Greek legend

hip·po·pot·a·mus \,hip-ə-'pät-ə-məs\ *n, pl* **-mus·es** *or* **-mi** \-,mī, -(,)mē\ [L, fr. Gk *hippopotamos,* fr. *hipp-* + *potamos* river, fr. *petesthai* to fly, rush — more at FEATHER] **:** any of several large herbivorous 4-toed chiefly aquatic mammals (family Hippopotamidae and esp. genus *Hippopotamus*) with an extremely large head and mouth, bare and very thick skin, and short legs

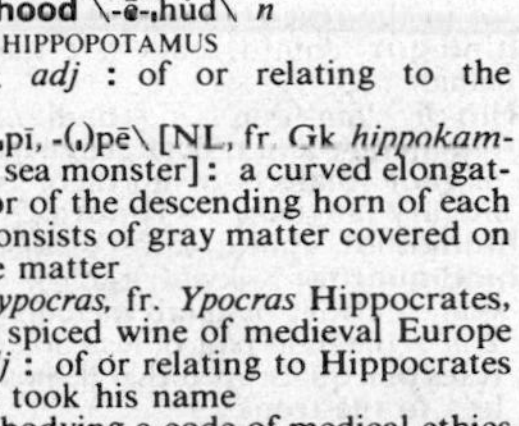

hippopotamus

-hip·pus \'hip-əs\ *n comb form* [NL, fr. Gk *hippos* — more at EQUINE] **:** horse — in generic names esp. in paleontology <Eo*hippus*>

hip roof *n* **:** a roof having sloping ends and sloping sides

hip·ster \'hip-stər\ *n* [5*hip*] **:** a person who is unusually aware of and interested in new and unconventional patterns esp. in jazz, in the use of stimulants (as narcotics), and in exotic religion

hip·ster·ism \-stə-,riz-əm\ *n* **1 :** HIPNESS **2 :** the way of life characteristic of hipsters

1hire \'hī(ə)r\ *n* [ME, fr. OE *hȳr;* akin to MD *hūre* hire] **1 a :** payment for the temporary use of something **b :** payment for labor or personal services **:** WAGES **2 a :** the act of hiring **b :** the state of being hired **:** EMPLOYMENT ***syn*** see WAGE

2hire *vb* **hired; hir·ing** *vt* **1 a :** to engage the personal services of for a set sum <~ on a new crew> **b :** to engage the temporary use of for a fixed sum <~ a hall> **2 :** to grant the personal services of or temporary use of for a fixed sum <~ themselves out> **3 :** to get done for pay <~ the mowing done> ~ *vi* **:** to take employment <~ out as a waitress during the tourist season> — **hir·er** *n*

syn HIRE, LET, LEASE, RENT, CHARTER *shared meaning element* **:** to engage or grant for use at a price. *Hire* and *let* are usually complementary terms, HIRE implying the act of engaging and LET the act of granting for use <we *hired* a house for the summer after some difficulty in persuading the owner to *let* it> Sometimes, and especially with relation to persons or their services, *hire* may be used in either situation <*hire* a servant> <he *hired* himself out as a servant> LEASE strictly implies a letting on contract <agreed to *lease* his farm to the young man on shares> but it may also be employed in the sense of to hire on a lease <we found it cheaper to *lease* than to buy a car> RENT stresses payment for the full use of property and may imply either a hiring or a letting. CHARTER applies to the hiring or letting of a conveyance (as a ship or bus) usually for exclusive use <*charter* an airplane to go to a football game>

hire·ling \'hī(ə)r-liŋ\ *n* **:** a person who serves for hire esp. for purely mercenary motives

hire purchase *n, chiefly Brit* **:** purchase on the installment plan

hiring hall *n* **:** a union-operated placement office where registered applicants are referred in rotation to jobs

hir·ple \'hir-pəl\ *vi* **hir·pled; hir·pling** \-p(ə-)liŋ\ [ME (Sc) *hirplen*] *Scot* **:** LIMP, HOBBLE

hir·sute \'hər-,süt, 'hi(ə)r-, ,hər-', hi(ə)r-'\ *adj* [L *hirsutus;* akin to L *horrēre* to bristle — more at HORROR] **:** roughly hairy; *esp* **:** pubescent with coarse stiff hairs — **hir·sute·ness** *n*

hir·sut·ism \'hər-sə-,tiz-əm, 'hi(ə)r-\ *n* **:** excessive growth of hair of normal or abnormal distribution

hir·su·tu·lous \,hər-'sü-chə-ləs, hi(ə)r-\ *adj* **:** minutely or slightly hirsute

hi·ru·din \hir-'üd-ᵊn, 'hir-(y)əd-ən\ *n* [fr. *Hirudin,* a trademark] **:** an anticoagulant extracted from the buccal glands of a leech

1his \(h)iz, ,hiz\ *adj* [ME, fr. OE, gen. of *hē* he] **:** of or relating to him or himself esp. as possessor, agent, or object of an action <~ house> <~ writings> <~ confirmation> — compare 1HE

2his \'hiz\ *pron, sing or pl in constr* **:** that which belongs to him — used without a following noun as a pronoun equivalent in meaning to the adjective *his*

His·pan·ic \his-'pan-ik\ *adj* [L *hispanicus,* fr. *Hispania* Iberian peninsula, Spain] **:** of or relating to the people, speech, or culture of Spain, Spain and Portugal, or Latin America — **His·pan·i·cism** \-'pan-ə-,siz-əm\ *n* — **His·pan·i·cist** \-səst\ *n* — **His·pan·i·cize** \-,sīz\ *vt*

his·pa·ni·dad \,is-,pan-i-'thä(th)\ *n* **:** HISPANISM 1

his·pa·nism \'his-pə-,niz-əm\ *n, often cap* **1 :** a movement to reassert the cultural unity of Spain and Latin America **2 :** a characteristic feature of Spanish occurring in another language

his·pid \'his-pəd\ *adj* [L *hispidus;* prob. akin to L *horrēre*] **:** rough or covered with bristles, stiff hairs, or minute spines <~ leaf> — **his·pid·i·ty** \his-'pid-ət-ē\ *n*

hiss \'his\ *vb* [ME *hissen,* of imit. origin] *vi* **:** to make a sharp sibilant sound often as an expression of disapproval ~ *vt* **1 :** to condemn by hissing **2 :** to utter with a hiss — **hiss** *n* — **hiss·er** *n*

1hist \s *often prolonged and usu with* p *preceding and* t *following; often read as* 'hist\ *interj* [origin unknown] — used to attract attention

2hist \'hīst\ *dial var of* HOIST

3hist *abbr* historian; historical; history

hist- *or* **histo-** *comb form* [F, fr. Gk *histos* mast, loom beam, web, fr. *histanai* to cause to stand] **:** tissue <*histo*physiology>

his·ta·mi·nase \his-'tam-ə-,nās, 'his-tə-mə-, -,nāz\ *n* [ISV] **:** a widely occurring flavoprotein enzyme that oxidizes histamine and various diamines

his·ta·mine \'his-tə-,mēn, -mən\ *n* [ISV] **:** a compound $C_5H_9N_3$ that is found in ergot and many animal tissues or made synthetically and is prob. responsible for the dilatation and increased permeability of blood vessels which play a major role in allergic reactions — **his·ta·min·ic** \,his-tə-'min-ik\ *adj*

his·ta·min·er·gic \,his-tə-mə-'nər-jik\ *adj* [ISV *histamine* + Gk *ergon* work — more at WORK] *of autonomic nerve fibers* **:** liberating or activated by histamine

his·ti·dine \'his-tə-,dēn\ *n* [ISV] **:** a crystalline basic amino acid $C_6H_9N_3O_2$ formed in the splitting of most proteins

his·tio·cyte \'his-tē-ə-,sīt\ *n* [Gk *histion* web (dim. of *histos*), + ISV *-cyte*] **:** a phagocytic tissue cell that may be fixed or freely motile, is derived from the reticuloendothelial system, and resembles the monocyte with which it is sometimes identified — **his·tio·cyt·ic** \,his-tē-ə-'sit-ik\ *adj*

his·to·chem·i·cal \,his-tō-'kem-i-kəl\ *adj* **:** of or relating to histochemistry — **his·to·chem·i·cal·ly** \-k(ə-)lē\ *adv*

his·to·chem·is·try \-'kem-ə-strē\ *n* [ISV] **:** a science dealing with the chemical makeup of cells and tissues

his·to·com·pat·i·bil·i·ty \'his-(,)tō-kəm-,pat-ə-'bil-ət-ē\ *n* **:** a state of mutual tolerance that allows some tissues to be grafted effectively to others

his·to·gen \'his-tə-jən\ *n* [ISV] **:** a zone or clearly delimited region of primary tissue in or from which the specific parts of a plant organ are believed to be produced

his·to·gen·e·sis \,his-tə-'jen-ə-səs\ *n* [NL] **:** the formation and differentiation of tissues — **his·to·ge·net·ic** \-jə-'net-ik\ *adj* — **his·to·ge·net·i·cal·ly** \-i-k(ə-)lē\ *adv*

his·to·gram \'his-tə-,gram\ *n* [*histo*ry + *-gram*] **:** a representation of a frequency distribution by means of rectangles whose widths represent class intervals and whose heights represent corresponding frequencies

his·tol·o·gy \his-'täl-ə-jē\ *n, pl* **-gies** [F *histologie,* fr. *hist-* + *-logie* -logy] **1 :** a branch of anatomy that deals with the minute structure of animal and plant tissues as discernible with the microscope **2 :** a treatise on histology **3 :** tissue structure or organization — **his·to·log·i·cal** \,his-tə-'läj-i-kəl\ *or* **his·to·log·ic** \-'läj-ik\ *adj* — **his·to·log·i·cal·ly** \-i-k(ə-)lē\ *adv* — **his·tol·o·gist** \his-'täl-ə-jəst\ *n*

his·tol·y·sis \his-'täl-ə-səs\ *n* [NL, fr. *hist-* + *-lysis*] **:** the breakdown of bodily tissues — **his·to·lyt·ic** \,his-tə-'lit-ik\ *adj*

his·tone \'his-,tōn\ *n* [ISV] **:** any of various simple water-soluble proteins that yield a high proportion of basic amino acids on hydrolysis and are found associated with DNA in cell nuclei

his·to·pa·thol·o·gy \,his-tō-pə-'thäl-ə-jē, -pa-\ *n* [ISV] **1 :** a branch of pathology concerned with the tissue changes characteristic of disease **2 :** the tissue changes that affect a part or accompany a disease — **his·to·path·o·log·ic** \-,path-ə-'läj-ik\ *or* **his·to·path·o·log·i·cal** \-i-kəl\ *adj* — **his·to·path·o·log·i·cal·ly** \-i-k(ə-)lē\ *adv* — **his·to·pa·thol·o·gist** \-pə-'thäl-ə-jəst, -pa-\ *n*

his·to·phys·i·ol·o·gy \-,fiz-ē-'äl-ə-jē\ *n* **1 :** a branch of physiology concerned with the function and activities of tissues **2 :** structural and functional tissue organization — **his·to·phys·i·o·log·ic** \-ē-ə-'läj-ik\ *or* **his·to·phys·i·o·log·i·cal** \-i-kəl\ *adj*

his·to·plas·mo·sis \ˌhis-tə-plaz-ˈmō-səs\ *n* [NL, fr. *Histoplasma,* genus of fungi] **:** a disease caused by infection with a fungus (*Histoplasma capsulatum*) and marked by benign involvement of lymph nodes of the trachea and bronchi or by severe progressive generalized involvement of the lymph nodes and the reticuloendothelial system

his·to·ri·an \his-ˈtōr-ē-ən, -ˈtȯr-, -ˈtär-\ *n* **1 :** a student or writer of history; *esp* **:** one that produces a scholarly synthesis **2 :** a writer or compiler of a chronicle

his·tor·ic \his-ˈtȯr-ik, -ˈtär-\ *adj* **:** HISTORICAL; *esp* **:** famous in history <~ battlefields>

his·tor·i·cal \-i-kəl\ *adj* **1 a :** of, relating to, or having the character of history **b :** based on history **c :** used in the past and reproduced in historical presentations **2 :** famous in history **3 a :** SECONDARY 1c **b :** DIACHRONIC — **his·tor·i·cal·ly** \-i-k(ə-)lē\ *adv* — **his·tor·i·cal·ness** \-i-kəl-nəs\ *n*

historical materialism *n* **:** the Marxist theory of history and society that holds that ideas and social institutions develop only as the superstructure of a material economic base — compare DIALECTICAL MATERIALISM

historical present *n* **:** the present tense used to relate past events

historical school *n* **:** a school esp. in economics, legal philosophy, or ethnology emphasizing evolutionary developments and historical methods of research, analysis, and interpretation

his·tor·i·cism \his-ˈtȯr-ə-ˌsiz-əm, -ˈtär-\ *n* **:** a theory that emphasizes the importance of history as a standard of value or as a determinant of events — **his·tor·i·cist** \-səst\ *adj or n*

his·to·ric·i·ty \ˌhis-tə-ˈris-ət-ē\ *n* **:** historical actuality **:** FACT

his·tor·i·cize \his-ˈtȯr-ə-ˌsīz, -ˈtär-\ *vb* **-cized; -ciz·ing** *vt* **:** to make historical ~ *vi* **:** to use historical material

his·tor·i·co- \his-ˈtȯr-i-(ˌ)kō, -ˈtär-\ *comb form* **:** historical **:** historical and <*historico*philosophical> <*historico*social>

his·to·ri·og·ra·pher \his-ˌtōr-ē-ˈäg-rə-fər, -ˌtȯr-\ *n* [MF *historiographeur,* fr. LL *historiographus,* fr. Gk *historiographos,* fr. *historia* + *graphein* to write — more at CARVE] **:** a usu. official writer of history **:** HISTORIAN

his·to·ri·og·ra·phy \-fē\ *n* **1 a :** the writing of history; *esp* **:** the writing of history based on the critical examination of sources, the selection of particulars from the authentic materials, and the synthesis of particulars into a narrative that will stand the test of critical methods **b :** the principles, theory, and history of historical writing <a course in ~> **2 :** the product of historical writing **:** a body of historical literature — **his·to·rio·graph·ic** \-ē-ə-ˈgraf-ik\ *or* **his·to·rio·graph·i·cal** \-i-kəl\ *adj* — **his·to·rio·graph·i·cal·ly** \-i-k(ə-)lē\ *adv*

his·to·ry \ˈhis-t(ə-)rē\ *n, pl* **-ries** [L *historia,* fr. Gk, inquiry, history, fr. *histōr, istōr* knowing, learned; akin to Gk *eidenai* to know — more at WIT] **1 :** TALE, STORY **2 a :** a chronological record of significant events (as affecting a nation or institution) usu. including an explanation of their causes **b :** a treatise presenting systematically related natural phenomena **c :** an account of a sick person's medical background **3 :** a branch of knowledge that records and explains past events <medieval ~> **4 a :** events that form the subject matter of a history **b :** past events <that's all ~ now> **c :** previous treatment, handling, or experience (as of a metal)
syn HISTORY, CHRONICLE, ANNALS *shared meaning element* **:** a written record of events

his·tri·on·ic \ˌhis-trē-ˈän-ik\ *adj* [LL *histrionicus,* fr. L *histrion-, histrio* actor, alter. of *hister,* fr. Etruscan] **1 :** of or relating to actors, acting, or the theater **2 :** deliberately affected **:** THEATRICAL — **his·tri·on·i·cal·ly** \-i-k(ə-)lē\ *adv*

his·tri·on·ics \-iks\ *n pl but sing or pl in constr* **1 :** theatrical performances **2 :** deliberate display of emotion for effect

1hit \ˈhit\ *vb* **hit; hit·ting** [ME *hitten,* fr. ON *hitta* to meet with, hit] *vt* **1 a :** to reach with or as if with a blow **b :** to come in contact with <the ball ~ the window> **2 a :** to cause to come into contact **b :** to deliver (as a blow) by action **3 :** to affect to the detriment of **4 :** to make a request of <~ his friend for 10 dollars> **5 :** to discover or meet esp. by chance **6 a :** to accord with **:** SUIT **b :** REACH, ATTAIN <prices ~ a new high> **c** *of fish* **:** to bite at or on **d :** to reflect accurately <~ the right note> **e :** to cause a propelled object to reach or strike (as a target) esp. for a score in a game or contest <couldn't seem to ~ the basket> **7 :** to indulge in excessively <~ the bottle> ~ *vi* **1 :** to strike a blow **2 a :** to come into contact with something **b :** ATTACK **c** *of a fish* **:** STRIKE *vi* 11b **d :** COME, HAPPEN **3 :** to succeed in attaining something — often used with *on* or *upon* <~ on a solution> **4** *obs* **:** to be in agreement **:** SUIT **5** *of an internal-combustion engine* **:** to fire the charge in the cylinders ***syn*** see STRIKE — **hit·ter** *n* — **hit it off :** to get along well — **hit the books :** to study esp. with intensity — **hit the hay** *or* **hit the sack :** to go to bed — **hit the high points** *or* **hit the high spots :** to touch on or at the most important or salient points or places — **hit the jackpot :** to be or become notably and unexpectedly successful — **hit the nail on the head :** to be exactly right — **hit the road :** LEAVE; *also* **:** to set out — **hit the roof** *or* **hit the ceiling :** to give vent to a burst of anger or angry protest — **hit the spot :** to give complete or special satisfaction — used esp. of food or drink

2hit *n* **1 a :** a blow striking an object aimed at **b :** COLLISION **2 a :** a stroke of luck **b :** something that is conspicuously successful <the show was a big ~> **3 :** a telling remark **4 :** BASE HIT — **hit·less** \ˈhit-ləs\ *adj*

hit–and–miss \ˌhit-ᵊn-ˈmis\ *adj* **:** sometimes successful and sometimes not **:** RANDOM

1hit–and–run \-ˈrən\ *adj* **1 :** being or relating to a baseball play in which a base runner starts for the next base as the pitcher starts to pitch and the batter attempts to hit the ball **2 :** being or involving a motor-vehicle driver who does not stop after being involved in an accident **3 :** involving or intended for quick specific action or results

2hit–and–run *vi* **:** to execute a hit-and-run play in baseball

1hitch \ˈhich\ *vb* [ME *hytchen*] *vt* **1 :** to move by jerks **2 a :** to catch or fasten by or as if by a hook or knot <~*ed* his horse to the top rail of the fence> **b (1) :** to connect (a vehicle or implement) with a source of motive power <~ a rake to a tractor> **(2) :** to attach (a source of motive power) to a vehicle or instrument <~ the horses to the wagon> **c :** to join in marriage **3 :** HITCHHIKE ~ *vi* **1 :** to move with halts and jerks **:** HOBBLE **2 a :** to become entangled, made fast, or linked **b :** to become joined in marriage **3 :** HITCHHIKE — **hitch·er** *n*

2hitch *n* **1 :** a sudden movement or pull **:** JERK <gave his trousers a ~> **2 :** LIMP **3 :** a sudden halt **:** STOPPAGE **4 :** the act or fact of catching hold **5 :** a connection between a vehicle or implement and a detachable source of power (as a tractor or horse) **6 :** a period usu. of military service **7 :** any of various knots used to form a temporary noose in a line or to secure a line temporarily to an object **8 :** LIFT 5b **9 :** CATCH 7

hitch·hike \ˈhich-ˌhīk\ *vi* **:** to travel by securing free rides ~ *vt* **:** to solicit and obtain (a free ride) esp. in a passing vehicle — **hitch·hik·er** *n*

hitch up *vi* **:** to harness and secure a draft animal or team to a vehicle (as a wagon) <we *hitched up* and were on our way before sunrise>

1hith·er \ˈhith-ər\ *adv* [ME *hider, hither,* fr. OE *hider;* akin to Goth *hidre* hither, L *citra* on this side — more at HE] **:** to this place

2hither *adj* **:** being on the near or adjacent side <the ~ side of the hill>

hith·er·most \-ˌmōst\ *adj* **:** nearest on this side

hith·er·to \-ˌtü, ˌhith-ər-ˈtü\ *adv* **:** up to this time

hith·er·ward \ˈhith-ə(r)-wərd\ *adv* **:** HITHER

Hit·le·ri·an \hit-ˈlir-ē-ən\ *adj* **:** of, relating to, or characteristic of Adolf Hitler or his regime in Germany

Hit·ler·ism \ˈhit-lə-ˌriz-əm\ *n* **1 :** the nationalistic and totalitarian principles and policies associated with Hitler **2 :** the Hitlerian movement — **Hit·ler·ite** \-ˌrīt\ *n or adj*

hit off *vt* **:** to characterize precisely and usu. satirically ~ *vi* **:** HARMONIZE, AGREE

hit–or–miss \ˌhit-ər-ˈmis\ *adj* **:** marked by a lack of care, forethought, system, or plan

hit or miss *adv* **:** in a hit-or-miss manner **:** HAPHAZARDLY

hit out *vi* **:** to aim angry and often random blows <*hitting out* at injustice and prejudice>

hit parade *n* **:** a group or listing of the most popular items of a particular kind (as popular songs)

Hitt *abbr* Hittite

Hit·tite \ˈhi-ˌtīt\ *n* [Heb *Ḥittī,* fr. Hitt *Hatti*] **1 :** a member of a conquering people in Asia Minor and Syria with an empire in the 2d millennium B.C. **2 :** the Indo-European language of the Hittites — see INDO-EUROPEAN LANGUAGES table — **Hittite** *adj*

1hive \ˈhīv\ *n* [ME, fr. OE *hȳf;* akin to Gk *kypellon* cup, OE *hēah* high — more at HIGH] **1 :** a container for housing honeybees **2 :** a colony of bees **3 :** a place swarming with busy occupants — **hive·less** \-ləs\ *adj*

2hive *vb* **hived; hiv·ing** *vt* **1 :** to collect into a hive **2 :** to store up in or as if in a hive ~ *vi* **1** *of bees* **:** to enter and take possession of a hive **2 :** to reside in close association

3hive *n* [back-formation fr. *hives*] **:** an urticarial wheal

hive off *vt* **:** to separate from a group <*hived off* the youngest campers into another room>

hives \ˈhīvz\ *n pl but sing or pl in constr* [origin unknown] **:** URTICARIA

hl *abbr* hectoliter

HL *abbr* House of Lords

hld *abbr* hold

HLF *abbr* Heart and Lung Foundation

hlqn *abbr* harlequin

HLS *abbr* **1** [L *hoc loco situs*] laid in this place **2** holograph letter signed

hlt *abbr* halt

hm *abbr* hectometer

HM *abbr* Her Majesty; His Majesty

HMAS *abbr* Her Majesty's Australian Ship; His Majesty's Australian Ship

HMBS *abbr* Her Majesty's British Ship; His Majesty's British Ship

HMC *abbr* **1** heroin, morphine, and cocaine **2** Her Majesty's Customs; His Majesty's Customs

HMCS *abbr* Her Majesty's Canadian Ship; His Majesty's Canadian Ship

HMF *abbr* Her Majesty's Forces; His Majesty's Forces

HMO *abbr* heart minute output

HMS *abbr* Her Majesty's Ship; His Majesty's Ship

HN *abbr* head nurse

HNS *abbr* Holy Name Society

hny *abbr* honey

ho \ˈhō\ *interj* [ME] — used esp. to attract attention to something specified <land ~>

Ho *symbol* holmium

hoa·gie *also* **hoa·gy** \ˈhō-gē\ *n, pl* **hoagies** [origin unknown] **:** SUBMARINE 2

1hoar \ˈhō(ə)r, ˈhȯ(ə)r\ *adj* [ME *hor,* fr. OE *hār;* akin to OHG *hēr* hoary] **:** HOARY

2hoar *n* [ME, hoariness, fr. *hor,* adj.] **:** FROST 1c

1hoard \ˈhō(ə)rd, ˈhȯ(ə)rd\ *n* [ME *hord,* fr. OE; akin to Gk *kysthos* vulva, OE *hȳdan* to hide] **:** a hidden supply or fund stored up

2hoard *vt* **1 :** to lay up a hoard of **2 :** to keep (as one's thoughts) to oneself **:** CHERISH <the people outside disperse their affections, you ~ yours —Joseph Conrad> ~ *vi* **:** to lay up a hoard

3hoard *n* **:** HOARDING 1

hoard·ing \'hōrd-iŋ, 'hȯrd-\ *n* [*hourd, hoard* (hoarding)] **1 :** a temporary board fence put about a building being erected or repaired — called also *hoard* **2** *Brit* **:** BILLBOARD

hoar·frost \'hō(ə)r-ˌfrȯst, 'hȯ(ə)r-\ *n* **:** FROST 1c

hoarse \'hō(ə)rs, 'hȯ(ə)rs\ *adj* **hoars·er; hoars·est** [ME *hos, hors,* fr. OE *hās;* akin to OE *hāt* hot — more at HOT] **1 :** rough or harsh in sound **:** GRATING <~ voice> **2 :** having a hoarse voice <shouted himself ~> — **hoarse·ly** *adv* — **hoarse·ness** *n*

hoars·en \'hōrs-ᵊn, 'hȯrs-\ *vb* **hoars·ened; hoars·en·ing** \'hōrs-niŋ, -ᵊn-iŋ, 'hȯrs-\ *vt* **:** to make hoarse ~ *vi* **:** to become hoarse

hoary \'hō(ə)r-ē, 'hȯ(ə)r-\ *adj* **hoar·i·er; -est** **1 a :** gray or white with age **b :** having grayish or whitish usu. pubescent leaves **2 :** impressively or venerably old **:** ANCIENT — **hoar·i·ness** *n*

hoa·tzin \wä(t)-'sēn\ *n* [AmerSp, fr. Nahuatl *uatzin*] **:** a crested So. American bird (*Opisthocomos cristatus* of the order Galliformes) smaller than a pheasant with olive-colored plumage marked with white above and with claws on the first and second fingers of the wing

¹hoax \'hōks\ *vt* [prob. contr. of *hocus*] **:** to trick into believing or accepting as genuine something false and often preposterous ***syn*** see DUPE — **hoax·er** *n*

²hoax *n* **1 :** an act intended to trick or dupe **:** IMPOSTURE **2 :** something accepted or established by fraud or fabrication

¹hob \'häb\ *n* [ME *hobbe,* fr. *Hobbe,* nickname for Robert] **1** *dial Eng* **:** HOBGOBLIN, ELF **2 :** MISCHIEF, TROUBLE <raise ~>

²hob *n* [origin unknown] **1 :** a projection at the back or side of a fireplace on which something may be kept warm **2 :** a cutting tool used for cutting the teeth of worm wheels or gear wheels

³hob *vt* **hobbed; hob·bing** **1 :** to furnish with hobnails **2 :** to cut with a hob

Hobbes·ian \'häb-zē-ən\ *adj* **:** of or relating to Hobbes or Hobbism

Hob·bism \'häb-ˌiz-əm\ *n* **:** the philosophical system of Hobbes; *esp* **:** the Hobbesian theory that absolutism in government is necessary to prevent the war of each against all to which natural selfishness inevitably leads mankind — **Hob·bist** \'häb-əst\ *n or adj*

¹hob·ble \'häb-əl\ *vb* **hob·bled; hob·bling** \-(ə-)liŋ\ [ME *hoblen;* akin to MD *hobbelen* to turn, roll] *vi* **:** to move along unsteadily or with difficulty; *esp* **:** to limp along ~ *vt* **1 :** to cause to limp **:** make lame **:** CRIPPLE **2** [prob. alter. of *hopple* (to hobble)] **a :** to fasten together the legs of (as a horse) to prevent straying **:** FETTER **b :** to place under handicap **:** HAMPER, IMPEDE — **hob·bler** \-(ə-)lər\ *n*

²hobble *n* **1 :** a hobbling movement **2** *archaic* **:** an awkward situation **3 :** something used to hobble an animal

hob·ble·de·hoy \'häb-əl-di-ˌhȯi\ *n* [origin unknown] **:** an awkward gawky youth

hobble skirt *n* **:** a skirt constricted at the bottom

¹hob·by \'häb-ē\ *n, pl* **hobbies** [short for *hobbyhorse*] **:** a pursuit outside one's regular occupation engaged in for relaxation — **hob·by·ist** \-ē-əst\ *n*

²hobby *n, pl* **hobbies** [ME *hoby,* fr. MF *hobé*] **:** a small Old World falcon (*Falco subbuteo*) formerly trained and flown at small birds (as larks)

hob·by·horse \'häb-ē-ˌhȯ(ə)rs\ *n* [*hobby* (small light horse)] **1 a :** a figure of a horse fastened about the waist in the morris dance **b :** a dancer wearing this figure **2** *obs* **:** BUFFOON **3 a :** a stick having an imitation horse's head at one end that a child pretends to ride **b :** ROCKING HORSE **c :** a toy horse suspended by springs from a frame **4 a :** a topic to which one constantly reverts **b :** ¹HOBBY

hob·gob·lin \'häb-ˌgäb-lən\ *n* **1 :** a mischievous goblin **2 :** BOGEY 2, BUGABOO

hob·nail \-ˌnāl\ *n* [²*hob*] **:** a short large-headed nail for studding shoe soles — **hob·nailed** \-ˌnāld\ *adj*

hob·nob \-ˌnäb\ *vi* **hob·nobbed; hob·nob·bing** [fr. the obs. phrase *drink hobnob* (to drink alternately to one another)] **1** *archaic* **:** to drink sociably **2 :** to associate familiarly — **hob·nob·ber** *n*

¹ho·bo \'hō-(ˌ)bō\ *n, pl* **hoboes** *also* **hobos** [perh. alter. of *ho, boy*] **1 :** a migratory worker **2 :** a homeless and usu. penniless vagrant **:** TRAMP

²hobo *vi* **:** to live or travel in the manner of a hobo

Hob·son's choice \ˌhäb-sənz-\ *n* [Thomas *Hobson* †1631 E liveryman, who required every customer to take the horse nearest the door] **:** a choice between undesirable alternatives

¹hock \'häk\ *n* [ME *hoch, hough,* fr. OE *hōh* heel; akin to ON *hāsin* hock, Skt *kaṅkāla* skeleton] **1 :** the tarsal joint or region in the hind limb of a digitigrade quadruped (as the horse) corresponding to the ankle of man but elevated and bending backward — see HORSE illustration **2 :** a joint of a fowl's leg that corresponds to the hock of a quadruped

²hock *n, often cap* [modif. of G *hochheimer,* fr. *Hochheim,* Germany] *chiefly Brit* **:** RHINE WINE 1

³hock *n* [D *hok* pen, prison] **1 a :** ¹PAWN 2 <got his watch out of ~> **b :** DEBT 2 <in ~ to the bank> **2 :** PRISON

⁴hock *vt* **:** PAWN — **hock·er** *n*

hock·ey \'häk-ē\ *n* [perh. fr. MF *hoquet* shepherd's crook, dim. of *hoc* hook, of Gmc origin; akin to OE *hōc* hook] **1 :** FIELD HOCKEY **2 :** ICE HOCKEY

hock·shop \'häk-ˌshäp\ *n* **:** PAWNSHOP

ho·cus \'hō-kəs\ *vt* **ho·cussed** *or* **ho·cused; ho·cus·sing** *or* **ho·cus·ing** [obs. *hocus,* n., short for *hocus-pocus*] **1 :** to perpetrate a trick or hoax on **:** DECEIVE **2 :** to befuddle often with drugged liquor; *also* **:** DOPE, DRUG <*hocussed* the favorite just before the race>

¹ho·cus–po·cus \ˌhō-kə-'spō-kəs\ *n* [prob. fr. *hocus pocus,* imitation Latin phrase used by jugglers] **1 :** SLEIGHT OF HAND **2 :** nonsense or sham used to cloak deception

²hocus–pocus *vt* **ho·cus–po·cussed** *or* **ho·cus–po·cused; ho·cus–po·cus·sing** *or* **ho·cus–po·cus·ing :** to play tricks on

hod \'häd\ *n* [prob. fr. MD *hodde;* akin to MHG *hotte* cradle, ME *schuderen* to shudder] **1 :** a tray or trough that has a pole handle and that is borne on the shoulder for carrying loads (as of mortar or brick) **2 :** a coal scuttle

ho·dad \'hō-ˌdad\ *also* **ho·dad·dy** \-ˌdad-ē\ *n* [perh. alter. of *hodag* (an ugly mythical animal)] **:** a nonsurfer who frequents surfing beaches and pretends to be a surfer

hod carrier *n* **:** a laborer employed in carrying supplies to bricklayers, stonemasons, cement finishers, or plasterers on the job

hodge·podge \'häj-ˌpäj\ *n* [alter. of *hotchpotch*] **:** a heterogeneous mixture **:** JUMBLE

Hodg·kin's disease \'häj-kənz-\ *n* [Thomas *Hodgkin* †1866 E physician] **:** a neoplastic disease that is characterized by progressive enlargement of lymph glands, spleen, and liver and by progressive anemia

ho·do·scope \'häd-ə-ˌskōp, 'hōd-\ *n* [Gk *hodos* road, path + E *-scope* — more at CEDE] **:** an instrument for tracing the paths of ionizing particles by means of ion counters in close array

¹hoe \'hō\ *n* [ME *howe,* fr. MF *houe,* of Gmc origin; akin to OHG *houwa* mattock, *houwan* to hew — more at HEW] **:** any of various implements for tilling, mixing, or raking; *esp* **:** an implement with a thin flat blade on a long handle used esp. for cultivating, weeding, or loosening the earth around plants

²hoe *vb* **hoed; hoe·ing** *vi* **:** to use a hoe **:** work with a hoe ~ *vt* **1 :** to weed, cultivate, or thin (a crop) with a hoe **2 :** to remove (weeds) by hoeing **3 :** to dress or cultivate (land) by hoeing — **ho·er** \'hō(-ə)r\ *n*

hoe·cake \'hō-ˌkāk\ *n* [fr. its formerly being baked on the blade of a hoe] **:** a small cake made of cornmeal

hoe·down \-ˌdaun\ *n* **1 :** SQUARE DANCE **2 :** a gathering featuring hoedowns

¹hog \'hȯg, 'häg\ *n, pl* **hogs** *also* **hog** [ME *hogge,* fr. OE *hogg*] **1 :** a domestic swine esp. when weighing more than 120 pounds; *broadly* **:** any of various wild and domestic swine **2** *usu* **hogg** *Brit* **:** a young unshorn sheep; *also* **:** wool from such a sheep **3 a :** a selfish, gluttonous, or filthy person **b :** one that uses something to excess <the . . . car becomes more of a gas ~ with each year —Don MacDonald>

²hog *vb* **hogged; hog·ging** *vt* **1 :** to cut (a horse's mane) short **:** ROACH **2 :** to cause to arch **3 :** to take in excess of one's due ~ *vi* **:** to become curved upward in the middle — used of a ship's bottom or keel

ho·gan \'hō-ˌgän\ *n* [Navaho] **:** a building usu. made of logs and mud and used as a dwelling by the Navaho Indians

hogan

HO gauge \(')ā-'chō-\ *n* [*half* + *O gauge*] **:** a gauge of track in model railroading in which the rails are approximately ⅝ inch apart

hog·back \'hȯg-ˌbak, 'häg-\ *n* **:** a ridge of land formed by the outcropping edges of tilted strata; *broadly* **:** a ridge with a sharp summit and steeply sloping sides

hog cholera *n* **:** a highly infectious often fatal virus disease of swine characterized by fever, loss of appetite, diarrhea, and petechial hemorrhages esp. in the kidneys and lymph glands

hog·fish \'hȯg-ˌfish, 'häg-\ *n* **1 :** a large West Indian and Florida wrasse (*Lachnolaimus maximus*) often used for food **2 :** PIGFISH 1

hog·gish \'hȯg-ish, 'häg-\ *adj* **:** grossly selfish, gluttonous, or filthy — **hog·gish·ly** *adv* — **hog·gish·ness** *n*

Hog·ma·nay \ˌhäg-mə-'nā\ *n* [origin unknown] **1** *Scot* **:** the eve of New Year's Day **2** *Scot* **:** a gift solicited or given at Hogmanay

hog·nose snake \ˌhȯg-ˌnōz, ˌhäg-\ *n* **:** any of several rather small harmless stout-bodied No. American colubrid snakes (genus *Heterodon*) — called also *hog-nosed snake*

hog score *n* [*hog* (curling stone that fails to reach the score)] **:** a line which is marked across a curling rink seven yards from the tee and beyond which a stone must pass or be removed from the ice — called also *hog line*

hogs·head \'hȯgz-ˌhed, 'hägz-\ *n* **1 :** a large cask or barrel; *esp* **:** one containing from 63 to 140 gallons **2 :** any of various units of capacity; *esp* **:** a U.S. unit equal to 63 gallons

hog sucker *n* **:** a No. American sucker (*Hypentelium nigricans*) that is brassy olive marked with brown and is sometimes used for food

hog–tie \'hȯg-ˌtī, 'häg-\ *vt* **1 :** to tie together the feet of **2 :** to make helpless

hog·wash \-ˌwȯsh, -ˌwäsh\ *n* **1 :** SWILL 1a, SLOP 4a **2 :** worthless or nonsensical language

hog–wild \-'wī(ə)ld\ *adj* **:** lacking in restraint of judgment or temper <would go ~ if unconfined by constitutional limitations —Leo Egan>

¹Ho·hen·stau·fen \'hō-ən-ˌs(h)tau-fən\ *adj* **:** of or relating to a princely German family that reigned over the Holy Roman Empire from 1138–1254 and over Sicily from 1194–1266

²Hohenstaufen *n* **:** a member of the Hohenstaufen family; *esp* **:** a Hohenstaufen monarch

¹Ho·hen·zol·lern \'hō-ən-ˌzäl-ərn\ *adj* **:** of or relating to a princely German family that reigned in Prussia from 1701–1918 and in Germany from 1871–1918

²Hohenzollern *n* **:** a member of the Hohenzollern family; *esp* **:** a Hohenzollern monarch

ho hum *interj* [imit.] — used to express weariness, boredom, or disdain

hoick \'hȯik\ *vt* [prob. alter. of ¹*hike*] **:** to move or pull abruptly **:** YANK <was ~*ed* out of my job —Vincent Sheean>

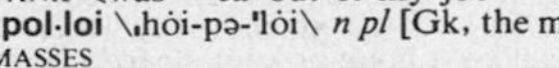

hoi pol·loi \ˌhȯi-pə-'lȯi\ *n pl* [Gk, the many] **:** the general populace **:** MASSES

hoise \ˈhȯiz\ *vt* **hoised** \ˈhȯizd\ *or* **hoist** \ˈhȯist\; **hois·ing** \ˈhȯi-ziŋ\ [origin unknown] : HOIST — **hoist with one's own petard** : victimized or hurt by one's own scheme

[1]**hoist** \ˈhȯist\ *vb* [alter. of *hoise*] *vt* : to raise into position by or as if by means of tackle ~ *vi* : to become hoisted : RISE *syn* see LIFT — **hoist·er** *n*

[2]**hoist** *n* **1** : an act of hoisting : LIFT **2** : an apparatus for hoisting **3** : the height of a flag when viewed flying

[1]**hoi·ty–toi·ty** \ˌhȯit-ē-ˈtȯit-ē, ˌhīt-ē-ˈtīt-ē\ *n* [irreg. redupl. of E dial. *hoit* (to play the fool)] : thoughtless giddy behavior

[2]**hoity–toity** *adj* **1** : thoughtlessly silly or frivolous : FLIGHTY **2** : marked by an air of assumed importance : POMPOUS

hoke \ˈhōk\ *vt* **hoked; hok·ing** [*hokum*] : to give a false value or quality to : FAKE — usu. used with *up* <used parts of B-grade movies to ~ up a film —Robert Sherrill>

hok·ey \ˈhō-kē\ *adj* **1** : sickly or affectedly sentimental : CORNY, MAWKISH <records on which she *didn't* sing ~ nursery rhymes —G. T. Simon> **2** : obviously contrived : PHONY <the plots are tricky but not ~ —Cleveland Amory> — **hok·ey·ness** *n*

ho·key·po·key \ˌhō-kē-ˈpō-kē\ *n* **1** : HOCUS-POCUS 2 **2** : ice cream sold by street vendors

hok·ku \ˈhō-(ˌ)kü\ *n, pl* **hokku** [Jap] **1** : HAIKU **2** : a lyric in hokku form

ho·kum \ˈhō-kəm\ *n* [prob. fr. *ho*cus-pocus + bun*kum*] **1** : a device used (as by showmen) to evoke a desired audience response **2** : pretentious nonsense : BUNKUM

hol- *or* **holo-** *comb form* [ME, fr. OF, fr. L, fr. Gk, fr. *holos* whole — more at SAFE] **1** : complete : total <*holo*hedral> **2** : completely : totally <*hol*andric>

hol·an·dric \hō-ˈlan-drik, hä-\ *adj* [ISV] **1** : inherited solely in the male line **2** : transmitted by a gene in the nonhomologous portion of the Y chromosome — **hol·an·dry** \ˈhō-ˌlan-drē, ˈhäl-ˌan-\ *n*

Hol·arc·tic \hō-ˈlärk-tik, hä-, -ˈlärt-ik\ *adj* : of, relating to, or being the biogeographic region including the northern parts of both hemispheres

[1]**hold** \ˈhōld\ *vb* **held** \ˈheld\; **hold·ing** [ME *holden*, fr. OE *healdan;* akin to OHG *haltan* to hold, L *celer* rapid] *vt* **1 a** : to maintain possession of : POSSESS **b** : to retain by force <troops ~*ing* the ridge> **c** : to keep control of or authority over **d** : to keep by way of threat or coercion <~*ing* the child for ransom> **2** : to impose restraint upon: as **a** : to refrain from producing **b** (1) : to keep under control <*held* his temper> (2) : STAY, ARREST <*held* his punches> (3) : to stop the action of temporarily <*held* the presses to insert a late story> **c** : to keep from advancing or succeeding in attack **d** : to restrict or limit by control or opposition <~ price increases to a minimum> **e** : to bind legally or morally <~ a man to his word> **f** : to tense muscles in order to brace (oneself) **3 a** : to have or keep in the grasp <*held* her hand> **b** : to cause to be or remain in a particular situation, position, or relation <~ a ladder steady> **c** : SUPPORT, SUSTAIN <the roof won't ~ much weight> **d** : to keep in custody <~*ing* him on a vagrancy charge> **e** : to have in reserve <~ a room> **4** : BEAR, CARRY, COMPORT <the soldierly way he ~*s* himself> **5 a** : to maintain in being or action : keep up without interruption, diminution, or flagging <~ silence> **b** : to keep the uninterrupted interest, attention, or devotion of <*held* the audience in suspense> **6 a** : to receive for storage : CONTAIN <the can ~*s* 5 gallons> **b** : to have in store <what the future ~*s*> **7 a** : to maintain by way of opinion or feeling : HARBOR <~ a theory> **b** : to have in regard <~*ing* money lightly, he spent it freely> **c** : to maintain in an expressed judgment or affirmation <~*ing* that it is nobody's business but his —Jack Olsen> **8 a** : to engage in with someone else or with others : do by concerted action <~ a conference> **b** : to cause to be conducted : CONVENE <~ a meeting of the council> **9 a** : to occupy as a result of an appointment, promotion, or election <~*s* a captaincy in the navy> **b** : to have earned or been awarded <~*s* a Ph.D.> **10** : AIM, POINT — used with *on* <*held* a gun on the druggist while an accomplice robbed the store> ~ *vi* **1 a** : to maintain position : refuse to give ground <the defensive line is ~*ing*> **b** : to continue in the same way or to the same degree : LAST <hopes the weather will ~> **2** : to maintain a grasp on something : remain fastened to something <the anchor *held* in the rough sea> **3** : to bear or carry oneself <asked him to ~ still> **4** : to be or remain valid : APPLY <the rule ~*s* in most cases> **5** : to go ahead as one has been going <*held* south for several miles> **6** : to forbear an intended or threatened action : HALT, PAUSE **7** : to stop counting during a countdown **8** : to have illicit drug material in one's possession *syn* see HAVE — **hold a candle to** : to qualify for comparison with — **hold forth** : to speak at length : EXPATIATE — **hold hands** : to engage one's hand with another's esp. as an expression of affection — **hold one's own** : to prove successful or competitive against opposition or in the face of difficulty — **hold the bag** **1** : to be left empty-handed **2** : to bear alone a responsibility that should have been shared by others — **hold the fort** **1** : to maintain a firm position **2** : to discharge usual responsibilities <is *holding the fort* until the manager returns> — **hold the line** : to operate within desirable limits <*holding the line* on prices —*Current Biog.*> — **hold to** : to give firm assent to : adhere to strongly <*holds to* his promise> — **hold to account** : to hold responsible — **hold water** : to stand up under criticism or analysis — **hold with** : to agree with or approve of

[2]**hold** *n* **1** : STRONGHOLD 1 **2 a** : CONFINEMENT, CUSTODY **b** : PRISON **3 a** (1) : the act or the manner of holding or grasping : GRIP <released his ~ on the handle> (2) : a manner of grasping an opponent in wrestling **b** : a nonphysical bond that attaches, restrains, or constrains or by which something is affected, controlled, or dominated <has lost its ~ on the broad public —Oscar Cargill> **c** : full comprehension <get ~ of exactly what is happening —J. P. Lyford> **d** : full or immediate control : POSSESSION <got ~ of himself> <wants to get ~ of a road map> **4** : something that may be grasped as a support **5 a** : FERMATA **b** : the time between the onset and the release of a vocal articulation **6** : a sudden motionless posture at the end of a dance **7 a** : an order or indication that something is to be reserved or delayed **b** : a delay in a countdown (as in launching a spacecraft)
syn HOLD, GRIP, CLASP, CLUTCH *shared meaning element* : a getting or keeping in control or possession

[3]**hold** *n* [alter. of *hole*] **1** : the interior of a ship below decks; *esp* : the cargo deck of a ship **2** : the cargo compartment of a plane

hold·all \ˈhōl-ˌdȯl\ *n* : a container for miscellaneous articles; *esp* : a traveling case or bag (as of cloth)

hold·back \ˈhōl(d)-ˌbak\ *n* **1** : something that retains or restrains **2 a** : the act of holding back **b** : something held back

hold back \(ˈ)hōl(d)-ˈbak\ *vt* **1** : to hinder the progress or achievement of : RESTRAIN **2** : to retain in one's keeping ~ *vi* : to keep oneself in check

hold–down \ˈhōl-ˌdau̇n\ *n* **1** : an act of holding down **2** : something used to fasten an object in place

hold down \(ˈ)hōl-ˈdau̇n\ *vt* **1** : to keep within limits <*hold* the noise *down*> **2** : to handle (a responsibility) continuously <*holding down* two jobs>

hold·en \ˈhōl-dən\ *archaic past part of* HOLD

hold·er \ˈhōl-dər\ *n* **1** : a person that holds: **a** (1) : OWNER (2) : TENANT **b** : a person in possession of and legally entitled to receive payment of a bill, note, or check **2** : a device that holds <cigarette ~>

holder in due course : one other than the original recipient who holds a legally effective negotiable instrument and who has a right to collect from and no responsibility toward the issuer

hold·fast \ˈhōl(d)-ˌfast\ *n* **1 a** : a part by which a plant clings to a flat surface **b** : an organ by which a parasitic animal attaches itself to its host **2** : something to which something else may be firmly secured

hold·ing \ˈhōl-diŋ\ *n* **1 a** : land held esp. as a vassal or tenant **b** : property (as land or securities) owned — usu. used in pl. **2** : a ruling of a court esp. upon an issue of law raised in a case — compare DICTUM **3** : something that holds

holding company *n* : a company whose primary business is holding a controlling interest in the securities of other companies — compare INVESTMENT COMPANY

holding pattern *n* : the usu. oval course flown (as over an airport) by aircraft awaiting clearance to land

hold off *vt* **1** : to fight to a standoff : WITHSTAND **2** : to block from an objective : DELAY **3** : to defer action on : POSTPONE ~ *vi* : to defer or temporarily stop doing something

hold on *vi* **1** : to persevere in difficult circumstances **2** : to await something (as a telephone connection) desired or requested — **hold on to** : to maintain possession of

hold·out \ˈhōl-ˌdau̇t\ *n* : one that holds out (as in negotiations)

hold out \(ˈ)hōl-ˈdau̇t\ *vt* **1** : to present as something realizable : PROFFER **2** : to represent to be ~ *vi* **1** : to remain unsubdued or operative : continue to cope **2** : to refuse to come to an agreement — **hold out for** : to insist on as the price for an agreement — **hold out on** : to withhold something (as information) from

hold·over \ˈhōl-ˌdō-vər\ *n* : one that is held over; *esp* : one that continues in office

hold over \(ˈ)hōl-ˈdō-vər\ *vi* : to continue (as in office) for a prolonged period ~ *vt* **1 a** : POSTPONE **b** : to keep in one's possession : RETAIN **2** : to prolong the engagement or tenure of

hold·up \ˈhōl-ˌdəp\ *n* **1** : an armed robbery **2** : DELAY

hold up \(ˈ)hōl-ˈdəp\ *vt* **1** : DELAY, IMPEDE **2** : to rob at gunpoint **3** : to present as an example <his work was *held up* to ridicule> <*hold* this *up* as perfection —*Times Lit. Supp.*> ~ *vi* : to endure a test

[1]**hole** \ˈhōl\ *n* [ME, fr. OE *hol* (fr. neut. of *hol*, adj., hollow) & *holh;* akin to OHG *hol*, adj., hollow, L *caulis* stalk, stem, Gk *kaulos*] **1** : an opening often forced into or through a thing **2 a** : a hollow place; *esp* : PIT **b** : a deep place in a body of water **c** : a defect in a crystal (as of a semiconductor) that is due to an electron's having left its normal position in one of the crystal bonds and that is equivalent in many respects to a positively charged particle **3** : an underground habitation : BURROW **4 a** : a serious discrepancy or flaw <gaping ~*s* in present political theory —W. H. Ferry> **b** : an opening in a defensive formation; *esp* : the area between the third baseman and the shortstop **5 a** : the unit of play from the tee to the hole in golf **b** : a usu. lined cavity in a putting green into which the ball is to be played in golf **6** : a mean or dreary place <a country whose capital was a provincial ~ —Frank O'Connor> **7** : an awkward position : FIX <heroes that got the rebels out of a ~ at the battle —Kenneth Roberts> — **in the hole** **1** : having a score below zero **2** : at a disadvantage

[2]**hole** *vb* **holed; hol·ing** *vt* **1** : to make a hole in **2** : to drive into a hole ~ *vi* : to make a hole in something

hole card *n* : a card in stud poker that is properly dealt facedown and that the holder need not expose before the showdown

hole in one : ACE 4

hole out *vi* : to play one's ball into the hole in golf

hole up *vi* : to take refuge or shelter in or as if in a hole or cave ~ *vt* : to place in or as if in a refuge or hiding place

hol·ey \ˈhō-lē\ *adj* : having holes

[1]**hol·i·day** \ˈhäl-ə-ˌdā\ *n* [ME, fr. OE *hāligdæg*, fr. *hālig* holy + *dæg* day] **1** : HOLY DAY **2** : a day on which one is exempt from work; *specif* : a day marked by a general suspension of work in commemoration of an event **3** : a period of relaxation : VACATION — often used in pl.

[2]**holiday** *vi* : to take or spend a holiday esp. in travel or at a resort — **hol·i·day·er** *n*

ə abut	ᵊ kitten	ər further	a back	ā bake	ä cot, cart
au̇ out	ch chin	e less	ē easy	g gift	i trip	ī life
j joke	ŋ sing	ō flow	ȯ flaw	ȯi coin	th thin	t͟h this
ü loot	u̇ foot	y yet	yü few	yu̇ furious	zh vision

hol·i·day·mak·er \'häl-ə-ˌdā-ˌmā-kər\ *n* : one who is on a holiday : VACATIONER

hol·i·days \-ˌdāz\ *adv* : on holidays repeatedly : on any holiday

ho·li·er–than–thou \ˌhō-lē-ər-t͟hən-'t͟haü\ *adj* : marked by an air of superior piety or morality

[1]ho·li·ness \'hō-lē-nəs\ *n* **1** : the quality or state of being holy — used as a title for various high religious dignitaries <His *Holiness* Pope Pius XII> **2** : SANCTIFICATION 2

[2]holiness *adj, often cap* : emphasizing the doctrine of the second blessing; *specif* : of or relating to a perfectionist movement arising in U.S. Protestantism in the late 19th century

ho·lism \'hō-ˌliz-əm\ *n* [*hol-* + *-ism*] : a theory that the universe and esp. living nature is correctly seen in terms of interacting wholes (as of living organisms) that are more than the mere sum of elementary particles

ho·lis·tic \hō-'lis-tik\ *adj* **1** : of or relating to holism **2** : emphasizing the organic or functional relation between parts and wholes — **ho·lis·ti·cal·ly** \-ti-k(ə-)lē\ *adv*

hol·land \'häl-ənd\ *n, often cap* [ME *holand,* fr. *Holand,* county in the Netherlands, fr. MD *Holland*] : a cotton or linen fabric in plain weave usu. heavily sized or glazed and used for window shades, bookbinding, and clothing

hol·lan·daise sauce \ˌhäl-ən-ˌdāz-\ *n* [F *sauce hollandaise,* lit., Dutch sauce] : a rich sauce made of butter, egg yolks, and lemon juice or vinegar

Hol·lands \'häl-ən(d)z\ *n* [D *hollandsch,* fr. *hollandsch genever* Dutch gin] : gin made in the Netherlands — called also *Holland gin*

[1]hol·ler \'häl-ər\ *vb* **hol·lered; hol·ler·ing** \-(ə-)riŋ\ [alter. of *hollo*] *vi* **1** : to cry out (as to attract attention or in pain) : SHOUT **2** : GRIPE, COMPLAIN ~ *vt* : to call out (a word or phrase)

[2]holler *n* **1** : SHOUT, CRY **2** : COMPLAINT **3** : a freely improvised American Negro work song

[3]holler *chiefly dial var of* HOLLOW

Hol·ler·ith \'häl-ə-ˌrith\ *n* [Herman *Hollerith* †1929 Am engineer] : a system for encoding alphanumeric information on punch cards — called also *Hollerith code*

Hol·ler·ith card \ˌhäl-ə-ˌrith-\ *n* : PUNCH CARD

[1]hol·lo \hä-'lō, hə-; 'häl-(ˌ)ō\ *also* **hol·loa** \hä-'lō, hə-\ *or* **hol·la** \hə-'lä, 'häl-(ˌ)ä\ *interj* [origin unknown] **1** — used to attract attention **2** — used as a call of encouragement or jubilation

[2]hol·lo *also* **hol·loa** \'häl-(ˌ)ō, -ə(-w)\ *or* **hol·la** \'häl-ə(-w)\ *vb* : to cry hollo : HOLLER

[3]hollo *also* **holloa** *or* **holla** *like*[2]\ *n, pl* **hollos** *also* **holloas** *or* **hollas** : an exclamation or call of hollo <every day for food or play, came to the mariner's ~ —S. T. Coleridge>

[1]hol·low \'häl-(ˌ)ō, -ə(-w)\ *adj* **hol·low·er** \'häl-ə-wər\; **hol·low·est** \-ə-wəst\ [ME *holw, holh,* fr. *holh* hole, den, fr. OE *holh* hole, hollow — more at HOLE] **1** : having an indentation or inward curve : CONCAVE, SUNKEN **2** : having a cavity within <~ tree> **3** : reverberating like a sound made in or by beating on a large empty enclosure : MUFFLED **4 a** : deceivingly lacking in real value or significance <a ~ victory> **b** : lacking in truth or substance : FALSE, DECEITFUL <~ promises> ***syn*** see VAIN — **hollow** *adv* — **hol·low·ly** \'häl-ō-lē, -ə-lē\ *adv* — **hol·low·ness** *n*

[2]hollow *vt* **1** : to make hollow **2** : to form by a hollowing action — usu. used with *out* <rain barrels ~*ed* out from trees —Robert Shaplen> ~ *vi* : to become hollow

[3]hollow *n* **1** : a depressed or low part of a surface; *esp* : a small valley or basin **2** : an unfilled space : CAVITY, HOLE

hollow organ *n* : a visceral organ that is a hollow tube or pouch (as the stomach or intestine) or that includes a cavity (as of the heart or bladder) which subserves a vital function

hol·low·ware *or* **hol·lo·ware** \'häl-ə-ˌwa(ə)r, -ˌwe(ə)r\ *n* : vessels (as bowls, cups, or vases) usu. of pottery, glass, or metal that have a significant depth and volume

hol·ly \'häl-ē\ *n, pl* **hollies** [ME *holin, holly,* fr. OE *holegn;* akin to OHG *hulis* holly, MIr *cuilenn*] **1 a** : any of a genus (*Ilex*) of trees and shrubs (family Aquifoliaceae, the holly family) having thick glossy spiny-margined leaves and usu. bright red berries **b** : the foliage or branches of the holly **2** : any of various trees with foliage resembling that of a holly

holly 1

hol·ly·hock \'häl-ē-ˌhäk, -ˌhȯk\ *n* [ME *holihoc,* fr. *holi* holy + *hoc* mallow, fr. OE] : a tall widely cultivated perennial Chinese herb (*Althaea rosea*) of the mallow family with large coarse rounded leaves and tall spikes of showy flowers

Hol·ly·wood \'häl-ē-ˌwu̇d\ *n* [*Hollywood,* district of Los Angeles, Calif.] : the American motion-picture industry — **Hol·ly·wood·ish** \-ish\ *adj*

Hollywood bed *n* : a mattress on a box spring supported by low legs sometimes with an upholstered headboard

holm \'hō(l)m\ *n* [ME, fr. OE, fr. ON *hōlmr;* akin to OE *hyll* hill] *Brit* : a small inland or inshore island; *also* : BOTTOMS

hol·mi·um \'hō(l)-mē-əm\ *n* [NL, fr. *Holmia* Stockholm, Sweden] : a metallic element of the rare-earth group that occurs with yttrium and forms highly magnetic compounds — see ELEMENT table

holm oak *n* : ILEX 1

holo- —see HOL-

ho·lo·blas·tic \ˌhō-lə-'blas-tik, ˌhäl-ə-\ *adj* [ISV] *of an egg* : having cleavage planes that divide the whole egg into distinct and separate though coherent blastomeres — compare MEROBLASTIC — **ho·lo·blas·ti·cal·ly** \-ti-k(ə-)lē\ *adv*

ho·lo·caust \'häl-ə-ˌkȯst, 'hō-lə- *also* 'hȯ-lə-\ *n* [ME, fr. OF *holocauste,* fr. LL *holocaustum,* fr. Gk *holokauston,* fr. neut. of *holokaustos* burnt whole, fr. *hol-* + *kaustos* burnt, fr. *kaiein* to burn — more at CAUSTIC] **1** : a sacrifice consumed by fire **2** : a thorough destruction esp. by fire

Ho·lo·cene \'hō-lə-ˌsēn, 'häl-ə-\ *adj* [ISV] : RECENT 2 — **Holocene** *n*

ho·lo·crine \-krən, -ˌkrīn, -ˌkrēn\ *adj* [ISV *hol-* + Gk *krinein* to separate — more at CERTAIN] : producing a secretion containing disintegrated secretory cells; *also* : produced by a holocrine gland

ho·lo·en·zyme \ˌhō-lō-'en-ˌzīm\ *n* [ISV] : a complete active enzyme consisting of an apoenzyme combined with its coenzyme

Ho·lo·fer·nes \ˌhäl-ə-'fər-(ˌ)nēz, ˌhō-lə-\ *n* [LL, fr. Gk *Holophernēs*] : a general of Nebuchadnezzar who led an Assyrian army against Israel and was beheaded while asleep by Judith

ho·log·a·mous \hō-'läg-ə-məs\ *adj* : having gametes of essentially the same size and structural features as vegetative cells — **ho·log·a·my** \-mē\ *n*

ho·lo·gram \'hō-lə-ˌgram, 'häl-ə-\ *n* : a three-dimensional picture that is made on a photographic film or plate without the use of a camera, that consists of a pattern of interference produced by a split coherent beam of light, and that for viewing is illuminated with coherent light from behind

ho·lo·graph \'hō-lə-ˌgraf, 'häl-ə-\ *n* [LL *holographus,* fr. LGk *holographos,* fr. Gk *hol-* + *graphein* to write — more at CARVE] : a document wholly in the handwriting of its author; *also* : the handwriting itself <a letter in the president's ~> — **holograph** *or* **ho·lo·graph·ic** \ˌhō-lə-'graf-ik, ˌhäl-ə-\ *adj*

ho·log·ra·phy \hō-'läg-rə-fē\ *n* : the process of making or using a hologram — **ho·lo·graph** \'hō-lə-ˌgraf, 'häl-ə-\ *vt* — **ho·lo·graph·ic** \ˌhō-lə-'graf-ik, ˌhäl-ə-\ *adj* — **ho·lo·graph·i·cal·ly** \-i-k(ə-)lē\ *adv*

ho·lo·gy·nic \ˌhō-lə-'jin-ik, ˌhäl-ə-, -'gī-nik\ *adj* [ISV *hol-* + *-gynic* (fr. Gk *gynē* woman) — more at QUEEN] : inherited solely in the female line presumably through transmission as a recessive factor in the nonhomologous portion of the X chromosome — **ho·log·y·ny** \hō-'läj-ə-nē\ *n*

ho·lo·he·dral \ˌhō-lə-'hē-drəl, ˌhäl-ə-\ *adj* [*hol-* + Gk *hedra* seat — more at SIT] *of a crystal* : having all the faces required by complete symmetry — compare HEMIHEDRAL, TETARTOHEDRAL

ho·lo·me·tab·o·lism \ˌhō-lō-mə-'tab-ə-ˌliz-əm, ˌhäl-ō-\ *n* : development of insects involving complete metamorphosis — **ho·lo·me·tab·o·lous** \-ləs\ *adj*

ho·lo·my·ar·i·an \-mī-'ar-ē-ən, -'er-\ *adj* [deriv. of Gk *holos* whole + *mys* muscle — more at SAFE, MOUSE] *of a nematode worm* : having the muscle layer continuous or divided into two longitudinal zones without true muscle cells

ho·lo·phras·tic \ˌhō-lə-'fras-tik, ˌhäl-ə-\ *adj* [ISV *hol-* + *-phrastic* (fr. Gk *phrazein* to point out, declare)] : expressing a complex of ideas in a single word or in a fixed phrase

ho·lo·phyt·ic \-'fit-ik\ *adj* : obtaining food after the manner of a green plant by photosynthetic activity

ho·lo·thu·ri·an \-'th(y)u̇r-ē-ən\ *n* [deriv. of Gk *holothourion* water polyp] : any of a class (Holothurioidea) of echinoderms having an elongate flexible tough muscular body : SEA CUCUMBER — **holothurian** *adj*

ho·lo·type \'hō-lə-ˌtīp, 'häl-ə-\ *n* **1** : the single specimen designated by an author as the type of a species or lesser taxon at the time of establishing the group **2** : the type of a species or lesser taxon designated at a date later than that of establishing a group or by another person than the author of the taxon — **ho·lo·typ·ic** \ˌhō-lə-'tip-ik, ˌhäl-ə-\ *adj*

ho·lo·zo·ic \ˌhō-lə-'zō-ik, ˌhäl-ə-\ *adj* : obtaining food after the manner of most animals by ingesting complex organic matter

holp \'hō(l)p\ *chiefly dial past of* HELP

hol·pen \'hō(l)-pən\ *chiefly dial past part of* HELP

hol·stein \'hōl-ˌstēn, -ˌstīn\ *n* [short for *holstein-friesian*] : any of a breed of large black-and-white dairy cattle orig. from northern Holland and Friesland that produce large quantities of comparatively low-fat milk

hol·stein–frie·sian \-'frē-zhən\ *n* [*Holstein,* Germany, its later locality + *Friesian* (var. of *Frisian*)] : HOLSTEIN

hol·ster \'hōl(t)-stər\ *n* [D; akin to OE *heolstor* cover, *helan* to conceal — more at HELL] : a usu. leather case for a pistol

holt \'hōlt\ *n* [ME, fr. OE; akin to OHG *holz* wood, Gk *klados* twig — more at GLADIATOR] *archaic* : a small woods : COPSE

ho·lus–bo·lus \ˌhō-ləs-'bō-ləs\ *adv* [prob. redupl. of *bolus*] : all at once

ho·ly \'hō-lē\ *adj* **ho·li·er; -est** [ME, fr. OE *hālig;* akin to OE *hāl* whole — more at WHOLE] **1** : set apart to the service of God or a god : SACRED <the ~ priesthood> **2 a** : characterized by perfection and transcendence : commanding absolute adoration and reverence <the ~ Trinity> **b** : spiritually pure : GODLY <a ~ man given to prayer and charitable works> **3 a** : evoking or meriting veneration or awe <the ~ cross> **b** : being awesome, frightening, or beyond belief <a ~ terror> **4** : filled with superhuman and potentially fatal power — **ho·li·ly** \-lə-lē\ *adv*

holy city *n* : a city that is the center of religious worship and traditions

Holy Communion *n* : COMMUNION 2a

holy day *n* : a day set aside for special religious observance

holy day of obligation : a feast on which Roman Catholics are duty-bound to hear mass

Holy Father *n* : POPE 1

Holy Ghost *n* : the third person of the Trinity : HOLY SPIRIT

Holy Grail *n* : GRAIL 1

Holy Hour *n* : an hour of prayer and meditation before the Blessed Sacrament esp. in memory of the Passion

Holy Joe \ˌhō-lē-'jō\ *n, slang* : PARSON, CHAPLAIN

Holy Office *n* : a congregation of the curia charged with protecting faith and morals

holy of holies [trans. of LL *sanctum sanctorum,* trans. of Heb *qōdhesh hag-qodhāshīm*] : the innermost and most sacred chamber of the Jewish tabernacle and temple

holy oil *n* : olive oil blessed by a bishop for use in a sacrament or sacramental

holy order *n, often cap H&O* **1** : MAJOR ORDER **2** : the rite or sacrament of ordination

Holy Roller *n* **:** a member of one of the Protestant sects whose worship meetings are characterized by frenzied excitement — often taken to be offensive
Holy Roman Empire *n* **:** an empire consisting primarily of a loose confederation of German and Italian territories under the suzerainty of an emperor and existing from the 9th or 10th century to 1806
Holy Saturday *n* **:** the Saturday before Easter
Holy See *n* **:** the see of the pope
Holy Spirit *n* **:** the active presence of God in human life constituting the third person of the Trinity
1ho·ly·stone \ˈhō-lē-ˌstōn\ *n* **:** a soft sandstone used to scrub a ship's decks
2holystone *vt* **:** to scrub with a holystone
Holy Synod *n* **:** the governing body of a national Eastern church
Holy Thursday *n* **1 :** ASCENSION DAY **2 :** MAUNDY THURSDAY
holy war *n* **:** a war waged by religious partisans to propagate or defend their faith
holy water *n* **:** water blessed by a priest and used as a purifying sacramental
Holy Week *n* **:** the week before Easter during which the last days of Christ's life are commemorated
holy writ *n, often cap H&W* **1 :** BIBLE 1 **2 :** a writing or utterance having unquestionable authority <its financial precepts were not necessarily *Holy Writ* —Herbert Stein>
Holy Year *n* **:** a Roman Catholic jubilee year
hom *abbr* homiletics; homily
hom- *or* **homo-** *comb form* [L, fr. Gk, fr. *homos* — more at SAME] **1 :** one and the same **:** similar **:** alike <*homo*graph> <*homo*sporous> **2 :** homologous with a (specified) chemical compound <*homo*gentisic acid>
hom·age \ˈ(h)äm-ij\ *n* [ME, fr. OF *hommage,* fr. *homme* man, vassal, fr. L *homin-, homo* man; akin to OE *guma* man, L *humus* earth — more at HUMBLE] **1 a :** a ceremony by which a man acknowledges himself the vassal of a lord **b :** the relationship between a feudal lord and his man **c :** an act done or payment made in meeting the obligations of vassalage **2 a :** reverential regard **:** DEFERENCE **b :** flattering attention **:** TRIBUTE ***syn*** see HONOR
hom·ag·er \ˈ(h)äm-ij-ər\ *n* **:** VASSAL
homalographic *var of* HOMOLOGRAPHIC
hom·bre \ˈäm-brē, ˈəm-, -ˌbrā\ *n* [Sp, man, fr. L *homin-, homo*] **:** GUY, FELLOW <a cabin occupied by a group of nasty-looking ~*s* —Philip Hamburger>
hom·burg \ˈhäm-ˌbərg\ *n* [*Homburg,* Germany] **:** a man's felt hat with a stiff curled brim and a high crown creased lengthwise
1home \ˈhōm\ *n* [ME *hom,* fr. OE *hām* village, home; akin to Gk *kōmē* village, L *civis* citizen, Gk *koiman* to put to sleep — more at CEMETERY] **1 a :** a family's place of residence **:** DOMICILE **b :** HOUSE **2 :** the social unit formed by a family living together **3 a :** a congenial environment **b :** HABITAT **4 a :** a place of origin <salmon returning to their ~ to spawn> **b :** HEADQUARTERS **5 :** an establishment providing residence and special care for disabled persons **6 :** the objective in various games; *esp* **:** HOME PLATE — **home·less** \-ləs\ *adj* — **at home 1 a :** relaxed and comfortable **:** at ease <felt completely *at home* on the stage> **b :** in harmony with the surroundings **2 :** on familiar ground **:** KNOWLEDGEABLE <teachers *at home* in their subject fields>

homburg

2home *adv* **1 :** to or at home **2 :** to a final, closed, or standard position <drive a nail ~> **3 a :** to an ultimate objective (as a goal or finish line) **b :** to a successful or rewarding end **4 :** to a vital sensitive core <the truth struck ~>
3home *adj* **1 :** of, relating to, or being a home, place of origin, or base of operations <~ office> **2 :** prepared, done, or designed for use in a home <~ remedies> <~ cooking> <a ~ aquarium> **3 :** operating or occurring in a home area <the ~ team> <~ games>
4home *vb* **homed; hom·ing** *vi* **1 a :** to go or return home **b** *of an animal* **:** to return accurately to one's home or natal area from a distance **c :** to proceed to or toward a source of radiated energy used as a guide <missiles ~ in on radar> **d :** to proceed or direct attention toward an objective <science is *homing* in on the mysterious human process —Sam Glucksberg> **2 :** to have a home ~ *vt* **:** to send to or provide with a home
home- *or* **homeo-** *also* **homoi-** *or* **homoio-** *comb form* [L&Gk; L *homoeo-,* fr. Gk *homoi-, homoio-,* fr. *homoios,* fr. *homos* same — more at SAME] **:** like **:** similar <*homeo*stasis> <*homoio*thermic>
home·body \ˈhōm-ˌbäd-ē\ *n* **:** one whose life centers in the home
1home·bound \ˈhōm-ˌbau̇nd\ *adj* [*home* + *1bound*] **:** going homeward <~ travelers>
2homebound *adj* [*home* + *4bound*] **:** confined to the home <~ invalids>
home·bred \ˈhōm-ˈbred\ *adj* **:** produced at home **:** INDIGENOUS
home brew *n* **:** an alcoholic beverage (as beer) made at home
home·com·ing \ˈhōm-ˌkəm-iŋ\ *n* **1 :** a return home **2 a :** the return of a group of people esp. on a special occasion to a place formerly frequented or regarded as home **b :** an annual celebration for alumni at a college or university
home economics *n pl but sing or pl in constr* **:** the theory and practice of homemaking — **home economist** *n*
home front *n* **:** the sphere of civilian activity in war
home·grown \ˈhōm-ˈgrōn\ *adj* **1 :** grown or produced at home **2 :** produced in or characteristic of the home country or place of origin <~ politicians>
home·land \-ˌland *also* -lənd\ *n* **:** native land **:** FATHERLAND
home·like \ˈhōm-ˌlīk\ *adj* **:** characteristic of a home: **a :** CHEERFUL, COZY **b :** SIMPLE, WHOLESOME
home·ly \ˈhōm-lē\ *adj* **home·li·er; -est 1 :** suggestive or characteristic of a home **2 :** frequently encountered **:** FAMILIAR <explained the problem in ~ terms> **3 :** of a sympathetic character **:** KINDLY **4 a :** unaffectedly natural **:** SIMPLE **b :** not elaborate or complex **5 :** lacking beauty of feature or grace of proportion **:** approaching ugliness <a ~ face redeemed by its smile> ***syn*** see PLAIN ***ant*** comely — **home·li·ness** *n*
home·made \ˈhōm-ˈ(m)ād\ *adj* **1 :** made in the home, on the premises, or by one's own efforts **2 :** of domestic manufacture
home·mak·er \ˈhōm-ˌmā-kər\ *n* **:** one who manages a household esp. as a wife and mother — **home·mak·ing** \-kiŋ\ *n or adj*
ho·meo·mor·phic \ˌhō-mē-ə-ˈmȯr-fik\ *adj* **:** characterized by homeomorphism
ho·meo·mor·phism \-ˌfiz-əm\ *n* [ISV] **1 :** a near similarity of crystalline forms between unlike chemical compounds **2 :** a one-to-one mapping in topology between two figures that is continuous in both directions
ho·meo·path \ˈhō-mē-ə-ˌpath\ *n* **:** a practitioner or adherent of homeopathy
ho·me·op·a·thy \ˌhō-mē-ˈäp-ə-thē, ˌhäm-ē-\ *n* [G *homöopathie,* fr. *homöo-* home- + *-pathie* -pathy] **:** a system of medical practice that treats a disease esp. by the administration of minute doses of a remedy that would in healthy persons produce symptoms of the disease treated — **ho·meo·path·ic** \ˌhō-mē-ə-ˈpath-ik\ *adj* — **ho·meo·path·i·cal·ly** \-i-k(ə-)lē\ *adv*
ho·meo·sta·sis \ˌhō-mē-ō-ˈstā-səs\ *n* [NL] **:** a relatively stable state of equilibrium or a tendency toward such a state between the different but interdependent elements or groups of elements of an organism or group — **ho·meo·stat·ic** \-ˈstat-ik\ *adj*
ho·meo·typ·ic \-ˈtip-ik\ *adj* **:** being or relating to the second or equational meiotic division
home plate *n* **:** a rubber slab at one corner of a baseball diamond at which a batter stands when batting and which must be touched by a base runner in order to score
home port *n* **:** the port from which a ship hails or from which it is documented
1ho·mer \ˈhō-mər\ *n* [Heb *hōmer*] **:** an ancient Hebrew unit of capacity equal to about 10½ or later 11½ bushels or 100 gallons
2hom·er \ˈhō-mər\ *n* **1 :** HOMING PIGEON **2 :** HOME RUN
3hom·er *vi* **:** to hit a home run
home range *n* **:** the area to which the activities of an animal are confined
Ho·mer·ic \hō-ˈmer-ik\ *adj* **1 :** of, relating to, or characteristic of the Greek poet Homer, his age, or his writings **2 :** of epic proportions **:** HEROIC <~ feats of reporting —Stanley Walker> — **Ho·mer·i·cal·ly** \-i-k(ə-)lē\ *adv*
home·room \ˈhōm-ˌrüm, -ˌru̇m\ *n* **:** a classroom where pupils of the same class report at the opening of school
home rule *n* **1 :** self-government in internal affairs by the people of a dependent political unit **2 :** limited autonomy in the organization and management of local affairs granted by a state to a county or municipality
home run *n* **:** a hit in baseball that enables the batter to make a complete circuit of the bases and score a run
home·sick \ˈhōm-ˌsik\ *adj* [back-formation fr. *homesickness*] **:** longing for home and family while absent from them — **home·sick·ness** *n*
home·site \-ˌsīt\ *n* **1 :** a location suitable for a home **2 :** the location of a home
1home·spun \-ˌspən\ *adj* **1 a :** spun or made at home **b :** made of homespun **2 :** SIMPLE, HOMELY <local ~ virtues —*Times Lit. Supp.*>
2homespun *n* **:** a loosely woven usu. woolen or linen fabric orig. made from homespun yarn
home stand *n* **:** a series of baseball games played at a team's home field
1home·stead \ˈhōm-ˌsted, -stəd\ *n* **1 a :** the home and adjoining land occupied by a family **b :** an ancestral home **c :** HOUSE **2 :** a tract of land acquired from U.S. public lands by filing a record and living on and cultivating the tract
2home·stead \-ˌsted\ *vt* **:** to acquire or occupy as a homestead ~ *vi* **:** to acquire or settle on land under a homestead law — **home·stead·er** \-ˌsted-ər\ *n*
homestead law *n* **1 :** a law exempting a homestead from attachment or sale under execution for general debts **2 :** any of several legislative acts authorizing the sale of public lands in homesteads to settlers
home·stretch \ˈhōm-ˈstrech\ *n* **1 :** the part of a racecourse between the last curve and the winning post **2 :** a final stage (as of a project)
home·town \-ˈtau̇n\ *n* **:** the city or town of one's birth or principal residence
home truth *n* **1 :** an unpleasant fact that jars the sensibilities **2 :** a statement of undisputed fact
1home·ward \ˈhōm-wərd\ *or* **home·wards** \-wərdz\ *adv* **:** toward home <look ~, angel —John Milton>
2homeward *adj* **:** being or going in the direction of home
home·work \ˈhōm-ˌwərk\ *n* **1 :** piecework done at home for pay **2 :** an assignment given to a student to be completed outside the regular class period **3 :** preparatory reading or research (as for a discussion) <had not done all his essential ~ in party and public relations —Arthur Krock>
hom·ey *also* **homy** \ˈhō-mē\ *adj* **hom·i·er; -est :** HOMELIKE <a restaurant with a ~ atmosphere> — **hom·ey·ness** *or* **hom·i·ness** *n*
ho·mi·cid·al \ˌhäm-ə-ˈsīd-ᵊl, ˌhō-mə-\ *adj* **:** of, relating to, or tending toward homicide — **ho·mi·cid·al·ly** \-ᵊl-ē\ *adv*
ho·mi·cide \ˈhäm-ə-ˌsīd, ˈhō-mə-\ *n* [in sense 1, fr. ME, fr. MF, fr. L *homicida,* fr. *homo* man + *-cida* -cide; in sense 2, fr. ME, fr. MF,

fr. L *homicidium,* fr. *homo* + *-cidium* -cide] **1 :** a person who kills another **2 :** a killing of one human being by another

hom·i·let·ic \ˌhäm-ə-ˈlet-ik\ *or* **hom·i·let·i·cal** \-i-kəl\ *adj* [LL *homileticus,* fr. Gk *homilētikos* of conversation, fr. *homilein*] **1 :** of, relating to, or resembling a homily **2 :** of or relating to homiletics — **hom·i·let·i·cal·ly** \-i-k(ə-)lē\ *adv*

hom·i·let·ics \-iks\ *n pl but sing in constr* **:** the art of preaching

hom·i·ly \ˈhäm-ə-lē\ *n, pl* **-lies** [ME *omelie,* fr. MF, fr. LL *homilia,* fr. LGk, fr. Gk, conversation, discourse, fr. *homilein* to consort with, address, fr. *homilos* crowd, assembly] **1 :** a religious discourse usu. delivered to a congregation **:** SERMON; *specif* **:** an informal exposition of Scripture **2 :** a lecture on moral conduct

homing pigeon *n* **:** a racing pigeon trained to return home

hom·i·nid \ˈhäm-ə-nəd, -ˌnid\ *n* [deriv. of L *homin-, homo* man] **:** any of a family (Hominidae) of bipedal primate mammals comprising recent man, his immediate ancestors, and related forms — **hominid** *adj*

hom·i·ni·za·tion \ˌhäm-ə-nə-ˈzā-shən\ *n* [L *homin-, homo* + E *-ization*] **:** the evolutionary development of human characteristics that differentiate man from his primate ancestors

hom·i·nized \ˈhäm-ə-ˌnīzd\ *adj* **:** characterized by hominization

hom·i·noid \-ˌnȯid\ *adj* **:** resembling or related to man — **hominoid** *n*

hom·i·ny \ˈhäm-ə-nē\ *n* [prob. of Algonquian origin; akin to Natick *-minne* grain] **:** hulled corn with the germ removed

hominy grits *n pl but sing or pl in constr* **:** hominy in uniform granular particles

[1]**ho·mo** \ˈhō-(ˌ)mō\ *n, pl* **homos** [NL *Homin-, Homo,* genus name, fr. L, man] **:** any of a genus (*Homo*) of primate mammals that usu. includes a single recent species (*H. sapiens*) comprising all surviving and various extinct men

[2]**homo** *n, pl* **homos** [by shortening] **:** HOMOSEXUAL

homo- — see HOM-

ho·mo·cer·cal \ˌhō-mə-ˈsər-kəl, ˌhäm-ə-\ *adj* **1 :** having the upper and lower lobes approximately symmetrical and the vertebral column ending at or near the middle of the base — used of the tail fin of a fish **2 :** having or relating to a homocercal tail fin

ho·mo·chro·mat·ic \-krō-ˈmat-ik\ *adj* **:** of or relating to one color

ho·mo·erot·ic \ˌhō-mō-i-ˈrät-ik\ *adj* **:** HOMOSEXUAL — **ho·mo·erot·i·cism** \-ˈrät-ə-ˌsiz-əm\ *n*

ho·mo·ga·met·ic \ˌhō-mō-gə-ˈmet-ik, ˌhäm-ō-\ *adj* **:** forming one kind of germ cell; *esp* **:** forming all gametes with one type of sex chromosome

ho·mog·a·my \hō-ˈmäg-ə-mē\ *n* [G *homogamie,* fr. *hom-* + *-gamie* -gamy] **1 a :** a state of having flowers alike throughout **b :** the maturing of stamens and pistils at the same period **2 :** reproduction within an isolated group perpetuating qualities by which it is differentiated from the larger group of which it is a part; *broadly* **:** the mating of like with like — **ho·mog·a·mous** \-məs\ *or* **ho·mo·gam·ic** \ˌhō-mə-ˈgam-ik, ˌhäm-ə-\ *adj*

ho·mog·e·nate \hō-ˈmäj-ə-ˌnāt, hə-\ *n* **:** a product of homogenizing

ho·mo·ge·ne·ity \ˌhō-mə-jə-ˈnē-ət-ē, -ˈnā-ət-; *esp Brit* ˌhäm-ə-\ *n* **1 :** the quality or state of being homogeneous **2 :** the state of having identical distribution functions or values <a test for ~ of variances> <~ of two statistical populations>

ho·mo·ge·neous \-ˈjē-nē-əs, -nyəs\ *adj* [ML *homogeneus, homogenus,* fr. Gk *homogenēs,* fr. *hom-* + *genos* kind — more at KIN] **1 :** of the same or a similar kind or nature **2 :** of uniform structure or composition throughout <a culturally ~ neighborhood> **3 :** having the property that if each variable is replaced by a constant times that variable the constant can be factored out **:** having each term of the same degree if all variables are considered <$x^2 + xy + y^2 = 0$ is a ~ equation> **4 :** HOMOGENOUS 1 — **ho·mo·ge·neous·ly** *adv* — **ho·mo·ge·neous·ness** *n*

ho·mog·e·ni·za·tion \hō-ˌmäj-ə-nə-ˈzā-shən, hə-\ *n* **1 :** the quality or state of being homogenized **2 :** the act or process of homogenizing

ho·mog·e·nize \hō-ˈmäj-ə-ˌnīz, hə-\ *vb* **-nized; -niz·ing** *vt* **1 a :** to blend (diverse elements) into a smooth mixture **b :** to make homogeneous **2 a :** to reduce to small particles of uniform size and distribute evenly usu. in a liquid **b :** to reduce the particles of so that they are uniformly small and evenly distributed; *specif* **:** to break up the fat globules of (milk) into very fine particles esp. by forcing through minute openings ~ *vi* **:** to become homogenized — **ho·mog·e·niz·er** *n*

ho·mog·e·nous \-nəs\ *adj* **1 :** of, relating to, or exhibiting homogeny **2 :** HOMOPLASTIC 2 **3 :** HOMOGENEOUS

ho·mog·e·ny \-nē\ *n* **:** correspondence between parts or organs due to descent from the same ancestral type

ho·mo·graft \ˈhō-mə-ˌgraft, ˈhäm-ə-\ *n* **:** a graft of tissue taken from a donor of the same species as the recipient — compare HETEROGRAFT

ho·mo·graph \ˈhäm-ə-ˌgraf, ˈhō-mə-\ *n* **:** one of two or more words spelled alike but different in meaning or derivation or pronunciation <the noun *conduct* and the verb *conduct* are ~*s*> — **ho·mo·graph·ic** \ˌhäm-ə-ˈgraf-ik, ˌhō-mə-\ *adj*

homoi- *or* **homoio-** — see HOME-

ho·moio·therm \hō-ˈmȯi-ə-ˌthərm\ *n* **:** a homoiothermic organism

ho·moio·ther·mic \-ˌmȯi-ə-ˈthər-mik\ *or* **ho·moio·ther·mal** \-məl\ *adj* **:** WARM-BLOODED

ho·moi·ou·si·an \hō-ˈmȯi-ˌü-zē-ən, hä-, -ˈü-sē-\ *n* [LGk *homoiousios* of like substance, fr. Gk *homoi-* home- + *ousia* essence, substance, fr. *ont-, ōn,* prp. of *einai* to be — more at IS] **:** an adherent of an ecclesiastical party of the 4th century holding that the Son is essentially like the Father but not of the same substance

ho·mo·lec·i·thal \ˌhō-mō-ˈles-ə-thəl, ˌhäm-ō-\ *adj* [*hom-* + Gk *lekithos* yolk] **:** having the yolk small in amount and nearly uniformly distributed

ho·mol·o·gate \hō-ˈmäl-ə-ˌgāt, hə-\ *vt* **-gat·ed; -gat·ing** [ML *homologatus,* pp. of *homologare* to agree, fr. Gk *homologein,* fr. *homologos*] **:** SANCTION, ALLOW; *esp* **:** to approve or confirm officially — **ho·mol·o·ga·tion** \-ˌmäl-ə-ˈgā-shən\ *n*

ho·mo·log·i·cal \ˌhō-mə-ˈläj-i-kəl, ˌhäm-ə-\ *adj* **:** HOMOLOGOUS — **ho·mo·log·i·cal·ly** \-i-k(ə-)lē\ *adv*

ho·mol·o·gize \hō-ˈmäl-ə-ˌjīz, hə-\ *vt* **-gized; -giz·ing** **1 :** to make homologous **2 :** to demonstrate the homology of — **ho·mol·o·giz·er** *n*

ho·mol·o·gous \hō-ˈmäl-ə-gəs, hə-\ *adj* [Gk *homologos* agreeing, fr. *hom-* + *legein* to say — more at LEGEND] **1 a :** having the same relative position, value, or structure **b** (1) **:** exhibiting biological homology (2) **:** having the same or allelic genes with genetic loci usu. arranged in the same order <~ chromosomes> **c :** belonging to or consisting of a chemical series whose members exhibit homology **2 :** derived from or developed in response to organisms of the same species <~ tissue graft>

hom·o·lo·graph·ic \ˌhäm-ə-lə-ˈgraf-ik\ *adj* [F *homalographique,* fr. Gk *homalos* even, level (akin to Gk *homos* same) + *graphein* to write — more at SAME, CARVE] **:** preserving the mutual relations of parts esp. as to size and form <a ~ map projection>

ho·mo·logue *or* **ho·mo·log** \ˈhō-mə-ˌlȯg, ˈhäm-ə-, -ˌläg\ *n* **:** something (as a chemical compound or a chromosome) that exhibits homology

ho·mol·o·gy \hō-ˈmäl-ə-jē, hə-\ *n, pl* **-gies** **1 :** a similarity often attributable to common origin **2 a :** likeness in structure between parts of different organisms due to evolutionary differentiation from the same or a corresponding part of a remote ancestor — compare ANALOGY, HOMOMORPHY **b :** correspondence in structure between different parts of the same individual **3 a :** the relation existing between chemical compounds in a series whose successive members have in composition a regular difference esp. of one carbon and two hydrogen atoms CH_2 **b :** the relation existing among elements in the same group of the periodic table **4 :** a classification of configurations in topology into distinct types

ho·mo·lo·sine projection \hō-ˈmäl-ə-ˌsīn-\ *n* [irreg. fr. Gk *homalos*] **:** an equal-area map projection that combines the sinusoidal projection for latitudes up to 40° with the homolographic for areas poleward of these latitudes

ho·mol·y·sis \hō-ˈmäl-ə-səs\ *n* [NL] **:** decomposition of a chemical compound into two uncharged atoms or radicals — **ho·mo·lyt·ic** \ˌhō-mə-ˈlit-ik, ˌhäm-ə-\ *adj*

ho·mo·mor·phism \ˌhō-mə-ˈmȯr-ˌfiz-əm, ˌhäm-ə-\ *n* [ISV] **1 :** likeness in form: as **a :** HOMOMORPHY **b :** the condition of having perfect flowers of only one type **2 :** a mapping of a mathematical group, ring, or vector space onto another in such a way that the result obtained by applying an operation to elements of the domain is mapped onto the result obtained by applying the operation to their images in the range — **ho·mo·mor·phic** \-fik\ *adj*

ho·mo·mor·phy \ˈhō-mə-ˌmȯr-fē, ˈhäm-ə-\ *n* [ISV] **:** similarity of form with different fundamental structure; *specif* **:** superficial resemblance between organisms of different groups due to convergence — compare HOMOLOGY, HOMOPHYLY

ho·mo·nu·cle·ar \ˌhō-mə-ˈn(y)ü-klē-ər, ˌhäm-ə-\ *adj* **:** of or relating to a molecule (as hydrogen gas) composed of identical nuclei

hom·onym \ˈhäm-ə-ˌnim, ˈhō-mə-\ *n* [L *homonymum,* fr. Gk *homōnymon,* fr. neut. of *homōnymos*] **1 a :** HOMOPHONE **b :** HOMOGRAPH **c :** one of two or more words spelled and pronounced alike but different in meaning <the noun *quail* and the verb *quail* are ~*s*> **2 :** NAMESAKE **3 :** a taxonomic designation rejected because the identical term has been used to designate another group of the same rank — compare SYNONYM — **hom·onym·ic** \ˌhäm-ə-ˈnim-ik, ˌhō-mə-\ *adj*

hom·on·y·mous \hō-ˈmän-ə-məs\ *adj* [L *homonymus* having the same name, fr. Gk *homōnymos,* fr. *hom-* + *onyma, onoma* name — more at NAME] **1 :** AMBIGUOUS **2 :** having the same designation **3 :** of, relating to, or being homonyms **:** HOMONYMIC — **hom·on·y·mous·ly** *adv*

hom·on·y·my \-mē\ *n* **:** the quality or state of being homonymous

ho·mo·ou·si·an \hō-ˈmō-ˌü-zē-ən, hä-, -ˌü-sē-\ *n* [LGk *homoousios* of the same substance, fr. Gk *hom-* + *ousia* substance — more at HOMOIOUSIAN] **:** an adherent of an ecclesiastical party of the 4th century holding to the doctrine of the Nicene Creed that the Son is of the same substance with the Father

ho·mo·phile \ˈhō-mə-ˌfīl\ *adj* [*hom-* + [2]*-phil*] **:** GAY 4b

ho·mo·phone \ˈhäm-ə-ˌfōn, ˈhō-mə-\ *n* [ISV] **1 :** one of two or more words pronounced alike but different in meaning or derivation or spelling <the words *to, too,* and *two* are ~*s*> **2 :** a character or group of characters pronounced the same as another character or group — **ho·moph·o·nous** \hō-ˈmäf-ə-nəs\ *adj*

ho·mo·phon·ic \ˌhäm-ə-ˈfän-ik, ˌhō-mə-, -ˈfō-nik\ *adj* [Gk *homophōnos* being in unison, fr. *hom-* + *phōnē* sound — more at BAN] **:** of, relating to, or being music consisting of a single accompanied melodic line — **ho·moph·o·ny** \hō-ˈmäf-ə-nē\ *n*

ho·mo·phy·ly \ˈhō-mə-ˌfī-lē, ˈhäm-ə-; hō-ˈmäf-ə-lē\ *n* [ISV *hom-* + *phyl-* + *-y*] **:** resemblance due to common ancestry — compare HOMOMORPHY

ho·mo·plas·tic \ˌhō-mə-ˈplas-tik, ˌhäm-ə-\ *adj* **1 :** of or relating to homoplasy **2 :** of, relating to, or derived from another individual of the same species <~ grafts> — **ho·mo·plas·ti·cal·ly** \-ti-k(ə-)lē\ *adv*

ho·mo·pla·sy \ˈhō-mə-ˌplā-sē, ˈhäm-ə-, -ˌplas-ē; hō-ˈmäp-lə-sē\ *n* **:** correspondence between parts or organs acquired as the result of parallel evolution or convergence

ho·mo·po·lar \ˌhō-mə-ˈpō-lər, ˌhäm-ə-\ *adj* **:** of or relating to a union of atoms of like polarity **:** NONIONIC

ho·mo·pol·y·mer \-ˈpäl-ə-mər\ *n* **:** a polymer (as polyethylene) consisting of identical monomer units

ho·mop·ter·an \hō-ˈmäp-tə-rən\ *n* **:** a homopterous insect — **homopteran** *adj*

ho·mop·ter·ous \-rəs\ *adj* [deriv. of Gk *hom-* + *pteron* wing — more at FEATHER] **:** of or relating to a large order or suborder (Homoptera) of insects (as cicadas, aphids, and scale insects) that have sucking mouthparts

Ho·mo sa·pi·ens \ˌhō-(ˌ)mō-ˈsap-ē-ənz, -ˈsā-pē-, -ˌenz\ *n* [NL, species name, fr. *Homo,* genus name + *sapiens,* specific epithet, fr. L, wise, intelligent — more at HOMO, SAPIENT] **:** MANKIND 1

ho·mo·sce·das·tic \ˌhō-mō-si-'das-tik, ˌhäm-ō-\ *adj* [*hom-* + Gk *skedastikos* able to scatter, fr. *skedannynai* to scatter] : having equal statistical variances <~ distributions> — **ho·mo·sce·das·tic·i·ty** \-ˌdas-'tis-ət-ē\ *n*

¹**ho·mo·sex·u·al** \ˌhō-mə-'seksh-(ə-)wəl, -'sek-shəl\ *adj* : of, relating to, or exhibiting sexual desire toward a member of one's own sex — **ho·mo·sex·u·al·ly** \-ē\ *adv*

²**homosexual** *n* : one who is inclined toward or practices homosexuality

ho·mo·sex·u·al·i·ty \ˌhō-mə-ˌsek-shə-'wal-ət-ē\ *n* **1** : the manifestation of sexual desire toward a member of one's own sex **2** : erotic activity with a member of one's own sex

ho·mo·spo·rous \ˌhō-mə-'spōr-əs, ˌhäm-ə-, -'spȯr-; hō-'mäs-pə-rəs\ *adj* : producing asexual spores of one kind only

ho·mo·spo·ry \'hō-mə-ˌspōr-ē, 'häm-ə-ˌspȯr-; hō-'mäs-pə-rē\ *n* : the production by various plants (as the club mosses and horsetails) of asexual spores of only one kind

ho·mo·thal·lic \ˌhō-mō-'thal-ik\ *adj* [*hom-* + Gk *thallein* to sprout, grow — more at THALLUS] **1** : having only one haploid phase that produces two kinds of gametes capable of fusing to form a zygote **2** : MONOECIOUS — **ho·mo·thal·lism** \-'thal-ˌiz-əm\ *n*

ho·mo·trans·plant \ˌhō-mō-'tran(t)-ˌsplant, ˌhäm-ō-\ *n* : HOMOGRAFT — **ho·mo·trans·plan·ta·tion** \-ˌtran(t)-ˌsplan-'tā-shən\ *n*

ho·mo·zy·go·sis \ˌhō-mə-zī-'gō-səs, ˌhäm-ə-\ *n* [NL] **1** : the union of gametes identical for one or more pairs of genes **2** : the state of being a homozygote — **ho·mo·zy·got·ic** \-'gät-ik\ *adj*

ho·mo·zy·gos·i·ty \-'gäs-ət-ē\ *n* : HOMOZYGOSIS 2

ho·mo·zy·gote \-'zī-ˌgōt\ *n* [ISV] : a homozygous individual

ho·mo·zy·gous \-'zī-gəs\ *adj* : containing either but not both members of a pair of alleles — **ho·mo·zy·gous·ly** *adv*

ho·mun·cu·lus \hō-'məŋ-kyə-ləs\ *n, pl* **-li** \-ˌlī, -ˌlē\ [L, dim. of *homin-, homo* man — more at HOMAGE] : a little man : MANIKIN

homy *var of* HOMEY

hon *abbr* honor; honorable; honorary

Hon *or* **Hond** *abbr* Honduras

hon·cho \'hän-(ˌ)chō\ *n, pl* **honchos** [Jap *hanchō* squad leader, fr. *han* squad + *chō* head, chief] : BOSS <the ~ of an elite state police force —H. F. Waters>

¹**hone** \'hōn\ *n* [ME, fr. OE *hān* stone; akin to ON *hein* whetstone, L *cot-, cos,* Gk *kōnos* cone] **1** : a fine-grit stone for sharpening a cutting implement **2** : a tool for enlarging holes to precise tolerances and controlling finishes by means of a mechanically rotated abrasive

²**hone** *vt* **honed; hon·ing 1** : to sharpen, enlarge, or smooth with a hone **2** : to make more acute, intense, or effective : WHET <helped her ~ her comic timing to perfection —Patricia Bosworth> — **hon·er** *n*

³**hone** *vi* **honed; hon·ing** [MF *hoigner* to grumble] **1** *dial* : GRUMBLE, MOAN **2** *dial* : YEARN

hon·est \'än-əst\ *adj* [ME, fr. OF *honeste,* fr. L *honestus* honorable, fr. *honos, honor* honor] **1 a** : free from fraud or deception : LEGITIMATE, TRUTHFUL <an ~ plea> **b** : GENUINE, REAL <making ~ stops at stop signs —*Christian Science Monitor*> **c** : HUMBLE, PLAIN **2 a** : REPUTABLE, RESPECTABLE <~ decent people> **b** *chiefly Brit* : GOOD, WORTHY **3** : CREDITABLE, PRAISEWORTHY <an ~ day's work> **4 a** : marked by integrity **b** : FRANK, SINCERE <an ~ appraisal> **c** : INNOCENT, SIMPLE ***syn*** see UPRIGHT ***ant*** dishonest — **hon·est** *adv* — **hon·est·ly** *adv*

honest broker *n* : a neutral mediator <an *honest broker* between the two Democrats —*Christian Science Monitor*>

hon·es·ty \'än-ə-stē\ *n, pl* **-ties 1** *obs* : CHASTITY **2 a** : fairness and straightforwardness of conduct **b** : adherence to the facts : SINCERITY **3** : any of a genus (*Lunaria*) of European plants of the mustard family with cordate leaves and broad siliques

syn HONESTY, HONOR, INTEGRITY, PROBITY *shared meaning element* : uprightness of character or action ***ant*** dishonesty

¹**hon·ey** \'hən-ē\ *n, pl* **honeys** [ME *hony,* fr. OE *hunig;* akin to OHG *honag* honey, L *canicae* bran] **1 a** : a sweet viscid material elaborated out of the nectar of flowers in the honey sac of various bees **b** : a sweet fluid resembling honey that is collected or elaborated by various insects **2 a** : SWEETHEART, DEAR **b** : a superlative example <a ~ of a girl —Philip Roth> **3** : the quality or state of being sweet : SWEETNESS

²**honey** *vb* **hon·eyed** *also* **hon·ied** \'hən-ēd\; **hon·ey·ing** *vt* **1** : to sweeten with or as if with honey **2** : to speak ingratiatingly to : FLATTER ~ *vi* : to use blandishments or cajolery

³**honey** *adj* **1** : of, relating to, or resembling honey **2** : much loved : DEAR

hon·ey·bee \'hən-ē-ˌbē\ *n* : a social honey-producing bee (*Apis* or related genera); *esp* : a native European bee (*A. mellifera*) kept for its honey and wax

honeybees: *1* worker, *2* queen, *3* drone

¹**hon·ey·comb** \-ˌkōm\ *n* **1** : a mass of hexagonal wax cells built by honeybees in their nest to contain brood and stores of honey **2** : something that resembles a honeycomb in structure or appearance; *esp* : a strong lightweight cellular structural material

²**honeycomb** *vt* **1 a** : to cause to be full of cavities like a honeycomb **b** : to make into a checkered pattern : FRET **2 a** : to penetrate into every part : FILL **b** : SUBVERT, WEAKEN ~ *vi* : to become pitted, checked, or cellular

hon·ey·creep·er \'hən-ē-ˌkrē-pər\ *n* **1** : any of numerous small bright-colored oscine birds (family Coerebidae) of tropical and subtropical America **2** : any of a family (Drepanididae) of oscine birds that are found only in Hawaii

hon·ey·dew \-ˌd(y)ü\ *n* : a saccharine deposit secreted on the leaves of plants usu. by aphids or scales or sometimes by a fungus

honeydew melon *n* : a pale smooth-skinned muskmelon with greenish sweet flesh

honey eater *n* : any of several oscine birds (family Meliphagidae) mostly of the South Pacific with a long protrusible tongue adapted for extracting nectar and small insects from flowers

honey guide *n* : any of several small plainly colored nonpasserine birds (family Indicatoridae and esp. genera *Indicator* and *Prodotiscus*) that inhabit Africa, the Himalayas, and the East Indies and lead men or lower animals to the nests of bees

honey locust *n* : a tall usu. spiny No. American leguminous tree (*Gleditsia triacanthos*) with very hard durable wood and long twisted pods containing a sweet edible pulp and seeds that resemble beans

hon·ey·moon \'hən-ē-ˌmün\ *n* [fr. the idea that the first month of marriage is the sweetest] **1** : a trip or vacation taken by a newly married couple **2** : a period of harmony immediately following marriage **3** : a period of unusual harmony following the establishment of a new relationship <the ~ between the new President and Congress —Arthur Blaustein> — **honeymoon** *vi* — **hon·ey·moon·er** *n*

honey sac *n* : a distension of the esophagus of a bee in which honey is elaborated — called also *honey stomach*

hon·ey·suck·le \'hən-ē-ˌsək-əl\ *n* [ME *honysoukel,* alter. of *honysouke,* fr. OE *hunisūce,* fr. *hunig* honey + *sūcan* to suck] : any of a genus (*Lonicera* of the family Caprifoliaceae, the honeysuckle family) of shrubs with opposite leaves and often showy flowers rich in nectar; *broadly* : any of various plants (as a columbine or azalea) with tubular flowers rich in nectar

hong \'häŋ, 'hȯŋ\ *n* [Chin (Cant) *hōng*] : a commercial establishment or house of foreign trade in China

¹**honk** \'häŋk, 'hȯŋk\ *n* [imit.] : the characteristic cry of a goose; *also* : a similar sound

²**honk** *vi* **1** : to make the characteristic cry of a goose **2** : to make a sound resembling the cry of a goose ~ *vt* : to cause (as a horn) to honk — **honk·er** *n*

hon·kie *or* **hon·ky** *also* **hon·key** \'hȯŋ-kē, 'häŋ-\ *n, pl* **honkies** *also* **honkeys** [origin unknown] : a white man — usu. used disparagingly

¹**hon·ky–tonk** \'häŋ-kē-ˌtäŋk, 'hȯŋ-kē-ˌtȯŋk\ *n* [origin unknown] : a cheap nightclub or dance hall : DIVE

²**honky–tonk** *adj* : of, used in, or being a form of ragtime piano playing performed typically on an upright piano

¹**hon·or** \'än-ər\ *n* [ME, fr. OF *honor,* fr. L *honos, honor*] **1 a** : good name or public esteem : REPUTATION **b** : a showing of usu. merited respect : RECOGNITION <a man worthy of all possible ~> **2** : PRIVILEGE **3** : a person of superior standing — now used esp. as a title for a holder of high office <if Your *Honor* please> **4** : one whose worth brings respect or fame : CREDIT <was an ~ to his profession> **5** : the center point of the upper half of an armorial escutcheon **6** : an evidence or symbol of distinction: as **a** : an exalted title or rank **b (1)** : BADGE, DECORATION **(2)** : a ceremonial rite or observance <buried with full military ~*s*> **c** *archaic* : a gesture of deference : BOW **d** *pl* **(1)** : an academic distinction conferred on a superior student **(2)** : a course of study for superior students supplementing or replacing a regular course **e** : an award in a contest or field of competition **7** : CHASTITY, PURITY <fought fiercely for her ~ and her life —Barton Black> **8 a** : a keen sense of ethical conduct : INTEGRITY **b** : one's word given as a guarantee of performance **9** *pl* : social courtesies or civilities extended by a host <did the ~*s* at the table> **10 a (1)** : an ace, king, queen, jack, or ten esp. of the trump suit in bridge **(2)** : the scoring value of honors held in bridge — usu. used in pl. **b** : the privilege of playing first from the tee in golf

syn **1** HONOR, HOMAGE, DEFERENCE, REVERENCE *shared meaning element* : respect and esteem shown to another
2 see HONESTY

²**honor** *vt* **hon·ored; hon·or·ing** \-(ə-)riŋ\ **1 a** : to regard or treat with honor or respect **b** : to confer honor on **2 a** : to live up to or fulfill the terms of <~ a commitment> **b** : to accept and pay when due <~ a draft> **3** : to salute with a bow in square dancing — **hon·or·er** \'än-ər-ər\ *n*

¹**hon·or·able** \'än-(ə-)rə-bəl, 'än-ər-bəl\ *adj* **1** : deserving of honor **2** : performed or accompanied with marks of honor or respect **3 a** : of great renown : ILLUSTRIOUS **b** : entitled to honor — used as a title for the children of certain British noblemen and for various government officials **4 a** : attesting to creditable conduct **b** : consistent with an untarnished reputation <an ~ withdrawal> **5** : characterized by integrity : guided by a high sense of honor and duty ***syn*** see UPRIGHT ***ant*** dishonorable — **hon·or·abil·i·ty** \ˌän-(ə-)rə-'bil-ət-ē\ *n* — **hon·or·able·ness** \'än-(ə-)rə-bəl-nəs, 'än-ər-bəl-\ *n* — **hon·or·ably** \-blē\ *adv*

²**honorable** *n* **1** : any of various members of British noble families **2** : any of various officials to whom the title of Honorable is applied

honorable mention *n* : a distinction conferred (as in a contest or exhibition) on works or persons of exceptional merit but not deserving of top honors

hon·o·rar·i·um \ˌän-ə-'rer-ē-əm\ *n, pl* **-ia** \-ē-ə\ *also* **-i·ums** [L, fr. neut. of *honorarius*] : a payment usu. for services on which custom or propriety forbids a price to be set <*honoraria* for the members of the committee —I. M. Price>

hon·or·ary \'än-ə-ˌrer-ē\ *adj* [L *honorarius,* fr. *honor*] **1 a** : having or conferring distinction **b** : COMMEMORATIVE **2 a** : conferred or elected in recognition of achievement or service without the usual prerequisites or obligations <an ~ degree> <an ~ member> **b** : UNPAID, VOLUNTARY <an ~ chairman> **3** : dependent on honor for fulfillment — **hon·or·ar·i·ly** \ˌän-ə-ˈrer-ə-lē\ *adv*

²**honorary** *n, pl* **-ar·ies** **1** *archaic* **:** HONORARIUM **2 :** an honorary society **3 :** an honorary degree or its recipient

hon·or·ee \ˌän-ə-ˈrē\ *n* **:** one who receives an honor

honor guard *n* **:** a guard assigned to greet or accompany a distinguished person or to accompany a casket at a military funeral — called also *guard of honor*

¹**hon·or·if·ic** \ˌän-ə-ˈrif-ik\ *adj* **1 :** conferring or conveying honor <~ titles> **2 :** belonging to or constituting a class of grammatical forms used in speaking to or about a social superior — **hon·or·if·i·cal·ly** \-i-k(ə-)lē\ *adv*

²**honorific** *n* **:** an honorific word, phrase, or form

honor roll *n* **:** a roster of names of persons deserving honor: as **a :** a list of students achieving academic distinction **b :** a publicly displayed list of the names of local citizens who have served in the armed forces

honor society *n* **:** a society for the recognition of scholarly achievement esp. of undergraduates

honor system *n* **:** a system (as at a college or prison) whereby persons are trusted to abide by the regulations without supervision or surveillance; *specif* **:** a system of conducting examinations without faculty supervision

hon·our \ˈän-ər\, **hon·our·able** *chiefly Brit var of* HONOR, HONORABLE

¹**hooch** \ˈhüch\ *n* [short for *hoochinoo* (a distilled liquor made by the Hoochinoo Indians, a Tlingit people)] *slang* **:** alcoholic liquor esp. when inferior or illicitly made or obtained

²**hooch** *or* **hootch** \ˈhüch\ *n* [modif. of Jap *uchi* house] *slang* **:** a usu. thatched hut; *broadly* **:** DWELLING <was awakened in his ~ at an air base . . . by a fellow pilot —M. D. Perry>

¹**hood** \ˈhu̇d\ *n* [ME, fr. OE *hōd;* akin to OHG *huot* head covering] **1 a** (1) **:** a flexible covering for the head and neck (2) **:** a protective covering for the head and face **b :** a covering for a hawk's head and eyes **c :** a covering for a horse's head; *also* **:** BLINDER **2 a :** an ornamental scarf worn over an academic gown that indicates by its color the wearer's college or university **b :** a color marking or crest on the head of an animal or an expansion of the head that suggests a hood **3 a :** something resembling a hood in form or use **b :** a cover for parts of mechanisms; *specif* **:** the movable metal covering over the engine of an automobile **c :** a top cover for the body of a vehicle designed to be folded back **d :** an enclosure or canopy provided with a draft for carrying off disagreeable or noxious fumes, sprays, smokes, or dusts **e :** a covering for an opening (as a companion hatch) on a boat — **hood** *vt* — **hood·like** \-ˌlīk\ *adj*

²**hood** \ˈhu̇d, ˈhüd\ *n* **:** HOODLUM

-hood \ˌhu̇d\ *n suffix* [ME *-hod,* fr. OE *-hād;* akin to OHG *-heit* state, condition, *heitar* bright, clear] **1 :** state **:** condition **:** quality **:** character <boy*hood*> <hardi*hood*> **2 :** time **:** period <child*hood*> <widow*hood*> **3 :** instance of a (specified) state or quality <false*hood*> **4 :** individuals sharing a (specified) state or character <brother*hood*>

hood·ed \ˈhu̇d-əd\ *adj* **1 :** having a hood **2 :** shaped like a hood <~ spathes> **3 a :** having the head conspicuously different in color from the rest of the body <~ bird> **b :** having a crest on the head that suggests a hood <~ seals> **c :** having the skin at each side of the neck capable of expansion by movements of the ribs <~ cobra> — **hood·ed·ness** *n*

hood·lum \ˈhüd-ləm, ˈhu̇d-\ *n* [origin unknown] **1 :** THUG; *esp* **:** one who commits acts of violence **2 :** a young ruffian — **hood·lum·ish** \-lə-mish\ *adj* — **hood·lum·ism** \-ˌmiz-əm\ *n*

hood·man-blind \ˌhu̇d-mən-ˈblīnd\ *n, archaic* **:** BLINDMAN'S BUFF

¹**hoo·doo** \ˈhüd-(ˌ)ü\ *n, pl* **hoodoos** [of African origin; akin to Hausa *hu³' du³' ba'* to arouse resentment] **1 :** VOODOO **2 :** something that brings bad luck **3 :** a natural column of rock in western No. America often in fantastic form — **hoo·doo·ism** \-ˌiz-əm\ *n*

²**hoodoo** *vt* **:** to cast a spell on; *broadly* **:** to be a source of misfortune to

hood·wink \ˈhu̇d-ˌwiŋk\ *vt* [¹*hood* + *wink*] **1** *archaic* **:** BLINDFOLD **2** *obs* **:** HIDE **3 :** to deceive by false appearance **:** impose upon — **hood·wink·er** *n*

hoo·ey \ˈhü-ē\ *n* [origin unknown] **:** NONSENSE

¹**hoof** \ˈhu̇f, ˈhüf\ *n, pl* **hooves** \ˈhu̇vz, ˈhüvz\ *or* **hoofs** [ME, fr. OE *hōf;* akin to OHG *huof* hoof, Skt *śapha*] **1 :** a curved covering of horn that protects the front of or encloses the ends of the digits of an ungulate mammal and that corresponds to a nail or claw **2 :** a hoofed foot esp. of a horse — **on the hoof** *of a meat animal* **:** before butchering **:** LIVING <10¢ a pound *on the hoof*>

hoof of a horse, unshod; *1, 2, 3, 4,* parts of wall (*1* toe, *2* side walls, *3* quarters, *4* buttresses) *5* bulbs, *6* sole, *7* white line, *8* frog, *9* bars

²**hoof** *vt* **1 :** WALK **2 :** KICK, TRAMPLE ~ *vi* **:** to move on the feet; *esp* **:** DANCE

hoof-and-mouth disease *n* **:** FOOT-AND-MOUTH DISEASE

hoof·beat \ˈhu̇f-ˌbēt, ˈhüf-\ *n* **:** the sound of a hoof striking a hard surface (as the ground)

hoofed \ˈhu̇ft, ˈhüft, ˈhu̇vd, ˈhüvd\ *adj* **:** furnished with hoofs **:** UNGULATE

hoof·er \ˈhu̇f-ər, ˈhü-fər\ *n* **:** a professional dancer

hoof·print \ˈhu̇f-ˌprint, ˈhüf-\ *n* **:** an impression or hollow made by a hoof

¹**hook** \ˈhu̇k\ *n* [ME, fr. OE *hōc;* akin to MD *hoec* fishhook, corner, Lith *kenge* hook] **1 :** a curved or bent device for catching, holding, or pulling **2 :** something curved or bent like a hook **3 :** a flight of a ball that deviates from a straight course in a direction opposite to the dominant hand of the player propelling it; *also* **:** a ball following such a course — compare SLICE **4 :** a short

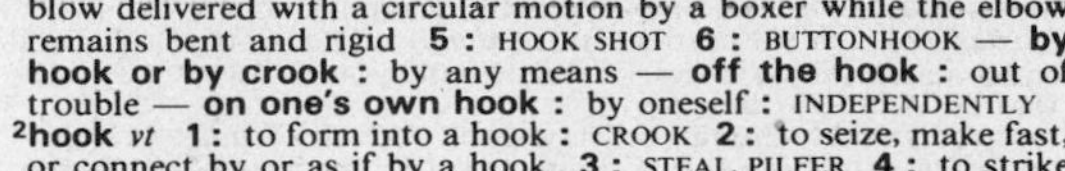

blow delivered with a circular motion by a boxer while the elbow remains bent and rigid **5 :** HOOK SHOT **6 :** BUTTONHOOK — **by hook or by crook :** by any means — **off the hook :** out of trouble — **on one's own hook :** by oneself **:** INDEPENDENTLY

²**hook** *vt* **1 :** to form into a hook **:** CROOK **2 :** to seize, make fast, or connect by or as if by a hook **3 :** STEAL, PILFER **4 :** to strike or pierce as if with a hook **5 :** to make (as a rug) by drawing loops of yarn, thread, or cloth through a coarse fabric with a hook **6 :** to hit or throw (a ball) so that a hook results ~ *vi* **1 :** to form a hook **:** CURVE **2 :** to become hooked

hoo·kah \ˈhu̇k-ə, ˈhü-kə\ *n* [Ar *ḥuqqah* bottle of a water pipe] **:** WATER PIPE

hook and eye *n* **:** a 2-part fastening device (as on a garment or a door) consisting of a metal hook that catches over a bar or into a loop

hook and ladder truck *n* **:** a piece of mobile fire apparatus carrying ladders and usu. other fire-fighting and rescue equipment — called also *hook and ladder, ladder truck*

hook-bill \ˈhu̇k-ˌbil\ *n* **:** PARROT; *also* **:** a closely related bird

hook check *n* **:** an act or instance of attempting to knock the puck away from an opponent in ice hockey by hooking it with the stick

hooked \ˈhu̇kt, *1 is also* ˈhu̇k-əd\ *adj* **1 :** having the form of a hook **2 :** provided with a hook **3 :** made by hooking <a ~ rug> **4 a :** addicted to narcotics **b :** fascinated by or devoted to something <~ on skiing> — **hooked·ness** \ˈhu̇k(t)-nəs, ˈhu̇k-əd-nəs\ *n*

¹**hook·er** \ˈhu̇k-ər\ *n* **1 :** one that hooks **2 :** PROSTITUTE

²**hooker** *n* [D *hoeker,* alter. of MD *hoecboot,* fr. *hoec* fishhook + *boot* boat] **1 :** a one-masted fishing boat used on the English and Irish coasts **2 :** an old, outmoded, or clumsy boat

hook·let \ˈhu̇k-lət\ *n* **:** a small hook

hook shot *n* **:** a shot in basketball made usu. while standing sideways to the basket by swinging the ball up through an arc with the far hand

hook·up \ˈhu̇k-ˌəp\ *n* **1 :** an assemblage (as of circuits) used for a specific purpose (as radio transmission); *also* **:** the plan of such an assemblage **2 :** an arrangement of mechanical parts; *also* **:** CONNECTION <a campsite with electric, water, and sewer ~*s*> **3 :** a state of cooperation or alliance often between antagonistic elements

hook·worm \ˈhu̇k-ˌwərm\ *n* **1 :** a parasitic nematode worm (family Ancylostomatidae) having strong buccal hooks or plates for attaching to the host's intestinal lining and including serious bloodsucking pests **2 :** ANCYLOSTOMIASIS

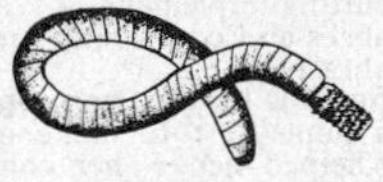

hookworm 1

hooky *or* **hook·ey** \ˈhu̇k-ē\ *n, pl* **hookies** *or* **hookeys** [prob. fr. slang *hook, hook it* (to make off)] **:** TRUANT — used chiefly in the phrase *play hooky*

hoo·li·gan \ˈhü-li-gən\ *n* [perh. fr. Patrick *Hooligan fl* 1898 Irish hoodlum in Southwark, London] **:** RUFFIAN, HOODLUM — **hoo·li·gan·ism** \-gə-ˌniz-əm\ *n*

¹**hoop** \ˈhüp, ˈhu̇p\ *n* [ME, fr. OE *hōp;* akin to MD *hoep* ring, hoop, Lith *kabe* hook] **1 :** a circular strip used esp. for holding together the staves of containers or as a plaything **2 a :** a circular figure or object **:** RING **b :** the rim of a basketball goal; *broadly* **:** the entire goal **3 :** a circle or series of circles of flexible material used to expand a woman's skirt — **hoop** *adj*

²**hoop** *vt* **:** to bind or fasten with or as if with a hoop — **hoop·er** *n*

hoop·la \ˈhü-ˌplä, ˈhu̇p-ˌlä\ *n* [F *houp-là,* interj.] **1 :** often gay and excited commotion **:** TO-DO **2 :** utterances designed to bewilder

hoo·poe \ˈhü-(ˌ)pü, -(ˌ)pō\ *n* [alter. of obs. *hoop,* fr. MF *huppe,* fr. L *upupa,* of imit. origin] **:** any of several Old World nonpasserine birds (family Upupidae) having a slender decurved bill

hoop·skirt \ˈhu̇p-ˈskərt, ˈhüp-\ *n* **:** a skirt stiffened with or as if with hoops

hoo·ray \hu̇-ˈrā\ *var of* HURRAH

hoose·gow \ˈhüs-ˌgau̇\ *n* [Sp *juzgado* panel of judges, courtroom, fr. pp. of *juzgar* to judge, fr. L *judicare*] *slang* **:** JAIL

Hoo·sier \ˈhü-zhər\ *n* [perh. alter. of E dial. *hoozer* anything large of its kind] **:** a native or resident of Indiana — used as a nickname — **Hoosier** *adj*

¹**hoot** \ˈhüt\ *vb* [ME *houten,* of imit. origin] *vi* **1 :** to utter a loud shout usu. in contempt **2 :** to make the natural throat noise of an owl or a similar cry **3 :** to make a loud clamorous mechanical sound ~ *vt* **1 :** to assail or drive out by hooting <~*ed* down the speaker> **2 :** to express in or by hoots <~*ed* their disapproval> — **hoot·er** *n*

²**hoot** *n* **1 :** a sound of hooting; *esp* **:** the cry of an owl **2 :** a minimum amount or degree (as of care or consideration) **:** the least bit <don't give a ~ what happens>

³**hoot** \ˈhüt\ *or* **hoots** \ˈhüts\ *interj* [origin unknown] *chiefly Scot* — used to express impatience, dissatisfaction, or objection

hoo·te·nan·ny \ˈhüt-ᵊn-ˌan-ē\ *n, pl* **-nies** [origin unknown] **1** *chiefly dial* **:** GADGET **2 :** a gathering at which folk singers entertain often with the audience joining in

¹**hop** \ˈhäp\ *vb* **hopped; hop·ping** [ME *hoppen,* fr. OE *hoppian;* akin to OE *hype* hip] *vi* **1 :** to move by a quick springy leap or in a series of leaps; *esp* **:** to jump on one foot **2 :** to make a quick trip esp. by air ~ *vt* **1 :** to jump over <~ a fence> **2 :** to ride on esp. surreptitiously and without authorization <~ a freight>

²**hop** *n* **1 a :** a short brisk leap esp. on one leg **b :** BOUNCE, REBOUND <shortstop took it on the first ~> **2 :** DANCE, BALL **3 a :** a flight in an aircraft **b :** a short trip **c :** a free ride

³**hop** *n* [ME *hoppe,* fr. MD; akin to OHG *hopfo* hop, OE *scēaf* sheaf — more at SHEAF] **1 :** a twining vine (*Humulus lupulus*) of the mulberry family with 3-lobed or 5-lobed leaves and inconspicuous flowers of which the pistillate ones are in glandular cone-shaped catkins **2** *pl* **:** the ripe dried pistillate catkins of a hop used esp. to impart a bitter flavor to malt liquors **3** *slang* **:** a narcotic drug; *esp* **:** OPIUM

[4]**hop** *vt* **hopped; hop·ping** **1 :** to impregnate with hops **2 a :** to drug or stimulate with drugs : DOPE — usu. used with *up* **b :** EXCITE, ROUSE — used with *up* **3 :** to increase the power of beyond an original rating — used with *up* <~ up an engine>
HOP *abbr* high oxygen pressure
[1]**hope** \ˈhōp\ *vb* **hoped; hop·ing** [ME *hopen,* fr. OE *hopian;* akin to MHG *hoffen* to hope] *vi* **1 :** to cherish a desire with expectation of fulfillment <~*s* for great things from his son> **2** *archaic* **:** TRUST ~ *vt* **1 :** to long for with expectation of obtainment **2 :** to expect with desire : TRUST ***syn*** see EXPECT ***ant*** despair (*of*), despond — **hop·er** *n* — **hope against hope :** to hope without any basis for expecting fulfillment
[2]**hope** *n* **1 :** TRUST, RELIANCE **2 a :** desire accompanied by expectation of or belief in fulfillment <are in ~*s* of an early recovery> **b :** someone or something on which hopes are centered <a fast halfback was the team's only ~ for victory> **c :** something hoped for
HOPE *abbr* Health Opportunity for People Everywhere
hope chest *n* **:** a young woman's accumulation of clothes and domestic furnishings (as silver and linen) kept in anticipation of her marriage; *also* **:** a chest for such an accumulation
[1]**hope·ful** \ˈhōp-fəl\ *adj* **1 :** full of or inclined to hope **2 :** having qualities which inspire hope — **hope·ful·ness** *n*
[2]**hopeful** *n* **:** a person who aspires to become or achieve something <political ~*s*>
hope·ful·ly \ˈhōp-fə-lē\ *adv* **1 :** in a hopeful manner **2 :** it is hoped <~ better coordinated and more effective programs may result —N. M. Pusey>
hope·less \ˈhō-pləs\ *adj* **1 a :** having no expectation of good or success : DESPAIRING **b :** not susceptible to remedy or cure : INCURABLE **2 a :** giving no ground for hope : DESPERATE **b :** incapable of solution, management, or accomplishment : IMPOSSIBLE ***syn*** see DESPONDENT ***ant*** hopeful — **hope·less·ly** *adv* — **hope·less·ness** *n*
hop·head \ˈhäp-ˌhed\ *n, slang* **:** a drug addict
hop hornbeam *n* **:** an American tree (*Ostrya virginiana*) with fruiting clusters resembling hops
Ho·pi \ˈhō-(ˌ)pē\ *n, pl* **Hopi** *also* **Hopis** [Hopi *Hópi,* lit., good, peaceful] **1 a :** an Amerindian people of northeastern Arizona **b :** a member of this people **2 :** the language of the Hopi people
hop·lite \ˈhäp-ˌlīt\ *n* [Gk *hoplitēs,* fr. *hoplon* tool, weapon, fr. *hepein* to care for, work at — more at SEPULCHER] **:** a heavily armed infantry soldier of ancient Greece
hop–o'–my–thumb \ˌhäp-ə-mə-ˈthəm\ *n* **:** a very small person
hop·per \ˈhäp-ər\ *n* **1 a :** one that hops **b :** a leaping insect; *specif* **:** an immature hopping form of an insect **2** [fr. the shaking motion of hoppers used to feed grain into a mill] **a :** a usu. funnel-shaped receptacle for delivering material (as grain or coal); *also* **:** any of various other receptacles for the temporary storage of material **b :** a freight car with a floor sloping to one or more hinged doors for discharging bulk materials — called also *hopper car* **c :** a box in which a bill to be considered by a legislative body is dropped **d :** a tank holding liquid and having a device for releasing its contents through a pipe
[1]**hop·ping** \ˈhäp-iŋ\ *adj* **1 :** journeying or flitting about from place to place — usu. used in combination <thus began a frenetic show-*hopping* existence — *N. Y. Times*> **2 :** intensely active **:** BUSY <they kept him ~> **3 :** extremely angry
[2]**hopping** *adv* **:** EXTREMELY, VIOLENTLY — used in the phrase *hopping mad*
hop·scotch \ˈhäp-ˌskäch\ *n* **:** a child's game in which a player tosses an object (as a stone) into areas of a figure outlined on the ground and hops through the figure and back to regain the object
hop, skip, and jump *n* **:** a short distance <only a *hop, skip, and jump* from home to work>
hop, step, and jump *n* **:** TRIPLE JUMP
hor *abbr* horizontal
ho·ra *also* **ho·rah** \ˈhȯr-ə, ˈhȯr-ə\ *n* [NHeb *hōrāh,* fr. Rum *horă*] **:** a circle dance of Rumania and Israel
Ho·rae \ˈhō(ə)r-ˌē, ˈhȯ(ə)r-, -ˌī\ *n pl* [L, fr. Gk *Hōrai*] **:** the Greek goddesses of the seasons
ho·ra·ry \ˈhȯr-ər-ē, ˈhȯr-, ˈhär-\ *adj* [ML *horarius,* fr. L *hora* hour — more at HOUR] **:** of or relating to an hour; *also* **:** HOURLY
Ho·ra·tian \hə-ˈrā-shən\ *adj* [L *Horatianus,* fr. *Horatius* Horace] **:** of, relating to, or characteristic of Horace or his poetry
Ho·ra·tio Al·ger \hə-ˌrā-shō-ˈal-jər\ *adj* **:** of, relating to, or resembling the fiction of Horatio Alger in which success is achieved through self-reliance and hard work
Ho·ra·tius \hə-ˈrā-sh(ē-)əs\ *n* [L] **:** a hero in Roman legend noted for his defense of a bridge over the Tiber against the Etruscans
horde \ˈhō(ə)rd, ˈhȯ(ə)rd\ *n* [MF, G & Pol; MF & G, fr. Pol *horda,* of Mongolic origin; akin to Mongolian *orda* camp, horde] **1 a :** a tribal group of Mongolian nomads **b :** a people or tribe of nomadic life **2 :** a loosely organized or disordered crowd or throng : SWARM <a ~ of flies buzzing about the table> ***syn*** see CROWD
hore·hound \ˈhō(ə)r-ˌhau̇nd, ˈhȯ(ə)r-\ *n* [ME *horhoune,* fr. OE *hārhūne,* fr. *hār* hoary + *hūne* horehound — more at HOAR] **1 a :** a bitter mint (*Marrubium vulgare*) with hoary downy leaves **b :** an extract or confection made from this plant **2 :** any of several mints resembling the horehound
ho·ri·zon \hə-ˈrīz-ᵊn\ *n* [ME *orizon,* fr. LL *horizont-, horizon,* fr. Gk *horizont-, horizōn,* fr. prp. of *horizein* to bound, define, fr. *horos* boundary; akin to L *urvus* circumference of a city] **1 a :** the apparent junction of earth and sky — called also *apparent horizon, visible horizon* **b (1) :** the plane tangent to the earth's surface at an observer's position — called also *sensible horizon* **(2) :** the plane parallel to the sensible horizon but passing through the earth's center; *also* **:** the great circle formed by the intersection of this plane with the celestial sphere — called also *celestial horizon, rational horizon* **c :** a level mirror (as the surface of mercury in a shallow vessel or a plane reflector adjusted to the true level artificially) used esp. in observing altitudes **d :** range of perception or experience **2 a :** the geological deposit of a particular time usu. identified by distinctive fossils **b :** any of the reasonably distinct layers of soil or its underlying material in a vertical section of land **c :** a cultural area or level of development indicated by separated groups of artifacts — **ho·ri·zon·al** \-ˈrīz-nəl, -ᵊn-əl\ *adj*
hor·i·zon·tal \ˌhȯr-ə-ˈzänt-ᵊl, ˌhär-\ *adj* **1 a :** of, relating to, or situated near the horizon **b :** parallel to, in the plane of, or operating in a plane parallel to the horizon or to a base line : LEVEL <~ distance> <~ engine> **2 :** relating to or consisting of individuals of similar status in a hierarchy <~ labor unions> — **horizontal** *n* — **hor·i·zon·tal·ly** \-ᵊl-ē\ *adv*
horizontal bar *n* **1 :** a steel bar supported in a horizontal position approximately eight feet above the floor and used for swinging feats in gymnastics **2 :** an event in gymnastics competition in which the horizontal bar is used
hor·mo·go·ni·um \ˌhȯr-mə-ˈgō-nē-əm\ *n, pl* **-nia** \-nē-ə\ [NL, fr. Gk *hormos* chain, necklace + NL *gonium* — more at SERIES] **:** a portion of a filament in many blue-green algae that becomes detached as a reproductive body
hor·mon·al \hȯr-ˈmōn-ᵊl\ *adj* **:** of, relating to, or effected by hormones — **hor·mon·al·ly** \-ᵊl-ē\ *adv*
hor·mone \ˈhȯr-ˌmōn\ *n* [Gk *hormōn,* prp. of *horman* to stir up, fr. *hormē* impulse, assault — more at SERUM] **1 :** a product of living cells that circulates in body fluids or sap and produces a specific effect on the activity of cells remote from its point of origin; *esp* **:** one exerting a stimulatory effect on a cellular activity **2 :** a synthetic substance that acts like a hormone — **hor·mone·like** \-ˌlīk\ *adj*
horn \ˈhȯ(ə)rn\ *n* [ME, fr. OE; akin to OHG *horn,* L *cornu,* Gk *keras*] **1 a :** one of the usu. paired bony processes that arise from the head of many ungulates and that are found in some extinct mammals and reptiles: as **(1) :** one of the permanent paired hollow sheaths of keratin usu. present in both sexes of cattle and their relatives that function chiefly for defense and arise from a bony core anchored to the skull — see COW illustration **(2) :** ANTLER **(3) :** a permanent solid horn of keratin that is attached to the nasal bone of a rhinoceros **(4) :** one of a pair of permanent bone protuberances from the skull of a giraffe or okapi that are covered with hairy skin **b :** a part like an animal's horn attributed esp. to the devil **c :** a natural projection or excrescence from an animal resembling or suggestive of a horn **d (1) :** the tough fibrous material consisting chiefly of keratin that covers or forms the horns of cattle and related animals, hooves, or other horny parts (as claws or nails) **(2) :** a manufactured product (as a plastic) resembling horn **e :** a hollow horn used to hold something **2 :** something resembling or suggestive of a horn: as **a :** one of the curved ends of a crescent **b :** a sharp mountain peak **c :** a body of land or water shaped like a horn **d :** a beak-shaped part of an anvil **e :** a high pommel of a saddle **3 a :** an animal's horn used as a wind instrument **b (1) :** HUNTING HORN **(2) :** FRENCH HORN **c :** a wind instrument used in a jazz band; *esp* **:** TRUMPET **d :** a usu. electrical device that makes a noise like that of a horn **4 :** a source of strength — **horn** *adj* — **horn·less** \-ləs\ *adj* — **horn·less·ness** *n* — **horn·like** \-ˌlīk\ *adj*
horn·beam \ˈhȯ(ə)rn-ˌbēm\ *n* **:** any of a genus (*Carpinus*) of trees of the birch family having smooth gray bark and hard white wood
horn·bill \-ˌbil\ *n* **:** any of a family (Bucerotidae) of large nonpasserine Old World birds having enormous bills

hornbill

horn·blende \-ˌblend\ *n* [G] **:** a mineral approximately $Ca_2Na(Mg,Fe)_4(Al,Fe,Ti)_3Si_6O_{22}(O,OH)_2$ that is the common dark variety of aluminous amphibole; *broadly* **:** AMPHIBOLE — **horn·blend·ic** \hȯrn-ˈblen-dik\ *adj*
horn·book \ˈhȯ(ə)rn-ˌbu̇k\ *n* **1 :** a child's primer consisting of a sheet of parchment or paper protected by a sheet of transparent horn **2 :** a rudimentary treatise
horned \ˈhȯ(ə)rnd\ *adj* **:** having a horn — often used in combination — **horned·ness** \ˈhȯr-nəd-nəs, ˈhȯ(ə)rn(d)-nəs\ *n*
horned owl *n* **:** any of various owls having conspicuous tufts of feathers on the head
horned pout *n* **:** a bullhead (genus *Ameiurus*); *esp* **:** a common bullhead (*A. nebulosus*) of the eastern U.S. that has been introduced into streams of the Pacific coast
horned toad *n* **:** any of several small harmless insectivorous lizards (genus *Phrynosoma*) of the western U.S. and Mexico having hornlike spines
horned viper *n* **:** CERASTES
hor·net \ˈhȯr-nət\ *n* [ME *hernet,* fr. OE *hyrnet;* akin to OHG *hornaz* hornet, L *crabro*] **:** any of the larger social wasps (family Vespidae) — compare YELLOW JACKET
hornet's nest *n* **1 :** a troublesome or hazardous situation **2 :** an angry reaction <must have known that his frank comments . . . would stir up a *hornet's nest* —*U.S. Investor*>
horn·fels \ˈhȯ(ə)rn-ˌfelz\ *n* [G, fr. *horn* horn + *fels* cliff, rock] **:** a fine-grained silicate rock produced by metamorphism esp. of slate
horn fly *n* **:** a small black European fly (*Haematobia irritans*) that has been introduced into No. America where it is a blood-sucking pest of cattle
horn in *vi* **:** to participate without invitation or consent : INTRUDE
horn–mad \ˈhȯ(ə)rn-ˈmad\ *adj* **:** furiously enraged

horn of plenty : CORNUCOPIA
horn·pipe \'hȯ(ə)rn-,pīp\ *n* **1** : a single-reed wind instrument consisting of a wooden or bone pipe with finger holes, a bell, and mouthpiece usu. of horn **2** : a lively folk dance of the British Isles orig. accompanied by hornpipe playing
horn-rims \-,rimz\ *n pl* : glasses with horn rims
horn·stone \'hȯ(ə)rn-,stōn\ *n* : a mineral that is a variety of quartz much like flint but more brittle
horn·swog·gle \-,swäg-əl\ *vt* **horn·swog·gled; horn·swog·gling** \-(ə-)liŋ\ [origin unknown] *slang* : BAMBOOZLE, HOAX
horn·tail \-,tāl\ *n* : any of various hymenopterous insects (family Siricidae) related to the typical sawflies but having larvae that burrow in woody plants and on the females a stout hornlike ovipositor for depositing the egg
horn·worm \-,wərm\ *n* : a hawkmoth caterpillar having a hornlike tail process
horn·wort \-,wərt, -,wȯ(ə)rt\ *n* : any of a genus (*Ceratophyllum*) of rootless thin-stemmed aquatic herbs that have flowers with a sepaloid perianth and a single carpel
horny \'hȯr-nē\ *adj* **horn·i·er; -est** **1 a** : of or made of horn **b** : HARD, CALLOUS <*horny*-handed> **c** : compact and homogeneous with a dull luster — used of a mineral **2** : having horns **3** [*horn* (erect penis) + *-y*] : excited sexually : LASCIVIOUS — sometimes considered vulgar
horol *abbr* horology
hor·o·loge \'hȯr-ə-,lōj, 'här-\ *n* [ME, fr. MF, fr. L *horologium*, fr. Gk *hōrologion*, fr. *hōra* hour + *legein* to gather — more at YEAR, LEGEND] : a timekeeping device
ho·rol·o·ger \hə-'räl-ə-jər\ *n* : HOROLOGIST
hor·o·log·ic \,hȯr-ə-'läj-ik, ,här-\ *also* **hor·o·log·i·cal** \-i-kəl\ *adj* : of or relating to a horologe or horology
ho·rol·o·gist \hə-'räl-ə-jəst\ *n* **1** : a person skilled in the practice or theory of horology **2** : a maker of clocks or watches
ho·rol·o·gy \-jē\ *n* [Gk *hōra* + E *-logy*] **1** : the science of measuring time **2** : the art of constructing instruments for indicating time
horo·scope \'hȯr-ə-,skōp, 'här-\ *n* [MF, fr. L *horoscopus*, fr. Gk *hōroskopos*, fr. *hōra* + *skopein* to look at — more at SPY] **1** : a diagram of the relative positions of planets and signs of the zodiac at a specific time (as at one's birth) for use by astrologers in inferring individual character and personality traits and in foretelling events of a person's life **2** : an astrological forecast
hor·ren·dous \hȯ-'ren-dəs, hä-, hə-\ *adj* [L *horrendus*, fr. gerundive of *horrēre*] : perfectly horrid : DREADFUL <the tax rate was ~> *syn* see HORRIBLE — **hor·ren·dous·ly** *adv*
hor·rent \'hȯr-ənt, 'här-\ *adj* [L *horrent-, horrens*, prp. of *horrēre*] **1** *archaic* : covered with bristling points : BRISTLED **2** *archaic* : standing up like bristles : BRISTLING
hor·ri·ble \'hȯr-ə-bəl, 'här-\ *adj* **1** : marked by or conducive to horror **2** : extremely unpleasant or disagreeable — **horrible** *n* — **hor·ri·ble·ness** *n* — **hor·ri·bly** \-blē\ *adv*
syn HORRIBLE, HORRID, HORRIFIC, HORRENDOUS *shared meaning element* : inspiring horror or abhorrence *ant* fascinating
hor·rid \'hȯr-əd, 'här-\ *adj* [L *horridus*, fr. *horrēre*] **1** *archaic* : ROUGH, BRISTLING **2** : innately offensive or repulsive: **a** : being such as to inspire horror : SHOCKING **b** : inspiring disgust or loathing : NASTY *syn* see HORRIBLE *ant* delightful — **hor·rid·ly** *adv* — **hor·rid·ness** *n*
hor·rif·ic \hȯ-'rif-ik, hä-\ *adj* : having the power to horrify <a ~ account of the tragedy> *syn* see HORRIBLE — **hor·rif·i·cal·ly** \-i-k(ə-)lē\ *adv*
hor·ri·fy \'hȯr-ə-,fī, 'här-\ *vt* **-fied; -fy·ing** **1** : to cause to feel horror **2** : to fill with distaste : SHOCK <his rough manner *horrified* his hostess> *syn* see DISMAY — **hor·ri·fy·ing·ly** \-,fī-iŋ-lē\ *adv*
¹hor·ror \'hȯr-ər, 'här-\ *n* [ME *horrour*, fr. MF *horror*, fr. L, action of trembling, fr. *horrēre* to tremble; akin to OE *gorst* gorse, Gk *chersos* dry land] **1 a** : painful and intense fear, dread, or dismay : CONSTERNATION <astonishment giving place to ~ on the faces of the people about me —H. G. Wells> **b** : intense aversion or repugnance **2 a** : the quality of inspiring horror : repulsive, horrible, or dismal quality or character <contemplating the ~ of their lives —Liam O'Flaherty> **b** : something that inspires horror **3** *pl* : a state of extreme depression or apprehension
²horror *adj* : calculated to inspire feelings of dread or horror : BLOODCURDLING <a ~ story>
hor·ror–struck \-,strək\ *adj* : struck with horror <stood ~ as they watched . . . their own city destroyed —*Nashville Tennessean*>
hors de com·bat \,ȯrd-ə-kōⁿ-'bä\ *adv or adj* [F] : out of combat : DISABLED
hors d'oeuvre \ȯr-'dərv\ *n, pl* **hors d'oeuvres** *also* **hors d'oeuvre** \-'dərv(z)\ [F *hors-d'œuvre*, lit., outside of work] : any of various savory foods usu. served as appetizers
¹horse \'hȯ(ə)rs\ *n, pl* **hors·es** *also* **horse** [ME *hors*, fr. OE; akin to OHG *hros* horse] **1 a** (1) : a large solid-hoofed herbivorous mammal (*Equus caballus*, family Equidae, the horse family) domesticated by man since a prehistoric period and used as a beast of burden, a draft animal, or for riding (2) : RACEHORSE <play the ~*s*> **b** : a male horse : STALLION *also* : a gelding as distinguished from an entire male **c** : a recent or extinct animal of the horse family **2 a** : JACKSTAY **b** : a frame usu. with legs used for supporting something (as planks or staging) **c** (1) : SIDE HORSE (2) : LONG HORSE **3** *horse pl* : CAVALRY **4** : a mass of the same geological character as the wall rock occurring within a vein **5** : HORSEPOWER **6** *slang* : HEROIN — **from the horse's mouth** : from the original source
²horse *vb* **horsed; hors·ing** *vt* **1** : to provide with a horse **2** : to move by brute force ~ *vi* **1** *of a mare* : to be in heat **2** : to engage in horseplay <*horsing* around too much>
³horse *adj* **1 a** : of or relating to a horse **b** : hauled or powered by a horse <a ~ barge> **2** : large or coarse of its kind **3** : mounted on horses <~ guards>
horse–and–buggy *adj* **1** : of or relating to the era before the advent of certain socially revolutionizing inventions (as the automobile) **2** : clinging to outdated attitudes or ideas : OLD-FASHIONED

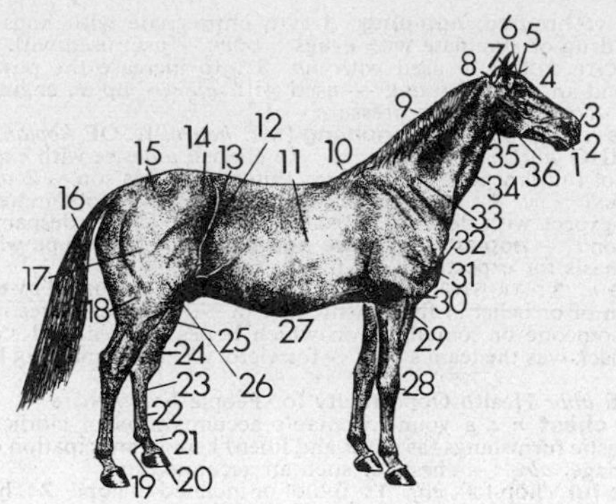

horse 1a: *1* mouth, *2* nose, *3* nostril, *4* face, *5* forehead, *6* forelock, *7* ear, *8* poll, *9* mane, *10* withers, *11* ribs, *12* flank, *13* loin, *14* haunch, *15* croup, *16* tail, *17* thigh, *18* buttock, *19* fetlock, *20* hoof, *21* coronet, *22* pastern, *23* cannon, *24* hock, *25* gaskin, *26* stifle, *27* belly, *28* knee, *29* forearm, *30* elbow, *31* shoulder, *32* breast, *33* neck, *34* throatlatch, *35* lower jaw, *36* cheek

¹horse·back \'hȯrs-,bak\ *n* **1** : the back of a horse **2** : a natural ridge : HOGBACK
²horseback *adv* : on horseback
horse·bean \'hȯrs-,bēn\ *n* **1** : BROAD BEAN **2** : JERUSALEM THORN 2
horse·car \-,kär\ *n* **1** : a streetcar drawn by horses **2** : a car fitted for transporting horses
horse chestnut *n* **1** : a large Asiatic tree (*Aesculus hippocastanum* of the family Hippocastanaceae, the horse-chestnut family) that has palmate leaves and erect conical clusters of showy flowers and is widely cultivated as an ornamental and shade tree and naturalized as an escape; *also* : BUCKEYE **2** : the large glossy brown seed of a horse chestnut
horse coper *n, Brit* : COPER
horse·flesh \'hȯrs-,flesh\ *n* : horses considered esp. with reference to riding, driving, or racing
horse·fly \-,flī\ *n* : any of a family (Tabanidae) of swift usu. large two-winged flies with bloodsucking females
horse gentian *n* : FEVERWORT
horse·hair \'hȯrs-,ha(ə)r, -,he(ə)r\ *n* **1** : the hair of a horse esp. from the mane or tail **2** : cloth made from horsehair
horsehair worm *n* : a free-living adult hairworm — called also *horsehair snake*
horse·hide \'hȯrs-,hīd\ *n* **1** : the dressed or raw hide of a horse **2** : the ball used in the game of baseball
horse latitudes *n pl* : either of two belts or regions in the neighborhood of 30° N and 30° S latitude characterized by high pressure, calms, and light baffling winds
horse·laugh \'hȯr-,slaf, -,släf\ *n* : a loud boisterous laugh : GUFFAW
horse·less carriage \,hȯr-sləs-\ *n* : AUTOMOBILE
horse mackerel *n* **1** : any of several large scombroid fishes (as a bluefin tuna) **2** : any of various large fishes (family Carangidae); *esp* : a large Atlantic food fish (*Trachurus trachurus*)
horse·man \'hȯr-smən\ *n* **1 a** : a rider on horseback **b** : one skilled in managing horses **2** : a breeder or raiser of horses — **horse·man·ship** \-,ship\ *n*
horse·mint \'hȯr-,smint\ *n* : any of various coarse mints; *esp* : MONARDA
horse nettle *n* : a coarse prickly weed (*Solanum carolinense*) of the nightshade family with bright yellow fruit resembling berries
horse opera *n* : WESTERN 2
horse·play \'hȯr-,splā\ *n* : rough or boisterous play
horse·play·er \-ər\ *n* : one who habitually bets on horse races
horse·pow·er \'hȯr-,spau̇(-ə)r\ *n* **1** : the power that a horse exerts in pulling **2** : a unit of power equal in the U.S. to 746 watts and nearly equivalent to the English gravitational unit of the same name that equals 550 foot-pounds of work per second
horsepower–hour *n* : the work performed or energy consumed by working at the rate of one horsepower for one hour that is equal to 1,980,000 foot-pounds
horse·rad·ish \'hȯrs-,rad-ish, -,red-\ *n* : a tall coarse white-flowered herb (*Armoracia lapathifolia*) of the mustard family; *also* : its pungent root used as a condiment
horse sense *n* : COMMON SENSE
horse·shit \'hȯrs(h)-,shit\ *n* : BUNK, NONSENSE — usu. considered vulgar
horse·shoe \'hȯrs(h)-,shü\ *n* **1** : a shoe for horses usu. consisting of a narrow plate of iron shaped to fit the rim of a horse's hoof and being somewhat U-shaped **2** : something (as a valley) shaped like a horseshoe **3** *pl* : a game like quoits played with horseshoes or with horseshoe-shaped pieces of metal — **horseshoe** *vt* — **horse·sho·er** \-,shü-ər\ *n*
horseshoe arch *n* : an arch having an intrados that widens above the springing before narrowing to a rounded or pointed crown — see ARCH illustration
horseshoe crab *n* : any of several closely related marine arthropods (order Xiphosura and class Merostomata) with a broad crescentic cephalothorax — called also *king crab*
horse show *n* : an exhibition of horses that usu. includes competition in riding, driving, and jumping
horse·tail \'hȯr-,stāl\ *n* : any of a genus (*Equisetum*) of perennial flowerless plants related to the ferns — called also *scouring rush*

horse trade *n* : negotiation accompanied by shrewd bargaining and reciprocal concessions <a political *horse trade*> — **horse-trade** *vi* — **horse trader** *n*
horse·weed \'hȯr-,swēd\ *n* **1** : a common No. American fleabane (*Erigeron canadensis*) with linear leaves and small discoid heads of yellowish flowers **2** : a coarse annual ragweed (*Ambrosia trifida*) **3** : a wild lettuce (*Lactuca canadensis*)
horse·whip \'hȯr-,swip, 'hȯrs-,hwip\ *vt* : to flog with or as if with a whip made to be used on a horse — **horse·whip·per** *n*
horse·wom·an \'hȯr-,swu̇m-ən\ *n* **1** : a woman horseback rider **2** : a woman skilled in caring for or managing horses
hors·ey *or* **horsy** \'hȯr-sē\ *adj* **hors·i·er; -est** **1** : of, relating to, or resembling a horse **2** : having to do with horses or horse racing **3** : characteristic of horsemen — **hors·i·ly** \-sə-lē\ *adv* — **hors·i·ness** \-sē-nəs\ *n*
horst \'hȯ(ə)rst\ *n* [G] : a block of the earth's crust separated by faults from adjacent relatively depressed blocks
hort *abbr* horticultural; horticulture
hor·ta·tive \'hȯrt-ət-iv\ *adj* [LL *hortativus*, fr. L *hortatus*, pp. of *hortari* to urge — more at YEARN] : giving exhortation : ADVISORY — **hor·ta·tive·ly** *adv*
hor·ta·to·ry \'hȯrt-ə-,tōr-ē, -,tȯr-\ *adj* : HORTATIVE, EXHORTATORY
hor·ti·cul·ture \'hȯrt-ə-,kəl-chər\ *n* [L *hortus* garden + E *-i-* + *culture* — more at YARD] : the science and art of growing fruits, vegetables, flowers, or ornamental plants — **hor·ti·cul·tur·al** \,hȯrt-ə-'kəlch(-ə)-rəl\ *adj* — **hor·ti·cul·tur·al·ly** \-rə-lē\ *adv* — **hor·ti·cul·tur·ist** \-rəst\ *n*
Ho·rus \'hōr-əs, 'hȯr-\ *n* [LL, fr. Gk *Hōros*, fr. Egypt *Ḥr*] : the Egyptian god of light and the son of Osiris and Isis
Hos *abbr* Hosea
[1]**ho·san·na** \hō-'zan-ə *also* -'zän-\ *interj* [ME *osanna*, fr. LL, fr. Gk *hōsanna*, fr. Heb *hōshī'āh-nnā* pray, save (us)!] — used as a cry of acclamation and adoration
[2]**hosanna** *n* : a cry of acclamation and adoration
HO scale \(')ā-'chō-\ *n* [fr. its fitness for rails of HO gauge] : a scale of ⅛ inch to one foot used esp. for model toys (as automobiles or trains)
[1]**hose** \'hōz\ *n, pl* **hose** *or* **hos·es** [ME, fr. OE *hosa* stocking, husk; akin to OHG *hosa* leg covering, Gk *kystis* bladder, OE *hӯd* hide] **1** *pl hose* **a** (1) : a cloth leg covering that sometimes covers the foot (2) : STOCKING, SOCK **b** (1) : a close-fitting garment covering the legs and waist that is usu. attached to a doublet by points (2) : short breeches reaching to the knee **2** : a flexible tube for conveying fluids (as from a faucet or hydrant)
[2]**hose** *vt* **hosed; hos·ing** : to spray, water, or wash with a hose — often used with *down* <~ down a stable floor>
Ho·sea \hō-'zē-ə, -'zā-\ *n* [Heb *Hōshēa'*] **1** : a Hebrew prophet of the 8th century B.C. **2** : a prophetic book of canonical Jewish and Christian Scripture — see BIBLE table
ho·sel \'hō-zəl\ *n* [dim. of [1]*hose*] : a socket in the head of a golf club into which the shaft is inserted
ho·siery \'hōzh(-ə)-rē, 'hōz(-ə)-\ *n* **1** : HOSE 1a **2** *chiefly Brit* : KNITWEAR
hosp *abbr* hospital
hos·pice \'häs-pəs\ *n* [F, fr. L *hospitium*, fr. *hospit-*, *hospes* host — more at HOST] : a lodging for travelers, young persons, or the underprivileged esp. when maintained by a religious order
hos·pi·ta·ble \hä-'spit-ə-bəl, 'häs-(,)pit-\ *adj* **1 a** : given to generous and cordial reception of guests **b** : promising or suggesting generous and cordial welcome **c** : offering a pleasant or sustaining environment **2** : readily receptive : OPEN <~ to new ideas> — **hos·pi·ta·bly** \-blē\ *adv*
hos·pi·tal \'häs-,pit-ᵊl\ *n* [ME, fr. OF, fr. ML *hospitale*, fr. LL, hospice, fr. L, guest room, fr. neut. of *hospitalis* of a guest, fr. *hospit-*, *hospes*] **1** : a charitable institution for the needy, aged, infirm, or young **2** : an institution where the sick or injured are given medical or surgical care — usu. used in British English without an article in the phrase *in hospital* **3** : a repair shop for specified small objects <clock ~>
Hos·pi·tal·er *or* **Hos·pi·tal·ler** \-ᵊl-ər\ *n* [ME *hospitalier*, fr. MF, fr. ML *hospitalarius*, fr. LL *hospitale*] : a member of a religious military order established in Jerusalem in the 12th century
hos·pi·tal·i·ty \,häs-pə-'tal-ət-ē\ *n, pl* **-ties** : hospitable treatment, reception, or disposition
hos·pi·tal·ize \'häs-,pit-ᵊl-,īz\ *vt* **-ized; -iz·ing** : to place in a hospital as a patient — **hos·pi·tal·iza·tion** \,häs-,pit-ᵊl-ə-'zā-shən\ *n*
hospital ship *n* : a ship equipped as a hospital; *esp* : one built or specifically assigned to assist the wounded, sick, and shipwrecked in time of war
[1]**host** \'hōst\ *n* [ME, fr. OF, fr. LL *hostis*, fr. L, stranger, enemy — more at GUEST] **1** : ARMY **2** : a very large number : MULTITUDE
[2]**host** *vi* : to assemble in a host usu. for a hostile purpose
[3]**host** *n* [ME *hoste* host, guest, fr. OF, fr. L *hospit-*, *hospes*, fr. *hostis*] **1 a** : one that receives or entertains guests socially, commercially, or officially **b** : one that provides facilities for an event or function <our college served as ~ for the basketball tournament> **2 a** : a living animal or plant affording subsistence or lodgment to a parasite **b** : the larger, stronger, or dominant member of a commensal or symbiotic pair **c** : an individual into which a tissue or part is transplanted from another **3** : a mineral or rock that is older than the minerals or rocks in it; *also* : substance that contains a usu. small amount of another substance incorporated in its structure **4** : a radio or television emcee
[4]**host** *vt* **1** : to receive or entertain socially : serve as host to <will ~ the cadets during their visit —*Springfield (Mass.) Daily News*> **2 a** : to serve as host at <the garden party he had ~*ed* last spring —*Saturday Rev.*> **b** : EMCEE <~*ed* a series of TV programs>
[5]**host** *n, often cap* [ME *hoste*, fr. MF *hoiste*, fr. LL & L; LL *hostia* Eucharist, fr. L, sacrifice] : the eucharistic bread
hos·tage \'häs-tij\ *n* [ME, fr. OF, fr. *hoste*] : a person held by one party in a conflict as a pledge that promises will be kept or terms met by the other party
[1]**hos·tel** \'häs-tᵊl\ *n* [ME, fr. OF, fr. LL *hospitale* hospice] **1** : INN **2** : a supervised lodging for usu. young travelers — called also *youth hostel*
[2]**hostel** *vi* : to stay at hostels overnight in the course of traveling (as by foot, bicycle, or motorcycle)
hos·tel·er \'häs-tə-lər\ *n* **1** : one that lodges guests or strangers **2** : a young traveler who stops at hostels overnight
hos·tel·ry \'häs-tᵊl-rē\ *n, pl* **-ries** : INN, HOTEL
[1]**host·ess** \'hō-stəs\ *n* **1** : a woman who entertains socially **2 a** : a woman in charge of a public dining room who seats diners **b** : a female employee on a ship, airplane, bus, or train who manages the provisioning of food and attends passengers **c** : a woman who acts as a dancing partner or companion to male patrons in a dance hall or bar
[2]**hostess** *vi* : to act as hostess ~ *vt* : to serve as hostess to <the guests will be ~*ed* before the encampment in councils —Alberta Schuckle>
hos·tile \'häs-tᵊl, -,tīl\ *adj* [MF or L; MF, fr. L *hostilis*, fr. *hostis*] **1** : of or relating to an enemy **2** : marked by esp. overt antagonism : UNFRIENDLY **3** : not hospitable <a ~ environment> — **hostile** *n* — **hos·tile·ly** \-tᵊl-(l)ē, -,tīl-lē\ *adv*
hos·til·i·ty \hä-'stil-ət-ē\ *n, pl* **-ties** **1 a** : a hostile state **b** (1) : hostile action (2) *pl* : overt acts of warfare : WAR **2** : antagonism, opposition, or resistance in thought or principle ***syn*** see ENMITY
hos·tler \'(h)äs-lər\ *n* [ME, innkeeper, hostler, fr. *hostel*] **1** : one who takes care of horses or mules **2** : one who services a vehicle (as a locomotive or truck) or machine (as a crane)
host·ly \'hōst-lē\ *adj* : of or appropriate to a host <so young-looking that people did not instinctively lay upon him ~ duties —John Updike>
host plant *n* : a plant upon which an organism (as an insect or mildew) lodges and subsists
[1]**hot** \'hät\ *adj* **hot·ter; hot·test** [ME, fr. OE *hāt*; akin to OHG *heiz* hot, Lith *kaisti* to get hot] **1 a** : having a relatively high temperature **b** : capable of giving a sensation of heat or of burning, searing, or scalding **c** : having heat in a degree exceeding normal body heat **2 a** : ARDENT, FIERY <a ~ temper> **b** : VIOLENT, RAGING <a ~ battle> **c** : LUSTFUL, LECHEROUS **d** : EAGER <~ for reform> **e** *of jazz* : ecstatic and emotionally exciting and marked by strong rhythms and free melodic improvisations **3** : having or causing the sensation of an uncomfortable degree of body heat <~ and tired> **4 a** : newly made : FRESH <a ~ scent> <~ off the press> **b** : close to something sought <guess again, you're getting *hotter*> **5 a** : suggestive of heat or of burning or glowing objects <~ colors> **b** : PUNGENT, PEPPERY **6 a** : of intense and immediate interest <a ~ scandal> **b** : unusually lucky or favorable <~ dice> **c** : temporarily capable of unusual performance (as in a sport) **d** : currently popular (as of merchandise) **e** : very good — used as a generalized term of approval <he's really ~ in math> **f** : ABSURD, UNBELIEVABLE <that's a ~ one> **7 a** : electrically energized esp. with high voltage **b** : RADIOACTIVE; *also* : dealing with radioactive material **c** *of an atom* : being in an excited state due usu. to nuclear processes **8 a** : recently and illegally obtained <~ jewels> **b** : wanted by the police; *also* : unsafe for a fugitive **9** *of a vehicle* : FAST — **hot·tish** \'hät-ish\ *adj*
[2]**hot** *adv* : HOTLY
hot air *n* : empty talk
hot·bed \'hät-,bed\ *n* **1** : a bed of soil enclosed in glass, heated esp. by fermenting manure, and used for forcing or for raising seedlings **2** : an environment that favors rapid growth or development <a ~ of crime>
hot·blood \-,bləd\ *n* : THOROUGHBRED 1
hot-blood·ed \-'bləd-əd\ *adj* **1** : EXCITABLE, ARDENT **2 a** *of a horse* : having Arab or Thoroughbred ancestors **b** *of livestock* : of pure or superior breeding — **hot-blood·ed·ness** *n*
hot·box \-,bäks\ *n* : a journal bearing (as of a railroad car) overheated by friction
hot·cake \-,kāk\ *n* : PANCAKE
hotch \'häch\ *vi* [prob. fr. MF *hocher* to shake, fr. OF *hochier*] *Scot* : WIGGLE, FIDGET
hotch·pot \'häch-,pät\ *n* [AF *hochepot*, fr. OF, hotchpotch] : the combining of properties into a common lot to ensure equality of division among heirs
hotch·potch \'häch-,päch\ *n* [ME *hochepot*, fr. MF, fr. OF, fr. *hochier* to shake + *pot*] **1 a** : a thick soup or stew of vegetables, potatoes, and usu. meat **b** : HODGEPODGE **2** : HOTCHPOT
hot corner *n* : the fielding position of the third baseman in baseball
hot-dog \'hät-,dȯg\ *vi* [[2]*hot dog*] : to perform in a conspicuous or often ostentatious manner; *esp* : to perform stunts and fancy maneuvers while riding a surfboard
[1]**hot dog** \'hät-,dȯg\ *n* **1** : FRANKFURTER; *esp* : a frankfurter heated and served in a long split roll **2** [prob. fr. [2]*hot dog*] : one that hotdogs; *also* : SHOW-OFF
[2]**hot dog** \'hät-,dȯg, -'dȯg\ *interj* — used to express approval or gratification
hot·dog·ger \-,dȯg-ər\ *n* : HOT DOG 2
ho·tel \hō-'tel\ *n* [F *hôtel*, fr. OF *hostel*] : an establishment that provides lodging and usu. meals, entertainment, and various personal services for the public : INN
Hotel — a communications code word for the letter *h*
ho·te·lier \hō-'tel-yər; ,ōt-ᵊl-'yā, ,ȯt-\ *n* [F *hôtelier*, fr. OF *hostelier*, fr. *hostel*] : a proprietor or manager of a hotel
ho·tel·man \hō-'tel-,man, -mən\ *n* : one who is engaged in the hotel business esp. in a supervisory or managerial capacity

hot flash *n* **:** a sudden brief flushing and sensation of heat caused by dilation of skin capillaries usu. associated with menopausal endocrine imbalance

1**hot·foot** \ˈhät-ˌfu̇t\ *adv* **:** in haste

2**hotfoot** *vi* **:** to go hotfoot **:** HURRY — usu. used with *it*

3**hotfoot** *n, pl* **hotfoots :** a practical joke in which a match is surreptitiously inserted between the upper and the sole of a victim's shoe and lighted

hot·head \ˈhät-ˌhed\ *n* **:** a hotheaded person

hot·head·ed \-ˈhed-əd\ *adj* **:** FIERY, IMPETUOUS — **hot·head·ed·ly** *adv* — **hot·head·ed·ness** *n*

1**hot·house** \-ˌhau̇s\ *n* **1** *obs* **:** BROTHEL **2 :** a greenhouse maintained at a high temperature esp. for the culture of tropical plants **3 :** HOTBED 2

2**hothouse** *adj* **1 :** grown in a hothouse **2 :** having the qualities of a plant raised in a hothouse; *esp.* **:** DELICATE

hot line *n* **:** a direct telephone line in constant operational readiness so as to facilitate immediate communication (as between heads of two governments)

hot·ly \ˈhät-lē\ *adv* **:** in a hot or fiery manner <a ~ debated issue> <~ colored paintings>

hot pepper *n* **1 :** any of various small and usu. thin-walled capsicum fruits of marked pungency **2 :** a pepper plant bearing hot peppers

hot plate *n* **1 :** a heated iron plate for cooking **2 :** a simple portable appliance for heating or for cooking in limited spaces

hot potato *n* **:** a controversial question or issue that involves unpleasant or dangerous consequences for anyone dealing with it

hot rod *n* **:** an automobile rebuilt or modified for high speed and fast acceleration — **hot-rod·der** \ˈhät-ˈräd-ər\ *n*

hot seat *n* **1** *slang* **:** ELECTRIC CHAIR **2 :** a position of uneasiness, embarrassment, or anxiety <on the *hot seat,* directing a half-million dollar gamble —Mark Stroock & Percy Knauth>

hot·shot \ˈhät-ˌshät\ *n* **1 :** a fast freight **2 :** a showily skillful person <a literary ~> — **hotshot** *adj*

hot spring *n* **:** THERMAL SPRING; *esp* **:** a spring with water above 98° F

Hot·ten·tot \ˈhät-ᵊn-ˌtät\ *n* [Afrik] **1 :** a member of a people of southern Africa apparently akin to both the Bushmen and the Bantus **2 :** the language of the Hottentot people

hot up *vi* **1 :** to grow hot, lively, or exciting <the gossip began to *hot up* —*Life*> **2 :** to speed up <air raids began to *hot up* about the beginning of February —George Orwell> ~ *vt* **:** to make livelier or speedier <the studios had *hotted up* her comeback —Kenneth Baily>

hot war *n* **:** a conflict involving actual fighting — compare COLD WAR

hot water *n* **:** a distressing predicament **:** DIFFICULTY

Hou·dan \ˈhü-ˌdan\ *n* [F, fr. *Houdan,* village in France] **:** any of a French breed of crested domestic fowls with black-and-white or white plumage and five toes

1**hound** \ˈhau̇nd\ *n* [ME, fr. OE *hund;* akin to OHG *hunt* dog, L *canis,* Gk *kyōn*] **1 a :** DOG **b :** a dog of any of various hunting breeds typically having large drooping ears and a deep voice and following their prey by scent **2 :** a mean or despicable person **3 :** DOGFISH **4 :** one markedly or unusually devoted to something **:** FAN <autograph ~*s*>

2**hound** *vt* **1 :** to pursue with or as if with hounds **2 :** to drive or affect by persistent harassing <~*ed* from office by rumors> ***syn*** see BAIT — **hound·er** *n*

hounds \ˈhau̇n(d)z\ *n pl* [ME *hune,* of Scand origin; akin to ON *hūnn* cube — more at CAVE] **:** the framing at the masthead of a ship that supports the heel of the topmast and the upper parts of the lower rigging

hound's-tongue \ˈhau̇n(d)z-ˌtəŋ\ *n* **:** any of various coarse plants (genus *Cynoglossum,* esp. *C. officinale*) of the borage family having tongue-shaped leaves and reddish flowers

hounds·tooth check *or* **hound's-tooth check** \ˌhau̇n(d)z-ˌtüth-\ *n* **:** a small broken-check textile pattern

houndstooth check

hour \ˈau̇(ə)r\ *n* [ME, fr. OF *heure,* fr. LL & L; LL *hora* canonical hour, fr. L, hour of the day, fr. Gk *hōra*] **1 :** a time or office for daily liturgical devotion; *esp* **:** CANONICAL HOUR **2 :** the 24th part of a day **3 a :** the time of day reckoned in two 12-hour periods **b** *pl* **:** the time reckoned in one 24-hour period from midnight to midnight using a 4-digit number of which the first two digits indicate the hour and the last two digits indicate the minute <attack at 0900 ~*s*> <in the military 4:30 p.m. is called 1630 ~*s*> **4 a :** a customary time <during his lunch ~> **b :** a particular time <in his ~ of need> **5 :** an angular unit of right ascension equal to 15 degrees measured along the equinoctial **6 :** the work done or distance traveled at normal rate in an hour <the city was two ~*s* away> **7 a :** a class session **b :** CREDIT HOUR, SEMESTER HOUR

hour angle *n* **:** the angle between the celestial meridian of an observer and the hour circle of a celestial object measured westward from the meridian

hour circle *n* **:** a circle on the celestial sphere that passes through both celestial poles

1**hour·glass** \ˈau̇(ə)r-ˌglas\ *n* **:** an instrument for measuring time consisting of a glass vessel having two compartments from the uppermost of which a quantity of sand, water, or mercury runs in an hour into the lower one

2**hourglass** *adj* **:** shaped like an hourglass <an ~ figure>

hou·ri \ˈhu̇(ə)r-ē, ˈhü-rē\ *n* [F, fr. Per *hūri,* fr. Ar *hūrīyah*] **1 :** one of the beautiful maidens that in Muslim belief live with the blessed in paradise **2 :** a voluptuously beautiful young woman

hour-long \ˈau̇(ə)r-ˈlȯŋ\ *adj* **:** lasting an hour

1**hour·ly** \ˈau̇(ə)r-lē\ *adv* **:** at or during every hour; *also* **:** FREQUENTLY, CONTINUALLY

hourglass

2**hourly** *adj* **1 a :** occurring hour by hour <~ bus service> **b :** FREQUENT, CONTINUAL <in ~ expectation of the rain's stopping> **2 :** computed in terms of an hour <an ~ wage>

1**house** \ˈhau̇s\ *n, pl* **hous·es** \ˈhau̇-zəz\ [ME *hous,* fr. OE *hūs;* akin to OHG *hūs* house] **1 :** a building that serves as living quarters for one or a few families **:** HOME **2 a (1) :** a shelter or refuge (as a nest or den) of a wild animal **(2) :** a natural covering (as a test or shell) that encloses and protects an animal or a colony of zooids **b :** a building in which something is housed <carriage ~> **3 a :** one of the 12 equal sectors in which the celestial sphere is divided in astrology **b :** a zodiacal sign that is the seat of a planet's greatest influence **c :** the circular area 12 feet in diameter surrounding the tee and within which a curling stone must rest in order to count **4 a :** HOUSEHOLD **b :** a family including ancestors, descendants, and kindred <the ~ of Tudor> **5 a :** a residence for a religious community or for students **b :** the community or students in residence **6 a :** a legislative, deliberative, or consultative assembly; *esp* **:** one constituting a division of a bicameral body **b :** the building or chamber where such an assembly meets **c :** a quorum of such an assembly **7 a :** a place of business or entertainment **b (1) :** a business organization <a publishing ~> **(2) :** a gambling establishment **c :** the audience in a theater or concert hall <a good ~ on opening night> — **house·ful** \ˈhau̇s-ˌfu̇l\ *n* — **on the house :** at the expense of an establishment or its management <have a drink on the ~>

2**house** \ˈhau̇z\ *vb* **housed; hous·ing** *vt* **1 a :** to provide with living quarters or shelter **b :** to store in a house **2 :** to encase, enclose, or shelter as if by putting in a house **3 :** to serve as shelter for **:** CONTAIN ~ *vi* **:** to take shelter **:** LODGE

house arrest *n* **:** confinement often under guard to one's house or quarters instead of in prison

1**house·boat** \ˈhau̇s-ˌbōt\ *n* **:** a barge fitted for use as a dwelling or for leisurely cruising; *also* **:** a dwelling supported on the water by floats

2**houseboat** *vi* **:** to live or cruise on a houseboat

house·bound \ˈhau̇s-ˌbau̇nd\ *adj* **:** confined to the house

house·boy \-ˌbȯi\ *n* **:** HOUSEMAN

1**house·break** \ˈhau̇s-ˌbrāk\ *vi* **-broke** \-ˌbrōk\; **-bro·ken** \-ˌbrō-kən\; **-break·ing** [back-formation fr. *housebreaker* & *housebreaking*] **:** to commit housebreaking — **house·break·er** *n*

2**housebreak** *vt* **-broke** \-ˌbrōk\; **-bro·ken** \-ˌbrō-kən\; **-break·ing** [back-formation fr. *housebroken*] **1 :** to make housebroken **2 a :** to teach acceptable social manners to **b :** TAME, SUBDUE

house·break·ing \ˈhau̇s-ˌbrā-kiŋ\ *n* **:** an act of breaking open and entering the dwelling house of another with a felonious purpose

house·bro·ken \-ˌbrō-kən\ *adj* **1 :** trained to excretory habits acceptable in indoor living **2 :** made tractable or polite

house·carl \-ˌkär(ə)l\ *n* [OE *hūscarl,* fr. ON *hūskarl,* fr. *hūs* house + *karl* man] **:** a member of the bodyguard of a Danish or early English king or noble

house cat *n* **:** CAT 1a

house·clean \ˈhau̇s-ˌklēn\ *vb* [back-formation fr. *housecleaning*] *vi* **1 :** to clean a house and its furniture **2 :** to get rid of unwanted or undesirable items or people ~ *vt* **1 :** to clean the surfaces and furnishings of **2 :** to improve or reform by ridding of undesirable people or practices — **house·clean·ing** *n*

house·coat \ˈhau̇-ˌskōt\ *n* **:** a woman's often long-skirted informal garment for wear around the house

house cricket *n* **:** any of various crickets living in or about dwellings; *esp* **:** a widely distributed American cricket (*Acheta domesticus*)

house detective *n* **:** one who is employed (as by a hotel) to prevent disorderly or improper conduct of patrons

house·dress \ˈhau̇s-ˌdres\ *n* **:** a dress with simple lines that is suitable for housework and is made usu. of a washable fabric

house·fa·ther \-ˌfät͟h-ər\ *n* **:** a man in charge of a dormitory, hall, or hostel for young people or children

house·fly \ˈhau̇s-ˌflī\ *n* **:** a cosmopolitan two-winged fly (*Musca domestica*) that is often about human habitations and acts as a mechanical vector of diseases (as typhoid fever); *also* **:** any of various flies of similar appearance or habitat

house·front \-ˌfrənt\ *n* **:** the facade of a house

house girl *n* **:** HOUSEMAID

house·guest \ˈhau̇s-ˌgest\ *n* **:** GUEST 1a

1**house·hold** \ˈhau̇s-ˌhōld, ˈhau̇-ˌsōld\ *n* **:** those who dwell under the same roof and compose a family; *also* **:** a social unit comprised of those living together in the same dwelling

2**household** *adj* **1 :** of or relating to a household **:** DOMESTIC **2 :** FAMILIAR, COMMON

household art *n* **:** one of the techniques (as cooking) used in the maintenance and care of a household

house·hold·er \ˈhau̇s-ˌhōl-dər, ˈhau̇-ˌsōl-\ *n* **:** one who occupies a house or tenement alone or as the head of a household

household troops *n pl* **:** troops appointed to attend and guard a sovereign or his residence

household word *n* **:** a common word or phrase

house·keep \ˈhau̇-ˌskēp\ *vi* **-kept** \-ˌskept\; **-keep·ing** [back-formation fr. *housekeeper*] **:** to keep house

house·keep·er \-ˌskē-pər\ *n* **1 :** a woman employed to keep house **2 :** HOUSEWIFE 1

house·keep·ing \-piŋ\ *n* **1 :** the management of a house and home affairs **2 :** the care and management of property and the provision of equipment and services (as for an industrial organization) **3 :** the routine tasks that have to be done in order for a system to function

1**hou·sel** \ˈhau̇-zəl\ *n* [ME, fr. OE *hūsel* sacrifice, Eucharist; akin to Goth *hunsl* sacrifice] *archaic* **:** the Eucharist or the act of administering or receiving it

2**housel** *vt, archaic* **:** to administer communion to

house·leek \'haů-,slēk\ *n* : a pink-flowered European plant (*Sempervivum tectorum*) of the orpine family found on old walls and roofs; *broadly* : SEMPERVIVUM
house·less \'haů-sləs, 'haůz-ləs\ *adj* **1** : destitute of the shelter of a house : HOMELESS <a ~ wanderer> **2** : destitute of houses <a ~ desert> — **house·less·ness** *n*
house·lights \'haů-,slīts\ *n pl* : the lights that illuminate the auditorium of a theater
house·maid \'haů-,smād\ *n* : a female servant employed to do housework
housemaid's knee *n* [so called fr. its frequent occurrence among servant girls who work a great deal on their knees] : a swelling over the knee due to an enlargement of the bursa in the front of the patella
house·man \'haů-smən, -,sman\ *n* : a person who performs general work about a house or hotel
house·mate \'haů-,smāt\ *n* : one that lives in the same house with another
house·moth·er \'haů-,sməth-ər\ *n* : a woman acting as hostess, chaperon, and often housekeeper in a residence for young people
house mouse *n* : a common nearly cosmopolitan usu. gray mouse (*Mus musculus*) that lives and breeds about buildings, is a vector of diseases, and is an important experimental animal
house of assembly : a legislative body or the lower house of a legislature (as in various British colonies, protectorates, and countries of the Commonwealth)
House of Burgesses : the colonial representative assembly of Virginia
house of cards : a structure or situation that is insubstantial, shaky, or in constant danger of collapse
House of Commons : the lower house of the British and Canadian parliaments
house of correction : an institution where persons who have committed a minor offense and are considered capable of reformation are confined
house of delegates : HOUSE 6a; *esp* : the lower house of the state legislature in Maryland, Virginia, and West Virginia
House of Lords : the upper house of the British Parliament composed of the peers temporal and spiritual
house of representatives : the lower house of a legislative body (as the U.S. Congress)
house of studies : an educational institution serving scholars of a religious order — called also *house of study*
house organ *n* : a periodical distributed by a business concern among its employees, sales personnel, and customers
house painter *n* : one whose business or occupation is painting houses
house party *n* : a party lasting over one or more nights at a residence (as a home or fraternity house)
house physician *n* : a physician who is employed by and lives in a hospital
house·plant \'haů-,splant\ *n* : a plant grown or kept indoors
house–proud \'haů-,spraůd\ *adj* : proud of one's house or housekeeping
hous·er \'haů-zər\ *n* [²*house*] : one that promotes or administers housing projects
house–rais·ing \'haůs-,rā-ziŋ\ *n* : the joint erection of a house or its framework by a gathering of neighbors
house·room \-,rüm, -,rům\ *n* : space for accommodation in or as if in a house <only two universities . . . gave the subject ~ —*Amer. Naturalist*>
house rule *n* : a rule that applies to a game only among a certain group or in a certain place
house seat *n* : a theater seat reserved by the management for special guests
house sparrow *n* : ENGLISH SPARROW
house–to–house \,haůs-tə-'haůs\ *adj* : DOOR-TO-DOOR 1
house·top \'haů-,stäp\ *n* : ROOF; *esp* : the level surface of a flat roof — **from the housetops** : for all to hear : OPENLY <shouting their grievances *from the housetops*>
house trailer *n* : TRAILER 3b
house–train \'haů-,strān\ *vt, chiefly Brit* : ²HOUSEBREAK
house·wares \'haů-,swā(ə)rz, -,swe(ə)rz\ *n pl* : furnishings for a house; *esp* : small articles of household equipment (as cooking utensils or small appliances)
house·warm·ing \'haů-,swȯr-miŋ\ *n* : a party to celebrate the taking possession of a house or premises
house·wife \'haů-,swīf; *an old pronunciation* 'həz-əf *or* 'həs-əf *survives for sense 2*\ *n* **1** : a married woman in charge of a household **2** : a small container for small articles (as thread) — **house·wife·li·ness** \-lē-nəs\ *n* — **house·wife·ly** \-lē\ *adj* — **house·wif·ery** \-,wī-f(ə-)rē\ *n*
house·work \'haů-,swərk\ *n* : the work of housekeeping
¹**hous·ing** \'haů-ziŋ\ *n* **1 a** : SHELTER, LODGING **b** : dwellings provided for people **2** : something that covers or protects: as **a** : a case or enclosure (as for a mechanical part or an instrument) **b** : a casing (as an enclosed bearing) in which a shaft revolves **c** : a support (as a frame) for mechanical parts **3** : a portion of a mast that is beneath the deck or of a bowsprit that is inboard **4 a** : the space taken out of a structural member (as a timber) to admit the insertion of part of another **b** : a niche for a sculpture
²**housing** *n* **1** : an ornamental cover for a saddle **2** *pl* : TRAPPINGS
housing development *n* : a group of individual dwellings or apartment houses typically of similar design that are built and leased under one management
housing estate *n, Brit* : HOUSING DEVELOPMENT
housing project *n* : a publically supported and administered housing development planned usu. for low-income families
Hou·yhn·hnm \hü-'in-əm, 'hwin-\ *n* [imit.] : a member of a race of horses endowed with reason in Swift's *Gulliver's Travels*
hove *past of* HEAVE
hov·el \'həv-əl, 'häv-\ *n* [ME] **1** : an open shed or shelter **2** : TABERNACLE **3** : a small, wretched, and often dirty house : HUT
hov·er \'həv-ər, 'häv-\ *vb* **hov·ered; hov·er·ing** \-(ə-)riŋ\ [ME *hoveren,* freq. of *hoven* to hover] *vi* **1 a** : to hang fluttering in the air or on the wing **b** : to remain suspended over a place or object **2 a** : to move to and fro near a place **b** : to be in a state of uncertainty, irresolution, or suspense ~ *vt* : to brood over <hen ~s her chicks> — **hover** *n* — **hov·er·er** \-ər-ər\ *n*
Hov·er·craft \-ər-,kraft\ *trademark* — used for a ground-effect machine
¹**how** \(')haů\ *adv* [ME, fr. OE *hū;* akin to OHG *hwuo* how, OE *hwā* who — more at WHO] **1 a** : in what manner or way **b** : with what meaning : to what effect **c** : by what name or title <~ art thou called —Shak.> **d** : for what reason : WHY **2** : to what degree or extent **3** : in what state or condition <~ are you> **4** : at what price <~ a score of ewes now —Shak.> — **how about** : what do you say to or think of <*how about* it, are you going>
²**how** *conj* **1 a** : the way or manner in which <remember ~ they fought>; *also* : the state or condition in which **b** : THAT <told them ~ he had a situation —Charles Dickens> **2** : HOWEVER, AS <a reader can shift his attention ~ he likes —William Empson>
³**how** \'haů\ *n* **1** : a question about manner or method **2** : MANNER, METHOD
¹**how·be·it** \haů-'bē-ət\ *adv* : NEVERTHELESS
²**howbeit** *conj* : ALTHOUGH
how·dah \'haůd-ə\ *n* [Hindi *hauda*] : a seat or covered pavilion on the back of an elephant or camel

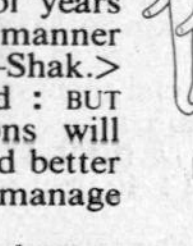
howdah

howe \'haů, 'hō\ *n* [ME (northern) *how, holl,* fr. OE *hol,* fr. *hol,* adj., hollow — more at HOLE] *Scot* : HOLLOW, VALLEY
¹**how·ev·er** \haů-'ev-ər\ *conj* **1** : in whatever manner or way <can go ~ he likes> **2** *archaic* : ALTHOUGH
²**however** *adv* **1 a** : to whatever degree or extent <has done this for ~ many thousands of years —Emma Hawkridge> **b** : in whatever manner or way <shall serve you, sir, truly, ~ else —Shak.> **2** : in spite of that : on the other hand : BUT <still seems possible, ~, that conditions will improve> <would like to go; ~, I think I'd better not> **3** : how in the world <~ did you manage to do it>
howff *or* **howf** \'haůf, 'hōf\ *n* [D *hof* enclosure; akin to OE *hof* enclosure, *hȳf* hive] *Scot* : HAUNT, RESORT
how·it·zer \'haů-ət-sər\ *n* [D *houwitser,* deriv. of Czech *houfnice* ballista] : a short cannon used to fire projectiles at medium muzzle velocities and with relatively high trajectories
howl \'haů(ə)l\ *vb* [ME *houlen;* akin to MHG *hiulen* to howl, Gk *kōkyein* to shriek] *vi* **1** : to emit a loud sustained doleful sound characteristic of dogs **2** : to cry loudly and without restraint under strong impulse (as pain or grief) **3** : to go on a spree or rampage ~ *vt* **1** : to utter with unrestrained outcry **2** : to affect, effect, or drive by adverse outcry — used esp. with *down* <~*ed* down the speaker> — **howl** *n*
howl·er \'haů-lər\ *n* **1** : one that howls **2** : a stupid and ridiculous blunder
howler monkey *n* : any of a genus (*Alouatta*) of So. and Central American monkeys that have a long prehensile tail and enlargement of the hyoid and laryngeal apparatus enabling them to make loud howling noises
howl·ing \'haů-liŋ\ *adj* **1** : marked by howling <a ~ storm> **2** : DESOLATE, WILD <a ~ wilderness> **3** : very great : PRONOUNCED <a ~ success>
how·so·ev·er \,haů-sə-'wev-ər\ *adv* **1** : in whatever manner **2** : to whatever degree or extent
how–to \'haů-'tü\ *adj* : giving practical instruction and advice (as on a craft) <~ books on all sorts of hobbies —Harry Milt>
¹**hoy** \'hȯi\ *interj* [ME] — used in attracting attention or in driving animals
²**hoy** *n* [ME, fr. MD *hoei*] **1** : a small usu. sloop-rigged coasting ship **2** : a heavy barge for bulky cargo
hoy·den \'hȯid-ᵊn\ *n* [perh. fr. obs D *heiden* country lout, fr. MD, heathen; akin to OE *hǣthen* heathen] : a girl or woman of saucy, boisterous, or carefree behavior — **hoy·den·ish** \-ish\ *adj*
hoyle \'hȯi(ə)l\ *n, often cap* [Edmond *Hoyle* †1769 E writer on games] : an encyclopedia of the rules of indoor games and esp. card games
HP *abbr* **1** half pay **2** high pressure **3** hire purchase **4** horsepower
HPA *abbr* high-power amplifier
HPF *abbr* **1** highest possible frequency **2** high power field
HPGC *abbr* heading per gyrocompass
HQ *abbr* headquarters
hr *abbr* **1** here **2** hour
HR *abbr* House of Representatives
hrdwre *abbr* hardware
H Rept *abbr* House report
H Res *abbr* House resolution
Hr factor \'ā-'chär-\ *n* [backward spelling of *Rh* (*factor*)] : a substance present in Rh-negative blood and apparently reciprocally related to the Rh factor
HRH *abbr* Her Royal Highness; His Royal Highness
HRI *abbr* height-range indicator
HRS *abbr* historical records survey
hrzn *abbr* horizon
HS *abbr* **1** high school **2** house surgeon

HSAA *abbr* Health Sciences Advancement Award

HSGT *abbr* high-speed ground transport

Hsia \shē-ˈä\ *n* [Chin (Pek) *hsia*4] **:** the legendary first dynasty of Chinese history traditionally dated from about 2200-1766 B.C.

HSL *abbr* high-speed launch

HST *abbr* **1** Hawaiian standard time **2** hypersonic transport

HSUS *abbr* Humane Society of the United States

ht *abbr* height

HT *abbr* **1** half time **2** halftone **3** hardtop **4** Hawaiian time **5** high-tension **6** high tide **7** [L *hoc tempore*] at this time **8** [L *hoc titulo*] under this title **9** hydrotherapy

hua·ra·che \wə-ˈräch-ē, hə-\ *n* [MexSp] **:** a low-heeled sandal having an upper made of interwoven leather thongs

hub \ˈhəb\ *n* [prob. alter. of 2*hob*] **1 :** the central part of a wheel, propeller, or fan **2 :** a center of activity **:** FOCAL POINT **3 :** a steel punch from which a working die for a coin or medal is made

hub·ble–bub·ble \ˈhəb-əl-ˌbəb-əl\ *n* [redupl. of *bubble*] **1 :** WATER PIPE **2 :** a flurry of sound or activity **:** COMMOTION

hub·bub \ˈhəb-ˌəb\ *n* [prob. of Celt origin; akin to ScGael *ub ub*, interj. of contempt] **1 :** NOISE, UPROAR **2 :** CONFUSION, TURMOIL

hub·by \ˈhəb-ē\ *n, pl* **hubbies** [by alter.] **:** HUSBAND — usu. used informally

hub·cap \ˈhəb-ˌkap\ *n* **:** a removable metal cap over the end of an axle; *esp* **:** one used on the wheel of a motor vehicle

hu·bris \ˈhyü-brəs\ *n* [Gk *hybris* — more at OUT] **:** exaggerated pride or self-confidence often resulting in retribution — **hu·bris·tic** \hyü-ˈbris-tik\ *adj*

huck \ˈhək\ *n* **:** HUCKABACK

huck·a·back \ˈhək-ə-ˌbak\ *n* [origin unknown] **:** an absorbent durable fabric of cotton, linen, or both used chiefly for towels

huck·le·ber·ry \ˈhək-əl-ˌber-ē\ *n* [perh. alter. of *hurtleberry* (huckleberry)] **1 :** any of a genus (*Gaylussacia*) of American shrubs of the heath family; *also* **:** the edible dark blue to black usu. acid berry (esp. of *G. baccata*) with 10 bony nutlets **2 :** BLUEBERRY

1**huck·ster** \ˈhək-stər\ *n* [ME *hukster*, fr. MD *hokester*, fr. *hoeken* to peddle; akin to MLG *hōken* to peddle — more at HAWKER] **1 :** HAWKER, PEDDLER **2 :** one who produces advertising material for commercial clients esp. for radio or television — **huck·ster·ism** \-stə-ˌriz-əm\ *n*

2**huckster** *vb* **huck·stered; huck·ster·ing** \-st(ə-)riŋ\ *vi* **:** HAGGLE ~ *vt* **1 :** to deal in or bargain over **2 :** to promote by showmanship

HUD *abbr* Department of Housing and Urban Development

1**hud·dle** \ˈhəd-ᵊl\ *vb* **hud·dled; hud·dling** \ˈhəd-liŋ, -ᵊl-iŋ\ [prob. fr. or akin to ME *hoderen* to huddle] *vt* **1** *Brit* **:** to arrange carelessly or hurriedly **2 a :** to crowd together <*huddled* masses of people> **b :** to draw (oneself) together **:** CROUCH **3** *archaic* **:** to herd into or out of a place in a disorderly mass **4 :** to wrap closely in (as clothes) ~ *vi* **1 a :** to gather in a close-packed group **b :** to curl up **:** CROUCH **2 a :** to hold a consultation **:** CONFER **b :** to gather in a huddle in football — **hud·dler** \ˈhəd-lər, -ᵊl-ər\ *n*

2**huddle** *n* **1 :** a close-packed group **:** BUNCH <~*s* of cattle> <a ~ of cottages> **2 a :** MEETING, CONFERENCE <secret ~*s* were held by five leading Republicans —*Newsweek*> **b :** a conference of football players away from the line of scrimmage to receive the strategy (as from the quarterback) for the next down

Hu·di·bras·tic \ˌhyüd-ə-ˈbras-tik\ *adj* [irreg. fr. *Hudibras*, satirical poem by Samuel Butler †1680] **1 :** written in humorous octosyllabic couplets **2 :** MOCK-HEROIC — **Hudibrastic** *n*

Hud·son seal \ˌhəd-sən-\ *n* [*Hudson* bay, sea in Canada] **:** the fur of the muskrat dressed to simulate seal

hue \ˈhyü\ *n* [ME *hewe*, fr. OE *hīw*; akin to OE *hār* hoary — more at HOAR] **1 :** COMPLEXION, ASPECT <political parties of every ~ —Louis Wasserman> **2 a :** gradation of color **b :** the attribute of colors that permits them to be classed as red, yellow, green, blue, or an intermediate between any contiguous pair of these colors — compare LIGHTNESS, SATURATION

hue and cry *n* [*hue* (outcry)] **1 a :** a loud outcry formerly used in the pursuit of one who is suspected of a crime **b :** the pursuit of a suspect or a written proclamation for the capture of a suspect **2 :** a clamor of alarm or protest **3 :** HUBBUB

hued \ˈhyüd\ *adj* **:** COLORED — usu. used in combination <green-*hued*>

1**huff** \ˈhəf\ *vb* [imit.] *vi* **1 :** to emit puffs (as of breath or steam) **2 a :** to make empty threats **:** BLUSTER <management ~*ed* about the chances of a lockout> **b :** to react or behave indignantly <refused to agree and ~*ed* off in anger> ~ *vt* **1 :** to puff up **:** INFLATE <their buying ~*ed* low-priced motor shares —*Time*> **2** *archaic* **:** to treat with contempt **:** BULLY **3 :** to make angry **:** PROVOKE

2**huff** *n* **:** a usu. peevish and transitory spell of anger or resentment

huff·ish \ˈhəf-ish\ *adj* **:** ARROGANT, SULKY

huffy \ˈhəf-ē\ *adj* **huff·i·er; -est 1 :** HAUGHTY, ARROGANT **2 a :** roused to indignation **:** IRRITATED **b :** easily offended **:** TOUCHY — **huff·i·ness** *n*

hug \ˈhəg\ *vt* **hugged; hug·ging** [perh. of Scand origin; akin to ON *hugga* to soothe] **1 :** to press tightly esp. in the arms **2 a :** CONGRATULATE **b :** to hold fast **:** CHERISH <*hugged* his miseries like a sulky child —John Buchan> **3 :** to stay close to <the road ~*s* the river> — **hug** *n* — **hug·ga·ble** \ˈhəg-ə-bəl\ *adj*

huge \ˈhyüj, ˈyüj\ *adj* **hug·er; hug·est** [ME, fr. OF *ahuge*] **:** very large or extensive; as **a :** of great size or area **b :** great in scale or degree <~ spending> **c :** great in scope or character <a man of ~ talent> — **huge·ly** *adv* — **huge·ness** *n*

syn HUGE, VAST, IMMENSE, ENORMOUS, GIGANTIC, COLOSSAL, MAMMOTH *shared meaning element* **:** exceedingly or excessively large. HUGE indicates extreme largeness, usually in size, bulk, or capacity <*huge* cities grow steadily *huger* —Aldous Huxley> VAST denotes extreme largeness or broadness, usually of extent or range <the *vast* varieties of religions ancient and modern —M. R. Cohen> <depleting our *vast* natural resources heedlessly> IMMENSE implies an exceeding of usual standards or measurements or accustomed concepts <an *immense* quill, plucked from a distended albatross' wing —Herman Melville> <the technical power of the human race has become *immense* —Michael Novak> ENORMOUS, often interchangeable with *immense*, is likely to be preferred when the idea of exceeding the reasonable, the normal, or the acceptable is to be conveyed <the burden of humiliation carried by most Africans over thirty is *enormous* —William Attwood> <some practitioners have attained *enormous* incomes as beneficiaries of the public systems of health care —T. R. McConnell> The remaining words graphically describe whatever is large beyond accustomed concepts, GIGANTIC calling up the image of the fabled giants of old, COLOSSAL that of the ancient Colossus, and MAMMOTH that of the ponderous prehistoric elephantine mammoth <*gigantic* jewels that a hundred Negroes could not carry —G. K. Chesterton> <the *colossal* speed of 15,000 miles a second —James Jeans> <the *mammoth* hydrogen bomb explosion —*N.Y. Times*> ***ant*** tiny

huge·ous \-əs\ *adj* **:** HUGE — **huge·ous·ly** *adv*

1**hug·ger–mug·ger** \ˈhəg-ər-ˌməg-ər\ *n* [origin unknown] **1 :** SECRECY **2 :** CONFUSION, MUDDLE

2**hugger–mugger** *adj* **1 :** SECRET **2 :** of a confused or disorderly nature **:** JUMBLED — **hugger–mugger** *adv*

3**hugger–mugger** *vb* **hug·ger–mug·gered; hug·ger–mug·ger·ing** \-ˌməg-(ə-)riŋ\ *vt* **:** to keep secret **:** hush up ~ *vi* **:** to act or confer stealthily

hug–me–tight \ˈhəg-mē-ˌtīt\ *n* **:** a woman's short usu. knitted sleeveless close-fitting jacket

Hu·gue·not \ˈhyü-gə-ˌnät\ *n* [MF, French Protestant, fr. MF dial. *huguenot*, adherent of a Swiss political movement, alter. (influenced by Besançon *Hugues* †1532 Swiss political leader) of *eidgnot*, fr. G dial. *eidgnoss* confederate] **:** a member of the French Reformed communion esp. of the 16th and 17th centuries — **Hu·gue·not·ic** \ˌhyü-gə-ˈnät-ik\ *adj* — **Hu·gue·not·ism** \ˈhyü-gə-ˌnät-ˌiz-əm\ *n*

hu·la \ˈhü-lə\ *also* **hu·la–hu·la** \ˌhü-lə-ˈhü-lə\ *n* [Hawaiian] **1 :** a sinuous Polynesian dance characterized by rhythmic movement of the hips and mimetic gestures with the hands and often accompanied by chants and rhythmic drumming **2 :** music to which a hula is performed

1**hulk** \ˈhəlk\ *n* [ME *hulke*, fr. OE *hulc*, fr. ML *holcas*, fr. Gk *holkas*, fr. *helkein* to pull — more at SULCUS] **1 a :** a heavy clumsy ship **b :** the body of an old ship unfit for service **c :** an abandoned wreck or shell **d :** a ship used as a prison — usu. used in pl. <every prisoner sent to the ~*s* —Kenneth Roberts> **2 :** one that is bulky or unwieldy <a big ~ of a man>

2**hulk** *vi* **1** *dial Eng* **:** to move ponderously **2 :** to appear impressively large or massive **:** LOOM

hulk·ing \ˈhəl-kiŋ\ *adj* **:** PONDEROUS, MASSIVE

1**hull** \ˈhəl\ *n* [ME, fr. OE *hulu*; akin to OHG *hala* hull, OE *helan* to conceal — more at HELL] **1 a :** the outer covering of a fruit or seed **b :** the persistent calyx or involucre that subtends some fruits **2 a :** the frame or body of a ship exclusive of masts, yards, sails, and rigging **b (1) :** the portion of a flying boat which furnishes buoyancy when in contact with the water and to which the main supporting surfaces and other parts are attached **(2) :** the main structure of a rigid airship **3 :** COVERING, CASING — **hull–less** \ˈhəl-ləs\ *adj*

2**hull** *vt* **:** to remove the hulls of **:** SHUCK — **hull·er** *n*

hul·la·ba·loo \ˈhəl-ə-bə-ˌlü\ *n, pl* **-loos** [perh. irreg. fr. *hallo* + Sc *balloo*, interj. used to hush children] **:** a confused noise **:** UPROAR

hull down *adv or adj, of a ship* **:** at such a distance that only the superstructure is visible

hul·lo \(ˌ)hə-ˈlō\ *chiefly Brit var of* HELLO

hum \ˈhəm\ *vb* **hummed; hum·ming** [ME *hummen*; akin to MHG *hummen* to hum, MD *hommel* bumblebee] *vi* **1 a :** to utter a sound like that of the speech sound \m\ prolonged **b :** to make the natural noise of an insect in motion or a similar sound **:** DRONE **c :** to give forth a low continuous blend of sound **2 :** to be busily active ~ *vt* **1 :** to sing with the lips closed and without articulation **2 :** to affect or express by humming <*hummed* me to sleep> <*hummed* his displeasure> — **hum** *n* — **hum·ma·ble** \ˈhəm-ə-bəl\ *adj* — **hum·mer** *n*

1**hu·man** \ˈhyü-mən, ˈyü-\ *adj* [ME *humain*, fr. MF, fr. L *humanus*; akin to L *homo* man — more at HOMAGE] **1 :** of, relating to, or characteristic of man **2 :** consisting of men **3 a :** having human form or attributes **b :** susceptible to or representative of the sympathies and frailties of man's nature <such an inconsistency is very ~ —P. E. More> — **hu·man·ness** \-mən-nəs\ *n*

2**human** *n* **:** a human being — **hu·man·like** \-mən-ˌlīk\ *adj*

hu·mane \hyü-ˈmān, yü-\ *adj* [ME *humain*] **1 :** marked by compassion, sympathy, or consideration for other human beings or animals **2 :** characterized by or tending to broad humanistic culture **:** HUMANISTIC <~ studies> — **hu·mane·ly** *adv* — **hu·mane·ness** \-ˈmān-nəs\ *n*

human ecology *n* **1 :** a branch of sociology concerned esp. with the study of the spatial and temporal interrelationships between men and their economic, social, and political organization **2 :** the ecology of man and of human communities and populations esp. as concerned with preservation of environmental quality (as of air or water) through proper application of conservation and civil engineering practices

human engineering *n* **1 :** management of human beings and affairs esp. in industry **2 :** a science that deals with the design of mechanical devices for efficient use by human beings

hu·man·ism \ˈhyü-mə-ˌniz-əm, ˈyü-\ *n* **1 a :** devotion to the humanities **:** literary culture **b :** the revival of classical letters, individualistic and critical spirit, and emphasis on secular concerns characteristic of the Renaissance **2 :** HUMANITARIANISM **3 :** a doctrine, attitude, or way of life centered on human interests or values; *esp* **:** a philosophy that asserts the dignity and worth of man and his capacity for self-realization through reason and that often rejects supernaturalism — **hu·man·ist** \-nəst\ *n or adj* — **hu·man·is·tic** \ˌhyü-mə-ˈnis-tik, ˌyü-\ *adj* — **hu·man·is·ti·cal·ly** \-ti-k(ə-)lē\ *adv*

hu·man·i·tar·i·an \hyü-ˌman-ə-ˈter-ē-ən, yü-\ *n* : a person promoting human welfare and social reform : PHILANTHROPIST — **humanitarian** *adj*

hu·man·i·tar·i·an·ism \-ē-ə-ˌniz-əm\ *n* : concern for human welfare esp. as expressed through philanthropic activities and interest in social reforms

hu·man·i·ty \hyü-ˈman-ət-ē, yü-\ *n, pl* **-ties** **1** : the quality or state of being humane **2 a** : the quality or state of being human **b** *pl* : human attributes or qualities <his work has the ripeness of the 18th century, and its rough *humanities* —Pamela H. Johnson> **3** *pl* : the branches of learning having primarily a cultural character **4** : MANKIND

hu·man·ize \ˈhyü-mə-ˌnīz, ˈyü-\ *vt* **-ized; -iz·ing** **1 a** : to represent as or endow with a human character **b** : to adapt to human nature or use **2** : to make humane <tried to ~ and regulate war —Vera M. Dean> — **hu·man·iza·tion** \ˌhyü-mə-nə-ˈzā-shən, ˌyü-\ *n* — **hu·man·iz·er** *n*

hu·man·kind \ˈhyü-mən-ˌkīnd, ˈyü-\ *n sing but sing or pl in constr* : MANKIND

hu·man·ly \ˈhyü-mən-lē, ˈyü-\ *adv* **1 a** : from the viewpoint of man <~ speaking, the process works . . . like this —Elizabeth Janeway> **b** : within the range of human capacity <a ~ impossible task> **2 a** : with regard to or in keeping with human proneness to error or weakness <had the temerity to be ~ inefficient a few times —Leonard Koppett> **b** : with regard to human needs and emotions <provide ~ for those who are not needed in the economy —E. F. Bacon>

human nature *n* : the nature of man: as **a** : the complex of behavioral patterns, attitudes, and ideas which man acquires socially **b** : the complex of fundamental dispositions and traits of man

hu·man·oid \ˈhyü-mə-ˌnȯid, ˈyü-\ *adj* : having human form or characteristics <~ dentition> <~ robots> — **humanoid** *n*

human relations *n pl but usu sing in constr* **1** : a study of human problems arising from organizational and interpersonal relations (as in industry) **2** : a course, study, or program designed to develop better interpersonal and intergroup adjustments

hu·mate \ˈhyü-ˌmāt, ˈyü-\ *n* : a salt or ester of a humic acid

[1]**hum·ble** \ˈhəm-bəl, ˈəm-\ *adj* **hum·bler** \-b(ə-)lər\; **hum·blest** \-b(ə-)ləst\ [ME, fr. OF, fr. L *humilis* low, humble, fr. *humus* earth; akin to Gk *chthōn* earth, *chamai* on the ground] **1** : not proud or haughty : not arrogant or assertive **2** : reflecting, expressing, or offered in a spirit of deference or submission <a ~ apology> **3** : ranking low in a hierarchy or scale : INSIGNIFICANT, UNPRETENTIOUS — **hum·ble·ness** \-bəl-nəs\ *n* — **hum·bly** \-blē\ *adv*

syn HUMBLE, MEEK, MODEST, LOWLY *shared meaning element* : lacking all signs of pride, aggressiveness, or self-assertiveness

[2]**humble** *vt* **hum·bled; hum·bling** \-b(ə-)liŋ\ **1** : to make humble in spirit or manner **2** : to destroy the power, independence, or prestige of ***syn*** see ABASE — **hum·bler** \-b(ə-)lər\ *n*

hum·ble–bee \ˈhəm-bəl-ˌbē\ *n* [ME *humbylbee*, fr. *humbyl-* (akin to MD *hommel* bumblebee) + *bee* — more at HUM] : BUMBLEBEE

humble pie *n* : submission, apology, or retraction usu. made under pressure : HUMILIATION — often used in the phrase *eat humble pie*

[1]**hum·bug** \ˈhəm-ˌbəg\ *n* [origin unknown] **1 a** : something designed to deceive and mislead **b** : a person who passes himself off as something that he is not **2** : an attitude or spirit of pretense and deception **3** : DRIVEL, NONSENSE ***syn*** see IMPOSTURE — **hum·bug·gery** \-ˌbəg-(ə-)rē\ *n*

[2]**humbug** *vb* **hum·bugged; hum·bug·ging** *vt* : DECEIVE, HOAX ~ *vi* : to engage in a hoax or deception

hum·ding·er \ˈhəm-ˈdiŋ-ər\ *n* [prob. alter. of *hummer* (humdinger)] : a striking or extraordinary person or thing

hum·drum \ˈhəm-ˌdrəm\ *adj* [irreg. redupl. of *hum*] : MONOTONOUS, DULL — **humdrum** *n*

hu·mec·tant \hyü-ˈmek-tənt\ *n* [L *humectant-, humectans*, prp. of *humectare* to moisten, fr. *humectus* moist, fr. *humēre* to be moist — more at HUMOR] : a substance that promotes retention of moisture — **humectant** *adj*

hu·mer·al \ˈhyüm-(ə-)rəl\ *adj* **1** : of, relating to, or situated in the region of the humerus or shoulder **2** : of, relating to, or being a body part analogous to the humerus or shoulder — **humeral** *n*

humeral veil *n* : an oblong vestment worn around the shoulders and over the hands by a priest or subdeacon holding a sacred vessel

hu·mer·us \ˈhyüm-(ə-)rəs\ *n, pl* **hu·meri** \ˈhyü-mə-ˌrī, -ˌrē\ [NL, fr. L, upper arm, shoulder; akin to Goth *ams* shoulder, Gk *ōmos*] : the long bone of the upper arm or forelimb extending from the shoulder to the elbow

hu·mic \ˈhyü-mik, ˈyü-\ *adj* : of, relating to, or derived at least in part from humus

humic acid *n* : any of various organic acids obtained from humus

hu·mid \ˈhyü-məd, ˈyü-\ *adj* [F or L; F *humide*, fr. L *humidus*, fr. *humēre*] : containing or characterized by perceptible moisture esp. to the point of being oppressive <a ~ climate> ***syn*** see WET — **hu·mid·ly** *adv*

hu·mid·i·fi·er \hyü-ˈmid-ə-ˌfī(-ə)r, yü-\ *n* : a device for supplying or maintaining humidity

hu·mid·i·fy \-ˌfī\ *vt* **-fied; -fy·ing** : to make humid — **hu·mid·i·fi·ca·tion** \-ˌmid-ə-fə-ˈkā-shən\ *n*

hu·mid·i·stat \hyü-ˈmid-ə-ˌstat, yü-\ *n* : an instrument for regulating or maintaining the degree of humidity

hu·mid·i·ty \hyü-ˈmid-ət-ē, yü-\ *n, pl* **-ties** : a moderate degree of wetness esp. of the atmosphere : DAMPNESS — compare RELATIVE HUMIDITY

hu·mi·dor \ˈhyü-mə-ˌdȯ(ə)r, ˈyü-\ *n* [*humid* + *-or* (as in *cuspidor*)] : a case usu. for storing cigars in which the air is kept properly humidified

hu·mi·fi·ca·tion \ˌhyü-mə-fə-ˈkā-shən, ˌyü-\ *n* : formation of or conversion into humus

hu·mi·fied \ˈhyü-mə-ˌfīd, ˈyü-\ *adj* : converted into humus

hu·mil·i·ate \hyü-ˈmil-ē-ˌāt, yü-\ *vt* **-at·ed; -at·ing** [LL *humiliatus*, pp. of *humiliare*, fr. L *humilis* low — more at HUMBLE] : to reduce to a lower position in one's own eyes or others' eyes : MORTIFY ***syn*** see ABASE — **hu·mil·i·a·tion** \-ˌmil-ē-ˈā-shən\ *n*

hu·mil·i·at·ing \hyü-ˈmil-ē-ˌāt-iŋ, yü-\ *adj* : extremely destructive to one's self-respect or dignity : HUMBLING — **hu·mil·i·at·ing·ly** \-iŋ-lē\ *adv*

hu·mil·i·ty \hyü-ˈmil-ət-ē, yü-\ *n* : the quality or state of being humble

hum·ming·bird \ˈhəm-iŋ-ˌbərd\ *n* : any of numerous tiny brightly colored nonpasserine birds (family Trochilidae) related to the swifts and like them having narrow wings with long primaries, a slender bill, and a very extensile tongue

hum·mock \ˈhəm-ək\ *n* [alter. of [2]*hammock*] **1** : a rounded knoll or hillock **2** : a ridge of ice **3** : [2]HAMMOCK 2 — **hum·mocky** \-ə-kē\ *adj*

[1]**hu·mor** \ˈ(h)yü-mər\ *n* [ME *humour*, fr. MF *humeur*, fr. ML & L; ML *humor*, fr. L, moisture; akin to ON *vökr* damp, L *humēre* to be moist, Gk *hygros* wet] **1 a** : a normal functioning bodily semifluid or fluid (as the blood or lymph) **b** : a secretion (as a hormone) that is an excitant of activity **2 a** *in medieval physiology* : a fluid or juice of an animal or plant; *specif* : one of the four fluids entering into the constitution of the body and determining by their relative proportions a person's health and temperament **b** : characteristic or habitual disposition or bent : TEMPERAMENT <a man of cheerful ~> **c** : an often temporary state of mind imposed esp. by circumstances <he was in no ~ to listen to further argument> **d** : a sudden, unpredictable, or unreasoning inclination : WHIM <beset by the uncertain ~*s* of nature> **3 a** : that quality which appeals to a sense of the ludicrous or absurdly incongruous **b** : the mental faculty of discovering, expressing, or appreciating the ludicrous or absurdly incongruous **c** : something that is or is designed to be comical or amusing ***syn*** see MOOD, WIT — **out of humor** : out of sorts

[2]**humor** *vt* **hu·mored; hu·mor·ing** \ˈ(h)yüm-(ə-)riŋ\ **1** : to soothe or content by indulgence **2** : to adapt oneself to ***syn*** see INDULGE

hu·mor·al \ˈ(h)yüm-(ə-)rəl\ *adj* : of, relating to, proceeding from, or involving a bodily humor (as a hormone)

hu·mor·esque \ˌ(h)yü-mə-ˈresk\ *n* [G *humoreske*, fr. *humor*, fr. E] : a musical composition typically whimsical or fanciful in character : CAPRICCIO

hu·mor·ist \ˈ(h)yüm-(ə-)rəst\ *n* **1** *archaic* : a person subject to whims **2** : a person specializing in or noted for humor

hu·mor·is·tic \ˌ(h)yü-mə-ˈris-tik\ *adj* : HUMOROUS

hu·mor·less \ˈ(h)yü-mər-ləs\ *adj* **1** : lacking a sense of humor **2** : lacking humorous characteristics — **hu·mor·less·ness** *n*

hu·mor·ous \ˈ(h)yüm-(ə-)rəs\ *adj* **1** *obs* : HUMID **2 a** : full of or characterized by humor : JOCULAR **b** : indicating or expressive of a sense of humor ***syn*** see WITTY — **hu·mor·ous·ly** *adv* — **hu·mor·ous·ness** *n*

hu·mour *chiefly Brit var of* HUMOR

[1]**hump** \ˈhəmp\ *n* [akin to MLG *hump* bump, L *incumbere* to lie down, Gk *kymbē* bowl, OE *hype* hip] **1** : a rounded protuberance: as **a** : HUMPBACK 1 **b** : a fleshy protuberance on the back of an animal (as a camel, bison, or whale) **c (1)** : MOUND, HUMMOCK **(2)** : MOUNTAIN, RANGE <the Himalayan ~> **2** *Brit* : a fit of depression or sulking **3** : a difficult, trying, or critical phase — often used in the phrase *over the hump*

[2]**hump** *vt* **1** : to exert (oneself) vigorously **2** : to make humpbacked : HUNCH **3** *chiefly Brit* : to put or carry on the back; *also* : TRANSPORT **4** : to copulate with — usu. considered vulgar ~ *vi* **1** : to exert oneself : HUSTLE **2** : to move swiftly : RACE

hump·back \-ˌbak, *for 1 also* -ˈbak\ *n* **1** : a humped or crooked back; *also* : KYPHOSIS **2** : HUNCHBACK 2 **3** : a large whalebone whale (genus *Megaptera*) related to the rorquals but having very long flippers

hump·backed \-ˈbakt\ *adj* **1** : having a humped back **2** : convexly curved <a ~ bridge>

humped \ˈhəm(p)t\ *adj* : having a hump; *esp* : HUMPBACKED

humped cattle *n* : domestic cattle developed from an Indian species (*Bos indicus*) and characterized by a hump of fat and muscle above the shoulders : Brahman cattle

[1]**humph** *a snort, or* h *followed by* m *or nasalized* ˈə; *often read as* ˈhəm(p)f\ *interj* [imit. of a grunt] — used to express doubt or contempt

[2]**humph** \ˈhəm(p)f\ *vi* : to utter a humph ~ *vt* : to utter (as a remark) in a tone suggestive of a humph

hump·ty–dump·ty \ˌhəm(p)-tē-ˈdəm(p)-tē\ *n, pl* **-dumpties** *often cap H&D* [*Humpty-Dumpty*, egg-shaped nursery-rhyme character who fell from a wall and broke into bits] : something that once damaged can never be repaired or made operative again

humpy \ˈhəm-pē\ *adj* **hump·i·er; -est** **1** : full of humps **2** : covered with humps

hu·mus \ˈhyü-məs, ˈyü-\ *n* [NL, fr. L, earth — more at HUMBLE] : a brown or black complex variable material resulting from partial decomposition of plant or animal matter and forming the organic portion of soil

Hun \ˈhən\ *n* [LL *Hunni*, pl.] **1** : a member of a nomadic Mongolian people gaining control of a large part of central and eastern Europe under Attila about A.D. 450 **2 a** *often not cap* : a person who is wantonly destructive : VANDAL **b** : GERMAN; *esp* : a German soldier — usu. used disparagingly

[1]**hunch** \ˈhənch\ *vb* [origin unknown] *vi* **1** : to thrust oneself forward **2** : to assume a bent or crooked posture ~ *vt* **1** : JOSTLE, SHOVE **2** : to thrust into a hump

[2]**hunch** *n* **1** : an act or instance of hunching : PUSH **2 a** : HUMP **b** : a thick piece : LUMP **3** : a strong intuitive feeling concerning a future event or result

---

ə abut ᵊ kitten ər further a back ā bake ä cot, cart
aù out ch chin e less ē easy g gift i trip ī life
j joke ŋ sing ō flow ȯ flaw ȯi coin th thin t͟h this
ü loot u̇ foot y yet yü few yu̇ furious zh vision

hunch·back \'hənch-ˌbak\ *n* **1 :** HUMPBACK 1 **2 :** a person with a humpback — **hunch·backed** \-'bakt\ *adj*

hun·dred \'hən-drəd, -dərd\ *n, pl* **hundreds** *or* **hundred** [ME, fr. OE; akin to ON *hundrath* hundred; both fr. a prehistoric WGmc-NGmc compound whose constituents were akin respectively to OE *hund* hundred and to Goth ga*rathjan* to count; akin to L *centum* hundred, Gk he*katon*, Av *satəm*, OE *tīen* ten — more at TEN, REASON] **1** — see NUMBER table **2 :** the number occupying the position three to the left of the decimal point in the arabic notation **3** **hundreds** *pl* **:** the numbers 100 to 999 **4 :** a 100-dollar bill **5 :** a subdivision of some English and American counties — **hundred** *adj* — **hun·dredth** \-drədth, -drətth\ *adj or n*

hun·dred–per·cent·er \ˌhən-drəd-pər-'sent-ər, -dərd-\ *n* [*hundred-percent (American)*] **:** a thoroughgoing nationalist — **hun·dred–per·cent·ism** \-'sent-ˌiz-əm\ *n*

hun·dred·weight \'hən-drə-ˌdwāt, -dər-ˌdwāt\ *n, pl* **hundredweight** *or* **hundredweights** **1 a :** a unit of weight equal to 100 pounds — called also *short hundredweight;* see WEIGHT table **b** *Brit* **:** a unit of weight equal to 112 pounds — called also *long hundredweight* **2 :** METRIC HUNDREDWEIGHT

hung *past of* HANG

Hung *abbr* Hungarian; Hungary

Hun·gar·i·an \ˌhəŋ-'ger-ē-ən, -'gar-\ *n* **1 a :** a native or inhabitant of Hungary **:** MAGYAR **b :** a person of Hungarian descent **2 :** MAGYAR 2 — **Hungarian** *adj*

1hun·ger \'həŋ-gər\ *n* [ME, fr. OE *hungor;* akin to OHG *hungar* hunger, Skt *kāṅkṣati* he desires] **1 a :** a craving or urgent need for food or a specific nutrient **b :** an uneasy sensation occasioned by the lack of food **c :** a weakened condition brought about by prolonged lack of food **2 :** a strong desire **:** CRAVING

2hunger *vb* **hun·gered; hun·ger·ing** \-g(ə-)riŋ\ *vi* **1 :** to feel or suffer hunger **2 :** to have an eager desire ~ *vt* **:** to make hungry *syn* see LONG

hunger strike *n* **:** refusal (as by a prisoner) to eat enough to sustain life

hung jury *n* **:** a jury that fails to reach a verdict

hung over *adj* **:** suffering from a hangover

hun·gry \'həŋ-grē\ *adj* **hun·gri·er; -est** **1 a :** feeling hunger **b :** characterized by or characteristic of hunger or appetite **2 :** EAGER, AVID **3 :** not rich or fertile **:** BARREN — **hun·gri·ly** \-grə-lē\ *adv* — **hun·gri·ness** \-grē-nəs\ *n*

hung up *adj* **1 :** delayed or detained for a time **2 :** anxiously nervous

hunk \'həŋk\ *n* [Flem *hunke*] **:** a large lump or piece

hun·ker \'həŋ-kər\ *vi* **hun·kered; hun·ker·ing** \-k(ə-)riŋ\ [perh. of Scand origin; akin to ON *hūka* to squat; akin to MLG *hōken* to squat — more at HAWKER] **:** CROUCH, SQUAT

hun·kers \'həŋ-kərz\ *n pl* **:** HAUNCHES

hunks \'həŋ(k)s\ *n pl but sing in constr* [origin unknown] **:** a surly ill-natured person; *esp* **:** MISER

hun·ky–do·ry \ˌhəŋ-kē-'dōr-ē, -'dȯr-\ *adj* [obs. E dial. *hunk* (home base) + *-dory* (origin unknown)] **:** quite satisfactory **:** FINE

Hun·nish \'hən-ish\ *adj* **:** relating to or resembling the Huns; *specif* **:** BARBAROUS

1hunt \'hənt\ *vb* [ME *hunten,* fr. OE *huntian;* akin to OHG heri*hunda* battle spoils] *vt* **1 a :** to pursue for food or in sport <~ buffalo> **b :** to manage in the search for game <~*s* a pack of dogs> **2 a :** to pursue with intent to capture <~*ed* the escaped prisoner> **b :** to search out **:** SEEK **3 :** to drive or chase esp. by harrying <members of the colonial council . . . were ~*ed* from their homes —J. T. Adams> **4 :** to traverse in search of prey <~*s* the woods> ~ *vi* **1 :** to take part in a hunt **2 :** to attempt to find something **3 :** to oscillate alternately to each side (as of a neutral point) or to run alternately faster and slower instead of steadily — used esp. of a device or machine

2hunt *n* **1 :** the act, the practice, or an instance of hunting **2 :** a group of mounted hunters and their hunting dogs

hunt·er \'hənt-ər\ *n* **1 a :** a person who hunts game **b :** a dog used or trained for hunting **c :** a horse used or adapted for use in hunting; *esp* **:** a fast strong horse trained for cross-country work and jumping **2 :** a person who searches for something

hunt·ing *n* **1 :** the act of one that hunts; *specif* **:** the pursuit of game **2 :** the process of hunting **3 a :** a periodic variation in speed of a synchronous electrical machine from that of the true synchronous speed **b :** a self-induced and undesirable oscillation of a variable above and below the desired value in an automatic control system **c :** a continuous attempt by an automatically controlled system to find a desired equilibrium condition

hunting horn *n* **:** a signal horn used in the chase; *specif* **:** a long conical tube coiled in a large circle and having a flared bell and a cup-shaped mouthpiece

hunt·ress \'hən-trəs\ *n* **:** a female hunter

Hunts *abbr* Huntingdonshire

hunts·man \'hən(t)-smən\ *n* **1 :** HUNTER 1a **2 :** a person who manages a hunt and looks after the hounds

hup \'həp\ *interj* [prob. alter. of *one*] — used to mark a marching cadence

hur·dies \'hərd-ēz\ *n pl* [origin unknown] *dial Brit* **:** BUTTOCKS, RUMP

1hur·dle \'hərd-ᵊl\ *n* [ME *hurdel,* fr. OE *hyrdel;* akin to OHG *hurd* hurdle, L *cratis* wickerwork, hurdle] **1 a :** a portable panel usu. of wattled withes and stakes used esp. for enclosing land or livestock **b :** a frame or sled formerly used in England for dragging traitors to execution **2 a :** an artificial barrier over which men or horses must leap in a race **b** *pl* **:** any of various track events in which a series of hurdles must be surmounted **3 :** BARRIER, OBSTACLE

2hurdle *vt* **hur·dled; hur·dling** \'hərd-liŋ, -ᵊl-iŋ\ **1 :** to leap over esp. while running **2 :** OVERCOME, SURMOUNT — **hur·dler** \'hərd-lər, -ᵊl-ər\ *n*

hur·dy–gur·dy \ˌhərd-ē-'gərd-ē, 'hərd-ē-ˌ\ *n, pl* **-gur·dies** [prob. imit.] **:** a musical instrument in which the sound is produced by turning a crank; *esp* **:** BARREL ORGAN

hurl \'hər(-ə)l\ *vb* **hurled; hurl·ing** \'hər-liŋ\ [ME *hurlen*] *vi* **1 :** RUSH, HURTLE **2 :** PITCH 4 ~ *vt* **1 :** to send or thrust with great vigor <the forces that were to be ~*ed* against the Turks —N. T. Gilroy> **2 :** to throw down with violence <~*ed* the tyrant from his throne> **3 a :** to throw forcefully **:** FLING <~*ed* the manuscript into the fire> <~*ed* himself over the fence> **b :** PITCH 2a *syn* see THROW — **hurl** *n* — **hurl·er** \'hər-lər\ *n*

hurdle 2a

hurl·ing *n* **:** an Irish game resembling field hockey played between two teams of 15 players each

hur·ly \'hər-lē\ *n* [prob. short for *hurly-burly*] **:** UPROAR, TUMULT

hur·ly–bur·ly \ˌhər-lē-'bər-lē\ *n* [prob. alter. & redupl. of *hurling,* gerund of *hurl*] **:** UPROAR, TUMULT

Hu·ron \'hyu̇r-ən, 'hyu̇(ə)r-ˌän, *or without* h\ *n, pl* **Hurons** *or* **Huron** [F, lit., boor] **1** *pl* **:** a confederacy of Amerindian peoples orig. of the St. Lawrence valley **2 :** a member of any of the Huron peoples

1hur·rah \hu̇-'rō, -'rä\ *also* **hur·ray** \hu̇-'rā\ *interj* [perh. fr. G *hurra*] — used to express joy, approbation, or encouragement

2hur·rah \hu̇-'rō, -'rä, 'hü-ˌ\ *n* **1 :** EXCITEMENT, FANFARE **2 :** FUSS, CONTROVERSY

Hur·ri·an \'hu̇r-ē-ən\ *n* **1 :** a member of an ancient non-Semitic people prominent in northern Mesopotamia, Syria, and eastern Asia Minor about 1500 B.C. **2 :** the language of the Hurrian people

hur·ri·cane \'hər-ə-ˌkān, -i-kən, 'hə-rə-, 'hə-ri-\ *n* [Sp *huracán,* fr. Taino *hurakán*] **:** a tropical cyclone with winds of 74 miles per hour or greater that is usu. accompanied by rain, thunder, and lightning and that sometimes moves into temperate latitudes — see BEAUFORT SCALE table

hurricane deck *n* **:** PROMENADE DECK

hurricane lamp *n* **:** a candlestick or an electric lamp equipped with a glass chimney

hur·ried \'hər-ēd, 'hə-rēd\ *adj* **1 :** going or working at speed **2 :** done in a hurry **:** HASTY — **hur·ried·ly** *adv* — **hur·ried·ness** *n*

1hur·ry \'hər-ē, 'hə-rē\ *vb* **hur·ried; hur·ry·ing** [perh. fr. ME *hory-en*] *vt* **1 a :** to carry or cause to go with haste <~ him to the hospital> **b :** to impel to rash or precipitate action **2 a :** to impel to greater speed **:** PROD <used spurs to ~ the horse> **b :** EXPEDITE **c :** to perform with undue haste <~ a minuet> ~ *vi* **:** to move or act with haste <please ~ up> — **hur·ri·er** *n*

2hurry *n* **1 :** disturbed or disorderly activity **:** COMMOTION **2 a :** flurried and often bustling or disorderly haste **b :** a state of eagerness or urgency **:** RUSH *syn* see HASTE — **in a hurry :** without delay **:** as rapidly as possible <the police got there *in a hurry*>

hur·ry–scur·ry *or* **hur·ry–skur·ry** \ˌhər-ē-'skər-ē, ˌhə-rē-'skə-rē\ *n* [redupl. of 2*hurry*] **:** a confused rush **:** TURMOIL — **hurry–scurry** *adj or adv*

1hurt \'hərt\ *vb* **hurt; hurt·ing** [ME *hurten*] *vt* **1 a :** to inflict with physical pain **:** WOUND **b :** to do substantial or material harm to **:** DAMAGE <the dry summer has ~ the land> **2 a :** to cause pain or anguish to **:** OFFEND **b :** to be detrimental to **:** HAMPER <charges of graft ~ his chances of being elected> ~ *vi* **1 a :** to feel pain **:** SUFFER **b** *chiefly Midland* **:** to be in need **:** WANT **2 :** to cause damage or distress <hit where it ~*s*> *syn* see INJURE — **hurt·er** *n*

2hurt *n* **1 :** a cause of injury or damage **:** BLOW **2 a :** a bodily injury or wound **b :** mental distress or anguish **:** SUFFERING **3 :** WRONG, HARM

hurt·ful \'hərt-fəl\ *adj* **:** causing injury or suffering **:** DAMAGING — **hurt·ful·ly** \-fə-lē\ *adv* — **hurt·ful·ness** *n*

hur·tle \'hərt-ᵊl\ *vb* **hur·tled; hur·tling** \'hərt-liŋ, -ᵊl-iŋ\ [ME *hurtlen* to collide, freq. of *hurten* to cause to strike, hurt] *vi* **:** to move with or as if with a rushing sound ~ *vt* **:** HURL, FLING — **hurtle** *n*

hurt·less \'hərt-ləs\ *adj* **:** causing no pain or injury **:** HARMLESS

1hus·band \'həz-bənd\ *n* [ME *husbonde,* fr. OE *hūsbonda* master of a house, fr. ON *hūsbōndi,* fr. *hūs* house + *bōndi* householder] **1 :** a married man **2** *Brit* **:** MANAGER, STEWARD **3 :** a frugal manager — **hus·band·ly** *adj*

2husband *vt* **1 a :** to manage prudently and economically **b :** to use sparingly **:** CONSERVE **2** *archaic* **:** to find a husband for **:** MATE — **hus·band·er** *n*

hus·band·man \'həz-bən(d)-mən\ *n* **1 :** one that plows and cultivates land **:** FARMER **2 :** a specialist in a branch of farm husbandry

hus·band·ry \'həz-bən-drē\ *n* **1** *obs* **:** the care of a household **2 :** the control or judicious use of resources **:** CONSERVATION **3 a :** the cultivation or production of plants and animals **:** AGRICULTURE **b :** the scientific control and management of a branch of farming and esp. of domestic animals

1hush \'həsh\ *vb* [back-formation fr. *husht* (hushed), fr. ME *hussht,* fr. *huissht,* interj. used to enjoin silence] *vt* **1 :** CALM, QUIET <~*ed* the children as they entered the library> **2 :** to put at rest **:** MOLLIFY <~ *ed* his conscience by bringing her flowers> **3 :** to keep from public knowledge **:** SUPPRESS <~ the story up> ~ *vi* **:** to become quiet

2hush *adj* **1** *archaic* **:** SILENT, STILL **2 :** intended to prevent the dissemination of certain information <~ money>

3hush *n* **:** a silence or calm esp. following noise **:** QUIET

hush–hush \'həsh-ˌhəsh\ *adj* **:** SECRET, CONFIDENTIAL

hush puppy *n, chiefly South* [fr. its occasional use as food for dogs] **:** cornmeal dough shaped into small balls and fried in deep fat — usu. used in pl.

1husk \'həsk\ *n* [ME] **1 a :** a typically dry or membranous outer covering (as of hulls, bracts, or pod) of a seed or fruit; *also* **:** one of the constituent parts **b :** a carob pod **2 a :** an outer layer **:** SHELL **b :** an emptied shell **:** REMNANT **c :** a supporting framework

2husk *vt* **:** to strip the husk from — **husk·er** *n*

husk·ing *n* : a gathering of farm families to husk corn
husk–tomato *n* : GROUND-CHERRY
1husky \ˈhəs-kē\ *adj* **husk·i·er; -est** : resembling, containing, or full of husks
2hus·ky \ˈhəs-kē\ *adj* **hus·ki·er; -est** [prob. fr. *husk* (huskiness), fr. obs. *husk* (to have a dry cough)] : hoarse with or as if with emotion — **hus·ki·ly** \-kə-lē\ *adv* — **hus·ki·ness** \-kē-nəs\ *n*
3hus·ky *adj* **hus·ki·er; -est** [prob. fr. *1husk*] **1** : BURLY, ROBUST **2** : LARGE
4hus·ky *n, pl* **huskies** : one that is husky
5hus·ky *n, pl* **huskies** [prob. by shortening & alter. fr. *Eskimo*] **1** : a heavy-coated working dog of the New World arctic region **2** : SIBERIAN HUSKY
hus·sar \(ˌ)hə-ˈzär, -ˈsär\ *n* [Hung *huszár* hussar, (obs.) highway robber, fr. Serb *husar* pirate, fr. ML *cursarius* — more at CORSAIR] : a member of any of various European units orig. modeled on the Hungarian light cavalry of the 15th century
Huss·ite \ˈhəs-ˌīt, ˈhu̇s-\ *n* [NL *Hussita*, fr. John *Huss*] : a member of the Bohemian religious and nationalist movement originating with John Huss — **Hussite** *adj* — **Huss·it·ism** \-ˌīt-ˌiz-əm\ *n*
hus·sy \ˈhəz-ē, ˈhəs-\ *n, pl* **hussies** [alter. of *housewife*] **1** : a lewd or brazen woman **2** : a saucy or mischievous girl
hus·tings \ˈhəs-tiŋz\ *n pl but sing or pl in constr* [ME, fr. OE *hūsting*, fr. ON *hūsthing*, fr. *hūs* house + *thing* assembly] **1 a** : a local court formerly held in various English municipalities and still held infrequently in London **b** : a local court in some cities in Virginia **2 a** : a raised platform used until 1872 for the nomination of candidates for the British Parliament and for election speeches **b** : an election platform : STUMP **c** : the proceedings or locale of an election campaign
hus·tle \ˈhəs-əl\ *vb* **hus·tled; hus·tling** \ˈhəs-(ə-)liŋ\ [D *husselen* to shake, fr. MD *hutselen*, freq. of *hutsen*; akin to MD *hodde* hod] *vt* **1 a** : JOSTLE, SHOVE **b** : to convey forcibly or hurriedly **c** : to urge forward precipitately **2 a** : to obtain by energetic activity **b** : to sell something to or obtain something from by energetic and esp. underhanded activity ~ *vi* **1** : SHOVE, PRESS **2** : HASTEN, HURRY **3 a** : to make strenuous efforts to secure money or business **b** : to obtain money by fraud or deception **c** : to engage in prostitution **4** : to play a game or sport in an alert aggressive manner — **hustle** *n* — **hus·tler** \ˈhəs-lər\ *n*
1hut \ˈhət\ *n* [MF *hutte*, of Gmc origin; akin to OHG *hutta* hut; akin to OE *hȳd* skin, hide] **1** : an often small and temporary dwelling of simple construction : SHACK **2** : a simple shelter from the elements — **hut** *vb*
2hut *interj* [prob. alter. of *one*] — used to mark a marching cadence
hutch \ˈhəch\ *n* [ME *huche*, fr. OF] **1 a** : a chest or compartment for storage **b** : a low cupboard usu. surmounted by open shelves **2** : a pen or coop for an animal **3** : SHACK, SHANTY
hut·ment \ˈhət-mənt\ *n* **1** : a collection of huts : ENCAMPMENT **2** : HUT
Hut·ter·ite \ˈhət-ə-ˌrīt, ˈhüt-\ *n* [Jakob *Hutter* †1536 Moravian Anabaptist] : a member of a Mennonite sect of northwestern U.S. and Canada living communally and holding property in common — **Hut·te·ri·an** \ˌhə-ˈtir-ē-ən, hü-\ *adj*
hutzpah *or* **hutzpa** *var of* CHUTZPAH
huz·zah *or* **huz·za** \(ˌ)hə-ˈzä\ *interj* — used to express joy or approbation
hv *abbr* have
HV *abbr* **1** high velocity **2** high-voltage
hvy *abbr* heavy
hw *abbr* how
HW *abbr* **1** high water **2** highway **3** hot water
hwan \ˈhwän\ *n, pl* **hwan** [Korean] **1** : a Korean monetary unit equal to 1/10 won **2** : a coin representing one hwan
HWM *abbr* high-water mark
hwy *abbr* highway
hy *abbr* henry
hy·a·cinth \ˈhī-ə-(ˌ)sin(t)th, -sən(t)th\ *n* [L *hyacinthus*, a precious stone, a flowering plant, fr. Gk *hyakinthos*] **1 a** : a precious stone of the ancients sometimes held to be the sapphire **b** : a gem zircon or essonite **2 a** : a plant of the ancients held to be a lily, iris, larkspur, or gladiolus **b** (1) : any of a genus (*Hyacinthus*) of bulbous herbs of the lily family; *esp* : a common garden plant (*H. orientalis*) widely grown for the beauty and fragrance of the flowers (2) : any of several other plants of the lily family **3** : a light violet to moderate purple — **hy·a·cin·thine** \ˌhī-ə-ˈsin(t)-thən\ *adj*

hyacinth 2b(1)

Hy·a·cin·thus \ˌhī-ə-ˈsin(t)-thəs\ *n* [L, fr. Gk *Hyakinthos*] : a youth loved and accidentally killed by Apollo who memorialized him with a hyacinth growing from the youth's blood
Hy·a·des \ˈhī-ə-ˌdēz\ *n pl* [L, fr. Gk] : a V-shaped cluster of stars in the head of the constellation Taurus held by the ancients to indicate rainy weather when they rise with the sun
hy·ae·na *var of* HYENA
hyal- *or* **hyalo-** *comb form* [LL, glass, fr. Gk, fr. *hyalos*] : glass : glassy : hyaline <*hyal*escent> <*hyalo*gen>
1hy·a·line \ˈhī-ə-lən, -ˌlīn\ *adj* [LL *hyalinus*, fr. Gk *hyalinos*, fr. *hyalos*] **1** : of or relating to glass **2 a** : transparent or nearly so and usu. homogeneous **b** *of a mineral* (1) : GLASSY (2) : lacking crystallinity : AMORPHOUS
2hy·a·line \ˈhī-ə-lən, -ˌlīn, *in sense 2* -lən *or* -ˌlēn\ *n* **1** : something (as the clear atmosphere) that is transparent **2** *or* **hy·a·lin** \-lən\ : any of several translucent nitrogenous substances related to chitin, found esp. around cells, and readily stained by eosin
hyaline cartilage *n* : translucent bluish white cartilage with the cells embedded in an apparently homogeneous matrix that is present in joints and respiratory passages and forms most of the fetal skeleton
hy·a·lite \ˈhī-ə-ˌlīt\ *n* [G *hyalit*, fr. Gk *hyalos*] : a colorless opal that is clear as glass or sometimes translucent or whitish
hy·a·loid \-ˌlȯid\ *adj* [Gk *hyaloeidēs*, fr. *hyalos*] : GLASSY, TRANSPARENT
hy·a·lo·plasm \hī-ˈal-ə-ˌplaz-əm, ˈhī-ə-lō-\ *n* [prob. fr. G *hyaloplasma*, fr. *hyal-* + *-plasma* -plasm] : the clear apparently homogeneous matrix of cytoplasm that is essentially the continuous phase of a multiple-phase colloidal system — called also *ground substance*
hy·al·uron·ic acid \ˌhī-əl-yu̇-ˌrän-ik-, ˌhī-əl-yü-\ *n* [ISV] : a viscous mucopolysaccharide acid that occurs esp. in the vitreous humor, the umbilical cord, and synovial fluid and as a cementing substance in the subcutaneous tissue
hy·al·uron·i·dase \-ˈrän-ə-ˌdās, -dāz\ *n* [ISV, irreg. fr. *hyaluronic* (*acid*) + *-ase*] : an enzyme that splits and lowers the viscosity of hyaluronic acid facilitating the spreading of fluids through tissues
hy·brid \ˈhī-brəd\ *n* [L *hybrida*] **1** : an offspring of two animals or plants of different races, breeds, varieties, species, or genera **2** : a person produced by the blending of two diverse cultures or traditions **3 a** : something heterogeneous in origin or composition : COMPOSITE <artificial ~*s* of DNA and RNA> **b** : a word composed of elements from different languages — **hybrid** *adj* — **hy·brid·ism** \-brə-ˌdiz-əm\ *n* — **hy·brid·i·ty** \hī-ˈbrid-ət-ē\ *n*
hybrid computer *n* : a computer system consisting of a combination of analog and digital computer systems
hy·brid·ize \ˈhī-brə-ˌdīz\ *vb* **-ized; -iz·ing** *vt* : to cause to produce hybrids : INTERBREED ~ *vi* : to produce hybrids — **hy·brid·iza·tion** \ˌhī-brəd-ə-ˈzā-shən\ *n* — **hy·brid·iz·er** *n*
hybrid perpetual rose *n* : any of numerous vigorous hardy bush roses derived from the bourbon rose and grown esp. for their sometimes recurrent often fragrant bloom
hybrid tea rose *n* : any of numerous moderately hardy cultivated bush roses derived chiefly from tea roses and hybrid perpetual roses and grown esp. for their strongly recurrent bloom of large usu. scentless flowers
hybrid vigor *n* : HETEROSIS
hy·bris \ˈhī-brəs, ˈhē-\ *var of* HUBRIS
hyd *abbr* **1** hydraulics **2** hydrostatics
hy·da·thode \ˈhīd-ə-ˌthōd\ *n* [ISV, fr. Gk *hydat-*, *hydōr* water + *hodos* road — more at CEDE] : an epidermal structure in higher plants functioning in the exudation of water
hy·da·tid \ˈhīd-ə-təd, -ˌtid\ *n* [Gk *hydatid-*, *hydatis* watery cyst, fr. *hydat-*, *hydōr*] : a larval tapeworm occurring as a fluid-filled sac containing daughter cysts and scolices or forming a proliferating spongy mass that actively invades and metastasizes in the host's tissues
hydr- *or* **hydro-** *comb form* [ME *ydr-*, *ydro-*, fr. OF, fr. L *hydr-*, *hydro-*, fr. Gk, fr. *hydōr* — more at WATER] **1 a** : water <*hydro*us> <*hydro*electricity> **b** : liquid <*hydro*kinetics> **2** : hydrogen : containing or combined with hydrogen <*hydro*carbon> <*hydr*oxyl> **3** : hydroid <*hydro*medusa>
Hy·dra \ˈhī-drə\ *n* [ME *Ydra*, fr. L *Hydra*, fr. Gk] **1** : a many-headed serpent or monster of Greek mythology slain by Hercules each head of which when cut off was replaced by two others **2** *not cap* : a multifarious evil not to be overcome by a single effort **3** [L (gen. *Hydrae*), fr. Gk] : a southern constellation of great length that lies south of Cancer, Sextans, Corvus, and Virgo and is represented on old maps by a serpent **4** *not cap* [NL, genus name, fr. L, Hydra] : any of numerous small tubular freshwater hydrozoan polyps (as of the genus *Hydra*) having at one end a mouth surrounded by tentacles

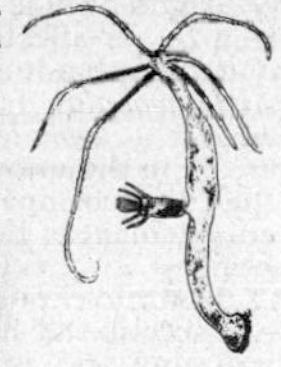
hydra 4

hy·dra–head·ed \ˌhī-drə-ˈhed-əd\ *adj* : having many centers or branches <a ~ organization>
hy·dral·azine \hī-ˈdral-ə-ˌzēn\ *n* [*hydr-* + phth*al*ic (acid) + *azine*] : a crystalline base $C_8H_8N_4$ used in the treatment of hypertension
hy·dran·gea \hī-ˈdrān-jə\ *n* [NL, genus name, fr. *hydr-* + Gk *angeion* vessel — more at ANGI-] : any of a genus (*Hydrangea*) of shrubs and one woody vine of the saxifrage family with opposite leaves and showy corymbose clusters of usu. sterile white or tinted flowers
hy·drant \ˈhī-drənt\ *n* **1** : a discharge pipe with a valve and spout at which water may be drawn from a water main (as for fighting fires) — called also *fireplug* **2** : FAUCET
hy·dranth \ˈhī-ˌdran(t)th\ *n* [ISV *hydr-* + Gk *anthos* flower — more at ANTHOLOGY] : one of the nutritive zooids of a hydroid colony
hy·drase \ˈhī-ˌdrās, -ˌdrāz\ *n* : an enzyme that promotes the addition or removal of water to or from its substrate
hy·dras·tine \hī-ˈdras-ˌtēn, -tən\ *n* : a bitter crystalline alkaloid $C_{21}H_{21}NO_6$ that is an active constituent of hydrastis
hy·dras·tis \-təs\ *n* [NL, genus name] : the dried rhizome and roots of a goldenseal (*Hydrastis canadensis*) formerly used as a bitter tonic, hemostatic, and antiseptic
1hy·drate \ˈhī-ˌdrāt\ *n* **1** : a compound or complex ion formed by the union of water with some other substance **2** : HYDROXIDE <calcium ~>
2hydrate *vb* **hy·drat·ed; hy·drat·ing** *vt* : to cause to take up or combine with water or the elements of water ~ *vi* : to become a hydrate — **hy·dra·tion** \hī-ˈdrā-shən\ *n* — **hy·dra·tor** \ˈhī-ˌdrāt-ər\ *n*
hy·drau·lic \hī-ˈdrȯ-lik\ *adj* [L *hydraulicus*, fr. Gk *hydraulikos*, fr. *hydraulis* hydraulic organ, fr. *hydr-* + *aulos* reed instrument — more at ALVEOLUS] **1** : operated, moved, or effected by means of water **2 a** : of or relating to hydraulics <~ engineer> **b** : of or relating to water or other liquid in motion <~ erosion> **3** : op-

erated by the resistance offered or the pressure transmitted when a quantity of liquid (as water or oil) is forced through a comparatively small orifice or through a tube <~ brakes> **4** : hardening or setting under water <~ cement> — **hy·drau·li·cal·ly** \-li-k(ə-)lē\ *adv*

hydraulic ram *n* : a pump that forces running water to a higher level by utilizing the kinetic energy of flow

hy·drau·lics \hī-ˈdrō-liks\ *n pl but sing in constr* : a branch of science that deals with practical applications (as the transmission of energy or the effects of flow) of liquid (as water) in motion

hy·dra·zide \ˈhī-drə-ˌzīd\ *n* : any of a class of compounds resulting from the replacement by an acid radical of hydrogen in hydrazine or in one of its derivatives

hy·dra·zine \ˈhī-drə-ˌzēn\ *n* [ISV] : a colorless fuming corrosive strongly reducing liquid base N_2H_4 used esp. in fuels for rocket and jet engines; *also* : an organic base derived from this compound

hy·dra·zo·ic acid \ˌhī-drə-ˌzō-ik-\ *n* [*hydr-* + *azo-* + *-ic*] : a colorless volatile poisonous explosive liquid HN_3 that has a foul odor and yields explosive salts of heavy metals

hy·dric \ˈhī-drik\ *adj* : characterized by, relating to, or requiring an abundance of moisture <a ~ habitat> <a ~ plant> — compare MESIC, XERIC — **hy·dri·cal·ly** \-dri-k(ə-)lē\ *adv*

-hy·dric \ˈhī-drik\ *adj suffix* **1** : containing acid hydrogen <mono*hydric*> **2** : containing hydroxyl <hexa*hydric* alcohols>

hy·dride \ˈhī-ˌdrīd\ *n* : a compound of hydrogen usu. with a more electropositive element or radical

hy·dri·od·ic acid \ˌhī-drē-ˌäd-ik-\ *n* [ISV] : an aqueous solution of hydrogen iodide HI that is a strong acid resembling hydrochloric acid chemically and that is also a strong reducing agent

¹hy·dro \ˈhī-(ˌ)drō\ *n, pl* **hydros** [short for *hydropathic establishment*] **1** *Brit* : a hotel that caters to people taking a water cure **2** *Brit* : an establishment that furnishes water cures : SPA

²hydro *adj* : HYDROELECTRIC <~ energy>

hy·dro·bi·ol·o·gy \ˌhī-drō-bī-ˈäl-ə-jē\ *n* : the biology of bodies or units of water; *esp* : LIMNOLOGY — **hy·dro·bi·o·log·i·cal** \-ˌbī-ə-ˈläj-i-kəl\ *adj* — **hy·dro·bi·ol·o·gist** \-bī-ˈäl-ə-jəst\ *n*

hy·dro·bro·mic acid \ˌhī-drə-ˌbrō-mik-\ *n* [ISV] : an aqueous solution of hydrogen bromide HBr that is a strong acid resembling hydrochloric acid chemically, that is a weak reducing agent, and that is used esp. for making bromides

hy·dro·car·bon \ˌhī-drə-ˈkär-bən\ *n* : an organic compound (as acetylene or benzene) containing only carbon and hydrogen and often occurring in petroleum, natural gas, coal, and bitumens — **hy·dro·car·bo·na·ceous** \-ˌkär-bə-ˈnā-shəs\ *or* **hy·dro·car·bon·ic** \-kär-ˈbän-ik\ *or* **hy·dro·car·bon·ous** \-ˈkär-bə-nəs\ *adj*

hy·dro·cele \ˈhī-drə-ˌsēl\ *n* [L, fr. Gk *hydrokēlē*, fr. *hydr-* + *kēlē* tumor — more at -CELE] : an accumulation of serous fluid in a sacculated cavity (as the scrotum)

hy·dro·ce·phal·ic \ˌhī-drō-sə-ˈfal-ik\ *adj* : relating to, characterized by, or affected with hydrocephalus — **hydrocephalic** *n*

hy·dro·ceph·a·lus \-ˈsef-ə-ləs\ *also* **hy·dro·ceph·a·ly** \-lē\ *n* [NL *hydrocephalus*, fr. LL, hydrocephalous, fr. Gk *hydrokephalos*, fr. *hydr-* + *kephalē* head — more at CEPHALIC] : an abnormal increase in the amount of cerebrospinal fluid within the cranial cavity that is accompanied by expansion of the cerebral ventricles, enlargement of the skull and esp. the forehead, and atrophy of the brain

hy·dro·chlo·ric acid \ˌhī-drə-ˌklōr-ik-, -ˌklȯr-\ *n* [ISV] : an aqueous solution of hydrogen chloride HCl that is a strong corrosive irritating acid, is normally present in dilute form in gastric juice, and is widely used in industry and in the laboratory

hy·dro·chlo·ride \-ˈklō(ə)r-ˌīd, -ˈklȯ(ə)r-\ *n* : a compound of hydrochloric acid esp. with an organic base (as an alkaloid)

hy·dro·chlo·ro·thi·a·zide \-ˌklōr-ə-ˈthī-ə-ˌzīd, -ˌklȯr-\ *n* [*hydr-* + *chlor-* + *thiazine* + *-ide*] : a diuretic and hypotensive drug $C_7H_8O_4N_3ClS_2$

hy·dro·col·loid \ˌhī-drə-ˈkäl-ˌȯid\ *n* : a substance that yields a gel with water — **hy·dro·col·loi·dal** \-kə-ˈlȯid-ᵊl, -kä-\ *adj*

hy·dro·cor·ti·sone \-ˈkȯrt-ə-ˌsōn, -ˌzōn\ *n* : CORTISOL

hy·dro·crack·ing \ˈhī-drə-ˌkrak-iŋ\ *n* : the cracking of hydrocarbons in the presence of hydrogen — **hy·dro·crack** \-ˌkrak\ *vt*

hy·dro·cy·an·ic acid \ˌhī-drō-sī-ˌan-ik-\ *n* [ISV] : an aqueous solution of hydrogen cyanide HCN that is a poisonous weak acid and is used chiefly in fumigating and in organic synthesis

hy·dro·dy·nam·ic \-dī-ˈnam-ik\ *also* **hy·dro·dy·nam·i·cal** \-i-kəl\ *adj* [NL *hydrodynamicus*, fr. *hydr-* + *dynamicus* dynamic] : of, relating to, or involving principles of hydrodynamics — **hy·dro·dy·nam·i·cal·ly** \-i-k(ə-)lē\ *adv*

hy·dro·dy·nam·ics \-iks\ *n pl but sing in constr* : a branch of science that deals with the motion of fluids and the forces acting on solid bodies immersed in fluids and in motion relative to them — compare HYDROSTATICS — **hy·dro·dy·nam·i·cist** \-ˈnam-ə-səst\ *n*

hy·dro·elec·tric \ˌhī-drō-i-ˈlek-trik\ *adj* [ISV] : of or relating to production of electricity by waterpower — **hy·dro·elec·tri·cal·ly** \-tri-k(ə-)lē\ *adv* — **hy·dro·elec·tric·i·ty** \-ˌlek-ˈtris-ət-ē, -ˈtris-tē\ *n*

hy·dro·flu·or·ic acid \ˌhī-drō-flü-ˌȯr-ik, -ˌär-\ *n* [ISV] : an aqueous solution of hydrogen fluoride HF that is a weak poisonous acid, that resembles hydrochloric acid chemically but attacks silica and silicates, and that is used esp. in finishing and etching glass

hy·dro·foil \ˈhī-drə-ˌfȯil\ *n* **1** : a body similar to an airfoil but designed for action in or on water **2** : a motorboat that has metal plates or fins attached by struts fore and aft for lifting the hull clear of the water as speed is attained

hy·dro·form·ing \-ˌfȯr-miŋ\ *n* [*hydr-* + *reforming*] : a process for producing high-octane gasoline from petroleum naphthas by catalytic dehydrogenation and aromatization in the presence of hydrogen — **hy·dro·form·er** \-mər\ *n*

hy·dro·gen \ˈhī-drə-jən\ *n* [F *hydrogène*, fr. *hydr-* + *-gène* -gen; fr. the fact that water is generated by its combustion] : a nonmetallic element that is the simplest and lightest of the elements, is normally a colorless odorless highly flammable diatomic gas, and is used esp. in synthesis — compare DEUTERIUM, TRITIUM; see ELEMENT table — **hy·drog·e·nous** \hī-ˈdräj-ə-nəs\ *adj*

hy·drog·e·nase \hī-ˈdräj-ə-ˌnās, -ˈnāz\ *n* : an enzyme of various microorganisms that promotes the formation and utilization of gaseous hydrogen

hy·dro·ge·nate \hī-ˈdräj-ə-ˌnāt, ˈhī-drə-jə-\ *vt* **-nat·ed; -nat·ing** : to combine or treat with or expose to hydrogen; *esp* : to add hydrogen to the molecule of (an unsaturated organic compound) — **hy·dro·ge·na·tion** \hī-ˌdräj-ə-ˈnā-shən, ˌhī-drə-jə-\ *n*

hydrogen bomb *n* : a bomb whose violent explosive power is due to the sudden release of atomic energy resulting from the union of light nuclei (as of hydrogen atoms) at very high temperature and pressure to form helium nuclei

hydrogen bond *n* : a linkage consisting of a hydrogen atom bonded between two electronegative atoms (as fluorine, oxygen, or nitrogen) with one side of the linkage being a covalent bond and the other being electrostatic in nature

hydrogen bromide *n* : a colorless irritating gas HBr that fumes in moist air and yields hydrobromic acid when dissolved in water

hydrogen chloride *n* : a colorless pungent poisonous gas HCl that fumes in moist air and yields hydrochloric acid when dissolved in water

hydrogen cyanide *n* **1** : a poisonous usu. gaseous compound HCN that has the odor of bitter almonds **2** : HYDROCYANIC ACID

hydrogen fluoride *n* : a colorless corrosive fuming usu. gaseous compound HI that yields hydrofluoric acid when dissolved in water

hydrogen iodide *n* : an acrid colorless gas HI that fumes in moist air and yields hydriodic acid when dissolved in water

hydrogen ion *n* **1** : the cation H^+ of acids consisting of a hydrogen atom whose electron has been transferred to the anion of the acid **2** : HYDRONIUM

hydrogen peroxide *n* : an unstable compound H_2O_2 used esp. as an oxidizing and bleaching agent, an antiseptic, and a propellant

hydrogen sulfide *n* : a flammable poisonous gas H_2S that has an odor suggestive of rotten eggs and is found esp. in many mineral waters and in putrefying matter

hy·drog·ra·phy \hī-ˈdräg-rə-fē\ *n* [MF *hydrographie*, fr. *hydr-* + *-graphie* -graphy] **1** : the description and study of bodies of water (as seas, lakes, and rivers): as **a** : the measurement of flow and investigation of the behavior of streams esp. with reference to the control of their waters **b** : the charting of bodies of water **2** : bodies of water — **hy·drog·ra·pher** \-fər\ n — **hy·dro·graph·ic** \ˌhī-drə-ˈgraf-ik\ *adj* — **hy·dro·graph·i·cal·ly** \-i-k(ə-)lē\ *adv*

¹hy·droid \ˈhī-ˌdrȯid\ *adj* [deriv. of NL *Hydra*] : of or relating to a hydrozoan; *esp* : resembling a typical hydra

²hydroid *n* : HYDROZOAN; *esp* : a hydrozoan polyp as distinguished from a medusa

hy·dro·ki·net·ic \ˌhī-drō-kə-ˈnet-ik, -(ˌ)kī-\ *adj* : of or relating to the motions of fluids or the forces which produce or affect such motions — compare HYDROSTATIC

hy·dro·lase \ˈhī-drə-ˌlās, -ˌlāz\ *n* : a hydrolytic enzyme (as an esterase)

hy·drol·o·gy \hī-ˈdräl-ə-jē\ *n* [NL *hydrologia*, fr. L *hydr-* + *-logia* -logy] : a science dealing with the properties, distribution, and circulation of water on the surface of the land, in the soil and underlying rocks, and in the atmosphere — **hy·dro·log·ic** \ˌhī-drə-ˈläj-ik\ *or* **hy·dro·log·i·cal** \-i-kəl\ *adj* — **hy·dro·log·i·cal·ly** \-i-k(ə-)lē\ *adv* — **hy·drol·o·gist** \hī-ˈdräl-ə-jəst\ *n*

hy·dro·ly·sate \hī-ˈdräl-ə-ˌsāt, ˌhī-drə-ˈlī-\ *also* **hy·dro·ly·zate** \-ˌzāt\ *n* : a product of hydrolysis

hy·dro·ly·sis \hī-ˈdräl-ə-səs, ˌhī-drə-ˈlī-\ *n* [NL] : a chemical process of decomposition involving splitting of a bond and addition of the elements of water — **hy·dro·lyt·ic** \ˌhī-drə-ˈlit-ik\ *adj* — **hy·dro·lyt·i·cal·ly** \-i-k(ə-)lē\ *adv*

hy·dro·lyze \ˈhī-drə-ˌlīz\ *vb* **-lyzed; -lyz·ing** [ISV, fr. NL *hydrolysis*] *vt* : to subject to hydrolysis ~ *vi* : to undergo hydrolysis — **hy·dro·lyz·able** \-ˌlī-zə-bəl\ *adj*

hy·dro·mag·net·ic \ˌhī-drō-mag-ˈnet-ik\ *adj* [*hydr-* + *magnetic*] **1** : MAGNETOHYDRODYNAMIC **2** : being a wave in an electrically conducting fluid immersed in a magnetic field

hy·dro·man·cy \ˈhī-drə-ˌman(t)-sē\ *n* [ME *ydromancie*, fr. MF, fr. L *hydromantia*, fr. *hydr-* + *-mantia* -mancy] : divination by the appearance or motion of liquids (as water)

hy·dro·me·chan·ics \ˌhī-drō-mi-ˈkan-iks\ *n pl but sing in constr* : a branch of mechanics that deals with the equilibrium and motion of fluids and of solid bodies immersed in them — **hy·dro·me·chan·i·cal** \-ˈkan-i-kəl\ *adj*

hy·dro·me·du·sa \ˌhī-drō-mi-ˈd(y)ü-sə, -zə\ *n, pl* **-sae** \-ˌsē, -ˌzē\ [NL] : a medusa (as of the orders Anthomedusae and Leptomedusae) produced as a bud from a hydroid — **hy·dro·me·du·san** \-ˈd(y)üs-ᵊn, -ˈd(y)üz-\ *adj or n* — **hy·dro·me·du·soid** \-ˈd(y)ü-ˌsȯid, -ˌzȯid\ *adj*

hy·dro·mel \ˈhī-drə-ˌmel\ *n* [ME *ydromel*, fr. MF & L; MF, fr. L *hydromeli*, fr. Gk, fr. *hydr-* + *meli* honey — more at MELLIFLUOUS] : a mixture of honey and water; *esp* : MEAD

hy·dro·met·al·lur·gy \ˌhī-drō-ˈmet-ᵊl-ˌər-jē\ *n* [ISV] : the treatment of ores by wet processes (as leaching) — **hy·dro·met·al·lur·gi·cal** \-ˌmet-ᵊl-ˈər-ji-kəl\ *adj*

hy·dro·me·te·or \ˌhī-drō-ˈmēt-ē-ər, -ē-ˌȯ(ə)r\ *n* [ISV] : a product (as fog, rain, or hail) formed by the condensation of atmospheric water vapor

hy·dro·me·te·o·rol·o·gy \-ˌmēt-ē-ə-ˈräl-ə-jē\ *n* : a branch of meteorology that deals with water in the atmosphere esp as precipitation — **hy·dro·me·te·o·ro·log·i·cal** \-ē-ˌȯr-ə-ˈläj-i-kəl, -ˌär-ə-, -ə-rə-\ *adj* — **hy·dro·me·te·o·rol·o·gist** \-e-ə-ˈräl-ə-jəst\ *n*

hy·drom·e·ter \hī-ˈdräm-ət-ər\ *n* : a floating instrument for determining specific gravities of liquids and hence the strength (as of spirituous liquors or saline solutions) — **hy·dro·met·ric** \ˌhī-drə-ˈme-trik\ *or* **hy·dro·met·ri·cal** \-tri-kəl\ *adj* — **hy·drom·e·try** \hī-ˈdräm-ə-trē\ *n*

hy·dro·mor·phic \ˌhī-drə-ˈmȯr-fik\ *adj, of a soil* : developed in the presence of an excess of moisture which tends to suppress aerobic factors in soil-building

hy·dron·ic \hī-ˈdrän-ik\ *adj* [*hydr-* + *-onic* (as in *electronic*)]

: of, relating to, or being a system of heating or cooling that involves transfer of heat by a circulating fluid (as water or vapor) in a closed system of pipes — **hy·dron·i·cal·ly** \-i-k(ə-)lē\ *adv*

hy·dro·ni·um \hī-'drō-nē-əm\ *n* [ISV *hydr-* + *-onium*] : a hydrated hydrogen ion H_3O^+

hy·drop·a·thy \hī-'dräp-ə-thē\ *n* [ISV] : the empirical use of water in the treatment of disease — compare HYDROTHERAPY — **hy·dro·path·ic** \ˌhī-drə-'path-ik\ *adj* — **hy·dro·path·i·cal·ly** \-i-k(ə-)lē\ *adv*

hy·dro·per·ox·ide \ˌhī-drō-pə-'räk-ˌsīd\ *n* : a compound containing an O_2H group

hy·dro·phane \'hī-drə-ˌfān\ *n* : a semitranslucent opal that becomes translucent or transparent on immersion in water

hy·dro·phil·ic \ˌhī-drə-'fil-ik\ *or* **hy·dro·phile** \'hī-drə-ˌfīl\ *adj* [NL *hydrophilus*, fr. Gk *hydr-* + *-philos* -philous] : of, relating to, or having a strong affinity for water — **hy·dro·phi·lic·i·ty** \ˌhī-drə-fil-'is-ət-ē\ *adv*

hy·dro·pho·bia \ˌhī-drə-'fō-bē-ə\ *n* [LL, fr. Gk, fr. *hydr-* + *-phobia* fear of something — more at PHOBIA] **1** : a morbid dread of water **2** : RABIES

hy·dro·pho·bic \-'fō-bik, -'fäb-ik\ *adj* **1** : of, relating to, or suffering from hydrophobia **2** : lacking affinity for water — **hy·dro·pho·bic·i·ty** \-fō-'bis-ət-ē\ *n*

hy·dro·phone \'hī-drə-ˌfōn\ *n* : an instrument for listening to sound transmitted through water

hy·dro·phyte \-ˌfīt\ *n* [ISV] **1** : a perennial vascular aquatic plant having its overwintering buds under water **2** : a plant growing in water or in soil too waterlogged for most plants to survive — **hy·dro·phyt·ic** \ˌhī-drə-'fit-ik\ *adj*

[1]**hy·dro·plane** \'hī-drə-ˌplān\ *n* **1** : HYDROFOIL **2 a** : a speedboat with hydrofoils or a stepped bottom so that the hull is raised wholly or partly out of the water **b** : a rudder on a horizontal axis on a submarine for steering it upward or downward **3** : SEAPLANE

[2]**hydroplane** *vi* **1 a** : to skim over the water with the hull more or less clear of the surface **b** *of a car* : to go out of control by skimming the surface of a wet road **2** : to drive or ride in a hydroplane — **hy·dro·plan·er** *n*

hy·dro·pon·ic \ˌhī-drə-'pän-ik\ *adj* : of or relating to hydroponics — **hy·dro·pon·i·cal·ly** \-i-k(ə-)lē\ *adv*

hy·dro·pon·ics \-'pän-iks\ *n pl but sing in constr* [*hydr-* + *-ponics* (as in *geoponics*)] : the growing of plants in nutrient solutions with or without an inert medium to provide mechanical support

hy·dro·qui·none \ˌhī-drō-kwin-'ōn, -'kwin-ˌōn\ *n* [ISV] : a white crystalline strongly reducing phenol $C_6H_6O_2$ used esp. as a photographic developer and as an antioxidant and stabilizer

hy·dro·scope \'hī-drə-ˌskōp\ *n* [ISV] : a mirror device for enabling a person to see an object at a considerable distance below the surface of water

hy·dro·sere \-ˌsi(ə)r\ *n* : an ecological sere originating in an aquatic habitat

hy·dro–ski \'hī-drō-ˌskē\ *n* : a hydrofoil attached below the fuselage of a seaplane to accelerate takeoffs

hy·dro·sol \'hī-drə-ˌsäl, -ˌsòl\ *n* [*hydr-* + *-sol* (fr. *solution*)] : a sol in which the liquid is water — **hy·dro·sol·ic** \ˌhī-drə-'säl-ik\ *adj*

hy·dro·space \-ˌspās\ *n* [*hydr-* + *space*] : the regions beneath the surface of the ocean

hy·dro·sphere \-ˌsfi(ə)r\ *n* [ISV] : the aqueous vapor of the atmosphere; *broadly* : the aqueous envelope of the earth including bodies of water and aqueous vapor in the atmosphere — **hy·dro·sphere·ic** \ˌhī-drə-'sfi(ə)r-ik, -'sfer\ *adj*

hy·dro·stat·ic \ˌhī-drə-'stat-ik\ *also* **hy·dro·stat·i·cal** \-i-kəl\ *adj* [prob. fr. NL *hydrostaticus*, fr. *hydr-* + *staticus* static] : of or relating to liquids at rest or to the pressures they exert or transmit — compare HYDROKINETIC — **hy·dro·stat·i·cal·ly** \-i-k(ə-)lē\ *adv*

hy·dro·stat·ics \-iks\ *n pl but sing in constr* : a branch of physics that deals with the characteristics of liquids at rest and esp. with the pressure in a liquid or exerted by a liquid on an immersed body — compare HYDRODYNAMICS

hy·dro·sul·fide \ˌhī-drə-'səl-ˌfīd\ *n* [ISV] : a compound that contains the radical SH and is derived from hydrogen sulfide by the replacement of one of its hydrogen atoms by an element or radical

hy·dro·sul·fite \-ˌfīt\ *n* [ISV] : a salt containing the radical S_2O_4; *esp* : a sodium salt used as a reducing and bleaching agent

hy·dro·tax·is \ˌhī-drə-'tak-səs\ *n* [NL] : a taxis in which moisture is the directive factor — **hy·dro·tac·tic** \-'tak-tik\ *adj*

hy·dro·ther·a·py \ˌhī-drə-'ther-ə-pē\ *n* [ISV] : the scientific use of water in the treatment of disease — compare HYDROPATHY

hy·dro·ther·mal \ˌhī-drə-'thər-məl\ *adj* [ISV] : of or relating to hot water — used esp. of the formation of minerals by hot solutions rising from a cooling magma — **hy·dro·ther·mal·ly** \-mə-lē\ *adv*

hy·dro·tho·rax \-'thō(ə)r-ˌaks, -'thò(ə)r-\ *n* [NL] : an excess of serous fluid in the pleural cavity; *esp* : an effusion resulting from failing circulation (as in heart disease or from lung infection)

hy·drot·ro·pism \hī-'drä-trə-ˌpiz-əm\ *n* [ISV] : a tropism (as in plant roots) in which water or water vapor is the orienting factor — **hy·dro·tro·pic** \ˌhī-drə-'trō-pik, -'träp-ik\ *adj* — **hy·dro·tro·pi·cal·ly** \-'trō-pi-k(ə-)lē, -'träp-i-\ *adv*

hy·drous \'hī-drəs\ *adj* : containing water usu. chemically combined (as in hydrates)

hy·drox·ide \hī-'dräk-ˌsīd\ *n* [ISV] **1** : a compound of hydroxyl with an element or radical **2** : any of various hydrated oxides regarded as containing hydroxyl

hydroxide ion *n* : the anion OH of basic hydroxides — called also *hydroxyl ion*

hy·droxy \hī-'dräk-sē\ *adj* [ISV, fr. *hydroxyl*] : HYDROXYL; *esp* : containing hydroxyl esp. in place of hydrogen — often used in combination <*hydroxy*acetic acid>

hy·droxy·ap·a·tite \hī-ˌdräk-sē-'ap-ə-ˌtīt\ *n* : a complex phosphate of calcium $Ca_5(PO_4)_3OH$ that occurs as a mineral and is the chief structural element of vertebrate bone

hy·droxy·bu·tyr·ic acid \-byü-ˌtir-ik-\ *n* : a hydroxy derivative $C_4H_8O_3$ of butyric acid

hy·drox·yl \hī-'dräk-səl\ *n* [*hydr-* + *ox-* + *-yl*] : the univalent group or radical OH consisting of one atom of hydrogen and one of oxygen that is characteristic esp. of hydroxides, oxygen acids, alcohols, glycols, and phenols — **hy·drox·yl·ic** \ˌhī-ˌdräk-'sil-ik\ *adj*

hy·drox·yl·amine \hī-ˌdräk-sə-lə-'mēn, ˌhī-ˌdräk-'sil-ə-ˌmēn\ *n* [ISV] : a colorless odorless nitrogenous base NH_3O that resembles ammonia in its reactions but is less basic and that is used esp. as a reducing agent

hy·drox·y·lase \hī-'dräk-sə-ˌlās, -ˌlāz\ *n* : an enzyme that catalyzes the coupled oxidation of two compounds with incorporation of oxygen into one of them

hy·drox·yl·ate \hī-'dräk-sə-ˌlāt\ *vt* **-at·ed; -at·ing** : to introduce hydroxyl into — **hy·drox·yl·ation** \-ˌdräk-sə-'lā-shən\ *n*

hy·droxy·pro·line \hī-ˌdräk-sē-'prō-ˌlēn\ *n* [*hydroxy-* + *proline*] : an amino acid $C_5H_9NO_3$ that occurs naturally as a constituent of collagen

hy·droxy·tryp·ta·mine \-'trip-tə-ˌmēn\ *n* : SEROTONIN

hy·droxy·urea \-yù-'rē-ə\ *n* : a compound $CH_4N_2O_2$ used as an antineoplastic agent in some forms of leukemia

hy·droxy·zine \hī-'dräk-sə-ˌzēn\ *n* [*hydroxy-* + pipera*zine*] : a compound $C_{21}H_{27}ClN_2O_2$ used as an antihistaminic and tranquilizer

hy·dro·zo·an \ˌhī-drə-'zō-ən\ *n* [deriv. of Gk *hydr-* + *zōion* animal — more at ZO-] : any of a class (Hydrozoa) of coelenterates that includes simple and compound polyps and jellyfishes having no stomodaeum or gastric tentacles — **hydrozoan** *adj*

hy·e·na \hī-'ē-nə\ *n* [L *hyaena*, fr. Gk *hyaina*, fr. *hys* hog — more at SOW] : any of several large strong nocturnal carnivorous Old World mammals (family Hyaenidae) that usu. feed as scavengers — **hy·e·nic** \-'ē-nik, -'en-ik\ *adj* — **hy·e·noid** \-'ē-ˌnòid\ *adj*

hyena

hyet- *or* **hyeto-** *comb form* [Gk, fr. *hyetos*, fr. *hyein* to rain — more at SUCK] : rain <*hyetology*>

Hy·ge·ia \hī-'jē-(y)ə\ *n* [L, fr. Gk *Hygieia*] : the goddess of health in Greek mythology

hy·giene \'hī-ˌjēn *also* hī-'\ *n* [F *hygiène* & NL *hygieina*, fr. Gk, neut. pl. of *hygieinos* healthful, fr. *hygiēs* healthy; akin to Skt *su* well and to L *vivus* living — more at QUICK] **1** : a science of the establishment and maintenance of health **2** : conditions or practices (as of cleanliness) conducive to health — **hy·gien·ic** \ˌhī-jē-'en-ik, hī-'jen-, hī-'jēn-\ *adj* — **hy·gien·i·cal·ly** \-i-k(ə-)lē\ *adv* — **hy·gien·ist** \hī-'jēn-əst, 'hī-ˌjēn-, hī-'jen-\ *n*

hy·gien·ics \ˌhī-jē-'en-iks, hī-'jen-, hī-'jēn-\ *n pl but sing in constr* : HYGIENE 1

hygr- *also* **hygro-** *comb form* [Gk, fr. *hygros* wet — more at HUMOR] : humidity : moisture <*hygro*scope>

hy·gro·graph \'hī-grə-ˌgraf\ *n* [ISV] : an instrument for recording automatically variations in atmospheric humidity

hy·grom·e·ter \hī-'gräm-ət-ər\ *n* [prob. fr. F *hygromètre*, fr. *hygr-* + *-mètre* -meter] : any of several instruments for measuring the humidity of the atmosphere — **hy·gro·met·ric** \ˌhī-grə-'me-trik\ *adj* — **hy·grom·e·try** \hī-'gräm-ə-trē\ *n*

hy·groph·i·lous \hī-'gräf-ə-ləs\ *adj* : living or growing in moist places

hy·gro·phyte \'hī-grə-ˌfīt\ *n* [ISV] : HYDROPHYTE — **hy·gro·phyt·ic** \ˌhī-grə-'fit-ik\ *adj*

hy·gro·scope \'hī-grə-ˌskōp\ *n* : an instrument that shows changes in humidity (as of the atmosphere)

hy·gro·scop·ic \ˌhī-grə-'skäp-ik\ *adj* [fr. the use of such materials in the hygroscope] **1** : readily taking up and retaining moisture **2** : taken up and retained under some conditions of humidity and temperature <~ water in clay> — **hy·gro·scop·i·cal·ly** \-i-k(ə-)lē\ *adv* — **hy·gro·scop·ic·i·ty** \-(ˌ)skäp-'is-ət-ē\ *n*

hying *pres part of* HIE

Hyk·sos \'hik-ˌsäs, -ˌsōs\ *adj* [Gk *Hyksōs*, dynasty ruling Egypt, fr. Egypt *hqꜣ ẖꜣswt* ruler of the countries of the nomads] : of or relating to a Semite dynasty that ruled Egypt from about the 18th to the 16th century B.C.

hyl- *or* **hylo-** *comb form* [Gk, fr. *hylē*, lit., wood] : matter : material <*hylo*morphous>

hy·la \'hī-lə\ *n* [NL, fr. Gk *hylē* wood] : any of a genus (*Hyla*) of tree frogs

hy·lo·zo·ism \ˌhī-lə-'zō-ˌiz-əm\ *n* [Gk *hylē* + *zōos* alive, living; akin to Gk *zōē* life — more at QUICK] : a doctrine held esp. by early Greek philosophers that all matter is animated — **hy·lo·zo·ist** \-'zō-əst\ *n* — **hy·lo·zo·is·tic** \-zō-'is-tik\ *adj*

hy·men \'hī-mən\ *n* [LL, fr. Gk *hymēn* membrane] : a fold of mucous membrane partly closing the orifice of the vagina — **hy·men·al** \-mən-ᵊl\ *adj*

Hymen *n* [L, fr. Gk *Hymēn*] : the Greek god of marriage

[1]**hy·me·ne·al** \ˌhī-mə-'nē-əl\ *adj* [L *hymenaeus* wedding song, wedding, fr. Gk *hymenaios*, fr. *Hymēn*] : NUPTIAL — **hy·me·ne·al·ly** \-'nē-ə-lē\ *adv*

[2]**hymeneal** *n* **1** *pl, archaic* : NUPTIALS **2** *archaic* : a wedding hymn

hy·me·ni·um \hī-'mē-nē-əm\ *n, pl* **-nia** \-nē-ə\ *or* **-ni·ums** [NL, fr. Gk *hymēn* membrane] : a spore-bearing layer in fungi consisting of a group of asci or basidia often interspersed with sterile structures — **hy·me·ni·al** \-nē-əl\ *adj*

[1]**hy·me·nop·ter·an** \ˌhī-mə-'näp-tə-rən\ *adj* : of or relating to hymenoptera

2**hymenopteran** *n* : HYMENOPTERON

hy·me·nop·ter·on \-tə-ˌrän, -rən\ *n, pl* **-tera** \-rə\ *also* **-ter·ons** [NL *hymenopteron*, fr. Gk, neut. of *hymenopteros* membrane-winged, fr. *hymēn* + *pteron* wing — more at FEATHER] : any of an order (Hymenoptera) of highly specialized insects with complete metamorphosis that include the bees, wasps, ants, ichneumon flies, sawflies, gall wasps, and related forms, often associate in large colonies with complex social organization, and have usu. four membranous wings and the abdomen generally borne on a slender pedicel — **hy·me·nop·ter·ous** \-rəs\ *adj*

1**hymn** \ˈhim\ *n* [ME *ymne*, fr. OF, fr. L *hymnus* song of praise, fr. Gk *hymnos*] **1 a** : a song of praise to God **b** : a metrical composition adapted for singing in a religious service **2** : a song of praise or joy **3** : something resembling a hymn : PAEAN

2**hymn** *vb* **hymned** \ˈhimd\; **hymn·ing** \ˈhim-iŋ\ *vt* : to praise or worship in hymns ~ *vi* : to sing a hymn

hym·nal \ˈhim-nəl\ *n* [ME *hymnale*, fr. ML, fr. L *hymnus*] : a collection of church hymns

hym·na·ry \ˈhim-nə-rē\ *n, pl* **-ries** : HYMNAL

hymn·book \ˈhim-ˌbu̇k\ *n* : HYMNAL

hym·no·dy \ˈhim-nəd-ē\ *n* [LL *hymnodia*, fr. Gk *hymnōidia*, fr. *hymnos* + *aeidein* to sing — more at ODE] **1** : hymn singing **2** : hymn writing **3** : the hymns of a time, place, or church

hym·nol·o·gy \him-ˈnäl-ə-jē\ *n* [Gk *hymnologia* singing of hymns, fr. *hymnos* + *-logia* -logy] **1** : HYMNODY **2** : the study of hymns

hy·oid \ˈhī-ˌȯid\ *adj* [NL *hyoides* hyoid bone] : of or relating to the hyoid bone

hyoid bone *n* [NL *hyoides*, fr. Gk *hyoeidēs* shaped like the letter upsilon (Υ, υ), being the hyoid bone, fr. *y, hy* upsilon] : a bone or complex of bones situated at the base of the tongue and supporting the tongue and its muscles

hy·o·scine \ˈhī-ə-ˌsēn\ *n* [ISV *hyoscyamine* + *-ine*] : SCOPOLAMINE; *esp* : the levorotatory form of scopolamine

hy·o·scy·a·mine \ˌhī-ə-ˈsī-ə-ˌmēn\ *n* [G *hyoscyamin*, fr. NL *Hyoscyamus* genus of herbs, fr. L, henbane, fr. Gk *hyoskyamos*, lit., swine's bean, fr. *hyos* (gen. of *hys* swine) + *kyamos* bean — more at SOW] : a poisonous crystalline alkaloid $C_{17}H_{23}NO_3$; *esp* : its levorotatory form found esp. in belladonna and henbane and used similarly to atropine

1**hyp** \ˈhip\ *n, archaic* : HYPOCHONDRIA — often used in pl.

2**hyp** *abbr* hypothesis; hypothetical

hyp- — see HYPO-

hyp·abys·sal \ˌhip-ə-ˈbis-əl, ˌhī-pə-\ *adj* [ISV] : of or relating to a fine-grained igneous rock usu. formed at a moderate distance below the surface — **hyp·abys·sal·ly** \-ə-lē\ *adv*

hy·pae·thral \hī-ˈpē-thrəl\ *adj* [L *hypaethrus* exposed to the open air, fr. Gk *hypaithros*, fr. *hypo-* + *aithēr* ether, air — more at ETHER] **1** : having a roofless central space <~ temple> **2** : open to the sky **3** : OUTDOOR

hy·pan·thi·um \hī-ˈpan(t)-thē-əm\ *n, pl* **-thia** \-thē-ə\ [NL, fr. *hypo-* + *anth-* + *-ium*] : an enlargement of the floral receptacle bearing on its rim the stamens, petals, and sepals and often enlarging and surrounding the fruits (as in the rose hip) — **hy·pan·thi·al** \-thē-əl\ *adj*

hype \ˈhīp\ *n* [by shortening & alter.] **1** *slang* : HYPODERMIC **2** *slang* : a narcotics addict **3** *slang* : DECEPTION, PUT-ON **4** *slang* : a statement to promote sales : BLURB

hyper- *prefix* [ME *iper-*, fr. L *hyper-*, fr. Gk, fr. *hyper* — more at OVER] **1** : above : beyond : SUPER- <*hyper*physical> **2 a** : excessively <*hyper*sensitive> **b** : excessive <*hyper*emia> **3** : that is or exists in a space of more than three dimensions <*hyper*cube> <*hyper*space>

hy·per·ac·id \ˌhī-pə-ˈras-əd\ *adj* : containing more than the normal amount of acid — **hy·per·acid·i·ty** \-rə-ˈsid-ət-ē\ *n*

hy·per·ac·tive \ˌhī-pə-ˈrak-tiv\ *adj* : excessively or pathologically active — **hy·per·ac·tiv·i·ty** \-ˌrak-ˈtiv-ət-ē\ *n*

hy·per·aes·the·sia *var of* HYPERESTHESIA

hy·per·al·do·ste·ron·ism \ˈhī-pə-ˌral-ˈdäs-tə-ˌrō-ˌniz-əm, -ˌral-dō-stə-ˈrō-\ *n* : ALDOSTERONISM

hy·per·bar·ic \ˌhī-pər-ˈbar-ik\ *adj* [*hyper-* + *bar-* + *-ic*] : of, relating to, or utilizing greater than normal pressure esp. of oxygen <~ oxygen chambers> <~ medicine> — **hy·per·bar·i·cal·ly** \-i-k(ə-)lē\ *adv*

hy·per·bo·la \hī-ˈpər-bə-lə\ *n, pl* **-las** *or* **-lae** \-(ˌ)lē\ [NL, fr. Gk *hyperbolē*] : a plane curve generated by a point so moving that the difference of the distances from two fixed points is a constant : a curve formed by the intersection of a double right circular cone with a plane that cuts both halves of the cone

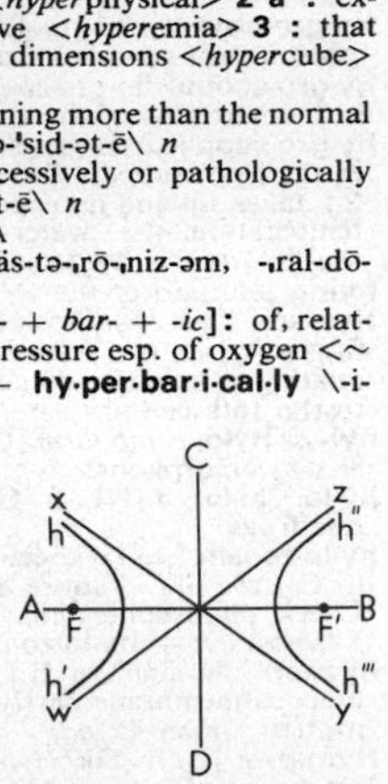

hyperbola: *AB, CD* axes; *F, F′* foci; *xy, zw* asymptotes; *h, h′, h″, h‴* hyperbola

hy·per·bo·le \hī-ˈpər-bə-(ˌ)lē\ *n* [L, fr. Gk *hyperbolē* excess, hyperbole, hyperbola, fr. *hyperballein* to exceed, fr. *hyper-* + *ballein* to throw — more at DEVIL] : extravagant exaggeration <"mile-high ice-cream cones" is an example of ~> — **hy·per·bo·list** \-ləst\ *n*

1**hy·per·bol·ic** \ˌhī-pər-ˈbäl-ik\ *also* **hy·per·bol·i·cal** \-i-kəl\ *adj* : of, characterized by, or given to hyperbole — **hy·per·bol·i·cal·ly** \-i-k(ə-)lē\ *adv*

2**hyperbolic** *also* **hyperbolical** *adj* **1** : of, relating to, or being analogous to a hyperbola **2** : of, relating to, or being a space in which more than one line parallel to a given line passes through a point <~ geometry>

hyperbolic function *n* : any of a set of six functions analogous to the trigonometric functions but related to the hyperbola in a way similar to that in which the trigonometric functions are related to a circle

hyperbolic paraboloid *n* : a saddle-shaped quadric surface whose sections by planes parallel to one coordinate plane are hyperbolas while those sections by planes parallel to the other two are parabolas if proper orientation of the coordinate axes is assumed

hy·per·bo·lize \hī-ˈpər-bə-ˌlīz\ *vb* **-lized; -liz·ing** *vi* : to indulge in hyperbole ~ *vt* : to exaggerate to a hyperbolic degree

hy·per·bo·loid \-ˌlȯid\ *n* : a quadric surface whose sections by planes parallel to one coordinate plane are ellipses while those sections by planes parallel to the other two are hyperbolas if proper orientation of the axes is assumed — **hy·per·bo·loi·dal** \(ˌ)hī-ˌpər-bə-ˈlȯid-ᵊl\ *adj*

1**hy·per·bo·re·an** \ˌhī-pər-ˈbȯr-ē-ən, -ˈbȯr-; -(ˌ)pər-bə-ˈrē-ən\ *adj* **1** : of or relating to an extreme northern region : FROZEN **2** : of or relating to any of the arctic peoples

2**hyperborean** *n* [L *Hyperborei* (pl.), fr. Gk *Hyperboreoi*, fr. *hyper-* + *Boreas*] **1** *often cap* : a member of a people held by the ancient Greeks to live beyond the north wind in a region of perpetual sunshine **2** : an inhabitant of a cool northern climate

hy·per·cal·ce·mia \ˌhī-pər-ˌkal-ˈsē-mē-ə\ *n* [NL] : an excess of calcium in the blood — **hy·per·cal·ce·mic** \-ˈsē-mik\ *adj*

hy·per·cap·nia \-ˈkap-nē-ə\ *n* [NL, fr. *hyper-* + Gk *kapnos* smoke] : the presence of excessive amounts of carbon dioxide in the blood — **hy·per·cap·nic** \-nik\ *adj*

hy·per·cat·a·lex·is \-ˌkat-ᵊl-ˈek-səs\ *n, pl* **-lex·es** \-ˈek-ˌsēz\ [NL, fr. *hyper-* + *catalexis*] : the occurrence of an additional syllable after the final complete foot or dipody in a line of verse — **hy·per·cat·a·lec·tic** \-ˈek-tik\ *adj*

hy·per·charge \ˈhī-pər-ˌchärj\ *n* : a quantum characteristic of a closely related group of strongly interacting particles represented by a number equal to twice the average value of the electric charge of the group

hy·per·cho·les·ter·emia \ˌhī-pər-kə-ˌles-tə-ˈrē-mē-ə\ *n* [NL] : HYPERCHOLESTEROLEMIA — **hy·per·cho·les·ter·emic** \-mik\ *adj*

hy·per·cho·les·ter·ol·emia \-tə-rə-ˈlē-mē-ə\ *n* [NL] : the presence of excess cholesterol in the blood — **hy·per·cho·les·ter·ol·emic** \-mik\ *adj*

hy·per·chro·mic anemia \ˈhī-pər-ˌkrō-mik-\ *n* [NL *hyperchromia* excessive coloring, fr. *hyper-* + Gk *chrōma* color — more at CHROMATIC] : an anemia with increase of hemoglobin in individual red blood cells and reduction in the number of red blood cells

hy·per·com·plex \ˌhī-pər-ˈkäm-ˌpleks\ *adj* : of, relating to, or being the most general form of number that extends the complex number to an expression of the same type involving a finite number of units or components in which addition is by components and multiplication does not have all of the properties of real or complex numbers <~ variable>

hy·per·crit·ic \ˌhī-pər-ˈkrit-ik\ *n* [NL *hypercriticus*, fr. *hyper-* + L *criticus* critic] : a carping or unduly censorious critic — **hy·per·crit·i·cism** \ˈkrit-ə-ˌsiz-əm\ *n*

hy·per·crit·i·cal \-ˈkrit-i-kəl\ *adj* : meticulously or excessively critical : censoriously critical ***syn*** see CRITICAL — **hy·per·crit·i·cal·ly** \-k(ə-)lē\ *adv*

hy·per·emia \ˌhī-pə-ˈrē-mē-ə\ *n* [NL] : excess of blood in a body part : CONGESTION — **hy·per·emic** \-mik\ *adj*

hy·per·es·the·sia \ˌhī-pə-res-ˈthē-zh(ē-)ə\ *n* [NL, fr. *hyper-* + *-esthesia* (as in *anesthesia*)] : unusual or pathological sensitivity of the skin or of a particular sense — **hy·per·es·thet·ic** \-ˈthet-ik\ *adj*

hy·per·eu·tec·tic \ˌhī-pər-yu̇-ˈtek-tik\ *adj* : containing the minor component in an amount in excess of that contained in the eutectic mixture

hy·per·eu·tec·toid \-ˌtȯid\ *adj* : containing the minor component in an amount in excess of that contained in the eutectoid

hy·per·ex·cit·abil·i·ty \ˌhī-pə-rik-ˌsīt-ə-ˈbil-ət-ē\ *n* : the state or condition of being unusually or excessively excitable

hy·per·fo·cal distance \ˌhī-pər-ˌfō-kəl-\ *n* [ISV] : the nearest distance upon which a photographic lens may be focused to produce satisfactory definition at infinity

hy·per·ga·my \hī-ˈpər-gə-mē\ *n, pl* **-mies** : marriage into an equal or higher caste or social group

hy·per·geo·met·ric distribution \ˈhī-pər-ˌjē-ə-ˌme-trik-\ *n* : a function of the form

$$f(x) = \frac{\binom{M}{x}\binom{N-M}{n-x}}{\binom{N}{n}} \quad \text{where} \quad \binom{M}{x} = \frac{M!}{x!(M-x)!}$$

that gives the probability of obtaining exactly x elements of one kind and $n - x$ elements of another if n elements are chosen at random without replacement from a finite population containing N elements of which M are of the first kind and $N - M$ are of the second kind

hy·per·gly·ce·mia \ˌhī-pər-glī-ˈsē-mē-ə\ *n* [NL] : excess of sugar in the blood — **hy·per·gly·ce·mic** \-mik\ *adj*

hy·per·gol \ˈhī-pər-ˌgōl, -ˌgȯl\ *n* [G, fr. *hyper-* + *erg-* + *-ol*] : a hypergolic fluid propellant

hy·per·gol·ic \ˌhī-pər-ˈgäl-ik\ *adj* **1** : igniting upon contact of components without external aid (as a spark) <~ rocket propellant> **2** : of, relating to, or using hypergolic fuel <a ~ engine> — **hy·per·gol·i·cal·ly** \-i-k(ə-)lē\ *adv*

hy·per·in·su·lin·ism \ˌhī-pə-ˈrin(t)-s(ə-)lə-ˌniz-əm\ *n* [ISV] : the presence of excess insulin in the body resulting in hypoglycemia

Hy·pe·ri·on \hī-ˈpir-ē-ən\ *n* [L, fr. Gk *Hyperiōn*] : a Titan and the father by Thea of Aurora, Selene, and Helios

hy·per·ir·ri·ta·bil·i·ty \ˌhī-pə-ˌrir-ət-ə-ˈbil-ət-ē\ *n* : abnormally great or uninhibited response to stimuli — **hy·per·ir·ri·ta·ble** \-ˈrir-ət-ə-bəl\ *adj*

hy·per·ker·a·to·sis \ˌhī-pər-ˌker-ə-ˈtō-səs\ *n, pl* **-to·ses** \-ˈtō-ˌsēz\ [NL] : hypertrophy of the corneous layer of the skin — **hy·per·ker·a·tot·ic** \-ˈtät-ik\ *adj*

hy·per·ki·ne·sia \-kə-ˈnē-zh(ē-)ə, -kī-\ *n* [NL, fr. *hyper-* + Gk *kinēsis* motion — more at KINESIS] : abnormally increased and usu. purposeless and uncontrollable muscular movement

hy·per·ki·net·ic \-ˈnet-ik\ *adj* : of, relating to, or marked by hyperkinesia

hy·per·li·pe·mia \ˌhī-pər-lī-ˈpē-mē-ə\ *n* [NL, fr. *hyper-* + *lip-* + *-emia*] : the presence of excess fat or lipids in the blood — **hy·per·li·pe·mic** \-mik\ *adj*

hy·per·lip·id·emia \-ˌlip-ə-ˈdē-mē-ə\ *n* [NL, fr. ISV *hyper-* + *lipid* + *-emia*] : HYPERLIPEMIA

hy·po·ther·mal \ˌhī-pō-ˈthər-məl\ *adj* : of or relating to a hydrothermal metalliferous ore vein deposited at high temperature

hy·po·ther·mia \-ˈthər-mē-ə\ *n* [NL, fr. *hypo-* + *therm-* + *-ia*] : subnormal temperature of the body — **hy·po·ther·mic** \-mik\ *adj*

hy·poth·e·sis \hī-ˈpäth-ə-səs\ *n, pl* **-e·ses** \-ˌsēz\ [Gk, fr. *hypotithenai* to put under, suppose, fr. *hypo-* + *tithenai* to put — more at DO] **1 :** a tentative assumption made in order to draw out and test its logical or empirical consequences **2 a :** an assumption or concession made for the sake of argument **b :** an interpretation of a practical situation or condition taken as the ground for action *syn* HYPOTHESIS, THEORY, LAW *shared meaning element* : a formulation of a natural principle based on inference from observed data

hy·poth·e·size \-ˌsīz\ *vb* **-sized; -siz·ing** *vi* : to make a hypothesis ~ *vt* : to adopt as a hypothesis

hy·po·thet·i·cal \ˌhī-pə-ˈthet-i-kəl\ *adj* **1 :** involving logical hypothesis : CONDITIONAL **2 :** of or depending on supposition : CONJECTURAL — **hy·po·thet·i·cal·ly** \-i-k(ə-)lē\ *adv*

hy·po·thy·roid \ˌhī-pō-ˈthī-ˌrȯid\ *adj* : of, relating to, or affected with hypothyroidism

hy·po·thy·roid·ism \-ˌiz-əm\ *n* [ISV] : deficient activity of the thyroid gland; *also* : a resultant lowered metabolic rate and general loss of vigor

hy·po·ton·ic \ˌhī-pə-ˈtän-ik, -pō-\ *adj* [ISV] **1 :** having deficient tone or tension <~ children> **2 :** having a lower osmotic pressure than a surrounding medium or a fluid under comparison <~ organisms> — **hy·po·ton·i·cal·ly** \-i-k(ə-)lē\ *adv* — **hy·po·to·nic·i·ty** \-tə-ˈnis-ət-ē\ *n*

hy·pot·ro·phy \hī-ˈpä-trə-fē\ *n* [ISV] : subnormal growth

hy·po·xan·thine \ˌhī-pō-ˈzan-ˌthēn\ *n* [ISV] : a purine base $C_5H_4N_4O$ found in plant and animal tissues that yields xanthine on oxidation

hyp·ox·emia \ˌhip-ˌäk-ˈsē-mē-ə, ˌhī-ˌpäk-\ *n* [NL, fr. *hypo-* + *ox-* + *-emia*] : deficient oxygenation of the blood — **hyp·ox·emic** \-mik\ *adj*

hyp·ox·ia \hip-ˈäk-sē-ə, hī-ˈpäk-\ *n* [NL, fr. *hypo-* + *ox-*] : a deficiency of oxygen reaching the tissues of the body — **hyp·ox·ic** \-sik\ *adj*

hyps- *or* **hypsi-** *or* **hypso-** *comb form* [Gk, fr. *hypsos* height; akin to OE *ūp* up] : height <*hypso*graphy>

hyp·sog·ra·phy \hip-ˈsäg-rə-fē\ *n, pl* **-phies** [ISV] **1 :** a branch of geography that deals with the measurement and mapping of the varying elevations of the earth's surface **2 :** topographic relief or the devices (as color shadings) by which it is indicated on maps

hyp·som·e·ter \hip-ˈsäm-ət-ər\ *n* [ISV] **1 :** an apparatus for estimating elevations in mountainous regions from the boiling points of liquids **2 :** any of various instruments for determining the height of trees by triangulation

hyp·som·e·try \hip-ˈsäm-ə-trē\ *n* : the measurement of heights (as with reference to sea level) — **hyp·so·met·ric** \ˌhip-sə-ˈme-trik\ *adj*

hy·rax \ˈhī-ˌraks\ *n, pl* **hy·rax·es** \-ˌrak-səz\ *also* **hy·ra·ces** \-rə-ˌsēz\ [Gk *hyrak-, hyrax* shrewmouse] : any of several small ungulate mammals (order Hyracoidea) characterized by thickset body with short legs and ears and rudimentary tail, feet with soft pads and broad nails, and teeth of which the molars resemble those of the rhinoceros and the incisors those of rodents — called also *coney*

hyrax

hy·son \ˈhīs-ᵊn\ *n* [Chin (Pek) *hsi*¹ *ch'un*¹, lit., flourishing spring] : a Chinese green tea made from thinly rolled and twisted leaves

hys·sop \ˈhis-əp\ *n* [ME *ysop*, fr. OE *ysope*, fr. L *hyssopus*, fr. Gk *hyssōpos*, of Sem origin; akin to Heb *ēzōbh* hyssop] **1 :** a plant used in purificatory sprinkling rites by the ancient Hebrews **2 :** a European mint (*Hyssopus officinalis*) that has highly aromatic and pungent leaves and is sometimes used as a potherb

hyster- *or* **hystero-** *comb form* [F or L; F *hystér-*, fr. L *hyster-*, fr. Gk, fr. *hystera*] **1 :** womb <*hystero*tomy> **2** [NL, fr. *hysteria*] **a :** hysteria <*hystero*genic> **b :** hysteria and <*hystero*neurasthenia>

hys·ter·ec·to·mize \ˌhis-tə-ˈrek-tə-ˌmīz\ *vt* **-mized; -miz·ing** : to remove the uterus of by surgery

hys·ter·ec·to·my \-mē\ *n, pl* **-mies** : surgical removal of the uterus

hys·ter·e·sis \ˌhis-tə-ˈrē-səs\ *n* [NL, fr. Gk *hysterēsis* shortcoming, fr. *hysterein* to be late, fall short, fr. *hysteros* later — more at OUT] : a retardation of the effect when the forces acting upon a body are changed (as if from viscosity or internal friction); *esp* : a lagging in the values of resulting magnetization in a magnetic material (as iron) due to a changing magnetizing force — **hys·ter·et·ic** \-ˈret-ik\ *adj*

hys·te·ria \his-ˈter-ē-ə, -ˈtir-\ *n* [NL, fr. E *hysteric*, adj., fr. L *hystericus*, fr. Gk *hysterikos*, fr. *hystera* womb; fr. the former notion that hysteric women were suffering from disturbances of the womb] **1 :** a psychoneurosis marked by emotional excitability and disturbances of the psychic, sensory, vasomotor, and visceral functions **2 :** unmanageable fear or emotional excess — **hys·ter·ic** \-ˈter-ik\ *n* — **hysteric** *or* **hys·ter·i·cal** \-ˈter-i-kəl\ *adj* — **hys·ter·i·cal·ly** \-i-k(ə-)lē\ *adv*

hys·ter·ics \-ˈter-iks\ *n pl but sing or pl in constr* : a fit of uncontrollable laughter or crying : HYSTERIA

hys·ter·oid \ˈhis-tə-ˌrȯid\ *adj* : resembling hysteria

hys·ter·on prot·er·on \ˌhis-tə-ˌrän-ˈprät-ə-ˌrän, -tə-rən-ˈprät-ə-rən\ *n* [LL, fr. Gk, lit., (the) later earlier, (the) latter first] **1 :** a figure of speech consisting of the reversal of a natural or rational order (as in "then came the thunder and the lightning") **2 :** a logical fallacy of assuming as a premise something that follows from what is to be proved

hys·tero·tely \ˈhis-tə-rō-ˌtel-ē\ *n* [Gk *hysteros* later + *telein* to complete, perfect, fr. *telos* end — more at WHEEL] : relatively retarded differentiation of a structure so as to exhibit a form usu. associated with an earlier stage of development

hys·ter·ot·o·my \ˌhis-tə-ˈrät-ə-mē\ *n, pl* **-mies** [NL *hysterotomia*, fr. *hyster-* + *-tomia* -tomy] : surgical incision of the uterus; *esp* : CESAREAN

Hz *abbr* hertz

¹i \ˈī\ *n, pl* **i's** *or* **is** \ˈīz\ *often cap, often attrib* **1 a :** the 9th letter of the English alphabet **b :** a graphic representation of this letter **c :** a speech counterpart of orthographic *i* **2 :** ONE — see NUMBER table **3 :** a graphic device for reproducing the letter *i* **4 :** one designated *i* esp. as the 9th in order or class **5 :** something shaped like the letter I **6 :** a unit vector parallel to the x-axis **7** [abbr. for *incomplete*] **a :** a grade rating a student's work as incomplete **b :** one graded or rated with an I **8 :** I FORMATION

²i *abbr, often cap* **1** Indian **2** industrial **3** initial **4** intelligence **5** intensity **6** interstate **7** intransitive **8** island; isle **9** Israeli

³i *symbol* positive square root of minus one

¹I \(ˈ)ī, ə\ *pron* [ME, fr. OE *ic*; akin to OHG *ih* I, L *ego*, Gk *egō*] : the one who is speaking or writing <~ feel fine> — compare ME, MINE, MY, WE

²I \ˈī\ *n, pl* **I's** *or* **Is** \ˈīz\ : someone aware of possessing a personal individuality : SELF

³I *symbol* **1** electric current **2** iodine

-i- [ME, fr. OF, fr. L, stem vowel of most nouns and adjectives in combination] — used as a connective vowel to join word elements esp. of Latin origin <matr*i*linear> <rat*i*cide>

Ia *or* **IA** *abbr* Iowa

¹-ia *n suffix* [NL, fr. L & Gk, suffix forming feminine nouns] **1 :** pathological condition <hyster*ia*> **2 :** genus of plants or animals <Fuchs*ia*> **3 :** territory : world : society <suburb*ia*>

²-ia *n pl suffix* [NL, fr. L (neut. pl. of *-ius*, adj. ending) & Gk, neut. pl. of *-ios*, adj. ending] **1 :** higher taxon (as class or order) consisting of (such plants or animals) <Saur*ia*> **2 :** things derived from or relating to (something specified) <tabloid*ia*>

[3]-ia *pl of* -IUM
IAA *abbr* indoleacetic acid
IAAF *abbr* International Amateur Athletic Federation
IABA *abbr* International Amateur Boxing Association
IACU *abbr* International Association of Catholic Universities
IADB *abbr* Inter-American Defense Board
IAEA *abbr* International Atomic Energy Agency
Ia·go \ē-'äg-(,)ō\ *n* : the villain of Shakespeare's tragedy *Othello*
-ial *adj suffix* [ME, fr. MF, fr. L *-ialis,* fr. *-i-* + *-alis* -al] : [1]-AL <manor*ial*>
IALC *abbr* instrument approach and landing chart
IAM *abbr* International Association of Machinists and Aerospace Workers
iamb \'ī-,am(b)\ *or* **iam·bus** \ī-'am-bəs\ *n, pl* **iambs** \'ī-,amz\ *or* **iam·bus·es** [L *iambus,* fr. Gk *iambos*] : a metrical foot consisting of one short syllable followed by one long syllable or of one unstressed syllable followed by one stressed syllable (as in *above*) — compare TROCHEE — **iam·bic** \ī-'am-bik\ *adj or n*
-ian — see -AN
-iana — see -ANA
IAP *abbr* international airport
IAPF *abbr* Inter-American Peacekeeping Force
IARU *abbr* International Amateur Radio Union
IAS *abbr* indicated airspeed
-i·a·sis \'ī-ə-səs\ *n suffix, pl* **-i·a·ses** \-,sēz\ [NL, fr. L, fr. Gk, suffix of action, fr. denominative verbs in *-ian, -iazein*] : disease having characteristics of or produced by (something specified) <hypochondr*iasis*> <ancylostom*iasis*>
IATA *abbr* International Air Transport Association
-i·at·ric \ē-'a-trik\ *also* **-i·at·ri·cal** \-tri-kəl\ *adj comb form* [NL *-iatria*] : of or relating to (such) medical treatment or healing <ped*iatric*>
-i·at·rics \ē-'a-triks\ *n pl comb form but sing or pl in constr* : medical treatment <ped*iatrics*>
iat·ro·gen·ic \(,)ī-,a-trə-'jen-ik\ *adj* [Gk *iatros* + E *-genic*] : induced inadvertently by a physician or his treatment <an ~ rash> — **iat·ro·gen·i·cal·ly** \-'jen-i-k(ə-)lē\ *adv*
-i·a·try \'ī-ə-trē, *in a few words* ē-,a-trē\ *n comb form* [F *-iatrie,* fr. NL *-iatria,* fr. Gk *iatreia* art of healing, fr. *iatros*] : medical treatment : healing <pod*iatry*>
IAU *abbr* **1** International Association of Universities **2** International Astronomical Union
ib *abbr* ibidem
IB *abbr* **1** in bond **2** incendiary bomb
I band \'ī-\ *n* : an isotropic band of a striated muscle fiber
I beam *n* : an iron or steel beam that is I-shaped in cross section
[1]**Ibe·ri·an** \ī-'bir-ē-ən\ *n* [*Iberia,* ancient region of the Caucasus] : a member of one or more peoples anciently inhabiting the Caucasus in Asia between the Black and Caspian seas — **Iberian** *adj*
[2]**Iberian** *n* [*Iberia,* peninsula in Europe] **1 a** : a member of one or more Caucasoid peoples anciently inhabiting the peninsula comprising Spain and Portugal and the Basque region about the Pyrenees and prob. related in origin to peoples of northern Africa **b** : a native or inhabitant of Spain or Portugal or the Basque region **2** : one or more of the languages of the ancient Iberians — **Iberian** *adj*
ibex \'ī-,beks\ *n, pl* **ibex** *or* **ibex·es** [L] **1** : any of several wild goats living chiefly in high mountain areas of the Old World and having large recurved horns transversely ridged in front **2** : a wild goat (*Capra aegagrus*) found in Asia Minor and believed to be the progenitor of the domestic goat

ibex 1

ibid \'ib-əd\ *abbr* ibidem
ibi·dem \'ib-ə-,dem, ib-'īd-əm\ *adv* [L] : in the same place
-ibil·i·ty \ə-'bil-ət-ē\ — see -ABILITY
ibis \'ī-bəs\ *n, pl* **ibis** *or* **ibis·es** [L, fr. Gk, fr. Egypt *hby*] : any of several wading birds (family Threskiornithidae) related to the herons but distinguished by a long slender downwardly curved bill
-ible \ə-bəl\ — see -ABLE
IBM *abbr* intercontinental ballistic missile
Ibo \'ē-(,)bō\ *n, pl* **Ibo** *or* **Ibos** **1** : a member of a Negro people of the area around the lower Niger **2** : a Kwa language used as a language of trade and education in a large area of southern Nigeria
Ib·sen·ism \'ib-sə-,niz-əm, 'ip-\ *n* **1** : dramatic invention or construction characteristic of Ibsen **2** : championship of Ibsen's plays and ideas — **Ib·sen·ite** \-,nīt\ *n or adj*
IBY *abbr* International Biological Year
[1]**IC** *n* : IMMEDIATE CONSTITUENT
[2]**IC** *n* : INTEGRATED CIRCUIT
[1]**-ic** \ik\ *adj suffix* [ME, fr. OF & L; OF *-ique,* fr. L *-icus* — more at -Y] **1** : having the character or form of : being <panoram*ic*> : consisting of <run*ic*> **2 a** : of or relating to <alderman*ic*> **b** : related to, derived from, or containing <alcohol*ic*> <ole*ic*> **3** : in the manner of : like that of : characteristic of <Byron*ic*> **4** : associated or dealing with <Ved*ic*> : utilizing <electron*ic*> **5** : characterized by : exhibiting <nostalg*ic*> : affected with <allerg*ic*> **6** : caused by <amoeb*ic*> **7** : tending to produce <analges*ic*> **8** : having a valence relatively higher than in compounds or ions named with an adjective ending in *-ous* <ferr*ic* iron>
[2]**-ic** *n suffix* : one having the character or nature of : one belonging to or associated with : one exhibiting or affected by : one that produces
ICA *abbr* **1** International Cooperation Administration **2** International Cooperative Alliance
-i·cal \i-kəl\ *adj suffix* [ME, fr. LL *-icalis* (as in *clericalis* clerical, *radicalis* radical)] : -IC <symmetr*ical*> <geolog*ical*> — sometimes differing from *-ic* in that adjectives formed with *-ical* have a wider or more transferred semantic range than corresponding adjectives in *-ic*
ICAO *abbr* International Civil Aviation Organization
Ic·a·rus \'ik-ə-rəs\ *n* [L, fr. Gk *Ikaros*] : the son of Daedalus who to escape imprisonment flies by means of artificial wings but falls into the sea and drowns when the wax of his wings melts as he flies too near the sun
ICBM \,ī-,sē-(,)bē-'em\ *n, pl* **ICBM's** *or* **ICBMs** \-'emz\ : an intercontinental ballistic missile
ICC *abbr* **1** Indian Claims Commission **2** International Chamber of Commerce **3** Interstate Commerce Commission
[1]**ice** \'īs\ *n, often attrib* [ME *is,* fr. OE *īs;* akin to OHG *īs* ice, Av *isu-* icy] **1 a** : frozen water **b** : a sheet or stretch of ice **2** : a state of coldness (as from formality or reserve) **3** : a substance resembling ice; *esp* : a substance reduced to the solid state by cold <ammonia ~ in the rings of Saturn> **4 a** : a frozen dessert containing a flavoring (as fruit juice); *esp* : one containing no milk or cream **b** *Brit* : a serving of ice cream **5** *slang* : DIAMONDS; *broadly* : JEWELRY **6** : an undercover premium paid to a theater employee for choice theater tickets — **ice·less** \'ī-sləs\ *adj* — **on ice** **1** : with every likelihood of being won or accomplished **2** : in reserve or safekeeping
[2]**ice** *vb* **iced; ic·ing** *vt* **1 a** : to coat with or convert into ice **b** : to chill with ice **c** : to supply with ice **2** : to cover with or as if with icing **3** : to put on ice **4** : to shoot (an ice hockey puck) the length of the rink and beyond the opponents' goal line ~ *vi* **1** : to become ice-cold **2 a** : to become covered with ice — often used with *up* **b** : to have ice form inside <the carburetor *iced* up>
Ice *abbr* Iceland
ICE *abbr* **1** internal-combustion engine **2** International Cultural Exchange
ice age *n* **1** : a time of widespread glaciation **2** *cap I&A* : the Pleistocene glacial epoch
ice ax *n* : a combination pick and adz with a spiked handle that is used in mountain climbing
ice bag *n* : a waterproof bag to hold ice for local application of cold to the body
ice·berg \'īs-,bərg\ *n* [prob. part trans. of Dan or Norw *isberg,* fr. *is* ice + *berg* mountain] **1** : a large floating mass of ice detached from a glacier **2** : an emotionally cold person
ice·blink \-,bliŋk\ *n* : a glare in the sky over an ice field
ice·boat \-,bōt\ *n* **1** : a skeleton boat or frame on runners propelled on ice usu. by sails **2** : ICEBREAKER 2
ice·boat·ing \-,bōt-iŋ\ *n* : the sport of sailing in iceboats — **ice·boat·er** \-,bōt-ər\ *n*
ice·bound \-,bau̇nd\ *adj* : surrounded or obstructed by ice
ice·box \-,bäks\ *n* : REFRIGERATOR
ice·break·er \-,brā-kər\ *n* **1** : a structure that protects a bridge pier from floating ice **2** : a ship equipped to make and maintain a channel through ice **3** : MIXER 1c
ice cap *n* **1** : an ice bag shaped to the head **2** : a cover of perennial ice and snow; *specif* : a glacier forming on an extensive area of relatively level land and flowing outward from its center — called also *ice sheet*
ice–cold \'ī-'skōld\ *adj* : extremely cold
ice–cream *adj* : of a color similar to that of vanilla ice cream — usu. used of clothing <an ~ suit>
ice cream \(')ī-'skrēm, 'ī-,\ *n* : a sweet variously flavored frozen food containing cream or butterfat and usu. eggs
ice–cream chair *n* [fr. its use in ice cream parlors] : a small armless chair with a circular seat for use at a table (as in a sidewalk café)
ice–cream cone *n* : a thin crisp edible cone for holding ice cream; *also* : one filled with ice cream
ice·fall \'īs-,fȯl\ *n* **1** : a frozen waterfall **2** : the mass of usu. jagged blocks into which a glacier may break when it moves down a steep declivity
ice field *n* **1** : an extensive sheet of sea ice **2** : ICE CAP
ice floe *n* : a flat free mass of floating sea ice; *broadly* : a large floating fragment of sheet ice
ice fog *n* : a fog composed of ice particles
ice hockey *n* : a game played on an ice rink by two teams of six players on skates whose object is to drive a puck into the opponent's goal with a hockey stick
ice·house \'īs-,hau̇s, 'ī-,sau̇s\ *n* : a building in which ice is made or stored
ice·kha·na \'īs-,kän-ə, -,kan-\ *n* [*ice* + gym*khana*] : an automobile gymkhana held on a frozen lake
Icel *abbr* Icelandic
[1]**Ice·lan·dic** \ī-'slan-dik\ *adj* : of, relating to, or characteristic of Iceland, the Icelanders, or Icelandic
[2]**Icelandic** *n* : the North Germanic language of the Icelandic people
Ice·land moss \,ī-slən(d)-, ,ī-,slan(d)-\ *n* : a lichen (*Cetraria islandica*) of mountainous and arctic regions sometimes used in medicine or as food
Iceland poppy *n* : any of various perennial cultivated poppies prob. derived from two species (*Papaver nudicaule* and *P. alpinum*) and characterized by rather small single or double chiefly pastel flowers
Iceland spar *n* : a doubly refracting transparent calcite
ice·man \'ī-,sman\ *n* **1** : a man skilled in traveling on ice **2** : one who sells or delivers ice
ice milk *n* : a sweetened frozen food made of skim milk
ice needle *n* : one of numerous slender ice particles that float in the air in clear cold weather — called also *ice crystal*
Ice·ni \ī-'sē-,nī\ *n pl* [L] : an ancient British people that under their queen Boadicea revolted against the Romans in A.D. 61 — **Ice·ni·an** \-'sē-nē-ən\ *or* **Ice·nic** \-'sē-nik, -'sen-ik\ *adj*
ice pack *n* : an expanse of pack ice
ice pick *n* : a hand tool ending in a spike for chipping ice

ice plant *n* : an Old World annual herb (*Mesembryanthemum crystallinum*) that is related to the carpetweed, has fleshy foliage covered with glistening papillate dots or vesicles, and is widely naturalized in warm regions; *broadly* : FIG MARIGOLD
ice point *n* : the temperature of 0° centigrade or 273.15° kelvin at which ice is in equilibrium with liquid water under air saturated with water at standard atmospheric pressure
ice show *n* : an entertainment consisting of various exhibitions by ice skaters usu. with musical accompaniment
ice–skate \ˈī(s)-ˌskāt\ *vi* : to skate on ice — **ice skater** *n*
ice skate *n* : a shoe with a metal runner attached for ice-skating
ice storm *n* : a storm in which falling rain freezes on contact
ice water *n* : chilled or iced water esp. for drinking
ICFTU *abbr* International Confederation of Free Trade Unions
ichn- *or* **ichno-** *comb form* [Gk, fr. *ichnos*] : footprint : track <*ichno*logy>
ich·neu·mon \ik-ˈn(y)ü-mən\ *n* [L, fr. Gk *ichneumōn*, lit., tracker, fr. *ichneuein* to track, fr. *ichnos*] **1** : MONGOOSE **2** : ICHNEUMON FLY
ichneumon fly *n* : any of a large superfamily (Ichneumonoidea) of hymenopterous insects whose larvae are usu. internal parasites of other insect larvae and esp. of caterpillars
ichor \ˈī-ˌkȯ(ə)r\ *n* [Gk *ichōr*] **1** : an ethereal fluid taking the place of blood in the veins of the ancient Greek gods **2** : a thin watery or blood-tinged discharge — **ichor·ous** \-kə-rəs\ *adj*
ichth *abbr* ichthyology
ichthy- *or* **ichthyo-** *comb form* [L, fr. Gk, fr. *ichthys*; akin to Arm *jukn* fish] : fish <*ichthy*ic>
ich·thyo·fau·na \ˌik-thē-ō-ˈfȯn-ə, -ˈfän-\ *n* [NL] : the fish life of a region — **ich·thyo·fau·nal** \-ˈfȯn-ᵊl, -ˈfän-\ *adj*
ich·thy·ol·o·gy \ˌik-thē-ˈäl-ə-jē\ *n* **1** : a branch of zoology that deals with fishes **2** : a treatise on fishes — **ich·thy·o·log·i·cal** \-thē-ə-ˈläj-i-kəl\ *adj* — **ich·thy·o·log·i·cal·ly** \-k(ə-)lē\ *adv* — **ich·thy·ol·o·gist** \-thē-ˈäl-ə-jəst\ *n*
ich·thy·oph·a·gous \ˌik-thē-ˈäf-ə-gəs\ *adj* [Gk *ichthyophagos*, fr. *ichthy-* + *-phagos* -phagous] : eating or subsisting on fish
ich·thy·or·nis \ˌik-thē-ˈȯr-nəs\ *n* [NL, genus name, fr. *ichthy-* + Gk *ornis* bird — more at ERNE] : any of a genus (*Ichthyornis*) of extinct toothed birds
ich·thyo·saur \ˈik-thē-ə-ˌsȯ(ə)r\ *n* [deriv. of Gk *ichthy-* + *sauros* lizard — more at SAURIAN] : any of an order (Ichthyosauria) of extinct marine reptiles with fish-shaped body and elongated snout — **ich·thyo·sau·ri·an** \ˌik-thē-ə-ˈsȯr-ē-ən\ *adj or n*

ichthyosaur

-i·cian \ˈish-ən\ *n suffix* [ME, fr. OF *-icien*, fr. L *-ica* (as in *rhetorica* rhetoric) + OF *-ien* -ian] : specialist : practitioner <beaut*ician*>
ici·cle \ˈī-ˌsik-əl\ *n* [ME *isikel*, fr. *is* ice + *ikel* icicle, fr. OE *gicel*; akin to OHG *ihilla* icicle, MIr *aig* ice] **1** : a pendent mass of ice formed by the freezing of dripping water **2** : an emotionally unresponsive person
[1]ic·ing \ˈī-siŋ\ *n* : a sweet, flavored, and usu. creamy mixture used to coat baked goods (as cupcakes) — called also *frosting*
[2]icing *n* : an act by an ice-hockey player of shooting a puck from within his defensive zone beyond the opponents' goal line
ICJ *abbr* International Court of Justice
ick·er \ˈik-ər\ *n* [deriv. of OE *ēar*, *eher* — more at EAR] *Scot* : a head of grain
icky \ˈik-ē\ *adj* **ick·i·er**; **-est** [perh. baby talk alter. of *sticky*] **1** : offensive to the senses or sensibilities : DISTASTEFUL <put off by her ~ triteness —Renata Adler> **2** : lacking sophistication
icon \ˈī-ˌkän\ *n* [L, fr. Gk *eikōn*, fr. *eikenai* to resemble] **1** : a usu. pictorial representation : IMAGE **2** [LGk *eikōn*, fr. Gk] : a conventional religious image typically painted on a small wooden panel and used in the devotions of Eastern Christians **3** : an object of uncritical devotion : IDOL — **icon·ic** \ī-ˈkän-ik\ *adj* — **icon·i·cal·ly** \-i-k(ə-)lē\ *adv* — **ico·nic·i·ty** \ˌī-kə-ˈnis-ət-ē\ *n*
icon- *or* **icono-** *comb form* [Gk *eikon-*, *eikono-*, fr. *eikon-*, *eikōn*] : image <*icono*later>
icon·o·clasm \ī-ˈkän-ə-ˌklaz-əm\ *n* : the doctrine, practice, or attitude of an iconoclast
icon·o·clast \-ˌklast\ *n* [ML *iconoclastes*, fr. MGk *eikonoklastēs*, lit., image destroyer, fr. Gk *eikono-* + *klan* to break — more at HALT] **1** : one who destroys religious images or opposes their veneration **2** : one who attacks established beliefs or institutions — **icon·o·clas·tic** \(ˌ)ī-ˌkän-ə-ˈklas-tik\ *adj* — **icon·o·clas·ti·cal·ly** \-ti-k(ə-)lē\ *adv*
ico·nog·ra·pher \ˌī-kə-ˈnäg-rə-fər\ *n* : a maker or designer of figures or drawings esp. of a conventional or mechanical type
icon·o·graph·ic \(ˌ)ī-ˌkän-ə-ˈgraf-ik\ *or* **icon·o·graph·i·cal** \-i-kəl\ *adj* **1** : of or relating to iconography **2** : representing something by pictures or diagrams — **icon·o·graph·i·cal·ly** \-i-k(ə-)lē\ *adv*
ico·nog·ra·phy \ˌī-kə-ˈnäg-rə-fē\ *n*, *pl* **-phies** [Gk *eikonographia* sketch, description, fr. *eikonographein* to describe, fr. *eikon-* + *graphein* to write — more at CARVE] **1** : pictorial material relating to or illustrating a subject : a pictorial record of a subject **2** : the traditional or conventional images or symbols associated with a subject and esp. a religious or legendary subject **3** : the imagery or symbolism of a work of art, an artist, or a body of art **4** : ICONOLOGY **5** : a published work dealing with or featuring iconography
ico·nol·a·try \-ˈnäl-ə-trē\ *n* : the worship of images or icons
ico·nol·o·gy \-ˈnäl-ə-jē\ *n* [F *iconologie*, fr. *icono-* icon- + *-logie* -logy] : the study of icons or artistic symbolism — **icon·o·log·i·cal** \(ˌ)ī-ˌkän-ᵊl-ˈäj-i-kəl\ *adj*
icon·o·scope \ī-ˈkän-ə-ˌskōp\ *n* [fr. *Iconoscope*, a trademark] : a camera tube containing an electron gun and a photoemissive mosaic screen each cell of which produces a charge proportional to the varying light intensity of the image focused on the screen
ico·nos·ta·sis \ˌī-kə-ˈnäs-tə-səs\ *n*, *pl* **-ta·ses** \-ˌsēz\ [MGk *eikonostasi*] : a screen or partition with doors and tiers of icons that separates the bema from the nave in Eastern churches
ico·sa·he·dral \(ˌ)ī-ˌkō-sə-ˈhē-drəl, -ˌkäs-ə-\ *adj* : of or having the form of an icosahedron
ico·sa·he·dron \-drən\ *n*, *pl* **-drons** *or* **-dra** \-drə\ [Gk *eikosaedron*, fr. *eikosi* twenty + *-edron* -hedron — more at VIGESIMAL] : a polyhedron having 20 faces

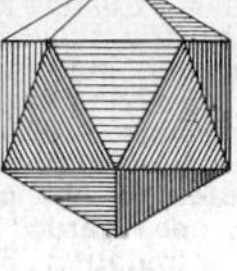

icosahedron

ICR *abbr* Institute for Cancer Research
-ics \(ˌ)iks\ *n pl suffix but sing or pl in constr* [*-ic* + *-s*; trans. of Gk *-ika*, fr. neut. pl. of *-ikos* -ic] **1** : study : knowledge : skill : practice <lingui*stics*> <electron*ics*> **2** : characteristic actions or activities <acrobat*ics*> **3** : characteristic qualities, operations, or phenomena <mechan*ics*>
ICSH *abbr* interstitial cell-stimulating hormone
ic·ter·ic \ik-ˈter-ik\ *adj* : of, relating to, or affected with jaundice
ic·ter·us \ˈik-tə-rəs\ *n* [NL, fr. Gk *ikteros*; akin to Gk *iktis* yellow-breasted marten] : JAUNDICE
ic·tus \ˈik-təs\ *n* [L, fr. *ictus*, pp. of *icere* to strike; akin to Gk *aichmē* lance] : the recurring stress or beat in a rhythmic or metrical series of sounds
ICU *abbr* intensive care unit
icy \ˈī-sē\ *adj* **ic·i·er**; **-est** **1 a** : covered with, abounding in, or consisting of ice **b** : intensely cold **2** : characterized by coldness : FRIGID <an ~ stare> — **ic·i·ly** \-sə-lē\ *adv* — **ic·i·ness** \-sē-nəs\ *n*
[1]id \ˈid\ *n* [NL, fr. L, it] : the one of the three divisions of the psyche in psychoanalytic theory that is completely unconscious and is the source of psychic energy derived from instinctual needs and drives — compare EGO, SUPEREGO
[2]id *n* [*-id*, fr. F *-ide*, fr. L *-id-*, *-is*, fem. patronymic suffix] : a skin rash that is an allergic reaction to an agent causing an infection
[3]id *abbr* idem
ID *abbr* **1** Idaho **2** identification **3** industrial design **4** inner diameter **5** inside dimensions **6** intelligence department **7** internal diameter **8** intradermal
[1]-id \əd, (ˌ)id\ *n suffix* [in sense 1, fr. L *-ides*, masc. patronymic suffix, fr. Gk *-idēs*; in sense 2, fr. It *-ide*, fr. L *-id-*, *is*, fem. patronymic suffix, fr. Gk] **1** : one belonging to a (specified) dynastic line <Fatim*id*> **2** : meteor associated with or radiating from a (specified) constellation or comet <Perse*id*>
[2]-id *n suffix* [prob. fr. L *-id-*, *-is*, fem. patronymic suffix, fr. Gk] : body : particle <energ*id*>
I'd \(ˌ)īd\ : I had : I should : I would
-i·dae \ə-ˌdē\ *n pl suffix* [NL, fr. L, fr. Gk *-idai*, pl. of *-idēs*] : members of the family of — in names of zoological families <Fel*idae*>
ID card \ī-ˈdē-\ *n* : a card bearing identifying data (as age or organizational membership) about the individual whose name appears thereon — called also *identification card*, *identity card*
-ide \ˌīd\ *also* **-id** \əd, (ˌ)id\ *n suffix* [G & F; G *-id*, fr. F *-ide* (as in *oxide*)] **1** : binary chemical compound — added to the contracted name of the nonmetallic or more electronegative element <hydrogen sulf*ide*> or radical <cyan*ide*> **2** : chemical compound derived from or related to another (usu. specified) compound <anhydr*ide*> <glucos*ide*>
idea \ī-ˈdē-ə, ˈīd-(ˌ)ē-ə, *esp South* ˈīd-ē\ *n* [L, fr. Gk, fr. *idein* to see — more at WIT] **1 a** : a transcendent entity that is a real pattern of which existing things are imperfect representations **b** : a standard of perfection : IDEAL **c** : a plan for action : DESIGN **2** *archaic* : a visible representation of a conception : a replica of a pattern **3 a** *obs* : an image recalled by memory **b** : an indefinite or unformed conception **c** : an entity (as a thought, concept, sensation, or image) actually or potentially present to consciousness **4** : a formulated thought or opinion **5** : whatever is known or supposed about something <a child's ~ of time> **6** : the central meaning or chief end of a particular action or situation **7** *Christian Science* : an image in Mind — **idea·less** \ī-ˈdē-ə-ləs\ *adj*
syn IDEA, CONCEPT, CONCEPTION, THOUGHT, NOTION, IMPRESSION *shared meaning element* : what exists in the mind as a representation (as of something comprehended) or as a formulation (as of a plan). IDEA is equally applicable to a mental image or formulation of something seen or known or imagined, to a pure abstraction, or to something assumed or vaguely sensed <that's not my *idea* of a good time> <try to get an *idea* of the complexity of the problem> CONCEPT in precise use applies to a generic idea conceived by the mind after acquaintance with instances of a category <the child as he grows develops such *concepts* as "chair", "dog", and "house"> but in frequent, if sometimes criticized use *concept* is applicable to any formulated and widely accepted idea of what a thing should be <we must expand the *concept* of conservation to meet the imperious problems of the new age —J. F. Kennedy> CONCEPTION, though often interchangeable with *concept* in the latter's more general use, can distinctively stress the process of imagining and formulating <too often a writer's *conception* exceeds his capacity for execution> THOUGHT is likely to suggest the result of reflection, meditation, or reasoning rather than of imagining <a child's *thought* about God> NOTION can apply to a vague, tentative, or chance idea <most of us retain the *notion* that all technical change is progress, is necessarily good —R. M. Hutchins> but in precise use it can come close to *concept* in

ə abut ᵊ kitten ər further a back ā bake ä cot, cart
aù out ch chin e less ē easy g gift i trip ī life
j joke ŋ sing ō flow ȯ flaw ȯi coin th thin th this
ü loot u̇ foot y yet yü few yu̇ furious zh vision

suggesting a general or universal idea <arriving at the *notion* of law —Irving Babbitt> or to *conception* in denoting the meaning content assigned by the mind to a term <[they] have no adequate *notion* of what we mean by causation —Edward Sapir> IMPRESSION usually implies the presence of external stimulation that gives rise to an often vague idea <I had an *impression* that the door opened softly>

[1]**ide·al** \ī-ˈdē(-ə)l\ *adj* [F or LL; F *idéal,* fr. LL *idealis,* fr. L *idea*] **1 a :** existing as a mental image or in fancy or imagination only; *broadly* : lacking practicality **b :** relating to or constituting mental images, ideas, or conceptions **2 a :** of, relating to, or embodying an ideal **b :** conforming exactly to an ideal, law, or standard : PERFECT **3 :** existing as an archetypal idea **4 :** of or relating to philosophical idealism

[2]**ideal** *n* **1 :** a standard of perfection, beauty, or excellence **2 :** one regarded as exemplifying an ideal and often taken as a model for imitation **3 :** an ultimate object or aim of endeavor : GOAL **4 :** a subset of a mathematical ring that is closed under addition and subtraction and contains the products of any given element of the subset with each element of the ring <the integers ending in 0 are an ~ in the ring of all integers> ***syn*** see MODEL — **ide·al·less** \ī-ˈdē(-ə)l-ləs\ *adj*

ide·al·ism \ī-ˈdē-(ə-)ˌliz-əm\ *n* **1 a (1) :** a theory that ultimate reality lies in a realm transcending phenomena **(2) :** a theory that the essential nature of reality lies in consciousness or reason **b (1) :** a theory that only the perceptible is real **(2) :** a theory that only mental states or entities are knowable **2 a :** the practice of forming ideals or living under their influence **b :** something that is idealized **3 :** literary or artistic theory or practice that affirms the preeminent value of imagination as compared with faithful copying of nature — compare REALISM

[1]**ide·al·ist** \-(ə-)ləst\ *n* **1 a :** an adherent of a philosophical theory of idealism **b :** an artist or author who advocates or practices idealism in art or writing **2 :** one guided by ideals; *esp* : one that places ideals before practical considerations

[2]**idealist** *adj* : IDEALISTIC

ide·al·is·tic \(ˌ)ī-ˌdē-(ə-)ˈlis-tik\ *adj* : of or relating to idealists or idealism — **ide·al·is·ti·cal·ly** \-ti-k(ə-)lē\ *adv*

ide·al·i·ty \ˌīd-ē-ˈal-ət-ē\ *n, pl* **-ties** **1 a :** the quality or state of being ideal **b :** existence only in idea **2 :** something imaginary or idealized

ide·al·ize \ī-ˈdē-(ə-)ˌlīz\ *vb* **-ized; -iz·ing** *vt* : to give an ideal form or value to **2 :** to treat idealistically ~ *vi* **1 :** to form ideals **2 :** to work idealistically — **ide·al·iza·tion** \-ˌdē-(ə-)lə-ˈzā-shən\ *n* — **ide·al·iz·er** \-ˈdē-(ə-)ˌlī-zər\ *n*

ide·al·ly \ī-ˈdē-ə-lē, -ˈdē(-ə)l-lē\ *adv* **1 :** in idea or imagination : MENTALLY **2 :** in relation to an exemplar **3 a :** conformably to or in respect to an ideal : PERFECTLY **b :** for best results <~, the counselor should vary his techniques for each applicant —T. M. Martinez> **c :** in accordance with an ideal or typical standard : CLASSICALLY

ideal point *n* : a point added to the plane or to space to eliminate special cases; *specif* : the point at infinity added in projective geometry as the assumed intersection of two parallel lines

ide·ate \ˈīd-ē-ˌāt\ *vb* **-at·ed; -at·ing** *vt* : to form an idea or conception of ~ *vi* : to form an idea

ide·ation \ˌīd-ē-ˈā-shən\ *n* : the capacity for or the act of forming or entertaining ideas

ide·ation·al \-shnəl, -shən-ᵊl\ *adj* : of, relating to, or produced by ideation; *broadly* : consisting of or referring to ideas or thoughts of objects not immediately present to the senses — **ide·ation·al·ly** \-ē\ *adv*

idem \ˈīd-ˌem, ˈēd-, ˈid-\ *pron* [L, same — more at IDENTITY] : something previously mentioned : SAME

idem·po·tent \ī-ˈdem-pət-ənt\ *adj* [ISV *idem-* (fr. L *idem* same) + L *potent-, potens* having power — more at POTENT] : relating to or being a mathematical quantity which is not zero and every positive power of which equals itself — **idempotent** *n*

iden·tic \ī-ˈdent-ik, ə-\ *adj* : IDENTICAL: as **a :** constituting a diplomatic action or expression in which two or more governments follow precisely the same course or employ an identical form **b :** constituting an action or expression in which a government follows precisely the same course or employs identical forms with reference to two or more other governments

iden·ti·cal \ī-ˈdent-i-kəl, ə-\ *adj* [prob. fr. ML *identicus,* fr. LL *identitas*] **1 :** being the same : SELFSAME <the ~ place we stopped before> **2 :** having such close resemblance as to be essentially the same <~ hats> <the copy was ~ with the original> **3 a :** having the same cause or origin <the infections appeared to be ~> **b :** MONOZYGOTIC ***syn*** **1** see SAME ***ant*** diverse **2** see SIMILAR ***ant*** different — **iden·ti·cal·ly** \-i-k(ə-)lē\ *adv* — **iden·ti·cal·ness** \-kəl-nəs\ *n*

iden·ti·fi·ca·tion \ī-ˌdent-ə-fə-ˈkā-shən, ə-\ *n* **1 a :** an act of identifying : the state of being identified **b :** evidence of identity **2 a :** psychological orientation of the self in regard to something (as a person or group) with a resulting feeling of close emotional association **b :** a mental mechanism whereby the individual attains gratification, emotional support, or relief from stress by consciously or unconsciously attributing to himself the characteristics of another person or a particular group ***syn*** see RECOGNITION

identification card *n* : ID CARD

iden·ti·fi·er \ī-ˈdent-ə-ˌfī(-ə)r, ə-\ *n* : one that identifies

iden·ti·fy \ī-ˈdent-ə-ˌfī, ə-\ *vb* **-fied; -fy·ing** *vt* **1 a :** to cause to be or become identical **b :** to conceive as united (as in spirit, outlook, or principle) <groups that are *identified* with conservation> **2 a :** to establish the identity of **b :** to determine the taxonomic position of (a biological specimen) ~ *vi* **1 :** to be or become the same **2 :** to practice psychological identification <~ with the hero of a novel> — **iden·ti·fi·able** \-ˌfī-ə-bəl\ *adj* — **iden·ti·fi·ably** \-blē\ *adv*

iden·ti·ty \ī-ˈden(t)-ət-ē, ə-ˈden(t)-\ *n, pl* **-ties** [MF *identité,* fr. LL *identitat-, identitas,* irreg. fr. L *idem* same, fr. *is* that — more at ITERATE] **1 a :** sameness of essential or generic character in different instances **b :** sameness in all that constitutes the objective reality of a thing : ONENESS **2 a :** the distinguishing character or personality of an individual : INDIVIDUALITY **b :** the relation established by psychological identification <a symbolic act . . . marking ~ and participation in a collective action —Paul Jacobs> **3 :** the condition of being the same with something described or asserted <establish the ~ of stolen goods> **4 :** an equation that is satisfied for all values of the symbols **5 :** IDENTITY ELEMENT

identity card *n* : ID CARD

identity crisis *n* : psychosocial confusion and maladjustment that arises esp. in adolescents when unable to attain psychological identification because of conflicting demands and pressures : personal anomie

identity element *n* : an element (as 0 in the group of integers under addition) that leaves any element of the set to which it belongs unchanged when combined with it by a specified operation (as addition or multiplication)

identity matrix *n* : a square matrix with numeral 1's along the principal diagonal and 0's elsewhere

ideo- *comb form* [F *idéo-,* fr. Gk *idea*] : idea <*ideo*gram>

ideo·gram \ˈīd-ē-ə-ˌgram, ˈid-\ *n* **1 :** a picture or symbol used in a system of writing to represent a thing or an idea but not a particular word or phrase for it; *esp* : one that represents not the object pictured but some thing or idea that the object pictured is supposed to suggest **2 :** LOGOGRAM — **ideo·gram·ic** *or* **ideo·gram·mic** \ˌīd-ē-ə-ˈgram-ik, ˌid-\ *adj* — **ideo·gram·mat·ic** \-ē-ō-grə-ˈmat-ik\ *adj*

ideo·graph \ˈīd-ē-ə-ˌgraf, ˈid-\ *n* : IDEOGRAM — **ideo·graph·ic** \ˌīd-ē-ə-ˈgraf-ik, ˌid-\ *adj* — **ideo·graph·i·cal·ly** \-i-k(ə-)lē\ *adv*

ide·og·ra·phy \ˌīd-ē-ˈäg-rə-fē, ˌid-\ *n* **1 :** the use of ideograms **2 :** the representation of ideas by graphic symbols

ideo·log·i·cal \ˌīd-ē-ə-ˈläj-i-kəl, ˌid-\ *also* **ideo·log·ic** \-ˈläj-ik\ *adj* **1 :** of, relating to, or based on ideology **2 :** relating to or concerned with ideas — **ideo·log·i·cal·ly** \-ˈläj-i-k(ə-)lē\ *adv*

ideo·logue \ˈīd-ē-ə-ˌlȯg, -ˌläg\ *n* [F *idéologue,* back-formation fr. *idéologie*] **1 :** an impractical idealist : THEORIST **2 :** an advocate or adherent of a particular ideology

ide·ol·o·gy \-ˈäl-ə-jē\ *also* **ide·al·o·gy** \-ˈäl-ə-jē, -ˈal-\ *n, pl* **-gies** [F *idéologie,* fr. *idéo-* ideo- + *-logie* -logy] **1 :** visionary theorizing **2 a :** a systematic body of concepts esp. about human life or culture **b :** a manner or the content of thinking characteristic of an individual, group, or culture **c :** the integrated assertions, theories, and aims that constitute a sociopolitical program — **ide·ol·o·gist** \-jəst\ *n*

ideo·mo·tor \ˌīd-ē-ə-ˈmōt-ər, ˌid-\ *adj* [ISV] : not reflex but resulting from the impingement of ideas on the system

ides \ˈīdz\ *n pl but sing or pl in constr* [MF, fr L *idus*] : the 15th day of March, May, July, or October or the 13th day of any other month in the ancient Roman calendar; *broadly* : this day and the seven days preceding it

-i·din \əd-ən, -ᵊn\ *or* **-i·dine** \ə-ˌdēn\ *n suffix* [ISV *-ide* + *-in, -ine*] : chemical compound related in origin or structure to another compound <tolu*idine*> <guan*idine*>

idio- *comb form* [Gk, fr. *idios* — more at IDIOT] : one's own : personal : separate : distinct <*idio*blast>

id·io·blast \ˈid-ē-ə-ˌblast\ *n* [ISV] : a plant cell (as a sclereid) that differs markedly from neighboring cells — **id·io·blas·tic** \ˌid-ē-ə-ˈblas-tik\ *adj*

id·i·o·cy \ˈid-ē-ə-sē\ *n, pl* **-cies** **1 :** extreme mental deficiency commonly due to incomplete or abnormal development of the brain **2 :** something notably stupid or foolish <the sort of ~ into which all forms of censorship fall —R. L. Weaver>

id·io·graph·ic \ˌid-ē-ə-ˈgraf-ik\ *adj* [ISV] : relating to or dealing with the concrete, individual, or unique

id·io·lect \ˈid-ē-ə-ˌlekt\ *n* [*idio-* + *-lect* (as in *dialect*)] : the language or speech pattern of one individual at a particular period of his life — **id·io·lec·tal** \ˌid-ē-ə-ˈlek-tᵊl\ *adj*

id·i·om \ˈid-ē-əm\ *n* [MF & LL; MF *idiome,* fr. LL *idioma* individual peculiarity of language, fr. Gk *idiōmat-, idiōma,* fr. *idiousthai* to appropriate, fr. *idios*] **1 a :** the language peculiar to a people or to a district, community, or class : DIALECT **b :** the syntactical, grammatical, or structural form peculiar to a language **2 :** an expression in the usage of a language that is peculiar to itself either grammatically (as *no, it wasn't me*) or in having a meaning that cannot be derived from the conjoined meanings of its elements (as *Monday week* for "the Monday a week after next Monday") **3 :** a style or form of artistic expression that is characteristic of an individual, a period or movement, or a medium or instrument <the modern jazz ~>

id·i·om·at·ic \ˌid-ē-ə-ˈmat-ik\ *adj* **1 :** of, relating to, or conforming to idiom **2 :** peculiar to a particular group, individual, or style — **id·i·om·at·i·cal·ly** \-i-k(ə-)lē\ *adv* — **id·i·om·at·ic·ness** \-ik-nəs\ *n*

id·io·mor·phic \ˌid-ē-ə-ˈmȯr-fik\ *adj* [Gk *idiomorphos,* fr. *idio-* + *-morphos* -morphous] : having the proper form or shape — used of minerals whose crystalline growth has not been interfered with — **id·io·mor·phi·cal·ly** \-fi-k(ə-)lē\ *adv*

id·io·path·ic \ˌid-ē-ə-ˈpath-ik\ *adj* **1 :** peculiar to the individual **2 :** arising spontaneously or from an obscure or unknown cause : PRIMARY — **id·io·path·i·cal·ly** \-ˈpath-i-k(ə-)lē\ *adv*

id·io·syn·cra·sy \ˌid-ē-ə-ˈsiŋ-krə-sē\ *n, pl* **-sies** [Gk *idiosynkrasia,* fr. *idio-* + *synkerannynai* to blend, fr. *syn-* + *kerannynai* to mingle, mix — more at CRATER] **1 :** characteristic peculiarity of habit or structure **2 a :** a peculiarity of constitution or temperament **b :** individual hypersensitiveness (as to a drug or food) ***syn*** see ECCENTRICITY — **id·io·syn·crat·ic** \ˌid-ē-ō-(ˌ)sin-ˈkrat-ik\ *adj* — **id·io·syn·crat·i·cal·ly** \-ˈkrat-i-k(ə-)lē\ *adv*

id·i·ot \ˈid-ē-ət\ *n* [ME, fr. L *idiota* ignorant person, fr. Gk *idiōtēs* one in a private station, layman, ignorant person, fr. *idios* one's own, private; akin to L *sed, se* without, *sui* of oneself] **1 :** a person afflicted with idiocy; *esp* : a feebleminded person having a mental age not exceeding three years and requiring complete custodial care

2 : a silly or foolish person **syn** see FOOL — **idiot** *adj*
id·i·ot·ic \ˌid-ē-ˈät-ik\ *also* **id·i·ot·i·cal** \-ˈät-i-kəl\ *adj* **1** : characterized by idiocy **2** : showing complete lack of thought or common sense : FOOLISH — **id·i·ot·i·cal·ly** \-i-k(ə-)lē\ *adv* — **id·i·ot·i·cal·ness** \-i-kəl-nəs\ *n*
¹id·i·o·tism \ˈid-ē-ə-ˌtiz-əm\ *n* [MF *idiotisme*, fr. L *idiotismus* common speech, fr. Gk *idiōtismos*, fr. *idiōtēs*] **1** *obs* : IDIOM 1 **2** : IDIOM 2
²id·i·ot·ism \ˈid-ē-ət-ˌiz-əm\ *n* [*idiot* + *-ism*] *archaic* : IDIOCY
idiot sa·vant \ˈē-ˌdyō-sä-ˈväⁿ\ *n, pl* **idiots savants** \-ˌdyō-sä-ˈväⁿ(z)\ *or* **idiot savants** \-ˈväⁿ(z)\ [F, lit., learned idiot] : a mentally defective person who exhibits exceptional skill or brilliance in some limited field
-id·i·um \ˈid-ē-əm\ *n suffix, pl* **-id·i·ums** *or* **-id·ia** \-ē-ə\ [NL, fr. Gk *-idion*, dim. suffix] : small one <anther*idium*>
¹idle \ˈīd-ᵊl\ *adj* **idler** \ˈīd-lər, -ᵊl-ər\; **idlest** \ˈīd-ləst, -ᵊl-əst\ [ME *idel*, fr. OE *īdel*; akin to OHG *ītal* worthless] **1** : lacking worth or basis : USELESS <~ rumor> **2** : not occupied or employed: as **a** : having no employment : INACTIVE <~ workmen> **b** : not turned to appropriate use <~ funds> **c** : not scheduled to compete <the team will be ~ tomorrow> **3 a** : SHIFTLESS, LAZY <~ fellows> **b** : having no evident lawful means of support <the charge of being an ~ person> **syn 1** see VAIN **2** see INACTIVE **ant** busy — **idle·ness** \ˈīd-ᵊl-nəs\ *n* — **idly** \ˈīd-lē\ *adv*
²idle *vb* **idled; idling** \ˈīd-liŋ, -ᵊl-iŋ\ *vi* **1 a** : to spend time in idleness **b** : to move idly **2** : to run disconnected so that power is not used for useful work <the engine is *idling*> ~ *vt* **1** : to pass in idleness **2** : to make idle <workers *idled* by a strike> **3** : to cause to idle — **idler** \ˈīd-lər, -ᵊl-ər\ *n*
idler pulley *n* : a guide or tightening pulley for a belt or chain
idler wheel *n* **1** : a wheel, gear, or roller used to transfer motion or to guide or support something **2** : IDLER PULLEY

idler wheel 1

idlesse \ˈīd-ləs, īd-ˈles\ *n* [*idle* + ME *-esse* (as in *richesse* wealth) — more at RICHES] : the quality or state of being idle : IDLENESS
ido·crase \ˈīd-ə-ˌkrās, ˈid-, -ˌkrāz\ *n* [F, fr. Gk *eidos* + *krasis* mixture fr. *kerannynai* to mix — more at CRATER] : a mineral $Ca_{10}(Mg,Fe)_2Al_4Si_9O_{34}(OH)_4$ that is a complex silicate of calcium, magnesium, iron, and aluminum
idol \ˈīd-ᵊl\ *n* [ME, fr. OF *idole*, fr. LL *idolum*, fr. Gk *eidōlon* phantom, idol; akin to Gk *eidos* form — more at IDYLL] **1** : a representation or symbol of an object of worship; *broadly* : a false god **2 a** : a likeness of something **b** *obs* : PRETENDER, IMPOSTOR **3** : a form or appearance visible but without substance <an enchanted phantom, a lifeless ~ —P. B. Shelley> **4** : an object of passionate devotion <a movie ~> **5** : a false conception : FALLACY
idol·a·ter \ī-ˈdäl-ət-ər\ *n* [ME *idolatrer*, fr. MF *idolatre*, fr. LL *idololatres*, fr. Gk *eidōlolatrēs*, fr. *eidōlon* + *-latrēs* -later] **1** : a worshiper of idols **2** : a person that admires or loves intensely and often blindly an object not usu. a subject of worship
idol·a·trous \ī-ˈdäl-ə-trəs\ *adj* **1** : of or relating to idolatry **2** : having the character of idolatry <the religion of ~ nationalism —Aldous Huxley> **3** : given to idolatry — **idol·a·trous·ly** *adv* — **idol·a·trous·ness** *n*
idol·a·try \-trē\ *n, pl* **-tries** **1** : the worship of a physical object as a god **2** : immoderate attachment or devotion to something
idol·ize \ˈīd-ᵊl-ˌīz\ *vb* **-ized; -iz·ing** *vt* : to worship idolatrously; *broadly* : to love or admire to excess <the common people whom he so *idolized* —*Times Lit. Supp.*> ~ *vi* : to practice idolatry — **idol·iza·tion** \ˌīd-ᵊl-ə-ˈzā-shən\ *n* — **idol·iz·er** \ˈīd-ᵊl-ˌī-zər\ *n*
IDP *abbr* **1** integrated data processing **2** international driving permit
idyll *or* **idyl** \ˈīd-ᵊl, *Brit also* ˈid-\ *n* [L *idyllium*, fr. Gk *eidyllion*, fr. dim. of *eidos* form; akin to Gk *idein* to see — more at WIT] **1 a** : a simple descriptive work either in poetry or prose that deals with rustic life or pastoral scenes or suggests a mood of peace and contentment **b** : a narrative poem (as Tennyson's *Idylls of the King*) treating an epic, romantic, or tragic theme **2 a** : a lighthearted carefree episode that is a fit subject for an idyll **b** : a romantic interlude **3** : a pastoral or romantic musical composition — **idyl·lic** \ī-ˈdil-ik\ *adj* — **idyl·li·cal·ly** \-i-k(ə-)lē\ *adv*
idyll·ist \ˈīd-ᵊl-əst\ *n* : a composer of idylls
i.e. \ˈthat-ˈiz, (ˈ)ī-ˈē\ *abbr* [L *id est*] that is
IE *abbr* industrial engineer
-ie *also* **-y** \ē\ *n suffix* [ME] **1** : little one : dear little one <bird*ie*> <sonn*y*> — sometimes in names of articles of apparel <pant*ie*> **2** : one belonging to : one having to do with <town*y*> **3** : one of (such) a kind or quality <cut*ie*> <tough*ie*>
IEA *abbr* International Education Association
IEEE *abbr* Institute of Electrical and Electronic Engineers
-ier — see -ER
¹if \(ˌ)if, əf\ *conj* [ME, fr. OE *gif*; akin to OHG *ibu* if] **1 a** : in the event that **b** : allowing that **c** : on condition that **2** : WHETHER <asked ~ the mail had come> **3** — used as a function word to introduce an exclamation expressing a wish <~ it would only rain> **4** : even though <an interesting ~ untenable argument> — **if anything** : on the contrary even : perhaps even <*if anything*, you ought to apologize>
²if \ˈif\ *n* **1** : CONDITION, STIPULATION <the question . . . depends on too many ~*s* to allow an answer —*Encounter*> **2** : SUPPOSITION
IF *abbr* intermediate frequency
IFC *abbr* International Finance Corporation
-if·er·ous \ˈif-(ə-)rəs\ *adj comb form* [ME, fr. L *-ifer*, fr. *-i-* + *-fer* -ferous] : -FEROUS
if·fy \ˈif-ē\ *adj* [ˡ*if*] : abounding in contingencies or unknown qualities or conditions <the situation is far too ~ for any predictions —*N.Y. Times*> — **if·fi·ness** *n*
IFIP *abbr* International Federation for Information Processing
IFO *abbr* identified flying object
-i·form \ə-ˌfȯrm\ *adj comb form* [MF & L; MF *-iforme*, fr. L *-iformis*, fr. *-i-* + *-formis* -form] : -FORM <ram*iform*>
I formation *n* : an offensive football formation in which the set backs line up in a line directly behind the quarterback — compare T FORMATION
IFR *abbr* instrument flight rules
-i·fy \ə-ˌfī\ *vb suffix* [ME *-ifien*, fr. OF *-ifier*, fr. L *-ificare*, fr. *-i-* + *-ficare* -fy] : -FY
Ig *abbr* immunoglobulin
IG *abbr* inspector general
Ig·bo \ˈig-(ˌ)bō\ *var of* IBO
ig·loo \ˈig-(ˌ)lü\ *n, pl* **igloos** [Esk *iglu*, *igdlu* house] **1** : an Eskimo dwelling often made of snow blocks and in the shape of a dome **2** : a building or structure shaped like a dome

igloo 1

ig·ne·ous \ˈig-nē-əs\ *adj* [L *igneus*, fr. *ignis* fire; akin to Skt *agni* fire] **1** : of, relating to, or resembling fire : FIERY **2 a** : relating to, resulting from, or suggestive of the intrusion or extrusion of magma or the activity of volcanoes **b** : formed by solidification of molten magma <~ rock>
ig·nes·cent \ig-ˈnes-ᵊnt\ *adj* **1** : capable of emitting sparks **2** : VOLATILE
igni- *comb form* [L, fr. *ignis*] : fire : burning <*igni*tron>
ig·nis fat·u·us \ˌig-nəs-ˈfach-(ə-)wəs\ *n, pl* **ig·nes fat·ui** \-ˌnēz-ˈfach-ə-ˌwī\ [ML, lit., foolish fire] **1** : a light that sometimes appears in the night over marshy ground and is often attributable to the combustion of gas from decomposed organic matter **2** : a deceptive goal or hope
ig·nite \ig-ˈnīt\ *vb* **ig·nit·ed; ig·nit·ing** [L *ignitus*, pp. of *ignire* to ignite, fr. *ignis*] *vt* **1** : to subject to fire or intense heat; *esp* : to render luminous by heat **2 a** : to set afire; *also* : KINDLE **b** : to cause (a fuel mixture) to burn **3** : to heat up : EXCITE <oppression that *ignited* the hatred of the people> ~ *vi* **1** : to catch fire **2** : to begin to glow **syn** see LIGHT — **ig·nit·able** *also* **ig·nit·ible** \-ˈnīt-ə-bəl\ *adj* — **ig·nit·er** *or* **ig·ni·tor** \-ˈnīt-ər\ *n*
ig·ni·tion \ig-ˈnish-ən\ *n* **1** : the act or action of igniting : KINDLING **2** : the process or means (as an electric spark) of igniting a fuel mixture
ig·ni·tron \ig-ˈnī-ˌträn\ *n* : a mercury-containing rectifier tube in which the arc is struck again at the beginning of each cycle by a special electrode separately energized by an auxiliary circuit
ig·no·ble \ig-ˈnō-bəl\ *adj* [L *ignobilis*, fr. *in-* + *nobilis* noble] **1** : of low birth or common origin : PLEBEIAN **2** : characterized by baseness or meanness **syn** see MEAN **ant** noble, magnanimous — **ig·no·bil·i·ty** \ˌig-nō-ˈbil-ət-ē\ *n* — **ig·no·ble·ness** \ig-ˈnō-bəl-nəs\ *n* — **ig·no·bly** \-blē *also* -bə-lē\ *adv*
ig·no·min·i·ous \ˌig-nə-ˈmin-ē-əs\ *adj* **1** : marked with or characterized by disgrace or shame : DISHONORABLE **2** : deserving of shame or infamy : DESPICABLE **3** : HUMILIATING, DEGRADING <suffered an ~ defeat> — **ig·no·min·i·ous·ly** *adv* — **ig·no·min·i·ous·ness** *n*
ig·no·mi·ny \ˈig-nə-ˌmin-ē, -mə-nē; ig-ˈnäm-ə-nē\ *n, pl* **-nies** [MF or L; MF *ignominie*, fr. L *ignominia*, fr. *ig-* (as in *ignorare* to be ignorant of, ignore) + *nomin-*, *nomen* name, repute — more at NAME] **1** : deep personal humiliation and disgrace **2** : disgraceful or dishonorable conduct, quality, or action **syn** see DISGRACE
ig·no·ra·mus \ˌig-nə-ˈrā-məs\ *n* [*Ignoramus*, ignorant lawyer in *Ignoramus* (1615), play by George Ruggle] : an utterly ignorant person : DUNCE
ig·no·rance \ˈig-n(ə-)rən(t)s\ *n* : the state of being ignorant
ig·no·rant \ˈig-n(ə-)rənt\ *adj* **1 a** : destitute of knowledge or education <an ~ society>; *also* : lacking knowledge or comprehension of the thing specified <parents ~ of modern mathematics> **b** : resulting from or showing lack of knowledge or intelligence <~ errors> **2** : UNAWARE, UNINFORMED — **ig·no·rant·ly** *adv* — **ig·no·rant·ness** *n*

syn IGNORANT, ILLITERATE, UNLETTERED, UNTUTORED, UNLEARNED *shared meaning element* : not having knowledge **ant** cognizant (*of something*), conversant, informed

ig·no·ra·tio elen·chi \ˌig-nə-ˌrät-ē-ˌō-i-ˈleŋ-ˌkē\ *n* [L, lit., ignorance of proof] : a fallacy in logic of supposing a point proved or disproved by an argument proving or disproving something not at issue
ig·nore \ig-ˈnō(ə)r, -ˈnȯ(ə)r\ *vt* **ig·nored; ig·nor·ing** [obs. *ignore* to be ignorant of, fr. F *ignorer*, fr. L *ignorare*, fr. *ignarus* ignorant, unknown, fr. *in-* + *gnoscere*, *noscere* to know — more at KNOW] **1** : to refuse to take notice of **2** : to reject (a bill of indictment) as ungrounded **syn** see NEGLECT **ant** heed, acknowledge — **ig·nor·able** \-ˈnōr-ə-bəl, -ˈnȯr-\ *adj* — **ig·nor·er** *n*
Igo·rot \ˌē-gə-ˈrōt\ *n, pl* **Igorot** *or* **Igorots** **1** : a member of any of several related peoples of northwestern Luzon, Philippines **2** : any of the Austronesian languages of the Igorot
Igraine \i-ˈgrān\ *n* : the wife of Uther and mother of Arthur in Arthurian legend
igua·na \i-ˈgwän-ə\ *n* [Sp, fr. Arawak *iwana*] : any of various large herbivorous typically dark-colored tropical American lizards (family Iguanidae) that have a serrated dorsal crest and are important as human food in their native habitat; *broadly* : any of various large lizards

ə abut	ᵊ kitten	ər further	a back	ā bake	ä cot, cart
au̇ out	ch chin	e less	ē easy	g gift	i trip	ī life
j joke	ŋ sing	ō flow	ȯ flaw	ȯi coin	th thin	t͟h this
ü loot	u̇ foot	y yet	yü few	yu̇ furious	zh vision

iguan·odon \i-ˈgwän-ə-ˌdän\ *n* [NL *Iguanodont-, Iguanodon,* genus name] : any of a genus (*Iguanodon*) of gigantic herbivorous dinosaurs from the early Cretaceous of Belgium and England

iguana

IGY *abbr* International Geophysical Year
IHD *abbr* International Hydrological Decade
IHP *abbr* indicated horsepower
IHS \ˌī-ˌā-ˈches\ [LL, part transliteration of Gk IHΣ, abbreviation for IHΣΟΥΣ *Iēsous* Jesus] — used as a Christian symbol and monogram for *Jesus*
ike·ba·na \ˌik-ā-ˈbän-ə, ˌik-i-, ˌēk-\ *n* [Jap, fr. *ikeru* to keep alive, arrange + *hana* flower] : the Japanese art of flower arranging that emphasizes form and balance
ikon *var of* ICON
IL *abbr* Illinois
il- — see IN-
ILA *abbr* International Longshoremen's Association
ilang–ilang \ˌē-ˌläŋ-ˈē-ˌläŋ\ *n* [Tag] **1 :** a tree (*Canangium odoratum*) of the custard-apple family of the Malay archipelago, the Philippines, and adjacent areas that has very fragrant greenish yellow flowers **2 :** a perfume distilled from the flowers of the ilang-ilang tree
ile- *also* **ileo-** *comb form* [NL *ileum*] **1 :** ileum <*ile*itis> **2 :** ileal and <*ileo*cecal>
1-ile \əl, ᵊl, ˌīl, (ˌ)īl\ *adj suffix* [ME, fr. MF, fr. L *-ilis*] : of, relating to, or capable of <contract*ile*>
2-ile *n suffix* [prob. fr. *-ile* (as in *quartile,* n.)] : segment of a (specified) size in a frequency distribution <dec*ile*>
il·e·itis \ˌil-ē-ˈīt-əs\ *n* [NL] : inflammation of the ileum
il·e·um \ˈil-ē-əm\ *n, pl* **il·ea** \-ē-ə\ [NL, fr. L, groin, viscera] : the last division of the small intestine extending between the jejunum and large intestine — **il·e·al** \-ē-əl\ *adj*
il·e·us \ˈil-ē-əs\ *n* [L, fr. Gk *eileos,* fr. *eilyein* to roll — more at VOLUBLE] : mechanical or functional obstruction of the bowel
ilex \ˈī-ˌleks\ *n* [L] **1 :** a southern European evergreen oak (*Quercus ilex*) — called also *holm oak* **2 :** HOLLY 1
ILGWU *abbr* International Ladies' Garment Workers' Union
il·i·ac \ˈil-ē-ˌak\ *also* **il·i·al** \ˈil-ē-əl\ *adj* [LL *iliacus,* fr. L *ilium*] : of, relating to, or located near the ilium
Il·i·ad \ˈil-ē-əd, -ē-ˌad\ *n* [*Iliad,* ancient Greek epic poem attributed to Homer, fr. L *Iliad-, Ilias,* fr. Gk] **1 :** a long narrative; *esp* : an epic in the Homeric tradition **2 a :** a series of exploits regarded as suitable for an epic **b :** a series of miseries or disastrous events — **Il·i·ad·ic** \ˌil-ē-ˈad-ik\ *adj*
ilio- *comb form* [NL *ilium*] : iliac and <*ilio*lumbar>
il·i·um \ˈil-ē-əm\ *n, pl* **il·ia** \-ē-ə\ [NL, fr. L *ilium, ileum*] : the dorsal, upper, and largest one of the three bones composing either lateral half of the pelvis
1ilk \ˈilk\ *pron* [ME, fr. OE *ilca,* fr. a prehistoric compound whose constituents are akin respectively to Goth *is* he (akin to L *is* he, that) and OE *gelīc* like — more at ITERATE, LIKE] *chiefly Scot* : SAME — used with *that* esp. in the names of landed families
2ilk *n* : SORT, KIND <the rejection of these books or others of like ~ —Kathleen Molz>
3ilk *pron* [ME, adj. & pron., fr. OE *ylc, ǣlc* — more at EACH] *chiefly Scot* : EACH
il·ka \ˈil-kə\ *adj* [ME, fr. *ilk* + *a* (indef. art.)] *chiefly Scot* : EACH, EVERY
1ill \ˈil\ *adj* **worse** \ˈwərs\; **worst** \ˈwərst\ [ME, fr. ON *illr*] **1 a** *chiefly Scot* : IMMORAL, VICIOUS **b :** resulting from, accompanied by, or indicative of an evil or malevolent intention <~ deeds> **c :** attributing evil or an objectionable quality <held an ~ opinion of his neighbors> **2 a :** causing suffering or distress <~ weather> **b** (1) **:** not normal or sound <~ health> (2) **:** not in good health; *also* : NAUSEATED **3 a :** not suited to circumstances or not to one's advantage : UNLUCKY <an ~ omen> **b :** involving difficulty : HARD <an ~ man to please> **4 a :** not meeting an accepted standard <~ manners> **b** *archaic* : notably unskillful or inefficient **5 a :** UNFRIENDLY, HOSTILE <~ feeling> **b :** HARSH, CRUEL <~ treatment> ***syn*** see BAD ***ant*** good
2ill *adv* **worse; worst 1 a :** with displeasure or hostility **b :** in a harsh manner **c :** so as to reflect unfavorably <spoke ~ of his neighbors> **2 :** in a reprehensible manner **3 :** HARDLY, SCARCELY <can ~ afford such extravagances> **4 a :** in an unfortunate manner : BADLY, UNLUCKILY <~ fares the land . . . where wealth accumulates, and men decay —Oliver Goldsmith> **b :** in a faulty, inefficient, or unpleasant manner — often used in combination <the methods used may be *ill*-adapted to the aims in view —R. M. Hutchins>
3ill *n* **1 :** the reverse of good : EVIL **2 a :** MISFORTUNE, DISTRESS **b** (1) **:** AILMENT, SICKNESS (2) **:** something that disturbs or afflicts : TROUBLE <economic and social ~*s*> **3 :** something that reflects unfavorably <spoke no ~ of him>
4ill *abbr* illustrated; illustration; illustrator
Ill *abbr* Illinois
I'll \(ˌ)ī(ə)l\ : I will : I shall
ill–ad·vised \ˌil-əd-ˈvīzd\ *adj* : resulting from or showing lack of wise and sufficient counsel or deliberation <an ~ decision> — **ill–ad·vis·ed·ly** \-ˈvī-zəd-lē\ *adv*
il·la·tion \il-ˈā-shən\ *n* [LL *illation-, illatio,* fr. L, action of bringing in, fr. *illatus* (pp. of *inferre* to bring in), fr. *in-* + *latus,* pp. of *ferre* to carry — more at TOLERATE, BEAR] **1 :** the action of inferring : INFERENCE **2 :** a conclusion inferred
1il·la·tive \ˈil-ət-iv, il-ˈāt-\ *n* **1 :** a word (as *therefore*) or phrase (as *as a consequence*) introducing an inference **2 :** ILLATION 2
2illative *adj* : INFERENTIAL — **il·la·tive·ly** *adv*
il·laud·able \(ˈ)il-ˈ(l)ȯd-ə-bəl\ *adj* [L *illaudabilis,* fr. *in-* + *laudabilis* laudable] : deserving no praise — **il·laud·ably** \-blē\ *adv*
ill–be·ing \ˈil-ˈbē-iŋ\ *n* : a condition of being deficient in health, happiness, or prosperity
ill–bod·ing \-ˈbōd-iŋ\ *adj* : boding evil : INAUSPICIOUS
ill–bred \-ˈbred\ *adj* **1 :** badly brought up or showing bad upbringing : IMPOLITE **2 :** inferior by reason of being the offspring of badly matched parents
il·le·gal \(ˈ)il-ˈ(l)ē-gəl\ *adj* [F or ML; F *illégal,* fr. ML *illegalis,* fr. L *in-* + *legalis* legal] : not according to or authorized by law : UNLAWFUL; *also* : not sanctioned by official rules (as of a game) — **il·le·gal·i·ty** \ˌil-i-ˈgal-ət-ē\ *n* — **il·le·gal·ly** \(ˈ)il-ˈ(l)ē-gə-lē\ *adv*
il·le·gal·ize \(ˈ)il-ˈ(l)ē-gə-ˌlīz\ *vt* : to make or declare illegal — **il·le·gal·iza·tion** \(ˌ)il-ˌ(l)ē-gə-lə-ˈzā-shən\ *n*
il·leg·i·ble \(ˈ)il-ˈ(l)ej-ə-bəl\ *adj* : not legible : UNDECIPHERABLE <~ writing> — **il·leg·i·bil·i·ty** \(ˌ)il-ˌ(l)ej-ə-ˈbil-ət-ē\ *n* — **il·leg·i·bly** \(ˈ)il-ˈ(l)ej-ə-blē\ *adv*
il·le·git·i·ma·cy \ˌil-i-ˈjit-ə-mə-sē\ *n* **1 :** the quality or state of being illegitimate **2 :** BASTARDY 2
il·le·git·i·mate \-ˈjit-ə-mət\ *adj* **1 :** not recognized as lawful offspring; *specif* : born of parents not married to each other **2 :** not rightly deduced or inferred : ILLOGICAL **3 :** departing from the regular : ERRATIC **4 a :** not sanctioned by law : ILLEGAL **b :** not authorized by good usage **c** *of a taxon* : published either validly or invalidly but not in accordance with the rules of the relevant international code — **il·le·git·i·mate·ly** *adv*
ill–fat·ed \ˈil-ˈfāt-əd\ *adj* **1 :** having or destined to an evil fate : UNFORTUNATE <an ~ expedition> **2 :** that causes or marks the beginning of misfortune
ill–fa·vored \-ˈfā-vərd\ *adj* **1 :** unattractive in physical appearance; *esp* : having an ugly face **2 :** OFFENSIVE, OBJECTIONABLE ***syn*** see UGLY ***ant*** well-favored, fair
ill–got·ten \-ˈgät-ᵊn\ *adj* : acquired by illicit or improper means <~ gains>
ill–hu·mored \ˈil-ˈ(h)yü-mərd\ *adj* : SURLY, IRRITABLE — **ill–hu·mored·ly** *adv*
il·lib·er·al \(ˈ)il-ˈ(l)ib(-ə)-rəl\ *adj* [MF or L; MF, fr. L *illiberalis* ignoble, stingy, fr. L *in-* + *liberalis* liberal] : not liberal: as **a** *archaic* (1) **:** lacking a liberal education (2) **:** lacking culture and refinement **b :** not requiring the background of a liberal arts education <trades and other ~ occupations> **c** *archaic* : not generous : STINGY **d** (1) **:** not broad-minded : BIGOTED (2) **:** opposed to liberalism — **il·lib·er·al·i·ty** \(ˌ)il-ˌib-ə-ˈral-ət-ē\ *n* — **il·lib·er·al·ly** \(ˈ)il-ˈ(l)ib(-ə)-rə-lē\ *adv* — **il·lib·er·al·ness** \-rəl-nəs\ *n*
il·lib·er·al·ism \-rə-ˌliz-əm\ *n* : opposition to or lack of liberalism
il·lic·it \(ˈ)il-ˈ(l)is-ət\ *adj* [L *illicitus,* fr. *in-* + *licitus* lawful — more at LICIT] : not permitted : UNLAWFUL <~ love affairs> — **il·lic·it·ly** *adv*
il·lim·it·able \(ˈ)il-ˈ(l)im-ət-ə-bəl\ *adj* : incapable of being limited or bounded : MEASURELESS <the ~ reaches of space and time> — **il·lim·it·abil·i·ty** \(ˌ)il-ˌ(l)im-ət-ə-ˈbil-ət-ē\ *n* — **il·lim·it·able·ness** \(ˈ)il-ˈ(l)im-ət-ə-bəl-nəs \ *n* — **il·lim·it·ably** \-blē\ *adv*
Il·li·nois \ˌil-ə-ˈnȯi *also* -ˈnȯiz\ *n, pl* **Illinois** [F, of Algonquian origin; akin to Shawnee *hilenawe* man] **1** *pl* **:** a confederacy of Amerindian peoples of Illinois, Iowa, and Wisconsin **2 :** a member of any of the Illinois peoples
il·liq·uid \(ˈ)il-ˈ(l)ik-wəd\ *adj* **1 :** not being cash or readily convertible into cash <~ holdings> **2 :** deficient in liquid assets <the position of the banks . . . was extremely ~. Deposits and cash reserves were falling, advances increasing —J. S. G. Wilson> — **il·li·quid·i·ty** \ˌil-(ˌ)(l)ik-ˈwid-ət-ē\ *n*
il·lite \ˈil-ˌīt\ *n* [*Illinois,* U.S.A.] : a group of clay minerals having essentially the crystal structure of muscovite; *also* : one of these minerals — **il·lit·ic** \il-ˈit-ik\ *adj*
il·lit·er·a·cy \(ˈ)il-ˈ(l)it-ə-rə-sē, -ˈ(l)i-trə-sē\ *n, pl* **-cies 1 :** the quality or state of being illiterate; *esp* : inability to read or write **2 :** a mistake or crudity (as in speaking) made by or typical of one who is illiterate
il·lit·er·ate \(ˈ)il-ˈ(l)it-ə-rət, -ˈ(l)i-trət\ *adj* [L *illiteratus,* fr. *in-* + *litteratus* literate] **1 :** having little or no education; *esp* : unable to read or write **2 a :** showing or marked by a lack of familiarity with language and literature **b :** violating approved patterns of speaking or writing **3 :** showing or marked by a lack of acquaintance with the fundamentals of a particular field of knowledge ***syn*** see IGNORANT ***ant*** literate — **illiterate** *n* — **il·lit·er·ate·ly** *adv* — **il·lit·er·ate·ness** *n*
ill–man·nered \ˈil-ˈman-ərd\ *adj* : having bad manners : RUDE
ill–na·tured \-ˈnā-chərd\ *adj* **1 :** MALEVOLENT, SPITEFUL **2 :** having a bad disposition : CROSS, SURLY — **ill–na·tured·ly** *adv*
ill·ness \ˈil-nəs\ *n* **1** *obs* **a :** WICKEDNESS **b :** UNPLEASANTNESS **2 :** an unhealthy condition of body or mind : SICKNESS
il·log·ic \(ˈ)il-ˈ(l)äj-ik\ *n* [back-formation fr. *illogical*] : the quality or state of being illogical : ILLOGICALITY
il·log·i·cal \-i-kəl\ *adj* **1 :** not observing the principles of logic **2 :** devoid of logic : SENSELESS — **il·log·i·cal·i·ty** \(ˌ)il-ˌ(l)äj-ə-ˈkal-ət-ē\ *n* — **il·log·i·cal·ly** \(ˈ)il-ˈ(l)äj-i-k(ə-)lē\ *adv* — **il·log·i·cal·ness** \-kəl-nəs\ *n*
ill–sort·ed \ˈil-ˈsȯrt-əd\ *adj* **1 :** not well matched <he and his wife were an ~ pair —Lord Byron> **2** *Scot* : much displeased
ill–starred \-ˈstärd\ *adj* : ILL-FATED, UNLUCKY <an ~ venture>
ill–tem·pered \-ˈtem-pərd\ *adj* : ILL-NATURED, QUARRELSOME — **ill–tem·pered·ly** \-lē\ *adv*
ill–treat \-ˈtrēt\ *vt* : to treat cruelly or improperly : MALTREAT — **ill–treat·ment** \-mənt\ *n*
il·lume \il-ˈüm\ *vt* **il·lumed; il·lum·ing :** ILLUMINATE
il·lu·mi·nance \-mə-nən(t)s\ *n* : ILLUMINATION 2
il·lu·mi·nant \-nənt\ *n* : an illuminating device or substance
1il·lu·mi·nate \il-ˈü-mə-nət\ *adj* **1** *archaic* : brightened with light **2** *archaic* : intellectually or spiritually enlightened
2il·lu·mi·nate \-ˌnāt\ *vt* **-nat·ed; -nat·ing** [L *illuminatus,* pp. of *illuminare,* fr. *in-* + *luminare* to light up, fr. *lumin-, lumen* light — more at LUMINARY] **1 a** (1) **:** to supply or brighten with light (2) **:** to make luminous or shining **b :** to enlighten spiritually or intellectually **c** *archaic* : to set alight **d :** to subject to radiation **2 :** to make clear : ELUCIDATE <~*s* a point by reference to current

life —J. F. T. Bugental> **3 :** to make illustrious or resplendent **4 :** to decorate (as a manuscript) with gold or silver or brilliant colors or with often elaborate designs or miniature pictures — **il·lu·mi·nat·ing·ly** \-ˌnāt-iŋ-lē\ *adv* — **il·lu·mi·na·tor** \-ˌnāt-ər\ *n*
[3]il·lu·mi·nate \-nət\ *n, archaic* **:** one having or claiming unusual enlightenment
il·lu·mi·na·ti \il-ˌü-mə-ˈnät-ē\ *n pl* [It & NL; It, fr. NL, fr. L, pl. of *illuminatus*] **1** *cap* **:** any of various groups claiming special religious enlightenment **2 :** persons who are or who claim to be unusually enlightened
il·lu·mi·na·tion \il-ˌü-mə-ˈnā-shən\ *n* **1 :** the action of illuminating or state of being illuminated: as **a :** spiritual or intellectual enlightenment **b** (1) **:** a lighting up (2) **:** decorative lighting or lighting effects **c :** decoration by the art of illuminating **2 :** the luminous flux per unit area on an intercepting surface at any given point **3 :** one of the decorative features used in the art of illuminating or in decorative lighting
il·lu·mi·na·tive \il-ˈü-mə-ˌnāt-iv\ *adj* **:** of, relating to, or producing illumination **:** ILLUMINATING
il·lu·mine \il-ˈü-mən\ *vt* **-mined; -min·ing :** ILLUMINATE — **il·lu·min·able** \-mə-nə-bəl\ *adj*
il·lu·mi·nism \-mə-ˌniz-əm\ *n* **1 :** belief in or claim to a personal enlightenment not accessible to mankind in general **2** *cap* **:** beliefs or claims viewed as forming doctrine or principles of Illuminati — **il·lu·mi·nist** \-nəst\ *n*
ill–us·age \ˈil-ˈyü-sij, -zij\ *n* **:** harsh, unkind, or abusive treatment
ill–use \-ˈyüz\ *vt* **:** to use badly **:** MALTREAT, ABUSE
il·lu·sion \il-ˈü-zhən\ *n* [ME, fr. MF, fr. LL *illusion-, illusio,* fr. L, action of mocking, fr. *illusus,* pp. of *illudere* to mock at, fr. *in-* + *ludere* to play, mock — more at LUDICROUS] **1 a** *obs* **:** the action of deceiving **b** (1) **:** the state or fact of being intellectually deceived or misled **:** MISAPPREHENSION (2) **:** an instance of such deception **2 a** (1) **:** a misleading image presented to the vision (2) **:** something that deceives or misleads intellectually **b** (1) **:** perception of something objectively existing in such a way as to cause misinterpretation of its actual nature (2) **:** HALLUCINATION 1 (3) **:** a pattern capable of reversible perspective **3 :** a fine plain transparent bobbinet or tulle usu. made of silk and used for veils, trimmings, and dresses ***syn*** see DELUSION — **il·lu·sion·al** \-ˈüzh-nəl, -ən-ᵊl\ *adj*

a
A
b
b
B
a
C
o

optical illusions: A: a equals b in length; B: either side a or side b may appear nearer the observer; C: o may be regarded as either the near or the far corner of the block

il·lu·sion·ary \il-ˈü-zhə-ˌner-ē\ *adj* **:** ILLUSORY ***syn*** see APPARENT ***ant*** factual, matter-of-fact
il·lu·sion·ism \il-ˈü-zhə-ˌniz-əm\ *n* **:** the use of artistic techniques (as perspective or shading) to create the illusion of reality esp. in a work of art — **il·lu·sion·ist** \-ˈüzh-(ə-)nəst\ *n or adj* — **il·lu·sion·is·tic** \-ˌü-zhə-ˈnis-tik\ *adj*
il·lu·sive \il-ˈü-siv, -ˈü-ziv\ *adj* **:** ILLUSORY — **il·lu·sive·ly** *adv* — **il·lu·sive·ness** *n*
il·lu·so·ry \il-ˈüs-(ə-)rē, -ˈüz-\ *adj* **:** based on or producing illusion **:** DECEPTIVE <~ hopes> ***syn*** see APPARENT ***ant*** factual, matter-of-fact — **il·lu·so·ri·ly** \-(ə-)rə-lē\ *adv* — **il·lu·so·ri·ness** \-(ə-)rē-nəs\ *n*
illust *or* **illus** *abbr* illustrated; illustration
il·lus·trate \ˈil-əs-ˌtrāt, il-ˈəs-\ *vb* **-trat·ed; -trat·ing** [L *illustratus,* pp. of *illustrare,* fr. *in-* + *lustrare* to purify, make bright — more at LUSTER] *vt* **1** *obs* **a :** ENLIGHTEN **b :** to light up **2 a** *archaic* **:** to make illustrious **b** *obs* (1) **:** to make bright (2) **:** ADORN **3 a :** to make clear **:** CLARIFY **b :** to make clear by giving or by serving as an example or instance **c :** to provide with visual features intended to explain or decorate <~ a book> **4 :** to show clearly **:** DEMONSTRATE ~ *vi* **:** to give an example or instance — **il·lus·tra·tor** \ˈil-əs-ˌtrāt-ər, il-ˈəs-\ *n*
il·lus·tra·tion \ˌil-əs-ˈtrā-shən, il-ˌəs-\ *n* **1 a :** the action of illustrating **:** the condition of being illustrated **b** *archaic* **:** the action of making illustrious or honored or distinguished **2 :** something that serves to illustrate: as **a :** an example or instance that helps make something clear **b :** a picture or diagram that helps make something clear or attractive ***syn*** see INSTANCE — **il·lus·tra·tion·al** \-shnəl, -shən-ᵊl\ *adj*
il·lus·tra·tive \il-ˈəs-trət-iv\ *adj* **:** serving, tending, or designed to illustrate <~ examples> — **il·lus·tra·tive·ly** *adv*
il·lus·tri·ous \il-ˈəs-trē-əs\ *adj* [L *illustris,* prob. back-formation fr. *illustrare*] **1 :** notably or brilliantly outstanding because of dignity or achievements or actions **:** EMINENT **2** *archaic* **a :** shining brightly with light **b :** clearly evident ***syn*** see FAMOUS ***ant*** infamous — **il·lus·tri·ous·ly** *adv* — **il·lus·tri·ous·ness** *n*
il·lu·vi·al \(ˈ)il-ˈü-vē-əl\ *adj* **:** of, relating to, or marked by illuviation or illuviated materials or areas
il·lu·vi·ate \-vē-ˌāt\ *vi* **-at·ed; -at·ing :** to undergo illuviation
il·lu·vi·a·tion \(ˌ)il-ˌü-vē-ˈā-shən\ *n* [*in-* + *-luviation* (as in *eluviation*)] **:** accumulation of dissolved or suspended soil materials in one area or horizon as a result of eluviation from another
il·lu·vi·um \(ˈ)il-ˈü-vē-əm\ *n, pl* **-vi·ums** *or* **-via** \-vē-ə\ [NL, fr. *in-* + *-luvium* (as in *alluvium*)] **:** material leached from one soil horizon and deposited in another
ill will *n* **:** unfriendly feeling ***syn*** see MALICE ***ant*** goodwill, charity
ill–wish·er \ˈil-ˌwish-ər, -ˈwish-\ *n* **:** one that wishes ill to another
il·ly \ˈil-(l)ē\ *adv* **:** not wisely or well **:** BADLY, ILL <his ~ concealed pride —Della Lutes>
Il·lyr·i·an \il-ˈir-ē-ən\ *n* **1 :** a native or inhabitant of ancient Illyria **2 :** the poorly attested Indo-European languages of the Illyrians — see INDO-EUROPEAN LANGUAGES table — **Illyrian** *adj*
il·men·ite \ˈil-mə-ˌnīt\ *n* [G *ilmenit,* fr. *Ilmen* range, Ural Mts., U.S.S.R.] **:** a usu. massive iron-black mineral $FeTiO_3$ composed of iron, titanium, and oxygen
ILO *abbr* International Labor Organization
Ilo·ca·no *or* **Ilo·ka·no** \ˌē-lə-ˈkän-(ˌ)ō, ˌil-ə-\ *n, pl* **Ilocano** *or* **Ilocanos** *or* **Ilokano** *or* **Ilokanos 1 a :** a major people of northern Luzon in the Philippines **b :** a member of this people **2 :** the Austronesian language of the Ilocano people
ILS *abbr* instrument landing system
IM *abbr* intramural
im- — see IN-
I'm \(ˌ)īm\ **:** I am
[1]im·age \ˈim-ij\ *n* [ME, fr. OF, short for *imagene,* fr. L *imagin-, imago;* akin to L *imitari* to imitate] **1 :** a reproduction or imitation of the form of a person or thing; *esp* **:** an imitation in solid form **:** STATUE **2 a :** the optical counterpart of an object produced by an optical device (as a lens or mirror) or an electronic device **b :** a likeness of an object produced on a photographic material **3 a :** exact likeness **:** SEMBLANCE <God created man in his own ~ —Gen 1:27 (RSV)> **b :** a person strikingly like another person <he is the ~ of his father> **4 a :** a tangible or visible representation **:** INCARNATION <he is the ~ of filial devotion> **b** *archaic* **:** an illusory form **:** APPARITION **5 a** (1) **:** a mental picture of something not actually present **:** IMPRESSION (2) **:** a mental conception held in common by members of a group and symbolic of a basic attitude and orientation <a disorderly courtroom can seriously tarnish a community's ~ of justice —Herbert Brownell> **b :** IDEA, CONCEPT **6 :** a vivid or graphic representation or description **7 :** FIGURE OF SPEECH **8 :** a popular conception (as of a person, institution, or nation) projected esp. through the mass media <promoting a corporate ~ of brotherly love and concern —R. C. Buck> **9 :** a set of values of a mathematical function (as a homomorphism) that corresponds to a particular subset of the domain
[2]image *vb* **im·aged; im·ag·ing** *vt* **1 :** to describe or portray in language esp. in a vivid manner **2 :** to call up a mental picture of **:** IMAGINE **3 a :** REFLECT, MIRROR **b :** to make appear **:** PROJECT **4 a :** to create a representation of; *also* **:** to form an image of **b :** to represent symbolically ~ *vi* **:** to form an image
image orthicon *n* **:** a highly sensitive television image tube that uses secondary emission and electron multiplication to produce the output signal
im·ag·ery \ˈim-ij-(ə-)rē\ *n* **1 :** the product of image makers **:** IMAGES; *also* **:** the art of making images **2 :** figurative language **3 :** mental images; *esp* **:** the products of imagination
image tube *n* **:** an electron tube in which incident electromagnetic radiation (as light or infrared) produces a visible image on its fluorescent screen duplicating the original pattern of radiation — called also *image converter*
imag·in·able \im-ˈaj-(ə-)nə-bəl\ *adj* **:** capable of being imagined **:** CONCEIVABLE — **imag·in·able·ness** *n* — **imag·in·ably** \-blē\ *adv*
[1]imag·i·nal \im-ˈaj-ən-ᵊl\ *adj* [*imagine* + *-al*] **:** of or relating to imagination, images, or imagery
[2]ima·gi·nal \im-ˈā-gən-ᵊl, -ˈäg-ən-\ *adj* [NL *imagin-, imago*] **:** of or relating to the insect imago
imag·i·nary \im-ˈaj-ə-ˌner-ē\ *adj* **1 :** existing only in imagination **:** lacking factual reality **2 :** containing or relating to the imaginary unit — **imag·i·nari·ly** \im-ˌaj-ə-ˈner-ə-lē\ *adv* — **imag·i·nari·ness** \-ˈaj-ə-ˌner-ē-nəs\ *n*
syn IMAGINARY, FANCIFUL, VISIONARY, FANTASTIC, CHIMERICAL *shared meaning element* **:** unreal or unbelievable ***ant*** real, actual
imaginary number *n* **:** a complex number (as 2 + 3i) whose imaginary part is not zero — called also *imaginary*
imaginary part *n* **:** the part of a complex number (as $3i$ in $2+3i$) that has the imaginary unit as a factor
imaginary unit *n* **:** the positive square root of minus 1 **:** $+\sqrt{-1}$
imag·i·na·tion \im-ˌaj-ə-ˈnā-shən\ *n* **1 :** the act or power of forming a mental image of something not present to the senses or never before wholly perceived in reality **2 a :** creative ability **b :** ability to confront and deal with a problem **:** RESOURCEFULNESS **3 a :** a creation of the mind; *esp* **:** an idealized or poetic creation **b :** fanciful or empty assumption **4 :** popular or traditional belief or conception
syn IMAGINATION, FANCY, FANTASY *shared meaning element* **:** the power to form mental images of things not before one
imag·i·na·tive \im-ˈaj-(ə-)nət-iv, -ˈaj-ə-ˌnāt-\ *adj* **1 a :** of, relating to, or characterized by imagination **b :** devoid of truth **:** FALSE **2 :** given to imagining **:** having a lively imagination **3 :** of or relating to images; *esp* **:** showing a command of imagery — **imag·i·na·tive·ly** *adv* — **imag·i·na·tive·ness** *n*
imag·ine \im-ˈaj-ən\ *vb* **imag·ined; imag·in·ing** \-ˈaj-(ə-)niŋ\ [ME *imaginen,* fr. MF *imaginer,* fr. L *imaginari,* fr. *imagin-, imago* image] *vt* **1 :** to form a mental image of (something not present) **2** *archaic* **:** PLAN, SCHEME **3 :** SUPPOSE, GUESS <I ~ it will rain> **4 :** to form a notion of without sufficient basis **:** FANCY <~s himself to be the reformer of the world> ~ *vi* **1 :** to use the imagination **2 :** SUPPOSE, THINK ***syn*** see THINK
im·ag·ism \ˈim-ij-ˌiz-əm\ *n, often cap* **:** a 20th century movement in poetry advocating free verse and the expression of ideas and emotions through clear precise images — **im·ag·ist** \-ij-əst\ *n* — **imagist** *or* **im·ag·is·tic** \ˌim-ij-ˈis-tik\ *adj* — **im·ag·is·ti·cal·ly** \-ti-k(ə-)lē\ *adv*
ima·go \im-ˈā-(ˌ)gō, -ˈäg-(ˌ)ō\ *n, pl* **imagoes** *or* **ima·gi·nes** \-ˈā-gə-ˌnēz, -ˈäg-ə-\ [NL, fr. L, image] **1 :** an insect in its final, adult, sexually mature, and typically winged state **2 :** an idealized mental image of another person or the self
imam \i-ˈmäm, -ˈmam\ *n* [Ar *imām*] **1 :** the prayer leader of a mosque **2** *cap* **:** a Muslim leader of the line of Ali held by Shiites

to be the divinely appointed, sinless, infallible successors of Muhammad **3** : any of various rulers that claim descent from Muhammad and exercise spiritual and temporal leadership over a Muslim region

imam·ate \-ˌāt\ *n, often cap* **1** : the office of an imam **2** : the region or country ruled over by an imam

ima·ret \i-ˈmär-ət\ *n* [Turk] : an inn or hospice in Turkey

im·bal·ance \(ˌ)im-ˈbal-ən(t)s\ *n* : lack of balance: as **a** : lack of functional balance between body parts or its effect **b** : lack of balance between segments of a nation's economy **c (1)** : numerical disproportion between males and females in a population **(2)** : numerical disproportion between racial elements (as in a school)

im·be·cile \ˈim-bə-səl, -ˌsil\ *n* [F *imbécile,* fr. *imbécile* weak, weak-minded, fr. L *imbecillus*] **1** : a mentally deficient person; *esp* : a feebleminded person having a mental age of three to seven years and requiring supervision in the performance of routine daily tasks of caring for himself **2** : FOOL, IDIOT ***syn*** see FOOL — **imbecile** *or* **im·be·cil·ic** \ˌim-bə-ˈsil-ik\ *adj* — **im·be·cile·ly** \ˈim-bə-sə(l)-lē, -ˌsil-lē\ *adv*

im·be·cil·i·ty \ˌim-bə-ˈsil-ət-ē\ *n, pl* **-ties** **1** : the quality or state of being imbecile or an imbecile **2 a** : utter foolishness; *also* : FUTILITY **b** : something that is foolish or nonsensical

imbed *var of* EMBED

im·bibe \im-ˈbīb\ *vb* **im·bibed; im·bib·ing** [in sense 1, fr. ME *enbiben,* fr. MF *embiber,* fr. L *imbibere* to drink in, conceive, fr. *in-* + *bibere* to drink; in other senses, fr. L *imbibere* — more at POTABLE] *vt* **1** *archaic* : SOAK, STEEP **2 a** : to receive into the mind and retain <~ moral principles> **b** : to assimilate or take into solution **3 a** : DRINK **b** : to take in or up <a sponge ~*s* moisture> ~ *vi* **1** : DRINK 2 **2 a** : to take in liquid **b** : to absorb or assimilate moisture, gas, light, or heat ***syn*** see ABSORB ***ant*** ooze, exude — **im·bib·er** *n*

im·bi·bi·tion \ˌim-bə-ˈbish-ən\ *n* : the act or action of imbibing; *esp* : the taking up of fluid by a colloidal system resulting in swelling — **im·bi·bi·tion·al** \-ˈbish-nəl, -ən-ᵊl\ *adj*

imbitter *var of* EMBITTER

imbosom *var of* EMBOSOM

¹im·bri·cate \ˈim-bri-kət\ *adj* [LL *imbricatus,* pp. of *imbricare* to cover with pantiles, fr. L *imbric-, imbrex* pantile, fr. *imbr-, imber* rain; akin to Gk *ombros* rain] : lying lapped over each other in regular order <~ scales> — **im·bri·cate·ly** *adv*

²im·bri·cate \ˈim-brə-ˌkāt\ *vb* **-cat·ed; -cat·ing** : OVERLAP; *esp* : to overlap like roof tiles

im·bri·ca·tion \ˌim-brə-ˈkā-shən\ *n* **1** : an overlapping of edges (as of tiles or scales) **2** : a decoration or pattern showing imbrication

imbrication 2

im·bro·glio \im-ˈbrōl-(ˌ)yō\ *n, pl* **-glios** [It, fr. *imbrogliare* to entangle, fr. MF *embrouiller* — more at EMBROIL] **1** : a confused mass **2 a** : an intricate or complicated situation (as in a drama or novel) **b** : an acutely painful or embarrassing misunderstanding **c** : a violently confused or bitterly complicated altercation : EMBROILMENT

imbrown *var of* EMBROWN

im·brue \im-ˈbrü\ *vt* **im·brued; im·bru·ing** [ME *enbrewen,* prob. fr. MF *abrevrer, embevrer* to soak, drench, deriv. of L *bibere* to drink — more at POTABLE] : DRENCH, STAIN

im·brute \-ˈbrüt\ *vb* **im·brut·ed; im·brut·ing** *vi* : to sink to the level of a brute ~ *vt* : to degrade to the level of a brute

im·bue \-ˈbyü\ *vt* **im·bued; im·bu·ing** [L *imbuere*] **1** : to tinge or dye deeply **2** : to cause to become penetrated : PERMEATE <a man *imbued* with a strong sense of duty> ***syn*** see INFUSE

IMCO *abbr* Inter-Governmental Maritime Consultative Organization

imdtly *abbr* immediately

IMF *abbr* International Monetary Fund

im·id·az·ole \ˌim-ə-ˈdaz-ˌōl\ *n* [ISV] : a white crystalline heterocyclic base $C_3H_4N_2$ that is an antimetabolite related to histidine; *broadly* : any of various derivatives of this

im·ide \ˈim-ˌīd\ *n* [ISV, alter. of *amide*] : a compound containing the NH group that is derived from ammonia by replacement of two hydrogen atoms by a metal or an equivalent of acid radicals — compare AMIDE — **im·id·ic** \im-ˈid-ik\ *adj*

im·i·do \ˈim-ə-ˌdō\ *adj* : relating to or containing the group NH or a substituted group NR united to one or two radicals of acid character

im·ine \ˈim-ˌēn\ *n* [ISV, alter. of *amine*] : a compound containing the NH group that is derived from ammonia by replacement of two hydrogen atoms by a hydrocarbon radical or other nonacid organic radical

im·i·no \ˈim-ə-ˌnō\ *adj* : relating to or containing the group NH or a substituted group NR united to a radical other than an acid radical

imip·ra·mine \im-ˈip-rə-ˌmēn\ *n* [*imide* + *propyl* + *amine*] : an antidepressant drug $C_{19}H_{24}N_2$

imit *abbr* imitative

im·i·ta·ble \ˈim-ət-ə-bəl\ *adj* : capable or worthy of being imitated or copied

im·i·tate \ˈim-ə-ˌtāt\ *vt* **-tat·ed; -tat·ing** [L *imitatus,* pp. of *imitari* — more at IMAGE] **1** : to follow as a pattern, model, or example **2** : to produce a copy of : REPRODUCE **3** : to be or appear like : RESEMBLE **4** : MIMIC, COUNTERFEIT <can ~ his father's booming voice> ***syn*** see COPY — **im·i·ta·tor** \-ˌtāt-ər\ *n*

¹im·i·ta·tion \ˌim-ə-ˈtā-shən\ *n* **1** : an act or instance of imitating **2** : something produced as a copy : COUNTERFEIT **3** : a literary work designed to reproduce the style of another author **4** : the repetition in a voice part of the melodic theme, phrase, or motive previously found in another part **5** : participation by a sensible object in a transcendent idea **6 a** : the execution of an act supposedly as a direct response to the perception of another person performing the act **b** : the assumption of the modes of behavior observed in other individuals — **im·i·ta·tion·al** \-shnəl, -shən-ᵊl\ *adj*

²imitation *adj* : resembling something else that is usu. genuine and of better quality : not real <~ leather>

im·i·ta·tive \ˈim-ə-ˌtāt-iv\ *adj* **1 a** : marked by imitation <acting is an ~ art> **b** : reproducing or representing a natural sound : ONOMATOPOEIC <"hiss" is an ~ word> **c** : exhibiting mimicry **2** : inclined to imitate **3** : imitating something superior : COUNTERFEIT — **im·i·ta·tive·ly** *adv* — **im·i·ta·tive·ness** *n*

im·mac·u·la·cy \im-ˈak-yə-lə-sē\ *n* : the quality or state of being immaculate

im·mac·u·late \im-ˈak-yə-lət\ *adj* [ME *immaculat,* fr. L *immaculatus,* fr. *in-* + *maculatus,* pp. of *maculare* to stain — more at MACULATE] **1** : having no stain or blemish : PURE **2** : containing no flaw or error **3 a** : spotlessly clean **b** : having no colored spots or marks <petals ~> — **im·mac·u·late·ly** *adv* — **im·mac·u·late·ness** *n*

Immaculate Conception *n* **1** : the conception of the Virgin Mary in which as decreed in Roman Catholic dogma her soul was preserved free from original sin by divine grace **2** : December 8 observed as a Roman Catholic festival in commemoration of the Immaculate Conception

im·mane \im-ˈān\ *adj* [L *immanis,* fr. *in-* + *manus* good — more at MATURE] *archaic* : HUGE; *also* : monstrous in character

im·ma·nence \ˈim-ə-nən(t)s\ *n* : the quality or state of being immanent : INHERENCE

im·ma·nen·cy \-nən-sē\ *n* : IMMANENCE

im·ma·nent \-nənt\ *adj* [LL *immanent-, immanens,* prp. of *immanēre* to remain in place, fr. L *in-* + *manēre* to remain — more at MANSION] : remaining or operating within a domain of reality or realm of discourse : INHERENT; *specif* : existing in consciousness or the mind and not in an extra-mental world — compare TRANSCENDENT — **im·ma·nent·ly** *adv*

im·ma·nent·ism \-ˌiz-əm\ *n* : any of several theories according to which God or an abstract mind or spirit is immanent in the world — **im·ma·nent·ist** \-nənt-əst, -ˌnent-\ *n* — **im·ma·nent·is·tic** \ˌim-ə-nənt-ˈis-tik\ *adj*

im·ma·te·ri·al \ˌim-ə-ˈtir-ē-əl\ *adj* [ME *immateriel,* fr. MF, fr. LL *immaterialis,* fr. L *in-* + LL *materialis* material] **1** : not consisting of matter : INCORPOREAL **2** : of no substantial consequence : UNIMPORTANT — **im·ma·te·ri·al·ly** \-ē-ə-lē\ *adv* — **im·ma·te·ri·al·ness** *n*

im·ma·te·ri·al·ism \-ē-ə-ˌliz-əm\ *n* : a theory that external bodies are in essence mental — **im·ma·te·ri·al·ist** \-ləst\ *n*

im·ma·te·ri·al·i·ty \ˌim-ə-ˌtir-ē-ˈal-ət-ē\ *n, pl* **-ties** **1** : the quality or state of being immaterial **2** : something immaterial

im·ma·te·ri·al·ize \-ˈtir-ē-ə-ˌlīz\ *vt* : to make immaterial or incorporeal

im·ma·ture \ˌim-ə-ˈt(y)u̇(ə)r *also* -ˈchu̇(ə)r\ *adj* [L *immaturus,* fr. *in-* + *maturus* mature] **1** *archaic* : PREMATURE **2 a** : lacking complete growth, differentiation, or development <a thin ~ soil> **b (1)** : having the potential capacity to attain a definitive form or state : CRUDE, UNFINISHED <a vigorous but ~ school of art> **(2)** *of a topographic feature* : predictably due to undergo further changes — used esp. of valleys and drainages while most of the area is well above baselevel **c** : exhibiting less than an expected degree of maturity <emotionally ~ adults> — **immature** *n* — **im·ma·ture·ly** *adv* — **im·ma·ture·ness** *n* — **im·ma·tu·ri·ty** \-ˈt(y)u̇r-ət-ē *also* -ˈchu̇r-\ *n*

im·mea·sur·able \(ˈ)im-ˈ(m)ezh-(ə-)rə-bəl, -ˈ(m)ezh-ər-bəl, -ˈ(m)āzh-\ *adj* : incapable of being measured; *broadly* : indefinitely extensive — **im·mea·sur·able·ness** *n* — **im·mea·sur·ably** \-blē\ *adv*

im·me·di·a·cy \im-ˈēd-ē-ə-sē, *Brit often* -ˈē-jə-sē\ *n, pl* **-cies** **1** : the quality or state of being immediate; *esp* : absence of a mediating agent **2** : something that is immediate — usu. used in pl.

im·me·di·ate \im-ˈēd-ē-ət, *Brit often* -ˈē-jit\ *adj* [LL *immediatus,* fr. L *in-* + LL *mediatus* intermediate — more at MEDIATE] **1 a** : acting or being without the intervention of another object, cause, or agency : DIRECT <the ~ cause of death> **b** : present to the mind independently of other states or factors <~ awareness> **c** : involving or derived from a single premise <an ~ inference> **2** : being next in line or relation <only the ~ family was present> **3 a** : made or done at once : INSTANT <an ~ need> **b (1)** *of time* : near to or related to the present <the ~ past> **(2)** : of or relating to the here and now : CURRENT <too busy with ~ concerns to worry about the future> **4 a** : existing without intervening space or substance <bring the chemicals into ~ contact very carefully> **b** : being near at hand <the ~ neighborhood> **5** : directly touching or concerning a person or thing <the child's ~ world is the classroom>

immediate constituent *n* : any of the meaningful constituents directly forming a larger linguistic construction (as a phrase or sentence)

¹im·me·di·ate·ly *adv* **1** : in direct connection or relation : DIRECTLY <the parties ~ involved in the case> <the house ~ beyond this one> **2** : without interval of time : STRAIGHTWAY

²immediately *conj* : as soon as

im·me·di·ate·ness *n* : IMMEDIACY 1

im·med·i·ca·ble \(ˈ)im-ˈ(m)ed-i-kə-bəl\ *adj* [L *immedicabilis,* fr. *in-* + *medicabilis* medicable] : INCURABLE <wounds ~ —John Milton> — **im·ned·i·ca·bly** \-blē\ *adv*

Im·mel·mann \ˈim-əl-mən\ *n* [Max *Immelmann*] : a turn in which an airplane in flight is first made to complete half of a loop and is then rolled half of a complete turn — called also *Immelmann turn*

im·me·mo·ri·al \ˌim-ə-ˈmōr-ē-əl, -ˈmȯr-\ *adj* [prob. fr. F *immémorial,* fr. MF, fr. *in-* + *memorial*] : extending beyond the reach of memory, record, or tradition <existing from time ~> — **im·me·mo·ri·al·ly** \-ē-ə-lē\ *adv*

im·mense \im-ˈen(t)s\ *adj* [MF, fr. L *immensus* immeasurable, fr. *in-* + *mensus,* pp. of *metiri* to measure — more at MEASURE] **1** : marked by greatness esp. in size or degree; *esp* : transcending ordinary means of measurement <the ~ and boundless universe>

2 : supremely good **:** EXCELLENT <her portrayal of the role was ~> ***syn*** see HUGE ***ant*** minute — **im·mense·ly** *adv* — **im·mense·ness** *n*

im·men·si·ty \im-ˈen(t)-sət-ē\ *n, pl* **-ties 1 :** the quality or state of being immense **2 :** something immense

im·men·su·ra·ble \(ˈ)im-ˈ(m)en(t)s-(ə-)rə-bəl, -ˈ(m)ench-(ə-)rə-\ *adj* [LL *immensurabilis,* fr. L *in-* + LL *mensurabilis* measurable] **:** IMMEASURABLE

im·merge \im-ˈərj\ *vi* **im·merged; im·merg·ing** [L *immergere*] **:** to plunge into or immerse oneself in something — **im·mer·gence** \-ˈər-jən(t)s\ *n*

im·merse \im-ˈərs\ *vt* **im·mersed; im·mers·ing** [L *immersus,* pp. of *immergere,* fr. *in-* + *mergere* to merge] **1 :** to plunge into something that surrounds or covers; *esp* **:** to plunge or dip into a fluid **2 :** to baptize by immersion **3 :** ENGROSS, ABSORB <completely *immersed* in his work>

im·mersed *adj, of a plant* **:** growing wholly under water

im·mers·ible \im-ˈər-sə-bəl\ *adj* **:** capable of being totally submerged in water without damage to the heating element <an ~ electric frying pan>

im·mer·sion \im-ˈər-zhən, -shən\ *n* **1 :** an act of immersing **:** a state of being immersed; *specif* **:** baptism by complete submersion of the person in water **2 :** disappearance of a celestial body behind or into the shadow of another

im·mesh \im-ˈesh\ *var of* ENMESH

im·me·thod·i·cal \ˌim-ə-ˈthäd-i-kəl\ *adj* **:** not methodical — **im·me·thod·i·cal·ly** \-k(ə-)lē\ *adv*

im·mi·grant \ˈim-i-grənt\ *n* **:** one that immigrates: **a :** a person who comes to a country to take up permanent residence **b :** a plant or animal that becomes established in an area where it was previously unknown ***syn*** see EMIGRANT — **immigrant** *adj*

im·mi·grate \ˈim-ə-ˌgrāt\ *vb* **-grat·ed; -grat·ing** [L *immigratus,* pp. of *immigrare* to remove, go in, fr. *in-* + *migrare* to migrate] *vi* **:** to enter and usu. become established; *esp* **:** to come into a country of which one is not a native for permanent residence ~ *vt* **:** to bring in or send as immigrants — **im·mi·gra·tion** \ˌim-ə-ˈgrā-shən\ *n* — **im·mi·gra·tion·al** \-shnəl, -shən-ᵊl\ *adj*

im·mi·nence \ˈim-ə-nən(t)s\ *n* **1 :** the quality or state of being imminent **2 :** something imminent; *esp* **:** impending evil or danger

im·mi·nen·cy \-nən-sē\ *n* **:** IMMINENCE 1

im·mi·nent \ˈim-ə-nənt\ *adj* [L *imminent-, imminens,* prp. of *imminēre* to project, threaten, fr. *in-* + *-minēre* (akin to L *mont-, mons* mountain) — more at MOUNT] **1 :** ready to take place; *esp* **:** hanging threateningly over one's head <was in ~ danger of being run over> **2 :** IMMANENT — **im·mi·nent·ly** *adv* — **im·mi·nent·ness** *n*

im·min·gle \im-ˈiŋ-gəl\ *vb* **:** BLEND, INTERMINGLE

im·mis·ci·ble \(ˈ)im-ˈ(m)is-ə-bəl\ *adj* **:** incapable of mixing or attaining homogeneity — **im·mis·ci·bil·i·ty** \(ˌ)im-ˌ(m)is-ə-ˈbil-ət-ē\ *n* — **im·mis·ci·bly** \(ˈ)im-ˈ(m)is-ə-blē\ *adv*

im·mit·i·ga·ble \(ˈ)im-ˈ(m)it-i-gə-bəl\ *adj* [LL *immitigabilis,* fr. L *in-* + *mitigare* to mitigate] **:** not capable of being mitigated — **im·mit·i·ga·ble·ness** *n* — **im·mit·i·ga·bly** \-blē\ *adv*

im·mit·tance \(ˈ)im-ˈ(m)it-ᵊn(t)s\ *n* [*im*pedance + ad*mittance*] **:** electrical admittance or impedance

im·mix \im-ˈiks\ *vt* [back-formation fr. *immixed* mixed in, fr. ME *immixte,* fr. L *immixtus,* pp. of *immiscēre,* fr. *in-* + *miscēre* to mix — more at MIX] **:** to mix intimately **:** COMMINGLE — **im·mix·ture** \-ˈiks-chər\ *n*

im·mo·bile \(ˈ)im-ˈ(m)ō-bəl, -ˌbēl, -ˌbīl\ *adj* [ME *in-mobill,* fr. L *immobilis,* fr. *in-* + *mobilis* mobile] **1 :** incapable of being moved **:** FIXED **2 :** not moving **:** MOTIONLESS <keep the patient ~> — **im·mo·bil·i·ty** \ˌim-(ˌ)ō-ˈbil-ət-ē\ *n*

im·mo·bi·lize \im-ˈō-bə-ˌlīz\ *vt* **:** to make immobile: as **a :** to prevent freedom of movement or effective use of <the planes were *immobilized* by bad weather> **b :** to reduce or eliminate motion of (the body or a part) by mechanical means or by strict bed rest **c :** to withhold (money or capital) from circulation — **im·mo·bi·li·za·tion** \-ˌō-bə-lə-ˈzā-shən\ *n* — **im·mo·bi·liz·er** \-ˈō-bə-ˌlī-zər\ *n*

im·mod·er·a·cy \(ˈ)im-ˈ(m)äd-(ə-)rə-sē\ *n* **:** lack of moderation

im·mod·er·ate \-(ə-)rət\ *adj* [ME *immoderat,* fr. L *immoderatus,* fr. *in-* + *moderatus,* pp. of *moderare* to moderate] **:** exceeding just, usual, or suitable bounds <~ pride> <an ~ appetite> ***syn*** see EXCESSIVE ***ant*** moderate — **im·mod·er·ate·ly** *adv* — **im·mod·er·ate·ness** *n* — **im·mod·er·a·tion** \(ˌ)im-ˌäd-ə-ˈrā-shən\ *n*

im·mod·est \(ˈ)im-ˈ(m)äd-əst\ *adj* [L *immodestus,* fr. *in-* + *modestus* modest] **:** not modest; *specif* **:** not conforming to the sexual mores of a particular time or place — **im·mod·est·ly** *adv* — **im·mod·es·ty** \-ə-stē\ *n*

im·mo·late \ˈim-ə-ˌlāt\ *vt* **-lat·ed; -lat·ing** [L *immolatus,* pp. of *immolare,* fr. *in-* + *mola* spelt grits; fr. the custom of sprinkling victims with sacrificial meal; akin to L *molere* to grind — more at MILL] **1 :** to offer in sacrifice; *esp* **:** to kill as a sacrificial victim **2 :** KILL, DESTROY — **im·mo·la·tor** \-ˌlāt-ər\ *n*

im·mo·la·tion \ˌim-ə-ˈlā-shən\ *n* **1 :** the act of immolating **:** the state of being immolated **2 :** something that is immolated

im·mor·al \(ˈ)im-ˈ(m)ȯr-əl, -ˈ(m)är-\ *adj* **:** not moral; *broadly* **:** conflicting with generally or traditionally held moral principles — **im·mor·al·ly** \-ə-lē\ *adv*

syn IMMORAL, UNMORAL, NONMORAL, AMORAL *shared meaning element* **:** not moral. In spite of their common element of meaning these words are rarely interchangeable without serious loss of precision. IMMORAL implies a positive and active opposition to what is *moral* and may designate whatever is discordant with accepted ethical principles or the dictates of conscience <*immoral* conduct> or, in weakened use, with accepted social custom or general practice <refusal to acknowledge the boundaries set by convention is the source of frequent denunciations of art as *immoral* —John Dewey> *Unmoral, nonmoral,* and *amoral* all, in contrast to *immoral,* imply a passive negation of what is moral. UNMORAL can imply a lack of ethical perception and moral awareness <infants and idiots are *unmoral* and without moral responsibility> or it can come close to *conscienceless* in implying disregard of moral principles <the great *unmoral* power of the modern industrial revolution —F. L. Wright> Occasionally, it, along with *nonmoral* and *amoral,* implies that the thing qualified is not a fit subject for ethical judgment. While *nonmoral* and *amoral* are frequently interchangeable, NONMORAL may be preferred when what is qualified is patently outside the realm of moral judgments, and AMORAL can be applied discriminatively to something not customarily or universally so exempt; thus, life in the abstract is a *nonmoral* concept but a particular human life may well be *amoral;* perspective is a *nonmoral* aspect of painting but a painter's approach is likely to be *amoral,* even though some critics consider the result *immoral.* ***ant*** moral

im·mor·al·ist \-ə-ləst\ *n* **:** an advocate of immorality

im·mo·ral·i·ty \ˌim-(ˌ)ȯ-ˈral-ət-ē, ˌim-ə-ˈral-\ *n* **1 :** the quality or state of being immoral; *esp* **:** UNCHASTITY **2 :** an immoral act or practice

¹im·mor·tal \(ˈ)im-ˈȯrt-ᵊl\ *adj* [ME, fr. L *immortalis,* fr. *in-* + *mortalis* mortal] **1 :** exempt from death <the ~ gods> **2 :** connected with or relating to immortality **3 :** exempt from oblivion **:** IMPERISHABLE <~ fame> — **im·mor·tal·ly** \-ᵊl-ē\ *adv*

²immortal *n* **1 a :** one exempt from death **b** *pl, often cap* **:** the gods of the Greek and Roman pantheon **2 a :** a person whose fame is lasting **b** *cap* **:** any of the 40 members of the Académie Française

im·mor·tal·i·ty \ˌim-ˌȯr-ˈtal-ət-ē\ *n* **:** the quality or state of being immortal: **a :** unending existence **b :** lasting fame

im·mor·tal·ize \im-ˈȯrt-ᵊl-ˌīz\ *vt* **-ized; -iz·ing :** to make immortal — **im·mor·tal·iza·tion** \-ˌȯrt-ᵊl-ə-ˈzā-shən\ *n* — **im·mor·tal·iz·er** \-ˈȯrt-ᵊl-ˌī-zər\ *n*

im·mor·telle \ˌim-ˌȯr-ˈtel\ *n* [F, fr. fem. of *immortel* immortal, fr. L *immortalis*] **:** EVERLASTING 3

im·mo·tile \(ˈ)im-ˈ(m)ōt-ᵊl, -ˈ(m)ō-ˌtīl\ *adj* **:** lacking motility — **im·mo·til·i·ty** \ˌim-ō-ˈtil-ət-ē\ *n*

¹im·mov·able \(ˈ)im-ˈ(m)ü-və-bəl\ *adj* **1 :** incapable of being moved; *broadly* **:** not moving or not intended to be moved **2 a :** STEADFAST, UNYIELDING **b :** not capable of being moved emotionally — **im·mov·abil·i·ty** \(ˌ)im-ˌ(m)ü-və-ˈbil-ət-ē\ *n* — **im·mov·able·ness** \(ˈ)im-ˈ(m)ü-və-bəl-nəs\ *n* — **im·mov·ably** \-blē\ *adv*

²immovable *n* **1 :** one that cannot be moved **2** *pl* **:** real property

immun *abbr* immunity; immunization

im·mune \im-ˈyün\ *adj* [L *immunis,* fr. *in-* + *munia* services, obligations; akin to L *munus* service] **1 a :** FREE, EXEMPT <~ from further taxation> **b :** marked by protection <some criminal leaders are ~ from arrest> **2 :** not susceptible or responsive <~ to all pleas>; *esp* **:** having a high degree of resistance to a disease <~ to diphtheria> **3 a :** having or producing antibodies to a corresponding antigen <an ~ serum> **b :** produced in response to the presence of a corresponding antigen <~ agglutinins> **c :** concerned with or involving immunity <~ globulins> <an ~ response> — **immune** *n*

im·mu·ni·ty \im-ˈyü-nət-ē\ *n, pl* **-ties :** the quality or state of being immune; *specif* **:** a condition of being able to resist a particular disease esp. through preventing development of a pathogenic microorganism or by counteracting the effects of its products

im·mu·nize \ˈim-yə-ˌnīz\ *vt* **-nized; -niz·ing :** to make immune — **im·mu·ni·za·tion** \ˌim-yə-nə-ˈzā-shən *also* im-ˌyü-nə-\ *n*

immuno- *comb form* [ISV, fr. *immune*] **:** immunity <*immuno*genetics>

im·mu·no·as·say \ˌim-yə-nō-ˈas-ˌā, im-ˌyü-nō-, -a-ˈsā\ *n* **:** the identification of a substance (as a protein) through its capacity to act as an antigen — **im·mu·no·as·say·able** \-a-ˈsā-ə-bəl\ *adj*

im·mu·no·chem·is·try \-ˈkem-ə-strē\ *n* [ISV] **:** a branch of chemistry that deals with the chemical aspects of immunology — **im·mu·no·chem·i·cal** \-ˈkem-i-kəl\ *adj* — **im·mu·no·chem·i·cal·ly** \-k(ə-)lē\ *adv* — **im·mu·no·chem·ist** \-ˈkem-əst\ *n*

im·mu·no·dif·fu·sion \-dif-ˈyü-zhən\ *n* **:** the separation of an antigen complex into discrete parts through differences in ability to pass through a semipermeable membrane or migrate through a medium

im·mu·no·elec·tro·pho·re·sis \ˈim-yə-nō-ə-ˌlek-trə-fə-ˈrē-səs, im-ˈyü-nō-\ *n, pl* **-re·ses** \-ˌsēz\ **:** electrophoretic separation of proteins followed by identification through specific immunologic reactions — **im·mu·no·elec·tro·pho·ret·ic** \-ˈret-ik\ *adj* — **im·mu·no·elec·tro·pho·ret·i·cal·ly** \-i-k(ə-)lē\ *adv*

im·mu·no·flu·o·res·cence \-(ˌ)flu̇(-ə)r-ˈes-ᵊn(t)s, -flōr-, -flȯr-\ *n* **:** antibody demonstration by use of a fluorescent dye to label the antibody — **im·mu·no·flu·o·res·cent** \-ᵊnt\ *adj*

im·mu·no·gen·e·sis \-ˈjen-ə-səs\ *n* **:** immunity production — **im·mu·no·gen·ic** \-ˈjen-ik\ *adj* — **im·mu·no·gen·i·cal·ly** \-i-k(ə-)lē\ *adv* — **im·mu·no·ge·nic·i·ty** \-jə-ˈnis-ət-ē\ *n*

im·mu·no·ge·net·ics \-jə-ˈnet-iks\ *n pl but sing in constr* **1 :** a branch of immunology that deals with the interrelation of immunity to disease and genetic makeup **2 :** a study of biological interrelationships by serological means — **im·mu·no·ge·net·ic** \-ik\ *adj* — **im·mu·no·ge·net·i·cal·ly** \-i-k(ə-)lē\ *adv*

im·mu·no·glob·u·lin \-ˈgläb-yə-lən\ *n* **:** a protein that behaves like an antibody or is formed in response to an antigen

im·mu·no·he·ma·tol·o·gy \-ˌhē-mə-ˈtäl-ə-jē\ *n* **:** a branch of immunology that deals with the immunologic properties of blood — **im·mu·no·he·ma·to·log·ic** \-ˌhē-mət-ᵊl-ˈäj-ik\ *or* **im·mu·no·he·ma·to·log·i·cal** \-ˈäj-i-kəl\ *adj*

immunol *abbr* immunology

im·mu·nol·o·gy \ˌim-yə-ˈnäl-ə-jē\ *n* [ISV] **:** a science that deals with the phenomena and causes of immunity — **im·mu·no·log·ic**

\-yən-ᵊl-ˈäj-ik\ *or* **im·mu·no·log·i·cal** \-ˈäj-i-kəl\ *adj* — **im·mu·no·log·i·cal·ly** \-i-k(ə-)lē\ *adv* — **im·mu·nol·o·gist** \ˌim-yə-ˈnäl-ə-jəst\ *n*

im·mu·no·pa·thol·o·gy \ˌim-yə-nō-pə-ˈthäl-ə-jē, im-ˌyü-nō-, -pa-\ *n* **:** a branch of medicine that deals with immunologic abnormalities and disease — **im·mu·no·path·o·log·ic** \-ˌpath-ə-ˈläj-ik\ *or* **im·mu·no·path·o·log·i·cal** \-i-kəl\ *adj* — **im·mu·no·pa·thol·o·gist** \-pə-ˈthäl-ə-jəst, -pa-\ *n*

im·mu·no·re·ac·tive \-rē-ˈak-tiv\ *adj* **:** reacting to particular antigens or haptens <serum ~ insulin> — **im·mu·no·re·ac·tiv·i·ty** \-(ˌ)rē-ˌak-ˈtiv-ət-ē\ *n*

im·mu·no·sup·pres·sion \-sə-ˈpresh-ən\ *n* **:** suppression (as by drugs) of natural immune responses — **im·mu·no·sup·pres·sant** \-ˈpres-ᵊnt\ *n or adj* — **im·mu·no·sup·pres·sive** \-ˈpres-iv\ *adj*

im·mu·no·ther·a·py \-ˈther-ə-pē\ *n* [ISV] **:** treatment of or prophylaxis against disease by means of antigens or antigenic preparations

im·mure \im-ˈyü(ə)r\ *vt* **im·mured; im·mur·ing** [ML *immurare*, fr. L *in-* + *murus* wall — more at MUNITION] **1 a :** to enclose within or as if within walls **b :** IMPRISON **2 :** to build into a wall; *esp* **:** to entomb in a wall — **im·mure·ment** \-ˈyü(ə)r-mənt\ *n*

im·mu·ta·ble \(ˈ)im-ˈ(m)yüt-ə-bəl\ *adj* [ME, fr. L *immutabilis*, fr. *in-* + *mutabilis* mutable] **:** not capable of or susceptible to change — **im·mu·ta·bil·i·ty** \(ˌ)im-ˌ(m)yüt-ə-ˈbil-ət-ē\ *n* — **im·mu·ta·ble·ness** \(ˈ)im-ˈ(m)yüt-ə-bəl-nəs\ *n* — **im·mu·ta·bly** \-blē\ *adv*

1**imp** \ˈimp\ *n* [ME *impe*, fr. OE *impa*, fr. *impian* to imp] **1** *obs* **:** SHOOT, BUD; *also* **:** GRAFT **2 a :** a small demon **:** FIEND **b :** a mischievous child **:** URCHIN

2**imp** *vt* [ME *impen*, fr. OE *impian;* akin to OHG *impfōn* to graft; both from a prehistoric WGmc word borrowed fr. (assumed) VL *imputare*, fr. L *in-* + *putare* to prune — more at PAVE] **1** *archaic* **:** to graft or repair (a wing, tail, or feather) with a feather to improve a falcon's flying capacity **2 :** to equip with wings

3**imp** *abbr* **1** imperative **2** imperfect **3** imperial **4** import; imported

1**im·pact** \im-ˈpakt\ *vb* [L *impactus*, pp. of *impingere* to push against — more at IMPINGE] *vt* **1 a :** to fix firmly by or as if by packing or wedging **b :** to press together **2 a :** to have an impact on **:** impinge on **b :** to strike forcefully; *also* **:** to cause to strike forcefully ~ *vi* **1 :** to have an impact **2 :** to impinge or make contact esp. forcefully — **im·pac·tive** \im-ˈpak-tiv\ *adj*

2**im·pact** \ˈim-ˌpakt\ *n* **1 a :** an impinging or striking esp. of one body against another **b :** a forceful contact, collision, or onset; *also* **:** the impetus communicated in or as if in a collision **2 :** the force of impression of one thing on another **:** an impelling or compelling effect <the ~ of modern science on our society>

im·pact·ed \im-ˈpak-təd\ *adj* **1** *of a tooth* **:** wedged between the jawbone and another tooth **2 :** of or relating to an area (as a school district) inhabited by a large number of employees of the federal government

im·pac·tion \im-ˈpak-shən\ *n* **:** the act of becoming or the state of being impacted; *esp* **:** lodgment of something (as feces) in a body passage or cavity

im·pac·tor *or* **im·pact·er** \im-ˈpak-tər\ *n* **:** one that impacts: as **a :** a machine or part that operates by striking blows **b :** an instrument for collecting samples of suspended particles (as dust in air) by directing a stream of the suspension onto a surface or into a liquid

im·paint \im-ˈpānt\ *vt, obs* **:** PAINT, DEPICT

im·pair \im-ˈpa(ə)r, -ˈpe(ə)r\ *vt* [ME *empeiren*, fr. MF *empeirer* fr. (assumed) VL *impejorare*, fr. L *in-* + LL *pejorare* to make worse — more at PEJORATIVE] **:** to make worse by or as if by diminishing in some material respect <his health was ~*ed* by overwork> <the strike seriously ~*ed* community services> ***syn*** see INJURE ***ant*** improve, amend — **im·pair·er** *n* — **im·pair·ment** \-ˈpa(ə)r-mənt\ *n*

im·pa·la \im-ˈpal-ə, -ˈpäl-\ *n* [Zulu] **:** a large brownish African antelope (*Aepyceros melampus*) that in the male has slender lyrate horns

impala

im·pale \im-ˈpā(ə)l\ *vt* **im·paled; im·pal·ing** [MF & ML; MF *empaler*, fr. ML *impalare*, fr. L *in-* + *palus* stake — more at POLE] **1 :** to pierce with or as if with something pointed; *esp* **:** to torture or kill by fixing on a sharp stake **2 :** to join coats of arms on a heraldic shield divided vertically by a pale — **im·pale·ment** \-mənt\ *n*

im·pal·pa·ble \(ˈ)im-ˈpal-pə-bəl\ *adj* **1 a :** incapable of being felt by touch **:** INTANGIBLE <the ~ aura of power that emanated from him —Osbert Sitwell> **b :** so finely divided that no grains or grit can be felt <rock worn to an ~ powder> **2 :** not readily discerned by the mind — **im·pal·pa·bil·i·ty** \(ˌ)im-ˌpal-pə-ˈbil-ət-ē\ *n* — **im·pal·pa·bly** \(ˌ)im-ˈpal-pə-blē\ *adv*

im·pan·el \im-ˈpan-ᵊl\ *vt* **:** to enroll in or on a panel <~ a jury>

im·par·a·dise \im-ˈpar-ə-ˌdīs, -ˌdīz\ *vt* **-dised; -dis·ing :** ENRAPTURE

im·par·i·ty \(ˈ)im-ˈpar-ət-ē\ *n, pl* **-ties** [LL *imparitas*, fr. L *impar* unequal, fr. *in-* + *par* equal] **:** INEQUALITY, DISPARITY

im·part \im-ˈpärt\ *vt* [MF & L; MF *impartir*, fr. L *impartire*, fr. *in-* + *partire* to divide, part] **1 :** to give, convey, or grant from or as if from a store <his assurance ~*ed* authority to his words> <the flavor ~*ed* by herbs> **2 :** to communicate the knowledge of **:** DISCLOSE ***syn*** see COMMUNICATE — **im·part·able** \-ə-bəl\ *adj* — **im·par·ta·tion** \ˌim-ˌpär-ˈtā-shən\ *n* — **im·part·ment** \im-ˈpärt-mənt\ *n*

im·par·tial \(ˈ)im-ˈpär-shəl\ *adj* **:** not partial or biased **:** treating or affecting all equally ***syn*** see FAIR ***ant*** partial — **im·par·tial·i·ty** \(ˌ)im-ˌpär-shē-ˈal-ət-ē, -ˌpär-ˈshal-\ *n* — **im·par·tial·ly** \(ˈ)im-ˈpärsh-(ə-)lē\ *adv*

im·par·ti·ble \(ˈ)im-ˈpärt-ə-bəl\ *adj* [LL *impartibilis*, fr. L *in-* + LL *partibilis* divisible, fr. L *partire*] **:** not partible **:** not subject to partition — **im·par·ti·bly** \-blē\ *adv*

im·pass·able \(ˈ)im-ˈpas-ə-bəl\ *adj* **:** incapable of being passed, traveled, crossed, or surmounted — **im·pass·abil·i·ty** \(ˌ)im-ˌpas-ə-ˈbil-ət-ē\ *n* — **im·pass·able·ness** \(ˈ)im-ˈpas-ə-bəl-nəs\ *n* — **im·pass·ably** \-blē\ *adv*

im·passe \ˈim-ˌpas, im-ˈ\ *n* [Fr, fr. *in-* + *passer* to pass] **1 :** an impassable road or way **:** CUL-DE-SAC **2 a :** a predicament affording no obvious escape **b :** DEADLOCK

im·pas·si·ble \(ˈ)im-ˈpas-ə-bəl\ *adj* [ME, fr. MF or LL; MF, fr. LL *impassibilis*, fr. L *in-* + LL *passibilis* passible] **1 a :** incapable of suffering or of experiencing pain **b :** inaccessible to injury **2 :** incapable of feeling **:** IMPASSIVE — **im·pas·si·bil·i·ty** \(ˌ)im-ˌpas-ə-ˈbil-ət-ē\ *n* — **im·pas·si·bly** \(ˈ)im-ˈpas-ə-blē\ *adv*

im·pas·sion \im-ˈpash-ən\ *vt* **im·pas·sioned; im·pas·sion·ing** \-(ə-)niŋ\ [prob. fr. It *impassionare*, fr. *in-* (fr. L) + *passione* passion, fr. LL *passion-*, *passio*] **:** to arouse the feelings or passions of

im·pas·sioned *adj* **:** filled with passion or zeal **:** showing great warmth or intensity of feeling
syn IMPASSIONED, PASSIONATE, ARDENT, FERVENT, FERVID, PERFERVID *shared meaning element* **:** showing intense feeling ***ant*** unimpassioned

im·pas·sive \(ˈ)im-ˈpas-iv\ *adj* **1 a** *archaic* **:** unsusceptible to pain **b :** unsusceptible to physical feeling **:** INSENSIBLE **c :** unsusceptible to or destitute of emotion **:** APATHETIC **2 :** giving no sign of feeling or emotion **:** EXPRESSIONLESS — **im·pas·sive·ly** *adv* — **im·pas·sive·ness** *n* — **im·pas·siv·i·ty** \ˌim-ˌpas-ˈiv-ət-ē\ *n*
syn IMPASSIVE, STOIC, PHLEGMATIC, APATHETIC, STOLID *shared meaning element* **:** unresponsive to what might normally excite interest or emotion ***ant*** responsive

im·paste \im-ˈpāst\ *vt* [It *impastare*, fr. *in-* (fr. L) + *pasta* paste, fr. LL] *obs* **:** to make into a paste or crust

im·pas·to \im-ˈpas-(ˌ)tō, -ˈpäs-\ *n* [It, fr. *impastare*] **1 :** the thick application of a pigment to a canvas or panel in painting; *also* **:** the body of pigment so applied **2 :** raised decoration on ceramic ware usu. of slip or enamel — **im·pas·toed** \-(ˌ)tōd\ *adj*

im·pa·tience \(ˈ)im-ˈpā-shən(t)s\ *n* **:** the quality or state of being impatient

im·pa·tiens \im-ˈpā-shənz, -shən(t)s\ *n* [NL, genus name, fr. L, impatient] **:** any of a widely distributed genus (*Impatiens*, family Balsaminaceae, the jewelweed family) of watery-juiced annual herbs with irregular spurred or saccate flowers and dehiscent capsules

im·pa·tient \(ˈ)im-ˈpā-shənt\ *adj* [ME *impacient*, fr. MF, fr. L *impatient-*, *impatiens*, fr. *in-* + *patient-*, *patiens* patient] **1 a :** not patient **:** restless or short of temper esp. under irritation, delay, or opposition **b :** INTOLERANT <~ of delay> **2 :** prompted or marked by impatience <an ~ reply> **3 :** eagerly desirous **:** ANXIOUS <~ to see his sweetheart> — **im·pa·tient·ly** *adv*

im·pawn \im-ˈpȯn, -ˈpän\ *vt, archaic* **:** to put in pawn **:** PLEDGE

1**im·peach** \im-ˈpēch\ *vt* [ME *empechen*, fr. MF *empeechier* to hinder, fr. LL *impedicare* to fetter, fr. L *in-* + *pedica* fetter, fr. *ped-*, *pes* foot — more at FOOT] **1 a :** to bring an accusation against **b :** to charge with a crime or misdemeanor; *specif* **:** to charge (a public official) before a competent tribunal with misconduct in office **2 :** to cast doubt on; *esp* **:** to challenge the credibility or validity of <~ the testimony of a witness> — **im·peach·able** \-ˈpē-chə-bəl\ *adj* — **im·peach·ment** \-ˈpēch-mənt\ *n*

2**impeach** *n, obs* **:** CHARGE, IMPEACHMENT

im·pearl \im-ˈpər(-ə)l\ *vt* [prob. fr. MF *emperler*, fr. *en-* + *perle* pearl] **:** to form into pearls; *also* **:** to form of or adorn with pearls

im·pec·ca·ble \(ˈ)im-ˈpek-ə-bəl\ *adj* [L *impeccabilis*, fr. *in-* + *peccare* to sin] **1 :** not capable of sinning or liable to sin **2 :** free from fault or blame **:** FLAWLESS <spoke ~ French> — **im·pec·ca·bil·i·ty** \(ˌ)im-ˌpek-ə-ˈbil-ət-ē\ *n* — **im·pec·ca·bly** \(ˈ)im-ˈpek-ə-blē\ *adv*

im·pe·cu·nious \ˌim-pi-ˈkyü-nyəs, -nē-əs\ *adj* [*in-* + obs. E *pecunious* (rich), fr. ME, fr. L *pecuniosus*, fr. *pecunia* money — more at FEE] **:** having very little or no money usu. habitually **:** PENNILESS — **im·pe·cu·ni·os·i·ty** \-ˌkyü-nē-ˈäs-ət-ē\ *n* — **im·pe·cu·nious·ly** *adv* — **im·pe·cu·nious·ness** *n*

im·ped·ance \im-ˈpēd-ᵊn(t)s\ *n* **:** something that impedes **:** HINDRANCE: as **a :** the apparent opposition in an electrical circuit to the flow of an alternating current that is analogous to the actual electrical resistance to a direct current and that is the ratio of effective electromotive force to the effective current **b :** the ratio of the pressure to the volume displacement at a given surface in a sound-transmitting medium

im·pede \im-ˈpēd\ *vt* **im·ped·ed; im·ped·ing** [L *impedire*, fr. *in-* + *ped-*, *pes* foot — more at FOOT] **:** to interfere with or slow the progress of ***syn*** see HINDER ***ant*** assist, promote — **im·ped·er** *n*

im·ped·i·ment \im-ˈped-ə-mənt\ *n* **1 :** something that impedes; *esp* **:** an organic obstruction to speech **2 :** a bar or hindrance (as lack of sufficient age) to a lawful marriage

im·ped·i·men·ta \(ˌ)im-ˌped-ə-ˈment-ə\ *n pl* [L, pl. of *impedimentum* impediment, fr. *impedire*] **1 :** APPURTENANCES, EQUIPMENT <silver candlesticks, diamond tiaras and other comforting ~ of a more stable past —*Life*> **2 :** things that impede

im·pel \im-ˈpel\ *vt* **im·pelled; im·pel·ling** [L *impellere*, fr. *in-* + *pellere* to drive — more at FELT] **1 :** to urge or drive forward or on by or as if by the exertion of strong moral pressure **:** FORCE **2 :** to impart motion to **:** PROPEL ***syn*** see MOVE

im·pel·ler *also* **im·pel·lor** \im-ˈpel-ər\ *n* **1 :** one that impels **2 :** ROTOR; *also* **:** a blade of a rotor

im·pend \im-ˈpend\ *vi* [L *impendēre*, fr. *in-* + *pendēre* to hang — more at PENDANT] **1** *archaic* **:** to hang suspended **2 a :** to hover threateningly **:** MENACE **b :** to be about to occur

im·pen·dent \im-ˈpen-dənt\ *adj* **:** being near at hand **:** APPROACHING

im·pen·e·tra·bil·i·ty \(ˌ)im-ˌpen-ə-trə-ˈbil-ət-ē\ *n* **1 :** the quality or state of being impenetrable **2 :** the inability of two portions of matter to occupy the same space at the same time

im·pen·e·tra·ble \(ˈ)im-ˈpen-ə-trə-bəl\ *adj* [ME *impenetrabel,* fr. MF *impenetrable,* fr. L *impenetrabilis,* fr. *in-* + *penetrabilis* penetrable] **1 a :** incapable of being penetrated or pierced **b :** inaccessible to knowledge, reason, or sympathy : IMPERVIOUS **2 :** incapable of being comprehended : INSCRUTABLE **3 :** having the property of impenetrability — **im·pen·e·tra·ble·ness** *n* — **im·pen·e·tra·bly** \-blē\ *adv*

im·pen·i·tence \(ˈ)im-ˈpen-ə-tən(t)s\ *n, archaic* **:** the quality or state of being impenitent

im·pen·i·tent \-tənt\ *adj* [LL *impaenitent-, impaenitens,* fr. L *in-* + *paenitent-, paenitens* penitent] **:** not penitent — **im·pen·i·tent·ly** *adv*

1im·per·a·tive \im-ˈper-ət-iv\ *adj* [LL *imperativus,* fr. L *imperatus,* pp. of *imperare* to command — more at EMPEROR] **1 a :** of, relating to, or constituting the grammatical mood that expresses the will to influence the behavior of another **b :** expressive of a command, entreaty, or exhortation **c :** having power to restrain, control, and direct **2 :** not to be avoided or evaded : URGENT <an ~ duty> ***syn*** see MASTERFUL — **im·per·a·tive·ly** *adv* — **im·per·a·tive·ness** *n*

2imperative *n* **1 :** the imperative mood or a verb form or verbal phrase expressing it **2 :** something that is imperative: as **a :** COMMAND, ORDER **b :** RULE, GUIDE **c :** an obligatory act or duty **d :** an imperative judgment or proposition

im·pe·ra·tor \ˌim-pə-ˈrät-ər, -ˈrä-ˌtȯ(ə)r\ *n* [L — more at EMPEROR] **:** a commander in chief or emperor of the ancient Romans — **im·per·a·to·ri·al** \(ˌ)im-ˌper-ə-ˈtōr-ē-əl, -ˈtȯr-\ *adj*

im·per·ceiv·able \ˌim-pər-ˈsē-və-bəl\ *adj, archaic* **:** IMPERCEPTIBLE

im·per·cep·ti·ble \ˌim-pər-ˈsep-tə-bəl\ *adj* [MF, fr. ML *imperceptibilis,* fr. L *in-* + LL *perceptibilis* perceptible] **:** not perceptible by a sense or by the mind : extremely slight, gradual, or subtle — **im·per·cep·ti·bil·i·ty** \-ˌsep-tə-ˈbil-ət-ē\ *n* — **im·per·cep·ti·bly** \-ˈsep-tə-blē\ *adv*

im·per·cep·tive \ˌim-pər-ˈsep-tiv\ *adj*: not perceptive — **im·per·cep·tive·ness** *n*

im·per·cip·i·ence \-ˈsip-ē-ən(t)s\ *n* **:** the quality or state of being unperceptive

im·per·cip·i·ent \-ənt\ *adj* **:** not percipient : UNPERCEPTIVE

imperf *abbr* imperfect

1im·per·fect \(ˈ)im-ˈpər-fikt\ *adj* [ME *imperfit,* fr. MF *imparfait,* fr. L *imperfectus,* fr. *in-* + *perfectus* perfect] **1 :** not perfect: as **a :** DEFECTIVE **b :** DICLINOUS <an ~ flower> **c :** lacking or not involving sexual reproduction <the ~ stage of a fungus> **2 :** of, relating to, or constituting a verb tense used to designate a continuing state or an incomplete action esp. in the past **3 :** not enforceable at law — **im·per·fect·ly** \-fik-(t)lē\ *adv* — **im·per·fect·ness** \-fik(t)-nəs\ *n*

2imperfect *n* **:** an imperfect tense; *also* **:** the verb form expressing it

imperfect fungus *n* **:** a fungus (order Fungi Imperfecti) of which only the conidial stage is known

im·per·fec·tion \ˌim-pər-ˈfek-shən\ *n* **:** the quality or state of being imperfect; *also* **:** FAULT, BLEMISH

im·per·fec·tive \ˌim-pər-ˈfek-tiv *also* (ˈ)im-ˈpər-fik-\ *adj, of a verb form or aspect* **:** expressing action as incomplete or without reference to completion or as reiterated — compare PERFECTIVE

im·per·fo·rate \(ˈ)im-ˈpər-f(ə-)rət, -fə-ˌrāt\ *adj* **1 :** having no opening or aperture; *specif* **:** lacking the usual or normal opening **2** *of a stamp or a sheet of stamps* **:** lacking perforations or rouletting

1im·pe·ri·al \im-ˈpir-ē-əl\ *adj* [ME, fr. MF, fr. LL *imperialis,* fr. L *imperium* command, empire] **1 a :** of, relating to, or befitting an empire or an emperor **b (1) :** of or relating to the United Kingdom as distinguished from the constituent parts **(2) :** of or relating to the British Commonwealth and Empire **2 a :** SOVEREIGN **b :** REGAL, IMPERIOUS **3 :** of superior or unusual size or excellence **4 :** belonging to the official British series of weights and measures — see WEIGHT table — **im·pe·ri·al·ly** \-ə-lē\ *adv*

2imperial *n* **1** *cap* **:** an adherent or soldier of the Holy Roman emperor **2 :** EMPEROR **3 :** a size of paper usu. 23 x 31 inches **4** [fr. the beard worn by Napoleon III] **:** a pointed beard growing below the lower lip **5 :** something of unusual size or excellence

imperial 4

im·pe·ri·al·ism \im-ˈpir-ē-ə-ˌliz-əm\ *n* **1 :** imperial government, authority, or system **2 :** the policy, practice, or advocacy of extending the power and dominion of a nation esp. by direct territorial acquisitions or by gaining indirect control over the political or economic life of other areas — **im·pe·ri·al·ist** \-ləst\ *n or adj* — **im·pe·ri·al·is·tic** \-ˌpir-ē-ə-ˈlis-tik\ *adj* — **im·pe·ri·al·is·ti·cal·ly** \-ti-k(ə-)lē\ *adv*

imperial moth *n* **:** a large American moth (*Eacles imperialis*) marked with yellow, lilac, or purplish brown

im·per·il \im-ˈper-əl\ *vt* **-iled** *or* **-illed; -il·ing** *or* **-il·ling :** to bring into peril : ENDANGER — **im·per·il·ment** \-əl-mənt\ *n*

im·pe·ri·ous \im-ˈpir-ē-əs\ *adj* [L *imperiosus,* fr. *imperium*] **1 :** befitting or characteristic of one of eminent rank or attainments : COMMANDING, DOMINANT <an ~ manner> **b :** marked by arrogant assurance : DOMINEERING <her ~ arbitrariness> **2 :** intensely compelling : URGENT <the ~ problems of the new age —J. F. Kennedy> ***syn*** see MASTERFUL ***ant*** abject — **im·pe·ri·ous·ly** *adv* — **im·pe·ri·ous·ness** *n*

im·per·ish·able \(ˈ)im-ˈper-ish-ə-bəl\ *adj* **1 :** not perishable or subject to decay **2 :** enduring permanently <~ fame> — **im·per·ish·abil·i·ty** \(ˌ)im-ˌper-ish-ə-ˈbil-ət-ē\ *n* — **imperishable** *n* — **im·per·ish·able·ness** \(ˈ)im-ˈper-ish-ə-bəl-nəs\ *n* — **im·per·ish·ably** \-blē\ *adv*

im·pe·ri·um \im-ˈpir-ē-əm\ *n* [L — more at EMPIRE] **1 a :** supreme power or absolute dominion : CONTROL **b :** EMPIRE **2 :** the right to command or to employ the force of the state : SOVEREIGNTY

im·per·ma·nence \(ˈ)im-ˈpərm(-ə)-nən(t)s\ *n* **:** the quality or state of being impermanent

im·per·ma·nen·cy \-nən-sē\ *n* **:** IMPERMANENCE

im·per·ma·nent \-nənt\ *adj* **:** not permanent : TRANSIENT — **im·per·ma·nent·ly** *adv*

im·per·me·able \(ˈ)im-ˈpər-mē-ə-bəl\ *adj* [LL *impermeabilis,* fr. L *in-* + LL *permeabilis* permeable] **:** not permitting passage (as of a fluid) through its substance : IMPERVIOUS — **im·per·me·abil·i·ty** \(ˌ)im-ˌpər-mē-ə-ˈbil-ət-ē\ *n* — **im·per·me·able·ness** \(ˈ) im-ˈpər-mē-ə-bəl-nəs\ *n* — **im·per·meably** \-blē\ *adv*

im·per·mis·si·ble \ˌim-pər-ˈmis-ə-bəl\ *adj* **:** not permissible — **im·per·mis·si·bil·i·ty** \-ˌmis-ə-ˈbil-ət-ē\ *n* — **im·per·mis·si·bly** \-ˈmis-ə-blē\ *adv*

im·per·son·al \(ˈ)im-ˈpərs-nəl, -ᵊn-əl\ *adj* [LL *impersonalis,* fr. L *in-* + LL *personalis* personal] **1 a :** denoting the verbal action of an unspecified agent and hence used with no expressed subject (as *methinks*) or with a merely formal subject (as *rained* in *it rained*) **b** *of a pronoun* **:** INDEFINITE **2 a :** having no personal reference or connection <~ criticism> **b :** not engaging the human personality or emotions <the machine as compared with the hand tool is an ~ agency —John Dewey> **c :** not existing as a person : not having personality — **im·per·son·al·i·ty** \(ˌ)im-ˌpərs-ᵊn-ˈal-ət-ē\ *n* — **im·per·son·al·ly** \(ˈ)im-ˈpərs-nə-lē, -ᵊn-ə-lē\ *adv*

im·per·son·al·ize \(ˈ)im-ˈpərs-nə-ˌlīz, -ᵊn-ə-\ *vt* **:** to make impersonal — **im·per·son·al·iza·tion** \(ˌ)im-ˌpərs-nə-lə-ˈzā-shən, -ᵊn-ə-\ *n*

im·per·son·ate \im-ˈpərs-ᵊn-ˌāt\ *vt* **-at·ed; -at·ing :** to assume or act the character of : PERSONATE — **im·per·son·ation** \-ˌpərs-ᵊn-ˈā-shən\ *n* — **im·per·son·ator** \-ˈpərs-ᵊn-ˌāt-ər\ *n*

im·per·ti·nence \(ˈ)im-ˈpərt-ᵊn-ən(t)s, -ˈpərt-nən(t)s\ *n* **1 :** the quality or state of being impertinent: as **a :** IRRELEVANCE, INAPPROPRIATENESS **b :** INCIVILITY, INSOLENCE **2 :** an instance of impertinence

im·per·ti·nen·cy \-ən-sē, -nən-\ *n, pl* **-cies :** IMPERTINENCE

im·per·ti·nent \(ˈ)im-ˈpərt-ᵊn-ənt, -ˈpərt-nənt\ *adj* [ME, fr. MF, fr. LL *impertinent-, impertinens,* fr. L *in-* + *pertinent-, pertinens,* prp. of *pertinēre* to pertain] **1 :** not pertinent : IRRELEVANT **2 :** not restrained within due or proper bounds esp. of propriety or good taste <~ curiosity>; *also* **:** given to or characterized by insolent rudeness <an ~ answer> — **im·per·ti·nent·ly** *adv*

syn IMPERTINENT, OFFICIOUS, MEDDLESOME, INTRUSIVE, OBTRUSIVE *shared meaning element* **:** inclined to thrust oneself into the affairs of others

im·per·turb·able \ˌim-pər-ˈtər-bə-bəl\ *adj* [ME, fr. LL *imperturbabilis,* fr. L *in-* + *perturbare* to perturb] **:** marked by extreme calm, impassivity, and steadiness : SERENE ***syn*** see COOL ***ant*** choleric, touchy — **im·per·turb·abil·i·ty** \-ˌtər-bə-ˈbil-ət-ē\ *n* — **im·per·turb·ably** \-ˈtər-bə-blē\ *adv*

im·per·vi·ous \(ˈ)im-ˈpər-vē-əs\ *adj* [L *impervius,* fr. *in-* + *pervius* pervious] **1 a :** not allowing entrance or passage : IMPENETRABLE <a coat ~ to rain> **b :** not capable of being damaged or harmed <a carpet ~ to rough treatment> **2 :** not capable of being affected or disturbed <~ to criticism> — **im·per·vi·ous·ly** *adv* — **im·per·vi·ous·ness** *n*

im·pe·tig·i·nous \ˌim-pə-ˈtij-ə-nəs\ *adj* **:** of, relating to, or like impetigo

im·pe·ti·go \ˌim-pə-ˈtē-(ˌ)gō, -ˈtī-\ *n* [L, fr. *impetere* to attack — more at IMPETUS] **:** an acute contagious skin disease characterized by vesicles, pustules, and yellowish crusts

im·pe·trate \ˈim-pə-ˌtrāt\ *vt* **-trat·ed; -trat·ing** [L *impetratus,* pp. of *impetrare,* fr. *in-* + *patrare* to accomplish — more at PERPETRATE] **1 :** to obtain by request or entreaty **2 :** to ask for : ENTREAT — **im·pe·tra·tion** \ˌim-pə-ˈtrā-shən\ *n*

im·pet·u·os·i·ty \im-ˌpech-ə-ˈwäs-ət-ē\ *n, pl* **-ties 1 :** the quality or state of being impetuous **2 :** an impetuous action or impulse

im·pet·u·ous \im-ˈpech-(ə-)wəs\ *adj* [ME, fr. MF *impetueux,* fr. LL *impetuosus,* fr. L *impetus*] **1 :** marked by force and violence of movement or action <an ~ wind> **2 :** marked by impulsive vehemence or passion <an ~ temperament> ***syn*** see PRECIPITATE — **im·pet·u·ous·ly** *adv* — **im·pet·u·ous·ness** *n*

im·pe·tus \ˈim-pət-əs\ *n* [L, assault, impetus, fr. *impetere* to attack, fr. *in-* + *petere* to go to, seek — more at FEATHER] **1 a :** a driving force : IMPULSE **b :** INCENTIVE, STIMULUS **2 :** the property possessed by a moving body in virtue of its mass and its motion — used of bodies moving suddenly or violently to indicate the origin and intensity of the motion

im·pi·ety \(ˈ)im-ˈpī-ət-ē\ *n, pl* **-eties 1 :** the quality or state of being impious : IRREVERENCE **2 :** an impious act

im·pinge \im-ˈpinj\ *vb* **im·pinged; im·ping·ing** [L *impingere,* fr. *in-* + *pangere* to fasten, drive in — more at PACT] *vi* **1 :** to strike or dash esp. with a sharp collision <I heard the rain ~ upon the earth —James Joyce> **2 :** to come into a relationship as if impinging : make an impression <waiting for the germ of a new idea to ~ upon my mind —Phyllis Bentley> **3 :** ENCROACH, INFRINGE <~ on other people's rights> ~ *vt* **:** to cause (as a gas or a flame) to strike — **im·pinge·ment** \-ˈpinj-mənt\ *n*

im·pi·ous \ˈim-pē-əs, (ˈ)im-ˈpī-\ *adj* [L *impius,* fr. *in-* + *pius* pious] **:** not pious : lacking in reverence or proper respect (as for God or one's parents) : IRREVERENT — **im·pi·ous·ly** *adv*

imp·ish \ˈim-pish\ *adj* **:** of, relating to, or befitting an imp; *esp* **:** MISCHIEVOUS — **imp·ish·ly** *adv* — **imp·ish·ness** *n*

im·pla·ca·ble \(ˈ)im-ˈplak-ə-bəl, -ˈplā-kə-\ *adj* [MF or L; MF, fr. L *implacabilis,* fr. *in-* + *placabilis* placable] **:** not placable : not capable of being appeased, significantly changed, or mitigated <an ~ enemy> — **im·pla·ca·bil·i·ty** \(ˌ)im-ˌplak-ə-ˈbil-ət-ē, -ˌplā-kə-\ *n*

— **im·pla·ca·ble·ness** \(ˈ)im-ˈplak-ə-bəl-nəs, -ˈplā-kə-\ *n* — **im·pla·ca·bly** \-blē\ *adv*

[1]**im·plant** \im-ˈplant\ *vt* **1 a :** to fix or set securely or deeply <a ruby ~*ed* in the idol's forehead> **b :** to set permanently in the consciousness or habit patterns : INCULCATE **2 :** to insert in a living site (as for growth, slow release, or formation of an organic union) <subcutaneously ~*ed* hormone pellets> — **im·plant·able** \-ə-bəl\ *adj* — **im·plan·ta·tion** \ˌim-ˌplan-ˈtā-shən\ *n* — **im·plant·er** \im-ˈplant-ər\ *n*

[2]**im·plant** \ˈim-ˌplant\ *n* **:** something (as a graft or pellet) implanted in tissue

im·plau·si·ble \(ˈ)im-ˈplȯ-zə-bəl\ *adj* **:** not plausible : provoking disbelief — **im·plau·si·bil·i·ty** \(ˌ)im-ˌplȯ-zə-ˈbil-ət-ē\ *n* — **im·plau·si·bly** \(ˈ)im-ˈplȯ-zə-blē\ *adv*

im·plead \im-ˈplēd\ *vt* [ME *empleden,* fr. MF *emplaider,* fr. OF *emplaidier,* fr. *en-* + *plaidier* to plead] **:** to sue or prosecute at law

[1]**im·ple·ment** \ˈim-plə-mənt\ *n* [ME, fr. LL *implementum* action of filling up, fr. L *implēre* to fill up, fr. *in-* + *plēre* to fill — more at FULL] **1 :** an article serving to equip <the ~*s* of religious worship> **2 :** a tool or utensil forming part of equipment for work **3 :** one that serves as an instrument or tool <the partnership agreement does not seem to be a very potent ~ —H. B. Hoffman>

[2]**im·ple·ment** \-ˌment\ *vt* **1 :** to carry out : ACCOMPLISH; *esp* **:** to give practical effect to and ensure of actual fulfillment by concrete measures <plans not yet ~*ed* due to lack of funds> **2 :** to provide instruments or means of expression for — **im·ple·men·tal** \ˌim-plə-ˈment-ᵊl\ *adj* — **im·ple·men·ta·tion** \ˌim-plə-mən-ˈtā-shən, -ˌmen-\ *n*

im·pli·cate \ˈim-plə-ˌkāt\ *vt* **-cat·ed; -cat·ing** [L *implicatus,* pp. of *implicare* — more at EMPLOY] **1** *archaic* **:** to fold or twist together : ENTWINE **2 :** to involve as a consequence, corollary, or natural inference : IMPLY **3 a :** to bring into intimate or incriminating connection **b :** to involve in the nature or operation of something ***syn*** see INVOLVE

im·pli·ca·tion \ˌim-plə-ˈkā-shən\ *n* **1 a :** the act of implicating : the state of being implicated **b :** close connection; *esp* **:** an incriminating involvement **2 a :** the act of implying : the state of being implied **b (1) :** a logical relation between two propositions that fails to hold only if the first is true and the second is false **(2) :** a logical relationship between two propositions in which if the first is true the second is true **(3) :** a statement exhibiting a relation of implication **3 :** something implied — **im·pli·ca·tive** \ˈim-plə-ˌkāt-iv, im-ˈplik-ət-\ *adj* — **im·pli·ca·tive·ly** *adv* — **im·pli·ca·tive·ness** *n*

im·plic·it \im-ˈplis-ət\ *adj* [L *implicitus,* pp. of *implicare*] **1 a :** capable of being understood from something else though unexpressed : IMPLIED <an ~ assumption> **b :** involved in the nature or essence of something though not revealed, expressed, or developed : POTENTIAL <a sculptor may see different figures ~ in a block of stone —John Dewey> **2 :** being without doubt or reserve : UNQUESTIONING, ABSOLUTE — **im·plic·it·ly** *adv* — **im·plic·it·ness** *n*

implicit differentiation *n* **:** the process of finding the derivative of a dependent variable in an implicit function by differentiating each term separately, by expressing the derivative of the dependent variable as a symbol, and by solving the resulting expression for the symbol

implicit function *n* **:** a mathematical function that is not expressed with the dependent variable on one side of an equation and the one or more independent variables on the other <in the expression $x^2 + 3xy + y^2 = 0$, *y* is an *implicit function* of *x*>

im·plode \im-ˈplōd\ *vb* **im·plod·ed; im·plod·ing** [*in-* + *-plode* (as in *explode*)] *vi* **1 a :** to burst inward <a blow causing a vacuum tube to ~> **b :** to undergo violent compression <massive stars which ~> **2 a :** CENTRALIZE **b :** INTEGRATE ~ *vt* **:** to cause to implode

im·plore \im-ˈplō(ə)r, -ˈplȯ(ə)r\ *vt* **im·plored; im·plor·ing** [MF or L; MF *implorer,* fr. L *implorare,* fr. *in-* + *plorare* to cry out] **1 :** to call upon in supplication : BESEECH **2 :** to call or pray for earnestly : ENTREAT ***syn*** see BEG

im·plo·sion \im-ˈplō-zhən\ *n* [*in-* + *-plosion* (as in *explosion*)] **1 :** the action of imploding **2 :** the inrush of air in forming a suction stop **3 :** the act or action of bringing to or as if to a center; *also* **:** INTEGRATION <this ~ of cultures makes realistic for the first time the age-old vision of a world culture —Kenneth Keniston> — **im·plo·sive** \-ˈplō-siv, -ziv\ *adj or n*

im·ply \im-ˈplī\ *vt* **im·plied; im·ply·ing** [ME *emplien,* fr. MF *emplier,* fr. L *implicare*] **1** *obs* **:** ENFOLD, ENTWINE **2 :** to involve or indicate by inference, association, or necessary consequence rather than by direct statement <rights ~ obligations> **3 :** to contain potentially **4 :** to express indirectly <his silence *implied* consent> ***syn*** see SUGGEST ***ant*** express

im·po·lite \ˌim-pə-ˈlīt\ *adj* [L *impolitus,* fr. *in-* + *politus* polite] **:** not polite : RUDE — **im·po·lite·ly** *adv* — **im·po·lite·ness** *n*

im·pol·i·tic \(ˈ)im-ˈpäl-ə-ˌtik\ *adj***:** not politic : UNWISE — **im·po·lit·i·cal** \ˌim-pə-ˈlit-i-kəl\ *adj* — **im·po·lit·i·cal·ly** \-ˈlit-i-k(ə-)lē\ *adv* — **im·pol·i·tic·ly** \(ˈ)im-ˈpäl-ə-ˌtik-lē\ *adv*

im·pon·der·a·ble \(ˈ)im-ˈpän-d(ə-)rə-bəl\ *adj* [ML *imponderabilis,* fr. L *in-* + LL *ponderabilis* ponderable] **:** not ponderable : incapable of being weighed or evaluated with exactness — **im·pon·der·abil·i·ty** \(ˌ)im-ˌpän-d(ə-)rə-ˈbil-ət-ē\ *n* — **imponderable** *n* — **im·pon·der·able·ness** \(ˈ)im-ˈpän-d(ə-)rə-bəl-nəs\ *n* — **im·pon·der·ably** \-blē\ *adv*

im·pone \im-ˈpōn\ *vt* **im·poned; im·pon·ing** [L *imponere* to put upon, fr. *in-* + *ponere* to put — more at POSITION] *obs* **:** WAGER, BET

[1]**im·port** \im-ˈpō(ə)rt, -ˈpȯ(ə)rt, ˈim-ˌ\ *vb* [ME *importen,* fr. L *importare* to bring into, fr. *in-* + *portare* to carry — more at FARE] *vt* **1 a :** to bear or convey as meaning or portent : SIGNIFY **b** *archaic* **:** EXPRESS, STATE **c :** IMPLY **2 :** to bring from a foreign or external source; *esp* **:** to bring (as merchandise) into a place or country from another country **3** *archaic* **:** to be of importance to : CONCERN ~ *vi* **:** to be of consequence : MATTER — **im·port·able** \im-ˈpōrt-ə-bəl, -ˈpȯrt-, ˈim-ˌ\ *adj* — **im·port·er** *n*

[2]**im·port** \ˈim-ˌpō(ə)rt, -ˌpȯ(ə)rt\ *n* **1 :** PURPORT, SIGNIFICATION **2 :** IMPORTANCE; *esp* **:** relative importance <it is hard to determine the ~ of this decision> **3 :** something that is imported **4 :** IMPORTATION ***syn*** see MEANING, IMPORTANCE

im·por·tance \im-ˈpȯrt-ᵊn(t)s, *oftenest in South* -ən(t)s\ *n* **1 a :** the quality or state of being important : CONSEQUENCE **b :** an important aspect or bearing : SIGNIFICANCE **2** *obs* **:** IMPORT, MEANING **3** *obs* **:** IMPORTUNITY **4** *obs* **:** a weighty matter

syn IMPORTANCE, CONSEQUENCE, MOMENT, WEIGHT, SIGNIFICANCE, IMPORT *shared meaning element* **:** a quality or aspect felt to have great worth, significance, or influence ***ant*** unimportance

im·por·tan·cy \-ᵊn-sē, -ən-\ *n, archaic* **:** IMPORTANCE

im·por·tant \im-ˈpȯrt-ᵊnt, -ənt\ *adj* [MF, fr. OIt *importante,* fr. L *important-, importans,* prp. of *importare*] **1 :** marked by or indicative of significant worth or consequence : valuable in content or relationship **2 :** giving evidence of a feeling of self-importance **3** *obs* **:** IMPORTUNATE, URGENT — **im·por·tant·ly** *adv*

im·por·ta·tion \ˌim-ˌpōr-ˈtā-shən, -ˌpȯr-, -pər-\ *n* **1 :** the act or practice of importing **2 :** something imported

imported cabbageworm *n* **:** a small cosmopolitan white butterfly (*Pieris rapae*) or its larva which is a pest of cruciferous plants and esp. cabbage

imported fire ant *n* **:** a small brown So. American fire ant (*Solenopsis saevissima richteri*) that is a destructive pest in the southeastern U.S.

im·por·tu·nate \im-ˈpȯrch-(ə-)nət\ *adj* **1 :** TROUBLESOME **2 :** troublesomely urgent : overly persistent in request or demand — **im·por·tu·nate·ly** *adv* — **im·por·tu·nate·ness** *n*

[1]**im·por·tune** \ˌim-pər-ˈt(y)ün, im-ˈpȯr-chən\ *adj* [ME, fr. MF & L; MF *importun,* fr. L *importunus,* fr. *in-* + *-portunus* (as in *opportunus* fit) — more at OPPORTUNE] **:** IMPORTUNATE — **im·por·tune·ly** *adv*

[2]**importune** *vb* **-tuned; -tun·ing** *vt* **1 a :** to press or urge with troublesome persistence **b** *archaic* **:** to request or beg for urgently **2 :** ANNOY, TROUBLE ~ *vi* **:** to beg, urge, or solicit persistently or troublesomely ***syn*** see BEG — **im·por·tun·er** *n*

im·por·tu·ni·ty \ˌim-pər-ˈt(y)ü-nət-ē\ *n* **:** the quality or state of being importunate

im·pose \im-ˈpōz\ *vb* **im·posed; im·pos·ing** [MF *imposer,* fr. L *imponere,* lit., to put upon (perf. indic. *imposui*), fr. *in-* + *ponere* to put — more at POSITION] *vt* **1 a :** to establish or apply as compulsory : LEVY <~ a tax> **b :** to establish or make prevail by force <*imposed* himself as their leader> **2 a** *archaic* **:** PLACE, SET **b :** to arrange (typeset or plated pages) in order for printing as a signature **3 :** to palm off <~ fake antiques on the public> **4 :** to force into the company or on the attention of another <~ oneself on others> ~ *vi* **1 :** to take unwarranted advantage of something <*imposed* on his good nature> **2 :** to practice deception — **im·pos·er** *n*

im·pos·ing \im-ˈpō-ziŋ\ *adj* **:** impressive because of size, bearing, dignity, or grandeur : COMMANDING ***syn*** see GRAND ***ant*** unimposing — **im·pos·ing·ly** \-ziŋ-lē\ *adv*

im·po·si·tion \ˌim-pə-ˈzish-ən\ *n* **1 :** the act of imposing **2 :** something imposed: as **a :** LEVY, TAX **b :** an excessive or uncalled-for requirement or burden **3 :** DECEPTION

im·pos·si·bil·i·ty \(ˌ)im-ˌpäs-ə-ˈbil-ət-ē\ *n* **1 :** the quality or state of being impossible **2 :** something impossible

im·pos·si·ble \(ˈ)im-ˈpäs-ə-bəl\ *adj* [ME, fr. MF & L; MF, fr. L *impossibilis,* fr. *in-* + *possibilis* possible] **1 a :** incapable of being or of occurring **b :** felt to be incapable of being done, attained, or fulfilled : insuperably difficult : HOPELESS **2 a :** extremely undesirable : UNACCEPTABLE **b :** extremely awkward or difficult to deal with — **im·pos·si·ble·ness** *n* — **im·pos·si·bly** \-blē\ *adv*

[1]**im·post** \ˈim-ˌpōst\ *n* [MF, fr. ML *impositum,* fr. L, neut. of *impositus,* pp. of *imponere*] **:** something imposed or levied : TAX

[2]**impost** *n* [F *imposte,* deriv. of L *impositus*] **:** a block, capital, or molding from which an arch springs — see ARCH illustration

1 imposts

im·pos·tor *or* **im·pos·ter** \im-ˈpäs-tər\ *n* [LL *impostor,* fr. *impostus,* pp.] **:** one that assumes an identity or title not his own for the purpose of deception

im·pos·tume \im-ˈpäs-ˌchüm\ *or* **im·pos·thume** \-ˌth(y)üm\ *n* [ME *emposteme,* deriv. of Gk *apostēma,* fr. *aphistanai* to remove, fr. *apo-* + *histanai* to cause to stand — more at STAND] *archaic* **:** ABSCESS

im·pos·ture \im-ˈpäs-chər\ *n* [LL *impostura,* fr. L *impositus, impostus,* pp. of *imponere*] **1 :** the act or practice of deceiving by means of an assumed character or name **2 :** an instance of imposture <his behavior was an ~ of true piety> ***syn*** IMPOSTURE, FRAUD, SHAM, FAKE, HUMBUG, COUNTERFEIT *shared meaning element* **:** a thing made to seem other than it is

im·po·tence \ˈim-pət-ən(t)s\ *n* **:** the quality or state of being impotent

im·po·ten·cy \-ən-sē\ *n* **:** IMPOTENCE

im·po·tent \ˈim-pət-ənt\ *adj* [ME, fr. MF & L; MF, fr. L *impotent-, impotens,* fr. *in-* + *potent-, potens* potent] **1 a :** not potent : lacking in power, strength, or vigor : HELPLESS **b :** unable to copulate; *broadly* **:** STERILE — usu. used in males **2** *obs* **:** incapable of self-restraint : UNGOVERNABLE ***syn*** see STERILE ***ant*** virile, potent — **impotent** *n* — **im·po·tent·ly** *adv*

im·pound \im-ˈpau̇nd\ *vt* **1 a :** to shut up in or as if in a pound : CONFINE **b :** to seize and hold in the custody of the law **2 :** to collect and confine (water) in or as if in a reservoir

im·pound·ment \-ˈpau̇n(d)-mənt\ *n* **1 :** the act of impounding : the state of being impounded **2 :** a body of water formed by impounding

im·pov·er·ish \im-ˈpäv-(ə-)rish\ *vt* [ME *enpoverisen,* fr. MF *empovriss-,* stem of *empovrir,* fr. *en-* + *povre* poor — more at POOR] **1**

: to make poor **2 :** to deprive of strength, richness, or fertility by depleting or draining of something essential ***syn*** see DEPLETE — **im·pov·er·ish·er** *n* — **im·pov·er·ish·ment** \-mənt\ *n*

im·pov·er·ished *adj* **:** POOR, DEPRIVED

im·prac·ti·ca·ble \(ˈ)im-ˈprak-ti-kə-bəl\ *adj* **1 a :** not practicable : incapable of being performed or accomplished by the means employed or at command **b :** IMPASSABLE <an ~ road> **2** *archaic* : INTRACTABLE, UNMANAGEABLE — **im·prac·ti·ca·bil·i·ty** \(ˌ)im-ˌprak-ti-kə-ˈbil-ət-ē\ *n* — **im·prac·ti·ca·ble·ness** \(ˈ)im-ˈprak-ti-kə-bəl-nəs\ *n* — **im·prac·ti·ca·bly** \-blē\ *adv*

im·prac·ti·cal \(ˈ)im-ˈprak-ti-kəl\ *adj* **:** not practical: as **a :** not wise to put into or keep in practice or effect **b :** incapable of dealing sensibly or prudently with practical matters **c :** IMPRACTICABLE **d :** IDEALISTIC — **im·prac·ti·cal·i·ty** \(ˌ)im-ˌprak-ti-ˈkal-ət-ē\ *n* — **im·prac·ti·cal·ly** \(ˈ)im-ˈprak-ti-k(ə-)lē\ *adv* — **im·prac·ti·cal·ness** \-kəl-nəs\ *n*

im·pre·cate \ˈim-pri-ˌkāt\ *vb* **-cat·ed; -cat·ing** [L *imprecatus*, pp. of *imprecari*, fr. *in-* + *precari* to pray — more at PRAY] *vt* **:** to invoke evil on **:** CURSE ~ *vi* **:** to utter curses

im·pre·ca·tion \ˌim-pri-ˈkā-shən\ *n* **1 :** the act of imprecating **2** : CURSE — **im·pre·ca·to·ry** \ˈim-pri-kə-ˌtōr-ē, im-ˈprek-ə-, -ˌtȯr-\ *adj*

im·pre·cise \ˌim-pri-ˈsīs\ *adj* **:** not precise **:** INEXACT, VAGUE — **im·pre·cise·ly** *adv* — **im·pre·cise·ness** *n* — **im·pre·ci·sion** \-ˈsizh-ən\ *n*

¹im·preg·na·ble \im-ˈpreg-nə-bəl\ *adj* [ME *imprenable*, fr. MF, fr. *in-* + *prenable* vulnerable to capture, fr. *prendre* to take — more at PRIZE] **1 :** incapable of being taken by assault **:** UNCONQUERABLE **2 :** being beyond criticism or question **:** UNASSAILABLE — **im·preg·na·bil·i·ty** \(ˌ)im-ˌpreg-nə-ˈbil-ət-ē\ *n* — **im·preg·na·ble·ness** \im-ˈpreg-nə-bəl-nəs\ *n* — **im·preg·na·bly** \-blē\ *adv*

²impregnable *adj* **:** capable of being impregnated

im·preg·nant \im-ˈpreg-nənt\ *n* **:** a substance used for impregnating another substance

¹im·preg·nate \im-ˈpreg-nət\ *adj* **:** being filled or saturated

²im·preg·nate \im-ˈpreg-ˌnāt, ˈim-ˌ\ *vt* **-nat·ed; -nat·ing** [LL *impraegnatus*, pp. of *impraegnare*, fr. L *in-* + *praegnas* pregnant] **1 a** (1) **:** to make pregnant (2) **:** to introduce sperm cells into **b** : FERTILIZE **2 a :** to cause to be filled, imbued, permeated, or saturated **b :** to permeate thoroughly **:** INTERPENETRATE ***syn*** see SOAK — **im·preg·na·tion** \(ˌ)im-ˌpreg-ˈnā-shən\ *n* — **im·preg·na·tor** \im-ˈpreg-ˌnāt-ər, ˈim-ˌ\ *n*

im·pre·sa \im-ˈprā-zə, -sə\ *n* [It, lit., undertaking] **:** a device with a motto used in the 16th and 17th centuries; *broadly* **:** EMBLEM

im·pre·sa·rio \ˌim-prə-ˈsär-ē-ˌō, -ˈsar-, -ˈzär-\ *n, pl* **-ri·os** [It, fr. *impresa* undertaking, fr. *imprendere* to undertake, fr. (assumed) VL *imprehendere* — more at EMPRISE] **1 :** the projector, manager, or conductor of an opera or concert company **2 :** one who puts on or sponsors an entertainment (as a television show or sports event) **3 :** MANAGER, DIRECTOR

¹im·press \im-ˈpres\ *vb* [ME *impressen*, fr. L *impressus*, pp. of *imprimere*, fr. *in-* + *premere* to press — more at PRESS] *vt* **1 a** : to apply with pressure so as to imprint **b :** to produce (as a mark) by pressure **c :** to mark by or as if by pressure or stamping **2 a :** to produce a vivid impression of **b :** to affect esp. forcibly or deeply **:** INFLUENCE **3 a :** TRANSFER, TRANSMIT **b :** to transmit (force or motion) by pressure; *esp* **:** to apply (as voltage) to a circuit from an outside source ~ *vi* **:** to produce an impression ***syn*** see AFFECT

²im·press \ˈim-ˌpres *also* im-ˈ\ *n* **1 :** the act of impressing **2 a** : a mark made by pressure **:** IMPRINT **b :** an image of something formed by or as if by pressure; *esp* **:** SEAL **c :** a product of pressure or influence **3 :** a characteristic or distinctive mark : STAMP <the ~ of a fresh and vital intelligence is stamped . . . in his work —Lytton Strachey> **4 :** IMPRESSION, EFFECT <made his strongest ~ upon the country by his . . . two speeches —G. H. Haynes>

³im·press \im-ˈpres\ *vt* [*in-* + *press*] **1 :** to levy or take by force for public service; *esp* **:** to force into naval service **2 a :** to procure or enlist by forcible persuasion **b :** FORCE <~*ed* him into a white coat for the Christmas festivities —Nancy Hale>

⁴im·press \ˈim-ˌpres *also* im-ˈ\ *n* **:** IMPRESSMENT

im·press·ible \im-ˈpres-ə-bəl\ *adj* **:** capable of being impressed : SENSITIVE — **im·press·ibil·i·ty** \-ˌpres-ə-ˈbil-ət-ē\ *n* — **im·press·ibly** \-ˈpres-ə-blē\ *adv*

im·pres·sion \im-ˈpresh-ən\ *n* **1 :** the act of impressing: as **a** : an affecting by stamping or pressing **b :** a communicating of a mold, trait, or character by an external force or influence **2 :** the effect produced by impressing: as **a :** a stamp, form, or figure resulting from physical contact **b :** an imprint of the teeth and adjacent portions of the jaw for use in dentistry **c :** an esp. marked influence or effect on feeling, sense, or mind **3 a :** a characteristic, trait, or feature resulting from some influence <the ~ on behavior produced by the social milieu> **b :** an effect of alteration or improvement <the settlement left little ~ on the wilderness> **c :** a telling image impressed on the senses or the mind **4 a :** the amount of pressure with which an inked printing surface deposits its ink on the paper **b :** one instance of the meeting of a printing surface and the material being printed; *also* : a single print or copy so made **c :** all the copies of a publication (as a book) printed in one continuous operation from a single makeready **5 :** a usu. indistinct or imprecise notion or remembrance **6 a :** the first coat of color in painting **b :** a coat of paint for ornament or preservation **7 :** an imitation or representation of salient features in an artistic or theatrical medium; *esp* **:** an imitation in caricature of a noted personality as a form of theatrical entertainment ***syn*** see IDEA — **im·pres·sion·al** \-ˈpresh-nəl, -ən-ᵊl\ *adj*

im·pres·sion·able \im-ˈpresh-(ə-)nə-bəl\ *adj* **:** capable of being easily impressed: **a :** easily influenced **b :** easily molded : PLASTIC — **im·pres·sion·abil·i·ty** \-ˌpresh-(ə-)nə-ˈbil-ət-ē\ *n* — **im·pres·sion·able·ness** \-ˈpresh-(ə-)nə-bəl-nəs\ *n* — **im·pres·sion·ably** \-blē\ *adv*

im·pres·sion·ism \im-ˈpresh-ə-ˌniz-əm\ *n* **1** *often cap* **:** a theory or practice in painting esp. among French painters of about 1870 of depicting the natural appearances of objects by means of dabs or strokes of primary unmixed colors in order to simulate actual reflected light **2 a :** the depiction of scene, emotion, or character by details intended to achieve a vividness or effectiveness more by evoking subjective and sensory impressions than by recreating an objective reality **b :** a style of musical composition designed to create vague impressions and moods through rich and varied harmonies and timbres **3 :** a practice of presenting and elaborating one's subjective reactions to a work of art

im·pres·sion·ist \im-ˈpresh-(ə-)nəst\ *n* **1** *often cap* **:** one (as a painter) who practices or adheres to the theories of impressionism **2 :** an entertainer who does impressions

im·pres·sion·is·tic \(ˌ)im-ˌpresh-ə-ˈnis-tik\ *adj* **1** *or* **im·pres·sion·ist** \im-ˈpresh-(ə-)nəst\ **:** of, relating to, or constituting impressionism **2 :** based on or involving impression as distinct from knowledge or fact <mankind has often had to resort to ~, intuitive truth —R. H. Wolf> — **im·pres·sion·is·ti·cal·ly** \(ˌ)im-ˌpresh-ə-ˈnis-ti-k(ə-)lē\ *adv*

im·pres·sive \im-ˈpres-iv\ *adj* **:** making or tending to make a marked impression **:** stirring deep feeling esp. of awe or admiration ***syn*** see MOVING ***ant*** unimpressive — **im·pres·sive·ly** *adv* — **im·pres·sive·ness** *n*

im·press·ment \im-ˈpres-mənt\ *n* **:** the act of seizing for public use or of impressing into public service

im·pres·sure \im-ˈpresh-ər\ *n, archaic* **:** a mark made by pressure : IMPRESSION

im·prest \ˈim-ˌprest\ *n* [obs. *imprest* (to lend), prob. fr. It *imprestare*] **:** a loan or advance of money

im·pri·ma·tur \ˌim-prə-ˈmä-ˌtu̇(ə)r, im-ˈprim-ə-ˌt(y)u̇(ə)r\ *n* [NL, let it be printed, fr. *imprimere* to print, fr. L, to imprint, impress — more at IMPRESS] **1 a :** a license to print or publish esp. by Roman Catholic episcopal authority **b :** approval of a publication under circumstances of official censorship **2 :** SANCTION, APPROVAL <placed his ~ on the . . . ensemble's work —Howard Taubman>

im·pri·mis \im-ˈprī-məs, -ˈprē-\ *adv* [ME *imprimis*, fr. L *in primis* among the first (things)] **:** in the first place — used to introduce a list of items or considerations

¹im·print \im-ˈprint, ˈim-ˌ\ *vt* **1 :** to mark by or as if by pressure : IMPRESS **2 :** to fix indelibly or permanently (as on the memory)

²im·print \ˈim-ˌprint\ *n* [MF *empreinte*, fr. fem. of *empreint*, pp. of *empreindre* to imprint, fr. L *imprimere*] **:** something imprinted or printed: as **a :** a mark or depression made by pressure <the fossil ~ of a dinosaur's foot> **b :** a publisher's name often with address and date of publication printed at the foot of a title page **c :** an indelible distinguishing effect or influence <their work bears a sort of regional ~ —Malcolm Cowley>

im·print·ing \ˈim-ˌprint-iŋ, im-ˈ\ *n* **:** a behavior pattern speedily established early in the life of a member of a social species that involves recognition of and attraction to identification characters for its own kind or for a surrogate

im·pris·on \im-ˈpriz-ᵊn\ *vt* [ME *imprisonen*, fr. OF *emprisoner*, fr. *en-* + *prison*] **:** to put in or as if in prison **:** CONFINE — **im·pris·on·able** \-ˈpriz-ᵊn-ə-bəl, -ˈpriz-nə-\ *adj* — **im·pris·on·ment** \im-ˈpriz-ən-mənt\ *n*

im·prob·a·bil·i·ty \(ˌ)im-ˌpräb-ə-ˈbil-ət-ē\ *n* **1 :** the quality or state of being improbable **2 :** something improbable

im·prob·a·ble \(ˈ)im-ˈpräb(-ə)-bəl\ *adj* [MF or L; MF, fr. L *improbabilis*, fr. *in-* + *probabilis* probable] **:** unlikely to be true or to occur — **im·prob·a·ble·ness** *n* — **im·prob·a·bly** \-blē\ *adv*

¹im·promp·tu \im-ˈpräm(p)-(ˌ)t(y)ü\ *adj* [F, fr. *impromptu* extemporaneously, fr. L *in promptu* in readiness] **1 :** made or done on or as if on the spur of the moment **:** IMPROVISED **2 :** composed or uttered without previous preparation **:** EXTEMPORANEOUS <a short ~ speech> — **impromptu** *adv*

²impromptu *n* **1 :** something that is impromptu **2 :** a musical composition suggesting improvisation

im·prop·er \(ˈ)im-ˈpräp-ər\ *adj* [MF *impropre*, fr. L *improprius*, fr. *in-* + *proprius* proper] **:** not proper: as **a :** not in accord with fact, truth, or right procedure **:** INCORRECT <~ inference> **b** : not regularly or normally formed or not properly so called **c** : not suited to the circumstances, design, or end <~ medicine> **d :** not in accord with propriety, modesty, good manners, or good taste ***syn*** see INDECOROUS ***ant*** proper — **im·prop·er·ly** *adv* — **im·prop·er·ness** *n*

improper fraction *n* **:** a fraction whose numerator is equal to, larger than, or of equal or higher degree than the denominator

improper integral *n* **:** a definite integral whose region of integration includes a point at which the integrand is undefined or tends to infinity or whose region of integration does not have all limits finite

im·pro·pri·ety \ˌim-p(r)ə-ˈprī-ət-ē\ *n, pl* **-eties** [F or LL; F *impropriété*, fr. LL *improprietat-*, *improprietas*, fr. L *improprius*] **1** : the quality or state of being improper **2 :** an improper or indecorous act or remark; *esp* **:** an unacceptable use of a word or of language

im·prov·able \im-ˈprü-və-bəl\ *adj* **:** capable of improving or being improved — **im·prov·abil·i·ty** \-ˌprü-və-ˈbil-ət-ē\ *n* — **im·prov·ably** \-ˈprü-və-blē\ *adv*

im·prove \im-ˈprüv\ *vb* **im·proved; im·prov·ing** [AF *emprouer* to invest profitably, fr. OF *en-* + *prou* advantage, fr. LL *prode* — more at PROUD] *vt* **1 a :** to enhance in value or quality **:** make better **b :** to increase the value of (land or property) by betterment (as cultivation or the erection of buildings) **c :** to grade and drain (a road) and apply surfacing material other than pavement **2** *archaic* : EMPLOY, USE **3** : to use to good purpose ~ *vi* **1** : to advance or make progress in what is desirable **2** : to make useful additions or amendments <the movie version ~*s* on the original play> — **im·prov·er** *n*

syn IMPROVE, BETTER, HELP, AMELIORATE *shared meaning element* : to make more acceptable or bring nearer to some standard ***ant*** impair, worsen

im·prove·ment \im-ˈprüv-mənt\ *n* **1** : the act or process of improving **2 a** : the state of being improved; *esp* : enhanced value or excellence **b** : an instance of such improvement : something that enhances value or excellence

im·prov·i·dence \(ˈ)im-ˈpräv-əd-ən(t)s, -ə-ˌden(t)s\ *n* : the quality or state of being improvident

im·prov·i·dent \-əd-ənt, -ə-ˌdent\ *adj* [LL *improvident-, improvidens*, fr. L *in-* + *provident-, providens* provident] : not provident : not foreseeing and providing for the future — **im·prov·i·dent·ly** *adv*

im·pro·vi·sa·tion \(ˌ)im-ˌpräv-ə-ˈzā-shən, ˌim-prə-və-\ *n* **1** : the act or art of improvising **2** : something (as a musical or dramatic composition) improvised — **im·pro·vi·sa·tion·al** \-shnəl, -shən-ᵊl\ *adj*

im·prov·i·sa·tor \im-ˈpräv-ə-ˌzāt-ər\ *n* : one that improvises — **im·prov·i·sa·to·ri·al** \(ˌ)im-ˌpräv-ə-zə-ˈtōr-ē-əl, -ˈtȯr-\ *adj* — **im·pro·vi·sa·to·ry** \im-ˈpräv-ə-zə-ˌtōr-ē, ˌim-prə-ˈvī-zə-, -ˌtȯr-\ *adj*

im·pro·vi·sa·to·re \(ˌ)im-ˌpräv-ə-zə-ˈtōr-ē, ˌim-prə-ˌvē-zə-, -ˈtȯr-\ *n, pl* **-to·ri** \-ˈtōr-ē, -ˈtȯr-\ *or* **-tores** [It *improvvisatore*, fr. *improvvisare*] : one that improvises (as verse) usu. extemporaneously

im·pro·vise \ˌim-prə-ˈvīz, ˈim-prə-ˌ\ *vb* **-vised; -vis·ing** [F *improviser*, fr. It *improvvisare*, fr. *improvviso* sudden, fr L *improvisus*, lit., unforeseen, fr. *in-* + *provisus*, pp. of *providēre* to see ahead — more at PROVIDE] *vt* **1** : to compose, recite, or sing extemporaneously : EXTEMPORIZE **2** : to make, invent, or arrange offhand **3** : to fabricate out of what is conveniently on hand ~ *vi* : to improvise something — **im·pro·vis·er** *or* **im·pro·vi·sor** \-ˈvī-zər, -ˌvī-\ *n*

im·pru·dence \(ˈ)im-ˈprüd-ᵊn(t)s\ *n* **1** : the quality or state of being imprudent **2** : an imprudent act

im·pru·dent \-ᵊnt\ *adj* [ME, fr. L *imprudent-, imprudens*, fr. *in-* + *prudent-, prudens* prudent] : not prudent : lacking discretion — **im·pru·dent·ly** *adv*

im·pu·dence \ˈim-pyəd-ən(t)s\ *n* : the quality or state of being impudent

im·pu·dent \-ənt\ *adj* [ME, fr. L *impudent-, impudens*, fr. *in-* + *pudent-, pudens*, prp. of *pudēre* to feel shame] **1** *obs* : lacking modesty **2** : marked by contemptuous or cocky boldness or disregard of others : INSOLENT — **im·pu·dent·ly** *adv*

im·pu·dic·i·ty \ˌim-pyü-ˈdis-ət-ē\ *n* : lack of modesty : SHAMELESSNESS

im·pugn \im-ˈpyün\ *vt* [ME *impugnen*, fr. MF *impugner*, fr. L *inpugnare*, fr. *in-* + *pugnare* to fight — more at PUGNACIOUS] **1** *obs* **a** : ASSAIL **b** : RESIST **2** : to assail by words or arguments : oppose or attack as false or lacking integrity <~ a rival's motives> ***syn*** see DENY ***ant*** authenticate, advocate — **im·pugn·able** \-ˈpyü-nə-bəl\ *adj* — **im·pugn·er** \-nər\ *n*

im·puis·sance \(ˈ)im-ˈpwis-ᵊn(t)s, (ˈ)im-ˈpyü-ə-sən(t)s; ˌim-pyü-ˈis-ᵊn(t)s\ *n* [MF, fr. *in-* + *puissance*] : WEAKNESS, POWERLESSNESS

im·puis·sant \-ᵊnt, -sənt\ *adj* [F] : WEAK, POWERLESS

¹im·pulse \ˈim-ˌpəls\ *n* [L *impulsus*, fr. *impulsus*, pp. of *impellere* to impel] **1 a** : the act of driving onward with sudden force : IMPULSION **b** : motion produced by such an impulsion : IMPETUS **c** : a wave of excitation transmitted through tissues and esp. nerve fibers and muscles that results in physiological activity or inhibition **2 a** : a force so communicated as to produce motion suddenly **b** : INCENTIVE **c** : INSPIRATION, MOTIVATION **3 a** : a sudden spontaneous inclination or incitement to some usu. unpremeditated action **b** : a propensity or natural tendency usu. other than rational **4 a** : the product of the average value of a force and the time during which it acts being a quantity equal to the change in momentum produced by the force **b** : PULSE 4a ***syn*** see MOTIVE

²im·pulse \ˈim-ˌpəls, im-ˈ\ *vt* **im·pulsed; im·puls·ing** : to give an impulse to

impulse buying *n* : the buying of merchandise on impulse

im·pul·sion \im-ˈpəl-shən\ *n* **1 a** : the act of impelling : the state of being impelled **b** : an impelling force **c** : an onward tendency derived from an impulsion : IMPETUS **2** : IMPULSE 3a **3** : COMPULSION 2

im·pul·sive \im-ˈpəl-siv\ *adj* **1** : having the power of or actually driving or impelling **2** : actuated by or prone to act on impulse **3** : acting momentarily ***syn*** see SPONTANEOUS ***ant*** deliberate — **im·pul·sive·ly** *adv* — **im·pul·sive·ness** *n*

im·pu·ni·ty \im-ˈpyü-nət-ē\ *n* [MF or L; MF *impunité*, fr. L *impunitat-, impunitas*, fr. *impune* without punishment, fr. *in-* + *poena* pain] : exemption or freedom from punishment, harm, or loss

im·pure \(ˈ)im-ˈpyu̇(ə)r\ *adj* [F & L; F, fr. L *impurus*, fr. *in-* + *purus* pure] : not pure: as **a** : LEWD, UNCHASTE **b** : containing something unclean : FOUL <~ water> **c** : ritually unclean **d** : marked by an intermixture of foreign elements or by substandard, incongruous, or objectionable locutions **e** : mixed or impregnated with an extraneous and usu. inferior substance : ADULTERATED <an ~ chemical> **f** : MIXED, BASTARD <an ~ style of ornamentation> — **im·pure·ly** *adv* — **im·pure·ness** *n*

im·pu·ri·ty \(ˈ)im-ˈpyu̇r-ət-ē\ *n, pl* **-ties** **1** : the quality or state of being impure **2** : something that is impure or makes something else impure

im·pu·ta·tion \ˌim-pyə-ˈtā-shən\ *n* **1** : the act of imputing: as **a** : ATTRIBUTION, ASCRIPTION **b** : ACCUSATION **c** : INSINUATION **2** : something imputed — **im·pu·ta·tive** \im-ˈpyüt-ət-iv\ *adj* — **im·pu·ta·tive·ly** *adv*

im·pute \im-ˈpyüt\ *vt* **im·puted; im·put·ing** [ME *inputen*, fr. L *imputare*, fr. *in-* + *putare* to consider — more at PAVE] **1** : to lay the responsibility or blame for often falsely or unjustly : CHARGE **2** : to credit to a person or a cause : ATTRIBUTE <our vices as well as our virtues have been *imputed* to bodily derangement —B. N. Cardozo> ***syn*** see ASCRIBE — **im·put·abil·i·ty** \-ˌpyüt-ə-ˈbil-ət-ē\ *n* — **im·put·able** \-ˈpyüt-ə-bəl\ *adj*

¹in \(ˈ)in, ən, ᵊn\ *prep* [ME, fr. OE; akin to OHG *in* in, L *in*, Gk *en*] **1 a** — used as a function word to indicate inclusion, location, or position within limits <~ the lake> <wounded ~ the leg> <~ the summer> **b** : INTO 1 <went ~ the house> **2** — used as a function word to indicate means or instrumentality <written ~ pencil> <bound ~ leather> **3 a** — used as a function word to indicate limitation, qualification, or circumstance <alike ~ some respects> <left ~ a hurry> **b** : INTO 2a <broke ~ pieces> **4** — used as a function word to indicate purpose <said ~ reply> **5** — used as a function word to indicate the larger member of a ratio <one ~ six is eligible>

²in \ˈin\ *adv* **1 a (1)** : to or toward the inside esp. of a house or other building <come ~> **(2)** : to or toward some destination or particular place <flew ~ on the first plane> **(3)** : at close quarters : NEAR <play close ~> **b** : so as to incorporate <mix ~ the flour> — often used in combination <built-*in* bookcases> **c** : to or at its place <fit a piece ~> **2 a** : within a particular place; *esp* : within the customary place of residence or business **b** : in the position of participant, insider, or officeholder **c (1)** : on good terms **(2)** : in a specified relation <~ bad with the boss> **(3)** : in a position of assured or definitive success **d** : in vogue or season **e** *of an oil well* : in production **f** : in one's presence, possession, or control <after harvests are ~> — **in for** : certain to experience <*in for* a rude awakening>

³in \ˈin\ *adj* **1 a** : that is located inside or within <the ~ part> **b** : that is in position, operation, or power <the ~ party> **c** : INSIDE 2 **2** : that is directed or bound inward : INCOMING <the ~ train> **3 a** : keenly aware of and responsive to what is new and smart <the ~ crowd> **b** : extremely fashionable <the ~ thing to do>

⁴in \ˈin\ *n* **1** : one who is in office or power or on the inside <a matter of ~*s* versus outs> **2** : INFLUENCE, PULL <enjoyed some sort of ~ with the commandant —Henriette Roosenburg>

⁵in *abbr* **1** inch **2** inlet

In *symbol* indium

IN *abbr* Indiana

¹in- *or* **il-** *or* **im-** *or* **ir-** *prefix* [ME, fr. MF, fr. L; akin to OE *un-*] : not : NON-, UN- — usu. *il-* before *l* <*il*logical> and *im-* before *b*, *m*, or *p* <*im*balance> <*im*moral> <*im*practical> and *ir-* before *r* <*ir*reducible> and *in-* before other sounds <*in*conclusive>

²in- *or* **il-** *or* **im-** *or* **ir-** *prefix* [ME, fr. MF, fr. L, fr. *in* in, into] **1** : in : within : into : toward : on <*il*luviation> <*im*mingle> <*ir*radiance> — usu. *il-* before *l*, *im-* before *b*, *m*, or *p*, *ir-* before *r*, and *in-* before other sounds **2** : ¹EN- <*im*brute> <*im*peril> <*in*spirit>

¹-in \ən, ᵊn, ˌin\ *n suffix* [F *-ine*, fr. L *-ina*, fem. of *-inus* of or belonging to — more at -EN] **1 a** : neutral chemical compound <insul*in*> **b** : enzyme <pancreat*in*> **c** : antibiotic <penicil*lin*> **2** : ²-INE 1a, 1b <epinephr*in*> **3** : pharmaceutical product <niac*in*>

²-in \-ˌin\ *comb form* [²*in-* (as in *sit-in*)] **1** : organized public protest by means of or in favor of : demonstration <teach-*in*> <love-*in*> **2** : public group activity <sing-*in*>

-i·na \ˈē-nə\ *n suffix* [prob. fr. It *-ina*, dim. suffix, fr. L *-ina*] : musical instrument <concert*ina*>

in·abil·i·ty \ˌin-ə-ˈbil-ət-ē\ *n* [ME *inabilite*, fr. MF *inhabilité*, fr. *in-* + *habilité* ability] : lack of sufficient power, resources, or capacity <his ~ to do math>

in ab·sen·tia \ˌin-ab-ˈsen-ch(ē-)ə\ *adv* [L] : in absence <gave him the award *in absentia*>

in·ac·ces·si·ble \ˌin-ik-ˈses-ə-bəl, (ˌ)in-ˌak-\ *adj* [MF or LL; MF, fr. LL *inaccessibilis*, fr. L *in-* + LL *accessibilis* accessible] : not accessible — **in·ac·ces·si·bil·i·ty** \-ˌses-ə-ˈbil-ət-ē\ *n* — **in·ac·ces·si·bly** \-ˈses-ə-blē\ *adv*

in·ac·cu·ra·cy \(ˈ)in-ˈak-yə-rə-sē\ *n, pl* **-cies** **1** : the quality or state of being inaccurate **2** : MISTAKE, ERROR

in·ac·cu·rate \-yə-rət\ *adj* : not accurate : FAULTY — **in·ac·cu·rate·ly** \-yə-rət-lē, -yərt-\ *adv*

in·ac·tion \(ˈ)in-ˈak-shən\ *n* : lack of action or activity : IDLENESS

in·ac·ti·vate \(ˈ)in-ˈak-tə-ˌvāt\ *vt* : to make inactive — **in·ac·ti·va·tion** \(ˌ)in-ˌak-tə-ˈvā-shən\ *n*

in·ac·tive \(ˈ)in-ˈak-tiv\ *adj* : not active: as **a (1)** : SEDENTARY **(2)** : INDOLENT, SLUGGISH **b (1)** : being out of use **(2)** : relating to members of the armed forces who are not performing or available for military duties **(3)** *of a disease* : QUIESCENT **c (1)** : chemically inert **(2)** : optically neutral in polarized light **d** : biologically inert esp. because of the loss of some quality (as infectivity or antigenicity) — **in·ac·tive·ly** *adv* — **in·ac·tiv·i·ty** \(ˌ)in-ˌak-ˈtiv-ət-ē\ *n*

syn INACTIVE, IDLE, INERT, PASSIVE, SUPINE *shared meaning element* : not engaged in work or activity ***ant*** active, live

in·ad·e·qua·cy \(ˈ)in-ˈad-i-kwə-sē\ *n, pl* **-cies** **1** : the quality or state of being inadequate **2** : INSUFFICIENCY, DEFICIENCY

in·ad·e·quate \-kwət\ *adj* : not adequate : INSUFFICIENT — **in·ad·e·quate·ly** *adv* — **in·ad·e·quate·ness** *n*

in·ad·mis·si·ble \ˌin-əd-ˈmis-ə-bəl\ *adj* : not admissible — **in·ad·mis·si·bil·i·ty** \-ˌmis-ə-ˈbil-ət-ē\ *n* — **in·ad·mis·si·bly** \-ˈmis-ə-blē\ *adv*

in·ad·ver·tence \ˌin-əd-ˈvərt-ᵊn(t)s\ *n* [ML *inadvertentia*, fr. L *in-* + *advertent-, advertens*, prp. of *advertere* to advert] **1** : the fact or action of being inadvertent : INATTENTION **2** : a result of inattention : OVERSIGHT

in·ad·ver·ten·cy \-ᵊn-sē\ *n, pl* **-cies** : INADVERTENCE

in·ad·ver·tent \-ᵊnt\ *adj* [back-formation of *inadvertence*] **1** : not turning the mind to a matter : INATTENTIVE **2** : UNINTENTIONAL — **in·ad·ver·tent·ly** *adv*

in·ad·vis·able \ˌin-əd-ˈvī-zə-bəl\ *adj* : not advisable — **in·ad·vis·abil·i·ty** \-ˌvī-zə-ˈbil-ət-ē\ *n*

-i·nae \ˈī-(ˌ)nē\ *n pl suffix* [NL *-inae*, fr. L, fem. pl. of *-inus*] : members of the subfamily of — in all names of zoological subfamilies in recent classifications <Fel*inae*>

in·alien·able \(ˈ)in-ˈāl-yə-nə-bəl, -ˈā-lē-ə-nə-\ *adj* [prob. fr. F *inaliénable,* fr. *in-* + *aliénable* alienable] : incapable of being alienated, surrendered, or transferred <~ rights> — **in·alien·abil·i·ty** \(ˌ)in-ˌāl-yə-nə-ˈbil-ət-ē, -ˌā-lē-ə-nə-\ *n* — **in·alien·ably** \(ˈ)in-ˈāl-yə-nə-blē, -ˈā-lē-ə-nə-\ *adv*

in·al·ter·able \(ˈ)in-ˈȯl-t(ə-)rə-bəl\ *adj*: not alterable : UNALTERABLE — **in·al·ter·abil·i·ty** \(ˌ)in-ˌȯl-t(ə-)rə-ˈbil-ət-ē\ *n* — **in·al·ter·able·ness** \(ˈ)in-ˈȯl-t(ə-)rə-bəl-nəs\ *n* — **in·al·ter·ably** \-blē\ *adv*

in·amo·ra·ta \in-ˌam-ə-ˈrät-ə\ *n* [It *innamorata,* fr. fem. of *innamorato,* pp. of *innamorare* to inspire with love, fr. *in-* (fr. L) + *amore* love, fr. L *amor* — more at AMOROUS] : a woman with whom one is in love or has intimate relations

in–and–in \in-ən-ˈ(d)in\ *adv or adj* : in repeated generations of the same or closely related stock <families . . . of one blood through mating or marrying ~ —F. H. Giddings> <this freak of color in range-bred horses is the result of ~ breeding —Andy Adams>

[1]**inane** \in-ˈān\ *adj* **inan·er; -est** [L *inanis*] **1** : EMPTY, INSUBSTANTIAL **2** : lacking significance, meaning, or point : SILLY ***syn*** see INSIPID — **inane·ly** *adv* — **inane·ness** \-ˈān-nəs\ *n*

[2]**inane** *n* : void or empty space <a voyage into the limitless ~ —V. G. Childe>

in·an·i·mate \(ˈ)in-ˈan-ə-mət\ *adj* [LL *inanimatus,* fr. L *in-* + *animatus,* pp. of *animare* to animate] **1** : not animate: **a** : not endowed with life or spirit **b** : lacking consciousness or power of motion **2** : not animated or lively : DULL — **in·an·i·mate·ly** *adv* — **in·an·i·mate·ness** *n*

in·a·ni·tion \ˌin-ə-ˈnish-ən\ *n* : the quality or state of being empty: **a** : the loss of vitality that results from lack of food and water **b** : the absence or loss of social, moral, or intellectual vitality or vigor : LETHARGY

inan·i·ty \in-ˈan-ət-ē\ *n, pl* **-ties 1** : the quality or state of being inane: as **a** : lack of substance : EMPTINESS **b** : vapid, pointless, or fatuous character : SHALLOWNESS **2** : something that is inane

in·ap·par·ent \ˌin-ə-ˈpar-ənt, -ˈper-\ *adj* : not apparent — **in·ap·par·ent·ly** *adv*

in·ap·peas·able \ˌin-ə-ˈpē-zə-bəl\ *adj* : UNAPPEASABLE

in·ap·pe·tence \(ˈ)in-ˈap-ət-ən(t)s\ *n* : loss or lack of appetite

in·ap·pli·ca·ble \(ˈ)in-ˈap-li-kə-bəl *also* ˌin-ə-ˈplik-ə-\ *adj* : not applicable : IRRELEVANT — **in·ap·pli·ca·bil·i·ty** \(ˌ)in-ˌap-li-kə-ˈbil-ət-ē *also* ˌin-ə-ˌplik-ə-\ *n* — **in·ap·pli·ca·bly** \(ˈ)in-ˈap-li-kə-blē *also* ˌin-ə-ˈplik-ə-\ *adv*

in·ap·po·site \(ˈ)in-ˈap-ə-zət\ *adj* : not apposite — **in·ap·po·site·ly** *adv* — **in·ap·po·site·ness** *n*

in·ap·pre·cia·ble \ˌin-ə-ˈprē-shə-bəl\ *adj* [prob. fr. F *inappréciable,* fr. MF *inappreciable,* fr. *in-* + *appreciable*] : too small to be perceived <an ~ difference in the temperature> — **in·ap·pre·cia·bly** \-blē\ *adv*

in·ap·pre·cia·tive \ˌin-ə-ˈprē-shət-iv *also* -shē-ˌāt-\ *adj* : not appreciative — **in·ap·pre·cia·tive·ly** *adv* — **in·ap·pre·cia·tive·ness** *n*

in·ap·proach·able \ˌin-ə-ˈprō-chə-bəl\ *adj* : not approachable : INACCESSIBLE

in·ap·pro·pri·ate \ˌin-ə-ˈprō-prē-ət\ *adj* : not appropriate : UNSUITABLE — **in·ap·pro·pri·ate·ly** *adv* — **in·ap·pro·pri·ate·ness** *n*

in·apt \(ˈ)in-ˈapt\ *adj* : not apt: **a** : not suitable **b** : INEPT — **in·apt·ly** \-ˈap-(t)lē\ *adv* — **in·apt·ness** \-ˈap(t)-nəs\ *n*

in·ap·ti·tude \-ˈap-tə-ˌt(y)üd\ *n* : lack of aptitude

in·ar·gu·able \(ˈ)in-ˈär-gyə-wə-bəl\ *adj* : not arguable — **in·ar·gu·ably** \-blē\ *adv*

in·ar·tic·u·late \ˌin-(ˌ)är-ˈtik-yə-lət\ *adj* [LL *inarticulatus,* fr. L *in-* + *articulatus,* pp. of *articulare* to utter distinctly — more at ARTICULATE] **1 a** *of a sound* : uttered or formed without the definite articulations of intelligible speech **b** (1) : incapable of speech esp. under stress of emotion : MUTE (2) : incapable of being expressed by speech <~ fear> (3) : not voiced or expressed : UNSPOKEN <society functions on many ~ premises> **2** : incapable of giving coherent, clear, or effective expression to one's ideas or feelings **3** [NL *inarticulatus,* fr. L *in-* + NL *articulatus* articulate] : lacking a shell hinge — used esp. of a brachiopod — **in·ar·tic·u·late·ly** *adv* — **in·ar·tic·u·late·ness** *n*

in·ar·tis·tic \ˌin-är-ˈtis-tik\ *adj* **1** : not conforming to the principles of art **2** : not appreciative of art — **in·ar·tis·ti·cal·ly** \-ti-k(ə-)lē\ *adv*

in·as·much as \ˌin-əz-ˌməch-əz\ *conj* **1** : in the degree that : insofar as **2** : in view of the fact that : SINCE

in·at·ten·tion \ˌin-ə-ˈten-chən\ *n* : failure to pay attention : DISREGARD

in·at·ten·tive \-ˈtent-iv\ *adj* : not attentive — **in·at·ten·tive·ly** *adv* — **in·at·ten·tive·ness** *n*

in·au·di·ble \(ˈ)in-ˈȯd-ə-bəl\ *adj* [LL *inaudibilis,* fr. L *in-* + LL *audibilis* audible] : not audible — **in·au·di·bil·i·ty** \(ˌ)in-ˌȯd-ə-ˈbil-ət-ē\ *n* — **in·au·di·bly** \(ˈ)in-ˈȯd-ə-blē\ *adv*

[1]**in·au·gu·ral** \in-ˈȯ-gyə-rəl, -g(ə-)rəl\ *adj* **1** : of or relating to an inauguration **2** : marking a beginning : first in a projected series

[2]**inaugural** *n* **1** : an inaugural address **2** : INAUGURATION

in·au·gu·rate \in-ˈȯ-g(y)ə-ˌrāt\ *vt* **-rat·ed; -rat·ing** [L *inauguratus,* pp. of *inaugurare,* lit., to practice augury, fr. *in-* + *augurare* to augur; fr. the rites connected with augury] **1** : to induct into an office with suitable ceremonies **2 a** : to dedicate ceremoniously : observe formally the beginning of **b** : to bring about the beginning of ***syn*** see BEGIN — **in·au·gu·ra·tor** \-ˌrāt-ər\ *n*

in·au·gu·ra·tion \-ˌȯ-g(y)ə-ˈrā-shən\ *n* : an act of inaugurating; *esp* : a ceremonial induction into office

Inauguration Day *n* : January 20 following a presidential election on which the president of the U.S. is inaugurated

in·aus·pi·cious \ˌin-ˌȯ-ˈspish-əs\ *adj* : not auspicious — **in·aus·pi·cious·ly** *adv* — **in·aus·pi·cious·ness** *n*

in·au·then·tic \ˌin-ˌȯ-ˈthent-ik\ *adj* : not authentic — **in·au·then·tic·i·ty** \ˌin-ˌȯ-ˌthen-ˈtis-ət-ē, -thən-\ *n*

[1]**in–be·tween** \ˌin-bi-ˈtwēn\ *n* : INTERMEDIATE <for the novice, expert, or ~>

[2]**in–between** *adj* : INTERMEDIATE <took an ~ stand on the issue>

[1]**in between** *adv* : BETWEEN <neither liberal nor conservative but fell somewhere *in between*>

[2]**in between** *prep* : BETWEEN <likes wine before, after, and *in between* meals>

[1]**in·board** \ˈin-ˌbō(ə)rd, -ˌbȯ(ə)rd\ *adv* **1** : inside the line of a ship's bulwarks or hull : toward the center line of a ship **2** : toward the inside **3** : in a position closer or closest to the longitudinal axis of an aircraft

[2]**inboard** *adj* : located, moving, or being inboard <an ~ engine>; *also* : having an inboard engine <~ boats>

in·born \ˈin-ˈbȯ(ə)rn\ *adj* **1** : born in or with one : NATURAL **2** : HEREDITARY, INHERITED ***syn*** see INNATE

in·bound \ˈin-ˌbau̇nd\ *adj* : inward bound

in·bounds \ˌin-ˌbau̇n(d)z\ *adj* : of or relating to putting a basketball in play by passing it onto the court from out of bounds <~ pass>

inbounds line *n* : either of two broken lines running the length of a football field at right angles to the yard lines and dividing the field into three parts

in·breathe \ˈin-ˈbrēth\ *vt* : to breathe (something) in : INHALE

in·bred \ˈin-ˈbred\ *adj* **1** : rooted and ingrained in one's nature as deeply as if implanted by heredity <an ~ love of freedom> **2 a** : produced by selective breeding **b** [fr. pp. of *inbreed*] : subjected to or produced by inbreeding ***syn*** see INNATE

in·breed \ˈin-ˈbrēd\ *vt* **-bred** \-ˈbred\; **-breed·ing** : to subject to or engage in inbreeding — **in·breed·er** \-ˌbrēd-ər\ *n*

in·breed·ing \ˈin-ˌbrēd-iŋ\ *n* **1** : the interbreeding of closely related individuals esp. to preserve and fix desirable characters of and to eliminate unfavorable characters from a stock **2** : confinement to a narrow range or a local or limited field of choice

in·built \ˈin-ˈbilt\ *adj* : BUILT-IN

inc *abbr* **1** incomplete **2** incorporated **3** increase

In·ca \ˈiŋ-kə\ *n* [Sp, fr. Quechua *inka* king, prince] **1 a** : a member of the Quechuan peoples of Peru maintaining an empire until the Spanish conquest **b** : a king or noble of this empire **2** : a member of any people under Inca influence — **In·ca·ic** \in-ˈkā-ik\ *adj* — **In·can** \ˈiŋ-kən\ *adj*

in·cal·cu·la·ble \(ˈ)in-ˈkal-kyə-lə-bəl\ *adj* : not capable of being calculated: as **a** : very great **b** : UNPREDICTABLE, UNCERTAIN — **in·cal·cu·la·bil·i·ty** \(ˌ)in-ˌkal-kyə-lə-ˈbil-ət-ē\ *n* — **in·cal·cu·la·bly** \(ˈ)in-ˈkal-kyə-lə-blē\ *adv*

in·ca·les·cence \ˌin-kə-ˈles-ᵊn(t)s, ˌiŋ-\ *n* [L *incalescere* to become warm, fr. *in-* + *calescere* to become warm, fr. *calēre* to be warm — more at LEE] : a growing warm or ardent — **in·ca·les·cent** \-ᵊnt\ *adj*

in camera *adv* [NL, lit., in a chamber] : in private : SECRETLY

in·can·desce \ˌin-kən-ˈdes\ *vb* **-desced; -desc·ing** [L *incandescere*] *vi* : to be or become incandescent ~ *vt* : to cause to become incandescent

in·can·des·cence \ˌin-kən-ˈdes-ᵊn(t)s\ *n* : the quality or state of being incandescent; *esp* : emission by a hot body of radiation that makes it visible

in·can·des·cent \-ᵊnt\ *adj* [prob. fr. F, fr. L *incandescent-, incandescens,* prp. of *incandescere* to become hot, fr. *in-* + *candescere* to become hot, fr. *candēre* to glow — more at CANDID] **1 a** : white, glowing, or luminous with intense heat **b** : strikingly bright, radiant, or clear **c** : marked by brilliance esp. of expression <~ wit> **d** : characterized by glowing zeal : ARDENT <~ affection> **2 a** : of, relating to, or being light produced by incandescence **b** : producing light by incandescence — **in·can·des·cent·ly** *adv*

incandescent lamp *n* : an electric lamp in which a filament gives off light when heated to incandescence by an electric current

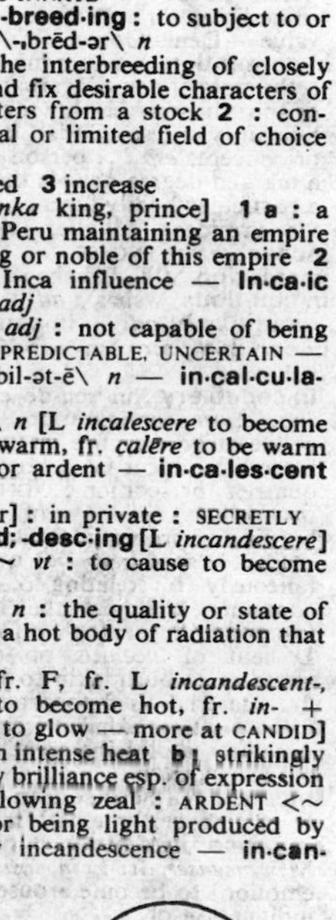

incandescent lamp: *1* gas or vacuum, *2* filament, *3* support, *4* button, *5* inner leads, *6* button rod, *7* exhaust tube, *8* base shell, *9* solder

in·can·ta·tion \ˌin-ˌkan-ˈtā-shən\ *n* [ME *incantacioun,* fr. MF *incantation,* fr. LL *incantation-, incantatio,* fr. L *incantatus,* pp. of *incantare* to enchant — more at ENCHANT] : a use of spells or verbal charms spoken or sung as a part of a ritual of magic; *also* : a written or recited formula of words designed to produce a particular effect — **in·can·ta·tion·al** \-shnəl, -shən-ᵊl\ *adj* — **in·can·ta·to·ry** \in-ˈkant-ə-ˌtōr-ē, -ˌtȯr-\ *adj*

in·ca·pa·ble \(ˈ)in-ˈkā-pə-bəl\ *adj* [MF, fr. *in-* + *capable*] **1** : lacking capacity, ability, or qualification for the purpose or end in view: as **a** *archaic* : not able to take in, hold, or keep **b** *archaic* : not receptive **c** : not being in a state or of a kind to admit : INSUSCEPTIBLE **d** : not able or fit for the doing or performance : INCOMPETENT **2** : lacking legal qualification or power (as by reason of mental incompetence) : DISQUALIFIED — **in·ca·pa·bil·i·ty** \(ˌ)in-ˌkā-pə-ˈbil-ət-ē\ *n* — **in·ca·pa·ble·ness** \(ˈ)in-ˈkā-pə-bəl-nəs\ *n* — **in·ca·pa·bly** \-blē\ *adv*

in·ca·pac·i·tate \ˌin-kə-ˈpas-ə-ˌtāt\ *vt* **-tat·ed; -tat·ing 1** : to deprive of capacity or natural power : DISABLE **2** : to make legally incapable or ineligible — **in·ca·pac·i·ta·tion** \-ˌpas-ə-ˈtā-shən\ *n* — **in·ca·pac·i·ta·tor** \-ˈpas-ə-ˌtāt-ər\ *n*

in·ca·pac·i·ty \ˌin-kə-ˈpas-ət-ē, -ˈpas-tē\ *n, pl* **-ties** [F *incapacité,* fr. MF, fr. *in-* + *capacité* capacity] : the quality or state of being incapable; *esp* : lack of physical or intellectual power or of natural or legal qualifications

ə abut	ᵊ kitten	ər further	a back	ā bake	ä cot, cart
au̇ out	ch chin	e less	ē easy	g gift	i trip
j joke	ŋ sing	ō flow	ȯ flaw	ȯi coin	th thin
ü loot	u̇ foot	y yet	yü few	yu̇ furious	zh vision

ī life; th̲ this

in·car·cer·ate \in-ˈkär-sə-ˌrāt\ *vt* **-at·ed; -at·ing** [L *incarceratus,* pp. of *incarcerare,* fr. *in-* + *carcer* prison] **1 :** to put in prison **2 :** to subject to confinement — **in·car·cer·a·tion** \(ˌ)in-ˌkär-sə-ˈrā-shən\ *n*

in·car·di·na·tion \(ˌ)in-ˌkärd-ᵊn-ˈā-shən\ *n* [LL *incardination-, incardinatio,* fr. *incardinatus,* pp. of *incardinare* to ordain as chief priest, fr. *in-* 2in- + *cardinalis* principal — more at CARDINAL] **:** the formal acceptance by a diocese of a clergyman from another diocese

1in·car·na·dine \in-ˈkär-nə-ˌdīn, -ˌdēn, -dən\ *adj* [MF *incarnadin,* fr. OIt *incarnadino,* fr. *incarnato* flesh-colored, fr. LL *incarnatus*] **1 :** of the color flesh **2 :** RED; *esp* **:** BLOODRED

2incarnadine *vt* **-dined; -din·ing :** to make incarnadine **:** REDDEN

1in·car·nate \in-ˈkär-nət, -ˌnāt\ *adj* [ME *incarnat,* fr. LL *incarnatus,* pp. of *incarnare* to incarnate, fr. L *in-* + *carn-, caro* flesh — more at CARNAL] **1 a :** invested with bodily and esp. human nature and form **b :** made manifest or comprehensible **:** EMBODIED <a fiend ~> **2 :** INCARNADINE <~ clover>

2in·car·nate \in-ˈkär-ˌnāt, ˈin-ˌ\ *vt* **-nat·ed; -nat·ing :** to make incarnate: as **a :** to give bodily form and substance to **b** (1) **:** to give a concrete or actual form to **:** ACTUALIZE <scientific laws were ~ in the Machine —Stringfellow Barr> (2) **:** to constitute an embodiment or type of <no one culture ~*s* every important human value —Denis Goulet>

in·car·na·tion \ˌin-ˌkär-ˈnā-shən\ *n* **1 :** the act of incarnating **:** the state of being incarnate **2 a** (1) **:** the embodiment of a deity or spirit in some earthly form (2) *cap* **:** the union of divinity with humanity in Jesus Christ **b :** a concrete or actual form of a quality or concept; *esp* **:** a person showing a trait or typical character to a marked degree <she is the ~ of goodness> **3 :** time passed in a particular bodily form or state <in another ~ he might be a first vice-president —Walter Teller>

incase *var of* ENCASE

in·cau·tion \(ˈ)in-ˈkȯ-shən\ *n* **:** lack of caution **:** HEEDLESSNESS

in·cau·tious \-shəs\ *adj* **:** lacking in caution **:** CARELESS — **in·cau·tious·ly** *adv* — **in·cau·tious·ness** *n*

in·cen·di·a·rism \in-ˈsen-dē-ə-ˌriz-əm\ *n* **:** incendiary action or behavior

1in·cen·di·ary \in-ˈsen-dē-ˌer-ē\ *n, pl* **-ar·ies** [L *incendiarius,* fr. *incendium* conflagration, fr. *incendere*] **1 a :** a person who deliberately sets fire to a building or other property **b :** an incendiary agent (as a bomb) **2 :** a person who excites factions, quarrels, or sedition **:** AGITATOR

2incendiary *adj* **1 :** of, relating to, or involving a deliberate burning of property **2 :** tending to excite or inflame **:** INFLAMMATORY <~ speeches> **3 a :** igniting combustible materials spontaneously **b :** relating to, being, or involving the use of a missile containing chemicals that ignite on bursting or on contact

1in·cense \ˈin-ˌsen(t)s\ *n* [ME *encens,* fr. OF, fr. LL *incensum,* fr. L, neut. of *incensus,* pp. of *incendere* to set on fire, fr. *in-* + *-cendere* to burn; akin to L *candēre* to glow — more at CANDID] **1 :** material used to produce a fragrant odor when burned **2 :** the perfume exhaled from some spices and gums when burned; *broadly* **:** a pleasing scent **3 :** pleasing attention **:** FLATTERY ***syn*** see FRAGRANCE

2incense *vt* **in·censed; in·cens·ing 1 :** to apply or offer incense to **2 :** to perfume with incense

3in·cense \in-ˈsen(t)s\ *vt* **in·censed; in·cens·ing** [ME *encensen,* fr. MF *incenser,* fr. L *incensus*] **1** *archaic* **:** to cause (a passion or emotion) to become aroused **2 :** to arouse the extreme anger or indignation of

in·cen·tive \in-ˈsent-iv\ *n* [ME, fr. LL *incentivum,* fr. neut. of *incentivus* stimulating, fr. L, setting the tune, fr. *incentus,* pp. of *incinere* to set the tune, fr. *in-* + *canere* to sing — more at CHANT] **:** something that incites or has a tendency to incite to determination or action ***syn*** see MOTIVE — **incentive** *adj*

in·cept \in-ˈsept\ *vt* [L *in-* + *-ceptus,* fr. *captus,* pp. of *capere* to take] **:** to take in; *esp* **:** INGEST — **in·cep·tor** \-ˈsep-tər\ *n*

in·cep·tion \in-ˈsep-shən\ *n* [L *inception, inceptio,* fr. *inceptus,* pp. of *incipere* to begin, fr. *in-* + *capere* to take — more at HEAVE] **:** an act, process, or instance of beginning **:** COMMENCEMENT ***syn*** see ORIGIN

1in·cep·tive \in-ˈsep-tiv\ *n* **:** an inchoative verb

2inceptive *adj* **1 :** of or relating to a beginning **2 :** INCHOATIVE 2 — **in·cep·tive·ly** *adv*

in·cer·ti·tude \(ˈ)in-ˈsərt-ə-ˌt(y)üd\ *n* [MF, fr. LL *incertitudo,* fr. L *in-* + LL *certitudo* certitude] **:** UNCERTAINTY: **a :** absence of assurance or confidence **:** DOUBT **b :** the quality or state of being unstable or insecure

in·ces·san·cy \(ˈ)in-ˈses-ᵊn-sē\ *n* **:** the quality or state of being incessant

in·ces·sant \(ˈ)in-ˈses-ᵊnt\ *adj* [ME *incessaunt,* fr. LL *incessant-, incessans,* fr. L *in-* + *cessant-, cessans,* prp. of *cessare* to delay — more at CEASE] **:** continuing or following without interruption **:** UNCEASING ***syn*** see CONTINUOUS ***ant*** intermittent — **in·ces·sant·ly** *adv*

in·cest \ˈin-ˌsest\ *n* [ME, fr. L *incestum,* fr. neut. of *incestus* impure, fr. *in-* + *castus* pure — more at CASTE] **:** sexual intercourse between persons so closely related that they are forbidden by law to marry; *also* **:** the statutory crime of such a relationship

in·ces·tu·ous \in-ˈses(h)-chə-wəs\ *adj* **1 :** constituting or involving incest **2 :** guilty of incest — **in·ces·tu·ous·ly** *adv* — **in·ces·tu·ous·ness** *n*

1inch \ˈinch\ *n* [ME, fr. OE *ynce,* fr. L *uncia* — more at OUNCE] **1 :** a unit of length equal to 1/36 yard — see WEIGHT table **2 :** a small amount, distance, or degree <is like cutting a dog's tail off by ~*es* —Milton Friedman> **3** *pl* **:** STATURE, HEIGHT **4 a :** a fall (as of rain or snow) sufficient to cover a surface or to fill a gauge to the depth of one inch **b :** a degree of atmospheric or other pressure sufficient to balance the weight of a column of liquid (as mercury) one inch high in a barometer or manometer **c :** WATER-INCH — **every inch :** to the utmost degree <looks *every inch* a winner> — **within an inch of one's life :** in a very thorough manner **:** SOUNDLY <trounced him *within an inch of his life*>

2inch *vi* **:** to move by small degrees <the long line of people ~*ing* up the stairs> ~ *vt* **:** to cause to move slowly <sooner or later they begin ~*ing* prices back up —*Forbes*>

3inch *n* [ME, fr. ScGael *innis*] *chiefly Scot* **:** ISLAND

inched \ˈincht\ *adj* **:** measuring a specified number of inches

-inch·er \ˈin-chər\ *comb form* **:** one that has a dimension of a specified number of inches

in chief *adv* **:** heading a staff **:** LEADING — usu. used in combination <general-*in-chief*> <physician-*in-chief*>

inch·meal \ˈinch-ˌmēl, -ˈmē(ə)l\ *adv* [1*inch* + *-meal* (as in *piecemeal*)] **:** little by little **:** GRADUALLY

in·cho·ate \in-ˈkō-ət, ˈin-kə-ˌwāt\ *adj* [L *inchoatus,* pp. of *inchoare,* lit., to hitch up, fr. *in-* + *cohum* strap fastening a plow beam to the yoke] **:** being only partly in existence or operation; *esp* **:** imperfectly formed or formulated <misty, ~ suspicions that all is not well with the nation —J. M. Perry> — **in·cho·ate·ly** *adv* — **in·cho·ate·ness** *n*

in·cho·ative \in-ˈkō-ət-iv\ *adj* **1 :** INITIAL, FORMATIVE <the ~ stages> **2 :** denoting the beginning of an action, state, or occurrence — used of verbs — **inchoative** *n* — **in·cho·ative·ly** *adv*

inch·worm \ˈinch-ˌwərm\ *n* **:** LOOPER 1

in·ci·dence \ˈin(t)-səd-ən(t)s, -sə-ˌden(t)s\ *n* **1 a :** an act or the fact or manner of falling upon or affecting **:** OCCURRENCE **b :** rate of occurrence or influence <a high ~ of crime> **2 a :** the arrival of something (as a projectile or a ray of light) at a surface **b :** ANGLE OF INCIDENCE

1in·ci·dent \ˈin(t)-səd-ənt, -sə-ˌdent\ *n* [ME, fr. MF, fr. ML *incident-, incidens,* fr. L, prp. of *incidere* to fall into, fr. *in-* + *cadere* to fall — more at CHANCE] **1 a :** an occurrence of an action or situation that is a separate unit of experience **:** HAPPENING **b :** an accompanying minor occurrence or condition **:** CONCOMITANT **2 :** an action likely to lead to grave consequences esp. in matters diplomatic <a serious border ~> **3 :** something dependent on or subordinate to something else of greater or principal importance ***syn*** see OCCURRENCE

2incident *adj* **1 :** occurring or likely to occur esp. as a minor consequence or accompaniment <the confusion ~ to moving day> **2 :** dependent on or relating to another thing in law **3 :** falling or striking on something <~ light rays>

1in·ci·den·tal \ˌin(t)-sə-ˈdent-ᵊl\ *adj* **1 :** occurring merely by chance or without intention or calculation **2 :** being likely to ensue as a chance or minor consequence <social obligations ~ to his job> ***syn*** see ACCIDENTAL ***ant*** essential

2incidental *n* **1 :** something that is incidental **2** *pl* **:** minor items (as of expense) that are not particularized

in·ci·den·tal·ly \-ˈdent-ᵊl-ē, *esp for 2* -ˈdent-lē\ *adv* **1 :** by chance **:** CASUALLY **2 :** by way of interjection or digression **:** PARENTHETICALLY

incidental music *n* **:** descriptive music played during a play to project a mood (as for a battle, a storm, or a death scene) or to accompany stage action

in·cin·er·ate \in-ˈsin-ə-ˌrāt\ *vt* **-at·ed; -at·ing** [ML *incineratus,* pp. of *incinerare,* fr. L *in-* + *ciner-, cinis* ashes; akin to Gk *konis* dust, ashes] **:** to cause to burn to ashes — **in·cin·er·a·tion** \-ˌsin-ə-ˈrā-shən\ *n*

in·cin·er·a·tor \in-ˈsin-ə-ˌrāt-ər\ *n* **:** one that incinerates; *esp* **:** a furnace or a container for incinerating waste materials

in·cip·ience \in-ˈsip-ē-ən(t)s\ *n* **:** INCIPIENCY

in·cip·i·en·cy \-ən-sē\ *n* **:** the state or fact of being incipient **:** BEGINNING

in·cip·i·ent \-ənt\ *adj* [L *incipient-, incipiens,* prp. of *incipere* to begin — more at INCEPTION] **:** beginning to come into being or to become apparent **:** COMMENCING <an ~ solar system> <evidence of ~ racial tension> — **in·cip·i·ent·ly** *adv*

in·ci·pit \ˈin(t)-sə-pət, ˈiŋ-kə-ˌpit\ *n* [L, it begins, fr. *incipere*] **:** the first part **:** BEGINNING; *specif* **:** the opening words of a text of a medieval manuscript or early printed book

in·cise \in-ˈsīz, -ˈsīs\ *vt* **in·cised; in·cis·ing** [MF or L; MF *inciser,* fr. L *incisus,* pp. of *incidere,* fr. *in-* + *caedere* to cut — more at CONCISE] **1 :** to cut into **2 a :** to carve figures, letters, or devices into **:** ENGRAVE **b :** to carve (as an inscription) into a surface

in·cised *adj* **1 a :** cut in **:** ENGRAVED; *esp* **:** decorated with incised figures **b** *of a wound* **:** made or as if made with a sharp knife **2 :** having a margin that is deeply and sharply notched <an ~ leaf>

in·ci·sion \in-ˈsizh-ən\ *n* **1 a :** a marginal notch (as in a leaf) **b :** CUT, GASH; *specif* **:** an incised wound made esp. in surgery into the body **2 :** an act of incising **3 :** the quality or state of being incisive

in·ci·sive \in-ˈsī-siv\ *adj* **:** impressively direct and decisive (as in manner or presentation) <~ writing> — **in·ci·sive·ly** *adv* — **in·ci·sive·ness** *n*

syn INCISIVE, TRENCHANT, CLEAR-CUT, CUTTING, BITING, CRISP *shared meaning element* **:** having or manifesting or suggesting a keen alertness of mind

in·ci·sor \in-ˈsī-zər\ *n* **:** a tooth adapted for cutting; *esp* **:** one of the cutting teeth in mammals in front of the canines — see TOOTH illustration

in·ci·ta·tion \ˌin-ˌsī-ˈtā-shən, ˌin(t)-sə-\ *n* **1 :** an act of inciting **:** STIMULATION **2 :** something that incites to action **:** INCENTIVE

in·cite \in-ˈsīt\ *vt* **in·cit·ed; in·cit·ing** [MF *inciter,* fr. L *incitare,* fr. *in-* + *citare* to put in motion — more at CITE] **:** to move to action **:** stir up **:** spur on **:** urge on — **in·cit·ant** \-ˈsīt-ᵊnt\ *n* — **in·cite·ment** \-mənt\ *n* — **in·cit·er** *n*

syn INCITE, INSTIGATE, ABET, FOMENT *shared meaning element* **:** to spur to action or excite into activity ***ant*** restrain

in·ci·vil·i·ty \ˌin(t)-sə-ˈvil-ət-ē\ *n* [MF *incivilité,* fr. LL *incivilitat-, incivilitas,* fr. *incivilis,* fr. L *in-* + *civilis* civil] **1 :** the quality or state of being uncivil **2 :** a rude or discourteous act

incl *abbr* including; inclusive

in·clem·en·cy \(ˈ)in-ˈklem-ən-sē\ *n* **:** the quality or state of being inclement

in·clem·ent \(ˈ)in-ˈklem-ənt\ *adj* [L *inclement-, inclemens,* fr. *in-* + *clement-, clemens* clement] **:** lacking clemency: as **a :** physically severe **:** STORMY <~ weather> **b** *archaic* **:** severe in temper or action **:** UNMERCIFUL — **in·clem·ent·ly** *adv*

in·clin·able \in-ˈklī-nə-bəl\ *adj* **:** having a tendency or inclination; *also* **:** disposed to favor or think well of

in·cli·na·tion \ˌin-klə-ˈnā-shən, ˌiŋ-\ *n* **1 :** an act or the action of bending or inclining: as **a :** BOW, NOD **b :** a tilting of something **2 a** *obs* **:** natural disposition **:** CHARACTER **b :** a particular disposition of mind or character **:** PROPENSITY; *esp* **:** LIKING <had little ~ for housekeeping> **3 a :** a deviation from the true vertical or horizontal **:** SLANT; *also* **:** the degree of such deviation **b :** an inclined surface **:** SLOPE **c (1) :** the angle determined by two lines or planes **(2) :** the angle made by a line with the x-axis measured counterclockwise from the positive direction of that axis **4 :** a tendency to a particular aspect, state, character, or action <the clutch has an ~ to slip> — **in·cli·na·tion·al** \-shnəl, -shən-ᵊl\ *adj*

¹in·cline \in-ˈklīn\ *vb* **in·clined; in·clin·ing** [ME *inclinen,* fr. MF *incliner,* fr. L *inclinare,* fr. *in-* + *clinare* to lean — more at LEAN] *vi* **1 :** to bend the head or body forward **:** BOW **2 :** to lean, tend, or become drawn toward an opinion or course of conduct **3 :** to deviate from a line, direction, or course; *specif* **:** to deviate from the vertical or horizontal ~ *vt* **1 :** to cause to stoop or bow **:** BEND **2 :** to have influence on **:** PERSUADE <his love of books *inclined* him toward a literary career> **3 :** to give a bend or slant to — **in·clin·er** *n*

***syn* 1** see SLANT

2 INCLINE, BIAS, DISPOSE, PREDISPOSE *shared meaning element* **:** to influence one to have or take an attitude toward something ***ant*** disincline

²in·cline \ˈin-ˌklīn\ *n* **:** an inclined plane **:** GRADE, SLOPE

in·clined \in-ˈklīnd, *2 also* ˈin-ˌ\ *adj* **1 :** having inclination, disposition, or tendency **2 a :** having a leaning or slope **b :** making an angle with a line or plane

inclined plane *n* **:** a plane surface that makes an oblique angle with the plane of the horizon

in·clin·ing \in-ˈklī-niŋ\ *n* **1 :** INCLINATION **2** *archaic* **:** PARTY, FOLLOWING

in·cli·nom·e·ter \ˌin-klə-ˈnäm-ət-ər, ˌiŋ-; ˌin-ˌklī-\ *n* **1 :** an apparatus for determining the direction of the earth's magnetic field with reference to the plane of the horizon **2 :** a machinist's clinometer **3 :** an instrument for indicating the inclination to the horizontal of an axis of a ship or an airplane

in·clip \in-ˈklip\ *vt, archaic* **:** CLASP, ENCLOSE

inclose, inclosure *var of* ENCLOSE, ENCLOSURE

in·clude \in-ˈklüd\ *vt* **in·clud·ed; in·clud·ing** [ME *includen,* fr. L *includere,* fr. *in-* + *claudere* to close — more at CLOSE] **1 :** to shut up **:** ENCLOSE **2 :** to take in or comprise as a part of a larger aggregate or principle — **in·clud·able** *or* **in·clud·ible** \-ˈklüd-ə-bəl\ *adj*

syn INCLUDE, COMPREHEND, EMBRACE, INVOLVE *shared meaning element* **:** to contain within as part of a whole ***ant*** exclude

in·clud·ed *adj* **:** that is enclosed or embraced; *esp* **:** not projecting beyond the mouth of the corolla — used of a stamen or pistil

in·clu·sion \in-ˈklü-zhən\ *n* [L *inclusion-, inclusio,* fr. *inclusus,* pp. of *includere*] **1 :** the act of including **:** the state of being included **2 :** something that is included: as **a :** a gaseous, liquid, or solid foreign body enclosed in a mass (as of a mineral) **b :** a passive product of cell activity (as a starch grain) within the protoplasm **3 :** a relation between two classes that obtains when all members of the first are also members of the second — compare MEMBERSHIP 3

inclusion body *n* **:** a rounded or oval intracellular body that consists of elementary bodies in a matrix, is characteristic of some virus diseases, and is believed to represent a stage in the multiplication of the virus

in·clu·sive \in-ˈklü-siv, -ziv\ *adj* **1 a :** broad in orientation or scope **b :** covering or intended to cover all items, costs, or services **2 :** comprehending the stated limits or extremes <from Monday to Friday ~> — **in·clu·sive·ly** *adv* — **in·clu·sive·ness** *n*

inclusive disjunction *n* **:** a statement of a logical proposition expressing alternatives that usu. takes the form *p* v *q* meaning *p* or *q* or both — see TRUTH TABLE table

inclusive of *prep* **:** taking into account <the cost of building *inclusive of* materials>

in·co·erc·ible \ˌin-kō-ˈər-sə-bəl\ *adj* **:** incapable of being controlled, checked, or confined

incog *abbr* incognito

in·cog·i·tant \in-ˈkäj-ət-ənt\ *adj* [L *incogitant-, incogitans,* fr. *in-* + *cogitant-, cogitans,* prp. of *cogitare* to cogitate] **:** THOUGHTLESS, INCONSIDERATE

in·cog·ni·ta \ˌin-ˌkäg-ˈnēt-ə, in-ˈkäg-nət-ə\ *adv or adj* [It, fem. of *incognito*] **:** INCOGNITO — used only of a woman — **incognita** *n*

¹in·cog·ni·to \ˌin-ˌkäg-ˈnēt-(ˌ)ō, in-ˈkäg-nə-ˌtō\ *adv or adj* [It, fr. L *incognitus* unknown, fr. *in-* + *cognitus,* pp. of *cognoscere* to know — more at COGNITION] **:** with one's identity concealed

²incognito *n, pl* **-tos 1 :** one appearing or living incognito **2 :** the state or disguise of an incognito or incognita

in·cog·ni·zant \(ˈ)in-ˈkäg-nə-zənt\ *adj* **:** lacking awareness or consciousness — **in·cog·ni·zance** \-zən(t)s\ *n*

in·co·her·ence \ˌin-kō-ˈhir-ən(t)s, -ˈher-\ *n* **1 :** the quality or state of being incoherent **2 :** something that is incoherent

in·co·her·ent \-ənt\ *adj* **:** lacking coherence: as **a :** lacking cohesion **:** LOOSE **b :** lacking orderly continuity, arrangement, or relevance **:** INCONSISTENT — **in·co·her·ent·ly** *adv*

in·com·bus·ti·ble \ˌin-kəm-ˈbəs-tə-bəl\ *adj* [ME, prob. fr. MF, fr. *in-* + *combustible*] **:** not combustible **:** incapable of being burned — **in·com·bus·ti·bil·i·ty** \-ˌbəs-tə-ˈbil-ət-ē\ *n* — **incombustible** *n*

in·come \ˈin-ˌkəm\ *n* **1 :** a coming in **:** ENTRANCE, INFLUX <fluctuations in the nutrient ~ of a body of water> **2 :** a gain or recurrent benefit usu. measured in money that derives from capital or labor; *also* **:** the amount of such gain received in a period of time <a small yearly ~>

income account *n* **:** a financial statement of a business showing the details of revenues, costs, expenses, losses, and profits for a given period — called also *income statement*

income bond *n* **:** a bond that pays interest at a rate based on the issuer's earnings

income tax \ˈin-(ˌ)kəm-\ *n* **:** a tax on the net income of an individual or a business

¹in·com·ing \ˈin-ˌkəm-iŋ\ *n* **1 :** the act of coming in **:** ARRIVAL **2 :** INCOME — usu. used in pl.

²incoming *adj* **1 a :** coming in **:** ARRIVING <an ~ ship> **b :** taking a new place or position <the ~ president> **c :** received at a usual, proper, or designated destination <~ mail> **2 :** just starting or beginning <the ~ freshman>

in·com·men·su·ra·ble \ˌin-kə-ˈmen(t)s(-ə)-rə-bəl, -ˈmench(-ə)-\ *adj* **:** not commensurable; *broadly* **:** lacking a common basis of comparison in respect to a quality normally subject to comparison — **in·com·men·su·ra·bil·i·ty** \-men(t)s(-ə)-rə-ˈbil-ət-ē, -ˌmench(-ə)-\ *n* — **incommensurable** *n* — **in·com·men·su·ra·bly** \-ˈmen(t)s(-ə)-rə-blē, -ˈmench(-ə)-\ *adv*

in·com·men·su·rate \-ˈmen(t)s(-ə)-rət, -ˈmench(-ə)-\ *adj* **:** not commensurate: as **a :** INCOMMENSURABLE **b :** INADEQUATE **c :** DISPROPORTIONATE

in·com·mode \ˌin-kə-ˈmōd\ *vt* **-mod·ed; -mod·ing** [MF *incommoder,* fr. L *incommodare,* fr. *incommodus* inconvenient, fr. *in-* + *commodus* convenient — more at COMMODE] **:** to give inconvenience or distress to **:** DISTURB

in·com·mo·di·ous \ˌin-kə-ˈmōd-ē-əs\ *adj* **:** not commodious **:** INCONVENIENT — **in·com·mo·di·ous·ly** *adv* — **in·com·mo·di·ous·ness** *n*

in·com·mod·i·ty \-ˈmäd-ət-ē\ *n* **:** a source of inconvenience **:** DISADVANTAGE

in·com·mu·ni·ca·ble \ˌin-kə-ˈmyü-ni-kə-bəl\ *adj* [MF or LL; MF, fr. LL *incommunicabilis,* fr. L *in-* + LL *communicabilis* communicable] **:** not communicable: as **a :** incapable of being communicated or imparted **b :** UNCOMMUNICATIVE — **in·com·mu·ni·ca·bil·i·ty** \-myü-ni-kə-ˈbil-ət-ē\ *n* — **in·com·mu·ni·ca·bly** \-ˈmyü-ni-kə-blē\ *adv*

in·com·mu·ni·ca·do \-ˌmyü-nə-ˈkäd-(ˌ)ō\ *adv or adj* [Sp *incomunicado,* fr. pp. of *incomunicar* to deprive of communication, fr. *in-* (fr. L) + *comunicar* to communicate, fr. L *communicare*] **:** without means of communication; *also* **:** in solitary confinement

in·com·mu·ni·ca·tive \-ˈmyü-nə-ˌkāt-iv, -ni-kət-\ *adj* **:** UNCOMMUNICATIVE

in·com·mut·able \ˌin-kə-ˈmyüt-ə-bəl\ *adj* [ME, fr. L *incommutabilis,* fr. *in-* + *commutabilis* commutable] **:** not commutable: as **a :** not interchangeable **b :** UNCHANGEABLE — **in·com·mut·ably** \-blē\ *adv*

in·com·pa·ra·ble \(ˈ)in-ˈkäm-p(ə-)rə-bəl\ *adj* [ME, fr. MF, fr. L *incomparabilis,* fr. *in-* + *comparabilis* comparable] **1 :** eminent beyond comparison **:** MATCHLESS **2 :** not suitable for comparison — **in·com·pa·ra·bil·i·ty** \(ˌ)in-ˌkäm-p(ə-)rə-ˈbil-ət-ē\ *n* — **in·com·pa·ra·bly** \(ˈ)in-ˈkäm-p(ə-)rə-blē\ *adv*

in·com·pat·i·bil·i·ty \ˌin-kəm-ˌpat-ə-ˈbil-ət-ē\ *n, pl* **-ties 1 a :** the quality or state of being incompatible **b :** lack of interfertility between two plants **2** *pl* **:** mutually antagonistic things or qualities

in·com·pat·i·ble \ˌin-kəm-ˈpat-ə-bəl\ *adj* [MF & ML; MF, fr. ML *incompatibilis,* fr. L *in-* + ML *compatibilis* compatible] **1 :** incapable of being held by one person at one time — used of offices that make conflicting demands on the holder **2 a :** incapable of association because incongruous, discordant, or disagreeing <~ colors> **b :** unsuitable for use together because of undesirable chemical or physiological effects <~ drugs> **c :** not both true <~ propositions> **d :** incapable of blending into a stable homogeneous mixture — **incompatible** *n* — **in·com·pat·i·bly** \-blē\ *adv*

in·com·pe·tence \(ˈ)in-ˈkäm-pət-ən(t)s\ *n* **:** the state or fact of being incompetent

in·com·pe·ten·cy \-ən-sē\ *n* **:** INCOMPETENCE

in·com·pe·tent \(ˈ)in-ˈkäm-pət-ənt\ *adj* [MF *incompétent,* fr. *in-* + *compétent* competent] **1 :** lacking the qualities needed for effective action **2 :** not legally qualified **3:** inadequate to or unsuitable for a particular purpose — **incompetent** *n* — **in·com·pe·tent·ly** *adv*

in·com·plete \ˌin-kəm-ˈplēt\ *adj* [ME *incompleet,* fr. LL *incompletus,* fr. L *in-* + *completus* complete] **:** not complete **:** UNFINISHED: as **a :** lacking a part; *esp* **:** lacking one or more sets of floral organs **b** *of a football pass* **:** not legally caught — **in·com·plete·ly** *adv* — **in·com·plete·ness** *n*

in·com·pli·ant \ˌin-kəm-ˈplī-ənt\ *adj* **:** not compliant or pliable **:** UNYIELDING

in·com·pre·hen·si·ble \(ˌ)in-ˌkäm-pri-ˈhen(t)-sə-bəl\ *adj* [ME, fr. L *incomprehensibilis,* fr. *in-* + *comprehensibilis* comprehensible] **1** *archaic* **:** having or subject to no limits **2 :** impossible to comprehend **:** UNINTELLIGIBLE — **in·com·pre·hen·si·bil·i·ty** \-ˌhen(t)-sə-ˈbil-ət-ē\ *n* — **in·com·pre·hen·si·ble·ness** *n* — **in·com·pre·hen·si·bly** \-ˈhen(t)-sə-blē\ *adv*

in·com·pre·hen·sion \-ˈhen-chən\ *n* **:** lack of comprehension or understanding

in·com·press·ible \in-kəm-ˈpres-ə-bəl\ *adj* **:** incapable of or resistant to compression — **in·com·press·ibil·i·ty** \-ˌpres-ə-ˈbil-ət-ē\ *n* — **in·com·press·ibly** \-blē\ *adv*

in·com·put·able \ˌin-kəm-ˈpyüt-ə-bəl\ *adj* **:** not computable **:** very great — **in·com·put·ably** \-blē\ *adv*

in·con·ceiv·able \ˌin-kən-ˈsē-və-bəl\ *adj* **:** not conceivable: as **a :** impossible to comprehend **b :** UNBELIEVABLE — **in·con·ceiv-**

abil·i·ty \-ˌsē-və-ˈbil-ət-ē\ *n* — **in·con·ceiv·able·ness** \-ˈsē-və-bəl-nəs\ *n* — **in·con·ceiv·ably** \-blē\ *adv*

in·con·cin·ni·ty \ˌin-kən-ˈsin-ət-ē\ *n* [L *inconcinnitas,* fr. *in-* + *concinnitas* concinnity] : lack of suitability or congruity : INELEGANCE

in·con·clu·sive \ˌin-kən-ˈklü-siv, -ziv\ *adj* : leading to no conclusion or definite result — **in·con·clu·sive·ly** *adv* — **in·con·clu·sive·ness** *n*

in·con·dens·able \ˌin-kən-ˈden(t)-sə-bəl\ *adj* : incapable of being condensed

in·con·dite \in-ˈkän-dət, -ˌdīt\ *adj* [L *inconditus,* fr. *in-* + *conditus,* pp. of *condere* to put together, fr. *com-* + *-dere* to put — more at DO] : badly put together : CRUDE

in·con·for·mi·ty \ˌin-kən-ˈfȯr-mət-ē\ *n* : NONCONFORMITY

in·con·gru·ence \ˌin-kən-ˈgrü-ən(t)s, (ˈ)in-ˈkäŋ-grə-wən(t)s\ *n* : INCONGRUITY

in·con·gru·ent \-ənt, -wənt\ *adj* [L *incongruent-, incongruens,* fr. *in-* + *congruent-, congruens* congruent] : not congruent <~ triangles> — **in·con·gru·ent·ly** *adv*

in·con·gru·ity \ˌin-kən-ˈgrü-ət-ē, -ˌkän-\ *n, pl* **-ities** **1 :** the quality or state of being incongruous **2 :** something that is incongruous

in·con·gru·ous \(ˈ)in-ˈkäŋ-grə-wəs\ *adj* [LL *incongruus,* fr. L *in-* + *congruus* congruous] : lacking congruity: as **a :** not harmonious : INCOMPATIBLE <~ colors> **b :** not conforming : DISAGREEING <conduct ~ with his principles> **c :** inconsistent within itself <an ~ story> **d :** lacking propriety : UNSUITABLE <~ manners> — **in·con·gru·ous·ly** *adv* — **in·con·gru·ous·ness** *n*

in·con·scient \(ˈ)in-ˈkän-chənt\ *adj* [prob. fr. F, fr. *in-* + *conscient* mindful, fr. L *conscient-, consciens,* prp. of *conscire* to be conscious — more at CONSCIENCE] : UNCONSCIOUS, MINDLESS

in·con·sec·u·tive \ˌin-kən-ˈsek-(y)ət-iv\ *adj* : not consecutive

in·con·se·quence \(ˈ)in-ˈkän(t)-sə-ˌkwen(t)s, -si-kwən(t)s\ *n* : the quality or state of being inconsequent

in·con·se·quent \-ˌkwent, -kwənt\ *adj* [LL *inconsequent-, inconsequens,* fr. L *in-* + *consequent-, consequens* consequent] **1 a :** lacking reasonable sequence : ILLOGICAL **b :** INCONSECUTIVE **2 :** IRRELEVANT **3 :** INCONSEQUENTIAL 2 — **in·con·se·quent·ly** *adv*

in·con·se·quen·tial \(ˌ)in-ˌkän(t)-sə-ˈkwen-chəl\ *adj* **1 a :** ILLOGICAL **b :** IRRELEVANT **2 :** of no significance : UNIMPORTANT — **in·con·se·quen·ti·al·i·ty** \-ˌkwen-chē-ˈal-ət-ē\ *n* — **in·con·se·quen·tial·ly** \-ˈkwench-(ə-)lē\ *adv*

in·con·sid·er·able \ˌin-kən-ˈsid-ər-(ə-)bəl, -ˈsid-rə-bəl\ *adj* [MF, fr. *in-* + *considerable,* fr. ML *considerabilis* considerable] : not considerable : TRIVIAL — **in·con·sid·er·able·ness** *n* — **in·con·sid·er·ably** \-blē\ *adv*

in·con·sid·er·ate \ˌin-kən-ˈsid-(ə-)rət\ *adj* [L *inconsideratus,* fr. *in-* + *consideratus* considerate] **1 :** not adequately considered : ILL-ADVISED **2 a :** HEEDLESS, THOUGHTLESS **b :** careless of the rights or feelings of others — **in·con·sid·er·ate·ly** *adv* — **in·con·sid·er·ate·ness** *n* — **in·con·sid·er·ation** \-ˌsid-ə-ˈrā-shən\ *n*

in·con·sis·tence \ˌin-kən-ˈsis-tən(t)s\ *n* : INCONSISTENCY

in·con·sis·ten·cy \ˌin-kən-ˈsis-tən-sē\ *n* **1 :** the quality or state of being inconsistent **2 :** an instance of being inconsistent

in·con·sis·tent \-tənt\ *adj* : lacking consistency: as **a :** not compatible with another fact or claim <~ statements> **b :** containing incompatible elements <an ~ argument> **c :** incoherent or illogical in thought or actions : CHANGEABLE **d :** not satisfiable by the same set of values for the unknowns <~ equations> <~ inequalities> — **in·con·sis·tent·ly** *adv*

in·con·sol·able \ˌin-kən-ˈsō-lə-bəl\ *adj* [L *inconsolabilis,* fr. *in-* + *consolabilis* consolable] : incapable of being consoled : DISCONSOLATE — **in·con·sol·able·ness** *n* — **in·con·sol·ably** \-blē\ *adv*

in·con·so·nance \(ˈ)in-ˈkän(t)-s(ə-)nən(t)s\ *n* : lack of consonance or harmony : DISAGREEMENT

in·con·so·nant \-s(ə-)nənt\ *adj* : not consonant : DISCORDANT

in·con·spic·u·ous \ˌin-kən-ˈspik-yə-wəs\ *adj* [L *inconspicuus,* fr. *in-* + *conspicuus* conspicuous] : not readily noticeable — **in·con·spic·u·ous·ly** *adv* — **in·con·spic·u·ous·ness** *n*

in·con·stan·cy \(ˈ)in-ˈkän(t)-stən-sē\ *n* : the quality or state of being inconstant

in·con·stant \-stənt\ *adj* [ME, fr. MF, fr. L *inconstant-, inconstans,* fr. *in-* + *constant-, constans* constant] : likely to change frequently without apparent or cogent reason — **in·con·stant·ly** *adv*

syn INCONSTANT, FICKLE, CAPRICIOUS, MERCURIAL, UNSTABLE *shared meaning element* : lacking firmness or steadiness (as in purpose or devotion) or indicative of such lack. INCONSTANT implies an incapacity for steadiness and an inherent tendency to change <swear not by the moon, the *inconstant* moon, that monthly changes in her circled orb —Shak.> FICKLE suggests unreliability because of perverse changeability and incapacity for steadfastness <lordly patrons are *fickle* and their favor not to be relied on —Aldous Huxley> CAPRICIOUS suggests motivation by sudden whim or fancy and stresses unpredictability <the *capricious* fluttering of . . . butterflies —Ludwig Bemelmans> MERCURIAL implies a rapid changeability of mood and suggests the mobility of spilled quicksilver <I was ardent in my temperament; quick, *mercurial,* impetuous —Washington Irving> UNSTABLE implies an incapacity for maintaining a fixed position or relationship and, when applied to persons, suggests a lack of emotional balance <*unstable* as water, thou shalt not excel —Gen 49:4 (AV)> ***ant*** constant

in·con·sum·able \ˌin-kən-ˈsü-mə-bəl\ *adj* : not capable of being consumed — **in·con·sum·ably** \-blē\ *adv*

in·con·test·able \ˌin-kən-ˈtes-tə-bəl\ *adj* [F, fr. *in-* + *contestable,* fr. *contester* to contest] : not contestable : INDISPUTABLE — **in·con·test·abil·i·ty** \-ˌtes-tə-ˈbil-ət-ē\ *n* — **in·con·test·ably** \-ˈtes-tə-blē\ *adv*

in·con·ti·nence \(ˈ)in-ˈkänt-ᵊn-ən(t)s\ *n* : the quality or state of being incontinent; as **a :** failure to restrain sexual appetite : UNCHASTITY **b :** inability of the body to control the evacuative functions

in·con·ti·nen·cy \-ən-sē\ *n* : INCONTINENCE

[1]**in·con·ti·nent** \(ˈ)in-ˈkänt-ᵊn-ənt\ *adj* [ME, fr. MF or L; MF, fr. L *incontinent-, incontinens,* fr. *in-* + *continent-, continens* continent] : not continent: as **a :** lacking self-restraint **b :** not being under control <that play . . . is singularly ~ and full of loose ends —*Times Lit. Supp.*>

[2]**incontinent** *adv* : [1]INCONTINENTLY

[1]**in·con·ti·nent·ly** *adv* : without delay : IMMEDIATELY

[2]**incontinently** *adv* : in an incontinent or unrestrained manner: as **a :** without moral restraint : LEWDLY **b :** without due or reasonable consideration

in·con·trol·la·ble \ˌin-kən-ˈtrō-lə-bəl\ *adj* : UNCONTROLLABLE

in·con·tro·vert·ible \(ˌ)in-ˌkän-trə-ˈvərt-ə-bəl\ *adj* : not open to question : INDISPUTABLE <~ evidence> — **in·con·tro·vert·ibly** \-blē\ *adv*

[1]**in·con·ve·nience** \ˌin-kən-ˈvē-nyən(t)s\ *n* **1 :** the quality or state of being inconvenient **2 :** something that is inconvenient

[2]**inconvenience** *vt* : to subject to inconvenience : put to trouble

in·con·ve·nien·cy \ˌin-kən-ˈvē-nyən-sē\ *n* : INCONVENIENCE

in·con·ve·nient \ˌin-kən-ˈvē-nyənt\ *adj* [ME, fr. MF, fr. L *inconvenient-, inconveniens,* fr. *in-* + *convenient-, conveniens* convenient] : not convenient esp. in giving trouble or annoyance : INOPPORTUNE — **in·con·ve·nient·ly** *adv*

in·con·vert·ible \-ˈvərt-ə-bəl\ *adj* [prob. fr. LL *inconvertibilis,* fr. L *in-* + *convertibilis* convertible] : not convertible: as **a** *of paper money* : not exchangeable on demand for specie **b** *of a currency* : not exchangeable for a foreign currency — **in·con·vert·ibil·i·ty** \-ˌvərt-ə-ˈbil-ət-ē\ *n* — **in·con·vert·ibly** \-ˈvərt-ə-blē\ *adv*

in·con·vinc·ible \ˌin-kən-ˈvin(t)-sə-bəl\ *adj* : incapable of being convinced

in·co·or·di·nate \ˌin-kō-ˈȯrd-nət, -ᵊn-ət, -ᵊn-ˌāt\ *also* **in·co·or·di·nat·ed** \-ˈȯrd-ᵊn-ˌāt-əd\ *adj* : not coordinate

in·co·or·di·na·tion \-ˌȯrd-ᵊn-ˈā-shən\ *n* : lack of coordination esp. of muscular movements resulting from loss of voluntary control

[1]**in·cor·po·rate** \in-ˈkȯr-pə-ˌrāt\ *vb* **-rat·ed; -rat·ing** [ME *incorporaten,* fr. LL *incorporatus,* pp. of *incorporare,* fr. L *in-* + *corpor-, corpus* body — more at MIDRIFF] *vt* **1 a :** to unite thoroughly with or work indistinguishably into something already existent **b :** to admit to membership in a corporate body **2 a :** to blend or combine thoroughly to form a consistent whole **b :** to form into a legal corporation **3 :** to give material form to : EMBODY ~ *vi* **1 :** to unite in or as one body **2 :** to form or become a corporation — **in·cor·po·ra·ble** \-p(ə-)rə-bəl\ *adj* — **in·cor·po·ra·tion** \ˌkȯr-pə-ˈrā-shən\ *n* — **in·cor·po·ra·tive** \-ˈkȯr-pə-ˌrāt-iv, -p(ə-)rət-\ *adj* — **in·cor·po·ra·tor** \-pə-ˌrāt-ər\ *n*

[2]**in·cor·po·rate** \in-ˈkȯr-p(ə-)rət\ *adj* : INCORPORATED

in·cor·po·rat·ed \-pə-ˌrāt-əd\ *adj* **1 :** united in one body **2 :** formed into a legal corporation

in·cor·po·re·al \ˌin-(ˌ)kȯr-ˈpōr-ē-əl, -ˈpȯr-\ *adj* [L *incorporeus,* fr. *in-* + *corporeus* corporeal] **1 :** not corporeal : having no material body or form **2 :** of, relating to, or constituting a right that is based upon property (as bonds or patents) which has no intrinsic value — **in·cor·po·re·al·ly** \-ə-lē\ *adv*

in·cor·po·re·ity \(ˌ)in-ˌkȯr-pə-ˈrē-ət-ē\ *n* : the quality or state of being incorporeal : IMMATERIALITY

in·cor·rect \ˌin-kə-ˈrekt\ *adj* [ME, fr. MF or L; MF, fr. L *incorrectus,* fr. *in-* + *correctus* correct] **1** *obs* : not corrected or chastened **2 a :** INACCURATE, FAULTY **b :** not true : WRONG **3 :** UNBECOMING, IMPROPER — **in·cor·rect·ly** \-ˈrek-(t)lē\ *adv* — **in·cor·rect·ness** \-ˈrek(t)-nəs\ *n*

in·cor·ri·gi·ble \(ˈ)in-ˈkȯr-ə-jə-bəl, -ˈkär-\ *adj* [ME, fr. LL *incorrigibilis,* fr. L *in-* + *corrigere* to correct — more at CORRECT] : incapable of being corrected or amended: as **a** (1) : not reformable : DEPRAVED (2) : DELINQUENT **b :** not manageable : UNCONTROLLABLE **c :** UNALTERABLE, DETERMINED — **in·cor·ri·gi·bil·i·ty** \(ˌ)in-ˌkȯr-ə-jə-ˈbil-ət-ē, ˌkär-\ *n* — **incorrigible** *n* — **in·cor·ri·gi·ble·ness** \(ˈ)in-ˈkȯr-ə-jə-bəl-nəs, -ˈkär-\ *n* — **in·cor·ri·gi·bly** \-blē\ *adv*

in·cor·rupt \ˌin-kə-ˈrəpt\ *also* **in·cor·rupt·ed** \-ˈrəp-təd\ *adj* [ME, fr. L *incorruptus,* fr. *in-* + *corruptus* corrupt] : free from corruption: as **a** *obs* : not affected with decay **b :** not defiled or depraved : UPRIGHT **c :** free from error — **in·cor·rupt·ly** \-ˈrəp-(t)lē\ *adv* — **in·cor·rupt·ness** \-ˈrəp(t)-nəs\ *n*

in·cor·rupt·ible \ˌin-kə-ˈrəp-tə-bəl\ *adj* : incapable of corruption: as **a :** not subject to decay or dissolution **b :** incapable of being bribed or morally corrupted — **in·cor·rupt·ibil·i·ty** \-ˌrəp-tə-ˈbil-ət-ē\ *n* — **incorruptible** *n* — **in·cor·rupt·ibly** \-ˈrəp-tə-blē\ *adv*

in·cor·rup·tion \ˌin-kə-ˈrəp-shən\ *n, archaic* : the quality or state of being free from physical decay

incr *abbr* increase; increased

[1]**in·crease** \in-ˈkrēs, ˈin-ˌ\ *vb* **in·creased; in·creas·ing** [ME *encresen,* fr. MF *encreistre,* fr. L *increscere,* fr. *in-* + *crescere* to grow — more at CRESCENT] *vi* **1 :** to become progressively greater (as in size, amount, number, or intensity) **2 :** to multiply by the production of young ~ *vt* **1 :** to make greater : AUGMENT **2** *obs* : ENRICH — **in·creas·able** \-ˈkrē-sə-bəl, -ˌkrē-\ *adj* — **in·creas·er** *n*

syn INCREASE, ENLARGE, AUGMENT, MULTIPLY *shared meaning element* : to become or to make greater or more numerous ***ant*** decrease

[2]**in·crease** \ˈin-ˌkrēs, in-ˈ\ *n* **1 :** the act or process of increasing: as **a :** addition or enlargement in size, extent, quantity **b** *obs* : PROPAGATION **2 :** something that is added to an original stock by augmentation or growth (as offspring, produce, profit)

in·creas·ing·ly \in-ˈkrē-siŋ-lē, ˈin-ˌkrē-\ *adv* : to an increasing degree

in·cre·ate \ˌin-krē-ˈāt, in-ˈkrē-ət\ *adj* [ME *increat,* fr. LL *increatus,* fr. L *in-* + *creatus,* pp. of *creare* to create — more at CRESCENT] : not created

in·cred·i·ble \(ˈ)in-ˈkred-ə-bəl\ *adj* [ME, fr. L *incredibilis,* fr. *in-* + *credibilis* credible] : too extraordinary and improbable to be believed; *also* : hard to believe — **in·cred·ibil·i·ty** \(ˌ)in-ˌkred-ə-ˈbil-ət-ē\ *n* — **in·cred·i·ble·ness** \(ˈ)in-ˈkred-ə-bəl-nəs\ *n* — **in·cred·i·bly** \-blē\ *adv*

in·cre·du·li·ty \ˌin-kri-ˈd(y)ü-lət-ē\ *n* **:** the quality or state of being incredulous **:** DISBELIEF ***syn*** see UNBELIEF

in·cred·u·lous \(ˈ)in-ˈkrej-ə-ləs\ *adj* [L *incredulus,* fr. *in-* + *credulus* credulous] **1 :** unwilling to admit or accept what is offered as true **:** not credulous **:** SKEPTICAL **2 :** expressing incredulity **3** *obs* **:** INCREDIBLE — **in·cred·u·lous·ly** *adv*

in·cre·ment \ˈiŋ-krə-mənt, ˈin-\ *n* [ME, fr. L *incrementum,* fr. *increscere*] **1 :** an increase esp. in quantity or value **:** ENLARGEMENT; *also* **:** QUANTITY **2 a :** something gained or added **b :** one of a series of regular consecutive additions **c :** a minute increase in quantity **3 :** a positive or negative change in the value of one or more of a set of variables — **in·cre·men·tal** \ˌiŋ-krə-ˈment-ᵊl, ˌin-\ *adj* — **in·cre·men·tal·ly** \-ᵊl-ē\ *adv*

in·cre·men·tal·ism \ˌiŋ-krə-ˈment-ᵊl-ˌiz-əm\ *n* **:** a policy or advocacy of a policy of political or social change in small increments **:** GRADUALISM — **in·cre·men·tal·ist** \-ᵊl-əst\ *n*

incremental repetition *n* **:** repetition in each stanza (as of a ballad) of part of the preceding stanza usu. with a slight change in wording for dramatic effect

in·cres·cent \in-ˈkres-ᵊnt\ *adj* [L *increscent-, increscens,* prp. of *increscere*] **:** becoming gradually greater **:** WAXING <the ~ moon>

in·crim·i·nate \in-ˈkrim-ə-ˌnāt\ *vt* **-nat·ed; -nat·ing** [LL *incriminatus,* pp. of *incriminare,* fr. L *in-* + *crimin-, crimen* crime] **:** to charge with or involve in a crime or fault — **in·crim·i·na·tion** \-ˌkrim-ə-ˈnā-shən\ *n* — **in·crim·i·na·to·ry** \-ˈkrim-(ə-)nə-ˌtōr-ē, -ˌtȯr-\ *adj*

in·cross \ˈin-ˌkrȯs\ *n* **:** an individual produced by crossing inbred lines of the same breed or strain

in·cross·bred \ˈin-ˈkrȯs-ˌbred\ *n* **:** an individual produced by crossing inbred lines of separate breeds or strains

incrust *var of* ENCRUST

in·crus·ta·tion \ˌin-ˌkrəs-ˈtā-shən\ *n* [L *incrustation-, incrustatio,* fr. *incrustatus,* pp. of *incrustare* to encrust] **1 :** the act of encrusting **:** the state of being encrusted **2 a :** a crust or hard coating **b :** a growth or accumulation (as of habits, opinions, or customs) resembling a crust **3 a :** OVERLAY a **b :** INLAY

in·cu·bate \ˈiŋ-kyə-ˌbāt, ˈin-\ *vb* **-bat·ed; -bat·ing** [L *incubatus,* pp. of *incubare,* fr. *in-* + *cubare* to lie — more at HIP] *vt* **1 :** to sit upon (eggs) so as to hatch by the warmth of the body; *also* **:** to maintain (as an embryo or a chemically active system) under conditions favorable for hatching, development, or reaction **2 :** to cause (as an idea) to develop ~ *vi* **1 :** to sit on eggs **2 :** to undergo incubation — **in·cu·ba·tive** \-ˌbāt-iv\ *adj* — **in·cu·ba·to·ry** \-kyə-bə-ˌtōr-ē, -ˌtȯr-; -ˌbāt-ə-rē\ *adj*

in·cu·ba·tion \ˌiŋ-kyə-ˈbā-shən, ˌin-\ *n* **1 :** the act or process of incubating **2 :** the period between the infection of an individual by a pathogen and the manifestation of the disease it causes — **in·cu·ba·tion·al** \-shnəl, -shən-ᵊl\ *adj*

in·cu·ba·tor \ˈiŋ-kyə-ˌbāt-ər, ˈin-\ *n* **:** one that incubates: as **a :** an apparatus by which eggs are hatched artificially **b :** an apparatus for the maintenance of controlled conditions esp. for the cultivation of microorganisms or the housing of premature or sick babies

in·cu·bus \ˈiŋ-kyə-bəs, ˈin-\ *n, pl* **-bi** \-ˌbī, -ˌbē\ *also* **-bus·es** [ME, fr. LL, fr. L *incubare*] **1 :** an evil spirit that lies on persons in their sleep; *esp* **:** one that has sexual intercourse with women while they are sleeping — compare SUCCUBUS **2 :** NIGHTMARE 2 **3 :** one that oppresses or burdens like a nightmare

in·cul·cate \in-ˈkəl-ˌkāt, ˈin-(ˌ)\ *vt* **-cat·ed; -cat·ing** [L *inculcatus,* pp. of *inculcare,* lit., to tread on, fr. *in-* + *calcare* to trample, fr. *calc-, calx* heel — more at CALK] **:** to teach and impress by frequent repetitions or admonitions — **in·cul·ca·tion** \ˌin-(ˌ)kəl-ˈkā-shən\ *n* — **in·cul·ca·tor** \in-ˈkəl-ˌkāt-ər, ˈin-(ˌ)\ *n*

in·cul·pa·ble \(ˈ)in-ˈkəl-pə-bəl\ *adj* **:** free from guilt **:** BLAMELESS

in·cul·pate \in-ˈkəl-ˌpāt, ˈin-(ˌ)\ *vt* **-pat·ed; -pat·ing** [LL *inculpatus,* fr. L *in-* + *culpatus,* pp. of *culpare* to blame — more at CULPABLE] **:** INCRIMINATE — **in·cul·pa·tion** \ˌin-(ˌ)kəl-ˈpā-shən\ *n* — **in·cul·pa·to·ry** \in-ˈkəl-pə-ˌtōr-ē, -ˌtȯr-\ *adj*

in·cult \in-ˈkəlt\ *adj* [L *incultus,* fr. *in-* + *cultus,* pp. of *colere* to cultivate — more at WHEEL] **:** COARSE, UNCULTURED

in·cum·ben·cy \in-ˈkəm-bən-sē\ *n, pl* **-cies 1 :** the quality or state of being incumbent **2 :** something that is incumbent **:** DUTY **3 :** the sphere of action or period of office of an incumbent

1**in·cum·bent** \in-ˈkəm-bənt\ *n* [ME, fr. L *incumbent-, incumbens,* prp. of *incumbere* to lie down on, fr. *in-* + *-cumbere* to lie down; akin to L *cubare* to lie — more at HIP] **:** the holder of an office or ecclesiastical benefice

2**incumbent** *adj* **1 a :** lying or resting on something else **b** *of a geologic stratum* **:** lying over other material **:** SUPERIMPOSED **2 :** imposed as a duty **:** OBLIGATORY **3 :** occupying a specified office **4 a** *archaic* **:** bending over **:** OVERHANGING **b** *archaic* **:** IMMINENT **c :** bent over so as to rest on or touch an underlying surface

incumber *var of* ENCUMBER

in·cu·na·ble \in-ˈkyü-nə-bəl\ *n* [F, fr. NL *incunabulum*] **:** INCUNABULUM

in·cu·nab·u·lum \ˌin-kyə-ˈnab-yə-ləm, ˌiŋ-\ *n, pl* **-la** \-lə\ [NL, fr. L *incunabula,* pl., swaddling clothes, cradle, fr. *in-* + *cunae* cradle — more at CEMETERY] **1 :** a book printed before 1501 **2 :** a work of art or of industry of an early period

in·cur \in-ˈkər\ *vt* **in·curred; in·cur·ring** [L *incurrere,* lit., to run into, fr. *in* + *currere* to run — more at CURRENT] **:** to become liable or subject to **:** bring down upon oneself <persons who adopt a child ~ great responsibilities>

syn INCUR, CONTRACT, CATCH *shared meaning element* **:** to bring (as something unwanted) upon oneself

in·cur·able \(ˈ)in-ˈkyu̇r-ə-bəl\ *adj* [ME, fr. MF or LL; MF, fr. LL *incurabilis,* fr. L *in-* + *curabilis* curable] **:** not curable — **in·cur·abil·i·ty** \(ˌ)in-ˌkyu̇r-ə-ˈbil-ət-ē\ *n* — **incurable** *n* — **in·cur·able·ness** \(ˈ)in-ˈkyu̇r-ə-bəl-nəs\ *n* — **in·cur·ably** \-blē\ *adv*

in·cu·ri·ous \(ˈ)in-ˈkyu̇r-ē-əs\ *adj* [L *incuriosus,* fr. *in-* + *curiosus* curious] **:** lacking a normal or usual curiosity **:** UNINTERESTED <a blank ~ stare> ***syn*** see INDIFFERENT ***ant*** curious, inquisitive — **in·cu·ri·os·i·ty** \(ˌ)in-ˌkyu̇r-ē-ˈäs-ət-ē\ *n* — **in·cu·ri·ous·ly** \(ˈ)in-ˈkyu̇r-ē-əs-lē\ *adv* — **in·cu·ri·ous·ness** *n*

in·cur·rence \in-ˈkər-ən(t)s, -ˈkə-rən(t)s\ *n* **:** the act or process of incurring

in·cur·rent \-ənt, -rənt\ *adj* [L *incurrent-, incurrens,* prp. of *incurrere*] **:** giving passage to a current that flows inward

in·cur·sion \in-ˈkər-zhən\ *n* [ME, fr. MF or L; MF, fr. L *incursion-, incursio,* fr. *incursus,* pp. of *incurrere*] **1 :** a hostile entrance into a territory **:** RAID **2 :** an entering in or into <his only ~ into the arts>

in·cur·vate \ˈin-ˌkər-ˌvāt, (ˈ)in-ˈkər-\ *vt* **-vat·ed; -vat·ing :** to cause to curve inward **:** BEND — **in·cur·vate** \ˈin-ˌkər-ˌvāt, (ˈ)in-ˈkər-vət\ *adj* — **in·cur·va·tion** \ˌin-ˌkər-ˈvā-shən\ *n* — **in·cur·va·ture** \(ˈ)in-ˈkər-və-ˌchu̇(ə)r, -chər, -ˌt(y)u̇(ə)r\ *n*

in·curve \(ˈ)in-ˈkərv, ˈin-ˌ\ *vt* [L *incurvare,* fr. *in-* + *curvare* to curve, fr. *curvus* curved — more at CROWN] **:** to bend so as to curve inward

in·cus \ˈiŋ-kəs\ *n, pl* **in·cu·des** \iŋ-ˈkyüd-(ˌ)ēz, ˈiŋ-kyə-ˌdēz\ [NL, fr. L, anvil, fr. *incudere*] **:** the middle of a chain of three small bones in the ear of a mammal — called also *anvil;* see EAR illustration

in·cuse \in-ˈkyüz, -ˈkyüs\ *adj* [L *incusus,* pp. of *incudere* to stamp, strike, fr. *in-* + *cudere* to beat — more at HEW] **:** formed by stamping or punching in — used chiefly of old coins or features of their design

ind *abbr* **1** independent **2** index **3** industrial; industry

1**Ind** \ˈind, ˈīnd\ *n* **1** *archaic* **:** India **2** *obs* **:** Indies

2**Ind** *abbr* **1** Indian **2** Indiana

IND *abbr* investigational new drug

ind- *or* **indi-** *or* **indo-** *comb form* [ISV, fr. L *indicum* — more at INDIGO] **1 :** indigo <*ind*oxyl> **2 :** resembling indigo (as in color) <*indo*phenol>

Ind- *or* **Indo-** *comb form* [Gk, fr. *Indos* India] **1 :** India or the East Indies <*Indo*phile> <*Indo*-Briton> **2 :** Indo-European <*Indo*-Hittite>

in·da·ba \in-ˈdäb-ə\ *n* [Zulu *in-daba* affair] *chiefly So Afr* **:** CONFERENCE, PARLEY

in·da·gate \ˈin-də-ˌgāt\ *vt* **-gat·ed; -gat·ing** [L *indagatus,* pp. of *indagare,* fr. *indago* act of enclosing, investigation, fr. OL *indu* in + L *agere* to drive — more at INDIGENOUS, AGENT] **:** to search into **:** INVESTIGATE — **in·da·ga·tion** \ˌin-də-ˈgā-shən\ *n* — **in·da·ga·tor** \ˈin-də-ˌgāt-ər\ *n*

ind·a·mine \ˈin-də-ˌmēn\ *n* [ISV *ind-* + *amine*] **:** any of a series of organic bases of which the simplest has the formula $C_{12}H_{11}N_3$ and which form salts that are unstable blue and green dyes

IndE *abbr* industrial engineer

in·debt·ed \in-ˈdet-əd\ *adj* [ME *indetted,* fr. OF *endeté,* pp. of *endeter* to involve in debt, fr. *en-* + *dete* debt] **1 :** owing money **2 :** owing gratitude or recognition to another **:** BEHOLDEN

in·debt·ed·ness *n* **1 :** the condition of being indebted **2 :** something (as an amount of money) that is owed

in·de·cen·cy \(ˈ)in-ˈdēs-ᵊn-sē\ *n* **1 :** the quality or state of being indecent **2 :** something (as a word or action) that is indecent

in·de·cent \-ᵊnt\ *adj* [MF or L; MF *indécent,* fr. L *indecent-, indecens,* fr. *in-* + *decent-, decens* decent] **:** not decent; *esp* **:** grossly unseemly or offensive to manners or morals ***syn*** see INDECOROUS ***ant*** decent — **in·de·cent·ly** *adv*

indecent assault *n* **:** an immoral act or series of acts exclusive of rape committed against another person without consent

indecent exposure *n* **:** intentional exposure of part of one's body (as the genitals) in a place where such exposure is likely to be an offense against the generally accepted standards of decency in a community

in·de·ci·pher·able \ˌin-di-ˈsī-f(ə-)rə-bəl\ *adj* **:** incapable of being deciphered

in·de·ci·sion \ˌin-di-ˈsizh-ən\ *n* [F *indécision,* fr. *indécis* undecided, fr. LL *indecisus,* fr. L *in-* + *decisus,* pp. of *decidere* to decide] **:** a wavering between two or more possible courses of action **:** IRRESOLUTION

in·de·ci·sive \ˌin-di-ˈsī-siv\ *adj* **1 :** not decisive **:** INCONCLUSIVE **2 :** marked by or prone to indecision **:** IRRESOLUTE **3 :** not clearly marked out **:** INDEFINITE — **in·de·ci·sive·ly** *adv* — **in·de·ci·sive·ness** *n*

in·de·clin·able \ˌin-di-ˈklī-nə-bəl\ *adj* [MF, fr. LL *indeclinabilis,* fr. L *in-* + LL *declinabilis* capable of being inflected, fr. L *declinare* to inflect — more at DECLINE] **:** having no grammatical inflections

in·de·com·pos·able \ˌin-ˌdē-kəm-ˈpō-zə-bəl\ *adj* **:** not capable of being broken up into component parts

in·de·co·rous \(ˈ)in-ˈdek-(ə-)rəs; ˌin-di-ˈkōr-əs, -ˈkȯr-\ *adj* [L *indecorus,* fr. *in-* + *decorus* decorous] **:** not decorous — **in·de·co·rous·ly** *adv* — **in·de·co·rous·ness** *n*

syn INDECOROUS, IMPROPER, UNSEEMLY, INDECENT, UNBECOMING, INDELICATE *shared meaning element* **:** not conforming to what is accepted as right, fitting, or in good taste ***ant*** decorous

in·de·co·rum \ˌin-di-ˈkōr-əm, -ˈkȯr-\ *n* [L, neut. of *indecorus*] **1 :** something that is indecorous **2 :** lack of decorum **:** IMPROPRIETY

in·deed \in-ˈdēd\ *adv* **1 :** without any question **:** TRULY, UNDENIABLY — often used interjectionally to express irony or disbelief or surprise **2 :** in reality **3 :** all things considered **:** as a matter of fact

indef *abbr* indefinite

in·de·fat·i·ga·ble \ˌin-di-ˈfat-i-gə-bəl\ *adj* [MF, fr. L *indefatigabilis,* fr. *in-* + *defatigare* to fatigue, fr. *de* down + *fatigare* to fatigue — more at DE-] **:** incapable of being fatigued **:** UNTIRING — **in-**

de·fa·ti·ga·bil·i·ty \-ˌfat-i-gə-ˈbil-ət-ē\ *n* — **in·de·fat·i·ga·ble·ness** \-ˈfat-i-gə-bəl-nəs\ *n* — **in·de·fat·i·ga·bly** \-blē\ *adv*

in·de·fea·si·ble \-ˈfē-zə-bəl\ *adj* **:** not capable of being annulled or voided or undone <an ~ right> — **in·de·fea·si·bil·i·ty** \-ˌfē-zə-ˈbil-ət-ē\ *n* — **in·de·fea·si·bly** \-ˈfē-zə-blē\ *adv*

in·de·fec·ti·ble \-ˈfek-tə-bəl\ *adj* **1 :** not subject to failure or decay **:** LASTING **2 :** free of faults **:** FLAWLESS — **in·de·fec·ti·bil·i·ty** \-ˌfek-tə-ˈbil-ət-ē\ *n* — **in·de·fec·ti·bly** \-ˈfek-tə-blē\ *adv*

in·de·fen·si·ble \-ˈfen(t)-sə-bəl\ *adj* **1 a :** incapable of being maintained as right or valid **:** UNTENABLE **b :** incapable of being justified or excused **:** INEXCUSABLE **2 :** incapable of being protected against physical attack — **in·de·fen·si·bil·i·ty** \-ˌfen(t)-sə-ˈbil-ət-ē\ *n* — **in·de·fen·si·bly** \-ˈfen(t)-sə-blē\ *adv*

in·de·fin·able \-ˈfī-nə-bəl\ *adj* **:** incapable of being precisely described or analyzed — **in·de·fin·abil·i·ty** \-ˌfī-nə-ˈbil-ət-ē\ *n* — **indefinable** *n* — **in·de·fin·able·ness** \-ˈfī-nə-bəl-nəs\ *n* — **in·de·fin·ably** \-blē\ *adv*

in·def·i·nite \(ˈ)in-ˈdef-(ə-)nət\ *adj* [L *indefinitus,* fr. *in-* + *definitus* definite]**:** not definite: as **a :** typically designating an unidentified or not immediately identifiable person or thing <the ~ articles *a* and *an*> **b :** not precise **:** VAGUE **c :** having no exact limits — **indefinite** *n* — **in·def·i·nite·ly** *adv* — **in·def·i·nite·ness** *n*

indefinite integral *n* **:** a function whose derivative is a given function

in·de·his·cent \ˌin-di-ˈhis-ᵊnt\ *adj* **:** remaining closed at maturity <~ fruits> — **in·de·his·cence** \-ᵊn(t)s\ *n*

in·del·i·ble \in-ˈdel-ə-bəl\ *adj* [ML *indelibilis,* alter. of L *indelebilis,* fr. *in-* + *delēre* to delete] **1 :** that cannot be removed, washed away, or erased **2 :** making marks that cannot easily be removed <an ~ pencil> — **in·del·i·bil·i·ty** \(ˌ)in-ˌdel-ə-ˈbil-ət-ē\ *n* — **in·del·i·bly** \in-ˈdel-ə-blē\ *adv*

in·del·i·ca·cy \-kə-sē\ *n* **1 :** the quality or state of being indelicate **2 :** something that is indelicate

in·del·i·cate \(ˈ)in-ˈdel-i-kət\ *adj* **:** not delicate: **a (1) :** lacking in or offending against propriety **:** IMPROPER **(2) :** verging on the indecent **:** COARSE **b :** marked by a lack of feeling for the sensibilities of others **:** TACTLESS ***syn*** see INDECOROUS ***ant*** delicate, refined — **in·del·i·cate·ly** *adv* — **in·del·i·cate·ness** *n*

in·dem·ni·fi·ca·tion \in-ˌdem-nə-fə-ˈkā-shən\ *n* **1 a :** the action of indemnifying **b :** the condition of being indemnified **2 :** INDEMNITY 2b

in·dem·ni·fy \in-ˈdem-nə-ˌfī\ *vt* **-fied; -fy·ing** [L *indemnis* unharmed, fr. *in-* + *damnum* damage] **1 :** to secure against hurt, loss, or damage **2 :** to make compensation to for incurred hurt, loss, or damage ***syn*** see PAY — **in·dem·ni·fi·er** \-ˌfī(-ə)r\ *n*

in·dem·ni·ty \in-ˈdem-nət-ē\ *n, pl* **-ties** **1 a :** security against hurt, loss, or damage **b :** exemption from incurred penalties or liabilities **2 a :** INDEMNIFICATION 1 **b :** something that indemnifies

in·de·mon·stra·ble \ˌin-di-ˈmän(t)-strə-bəl, (ˌ)in-ˈdem-ən-strə-\ *adj* **:** incapable of being demonstrated **:** not subject to proof — **in·de·mon·stra·bly** \-blē\ *adv*

in·dene \ˈin-ˌdēn\ *n* [ISV, fr. *indole*]**:** a liquid hydrocarbon C_9H_8 obtained from coal tar and used esp. in making resins

[1]**in·dent** \in-ˈdent\ *vb* [ME *indenten,* fr. MF *endenter,* fr. OF, fr. *en-* + *dent* tooth, fr. L *dent-, dens* — more at TOOTH] *vt* **1 a :** to cut or otherwise divide (a document carrying two or more copies) to produce sections with irregular edges that can be matched for authentication **b :** to draw up (as a deed) in two or more exactly corresponding copies **2 a :** to notch the edge of **:** make jagged **b :** to cut into for the purpose of mortising or dovetailing **3 :** INDENTURE **4 :** to set (as a line of a paragraph) in from the margin **5 :** to join together by or as if by mortises or dovetails **6** *chiefly Brit* **:** to order by an indent ~ *vi* **1** *obs* **:** to make a formal or express agreement **2 :** to form an indentation **3** *chiefly Brit* **:** to make out an indent for something — **in·dent·er** *n* — **indent on 1** *chiefly Brit* **:** to make a requisition on **2** *chiefly Brit* **:** to draw on

[2]**in·dent** \in-ˈdent, ˈin-ˌ\ *n* **1 a :** INDENTURE 1 **b :** a certificate issued by the U.S. at the close of the American Revolution for the principal or interest on the public debt **2** *chiefly Brit* **a :** an official requisition **b :** a purchase order for goods esp. when sent from a foreign country **3 :** INDENTION

[3]**in·dent** \in-ˈdent\ *vt* [ME *endenten,* fr. *en-* + *denten* to dent] **1 :** to force inward so as to form a depression **2 :** to form a dent in — **in·dent·er** *n*

[4]**in·dent** \in-ˈdent, ˈin-ˌ\ *n* **:** INDENTATION

in·den·ta·tion \ˌin-ˌden-ˈtā-shən\ *n* **1 a :** an angular cut in an edge **:** NOTCH **b :** a recess in a surface **2 :** the action of indenting **:** the condition of being indented **3 :** DENT **4 :** INDENTION 2b

in·den·tion \in-ˈden-chən\ *n* **1** *archaic* **:** INDENTATION 1 **2 a :** the action of indenting **:** the condition of being indented **b :** the blank space produced by indenting

[1]**in·den·ture** \in-ˈden-chər\ *n* **1 a (1) :** a document or a section of a document that is indented **(2) :** a formal or official document usu. executed in two or more copies **(3) :** a contract binding one person to work for another for a given period of time — usu. used in pl. **b :** a formal certificate (as an inventory or voucher) prepared for purposes of control **c :** a document stating the terms under which a security (as a bond) is issued **2 :** INDENTATION 1 **3** [[3]*indent*] **:** DENT

[2]**indenture** *vt* **in·den·tured; in·den·tur·ing** \-ˈdench-(ə-)riŋ\ **1 :** to bind (as an apprentice) by indentures **2** *archaic* **:** to make a dent in

indentured servant *n* **:** a person who binds himself by indentures to work for another for a specified time esp. in return for payment of his travel expenses and maintenance

in·de·pen·dence \ˌin-də-ˈpen-dən(t)s\ *n* **1 :** the quality or state of being independent **:** FREEDOM **2** *archaic* **:** COMPETENCE 1

Independence Day *n* **:** a day set aside for public celebration of an anniversary connected with the beginnings of national independence; *specif* **:** July 4 observed as a legal holiday in the U.S. in commemoration of the adoption of the Declaration of Independence in 1776

in·de·pen·den·cy \ˌin-də-ˈpen-dən-sē\ *n* **1 :** INDEPENDENCE 1 **2** *cap* **:** the Independent polity or movement **3 :** an independent political unit

[1]**in·de·pen·dent** \ˌin-də-ˈpen-dənt\ *adj* **1 :** not dependent: as **a (1) :** not subject to control by others **:** SELF-GOVERNING **(2) :** not affiliated with a larger controlling unit **b (1) :** not requiring or relying on something else **:** not contingent <an ~ conclusion> **(2) :** not looking to others for one's opinions or for guidance in conduct **(3) :** not bound by or committed to a political party **c (1) :** not requiring or relying on others (as for care or livelihood) <~ of his parents> **(2) :** being enough to free one from the necessity of working for a living <a man of ~ means> **d (1) :** refusing to accept help from or to be under obligation to others **(2) :** showing a desire for freedom <an ~ manner> **e (1) :** having linear independence <an ~ set of vectors> **(2) :** having the property that the joint probability (as of events or samples) or the joint probability density function (as of random variables) equals the product of the probabilities or probability density functions of separate occurrence **2** *cap* **:** of or relating to the Independents **3 a :** MAIN 5 <the ~ clause> **b :** neither deducible from nor incompatible with another statement <~ postulates> ***syn*** see FREE ***ant*** dependent — **in·de·pen·dent·ly** *adv*

[2]**independent** *n* **1** *cap* **:** a sectarian of an English religious movement for congregational autonomy originating in the late 16th century, giving rise to Congregationalists, Baptists, and Friends, and forming one of the major political groupings of the period of Cromwell **2 :** one that is independent; *esp, often cap* **:** one that is not bound by or definitively committed to a political party

independent assortment *n* **:** formation of combinations of chromosomes in meiosis with one of each diploid pair of homologous chromosomes passing at random into each gamete independently of each other pair; *also* **:** the similar process when genes on different pairs of homologous chromosomes are considered

independent variable *n* **:** a mathematical variable whose value determines that of one or more other variables in a function <in $z = x^2 + 3xy + y^2$, *x* and *y* are *independent variables*>

in–depth \(ˌ)in-ˌdepth\ *adj* **:** COMPREHENSIVE, THOROUGH <an ~ study>

in·de·scrib·able \ˌin-di-ˈskrī-bə-bəl\ *adj* **1 :** that cannot be described <an ~ sensation> **2 :** surpassing description <~ joy> — **in·de·scrib·able·ness** *n* — **in·de·scrib·ably** \-blē\ *adv*

in·de·struc·ti·ble \-ˈstrək-tə-bəl\ *adj* [prob. fr. LL *indestructibilis,* fr. L *in-* + *destructus,* pp. of *destruere* to tear down — more at DESTROY] **:** not destructible — **in·de·struc·ti·bil·i·ty** \-ˌstrək-tə-ˈbil-ət-ē\ *n* — **in·de·struc·ti·ble·ness** \-ˈstrək-tə-bəl-nəs\ *n* — **in·de·struc·ti·bly** \-blē\ *adv*

in·de·ter·min·able \ˌin-di-ˈtərm-(ə-)nə-bəl\ *adj* **1 :** incapable of being definitely decided or settled **2 :** incapable of being definitely fixed or ascertained — **in·de·ter·min·able·ness** *n* — **in·de·ter·min·ably** \-blē\ *adv*

in·de·ter·mi·na·cy \-ˈtərm-(ə-)nə-sē\ *n* **:** the quality or state of being indeterminate

indeterminacy principle *n* **:** UNCERTAINTY PRINCIPLE

in·de·ter·mi·nate \ˌin-di-ˈtərm-(ə-)nət\ *adj* [ME *indeterminat,* fr. LL *indeterminatus,* fr. L *in-* + *determinatus,* pp. of *determinare* to determine] **1 a :** not definitely or precisely determined or fixed **:** VAGUE **b :** not known in advance **c :** not leading to a definite end or result **2 :** having an infinite number of solutions <a system of ~ equations> **3 :** being one of the seven undefined mathematical expressions $\frac{0}{0}, \frac{\infty}{\infty}, \infty \cdot 0, 1^\infty, 0^0, \infty^0, \infty - \infty$ **4 :** RACEMOSE — **in·de·ter·mi·nate·ly** *adv* — **in·de·ter·mi·nate·ness** *n* — **in·de·ter·mi·na·tion** \-ˌtər-mə-ˈnā-shən\ *n*

in·de·ter·min·ism \-ˈtər-mə-ˌniz-əm\ *n* **1 a :** a theory that the will is free and that deliberate choice and actions are not determined by or predictable from antecedent causes **b :** a theory that holds that not every event has a cause **2 :** the quality or state of being indeterminate; *esp* **:** UNPREDICTABILITY — **in·de·ter·min·ist** \-ˈtərm-(ə-)nəst\ *n* — **in·de·ter·min·is·tic** \-ˌtər-mə-ˈnis-tik\ *adj*

[1]**in·dex** \ˈin-ˌdeks\ *n, pl* **in·dex·es** *or* **in·di·ces** \-də-ˌsēz\ [L *indic-, index,* fr. *indicare* to indicate] **1 :** a list (as of bibliographical information or citations to a body of literature) arranged usu. in alphabetical order of some specified datum (as author, subject, or keyword): as **a :** a list of items (as topics or names) treated in a printed work that gives for each item the page number where it may be found **b :** THUMB INDEX **c :** a bibliographical analysis of groups of publications that is usu. published periodically **2 a :** a device (as the pointer on a scale or the gnomon of a sundial) that serves to indicate a value or quantity **b :** something (as a physical feature or a mode of expression) that points toward a particular fact or conclusion <the fertility of the land is an ~ of the country's wealth> **3 :** a list of restricted or prohibited material; *specif, cap* **:** a list of books the reading of which is prohibited or restricted for Roman Catholics by the church authorities **4** *pl usu indices* **:** a number or symbol or expression (as an exponent) associated with another to indicate a mathematical operation to be performed or to indicate use or position in an arrangement <the *indices* 2 and 3 locate the element a_{23} in the second row and third column of a determinant> **5 :** a character ☞ used to direct attention to a note or paragraph — called also *fist* **6 a :** a ratio or other number derived from a series of observations and used as an indicator or measure (as of a condition, property, or phenomenon); *specif* **:** INDEX NUMBER **b :** the ratio of one dimension of a thing (as an anatomical structure) to another dimension — **in·dex·i·cal** \in-ˈdek-si-kəl\ *adj*

[2]**index** *vt* **1 a :** to provide with an index **b :** to list in an index **2 :** to serve as an index of ~ *vi* **:** to index something — **in·dex·er** *n*

index finger *n* **:** FOREFINGER

index fossil *n* **:** a fossil usu. with a narrow time range and wide spatial distribution that is used in the identification of related geologic formations

index number *n* **:** a number used to indicate change in magnitude (as of cost or price) as compared with the magnitude at some specified time usu. taken as 100

index of refraction : the ratio of the velocity of radiation (as light) in the first of two media to its velocity in the second as it passes from one into the other

indi- — see IND-

In·dia \ˈin-dē-ə\ — a communications code word for the letter *i*

india ink *n, often cap 1st I* **1 :** a solid black pigment (as specially prepared lampblack) used in drawing and lettering **2 :** a fluid ink consisting usu. of a fine suspension of india ink in a liquid

In·dia·man \ˈin-dē-ə-mən\ *n* **:** a merchant ship formerly used in trade with India; *esp* **:** a large sailing ship used in this trade

In·di·an \ˈin-dē-ən, *nonstandard* ˈin-jən\ *n* **1 :** a native or inhabitant of the subcontinent of India or of the East Indies **2 a** [fr. the belief held by Columbus that the lands he discovered were part of Asia] **:** AMERICAN INDIAN **b :** one of the native languages of American Indians — **Indian** *adj*

Indian agent *n* **:** an official representative of the U.S. federal government to American Indian tribes esp. on reservations

Indian club *n* **:** a usu. wooden club shaped like a large bottle or tenpin that is swung for gymnastic exercise

Indian corn *n* **1 :** a tall widely cultivated American cereal grass (*Zea mays*) bearing seeds on elongated ears **2 :** the ears of Indian corn; *also* **:** its edible seeds

Indian file *n* **:** SINGLE FILE

Indian giver *n* **:** one that gives something to another and then takes it back or expects an equivalent in return — **Indian giving** *n*

Indian hemp *n* **1 :** an American dogbane (*Apocynum cannabinum*) with milky juice, tough fibrous bark, and an emetic and cathartic root **2 :** HEMP 1

Indian licorice *n* **:** ROSARY PEA 1

Indian meal *n* **:** CORNMEAL

Indian paintbrush *n* **1 :** any of a genus (*Castilleja*) of herbaceous plants of the figwort family that have brightly colored bracts — called also *painted cup* **2 :** ORANGE HAWKWEED

Indian pipe *n* **:** a waxy white leafless saprophytic herb (*Monotropa uniflora* of the family Monotropaceae, the Indian-pipe family) of Asia and the U.S.

Indian pipe

Indian pudding *n* **:** a pudding made chiefly of cornmeal, milk, and molasses

Indian red *n* **1 a :** a yellowish red earth containing hematite and used as a pigment **b :** any of various light red to purplish brown pigments made by calcining iron salts **2 :** a strong or moderate reddish brown

Indian sign *n* **:** HEX, SPELL

Indian summer *n* **1 :** a period of warm or mild weather in late autumn or early winter **2 :** a happy or flourishing period occurring toward the end of something <life in the *Indian summer* of Czarist Russia —John Davenport>

Indian tobacco *n* **1 :** an American wild lobelia (*Lobelia inflata*) with small blue flowers **2 :** a wild tobacco (*Nicotiana rustica*) **3 :** a common cat's-foot (*Antennaria plantaginifolia*) of eastern No. America

In·di·an–wres·tle \ˈin-dē-ən-ˌres-əl, -ˌras-\ *vi* [back-formation fr. *Indian wrestling*] **:** to engage in Indian wrestling

Indian wrestling *n* **1 :** wrestling in which two wrestlers lie side by side on their backs in reversed position locking their near arms and raising and locking the corresponding legs and attempt to force each other's leg down and turn the other wrestler on his face **2 :** wrestling in which two wrestlers stand face to face gripping usu. their right hands and setting the outsides of the corresponding feet together and attempt to force each other off balance **3 :** ARM WRESTLING

India paper *n* **1 :** a thin absorbent paper used esp. for proving inked intaglio surfaces (as steel engravings) **2 :** a thin tough opaque printing paper

india rubber *n, often cap I* **:** [1]RUBBER 2a

indic *abbr* indicative

In·dic \ˈin-dik\ *adj* **1 :** of or relating to the subcontinent of India **:** INDIAN **2 :** of, relating to, or constituting the Indian branch of the Indo-European languages — see INDO-EUROPEAN LANGUAGES table — **Indic** *n*

in·di·can \ˈin-də-ˌkan\ *n* [L *indicum* indigo — more at INDIGO] **1 :** a glucoside $C_{14}H_{17}NO_6$ occurring esp. in the indigo plant and being a source of natural indigo **2 :** an indigo-forming substance $C_8H_7NO_4S$ found as a salt in urine and other animal fluids

in·di·cant \ˈin-di-kənt\ *n* **:** something that serves to indicate

in·di·cate \ˈin-də-ˌkāt\ *vt* **-cat·ed; -cat·ing** [L *indicatus,* pp. of *indicare,* fr. *in-* + *dicare* to proclaim, dedicate — more DICTION] **1 a :** to point out or point to **b :** to be a sign, symptom, or index of <the high fever ~*s* a serious condition> **c :** to demonstrate or suggest the necessity or advisability of <*indicated* the need for a new school> **2 :** to state or express briefly **:** SUGGEST <*indicated* his desire to cooperate>

in·di·ca·tion \ˌin-də-ˈkā-shən\ *n* **1 :** the action of indicating **2 a :** something that serves to indicate **b :** something that is indicated as advisable or necessary **3 :** the degree indicated on a graduated instrument **:** READING — **in·di·ca·tion·al** \-shnəl, -shən-ᵊl\ *adj*

[1]**in·dic·a·tive** \in-ˈdik-ət-iv\ *adj* **1 :** of, relating to, or constituting a verb form or set of verb forms that represents the denoted act or state as an objective fact <the ~ mood> <an ~ verb form> **2 :** serving to indicate <actions ~ of fear> — **in·dic·a·tive·ly** *adv*

[2]**indicative** *n* **1 :** the indicative mood of a language **2 :** a form in the indicative mood

in·di·ca·tor \ˈin-də-ˌkāt-ər\ *n* **1 :** one that indicates: as **a :** an index hand (as on a dial) **:** POINTER **b (1) :** a pressure gauge **(2) :** an instrument for automatically making a diagram that indicates the pressure in and volume of the working fluid of an engine throughout the cycle **c :** a dial that registers something (as the movement of an elevator) **2 a :** a substance (as litmus) used to show visually (as by change of color) the condition of a solution with respect to the presence of a particular material (as a free acid or alkali) **b :** TRACER 4b **3 :** an organism or ecological community so strictly associated with particular environmental conditions that its presence is indicative of the existence of these conditions — **in·dic·a·to·ry** \in-ˈdik-ə-ˌtōr-ē, -ˌtȯr-\ *adj*

indices *pl of* INDEX

in·di·cia \in-ˈdish-(ē-)ə\ *n pl* [L, pl. of *indicium* sign, fr. *indicare*] **1 :** distinctive marks **:** INDICATIONS **2 :** postal markings often imprinted on mail or on labels to be affixed to mail

in·dict \in-ˈdīt\ *vt* [alter. of earlier *indite,* fr. ME *inditen,* fr. AF *enditer,* fr. OF, to write down — more at INDITE] **1 :** to charge with some offense **:** ACCUSE **2 :** to charge with a crime by the finding or presentment of a jury (as a grand jury) in due form of law — **in·dict·er** *or* **in·dict·or** \-ˈdīt-ər\ *n*

in·dict·able \-ˈdīt-ə-bəl\ *adj* **1 :** subject to being indicted **:** liable to indictment **2 :** making one liable to indictment <an ~ offense>

in·dic·tion \in-ˈdik-shən\ *n* [ME *indiccioun,* fr. LL *indiction-, indictio,* fr. L, proclamation, fr. *indictus,* pp. of *indicere* to proclaim, fr. *in-* + *dicere* to say — more at DICTION] **:** a 15-year cycle used as a chronological unit in several ancient and medieval systems

in·dict·ment \in-ˈdīt-mənt\ *n* **1 a :** the action or the legal process of indicting **b :** the state of being indicted **2 :** a formal written statement framed by a prosecuting authority and found by a jury (as a grand jury) charging a person with an offense

in·dif·fer·ence \in-ˈdif-ərn(t)s, -ˈdif-(ə-)rən(t)s\ *n* **1 :** the quality, state, or fact of being indifferent **2 a** *archaic* **:** lack of difference or distinction between two or more things **b :** absence of compulsion to or toward one thing or another

in·dif·fer·en·cy \-ərn-sē, -(ə-)rən-sē\ *n, archaic* **:** INDIFFERENCE

in·dif·fer·ent \in-ˈdif-ərnt, -ˈdif-(ə-)rənt\ *adj* [ME, fr. MF or L; MF, regarded as neither good nor bad, fr. L *indifferent-, indifferens,* fr. *in-* + *different-, differens,* prp. of *differre* to be different — more at DIFFERENT] **1 :** marked by impartiality **:** UNBIASED **2 a :** that does not matter one way or the other **b :** that has nothing that calls for sanction or condemnation in either observance or neglect **:** of no importance or value one way or the other **3 a :** marked by no special liking for or dislike of something <was ~ about which book he was given> **b :** marked by a lack of interest in or concern about something **:** APATHETIC <was ~ to suffering and poverty> **4 :** being neither excessive nor defective **5 a :** being neither good nor bad **:** MEDIOCRE **b :** being neither right nor wrong **6 :** characterized by lack of active quality **:** NEUTRAL **7 a :** not differentiated **b :** capable of development in more than one direction; *esp* **:** not yet embryologically determined — **in·dif·fer·ent·ly** *adv*

syn INDIFFERENT, UNCONCERNED, INCURIOUS, ALOOF, DETACHED, DISINTERESTED ***shared meaning element*** **:** not showing or feeling interest ***ant*** avid

in·dif·fer·ent·ism \-ərnt-ˌiz-əm, -(ə-)rənt-\ *n* **:** INDIFFERENCE; *specif* **:** belief that all religions are equally valid — **in·dif·fer·ent·ist** \-əst\ *n*

in·di·gence \ˈin-di-jən(t)s\ *n* **:** a level of poverty in which real hardship and deprivation are suffered and comforts of life are wholly lacking ***syn*** see POVERTY

in·di·gene \ˈin-də-ˌjēn\ *also* **in·di·gen** \-di-jən, -də-ˌjen\ *n* [L *indigena*] **:** NATIVE

in·dig·e·nous \in-ˈdij-ə-nəs\ *adj* [LL *indigenus,* fr. L *indigena,* n., native, fr. OL *indu, endo* in, within (akin to L *in* and to L *de* down) + L *gignere* to beget — more at DE-, KIN] **1 :** having originated in and being produced, growing, or living naturally in a particular region or environment **2 :** INNATE, INBORN ***syn*** see NATIVE ***ant*** naturalized, exotic — **in·dig·e·nous·ly** *adv* — **in·dig·e·nous·ness** *n*

in·di·gent \ˈin-di-jənt\ *adj* [ME, fr. MF, fr. L *indigent-, indigens,* prp. of *indigēre* to need, fr. OL *indu* + L *egēre* to need; akin to OHG *ekrōdi* thin] **1 :** suffering from indigence **:** IMPOVERISHED **2 a** *archaic* **:** DEFICIENT **b** *archaic* **:** totally lacking in something specified — **indigent** *n*

in·di·gest·ed \ˌin-(ˌ)dī-ˈjes-təd, -də-\ *adj* **:** not carefully thought out or arranged **:** FORMLESS

in·di·gest·ible \-ˈjes-tə-bəl\ *adj* [LL *indigestibilis,* fr. L *in-* + LL *digestibilis* digestible] **:** not digestible **:** not easily digested — **in·di·gest·ibil·i·ty** \-ˌjes-tə-ˈbil-ət-ē\ *n* — **indigestible** *n*

in·di·ges·tion \-ˈjes(h)-chən\ *n* **1 :** inability to digest or difficulty in digesting something **2 :** a case or attack of indigestion

in·dign \in-ˈdīn\ *adj* [ME *indigne,* fr. MF, fr. L *indignus*] **1** *archaic* **:** UNWORTHY, UNDESERVING **2** *obs* **:** UNBECOMING, DISGRACEFUL

in·dig·nant \in-ˈdig-nənt\ *adj* [L *indignant-, indignans,* prp. of *indignari* to be indignant, fr. *indignus* unworthy, fr. *in-* + *dignus* worthy — more at DECENT] **:** filled with or marked by indignation <became ~ at the accusation> — **in·dig·nant·ly** *adv*

in·dig·na·tion \ˌin-dig-ˈnā-shən\ *n* **:** anger aroused by something unjust, unworthy, or mean ***syn*** see ANGER

in·dig·ni·ty \in-ˈdig-nət-ē\ *n, pl* **-ties** [L *indignitat-, indignitas,* fr. *indignus*] **1** *obs* **:** lack or loss of dignity or honor **2 a :** an act that offends against a person's dignity or self-respect **:** INSULT **b :** humiliating treatment

in·di·go \ˈin-di-ˌgō\ *n, pl* **-gos** *or* **-goes** [It dial., fr. L *indicum,* fr. Gk *indikon,* fr. neut. of *indikos* Indic, fr. *Indos* India] **1 a :** a blue vat dye obtained from plants (as indigo plants) **b :** the principal

ə abut ᵊ kitten ər further a back ā bake ä cot, cart
au̇ out ch chin e less ē easy g gift i trip ī life
j joke ŋ sing ō flow ȯ flaw ȯi coin th thin t͟h this
ü loot u̇ foot y yet yü few yu̇ furious zh vision

coloring matter $C_{16}H_{10}N_2O_2$ of natural indigo usu. synthesized as a blue powder with a coppery luster **c :** any of several blue vat dyes derived from or closely related to indigo **2 :** a variable color averaging a dark grayish blue **3 :** INDIGO PLANT

indigo bunting *n* **:** a common small finch (*Passerina cyanea*) of the eastern U.S. of which the male is largely indigo-blue

indigo plant *n* **:** a plant that yields indigo; *esp* **:** any of a genus (*Indigofera*) of leguminous herbs

indigo snake *n* **:** a large harmless blue-black snake (*Drymarchon corais couperi*) of the southern U.S. — called also *gopher snake*

in·di·go·tin \in-ˈdig-ət-ən, ˌin-di-ˈgōt-ᵊn\ *n* [ISV *indigo* + connective *-t-* + *-in*] **:** INDIGO 1b

in·di·rect \ˌin-də-ˈrekt, -(ˌ)dī-\ *adj* [ME, fr. ML *indirectus,* fr. L *in-* + *directus* direct] **:** not direct: as **a (1) :** deviating from a direct line or course **:** ROUNDABOUT (2) **:** not going straight to the point <an ~ accusation> **b :** not straightforward and open **:** DECEITFUL **c :** not directly aimed at or achieved <~ consequences> **d :** stating what a real or supposed original speaker said with changes in wording that conform the statement grammatically to the sentence in which it is included <~ discourse> **e :** not effected by the action of the people or the electorate <~ government representation> — **in·di·rect·ly** \-ˈrek-(t)lē\ *adv* — **in·di·rect·ness** \-ˈrek(t)-nəs\ *n*

indirect cost *n* **:** a cost that is not identifiable with a specific product, function, or activity

indirect evidence *n* **:** evidence that establishes immediately collateral facts from which the main fact may be inferred **:** CIRCUMSTANTIAL EVIDENCE

indirect fire *n* **:** gunfire by indirect aiming at a target not visible from the gun

in·di·rec·tion \ˌin-də-ˈrek-shən, -(ˌ)dī-\ *n* **1 a :** lack of straightforwardness and openness **:** DECEITFULNESS **b :** something (as an act or statement) marked by lack of straightforwardness <hated diplomatic ~*s* —*Rev. of Reviews*> **2 a :** indirect action or procedure **b :** lack of direction **:** AIMLESSNESS

indirect lighting *n* **:** lighting in which the light emitted by a source is diffusely reflected (as by the ceiling)

indirect object *n* **:** a grammatical object representing the secondary goal of the action of its verb <*her* in "I gave her the book" is an *indirect object*>

indirect proof *n* **:** REDUCTIO AD ABSURDUM

indirect tax *n* **:** a tax exacted from a person other than the one on whom the ultimate burden of the tax is expected to fall

in·dis·cern·ible \ˌin-dis-ˈər-nə-bəl, -diz-\ *adj* **:** incapable of being discerned **:** not recognizable as distinct

in·dis·ci·plin·able \(ˌ)in-ˌdis-ə-ˈplin-ə-bəl; (ˈ)in-ˈdis-ə-plən-\ *adj* **:** not subject to or capable of being disciplined

in·dis·ci·pline \(ˈ)in-ˈdis-ə-plən\ *n* **:** lack of discipline

in·dis·ci·plined \-ˌplənd, -(ˌ)plind\ *adj* **:** lacking in discipline **:** WILD

in·dis·cov·er·able \ˌin-dis-ˈkəv-(ə-)rə-bəl\ *adj* **:** not discoverable

in·dis·creet \ˌin-dis-ˈkrēt\ *adj* [ME *indiscrete,* fr. MF & LL; MF *indiscret,* fr. LL *indiscretus,* fr. L, indistinguishable, fr. *in-* + *discretus,* pp. of *discernere* to separate — more at DISCERN] **:** not discreet **:** IMPRUDENT — **in·dis·creet·ly** *adv* — **in·dis·creet·ness** *n*

in·dis·crete \ˌin-dis-ˈkrēt, (ˈ)in-ˈdis-ˌ\ *adj* [L *indiscretus*] **:** not separated into distinct parts <an ~ mass>

in·dis·cre·tion \ˌin-dis-ˈkresh-ən\ *n* **1 :** lack of discretion **:** IMPRUDENCE **2 :** something (as an act or remark) marked by lack of discretion; *specif* **:** an act at variance with the accepted morality of a society

in·dis·crim·i·nate \ˌin-dis-ˈkrim-(ə-)nət\ *adj* **1 a :** not marked by careful distinction **:** deficient in discrimination and discernment <~ reading habits> **b :** HAPHAZARD, RANDOM <their language is an ~ mixture of French and English> **2 a :** PROMISCUOUS, UNRESTRAINED <~ sexual behavior> **b :** HETEROGENEOUS, CONFUSED <clothes tossed in an ~ heap> — **in·dis·crim·i·nate·ly** *adv* — **in·dis·crim·i·nate·ness** *n*

syn INDISCRIMINATE, WHOLESALE, SWEEPING *shared meaning element* **:** including all or nearly all within the range of choice, operation, or effectiveness ***ant*** discriminate, selective

in·dis·crim·i·nat·ing \-ˈkrim-ə-ˌnāt-iŋ\ *adj* **:** not discriminating — **in·dis·crim·i·nat·ing·ly** \-iŋ-lē\ *adv*

in·dis·crim·i·na·tion \-ˌkrim-ə-ˈnā-shən\ *n* **:** lack of discrimination

in·dis·cuss·ible \ˌin-dis-ˈkəs-ə-bəl\ *adj* **:** not capable of being discussed

in·dis·pens·able \ˌin-dis-ˈpen(t)-sə-bəl\ *adj* **1 :** not subject to being set aside or neglected <an ~ obligation> **2 :** absolutely necessary **:** ESSENTIAL <carbon dioxide is ~ for plants> — **in·dis·pens·abil·i·ty** \-ˌpen(t)-sə-ˈbil-ət-ē\ *n* — **indispensable** *n* — **in·dis·pens·able·ness** \-ˈpen(t)-sə-bəl-nəs\ *n* — **in·dis·pens·ably** \-blē\ *adv*

in·dis·pose \ˌin-dis-ˈpōz\ *vt* **-posed; -pos·ing** [prob. back-formation fr. *indisposed*] **1 a :** to make unfit **:** DISQUALIFY **b :** to make averse **:** DISINCLINE **2** *archaic* **:** to cause to be in poor physical health

in·dis·posed \-ˈpōzd\ *adj* **1 :** slightly ill **2 :** AVERSE

in·dis·po·si·tion \(ˌ)in-ˌdis-pə-ˈzish-ən\ *n* **:** the condition of being indisposed: **a :** DISINCLINATION **b :** a usu. slight illness

in·dis·put·able \ˌin-dis-ˈpyüt-ə-bəl, (ˈ)in-ˈdis-pyət-\ *adj* [LL *indisputabilis,* fr. L *in-* + *disputabilis* disputable] **:** not disputable **:** UNQUESTIONABLE <~ proof> — **in·dis·put·able·ness** *n* — **in·dis·put·ably** \-blē\ *adv*

in·dis·so·cia·ble \ˌin-dis-ˈō-sh(ē-)ə-bəl, -sē-ə-\ *adj* **:** not dissociated **:** INSEPARABLE — **in·dis·so·cia·bly** \-blē\ *adv*

in·dis·sol·u·ble \ˌin-dis-ˈäl-yə-bəl\ *adj***:** not dissoluble; as **a :** incapable of being annulled, undone, or broken **:** PERMANENT <an ~ contract> **b :** incapable of being dissolved, decomposed, or disintegrated — **in·dis·sol·u·bil·i·ty** \-ˌäl-yə-ˈbil-ət-ē\ *n* — **in·dis·sol·u·ble·ness** \-ˈäl-yə-bəl-nəs\ *n* — **in·dis·sol·u·bly** \-blē\ *adv*

in·dis·tinct \ˌin-dis-ˈtiŋ(k)t\ *adj* [L *indistinctus,* fr. *in-* + *distinctus* distinct] **:** not distinct: as **a :** not sharply outlined or separable **:** BLURRED <~ figures in the fog> **b :** FAINT, DIM <an ~ light in the distance> **c :** not clearly recognizable or understandable **:** UNCERTAIN — **in·dis·tinct·ly** \-ˈtiŋ(k)-tlē, -ˈtiŋ-klē\ *adv* — **in·dis·tinct·ness** \-ˈtiŋt-nəs, -ˈtiŋk-nəs\ *n*

in·dis·tinc·tive \-ˈtiŋ(k)-tiv\ *adj* **:** lacking distinctive qualities

in·dis·tin·guish·able \ˌin-dis-ˈtiŋ-(g)wish-ə-bəl\ *adj* **:** not distinguishable: as **a :** indeterminate in shape or structure **b :** not clearly recognizable or understandable **c :** lacking identifying or individualizing qualities — **in·dis·tin·guish·abil·i·ty** \-ˌtiŋ-(g)wish-ə-ˈbil-ət-ē\ *n* — **in·dis·tin·guish·able·ness** \-ˈtiŋ-(g)wish-ə-bəl-nəs\ *n* — **in·dis·tin·guish·ably** \-blē\ *adv*

in·dite \in-ˈdīt\ *vt* **in·dit·ed; in·dit·ing** [ME *enditen,* fr. OF *enditer* to write down, proclaim, fr. (assumed) VL *indictare* to proclaim, fr. L *indictus,* pp. of *indicere* to proclaim, fr. *in-* + *dicere* to say — more at DICTION] **1 a :** to make up **:** COMPOSE <~ a poem> **b :** to give literary or formal expression to **c :** to put down in writing <~ a message> **2** *obs* **:** DICTATE — **in·dit·er** *n*

in·di·um \ˈin-dē-əm\ *n* [ISV *ind-* + NL *-ium*] **:** a malleable fusible silvery metallic element that is chiefly trivalent, occurs esp. in sphalerite ores, and is used as a plating for bearings, in alloys melting at a low temperature, and in the making of transistors — see ELEMENT table

indiv *abbr* individual

in·di·vert·ible \ˌin-də-ˈvərt-ə-bəl, -(ˌ)dī-\ *adj* **:** not to be diverted or turned aside — **in·di·vert·ibly** \-blē\ *adv*

[1]**in·di·vid·u·al** \ˌin-də-ˈvij-(ə-)wəl, -ˈvij-əl\ *adj* [ML *individualis,* fr. L *individuus* indivisible, fr. *in-* + *dividuus* divided, fr. *dividere* to divide] **1** *obs* **:** INSEPARABLE **2 a :** of, relating to, or distinctively associated with an individual <~ turns of phrase that identify his writing> **b :** being an individual or existing as an indivisible whole **c :** intended for one person <an ~ serving> **3 :** existing as a distinct entity **:** SEPARATE **4 :** having marked individuality <an ~ style> ***syn* 1** see SPECIAL ***ant*** general **2** see CHARACTERISTIC ***ant*** common — **in·di·vid·u·al·ly** \-ē\ *adv*

[2]**individual** *n* **1 a :** a particular being or thing as distinguished from a class, species, or collection: as **(1) :** a single human being as contrasted with a social group or institution <though he works with ~*s* . . . he is always aware of the world which surrounds his patient —Norman Mailer> **(2) :** a single organism as distinguished from a group **b :** a particular person <an odd ~> **2 :** an indivisible entity **3 :** the reference of a name or variable of the lowest logical type in a calculus

in·di·vid·u·al·ism \ˌin-də-ˈvij-(ə-)wə-ˌliz-əm, -ˈvij-ə-ˌliz-\ *n* **1 a (1) :** a doctrine that the interests of the individual are or ought to be ethically paramount; *also* **:** conduct guided by such a doctrine **(2) :** the conception that all values, rights, and duties originate in individuals **b :** a theory maintaining the political and economic independence of the individual and stressing individual initiative, action, and interests; *also* **:** conduct or practice guided by such a theory **2 a :** INDIVIDUALITY **b :** an individual peculiarity **:** IDIOSYNCRASY

in·di·vid·u·al·ist \-ləst\ *n* **1 :** one that pursues a markedly independent course in thought or action **2 :** one that advocates or practices individualism — **individualist** *or* **in·di·vid·u·al·is·tic** \-ˌvij-(ə-)wə-ˈlis-tik, -ˌvij-ə-ˈlis-\ *adj* — **in·di·vid·u·al·is·ti·cal·ly** \-ˈlis-ti-k(ə-)lē\ *adv*

in·di·vid·u·al·i·ty \-ˌvij-ə-ˈwal-ət-ē\ *n, pl* **-ties 1 a :** total character peculiar to and distinguishing an individual from others **b :** PERSONALITY **2** *archaic* **:** the quality or state of being indivisible **:** INSEPARABILITY **3 :** INDIVIDUAL, PERSON **4 :** separate or distinct existence

in·di·vid·u·al·ize \-ˈvij-(ə-)wə-ˌlīz, -ˈvij-ə-ˌlīz\ *vt* **-ized; -iz·ing 1 :** to make individual in character **2 :** to treat or notice individually **:** PARTICULARIZE **3 :** to adapt to the needs or special circumstances of an individual <efforts to ~ teaching according to student ability and interest> — **in·di·vid·u·al·iza·tion** \-ˌvij-(ə-)wə-lə-ˈzā-shən, -ˌvij-ə-lə-\ *n*

individual medley *n* **:** a swimming race in which each contestant swims each quarter of the course with a different stroke

in·di·vid·u·ate \ˌin-də-ˈvij-ə-ˌwāt\ *vt* **-at·ed; -at·ing 1 :** to give individuality to **2 :** to form into a distinct entity

in·di·vid·u·a·tion \-ˌvij-ə-ˈwā-shən\ *n* **1 :** the act or process of individuating: as **a (1) :** the development of the individual from the universal **(2) :** the determination of the individual in the general **b :** the process by which individuals in society become differentiated from one another **c :** regional differentiation along a primary embryonic axis **2 :** the state of being individuated; *specif* **:** INDIVIDUALITY

in·di·vis·i·ble \ˌin-də-ˈviz-ə-bəl\ *adj* [ME, fr. LL *indivisibilis,* fr. L *in-* + LL *divisibilis* divisible] **:** not divisible — **in·di·vis·i·bil·i·ty** \-ˌviz-ə-ˈbil-ət-ē\ *n* — **indivisible** *n* — **in·di·vis·i·ble·ness** \-ˈviz-ə-bəl-nəs\ *n* — **in·di·vis·i·bly** \-blē\ *adv*

indn *abbr* indication

indo- — see IND-

Indo- — see IND-

In·do–Ar·y·an \ˌin-dō-ˈar-ē-ən, -ˈer-; -ˈär-yən\ *n* **1 :** a member of one of the peoples of India of Aryan speech and physique **2 :** one of the early Indo-European invaders of Persia, Afghanistan, and India **3 :** the Indo-European languages of India and Pakistan as a group — **Indo–Aryan** *adj*

In·do–Chi·nese \-ˌchī-ˈnēz, -ˈnēs\ *n* **1 :** a native or inhabitant of Indochina **2 :** SINO-TIBETAN — **Indo–Chinese** *adj*

in·doc·ile \(ˈ)in-ˈdäs-əl *also* -ˌīl, *esp Brit* -ˈdō-ˌsīl\ *adj* [MF, fr. L *indocilis,* fr. *in-* + *docilis* docile] **:** unwilling or indisposed to be taught or disciplined **:** INTRACTABLE — **in·do·cil·i·ty** \ˌin-dä-ˈsil-ət-ē, -dō-\ *n*

in·doc·tri·nate \in-ˈdäk-trə-ˌnāt\ *vt* **-nat·ed; -nat·ing** [prob. fr. ME *endoctrinen,* fr. MF *endoctriner,* fr. OF, fr. *en-* + *doctrine*] **1 :** to instruct esp. in fundamentals or rudiments **:** TEACH **2 :** to imbue with a usu. partisan or sectarian opinion, point of view, or principle — **in·doc·tri·na·tion** \(ˌ)in-ˌdäk-trə-ˈnā-shən\ *n* — **in·doc·tri·na·tor** \in-ˈdäk-trə-ˌnāt-ər\ *n*

In·do–Eu·ro·pe·an \ˌin-dō-ˌyu̇r-ə-ˈpē-ən\ *adj* **:** of, relating to, or constituting the Indo-European languages — **Indo–European** *n*

Indo-European languages *n pl* **:** a family of languages comprising those spoken in most of Europe and in the parts of the world colonized by Europeans since 1500 and also in Persia, the subcontinent of India, and some other parts of Asia

In·do-Ger·man·ic \ˌin-dō-jər-ˈman-ik\ *n* **:** INDO-EUROPEAN — **Indo-Germanic** *adj*

In·do-Hit·tite \-ˈhi-ˌtīt\ *n* **1 :** a language family including Indo-European and Anatolian **2 :** a hypothetical parent language of Indo-European and Anatolian — **Indo-Hittite** *adj*

In·do-Ira·ni·an \-ir-ˈā-nē-ən\ *adj* **:** of, relating to, or constituting a subfamily of the Indo-European languages that consists of the Indic and the Iranian branches — see INDO-EUROPEAN LANGUAGES table — **Indo-Iranian** *n*

in·dole \ˈin-ˌdōl\ *n* [ISV *ind-* + *-ole*] **:** a crystalline compound C_8H_7N that is a decomposition product of proteins containing tryptophan, often formed by reduction distillation of indigo, and used in perfumes; *also* **:** a derivative of indole

in·dole·ace·tic acid \ˈin-ˌdōl-ə-ˌsēt-ik-\ *n* **:** a crystalline plant hormone $C_{10}H_9NO_2$ that promotes growth and rooting of plants — called also *heteroauxin*

in·dole·bu·tyr·ic acid \-byü-ˌtir-ik-\ *n* **:** a crystalline acid $C_{12}H_{13}NO_2$ similar to indoleacetic acid in its effects on plants

in·do·lence \ˈin-də-lən(t)s\ *n* **1 :** a condition of causing little or no pain **2 :** indisposition to labor **:** SLOTH

in·do·lent \-lənt\ *adj* [LL *indolent-, indolens* insensitive to pain, fr. L *in-* + *dolent-, dolens,* prp. of *dolēre* to feel pain — more at CONDOLE] **1 a :** causing little or no pain **b :** slow to develop or heal **2 a :** averse to activity, effort, or movement **:** habitually lazy **b :** conducing to or encouraging laziness <~ heat> **c :** exhibiting indolence <an ~ sigh> ***syn*** see LAZY ***ant*** industrious — **in·do·lent·ly** *adv*

in·do·meth·a·cin \ˌin-dō-ˈmeth-ə-sən\ *n* [*indole* + *meth-* + *acetic acid* + *-in*] **:** a nonsteroidal analgesic drug $C_{19}H_{16}ClNO_4$ used esp. in treating arthritis

in·dom·i·ta·ble \in-ˈdäm-ət-ə-bəl\ *adj* [LL *indomitabilis,* fr. L *in-* + *domitare* to tame — more at DAUNT] **:** incapable of being subdued **:** UNCONQUERABLE <~ courage> — **in·dom·i·ta·bil·i·ty** \(ˌ)in-ˌdäm-ət-ə-ˈbil-ət-ē\ *n* — **in·dom·i·ta·ble·ness** \in-ˈdäm-ət-ə-bəl-nəs\ *n* — **in·dom·i·ta·bly** \-blē\ *adv*

Indon *abbr* Indonesia; Indonesian

In·do·ne·sian \ˌin-də-ˈnē-zhən, -shən\ *n* **1 :** a native or inhabitant of the Malay archipelago **2 a :** a native or inhabitant of the Republic of Indonesia **b :** the language based on Malay that is the national language of the Republic of Indonesia — **Indonesian** *adj*

in·door \ˌin-ˌdō(ə)r, -ˌdȯ(ə)r\ *adj* **1 :** of or relating to the interior of a building **2 :** done, living, or belonging within doors <an ~ sport>

in·doors \(ˈ)in-ˈdō(ə)rz, -ˈdȯ(ə)rz\ *adv* **:** in or into a building

in·do·phe·nol \ˌin-dō-ˈfē-ˌnōl, ˌin-(ˌ)dō-fi-ˈ\ *n* [ISV] **:** any of various blue or green dyes

indorse *var of* ENDORSE

in·dox·yl \in-ˈdäk-səl\ *n* [ISV *ind-* + hydr*oxyl*] **:** a crystalline compound C_8H_7NO found in plants and animals or synthesized as a step in indigo manufacture

in·draft \ˈin-ˌdraft, -ˌdrȧft\ *n* **1 :** a drawing or pulling in **2 :** an inward flow or current (as of air or water)

in·drawn \ˈin-ˌdrȯn\ *adj* **1 :** drawn in **2 :** ALOOF, RESERVED

in·du·bi·ta·ble \(ˈ)in-ˈd(y)ü-bət-ə-bəl\ *adj* [F or L; F, fr. L *indubitabilis,* fr. *in-* + *dubitabilis* dubitable] **:** too evident to be doubted **:** UNQUESTIONABLE — **in·du·bi·ta·bil·i·ty** \(ˌ)in-ˌdyü-bət-ə-ˈbil-ət-ē\ *n* — **in·du·bi·ta·ble·ness** \(ˈ)in-ˈd(y)ü-bət-ə-bəl-nəs\ *n* — **in·du·bi·ta·bly** \-blē\ *adv*

in·duce \in-ˈd(y)üs\ *vt* **in·duced; in·duc·ing** [ME *inducen,* fr. L *inducere,* fr. *in-* + *ducere* to lead — more at TOW] **1 a :** to lead on **:** move by persuasion or influence **b :** to call forth or bring about by influence or stimulation **2 a :** EFFECT, CAUSE **b :** to cause the formation of **c :** to produce (as an electric current) by induction **d :** to arouse by indirect stimulation <~ a contrast color> **3 :** to determine by induction; *specif* **:** to infer from particulars — compare DEDUCE — **in·duc·ibil·i·ty** \-ˌd(y)ü-sə-ˈbil-ət-ē\ *n* — **in·duc·ible** \-ˈd(y)ü-sə-bəl\ *adj*

syn INDUCE, PERSUADE, PREVAIL, GET *shared meaning element* **:** to move one to act or decide in a certain way

in·duce·ment \in-ˈd(y)ü-smənt\ *n* **1 :** the act or process of inducing **2 :** a motive or consideration that leads one to action or to additional or more effective actions <prizes offered as ~*s* to students to do better work> **3 :** matter presented by way of introduction or background to explain the principal allegations of a legal cause, plea, or defense ***syn*** see MOTIVE

in·duc·er \-ˈd(y)ü-sər\ *n* **:** one that induces; *specif* **:** a substance that is capable of activating a structural gene by combining with and inactivating a genetic repressor

in·duct \in-ˈdəkt\ *vt* [ME *inducten,* fr. ML *inductus,* pp. of *inducere,* fr. L] **1 :** to put in formal possession (as of a benefice or office) **:** INSTALL <was ~*ed* as president of the college> **2 a :** to admit as a member <~*ed* into a scholastic society> **b :** INTRODUCE, INITIATE **c :** to enroll for military training or service (as under a selective-service act) **3 :** LEAD, CONDUCT

in·duc·tance \in-ˈdək-tən(t)s\ *n* **1 :** a property of an electric circuit by which an electromotive force is induced in it by a variation of current either (1) in the circuit itself or (2) in a neighboring circuit **2 :** a circuit or a device possessing inductance

in·duct·ee \(ˌ)in-ˌdək-ˈtē, in-ˈdək-ˌ\ *n* **:** a person inducted into military service

in·duc·tion \in-ˈdək-shən\ *n* **1 a :** the act or process of inducting (as into office) **b :** an initial experience **:** INITIATION **c :** the formality by which a civilian is inducted into military service **2 a :** the act, process, or result or an instance of reasoning from a part to a whole, from particulars to generals, or from the individual to the universal **b :** mathematical demonstration of the validity of a law concerning all the positive integers by proving that it holds for the first integer and that if it holds for all the integers preceding a given integer it must hold for the next following integer **3 :** a preface, prologue, or introductory scene esp. of an early English play **4 a :** the act of bringing forward or adducing (as facts or particulars) **b :** the act of causing or bringing on or about **c :** the process by which an electrical conductor becomes electrified when near a charged body, by which a magnetizable body becomes magnetized when in a magnetic field or in the magnetic flux set up by a magnetomotive force, or by which an electromotive force is produced in a circuit by varying the magnetic field linked with the circuit **d :** the inspiration of the fuel-air charge from the carburetor into the combustion chamber of an internal-combustion engine **e :** the sum of the processes by which the fate of embryonic cells is determined and morphogenetic differentiation brought about

induction coil *n* **:** an apparatus for obtaining intermittent high voltage consisting of a primary coil through which the direct current flows, an interrupter, and a secondary coil of a larger number of turns in which the high voltage is induced

induction heating *n* **:** heating of material by means of an electric current that is caused to flow through the material or its container by electromagnetic induction

in·duc·tive \in-ˈdək-tiv\ *adj* **1 :** leading on **:** INDUCING **2 :** of, relating to, or employing mathematical or logical induction <~ reasoning> **3 :** of or relating to inductance or electrical induction **4 :** INTRODUCTORY **5 :** involving the action of an embryological inductor **:** tending to produce induction — **in·duc·tive·ly** *adv* — **in·duc·tive·ness** *n*

in·duc·tor \in-ˈdək-tər\ *n* **1 :** one that inducts **2 a :** a part of an electrical apparatus that acts upon another or is itself acted upon by induction **b :** REACTOR 2 **3 :** ORGANIZER 2

indue *var of* ENDUE

in·dulge \in-ˈdəlj\ *vb* **in·dulged; in·dulg·ing** [L *indulgēre* to be complaisant] *vt* **1 a :** to give free rein to **b :** to take unrestrained pleasure in **:** GRATIFY **2 a :** to yield to the desire of **:** HUMOR **b :** to treat with excessive leniency, generosity, or consideration ~ *vi* **:** to indulge oneself — **in·dulg·er** *n*

syn INDULGE, PAMPER, HUMOR, SPOIL, BABY, MOLLYCODDLE *shared meaning element* **:** to show undue favor to a person or his wishes ***ant*** discipline

[1]in·dul·gence \in-ˈdəl-jən(t)s\ *n* **1 :** remission of part or all of the temporal and esp. purgatorial punishment that according to Roman Catholicism is due for sins whose eternal punishment has been remitted and whose guilt has been pardoned (as through the sacrament of penance) **2 :** the act of indulging **:** the state of being indulgent <treated her moody child with ~> **3 a :** an indulgent act **b :** an extension of time for payment or performance granted as a favor **4 a :** the act of indulging in something **:** the thing indulged in **b :** SELF-INDULGENCE

[2]indulgence *vt* **-genced; -genc·ing :** to attach an indulgence to <*indulgenced* prayers>

in·dul·gent \in-ˈdəl-jənt\ *adj* [L *indulgent-, indulgens,* prp. of *indulgēre*] **:** indulging or characterized by indulgence **:** LENIENT — **in·dul·gent·ly** *adv*

in·du·line \ˈin-d(y)ə-ˌlēn\ *n* [ISV *ind-* + *-ule* + *-ine*] **:** any of numerous blue or violet dyes related to the safranines

in·dult \ˈin-ˌdəlt, in-ˈ\ *n* [ME (Sc), fr. ML *indultum,* fr. LL, grant, fr. L, neut. of *indultus,* pp. of *indulgēre*] **:** a special often temporary dispensation granted in the Roman Catholic Church

[1]in·du·rate \ˈin-d(y)ə-rət, in-ˈd(y)u̇r-ət\ *adj* **:** physically or morally hardened

[2]in·du·rate \ˈin-d(y)ə-ˌrāt\ *vb* **-rat·ed; -rat·ing** [L *induratus,* pp. of *indurare,* fr. *in-* + *durare* to harden, fr. *durus* hard — more at DURING] *vt* **1 :** to make unfeeling, stubborn, or obdurate **2 :** to make hardy **:** INURE **3 a :** to make hard <great heat ~*s* clay> **b :** to increase the fibrous elements of <*indurated* tissue> **4 :** to establish firmly **:** CONFIRM ~ *vi* **1 :** to grow hard **:** HARDEN **2 :** to become established — **in·du·ra·tion** \ˌin-d(y)ə-ˈrā-shən\ *n* — **in·du·ra·tive** \ˈin-d(y)ə-ˌrāt-iv, in-ˈd(y)u̇r-ət-\ *adj*

indus *abbr* industrial; industry

in·du·si·um \in-ˈd(y)ü-z(h)ē-əm\ *n, pl* **-sia** \-z(h)ē-ə\ [NL, fr. L, tunic] **:** an investing outgrowth or membrane: as **a :** an outgrowth of a fern frond that invests the sori **b :** the annulus of a fungus esp. when large and full

[1]in·dus·tri·al \in-ˈdəs-trē-əl\ *adj* **1 :** of or relating to industry **2 :** characterized by highly developed industries <an ~ nation> **3 :** engaged in industry <the ~ classes> **4 :** derived from human industry <~ wealth> **5 :** used in industry <~ diamonds> — **in·dus·tri·al·ly** \-trē-ə-lē\ *adv*

[2]industrial *n* **1 a :** one that is employed in industry **b :** a company engaged in industrial production or service **2 :** a stock or bond issued by an industrial corporation or enterprise

industrial arts *n pl but sing in constr* **:** a subject taught in elementary and secondary schools that aims at developing manual skill and familiarity with tools and machines

industrial engineering *n* **:** engineering that deals with the development and application of cost and work standards for the various operations involved in manufacture

in·dus·tri·al·ism \in-ˈdəs-trē-ə-ˌliz-əm\ *n* **:** social organization in which industries and esp. large-scale industries are dominant

in·dus·tri·al·ist \-ləst\ *n* **:** one owning or engaged in the management of an industry **:** MANUFACTURER

in·dus·tri·al·ize \in-ˈdəs-trē-ə-ˌlīz\ *vb* **-ized; -iz·ing** *vt* **:** to make industrial <~ an agricultural region> ~ *vi* **:** to become industrial — **in·dus·tri·al·iza·tion** \-ˌdəs-trē-ə-lə-ˈzā-shən\ *n*

industrial melanism *n* **:** genetically determined melanism esp. in insect populations that occurs in areas darkened by industrial pollutants

---

ə abut	ᵊ kitten	ər further	a back	ā bake	ä cot, cart
au̇ out	ch chin	e less	ē easy	g gift	i trip
ī life	j joke	ŋ sing	ō flow	ȯ flaw	ȯi coin
th thin	t͟h this	ü loot	u̇ foot	y yet	yü few
yu̇ furious	zh vision				

INDO-EUROPEAN LANGUAGES

BRANCH	GROUP	LANGUAGES AND MAJOR DIALECTS[1]: ANCIENT	MEDIEVAL	MODERN	PROVENIENCE
GERMANIC	East		*Gothic*		eastern Europe
	North		*Old Norse*	Icelandic	Iceland
				Faeroese	Faeroe Islands
				Norwegian	Norway
				Swedish	Sweden
				Danish	Denmark
	West		*Old High German*	German	Germany, Switzerland, Austria
			Middle High German		
				Yiddish	Germany, eastern Europe
			Old Saxon	Low German	northern Germany
			Middle Low German		
			Middle Dutch	Dutch	Netherlands
				Afrikaans	South Africa
			Middle Flemish	Flemish	Belgium
			Old Frisian	Frisian	Netherlands, Germany
			Old English	English	England
			Middle English		
CELTIC	Continental	*Gaulish*			Gaul
	Goidelic		*Old Irish*	Irish Gaelic	Ireland
			Middle Irish		
				Scottish Gaelic	Scotland
				Manx	Isle of Man
	Brythonic		*Old Welsh*	Welsh	Wales
			Middle Welsh		
			Old Cornish	*Cornish*	Cornwall
			Middle Breton	Breton	Brittany
ITALIC	Osco-Umbrian	*Oscan, Sabellian*			ancient Italy
		Umbrian			
	Latinian or Romance[2]	*Venetic, Faliscan,*			ancient Italy
		Lanuvian, Praenestine			
		Latin		Portuguese	Portugal
				Spanish	Spain
				Judeo-Spanish	Mediterranean lands
				Catalan	Spain (Catalonia)
			Old Provencal	Provençal	southern France
			Old French	French	France, Belgium, Switzerland
			Middle French		
				Haitian Creole	Haiti
				Italian	Italy, Switzerland
				Rhaeto-Romanic	Switzerland, Italy
				Sardinian	Sardinia
				Dalmatian	Adriatic Coast
				Rumanian	Rumania, Balkans
Scantily recorded and of uncertain affinities within Indo-European		*Ligurian, Messapian,*			ancient Italy
		Illyrian, Thracian,			Balkans
		Phrygian			Asia Minor
Albanian				Albanian	Albania, southern Italy
Greek or Hellenic		Greek	Greek	Greek	Greece, the eastern Mediterranean
BALTO-SLAVIC	Baltic		*Old Prussian*		East Prussia
				Lithuanian	Lithuania
				Latvian	Latvia
	Slavic: South		Old Church Slavonic		
				Slovene	Yugoslavia
				Serbo-Croatian	Yugoslavia
				Macedonian	Macedonia
				Bulgarian	Bulgaria
	Slavic: West		*Old Czech*	Czech, Slovak	Czechoslovakia
				Polish, Kashubian	Poland
				Wendish, *Polabian*	Germany
	Slavic: East		*Old Russian*	Russian	Russia
				Ukrainian	Ukraine
				Belorussian	White Russia
Armenian			Armenian	Armenian	Asia Minor, Caucasus
Anatolian		*Hittite, Lydian, Lycian*			ancient Asia Minor
		Luwian			
		Palaic			
		Hieroglyphic Hittite			
INDO-IRANIAN	Iranian: West	*Old Persian*	*Pahlavi*		Persia
			Persian	Persian	Persia (Iran)
				Kurdish	Persia, Iraq, Turkey
				Baluchi	Pakistan
				Tajiki	central Asia
	Iranian: East	Avestan			ancient Persia
			Sogdian		central Asia
			Khotanese		central Asia
				Pashto	Afghanistan, Pakistan
				Ossetic	Caucasus
	Indic: Dard			Shina, Khowar, Kafiri	upper Indus valley
				Kashmiri	Kashmir
	Indic: Sanskritic	Sanskrit, Pali			India
		Prakrits	*Prakrits*		
				Lahnda	western Punjab
				Sindhi	Sind
				Panjabi	Punjab
				Rajasthani	Rajasthan
				Gujarati	Gujarat
				Marathi	western India
				Konkani	western India
				Oriya	Orissa
				Bengali	Bengal
				Assamese	Assam
				Bihari	Bihar
				Hindi	northern India
				Urdu	Pakistan, India
				Nepali	Nepal
				Sinhalese	Ceylon
				Romany	uncertain
Tocharian			*Tocharian A*		central Asia
			Tocharian B		

[1] Italics denote dead languages. Languages listed in roman type in the ancient or medieval column are those which survive only in some special use, as in literary composition or liturgy.

[2] Romance is normally applied only to medieval and modern languages; Latinian is normally applied only to ancient languages.

industrial park *n* : an area that is at a distance from the center of a city and that is designed esp. for a community of industries and businesses

industrial psychology *n* : the application of the findings and methods of experimental, clinical, and social psychology to industrial problems (as personnel selection and training) — **industrial psychologist** *n*

industrial relations *n pl* : the dealings or relationships of a usu. large business or industrial enterprise with its own workers, with labor in general, with governmental agencies, or with the public

industrial revolution *n* : a rapid major change in an economy (as in England in the late 18th century) marked by the general introduction of power-driven machinery or by an important change in the prevailing types and methods of use of such machines

industrial school *n* : a school specializing in the teaching of industrial arts; *specif* : a public institution of this kind for juvenile delinquents

industrial sociology *n* : sociological analysis directed at institutions and social relationships within and largely controlled or affected by industry

industrial union *n* : a labor union that admits to membership workmen in an industry irrespective of their occupation or craft — compare CRAFT UNION

in·dus·tri·ous \in-ˈdəs-trē-əs\ *adj* **1** *obs* : SKILLFUL, INGENIOUS **2** : persistently active : ZEALOUS **3** : constantly, regularly, or habitually occupied : DILIGENT ***syn*** see BUSY ***ant*** slothful, indolent — **in·dus·tri·ous·ly** *adv* — **in·dus·tri·ous·ness** *n*

in·dus·try \ˈin-(ˌ)dəs-trē\ *n, pl* **-tries** [MF *industrie* skill, employment involving skill, fr. L *industria* diligence, fr. *industrius* diligent, fr. OL *indostruus,* fr. *indu* in + *-struus* (akin to L *struere* to build) — more at INDIGENOUS, STRUCTURE] **1** : diligence in an employment or pursuit **2 a** : systematic labor esp. for the creation of value **b** : a department or branch of a craft, art, business, or manufacture; *esp* : one that employs a large personnel and capital esp. in manufacturing **c** : a distinct group of productive or profit-making enterprises <the automobile ~> **d** : manufacturing activity as a whole <the nation's ~> ***syn*** see BUSINESS

in·dwell \(ˈ)in-ˈdwel\ *vi* : to exist as an inner activating spirit, force, or principle ~ *vt* : to exist within as an activating spirit, force, or principle — **in·dwell·er** *n*

in·dwell·ing \ˈin-ˌdwel-iŋ\ *adj* : left within a bodily organ or passage esp. to promote drainage — used of an implanted tube (as a catheter)

1**-ine** \ˌīn, ən, (ˌ)in, ˌēn\ *adj suffix* **1** [ME *-in, -ine,* fr. MF&L; MF *-in,* fr. L *-inus* — more at -EN] : of or relating to <estuar*ine*> **2** [ME *-in, -ine,* fr. MF&L; MF *-in,* fr. L *-īnus,* fr. Gk *-inos* — more at -EN] : made of : like <opal*ine*>

2**-ine** \ˌēn, ˈēn, ən, (ˌ)in\ *n suffix* [ME *-ine, -in,* fr. MF&L; MF *-ine,* fr. L *-ina,* fr. fem. of *-īnus* adj suffix] **1** : chemical substance: as **a** : halogen element <chlor*ine*> **b** : basic or base-containing carbon compound that contains nitrogen <quin*ine*> <cyst*ine*> **c** : mixture of compounds (as of hydrocarbons) <gasol*ine*> **d** : hydride <ars*ine*> **2** : -IN 1a **3** : commercial product or material <glass*ine*>

ine·bri·ant \in-ˈē-brē-ənt\ *n* : INTOXICANT — **inebriant** *adj*

1**ine·bri·ate** \in-ˈē-brē-ˌāt\ *vt* **-at·ed; -at·ing** [L *inebriatus,* pp. of *inebriare,* fr. *in-* + *ebriare* to intoxicate, fr. *ebrius* drunk — more at SOBER] **1** : to make drunk : INTOXICATE **2** : to exhilarate or stupefy as if by liquor — **ine·bri·a·tion** \-ˌē-brē-ˈā-shən\ *n*

2**ine·bri·ate** \in-ˈē-brē-ət\ *adj* **1** : affected by alcohol : DRUNK **2** : addicted to excessive drinking

3**ine·bri·ate** \-ət\ *n* : one who is drunk; *esp* : an habitual drunkard

ine·bri·at·ed \-brē-ˌāt-əd\ *adj* : exhilarated or confused by or as if by alcohol : INTOXICATED

in·ebri·ety \ˌin-i-ˈbrī-ət-ē\ *n* [prob. blend of *inebriation* and *ebriety* (drunkenness)] : the state of being inebriated : DRUNKENNESS

in·ed·i·ble \(ˈ)in-ˈed-ə-bəl\ *adj* : not fit to be eaten

in·ed·it·ed \(ˈ)in-ˈed-ət-əd\ *adj* [NL *ineditus,* fr. L, not made known, fr. *in-* + *editus,* pp. of *edere* to proclaim — more at EDITION] **1** : not edited; *esp* : published without editorial alteration **2** : not published

in·ed·u·ca·ble \(ˈ)in-ˈej-ə-kə-bəl\ *adj* : incapable of being educated — **in·ed·u·ca·bil·i·ty** \(ˌ)in-ˌej-ə-kə-ˈbil-ət-ē\ *n*

in·ef·fa·ble \(ˈ)in-ˈef-ə-bəl\ *adj* [ME, fr. MF, fr. L *ineffabilis,* fr. *in-* + *effabilis* capable of being expressed, fr. *effari* to speak out, fr. *ex-* + *fari* to speak — more at BAN] **1 a** : incapable of being expressed in words : INDESCRIBABLE <~ joy> **b** : UNSPEAKABLE <~ disgust> **2** : not to be uttered : TABOO <the ~ name of Jehovah> — **in·ef·fa·bil·i·ty** \(ˌ)in-ˌef-ə-ˈbil-ət-ē\ *n* — **in·ef·fa·ble·ness** \(ˈ)in-ˈef-ə-bəl-nəs\ *n* — **in·ef·fa·bly** \-blē\ *adv*

in·ef·face·able \ˌin-ə-ˈfā-sə-bəl\ *adj* [prob. fr. F *ineffaçable,* fr. MF, fr. *in-* + *effaçable* effaceable] : not effaceable : INERADICABLE — **in·ef·face·abil·i·ty** \-ˌfā-sə-ˈbil-ət-ē\ *n* — **in·ef·face·ably** \-ˈfā-sə-blē\ *adv*

in·ef·fec·tive \ˌin-ə-ˈfek-tiv\ *adj* **1** : not producing an intended effect : INEFFECTUAL <~ lighting> **2** : not capable of performing efficiently or as expected : INCAPABLE <an ~ executive> — **in·ef·fec·tive·ly** *adv* — **in·ef·fec·tive·ness** *n*

in·ef·fec·tu·al \ˌin-ə-ˈfek-chə(-wə)l, -ˈfeksh-wəl\ *adj* **1** : not producing the proper or intended effect : FUTILE **2** : INEFFECTIVE 2 — **in·ef·fec·tu·al·i·ty** \-ˌfek-chə-ˈwal-ət-ē\ *n* — **in·ef·fec·tu·al·ly** \-ˈfek-chə(-wə)-lē, -ˈfeksh-wə-\ *adv* — **in·ef·fec·tu·al·ness** *n*

in·ef·fi·ca·cious \(ˌ)in-ˌef-ə-ˈkā-shəs\ *adj* : lacking the power to produce a desired effect : INEFFECTIVE — **in·ef·fi·ca·cious·ly** *adv* — **in·ef·fi·ca·cious·ness** *n*

in·ef·fi·ca·cy \(ˈ)in-ˈef-i-kə-sē\ *n* [LL *inefficacia,* fr. L *inefficac-, inefficax* inefficacious, fr. *in-* + *efficac-, efficax* efficacious] : lack of power to produce a desired effect

in·ef·fi·cien·cy \ˌin-ə-ˈfish-ən-sē\ *n, pl* **-cies 1** : the quality or state of being inefficient **2** : something that is inefficient

in·ef·fi·cient \-ˈfish-ənt\ *adj* : not efficient: **a** : not producing the effect intended or desired : INEFFICACIOUS <the scare technique proved to be ~> **b** : wasteful of time or energy <~ operating procedures> **c** : INCAPABLE, INCOMPETENT <an ~ worker> — **inefficient** *n* — **in·ef·fi·cient·ly** *adv*

in·e·gal·i·tar·i·an \ˌin-i-ˌgal-ə-ˈter-ē-ən\ *adj* : marked by disparity in social and economic standing

in·elas·tic \ˌin-ə-ˈlas-tik\ *adj* : not elastic: **a** : slow to react or respond to changing conditions **b** : INFLEXIBLE, UNYIELDING — **in·elas·tic·i·ty** \ˌin-i-ˌlas-ˈtis-ət-ē, (ˌ)in-ˌē-ˌlas-, -ˈtis-tē\ *n*

inelastic collision *n* : a collision in which part of the kinetic energy of the colliding particles changes into another form of energy (as radiation)

inelastic scattering *n* : a scattering of particles as the result of inelastic collision in which the total kinetic energy of the colliding particles changes

in·el·e·gance \(ˈ)in-ˈel-i-gən(t)s\ *n* : lack of elegance

in·el·e·gant \-gənt\ *adj* [MF, fr. L *inelegant-, inelegans,* fr. *in-* + *elegant-, elegans* elegant] : lacking in refinement, grace, or good taste — **in·el·e·gant·ly** *adv*

in·el·i·gi·ble \(ˈ)in-ˈel-ə-jə-bəl\ *adj* [F *inéligible,* fr. *in-* + *éligible* eligible] **1** : not qualified to be chosen for an office **2** : not worthy to be chosen or preferred **3** : not being allowed under football rules to catch a forward pass — **in·el·i·gi·bil·i·ty** \(ˌ)in-ˌel-ə-jə-ˈbil-ət-ē\ *n* — **ineligible** *n*

in·el·o·quent \(ˈ)in-ˈel-ə-kwənt\ *adj* : not eloquent — **in·el·o·quent·ly** *adv*

in·eluc·ta·ble \ˌin-i-ˈlək-tə-bəl\ *adj* [L *ineluctabilis,* fr. *in-* + *eluctari* to struggle out, fr. *ex-* + *luctari* to struggle — more at LOCK] : not to be avoided, changed, or resisted : INEVITABLE — **in·eluc·ta·bil·i·ty** \-ˌlək-tə-ˈbil-ət-ē\ *n* — **in·eluc·ta·bly** \-ˈlək-tə-blē\ *adv*

in·elud·ible \ˌin-i-ˈlüd-ə-bəl\ *adj* : INESCAPABLE

in·enar·ra·ble \ˌin-i-ˈnar-ə-bəl\ *adj* [ME, fr. MF, fr. L *inenarrabilis,* fr. *in-* + *enarrare* to explain in detail, fr. *e-* + *narrare* to narrate] : incapable of being narrated : INDESCRIBABLE

in·ept \in-ˈept\ *adj* [F *inepte,* fr. L *ineptus,* fr. *in-* + *aptus* apt] **1** : lacking in fitness or aptitude : UNFIT **2** : not suitable to the time, place, or occasion : inappropriate often to an absurd degree **3** : lacking sense or reason : FOOLISH **4** : generally incompetent : BUNGLING ***syn*** see AWKWARD ***ant*** apt, adept — **in·ep·ti·tude** \-ˈep-tə-ˌt(y)üd\ *n* — **in·ept·ly** \-ˈep-(t)lē\ *adv* — **in·ept·ness** \-ˈep(t)-nəs\ *n*

in·equal·i·ty \ˌin-i-ˈkwäl-ət-ē\ *n* [MF *inequalité,* fr. L *inaequalitat-, inaequalitas,* fr. *inaequalis* unequal, fr. *in-* + *aequalis* equal] **1** : the quality of being unequal or uneven: as **a** : lack of evenness **b** : social disparity **c** : disparity of distribution or opportunity **d** : the condition of being variable : CHANGEABLENESS **2** : an instance of being unequal **3** : a formal statement of inequality between two quantities usu. with a sign of inequality (as <, >, or ≠ signifying respectively *is less than, is greater than,* or *is not equal to*) between them <2<3, 4>1, and $a \neq b$ are *inequalities*>

in·eq·ui·ta·ble \(ˈ)in-ˈek-wət-ə-bəl\ *adj* : not equitable : UNFAIR — **in·eq·ui·ta·bly** \-blē\ *adv*

in·eq·ui·ty \(ˈ)in-ˈek-wət-ē\ *n* **1** : INJUSTICE, UNFAIRNESS **2** : an instance of injustice or unfairness

in·equi·valve \(ˈ)in-ˈē-kwə-ˌvalv\ *also* **in·equi·valved** \-ˌvalvd\ *adj* : having the valves unequal in size and form — used of a bivalve mollusk or shell

in·erad·i·ca·ble \ˌin-i-ˈrad-i-kə-bəl\ *adj* : incapable of being eradicated — **in·erad·i·ca·bil·i·ty** \-ˌrad-i-kə-ˈbil-ət-ē\ *n* — **in·erad·i·ca·bly** \-ˈrad-i-kə-blē\ *adv*

in·er·ran·cy \(ˈ)in-ˈer-ən-sē\ *n* : exemption from error : INFALLIBILITY <the concept of the verbal ~ of the Scriptures —George Hedley>

in·er·rant \-ənt\ *adj* [L *inerrant-, inerrans,* fr. *in-* + *errant-, errans,* prp. of *errare* to err] : free from error : INFALLIBLE

in·ert \in-ˈərt\ *adj* [L *inert-, iners* unskilled, idle, fr. *in-* + *art-, ars* skill — more at ARM] **1** : lacking the power to move **2** : deficient in active properties; *esp* : lacking a usual or anticipated chemical or biological action **3** : very slow to move or act : SLUGGISH ***syn*** see INACTIVE ***ant*** dynamic, animated — **inert** *n* — **in·ert·ly** *adv* — **in·ert·ness** *n*

inert gas *n* : NOBLE GAS

in·er·tia \in-ˈər-shə, -shē-ə\ *n* [NL, fr. L, lack of skill, fr. *inert-, iners*] **1 a** : a property of matter by which it remains at rest or in uniform motion in the same straight line unless acted upon by some external force **b** : an analogous property of other physical quantities (as electricity) **2** : indisposition to motion, exertion, or change : INERTNESS <failed to make a needed change in the system through sheer ~> — **in·er·tial** \-shəl\ *adj* — **in·er·tial·ly** \-ˈərsh-(ə-)lē\ *adv*

inertial guidance *n* : guidance (as of an aircraft or spacecraft) by means of self-contained automatically controlling devices that respond to inertial forces — called also *inertial navigation*

in·es·cap·able \ˌin-ə-ˈskā-pə-bəl\ *adj* : incapable of being avoided, ignored, or denied : INEVITABLE — **in·es·cap·ably** \-blē\ *adv*

in·es·sen·tial \ˌin-ə-ˈsen-chəl\ *adj* **1** : having no essence **2** : not essential : UNESSENTIAL

in·es·ti·ma·ble \(ˈ)in-ˈes-tə-mə-bəl\ *adj* [ME, fr. MF, fr. L *inaestimabilis,* fr. *in-* + *aestimabilis* estimable] **1** : incapable of being estimated or computed <storms caused ~ damage along the coast> **2** : too valuable or excellent to be measured or appreciated <has performed an ~ service for his country> — **in·es·ti·ma·bly** \-blē\ *adv*

in·ev·i·ta·ble \in-ˈev-ət-ə-bəl\ *adj* [ME, fr. L *inevitabilis,* fr. *in-* + *evitabilis* evitable] : incapable of being avoided or evaded — **in·ev·i·ta·bil·i·ty** \(ˌ)in-ˌev-ət-ə-ˈbil-ət-ē\ *n* — **in·ev·i·ta·ble·ness** \(ˈ)in-ˈev-ət-ə-bəl-nəs\ *n* — **in·ev·i·ta·bly** \-blē\ *adv*

ə abut ᵊ kitten ər further a back ā bake ä cot, cart
aú out ch chin e less ē easy g gift i trip ī life
j joke ŋ sing ō flow ȯ flaw ȯi coin th thin t͟h this
ü loot ú foot y yet yü few yú furious zh vision

in·ex·act \ˌin-ig-ˈzakt\ *adj* [F, fr. *in-* + *exact*] **1 :** not precisely correct or true : INACCURATE <an ~ translation> **2 :** not rigorous and careful <an ~ thinker> — **in·ex·ac·ti·tude** \-ˈzak-tə-ˌt(y)üd\ *n* — **in·ex·act·ly** \-ˈzak-(t)lē\ *adv* — **in·ex·act·ness** \-ˈzak(t)-nəs\ *n*

in·ex·cus·able \ˌin-ik-ˈskyü-zə-bəl\ *adj* [L *inexcusabilis*, fr. *in-* + *excusabilis* excusable] : being without excuse or justification — **in·ex·cus·able·ness** *n* — **in·ex·cus·ably** \-blē\ *adv*

in·ex·haust·ible \ˌin-ig-ˈzȯ-stə-bəl\ *adj* : not exhaustible: as **a** : incapable of being used up <~ riches> **b :** incapable of being wearied or worn out <an ~ hiker> — **in·ex·haust·ibil·i·ty** \-ˌzȯ-stə-ˈbil-ət-ē\ *n* — **in·ex·haust·ible·ness** \-ˈzȯ-stə-bəl-nəs\ *n* — **in·ex·haust·ibly** \-blē\ *adv*

in·ex·is·tence \ˌin-ig-ˈzis-tən(t)s\ *n* : absence of existence : NONEXISTENCE

in·ex·is·tent \-tənt\ *adj* [LL *inexsistent-*, *inexsistens*, fr. L *in-* + *exsistent-*, *exsistens*, prp. of *exsistere* to exist] : not having existence : NONEXISTENT

in·ex·o·ra·ble \(ˈ)in-ˈeks-(ə-)rə-bəl, -ˈegz-ə-rə-\ *adj* [L *inexorabilis*, fr. *in-* + *exorabilis* pliant, fr. *exorare* to prevail upon, fr. *ex-* + *orare* to speak — more at ORATION] : not to be persuaded or moved by entreaty : RELENTLESS ***syn*** see INFLEXIBLE — **in·ex·o·ra·bil·i·ty** \(ˌ)in-ˌeks-(ə-)rə-ˈbil-ət-ē, -ˌegz-ə-rə-\ *n* — **in·ex·o·ra·ble·ness** \(ˈ)in-ˈeks-(ə-)rə-bəl-nəs, -ˈegz-ə-rə-\ *n* — **in·ex·o·ra·bly** \-blē\ *adv*

in·ex·pe·di·ence \ˌin-ik-ˈspēd-ē-ən(t)s\ *n* : INEXPEDIENCY

in·ex·pe·di·en·cy \-ən-sē\ *n* : the quality or fact of being inexpedient

in·ex·pe·di·ent \-ənt\ *adj* : not expedient : INADVISABLE — **in·ex·pe·di·ent·ly** *adv*

in·ex·pen·sive \ˌin-ik-ˈspen(t)-siv\ *adj* : reasonable in price : CHEAP — **in·ex·pen·sive·ly** *adv* — **in·ex·pen·sive·ness** *n*

in·ex·pe·ri·ence \ˌin-ik-ˈspir-ē-ən(t)s\ *n* [MF, fr. LL *inexperientia*, fr. L *in-* + *experientia* experience] **1 :** lack of practical experience **2 :** lack of knowledge of the ways of the world — **in·ex·pe·ri·enced** \-ən(t)st\ *adj*

in·ex·pert \(ˈ)in-ˈek-ˌspərt, ˌin-ik-ˈ\ *adj* [ME, fr. MF, fr. L *inexpertus*, fr. *in-* + *expertus* expert] : not expert : UNSKILLED — **in·ex·pert** \(ˈ)in-ˈek-ˌspərt\ *n* — **in·ex·pert·ly** \(ˈ)in-ˈek-ˌspərt-lē, ˌin-ik-ˈ\ *adv* — **in·ex·pert·ness** *n*

in·ex·pi·a·ble \(ˈ)in-ˈek-spē-ə-bəl\ *adj* [L *inexpiabilis*, fr. *in-* + *expiare* to expiate] **1 :** not capable of being atoned for **2** *obs* : IMPLACABLE, UNAPPEASABLE — **in·ex·pi·a·bly** \-blē\ *adv*

in·ex·plain·able \ˌin-ik-ˈsplā-nə-bəl\ *adj* : INEXPLICABLE

in·ex·pli·ca·ble \ˌin-ik-ˈsplik-ə-bəl, (ˈ)in-ˈek-(ˌ)splik-\ *adj* [MF, fr. L *inexplicabilis*, fr. *in-* + *explicabilis* explicable] : incapable of being explained, interpreted, or accounted for — **in·ex·pli·ca·bil·i·ty** \ˌin-ik-ˌsplik-ə-ˈbil-ət-ē, (ˌ)in-ˌek-(ˌ)splik-\ *n* — **in·ex·pli·ca·ble·ness** \ˌin-ik-ˌsplik-ə-bəl-nəs, (ˈ)in-ˈek-(ˌ)splik-\ *n* — **in·ex·pli·ca·bly** \-blē\ *adv*

in·ex·plic·it \ˌin-ik-ˈsplis-ət\ *adj* : not explicit

in·ex·press·ible \-ˈspres-ə-bəl\ *adj* : not capable of being expressed : INDESCRIBABLE — **in·ex·press·ibil·i·ty** \-ˌspres-ə-ˈbil-ət-ē\ *n* — **in·ex·press·ible·ness** \-ˈspres-ə-bəl-nəs\ *n* — **in·ex·press·ibly** \-blē\ *adv*

in·ex·pres·sive \-ˈspres-iv\ *adj* **1** *archaic* : INEXPRESSIBLE **2** : lacking expression or meaning <an ~ face> — **in·ex·pres·sive·ly** *adv* — **in·ex·pres·sive·ness** *n*

in·ex·pug·na·ble \ˌin-ik-ˈspəg-nə-bəl, -ˈspyü-nə-\ *adj* [MF, fr. L *inexpugnabilis*, fr. *in-* + *expugnare* to take by storm, fr. *ex-* + *pugnare* to fight — more at PUNGENT] **1 :** incapable of being subdued or overthrown : IMPREGNABLE <an ~ position> **2** : STABLE, FIXED <~ hatred> — **in·ex·pug·na·ble·ness** *n* — **in·ex·pug·na·bly** \-blē\ *adv*

in·ex·pung·ible \ˌin-ik-ˈspən-jə-bəl\ *adj* [*in-* + *expunge*] : incapable of being obliterated <~ scent of a bottle of perfume he had . . . broken —Louis Auchincloss>

in ex·ten·so \ˌin-ik-ˈsten(t)-(ˌ)sō\ *adv* [ML] : at full length

in·ex·tin·guish·able \ˌin-ik-ˈstiŋ-(g)wish-ə-bəl\ *adj* : not extinguishable : UNQUENCHABLE <an ~ flame> <an ~ longing> — **in·ex·tin·guish·ably** \-blē\ *adv*

in ex·tre·mis \ˌin-ik-ˈstrā-məs, -ˈstrē-\ *adv* [L] : in extreme circumstances; *esp* : at the point of death

in·ex·tri·ca·ble \ˌin-ik-ˈstrik-ə-bəl, (ˈ)in-ˈek-(ˌ)strik-\ *adj* [MF or L; MF, fr. L *inextricabilis*, fr. *in-* + *extricabilis* extricable] **1** : forming a maze or tangle from which it is impossible to get free **2 a :** incapable of being disentangled or untied <an ~ knot> **b** : not capable of being solved — **in·ex·tri·ca·bil·i·ty** \ˌin-ik-ˌstrik-ə-ˈbil-ət-ē, (ˈ)in-ˌek-(ˌ)strik-\ *n* — **in·ex·tri·ca·bly** \ˌin-ik-ˈstrik-ə-blē, (ˈ)in-ˈek-(ˌ)strik-\ *adv*

inf *abbr* **1** infantry **2** infinitive

in·fal·li·ble \(ˈ)in-ˈfal-ə-bəl\ *adj* [ML *infallibilis*, fr. L *in-* + LL *fallibilis* fallible] **1 :** incapable of error : UNERRING <an ~ memory> **2 :** not liable to mislead, deceive, or disappoint : CERTAIN <an ~ remedy> **3 :** incapable of error in defining doctrines touching faith or morals — **in·fal·li·bil·i·ty** \(ˌ)in-ˌfal-ə-ˈbil-ət-ē\ *n* — **in·fal·li·bly** \(ˈ)in-ˈfal-ə-blē\ *adv*

in·fa·mous \ˈin-fə-məs\ *adj* [ME, fr. L *infamis*, fr. *in-* + *fama* fame] **1 :** having a reputation of the worst kind **2 :** causing or bringing infamy : DISGRACEFUL **3 :** convicted of an offense bringing infamy ***syn*** see VICIOUS ***ant*** illustrious — **in·fa·mous·ly** *adv*

in·fa·my \-mē\ *n, pl* **-mies 1 :** evil reputation brought about by something grossly criminal, shocking, or brutal **2 a :** an extreme and publicly known criminal or evil act **b :** the state of being infamous ***syn*** see DISGRACE

in·fan·cy \ˈin-fən-sē\ *n, pl* **-cies 1 :** early childhood **2 :** a beginning or early period of existence **3 :** the legal status of an infant

¹in·fant \ˈin-fənt\ *n* [ME *enfaunt*, fr. MF *enfant*, fr. L *infant-*, *infans*, fr. *infant-*, *infans*, incapable of speech, young, fr. *in-* + *fant-*, *fans*, prp. of *fari* to speak — more at BAN] **1 :** a child in the first period of life **2 :** a person who is not of full age : MINOR

²infant *adj* **1 :** of, relating to, or being in infancy **2 :** being in an early stage of development **3 :** intended for young children

in·fan·ta \in-ˈfant-ə, -ˈfänt-\ *n* [Sp & Pg, fem. of *infante*] : a daughter of a Spanish or Portuguese monarch

in·fan·te \in-ˈfant-ē, -ˈfän-(ˌ)tā\ *n* [Sp & Pg, lit., infant, fr. L *infant-*, *infans*] : a younger son of a Spanish or Portuguese monarch

in·fan·ti·cide \in-ˈfant-ə-ˌsīd\ *n* [LL *infanticidium*, fr. L *infant-*, *infans* + *-i-* + *-cidium* -cide] **1 :** the killing of an infant **2** : one who kills an infant

in·fan·tile \ˈin-fən-ˌtīl, -tᵊl, -ˌtēl, -(ˌ)til\ *adj* **1 :** of or relating to infants or infancy **2 :** suitable to or characteristic of an infant; *esp* : very immature <the immature parents . . . who have so many ~ traits themselves —H. B. Peck> **3** *of topography* **:** being in a very early stage of development following an uplift or equivalent change — **in·fan·til·i·ty** \ˌin-fən-ˈtil-ət-ē\ *n*

infantile paralysis *n* : POLIOMYELITIS

in·fan·til·ism \ˈin-fən-ˌtīl-ˌiz-əm, -tə-ˌliz-; in-ˈfan-tᵊl-ˌiz-\ *n* **1 :** retention of childish physical, mental, or emotional qualities in adult life; *esp* : failure to attain sexual maturity **2 :** an act or expression that indicates lack of maturity

in·fan·tine \ˈin-fən-ˌtīn, -ˌtēn\ *adj* : INFANTILE, CHILDISH

in·fan·try \ˈin-fən-trē\ *n, pl* **-tries** [MF & OIt; MF *infanterie*, fr. OIt *infanteria*, fr. *infante* boy, foot soldier, fr. L *infant-*, *infans*] **1 a :** soldiers trained, armed, and equipped to fight on foot **b** : a branch of an army composed of these soldiers **2 :** an infantry regiment

in·fan·try·man \-trē-mən\ *n* : an infantry soldier

infant school *n, Brit* : KINDERGARTEN

in·farct \ˈin-ˌfärkt, in-ˈ\ *n* [L *infarctus*, pp. of *infarcire* to stuff, fr. *in-* + *farcire* to stuff — more at FARCE] : an area of necrosis in a tissue or organ resulting from obstruction of the local circulation by a thrombus or embolus — **in·farct·ed** \in-ˈfärk-təd\ *adj* — **in·farc·tion** \in-ˈfärk-shən\ *n*

in·fare \ˈin-ˌfa(ə)r, -ˌfe(ə)r\ *n* [ME *infer*, fr. OE *infær* entrance, fr. *in* + *fær* way, fr. *faran* to go — more at FARE] *chiefly dial* : a reception for a newly married couple

¹in·fat·u·ate \in-ˈfach-ə-wət\ *adj* : being in an infatuated state or condition

²in·fat·u·ate \-ˌwāt\ *vt* **-at·ed; -at·ing** [L *infatuatus*, pp. of *infatuare*, fr. *in-* + *fatuus* fatuous] **1 :** to affect with folly **2** : to inspire with a foolish or extravagant love or admiration — **in·fat·u·at·ed** *adj* — **in·fat·u·a·tion** \-ˌfach-ə-ˈwā-shən\ *n*

in·fau·na \ˈin-ˌfȯn-ə, -ˌfän-\ *n* [NL, fr. ²*in-* + *fauna*] : benthic fauna living on the substrate and esp. in a soft sea bottom — compare EPIFAUNA — **in·fau·nal** \-ˌfȯn-ᵊl, -ˌfän-\ *adj*

in·fea·si·ble \(ˈ)in-ˈfē-zə-bəl\ *adj* : not feasible : IMPRACTICABLE

in·fect \in-ˈfekt\ *vt* [ME *infecten*, fr. L *infectus*, pp. of *inficere*, fr. *in-* + *facere* to make, do — more at DO] **1 :** to contaminate with a disease-producing substance or agent (as bacteria) **2 a :** to communicate a pathogen or a disease to **b** *of a pathogenic organism* : to invade (an individual or organ) usu. by penetration **3 a** : CONTAMINATE, CORRUPT <manages to ~ her with a sense of guilt> **b :** to work upon or seize upon so as to induce sympathy, belief, or support <the teacher ~*ed* his pupils with his enthusiasm> — **in·fec·tor** \-ˈfek-tər\ *n*

in·fec·tion \in-ˈfek-shən\ *n* **1 :** the act or result of affecting injuriously **2 :** an act or process of infecting; *also* : the establishment of a pathogen in its host after invasion **3 :** the state produced by the establishment of an infective agent in or on a suitable host; *also* : a contagious or infectious disease **4 :** an infective agent or material contaminated with an infective agent **5** : the communication of emotions or qualities through example or contact

in·fec·tious \-shəs\ *adj* **1 a :** capable of causing infection **b** : communicable by infection — compare CONTAGIOUS **2 :** that corrupts or contaminates **3 :** capable of being easily diffused or spread : readily communicated <~ excitement> — **in·fec·tious·ly** *adv* — **in·fec·tious·ness** *n*

infectious hepatitis *n* : an acute virus inflammation of the liver characterized by jaundice, fever, nausea, vomiting, and abdominal discomfort

infectious mononucleosis *n* : an acute infectious disease characterized by fever, swelling of lymph glands, and lymphocytosis

in·fec·tive \in-ˈfek-tiv\ *adj* **1 :** producing or capable of producing infection **2 :** affecting others : INFECTIOUS — **in·fec·tiv·i·ty** \(ˌ)in-ˌfek-ˈtiv-ət-ē\ *n*

in·fe·lic·i·tous \ˌin-fi-ˈlis-ət-əs\ *adj* : not appropriate in application or expression <essays written in an ~ style> — **in·fe·lic·i·tous·ly** *adv*

in·fe·lic·i·ty \-ət-ē\ *n, pl* **-ties** [ME *infelicite*, fr. L *infelicitas*, fr. *infelic-*, *infelix* unhappy, fr. *in-* + *felic-*, *felix* fruitful — more at FEMININE] **1 :** the quality or state of being infelicitous **2** : something that is infelicitous

in·fer \in-ˈfər\ *vb* **in·ferred; in·fer·ring** [MF or L; MF *inferer*, fr. L *inferre*, lit., to carry or bring into, fr. *in-* + *ferre* to carry — more at BEAR] *vt* **1 :** to derive as a conclusion from facts or premises <we see smoke and ~ fire —L. A. White> — compare IMPLY **2** : GUESS, SURMISE <your letter . . . allows me to ~ that you are as well as ever —O. W. Holmes †1935> **3 a :** to involve as a normal outcome of thought **b :** to point out : INDICATE <this doth ~ the zeal I had to see him —Shak.> **4 :** SUGGEST, HINT <another survey . . . ~*s* that two-thirds of all present computer installations are not paying for themselves —H. R. Chellman> ~ *vi* : to draw inferences <men . . . have observed, *inferred*, and reasoned . . . to all kinds of results —John Dewey> — **in·fer·able** *or* **in·fer·ri·ble** \in-ˈfər-ə-bəl\ *adj* — **in·fer·rer** \-ˈfər-ər\ *n*

syn INFER, DEDUCE, CONCLUDE, JUDGE, GATHER *shared meaning element* : to arrive at a mental conclusion

in·fer·ence \ˈin-f(ə-)rən(t)s, -fərn(t)s\ *n* **1 :** the act or process of inferring: as **a :** the act of passing from one proposition, statement, or judgment considered as true to another whose truth is believed to follow from that of the former **b :** the act of passing from statistical sample data to generalizations (as of the value of population parameters) usu. with calculated degrees of certainty **2** : something that is inferred; *esp* : a proposition arrived at by inference **3 :** the premises and conclusion of a process of inferring

in·fer·en·tial \ˌin-fə-ˈren-chəl\ *adj* [ML *inferentia,* fr. L *inferent-, inferens,* prp. of *inferre*] **1 :** relating to, involving, or resembling inference **2 :** deduced or deducible by inference — **in·fer·en·tial·ly** \-ˈrench-(ə-)lē\ *adv*

in·fe·ri·or \in-ˈfir-ē-ər\ *adj* [ME, fr. L, compar. of *inferus* — more at UNDER] **1 :** situated lower down : LOWER **2 :** of low or lower degree or rank **3 :** of little or less importance, value, or merit <always felt ~ to his older brother> **4 a :** situated below another and esp. another similar superior part of an upright body **b :** situated in a relatively low posterior or ventral position in a quadrupedal body **c** (1) **:** situated below another plant part or organ (2) **:** ABAXIAL **5 :** relating to or being a subscript **6 a :** nearer the sun than the earth is <~ planets> **b :** nearer the earth than the sun is <~ conjunction of Venus> — **inferior** *n* — **in·fe·ri·or·i·ty** \(ˌ)in-ˌfir-ē-ˈór-ət-ē, -ˈär-\ *n* — **in·fe·ri·or·ly** \in-ˈfir-ē-ər-lē\ *adv*

inferiority complex *n* **:** an acute sense of personal inferiority resulting either in timidity or through overcompensation in exaggerated aggressiveness

in·fer·nal \in-ˈfərn-ᵊl\ *adj* [ME, fr. OF, fr. LL *infernalis,* fr. *infernus* hell, fr. L, lower; akin to L *inferus* inferior] **1 :** of or relating to a nether world of the dead **2 a :** of or relating to hell **b :** HELLISH, DIABOLICAL <~ wickedness> **3 :** DAMNABLE <an ~ nuisance> — **in·fer·nal·ly** \-ᵊl-ē\ *adv*

infernal machine *n* **:** a machine or apparatus maliciously designed to explode and destroy life or property; *esp* **:** a concealed or disguised bomb

in·fer·no \in-ˈfər-(ˌ)nō\ *n, pl* **-nos** [It, hell, fr. LL *infernus*]**:** a place or a state that resembles or suggests hell <the ~ of war>; *also* **:** intense heat <the roaring ~ of the blast furnace>

in·fero- \ˌin-fə-(ˌ)rō\ *comb form* [L *inferus*]**:** below and <*infero*lateral>

in·fer·tile \(ˈ)in-ˈfərt-ᵊl\ *adj* [MF, fr. LL *infertilis,* fr. L *in-* + *fertilis* fertile] **:** not fertile or productive <~ eggs> <~ fields> ***syn*** see STERILE ***ant*** fertile — **in·fer·til·i·ty** \ˌin-(ˌ)fər-ˈtil-ət-ē\ *n*

in·fest \in-ˈfest\ *vt* [MF *infester,* fr. L *infestare,* fr. *infestus* hostile] **1 :** to spread or swarm in or over in a troublesome manner <a slum ~*ed* with crime> <shark-*infested* waters> **2 :** to live in or on as a parasite — **in·fes·tant** \-ˈfes-tənt\ *n* — **in·fes·ta·tion** \ˌin-ˌfes-ˈtā-shən\ *n* — **in·fest·er** \in-ˈfes-tər\ *n*

in·fi·del \ˈin-fəd-ᵊl, -fə-ˌdel\ *n* [MF *infidele,* fr. LL *infidelis* unbelieving, fr. L, unfaithful, fr. *in-* + *fidelis* faithful — more at FEAL] **1 :** one who is not a Christian or who opposes Christianity **2 a :** an unbeliever in respect to a particular religion **b :** one who acknowledges no religious belief **3 :** a disbeliever in something specified or understood ***syn*** see ATHEIST — **infidel** *adj*

in·fi·del·i·ty \ˌin-fə-ˈdel-ət-ē, -(ˌ)fī-\ *n, pl* **-ties** **1 :** lack of belief in a religion **2 a :** unfaithfulness to a moral obligation : DISLOYALTY **b :** marital unfaithfulness or an instance of it

in·field \ˈin-ˌfēld\ *n* **1 :** a field near a farmhouse **2 a :** the area of a baseball field enclosed by the three bases and home plate **b :** the defensive positions comprising first base, second base, shortstop, and third base; *also* **:** the players who play these positions **3 :** the area enclosed by a racetrack or running track

in·field·er \-ˌfēl-dər\ *n* **:** a baseball player who plays in the infield

infield hit *n* **:** a base hit that does not leave the infield

infield out *n* **:** a ground ball on which the batter is retired by an infielder

in·fight·ing \ˈin-ˌfīt-iŋ\ *n* **1 :** fighting or boxing at close quarters **2 :** rough-and-tumble fighting **3 :** prolonged and often bitter dissension among members of a group or organization <bureaucratic ~ and departmental jealousies —H. H. Ransom> — **in·fight·er** \-ər\ *n*

in·fil·trate \in-ˈfil-ˌtrāt, ˈin-(ˌ)\ *vb* **-trat·ed; -trat·ing** *vt* **1 :** to cause (as a liquid) to permeate something by penetrating its pores or interstices **2 :** to pass into or through (a substance) by filtering or permeating **3 :** to pass (troops) singly or in small groups through gaps in the enemy line **4 :** to enter or become established in gradually or unobtrusively <the intelligence staff had been *infiltrated* by spies> ~ *vi* **:** to enter, permeate, or pass through a substance or area by filtering or by insinuating gradually <police can't ~ into the closely-knit organization> — **in·fil·tra·tion** \ˌin-(ˌ)fil-ˈtrā-shən\ *n* — **in·fil·tra·tive** \ˈin-(ˌ)fil-ˌtrāt-iv, in-ˈfil-trət-\ *adj* — **in·fil·tra·tor** \in-ˈfil-ˌtrat-ər, ˈin-(ˌ)\ *n*

¹in·fi·nite \ˈin-fə-nət\ *adj* [ME *infinit,* fr. MF or L; MF, fr. L *infinitus,* fr. *in-* + *finitus* finite] **1 :** subject to no limitation or external determination **2 :** extending indefinitely : ENDLESS <~ space> **3 :** immeasurably or inconceivably great or extensive : INEXHAUSTIBLE <~ patience> **4 a :** extending beyond, lying beyond, or being greater than any preassigned finite value however large <~ number of positive numbers> **b :** extending to infinity <~ plane surface> **c :** characterized by an infinite number of elements or terms <an ~ set> <an ~ series> — **in·fi·nite·ly** *adv* — **in·fi·nite·ness** *n*

²infinite *n* **1 :** boundless space or duration **2 :** an incalculable or very great number **3 :** an infinite quantity or magnitude

¹in·fin·i·tes·i·mal \(ˌ)in-ˌfin-ə-ˈtes-ə-məl, -ˈtez-\ *n* [NL *infinitesimus* infinite in rank, fr. L *infinitus*] **1 :** a variable that takes on values arbitrarily close to zero **2 :** an infinitesimal quantity

²infinitesimal *adj* **1 :** taking on values arbitrarily close to zero **2 :** immeasurably or incalculably small — **in·fin·i·tes·i·mal·ly** \-mə-lē\ *adv*

infinitesimal calculus *n* **:** CALCULUS 3b

in·fin·i·ti·val \(ˌ)in-ˌfin-ə-ˈtī-vəl\ *adj* **:** relating to the infinitive

¹in·fin·i·tive \in-ˈfin-ət-iv\ *adj* [LL *infinitivus,* fr. L *infinitus*] **:** formed with the infinitive — **in·fin·i·tive·ly** *adv*

²infinitive *n* **:** a verb form normally identical in English with the first person singular that performs some functions of a noun and at the same time displays some characteristics of a verb and that is used with *to* (as in "I asked him *to go*") except with auxiliary and various other verbs (as in "no one saw him *leave*")

in·fin·i·tude \in-ˈfin-ə-ˌt(y)üd\ *n* **1 :** the quality or state of being infinite : INFINITENESS **2 :** something that is infinite esp. in extent **3 :** an infinite number or quantity

in·fin·i·ty \in-ˈfin-ət-ē\ *n, pl* **-ties** **1 a :** the quality of being infinite **b :** unlimited extent of time, space, or quantity : BOUNDLESSNESS **2 :** an indefinitely great number or amount **3 a :** the limit of a function when its value tends to become numerically larger than any preassigned value **b :** a part of a geometric magnitude that lies beyond any part whose distance from a given reference position is finite <do parallel lines ever meet if they extend to ~> **c :** a transfinite number (as aleph-null) **4 :** a distance so great that the rays of light from a point source at that distance may be regarded as parallel

in·firm \in-ˈfərm\ *adj* [ME, fr. L *infirmus,* fr. *in-* + *firmus* firm] **1 :** of poor or deteriorated vitality; *esp* **:** feeble from age **2 :** weak of mind, will, or character : IRRESOLUTE, VACILLATING **3 :** not solid or stable : INSECURE ***syn*** see WEAK ***ant*** hale — **in·firm·ly** *adv*

in·fir·ma·ry \in-ˈfərm-(ə-)rē\ *n, pl* **-ries** **:** a place where the infirm or sick are lodged for care and treatment

in·fir·mi·ty \in-ˈfər-mət-ē\ *n, pl* **-ties** **1 a :** the quality or state of being infirm **b :** the condition of being feeble : FRAILTY **2 :** DISEASE, MALADY **3 :** a personal failing : FOIBLE <one of the besetting *infirmities* of living creatures is egotism —A. J. Toynbee>

¹in·fix \ˈin-ˌfiks, in-ˈ\ *vt* [L *infixus,* pp. of *infigere,* fr. *in-* + *figere* to fasten — more at DIKE] **1 :** to fasten or fix by piercing or thrusting in **2 :** INSTILL, INCULCATE **3 :** to insert (as a sound or letter) as an infix

²in·fix \ˈin-ˌfiks\ *n* **:** a derivational or inflectional affix appearing in the body of a word <Sanskrit *-n-* is an ~ in *vindami* "I know" as contrasted with *vid* "to know">

infl *abbr* influenced

in fla·gran·te de·lic·to \ˌin-flə-ˌgrant-ē-di-ˈlik-(ˌ)tō\ *adv* **:** FLAGRANTE DELICTO

in·flame \in-ˈflām\ *vb* **in·flamed; in·flam·ing** [ME *enflamen,* fr. MF *enflamer,* fr. L *inflammare,* fr. *in-* + *flamma* flame] *vt* **1 :** to set on fire : KINDLE **2 a :** to excite to excessive or unnatural action or feeling **b :** to make more heated or violent : INTENSIFY <insults served only to ~ the feud> **3 :** to cause to redden or grow hot from anger or excitement **4 :** to cause inflammation in (bodily tissue) ~ *vi* **1 :** to burst into flame **2 :** to become excited or angered **3 :** to become affected with inflammation — **in·flam·er** *n*

in·flam·ma·ble \in-ˈflam-ə-bəl\ *adj* [F, fr. ML *inflammabilis,* fr. L *inflammare* to inflame] **1 :** FLAMMABLE **2 :** easily inflamed, excited, or angered : IRASCIBLE — **in·flam·ma·bil·i·ty** \-ˌflam-ə-ˈbil-ət-ē\ *n* — **inflammable** *n* — **in·flam·ma·ble·ness** \-ˈflam-ə-bəl-nəs\ *n* — **in·flam·ma·bly** \-blē\ *adv*

in·flam·ma·tion \ˌin-flə-ˈmā-shən\ *n* **1 :** the act of inflaming **:** the state of being inflamed **2 :** a local response to cellular injury that is marked by capillary dilatation, leukocytic infiltration, redness, heat, and pain and that serves as a mechanism initiating the elimination of noxious agents and of damaged tissue

in·flam·ma·to·ry \in-ˈflam-ə-ˌtōr-ē, -ˌtór-\ *adj* **1 :** tending to inflame or excite the senses **2 :** tending to excite anger, disorder, or tumult : SEDITIOUS **3 :** accompanied by or tending to cause inflammation — **in·flam·ma·to·ri·ly** \-ˌflam-ə-ˈtōr-ə-lē, -ˈtór-\ *adv*

in·flat·able \in-ˈflāt-ə-bəl\ *adj* **:** capable of being inflated <an ~ boat> — **inflatable** *n*

in·flate \in-ˈflāt\ *vb* **in·flat·ed; in·flat·ing** [L *inflatus,* pp. of *inflare,* fr. *in-* + *flare* to blow — more at BLOW] *vt* **1 :** to swell or distend with air or gas **2 :** to puff up : ELATE **3 :** to expand or increase abnormally or imprudently ~ *vi* **:** to become inflated ***syn*** see EXPAND ***ant*** deflate — **in·fla·tor** *or* **in·flat·er** \-ˈflāt-ər\ *n*

in·flat·ed *adj* **1 :** distended with air or gas **2 :** BOMBASTIC, EXAGGERATED <an ~ style of writing> **3 :** expanded to an abnormal or unjustifiable volume or level <~ prices> **4 a :** being hollow and distended **b :** open and swelled out or enlarged

in·fla·tion \in-ˈflā-shən\ *n* **1 :** an act of inflating **:** a state of being inflated: as **a :** DISTENSION **b :** empty pretentiousness : POMPOSITY **2 :** an increase in the volume of money and credit relative to available goods resulting in a substantial and continuing rise in the general price level

in·fla·tion·ary \-shə-ˌner-ē\ *adj* **:** of, characterized by, or productive of inflation

inflationary spiral *n* **:** a continuous rise in prices that is sustained by the tendency of wage increases and cost increases to react on each other

in·fla·tion·ism \in-ˈflā-shə-ˌniz-əm\ *n* **:** the policy of economic inflation — **in·fla·tion·ist** \-sh(ə-)nəst\ *n or adj*

in·flect \in-ˈflekt\ *vb* [ME *inflecten,* fr. L *inflectere,* fr. *in-* + *flectere* to bend] *vt* **1 :** to turn from a direct line or course : CURVE **2 :** to vary (a word) by inflection : DECLINE, CONJUGATE **3 :** to change or vary the pitch of (as the voice) : MODULATE ~ *vi* **:** to become modified by inflection — **in·flec·tive** \-ˈflek-tiv\ *adj*

in·flec·tion \in-ˈflek-shən\ *n* **1 :** the act or result of curving or bending : BEND **2 :** change in pitch or loudness of the voice **3 a :** the change of form that words undergo to mark such distinctions as those of case, gender, number, tense, person, mood, or voice **b :** a form, suffix, or element involved in such variation **c :** ACCIDENCE **4 a :** change of curvature with respect to a fixed line from concave to convex or conversely **b :** INFLECTION POINT

in·flec·tion·al \-shnəl, -shən-ᵊl\ *adj* **:** of, relating to, or characterized by inflection <an ~ suffix> — **in·flec·tion·al·ly** \-ē\ *adv*

inflection point *n* **:** a point on a curve that separates an arc concave upward from one concave downward and vice versa

in·flexed \ˈin-ˌflekst\ *adj* [L *inflexus,* pp. of *inflectere*] **:** bent or turned abruptly inward or downward or toward the axis <~ petals>

---

in·flex·i·ble \(ˈ)in-ˈflek-sə-bəl\ *adj* [ME, fr. L *inflexibilis,* fr. *in-* + *flexibilis* flexible] **1 :** not readily bent : lacking or deficient in suppleness **2 :** rigidly firm in will or purpose : UNYIELDING **3 :** incapable of change : UNALTERABLE — **in·flex·i·bil·i·ty** \(ˌ)in-ˌflek-sə-ˈbil-ət-ē\ *n* — **in·flex·i·ble·ness** \(ˈ)in-ˈflek-sə-bəl-nəs\ *n* — **in·flex·i·bly** \-blē\ *adv*

syn **1** see STIFF ***ant*** flexible

2 INFLEXIBLE, INEXORABLE, OBDURATE, ADAMANT *shared meaning element* : unwilling to alter a predetermined course or purpose ***ant*** flexible

in·flex·ion *chiefly Brit var of* INFLECTION

in·flict \in-ˈflikt\ *vt* [L *inflictus,* pp. of *infligere,* fr. *in-* + *fligere* to strike — more at PROFLIGATE] **1 a :** to give by striking <~*s* a blow on his opponent's jaw> **b :** to cause (something damaging or painful) to be endured : IMPOSE <~ punishment> **2 :** AFFLICT — **in·flict·er** *or* **in·flic·tor** \-ˈflik-tər\ *n* — **in·flic·tive** \-tiv\ *adj*

in·flic·tion \in-ˈflik-shən\ *n* **1 :** the act of inflicting **2 :** something (as punishment or suffering) that is inflicted

in–flight \ˈin-ˈflīt\ *adj* : made, carried out, or provided for use or enjoyment while in flight <~ movies>

in·flo·res·cence \ˌin-flə-ˈres-ᵊn(t)s\ *n* [NL *inflorescentia,* fr. LL *inflorescent-, inflorescens,* prp. of *inflorescere* to begin to bloom, fr. L *in-* + *florescere* to begin to bloom — more at FLORESCENCE] **1 a (1) :** the arrangement and order of development of flowers on an axis **(2) :** a floral axis with its appendages; *also* : a flower cluster or sometimes a solitary flower **b :** a cluster of reproductive organs on a moss usu. subtended by a bract **2 :** the budding and unfolding of blossoms : FLOWERING — **in·flo·res·cent** \-ᵊnt\ *adj*

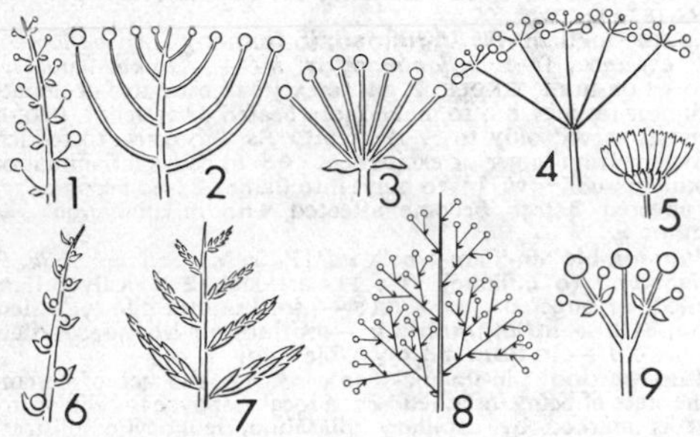

types of inflorescence 1a(1): *1* raceme, *2* corymb, *3* umbel, *4* compound umbel, *5* capitulum, *6* spike, *7* compound spike, *8* panicle, *9* cyme

in·flow \ˈin-ˌflō\ *n* : INFLUX

¹in·flu·ence \ˈin-ˌflü-ən(t)s, *esp South* in-ˈ\ *n* [ME, fr. MF, fr. ML *influentia,* fr. L *influent-, influens,* prp. of *influere* to flow in, fr. *in-* + *fluere* to flow — more at FLUID] **1 a :** an ethereal fluid held to flow from the stars and to affect the actions of men **b :** an emanation of occult power held to derive from stars **2 :** an emanation of spiritual or moral force **3 a :** the act or power of producing an effect without apparent exertion of force or direct exercise of command **b :** corrupt interference with authority for personal gain **4 :** the power or capacity of causing an effect in indirect or intangible ways : SWAY **5 :** one that exerts influence **6 :** INDUCTION 4c

syn INFLUENCE, AUTHORITY, PRESTIGE, WEIGHT, CREDIT *shared meaning element* : power exerted over the minds or behavior of others — **under the influence :** affected by liquor : DRUNK <was arrested for driving *under the influence*>

²influence *vt* **-enced; -enc·ing 1 :** to affect or alter by indirect or intangible means : SWAY **2 :** to have an effect on the condition or development of : MODIFY ***syn*** see AFFECT — **in·flu·enc·er** *n*

¹in·flu·ent \ˈin-ˌflü-ənt, in-ˈ\ *adj* : flowing in

²influent *n* **1 :** a tributary stream **2 :** a factor (as a kind of animal) modifying the balance and stability of an ecological community

¹in·flu·en·tial \ˌin-(ˌ)flü-ˈen-chəl\ *adj* : exerting or possessing influence — **in·flu·en·tial·ly** \-ˈench-(ə-)lē\ *adv*

²influential *n* : one who has great influence <~*s* from the worlds of finance, politics and the arts —Thomas Meehan>

in·flu·en·za \ˌin-(ˌ)flü-ˈen-zə\ *n* [It, lit., influence, fr. ML *influentia;* fr. the belief that epidemics were due to the influence of the stars] **1 :** an acute highly contagious virus disease characterized by sudden onset, fever, prostration, severe aches and pains, and progressive inflammation of the respiratory mucous membrane; *broadly* : a human respiratory infection of undetermined cause **2 :** any of numerous febrile usu. virus diseases of domestic animals marked by respiratory symptoms, inflammation of mucous membranes, and often systemic involvement

in·flux \ˈin-ˌfləks\ *n* [LL *influxus,* fr. L, pp. of *influere*] : a flowing in : INFLOW <an ~ of foreign capital>

in·fo \ˈin-(ˌ)fō\ *n* : INFORMATION

in·fold \in-ˈfōld\ *vt* : ENFOLD, ENVELOP ~ \ˈin-ˌ\ *vi* : to fold inward or toward one another

in·form \in-ˈfȯ(ə)rm\ *vb* [ME *informen,* fr. MF *enformer,* fr. L *informare,* fr. *in-* + *forma* form] *vt* **1** *obs* : to give material form to **2 a :** to give character or essence to <the principles which ~ modern teaching> **b :** to be the characteristic quality of : ANIMATE <the compassion that ~*s* his work> **3** *obs* : GUIDE, DIRECT **4** *obs* : to make known **5 :** to communicate knowledge to <~ a prisoner of his rights> ~ *vi* **1 :** to give information or knowledge **2 :** to act as an informer

syn INFORM, ACQUAINT, APPRISE, NOTIFY *shared meaning element* : to make one aware of something

in·for·mal \(ˈ)in-ˈfȯr-məl\ *adj* **1 :** marked by the absence of formality or ceremony <an ~ meeting> <an ~ group> **2 :** characteristic of or appropriate to ordinary, casual, or familiar use <~ English> <~ clothes> — **in·for·mal·i·ty** \ˌin-(ˌ)fȯr-ˈmal-ət-ē, -fər-\ *n* — **in·for·mal·ly** \(ˈ)in-ˈfȯr-mə-lē\ *adv*

in·for·mant \in-ˈfȯr-mənt\ *n* : one who gives information: as **a :** INFORMER **b :** one who supplies cultural or linguistic data in response to interrogation by an investigator

in for·ma pau·pe·ris \ˌin-ˌfȯr-mə-ˈpȯ-pə-rəs, -ˈpau̇-\ *adv or adj* [L, in the form of a pauper] : as a poor man

in·for·mat·ics \ˌin-fər-ˈmat-iks\ *n pl but sing in constr* [ISV *informat*ion + *-ics*] : INFORMATION SCIENCE

in·for·ma·tion \ˌin-fər-ˈmā-shən\ *n* **1 :** the communication or reception of knowledge or intelligence **2 a :** knowledge obtained from investigation, study, or instruction **b :** INTELLIGENCE, NEWS **c :** FACTS, DATA **d :** a signal or character (as in a communication system or computer) representing data **e :** something (as a message, experimental data, or a picture) which justifies change in a construct (as a plan or theory) that represents physical or mental experience or another construct **f :** a quantitative measure of the content of information; *specif* : a numerical quantity that measures the uncertainty in the outcome of an experiment to be performed **3 :** the act of informing against a person **4 :** a formal accusation of a crime made by a prosecuting officer as distinguished from an indictment presented by a grand jury — **in·for·ma·tion·al** \-shnəl, -shən-ᵊl\ *adj*

information retrieval *n* : the techniques of storing and recovering and often disseminating recorded data esp. through the use of a computerized system

information science *n* : the collection, classification, storage, retrieval, and dissemination of recorded knowledge treated both as a pure and as an applied science

information theory *n* : a theory that deals statistically with information, the measurement of its content in terms of its distinguishing essential characteristics or by the number of alternatives from which it makes a choice possible, and with the efficiency of processes of communication between men and machines (as in telecommunication or in computing machines)

in·for·ma·tive \in-ˈfȯr-mət-iv\ *adj* : imparting knowledge : INSTRUCTIVE — **in·for·ma·tive·ly** *adv* — **in·for·ma·tive·ness** *n*

in·for·ma·to·ry \-mə-ˌtōr-ē, -ˌtȯr-\ *adj* : conveying information : INFORMATIVE

in·formed \in-ˈfȯ(ə)rmd\ *adj* **1 a :** having information <~ sources> <~ observers> **b :** based on possession of information <an ~ estimate of next year's tax receipts> **2 :** EDUCATED, INTELLIGENT <what the ~ person should know about psychology>

in·form·er \-ˈfȯr-mər\ *n* **1 :** one that imparts knowledge or news **2 :** one that informs against another; *specif* : one who makes a practice esp. for a financial reward of informing against others for violations of penal laws — called also *common informer*

in·fra \ˈin-frə, -ˌfrä\ *adv* [L] : BELOW : later in this writing <for additional examples see ~>

infra- *prefix* [L *infra* — more at UNDER] **1 :** below <*infra*human> <*infra*sonic> **2 :** within <*infra*specific> **3 :** below in a scale or series <*infra*red>

in·fract \in-ˈfrakt\ *vt* [L *infractus,* pp. of *infringere* to break off — more at INFRINGE] : INFRINGE, VIOLATE — **in·frac·tor** \-ˈfrak-tər\ *n*

in·frac·tion \in-ˈfrak-shən\ *n* : the act or an instance of infringing : VIOLATION <an ~ of the law>

in·fra dig \ˌin-frə-ˈdig\ *adj* [short for L *infra dignitatem*] : being beneath one's dignity : UNDIGNIFIED <while his work . . . was financially profitable, it was just a bit *infra dig* —John McCarten>

in·fra·hu·man \ˌin-frə-ˈhyü-mən, -(ˌ)frä-, -ˈyü-\ *adj* : less or lower than human; *esp* : ANTHROPOID — **infrahuman** *n*

in·fran·gi·bil·i·ty \(ˌ)in-ˌfran-jə-ˈbil-ət-ē\ *n* : the quality or state of being infrangible

in·fran·gi·ble \(ˈ)in-ˈfran-jə-bəl\ *adj* [MF, fr. LL *infrangibilis,* fr. L *in-* + *frangere* to break — more at BREAK] **1 :** not capable of being broken or separated into parts **2 :** not to be infringed or violated — **in·fran·gi·ble·ness** *n* — **in·fran·gi·bly** \-blē\ *adv*

in·fra·red \ˌin-frə-ˈred, -(ˌ)frä-\ *adj* **1 :** lying outside the visible spectrum at its red end — used of thermal radiation of wavelengths longer than those of visible light **2 :** relating to, producing, or employing infrared radiation <~ therapy> **3 :** sensitive to infrared radiation <~ photographic film> — **infrared** *n*

in·fra·son·ic \-ˈsän-ik\ *adj* **1 :** having or relating to a frequency below the audibility range of the human ear **2 :** utilizing or produced by infrasonic waves or vibrations

in·fra·spe·cif·ic \-spi-ˈsif-ik\ *adj* : included within a species <~ categories>

in·fra·struc·ture \ˈin-frə-ˌstrək-chər, -(ˌ)frä-\ *n* **1 :** the underlying foundation or basic framework (as of a system or organization) **2 :** the permanent installations required for military purposes

in·fre·quence \(ˈ)in-ˈfrē-kwən(t)s\ *n* : INFREQUENCY

in·fre·quen·cy \-kwən-sē\ *n* : rarity of occurrence

in·fre·quent \(ˈ)in-ˈfrē-kwənt\ *adj* [L *infrequent-, infrequens,* fr. *in-* + *frequent-, frequens* frequent] **1 :** seldom happening or occurring : RARE **2 :** placed or occurring at wide intervals in space or time <a slope scattered with ~ pines> <his ~ complaints> — **in·fre·quent·ly** *adv*

syn INFREQUENT, UNCOMMON, SCARCE, RARE, SPORADIC *shared meaning element* : not common or abundant ***ant*** frequent

in·fringe \in-ˈfrinj\ *vb* **in·fringed; in·fring·ing** [L *infringere,* lit., to break off, fr. *in-* + *frangere* to break — more at BREAK] *vt* **1** *obs* : DEFEAT, FRUSTRATE **2 :** to encroach upon in a way that violates law or the rights of another <~ a patent> ~ *vi* : to infringe on something : ENCROACH ***syn*** see TRESPASS — **in·fring·er** *n*

in·fringe·ment \in-ˈfrinj-mənt\ *n* **1 :** the act of infringing : VIOLATION **2 :** an encroachment or trespass on a right or privilege

in·fun·dib·u·lar \ˌin-(ˌ)fən-ˈdib-yə-lər\ *or* **in·fun·dib·u·late** \-lət\ *adj* **1 :** INFUNDIBULIFORM **2 :** of, relating to, or having an infundibulum

in·fun·dib·u·li·form \-lə-ˌfȯrm\ *adj* [NL *infundibulum* + E *-iform*] : having the form of a funnel or cone

in·fun·dib·u·lum \ˌin-(ˌ)fən-ˈdib-yə-ləm\ *n, pl* **-la** \-lə\ [NL, fr. L, funnel — more at FUNNEL] **:** any of various conical or dilated organs or parts: as **a :** the hollow conical process of gray matter by which the pituitary body is continuous with the brain **b :** the calyx of a kidney **c :** the abdominal opening of a fallopian tube

¹in·fu·ri·ate \in-ˈfyu̇r-ē-ˌāt\ *vt* **-at·ed; -at·ing** [ML *infuriatus,* pp. of *infuriare,* fr. L *in-* + *furia* fury] **:** to make furious **:** ENRAGE — **in·fu·ri·at·ing·ly** \-ˌāt-iŋ-lē\ *adv* — **in·fu·ri·a·tion** \-ˌfyu̇r-ē-ˈā-shən\ *n*

²in·fu·ri·ate \in-ˈfyu̇r-ē-ət\ *adj* **:** furiously angry — **in·fu·ri·ate·ly** *adv*

in·fuse \in-ˈfyüz\ *vt* **in·fused; in·fus·ing** [ME *infusen,* fr. MF & L; MF *infuser,* fr. L *infusus,* pp. of *infundere* to pour in, fr. *in-* + *fundere* to pour — more at FOUND] **1 a :** to cause to be permeated with something (as a principle or quality) that alters usu. for the better <attributes the fine spirit of the whole project to the self-respect with which men had been *infused* —Dixon Wecter> **b :** INTRODUCE, INSINUATE <a new spirit was *infused* into American art —*Amer. Guide Series: N.Y.*> **2 :** INSPIRE, ANIMATE <the sense of purpose that *infuses* scientific research> **3 :** to steep in liquid (as water) without boiling for extracting useful qualities — **in·fus·er** *n*

syn INFUSE, SUFFUSE, IMBUE, INGRAIN, INOCULATE, LEAVEN *shared meaning element* **:** to introduce one thing into another so as to affect it throughout

in·fus·ible \(ˈ)in-ˈfyü-zə-bəl\ *adj* **:** incapable of being fused **:** very difficult to fuse — **in·fus·ibil·i·ty** \(ˌ)in-ˌfyü-zə-ˈbil-ət-ē\ *n* — **in·fus·ible·ness** \(ˈ)in-ˈfyü-zə-bəl-nəs\ *n*

in·fu·sion \in-ˈfyü-zhən\ *n* **1 :** the act or process of infusing **2 :** the continuous slow introduction of a solution esp. into a vein **3 :** a product obtained by infusing

in·fu·so·ri·al \ˌin-fyü-ˈzōr-ē-əl, -ˈsōr-, -ˈzȯr-, -ˈsȯr-\ *adj* **:** of, relating to, or being infusorians

in·fu·so·ri·an \-ē-ən\ *n* [deriv. of L *infusus*] **:** any of a heterogeneous group of minute organisms found esp. in decomposing infusions of organic matter; *esp* **:** a ciliated protozoan — **infusorian** *adj*

¹-ing \iŋ; *in some dialects usu., in other dialects informally,* ən, in, *or (after certain consonants)* ᵊn, ᵊm, ᵊŋ\ *vb suffix or adj suffix* [ME, alter. of *-ende,* fr. OE, fr. *-e-,* verb stem vowel + *-nde,* prp. suffix — more at -ANT] — used to form the present participle <sail*ing*> and sometimes to form an adjective resembling a present participle but not derived from a verb <swashbuckl*ing*>

²-ing *n suffix* [ME, fr. OE; akin to OHG *-ing* one of a (specified) kind] **:** one of a (specified) kind <sweet*ing*>

³-ing *n suffix* [ME, fr. OE, suffix forming nouns from verbs; akin to OHG *-ung,* suffix forming nouns from verbs] **1 :** action or process <runn*ing*> <sleep*ing*> **:** instance of an action or process <a meet*ing*> **2 a :** product or result of an action or process <an engrav*ing*> — often in pl. <earn*ings*> **b :** something used in an action or process <a bed cover*ing*> <the lin*ing* of a coat> **3 :** action or process connected with (a specified thing) <boat*ing*> **4 :** something connected with, consisting of, or used in making (a specified thing) <scaffold*ing*> <shirt*ing*> **5 :** something related to (a specified concept) <off*ing*>

in·gath·er \ˈin-ˌgath̲-ər, -ˌgeth̲-\ *vt* **:** to gather in ~ *vi* **:** ASSEMBLE — **in·gath·er·ing** \-ˌgath̲-(ə-)riŋ, -ˌgeth̲-\ *n*

in·ge·nious \in-ˈjēn-yəs\ *adj* [MF *ingenieux,* fr. L *ingeniosus,* fr. *ingenium* natural capacity — more at ENGINE] **1** *obs* **:** showing or calling for intelligence, aptitude, or discernment **2 :** marked by especial aptitude at discovering, inventing, or contriving **3 :** marked by originality, resourcefulness, and cleverness in conception or execution ***syn*** see CLEVER — **in·ge·nious·ly** *adv* — **in·ge·nious·ness** *n*

in·ge·nue *or* **in·gé·nue** \ˈan-jə-ˌnü, ˈän-; ˈaⁿ-zhə-, ˈäⁿ-\ *n* [F *ingénue,* fem. of *ingénu* ingenuous, fr. L *ingenuus*] **1 :** a naive girl or young woman **2 :** the stage role of an ingenue; *also* **:** an actress playing such a role

in·ge·nu·ity \ˌin-jə-ˈn(y)ü-ət-ē\ *n, pl* **-ities 1** *obs* **:** CANDOR, INGENUOUSNESS **2 a :** skill or cleverness in devising or combining **:** INVENTIVENESS **b :** cleverness or aptness of design or contrivance **3 :** an ingenious device or contrivance

in·gen·u·ous \in-ˈjen-yə-wəs\ *adj* [L *ingenuus* native, free born, fr. *in-* + *gignere* to beget — more at KIN] **1** *obs* **:** NOBLE, HONORABLE **2 a :** showing innocent or childlike simplicity and candidness **b :** lacking craft or subtlety **3** [by alter.] *obs* **:** INGENIOUS ***syn*** see NATURAL ***ant*** disingenuous, cunning — **in·gen·u·ous·ly** *adv* — **in·gen·u·ous·ness** *n*

in·gest \in-ˈjest\ *vt* [L *ingestus,* pp. of *ingerere* to carry in, fr. *in-* + *gerere* to bear — more at CAST] **:** to take in for or as if for digestion **:** ABSORB — **in·gest·ible** \-ˈjes-tə-bəl\ *adj* — **in·ges·tion** \-ˈjes(h)-chən\ *n* — **in·ges·tive** \-ˈjes-tiv\ *adj*

in·ges·ta \in-ˈjes-tə\ *n pl* [NL, fr. L, neut. pl. of *ingestus*] **:** material taken into the body by way of the digestive tract

in·gle \ˈiŋ-(g)əl\ *n* [ScGael *aingeal*] **1 :** FLAME, BLAZE **2 :** FIREPLACE **3 :** CORNER, ANGLE

in·gle·nook \-ˌnu̇k\ *n* **:** a nook by a large open fireplace; *also* **:** a bench or settle occupying this nook

in·glo·ri·ous \(ˈ)in-ˈglōr-ē-əs, -ˈglȯr-\ *adj* [L *inglorius,* fr. *in-* + *gloria* glory] **1 :** not glorious **:** lacking fame or honor **2 :** SHAMEFUL, IGNOMINIOUS — **in·glo·ri·ous·ly** *adv* — **in·glo·ri·ous·ness** *n*

in·got \ˈiŋ-gət\ *n* [ME, prob. modif. of MF *lingot* ingot of metal, incorrectly divided as *l'ingot,* as if fr. *le* the, fr. L *ille* that] **1 :** a mold in which metal is cast **2 :** a mass of metal cast into a convenient shape for storage or transportation to be later processed

ingot iron *n* **:** iron containing only small proportions of impurities (as less than 0.05 percent carbon)

¹in·grain \(ˈ)in-ˈgrān\ *vt* **:** to work indelibly into the natural texture or mental or moral constitution ***syn*** see INFUSE

²in·grain \ˌin-ˌgrān\ *adj* **1 a :** made of fiber that is dyed before being spun into yarn **b :** made of yarn that is dyed before being woven or knitted **2 :** thoroughly worked in **:** INNATE

³in·grain \ˈin-ˌgrān\ *n* **1 :** an article made with ingrain yarns **2 :** innate quality or character

in·grained \ˈin-ˌgrānd, (ˈ)in-ˈ\ *adj* **1 :** worked into the grain or fiber **2 :** forming a part of the essence or inmost being **:** DEEP-SEATED <~ prejudice> — **in·grained·ly** \ˈin-ˌgrā-nəd-lē, ˈin-ˌgrānd-lē, (ˈ)in-ˈ\ *adv*

in·grate \ˈin-ˌgrāt\ *n* [L *ingratus* ungrateful, fr. *in-* + *gratus* grateful — more at GRACE] **:** an ungrateful person

in·gra·ti·ate \in-ˈgrā-shē-ˌāt\ *vt* **-at·ed; -at·ing** [*in-* + L *gratia* grace] **:** to gain favor or favorable acceptance for by deliberate effort — usu. used with *with* <~ themselves with the community leaders —William Attwood> — **in·gra·ti·a·tion** \-ˌgrā-shē-ˈā-shən\ *n* — **in·gra·tia·to·ry** \-ˈgrā-sh(ē-)ə-ˌtōr-ē, -ˌtȯr-\ *adj*

in·gra·ti·at·ing *adj* **1 :** capable of winning favor **:** PLEASING <an ~ smile> **2 :** intended or adopted in order to gain favor **:** FLATTERING — **in·gra·ti·at·ing·ly** \-ˈgrā-shē-ˌāt-iŋ-lē\ *adv*

in·grat·i·tude \(ˈ)in-ˈgrat-ə-ˌt(y)üd\ *n* [ME, fr. MF, fr. ML *ingratitudo,* fr. L *in-* + LL *gratitudo* gratitude] **:** forgetfulness of or poor return for kindness received **:** UNGRATEFULNESS

in·gre·di·ent \in-ˈgrēd-ē-ənt\ *n* [ME, fr. L *ingredient-, ingrediens,* prp. of *ingredi* to go into, fr. *in-* + *gradi* to go — more at GRADE] **:** something that enters into a compound or is a component part of any combination or mixture **:** CONSTITUENT ***syn*** see ELEMENT — **ingredient** *adj*

in·gress \ˈin-ˌgres\ *n* [ME, fr. L *ingressus,* fr. *ingressus,* pp. of *ingredi*] **1 :** the act of entering **:** ENTRANCE; *specif* **:** the entrance of a celestial object into eclipse, occultation, or transit **2 :** the power or liberty of entrance or access — **in·gres·sion** \in-ˈgresh-ən\ *n*

in·gres·sive \in-ˈgres-iv\ *adj* **1 :** of, relating to, or involving ingress <an ~ current of air> **2 :** INCHOATIVE 2 — **ingressive** *n* — **in·gres·sive·ness** *n*

in–group \ˈin-ˌgrüp\ *n* **:** a group with which one feels a sense of solidarity or community of interests — compare OUT-GROUP

in·grow·ing \ˈin-ˌgrō-iŋ\ *adj* **:** growing or tending inward

in·grown \-ˌgrōn\ *adj* **1 :** grown in; *specif* **:** having the free tip or edge embedded in the flesh <an ~ toenail> **2 :** having the direction of growth or activity or interest inward rather than outward **:** WITHDRAWN — **in·grown·ness** \-ˈgrōn-nəs\ *n*

in·growth \ˈin-ˌgrōth\ *n* **1 :** a growing inward (as to fill a void) **2 :** something that grows in or into a space

in·gui·nal \ˈiŋ-gwən-ᵊl\ *adj* [L *inguinalis,* fr. *inguin-, inguen* groin — more at ADEN-] **:** of, relating to, or situated in the region of the groin or in either of the lowest lateral regions of the abdomen

in·gur·gi·tate \in-ˈgər-jə-ˌtāt\ *vt* **-tat·ed; -tat·ing** [L *ingurgitatus,* pp. of *ingurgitare,* fr. *in-* + *gurgit-, gurges* whirlpool — more at VORACIOUS] **:** to swallow greedily or in large quantities **:** GUZZLE — **in·gur·gi·ta·tion** \(ˌ)in-ˌgər-jə-ˈtā-shən\ *n*

INH \ˌī-ˌen-ˈāch\ *abbr* [*iso*nicotinic acid *h*ydrazide] isoniazid

in·hab·it \in-ˈhab-ət\ *vb* [ME *enhabiten,* fr. MF & L; MF *enhabiter,* fr. L *inhabitare,* fr. *in-* + *habitare* to dwell, fr. *habitus,* pp. of *habēre* to have — more at GIVE] *vt* **1 :** to occupy as a place of settled residence or habitat **:** live in <~*ed* a small two-room apartment> **2 :** to occupy or be present in any manner or form <the human beings who ~ this tale —Al Newman> ~ *vi, archaic* **:** to have residence in a place **:** DWELL — **in·hab·it·able** \-ə-bəl\ *adj* — **in·hab·it·er** *n*

in·hab·it·an·cy \in-ˈhab-ət-ən-sē\ *n* **:** INHABITATION

in·hab·it·ant \in-ˈhab-ət-ənt\ *n* **:** one that occupies a particular place regularly, routinely, or for a period of time <~*s* of large cities> <the tapeworm is an ~ of the intestine>

in·hab·i·ta·tion \in-ˌhab-ə-ˈtā-shən\ *n* **:** the act of inhabiting **:** the state of being inhabited

in·hab·it·ed *adj* **:** having inhabitants

in·hal·ant \in-ˈhā-lənt\ *n* **:** something (as an allergen or medication) that is inhaled — **inhalant** *adj*

in·ha·la·tion \ˌin-(h)ə-ˈlā-shən, ˌin-ᵊl-ˈā-\ *n* **1 :** the act or an instance of inhaling **2 :** material (as medication) to be taken in by inhaling — **in·ha·la·tion·al** \-shnəl, -shən-ᵊl\ *adj*

in·ha·la·tor \ˈin-(h)ə-ˌlāt-ər, ˈin-ᵊl-ˌāt-\ *n* **:** a device providing a mixture of oxygen and carbon dioxide for breathing that is used esp. in conjunction with artificial respiration

in·hale \in-ˈhā(ə)l\ *vb* **in·haled; in·hal·ing** [*in-* + *-hale* (as in *exhale*)] *vt* **1 :** to draw in by breathing **2 :** to take in eagerly or greedily <*inhaled* about four meals at once —Ring Lardner> ~ *vi* **:** to breathe in — **in·hale** \in-ˈ, ˈin-ˌ\ *n*

in·hal·er \in-ˈhā-lər\ *n* **1 :** one that inhales **2 :** a device by means of which medicinal material is inhaled **3 :** SNIFTER

in·har·mon·ic \ˌin-(ˌ)här-ˈmän-ik\ *adj* **:** not harmonic **:** DISCORDANT

in·har·mo·ni·ous \-ˈmō-nē-əs\ *adj* **1 :** not harmonious **:** DISCORDANT **2:** not fitting or congenial **:** CONFLICTING — **in·har·mo·ni·ous·ly** *adv* — **in·har·mo·ni·ous·ness** *n*

in·har·mo·ny \(ˈ)in-ˈhär-mə-nē\ *n* **:** DISCORD

in·here \in-ˈhi(ə)r\ *vi* **in·hered; in·her·ing** [L *inhaerēre,* fr. *in-* + *haerēre* to adhere — more at HESITATE] **:** to be inherent **:** BELONG

in·her·ence \in-ˈhir-ən(t)s, -ˈher-\ *n* **:** the quality, state, or fact of inhering

in·her·ent \-ənt\ *adj* [L *inhaerent-, inhaerens,* prp. of *inhaerēre*] **:** involved in the constitution or essential character of something **:** belonging by nature or settled habit **:** INTRINSIC — **in·her·ent·ly** *adv*

in·her·it \in-ˈher-ət\ *vb* [ME *enheriten* to make heir, inherit, fr. MF *enheriter* to make heir, fr. LL *inhereditare,* fr. L *in-* + *hereditas* inheritance — more at HEREDITY] *vt* **1 :** to come into possession of or receive esp. as a right or divine portion <and every one who has left houses or brothers or sisters . . . for my name's sake, will receive a hundredfold, and ~ eternal life —Mt 19:29 (RSV)> **2**

ə abut ᵊ kitten ər further a back ā bake ä cot, cart
au̇ out ch chin e less ē easy g gift i trip ī life
j joke ŋ sing ō flow ȯ flaw ȯi coin th thin th̲ this
ü loot u̇ foot y yet yü few yu̇ furious zh vision

: to receive as a right or title descendible by law from an ancestor at his death **3 :** to receive from ancestors by genetic transmission <~ a strong constitution> **4 :** to have in turn or receive as if from an ancestor <~*ed* the problem from his predecessor> ~ *vi* : to take or hold a possession or rights by inheritance — **in·her·i·tor** \-ət-ər\ *n* — **in·her·i·tress** \-ə-trəs\ *or* **in·her·i·trix** \-ə-(ˌ)triks\ *n*

in·her·it·able \in-ˈher-ət-ə-bəl\ *adj* **1 :** capable of being inherited : TRANSMISSIBLE **2 :** capable of taking by inheritance — **in·her·it·abil·i·ty** \-ˌher-ət-ə-ˈbil-ət-ē\ *n* — **in·her·it·able·ness** \-ˈher-ət-ə-bəl-nəs\ *n*

in·her·i·tance \in-ˈher-ət-ən(t)s\ *n* **1 a :** the act of inheriting property **b :** the reception of genetic qualities by transmission from parent to offspring **c :** the acquisition of a possession, condition, or trait from past generations **2 :** something that is or may be inherited **3 a :** TRADITION **b :** a valuable possession that is a common heritage from nature **4** *obs* **:** POSSESSION ***syn*** see HERITAGE

inheritance tax *n* **1 :** an excise in the form of a percentage of the value of the property received that is levied on the privilege of an heir to receive property as an inheritance **2 :** DEATH TAX; *esp* : ESTATE TAX

in·hib·it \in-ˈhib-ət\ *vb* [ME *inhibiten,* fr. L *inhibitus,* pp. of *inhibēre,* fr. *in-* + *habēre* to have — more at HABIT] *vt* **1 :** to prohibit from doing something **2 a :** to hold in check : RESTRAIN **b :** to discourage from free or spontaneous activity esp. through the operation of inner psychological impediments or of social controls ~ *vi* **:** to cause inhibition ***syn*** see FORBID ***ant*** allow — **in·hib·i·tive** \-ət-iv\ *adj* — **in·hib·i·to·ry** \-ə-ˌtōr-ē, -ˌtȯr-\ *adj*

in·hi·bi·tion \ˌin-(h)ə-ˈbish-ən\ *n* **1 a :** the act of inhibiting : the state of being inhibited **b :** something that forbids, debars, or restricts **2 :** an inner impediment to free activity, expression, or functioning: as **a :** a psychical activity imposing restraint upon another activity **b :** a restraining of the function of a bodily organ or an agent (as an enzyme)

in·hib·i·tor *or* **in·hib·it·er** \in-ˈhib-ət-ər\ *n* **:** one that inhibits; *esp* : an agent that slows or interferes with a chemical action (as rusting)

in·hos·pi·ta·ble \ˌin-(ˌ)häs-ˈpit-ə-bəl, (ˈ)in-ˈhäs-(ˌ)pit-\ *adj* **1 :** not showing hospitality : not friendly or receptive **2 :** providing no shelter or sustenance : BARREN — **in·hos·pi·ta·ble·ness** *n* — **in·hos·pi·ta·bly** \-blē\ *adv*

in·hos·pi·tal·i·ty \(ˌ)in-ˌhäs-pə-ˈtal-ət-ē\ *n* **:** the quality or state of being inhospitable

in-house \ˌin-ˌhau̇s, ˈin-ˈ\ *adj* **:** of, relating to, or carried on within a group or organization <can be an outside or an ~ job —*Book Production Industry*> — **in-house** *adv*

in·hu·man \(ˈ)in-ˈhyü-mən, -ˈyü-\ *adj* [MF & L; MF *inhumain,* fr. L *inhumanus,* fr. *in-* + *humanus* human] **1 a :** lacking pity, kindness, or mercy : SAVAGE <an ~ tyrant> **b :** COLD, IMPERSONAL <his usual quiet, almost ~ courtesy —F. Tennyson Jesse> **c** : not worthy of or conforming to the needs of human beings <~ living conditions> **2 :** of or suggesting a nonhuman class of beings — **in·hu·man·ly** *adv* — **in·hu·man·ness** \-mən-nəs\ *n*

in·hu·mane \ˌin-(ˌ)hyü-ˈmān, -(ˌ)yü-\ *adj* [MF *inhumain* & L *inhumanus*] **:** not humane : INHUMAN 1 — **in·hu·mane·ly** *adv*

in·hu·man·i·ty \-ˈman-ət-ē\ *n, pl* **-ities** **1 a :** the quality or state of being cruel or barbarous **b :** a cruel or barbarous act **2** : absence of warmth or geniality : IMPERSONALITY

in·hume \in-ˈhyüm\ *vt* **in·humed; in·hum·ing** [prob. fr. F *inhumer,* fr. L *inhumare,* fr. *in-* + *humus* earth — more at HUMBLE] : BURY, INTER — **in·hu·ma·tion** \ˌin-hyü-ˈmā-shən\ *n*

in·im·i·cal \in-ˈim-i-kəl\ *adj* [LL *inimicalis,* fr. L *inimicus* enemy — more at ENEMY] **1 a :** having the disposition of an enemy : HOSTILE **b :** reflecting or indicating hostility : UNFRIENDLY **2** : being adverse usu. by reason of hostility or malevolence ***syn*** see ADVERSE — **in·im·i·cal·ly** \-i-k(ə-)lē\ *adv*

in·im·i·ta·ble \(ˈ)in-ˈim-ət-ə-bəl\ *adj* [MF or L; MF, fr. L *inimitabilis,* fr. *in-* + *imitabilis* imitable] **:** not capable of being imitated : MATCHLESS — **in·im·i·ta·ble·ness** *n* — **in·im·i·ta·bly** \-blē\ *adv*

in·iq·ui·tous \in-ˈik-wət-əs\ *adj* **:** characterized by iniquity ***syn*** see VICIOUS ***ant*** righteous — **in·iq·ui·tous·ly** *adv* — **in·iq·ui·tous·ness** *n*

in·iq·ui·ty \-wət-ē\ *n, pl* **-ties** [ME *iniquite,* fr. MF *iniquité,* fr. L *iniquitat-, iniquitas,* fr. *iniquus* uneven, fr. *in-* + *aequus* equal] **1** : gross injustice : WICKEDNESS **2 :** an iniquitous act or thing : SIN

¹ini·tial \in-ˈish-əl\ *adj* [MF & L; MF, fr. L *initialis,* fr. *initium* beginning, fr. *initus,* pp. of *inire* to go into, fr. *in-* + *ire* to go — more at ISSUE] **1 :** of or relating to the beginning : INCIPIENT **2** : placed at the beginning : FIRST — **ini·tial·ly** \-ˈish-(ə-)lē\ *adv* — **ini·tial·ness** \-ˈish-əl-nəs\ *n*

²initial *n* **1 a :** the first letter of a name **b** *pl* **:** the first letter of each word in a full name <found that their ~*s* were identical> **2 :** a large letter beginning a text or a division or paragraph **3** : ANLAGE, PRECURSOR; *specif* **:** a meristematic cell

³initial *vt* **ini·tialed** *or* **ini·tialled; ini·tial·ing** *or* **ini·tial·ling** \-ˈish-(ə-)liŋ\ **1 :** to affix an initial to **2 :** to authenticate or give preliminary approval to by affixing the initials of an authorizing representative

ini·tial·ism \in-ˈish-ə-ˌliz-əm\ *n* **:** an acronym formed from initial letters

ini·tial·ize \-ˌlīz\ *vt* **-ized; -iz·ing :** to set (as a computer program counter) to a starting position or value — **ini·tial·iza·tion** \-in-ˌish-(ə-)lə-ˈzā-shən\ *n*

initial rhyme *n* **1 :** ALLITERATION **2 :** BEGINNING RHYME

initial side *n* **:** the stationary straight line that contains the point about which another straight line is revolved in forming a trigonometric figure

initial teaching alphabet *n* **:** a 44-symbol alphabet designed esp. for use in the initial stages of teaching children to read English

¹ini·ti·ate \in-ˈish-ē-ˌāt\ *vt* **-at·ed; -at·ing** [LL *initiatus,* pp. of *initiare,* fr. L, to induct, fr. *initium*] **1 :** to cause or facilitate the beginning of : set going <~ a program of reform> <enzymes that ~ fermentation> **2 :** to instruct in the rudiments or principles of something : INTRODUCE **3 :** to induct into membership by or as if by special rites ***syn*** see BEGIN ***ant*** consummate — **ini·ti·a·tor** \-ˌāt-ər\ *n*

²ini·tiate \in-ˈish-(ē-)ət\ *adj* **1 a :** initiated or properly admitted (as to membership or an office) **b :** instructed in some secret knowledge **2** *obs* **:** relating to an initiate

³ini·tiate \in-ˈish-(ē-)ət\ *n* **1 :** a person who is undergoing or has undergone an initiation **2 :** a person who is instructed or adept in some special field

ini·ti·a·tion \in-ˌish-ē-ˈā-shən\ *n* **1 a :** the act or an instance of initiating **b :** the process of being initiated **c :** the rites, ceremonies, ordeals, or instructions with which one is made a member of a sect or society or is invested with a particular function or status **2 :** the condition of being initiated into some experience or sphere of activity : KNOWLEDGEABLENESS <clear to a reader of any degree of ~ —J. W. Beach>

¹ini·tia·tive \in-ˈish-ət-iv\ *adj* **:** of or relating to initiation : INTRODUCTORY, PRELIMINARY

²initiative *n* **1 :** an introductory step <he took the ~ in attempting to settle the issue> **2 :** energy or aptitude displayed in initiation of action : ENTERPRISE <a man of great ~> **3 a :** the right to initiate legislative action **b :** a procedure enabling a specified number of voters by petition to propose a law and secure its submission to the electorate or to the legislature for approval — compare REFERENDUM — **on one's own initiative :** at one's own discretion : independently of outside influence or control

ini·tia·to·ry \in-ˈish-(ē-)ə-ˌtōr-ē, -ˌtȯr-\ *adj* **1 :** constituting a beginning **2 :** tending or serving to initiate

in·ject \in-ˈjekt\ *vt* [L *injectus,* pp. of *inicere,* fr. *in-* + *jacere* to throw — more at JET] **1 a :** to throw, drive, or force into something <~ fuel into an engine> **b :** to force a fluid into (as for medical purposes) **2 :** to introduce as an element or factor in or into some situation or subject <condemning any attempt to ~ religious bigotry into the campaign —*Current Biog.*> — **in·ject·able** \-ˈjek-tə-bəl\ *adj* — **in·jec·tor** \-ˈjek-tər\ *n*

in·jec·tant \-ˈjek-tənt\ *n* **:** a substance that is injected into something

in·jec·tion \in-ˈjek-shən\ *n* **1 a :** an act or instance of injecting <the ~ of academic values into that aspect of our national life is a highly desirable . . . development —Goodwin Watson> **b :** the placing of an artificial satellite or a spacecraft into an orbit or on a trajectory; *also* **:** the time or place at which injection occurs **2** : something (as a medication) that is injected

in·jec·tor razor \in-ˌjek-tər-\ *n* **:** a safety razor with a narrow single-edged blade that is forced into place by a blade dispenser

in·ju·di·cious \ˌin-jü-ˈdish-əs\ *adj* **:** not judicious : INDISCREET, UNWISE — **in·ju·di·cious·ly** *adv* — **in·ju·di·cious·ness** *n*

in·junc·tion \in-ˈjəŋ(k)-shən\ *n* [MF & LL; MF *injonction,* fr. LL *injunction-, injunctio,* fr. L *injunctus,* pp. of *injungere* to enjoin — more at ENJOIN] **1 :** the act or an instance of enjoining : ORDER, ADMONITION **2 :** a writ granted by a court of equity whereby one is required to do or to refrain from doing a specified act — **in·junc·tive** \-ˈjəŋ(k)-tiv\ *adj*

in·jure \ˈin-jər\ *vt* **in·jured; in·jur·ing** \ˈinj-(ə-)riŋ\ [back-formation fr. *injury*] **1 a :** to do an injustice to : WRONG **b :** to harm, impair, or tarnish the standing of **c :** to give pain to <~ a man's pride> **2 a :** to inflict bodily hurt on **b :** to impair the soundness of **c :** to inflict material damage or loss on — **in·jur·er** \ˈin-jər-ər\ *n*

syn INJURE, HARM, HURT, DAMAGE, IMPAIR, MAR *shared meaning element* **:** to affect injuriously ***ant*** aid

in·ju·ri·ous \in-ˈju̇r-ē-əs\ *adj* **1 :** inflicting or tending to inflict injury : DETRIMENTAL <~ to health> **2 :** ABUSIVE, DEFAMATORY <speak not ~ words —George Washington> — **in·ju·ri·ous·ly** *adv* — **in·ju·ri·ous·ness** *n*

in·ju·ry \ˈinj-(ə-)rē\ *n, pl* **-ries** [ME *injurie,* fr. L *injuria,* fr. *injurus* injurious, fr. *in-* + *jur-, jus* right — more at JUST] **1 a :** an act that damages or hurts : WRONG **b :** violation of another's rights for which the law allows an action to recover damages **2 :** hurt, damage, or loss sustained ***syn*** see INJUSTICE

in·jus·tice \(ˈ)in-ˈjəs-təs\ *n* [ME, fr. MF, fr. L *injustitia,* fr. *injustus* unjust, fr. *in-* + *justus* just] **1 :** absence of justice : violation of right or of the rights of another : UNFAIRNESS **2 :** an unjust act

syn INJUSTICE, INJURY, WRONG, GRIEVANCE *shared meaning element* : an act that inflicts undeserved hurt

¹ink \ˈiŋk\ *n, often attrib* [ME *enke,* fr. OF, fr. LL *encaustum,* fr. neut. of L *encaustus* burned in, fr. Gk *enkaustos,* verbal of *enkaiein* to burn in — more at ENCAUSTIC] **1 :** a colored usu. liquid material for writing and printing **2 :** the black protective secretion of a cephalopod — **ink·i·ness** \ˈiŋ-kē-nəs\ *n* — **inky** \ˈiŋ-kē\ *adj*

²ink *vt* **:** to put ink on <~ a pen>; *also* **:** to write on, draw, or sign in ink <~*ed* a new contract>

ink·ber·ry \ˈiŋk-ˌber-ē\ *n* [fr. the use of the berries for making ink] **1 a :** a holly (*Ilex glabra*) of eastern No. America with evergreen oblong leathery leaves and small black berries **b :** POKEWEED **2** : the fruit of an inkberry

ink·blot test \ˈiŋk-ˌblät-\ *n* **:** any of several psychological tests based on the interpretation of irregular figures (as blots of ink)

¹ink·horn \ˈiŋk-ˌhȯ(ə)rn\ *n* **:** a small portable bottle (as of horn) for holding ink

²inkhorn *adj* **:** ostentatiously learned : PEDANTIC <~ terms>

in·kle \ˈiŋ-kəl\ *n* [origin unknown] **:** a colored linen tape or braid woven on a very narrow loom and used for trimming; *also* **:** the thread used

in·kling \ˈiŋ-kliŋ\ *n* [ME *yngkiling,* prob. fr. *inclen* to hint at; akin to OE *inca* suspicion, Lith *ingis* sluggard] **1 :** a slight indication or suggestion : HINT, CLUE <there was no path — no ~ even of a track —*New Yorker*> **2 :** a slight knowledge or vague notion <had not the faintest ~ of what it was all about —H. W. Carter>

ink·stand \ˈiŋk-ˌstand\ *n* **:** INKWELL; *also* **:** a stand with fittings for holding ink and pens

ink·well \ˈiŋ-ˌkwel\ *n* **:** a container (as in a school desk) for ink

inky cap *n* : a mushroom (genus *Coprinus,* esp. *C. atramentarius*) whose pileus melts into an inky fluid after the spores have matured

inky cap

in·laid \ˈin-ˈlād\ *adj* **1 a** : set into a surface in a decorative design <tables with ~ marble> **b** : decorated with a design or material set into a surface <a table with an ~ top> **2** *of linoleum* : having a design that goes all the way through to the backing

¹in·land \ˈin-ˌland, -lənd\ *n* : the interior part of a country

²inland *adj* **1** *chiefly Brit* : not foreign : DOMESTIC **2** : of or relating to the interior of a country

³inland *adv* : into or toward the interior

in·land·er \ˈin-ˌlan-dər, -lən-\ *n* : one who lives inland

in–law \ˈin-ˌlȯ\ *n* [back-formation fr. *mother-in-law,* etc.] : a relative by marriage

¹in·lay \(ˈ)in-ˈlā, ˈin-ˌ\ *vt* **in·laid** \-ˈlād\; **in·lay·ing** **1 a** : to set into a surface or ground material **b** : to adorn with insertions **c** : to insert (as a color plate) into a mat or other reinforcement **d** : to reinforce (silver-plated ware) at points of wear with additional silver **2** : to rub, beat, or fuse (as wire) into an incision in metal, wood, or stone — **in·lay·er** *n*

²in·lay \ˈin-ˌlā\ *n* **1** : inlaid work or a decorative inlaid pattern **2** : a tooth filling shaped to fit a cavity and then cemented into place

in·let \ˈin-ˌlet, -lət\ *n* [fr. its letting water in] **1 a** : a bay or recess in the shore of a sea, lake, or river; *also* : CREEK **b** : a narrow water passage between peninsulas or through a barrier island leading to a bay or lagoon **2** : a way of entering; *esp* : an opening for intake <a fuel ~>

in·li·er \ˈin-ˌlī(-ə)r\ *n* [³*in* + *-lier* (as in *outlier*)] **1** : a mass of rock whose outcrop is surrounded by rock of younger age **2** : a distinct area or formation completely surrounded by another; *also* : ENCLAVE

in–line engine \(ˌ)in-ˌlīn-\ *n* : an internal-combustion engine in which the cylinders are arranged in one or more straight lines

¹in lo·co pa·ren·tis \in-ˌlō-kō-pə-ˈrent-əs\ *adv* [L] : in the place of a parent

²in loco parentis *n* : regulation or supervision by an administrative body (as at a university) acting in loco parentis <the concept of *in loco parentis* is a dead issue as far as these faculty members are concerned —*Change*>

in·ly \ˈin-lē\ *adv* **1** : INWARDLY **2** : in a manner suggesting great depth of knowledge or understanding : THOROUGHLY

in·mate \ˈin-ˌmāt\ *n* : one of a group occupying a single place of residence; *esp* : a person confined (as in a prison or hospital)

in me·di·as res \in-ˌmed-ē-əs-ˈrās, -ˌmēd-ē-əs-ˈrēz\ *adv* [L, lit., into the midst of things] : in or into the middle of a narrative or plot <the script . . . hops from one thing to another, starting *in medias res* —H. C. Schonberg>

in me·mo·ri·am \ˌin-mə-ˈmōr-ē-əm, -ˈmȯr-\ *prep* [L] : in memory of — used esp. in epitaphs

in–mi·grant \ˈin-ˌmī-grənt\ *n* : one that in-migrates

in–migrate \ˈin-ˌmī-ˌgrāt\ *vi* : to move into or come to live in a region or community esp. as part of a large-scale and continuing movement of population — compare OUT-MIGRATE — **in–mi·gra·tion** \-ˌgrā-shən\ *n*

in·most \ˈin-ˌmōst\ *adj* [ME, fr. OE *innemest,* superl. of *inne,* adv., in, within, fr. *in,* adv.] : deepest within : farthest from the outside

¹inn \ˈin\ *n* [ME, fr. OE; akin to ON *inni* dwelling, inn, OE *in,* adv.] **1 a** : a public house for the lodging and entertaining of travelers **b** : TAVERN **2** : a residence formerly provided for British students in London and esp. for students of law

²inn *vi* : to put up at an inn

in·nards \ˈin-ərdz\ *n pl* [alter. of *inwards*] **1** : the internal organs of a man or animal; *esp* : VISCERA **2** : the internal parts of a structure or mechanism

in·nate \in-ˈāt, ˈin-ˌ\ *adj* [ME *innat,* fr. L *innatus,* pp. of *innasci* to be born in, fr. *in-* + *nasci* to be born — more at NATION] **1 a** : existing in or belonging to an individual from birth : NATIVE **b** : belonging to the essential nature of something : INHERENT **c** : originating in or derived from the mind or the constitution of the intellect rather than from experience **2 a** : attached to the apex of the support — compare ADNATE **b** : ENDOGENOUS **c** : immersed or embedded in — **in·nate·ly** *adv* — **in·nate·ness** *n*

syn INNATE, INBORN, INBRED, CONGENITAL, HEREDITARY *shared meaning element* : not acquired after birth

in·ner \ˈin-ər\ *adj* [ME, fr. OE *innera,* compar. of *inne* within — more at INMOST] **1 a** : situated farther in <the ~ bark> **b** : being near a center esp. of influence <the life and soul of the government, the ~ cabinet of deputy prime ministers, has disappeared —Richard Lowenthal> **2** : of or relating to the mind or spirit <the ~ life of man> — **inner** *n* — **in·ner·ly** *adv*

inner city *n* : the usu. older and more densely populated central section of a city — **inner–city** *adj*

in·ner–di·rect·ed \ˌin-ər-də-ˈrek-təd, -(ˌ)dī-\ *adj* : directed in thought and action by one's own scale of values as opposed to external norms

inner ear *n* : the essential organ of hearing and equilibrium located in the temporal bone and innervated by the auditory nerve

inner light *n, often cap I & L* : a divine presence held (as in Quaker doctrine) to enlighten and guide the soul

¹in·ner·most \ˈin-ər-ˌmōst\ *adj* : farthest inward : INMOST

²innermost *n* : the inmost part

inner planet *n* : any of the planets Mercury, Venus, Earth, and Mars that as a group have orbits nearer the sun than the outer planets

inner product *n* : SCALAR PRODUCT

in·ner·sole \ˌin-ər-ˈsōl\ *n* : INSOLE

inner space *n* : space at or near the earth's surface and esp. under the sea

in·ner·spring \ˌin-ər-ˌspriŋ\ *adj* : having coil springs inside a padded casing <~ mattress>

inner tube *n* : TUBE 3

in·ner·vate \in-ˈər-ˌvāt, ˈin-(ˌ)ər-\ *vt* **-vat·ed**; **-vat·ing** : to supply with nerves — **in·ner·va·tion** \ˌin-(ˌ)ər-ˈvā-shən, in-ˌər-\ *n* — **in·ner·va·tion·al** \-shnəl, -shən-ᵊl\ *adj*

in·nerve \in-ˈərv\ *vt* : to give nervous energy or power to

inn·hold·er \ˈin-ˌhōl-dər\ *n* : INNKEEPER

in·ning \ˈin-iŋ\ *n* [in sense 1, fr. E dial. *in* to reclaim; in other senses, fr. ²*in*] **1** : the reclaiming of land esp. from the sea **2 a** : a division of a baseball game consisting of a turn at bat for each team; *also* : a baseball team's turn at bat ending with the third out **b** *pl but sing or pl in constr* : a division of a cricket match **c** : a player's turn (as in horseshoes, pool, or croquet) **3** : a chance or opportunity for action or accomplishment — usu. used in pl. but sing. or pl. in constr. <on the verge of that momentous ~*s* which was to project him into world politics —*Times Lit. Supp.*>

inn·keep·er \ˈin-ˌkē-pər\ *n* : the landlord of an inn

in·no·cence \ˈin-ə-sən(t)s\ *n* **1 a** : freedom from guilt or sin through being unacquainted with evil : BLAMELESSNESS **b** : CHASTITY **c** : freedom from legal guilt of a particular crime or offense **d** (1) : freedom from guile or cunning : SIMPLICITY (2) : lack of worldly experience or sophistication **e** : lack of knowledge : IGNORANCE <written in entire ~ of the Italian language —E. R. Bentley> **2** : one that is innocent **3 a** : BLUET **b** (1) : a small herb (*Collinsia verna* of the figwort family) of the central U.S. (2) : a related California herb (*C. bicolor*)

in·no·cen·cy \-sən-sē\ *n, pl* **-cies** : INNOCENCE; *also* : an innocent action or quality

in·no·cent \ˈin-ə-sənt\ *adj* [ME, fr. MF, fr. L *innocent-, innocens,* fr. *in-* + *nocent-, nocens,* wicked, fr. pp. of *nocēre* to harm — more at NOXIOUS] **1 a** : free from guilt or sin esp. through lack of knowledge of evil : BLAMELESS <an ~ child> **b** : harmless in effect or intention <searching for a hidden motive in even the most ~ conversation —Leonard Wibberley>; *also* : CANDID <gave me an ~ gaze> **c** : free from legal guilt or fault; *also* : LAWFUL <a wholly ~ transaction> **2** : lacking or deprived of something <her face ~ of cosmetics —Marcia Davenport> **3 a** : lacking or reflecting a lack of sophistication, guile, or self-consciousness : ARTLESS, INGENUOUS **b** : IGNORANT <almost entirely ~ of Latin —C. L. Wrenn>; *also* : UNAWARE <perfectly ~ of the confusion he had created —B. R. Haydon> — **innocent** *n* — **in·no·cent·ly** *adv*

in·noc·u·ous \in-ˈäk-yə-wəs\ *adj* [L *innocuus,* fr. *in-* + *nocēre*] **1** : producing no injury : HARMLESS **2** : not likely to give offense or to arouse strong feelings or hostility : INOFFENSIVE, INSIPID — **in·noc·u·ous·ly** *adv* — **in·noc·u·ous·ness** *n*

Inn of Court **1** : one of four sets of buildings in London belonging to four societies of students and practitioners of the law **2** : one of four societies that alone admit to practice at the English bar

in·nom·i·nate \in-ˈäm-ə-nət\ *adj* [LL *innominatus,* fr. L *in-* + *nominatus,* pp. of *nominare* to nominate] : having no name : UNNAMED; *also* : ANONYMOUS

innominate artery *n* : a short artery that arises from the arch of the aorta and divides into the carotid and subclavian arteries of the right side

innominate bone *n* : the large flaring bone that makes a lateral half of the pelvis in mammals and is composed of the ilium, ischium, and pubis which are consolidated into one bone in the adult

innominate vein *n* : either of a pair of veins that receive blood from the head and neck and fuse to form the superior vena cava

in·no·vate \ˈin-ə-ˌvāt\ *vb* **-vat·ed**; **-vat·ing** [L *innovatus,* pp. of *innovare,* fr. *in-* + *novus* new — more at NEW] *vt* **1** : to introduce as or as if new **2** *archaic* : to effect a change in <the dictates of my father were . . . not to be altered, *innovated,* or even discussed —Sir Walter Scott> ~ *vi* : to make changes — **in·no·va·tor** \-ˌvāt-ər\ *n* — **in·no·va·to·ry** \ˈin-ə-və-ˌtōr-ē, in-ˈō-və-, -ˌtȯr-; ˈin-ə-ˌvāt-ə-rē\ *adj*

in·no·va·tion \ˌin-ə-ˈvā-shən\ *n* **1** : the introduction of something new **2** : a new idea, method, or device : NOVELTY — **in·no·va·tion·al** \-shnəl, -shən-ᵊl\ *adj*

in·no·va·tive \ˈin-ə-ˌvāt-iv\ *adj* : characterized by, tending to, or introducing innovations — **in·no·va·tive·ness** *n*

¹in·nu·en·do \ˌin-yə-ˈwen-(ˌ)dō\ *n, pl* **-dos** *or* **-does** [L, by hinting, fr. *innuere* to hint, fr. *in-* + *nuere* to nod — more at NUMEN] **1** : an oblique allusion : HINT, INSINUATION; *esp* : a veiled or equivocal reflection on character or reputation **2** : a parenthetical explanation introduced into the text of a legal document

²innuendo *vi* : to make an innuendo ~ *vt* : to insinuate by an innuendo

in·nu·mer·a·ble \in-ˈ(y)üm(-ə)-rə-bəl\ *adj* [ME, fr. L *innumerabilis,* fr. *in-* + *numerabilis* numerable] : too many to be numbered : COUNTLESS — **in·nu·mer·a·ble·ness** *n* — **in·nu·mer·a·bly** \-blē\ *adv*

in·nu·mer·ous \-rəs\ *adj* [L *innumerus,* fr. *in-* + *numerus* number — more at NIMBLE] : INNUMERABLE

in·nu·tri·tion \ˌin-(n)(y)ü-ˈtrish-ən\ *n* : failure of nourishment

in·ob·ser·vance \ˌin-əb-ˈzər-vən(t)s\ *n* [F & L; F, fr. L *inobservantia,* fr. *in-* + *observantia* observance] **1** : lack of attention : HEEDLESSNESS **2** : failure to fulfill : NONOBSERVANCE — **in·ob·ser·vant** \-vənt\ *adj*

in·oc·u·lant \in-ˈäk-yə-lənt\ *n* : INOCULUM

in·oc·u·late \in-ˈäk-yə-ˌlāt\ *vt* **-lat·ed**; **-lat·ing** [ME *inoculaten* to insert a bud in a plant, fr. L *inoculatus,* pp. of *inoculare,* fr. *in-* +

ə abut ᵊ kitten ər further a back ā bake ä cot, cart
aü out ch chin e less ē easy g gift i trip ī life
j joke ŋ sing ō flow ȯ flaw ȯi coin th thin th this
ü loot u̇ foot y yet yü few yu̇ furious zh vision

oculus eye, bud — more at EYE] **1 a :** to introduce a microorganism into <~ mice with anthrax> <beans *inoculated* with nitrogen-fixing bacteria> **b :** to introduce (as a microorganism) into a suitable situation for growth **c :** to introduce immunologically active material (as an antibody or antigen) into esp. in order to treat or prevent a disease <~ children against diphtheria> **2 :** to introduce something into the mind of ***syn*** see INFUSE — **in·oc·u·la·tive** \-ˌlāt-iv\ *adj* — **in·oc·u·la·tiv·i·ty** \-ˌäk-yə-lə-ˈtiv-ət-ē\ *n* — **in·oc·u·la·tor** \-ˈäk-yə-ˌlāt-ər\ *n*

in·oc·u·la·tion \in-ˌäk-yə-ˈlā-shən\ *n* **1 :** the act or process or an instance of inoculating; *esp* **:** the introduction of a pathogen or antigen into a living organism to stimulate the production of antibodies **2 :** INOCULUM

in·oc·u·lum \in-ˈäk-yə-ləm\ *n, pl* **-la** \-lə\ [NL, fr. L *inoculare*] **:** material used for inoculation

in·of·fen·sive \ˌin-ə-ˈfen(t)-siv\ *adj* **1 :** causing no harm or injury **2 a :** giving no provocation **:** PEACEABLE **b :** not objectionable to the senses — **in·of·fen·sive·ly** *adv* — **in·of·fen·sive·ness** *n*

in·op·er·a·ble \(ˈ)in-ˈäp-(ə-)rə-bəl\ *adj* [prob. fr. F *inopérable*] **1 :** not suitable for surgery **2 :** not operable

in·op·er·a·tive \-ˈäp-(ə-)rət-iv, -ˈäp-ə-ˌrāt-\ *adj* **:** not functioning **:** not operable — **in·op·er·a·tive·ness** *n*

in·oper·cu·late \ˌin-ō-ˈpər-kyə-lət\ *adj* **:** having no operculum — **inoperculate** *n*

in·op·por·tune \(ˌ)in-ˌäp-ər-ˈt(y)ün\ *adj* [L *inopportunus,* fr. *in-* + *opportunus* opportune] **:** INCONVENIENT, UNSEASONABLE — **in·op·por·tune·ly** *adv* — **in·op·por·tune·ness** \-ˈt(y)ün-nəs\ *n*

in order that *conj* **:** THAT 2a(1)

in·or·di·nate \in-ˈȯrd-ᵊn-ət, -ˈȯrd-nət\ *adj* [ME *inordinat,* fr. L *inordinatus,* fr. *in-* + *ordinatus,* pp. of *ordinare* to arrange — more at ORDAIN] **1 :** DISORDERLY, UNREGULATED **2 :** exceeding reasonable limits **:** IMMODERATE ***syn*** see EXCESSIVE ***ant*** temperate — **in·or·di·nate·ly** *adv* — **in·or·di·nate·ness** *n*

inorg *abbr* inorganic

in·or·gan·ic \ˌin-ˌȯr-ˈgan-ik\ *adj* **1 a (1) :** being or composed of matter other than plant or animal **:** MINERAL **(2) :** forming or belonging to the inanimate world **b :** of, relating to, or dealt with by a branch of chemistry concerned with substances not usu. classed as organic **2 :** not arising from natural growth **:** ARTIFICIAL; *also* **:** lacking structure, character, or vitality <dull ~ things, without individuality or prestige —John Buchan> — **in·or·gan·i·cal·ly** \-i-k(ə-)lē\ *adv*

in·os·cu·late \in-ˈäs-kyə-ˌlāt\ *vb* **-lat·ed; -lat·ing :** to unite by apposition or contact **:** BLEND — **in·os·cu·la·tion** \(ˌ)in-ˌäs-kyə-ˈlā-shən\ *n*

ino·si·tol \in-ˈō-sə-ˌtȯl, ī-ˈnō-, -ˌtōl\ *n* [ISV, fr. *inosite* inositol, fr. Gk *inos,* gen. of *is* sinew — more at WITHY] **:** any of several crystalline stereoisomeric cyclic alcohols $C_6H_{12}O_6$; *esp* **:** MYOINOSITOL

ino·tro·pic \ˌē-nə-ˈtrō-pik, ˌī-nə-, -ˈträp-ik\ *adj* [ISV *ino-* (fr. Gk *in-, is* sinew) + *-tropic*] **:** influencing muscular contractility

INP *abbr* International News Photo

in·pa·tient \ˈin-ˌpā-shənt\ *n* **:** a hospital patient who receives lodging and food as well as treatment — compare OUTPATIENT

in–per·son \ˌin-ˌpərs-ᵊn\ *adj* **:** of or relating to the actual presence of the subject **:** LIVE <an ~ performance>

in per·so·nam \ˌin-pər-ˈsō-ˌnam, -ˌnäm\ *adv or adj* [LL, against a person] **:** against a person for the purpose of imposing a liability or obligation — used esp. of legal actions or judgments; compare IN REM

in pet·to \in-ˈpet-(ˌ)ō\ *adv or adj* [It, lit., in the breast] **1 :** in private **:** SECRETLY **2 :** in miniature

in·phase \(ˌ)in-ˌfāz\ *adj* [fr. the phrase *in phase*] **:** being of the same electrical phase

in·pour \(ˈ)in-ˈpō(ə)r, -ˈpȯ(ə)r\ *vi* **:** to pour in <goods and money ~*ed* . . . and cheered the population —J. J. Mallon>

in–print \(ˌ)in-ˌprint\ *adj* **:** being in print

in–pro·cess \(ˌ)in-ˌpräs-ˌes, -ˌprōs-, -əs\ *adj* **:** of, relating to, or being goods in manufacture as distinguished from raw materials or from finished products

in pro·pria per·so·na \in-ˌprō-prē-ə-pər-ˈsō-nə\ *adv* [ML] **:** in one's own person or character **:** PERSONALLY; *specif* **:** without the assistance of an attorney

¹in·put \ˈin-ˌpu̇t\ *n* **1 :** something that is put in: as **a :** an amount put in <increased ~ of fertilizer increases crop yield> **b :** power or energy put into a machine or system for storage, conversion in kind, or conversion of characteristics usu. with the intent of sizable recovery in the form of output **c :** a component of production (as land, labor, or raw materials) **d :** information fed into a data processing system or computer **2 :** the point at which an input (as of energy, material, or data) is made **3 :** the act or process of putting in

²input *vt* **in·put·ted; in·put·ting :** to enter (as data) into a computer or data processing system

inq *abbr* inquire

in·quest \ˈin-ˌkwest\ *n* [ME, fr. OF *enqueste,* fr. (assumed) VL *inquaestus,* pp. of *inquaerere* to inquire] **1 a :** a judicial or official inquiry or examination esp. before a jury <a coroner's ~> **b :** a body of men (as a jury) assembled to hold such an inquiry **c :** the finding of the jury upon such inquiry or the document recording it **2 :** INQUIRY, INVESTIGATION

in·qui·etude \(ˈ)in-ˈkwī-ə-ˌt(y)üd\ *n* [ME, fr. MF or LL; MF, fr. LL *inquietudo,* fr. L *inquietus* disturbed, fr. *in-* + *quietus* quiet] **:** disturbed state **:** DISQUIETUDE

in·qui·line \ˈin-kwə-ˌlīn, ˈiŋ-, -lən\ *n* [L *inquilinus* tenant, lodger, fr. *in-* + *colere* to cultivate, dwell — more at WHEEL] **:** an animal that lives habitually in the nest or abode of some other species — **inquiline** *adj* — **in·qui·lin·ism** \-lə-ˌniz-əm\ *n* — **in·qui·lin·i·ty** \ˌin-kwə-ˈlin-ət-ē, ˌiŋ-\ *n* — **in·qui·li·nous** \-ˈlī-nəs\ *adj*

in·quire \in-ˈkwī(ə)r\ *vb* **in·quired; in·quir·ing** [ME *enquiren,* fr. OF *enquerre,* fr. (assumed) VL *inquaerere,* alter. of L *inquirere,* fr. *in-* + *quaerere* to seek] *vt* **1 :** to ask about <some kindred spirit shall ~ thy fate —Thomas Gray> **2 :** to search into esp. by asking questions **:** INVESTIGATE ~ *vi* **1 :** to put a question **:** seek for information by questioning <*inquired* about the horses —*Amer. Guide Series: La.*> **2 :** to make investigation or inquiry — often used with *into* <a government cannot ~ into religious conviction —W. R. Inge> ***syn*** see ASK — **in·quir·er** *n* — **in·quir·ing·ly** \-ˈkwī-riŋ-lē\ *adv* — **inquire after :** to ask about the health of

in·qui·ry \ˈin-ˌkwī(ə)r-ē, in-ˈ; ˈin-kwə-rē, ˈiŋ-\ *n, pl* **-ries 1 :** a request for information **2 :** a systematic investigation often of a matter of public interest

in·qui·si·tion \ˌin-kwə-ˈzish-ən, ˌiŋ-\ *n* [ME *inquisicioun,* fr. MF *inquisition,* fr. L *inquisition-, inquisitio,* fr. *inquisitus,* pp. of *inquirere*] **1 :** the act of inquiring **:** EXAMINATION **2 :** a judicial or official inquiry or examination usu. before a jury; *also* **:** the finding of the jury **3 a** *cap* **:** a former Roman Catholic tribunal for the discovery and punishment of heresy **b :** an investigation conducted with little regard for individual rights **c :** a severe questioning — **in·qui·si·tion·al** \-ˈzish-nəl, -ən-ᵊl\ *adj*

in·quis·i·tive \in-ˈkwiz-ət-iv\ *adj* **1 :** given to examination or investigation **2 :** inclined to ask questions; *esp* **:** inordinately or improperly curious about the affairs of others ***syn*** see CURIOUS ***ant*** incurious — **in·quis·i·tive·ly** *adv* — **in·quis·i·tive·ness** *n*

in·quis·i·tor \in-ˈkwiz-ət-ər\ *n* **:** one who inquires or makes inquisition; *esp* **:** one who is unduly harsh, severe, or hostile in making an inquiry — **in·quis·i·to·ri·al** \-ˌkwiz-ə-ˈtōr-ē-əl, -ˈtȯr-\ *adj* — **in·quis·i·to·ri·al·ly** \-ē-ə-lē\ *adv*

in re \in-ˈrā, -ˈrē\ *prep* [L] **:** in the matter of **:** CONCERNING, RE — often used in the title or name of a law case

in rem \in-ˈrem\ *adv or adj* [LL] **:** against a thing (as a right, status, or property) — used esp. of legal actions or judgments; compare IN PERSONAM

in–res·i·dence *adj* **:** being officially associated with an organization in a specified capacity — usu. used in combination <writer-*in-residence* at the university>

INRI *abbr* [L *Iesus Nazarenus Rex Iudaeorum*] Jesus of Nazareth, King of the Jews

in·road \ˈin-ˌrōd\ *n* **1 :** a sudden hostile incursion **:** RAID **2 :** an advance or penetration often at the expense of someone or something <ready to defend himself and his property from the ~*s* of others —Audrey Butt> <power to make dramatic ~*s* against an injustice of long standing —M. S. Eisenhower>

in·rush \ˈin-ˌrəsh\ *n* **:** a crowding or flooding in **:** INFLUX

ins *abbr* **1** inches **2** insurance

in·sa·lu·bri·ous \ˌin(t)-sə-ˈlü-brē-əs\ *adj* [L *insalubris,* fr. *in-* + *salubris* healthful — more at SAFE] **:** not conducive to health **:** UNWHOLESOME <an ~ climate> — **in·sa·lu·bri·ty** \-brət-ē\ *n*

in·sane \(ˈ)in-ˈsān\ *adj* [L *insanus,* fr. *in-* + *sanus* sane] **1 :** mentally disordered **:** exhibiting insanity **2 :** used by, typical of, or intended for insane persons <an ~ asylum> **3 :** ABSURD <an ~ scheme for making money> — **in·sane·ly** *adv* — **in·sane·ness** \-ˈsān-nəs\ *n*

in·san·i·tary \(ˈ)in-ˈsan-ə-ˌter-ē\ *adj* **:** unclean enough to endanger health **:** FILTHY, CONTAMINATED — **in·san·i·ta·tion** \in-ˌsan-ə-ˈtā-shən\ *n*

in·san·i·ty \in-ˈsan-ət-ē\ *n, pl* **-ties 1 a :** a deranged state of the mind usu. occurring as a specific disorder (as schizophrenia) and usu. excluding such states as mental deficiency, psychoneurosis, and various character disorders **b :** a mental disorder **2 :** such unsoundness of mind or lack of understanding as prevents one from having the mental capacity required by law to enter into a particular relationship, status, or transaction or as removes one from criminal or civil responsibility **3 a :** extreme folly or unreasonableness **b :** something utterly foolish or unreasonable

in·sa·tia·ble \(ˈ)in-ˈsā-shə-bəl\ *adj* [ME *insaciable,* fr. MF, fr. L *insatiabilis,* fr. *in-* + *satiare* to satisfy — more at SATIATE] **:** incapable of being satisfied **:** QUENCHLESS <had an ~ desire for wealth> — **in·sa·tia·bil·i·ty** \(ˌ)in-ˌsā-shə-ˈbil-ət-ē\ *n* — **in·sa·tia·ble·ness** \(ˈ)in-ˈsā-shə-bəl-nəs\ *n* — **in·sa·tia·bly** \-blē\ *adv*

in·sa·tiate \(ˈ)in-ˈsā-sh(ē-)ət\ *adj* **:** INSATIABLE — **in·sa·tiate·ly** *adv* — **in·sa·tiate·ness** *n*

in·scribe \in-ˈskrīb\ *vt* [L *inscribere,* fr. *in-* + *scribere* to write — more at SCRIBE] **1 a :** to write, engrave, or print as a lasting record **b :** to enter on a list **:** ENROLL **c :** to write (characters) in a particular format in cryptography **2 a :** to write, engrave, or print characters upon **b :** to autograph or address as a gift **3 :** to dedicate to someone **4 :** to draw within a figure so as to touch in as many places as possible <a regular polygon *inscribed* in a circle> **5** *Brit* **:** to register the name of the holder of (a security) — **in·scrib·er** *n*

in·scrip·tion \in-ˈskrip-shən\ *n* [ME *inscripcioun,* fr. L *inscription-, inscriptio,* fr. *inscriptus,* pp. of *inscribere*] **1 a :** something that is inscribed; *also* **:** SUPERSCRIPTION **b :** EPIGRAPH 2 **c :** the wording on a coin, medal, or seal **:** LEGEND **2 :** the dedication of a book or work of art **3 a :** the act of inscribing **b :** the entering of a name on or as if on a list **:** ENROLLMENT **4** *Brit* **a :** the act of inscribing securities **b** *pl* **:** inscribed securities — **in·scrip·tion·al** \-shnəl, -shən-ᵊl\ *adj*

in·scrip·tive \in-ˈskrip-tiv\ *adj* **:** relating to or constituting an inscription — **in·scrip·tive·ly** *adv*

in·scroll \in-ˈskrōl\ *vt* **:** to write on a scroll **:** RECORD

in·scru·ta·ble \in-ˈskrüt-ə-bəl\ *adj* [ME, fr. LL *inscrutabilis,* fr. L *in-* + *scrutari* to search — more at SCRUTINY] **:** not readily investigated or interpreted **:** hard to grasp <God, thy judgments are ~ —Robert Browning> ***syn*** see MYSTERIOUS — **in·scru·ta·bil·i·ty** \-ˌskrüt-ə-ˈbil-ət-ē\ *n* — **in·scru·ta·ble·ness** \-ˈskrüt-ə-bəl-nəs\ *n* — **in·scru·ta·bly** \-blē\ *adv*

in·sculp \in-ˈskəlp\ *vt* [ME *insculpen,* fr. L *insculpere,* fr. *in-* + *sculpere* to carve — more at SHELF] *archaic* **:** ENGRAVE, SCULPTURE

in·seam \ˈin-ˌsēm\ *n* **:** an inner seam of a garment or shoe

in·sect \ˈin-ˌsekt\ *n* [L *insectum,* fr. neut. of *insectus,* pp. of *insecare* to cut into, fr. *in-* + *secare* to cut — more at SAW] **1 a :** any of numerous small invertebrate animals (as spiders or centipedes) that are more or less obviously segmented **b :** any of a class (Insecta) of arthropods (as bugs or bees) with well-defined head, thorax, and abdomen, only three pairs of legs, and typically one or two pairs of wings **2 :** any of various small animals (as earthworms or turtles) <whatever creeps the ground, ~ or worm —John Milton>

3 : a trivial or contemptible person — **insect** *adj* — **in·sec·tan** \in-ˈsek-tən\ *adj*

in·sec·ta·ry \ˈin-ˌsek-tə-rē, in-ˈ\ *n, pl* **-ries :** a place for the keeping or rearing of living insects

in·sec·ti·cid·al \(ˌ)in-ˌsek-tə-ˈsīd-ᵊl\ *adj* **1 :** destroying or controlling insects **2 :** of or relating to an insecticide — **in·sec·ti·cid·al·ly** \-ᵊl-ē\ *adv*

in·sec·ti·cide \in-ˈsek-tə-ˌsīd\ *n* [ISV] **:** an agent that destroys insects

in·sec·ti·fuge \-tə-ˌfyüj\ *n* **:** an insect repellent

in·sec·tile \in-ˈsek-tᵊl, -ˌtīl\ *adj***:** resembling or being an insect; *also* **:** consisting of insects <an ~ population>

external parts of an insect 1b: *1* labial palpus, *2* maxillary palpus, *3* simple eye, *4* antenna, *5* compound eye, *6* prothorax, *7* tympanum, *8* wing, *9* ovipositor, *10* spiracles, *11* abdomen, *12* metathorax, *13* mesothorax

in·sec·ti·vore \in-ˈsek-tə-ˌvō(ə)r, -ˌvȯ(ə)r\ *n* [deriv. of L *insectum* + *-vorus* -vorous] **1 :** any of an order (Insectivora) of mammals comprising forms (as moles, shrews, and hedgehogs) that are mostly small, insectivorous, and nocturnal **2 :** an insectivorous plant or animal

in·sec·tiv·o·rous \ˌin-ˌsek-ˈtiv-(ə-)rəs\ *adj* **:** depending on insects as food — **in·sec·tiv·o·ry** \-ˈtiv-ə-rē\ *n*

in·se·cure \ˌin(t)-si-ˈkyu̇(ə)r\ *adj* [ML *insecurus,* fr. L *in-* + *securus* secure] **1 :** not confident or sure **:** UNCERTAIN <feeling somewhat ~ of his reception> **2 :** not adequately guarded or sustained **:** UNSAFE <an ~ investment> **3 :** not firmly fastened or fixed **:** SHAKY <the hinge is loose and ~> **4 a :** not highly stable or well-adjusted <an ~ marriage> **b :** deficient in assurance **:** beset by fear and anxiety <always felt ~ in a group of strangers> — **in·se·cure·ly** *adv* — **in·se·cure·ness** *n* — **in·se·cu·ri·ty** \-ˈkyu̇r-ət-ē\ *n*

in·sem·i·nate \in-ˈsem-ə-ˌnāt\ *vt* **-nat·ed; -nat·ing** [L *inseminatus,* pp. of *inseminare,* fr. *in-* + *semin-, semen* seed — more at SEMEN] **1 :** SOW **2 :** to introduce semen into the genital tract of (a female) — **in·sem·i·na·tion** \-ˌsem-ə-ˈnā-shən\ *n*

in·sem·i·na·tor \-ˈsem-ə-ˌnāt-ər\ *n* **:** one that inseminates cattle artificially

in·sen·sate \(ˈ)in-ˈsen-ˌsāt, -sət\ *adj* [LL *insensatus,* fr. L *in-* + LL *sensatus* having sense, fr. L *sensus* sense] **1 :** lacking animate awareness or sensation **2 :** lacking sense or understanding; *also* **:** FOOLISH **3 :** lacking humane feeling **:** BRUTAL — **in·sen·sate·ly** *adv* — **in·sen·sate·ness** *n*

in·sen·si·ble \(ˈ)in-ˈsen(t)-sə-bəl\ *adj* [ME, fr. MF & L; MF, fr. L *insensibilis,* fr. *in-* + *sensibilis* sensible] **1 :** incapable or bereft of feeling or sensation: as **a :** not endowed with life or spirit **:** INSENTIENT <~ earth> **b :** UNCONSCIOUS <knocked ~ by a sudden blow> **c :** lacking sensory perception <~ to pain>; *also* **:** deprived of such perception or ability to react <hands ~ from cold> **2 :** IMPERCEPTIBLE <dampened by an ~ dew>; *broadly* **:** SLIGHT, GRADUAL <~ motion> **3** *archaic* **:** STUPID, SENSELESS **4 a :** lacking emotional response **:** APATHETIC, INDIFFERENT <~ to fear> **b :** UNAWARE <~ of their danger> **5 :** not intelligible **:** MEANINGLESS **6 :** lacking delicacy or refinement — **in·sen·si·bil·i·ty** \(ˌ)in-ˌsen(t)-sə-ˈbil-ət-ē\ *n* — **in·sen·si·ble·ness** \(ˈ)in-ˈsen(t)-sə-bəl-nəs\ *n* — **in·sen·si·bly** \-blē\ *adv*

in·sen·si·tive \(ˈ)in-ˈsen(t)-sət-iv, -ˈsen(t)-stiv\ *adj* **1 a :** not responsive or susceptible <~ to the demands of the public> **b :** lacking feeling or tact <so ~ as to laugh at someone in pain> **2 :** not physically or chemically sensitive — **in·sen·si·tive·ly** *adv* — **in·sen·si·tive·ness** *n* — **in·sen·si·tiv·i·ty** \(ˌ)in-ˌsen(t)-sə-ˈtiv-ət-ē\ *n*

in·sen·tient \(ˈ)in-ˈsen-ch(ē-)ənt\ *adj* **:** lacking perception, consciousness, or animation — **in·sen·tience** \-ch(ē-)ən(t)s\ *n*

in·sep·a·ra·ble \(ˈ)in-ˈsep-(ə-)rə-bəl\ *adj* [ME, fr. L *inseparabilis,* fr. *in-* + *separabilis* separable] **:** incapable of being separated or disjoined — **in·sep·a·ra·bil·i·ty** \(ˌ)in-ˌsep-(ə-)rə-ˈbil-ət-ē\ *n* — **inseparable** *n* — **in·sep·a·ra·ble·ness** \(ˈ)in-ˈsep-(ə-)rə-bəl-nəs\ *n* — **in·sep·a·ra·bly** \-blē\ *adv*

[1]**in·sert** \in-ˈsərt\ *vb* [L *insertus,* pp. of *inserere,* fr. *in-* + *serere* to join — more at SERIES] *vt* **1 :** to put or thrust in <~ the key in the lock> <~ a spacecraft into orbit> **2 :** to put or introduce into the body of something **:** INTERPOLATE <~ a change in a manuscript> **3 :** to set in and make fast; *esp* **:** to insert by sewing between two cut edges ~ *vi, of a muscle* **:** to be in attachment to the part to be moved ***syn*** see INTRODUCE ***ant*** abstract — **in·sert·er** *n*

[2]**in·sert** \ˈin-ˌsərt\ *n* **:** something that is inserted or is for insertion; *esp* **:** written or printed material inserted (as between the leaves of a book)

in·ser·tion \in-ˈsər-shən\ *n* **1 :** the act or process of inserting **2 :** something that is inserted: as **a :** the part of a muscle that inserts **b :** the mode or place of attachment of an organ or part **c :** embroidery or needlework inserted as ornament between two pieces of fabric **d :** a single appearance of an advertisement — **in·ser·tion·al** \-shnəl, -shən-ᵊl\ *adj*

in–ser·vice \(ˌ)in-ˌsər-vəs\ *adj* **1 :** of, relating to, or being one that is fully employed <~ teachers> <~ police officers> **2 :** going on or continuing while one is fully employed <~ teacher education workshops>

in·ses·so·ri·al \ˌin-(ˌ)se-ˈsōr-ē-əl, -ˈsȯr-\ *adj* [L *insessus,* pp. of *insidēre* to sit on — more at INSIDIOUS] **:** perching or adapted for perching

[1]**in·set** \ˈin-ˌset\ *n* **1 a :** a place where something flows in **:** CHANNEL **b :** a setting or flowing in **2 :** something that is inset: as **a :** a small graphic representation (as a map or picture) set within the compass of a larger one **b :** a piece of cloth set into a garment for decoration **c :** a part or section of a utensil that fits into an outer part

[2]**in·set** \ˈin-ˌset, in-ˈ\ *vt* **inset** *or* **in·set·ted; in·set·ting :** to insert as an inset

[1]**in·shore** \ˈin-ˈshō(ə)r, -ˈshȯ(ə)r\ *adj* **1 :** situated or carried on near shore **2 :** moving toward shore <an ~ current>

[2]**inshore** *adv* **:** to or toward shore <boats driven ~ by the storm>

[1]**in·side** \(ˈ)in-ˈsīd, ˈin-ˌ\ *n* **1 :** an inner side or surface **2 a :** an interior or internal part **:** the part within **b :** inward nature, thoughts, or feeling **c :** VISCERA, ENTRAILS — usu. used in pl. **3 a :** a position of power or confidence <only someone on the ~ could have told> **b :** confidential information <has the ~ on what happened at the convention> **4 :** the area nearest a specified or implied point of reference: as **a :** the side of home plate nearest the batter **b :** the middle portion of a playing area **c :** the area near or underneath the basket in basketball

[2]**inside** *adj* **1 :** of, relating to, or being on or near the inside <an ~ pitch> **2 :** relating or known to a select group <an ~ joke>

[3]**inside** *prep* **1 a :** in or into the interior of **b :** on the inner side of **2 :** WITHIN <~ an hour>

[4]**inside** *adv* **1 :** on the inner side **2 :** in or into the interior **3 :** to or on the inside

inside address *n* **:** ADDRESS 5c

inside of *prep* **:** INSIDE

inside out *adv* **1 :** in such a manner that the inner surface becomes the outer <turned the shirt *inside out*> **2 :** in a thorough manner <knows his subject *inside out*>

in·sid·er \(ˈ)in-ˈsīd-ər\ *n* **:** a person recognized or accepted as a member of a group, category, or organization: as **a :** a person who is in a position of power or has access to confidential information **b :** one (as an officer or director or a holder of 10 percent or more of an equity security) who is in a position to have special knowledge of the affairs of or to influence the decisions of a company

inside track *n* **1 :** the inner side of a curved racecourse **2 :** an advantageous competitive position <the owner's son has the *inside track* for the job>

in·sid·i·ous \in-ˈsid-ē-əs\ *adj* [L *insidiosus,* fr. *insidiae* ambush, fr. *insidēre* to sit in, sit on, fr. *in-* + *sedēre* to sit — more at SIT] **1 a :** awaiting a chance to entrap **:** TREACHEROUS **b :** harmful but enticing **:** SEDUCTIVE <~ drugs that destroy the young> **2 a :** having a gradual and cumulative effect **:** SUBTLE <the ~ pressures of modern life> **b** *of a disease* **:** developing so gradually as to be well established before becoming apparent — **in·sid·i·ous·ly** *adv* — **in·sid·i·ous·ness** *n*

in·sight \ˈin-ˌsīt\ *n* **1 :** the power or act of seeing into a situation **:** PENETRATION **2 :** the act or result of apprehending the inner nature of things or of seeing intuitively ***syn*** see DISCERNMENT

in·sight·ful \ˈin-ˌsīt-fəl, in-ˈ\ *adj* **:** exhibiting or characterized by insight — **in·sight·ful·ly** *adv*

in·sig·nia \in-ˈsig-nē-ə\ *or* **in·sig·ne** \-(ˌ)nē\ *n, pl* **-nia** *or* **-ni·as** [L *insignia,* pl. of *insigne* mark, badge, fr. neut. of *insignis* marked, distinguished, fr. *in-* + *signum* mark, sign] **1 :** a badge of authority or honor **:** EMBLEM **2 :** a distinguishing mark or sign

in·sig·nif·i·cance \ˌin(t)-sig-ˈnif-i-kən(t)s\ *n* **:** the quality or state of being insignificant

in·sig·nif·i·can·cy \-kən-sē\ *n* **1 :** INSIGNIFICANCE **2 :** an insignificant thing or person

in·sig·nif·i·cant \-kənt\ *adj* **:** not significant: as **a :** lacking meaning or import **:** INCONSEQUENTIAL **b :** not worth considering **:** UNIMPORTANT **c :** lacking weight, position, or influence **:** CONTEMPTIBLE **d :** small in size, quantity, or number — **in·sig·nif·i·cant·ly** *adv*

in·sin·cere \ˌin(t)-sin-ˈsi(ə)r, -sən-\ *adj* [L *insincerus,* fr. *in-* + *sincerus* sincere] **:** not sincere **:** HYPOCRITICAL — **in·sin·cere·ly** *adv* — **in·sin·cer·i·ty** \-ˈser-ət-ē *also* -ˈsir-\ *n*

in·sin·u·ate \in-ˈsin-yə-ˌwāt\ *vb* **-at·ed; -at·ing** [L *insinuatus,* pp. of *insinuare,* fr. *in-* + *sinuare* to bend, curve, fr. *sinus* curve] *vt* **1 a :** to introduce (as an idea) gradually or in a subtle, indirect, or covert way <~ doubts into a trusting mind> **b :** to impart or communicate with artful or oblique reference <~ an evil one dares not charge openly> **2 :** to introduce (as oneself) by stealthy, smooth, or artful means ~ *vi* **1** *archaic* **:** to enter gently, slowly, or imperceptibly **:** CREEP **2** *archaic* **:** to ingratiate oneself ***syn*** see INTRODUCE, SUGGEST — **in·sin·u·a·tive** \-ˌwāt-iv\ *adj* — **in·sin·u·a·tor** \-ˌwāt-ər\ *n*

in·sin·u·at·ing *adj* **1 :** tending gradually to cause doubt, distrust, or change of outlook <~ remarks> **2 :** winning favor and confidence by imperceptible degrees **:** INGRATIATING — **in·sin·u·at·ing·ly** \-ˌwāt-iŋ-lē\ *adv*

in·sin·u·a·tion \(ˌ)in-ˌsin-yə-ˈwā-shən\ *n* **1 :** the act or process of insinuating **2 :** something that is insinuated; *esp* **:** a sly, subtle, and usu. derogatory utterance

in·sip·id \in-ˈsip-əd\ *adj* [F & LL; F *insipide,* fr. LL *insipidus,* fr. L *in-* + *sapidus* savory, fr. *sapere* to taste — more at SAGE] **1 :** lacking taste or savor **:** TASTELESS **2 :** lacking in qualities that interest, stimulate, or challenge **:** DULL, FLAT — **in·si·pid·i·ty** \-ˌin(t)-sə-ˈpid-ət-ē\ *n* — **in·sip·id·ly** \in-ˈsip-əd-lē\ *adv*

syn INSIPID, VAPID, FLAT, JEJUNE, BANAL, INANE *shared meaning element* **:** devoid of qualities that make for spirit and character ***ant*** sapid, zestful

in·sist \in-ˈsist\ *vb* [MF or L; MF *insister,* fr. L *insistere* to stand upon, persist, fr. *in-* + *sistere* to stand; akin to L *stare* to stand — more at STAND] *vi* **1 :** to take a resolute stand or course <they ~ upon going> **2** *archaic* **:** PERSIST ~ *vt* **:** to maintain in a persistent or positive manner <~*ed* that his story was true>

in·sis·tence \in-ˈsis-tən(t)s\ *n* **1 :** the act or an instance of insisting **2 :** the quality or state of being insistent **:** URGENCY

in·sis·ten·cy \-tən-sē\ *n, pl* **-cies :** INSISTENCE

in·sis·tent \in-ˈsis-tənt\ *adj* [L *insistent-, insistens,* prp. of *insistere*] **:** disposed to insist **:** PERSISTENT — **in·sis·tent·ly** *adv*

ə abut	ᵊ kitten	ər further	a back	ā bake	ä cot, cart
au̇ out	ch chin	e less	ē easy	g gift	i trip ī life
j joke	ŋ sing	ō flow	ȯ flaw	ȯi coin	th thin th this
ü loot	u̇ foot	y yet	yü few	yu̇ furious	zh vision

in si·tu \(ˈ)in-ˈsī-(ˌ)tü *also* -ˈsi- *or* -(ˌ)chü *or* -(ˌ)tyü; *also* -ˈsē-(ˌ)tü\ *adv or adj* [L, in position] : in the natural or original position

in·so·bri·ety \ˌin(t)-sə-ˈbrī-ət-ē, -sō-\ *n* : lack of sobriety or moderation; *esp* : intemperance in drinking

in·so·cia·ble \(ˈ)in-ˈsō-shə-bəl\ *adj* [L *insociabilis,* fr. *in-* + *sociabilis* sociable] : not sociable — **in·so·cia·bil·i·ty** \(ˌ)in-(ˌ)sō-shə-ˈbil-ət-ē\ *n* — **in·so·cia·bly** \(ˈ)in-ˈsō-shə-blē\ *adv*

in·so·far \ˌin(t)-sə-ˈfär\ *adv* : to such extent or degree

insofar as \ˌin(t)-sə-ˌfär-əz\ *conj* : to the extent or degree that

insol *abbr* insoluble

in·so·late \ˈin(t)-(ˌ)sō-ˌlāt, in-ˈ\ *vt* **-lat·ed; -lat·ing** [L *insolatus,* pp. of *insolare,* fr. *in-* + *sol* sun — more at SOLAR] : to expose to the sun's rays

in·so·la·tion \ˌin(t)-(ˌ)sō-ˈlā-shən, in-ˌsō-\ *n* **1** : the act or an instance of insolating **2** : SUNSTROKE **3 a** : solar radiation that has been received **b** : the rate of delivery of all direct solar energy per unit of horizontal surface

in·sole \ˈin-ˌsōl\ *n* **1** : an inside sole of a shoe **2** : a loose thin strip placed inside a shoe for warmth or comfort

in·so·lence \ˈin(t)-s(ə-)lən(t)s\ *n* **1** : the quality or state of being insolent **2** : an instance of insolent conduct or treatment

in·so·lent \-s(ə-)lənt\ *adj* [ME, fr. L *insolent-, insolens;* akin to L *insolescere* to grow haughty] **1** : insultingly contemptuous in speech or conduct : OVERBEARING **2** : exhibiting boldness or effrontery : IMPUDENT ***syn*** see PROUD ***ant*** deferential — **insolent** *n* — **in·so·lent·ly** *adv*

in·sol·u·bi·lize \(ˈ)in-ˈsäl-yə-bə-ˌlīz\ *vt* : to make insoluble — **in·sol·u·bi·li·za·tion** \(ˌ)in-ˌsäl-yə-bə-lə-ˈzā-shən\ *n*

in·sol·u·ble \(ˈ)in-ˈsäl-yə-bəl\ *adj* [ME *insolible,* fr. L *insolubilis,* fr. *in-* + *solvere* to free, dissolve — more at SOLVE] : not soluble: as **a** *archaic* : INDISSOLUBLE **b** : having or admitting of no solution or explanation **c** : incapable of being dissolved in a liquid; *also* : soluble only with difficulty or to a slight degree — **in·sol·u·bil·i·ty** \(ˌ)in-ˌsäl-yə-ˈbil-ət-ē\ *n* — **insoluble** *n* — **in·sol·u·ble·ness** \(ˈ)in-ˈsäl-yə-bəl-nəs\ *n* — **in·sol·u·bly** \-blē\ *adv*

in·solv·able \(ˈ)in-ˈsäl-və-bəl, -ˈsȯl-\ *adj* : admitting no solution <an apparently ~ problem> — **in·solv·ably** \-blē\ *adv*

in·sol·vent \(ˈ)in-ˈsäl-vənt, -ˈsȯl-\ *adj* **1 a** : unable to pay debts as they fall due in the usual course of business; *specif* : having liabilities in excess of a reasonable market value of assets held **b** : insufficient to pay all debts <an ~ estate> **c** : not up to a normal standard or complement : IMPOVERISHED **2** : relating to or for the relief of insolvents — **in·sol·ven·cy** \-vən-sē\ *n* — **insolvent** *n*

in·som·nia \in-ˈsäm-nē-ə\ *n* [L, fr. *insomnis* sleepless, fr. *in-* + *somnus* sleep — more at SOMNOLENT] : prolonged and usu. abnormal inability to obtain adequate sleep — **in·som·ni·ac** \-nē-ˌak\ *adj or n*

in·so·much \ˌin(t)-sə-ˌməch-əz\ *conj* : inasmuch as

insomuch that *conj* : SO 1

in·sou·ci·ance \in-ˈsü-sē-ən(t)s, a^{n}-süs-yä^{n}s\ *n* [F] : lighthearted unconcern : NONCHALANCE — **in·sou·ci·ant** \in-ˈsü-sē-ənt, a^{n}-süs-yä^{n}\ *adj* — **in·sou·ci·ant·ly** \in-ˈsü-sē-ənt-lē\ *adv*

insoul *var of* ENSOUL

insp *abbr* inspector

in·span \in-ˈspan, ˈin-ˌ\ *vb* [Afrik, fr. D *inspannen*] *chiefly So Afr* : YOKE, HARNESS

in·spect \in-ˈspekt\ *vb* [L *inspectus,* pp. of *inspicere,* fr. *in-* + *specere* to look — more at SPY] *vt* **1** : to view closely in critical appraisal : look over **2** : to examine officially <~*s* the barracks every Friday> ~ *vi* : to make an inspection ***syn*** see SCRUTINIZE — **in·spec·tive** \-ˈspek-tiv\ *adj*

in·spec·tion \in-ˈspek-shən\ *n* **1** : the act of inspecting **2** : a checking or testing of an individual against established standards

inspection arms *n* [fr. the command *inspection arms!*] : a position in the manual of arms in which the rifle is held at port arms with the chamber open for inspection; *also* : a command to assume this position

in·spec·tor \in-ˈspek-tər\ *n* **1** : a person employed to inspect something **2 a** : a police officer who is in charge of several precincts and ranks below a superintendent or deputy superintendent **b** : a person appointed to oversee a polling place — **in·spec·tor·ate** \-t(ə-)rət\ *n* — **in·spec·tor·ship** \-tər-ˌship\ *n*

inspector general *n* : an officer of a military or naval corps of inspectors that investigates and reports on organizational matters

insphere *var of* ENSPHERE

in·spi·ra·tion \ˌin(t)-spə-ˈrā-shən, -(ˌ)spir-ˈā-\ *n* **1 a** : a divine influence or action on a person held to qualify him to receive and communicate sacred revelation **b** : the action or power of moving the intellect or emotions **c** : the act of influencing or suggesting opinions <the ~ of this rumor was traced to a source near the governor> **2** : the act of drawing in; *specif* : the drawing of air into the lungs **3 a** : the quality or state of being inspired **b** : something that is inspired <a scheme that was pure ~> **4** : an inspiring agent or influence — **in·spi·ra·tion·al** \-shnəl, -shən-^{ə}l\ *adj* — **in·spi·ra·tion·al·ly** \-ē\ *adv*

in·spi·ra·tor \ˈin(t)s-pə-ˌrāt-ər, -(ˌ)pir-ˌāt-\ *n* **1** : one that inspires <teachers who are ~*s* of the young> **2** : a device (as an injector or respirator) by which something (as gas or vapor) is drawn in

in·spi·ra·to·ry \in-ˈspī-rə-ˌtōr-ē, ˈin(t)-sp(ə-)rə-, -ˌtȯr-\ *adj* : relating to, used for, or associated with inspiration

in·spire \in-ˈspī(ə)r\ *vb* **in·spired; in·spir·ing** [ME *inspiren,* fr. MF & L; MF *inspirer,* fr. L *inspirare,* fr. *in-* + *spirare* to breathe — more at SPIRIT] *vt* **1 a** *archaic* : to breathe or blow into or upon **b** *archaic* : to infuse (as life) by breathing **2** : INHALE 1 **3 a** : to influence, move, or guide by divine or supernatural inspiration <the gods were believed to ~ the oracles> **b** : to exert an animating, enlivening, or exalting influence on <was particularly *inspired* by the Romanticists> **c** : to spur on : IMPEL, MOTIVATE <threats don't necessarily ~ people to work> **d** : AFFECT <seeing the old room again *inspired* him with nostalgia> **4 a** : to communicate to an agent supernaturally **b** : to draw forth or bring out <thoughts *inspired* by his visit to the cathedral> **5 a** : to bring about : OCCASION <the book was *inspired* by his travels in the Far East> **b** : INCITE **6** : to spread (rumor) by indirect means or through the agency of another ~ *vi* : INHALE — **in·spir·er** *n*

in·spired *adj* : outstanding or brilliant in a way or to a degree suggestive of divine inspiration <gave an ~ performance as the protagonist of the tragedy>

in·spir·ing *adj* : having an animating or exalting effect <the minister delivered an ~ sermon>

in·spir·it \in-ˈspir-ət\ *vt* : to fill with spirit : ANIMATE

^{1}**in·spis·sate** \in-ˈspis-ət, ˈin(t)-spə-ˌsāt\ *or* **in·spis·sat·ed** \in-ˈspis-ˌāt-əd, ˈin(t)-spə-ˌsāt-\ *adj* [LL *inspissatus,* pp. of *inspissare,* fr. L *in-* + *spissus* thick; akin to Gk *spidios* extended, L *spatium* space — more at SPEED] : thickened in consistency; *broadly* : made thick, heavy, or intense

^{2}**in·spis·sate** \in-ˈspis-ˌāt, ˈin(t)-spə-ˌsāt\ *vt* **-sat·ed; -sat·ing** : to make thick or thicker — **in·spis·sa·tion** \ˌin(t)-spə-ˈsā-shən, (ˌ)in-ˌspis-ˈā-\ *n* — **in·spis·sa·tor** \in-ˈspis-ˌāt-ər, ˈin(t)-spə-ˌsāt-\ *n*

inst *abbr* **1** instant **2** institute; institution; institutional

in·sta·bil·i·ty \ˌin(t)-stə-ˈbil-ət-ē\ *n* : the quality or state of being unstable; *esp* : lack of emotional or mental stability

in·sta·ble \(ˈ)in-ˈstā-bəl\ *adj* [MF or L; MF, fr. L *instabilis,* fr. *in-* + *stabilis* stable] : UNSTABLE

in·stall *or* **in·stal** \in-ˈstȯl\ *vt* **in·stalled; in·stall·ing** [MF *installer,* fr. ML *installare,* fr. L *in-* + ML *stallum* stall, fr. OHG *stal*] **1 a** : to place in an office or dignity by seating in a stall or official seat **b** : to induct into an office, rank, or order <~*ed* the new department chairman> **2** : to establish in an indicated place, condition, or status <~*ing* herself in front of the fireplace> **3** : to set up for use or service <had an exhaust fan ~*ed* in the kitchen> — **in·stall·er** *n*

in·stal·la·tion \ˌin(t)-stə-ˈlā-shən\ *n* **1** : the act of installing : the state of being installed **2** : something that is installed for use **3** : a military camp, fort, or base

^{1}**in·stall·ment** *or* **in·stal·ment** \in-ˈstȯl-mənt\ *n* : INSTALLATION 1

^{2}**installment** *also* **instalment** *n* [alter. of earlier *estallment* payment by installment, deriv. of OF *estaler* to place, fix, fr. *estal* place, of Gmc origin; akin to OHG *stal* place, stall] **1** : one of the parts into which a debt is divided when payment is made at intervals **2 a** : one of several parts (as of a publication) presented at intervals **b** : one part of a serial story — **installment** *adj*

installment plan *n* : a system of paying for goods by installments

^{1}**in·stance** \ˈin(t)-stən(t)s\ *n* **1 a** *archaic* : urgent or earnest solicitation **b** : INSTIGATION, REQUEST <am writing to you at the ~ of my client> **c** *obs* : an impelling cause or motive **2 a** *archaic* : EXCEPTION **b** : an individual illustrative of a category or brought forward in support or disproof of a generalization **c** *obs* : TOKEN, SIGN **3** : the institution and prosecution of a lawsuit : SUIT **4** : a step, stage, or situation viewed as part of a process or series of events <prefers, in this ~, to remain anonymous —*Times Lit. Supp.*>
syn INSTANCE, CASE, ILLUSTRATION, EXAMPLE, SAMPLE, SPECIMEN *shared meaning element* : something that exhibits distinguishing characteristics of the category to which it belongs
— **for instance** : as an example

^{2}**instance** *vt* **in·stanced; in·stanc·ing** **1** : to illustrate or demonstrate by an instance **2** : to mention as a case or example : CITE ***syn*** see MENTION

in·stan·cy \ˈin(t)-stən-sē\ *n, pl* **-cies** **1** : URGENCY, INSISTENCE **2** : nearness of approach : IMMINENCE **3** : immediacy of occurrence or action : INSTANTANEOUSNESS

^{1}**in·stant** \ˈin(t)-stənt\ *n* [ME, fr. ML *instant-, instans,* fr. *instant-, instans,* adj., instant, fr. L] **1** : an infinitesimal space of time; *esp* : a point in time separating two states <at the ~ of death> **2** : the present or current month

^{2}**instant** *adj* [ME, fr. MF or L; MF, fr. L *instant-, instans,* fr. prp. of *instare* to stand upon, urge, fr. *in-* + *stare* to stand — more at STAND] **1** : IMPORTUNATE, URGENT **2 a** : PRESENT, CURRENT <previous felonies not related to the ~ crime> **b** : of or occurring in the present month **3** : IMMEDIATE, DIRECT <the play was an ~ success> **4 a** (1) : premixed or precooked for easy final preparation <~ mashed potatoes> (2) : appearing in or as if in ready-to-use form <~ culture> <updating . . . your image with ~ beards, mustaches, and sideburns —*Playboy*> **b** : immediately soluble in water <~ coffee> — **in·stant·ness** *n*

in·stan·ta·neous \ˌin(t)-stən-ˈtā-nē-əs, -nyəs\ *adj* [ML *instantaneus,* fr. *instant-, instans* n.] **1** : done, occurring, or acting without any perceptible duration of time <death was ~> **2** : done without any delay being purposely introduced <took ~ action to correct the abuse> **3** : occurring or present at a particular instant <~ velocity> — **in·stan·ta·ne·ity** \in-ˌstant-^{ə}n-ˈē-ət-ē, ˌin(t)-stən-tə-ˈnē-\ *n* — **in·stan·ta·neous·ly** \ˌin(t)-stən-ˈtā-nē-ə-slē, -nyə-slē\ *adv* — **in·stan·ta·neous·ness** *n*

in·stan·ter \in-ˈstant-ər\ *adv* [ML, fr. *instant-, instans*] : at once

in·stan·ti·ate \in-ˈstan-chē-ˌāt\ *vt* **-at·ed; -at·ing** : to represent (an abstraction) by a concrete instance — **in·stan·ti·a·tion** \-ˌstan-chē-ˈā-shən\ *n*

^{1}**in·stant·ly** \ˈin(t)-stənt-lē\ *adv* **1** : with importunity : URGENTLY **2** : without the least delay : IMMEDIATELY

^{2}**instantly** *conj* : as soon as <he ran across the grass ~ he perceived his mother —W. P. Thackeray>

instant replay *n* : a videotape recording of an action (as a play in football) that can be played back (as in slow motion) immediately after the action has been completed

in·star \ˈin-ˌstär\ *n* [NL, fr. L, equivalent, figure; akin to L *instare* to stand upon] : a stage in the life of an arthropod (as an insect) between two successive molts; *also* : an individual in a specified instar

in·state \in-ˈstāt\ *vt* **1** : to set or establish in a rank or office : INSTALL **2** *obs* **a** : INVEST, ENDOW **b** : BESTOW, CONFER

in sta·tu quo \in-ˌstā-(ˌ)tü-ˈkwō, -ˌsta-; -ˌstach-(ˌ)ü-\ *adv* [NL, lit., in the state in which] : in the former or same state

in·stau·ra·tion \in-ˌstȯ-ˈrā-shən, ˌin(t)-stə-\ *n* [L *instauration-, instauratio,* fr. *instauratus,* pp. of *instaurare* to renew, restore —

more at STORE] **1 :** restoration after decay, lapse, or dilapidation **2 :** an act of instituting or establishing something

in·stead \in-ˈsted\ *adv* **1 :** as a substitute or equivalent <was going to write but called ~> **2 :** as an alternative to something expressed or implied : RATHER <longed ~ for a quiet country life>

instead of \in-ˌsted-ə(v), -ˌstid-\ *prep* [ME *in sted of*] **:** in place of : as a substitute for or alternative to

in·step \ˈin-ˌstep\ *n* **1 :** the arched middle portion of the human foot in front of the ankle joint; *esp* **:** its upper surface **2 :** the part of the hind leg of the horse between the hock and the pastern joint **3 :** the part of a shoe or stocking over the instep

in·sti·gate \ˈin(t)-stə-ˌgāt\ *vt* **-gat·ed; -gat·ing** [L *instigatus*, pp. of *instigare* — more at STICK] **:** to goad or urge forward : PROVOKE ***syn*** see INCITE — **in·sti·ga·tion** \ˌin(t)-stə-ˈgā-shən\ *n* — **in·sti·ga·tive** \ˈin(t)-stə-ˌgāt-iv\ *adj* — **in·sti·ga·tor** \-ˌgāt-ər\ *n*

in·still *also* **in·stil** \in-ˈstil\ *vt* **in·stilled; in·still·ing** [MF & L; MF *instiller*, fr. L *instillare*, fr. *in-* + *stillare* to drip — more at DISTILL] **1 :** to cause to enter drop by drop <~ medication into the infected eye> **2 :** to impart gradually <~*ing* in children a love of learning> — **in·stil·la·tion** \ˌin(t)-stə-ˈlā-shən, -(ˌ)stil-ˈā-\ *n* — **in·still·er** \in-ˈstil-ər\ *n* — **in·still·ment** \-mənt\ *n*

¹in·stinct \ˈin-ˌstiŋ(k)t\ *n* [ME, fr. L *instinctus* impulse, fr. *instinctus*, pp. of *instinguere* to incite; akin to L *instigare* to instigate] **1 :** a natural or inherent aptitude, impulse, or capacity <had an ~ for the right word> **2 a :** a largely inheritable and unalterable tendency by an organism to make a complex and specific response to environmental stimuli without involving reason and for the purpose of removing somatic tension **b :** behavior that is mediated by reactions below the conscious level — **in·stinc·tu·al** \in-ˈstiŋ(k)-chə(-wə)l, -ˈstiŋ(k)sh-wəl\ *adj*

²in·stinct \in-ˈstiŋ(k)t, ˈin-ˌ\ *adj* **1** *obs* **:** impelled by an inner or animating or exciting agency **2 :** profoundly imbued : INFUSED <a man ~ with patriotism>

in·stinc·tive \in-ˈstiŋ(k)-tiv\ *adj* **1 :** of, relating to, or being instinct **2 :** prompted by natural instinct or propensity **:** arising spontaneously and being independent of judgment or will <an ~ doubt of his honesty> ***syn*** see SPONTANEOUS ***ant*** intentional — **in·stinc·tive·ly** *adv*

¹in·sti·tute \ˈin(t)-stə-ˌt(y)üt\ *vt* **-tut·ed; -tut·ing** [ME *instituten*, fr. L *institutus*, pp. of *instituere*, fr. *in-* + *statuere* to set up — more at STATUTE] **1 :** to establish in a position or office **2 a :** to originate and get established : ORGANIZE <*instituted* many social reforms> **b :** to set going : INAUGURATE <*instituting* an investigation of the charges> — **in·sti·tut·er** *or* **in·sti·tu·tor** \-ˌt(y)üt-ər\ *n*

²institute *n* **1** *obs* **:** an act of instituting **2 :** something that is instituted: as **a** (1) **:** an elementary principle recognized as authoritative (2) *pl* **:** a collection of such principles and precepts; *esp* **:** a legal compendium **b :** an organization for the promotion of a cause : ASSOCIATION <a research ~> <an ~ for the blind> **c :** an educational institution **d :** a usu. brief intensive course of instruction on selected topics relating to a particular field <an urban studies ~>

in·sti·tu·tion \ˌin(t)-stə-ˈt(y)ü-shən\ *n* **1 :** an act of instituting : ESTABLISHMENT **2** *archaic* **:** something that serves to instruct; *also* **:** INSTRUCTION, TRAINING **3 a :** a significant practice, relationship, or organization in a society or culture <the ~ of marriage> **b :** an established organization or corporation (as a college or university) esp. of a public or eleemosynary character — **in·sti·tu·tion·al** \-shnəl, -shən-ᵊl\ *adj* — **in·sti·tu·tion·al·ly** \-ē\ *adv*

in·sti·tu·tion·al·ism \-shnəl-ˌiz-əm, -shən-ᵊl-\ *n* **1 :** emphasis on organization (as in religion) at the expense of other factors **2 :** public institutional care of defective, delinquent, or dependent persons **3 :** an economic school of thought that emphasizes the role of social institutions in influencing economic behavior — **in·sti·tu·tion·al·ist** \-əst\ *n*

in·sti·tu·tion·al·ize \-ˌīz\ *vt* **-ized; -iz·ing** **1 :** to make into or give the character of an institution to <*institutionalized* housing> **2 :** to put in the care of an institution <~ alcoholics> — **in·sti·tu·tion·al·iza·tion** \-ˌt(y)ü-shnəl-ə-ˈzā-shən, -shən-ᵊl-\ *n*

instr *abbr* **1** instructor **2** instrument; instrumental

in·struct \in-ˈstrəkt\ *vt* [ME *instructen*, fr. L *instructus*, pp. of *instruere*, fr. *in-* + *struere* to build — more at STRUCTURE] **1 :** to give knowledge or information to; *esp* **:** to impart knowledge to in a systematic manner <she had ~*ed* three generations of village children> **2 a :** to direct authoritatively and on the basis of informed awareness **b :** to give an order precisely and clearly ***syn*** see TEACH, COMMAND

in·struct·ed *adj* **1 :** being informed : TAUGHT **2 :** subject to specific instructions <sent ~ delegates to the convention>

in·struc·tion \in-ˈstrək-shən\ *n* **1 a :** LESSON, PRECEPT **b :** a direction calling for compliance : ORDER <had ~*s* not to admit strangers> **c** *pl* **:** an outline or manual of technical procedure : DIRECTIONS **d :** a code that tells a computer to perform a particular operation **2 :** the action, practice, or profession of a teacher : TEACHING — **in·struc·tion·al** \-shnəl, -shən-ᵊl\ *adj*

in·struc·tive \in-ˈstrək-tiv\ *adj* **:** carrying a lesson : ENLIGHTENING — **in·struc·tive·ly** *adv* — **in·struc·tive·ness** *n*

in·struc·tor \in-ˈstrək-tər\ *n* **:** one that instructs : TEACHER; *specif* **:** a college teacher below professorial rank — **in·struc·tor·ship** \-ˌship\ *n* — **in·struc·tress** \-ˈstrək-trəs\ *n*

¹in·stru·ment \ˈin(t)-strə-mənt\ *n* [ME, fr. L *instrumentum*, fr. *instruere* to arrange, instruct] **1 a :** a means whereby something is achieved, performed, or furthered **b :** one used by another as a means or aid : DUPE, TOOL **2 :** UTENSIL, IMPLEMENT **3 :** a device used to produce music **4 :** a formal legal document (as a deed, bond, or agreement) **5 a :** a measuring device for determining the present value of a quantity under observation **b :** an electrical or mechanical device used in navigating an airplane; *esp* **:** such a device used as the sole means of navigating ***syn*** see MEAN, IMPLEMENT

²in·stru·ment \-ˌment\ *vt* **1 :** to address a legal instrument to **2 :** to score for musical performance : ORCHESTRATE **3 :** to equip with instruments

in·stru·men·tal \ˌin(t)-strə-ˈment-ᵊl\ *adj* **1 a :** serving as a means, agent, or tool <was ~ in organizing the strike> **b :** of, relating to, or done with an instrument or tool **2 :** relating to, composed for, or performed on a musical instrument **3 :** of or relating to a grammatical case or form expressing means or agency **4 :** of or relating to instrumentalism **5 :** based on or involving reward or avoidance of distress <~ learning> <~ conditioning> — **instrumental** *n* — **in·stru·men·tal·ly** \-ᵊl-ē\ *adv*

in·stru·men·tal·ism \-ˌiz-əm\ *n* **:** a doctrine that ideas are instruments of action and that their usefulness determines their truth

in·stru·men·tal·ist \-əst\ *n* **1 :** a player on a musical instrument **2 :** a student or exponent of instrumentalism — **instrumentalist** *adj*

in·stru·men·tal·i·ty \ˌin(t)-strə-mən-ˈtal-ət-ē, -ˌmen-\ *n, pl* **-ties** **1 :** the quality or state of being instrumental **2 :** MEANS, AGENCY

in·stru·men·ta·tion \ˌin(t)-strə-mən-ˈtā-shən, -ˌmen-\ *n* **1 a :** the use of instruments **b :** the application of instruments for observation, measurement, or control **2 :** the arrangement or composition of music for instruments esp. for a band or orchestra **3 a :** a science concerned with the development and manufacture of instruments **b :** instruments for a particular purpose

instrument flying *n* **:** navigation of an airplane by instruments only

instrument landing *n* **:** a landing made with little or no external visibility by means of instruments and by ground radio directive devices

instrument panel *n* **:** a panel on which instruments are mounted; *esp* **:** DASHBOARD 2

in·sub·or·di·nate \ˌin(t)-sə-ˈbȯrd-ᵊn-ət, -ˈbȯrd-nət\ *adj* **:** unwilling to submit to authority : REFRACTORY — **insubordinate** *n* — **in·sub·or·di·nate·ly** *adv* — **in·sub·or·di·na·tion** \-ˌbȯrd-ᵊn-ˈā-shən\ *n*

in·sub·stan·tial \ˌin(t)-səb-ˈstan-chəl\ *adj* [prob. fr. F *insubstantiel*, fr. LL *insubstantialis*, fr. L *in-* + LL *substantialis* substantial] **1 :** lacking substance or material nature : SPECTRAL, IMAGINARY **2 :** lacking firmness or solidity : FLIMSY — **in·sub·stan·ti·al·i·ty** \-ˌstan-chē-ˈal-ət-ē\ *n*

in·suf·fer·able \(ˈ)in-ˈsəf-(ə-)rə-bəl\ *adj* **:** incapable of being endured : INTOLERABLE <an ~ bore> — **in·suf·fer·able·ness** *n* — **in·suf·fer·ably** \-blē\ *adv*

in·suf·fi·cience \ˌin(t)-sə-ˈfish-ən(t)s\ *n* **:** INSUFFICIENCY

in·suf·fi·cien·cy \-ən-sē\ *n, pl* **-cies** **1 :** the quality or state of being insufficient: as **a :** lack of mental or moral fitness : INCOMPETENCE <the ~ of this man for public office> **b :** lack of adequate supply <~ of provisions> **c :** lack of physical power or capacity; *specif* **:** inability of an organ or body part to function normally **2 :** something insufficient <he was aware of his *insufficiencies*>

in·suf·fi·cient \ˌin(t)-sə-ˈfish-ənt\ *adj* [ME, fr. MF, fr. LL *insufficient-, insufficiens*, fr. L *in-* + *sufficient-, sufficiens* sufficient] **:** not sufficient; *esp* **:** deficient in power, capacity, or competence <life is often held to be an ~ begetter of fiction —Anthony Quinton> — **in·suf·fi·cient·ly** *adv*

in·suf·flate \ˈin(t)-sə-ˌflāt, in-ˈsəf-ˌlāt\ *vt* **-flat·ed; -flat·ing** [LL *insufflatus*, pp. of *insufflare*, fr. L *in-* + *sufflare* to blow up, fr. *sub-* up + *flare* to blow — more at SUB-, BLOW] **1 :** to blow on or into <~ a room with insecticide> **2 :** to disseminate (as a powder or gas) by blowing — **in·suf·fla·tor** \-ˌflāt-ər, -ˌlāt-\ *n*

in·suf·fla·tion \ˌin(t)-sə-ˈflā-shən, in-ˌsəf-ˈlā-\ *n* **:** an act or instance of insufflating; *also* **:** a Christian ceremonial rite of exorcism performed by breathing on a person

in·su·lant \ˈin(t)-sə-lənt\ *n* **:** an insulating material

in·su·lar \ˈin(t)s-(y)ə-lər, ˈin-shə-lər\ *adj* [LL *insularis*, fr. L *insula* island] **1 a :** of, relating to, or constituting an island **b :** dwelling or situated on an island <~residents> **2** *of a plant or animal* **:** having a restricted or isolated natural range or habitat **3 a :** of or relating to island people <surviving ~ customs> **b :** that results from isolation or is characteristic of isolated people <~ prejudices> **4 :** of or relating to an island of cells or tissue — **in·su·lar·ism** \-lə-ˌriz-əm\ *n* — **in·su·lar·i·ty** \ˌin(t)s-(y)ə-ˈlar-ət-ē, ˌin-shə-ˈlar-\ *n* — **in·su·lar·ly** \ˈin(t)s-(y)ə-lər-lē, ˈin-shə-\ *adv*

in·su·late \ˈin(t)-sə-ˌlāt\ *vt* **-lat·ed; -lat·ing** [L *insula* island] **:** to place in a detached situation : ISOLATE; *esp* **:** to separate from conducting bodies by means of nonconductors so as to prevent transfer of electricity, heat, or sound

in·su·la·tion \ˌin(t)-sə-ˈlā-shən\ *n* **1 :** the action of insulating : the state of being insulated **2 :** material used in insulating

in·su·la·tor \ˈin(t)-sə-ˌlāt-ər\ *n* **:** one that insulates; *esp* **:** a material that is a poor conductor of electricity or a device made of such material and used for separating or supporting conductors to prevent undesired flow of electricity

in·su·lin \ˈin(t)-s(ə-)lən\ *n* [NL *insula* islet (of Langerhans), fr. L, island] **:** a protein pancreatic hormone secreted by the islets of Langerhans that is essential esp. for the metabolism of carbohydrates and is used in the treatment and control of diabetes mellitus

insulin shock *n* **:** hypoglycemia associated with the presence of excessive insulin in the system and characterized by progressive development of coma

¹in·sult \in-ˈsəlt\ *vb* [MF or L; MF *insulter*, fr. L *insultare*, lit., to spring upon, fr. *in-* + *saltare* to leap — more at SALTATION] *vi, archaic* **:** to behave with pride or arrogance : VAUNT ~ *vt* **:** to treat with insolence, indignity, or contempt : AFFRONT; *also* **:** to affect offensively or damagingly <doggerel that ~*s* the reader's

intelligence> <foods that ~ the body> ***syn*** see OFFEND — **in·sult·er** *n* — **in·sult·ing·ly** \in-ˈsəl-tiŋ-lē\ *adv*

²in·sult \ˈin-ˌsəlt\ *n* **1** *archaic* **:** an act of attacking **2 :** a gross indignity **:** INSOLENCE **3 :** injury to the body or one of its parts; *also* **:** something that causes or has a potential for causing such insult <pollution and other environmental ~*s*>

in·su·per·a·ble \(ˈ)in-ˈsü-p(ə-)rə-bəl\ *adj* [ME, fr. MF & L; MF, fr. L *insuperabilis,* fr. *in-* + *superare* to surmount, fr. *super* over — more at OVER] **:** incapable of being surmounted, overcome, or passed over <~ difficulties> — **in·su·per·a·bly** \-blē\ *adv*

in·sup·port·able \ˌin(t)-sə-ˈpōrt-ə-bəl, -ˈpȯrt-\ *adj* [MF or LL; MF, fr. LL *insupportabilis,* fr. L *in-* + *supportare* to support] **:** not supportable: **a :** incapable of being borne **:** UNENDURABLE <~ pain> **b :** incapable of being sustained **:** UNJUSTIFIABLE <~ charges> — **in·sup·port·able·ness** *n* — **in·sup·port·ably** \-blē\ *adv*

in·sup·press·ible \ˌin(t)-sə-ˈpres-ə-bəl\ *adj* **:** IRREPRESSIBLE — **in·sup·press·ibly** \-blē\ *adv*

in·sur·able \in-ˈshu̇r-ə-bəl\ *adj* **:** that may be insured — **in·sur·abil·i·ty** \-ˌshu̇r-ə-ˈbil-ət-ē\ *n*

in·sur·ance \in-ˈshu̇r-ən(t)s, *chiefly South* ˈin-ˌ\ *n* **1 a :** the action or process of insuring **:** the state of being insured **b :** means of insuring <shelters designed to provide ~ against enemy attack> **2 a :** the business of insuring persons or property **b :** coverage by contract whereby one party undertakes to indemnify or guarantee another against loss by a specified contingency or peril **c :** the sum for which something is insured

insurance run *n* **:** a run in baseball that increases a winning team's lead

in·sure \in-ˈshu̇(ə)r\ *vb* **in·sured; in·sur·ing** [ME *insuren,* prob. alter. of *assuren* to assure] *vt* **1 :** to give, take, or procure insurance on or for **2 :** to make certain esp. by taking necessary measures and precautions ~ *vi* **:** to contract to give or take insurance; *specif* **:** UNDERWRITE ***syn*** see ENSURE

in·sured *n* **:** a person whose life or property is insured

in·sur·er \in-ˈshu̇r-ər\ *n* **:** one that insures; *specif* **:** an insurance underwriter

in·sur·gence \in-ˈsər-jən(t)s\ *n* **:** an act or the action of being insurgent **:** INSURRECTION

in·sur·gen·cy \-jən-sē\ *n, pl* **-cies 1 :** the quality or state of being insurgent; *specif* **:** a condition of revolt against a government that is less than an organized revolution and that is not recognized as belligerency **2 :** INSURGENCE

¹in·sur·gent \-jənt\ *n* [L *insurgent-, insurgens,* prp. of *insurgere* to rise up, fr. *in-* + *surgere* to rise — more at SURGE] **1 :** a person who revolts against civil authority or an established government; *esp* **:** a rebel not recognized as a belligerent **2 :** one who acts contrary to the policies and decisions of his political party

²insurgent *adj* **:** rising in opposition to civil authority or established leadership **:** REBELLIOUS — **in·sur·gent·ly** *adv*

in·sur·mount·able \ˌin(t)-sər-ˈmau̇nt-ə-bəl\ *adj* **:** incapable of being surmounted **:** INSUPERABLE <~ problems> — **in·sur·mount·ably** \-blē\ *adv*

in·sur·rec·tion \ˌin(t)-sə-ˈrek-shən\ *n* [ME, fr. MF, fr. LL *insurrection-, insurrectio,* fr. *insurrectus,* pp. of *insurgere*] **:** an act or instance of revolting against civil authority or an established government ***syn*** see REBELLION — **in·sur·rec·tion·al** \-shnəl, -shən-ᵊl\ *adj* — **in·sur·rec·tion·ary** \-shə-ˌner-ē\ *adj or n* — **in·sur·rec·tion·ist** \-sh(ə-)nəst\ *n*

in·sus·cep·ti·ble \ˌin(t)-sə-ˈsep-tə-bəl\ *adj* **:** not susceptible <~ to flattery> — **in·sus·cep·ti·bil·i·ty** \-ˌsep-tə-ˈbil-ət-ē\ *n* — **in·sus·cep·ti·bly** \ˌin(t)-sə-ˈsep-tə-blē\ *adv*

int *abbr* **1** intelligence **2** intercept **3** interest **4** interim **5** interior **6** interjection **7** interleaved **8** intermediate **9** internal **10** international **11** interpreter **12** intersection **13** interval **14** interview **15** intransitive

in·tact \in-ˈtakt\ *adj* [ME *intacte,* fr. L *intactus,* fr. *in-* + *tactus,* pp. of *tangere* to touch — more at TANGENT] **1 :** untouched esp. by anything that harms or diminishes **:** ENTIRE, UNINJURED **2** *of a living body or its parts* **:** having no relevant component removed or destroyed: **a :** physically virginal **b :** not castrated — **in·tact·ness** \-ˈtak(t)-nəs\ *n*

in·ta·glio \in-ˈtal-(ˌ)yō, -ˈtäl-; -ˈtag-lē-ˌō, -ˈtäg-\ *n, pl* **-glios** [It, fr. *intagliare* to engrave, cut, fr. ML *intaliare,* fr. L *in-* + LL *taliare* to cut — more at TAILOR] **1 a :** an engraving or incised figure in stone or other hard material depressed below the surface of the material so that an impression from the design yields an image in relief **b :** the art or process of executing intaglios **c :** printing (as in die stamping and gravure) done from a plate in which the image is sunk below the surface **2 :** something (as a gem) carved in intaglio

in·take \ˈin-ˌtāk\ *n* **1 :** an opening through which fluid enters an enclosure **2 a :** a taking in **b** (1) **:** the amount taken in (2) **:** something (as energy) taken in **:** INPUT

¹in·tan·gi·ble \(ˈ)in-ˈtan-jə-bəl\ *adj* [F or ML; F, fr. ML *intangibilis,* fr. L *in-* + LL *tangibilis* tangible] **:** not tangible **:** IMPALPABLE — **in·tan·gi·bil·i·ty** \(ˌ)in-ˌtan-jə-ˈbil-ət-ē\ *n* — **in·tan·gi·ble·ness** \(ˈ)in-ˈtan-jə-bəl-nəs\ *n* — **in·tan·gi·bly** \-blē\ *adv*

²intangible *n* **:** something intangible; *specif* **:** an asset (as goodwill) that is not corporeal

in·tar·sia \in-ˈtär-sē-ə\ *n* [G, modif. of It *intarsio*] **:** a mosaic usu. of wood fitted into a support; *also* **:** the art or process of making such a mosaic

in·te·ger \ˈint-i-jər\ *n* [L, adj., whole, entire — more at ENTIRE] **1 :** any of the natural numbers, the negatives of these numbers, or zero **2 :** a complete entity

in·te·gra·ble \ˈint-i-grə-bəl\ *adj* **:** capable of being integrated — **in·te·gra·bil·i·ty** \ˌint-i-grə-ˈbil-ət-ē\ *n*

¹in·te·gral \ˈint-i-grəl (*usu so in mathematics*); in-ˈteg-rəl *also* -ˈtēg-\ *adj* **1 a :** essential to completeness **:** CONSTITUENT **b** (1) **:** being or relating to a mathematical integer (2) **:** relating to or concerned with mathematical integrals or integration **c :** formed as a unit with another part **2 :** composed of integral parts **:** INTEGRATED **3 :** lacking nothing essential **:** ENTIRE — **in·te·gral·i·ty** \ˌint-ə-ˈgral-ət-ē\ *n* — **in·te·gral·ly** \ˈint-i-grə-lē; in-ˈteg-rə- *also* -ˈtēg-\ *adv*

²integral *n* **:** the result of a mathematical integration — compare DEFINITE INTEGRAL, INDEFINITE INTEGRAL

integral calculus *n* **:** a branch of mathematics dealing with methods of finding indefinite integrals and with their applications (as to the determination of lengths, areas, and volumes and to the solution of differential equations)

integral domain *n* **:** a mathematical ring in which multiplication is commutative, which has a multiplicative identity element, and which contains no pair of nonzero elements whose product is zero <the integers under the operations of addition and multiplication form an *integral domain*>

in·te·grand \ˈint-ə-ˌgrand\ *n* [L *integrandus,* gerundive of *integrare*] **:** a mathematical expression to be integrated

in·te·grate \ˈint-ə-ˌgrāt\ *vb* **-grat·ed; -grat·ing** [L *integratus,* pp. of *integrare,* fr. *integr-, integer*] *vt* **1 :** to form or blend into a whole **:** UNITE **2 a :** to unite with something else **b :** to incorporate into a larger unit **3 :** to find the integral of (as a function or equation) **4 a :** to end the segregation of and bring into common and equal membership in society or an organization **b :** DESEGREGATE <~ school districts> ~ *vi* **:** to become integrated

integrated circuit *n* **:** a tiny complex of electronic components and their connections that is produced in or on a small slice of material (as silicon) — **integrated circuitry** *n*

in·te·gra·tion \ˌint-ə-ˈgrā-shən\ *n* **1 :** the act or process or an instance of integrating: as **a :** incorporation as equals into society or an organization of individuals of different groups (as races) **b :** coordination of mental processes into a normal effective personality or with the individual's environment **2 a :** the operation of finding a function whose differential is known **b :** the operation of solving a differential equation

in·te·gra·tion·ist \-sh(ə-)nəst\ *n* **:** a person who believes in, advocates, or practices social integration — **integrationist** *adj*

in·te·gra·tive \ˈint-ə-ˌgrāt-iv\ *adj* **:** serving to integrate or favoring integration **:** directed toward integration <~ forces in a fragmented society>

in·te·gra·tor \-ˌgrāt-ər\ *n* **:** one that integrates; *esp* **:** a device or computer unit that totalizes variable quantities in a manner comparable to the mathematical integrating or solution of differential equations

in·teg·ri·ty \in-ˈteg-rət-ē\ *n* **1 :** an unimpaired condition **:** SOUNDNESS **2 :** firm adherence to a code of esp. moral or artistic values **:** INCORRUPTIBILITY **3 :** the quality or state of being complete or undivided **:** COMPLETENESS ***syn* 1** see HONESTY ***ant*** duplicity **2** see UNITY

in·teg·u·ment \in-ˈteg-yə-mənt\ *n* [L *integumentum,* fr. *integere* to cover, fr. *in-* + *tegere* to cover — more at THATCH] **:** something that covers or encloses; *esp* **:** an enveloping layer (as a skin, membrane, or husk) of an organism or one of its parts — **in·teg·u·men·tal** \-ˌteg-yə-ˈment-ᵊl\ *adj* — **in·teg·u·men·ta·ry** \-ˈment-ə-rē, -ˈmen-trē\ *adj*

in·tel·lect \ˈint-ᵊl-ˌekt\ *n* [ME, fr. MF or L; MF, fr. L *intellectus,* fr. *intellectus,* pp. of *intellegere* to understand — more at INTELLIGENT] **1 a :** the power of knowing as distinguished from the power to feel and to will **:** the capacity for knowledge **b :** the capacity for rational or intelligent thought esp. when highly developed **2 :** a person with great intellectual powers

in·tel·lec·tion \ˌint-ᵊl-ˈek-shən\ *n* **1 :** exercise of the intellect **:** REASONING **2 :** an act of the intellect **:** THOUGHT

in·tel·lec·tive \-ˈek-tiv\ *adj* **:** having, relating to, or belonging to the intellect **:** RATIONAL — **in·tel·lec·tive·ly** *adv*

¹in·tel·lec·tu·al \ˌint-ᵊl-ˈek-chə(-wə)l, -ˈeksh-wəl\ *adj* **1 a :** of or relating to the intellect or its use **b :** developed or chiefly guided by the intellect rather than by emotion or experience **:** RATIONAL **c :** requiring use of the intellect **2 a :** given to study, reflection, and speculation **b :** engaged in activity requiring the creative use of the intellect — **in·tel·lec·tu·al·i·ty** \-ˌek-chə-ˈwal-ət-ē\ *n* — **in·tel·lec·tu·al·ly** \-ˈek-chə-(wə-)lē, -ˈeksh-wə-lē\ *adv* — **in·tel·lec·tu·al·ness** \-ˈek-chə(-wə)l-nəs, -ˈeksh-wəl-\ *n*

²intellectual *n* **1** *pl, archaic* **:** intellectual powers **2 :** an intellectual person

in·tel·lec·tu·al·ism \ˌint-ᵊl-ˈek-chə(-wə)-ˌliz-əm, -ˈeksh-wə-\ *n* **:** devotion to the exercise of intellect or to intellectual pursuits — **in·tel·lec·tu·al·ist** \-ləst\ *n* — **in·tel·lec·tu·al·is·tic** \-ˌek-chə-(-wə)-ˈlis-tik, -ˌeksh-wə-\ *adj*

in·tel·lec·tu·al·ize \ˌint-ᵊl-ˈek-chə(-wə)-ˌlīz, -ˈeksh-wə-\ *vt* **-ized; -iz·ing :** to give rational form or content to — **in·tel·lec·tu·al·iza·tion** \-ˌek-chə(-wə)-lə-ˈzā-shən, -ˌeksh-wə-\ *n* — **in·tel·lec·tu·al·iz·er** \-ˈek-chə(-wə)-ˌlī-zər, -ˈeksh-wə-\ *n*

in·tel·li·gence \in-ˈtel-ə-jən(t)s\ *n* [ME, fr. MF, fr. L *intelligentia,* fr. *intelligent-, intelligens* intelligent] **1 a** (1) **:** the ability to learn or understand or to deal with new or trying situations **:** REASON; *also* **:** the skilled use of reason (2) **:** the ability to apply knowledge to manipulate one's environment or to think abstractly as measured by objective criteria (as tests) **b** *Christian Science* **:** the basic eternal quality of divine Mind **c :** mental acuteness **:** SHREWDNESS **2 a :** an intelligent entity; *esp* **:** ANGEL **b :** intelligent minds or mind <cosmic ~> **3 :** the act of understanding **:** COMPREHENSION **4 a :** INFORMATION, NEWS **b :** information concerning an enemy or possible enemy or an area; *also* **:** an agency engaged in obtaining such information

intelligence quotient *n* **:** a number used to express the apparent relative intelligence of a person determined by dividing his mental age as reported on a standardized test by his chronological age and multiplying by 100

in·tel·li·genc·er \in-ˈtel-ə-jən-sər; -ˈtel-ə-ˌjen(t)-, -ˌtel-ə-ˈ\ *n* **1 :** a secret agent **:** SPY **2 :** a bringer of news **:** REPORTER

intelligence test *n* **:** a test designed to determine the relative mental capacity of a person

in·tel·li·gent \in-ˈtel-ə-jənt\ *adj* [L *intelligent-, intelligens,* prp. of *intelligere, intellegere* to understand, fr. *inter-* + *legere* to gather, select — more at LEGEND] **1 a :** possessing intelligence **b :** guided or directed by intellect **:** RATIONAL **2 a:** having or indicating a high or satisfactory degree of intelligence and mental capacity **b :** revealing or reflecting good judgment or sound thought : SKILLFUL **3 :** able to perform some of the functions of a computer <an ~ computer terminal> — **in·tel·li·gen·tial** \-ˌtel-ə-ˈjen-chəl\ *adj* — **in·tel·li·gent·ly** \-ˈtel-ə-jənt-lē\ *adv*

syn INTELLIGENT, CLEVER, ALERT, QUICK-WITTED, KNOWING *shared meaning element* : mentally keen or quick ***ant*** unintelligent

in·tel·li·gen·tsia \in-ˌtel-ə-ˈjen(t)-sē-ə, -ˈgen(t)-\ *n* [Russ *intelligentsiya,* fr. L *intelligentia* intelligence] : intellectuals who form an artistic, social, or political vanguard or elite

in·tel·li·gi·ble \in-ˈtel-ə-jə-bəl\ *adj* [ME, fr. L *intelligibilis;* fr. *intelligere*] **1 :** capable of being understood or comprehended **2 :** apprehensible by the intellect only — **in·tel·li·gi·bil·i·ty** \-ˌtel-ə-jə-ˈbil-ət-ē\ *n* — **in·tel·li·gi·ble·ness** \-ˈtel-ə-jə-bəl-nəs\ *n* — **in·tel·li·gi·bly** \-blē\ *adv*

in·tem·per·ance \(ˈ)in-ˈtem-p(ə-)rən(t)s\ *n* : lack of moderation esp. in satisfying an appetite or passion; *esp* : habitual or excessive drinking of intoxicants

in·tem·per·ate \-p(ə-)rət\ *adj* [ME *intemperat,* fr. L *intemperatus,* fr. *in-* + *temperatus,* pp. of *temperare* to temper] : not temperate; *esp* : given to excessive use of intoxicating liquors — **in·tem·per·ate·ly** *adv* — **in·tem·per·ate·ness** *n*

in·tend \in-ˈtend\ *vb* [ME *entenden, intenden,* fr. MF *entendre* to purpose, fr. L *intendere* to stretch out, to purpose, fr. *in-* + *tendere* to stretch — more at THIN] *vt* **1 a :** SIGNIFY, MEAN **b :** to refer to **2 a :** to have in mind as a purpose or goal : PLAN **b :** to design for a specified use or future **3** *archaic* : to proceed on (a course) **4 :** to direct the mind on ~ *vi, archaic* : to set out : START — **in·tend·er** *n*

in·ten·dance \in-ˈten-dən(t)s\ *n* **1 :** MANAGEMENT, SUPERINTENDENCE **2 :** an administrative department

in·ten·dant \-dənt\ *n* [F, fr. MF, fr. L *intendent-, intendens,* prp. of *intendere* to intend, attend] : an administrative official (as a governor) esp. under the French, Spanish, or Portuguese monarchies

[1]in·tend·ed *adj* **1 :** planned for the future : PROPOSED; *esp* : chosen for marriage at some future time <his ~ bride> **2 :** INTENTIONAL — **in·tend·ed·ly** *adv* — **in·tend·ed·ness** *n*

[2]intended *n* : an affianced person : BETROTHED

in·tend·ing *adj* : PROSPECTIVE, ASPIRING <an ~ teacher>

in·tend·ment \in-ˈten(d)-mənt\ *n* : the true meaning or intention esp. of a law

in·ten·er·ate \in-ˈten-ə-ˌrāt\ *vt* **-at·ed; -at·ing** [[2]*in-* + L *tener* soft, tender — more at TENDER] : to make tender : SOFTEN — **in·ten·er·a·tion** \-ˌten-ə-ˈrā-shən\ *n*

in·tense \in-ˈten(t)s\ *adj* [ME, fr. MF, fr. L *intensus,* fr. pp. of *intendere* to stretch out] **1 a :** existing in an extreme degree **b :** having or showing a characteristic in extreme degree **c :** very large : CONSIDERABLE **2 :** strained or straining to the utmost **3 a :** feeling deeply esp. by nature or temperament **b :** deeply felt — **in·tense·ly** *adv* — **in·tense·ness** *n*

in·ten·si·fi·er \in-ˈten(t)-sə-ˌfī(-ə)r\ *n* : one that intensifies; *esp* : INTENSIVE

in·ten·si·fy \in-ˈten(t)-sə-ˌfī\ *vb* **-fied; -fy·ing** *vt* **1 :** to make intense or more intensive : STRENGTHEN **2 a :** to increase the density and contrast of (a photographic image) by chemical treatment **b :** to make more acute : SHARPEN ~ *vi* : to become intense or more intensive : grow stronger or more acute — **in·ten·si·fi·ca·tion** \-ˌten(t)s-(ə-)fə-ˈkā-shən\ *n*

syn INTENSIFY, AGGRAVATE, HEIGHTEN, ENHANCE *shared meaning element* : to increase markedly in measure or degree ***ant*** temper, mitigate, abate

in·ten·sion \in-ˈten-chən\ *n* **1 :** INTENSITY **2 :** CONNOTATION 3 — **in·ten·sion·al** \-ˈtench-nəl, -ˈten-chən-ᵊl\ *adj* — **in·ten·sion·al·ly** \-ē\ *adv*

in·ten·si·ty \in-ˈten(t)-sət-ē\ *n, pl* **-ties** **1 :** the quality or state of being intense; *esp* : extreme degree of strength, force, or energy **2 :** the magnitude of force or energy per unit (as of surface, charge, mass, or time) **3 :** SATURATION 4a

[1]in·ten·sive \in-ˈten(t)-siv\ *adj* : of, relating to, or marked by intensity or intensification: as **a :** highly concentrated <~ study> **b :** tending to strengthen or increase; *esp* : tending to give force or emphasis <~ adverb> **c :** constituting or relating to a method designed to increase productivity by the expenditure of more capital and labor rather than by increase in scope <~ farming> — **in·ten·sive·ly** *adv* — **in·ten·sive·ness** *n*

[2]intensive *n* : an intensive linguistic element

[1]in·tent \in-ˈtent\ *n* [ME *entent,* fr. OF, fr. LL *intentus,* fr. L, act of stretching out, fr. *intentus,* pp. of *intendere*] **1 a :** the act or fact of intending : PURPOSE **b :** the state of mind with which an act is done : VOLITION **2 :** a usu. clearly formulated or planned intention : AIM **3 a :** MEANING, SIGNIFICANCE **b :** CONNOTATION 3 ***syn*** see INTENTION

[2]intent *adj* [L *intentus,* fr. pp. of *intendere*] **1 :** directed with strained or eager attention : CONCENTRATED **2 :** having the mind, attention, or will concentrated on something or some end or purpose <~ on his work> — **in·tent·ly** *adv* — **in·tent·ness** *n*

in·ten·tion \in-ˈten-chən\ *n* **1 :** a determination to act in a certain way : RESOLVE **2** *pl* : purpose with respect to marriage **3 a :** what one intends to do or bring about **b :** the object for which a prayer, mass, or pious act is offered **4 :** IMPORT, SIGNIFICANCE **5 :** CONCEPT; *esp* : a concept considered as the product of attention directed to an object of knowledge **6 :** a process or manner of healing of incised wounds

syn INTENTION, INTENT, PURPOSE, DESIGN, AIM, END, OBJECT, OBJECTIVE, GOAL *shared meaning element* : what one purposes to accomplish or attain

in·ten·tion·al \in-ˈtench-nəl, -ˈten-chən-ᵊl\ *adj* **1 :** done by intention or design : INTENDED <~ damage> **2 a :** of or relating to epistemological intention **b :** having external reference ***syn*** see VOLUNTARY ***ant*** instinctive — **in·ten·tion·al·i·ty** \-ˌten-chə-ˈnal-ət-ē\ *n* — **in·ten·tion·al·ly** \in-ˈtench-nə-lē, -ˈten-chən-ᵊl-ē\ *adv*

in·ter \in-ˈtər\ *vt* **in·terred; in·ter·ring** [ME *enteren,* fr. OF *enterrer,* fr. (assumed) VL *interrare,* fr. *in-* + L *terra* earth — more at TERRACE] : to deposit (a dead body) in the earth or in a tomb : BURY

inter- *prefix* [ME *inter-, enter-,* fr. MF & L; MF *inter-, entre-,* fr. L *inter-,* fr. *inter;* akin to OHG *untar* between, among, Gk *enteron* intestine, OE *in* in] **1 :** between : among : in the midst <*inter*crop> <*inter*penetrate> <*inter*stellar> **2 :** reciprocal <*inter*relation> : reciprocally <*inter*marry> **3 :** located between <*inter*face> **4 :** carried on between <*inter*national> **5 :** occurring between : intervening <*inter*glacial> **6 :** shared by or derived from two or more <*inter*faith> **7 :** between the limits of : within <*inter*tropical>

in·ter·act \ˌint-ə-ˈrakt\ *vi* : to act upon one another — **in·ter·ac·tive** \-ˈrak-tiv\ *adj*

in·ter·ac·tant \-ˈrak-tənt\ *n* : one that interacts; *specif* : a chemical reactant

in·ter·ac·tion \ˌint-ə-ˈrak-shən\ *n* : mutual or reciprocal action or influence — **in·ter·ac·tion·al** \-shnəl, -shən-ᵊl\ *adj*

in·ter alia \ˌint-ə-ˈrā-lē-ə, -ˈrä-\ *adv* [L] : among other things

in·ter ali·os \-lē-ˌōs\ *adv* [L] : among other persons

in·ter·atom·ic \ˌint-ə-rə-ˈtäm-ik\ *adj* : existing or acting between atoms

in·ter·brain \ˈint-ər-ˌbrān\ *n* : DIENCEPHALON

in·ter·breed \ˌint-ər-ˈbrēd\ *vb* **-bred** \-ˈbred\; **-breed·ing** *vi* : to breed together: as **a :** CROSSBREED **b :** to breed within a closed population ~ *vt* : to cause to breed together

in·ter·ca·la·ry \in-ˈtər-kə-ˌler-ē, ˌint-ər-ˈkal-ə-rē\ *adj* [L *intercalarius,* fr. *intercalare*] **1 a :** inserted in a calendar <an ~ day> **b** *of a year* : containing an intercalary period **2 :** inserted between other things or parts : INTERPOLATED

in·ter·ca·late \in-ˈtər-kə-ˌlāt\ *vt* **-lat·ed; -lat·ing** [L *intercalatus,* pp. of *intercalare,* fr. *inter-* + *calare* to call, summon — more at LOW] **1 :** to insert (as a day) in a calendar **2 :** to insert between or among existing elements or layers ***syn*** see INTRODUCE — **in·ter·ca·la·tion** \-ˌtər-kə-ˈlā-shən\ *n*

in·ter·cede \ˌint-ər-ˈsēd\ *vi* **-ced·ed; -ced·ing** [L *intercedere,* fr. *inter-* + *cedere* to go — more at CEDE] : to intervene between parties with a view to reconciling differences : MEDIATE ***syn*** see INTERPOSE — **in·ter·ced·er** *n*

in·ter·cel·lu·lar \ˌint-ər-ˈsel-yə-lər\ *adj* : occurring between cells <~ spaces> — **in·ter·cel·lu·lar·ly** *adv*

[1]in·ter·cept \ˌint-ər-ˈsept\ *vt* [L *interceptus,* pp. of *intercipere,* fr. *inter-* + *capere* to take, seize — more at HEAVE] **1 :** to stop, seize, or interrupt in progress or course or before arrival **2** *obs* : PREVENT, HINDER **3** *obs* : to interrupt communication or connection with **4 :** INTERSECT **5 :** to gain possession of (an opponent's pass)

[2]in·ter·cept \ˈint-ər-ˌsept\ *n* **1 :** the distance from the origin to a point where a graph crosses a coordinate axis **2 :** INTERCEPTION; *esp* : the interception of a missile by an interceptor or of a target by a missile

in·ter·cept·er \ˌint-ər-ˈsep-tər\ *n* : INTERCEPTOR

in·ter·cep·tion \ˌint-ər-ˈsep-shən\ *n* **1 a :** the action of intercepting **b :** the state of being intercepted **2 :** something that is intercepted; *esp* : an intercepted forward pass <threw three ~*s* in one game>

in·ter·cep·tor \-ˈsep-tər\ *n* : one that intercepts; *specif* : a light high-speed fast-climbing fighter plane or missile designed for defense against raiding bombers or missiles

in·ter·ces·sion \ˌint-ər-ˈsesh-ən\ *n* [MF or L; MF, fr. L *intercession-, intercessio,* fr. *intercessus,* pp. of *intercedere*] **1 :** the act of interceding **2 :** prayer, petition, or entreaty in favor of another — **in·ter·ces·sion·al** \-ˈsesh-nəl, -ən-ᵊl\ *adj* — **in·ter·ces·sor** \-ˈses-ər\ *n* — **in·ter·ces·so·ry** \-ˈses-(ə-)rē\ *adj*

[1]in·ter·change \ˌint-ər-ˈchānj\ *vb* [ME *entrechaungen,* fr. MF *entrechangier,* fr. OF, fr. *entre-* inter- + *changier* to change] *vt* **1 :** to put each of (two things) in the place of the other **2 :** EXCHANGE ~ *vi* : to change places mutually — **in·ter·chang·er** *n*

[2]in·ter·change \ˈint-ər-ˌchānj\ *n* **1 :** the act, process, or an instance of interchanging : EXCHANGE **2 :** a junction of two or more highways by a system of separate levels that permit traffic to pass from one to another without the crossing of traffic streams

in·ter·change·able \ˌint-ər-ˈchān-jə-bəl\ *adj* : capable of being interchanged; *esp* : permitting mutual substitution <~ parts> — **in·ter·change·abil·i·ty** \-ˌchān-jə-ˈbil-ət-ē\ *n* — **in·ter·change·able·ness** \-ˈchān-jə-bəl-nəs\ *n* — **in·ter·change·ably** \-blē\ *adv*

in·ter·clav·i·cle \ˌint-ər-ˈklav-i-kəl\ *n* : a bone lying in front of the sternum and between the clavicles (as in a reptile) — **in·ter·cla·vic·u·lar** \-kla-ˈvik-yə-lər, -klə-\ *adj*

in·ter·col·le·giate \ˌint-ər-kə-ˈlē-j(ē-)ət\ *adj* : existing, carried on, or participating in activities between colleges <~ athletics>

in·ter·co·lum·ni·a·tion \ˌint-ər-kə-ˌləm-nē-ˈā-shən\ *n* [L *intercolumnium* space between two columns, fr. *inter-* + *columna* column] **1 :** the clear space between the columns of a series **2 :** the system of spacing of the columns of a colonnade

in·ter·com \ˈint-ər-ˌkäm\ *n* : INTERCOMMUNICATION SYSTEM

in·ter·com·mu·ni·cate \ˌint-ər-kə-ˈmyü-nə-ˌkāt\ *vi* **1 :** to exchange communication with one another **2 :** to afford passage from one to another — **in·ter·com·mu·ni·ca·tion** \-ˌmyü-nə-ˈkā-shən\ *n*

intercommunication system *n* : a two-way communication system with microphone and loudspeaker at each station for localized use

in·ter·com·mu·nion \ˌint-ər-kə-ˈmyü-nyən\ *n* : interdenominational participation in communion

in·ter·con·nect \ˌint-ər-kə-ˈnekt\ *vt* **:** to connect with one another — **in·ter·con·nec·tion** \-ˈnek-shən\ *n*

in·ter·con·ti·nen·tal \ˌint-ər-ˌkänt-ᵊn-ˈent-ᵊl\ *adj* **1 :** extending among continents or carried on between continents **2 :** capable of traveling between continents <~ ballistic missile>

in·ter·con·ver·sion \ˌint-ər-kən-ˈvər-zhən, -shən\ *n* **:** mutual conversion <~ of chemical compounds> — **in·ter·con·vert** \-ˈvərt\ *vt* — **in·ter·con·vert·ibil·i·ty** \-ˌvərt-ə-ˈbil-ət-ē\ *n* — **in·ter·con·vert·ible** \-ˈvərt-ə-bəl\ *adj*

in·ter·cool·er \ˌint-ər-ˈkü-lər\ *n* **:** a device for cooling a fluid (as air) between successive heat-generating processes

in·ter·cos·tal \ˌint-ər-ˈkäs-tᵊl\ *adj* [NL *intercostalis,* fr. L *inter-* + *costa* rib] **:** situated between the ribs; *also* **:** of or relating to an intercostal part — **intercostal** *n* — **in·ter·cos·tal·ly** \-tə-lē\ *adv*

in·ter·course \ˈint-ər-ˌkō(ə)rs, -ˌkȯ(ə)rs\ *n* [ME *intercurse,* prob. fr. MF *entrecours,* fr. ML *intercursus,* fr. L, act of running between, fr. *intercursus,* pp. of *intercurrere* to run between, fr. *inter-* + *currere* to run — more at CURRENT] **1 :** connection or dealings between persons or groups **2 :** exchange esp. of thoughts or feelings **:** COMMUNION **3 :** COITUS, COPULATION

in·ter·crop \ˌint-ər-ˈkräp, ˈint-ər-ˌ\ *vt* **:** to grow a crop in between elements (as rows) of (another) ~ *vi* **:** to grow two or more crops simultaneously (as in alternate rows) on the same plot — **in·ter·crop** \ˈint-ər-ˌkräp\ *n*

1**in·ter·cross** \ˌint-ər-ˈkrȯs\ *vb* **:** CROSS

2**in·ter·cross** \ˈint-ər-ˌkrȯs\ *n* **:** an instance or a product of crossbreeding

in·ter·cul·tur·al \ˌint-ər-ˈkəlch(-ə)-rəl\ *adj* **:** occurring between or relating to two or more cultures — **in·ter·cul·tur·al·ly** \-rə-lē\ *adv*

in·ter·cur·rent \ˌint-ər-ˈkər-ənt, -ˈkə-rənt\ *adj* [L *intercurrent-, intercurrens,* prp. of *intercurrere*] **:** occurring in the midst of a process **:** INTERRUPTING — **in·ter·cur·rent·ly** *adv*

in·ter·cut \ˌint-ər-ˈkət\ *vt* **1 :** to insert a contrasting camera shot into (a take) by cutting **2 :** to insert (a contrasting camera shot) into a take by cutting ~ *vi* **:** to alternate contrasting camera shots by cutting

in·ter·de·nom·i·na·tion·al \ˌint-ər-di-ˌnäm-ə-ˈnā-shnəl, -shən-ᵊl\ *adj* **:** involving or occurring between different denominations — **in·ter·de·nom·i·na·tion·al·ism** \-ˌiz-əm\ *n*

in·ter·den·tal \ˌint-ər-ˈdent-ᵊl\ *adj* **1 :** situated or intended for use between the teeth **2 :** formed with the tip of the tongue between the upper and lower front teeth — **in·ter·den·tal·ly** \-ᵊl-ē\ *adv*

in·ter·de·part·men·tal \ˌint-ər-di-ˌpärt-ˈment-ᵊl, -ˌdē-\ *adj* **:** carried on between or involving departments (as of an educational institution) — **in·ter·de·part·men·tal·ly** \-ᵊl-ē\ *adv*

in·ter·de·pend \ˌint-ər-di-ˈpend\ *vi* **:** to depend upon one another

in·ter·de·pen·dence \-ˈpen-dən(t)s\ *n* **:** mutual dependence

in·ter·de·pen·den·cy \-dən-sē\ *n* **:** INTERDEPENDENCE

in·ter·de·pen·dent \-dənt\ *adj* **:** mutually dependent — **in·ter·de·pen·dent·ly** \-lē\ *adv*

1**in·ter·dict** \ˈint-ər-ˌdikt\ *n* [ME *entredit,* fr. OF, fr. L *interdictum* prohibition, praetorian interdict, fr. neut. of *interdictus,* pp. of *interdicere* to interpose, forbid, fr. *inter-* + *dicere* to say — more at DICTION] **1 :** a Roman Catholic ecclesiastical censure withdrawing most sacraments and Christian burial from a person or district **2 :** a prohibitory decree **:** PROHIBITION

2**in·ter·dict** \ˌint-ər-ˈdikt\ *vt* **1 :** to lay under or prohibit by an interdict **2 :** to forbid in a usu. formal or authoritative manner **3 :** to destroy, cut, or damage (as an enemy line of supply) by firepower to stop or hamper an enemy ***syn*** see FORBID ***ant*** sanction — **in·ter·dic·tion** \-ˈdik-shən\ *n* — **in·ter·dic·tive** \-ˈdik-tiv\ *adj* — **in·ter·dic·tor** \-tər\ *n* — **in·ter·dic·to·ry** \-t(ə-)rē\ *adj*

in·ter·dif·fuse \-dif-ˈyüz\ *vi* **:** to diffuse and mix freely so as to approach a homogeneous mixture — **in·ter·dif·fu·sion** \-ˈyü-zhən\ *n*

in·ter·dig·i·tate \-ˈdij-ə-ˌtāt\ *vi* **-tat·ed; -tat·ing** [*inter-* + L *digitus* finger — more at TOE] **:** to become interlocked like the fingers of folded hands — **in·ter·dig·i·ta·tion** \-ˌdij-ə-ˈtā-shən\ *n*

in·ter·dis·ci·plin·ary \-ˈdis-ə-plə-ˌner-ē\ *adj* **:** involving two or more academic, scientific, or artistic disciplines

1**in·ter·est** \ˈin-trəst; ˈint-ə-rəst, -ə-ˌrest, -ərst; ˈin-ˌtrest\ *n* [ME, prob. alter. of earlier *interesse,* fr. AF & ML; AF, fr. ML, fr. L, to be between, make a difference, concern, fr. *inter-* + *esse* to be — more at IS] **1 a (1) :** right, title, or legal share in something **(2) :** participation in advantage and responsibility **b :** a business in which one has an interest **2 :** WELFARE, BENEFIT; *specif* **:** SELF-INTEREST **3 a :** a charge for borrowed money generally a percentage of the amount borrowed **b :** an excess above what is due **4 :** a group financially interested in an industry or enterprise **5 a :** readiness to be concerned with or moved by an object or class of objects **b :** the quality in a thing that arouses interest

2**interest** *vt* **1 :** to induce or persuade to participate or engage **2 :** to engage the attention or arouse the interest of

in·ter·est·ed *adj* **1 :** having the attention engaged <~ listeners> **2 :** being affected or involved <~ parties> — **in·ter·est·ed·ly** *adv*

interest group *n* **:** a group of persons having a common identifying interest that often provides a basis for action

in·ter·est·ing *adj* **:** holding the attention **:** arousing interest — **in·ter·est·ing·ly** *adv*

1**in·ter·face** \ˈint-ər-ˌfās\ *n* **1 :** a surface forming a common boundary of two bodies, spaces, or phases <an oil-water ~> **2 a :** the place at which independent systems meet and act on or communicate with each other <the man-machine ~>; *broadly* **:** an area in which diverse things interact <the high school-college ~> **b :** the means by which interaction or communication is effected at an interface — **in·ter·fa·cial** \ˌint-ər-ˈfā-shəl\ *adj*

2**interface** *vt* **1 :** to connect by means of an interface <~ a machine with a computer> **2 :** to serve as an interface for ~ *vi* **1 :** to become interfaced **2 :** to serve as an interface

in·ter·faith \ˌint-ər-ˈfāth\ *adj* **:** involving persons of different religious faiths

in·ter·fas·cic·u·lar \ˌint-ər-fə-ˈsik-yə-lər, -fa-\ *adj* **:** situated between fascicles

in·ter·fere \ˌint-ə(r)-ˈfi(ə)r\ *vi* **-fered; -fer·ing** [MF *(s')entreferir* to strike one another, fr. OF, fr. *entre-* inter- + *ferir* to strike, fr. L *ferire* — more at BORE] **1 :** to strike one foot against the opposite foot or ankle in walking or running — used esp. of horses **2 :** to interpose in a way that hinders or impedes **:** come into collision or be in opposition **3 :** to enter into or take a part in the concerns of others **4 :** to act reciprocally so as to augment, diminish, or otherwise affect one another — used of waves **5 :** to claim substantially the same invention and thus question the priority of invention between the claimants **6 :** to hinder illegally an attempt of a player to catch or hit a ball or puck — usu. used with *with* ***syn*** see INTERPOSE, MEDDLE — **in·ter·fer·er** *n*

in·ter·fer·ence \-ˈfir-ən(t)s\ *n* **1 a :** the act or process of interfering **b :** something that interferes **:** OBSTRUCTION **2 :** the mutual effect on meeting of two wave trains of the same type so that such light waves produce lines, bands, or fringes either alternately light and dark or variously colored and sound waves produce silence, increased intensity, or beats **3 a :** the legal blocking of an opponent in football to make way for the ballcarrier **b :** the illegal hindering of an opponent in sports **4 a :** confusion of received radio signals due to strays or undesired signals **b :** something that produces such confusion — **in·ter·fer·en·tial** \-fə-ˈren-chəl, -ˌfir-ˈen-\ *adj*

in·ter·fer·o·gram \ˌint-ə(r)-ˈfir-ə-ˌgram\ *n* **:** a photographic record made by an apparatus for recording optical interference phenomena

in·ter·fer·om·e·ter \ˌint-ə(r)-fə-ˈräm-ət-ər, -ˌfir-ˈäm-\ *n* [ISV] **:** an instrument that utilizes light interference phenomena for precise determinations of wavelength, spectral fine structure, indices of refraction, and very small linear displacements — **in·ter·fer·o·met·ric** \-ˌfir-ə-ˈme-trik\ *adj* — **in·ter·fer·o·met·ri·cal·ly** \-tri-k(ə-)lē\ *adv* — **in·ter·fer·om·e·try** \-fə-ˈräm-ə-trē, -ˌfir-ˈäm-\ *n*

in·ter·fer·on \ˌint-ə(r)-ˈfi(ə)r-ˌän\ *n* [*interfer*ence + *-on*] **:** a heat-stable soluble basic antiviral protein of low molecular weight produced by cells exposed to the action of a virus, sometimes to that of another intracellular parasite (as a brucella), or experimentally to that of certain chemicals

in·ter·fer·tile \ˌint-ər-ˈfərt-ᵊl\ *adj* **:** capable of interbreeding — **in·ter·fer·til·i·ty** \-(ˌ)fər-ˈtil-ət-ē\ *n*

in·ter·file \ˌint-ər-ˈfī(ə)l\ *vt* **:** 4FILE 1 ~ *vi* **:** 4FILE 2; *also* **:** to fit in with an existing file

in·ter·fuse \ˌint-ər-ˈfyüz\ *vt* [L *interfusus,* pp. of *interfundere* to pour between, fr. *inter-* + *fundere* to pour — more at FOUND] **1 :** to combine by fusing **:** BLEND **2 :** to cause to pass into or through others **:** INFUSE **3 :** PERVADE, PERMEATE <wit that *interfused* all his writings> — **in·ter·fu·sion** \-ˈfyü-zhən\ *n*

in·ter·ga·lac·tic \ˌint-ər-gə-ˈlak-tik\ *adj* **:** situated or occurring in the spaces between galaxies

in·ter·gen·er·a·tion·al \-ˌjen-ə-ˈrā-shnəl, -shən-ᵊl\ *adj* **:** existing or occurring between two or more generations <~ conflicts>

in·ter·ge·ner·ic \-jə-ˈner-ik\ *adj* **:** existing or occurring between genera <~ hybridization>

in·ter·gla·cial \-ˈglā-shəl\ *adj* **:** occurring or formed between glacial epochs

in·ter·gov·ern·men·tal \-ˌgəv-ər(n)-ˈment-ᵊl\ *adj* **:** existing or occurring between two or more governments or levels of government

in·ter·gra·da·tion \-grā-ˈdā-shən, -grə-\ *n* **:** the condition of one that intergrades — **in·ter·gra·da·tion·al** \-shnəl, -shən-ᵊl\ *adj*

1**in·ter·grade** \ˌint-ər-ˈgrād\ *vi* **:** to merge gradually one with another through a continuous series of intermediate forms

2**in·ter·grade** \ˈint-ər-ˌgrād\ *n* **:** an intermediate or transitional form

in·ter·group \ˌint-ər-ˈgrüp\ *adj* **:** existing or occurring between two or more social groups

in·ter·growth \ˈint-ər-ˌgrōth\ *n* **:** a growing between or together; *also* **:** the product of such growth

in·ter·hemi·spher·ic \ˈint-ər-ˌhem-ə-ˈsfi(ə)r-ik, -ˈsfer-\ *adj* **:** extending or occurring between hemispheres

1**in·ter·im** \ˈint-ə-rəm\ *n* [L, adv., meanwhile, fr. *inter* between — more at INTER-] **:** an intervening time **:** INTERVAL

2**interim** *adj* **:** done, made, or occurring for an interim **:** TEMPORARY, PROVISIONAL

in·ter·ion·ic \ˌint-ə-(ˌ)rī-ˈän-ik\ *adj* **:** situated or acting between ions <~ distance>

1**in·te·ri·or** \in-ˈtir-ē-ər\ *adj* [MF & L; MF, fr. L, compar. of (assumed) OL *interus* inward, on the inside; akin to L *inter*] **1 :** lying, occurring, or functioning within the limits **:** INNER **2 :** lying away or remote from the border or shore **3 :** belonging to the inner constitution or concealed nature of something <~ meaning of a poem> **4 :** belonging to mental or spiritual life <a simple ~ piety> — **in·te·ri·or·i·ty** \(ˌ)in-ˌtir-ē-ˈȯr-ət-ē, -ˈär-\ *n* — **in·te·ri·or·ly** \in-ˈtir-ē-ər-lē\ *adv*

2**interior** *n* **1 :** the internal or inner part of a thing **:** INSIDE **2 :** the interior part (as of a country or island) **3 :** the inner or spiritual nature **:** CHARACTER **4 :** the internal affairs of a state or nation **5 :** a representation of the interior of a building

interior decoration *n* **:** INTERIOR DESIGN

interior decorator *n* **1 :** INTERIOR DESIGNER **2 :** one who supplies house furnishings **3 :** one who paints or wallpapers architectural interiors

interior design *n* **:** the art or practice of planning and supervising the design and execution of architectural interiors and their furnishings

interior designer *n* **:** one who specializes in interior design

in·te·ri·or·ize \in-ˈtir-ē-ə-ˌrīz\ *vt* **-ized; -iz·ing :** to make interior; *esp* **:** to make a part of one's own inner being or mental structure — **in·te·ri·or·iza·tion** \-ˌtir-ē-ə-rə-ˈzā-shən\ *n*

interior monologue *n* **:** a usu. extended representation in monologue of a fictional character's sequence of thought and feeling

interj *abbr* interjection

in·ter·ject \ˌint-ər-ˈjekt\ *vt* [L *interjectus,* pp. of *intericere,* fr. *inter-* + *jacere* to throw — more at JET] **:** to throw in between or among other things **:** INTERPOLATE <~ a remark> ***syn*** see INTRODUCE — **in·ter·jec·tor** \-ˈjek-tər\ *n* — **in·ter·jec·to·ry** \-t(ə-)rē\ *adj*

in·ter·jec·tion \ˌint-ər-ˈjek-shən\ *n* **1 a** : the act of uttering exclamations : EJACULATION **b** : the act of putting in between : INTERPOSITION **2** : something that is interjected or that interrupts **3 a** : an ejaculatory word (as *Wonderful*) or form of speech (as *ah*) **b** : a cry or inarticulate utterance (as *ouch*) expressing an emotion

in·ter·jec·tion·al \-shnəl, -shən-ᵊl\ *adj* **1** : thrown in between other words : PARENTHETICAL **2** : of, relating to, or constituting an interjection : EJACULATORY — **in·ter·jec·tion·al·ly** \-ē\ *adv*

in·ter·lace \ˌint-ər-ˈlās\ *vb* [ME *entrelacen,* fr. MF *entrelacer,* fr. OF *entrelacier,* fr. *entre-* inter- + *lacier* to lace] *vt* **1** : to unite by or as if by lacing together : INTERWEAVE **2** : to vary by alternation or intermixture : INTERSPERSE <narrative *interlaced* with anecdotes> ~ *vi* : to cross one another as if woven together : INTERTWINE — **in·ter·lace·ment** \-ˈlā-smənt\ *n*

in·ter·lam·i·nate \-ˈlam-ə-ˌnāt\ *vt* **1** : to insert between laminae **2** : to arrange in alternate laminae — **in·ter·lam·i·na·tion** \-ˌlam-ə-ˈnā-shən\ *n*

in·ter·lard \ˌint-ər-ˈlärd\ *vt* [MF *entrelarder,* fr. OF, fr. *entre* inter- + *larder* to lard, fr. *lard,* n.] : to intersperse something often foreign or irrelevant into <text ~*ed* with photographs>

in·ter·lay·er \ˈint-ər-ˌlā-ər, -ˌle(-ə)r\ *n* : a layer placed between other layers — **in·ter·lay·er·ing** \ˌint-ər-ˈlā-ə-riŋ, -ˈle-ə-\ *n*

¹**in·ter·leaf** \ˌint-ər-ˈlēf\ *vt* : INTERLEAVE

²**in·ter·leaf** \ˈint-ər-ˌlēf\ *n* **1** : a usu. blank leaf inserted between two leaves of a book (as for protecting color plates) **2** : SLIP SHEET

in·ter·leave \ˌint-ər-ˈlēv\ *vt* **-leaved; -leav·ing 1 a** : to equip with an interleaf **b** : SLIP-SHEET **2** : INTERLAMINATE **3** : to arrange in or as if in alternate layers

in·ter·li·brary \-ˈlī-ˌbrer-ē\ *adj* : taking place between libraries <an ~ loan>

¹**in·ter·line** \ˌint-ər-ˈlīn\ *vt* [ME *enterlinen,* fr. ML *interlineare,* fr. L *inter-* + *linea* line] : to insert between lines already written or printed — **in·ter·lin·ea·tion** \-ˌlin-ē-ˈā-shən\ *n*

²**interline** *vt* [ME *interlinen,* fr. *inter-* + *linen* to line] : to provide (a garment) with an interlining

³**interline** *adj* : relating to, involving, or carried by two or more transportation lines

¹**in·ter·lin·ear** \ˌint-ər-ˈlin-ē-ər\ *adj* [ME *interliniare,* fr. ML *interlinearis,* fr. L *inter-* + *linea* line] **1** : inserted between lines already written or printed **2** : written or printed in different languages or texts in alternate lines — **in·ter·lin·ear·ly** *adv*

²**interlinear** *n* : a book having interlinear matter; *esp* : a book in a foreign language with interlinear translation

in·ter·lin·ing \ˈint-ər-ˌlī-niŋ\ *n* : a lining (as of a coat) sewn between the ordinary lining and the outside fabric

in·ter·link \ˌint-ər-ˈliŋk\ *vt* : to link together — **in·ter·link** \ˈint-ər-ˌliŋk\ *n*

in·ter·lo·cal \ˌint-ər-ˈlō-kəl\ *adj* : existing between localities

in·ter·lock \ˌint-ər-ˈläk\ *vi* : to become engaged or interrelated with one another ~ *vt* **1** : to lock together : UNITE **2** : to connect so that motion of any part is constrained by another; *esp* : to arrange the connections of (as railroad signals) to ensure movement in proper sequence — **in·ter·lock** \ˈint-ər-ˌläk\ *n* — **in·ter·lock·er** \ˌint-ər-ˈläk-ər\ *n*

in·ter·lo·cu·tion \ˌint-ər-lō-ˈkyü-shən\ *n* [L *interlocution-, interlocutio,* fr. *interlocutus,* pp. of *interloqui* to speak between, fr. *inter-* + *loqui* to speak] : interchange of speech : CONVERSATION

in·ter·loc·u·tor \ˌint-ər-ˈläk-yət-ər\ *n* **1** : one who takes part in dialogue or conversation **2** : a man in the middle of the line in a minstrel show who questions the end men and acts as leader

in·ter·loc·u·to·ry \-ˌtōr-ē, -ˌtȯr-\ *adj* : pronounced during the progress of a legal action and having only provisional force <~ decree>

in·ter·lope \ˌint-ər-ˈlōp, ˈint-ər-ˌ\ *vi* **-loped; -lop·ing** [prob. back-formation fr. *interloper,* fr. *inter-* + *-loper* (akin to MD *lopen* to run, OE *hlēapan* to leap) — more at LEAP] **1** : to encroach on the rights (as in trade) of others **2** : INTRUDE, INTERFERE — **in·ter·lop·er** *n*

in·ter·lude \ˈint-ər-ˌlüd\ *n* [ME *enterlude,* fr. ML *interludium,* fr. L *inter-* + *ludus* play — more at LUDICROUS] **1 a** : a light or farcical entertainment presented between the acts of a mystery or morality play or at a fete **b** : a farce or comedy derived from these entertainments **2** : a performance or entertainment between the acts of a play **3** : an intervening or interruptive period, space, or event : INTERVAL **4** : a musical composition inserted between the parts of a longer composition, a drama, or a religious service

in·ter·lu·nar \ˌint-ər-ˈlü-nər\ *also* **in·ter·lu·na·ry** \-nə-rē\ *adj* [prob. fr. MF *interlunaire,* fr. L *interlunium* interlunary period, fr. *inter-* + *luna* moon — more at LUNAR] : relating to the interval between old and new moon when the moon is invisible

in·ter·mar·riage \ˌint-ər-ˈmar-ij\ *n* **1** : marriage between members of different groups **2** : ENDOGAMY 1

in·ter·mar·ry \-ˈmar-ē\ *vi* **1 a** : to marry each other **b** : to marry within a group **2** : to become connected by marriage between members

in·ter·med·dle \ˌint-ər-ˈmed-ᵊl\ *vi* [ME *entermedlen,* fr. MF *entremedler,* fr. OF, fr. *entre-* inter- + *medler* to mix — more at MEDDLE] : to meddle impertinently and officiously and usu. so as to interfere ***syn*** see MEDDLE — **in·ter·med·dler** \-ˈmed-lər, -ᵊl-ər\ *n*

in·ter·me·di·a·cy \ˌint-ər-ˈmēd-ē-ə-sē\ *n* **1** : the act or action of intermediating **2** : the quality or state of being intermediate

¹**in·ter·me·di·ary** \ˌint-ər-ˈmēd-ē-ˌer-ē\ *adj* **1** : INTERMEDIATE **2** : acting as a mediator <an ~ agent>

²**intermediary** *n, pl* **-ar·ies 1 a** : MEDIATOR, GO-BETWEEN **b** : MEDIUM, MEANS **2** : an intermediate form or stage

¹**in·ter·me·di·ate** \ˌint-ər-ˈmēd-ē-ˌāt\ *vi* [ML *intermediatus,* pp. of *intermediare,* fr. L *inter-* + LL *mediare* to mediate] **1** : INTERPOSE, INTERVENE **2** : to act as an intermediate

²**in·ter·me·di·ate** \-ē-ət\ *adj* [ML *intermediatus,* fr. L *intermedius,* fr. *inter-* + *medius* mid, middle — more at MID] **1** : being or occurring at the middle place, stage, or degree or between extremes **2** : of or relating to an intermediate school <an ~ curriculum> — **in·ter·me·di·ate·ly** *adv* — **in·ter·me·di·ate·ness** *n*

³**in·ter·me·di·ate** \-ē-ət\ *n* **1** : an intermediate term, object, or class **2** : MEDIATOR, GO-BETWEEN **3** : a chemical compound formed as an intermediate step between the starting material and the final product **4** : an automobile larger than a compact but smaller than a full-sized automobile

intermediate host *n* **1** : a host which is normally used by a parasite in the course of its life cycle and in which it may multiply asexually but not sexually **2 a** : RESERVOIR 3 **b** : VECTOR

intermediate school *n* **1** : JUNIOR HIGH SCHOOL **2** : a school usu. comprising grades 4-6

in·ter·me·di·a·tion \ˌint-ər-ˌmēd-ē-ˈā-shən\ *n* : the act of coming between : INTERVENTION, MEDIATION

in·ter·me·din \ˌint-ər-ˈmēd-ᵊn\ *n* : a hormone secreted by the intermediate part or anterior lobe of the pituitary body that induces expansion of vertebrate chromatophores

in·ter·ment \in-ˈtər-mənt\ *n* : the act or ceremony of interring

in·ter·me·tal·lic \ˌint-ər-mə-ˈtal-ik\ *adj* : composed of two or more metals or of a metal and a nonmetal; *esp* : being an alloy having a characteristic crystal structure and usu. a definite composition — **intermetallic** *n*

in·ter·mez·zo \ˌint-ər-ˈmets-(ˌ)ō, -ˈmedz-\ *n, pl* **-zi** \-(ˌ)ē\ *or* **-zos** [It, deriv. of L *intermedius* intermediate] **1** : a short light entr'acte **2 a** : a movement coming between the major sections of an extended musical work (as an opera) **b** : a short independent instrumental composition

in·ter·mi·na·ble \(ˈ)in-ˈtərm-(ə-)nə-bəl\ *adj* [ME, fr. LL *interminabilis,* fr. L *in-* + *terminare* to terminate] : having or seeming to have no end; *esp* : wearisomely protracted <an ~ sermon> — **in·ter·mi·na·ble·ness** *n* — **in·ter·mi·na·bly** \-blē\ *adv*

in·ter·min·gle \ˌint-ər-ˈmiŋ-gəl\ *vb* : INTERMIX

in·ter·mis·sion \ˌint-ər-ˈmish-ən\ *n* [L *intermission-, intermissio,* fr. *intermissus,* pp. of *intermittere*] **1** : the act of intermitting : the state of being intermitted **2** : an intervening period of time (as between acts of a performance or paroxysms of a disease) ***syn*** see PAUSE

in·ter·mit \-ˈmit\ *vb* **-mit·ted; -mit·ting** [L *intermittere,* fr. *inter-* + *mittere* to send — more at SMITE] *vt* : to cause to cease for a time or at intervals : DISCONTINUE ~ *vi* : to be intermittent ***syn*** see DEFER — **in·ter·mit·ter** *n*

in·ter·mit·tent \-ˈmit-ᵊnt\ *adj* [L *intermittent-, intermittens,* prp. of *intermittere*] : coming and going at intervals : not continuous <~ rain> — **in·ter·mit·tence** \-ᵊn(t)s\ *n* — **in·ter·mit·tent·ly** *adv*

syn INTERMITTENT, RECURRENT, PERIODIC, ALTERNATE *shared meaning element* : occurring or appearing in interrupted sequence. INTERMITTENT stresses breaks in continuity <an *intermittent* correspondence with a distant relative> <*intermittent* conflict> RECURRENT stresses repetition; thus, a *recurrent* problem can be counted on to come up again and again; a *recurrent* fever tends to reappear at more or less regular intervals. PERIODIC implies recurrence at regular intervals <the *periodic* reappearance of a comet> ALTERNATE may apply to two contrasting things appearing repeatedly one after the other <*alternate* fits of false confidence and secret misgivings —Mildred S. Fenner> or to every second member of a series <the club meets on *alternate* Tuesdays> ***ant*** incessant, continued

intermittent current *n* : an electric current that flows and ceases to flow at intervals but is not reversed

in·ter·mix \ˌint-ər-ˈmiks\ *vb* [back-formation fr. obs. *intermixt* (intermingled), fr. L *intermixtus,* pp. of *intermiscēre* to intermix, fr. *inter-* + *miscēre* to mix — more at MIX] *vt* : to mix together ~ *vi* : to become mixed together — **in·ter·mix·ture** \-ˈmiks-chər\ *n*

in·ter·mo·lec·u·lar \ˌint-ər-mə-ˈlek-yə-lər\ *adj* : existing or acting between molecules — **in·ter·mo·lec·u·lar·ly** *adv*

¹**in·tern** *or* **in·terne** \in-ˈtərn, ˈin-ˌ\ *adj* [MF *interne,* fr. L *internus*] *archaic* : INTERNAL

²**in·tern** \ˈin-ˌtərn, in-ˈ\ *vt* : to confine or impound esp. during a war <~ enemy aliens>

³**in·tern** *or* **in·terne** \ˈin-ˌtərn\ *n* [F *interne,* fr. *interne,* adj.] : an advanced student or graduate usu. in a professional field (as medicine or teaching) gaining supervised practical experience (as in a hospital or classroom) — **in·tern·ship** \-ˌship\ *n*

⁴**in·tern** \ˈin-ˌtərn\ *vi* : to act as an intern

in·ter·nal \in-ˈtərn-ᵊl\ *adj* [L *internus;* akin to L *inter* between] **1 a** : existing or situated within the limits or surface of something **b (1)** : situated near the inside of the body **(2)** : situated on the side toward the median plane of the body **2** : capable of being applied through the stomach by being swallowed <an ~ remedy> **3** : relating or belonging to or existing within the mind **4** : INTRINSIC, INHERENT <~ evidence of forgery in a document> **5** : present or arising within an organism or one of its parts <~ stimulus> **6** : of or relating to the domestic affairs of a state <~ strife> — **in·ter·nal·i·ty** \ˌin-ˌtər-ˈnal-ət-ē\ *n* — **in·ter·nal·ly** \in-ˈtərn-ᵊl-ē\ *adv*

internal–combustion engine *n* : a heat engine in which the combustion that generates the heat takes place inside the engine proper instead of in a furnace

in·ter·nal·ize \in-ˈtərn-ᵊl-ˌīz\ *vt* **-ized; -iz·ing** : to give a subjective character to; *specif* : to incorporate (as values or patterns of culture) within the self as conscious or subconscious guiding principles through learning or socialization — **in·ter·nal·iza·tion** \-ˌtərn-ᵊl-ə-ˈzā-shən\ *n*

internal medicine *n* : a branch of medicine that deals with the diagnosis and treatment of nonsurgical diseases

internal respiration *n* : exchange of gases between the cells of the body and the blood by way of the fluid bathing the cells
internal rhyme *n* : rhyme between a word within a line and another either at the end of the same line or within another line
internal secretion *n* : HORMONE
1in·ter·na·tion·al \ˌint-ər-ˈnash-nəl, -ən-ᵊl\ *adj* **1** : affecting or involving two or more nations <~ trade> **2** : of, relating to, or constituting a group or association having members in two or more nations <~ movement> **3** : of or relating to one whose activities extend across national boundaries <an ~ celebrity> — **in·ter·na·tion·al·i·ty** \-ˌnash-ə-ˈnal-ət-ē\ *n* — **in·ter·na·tion·al·ly** \-ˈnash-nə-lē, -ən-ᵊl-ē\ *adv*
2in·ter·na·tion·al \-ˈnash-nəl, -ən-ᵊl, *in sense a often* -ˌnash-ə-ˈnal, -ˈnäl\ *n* : an organized group that transcends national limits: as **a** *also* **in·ter·na·tio·nale** \-ˌnash-ə-ˈnal, -ˈnäl\ : one of several socialist or communist organizations of international scope **b** : a labor union having locals in more than one country
international date line *n* : DATE LINE
in·ter·na·tion·al·ism \-ˈnash-nəl-ˌiz-əm, -ˈnash-ən-ᵊl-\ *n* **1** : international character, principles, interests, or outlook **2 a** : a policy of cooperation among nations and esp. of the development of close international political and economic relations **b** : an attitude or belief favoring such a policy — **in·ter·na·tion·al·ist** \-əst\ *n or adj*
in·ter·na·tion·al·ize \ˌint-ər-ˈnash-nəl-ˌīz, -ˈnash-ən-ᵊl-\ *vt* : to make international; *specif* : to place under international control — **in·ter·na·tion·al·iza·tion** \-ˌnash-nəl-ə-ˈzā-shən, -ən-ᵊl-\ *n*
international law *n* : a body of rules that control or affect the rights of nations in their relations with each other
International Phonetic Alphabet *n* : IPA
international pitch *n* : a tuning standard of 440 vibrations per second for A above middle C
international relations *n pl but sing in constr* : a branch of political science concerned with relations between nations and primarily with foreign policies
International Scientific Vocabulary *n* : a part of the vocabulary of the sciences and other specialized studies that consists of words or other linguistic forms current in two or more languages and differing from New Latin in being adapted to the structure of the individual languages in which they appear — abbr. *ISV*
international unit *n* : a quantity of a biological (as a vitamin) that produces a particular biological effect agreed upon as an international standard
international volt *n* : 2VOLT 2
internatl *abbr* international
in·ter·ne·cine \ˌint-ər-ˈnes-ˌēn, -ˈnēs-ˌīn, -ᵊn; in-ˈtər-nə-ˌsēn, -sən; ˌint-ər-nə-ˈsēn\ *adj* [L *internecinus,* fr. *internecare* to destroy, kill, fr. *inter-* + *necare* to kill, fr. *nec-, nex* violent death — more at NOXIOUS] **1** : marked by slaughter : DEADLY; *esp* : mutually destructive **2** : of, relating to, or involving conflict within a group <bitter ~ feuds>
in·tern·ee \(ˌ)in-ˌtər-ˈnē\ *n* : an interned person
in·ter·neu·ron \ˌint-ər-ˈn(y)ü-ˌrän, -ˈn(y)u̇(ə)r-ˌän\ *n* : an internuncial neuron — **in·ter·neu·ro·nal** \-ˈn(y)u̇r-ən-ᵊl, -nyu̇-ˈrōn-\ *adj*
in·ter·nist \ˈin-ˌtər-nəst\ *n* : a specialist in internal medicine esp. as distinguished from a surgeon
in·tern·ment \in-ˈtərn-mənt\ *n* : the act of interning : the state of being interned
in·ter·node \ˈint-ər-ˌnōd\ *n* [L *internodium,* fr. *inter-* + *nodus* knot] : an interval or part between two nodes (as of a stem) — **in·ter·nod·al** \ˌint-ər-ˈnōd-ᵊl\ *adj*
in·ter·nu·cle·ar \ˌint-ər-ˈn(y)ü-klē-ər\ *adj* : situated or occurring between atomic or biological nuclei
in·ter·nun·ci·al \ˌint-ər-ˈnən(t)-sē-əl, -ˈnu̇n(t)-\ *adj* **1** : of or relating to an internuncio **2** : serving to link sensory and motor neurons — **in·ter·nun·ci·al·ly** \-ə-lē\ *adv*
in·ter·nun·cio \ˌint-ər-ˈnən(t)-sē-ˌō, -ˈnu̇n(t)-\ *n* [It *internunzio,* fr. L *internuntius, internuncius,* fr. *inter-* + *nuntius, nuncius* messenger] **1** : a messenger between two parties : GO-BETWEEN **2** : a papal legate of lower rank than a nuncio
in·tero·cep·tive \ˌint-ə-rō-ˈsep-tiv\ *adj* [*inter-* (as in *interior*) + *-o-* + *-ceptive* (as in *receptive*)] : of, relating to, or being stimuli arising within the body and esp. the viscera
in·tero·cep·tor \-tər\ *n* : a sensory receptor excited by interoceptive stimuli
in·ter·of·fice \ˌint-ə-ˈrȯf-əs, -ˈräf-\ *adj* : taking place or communicating between or in the offices of an organization
in·ter·pel·late \ˌint-ər-ˈpel-ˌāt, -pə-ˈlāt\ *vt* **-lat·ed; -lat·ing** [L *interpellatus,* pp. of *interpellare* to interrupt, fr. *inter-* + *-pellare* (fr. *pellere* to drive)] : to question (as a foreign minister) formally concerning an official action or policy or personal conduct — **in·ter·pel·la·tion** \-pə-ˈlā-shən\ *n* — **in·ter·pel·la·tor** \-ˈpel-ˌāt-ər, -pə-ˈlāt-\ *n*
in·ter·pen·e·trate \ˌint-ər-ˈpen-ə-ˌtrāt\ *vt* : to penetrate between, within, or throughout : PERMEATE ~ *vi* : to penetrate mutually — **in·ter·pen·e·tra·tion** \-ˌpen-ə-ˈtrā-shən\ *n*
in·ter·per·son·al \-ˈpərs-nəl, -ᵊn-əl\ *adj* : being, relating to, or involving relations between persons — **in·ter·per·son·al·ly** \-ē\ *adv*
in·ter·phase \ˈint-ər-ˌfāz\ *n* : the interval between the end of one mitotic or meiotic division and the beginning of another
in·ter·plan·e·tary \ˌint-ər-ˈplan-ə-ˌter-ē\ *adj* : existing, carried on, or operating between planets <~ space>
in·ter·plant \-ˈplant\ *vt* : to plant a crop between (plants of another kind); *also* : to set out young trees among (existing growth)
in·ter·play \ˈint-ər-ˌplā\ *n* : INTERACTION — **in·ter·play** \ˌint-ər-ˈ, ˈint-ər-ˌ\ *vi*
in·ter·plead \ˌint-ər-ˈplēd\ *vi* [AF *enterpleder,* fr. *enter-* inter- + *pleder* to plead, fr. OF *plaidier* — more at PLEAD] : to go to trial with each other in order to determine a right on which the action of a third party depends
1in·ter·plead·er \-ər\ *n* [AF *enterpleder,* fr. *enterpleder,* v.] : a proceeding to enable a person to compel parties making the same claim against him to litigate the matter between themselves
2interpleader *n* : one that interpleads
in·ter·po·late \in-ˈtər-pə-ˌlāt\ *vb* **-lat·ed; -lat·ing** [L *interpolatus,* pp. of *interpolare* to refurbish, alter, interpolate, fr. *inter-* + *-polare* (fr. *polire* to polish)] *vt* **1 a** : to alter or corrupt (as a text) by inserting new or foreign matter **b** : to insert (words) into a text or into a conversation **2** : to insert between other things or parts : INTERCALATE **3** : to estimate values of (a function) between two known values ~ *vi* : to make insertions ***syn*** see INTRODUCE — **in·ter·po·la·tion** \-ˌtər-pə-ˈlā-shən\ *n* — **in·ter·po·la·tive** \-ˈtər-pə-ˌlāt-iv\ *adj* — **in·ter·po·la·tor** \-ˌlāt-ər\ *n*
in·ter·pose \ˌint-ər-ˈpōz\ *vb* **-posed; -pos·ing** [MF *interposer,* fr. L *interponere* (perf. indic. *interposui*), fr. *inter-* + *ponere* to put — more at POSITION] *vt* **1 a** : to place in an intervening position **b** : to put (oneself) between : INTRUDE **2** : to put forth by way of interference or intervention **3** : to introduce or throw in between the parts of a conversation or argument ~ *vi* **1** : to be or come between **2** : to step in between parties at variance : INTERVENE **3** : INTERRUPT — **in·ter·pos·er** *n*
syn **1** see INTRODUCE
2 INTERPOSE, INTERFERE, INTERVENE, MEDIATE, INTERCEDE *shared meaning element* : to come or go between
in·ter·po·si·tion \-pə-ˈzish-ən\ *n* **1 a** : the act of interposing **b** : the action of a state whereby its sovereignty is placed between its citizens and the federal government **2** : something interposed
in·ter·pret \in-ˈtər-prət, *rapid* -pət\ *vb* [ME *interpreten,* fr. MF&L; MF *interpreter,* fr. L *interpretari,* fr. *interpret-, interpres* agent, negotiator, interpreter] *vt* **1** : to explain or tell the meaning of : present in understandable terms **2** : to conceive in the light of individual belief, judgment, or circumstance : CONSTRUE **3** : to represent by means of art : bring to realization by performance <~*s* a role> ~ *vi* : to act as an interpreter between speakers of different languages ***syn*** see EXPLAIN — **in·ter·pret·abil·i·ty** \-ˌtər-prət-ə-ˈbil-ət-ē, -pət-\ *n* — **in·ter·pret·able** \-ˈtər-prət-ə-bəl, -pət-\ *adj* — **in·ter·pret·er** \-ər\ *n*
in·ter·pre·ta·tion \in-ˌtər-prə-ˈtā-shən, *rapid* -pə-\ *n* **1** : the act or the result of interpreting : EXPLANATION **2** : an instance of artistic interpretation in performance or adaptation — **in·ter·pre·ta·tion·al** \-shnəl, -shən-ᵊl\ *adj*
in·ter·pre·ta·tive \in-ˈtər-prə-ˌtāt-iv, *rapid* -pə-\ *adj* : of, relating to, or concerning interpretation : EXPLANATORY — **in·ter·pre·ta·tive·ly** *adv*
in·ter·pret·er \in-ˈtər-prət-ər, *rapid* -pət-\ *n* **1** : one that interprets; *esp* : a person who translates orally for parties conversing in different languages **2** : a computer program that translates an instruction into machine language and executes it before going to the next instruction
in·ter·pre·tive \-prət-iv, *rapid* -pət-\ *adj* : INTERPRETATIVE — **in·ter·pre·tive·ly** *adv*
in·ter·pu·pil·lary \ˌint-ər-ˈpyü-pə-ˌler-ē\ *adj* : extending between the pupils of the eyes; *also* : extending between the centers of a pair of spectacle lenses <~ distance>
in·ter·ra·cial \-ˈrā-shəl\ *adj* : of, involving, or designed for members of different races
interred *past of* INTER
in·ter·reg·num \ˌint-ə-ˈreg-nəm\ *n, pl* **-nums** *or* **-na** \-nə\ [L, fr. *inter-* + *regnum* reign — more at REIGN] **1** : the time during which a throne is vacant between two successive reigns or regimes **2** : a period during which the normal functions of government or control are suspended **3** : a lapse or pause in a continuous series
in·ter·re·late \ˌint-ə(r)-ri-ˈlāt\ *vt* : to bring into mutual relation ~ *vi* : to have mutual relationship — **in·ter·re·la·tion** \-ˈlā-shən\ *n* — **in·ter·re·la·tion·ship** \-ˌship\ *n*
in·ter·re·lat·ed \-ˈlāt-əd\ *adj* : having a mutual or reciprocal relation or parallelism — **in·ter·re·lat·ed·ly** *adv* — **in·ter·re·lat·ed·ness** *n*
in·ter·re·li·gious \ˌint-ə(r)-ri-ˈlij-əs\ *adj* : existing between or involving different religions or members of different religions
interring *pres part of* INTER
in·ter·ro·bang *also* **in·tera·bang** \in-ˈter-ə-ˌbaŋ\ *n* [*interro*gation point + *bang* (printers' slang for *exclamation point*)] : a punctuation mark ‽ designed for use esp. at the end of an exclamatory rhetorical question
interrog *abbr* interrogative
in·ter·ro·gate \in-ˈter-ə-ˌgāt\ *vt* **-gat·ed; -gat·ing** [L *interrogatus,* pp. of *interrogare,* fr. *inter-* + *rogare* to ask — more at RIGHT] **1** : to question formally and systematically **2** : to give or send out a signal to (as a transponder or computer) for triggering an appropriate response ***syn*** see ASK — **in·ter·ro·ga·tion** \-ˌter-ə-ˈgā-shən\ *n* — **in·ter·ro·ga·tion·al** \-shnəl, -shən-ᵊl\ *adj*
interrogation point *n* : QUESTION MARK
1in·ter·rog·a·tive \ˌint-ə-ˈräg-ət-iv\ *adj* **1 a** : having the form or force of a question **b** : used in a question **2** : INQUISITIVE, QUESTIONING — **in·ter·rog·a·tive·ly** *adv*
2interrogative *n* **1** : an interrogative utterance **2** : a word (as *who, what, which*) or a particle (as Latin *-ne*) used in asking questions
in·ter·ro·ga·tor \in-ˈter-ə-ˌgāt-ər\ *n* **1** : one that interrogates **2** : a radio transmitter and receiver for sending out a signal that triggers a transponder and for receiving and displaying the reply
1in·ter·rog·a·to·ry \ˌint-ə-ˈräg-ə-ˌtōr-ē, -ˌtȯr-\ *n, pl* **-ries** : a formal question or inquiry; *esp* : a written question required to be answered under direction of a court
2interrogatory *adj* : INTERROGATIVE
in·ter·ro·gee \in-ˌter-ə-ˈgē\ *n* : one who is interrogated
1in·ter·rupt \ˌint-ə-ˈrəpt\ *vb* [ME *interrupten,* fr. L *interruptus,* pp. of *interrumpere,* fr. *inter-* + *rumpere* to break — more at REAVE] *vt* **1** : to stop or hinder by breaking in **2** : to break the uniformity or continuity of ~ *vi* : to break in upon an action; *esp* : to break in with questions or remarks while another is speaking — **in·ter·rupt·ible** \-ˈrəp-tə-bəl\ *adj* — **in·ter·rup·tion** \-ˈrəp-shən\ *n* — **in·ter·rup·tive** \-ˈrəp-tiv\ *adj*
2in·ter·rupt \ˌint-ə-ˈrəpt, ˈint-ə-ˌ\ *n* : a signal to a computer that stops the execution of an ongoing program while a higher priority program is executed; *also* : a circuit that conveys such a signal

in·ter·rupt·er \ˌint-ə-ˈrəp-tər\ *n* : one that interrupts; *esp* : a device for periodically and automatically interrupting an electric current

in·ter·scho·las·tic \ˌint-ər-skə-ˈlas-tik\ *adj* : existing or carried on between schools <~ athletics>

in·ter se \ˌint-ər-ˈsā, -ˈsē\ *adv or adj* [L] : among or between themselves

in·ter·sect \ˌint-ər-ˈsekt\ *vb* [L *intersectus,* pp. of *intersecare,* fr. *inter-* + *secare* to cut — more at SAW] *vt* : to pierce or divide by passing through or across : CROSS ~ *vi* **1** : to meet and cross at a point **2** : to share a common area : OVERLAP

in·ter·sec·tion \ˌint-ər-ˈsek-shən, *esp in sense 2* ˈint-ər-ˌ\ *n* **1** : the act or process of intersecting **2** : a place or area where two or more things (as streets) intersect **3** : the set of elements common to two sets; *esp* : the set of points common to two geometric configurations

in·ter·ser·vice \ˌint-ər-ˈsər-vəs\ *adj* : existing between or relating to two or more of the armed services <~ rivalry>

in·ter·ses·sion \ˈint-ər-ˌsesh-ən\ *n* : a period between two academic sessions or terms sometimes utilized for brief concentrated courses

in·ter·sex \ˈint-ər-ˌseks\ *n* [ISV] : an intersexual individual

in·ter·sex·u·al \ˌint-ər-ˈseksh-(ə-)wəl, -ˈsek-shəl\ *adj* [ISV] **1** : existing between sexes <~ hostility> **2** : intermediate in sexual characters between a typical male and a typical female — **in·ter·sex·u·al·i·ty** \-ˌsek-shə-ˈwal-ət-ē\ *n* — **in·ter·sex·u·al·ly** \-ˈseksh-(ə-)wə-lē, -(ə-)lē\ *adv*

[1]**in·ter·space** \ˈint-ər-ˌspās\ *n* : an intervening space : INTERVAL

[2]**in·ter·space** \ˌint-ər-ˈspās\ *vt* **1** : to separate (as printed letters) by spaces **2** : to occupy or fill the space between

in·ter·spe·cif·ic \ˌint-ər-spi-ˈsif-ik\ *or* **in·ter·spe·cies** \-ˈspē-(ˌ)shēz, -(ˌ)sēz\ *adj* : existing or arising between species <~ hybrid>

in·ter·sperse \ˌint-ər-ˈspərs\ *vt* **-spersed; -spers·ing** [L *interspersus* interspersed, fr. *inter-* + *sparsus* pp. of *spargere* to scatter — more at SPARK] **1** : to insert at intervals among other things <*interspersing* drawings throughout the text> **2** : to place something at intervals in or among <the street was full of country folk, *interspersed* with visitors —Mary Webb> — **in·ter·sper·sion** \-ˈspər-zhən, -shən\ *n*

in·ter·sta·di·al \ˌint-ər-ˈstād-ē-əl\ *n* [ISV *inter-* + NL *stadium* stage, phase] : a subdivision within a glacial stage marking a temporary retreat of the ice

in·ter·state \ˌint-ər-ˈstāt\ *adj* : of, connecting, or existing between two or more states esp. of the U.S. <an ~ highway>

in·ter·stel·lar \-ˈstel-ər\ *adj* : located or taking place among the stars

in·ter·ster·ile \-ˈster-əl, *chiefly Brit* -ˌīl\ *adj* : incapable of producing offspring by interbreeding — **in·ter·ste·ril·i·ty** \-stə-ˈril-ət-ē\ *n*

in·ter·stice \in-ˈtər-stəs\ *n, pl* **-stic·es** \-stə-ˌsēz, -stə-səz\ [F, fr. LL *interstitium,* fr. L *interstitus,* pp. of *intersistere* to stand still in the middle, fr. *inter-* + *sistere* to come to a stand; akin to L *stare* to stand] : a space that intervenes between things : INTERVAL; *esp* : one between closely spaced things ***syn*** see APERTURE

in·ter·sti·tial \ˌint-ər-ˈstish-əl\ *adj* **1** : relating to or situated in the interstices **2 a** : situated within but not restricted to or characteristic of a particular organ or tissue — used esp. of fibrous tissue **b** : affecting the interstitial tissues of an organ or part **3** : being or relating to a crystalline compound in which usu. small atoms or ions of a nonmetal occupy holes between the larger metal atoms or ions in the crystal lattice — **in·ter·sti·tial·ly** \-ə-lē\ *adv*

in·ter·sub·jec·tive \ˌint-ər-səb-ˈjek-tiv\ *adj* **1** : involving or occurring between separate conscious minds <~ communication> **2** : accessible to or capable of being established for two or more subjects : OBJECTIVE — **in·ter·sub·jec·tive·ly** *adv* — **in·ter·sub·jec·tiv·i·ty** \-(ˌ)səb-ˌjek-ˈtiv-ət-ē\ *n*

in·ter·tes·ta·men·tal \-ˌtes-tə-ˈment-ᵊl\ *adj* : of, relating to, or forming the period of two centuries between the composition of the last book of the Old Testament and the first book of the New Testament

in·ter·tid·al \-ˈtīd-ᵊl\ *adj* : of, relating to, or being the part of the littoral zone above low-tide mark — **in·ter·tid·al·ly** \-ᵊl-ē\ *adv*

in·ter·tie \ˈint-ər-ˌtī\ *n* : an interconnection permitting passage of current between two or more electric utility systems

in·ter·till \ˌint-ər-ˈtil\ *vt* : to cultivate between the rows of (a crop) — **in·ter·till·age** \-ˈtil-ij\ *n*

in·ter·trop·i·cal \-ˈträp-i-kəl\ *adj* **1** : situated between or within the tropics **2** : relating to regions within the tropics : TROPICAL

in·ter·twine \-ˈtwīn\ *vt* : to unite by twining one with another ~ *vi* : to twine about one another; *also* : to become mutually involved — **in·ter·twine·ment** \-mənt\ *n*

in·ter·twist \-ˈtwist\ *vb* : INTERTWINE — **in·ter·twist** \ˈint-ər-ˌtwist\ *n*

in·ter·ur·ban \ˌint-ər-ˈər-bən\ *adj* : connecting cities or towns

in·ter·val \ˈint-ər-vəl\ *n* [ME *intervalle,* fr. MF, fr. L *intervallum* space between ramparts, interval, fr. *inter-* + *vallum* rampart — more at WALL] **1 a** : a space of time between events or states : PAUSE **b** *Brit* : INTERMISSION **2 a** : a space between objects, units, or states **b** : difference in pitch between tones **3** : a set of real numbers between two numbers either including or excluding one or both of them; *also* : the set of real numbers greater or less than and including or excluding a real number

in·ter·vale \ˈint-ər-vəl, -ˌvāl\ *n* [obs. *intervale* interval] *chiefly NewEng* : BOTTOM 5

in·ter·val·om·e·ter \ˌint-ər-və-ˈläm-ət-ər\ *n* : a device that operates a control (as for a camera shutter) at regular intervals

in·ter·vene \ˌint-ər-ˈvēn\ *vi* **-vened; -ven·ing** [L *intervenire* to come between, fr. *inter-* + *venire* to come — more at COME] **1** : to enter or appear as an irrelevant or extraneous feature or circumstance **2** : to occur, fall, or come between points of time or events **3** : to come in or between by way of hindrance or modification <~ to settle a quarrel> **4** : to occur or lie between two things **5 a** : to become a third party to a legal proceeding begun by others for the protection of an alleged interest **b** : to interfere usu. by force or threat of force in another nation's internal affairs esp. to compel or prevent an action or to maintain or alter a condition ***syn*** see INTERPOSE — **in·ter·ven·tion** \-ˈven-chən\ *n*

in·ter·ve·nor \-ˈvē-nər, -ˌnȯ(ə)r\ *or* **in·ter·ven·er** \-ˈvē-nər\ *n* : one who intervenes; *esp* : one who intervenes as a third party in a legal proceeding

in·ter·ven·tion·ism \-ˈven-chə-ˌniz-əm\ *n* : the theory or practice of intervening; *specif* : governmental interference in economic affairs at home or in political affairs of another country — **in·ter·ven·tion·ist** \-ˈvench-(ə-)nəst\ *n or adj*

in·ter·ver·te·bral \ˌint-ər-ˈvərt-ə-brəl, -(ˌ)vər-ˈtē-\ *adj* : situated between vertebrae — **in·ter·ver·te·bral·ly** \-brə-lē\ *adv*

intervertebral disk *n* : one of the tough elastic disks that are interposed between the centra of adjoining vertebrae and that consist of an outer fibrous ring enclosing an inner pulpy nucleus

in·ter·view \ˈint-ər-ˌvyü\ *n* [MF *entrevue,* fr. *(s')entrevoir* to see one another, meet, fr. *entre-* inter- + *voir* to see — more at VIEW] **1** : a formal consultation usu. to evaluate qualifications (as of a prospective student or employee) **2 a** : a meeting at which information is obtained (as by a reporter, television commentator, or pollster) from a person **b** : a report or reproduction of information so obtained — **interview** *vt* — **in·ter·view·er** *n*

in·ter·view·ee \ˌint-ər-(ˌ)vyü-ˈē\ *n* : one who is interviewed

in·ter vi·vos \ˌint-ər-ˈvē-ˌvōs, -ˈvī-\ *adv or adj* [LL] : between living persons <transaction *inter vivos*>; *esp* : from one living person to another <*inter vivos* gifts> <property transferred *inter vivos*>

in·ter·vo·cal·ic \ˌint-ər-vō-ˈkal-ik\ *adj* : immediately preceded and immediately followed by a vowel

in·ter·war \ˌint-ər-ˌwȯ(ə)r\ *adj* : occurring or falling between wars <the ~ years>

in·ter·weave \ˌint-ər-ˈwēv\ *vb* **-wove** \-ˈwōv\ *also* **-weaved; -wo·ven** \-ˈwō-vən\ *also* **-weaved; -weav·ing** *vt* **1** : to weave together **2** : to intermingle or blend together <*interweaving* his own insights . . . with letters and memoirs —Phoebe Adams> ~ *vi* : INTERTWINE, INTERMINGLE — **in·ter·weave** \ˈint-ər-ˌwēv\ *n* — **in·ter·wo·ven** \ˌint-ər-ˈwō-vən\ *adj*

in·ter·zon·al \ˌint-ər-ˈzōn-ᵊl\ *or* **in·ter·zone** \-ˌzōn\ *adj* : occurring or carried on between zones <an ~ competition>

in·tes·ta·cy \in-ˈtes-tə-sē\ *n* : the quality or state of being or dying intestate

[1]**in·tes·tate** \in-ˈtes-ˌtāt, -tət\ *adj* [ME, fr. L *intestatus,* fr. *in-* + *testatus* testate] **1** : having made no valid will <he died ~> **2** : not disposed of by will <an ~ estate>

[2]**intestate** *n* : one who dies intestate

in·tes·ti·nal \in-ˈtes-tən-ᵊl, -ˈtes(t)-nəl\ *adj* **1** : of, relating to, or being the intestine **2** : affecting or occurring in the intestine; *also* : living in the intestine — **in·tes·ti·nal·ly** \-ē\ *adv*

intestinal fortitude *n* [euphemism for *guts*] : COURAGE, STAMINA

[1]**in·tes·tine** \in-ˈtes-tən\ *adj* [MF or L; MF *intestin,* fr. L *intestinus,* fr. *intus* within — more at ENT-] : INTERNAL; *specif* : of or relating to the internal affairs of a state or country <~ war>

[2]**intestine** *n* [MF *intestin,* fr. L *intestinum,* fr. neut. of *intestinus*] : the tubular part of the alimentary canal that extends from the stomach to the anus

in·ti·ma \ˈint-ə-mə\ *n, pl* **-mae** \-ˌmē, -ˌmī\ *or* **-mas** [NL, fr. L, fem. of *intimus*] : the innermost coat of an organ consisting usu. of an endothelial layer backed by connective tissue and elastic tissue — **in·ti·mal** \-məl\ *adj*

in·ti·ma·cy \ˈint-ə-mə-sē\ *n* : the state of being intimate : FAMILIARITY

[1]**in·ti·mate** \ˈint-ə-ˌmāt\ *vt* **-mat·ed; -mat·ing** [LL *intimatus,* pp. of *intimare* to put in, announce, fr. L *intimus* innermost, superl. of (assumed) OL *interus* inward — more at INTERIOR] **1** : to make known esp. publicly or formally : ANNOUNCE **2** : to communicate delicately and indirectly : HINT ***syn*** see SUGGEST — **in·ti·mat·er** *n* — **in·ti·ma·tion** \ˌint-ə-ˈmā-shən\ *n*

[2]**in·ti·mate** \ˈint-ə-mət\ *adj* [alter. of obs. *intime,* fr. L *intimus*] **1 a** : INTRINSIC, ESSENTIAL **b** : belonging to or characterizing one's deepest nature **2** : marked by very close association, contact, or familiarity <~ knowledge of the law> **3 a** : marked by a warm friendship developing through long association **b** : suggesting informal warmth or privacy <~ clubs> **4** : of a very personal or private nature — **in·ti·mate·ly** *adv* — **in·ti·mate·ness** *n*

[3]**in·ti·mate** \ˈint-ə-mət\ *n* : an intimate friend or confidant

in·tim·i·date \in-ˈtim-ə-ˌdāt\ *vt* **-dat·ed; -dat·ing** [ML *intimidatus,* pp. of *intimidare,* fr. L *in-* + *timidus* timid] : to make timid or fearful : FRIGHTEN; *esp* : to compel or deter by or as if by threats — **in·tim·i·da·tion** \-ˌtim-ə-ˈdā-shən\ *n* — **in·tim·i·da·tor** \-ˈtim-ə-ˌdāt-ər\ *n*

in·tim·i·da·to·ry \-ˈtim-ə-də-ˌtōr-ē, -ˌtȯr-\ *adj* : tending to intimidate

in·tinc·tion \in-ˈtiŋ(k)-shən\ *n* [LL *intinction-, intinctio* baptism, fr. L *intinctus,* pp. of *intingere* to dip in, fr. *in-* + *tingere* to dip, moisten — more at TINGE] : the administration of the sacrament of Communion by dipping the bread in the wine and giving both together to the communicant

in·tine \ˈin-ˌtēn\ *n* [prob. fr. G, fr. L *intus* within + NL *in-* fibrous tissue, fr. Gk *in-, is* tendon] : the inner mostly cellulose wall of a spore (as a pollen grain)

in·tit·ule \in-ˈtich-(ˌ)ü(ə)l\ *vt* **-uled; -ul·ing** [MF *intituler,* fr. LL *intitulare,* fr. L *in-* + *titulus* title] *Brit* : to furnish (as a legislative act) with a title or designation

intl *abbr* international

intnl *abbr* international

in·to \ˌin-tə(-w), ˈin-(ˌ)tü\ *prep* [ME, fr. OE *intō,* fr. [2]*in* + *tō* to] **1** — used as a function word to indicate entry, introduction,

ə abut ᵊ kitten ər further a back ā bake ä cot, cart
aú out ch chin e less ē easy g gift i trip ī life
j joke ŋ sing ō flow ȯ flaw ȯi coin th thin t͟h this
ü loot ú foot y yet yü few yú furious zh vision

insertion, or inclusion <came ~ the house> <enter ~ an alliance> **2 a :** to the state, condition, or form of <got ~ trouble> **b :** to the occupation, action, or possession of <go ~ farming> **c :** involved with <they were ~ hard drugs> **3** — used as a function word to indicate a period of time or an extent of space part of which is passed or occupied <far ~ the night> **4 :** in the direction of <looking ~ the sun> **5 :** to a position of contact with : AGAINST <ran ~ a wall>

in·tol·er·a·ble \(ˈ)in-ˈtäl-(ə-)rə-bəl, -ˈtäl-ər-bəl\ *adj* [ME, fr. L *intolerabilis,* fr. *in-* + *tolerabilis* tolerable] **1 :** not tolerable : UNBEARABLE <~ pain> **2 :** EXCESSIVE — **in·tol·er·a·bil·i·ty** \(ˌ)in-ˌtäl-(ə-)rə-ˈbil-ət-ē\ *n* — **in·tol·er·a·ble·ness** \(ˈ)in-ˈtäl-(ə-)rə-bəl-nəs, -ˈtäl-ər-bəl-\ *n* — **in·tol·er·a·bly** \-blē\ *adv*

in·tol·er·ance \(ˈ)in-ˈtäl(-ə)-rən(t)s\ *n* **:** the quality or state of being intolerant; *esp* **:** exceptional sensitivity (as to a drug)

in·tol·er·ant \-rənt\ *adj* **1 :** unable or unwilling to endure <a plant ~ of direct sunlight> <~ of criticism> **2 a :** unwilling to grant equal freedom of expression esp. in religious matters **b :** unwilling to grant or share social, political, or professional rights : BIGOTED — **in·tol·er·ant·ly** *adv* — **in·tol·er·ant·ness** *n*

in·to·nate \ˈin-tə-ˌnāt\ *vt* **-nat·ed; -nat·ing :** INTONE, UTTER

in·to·na·tion \ˌin-tə-ˈnā-shən, -(ˌ)tō-\ *n* **1 :** the act of intoning and esp. of chanting **2 :** something that is intoned; *specif* **:** the opening tones of a Gregorian chant **3 :** the manner of singing, playing, or uttering tones **4 :** the rise and fall in pitch of the voice in speech — **in·to·na·tion·al** \-shnəl, -shən-ᵊl\ *adj*

intonation pattern *n* **:** a combination of pitch and terminal juncture that contributes to the total meaning of an utterance <a falling *intonation pattern* makes *He is* a statement, a rising one makes it a question> — called also *intonation contour*

in·tone \in-ˈtōn\ *vb* **in·toned; in·ton·ing** [ME *entonen,* fr. MF *entoner,* fr. ML *intonare,* fr. L *in-* + *tonus* tone] *vt* **:** to utter in musical or prolonged tones **:** recite in singing tones or in a monotone ~ *vi* **:** to utter something in singing tones or in monotone — **in·ton·er** *n*

in to·to \in-ˈtōt-(ˌ)ō\ *adv* [L, on the whole] **:** TOTALLY, ENTIRELY <accepted the plan *in toto*>

in·tox·i·cant \in-ˈtäk-si-kənt\ *n* **:** something that intoxicates; *esp* **:** an alcoholic drink — **intoxicant** *adj*

¹in·tox·i·cate \-si-kət\ *adj, archaic* **:** INTOXICATED

²in·tox·i·cate \-sə-ˌkāt\ *vt* **-cat·ed; -cat·ing** [ML *intoxicatus,* pp. of *intoxicare,* fr. L *in-* + *toxicum* poison — more at TOXIC] **1 :** POISON **2 a :** to excite or stupefy by alcohol or a drug esp. to the point where physical and mental control is markedly diminished **b :** to excite or elate to the point of enthusiasm or frenzy <*intoxicated* with joy>

in·tox·i·cat·ed \-sə-ˌkāt-əd\ *adj* **:** affected by or as if by alcohol — **in·tox·i·cat·ed·ly** \-ˌkāt-əd-lē\ *adv*

in·tox·i·ca·tion \in-ˌtäk-sə-ˈkā-shən\ *n* **1 :** an abnormal state that is essentially a poisoning <intestinal ~> **2 a :** the condition of being drunk **:** INEBRIATION **b :** a strong excitement or elation

intra- \ˌin-trə, -(ˌ)trä\ *prefix* [LL, fr. L *intra,* fr. (assumed) OL *interus,* adj., inward — more at INTERIOR] **1 a :** within <*intra*continental> **b :** during <*intra*natal> **c :** between layers of <*intra*dermal> **2 :** INTRO- <an *intra*muscular injection>

in·tra·ar·te·ri·al \-är-ˈtir-ē-əl\ *adj* **:** situated within or entering by way of an artery; *also* **:** used in intraarterial procedures — **in·tra·ar·te·ri·al·ly** \-ē-ə-lē\ *adv*

in·tra·car·di·ac \-ˈkärd-ē-ˌak\ *also* **in·tra·car·di·al** \-ē-əl\ *adj* **:** existing or occurring within the heart <~ surgery>; *also* **:** used in intracardial procedures <an ~ catheter> — **in·tra·car·di·al·ly** \-ē-ə-lē\ *adv*

in·tra·cel·lu·lar \-ˈsel-yə-lər\ *adj* **:** existing, occurring, or functioning within a protoplasmic cell <~ enzymes> — **in·tra·cel·lu·lar·ly** *adv*

in·tra·cra·ni·al \-ˈkrā-nē-əl\ *adj* **:** existing or occurring within the cranium; *also* **:** affecting or involving intracranial structures — **in·tra·cra·ni·al·ly** \-nē-ə-lē\ *adv*

in·trac·ta·ble \(ˈ)in-ˈtrak-tə-bəl\ *adj* [L *intractabilis,* fr. *in-* + *tractabilis* tractable] **1 :** not easily governed, managed, or directed **:** OBSTINATE **2 :** not easily manipulated or wrought <~ metal> **3 :** not easily relieved or cured <~ pain> ***syn*** see UNRULY ***ant*** tractable — **in·trac·ta·bil·i·ty** \(ˌ)in-ˌtrak-tə-ˈbil-ət-ē\ *n* — **in·trac·ta·ble·ness** \(ˈ)in-ˈtrak-tə-bəl-nəs\ *n* — **in·trac·ta·bly** \-blē\ *adv*

in·tra·cu·ta·ne·ous \ˌin-trə-kyu̇-ˈtā-nē-əs, -(ˌ)trä-\ *adj* **:** INTRADERMAL — **in·tra·cu·ta·ne·ous·ly** *adv*

in·tra·der·mal \-ˈdər-məl\ *adj* **:** situated or done within or between the layers of the skin — **in·tra·der·mal·ly** \-mə-lē\ *adv*

intradermal test *n* **:** a test for immunity or hypersensitivity made by injecting a minute amount of diluted antigen into the skin

in·tra·dos \ˈin-trə-ˌdäs, -ˌdō; in-ˈtrā-ˌdäs\ *n, pl* **-dos** \-ˌdōz, -ˌdäs\ *or* **-dos·es** \-ˌdäs-əz\ [F, fr. L *intra* within + F *dos* back — more at DOSSIER] **:** the interior curve of an arch

1 intrados

in·tra·ga·lac·tic \ˌin-trə-gə-ˈlak-tik, -(ˌ)trä-\ *adj* **:** situated or occurring within the confines of a single galaxy

in·tra·mo·lec·u·lar \-mə-ˈlek-yə-lər\ *adj* [ISV] **:** existing or acting within the molecule; *also* **:** formed by reaction between different parts of the same molecule — **in·tra·mo·lec·u·lar·ly** *adv*

in·tra·mu·ral \-ˈmyu̇r-əl\ *adj* **1 a :** being or occurring within the limits usu. of a community or institution **b :** competitive only within the student body <~ sports> **2 :** situated or occurring within the substance of the walls of an organ — **in·tra·mu·ral·ly** \-ə-lē\ *adv*

in·tra·mus·cu·lar \-ˈməs-kyə-lər\ *adj* [ISV] **:** situated within or going into a muscle — **in·tra·mus·cu·lar·ly** *adv*

intrans *abbr* intransitive

in trans *abbr* [L *in transitu*] in transit

in·tran·si·geance \in-ˈtran(t)s-ə-jən(t)s, -ˈtranz-\ *n* [F] **:** INTRANSIGENCE — **in·tran·si·geant** \-jənt\ *adj or n* — **in·tran·si·geant·ly** *adv*

in·tran·si·gence \-jən(t)s\ *n* **:** the quality or state of being intransigent

in·tran·si·gent \-jənt\ *adj* [Sp *intransigente,* fr. *in-* + *transigente,* prp. of *transigir* to compromise, fr. L *transigere* to transact — more at TRANSACT] **1 a :** refusing to compromise or to abandon an extreme position or attitude **:** UNCOMPROMISING **b :** IRRECONCILABLE **2 :** characteristic of an intransigent person — **intransigent** *n* — **in·tran·si·gent·ly** *adv*

in·tran·si·tive \(ˈ)in-ˈtran(t)s-ət-iv, -ˈtranz-; -ˈtran(t)s-tiv\ *adj* [LL *intransitivus,* fr. L *in-* + LL *transitivus* transitive] **:** not transitive; *esp* **:** characterized by not having or containing a direct object <an ~ verb> — **in·tran·si·tive·ly** *adv* — **in·tran·si·tive·ness** *n*

in·trant \ˈin-trənt\ *n* [L *intrant-, intrans,* prp. of *intrare* to enter — more at ENTER] **:** ENTRANT; *esp* **:** one entering an educational institution or a holy order

in·tra·per·i·to·ne·al \ˌin-trə-ˌper-ət-ᵊn-ˈē-əl\ *adj* **:** existing within or going into the peritoneal cavity; *also* **:** introduced through the peritoneum — **in·tra·per·i·to·ne·al·ly** \-ē-ə-lē\ *adv*

in·tra·per·son·al \-ˈpərs-nəl, -ᵊn-əl\ *adj* **:** occurring within the individual mind or self <~ concerns of the aged>

in·tra·pop·u·la·tion \ˈin-trə-ˌpäp-yə-ˈlā-shən, -(ˌ)trä-\ *adj* **:** occurring within or taking place between members of a population

in·tra·psy·chic \ˌin-trə-ˈsī-kik, -(ˌ)trä-\ *adj* **:** being or occurring within the psyche, mind, or personality — **in·tra·psy·chi·cal·ly** \-ki-k(ə-)lē\ *adv*

in·tra·spe·cies \-ˈspē-(ˌ)shēz, -(ˌ)sēz\ *adj* **:** INTRASPECIFIC

in·tra·spe·cif·ic \-spi-ˈsif-ik\ *adj* **:** occurring within a species or involving members of one species — **in·tra·spe·cif·i·cal·ly** \-i-k(ə-)lē\ *adv*

in·tra·state \-ˈstāt\ *adj* **:** existing or occurring within a state <interstate and ~ commerce>

in·tra·uter·ine \-ˈyüt-ə-rən, -ˌrīn\ *adj* [ISV] **:** situated, used, or occurring within the uterus; *also* **:** involving the part of development that takes place in the uterus

intrauterine device *n* **:** a device inserted and left in the uterus to prevent effective conception — called also *intrauterine contraceptive device, IUD*

in·tra·vas·cu·lar \ˌin-trə-ˈvas-kyə-lər, -(ˌ)trä-\ *adj* **:** situated or occurring within a vessel and esp. a blood vessel <~ thrombosis> — **in·tra·vas·cu·lar·ly** *adv*

in·tra·ve·nous \ˌin-trə-ˈvē-nəs\ *adj* [ISV] **:** situated within or entering by way of a vein; *also* **:** used in intravenous procedures — **in·tra·ve·nous·ly** *adv*

in·tra·vi·tal \ˌin-trə-ˈvīt-ᵊl, -(ˌ)trä-\ *adj* [ISV] **:** INTRAVITAM — **in·tra·vi·tal·ly** \-ᵊl-ē\ *adv*

in·tra·vi·tam \-ˈvī-ˌtam, -ˈwē-ˌtäm\ *adj* [NL *intra vitam* during life] **1 :** performed upon or found in a living subject **2** *of a stain* **:** having the property of tinting living cells without killing them — compare SUPRAVITAL

in·tra·zon·al \ˌin-trə-ˈzōn-ᵊl, -(ˌ)trä-\ *adj* **:** of, relating to, or being a soil or a major soil group marked by relatively well-developed characteristics that are determined primarily by essentially local factors (as the parent material) rather than climate and vegetation — compare AZONAL, ZONAL

intreat *archaic var of* ENTREAT

intrench *var of* ENTRENCH

in·trep·id \in-ˈtrep-əd\ *adj* [L *intrepidus,* fr. *in-* + *trepidus* alarmed — more at TREPIDATION] **:** characterized by resolute fearlessness, fortitude, and endurance <an ~ explorer> — **in·tre·pid·i·ty** \ˌin-trə-ˈpid-ət-ē\ *n* — **in·trep·id·ly** \in-ˈtrep-əd-lē\ *adv* — **in·trep·id·ness** *n*

in·tri·ca·cy \ˈin-tri-kə-sē\ *n, pl* **-cies** **1 :** the quality or state of being intricate **2 :** something intricate <the *intricacies* of a plot>

in·tri·cate \ˈin-tri-kət\ *adj* [ME, fr. L *intricatus,* pp. of *intricare* to entangle, fr. *in-* + *tricae* trifles, impediments] **1 :** having many complexly interrelating parts or elements **:** COMPLICATED **2 :** difficult to resolve or analyze ***syn*** see COMPLEX — **in·tri·cate·ly** *adv* — **in·tri·cate·ness** *n*

in·tri·gant *or* **in·tri·guant** \ˌin-trē-ˈgänt, ˌan-, -ˈgäⁿ\ *n* [F *intrigant,* fr. It *intrigante,* prp. of *intrigare*] **:** one that intrigues **:** INTRIGUER

¹in·trigue \in-ˈtrēg\ *vb* **in·trigued; in·trigu·ing** [F *intriguer,* fr. It *intrigare,* fr. L *intricare* to entangle, perplex] *vt* **1 :** CHEAT, TRICK **2 :** to accomplish by intrigue <*intrigued* themselves into office —F. M. Ford> **3** *obs* **:** ENTANGLE **4 :** to arouse the interest, desire, or curiosity of <*intrigued* by the tale> ~ *vi* **:** to carry on an intrigue; *esp* **:** PLOT, SCHEME — **in·trigu·er** *n*

²in·trigue \ˈin-ˌtrēg, in-ˈ\ *n* **1 a :** a secret scheme **:** MACHINATION **b :** the practice of engaging in intrigues **2 :** a clandestine love affair

in·trigu·ing \in-ˈtrē-giŋ\ *adj* **:** engaging the interest to a marked degree **:** FASCINATING <a thoroughly ~ young woman> — **in·trigu·ing·ly** \-giŋ-lē\ *adv*

in·trin·sic \in-ˈtrin-zik, -ˈtrin(t)-sik\ *adj* [MF *intrinsèque* internal, fr. LL *intrinsecus,* fr. L, adv., inwardly; akin to L *intra* within — more at INTRA-] **1 a :** belonging to the essential nature or constitution of a thing <the ~ worth of a gem> **b :** being or relating to a semiconductor in which the concentration of charge carriers is characteristic of the material itself instead of the content of any impurities it contains **2 :** originating or situated within the body or part acted on — **in·trin·si·cal·ly** \-zi-k(ə-)lē, -si-\ *adv* — **in·trin·si·cal·ness** \-kəl-nəs\ *n*

in·trin·si·cal \-zi-kəl, -si-\ *adj, archaic* **:** INTRINSIC

intrinsic factor *n* **:** a substance produced by normal gastrointestinal mucosa that facilitates absorption of vitamin B_{12}

intro- *prefix* [ME, fr. MF, fr. L, fr. *intro* inside, to the inside, fr. (assumed) OL *interus,* adj., inward] **1 :** in **:** into <*intro*jection> **2 :** inward **:** within <*intro*vert> — compare EXTRO-

introd *abbr* introduction

in·tro·duce \ˌin-trə-ˈd(y)üs\ *vt* **-duced; -duc·ing** [L *introducere,* fr. *intro-* + *ducere* to lead — more at TOW] **1 :** to lead or bring in esp. for the first time **2 a :** to bring into play **b :** to bring into practice or use : INSTITUTE <*introduced* reforms in court practice> **3 :** to lead to or make known by a formal act, announcement, or recommendation: as **a :** to cause to be acquainted **b :** to present formally at court or into society **c :** to present or announce formally or officially or by an official reading **d :** to make preliminary explanatory or laudatory remarks about **e :** to bring (as an actor or singer) before the public for the first time **4 :** PLACE, INSERT <the risk of *introducing* harmful substances into the body> **5 :** to bring to a knowledge of something — **in·tro·duc·er** *n*

syn INTRODUCE, INSERT, INSINUATE, INTERPOLATE, INTERCALATE, INTERPOSE, INTERJECT *shared meaning element* : to put among or between others ***ant*** withdraw, abstract

in·tro·duc·tion \ˌin-trə-ˈdək-shən\ *n* [ME *introduccioun* act of introducing, fr. MF *introduction,* fr. L *introduction-, introductio,* fr. *introductus,* pp. of *introducere*] **1 :** something that introduces: as **a** (1) **:** a part of a book or treatise preliminary to the main portion (2) **:** a preliminary treatise or course of study **b :** a short introductory musical passage **2 :** the act or process of introducing **:** the state of being introduced **3 :** a putting in **:** INSERTION **4 :** something introduced; *specif* **:** a new or exotic plant or animal

in·tro·duc·to·ry \ˌin-trə-ˈdək-t(ə-)rē\ *adj* **:** of, relating to, or being a first step that sets something going or in proper perspective <the speaker's ~ remarks established his point of view> <an ~ course in calculus> ***syn*** see PRELIMINARY — **in·tro·duc·to·ri·ly** \-t(ə-)rə-lē\ *adv*

in·tro·gres·sion \ˌin-trə-ˈgresh-ən\ *n* [*intro-* + *-gression* (as in *regression*)] **:** the entry or introduction of a gene from one gene complex into another — **in·tro·gres·sant** \-ˈgres-ᵊnt\ *adj or n* — **in·tro·gres·sive** \-ˈgres-iv\ *adj*

in·troit \ˈin-ˌtrō-ət, -ˌtrȯit, in-ˈ\ *n* [MF *introite,* fr. ML *introitus,* fr. L, entrance, fr. *introitus,* pp. of *introire* to go in, fr. *intro-* + *ire* to go — more at ISSUE] **1** *often cap* **:** the first part of the traditional proper of the mass consisting of an antiphon, verse from a psalm, and the Gloria Patri **2 :** a piece of music sung or played at the beginning of a worship service

in·tro·ject \ˌin-trə-ˈjekt\ *vt* [*intro-* + *-ject* (as in *project,* v.)] **:** to incorporate (attitudes or ideas) into one's personality unconsciously — **in·tro·jec·tion** \-ˈjek-shən\ *n*

in·tro·mis·sion \ˌin-trə-ˈmish-ən\ *n* [F, fr. MF, fr. L *intromissus,* pp. of *intromittere*] **:** the act or process of intromitting; *esp* **:** the insertion or period of insertion of the penis in the vagina in copulation

in·tro·mit \-ˈmit\ *vt* **-mit·ted; -mit·ting** [L *intromittere,* fr. *intro-* + *mittere* to send] **:** to send or put in **:** INSERT — **in·tro·mit·tent** \-ˈmit-ᵊnt\ *adj* — **in·tro·mit·ter** \-ər\ *n*

in·trorse \ˈin-ˌtrȯ(ə)rs\ *adj* [L *introrsus,* adv., inward, fr. *intro-* + *versus* toward, fr. pp. of *vertere* to turn — more at WORTH] **:** facing inward or toward the axis of growth — **in·trorse·ly** *adv*

in·tro·spect \ˌin-trə-ˈspekt\ *vb* [L *introspectus,* pp. of *introspicere* to look inside, fr. *intro-* + *specere* to look — more at SPY] *vt* **:** to examine (one's own mind or its contents) reflectively ~ *vi* **:** to engage in an examination of one's thought process and sensory experience — **in·tro·spec·tive** \-ˈspek-tiv\ *adj* — **in·tro·spec·tive·ly** *adv* — **in·tro·spec·tive·ness** *n*

in·tro·spec·tion \-ˈspek-shən\ *n* **:** the examination of one's own thought and feeling **:** SELF-EXAMINATION — **in·tro·spec·tion·al** \-shnəl, -shən-ᵊl\ *adj*

in·tro·spec·tion·ism \-shə-ˌniz-əm\ *n* **:** a doctrine that psychology must be based essentially on data derived from introspection — compare BEHAVIORISM — **in·tro·spec·tion·ist** \-sh(ə-)nəst\ *or* **in·tro·spec·tion·is·tic** \-ˌspek-shə-ˈnis-tik\ *adj* — **introspectionist** *n*

in·tro·ver·sion \ˌin-trə-ˈvər-zhən, -shən\ *n* [*intro-* + *-version* (as in *diversion*)] **1 :** the act of introverting **:** the state of being introverted **2:** the state or tendency toward being wholly or predominantly concerned with and interested in one's own mental life — **in·tro·ver·sive** \-ˈvər-siv, -ziv\ *adj* — **in·tro·ver·sive·ly** *adv*

¹in·tro·vert \ˈin-trə-ˌvərt\ *vt* [*intro-* + *-vert* (as in *divert*)] **:** to turn inward or in upon itself: as **a :** to bend inward; *also* **:** to draw in (a tubular part) usu. by invagination **b :** to concentrate or direct upon oneself <his ~*ed* despair and his irrational destructiveness —*Current Biog.*>; *also* **:** to produce psychological introversion in

²introvert *n* **1 :** something (as the eyestalk of a snail) that is or can be introverted **2 :** one whose personality is characterized by introversion

in·trude \in-ˈtrüd\ *vb* **in·trud·ed; in·trud·ing** [L *intrudere* to thrust in, fr. *in-* + *trudere* to thrust — more at THREAT] *vi* **1 :** to thrust oneself in without invitation, permission, or welcome **2 :** to enter as a geological intrusion ~ *vt* **1 :** to thrust or force in or upon esp. without permission, welcome, or fitness <*intruded* a trite moral into his play> **2 :** to cause to enter as if by force — **in·trud·er** *n*

in·tru·sion \in-ˈtrü-zhən\ *n* [ME, fr. MF, fr. ML *intrusion-, intrusio,* fr. L *intrusus,* pp. of *intrudere*] **1 :** the act of intruding or the state of being intruded; *specif* **:** the act of wrongfully entering upon, seizing, or taking possession of the property of another **2 :** the forcible entry of molten rock or magma into or between other rock formations; *also* **:** the intruded magma

in·tru·sive \in-ˈtrü-siv, -ziv\ *adj* **1 a :** characterized by intrusion **b :** intruding where one is not welcome or invited **2 a :** projecting inward <an ~ arm of the sea> **b** (1) *of a rock* **:** having been forced while in a plastic state into cavities or between layers (2) **:** PLUTONIC **3 :** having nothing that corresponds to a sound or letter in orthography or etymon <~ \t\ in \ˈmints\ for *mince*> ***syn*** see IMPERTINENT ***ant*** retiring, unintrusive — **in·tru·sive·ly** *adv* — **in·tru·sive·ness** *n*

intrust *var of* ENTRUST

intsv *abbr* intensive

in·tu·ba·tion \ˌin-(ˌ)t(y)ü-ˈbā-shən, -tə-\ *n* **:** the introduction of a tube into a hollow organ (as the trachea) — **in·tu·bate** \ˈin-(ˌ)tyü-ˌbāt, -tə-\ *vt*

in·tu·it \in-ˈt(y)ü-ət\ *vt* **:** to apprehend by intuition — **in·tu·it·able** \-ə-bəl\ *adj*

in·tu·ition \ˌin-t(y)ü-ˈish-ən\ *n* [LL *intuition-, intuitio* act of contemplating, fr. L *intuitus,* pp. of *intueri* to look at, contemplate, fr. *in-* + *tueri* to look at] **1 a :** immediate apprehension or cognition **b :** knowledge or conviction gained by intuition **c :** the power or faculty of attaining to direct knowledge or cognition without evident rational thought and inference **2 :** quick and ready insight ***syn*** see REASON — **in·tu·ition·al** \-ˈish-nəl, -ən-ᵊl\ *adj*

in·tu·ition·ism \-ˈish-ə-ˌniz-əm\ *n* **1 a :** a doctrine that there are basic truths intuitively known **b :** a doctrine that objects of perception are intuitively known to be real **2 :** a doctrine that right or wrong or fundamental principles about what is right and wrong can be intuited — **in·tu·ition·ist** \-ˈish-(ə-)nəst\ *adj or n*

in·tu·itive \in-ˈt(y)ü-ət-iv\ *adj* **1 :** knowing or perceiving by intuition **2 a :** known or perceived by intuition **:** directly apprehended <had an ~ awareness of his sister's feelings> **b :** knowable by intuition **3 :** possessing or given to intuition or insight <an ~ mind> — **in·tu·itive·ly** *adv* — **in·tu·itive·ness** *n*

in·tu·mesce \ˌin-t(y)ü-ˈmes\ *vi* **-mesced; -mesc·ing** [L *intumescere* to swell up, fr. *in-* + *tumescere,* incho. of *tumēre* to swell — more at THUMB] **:** ENLARGE, SWELL

in·tu·mes·cence \-ˈmes-ᵊn(t)s\ *n* **1 a :** an enlarging, swelling, or bubbling up (as under the action of heat) **b :** the state of being swollen **2 :** something swollen or enlarged

in·tu·mes·cent \-ᵊnt\ *adj* [L *intumescent-, intumescens,* prp. of *intumescere*] **1 :** marked by intumescence **2** *of paint* **:** swelling and charring when exposed to flame

in·tus·sus·cept \ˌint-ə-sə-ˈsept\ *vb* [prob. fr. (assumed) NL *intussusceptus,* pp. of *intussuscipere,* fr. L *intus* within + *suscipere* to take up — more at ENT-, SUSCEPTIBLE] *vt* **:** to take in by or cause to undergo intussusception; *esp* **:** INVAGINATE ~ *vi* **:** to undergo intussusception

in·tus·sus·cep·tion \-ˈsep-shən\ *n* **:** a drawing in of something from without: as **a :** INVAGINATION; *esp* **:** the slipping of a length of intestine into an adjacent portion usu. producing obstruction **b :** the assimilation of new material and its dispersal among preexistent matter — **in·tus·sus·cep·tive** \-ˈsep-tiv\ *adj*

in·u·lin \ˈin-yə-lən\ *n* [prob. fr. G *inulin,* fr. L *inula* elecampane] **:** a tasteless white polysaccharide found esp. dissolved in the sap of the roots and rhizomes of composite plants

in·unc·tion \in-ˈəŋ(k)-shən\ *n* [ME, fr. L *inunction-, inunctio,* fr. *inunctus,* pp. of *inunguere* to anoint — more at ANOINT] **:** an act of applying oil or ointment **:** ANOINTING

in·un·date \ˈin-(ˌ)ən-ˌdāt\ *vt* **-dat·ed; -dat·ing** [L *inundatus,* pp. *inundare,* fr. *in-* + *unda* wave — more at WATER] **1 :** to cover with a flood **:** OVERFLOW **2 :** OVERWHELM — **in·un·da·tion** \ˌin-(ˌ)ən-ˈdā-shən\ *n* — **in·un·da·tor** \ˈin-(ˌ)ən-ˌdāt-ər\ *n* — **in·un·da·to·ry** \in-ˈən-də-ˌtōr-ē, -ˌtȯr-\ *adj*

in·ure \in-ˈ(y)ů(ə)r\ *vb* **in·ured; in·ur·ing** [ME *enuren,* fr. *en-* + *ure,* n., use, custom, fr. MF *uevre* work, practice, fr. L *opera* work — more at OPERA] *vt* **:** to accustom to accept something undesirable **:** HABITUATE ~ *vi* **:** to become of advantage **:** ACCRUE — **in·ure·ment** \-mənt\ *n*

in·urn \in-ˈərn\ *vt* **1 :** to place (as cremated remains) in an urn **2 :** ENTOMB

in·utile \(ˈ)in-ˈyüt-ᵊl, -ˈyü-ˌtīl\ *adj* [ME, fr. MF, fr. L *inutilis,* fr. *in-* + *utilis* useful — more at UTILITY] **:** USELESS, UNUSABLE — **in·util·i·ty** \ˌin-yü-ˈtil-ət-ē\ *n*

inv *abbr* **1** inventor **2** invoice

in vac·uo \in-ˈvak-yə-ˌwō\ *adv* [NL] **:** in a vacuum

in·vade \in-ˈvād\ *vt* **in·vad·ed; in·vad·ing** [ME *invaden,* fr. L *invadere,* fr. *in-* + *vadere* to go — more at WADE] **1 :** to enter for conquest or plunder **2 :** to encroach upon **:** INFRINGE **3 a :** to spread over or into as if invading **:** PERMEATE <doubts ~ his mind> **b :** to affect injuriously and progressively <gangrene ~*s* healthy tissue> ***syn*** see TRESPASS — **in·vad·er** *n*

in·vag·i·nate \in-ˈvaj-ə-ˌnāt\ *vb* **-nat·ed; -nat·ing** [ML *invaginatus,* pp. of *invaginare,* fr. L *in-* + *vagina* sheath] *vt* **1 :** ENCLOSE, SHEATHE **2 :** to fold in so that an outer becomes an inner surface ~ *vi* **:** to undergo invagination

in·vag·i·na·tion \-ˌvaj-ə-ˈnā-shən\ *n* **1 :** an act or process of invaginating: as **a :** the formation of a gastrula by an infolding of part of the wall of the blastula **b :** intestinal intussusception **2 :** an invaginated part

¹in·val·id \(ˈ)in-ˈval-əd\ *adj* [L *invalidus* weak, fr. *in-* + *validus* strong — more at VALID] **:** not valid: **a :** being without foundation or force in fact, truth, or law **b :** logically inconsequent — **in·va·lid·i·ty** \ˌin-və-ˈlid-ət-ē, -va-\ *n* — **in·val·id·ly** \(ˈ)in-ˈval-əd-le\ *adv* — **in·val·id·ness** *n*

²in·va·lid \ˈin-və-ləd, *Brit usu* -ˌlēd\ *adj* [L & F; F *invalide,* fr. L *invalidus*] **1 :** suffering from disease or disability **:** SICKLY **2 :** of, relating to, or suited to one that is sick

³invalid *like*²\ *n* **:** one that is sickly or disabled

⁴in·va·lid \ˈin-və-ləd, -ˌlid, *Brit usu* ˌin-və-ˈlēd\ *vt* **1 :** to make sickly or disabled **2 :** to remove from active duty by reason of sickness or disability

in·val·i·date \(ˈ)in-ˈval-ə-ˌdāt\ *vt* **:** to make invalid; *esp* **:** to weaken or destroy the cogency of ***syn*** see NULLIFY — **in·val·i·da·tion** \(ˌ)in-ˌval-ə-ˈdā-shən\ *n* — **in·val·i·da·tor** \in-ˈval-ə-ˌdāt-ər\ *n*

in·va·lid·ism \ˈin-və-ləd-ˌiz-əm\ *n* **:** a chronic condition of being an invalid

in·valu·able \(ˈ)in-ˈval-yə(-wə)-bəl\ *adj* [¹*in-* + *value,* v. + *-able*] **:** valuable beyond estimation **:** PRICELESS ***syn*** see COSTLY ***ant*** worthless — **in·valu·able·ness** *n* — **in·valu·ably** \-blē\ *adv*

in·vari·able \(ˈ)in-ˈver-ē-ə-bəl, -ˈvar-\ *adj* **:** not changing or capable of change **:** CONSTANT — **in·vari·abil·i·ty** \(ˌ)in-ˌver-ē-ə-ˈbil-ət-ē,

-ˌvar-\ *n* — **invariable** *n* — **in·vari·able·ness** *n* — **in·vari·ably** \-blē\ *adv*

in·vari·ance \(ˈ)in-ˈver-ē-ən(t)s, -ˈvar-\ *n* : the quality or state of being invariant

in·vari·ant \-ənt\ *adj* : CONSTANT, UNCHANGING; *specif* : unaffected by the group of mathematical operations under consideration <~ factor> — **invariant** *n*

in·va·sion \in-ˈvā-zhən\ *n* [ME *invasioune*, fr. MF *invasion*, fr. LL *invasion-, invasio*, fr. L *invasus*, pp. of *invadere*] **1** : an act of invading; *esp* : incursion of an army for conquest or plunder **2** : the incoming or spread of something usu. hurtful

in·va·sive \-siv, -ziv\ *adj* **1** : of, relating to, or characterized by military aggression **2** : tending to spread; *esp* : tending to invade healthy tissue <~ cancer cells> **3** : tending to infringe — **in·va·sive·ness** *n*

¹in·vec·tive \in-ˈvek-tiv\ *adj* [ME *invectif*, fr. MF, fr. L *invectivus*, fr. *invectus*, pp. of *invehere*] : of, relating to, or characterized by insult or abuse : DENUNCIATORY — **in·vec·tive·ly** *adv* — **in·vec·tive·ness** *n*

²invective *n* **1** : an abusive expression or speech **2** : insulting or abusive language : VITUPERATION ***syn*** see ABUSE

in·veigh \in-ˈvā\ *vi* [L *invehi* to attack, inveigh, pass. of *invehere* to carry in, fr. *in-* + *vehere* to carry — more at WAY] : to protest or complain bitterly or vehemently : RAIL — **in·veigh·er** *n*

in·vei·gle \in-ˈvā-gəl, -ˈvē-\ *vt* **in·vei·gled; in·vei·gling** \-g(ə-)liŋ\ [modif. of MF *aveugler* to blind, hoodwink, fr. OF *avogler*, fr. *avogle* blind, fr. ML *ab oculis*, lit., lacking eyes] **1** : to win over by wiles : ENTICE **2** : to acquire by ingenuity or flattery ***syn*** see LURE — **in·vei·gle·ment** \-gəl-mənt\ *n* — **in·vei·gler** \-g(ə-)lər\ *n*

in·vent \in-ˈvent\ *vt* [ME *inventen*, fr. L *inventus*, pp. of *invenire* to come upon, find, fr. *in-* + *venire* to come — more at COME] **1** *archaic* : FIND, DISCOVER **2** : to think up or imagine : FABRICATE **3** : to produce (as something useful) for the first time through the use of the imagination or of ingenious thinking and experiment <~ a new machine> — **in·ven·tor** \-ˈvent-ər\ *n* — **in·ven·tress** \-ˈven-trəs\ *n*

syn INVENT, CREATE, DISCOVER *shared meaning element* : to bring into existence or make known something new

in·ven·tion \in-ˈven-chən\ *n* **1** : DISCOVERY, FINDING **2** : productive imagination : INVENTIVENESS **3 a** : something invented: as (1) : a product of the imagination; *esp* : a false conception (2) : a device, contrivance, or process originated after study and experiment **b** : a short keyboard composition usu. in double counterpoint **4** : the act or process of inventing

in·ven·tive \in-ˈvent-iv\ *adj* **1** : adept or prolific at producing inventions : CREATIVE **2** : characterized by invention — **in·ven·tive·ly** *adv* — **in·ven·tive·ness** *n*

¹in·ven·to·ry \ˈin-vən-ˌtōr-ē, -ˌtȯr-\ *n, pl* **-ries** **1 a** : an itemized list of current assets: as (1) : a catalog of the property of an individual or estate (2) : a list of goods on hand **b** : a survey of natural resources **c** : a list of traits, preferences, attitudes, interests, or abilities used to evaluate personal characteristics or skills **2** : the quantity of goods or materials on hand : STOCK **3** : the act or process of taking an inventory — **in·ven·to·ri·al** \ˌin-vən-ˈtōr-ē-əl\ *adj* — **in·ven·to·ri·al·ly** \-ē-ə-lē\ *adv*

²inventory *vt* **-ried; -ry·ing** : to make an inventory of : CATALOG

in·ver·ness \ˌin-vər-ˈnes\ *n* [*Inverness*, Scotland] : a loose belted coat having a cape with a close-fitting round collar

¹in·verse \(ˈ)in-ˈvərs, ˈin-ˌ\ *adj* [L *inversus*, fr. pp. of *invertere*] **1** : opposite in order, nature, or effect **2** : being an inverse function <~ sine> — **in·verse·ly** *adv*

²in·verse \ˈin-ˌvərs, (ˈ)in-ˈ\ *n* **1** : something of a contrary nature or quality : OPPOSITE, REVERSE **2** : the result of an inversion; *specif* : a proposition which is inferred immediately from another and in which the subject term is the negative of the subject of the given proposition and the predicate term is unchanged **3 a** : an inverse function, operation, or point **b** : a set element that is related to another element in such a way that the result of applying a given binary operation to them is an identity element of the set

1 inverness

inverse function *n* : the mathematical function that expresses the independent variable of another function in terms of its dependent variable

in·ver·sion \in-ˈvər-zhən, -shən\ *n* **1** : the act or process of inverting **2** : a reversal of position, order, form, or relationship: as **a** (1) : a change in normal word order; *esp* : the placement of a verb before its subject (2) : the process or result of changing or reversing the relative positions of the elements of a musical interval, chord, or phrase (as by repeating a phrase with its intervals in the contrary order) **b** : the condition of being turned inward or inside out <~ of the foot> <~ of the uterus> **c** : a breaking off of a chromosome section and its subsequent reattachment in inverted position; *also* : a chromosomal section that has undergone this process **3 a** : a change in the order of the terms of a mathematical proportion effected by inverting each ratio **b** : the operation of inverting or forming the inverse of a magnitude, an operation, or an element **4** : HOMOSEXUALITY **5** : a conversion of a substance showing dextrorotation into one showing levorotation or vice versa <~ of sucrose> **6** : a conversion of direct current into alternating current **7** : a reversal of the normal atmospheric temperature gradient

in·ver·sive \-ˈvər-siv, -ziv\ *adj* : marked by inversion

¹in·vert \in-ˈvərt\ *vt* [L *invertere*, fr. *in-* + *vertere* to turn — more at WORTH] **1 a** : to turn inside out or upside down **b** : to turn inward **2 a** : to reverse in position, order, or relationship **b** : to subject to musical inversion **c** : to subject to chemical inversion — **in·vert·ible** \-ə-bəl\ *adj*

²in·vert \ˈin-ˌvərt\ *n* : one characterized by inversion; *esp* : HOMOSEXUAL

³in·vert \ˈin-ˌvərt\ *adj* : subjected to chemical inversion

in·ver·tase \in-ˈvərt-ˌās, -ˌāz; ˈin-vər-ˌtās, -ˌtāz\ *n* [ISV] : an enzyme capable of inverting sucrose

in·ver·te·brate \(ˈ)in-ˈvərt-ə-brət, -ˌbrāt\ *adj* [NL *invertebratus*, fr. L *in-* + NL *vertebratus* vertebrate] **1** : lacking a spinal column; *also* : of or relating to invertebrate animals **2** : lacking in strength or vitality : WEAK — **invertebrate** *n*

inverted comma *n* **1** : a comma in type turned to print upside down at the top of the line **2** *chiefly Brit* : QUOTATION MARK

in·vert·er \in-ˈvərt-ər\ *n* **1** : one that inverts **2** : a device for converting direct current into alternating current by mechanical or electronic means

in·vert·ible \in-ˈvərt-ə-bəl\ *adj* : capable of being inverted or subjected to inversion <an ~ matrix>

invert sugar *n* : a mixture of dextrose and levulose found in fruits or produced artificially by the inversion of sucrose; *also* : dextrose obtained from starch

¹in·vest \in-ˈvest\ *vt* [L *investire* to clothe, surround, fr. *in-* + *vestis* garment — more at WEAR] **1** [ML *investire*, fr. L, to clothe] **a** : to array in the symbols of office or honor **b** : to furnish with power or authority **c** : to grant someone control or authority over : VEST **2** : to cover completely : ENVELOP **3** : CLOTHE, ADORN **4** [MF *investir*, fr. OIt *investire*, fr. L, to surround] : to surround with troops or ships so as to prevent escape or entry **5** : to endow with a quality or characteristic : INFUSE

²invest *vb* [It *investire* to clothe, invest money, fr. L, to clothe] *vt* **1** : to commit (money) in order to earn a financial return **2** : to make use of for future benefits or advantages <~*ed* his time well> ~ *vi* : to make an investment — **in·vest·able** \-ˈves-tə-bəl\ *adj* — **in·ves·tor** \-tər\ *n*

in·ves·ti·gate \in-ˈves-tə-ˌgāt\ *vb* **-gat·ed; -gat·ing** [L *investigatus*, pp. of *investigare* to track, investigate, fr. *in-* + *vestigium* footprint, track] *vt* : to observe or study by close examination and systematic inquiry ~ *vi* : to make a systematic examination; *esp* : to conduct an official inquiry — **in·ves·ti·ga·tion** \-ˌves-tə-ˈgā-shən\ *n* — **in·ves·ti·ga·tion·al** \-shnəl, -shən-ᵊl\ *adj* — **in·ves·ti·ga·tive** \-ˈves-tə-ˌgāt-iv\ *adj* — **in·ves·ti·ga·tor** \-ˌgāt-ər\ *n* — **in·ves·ti·ga·to·ry** \-ˈves-ti-gə-ˌtōr-ē, -ˌtȯr-\ *adj*

in·ves·ti·ture \in-ˈves-tə-ˌchu̇(ə)r, -chər, -ˌt(y)u̇(ə)r\ *n* [ME, fr. ML *investitura*, fr. *investitus*, pp. of *investire*] **1** : the act of establishing in office or ratifying : CONFIRMATION **2** : something that covers or adorns

¹in·vest·ment \in-ˈves(t)-mənt\ *n* [¹*invest*] **1 a** *archaic* : VESTMENT **b** : an outer layer : ENVELOPE **2** : INVESTITURE 1 **3** : BLOCKADE, SIEGE

²investment *n* [²*invest*] : the outlay of money usu. for income or profit : capital outlay; *also* : the sum invested or the property purchased

investment company *n* : a company whose primary business is holding securities of other companies purely for investment purposes — compare HOLDING COMPANY

in·vet·er·a·cy \in-ˈvet-ə-rə-sē, -ˈve-trə-sē\ *n* [*inveterate* + *-cy*] : the quality or state of being obstinate or persistent : TENACITY

in·vet·er·ate \in-ˈvet-ə-rət, -ˈve-trət\ *adj* [L *inveteratus*, fr. pp. of *inveterare* to age (v.t.), fr. *in-* + *veter-, vetus* old — more at WETHER] **1** : firmly established by long persistence <the ~ tendency to overlook the obvious> **2** : confirmed in a habit : HABITUAL <an ~ smoker> — **in·vet·er·ate·ly** *adv*

syn INVETERATE, CONFIRMED, CHRONIC, DEEP-SEATED, DEEP-ROOTED *shared meaning element* : firmly established or having something firmly established

in·vi·a·ble \(ˈ)in-ˈvī-ə-bəl\ *adj* [ISV] : incapable of surviving esp. because of genetic constitution — **in·vi·a·bil·i·ty** \(ˌ)in-ˌvī-ə-ˈbil-ət-ē\ *n*

in·vid·i·ous \in-ˈvid-ē-əs\ *adj* [L *invidiosus* envious, invidious, fr. *invidia* envy — more at ENVY] **1** : tending to cause discontent, animosity, or envy **2** : ENVIOUS **3 a** : of an unpleasant or objectionable nature : OBNOXIOUS <subtle and ~ criticism> **b** : of a kind to cause harm or resentment <a most ~ comparison> ***syn*** see REPUGNANT — **in·vid·i·ous·ly** *adv* — **in·vid·i·ous·ness** *n*

in·vig·o·rate \in-ˈvig-ə-ˌrāt\ *vt* **-rat·ed; -rat·ing** [prob. fr. *in-* + *vigor*] : to give life and energy to : ANIMATE — **in·vig·o·rat·ing·ly** \-ˌrāt-iŋ-lē\ *adv* — **in·vig·o·ra·tion** \-ˌvig-ə-ˈrā-shən\ *n* — **in·vig·o·ra·tor** \-ˈvig-ə-ˌrāt-ər\ *n*

in·vin·ci·ble \(ˈ)in-ˈvin(t)-sə-bəl\ *adj* [ME, fr. MF, fr. LL *invincibilis*, fr. L *in-* + *vincere* to conquer — more at VICTOR] : incapable of being conquered, overcome, or subdued — **in·vin·ci·bil·i·ty** \(ˌ)in-ˌvin(t)-sə-ˈbil-ət-ē\ *n* — **in·vin·ci·ble·ness** \(ˈ)in-ˈvin(t)-sə-bəl-nəs\ *n* — **in·vin·ci·bly** \-blē\ *adv*

in·vi·o·la·ble \(ˈ)in-ˈvī-ə-lə-bəl\ *adj* [MF or L; MF, fr. L *inviolabilis*, fr. *in-* + *violare* to violate] **1** : secure from violation or profanation **2** : secure from assault or trespass : UNASSAILABLE ***syn*** see SACRED — **in·vi·o·la·bil·i·ty** \(ˌ)in-ˌvī-ə-lə-ˈbil-ət-ē\ *n* — **in·vi·o·la·ble·ness** \(ˈ)in-ˈvī-ə-lə-bəl-nəs\ *n* — **in·vi·o·la·bly** \-blē\ *adv*

in·vi·o·la·cy \(ˈ)in-ˈvī-ə-lə-sē\ *n* : the quality or state of being inviolate

in·vi·o·late \(ˈ)in-ˈvī-ə-lət\ *adj* : not violated or profaned; *esp* : PURE ***syn*** see SACRED ***ant*** violated — **in·vi·o·late·ly** *adv* — **in·vi·o·late·ness** *n*

in·vis·cid \(ˈ)in-ˈvis-əd\ *adj* **1** : having zero viscosity **2** : of or relating to an inviscid fluid <~ flow>

in·vis·i·ble \(ˈ)in-ˈviz-ə-bəl\ *adj* [ME, fr. MF, fr. L *invisibilis*, fr. *in-* + *visibilis* visible] **1 a** : incapable by nature of being seen **b** : inaccessible to view : HIDDEN **2 a** : not appearing in published financial statements **b** : not reflected in statistics **3** : IMPERCEPTIBLE, INCONSPICUOUS — **in·vis·i·bil·i·ty** \(ˌ)in-ˌviz-ə-ˈbil-ət-ē\ *n* — **invisible** *n* — **in·vis·i·ble·ness** \(ˈ)in-ˈviz-ə-bəl-nəs\ *n* — **in·vis·i·bly** \-blē\ *adv*

in·vi·ta·tion \ˌin-və-ˈtā-shən\ *n* **1 a** : the act of inviting **b** : an often formal request to be present or participate **2** : INCENTIVE, INDUCEMENT

in·vi·ta·tion·al \-shnəl, -shən-ᵊl\ *adj* **1** : prepared or entered in response to a request <an ~ article> **2** : limited to invited participants <an ~ tournament>

1in·vi·ta·to·ry \in-'vīt-ə-ˌtōr-ē, -ˌtȯr-\ *adj* : containing an invitation
2invitatory *n, pl* **-ries** : an invitatory psalm or antiphon
1in·vite \in-'vīt\ *vt* **in·vit·ed; in·vit·ing** [MF or L; MF *inviter,* fr. L *invitare*] **1 a** : to offer an incentive or inducement to : ENTICE **b** : to increase the likelihood of **2 a** : to request the presence or participation of **b** : to request formally **c** : to urge politely : WELCOME — **in·vit·er** *n*
syn INVITE, SOLICIT, COURT *shared meaning element* : to request or encourage to respond or act
2in·vite \'in-ˌvīt\ *n, chiefly dial* : INVITATION 1
in·vi·tee \ˌin-və-'tē, -ˌvī-\ *n* : an invited person
in·vit·ing \in-'vīt-iŋ\ *adj* : ATTRACTIVE, TEMPTING — **in·vit·ing·ly** \-iŋ-lē\ *adv*
in vi·tro \in-'vē-(ˌ)trō\ *adv or adj* [NL, lit., in glass] : outside the living body and in an artificial environment
in vi·vo \in-'vē-(ˌ)vō\ *adv or adj* [NL, lit., in the living] : in the living body of a plant or animal
in·vo·cate \'in-və-ˌkāt\ *vt, archaic* : INVOKE
in·vo·ca·tion \ˌin-və-'kā-shən\ *n* [ME *invocacioun,* fr. MF *invocation,* fr. L *invocation-, invocatio,* fr. *invocatus,* pp. of *invocare*] **1 a** : the act or process of petitioning for help or support : SUPPLICATION; *specif, often cap* : an invocatory prayer (as at the beginning of a service of worship) **b** : a calling upon for authority or justification **2** : a formula for conjuring : INCANTATION **3** : an act of legal or moral implementation : ENFORCEMENT — **in·vo·ca·tion·al** \-shnəl, -shən-ᵊl\ *adj* — **in·voc·a·to·ry** \in-'väk-ə-ˌtōr-ē, -ˌtȯr-\ *adj*
1in·voice \'in-ˌvȯis\ *n* [modif. of MF *envois,* pl. of *envoi* message — more at ENVOI] **1** : an itemized list of goods shipped usu. specifying the price and the terms of sale : BILL **2** : a consignment of merchandise
2invoice *vt* **in·voiced; in·voic·ing** : to submit an invoice for or to : BILL
in·voke \in-'vōk\ *vt* **in·voked; in·vok·ing** [ME *invoken,* fr. MF *invoquer,* fr. L *invocare,* fr. *in-* + *vocare* to call — more at VOICE] **1 a** : to petition for help or support **b** : to appeal to or cite as authority **2** : to call forth by incantation : CONJURE **3** : to make an earnest request for : SOLICIT <*invoked* their forgiveness> **4** : to put into effect or operation : IMPLEMENT **5** : to bring about : CAUSE — **in·vok·er** *n*
in·vo·lu·cre \'in-və-ˌlü-kər\ *n* [F, fr. NL *involucrum*] : one or more whorls of bracts situated below and close to a flower, flower cluster, or fruit — **in·vo·lu·cral** \ˌin-və-'lü-krəl\ *adj* — **in·vo·lu·crate** \-krət, -ˌkrāt\ *adj* — **in·vo·lu·cred** \'in-və-ˌlü-kərd\ *adj*
in·vo·lu·crum \ˌin-və-'lü-krəm\ *n, pl* **-cra** \-krə\ [NL, sheath, involucre, fr. L, sheath, fr. *involvere* to wrap] : a surrounding envelope or sheath; *esp* : INVOLUCRE
in·vol·un·tary \(ˈ)in-'väl-ən-ˌter-ē\ *adj* [LL *involuntarius,* fr. L *in-* + *voluntarius* voluntary] **1** : done contrary to or without choice **2** : COMPULSORY **3** : not subject to control of the will : REFLEX — **in·vol·un·tari·ly** \(ˌ)in-ˌväl-ən-'ter-ə-lē\ *adv* — **in·vol·un·tari·ness** \(ˈ)in-'väl-ən-ˌter-ē-nəs\ *n*
1in·vo·lute \'in-və-ˌlüt\ *adj* [L *involutus* involved, fr. pp. of *involvere*] **1 a** (1) : curled spirally (2) : having the whorls closely coiled <~ shell> **b** (1) : curled or curved inward (2) : having the edges rolled over the upper surface toward the midrib <an ~ leaf> **c** : having the form of an involute <a gear with ~ teeth> **2** : INVOLVED, INTRICATE — **in·vo·lute·ly** *adv*
2involute *n* : a curve traced by a point on a thread kept taut as it is unwound from another curve
3in·vo·lute \ˌin-və-'lüt\ *vi* **-lut·ed; -lut·ing** **1** : to become involute **2 a** : to return to a former condition **b** : to become cleared up : DISAPPEAR
in·vo·lu·tion \ˌin-və-'lü-shən\ *n* [L *involution-, involutio,* fr. *involutus,* pp. of *involvere*] **1 a** (1) : the act or an instance of enfolding or entangling : INVOLVEMENT (2) : an involved grammatical construction usu. characterized by the insertion of clauses between the subject and predicate **b** : COMPLEXITY, INTRICACY **2** : the act or process of raising a quantity to a power **3 a** : an inward curvature or penetration **b** : the formation of a gastrula by ingrowth of cells formed at the dorsal lip **4** : a shrinking or return to a former size **5** : the regressive alterations of a body or its parts characteristic of the aging process; *specif* : decline marked by a decrease of bodily vigor and in women by the menopause — **in·vo·lu·tion·al** \-shnəl, -shən-ᵊl\ *adj* — **in·vo·lu·tion·ary** \-shə-ˌner-ē\ *adj*

involute *a, p, p, p, p* traced by any point *p* of the thread *t* unwinding from curve *c*

in·volve \in-'välv, -'vȯlv\ *vt* **in·volved; in·volv·ing** [ME *involven* to roll up, wrap, fr. L *involvere,* fr. *in-* + *volvere* to roll — more at VOLUBLE] **1** *archaic* : to enfold or envelop so as to encumber **2 a** : to engage as a participant <workmen *involved* in building a house> **b** : to oblige to take part <the questionable right of an executive to ~ the nation in war> **c** : to occupy (as oneself) absorbingly; *esp* : to commit (as oneself) emotionally <she became *involved* with a married man> **3** : to surround as if with a wrapping : ENVELOP **4 a** *archaic* : to wind, coil, or wreathe about : ENTWINE **b** : to relate closely : CONNECT **5 a** : to have within or as part of itself : INCLUDE **b** : to require as a necessary accompaniment : ENTAIL **c** : to have an effect on : AFFECT — **in·volve·ment** \-'välv-mənt, -'vȯlv-\ *n* — **in·volv·er** *n*
syn **1** see INCLUDE
2 INVOLVE, IMPLICATE *shared meaning element* : to bring into a situation from which escape is difficult
in·volved \-'välvd, -'vȯlvd\ *adj* **1** : INVOLUTE, TWISTED **2 a** : marked by extreme and often needless or excessive complexity <a story with an ~ plot> **b** : difficult to deal with because of complexity or disorder <his affairs were found to be dangerously ~ when he died> **3** : being affected or implicated *syn* see COMPLEX — **in·volv·ed·ly** \-'väl-vəd-lē, -'vȯl-\ *adv*
in·vul·ner·a·ble \(ˈ)in-'vəln-(ə-)rə-bəl, -'vəl-nər-bəl\ *adj* [L *invulnerabilis,* fr. *in-* + *vulnerare* to wound — more at VULNERABLE] **1** : incapable of being wounded, injured, or harmed **2** : immune to or proof against attack : IMPREGNABLE — **in·vul·ner·a·bil·i·ty** \(ˌ)in-ˌvəln-(ə-)rə-'bil-ət-ē\ *n* — **in·vul·ner·a·ble·ness** \(ˈ)in-'vəln-(ə-)rə-bəl-nəs, -'vəl-nər -bəl-\ *n* — **in·vul·ner·a·bly** \-blē\ *adv*
1in·ward \'in-wərd\ *adj* [ME, fr. OE *inweard;* akin to OHG *inwert* inward; both fr. a prehistoric WGmc compound whose constituents are represented by OE *in* & OE *-weard* -ward] **1** : situated on the inside : INNER **2** : of or relating to the mind or spirit <struggled to achieve ~ peace> **3** : marked by close acquaintance : FAMILIAR **4** : directed toward the interior
2inward *or* **in·wards** \-wərdz\ *adv* **1** : toward the inside, center, or interior **2** : toward the inner being
3inward *n* **1** : something that is inward **2 in·wards** \'in-ərdz, -wərdz\ *pl* : INNARDS
Inward Light *n* : INNER LIGHT
in·ward·ly \'in-wərd-lē\ *adv* **1** : in the innermost being : MENTALLY, SPIRITUALLY **2 a** : beneath the surface : INTERNALLY <bled ~> **b** : to oneself : PRIVATELY <cursed ~>
in·ward·ness *n* **1** : close acquaintance : FAMILIARITY **2** : fundamental nature : ESSENCE **3** : internal quality or substance **4** : absorption in one's own mental or spiritual life
in·weave \(ˈ)in-'wēv\ *vt* **-wove** \-'wōv\ *also* **-weaved; -wo·ven** \-'wō-vən\ *also* **-weaved; -weav·ing** : INTERWEAVE, INTERLACE
in–wrought \(ˈ)in-'rȯt, 'in-ˌ\ *adj* **1** : having decoration worked in : ORNAMENTED; *esp* : decorated with embroidery **2** : worked in esp. as decoration
Io \'ī-(ˌ)ō\ *n* [L, fr. Gk *Iō*] : a maiden loved by Zeus and changed by him into a heifer so that she might escape the jealous rage of Hera
I/O *abbr* input/output
IOC *abbr* International Olympic Committee
iod- *or* **iodo-** *comb form* [F *iode*] : iodine <*iod*ize> <*iodo*form>
1io·date \'ī-ə-ˌdāt, -əd-ət\ *n* [F, fr. *iode*] : a salt of iodic acid
2io·date \'ī-ə-ˌdāt\ *vt* **io·dat·ed; io·dat·ing** [*iod-* + *-ate*] : to impregnate or treat with iodine — **io·da·tion** \ˌī-ə-'dā-shən\ *n*
iod·ic \ī-'äd-ik\ *adj* [F *iodique,* fr. *iode*] : of, relating to, or containing iodine; *esp* : containing iodine with a valence of five
iodic acid *n* : a crystalline oxidizing solid HIO_3 formed by oxidation of iodine
io·dide \'ī-ə-ˌdīd\ *n* [ISV] : a compound of iodine usu. with a more electropositive element or radical; *esp* : a salt or ester of hydriodic acid
io·din·ate \'ī-ə-də-ˌnāt\ *vt* **-at·ed; -at·ing** : to treat or cause to combine with iodine or a compound of iodine — **io·din·ation** \ˌī-ə-də-'nā-shən\ *n*
io·dine *also* **io·din** \'ī-ə-ˌdīn, -əd-ᵊn, -ə-ˌdēn\ *n, often attrib* [F *iode,* fr. Gk *ioeidēs* violet colored, fr. *ion* violet] : a nonmetallic halogen element obtained usu. as heavy shining blackish gray crystals and used esp. in medicine, photography, and analysis — see ELEMENT table
io·dize \'ī-ə-ˌdīz\ *vt* **io·dized; io·diz·ing** : to treat with iodine or an iodide <*iodized* salt>
io·do·form \ī-'ōd-ə-ˌfȯrm, -'äd-\ *n* [ISV *iod-* + *-form* (as in *chloroform*)] : a yellow crystalline volatile compound CHI_3 with a penetrating persistent odor that is used as an antiseptic dressing
io·do·phor \-ˌfō(ə)r\ *n* [*iod-* + Gk *-phoros* carrier — more at -PHORE] : a complex of iodine and an organic compound that releases iodine gradually and serves as a disinfectant
io·dop·sin \ˌī-ə-'däp-sən\ *n* [*iod-* (fr. Gk *ioeidēs* violet colored) + Gk *opsis* sight, vision + E *-in* — more at OPTIC] : a photosensitive violet pigment in the retinal cones that is similar to rhodopsin but more labile, is formed from vitamin A, and is important in daylight vision
io·dous \ī-'ōd-əs, 'ī-əd-\ *adj* [ISV] : relating to or containing iodine and esp. iodine with a valence of three
io moth \ˌī-(ˌ)ō-\ *n* [L *Io*] : a large yellowish American moth (*Automeris io*) having a large ocellated spot on each hind wing and a larva with stinging spines
ion \'ī-ən, 'ī-ˌän\ *n* [Gk, neut. of *iōn,* prp. of *ienai* to go — more at ISSUE] **1** : an atom or group of atoms that carries a positive or negative electric charge as a result of having lost or gained one or more electrons **2** : a free electron or other charged subatomic particle
Ion *abbr* Ionic

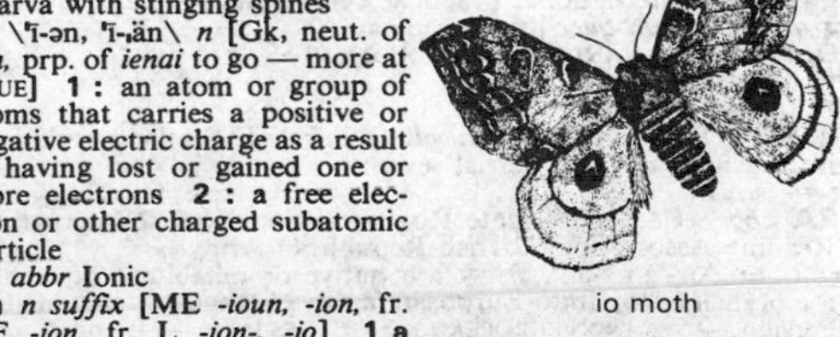
io moth

-ion *n suffix* [ME *-ioun, -ion,* fr. OF *-ion,* fr. L *-ion-, -io*] **1 a** : act or process <validat*ion*> **b** : result of an act or process <regulat*ion*> **2** : state or condition <hydrat*ion*>
ion engine *n* : a reaction engine deriving thrust from the ejection of a stream of ionized particles
ion exchange *n* : a reversible interchange of one kind of ion present on an insoluble solid with another of like charge present in a solution surrounding the solid with the reaction being used esp. for softening or demineralizing water, the purification of chemicals, or the separation of substances — **ion–ex·chang·er** *n*

ion·ic \ī-ˈän-ik\ *adj* [ISV] **1** : of, relating to, existing as, or characterized by ions <~ gases> <the ~ charge> **2** : based on or functioning by means of ions <~ conduction> <an ~ lattice> — **ion·ic·i·ty** \ˌī-ə-ˈnis-ət-ē\ *n*

[1]**Ion·ic** \ī-ˈän-ik\ *adj* [L & MF; MF *ionique,* fr. L *ionicus,* fr. Gk *iōnikos,* fr. *Iōnia* Ionia] **1** : of or relating to Ionia or the Ionians **2** : belonging to or resembling the Ionic order of architecture characterized esp. by the spiral volutes of its capital

[2]**Ionic** *n* : a dialect of ancient Greek used in Ionia that is the vehicle of an important body of literature

ionic bond *n* : ELECTROVALENT BOND

io·ni·um \ī-ˈō-nē-əm\ *n* [*ion;* fr. its ionizing action] : a natural radioactive isotope of thorium having a mass number of 230

ionization chamber *n* : a partially evacuated tube provided with electrodes so that its conductivity due to the ionization of the residual gas reveals the presence of ionizing radiation

ion·ize \ˈī-ə-ˌnīz\ *vb* **ion·ized; ion·iz·ing** [ISV] *vt* : to convert wholly or partly into ions ~ *vi* : to become ionized — **ion·iz·able** \-ˌnī-zə-bəl\ *adj* — **ion·iza·tion** \ˌī-ə-nə-ˈzā-shən\ *n* — **ion·iz·er** \ˈī-ə-ˌnī-zər\ *n*

ion·o·sphere \ī-ˈän-ə-ˌsfi(ə)r\ *n* : the part of the earth's atmosphere beginning at an altitude of about 25 miles and extending outward 250 miles or more, containing free electrically charged particles by means of which radio waves are transmitted to great distances around the earth, and consisting of several regions within which occur one or more layers that vary in height and ionization with time of day, season, and the solar cycle; *also* : a comparable region of charged particles surrounding a celestial body (as Venus or Mars) — **ion·o·spher·ic** \(ˌ)ī-ˌän-ə-ˈsfi(ə)r-ik, -ˈsfer-\ *adj* — **ion·o·spher·i·cal·ly** \-i-k(ə-)lē\ *adv*

IOOF *abbr* Independent Order of Odd Fellows

IORM *abbr* Improved Order of Red Men

io·ta \ī-ˈōt-ə\ *n* [L, fr. Gk *iōta,* of Sem origin; akin to Heb *yōdh* yod] **1** : the 9th letter of the Greek alphabet — see ALPHABET table **2** : an infinitesimal amount : JOT

io·ta·cism \ī-ˈōt-ə-ˌsiz-əm\ *n* [LL *iotacismus* repetition of iota, fr. Gk *iōtakismos,* fr. *iōta*] : excessive use of the letter iota or I or of its sound; *specif* : the use in modern Greek of the sound \ē\ of iota in speaking words written with other vowels or diphthongs (as *ē, y, ei, oi*)

IOU \ˌī-(ˌ)ō-ˈyü\ *n* [fr. the pronunciation of *I owe you*] **1** : a paper that has on it the letters IOU, a stated sum, and a signature and that is given as an acknowledgment of debt **2** : DEBT, OBLIGATION

-ious *adj suffix* [ME, partly fr. OF *-ious, -ieux,* fr. L *-iosus,* fr. *-i-* (penultimate vowel of some noun stems) + *-osus* -ous; partly fr. L *-ius,* adj. suffix] : -OUS <edac*ious*>

IP *abbr* **1** initial point **2** intermediate pressure

IPA \ˌī-ˌpē-ˈā\ *n* [*I*nternational *P*honetic *A*lphabet] : an alphabet designed to represent each human speech sound with a unique symbol

ip·e·cac \ˈip-i-ˌkak\ *or* **ipe·ca·cu·a·nha** *Pg* ē-ˌpek-ə-kü-ˈa-nʸə\ *n* [Pg *ipecacuanha,* fr. Tupi *ipekaaguéne*] **1** : a tropical So. American creeping plant (*Cephaelis ipecacuanha*) of the madder family with drooping flowers **2** : the dried rhizome and roots of ipecac valued esp. as a source of emetine; *also* : any of several roots similarly used

Iph·i·ge·nia \ˌif-ə-jə-ˈnī-ə\ *n* [L, fr. Gk *Iphigeneia*] : a daughter of Agamemnon nearly sacrificed by him to Artemis but saved by her and made a priestess

IPM *abbr* inches per minute

IPPF *abbr* International Planned Parenthood Federation

ipro·ni·a·zid \ˌī-prə-ˈnī-ə-zəd\ *n* [blend of *isoniazid* and *propyl*] : a derivative $C_9H_{13}N_3O$ of isoniazid that is used as a monoamine oxidase inhibitor and was formerly used in treating tuberculosis

IPS *abbr* inches per second

ip·se dix·it \ˌip-sē-ˈdik-sət\ *n* [L, he himself said it] : an assertion made but not proved : DICTUM

ip·si·lat·er·al \ˌip-si-ˈlat-ə-rəl, -ˈla-trəl\ *adj* [ISV, fr. L *ipse* self, himself + *later-, latus* side] : situated or appearing on or affecting the same side of the body — **ip·si·lat·er·al·ly** \-ē\ *adv*

ip·sis·si·ma ver·ba \ip-ˌsis-ə-mə-ˈvər-bə\ *n pl* [NL, lit., the selfsame words] : the exact language used by someone quoted

ip·so fac·to \ˌip-(ˌ)sō-ˈfak-(ˌ)tō\ *adv* [NL, lit., by the fact itself] : by the very nature of the case

IPTS *abbr* International Practical Temperature Scale

iq *abbr* [L *idem quod*] the same as

IQ \ˈī-ˈkyü\ *n* : INTELLIGENCE QUOTIENT

[1]**Ir** *abbr* Irish

[2]**Ir** *symbol* iridium

IR *abbr* **1** information retrieval **2** infrared **3** inland revenue **4** intelligence ratio **5** internal revenue

ir- — see IN-

IRA *abbr* **1** Intercollegiate Rowing Association **2** International Reading Association **3** Irish Republican Army

Ira·ni·an \ir-ˈā-nē-ən\ *n* **1** : a native or inhabitant of Iran **2** : a branch of the Indo-European family of languages that includes Persian — see INDO-EUROPEAN LANGUAGES table — **Iranian** *adj*

Iraqi \i-ˈräk-ē, -ˈrak-\ *n* [Ar *ʽirāqīy,* fr. *ʽIrāq* Iraq] **1** : a native or inhabitant of Iraq **2** : the dialect of Modern Arabic spoken in Iraq — **Iraqi** *adj*

iras·ci·ble \ir-ˈas-ə-bəl, ī-ˈras-\ *adj* [MF, fr. LL *irascibilis,* fr. L *irasci* to become angry, be angry, fr. *ira*] : marked by hot temper and easily provoked anger — **iras·ci·bil·i·ty** \-ˌas-ə-ˈbil-ət-ē, -ˌras-\ *n* — **iras·ci·ble·ness** \ir-ˈas-ə-bəl-nəs, ī-ˈras-\ *n* — **iras·ci·bly** \-blē\ *adv*

syn IRASCIBLE, CHOLERIC, SPLENETIC, TESTY, TOUCHY, CRANKY, CROSS *shared meaning element* : easily angered or upset

irate \ī-ˈrāt\ *adj* **1** : roused to or given to ire : INCENSED <an ~ taxpayer> **2** : arising from anger <~ words> — **irate·ly** *adv* — **irate·ness** *n*

IRBM *abbr* intermediate range ballistic missile

ire \ˈī(ə)r\ *n* [ME, fr. OF, fr. L *ira;* akin to OE *ofost* haste, zeal, Gk *hieros* holy, *oistros* gadfly, frenzy] : intense and usu. openly displayed anger ***syn*** see ANGER — **ire** *vt* — **ire·ful** \-fəl\ *adj*

Ire *abbr* Ireland

ire·nic \ī-ˈren-ik, -ˈrē-nik\ *adj* [Gk *eirēnikos,* fr. *eirēnē* peace] : conducive to or operating toward peace or conciliation ***syn*** see PACIFIC ***ant*** acrimonious — **ire·ni·cal·ly** \-ˈren-i-k(ə-)lē, -ˈrē-ni-\ *adv*

irid *abbr* iridescent

irid- *or* **irido-** *comb form* **1** [L *irid-, iris*] : rainbow <*irid*escent> **2** [NL *irid-, iris*] : iris of the eye <*irid*ectomy> **3** [NL *iridium*] : iridium <*irid*ic> : iridium and <*irid*osmium>

iri·da·ceous \ˌir-ə-ˈdā-shəs, ˌī-rə-\ *adj* : of or relating to the iris family

ir·i·des·cence \ˌir-ə-ˈdes-ᵊn(t)s\ *n* **1** : a play of colors producing rainbow effects (as in a soap bubble) **2** : a display or effect suggestive of iridescence (as in brilliance) : GLITTER <a certain ~ of glamor and superiority —Margaret Landon>

ir·i·des·cent \-ᵊnt\ *adj* : having or exhibiting iridescence — **ir·i·des·cent·ly** *adv*

irid·ic *1 usu* ir-ˈid-ik, *2 usu* ī-ˈrid-\ *adj* **1** : of or relating to iridium; *esp* : containing tetravalent iridium **2** : of or relating to the iris of the eye

irid·i·um \ir-ˈid-ē-əm\ *n* [NL, fr. L *irid-, iris;* fr. the colors produced by its dissolving in hydrochloric acid] : a silver-white hard brittle very heavy metallic element of the platinum group — see ELEMENT table

ir·id·os·mine \ˌir-ə-ˈdäz-ˌmēn\ *n* [G, fr. *irid-* + NL *osmium*] : a mineral that is a native iridium osmium alloy usu. containing some rhodium and platinum

[1]**iris** \ˈī-rəs\ *n, pl* **iris·es** *or* **iri·des** \ˈī-rə-ˌdēz, ˈir-ə-\ [ME, fr. L *irid-, iris* rainbow, iris plant, fr. Gk, rainbow, iris plant, iris of the eye — more at WIRE] **1** : RAINBOW **2** [NL *irid-, iris,* fr. Gk] **a** : the opaque contractile diaphragm perforated by the pupil and forming the colored portion of the eye — see EYE illustration **b** : IRIS DIAPHRAGM; *also* : a similar device with a circular opening that can be varied in size **3** [NL *Irid-, Iris,* genus name, fr. L] : any of a large genus (*Iris* of the family Iridaceae, the iris family) of perennial herbaceous plants with linear usu. basal leaves and large showy flowers

[2]**iris** *vt* **1** : to make iridescent : give the form or appearance of a rainbow to **2** : to operate the iris of a motion-picture camera so as to fade (a picture) — used with *in* or *out*

Iris \ˈī-rəs\ *n* [L, fr. Gk] : the Greek goddess of the rainbow and a messenger of the gods

iris diaphragm *n* : an adjustable diaphragm of thin opaque plates that can be turned by a ring so as to change the diameter of a central opening usu. to regulate the aperture of a lens

Irish \ˈī(ə)r-ish\ *n* **1** *pl in constr* : natives or inhabitants of Ireland or their immediate descendants esp. when of Celtic speech or culture **2 a** : the Celtic language of Ireland : IRISH GAELIC **b** : English spoken by the Irish — **Irish** *adj*

Irish bull *n* : an apparently congruous but actually incongruous expression (as "it was hereditary in his family to have no children")

Irish coffee *n* : hot sugared coffee with Irish whiskey and whipped cream

Irish confetti *n* : a rock, brick, or fragment of rock or brick used as a missile

Irish Gaelic *n* : the Celtic language of Ireland esp. as used since the end of the medieval period

Irish·ism \ˈī-rish-ˌiz-əm\ *n* : a word, phrase, or expression characteristic of the Irish

Irish mail *n* : a 3- or 4-wheeled toy vehicle activated by a hand lever

Irish·man \ˈī-rish-mən\ *n* **1** : a native or inhabitant of Ireland **2** : one that is of Irish descent

Irish moss *n* **1** : the dried and bleached plants of two red algae (*Chondrus crispus* and *Gigartina mamillosa*) used as an agent for thickening or emulsifying or as a demulcent **2** : CARRAGEEN

Irish moss 1

Irish potato *n* : POTATO 2b

Irish·ry \ˈī-rish-rē\ *n, pl* **-ries** **1** : IRISH 1 **2 a** : Irish quality or character **b** : an Irish peculiarity or trait

Irish setter *n* : any of a breed of bird dogs generally comparable to English setters but with a chestnut-brown or mahogany-red coat

Irish stew *n* : a stew having as its principal ingredients meat (as lamb), potatoes, and onions in a thick gravy

Irish terrier *n* : any of a breed of active medium-sized terriers developed in Ireland and characterized by a dense close usu. reddish wiry coat

Irish water spaniel *n* : any of a breed of large retrievers developed in Ireland and characterized by a heavy curly liver-colored coat and a nearly hairless tail

Irish whiskey *n* : whiskey made in Ireland chiefly of barley

Irish wolfhound *n* : a very large tall hound that resembles the Scottish deerhound but is much larger and stronger

Irish·wom·an \ˈī-rish-ˌwu̇m-ən\ *n* : a woman born in Ireland or of Irish descent

[1]**irk** \ˈərk\ *n* [ME *irken*] : to make weary, irritated, or bored ***syn*** see ANNOY

[2]**irk** *n* **1** : TEDIUM, IRKSOMENESS **2** : a cause or source of annoyance or disgust

irk·some \ˈərk-səm\ *adj* : tending to irk : TEDIOUS <an ~ task> — **irk·some·ly** *adv* — **irk·some·ness** *n*

[1]**iron** \ˈī(-ə)rn\ *n* [ME, fr. OE *īsern, īren;* akin to OHG *īsarn* iron] **1** : a heavy malleable ductile magnetic silver-white metallic element that readily rusts in moist air, occurs native in meteorites and combined in most igneous rocks, is the most used of metals, and is vital to biological processes — see ELEMENT table **2** : something made of iron: as **a** : something (as handcuffs) used to bind or restrain — usu. used in pl. **b** : a heated metal implement used for

branding or cauterizing **c :** HARPOON **d :** a heatable device usu. with a flat metal base that is used to smooth, finish, or press (as cloth) **:** FLATIRON **e :** STIRRUP **f :** any of a series of numbered golf clubs having metal heads **3 :** great strength or hardness — **iron in the fire 1 :** a matter requiring close attention **:** ENTERPRISE <was a businessman and had other *irons in the fire* — J. D. Beresford> **2 :** a prospective course of action **:** a project not yet realized <got several *irons in the fire* and I'm hoping to land something before very long —W. S. Maugham>

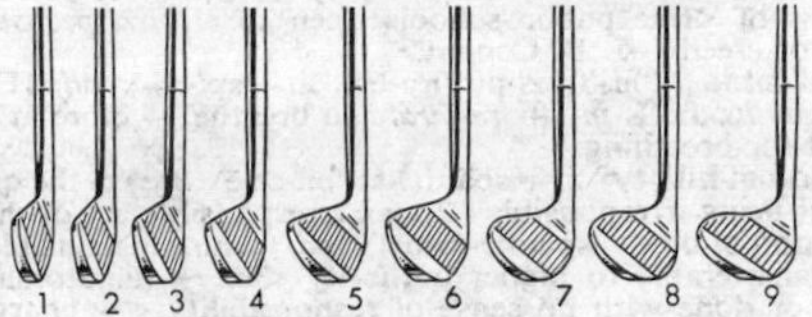

irons 2f

²iron *adj* **1 :** of, relating to, or made of iron **2 :** resembling iron **3 a :** strong and healthy **:** ROBUST **b :** INFLEXIBLE, UNRELENTING <~ determination> **c :** holding or binding fast <the ~ ties of kinship> — **iron·ness** \ˈī(-ə)rn-nəs\ *n*

³iron *vt* **1 :** to furnish or cover with iron **2 :** to shackle with irons **3 a :** to smooth with or as if with a heated iron <~ *ed* his shirt> **b :** to remove (as wrinkles) by ironing ~ *vi* **:** to smooth or press cloth or clothing with a heated iron

Iron Age *n* **:** the period of human culture characterized by the smelting of iron and its use in industry beginning somewhat before 1000 B.C. in western Asia and Egypt

iron·bound \ˈī(-ə)rn-ˈbau̇nd\ *adj* **:** bound with or as if with iron: as **a :** HARSH, RUGGED <~ coast> **b :** STERN, RIGOROUS <~ traditions>

¹iron·clad \-ˈklad\ *adj* **1 :** sheathed in iron armor — used esp. of naval vessels **2 a :** RIGOROUS, EXACTING <an ~ oath> **b :** being fixed and unshakable **:** INFLEXIBLE <an ~ rule>

²iron·clad \-ˌklad\ *n* **:** an armored naval vessel

iron curtain *n* **1 :** a political, military, and ideological barrier that cuts off and isolates an area; *specif* **:** one between an area under Soviet control and other areas **2 a :** an intangible barrier against communication of information or ideas; *esp* **:** one that is set up for concealment and bars any opportunity for penetration **b :** a bar to the crossing of a mental or cultural border line

iron·er \ˈī(-ə)r-nər\ *n* **:** one that irons; *specif* **:** MANGLE

iron·fisted \ˈī(-ə)rn-ˈfis-təd\ *adj* **1 :** STINGY, MISERLY **2 :** being both harsh and ruthless <~ methods>

iron gray *n* **:** a nearly neutral very slightly greenish dark gray

iron hand *n* **:** stern or rigorous control <ruled with an *iron hand*> — **iron·hand·ed** \ˌī(-ə)rn-ˈhan-dəd\ *adj* — **iron·hand·ed·ly** *adv* — **iron·hand·ed·ness** *n*

iron·heart·ed \ˌī(-ə)rn-ˈhärt-əd\ *adj* **:** CRUEL, HARDHEARTED

iron horse *n* **:** a locomotive engine

iron·ic \ī-ˈrän-ik\ *or* **iron·i·cal** \-i-kəl\ *adj* **1 :** relating to, containing, or constituting irony **2 :** given to irony ***syn*** see SARCASTIC — **iron·i·cal·ly** \-i-k(ə-)lē\ *adv* — **iron·i·cal·ness** \-i-kəl-nəs\ *n*

iron·ing \ˈī(-ə)r-niŋ\ *n* **1 :** the action or process of smoothing or pressing with or as if with a heated iron **2 :** clothes ironed or to be ironed

ironing board *n* **:** a flat padded cloth-covered surface on which clothes are ironed

iro·nist \ˈī-rə-nəst\ *n* **:** one who uses irony esp. in the development of a literary work or theme

iron lung *n* **:** a device for artificial respiration in which rhythmic alternations in the air pressure in a chamber surrounding a patient's chest force air into and out of the lungs

iron·mas·ter \ˈī(-ə)rn-ˌmas-tər\ *n* **:** a manufacturer of iron

iron·mon·ger \-ˌməŋ-gər, -ˌmäŋ-\ *n, Brit* **:** a dealer in iron and hardware — **iron·mon·gery** \-g(ə-)rē\ *n*

iron out *vt* **1 :** REMOVE **2 :** to make tolerable or harmonious by suppression or modification of extremes <*ironed out* their differences>

iron oxide *n* **:** any of several oxides of iron: as **a :** FERRIC OXIDE **b :** FERROUS OXIDE

iron pyrites *n* **:** PYRITE — called also *iron pyrite*

iron ration *n* **:** an emergency ration

iron·side \-ˌsīd\ *n* **:** a man of great strength or bravery

iron·stone \ˈī(-ə)rn-ˌstōn\ *n* **1 :** a hard sedimentary rock rich in iron; *esp* **:** a siderite in a coal region **2 :** IRONSTONE CHINA

ironstone china *n* **:** a hard heavy durable white pottery developed in England early in the 19th century — called also *ironstone*

iron·ware \ˈī(-ə)rn-ˌwa(ə)r, -ˌwe(ə)r\ *n* **:** articles made of iron

iron·weed \-ˌwēd\ *n* **:** any of several mostly weedy American composite plants (genus *Veronia*) with alternate leaves and perfect red or purple tubular flowers in terminal cymose heads

iron·wood \-ˌwu̇d\ *n* **1 :** any of numerous trees and shrubs with exceptionally tough or hard wood **2 :** the wood of an ironwood

iron·work \-ˌwərk\ *n* **1 :** work in iron **2** *pl but sing or pl in constr* **:** a mill or building where iron or steel is smelted or heavy iron or steel products are made — **iron·work·er** \-ˌwər-kər\ *n*

iro·ny \ˈī-rə-nē\ *n, pl* **-nies** [L *ironia,* fr. Gk *eirōnia,* fr. *eirōn* dissembler] **1 :** a pretense of ignorance and of willingness to learn from another assumed in order to make the other's false conceptions conspicuous by adroit questioning — called also *Socratic irony* **2 a :** the use of words to express something other than and esp. the opposite of the literal meaning **b :** a usu. humorous or sardonic literary style or form characterized by irony **c :** an ironic expression or utterance **3 a (1) :** incongruity between the actual result of a sequence of events and the normal or expected result **(2) :** an event or result marked by such incongruity **b :** incongruity between a situation developed in a drama and the accompanying words or actions that is understood by the audience but not by the characters in the play — called also *dramatic irony, tragic irony* **4 :** an attitude of detached awareness of incongruity <looked with ~ on the craze for overkill> ***syn*** see WIT

Ir·o·quoi·an \ˌir-ə-ˈkwȯi-ən\ *n* **1 :** a language family of eastern No. America including Cayuga, Cherokee, Erie, Mohawk, Onondaga, Oneida, Seneca, and Tuscarora **2 :** a member of any of the peoples constituting the Iroquois — **Iroquoian** *adj*

Ir·o·quois \ˈir-ə-ˌkwȯi *also* -ˌkwä\ *n, pl* **Iroquois** \-ˌkwȯi(z), -ˌkwä(z)\ [F, fr. Algonquin *Irinakhoiw,* lit., real adders] **1** *pl* **:** an Amerindian confederacy of New York that consisted of the Cayuga, Mohawk, Oneida, Onondaga, and Seneca and later included the Tuscarora **2 :** a member of any of the Iroquois peoples

ir·ra·di·ance \ir-ˈād-ē-ən(t)s\ *n* **1 :** RADIANCE 1 **2 :** radiant flux density on a given surface usu. expressed in watts per square centimeter or square meter

ir·ra·di·ate \ir-ˈād-ē-ˌāt\ *vb* **-at·ed; -at·ing** [L *irradiatus,* pp. of *irradiare,* fr. *in-* + *radius* ray] *vt* **1 a :** to cast rays of light upon **:** ILLUMINATE **b :** to enlighten intellectually or spiritually **c :** to affect or treat by radiant energy (as heat); *specif* **:** to treat by exposure to radiation **2 :** to emit like rays of light **:** RADIATE <*irradiating* strength and comfort> ~ *vi, archaic* **:** to emit rays **:** SHINE — **ir·ra·di·a·tive** \-ˌāt-iv\ *adj* — **ir·ra·di·a·tor** \-ˌāt-ər\ *n*

ir·ra·di·a·tion \ir-ˌād-ē-ˈā-shən\ *n* **1 :** emission of radiant energy (as heat or light) **2 :** exposure to radiation (as X rays or alpha rays) **3 :** IRRADIANCE 2

ir·rad·i·ca·ble \ˈi(ə)r-ˈrad-i-kə-bəl\ *adj* [ML *irradicabilis,* fr. L *in-* + *radic-, radix* root — more at ROOT] **:** impossible to eradicate **:** DEEP-ROOTED — **ir·rad·i·ca·bly** \-blē\ *adv*

¹ir·ra·tio·nal \(ˈ)ir-ˈ(r)ash-nəl, -ən-ᵊl\ *adj* [ME, fr. L *irrationalis,* fr. *in-* + *rationalis* rational] **:** not rational: as **a (1) :** not endowed with reason or understanding **(2) :** lacking usual or normal mental clarity or coherence **b :** not governed by or according to reason <~ fears> **c** *Greek & Latin prosody* **(1)** *of a syllable* **:** having a quantity other than that required by the meter **(2)** *of a foot* **:** containing such a syllable **d (1) :** being an irrational number <an ~ root of an equation> **(2) :** having a numerical value that is an irrational number <a length that is ~> — **ir·ra·tio·nal·i·ty** \(ˌ)ir-ˌ(r)ash-ə-ˈnal-ət-ē\ *n* — **ir·ra·tio·nal·ly** \(ˈ)ir-ˈ(r)ash-nə-lē, -ən-ᵊl-ē\ *adv* — **ir·ra·tio·nal·ness** \-nəl-nəs, -ən-ᵊl-\ *n*

²irrational *n* **1 :** an irrational being **2 :** IRRATIONAL NUMBER

ir·ra·tio·nal·ism \(ˈ)ir-ˈ(r)ash-nəl-ˌiz-əm, -ən-ᵊl-\ *n* **1 :** a system emphasizing intuition, instinct, feeling, or faith rather than reason or holding that the universe is governed by irrational forces **2 :** the quality or state of being irrational — **ir·ra·tio·nal·ist** \-əst\ *n or adj* — **ir·ra·tio·nal·is·tic** \(ˌ)ir-ˌ(r)ash-nəl-ˈis-tik, -ən-ᵊl-\ *adj*

irrational number *n* **:** a number that can be expressed as an infinite decimal with no set of consecutive digits repeating itself indefinitely and that cannot be expressed as the quotient of two integers

ir·re·al \(ˈ)ir-ˈrē(-ə)l, -ˈri(-ə)l\ *adj* **:** not real

ir·re·al·i·ty \ˌir-ē-ˈal-ət-ē\ *n* **:** UNREALITY

ir·re·claim·able \ˌir-i-ˈklā-mə-bəl\ *adj* **:** incapable of being reclaimed — **ir·re·claim·ably** \-blē\ *adv*

¹ir·rec·on·cil·able \(ˌ)ir-ˌ(r)ek-ən-ˈsī-lə-bəl, (ˈ)ir-ˈ(r)ek-ən-ˌ\ *adj* **:** impossible to reconcile — **ir·rec·on·cil·abil·i·ty** \(ˌ)ir-ˌ(r)ek-ən-ˌsī-lə-ˈbil-ət-ē\ *n* — **ir·rec·on·cil·able·ness** \(ˌ)ir-ˌ(r)ek-ən-ˈsī-lə-bəl-nəs, (ˈ)ir-ˈ(r)ek-ən-ˌ\ *n* — **ir·rec·on·cil·ably** \-blē\ *adv*

²irreconcilable *n* **:** one that is irreconcilable; *esp* **:** a member of a group (as a political party) that opposes compromise or collaboration

ir·re·cov·er·able \ˌir-i-ˈkəv-(ə-)rə-bəl\ *adj* **:** not capable of being recovered or rectified **:** IRREPARABLE — **ir·re·cov·er·able·ness** *n* — **ir·re·cov·er·ably** \-blē\ *adv*

ir·re·cu·sa·ble \ˌir-i-ˈkyü-zə-bəl\ *adj* [LL *irrecusabilis,* fr. L *in-* + *recusare* to reject, refuse — more at RECUSANCY] **:** not subject to exception or rejection — **ir·re·cu·sa·bly** \-blē\ *adv*

irred *abbr* irredeemable

ir·re·deem·able \ˌir-i-ˈdē-mə-bəl\ *adj* **1 :** not redeemable: as **a :** not terminable by payment of the principal <~ bond> **b :** INCONVERTIBLE a **2 :** being beyond remedy **:** HOPELESS <~ mistakes> — **ir·re·deem·ably** \-blē\ *adv*

ir·re·den·ta \ˌir-i-ˈdent-ə\ *n* [It *Italia irredenta* Italian-speaking territory not incorporated in Italy, lit., unredeemed Italy] **:** a territory historically or ethnically related to one political unit but presently subject to another

ir·re·den·tism \-ˈden-ˌtiz-əm\ *n* **:** a political principle or policy directed toward the incorporation of irredentas within the boundaries of their historically or ethnically related political unit — **ir·re·den·tist** \-ˈdent-əst\ *n or adj*

ir·re·duc·ible \ˌir-i-ˈd(y)ü-sə-bəl\ *adj* **:** impossible to bring into a desired, normal, or simpler state <an ~ matrix>; *specif* **:** incapable of being factored into polynomials of lower degree with coefficients in some given field (as the rational numbers) or integral domain (as the integers) <~ polynomials> <an ~ equation> — **ir·re·duc·ibil·i·ty** \-ˌd(y)ü-sə-ˈbil-ət-ē\ *n* — **ir·re·duc·i·bly** \-ˈd(y)ü-sə-blē\ *adv*

ir·re·flex·ive \ˌir-i-ˈflek-siv\ *adj* **:** not reflexive

ir·re·form·able \ˌir-i-ˈfȯr-mə-bəl\ *adj* **1 :** incapable of being reformed **:** INCORRIGIBLE **2 :** not subject to revision or alteration <~ dogma> — **ir·re·form·abil·i·ty** \-ˌfȯr-mə-ˈbil-ət-ē\ *n*

ir·re·fra·ga·ble \(ˈ)ir-ˈ(r)ef-rə-gə-bəl, ˌir-i-ˈfrag-ə-\ *adj* [LL *irrefragabilis,* fr. L *in-* + *refragari* to oppose, fr. *re-* + *-fragari* (as in *suffragari* to vote for); akin to L *suffragium* suffrage] **1 :** impossible to deny or refute <~ arguments> **2 :** impossible to break or alter <~ rules> <an ~ cement> — **ir·re·fra·ga·bil·i·ty** \(ˌ)ir-ˌ(r)ef-rə-gə-ˈbil-ət-ē, ˌir-i-ˌfrag-ə-\ *n* — **ir·ref·ra·ga·bly** \(ˈ)ir-ˈ(r)ef-rə-gə-blē, ˌir-i-ˈfrag-ə-\ *adv*

ir·re·fran·gi·ble \ˌir-i-ˈfran-jə-bəl\ *adj* : not capable of being refracted — used of radiations (as visible light)

ir·re·fut·able \ˌir-i-ˈfyüt-ə-bəl, (ˈ)ir-ˈ(r)ef-yət-\ *adj* [LL *irrefutabilis*, fr. L *in-* + *refutare* to refute] : impossible to refute : INCONTROVERTIBLE <~ proof> — **ir·re·fut·abil·i·ty** \ˌir-i-ˌfyüt-ə-ˈbil-ət-ē, (ˌ)ir-ˌ(r)ef-yət-\ *n* — **ir·re·fut·ably** \ˌir-i-ˈfyüt-ə-blē, (ˈ)ir-ˈ(r)ef-yət-\ *adv*

irreg *abbr* irregular

ir·re·gard·less \ˌir-i-ˈgärd-ləs\ *adv* [prob. blend of *irrespective* and *regardless*] *nonstand* : REGARDLESS

1ir·reg·u·lar \(ˈ)ir-ˈ(r)eg-yə-lər\ *adj* [ME *irreguler*, fr. MF, fr. LL *irregularis* not in accordance with rule, fr. L *in-* + *regularis* regular] **1 a :** behaving without regard to established laws, customs, or moral principles **b :** not belonging to or qualified under the rules of some particular group or organized body <~ practitioners of medicine> **2 a :** failing to accord with what is usual, proper, accepted, or right <~ behavior> **b :** not conforming to the normal or usual manner of inflection <*sell, put, feed* are ~ verbs>; *specif* : STRONG **c** (1) **:** improper or inadequate because of failure to conform to a prescribed course (2) *Brit* : celebrated without either proclamation of the banns or publication of intention to marry : CLANDESTINE <~ marriage> **d :** not belonging to the regular army organization but raised for a special purpose <~ troops> **3 :** lacking perfect symmetry or evenness <an ~ coastline>; *esp* : ZYGOMORPHIC <~ flowers> **4 :** lacking continuity or regularity esp. of occurrence or activity <~ employment> — **ir·reg·u·lar·ly** *adv*

syn IRREGULAR, ANOMALOUS, UNNATURAL *shared meaning element* : not according with or explainable by law, rule, or custom. IRREGULAR implies a lack of accord with a law or regulation imposed for the sake of uniformity in method, practice, or conduct; thus, an *irregular* marriage fails to conform to the regulations of church or state; *irregular* verse departs from accepted metrical patterns; *irregular* behavior deviates from the code of conduct of the community. ANOMALOUS implies a failure to conform to what is expected of the thing in question because of the class to which it belongs or the laws which govern its existence <an *anomalous* piece of domestic architecture, combining the small, familiar pleasures of the hearth with the headier excitements of Doomsday —*New Yorker*> and may specifically suggest an unclassifiable state or a conflict between mutually exclusive or mutually antagonistic classes <the *anomalous* position of the free Negro in the slave states — E. T. Price> UNNATURAL implies contravention of natural law or of those principles held essential to the well-being of civilized society and is likely to suggest reprehensible abnormality <thy deed, inhuman and *unnatural* provokes this deluge most *unnatural* —Shak.> ***ant*** regular

2irregular *n* : one that is irregular: as **a :** a soldier who is not a member of a regular military force **b** *pl* **:** merchandise that has minor imperfections or that falls next below the manufacturer's standard for firsts

ir·reg·u·lar·i·ty \(ˌ)ir-ˌ(r)eg-yə-ˈlar-ət-ē\ *n, pl* **-ties 1 :** the quality or state of being irregular **2 :** something (as dishonest conduct) that is irregular <alleged *irregularities* in the city government> **3** : CONSTIPATION

ir·rel·a·tive \(ˈ)ir-ˈ(r)el-ət-iv\ *adj* : not relative: **a :** not related **b** : IRRELEVANT — **ir·rel·a·tive·ly** *adv*

ir·rel·e·vance \(ˈ)ir-ˈ(r)el-ə-vən(t)s\ *n* **1 :** the quality or state of being irrelevant **2 :** something irrelevant

ir·rel·e·van·cy \-vən-sē\ *n, pl* **-cies** : IRRELEVANCE

ir·rel·e·vant \-vənt\ *adj* : not relevant : INAPPLICABLE <that statement is ~ to your argument> — **ir·rel·e·vant·ly** *adv*

ir·re·li·gion \ˌir-i-ˈlij-ən\ *n* [MF or L; MF, fr. L *irreligion-, irreligio*, fr. *in-* + *religion-, religio* religion] : the quality or state of being irreligious — **ir·re·li·gion·ist** \-ˈlij-(ə-)nəst\ *n*

ir·re·li·gious \-ˈlij-əs\ *adj* **1 :** neglectful of religion : lacking religious emotions, doctrines, or practices <so ~ that they exploit popular religion for professional purposes —G. B. Shaw> **2** : indicating lack of religion — **ir·re·li·gious·ly** *adv*

ir·re·me·able \(ˈ)ir-ˈ(r)ē-mē-ə-bəl\ *adj* [L *irremeabilis*, fr. *in-* + *remeare* to go back, fr. *re-* + *meare* to go — more at PERMEATE] *archaic* : offering no possibility of return

ir·re·me·di·a·ble \ˌir-i-ˈmēd-ē-ə-bəl\ *adj* [L *irremediabilis*, fr. *in-* + *remediabilis* remediable] : not remediable; *specif* : INCURABLE — **ir·re·me·di·a·ble·ness** *n* — **ir·re·me·di·a·bly** \-blē\ *adv*

ir·re·mov·able \-ˈmü-və-bəl\ *adj* : not removable — **ir·re·mov·abil·i·ty** \-ˌmü-və-ˈbil-ət-ē\ *n* — **ir·re·mov·ably** \-ˈmü-və-blē\ *adv*

ir·rep·a·ra·ble \(ˈ)ir-ˈ(r)ep-(ə-)rə-bəl\ *adj* [ME, fr. MF, fr. L *irreparabilis*, fr. *in-* + *reparabilis* reparable] : not reparable : IRRETRIEVABLE <~ damage> — **ir·rep·a·ra·ble·ness** *n* — **ir·rep·a·ra·bly** \-blē\ *adv*

ir·re·peal·able \ˌir-i-ˈpē-lə-bəl\ *adj* : not repealable — **ir·re·peal·abil·i·ty** \-ˌpē-lə-ˈbil-ət-ē\ *n*

ir·re·place·able \-ˈplā-sə-bəl\ *adj* : not replaceable — **ir·re·place·abil·i·ty** \-ˌplā-sə-ˈbil-ət-ē\ *n* — **ir·re·place·able·ness** \-ˈplā-sə-bəl-nəs\ *n* — **ir·re·place·ably** \-blē\ *adv*

ir·re·press·ible \-ˈpres-ə-bəl\ *adj* : impossible to repress, restrain, or control <~ curiosity> — **ir·re·press·ibil·i·ty** \-ˌpres-ə-ˈbil-ət-ē\ *n* — **ir·re·press·ibly** \-ˈpres-ə-blē\ *adv*

ir·re·proach·able \-ˈprō-chə-bəl\ *adj* : not reproachable : BLAMELESS <~ conduct> — **ir·re·proach·abil·i·ty** \-ˌprō-chə-ˈbil-ət-ē\ *n* — **ir·re·proach·able·ness** \-ˈprō-chə-bəl-nəs\ *n* — **ir·re·proach·ably** \-blē\ *adv*

ir·re·pro·duc·ible \(ˈ)ir-ˌrē-prə-ˈd(y)ü-sə-bəl\ *adj* : not reproducible — **ir·re·pro·duc·ibil·i·ty** \-ˌd(y)ü-sə-ˈbil-ət-ē\ *n*

ir·re·sist·ible \ˌir-i-ˈzis-tə-bəl\ *adj* : impossible to resist successfully <an ~ attraction> — **ir·re·sist·ibil·i·ty** \-ˌzis-tə-ˈbil-ət-ē\ *n* — **ir·re·sist·ible·ness** \-ˈzis-tə-bəl-nəs\ *n* — **ir·re·sist·ibly** \-blē\ *adv*

ir·re·sol·u·ble \-ˈzäl-yə-bəl\ *adj* [L *irresolubilis*, fr. *in-* + *resolvere* to resolve] **1** *archaic* : INDISSOLUBLE **2 :** having or admitting of no solution or explanation

ir·res·o·lute \(ˈ)ir-ˈ(r)ez-ə-ˌlüt, -lət\ *adj* : uncertain how to act or proceed : VACILLATING — **ir·res·o·lute·ly** \-ˌlüt-lē, -lət-; (ˌ)ir-ˌ(r)ez-ə-ˈlüt-\ *adv* — **ir·res·o·lute·ness** \-ˌlüt-nəs, -lət-, -ˈlüt-\ *n* — **ir·res·o·lu·tion** \(ˌ)ir-ˌ(r)ez-ə-ˈlü-shən\ *n*

ir·re·solv·able \ˌir-i-ˈzäl-və-bəl, -ˈzȯl-\ *adj* : incapable of being resolved; *esp* : not analyzable

ir·re·spec·tive of \ˌir-i-ˈspek-tiv-\ *prep* : without regard to : regardless of <free public schools open to all *irrespective of* race, color, or creed —J. B. Conant>

ir·re·spi·rable \(ˈ)ir-ˈ(r)es-p(ə-)rə-bəl, ˌir-i-ˈspī-rə-\ *adj* [F, fr. LL *irrespirabilis*, fr. L *in-* + *respirare* to breathe — more at RESPIRE] : unfit for breathing

ir·re·spon·si·bil·i·ty \ˌir-i-ˌspän(t)-sə-ˈbil-ət-ē\ *n* **1 :** the quality or state of being irresponsible **2 :** an irresponsible act or individual

1ir·re·spon·si·ble \-ˈspän(t)-sə-bəl\ *adj* : not responsible: as **a** : not answerable to higher authority <an ~ dictatorship> **b** : said or done with no sense of responsibility <~ charges> **c** : lacking a sense of responsibility **d :** unable esp. mentally or financially to bear responsibility — **ir·re·spon·si·ble·ness** *n* — **ir·re·spon·si·bly** \-blē\ *adv*

2irresponsible *n* : one that is irresponsible

ir·re·spon·sive \ˌir-i-ˈspän(t)-siv\ *adj* : not responsive; *esp* : not able, ready, or inclined to respond — **ir·re·spon·sive·ness** *n*

ir·re·triev·able \ˌir-i-ˈtrē-və-bəl\ *adj* : not retrievable : IRRECOVERABLE — **ir·re·triev·abil·i·ty** \-ˌtrē-və-ˈbil-ət-ē\ *n* — **ir·re·triev·ably** \ˌir-i-ˈtrē-və-blē\ *adv*

ir·rev·er·ence \(ˈ)ir-ˈ(r)ev-(ə-)rən(t)s, -ˈ(r)ev-ərn(t)s\ *n* **1 :** lack of reverence **2 :** an irreverent act or utterance

ir·rev·er·ent \-(ə-)rənt, -ərnt\ *adj* [L *irreverent-, irreverens*, fr. *in-* + *reverent-, reverens* reverent] : not reverent: as **a :** lacking proper respect in speech or action **b :** characterized by a lightly pert quality or manner — **ir·rev·er·ent·ly** *adv*

ir·re·vers·ible \ˌir-i-ˈvər-sə-bəl\ *adj* : incapable of being reversed — **ir·re·vers·ibil·i·ty** \-ˌvər-sə-ˈbil-ət-ē\ *n* — **ir·re·vers·ibly** \-ˈvər-sə-blē\ *adv*

ir·rev·o·ca·ble \(ˈ)ir-ˈ(r)ev-ə-kə-bəl\ *adj* [ME, fr. L *irrevocabilis*, fr. *in-* + *revocabilis* revocable] : incapable of being revoked : UNALTERABLE <an ~ decision> — **ir·rev·o·ca·bil·i·ty** \(ˌ)ir-ˌ(r)ev-ə-kə-ˈbil-ət-ē\ *n* — **ir·re·vo·ca·ble·ness** \(ˈ)ir-ˈ(r)ev-ə-kə-bəl-nəs\ *n* — **ir·re·vo·ca·bly** \-blē\ *adv*

irridenta *var of* IRREDENTA

ir·ri·gate \ˈir-ə-ˌgāt\ *vb* **-gat·ed; -gat·ing** [L *irrigatus*, pp. of *irrigare*, fr. *in-* + *rigare* to water] *vt* **1 :** WET, MOISTEN: as **a** : to supply (as land) with water by artificial means **b :** to flush (a body part) with a stream of liquid (as in removing a foreign body or medicating) **2 :** to refresh as if by watering ~ *vi* : to practice irrigation — **ir·ri·ga·tion** \ˌir-ə-ˈgā-shən\ *n* — **ir·ri·ga·tor** \ˈir-ə-ˌgāt-ər\ *n*

ir·ri·ta·bil·i·ty \ˌir-ət-ə-ˈbil-ət-ē\ *n, pl* **-ties 1 :** the quality or state of being irritable: as **a :** quick excitability to annoyance, impatience, or anger : PETULANCE **b :** abnormal or excessive excitability of an organ or part of the body **2 :** the property of protoplasm and of living organisms that permits them to react to stimuli

ir·ri·ta·ble \ˈir-ət-ə-bəl\ *adj* : capable of being irritated: as **a** : easily exasperated or excited **b :** responsive to stimuli — **ir·ri·ta·ble·ness** *n* — **ir·ri·ta·bly** \-blē\ *adv*

1ir·ri·tant \ˈir-ə-tənt\ *adj* : causing irritation; *specif* : tending to produce physical irritation

2irritant *n* : something that irritates or excites

ir·ri·tate \ˈir-ə-ˌtāt\ *vb* **-tat·ed; -tat·ing** [L *irritatus*, pp. of *irritare*] *vt* **1 :** to excite impatience, anger, or displeasure in : ANNOY **2** : to induce irritability in or of ~ *vi* : to cause or induce displeasure or irritation — **ir·ri·tat·ing·ly** \-ˌtāt-iŋ-lē\ *adv*

syn IRRITATE, EXASPERATE, NETTLE, PROVOKE, AGGRAVATE, RILE, PEEVE *shared meaning element* : to excite to angry annoyance

ir·ri·tat·ed *adj* : subjected to irritation; *esp* : roughened, reddened, or inflamed by an irritant <~ eyes>

ir·ri·ta·tion \ˌir-ə-ˈtā-shən\ *n* **1 a :** the act of irritating **b** : something that irritates **c :** the state of being irritated **2** : a condition of irritability, soreness, roughness, or inflammation of a bodily part

ir·ri·ta·tive \ˈir-ə-ˌtāt-iv\ *adj* **1 :** serving to excite : IRRITATING **2** : accompanied with or produced by irritation <~ coughing>

ir·ro·ta·tion·al \ˌir-(r)ō-ˈtā-shnəl, -shən-ᵊl\ *adj* **1 :** not rotating or involving rotation <an ~ electric field> **2 :** free of vortices <~ flow>

ir·rupt \(ˈ)i(ə)r-ˈ(r)əpt\ *vi* [L *irruptus*, pp. of *irrumpere*, lit., to break in, fr. *in-* + *rumpere* to break — more at RUPTURE] **1 :** to rush in forcibly or violently **2** *of a natural population* : to undergo a sudden upsurge in numbers esp. when natural ecological balances and checks are disturbed **3 :** ERUPT 1c <the crowd ~*ed* in a fervor of patriotism —*Time*> — **ir·rup·tion** \-ˈ(r)əp-shən\ *n*

ir·rup·tive \-ˈ(r)əp-tiv\ *adj* **1 :** irrupting or tending to irrupt **2** *of an igneous rock* : INTRUSIVE — **ir·rup·tive·ly** *adv*

IRS *abbr* Internal Revenue Service

1is [ME, fr. OE; akin to OHG *ist* is (fr. *sīn* to be), L *est* (fr. *esse* to be), Gk *esti* (fr. *einai* to be)] *pres 3d sing of* BE, *dial pres 1st & 2d sing of* BE, *substand pres pl of* BE

2is *abbr* island; isle

is- *or* **iso-** *comb form* [LL, fr. Gk, fr. *isos* equal] **1 :** equal : homogeneous : uniform <*is*acoustic> **2 :** isomeric <*iso*propyl> **3 :** for or from different individuals of the same species <*iso*agglutination>

Isa *or* **Is** *abbr* Isaiah

Isaac \ˈī-zik, -zək\ *n* [LL, fr. Heb *Yiṣḥāq*] : the son of Abraham and father of Jacob according to the account in Genesis

Isa·iah \ī-ˈzā-ə, *chiefly Brit* -ˈzī-\ *n* [Heb *Yĕsha'yāhū*] **1 :** a major Hebrew prophet in Judah about 740 to 701 B.C. **2 :** a prophetic book of canonical Jewish and Christian Scripture — see BIBLE table

Isa·ias \-əs\ *n* [LL, fr. Gk *Esaias*, fr. Heb *Yĕshaʻyāhū*] : ISAIAH

is·al·lo·bar \(ˈ)ī-ˈsal-ə-ˌbär\ *n* [ISV *is-* + *all-* + *-bar* (as in *isobar*)] : an imaginary line or a line on a chart connecting the places of equal change of atmospheric pressure within a specified time — **is·al·lo·bar·ic** \ˌī-ˌsal-ə-ˈbär-ik, -ˈbar-\ *adj*

is·ba \iz-ˈbä\ *n* [Russ *izba*] : a Russian log hut

ISBN *abbr* International Standard Book Number

ISC *abbr* **1** International Space Congress **2** International Student Conference **3** interstate commerce

isch·emia \is-ˈkē-mē-ə\ *n* [NL *ischaemia*, fr. *ischaemus* styptic, fr. Gk *ischaimos*, fr. *ischein* to restrain + *haima* blood; akin to Gk *echein* to hold — more at SCHEME] : localized tissue anemia due to obstruction of the inflow of arterial blood — **isch·emic** \-mik\ *adj*

is·chi·um \ˈis-kē-əm\ *n, pl* **is·chia** \-ə\ [L, hip joint, fr. Gk *ischion*] : the dorsal and posterior of the three principal bones composing either half of the pelvis — **is·chi·al** \-əl\ *adj*

-ise \ˌīz\ *vb suffix, chiefly Brit* : -IZE

is·en·tro·pic \ˌīs-ᵊn-ˈtrō-pik, -ˈträp-ik\ *adj* : of or relating to equal or constant entropy; *esp* : taking place without change of entropy <an ~ expansion> — **is·en·tro·pi·cal·ly** \-ˈtrō-pi-k(ə-)lē, -ˈträp-i-\ *adv*

Iseult \is-ˈült, iz-\ *n* [OF *Isolt*, *Iseut*] : ISOLDE

-ish \ish\ *adj suffix* [ME, fr. OE *-isc*; akin to OHG *-isc*, -ish, Gk *-iskos*, dim. suffix] **1** : of, relating to, or being — chiefly in adjectives indicating nationality or ethnic group <Finn*ish*> **2 a** : characteristic of <boy*ish*> <mul*ish*> **b (1)** : having a touch or trace of <summer*ish*> : somewhat <purpl*ish*> **(2)** : having the approximate age of <forty*ish*> **(3)** : being or occurring at the approximate time of <eight*ish*>

Ish·ma·el \ˈish-mē-əl\ *n* [Heb *Yishmāʻēl*] **1** : the outcast son of Abraham and Hagar according to the account in Genesis **2** : a social outcast

Ish·ma·el·ite \-ə-ˌlīt\ *n* **1** : a descendant of Ishmael **2** : ISHMAEL 2 — **Ish·ma·el·it·ish** \-ˌlīt-ish\ *adj* — **Ish·ma·el·it·ism** \-ˌlīt-ˌiz-əm\ *n*

isin·glass \ˈīz-ᵊn-ˌglas, ˈī-ziŋ-\ *n* [prob. by folk etymology fr. obs. D *huizenblas*, fr. MD *huusblase*, fr. *huus* sturgeon + *blase* bladder] **1** : a semitransparent whitish very pure gelatin prepared from the air bladders of fishes (as sturgeons) and used esp. as a clarifying agent and in jellies and glue **2** : MICA

Isis \ˈī-səs\ *n* [L *Isid-*, *Isis*, fr. Gk, fr. Egypt *ist*] : an Egyptian nature goddess and wife of Osiris

isl *abbr* island

Is·lam \is-ˈläm, iz-, -ˈlam, ˈis-ˌ, ˈiz-ˌ\ *n* [Ar *islām* submission (to the will of God)] **1** : the religious faith of Muslims including belief in Allah as the sole deity and in Muhammad as his prophet **2 a** : the civilization erected upon Islamic faith **b** : the group of modern nations in which Islam is the dominant religion — **Is·lam·ic** \is-ˈläm-ik, iz-, -ˈlam-\ *adj* — **Is·lam·ics** \-iks\ *n pl but sing or pl in constr*

Is·lam·ism \is-ˈläm-ˌiz-əm, iz-ˈläm-, -ˈlam-; ˈiz-ləm-\ *n* : the faith, doctrine, or cause of Islam — **Is·lam·ist** \-əst\ *n*

Is·lam·ize \ˈiz-lə-ˌmīz; is-ˈläm-ˌīz, iz-ˈläm-, -ˈlam-\ *vt* **-ized; -iz·ing** : to make Islamic; *esp* : to convert to Islam — **Is·lam·iza·tion** \ˌiz-lə-mə-ˈzā-shən; is-ˌläm-ə-, iz-ˌläm-, -ˌlam-\ *n*

¹is·land \ˈī-lənd\ *n* [alter. of earlier *iland*, fr. ME, fr. OE *īgland*; akin to ON *eyland* island; both fr. a prehistoric NGmc-WGmc compound whose first constituent is represented by OE *īg* island (akin to OE *ēa* river, L *aqua* water) and whose second constituent is represented by OE *land*] **1** : a tract of land surrounded by water and smaller than a continent **2** : something resembling an island esp. in its isolated or surrounded position **3 a** : SAFETY ISLAND **b** : SAFETY ZONE **4** : a superstructure on the deck of a ship (as an aircraft carrier) **5** : an isolated group or area; *esp* : an isolated ethnological group

²island *vt* **1 a** : to make into or as if into an island **b** : to dot with or as if with islands **2** : ISOLATE

is·land·er \ˈī-lən-dər\ *n* : a native or inhabitant of an island

island universe *n* : a galaxy other than the Milky Way

¹isle \ˈī(ə)l\ *n* [ME, fr. OF, fr. L *insula*] : ISLAND; *esp* : a small island

²isle *vt* **isled; isl·ing** **1** : to make an isle of **2** : to place on or as if on an isle

is·let \ˈī-lət\ *n* : a little island

islet of Lang·er·hans \-ˈläŋ-ər-ˌhänz, -ˌhän(t)s\ [Paul *Langerhans* †1888 G physician] : any of the groups of small slightly granular endocrine cells that form anastomosing trabeculae among the tubules and alveoli of the pancreas and secrete insulin

ism \ˈiz-əm\ *n* [*-ism*] : a distinctive doctrine, cause, or theory

-ism \ˌiz-əm\ *n suffix* [ME *-isme*, fr. MF & L; MF, partly fr. L *-isma* (fr. Gk) & partly fr. L *-ismus*, fr. Gk *-ismos*; Gk *-isma* & *-ismos*, fr. verbs in *-izein* -ize] **1 a** : act : practice : process <critic*ism*> <plagiar*ism*> **b** : manner of action or behavior characteristic of a (specified) person or thing <animal*ism*> **2 a** : state : condition : property <barbarian*ism*> **b** : abnormal state or condition resulting from excess of a (specified) thing <alcohol*ism*> or marked by resemblance to (such) a person or thing <mongol*ism*> **3 a** : doctrine : theory : cult <Buddh*ism*> **b** : adherence to a system or a class of principles <stoic*ism*> **4** : characteristic or peculiar feature or trait <colloquial*ism*>

isn't \ˈiz-ᵊnt\ : is not

iso·ag·glu·ti·na·tion \ˈī-(ˌ)sō-ə-ˌglüt-ᵊn-ˈā-shən\ *n* : agglutination of an agglutinogen of one individual by the serum of another of the same species — **iso·ag·glu·ti·na·tive** \-ˈglüt-ᵊn-ˌāt-iv\ *adj*

iso·ag·glu·ti·nin \ˌī-(ˌ)sō-ə-ˈglüt-ᵊn-ən\ *n* : an agglutinin specific for the cells of another individual of the same species

iso·ag·glu·tin·o·gen \ˈī-(ˌ)sō-ˌag-lü-ˈtin-ə-jən\ *n* : a substance capable of provoking formation of or reacting with an isoagglutinin

iso·al·lox·a·zine \ˌī-(ˌ)sō-ə-ˈläk-sə-ˌzēn\ *n* [*iso-* + *all*antoic + *ox*alic + *azine*] : a yellow solid $C_{10}H_6N_4O_2$ that is the parent compound of various flavins (as riboflavin)

iso·an·ti·body \ˌī-(ˌ)sō-ˈant-i-ˌbäd-ē\ *n* : an antibody against an antigen present in some members of a species that is produced by a member of the species lacking that antigen

iso·an·ti·gen \-ˈant-i-jən\ *n* [ISV] : an antigen capable of inducing the production of an isoantibody — **iso·an·ti·gen·ic** \ˈī-(ˌ)sō-ˌant-i-ˈjen-ik\ *adj* — **iso·an·ti·ge·nic·i·ty** \-jə-ˈnis-ət-ē\ *n*

iso·bar \ˈī-sə-ˌbär\ *n* [ISV *is-* + *-bar* (fr. Gk *baros* weight); akin to Gk *barys* heavy — more at GRIEVE] **1** : an imaginary line or a line on a map or chart connecting or marking places on the surface of the earth where the height of the barometer reduced to sea level is the same either at a given time or for a certain period **2** : one of two or more atoms or elements having the same atomic weights or mass numbers but different atomic numbers — **iso·bar·ic** \ˌī-sə-ˈbär-ik, -ˈbar-\ *adj*

iso·bu·tyl·ene \ˌī-sō-ˈbyüt-ᵊl-ˌēn\ *n* [ISV] : a gaseous butylene C_4H_8 used esp. in making butyl rubber and gasoline components

iso·chro·mat·ic \ˌī-sə-krō-ˈmat-ik\ *adj* : ORTHOCHROMATIC

iso·chron \ˈī-sə-ˌkrän\ *or* **iso·chrone** \-ˌkrōn\ *n* [ISV *is-* + *-chron* (fr. Gk *chronos* time)] : a line on a chart connecting points at which an event occurs simultaneously or which represents the same time or time difference

iso·chro·nal \ī-ˈsäk-rən-ᵊl, ˌī-sə-ˈkrōn-\ *adj* [Gk *isochronos*, fr. *is-* + *chronos* time] : uniform in time : having equal duration : recurring at regular intervals — **iso·chro·nal·ly** \-ᵊl-ē\ *adv* — **iso·chro·nism** \ī-ˈsäk-rə-ˌniz-əm, ˌī-sə-ˈkrō-\ *n*

iso·chro·nous \ī-ˈsäk-rə-nəs, ˌī-sə-ˈkrō-\ *adj* [Gk *isochronos*] : ISOCHRONAL — **iso·chro·nous·ly** *adv*

¹iso·cli·nal \ˌī-sə-ˈklīn-ᵊl\ *adj* [ISV] : relating to, having, or indicating equality of inclination or dip — **iso·cli·nal·ly** \-ᵊl-ē\ *adv*

²isoclinal *n* : ISOCLINIC LINE

iso·cline \ˈī-sə-ˌklīn\ *n* : an anticline or syncline so closely folded that the rock beds of the two sides have the same dip

iso·clin·ic \ˌī-sə-ˈklin-ik\ *adj* [ISV] : ISOCLINAL — **iso·clin·i·cal·ly** \-ˈklin-i-k(ə-)lē\ *adv*

isoclinic line *n* : a line on a map or chart joining points on the earth's surface at which a magnetic needle has the same inclination to the plumb line

iso·cy·a·nate \ˌī-sō-ˈsī-ə-ˌnāt, -nət\ *n* [ISV] : a salt or ester of isomeric cyanic acid HNCO used esp. in plastics and adhesives

iso·cy·clic \-ˈsī-klik, -ˈsik-lik\ *adj* [ISV] : having or being a ring composed of atoms of only one element; *esp* : CARBOCYCLIC

iso·di·a·met·ric \-ˌdī-ə-ˈme-trik\ *adj* [ISV] : having equal diameters <~ cells of plant parenchymatous tissue>

iso·dose \ˈī-sə-ˌdōs\ *adj* [ISV] : of or relating to points or zones in a medium that receive equal doses of radiation

iso·dy·nam·ic \ˌī-sō-dī-ˈnam-ik\ *adj* [ISV] **1** : of or relating to equality or uniformity of force **2** : connecting points at which the magnetic intensity is the same <~ line>

iso·elec·tric \ˌī-sō-i-ˈlek-trik\ *adj* [ISV] **1** : having or representing zero difference of electric potential **2** : being the pH at which the electrolyte will not migrate in an electrical field <the ~ point of a protein>

iso·elec·tron·ic \-i-ˌlek-ˈträn-ik\ *adj* [ISV] : having the same number of electrons or valency electrons — **iso·elec·tron·i·cal·ly** \-i-k(ə-)lē\ *adv*

iso·en·zyme \-ˈen-ˌzīm\ *n* : ISOZYME — **iso·en·zy·mat·ic** \ˈī-sō-ˌen-zə-ˈmat-ik, -zī-\ *adj* — **iso·en·zy·mic** \-en-ˈzī-mik\ *adj*

iso·ga·mete \ˌī-sō-gə-ˈmēt, -ˈgam-ˌēt\ *n* [ISV] : a gamete indistinguishable in form or size or behavior from another gamete with which it can unite to form a zygote — **iso·ga·met·ic** \-gə-ˈmet-ik\ *adj*

isog·a·mous \ī-ˈsäg-ə-məs\ *adj* [prob. fr. (assumed) NL *isogamus*, fr. *is-* + *-gamus* -gamous] : having or involving isogametes — compare HETEROGAMOUS — **isog·a·my** \-mē\ *n*

iso·ge·ne·ic \ˌī-sō-jə-ˈnē-ik\ *adj* [*is-* + *-geneic* (as in *syngeneic*)] : genetically too similar to react antigenically <an ~ graft>

iso·gen·ic \-ˈjen-ik\ *adj* [*is-* + *gene* + *-ic*] : characterized by essentially identical genes <identical twins are ~>

iso·gloss \ˈī-sə-ˌgläs, -ˌglȯs\ *n* [ISV *is-* + Gk *glōssa* language — more at GLOSS] **1** : a boundary line between places or regions that differ in a particular linguistic feature **2** : a line on a map representing an isogloss — **iso·gloss·al** \ˌī-sə-ˈgläs-əl, -ˈglȯ-səl\ *adj*

¹iso·gon·ic \ˌī-sə-ˈgän-ik\ *or* **isog·o·nal** \ī-ˈsäg-ən-ᵊl, ˌī-sə-ˈgōn-\ *adj* [ISV *is-* + Gk *gōnia* angle — more at -GON] : of, relating to, or having equal angles

²isogonic *or* **isogonal** *n* : ISOGONIC LINE

³isogonic *adj* [*isogony*, fr. *is-* + *-gony*] : exhibiting equivalent relative growth of parts such that size relations remain constant — **isog·o·ny** \ī-ˈsäg-ə-nē\ *n*

isogonic line *n* : an imaginary line or a line on a map joining points on the earth's surface at which the magnetic declination is the same

iso·gram \ˈī-sə-ˌgram\ *n* : a line on a map or chart along which there is a constant value (as of temperature, pressure, or rainfall)

iso·hel \ˈī-sō-ˌhel\ *n* [*is-* + Gk *hēlios* sun — more at SOLAR] : a line drawn on a map or chart connecting places of equal duration of sunshine

iso·he·mol·y·sis \ˌī-sō-hi-ˈmäl-ə-səs\ *n* [NL] : lysis of the red blood cells of one individual by antibodies in the serum of another of the same species

iso·hy·et \ˌī-sō-ˈhī-ət\ *n* [ISV *is-* + Gk *hyetos* rain — more at HYET-] : a line on a map or chart connecting areas of equal rainfall — **iso·hy·et·al** \-ət-əl\ *adj*

iso·la·ble \ˈī-sə-lə-bəl *also* ˈis-ə-\ *also* **iso·lat·able** \-ˌlāt-ə-bəl\ *adj* : capable of being isolated

¹iso·late \ˈī-sə-ˌlāt *also* ˈis-ə-\ *vt* **-lat·ed; -lat·ing** [back-formation fr. *isolated* set apart, fr. F *isolé*, fr. It *isolato*, fr. *isola* island, fr. L *insula*] **1** : to set apart from others; *also* : QUARANTINE **2** : to select from among others; *esp* : to separate from another substance so as to obtain pure or in a free state **3 :** INSULATE — **iso·la·tor** \-ˌlāt-ər\ *n*

²**iso·late** \-lət, -ˌlāt\ *adj* **:** being alone **:** SOLITARY, ISOLATED <standing there, ~, and still —D. H. Lawrence>

³**iso·late** \-lət, -ˌlāt\ *n* **:** a product of isolating **:** an individual or kind obtained by selection or separation

iso·la·tion \ˌī-sə-ˈlā-shən *also* ˌis-ə-\ *n* **:** the action of isolating **:** the condition of being isolated ***syn*** see SOLITUDE

iso·la·tion·ism \-shə-ˌniz-əm\ *n* **:** a policy of national isolation by abstention from alliances and other international political and economic relations — **iso·la·tion·ist** \-sh(ə-)nəst\ *n or adj*

Isol·de \i-ˈzōl-də\ *n* [G, fr. OF *Isolt, Iseut*] **1 :** an Irish princess married to King Mark of Cornwall and loved by Tristram **2 :** the daughter of the King of Brittany and wife of Tristram

iso·leu·cine \ˌī-sō-ˈlü-ˌsēn\ *n* [ISV] **:** a crystalline essential amino acid $C_6H_{13}NO_2$ isomeric with leucine

iso·line \ˈī-(ˌ)sō-ˌlīn\ *n* **:** ISOGRAM

isoln *abbr* isolation

isol·o·gous \ī-ˈsäl-ə-gəs\ *adj* [ISV *is-* + *-logous* (as in *homologous*)] **:** relating to or being any of two or more compounds of related structure and a characteristic difference of composition other than CH_2 or a multiple thereof — **iso·logue** *or* **iso·log** \ˈī-sə-ˌlȯg, -ˌläg\ *n*

iso·mag·net·ic \ˌī-sō-mag-ˈnet-ik\ *adj* [ISV] **1 :** of or relating to points of equal magnetic intensity or of equal value of a component of such intensity **2 :** connecting isomagnetic points <~ line on a map>

iso·mer \ˈī-sə-mər\ *n* [ISV, back-formation fr. *isomeric*] **:** a compound, radical, ion, or nuclide isomeric with one or more others

isom·er·ase \ī-ˈsäm-ə-ˌrās, -ˌrāz\ *n* **:** an enzyme that catalyzes the conversion of its substrate to an isomeric form

iso·mer·ic \ˌī-sə-ˈmer-ik\ *adj* [ISV, fr. Gk *isomerēs* equally divided, fr. *is-* + *meros* part — more at MERIT] **:** of, relating to, or exhibiting isomerism

isom·er·ism \ī-ˈsäm-ə-ˌriz-əm\ *n* **1 :** the relation of two or more compounds, radicals, or ions that contain the same numbers of atoms of the same elements but differ in structural arrangement and properties **2 :** the relation of two or more nuclides with the same mass numbers and atomic numbers but different energy states and rates of radioactive decay **3 :** the condition of being isomerous

isom·er·ize \ī-ˈsäm-ə-ˌrīz\ *vb* **-ized; -iz·ing** *vi* **:** to become changed into an isomeric form ~ *vt* **:** to cause to isomerize — **isom·er·i·za·tion** \-ˌsäm-ə-rə-ˈzā-shən\ *n*

isom·er·ous \ī-ˈsäm-ə-rəs\ *adj* **:** having an equal number of parts (as ridges or markings); *esp* **:** having the members of each floral whorl equal in number

iso·met·ric \ˌī-sə-ˈme-trik\ *also* **iso·met·ri·cal** \-tri-kəl\ *adj* **1 :** of, relating to, or characterized by equality of measure: as **a :** of, relating to, or being an isometric drawing or projection **b :** relating to or being a crystallographic system characterized by three equal axes at right angles **2 :** of, relating to, or involving isometrics — **iso·met·ri·cal·ly** \-tri-k(ə-)lē\ *adv*

isometric drawing *n* **:** the representation of an object in isometric projection but with lines parallel to the edges drawn in true length — see ISOMETRIC PROJECTION illustration

isometric line *n* **1 :** a line (as a contour line) drawn on a map and indicating a true constant value throughout its extent **2 :** a line representing changes of pressure or temperature under conditions of constant volume

isometric projection *n* **:** axonometric projection in which all three faces are equally inclined to the drawing surface so that all the edges are equally foreshortened

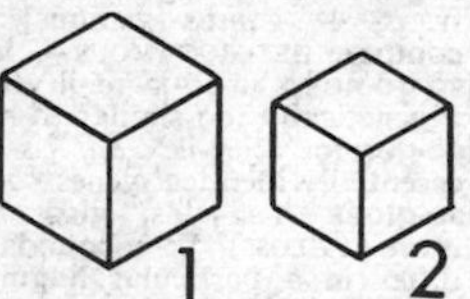

1 isometric drawing, in which the lines of the cube are drawn in their actual length; *2* isometric projection, in which the lines of the cube are foreshortened

iso·met·rics \-ˈme-triks\ *n pl but sing or pl in constr* **:** exercise or a system of exercises in which opposing muscles are so contracted that there is little shortening but great increase in tone of muscle fibers involved

isom·e·try \ī-ˈsäm-ə-trē\ *n, pl* **-tries :** a mapping of a metric space onto another or onto itself so that the distance between any two points in the original space is the same as the distance between their images in the second space <rotation and translation are *isometries* of the plane>

iso·morph \ˈī-sə-ˌmȯrf\ *n* [ISV] **:** something identical with or similar to something else in form or structure: as **a :** one of two or more substances related by isomorphism **b :** an individual or group exhibiting isomorphism — **iso·mor·phous** \ˌī-sə-ˈmȯr-fəs\ *adj*

iso·mor·phic \ˌī-sə-ˈmȯr-fik\ *adj* **1 :** being of identical or similar form or shape or structure; *esp* **:** having sporophytic and gametophytic generations alike in size and shape <some algae and fungi are ~> **2 :** related by an isomorphism <~ mathematical rings> — **iso·mor·phi·cal·ly** \-fi-k(ə-)lē\ *adv*

iso·mor·phism \ˌī-sə-ˈmȯr-ˌfiz-əm\ *n* [ISV] **1 :** similarity in organisms of different ancestry resulting from convergence **2 a :** similarity of crystalline form between substances of similar composition **b :** HOMEOMORPHISM 1 **3 :** a one-to-one correspondence between two mathematical sets; *esp* **:** a homomorphism that is one-to-one — compare ENDOMORPHISM

iso·ni·a·zid \ˌī-sə-ˈnī-ə-zəd\ *n* [*isoni*cotinic acid hydr*azide*] **:** a crystalline compound $C_6H_7N_3O$ used in treating tuberculosis

ison·o·my \ī-ˈsän-ə-mē\ *n* [Gk *isonomia,* fr. *isonomos* characterized by isonomy, fr. *is-* + *nomos* right, law] **:** equality before the law

iso·oc·tane \ˌī-sō-ˈäk-ˌtān\ *n* [ISV] **:** an octane of branched-chain structure or a mixture of such octanes; *esp* **:** a flammable liquid octane used to determine the octane number of fuels

iso·phote \ˈī-sə-ˌfōt\ *n* [ISV *is-* + *-phote* (fr. Gk *phōt-, phōs* light) — more at FANCY] **:** a curve on a chart joining points of equal light intensity from a given source — **iso·phot·al** \ˌī-sə-ˈfōt-əl\ *adj*

iso·pi·es·tic \ˌī-sō-pē-ˈes-tik, -pī-\ *adj* [*is-* + Gk *piestos,* verbal of *piezein* to press] **:** of, relating to, or marked by equal pressure

iso·pleth \ˈī-sə-ˌpleth\ *n* [ISV *is-* + Gk *plēthos* quantity; akin to Gk *plēthein* to be full — more at FULL] **1 :** an isogram on a graph showing the occurrence or frequency of a phenomenon as a function of two variables **2 :** a line on a map connecting points at which a given variable has a specified constant value — **iso·pleth·ic** \ˌī-sə-ˈpleth-ik\ *adj*

iso·pod \ˈī-sə-ˌpäd\ *n* [deriv. of Gk *is-* + *pod-, pous* foot — more at FOOT] **:** any of a large order (Isopoda) of small sessile-eyed crustaceans with the body composed of seven free thoracic segments each bearing a pair of similar legs — **isopod** *adj* — **isop·o·dan** \ī-ˈsäp-əd-ən\ *adj or n*

iso·pren·a·line \ˌī-sə-ˈpren-ᵊl-ən\ *n* [prob. fr. *isopro*pyl + adr*enaline*] **:** ISOPROTERANOL

iso·prene \ˈī-sə-ˌprēn\ *n* [prob. fr. *is-* + *propyl* + *-ene*] **:** a flammable liquid unsaturated hydrocarbon C_5H_8 used esp. in synthetic rubber

iso·pren·oid \ˌī-sə-ˈprē-ˌnȯid\ *adj* **:** relating to, containing, or being a branched-chain grouping characteristic of isoprene

iso·pro·pyl \ˌī-sə-ˈprō-pəl\ *n* [ISV] **:** the alkyl radical isomeric with normal propyl

isopropyl alcohol *n* **:** a volatile flammable alcohol C_3H_8O used esp. as a solvent and rubbing alcohol

iso·pro·ter·e·nol \ˌī-sə-prō-ˈter-ə-ˌnȯl, -ˌnōl\ *n* [*isopro*pyl + ar*terenol* (norepinephrine), fr. *Arterenol,* a trademark] **:** a drug $C_{11}H_{17}NO_3$ used in the treatment of asthma

isos·ce·les triangle \ī-ˌsäs-(ə-)ˌlēz-\ *n* [LL *isosceles* having two equal sides, fr. Gk *isoskelēs,* fr. *is-* + *skelos* leg — more at CYLINDER] **:** a triangle having two equal sides — see TRIANGLE illustration

iso·seis·mal \ˌī-sə-ˈsīz-məl, -ˈsīs-\ *adj* **:** of, relating to, or marked by equal intensity of earthquake shock

is·os·mot·ic \ˌī-ˌsäz-ˈmät-ik, -ˌsäs-\ *adj* [ISV] **:** of, relating to, or exhibiting equal osmotic pressure <~ solutions> — **is·os·mot·i·cal·ly** \-ˈmät-i-k(ə-)lē\ *adv*

iso·spin \ˈī-sə-ˌspin\ *n* **:** a quantum characteristic of a group of closely related elementary particles (as a proton and a neutron) handled mathematically like ordinary spin with the possible orientations in a hypothetical space specifying the number of particles of different electric charge comprising the group — called also *isotopic spin*

iso·spon·dy·lous \ˌī-sō-ˈspän-də-ləs\ *adj* [deriv. of Gk *isos* equal + Gk *spondylos* vertebra — more at SPONDYLITIS] **:** of or relating to an order (Isospondyli) of primitive soft-finned teleost fishes

iso·spo·rous \ˌī-sə-ˈspōr-əs, -ˈspȯr-; ī-ˈsäs-pə-rəs\ *adj* **:** producing sexual or asexual spores of but one kind — **iso·spo·ry** \ˈī-sə-ˌspōr-ē, -ˌspȯr-; ī-ˈsäs-pə-rē\ *n*

isos·ta·sy \ī-ˈsäs-tə-sē\ *n* [ISV *is-* + Gk *-stasia* condition of standing, fr. *histanai* to cause to stand — more at STAND] **1 :** the quality or state of being subjected to equal pressure from every side **2 :** general equilibrium in the earth's crust maintained by a yielding flow of rock material beneath the surface under gravitative stress — **iso·stat·ic** \ˌī-sə-ˈstat-ik\ *adj* — **iso·stat·i·cal·ly** \-ˈstat-i-k(ə-)lē\ *adv*

iso·tach \ˈī-sə-ˌtak\ *n* [ISV *is-* + *-tach* (fr. Gk *tachys* quick)] **:** a line on a map or chart connecting points of equal wind velocity

iso·therm \ˈī-sə-ˌthərm\ *n* [F *isotherme,* adj.] **1 :** a line on a map or chart of the earth's surface connecting points having the same temperature at a given time or the same mean temperature for a given period **2 :** a line on a chart representing changes of volume or pressure under conditions of constant temperature

iso·ther·mal \ˌī-sə-ˈthər-məl\ *adj* [F *isotherme,* fr. *is-* + Gk *thermos* hot — more at WARM] **1 :** of, relating to, or marked by equality of temperature **2 :** of, relating to, or marked by changes of volume or pressure under conditions of constant temperature — **iso·ther·mal·ly** \-mə-lē\ *adv*

iso·ton·ic \ˌī-sə-ˈtän-ik\ *adj* [ISV] **1 :** of, relating to, or exhibiting equal tension **2 :** ISOSMOTIC — used of solutions — **iso·ton·i·cal·ly** \-i-k(ə-)lē\ *adv* — **iso·to·nic·i·ty** \-tō-ˈnis-ət-ē\ *n*

iso·tope \ˈī-sə-ˌtōp\ *n* [*is-* + Gk *topos* place — more at TOPIC] **1 :** any of two or more species of atoms of a chemical element with the same atomic number and position in the periodic table and nearly identical chemical behavior but with differing atomic mass or mass number and different physical properties **2 :** NUCLIDE — **iso·to·pic** \ˌī-sə-ˈtäp-ik, -ˈtō-pik\ *adj* — **iso·to·pi·cal·ly** \-ˈtäp-i-k(ə-)lē, -ˈtō-pi-\ *adv* — **iso·to·py** \ˈī-sə-ˌtō-pē, ī-ˈsät-ə-pē\ *n*

iso·tro·pic \ˌī-sə-ˈtrō-pik, -ˈträp-ik\ *adj* [ISV] **1 :** exhibiting properties (as velocity of light transmission) with the same values when measured along axes in all directions <an ~ crystal> **2 :** lacking predetermined axes <an ~ egg> — **isot·ro·py** \ī-ˈsä-trə-pē\ *n*

iso·zyme \ˈī-sə-ˌzīm\ *n* **:** any of two or more chemically distinct but functionally like enzymes — **iso·zy·mic** \ˌī-sə-ˈzī-mik\ *adj*

Isr *abbr* Israel; Israeli

Is·ra·el \ˈiz-rē-əl\ *n* [ME, fr. OE, fr. LL, fr. Gk *Israēl,* fr. Heb *Yiśrāʼēl*] **1 :** JACOB **2 :** the Jewish people **3 :** a people chosen by God — **Israel** *adj*

¹**Is·rae·li** \iz-ˈrā-lē\ *adj* [NHeb *yiśrēʼēlī,* fr. Heb, Israelite, n. & adj., fr. *Yiśrāʼēl*] **:** of or relating to the republic of Israel

²**Israeli** *n, pl* **Israelis** *also* **Israeli :** a native or inhabitant of the republic of Israel

Is·ra·el·ite \ˈiz-rē-ə-ˌlīt\ *n* [ME, fr. LL *Israelita,* fr. Gk *Israēlitēs,* fr. *Israēl*] **:** a descendant of the Hebrew patriarch Jacob; *specif* **:** a native or inhabitant of the ancient northern kingdom of Israel — **Israelite** *or* **Is·ra·el·it·ish** \-ˌlīt-ish\ *adj*

Is·sa \ē-ˈsä\ *n, pl* **Issa** *or* **Is·sas** \-ˈsä(z)\ **:** a member of a Somali people of eastern Ethiopia, Somalia, and the French Territory of the Afars and the Issas

Is·sa·char \ˈis-ə-ˌkär\ *n* [LL, fr. Gk, fr. Heb *Yiśśākhār*] **:** a son of Jacob and the traditional eponymous ancestor of one of the tribes of Israel

is·su·able \ˈish-ü-ə-bəl\ *adj* **1 :** open to contest, debate, or litigation **2 :** authorized for issue <bonds ~ under the merger

terms> **3 :** possible as a result or consequence — **is·su·ably** \-blē\ *adv*

is·su·ance \ˈish-ə-wən(t)s\ *n* **:** ISSUE

is·su·ant \-wənt\ *adj* **1** *archaic* **:** coming forth **:** EMERGING **2** *of a heraldic animal* **:** rising with only the upper part visible

[1]**is·sue** \ˈish-(ˌ)ü, ˈish-ə(-w), *chiefly Brit* ˈis-(ˌ)yü\ *n* [ME, exit, proceeds, fr. MF, fr. OF, fr. *issir* to come out, go out, fr. L *exire* to go out, fr. *ex-* + *ire* to go; akin to Goth *iddja* he went, Gk *ienai* to go, Skt *eti* he goes] **1** *pl* **:** proceeds from a source of revenue (as an estate) **2 :** the action of going, coming, or flowing out **:** EGRESS, EMERGENCE **3 :** a means or place of going out **:** EXIT, OUTLET **4 :** OFFSPRING, PROGENY <died without ~> **5 a :** a final outcome that usu. constitutes a solution (as of a problem) or resolution (as of a difficulty) **b** *obs* **:** a final conclusion or decision about something arrived at after consideration **c** *archaic* **:** TERMINATION, END <hope that his enterprise would have a prosperous ~ —T. B. Macaulay> **6 a :** a matter that is in dispute between two or more parties **:** a point of debate or controversy **b :** the point at which an unsettled matter is ready for a decision <brought the matter to an ~> **7 :** a discharge (as of blood) from the body **8 a :** something coming forth from a specified source <~*s* of a disordered imagination> **b** *obs* **:** DEED **9 a :** the act of publishing or officially giving out or making available <the next ~ of commemorative stamps> <~ of supplies by the quartermaster> **b :** the thing or the whole quantity of things given out at one time <read the latest ~> ***syn*** see EFFECT — **is·sue·less** \ˈish-ü-ləs\ *adj* — **at issue 1 :** in a state of controversy **:** in disagreement **2** *also* **in issue :** under discussion or in dispute

[2]**issue** *vb* **is·sued; is·su·ing** *vi* **1 a :** to go, come, or flow out **b :** to come forth **:** EMERGE **c :** to come to an issue of law or fact in pleading **2 :** ACCRUE <profits *issuing* from the sale of the stock> **3 :** to descend from a specified parent or ancestor **4 :** to be a consequence or final outcome **:** EMANATE, RESULT **5 :** to appear or become available through being officially put forth or distributed **:** appear through issuance or publication <no new editions are expected to ~ from that press> **6 :** EVENTUATE, TERMINATE ~ *vt* **1 :** to cause to come forth **:** DISCHARGE, EMIT **2 a :** to put forth or distribute officially <government *issued* a new airmail stamp> <~ orders to advance> **b :** to send out for sale or circulation **:** PUBLISH ***syn*** see SPRING — **is·su·er** *n*

IST *abbr* insulin shock therapy

[1]**-ist** \əst\ *n suffix* [ME *-iste,* fr. OF & L; OF *-iste,* fr. L *-ista, -istes,* fr. Gk *-istēs,* fr. verbs in *-izein* -ize] **1 a :** one that performs a (specified) action <cycl*ist*> **:** one that makes or produces a (specified) thing (novel*ist*> **b :** one that plays a (specified) musical instrument <harp*ist*> **c :** one that operates a (specified) mechanical instrument or contrivance <automobil*ist*> **2 :** one that specializes in a (specified) art or science or skill <geolog*ist*> <ventriloqu*ist*> **3 :** one that adheres to or advocates a (specified) doctrine or system or code of behavior <social*ist*> <royal*ist*> <hedon*ist*> or that of a (specified) individual (Calvin*ist*> <Darwin*ist*>

[2]**-ist** *adj suffix* **:** of, relating to, or characteristic of <dilettant*ist*>

isth *abbr* isthmus

[1]**isth·mi·an** \ˈis-mē-ən\ *n* **1 :** a native or inhabitant of an isthmus **2** *cap* **:** a native or inhabitant of the Isthmus of Panama

[2]**isthmian** *adj* **:** of, relating to, or situated in or near an isthmus: as **a** *often cap* **:** of or relating to the Isthmus of Corinth in Greece or the games held there in ancient times **b** *often cap* **:** of or relating to the Isthmus of Panama connecting the No. American and So. American continents

isth·mic \ˈis-mik\ *adj* **:** ISTHMIAN

isth·mus \ˈis-məs\ *n* [L, fr. Gk *isthmos*] **1 :** a narrow strip of land connecting two larger land areas **2 :** a contracted anatomical part or passage connecting two larger structures or cavities

is·tle \ˈist-lē\ *n* [AmerSp *ixtle,* fr. Nahuatl *ichtli*] **:** a strong fiber (as for cordage or basketry) from various tropical American plants

ISV *abbr* International Scientific Vocabulary

[1]**it** \(ˈ)it, ət\ *pron* [ME, fr. OE *hit* — more at HE] **1 :** that one — used as subject or direct object or indirect object of a verb or object of a preposition usu. in reference to a lifeless thing <took a quick look at the house and noticed ~ was very old>, a plant <there is a rosebush near the fence and ~ is now blooming>, a person or animal whose sex is unknown or disregarded <don't know who ~ is>, a group of individuals or things, or an abstract entity <beauty is everywhere and ~ is a source of joy>; compare HE, ITS, SHE, THEY **2** — used as subject of an impersonal verb that expresses a condition or action without reference to an agent <~ is raining> **3 a** — used as anticipatory subject or object of a verb <~ is necessary to repeat the whole thing>; often used to shift emphasis to a part of a statement other than the subject <~ was in this city that the treaty was signed> **b** — used with many verbs as a direct object with little or no meaning <footed ~ back to camp> **4** — used to refer to an explicit or implicit state of affairs or circumstances <how is ~ going>

[2]**it** \ˈit\ *n* **:** the player in a game who performs a function (as trying to catch others in a game of tag) essential to the nature of the game

It *abbr* Italian; Italy

ITA \ˌī-ˌtē-ˈā\ *abbr* Initial Teaching Alphabet

it·a·col·u·mite \ˌit-ə-ˈkäl-(y)ə-ˌmīt\ *n* [*Itacolumi,* mountain in Brazil] **:** a quartzite resembling mica and flexible when split into thin slabs

it·a·con·ic acid \ˌit-ə-ˌkän-ik-\ *n* [ISV, anagram of *aconitic acid,* $C_3H_3(COOH)_3$] **:** a crystalline dicarboxylic acid $C_5H_6O_4$ obtained usu. by fermentation of sugars with molds (genus *Aspergillus*) and used as a monomer for vinyl-type polymers and polyesters

ital *abbr* italic; italicized

Ital *abbr* Italian

Ital·ian \ə-ˈtal-yən, i-\ *n* **1 a :** a native or inhabitant of Italy **b :** a person of Italian descent **2 :** the Romance language of the Italians — **Italian** *adj*

ital·ian·ate \-yə-ˌnāt\ *vt* **-at·ed; -at·ing :** ITALIANIZE

Ital·ian·ate \-nət, -ˌnāt\ *adj* **:** Italian in quality or characteristics

Italian greyhound *n* **:** any of a breed of toy dogs developed by selective breeding from standard greyhounds

Ital·ian·ism \ə-ˈtal-yə-ˌniz-əm, i-\ *n* **1 a :** a quality characteristic of Italy or the Italian people **b :** a characteristic feature of Italian occurring in another language **2 a :** specialized interest in or emulation of Italian qualities or achievements **b :** promotion or love of Italian policies or ideals

ital·ian·ize \ə-ˈtal-yə-ˌnīz, i-\ *vb* **-ized; -iz·ing** *vi, often cap* **:** to act Italian; *specif* **:** to follow the style or technique of recognized Italian painters ~ *vt, often cap* **:** to make Italian (as in appearance or behavior) — **ital·ian·iza·tion** \-ˌtal-yə-nə-ˈzā-shən\ *n*

Italian sandwich *n* **:** SUBMARINE 2

Italian sonnet *n* **:** a sonnet consisting of an octave rhyming *abba abba* and a sestet rhyming in any of various patterns (as *cde cde* or *cdc dcd*) — called also *Petrarchan sonnet*

[1]**ital·ic** \ə-ˈtal-ik, i-, ī-\ *adj* **1** *cap* **:** of or relating to ancient Italy, its peoples, or their Indo-European languages **2 :** of or relating to a type style with characters that slant upward to the right (as in "*these words are italic*")

[2]**italic** *n* **1 :** an italic character or type **2** *cap* **:** the Italic branch of the Indo-European language family — see INDO-EUROPEAN LANGUAGES table

Ital·i·cism \ə-ˈtal-ə-ˌsiz-əm, i-\ *n* **:** ITALIANISM 1b

ital·i·cize \ə-ˈtal-ə-ˌsīz, i-, ī-\ *vt* **-cized; -ciz·ing :** to print in italics or underscore with a single line — **ital·i·ci·za·tion** \-ˌtal-ə-sə-ˈzā-shən\ *n*

Ita·lo- *comb form* **1 :** Italian **2** \ˈit-ᵊl-ō *also* ə-ˈtal-ō *or* i-ˈtal-ō\ **:** Italian and <*Italo*-Austrian>

Italo·phile \ə-ˈtal-ə-ˌfīl, i-\ *adj* **:** friendly to or favoring what is Italian — **Italophile** *n*

[1]**itch** \ˈich\ *vb* [ME *icchen,* fr. OE *giccan;* akin to OHG *jucchen* to itch] *vi* **1 a :** to have an itch <her arm ~*ed*> **b :** to produce such a sensation <long underwear that ~*es*> **2 :** to have a restless desire or hankering for something <were ~*ing* to go outside> ~ *vt* **1 :** to cause to itch **2 :** VEX, IRRITATE

[2]**itch** *n* **1 a :** an uneasy irritating sensation in the upper surface of the skin usu. held to result from mild stimulation of pain receptors **b :** a skin disorder accompanied by such a sensation; *esp* **:** a contagious eruption caused by a mite (*Sarcoptes scabiei*) that burrows in the skin and causes intense itching **2 a :** a restless usu. constant often compulsive desire <an ~ to travel> **b :** LUST, PRURIENCE — **itch·i·ness** \ˈich-ē-nəs\ *n* — **itchy** \-ē\ *adj*

it'd \ˌit-əd\ **:** it had **:** it would

[1]**-ite** \ˌīt\ *n suffix* [ME, fr. OF & L; OF, fr. L *-ita, -ites,* fr. Gk *-itēs*] **1 a :** native **:** resident <Brooklyn*ite*> **b :** decendant <Ephraim*ite*> **c:** adherent **:** follower <Jacob*ite*> <Pusey*ite*> **2 a** (1) **:** product <metabol*ite*> (2) **:** commercially manufactured product <ebon*ite*> **b :** -ITOL <inos*ite*> **3** [NL *-ites,* fr. L] **:** fossil <ammon*ite*> **4 :** mineral <erythr*ite*> **:** rock <anorthos*ite*> **5** [F, fr. L *-ita, -ites*] **:** segment or constituent part of a body or of a bodily part <som*ite*> <dendr*ite*>

[2]**-ite** *n suffix* [F, alter. of *-ate* -ate, fr. NL *-atum*] **:** salt or ester of an acid with a name ending in *-ous*

[1]**item** \ˈī-ˌtem, ˈīt-əm\ *adv* [ME, fr. L, fr. *ita* thus] **:** and in addition **:** ALSO — used to introduce each article in a list or enumeration

[2]**item** \ˈīt-əm\ *n* **1** *obs* **:** WARNING, HINT **2 :** a separate particular in an enumeration, account, or series **:** ARTICLE **3 :** a separate piece of news or information <column of local ~*s*>
syn ITEM, DETAIL, PARTICULAR *shared meaning element* **:** one of the distinct parts of a whole

[3]**item** \ˈīt-əm\ *vt* **1** *archaic* **:** COMPUTE, RECKON **2** *archaic* **:** to set down the particular details of

item·iza·tion \ˌīt-ə-mə-ˈzā-shən\ *n* **:** the act of itemizing; *also* **:** an itemized list

item·ize \ˈīt-ə-ˌmīz\ *vt* **-ized; -iz·ing :** to set down in detail or by particulars **:** LIST <*itemized* all expenses>

it·er·ance \ˈit-ə-rən(t)s\ *n* **:** REPETITION

it·er·ant \-rənt\ *adj* **:** marked by repetition, reiteration, or recurrence <~ echoes>

it·er·ate \ˈit-ə-ˌrāt\ *vt* **-at·ed; -at·ing** [L *iteratus,* pp. of *iterare,* fr. *iterum* again; akin to L *is* he, that, *ita* thus, Skt *itara* the other, *iti* thus] **:** to say or do again or again and again **:** REITERATE ***syn*** see REPEAT — **it·er·a·tion** \ˌit-ə-ˈrā-shən\ *n*

it·er·a·tive \ˈit-ə-ˌrāt-iv, -rət-\ *adj* **:** involving repetition: as **a :** expressing repetition of a verbal action **b :** relating to or being a computational procedure in which replication of a cycle of operations produces results which approximate the desired result more and more closely — **it·er·a·tive·ly** *adv*

ithy·phal·lic \ˌith-i-ˈfal-ik\ *adj* [LL *ithyphallicus,* fr. Gk *ithyphallikos,* fr. *ithyphallos* erect phallus, fr. *ithys* straight + *phallos* phallus; akin to Skt *sādhati* he reaches the goal] **1 :** of or relating to the phallus carried in procession in ancient festivals of Bacchus **2 a :** having an erect penis — usu. used of figures in an art representation **b :** LEWD, OBSCENE

itin·er·a·cy \ī-ˈtin-ə-rə-sē, ə-\ *n* [*itinerate,* adj. (itinerant)] **:** ITINERANCY

itin·er·an·cy \-rən-sē\ *n* **1 a :** the act of itinerating **b :** the state of being itinerant **2 :** a system (as in the Methodist Church) of rotating ministers who itinerate

itin·er·ant \-rənt\ *adj* [LL *itinerant-, itinerans,* prp. of *itinerari* to journey, fr. L *itiner-, iter* journey, way, fr. *ire* to go — more at ISSUE] **:** traveling from place to place; *esp* **:** covering a circuit <~ preacher> — **itinerant** *n* — **itin·er·ant·ly** *adv*

itin·er·ary \ī-ˈtin-ə-ˌrer-ē, ə- *also* -ˈtin-ə-rē\ *n, pl* **-ar·ies 1 :** the route of a journey or the proposed outline of one **2 :** a travel diary **3 :** a traveler's guidebook — **itinerary** *adj*

ə abut ᵊ kitten ər further a back ā bake ä cot, cart
au̇ out ch chin e less ē easy g gift i trip ī life
j joke ŋ sing ō flow ȯ flaw ȯi coin th thin t͟h this
ü loot u̇ foot y yet yü few yu̇ furious zh vision

itin·er·ate \ī-ˈtin-ə-ˌrāt, ə-\ *vi* **-at·ed; -at·ing :** to travel a preaching or judicial circuit — **itin·er·a·tion** \-ˌtin-ə-ˈrā-shən, ə-\ *n*

-i·tious \ˈish-əs\ *adj suffix* [L *-icius, -itius*] **:** of, relating to, or having the characteristics of <excrement*itious*>

-i·tis \ˈīt-əs *also but not shown at individual entries* ˈēt-\ *n suffix, pl* **-i·tis·es** *also* **-it·i·des** \ˈit-ə-ˌdēz\ *sometimes* **-i·tes** \ˈīt-(ˌ)ēz, ˈēt-\ [NL, fr. L & Gk; L, fr. Gk, fr. fem. of *-itēs* -ite] **1 :** disease or inflammation <bronch*itis*> **2** *pl usu* **-itises a** (1) **:** malady arising from <vacation*itis*> (2) **:** forced endurance of <television*itis*> **b** (1) **:** marked proneness to <accident*itis*> (2) infatuation with <jazz*itis*> (3) **:** excessive advocacy of or reliance on <education*itis*> **c :** excess of the qualities of <big-business*itis*>

it'll \ˌit-ᵊl\ **:** it will **:** it shall

ITO *abbr* International Trade Organization

-i·tol \ə-ˌtȯl, -ˌtōl\ *n suffix* [ISV *-ite* (fr. ¹*-ite*) + *-ol*] **:** polyhydroxy alcohol usu. related to a sugar <mann*itol*>

its \(ˌ)its, əts\ *adj* **:** of or relating to it or itself esp. as possessor, agent, or object of an action <going to ~ kennel> <a child proud of ~ first drawings> <~ final enactment into law>

it's \(ˌ)its, əts\ **1 :** it is **2 :** it has

it·self \it-ˈself, ət-\ *pron* **1 :** that identical one — compare ¹IT 1; used reflexively <watched the cat giving ~ a bath>, for emphasis <the letter ~ was missing>, or in absolute constructions <~ a splendid specimen of classic art, it is sure to be exhibited throughout the world> **2 :** its normal, healthy, or sane condition

ITT *abbr* insulin tolerance test

it·ty-bit·ty \ˌit-ē-ˈbit-ē\ *or* **it·sy-bit·sy** \ˌit-sē-ˈbit-sē\ *adj* [prob. fr. baby talk for *little bit*] **:** extremely small **:** TINY

ITU *abbr* **1** International Telecommunication Union **2** International Typographical Union

ITV *abbr* instructional television

-ity \ət-ē\ *n suffix* [ME *-ite*, fr. OF or L; OF *-ité*, fr. L *-itat-, -itas*, fr. *-i-* (stem vowel of adjs.) + *-tat-, -tas* -ity; akin to Gk *-tēt-, -tēs* -ity] **:** quality **:** state **:** degree <alkalin*ity*> <theatrical*ity*>

IU *abbr* international unit

IUD \ˌī-ˌyü-ˈdē\ *n* **:** INTRAUTERINE DEVICE

-ium *n suffix* **1** [NL, fr. L, ending of some neut. nouns] **a** (1) **:** a chemical element <sod*ium*> (2) **:** chemical radical <ammon*ium*> **b :** positive ion <imidazol*ium* $[C_3H_4N_2H]^+$> **2** *pl* **-iums** *or* **-ia** [NL, fr. L, fr. Gk *-ion*] **:** small one **:** mass — esp. in botanical terms <pollin*ium*>

IUPAC *abbr* International Union of Pure and Applied Chemistry

IV *abbr* intravenous; intravenously

-ive \iv\ *adj suffix* [ME *-if, -ive*, fr. MF & L; MF *-if*, fr. L *-ivus*] **:** that performs or tends toward an (indicated) action <amus*ive*>

I've \(ˌ)īv\ **:** I have

ivied \ˈī-vēd\ *adj* **:** overgrown with ivy <~ walls>

ivo·ry \ˈīv-(ə-)rē\ *n, pl* **-ries** [ME *ivorie*, fr. OF *ivoire*, fr. L *eboreus* of ivory, fr. *ebor-, ebur* ivory, fr. Egypt ꜣ*b*, ꜣ*bw* elephant, ivory] **1 a :** the hard creamy-white modified dentine that composes the tusks of a tusked mammal and esp. the elephant **b :** a tusk (as of an elephant) that yields ivory **2 :** a variable color averaging a pale yellow **3** *slang* **:** TOOTH **4 :** something (as dice or piano keys) made of ivory or of a similar substance — **ivory** *adj*

ivo·ry·bill \ˈīv-(ə-)rē-ˌbil\ *n* **:** IVORY-BILLED WOODPECKER

ivo·ry-billed woodpecker \ˌīv-(ə-)rē-ˌbild-\ *n* **:** a very large, nearly extinct, black-and-white woodpecker (*Campephilus principalis*) of the southeastern U.S. that has a showy red crest in the male

ivory black *n* **:** a fine black pigment made by calcining ivory

ivory nut *n* **:** the nutlike seed of a So. American palm (*Phytelephas macrocarpa*) containing a very hard endosperm used for carving and turning — compare VEGETABLE IVORY

ivory tower *n* [trans. of F *tour d'ivoire*] **1 :** an impractical often escapist attitude marked by aloof lack of concern with or interest in practical matters or urgent problems **2 :** a secluded place for meditation **:** RETREAT <viewing college as an *ivory tower*> — **ivory-tower** *adj* — **ivo·ry-tow·er·ish** \ˌīv-(ə-)rē-ˈtau̇-(ə-)rish\ *adj*

ivo·ry-tow·ered \ˌīv-(ə-)rē-ˈtau̇(-ə)rd\ *adj* **:** divorced from reality and practical matters <an ~ recluse>

¹ivy \ˈī-vē\ *n, pl* **ivies** [ME, fr. OE *īfig*; akin to OHG *ebah* ivy] **1 :** a widely cultivated ornamental climbing or prostrate or sometimes shrubby Eurasian vine (*Hedera helix*) of the ginseng family with evergreen leaves, small yellowish flowers, and black berries **2 :** POISON IVY

²ivy *adj* [fr. the prevalence of ivy-covered buildings on the campuses of the older U.S. colleges] **1 :** ACADEMIC **2 :** IVY LEAGUE

Ivy League *adj* **1 :** of, relating to, or characteristic of a group of long-established eastern U.S. colleges widely regarded as high in scholastic and social prestige **2 :** of, relating to, or characteristic of the students of Ivy League colleges

ivy 1

Ivy Leaguer *n* **:** a student at or a graduate of an Ivy League college

IW *abbr* **1** index word **2** inside width **3** Isle of Wight **4** isotopic weight

iwis \ē-ˈwis, ī-\ *adv* [ME, fr. OE *gewis* certain; akin to OHG *giwisso* certainly, OE *witan* to know — more at WIT] *archaic* **:** CERTAINLY

IWW *abbr* Industrial Workers of the World

Ix·i·on \ik-ˈsī-ən\ *n* [L, fr. Gk *Ixiōn*] **:** a Thessalian king bound on a burning wheel in Tartarus for attempting while a guest of Zeus to seduce Hera

ix·o·did \ˈik-sə-ˌdid, ik-ˈsōd-əd\ *adj* [deriv. of Gk *ixōdēs* sticky, fr. *ixos* birdlime] **:** of, relating to, or being a typical tick (family Ixodidae) — **ixodid** *n*

Iyar \ˈē-ˌyär\ *n* [Heb *Iyyār*] **:** the 8th month of the civil year or the 2d month of the ecclesiastical year in the Jewish calendar — see MONTH table

-iza·tion \ə-ˈzā-shən *also esp when an unstressed syllable precedes but not shown at individual entries* (ˌ)ī-ˈzā-\ *n suffix* **:** action, process, or result of making <social*ization*>

-ize \ˌīz\ *vb suffix* [ME *-isen*, fr. OF *-iser*, fr. LL *-izare*, fr. Gk *-izein*] **1 a** (1) **:** cause to be or conform to or resemble <system*ize*> <American*ize*> **:** cause to be formed into <union*ize*> (2) **:** subject to a (specified) action <plagiar*ize*> (3) **:** impregnate or treat or combine with <albumin*ize*> **b :** treat like <idol*ize*> **c :** treat according to the method of <bowdler*ize*> **2 a :** become **:** become like <crystall*ize*> **b :** be productive in or of <hypothes*ize*> **:** engage in a (specified) activity <philosoph*ize*> **c :** adopt or spread the manner of activity or the teaching of <calvin*ize*>

iz·zard \ˈiz-ərd\ *n* [alter. of earlier *ezod, ezed*, prob. fr. MF *et zede* and Z] *chiefly dial* **:** the letter *z*

J

¹j \ˈjā\ *n, pl* **j's** *or* **js** \ˈjāz\ *often cap, often attrib* **1 a :** the 10th letter of the English alphabet **b :** a speech counterpart of orthographic *j* **2 a :** a graphic device for reproducing the letter *j* **b :** a unit vector parallel to the y-axis **3 :** one designated *j* esp. as the 10th in order or class **4 :** something shaped like the letter J

²j *abbr, often cap* **1** jack **2** joule **3** journal **4** judge **5** justice

JA *abbr* **1** joint account **2** judge advocate

¹jab \ˈjab\ *vb* **jabbed; jab·bing** [alter. of *job* (to strike)] *vt* **1 a :** to pierce with or as if with a sharp object **:** STAB **b :** to poke quickly or abruptly **:** THRUST **2 :** to strike with a short straight blow ~ *vi* **1 :** to make quick or abrupt thrusts with a sharp object **2 :** to strike a person with a short straight blow

²jab *n* **:** an act of jabbing; *specif* **:** a short straight boxing punch delivered with the leading hand

¹jab·ber \ˈjab-ər\ *vb* **jab·bered; jab·ber·ing** \ˈjab-(ə-)riŋ\ [ME *jaberen*, of imit. origin] *vi* **:** to talk rapidly, indistinctly, or unintelligibly ~ *vt* **:** to speak rapidly or indistinctly — **jab·ber·er** \ˈjab-ər-ər\ *n*

²jabber *n* **:** GIBBERISH, CHATTER

³jabber *n* **:** one that jabs

jab·ber·wocky \ˈjab-ər-ˌwäk-ē\ *n* [*Jabberwocky*, nonsense poem by Lewis Carroll] **:** meaningless speech or writing

jab·i·ru \ˌzhab-ə-ˈrü\ *n* [Pg, fr. Tupi & Guarani *jabirú*] **:** any of several large tropical storks

jab·o·ran·di \ˌzhab-ə-ˌran-ˈdē, -ˈran-dē\ *n* [Pg, fr. Tupi *yaborandi*] **:** the dried leaves of two So. American shrubs (*Pilocarpus jaborandi* and *P. microphyllus*) of the rue family that are a source of pilocarpine

ja·bot \zha-ˈbō, ˈjab-ˌō\ *n* [F] **1 :** a fall of lace or cloth attached to the front of a neckband and worn esp. by men in the 18th century **2 :** a pleated frill of cloth or lace attached down the center front of a woman's blouse or dress

ja·bo·ti·ca·ba \zhə-ˌbüt-i-ˈkäb-ə\ *n* [Pg, fr. Tupi] : a tropical American shrubby tree (*Myrciaria cauliflora*) of the myrtle family cultivated in warm regions for its edible purplish fruit

ja·cal \hə-ˈkäl\ *n, pl* **ja·ca·les** \-ˈkäl-(ˌ)ās\ *also* **ja·cals** [MexSp, fr. Nahuatl *xacalli*] : a hut in Mexico and southwestern U.S. with a thatched roof and walls made of upright poles or sticks covered and chinked with mud or clay

jac·a·mar \ˈzhak-ə-ˌmär\ *n* [F, fr. Tupi *jacamá-ciri*] : any of a family (Galbulidae) of usu. iridescent green or bronze insectivorous birds of American tropical forests

ja·ca·na \ˌzhas-ən-ˈän\ *n* [Pg *jaçanã*, fr. Tupi & Guarani] : any of several long-legged and long-toed wading birds (family Jacanidae) that frequent coastal freshwater marshes and ponds in warm regions

jac·a·ran·da \ˌjak-ə-ˈran-də\ *n* [NL, genus name, fr. Pg, a tree of this genus] : any of a genus (*Jacaranda*) of pinnate-leaved tropical American trees of the trumpet-creeper family with showy blue flowers in panicles

ja·cinth \ˈjās-ən(t)th, ˈjas-\ *n* [ME *iacinct*, fr. OF *jacinthe*, fr. L *hyacinthus*, a flowering plant, a gem] **1** : HYACINTH **2** : a gem more nearly orange in color than a hyacinth

ja·cinthe \ˈjās-ən(t)th, ˈjas-; zhä-ˈsant\ *n* [F] : a moderate orange

[1]**jack** \ˈjak\ *n* [ME *jacke*, fr. *Jacke*, nickname for *Johan* John] **1** **a** : MAN — usually used as an intensive in such phrases as *every man jack* **b** *often cap* : SAILOR **c** (1) : SERVANT, LABORER (2) : LUMBERJACK **2** : any of various mechanical devices: as **a** : a device for turning a spit **b** : any of various portable mechanisms for exerting pressure or lifting a heavy body a short distance **3** : something that supports or holds in position: as **a** : a bar of iron at a topgallant masthead to support a royal mast and spread the royal shrouds **b** : a wooden brace fastened behind a scenic unit in a stage set to prop it up **4 a** : any of several fishes; *esp* : any of various carangids **b** : a male donkey **c** : any of several birds (as a jackdaw) **5 a** : a small white target ball in lawn bowling **b** : a small national flag flown by a ship **c** (1) *pl but sing in constr* : a game played with a set of small objects that are tossed, caught, and moved in various figures (2) : a small 6-pointed metal object used in the game of jacks **6 a** : a playing card carrying the figure of a soldier or servant and ranking usu. below the queen **b** [by shortening] : JACKPOT 1a(2) **7** *slang* : MONEY **8** : a female fitting in an electric circuit used with a plug to make a connection with another circuit **9 a** [by shortening] : APPLEJACK **b** : BRANDY **10** [by shortening] : JACKKNIFE 2

[2]**jack** *vi* : to hunt or fish at night with a jacklight ~ *vt* **1** : to hunt or fish for at night with a jacklight **2 a** : to move or lift by or as if by a jack **b** : to raise the level or quality of <~ up the price> **c** : to take to task — **jack·er** *n*

jack·al \ˈjak-əl, -ˌȯl\ *n* [Turk *çakal*, fr. Per *shagāl*, fr. Skt *sṛgāla*] **1** : any of several Old World wild dogs smaller than the related wolves **2 a** : a person who performs routine or menial tasks for another **b** : a person who serves or collaborates with another esp. in the commission of base acts

jackal 1

Jack-a-Lent \ˈjak-ə-ˌlent\ *n* [[1]*jack* + *a* (of) + *Lent*] **1** : a small stuffed puppet set up to be pelted for fun in Lent **2** : a simple or insignificant person

jack·a·napes \ˈjak-ə-ˌnāps\ *n* [ME *Jack Napis*, nickname for William de la Pole †1450 duke of Suffolk] **1** : MONKEY, APE **2 a** : an impudent or conceited fellow **b** : a saucy or mischievous child

jack·ass \ˈjak-ˌas\ *n* **1** : a male ass; *also* : DONKEY **2** : a stupid person : FOOL

jack·ass·ery \ˈjak-ˌas-(ə-)rē\ *n, pl* **-er·ies** : a stupid or foolish act

jack bean *n* : a bushy annual tropical American legume (genus *Canavalia*); *esp* : a plant (*C. ensiformis*) grown esp. for forage

jack·boot \ˈjak-ˌbüt\ *n* **1** : a heavy military boot made of glossy black leather extending above the knee and worn esp. during the 17th and 18th centuries **2** : a laceless military boot reaching to the calf

jack crevalle *n* [[1]*jack* + *crevalle*] : a carangid fish (*Caranx hippos*) that is an important food fish along the west coast of Florida

jack·daw \ˈjak-ˌdȯ\ *n* **1** : a common black and gray Eurasian bird (*Corvus monedula*) that is related to but smaller than the common crow **2** : GRACKLE 2

[1]**jack·et** \ˈjak-ət\ *n* [ME *jaket*, fr. MF *jaquet*, dim. of *jaque* short jacket, fr. *jacque* peasant, fr. the name *Jacques* James] **1 a** : a garment for the upper body usu. having a front opening, collar, lapels, sleeves, and pockets **b** : something worn or fastened around the body but not for use as clothing **2 a** (1) : the natural covering of an animal (2) : the fur or wool of a mammal **b** : the skin of a potato **3** : an outer covering or casing: as **a** (1) : a thermally nonconducting cover (2) : a covering that encloses an intermediate space through which a temperature-controlling fluid circulates (3) : a tough cold-worked metal casing that forms the outer shell of a built-up bullet **b** (1) : a wrapper or open envelope for a document (2) : an envelope for enclosing registered mail during delivery from one post office to another **c** (1) : a detachable protective cover for a book (2) : the cover of a paperback book (3) : the outside leaves for a booklet, pamphlet, or catalog that is to be stitched or wired through the center of the fold (4) : a paper or paperboard envelope for a phonograph record

[2]**jacket** *vt* : to put a jacket on : enclose in or with a jacket

Jack Frost *n* : frost or frosty weather personified

jack·fruit \ˈjak-ˌfrüt\ *n* [Pg *jaca* jackfruit + E *fruit*] **1 a** : a large widely cultivated tropical tree (*Artocarpus heterophyllus*) related to the breadfruit that yields a fine-grained yellow wood and immense fruits which contain an edible pulp and nutritious seeds **b** : the fruit of this tree **2** : DURIAN

jack·ham·mer \ˈjak-ˌham-ər\ *n* **1** : a pneumatically operated percussive rock-drilling tool usu. held in the hands **2** : a device in which a tool (as a chisel for breaking up pavements) is driven percussively by compressed air

jack-in-the-box \ˈjak-ən-t͟hə-ˌbäks\ *n, pl* **jack-in-the-box·es** *or* **jacks-in-the-box** : a small box out of which a figure (as of a clown's head) springs when the lid is raised

jack-in-the-pul·pit \ˌjak-ən-t͟hə-ˈpu̇l-ˌpit, -pət *also* -ˈpəl-\ *n, pl* **jack-in-the-pulpits** *or* **jacks-in-the-pulpit** : any of several plants (genus *Arisaema*) of the arum family; *esp* : an American spring-flowering woodland herb (*A. atrorubens*) having an upright club-shaped spadix arched over by a green and purple spathe

[1]**jack·knife** \ˈjak-ˌnīf\ *n* **1** : a large strong clasp knife for the pocket **2** : a dive executed headfirst in which the diver bends from the waist and touches his ankles while holding his knees unflexed and then straightens out

[2]**jackknife** *vt* **1** : to cut with a jackknife **2** : to cause to double up like a jackknife ~ *vi* **1** : to double up like a jackknife **2** : to turn or rise and form an angle of 90 degrees or less with each other — used esp. of a pair of vehicles (as a tractor and its trailer) that are fastened together

jack·leg \ˈjak-ˌleg, -ˌläg\ *adj* [[1]*jack* + *-leg* (as in *blackleg*)] **1 a** : lacking skill or training : AMATEUR <a ~ carpenter> **b** : characterized by unscrupulousness, dishonesty, or lack of professional standards <a ~ lawyer> **2** : designed as a temporary expedient : MAKESHIFT — **jackleg** *n*

jack·light \-ˌlīt\ *n* : a light used esp. in hunting or fishing at night

jack mackerel *n* : a California market fish (*Trachurus symmetricus*) that is iridescent green or bluish above and silvery below; *also* : a closely related Australian fish (*T. novaezelandiae*)

jack-of-all-trades \ˌjak-ə-ˈvȯl-ˌtrādz\ *n, pl* **jacks-of-all-trades** : a person who can do passable work at various tasks : a handy versatile person

jack off *vb* [prob. alter. of *jerk off*] : MASTURBATE — usu. considered vulgar

jack-o'-lan·tern \ˈjak-ə-ˌlant-ərn\ *n* **1 a** : IGNIS FATUUS **b** : SAINT ELMO'S FIRE **2** : a lantern made of a pumpkin cut to look like a human face

jack pine *n* : a slender No. American pine (*Pinus banksiana*) that has two stout twisted leaves in each fascicle and wood used esp. for pulpwood

jack·pot \ˈjak-ˌpät\ *n* **1 a** (1) : a hand or game of draw poker in which a pair of jacks or better is required to open (2) : a large pot (as in poker) formed by the accumulation of stakes from previous play **b** (1) : a combination on a slot machine that wins a top prize or all the coins in the machine (2) : the sum so won **c** : a large fund of money or other reward formed by the accumulation of unwon prizes **2** : an impressive often unexpected success or reward **3** *chiefly West* : a tight spot : JAM

jack·rab·bit \-ˌrab-ət\ *n* [[1]*jack* (jackass) + *rabbit*; fr. its long ears] : any of several large hares (genus *Lepus*) of western No. America having very long ears and long hind legs

jackrabbit

jack salmon *n* **1** : WALLEYE 4 **2** : GRILSE

jack·screw \ˈjak-ˌskrü\ *n* : a screw-operated jack for lifting or for exerting pressure

jack·smelt \-ˌsmelt\ *n* : a large silversides (*Atherinopsis californiensis*) of the Pacific coast of No. America that is the chief commercial smelt of the California markets

jack·snipe \-ˌsnīp\ *n* : an Old World true snipe (*Limnocryptes minima*) that is smaller and more highly colored than the common snipe

Jack·son Day \ˈjak-sən-\ *n* [Andrew *Jackson*, defender of New Orleans] : January 8 celebrated as a legal holiday in Louisiana commemorating the successful defense of New Orleans in 1815

Jack·so·ni·an \jak-ˈsō-nē-ən\ *adj* : of, relating to, or characteristic of Andrew Jackson or his political principles or policies — **Jacksonian** *n*

jack·stay \-ˌstā\ *n* **1** : an iron rod, wooden bar, or wire rope along a yard of a ship to which the sails are fastened **2** : a support of wood, iron, or rope running up a mast on which the parrel of a yard travels

jack·straw \ˈjak-ˌstrȯ\ *n* **1** : one of the pieces used in the game jackstraws **2** *pl but sing in constr* : a game in which a set of straws or thin strips are let fall in a heap with each player in turn trying to remove them one at a time without disturbing the rest

jack-tar \-ˈtär\ *n, often cap* : SAILOR

Ja·cob \ˈjā-kəb\ *n* [LL, fr. Gk *Iacōb*, fr. Heb *Yaʽaqōbh*] **1** : a son of Isaac and Rebekah, the twin brother of Esau, and heir of God's promise of blessing to Abraham **2** : the ancient Hebrew nation

Jac·o·be·an \ˌjak-ə-ˈbē-ən\ *adj* [NL *Jacobaeus*, fr. *Jacobus* James] : of, relating to, or characteristic of James I of England or his age — **Jacobean** *n*

jacobean lily *n, often cap J* [LL *Jacobus* (St. James)] : a Mexican bulbous herb (*Sprekelia formosissima*) of the amaryllis family cultivated for its bright red solitary flower

Ja·co·bi·an \jə-ˈkō-bē-ən, yä-\ *n* [K. G. J. *Jacobi* †1851 G mathematician] : a determinant defined for a finite number of

ə abut   ə kitten   ər further   a back   ā bake   ä cot, cart
au̇ out   ch chin   e less   ē easy   g gift   i trip   ī life
j joke   ŋ sing   ō flow   ȯ flaw   ȯi coin   th thin   t͟h this
ü loot   u̇ foot   y yet   yü few   yu̇ furious   zh vision

functions of the same number of variables in which each row consists of the first partial derivatives of the same function with respect to each of the variables

Jac·o·bin \ˈjak-ə-bən\ *n* [ME, fr. MF, fr. ML *Jacobinus*, fr. LL *Jacobus* (St. James); fr. the location of the first Dominican convent in the street of St. James, Paris] **1 :** DOMINICAN **2** [F, fr. *Jacobin* Dominican; fr. the group's founding in the Dominican convent in Paris] **:** a member of an extremist or radical political group; *esp* **:** a member of such a group advocating egalitarian democracy and engaging in terrorist activities during the French Revolution of 1789 — **Jac·o·bin·ic** \ˌjak-ə-ˈbin-ik\ *or* **Jac·o·bin·i·cal** \-i-kəl\ *adj* — **Jac·o·bin·ism** \ˈjak-ə-bə-ˌniz-əm\ *n* — **jac·o·bin·ize** \-ˌnīz\ *vt, often cap*

[1]**Jac·o·bite** \ˈjak-ə-ˌbīt\ *n* [ME, fr. ML *Jacobita*, fr. *Jacobus* Baradaeus (Jacob Baradai) †578 Syrian monk] **:** a member of any of various Monophysite Eastern churches; *esp* **:** a member of the Monophysite Syrian church

[2]**Jacobite** *n* [*Jacobus* (James II)] **:** a partisan of James II of England or of the Stuarts after the revolution of 1688 — **Jac·o·bit·i·cal** \ˌjak-ə-ˈbit-i-kəl\ *adj* — **Jac·o·bit·ism** \ˈjak-ə-ˌbīt-ˌiz-əm\ *n*

Ja·cob's ladder \ˌjā-kəbz-\ *n* [fr. the ladder seen in a dream by Jacob in Gen 28:12] **1 :** any of a genus (*Polemonium*) of herbs of the phlox family that have pinnate leaves, an herbaceous calyx, a bell-shaped corolla with declinate stamens, and a several-seeded capsule; *esp* **:** a perennial (*P. caeruleum*) of European origin with bright blue or white flowers **2 :** a marine ladder of rope or chain with wooden or iron rungs

Ja·co·bus \jə-ˈkō-bəs\ *n* [*Jacobus* (James I), during whose reign unites were coined] **:** UNITE

jac·o·net \ˈjak-ə-ˌnet\ *n* [modif. of Urdu *jagannāthī*] **:** a lightweight cotton cloth used for clothing and bandages

jac·quard \ˈjak-ˌärd\ *n, often cap* [Joseph *Jacquard*] **1 a :** a loom apparatus or head for weaving figured fabrics **b :** a loom having a jacquard **2 :** a fabric of intricate variegated weave or pattern

jac·que·rie \ˌzhäk-ə-ˈrē, ˌzhak-\ *n, often cap* [F, fr. the French peasant revolt in 1358, fr. MF, fr. *jacque* peasant — more at JACKET] **:** a peasants' revolt

jac·ti·ta·tion \ˌjak-tə-ˈtā-shən\ *n* [LL *jactitation-, jactitatio*, fr. *jactitatus*, pp. of *jactitare*, freq. of *jactare* to throw — more at JET] **:** a tossing to and fro or jerking and twitching of the body

[1]**jade** \ˈjād\ *n* [ME] **1 :** a broken-down, vicious, or worthless horse **2 a :** a disreputable woman **b :** a flirtatious girl

[2]**jade** *vb* **jad·ed; jad·ing** *vt* **1 a :** to wear out by overwork or abuse **b :** to tire by severe or tedious tasks **2** *obs* **:** to make ridiculous ~ *vi* **:** to become weary or dulled ***syn*** see TIRE

[3]**jade** *n* [F, fr. obs. Sp (*piedra de la*) *ijada*, lit., loin stone; fr. the belief that jade cures renal colic] **:** either of two tough compact typically green gemstones that take a high polish: **a :** JADEITE **b :** NEPHRITE

jad·ed *adj* **1 :** fatigued by overwork **:** EXHAUSTED **2 :** dulled by surfeit or excess — **jad·ed·ly** *adv* — **jad·ed·ness** *n*

jade green *n* **:** a variable color averaging a light bluish green

jade·ite \ˈjā-ˌdīt\ *n* [F] **:** a monoclinic mineral that is a jade — **ja·dit·ic** \jā-ˈdit-ik\ *adj*

jade plant *n* **:** any of several stonecrops (genus *Crassula*) cultivated as foliage plants

jae·ger \ˈyā-gər\ *n* [G *jäger*] **1 a :** HUNTER, HUNTSMAN **b :** one attending a person of rank or wealth and wearing hunter's costume **2 :** any of several large dark-colored birds (genus *Stercorarius* of the family Stercorariidae) of northern seas that are strong fliers and that tend to harass weaker birds until they drop or disgorge their prey

[1]**jag** \ˈjag\ *vb* **jagged; jag·ging** [ME *jaggen*] *vt* **1** *chiefly dial* **:** PRICK, STAB **2 :** to cut indentations into; *also* **:** to form teeth on (a saw) by cutting indentations ~ *vi* **1 :** PRICK, THRUST **2 :** to move in jerks — **jag·ger** *n*

[2]**jag** *n* **:** a sharp projecting part **:** BARB

[3]**jag** *n* [origin unknown] **1 :** a small load **2 a :** a state or feeling of exhilaration or intoxication usu. induced by liquor **b :** SPREE

JAG *abbr* judge advocate general

jag·ged \ˈjag-əd\ *adj* **1 :** having a sharply uneven edge or surface **2 :** having a harsh, rough, or irregular quality — **jag·ged·ly** *adv* — **jag·ged·ness** *n*

jag·gery \ˈjag-ə-rē\ *n* [Hindi *jāgrī*] **:** an unrefined brown sugar made from palm sap

jag·gy \ˈjag-ē\ *adj* **:** JAGGED, NOTCHED

jag·uar \ˈjag(-yə)-ˌwär, *esp Brit* -wər\ *n* [Sp *yaguar* & Pg *jaguar*, fr. Guarani *yaguara* & Tupi *jaguara*] **:** a large cat (*Felis onca*) of tropical America that is larger and stockier than the leopard and is brownish yellow or buff with black spots

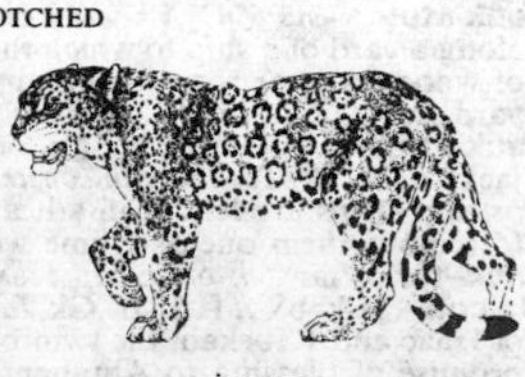

jaguar

jag·ua·run·di \ˌzhag-wə-ˈrən-dē\ *n* [AmerSp & Pg, fr. Tupi *jaguarundi* & Guarani *yaguarundi*] **:** a slender long-tailed short-legged grayish wildcat (*Felis jaguarondi*) of Central and So. America

Jah·veh \ˈyä-(ˌ)vā\ *var of* YAHWEH

jai alai \ˈhī-ˌlī, ˌhī-ə-ˈlī\ *n* [Sp, fr. Basque, fr. *jai* festival + *alai* merry] **:** a court game somewhat like handball played by two or four players with a ball and a long curved wicker basket strapped to the right wrist

[1]**jail** \ˈjā(ə)l\ *n* [ME *jaiole*, fr. OF, fr. (assumed) VL *caveola*, dim. of L *cavea* cage — more at CAGE] **:** PRISON; *esp* **:** a building for the confinement of persons held in lawful custody

[2]**jail** *vt* **:** to confine in or as if in a jail

jail·bait \ˈjā(ə)l-ˌbāt\ *n* **:** a girl under the age of consent with whom unlawful sexual intercourse constitutes statutory rape

jail·bird \-ˌbərd\ *n* **:** a person confined in jail; *specif* **:** an habitual criminal

jail·break \-ˌbrāk\ *n* **:** a forcible escape from jail

jail delivery *n* **1 :** the clearing of a jail by bringing the prisoners to trial **2 :** the freeing of prisoners by force

jail·er *or* **jail·or** \ˈjā-lər\ *n* **1 :** a keeper of a jail **2 :** one that restricts another's liberty as if by imprisonment

Jain \ˈjīn\ *or* **Jai·na** \ˈjī-nə\ *n* [Hindi *Jain*, fr. Skt *Jaina*] **:** an adherent of Jainism

Jain·ism \ˈjī-ˌniz-əm\ *n* **:** a religion of India originating in the 6th century B.C. and teaching liberation of the soul by right knowledge, right faith, and right conduct

jake leg \ˈjā-ˌkleg, -ˌklāg\ *n* [*jake* (strong liquor)] **:** a paralysis caused by drinking strong liquor

jakes \ˈjāks\ *n pl but sing or pl in constr* [perh. fr. F *Jacques* James] *archaic* **:** PRIVY 2

jal·ap \ˈjal-əp, ˈjäl-\ *n* [F & Sp; F *jalap*, fr. Sp *jalapa*, fr. *Jalapa*, Mexico] **1 a :** the dried purgative tuberous root of a Mexican plant (*Exogonium purga*) of the morning-glory family; *also* **:** a powdered drug prepared from it that contains resinous glycosides **b :** the root or derived drug of plants related to the one supplying jalap **2 :** a plant yielding jalap

ja·lopy \jə-ˈläp-ē\ *n, pl* **jalopies** [origin unknown] **:** a dilapidated old automobile or airplane

jal·ou·sie \ˈjal-ə-sē\ *n* [F, lit., jealousy, fr. OF *jelous* jealous] **1 :** a blind with adjustable horizontal slats for admitting light and air while excluding sun and rain **2 :** a window made of adjustable glass louvers that control ventilation

[1]**jam** \ˈjam\ *vb* **jammed; jam·ming** [perh. of imit. origin] *vt* **1 a :** to press into a close or tight position <~ his hat on> **b** (1) **:** to cause to become wedged so as to be unworkable <~ the typewriter keys> (2) **:** to make unworkable by jamming **c :** to block passage of **:** OBSTRUCT **d :** to fill often to excess **:** PACK **2 :** to push forcibly; *esp* **:** to apply (brakes) suddenly and forcibly — used with *on* **3 :** CRUSH, BRUISE **4 a :** to make unintelligible by sending out interfering signals or messages **b :** to make (as a radar apparatus) ineffective by jamming signals or by causing reflection of radar waves ~ *vi* **1 a :** to become blocked or wedged **b :** to become unworkable through the jamming of a movable part **2 :** to force one's way into a restricted space **3 :** to take part in a jam session

[2]**jam** *n* **1 a :** an act or instance of jamming **b :** a crowded mass that impedes or blocks **2 a :** the quality or state of being jammed **b :** the pressure or congestion of a crowd **:** CRUSH **3 :** a difficult state of affairs **4 :** JAM SESSION **5 :** a round in roller derby in which a jammer from each team tries to lap members of the opposing team and score points ***syn*** see PREDICAMENT

[3]**jam** *n* [prob. fr. [1]*jam*] **:** a food made by boiling fruit and sugar to a thick consistency

Jam *abbr* Jamaica

Ja·mai·ca ginger \jə-ˌmā-kə-\ *n* [*Jamaica*, W. Indies] **1 :** an alcoholic extract of ginger used as a flavoring essence **2 :** the powdered root of ginger used as an intestinal stimulant and carminative

Jamaica rum *n* **:** a heavy-bodied rum made by slow fermentation and marked by a pungent bouquet

jamb \ˈjam\ *n* [ME *jambe*, fr. MF, lit., leg, fr. LL *gamba* — more at GAMBIT] **1 :** an upright piece or surface forming the side of an opening (as for a door, window, or fireplace) **2 :** a projecting columnar part or mass

jam·ba·laya \ˌjəm-bə-ˈlī-ə\ *n* [LaF, fr. Prov *jambalaia*] **1 :** rice cooked with ham, sausage, chicken, shrimp, or oysters and seasoned with herbs **2 :** a mixture of diverse elements

jam·beau \ˈjam-(ˌ)bō\ *n, pl* **jam·beaux** \-(ˌ)bōz\ [ME, fr. (assumed) AF, fr. MF *jambe*] **:** a piece of medieval armor for the leg below the knee — see ARMOR illustration

jam·bo·ree \ˌjam-bə-ˈrē\ *n* [origin unknown] **1 :** a noisy or unrestrained carousal **2 a :** a large festive gathering **b :** a national or international camping assembly of boy scouts **3 :** a long mixed program of entertainment

James \ˈjāmz\ *n* [F, fr. LL *Jacobus*] **1 :** an apostle, son of Zebedee, and brother of the apostle John according to the Gospel accounts **2 :** an apostle and son of Alphaeus according to the Gospel accounts — called also *James the Less* **3 :** a brother of Jesus traditionally held to be the author of the New Testament Epistle of James **4 :** a moral lecture addressed to early Christians and included as a book in the New Testament — see BIBLE table

James·ian \ˈjām-zē-ən\ *adj* **1 :** of, relating to, or characteristic of William James or his teachings **2 :** of, relating to, or characteristic of Henry James or his writings

jam·mer \ˈjam-ər\ *n* **1 :** one that jams; *esp* **:** a usu. modulated transmitter that emits a signal that is intended to interfere with or make unintelligible radio or radar signals **2 :** a player on a roller derby team who attempts to lap members of the opposing team in order to score points

jams \ˈjamz\ *n pl* [prob. by shortening fr. *pajamas*] **:** knee-length loose-fitting swim trunks usu. having a drawstring waist and large brightly colored patterns

jam session *n* [[2]*jam*] **:** an impromptu performance engaged in by a group of jazz musicians and characterized by group improvisation

Jam·shid *or* **Jam·shyd** \jam-ˈshēd\ *n* [Per *Jamshīd*] **:** an early legendary king of Persia who reigned for 700 years

Jan *abbr* January

Jane Doe \ˈjān-ˈdō\ *n* **:** a female party to legal proceedings whose true name is unknown

[1]**jan·gle** \ˈjaŋ-gəl\ *vb* **jan·gled; jan·gling** \-g(ə-)liŋ\ [ME *janglen*, fr. OF *jangler*, of Gmc origin; akin to MD *jangelen* to grumble] *vi* **1** *archaic* **:** to talk idly **2 :** to quarrel verbally **3 :** to make a harsh or discordant often ringing sound ~ *vt* **1 :** to utter or sound in a discordant, babbling, or chattering way **2 a :** to cause to sound harshly or inharmoniously **b :** to excite to tense irritation — **jan·gler** \-g(ə-)lər\ *n*

[2]**jangle** *n* **1 :** idle talk **2 :** noisy quarreling **3 :** a discordant often ringing sound

jan·is·sary *or* **jan·i·zary** \ˈjan-ə-ˌser-ē, -ˌzer-\ *n, pl* **-saries** *or* **-zaries** [It *gianizzero*, fr. Turk *yeniçeri*] **1** *often cap* **:** a soldier of an elite corps of Turkish troops organized in the 14th century and

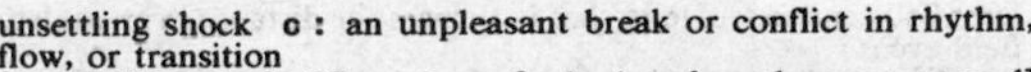

abolished in 1826 **2 :** a member of a group of loyal or subservient troops, officials, or supporters

jan·i·tor \'jan-ət-ər\ *n* [L, fr. *janua* door, fr. *janus* arch, gate] **1 :** DOORKEEPER **2 :** one who keeps the premises of an apartment, office, or other building clean, tends the heating system, and makes minor repairs — **jan·i·to·ri·al** \ˌjan-ə-'tōr-ē-əl, -'tȯr-\ *adj* — **jan·i·tress** \'jan-ə-trəs\ *n*

Jan·sen·ism \'jan(t)-sə-ˌniz-əm\ *n* [F *jansénisme*, fr. Cornelis *Jansen*] **1 :** a system of doctrine based on moral determinism, defended by various reformist factions among 17th and 18th century western European Roman Catholic clergy, religious, and scholars, and condemned as heretical by papal authority **2 :** a puritanical attitude (as toward sex) — **Jan·sen·ist** \-nəst\ *n* — **Jan·sen·is·tic** \ˌjan(t)-sə-'nis-tik\ *adj*

Jan·u·ary \'jan-yə-ˌwer-ē\ *n* [ME *Januarie*, fr. L *Januarius*, 1st month of the ancient Roman year, fr. *Janus*] **:** the 1st month of the Gregorian calendar

Ja·nus \'jā-nəs\ *n* [L] **:** a Roman god that is identified with doors, gates, and all beginnings and that is represented artistically with two opposite faces

the head of Janus on a Roman coin

Janus green *n* [prob. fr. *Janus*, a trademark] **:** a basic azine dye used esp. as a biological stain (as for mitochondria)

Jap *abbr* Japan; Japanese

¹ja·pan \jə-'pan\ *adj* **:** of, relating to, or originating in Japan **:** of a kind or style typical of or imitative of Japanese workmanship

²japan *n* **1 a :** any of several varnishes yielding a hard brilliant finish **b :** a hard dark coating containing asphalt and a drier that is used esp. on metal and fixed by heating — called also *japan black* **2 :** work (as lacquer ware) finished and decorated in the Japanese manner

³japan *vt* **ja·panned; ja·pan·ning 1 :** to cover with or as if with a coat of japan **2 :** to give a high gloss to — **ja·pan·ner** *n*

Japan allspice *n* **:** a Japanese shrub (*Chimonanthus praecox*) cultivated for its fragrant yellow flowers

Japan clover *n* **:** an annual lespedeza (*Lespedeza striata*) used as a forage, soil-improving, and pasture crop esp. in the southeastern U.S. — called also *Japanese clover*

Jap·a·nese \ˌjap-ə-'nēz, -'nēs\ *n, pl* **Japanese 1 a :** a native or inhabitant of Japan **b :** a person of Japanese descent **2 :** the language of the Japanese — **Japanese** *adj*

Japanese an·drom·e·da \-ˌan-'dräm-əd-ə\ *n* [NL *Andromeda* (genus of plants), fr. L *Andromeda*, Ethiopian princess, fr. Gk *Andromedē*] **:** a shrubby evergreen Asiatic heath (*Pieris japonica*) with glossy leaves and drooping clusters of whitish flowers

Japanese barnyard millet *n* **:** JAPANESE MILLET

Japanese beetle *n* **:** a small metallic green and brown scarab beetle (*Popillia japonica*) that has been introduced into America from Japan and as a grub feeds on the roots of grasses and decaying vegetation and as an adult eats foliage and fruits

Japanese beetle

Japanese cedar *n* **:** a large evergreen tree (*Cryptomeria japonica*) grown esp. in China and Japan for its valuable soft wood

Japanese iris *n* **:** any of various beardless garden irises with very large showy flowers

Japanese lacquer *n* **:** LACQUER 1b

Japanese millet *n* **:** a coarse annual grass (*Echinochloa frumentacea*) cultivated esp. in Asia for its edible seeds

Japanese mink *n* **:** an Asiatic weasel (*Mustela sibirica*); *also* **:** its pale yellowish brown fur

Japanese persimmon *n* **:** an Asiatic persimmon (*Diospyros kaki*) widely cultivated for its large edible fruits; *also* **:** its fruit

Japanese plum *n* **1 :** any of numerous large showy usu. yellow to light red cultivated plums **2 :** a tree that bears Japanese plums and is derived from a Chinese tree (*Prunus salicina*)

Japanese quail *n* **:** any of a subspecies (*Coturnix coturnix japonica*) of Old World quail from China and Japan that are used extensively in laboratory research

Japanese quince *n* **:** a hardy Chinese ornamental shrub (*Chaenomeles lagenaria*) of the rose family with scarlet flowers

Japanese spaniel *n* **:** any of a Japanese breed of toy dogs that have a silky undercoat and black and white or red and white coloring

Japanese spurge *n* **:** a low Japanese herb or subshrub (*Pachysandra terminales*) of the box family often used as a ground cover

jap·a·nize \'jap-ə-ˌnīz\ *vt* **-nized; -niz·ing** *often cap* **1 :** to make Japanese **2 :** to bring (an area) under the influence of Japan — **jap·a·ni·za·tion** \ˌjap-ə-nə-'zā-shən\ *n, often cap*

Japan wax *n* **:** a yellowish fat obtained from the berries of several sumacs (as *Rhus verniciflua* and *R. succedanea*) and used chiefly in polishes

¹jape \'jāp\ *vb* **japed; jap·ing** [ME *japen*] *vi* **:** to say or do something jokingly or mockingly ~ *vt* **:** to make mocking fun of — **jap·er** \'jā-pər\ *n* — **jap·ery** \'jā-p(ə-)rē\ *n*

²jape *n* **:** something designed to arouse amusement or laughter: as **a :** an amusing literary or dramatic production **b :** GIBE

Ja·pheth \'jā-fəth\ *n* [L *Japheth* or Gk *Iapheth*, fr. Heb *Yepheth*] **:** a son of Noah and progenitor of the Medes and Greeks

ja·pon·i·ca \jə-'pän-i-kə\ *n* [NL, fr. fem. of *Japonicus* Japanese, fr. *Japonia* Japan] **:** JAPANESE QUINCE

¹jar \'jär\ *vb* **jarred; jar·ring** [prob. of imit. origin] *vi* **1 a :** to make a harsh or discordant sound **b :** to be out of harmony; *specif* **:** BICKER **c :** to have a harshly disagreeable or disconcerting effect **2 :** to undergo severe vibration ~ *vt* **:** to cause to jar: as **a :** to affect disagreeably **b :** to make unstable **:** SHAKE — **jar·ring·ly** \'jär-iŋ-lē\ *adv*

²jar *n* **1 a :** a harsh grating sound **b :** a state or manifestation of discord or conflict **2 a :** a sudden or unexpected shake **b :** an unsettling shock **c :** an unpleasant break or conflict in rhythm, flow, or transition

³jar *n* [MF *jarre*, fr. OProv *jarra*, fr. Ar *jarrah* earthen water vessel] **1 :** a widemouthed container made typically of earthenware or glass **2 :** as much as a jar will hold — **jar·ful** \-ˌfu̇l\ *n*

⁴jar *n* [alter. of earlier *char* turn, fr. ME — more at CHARE] *archaic* **:** the position of being ajar — usu. used in the phrase *on the jar*

jar·di·niere \ˌjärd-ᵊn-'i(ə)r, ˌzhärd-ᵊn-'(y)e(ə)r\ *n* [F *jardinière*, lit., female gardener] **1 a :** an ornamental stand for plants or flowers **b :** a large usu. ceramic flowerpot holder **2 :** a garnish for meat consisting of several cooked vegetables cut into pieces

¹jar·gon \'jär-gən, -ˌgän\ *n* [ME, fr. MF] **1 a :** confused unintelligible language **b :** a strange, outlandish, or barbarous language or dialect **c :** a hybrid language or dialect simplified in vocabulary and grammar and used for communication between peoples of different speech **2 :** the technical terminology or characteristic idiom of a special activity or group **3 :** obscure and often pretentious language marked by circumlocutions and long words ***syn*** see DIALECT — **jar·gon·is·tic** \ˌjär-gə-'nis-tik\ *adj*

²jargon *vi* **1 :** TWITTER, WARBLE **2 :** JARGONIZE

jar·gon·ize \'jär-gə-ˌnīz\ *vb* **-ized; -iz·ing** *vi* **:** to speak or write jargon ~ *vt* **1 :** to express in jargon **2 :** to make into jargon

jar·goon \jär-'gün\ *or* **jar·gon** \-'gän\ *n* [F *jargon* — more at ZIRCON] **:** a colorless, pale yellow, or smoky zircon

jarl \'yär(-ə)l\ *n* [ON — more at EARL] **:** a Scandinavian noble ranking immediately below the king

jar·rah \'jar-ə\ *n* [native name in Australia] **:** an Australian eucalypt (*Eucalyptus marginata*) with rough bark and ovate leaves; *also* **:** its wood

Jas *abbr* James

jas·mine \'jaz-mən\ *n* [F *jasmin*, fr. Ar *yāsamīn*, fr. Per] **1 a :** any of numerous often climbing shrubs (genus *Jasminum*) of the olive family that usu. have extremely fragrant flowers; *esp* **:** a tall-climbing half-evergreen Asiatic shrub (*J. officinale*) with fragrant white flowers from which a perfume is extracted **b :** any of numerous plants having sweet-scented flowers; *esp* **:** YELLOW JESSAMINE 2 **2 :** a light yellow

Ja·son \'jās-ᵊn\ *n* [L *Iason*, fr. Gk *Iasōn*] **:** a legendary Greek hero distinguished for his successful quest of the Golden Fleece

jas·per \'jas-pər\ *n* [ME *jaspre*, fr. MF, fr. L *jaspis*, fr. Gk *iaspis*, of Sem origin; akin to Heb *yāshĕpheh* jasper] **1 :** an opaque cryptocrystalline quartz of any of several colors; *esp* **:** green chalcedony **2 :** colored stoneware with raised white decoration **3 :** a blackish green — **jas·pery** \-pə-rē\ *adj*

jas·per·ware \'jas-pər-ˌwa(ə)r, -ˌwe(ə)r\ *n* **:** JASPER 2

jas·sid \'jas-əd\ *n* [deriv. of Gk *Iasos*, town in Asia Minor] **:** any of a large cosmopolitan family (Jassidae) of small leafhoppers that include many economically significant pests of cultivated plants; *broadly* **:** LEAFHOPPER

Jat \'jät\ *n* [Hindi *Jāt*] **:** a member of an Indo-Aryan people of the Punjab and Uttar Pradesh

ja·to unit \'jāt-(ˌ)ō-\ *n* [*j*et-*a*ssisted *t*ake*o*ff] **:** a unit for assisting the takeoff of an airplane consisting of one or more rocket engines

jaunce \'jȯn(t)s, 'jän(t)s\ *vi* [origin unknown] *archaic* **:** PRANCE

jaun·dice \'jȯn-dəs, 'jän-\ *n* [ME *jaundis*, fr. MF *jaunisse*, fr. *jaune* yellow, fr. L *galbinus* yellowish green, fr. *galbus* yellow] **1 :** yellowish pigmentation of the skin, tissues, and body fluids caused by the deposition of bile pigments **2 :** a disease or abnormal condition characterized by jaundice **3 :** a state or attitude characterized by satiety, distaste, or hostility

jaun·diced \-dəst\ *adj* **1 :** affected with or as if with jaundice **2 :** exhibiting or influenced by envy, distaste, or hostility

¹jaunt \'jȯnt, 'jänt\ *vi* [origin unknown] **1** *archaic* **:** to trudge about **2 :** to make a short journey for pleasure

²jaunt *n* **1** *archaic* **:** a tiring trip **2 :** an excursion undertaken for pleasure

jaunting car *n* **:** a light two-wheeled open horse-drawn vehicle used esp. in Ireland with lengthwise seats placed face to face or back to back

jaunting car

jaun·ty \'jȯnt-ē, 'jänt-\ *adj* **jaun·ti·er; -est** [modif. of F *gentil*] **1** *archaic* **a :** GENTEEL **b :** STYLISH **2 :** sprightly in manner or appearance **:** LIVELY — **jaun·ti·ly** \'jȯnt-ᵊl-ē, 'jänt-\ *adv* — **jaun·ti·ness** \'jȯnt-ē-nəs, 'jänt-\ *n*

Jav *abbr* Javanese

Ja·va *n* [*Java*, island of Indonesia] **1** \'jav-ə, -ē\ *often not cap* **:** COFFEE **2** \'jäv-ə, 'jav-ə\ **:** any of a breed of large general-purpose domestic fowls

Ja·va man \ˌjäv-ə-, ˌjav-ə-\ *n* **:** either of two small-brained prehistoric men (*Pithecanthropus erectus* and *P. robustus*) known chiefly from more or less fragmentary skulls found in Trinil, Java

Ja·va·nese \ˌjav-ə-'nēz, ˌjäv-, -'nēs\ *n, pl* **Javanese** [*Java* + *-nese* (as in *Japanese*)] **1 :** a member of an Indonesian people inhabiting the island of Java **2 :** an Austronesian language of the Javanese people — **Javanese** *adj*

Java sparrow *n* **:** a Javanese weaverbird (*Padda oryzivora*) that is glaucous gray and black above with pinkish underparts, white cheeks, and large pink bill and that is a common cage bird

jav·e·lin \'jav-(ə-)lən\ *n* [MF *javeline*, alter. of *javelot*, of Celt origin; akin to OIr *gabul* forked stick] **1 :** a light spear thrown as a weapon of war or in hunting **2 :** a slender usu. metal shaft at least 260 centimeters long that is thrown for distance in an athletic field event

ja·ve·li·na \ˌhäv-ə-ˈlē-nə\ *n* [AmerSp *jabalina,* fr. Sp, fem. of *jabalí* wild boar, fr. Ar *jabalīy*] : PECCARY

Ja·velle water \zha-ˈvel, zhə-\ *n* [*Javel,* former village in France] : an aqueous solution of sodium hypochlorite used as a disinfectant or a bleaching agent and in photography

[1]**jaw** \ˈjȯ\ *n* [ME] **1 a :** either of two complex cartilaginous or bony structures in most vertebrates that border the mouth, support the soft parts enclosing it, usu. bear teeth on their oral margin, and are an upper that is more or less firmly fused with the skull and a lower that is hinged, movable, and articulated with the temporal bone of either side **b :** the parts constituting the walls of the mouth and serving to open and close it — usu. used in pl. **c :** any of various organs of invertebrates that perform the function of the vertebrate jaws **2 :** something resembling the jaw of an animal: as **a :** one of the sides of a narrow pass or channel **b :** either of two or more opposable parts that open and close for holding or crushing something between them **3** *slang* **a :** impudent or offensive talk **b :** a friendly chat

[2]**jaw** *vt* **:** to talk to in a scolding or boring manner ~ *vi* **:** to talk abusively, indignantly, or longwindedly

jaw·bone \ˈjȯ-ˈbōn, -ˌbōn\ *n* **:** JAW 1a; *esp* **:** MANDIBLE

jaw·break·er \-ˌbrā-kər\ *n* **1 :** a word difficult to pronounce **2 :** a round hard candy

jawed \ˈjȯd\ *adj* **:** having jaws <~ fishes> — usu. used in combination <square-*jawed*> <a 3-*jawed* chuck>

jaw·less fish \ˌjȯ-ləs-\ *n* **:** any of the taxonomic group (Agnatha) of primitive vertebrates without jaws that is comprised of cyclostomes and extinct related forms

jaw·line \ˈjȯ-ˌlīn\ *n* **:** the outline of the lower jaw

[1]**jay** \ˈjā\ *n* [ME, fr. MF *jai,* fr. LL *gaius*] **1 a :** a predominantly fawn-colored Old World bird (*Garrulus glandarius*) of the crow family with a black-and-white crest and wings marked with black, white, and blue **b :** any of various usu. crested and largely blue birds that with the common Old World jay constitute a subfamily of the crow family, have roving habits and harsh voices, and are often destructive to the eggs and young of other birds **2 a :** an impertinent chatterer **b :** DANDY 1 **c :** GREENHORN **3 :** a moderate blue

[2]**jay** *n* **:** the letter *j*

jay·bird \ˈjā-ˌbərd\ *n* **:** JAY 1, 2

Jay·cee \ˈjā-ˈsē\ *n* [*j*unior *c*hamber] **:** a member of a junior chamber of commerce

jay·gee \ˈjā-ˈjē\ *n* [*j*unior *g*rade] **:** LIEUTENANT JUNIOR GRADE

jay·hawk·er \ˈjā-ˌhȯ-kər\ *n* [*jayhawk* (fictitious bird of Kansas)] **1 a** *often cap* **:** a member of a band of antislavery guerrillas in Kansas and Missouri before and during the Civil War **b :** BANDIT **2** *cap* **:** a native or resident of Kansas — used as a nickname

jay·vee \ˈjā-ˈvē\ *n* [*j*unior *v*arsity] **1 :** JUNIOR VARSITY **2 :** a member of a junior varsity team

jay·walk \ˈjā-ˌwȯk\ *vi* **:** to cross a street carelessly or in an illegal manner so as to be endangered by traffic — **jay·walk·er** *n*

[1]**jazz** \ˈjaz\ *vb* [E slang *jazz* to copulate with, of unknown origin] *vt* **1 a :** ENLIVEN — usu. used with *up* **b :** ACCELERATE **2 :** to play in the manner of jazz ~ *vi* **1 :** to go here and there **:** GAD **2 :** to dance to or play jazz

[2]**jazz** *n, often attrib* **1 a :** American music developed esp. from ragtime and blues and characterized by syncopated rhythms, contrapuntal ensemble playing, and usu. improvisation often with special melodic features (as blue notes) peculiar to the individual interpretation of the player **b :** popular dance music influenced by jazz and played in a loud rhythmic manner **2 :** empty talk **:** HUMBUG <spouted all the scientific ~ —Pete Martin> **3 :** similar but unspecified things **:** STUFF <that wind, and the waves, and all that ~ —John Updike>

jazz·man \ˈjaz-ˌman, -mən\ *n* **:** a jazz musician

jazzy \ˈjaz-ē\ *adj* **jazz·i·er; -est 1 :** having the characteristics of jazz **2 :** marked by unrestraint, animation, or flashiness — **jazz·i·ly** \ˈjaz-ə-lē\ *adv* — **jazz·i·ness** \ˈjaz-ē-nəs\ *n*

J-bar lift \ˌjā-ˌbär-\ *n* **:** a ski lift having a series of J-shaped bars each of which pulls one skier

JBS *abbr* John Birch Society

JCB *abbr* **1** junior college of business **2** [NL *juris canonici baccalaureus*] bachelor of canon law

JCC *abbr* junior chamber of commerce

JCD *abbr* [NL *juris canonici doctor*] doctor of canon law

JCL *abbr* [NL *juris canonici licentiatus*] licentiate in canon law

JCS *abbr* joint chiefs of staff

jct *abbr* junction

JD *abbr* **1** junior dean **2** [L *juris doctor*] doctor of jurisprudence; doctor of law **3** [L *jurum doctor*] doctor of laws **4** justice department **5** juvenile delinquent

jeal·ous \ˈjel-əs\ *adj* [ME *jelous,* fr. OF, fr. (assumed) VL *zelosus,* fr. LL *zelus* zeal — more at ZEAL] **1 a :** intolerant of rivalry or unfaithfulness **b :** disposed to suspect rivalry or unfaithfulness **:** apprehensive of the loss of another's exclusive devotion **2 :** hostile toward a rival or one believed to enjoy an advantage **3 :** vigilant in guarding a possession <his ~ love of privacy —J. W. Beach> **4 :** distrustfully watchful **:** SUSPICIOUS <kept a ~ eye on her husband> *syn* see ENVIOUS — **jeal·ous·ly** *adv* — **jeal·ous·ness** *n*

jeal·ou·sy \ˈjel-ə-sē\ *n* **1 :** a jealous disposition, attitude, or feeling **2 :** zealous vigilance

jean \ˈjēn\ *n* [short for *jean fustian,* fr. ME *Gene* Genoa, Italy + *fustian*] **1 :** a durable twilled cotton cloth used esp. for sportswear and work clothes **2** *pl* **a :** pants made of jean or denim **b :** TROUSERS

jeep \ˈjēp\ *n* [alter. of *gee pee,* fr. general-*purpose*] **:** a small general-purpose motor vehicle with 80-inch wheelbase, ¼-ton capacity, and four-wheel drive used by the U.S. army in World War II; *also* **:** a similar but larger and more powerful U.S. army vehicle

[1]**jeer** \ˈji(ə)r\ *vb* [origin unknown] *vi* **:** to speak or cry out with derision or mockery ~ *vt* **:** to deride with jeers **:** TAUNT *syn* see SCOFF — **jeer·er** *n* — **jeer·ing·ly** \-iŋ-lē\ *adv*

[2]**jeer** *n* **:** a jeering remark or sound **:** TAUNT

Jef·fer·son Da·vis's Birthday \ˌjef-ər-sən-ˌdā-və-səz-\ *n* **:** June 3 observed as a legal holiday in many southern states

Jef·fer·son Day \ˈjef-ər-sən-\ *n* **:** April 13 observed as a holiday in some states in commemoration of Thomas Jefferson's birthday

Jef·fer·so·nian \ˌjef-ər-ˈsō-nē-ən, -nyən\ *adj* **:** of, relating to, or characteristic of Thomas Jefferson or his political principles or policies — **Jeffersonian** *n* — **Jef·fer·so·nian·ism** \-ˌiz-əm\ *n*

Jef·frey pine \ˌjef-rē-\ *n* [John *Jeffrey,* 19th cent. Sc botanical explorer] **:** a pine (*Pinus jeffreyi*) of western No. America with long needles in groups of three

jehad *var of* JIHAD

Je·hosh·a·phat \ji-ˈhäs(h)-ə-ˌfat\ *n* [Heb *Yĕhōshāphāth*] **:** a king of Judah who brought Judah into an alliance with the northern kingdom of Israel in the 9th century B.C.

Je·ho·vah \ji-ˈhō-və\ *n* [NL, false reading (as *Yĕhōwāh*) of Heb *Yahweh*] **:** GOD 1 <in the Lord ~ is everlasting strength —Isa 26:4 (AV)>

Jehovah's Witness *n* **:** a member of a group that witness by distributing literature and by personal evangelism to beliefs in the theocratic rule of God, the sinfulness of organized religions and governments, and an imminent millennium

je·hu \ˈjē-(ˌ)h(y)ü\ *n* [Heb *Yēhū*] **1** *cap* **:** a king of Israel in the 9th century B.C. who according to the account in II Kings had Jezebel killed in accordance with Elijah's prophecy **2 :** a driver of a coach or cab

jejun- *or* **jejuno-** *comb form* [L *jejunum*] **:** jejunum <*jejunectomy*>

je·ju·nal \ji-ˈjün-ᵊl\ *adj* **:** of or relating to the jejunum

je·june \ji-ˈjün\ *adj* [L *jejunus*] **1 :** lacking nutritive value <~ diets> **2 :** lacking interest or significance **:** DULL, UNSATISFYING <~ lectures> **3 :** lacking maturity **:** PUERILE <~ remarks on world affairs> *syn* see INSIPID — **je·june·ly** *adv* — **je·june·ness** \-ˈjün-nəs\ *n*

je·ju·num \ji-ˈjü-nəm\ *n* [L, fr. neut. of *jejunus*] **:** the section of the small intestine that comprises the first two fifths beyond the duodenum and that is larger, thicker-walled, and more vascular and has more circular folds than the ileum

Je·kyll and Hyde \ˌjek-ə-lən-ˈhīd, ˌjē-kə-, ˌjā-kə-\ *n* [Dr. *Jekyll* & Mr. *Hyde,* representing the split personality of the protagonist in *The Strange Case of Dr. Jekyll and Mr. Hyde* (1886) by R. L. Stevenson] **:** a person having a split personality one side of which is good and the other evil

jell \ˈjel\ *vb* [back-formation fr. *jelly*] *vi* **1 :** to come to the consistency of jelly **2 :** to take shape **:** CRYSTALLIZE ~ *vt* **:** to cause to take form

jellied gasoline *n* **:** NAPALM

Jell-O \ˈjel-(ˌ)ō\ *trademark* — used for a gelatin dessert usu. with the flavor and color of fruit

[1]**jel·ly** \ˈjel-ē\ *n, pl* **jellies** [ME *gelly,* fr. MF *gelee,* fr. fem. of *gelé,* pp. of *geler* to freeze, congeal, fr. L *gelare* — more at COLD] **1 :** a soft somewhat elastic food product made usu. with gelatin or pectin; *esp* **:** a fruit product made by boiling sugar and the juice of fruit **2 :** a substance resembling jelly in consistency **3 :** a state of fear or irresolution **4 :** a shapeless structureless mass **:** PULP — **jel·ly·like** \-ˌlīk\ *adj*

[2]**jelly** *vb* **jel·lied; jel·ly·ing** *vi* **1 :** JELL **2 :** to make jelly ~ *vt* **:** to bring to the consistency of jelly

jelly bean *n* **1 :** a sugar-glazed bean-shaped candy **2 :** a weak, spineless, or effeminate person

jel·ly·fish \ˈjel-ē-ˌfish\ *n* **1 a :** a free-swimming marine coelenterate that is the sexually reproducing form of a hydrozoan or scyphozoan and has a nearly transparent saucer-shaped body and extensile marginal tentacles studded with stinging cells **b :** SIPHONOPHORE **c :** CTENOPHORE **2 :** a person lacking backbone or firmness

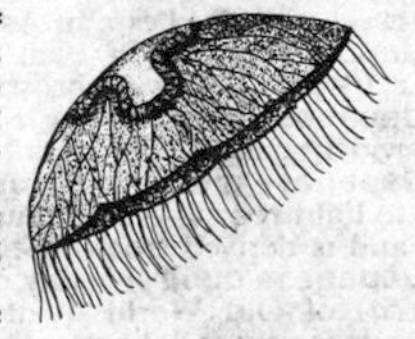

jellyfish 1a

jelly roll *n* **:** a thin sheet of sponge cake spread with jelly and rolled up

jel·u·tong \ˈjel-ə-ˌtȯŋ\ *n* [Malay *jĕlutong*] **1 :** any of several trees (genus *Dyera*) of the dogbane family **2 :** the resinous rubbery latex of a jelutong (esp. *Dyera costulata*) used esp. as a chicle substitute

je ne sais quoi \zhə-nə-ˌsā-ˈkwä\ *n* [F, lit., I know not what] **:** something that cannot be adequately described or expressed

jen·net \ˈjen-ət\ *n* [ME *genett,* fr. MF *genet,* fr. Catal, Zenete (member of a Berber people), horse] **1 :** a small Spanish horse **2 a :** a female donkey **b :** HINNY

jen·ny \ˈjen-ē\ *n, pl* **jennies** [fr. the name *Jenny*] **1 a :** a female bird <~ wren> **b :** a female donkey **2 :** SPINNING JENNY

jeop·ard \ˈjep-ərd\ *vt* [ME *jeoparden,* back-formation fr. *jeopardie*] **:** JEOPARDIZE

jeop·ar·dize \ˈjep-ər-ˌdīz\ *vt* **-dized; -diz·ing :** to expose to danger **:** IMPERIL

jeop·ar·dy \ˈjep-ərd-ē\ *n* [ME *jeopardie,* fr. AF *juparti,* fr. OF *jeu parti* alternative, lit., divided game] **1 :** exposure to or imminence of death, loss, or injury **:** DANGER **2 :** the danger that an accused person is subjected to when on trial for a criminal offense

je·quir·i·ty bean \jə-ˈkwir-ət-ē-\ *n* [Pg *jequiriti*] **1 :** the poisonous scarlet and black seed of the rosary pea often used for beads **2 :** ROSARY PEA 1

Jer *abbr* Jeremiah; Jeremias

jer·boa \jər-ˈbō-ə, jer-\ *n* [Ar *yarbū'*] **:** any of several social nocturnal Old World jumping rodents (family Dipodidae) with long hind legs and long tail

jerboa mouse *n* **:** any of various leaping rodents usu. with elongated hind legs

jer·e·mi·ad \ˌjer-ə-ˈmī-əd, -ˌad\ *n* [F *jérémiade,* fr. *Jérémie* Jeremiah, fr. LL *Jeremias*] **:** a prolonged lamentation or complaint

Jer·e·mi·ah \ˌjer-ə-ˈmī-ə\ *n* [LL *Jeremias*, fr. Gk *Hieremias*, fr. Heb *Yirmĕyāh*] **1 :** a major Hebrew prophet of the 6th and 7th centuries B.C. **2 :** one who is pessimistic about the present and foresees a calamitous future **3 :** a prophetic book of canonical Jewish and Christian Scripture — see BIBLE table

Jer·e·mi·as \-ˈmī-əs\ *n* [LL] **:** JEREMIAH

[1]**jerk** \ˈjərk\ *vb* [prob. alter. of *yerk*] *vt* **1 :** to give a quick suddenly arrested push, pull, or twist to **2 :** to propel with a quick suddenly arrested motion **3 :** to utter in an abrupt, snappy, or sharply broken manner **4 :** to mix and dispense (as sodas) behind a soda fountain ~ *vi* **1 :** to make a sudden spasmodic motion **2 :** to move in short abrupt motions or with frequent jolts **3 :** to throw an object with a jerk — **jerk·er** *n*

syn JERK, SNAP, TWITCH, YANK *shared meaning element* **:** to make or act on with a sudden sharp quick movement

[2]**jerk** *n* **1 :** a single quick motion of short duration **2 a :** jolting, bouncing, or thrusting motions **b :** a tendency to produce spasmodic motions **3 a :** an involuntary spasmodic muscular movement due to reflex action **b** *pl* (1) **:** CHOREA (2) **:** involuntary twitchings due to nervous excitement **4 :** a stupid, foolish, or unconventional person **5 :** the pushing of a weight from shoulder height to a position overhead in weight lifting ; the second phase of the clean and jerk

[3]**jerk** *vt* [back-formation fr. [2]*jerky*] **:** to cut (meat) into long slices or strips and dry in the sun

jer·kin \ˈjər-kən\ *n* [origin unknown] **:** a close-fitting hip-length sleeveless jacket

jerk off *vb* **:** MASTURBATE — usu. considered vulgar

jerk·wa·ter \ˈjər-ˌkwȯt-ər, -ˌkwät-\ *adj* [fr. *jerkwater* (rural train); fr. the fact that it took on water carried in buckets from the source of supply] **1:** remote and unimportant <~ towns> **2:** PIDDLING

[1]**jerky** \ˈjər-kē\ *adj* **jerk·i·er; -est** **1 a :** moving along with or marked by fits and starts **b :** characterized by abrupt transitions **2 :** INANE, FOOLISH — **jerk·i·ly** \-kə-lē\ *adv* — **jerk·i·ness** \-kē-nəs\ *n*

[2]**jer·ky** \ˈjər-kē\ *n* [Sp *charqui*] **:** jerked meat

jer·o·bo·am \ˌjer-ə-ˈbō-əm\ *n* [*Jeroboam* I †*ab*912 B.C. king of the northern kingdom of Israel] **:** an oversize wine bottle holding about four 26-ounce quarts <a ~ of champagne>

jer·ri·can *or* **jerry can** \ˈjer-ē-ˌkan\ *n* [*Jerry* + *can;* fr. its German design] **:** a narrow flat-sided 5-gallon liquid container

Jer·ry \ˈjer-ē\ *n, pl* **Jerries** [by shortening & alter.] *chiefly Brit* **:** GERMAN

jer·ry–build \ˈjer-ē-ˌbild\ *vt* **-built** \-ˌbilt\; **-build·ing** [back-formation fr. *jerry-built*] **:** to build cheaply and flimsily — **jer·ry–build·er** *n*

jer·ry–built *adj* [origin unknown] **1 :** built cheaply and unsubstantially **2 :** carelessly or hastily put together

jer·sey \ˈjər-zē\ *n, pl* **jerseys** [*Jersey*, one of the Channel islands] **1 :** a plain weft-knitted fabric made of wool, cotton, nylon, rayon, or silk and used esp. for clothing **2 :** any of various close-fitting usu. circular-knitted garments esp. for the upper body **3 :** any of a breed of small short-horned predominantly yellowish brown or fawn dairy cattle noted for their rich milk

Jersey giant *n* [*New Jersey*, state of U.S.] **:** any of a breed of large usu. black domestic fowls developed by interbreeding large Asiatic fowls with Langshans

Jersey pine *n* **:** VIRGINIA PINE

Je·ru·sa·lem artichoke \jə-ˌrü-s(ə-)ləm, -ˌrüz-(ə-)ləm-\ *n* [*Jerusalem* by folk etymology fr. It *girasole* girasol] **:** a perennial American sunflower (*Helianthus tuberosus*) widely cultivated for its tubers that are used as a vegetable, a livestock feed, and a source of levulose

Jerusalem cherry *n* [*Jerusalem*, Palestine] **:** either of two plants (*Solanum pseudo-capsicum* or *S. capsicastrum*) of the nightshade family cultivated as ornamental houseplants for their orange to red berries

Jerusalem cricket *n* **:** a large-headed burrowing nocturnal insect (*Stenopelmatus fuscus*) of the southwestern U.S. related to the katydids

Jerusalem thorn *n* **1 :** CHRIST'S-THORN **2 :** a tropical American leguminous spiny shrub or shrubby tree (*Parkinsonia aculeata*) with pinnate leaves and showy racemose yellow flowers that is used for hedging and as emergency food for livestock — called also *horsebean*

jess \ˈjes\ *n* [ME *ges*, fr. MF *gies*, fr. pl. of *jet* throw, fr. *jeter* to throw — more at JET] **:** a short strap secured on the leg of a hawk and usu. provided with a ring for attaching a leash — **jessed** \ˈjest\ *adj*

jes·sa·mine \ˈjes-(ə-)mən\ *var of* JASMINE

Jes·se \ˈjes-ē\ *n* [Heb *Yishay*] **:** the father of David, king of Israel according to the account in I Samuel

[1]**jest** \ˈjest\ *n* [ME *geste*, fr. OF, fr. L *gesta* deeds, fr. neut. pl. of *gestus*, pp. of *gerere* to bear, wage — more at CAST] **1 a :** an act intended to provoke laughter **:** PRANK **b :** a comic incident **2 :** an utterance (as a jeer or a witty quip) intended to be taken as mockery or humor rather than literal truth **3 a :** a frivolous mood or manner <spoken in ~> **b :** gaiety and merriment **4 :** LAUGHINGSTOCK

syn **1** JEST, JOKE, QUIP, WITTICISM, WISECRACK, GAG *shared meaning element* **:** a remark, story, or action intended to evoke laughter **2** see FUN

[2]**jest** *vi* **1 :** to utter taunts **:** GIBE **2 :** to speak or act without seriousness **3:** to make a witty remark **:** JOKE ~ *vt* **:** to make fun of

jest·er \ˈjes-tər\ *n* **1 :** FOOL 2a **2 :** one given to jests

Je·su·it \ˈjezh-(ə-)wət, ˈjez-\ *n* [NL *Jesuita*, fr. LL *Jesus*] **1 :** a member of the Roman Catholic Society of Jesus founded by St. Ignatius Loyola in 1534 and devoted to missionary and educational work **2 :** one given to intrigue or equivocation — **je·su·it·ic** \ˌjezh(-)ə-ˈwit-ik\ *or* **je·su·it·i·cal** \-i-kəl\ *adj, often cap* — **je·su·it·i·cal·ly** \-i-k(ə-)lē\ *adv, often cap* — **je·su·it·ism** \ˈjezh-(ə-)wət-ˌiz-əm, ˈjez-\ *or* **je·su·it·ry** \-(ə-)wə-trē\ *n, often cap* — **je·su·it·ize** \-(ə-)wət-ˌīz\ *vb, often cap*

Je·sus \ˈjē-zəs, -zəz *clerically also* -ˌzəs *and* -ˌzəz\ *n* [LL, fr. Gk *Iēsous*, fr. Heb *Yēshūaʿ*] **1 :** the Jewish religious teacher whose life, death, and resurrection as reported by the Evangelists are the basis of the Christian message of salvation — called also *Jesus Christ* **2** *Christian Science* **:** the highest human corporeal concept of the divine idea rebuking and destroying error and bringing to light man's immortality

[1]**jet** \ˈjet\ *n* [ME, fr. MF *jaiet*, fr. L *gagates*, fr. Gk *gagatēs*, fr. *Gagas*, town and river in Asia Minor] **1 :** a compact velvet-black coal that takes a good polish and is often used for jewelry **2 :** an intense black

[2]**jet** *vb* **jet·ted; jet·ting** [MF *jeter*, lit., to throw, fr. L *jactare* to throw, fr. *jactus*, pp. of *jacere* to throw; akin to Gk *hienai* to send] *vi* **:** to spout forth **:** GUSH ~ *vt* **1 :** to emit in a stream **:** SPOUT **2 :** to place (as a pile) in the ground by means of a jet of water

[3]**jet** *n* **1 a :** a usu. forceful stream of fluid (as water or gas) discharged from a narrow opening or a nozzle **b :** a nozzle for a jet of fluid **2 :** something issuing as if in a jet <talk poured from her in a brilliant ~ —*Time*> **3 a :** JET ENGINE **b :** JET AIRPLANE **4 :** JET STREAM

[4]**jet** *vi* **jet·ted; jet·ting :** to travel by jet airplane

jet airplane *n* **:** an airplane powered by a jet engine that utilizes the surrounding air in the combustion of fuel or by a rocket-type jet engine that carries its fuel and all the oxygen needed for combustion

jet·bead \ˈjet-ˌbēd\ *n* **:** a shrub (*Rhodotypos scandens*) that has black shining fruit and is used as an ornamental

je·té \zhə-ˈtā\ *n* [F, fr. pp. of *jeter*] **:** a broad leap in ballet with one leg stretched forward and the other leg backward

jet engine *n* **:** an engine that produces motion as a result of the rearward discharge of a jet of fluid; *specif* **:** an airplane engine having one or more exhaust nozzles for discharging rearwardly a jet of heated air and exhaust gases to produce forward propulsion

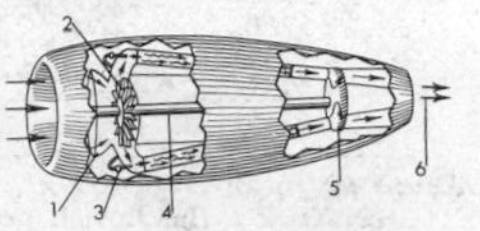

jet engine, simplified cutaway: *1* air intake, *2* compressor, *3* fuel injection, *4* drive shaft, *5* turbine, *6* exhaust

Jeth \ˈjet\ *n* [Hindi *Jēth*, fr. Skt *Jyaiṣṭha*] **:** a month of the Hindu year — see MONTH table

jet·port \ˈjet-ˌpō(ə)rt, -ˌpȯ(ə)rt\ *n* **:** an airport designed to handle jet airplanes

jet–pro·pelled \ˌjet-prə-ˈpeld\ *adj* **1 :** moving by jet propulsion **2 :** suggestive of the speed and force of a jet airplane

jet propulsion *n* **:** propulsion of a body produced by the forwardly directed forces of the reaction resulting from the rearward discharge of a jet of fluid; *specif* **:** propulsion of an airplane by jet engines

jet·sam \ˈjet-səm\ *n* [alter. of *jettison*] **1 :** the part of a ship, its equipment, or cargo that is cast overboard to lighten the load in time of distress and that sinks or is washed ashore **2 :** FLOTSAM 2

jet set *n* [fr. the surpassing speed of jet airplanes] **:** an international social group of wealthy individuals who frequent fashionable resorts — **jet–set·ter** \-ˌset-ər\ *n*

jet stream *n* **:** a long narrow meandering current of high-speed winds near the tropopause blowing from a generally westerly direction and often exceeding a speed of 250 miles per hour

[1]**jet·ti·son** \ˈjet-ə-sən, -ə-zən\ *n* [ME *jetteson*, fr. AF *getteson*, fr. OF *getaison* action of throwing, fr. L *jactation-*, *jactatio*, fr. *jactatus*, pp. of *jactare* — more at JET] **1 :** a voluntary sacrifice of cargo to lighten a ship's load in time of distress **2 :** ABANDONMENT

[2]**jettison** *vt* **1 :** to make jettison of **2 :** to cast off as superfluous or encumbering **:** DISCARD **3 :** to drop from an airplane or spacecraft in flight — **jet·ti·son·able** \-sə-nə-bəl, -zə-\ *adj*

[1]**jet·ty** \ˈjet-ē\ *n, pl* **jetties** [ME *jette*, fr. MF *jetee*, fr. fem. of *jeté*, pp. of *jeter* to throw — more at JET] **1 a :** a structure extended into a sea, lake, or river to influence the current or tide or to protect a harbor **b :** a protecting frame of a pier **2 :** a landing wharf **:** PIER

[2]**jetty** *vi* **jet·tied; jet·ty·ing :** PROJECT, JUT

[3]**jetty** *adj* **:** black as jet

jeu d'es·prit \zhœ̄-des-prē\ *n, pl* **jeux d'esprit** *same*\ [F, lit., play of the mind] **:** a witty comment or composition

jeu·nesse do·rée \zhœ-nes-dȯ-rā\ *n* [F, gilded youth] **:** young people of wealth and fashion

Jew \ˈjü\ *n* [ME, fr. OF *gyu*, fr. L *Judaeus*, fr. Gk *Ioudaios*, fr. Heb *Yĕhūdhī*, fr. *Yĕhūdhāh* Judah, Jewish kingdom] **1 a :** a member of the tribe of Judah **b :** ISRAELITE **2 :** a member of a nation existing in Palestine from the 6th century B.C. to the 1st century A.D. **3 :** a person belonging to a continuation through descent or conversion of the ancient Jewish people **4 :** one whose religion is Judaism

[1]**jew·el** \ˈjü-əl\ *n, often attrib* [ME *juel*, fr. OF, dim. of *jeu* game, play, fr. L *jocus* game, joke — more at JOKE] **1 :** an ornament of precious metal often set with stones or decorated with enamel and worn as an accessory of dress **2 :** one that is highly esteemed **3 :** a precious stone **:** GEM **4 :** a bearing for a pivot (as in a watch or compass) made of crystal, precious stone, or glass

[2]**jewel** *vt* **-eled** *or* **-elled; -el·ing** *or* **-el·ling** **1 :** to adorn or equip with jewels **2 :** to give beauty to as if with jewels

jew·el·er *or* **jew·el·ler** \ˈjü-ə-lər\ *n* **1 :** one who makes or repairs jewelry **2 :** one who deals in jewelry, precious stones, watches, and usu. silverware and china

jew·el·ry \ˈjü-əl-rē\ *n* **:** JEWELS; *esp* **:** objects of precious metal often set with gems and worn for personal adornment

jew·el·weed \-ˌwēd\ *n* **:** IMPATIENS

ə abut	ᵊ kitten	ər further	a back	ā bake	ä cot, cart
au̇ out	ch chin	e less	ē easy	g gift	i trip ī life
j joke	ŋ sing	ō flow	ȯ flaw	ȯi coin	th thin t͟h this
ü loot	u̇ foot	y yet	yü few	yu̇ furious	zh vision

Jew·ess \'jü-əs\ *n* **:** a female Jew
jew·fish \'jü-ˌfish\ *n* **:** any of various large groupers that are usu. dusky green or blackish, thickheaded, and rough-scaled
Jew·ish \'jü-ish\ *adj* **:** of, relating to, or characteristic of the Jews — **Jew·ish·ly** *adv* — **Jew·ish·ness** *n*
Jewish calendar *n* **:** a calendar in use among Jewish peoples that is reckoned from the year 3761 B.C. and dates in its present form from about A.D. 360 — see MONTH table

JEWISH YEARS 5734 – 5753

JEWISH YEAR		A.D.
5734	begins	Sept. 27, 1973
5735	"	Sept. 17, 1974
5736	"	Sept. 6, 1975
5737	"	Sept. 25, 1976
5738	"	Sept. 13, 1977
5739	"	Oct. 2, 1978
5740	"	Sept. 22, 1979
5741	"	Sept. 11, 1980
5742	"	Sept. 29, 1981
5743	"	Sept. 18, 1982
5744	"	Sept. 8, 1983
5745	"	Sept. 27, 1984
5746	"	Sept. 16, 1985
5747	"	Oct. 4, 1986
5748	"	Sept. 24, 1987
5749	"	Sept. 12, 1988
5750	"	Sept. 30, 1989
5751	"	Sept. 20, 1990
5752	"	Sept. 9, 1991
5753	"	Sept. 28, 1992

Jew·ry \'jů(ə)r-ē, 'jü-rē\ *n* **1** *pl* **Jewries :** a community of Jews **:** GHETTO **2 :** the Jewish people
Jew's harp *or* **Jews' harp** \'jüz-ˌhärp, 'jüs-\ *n* **:** a small lyre-shaped instrument that when placed between the teeth gives tones from a metal tongue struck by the finger

Jew's harp

Jez·e·bel \'jez-ə-ˌbəl\ *n* [Heb *Izebhel*] **1 :** the Phoenician wife of Ahab who according to the account in I and II Kings pressed the cult of Baal on the Israelite kingdom but was finally killed in accordance with Elijah's prophecy **2** *often not cap* **:** an impudent, shameless, or abandoned woman
jg *abbr* junior grade
JHVH *var of* YHWH
1jib \'jib\ *n* [origin unknown] **:** a triangular sail set on a stay extending from the head of the foremast to the bowsprit or the jibboom — see SAIL illustration
2jib *vb* **jibbed; jib·bing** *vt* **:** to cause (as a sail or yard) to swing from one side of a ship to the other ~ *vi* **:** to shift across or swing round from one side of a ship to the other
3jib *n* [prob. by shortening & alter. fr. *gibbet*] **1 :** the projecting arm of a crane **2 :** a derrick boom
4jib *vi* **jibbed; jib·bing** [prob. fr. *2jib*] **:** to refuse to proceed further **:** BALK — **jib·ber** *n*
jib·boom \ˌjib-'(b)üm\ *n* [*1jib* + *boom*] **:** a spar that forms an extension of the bowsprit
1jibe \'jīb\ *vb* **jibed; jib·ing** [perh. modif. of D *gijben*] *vi* **1 :** to shift suddenly and forcibly from one side to the other — used of a fore-and-aft sail **2 :** to change a ship's course so that the sail jibes ~ *vt* **:** to cause to jibe
2jibe *var of* GIBE
3jibe *vi* **jibed; jib·ing** [origin unknown] **:** to be in accord **:** AGREE <moral claims do not ~ with . . . actual traditions —John Cogley>
jiff \'jif\ *n* [by shortening] **:** JIFFY
jif·fy \'jif-ē\ *n, pl* **jiffies** [origin unknown] **:** MOMENT, INSTANT <ready in a ~>
1jig \'jig\ *n* [prob. fr. MF *giguer* to dance, fr. *gigue* fiddle, of Gmc origin; akin to OHG *gīga* fiddle; akin to ON *geiga* to turn aside — more at GIG] **1 a :** any of several lively springy dances in triple rhythm **b :** music to which a jig may be danced **2 :** TRICK, STRATAGEM <the ~ is up> **3 a :** any of several fishing devices that are jerked up and down or drawn through the water **b :** a device used to maintain mechanically the correct positional relationship between a piece of work and the tool or between parts of work during assembly **c :** a device in which crushed ore is concentrated or coal is cleaned by agitating in water
2jig *vb* **jigged; jig·ging** *vt* **1 :** to dance in the rapid lively manner of a jig **2 a :** to give a rapid jerky motion to **b :** to separate (a mineral or ore from waste) with a jig **3 :** to catch (a fish) with a jig **4 :** to machine by means of a jig-controlled tool operation ~ *vi* **1 a :** to dance a jig **b :** to move with rapid jerky motions **2 :** to fish with a jig **3 :** to work with the aid of a jig
1jig·ger \'jig-ər\ *n* **1 :** one that jigs or operates a jig **2 :** any of several sails **3 :** 1JIG 3a **4 a** (1) **:** a mechanical device usu. with a jerky reciprocating motion (2) **:** a mold or a machine incorporating a revolving mold on which ceramic items (as plates) are formed **b :** something too complex, tricky, or trivial to designate accurately **:** GADGET **5 :** a measure that is used in mixing drinks and that usu. holds 1½ ounces
2jigger *n* [of African origin; akin to Wolof *jiga* insect] **:** CHIGGER
1jig·gle \'jig-əl\ *vb* **jig·gled; jig·gling** \-(ə-)liŋ\ [freq. of *2jig*] *vi* **:** to move with quick little jerks or oscillating motions ~ *vt* **:** to cause to jiggle
2jiggle *n* **:** a jiggling motion
jig·gly \'jig-(ə-)lē\ *adj* **jig·gli·er; -est :** UNSTEADY, JIGGLING
1jig·saw \'jig-ˌsȯ\ *n* **1 :** a machine saw with a narrow vertically reciprocating blade for cutting curved and irregular lines or ornamental patterns in openwork **2 :** SCROLL SAW 1
2jigsaw *vt* **1 :** to cut or form by or as if by a jigsaw **2 :** to arrange or place in an intricate or interlocking way
jigsaw puzzle *n* **:** a puzzle consisting of small irregularly cut pieces that are to be fitted together to form a picture
ji·had \ji-'häd, -'had\ *n* [Ar *jihād*] **1 :** a holy war waged on behalf of Islam as a religious duty **2 :** a crusade for a principle or belief
jil·lion \'jil-yən\ *n* [*j* + *-illion* (as in *million*)] **:** an indeterminately large number — **jillion** *adj*
1jilt \'jilt\ *n* [alter. of *jillet* (flirtatious girl)] **:** a woman who capriciously or unfeelingly drops her lover
2jilt *vt* **:** to drop (one's lover) capriciously or unfeelingly — **jilt·er** *n*
jim crow \'jim-'krō\ *n, often cap J & C* [*Jim Crow,* stereotype Negro in a 19th cent. song-and-dance act] **1 :** NEGRO — usu. taken to be offensive **2 :** ethnic discrimination esp. against the Negro by legal enforcement or traditional sanctions — **jim crow** *adj, often cap J & C* — **jim crow·ism** \-ˌiz-əm\ *n, often cap J & C*
jim-dan·dy \'jim-'dan-dē\ *n* [fr. the name *Jim*] **:** something excellent of its kind
jim·jams \'jim-ˌjamz\ *n pl* [perh. alter. of *delirium tremens*] **1 :** DELIRIUM TREMENS **2 :** JITTERS
1jim·my \'jim-ē\ *n, pl* **jimmies** [fr. the name *Jimmy*] **:** a short crowbar
2jimmy *vt* **jim·mied; jim·my·ing :** to force open with or as if with a jimmy <the burglar *jimmied* a window>
jim·son·weed \'jim(p)-sən-ˌwēd\ *n, often cap* [*Jamestown,* Va.] **:** a poisonous tall coarse annual weed (*Datura stramonium*) of the nightshade family with rank-smelling foliage and large white or violet trumpet-shaped flowers succeeded by globose prickly fruits
1jin·gle \'jiŋ-gəl\ *vb* **jin·gled; jin·gling** \-g(ə-)liŋ\ [ME *ginglen,* of imit. origin] *vi* **1 :** to make a light clinking or tinkling sound **2 :** to rhyme or sound in a catchy repetitious manner ~ *vt.* **:** to cause to jingle — **jin·gler** \-g(ə-)lər\ *n*
2jingle *n* **1 a :** a light clinking or tinkling sound **b :** a catchy repetition of sounds in a poem **2 a :** something that jingles **b :** a short verse or song marked by catchy repetition **3 :** a 2-wheeled horse-drawn covered vehicle used esp. in Ireland and Australia as a public conveyance — **jin·gly** \-g(ə-)lē\ *adj*
1jin·go \'jiŋ-(ˌ)gō\ *interj* [prob. euphemism for *Jesus*] — used as a mild oath usu. in the phrase *by jingo*
2jingo *n, pl* **jingoes** [fr. the fact that the phrase *by jingo* appeared in the refrain of a chauvinistic song] **:** one characterized by jingoism — **jin·go·ish** \-ish\ *adj*
jin·go·ism \'jiŋ-(ˌ)gō-ˌiz-əm\ *n* **:** extreme chauvinism or nationalism marked esp. by a belligerent foreign policy — **jin·go·ist** \-əst\ *n* — **jin·go·is·tic** \ˌjiŋ-gō-'is-tik\ *adj* — **jin·go·is·ti·cal·ly** \-ti-k(ə-)lē\ *adv*
1jink \'jiŋk\ *n* [origin unknown] **1 :** a quick evasive turn **:** SLIP **2** *pl* **:** PRANKS, FROLICS <high ~*s*>
2jink *vi* **:** to move quickly or unexpectedly with sudden turns and shifts (as in dodging)
jinn \'jin\ *or* **jin·ni** \jə-'nē, 'jin-ē\ *n, pl* **jinns** *or* **jinn** [Ar *jinnīy* demon] **1 :** one of a class of spirits that according to Muslim demonology inhabit the earth, assume various forms, and exercise supernatural power **2 :** a supernatural spirit that often takes human form and serves his summoner
jin·rik·i·sha \jin-'rik-ˌshȯ\ *n* [Jap] **:** RICKSHA
1jinx \'jiŋ(k)s\ *n* [prob. alter. of *jynx* (wryneck); fr. the use of wrynecks in witchcraft] **:** one that brings bad luck
2jinx *vt* **:** to foredoom to failure or misfortune **:** bring bad luck to
ji·pi·ja·pa \ˌhē-pē-'häp-ə\ *n* [Sp, fr. *Jipijapa,* Ecuador] **1 :** a Central and So. American plant (*Carludovica palmata* of the family Cyclanthaceae) resembling a palm **2 :** PANAMA
JIT *abbr* job instruction training
jit·ney \'jit-nē\ *n, pl* **jitneys** [origin unknown] **1** *slang* **:** NICKEL 2a(1) **2** [fr. the original 5 cent fare] **:** BUS 1a; *esp* **:** a small bus that carries passengers over a regular route according to a flexible schedule
1jit·ter \'jit-ər\ *vi* [origin unknown] **1 :** to be nervous or act in a nervous way **2 :** to make continuous fast repetitive movements
2jitter *n* **1 :** the state of mind or the movement of one that jitters **2** *pl* **:** a sense of panic or extreme nervousness <had a bad case of the ~*s* before his performance> **3 :** irregular random movement (as of a pointer or an image on a screen)
1jit·ter·bug \'jit-ər-ˌbəg\ *n* **1 :** a jazz variation of the two-step in which couples swing, balance, and twirl in standardized patterns and often with vigorous acrobatics **2 :** one who dances the jitterbug
2jitterbug *vi* **1 :** to dance the jitterbug **2 :** to move around or back and forth with quick often jerky movements esp. to confuse or disconcert an opponent in sports
jit·tery \'jit-ə-rē\ *adj* **1 :** suffering from the jitters **2 :** marked by jittering movements
jiu·jit·su *or* **jiu·jut·su** *var of* JUJITSU
1jive \'jīv\ *n* [origin unknown] **1 :** swing music or the dancing performed to it **2 a :** glib, deceptive, or foolish talk **b :** the jargon of hipsters **c :** a special jargon of difficult or slang terms
2jive *vb* **jived; jiv·ing** *vi* **1 :** KID **2 :** to dance to or play jive ~ *vt* **1 :** TEASE 3, CAJOLE **2 :** SWING 5
3jive *adj, slang* **:** PHONY
Jn *or* **Jno** *abbr* John
JND *abbr* just noticeable difference
jnr *abbr, Brit* junior
jo \'jō\ *n, pl* **joes** [alter. of *joy*] *chiefly Scot* **:** SWEETHEART, DEAR
Jo *abbr* Joel
1job \'jäb\ *n* [perh. fr. obs. E *job* (lump)] **1 a :** a piece of work; *esp* **:** a small miscellaneous piece of work undertaken on order at a stated rate **b :** the object or material on which work is being done **c :** something produced by or as if by work <do a better ~ next time> **d :** an example of a usu. specified type **:** ITEM <this ~ is round-necked and sleeveless —Lois Long> **2 a :** something done for private advantage <suspected the whole incident was a put-up ~> **b :** a criminal enterprise; *specif* **:** ROBBERY **c :** a damaging or destructive bit of work <did a ~ on him> **3 a** (1)

: something that has to be done : TASK (2) : an undertaking requiring unusual exertion <it was a real ~ to talk over that noise> **b** : a specific duty, role, or function **c** : a regular remunerative position **d** *chiefly Brit* : state of affairs — used with *bad* or *good* <it was a good ~ you didn't hit the old man —E. L. Thomas> ***syn*** see TASK — **on the job** : on the alert : on duty <safety devices that are constantly *on the job*>

[2]**job** *vb* **jobbed; job·bing** *vi* **1** : to do odd or occasional pieces of work for hire **2** : to carry on public business for private gain **3** : to carry on the business of a middleman or wholesaler <his company ~*s* and doesn't sell to the homeowner> ~ *vt* **1** : to buy and sell (as stock) for profit : SPECULATE **2** : to hire or let by the job or for a period of service **3** : to get, deal with, or effect by jobbery **4** : to do or cause to be done by separate portions or lots : SUBCONTRACT **5** : SWINDLE, TRICK

[3]**job** *adj* **1** *Brit* : that is for hire for a given service or period **2** : used in, engaged in, or done as job work <a ~ shop> **3** : of or relating to a job or to employment <a guarantee of ~ security>

Job \ˈjōb\ *n* [L, fr. Gk *Iōb*, fr. Heb *Iyyōbh*] **1** : the hero of the book of Job who endures afflictions with fortitude and faith **2** : a narrative and poetic book of canonical Jewish and Christian Scripture — see BIBLE table

job action *n* : a temporary refusal (as by policemen) to work as a means of enforcing compliance with demands

job·ber \ˈjäb-ər\ *n* : one that jobs: as **a** (1) : STOCKJOBBER (2) : WHOLESALER; *specif* : a wholesaler who operates on a small scale or who sells only to retailers and institutions **b** : one who works by the job or on job work

job·bery \ˈjäb-(ə-)rē\ *n* : the act or practice of jobbing; *esp* : corruption in public office

job·hold·er \ˈjäb-ˌhōl-dər\ *n* : one having a regular job

job–hop·ping \-ˌhäp-iŋ\ *n* : the practice of moving (as for immediate financial gain) from job to job — **job–hop·per** \-ˌhäp-ər\ *n*

job·less \ˈjäb-ləs\ *adj* **1** : having no job **2** : of or relating to those having no job — **job·less·ness** *n*

job lot *n* **1** : a miscellaneous collection of goods for sale as a lot usu. to a retailer **2** : a miscellaneous and usu. inferior collection or group

Job's comforter \ˈjōbz-\ *n* [fr. the tone of the speeches made to Job by his friends] : one who discourages or depresses while seemingly giving comfort and consolation

Job's tears *n pl* **1** : hard pearly white seeds often used as beads **2** *sing in constr* : an Asiatic grass (*Coix lacryma-jobi*) whose seeds are Job's tears

Jo·cas·ta \jō-ˈkas-tə\ *n* [L, fr. Gk *Iokastē*] : a queen of Thebes and mother of Oedipus who unknowingly becomes her husband

[1]**jock** \ˈjäk\ *n* **1** : JOCKEY 1 **2** : DISC JOCKEY

[2]**jock** *n* [*jockstrap*] **1** : ATHLETIC SUPPORTER **2** : ATHLETE; *esp* : a college athlete

[1]**jock·ey** \ˈjäk-ē\ *n, pl* **jockeys** [*Jockey*, Sc nickname for *John*] **1** : one who rides a horse esp. as a professional in a race **2** : one who operates or works with a specified vehicle, device, or object : OPERATOR <an accountant, a pencil ~ — with almost no association with the out-of-doors —James Selder> <switchboard ~>

[2]**jockey** *vb* **jock·eyed; jock·ey·ing** *vt* **1** : to deal shrewdly or fraudulently with **2 a** : to ride (a horse) as a jockey **b** : DRIVE, OPERATE **3 a** : to maneuver or manipulate by adroit or devious means <was ~*ed* out of a political job> **b** : to change the position of by a series of movements <~ a truck into position> ~ *vi* **1** : to act as a jockey **2** : to maneuver for advantage <~ for a starting position on the team>

jockey club *n* : an association for the promotion and regulation of horse racing

jock itch *n* [[2]*jock*] : ringworm of the crotch : TINEA CRURIS

jock·strap \ˈjäk-ˌstrap\ *n* [E slang *jock* (penis) + E *strap*] : ATHLETIC SUPPORTER

jo·cose \jō-ˈkōs\ *adj* [L *jocosus*, fr. *jocus* joke] **1** : given to joking : MERRY **2** : characterized by joking : HUMOROUS ***syn*** see WITTY — **jo·cose·ly** *adv* — **jo·cose·ness** *n* — **jo·cos·i·ty** \jō-ˈkäs-ət-ē\ *n*

joc·u·lar \ˈjäk-yə-lər\ *adj* [L *jocularis*, fr. *joculus*, dim. of *jocus*] **1** : given to jesting : habitually jolly or jocund **2** : characterized by jesting : PLAYFUL ***syn*** see WITTY — **joc·u·lar·i·ty** \ˌjäk-yə-ˈlar-ət-ē\ *n* — **joc·u·lar·ly** \ˈjäk-yə-lər-lē\ *adv*

jo·cund \ˈjäk-ənd *also* ˈjōk-(ˌ)ənd\ *adj* [ME, fr. LL *jocundus*, alter. of L *jucundus*, fr. *juvare* to help] : marked by or suggestive of high spirits and lively mirthfulness <a poet could not but be gay, in such a ~ company —William Wordsworth> ***syn*** see MERRY — **jo·cun·di·ty** \jō-ˈkən-dət-ē, jä-\ *n* — **jo·cund·ly** \ˈjäk-ən-dlē, ˈjōk-(ˌ)\ *adv*

jodh·pur \ˈjäd-pər\ *n* [*Jodhpur*, India] **1** *pl* : riding breeches cut full through the hips and close-fitting from knee to ankle **2** : an ankle-high boot fastened with a strap that is buckled at the side

Jo·el \ˈjō-əl\ *n* [L, fr. Gk *Iōēl*, fr. Heb *Yō'ēl*] **1** : the traditionally assumed author of the book of Joel **2** : a narrative and apocalyptic book of canonical Jewish and Christian Scripture — see BIBLE table

joe–pye weed \ˌjō-ˈpī-\ *n* [perh. alter. of earlier *eupatory*, fr. NL *Eupatorium*, genus name] : any of several tall American perennial composite herbs (genus *Eupatorium*) with whorled leaves and corymbose heads of typically purple tubular flowers

[1]**jog** \ˈjäg\ *vb* **jogged; jog·ging** [prob. alter. of *shog*] *vt* **1** : to give a slight shake or push to : NUDGE **2** : to rouse to alertness <*jogged* his memory> **3** : to cause (as a horse) to go at a jog **4** : to align the edges of (piled sheets of paper) by hitting or shaking against a flat surface ~ *vi* **1** : to move up and down or about with a short heavy motion <his . . . holster *jogging* against his hip —Thomas Williams> **2 a** : to run or ride at a slow trot **b** : to go at a slow, leisurely, or monotonous pace : TRUDGE

[2]**jog** *n* **1** : a slight shake : PUSH **2 a** : a jogging movement, pace, or trip **b** : a horse's slow gait with marked beats

[3]**jog** *n* [prob. alter. of [2]*jag*] **1 a** : a projecting or retreating part (as of a line or surface) **b** : the space in the angle of a jog **2** : a brief abrupt change in direction

[4]**jog** *vi* **jogged; jog·ging** : to make a jog <the road ~*s* to the right>

jog·ger \ˈjäg-ər\ *n* **1** : one that jogs **2** : a device for jogging piled sheets of paper

[1]**jog·gle** \ˈjäg-əl\ *vb* **jog·gled; jog·gling** \-(ə-)liŋ\ [freq. of [1]*jog*] *vt* : to shake slightly ~ *vi* : to move shakily or jerkily — **jog·gler** \-(ə-)lər\ *n*

[2]**joggle** *n* : [2]JOG 2a

[3]**joggle** *n* [dim. of [3]*jog*] **1** : a notch or tooth in a joining surface (as of a piece of building material) to prevent slipping **2** : a dowel for joining two adjacent blocks of masonry

[4]**joggle** *vt* **jog·gled; jog·gling** \ˈjäg-(ə-)liŋ\ : to join by means of a joggle so as to prevent sliding apart

jog trot *n* **1** : a slow regular jolting gait (as of a horse) **2** : a routine habit or course of action

jo·han·nes \jō-ˈhan-əs\ *n, pl* **johannes** [*Johannes* John V †1750 king of Portugal] : a Portuguese gold coin of the 18th and 19th centuries equivalent to 6400 reis

Jo·han·nine \jō-ˈhan-ˌīn, -ən\ *adj* [LL *Johannes* John] : of, relating to, or characteristic of the apostle John or the New Testament books ascribed to him

john \ˈjän\ *n* [fr. the name *John*] **1** : TOILET **2** : a prostitute's client

John \ˈjän\ *n* [LL *Johannes*, fr. Gk *Iōannēs*, fr. Heb *Yōḥānān*] **1** : a Jewish prophet who according to Gospel accounts foretold Jesus's messianic ministry and baptized him — called also *John the Baptist* **2** : an apostle who according to various Christian traditions wrote the fourth Gospel, the three Johannine Epistles, and the Book of Revelation **3** : the fourth Gospel in the New Testament — see BIBLE table **4** : any of three short didactic letters addressed to early Christians and included in the New Testament — see BIBLE table

John Barleycorn *n* : alcoholic liquor personified

john·boat \ˈjän-ˌbōt\ *n* [fr. the name *John*] : a narrow flat-bottomed square-ended boat usu. propelled by a pole or paddle and used on inland waterways

John Bull \-ˈbu̇l\ *n* [*John Bull*, character typifying the English nation in *The History of John Bull* (1712) by John Arbuthnot] **1** : the English nation personified : the English people **2** : a typical Englishman — **John Bull·ish** \-ish\ *adj* — **John Bull·ish·ness** *n* — **John Bull·ism** \-ˌiz-əm\ *n*

John Doe \-ˈdō\ *n* **1** : a party to legal proceedings whose true name is unknown **2** : an average man <brilliant educators and plain *John Does* —K. D. Wells>

John Do·ry \-ˈdōr-ē, -ˈdȯr-\ *n, pl* **John Dories** [earlier *dory*, fr. ME *dorre*, fr. MF *doree*, lit., gilded one] : a common yellow to olive European food fish (*Zeus faber*) with an oval compressed body, long dorsal spines, and a dark spot on each side; *also* : a closely related and possibly identical fish (*Z. capensis*) widely distributed in southern seas

Joh·ne's disease \ˈyō-nəz-\ *n* [Heinrich A. *Johne* †1910 G bacteriologist] : a chronic often fatal enteritis esp. of cattle that is caused by a bacillus (*Mycobacterium paratuberculosis*) and is characterized by persistent diarrhea and gradual emaciation

John Han·cock \ˈjän-ˈhan-ˌkäk\ *n* [*John Hancock*; fr. the prominence of his signature on the Declaration of Independence] : an autograph signature

John Hen·ry \-ˈhen-rē\ *n* [fr. the name *John Henry*] : an autograph signature

John Mark *n* : MARK 1a

john·ny \ˈjän-ē\ *n, pl* **johnnies** [fr. the name *Johnny*] **1** *often cap* : FELLOW, GUY **2** : a short-sleeved collarless gown with an opening in the back for wear by persons (as hospital patients) undergoing medical examination or treatment

john·ny·cake \ˈjän-ē-ˌkāk\ *n* [prob. fr. the name *Johnny*] : a bread made with cornmeal

John·ny–come–late·ly \ˌjän-ē-(ˌ)kəm-ˈlāt-lē\ *n, pl* **Johnny–come–latelies** *or* **Johnnies–come–lately** **1** : a late or recent arrival : NEWCOMER **2** : UPSTART <established families tend to hold themselves above the *Johnny-come-latelies* —William Zeckendorf *b*1905>

John·ny–jump–up \ˌjän-ē-ˈjəm-ˌpəp\ *n* **1** : WILD PANSY; *broadly* : any of various small-flowered cultivated pansies **2** : any of various American violets

John·ny–on–the–spot \ˌjän-ē-ˌȯn-t͟hə-ˈspät, -ē-ˌän-\ *n* : one who is on hand and ready to perform a service or respond to an emergency

Johnny Reb \-ˈreb\ *n* [fr. the name *Johnny* + *reb* (rebel)] : a Confederate soldier

John·son·ese \ˌjän(t)-sə-ˈnēz, -ˈnēs\ *n* [Samuel *Johnson*] : a literary style characterized by balanced phraseology and Latinate diction

John·son grass \ˈjän(t)-sən-\ *n* [William *Johnston* †1859 Am agriculturist] : a tall perennial sorghum (*Sorghum halepense*) naturalized as a hay and forage grass in warm regions

joie de vi·vre \ˌzhwäd-ə-ˈvēvrᵊ\ *n* [F, lit., joy of living] : keen or buoyant enjoyment of life

[1]**join** \ˈjȯin\ *vb* [ME *joinen*, fr. OF *joindre*, fr. L *jungere* — more at YOKE] *vt* **1 a** : to put or bring together so as to form a unit <~ two blocks of wood with glue> **b** : to connect (as points) by a line **c** : ADJOIN **2** : to put or bring into close association or relationship <~*ed* in marriage> **3** : to engage in (battle) **4 a** : to come into the company of <~*ed* us for lunch> **b** : to associate oneself

with <~*ed* the church> ~ *vi* **1 a :** to come together so as to be connected <nouns ~ to form compounds> **b :** ADJOIN <the two estates ~> **2 :** to come into close association or relationship: as **a :** to form an alliance <~*ed* to combat crime> **b :** to become a member of a group **c :** to take part in a collective activity <~ in singing> — **join·able** \ˈjȯi-nə-bəl\ *adj*

syn JOIN, COMBINE, UNITE, CONNECT, LINK, ASSOCIATE, RELATE *shared meaning element* **:** to bring or come together into some manner of union ***ant*** disjoin, part

[2]**join** *n* **1 :** JOINT **2 :** UNION 2d

join·der \ˈjȯin-dər\ *n* [F *joindre* to join] **1 :** CONJUNCTION **2 a** (1) **:** a joining of parties as plaintiffs or defendants in a suit (2) **:** a joining of causes of action or defense **b :** acceptance of an issue tendered

join·er \ˈjȯi-nər\ *n* **:** one that joins: as **a :** a person whose occupation is to construct articles by joining pieces of wood **b :** a gregarious or civic-minded person who joins many organizations

join·ery \ˈjȯin-(ə-)rē\ *n* **1 :** the art or trade of a joiner **2 :** work done by a joiner

join·ing \ˈjȯi-niŋ\ *n* **:** the act or instance of joining one thing to another **:** JUNCTURE

[1]**joint** \ˈjȯint\ *n* [ME *jointe,* fr. OF, fr. *joindre*] **1 a** (1) **:** the point of contact between elements of an animal skeleton with the parts that surround and support it (2) **:** NODE 4b **b :** a part or space included between two articulations, knots, or nodes **c :** a large piece of meat for roasting **2 a :** a place where two things or parts are joined **b :** a space between the adjacent surfaces of two bodies joined and held together (as by cement or mortar) **c :** a fracture or crack in rock not accompanied by dislocation **d :** the flexing part of a cover along either backbone edge of a book **e :** the junction of two or more members of a framed structure **f :** a union formed by two abutting rails in a track including the elements (as bars and bolts) necessary to hold the abutting rails together **g :** an area at which two ends, surfaces, or edges are attached **3 a :** a shabby or disreputable place of entertainment **b :** PLACE, ESTABLISHMENT **4 :** a marijuana cigarette — **joint·ed** \-əd\ *adj* — **joint·ed·ly** *adv* — **joint·ed·ness** *n* — **out of joint** **1 a** *of a bone* **:** having the head slipped from its socket **b :** at variance **2 a :** DISORDERED 2a **b :** being out of humor **:** DISSATISFIED

[2]**joint** *adj* [ME, fr. MF, fr. pp. of *joindre*] **1 :** UNITED, COMBINED <the ~ influences of culture and climate> **2 :** common to two or more: as **a** (1) **:** involving the united activity of two or more <a ~ effort> (2) **:** constituting an activity, operation, or organization in which elements of more than one armed service participate <~ maneuvers> (3) **:** constituting an action or expression of two or more governments <~ peace talks> **b :** shared by or affecting two or more <a ~ fine> **3 :** united, joined, or sharing with another (as in a right or status) <~ heirs> **4 :** being a function of or involving two or more variables and esp. random variables <a ~ probability density function>

[3]**joint** *vb* [[1]*joint*] *vt* **1 a :** to unite by a joint **:** fit together **b :** to provide with a joint **:** ARTICULATE **c :** to prepare (as a board) for joining by planing the edge **2 :** to separate the joints of (as meat) ~ *vi* **1 :** to fit as if by joints <the stones ~ neatly> **2 :** to form joints as a stage in growth — used esp. of small grains

Joint Chiefs of Staff : a military advisory group composed of the chiefs of staff of the army and air force, the chief of naval operations, and sometimes the commandant of the marine corps

joint·er \ˈjȯint-ər\ *n* **:** one that joints; *esp* **:** any of various tools used in making joints

joint grass *n* **:** a coarse creeping grass (*Paspalum distichum*) with jointed stems that is used for fodder and for erosion control

joint·ly *adv* **:** in a joint manner **:** TOGETHER

joint resolution *n* **:** a resolution passed by both houses of a legislative body that has the force of law when signed by or passed over the veto of the executive

join·tress \ˈjȯin-trəs\ *n* **:** a woman having a legal jointure

joint–stock company *n* **:** a company or association consisting of individuals organized to conduct a business for gain and having a joint stock of capital represented by shares owned individually by the members and transferable without the consent of the group

join·ture \ˈjȯin-chər\ *n* **1 a :** an act of joining **:** the state of being joined **b :** JOINT **2 a :** an estate settled on a wife to be taken by her in lieu of dower **b :** a settlement on the wife of a freehold estate for her lifetime

joint·worm \ˈjȯint-ˌwərm\ *n* **:** the larva of any of several small chalcid wasps (genus *Harmolita*) that attack the stems of grain and cause swellings like galls at or just above the first joint

joist \ˈjȯist\ *n* [ME *giste,* fr. MF, fr. (assumed) VL *jacitum,* fr. L *jacēre* to lie — more at ADJACENT] **:** any of the small timbers or metal beams ranged parallel from wall to wall in a structure to support a floor or ceiling

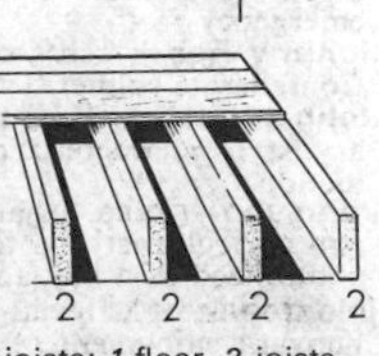

joists: *1* floor, *2* joists

jo·jo·ba \hə-ˈhō-bə\ *n* [MexSp] **:** a shrub or small tree (*Simmondsia californica*) of the box family of southwestern No. America with edible seeds that yield a valuable liquid wax

[1]**joke** \ˈjōk\ *n* [L *jocus;* akin to OHG *gehan* to say, Skt *yācati* he implores] **1 a :** something said or done to provoke laughter; *esp* **:** a brief oral narrative with a climactic humorous twist **b** (1) **:** the humorous or ridiculous element in something (2) **:** an instance of jesting **:** KIDDING <can't take a ~> **c :** PRACTICAL JOKE **d :** LAUGHINGSTOCK **2 a :** something not to be taken seriously **:** a trifling matter <consider his skiing a ~ —Harold Callender> — often used in negative construction <it is no ~ to be lost in the desert> **b :** something presenting no difficulty <that exam was a ~> ***syn*** see JEST

[2]**joke** *vb* **joked; jok·ing** *vi* **:** to make jokes **:** JEST ~ *vt* **:** to make the object of a joke **:** KID — **jok·ing·ly** \ˈjō-kiŋ-lē\ *adv*

jok·er \ˈjō-kər\ *n* **1 a :** a person given to joking **:** WAG **b :** FELLOW, GUY; *esp* **:** an insignificant, obnoxious, or incompetent person <a shame to let a ~ like this win —Harold Robbins> **2 :** a playing card added to a pack as a wild card or as the highest-ranking card **3 a** (1) **:** an ambiguous or apparently immaterial clause inserted in a legislative bill to make it inoperative or uncertain in some respect (2) **:** an unsuspected, misleading, or misunderstood clause, phrase, or word in a document that nullifies or greatly alters it **b :** something (as an expedient or stratagem) held in reserve to gain an end or escape from a predicament **c :** an unsuspected or not readily apparent fact, factor, or condition that thwarts or nullifies a seeming advantage

jol·li·fi·ca·tion \ˌjäl-i-fə-ˈkā-shən\ *n* **:** FESTIVITY, MERRYMAKING

jol·li·ty \ˈjäl-ət-ē\ *n, pl* **-ties** **1 :** the quality or state of being jolly **:** MERRIMENT **2** *Brit* **:** a festive gathering ***syn*** see MIRTH

[1]**jol·ly** \ˈjäl-ē\ *adj* **jol·li·er; -est** [ME *joli,* fr. OF] **1 a** (1) **:** full of high spirits **:** JOYOUS (2) **:** given to conviviality **:** JOVIAL **b :** expressing, suggesting, or inspiring gaiety **:** CHEERFUL **2 :** extremely pleasant or agreeable **:** SPLENDID ***syn*** see MERRY

[2]**jolly** *adv* **:** VERY <would . . . do as they were ~ well told —John Stockbridge>

[3]**jolly** *vb* **jol·lied; jol·ly·ing** *vi* **:** to engage in good-natured banter **:** KID ~ *vt* **:** to put or try to put in good humor esp. to gain an end **:** WHEEDLE

[4]**jolly** *n, pl* **jollies** **1** *chiefly Brit* **:** a good time **:** JOLLIFICATION **2** *pl* **:** KICKS <get their *jollies* by reenacting famous murders —H. F. Waters>

jol·ly boat \ˈjäl-ē-\ *n* [origin unknown] **:** a ship's boat of medium size used for general rough or small work

Jol·ly Rog·er \ˌjäl-ē-ˈräj-ər\ *n* [prob. fr. [1]*jolly* + the name *Roger*] **:** a black flag with a white skull and crossbones

[1]**jolt** \ˈjōlt\ *vb* [prob. blend of obs. *joll* (to strike) and *jot* (to bump)] *vt* **1 :** to cause to move with a sudden jerky motion **2 :** to give a knock or blow to; *specif* **:** to jar with a quick or hard blow **3 a :** to disturb the composure of <crudely ~*ed* out of that mood —Virginia Woolf> **b :** to interfere with roughly, abruptly, and disconcertingly <determination to pursue his own course was ~*ed* badly —F. L. Paxson> ~ *vi* **:** to move with a sudden jerky motion — **jolt·er** *n*

[2]**jolt** *n* **1 :** an abrupt sharp jerky blow or movement knocking or shaking violently and tending to unsettle or dislodge **:** JOUNCE **2 a** (1) **:** a sudden feeling of shock, surprise, or disappointment (2) **:** an event or development causing such a feeling <his defeat was quite a ~ to him> **b :** a serious check or reverse <had a severe financial ~> **3 :** a small potent or bracing portion **:** SHOT <a ~ of fresh air> — **jolty** \ˈjōl-tē\ *adj*

jolt–wag·on \ˈjōlt-ˌwag-ən\ *n, Midland* **:** a farm wagon

Jo·nah \ˈjō-nə, *3 is also* -nər\ *n* [Heb *Yōnāh*] **1 :** an Israelite prophet who according to the account in the book of Jonah resisted a divine call to preach repentance to the people of Nineveh, was swallowed and vomited by a great fish, and eventually carried out his mission **2 :** a narrative book of canonical Jewish and Christian Scripture — see BIBLE table **3 :** one believed to bring bad luck

Jo·nas \ˈjō-nəs\ *n* [LL, fr. Heb *Yōnāh*] **:** JONAH

Jon·a·than \ˈjän-ə-thən\ *n* [Heb *Yōnāthān*] **1 :** a son of Saul and friend of David according to the account in I Samuel **2 :** AMERICAN; *esp* **:** a New Englander

jon·gleur \zhō^{n}-ˈglər\ *n* [F, fr. OF *jogleour* — more at JUGGLER] **:** an itinerant medieval minstrel providing entertainment chiefly by song or recitation

jon·quil \ˈjän-kwəl, ˈjäŋ-\ *n* [F *jonquille,* fr. Sp *junquillo,* dim. of *junco* reed, fr. L *juncus;* akin to ON *einir* juniper, L *juniperus*] **:** a Mediterranean perennial bulbous herb (*Narcissus jonquilla*) of the amaryllis family with long linear leaves that is widely cultivated for its yellow or white fragrant short-tubed clustered flowers — compare DAFFODIL

Jor·dan almond \ˌjȯrd-^{ə}n-\ *n* [ME *jardin almande,* fr. MF *jardin* garden + ME *almande* almond] **:** a large Spanish almond that is salted or coated with sugar of various colors

Jor·dan curve \zhȯr-ˌdä^{n}-, ˌjȯrd-^{ə}n-\ *n* [Camille *Jordan* †1922 F mathematician] **:** SIMPLE CLOSED CURVE

Jordan curve theorem *n* **:** a fundamental theorem of topology: every simple closed curve divides the plane into two regions for which it is the common boundary

jo·rum \ˈjōr-əm, ˈjȯr-\ *n* [perh. fr. *Joram* in the Bible who "brought with him vessels of silver" (2 Sam 8:10—AV)] **:** a large drinking vessel or its contents

jo·seph \ˈjō-zəf *also* -səf\ *n* [L, fr. Gk *Iōsēph,* fr. Heb *Yōsēph*] **1** *cap* **a :** a son of Jacob who according to the account in Genesis rose to high political office in Egypt after being sold into slavery by his brothers **b :** the husband of Mary the mother of Jesus according to the Gospel accounts **2 :** a long cloak worn esp. by women in the 18th century

Jo·seph·ite \-ˌīt\ *n* **:** a member of St. Joseph's Society of the Sacred Heart founded in 1871 in Baltimore, Md. and devoted to missionary work among American Negroes

Joseph of Ar·i·ma·thea \-ˌar-ə-mə-ˈthē-ə\ **:** a rich councillor of the Sanhedrin who according to the Gospel accounts placed the body of Jesus in his own tomb and according to medieval legend took the Holy Grail to England

[1]**josh** \ˈjäsh\ *vb* [origin unknown] *vt* **:** to make fun of **:** TEASE ~ *vi* **:** to engage in banter **:** JOKE — **josh·er** *n*

[2]**josh** *n* **:** a good-humored joke **:** JEST

Josh *abbr* Joshua

Josh·ua \ˈjäsh-(ə-)wə\ *n* [Heb *Yehōshūa'*] **1 :** the divinely commissioned successor of Moses and military leader of the Israelites during the conquest of Canaan according to the account in the book of Joshua **2 :** a mainly narrative book of canonical Jewish and Christian Scripture — see BIBLE table

Joshua tree *n* **:** a tall branched arborescent yucca (*Yucca brevifolia*) of the southwestern U.S. that has short leaves and clustered greenish white flowers

joss \ˈjäs, ˈjȯs\ *n* [Pidgin E, fr. Pg *deus* god, fr. L — more at DEITY] **:** a Chinese idol or cult image

joss house *n* **:** a Chinese temple or shrine

joss stick *n* : a slender stick of incense burned in front of a joss

Joshua tree

¹jos·tle \'jäs-əl\ *vb* **jos·tled; jos·tling** \-(ə-)liŋ\ [alter. of *justle,* freq. of *¹joust*] *vi* **1 a** : to come in contact or into collision **b** : to make one's way by pushing and shoving **c** : to exist in close proximity **2** : to vie in gaining an objective : CONTEND ~ *vt* **1 a** : to come in contact or into collision with **b** : to force by pushing : ELBOW **c** : to stir up : AGITATE **d** : to exist in close proximity with **2** : to vie with in attaining an objective

²jostle *n* **1** : a jostling encounter or experience **2** : the state of being crowded or jostled together

Jos·ue \'jäsh-ə-,wā\ *n* [LL, fr. Heb *Yĕhōshūa'*] : JOSHUA

¹jot \'jät\ *n* [L *iota, jota* iota] : the least bit : IOTA <nothing ... has caused the author to change his mind one ~ —*Times Lit. Supp.*>

²jot *vt* **jot·ted; jot·ting** : to write briefly or hurriedly : set down in the form of a note <~ this down>

jot·ting \'jät-iŋ\ *n* : a brief note : MEMORANDUM

Jo·tun *also* **Jo·tunn** \'yōt-ᵊn, 'yō-,tün\ *n* [ON *jötunn*] : a member of a race of giants in Norse mythology

Jo·tun·heim *also* **Jo·tunn·heim** \'yōt-ᵊn-,hīm, -,hām\ *n* [ON *Jötunheimar*] : the home of the Jotuns in Norse mythology

joule \'jü(ə)l, 'jaü(ə)l\ *n* [James P. *Joule*] : the absolute mks unit of work or energy equal to 10^7 ergs or approximately 0.7375 foot-pounds

¹jounce \'jaün(t)s\ *vb* **jounced; jounc·ing** [ME *jouncen*] *vi* : to move in an up-and-down manner : BOUNCE ~ *vt* : to cause to jounce

²jounce *n* : JOLT

jouncy \'jaün(t)-sē\ *adj* **jounc·i·er; -est** : marked by a jouncing motion or effect

jour *abbr* **1** journal **2** journeyman

jour·nal \'jərn-ᵊl\ *n* [ME, service book containing the day hours, fr. MF, fr. *journal* daily, fr. L *diurnalis,* fr. *diurnus* of the day, fr. *dies* day — more at DEITY] **1 a** : a record of current transactions: as (1) : DAYBOOK 2 (2) : a book of original entry in double-entry bookkeeping **b** : an account of day-to-day events **c** : a record of experiences, ideas, or reflections kept regularly for private use **d** : a record of transactions kept by a deliberative or legislative body **e** : LOG 3, 4 **2 a** : a daily newspaper **b** : a periodical dealing esp. with matters of current interest **3** : the part of a rotating shaft, axle, roll, or spindle that turns in a bearing

journal box *n* : a metal housing to support and protect a journal bearing

jour·nal·ese \,jərn-ᵊl-'ēz, -'ēs\ *n* : a style of writing held to be characteristic of newspapers

jour·nal·ism \'jərn-ᵊl-,iz-əm\ *n* **1 a** : the collection and editing of material of current interest for presentation through news media **b** : the editorial or business management of an agency engaged in the collection and dissemination of news **c** : an academic study concerned with the collection and editing of news or the management of a news medium **2 a** : writing designed for publication in a newspaper or popular magazine **b** : writing characterized by a direct presentation of facts or description of events without an attempt at interpretation **c** : writing designed to appeal to current popular taste or public interest **3** : newspapers and magazines

jour·nal·ist \-ᵊl-əst\ *n* **1 a** : one engaged in journalism; *esp* : a writer or editor for a news medium **b** : a writer who aims at a mass audience **2** : one who keeps a journal

jour·nal·is·tic \,jərn-ᵊl-'is-tik\ *adj* : of, relating to, or characteristic of journalism or journalists — **jour·nal·is·ti·cal·ly** \-ti-k(ə-)lē\ *adv*

jour·nal·ize \'jərn-ᵊl-,īz\ *vb* **-ized; -iz·ing** *vt* : to record in a journal ~ *vi* **1** : to keep a journal in accounting **2** : to keep a personal journal — **jour·nal·iz·er** *n*

¹jour·ney \'jər-nē\ *n, pl* **journeys** [ME, fr. OF *journee* day's journey, fr. *jour* day, fr. LL *diurnum,* fr. L, neut. of *diurnus*] **1** : travel or passage from one place to another : TRIP **2** *chiefly dial* : a day's travel **3** : something suggesting travel or passage from one place to another <the ... ~ from childhood through adolescence to maturity —Peter Marin>

²journey *vb* **jour·neyed; jour·ney·ing** *vi* : to go on a journey : TRAVEL ~ *vt* : to travel over or through : TRAVERSE — **jour·ney·er** *n*

jour·ney·man \-nē-mən\ *n* [ME, fr. *journey* journey, a day's labor + *man*] **1** : a worker who has learned a trade and works for another person usu. by the day **2** : an experienced reliable worker or performer esp. as distinguished from one who is brilliant or colorful <a good ~ trumpeter —*New Yorker*> <a ~ outfielder>

jour·ney·work \-,wərk\ *n* **1** : work done by a journeyman **2** : HACKWORK

¹joust \'jaüst *sometimes* 'jəst *or* 'jüst\ *vi* [ME *jousten,* fr. OF *juster,* fr. (assumed) VL *juxtare,* fr. L *juxta* near; akin to L *jungere* to join — more at YOKE] **1 a** : to fight on horseback as a knight or man-at-arms **b** : to engage in combat with lances on horseback **2** : to engage in personal combat or competition — **joust·er** *n*

²joust *n* **1 a** : a combat on horseback between two knights with lances esp. as part of a tournament **b** *pl* : TOURNAMENT **2** : a personal combat or competition : STRUGGLE

Jove \'jōv\ *n* [L *Jov-, Juppiter*] : JUPITER — often used interjectionally to express surprise or agreement esp. in the phrase *by Jove*

jo·vial \'jō-vē-əl, -vyəl\ *adj* **1** *cap* : of or relating to Jove **2** : markedly good-humored esp. as evidenced by jollity and conviviality ***syn*** see MERRY — **jo·vi·al·i·ty** \,jō-vē-'al-ət-ē\ *n* — **jo·vial·ly** \'jō-vē-ə-lē, -vyə-\ *adv*

Jo·vi·an \'jō-vē-ən\ *adj* : of, relating to, or characteristic of the god or planet Jupiter

jow \'jaü\ *n* [E dial. *jow* (to strike, toll)] *chiefly Scot* : STROKE, TOLL

¹jowl \'jaü(ə)l *sometimes* 'jōl\ *n* [alter. of ME *chavel,* fr. OE *ceafl;* akin to MHG *kivel* jaw, Av *zafar-* mouth] **1 a** : JAW; *esp* : MANDIBLE **b** : one of the lateral halves of the mandible **2 a** : CHEEK **1 b** : the cheek meat of a hog <a dinner of boiled ~*s*> — see PORK illustration

²jowl *n* [ME *cholle*] : usu. slack flesh (as a dewlap, wattle, or the pendulous part of a double chin) associated with the lower jaw or throat

³jowl *n* [ME *choll*] : a cut of fish consisting of the head and usu. adjacent parts

jowly \'jaü-lē *sometimes* 'jō-\ *adj* **jowl·i·er; -est** : having marked jowls : having full or saggy flesh about the lower cheeks and jaw area <elderly man with a disillusioned ~ face —John Dos Passos>

¹joy \'jói\ *n* [ME, fr. OF *joie,* fr. L *gaudia,* pl. of *gaudium,* fr. *gaudēre* to rejoice; akin to Gk *gēthein* to rejoice] **1 a** : the emotion evoked by well-being, success, or good fortune or by the prospect of possessing what one desires : DELIGHT **b** : the expression or exhibition of such emotion : GAIETY **2** : a state of happiness or felicity : BLISS **3** : a source or cause of delight — **joy·less** \-ləs\ *adj* — **joy·less·ly** *adv* — **joy·less·ness** *n*

²joy *vi* : to experience great pleasure or delight : REJOICE ~ *vt* **1** *archaic* : GLADDEN **2** *archaic* : ENJOY

joy·ance \'jói-ən(t)s\ *n* : DELIGHT, ENJOYMENT

joy·ful \'jói-fəl\ *adj* : experiencing, causing, or showing joy : HAPPY ***syn*** see GLAD ***ant*** joyless — **joy·ful·ly** \-fə-lē\ *adv* — **joy·ful·ness** *n*

joy·ous \'jói-əs\ *adj* : filled with or expressive of joy <a ~ heart> ***syn*** see GLAD ***ant*** lugubrious — **joy·ous·ly** *adv* — **joy·ous·ness** *n*

joy·pop \'jói-,päp\ *vi* : to use habit-forming drugs occasionally or irregularly without becoming addicted — **joy·pop·per** *n*

joy·ride \'jói-,rīd\ *n* **1** : a ride taken for pleasure and often marked by reckless driving **2** : conduct or action resembling a joyride esp. in disregard of cost or consequences — **joy·rid·er** \-,rīd-ər\ *n* — **joy·rid·ing** *n*

joy·stick \-,stik\ *n* [perh. fr. E slang *joystick* penis] **1** : a lever in an airplane that operates the elevators by a fore-and-aft motion and the ailerons by a side-to-side motion **2** : a control for any of various devices that resembles an airplane's joystick esp. in being capable of motion in two or more directions

JP *abbr* **1** jet propulsion **2** justice of the peace

JPS *abbr* Jewish Publication Society

Jr *abbr* junior

JRC *abbr* Junior Red Cross

JSD *abbr* [NL *juris scientiae doctor*] doctor of science of law

jt *or* **jnt** *abbr* joint

ju·ba \'jü-bə\ *n* [origin unknown] : a dance of Southern plantation Negroes accompanied by complexly rhythmic hand clapping and slapping of the knees and thighs

Ju·bal \'jü-bəl\ *n* [Heb *Yūbhāl*] : a descendant of Cain who according to the account in Genesis is the father of those who play the harp and organ

ju·bi·lant \'jü-bə-lənt\ *adj* : filled with or expressing great joy : EXULTANT — **ju·bi·lant·ly** *adv*

ju·bi·lar·i·an \,jü-bə-'ler-ē-ən, -'lar-\ *n* : one celebrating a jubilee

ju·bi·late \'jü-bə-,lāt\ *vi* **-lat·ed; -lat·ing** [L *jubilatus,* pp. of *jubilare;* akin to MHG *jū* (exclamation of joy), Gk *iygē* shout] : REJOICE

Ju·bi·la·te \,yü-bə-'lä-,tā, ,jü-\ *n* [L, 2d pers. pl. imper. of *jubilare*] **1 a** : the 100th Psalm in the Authorized Version **b** *not cap* : a joyous song or outburst **2** : the third Sunday after Easter

ju·bi·la·tion \,jü-bə-'lā-shən\ *n* **1** : an act of rejoicing : the state of being jubilant **2** : an expression of great joy

ju·bi·lee \'jü-bə-(,)lē, ,jü-bə-'lē\ *n* [ME, fr. MF & LL; MF *jubilé,* fr. LL *jubilaeus,* modif. of LGk *iōbēlaios,* fr. Heb *yōbhēl* ram's horn, jubilee] **1** *often cap* : a year of emancipation and restoration provided by ancient Hebrew law to be kept every 50 years by the emancipation of Hebrew slaves, restoration of alienated lands to their former owners, and omission of all cultivation of the land **2 a** : a special anniversary; *esp* : a 50th anniversary **b** : a celebration of such an anniversary **3 a** : a period of time proclaimed by the Roman Catholic pope ordinarily every 25 years as a time of special solemnity **b** : a special plenary indulgence granted during a year of jubilee to Roman Catholics who perform certain specified works of repentance and piety **4 a** : JUBILATION **b** : a season of celebration **5** : a Negro folk song with references to a future happy time

Jud *abbr* Judith

Ju·dah \'jüd-ə\ *n* [Heb *Yĕhūdhāh*] : a son of Jacob and the traditional eponymous ancestor of one of the tribes of Israel

Ju·da·ic \jü-'dā-ik\ *also* **Ju·da·ical** \-'dā-ə-kəl\ *adj* [L *judaicus,* fr. Gk *ioudaikos,* fr. *Ioudaios* Jew — more at JEW] : of, relating to, or characteristic of Jews or Judaism

Ju·da·ica \-'dā-ə-kə\ *n pl* [L, neut. pl. of *Judaicus*] : literary or historical materials relating to Jews or Judaism

Ju·da·ism \'jüd-ə-,iz-əm, 'jüd-ē-,iz-\ *n* **1** : a religion developed among the ancient Hebrews and characterized by belief in one transcendent God who has revealed himself to Abraham, Moses, and the Hebrew prophets and by a religious life in accordance with Scriptures and rabbinic traditions **2** : conformity to Jewish rites, ceremonies, and practices **3** : the cultural, social, and religious beliefs and practices of the Jews **4** : the whole body of Jews : the Jewish people

Ju·da·ist \'jüd-ə-əst, 'jüd-ē-, jü-'dā-\ *n* : one that believes in or practices Judaism — **Ju·da·is·tic** \,jüd-ə-'is-tik, ,jüd-ē-\ *adj*

Ju·da·ize \'jüd-ə-,īz, 'jüd-ē-\ *vb* **-ized; -iz·ing** *vi* : to adopt the customs, beliefs, or character of a Jew ~ *vt* : to make Jewish —

Ju·da·iza·tion \ˌjüd-ə-ə-ˈzā-shən, ˌjüd-ē-ə-\ *n* — **Ju·da·iz·er** \ˈjüd-ə-ˌiz-ər, ˈjüd-ē-\ *n*

Ju·das \ˈjüd-əs\ *n* [LL, fr. Gk *Ioudas*, fr. Heb *Yĕhūdhāh*] **1 a** : the apostle who in the Gospel accounts betrayed Jesus **b** : a son of James and one of the twelve apostles **2** : TRAITOR; *esp* : one who betrays under the guise of friendship **3** *not cap* : PEEPHOLE — called also *judas hole, judas window*

Judas Is·car·i·ot \-is-ˈkar-ē-ət\ *n* [LL *Judas Iscariotes*, fr. Gk *Ioudas Iskariōtēs*] : JUDAS 1a

Judas tree *n* [fr. the belief that Judas Iscariot hanged himself from a tree of this kind] : any of a genus (*Cercis*) of leguminous trees and shrubs, often cultivated for their showy flowers; *esp* : a Eurasian tree (*C. siliquastrum*) with purplish rosy flowers

[1]jud·der \ˈjəd-ər\ *vi* [prob. alter. of *shudder*] *chiefly Brit* : to vibrate with intensity <the engine stalled and kept ~*ing* — Roy Spicer>

[2]judder *n, chiefly Brit* : the action or sound of juddering

Jude \ˈjüd\ *n* [LL *Judas*] **1** : the author of the New Testament Epistle of Jude **2** : a short hortatory epistle addressed to early Christians and included as a book in the New Testament — see BIBLE table

Ju·deo–Chris·tian \jü-ˌdā-ō-ˈkris(h)-chən *also* ˌjüd-ē-ō- *or* jü-ˌdē-ō-\ *adj* [L *Judaeus* Jew — more at JEW] : having historical roots in both Judaism and Christianity

Ju·deo–Span·ish \-ˈspan-ish\ *n* : the Romance language of Sephardic Jews in the Balkans and Asia Minor

Judg *abbr* Judges

[1]judge \ˈjəj\ *vb* **judged; judg·ing** [ME *juggen*, fr. OF *jugier*, fr. L *judicare*, fr. *judic-*, *judex* judge, fr. *jus* right, law + *dicere* to decide, say — more at JUST, DICTION] *vt* **1** : to form an opinion about through careful weighing of evidence and testing of premises **2** : to sit in judgment on : TRY **3** : to determine or pronounce after inquiry and deliberation **4** : GOVERN, RULE — used of a Hebrew tribal leader **5** : to form an estimate or evaluation of **6** : to hold as an opinion : GUESS, THINK <I ~ she knew what she was doing> ~ *vi* **1** : to form an opinion **2** : to decide as a judge ***syn*** see INFER — **judg·er** *n*

[2]judge *n* [ME *juge*, fr. MF, fr. L *judex*] : one who judges: as **a** : a public official authorized to decide questions brought before a court **b** *often cap* : a tribal hero exercising leadership among the Hebrews after the death of Joshua **c** : one appointed to decide in a contest or competition : UMPIRE **d** : one who gives an authoritative opinion **e** : CRITIC — **judge·ship** \-ˌship\ *n*

judge advocate *n* **1** : an officer assigned to the judge advocate general's corps or department **2** : a staff officer serving as legal adviser to a military commander

judge advocate general *n* : the senior legal officer and chief legal adviser in the army, air force, or navy

Judg·es \ˈjəj-əz\ *n* : a narrative and historical book of Jewish and Christian Scripture — see BIBLE table

judg·mat·ic \ˌjəj-ˈmat-ik\ *or* **judg·ma·ti·cal** \-i-kəl\ *adj* [prob. irreg. fr. *judgment*] : JUDICIOUS — **judg·mat·i·cal·ly** \-i-k(ə-)lē\ *adv*

judg·ment *or* **judge·ment** \ˈjəj-mənt\ *n* **1 a** : a formal utterance of an authoritative opinion **b** : an opinion so pronounced **2 a** : a formal decision given by a court **b** (1) : an obligation (as a debt) created by the decree of a court (2) : a certificate evidencing such a decree **3 a** *cap* : the final judging of mankind by God **b** : a divine sentence or decision; *specif* : a calamity held to be sent by God **4 a** : the process of forming an opinion or evaluation by discerning and comparing **b** : an opinion or estimate so formed **5 a** : the capacity for judging : DISCERNMENT **b** : the exercise of this capacity **6** : a proposition stating something believed or asserted ***syn*** see SENSE — **judg·men·tal** \ˌjəj-ˈment-ᵊl\ *adj*

judgment day *n* **1** *cap J&D* : the day of God's judgment of mankind at the end of the world according to various theologies **2** : a day of final judgment

ju·di·ca·to·ry \ˈjüd-i-kə-ˌtōr-ē, -ˌtȯr-\ *n, pl* **-ries** **1** : JUDICIARY 1a **2** : JUDICATURE 2

ju·di·ca·ture \ˈjüd-i-kə-ˌchu̇(ə)r, -chər, -ˌt(y)u̇(ə)r\ *n* [MF, fr. ML *judicatura*, fr. L *judicatus*, pp. of *judicare*] **1** : the action of judging : the administration of justice **2** : a court of justice **3** : JUDICIARY 1

ju·di·cial \ju̇-ˈdish-əl\ *adj* [ME, fr. L *judicialis*, fr. *judicium* judgment, fr. *judex*] **1 a** : of or relating to a judgment, the function of judging, the administration of justice, or the judiciary <~ processes> **b** : belonging to the branch of government that is charged with trying all cases that involve the government and with the administration of justice within its jurisdiction — compare EXECUTIVE, LEGISLATIVE **2** : ordered or enforced by a court <~ decisions> **3** : of, characterized by, or expressing judgment : CRITICAL 1c **4** : arising from a judgment of God **5** : belonging or appropriate to a judge or the judiciary — **ju·di·cial·ly** \-ˈdish-(ə-)lē\ *adv*

judicial review *n* **1** : REVIEW 5 **2** : a constitutional doctrine that gives to a court system the power to annul legislative or executive acts which the judges declare to be unconstitutional

ju·di·cia·ry \ju̇-ˈdish-ē-ˌer-ē, -ˈdish-ə-rē\ *n* [*judiciary*, adj., fr. L *judiciarius* judicial, fr. *judicium*] **1 a** : a system of courts of law **b** : the judges of these courts **2** : a branch of government in which judicial power is vested — **judiciary** *adj*

ju·di·cious \ju̇-ˈdish-əs\ *adj* : having, exercising, or characterized by sound judgment : DISCREET ***syn*** see WISE ***ant*** injudicious, asinine — **ju·di·cious·ly** *adv* — **ju·di·cious·ness** *n*

Ju·dith \ˈjüd-əth\ *n* [LL, fr. Gk *Ioudith*, fr. Heb *Yĕhūdhīth*] **1** : the Jewish heroine who saves the city of Bethulia in the book of Judith **2** : a book of Scripture included in the Roman Catholic canon of the Old Testament and in the Protestant Apocrypha — see BIBLE table

ju·do \ˈjüd-(ˌ)ō\ *n* [Jap *jūdō*, fr. *jū* weakness, gentleness + *dō* art] : a Japanese sport developed from jujitsu that emphasizes the use of quick movement and leverage to throw an opponent — **judo·ist** \-ˌō-əst, -ə-wəst\ *n*

[1]jug \ˈjəg\ *n* [perh. fr. *Jug*, nickname for *Joan*] **1 a** *chiefly Brit* : a small pitcher **b** (1) : a large deep earthenware or glass container with a narrow mouth and a handle (2) : the contents of such a container : JUGFUL **2** : JAIL, PRISON

[2]jug *vt* **jugged; jug·ging** **1** : to stew (as a hare) in an earthenware vessel **2** : JAIL, IMPRISON

ju·gate \ˈjü-ˌgāt, -gət\ *adj* [NL *jugum*] **1** : having parts arranged in pairs : PAIRED **2** : having a jugum

jug band *n* : a band that uses crude improvised instruments (as jugs, washboards, and stovepipes)

jug·ful \ˈjəg-ˌfu̇l\ *n* **1** : as much as a jug will hold **2** : a great deal — used in the phrase *not by a jugful*

jug·ger·naut \ˈjəg-ər-ˌnȯt, -ˌnät\ *n* [Hindi *Jagannāth*, title of Vishnu, lit., lord of the world] : a massive inexorable force or object that crushes whatever is in its path

[1]jug·gle \ˈjəg-əl\ *vb* **jug·gled; jug·gling** \-(ə-)liŋ\ [ME *jogelen*, fr. MF *jogler* to joke, fr. L *joculari*, fr. *joculus*, dim. of *jocus* joke] *vi* **1** : to perform the tricks of a juggler **2** : to engage in manipulation esp. in order to achieve a desired end ~ *vt* **1 a** : to practice deceit or trickery on : BEGUILE **b** : to manipulate esp. in order to achieve a desired end <~ an account to hide a loss> **2 a** : to toss in the manner of a juggler **b** : to hold or balance precariously

[2]juggle *n* : an act or instance of juggling: **a** : a trick of magic **b** : a show of manual dexterity **c** : an act of manipulation esp. to achieve a desired end

jug·gler \ˈjəg-(ə-)lər\ *n* [ME *jogelour*, fr. OE *geogelere*, fr. OF *jogleour*, fr. L *joculator*, fr. *joculatus*, pp. of *joculari*] **1 a** : one who performs tricks or acts of magic **b** : one skilled in keeping several objects in motion in the air at the same time by alternately tossing and catching them **2** : one who manipulates esp. in order to achieve a desired end

jug·glery \ˈjəg-lə-rē\ *n* **1** : the art or practice of a juggler **2** : manipulation or trickery esp. to achieve a desired end <advertising agencies with all their ~ of public sentiment —Gilbert Seldes>

[1]jug·u·lar \ˈjəg-yə-lər *also* ˈjüg-\ *adj* [LL *jugularis*, fr. L *jugulum* collarbone, throat; akin to L *jungere* to join — more at YOKE] **1 a** : of or relating to the throat or neck **b** : of or relating to the jugular vein **2 a** *of a fish* : having the ventral fins on the throat anterior to the pectoral fins **b** *of a fin* : located on the throat

[2]jugular *n* : JUGULAR VEIN

jugular vein *n* : any of several veins of each side of the neck that return blood from the head

jug·u·lum \ˈjəg-yə-ləm, ˈjüg-\ *n, pl* **-la** \-lə\ [NL, fr. L] **1** : the part of the neck just above the breast of a bird **2** : JUGUM 2

ju·gum \ˈjü-gəm\ *n, pl* **ju·ga** \-gə\ *or* **jugums** [NL, fr. L, yoke — more at YOKE] **1** : a pair of the opposite leaflets of a pinnate leaf **2** : the most posterior and basal region of an insect's wing modified in some lepidopterans into a lobe that couples the fore and hind wings during flight

[1]juice \ˈjüs\ *n* [ME *jus*, fr. OF, broth, juice, fr. L; akin to Skt *yūṣa* broth] **1** : the extractable fluid contents of cells or tissues **2 a** *pl* : the natural fluids of an animal body **b** : the liquid or moisture contained in something **3 a** : the inherent quality of a thing : ESSENCE **b** : virile strength and vigor <pioneers . . . full of ~ and jests —Sinclair Lewis> **4** : a medium (as electricity or gasoline) that supplies power **5** *slang* : LIQUOR **6** : exorbitant interest exacted of a borrower under the threat of violence — **juice·less** \ˈjü-sləs\ *adj*

[2]juice *vt* **juiced; juic·ing** **1** : to extract the juice of **2** : to add juice to

juiced \ˈjüst\ *adj* **1** : containing juice — usu. used in combination <precious-*juiced* flowers —Shak.> **2** *slang* : DRUNK 1

juice·head \ˈjüs-ˌhed\ *n, slang* : ALCOHOLIC

juic·er \ˈjü-sər\ *n* **1** : ELECTRICIAN; *esp* : one who arranges the lighting for a stage set **2** : an appliance for extracting juice from fruit or vegetables **3** *slang* : a heavy or habitual drinker

juice up *vt* : to give life, energy, or spirit to

juicy \ˈjü-sē\ *adj* **juic·i·er; -est** **1** : having much juice : SUCCULENT **2** : financially rewarding <a ~ contract> **3 a** : rich in interest : COLORFUL <~ details> **b** : PIQUANT, RACY <a ~ scandal> **c** : full of vitality — **juic·i·ly** \-sə-lē\ *adv* — **juic·i·ness** \-sē-nəs\ *n*

ju·jit·su *or* **ju·jut·su** \jü-ˈjit-(ˌ)sü\ *n* [Jap *jūjutsu*, fr. *jū* weakness, gentleness + *jutsu* art, skill] : an ancient Japanese art of weaponless fighting employing holds, throws, and paralyzing blows to subdue or disable an opponent

ju·ju \ˈjü-(ˌ)jü\ *n* [of W. African origin; akin to Hausa *djudju* fetish] **1** : a fetish, charm, or amulet of West African peoples **2** : the magic attributed to or associated with jujus

ju·jube \ˈjü-ˌjüb, *esp for 2 often* ˈjü-ju̇-ˌbē\ *n* [ME, fr. ML *jujuba*, alter. of L *zizyphum*, fr. Gk *zizyphon*] **1 a** : an edible drupaceous fruit of any of several trees (genus *Ziziphus*) of the buckthorn family; *esp* : CHINESE DATE **b** : a tree producing this fruit **2** : a fruit-flavored gumdrop or lozenge

juke \ˈjük\ *vt* **juked; juk·ing** [prob. alter. of E dial. *jouk* (to cheat, deceive)] : to fake out of position (as in football)

juke·box \ˈjük-ˌbäks, ˈjüt-\ *n* [Gullah *juke* disorderly, of W. African origin; akin to Bambara *dzugu* wicked] : a coin-operated phonograph that automatically plays records selected from its list

juke joint *n* : a small inexpensive establishment for eating, drinking, or dancing to the music of a jukebox

ju·lep \ˈjü-ləp\ *n* [ME, fr. MF, fr. Ar *julāb*, fr. Per *gulāb*, fr. *gul* rose + *āb* water] **1** : a drink consisting of sweet syrup, flavoring, and water **2** : a drink consisting of a liquor (as bourbon or brandy) and sugar poured over crushed ice and garnished with mint

Ju·lian calendar \ˌjül-yən-\ *n* [L *julianus*, fr. Gaius *Julius* Caesar] : a calendar introduced in Rome in 46 B.C. establishing the 12-month year of 365 days with each fourth year having 366 days the the months each having 31 or 30 days except for February which has 28 or in leap years 29 days — compare GREGORIAN CALENDAR

[1]ju·li·enne \ˌjü-lē-ˈen, ˌzhü-\ *n* [F] : a clear soup containing julienne vegetables

[2]julienne *adj* : cut in long thin strips <~ potatoes> <green beans ~>

Ju·liet \'jül-yət; ˌjü-lē-'et, 'jü-lē-ˌ\ *n* **:** the heroine of Shakespeare's tragedy *Romeo and Juliet*

Ju·li·ett \ˌjül-ē-'et\ [prob. irreg. fr. *Juliet*] — a communications code word for the letter *j*

Ju·ly \jù-'lī\ *n* [ME *Julie*, fr. OE *Julius*, fr. L, fr. Gaius *Julius* Caesar] **:** the 7th month of the Gregorian calendar

Ju·ma·da \jù-'mäd-ə\ *n* [Ar *Jumāda*] **:** either of two months of the Muhammadan year: **a :** the 5th month **b :** the 6th month — see MONTH table

[1]**jum·ble** \'jəm-bəl\ *vb* **jum·bled; jum·bling** \-b(ə-)liŋ\ [perh. imit.] *vi* **:** to move or mingle in a confused or disordered manner ~ *vt* **:** to mix in a confused or disordered mass — often used with *up*

[2]**jumble** *n* **1 a :** a mass of things mingled together without order or plan **:** HODGEPODGE **b :** a state of confusion **2** *Brit* **:** articles for a rummage sale

[3]**jumble** *n* [origin unknown] **:** a small thin usu. ring-shaped sugared cookie or cake

jumble sale *n, Brit* **:** RUMMAGE SALE

jum·bo \'jəm-(ˌ)bō\ *n, pl* **jumbos** [*Jumbo*, a huge elephant exhibited by P. T. Barnum] **:** a very large specimen of its kind — **jumbo** *adj*

[1]**jump** \'jəmp\ *vb* [prob. akin to LG *gumpen* to jump] *vi* **1 a :** to spring into the air **:** LEAP; *esp* **:** to spring free from the ground or other base by the muscular action of feet and legs **b :** to move suddenly or involuntarily **:** START **c :** to move over a position occupied by an opponent's man in a board game often thereby capturing the man **d :** SKIP <his typewriter ~*s*> **e :** to undergo a vertical or lateral displacement owing to improper alignment of the film on a projector mechanism **f :** to begin a forward movement — usu. used with *off* **g :** to move energetically **:** HUSTLE **h :** to go from one sequence of instructions in a computer program to another <~ to a subroutine> **2 :** COINCIDE, AGREE **3 a :** to move haphazardly or aimlessly <~*ed* from job to job> **b :** to change employment in violation of contract **c :** to rise suddenly in rank or status **d :** to undergo a sudden sharp increase <prices ~*ed*> **e :** to make a jump in bridge **f :** to make a hurried judgment <~ to conclusions> **g :** to show eagerness <~*ed* at the chance> **h :** to enter eagerly — usu. used with *in* or *into* **4 :** to make a sudden physical or verbal attack <~*ed* on him for his criticism> **5 :** to bustle with activity ~ *vt* **1 a :** to leap over <~ a hurdle> **b :** to move over (a man) in a board game **c :** BYPASS <~ electrical connections> **d :** to act, move, or begin before (as a signal) <~ the green light> **e :** to leap aboard <~ a freight> **2** *obs* **:** RISK, HAZARD **3 a :** to escape from **b :** to leave hastily or in violation of contract <~ town without paying their bills —Hamilton Basso> **c :** to depart from (a normal course) <~ the track> **4 a :** to make a sudden physical or verbal attack on **b :** to occupy illegally <~ a mining claim> **5 a (1) :** to cause to leap **(2) :** to cause (game) to break cover **:** START, FLUSH **b :** to elevate in rank or status **c :** to raise (a bridge partner's bid) by more than one rank **d :** to increase suddenly and sharply — **jump the gun 1 :** to start in a race before the starting signal **2 :** to act, move, or begin something before the proper time

[2]**jump** *adv, obs* **:** EXACTLY, PAT

[3]**jump** *n* **1 a (1) :** an act of jumping **:** LEAP **(2) :** any of several sports competitions featuring a leap, spring, or bound **(3) :** a space cleared or covered by a leap **(4) :** an obstacle to be jumped over **b (1) :** a sudden involuntary movement **:** START **(2)** *pl* **:** FIDGETS **c :** a move made in a board game by jumping **d :** a transfer from one sequence of instructions in a computer program to a different sequence <conditional ~> **2** *obs* **:** VENTURE **3 a (1) :** a sharp sudden increase **(2) :** a bid in bridge of more tricks than are necessary to overcall the preceding bid — compare SHIFT **b :** a sudden change **c (1) :** a quick short journey **(2) :** one in a series of moves from one place to another **4 :** an advantage at the start <desirous of getting the ~ on the competition —Elmer Davis>

jump ball *n* **:** a method of putting a basketball into play by tossing it into the air between two opponents who jump up and attempt to tap the ball to a teammate

jump boot *n* **:** a boot worn esp. by paratroopers

jump cut *n* **:** a discontinuity or acceleration in the action of a filmed scene brought about by removal of medial portions of the shot

[1]**jump·er** \'jəm-pər\ *n* **1 :** a person who jumps **2 a :** any of various devices operating with a jumping motion **b :** any of several sleds **c :** a short wire used to close a break or cut out part of a circuit **3 :** any of several jumping animals; *esp* **:** a saddle horse trained to jump obstacles **4 :** JUMP SHOT

[2]**jum·per** \'jəm-pər\ *n* [prob. fr. E dial. *jump* (jumper)] **1 :** a loose blouse or jacket worn by workmen **2 :** a sleeveless one-piece dress worn usu. with a blouse **3 :** a child's one-piece coverall — usu. used in pl.

jumping bean *n* **:** a seed of any of several Mexican shrubs (genera *Sebastiania* and *Sapium*) of the spurge family that tumbles about because of the movements of the larva of a small moth (*Carpocapsa saltitans*) inside it

cross section of jumping beans

jumping jack *n* **1 :** a toy figure of a man jointed and made to jump or dance by means of strings or a sliding stick **2 :** a conditioning exercise performed from a standing position by jumping to a position with legs spread and hands touching overhead and then to the original position — called also *side-straddle hop*

jumping mouse *n* **:** any of several small hibernating No. American rodents (family Zapodidae) with long hind legs and tail and no cheek pouches

jumping–off place \ˌjəm-piŋ-'òf-\ *n* **1 :** a remote or isolated place **2 :** a place from which an enterprise is launched — called also *jumping–off point*

jumping plant louse *n* **:** any of numerous plant lice (family Psyllidae) with the femurs thickened and adapted for leaping

jumping spider *n* **:** any of a family (Salticidae) of small spiders that stalk and leap upon their prey

jump–off \'jəm-ˌpòf\ *n* **1 :** the start of a race or an attack **2 :** the jumping competition in a horse show

jump pass *n* **:** a pass made by a player (as in football or basketball) while jumping

jump seat *n* **1 :** a movable carriage seat **2 :** a folding seat between the front and rear seats of a passenger automobile

jump shot *n* **:** a shot in basketball made by jumping into the air and releasing the ball with one or both hands at the peak of the jump

jump suit *n* **1 :** a uniform worn by parachutists for jumping **2 :** a one-piece garment consisting of a blouse or shirt with attached trousers or shorts

jumpy \'jəm-pē\ *adj* **jump·i·er; -est 1 :** characterized by jumps or sudden variations **2 :** NERVOUS, JITTERY — **jump·i·ness** *n*

[1]**jun** \'jən\ *n, pl* **jun** [Korean] — see *won* at MONEY table

[2]**jun** *abbr* junior

Jun *abbr* June

junc *abbr* junction

jun·co \'jəŋ-(ˌ)kō\ *n, pl* **juncos** *or* **juncoes** [NL, genus name, fr. Sp, reed — more at JONQUIL] **:** any of a genus (*Junco*) of small widely distributed American finches usu. having a pink bill, ashy gray head and back, and conspicuous white lateral tail feathers

junc·tion \'jəŋ(k)-shən\ *n* [L *junction-, junctio*, fr. *junctus*, pp. of *jungere* to join — more at YOKE] **1 :** an act of joining **:** the state of being joined **2 a :** a place or point of meeting **b :** an intersection of roads esp. where one terminates **c :** a point (as in a thermocouple) at which dissimilar metals make contact **d :** an interface in a semiconductor device between regions with different electrical characterisitcs **3 :** something that joins — **junc·tion·al** \-shnəl, -shən-ᵊl\ *adj*

syn JUNCTION, CONFLUENCE, CONCOURSE *shared meaning element* **:** an act, state, or place of meeting or uniting

junc·tur·al \'jəŋ(k)-chə-rəl, 'jəŋ(k)-shrəl\ *adj* **:** of or relating to grammatical juncture

junc·ture \'jəŋ(k)-chər\ *n* **1 :** an instance of joining **:** UNION **2 a :** JOINT, CONNECTION **b :** the manner of transition or mode of relationship between two consecutive sounds in speech **3 :** a point of time; *esp* **:** one made critical by a concurrence of circumstances

syn JUNCTURE, PASS, EXIGENCY, EMERGENCY, CONTINGENCY, PINCH, STRAIT, CRISIS *shared meaning element* **:** a critical or crucial time or state of affairs

June \'jün\ *n* [ME, fr. MF & L; MF *Juin*, fr. L *Junius*] **:** the 6th month of the Gregorian calendar

june beetle *n, often cap J* **:** any of numerous rather large leaf-eating beetles (family Melolonthidae) that fly chiefly in late spring and have as larvae white grubs that live in soil and feed chiefly on the roots of grasses and other plants — called also *june bug*

June·ber·ry \'jün-ˌber-ē\ *n* **:** SERVICEBERRY 2

[1]**Jung·ian** \'yùŋ-ē-ən\ *n* **:** an adherent of the psychological doctrines of C. G. Jung

[2]**Jungian** *adj* **:** of, relating to, or characteristic of C. G. Jung or his psychological doctrines

jun·gle \'jəŋ-gəl\ *n, often attrib* [Hindi *jaṅgal*] **1 a :** an impenetrable thicket or tangled mass of tropical vegetation **b :** a tract overgrown with thickets or masses of vegetation **2 :** a hobo camp **3 a (1) :** a confused or disordered mass of objects **:** JUMBLE **(2) :** something that baffles or frustrates by its tangled or complex character **:** MAZE <the ~ of housing laws —Bernard Taper> **b :** a place of ruthless struggle for survival <the city is a ~ where no one is safe after dark —Stuart Chase> — **jun·gly** \-g(ə-)lē\ *adj*

jungle fowl *n* **:** any of several Asiatic wild birds (genus *Gallus*); *esp* **:** a bird (*G. gallus*) of southeastern Asia from which domestic fowls have prob. descended

jungle gym *n* [fr. *Junglegym*, a trademark] **:** a structure of vertical and horizontal bars for use by children at play

[1]**ju·nior** \'jü-nyər\ *n* [L, n. & adj.] **1 a (1) :** a person who is younger than another **(2) :** a male child **:** SON **b :** a clothing size for women and girls with slight figures **2 a :** a person holding a lower position in a hierarchy of ranks **b :** a student in his next-to-the-last year before graduating from an educational institution

[2]**junior** *adj* [L, compar. of *juvenis* young — more at YOUNG] **1 a :** YOUNGER — used chiefly to distinguish a son with the same given name as his father **b (1) :** YOUTHFUL **(2) :** designed esp. for adolescents **c :** of more recent date and therefore inferior or subordinate <a ~ lien> **2 :** lower in standing or rank <~ partners> **3 :** of or relating to juniors or the class of juniors at an educational institution <the ~ prom>

ju·nior·ate \'jü-nyə-ˌrāt, -rət\ *n* **1 :** a course of high school or college study for candidates for the priesthood, brotherhood, or sisterhood; *specif* **:** one preparatory to the course in philosophy **2 :** a seminary for juniorate training

junior college *n* **:** an educational institution that offers two years of studies corresponding to those in the first two years of a four-year college and that often offers technical, vocational, and liberal studies to the adults of a community

junior high school *n* **:** a school usu. including grades 7-9

Junior Leaguer *n* **:** a member of a league of young women organized for volunteer service to civic and social organizations

junior miss *n* **1 :** an adolescent girl **2 :** JUNIOR 1b

junior varsity *n* **:** a team composed of members lacking the experience or qualification required for the varsity

---

ə abut   ᵊ kitten   ər further   a back   ā bake   ä cot, cart
aù out   ch chin   e less   ē easy   g gift   i trip   ī life
j joke   ŋ sing   ō flow   ò flaw   òi coin   th thin   t͟h this
ü loot   ù foot   y yet   yü few   yù furious   zh vision

ju·ni·per \'jü-nə-pər\ *n* [ME *junipere*, fr. L *juniperus* — more at JONQUIL] **1 :** an evergreen shrub or tree (genus *Juniperus*) of the pine family; *esp* : one having a prostrate or shrubby habit **2 :** any of several coniferous trees resembling true junipers
juniper oil *n* **:** an acrid essential oil obtained from the fruit of the common juniper and used esp. in gin and liqueurs
[1]**junk** \'jəŋk\ *n* [ME *jonke*] **1 :** pieces of old cable or cordage used esp. to make gaskets, mats, swabs, or oakum **2 :** hard salted beef for use on shipboard **3 a** (1) **:** old iron, glass, paper, or other waste that may be used again in some form (2) **:** secondhand, worn, or discarded articles **b :** a shoddy product : TRASH **c :** something of little meaning or significance **4** *slang* **:** NARCOTICS; *esp* **:** HEROIN — **junky** \'jəŋ-kē\ *adj*
[2]**junk** *vt* **:** to get rid of as worthless **:** SCRAP *syn* see DISCARD
[3]**junk** *n* [Pg *junco*, fr. Jav *joṅ*] **:** any of various ships of Chinese waters with bluff lines, a high poop and overhanging stem, little or no keel, high pole masts, and a deep rudder

junk

junk art *n* **:** three-dimensional art made from discarded material (as metal, mortar, glass, or wood) — **junk artist** *n*
junk·er \'jəŋ-kər\ *n* [[1]*junk* + *-er*]**:** something (as an automobile) of such age and condition as to be ready for scrapping
Jun·ker \'yůŋ-kər\ *n* [G, fr. OHG *junchērro*, lit., young lord]**:** a member of the Prussian landed aristocracy — **Jun·ker·dom** \-kərd-əm\ *n* — **Jun·ker·ism** \-kə-ˌriz-əm\ *n*
[1]**jun·ket** \'jəŋ-kət\ *n* [ME *ioncate*, deriv. of (assumed) VL *juncata*, fr. L *juncus* rush] **1 :** a dessert of sweetened flavored milk set with rennet **2 a :** a festive social affair **b :** TRIP, JOURNEY; *esp* **:** a trip made by an official at public expense
[2]**junket** *vi* **1 :** FEAST, BANQUET **2 :** to go on a junket — **jun·ke·teer** \ˌjəŋ-kə-'ti(ə)r\ *or* **jun·ket·er** \'jəŋ-kət-ər\ *n*
junk·ie *or* **junky** \'jəŋ-kē\ *n, pl* **junk·ies** **1 :** a junk dealer **2** *slang* **:** a narcotics peddler or addict
junk mail *n* **:** third-class mail (as advertising circulars) that is often addressed to "occupant" or "resident"
junk·yard \'jəŋk-ˌyärd\ *n* **:** a yard used to store usu. resalable junk
Ju·no \'jü-(ˌ)nō\ *n* **:** the wife of Jupiter, queen of heaven, and goddess of light, beginnings, birth, women, and marriage — compare HERA
Ju·no·esque \ˌjü-(ˌ)nō-'esk\ *adj* **:** marked by stately beauty
jun·ta \'hůn-tə, 'jənt-ə, 'hən-tə\ *n* [Sp, fr. fem. of *junto* joined, fr. L *junctus*, pp. of *jungere* to join — more at YOKE] **1 :** a council or committee for political or governmental purposes; *esp* **:** a group of persons controlling a government esp. after a revolutionary seizure of power **2 :** JUNTO
jun·to \'jənt-(ˌ)ō\ *n, pl* **juntos** [prob. alter. of *junta*] **:** a group of persons joined for a common purpose
Ju·pi·ter \'jü-pət-ər\ *n* [L] **1 :** the chief Roman god, husband of Juno, and god of light, of the sky and weather, and of the state and its welfare and its laws — compare ZEUS **2 :** the largest of the planets and fifth in order from the sun — see PLANET table
Ju·ra \'jůr-ə\ *n* [prob. G, fr. the *Jura* mountain range]**:** the Jurassic geological period or the rocks belonging to it
ju·ral \'jůr-əl\ *adj* [L *jur-*, *jus* law] **1 :** of or relating to law **2 :** of or relating to rights or obligations — **ju·ral·ly** \-ə-lē\ *adv*
Ju·ras·sic \jů-'ras-ik\ *adj* [F *jurassique*, fr. *Jura* mountain range] **:** of, relating to, or being the period of the Mesozoic era between the Comanchean and the Triassic or the corresponding system of rocks marked by the presence of dinosaurs and the first appearance of birds — **Jurassic** *n*
ju·rat \'jů(ə)r-ˌat\ *n* [short for L *juratum (est)* it has been sworn, 3d sing. perf. pass. of *jurare* to swear] **:** a certificate added to an affidavit stating when, before whom, and where it was made
ju·rel \hü-'rel\ *n* [Sp] **:** any of several food fishes (family Carangidae) of warm seas
ju·rid·i·cal \jů-'rid-i-kəl\ *or* **ju·rid·ic** \-ik\ *adj* [L *juridicus*, fr. *jur-*, *jus* + *dicere* to say — more at DICTION] **1 :** of or relating to the administration of justice or the office of a judge **2 :** of or relating to law in general or jurisprudence **:** LEGAL <~ terms> — **ju·rid·i·cal·ly** \-i-k(ə-)lē\ *adv*
ju·ris·con·sult \ˌjůr-ə-'skän-ˌsəlt, -skən-'\ *n* [L *jurisconsultus*, fr. *juris* (gen. of *jus*) + *consultus*, pp. of *consulere* to consult]**:** JURIST; *esp* **:** one learned in international and public law
ju·ris·dic·tion \ˌjůr-əs-'dik-shən\ *n* [ME *jurisdiccioun*, fr. OF & L; OF *juridiction*, fr. L *jurisdiction-*, *jurisdictio*, fr. *juris* + *diction-*, *dictio* act of saying — more at DICTION] **1 :** the power, right, or authority to interpret and apply the law **2 :** the authority of a sovereign power to govern or legislate **3 :** the limits or territory within which authority may be exercised **:** CONTROL — **ju·ris·dic·tion·al** \-shnəl, -shən-ᵊl\ *adj* — **ju·ris·dic·tion·al·ly** \-ē\ *adv*
ju·ris·pru·dence \ˌjůr-ə-'sprüd-ᵊn(t)s\ *n* **1 a :** a system or body of law **b :** the course of court decisions **2 :** the science or philosophy of law **3 :** a department of law <medical ~> — **ju·ris·pru·den·tial** \-sprü-'den-chəl\ *adj* — **ju·ris·pru·den·tial·ly** \-'dench-(ə-)lē\ *adv*
ju·ris·pru·dent \-'sprüd-ᵊnt\ *n* [LL *jurisprudent-*, *jurisprudens*, fr. L *juris* + *prudent-*, *prudens* skilled, prudent] **:** JURIST
ju·rist \'jů(ə)r-əst\ *n* [MF *juriste*, fr. ML *jurista*, fr. L *jur-*, *jus*] **:** one having a thorough knowledge of law: **a :** LAWYER **b :** JUDGE
ju·ris·tic \jů-'ris-tik\ *adj* **1 :** of or relating to a jurist or jurisprudence **2 :** of, relating to, or recognized in law — **ju·ris·ti·cal·ly** \-ti-k(ə-)lē\ *adv*
ju·ror \'jůr-ər, 'jů(ə)r-ˌȯ(ə)r\ *n* **1 a :** a member of a jury **b :** a person summoned to serve on a jury **2 :** a person who takes an oath (as of allegiance)
[1]**ju·ry** \'jů(ə)r-ē\ *n, pl* **juries** [ME *jure*, fr. AF *juree*, fr. OF *jurer* to swear, fr. L *jurare*, fr. *jur-*, *jus*] **1 :** a body of men sworn to give a verdict on some matter submitted to them; *esp* **:** a body of men legally selected and sworn to inquire into any matter of fact and to give their verdict according to the evidence **2 :** a committee for judging and awarding prizes at a contest or exhibition
[2]**jury** *adj* [origin unknown] **:** improvised for temporary use esp. in an emergency **:** MAKESHIFT <a ~ mast> <a ~ rig>
jus gen·ti·um \'yüs-'gent-ē-əm\ *n* [L, law of nations] **:** INTERNATIONAL LAW
jus san·gui·nis \-'säŋ-gwə-nəs\ *n* [L, right of blood] **:** a rule that a child's citizenship is determined by its parents' citizenship
jus·sive \'jəs-iv\ *n* [L *jussus*, pp. of *jubēre* to order; akin to Gk *hysminē* battle] **:** a word, form, case, or mood expressing command — **jussive** *adj*
jus so·li \'yüs-'sō-ˌlē\ *n* [L, right of the soil] **:** a rule that the citizenship of a child is determined by the place of its birth
[1]**just** \'jəst, 'jüst\ *var of* JOUST
[2]**just** \'jəst\ *adj* [ME, fr. MF & L; MF *juste*, fr. L *justus*, fr. *jus* right, law; akin to Skt *yos* welfare] **1 a :** having a basis in or conforming sometimes rigidly to fact or reason **:** REASONABLE <a ~ but not a generous decision> <~ anger> **b** *archaic* **:** faithful to an original **c :** conforming to a standard of correctness **:** PROPER <~ proportions> **2 a** (1) **:** acting or being in conformity with what is morally upright or good **:** RIGHTEOUS <a ~ ruler rules for the good of the people> (2) **:** being what is merited **:** DESERVED <a ~ punishment> **b :** legally correct **:** LAWFUL <~ title to an estate> ***syn* 1** see UPRIGHT **2** see FAIR ***ant*** unjust — **just·ly** *adv* — **just·ness** \'jəs(t)-nəs\ *n*
[3]**just** \(ˌ)jəst, (ˌ)jist, (ˌ)jest\ *adv* **1 a :** EXACTLY, PRECISELY <~ right> **b :** very recently <the bell ~ rang> **2 a :** by a very small margin **:** BARELY <~ too late> **b :** IMMEDIATELY, DIRECTLY <~ west of here> **3 a :** ONLY, SIMPLY <~ a note> **b :** QUITE, VERY <~ wonderful> **4 :** POSSIBLY, PERHAPS <it ~ might work> — **just about :** ALMOST <the work is *just about* done> — **just in case :** by way of precaution against a possible eventuality — **just the same :** even so **:** NEVERTHELESS
jus·tice \'jəs-təs\ *n* [ME, fr. OF, fr. L *justitia*, fr. *justus*] **1 a :** the maintenance or administration of what is just esp. by the impartial adjustment of conflicting claims or the assignment of merited rewards or punishments **b :** JUDGE **c :** the administration of law; *esp* **:** the establishment or determination of rights according to the rules of law or equity **2 a :** the quality of being just, impartial, or fair **b** (1) **:** the principle or ideal of just dealing or right action (2) **:** conformity to this principle or ideal **:** RIGHTEOUSNESS **c :** the quality of conforming to law **3 :** conformity to truth, fact, or reason **:** CORRECTNESS — **do justice 1 a :** to act justly **b :** to treat fairly or adequately **c :** to show due appreciation for **2 :** to acquit in a way worthy of one's powers
justice court *n* **:** an inferior court not of record that has limited criminal or civil jurisdiction and that is presided over by a justice of the peace
justice of the peace : a local magistrate empowered chiefly to administer summary justice in minor cases, to commit for trial, and to administer oaths and perform marriages
jus·ti·cia·ble \ˌjəs-'tish-(ē-)ə-bəl\ *adj* **1 :** liable to trial in a court of justice <a ~ offense> **2 :** capable of being decided by legal principles or by a court of justice — **jus·ti·cia·bil·i·ty** \ˌjəs-ˌtish-(ē-)ə-'bil-ət-ē\ *n*
jus·ti·ci·ar \ˌjəs-'tish-ē-ər, -ē-ˌär\ *n* [ME, fr. ML *justitiarius*, fr. L *justitia*] **:** the chief political and judicial officer of the Norman and later kings of England until the 13th century
jus·ti·fi·able \'jəs-tə-ˌfī-ə-bəl\ *adj* **:** capable of being justified **:** EXCUSABLE <~ family pride —*Current Biog.*> — **jus·ti·fi·abil·i·ty** \ˌjəs-tə-ˌfī-ə-'bil-ət-ē\ *n* — **jus·ti·fi·ably** \'jəs-tə-ˌfī-ə-blē\ *adv*
jus·ti·fi·ca·tion \ˌjəs-tə-fə-'kā-shən\ *n* **1 :** the act, process, or state of being justified by God **2 a :** the act or an instance of justifying **:** VINDICATION **b :** something that justifies
jus·ti·fi·ca·tive \'jəs-tə-fə-ˌkāt-iv\ *adj* **:** JUSTIFICATORY
jus·ti·fi·ca·to·ry \ˌjəs-'tif-i-kə-ˌtōr-ē, -ˌtȯr-; 'jəs-tə-fə-ˌkāt-ə-rē\ *adj* **:** tending or serving to justify **:** VINDICATORY
jus·ti·fy \'jəs-tə-ˌfī\ *vb* **-fied; -fy·ing** [ME *justifien*, fr. MF or LL; MF *justifier*, fr. LL *justificare*, fr. L *justus*] *vt* **1 a :** to prove or show to be just, right, or reasonable **b** (1) **:** to show to have had a sufficient legal reason (2) **:** to qualify (oneself) as a surety by taking oath to the ownership of sufficient property **2 a** *archaic* **:** to administer justice to **b** *archaic* **:** ABSOLVE **c :** to judge, regard, or treat as righteous and worthy of salvation **3 :** to adjust or arrange exactly; *specif* **:** to set (type) so as to fill a full line ~ *vi* **1 a :** to show a sufficient lawful reason for an act done **b :** to qualify as bail or surety **2 :** to fit exactly; *specif* **:** to fill a full line — **jus·ti·fi·er** \-ˌfī(-ə)r\ *n*
***syn* 1** see MAINTAIN
2 JUSTIFY, WARRANT *shared meaning element* **:** to be what constitutes sufficient grounds (as for doing, using, saying, or preferring something). JUSTIFY may be preferred when the emphasis is on provision of grounds that satisfy both conscience and reason; often it suggests that in the absence of such grounds the thing in question would draw down disapproval <we know that the pursuit of good ends does not *justify* the employment of bad means —Aldous Huxley> <your behavior *justified* his harsh rebuke> WARRANT is especially appropriate when the emphasis is to be placed on explanation or reason rather than excuse; it is likely to suggest support by the authority of precedent, experience, or logic <the deposit has shown enough ore to *warrant* further testing> <the history and appearance clearly *warrant* such assumption —H. G. Armstrong>
[1]**jut** \'jət\ *vb* **jut·ted; jut·ting** [perh. short for [2]*jutty*] *vi* **:** to shoot out, up, or forward **:** PROJECT <mountains *jutting* into the sky> ~ *vt* **:** to cause to project
[2]**jut** *n* **:** something that juts **:** PROJECTION
jute \'jüt\ *n* [Hindi & Bengali *jūṭ*] **:** the glossy fiber of either of two East Indian plants (*Corchorus olitorius* and *C. capsularis*) of the linden family used chiefly for sacking, burlap, and twine; *also*

: a plant producing jute

Jute \ˈjüt\ *n* [ME, fr. ML *Jutae* Jutes] **:** a member of a Germanic people invading England from the Continent and settling in Kent in the 5th century — **Jut·ish** \ˈjüt-ish\ *adj*

[1]**jut·ty** \ˈjət-ē\ *n, pl* **jutties** [ME] **1** *archaic* **:** JETTY **2 :** a projecting part of a building

[2]**jutty** *vt* **jut·tied; jut·ty·ing** *obs* **:** to project beyond

juv *abbr* juvenile

ju·ve·nes·cence \ˌjü-və-ˈnes-ᵊn(t)s\ *n* **:** the state of being youthful or of growing young — **ju·ve·nes·cent** \-ᵊnt\ *adj*

[1]**ju·ve·nile** \ˈjü-və-ˌnīl, -vən-ᵊl\ *adj* [F or L; F *juvénile,* fr. L *juvenilis,* fr. *juvenis* young person — more at YOUNG] **1 a :** physiologically immature or undeveloped **:** YOUNG **b :** derived from sources within the earth and coming to the surface for the first time — used esp. of water and gas **2 :** of, relating to, characteristic of, or suitable for children or young people <~ books> **3 :** reflecting psychological or intellectual immaturity **:** CHILDISH

[2]**juvenile** *n* **1 a :** a young person **:** YOUTH **b :** a book for children or young people **2 :** a young individual resembling an adult of its kind except in size and reproductive activity: as **a :** a fledged bird not yet in adult plumage **b :** a 2-year-old racehorse **3 :** an actor or actress who plays youthful parts

juvenile court *n* **:** a court that has special jurisdiction over delinquent and dependent children usu. up to the age of 18

juvenile delinquency *n* **1 :** a status in a juvenile characterized by antisocial behavior that is beyond parental control and therefore subject to legal action **2 :** a violation of the law committed by a juvenile and not punishable by death or life imprisonment — **juvenile delinquent** *n*

juvenile hormone *n* **:** an insect hormone that is secreted by the corpora allata, inhibits maturation to the imago, and plays a role in reproduction

juvenile officer *n* **:** a police officer charged with the detection, prosecution, and care of juvenile delinquents

ju·ve·nil·ia \ˌjü-və-ˈnil-ē-ə\ *n pl* [L, neut. pl. of *juvenilis*] **1 :** artistic or literary compositions produced in the artist's or author's youth **2 :** artistic or literary compositions suited to or designed for the young

ju·ve·nil·i·ty \ˌjü-və-ˈnil-ət-ē\ *n, pl* **-ties 1 :** the quality or state of being juvenile **:** YOUTHFULNESS **2 a :** immaturity of thought or conduct **b :** an instance of being juvenile

ju·ve·noc·ra·cy \ˌjü-və-ˈnäk-rə-sē\ *n, pl* **-cies** [L *juvenis* + E *-o-* + *-cracy*] **:** a state ruled or greatly influenced by youth

jux·ta- \ˌjək-stə\ *comb form* [L *juxta* near] **:** situated near <*juxta*glomerular cells>

jux·ta·pose \ˈjək-stə-ˌpōz\ *vt* **-posed; -pos·ing** [prob. back-formation fr. *juxtaposition*] **:** to place side by side <~ unexpected combinations of colors, shapes and ideas —J. F. T. Bugental>

jux·ta·po·si·tion \ˌjək-stə-pə-ˈzish-ən\ *n* [L *juxta* near + E *position* — more at JOUST] **:** the act or an instance of placing two or more things side by side; *also* **:** the state of being so placed — **jux·ta·po·si·tion·al** \-ˈzish-nəl, -ən-ᵊl\ *adj*

JV *abbr* junior varsity

JWB *abbr* Jewish Welfare Board

K L

[1]**k** \ˈkā\ *n, pl* **k's** *or* **ks** \ˈkāz\ *often cap, often attrib* **1 a :** the 11th letter of the English alphabet **b :** a graphic representation of this letter **c :** a speech counterpart of orthographic *k* **2 :** a graphic device for reproducing the letter *k* **3 :** one designated *k* esp. as the 11th in order or class **4 :** something shaped like the letter K **5 :** a unit vector parallel to the z-axis **6** [*kilo-*] **:** THOUSAND <a salary of $14*K*> **7** [*kilo-*] **:** a unit of computer storage capacity equal to 1024 bytes <a computer memory of 64*K*>

[2]**k** *abbr, often cap* **1** karat **2** kelvin **3** kilogram **4** kindergarten **5** kitchen **6** knit **7** knot **8** koruna **9** kosher **10** kyat

K *symbol* [NL *kalium*] potassium

ka *abbr* [G *kathode*] cathode

Kaa·ba \ˈkäb-ə\ *n* [Ar *kaʽbah,* lit., square building] **:** a small stone building in the court of the Great Mosque at Mecca that contains a sacred black stone and is the goal of Islamic pilgrimage and the point toward which Muslims turn in praying

KAB *abbr* Keep America Beautiful

kabala *or* **kabbala** *or* **kabbalah** *var of* CABALA

ka·bob \ˈkä-ˌbäb, kə-ˈ\ *n* [Per, Hindi, Ar & Turk; Per & Hindi *kabāb,* fr. Ar, fr. Turk *kebap*] **:** cubes of meat (as lamb or beef) marinated and cooked with vegetables (as onions, tomatoes, and green peppers) usu. on a skewer

Ka·bu·ki \kə-ˈbü-kē, ˈkäb-ü-(ˌ)kē\ *n* [Jap, lit., art of singing and dancing] **:** traditional Japanese popular drama with singing and dancing performed in a highly stylized manner

Ka·byle \kə-ˈbī(ə)l\ *n* [Ar *qabāʼil,* pl. of *qabīlah* tribe] **1 :** a Berber of the mountainous coastal area east of Algiers **2 :** the Berber language of the Kabyles

kad·dish \ˈkäd-ish\ *n, often cap* [Aram *qaddīsh* holy] **:** a Jewish prayer recited in the daily ritual of the synagogue and by mourners at public services after the death of a close relative

kaf·fee·klatsch \ˈkö-fē-ˌklach; ˈkäf-ē-ˌklach, -ˌkläch\ *n, often cap* [G, fr. *kaffee* coffee + *klatsch* gossip] **:** an informal social gathering for coffee and conversation

Kaf·fir *or* **Kaf·ir** \ˈkaf-ər\ *n* [Ar *kāfir* infidel] **:** a member of a group of southern African Bantu-speaking peoples

kaf·ir \ˈkaf-ər\ *n* **:** a grain sorghum with stout short-jointed somewhat juicy stalks and erect heads

Kaf·ir \ˈkaf-ər\ *n* [Ar *kāfir*] **:** a member of a people of the Hindu Kush in northeastern Afghanistan

Kaf·iri \ˈkaf-ə-rē\ *n* **:** the Dard language of the Kafir people

kaftan *var of* CAFTAN

ka·hu·na \kə-ˈhü-nə\ *n* [Hawaiian] **:** a Hawaiian witch doctor

kail·yard school \ˈkā(ə)l-ˌyärd-\ *n, often cap K* [Sc *kailyard* (kitchen garden), fr. *kail, kale* + E *yard*] **:** a group of writers whose work is characterized by sentimental description of Scottish life and considerable use of Scots dialect

kai·nite \ˈkī-ˌnīt, ˈkā-\ *also* **kai·nit** \kī-ˈnēt\ *n* [G *kainit,* fr. Gk *kainos* new — more at RECENT] **:** a natural salt $KMg(SO_4)Cl.3H_2O$ consisting of a hydrous sulfate and chloride of magnesium and potassium that is used as a fertilizer and as a source of potassium and magnesium compounds

kai·ser \ˈkī-zər\ *n* [ME, fr. ON *keisari;* akin to OHG *keisur* emperor; both fr. a prehistoric Gmc word borrowed fr. L *Caesar,* cognomen of the Emperor Augustus] **:** EMPEROR; *esp* **:** the ruler of Germany from 1871 to 1918 — **kai·ser·dom** \-ərd-əm\ *n* — **kai·ser·ism** \-zə-ˌriz-əm\ *n*

kale 1b

kai·se·rin \ˈkī-zə-rən\ *n* [G, fem. of *kaiser*] **:** the wife of a kaiser

ka·ka \ˈkäk-ə\ *n* [Maori] **:** an olive brown New Zealand parrot (*Nestor meridionalis*) with gray and red markings

ka·ka·po \ˌkäk-ə-ˈpō\ *n, pl* **-pos** [Maori] **:** a chiefly nocturnal burrowing New Zealand parrot (*Strigops habroptilus*) with green and brown barred plumage

ka·ke·mo·no \ˌkäk-i-ˈmō-(ˌ)nō\ *n, pl* **-nos** [Jap] **:** a vertical Japanese ornamental pictorial or calligraphic scroll

kala–azar \ˌkäl-ə-ə-ˈzär, ˌkal-\ *n* [Hindi *kālā-āzār* black disease, fr. Hindi *kālā* black + Per *āzār* disease] **:** a severe infectious disease chiefly of Asia marked by fever, progressive anemia, leukopenia, and enlargement of the spleen and liver and caused by a flagellate (*Leishmania donovani*) transmitted by the bite of sand flies

kale \ˈkā(ə)l\ *n* [Sc, fr. ME (northern) *cal,* fr. OE *cāl* — more at COLE] **1 a :** COLE **b :** a hardy cabbage (*Brassica oleracea acephala*) with curled often finely incised leaves that do not form a dense head **2** *slang* **:** MONEY

ka·lei·do·scope \kə-ˈlīd-ə-ˌskōp\ *n* [Gk *kalos* beautiful + *eidos* form + E *-scope* — more at CALLIGRAPHY, IDOL] **1 :** an instrument containing loose bits of colored glass between two flat plates and two plane mirrors so placed that changes of position of the bits of glass are reflected in an endless variety of patterns **2 a :** a variegated changing pattern or scene <the lake a ~ of changing colors —Robert Gibbings> **b :** a succession of changing phases or actions <a . . . ~ of shifting values, information, fashions

—Frank McLaughlin> — **ka·lei·do·scop·ic** \-ˌlīd-ə-ˈskäp-ik\ *or* **ka·lei·do·scop·i·cal** \-i-kəl\ *adj* — **ka·lei·do·scop·i·cal·ly** \-i-k(ə-)lē\ *adv*

kalends *var of* CALENDS

ka·lim·ba \kə-ˈlim-bə\ *n* [of Bantu origin; akin to Bemba *akalimba* zanza, Kimbundu *marimba* xylophone] **:** an African musical instrument derived from the zanza

kal·li·din \ˈkal-əd-ən\ *n* [G, fr. *kalli*krein + *-d-* (prob. fr. *deka-*) + *-in*] **:** any of several kinins formed from blood plasma globulin by the action of kallikrein

kal·li·krein \ˈkal-ə-ˌkrīn\ *n* [G, fr. *kalli-* beautiful (fr. Gk) + pan*kreas* pancreas + *-in;* prob. fr. its therapeutic use in pancreatic disorders — more at CALLIGRAPHY] **:** an enzyme that liberates kinins from blood plasma

Kal·muck *or* **Kal·muk** \ˈkal-ˌmək, kal-ˈ\ *or* **Kal·myk** \kal-ˈmik\ *n* [Russ *Kalmyk,* fr. Kazan Tatar] **1 :** a member of a Buddhist Mongol people orig. of Dzungaria **2 :** the Mongolian language of the Kalmucks

kal·pa \ˈkäl-pə\ *n* [Skt] **:** a period in which according to Hindu cosmology the universe undergoes a cycle of creation and destruction

kalsomine *var of* CALCIMINE

Ka·ma \ˈkäm-ə\ *n* [Skt *Kāma,* fr. *kāma* love] **:** the Hindu god of love

ka·ma·ai·na \ˌkäm-ə-ˈī-nə\ *n* [Hawaiian *kamaʻāina,* fr. *kama* child + *ʻāina* land] **:** one who has lived in Hawaii for a long time

ka·ma·la \ˈkäm-ə-lə\ *n* [Skt] **1 :** an East Indian tree (*Mallotus philippinensis*) of the spurge family **2 :** an orange red powder from kamala capsules used for dyeing silk and wool or as a vermifuge

kame \ˈkām\ *n* [Sc, kame, comb, fr. ME (northern) *camb* comb, fr. OE] **:** a short ridge, hill, or mound of stratified drift deposited by glacial meltwater

Ka·me·ha·me·ha Day \kə-ˌmā-ə-ˈmā-(ˌ)hä-\ *n* **:** June 11 observed as a holiday in Hawaii in commemoration of the birthday of Kamehameha I

[1]**ka·mi·ka·ze** \ˌkäm-i-ˈkäz-ē\ *n* [Jap, lit., divine wind] **1 :** a member of a Japanese air attack corps in World War II assigned to make a suicidal crash on a target (as a ship) **2 :** an airplane containing explosives to be flown in a suicide crash on a target

[2]**kamikaze** *adj* **1 :** of, relating to, or being a kamikaze **2 :** SUICIDAL <the city's ~ taxi drivers>

kam·pong \ˈkäm-ˌpȯŋ, ˈkam-\ *n* [Malay] **:** a native hamlet or village in a Malay-speaking country

kana·my·cin \ˌkan-ə-ˈmīs-ᵊn\ *n* [NL *kanamyceticus,* specific epithet of *Streptomyces kanamyceticus*] **:** a broad-spectrum antibiotic from a Japanese soil actinomycete (*Streptomyces kanamyceticus*)

Kan·a·rese \ˌkan-ə-ˈrēz, -ˈrēs\ *n, pl* **Kanarese** [*Kanara,* India] **1 :** a member of a Kannada-speaking people of Mysore, southern India **2 :** KANNADA

kan·ga·roo \ˌkaŋ-gə-ˈrü\ *n, pl* **-roos** [prob. native name in Australia] **:** any of various herbivorous leaping marsupial mammals (family Macropodidae) of Australia, New Guinea, and adjacent islands with a small head, large ears, long powerful hind legs, a long thick tail used as a support and in balancing, and rather small forelegs not used in progression

kangaroo

kangaroo court *n* **1 :** a mock court in which the principles of law and justice are disregarded or perverted **2 :** a court characterized by irresponsible, unauthorized, or irregular status or procedures **3 :** judgment or punishment given outside of legal procedure

kangaroo rat *n* **:** any of numerous pouched nocturnal burrowing rodents (genus *Dipodomys*) of arid parts of the western U.S.

Kan·na·da \ˈkän-əd-ə\ *n* [Kannada *Kannaḍa*] **:** the major Dravidian language of Mysore, southern India

Kans *abbr* Kansas

kan·te·le \ˈkän-tə-lə\ *n* [Finn] **:** a traditional Finnish harp orig. having 5 strings but now having as many as 30

Kant·ian \ˈkant-ē-ən, ˈkänt-\ *adj* **:** of, relating to, or characteristic of Kant or his philosophy — **Kantian** *n* — **Kant·ian·ism** \-ē-ə-ˌniz-əm\ *n*

ka·olin *also* **ka·oline** \ˈkā-ə-lən\ *n* [F *kaolin,* fr. *Kao-ling,* hill in China] **:** a fine usu. white clay that is used in ceramics and refractories, as an adsorbent, and as a filler or extender

ka·olin·ite \-lə-ˌnīt\ *n* **:** a mineral $Al_2Si_2O_5(OH)_4$ consisting of a hydrous silicate of aluminum that constitutes the principal mineral in kaolin — **ka·olin·it·ic** \ˌkā-ə-lə-ˈnit-ik\ *adj*

ka·on \ˈkā-ˌän\ *n* [ISV *ka* kay (fr. *K-meson,* its earlier name) + [2]*-on*] **:** an unstable meson produced in high-energy particle collisions with its electrically charged forms being 966.3 times more massive than the electron and its neutral form being 974.6 times more massive than the electron

ka·pell·mei·ster \kə-ˈpel-ˌmī-stər, kä-\ *n, often cap* [G, fr. *kapelle* choir + *meister* master] **:** the director of a choir or orchestra

kaph \ˈkäf, ˈkȯf\ *n* [Heb, lit., palm of the hand] **:** the 11th letter of the Hebrew alphabet — see ALPHABET table

ka·pok \ˈkā-ˌpäk\ *n* [Malay] **:** a mass of silky fibers that clothe the seeds of the ceiba tree and are used esp. as a filling for mattresses, life preservers, and sleeping bags and as insulation

kap·pa \ˈkap-ə\ *n* [Gk, of Sem origin; akin to Heb *kaph*] **:** the 10th letter of the Greek alphabet — see ALPHABET table

ka·put *also* **ka·putt** \kä-ˈpu̇t, kə-, -ˈpüt *adj* [G, fr. F *capot* not having made a trick at piquet] **1 :** utterly finished, defeated, or destroyed **2 :** unable to function **:** USELESS <my battery went ~ —Henry James Jr.> **3 :** hopelessly outmoded

karabiner *var of* CARABINER

Kara·ism \ˈkar-ə-ˌiz-əm\ *n* [LHeb *qĕrāīm* Karaites] **:** a Jewish doctrine originating in Baghdad in the 8th century that rejects rabbinism and talmudism and bases its tenets on scripture alone — **Kara·ite** \-ˌīt\ *n*

kar·a·kul \ˈkar-ə-kəl\ *n* [*Karakul,* village in Bukhara] **1** *often cap* **:** any of a breed of hardy fat-tailed sheep from Bukhara with a narrow body and coarse wiry brown fur **2 :** the tightly curled glossy black coat of the newborn lamb of a karakul valued as fur

kar·at \ˈkar-ət\ *n* [prob. fr. MF *carat,* fr. ML *carratus* unit of weight for precious stones — more at CARAT] **:** a unit of fineness for gold equal to $^1/_{24}$ part of pure gold in an alloy

ka·ra·te \kə-ˈrät-ē\ *n* [Jap, lit., empty hand] **:** an oriental art of self-defense in which an attacker is disabled by crippling kicks and punches — **ka·ra·te·ist** \-ē-əst\ *n*

ka·ra·ya gum \kə-ˌrī-ə-\ *n* [Hindi *karāyal* resin] **:** STERCULIA GUM; *esp* **:** a gum derived from an Indian tree (*Sterculia urens*)

Ka·re·lian \kə-ˈrē-lē-ən, -ˈrēl-yən\ *n* **1 :** a native or inhabitant of Karelia **2 :** the Finno-Ugric language of the Karelians — **Karelian** *adj*

Ka·ren \kə-ˈren\ *n, pl* **Karen** *or* **Karens** **1 a :** a group of peoples of eastern and southern Burma **b :** a member of any of these peoples **2 a :** a group of languages spoken by the Karen peoples **b :** a language of this group

kar·ma \ˈkär-mə, ˈkər-\ *n, often cap* [Skt *karman* (nom. *karma*), lit., work] **1 :** the force generated by a person's actions held in Hinduism and Buddhism to perpetuate transmigration and in its ethical consequences to determine his destiny in his next existence **2 :** VIBRATION 4 — **kar·mic** \-mik\ *adj, often cap*

ka·roo *or* **kar·roo** \kə-ˈrü\ *n, pl* **karoos** *or* **karroos** [Afrik *karo*] **:** a dry tableland of southern Africa

ka·ross \kə-ˈräs\ *n* [Afrik *karos*] **:** a simple garment or rug of skins used esp. by native tribesmen of southern Africa

karst \ˈkärst\ *n* [G] **:** an irregular limestone region with sinks, underground streams, and caverns — **karst·ic** \ˈkär-stik\ *adj*

kart \ˈkärt\ *n* [prob. fr. *GoKart,* a trademark] **:** a miniature motorcar used esp. in racing

Kar·tik \ˈkärt-ik\ *n* [Hindi *Kārtik,* fr. Skt *Kārttika*] **:** a month of the Hindu year — see MONTH table

kart·ing \ˈkärt-iŋ\ *n* **:** the sport of racing miniature motorcars

kary- *or* **karyo-** *also* **cary-** *or* **caryo-** *comb form* [NL, fr. Gk *karyon* nut — more at CAREEN] **1 :** nucleus of a cell <*karyo*kinesis> **2 :** nut **:** kernel <*cary*opsis>

karyo·ki·ne·sis \ˌkar-ē-ō-kə-ˈnē-səs, -kī-\ *n* [NL, fr. *kary-* + Gk *kinēsis* motion — more at KINESIOLOGY] **1 :** the nuclear phenomena characteristic of mitosis **2 :** the whole process of mitosis — **karyo·ki·net·ic** \-ˈnet-ik\ *adj*

kary·ol·o·gy \ˌkar-ē-ˈäl-ə-jē\ *n* [ISV] **:** a branch of cytology that deals with the minute anatomy of cell nuclei and esp. the nature and structure of chromosomes — **kary·o·log·i·cal** \-ē-ə-ˈläj-i-kəl\ *also* **kary·o·log·ic** \-ik\ *adj*

karyo·lymph \ˈkar-ē-ō-ˌlim(p)f\ *n* [ISV] **:** NUCLEAR SAP

karyo·some \ˈkar-ē-ə-ˌsōm\ *n* [ISV] **:** a mass of chromatin in a cell nucleus that resembles a nucleolus

karyo·sys·tem·at·ics \ˌkar-ē-ō-ˌsis-tə-ˈmat-iks\ *n pl but sing in constr* **:** a branch of systematics that seeks to determine natural relationships by the study of karyotypes

karyo·type \ˈkar-ē-ə-ˌtīp\ *n* [ISV] **:** the sum of the specific characteristics of the chromosomes of a cell; *also* **:** the chromosomes themselves — **karyo·typ·ic** \ˌkar-ē-ə-ˈtip-ik\ *or* **karyo·typ·i·cal** \-i-kəl\ *adj*

Kasbah *var of* CASBAH

Kash·mir goat \ˌkash-ˌmi(ə)r-, ˌkazh-\ *n* [*Kashmir,* region in India] **:** an Indian goat raised esp. for its undercoat of fine soft wool that constitutes the cashmere wool of commerce

Kash·miri \kash-ˈmi(ə)r-ē, kazh-\ *n, pl* **Kashmiris** *or* **Kashmiri** **1 :** a native or inhabitant of Kashmir **2 :** the Indic language of Kashmir

kash·ruth *or* **kash·rut** \kä-ˈshrüt(h)\ *n* [Heb *kashrūth,* lit., fitness] **1 :** the state of being kosher **2 :** the Jewish dietary laws

Ka·shu·bi·an \kə-ˈshü-bē-ən\ *n* [*Kashube* (a member of a Slavic people)] **:** a West Slavic language spoken in the vicinity of Gdansk

kat \ˈkät\ *n* [Ar *qāt*] **:** a shrub (*Caltha edulis*) cultivated by the Arabs for its leaves and buds that are the source of an habituating stimulant when chewed or used as a tea

Ka·tha·re·vu·sa \ˌkäth-ə-ˈrev-ə-ˌsä\ *n* [NGk *kathareuousa,* fr. Gk, fem. of *kathareuōn,* prp. of *kathareuein* to be pure, fr. *katharos* pure] **:** modern Greek conforming to classic Greek usage

katharsis *var of* CATHARSIS

ka·ty·did \ˈkāt-ē-ˌdid\ *n* [imit.] **:** any of several large green American long-horned grasshoppers usu. having stridulating organs on the fore wings of the males that produce a loud shrill sound

katydid

kat·zen·jam·mer \ˈkat-sən-ˌjam-ər\ *n* [G, fr. *katzen* cats + *jammer* distress] **1 :** HANGOVER **2 :** DISTRESS, DEPRESSION **3 :** a discordant clamor

kau·ri \ˈkau̇(ə)r-ē\ *n* [Maori *kawri*] **1 :** any of various trees (genus *Agathis*) of the pine family; *esp* **:** a tall timber tree (*A. australis*) of New Zealand having fine white straight-grained wood **2 :** a light-colored to brown resin from the kauri tree found as a fossil in the ground or collected from living trees and used esp. in varnishes and linoleum — called also *kauri gum, kauri copal, kauri resin*

ka·va \ˈkäv-ə\ *n* [Tongan & Marquesan, lit., bitter] **1 :** an Australasian shrubby pepper (*Piper methysticum*) from whose crushed root an intoxicating beverage is made **2 :** the beverage made from kava

kay \ˈkā\ *n* **:** the letter *k*

Kay \ˈkā\ *n* **:** a boastful malicious knight of the Round Table who in Arthurian legend is foster brother and seneschal of King Arthur

kay·ak \ˈkī-ˌak\ *n* [Esk *qajaq*] **1 :** an Eskimo canoe made of a frame covered with skins except for a small opening in the center and propelled by a double-bladed paddle **2 :** a portable boat styled like an Eskimo kayak and used widely in the U.S. — **kay·ak·er** \-ˌak-ər\ *n*

[1]**kayo** \(ˈ)kā-ˈō, ˈkā-(ˌ)ō\ *n* [pronunciation of *KO,* abbr.] **:** KNOCKOUT

[2]kayo *vt* **kay·oed; kayo·ing 1 :** to knock out **2 :** to cause the removal of (a baseball pitcher) by a batting rally

kayak 1

ka·zoo \kə-ˈzü\ *n, pl* **kazoos** [imit.] **:** a toy musical instrument consisting of a tube with a membrane sealing one end and a side hole into which one sings or hums

kb *or* **kbar** *abbr* kilobar

kc *abbr* kilocycle

KC *abbr* **1** Kansas City **2** King's Counsel **3** Knights of Columbus

kcal *abbr* kilocalorie; kilogram calorie

KCB *abbr* knight commander of the Order of the Bath

kc/s *abbr* kilocycles per second

KD *abbr* **1** kiln-dried **2** knocked down

kea \ˈkē-ə\ *n* [Maori] **:** a large predominantly green New Zealand parrot (*Nestor notabilis*) that is normally insectivorous but sometimes destroys sheep by slashing the back to feed on the kidney fat

ke·bab *or* **ke·bob** \ˈkā-ˌbäb, kə-ˈ\ *var of* KABOB

keb·buck *or* **keb·bock** \ˈkeb-ək\ *n* [ME (Sc dial.) *cabok,* fr. ScGael *ceapag*] *dial Brit* **:** a whole cheese

Ke·chu·ma·ran \ˌkech-ə-mə-ˈrän, kə-ˌchü-\ *n* [*Kechu*a (Quechua) + A*ymara* + *-an*] **:** a language stock comprising Aymara and Quechua

[1]kedge \ˈkej\ *vt* **kedged; kedg·ing** [ME *caggen*] **:** to move (a ship) by means of a line attached to a kedge dropped at the distance and in the direction desired

[2]kedge *n* **:** a small anchor used esp. in kedging

[1]keek \ˈkēk\ *vi* [ME *kiken*] *chiefly Scot* **:** PEEP, LOOK

[2]keek *n, chiefly Scot* **:** PEEP, LOOK

[1]keel \ˈkē(ə)l\ *vb* [ME *kelen,* fr. OE *cēlan,* fr. *cōl* cool] *chiefly dial* **:** COOL

[2]keel *n* [ME *kele,* fr. MD *kiel;* akin to OE *cēol* ship, *cot* small house — more at COT] **1 a :** a flat-bottomed ship; *esp* **:** a barge used on the Tyne to carry coal **b :** a barge load of coal **2 :** a British unit of weight for coal equal to 21.2 long tons

[3]keel *n* [ME *kele,* fr. ON *kjölr;* akin to OE *ceole* throat, beak of a ship — more at GLUTTON] **1 a :** a longitudinal timber or plate extending along the center of the bottom of a ship and often projecting from the bottom **b :** SHIP **c :** the assembly of members at the bottom of the hull of a semirigid or rigid airship **2 :** a projection suggesting a keel; *esp* **:** CARINA — **keeled** \ˈkē(ə)ld\ *adj* — **keel·less** \ˈkē(ə)l-ləs\ *adj*

[4]keel *vt* **:** to cause to turn over ~ *vi* **1 :** to turn over **2 :** to fall in or as if in a faint — usu. used with *over* <~*ed* over with laughter —Bud Freeman>

[5]keel *n* [ME (Sc dial.) *keyle*] **1** *chiefly dial* **:** RED OCHER **2 :** a colored marking crayon used esp. for chalking lines or marking lumber

keel·boat \ˈkē(ə)l-ˌbōt\ *n* **:** a shallow covered keeled riverboat that is usu. rowed, poled, or towed and that is used for freight

keel·haul \-ˌhȯl\ *vt* [D *kielhalen,* fr. *kiel* keel + *halen* to haul] **1 :** to haul under the keel of a ship as punishment or torture **2 :** to rebuke severely

keel·son \ˈkel-sən, ˈkē(ə)l-\ *n* [prob. of Scand origin; akin to Sw *kölsvin* keelson] **:** a longitudinal structure running above and fastened to the keel of a ship in order to stiffen and strengthen its framework

[1]keen \ˈkēn\ *adj* [ME *kene* brave, sharp, fr. OE *cēne* brave; akin to OHG *kuoni* brave, OE *cnāwan* to know — more at KNOW] **1 a :** having a fine edge or point **:** SHARP <a ~ sword> **b :** affecting one as if by cutting <~ sarcasm> **c :** pungent to the sense <a ~ scent> **2 a :** showing a quick and ardent responsiveness **:** ENTHUSIASTIC <a ~ swimmer> **b** *of emotion or feeling* **:** INTENSE <the ~ delight in the chase —F. W. Maitland> **3 a :** intellectually alert **:** having or characteristic of a quick penetrating mind <a ~ student> <had a ~ awareness of the problem>; *also* **:** shrewdly astute <~ bargainers> **b :** sharply contested <~ debate> **c :** extremely sensitive in perception <~ eyesight> **4 :** WONDERFUL, EXCELLENT ***syn* 1** see SHARP ***ant*** blunt **2** see EAGER — **keen·ly** *adv* — **keen·ness** \ˈkēn-nəs\ *n*

[2]keen *vb* [IrGael *caoinim* I lament] *vi* **1 a :** to lament with a keen **b :** to make a sound suggestive of a keen **2 :** to lament, mourn, or complain loudly ~ *vt* **:** to utter by keening — **keen·er** *n*

[3]keen *n* **:** a lamentation for the dead uttered in a loud wailing voice or sometimes in a wordless cry

[1]keep \ˈkēp\ *vb* **kept** \ˈkept\; **keep·ing** [ME *kepen,* fr. OE *cēpan;* akin to OHG *chapfēn* to look] *vt* **1 :** to take notice of by appropriate conduct **:** FULFILL: as **a :** to be faithful to <~ a promise> **b :** to act fittingly in relation to <~ the Sabbath> **c :** to conform to in habits or conduct <~ late hours> **d :** to stay in accord with (a beat) <~ time> **2 :** PRESERVE, MAINTAIN: as **a :** to watch over and defend <~ us from harm> **b (1) :** to take care of **:** TEND <~ a garden> **(2) :** SUPPORT <~ a wife> **(3) :** to maintain in a good, fitting, or orderly condition <~ house> **c :** to continue to maintain <~ silence> **d (1) :** to cause to remain in a given place, situation, or condition <~ him waiting> **(2) :** to preserve (food) in an unspoiled condition **e :** to have or maintain in one's service or at one's disposal <~ a mistress> — often used with *on* <*kept* the cook on until he found another job>; *also* **:** to lodge or feed for pay <~ boarders> **f (1) :** to maintain a record in <~ a diary> **(2) :** to enter in a book <~ records> **g :** to have customarily in stock for sale **3 a :** to restrain from departure or removal **:** DETAIN <~ children in after school> **b :** to hold back **:** RESTRAIN <~ him from going> <*kept* him back with difficulty> **c :** SAVE, RESERVE <~ some for later> <*kept* some out for a friend> **d :** to refrain from revealing <~ a secret> **4 a :** to retain in one's possession or power <*kept* the money he found> **b :** to refrain from granting, giving, or allowing <*kept* the news back> **c :** to have in control <~ your temper> **5 :** to confine oneself to <~*s* her room> **6 a :** to stay or continue in <~ the path> <~ your seat> **b :** to stay or remain on or in usu. against opposition **:** HOLD <*kept* his ground> **7 :** to carry on **:** CONDUCT, MANAGE <~ a tearoom> ~ *vi* **1** *chiefly Brit* **:** LIVE, LODGE **2 a :** to maintain a course, direction, or progress <~ to the right> **b :** to continue usu. without interruption <~ talking> <~ on smiling> **c :** to persist in a practice <*kept* bothering them> <*kept* on smoking in spite of warnings> **3 :** STAY, REMAIN <~ out of the way> <~ off the grass>: as **a :** to stay even — usu. used with *up* <~ up with the Joneses> **b :** to remain in good condition <meat will ~ in the freezer> **c :** to remain undivulged <the secret would ~> **d :** to call for no immediate action <the matter will ~ until morning> **4 :** ABSTAIN, REFRAIN <can't ~ from talking> **5 :** to be in session <school will ~ through the winter —W. M. Thayer> **6** *of a quarterback* **:** to retain possession of a football esp. after faking a handoff

syn* 1** KEEP, OBSERVE, CELEBRATE, COMMEMORATE *shared meaning element* **:** to notice or honor a day, occasion, or deed ***ant break **2** KEEP, RETAIN, DETAIN, WITHHOLD, RESERVE *shared meaning element* **:** to hold in one's possession or under one's control ***ant*** relinquish

— **keep an eye on :** WATCH — **keep at :** to persist in doing or concerning oneself with — **keep company :** to go together as frequent companions or in courtship — **keep one's distance** *or* **keep at a distance :** to stay aloof **:** maintain a reserved attitude — **keep one's eyes open** *or* **keep one's eyes peeled :** to be on the alert **:** be watchful — **keep one's hand in :** to keep in practice — **keep pace :** to stay even — **keep step :** to keep in step — **keep to 1a :** to stay in **b :** to limit oneself to **2 :** to abide by — **keep to oneself 1 :** to keep secret <*kept* the facts *to himself*> **2 :** to remain solitary or apart from other people

[2]keep *n* **1 a** *archaic* **:** CUSTODY, CHARGE **b :** MAINTENANCE **2 :** one that keeps or protects: as **a :** FORTRESS, CASTLE; *specif* **:** the strongest and securest part of a medieval castle **b :** one whose job is to keep or tend **c :** PRISON, JAIL **3 :** the means or provisions by which one is kept <earned his ~> **4 :** KEEPER 4 — **for keeps 1 a :** with the provision that one keep what he has won <played marbles *for keeps*> **b :** with deadly seriousness **2 :** for an indefinitely long time **:** PERMANENTLY **3 :** with the result of ending the matter

keep back *vi* **:** to refrain from approaching or advancing near something <policemen asked the spectators to *keep back*>

keep down *vt* **1 :** to keep in control <*keep* expenses *down*> **2 :** to prevent from growing, advancing, or succeeding <can't *keep* a good man *down*>

keep·er \ˈkē-pər\ *n* **1 :** one that keeps: as **a :** PROTECTOR **b :** GAMEKEEPER **c :** WARDEN **d :** CUSTODIAN **e :** CURATOR **2 :** any of various devices for keeping something in position **3 :** one fit or suitable for keeping; *esp* **:** a fish large enough to be legally caught **4 :** an offensive football play in which the quarterback runs with the ball

keep·ing \ˈkē-piŋ\ *n* **1 :** the act of one that keeps: as **a :** CUSTODY, MAINTENANCE **b :** OBSERVANCE **c :** a reserving or preserving for future use **2 a :** the means by which something is kept **:** SUPPORT, PROVISION **b :** the state of being kept or the condition in which something is kept <the house is in good ~> **3 :** CONFORMITY <in ~ with good taste> <out of ~ with accepted standards>

keep·sake \ˈkēp-ˌsāk\ *n* [[1]*keep* + *-sake* (as in *namesake*)] **:** something kept or given to be kept as a memento

keep up *vt* **:** to persist or persevere in <*kept up* the good work>; *also* **:** MAINTAIN, SUSTAIN <*keep* standards *up*> ~ *vi* **1 a :** to keep adequately informed <*keep up* on international affairs> **b :** to maintain a harmonious relationship <*keep up* with the times> **2 :** to continue without interruption <rain *kept up* all night>

kees·hond \ˈkās-ˌhȯnt\ *n, pl* **kees·hon·den** \-ˌhȯn-dən\ [D, prob. fr. *Kees* (nickname for *Cornelis* Cornelius) + *hond* dog, fr. MD; akin to OE *hund* hound] **:** any of a breed of small gray heavy-coated dogs that have a thick coat around the neck, shoulders, and chest, a face and head suggesting those of a fox, and small pointed ears

keet \ˈkēt\ *n* [imit.] **:** GUINEA FOWL; *esp* **:** a young guinea fowl

kef \ˈkef, ˈkēf, ˈkāf\ *n* [Ar *kayf* pleasure] **1 :** a state of dreamy tranquillity **2 :** a smoking material (as marijuana) that produces kef

ke·fir \ke-ˈfi(ə)r\ *n* [Russ] **:** a slightly effervescent acidulous beverage made of fermented cow's milk

keg \ˈkeg, ˈkag, ˈkāg\ *n* [ME *kag,* of Scand origin; akin to ON *kaggi* keg] **1 :** a small cask or barrel having a capacity of 30 gallons or less **2 :** the contents of a keg

keg·ler \ˈkeg-lər, ˈkāg-\ *n* [G] **:** [1]BOWLER

keg·ling \ˈkeg-liŋ, ˈkāg-\ *n* **:** BOWLING

kelly green \ˈkel-ē-\ *n, often cap K* [fr. the common Irish name *Kelly;* fr. green's being a traditional Irish color] **:** a variable color averaging a strong yellowish green

kelp 1a

ke·loid \ˈkē-ˌlȯid\ *n* [F *kiloïde,* fr. Gk *chēlē* claw] **:** a thick scar resulting from excessive growth of fibrous tissue — **ke·loi·dal** \kē-ˈlȯid-ᵊl\ *adj*

kelp \ˈkelp\ *n* [ME *culp*] **1 a :** any of various large brown seaweeds (orders Laminariales and Fucales) **b :** a mass of large seaweeds **2 :** the ashes of seaweed used esp. as a source of iodine

kelp bass *n* **:** a mottled California sea bass (*Paralabrax clathratus*) that is an important sport fish

---

[1]kel·pie \ˈkel-pē\ *n* [prob. of Celt origin; akin to ScGael *cailpeach* colt] **:** a water sprite of Scottish folklore that delights in or brings about the drowning of wayfarers

[2]kelpie *n* [*Kelpie,* a dog of this breed] **:** an Australian sheep dog of a breed developed by crossing the dingo with various British sheep dogs

Kelt \ˈkelt\, **Kelt·ic** \ˈkel-tik\ *var of* CELT, CELTIC

kel·vin \ˈkel-vən\ *n* **:** a unit of temperature equal to 1/273.16 of the Kelvin scale temperature of the triple point of water

Kelvin *adj* [William Thomson, Lord *Kelvin*] **:** relating to, conforming to, or having a thermometric scale on which the unit of measurement equals the centigrade degree and according to which absolute zero is 0°, the equivalent of –273.16°C

kemp \ˈkemp\ *n* [ME *kempe,* fr. OE *cempa;* akin to OHG *kempho* warrior] *dial Brit* **:** CHAMPION

kempt \ˈkem(p)t\ *adj* [ME, fr. pp. of *kemben* to comb, fr. OE *cemban;* akin to OE *camb* comb] **:** neatly kept **:** TRIM <old but ~ homes —David Bourdon>

[1]ken \ˈken\ *vb* **kenned; ken·ning** [ME *kennen,* fr. OE *cennan* to make known & ON *kenna* to perceive; both akin to OE *can* know — more at CAN] *vt* **1** *archaic* **:** SEE **2** *chiefly dial* **:** RECOGNIZE **3** *chiefly Scot* **:** KNOW ~ *vi, chiefly Scot* **:** KNOW

[2]ken *n* **1 a :** the range of vision **b :** SIGHT, VIEW <'tis double death to drown in ~ of shore —Shak.> **2 :** the range of perception, understanding, or knowledge <abstract words that are beyond the ~ of young children —Lois M. Rettie>

ke·naf \kə-ˈnaf\ *n* [Per] **:** an East Indian hibiscus (*Hibiscus cannabinus*) widely cultivated for its fiber; *also* **:** the fiber used esp. for cordage

Ken·dal green \ˌken-dᵊl-\ *n* [ME, fr. *Kendal,* England] **:** a green woolen cloth resembling homespun or tweed

ken·do \ˈken-(ˌ)dō\ *n* [Jap *kendō,* fr. *ken* sword + *dō* art] **:** a Japanese sport of fencing with bamboo staves

[1]ken·nel \ˈken-ᵊl\ *n* [ME *kenel,* deriv. of (assumed) VL *canile,* fr. L *canis* dog — more at HOUND] **1 a :** a shelter for a dog **b :** an establishment for the breeding or boarding of dogs **2 :** a pack of dogs

[2]kennel *vb* **-neled** *or* **-nelled; -nel·ing** *or* **-nel·ling** *vi* **:** to take shelter in or as if in a kennel ~ *vt* **:** to put or keep in or as if in a kennel

[3]kennel *n* [alter. of *cannel* (gutter)] **:** a gutter in a street

[1]ken·ning \ˈken-iŋ\ *n* [ME, sight, view, fr. gerund of *kennen*] *chiefly Scot* **:** a perceptible but small amount <his father was . . . a ~ on the wrong side of the law —R. L. Stevenson>

[2]kenning *n* [ON, fr. *kenna*] **:** a metaphorical compound word or phrase used esp. in Old English and Old Norse poetry <*swan-road* for *ocean* is an example of a ~>

Ken·ny method \ˈken-ē-\ *n* [Elizabeth *Kenny*] **:** a method of treating poliomyelitis consisting basically of application of hot fomentations and reeducation — called also *Kenny treatment*

ke·no \ˈkē-(ˌ)nō\ *n* [F *quine,* set of five winning numbers in a lottery + E *-o* (as in *lotto*)] **:** a game resembling bingo

ken·speck·le \ˈken-ˌspek-əl\ *adj* [prob. of Scand origin; akin to Norw *kjennspak* quick to recognize] *chiefly Scot* **:** CONSPICUOUS

kent·ledge \ˈkent-lij\ *n* [origin unknown] **:** pig iron or scrap metal used as ballast

Ken·tucky bluegrass \kən-ˌtək-ē-\ *n* [*Kentucky,* U.S.] **:** a valuable pasture and meadow grass (*Poa pratensis*) of both Europe and America — called also *bluegrass*

Kentucky coffee tree *n* **:** a tall No. American leguminous tree (*Gymnocladus dioica*) with bipinnate leaves and large woody brown pods whose seeds have been used as a substitute for coffee

Kentucky rifle *n* **:** a muzzle-loading long-barreled flintlock rifle developed in the 18th century in Pennsylvania and used extensively on the American frontier

ke·pi \ˈkā-pē, ˈkep-ē\ *n* [F *képi*] **:** a military cap with a round flat top sloping toward the front and a visor

Kep·le·ri·an \kep-ˈlir-ē-ən\ *adj* **:** of or relating to the astronomer Kepler or his laws concerning the motions of the planets in their orbits

kept *past of* KEEP

Ker *abbr* Kerry

kerat- *or* **kerato-** — see CERAT-

ker·a·tin \ˈker-ət-ᵊn\ *n* [ISV] **:** any of various sulfur-containing fibrous proteins that form the chemical basis of horny epidermal tissues — **ke·ra·ti·nous** \kə-ˈrat-ᵊn-əs, ˌker-ə-ˈtī-nəs\ *adj*

ke·ra·ti·ni·za·tion \ˌker-ə-tə-nə-ˈzā-shən, kə-ˌrat-ᵊn-ə-\ *n* **:** conversion into keratin or keratinous tissue

ke·ra·ti·no·phil·ic \ˌker-ə-tə-nə-ˈfil-ik, kə-ˌrat-ᵊn-ə-\ *adj* **:** exhibiting affinity for keratin (as in hair, skin, feathers, or horns) — used chiefly of fungi capable of growing on such materials

ker·a·ti·tis \ˌker-ə-ˈtīt-əs\ *n, pl* **-tit·i·des** \-ˈtit-ə-ˌdēz\ [NL] **:** inflammation of the cornea of the eye

ker·a·to·con·junc·ti·vi·tis \ˈker-ə-(ˌ)tō-kən-ˌjəŋ(k)-tə-ˈvīt-əs\ *n* [NL] **:** combined inflammation of the cornea and conjunctiva

ker·a·to·sis \ˌker-ə-ˈtō-səs\ *n, pl* **-to·ses** \-ˌsēz\ [NL] **:** an area of skin marked by overgrowth of horny tissue — **ker·a·tot·ic** \-ˈtät-ik\ *adj*

kerb \ˈkərb\ *n, Brit* **:** CURB 5

ker·chief \ˈkər-chəf, -ˌchēf\ *n, pl* **kerchiefs** \-chəfs, -ˌchēfs\ *also* **ker·chieves** \-ˌchēvz\ [ME *courchef,* fr. OF *cuevrechief,* fr. *covrir* to cover + *chief* head — more at CHIEF] **1 :** a square of cloth used by women as a head covering or worn as a scarf around the neck **2 :** HANDKERCHIEF 1 — **ker·chiefed** \-chəft, -ˌchēft \ *adj*

kerf \ˈkərf\ *n* [ME, fr. OE *cyrf* action of cutting; akin to OE *ceorfan* to carve — more at CARVE] **1 :** a slit or notch made by a saw or cutting torch **2 :** the width of cut made by a saw or cutting torch

Ker·man \kər-ˈmän, ke(ə)r-\ *var of* KIRMAN

ker·mes \ˈkər-(ˌ)mēz\ *n* [F *kermès,* fr. Ar *qirmiz*] **:** the dried bodies of the females of various scale insects (genus *Kermes*) that are found on a Mediterranean oak (*Quercus coccinea*) and constitute a red dyestuff

ker·mis \ˈkər-məs\ *or* **ker·mess** \ˈkər-məs, (ˌ)kər-ˈmes\ *n* [D *kermis*] **1 :** an outdoor festival of the Low Countries **2 :** a fair held usu. for charitable purposes

[1]kern *or* **kerne** \ˈkərn, ˈke(ə)rn\ *n* [ME *kerne,* fr. MIr *cethern* band of soldiers] **1 :** a light-armed foot soldier of medieval Ireland or Scotland **2 :** YOKEL

[2]kern \ˈkərn\ *n* [F *carne* corner, fr. L *cardin-, cardo* hinge — more at CARDINAL] **:** a part of a typeset letter that projects beyond its side bearings

kern

[3]kern *vt* **:** to form or set with a kern <~*ed* letters> ~ *vi* **:** to become kerned

ker·nel \ˈkərn-ᵊl\ *n* [ME, fr. OE *cyrnel,* dim. of *corn*] **1** *chiefly dial* **:** a fruit seed **2 :** the inner softer part of a seed, fruit stone, or nut **3 :** a whole seed of a cereal **4 :** a central or essential part <like many stereotypes . . . this one too contains some ~*s* of truth —S. M. Lyman> **5 :** a subset of the elements of one set (as a group) that a function (as a homomorphism) maps onto an identity element of another set

kern·ite \ˈkər-ˌnīt\ *n* [*Kern* co., Calif.] **:** a mineral $Na_2B_4O_7.4H_2O$ that consists of a hydrous sodium borate and is an important source of borax

ker·o·gen \ˈker-ə-jən\ *n* [Gk *kēros* wax + E *-gen* — more at CERUMEN] **:** bituminous material occurring in shale and yielding oil when heated

ker·o·sine *or* **ker·o·sene** \ˈker-ə-ˌsēn, ˌker-ə-ˈ, ˈkar-, ˌkar-\ *n* [Gk *kēros* + E *-ene* (as in *camphene*)] **:** a flammable hydrocarbon oil usu. obtained by distillation of petroleum and used for a fuel and as a solvent and thinner

ker·ria \ˈker-ē-ə\ *n* [NL, genus name, fr. William *Kerr* †1814 E gardener] **:** any of a genus (*Kerria*) of Chinese shrubs of the rose family with solitary yellow and often double flowers

ker·ry \ˈker-ē\ *n, pl* **kerries** *often cap* [County *Kerry,* Ireland] **:** any of an Irish breed of small hardy long-lived black dairy cattle

Kerry blue terrier *n* **:** any of an Irish breed of medium-sized terriers with a long head, deep chest, and silky bluish coat

ker·sey \ˈkər-zē\ *n, pl* **kerseys** [ME, fr. *Kersey,* England] **1 a :** a coarse ribbed woolen cloth for hose and work clothes **b :** a heavy wool or wool and cotton fabric used esp. for uniforms and coats **2 :** a garment of kersey

ker·sey·mere \ˈkər-zē-ˌmi(ə)r\ *n* [alter. of *cassimere*] **:** a fine woolen fabric with a close nap made in fancy twill weaves

ke·ryg·ma \kə-ˈrig-mə\ *n* [Gk *kērygma,* fr. *kēryssein* to proclaim, fr. *kēryx* herald — more at CADUCEUS] **:** the apostolic proclamation of salvation through Jesus Christ — **ker·yg·mat·ic** \ˌker-ig-ˈmat-ik\ *adj*

kes·trel \ˈkes-trəl\ *n* [ME *castrel,* fr. MF *crecerelle*] **:** a small European falcon (*Falco tinnunculus*) that is noted for its habit of hovering in the air against a wind and that is about a foot long, bluish gray above in the male, and reddish brown in the female; *broadly* **:** any of various small Old World falcons

ket- *or* **keto-** *comb form* [ISV] **:** ketone <*ketosis*>

ketch \ˈkech\ *n* [ME *cache*] **:** a fore-and-aft rigged ship similar to a yawl but with a larger mizzen and with the mizzenmast stepped farther forward

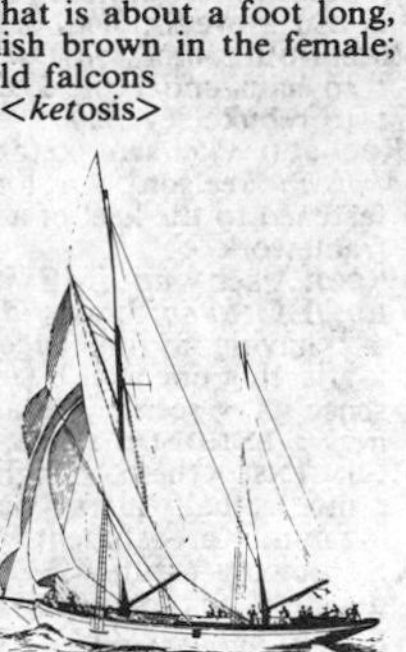

ketch

ketch·up *var of* CATSUP

ke·tene \ˈkē-ˌtēn\ *n* [ISV] **:** a colorless poisonous gas C_2H_2O of penetrating odor used esp. as an acetylating agent

ke·to \ˈkēt-(ˌ)ō\ *adj* [*ket-*] **:** of or relating to a ketone; *also* **:** containing a ketone group

ke·to·gen·e·sis \ˌkēt-ō-ˈjen-ə-səs\ *n* [NL] **:** the production of ketone bodies (as in diabetes) — **ke·to·gen·ic** \-ˈjen-ik\ *adj*

ke·to·glu·tar·ic acid \-glü-ˌtar-ik-\ *n* **:** either of two crystalline keto derivatives $C_5H_6O_5$ of glutaric acid; *esp* **:** the alpha keto isomer formed in various metabolic processes (as the Krebs cycle)

ke·tone \ˈkē-ˌtōn\ *n* [G *keton,* alter. of *aceton* acetone] **:** an organic compound (as acetone) with a carbonyl group attached to two carbon atoms — **ke·ton·ic** \kē-ˈtän-ik\ *adj*

ketone body *n* **:** any of the three compounds acetoacetic acid, acetone, and beta-hydroxybutyric acid found in the blood and urine in abnormal amounts in conditions of impaired metabolism (as diabetes mellitus)

ke·tose \ˈkē-ˌtōs, -ˌtōz\ *n* [ISV] **:** a sugar (as fructose) containing one ketone group per molecule

ke·to·sis \kē-ˈtō-səs\ *n* [NL] **:** an abnormal increase of ketone bodies in the body — **ke·tot·ic** \-ˈtät-ik\ *adj*

ke·to·ste·roid \ˌkēt-ō-ˈsti(ə)r-ˌȯid *also* -ˈste(ə)r-\ *n* [ISV] **:** a steroid (as cortisone or estrone) containing a ketone group

ket·tle \ˈket-ᵊl\ *n* [ME *ketel,* fr. ON *ketill;* akin to OE *cietel* kettle; both fr. a prehistoric Gmc word borrowed fr. L *catillus,* dim. of *catinus* bowl] **1 :** a metallic vessel for boiling liquids; *esp* **:** TEAKETTLE **2 :** KETTLEDRUM **3 a :** POTHOLE **b :** a steep-sided hollow without surface drainage esp. in a deposit of glacial drift

ket·tle·drum \-ˌdrəm\ *n* **:** a percussion instrument that consists of a hollow brass or copper hemisphere with a parchment head whose tension can be changed to vary the pitch

kettle of fish **1 :** a bad state of affairs **:** MESS **2 :** something to be considered or reckoned with **:** MATTER <books and discs . . . were two very different *kettles of fish* —Roland Gelatt>

keV *abbr* kilo-electron volt

Kew·pie \ˈkyü-pē\ *trademark* — used for a small chubby doll with a topknot of hair

[1]key \ˈkē\ *n* [ME, fr. OE *cǣg;* akin to MLG *keige* spear] **1 a**

: a usu. metal instrument by which the bolt of a lock is turned **b :** any of various devices having the form or function of such a key **2 a :** a means of gaining or preventing entrance, possession, or control **b :** an instrumental or deciding factor **3 a :** something that gives an explanation or identification or provides a solution <the ~ to a riddle> **b :** a list of words or phrases giving an explanation of symbols or abbreviations **c :** an aid to interpretation or identification : CLUE <can spot a zone defense by the one ~ of the strong-side safety who plays . . . more to the outside —John Unitas> **d :** an arrangement of the salient characters of a group of plants or animals or of taxa designed to facilitate identification **e :** a map legend **4 a (1) :** COTTER PIN **(2) :** 2COTTER **b :** a keystone in an arch **c :** a small piece of wood or metal used as a wedge or for preventing motion between parts **5 a :** one of the levers of a keyboard musical instrument that actuates the mechanism and produces the tones **b :** a lever that controls a vent in the side of a woodwind instrument or a valve in a brass instrument **c :** a digital that serves as one unit of a keyboard and that works usu. by lever action to set in motion a character or an escapement (as in some typesetting machines) **d :** KEYBUTTON **6 :** SAMARA **7 :** a system of seven tones based on their relationship to a tonic; *specif* **:** the tonality of a scale **8 a :** characteristic style or tone **b :** the tone or pitch of a voice **c :** the predominant tone of a photograph with respect to its lightness or darkness **9 :** a decoration or charm resembling a key **10 :** a small switch for opening or closing an electric circuit **11 :** the set of instructions governing the encipherment and decipherment of messages **12 :** KEYHOLE 2 — **keyed** \ˈkēd\ *adj* — **key·less** \ˈkē-ləs\ *adj*

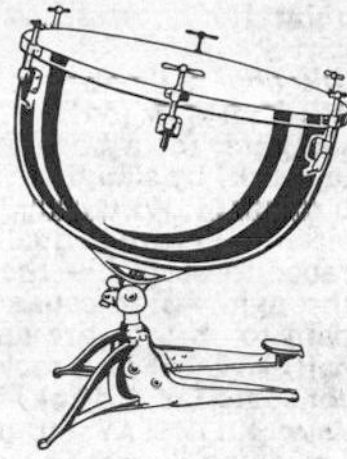
kettledrum

2key *vt* **1 :** to lock with or as if with a key : FASTEN: as **a :** to secure (as a pulley on a shaft) by a key **b :** to finish off (an arch) by inserting a keystone **2 :** to regulate the musical pitch of **3 :** to bring into harmony or conformity : make appropriate : ATTUNE <remarks ~*ed* to a situation> **4 :** to identify (a biological specimen) by a key **5 :** to provide with identifying or explanatory cross-references <instructions ~*ed* to accompanying drawings —John Gartner> **6 :** to make nervous, tense, or excited — usu. used with *up* <was ~*ed* up over her impending operation> **7 :** KEYBOARD ~ *vi* **1 :** to use a key **2 :** to observe the position or movement of an opposing player in football in order to anticipate the play — usu. used with *on* <the middle linebacker was ~*ing* on the halfback>

3key *adj* **:** of basic importance : FUNDAMENTAL <~ issues>

4key *n* [Sp *cayo,* fr. Lucayo] **:** a low island or reef; *specif* **:** one of the coral islets off the southern coast of Florida

5key *n* [prob. fr. Sp *kilogramo* kilogram] *slang* **:** a kilogram of marijuana

1key·board \ˈkē-ˌbō(ə)rd, -ˌbȯ(ə)rd\ *n* **1 :** a bank of keys on a musical instrument (as a piano) that consists of seven white and five raised black keys to the octave **2 :** an assemblage of systematically arranged keys by which a machine is operated **3 :** a board on which keys for locks are hung

2keyboard *vi* **:** to operate a machine (as for typesetting) by means of a keyboard ~ *vt* **:** to capture or set (as data or text) by means of a keyboard — **key·board·er** *n*

key·but·ton \ˈkē-ˌbət-ᵊn\ *n* **:** any of the small buttons or knobs depressed by the fingers in operating a keyboard machine

key club *n* [so called because each member is provided with a key to the premises] **:** an informal private club serving liquor and providing entertainment

1key·hole \ˈkē-ˌhōl\ *n* **1 :** a hole for receiving a key **2 :** a free-throw area in basketball

2keyhole *adj* **1 :** revealingly intimate <a ~ report> **2 :** intent on revealing intimate details <~ columnists>

keyhole saw *n* **:** a narrow pointed fine-toothed saw used for cutting curves of short radius

keying sequence *n* **:** a sequence of letters or numbers that enciphers or deciphers a polyalphabetic substitution cipher letter by letter

key light *n* **:** the main light illuminating a subject in photography

Keynes·ian \ˈkān-zē-ən\ *adj* **:** of, relating to, or characteristic of John M. Keynes or his economic theories and programs — **Keynes·ian** *n*

Keynes·ian·ism \-ə-ˌniz-əm\ *n* **:** the economic theories and programs ascribed to John M. Keynes and his followers; *specif* **:** the advocacy of monetary and fiscal programs by government to increase employment

1key·note \ˈkē-ˌnōt\ *n* **1 :** the first and harmonically fundamental tone of a scale **2 :** the fundamental or central fact, idea, or mood <sadness is the ~ of this little collection —*Books Abroad*>

2keynote *vt* **1 :** to set the keynote of **2 :** to deliver the keynote address at — **key·not·er** *n*

keynote address *n* **:** an address designed to present the issues of primary interest to an assembly (as a political convention) and often to arouse unity and enthusiasm — called also *keynote speech*

keynote speaker *n* **:** one who delivers a keynote address : KEYNOTER

1key·punch \ˈkē-ˌpənch\ *n* **:** a machine with a keyboard used to cut holes or notches in punch cards

2keypunch *vt* **:** to cut holes or notches in (a punch card) with a keypunch — **key·punch·er** *n*

key·set \ˈkē-ˌset\ *n* **:** KEYBOARD 2

key signature *n* **:** the sharps or flats placed after a clef in music to indicate the key

key·stone \ˈkē-ˌstōn\ *n* **1 :** the wedge-shaped piece at the crown of an arch that locks the other pieces in place **2 :** something on which associated things depend for support <collective bargaining — the ~ of industrial democracy —A. E. Stevenson †1965>

key·stroke \-ˌstrōk\ *n* **:** the act or an instance of depressing a key on a keyboard — **keystroke** *vb*

key signatures

key·way \-ˌwā\ *n* **1 :** a groove or channel for a key **2 :** the aperture for the key in a lock having a flat metal key

key word *n* **:** a word that is a key: as **a :** a word exemplifying the meaning or value of a letter or symbol **b** *usu* **key·word :** a significant word from a title or document that is used as an index to content

kg *abbr* **1** keg **2** kilogram **3** king

KG *abbr* **1** kilogauss **2** knight of the Order of the Garter

KGB *abbr* [Russ *Komitet Gosudarstvennoye Bezopastnosti*] (Soviet) State Security Committee

KGPS *abbr* kilograms per second

khad·dar \ˈkäd-ər\ *or* **kha·di** \ˈkäd-ē\ *n* [Hindi *khādar, khādī*] **:** homespun cotton cloth of India

kha·ki \ˈkak-ē, ˈkäk-, *in Canada often* ˈkärk-\ *n* [Hindi *khākī* dust-colored, fr. *khāk* dust, fr. Per] **1 a :** a khaki-colored cloth made usu. of cotton or wool and used esp. for military uniforms **b :** a garment of this cloth; *esp* **:** a military uniform **2 :** a light yellowish brown — **khaki** *adj*

1, keystone 1

Khal·kha \ˈkal-kə\ *n* **1 :** a member of a Mongol people of Outer Mongolia **2 :** the language of the Khalkha people used as the official language of the Mongolian People's Republic

kham·sin \kam-ˈsēn\ *n* [Ar *rīḥ al-khamsīn* the wind of the fifty (days between Easter and Pentecost)] **:** a hot southerly Egyptian wind coming from the Sahara

1khan \ˈkän, ˈkan\ *n* [ME *caan,* fr. MF, of Turkic origin; akin to Turk *han* prince] **1 :** a medieval sovereign of China and ruler over the Turkish, Tatar, and Mongol tribes **2 :** a local chieftain or man of rank in some countries of central Asia — **khan·ate** \-ˌāt\ *n*

2khan *n* [Ar *khān*] **:** a caravansary or rest house in some Asian countries

khap·ra beetle \ˌkap-rə-, ˌkäp-\ *n* [Hindi *khaprā,* lit., destroyer] **:** a dermestid beetle (*Trogoderma granarium*) that is native to the Indian subcontinent and is now a serious pest of stored grain in most parts of the world

khat *var of* KAT

khe·dive \kə-ˈdēv\ *n* [F *khédive,* fr. Turk *hidiv*] **:** a ruler of Egypt from 1867 to 1914 governing as a viceroy of the sultan of Turkey — **khe·div·al** \-ˈdē-vəl\ *or* **khe·div·i·al** \-ˈdē-vē-əl\ *adj*

Khmer \kə-ˈme(ə)r\ *n, pl* **Khmer** *or* **Khmers 1 :** a member of an aboriginal people of Cambodia **2 :** the Mon-Khmer language of the Khmer people that is the official language of Cambodia — **Khmer·ian** \-ˈmer-ē-ən\ *adj*

Khoi·san \ˈkȯi-ˌsän\ *n* **1 :** a group of African peoples speaking Khoisan languages **2 :** a subfamily of African languages comprising Hottentot and the several languages known as Bushman

Kho·war \ˈkō-ˌwär\ *n* **:** a Dard language of northwest Pakistan

kHz *abbr* kilohertz

KIA *abbr* killed in action

ki·ang \kē-ˈäŋ\ *n* [Tibetan *rkyaṅ*] **:** an Asiatic wild ass (*Equus hemionus*) usu. with reddish back and sides and white underparts, muzzle, and legs

kiaugh \ˈkyäk\ *n* [prob. fr. ScGael *cabhag*] *Scot* **:** TROUBLE, ANXIETY

1kib·ble \ˈkib-əl\ *vt* **kib·bled; kib·bling** \-(ə-)liŋ\ [origin unknown] **:** to grind coarsely <*kibbled* dog biscuit> <*kibbled* grain>

2kibble *n* **:** coarsely ground meal or grain

kib·butz \kib-ˈu̇ts, -ˈüts\ *n, pl* **kib·but·zim** \-ˌu̇t-ˈsēm, -ˌüt-\ [NHeb *qibbūṣ*] **:** a collective farm or settlement in Israel

kib·butz·nik \-ˈu̇t-snik, -ˈüt-\ *n* [Yiddish, fr. *kibbutz* (fr. Heb *qibbūṣ*) + *-nik*] **:** a member of a kibbutz

kibe \ˈkīb\ *n* [ME] **:** an ulcerated chilblain esp. on the heel

ki·bitz \ˈkib-əts, kə-ˈbits\ *vb* [Yiddish *kibitsen,* fr. G *kiebitzen,* fr. *kiebitz,* lit., pewit] *vi* **:** to act as a kibitzer ~ *vt* **:** to observe as a kibitzer; *esp* **:** to be a kibitzer at <~ a card game>

ki·bitz·er \ˈkib-ət-sər, kə-ˈbit-\ *n* **:** one who looks on and often offers unwanted advice or comment esp. at a card game

ki·bosh \ˈkī-ˌbäsh, kī-ˈ; kib-ˈäsh\ *n* [origin unknown] **:** something that serves as a check or stop <put the ~ on that> — **kibosh** *vt*

1kick \ˈkik\ *vb* [ME *kiken*] *vi* **1 a :** to strike out with the foot or feet **b :** to make a kick in football **2 a :** to show opposition : RESIST, REBEL **b :** to protest strenuously or urgently : express grave discontent; *broadly* **:** COMPLAIN **3** *of a firearm* **:** to recoil when fired **4 :** to go from one place to another as circumstance or whim dictates ~ *vt* **1 a :** to strike, thrust, or hit with the foot **b :** to strike suddenly and forcefully as if with the foot **2 :** to score by kicking a ball **3** *slang* **:** to free oneself of (a drug habit) *syn* see OBJECT — **kick over the traces :** to cast off restraint, authority, or control — **kick the bucket :** DIE — **kick up one's heels 1 :** to show sudden delight **2 :** to have a lively time — **kick upstairs :** to promote to a higher but less desirable position

2kick *n* **1 a :** a blow or sudden forceful thrust with the foot; *specif* **:** a sudden propelling of a ball with the foot **b :** the power to kick **c :** a rhythmic motion of the legs used in swimming **d :** a burst of speed in racing **2 :** a sudden forceful jolt or thrust suggesting a kick; *specif* **:** the recoil of a gun **3 a :** a feeling or expression of opposition or objection <all sorts of ~*s* against the administra-

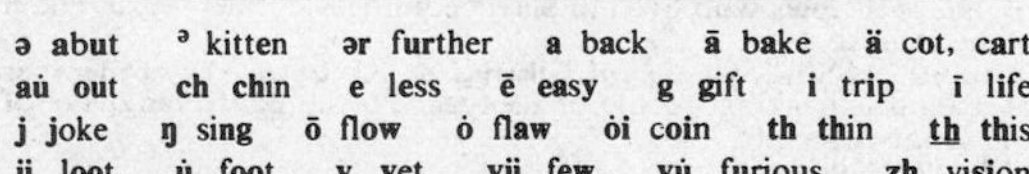
ə abut ᵊ kitten ər further a back ā bake ä cot, cart
au̇ out ch chin e less ē easy g gift i trip ī life
j joke ŋ sing ō flow ȯ flaw ȯi coin th thin t͟h this
ü loot u̇ foot y yet yü few yu̇ furious zh vision

tion> **b** : the grounds for objection **4 a** : a stimulating or pleasurable effect or experience **b** : pursuit of an absorbing or obsessive new interest <went on a mystery-reading ~ —*Time*> **5** : a sudden and striking surprise, revelation, or turn of events : TWIST

kick around *vt* **1** : to treat in an inconsiderate or high-handed fashion **2** : to consider, examine, or discuss from various angles

kick·back \ˈkik-ˌbak\ *n* **1** : a sharp violent reaction **2** : a return of a part of a sum received often because of confidential agreement or coercion <appointees paid a ~ to the ward boss out of each paycheck>

kick·er *n* **1** : one that kicks or kicks something **2** : KICK 5

kick in *vt* : CONTRIBUTE ~ *vi* **1** *slang* : DIE **2** : to make a contribution

kick·off \ˈkik-ˌȯf\ *n* **1** : a kick that puts the ball into play in a football or soccer game **2** : COMMENCEMENT 1

kick off *vi* **1** : to start or resume play in football by a placekick **2** : to begin proceedings **3** *slang* : DIE ~ *vt* : to mark the beginning of

kick out *vt* : to dismiss or eject forcefully or summarily

kick over *vi* : to begin to fire — used of an internal-combustion engine ~ *vt* : to cause (an internal-combustion engine) to turn over and usu. begin to fire

kick·shaw \ˈkik-ˌshȯ\ *n* [by folk etymology fr. F *quelque chose* something] **1** : a fancy dish : DELICACY **2** : BAUBLE, GEWGAW

kick·stand \ˈkik-ˌstand\ *n* [fr. its being put in position by a kick] : a swiveling metal bar or rod for holding up a 2-wheeled vehicle when not in use

kick turn *n* : a standing half turn in skiing made by swinging one ski high with a jerk and planting it in the desired direction and then lifting the other ski into a parallel position

kick·up \ˈkik-ˌəp\ *n* : a noisy quarrel : ROW

kick up \(ˈ)kik-ˈəp\ *vt* **1** : to cause to rise upward <clouds of dust *kicked up* by passing cars> **2** : to stir up : PROVOKE <*kick up* a fuss> ~ *vi* : to give evidence of disorder

¹kid \ˈkid\ *n* [ME *kide*, of Scand origin; akin to ON *kith* kid] **1 a** : a young goat **b** : a young individual of various animals related to the goat **2 a** : the flesh, fur, or skin of a kid **b** : something made of kid **3** : a young person : CHILD — **kid·dish** \ˈkid-ish\ *adj*

²kid *vi* **kid·ded; kid·ding** : to bring forth young — used of a goat or an antelope

³kid *vb* **kid·ded; kid·ding** [prob. fr. ¹*kid*] *vt* **1** : to deceive as a joke : FOOL <it's the truth; I wouldn't ~ you> **2** : to make fun of : TEASE ~ *vi* : to engage in good-humored fooling or horseplay : JOKE — often used with *around* — **kid·der** *n* — **kid·ding·ly** \ˈkid-iŋ-lē\ *adv*

Kid·der·min·ster \ˈkid-ər-ˌmin(t)-stər\ *n* [*Kidderminster*, England] : an ingrain carpet

kid·die *or* **kid·dy** \ˈkid-ē\ *n, pl* **kiddies** [¹*kid*] : a small child

kid·dush \ˈkid-əsh, -ish; kid-ˈüsh\ *n* [LHeb *qiddūsh* sanctification] : a ceremonial blessing pronounced over wine or bread in a Jewish home or synagogue on a sabbath or other holy day

kiddush ha·shem \-hə-ˈshām\ *n, often cap K & H* [LHeb *qiddūsh hash-shēm* sanctification of the name (of God)] : an act of moral uprightness or religious heroism that reflects credit on a Jew's commitment to Judaism; *specif* : martyrdom in the cause of Judaism

kid glove *n* : a dress glove made of kid leather — **kid–gloved** \ˈkid-ˈgləvd\ *adj* — **with kid gloves** : with special consideration

kid leather *n* **1** : a soft pliable leather made from kidskin **2** : a glove leather made from lambskin or goatskin

kid·nap \ˈkid-ˌnap\ *vt* **-napped** *or* **-naped** \-ˌnapt\; **-nap·ping** *or* **-nap·ing** [prob. back-formation fr. *kidnapper*, fr. *kid* + obs. *napper* (thief)] : to seize and detain or carry away by unlawful force or fraud and often with a demand for ransom — **kid·nap·per** *or* **kid·nap·er** *n*

kid·ney \ˈkid-nē\ *n, pl* **kidneys** [ME] **1 a** : one of a pair of vertebrate organs situated in the body cavity near the spinal column that excrete waste products of metabolism, in man are bean-shaped organs about 4½ inches long lying behind the peritoneum in a mass of fatty tissue, and consist chiefly of nephrons by which urine is secreted, collected, and discharged into a main cavity whence it is conveyed by the ureter to the bladder **b** : any of various excretory organs of invertebrate animals **2** : the kidney of an animal eaten as food by man **3** : sort or kind esp. with regard to temperament <a nice helpful guy, of a different ~ entirely from the ubiquitous Secret Police functionaries —Paula Lecler>

kidney bean *n* **1** : an edible and nutritious seed of any cultivated bean of the common species (*Phaseolus vulgaris*); *esp* : a large dark-red bean seed **2** : a plant bearing kidney beans

kidney stone *n* : a calculus in the kidney

kid·skin \ˈkid-ˌskin\ *n* : the skin of a young or sometimes a mature goat; *also* : KID LEATHER

kid stuff *n* **1** : something befitting or appropriate only to children **2** : something extremely simple or easy

kiel·ba·sa \k(y)el-ˈbäs-ə, kil-\ *n, pl* **-basas** *also* **-ba·sy** \-ˈbäs-ē\ [Pol *kiełbasa*; akin to Russ *kolbasa* sausage] : a smoked sausage of Polish origin

kie·sel·guhr *or* **kie·sel·gur** \ˈkē-zəl-ˌgü(ə)r\ *n* [G *kieselgur*] : loose or porous diatomite

kie·ser·ite \ˈkē-zə-ˌrīt\ *n* [G *kieserit*, fr. Dietrich *Kieser* †1862 G physician] : a mineral $MgSO_4H_2O$ that is a white hydrous magnesium sulfate

kif \ˈkif, ˈkēf\ *var of* KEF

kike \ˈkīk\ *n* [prob. alter. of *kiki*, redupl. of *-ki* common ending of names of Jews who lived in Slavic countries] : JEW — usu. taken to be offensive

Ki·ku·yu \ki-ˈkü-(ˌ)yü\ *n, pl* **Kikuyu** *or* **Kikuyus** **1** : a member of a Bantu-speaking people of Kenya **2** : the Bantu language of the Kikuyu people

Kild *abbr* Kildare

kil·der·kin \ˈkil-dər-kən\ *n* [ME, fr. MD *kindekijn*, fr. ML *quintale* quintal] **1** : CASK **2** : an English unit of capacity equal to ½ barrel

Kilk *abbr* Kilkenny

¹kill \ˈkil\ *vb* [ME *killen*] *vt* **1 a** : to deprive of life **b** (1) : to slaughter (as a hog) for food (2) : to convert a food animal into (as pork) by slaughtering **2 a** : to put an end to <~ competition> **b** : DEFEAT, VETO **c** : to mark for omission **3 a** : to destroy the vital or essential quality of <~*ed* the pain with drugs> **b** : to cause to stop <~ the motor> **c** : to check the flow of current through **4** : to cause to elapse <~ time> **5 a** : to cause extreme pain to **b** : to tire almost to the point of collapse **6** : to hit (a ball) so hard in a racket game that a return is impossible **7** : to consume (as a drink) totally ~ *vi* : to deprive one of life

syn KILL, SLAY, MURDER, ASSASSINATE, DISPATCH, EXECUTE *shared meaning element* : to deprive of life

²kill *n* **1** : an act or instance of killing **2** : something killed: as **a** (1) : an animal shot in a hunt (2) : animals killed in a hunt, season, or particular period of time **b** : an enemy airplane, submarine, or ship destroyed by military action **c** : a return shot in a racket game that is too hard for an opponent to handle

³kill *n, often cap* [D *kil*] : CHANNEL, CREEK — used chiefly in place names in Delaware and New York

kill·deer \ˈkil-ˌdi(ə)r\ *n, pl* **killdeers** *or* **killdeer** [imit.] : a plover (*Charadrius vociferus* syn. *Oxyechus vociferus*) of temperate No. America characterized by a plaintive penetrating cry

kill·er \ˈkil-ər\ *n* **1** : one that kills **2** : KILLER WHALE

killer whale *n* : a carnivorous gregarious largely black whale (*Orcinus orca* syn. *Orca orca*) 20 to 30 feet long

killer whale

kil·lick \ˈkil-ik\ *n* [origin unknown] : a small anchor; *also* : an anchor formed by a stone usu. enclosed by pieces of wood

kil·li·fish \ˈkil-ē-ˌfish\ *n* [*killie* (killifish) + *fish*] **1** : any of numerous small oviparous fishes (family Cyprinodontidae) much used as bait and in mosquito control **2** : TOPMINNOW 1

¹kill·ing \ˈkil-iŋ\ *n* **1** : the act of one that kills **2** : KILL 2a **3** : a sudden notable gain or profit

²killing *adj* **1** : that kills or relates to killing **2** : highly amusing

kill·joy \ˈkil-ˌjȯi\ *n* : one who spoils the pleasure of others

kill off *vt* : to destroy in large numbers or totally <hunters *killed* the buffalo *off* rapidly until only a few were left>

¹kiln \ˈkiln, ˈkil\ *n* [ME *kilne*, fr. OE *cyln*, fr. L *culina* kitchen, fr. *coquere* to cook — more at COOK] : an oven, furnace, or heated enclosure used for processing a substance by burning, firing, or drying

²kiln *vt* : to process in a kiln

ki·lo \ˈkē-(ˌ)lō\ *n, pl* **kilos** **1** : KILOGRAM **2** : KILOMETER

Kilo — a communications code word for the letter *k*

kilo- *comb form* [F, modif. of Gk *chilioi* — more at MILE] : thousand <*kiloton*>

ki·lo·bar \ˈkē-lə-ˌbär, ˈkil-ə-\ *n* [ISV] : a unit of pressure equal to 1000 bars

ki·lo·bit \-ˌbit\ *n* [ISV] : 1000 bits

ki·lo·cal·o·rie \-ˌkal-(ə-)rē\ *n* [ISV] : CALORIE 1b

ki·lo·cu·rie \-ˌkyu̇(ə)r-(ˌ)ē, -kyu̇-ˌrē\ *n* [ISV] : 1000 curies

kilo·cy·cle \ˈkil-ə-ˌsī-kəl\ *n* [ISV] : 1000 cycles; *esp* : 1000 cycles per second

ki·lo·gauss \ˈkē-lə-ˌgau̇s, ˈkil-ə-\ *n* [ISV] : 1000 gauss

ki·lo·gram \ˈkē-lə-ˌgram, ˈkil-ə-\ *n* [F *kilogramme*, fr. *kilo-* + *gramme* gram] **1** : the basic metric unit of mass and weight equal to the mass of a platinum-iridium cylinder kept at the International Bureau of Weights and Measures near Paris and nearly equal to 1000 cubic centimeters of water at the temperature of its maximum density — see METRIC SYSTEM table **2** : a unit of force equal to the weight of a kilogram mass under a gravitational attraction of approximately 980.1 centimeters per second per second

kilogram calorie *n* : CALORIE 1b

kilogram–meter *n* : the mks gravitational unit of work and energy equal to the work done by a kilogram force acting through a distance of one meter in the direction of the force : about 7.235 foot-pounds

ki·lo·hertz \ˈkil-ə-ˌhərts, ˈkē-lə-, -ˌhe(ə)rts\ *n* [ISV] : 1000 hertz

kilo·li·ter \ˈkil-ə-ˌlēt-ər\ *n* [F *kilolitre*, fr. *kilo-* + *litre* liter] — see METRIC SYSTEM table

ki·lo·me·ter \kil-ˈäm-ət-ər (*not parallel with other metric-system compounds*), ˈkil-ə-ˌmēt-\ *n* [F *kilomètre*, fr. *kilo-* + *mètre* meter] — see METRIC SYSTEM table

ki·lo·oer·sted \ˈkē-lō-ˌər-stəd, ˈkil-ō-, -ˌȯr-\ *n* [ISV] : 1000 oersteds

ki·lo·par·sec \-ˌpär-ˌsek\ *n* : 1000 parsecs

ki·lo·rad \-ˌrad\ *n* [ISV] : 1000 rads

ki·lo·ton \-ˌtən\ *n* **1** : 1000 tons **2** : an explosive force equivalent to that of 1000 tons of TNT

ki·lo·volt \-ˌvōlt\ *n* [ISV] : a unit of potential difference equal to 1000 volts

kilo·watt \ˈkil-ə-ˌwät\ *n* [ISV] : 1000 watts

kilowatt–hour *n* : a unit of work or energy equal to that expended by one kilowatt in one hour

¹kilt \ˈkilt\ *vb* [ME *kilten*, of Scand origin; akin to ON *kjalta* fold of a gathered skirt] *vt* **1** *chiefly dial* : to tuck up (as a skirt) **2** : to equip with a kilt ~ *vi* : to move nimbly

²kilt *n* **1** : a knee-length pleated skirt usu. of tartan worn by men in Scotland and by Scottish regiments in the British armies **2** : a garment that resembles a Scottish kilt

kil·ter \ˈkil-tər\ *n* [origin unknown] : proper condition : ORDER <out of ~>

Kim·bun·du \kim-ˈbu̇n-(ˌ)dü\ *n* : a Bantu language of northern Angola

ki·mo·no \kə-ˈmō-nə *also* -(ˌ)nō\ *n, pl* **-nos** [Jap, clothes] **1 :** a loose robe with wide sleeves and a broad sash traditionally worn as an outer garment by the Japanese **2 :** a loose dressing gown worn chiefly by women

kimono 1

[1]**kin** \ˈkin\ *n* [ME, fr. OE *cyn;* akin to OHG *chunni* race, L *genus* birth, race, kind, Gk *genos,* L *gignere* to beget, Gk *gignesthai* to be born] **1 :** a group of persons of common ancestry **:** CLAN **2 a :** one's relatives **:** KINDRED **b :** KINSMAN <he wasn't any ~ to you —Jean Stafford> **3** *archaic* **:** KINSHIP

[2]**kin** *adj* **:** KINDRED, RELATED

Kin *abbr* Kinross-shire

-kin \kən\ *also* **-kins** \kənz\ *n suffix* [ME, fr. MD *-kin;* akin to OHG *-chīn,* dim. suffix] **:** little <cat*kin*> <baby*kins*>

ki·nase \ˈkī-ˌnās, -ˌnāz\ *n* [ISV, fr. *kinetic*] **:** an enzyme that catalyzes the transfer of phosphate groups from ATP or ADP to a substrate

Kinc *abbr* Kincardineshire

[1]**kind** \ˈkīnd\ *n* [ME *kinde,* fr. OE *cynd;* akin to OE *cyn* kin] **1 a** *archaic* **:** NATURE **b** *archaic* **:** FAMILY, LINEAGE **2** *archaic* **:** MANNER **3 :** fundamental nature or quality **:** ESSENCE **4 a :** a group united by common traits or interests **:** CATEGORY <biting insects with habits characteristic of their ~> **b :** a specific or recognized variety <what ~ of car do you drive> **c :** a doubtful or barely admissible member of a category <a ~ of gray> **5 a :** goods or commodities as distinguished from money <payment in ~ rather than in cash> **b :** the equivalent of what has been offered or received ***syn*** see TYPE — **all kinds of 1 :** MANY <likes *all kinds of* sports> **2 :** plenty of <has *all kinds of* time to get there>

[2]**kind** *adj* **1** *chiefly dial* **:** AFFECTIONATE, LOVING **2 a :** of a sympathetic nature **:** disposed to be helpful and solicitous **b :** of a forbearing nature **:** GENTLE **c :** arising from or characterized by sympathy or forbearance <a ~ act> **3 :** of a kind to give pleasure or relief **:** AGREEABLE

syn KIND, KINDLY, BENIGN, BENIGNANT *shared meaning element* **:** showing or having a gentle considerate nature ***ant*** unkind

kin·der·gar·ten \ˈkin-də(r)-ˌgärt-ᵊn, -ˌgärd-\ *n* [G, fr. *kinder* children + *garten* garden] **:** a school or class for children usu. from four to six years old

kin·der·gart·ner \-ˌgärt-nər\ *n* **1 :** a child attending or of an age to attend kindergarten **2 :** a teacher at a kindergarten

kind·heart·ed \ˈkīnd-ˈhärt-əd\ *adj* **:** marked by a sympathetic nature — **kind·heart·ed·ly** *adv* — **kind·heart·ed·ness** *n*

[1]**kin·dle** \ˈkin-dᵊl\ *vb* **kin·dled; kin·dling** \-(d)liŋ, -dᵊl-iŋ\ [ME *kindlen,* fr. ON *kynda;* akin to OHG *cuntesal* fire] *vt* **1 :** to start (a fire) burning **:** LIGHT **2 :** to stir up **:** AROUSE **3 :** to cause to glow **:** ILLUMINATE ~ *vi* **1 :** to catch fire **2 a :** to flare up **b :** to become animated **3 :** to become illuminated ***syn*** see LIGHT — **kin·dler** \-(d)lər, -dᵊl-ər\ *n*

[2]**kindle** *vb* **kin·dled; kin·dling** [ME *kindlen*] *vt* **:** BEAR — used esp. of a rabbit ~ *vi* **:** to bring forth young — used esp. of a rabbit

kind·less \ˈkīn-(d)ləs\ *adj* **1** *obs* **:** INHUMAN **2 :** DISAGREEABLE, UNCONGENIAL — **kind·less·ly** *adv*

kind·li·ness \ˈkīn-(d)lē-nəs\ *n* **1 :** the quality or state of being kindly **2 :** a kindly deed

kin·dling \ˈkin-(d)liŋ, ˈkin-lən\ *n* **:** easily combustible material for starting a fire

[1]**kind·ly** \ˈkīn-(d)lē\ *adj* **kind·li·er; -est 1 a** *obs* **:** NATURAL **b** *archaic* **:** LAWFUL **2 :** of an agreeable or beneficial nature **:** PLEASANT <~ climate> **3 :** of a sympathetic or generous nature **:** FRIENDLY <~ men> ***syn*** see KIND ***ant*** unkindly, acrid (*as of attitudes, comments*)

[2]**kindly** *adv* **1 a :** in the normal way **:** NATURALLY <old wounds which had healed ~ —*Amer. Mercury*> **b :** READILY <did not take ~ to suggestions> **2 a :** in a kind manner **:** SYMPATHETICALLY **b :** as a gesture of goodwill <would take it ~ if you would put in a good word for the boy> **c :** in a gracious manner **:** COURTEOUSLY, OBLIGINGLY <~ fill out the attached questionnaire>

kind·ness \ˈkīn(d)-nəs\ *n* **1 :** a kind deed **:** FAVOR **2 a :** the quality or state of being kind **b** *archaic* **:** AFFECTION

kind of \ˌkīn-də(v)\ *adv* **:** to a moderate degree **:** SOMEWHAT <it's *kind of* late to begin>

[1]**kin·dred** \ˈkin-drəd\ *n* [ME, fr. *kin* + OE *rǣden* condition, fr. *rǣdan* to advise, read] **1 a :** a group of related individuals **b :** one's relatives **2 :** family relationship **:** KINSHIP

[2]**kindred** *adj* **1 :** of a similar nature or character **:** LIKE **2 :** of the same ancestry ***syn*** see RELATED

kine \ˈkīn\ *archaic pl of* COW

kin·e·ma \ˈkin-ə-mə\ *Brit var of* CINEMA

ki·ne·mat·ics \ˌkin-ə-ˈmat-iks, ˌkī-nə-\ *n pl but sing in constr* [F *cinématique,* fr. Gk *kinēmat-, kinēma* motion — more at CINEMATOGRAPH] **:** a branch of dynamics that deals with aspects of motion apart from considerations of mass and force — **ki·ne·mat·ic** \-ik\ *or* **ki·ne·mat·i·cal** \-i-kəl\ *adj* — **ki·ne·mat·i·cal·ly** \-i-k(ə-)lē\ *adv*

[1]**kin·e·scope** \ˈkin-ə-ˌskōp, ˈkī-nə-\ *n* [fr. *Kinescope,* a trademark] **1 :** PICTURE TUBE **2 :** a motion picture made from an image on a picture tube

[2]**kinescope** *vt* **-scoped; -scop·ing :** to make a kinescope of

ki·ne·sics \kə-ˈnē-siks, kī-, -ziks\ *n pl but sing in constr* [Gk *kinēsis* + E *-ics*] **:** a systematic study of the relationship between nonlinguistic body motions (as blushes, shrugs, or eye movement) and communication

ki·ne·si·ol·o·gy \kə-ˌnē-sē-ˈäl-ə-jē, kī-, -zē-\ *n* [Gk *kinēsis* motion] **:** the study of the principles of mechanics and anatomy in relation to human movement

ki·ne·sis \kə-ˈnē-səs, kī-\ *n, pl* **ki·ne·ses** \-ˌsēz\ [NL, fr. Gk *kinēsis* motion] **:** a movement that lacks directional orientation and depends upon the intensity of stimulation

-ki·ne·sis \kə-ˈnē-səs, (ˌ)kī-\ *n comb form, pl* **-ki·ne·ses** \-ˈnē-ˌsēz\ [NL, fr. Gk *kinēsis* motion, fr. *kinein* to move — more at HIGHT] **:** division <karyo*kinesis*>

kin·es·the·sia \ˌkin-əs-ˈthē-zh(ē-)ə, ˌkī-nəs-\ *or* **kin·es·the·sis** \-ˈthē-səs\ *n, pl* **-the·sias** *or* **-the·ses** \-ˌsēz\ [NL, fr. Gk *kinein* + *aisthēsis* perception — more at ANESTHESIA] **:** a sense mediated by end organs located in muscles, tendons, and joints and stimulated by bodily movements and tensions; *also* **:** sensory experience derived from this sense — **kin·es·thet·ic** \-ˈthet-ik\ *adj* — **kin·es·thet·i·cal·ly** \-i-k(ə-)lē\ *adv*

kinet- *or* **kineto-** *comb form* [Gk *kinētos* moving] **:** movement **:** motion <*kineto*genic>

ki·net·ic \kə-ˈnet-ik, kī-\ *adj* [Gk *kinētikos,* fr. *kinētos* moving, fr. *kinein*] **1 :** of or relating to the motion of material bodies and the forces and energy associated therewith **2 a :** ACTIVE, LIVELY **b :** DYNAMIC, ENERGIZING

kinetic art *n* **:** art (as sculpture or assemblage) having mechanical parts which can be set in motion (as by a motor) — **kinetic artist** *n*

kinetic energy *n* **:** energy associated with motion

ki·net·i·cist \kə-ˈnet-ə-səst, kī-\ *n* **1 :** a specialist in kinetics **2 :** one who works in kinetic art **:** KINETIC ARTIST

kinetic potential *n* **:** LAGRANGIAN

ki·net·ics \kə-ˈnet-iks, kī-\ *n pl but sing or pl in constr* **1 a :** a branch of science that deals with the effects of forces upon the motions of material bodies or with changes in a physical or chemical system **b :** the rate of change in such a system **2 :** the mechanism by which a physical or chemical change is effected

kinetic theory *n* **:** either of two theories in physics based on the fact that the minute particles of a substance are in vigorous motion: **a :** a theory that the particles of a gas move in straight lines with high average velocity, continually encounter one another and thus change their individual velocities and directions, and cause pressure by their impact against the walls of a container — called also *kinetic theory of gases* **b :** a theory that the temperature of a substance increases with an increase in either the average kinetic energy of the particles or the average potential energy of separation (as in fusion) of the particles or in both when heat is added — called also *kinetic theory of heat*

ki·ne·tin \ˈkī-nə-tən\ *n* [*kinet-* + *-in*] **:** a plant growth substance that increases mitosis and callus formation

ki·net·o·chore \kə-ˈnet-ə-ˌkō(ə)r, kī-, -ˌkȯ(ə)r\ *n* [*kinet-* + Gk *chōros* place] **:** CENTROMERE

ki·neto·nu·cle·us \kə-ˌnet-ō-ˈn(y)ü-klē-əs, kī-\ *n* [NL, fr. Gk *kinētos* + NL *nucleus*] **:** KINETOPLAST

ki·neto·plast \kə-ˈnet-ə-ˌplast, kī-\ *n* [ISV] **:** an extranuclear cell organelle esp. of trypanosomes that contains DNA and has some mitochondrial characteristics — **ki·neto·plas·tic** \-ˌnet-ə-ˈplas-tik\ *adj*

ki·neto·scope \kə-ˈnet-ə-ˌskōp, kī-\ *n* [fr. *Kinetoscope,* a trademark] **:** a device for viewing through a magnifying lens a sequence of pictures on an endless band of film moved continuously over a light source and a rapidly rotating shutter that creates an illusion of motion

ki·neto·some \-ˌsōm\ *n* **:** BASAL BODY

kin·folk \ˈkin-ˌfōk\ *or* **kinfolks** *n pl* **:** RELATIVES

king \ˈkiŋ\ *n* [ME, fr. OE *cyning;* akin to OHG *kuning* king, OE *cyn* kin] **1 a :** a male monarch of a major territorial unit; *esp* **:** one who inherits his position and rules for life **b :** a paramount chief **2** *cap* **:** GOD, CHRIST **3 :** one that holds a preeminent position; *esp* **:** a chief among competitors **4 :** the principal piece of each color in a set of chessmen having the power to move ordinarily one square in any direction and to capture opposing men but being obliged never to enter or remain in check **5 :** a playing card that is marked with a stylized figure of a king **6 :** a checker that has been crowned

king·bird \-ˌbərd\ *n* **:** any of various American tyrant flycatchers (genus *Tyrannus*)

king·bolt \-ˌbōlt\ *n* **:** a vertical bolt by which the forward axle and wheels of a vehicle or the trucks of a railroad car are connected with the other parts

King Charles spaniel \kiŋ-ˌchärlz-\ *n* [*Charles* II of England] **:** a dog of a black and tan variety of the English toy spaniel

king cobra *n* **:** a large venomous elapid snake (*Naja hannah*) of southeastern Asia and the Philippines — called also *hamadryad*

king crab *n* **1 :** HORSESHOE CRAB **2 :** any of several very large crabs

king·craft \ˈkiŋ-ˌkraft\ *n* **:** the art of governing as a king

king·cup \-ˌkəp\ *n* **:** any of various buttercups

king·dom \ˈkiŋ-dəm\ *n* **1** *archaic* **:** KINGSHIP **2 :** a politically organized community or major territorial unit having a monarchical form of government headed by a king or queen **3** *often cap* **a :** the eternal kingship of God **b :** the realm in which God's will is fulfilled **4 a :** a realm or region in which something is dominant **b :** an area or sphere in which one holds a preeminent position **5 :** one of the three primary divisions into which natural objects are commonly classified — compare ANIMAL KINGDOM, MINERAL KINGDOM, PLANT KINGDOM

king·fish \ˈkiŋ-ˌfish\ *n* **1 a :** any of several marine croakers (family Sciaenidae and esp. genus *Menticirrhus*) **b :** any of various scombroid fishes; *esp* **:** CERO **c :** any of various marine percoid fishes (as of the family Carangidae) **2 :** an undisputed master in an area or group

king·fish·er \-ˌfish-ər\ *n* **:** any of numerous nonpasserine birds (family Alcedinidae) that are usu. crested and bright-colored with a short tail and a long stout sharp bill

King James Version \kiŋ-ˈjāmz-\ *n* [*James* I of England] : AUTHORIZED VERSION

king·let \ˈkiŋ-lət\ *n* **1 :** a weak or petty king **2 :** any of several small birds (genus *Regulus*) that resemble warblers but have some of the habits of titmice

king·ly \ˈkiŋ-lē\ *adj* **king·li·er; -est 1 :** having royal rank **2 :** of, relating to, or befitting a king **3 :** MONARCHICAL — **king·li·ness** *n* — **kingly** *adv*

king mackerel *n* **:** a cero (*Scomberomorus cavalla*) that is noted esp. as a fighting sport fish

king·mak·er \ˈkiŋ-ˌmā-kər\ *n* **:** one having great influence over the choice of candidates for political office

king of arms : an officer of arms of the highest rank

king·pin \ˈkiŋ-ˌpin\ *n* **1 :** any of several bowling pins: as **a :** HEADPIN **b :** the number 5 pin **2 :** the chief person in a group or undertaking **3 a :** KINGBOLT **b :** a pin connecting the two parts of a knuckle joint

king post *n* **:** a vertical member connecting the apex of a triangular truss (as of a roof) with the base

Kings \ˈkiŋz\ *n pl but sing in constr* **1 :** either of two narrative and historical books of canonical Jewish and Protestant Scripture — see BIBLE table **2 :** any of four narrative and historical books in the Roman Catholic canon of the Old Testament — see BIBLE table

King's Bench *n* **:** a division in the English superior courts system that hears civil and criminal cases

king's blue *n* **:** COBALT BLUE

King's Counsel *n* **:** a barrister selected to serve as counsel to the British crown

King's English *n* **:** standard, pure, or correct English speech or usage

king's evil *n, often cap K&E* [fr. the former belief that it could be healed by a king's touch] **:** SCROFULA

king·ship \ˈkiŋ-ˌship\ *n* **1 :** the position, office, or dignity of a king **2 :** the personality of a king **:** MAJESTY **3 :** government by a king

king·side \-ˌsīd\ *n* **:** the side of a chessboard containing the file on which the king sits at the beginning of the game

king–size \-ˌsīz\ *or* **king–sized** \-ˌsīzd\ *adj* **1 :** longer than the regular or standard size <a ~ cigarette> **2 :** unusually large **3 a :** having dimensions of approximately 76 inches by 80 inches — used of a bed; compare FULL-SIZE, QUEEN-SIZE, TWIN-SIZE **b :** of a size that fits a king-size bed <~ sheets>

king snake *n* **:** any of numerous brightly marked colubrid snakes (genus *Lampropeltis*) of the southern and central U.S. that are voracious consumers of rodents

king's yellow *n* **:** arsenic trisulfide used as a pigment

ki·nin \ˈkī-nən\ *n* [Gk *kinein* to move, stimulate + E *-in* — more at HIGHT] **1 :** any of various polypeptide hormones that are formed locally in the tissues and have their chief effect on smooth muscle **2 :** any of various plant growth factors that are related to adenine and play a part in fundamental growth processes

ki·nin·o·gen \kī-ˈnin-ə-jən\ *n* **:** an inactive precursor of a kinin — **ki·nin·o·gen·ic** \(ˌ)kī-ˌnin-ə-ˈjen-ik\ *adj*

1**kink** \ˈkiŋk\ *n* [D; akin to MLG *kinke* kink] **1 :** a short tight twist or curl caused by a doubling or winding of something upon itself **2 a :** a mental or physical peculiarity **:** ECCENTRICITY, QUIRK **b :** WHIM **3 :** a clever unusual way of doing something **4 :** a cramp in some part of the body **5 :** an imperfection likely to cause difficulties in the operation of something

2**kink** *vi* **:** to form a kink ~ *vt* **:** to make a kink in

kin·ka·jou \ˈkiŋ-kə-ˌjü\ *n* [F, of Algonquian origin; akin to Ojibwa *qwĭngwâage* wolverine] **:** a slender nocturnal arboreal carnivorous mammal (*Potos caudivolvulus,* family Procyonidae) of Mexico and Central and So. America that is about three feet long and has a long prehensile tail, large lustrous eyes, and soft woolly yellowish brown fur

kinky \ˈkiŋ-kē\ *adj* **kink·i·er; -est** [1*kink* + *-y*] **1 :** closely twisted or curled <~ hair> **2 :** FAR-OUT, OFFBEAT — **kink·i·ness** *n*

kin·ni·kin·nick *also* **kin·ni·ki·nic** \ˌkin-i-kə-ˈnik, ˈkin-i-kə-ˌ\ *n* [of Algonquian origin; akin to Natick *kinukkinuk* mixture] **:** a mixture of dried leaves and bark and sometimes tobacco smoked by the Indians and pioneers esp. in the Ohio valley; *also* **:** a plant (as a sumac or dogwood) used in it

-kins — see -KIN

kins·folk \ˈkinz-ˌfōk\ *n pl* **:** RELATIVES

kin·ship \ˈkin-ˌship\ *n* **:** the quality or state of being kin **:** RELATIONSHIP

kins·man \ˈkinz-mən\ *n* **:** RELATIVE; *specif* **:** a male relative

kins·wom·an \-ˌwu̇m-ən\ *n* **:** a female relative

ki·osk \ˈkē-ˌäsk, kē-ˈ\ *n* [Turk *kösk,* fr. Per *kūshk* portico] **1 :** an open summerhouse or pavilion **2 :** a small light structure with one or more open sides used esp. as a newsstand or a telephone booth

Ki·o·wa \ˈkī-ə-ˌwȯ, -ˌwä, -ˌwā\ *n, pl* **Kiowa** *or* **Kiowas 1 :** a member of an Amerindian people of Colorado, Kansas, New Mexico, Oklahoma, and Texas **2 :** the language of the Kiowa people

1**kip** \ˈkip\ *n* [obs. D; akin to MLG *kip* bundle of hides] **:** a bundle of undressed hides of young or small animals; *also* **:** one of the hides

2**kip** *n* [*ki*lo- + *p*ound] **:** a unit of weight equal to 1000 pounds used to express deadweight load

3**kip** \ˈkip, ˈgip\ *n, pl* **kip** *or* **kips** [Thai] — see MONEY table

1**kip·per** \ˈkip-ər\ *n* [ME *kypre,* fr. OE *cypera;* akin to OE *coper* copper] **1 :** a male salmon or sea trout during or after the spawning season **2 :** a kippered herring or salmon

2**kipper** *vt* **kip·pered; kip·per·ing** \-(ə-)riŋ\ **:** to cure (split dressed fish) by salting and smoking

Kir·ghiz \ki(ə)r-ˈgēz\ *n, pl* **Kirghiz** *or* **Kir·ghiz·es** [Kirghiz *Kyrghyz*] **1 :** a member of a people of Mongolian ancestry prob. with some Caucasian intermixture who inhabit chiefly the Central Asian steppes **2 :** the Turkic language of the Kirghiz

kirk \ˈki(ə)rk, ˈkərk\ *n* [ME (northern dial.), fr. ON *kirkja,* fr. OE *cirice* — more at CHURCH] **1** *chiefly Scot* **:** CHURCH **2** *cap* **:** the national church of Scotland as distinguished from the Church of England or the Episcopal Church in Scotland

Kirk *abbr* Kirkudbrightshire

Kir·man \kər-ˈmän, ki(ə)r-\ *n* [*Kirman,* province in Iran] **:** a Persian carpet or rug characterized by elaborate fluid designs and soft colors

kir·mess \ˈkər-məs, (ˌ)kər-ˈmes\ *var of* KERMIS

kirsch \ˈki(ə)rsh\ *n* [G, short for *kirschwasser,* fr. *kirsche* cherry + *wasser* water] **:** a dry colorless brandy distilled from the fermented juice of the black morello cherry

kir·tle \ˈkərt-ᵊl\ *n* [ME *kirtel,* fr. OE *cyrtel,* fr. (assumed) OE *curt* short, fr. L *curtus* shortened — more at SHEAR] **1 :** a tunic or coat worn by men esp. in the Middle Ages **2 :** a long gown or dress worn by women

kish·ke *also* **kish·ka** \ˈkish-kə\ *n* [Yiddish *kishke* gut, sausage, of Slavic origin; akin to Pol *kiszka* gut, sausage; akin to OE *hord* hoard] **:** beef or fowl casing stuffed (as with meat, flour, and spices) and cooked

Kis·lev \ˈkis-ləf\ *n* [Heb *Kislēw*] **:** the 3d month of the civil year or the 9th month of the ecclesiastical year in the Jewish calendar — see MONTH table

kis·met \ˈkiz-ˌmet, -mət\ *n, often cap* [Turk, fr. Ar *qismah* portion, lot] **:** FATE 1, 2a

1**kiss** \ˈkis\ *vb* [ME *kissen,* fr. OE *cyssan;* akin to OHG *kussen* to kiss] *vt* **1 :** to touch with the lips esp. as a mark of affection or greeting **2 :** to touch gently or lightly <wind gently ~*ing* the trees> ~ *vi* **1 :** to salute or caress one another with the lips **2 :** to come in gentle contact — **kiss·able** \-ə-bəl\ *adj* — **kiss good–bye :** LEAVE **2 :** to resign oneself to the loss of <you might as well *kiss* the money you loaned him *good-bye*>

2**kiss** *n* **1 :** a caress with the lips **2 :** a gentle touch or contact **3 a :** a small drop cookie made of meringue **b :** a bite-size piece of candy often wrapped in paper or foil

kiss·er \ˈkis-ər\ *n* **1 :** one that kisses **2** *slang* **a :** MOUTH **b :** FACE

kissing bug *n* **:** CONENOSE

kissing cousin *n* **:** a relative whom one knows well enough to kiss more or less formally upon meeting

kissing disease *n* [fr. the belief that it is frequently transmitted by kissing] **:** INFECTIOUS MONONUCLEOSIS

kiss of death [fr. the kiss with which Judas betrayed Jesus (Mk 14:44-46)] **:** an act or association ultimately causing ruin

kiss off *vt* **:** DISMISS <*kisses* the other performers *off* as mere amateurs>

kiss of peace : a ceremonial kiss, embrace, or handclasp used in Christian liturgies and esp. the Eucharist as a sign of fraternal unity

kist \ˈkist\ *n* [ME *kiste,* fr. ON *kista* — more at CHEST] *chiefly dial* **:** CHEST

1**kit** \ˈkit\ *n* [ME] **1** *dial Brit* **:** a wooden tub **2 a** (1) **:** a collection of articles usu. for personal use <a travel ~> (2) **:** a set of tools or implements <a carpenter's ~> (3) **:** a set of parts to be assembled <model-airplane ~> (4) **:** a packaged collection of related material <convention ~> **b :** a container for any of such sets or collections **3 :** a group of persons or things — usu. used in the phrase *the whole kit and caboodle*

2**kit** *n* [origin unknown] **:** a small narrow violin

3**kit** *n* **1 :** KITTEN **2 :** a young or undersized fur-bearing animal; *also* **:** its pelt

kit bag *n* [1*kit*] **1 :** KNAPSACK **2 :** a traveling bag with sides that fasten at the top or open to the full width of the bag

kitch·en \ˈkich-ən\ *n* [ME *kichene,* fr. OE *cycene;* akin to OHG *chuhhina* kitchen; both fr. a prehistoric WGmc word borrowed fr. LL *coquina,* fr. L *coquere* to cook — more at COOK] **1 :** a place (as a room) with cooking facilities **2 :** the personnel that prepares, cooks, and serves food

kitchen cabinet *n* **1 :** a cupboard with drawers and shelves for use in a kitchen **2 :** an informal group of advisers to the head of a government

kitch·en·ette \ˌkich-ə-ˈnet\ *n* **:** a small kitchen or an alcove containing cooking facilities

kitchen garden *n* **:** a garden in which vegetables are cultivated

kitchen midden *n* **:** a refuse heap; *specif* **:** a mound marking the site of a primitive human habitation

kitchen police *n* **1 :** enlisted men detailed to assist the cooks in a military mess **2 :** the work of kitchen police

kitch·en·ware \ˈkich-ən-ˌwa(ə)r, -ˌwe(ə)r\ *n* **:** utensils and appliances for use in a kitchen

1**kite** \ˈkīt\ *n* [ME, fr. OE *cȳta;* akin to MHG *kūze* owl, Gk *goan* to lament] **1 :** any of various hawks (family Accipitridae) with long narrow wings, a deeply forked tail, and feet adapted for taking insects and small reptiles as prey **2 :** a person who preys on others **3 :** a light frame covered with paper or cloth, often provided with a balancing tail, and designed to be flown in the air at the end of a long string **4 a :** ACCOMMODATION PAPER **b :** a check drawn against uncollected funds in a bank account or fraudulently raised before cashing **5** *pl* **:** the lightest and usu. the loftiest sails carried only in a light breeze

kite 1

2**kite** *vb* **kit·ed; kit·ing** *vi* **1 a :** to go in a rapid, carefree, or flighty manner **b :** to rise rapidly **:** SOAR <the prices of necessities continue to ~> **2 :** to get money or credit by a kite ~ *vt* **1 :** to cause to soar **2 :** to use (a kite) to get credit or money

kit fox *n* [3*kit*] **1 a :** a small fox (*Vulpes velox*) of the plains of western No. America **b :** a fox (*Vulpes macrotis*) of the southwestern U.S. and Mexico **2 :** the fur or pelt of a kit fox

kith \ˈkith\ *n* [ME, fr. OE *cȳthth,* fr. *cūth* known — more at UNCOUTH] **:** familiar friends, neighbors, or relatives <~ and kin>

kithe \'kīth\ *vb* **kithed; kith·ing** [ME *kithen,* fr. OE *cȳthan,* fr. *cūth*] *vt, chiefly Scot* : to make known ~ *vi, chiefly Scot* : to become known

kitsch \'kich\ *n* [G] : artistic or literary material designed to appeal to current popular tastes and interests — **kitschy** \-ē\ *adj*

[1]**kit·ten** \'kit-ᵊn\ *n* [ME *kitoun,* fr. (assumed) ONF *caton,* dim. of *cat,* fr. LL *cattus*] : a young cat; *also* : an immature individual of various other small mammals

[2]**kitten** *vi* **kit·tened; kit·ten·ing** \'kit-niŋ, -ᵊn-iŋ\ : to give birth to kittens

kit·ten·ish \'kit-nish, -ᵊn-ish\ *adj* : resembling a kitten; *esp* : coyly playful — **kit·ten·ish·ly** *adv* — **kit·ten·ish·ness** *n*

kit·ti·wake \'kit-ē-ˌwāk\ *n* [*imit.*] : any of various gulls (genus *Rissa*) having the hind toe short or rudimentary

[1]**kit·tle** \'kit-ᵊl\ *vt* **kit·tled; kit·tling** \'kit-liŋ, -ᵊl-iŋ\ [ME (northern dial.) *kytyllen*] **1** *chiefly Scot* : TICKLE **2** *chiefly Scot* : PERPLEX

[2]**kittle** *adj* **1** *chiefly Scot* **a** : SKITTISH **b** : APT **c** : CAPRICIOUS **2** *chiefly Scot* : TICKLISH

[1]**kit·ty** \'kit-ē\ *n, pl* **kitties** : CAT 1a; *esp* : KITTEN

[2]**kitty** *n, pl* **kitties** [[1]*kit*] **1** : a fund in a poker game made up of contributions from each pot and used (as to pay expenses or buy refreshments) for the players **2** : a sum of money or collection of goods made up of small contributions : POOL

kit·ty–cor·ner *or* **kit·ty–cor·nered** *var of* CATERCORNER

ki·va \'kē-və\ *n* [Hopi] : a Pueblo Indian ceremonial structure that is usu. round and partly underground

Ki·wa·ni·an \kə-'wän-ē-ən\ *n* [*Kiwanis* (*club*)] : a member of a major national and international service club

ki·wi \'kē-(ˌ)wē\ *n* [Maori, of imit. origin] **1** : a flightless New Zealand bird (genus *Apteryx*) with rudimentary wings, stout legs, a long bill, and grayish brown hairlike plumage **2** *cap* : a native or resident of New Zealand — used as a nickname

kiwi

KJV *abbr* King James Version

KKK *abbr* Ku Klux Klan

kl *abbr* kiloliter

Klam·ath weed \'klam-əth-\ *n* [*Klamath* (*river*)] : a cosmopolitan yellow-flowered perennial St.-John's-wort (*Hypericum perforatum*) that is often a noxious weed esp. in rangelands

Klan \'klan\ *n* [(*Ku Klux*) *Klan*] : an organization of Ku Kluxers; *also* : a subordinate unit of such an organization — **Klan·ism** \-ˌiz-əm\ *n* — **Klans·man** \'klanz-mən\ *n*

klatch *or* **klatsch** \'klach, 'kläch\ *n* [G *klatsch* gossip] : a gathering characterized by informal conversation

Klax·on \'klak-sən\ *trademark* — used for an electrically operated horn or warning signal

kleb·si·el·la \ˌkleb-zē-'el-ə\ *n* [NL, genus name, fr. Edwin *Klebs* †1913 G pathologist] : any of a genus (*Klebsiella*) of plump nonmotile gram-negative frequently encapsulated bacterial rods

Klee·nex \'klē-ˌneks\ *trademark* — used for a cleansing tissue

Klein bottle \'klīn-\ *n* [Felix *Klein* †1925 G mathematician] : a one-sided surface that is formed by passing the narrow end of a tapered tube through the side of the tube and flaring this end out to join the other end

klepht \'kleft\ *n, often cap* [NGk *klephtēs,* lit., robber, fr. Gk *kleptēs,* fr. *kleptein* to steal] : a Greek belonging to one of several independent guerrilla communities formed after the Turkish conquest of Greece — **kleph·tic** \'klef-tik\ *adj, often cap*

klept- *or* **klepto-** *comb form* [Gk, fr. *kleptein* to steal; akin to Goth *hlifan* to steal, L *clepere*] : stealing : theft <*klepto*mania>

klep·to·ma·nia \ˌklep-tə-'mā-nē-ə, -nyə\ *n* [NL] : a persistent neurotic impulse to steal esp. without economic motive

klep·to·ma·ni·ac \-nē-ˌak\ *n* : a person evidencing kleptomania

klieg eyes *or* **kleig eyes** \'klēg-\ *n pl* [*klieg* or *kleig* (*light*)] : a condition marked by conjunctivitis and watering of the eyes resulting from excessive exposure to intense light

klieg light *or* **kleig light** *n* [John H. *Kliegl* †1959 & Anton T. *Kliegl* †1927 German-born Am lighting experts] : a carbon arc lamp used in taking motion pictures

Kline·fel·ter's syndrome \'klīn-ˌfel-tərz-\ *n* [Harry F. *Klinefelter b*1912 Am physician] : an abnormal condition characterized by two X and one Y chromosomes and an infertile male phenotype with small testicles

kloof \'klüf\ *n* [Afrik] *South Africa* : a deep glen : RAVINE

kludge \'klüj\ *n* [origin unknown] : a system and esp. a computer system made up of components that are poorly matched or were orig. intended for some other use

kly·stron \'klī-ˌsträn\ *n* [fr. *Klystron,* a trademark] : an electron tube in which bunching of electrons is produced by electric fields and which is used for the generation and amplification of ultrahigh-frequency current

km *abbr* kilometer

KMPS *abbr* kilometers per second

kn *abbr* knot

knack \'nak\ *n* [ME *knak*] **1 a** : a task requiring adroitness and dexterity **b** : a clever way of doing something **c** : TRICK, STRATAGEM **2** : a special ready capacity that is hard to analyze or teach **3** *archaic* : an ingenious device; *broadly* : TOY, KNICKKNACK *syn* see GIFT

knack·er \'nak-ər\ *n* [prob. fr. E dial., saddlemaker] **1** *Brit* : a buyer of worn-out domestic animals or their carcasses for use esp. as animal food or fertilizer **2** *Brit* : a buyer of old structures for their constituent materials — **knack·ery** \'nak-ə-rē\ *n*

[1]**knap** \'nap\ *n* [ME, fr. OE *cnæp;* akin to OE *cnotta* knot] **1** *chiefly dial* : a crest of a hill : SUMMIT **2** *chiefly dial* : a small hill

[2]**knap** *vt* **knapped; knap·ping** [ME *knappen,* of imit. origin] **1** *dial Brit* : [2]RAP **2** : to break with a quick blow; *esp* : to shape (as flints) by breaking off pieces **3** *dial Brit* : SNAP, CROP **4** *dial Brit* : CHATTER — **knap·per** *n*

knap·sack \'nap-ˌsak\ *n* [LG *knappsack* or D *knapzak,* fr. LG & D *knappen* to make a snapping noise, eat + LG *sack* or D *zak* sack] : a bag (as of canvas or nylon) strapped on the back and used (as on a hike) for carrying supplies or personal belongings

knap·weed \-ˌwēd\ *n* [ME *knopwed,* fr. *knop* + *wed* weed] : any of various weedy centaureas; *esp* : a widely naturalized European perennial (*C. nigra*) with tough wiry stems and knobby heads of purple flowers

knave \'nāv\ *n* [ME, fr. OE *cnafa;* akin to OHG *knabo* boy] **1** *archaic* **a** : a boy servant **b** : a male servant **c** : a man of humble birth or position **2** : a tricky deceitful fellow : ROGUE **3** : JACK 6a

knav·ery \'nāv-(ə-)rē\ *n, pl* **-er·ies** **1 a** : the practices of a knave : RASCALITY **b** : a roguish or mischievous act **2** *obs* : roguish mischief

knav·ish \'nā-vish\ *adj* : of, relating to, or characteristic of a knave; *esp* : DISHONEST — **knav·ish·ly** *adv*

knead \'nēd\ *vt* [ME *kneden,* fr. OE *cnedan;* akin to OHG *knetan* to knead, OE *cnotta* knot] **1** : to work and press into a mass with or as if with the hands <~*ing* dough> **2** : to form or shape by or as if by kneading <~ and mold public opinion> — **knead·able** \-ə-bəl\ *adj* — **knead·er** *n*

[1]**knee** \'nē\ *n, often attrib* [ME, fr. OE *cnēow;* akin to OHG *kneo* knee, L *genu,* Gk *gony*] **1 a** : a joint in the middle part of the human leg that is the articulation between the femur, tibia, and patella; *also* : the part of the leg that includes this joint **b** (1) : the joint in the hind leg of a four-footed vertebrate that corresponds to the human knee (2) : the carpal joint of the foreleg of a four-footed vertebrate **c** : the tarsal joint of a bird **d** : the joint between the femur and tibia of an insect **2 a** : something resembling the human knee **b** : a rounded or conical process rising from the roots of various swamp-growing trees <cypress ~> **3** : the part of a garment covering the knee **4** : a blow with the bent knee — **kneed** \'nēd\ *adj* — **to one's knees** : into a state of submission or defeat <forced *to his knees* by competition>

[2]**knee** *vt* **kneed; knee·ing** **1** *archaic* : to bend the knee to **2** : to strike with the knee

knee action *n* : a front-wheel suspension of an automobile permitting independent vertical movement of each front wheel

knee·cap \'nē-ˌkap\ *n* : PATELLA

knee–deep \-'dēp\ *adj* **1** : KNEE-HIGH **2 a** : sunk to the knees <~ in mud> **b** : deeply engaged or occupied <~ in work>

knee–high \-'hī\ *adj* : rising or reaching upward to the knees

knee·hole \-ˌhōl\ *n* : an open space (as under a desk) for the knees

knee jerk *n* : an involuntary forward kick produced by a light blow on the tendon below the patella

kneel \'nē(ə)l\ *vi* **knelt** \'nelt\ *or* **kneeled; kneel·ing** [ME *knelen,* fr. OE *cnēowlian;* akin to OE *cnēow* knee] : to bend the knee : fall or rest on the knees — **kneel·er** *n*

knee·pan \'nē-ˌpan\ *n* : PATELLA

[1]**knell** \'nel\ *vb* [ME *knellen,* fr. OE *cnyllan;* akin to MHG er*knellen* to toll] *vi* **1** : to ring esp. for a death, funeral, or disaster : TOLL **2** : to sound in an ominous manner or with an ominous effect ~ *vt* : to summon, announce, or proclaim by or as if by a knell

knickers

[2]**knell** *n* **1** : a stroke or sound of a bell esp. when rung slowly (as for a death, funeral, or disaster) **2** : an indication of the end or the failure of something <this decision sounded the death ~ for our hopes>

knew *past of* KNOW

knick·er·bock·er \'nik-ə(r)-ˌbäk-ər\ *n* [Diedrich *Knickerbocker,* fictitious author of *History of New York* (1809) by Washington Irving] **1** *cap* : a descendant of the early Dutch settlers of New York; *broadly* : a native or resident of the city or state of New York — used as a nickname **2** *pl* : KNICKERS

knick·ers \'nik-ərz\ *n pl* [short for *knickerbockers*] : loose-fitting short pants gathered at the knee

knick·knack \'nik-ˌnak\ *n* [redupl. of *knack*] : a small trivial article intended for ornament

[1]**knife** \'nīf\ *n, pl* **knives** \'nīvz\ *often attrib* [ME *knif,* fr. OE *cnīf;* akin to MLG *knīf* knife, OE *cnotta* knot] **1 a** : a cutting instrument consisting of a sharp blade fastened to a handle **b** : a weapon resembling a knife **2** : a sharp cutting blade or tool in a machine — **knife·like** \'nī-ˌflīk\ *adj* — **under the knife** : undergoing surgery <was *under the knife* for 3 hours>

[2]**knife** *vb* **knifed; knif·ing** *vt* **1** : to use a knife on; *specif* : to stab, slash, or wound with a knife **2** : to cut, mark, or spread with a knife **3** : to try to defeat by underhand means **4** : to move like a knife in <prows *knifing* the water> ~ *vi* : to cut a way with or as if with a knife blade <the cruiser *knifed* through the heavy seas>

knife–edge \'nī-ˌfej\ *n* **1** : a sharp narrow knifelike edge **2** : a sharp wedge of steel or other hard material used as a fulcrum for a lever beam in a precision instrument

[1]**knight** \'nīt\ *n* [ME, fr. OE *cniht;* akin to OHG *kneht* youth, military follower, OE *cnotta* knot] **1 a** (1) : a mounted man-at-arms serving a feudal superior; *esp* : a man ceremonially inducted into special military rank usu. after completing service as page and squire (2) : a man honored by a sovereign for merit and in Great Britain ranking below a baronet (3) : a person of antiquity equal to a knight in rank **b** : a man devoted to the service of a lady as her attendant or champion **c** : a member of an order or society **2** : either of two pieces of the same color in a set of chessmen having an L-shaped move of two squares in one row and one square in a perpendicular row over squares that may be occupied

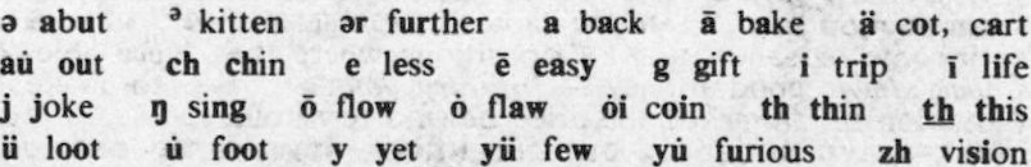

ə abut ᵊ kitten ər further a back ā bake ä cot, cart
au̇ out ch chin e less ē easy g gift i trip ī life
j joke ŋ sing ō flow ȯ flaw ȯi coin th thin th this
ü loot u̇ foot y yet yü few yu̇ furious zh vision

[2]**knight** *vt* : to make a knight of
knight bachelor *n, pl* **knights bachelors** *or* **knights bachelor** : a knight of the most ancient and lowest order of English knights
knight–er·rant \ˈnīt-ˈer-ənt\ *n, pl* **knights–errant** : a knight traveling in search of adventures in which to exhibit military skill, prowess, and generosity
knight–er·rant·ry \ˈnīt-ˈer-ən-trē\ *n, pl* **knight–errantries** 1 : the practice or actions of a knight-errant 2 : quixotic conduct
knight·hood \ˈnīt-ˌhu̇d\ *n* 1 : the rank, dignity, or profession of a knight 2 : the qualities befitting a knight : CHIVALRY 3 : knights as a class or body
knight·ly \ˈnīt-lē\ *adj* 1 : of, relating to, or characteristic of a knight 2 : made up of knights — **knight·li·ness** *n* — **knightly** *adv*
Knight of Co·lum·bus \-kə-ˈləm-bəs\ *n, pl* **Knights of Columbus** [Christopher *Columbus*] : a member of a benevolent and fraternal society of Roman Catholic men
Knight of Pyth·i·as \-ˈpith-ē-əs\ *n, pl* **Knights of Pythias** : a member of a secret benevolent and fraternal order
Knight of the Mac·ca·bees \-ˈmak-ə-ˌbēz\ *n, pl* **Knights of the Maccabees** : a member of a secret benevolent society
Knight Templar *n, pl* **Knights Templars** *or* **Knights Templar** 1 : TEMPLAR 1 2 : a member of an order of Freemasonry conferring three degrees in the York rite
knish \kə-ˈnish\ *n* [Yiddish, fr. Russ] : a small round or square of dough stuffed with a filling (as of meat, cheese, or fruit) and baked or fried
[1]**knit** \ˈnit\ *vb* **knit** *or* **knit·ted; knit·ting** [ME *knitten,* fr. OE *cnyttan;* akin to OE *cnotta* knot] *vt* 1 *chiefly dial* : to tie together 2 a : to link firmly or closely <*knitted* her hands until the knuckles blanched> b : to cause to grow together <time and rest will ~ a fractured bone> c : to contract into wrinkles <*knitted* her brow in thought> 3 : to form by interlacing yarn or thread in a series of connected loops with needles ~ *vi* 1 : to make knitted fabrics or objects 2 a : to become compact b : to grow together c : to become drawn together <closely ~ by common interests> — **knit·ter** *n*
[2]**knit** *n* : KNIT STITCH
knit stitch *n* : a basic knitting stitch usu. made with the yarn at the back of the work by inserting the right needle into the front part of a loop on the left needle from the left side, catching the yarn with the point of the right needle, and bringing it through the first loop to form a new loop — compare PURL STITCH
knit·ting *n* 1 : the action or method of one that knits 2 : work done or being done by one that knits
knit·wear \ˈnit-ˌwa(ə)r, -ˌwe(ə)r\ *n* : knitted clothing
knob \ˈnäb\ *n* [ME *knobbe;* akin to MLG *knubbe* knob, OE *-cnoppa* — more at KNOP] 1 a : a rounded protuberance : LUMP b : a small rounded ornament or handle 2 : a rounded usu. isolated hill or mountain — **knobbed** \ˈnäbd\ *adj* — **knob·by** \ˈnäb-ē\ *adj*
knob·ker·rie \ˈnäb-ˌker-ē\ *n* [Afrik *knopkierie,* fr. *knop* knob + *kierie* club] : a short wooden club with a knob at one end used as a missile or in close attack esp. by Zulus of southern Africa
[1]**knock** \ˈnäk\ *vb* [ME *knoken,* fr. OE *cnocian;* akin to MHG *knochen* to press] *vi* 1 : to strike something with a sharp blow 2 : to collide with something 3 a : BUSTLE <heard him ~*ing* around in the kitchen most of the morning> b : WANDER <~*ed* about Europe all summer> 4 a : to make a pounding noise b : to have engine knock 5 : to find fault ~ *vt* 1 a (1) : to strike sharply (2) : to drive, force, or make by so striking b : to set forcibly in motion with a blow 2 : to cause to collide 3 : to find fault with <always ~*ing* those in authority> — **knock cold** : to knock out <was *knocked cold* in the third round> — **knock dead** : to move strongly esp. to admiration or applause <a comedian who really *knocks* them *dead*> — **knock for a loop** 1 a : OVERCOME <*knocked* his opponent *for a loop*> b : DEMOLISH <*knocked* his faith in human nature *for a loop*> 2 : DUMBFOUND, AMAZE <the news *knocked* them *for a loop*> — **knock out of the box** : to cause (an opposing pitcher) to be retired from a baseball game by hitting pitched balls with marked effectiveness — **knock together** : to make or assemble esp. hurriedly or in a makeshift way <*knocked together* his own desk and bookcase>
[2]**knock** *n* 1 a : a sharp blow : RAP b (1) : a severe misfortune or hardship (2) : SETBACK, REVERSAL 2 a : a pounding noise b : a sharp metallic noise caused by abnormal ignition in an automobile engine 3 : a harsh and often petty criticism <likes praise but can't stand the ~*s*>
[1]**knock·about** \ˈnäk-ə-ˌbau̇t\ *adj* 1 : suitable for rough use <~ clothing> 2 a : being noisy and rough : BOISTEROUS <~ games> b : characterized by boisterous antics and often extravagant burlesque <~ comedy>
[2]**knockabout** *n* 1 : a performer or performance of knockabout comedy 2 : a sloop with a simplified rig marked by absence of bowsprit and topmast 3 : something (as an article of clothing) suitable for rough use
knock back *vt, chiefly Brit* : SWALLOW; *specif* : to toss down (an alcoholic beverage) <you *knock back* a pint in the pub —John Braine>
[1]**knock·down** \ˈnäk-ˌdau̇n\ *n* 1 : the action of knocking down 2 : something (as a blow) that strikes down or overwhelms 3 : something (as a piece of furniture) that can be easily assembled or disassembled
[2]**knockdown** *adj* 1 : having such force as to strike down or overwhelm <a bewildering assortment of ~ arguments —J. W. Krutch> 2 : that can easily be assembled or disassembled <a ~ table>
knock down \-ˈdau̇n\ *vt* 1 : to strike to the ground with or as if with a sharp blow : FELL 2 : to dispose of (an item) to a bidder at an auction sale 3 : to take apart : DISASSEMBLE 4 : to receive as income or salary : EARN <positions where they were able to *knock down* good money —*Infantry Jour.*> 5 : to make a reduction in <*knocked* the price *down* a few dollars>
knock–down–and–drag–out *also* **knock–down–drag–out** *adj* : marked by extreme violence or bitterness and by the giving of no quarter <~ political debates> — **knock–down–and–drag–out** *n*
knock·er \ˈnäk-ər\ *n* : one that knocks: as a : a metal ring, bar, or hammer hinged to a door for use in knocking b : a persistently pessimistic critic
knock–knee \ˈnäk-ˈnē, -ˌnē\ *n* : a condition in which the legs curve inward at the knees — **knock–kneed** \-ˈnēd\ *adj*
knock·off \ˈnäk-ˌȯf\ *n* : a copy (as of a dress design) that sells for less than the original
knock off \-ˈȯf\ *vi* : to stop doing something ~ *vt* 1 : to do hurriedly or routinely <*knocked off* one painting after another> 2 : DISCONTINUE, STOP <they *knocked off* work at five> 3 : DEDUCT <*knocked off* a few cents to make the price more attractive> 4 a : KILL <*knocked off* two men . . . on mercenary grounds —Lewis Baker> b : OVERCOME <*knocked off* each center of rebellion> 5 : ROB <*knocked off* a couple of banks>
knock·out \ˈnäk-ˌau̇t\ *n* 1 a : the act of knocking out : the condition of being knocked out b (1) : the termination of a boxing match when one boxer has been knocked unconscious or has been knocked down and is unable to rise and resume boxing within a specified time (2) : TECHNICAL KNOCKOUT c : a blow that knocks out an opponent 2 : something sensationally striking or attractive — **knockout** *adj*
knock out \-ˈau̇t\ *vt* 1 : to produce roughly or hastily 2 a (1) : to defeat (a boxing opponent) by a knockout (2) : to make unconscious <the drug *knocked* him *out*> b : to make inoperative or useless <telephone communications were *knocked out* by the storm> 3 : to tire out : EXHAUST <*knocked* themselves *out* with work> 4 : to cause (an opposing pitcher) to be retired from a baseball game by a batting rally
knockout drops *n pl* : drops of a solution of a drug (as chloral hydrate) put into a drink and designed to produce unconsciousness or stupefaction
knock over *vt* 1 a (1) : to strike to the ground : FELL (2) : OVERWHELM <was *knocked over* by the news> b : ELIMINATE <*knocked over* every difficulty> 2 a : STEAL; *esp* : HIJACK <*knocks over* a truckload of merchandise —J. B. Martin> b : ROB <*knocking over* a bank> 3 : to move strongly esp. to admiration or applause <his perception really *knocks* me *over*>
knock up *vt* 1 *Brit* : ROUSE, SUMMON 2 : to make pregnant
knock·wurst *or* **knack·wurst** \ˈnäk-(ˌ)wərst, -ˌvu̇(ə)rst, -ˌvu̇s(h)t\ *n* [G *knackwurst,* fr. *knacken* to crackle (of imit. origin) + *wurst*] : a short thick heavily seasoned sausage
[1]**knoll** \ˈnōl\ *n* [ME *knol,* fr. OE *cnoll;* akin to ON *knollr* mountaintop, OE *cnotta* knot] : a small round hill : MOUND
[2]**knoll** *vb* [ME *knollen*] *archaic* : KNELL
knop \ˈnäp\ *n* [ME, fr. OE *-cnoppa* knob; akin to OE *cnotta*] : a usu. ornamental knob — **knopped** \ˈnäpt\ *adj*
[1]**knot** \ˈnät\ *n* [ME, fr. OE *cnotta;* akin to OHG *knoto* knot, Lith *gniusti* to press] 1 a : an interlacement of the parts of one or more flexible bodies forming a lump or knob b : the lump or knob so formed c : a tight constriction or the sense of constriction <his stomach was all in ~*s*> 2 : something hard to solve : PROBLEM <a matter full of legal ~*s*> 3 : a bond of union; *esp* : the marriagebond 4 a : a protuberant lump or swelling in tissue <a ~ in a gland> b : the base of a woody branch enclosed in the stem from which it arises; *also* : its section in lumber 5 : a cluster of persons or things : GROUP 6 : an ornamental bow of ribbon : COCKADE 7 a : a division of the log's line serving to measure a ship's speed b (1) : one nautical mile per hour (2) : one nautical mile

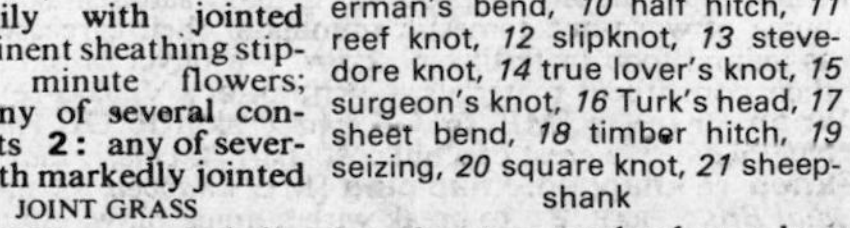

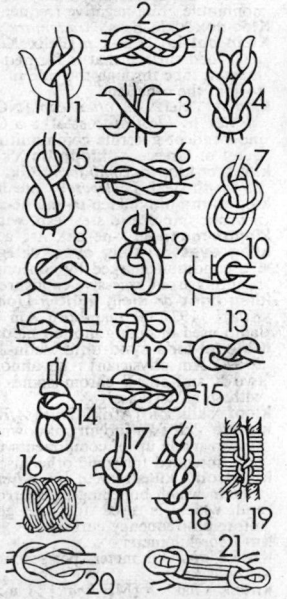

knots 1b: *1* Blackwall hitch, *2* carrick bend, *3* clove hitch, *4* cat's-paw, *5* figure eight, *6* granny knot, *7* bowline, *8* overhand knot, *9* fisherman's bend, *10* half hitch, *11* reef knot, *12* slipknot, *13* stevedore knot, *14* true lover's knot, *15* surgeon's knot, *16* Turk's head, *17* sheet bend, *18* timber hitch, *19* seizing, *20* square knot, *21* sheepshank

[2]**knot** *vb* **knot·ted; knot·ting** *vt* 1 : to tie in or with a knot : form knots in 2 : to unite closely or intricately : ENTANGLE ~ *vi* : to form knots — **knot·ter** *n*
[3]**knot** *n, pl* **knots** *or* **knot** [ME *knott*] : any of several sandpipers (genus *Calidris*) that breed in the Arctic and winter in temperate or warm parts of the New and Old World
knot·grass \ˈnät-ˌgras\ *n* 1 : a cosmopolitan weed (*Polygonum aviculare*) of the buckwheat family with jointed stems, prominent sheathing stipules, and minute flowers; *broadly* : any of several congeneric plants 2 : any of several grasses with markedly jointed stems; *esp* : JOINT GRASS
knot·hole \-ˌhōl\ *n* : a hole in a board or tree trunk where a knot or branch has come out
knot·ted \ˈnät-əd\ *adj* 1 : tied in or with a knot 2 : full of knots : GNARLED 3 : KNOTTY 4 : ornamented with knots or knobs

knot·ty \'nät-ē\ *adj* **knot·ti·er; -est :** marked by or full of knots; *esp* **:** so full of difficulties and complications as to be likely to defy solution *syn* see COMPLEX — **knot·ti·ness** *n*

knotty pine *n* **:** pine wood that has a decorative distribution of knots and is used esp. for interior finish

knot·weed \'nät-,wēd\ *n* **:** any of several herbs (genus *Polygonum*) of the buckwheat family with leaves and bracts jointed and having a very short petiole; *broadly* **:** POLYGONUM

knout \'naůt, 'nüt\ *n* [Russ *knut,* of Scand origin; akin to ON *knūtr* knot; akin to OE *cnotta*] **:** a whip for flogging criminals — **knout** *vt*

1know \'nō\ *vb* **knew** \'n(y)ü\; **known** \'nōn\; **know·ing** [ME *knowen,* fr. OE *cnāwen;* akin to OHG bi*chnāan* to recognize, L *gnoscere, noscere* to come to know, Gk *gignōskein*] *vt* **1 a** (1) **:** to perceive directly **:** have direct cognition of (2) **:** to have understanding of <importance of ~*ing* oneself> (3) **:** to recognize the nature of **:** DISCERN **b** (1) **:** to recognize as being the same as something previously known (2) **:** to be acquainted or familiar with (3) **:** to have experience of **2 a :** to be aware of the truth or factuality of **:** be convinced or certain of **b :** to have a practical understanding of <~*s* how to write> **3** *archaic* **:** to have sexual intercourse with ~ *vi* **1 :** to have knowledge **2 :** to be or become cognizant — **know·able** \'nō-ə-bəl\ *adj* — **know·er** \'nō(-ə)r\ *n*

syn KNOW, BELIEVE, THINK *shared meaning element* **:** to hold something in one's mind as true or as being what it purports to be. These words are often used interchangeably with little thought of their basic signification but it is possible to employ them with discrimination so as to convey quite distinct ideas. In such use KNOW stresses assurance and implies a sound logical or factual basis; BELIEVE, too, stresses assurance but implies trust and faith (as in a higher power) as its basis; while THINK suggests probability rather than firm assurance and implies mental appraisal of pertinent circumstances as its basis. Thus, "I *know* he is telling the truth" implies such factual information in the hands of the speaker as fully confirms the questioned statement; "I *believe* he is telling the truth" can imply such knowledge of the character and personality of the one challenged as to inspire perfect trust; "I *think* he is telling the truth" implies no more than an acceptance of the probability of truthfulness in light of the circumstances <every man *knows* he must die; many men *believe* in an afterlife; some men *think* life is not worth living>

2know *n* **:** KNOWLEDGE — **in the know :** in possession of confidential or otherwise exclusive knowledge or information

know-how \'nō-,haů\ *n* **:** knowledge of how to do something smoothly and efficiently **:** EXPERTISE

1know·ing \'nō-iŋ\ *n* **:** ACQUAINTANCE, COGNIZANCE

2knowing *adj* **1 :** having or reflecting knowledge, information, or intelligence **2 :** shrewdly and keenly alert **:** ASTUTE **3 :** COGNITIVE **4 :** DELIBERATE <~ interference in the affairs of another> *syn* see INTELLIGENT — **know·ing·ly** \-iŋ-lē\ *adv*

know-it-all \'nō-ət-,ȯl\ *n* **:** one who claims to know everything **:** one who disdains advice — **know-it-all** *adj*

knowl·edge \'näl-ij\ *n* [ME *knowlege,* fr. *knowlechen* to acknowledge, irreg. fr. *knowen*] **1** *obs* **:** COGNIZANCE **2 a** (1) **:** the fact or condition of knowing something with familiarity gained through experience or association (2) **:** acquaintance with or understanding of a science, art, or technique **b** (1) **:** the fact or condition of being aware of something (2) **:** the range of one's information or understanding <answered to the best of his ~> **c :** the fact or condition of apprehending truth or fact **:** COGNITION **d :** the fact or condition of having information or of being learned <a man of unusual ~> **3** *archaic* **:** SEXUAL INTERCOURSE **4 a :** the sum of what is known **:** the body of truth, information, and principles acquired by mankind **b** *archaic* **:** a branch of learning

syn KNOWLEDGE, LEARNING, ERUDITION, SCHOLARSHIP *shared meaning element* **:** what is or can be known by an individual or by mankind *ant* ignorance

knowl·edge·able \'näl-ij-ə-bəl\ *adj* **:** having or exhibiting knowledge or intelligence **:** KEEN — **knowl·edge·abil·i·ty** \,näl-ij-ə-'bil-ət-ē\ *n* — **knowl·edge·able·ness** *n* — **knowl·edge·ably** \-blē\ *adv*

known \'nōn\ *adj* **:** generally recognized <a ~ authority on this topic>

know-noth·ing \'nō-,nəth-iŋ\ *n* **1 a :** IGNORAMUS **b :** AGNOSTIC **2** *cap K & N* **:** a member of a 19th century secret American political organization hostile to the political influence of recent immigrants and Roman Catholics

know-noth·ing·ism \-iŋ-,iz-əm\ *n* **1** *cap K & N* **:** the principles and policies of the Know-Nothings **2 :** the condition of knowing nothing or desiring to know nothing or the conviction that nothing can be known with certainty esp. in religion or morality **3** *often cap K&N* **:** a mid-twentieth century political attitude characterized by anti-intellectualism, exaggerated patriotism, and fear of foreign subversive influences

1knuck·le \'nək-əl\ *n* [ME *knokel;* akin to MHG *knöchel* knuckle, OE *cnotta* knot] **1 a :** the rounded prominence formed by the ends of the two adjacent bones at a joint — used esp. of those at the joints of the fingers **b :** the joint of a knuckle **2 :** a cut of meat consisting of the tarsal or carpal joint with the adjoining flesh **3 :** something resembling a knuckle: as **a** (1) **:** one of the joining parts of a hinge through which a pin or rivet passes (2) **:** KNUCKLE JOINT **b :** the meeting of two surfaces at a sharp angle (as in a roof) **c :** a pivotal point **4** *pl* **:** a set of metal finger rings or guards attached to a transverse piece and worn over the front of the doubled fist for use as a weapon — called also *brass knuckles*

2knuckle *vb* **knuck·led; knuck·ling** \'nək-(ə-)liŋ\ *vi* **:** to place the knuckles on the ground in shooting a marble ~ *vt* **:** to press or rub with the knuckles

knuck·le·ball \'nək-əl-,bȯl\ *n* **:** a baseball pitch in which the ball is gripped with the knuckles or the tips of the fingers pressed against the top and thrown with little speed or spin — called also *knuckler*

knuck·le·ball·er \-,bȯ-lər\ *n* **:** a pitcher who specializes in throwing knuckleballs

knuck·le·bone \,nək-əl-'bōn, 'nək-əl-,\ *n* **:** one of the bones forming a knuckle; *esp* **:** a metacarpal or metatarsal bone of a sheep formerly used in gaming or divination

knuckle down *vi* **:** to apply oneself earnestly <let's *knuckle down* to business>

knuck·le-dust·er \'nək-əl-,dəs-tər\ *n* **:** KNUCKLE 4

knuck·le·head \-,hed\ *n* **:** DUMBBELL 2 — **knuck·le·head·ed** \,nək-əl-'hed-əd\ *adj*

knuckle joint *n* **:** a hinge joint in which a projection with an eye on one piece enters a jaw between two corresponding projections with eyes on another piece and is retained by a pin or rivet

knuckle under *vi* **:** to give in **:** SUBMIT <refused to *knuckle under* to any dictatorship>

knur \'nər\ *n* [ME *knorre;* akin to OE *cnotta* knot] **:** a hard excrescence (as on a tree trunk) **:** GNARL

knurl \'nər(-ə)l\ *n* [prob. blend of *knur* and *gnarl*] **1 :** a small protuberance, excrescence, or knob **2 :** one of a series of small ridges or beads on a metal surface to aid in gripping — **knurled** \'nər(-ə)ld\ *adj* — **knurly** \'nər-lē\ *adj*

1KO \(')kā-'ō, 'kā-(,)ō\ *n* [*k*nock *o*ut] **:** KNOCKOUT

2KO *vt* **KO'd** \kā-'ōd, 'kā-(,)ōd\; **KO'·ing** \-'ō-iŋ, -(,)ō-\ **:** to knock out (as in boxing)

koa \'kō-ə\ *n* [Hawaiian] **1 :** a Hawaiian timber tree (*Acacia Koa*) with crescent-shaped leaves and white flowers borne in small round heads **2 :** the fine-grained red wood of the koa used esp. for furniture

ko·ala \kō-'äl-ə, kə-'wäl-\ *n* [native name in Australia] **:** an Australian arboreal marsupial (*Phascolarctos cinereus*) about two feet long that has large hairy ears, gray fur, and sharp claws and feeds on eucalyptus leaves

koala

ko·an \'kō-,än\ *n* [Jap *kōan,* fr. *kō* public + *an* proposition] **:** a paradox to be meditated upon that is used to train Zen Buddhist monks to abandon ultimate dependence on reason and to force them into gaining sudden intuitive enlightenment

ko·bold \'kō-,bȯld\ *n* [G — more at COBALT] **1 :** a gnome that in German folklore inhabits underground places **2 :** an often mischievous domestic spirit of German folklore

Ko·dak \'kō-,dak\ *trademark* — used for a small hand camera

K of C *abbr* Knights of Columbus

K of P *abbr* Knights of Pythias

Koh-i-noor \'kō-ə-,nů(ə)r\ *n* [Per *Kōh-i-nūr,* lit., mountain of light] **:** a large diamond discovered in India and made one of the British crown jewels

kohl \'kōl\ *n* [Ar *kuḥl*] **:** a preparation used by women esp. in Arabia and Egypt to darken the edges of the eyelids

kohl·ra·bi \kōl-'rab-ē, -'räb-\ *n, pl* **-bies** [G, fr. It *cavolo rapa,* fr. *cavolo* cabbage + *rapa* turnip] **:** any of a race of cabbages having a greatly enlarged, fleshy, turnip-shaped edible stem

koi·ne \kȯi-'nā, 'kȯi-,; kē-'nē\ *n* [Gk *koinē,* fem. of *koinos* common] **1** *cap* **:** the Greek language commonly spoken and written in eastern Mediterranean countries in the Hellenistic and Roman periods **2 :** a dialect or language of a region that has become the common or standard language of a larger area

ko·kan·ee \kō-'kan-ē\ *n* [prob. fr. *Kokanee* creek, British Columbia] **:** a small landlocked sockeye salmon — called also *kokanee salmon*

kok-sa·ghyz *or* **kok-sa·gyz** \,kōk-sə-'gēz, ,käk-, -'giz\ *n* [Russ *kok-sagyz*] **:** a perennial Asiatic dandelion (*Taraxacum kok-saghyz*) cultivated for its fleshy roots that have a high rubber content

kola *var of* COLA

ko·la nut \'kō-lə-\ *n* **:** the bitter caffeine-containing seed of a kola tree used esp. as a masticatory and in beverages

kola tree *n* **:** an African tree (genus *Cola,* esp. *C. nitida*) of the chocolate family cultivated in various tropical areas for its kola nuts

ko·lin·sky *or* **ko·lin·ski** \kə-'lin(t)-skē\ *n, pl* **-skies** [Russ *kolinskiĭ* of Kola, fr. *Kola,* town and peninsula in U.S.S.R.] **1 :** any of several Asiatic minks (esp. *Mustela siberica*) **2 :** the fur or pelt of a kolinsky

kol·khoz \käl-'kȯz, -'kȯs\ *n, pl* **kol·kho·zy** \-'kȯ-zē\ *or* **kol·khoz·es** \-'kȯ-zəz\ [Russ, fr. *kol*lektivnoe *khoz*yaĭstvo collective farm] **:** a collective farm of the U.S.S.R.

kol·khoz·nik \käl-'kȯz-nik\ *n, pl* **-ni·ki** \-ni-kē\ *or* **-niks** [Russ, fr. *kolkhoz* + *-nik*] **:** a member of a kolkhoz

Kol Ni·dre \kōl-'nid-(,)rā, kōl-, -rə\ *n* [Aram *kol nidhrē* all the vows; fr. the opening phrase of the prayer] **:** a formula for the annulment of private vows chanted in the synagogue on the eve of Yom Kippur

ko·lo \'kō-(,)lō\ *n, pl* **kolos** [Serbo-Croatian, fr. OSlav, wheel; akin to OE *hwēol* wheel] **:** a central European folk dance in which dancers form a circle and progress slowly to right or left while one or more dancers perform elaborate steps in the center of the circle

ko·mat·ik \kō-'mat-ik\ *n* [Esk (Labrador dial.)] **:** an Eskimo sledge with wooden runners and crossbars lashed with rawhide

kom·man·da·tu·ra \kə-,man-də-'tůr-ə\ *n* [prob. fr. G *kommandantur* command post] **:** a military government headquarters

ko·mon·dor \'käm-ən-,dȯ(ə)r, 'kō-mən-\ *n* [Hung] **:** any of a Hungarian breed of large powerful shaggy-coated white dogs with

---

ə abut ə kitten ər further a back ā bake ä cot, cart
aů out ch chin e less ē easy g gift i trip ī life
j joke ŋ sing ō flow ȯ flaw ȯi coin th thin t͟h this
ü loot ů foot y yet yü few yů furious zh vision

a black nose and dark brown eyes that are used as guard dogs and as herd dogs
Kon·go \'käŋ-(ˌ)gō\ *n, pl* **Kongo** *or* **Kongos** **1 :** a member of a Bantu people of the lower Congo river **2 :** the Bantu language of the Kongo people used as a trade language
Kon·ka·ni \'käŋ-kə-(ˌ)nē\ *n* [Marathi *Koṅkaṇī*] **:** an Indic language of the west coast of India
koo·doo *var of* KUDU
kook \'kük\ *n* [by shortening and alter. fr. *cuckoo*] **:** one whose ideas or actions are eccentric, fantastic, or insane **:** SCREWBALL
kook·a·bur·ra \'ku̇k-ə-ˌbər-ə, -ˌbə-rə\ *n* [native name in Australia] **:** a kingfisher (*Dacelo gigas*) of Australia that is about the size of a crow and has a call resembling loud laughter — called also *laughing jackass*
kooky *also* **kook·ie** \'kü-kē\ *adj* **kook·i·er; -est :** having the characteristics of a kook **:** CRAZY, OFFBEAT — **kook·i·ness** *n*
kop *abbr* kopeck
ko·peck *also* **ko·pek** \'kō-ˌpek\ *n* [Russ *kopeĭka*] — see *ruble* at MONEY table
koph *var of* QOPH
kop·je *or* **kop·pie** \'käp-ē\ *n* [Afrik *koppie*] **:** a small hill esp. on the African veld
kor \'kȯ(ə)r\ *n* [Heb *kōr*] **:** an ancient Hebrew and Phoenician unit of measure of capacity
Kor *abbr* Korea; Korean
Ko·ran \kə-'ran, -'rän; 'kō(ə)r-ˌan, 'kȯ(ə)r-\ *n* [Ar *qur'ān*] **:** the book composed of writings accepted by Muslims as revelations made to Muhammad by Allah through the angel Gabriel — **Ko·ran·ic** \kə-'ran-ik\ *adj*
Ko·re·an \kə-'rē-ən, *esp South* (')kō-\ *n* **1 :** a native or inhabitant of Korea **2 :** the language of the Korean people — **Korean** *adj*
ko·ru·na \'kȯr-ə-ˌnä, 'kär-\ *n, pl* **ko·ru·ny** \-ə-nē\ *or* **korunas** [Czech, lit., crown, fr. L *corona*] — see MONEY table
1**ko·sher** \'kō-shər\ *adj* [Yiddish, fr. Heb *kāshēr* fit, proper] **1 a :** sanctioned by Jewish law; *esp* **:** ritually fit for use <~ meat> **b :** selling or serving food ritually fit according to Jewish law <a ~ restaurant> **2 :** PROPER <found things going on that were not ~ —Homer Bigart>
2**kosher** *vt* **ko·shered; ko·sher·ing** \-sh(ə-)riŋ\ **:** to make kosher
ko·to \'kōt-(ˌ)ō\ *n* [Jap] **:** a long Japanese zither having 13 silk strings
kou·miss *or* **ku·miss** \kü-'mis, 'kü-məs\ *n* [Russ *kumys*] **:** a fermented beverage made orig. by the nomadic peoples of central Asia from mare's milk
1**kow·tow** \(')kau̇-'tau̇, 'kau̇-ˌ\ *n* [Chin (Pek) *k'o¹ t'ou²*, fr. *k'o¹* to bump + *t'ou²* head] **:** an act of kowtowing
2**kowtow** *vi* **1 :** to kneel and touch the forehead to the ground in token of homage, worship, or deep respect **2 :** to show obsequious deference **:** FAWN
KP *abbr* kitchen police
kpc *abbr* kiloparsec
kr *abbr* **1** krona **2** krone
Kr *symbol* krypton
1**kraal** \'krȯl, 'kräl\ *n* [Afrik, fr. Pg *curral* pen for cattle, enclosure, fr. (assumed) VL *currale* enclosure for vehicles — more at CORRAL] **1 a :** a village of southern African natives **b :** the native village community **2 :** an enclosure for domestic animals in southern Africa
2**kraal** *vt* **:** to pen in a kraal
kraft \'kraft\ *n, often attrib* [G, lit., strength, fr. OHG — more at CRAFT] **:** a strong paper or board made from wood pulp derived from wood chips boiled in an alkaline solution containing sodium sulfate
krait \'krīt\ *n* [Hindi *karait*] **:** any of several brightly banded extremely venomous nocturnal elapid snakes (genus *Bungarus*) of eastern Asia and adjacent islands
kra·ken \'kräk-ən\ *n* [Norw dial.] **:** a fabulous Scandinavian sea monster
kra·ter \'krāt-ər, krä-'te(ə)r\ *n* [Gk *kratēr* — more at CRATER] **:** a jar or vase of classical antiquity having a large round body and a wide mouth, and used for mixing wine and water
K ration \'kā-\ *n* [A. B. *K*eys *b*1904 Am physiologist] **:** a lightweight packaged ration of emergency foods developed for the U.S. armed forces in World War II
kraut \'krau̇t\ *n* [G — more at SAUERKRAUT] **:** SAUERKRAUT
Krebs cycle \'krebz-\ *n* [H. A. *Krebs*] **:** a sequence of reactions in the living organism in which oxidation of acetic acid or acetyl equivalent provides energy for storage in phosphate bonds — called also *citric acid cycle, tricarboxylic acid cycle*

1 krater

krem·lin \'krem-lən\ *n* [prob. fr. obs. G *kremelin*, fr. Russ *kreml'*] **1 :** the citadel of a Russian city **2** [the *Kremlin*, citadel of Moscow and governing center of the U.S.S.R.] *cap* **:** the Russian government
krem·lin·ol·o·gy \ˌkrem-lə-'näl-ə-jē\ *n, often cap* **:** the study of the policies and practices of the Soviet government — **krem·lin·ol·o·gist** \-jəst\ *n, often cap*
kreu·zer \'krȯit-sər\ *n* [G] **:** a small coin formerly used in Austria and Germany
krill \'kril\ *n* [Norw *kril* fry of fish] **:** planktonic crustaceans and larvae that constitute the principal food of whalebone whales
krim·mer \'krim-ər\ *n* [G, fr. *Krim* Crimea] **:** a gray fur made from the pelts of young lambs of the Crimean peninsula region
kris \'krēs\ *n* [Malay *kĕris*] **:** a Malay or Indonesian dagger with a ridged serpentine blade
Krish·na \'krish-nə\ *n* [Skt *Kṛṣṇa*] **:** a deity or deified hero of later Hinduism worshiped as an incarnation of Vishnu
Krish·na·ism \-ˌiz-əm\ *n* **:** a widespread form of Hindu religion characterized by the worship of Krishna
Kriss Krin·gle \'kris-'kriŋ-gəl\ *n* [G *Christkindl* Christ child, Christmas gift, dim. of *Christkind* Christ child] **:** SANTA CLAUS
1**kro·na** \'krō-nə\ *n, pl* **kro·nur** \-nər\ [Icel *krōna*, lit., crown] — see MONEY table
2**kro·na** \'krō-nə\ *n, pl* **kro·nor** \-ˌnȯ(ə)r, -nər\ [Sw, lit., crown] — see MONEY table
1**kro·ne** \'krō-nə\ *n, pl* **kro·nen** \-nən\ [G, lit., crown] **1 :** the basic monetary unit of Austria from 1892 to 1925 **2 :** a coin representing one krone
2**kro·ne** \'krō-nə\ *n, pl* **kro·ner** \-nər\ [Dan, lit., crown] — see MONEY table
Kro·neck·er delta \ˌkrō-ˌnek-ər-\ *n* [Leopold *Kronecker* †1891 G mathematician] **:** a function of two variables that is 1 when the variables have the same value and is 0 when they have different values
Kru·ger·rand \'krü-gə(r)-ˌrand, -ˌränd, -ˌränt\ *n* [S.J.P. *Kruger* + *rand*] **:** a one-ounce gold coin of the Republic of So. Africa equal in bullion value to 25 rand and having an official price of 31 rand
krumm·holz \'kru̇m-ˌhōlts\ *n, pl* **krummholz** [G, fr. *krumm* crooked + *holz* wood] **:** stunted forest characteristic of timberline
kryp·ton \'krip-ˌtän\ *n* [Gk, neut. of *kryptos* hidden — more at CRYPT] **:** a colorless relatively inert gaseous element found in air at about one volume per million and used esp. in electric lamps — see ELEMENT table
KS *abbr* Kansas
Ksha·tri·ya \(kə-)'sha-trē-(y)ə, 'cha-\ *n* [Skt *kṣatriya*] **:** a Hindu of an upper caste traditionally assigned to governing and military occupations
kt *abbr* **1** karat **2** knight
Ku·che·an \kü-'chē-ən\ *n* [*Kuche, Kucha*, Sinkiang, China] **:** TOCHARIAN B
ku·chen \'kü-kən, -kən\ *n, pl* **kuchen** [G, cake, fr. OHG *kuocho* — more at CAKE] **:** any of various coffee cakes made from sweet yeast dough
ku·do \'kyüd-(ˌ)ō\ *n, pl* **kudos** [back-formation fr. *kudos* (taken as a pl.)] **1 :** AWARD, HONOR <a score of honorary degrees and . . . other ~*s* —*Time*> **2 :** COMPLIMENT, PRAISE <to all three should go some kind of special ~ for refusing to succumb —Al Hine>
ku·dos \'k(y)ü-ˌdäs\ *n* [Gk *kydos*; akin to Gk *akouein* to hear — more at HEAR] **:** fame and renown resulting from an act or achievement **:** PRESTIGE
ku·du \'küd-(ˌ)ü\ *n* [Afrik *koedoe*] **:** a large grayish brown African antelope (*Strepsiceros strepsiceros*) with large annulated spirally twisted horns

kudu

kud·zu \'ku̇d-(ˌ)zü\ *n* [Jap *kuzu*] **:** a prostrate Asiatic leguminous vine (*Pueraria thunbergiana*) used widely for hay and forage and for erosion control
Ku Klux·er \'k(y)ü-ˌklək-sər *also* 'klü-\ *n* **:** a member of the Ku Klux Klan — **Ku Klux·ism** \-ˌklək-ˌsiz-əm\ *n*
Ku Klux Klan \ˌk(y)ü-ˌklək-'sklan *also* ˌklü-\ *n* **1 :** a post-Civil War secret society advocating white supremacy **2 :** a 20th-century secret fraternal group held to confine its membership to American-born Protestant whites
ku·lak \k(y)ü-'lak, -'läk, 'k(y)ü-ˌ\ *n* [Russ, lit., fist] **1 :** a prosperous or wealthy peasant farmer in 19th century Russia **2 :** a farmer characterized by Communists as having excessive wealth
kul·tur \ku̇l-'tu̇(ə)r\ *n, often cap* [G, fr. L *cultura* culture] **1 :** CULTURE 5 **2 :** culture emphasizing practical efficiency and individual subordination to the state **3 :** German culture held to be superior esp. by militant Nazi and Hohenzollern expansionists
Kul·tur·kampf \-ˌkäm(p)f\ *n* [G, fr. *kultur* + *kampf* conflict] **:** conflict between civil government and religious authorities esp. over control of education and church appointments
küm·mel \'kim-əl\ *n* [G, lit., caraway seed, fr. OHG *kumīn* cumin] **:** a colorless aromatic liqueur flavored principally with caraway seeds
kum·quat \'kəm-ˌkwät\ *n* [Chin (Cant) *kam kwat*, fr. *kam* gold + *kwat* orange] **:** any of several small citrus fruits with sweet spongy rind and somewhat acid pulp that are used chiefly for preserves; *also* **:** a tree or shrub (genus *Fortunella*) of the rue family that bears kumquats
kung fu \'ku̇ŋ-'fü, 'gu̇ŋ-\ *n* [Chin dial., alter. of Pek *ch'üan² fa³*, lit., boxing principles] **:** a Chinese art of self-defense resembling karate
kunz·ite \'ku̇n(t)-ˌsīt\ *n* [G. F. *Kunz* †1932 Am gem expert] **:** a spodumene that occurs in pinkish lilac crystals and is used as a gem
Kurd \'ku̇(ə)rd, 'kərd\ *n* **:** a member of a pastoral and agricultural people who inhabit a plateau region in adjoining parts of Turkey, Iran, Iraq, and Syria and in the Armenian and Azerbaidzhan sectors of the Soviet Caucasus — **Kurd·ish** \-ish\ *adj*
Kurdish *n* **:** the Iranian language of the Kurds
Kur·di·stan \ˌku̇rd-ə-'stan, ˌkərd-\ *n* [*Kurdistan*, Asia] **:** an oriental rug woven by the Kurds and noted for fine colors and durability
kur·gan \ku̇(ə)r-'gän, -'gan\ *n* [Russ, of Turkic origin; akin to Turk *kurgan* fortress, castle] **:** a burial mound of eastern Europe or Siberia
kur·ra·jong \'kər-ə-ˌjȯŋ, 'kə-rə-, -ˌjäŋ\ *n* [native name in Australia] **:** any of several Australian trees or shrubs (family Sterculiaceae) having strong bast fiber used by Australian aborigines; *esp* **:** a widely planted shelter and forage tree (*Brachychiton populneum*)
kur·to·sis \(ˌ)kər-'tō-səs\ *n* [Gk *kyrtōsis* convexity, fr. *kyrtos* convex; akin to L *curvus* curved — more at CROWN] **:** the peakedness or flatness of the graph of a frequency distribution esp. as determining the concentration of values near the mean as compared with the normal distribution

ku·ru \ˈkü(ə)r-(ˌ)ü\ *n* [native name in New Guinea, lit., trembling] : a fatal disease of the nervous system that occurs among tribesmen in eastern New Guinea
ku·rus \kə-ˈrüsh\ *n, pl* **kurus** [Turk *kuruş*]: the Turkish piaster
kv *abbr* kilovolt
kvar *abbr* kilovar
kvass \kə-ˈväs, ˈkfäs\ *n* [Russ *kvas*] : a sour-sweet beverage of slight alcoholic content made in eastern Europe usu. by fermenting mixed cereals and adding flavoring (as fruit or peppermint)
kw *abbr* kilowatt
Kwa \ˈkwä\ *n* : a branch of the Niger-Congo language family that is spoken along the African coast and a short distance inland from Liberia to Nigeria
kwa·cha \ˈkwäch-ə\ *n, pl* **kwacha** [native name in Zambia, lit., dawn] — see MONEY table
kwash·i·or·kor \ˌkwäsh-ē-ˈȯr-kər, -ȯr-ˈkȯ(ə)r\ *n* [native name in Ghana, lit., red boy] : severe malnutrition in infants and children that is caused by a diet high in carbohydrate and low in protein
kwhr *or* **kwh** *abbr* kilowatt-hour
KWIC \ˈkwik\ *n* [*key word in context*] : a computer-generated index alphabetized on a keyword that appears within a portion of its context
KWOC \ˈkwäk\ *n* [*key word out of context*] : a computer-generated index in which the keyword is followed by its context
Ky *or* **KY** *abbr* Kentucky
ky·ack \ˈkī-ˌak\ *n* [origin unknown] : a packsack to be swung on either side of a packsaddle
ky·a·nite \ˈkī-ə-ˌnīt\ *n* [G *zyanit*, fr. Gk *kyanos* dark blue enamel, lapis lazuli] : an aluminum silicate Al_2SiO_5 that occurs usu. in blue thin-bladed triclinic crystals and crystalline aggregates and is sometimes used as a gemstone
kyat \ˈchät\ *n* [Burmese] — see MONEY table
ky·mo·gram \ˈkī-mə-ˌgram\ *n* [ISV] : a record made by a kymograph
ky·mo·graph \-ˌgraf\ *n* [Gk *kyma* wave + ISV *-graph* — more at CYME] : a device which graphically records motion or pressure (as of blood) — **ky·mo·graph·ic** \ˌkī-mə-ˈgraf-ik\ *adj*
Kymric *var of* CYMRIC
ky·pho·sis \kī-ˈfō-səs\ *n* [NL, fr. Gk *kyphōsis*, fr. *kyphos* humpbacked; akin to OE *hēah* high] : abnormal backward curvature of the spine — **ky·phot·ic** \-ˈfät-ik\ *adj*
ky·rie \ˈkir-ē-ˌā\ *n, often cap* [NL, fr. LL *kyrie eleison*, transliteration of Gk *kyrie eleēson* Lord, have mercy] : a short liturgical prayer that begins with or consists of the words "Lord, have mercy"
ky·rie elei·son \ˈkir-ē-ˌā-ə-ˈlā-(ə-)ˌsän, -(ə-)sən *also* ˌkir-ē-ə-ˈlā-\ *n, often cap K & E* : KYRIE
kyte \ˈkīt\ *n* [prob. fr. LG *küt* bowel] *chiefly Scot* : STOMACH, BELLY
kythe *var of* KITHE

¹l \ˈel\ *n, pl* **l's** *or* **ls** \ˈelz\ *often cap, often attrib* **1 a** : the 12th letter of the English alphabet **b** : a graphic representation of this letter **c** : a speech counterpart of orthographic *l* **2** : fifty — see NUMBER table **3** : a graphic device for reproducing the letter *l* **4** : one designated *l* esp. as the 12th in order or class **5** : something shaped like the letter L; *specif* : ELL **6** : ELEVATED RAILROAD
²l *abbr, often cap* **1** lady **2** lake **3** lambert **4** land **5** late **6** Latin **7** left **8** [L *libra*] pound **9** liquid **10** lira; lire **11** liter **12** little **13** low
L *symbol* **1** inductance **2** Lagrangian
l- *prefix* [ISV, fr. *lev-*] **1** \ˌlē-(ˌ)vō, ˌel, ˈel\ : levorotatory <*l*-tartaric acid> **2** \ˌel, ˈel\ : having a similar configuration at a selected carbon atom to the configuration of levorotatory glyceraldehyde <L-fructose>
¹la \ˈlä\ *n* [ME, fr. ML, fr. the syllable sung to this note in a medieval hymn to St. John the Baptist] : the 6th tone of the diatonic scale in solmization
²la \ˈlō, ˈlä\ *interj* [ME (northern dial.), fr. OE *lā*] *chiefly dial* — used for emphasis or expressing surprise
¹La *abbr* Louisiana
²La *symbol* lanthanum
LA *abbr* **1** law agent **2** Los Angeles **3** Louisiana
laa·ger \ˈläg-ər\ *n* [obs. Afrik *lager* (now *laer*), fr. G] *South Africa* : CAMP; *esp* : an encampment protected by a circle of wagons or armored vehicles — **laager** *vi*
lab \ˈlab\ *n* : LABORATORY
Lab *abbr* Labrador
lab·a·rum \ˈlab-ə-rəm\ *n* [LL] : an imperial standard of the later Roman emperors resembling the vexillum; *esp* : the standard adopted by Constantine after his conversion to Christianity
lab·da·num \ˈlab-də-nəm\ *n* [ML *lapdanum*] : a soft dark fragrant bitter oleoresin derived from various rockroses (genus *Cistus*) and used in making perfumes
¹la·bel \ˈlā-bəl\ *n* [ME, fr. MF] **1** *archaic* : BAND, FILLET; *specif* : one attached to a document to hold an appended seal **2** : a heraldic charge that consists of a narrow horizontal band with usu. three pendants **3 a** : a slip (as of paper or cloth) inscribed and affixed to something for identification or description **b** : written or printed matter accompanying an article to furnish identification or other information **c** : a descriptive or identifying word or phrase: as (1) : EPITHET (2) : a word or phrase used with a dictionary definition to provide additional information **d** : material used in isotopic labeling **4** : a projecting molding by the sides and over the top of an opening **5** : an adhesive stamp (as for postage or revenue) **6** : BRAND 4a: as **a** : a brand of commercial recordings issued under a usu. trademarked name; *also* : a recording so issued **b** : the brand name of a retail store selling clothing, a clothing manufacturer, or a fashion designer
²label *vt* **la·beled** *or* **la·belled; la·bel·ing** *or* **la·bel·ling** \ˈlā-b(ə-)liŋ\ **1 a** : to affix a label to **b** : to describe or designate with a label **2 a** : to distinguish (an element or atom) by using a radioactive isotope or an isotope of unusual mass for tracing through chemical reactions or biological processes **b** : to distinguish (as a compound or molecule) by introducing a labeled atom — **la·bel·able** \ˈlā-bə-lə-bəl\ *adj* — **la·bel·er** \ˈlā-b(ə-)lər\ *n*
la·bel·lum \lə-ˈbel-əm\ *n, pl* **la·bel·la** \-ˈbel-ə\ [NL, fr. L, dim. of *labrum* lip — more at LIP] **1** : the median member of the corolla of an orchid **2** : a terminal part of the labium or labrum of various insects — **la·bel·late** \lə-ˈbel-ət\ *adj*
¹la·bi·al \ˈlā-bē-əl\ *adj* [ML *labialis*, fr. L *labium* lip] **1** : of or relating to the lips or labia **2** : uttered with the participation of one or both lips <the ~ sounds \f\, \p\, and \ü\> — **la·bi·al·ly** \-ə-lē\ *adv*
²labial *n* : a labial consonant
la·bi·al·ize \ˈlā-bē-ə-ˌlīz\ *vt* **-ized; -iz·ing** : to make labial : ROUND — **la·bi·al·iza·tion** \ˌlā-bē-ə-lə-ˈzā-shən, -byə-lə-\ *n*
la·bia ma·jo·ra \ˌlā-bē-ə-mə-ˈjōr-ə, -ˈjȯr-\ *n pl* [NL, lit., larger lips] : the outer fatty folds bounding the vulva
labia mi·no·ra \-mə-ˈnōr-ə, -ˈnȯr-\ *n pl* [NL, lit., smaller lips] : the inner highly vascular largely connective-tissue folds bounding the vulva
¹la·bi·ate \ˈlā-bē-ət, -bē-ˌāt\ *adj* [NL *labiatus*, fr. L *labium*] **1** : having the limb of a tubular corolla or calyx divided into two

unequal parts projecting one over the other like lips <mints and the snapdragon are ~> **2 :** of or relating to the mint family

2labiate *n* **:** a plant of the mint family

la·bile \ˈlā-ˌbīl, -bəl\ *adj* [F, fr. MF, prone to err, fr. LL *labilis,* fr. L *labi* to slip — more at SLEEP] **1 :** readily open to change **:** PLASTIC **2 :** readily or continually undergoing chemical, physical, or biological change or breakdown **:** UNSTABLE <a ~ mineral> — **la·bil·i·ty** \lā-ˈbil-ət-ē\ *n*

labio- *comb form* [L *labium*] **:** labial and <*labio*dental>

la·bio·den·tal \ˌlā-bē-ō-ˈdent-ᵊl\ *adj* **:** uttered with the participation of the lip and teeth <the ~ sounds \f\ and \v\> — **labiodental** *n*

la·bio·ve·lar \-ˈvē-lər\ *adj* [ISV] **:** both labial and velar <the ~ sound \w\> — **labiovelar** *n*

la·bi·um \ˈlā-bē-əm\ *n, pl* **la·bia** \-ə\ [NL, fr. L, lip — more at LIP] **1 :** any of the folds at the margin of the vulva — compare LABIA MAJORA, LABIA MINORA **2 :** the lower lip of a labiate corolla **3 a :** a lower mouthpart of an insect that is formed by the second pair of maxillae united in the middle line **b :** a liplike part of various invertebrates

1la·bor \ˈlā-bər\ *n* [ME, fr. OF, fr. L *labor*] **1 a :** expenditure of physical or mental effort esp. when difficult or compulsory **b (1) :** human activity that provides the goods or services in an economy **(2) :** the services performed by workers for wages as distinguished from those rendered by entrepreneurs for profits **c :** the physical activities involved in parturition; *also* **:** the period of such labor **2 :** an act or process requiring labor **:** TASK **3 :** a product of labor **4 a :** an economic group comprising those who do manual labor or work for wages **b (1) :** workers employed in an establishment **(2) :** workers available for employment **c :** the organizations or officials representing groups of workers **5** *usu Labour* **:** the Labour party of the United Kingdom or of another nation of the British Commonwealth ***syn*** see WORK

2labor *vb* **la·bored; la·bor·ing** \-b(ə-)riŋ\ *vi* **1 :** to exert one's powers of body or mind esp. with painful or strenuous effort **:** WORK **2 :** to move with great effort <a fat man ~*ing* up the stairs> **3 :** to be in the labor of giving birth **4 :** to suffer from some disadvantage or distress <~ under a delusion> **5** *of a ship* **:** to pitch or roll heavily ~ *vt* **1** *archaic* **a :** to spend labor on or produce by labor **b :** to strive to effect or achieve **2 :** to treat or work out in often laborious detail <~ the obvious> **3 :** BURDEN, DISTRESS **4 :** to cause to labor — **la·bor·er** \-bər-ər, -brər\ *n*

3labor *adj* **1 :** of or relating to labor **2** *cap* **:** of, relating to, or constituting a political party held to represent the interests of workingmen or characterized by a membership in which organized labor groups predominate

lab·o·ra·to·ry \ˈlab-(ə-)rə-ˌtōr-ē, -ˌtȯr-, *Brit usu* lə-ˈbär-ə-t(ə-)rē\ *n, pl* **-ries** *often attrib* [ML *laboratorium,* fr. L *laboratus,* pp. of *laborare* to labor, fr. *labor*] **1 :** a place equipped for experimental study in a science or for testing and analysis; *broadly* **:** a place providing opportunity for experimentation, observation, or practice in a field of study **2 :** an academic period set aside for laboratory work

labor camp *n* **1 :** a penal colony where forced labor is performed **2 :** a camp for migratory laborers

Labor Day *n* **:** a day set aside for special recognition of the workingman: as **a :** the first Monday in September observed in the U.S. and Canada as a legal holiday **b :** May 1 in many countries

la·bored *adj* **1 :** produced or performed with labor **2 :** bearing marks of labor and effort; *esp* **:** lacking ease of expression <a ~ speech>

la·bo·ri·ous \lə-ˈbōr-ē-əs, -ˈbȯr-\ *adj* **1 :** devoted to labor **:** INDUSTRIOUS **2 :** involving or characterized by hard or toilsome effort **:** LABORED — **la·bo·ri·ous·ly** *adv* — **la·bo·ri·ous·ness** *n*

la·bor·ite \ˈlā-bə-ˌrīt\ *n* **1 :** a member of a group favoring the interests of labor **2** *cap* **a :** a member of a political party devoted chiefly to the interests of labor **b** *usu* **La·bour·ite :** a member of the British Labour party

la·bor·sav·ing \ˈlā-bər-ˌsā-viŋ\ *adj* **:** adapted to replace or decrease human and esp. manual labor

labor union *n* **:** an organization of workers formed for the purpose of advancing its members' interests in respect to wages, benefits, and working conditions

la·bour *chiefly Brit var of* LABOR

lab·ra·dor·ite \ˈlab-rə-ˌdȯ(ə)r-ˌīt\ *n* [*Labrador* peninsula, Canada] **:** a triclinic feldspar showing a play of several colors

Lab·ra·dor retriever \ˌlab-rə-ˌdȯr-\ *n* [*Labrador,* Newfoundland] **:** a retriever largely developed in England from stock originating in Newfoundland and characterized by a short dense usu. black coat and notable breadth of head and chest — called also *Labrador*

la·bret \ˈlā-brət\ *n* [L *labrum*] **:** an ornament worn in a perforation of the lip

la·brum \ˈlā-brəm\ *n* [NL, fr. L, lip, edge — more at LIP] **:** an upper or anterior mouthpart of an arthropod consisting of a single median piece in front of or above the mandibles

la·bur·num \lə-ˈbər-nəm\ *n* [NL, genus name, fr. L, laburnum] **:** any of a small genus (*Laburnum*) of poisonous Eurasian leguminous shrubs and trees with pendulous racemes of bright yellow flowers; *esp* **:** an ornamental tree (*L. anagyroides*) often cultivated for Easter decoration

lab·y·rinth \ˈlab-ə-ˌrin(t)th, -rən(t)th\ *n* [ME *laborintus,* fr. L *labyrinthus,* fr. Gk *labyrinthos*] **1 a :** a place constructed of or full of intricate passageways and blind alleys **b :** a maze (as in a garden) formed by paths separated by high hedges **2 :** something extremely complex or tortuous in structure, arrangement, or character **:** INTRICACY, PERPLEXITY <a ~ of swamps and channels> <guided them through the ~*s* of city life —Paul Blanshard> **3 :** a tortuous anatomical structure; *esp* **:** the internal ear or its bony or membranous part

lab·y·rin·thi·an \ˌlab-ə-ˈrin(t)-thē-ən\ *adj* **:** LABYRINTHINE

lab·y·rin·thine \-ˈrin(t)-thən; -ˈrin-ˌthīn, -ˌthēn\ *adj* **1 :** of, relating to, or resembling a labyrinth **:** INTRICATE, INVOLVED **2 :** of, relating to, affecting, or originating in the internal ear <human ~ lesions>

1lac \ˈlak\ *n* [Per *lak* & Hindi *lākh,* fr. Skt *lākṣā*] **:** a resinous substance secreted by a scale insect (*Laccifer lacca*) and used chiefly in the form of shellac

2lac *var of* LAKH

lac·co·lith \ˈlak-ə-ˌlith\ *n* [Gk *lakkos* cistern + E *-lith*] **:** a mass of igneous rock that is intruded between sedimentary beds and produces a domical bulging of the overlying strata

1lace \ˈlās\ *n* [ME, fr. OF *laz,* fr. L *laqueus* snare — more at DELIGHT] **1 :** a cord or string used for drawing together two edges (as of a garment or a shoe) **2 :** an ornamental braid for trimming coats or uniforms **3 :** an openwork usu. figured fabric made of thread or yarn and used for trimmings, household coverings, and entire garments — **laced** \ˈlāst\ *adj* — **lace·less** \ˈlā-sləs\ *adj* — **lace·like** \ˈlā-ˌslīk\ *adj*

2lace *vb* **laced; lac·ing** [ME *lacen,* fr. OF *lacier,* fr. L *laqueare* to ensnare, fr. *laqueus*] *vt* **1 :** to draw together the edges of by or as if by a lace passed through eyelets **2 :** to draw or pass (as a lace) through something (as eyelets) **3 :** to confine or compress by tightening laces esp. of a corset **4 a :** to adorn with or as if with lace **b :** to mark with streaks of color **5 :** BEAT, LASH **6 a :** to add a dash of an alcoholic liquor to **b :** to give savor or zest to ~ *vi* **:** to admit of being tied or fastened with a lace — **lac·er** *n*

lace–curtain *adj* **:** copying middle-class attributes **:** aspiring to middle-class standing

1lac·er·ate \ˈlas-ə-rət, -ˌrāt\ *or* **lac·er·at·ed** \-ˌrāt-əd\ *adj* **1 a :** TORN, MANGLED **b :** extremely harrowed or distracted **2 :** having the edges deeply and irregularly cut <a ~ petal>

2lac·er·ate \-ˌrāt\ *vt* **-at·ed; -at·ing** [L *laceratus,* pp. of *lacerare* to tear; akin to L *lacer* mangled, Gk *lakis* rent] **1 :** to tear or rend roughly **2 :** to cause sharp mental or emotional pain to **:** DISTRESS — **lac·er·a·tive** \-ˌrāt-iv\ *adj*

lac·er·a·tion \ˌlas-ə-ˈrā-shən\ *n* **1 :** the act of lacerating **2 :** a torn and ragged wound

lace·wing \ˈlā-ˌswiŋ\ *n* **:** any of various neuropterous insects (as genera *Chrysopa* and *Hemerobius*) having delicate lacelike wing venation, long antennae, and brilliant eyes

lacewing

lace·work \ˈlā-ˌswərk\ *n* **:** objects or patterns consisting of or resembling lace

lac·ey *var of* LACY

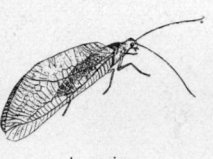

la·ches \ˈlach-əz, ˈlā-chəz\ *n, pl* **laches** [ME *lachesse,* fr. MF *laschesse*] **:** negligence in the observance of duty or opportunity; *specif* **:** undue delay in asserting a legal right or privilege

lach·ry·mal *or* **lac·ri·mal** \ˈlak-rə-məl\ *adj* [MF or ML; MF *lacrymal,* fr. ML *lacrimalis,* fr. L *lacrima* tear — more at TEAR] **1** *usu lacrimal* **:** of, relating to, or constituting the glands that produce tears **2 :** of, relating to, or marked by tears

lach·ry·mose \-ˌmōs\ *adj* **1 :** given to tears or weeping **:** TEARFUL **2 :** tending to cause tears **:** MOURNFUL — **lach·ry·mose·ly** *adv*

lac·ing \ˈlā-siŋ\ *n* **1 :** the action of one that laces **2 :** something that laces **:** LACE **3 :** a contrasting marginal band of color (as on a feather) **4 a :** a dash of alcoholic liquor in a food or beverage **b :** a trace or sprinkling that adds spice or savor **5 :** an act or instance of beating or trouncing

la·cin·i·ate \lə-ˈsin-ē-ət, -ˌāt\ *adj* [L *lacinia* flap; akin to L *lacer*] **:** bordered with a fringe; *esp* **:** cut into deep irregular usu. pointed lobes <~ petals> — **la·cin·i·a·tion** \-ˌsin-ē-ˈā-shən\ *n*

1lack \ˈlak\ *vb* [ME *laken,* fr. MD; akin to ON *leka* to leak] *vi* **1 :** to be deficient or missing <time ~*s* for a full explanation> **2 :** to be short or have need of something <he will not ~ for advisers> ~ *vt* **:** to stand in need of **:** suffer from the absence or deficiency of <~ the necessities of life> <he ~*s* skill in debate> ***syn*** LACK, WANT, NEED, REQUIRE *shared meaning element* **:** to be without something essential or greatly desired. LACK can imply either an absence or a shortage in supply <good counselors *lack* no clients —Shak.> WANT adds to *lack* the notion of urgency in needing or desiring <the whole place *wanted* painting> <they *want* the very necessities of life> NEED stresses urgent necessity more than absence or shortage <all children *need* to succeed —John Holt> <felt he *needed* a change> REQUIRE, often interchangeable with *need,* may heighten the implication of urgent necessity to the point of suggesting an imperativeness of needing or desiring <they *require* help if they are to survive> <great acts *require* great means of enterprise —John Milton>

2lack *n* **1 :** the fact or state of being wanting or deficient **2 :** something that is lacking or is needed

lack·a·dai·si·cal \ˌlak-ə-ˈdā-zi-kəl\ *adj* [by folk etymology fr. *lackaday* + *-ical*] **:** lacking life, spirit, or zest **:** LANGUID — **lack·a·dai·si·cal·ly** \-k(ə-)lē\ *adv*

lack·a·day \ˈlak-ə-ˌdā\ *interj* [by alter. & shortening of *alack the day*] *archaic* — used to express regret or deprecation

1lack·ey \ˈlak-ē\ *n, pl* **lackeys** [MF *laquais*] **1 :** a liveried retainer **:** FOOTMAN **2 :** a servile follower **:** TOADY

2lackey *vb* **lack·eyed; lack·ey·ing** *vi, obs* **:** to act as a lackey **:** TOADY ~ *vt* **:** to wait upon or serve obsequiously

lack·lus·ter \ˈlak-ˌləs-tər\ *adj* **:** lacking in sheen, radiance, or vitality **:** DULL — **lackluster** *n*

La·combe \lə-ˈkōm\ *n* [*Lacombe* Experiment Station, Lacombe, Alta., Canada] **:** any of a breed of white bacon-type swine developed in Canada from Landrace, Chester White, and Berkshire stock

la·con·ic \lə-ˈkän-ik\ *adj* [L *laconicus* Spartan, fr. Gk *lakōnikos;* fr. the Spartan reputation for terseness of speech] **:** using or involving the use of a minimum of words **:** concise to the point of seeming rude or mysterious ***syn*** see CONCISE ***ant*** verbose — **la·con·i·cal·ly** \-i-k(ə-)lē\ *adv*

lac·o·nism \ˈlak-ə-ˌniz-əm\ *n* **:** brevity or terseness of expression or style

1lac·quer \ˈlak-ər\ *n* [Pg *lacré* sealing wax, fr. *laca* lac, fr. Ar *lakk,* fr. Per *lak*] **1 a :** a spirit varnish (as shellac) **b :** any of various durable natural varnishes; *esp* **:** a varnish obtained from an Asiatic sumac (*Rhus verniciflua*) — called also *Chinese lacquer, Japanese*

lacquer **2 :** any of various clear or colored synthetic organic coatings that typically dry to form a film by evaporation of the solvent; *esp* **:** a solution of a cellulose derivative (as nitrocellulose)
[2]**lacquer** *vt* **lac·quered; lac·quer·ing** \-(ə-)riŋ\ **1 :** to coat with lacquer **2 :** to give a smooth finish or appearance to — **lac·quer·er** \-ər-ər\ *n*
lac·ri·ma·tion \ˌlak-rə-ˈmā-shən\ *n* **:** the secretion of tears esp. when abnormal or excessive
lac·ri·ma·tor *or* **lach·ry·ma·tor** \ˈlak-rə-ˌmāt-ər\ *n* [L *lacrimatus,* pp. of *lacrimare* to weep, fr. *lacrima* tear — more at TEAR] **:** a tear-producing substance (as tear gas)
la·crosse \lə-ˈkrȯs\ *n* [CanF *la crosse,* lit., the crosier] **:** a goal game in which players use a long-handled stick that has a triangular head with a loose mesh pouch for catching and carrying the ball
lact- *or* **lacti-** *or* **lacto-** *comb form* [F & L; F, fr. L, fr. *lact-, lac* — more at GALAXY] **1 :** milk <*lacto*flavin> **2 a :** lactic acid <*lactate*> **b :** lactose <*lact*ase>
lact·al·bu·min \ˌlak-ˌtal-ˈbyü-mən\ *n* [ISV] **:** an albumin that is obtained from whey and is similar to serum albumin
lac·tase \ˈlak-ˌtās, -ˌtāz\ *n* [ISV] **:** an enzyme that hydrolyzes lactose and other beta-galactosides and occurs esp. in the intestines of young mammals and in yeasts
[1]**lac·tate** \ˈlak-ˌtāt\ *n* **:** a salt or ester of lactic acid
[2]**lactate** *vi* **lac·tat·ed; lac·tat·ing** [L *lactatus,* pp. of *lactare,* fr. *lact-, lac*] **:** to secrete milk — **lac·ta·tion** \lak-ˈtā-shən\ *n* — **lac·ta·tion·al** \-shnəl, -shən-ᵊl\ *adj* — **lac·ta·tion·al·ly** \-ē\ *adv*
[1]**lac·te·al** \ˈlak-tē-əl\ *adj* [L *lacteus* of milk, fr. *lact-, lac*] **1 :** consisting of, producing, or resembling milk **2 a :** conveying or containing a milky fluid **b :** of or relating to the lacteals
[2]**lacteal** *n* **:** one of the lymphatic vessels arising from the villi of the small intestine and conveying chyle to the thoracic duct
lac·tic \ˈlak-tik\ *adj* **1 a :** of or relating to milk **b :** obtained from sour milk or whey **2 :** involving the production of lactic acid
lactic acid *n* **:** a hygroscopic organic acid $C_3H_6O_3$ present normally in tissue, produced in carbohydrate matter usu. by bacterial fermentation, and used esp. in food and medicine and in industry
lac·tif·er·ous \lak-ˈtif-(ə-)rəs\ *adj* [F or LL; F *lactifère,* fr. LL *lactifer,* fr. L *lact-, lac* + *-fer*] **1 :** secreting or conveying milk **2 :** yielding a milky juice <~ plants> — **lac·tif·er·ous·ness** *n*
lac·to·ba·cil·lus \ˌlak-tō-bə-ˈsil-əs\ *n* [NL] **:** any of a genus (*Lactobacillus*) of lactic-acid-forming bacteria
lac·to·gen·ic \ˌlak-tə-ˈjen-ik\ *adj* **:** inducing lactation
lac·to·glob·u·lin \-ˈgläb-yə-lən\ *n* **:** a crystalline protein fraction that is obtained from the whey of milk
lac·tone \ˈlak-ˌtōn\ *n* [ISV] **:** any of various cyclic anhydrides formed from hydroxy acids — **lac·ton·ic** \lak-ˈtän-ik\ *adj*
lac·tose \ˈlak-ˌtōs, -ˌtōz\ *n* [ISV] **:** a disaccharide sugar $C_{12}H_{22}O_{11}$ that is present in milk and yields glucose and galactose upon hydrolysis and yields esp. lactic acid upon fermentation
la·cu·na \lə-ˈk(y)ü-nə\ *n, pl* **la·cu·nae** \-ˈkyü-(ˌ)nē, -ˈkü-ˌnī\ *or* **la·cu·nas** \-ˈk(y)ü-nəz\ [L, pool, pit, gap — more at LAGOON] **1 :** a blank space or a missing part **:** GAP **2 :** a small cavity, pit, or discontinuity in an anatomical structure — **la·cu·nal** \-ˈk(y)ün-ᵊl\ *adj* — **la·cu·nar** \-ˈk(y)ü-nər\ *adj* — **la·cu·nary** \ˈlak-yə-ˌner-ē, lə-ˈk(y)ü-nə-rē\ *adj* — **la·cu·nate** \lə-ˈk(y)ü-nət, -ˌnāt; ˈlak-yə-ˌnāt\ *adj*
la·cu·nar \lə-ˈk(y)ü-nər\ *n* [L, fr. *lacuna* pit] **1 :** a ceiling with recessed panels **2** *pl* **lac·u·nar·ia** \ˌlak-yə-ˈner-ē-ə\ **:** a recessed panel in a patterned ceiling or soffit
la·cus·trine \lə-ˈkəs-trən\ *adj* [prob. fr. F or It *lacustre,* fr. L *lacus* lake] **:** of, relating to, or growing in lakes
lacy \ˈlā-sē\ *adj* **lac·i·er; -est :** resembling or consisting of lace
lad \ˈlad\ *n* [ME *ladde*] **1 :** a male person of any age between early boyhood and maturity **:** BOY, YOUTH **2 :** FELLOW, CHAP
lad·a·num \ˈlad-ᵊn-əm, ˈlad-nəm\ *var of* LABDANUM
lad·der \ˈlad-ər\ *n, often attrib* [ME, fr. OE *hlǣder;* akin to OHG *leitara* ladder, OE *hlinian* to lean — more at LEAN] **1 :** a structure for climbing up or down that consists essentially of two long sidepieces joined at intervals by crosspieces on which one may step **2 :** something that resembles or suggests a ladder in form or use; *esp* **:** RUN 11a **3 :** a series of usu. ascending steps or stages **:** SCALE
lad·der–back \-ˌbak\ *adj, of furniture* **:** having a back consisting of two upright posts connected by horizontal slats
ladder truck *n* **:** HOOK AND LADDER TRUCK
lad·die \ˈlad-ē\ *n* **:** a young lad
lade \ˈlād\ *vb* **lad·ed; laded** *or* **lad·en** \ˈlād-ᵊn\; **lad·ing** [ME *laden,* fr. OE *hladan;* akin to OHG *hladan* to load, OSlav *klasti*] *vt* **1 a :** to put a load or burden on or in **:** LOAD **b :** to put or place as a load esp. for shipment **:** SHIP **c :** to load heavily or oppressively **2 :** DIP, LADLE ~ *vi* **1 :** to take on cargo **:** LOAD **2 :** to take up or convey a liquid by dipping
[1]**lad·en** \ˈlād-ᵊn\ *vt* **lad·ened; lad·en·ing** \ˈlād-niŋ, -ᵊn-iŋ\ **:** LADE
[2]**laden** *adj* **:** carrying a load or burden
la–di–da \ˌläd-ē-ˈdä\ *adj* [perh. alter. of *lardy-dardy* (foppish)] **:** affectedly refined or polished **:** PRETENTIOUS, ELEGANT
ladies' man *also* **lady's man** *n* **:** a man who shows a marked fondness for the company of women or is esp. attentive to women
ladies' room *n* **:** a room equipped with lavatories and toilets for the use of women
ladies' tresses *n pl but sing or pl in constr* **:** any of a widely distributed genus (*Spiranthes*) of terrestrial orchids with slender often twisted spikes of white irregular flowers
La·din \lə-ˈdēn\ *n* [Rhaeto-Romanic, fr. L *Latinum* Latin] **1 :** ROMANSH **2 :** one speaking Romansh as a mother tongue
lad·ing \ˈlād-iŋ\ *n* **1 a :** LOADING 1 **b :** an act of bailing, dipping, or ladling **2 :** CARGO, FREIGHT
[1]**la·di·no** \lə-ˈdē-(ˌ)nō\ *n, pl* **-nos** [Sp, fr. *ladino* cunning, learned, lit., Latin, fr. L *latinus*] **1 :** JUDEO-SPANISH **2** *often cap* [AmerSp] **:** a westernized Spanish-speaking Latin American; *esp* **:** MESTIZO **3** [AmerSp] *Southwest* **:** a cunningly vicious horse or steer

[2]**la·di·no** \lə-ˈdī-(ˌ)nō, -nə\ *n, pl* **-nos** [perh. irreg. fr. *Lodi,* Italy + It *-ino,* adj. suffix] **:** a large nutritious rapidly growing clover that is a variety of white clover and is widely planted for hay or silage
[1]**la·dle** \ˈlād-ᵊl\ *n* [ME *ladel,* fr. OE *hlædel,* fr. *hladan*] **1 :** a deep-bowled long-handled spoon used esp. for dipping up and conveying liquids **2 :** an instrument or device resembling a ladle in form or function
[2]**ladle** *vt* **la·dled; la·dling** \ˈlād-liŋ, -ᵊl-iŋ\ **:** to take up and convey in or as if in a ladle
la·dy \ˈlād-ē\ *n, pl* **ladies** *often attrib* [ME, fr. OE *hlǣfdīge,* fr. *hlāf* bread + *-dīge* (akin to *dǣge* kneader of bread) — more at LOAF, DAIRY] **1 a :** a woman having proprietary rights or authority esp. as a feudal superior **b :** a woman receiving the homage or devotion of a knight or lover **2** *cap* **:** VIRGIN MARY — usu. used with *Our* **3 a :** a woman of superior social position **b :** a woman of refinement and gentle manners **c :** WOMAN, FEMALE — often used in a courteous reference <show the ~ to a seat> or usu. in the pl. in address <*ladies* and gentlemen> **4 :** WIFE **5 a :** any of various titled women in Great Britain — used as the customary title of (1) a marchioness, countess, viscountess, or baroness or (2) the wife of a knight, baronet, member of the peerage, or one having the courtesy title of *lord* and used as a courtesy title for the daughter of a duke, marquess, or earl **b :** a female member of an order of knighthood — compare DAME
lady beetle *n* **:** LADYBUG
la·dy·bird \ˈlād-ē-ˌbərd\ *n* **:** LADYBUG
la·dy·bug \-ˌbəg\ *n* [Our *Lady,* the Virgin Mary] **:** any of numerous small nearly hemispherical often brightly colored beetles (family Coccinellidae) of temperate and tropical regions that usu. feed both as larvae and adults on other insects

ladybug

lady chapel *n, often cap L&C* **:** a chapel dedicated to the Virgin Mary
Lady Day *n* **:** the feast of the Annunciation
la·dy·fin·ger \ˈlād-ē-ˌfiŋ-gər\ *n* **:** a small finger-shaped sponge cake
la·dy·fish \-ˌfish\ *n* **1 :** BONEFISH 1a **2 :** a large silvery food and sport fish (*Elops saurus*) that resembles a herring but is related to the tarpon
la·dy–in–wait·ing \ˌlād-ē-in-ˈwāt-iŋ\ *n, pl* **ladies–in–waiting :** a lady of a queen's or a princess's household appointed to wait on her
la·dy·kin \ˈlād-ē-kən\ *n* **:** a little lady
la·dy·like \-ˌlīk\ *adj* **1 :** resembling a lady in appearance or manners **:** WELL-BRED **2 :** becoming or suitable to a lady **3 a :** feeling or showing too much concern about elegance or propriety <~ embarrassment at not being the wife of a real doctor —Lewis Vogler> **b :** lacking in strength, force, or virility
la·dy·love \ˈlād-ē-ˌləv, ˌlād-ē-ˈ\ *n* **:** SWEETHEART, MISTRESS
lady of the house : the chief female in a household
Lady of the Lake : VIVIAN
la·dy's–ear·drop \ˌlād-ē-ˈzi(ə)r-ˌdräp\ *n* **:** any of several plants (as a fuchsia or bleeding heart) with flowers resembling eardrops — called also *ladies'-eardrops*
la·dy·ship \ˈlād-ē-ˌship\ *n* **:** the condition of being a lady **:** rank of lady — used as a title for a woman having the rank of lady <her *Ladyship* is not at home> <if your *Ladyship* please>
lady's slipper \ˈlād-ē(z)-ˌslip-ər\ *n* **:** any of several No. American temperate-zone orchids (as of the genus *Cypripedium*) having flowers whose shape suggests a slipper — called also *lady slipper*
la·dy's–smock \ˈlād-ē(z)-ˌsmäk\ *n* **:** CUCKOOFLOWER 1
lady's thumb *n* **:** a widely distributed weedy annual herb (*Polygonum persicaria*) that has large lanceolate leaves often with a blackish blotch suggesting a thumbprint
La·er·tes \lā-ˈərt-ēz\ *n* [L, fr. Gk *Laertēs*] **1 :** the father of Odysseus in Greek legend **2 :** the son of Polonius and brother of Ophelia in Shakespeare's *Hamlet*

lady's slipper

Lae·ta·re Sunday \lā-ˌtär-ē-, -ˌtar-ē-\ *n* [L *laetare,* sing. imper. of *laetari* to rejoice] **:** the fourth Sunday in Lent
LaF *abbr* Louisiana French
[1]**lag** \ˈlag\ *vb* **lagged; lag·ging** [prob. of Scand origin; akin to Norw *lagga* to go slowly] *vi* **1 a :** to stay or fall behind **:** LINGER, LOITER **b :** to move, function, or develop with comparative slowness **c :** to become retarded in attaining maximum value **2 :** to slacken or weaken gradually **:** FLAG **3 :** to toss or roll a marble toward a line or a cue ball toward the head cushion to determine order of play ~ *vt* **1 :** to lag behind <current that ~*s* the voltage> **2 :** to pitch or shoot (as a coin or marble) at a mark — **lag·ger** *n*
[2]**lag** *n* **1 :** one that lags or is last **2 a :** the act or the condition of lagging **b :** comparative slowness or retardation **c** (1) **:** an amount of lagging or the time during which lagging continues (2) **:** a space of time esp. between related events or phenomena **:** INTERVAL **3 :** the action of lagging for opening shot (as in marbles or billiards)
[3]**lag** *adj* **:** LAST, HINDMOST
[4]**lag** *vt* **lagged; lag·ging** [origin unknown] **1** *slang* **:** to transport for crime or send to jail **2** *slang* **:** ARREST

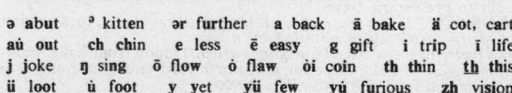

[5]lag *n* **1** *slang* **a :** a person transported for crime **b :** CONVICT **c :** an ex-convict **2** *slang* **:** a jail sentence **:** STRETCH

[6]lag *n* [prob. of Scand origin; akin to ON *lögg* rim of a barrel] **1 :** a barrel stave **2 :** a stave, slat, or strip (as of wood or asbestos) forming part of a covering for a cylindrical object

[7]lag *vt* **lagged; lag·ging :** to cover or provide with lags

lag·an \'lag-ən\ *also* **lag·end** \-ənd\ *n* [MF *lagan* or ML *laganum* debris washed up from the sea] **:** goods thrown into the sea with a buoy attached so that they may be found again

Lag b'Omer \'läg-'bō-mər, ˌläg-bə-'ō-\ *n* [Heb, 33d in omer] **:** a Jewish holiday falling on the 33d day of the omer and commemorating the heroism of Bar Cocheba and Akiba

la·ger \'läg-ər\ *n* [G *lagerbier* beer made for storage, fr. *lager* storehouse + *bier* beer] **:** a beer brewed by slow fermentation and stored in refrigerated cellars for maturing

[1]lag·gard \'lag-ərd\ *adj* **:** lagging or tending to lag **:** DILATORY — **lag·gard·ly** *adv or adj* — **lag·gard·ness** *n*

[2]laggard *n* **:** one that lags or lingers; *esp* **:** a security whose price has lagged for no obvious reason behind the average of its group or of the market

lag·ging \'lag-iŋ\ *n* **:** a lag or material used for making lags: as **a :** material for thermal insulation esp. around a cylindrical object **b :** planking used esp. for preventing cave-ins in earthwork or for supporting an arch during construction

la·gniappe \'lan-ˌyap, lan-'\ *n* [AmerF, fr. AmerSp *la ñapa* the lagniappe] **:** a small gift given a customer by a merchant at the time of a purchase; *broadly* **:** something given or obtained gratuitously or by way of good measure

lago·morph \'lag-ə-ˌmȯrf\ *n* [deriv. of Gk *lagōs* hare + *morphē* form] **:** any of an order (Lagomorpha) of gnawing mammals having two pairs of incisors in the upper jaw one behind the other and comprising the rabbits, hares, and pikas — **lago·mor·phic** \ˌlag-ə-'mȯr-fik\ *adj* — **lago·mor·phous** \-fəs\ *adj*

la·goon \lə-'gün\ *n* [F & It; F *lagune*, fr. It *laguna*, fr. L *lacuna* pit, pool, fr. *lacus* lake] **1 :** a shallow sound, channel, or pond near or communicating with a larger body of water **2 :** a shallow artificial pool or pond (as for the processing of sewage or storage of a liquid) — **la·goon·al** \-ᵊl\ *adj*

La·grang·ian \lə-'grän-jē-ən, -'grän-zhē-\ *n* [Joseph Louis *Lagrange*] **:** a function that describes the state of a dynamic system in terms of position coordinates and their time derivatives and that is equal to the difference between the potential energy and kinetic energy — called also *kinetic potential;* compare HAMILTONIAN

la·gu·na \lə-'gü-nə\ *n* [Sp, fr. L *lacuna*] **:** a small lake or pond

Lahn·da \'län-də\ *n* **:** an Indic language of West Punjab

la·ical \'lā-ə-kəl\ *or* **la·ic** \'lā-ik\ *adj* [LL *laicus*, fr. LGk *laikos*, fr. Gk, of the people, fr. *laos* people] **:** of or relating to the laity **:** SECULAR — **laic** *n* — **la·ical·ly** \'lā-ə-k(ə-)lē\ *adv*

la·icism \'lā-ə-ˌsiz-əm\ *n* **:** a political system characterized by the exclusion of ecclesiastical control and influence

la·icize \'lā-ə-ˌsīz\ *vt* **la·icized; la·iciz·ing 1 :** to reduce to lay status **2 :** to put under the direction of or open to laymen — **la·ici·za·tion** \ˌlā-ə-sə-'zā-shən\ *n*

laid *past of* LAY

laid paper \'lād-\ *n* **:** paper watermarked with fine lines running across the grain — compare WOVE PAPER

laigh \'lāk\ *Scot var of* LOW

lain *past part of* LIE

[1]lair \'la(ə)r, 'le(ə)r\ *n* [ME, fr. OE *leger;* akin to OHG *legar* bed, OE *licgan* to lie — more at LIE] **1** *dial Brit* **:** a resting or sleeping place **:** BED **2 a :** the resting or living place of a wild animal **:** DEN **b :** a refuge or place for hiding

[2]lair *vb* [Sc *lair* (mire)] *vt, chiefly Scot* **:** to cause to sink in mire ~ *vi, chiefly Scot* **:** WALLOW

laird \'la(ə)rd, 'le(ə)rd\ *n* [ME (northern dial.) *lord, lard* lord] *Scot* **:** a landed proprietor — **laird·ly** \-lē\ *adj*

lais·ser–faire *chiefly Brit var of* LAISSEZ-FAIRE

lais·sez–faire \ˌle-ˌsā-'fa(ə)r, ˌlā-, -ˌzā-, -'fe(ə)r\ *n* [F *laissez faire*, imper. of *laisser faire* to let (people) do (as they choose)] **1 :** a doctrine opposing governmental interference in economic affairs beyond the minimum necessary for the maintenance of peace and property rights **2 :** a philosophy or practice characterized by a usu. deliberate abstention from direction or interference esp. with individual freedom of choice and action — **laissez–faire** *adj*

lais·sez–pas·ser \-ˌpa-'sā\ *n* [F, fr. *laissez passer* let (someone) pass] **:** PERMIT, PASS

lai·tance \'lāt-ᵊn(t)s\ *n* [F, fr. *lait* milk, fr. L *lact-, lac* — more at GALAXY] **:** an accumulation of fine particles on the surface of fresh concrete due to an upward movement of water (as when excessive mixing water is used)

la·ity \'lā-ət-ē\ *n* [[5]*lay*] **1 :** the people of a religious faith as distinguished from its clergy **2 :** the mass of the people as distinguished from those of a particular profession or those specially skilled

La·ius \'lā-(y)əs, 'lī-əs\ *n* [L, fr. Gk *Laïos*] **:** a king of Thebes slain by his son Oedipus in fulfillment of an oracle

[1]lake \'lāk\ *n, often attrib* [ME, fr. OF *lac* lake, fr. L *lacus;* akin to OE *lagu* sea, Gk *lakkos* pond] **:** a considerable inland body of standing water; *also* **:** a pool of other liquid (as lava, oil, or pitch)

[2]lake *n* [F *laque* lac, fr. OProv *laca*, fr. Ar *lakk* — more at LACQUER] **1 a :** a purplish red pigment prepared from lac or cochineal **b :** any of numerous usu. bright translucent organic pigments composed essentially of a soluble dye absorbed on or combined with an inorganic carrier **2 :** CARMINE 2 — **laky** \'lā-kē\ *adj*

[3]lake *vb* **laked; lak·ing** *vi, of blood* **:** to alter so that the hemoglobin is dissolved in the plasma ~ *vt* **:** to cause (blood) to lake

lake dweller *n* **:** one that lives in a lake dwelling

lake dwelling *n* **:** a dwelling built on piles in a lake; *specif* **:** one built in prehistoric times

lake·front \'lāk-ˌfrənt\ *n* **:** land, land with buildings, or a section of a town fronting or abutting on a lake

lake herring *n* **:** a cisco (*Coregonus artedii*) found from Lake Memphremagog to Lake Superior and northward and important as a commercial food fish; *broadly* **:** CISCO

Lake·land terrier \'lā-ˌklan(d)-, -klən(d)-\ *n* [*Lakeland*, England] **:** any of an English breed of rather small harsh-coated straight-legged terriers

lak·er \'lā-kər\ *n* **:** one associated with a lake; *esp* **:** a fish living in or taken from a lake

lake·shore \-ˌshō(ə)r, -ˌshȯ(ə)r\ *n* **:** the shore of a lake; *also* **:** LAKEFRONT

lake·side \-ˌsīd\ *n* **:** LAKEFRONT

lake trout *n* **:** any of various salmon and trout found in lakes; *esp* **:** a large dark No. American char (*Salvelinus namaycush*) that is an important commercial food fish in northern lakes

lakh \'läk, 'lak\ *n* [Hindi *lākh*] **1 :** one hundred thousand <50 ~*s* of rupees> **2 :** a great number — **lakh** *adj*

-la·lia \'lā-lē-ə\ *n comb form* [NL, fr. Gk *lalia* chatter, fr. *lalein* to chat] **:** speech disorder (of a specified type) <echo*lalia*>

lal·lan \'lal-ən\ *or* **lal·land** \-ən(d)\ *Scot var of* LOWLAND

Lal·lans \'lal-ənz\ *n* **:** Scots as spoken in the southern and eastern part of Scotland

Lal·ly \'läl-ē\ *trademark* — used for a concrete-filled cylindrical steel structural column

lal·ly·gag \'läl-\ *var of* LOLLYGAG

[1]lam \'lam\ *vb* **lammed; lam·ming** [of Scand origin; akin to ON *lemja* to thrash; akin to OE *lama* lame] *vt* **:** to beat soundly **:** THRASH ~ *vi* **1 :** STRIKE, THRASH **2 :** to flee hastily **:** SCRAM

[2]lam *n* **:** sudden or hurried flight esp. from the law <on the ~>

[3]lam *abbr* laminated

Lam *abbr* Lamentations

la·ma \'läm-ə\ *n* [Tibetan *blama*] **:** a Lamaist monk

La·ma·ism \'läm-ə-ˌiz-əm\ *n* **:** the Mahayana Buddhism of Tibet and Mongolia marked by tantric and shamanistic ritual and a dominant monastic hierarchy headed by the Dalai Lama — **La·ma·ist** \-ə-əst\ *n or adj* — **La·ma·is·tic** \ˌläm-ə-'is-tik\ *adj*

La·marck·ian \lə-'mär-kē-ən\ *adj* **:** of or relating to Lamarckism

La·marck·ism \lə-'mär-ˌkiz-əm\ *n* [J. B. de Monet *Lamarck*] **:** a theory of organic evolution asserting that environmental changes cause structural changes in animals and plants that are transmitted to offspring

la·ma·sery \'läm-ə-ˌser-ē\ *n, pl* **-ser·ies** [F *lamaserie*, fr. *lama* + Per *sarāi* palace] **:** a monastery of lamas

[1]lamb \'lam\ *n* [ME, fr. OE; akin to OHG *lamb* lamb, *elaho* elk — more at ELK] **1 a :** a young sheep; *esp* **:** one that is less than one year old or without permanent teeth **b :** the young of various animals (as the smaller antelopes) other than sheep **2 a :** a person as gentle or weak as a lamb **b :** DEAR, PET **c :** a person easily cheated or deceived esp. in trading securities **3 a :** the flesh of a lamb used as food **b :** LAMBSKIN

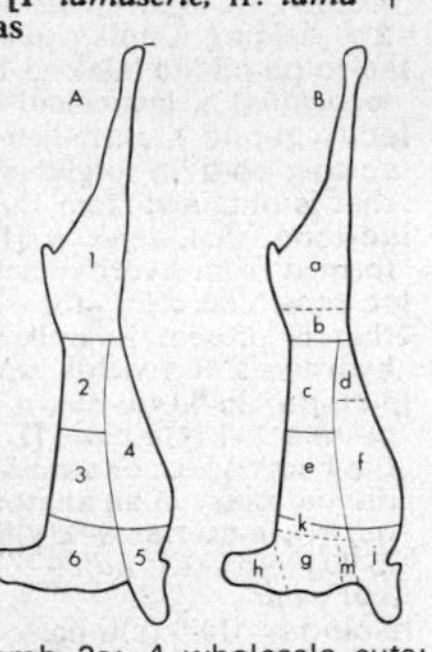

lamb 3a: *A* wholesale cuts: *1* leg, *2* loin, *3* rack, *4* breast, *5* shank, *6* shoulder; *B* retail cuts: *a* leg, *b* sirloin chops and roast, *c* loin chops and rolled loin roast, *d* patties and chopped roast, *e* rib chops and crown roast, *f* riblets, stew, and stuffed or rolled breast, *g* shoulder roast, shoulder chops, *h* neck slices, *i* shanks, *k* blade chops, *m* arm chops

[2]lamb *vi* **:** to bring forth a lamb ~ *vt* **1 :** to bring forth (a lamb) **2 :** to tend (ewes) at lambing time — **lamb·er** \'lam-ər\ *n*

lam·baste *or* **lam·bast** \(')lam-'bāst, -'bast\ *vt* [prob. fr. [1]*lam* + *baste*] **1 :** to assault violently **:** BEAT, WHIP **2 :** to attack verbally **:** CENSURE

lamb·da \'lam-də\ *n* [Gk, of Sem origin; akin to Heb *lāmedh* lamed] **1 :** the 11th letter of the Greek alphabet — see ALPHABET table **2 :** one thousandth of a cubic centimeter **3 :** an uncharged unstable elementary particle that has a mass 2183 times that of an electron and that decays typically into a nucleon and a pion

lam·ben·cy \'lam-bən-sē\ *n, pl* **-cies :** the quality, state, or an instance of being lambent

lam·bent \'lam-bənt\ *adj* [L *lambent-, lambens*, prp. of *lambere* to lick — more at LAP] **1 :** playing lightly on or over a surface **:** FLICKERING **2 :** softly bright or radiant **3 :** marked by lightness or brilliance esp. of expression — **lam·bent·ly** *adv*

lam·bert \'lam-bərt\ *n* [Johann H. *Lambert* †1777 G physicist & philosopher] **:** the cgs unit of brightness equal to the brightness of a perfectly diffusing surface that radiates or reflects one lumen per square centimeter

lamb·kill \'lam-ˌkil\ *n* **:** SHEEP LAUREL

lam·bre·quin \'lam-bər-kən, -bri-kən\ *n* [F] **1 :** a scarf used to cover a knight's helmet **2 :** a short decorative drapery for a shelf edge or for the top of a window casing **:** VALANCE

lamb·skin \'lam-ˌskin\ *n* **:** a lamb's skin or a small fine-grade sheepskin or the leather made from either; *specif* **:** such a skin dressed with the wool on and used esp. for winter clothing

lamb's–quar·ters \'lamz-ˌkwȯ(r)t-ərz\ *n pl but sing or pl in constr* **1 :** a goosefoot (*Chenopodium album*) with glaucous foliage that is sometimes used as a potherb **2 :** any of several oraches

[1]lame \'lām\ *adj* **lam·er; lam·est** [ME, fr. OE *lama;* akin to OHG *lam* lame, Lith *limti* to break down] **1 a :** having a body part and esp. a limb so disabled as to impair freedom of movement <a ~ old man> **b :** marked by stiffness and soreness <a ~ shoulder> **2 :** lacking needful or desirable substance **:** WEAK <a ~ excuse> **3** *slang* **:** not in the know **:** SQUARE — **lame·ly** *adv* — **lame·ness** *n*

[2]lame *vt* **lamed; lam·ing 1 :** to make lame **:** CRIPPLE **2 :** to make weak or ineffective **:** DISABLE

[3]lame *n, slang* **:** a person who is not in the know **:** SQUARE

[4]lame \'lām, 'lam\ *n* [MF, fr. L *lamina*] **1 :** a thin plate esp. of metal **:** LAMINA **2** *pl* **:** small overlapping steel plates joined to slide on one another (as in medieval armor)

la·mé \lä-ˈmā, la-\ *n* [F] **:** a brocaded clothing fabric made from any of various fibers combined with tinsel filling threads often of gold or silver

lame·brain \ˈlām-ˌbrān\ *n* **:** a dull-witted or erratic person **:** CRACKPOT, DOLT — **lamebrain** *or* **lame·brained** \-ˈbrānd\ *adj*

la·med \ˈläm-ˌed\ *n* [Heb *lāmedh,* lit., ox goad] **:** the 12th letter of the Hebrew alphabet — see ALPHABET table

lame duck *n* **1 :** an elected officer or group continuing to hold political office during a usu. brief interim between defeat for reelection and the inauguration of a successor **2 :** one that falls behind in achievement **:** WEAKLING

lamell- *or* **lamelli-** *comb form* [NL, fr. *lamella*] **:** lamella <*lamelli*form> <*lamell*ose>

la·mel·la \lə-ˈmel-ə\ *n, pl* **la·mel·lae** \-ˈmel-(ˌ)ē, -ˌī\ *also* **lamellas** [NL, fr. L, dim. of *lamina* thin plate] **:** a thin flat scale, membrane, or part: as **a :** one of the thin plates composing the gills of a bivalve mollusk **b :** a gill of a mushroom — **la·mel·lar** \-ˈmel-ər\ *adj* — **la·mel·lar·ly** *adv*

la·mel·late \lə-ˈmel-ət, ˈlam-ə-ˌlāt\ *adj* **1 :** composed of or furnished with lamellae **2 :** LAMELLIFORM — **la·mel·late·ly** *adv*

lam·el·la·tion \ˌlam-ə-ˈlā-shən\ *n* **1 :** formation or division into lamellae **2 :** LAMELLA

la·mel·li·branch \lə-ˈmel-ə-ˌbraŋk\ *n, pl* **-branchs** [NL *Lamellibranchia,* class name, fr. *lamell-* + L *branchia* gill — more at BRANCHIA] **:** any of a class (Lamellibranchia) of bivalve mollusks (as clams, oysters, and mussels) that have the body bilaterally symmetrical, compressed, and enclosed within the mantle and that build up a shell whose right and left parts are connected by a hinge over the animal's back — **lamellibranch** *adj* — **la·mel·li·bran·chi·ate** \lə-ˌmel-ə-ˈbraŋ-kē-ət\ *adj or n*

la·mel·li·corn \lə-ˈmel-ə-ˌkȯrn\ *adj* **:** of, relating to, or belonging to a taxonomic group (Lamellicornia) of beetles (as a dung beetle and a stag beetle) that are characterized by 5-jointed tarsi and club-shaped antennae — **lamellicorn** *n*

la·mel·li·form \-ˌfȯrm\ *adj* **:** having the form of a thin plate

¹la·ment \lə-ˈment\ *vb* [MF & L; MF *lamenter,* fr. L *lamentari,* fr. *lamentum,* n., lament; akin to ON *lōmr* loon, L *latrare* to bark, Gk *lēros* nonsense] *vi* **:** to mourn aloud **:** WAIL ~ *vt* **1 :** to express sorrow or mourning for often demonstratively **:** MOURN **2 :** to regret strongly ***syn*** see DEPLORE

²lament *n* **1 :** a crying out in grief **:** WAILING **2 :** DIRGE, ELEGY **3 :** COMPLAINT

la·men·ta·ble \ˈlam-ən-tə-bəl, lə-ˈment-ə-\ *adj* **1 :** that is to be regretted or lamented **:** DEPLORABLE **2 :** expressing grief **:** MOURNFUL — **la·men·ta·ble·ness** *n* — **la·men·ta·bly** \-blē\ *adv*

lam·en·ta·tion \ˌlam-ən-ˈtā-shən\ *n* **:** an act or instance of lamenting

Lam·en·ta·tions \-shənz\ *n pl but sing in constr* **:** a poetic book on the fall of Jerusalem in canonical Jewish and Christian Scripture — see BIBLE table

la·ment·ed \lə-ˈment-əd\ *adj* **:** mourned for — **la·ment·ed·ly** *adv*

la·mia \ˈlā-mē-ə\ *n* [ME, fr. L, fr. Gk, devouring monster — more at LEMUR] **:** a female demon **:** VAMPIRE

lamin- *or* **lamini-** *or* **lamino-** *comb form* **:** lamina <*lamin*ar>

lam·i·na \ˈlam-ə-nə\ *n, pl* **-nae** \-ˌnē, -ˌnī\ *or* **-nas** [L] **1 :** a thin plate or scale **2 :** the expanded part of a foliage leaf **3 :** one of the narrow thin parallel plates of soft vascular sensitive tissue that cover the flesh within the wall of a hoof

lam·i·nal \ˈlam-ən-ᵊl\ *adj* **:** LAMINAR

lamina pro·pria \-ˈprō-prē-ə\ *n, pl* **laminae pro·pri·ae** \-prē-ˌē, -ˌī\ [NL, lit., lamina proper] **:** BASEMENT MEMBRANE

lam·i·nar \ˈlam-ə-nər\ *adj* **:** arranged in, consisting of, or resembling laminae

laminar flow *n* **:** streamline flow in a viscous fluid near a solid boundary — compare TURBULENT FLOW

lam·i·nar·ia \ˌlam-ə-ˈner-ē-ə, -ˈnar-\ *n* [NL, genus name] **:** any of a genus (*Laminaria*) of large chiefly perennial kelps with an unbranched cylindrical or flattened stipe and a smooth or convoluted blade; *broadly* **:** any of various related kelps (order Laminariales) — **lam·i·nar·i·an** \-ē-ən\ *adj*

laminaria

lam·i·nar·i·an \-ē-ən\ *n* **:** LAMINARIA

lam·i·nar·in \ˌlam-ə-ˈner-ən, -ˈnar-\ *n* [ISV *laminar-* (fr. NL *Laminaria*) + *-in*] **:** a polysaccharide that is found in various brown algae and yields only glucose on hydrolysis

¹lam·i·nate \ˈlam-ə-ˌnāt\ *vb* **-nat·ed; -nat·ing** *vt* **1 :** to roll or compress into a thin plate **2 :** to separate into laminae **3 :** to make by uniting superposed layers of one or more materials ~ *vi* **:** to divide into laminae — **lam·i·na·tor** \-ˌnāt-ər\ *n*

²lam·i·nate \-nət, -ˌnāt\ *adj* **1 :** consisting of laminae **2 :** bearing or covered with laminae

³lam·i·nate \-nət, -ˌnāt\ *n* **:** a product made by laminating

lam·i·nat·ed \-ˌnāt-əd\ *adj* **1 :** LAMINATE 1 **2 a :** composed of layers of firmly united material **b :** made by bonding or impregnating superposed layers (as of paper, wood, or fabric) with resin and compressing under heat

lam·i·na·tion \ˌlam-ə-ˈnā-shən\ *n* **1 :** the process of laminating **2 :** the state of being laminated **3 :** a laminate structure **4 :** LAMINA

Lam·mas \ˈlam-əs\ *n* [ME *Lammasse,* fr. OE *hlāfmæsse,* fr. *hlāf* loaf, bread + *mæsse* mass; fr. the fact that formerly loaves from the first ripe grain were consecrated on this day] **1 :** August 1 orig. celebrated in England as a harvest festival — called also *Lammas Day* **2 :** the time of the year around Lammas Day

Lammastide *n* **:** LAMMAS 2

lam·mer·gei·er *or* **lam·mer·gey·er** \ˈlam-ər-ˌgī(-ə)r\ *n* [G *lämmergeier*] **:** a large Eurasian vulture (*Gypaetus barbatus aureus*) that occurs in mountain regions from the Pyrenees to northern China and in flight resembles a huge falcon

lamp \ˈlamp\ *n* [ME, fr. OF *lampe,* fr. L *lampas,* fr. Gk, fr. *lampein* to shine; akin to ON *leiptr* lightning] **1 a :** a vessel with a wick for burning an inflammable liquid (as oil) to produce artificial light **b :** any of various devices for producing light or heat **2 :** a celestial body **3 :** a source of intellectual or spiritual illumination

lamp·black \-ˌblak\ *n* **:** a finely powdered black soot deposited in incomplete combustion of carbonaceous materials and used chiefly as a pigment (as in paints, enamels, and printing inks)

lamp·brush chromosome \ˌlamp-ˌbrəsh-\ *n* [*lampbrush* prob. trans. of (assumed) G *lampebürste* brush for cleaning oil lamps] **:** a greatly enlarged pachytene chromosome that has apparently filamentous granular loops extending from the chromomeres and is characteristic of some animal oocytes

lam·per eel \ˌlam-pər-\ *n* [alter. of *lamprey*] **1 :** LAMPREY **2 :** CONGO SNAKE

lamp·light \ˈlam-ˌplīt\ *n* **:** the light of a lamp

lamp·light·er \-ər\ *n* **:** one that lights a lamp

¹lam·poon \lam-ˈpün\ *n* [F *lampon*] **1 :** a harsh satire usu. directed against an individual **2 :** a light mocking satire

²lampoon *vt* **:** to make the subject of a lampoon **:** RIDICULE — **lam·poon·er** *n* — **lam·poon·ery** \-ˈpün-(ə-)rē\ *n*

lam·prey \ˈlam-prē, -ˌprā\ *n, pl* **lampreys** [ME, fr. OF *lampreie,* fr. ML *lampreda*] **:** any of an order (Hyperoartia) of aquatic vertebrates that are widely distributed in temperate and subarctic regions in both fresh and salt water and resemble eels but have a large suctorial mouth — called also *lamprey eel*

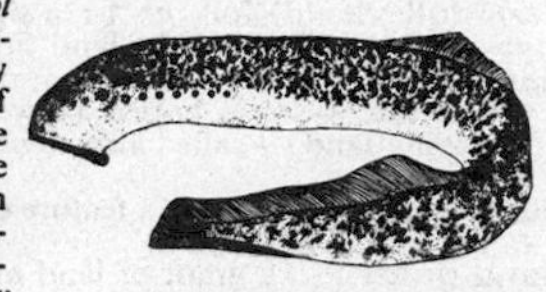
lamprey

lamp·shell \ˈlamp-ˌshel\ *n* [fr. the resemblance of the shell and its protruding peduncle to an ancient oil lamp with the wick protruding] **:** BRACHIOPOD

lam·ster \ˈlam(p)-stər\ *also* **lam·is·ter** \ˈlam-ə-stər\ *n* [²*lam* + *-ster*] **:** a fugitive esp. from the law

la·nai \lə-ˈnī, lä-\ *n* [Hawaiian] **:** PORCH, VERANDA

Lan·cas·tri·an \lan-ˈkas-trē-ən, laŋ-\ *adj* [John of Gaunt, duke of *Lancaster* †1399] **:** of or relating to the English royal house that ruled from 1399 to 1461

¹lance \ˈlan(t)s\ *n* [ME, fr. OF, fr. L *lancea*] **1 :** a weapon of war consisting of a long shaft with a sharp steel head carried by mounted knights or light cavalry **2 :** any of various sharp objects suggestive of a lance: as **a :** LANCET **b :** a spear used for killing whales **3 :** LANCER 1b

²lance *vb* **lanced; lanc·ing** [ME *launcen,* fr. MF *lancer,* fr. LL *lanceare,* fr. L *lancea*] *vt* **1 a :** to pierce with or as if with a lance **b :** to open with or as if with a lancet <~ a boil> **2 :** to throw forward **:** HURL ~ *vi* **:** to move forward quickly

lance corporal *n* [*lance* (as in obs. *lancepesade* lance corporal, fr. MF *lancepessade*)] **:** an enlisted man in the marine corps ranking above a private first class and below a corporal

lance·let \ˈlan(t)-slət\ *n* **:** any of various small translucent marine animals (subphylum Cephalochordata) related to the vertebrates — called also *amphioxus*

Lan·ce·lot \ˈlan(t)-sə-ˌlät, ˈlän(t)-, -s(ə-)lət\ *n* [F] **:** a knight of the Round Table and lover of Queen Guinevere

lan·ceo·late \ˈlan(t)-sē-ə-ˌlāt\ *adj* [LL *lanceolatus,* fr. L *lanceola,* dim. of *lancea*] **:** shaped like a lance head; *specif* **:** tapering to a point at the apex and sometimes at the base <~ leaves> <~ prisms> — **lan·ceo·late·ly** *adv*

lanc·er \ˈlan(t)-sər\ *n* **1 a :** one who carries a lance **b :** a member of a military unit formerly composed of light cavalry armed with lances **2** *pl but sing in constr* **a :** a set of five quadrilles each in a different meter **b :** the music for such dances

lan·cet \ˈlan(t)-sət\ *n* **1 :** a sharp-pointed and commonly two-edged surgical instrument used to make small incisions **2 a :** LANCET WINDOW **b :** LANCET ARCH

lancet arch *n* **:** an acutely pointed arch — see ARCH illustration

lan·cet·ed \ˈlan(t)-sət-əd\ *adj* **:** having a lancet arch or lancet windows

lancet window *n* **:** a high narrow window with an acutely pointed head and without tracery

lance·wood \ˈlan(t)-ˌswu̇d\ *n* **:** a tough elastic wood used esp. for shafts, fishing rods, and bows; *also* **:** a tree (esp. *Oxandra lanceolata*) yielding this wood

lan·ci·nate \ˈlan(t)-sə-ˌnāt\ *vb* **-nat·ed; -nat·ing** [L *lancinatus,* pp. of *lancinare;* akin to L *lacer* mangled — more at LACERATE] **:** PIERCE, STAB — **lan·ci·na·tion** \ˌlan(t)-sə-ˈnā-shən\ *n*

Lancs *abbr* Lancashire

¹land \ˈland\ *n, often attrib* [ME, fr. OE; akin to OHG *lant* land, OIr *land* open space] **1 a :** the solid part of the surface of the earth; *also* **:** a corresponding part of another celestial body (as the moon) **b :** ground or soil of a specified situation, nature, or quality <wet ~> **c :** the surface of the earth and all its natural resources **2 :** a portion of the earth's solid surface distinguishable by boundaries or ownership: as **a :** COUNTRY <campaigned in every corner of the ~> **b :** privately or publicly owned land <had some ~ in the country> **3 :** REALM, DOMAIN <in the ~ of dreams> **4 :** the people of a country <the ~ rose in rebellion> **5 :** an area of a partly machined surface that is left without machining — **land·less** \ˈlan-dləs\ *adj*

²land *vt* **1 :** to set or put on shore from a ship **:** DISEMBARK **2 a :** to set down after conveying **b :** to cause to reach or come to rest in a particular place <never ~*ed* a punch> **c :** to bring to a specified condition <his carelessness ~*ed* him in trouble> **d** : to bring (as an airplane) to a landing **3 a** : to catch and bring in (as a fish) **b** : GAIN, SECURE <~ a job> ~ *vi* **1 a** : to go ashore from a ship : DISEMBARK **b** *of a ship or boat* : to touch at a place on shore **2 a** : to come to the end of a course or to a stage in a journey : ARRIVE <took the wrong subway and ~*ed* on the other side of town> **b** : to strike or meet a surface (as after a fall) <~*ed* on his head> **c** *of an airplane or spacecraft* : to alight on a surface

lan·dau \ˈlan-ˌdau̇, -ˌdȯ\ *n* [*Landau,* Bavaria, Germany] **1** : a four-wheeled carriage with a top divided into two sections that can be let down, thrown back, or removed and with a raised seat outside for the driver **2** : a closed automobile body with a folding top over the rear passenger compartment

lan·dau·let \ˌlan-dᵊl-ˈet\ *n* **1** : a small landau **2** : an automobile body with an open driver's seat and an enclosed rear section having one cross seat and a collapsible roof

land·ed \ˈlan-dəd\ *adj* **1** : having an estate in land <~ proprietors> **2** : consisting in or derived from land or real estate <~ property>

land·er \ˈlan-dər\ *n* : one that lands; *esp* : a space vehicle that is designed to land on a celestial body (as the moon or a planet)

land·fall \ˈlan(d)-ˌfȯl\ *n* **1** : a sighting or making of land after a voyage or flight **2** : the land first sighted on a voyage or flight

land·fill \-ˌfil\ *n* **1** : a system of trash and garbage disposal in which the waste is buried between layers of earth to build up low-lying land — called also *sanitary landfill* **2** : an area built up by landfill

land·form \-ˌfȯrm\ *n* : a feature of the earth's surface attributable to natural causes

land grant *n* : a grant of land made by the government esp. for roads, railroads, or agricultural colleges

land·hold·er \ˈland-ˌhōl-dər\ *n* : a holder or owner of land — **land·hold·ing** \-diŋ\ *adj or n*

land·ing *n* **1** : an act or process of one that lands; *esp* : a going or bringing to a surface (as land or shore) after a voyage or flight **2** : a place for discharging and taking on passengers and cargo **3** : a level part of a staircase (as at the end of a flight of stairs)

landing craft *n* : any of numerous naval craft designed for putting troops and equipment ashore

landing field *n* : a field where aircraft may land and take off

landing gear *n* : the part that supports the weight of an airplane or spacecraft when in contact with the land or water — see AIRPLANE illustration

landing net *n* : a small net with a handle used to take hooked fish from the water

landing strip *n* : AIRSTRIP

land·la·dy \ˈlan-ˌ(d)lād-ē\ *n* : a female landlord

land·locked \ˈlan-ˌ(d)läkt\ *adj* **1** : enclosed or nearly enclosed by land <a ~ country> **2** : confined to fresh water by some barrier <~ salmon>

land·lord \ˈlan-ˌ(d)lȯ(ə)rd\ *n* **1** : the owner of property (as land, houses, or apartments) which is leased or rented to another **2** : the master of an inn or lodging house : INNKEEPER

land·lord·ism \-ˌiz-əm\ *n* : an economic system or practice by which ownership of land is vested in one who leases it to cultivators

land·lub·ber \ˈlan-ˌ(d)ləb-ər\ *n* **1** : LANDSMAN 2 **2** : a person unacquainted with the sea or seamanship — **land·lub·ber·ly** \-ər-lē\ *adj*

land·mark \ˈlan(d)-ˌmärk\ *n* **1** : an object (as a stone or tree) that marks the boundary of land **2 a** : a conspicuous object on land that marks a locality **b** : an anatomical structure used as a point of orientation in locating other structures **3** : an event or development that marks a turning point or a stage <this novel is a ~ in modern literature> **4** : a structure (as a building) of unusual historical and usu. aesthetic interest; *esp* : one that is officially designated and set aside for preservation

land·mass \-ˌmas\ *n* : a large area of land <continental ~*es*>

land office *n* : a government office in which entries upon and sales of public land are registered

land–office business *n* : extensive and rapid business <money changers . . . did a *land-office business* on payday —F. J. Haskin>

land·own·er \ˈlan-ˌdō-nər\ *n* : an owner of land — **land·own·er·ship** \-ˌship\ *n* — **land·own·ing** \-ˌdō-niŋ\ *adj or n*

land plaster *n* : gypsum or gypsiferous rock ground fine for use as a fertilizer and soil amendment

land–poor \ˈlan(d)-ˌpu̇(ə)r\ *adj* : owning so much unprofitable or encumbered land as to lack funds to develop the land or pay the charges due thereon

Land·ra·ce \ˈlän-ˌ(d)räs-ə\ *n* [Dan, fr. *land* + *race*] : a swine of any of several breeds locally developed in northern Europe

land rail *n* : CORNCRAKE

land reform *n* : measures designed to effect a more equitable distribution of agricultural land esp. by governmental action; *also* : the resulting redistribution

¹land·scape \ˈlan(d)-ˌskāp\ *n, often attrib* [D *landschap,* fr. *land* + *-schap* -ship] **1 a** : a picture representing a view of natural inland scenery **b** : the art of depicting such scenery **2 a** : the landforms of a region in the aggregate **b** : a portion of territory that the eye can comprehend in a single view **3** *obs* : VISTA, PROSPECT

²landscape *vb* **land·scaped; land·scap·ing** *vt* : to modify or ornament (a natural landscape) by altering the plant cover ~ *vi* : to engage in the occupation of landscape gardening — **land·scap·er** *n*

landscape architect *n* : one whose profession is the arrangement of land for human use and enjoyment involving the placement of structures, vehicular and pedestrian ways, and plantings — **landscape architecture** *n*

landscape gardener *n* : one skilled in the development and decorative planting of gardens and grounds — **landscape gardening** *n*

land·side \ˈlan(d)-ˌsīd\ *n* : a sidepiece opposite the moldboard in a plow that guides the plow and takes the side pressure when the furrow is turned

¹land·slide \ˈlan(d)-ˌslīd\ *n* **1** : the usu. rapid downward movement of a mass of rock, earth, or artificial fill on a slope; *also* : the mass that moves down **2 a** : a great majority of votes for one side **b** : an overwhelming victory

²landslide *vi* **-slid** \-ˌslid\; **-slid·ing** \-ˌslīd-iŋ\ **1** : to produce a landslide **2** : to win an election by a heavy majority

land·slip \-ˌslip\ *n* : LANDSLIDE 1

Lands·mål *or* **Lands·maal** \ˈlän(t)s-ˌmȯl\ *n* [Norw, lit., language of the country] : NYNORSK

lands·man \ˈlan(d)z-mən\ *n* **1** : a fellow countryman **2** : one who lives on the land; *esp* : one who knows little or nothing of the sea or seamanship

¹land·ward \ˈlan-dwərd\ *also* **land·wards** \-dwərdz\ *adv* : to or toward the land

²landward *adj* : lying or being toward the land or on the side toward the land

¹lane \ˈlān\ *n* [ME, fr. OE *lanu;* akin to MD *lane* lane] **1** : a narrow passageway between fences or hedges **2** : a relatively narrow way or track: as **a** : an ocean route used by or prescribed for ships **b** : a strip of roadway for a single line of vehicles **c** : AIR LANE **d** : any of several parallel courses in which a competitor must stay during a race **e** : a narrow hardwood surface having pins at one end and a shallow channel along each side that is used in bowling **f** : FREE THROW LANE

²lane *Scot var of* LONE

lang *abbr* language

lang·bein·ite \ˈlaŋ-ˌbī-ˌnīt\ *n* [G *langbeinit,* fr. A. *Langbein,* 19th cent. G chemist] : a mineral $K_2Mg_2(SO_4)_3$ that is a double sulfate of potassium and magnesium much used in the fertilizer industry

lang·lauf \ˈläŋ-ˌlau̇f\ *n* [G, fr. *lang* long + *lauf* race] : cross-country running or racing on skis — **lang·lauf·er** \-ˌlau̇-fər\ *n*

lang·ley \ˈlaŋ-lē\ *n, pl* **langleys** [Samuel P. *Langley*] : a unit of solar radiation equivalent to one gram calorie per square centimeter of irradiated surface

Lan·go·bard \ˈlaŋ-gə-ˌbärd\ *n* [L *Langobardus*] : LOMBARD 1a — **Lan·go·bar·dic** \ˌlaŋ-gə-ˈbär-dik\ *adj*

lan·gouste \läⁿ-ˈgüst\ *n* [F] : SPINY LOBSTER

Lang·shan \ˈlaŋ-ˌshan\ *n* [*Langshan,* locality near Shanghai, China] : any of an Asiatic breed of large single-combed usu. black or white domestic fowls resembling the Cochin Chinas

¹lang syne \(ˈ)laŋ-ˈzīn\ *adv* [ME(Sc), fr. *lang* long + *syne* since] *chiefly Scot* : at a distant time in the past

²lang syne *n, chiefly Scot* : times past <should auld acquaintance be forgot, and days o' auld *lang syne* —Robert Burns>

lan·guage \ˈlaŋ-gwij\ *n* [ME, fr. OF, fr. *langue* tongue, language, fr. L *lingua* — more at TONGUE] **1 a** : the words, their pronunciation, and the methods of combining them used and understood by a considerable community **b (1)** : audible, articulate, meaningful sound as produced by the action of the vocal organs **(2)** : a systematic means of communicating ideas or feelings by the use of conventionalized signs, sounds, gestures, or marks having understood meanings **(3)** : the suggestion by objects, actions, or conditions of associated ideas or feelings <body ~> **(4)** : the means by which animals communicate **(5)** : a formal system of signs and symbols (as a logical calculus or FORTRAN) including rules for the formation and transformation of admissible expressions **(6)** : MACHINE LANGUAGE **2 a** : form or manner of verbal expression; *specif* : STYLE **b** : the vocabulary and phraseology belonging to an art or department of knowledge <legal ~> <indexing ~> **c** : abusive epithets : PROFANITY **3** : the study of language esp. as a school subject

LANGUAGES WITH OVER THIRTY MILLION NATIVE SPEAKERS[1]

LANGUAGE	MILLIONS	LANGUAGE	MILLIONS
Mandarin Chinese	585[2]	Telugu	55
English	275	Cantonese	55
Spanish	185	Korean	50
Russian	140	Panjabi	49
Bengali	125	Marathi	48
Hindi with Urdu	125	Tamil	47
Arabic	115	Ukrainian	46
Portuguese	110	Eastern Hindi	40
Japanese	105	Bhojpuri	39
German	100	Polish	38
Wu [Shanghai] Chinese	65	Vietnamese	37
Italian	60	Amoy-Swatow Chinese	36
Javanese	60	Thai with Lao	34
French	55	Turkish	34

[1] By permission of the Center for Applied Linguistics, Arlington, Va.
[2] Figures 50 million or above are given to the nearest 5 million.

language arts *n pl* : the subjects (as reading, spelling, literature, and composition) that aim at developing the student's comprehension and capacity for use of written and oral language

langue \ˈläⁿg\ *n* [F, lit., language] : language that is a system of elements or a set of habits common to a community of speakers — compare PAROLE

langue d'oc \läŋ-ˈdȯk, läⁿg-dȯk\ *n* [F, fr. OF, lit., language of *oc;* fr. the Provençal use of the word *oc* for "yes"] : PROVENÇAL 2

langue d'oïl \läŋ-ˈdȯi(ə)l, -ˈdȯi; läⁿg-dȯ-ēl, -dȯi\ *n* [F, fr. OF, lit., language of *oïl;* fr. the French use of the word *oïl* for "yes"] : FRENCH 1

lan·guet \ˈlaŋ-gwət, laŋ-ˈgwet\ *n* [ME, fr. MF *languete,* dim. of *langue*] : something resembling the tongue in form or function

lan·guid \ˈlaŋ-gwəd\ *adj* [MF *languide,* fr. L *languidus,* fr. *languēre* to languish — more at SLACK] **1** : drooping or flagging from or as if from exhaustion : WEAK **2** : sluggish in character or disposition : LISTLESS **3** : lacking force or quickness of movement : SLOW — **lan·guid·ly** *adv* — **lan·guid·ness** *n*

lan·guish \ˈlaŋ-gwish\ *vi* [ME *languishen,* fr. MF *languiss-,* stem of *languir,* fr. (assumed) VL *languire,* fr. L *languēre*] **1 a** : to be or become feeble, weak, or enervated **b** : to be or live in a state of depression or decreasing vitality **2 a :** to become dispirited : PINE <~*ing* in prison> **b :** to suffer neglect <the bill ~*ed* in the Senate for eight months> **3 :** to assume an expression of grief or emotion appealing for sympathy — **lan·guish·er** *n* — **lan·guish·ing·ly** \-gwish-iŋ-lē\ *adv* — **lan·guish·ment** \-gwish-mənt\ *n*

lan·guor \ˈlaŋ-(g)ər\ *n* [ME, fr. OF, fr. L, fr. *languēre*] **1 :** weakness or weariness of body or mind **2 :** listless indolence : DREAMINESS

lan·guor·ous \ˈlaŋ-(g)ə-rəs, -grəs\ *adj* **1 :** full of or characterized by languor **2 :** producing or tending to produce languor <a ~ climate> — **lan·guor·ous·ly** *adv*

lan·gur \läŋ-ˈgü(ə)r\ *n* [Hindi *lãgūr*] **:** any of various Asiatic slender long-tailed monkeys (family Colobidae) with bushy eyebrows and a chin tuft

lank \ˈlaŋk\ *adj* [(assumed) ME, fr. OE *hlanc;* akin to OHG *hlanca* loin, L *clingere* to girdle] **1 :** not well filled out : SLENDER, THIN <~ cattle> **2 :** insufficient in quantity, degree, or extent <~ grass> **3 :** hanging straight and limp without spring or curl <~ hair> ***syn*** see LEAN ***ant*** burly — **lank·ly** *adv* — **lank·ness** *n*

lanky \ˈlaŋ-kē\ *adj* **lank·i·er; -est :** ungracefully tall and thin ***syn*** see LEAN — **lank·i·ly** \-kə-lē\ *adv* — **lank·i·ness** \-kē-nəs\ *n*

lan·ner \ˈlan-ər\ *n* [ME *laner,* fr. MF *lanier*] **:** a falcon (*Falco biarmicus*) of southern Europe, southwestern Asia, or Africa; *specif* **:** a female lanner

lan·ner·et \ˌlan-ə-ˈret\ *n* **:** a male lanner

lan·o·lin \ˈlan-ᵊl-ən\ *n* [L *lana* wool + ISV *-ol* + *-in*] **:** wool grease esp. when refined for use in ointments and cosmetics

lan·ta·na \lan-ˈtän-ə\ *n* [NL, genus name, deriv. of It dial., viburnum] **:** any of a genus (*Lantana*) of tropical shrubs of the vervain family with showy heads of small bright flowers

lan·tern \ˈlant-ərn\ *n, often attrib* [ME *lanterne,* fr. MF, fr. L *lanterna,* fr. Gk *lamptēr,* fr. *lampein* to shine — more at LAMP] **1 :** a usu. portable protective case for a light with transparent openings **2 a** *obs* **:** LIGHTHOUSE **b :** the chamber in a lighthouse containing the light **c :** a structure with glazed or open sides above an opening in a roof for light or ventilation **d :** a small tower or cupola or one stage of a cupola **3 :** PROJECTOR 2b

lanterns 1: *1* barn, *2* bull's-eye

lantern fly *n* **:** any of several large brightly marked homopterous insects (family Fulgoridae) having the front of the head prolonged into a hollow structure

lantern jaw *n* **:** an undershot jaw — **lan·tern-jawed** \ˌlant-ərn-ˈjȯd\ *adj*

lantern pinion *n* **:** a gear pinion having cylindrical bars instead of teeth

lan·tha·nide \ˈlan(t)-thə-ˌnīd\ *n* [ISV] **:** any element in a series of elements of increasing atomic numbers beginning with lanthanum (57) or cerium (58) and ending with lutetium (71) — see PERIODIC TABLE table

lan·tha·non \-ˌnän\ *n* **:** LANTHANIDE

lan·tha·num \-nəm\ *n* [NL, fr. Gk *lanthanein* to escape notice] **:** a white soft malleable metallic element that occurs in rare-earth minerals — see ELEMENT table

lant·horn \ˈlant-ərn\ *n, chiefly Brit* **:** LANTERN

la·nu·gi·nous \lə-ˈn(y)ü-jə-nəs\ *adj* [L *lanuginosus,* fr. *lanugin-, lanugo*]**:** covered with down or fine soft hair : DOWNY — **la·nu·gi·nous·ness** *n*

la·nu·go \lə-ˈn(y)ü-(ˌ)gō\ *n* [L, down — more at WOOL] **:** a dense cottony or downy growth; *specif* **:** the soft woolly hair that covers the fetus of some mammals

lan·yard \ˈlan-yərd\ *n* [ME *lanyer,* fr. MF *laniere*] **1 :** a piece of rope or line for fastening something in a ship; *esp* **:** one of the pieces passing through deadeyes to extend shrouds or stays **2 a :** a cord worn around the neck to hold something (as a knife or a whistle) **b :** a cord worn as a symbol of a military citation **3 :** a strong line used to activate a system (as in firing a cannon or sounding a whistle)

Lao \ˈlau̇\ *n, pl* **Lao** *or* **Laos** \ˈlau̇z\ **1 :** a member of a Buddhist people living in Laos and adjacent parts of northeastern Thailand and constituting an important branch of the Tai race **2 :** the Thai language of the Lao people — **Lao** *adj*

La·oc·o·ön \lā-ˈäk-ə-ˌwän\ *n* [L, fr. Gk *Laokoōn*] **:** a Trojan priest killed with his sons by two sea serpents after warning the Trojans against the wooden horse

La·od·i·ce·an \(ˌ)lā-ˌäd-ə-ˈsē-ən\ *adj* [fr. the reproach to the church of the Laodiceans in Rev 3:15-16] **:** lukewarm or indifferent in religion or politics — **Laodicean** *n*

Lao·tian \lā-ˈō-shən, ˈlau̇-shən\ *n* [prob. fr. F *laotien,* adj. & n., irreg. fr. *Lao*] **:** LAO — **Laotian** *adj*

¹lap \ˈlap\ *n* [ME *lappe,* fr. OE *læppa;* akin to OHG *lappa* flap, L *labi* to slide — more at SLEEP] **1 a :** a loose panel or hanging flap esp. of a garment **b** *archaic* **:** the skirt of a coat or dress **2 a :** the clothing that lies on the knees, thighs, and lower part of the trunk when one sits **b :** the front part of the lower trunk and thighs of a seated person **3 :** responsible custody : CONTROL <going to drop the whole thing in your ~ —Hamilton Basso> — **lap·ful** \ˈlap-ˌfu̇l\ *n* — **the lap of luxury :** an environment of great ease, comfort, and wealth <was reared in *the lap of luxury*>

²lap *vb* **lapped; lap·ping** *vt* **1 a :** to fold over or around something : WIND **b :** to envelop entirely : SWATHE **2 :** to fold over esp. into layers **3 :** to hold protectively in or as if in the lap : CUDDLE **4 a :** to place over and cover a part of : OVERLAP <~ shingles on a roof> **b :** to unite (as beams or timbers) so as to preserve the same breadth and depth throughout **5 a :** to dress, smooth, or polish (as a metal surface) to a high degree of refinement or accuracy **b :** to work two surfaces together with or without abrasives until a very close fit is produced **6 a :** to overtake and thereby lead or increase the lead over (another contestant) by a full circuit of a racecourse **b :** to complete the circuit of (a racecourse) ~ *vi* **1 :** FOLD, WIND **2 a :** to project beyond or spread over something **b :** to lie partly over or alongside of something or of one another **3 :** to traverse a course — **lap·per** *n*

³lap *n* **1 a :** the amount by which one object overlaps or projects beyond another **b :** the part of an object that overlaps another **2 :** a smoothing and polishing tool usu. comprising a piece of wood, leather, felt, or soft metal used with or without an embedded abrasive **3 :** a doubling or layering of a flexible substance (as fibers or paper) **4 a :** the act or an instance of moving once around a closed course (as a racing track); *also* **:** the distance covered **b :** the act or an instance of traversing the length of a straight course (as a swimming pool); *also* **:** the distance covered **c :** one segment of a larger unit (as a journey) **d :** one complete turn (as of a rope around a drum)

⁴lap *vb* **lapped; lap·ping** [ME *lapen,* fr. OE *lapian;* akin to OHG *laffan* to lick, L *lambere,* Gk *laphyssein* to devour] *vi* **1 :** to take in food or drink with the tongue **2 a :** to make a gentle intermittent splashing sound **b :** to move in little waves : WASH ~ *vt* **1 a :** to take in (food or drink) with the tongue **b :** to take in or absorb eagerly or quickly — used with *up* <the crowd *lapped* up every word he said> **2 :** to flow or splash against in little waves — **lap·per** *n*

⁵lap *n* **1 a :** an act or instance of lapping **b :** the amount that can be carried to the mouth by one lick or scoop of the tongue **2 :** a thin or weak beverage or food **3 :** a gentle splashing sound

lap·a·rot·o·my \ˌlap-ə-ˈrät-ə-mē\ *n, pl* **-mies** [Gk *lapara* flank + ISV *-tomy*] **:** surgical section of the abdominal wall

lap belt *n* **:** a seat belt that fastens across the lap

lap·board \ˈlap-ˌbō(ə)rd, -ˌbȯ(ə)rd\ *n* **:** a board used on the lap as a table or desk

lap·dog \-ˌdȯg\ *n* **:** a small dog that may be held in the lap

la·pel \lə-ˈpel\ *n* [dim. of ¹*lap*] **:** the part of a garment that is turned back; *specif* **:** the fold of the front of a coat that is usu. a continuation of the collar

lap·i·dar·i·an \ˌlap-ə-ˈder-ē-ən\ *adj* **:** LAPIDARY 2

¹lap·i·dary \ˈlap-ə-ˌder-ē\ *n, pl* **-dar·ies 1 :** a cutter, polisher, or engraver of precious stones usu. other than diamonds **2 :** the art of cutting gems

²lapidary *adj* [L *lapidarius* of stone, fr. *lapid-, lapis* stone; akin to Gk *lepas* crag] **1 a :** sculptured in or engraved on stone **b :** of or relating to precious stones or the art of cutting them **2 :** having the elegance and precision associated with inscriptions on monumental stone <the ~ phrasing . . . and subtle condensations of emotions . . . reward attentive reading —G. A. Cardwell>

la·pil·lus \lə-ˈpil-əs\ *n, pl* **-li** \-ˌī, -(ˌ)ē\ [L, dim. of *lapis*] **:** a small stony or glassy fragment of lava thrown out in a volcanic eruption

lap·in \ˈlap-ən\ *n* [F] **1 :** RABBIT; *specif* **:** a castrated male rabbit **2 :** rabbit fur usu. sheared and dyed

la·pis la·zu·li \ˌlap-ə-ˈslaz(h)-ə-lē\ *n* [ME, fr. ML, fr. L *lapis* + ML *lazuli,* gen. of *lazulum* lapis lazuli, fr. Ar *lāzaward* — more at AZURE] **:** a semiprecious stone that is usu. rich azure blue and is essentially a complex silicate often with spangles of iron pyrites

lap joint *n* **:** a joint made by overlapping two ends or edges and fastening them together — **lap-joint·ed** \ˈlap-ˈjȯint-əd\ *adj*

Lapp \ˈlap\ *n* [Sw] **1 :** a member of a people of northern Scandinavia, Finland, and the Kola peninsula of northern Russia who are typically nomadic herders of reindeer, fishermen, and hunters of sea mammals **2 :** any or all of the closely related Finno-Ugric languages of the Lapps

lap·pet \ˈlap-ət\ *n* **1 :** a fold or flap on a garment or headdress **2 :** a flat overlapping or hanging piece (as a roofing tile or the wattle of a bird)

lap robe *n* **:** a covering (as a blanket) for the legs, lap, and feet esp. of a passenger in a car or carriage

¹lapse \ˈlaps\ *n* [L *lapsus,* fr. *lapsus,* pp. of *labi* to slip — more at SLEEP] **1 a :** a slight error typically due to forgetfulness or inattention <a ~ in table manners> **b :** a temporary deviation or fall esp. from a higher to a lower state <a ~ from grace> **2 a :** DROP; *specif* **:** a decrease of temperature or pressure as the height increases — compare LAPSE RATE **b :** a becoming less : DECLINE **3 a (1) :** the termination of a right or privilege through neglect to exercise it within some limit of time **(2) :** termination of coverage for nonpayment of premiums **b :** INTERRUPTION, DISCONTINUANCE <returned to college after a ~ of several years> **4 :** an abandonment of religious faith : APOSTASY **5 :** a passage of time; *also* **:** INTERVAL ***syn*** see ERROR

²lapse *vb* **lapsed; laps·ing** *vi* **1 a :** to fall from an attained and usu. high level (as of morals or manners) to one much lower : depart from an accepted standard **b :** to sink or slip gradually : SUBSIDE <the guests *lapsed* into silence when the speech began> **2 :** to go out of existence : CEASE <the experiment *lapsed* last year> **3 :** to pass from one proprietor to another by omission or negligence **4 a** *of time* **:** to run its course : PASS **b :** to glide past or along ~ *vt* **:** to let slip : FORFEIT <all of those who have *lapsed* their membership —*AAUP Bull.*> — **laps·er** *n*

syn LAPSE, RELAPSE, BACKSLIDE ***shared meaning element*** **:** to fall from a better or higher state into a lower or poorer one

lapse rate *n* **:** the adiabatic rate of change of a meteorological element (as temperature) associated with a change in height

lap·strake \ˈlap-ˌstrāk\ *also* **lap·streak** \-ˌstrēk\ *adj* **:** CLINKER-BUILT

La·pu·tan \lə-ˈpyüt-ᵊn\ *n* **:** an inhabitant of a flying island in Swift's *Gulliver's Travels* characterized by a neglect of useful occupations and a devotion to visionary projects — **Laputan** *adj*

lap·wing \'lap-ˌwiŋ\ *n* [ME, by folk etymology fr. OE *hlēapewince;* akin to OE *hlēapan* to leap and to OE *wincian* to wink] **:** a crested Old World plover (*Vanellus vanellus*) noted for its slow irregular flapping flight and its shrill wailing cry; *also* **:** any of several related plovers

Lar \'lär\ *n, pl* **Lar·es** \'la(ə)r-(ˌ)ēz, 'le(ə)r-\ [L — more at LARVA] **:** a tutelary god or spirit associated with Vesta and the Penates as a guardian of the household by the ancient Romans

lar·board \'lär-bərd\ *n* [ME *ladeborde*] **:** PORT — **larboard** *adj*

lar·ce·ner \'lärs-nər, -ᵊn-ər\ *n* **:** LARCENIST

lar·ce·nist \'lärs-nəst, -ᵊn-əst\ *n* **:** one who commits larceny

lar·ce·nous \'lärs-nəs, -ᵊn-əs\ *adj* **1 :** having the character of or constituting larceny **2 :** committing larceny **:** THIEVISH — **lar·ce·nous·ly** *adv*

lar·ce·ny \'lärs-nē, -ᵊn-ē\ *n, pl* **-nies** [ME, fr. MF *larcin* theft, fr. L *latrocinium* robbery, fr. *latron-, latro* mercenary soldier; akin to OE un*lǣd* poor, Gk *latron* pay] **1 :** the unlawful taking and carrying away of personal property with intent to deprive the rightful owner of his property permanently **:** THEFT **2 :** any of various statutory offenses whereby property is illegally obtained

larch \'lärch\ *n* [prob. fr. G *lärche,* fr. L *laric-, larix*] **1 :** any of a genus (*Larix*) of trees of the pine family with short fascicled deciduous leaves; *also* **:** any of several related trees (as of the genus *Abies*) **2 :** the wood of a larch

larch 1

¹lard \'lärd\ *vt* **1 a :** to dress (meat) for cooking by inserting or covering with something (as strips of fat) **b :** to cover or soil with grease **2 :** to decorate or intersperse with something **:** GARNISH <the book is well ~*ed* with anecdotes> **3** *obs* **:** to make rich with or as if with fat **:** ENRICH

²lard *n* [ME, fr. OF, fr. L *lardum;* akin to L *laetus* glad, *largus* abundant, Gk *larinos* fat] **:** a soft white solid or semisolid fat obtained by rendering fatty tissue of the hog — **lardy** \'lärd-ē\ *adj*

lar·der \'lärd-ər\ *n* [ME, fr. MF *lardier,* fr. OF, fr. *lard*] **1 :** a place where food is stored **:** PANTRY **2 :** a supply of food

lar·doon \lär-'dün\ *or* **lar·don** \'lär-ˌdän\ *n* [F *lardon* piece of fat pork, fr. OF, fr. *lard*] **:** a strip (as of salt pork) with which meat is larded

lard type *n* **:** a type of hog adapted to converting feed (as corn) into fat — compare MEAT TYPE

lares and penates *see* LAR, PENATES\ *n pl* **1 :** household gods **2 :** personal or household effects

¹large \'lärj\ *adj* **larg·er; larg·est** [ME, fr. OF, fr. L *largus*] **1** *obs* **:** liberal in giving **:** LAVISH **2** *obs* **a :** AMPLE, ABUNDANT **b :** EXTENSIVE, BROAD **3 :** having more than usual power, capacity, or scope **:** COMPREHENSIVE <establishing a *larger* social justice> **4 a :** exceeding most other things of like kind esp. in quantity or size **:** BIG **b :** dealing in great numbers or quantities <a ~ and highly profitable business> **5** *obs* **a** *of language or expression* **:** COARSE, VULGAR **b :** lax in conduct **:** LOOSE **6** *of a wind* **:** FAVORABLE **7 :** EXTRAVAGANT, BOASTFUL <~ talk> — **large·ness** *n* — **larg·ish** \'lär-jish\ *adj*

syn LARGE, BIG, GREAT *shared meaning element* **:** above average in magnitude ***ant*** small

²large *adv* **1** *obs* **:** in abundance **:** AMPLY, LIBERALLY **2 :** with the wind abaft the beam

³large *n, obs* **:** LIBERALITY, GENEROSITY — **at large 1 :** without restraint or confinement <the escaped prisoner is still *at large*> **2 :** at length **3 :** in a general way **:** at random **4 :** as a whole <society *at large*> **5 :** as the political representative of or to a whole area rather than of one of its subdivisions — used in combination with a preceding noun <a congressman-*at-large*>

large calorie *n* **:** CALORIE 1b

large·heart·ed \'lärj-'härt-əd\ *adj* **:** having a generous disposition **:** SYMPATHETIC — **large·heart·ed·ness** *n*

large intestine *n* **:** the posterior division of the vertebrate intestine that is wider and shorter than the small intestine, typically divided into cecum, colon, and rectum, and concerned esp. with the dehydration of digestive residues into feces

large·ly \'lärj-lē\ *adv* **1 :** to a large extent **:** EXTENSIVELY **2 :** in a general or wide sense **:** COMPREHENSIVELY

large–mind·ed \'lärj-'mīn-dəd\ *adj* **:** generous or comprehensive in outlook, range, or capacity — **large–mind·ed·ly** *adv* — **large–mind·ed·ness** *n*

large·mouth bass \ˌlärj-ˌmau̇th-\ *n* **:** a large black bass (*Micropterus salmoides*) that is blackish green above and lighter below and has the angle of the jaw falling behind the eye — called also *largemouth, largemouth black bass*

large–print \-'print\ *adj* **:** being set in a large size of type (as 14 point or larger) esp. for use by the partially sighted <~ books>

large–scale \'lärj-'skā(ə)l\ *adj* **:** larger than others of its kind: as **a :** involving great numbers or quantities **:** EXTENSIVE **b** *of a map* **:** having a scale that permits the plotting of much detail

lar·gess *or* **lar·gesse** \lär-'zhes, lär-'jes *also* 'lär-ˌjes\ *n* [ME *largesse,* fr. OF, fr. *large*] **1 :** liberal giving to or as if to an inferior **2 :** excessive or ostentatious gratuities **3 :** an innate generosity of mind or spirit

large–type \-'tīp\ *adj* **:** LARGE-PRINT

large white *n* **:** any of a British breed of large long-bodied white swine

¹lar·ghet·to \lär-'get-(ˌ)ō\ *adv or adj* [It, somewhat slow, fr. *largo*] **:** slower than andante but not so slow as largo — used as a direction in music

²larghetto *n, pl* **-tos :** a larghetto movement

¹lar·go \'lär-(ˌ)gō\ *adv or adj* [It, slow, broad, fr. L *largus* abundant — more at LARD] **:** in a very slow and broad manner — used as a direction in music

²largo *n, pl* **largos :** a largo movement

lar·i·at \'lar-ē-ət, 'ler-\ *n* [AmerSp *la reata* the lasso, fr. Sp *la* the (fem. of *el,* fr. L *ille* that; akin to L *uls* beyond) + AmerSp *reata* lasso, fr. Sp *reatar* to tie again, fr. *re-* + *atar* to tie, fr. L *aptare* to fit — more at ALL, ADAPT] **:** a long light rope (as of hemp or leather) used with a running noose to catch livestock or with or without the noose to picket grazing animals **:** LASSO

¹lark \'lärk\ *n* [ME, fr. OE *lāwerce;* akin to OHG *lērihha* lark] **1 :** any of numerous singing birds (family Alaudidae) mostly of Europe, Asia, and northern Africa; *esp* **:** SKYLARK **2 :** any of various usu. ground-living birds <meadow*lark*> <tit*lark*>

²lark *vi* [prob. alter. of *lake* (to frolic)] **:** FROLIC, SPORT — **lark·er** *n*

³lark *n* **:** a merry adventure **:** FROLIC; *also* **:** PRANK

lark·spur \'lärk-ˌspər\ *n* **:** any of a genus (*Delphinium*) of plants of the buttercup family; *esp* **:** a cultivated annual delphinium grown for its showy irregular flowers with spurred calyxes

larky \'lär-kē\ *adj* **lark·i·er; -est :** FROLICSOME

lar·ri·gan \'lar-i-gən\ *n* [origin unknown] **:** an oil-tanned moccasin with a leg often reaching the knee

lar·ri·kin \'lar-i-kən\ *n* [origin unknown] *chiefly Austral* **:** HOODLUM, ROWDY — **larrikin** *adj*

¹lar·rup \'lar-əp\ *vb* [perh. imit.] *vt* **1** *dial* **:** to flog soundly **:** WHIP **2** *dial* **:** to defeat decisively **:** TROUNCE ~ *vi, dial* **:** to move indolently or clumsily **:** SLOUCH

²larrup *n, dial* **:** BLOW

la·rum \'lär-əm, 'lar-\ *n* [short for *alarum*] **:** ALARM

lar·va \'lär-və\ *n, pl* **lar·vae** \-(ˌ)vē, -ˌvī\ *also* **larvas** [NL, fr. L, specter, mask; akin to L *lar*] **1 :** the immature, wingless, and often vermiform feeding form that hatches from the egg of many insects, alters chiefly in size while passing through several molts, and is finally transformed into a pupa or chrysalis from which the adult emerges **2 :** the early form of an animal (as a frog) that at birth or hatching is fundamentally unlike its parent and must metamorphose before assuming the adult characters — **lar·val** \-vəl\ *adj*

larvi- *comb form* [NL, fr. *larva*] **:** larva <*larvi*cide>

¹lar·vi·cide \'lär-və-ˌsīd\ *n* **:** an agent for killing larval pests — **lar·vi·cid·al** \ˌlär-və-'sīd-ᵊl\ *adj*

²larvicide *vt* **-cid·ed; -cid·ing :** to treat with a larvicide

laryng- *or* **laryngo-** *comb form* [NL, fr. Gk, fr. *laryng-, larynx*] **1 :** larynx <*laryng*itis> **2** \lə-ˌriŋ-gō, -ˌrin-jō\ **:** laryngeal and <*laryngo*pharyngeal>

¹la·ryn·geal \ˌlar-ən-'jē-əl, lə-'rin-j(ē-)əl\ *adj* **1 :** of, relating to, or used on the larynx **2 :** produced by or with constriction of the larynx <~ articulation of sounds> — **la·ryn·geal·ly** \-ē\ *adv*

²laryngeal *n* **1 :** an anatomical part (as a nerve or artery) that supplies or is associated with the larynx **2 a :** a laryngeal sound **b :** any of a set of several phonemes reconstructed for Proto-Indo-European chiefly on indirect evidence

lar·yn·gec·to·mee \ˌlar-ən-ˌjek-tə-'mē\ *n* **:** a person who has undergone laryngectomy

lar·yn·gec·to·my \-'jek-to-mē\ *n, pl* **-mies :** surgical removal of all or part of the larynx

lar·yn·git·ic \ˌlar-ən-'jit-ik\ *adj* **1 :** of, relating to, or characteristic of laryngitis **2 :** affected with laryngitis

lar·yn·gi·tis \ˌlar-ən-'jīt-əs\ *n* [NL] **:** inflammation of the larynx

lar·yn·gol·o·gy \ˌlar-ən-'gäl-ə-jē\ *n* [ISV] **:** a branch of medicine dealing with diseases of the larynx and nasopharynx

la·ryn·go·scope \lə-'riŋ-gə-ˌskōp, -'rin-jə-\ *n* [ISV] **:** an instrument for examining the interior of the larynx — **la·ryn·go·scop·ic** \-ˌriŋ-gə-'skäp-ik, -ˌrin-jə-\ *or* **la·ryn·go·scop·i·cal** \-i-kəl\ *adj* — **la·ryn·go·scop·i·cal·ly** \-i-k(ə-)lē\ *adv* — **lar·yn·gos·co·py** \ˌlar-ən-'gäs-kə-pē\ *n*

lar·ynx \'lar-iŋ(k)s\ *n, pl* **la·ryn·ges** \lə-'rin-(ˌ)jēz\ *or* **lar·ynx·es** [NL *laryng-, larynx,* fr. Gk] **:** the modified upper part of the trachea of air-breathing vertebrates that in man, most other mammals, and a few lower forms contains the vocal cords

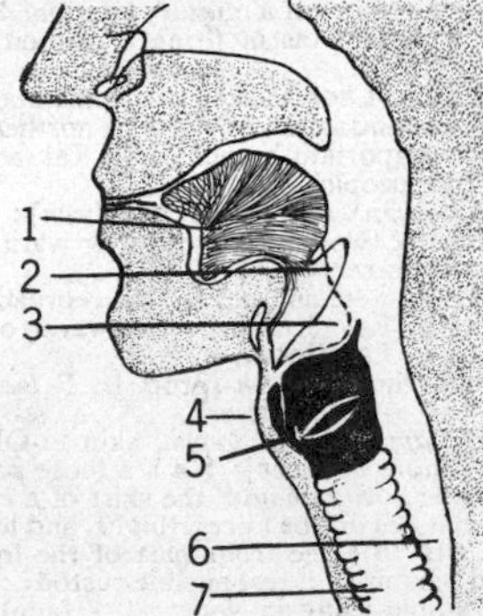

larynx: *1* tongue, *2* epiglottis, *3* epiglottis closing larynx, *4* Adam's apple, *5* vocal cords, *6* esophagus, *7* trachea

la·sa·gna \lə-'zän-yə\ *n* [It *lasagna* (pl. *lasagne*), fr. (assumed) VL *lasania,* fr. L *lasanum* cooking pot, fr. Gk *lasanon* chamber pot] **1** *also* **la·sa·gne** \-yə, -(ˌ)yä\ **:** broad flat noodles **2 :** boiled lasagna noodles baked with a sauce usu. of tomatoes, cheese, and meat (as ground beef)

las·car \'las-kər\ *n* [Hindi *lashkar* army] **:** an East Indian sailor, army servant, or native artilleryman

las·civ·i·ous \lə-ˈsiv-ē-əs\ *adj* [L *lascivia* wantonness, fr. *lascivus* wanton — more at LUST] **:** LEWD, LUSTFUL — **las·civ·i·ous·ly** *adv* — **las·civ·i·ous·ness** *n*

lase \ˈlāz\ *vi* **lased; las·ing** [back-formation fr. *laser*] **:** to emit coherent light

la·ser \ˈlā-zər\ *n* [*l*ight *a*mplification by *s*timulated *e*mission of *r*adiation] **:** a device that utilizes the natural oscillations of atoms or molecules between energy levels for generating coherent electromagnetic radiation in the ultraviolet, visible, or infrared regions of the spectrum

1lash \ˈlash\ *vb* [ME *lashen*] *vi* **1 :** to move violently or suddenly **:** DASH **2 :** to strike with or as if with a whip **3 :** to make a verbal attack or retort — usu. used with *out* **4** *Brit* **:** to spend money recklessly — usu. used with *out* ~ *vt* **1 a :** to strike with a lash **:** WHIP **b :** to strike quickly and forcibly <rain ~*es* the window> **2 a :** to assail with stinging words **b :** DRIVE, GOAD <~*ed* them into a fury with his fiery speech> **c :** to cause to lash — **lash·er** *n*

2lash *n* **1 a** (1) **:** a stroke with or as if with a whip (2) **:** the flexible part of a whip; *also* **:** WHIP **b :** a sudden swinging blow **2 :** a verbal blow **3 :** EYELASH **4 :** the clearance or play between adjacent movable mechanical parts

3lash *vt* [ME *lasschen* to lace, fr. MF *lacier* — more at LACE] **:** to bind with a line (as of rope, cord, or chain) — **lash·er** *n*

lash·ing *n* **:** something used for binding, wrapping, or fastening

lash·ings \ˈlash-iŋz, -ənz\ *also* **lash·ins** \-ənz\ *n pl* [fr. gerund of 1*lash*] **:** a great plenty **:** ABUNDANCE <piles of bread and butter and ~ of tea —Molly Weir>

lash–up \ˈlash-ˌəp\ *n* [3*lash*] **1 :** something improvised **:** CONTRIVANCE **2 :** SETUP, LAYOUT

L–as·pa·rag·i·nase \ˈel-ˌas-pə-ˈraj-ə-ˌnās, -ˌnāz\ *n* **:** an enzyme that breaks down the physiologically commoner form of asparagine, is obtained esp. from bacteria, and is used esp. to treat leukemia

lass \ˈlas\ *n* [ME *las*] **1 :** young woman **:** GIRL **2 :** SWEETHEART

lass·ie \ˈlas-ē\ *n* **:** LASS, GIRL

las·si·tude \ˈlas-ə-ˌt(y)üd\ *n* [MF, fr. L *lassitudo*, fr. *lassus* weary — more at LET] **1 :** a condition of weariness or debility **:** FATIGUE **2 :** a condition of listlessness **:** LANGUOR

1las·so \ˈlas-(ˌ)ō, la-ˈsü\ *n, pl* **lassos** *or* **lassoes** [Sp *lazo*, fr. L *laqueus* snare — more at DELIGHT] **:** a rope or long thong of leather with a running noose that is used esp. for catching horses and cattle **:** LARIAT

2lasso *vt* **:** to catch with or as if with a lasso **:** ROPE — **las·so·er** *n*

1last \ˈlast\ *vb* [ME *lasten*, fr. OE *lǣstan* to last, follow; akin to OE *lāst* footprint] *vi* **1 :** to continue in time **:** go on **2 a :** to remain fresh or unimpaired **:** ENDURE **b :** to manage to continue (as in a course of action) **c :** to continue to live <he won't ~ much longer> ~ *vt* **1 :** to continue in existence or action as long as or longer than — often used with *out* <couldn't ~ out the training program> **2 :** to be enough for the needs of <the supplies will ~ them a week> **syn** see CONTINUE — **last·er** *n*

2last *adj* [ME, fr. OE *latost*, superl. of *læt* late] **1 a :** following all the rest <he was the ~ one out> **b :** being the only remaining <his ~ dollar> **2 a :** belonging to the final stage (as of life) <his ~ hours on earth> **b :** administered to the seriously sick or dying <the ~ rites of the church> **3 a :** next before the present **:** most recent <~ week> <his ~ book was a failure> **b :** most up-to-date **:** LATEST <it's the ~ thing in fashion> **4 a :** lowest in rank or standing; *also* **:** WORST **b :** farthest from a specified quality, attitude, or likelihood <he'd be the ~ person to fall for flattery> **5 a :** CONCLUSIVE <there is no ~ answer to a problem of human relations> **b :** highest in degree **:** SUPREME **c :** DISTINCT, SEPARATE — used as an intensive <ate every ~ piece of food on his plate> — **last·ly** *adv*

syn LAST, FINAL, TERMINAL, EVENTUAL, ULTIMATE *shared meaning element* **:** following all relevant others (as in time, order, or importance) **ant** first

3last *adv* **1 :** after all others **:** at the end <came ~ and left first> **2 :** most lately <saw him ~ in New York> **3 :** in conclusion <and ~, I'd like to consider the economic aspect>

4last *n* **:** something that is last — **at last** *or* **at long last :** at the end of a period of time **:** FINALLY <*at last* you've come home>

5last *n* [ME, fr. OE *lǣste*, fr. *lāst* footprint; akin to OHG *leist* shoemaker's last, L *lira* furrow — more at LEARN] **:** a form (as of metal or plastic) which is shaped like the human foot and over which a shoe is shaped or repaired

6last *vt* **:** to shape with a last — **last·er** *n*

last–ditch *adj* **:** made as a final effort esp. to avert disaster <a ~ attempt to raise the money>

last ditch *n* **:** a place of final defense <the anti-liquor groups fought the changes to the *last ditch* —*N.Y. Times*>

Las·tex \ˈlas-ˌteks\ *trademark* — used for an elastic yarn consisting of a core of latex thread wound with threads of cotton, rayon, nylon, or silk

Last Gospel *n* **:** the liturgical Gospel usu. comprising John 1:1-14 that is read by the celebrant following the close of the Mass in Roman Catholic churches and the Holy Communion in many Episcopal churches

last hurrah *n* **:** a last effort or attempt <his unsuccessful Senate run was his *last hurrah* —R. W. Daly>

1last·ing *adj* **:** existing or continuing a long while **:** ENDURING — **last·ing·ly** \ˈlas-tiŋ-lē\ *adv* — **last·ing·ness** *n*

2lasting *n* **1** *archaic* **:** long life **2** [1*lasting*] **:** a sturdy cotton or worsted cloth used esp. in shoes and luggage

last minute *n* **:** the moment just before some climactic, decisive, or disastrous event

last name *n* **:** SURNAME 2

last straw *n* [fr. the fable of the last straw that broke the camel's back when added to his burden] **:** the last of a series (as of events or indignities) that brings one beyond the point of endurance

Last Supper *n* **:** the supper eaten by Jesus and his disciples on the night of his betrayal

Last Things *n pl* [trans. of ML *Novissima*] **:** events (as the resurrection and divine judgment of all humankind) marking the end of the world **:** eschatological happenings

last word *n* **1 :** the final remark in a verbal exchange **2 a :** the power of final decision **b :** a definitive statement or treatment <his study will surely be the *last word* on the subject for many years> **3 :** the most advanced, up-to-date, or fashionable exemplar of its kind <the *last word* in sports cars>

lat *abbr* latitude

Lat *abbr* **1** Latin **2** Latvia

LAT *abbr* local apparent time

lat·a·kia \ˌlat-ə-ˈkē-ə\ *n* [*Latakia*, seaport in Syria] **:** a highly aromatic Turkish smoking tobacco

1latch \ˈlach\ *vi* [ME *lachen*, fr. OE *læccan*; akin to Gk *lambanein* to take, seize] **1 :** to catch or get hold — used with *on* or *onto* **2 :** to attach oneself <~*ed* onto a rich widow>

2latch *n* **:** any of various devices in which mating mechanical parts engage to fasten but usu. not to lock something: **a :** a fastener (as for a door) consisting essentially of a pivoted bar that falls into a notch **b :** a fastener (as for a door) in which a spring slides a bolt into a hole; *also* **:** NIGHT LATCH

3latch *vt* **:** to make fast with or as if with a latch

latch·et \ˈlach-ət\ *n* [ME *lachet*, fr. MF, shoestring, fr. *laz* snare, fr. L *laqueus* — more at DELIGHT] **:** a narrow leather strap, thong, or lace that fastens a shoe or sandal on the foot

latch·key \ˈlach-ˌkē\ *n* **:** a key to an outside and esp. a front door

latch·string \-ˌ(s)triŋ\ *n* **:** a string on a latch that may be left hanging outside the door to permit the raising of the latch from the outside or drawn inside to prevent intrusion

1late \ˈlāt\ *adj* **lat·er; lat·est** [ME, late, slow, fr. OE *læt*; akin to OHG *laz* slow, OE *lǣtan* to let] **1 a** (1) **:** coming or remaining after the due, usual, or proper time <a ~ spring> (2) **:** of, relating to, or imposed because of tardiness **b :** of or relating to an advanced stage in point of time or development <the ~ Middle Ages>; *esp* **:** far advanced toward the close of the day or night <~ hours> **2 a :** living comparatively recently — used of persons with reference to a specific relationship or status <his ~ wife> <the ~ chairman of the board> **b :** being something or holding some position or relationship recently but not now <the ~ belligerents> **c :** made, appearing, or happening just previous to the present time esp. as the most recent of a succession <our ~ quarrel> **syn 1** see TARDY **ant** early, punctual, prompt **2** see DEAD **3** see MODERN — **late·ness** *n*

2late *adv* **lat·er; lat·est 1 a :** after the usual or proper time <got to work ~> **b :** at or to an advanced point of time <saw her ~ in the day> — often used with *on* **2 :** not long ago **:** RECENTLY <a man ~ of Chicago> — **of late :** in the period shortly or immediately preceding **:** RECENTLY <have not seen him *of late*>

late blight *n* **:** a disease of solanaceous plants (as the potato and tomato) that is caused by a fungus (*Phytophthora infestans*) and is characterized by decay of stems, leaves, and in the potato also of tubers

late·com·er \ˈlāt-ˌkəm-ər\ *n* **:** one that arrives late; *also* **:** a recent arrival

lat·ed \ˈlāt-əd\ *adj* **:** BELATED

1la·teen \lə-ˈtēn\ *adj* [F (*voile*) *latine* lateen sail] **:** being or relating to a rig used esp. on the north coast of Africa and characterized by a triangular sail extended by a long spar slung to a low mast

2lateen *n* **1** *also* **la·teen·er** \-ˈtē-nər\ **:** a lateen-rigged ship **2 :** a lateen sail

Late Greek *n* **:** the Greek language as used in the 3d to 6th centuries

Late Latin *n* **:** the Latin language used by writers in the 3d to 6th centuries

late·ly \ˈlāt-lē\ *adv* **:** of late **:** RECENTLY <has been friendlier ~>

lat·en \ˈlāt-ᵊn\ *vb* **lat·ened; lat·en·ing** \ˈlāt-niŋ, -ᵊn-iŋ\ *vi* **:** to grow late ~ *vt* **:** to cause to grow late

la·ten·cy \ˈlāt-ᵊn-sē\ *n, pl* **-cies 1 :** the quality or state of being latent **:** DORMANCY **2 :** something latent **3 :** a stage of personality development that extends from about the age of five to the beginning of puberty and during which sexual urges often appear to lie dormant **4 :** LATENT PERIOD 2

latency period *n* **1 :** LATENCY 3 **2 :** LATENT PERIOD 2

La Tène \lä-ˈten, -ˈtān\ *adj* [*La Tène*, shallows of the Lake of Neuchâtel, Switzerland] **:** of or relating to the later period of the Iron Age in Europe assumed to date from 500 B.C. to A.D. 1

la·ten·si·fi·ca·tion \lā-ˌten(t)-sə-fə-ˈkā-shən, lə-\ *n* [blend of 1*latent* and *intensification*] **:** intensification of a latent photographic image by chemical treatment or exposure to light of low intensity — **la·ten·si·fy** \-ˈten(t)-sə-ˌfī\ *vt*

1la·tent \ˈlāt-ᵊnt\ *adj* [L *latent-*, *latens*, fr. prp. of *latēre* to lie hidden; akin to OHG *luog* den, Gk *lanthanein* to escape notice] **:** present and capable of becoming though not now visible or active <a ~ infection> <his desire for success remained ~>

syn LATENT, DORMANT, QUIESCENT, POTENTIAL, ABEYANT *shared meaning element* **:** not now manifest or showing signs of existence or activity **ant** patent

2latent *n* **:** a fingerprint (as at the scene of a crime) that is scarcely visible but can be developed for study

latent heat *n* **:** heat given off or absorbed in a process (as fusion or vaporization) other than a change of temperature

latent period *n* **1 :** the incubation period of a disease **2 :** the interval between stimulation and response

latent root *n* **:** a characteristic root of a matrix

-la·ter \l-ət-ər\ *n comb form* [ME *-latrer,* fr. MF *-latre,* fr. LL *-latres,* fr. Gk *-latrēs;* akin to Gk *latron* pay — more at LARCENY] : worshiper <icono*later*>
lat·er·ad \ˈlat-ə-ˌrad\ *adv* [L *later-, latus*] : toward the side
1lat·er·al \ˈlat-ə-rəl, ˈla-trəl\ *adj* [L *lateralis,* fr. *later-, latus* side] : of or relating to the side : situated on, directed toward, or coming from the side — **lat·er·al·ly** \-ē\ *adv*
2lateral *n* **1** : a side ditch or conduit (as in a water system) **2** : a mining drift to one side of and parallel to a main drift **3** : a pass in football thrown parallel to the line of scrimmage or in a direction away from the opponent's goal
3lateral *vi* : to throw a lateral
lateral bud *n* : a bud that develops in the axil between a petiole and a stem — called also *axillary bud*
lateral line *n* : a canal along the side of a fish containing pores that open into tubes supplied with sense organs sensitive to low vibrations; *also* : one of these tubes or sense organs
lat·er·ite \ˈlat-ə-ˌrīt\ *n* [L *later* brick] : a residual product of rock decay that is red in color and has a high content in the oxides of iron and hydroxide of aluminum — **lat·er·it·ic** \ˌlat-ə-ˈrit-ik\ *adj*
lat·er·i·za·tion \ˌlat-ə-rə-ˈzā-shən\ *n* : the process of conversion of rock to laterite
lat·est \ˈlāt-əst\ *n* **1** : the most recent or currently fashionable style or development <the ~ in diving techniques> **2** : the latest acceptable time — usu. used in the phrase *at the latest* <be home by one *at the latest*>
late·wood \ˈlāt-ˌwu̇d\ *n* : SUMMERWOOD
la·tex \ˈlā-ˌteks\ *n, pl* **la·ti·ces** \ˈlāt-ə-ˌsēz, ˈlat-\ *or* **la·tex·es** [NL *latic-, latex,* fr. L, fluid] **1** : a milky usu. white fluid that is produced by cells of various seed plants (as of the milkweed, spurge, and poppy families) and is the source of rubber, gutta-percha, chicle, and balata **2** : a water emulsion of a synthetic rubber or plastic obtained by polymerization and used esp. in coatings (as paint) and adhesives — **la·ti·cif·er·ous** \ˌlāt-ə-ˈsif-(ə-)rəs, ˌlat-\ *adj*
1lath \ˈlath *also* ˈlat͟h\ *n, pl* **laths** *or* **lath** [ME, fr. OE *lætt;* akin to OHG *latta* lath, W *llath* yard] **1** : a thin narrow strip of wood nailed to rafters, joists, or studding as a groundwork for slates, tiles, or plaster **2** : a building material in sheets used as a base for plaster **3** : a quantity of laths
2lath *vt* : to cover or line with laths
1lathe \ˈlāt͟h\ *n* [prob. fr. ME *lath* supporting stand] : a machine in which work is rotated about a horizontal axis and shaped by a fixed tool
2lathe *vt* **lathed; lath·ing** : to cut or shape with a lathe
1lath·er \ˈlat͟h-ər\ *n* [(assumed) ME, fr. OE *lēathor;* akin to OE *lēag* lye — more at LYE] **1 a** : a foam or froth formed when a detergent (as soap) is agitated in water **b** : foam or froth from profuse sweating (as on a horse) **2** : an agitated or overwrought state : DITHER — **lath·ery** \-(ə-)rē\ *adj*
2lather *vb* **lath·ered; lath·er·ing** \-(ə-)riŋ\ *vt* **1** : to spread lather over **2** : to beat severely : FLOG ~ *vi* : to form a lather or a froth like lather — **lath·er·er** \-ər-ər\ *n*
lath·ing \ˈlath-iŋ, ˈlat͟h-\ *n* **1** : the action or process of placing laths **2** : a quantity or an installation of laths
lath·y·rism \ˈlath-ə-ˌriz-əm\ *n* [NL *Lathyrus,* genus name, fr. Gk *lathyros,* a type of pea] : a diseased condition of man, domestic animals, and esp. horses that results from poisoning by a substance found in some legumes (genus *Lathyrus* and esp. *L. sativus*) and is characterized esp. by spastic paralysis of the hind or lower limbs
lath·y·rit·ic \ˌlath-ə-ˈrit-ik\ *adj* : of, relating to, affected with, or characteristic of lathyrism <~ rats> <~ cartilage>
latices *pl of* LATEX
la·tic·i·fer \lā-ˈtis-ə-fər\ *n* [ISV *latici-* (fr. NL *latic-, latex*) + *-fer*] : a plant cell or vessel that contains latex
la·ti·fun·dio \ˌlät-ə-ˈfün-dē-ˌō\ *n, pl* **-di·os** [Sp, fr. L *latifundium*] : a latifundium in Spain or Latin America
lat·i·fun·di·um \ˌlat-ə-ˈfən-dē-əm\ *n, pl* **-dia** \-dē-ə\ [L, fr. *latus* wide + *fundus* piece of landed property — more at BOTTOM] : a great landed estate with primitive agriculture and labor often in a state of partial servitude
lat·i·go \ˈlat-i-ˌgō\ *n, pl* **-gos** *also* **-goes** [Sp *látigo*] *chiefly West* : a long strap on a saddletree to tighten and fasten the cinch
lat·i·me·ria \ˌlat-ə-ˈmir-ē-ə\ *n* [NL, genus name, fr. Marjorie E. D. Courtenay-*Latimer b*1907 So. African museum director] : any of a genus (*Latimeria*) of living coelacanth fishes of deep seas off southern Africa
1Lat·in \ˈlat-ᵊn\ *adj* [ME, fr. OE, fr. L *Latinus,* fr. *Latium,* ancient country of Italy] **1** : of or relating to Latium or the Latins **2 a** : of, relating to, or composed in Latin **b** : ROMANCE **3** : of or relating to the part of the Catholic Church that until recently used a Latin rite and forms the patriarchate of the pope **4** : of or relating to the peoples or countries using Romance languages; *specif* : of or relating to the peoples or countries of Latin America
2Latin *n* **1** : the Italic language of ancient Latium and of Rome and until modern times the dominant language of school, church, and state in western Europe — see INDO-EUROPEAN LANGUAGES table **2** : a member of the people of ancient Latium **3** : a Catholic of the Latin rite **4** : a member of one of the Latin peoples; *specif* : a native or inhabitant of Latin America **5** : the Latin alphabet
Lat·in·ate \ˈlat-ᵊn-ˌāt\ *adj* : of, relating to, resembling, or derived from Latin
Latin cross *n* : a figure of a cross having a long upright shaft and a shorter crossbar traversing it above the middle — see CROSS illustration
La·tin·i·an \la-ˈtin-ē-ən, lə-\ *n* : a division of the Italic languages that includes Latin — see INDO-EUROPEAN LANGUAGES table
Lat·in·ism \ˈlat-ᵊn-ˌiz-əm\ *n* **1** : a characteristic feature of Latin occurring in another language **2** : Latin quality, character, or mode of thought
Lat·in·ist \ˈlat-ᵊn-əst, ˈlat-nəst\ *n* : a specialist in the Latin language or Roman culture
la·tin·i·ty \la-ˈtin-ət-ē, lə-\ *n, often cap* **1** : a manner of speaking or writing Latin **2** : LATINISM 2
lat·in·ize \ˈlat-ᵊn-ˌīz\ *vb* **-ized; -iz·ing** *often cap, vt* **1 a** *obs* : to translate into Latin **b** : to give a Latin form to **c** : to introduce Latinisms into **d** : ROMANIZE 2 **2** : to make Latin or Italian in doctrine, ideas, or traits; *specif* : to cause to resemble the Roman Catholic Church ~ *vi* **1** : to use Latinisms **2** : to exhibit the influence of the Romans or of the Roman Catholic Church — **lat·in·iza·tion** \ˌlat-ᵊn-ə-ˈzā-shən, ˌlat-nə-\ *n*
Latin Quarter *n* [trans. of F *Quartier Latin*] : a section of Paris south of the Seine frequented by students and artists
Latin square *n* : a square array in which the number of elements is the same as the number of columns and no element occurs twice in the same column or row and which is used esp. in the statistical design of experiments (as in agriculture)
lat·ish \ˈlāt-ish\ *adj* : being somewhat late
lat·i·tude \ˈlat-ə-ˌt(y)üd\ *n* [ME, fr. L *latitudin-, latitudo,* fr. *latus* wide; akin to Arm *lain* wide] **1** *archaic* : extent or distance from side to side : WIDTH **2** : angular distance from some specified circle or plane of reference: as **a** : angular distance north or south from the earth's equator measured through 90 degrees **b** : angular distance of a celestial body from the ecliptic **c** : a region or locality as marked by its latitude **3 a** *archaic* : SCOPE, RANGE **b** : the range of exposures within which a film or plate will produce a negative or positive of satisfactory quality **4** : freedom of action or choice — **lat·i·tu·di·nal** \ˌlat-ə-ˈt(y)üd-nəl, -ᵊn-əl\ *adj* — **lat·i·tu·di·nal·ly** \-ē\ *adv*

latitude 2a: hemisphere marked with parallels of latitude

lat·i·tu·di·nar·i·an \ˌlat-ə-ˌt(y)üd-ᵊn-ˈer-ē-ən\ *n* : a person who is broad and liberal in his standards of religious belief and conduct — **latitudinarian** *adj* — **lat·i·tu·di·nar·i·an·ism** \-ē-ə-ˌniz-əm\ *n*
lat·o·sol \ˈlat-ə-ˌsȯl\ *n* [irreg. fr. L *later* brick + E *-sol* (as in *podsol,* var. of *podzol*)] : a leached red and yellow tropical soil — **lat·o·sol·ic** \ˌlat-ə-ˈsȯ-lik\ *adj*
la·trine \lə-ˈtrēn\ *n* [F, fr. L *latrina,* contr. of *lavatrina,* fr. *lavere* to wash — more at LYE] **1** : a receptacle (as a pit in the earth) for use as a toilet **2** : TOILET
-la·try \l-ə-trē\ *n comb form* [ME *-latrie,* fr. OF, fr. LL *-latria,* fr. Gk, fr. *latreia*] : worship <helio*latry*>
lat·ten *or* **lat·tin** \ˈlat-ᵊn\ *n* [ME *laton,* fr. MF] **1** : a yellow alloy identical to or resembling brass typically hammered into thin sheets and formerly much used for church utensils **2 a** : iron plate covered with tin **b** : metal in thin sheets <gold ~>
lat·ter \ˈlat-ər\ *adj* [ME, fr. OE *lætra,* compar. of *læt* late] **1 a** : more recent : LATER <the ~ stages of a process> **b** : of or relating to the end : FINAL **c** : RECENT, PRESENT **2** : of, relating to, or being the second of two groups or things or the last of several groups or things referred to <of ham and beef the ~ meat is cheaper today>
lat·ter–day \ˌlat-ər-ˌdā\ *adj* **1** : of a later or subsequent time **2** : of present or recent times
Latter–Day Saint *n* : a member of a religious body tracing its origin to Joseph Smith in 1830 and accepting the Book of Mormon as divine revelation : MORMON
lat·ter·ly *adv* **1** : at a subsequent time : LATER **2** : of late : RECENTLY
lat·tice \ˈlat-əs\ *n* [ME *latis,* fr. MF *lattis*] **1 a** : a framework or structure of crossed wood or metal strips **b** : a window, door, or gate having a lattice **c** : a network or design resembling a lattice **2** : a regular geometrical arrangement of points or objects over an area or in space: as **a** : SPACE LATTICE **b** : a geometrical arrangement of fissionable material in a nuclear reactor **c** : a mathematical set that has some elements ordered and that is such that for any two elements there exists a least element greater than or equal to both and a greatest element less than or equal to both — **lattice** *vt* — **lat·ticed** \-əst\ *adj*
lattice girder *n* : a girder with top and bottom flanges connected by a latticework web
lat·tice·work \ˈlat-ə-ˌswərk\ *n* : a lattice or work made of lattices
la·tus rec·tum \ˌlat-əs-ˈrek-təm\ *n* [NL, lit., straight side] : a chord of a conic section (as an ellipse) that passes through a focus and is parallel to the directrix
Lat·vi·an \ˈlat-vē-ən\ *n* **1** : a native or inhabitant of Latvia **2** : the Baltic language of the Latvian people — **Latvian** *adj*
lau·an \ˈlü-ˌän, lü-ˈ; lau̇-ˈän\ *n* [Tag *lawaan*] : any of various Philippine timbers (as of the genera *Shorea* and *Parashorea*) that are light yellow to reddish brown or brown, are of moderate strength and durability, and include some which enter commerce as Philippine mahogany
1laud \ˈlȯd\ *n* [ME *laudes* (pl.), fr. ML, fr. L, pl. of *laud-, laus* praise; akin to OHG *liod* song] **1** *pl but sing or pl in constr, often cap* : an office of solemn praise to God forming with matins the first of the canonical hours **2** : ACCLAIM, PRAISE
2laud *vt* [L *laudare,* fr. *laud-, laus*] : PRAISE, EXTOL
laud·able \ˈlȯd-ə-bəl\ *adj* : worthy of praise : COMMENDABLE — **laud·abil·i·ty** \ˌlȯd-ə-ˈbil-ət-ē\ *n* — **laud·able·ness** \ˈlȯd-ə-bəl-nəs\ *n* — **laud·ably** \-blē\ *adv*
lau·da·num \ˈlȯd-nəm, -ᵊn-əm\ *n* [NL] **1** : any of various formerly used preparations of opium **2** : a tincture of opium
lau·da·tion \lȯ-ˈdā-shən\ *n* : the act of praising : EULOGY
lau·da·tive \ˈlȯd-ət-iv\ *adj* : LAUDATORY
lau·da·to·ry \ˈlȯd-ə-ˌtōr-ē, -ˌtȯr-\ *adj* : of, relating to, or expressing praise
1laugh \ˈlaf, ˈläf\ *vb* [ME *laughen,* fr. OE *hliehhan;* akin to OHG *lachēn* to laugh, OE *hlōwan* to moo — more at LOW] *vi* **1 a** : to show mirth, joy, or scorn with a smile and chuckle or explosive sound **b** : to find amusement or pleasure in something <~*ed* at his own clumsiness> **c** : to become amused or derisive <a very skeptical public ~*ed* at our early efforts —Graenum Berger> **2 a** : to produce the sound or appearance of laughter <a ~*ing* brook> **b** : to be of a kind that inspires joy ~ *vt* **1** : to influence

or move by laughter <~*ed* the bad singer off the stage> **2** : to utter with a laugh — **laugh·er** *n* — **laugh·ing·ly** \-iŋ-lē\ *adv*

[2]**laugh** *n* **1 :** the act of laughing **2 a :** a cause for derision or merriment : JOKE <swim in that current? That's a ~ > **b :** an expression of scorn or mockery : JEER **3** *pl* : DIVERSION, SPORT <play baseball just for ~*s*>

laugh·able \'laf-ə-bəl, 'láf-\ *adj* **:** of a kind to provoke laughter or sometimes derision : amusingly ridiculous — **laugh·able·ness** *n* — **laugh·ably** \-blē\ *adv*

syn LAUGHABLE, LUDICROUS, RIDICULOUS, COMIC, COMICAL, DROLL, FUNNY *shared meaning element* : provoking laughter or mirth

laughing gas *n* **:** NITROUS OXIDE

laughing jackass *n* **:** KOOKABURRA

laugh·ing·stock \'laf-iŋ-ˌstäk, 'láf-\ *n* **:** an object of ridicule : BUTT

laugh off *vt* **:** to minimize by treating as amusingly or absurdly trivial

laugh·ter \'laf-tər, 'láf-\ *n* [ME, fr. OE *hleahtor;* akin to OE *hliehhan*] **1 :** a sound of or as if of laughing **2** *archaic* **:** a cause of merriment

launce \'lȯn(t)s, 'län(t)s\ *n* [prob. fr. [1]*lance*] **:** SAND LANCE

[1]**launch** \'lȯnch, 'länch\ *vb* [ME *launchen,* fr. ONF *lancher,* fr. LL *lanceare* to wield a lance — more at LANCE] *vt* **1 a :** to throw forward : HURL **b :** to release, catapult, or send off (a self-propelled object) <~ a rocket> **2 a :** to set (a boat or ship) afloat **b :** to give (a person) a start **c (1) :** to originate or set in motion : INITIATE **(2) :** to get off to a good start ~ *vi* **1 a :** to spring forward or take off **b :** to throw oneself energetically : PLUNGE **2 a** *archaic* **:** to slide down the ways **b :** to make a start

[2]**launch** *n* **:** an act or instance of launching

[3]**launch** *n* [Sp or Pg; Sp *lancha,* fr. Pg] **1 :** a large boat that operates from a ship **2 :** a small motorboat that is open or that has the forepart of the hull covered

launch·er \'lȯn-chər, 'län-\ *n* **:** one that launches: as **a :** a device for firing a grenade from a rifle **b :** a device for launching a rocket or rocket shell **c :** CATAPULT

launch·pad \'lȯnch-ˌpad, 'länch-\ *n* **:** a nonflammable platform from which a rocket, launch vehicle, or guided missile can be launched — called also *launching pad*

launch vehicle *n* **:** the rocket power source by which a spacecraft is hurled toward its objective

launch window *n* **:** WINDOW 8

[1]**laun·der** \'lȯn-dər, 'län-\ *n* [ME, launderer, fr. MF *lavandier,* fr. ML *lavandarius,* fr. L *lavandus,* gerundive of *lavare* to wash — more at LYE] **:** TROUGH; *esp* **:** a box conduit conveying particulate material suspended in water in ore dressing

[2]**launder** *vb* **laun·dered; laun·der·ing** \-d(ə-)riŋ\ [ME *launder,* n.] *vt* **1 :** to wash (as clothes) in water **2 :** to make ready for use by washing and ironing <a freshly ~*ed* shirt> ~ *vi* **:** to wash or wash and iron clothing or household linens — **laun·der·er** \-dər-ər\ *n* — **laun·dress** \-drəs\ *n*

laun·der·ette \ˌlȯn-də-'ret, ˌlän-\ *n* [fr. *Launderette,* a service mark] **:** a self-service laundry

Laun·dro·mat \'lȯn-drə-ˌmat, 'län-\ *service mark* — used for a self-service laundry

laun·dry \'lȯn-drē, 'län-\ *n, pl* **laundries** **1 :** clothes or linens that have been or are to be laundered **2 a :** a room for doing the family wash **b :** a commercial laundering establishment

laun·dry·man \-mən\ *n* **:** a male laundry worker

laun·dry·wom·an \-ˌwu̇m-ən\ *n* **:** a female who does laundry

Laun·fal \'lȯn-fəl, 'län-\ *n* **:** a knight of the Round Table in late Arthurian legend

lau·ra \'läv-rə\ *n* [LGk, fr. Gk, lane] **:** a monastery of an Eastern church

[1]**lau·re·ate** \'lȯr-ē-ət, 'lär-\ *n* [L *laureatus* crowned with laurel, fr. *laurea* laurel wreath, fr. fem. of *laureus* of laurel, fr. *laurus*] **:** the recipient of honor for achievement in an art or science; *specif* **:** POET LAUREATE — **laureate** *adj* — **lau·re·ate·ship** \-ˌship\ *n*

[2]**lau·re·ate** \-ē-ˌāt\ *vt* **-at·ed; -at·ing** **1 :** to crown with or as if with a laurel wreath for excellence or achievement **2 :** to appoint to the office of poet laureate — **lau·re·ation** \ˌlȯr-ē-'ā-shən, ˌlär-\ *n*

[1]**lau·rel** \'lȯr-əl, 'lär-\ *n* [ME *lorel,* fr. OF *lorier,* fr. *lor* laurel, fr. L *laurus*] **1 :** any of a genus (*Laurus* of the family Lauraceae, the laurel family) of trees or shrubs that have alternate entire leaves, small tetramerous flowers surrounded by bracts, and fruits that are ovoid berries; *specif* **:** a tree (*L. nobilis*) of southern Europe with foliage used by the ancient Greeks to crown victors in the Pythian games **2 :** a tree or shrub that resembles the true laurel; *esp* **:** MOUNTAIN LAUREL **3 :** a crown of laurel : HONOR — usu. used in pl.

[2]**laurel** *vt* **-reled** *or* **-relled; -rel·ing** *or* **-rel·ling** **:** to deck or crown with laurel

lau·ric acid \ˌlȯr-ik-, ˌlär-\ *n* [ISV, fr. L *laurus*] **:** a crystalline fatty acid $C_{12}H_{24}O_2$ found esp. in coconut oil and used in making soaps, esters, and lauryl alcohol

lau·ryl alcohol \ˌlȯr-əl-, ˌlär-\ *n* **:** a compound $C_{12}H_{26}O$; *also* **:** a liquid mixture of this and other alcohols used esp. in making detergents

lav *abbr* lavatory

la·va \'läv-ə, 'lav-\ *n* [It, fr. L *labes* fall; akin to L *labi* to slide — more at SLEEP] **:** fluid rock that issues from a volcano or from a fissure in the earth's surface; *also* **:** such rock solidified — **la·va·like** \-ˌlīk\ *adj*

la·va·bo \lə-'väb-(ˌ)ō\ *n, pl* **-bos** [L, I shall wash, fr. *lavare*] **1** *often cap* **:** a ceremony at Mass in which the celebrant washes his hands after offering the oblations and says Psalm 25:6–12 **2 a :** a washbasin and a tank with a spigot that are fastened to a wall **b :** this combination used as a planter

la·vage \lə-'väzh\ *n* [F, fr. MF, fr. *laver* to wash, fr. L *lavare*] **:** WASHING; *esp* **:** the therapeutic washing out of an organ

la·va·la·va \ˌläv-ə-'läv-ə\ *n* [Samoan, clothing] **:** a rectangular cloth of cotton print worn like a kilt or skirt in Polynesia and esp. in Samoa

la·va·liere *or* **la·val·liere** \ˌläv-ə-'li(ə)r, ˌlav-\ *n* [F *lavallière* necktie with a large bow] **:** a pendant on a fine chain that is worn as a necklace

la·va·tion \lā-'vā-shən\ *n* [L *lavation-, lavatio,* fr. *lavatus*] **:** the act or an instance of washing or cleansing — **la·va·tion·al** \-shnəl, -shən-ᵊl\ *adj*

lav·a·to·ry \'lav-ə-ˌtōr-ē, -ˌtȯr-\ *n, pl* **-ries** [ME *lavatorie,* fr. ML *lavatorium,* fr. L *lavatus,* pp. of *lavare* to wash — more at LYE] **1 :** a vessel (as a basin) for washing; *esp* **:** a fixed bowl or basin with running water and drainpipe for washing **2 :** a room with conveniences for washing and usu. with one or more toilets **3 :** TOILET — **lavatory** *adj*

[1]**lave** \'lāv\ *n* [ME (northern dial.), fr. OE *lāf;* akin to OE be*lifan* to remain — more at LEAVE] *chiefly dial* **:** something that is left : RESIDUE

[2]**lave** *vb* **laved; lav·ing** [ME *laven,* fr. OE *lafian;* akin to OHG *labōn* to wash; both fr. a prehistoric WGmc word borrowed fr. L *lavare*] *vt* **1 a :** WASH, BATHE **b :** to flow along or against **2 :** POUR ~ *vi, archaic* **:** to wash oneself : BATHE

la·veer \lə-'vi(ə)r\ *vi* [D *laveren*] **:** to sail against the wind : TACK

[1]**lav·en·der** \'lav-ən-dər\ *n* [ME *lavendre,* fr. AF, fr. ML *lavandula*] **1 a :** a Mediterranean mint (*Lavandula officinalis*) widely cultivated for its narrow aromatic leaves and spikes of lilac-purple flowers which are dried and used in sachets **b :** any of several plants congeneric with true lavender and used similarly but often considered inferior **2 :** a variable color averaging a pale purple

[2]**lavender** *vt* **lav·en·dered; lav·en·der·ing** \-d(ə-)riŋ\ **:** to sprinkle or perfume with lavender

[1]**la·ver** \'lā-vər\ *n* [ME *lavour,* fr. MF *lavoir*] **:** a large basin used for ceremonial ablutions in the ancient Jewish Tabernacle and Temple worship

[2]**laver** *n* [NL, fr. L, a water plant] **:** any of several mostly edible seaweeds: as **a :** SEA LETTUCE **b :** any of several common red algae (genus *Porphyra* and esp. *P. laciniata* and *P. vulgaris*) with fronds that are stewed or pickled

la·ver·ock *or* **lav·rock** \'lāv-rək, 'lav-(ə-)rək\ *n* [ME *laverok,* fr. OE *lāwerce*] *chiefly Scot* **:** LARK

La·vin·ia \lə-'vin-ē-ə\ *n* [L] **:** a daughter of King Latinus in Vergil's *Aeneid* who is betrothed to Turnus but marries Aeneas

[1]**lav·ish** \'lav-ish\ *adj* [ME *lavas* abundance, fr. MF *lavasse* downpour of rain, fr. *laver* to wash — more at LAVAGE] **1 :** expending or bestowing profusely : PRODIGAL **2 :** expended or produced in abundance ***syn*** see PROFUSE ***ant*** sparing — **lav·ish·ly** *adj* — **lav·ish·ness** *n*

[2]**lavish** *vt* **:** to expend or bestow with profusion : SQUANDER

[1]**law** \'lȯ\ *n* [ME, fr. OE *lagu,* of Scand origin; akin to ON *lög* law; akin to OE *licgan* to lie — more at LIE] **1 a (1) :** a binding custom or practice of a community : a rule of conduct or action prescribed or formally recognized as binding or enforced by a controlling authority **(2) :** the whole body of such customs, practices, or rules **(3) :** COMMON LAW **b (1) :** the control brought about by the existence or enforcement of such law **(2) :** the action of laws considered as a means of redressing wrongs; *also* **:** LITIGATION **(3) :** the agency of or an agent of established law **c :** a rule or order that it is advisable or obligatory to observe **d :** something compatible with or enforceable by established law **e :** CONTROL, AUTHORITY **2 a** *often cap* **:** the revelation of the will of God set forth in the Old Testament **b** *cap* **:** the first part of the Jewish scriptures : PENTATEUCH — see BIBLE table **3 :** a rule of construction or procedure <the ~*s* of poetry> **4 :** the whole body of laws relating to one subject **5 a :** the legal profession **b :** law as a department of knowledge : JURISPRUDENCE **c :** legal knowledge **6 a :** a statement of an order or relation of phenomena that so far as is known is invariable under the given conditions **b :** a relation proved or assumed to hold between mathematical or logical expressions **c :** the observed regularity of nature ***syn*** see HYPOTHESIS — **at law :** under or within the provisions of the law <enforceable *at law*>

[2]**law** *vi* **:** LITIGATE ~ *vt, chiefly dial* **:** to sue or prosecute at law

law–abid·ing \'lȯ-ə-ˌbīd-iŋ\ *adj* **:** abiding by or obedient to the law — **law–abid·ing·ness** *n*

law·break·er \'lȯ-ˌbrā-kər\ *n* **:** one who violates the law — **law·break·ing** \-kiŋ\ *adj*

law·ful \'lȯ-fəl\ *adj* **1 a :** being in harmony with the law <a ~ judgment> **b :** constituted, authorized, or established by law : RIGHTFUL <~ institutions> **2 :** LAW-ABIDING <~ citizens> — **law·ful·ly** \-f(ə-)lē\ *adv* — **law·ful·ness** \-fəl-nəs\ *n*

syn LAWFUL, LEGAL, LEGITIMATE, LICIT *shared meaning element* : being in accordance with law. LAWFUL can imply conformity with law of any sort (as natural, divine, common, or canon) and may come close in meaning to *allowable* or *permissible* <all things are *lawful* unto me, but all things are not expedient —1 Cor 6:12 (AV)> or to *rightful* or *proper* <the *lawful* heir> LEGAL implies a reference to law as it appears in statute books or is administered by the courts; thus, the *lawful* owner of a piece of property is one whose *legal* right to it is certain. Often *legal* stresses conformity with or sanction by law; thus, a *legal* marriage is one carried out with all the observances called for by law; a *lawful* marriage is one to which no compelling *legal* impediment (as close consanguinity) exists. LEGITIMATE can imply a legal right or status <his *legitimate* children> or in more general use a right or status supported by tradition, custom, or accepted standards <language is a *legitimate* part of the subject matter or content of English —A. H. Marckwardt> LICIT usually implies strict conformity to the provisions of the law and applies especially to what is regulated by law <*licit* use of property does not include creating a neighborhood nuisance> ***ant*** unlawful

law·giv·er \ˈlȯ-ˌgiv-ər\ *n* **1 :** one who gives a code of laws to a people **2 :** LEGISLATOR

law–hand \-ˌhand\ *n* **:** a special style of handwriting used in engrossing old legal documents in England

law·less \ˈlȯ-ləs\ *adj* **1 :** not regulated by or based on law **2 a :** not restrained or controlled by law **:** UNRULY **b :** ILLEGAL — **law·less·ly** *adv* — **law·less·ness** *n*

law·mak·er \ˈlȯ-ˌmā-kər\ *n* **:** one that makes laws **:** LEGISLATOR — **law·mak·ing** \-kiŋ\ *n*

law·man \ˈlȯ-mən\ *n* **:** a law-enforcement officer (as a sheriff or marshal)

law merchant *n, pl* **laws merchant :** the legal rules formerly applied to cases arising in commercial transactions

¹lawn \ˈlȯn, ˈlän\ *n* [ME, fr. *Laon,* France] **:** a fine sheer linen or cotton fabric of plain weave that is thinner than cambric — **lawny** \-ē\ *adj*

²lawn *n* [ME *launde,* fr. MF *lande* heath, of Celt origin; akin to OIr *land* open space — more at LAND] **1** *archaic* **:** an open space between woods **:** GLADE **2 :** ground (as around a house or in a garden or park) that is covered with grass and is kept mowed — **lawn** *or* **lawny** \-ē\ *adj*

lawn bowling *n* **:** a bowling game played on a green with wooden balls which are rolled at a jack

lawn mower *n* **:** a machine for cutting grass on lawns

lawn tennis *n* **:** TENNIS 2; *specif* **:** tennis played on a grass court

law of dominance : MENDEL'S LAW 3

law of independent assortment : MENDEL'S LAW 2

law of large numbers : a theorem in mathematical statistics: the probability that the mean of a random sample differs from the mean of the population from which the sample is drawn by more than a given amount approaches zero as the size of the sample approaches infinity

Law of Moses : PENTATEUCH

law of nations : INTERNATIONAL LAW

law of parsimony : OCCAM'S RAZOR

law of segregation : MENDEL'S LAW 1

law of war : the code that governs or one of the rules that govern the rights and duties of belligerents in international war

law·ren·ci·um \lȯ-ˈren(t)-sē-əm\ *n* [NL, fr. Ernest O. *Lawrence*] **:** a short-lived radioactive element that is produced artificially from californium — see ELEMENT table

law·suit \ˈlȯ-ˌsüt\ *n* **:** a suit in law **:** a case before a court

law·yer \ˈlȯ-yər, ˈlȯi-ər\ *n* **:** one whose profession is to conduct lawsuits for clients or to advise as to legal rights and obligations in other matters — **law·yer·ly** \-lē\ *adv*

lax \ˈlaks\ *adj* [ME, fr. L *laxus* loose — more at SLACK] **1 a** *of the bowels* **:** LOOSE, OPEN **b :** having loose bowels **2 :** deficient in firmness **:** not stringent <~ control> <a ~ foreman> **3 a :** not tense, firm, or rigid **:** SLACK <a ~ rope> **b :** having an open or loose texture **c :** having the constituents spread apart <a ~ flower cluster> **4 :** articulated with the muscles involved in a relatively relaxed state (as the vowel \i\ in contrast with the vowel \ē\) ***syn*** **1** see LOOSE ***ant*** rigid **2** see NEGLIGENT ***ant*** strict, stringent — **lax·a·tion** \lak-ˈsā-shən\ *n* — **lax·ly** \ˈlak-slē\ *adv* — **lax·ness** *n*

¹lax·a·tive \ˈlak-sət-iv\ *adj* [ME *laxatif,* fr. ML *laxativus,* fr. L *laxatus,* pp. of *laxare* to loosen, fr. *laxus*] **1 :** having a tendency to loosen or relax; *specif* **:** relieving constipation **2 :** having loose bowels — **lax·a·tive·ly** *adv* — **lax·a·tive·ness** *n*

²laxative *n* **:** a usu. mild laxative drug

lax·ity \ˈlak-sət-ē\ *n* **:** the quality or state of being lax

¹lay \ˈlā\ *vb* **laid** \ˈlād\; **lay·ing** [ME *leyen,* fr. OE *lecgan;* akin to OE *licgan* to lie — more at LIE] *vt* **1 :** to beat or strike down with force **2 a :** to put or set down **b :** to place for rest or sleep; *esp* **:** BURY **3 :** to bring forth and deposit (an egg) **4 :** CALM, ALLAY <~ the dust> **5 :** BET, WAGER **6 :** to press down giving a smooth and even surface **7 a :** to dispose or spread over or on a surface <~ track> <~ plaster> **b :** to set in order or position <~ a table for dinner> <~ brick> **c :** to put (strands) in place and twist to form a rope, hawser, or cable; *also* **:** to make by so doing <~ up rope> **8 a :** to impose as a duty, burden, or punishment <~ a tax> **b :** to put as a burden of reproach <*laid* the blame on him> **c :** to advance as an accusation **:** IMPUTE <the disaster was *laid* to faulty inspection> **9 :** to place (something immaterial) on something <~ stress on grammar> **10 :** PREPARE, CONTRIVE <a well-*laid* plan> **11 a :** to bring against or into contact with something **:** APPLY <*laid* the watch to his ear> **b :** to prepare or position for action or operation <~ a fire in the fireplace>; *also* **:** to adjust (a gun) to the proper direction and elevation **12 :** to bring to a specified condition <~ waste the land> **13 a :** ASSERT, ALLEGE <~ claim to an estate> **b :** to submit for examination and judgment <*laid* his case before the commission> **14 :** to copulate with — sometimes considered vulgar ~ *vi* **1 :** to produce and deposit eggs **2** *nonstand* **:** ¹LIE **3 :** WAGER, BET **4** *dial* **:** PLAN, PREPARE <~ for a chance> **5 a :** to apply oneself vigorously <*laid* to his oars> **b :** to proceed to a specified place or position on a ship <~ aloft> — **lay on the table 1 :** to remove (a parliamentary motion) from consideration indefinitely **2** *Brit* **:** to put (as legislation) on the agenda

²lay *n* **1 :** something (as a layer) that lies or is laid **2 :** COVERT, LAIR **3 a :** line of action **:** PLAN **b :** line of work **:** OCCUPATION **4 a :** terms of sale or employment **:** PRICE **b :** share of profit (as on a whaling voyage) paid in lieu of wages **5 a :** the amount of advance of any point in a rope strand for one turn **b :** the nature of a fiber rope as determined by the amount of twist, the angle of the strands, and the angle of the threads in the strands **6 :** the way in which a thing lies or is laid in relation to something else <the ~ of the land> **7 :** the state of one that lays eggs <hens coming into ~> **8 a :** a partner in sexual intercourse — usu. considered vulgar **b :** SEXUAL INTERCOURSE — usu. considered vulgar

³lay *past of* LIE

⁴lay *n* [ME, fr. OF *lai*] **1 :** a simple narrative poem **:** BALLAD **2 :** MELODY, SONG

⁵lay *adj* [ME, fr. OF *lai,* fr. LL *laicus,* fr. Gk *laikos* of the people, fr. *laos* people] **1 :** of or relating to the laity **:** not ecclesiastical **2 :** of or relating to members of a religious house occupied with domestic or manual work <a ~ brother> **3 :** not of or from a particular profession **:** UNPROFESSIONAL <the ~ public>

lay·about \ˈlā-ə-ˌbau̇t\ *n, chiefly Brit* **:** a lazy shiftless person **:** IDLER

lay·away \ˈlā-ə-ˌwā\ *n* **:** an article of merchandise reserved for future delivery to a customer who pays a deposit and agrees to complete payment when the article is called for

lay away *vt* **:** to put aside for future use or delivery

lay–by \ˈlā-ˌbī\ *n* **1 :** the final operation (as a last cultivating) in the growing of a field crop **2** *Brit* **:** a branch from or a widening of a road to permit vehicles to stop without obstructing traffic

lay by *vt* **1 :** to lay aside **:** DISCARD **2 :** to store for future use **:** SAVE **3 :** to cultivate (as corn) for the last time

lay day *n* **1 :** one of the days allowed by the charter for loading or unloading a vessel **2 :** a day of delay in port

lay down *vt* **1 :** to give up **:** SURRENDER <*lay down* your arms> **2 a :** ESTABLISH, PRESCRIBE <*lay down* a scale for a map> **b :** to assert or command dogmatically <*lay down* the law> **3 :** STORE, PRESERVE **4 a :** to direct toward a target <*lay down* a barrage> **b :** to hit along the ground <*laid down* a sacrifice bunt> ~ *vi, nonstand* **:** to lie down

¹lay·er \ˈlā-ər, ˈle(-ə)r\ *n* **1 :** one that lays (as a workman who lays brick or a hen that lay eggs) **2 a :** one thickness, course, or fold laid or lying over or under another **b :** STRATUM **c :** HORIZON 2 **3 a :** a branch or shoot of a plant treated to induce rooting while still attached to the parent plant **b :** a plant developed by layering — **lay·ered** \ˈlā-ərd, ˈle-ərd\ *adj*

²layer *vt* **:** to propagate (a plant) by means of layers ~ *vi* **1 a :** to separate into layers **b :** to form out of superimposed layers **2** *of a plant* **:** to form roots where a stem comes in contact with the ground

lay·er·age \ˈlā-ə-rij, ˈle-ə-\ *n* **:** the practice or art of layering plants

lay·ette \lā-ˈet\ *n* [F, fr. MF, dim. of *laye* box, fr. MD *lade;* akin to OE *hladan* to load — more at LADE] **:** a complete outfit of clothing and equipment for a newborn infant

lay figure \ˈlā-\ *n* [obs. E *layman* (lay figure), fr. D *leeman*] **1 :** a jointed model of the human body used by artists to show the disposition of drapery **2 :** a person likened to a dummy or puppet

lay in *vt* **:** to lay by **:** SAVE

laying on of hands : the act of laying hands on a person's head to confer a spiritual blessing (as in Christian ordination, confirmation, or faith healing)

lay·man \ˈlā-mən\ *n* **1 :** a person who is not a clergyman **2 :** a person who does not belong to a particular profession or who is not expert in some field

lay·off \ˈlā-ˌȯf\ *n* **1 :** the act of laying off an employee or a work force; *also* **:** SHUTDOWN **2 :** a period of inactivity or idleness

lay off \(ˈ)lā-ˈȯf\ *vt* **1 :** to mark or measure off **2 :** to cease to employ (a worker) usu. temporarily **3 a :** to let alone **b :** AVOID, QUIT ~ *vi* **:** to stop or rest from work

lay on *vt* **1** *chiefly Brit* **:** to supply (as water or gas) to a building **2** *chiefly Brit* **:** to provide facilities for <*lay on* a banquet> **3** *chiefly Brit* **:** HIRE ~ *vi* **:** ATTACK, BEAT

lay·out \ˈlā-ˌau̇t\ *n* **1 :** the act or process of planning or laying out in detail **2 :** the plan or design or arrangement of something that is laid out: as **a :** DUMMY 6 **b :** final arrangement of matter to be reproduced esp. by printing **c :** the placing of men, machines, and materials in a manufacturing plant **3 a :** something that is laid out <a model train ~> **b :** land and structures or rooms used for a particular purpose <a cattle-ranching ~>; *also* **:** PLACE **c :** a set or outfit esp. of tools

lay out \(ˈ)lā-ˈau̇t\ *vt* **1 a :** to prepare (a corpse) for viewing **b :** to knock flat or unconscious **2 :** to plan in detail <*lay out* a campaign> **3 :** to mark (work) for drilling, machining, or filing **4 :** ARRANGE, DESIGN **5 :** SPEND

lay·over \ˈlā-ˌō-vər\ *n* **:** STOPOVER

lay over \(ˈ)lā-ˈō-vər\ *vt* **:** POSTPONE ~ *vi* **:** to make a stopover

lay reader *n* **:** an Anglican or Roman Catholic layman authorized to conduct parts of the church services not requiring a clergyman

lay to \(ˈ)lā-ˈtü\ *vt* **:** to bring (a ship) into the wind and hold stationary ~ *vi* **:** to lie to

lay–up \ˈlā-ˌəp\ *n* **1 :** the action of laying up or the condition of being laid up **2 :** a shot in basketball made from near the basket usu. by playing the ball off the backboard

lay up \(ˈ)lā-ˈəp\ *vt* **1 :** to store up **:** lay by **2 :** to disable or confine with illness or injury **3 :** to take out of active service

lay·wom·an \ˈlā-ˌwu̇m-ən\ *n* **:** a woman who is a member of the laity

la·zar \ˈlaz-ər, ˈlā-zər\ *n* [ME, fr. ML *lazarus,* fr. LL *Lazarus*] **:** a person afflicted with a repulsive disease; *specif* **:** LEPER

laz·a·ret·to \ˌlaz-ə-ˈret-(ˌ)ō\ *or* **laz·a·ret** \-ˈret, -ˈrēt\ *n, pl* **-rettos** *or* **-rets** [It dial. *lazareto,* alter. of *nazareto,* fr. *Santa Maria di Nazaret,* church in Venice that maintained a hospital] **1** *usu lazaretto* **:** a hospital for contagious diseases **2 :** a building or a ship used for detention in quarantine **3** *usu lazaret* **:** a space in a ship between decks used as a storeroom

La·za·rist \ˈlaz-ə-rəst, lə-ˈzär-əst\ *n* [College of St. *Lazare,* Paris, former home of the congregation] **:** VINCENTIAN

Laz·a·rus \ˈlaz-(ə-)rəs\ *n* [LL, fr. Gk *Lazaros,* fr. Heb *El'āzār*] **1 :** a brother of Mary and Martha raised by Jesus from the dead according to the account in John 11 **2 :** the diseased beggar in the parable of the rich man and the beggar found in Luke 16

laze \ˈlāz\ *vb* **lazed; laz·ing** [back-formation fr. *lazy*] *vi* **:** to act or lie lazily **:** IDLE ~ *vt* **:** to pass (time) in idleness or relaxation — **laze** *n*

la·zu·lite \ˈlaz(h)-ə-ˌlīt\ *n* [G *lazulith,* fr. ML *lazulum* lapis lazuli] **:** an often crystalline azure-blue mineral $(Mg,Fe)Al_2(PO_4)_2(OH)_2$ that is a hydrous phosphate of aluminum, iron, and magnesium — **la·zu·lit·ic** \ˌlaz(h)-ə-ˈlit-ik\ *adj*

[1]**la·zy** \'lā-zē\ *adj* **la·zi·er; -est** [perh. fr. MLG *lasich* feeble; akin to MHG *erleswen* to become weak] **1 a :** disinclined to activity or exertion **:** not energetic or vigorous **b :** encouraging inactivity or indolence **2 :** moving slowly **:** SLUGGISH **3 :** DROOPY, LAX **4 :** placed on its side <~ E livestock brand> — **la·zi·ly** \-zə-lē\ *adv* — **la·zi·ness** \-zē-nəs\ *n*

syn LAZY, INDOLENT, SLOTHFUL *shared meaning element* **:** not easily aroused to action or activity

[2]**lazy** *vi* **la·zied; la·zy·ing :** to move or lie lazily **:** LAZE

la·zy·bones \'lā-zē-ˌbōnz\ *n pl but sing or pl in constr* **:** a lazy person

lazy eye *n* **:** AMBLYOPIA

la·zy·ish \'lā-zē-ish\ *adj* **:** somewhat lazy

lazy Su·san \-'süz-ᵊn\ *n* **:** a revolving tray placed on a dining table for serving food, condiments, or relishes

lazy tongs *n pl* **:** a series of jointed and pivoted bars capable of great extension used for picking up or handling something at a distance

laz·za·ro·ne \ˌlaz-ə-'rō-nē, ˌläd-zə-\ *n, pl* **-ro·ni** \-(ˌ)nē\ [It, aug. of *lazzaro* lazar, beggar, fr. ML *lazarus*] **:** one of the homeless idlers of Naples

lb *abbr* [L *libra*] pound

lc *abbr* lowercase

LC *abbr* **1** landing craft **2** left center **3** letter of credit **4** Library of Congress

LCD *abbr* least common denominator; lowest common denominator

LCDR *abbr* lieutenant commander

LCL *abbr* less-than-carload lot

LCM *abbr* **1** least common multiple; lowest common multiple **2** [NL *legis comparativae magister*] master of comparative law

LCpl *abbr* lance corporal

LCS *abbr* landing craft, support

LCT *abbr* **1** landing craft, tank **2** local civil time

ld *abbr* **1** load **2** lord

LD *abbr* **1** lethal dose — often used with a numerical subscript to indicate the percent of a test group of organisms the dose is expected to kill <LD_{50}> **2** line of departure

ldg *abbr* **1** landing **2** loading

LDH *abbr* **1** lactate dehydrogenase **2** lactic dehydrogenase

L–do·pa \'el-'dō-pə\ *n* [*l-* + *dopa*] **:** the levorotatory form of dopa found esp. in broad beans or prepared synthetically and used in treating Parkinson's disease

ldr *abbr* leader

LDS *abbr* Latter-Day Saints

LE *abbr* leading edge

[1]**lea** *or* **ley** \'lē, 'lā\ *n* [ME *leye*, fr. OE *lēah*; akin to OHG *lōh* thicket, L *lucus* grove, *lux* light — more at LIGHT] **1 :** GRASSLAND, PASTURE **2** *usu ley* **:** arable land used temporarily for hay or grazing

[2]**lea** *abbr* leather

LEA *abbr* local education authority

[1]**leach** \'lēch\ *var of* LEECH

[2]**leach** *n* [prob. alter. of *letch* (muddy ditch)] **1 :** a perforated vessel to hold wood ashes through which water is passed to extract the lye **2 :** LEACHATE **3** [[3]*leach*] **:** the process of leaching

[3]**leach** *vt* **1 :** to subject to the action of percolating liquid (as water) in order to separate the soluble components **2 :** to dissolve out by the action of a percolating liquid <~ out alkali from ashes> ~ *vi* **:** to pass out or through by percolation — **leach·abil·i·ty** \ˌlē-chə-'bil-ət-ē\ *n* — **leach·able** \'lē-chə-bəl\ *adj* — **leach·er** *n*

leach·ate \'lē-ˌchāt\ *n* **:** a solution or product obtained by leaching

[1]**lead** \'lēd\ *vb* **led** \'led\; **lead·ing** [ME *leden*, fr. OE *lǣdan*; akin to OHG *leiten* to lead, OE *līthan* to go] *vt* **1 a :** to guide on a way esp. by going in advance **b :** to direct on a course or in a direction **c :** to serve as a channel for <a pipe ~*s* water to the house> **2 :** to go through **:** LIVE <~ a quiet life> **3 a** (1) **:** to direct the operations, activity, or performance of <~ an orchestra> (2) **:** to have charge of <~ a campaign> **b** (1) **:** to go at the head of <~ a parade> (2) **:** to be first in or among <~ the league> (3) **:** to have a margin over <*led* his opponent> **4 :** to begin play with <~ trumps> **5 a :** to aim in front of (a moving object) <~ a duck> **b :** to pass a ball or puck just in front of (a moving teammate) **6 :** to begin a series of blows with <*led* a short jab to the head> ~ *vi* **1 a :** to guide someone or something along a way **b :** to lie, run, or open in a specified place or direction <path ~*s* uphill> **2 a :** to be first **b** (1) **:** BEGIN, OPEN <~ off for the home team> (2) **:** to play the first card of a trick, round, or game **3 :** to tend toward a definite result <study ~*ing* to a degree> **4 :** to direct the first of a series of blows at an opponent in boxing; *also* **:** to punch with the leading hand ***syn*** see GUIDE ***ant*** follow

[2]**lead** *n* **1 a** (1) **:** position at the front **:** VANGUARD (2) **:** INITIATIVE (3)**:** the act or privilege of leading in cards; *also* **:** the card or suit led **b** (1) **:** LEADERSHIP (2) **:** EXAMPLE, PRECEDENT **c :** a margin or measure of advantage or superiority or position in advance **2 :** one that leads: as **a** (1) **:** LODE 2 (2) **:** an auriferous gravel deposit in an old river bed; *esp* **:** one buried under lava **b :** a channel of water esp. through a field of ice **c :** INDICATION, CLUE **d :** a principal role in a dramatic production; *also* **:** one who plays such a role **e :** LEASH 1 **f** (1) **:** an introductory section of a news story (2) **:** a news story of chief importance **3 :** an insulated electrical conductor **4 :** the length of a rope from end to end **5 :** the amount of axial advance of a point accompanying a complete turn of a thread (as of a screw or worm) **6 :** a position taken by a base runner off a base toward the next

[3]**lead** *adj* **:** acting or serving as a lead or leader <a ~ article>

[4]**lead** \'led\ *n, often attrib* [ME *leed*, fr. OE *lēad*; akin to MHG *lōt* lead] **1 :** a heavy soft malleable ductile plastic but inelastic bluish white metallic element found mostly in combination and used esp. in pipes, cable sheaths, batteries, solder, type metal, and shields against radioactivity — see ELEMENT table **2 a :** a plummet for sounding at sea **b** *pl, Brit* **:** a usu. flat lead roof **c** *pl* **:** lead framing for panes in windows **d :** a thin strip of metal used to separate lines of type in printing **3 a :** a thin stick of marking substance in or for a pencil **b :** WHITE LEAD **4 :** BULLETS, PROJECTILES **5 :** TETRAETHYLLEAD

[5]**lead** \'led\ *vt* **1 :** to cover, line, or weight with lead **2 :** to fix (window glass) in position with leads **3 :** to place leads or other spacing material between the lines of (type matter) **4 :** to treat or mix with lead or a lead compound <~*ed* gasoline>

lead acetate *n* **:** an acetate of lead; *esp* **:** a poisonous soluble salt $PbC_4H_6O_4 \cdot 3H_2O$

lead arsenate *n* **:** an arsenate of lead; *esp* **:** an acid salt $PbHAsO_4$ used as an insecticide

lead azide *n* **:** a crystalline explosive compound $Pb(N_3)_2$ used as a detonating agent

lead back *vt* **:** to lead (a card) from a suit that one's partner has orig. led

lead carbonate *n* **:** a carbonate of lead; *esp* **:** a poisonous basic salt $Pb_3(OH)_2(CO_3)_2$ used esp. as a white pigment

lead chromate *n* **:** a chromate of lead; *esp* **:** CHROME YELLOW

lead colic *n* **:** intestinal colic associated with obstinate constipation due to chronic lead poisoning — called also *painter's colic*

lead dioxide *n* **:** a poisonous compound PbO_2 used esp. as an oxidizing agent and as an electrode in batteries

lead·en \'led-ᵊn\ *adj* **1 a :** made of lead **b :** of the color of lead **:** dull gray **2 :** low in quality **:** POOR **3 a :** oppressively heavy **b :** SLUGGISH **c :** lacking spirit or animation **:** DULL — **lead·en·ly** *adv* — **lead·en·ness** \-ᵊn-(n)əs\ *n*

lead·er \'lēd-ər\ *n* **1 :** something that leads: as **a :** a primary or terminal shoot of a plant **b :** TENDON, SINEW **c** *pl* **:** dots or hyphens (as in an index) used to lead the eye horizontally **:** ELLIPSIS 2 **d** *chiefly Brit* **:** a newspaper editorial **e** (1) **:** something for guiding fish into a trap (2) **:** a short length of material for attaching the end of a fishing line to a lure or hook **f :** a pipe for conducting fluid **g :** an article offered at an attractive special low price to stimulate business **h :** something that ranks first **i :** a blank section at the beginning of a reel of film or recorded tape **2 :** a person that leads: as **a :** GUIDE, CONDUCTOR **b** (1) **:** a person who directs a military force or unit (2) **:** a person who has commanding authority or influence **c** (1)**:** the principal officer of a British political party (2) **:** a member chosen by his party to manage party activities in a legislative body (3) **:** such a member presiding over the whole legislative body when his party constitutes a majority (4) **:** one that exercises paramount but responsible authority over a state or local party organization (5) **:** the principal member of the party elite in a totalitarian system endowed by official ideology with a heroic or mystical character and who governs with a minimum of formal constitutional restraints, extreme nationalist demagogy, and claims to be above narrow class or group interests **d** (1) **:** CONDUCTOR c (2) **:** a first or principal performer of a group **e :** STRAW BOSS, FOREMAN **3 :** a horse placed in advance of the other horses of a team — **lead·er·less** \-ləs\ *adj*

leader of the opposition : the principal member of the opposition party in a British legislative body who is given the status of a salaried government official and an important role in organizing the business of the house

lead·er·ship \'lēd-ər-ˌship\ *n* **1 :** the office or position of a leader **2 :** the quality of a leader **:** capacity to lead

lead glass *n* **:** glass of high refractive index containing lead oxide

lead–in \'lēd-ˌin\ *n* **:** something that leads in; *esp* **:** the part of a radio or television antenna that runs to the transmitting or receiving set — **lead–in** *adj*

lead·ing \'lēd-iŋ\ *adj* **1 :** coming or ranking first **:** FOREMOST **2 :** exercising leadership **3 :** providing direction or guidance <a ~ question> **4 :** given most prominent display <the ~ story>

leading article *n* **1** *chiefly Brit* **:** EDITORIAL **2 :** the article given the most significant position or most prominent display in a periodical

leading edge *n* **1 :** the foremost edge of an airfoil or propeller blade **2 :** the forward part of a vehicle or of something that itself moves

leading lady *n* **:** an actress who plays the leading feminine role in a play or movie

leading man *n* **:** an actor who plays the leading male role in a play or movie

leading strings *n pl* **1 :** strings by which children are supported when beginning to walk **2 :** a state of dependence or tutelage **:** GUIDANCE — usu. used in the phrase *in leading strings*

leading tone *n* **:** the seventh tone of a diatonic scale — called also *leading note*

lead·less \'led-ləs\ *adj* **:** being without lead <~ gasoline>

lead line \'led-\ *n* **:** SOUNDING LINE

lead monoxide *n* **:** a yellow to brownish red poisonous compound PbO used in rubber manufacture and glassmaking

[1]**lead·off** \'lēd-ˌȯf\ *n* **1 :** a beginning or leading action **2 :** one that leads off

[2]**leadoff** *adj* **1 :** leading off **:** OPENING **2 :** of, being, or made by the first batter in an inning <~ hitter> <~ single>

lead off \(')lēd-'ȯf\ *vt* **1 :** to make a start on **:** OPEN **2 :** to bat first for a baseball team in (an inning)

lead on *vt* **:** to entice or induce to proceed in a course esp. when unwise or mistaken

lead pencil \'led-\ *n* **:** a pencil using graphite as the marking material

lead·plant \'led-ˌplant\ *n* **:** a leguminous shrub (*Amorpha canescens*) of the western U.S. that has hoary pinnate leaves and bears dull-colored racemose flowers

lead poisoning *n* **:** chronic intoxication that is produced by the absorption of lead into the system and is characterized by severe colicky pains, a dark line along the gums, and local muscular paralysis

leads·man \ˈledz-mən\ *n* **:** a man who uses a sounding lead to determine depth of water

lead time \ˈlēd-\ *n* **:** the period between the decision to begin a process (as the development of a new product) and the completion of the process <a long *lead time* on a new aircraft>

lead–up \ˈlēd-ˌəp\ *n* **:** something that leads up to or prepares the way for something else

lead up \(ˈ)lēd-ˈəp\ *vi* **1 :** to prepare the way **2 :** to make a gradual or indirect approach to a topic

lead·work \ˈled-ˌwərk\ *n* **1 :** something made of lead **2 :** work that is done with lead

leady \ˈled-ē\ *adj* **lead·i·er; -est :** containing or resembling lead

[1]**leaf** \ˈlēf\ *n, pl* **leaves** \ˈlēvz\ *often attrib* [ME *leef,* fr. OE *lēaf;* akin to OHG *loub* leaf, L *liber* bast, book] **1 a (1) :** a lateral outgrowth from a stem that constitutes a unit of the foliage of a plant and functions primarily in food manufacture by photosynthesis **(2) :** a modified leaf primarily engaged in functions other than food manufacture **b (1) :** FOLIAGE **(2) :** the leaves of a plant as an article of commerce **2 :** something suggestive of a leaf: as **a :** a part of a book or folded sheet containing a page on each side **b (1) :** a part (as of window shutters, folding doors, or gates) that slides or is hinged **(2) :** the movable parts of a table top **c (1) :** a thin sheet or plate of any substance **:** LAMINA **(2) :** metal (as gold or silver) in sheets usu. thinner than foil **(3) :** one of the plates of a leaf spring — **leaf·less** \ˈlē-fləs\ *adj* — **leaf·like** \ˈlē-ˌflīk\ *adj*

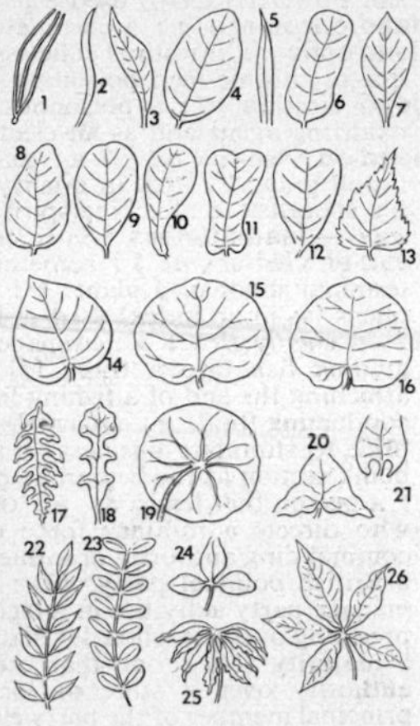

forms of leaves 1a(1): *1* acerate; *2* linear; *3* lanceolate; *4* elliptic; *5* ensiform; *6* oblong; *7* oblanceolate, with acuminate tip; *8* ovate, with acute tip; *9* obovate; *10* spatulate; *11* pandurate; *12* cuneate; *13* deltoid; *14* cordate; *15* reniform; *16* orbiculate; *17* runcinate; *18* lyrate; *19* peltate; *20* hastate; *21* sagittate; *22* odd-pinnate; *23* abruptly pinnate; *24* palmate (trifoliolate); *25* palmate (pedate in form, with margin incised); *26* palmate (quinquefoliolate)

[2]**leaf** *vi* **1 :** to shoot out or produce leaves **2 :** to turn over pages <~ through a book> ~ *vt* **:** to turn over the pages of

leaf·age \ˈlē-fij\ *n* **1 :** FOLIAGE 1 **2 :** the representation of leafage (as in architecture)

leaf bud *n* **:** a bud that develops into a leafy shoot and does not produce flowers

leaf butterfly *n* **:** any of a genus (*Kallima*) of nymphalid butterflies of southern Asia and the East Indies that mimic leaves

leaf curl *n* **:** a plant disease characterized by curling of leaves; *esp* **:** PEACH LEAF CURL

leafed \ˈlēft\ *adj* **:** LEAVED

leaf fat *n* **:** the fat that lines the abdominal cavity and encloses the kidneys; *esp* **:** that of a hog used in the manufacture of lard

leaf·hop·per \ˈlēf-ˌhäp-ər\ *n* **:** any of numerous small leaping homopterous insects (family Cicadellidae) that suck the juices of plants

leaf lard *n* **:** high-quality lard made from leaf fat

leaf·let \ˈlē-flət\ *n* **1 a :** one of the divisions of a compound leaf **b :** a small or young foliage leaf **2 :** a leaflike organ or part **3 a :** a single printed sheet of paper unfolded or folded but not trimmed at the fold **b :** a sheet of small pages folded but not stitched

leaf miner *n* **:** any of various small insects (as moths or two-winged flies) that in the larval stages burrow in and eat the parenchyma of leaves

leaf mold *n* **1 :** a compost or layer composed chiefly of decayed vegetable matter **2 :** a mold or mildew of foliage

leaf roll *n* **:** a virus disease of the potato that is transmitted by aphids and is characterized by an upward rolling of the leaf margins, smaller tubers, and netlike necrotic areas in the phloem

leaf roller *n* **:** any of various lepidopterans whose larvae make a nest by rolling up plant leaves

leaf rust *n* **:** a rust disease of plants and esp. of wheat that affects primarily the leaves

leaf spot *n* **:** any of various plant diseases characterized by discolored often circular spots on the leaves

leaf spring *n* **:** a spring made of superposed strips, plates, or leaves

leaf·stalk \ˈlēf-ˌstȯk\ *n* **:** PETIOLE

leaf trace *n* [[3]*trace*] **:** a trace associated with a leaf

leafy \ˈlē-fē\ *adj* **leaf·i·er; -est 1 a :** furnished with or abounding in leaves <~ woodlands> **b :** having broad-bladed leaves <mosses, grasses, and ~ plants> **c :** consisting chiefly of leaves <~ vegetables> **2 :** resembling a leaf; *specif* **:** LAMINATE

leafy liverwort *n* **:** any of an order (Jungermanniales) of usu. epiphytic liverworts with a leafy gametophyte that has one ventral and two dorsal rows of leaves on the stem

leafy spurge *n* **:** a tall perennial European herb (*Euphorbia esula*) that is naturalized and troublesome as a weed in the northern U.S. and Canada

[1]**league** \ˈlēg\ *n* [ME *leuge, lege,* fr. LL *leuga*] **1 :** any of various units of distance from about 2.4 to 4.6 statute miles **2 :** a square league

[2]**league** *n* [ME (Sc) *ligg,* fr. MF *ligue,* fr. OIt *liga,* fr. *ligare* to bind, fr. L — more at LIGATURE] **1 a :** an association of nations or other political entities for a common purpose **b :** an association of persons or groups united by common interests or goals; *specif* **:** an association of ball clubs **c :** an informal alliance **2 :** CLASS, CATEGORY

[3]**league** *vb* **leagued; leagu·ing** *vt* **:** to unite in a league ~ *vi* **:** to form a league

[1]**lea·guer** \ˈlē-gər\ *n* [D *leger;* akin to OHG *legar* act of lying down — more at LAIR] **1 :** a military camp **2 :** SIEGE

[2]**leaguer** *vt, archaic* **:** BESIEGE, BELEAGUER

[3]**leagu·er** \ˈlē-gər\ *n* **:** a member of a league

[1]**leak** \ˈlēk\ *vb* [ME *leken,* fr. ON *leka;* akin to OE *leccan* to moisten, OIr *legaim* I melt] *vi* **1 a :** to enter or escape through an opening usu. by a fault or mistake <fumes ~ in> **b :** to let a substance or light in or out through an opening **2 :** to become known despite efforts at concealment ~ *vt* **1 :** to permit to enter or escape through or as if through a leak **2 :** to give out (information) surreptitiously <~*ed* the story to the press>

[2]**leak** *n* **1 a :** a crack or hole that usu. by mistake admits or lets escape **b :** something that permits the admission or escape of something else usu. with prejudicial effect **c :** a loss of electricity due to faulty insulation; *also* **:** the point or the path at which such loss occurs **2 :** the act, process, or an instance of leaking **3 :** an act of urinating — usu. used with *take;* sometimes considered vulgar

leak·age \ˈlē-kij\ *n* **1 :** the act, process, or an instance of leaking **2 :** something or the amount that leaks

leaky \ˈlē-kē\ *adj* **leak·i·er; -est :** permitting fluid to leak in or out — **leak·i·ly** \-kə-lē\ *adv* — **leak·i·ness** \-kē-nəs\ *n*

leal \ˈlē(ə)l\ *adj* [ME *leel,* fr. OF *leial, leel* — more at LOYAL] *chiefly Scot* **:** LOYAL, TRUE — **leal·ly** \ˈlē-əl-(l)ē, ˈlēl-lē\ *adv*

[1]**lean** \ˈlēn\ *vb* **leaned** \ˈlēnd, *chiefly Brit* ˈlent\; **lean·ing** \ˈlē-niŋ\ [ME *lenen,* fr. OE *hleonian;* akin to OHG *hlinēn* to lean, Gk *klinein,* L *clinare*] *vi* **1 a :** to incline, deviate, or bend from a vertical position **b :** to cast one's weight to one side for support **2 :** to rely for support or inspiration **3 :** to incline in opinion, taste, or desire ~ *vt* **:** to cause to lean **:** INCLINE ***syn*** see SLANT

[2]**lean** *n* **:** the act or an instance of leaning **:** INCLINATION

[3]**lean** *adj* [ME *lene,* fr. OE *hlǣne*] **1 a :** lacking or deficient in flesh **b :** containing little or no fat **2 :** lacking richness, sufficiency, or productiveness **3 :** deficient in an essential or important quality or ingredient: as **a** *of ore* **:** containing little valuable mineral **b :** low in combustible component — used esp. of fuel mixtures **4 :** characterized by economy of style or expression — **lean·ly** *adv* — **lean·ness** \ˈlēn-nəs\ *n*

syn LEAN, SPARE, LANK, LANKY, GAUNT, RAWBONED, SCRAWNY, SKINNY *shared meaning element* **:** thin because of absence of superfluous flesh ***ant*** fleshy

[4]**lean** *vt* **:** to make lean

[5]**lean** *n* **:** the part of meat that consists principally of fat-free muscle

Le·an·der \lē-ˈan-dər\ *n* [L, fr. Gk *Leandros*] **:** a legendary Greek youth who swam the Hellespont nightly to visit Hero but ultimately was drowned in one of the crossings

lean·ing \ˈlē-niŋ\ *n* **:** a definite but not decisive attraction or tendency

syn LEANING, PROCLIVITY, PROPENSITY, PENCHANT, FLAIR *shared meaning element* **:** a strong attraction to or liking for someone or something

leant \ˈlent\ *chiefly Brit past of* LEAN

[1]**lean–to** \ˈlēn-ˌtü\ *n, pl* **lean–tos** \-ˌtüz\ **1 :** a wing or extension of a building having a lean-to roof **2 :** a rough shed or shelter with a lean-to roof

[2]**lean–to** *adj* **:** having only one slope or pitch <~ roof>

[1]**leap** \ˈlēp\ *vb* **leaped** *or* **leapt** \ˈlept *also* ˈlēpt\; **leap·ing** \ˈlē-piŋ\ [ME *lepen,* fr. OE *hlēapan;* akin to OHG *hlouffan* to run] *vi* **1 :** to spring free from or as if from the ground **:** JUMP <~ over a fence> <a fish ~*s* out of the water> **2 a :** to pass abruptly from one state or topic to another **b :** to act precipitately <~*ed* at the chance> ~ *vt* **:** to pass over by leaping — **leap·er** \ˈlē-pər\ *n*

[2]**leap** *n* **1 a :** an act of leaping **:** SPRING, BOUND **b (1) :** a place leaped over or from **(2) :** the distance covered by a leap **2 :** a sudden transition

[1]**leap·frog** \ˈlēp-ˌfrȯg, -ˌfräg\ *n* **:** a game in which one player bends down and another leaps over him

[2]**leapfrog** *vb* **leap·frogged; leap·frog·ging** *vi* **:** to leap or progress in or as if in leapfrog ~ *vt* **1 :** to go ahead of (each other) in turn; *specif* **:** to advance (two military units) by keeping one unit in action while moving the other unit past it to a position farther in front **2 :** to evade by or as if by a bypass

leap year *n* **1 :** a year in the Gregorian calendar containing 366 days with February 29 as the extra day **2 :** an intercalary year in any calendar

Lear \ˈli(ə)r\ *n* **:** a legendary king of Britain and hero of Shakespeare's tragedy *King Lear*

learn \ˈlərn\ *vb* **learned** \ˈlərnd, ˈlərnt\ *also* **learnt** \ˈlərnt\; **learn·ing** [ME *lernen,* fr. OE *leornian;* akin to OHG *lernen* to learn, L *lira* furrow, track] *vt* **1 a (1) :** to gain knowledge or understanding of or skill in by study, instruction, or experience <~ a trade> **(2) :** MEMORIZE <~ the lines of a play> **b :** to come to be able <~ to dance> **c :** to come to realize <~*ed* that honesty paid> **2 a** *substand* **:** TEACH **b** *obs* **:** to inform of something **3 :** to come to know **:** HEAR <we just ~*ed* that he was ill> ~ *vi* **:** to acquire knowledge or skill or a behavioral tendency ***syn*** see DISCOVER — **learn·able** \ˈlər-nə-bəl\ *adj* — **learn·er** *n*

learned *adj* **1** \ˈlər-nəd\ **:** characterized by or associated with learning **:** ERUDITE **2** \ˈlərnd, ˈlərnt\ **:** acquired by learning <~ versus innate behavior patterns> — **learn·ed·ly** \ˈlər-nəd-lē\ *adv* — **learn·ed·ness** \-nəd-nəs\ *n*

learn·ing *n* **1 :** the act or experience of one that learns **2 :** knowledge or skill acquired by instruction or study **3 :** modification of a behavioral tendency by experience (as exposure to conditioning) ***syn*** see KNOWLEDGE

[1]**lease** \ˈlēs\ *n* **1 :** a contract by which one conveys real estate, equipment, or facilities for a specified term and for a specified rent; *also* **:** the act of such conveyance or the term for which it is made **2 :** a piece of land or property that is leased **3 :** a continuance or opportunity for continuance — used esp. in the phrase *lease on life*

2**lease** *vt* **leased; leas·ing** [AF *lesser,* fr. OF *laissier* to let go, fr. L *laxare* to loosen, fr. *laxus* slack — more at SLACK] **1 :** to grant by lease **2 :** to hold under a lease *syn* see HIRE

lease·hold \ˈlēs-ˌhōld\ *n* **1 :** a tenure by lease **2 :** property held by lease — **lease·hold·er** *n*

leash \ˈlēsh\ *n* [ME *lees, leshe,* fr. OF *laisse,* fr. *laissier*] **1 :** a line for leading or restraining an animal **2 a :** a set of three animals (as greyhounds, foxes, bucks, or hares) **b :** a set of three — **leash** *vt*

leas·ing \ˈlē-siŋ, -ziŋ\ *n* [ME *lesing,* fr. OE *lēasung,* fr. *lēasian* to lie, fr. *lēas* false] *archaic* **:** the act of lying; *also* **:** LIE, FALSEHOOD

1**least** \ˈlēst\ *adj* [ME *leest,* fr. OE *lǣst* superl. of *lǣssa* less] **1 :** lowest in importance or position **2 a :** smallest in size or degree **b :** being a member of a kind distinguished by diminutive size <~ bittern> **c :** smallest possible **:** SLIGHTEST

2**least** *n* **:** one that is least — **at least 1 :** at the minimum **2 :** in any case

3**least** *adv* **:** in the smallest or lowest degree — **least of all :** especially not <no one, *least of all* the children, paid attention>

least common denominator *n* **:** the least common multiple of two or more denominators

least common multiple *n* **1 :** the smallest common multiple of two or more numbers **2 :** the common multiple of lowest degree of two or more polynomials

least squares *n pl* **:** a method of fitting a curve to a set of points representing statistical data in such a way that the sum of the squares of the distances of the points from the curve is a minimum

least·ways \ˈlēs-ˌtwāz\ *adv, dial* **:** at least

least·wise \-ˌtwīz\ *adv* **:** at least

1**leath·er** \ˈleth-ər\ *n* [ME *lether,* fr. OE *lether-;* akin to OHG *leder* leather] **1 :** animal skin dressed for use **2 :** the pendulous part of the ear of a dog — see DOG illustration **3 :** something wholly or partly made of leather — **leath·er·like** \-ˌlīk\ *adj*

2**leather** *vt* **leath·ered; leath·er·ing** \ˈleth-(ə-)riŋ\ **1 :** to cover with leather **2 :** to beat with a strap **:** THRASH

leath·er·back \ˈleth-ər-ˌbak\ *n* **:** the largest existing sea turtle (*Dermochelys coriacea*) distinguished by its flexible carapace composed of a mosaic of small bones embedded in a thick leathery skin

Leath·er·ette \ˌleth-ə-ˈret\ *trademark* — used for a product colored, finished, and embossed in imitation of leather grains

leath·er·leaf \ˈleth-ər-ˌlēf\ *n* **:** a north temperate ericaceous bog shrub (*Chamaedaphne calyculata*) with evergreen coriaceous leaves and small white cylindrical flowers

leath·ern \ˈleth-ərn\ *adj* **:** made of, consisting of, or resembling leather

leath·er·neck \-ər-ˌnek\ *n* [fr. the leather neckband formerly part of the uniform] **:** a member of the U.S. Marine Corps

Leath·er·oid \-ə-ˌrȯid\ *trademark* — used for an artificial leather consisting of chemically treated paper combined with rubber and sandarac

leath·er·wood \ˈleth-ər-ˌwu̇d\ *n* **:** a small tree (*Dirca palustris*) of the mezereon family with pliant stems and yellow flowers

leath·ery \ˈleth-(ə-)rē\ *adj* **:** resembling leather in appearance or consistency **:** TOUGH

1**leave** \ˈlēv\ *vb* **left** \ˈleft\; **leav·ing** [ME *leven,* fr. OE *lǣfan;* akin to OHG *verleiben* to leave, OE *belīfan* to be left over, Gk *lipos* fat] *vt* **1 a** (1) **:** BEQUEATH, DEVISE <*left* a fortune to his son> (2) **:** to have remaining after one's death <~*s* a widow and two children> **b :** to cause to remain as a trace or aftereffect <oil ~*s* a stain> <the wound *left* an ugly scar> **2 a :** to cause or allow to be or remain in a specified condition <~ the door open> <his manner *left* me cold> **b :** to fail to include or take along <*left* his notes at home> **c :** to have as a remainder <4 from 7 ~*s* 3> **d :** to permit to be or remain subject to another's action or control <just ~ everything to me> **3 a :** to go away from **:** DEPART <told him to ~ the room> **b :** DESERT, ABANDON <*left* his wife> **c :** to terminate association with **:** withdraw from <*left* school a month before graduation> **4 :** to put, deposit, or deliver before or in the process of departing <the postman *left* a package for you> **5 :** to fall short of being satisfactory by (an indicated amount) <his solution to the problem ~*s* something to be desired —*Wall Street Jour.*> **6 :** to provide someone with (information) <~ your name and address with the receptionist> ~ *vi* **:** to set out **:** DEPART *syn* see GO — **leav·er** *n*

2**leave** *n* [ME *leve,* fr. OE *lēaf;* akin to MHG *loube* permission, OE *alȳfan* to allow — more at BELIEVE] **1 a :** permission to do something **b :** authorized esp. extended absence from duty or employment **2 :** an act of leaving **:** DEPARTURE *syn* see PERMISSION

3**leave** *vi* **leaved; leav·ing** [ME *leven,* fr. *leef* leaf] **:** LEAF

leaved *adj* **1 :** having leaves <a ~ branch> **2 :** having (such or so many) leaves — used in combination <palmate-*leaved*> <a four-*leaved* clover>

1**leav·en** \ˈlev-ən\ *n* [ME *levain,* fr. MF, fr. (assumed) VL *levamen,* fr. L *levare* to raise — more at LEVER] **1 a :** a substance (as yeast) used to produce fermentation in dough or a liquid; *esp* **:** SOURDOUGH **b :** a material (as baking powder) used to produce a gas that lightens dough or batter **2 :** something that modifies or lightens a mass or aggregate

2**leaven** *vt* **leav·ened; leav·en·ing** \ˈlev-(ə-)niŋ\ **1 :** to raise (as bread) with a leaven **2 :** to mingle or permeate with some modifying, alleviating, or vivifying element *syn* see INFUSE

leav·en·ing *n* **:** a leavening agent **:** LEAVEN

leave off *vb* **:** STOP, CEASE

leaves *pl of* LEAF

leave–tak·ing \ˈlēv-ˌtā-kiŋ\ *n* **:** DEPARTURE, FAREWELL

leav·ings \ˈlē-viŋz\ *n pl* **:** REMNANT, RESIDUE

Leb *abbr* Lebanese; Lebanon

leb·en \ˈleb-ən\ *n* [Ar *laban*] **:** a liquid or semiliquid solid food made from curdled milk by the peoples of the Levant and No. Africa

le·bens·raum \ˈlā-bənz-ˌrau̇m, -bən(t)s-\ *n, often cap* [G, fr. *leben* living, life + *raum* space] **1 :** territory believed esp. by Nazis to be necessary for national existence or economic self-sufficiency **2 :** space required for life, growth, or activity

lech·er \ˈlech-ər\ *n* [ME *lechour,* fr. OF *lecheor,* fr. *lechier* to lick, live in debauchery, of Gmc origin; akin to OHG *leckōn* to lick — more at LICK] **:** a man who engages in lechery

lech·er·ous \ˈlech-(ə-)rəs\ *adj* **:** given to or suggestive of lechery — **lech·er·ous·ly** *adv* — **lech·er·ous·ness** *n*

lech·ery \ˈlech-(ə-)rē\ *n* **:** inordinate indulgence in sexual activity **:** LASCIVIOUSNESS

lec·i·thin \ˈles-ə-thən\ *n* [ISV, fr. Gk *lekithos* yolk of an egg] **:** any of several waxy hygroscopic phosphatides that are widely distributed in animals and plants, form colloidal solutions in water, and have emulsifying, wetting, and antioxidant properties; *also* **:** a mixture of or substance rich in lecithins

lec·i·thin·ase \-thə-ˌnās, -ˌnāz\ *n* **:** any of several enzymes that hydrolyze lecithins or cephalins

lect *abbr* lecture; lecturer

lec·tern \ˈlek-tərn\ *n* [ME *lettorne,* fr. MF *letrun,* fr. ML *lectorinum,* fr. L *lector* reader, fr. *lectus,* pp. of *legere* to read — more at LEGEND] **:** READING DESK; *esp* **:** one from which scripture lessons are read in a church service

lec·tion \ˈlek-shən\ *n* [LL *lection-, lectio,* fr. L, act of reading — more at LESSON] **1 :** a liturgical lesson for a particular day **2** [NL *lection-, lectio,* fr. L] **:** a variant reading of a text

lec·tion·ary \ˈlek-shə-ˌner-ē\ *n, pl* **-ar·ies :** a book or list of lections for the church year

lec·tor \ˈlek-tər, -ˌtȯ(ə)r\ *n* [LL, reader of the lessons in a church service, fr. L, reader, fr. *lectus,* pp.] **:** one who assists at a worship service (as a Eucharist) chiefly by reading a lesson

lec·to·type \ˈlek-tə-ˌtīp\ *n* [Gk *lektos* chosen (fr. *legein* to gather, choose) + E *type* — more at LEGEND] **:** a specimen chosen as the type of a species or subspecies if the author of the name fails to designate a type

1**lec·ture** \ˈlek-chər\ *n* [ME, act of reading, fr. LL *lectura,* fr. L *lectus,* pp. of *legere* to read — more at LEGEND] **1 :** a discourse given before an audience or class esp. for instruction **2 :** a formal reproof **:** REPRIMAND — **lec·ture·ship** \-ˌship\ *n*

2**lecture** *vb* **lec·tured; lec·tur·ing** \ˈlek-chə-riŋ, ˈled-shriŋ\ *vi* **:** to deliver a lecture or a course of lectures ~ *vt* **1 :** to deliver a lecture to **2 :** to reprove formally — **lec·tur·er** \-chər-ər, -shrər\ *n*

led *past of* LEAD

Le·da \ˈlēd-ə\ *n* [L, fr. Gk *Lēdā*] **:** a legendary Spartan princess visited by Zeus in the form of a swan and mother by him of Pollux and Helen and at the same time mother of Castor and Clytemnestra by her husband Tyndareus

le·der·ho·sen \ˈlād-ər-ˌhōz-ᵊn\ *n pl* [G, fr. MHG *lederhose,* fr. *leder* leather + *hose* trousers] **:** leather shorts often with suspenders worn esp. in Bavaria

ledge \ˈlej\ *n* [ME *legge* bar of a gate] **1 :** a raised or projecting edge or molding intended to protect or check <a window ~> **2 :** an underwater ridge or reef esp. near the shore **3 a :** a narrow flat surface or shelf; *esp* **:** one that projects from a wall of rock **b :** rock solid or continuous enough to form ledges <the field was full of ~> **4 :** LODE, VEIN — **ledgy** \ˈlej-ē\ *adj*

led·ger \ˈlej-ər\ *n* [ME *legger,* prob. fr. *leyen, leggen* to lay] **1 :** a book containing accounts to which debits and credits are posted from books of original entry **2 :** a horizontal timber secured to the uprights of scaffolding to support the putlog

ledger board *n* **1 :** a horizontal board forming the top rail of a simple fence or the handrail of a balustrade **2 :** RIBBON 2a

ledger line *n* **:** a short line added above or below a musical staff to extend its range

1**lee** \ˈlē\ *n* [ME, fr. OE *hlēo;* akin to OHG *lāo* lukewarm, L *calēre* to be warm] **1 :** protecting shelter **2 :** the side (as of a ship) that is sheltered from the wind

2**lee** *adj* **1 :** of or relating to the lee — compare WEATHER **2 :** facing in the direction of motion of an overriding glacier — used esp. of a hillside

lee·board \ˈlē-ˌbō(ə)rd, -ˌbȯ(ə)rd\ *n* **:** either of the wood or metal planes attached outside the hull of a sailboat to prevent leeway

leek

1**leech** \ˈlēch\ *n* [ME *leche,* fr. OE *lǣce;* akin to OHG *lāhhi* physician] **1** *archaic* **:** PHYSICIAN, SURGEON **2** [fr. its former use by physicians for bleeding patients] **:** any of numerous carnivorous or bloodsucking usu. freshwater annelid worms (class Hirudinea) that have typically a flattened lanceolate segmented body with a sucker at each end — see ANNELID illustration **3 :** a hanger-on who seeks advantage or gain

2**leech** *vt* **1 :** to bleed by the use of leeches **2 :** to drain the substance of **:** EXHAUST ~ *vi* **:** to attach oneself to a person as a leech

3**leech** *n* [ME *leche,* fr. MLG *līk* boltrope; akin to MHG *geleich* joint — more at LIGATURE] **1 :** either vertical edge of a square sail **2 :** the after edge of a fore-and-aft sail

leek \ˈlēk\ *n* [ME, fr. OE *lēac;* akin to OHG *louh* leek] **:** a biennial garden herb (*Allium porrum*) of the lily family grown for its mildly pungent succulent linear leaves and esp. for its thick cylindrical stalk

1**leer** \ˈli(ə)r\ *vi* [prob. fr. obs. *leer* (cheek)] **:** to cast a sidelong glance; *esp* **:** to give a leer

2leer *n* : a lascivious, knowing, or wanton look

leery \'li(ə)r-ē\ *adj* : SUSPICIOUS, WARY

lees \'lēz\ *n pl* [ME *lie,* fr. MF, fr. ML *lia*] : the settlings of liquor during fermentation and aging : DREGS

Lee's Birthday \'lēz-\ *n* [Robert E. *Lee*] : January 19 observed as a legal holiday in many southern states

lee shore *n* : a shore lying off a ship's leeward side and constituting a severe danger in storm

1lee·ward \'lē-wərd, *esp naut* 'lü-ərd\ *adj* : being in or facing the direction toward which the wind is blowing; *also* : being the side opposite the windward

2leeward *n* : the lee side

lee·way \'lē-ˌwā\ *n* **1 a** : off-course lateral movement of a ship when under way **b** : the angle between the heading and the track of an airplane **2** : an allowable margin of freedom or variation : TOLERANCE

1left \'left\ *adj* [ME, fr. OE, weak; akin to MLG *lucht* left; fr. the left hand's being the weaker in most individuals] **1 a** : relating to or being a bodily part and esp. the hand on the side of the body in which the heart is mostly located **b** : located nearer to the left hand than to the right: as (1) : located on the left when facing in the same direction as an observer (2) : located on the left when facing downstream **2** *often cap* : of, adhering to, or constituted by the left esp. in politics — **left** *adv*

2left *n* **1 a** : the left hand **b** : the location or direction of the left side **c** : the part on the left side **2** *often cap* **a** : the part of a legislative chamber located to the left of the presiding officer **b** : the members of a continental European legislative body occupying the left as a result of holding more radical political views than other members **3** *cap* **a** : those professing views usu. characterized by desire to reform or overthrow the established order esp. in politics and usu. advocating change in the name of the greater freedom or well-being of the common man **b** : a radical as distinguished from a conservative position

3left *past of* LEAVE

Left Bank *n* : the bohemian district of Paris situated on the left bank of the Seine river

left field *n* **1** : the part of the baseball outfield to the left looking out from the plate **2** : the position of the player defending left field — **left fielder** *n*

left–hand \ˌleft-ˌhand, ˌlef-ˌtand\ *adj* **1** : situated on the left **2** : LEFT-HANDED

left–hand·ed \'left-'han-dəd, 'lef-'tan-\ *adj* **1** : using the left hand habitually or more easily than the right; *also* : swinging from left to right <a ~ batter> **2** : relating to, designed for, or done with the left hand **3** : MORGANATIC **4** : CLUMSY, AWKWARD; *also* : INSINCERE, MALICIOUS **5 a** : having a direction contrary to that of the hands of a watch viewed from in front : COUNTERCLOCKWISE **b** : having a structure involving a counterclockwise direction **c** *of a rope* : formed of strands twisted counterclockwise so that if held vertically the strands spiral upward to the left — **left–handed** *adv* — **left–hand·ed·ly** *adv* — **left–hand·ed·ness** *n*

left–hand·er \-'han-dər, -'tan-\ *n* : a left-handed person : SOUTHPAW

left heart *n* : the half of the heart containing oxygenated blood and consisting of the left auricle and ventricle

left·ism \'lef-ˌtiz-əm\ *n* **1** : the principles and views of the Left; *also* : the movement embodying these principles **2** : advocacy of or adherence to the doctrines of the Left — **left·ist** \-təst\ *n or adj*

1left·over \ˌlef-ˌtō-vər\ *adj* : remaining as unused residue

2left·over \'lef-ˌtō-vər\ *n* : an unused or unconsumed residue; *esp* : leftover food served at a later meal

left shoulder arms *n* [fr. the command *left shoulder arms!*] : a position in the manual of arms in which the butt of the rifle is held in the left hand with the barrel resting on the left shoulder; *also* : a command to assume this position

left·ward \'lef-twərd\ *adj* : being toward or on the left

left wing *n* **1** : the leftist division of a group **2** : LEFT 3a — **left–wing** *adj* — **left–wing·er** \'lef-'twiŋ-ər\ *n*

lefty \'lef-tē\ *n, pl* **left·ies** **1** : LEFT-HANDER **2** : an advocate of leftism

1leg \'leg, 'lāg\ *n* [ME, fr. ON *leggr;* akin to OE *līra* muscle, calf, L *lacertus* muscle, upper arm] **1** : a limb of an animal used esp. for supporting the body and for walking: as **a** : the part of the vertebrate limb between the knee and foot **b** : the back half of a hindquarter of a meat animal **c** : one of the rather generalized segmental appendages of an arthropod used in walking and crawling **2 a** : a pole or bar serving as a support or prop <the ~s of a tripod> **b** : a branch of a forked or jointed object <the ~s of a compass> **3 a** : the part of an article of clothing that covers the leg **b** : the part of the upper (as of a boot) that extends above the ankle **4** : OBEISANCE, BOW — used chiefly in the phrase *to make a leg* **5** : either side of a triangle as distinguished from the base or hypotenuse **6 a** : the course and distance sailed by a boat on a single tack **b** : a portion of a trip : STAGE **c** : one section of a relay race **d** : one of several events or games necessary to be won to decide a competition <won the first two ~s of horse racing's Triple Crown> **7** : a branch or part of an object or system — **leg·less** \-ləs\ *adj* — **a leg to stand on** : SUPPORT; *esp* : a basis for one's position in a controversy — **on one's last legs** : at or near the end of one's resources : on the verge of failure, exhaustion, or ruin

2leg *vi* **legged; leg·ging** : to use the legs in walking; *esp* : RUN

3leg *abbr* **1** legal **2** legato **3** legislative; legislature

leg·a·cy \'leg-ə-sē\ *n, pl* **-cies** [ME *legacie* office of a legate, bequest, fr. MF or ML; MF, office of a legate, fr. ML *legatia,* fr. L *legatus*] **1** : a gift by will esp. of money or other personal property : BEQUEST **2** : something received from an ancestor or predecessor or from the past <the ~ of the ancient philosophers>

1le·gal \'lē-gəl\ *adj* [ME, fr. MF, fr. L *legalis,* fr. *leg-, lex* law] **1** : of or relating to law **2 a** : deriving authority from or founded on law : de jure **b** : having a formal status derived from law often without a basis in actual fact : TITULAR <a corporation is a ~ but not a real person> **c** : established by law; *esp* : STATUTORY **3** : conforming to or permitted by law or established rules **4** : recognized or made effective by a court of law as distinguished from a court of equity **5** : of, relating to, or having the characteristics of the profession of law or of one of its members **6** : created by the constructions of the law <a ~ fiction> ***syn*** see LAWFUL ***ant*** illegal — **le·gal·ly** \-gə-lē\ *adv*

2legal *n* : one that conforms to rules or the law

legal age *n* : the age at which a person enters into full adult legal rights and responsibilities (as of making contracts or wills)

legal aid *n* : aid provided by an organization established esp. to serve the legal needs of the poor

legal cap *n* [*-cap* (as in *foolscap*)] : a white often ruled writing paper for legal use that is usu. 8½ inches wide and 13 or 14 inches long

le·gal·ese \ˌlē-gə-'lēz, -'lēs\ *n* : the specialized language of the legal profession <befogged far beyond . . . ~; it is one of the least comprehensible documents —Bernard De Voto>

legal holiday *n* : a holiday established by legal authority and characterized by legal restrictions on work and transaction of official business

le·gal·ism \'lē-gə-ˌliz-əm\ *n* **1** : strict, literal, or excessive conformity to the law or to a religious or moral code <that mixture of arid ~ and semantic pretentiousness that so often passes . . . for statesmanship —G. F. Kennan> **2** : a legal term or rule

le·gal·ist \-ləst\ *n* **1** : an advocate or adherent of moral legalism **2** : one that views things from a legal standpoint; *esp* : one that places primary emphasis on legal principles or on the formal structure of governmental institutions — **le·gal·is·tic** \ˌlē-gə-'lis-tik\ *adj* — **le·gal·is·ti·cal·ly** \-ti-k(ə-)lē\ *adv*

le·gal·i·ty \li-'gal-ət-ē\ *n, pl* **-ties** **1** : attachment to or observance of law **2** : the quality or state of being legal : LAWFULNESS **3** *pl* : obligations imposed by law

le·gal·ize \'lē-gə-ˌlīz\ *vt* **-ized; -iz·ing** : to make legal; *esp* : to give legal validity or sanction to — **le·gal·iza·tion** \ˌlē-gə-lə-'zā-shən\ *n*

legal reserve *n* : the minimum amount of bank deposits or life insurance company assets required by law to be kept as reserves

legal tender *n* : money that may be offered legally in satisfaction of a money debt and that must be accepted by a creditor to that end when so offered

1leg·ate \'leg-ət\ *n* [ME, fr. OF & L; OF *legat,* fr. L *legatus* deputy, emissary, fr. pp. of *legare* to depute, send as emissary, bequeath, fr. *leg-, lex*] : a usu. official emissary — **leg·ate·ship** \-ˌship\ *n*

2le·gate \li-'gāt\ *vt* **le·gat·ed; le·gat·ing** [*legatus,* pp. of *legare* to bequeath] : BEQUEATH 1 — **le·ga·tor** \-'gāt-ər\ *n*

leg·a·tee \ˌleg-ə-'tē\ *n* : one to whom a legacy is bequeathed or a devise is given

leg·a·tine \'leg-ə-ˌtēn, -ˌtīn\ *adj* : of, headed by, or enacted under the authority of a legate

le·ga·tion \li-'gā-shən\ *n* **1** : the sending forth of a legate **2** : a body of deputies sent on a mission; *specif* : a diplomatic mission in a foreign country headed by a minister **3** : the official residence and office of a diplomatic minister in a foreign country

1le·ga·to \li-'gät-(ˌ)ō\ *adv or adj* [It, lit., tied] : in a manner that is smooth and connected (as between successive tones) — used esp. as a direction in music

2legato *n* : a smooth and connected manner of performance (as of music); *also* : a passage of music so performed

leg·end \'lej-ənd\ *n* [ME *legende,* fr. MF & ML; MF *legende,* fr. ML *legenda,* fr. L, fem. of *legendus,* gerundive of *legere* to gather, select, read; akin to Gk *legein* to gather, say, *logos* speech, word, reason] **1 a** : a story coming down from the past; *esp* : one popularly regarded as historical although not verifiable **b** : a body of such stories <a place in the ~ of the frontier> **c** : a popular myth of recent origin **d** : a person or thing that inspires legends **2 a** : an inscription or title on an object (as a coin) **b** : CAPTION 2b **c** : an explanatory list of the symbols on a map or chart ***syn*** see MYTH

leg·end·ary \'lej-ən-ˌder-ē\ *adj* : of, relating to, or characteristic of legend or a legend ***syn*** see FICTITIOUS — **leg·en·dari·ly** \ˌlej-ən-'der-ə-lē\ *adv*

leg·end·ry \'lej-ən-drē\ *n* : a body of legends <a life which is built on ~ and myth —Irene C. Edmonds>

leg·er·de·main \ˌlej-ərd-ə-'mān\ *n* [ME, fr. MF *leger de main* light of hand] **1** : SLEIGHT OF HAND **2** : a display of skill or adroitness

le·ger·i·ty \lə-'jer-ət-ē, le-\ *n* [MF *legereté,* fr. OF, lightness, fr. *leger* light, fr. (assumed) VL *leviarius,* fr. L *levis* — more at LIGHT] : alert facile quickness of mind or body ***syn*** see CELERITY ***ant*** deliberateness, sluggishness

leges *pl of* LEX

legged \'leg-əd, 'lāg-, *Brit usu* 'legd\ *adj* : having a leg or legs esp. of a specified kind or number — often used in combination <a four-*legged* animal>

leg·ging *or* **leg·gin** \'leg-ən, 'lāg-, -iŋ\ *n* : a covering (as of leather or cloth) for the leg — usu. used in pl.

leg·gy \'leg-ē, 'lāg-\ *adj* **leg·gi·er; -est** **1** : having disproportionately long legs **2** : having attractive legs **3** : SPINDLY — used of a plant

leg·horn \'leg-ˌ(h)ò(ə)rn, 'leg-ərn\ *n* [*Leghorn,* Italy] **1 a** : a fine plaited straw made from an Italian wheat **b** : a hat of this straw **2** : any of a Mediterranean breed of small hardy fowls noted for their large production of white eggs

leg·i·ble \'lej-ə-bəl\ *adj* [ME, fr. LL *legibilis,* fr. L *legere* to read] : capable of being read or deciphered : PLAIN — **leg·i·bil·i·ty** \ˌlej-ə-'bil-ət-ē\ *n* — **leg·i·bly** \'lej-ə-blē\ *adv*

1le·gion \'lē-jən\ *n* [ME, fr. OF, fr. L *legion-, legio,* fr. *legere* to gather — more at LEGEND] **1** : the principal unit of the Roman army comprising 3000 to 6000 foot soldiers with cavalry **2** : a large military force; *esp* : ARMY 1a **3** : a very large number : MULTITUDE **4** : a national association of ex-servicemen

2legion *adj* : MANY, NUMEROUS <the problems are ~>

1le·gion·ary \'lē-jə-ˌner-ē\ *adj* [L *legionarius,* fr. *legion-, legio*] : of, relating to, or constituting a legion

2legionary *n, pl* **-ar·ies** : LEGIONNAIRE

le·gion·naire \ˌlē-jə-ˈna(ə)r, -ˈne(ə)r\ *n* [F *légionnaire,* fr. L *legionarius*] **:** a member of a legion

Legion of Honor : a French order conferred as a reward for civil or military merit

Legion of Merit : a U.S. military decoration awarded for exceptionally meritorious conduct in the performance of outstanding services

legis *abbr* legislation; legislative; legislature

leg·is·late \ˈlej-ə-ˌslāt\ *vb* **-lat·ed; -lat·ing** [back-formation fr. *legislator*] *vi* **:** to perform the function of legislation; *specif* **:** to make or enact laws ~ *vt* **:** to cause, create, provide, or bring about by legislation

leg·is·la·tion \ˌlej-ə-ˈslā-shən\ *n* **1 :** the action of legislating; *specif* **:** the exercise of the power and function of making rules (as laws) that have the force of authority by virtue of their promulgation by an official organ of a state or other organization **2 :** the enactments of a legislator or a legislative body **3 :** a matter of business for or under consideration by a legislative body

[1]**leg·is·la·tive** \ˈlej-ə-ˌslāt-iv\ *adj* **1 a :** having the power or performing the function of legislating **b :** belonging to the branch of government that is charged with such powers as making laws, levying and collecting taxes, and making financial appropriations — compare EXECUTIVE, JUDICIAL **2 a :** of or relating to a legislature <~ committees> <~ immunity> **b :** composed of members of a legislature <~ caucus> **c :** created by a legislature esp. as distinguished from an executive or judicial body **d :** designed to assist a legislature or its members <a ~ research agency> **3 :** of, concerned with, or created by legislation — **leg·is·la·tive·ly** *adv*

[2]**legislative** *n* **:** the body or department exercising the power and function of legislating **:** LEGISLATURE

legislative assembly *n, often cap L&A* **1 :** a bicameral legislature (as in an American state) **2 :** the lower house of a bicameral legislature **3 :** a unicameral legislature; *esp* **:** one in a Canadian province

legislative council *n, often cap L&C* **1 :** the upper house of a British bicameral legislature **2 :** a unicameral legislature (as in a British colony) **3 :** a permanent committee chosen from both houses that meets between sessions of a state legislature to study state problems and plan a legislative program

leg·is·la·tor \ˈlej-ə-ˌslāt-ər\ *n* [L *legis lator,* lit., proposer of a law, fr. *legis,* gen. of *lex* law + *lator* proposer, fr. *latus* suppletive pp. of *ferre* to carry, propose — more at TOLERATE, BEAR] **:** one that makes laws esp. for a political unit; *esp* **:** a member of a legislative body — **leg·is·la·to·ri·al** \ˌlej-ə-slə-ˈtōr-ē-əl, -ˈtȯr-\ *adj* — **leg·is·la·tor·ship** \ˈlej-ə-ˌslāt-ər-ˌship\ *n* — **leg·is·la·tress** \ˌlej-ə-ˈslā-trəs\ *n* — **leg·is·la·trix** \-triks\ *n*

leg·is·la·ture \ˈlej-ə-ˌslā-chər\ *n* **:** a body of persons having the power to legislate; *specif* **:** an organized body having the authority to make laws for a political unit

le·gist \ˈlē-jəst\ *n* [MF *legiste,* fr. ML *legista,* fr. L *leg-, lex*] **:** a specialist in law; *esp* **:** one learned in Roman or civil law

le·git \li-ˈjit\ *adj, slang* **:** LEGITIMATE <a racket boy with a lot of ~ business —Harold Robbins>

le·git·i·ma·cy \li-ˈjit-ə-mə-sē\ *n* **:** the quality or state of being legitimate

[1]**le·git·i·mate** \li-ˈjit-ə-mət\ *adj* [ML *legitimatus,* pp. of *legitimare* to legitimate, fr. L *legitimus* legitimate, fr. *leg-, lex* law] **1 a :** lawfully begotten; *specif* **:** born in wedlock **b :** having full filial rights and obligations by birth <a ~ child> **2 :** being exactly as purposed **:** neither spurious nor false <~ grievance> **3 a :** accordant with law or with established legal forms and requirements <a ~ government> **b :** ruling by or based on the strict principle of hereditary right <a ~ king> **4 :** conforming to recognized principles or accepted rules and standards <~ advertising expenditure> <~ inference> **5 :** relating to plays acted by professional actors but not including revues, burlesque, or some forms of musical comedy <the ~ theater> ***syn*** see LAWFUL ***ant*** illegitimate — **le·git·i·mate·ly** *adv*

[2]**le·git·i·mate** \-ˌmāt\ *vt* **-mat·ed; -mat·ing :** to make legitimate: **a** (1) **:** to give legal status or authorization to (2) **:** to show or affirm to be justified **b :** to put (a bastard) in the state of a legitimate child before the law by legal means — **le·git·i·ma·tion** \-ˌjit-ə-ˈmā-shən\ *n*

le·git·i·ma·tize \li-ˈjit-ə-mə-ˌtīz\ *vt* **-tized; -tiz·ing :** LEGITIMATE

le·git·i·mism \li-ˈjit-ə-ˌmiz-əm\ *n, often cap* **:** adherence to the principles of political legitimacy or to a person claiming legitimacy — **le·git·i·mist** \-məst\ *n, often cap* — **legitimist** *adj*

le·git·i·mize \-ˌmīz\ *vt* **-mized; -miz·ing :** LEGITIMATE — **le·git·i·mi·za·tion** \-ˌjit-ə-mə-ˈzā-shən\ *n* — **le·git·i·miz·er** \-ˈjit-ə-ˌmī-zər\ *n*

leg·man \ˈleg-ˌman, ˈlāg-\ *n* **1 :** a newspaperman assigned usu. to gather information **2 :** an assistant who performs various subordinate tasks (as gathering information or running errands)

leg–of–mut·ton *or* **leg–o'–mut·ton** \ˌleg-ə(v)-ˈmət-ᵊn, ˌlāg-\ *adj* **:** having the approximately triangular shape or outline of a leg of mutton <~ sleeve> <~ sail>

leg out *vt* **:** to make (as a base hit) by fast running

leg–pull \ˈleg-ˌpu̇l, ˈlāg-\ *n* [fr. the phrase *pull one's leg*] **:** a humorous deception or hoax

leg·room \-ˌrüm, -ˌru̇m\ *n* **:** space in which to extend the legs while seated

le·gume \ˈleg-ˌyüm, li-ˈgyüm\ *n* [F *légume,* fr. L *legumin-, legumen* leguminous plant, fr. *legere* to gather — more at LEGEND] **1 a :** the fruit or seed of leguminous plants (as peas or beans) used for food **b :** a vegetable used for food **2 :** any of a large family (Leguminosae) of dicotyledonous herbs, shrubs, and trees having fruits that are legumes or loments, bearing nodules on the roots that contain nitrogen-fixing bacteria, and including important food and forage plants (as peas, beans, or clovers) **3 :** a dry dehiscent one-celled fruit developed from a simple superior ovary and usu. dehiscing into two valves with the seeds attached to the ventral suture **:** POD

le·gu·mi·nous \li-ˈgyü-mə-nəs, le-\ *adj* **1 :** of, relating to, or consisting of plants that are legumes **2 :** resembling a legume

leg up *n* **1 :** a helping hand **:** BOOST **2 :** HEAD START

leg·work \ˈleg-ˌwərk, ˈlāg-\ *n* **:** work (as gathering information) that involves a preponderance of physical activity and that forms the basis of more creative or mentally exacting work (as writing a book)

le·hua \lā-ˈhü-ə\ *n* [Hawaiian] **:** a common very showy tree (*Metrosideros villosa*) of the myrtle family of the Pacific islands having bright red corymbose flowers and a hard wood; *also* **:** its flower

[1]**lei** \ˈlā, ˈlā-ˌē\ *n* [Hawaiian] **:** a wreath or necklace usu. of flowers or leaves

[2]**lei** \ˈlā\ *pl of* LEU

Leib·niz·ian \līp-ˈnit-sē-ən\ *adj* **:** of, relating to, or characteristic of Leibniz or his philosophy — **Leib·niz·ian·ism** \-ē-ə-ˌniz-əm\ *n*

Leices·ter \ˈles-tər\ *n* [*Leicester,* county in England] **:** any of a breed of white-faced long-wool mutton-type sheep originating in England and having white fleece finer than that of most long-wool sheep

Leics *or* **Leic** *abbr* Leicestershire

Lei Day *n* **:** May Day in Hawaii celebrated with pageants and prizes for the most beautiful or distinctive leis

leish·man·ia \lēsh-ˈman-ē-ə\ *n* [NL, genus name, fr. Sir W. B. *Leishman* †1926 Brit medical officer] **:** any of a genus (*Leishmania*) of flagellate protozoans that are parasitic in the tissues of vertebrates; *broadly* **:** an organism resembling the leishmanias that is included in the family (Trypanosomatidae) to which they belong

leish·man·i·a·sis \ˌlēsh-mə-ˈnī-ə-səs\ *n* [NL] **:** infection with or disease caused by leishmanias

[1]**leis·ter** \ˈlē-stər\ *n* [of Scand origin; akin to ON *ljōstr* leister] **:** a spear armed with three or more barbed prongs for catching fish

[2]**leister** *vt* **:** to spear with a leister

lei·sure \ˈlēzh-ər, ˈlezh-, ˈlāzh-\ *n* [ME *leiser,* fr. OF *leisir,* fr. *leisir* to be permitted, fr. L *licēre* — more at LICENSE] **1 :** freedom provided by the cessation of activities; *esp* **:** time free from work or duties **2 :** EASE, LEISURELINESS — **leisure** *adj* — **at leisure** *or* **at one's leisure :** in one's leisure time **:** at one's convenience <finished the book *at his leisure*>

lei·sured \-ərd\ *adj* **:** having leisure **:** characterized by leisureliness

[1]**lei·sure·ly** \-ər-lē\ *adv* **:** without haste **:** DELIBERATELY

[2]**leisurely** *adj* **:** characterized by leisure **:** UNHURRIED — **lei·sure·li·ness** *n*

Leit *abbr* Leitrim

leit·mo·tiv *or* **leit·mo·tif** \ˈlīt-mō-ˌtēf\ *n* [G *leitmotiv,* fr. *leiten* to lead + *motiv* motive] **1 :** an associated melodic phrase or figure that accompanies the reappearance of an idea, person, or situation esp. in a Wagnerian music drama **2 :** a dominant recurring theme

[1]**lek** \ˈlek\ *n* [Alb] — see MONEY table

[2]**lek** *n* [prob. fr. Sw, sport, play] **:** an assembly area where birds and esp. black grouse carry on display and courtship behavior

LEM *abbr* lunar excursion module

le·man \ˈlem-ən, ˈlē-mən\ *n* [ME *lefman, leman,* fr. *lef* lief] *archaic* **:** SWEETHEART, LOVER; *esp* **:** MISTRESS

[1]**lem·ma** \ˈlem-ə\ *n, pl* **lemmas** *or* **lem·ma·ta** \-ət-ə\ [L, fr. Gk *lēmma* thing taken, assumption, fr. *lambanein* to take — more at LATCH] **1 :** an auxiliary proposition accepted as true for use in the demonstration of another proposition **2 :** the argument or theme of a composition prefixed as a title or introduction; *also* **:** the heading or theme of a comment or note on a text **3 :** a glossed word or phrase

[2]**lemma** *n* [Gk, husk, fr. *lepein* to peel — more at LEPER] **:** the lower of the two bracts enclosing the flower in the spikelet of grasses

lem·ming \ˈlem-iŋ\ *n* [Norw; akin to ON *lōmr* guillemot, L *latrare* to bark — more at LAMENT] **:** any of several small short-tailed furry-footed rodents (genera *Lemmus* and *Dicrostonyx*) of circumpolar distribution that are notable for the recurrent mass migrations of a European form (*L. lemmus*) which often continue into the sea where vast numbers are drowned

lemming

lem·nis·cate \lem-ˈnis-kət\ *n* [NL *lemniscata,* fr. fem. of L *lemniscatus* with hanging ribbons, fr. *lemniscus*] **:** a figure-eight shaped curve whose equation in polar coordinates is $\rho^2 = a^2 \cos 2\theta$

lem·nis·cus \lem-ˈnis-kəs\ *n, pl* **-nis·ci** \-ˈnis-ˌ(k)ī, -ˈnis-ˌkē\ [NL, fr. L, ribbon, fr. Gk *lēmniskos*] **:** a band of fibers and esp. nerve fibers

[1]**lem·on** \ˈlem-ən\ *n* [ME *lymon,* fr. MF *limon,* fr. ML *limon-, limo,* fr. Ar *laymūn*] **1 a :** an acid fruit that is botanically a many-seeded pale yellow oblong berry and is produced by a stout thorny tree (*Citrus limon*) **b :** a tree that bears lemons **2 :** one (as an automobile) that is unsatisfactory **:** DUD

[2]**lemon** *adj* **1 a :** containing lemon **b :** having the flavor or scent of lemon **2 :** of the color lemon yellow

lem·on·ade \ˌlem-ə-ˈnād\ *n* **:** a beverage of sweetened lemon juice mixed with water

lemon balm *n* **:** a bushy perennial Old World mint (*Melissa officinalis*) often cultivated for its fragrant lemon-flavored leaves

lem·on·grass \ˈlem-ən-ˌgras\ *n* **:** a grass (*Cymbopogon citratus*) of robust habit that grows in tropical regions (as the West Indies) and is the source of an essential oil with an odor of lemon or verbena; *also* **:** a similar tropical grass (*C. flexuosus*)

ə abut	ᵊ kitten	ər further	a back	ā bake	ä cot, cart	
au̇ out	ch chin	e less	ē easy	g gift	i trip	ī life
j joke	ŋ sing	ō flow	ȯ flaw	ȯi coin	th thin	t͟h this
ü loot	u̇ foot	y yet	yü few	yu̇ furious	zh vision	

lem·ony \ˈlem-ə-nē\ *adj* : suggestive of lemon : LEMON <a ~ taste>
lemon yellow *n* : a variable color averaging a brilliant greenish yellow
lem·pi·ra \lem-ˈpir-ə\ *n* [AmerSp, fr. *Lempira,* 16th cent. Indian chief] — see MONEY table
le·mur \ˈlē-mər\ *n* [L *lemures,* pl., ghosts; akin to Gk *lamia* devouring monster] : any of numerous arboreal chiefly nocturnal mammals that were formerly widespread but are now largely confined to Madagascar, are related to the monkeys but are usu. regarded as constituting a distinct superfamily (Lemuroidea), and usu. have a muzzle like a fox, large eyes, very soft woolly fur, and a long furry tail

lemur

le·mu·res \ˈlem-ə-ˌrās, ˈlem-yə-ˌrēz\ *n pl* [L] : spirits of the unburied dead exorcised from homes in early Roman religious observances
lend \ˈlend\ *vb* **lent** \ˈlent\; **lend·ing** [ME *lenen, lenden,* fr. OE *lǣnan,* fr. *lǣn* loan — more at LOAN] *vt* **1 a :** to give for temporary use on condition that the same or its equivalent be returned **b :** to let out (money) for temporary use on condition of repayment with interest **2 a :** to give the assistance or support of : AFFORD, FURNISH <a dispassionate and scholarly manner which ~*s* great force to his criticisms —*Times Lit. Supp.*> **b :** to adapt or apply (oneself) : ACCOMMODATE <a topic that ~*s* itself admirably to class discussion> ~ *vi* : to make a loan — **lend·er** *n*
lending library *n* : RENTAL LIBRARY
lend–lease \ˈlen-ˈdlēs\ *n* [U.S. *Lend-Lease* Act (1941)] : the transfer of goods and services to an ally to aid in a common cause with payment being made by a return of the original items or their use in the common cause or by a similar transfer of other goods and services — **lend–lease** *vt*
length \ˈleŋ(k)th\ *n* [ME *lengthe,* fr. OE *lengthu,* fr. *lang* long] **1 a :** the longer or longest dimension of an object **b :** a measured distance or dimension <10-inch ~> — see METRIC SYSTEM table, WEIGHT table **c :** the quality or state of being long <was unconcerned about the ~ or shortness of her visit> **2 a :** duration or extent in time **b :** relative duration or stress of a sound **3 a :** distance or extent in space **b :** the length of something taken as a unit of measure <his horse led by a ~> **4 :** the degree to which something (as a course of action or a line of thought) is carried — often used in pl. <went to great ~*s* to learn the truth> **5 a :** a long expanse or stretch **b :** a piece constituting or usable as part of a whole or of a connected series : SECTION <a ~ of pipe> **6 :** a vertical dimension of an article of clothing — **at length 1 :** FULLY, COMPREHENSIVELY **2 :** at last : FINALLY
length·en \ˈleŋ(k)-thən\ *vb* **length·ened; length·en·ing** \ˈleŋ(k)th-(ə-)niŋ\ *vt* : to make longer ~ *vi* : to grow longer ***syn*** see EXTEND ***ant*** shorten — **length·en·er** \ˈleŋ(k)th-(ə-)nər\ *n*
length·ways \ˈleŋ(k)th-ˌwāz\ *adv* : LENGTHWISE
length·wise \-ˌwīz\ *adv* : in the direction of the length : LONGITUDINALLY — **lengthwise** *adj*
lengthy \ˈleŋ(k)-thē\ *adj* **length·i·er; -est 1 :** protracted excessively : OVERLONG **2 :** EXTENDED, LONG — **length·i·ly** \-thə-lē\ *adv* — **length·i·ness** \-thē-nəs\ *n*
le·nience \ˈlē-nyən(t)s, -nē-ən(t)s\ *n* : LENIENCY
le·nien·cy \ˈlē-nē-ən-sē, -nyən-sē\ *n, pl* **-cies 1 :** the quality or state of being lenient **2 :** a lenient disposition or practice
le·nient \ˈlē-nē-ənt, -nyənt\ *adj* [L *lenient-, leniens,* prp. of *lenire* to soften, soothe, fr. *lenis* soft, mild — more at LET] **1 :** exerting a soothing or easing influence : relieving pain or stress **2 :** of mild and tolerant disposition; *esp* : INDULGENT ***syn*** see SOFT ***ant*** caustic — **le·nient·ly** *adv*
Leni–Le·nape *or* **Len·ni–Le·nape** \ˌlen-ē-lə-ˈnäp-ē, ˌlen-ē-ˈlen-ə-pē, ˌlen-ē-lə-ˈnäp\ *n* [Delaware] : DELAWARE 1
Le·nin·ism \ˈlen-ə-ˌniz-əm\ *n* : the political, economic, and social principles and policies advocated by Lenin; *esp* : the theory and practice of communism developed by or associated with Lenin — **Le·nin·ist** \-nəst\ *n or adj* — **Le·nin·ite** \-ˌnīt\ *n or adj*
le·nis \ˈlē-nəs, ˈlā-\ *adj* [NL, fr. L, mild, smooth] : produced with relatively lax articulation and weak expiration <\d\ in *doe* is ~, \t\ in *toe* is fortis>
len·i·tive \ˈlen-ət-iv\ *adj* [MF *lenitif,* fr. ML *lenitivus,* fr. L *lenitus,* pp. of *lenire*] : alleviating pain or harshness : SOOTHING — **lenitive** *n* — **len·i·tive·ly** *adv*
len·i·ty \ˈlen-ət-ē\ *n* : usu. unmerited or excessive clemency <errors which . . . regarded with a less affectionate ~, would have stood against his official account —S. H. Adams> ***syn*** see MERCY ***ant*** severity
lens *also* **lense** \ˈlenz\ *n* [NL *lent-, lens,* fr. L, lentil; fr. its shape — more at LENTIL] **1 a :** a piece of transparent material (as glass) that has two opposite regular surfaces either both curved or one curved and the other plane and that is used either singly or combined in an optical instrument for forming an image by focusing rays of light **b :** a combination of two or more simple lenses **2 :** a device for directing or focusing radiation other than light (as sound waves, radio microwaves, or electrons) **3 :** something shaped like a double-convex optical lens **4 :** a highly transparent biconvex lens-shaped or nearly spherical body in the eye that focuses light rays (as upon the retina) — see EYE illustration — **lensed** \ˈlenzd\ *adj* — **lens·less** \ˈlenz-ləs\ *adj*

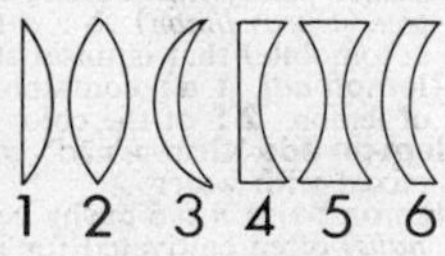

lens 1a: *1* plano-convex, *2* biconvex, *3* converging meniscus, *4* plano-concave, *5* biconcave, *6* diverging meniscus

Lent \ˈlent\ *n* [ME *lente* springtime, Lent, fr. OE *lengten;* akin to OHG *lenzin* spring] : the 40 weekdays from Ash Wednesday to Easter observed by the Roman Catholic, Eastern, and some Protestant churches as a period of penitence and fasting
len·ta·men·te \ˌlent-ə-ˈmen-(ˌ)tā\ *adv or adj* [It, fr. *lento* slow] : SLOWLY —used as a direction in music
len·tan·do \len-ˈtän-(ˌ)dō\ *adv or adj* [It] : in a retarding manner — used as a direction in music
Lent·en \ˈlent-ᵊn\ *adj* **1 :** of or relating to Lent **2 :** suitable to Lent; *esp* : MEAGER <~ fare>
len·tic \ˈlent-ik\ *adj* [L *lentus* sluggish] : of, relating to, or living in still waters (as lakes, ponds, or swamps) — compare LOTIC
len·ti·cel \ˈlent-ə-ˌsel\ *n* [NL *lenticella,* dim. of L *lent-, lens* lentil] : a pore in the stems of woody plants through which gases are exchanged between the atmosphere and the stem tissues
len·tic·u·lar \len-ˈtik-yə-lər\ *adj* [L *lenticularis* lentil-shaped, fr. *lenticula* lentil] **1 :** having the shape of a double-convex lens **2 :** of or relating to a lens **3 :** provided with or utilizing lenticules <a ~ screen>
len·tic·u·late \-lət\ *vt* **-lat·ed; -lat·ing :** to provide with lenticules (as by embossing, molding, or coating) <*lenticulated* film> — **len·tic·u·la·tion** \-ˌtik-yə-ˈlā-shən\ *n*
len·ti·cule \ˈlent-ə-ˌkyü(ə)l\ *n* [L *lenticula* lentil] **1 :** any of the minute lenses on the base side of a film used in stereoscopic or color photography **2 :** any of the tiny corrugations or grooves molded or embossed into the surface of a projection screen
len·til \ˈlent-ᵊl\ *n* [ME, fr. OF *lentille,* fr. L *lenticula,* dim. of *lent-, lens;* akin to Gk *lathyros* vetch] **1 :** a widely cultivated Eurasian annual leguminous plant (*Lens culinaris*) with flattened edible seeds and leafy stalks used as fodder **2 :** the seed of the lentil
len·tis·si·mo \len-ˈtis-ə-ˌmō\ *adv or adj* [It, superl. of *lento*] : in a very slow manner — used as a direction in music
len·to \ˈlen-(ˌ)tō\ *adv or adj* [It, fr. *lento,* adj., slow, fr. L *lentus* pliant, sluggish, slow — more at LITHE] : in a slow manner — used as a direction in music
Leo \ˈlē-(ˌ)ō\ *n* [L (gen. *Leonis*), lit., lion — more at LION] **1 :** a northern constellation east of Cancer **2 a :** the 5th sign of the zodiac in astrology — see ZODIAC table **b :** one born under this sign
Le·o·nar·desque \ˌlē-ə-ˌnär-ˈdesk, ˌlā-\ *adj* [*Leonardo* da Vinci] : of, relating to, or suggesting Leonardo or his style of painting
le·one \lē-ˈōn\ *n* [*Sierra Leone*] — see MONEY table
Leo·nid \ˈlē-ə-nəd\ *n, pl* **Leo·nids** *or* **Le·on·i·des** \lē-ˈän-ə-ˌdēz\ [L *Leon-, Leo;* fr. their appearing to radiate from a point in Leo] : one of the shooting stars constituting the meteoric shower that recurs near the 14th of November
le·o·nine \ˈlē-ə-ˌnīn\ *adj* [ME, fr. L *leoninus,* fr. *leon-, leo*] : of, relating to, or resembling a lion
leop·ard \ˈlep-ərd\ *n* [ME, fr. OF *leupart,* fr. LL *leopardus,* fr. Gk *leopardos,* fr. *leōn* lion + *pardos* leopard] **1 :** a large strong cat (*Felis pardus*) of southern Asia and Africa that is usu. tawny or buff with black spots arranged in broken rings or rosettes — called also *panther* **2 :** a heraldic representation of a lion passant guardant — **leop·ard·ess** \-ərd-əs\ *n*

leopard 1

leopard frog *n* : a common American frog (*Rana pipiens*) that is bright green with large black white-margined blotches on the back; *also* : a similar frog (*R. sphenocephala*) of the southeastern U.S.
le·o·tard \ˈlē-ə-ˌtärd\ *n* [Jules *Léotard,* 19th cent. F aerial gymnast] : a close-fitting garment usu. with long sleeves, a high neck, and ankle-length legs worn for practice or performance by dancers, acrobats, and aerialists; *also* : TIGHTS
Lep·cha \ˈlep-chə\ *n, pl* **Lepcha** *or* **Lepchas 1 :** a member of a Mongoloid people of Sikkim, India **2 :** the Tibeto-Burman language of the Lepcha people
lep·er \ˈlep-ər\ *n* [ME, fr. *lepre* leprosy, fr. OF, fr. LL *lepra,* fr. Gk, fr. *lepein* to peel; akin to OE *lǣfer* reed] **1 :** a person affected with leprosy **2 :** a person shunned for moral or social reasons : OUTCAST
lepid- *or* **lepido-** *comb form* [NL, fr. Gk, fr. *lepid-, lepis* scale, fr. *lepein*] : flake : scale <*Lepido*ptera>
le·pid·o·lite \li-ˈpid-ᵊl-ˌīt\ *n* [G *lepidolith,* fr. *lepid-* + *-lith*] : a variable mineral typically $K(Li,Al)_3(Si,Al)_4O_{10}(F, OH)_2$ that consists of a mica containing lithium and is used esp. in glazes and enamels
lep·i·dop·ter·an \ˌlep-ə-ˈdäp-tə-rən\ *n* [NL *Lepidoptera* order of insects, fr. *lepid-* + Gk *pteron* wing — more at FEATHER] : any of a large order (Lepidoptera) of insects comprising the butterflies, moths, and skippers that as adults have four broad or lanceolate wings usu. covered with minute overlapping and often brightly colored scales and that as larvae are caterpillars — **lepidopteran** *adj* — **lep·i·dop·ter·ous** \-tə-rəs\ *adj*
lep·i·dop·ter·ist \-tə-rəst\ *n* : a specialist in lepidopterology
lep·i·dop·ter·ol·o·gy \-ˌdäp-tə-ˈräl-ə-jē\ *n* : a branch of entomology concerned with lepidopterans — **lep·i·dop·ter·o·log·i·cal** \-tə-rə-ˈläj-i-kəl\ *adj* — **lep·i·dop·ter·ol·o·gist** \-tə-ˈräl-ə-jəst\ *n*
lep·i·dop·ter·on \ˌlep-ə-ˈdäp-tə-rən, -ˌrän\ *n, pl* **-tera** \-tə-rə\ *also* **-ter·ons** [NL, sing. of *Lepidoptera*] : LEPIDOPTERAN
lep·i·do·sis \ˌlep-ə-ˈdō-səs\ *n, pl* **-do·ses** \-ˌsēz\ [NL] : the arrangement and character of scales or shields (as on a snake)
lep·i·dote \ˈlep-ə-ˌdōt\ *adj* [Gk *lepidōtos* scaly, fr. *lepid-, lepis*] : covered with scurf or scurfy scales <~ rhododendrons>
lep·re·chaun \ˈlep-rə-ˌkän, -ˌkȯn\ *n* [IrGael *leipreachān*] : a mischievous elf of Irish folklore usu. believed to reveal the hiding place of treasure if caught
lep·ro·sar·i·um \ˌlep-rə-ˈser-ē-əm\ *n, pl* **-i·ums** *or* **-ia** \-ē-ə\ [ML, fr. LL *leprosus*] : a hospital for leprosy patients
lep·ro·sy \ˈlep-rə-sē\ *n* [*leprous* + *-y*] **1 :** a chronic disease caused by a bacillus (*Mycobacterium leprae*) and characterized by the formation of nodules or of macules that enlarge and spread accompanied by loss of sensation with eventual paralysis, wasting

of muscle, and production of deformities and mutilations **2 :** a morally or spiritually harmful influence <the ~ of poverty> — **lep·rot·ic** \le-'prät-ik\ *adj*

lep·rous \'lep-rəs\ *adj* [ME, fr. LL *leprosus* leprous, fr. *lepra* leprosy] **1 a :** infected with leprosy **b :** of, relating to, or resembling leprosy or a leper **2 :** SCALY, SCURFY — **lep·rous·ly** *adv* — **lep·rous·ness** *n*

-lep·sy \,lep-sē\ *n comb form* [MF *-lepsie*, fr. LL *-lepsia*, fr. Gk *-lēpsia*, fr. *lēpsis*, fr. *lambanein* to take, seize — more at LATCH] **:** taking **:** seizure <nympho*lepsy*>

lep·to·ceph·a·lus \,lep-tə-'sef-ə-ləs\ *n, pl* **-li** \-,lī, -,lē\ [NL, fr. Gk *leptos* + *kephalē* head — more at CEPHALIC] **:** a long thin small-headed transparent pelagic first larva of various eels

[1]lep·ton \lep-'tän\ *n, pl* **lep·ta** \-'tä\ [NGk, fr. Gk, a small coin, fr. neut. of *leptos* peeled, slender, small, fr. *lepein* to peel — more at LEPER] — see *drachma* at MONEY table

[2]lep·ton \'lep-,tän\ *n* [GK *leptos* + E [2]*-on*] **:** any of a group of particles consisting of electrons, muons, and neutrinos that experience no strong interactions and are less massive than mesons and baryons — **lep·ton·ic** \lep-'tän-ik\ *adj*

lep·to·some \'lep-tə-,sōm\ *adj* [G *leptosom*, fr. Gk *leptos* slender + *sōma* body] **:** ASTHENIC 2, ECTOMORPHIC — **leptosome** *n*

lep·to·spire \-,spī(ə)r\ *n* [NL *Leptospira*, genus name, fr. Gk *leptos* + L *spira* coil — more at SPIRE] **:** any of a genus (*Leptospira*) of slender aerobic spirochetes that are free-living or parasitic in mammals — **lep·to·spir·al** \,lep-tə-'spī-rəl\ *adj*

lep·to·spi·ro·sis \,lep-tə-spī-'rō-səs\ *n, pl* **-ro·ses** \-,sēz\ [NL] **:** any of several diseases of man and domestic animals that are caused by infection with leptospires

lep·to·tene \'lep-tə-,tēn\ *n* [ISV] **:** a stage of meiotic prophase immediately preceding synapsis in which the chromosomes appear as fine discrete threads — **leptotene** *adj*

[1]les·bi·an \'lez-bē-ən\ *adj, often cap* **1 :** of or relating to Lesbos **2** [fr. the reputed homosexual band associated with Sappho of Lesbos] **:** of or relating to homosexuality between females

[2]lesbian *n, often cap* **:** a female homosexual

les·bi·an·ism \'lez-bē-ə-,niz-əm\ *n* **:** female homosexuality

lese maj·es·ty *or* **lèse ma·jes·té** \(')lēz-'maj-ə-stē\ *n* [MF *lese majesté*, fr. L *laesa majestas*, lit., injured majesty] **1 a :** a crime (as treason) committed against a sovereign power **b :** an offense violating the dignity of a ruler as the representative of a sovereign power **2 :** a detraction from or affront to dignity or importance

le·sion \'lē-zhən\ *n* [ME, fr. MF, fr. L *laesion-*, *laesio*, fr. *laesus*, pp. of *laedere* to injure] **1 :** INJURY, HARM **2 :** an abnormal change in structure of an organ or part due to injury or disease; *esp* **:** one that is circumscribed and well defined

les·pe·de·za \,les-pə-'dē-zə\ *n* [NL, irreg. fr. V. M. de *Zespedes* *fl*1785 Sp governor of East Florida] **:** any of a genus (*Lespedeza*) of herbaceous or shrubby leguminous plants including some widely used for forage, soil improvement, and esp. hay

[1]less \'les\ *adj* [ME, partly fr. OE *lǣs*, adv. & n.; partly fr. *lǣssa*, adj.; akin to OFris *lēs* less, Gk *limos* hunger] **1 :** constituting a more limited number <~ than three> **2 :** of lower rank, degree, or importance <no ~ a person than the president himself> **3 a :** of reduced size, extent, or degree **b :** more limited in quantity <in ~ time>

syn LESS, LESSER, SMALLER, FEWER *shared meaning element* **:** not as great (as in size, number, worth, or significance) as some expressed or implied other. In spite of the common element of meaning these terms are rarely interchangeable without loss of precision. LESS in its most characteristic use applies to matters of degree, value, or amount, is opposed to *more*, and chiefly modifies collective nouns or nouns denoting a mass or an abstract whole <the moon gives *less* light than the sun> *Less* is sometimes applied to matters of number, but the usage is decried by many careful writers and speakers. LESSER applies especially to matters of quality, worth, or significance and is opposed to *greater* or *major* <God made . . . the *lesser* light to rule the night —Gen 1:16 (AV)> In vernacular names of plants and animals *lesser* specifically implies distinction based on relative smallness <the *lesser* yellowlegs> <*lesser* celandine> SMALLER is applicable especially to matters of size, dimension, or quantity and is opposed to *larger* <the advantage of *smaller* cars> <use a *smaller* amount of seasoning> FEWER applies specifically to matters of number and therefore regularly modifies a plural noun. Thus, "he has *fewer* (not *less*) spendable dollars this year," but "he has *less* (not *fewer*) money to spend than he used to." Occasionally the distinction between quantity and number is obscured and either *fewer* or *less* is appropriate <seasonal workers who average *fewer* (or *less*) than six months' work a year> ***ant*** more

[2]less *adv* **:** to a lesser extent or degree — **less and less :** to a progressively smaller size or extent — **less than :** by no means **:** not at all <was being *less than* honest in his replies>

[3]less *prep* **:** diminished by **:** MINUS

[4]less *n, pl* **less** **1 :** a smaller portion or quantity **2 :** something of less importance

-less \ləs\ *adj suffix* [ME *-les, -lesse*, fr. OE *-lēas*, fr. *lēas* devoid, false; akin to OHG *lōs* loose, OE *losian* to get lost — more at LOSE] **1 :** destitute of **:** not having <wit*less*> <child*less*> **2 :** unable to be acted on or to act (in a specified way) <daunt*less*> <fade*less*>

les·see \le-'sē\ *n* [ME, fr. AF, fr. *lessé*, pp. of *lesser* to lease — more at LEASE] **:** one that holds real or personal property under a lease

less·en \'les-ᵊn\ *vb* **less·ened; less·en·ing** \'les-niŋ, -ᵊn-iŋ\ *vi* **:** to shrink in size, number, or degree **:** DECREASE — *vt* **1 :** to reduce in size, extent, or degree **2 a** *archaic* **:** to represent as of little value **:** MINIMIZE **b :** to lower in status or dignity **:** DEGRADE ***syn*** see DECREASE

[1]less·er \'les-ər\ *adj* **:** of less size, quality, or significance ***syn*** see LESS ***ant*** greater, major

[2]lesser *adv* **:** LESS <*lesser*-known>

Lesser Bear *n* **:** URSA MINOR

lesser celandine *n* **:** CELANDINE 2

lesser cornstalk borer *n* **:** a pyralid moth (*Elasmopalpus lignosellus*) whose slender greenish larva is a destructive pest that burrows in the stalk esp. of Indian corn near ground level

Lesser Dog *n* **:** CANIS MINOR

lesser peach tree borer *n* **:** a moth (*Synanthedon pictipes* family Aegeriidae) whose larva is a borer in the forks and crotches of stone-fruit trees and esp. the peach

lesser scaup *n* **:** a common No. American diving duck (*Athya affinis*) similar to but smaller than the greater scaup with a purplish iridescence on the head of the adult male — called also *lesser scaup duck*

lesser yellowlegs *n pl but sing or pl in constr* **:** a common American marsh and shore bird (*Tringa flavipes*) that closely resembles the greater yellowlegs in color and markings but is smaller with a shorter more slender bill

[1]les·son \'les-ᵊn\ *n* [ME, fr. OF *leçon*, fr. LL *lection-*, *lectio*, fr. L, act of reading, fr. *lectus*, pp. of *legere* to read — more at LEGEND] **1 :** a passage from sacred writings read in a service of worship **2 a :** a piece of instruction **:** TEACHING **b :** a reading or exercise to be studied by a pupil **c :** a division of a course of instruction **3 a :** something learned by study or experience <his years of travel had taught him valuable ~*s*> **b :** an instructive example <the ~*s* history has for us> **c :** REPRIMAND

[2]lesson *vt* **les·soned; les·son·ing** \'les-ə-niŋ, 'les-niŋ\ **1 :** to give a lesson to **:** INSTRUCT **2 :** LECTURE, REBUKE

les·sor \'les-,ó(ə)r, le-'só(ə)r\ *n* [ME *lessour*, fr. AF, fr. *lesser* to lease] **:** one that conveys property by lease

lest \(,)lest\ *conj* [ME *les the, leste*, fr. OE *thȳ lǣs the*, fr. *thȳ* (instrumental of *thæt* that) + *lǣs* + *the*, relative particle] **:** for fear that — used after an expression denoting fear or apprehension <worried ~ he should be late> <hesitant to speak out ~ he be branded a troublemaker>

[1]let \'let\ *vt* **let·ted; letted** *or* **let; let·ting** [ME *letten*, fr. OE *lettan* to delay, hinder; akin to OHG *lezzen* to delay, hurt, OE *lǣt* late] *archaic* **:** HINDER, PREVENT

[2]let *n* **1 :** something that impedes **:** OBSTRUCTION **2 :** a stroke in racket games that does not count and must be replayed

[3]let *vb* **let; let·ting** [ME *leten*, fr. OE *lǣtan*; akin to OHG *lāzzan* to permit, L *lassus* weary, *lenis* soft, mild] *vt* **1 :** to cause to **:** MAKE <~ it be known> **2 a :** to offer or grant for rent or lease <~ rooms> **b :** to assign esp. after bids <~ a contract> **3 a :** to give opportunity to whether by positive action or by failure to prevent <live and ~ live> <a break in the clouds ~ him see his objective> **b** — used in the imperative to introduce a request or proposal <~ us pray> **c** — used as an auxiliary to express a warning <~ him try> **4 :** to free from or as if from confinement **:** RELEASE <~ the prisoner go> <she ~ out a scream> **5 :** to permit to enter, pass, or leave <~ them through> ~ *vi* **1 :** to become rented or leased **2 :** to become awarded to a contractor

syn **1** see HIRE

2 LET, ALLOW, PERMIT, SUFFER *shared meaning element* **:** to neither forbid nor prevent

-let \lət\ *n suffix* [ME, fr. MF *-elet*, fr. *-el*, dim. suffix (fr. L *-ellus*) + *-et*] **1 :** small one <book*let*> **2 :** article worn on <wrist*let*>

let alone *prep* **:** to say nothing of **:** not to mention <lacked the courage, *let alone* the skill, to be effective>

let·down \'let-,daún\ *n* **1 a :** DISCOURAGEMENT, DISAPPOINTMENT **b :** a slackening of effort **:** RELAXATION **2 :** the descent of an aircraft or spacecraft to the point at which a landing approach is begun

[1]le·thal \'lē-thəl\ *adj* [L *letalis, lethalis*, fr. *letum* death] **1 a :** of, relating to, or causing death <a ~ injury> **b :** capable of causing death <~ chemicals> **2 :** gravely damaging or destructive **:** DEVASTATING <a ~ attack on his reputation> ***syn*** see DEADLY — **le·thal·i·ty** \lē-'thal-ət-ē\ *n* — **le·thal·ly** \'lē-thə-lē\ *adv*

[2]lethal *n* **1 :** an abnormality of genetic origin causing the death of the organism possessing it **2 :** LETHAL GENE

lethal gene *n* **:** a gene that in some (as homozygous) conditions may prevent development or cause the death of an organism or its germ cells — called also *lethal factor, lethal mutant, lethal mutation*

le·thar·gic \lə-'thär-jik, le-\ *adj* **1 :** of, relating to, or characterized by lethargy **:** SLUGGISH **2 :** INDIFFERENT, APATHETIC — **le·thar·gi·cal·ly** \-ji-k(ə-)lē\ *adv*

syn LETHARGIC, SLUGGISH, TORPID, COMATOSE *shared meaning element* **:** deficient in alertness or activity ***ant*** energetic

leth·ar·gy \'leth-ər-jē\ *n* [ME *litargie*, fr. ML *litargia*, fr. LL *lethargia*, fr. Gk *lēthargia*, fr. *lēthargos* forgetful, lethargic, fr. *lēthē* + *argos* lazy — more at ARGON] **1 :** abnormal drowsiness **2 :** the quality or state of being lazy or indifferent

le·the \'lē-thē\ *n* [L, fr. Gk *Lēthē*, fr. *lēthē* forgetfulness; akin to Gk *lanthanein* to escape notice, *lanthanesthai* to forget — more at LATENT] **1** *cap* **:** a river in Hades whose waters cause drinkers to forget their past **2 :** OBLIVION, FORGETFULNESS — **le·the·an** \'lē-thē-ən, li-'thē-\ *adj, often cap*

let on *vi* **1 :** to make acknowledgment **:** ADMIT <knows more than he *lets on*> **2 :** to reveal a secret <nobody *let on* about the surprise party> **3 :** PRETEND <*let on* to being a stranger>

let's \(,)lets, *rapid* (,)les\ **:** let us

Lett \'let\ *n* [G *Lette*, fr. Latvian *Latvi*] **:** a member of a people closely related to the Lithuanians and mainly inhabiting Latvia

[1]let·ter \'let-ər\ *n* [ME, fr. OF *lettre*, fr. L *littera* letter of the alphabet, *litterae*, pl., epistle, literature] **1 :** a symbol usu. written or printed representing a speech sound and constituting a unit of an alphabet **2 a :** a direct or personal written or printed message addressed to a person or organization **b :** a written communication containing a grant — usu. used in pl. **3** *pl but sing or pl in* *constr* **a** : LITERATURE, BELLES LETTRES **b** : LEARNING **4** : the strict or outward sense or significance <the ~ of the law> **5 a** : a single piece of type **b** : a style of type **c** : TYPE; *esp* : a supply of type **6** : the initial of a school awarded to a student for achievement usu. in athletics

[2]**letter** *vt* **1** : to set down in letters : PRINT **2** : to mark with letters : INSCRIBE ~ *vi* : to win an athletic letter — **let·ter·er** \-ər-ər\ *n*

[3]**let·ter** \'let-ər\ *n* : one that rents or leases

letter carrier *n* : MAILMAN

let·tered \'let-ərd\ *adj* **1 a** : LEARNED, EDUCATED **b** : of, relating to, or characterized by learning : CULTURED **2** : inscribed with or as if with letters

let·ter·form \-ər-ˌfȯrm\ *n* : the shape of a letter of an alphabet esp. when considered from the standpoint of design or development

let·ter·head \'let-ər-ˌhed\ *n* **1** : a sheet of stationery printed or engraved usu. with the name and address of an organization **2** : the heading at the top of a letterhead

let·ter·ing \'let-ə-riŋ\ *n* : letters used in an inscription

letter missive *n, pl* **letters missive** [ME, fr. MF *lettre missive* letter intended to be sent] : a letter from a superior authority conveying a command, recommendation, permission, or invitation

letter of credence : a formal document furnished a diplomatic agent attesting to his power to act for his government — called also *letters of credence*

letter of credit **1** : a letter addressed by a banker to a correspondent certifying that a person named therein is entitled to draw on him or his credit up to a certain sum **2** : a letter addressed by a banker to a person to whom credit is given authorizing him to draw on the issuing bank or on a bank in his country up to a certain sum and guaranteeing to accept the drafts if duly made

let·ter–per·fect \ˌlet-ər-'pər-fikt\ *adj* : correct to the smallest detail; *esp* : VERBATIM

let·ter·press \'let-ər-ˌpres\ *n* **1 a** : the process of printing from an inked raised surface esp. when the paper is impressed directly upon the surface **b** : work done by this process **c** : a press for letterpress printing **2** *chiefly Brit* : text (as of a book) distinct from pictorial illustrations

letter sheet *n* : a sheet of stationery that can be folded and sealed with the message inside to form its own envelope

letters of administration : a letter evidencing the right of an administrator to administer the goods or estate of a deceased person

letters of marque \-'märk\ : written authority granted to a private person by a government to seize the subjects of a foreign state or their goods; *specif* : a license granted to a private person to fit out an armed ship to plunder the enemy

letters patent *n pl* : a writing (as from a sovereign) that confers on a designated person a grant in a form readily open for inspection by all

letters testamentary *n pl* : a written communication from a court or officer informing an executor of his appointment and authority to execute the will of the testator

[1]**Lett·ish** \'let-ish\ *adj* : of or relating to the Latvians or their language

[2]**Lettish** *n* : LATVIAN 2

let·tre de ca·chet \ˌle-trə-də-ˌka-'shā\ *n, pl* **lettres de cachet** \-trə(z)-\ [F] : a letter bearing an official seal and usu. authorizing imprisonment without trial of a named person

let·tuce \'let-əs\ *n* [ME *letuse,* fr. OF *laitues,* pl. of *laitue,* fr. L *lactuca,* fr. *lact-, lac* milk; fr. its milky juice — more at GALAXY] : any of a genus (*Lactuca*) of composite plants; *esp* : a common garden vegetable (*L. sativa*) whose succulent leaves are used esp. in salads

let·up \'let-ˌəp\ *n* : a lessening of effort

let up \(ˈ)let-'əp\ *vi* **1 a** : to diminish or slow down **b** : CEASE, STOP **2** : to become less severe — used with *on*

leu \'leu̇\ *n, pl* **lei** \'lā\ [Rum, lit., lion, fr. L *leo* — more at LION] — see MONEY table

leu·cine \'lü-ˌsēn\ *n* [ISV *leuc-* + *-ine*] : a white crystalline essential amino acid $C_6H_{13}NO_2$ obtained by the hydrolysis of most dietary proteins

leu·cite \'lü-ˌsīt\ *n* [G *leuzit,* fr. *leuz-* leuk-] : a white or gray mineral $KAlSi_2O_6$ consisting of a potassium aluminum silicate and occurring in igneous rocks — **leu·cit·ic** \lü-'sit-ik\ *adj*

leu·co·ci·din \ˌlü-kə-'sīd-ᵊn\ *n* [ISV *leuc-* + *-cide* + *-in*] : a bacterial substance that destroys leukocytes

leu·co·ma \lü-'kō-mə\ *n* [LL, fr. Gk *leukōma,* fr. *leukos* white] : a dense white opacity in the cornea of the eye

leu·co·plast \'lü-kə-ˌplast\ *also* **leu·co·plas·tid** \ˌlü-kə-'plas-təd\ *n* [ISV] : a colorless plastid esp. in the cytoplasm of interior plant tissues that is potentially capable of developing into a chromoplast

leuk- *or* **leuko-** *also* **leuc-** *or* **leuco-** *comb form* [NL *leuc-, leuco-,* fr. Gk *leuk-, leuko-,* fr. *leukos* — more at LIGHT] **1** : white : colorless : weakly colored <*leuko*cyte> <*leuko*rrhea> **2** : leukocyte <*leuk*emia> **3** : white matter of the brain <*leuco*tomy>

leu·ke·mia \lü-'kē-mē-ə\ *n* [NL] : an acute or chronic disease in man and other warm-blooded animals characterized by an abnormal increase in the number of leukocytes in the tissues and often in the blood — **leu·ke·mic** \-mik\ *adj or n*

leu·ke·moid \-ˌmȯid\ *adj* : resembling leukemia but not involving the same changes in the blood-forming organs <a ~ reaction in malaria>

leukocyt- *or* **leukocyto-** *also* **leucocyt-** *or* **leucocyto-** *comb form* [ISV] : leukocyte <*leukocyt*osis>

leu·ko·cyte *also* **leu·co·cyte** \'lü-kə-ˌsīt\ *n* [ISV] : any of the white or colorless nucleated cells that occur in blood — **leu·ko·cyt·ic** \ˌlü-kə-'sit-ik\ *adj* — **leu·ko·cyt·oid** \'lü-kə-ˌsīt-ˌȯid\ *adj*

leu·ko·cy·to·sis \ˌlü-kə-sī-'tō-səs, -kə-sə-\ *n* [NL] : an increase in the number of leukocytes in the circulating blood — **leu·ko·cy·tot·ic** \-'tät-ik\ *adj*

leu·ko·dys·tro·phy \ˌlü-kō-'dis-trə-fē\ *n, pl* **-phies** : any of several genetically determined diseases characterized by degeneration of the white matter of the brain

leu·kon \'lü-ˌkän\ *n* [NL, fr. Gk, neut. of *leukos*] : the white blood cells and their precursors

leu·ko·pe·nia \ˌlü-kə-'pē-nē-ə\ *n* [NL, fr. *leuc-* + Gk *penia* poverty, lack] : a condition in which the number of leukocytes circulating in the blood is abnormally low — **leu·ko·pe·nic** \-nik\ *adj*

leu·ko·poi·e·sis \-pȯi-'ē-səs\ *n* [NL] : the formation of white blood cells — **leu·ko·poi·et·ic** \-'et-ik\ *adj*

leu·kor·rhea \ˌlü-kə-'rē-ə\ *n* [NL] : a whitish viscid discharge from the vagina resulting from inflammation or congestion of the mucous membrane — **leu·kor·rhe·al** \-'rē-əl\ *adj*

leu·ko·sis \lü-'kō-səs\ *n, pl* **-ko·ses** \-ˌsēz\ [NL] : LEUKEMIA — **leu·kot·ic** \-'kät-ik\ *adj*

lev \'lef\ *n, pl* **le·va** \'lev-ə\ [Bulg, lit., lion] — see MONEY table

Lev *abbr* Leviticus

lev- *or* **levo-** *comb form* [F *lévo-,* fr. L *laevus* left; akin to Gk *laios* left] **1** : levorotatory <*lev*ulose> **2** : to the left <*levo*rotatory>

Le·val·loi·si·an \ˌlev-ə-'lȯi-zē-ən, lə-ˌval-'wä-zē-\ *adj* [*Levallois*-Perret, suburb of Paris, France] : of or relating to a lower Paleolithic culture characterized by a technique of manufacturing tools by striking flakes from a flat flint nodule

le·vant \lə-'vant\ *vi* [perh. fr. Sp *levantar* to break camp, deriv. of L *levare*] *chiefly Brit* : to run away from a debt

le·vant·er \lə-'vant-ər\ *n* **1** *cap* : a native or inhabitant of the Levant **2** : a strong easterly Mediterranean wind

Le·vant storax \lə-'vant-\ *n* : STORAX 1a

le·va·tor \li-'vāt-ər\ *n, pl* **lev·a·to·res** \ˌlev-ə-'tōr-(ˌ)ēz\ *or* **le·va·tors** \li-'vāt-ərz\ [NL, fr. L *levatus,* pp. of *levare* to raise — more at LEVER] : a muscle that serves to raise a body part — compare DEPRESSOR

[1]**le·vee** \'lev-ē; lə-'vē, -'vā\ *n* [F *lever,* fr. MF, act of arising, fr. (*se*) *lever* to rise] **1** : a reception held by a person of distinction on rising from bed **2** : an afternoon assembly at which the British sovereign or his representative receives only men **3** : a reception usu. in honor of a particular person

[2]**lev·ee** \'lev-ē\ *n* [F *levée,* fr. OF, act of raising, fr. *lever* to raise — more at LEVER] **1 a** : an embankment for preventing flooding **b** : a river landing place : PIER **2** : a continuous dike or ridge (as of earth) for confining the irrigation areas of land to be flooded

[3]**lev·ee** \'lev-ē\ *vt* **lev·eed; lev·ee·ing** : to provide with a levee

[1]**lev·el** \'lev-əl\ *n* [ME, fr. MF *livel,* fr. (assumed) VL *libellum,* alter. of L *libella,* fr. dim. of *libra* weight, balance] **1** : a device for establishing a horizontal line or plane by means of a bubble in a liquid that shows adjustment to the horizontal by movement to the center of a slightly bowed glass tube **2** : a measurement of the difference of altitude of two points by means of a level **3** : horizontal condition; *esp* : equilibrium of a fluid marked by a horizontal surface of even altitude <water seeks its own ~> **4 a** : an approximately horizontal line or surface taken as an index of altitude **b** : a practically horizontal surface or area (as of land) **5** : a position in a scale or rank (as of value or achievement) <the top 10 percent ~> **6 a** : a line or surface that cuts perpendicularly all plumb lines that it meets and hence would everywhere coincide with a surface of still water **b** : the plane of the horizon or a line in it **7** : a horizontal passage in a mine intended for regular working and transportation **8** : a concentration of a constituent esp. of a body fluid (as blood) **9** : the magnitude of a quantity considered in relation to an arbitrary reference value — **on the level** : bona fide : HONEST

[2]**level** *vb* **-eled** *or* **-elled; -el·ing** *or* **-el·ling** \'lev-(ə-)liŋ\ *vt* **1** : to make (a line or surface) horizontal : make flat or level <~ a field for planting> <~ off a house lot> **2 a** : to bring to a horizontal aiming position **b** : AIM, DIRECT <~*ed* a charge of fraud at him> **3** : to bring to a common level or plane : EQUALIZE <love ~*s* all ranks —W. S. Gilbert> **4** : to lay level with the ground : RAZE **5** : to make (as color) even or uniform **6** : to find the heights of different points in (a piece of land) esp. with a surveyor's level ~ *vi* **1** : to attain or come to a level <the plane ~*ed* off at 10,000 ft.> **2** : to aim a gun or other weapon horizontally **3** : to bring persons or things to a level **4** : to deal frankly and openly

[3]**level** *adj* **1 a** : having no part higher than another : conforming to the curvature of the liquid parts of the earth's surface **b** : parallel with the plane of the horizon : HORIZONTAL **2 a** : even or unvarying in height **b** : equal in advantage, progression, or standing **c** : proceeding monotonously or uneventfully **d** (1) : STEADY, UNWAVERING <gave him a ~ look> (2) : CALM, UNEXCITED <spoke in ~ tones> **3** : REASONABLE, BALANCED <arrive at a justly proportional and ~ judgment on this affair — Sir Winston Churchill> **4** : distributed evenly <~ stress> **5** : being a surface perpendicular to all lines of force in a field of force : EQUIPOTENTIAL **6** : suited to a particular rank or plane of ability or achievement <top-*level* thinking> **7** : bona fide **8** : of or relating to the spreading out of a cost or charge in even payments over a period of time — **lev·el·ly** \'lev-əl-(l)ē\ *adv* — **lev·el·ness** \-əl-nəs\ *n*

syn LEVEL, FLAT, PLANE, EVEN, SMOOTH *shared meaning element* : having a surface without bends, curves, or irregularities

— **level best** : very best

level crossing *n, Brit* : GRADE CROSSING

lev·el·er *or* **lev·el·ler** \'lev-(ə-)lər\ *n* **1** : one that levels **2 a** *cap* : one of a group of radicals arising during the English Civil War and advocating equality before the law and religious toleration **b** : one favoring the removal of political, social, or economic social inequalities **c** : something that tends to reduce or eliminate differences among men

lev·el·head·ed \ˌlev-əl-'hed-əd\ *adj* : having sound judgment : SENSIBLE — **lev·el·head·ed·ness** *n*

leveling rod *n* : a graduated rod used in measuring the vertical distance between a point on the ground and the line of sight of a surveyor's level

level of significance : the probability of rejecting the null hypothesis in a statistical test when it is true — called also *significance level*

[1]le·ver \ˈlev-ər, ˈlē-vər\ *n* [ME, fr. OF *levier,* fr. *lever* to raise, fr. L *levare;* akin to L *levis* light in weight — more at LIGHT] **1 a :** a bar used for prying or dislodging something **b :** an inducing or compelling force **:** TOOL <attempts to use food as a political ~ —*Time*> **2 a :** a rigid piece that transmits and modifies force or motion when forces are applied at two points and it turns about a third; *specif* **:** a rigid bar used to exert a pressure or sustain a weight at one point of its length by the application of a force at a second and turning at a third on a fulcrum **b :** a projecting piece by which a mechanism is operated or adjusted

[2]lever *vt* **le·vered; le·ver·ing** \ˈlev-(ə-)riŋ, ˈlēv-\ **1 :** to pry, raise, or move with or as if with a lever **2 :** to operate (a device) in the manner of a lever

[1]le·ver·age \ˈlev-(ə-)rij, ˈlēv-\ *n* **1 :** the action of a lever or the mechanical advantage gained by it **2 :** POWER, EFFECTIVENESS <organizing . . . to gain greater professional, economic, and political ~ —*Change*> **3 :** the use of supplementary non-equity capital (as senior securities or borrowed money) to increase the returns on equity; *also* **:** the resultant economic advantage

[2]leverage *vt* **-aged; -ag·ing :** to provide (as a corporation) with leverage

lev·er·et \ˈlev-(ə-)rət\ *n* [ME, fr. (assumed) MF *levret,* fr. MF *levre* hare, fr. L *lepor-, lepus*] **:** a hare in its first year

Le·vi \ˈlē-ˌvī\ *n* [LL, from Heb *Lēwī*] **:** a son of Jacob and the traditional eponymous ancestor of the priestly tribe of Levi

levi·able \ˈlev-ē-ə-bəl\ *adj* **:** capable of being levied or levied upon

le·vi·a·than \li-ˈvī-ə-thən\ *n* [ME, fr. LL, fr. Heb *liwyāthān*] **1 a** *often cap* **:** a sea monster represented as an adversary defeated by Yahweh in various Scriptural accounts **b (1) :** a large sea animal **(2) :** a large oceangoing ship **2** *cap* **:** the political state; *esp* **:** a totalitarian state having a vast bureaucracy **3 :** something large or formidable — **leviathan** *adj*

levi·er \ˈlev-ē-ər\ *n* **:** one that levies

lev·i·gate \ˈlev-ə-ˌgāt\ *vt* **-gat·ed; -gat·ing** [L *levigatus,* pp. of *levigare,* fr. *levis* smooth + *-igare* (akin to *agere* to drive) — more at LIME, AGENT] **1 :** POLISH, SMOOTH **2 a :** to grind to a fine smooth powder while in moist condition **b :** to separate (fine powder) from coarser material by suspending in a liquid — **lev·i·ga·tion** \ˌlev-ə-ˈgā-shən\ *n*

lev·in \ˈlev-ən\ *n* [ME *levene*] *archaic* **:** LIGHTNING

le·vi·rate \ˈlev-ə-rət, ˈlē-və-, -ˌrāt\ *n* [L *levir* husband's brother; akin to OE *tācor* husband's brother, Gk *daēr*] **:** the sometimes compulsory marriage of a widow by a brother of her deceased husband — **le·vi·rat·ic** \ˌlev-ə-ˈrat-ik, ˌlē-və-\ *adj*

Le·vi's \ˈlē-ˌvīz\ *trademark* — used esp. for blue denim jeans

Levit *abbr* Leviticus

lev·i·tate \ˈlev-ə-ˌtāt\ *vb* **-tat·ed; -tat·ing** [*levity*] *vi* **:** to rise or float in the air esp. in seeming defiance of gravitation <objects *levitating* during a spiritualistic seance> ~ *vt* **:** to cause to levitate <a particle *levitated* by an electromagnetic device>

lev·i·ta·tion \ˌlev-ə-ˈtā-shən\ *n* **:** the act or process of levitating; *esp* **:** the rising or lifting of a person or thing by means held to be supernatural — **lev·i·ta·tion·al** \-shnəl, -shən-ᵊl\ *adj*

Le·vite \ˈlē-ˌvīt\ *n* **:** a member of the priestly Hebrew tribe of Levi; *specif* **:** a Levite of non-Aaronic descent assigned to lesser ceremonial offices under the Levitical priests of the family of Aaron

Le·vit·i·cal \li-ˈvit-i-kəl\ *adj* [LL *Leviticus*] **:** of or relating to the Levites or to Leviticus

Le·vit·i·cus \-kəs\ *n* [LL, lit., of the Levites] **:** the third book of canonical Jewish and Christian Scripture consisting mainly of priestly legislation — see BIBLE table

lev·i·ty \ˈlev-ət-ē\ *n* [L *levitat-, levitas,* fr. *levis* light in weight — more at LIGHT] **1 a :** excessive or unseemly frivolity **b :** lack of steadiness **:** CHANGEABLENESS **2 :** the quality or state of being light in weight **:** BUOYANCY ***syn*** see LIGHTNESS ***ant*** gravity

le·vo \ˈlē-(ˌ)vō\ *adj* **:** LEVOROTATORY

levo- — see LEV-

le·vo·ro·ta·tion \ˌlē-və-rō-ˈtā-shən\ *n* **:** left-handed or counterclockwise rotation — used of the plane of polarization of light

le·vo·ro·ta·to·ry \-ˈrōt-ə-ˌtōr-ē, -ˌtȯr-\ *or* **le·vo·ro·ta·ry** \-ˈrōt-ə-rē\ *adj* **:** turning toward the left or counterclockwise; *esp* **:** rotating the plane of polarization of light to the left — compare DEXTROROTATORY

lev·u·lose \ˈlev-yə-ˌlōs, -ˌlōz\ *n* [ISV, irreg. fr. *lev-* + *-ose*] **:** FRUCTOSE 2

[1]levy \ˈlev-ē\ *n, pl* **lev·ies** [ME, fr. MF *levee,* fr. OF, act of raising — more at LEVEE] **1 a :** the imposition or collection of an assessment **b :** an amount levied **2 a :** the enlistment or conscription of men for military service **b :** troops raised by levy

[2]levy *vb* **lev·ied; levy·ing** *vt* **1 a :** to impose or collect by legal authority <~ a tax> **b :** to require by authority **2 :** to enlist or conscript for military service **3 :** to carry on (war) **:** WAGE ~ *vi* **:** to seize property

levy en masse *n* **:** the spontaneous act of the people of a territory of taking up arms for self-defense upon the approach of an enemy without having had time to organize in accordance with recognized rules of warfare

lewd \ˈlüd\ *adj* [ME *lewed* vulgar, fr. OE *lǣwede* laical, ignorant] **1** *obs* **:** EVIL, WICKED **2 a :** sexually unchaste or licentious **b :** OBSCENE, SALACIOUS — **lewd·ly** *adv* — **lewd·ness** *n*

lew·is \ˈlü-əs\ *n* [prob. fr. the name *Lewis*] **:** an iron dovetailed tenon that is made in sections, can be fitted into a dovetail mortise, and is used in hoisting large stones

lew·is·ite \ˈlü-ə-ˌsīt\ *n* [Winford L. *Lewis* †1943 Am chemist] **:** a colorless or brown vesicant liquid $C_2H_2AsCl_3$ developed as a poison gas for war use

lew·is·son \ˈlü-ə-sən\ *n* **:** LEWIS

lex \ˈleks\ *n, pl* **le·ges** \ˈlā-(ˌ)gās\ [L *leg-, lex*] **:** LAW

lex·i·cal \ˈlek-si-kəl\ *adj* **1 :** of or relating to words or the vocabulary of a language as distinguished from its grammar and construction **2 :** of or relating to a lexicon or to lexicography — **lex·i·cal·i·ty** \ˌlek-sə-ˈkal-ət-ē\ *n* — **lex·i·cal·ly** \ˈlek-si-k(ə-)lē\ *adv*

lexical meaning *n* **:** the meaning of the base (as the word *play*) in a paradigm (as *plays, played, playing*) — compare GRAMMATICAL MEANING

lex·i·cog·ra·pher \ˌlek-sə-ˈkäg-rə-fər\ *n* [LGk *lexikographos,* fr. *lexikon* + Gk *-graphos* -grapher] **:** an author or editor of a dictionary

lex·i·co·graph·i·cal \ˌlek-sə-kō-ˈgraf-i-kəl\ *or* **lex·i·co·graph·ic** \-ik\ *adj* **:** of or relating to lexicography — **lex·i·co·graph·i·cal·ly** \-i-k(ə-)lē\ *adv*

lex·i·cog·ra·phy \ˌlek-sə-ˈkäg-rə-fē\ *n* **1 :** the editing or making of a dictionary **2 :** the principles and practices of dictionary making

lex·i·col·o·gy \ˌlek-sə-ˈkäl-ə-jē\ *n* [F *lexicologie,* fr. *lexico-* (fr. LGk *lexiko-,* fr. *lexikon*) + *-logie* -logy] **:** a branch of linguistics concerned with the signification and application of words — **lex·i·col·o·gist** \-jəst\ *n*

lex·i·con \ˈlek-sə-ˌkän, -si-kən\ *n, pl* **lex·i·ca** \-si-kə\ *or* **lexicons** [LGk *lexikon,* fr. neut. of *lexikos* of words, fr. Gk *lexis* word, speech, fr. *legein* to say — more at LEGEND] **1 :** a book containing an alphabetical arrangement of the words in a language and their definitions **:** DICTIONARY **2 :** the vocabulary of a language, an individual speaker, or a subject **3 :** the total stock of morphemes in a language

lex·is \ˈlek-səs\ *n, pl* **lex·es** \-ˌsēz\ [Gk, speech, word] **:** LEXICON 2

ley *var of* LEA

Ley·den jar \ˌlīd-ᵊn-\ *n* [*Leiden, Leyden,* Netherlands] **:** an electrical condenser consisting of a glass jar coated inside and outside with metal foil and having the inner coating connected to a conducting rod passed through the insulating stopper

Leyden jar

lf *abbr* lightface

LF *abbr* **1** ledger folio **2** low frequency

L–form \ˈel-ˌfȯrm\ *n* [*L*ister Institute, London, where it was first isolated] **:** a filterable form of some bacteria that may be a specialized reproductive body appearing chiefly when the environment is unfavorable and resembling typical pleuropneumonia organisms

lg *abbr* **1** large **2** long

LH *abbr* **1** left hand **2** lower half **3** luteinizing hormone

Lha·sa ap·so \ˌläs-ə-ˈäp-(ˌ)sō, ˌlas-ə-ˈap-\ *n, pl* **Lhasa apsos** [*Lhasa,* Tibet + Tibetan *apso*] *often cap A* **:** any of a Tibetan breed of small terriers that have a dense coat of long hard straight hair, a heavy fall over the eyes, heavy whiskers and beard, and a well-feathered tail curled over the back

LHD *abbr* [L *litterarum humaniorum doctor*] doctor of humane letters; doctor of humanities

[1]li \ˈlē\ *n, pl* **li** *also* **lis** \ˈlēz\ [Chin (Pek) *li*[3]] **:** any of various Chinese units of distance; *esp* **:** one equal to about ⅓ mile

[2]li *abbr* link

Li *symbol* lithium

LI *abbr* Long Island

li·a·bil·i·ty \ˌlī-ə-ˈbil-ət-ē\ *n, pl* **-ties** **1 a :** the quality or state of being liable **b :** LIKELIHOOD **2 :** something for which one is liable; *esp, pl* **:** pecuniary obligations **:** DEBTS **3 :** one that works as a disadvantage **:** DRAWBACK

li·a·ble \ˈlī-ə-bəl, *esp in sense 2b also* ˈlī-bəl\ *adj* [(assumed) AF, fr. OF *lier* to bind, fr. L *ligare* — more at LIGATURE] **1 a :** obligated according to law or equity **:** RESPONSIBLE **b :** subject to appropriation or attachment **2 a :** being in a position to incur — used with *to* <~ to diseases> **b :** exposed or subject to some usu. adverse contingency or action <watch out or you're ~ to fall>

li·aise \lē-ˈāz\ *vi* **li·aised; li·ais·ing** [back-formation fr. *liaison*] **1 :** to establish liaison **2 :** to act as a liaison officer

li·ai·son \ˈlē-ə-ˌzän, lē-ˈā-\ *n* [F, fr. MF, fr. *lier*] **1 a :** a close bond or connection **:** INTERRELATIONSHIP **b :** an illicit sexual relationship **:** AFFAIR 3a **2 :** the pronunciation of an otherwise absent consonant sound at the end of the first of two consecutive words the second of which begins with a vowel sound and follows without pause **3 :** communication for establishing and maintaining mutual understanding esp. between parts of an armed force

li·a·na \lē-ˈän-ə, -ˈan-ə\ *or* **li·ane** \-ˈän, -ˈan\ *n* [F *liane*] **:** a climbing herbaceous or woody vine esp. of tropical rain forests that roots in the ground — **li·a·noid** \-ˈän-ˌȯid, -ˈan-\ *adj*

li·ang \lē-ˈäŋ\ *n, pl* **liang** *also* **liangs** [Chin (Pek) *liang*[3]] **:** an old Chinese unit of weight equal to $\frac{1}{16}$ catty

li·ar \ˈlī(-ə)r\ *n* [ME, fr. OE *lēogere,* fr. *lēogan* to lie — more at LIE] **:** one that tells lies

Li·as \ˈlī-əs\ *adj* [*Lias,* division of the European Jurassic, fr. F, fr. E (a limestone rock)] **:** of, relating to, or being a subdivision of the European Jurassic

Li·as·sic \lī-ˈas-ik\ *adj* [modif. (influenced by *Jurassic*) of F *liasique,* fr. *Lias*] **:** LIAS

[1]lib \ˈlib\ *n* **:** LIBERATION 2

[2]lib *abbr* **1** liberal **2** librarian; library

li·ba·tion \lī-ˈbā-shən\ *n* [L *libation-, libatio,* fr. *libatus,* pp. of *libare* to pour as an offering; akin to Gk *leibein* to pour] **1 a :** an act of pouring a liquid as a sacrifice (as to a deity) **b :** a liquid (as wine) used as a libation **2 a :** an act or instance of drinking often ceremoniously **b :** BEVERAGE; *esp* **:** a drink containing alcohol — **li·ba·tion·ary** \-shə-ˌner-ē\ *adj*

li·bec·cio \li-ˈbech-(ē-ˌ)ō\ *or* **li·bec·chio** \-ˈbek-ē-ˌō\ *n* [It] **:** a southwest wind

[1]li·bel \ˈlī-bəl\ *n* [ME, written declaration, fr. MF, fr. L *libellus,* dim. of *liber* book — more at LEAF] **1 a** *archaic* **:** a handbill esp. attacking or defaming someone **b :** a written statement in which a plaintiff in certain courts sets forth his cause of action or the relief he seeks **2 a :** a written or oral defamatory statement or representation that conveys an unjustly unfavorable impression **b (1) :** a statement or representation published without just cause and tending to expose another to public contempt (2) : defamation of a person by written or representational means (3) : the publication of blasphemous, treasonable, seditious, or obscene writings or pictures (4) : the act, tort, or crime of publishing such a libel

2**libel** *vb* **-beled** *or* **-belled; -bel·ing** *or* **-bel·ling** \-b(ə-)liŋ\ *vi* : to make libelous statements ~ *vt* : to make or publish a libel against — **li·bel·er** \-b(ə-)lər\ *n* — **li·bel·ist** \-bə-ləst\ *n*

li·bel·ant *or* **li·bel·lant** \'lī-bə-lənt\ *n* : one that institutes a suit by a libel

li·bel·ee *or* **li·bel·lee** \ˌlī-bə-'lē\ *n* : one against whom a libel has been filed in a court

li·bel·ous *or* **li·bel·lous** \'lī-b(ə-)ləs\ *adj* : constituting or including a libel : DEFAMATORY <a ~ statement>

Li·be·ra \'lē-bə-ˌrä, 'lē-brə\ *n* [L, lit., deliver, imper. of *liberare* to liberate; fr. the first word of the responsory] : a Roman Catholic funeral responsory

1**lib·er·al** \'lib(-ə)-rəl\ *adj* [ME, fr. MF, fr. L *liberalis* suitable for a freeman, generous, fr. *liber* free; akin to OE *lēodan* to grow, Gk *eleutheros* free] **1 a** : of, relating to, or based on the liberal arts <~ education> **b** *archaic* : of or befitting a man of free birth **2 a** : marked by generosity and openhandedness <a ~ giver> **b** : given or provided in a generous and openhanded way <a ~ meal> **c** : AMPLE, FULL **3** *obs* : lacking moral restraint : LICENTIOUS **4** : not literal : LOOSE <a ~ translation> **5** : BROAD-MINDED, TOLERANT; *esp* : not bound by authoritarianism, orthodoxy, or traditional forms **6 a** : of, favoring, or based upon the principles of liberalism **b** *cap* : of or constituting a political party advocating or associated with the principles of political liberalism; *esp* : of or constituting a political party in the United Kingdom associated with ideals of individual esp. economic freedom, greater individual participation in government, and constitutional, political, and administrative reforms designed to secure these objectives — **lib·er·al·ly** \-rə-lē\ *adv* — **lib·er·al·ness** *n*

syn LIBERAL, GENEROUS, BOUNTIFUL, MUNIFICENT *shared meaning element* : giving freely and unstintingly ***ant*** close

2**liberal** *n* : one who is liberal: as **a** : one who is open-minded or not strict in the observance of orthodox, traditional or established forms or ways **b** *cap* : a member or supporter of a liberal political party **c** : an advocate or adherent of liberalism esp. in individual rights

liberal arts *n pl* **1** : the medieval studies comprising the trivium and quadrivium **2** : the studies (as language, philosophy, history, literature, abstract science) in a college or university intended to provide chiefly general knowledge and to develop the general intellectual capacities (as reason and judgment) as opposed to professional or vocational skills

lib·er·al·ism \'lib(-ə)-rə-ˌliz-əm\ *n* **1** : the quality or state of being liberal **2 a** *often cap* : a movement in modern Protestantism emphasizing intellectual liberty and the spiritual and ethical content of Christianity **b** : a theory in economics emphasizing individual freedom from restraint and usu. based on free competition, the self-regulating market, and the gold standard **c** : a political philosophy based on belief in progress, the essential goodness of man, and the autonomy of the individual and standing for the protection of political and civil liberties **d** *cap* : the principles and policies of a Liberal party — **lib·er·al·ist** \-rə-ləst\ *n or adj* — **lib·er·al·is·tic** \ˌlib(-ə)-rə-'lis-tik\ *adj*

lib·er·al·i·ty \ˌlib-ə-'ral-ət-ē\ *n, pl* **-ties** : the quality or state of being liberal; *also* : an instance of this

lib·er·al·ize \'lib(-ə)-rə-ˌlīz\ *vb* **-ized; -iz·ing** *vt* : to make liberal or more liberal ~ *vi* : to become liberal or more liberal — **lib·er·al·iza·tion** \ˌlib(-ə)-rə-lə-'zā-shən\ *n* — **lib·er·al·iz·er** \'lib(-ə)-rə-ˌlī-zər\ *n*

lib·er·ate \'lib-ə-ˌrāt\ *vt* **-at·ed; -at·ing** [L *liberatus*, pp. of *liberare*, fr. *liber*] **1** : to set at liberty : RELEASE; *specif* : to free (as a country) from domination by a foreign power **2** : to free from combination **3** : to take or take over illegally <a . . . barricade was constructed . . . with material *liberated* from a nearby construction site —Thorne Dreyer> ***syn*** see FREE — **lib·er·a·tor** \-ˌāt-ər\ *n*

lib·er·a·tion \ˌlib-ə-'rā-shən\ *n* **1** : the act of liberating : the state of being liberated **2** : the action of seeking equal rights and status <women's ~> — **lib·er·a·tion·ist** \-sh(ə-)nəst\ *n*

lib·er·tar·i·an \ˌlib-ər-'ter-ē-ən\ *n* **1** : an advocate of the doctrine of free will **2** : one who upholds the principles of absolute and unrestricted liberty esp. of thought and action — **libertarian** *adj* — **lib·er·tar·i·an·ism** \-ē-ə-ˌniz-əm\ *n*

lib·er·tin·age \'lib-ər-ˌtē-nij\ *n* : LIBERTINISM

1**lib·er·tine** \'lib-ər-ˌtēn\ *n* [ME *libertyn*, freedman, fr. L *libertinus*, fr. *libertinus*, adj., of a freedman, fr. *libertus* freedman, fr. *liber*] **1** : a freethinker esp. in religious matters — usu. used disparagingly **2** : a person who is unrestrained by convention or morality; *specif* : one leading a dissolute life

2**libertine** *adj* : of, relating to, or characteristic of a libertine

lib·er·tin·ism \'lib-ər-ˌtē-ˌniz-əm, -tə-\ *n* : the quality or state of being libertine : the behavior of a libertine

lib·er·ty \'lib-ərt-ē\ *n, pl* **-ties** [ME, fr. MF *liberté*, fr. L *libertat-, libertas*, fr. *liber* free — more at LIBERAL] **1** : the quality or state of being free: **a** : the power to do as one pleases **b** : freedom from physical restraint **c** : freedom from arbitrary or despotic control **d** : the positive enjoyment of various social, political, or economic rights and privileges **e** : the power of choice **2 a** : a right or immunity enjoyed by prescription or by grant : PRIVILEGE **b** : permission esp. to go freely within specified limits **3** : an action going beyond normal limits: as **a** : a breach of etiquette or propriety : FAMILIARITY **b** : RISK, CHANCE <took foolish *liberties* with his health> **c** : a violation of rules or standard practice **d** : a distortion of fact **4** : a short authorized absence from naval duty usu. for less than 48 hours ***syn*** see FREEDOM ***ant*** restraint — **at liberty 1** : FREE **2** : at leisure : UNOCCUPIED

liberty cap *n* : a close-fitting conical cap used as a symbol of liberty by the French revolutionists and in the U.S. before 1800

liberty pole *n* : a tall flagstaff surmounted by a liberty cap or the flag of a republic and set up as a symbol of liberty

li·bid·i·nal \lə-'bid-ᵊn-əl, -'bid-nᵊl\ *adj* : of or relating to the libido — **li·bid·i·nal·ly** \-ē\ *adv*

li·bid·i·nous \-ᵊn-əs, -'bid-nəs\ *adj* [ME, fr. MF *libidineus*, fr. L *libidinosus*, fr. *libidin-, libido*] **1** : having or marked by lustful desires : LASCIVIOUS **2** : LIBIDINAL — **li·bid·i·nous·ly** *adv* — **li·bid·i·nous·ness** *n*

li·bi·do \lə-'bēd-(ˌ)ō *also* 'lib-ə-ˌdō *or* lə-'bī-(ˌ)dō\ *n, pl* **-dos** [NL *libidin-, libido*, fr. L, desire, lust, fr. *libēre* to please — more at LOVE] **1** : emotional or psychic energy that in psychoanalytic theory is derived from primitive biological urges and that is usu. goal-directed **2** : sexual drive

li·bra *for 1 & 2a* 'lī-brə *or* 'lē-brə, *for 2b* 'lē-brə *or* 'lēv-rə\ *n* [ME, fr. L (gen. *Librae*), lit., scales, pound] **1** *cap* **a** : a southern zodiacal constellation between Virgo and Scorpio represented by a pair of scales **b** (1) : the 7th sign of the zodiac in astrology — see ZODIAC table (2) : one born under this sign **2 a** *pl* **li·brae** \'lī-ˌbrē, 'lē-ˌbrī\ [L] : an ancient Roman unit of weight equal to 327.45 grams **b** [Sp & Pg, fr. L] : any of various Spanish, Portuguese, Colombian, or Venezuelan units of weight

li·brar·i·an \lī-'brer-ē-ən\ *n* : a specialist in the care or management of a library — **li·brar·i·an·ship** \-ˌship\ *n*

li·brary \'lī-ˌbrer-ē\ *n, pl* **-brar·ies** [ME, fr. ML *librarium*, fr. L, neut. of *librarius* of books, fr. *libr-, liber* book — more at LEAF] **1 a** : a place in which literary, musical, artistic, or reference materials (as books, manuscripts, recordings, or films) are kept for use but not for sale **b** : a collection of such literary, musical, artistic, or reference materials **2 a** : a collection resembling or suggesting a library <a ~ of computer programs> <every respectable liquor ~ should have two bottles of cognac —Maurice Zolotow> **b** : MORGUE 2 **3** : a series of related books issued by a publisher

library paste *n* : a thick white adhesive made from starch

library science *n* : the study or the principles and practices of library care and administration

li·bra·tion \lī-'brā-shən\ *n* [L *libration-, libratio*, fr. *libratus*, pp. of *librare* to balance, fr. *libra* scales] : an oscillation in the apparent aspect of a secondary body (as a planet or a satellite) as seen from the primary object around which it revolves — **li·bra·tion·al** \-shnəl, -shən-ᵊl\ *adj* — **li·bra·to·ry** \'lī-brə-ˌtōr-ē, -ˌtȯr-\ *adj*

li·bret·tist \lə-'bret-əst\ *n* : the writer of a libretto

li·bret·to \lə-'bret-(ˌ)ō\ *n, pl* **-tos** *or* **-ti** \-(ˌ)ē\ [It, dim. of *libro* book, fr. L *libr-, liber*] **1** : the text of a work (as an opera) for the musical theater **2** : the book containing a libretto

li·bri·form \'lī-brə-ˌfȯrm\ *adj* [L *libr-, liber* + ISV *-iform*] : resembling phloem fibers

Lib·y·an \'lib-ē-ən\ *n* **1** : a native or inhabitant of Libya **2** : a Berber language of ancient No. Africa — **Libyan** *adj*

lice *pl of* LOUSE

1**li·cense** *or* **li·cence** \'līs-ᵊn(t)s\ *n* [ME, fr. MF *licence*, fr. L *licentia*, fr. *licent-, licens*, prp. of *licēre* to be permitted; akin to Latvian *likt* to come to terms] **1 a** : permission to act **b** : freedom of action **2 a** : a permission granted by competent authority to engage in a business or occupation or in an activity otherwise unlawful **b** : a document, plate, or tag evidencing a license granted **3 a** : freedom that allows or is used with irresponsibility **b** : disregard for rules of personal conduct : LICENTIOUSNESS **4** : deviation from fact, form, or rule by an artist or writer for the sake of the effect gained ***syn*** see FREEDOM

2**license** *also* **licence** *vt* **li·censed; li·cens·ing 1** : to issue a license to **2** : to permit or authorize esp. by formal license — **li·cens·able** \-ᵊn-sə-bəl\ *adj* — **li·cens·er** \-sər\ *or* **li·cen·sor** \-sər, ˌlīs-ᵊn-'sȯ(ə)r\ *n*

licensed practical nurse *n* : a person who has undergone training and obtained a license (as from a state) conferring authorization to provide routine care for the sick

li·cens·ee \ˌlīs-ᵊn-'sē\ *n* : one that is licensed

license plate *n* : a plate or tag (as of metal) attesting that a license has been secured and usu. bearing a registration number

li·cen·sure \'līs-ᵊn-shər, -ˌshu̇(ə)r\ *n* : the granting of licenses esp. to practice a profession

li·cen·ti·ate \lī-'sen-chē-ət, *esp in sense 2* li-\ *n* [ML *licentiatus*, fr. pp. of *licentiare* to allow, fr. L *licentia*] **1** : one who has a license granted esp. by a university to practice a profession **2** : an academic degree ranking below that of doctor given by some European universities

li·cen·tious \lī-'sen-chəs\ *adj* [L *licentiosus*, fr. *licentia*] **1** : lacking legal or moral restraints; *esp* : disregarding sexual restraints **2** : marked by disregard for strict rules of correctness — **li·cen·tious·ly** *adv* — **li·cen·tious·ness** *n*

li·chee *var of* LITCHI

li·chen \'lī-kən\ *n* [L, fr. Gk *leichēn, lichēn*] **1** : any of numerous complex thallophytic plants (group Lichenes) made up of an alga and a fungus growing in symbiotic association on a solid surface (as a rock) **2** : any of several skin diseases characterized by a papular eruption — **li·chened** \-kənd\ *adj* — **li·chen·ous** \-kə-nəs\ *adj*

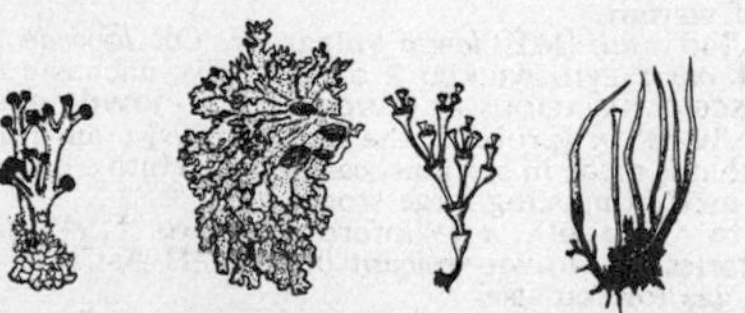

lichens 1

lich–gate *var of* LYCH-GATE

licht \'likt\ *Scot var of* LIGHT

lic·it \'lis-ət\ *adj* [MF *licite*, fr. L *licitus*, fr. pp. of *licēre* to be permitted — more at LICENSE] : conforming to the requirements of the law : not forbidden by law : PERMISSIBLE ***syn*** see LAWFUL ***ant*** illicit — **lic·it·ly** *adv*

1lick \'lik\ *vb* [ME *licken,* fr. OE *liccian;* akin to OHG *leckōn* to lick, L *lingere,* Gk *leichein*] *vt* **1 a** (1) : to draw the tongue over <~ a stamp> (2) : to flicker over like a tongue **b** : to take into the mouth with the tongue : LAP **2 a** : to strike repeatedly : THRASH **b** : to get the better of : OVERCOME <has ~*ed* every problem> ~ *vi* **1** : to lap with or as if with the tongue **2** : to dart like a tongue <flames ~*ing* out of windows> **3** : to move at top speed — **lick into shape** : to put into proper form or condition — **lick one's wounds** : to recover from injury

2lick *n* **1 a** : an act or instance of licking **b** : a small amount : BIT **c** : a hasty careless effort **2 a** : a sharp hit : BLOW **b** : OPPORTUNITY, TURN — usu. used in pl. **3** : a place (as a salt spring) to which animals regularly resort to lick a salt deposit **4** : a musical figure; *specif* : an interpolated and usu. improvised figure or flourish — **lick and a promise** : a perfunctory performance of a task

lick·er·ish \'lik-(ə-)rish\ *adj* [alter. of *lickerous,* fr. ME *likerous,* fr. (assumed) ONF, fr. ONF *leckeur* lecher; akin to OF *lecheor* lecher] **1 a** *archaic* : fond of good food : eager to taste or enjoy **b** : GREEDY, DESIROUS **2** *obs* : tempting to the appetite **3** : LECHEROUS — **lick·er·ish·ly** *adv* — **lick·er·ish·ness** *n*

lick·e·ty-split \ˌlik-ət-ē-'split\ *adv* [prob. irreg. fr. **1***lick* + *split*] : at great speed

lick·ing *n* **1** : a sound thrashing : DRUBBING **2** : a severe setback : DEFEAT

lick·spit·tle \'lik-ˌspit-ᵊl\ *n* : a fawning subordinate : TOADY

lic·o·rice \'lik(-ə)-rish, -rəs\ *n* [ME *licorice,* fr. OF, fr. LL *liquiritia,* alter. of L *glycyrrhiza,* fr. Gk *glykyrrhiza,* fr. *glykys* sweet + *rhiza* root — more at ROOT] **1** : a European leguminous plant (*Glycyrrhiza glabra*) with pinnate leaves and spikes of blue flowers **2 a** : the dried root of licorice; *also* : an extract of this used esp. in medicine, brewing, and confectionery **b** : a candy flavored with licorice

lic·tor \'lik-tər\ *n* [L] : a Roman officer who bears the fasces as the insignia of his office and whose duties include accompanying the chief magistrates in public appearances

1lid \'lid\ *n* [ME, fr. OE *hlid;* akin to OHG *hlit* cover, OE *hlinian* to lean — more at LEAN] **1** : a movable cover for the opening of a hollow container (as a vessel or box) **2** : EYELID **3** : the operculum in mosses **4** *slang* : HAT **5** : RESTRAINT, CURB <put a ~ on further release of information> **6** : an ounce of marijuana

2lid *vt* **lid·ded; lid·ding** : to cover or supply with a lid

li·dar \'lī-ˌdär\ *n* [*li*ght + ra*dar*] : a device that is similar in operation to radar but emits pulsed laser light instead of microwaves

lid·less \'lid-ləs\ *adj* **1** : having no lid **2** *archaic* : WATCHFUL

li·do \'lēd-(ˌ)ō\ *n, pl* **lidos** [*Lido,* Italy] : a fashionable beach resort

li·do·caine \'līd-ə-ˌkān\ *n* [acetani*lid* + *-o-* + *-caine*] : a crystalline compound that is used in the form of its hydrochloride as a local anesthetic

1lie \'lī\ *vi* **lay** \'lā\; **lain** \'lān\; **ly·ing** \'lī-iŋ\ [ME *lien,* fr. OE *licgan;* akin to OHG *ligen* to lie, L *lectus* bed, Gk *lechos*] **1 a** : to be or to stay at rest in a horizontal position : be prostrate : REST, RECLINE <~ motionless> <~ asleep> **b** : to assume a horizontal position — often used with *down* **c** *archaic* : to reside temporarily : stay for the night : LODGE **d** *archaic* : to have sexual intercourse — used with *with* **e** : to stay in concealment <~ in wait> **2** : to be in a helpless or defenseless state <the town *lay* at the mercy of the invaders> **3** *of an inanimate thing* : to be or remain in a flat or horizontal position upon a broad support <books *lying* on the table> **4** : to have direction : EXTEND <the route *lay* to the west> **5 a** : to occupy a certain relative place or position <hills ~ behind us> **b** : to have a place in relation to something else <the real reason ~*s* deeper> **c** : to have an effect through mere presence, weight, or relative position <remorse *lay* heavily on him> **d** : to be sustainable or admissible **6** : to remain at anchor or becalmed **7** : REMAIN; *esp* : to remain unused, unsought, or uncared for — **li·er** \'lī(-ə)r\ *n* — **lie low 1** : to lie prostrate, defeated, or disgraced **2** : to stay in hiding : strive to avoid notice **3** : to bide one's time : remain secretly ready for action

2lie *n* **1** : the position or situation in which something lies **2** *chiefly Brit* : LAY 6 **3** : the haunt of an animal (as a fish) : COVERT **4** *Brit* : an act or instance of lying or resting

3lie *vb* **lied; ly·ing** \'lī-iŋ\ [ME *lien,* fr. OE *lēogan;* akin to OHG *liogan* to lie, OSlav *lŭgati*] *vi* **1** : to make an untrue statement with intent to deceive **2** : to create a false or misleading impression ~ *vt* : to affect by telling lies <managed to ~ his way out of trouble>
syn LIE, PREVARICATE, EQUIVOCATE, PALTER, FIB *shared meaning element* : to be untruthful

4lie *n* **1 a** : an assertion of something known or believed by the speaker to be untrue with intent to deceive **b** : an untrue or inaccurate statement that may or may not be believed true by the speaker **2** : something that misleads or deceives **3** : a charge of lying

lieb·frau·milch \'lēp-ˌfraů-ˌmilk\ *n* [G, alter. of *liebfrauenmilch,* fr. *Liebfrauenstift,* religious foundation in Worms, Germany + *milch* milk] : a dry white Rhine wine; *also* : a similar wine made elsewhere

lie by *vi* : to remain inactive : REST

lied \'lēt\ *n, pl* **lie·der** \'lēd-ər\ [G, song, fr. OHG *liod* — more at LAUD] : a German art song esp. of the 19th century

Lie·der·kranz \'lēd-ər-ˌkran(t)s, -ˌkrän(t)s\ *trademark* — used for a soft surface-ripened cheese with a fairly strong pungent flavor and odor

lie detector *n* : an instrument for detecting physical evidences of the tension that accompanies lying

lie down *vi* **1** : to submit meekly or abjectly to defeat, disappointment, or insult <won't take that criticism *lying down*> **2** : to fail to perform or to neglect one's part deliberately <*lying down* on the job>

1lief \'lēf, 'lēv\ *adj* [ME *lief, lef,* fr. OE *lēof;* akin to OE *lufu* love — more at LOVE] **1** *archaic* : DEAR, BELOVED **2** *archaic* : WILLING, GLAD

2lief \'lēv, 'lēf\ *adv* : SOON, GLADLY <I'd as ~ go as not>

1liege \'lēj\ *adj* [ME, fr. OF, fr. LL *laeticus,* fr. *laetus* serf, of Gmc origin; akin to OFris *let* serf] **1 a** : having the right to feudal allegiance or service <his ~ lord> **b** : obligated to render feudal allegiance and service **2** : FAITHFUL, LOYAL <master of his own impulses, as a soloist should be, and not ~ to the conductor —Irving Kolodin>

2liege *n* **1 a** : a vassal bound to feudal service and allegiance **b** : a loyal subject **2** : a feudal superior to whom allegiance and service are due

liege man *n* **1** : VASSAL **2** : a devoted follower

lie-in \'lī-ˌin\ *n* : an act of lying down (as on a public thoroughfare) in organized protest and as a means of forcing compliance with demands

lie in \(ˈ)lī-'in\ *vi* : to be confined to give birth to a child

lien \'lēn, 'lē-ən\ *n* [MF, tie, band, fr. L *ligamen,* fr. *ligare* to bind — more at LIGATURE] **1** : a charge upon real or personal property for the satisfaction of some debt or duty ordinarily arising by operation of law **2** : the security interest created by a mortgage

lie off *vi* **1** : to keep a little away from the shore or another ship **2** : to cease work for a time **3** : to hold back in the early part of a race

lie over *vi* : to await disposal or attention at a later time <several jobs *lying over* from last week>

li·erne \lē-'ərn, -'e(ə)rn\ *n* [F] : a rib in Gothic vaulting that passes from one intersection of the principal ribs to another

lie to \(ˈ)lī-'tü\ *vi, of a ship* : to stay stationary with head to windward

lieu \'lü\ *n* [MF, fr. L *locus* — more at STALL] *archaic* : PLACE, STEAD — **in lieu** : INSTEAD — **in lieu of** : in the place of : instead of

lie up *vi* **1** : to stay in bed or at rest **2** : to go into or remain in a dock

lieut *abbr* lieutenant

lieu·ten·an·cy \lü-'ten-ən-sē, *Brit* le(f)-'ten-\ *n* : the office, rank, or commission of a lieutenant

lieu·ten·ant \-'ten-ənt\ *n* [ME, fr. MF, fr. *lieu* + *tenant* holding, fr. *tenir* to hold, fr. L *tenēre* — more at THIN] **1 a** : an official empowered to act for a higher official **b** : a representative of another in the performance of duty : ASSISTANT **2 a** (1) : FIRST LIEUTENANT (2) : SECOND LIEUTENANT **b** : a commissioned officer in the navy or coast guard ranking above a lieutenant junior grade and below a lieutenant commander **c** : a fire or police department officer ranking below a captain

lieutenant colonel *n* : a commissioned officer in the army, air force, or marine corps ranking above a major and below a colonel

lieutenant commander *n* : a commissioned officer in the navy or coast guard ranking above a lieutenant and below a commander

lieutenant general *n* : a commissioned officer in the army, air force, or marine corps who ranks above a major general and whose insignia is three stars

lieutenant governor *n* : a deputy or subordinate governor: as **a** : an elected official serving as deputy to the governor of an American state **b** : the formal head of the government of a Canadian province appointed by the federal government as the representative of the crown — **lieutenant governorship** *n*

lieutenant junior grade *n, pl* **lieutenants junior grade** : a commissioned officer in the navy or coast guard ranking above an ensign and below a lieutenant

1life \'līf\ *n, pl* **lives** \'līvz\ [ME *lif,* fr. OE *līf;* akin to OE *libban* to live — more at LIVE] **1 a** : the quality that distinguishes a vital and functional being from a dead body **b** : a principle or force that is considered to underlie the distinctive quality of animate beings — compare VITALISM 1 **c** : an organismic state characterized by capacity for metabolism, growth, reaction to stimuli, and reproduction **2 a** : the sequence of physical and mental experiences that make up the existence of an individual **b** : one or more aspects of the process of living <sex ~ of the frog> **3** : BIOGRAPHY 1 **4** : spiritual existence transcending physical death **5 a** : the period from birth to death **b** : a specific phase of earthly existence <adult ~> **c** : the period from an event until death <a judge appointed for ~> **d** : a sentence of imprisonment for the remainder of a convict's life **6** : a way or manner of living **7** : LIVELIHOOD **8** : a vital or living being; *specif* : PERSON <many *lives* were lost in the disaster> **9** : an animating and shaping force or principle **10** : SPIRIT, ANIMATION <there was no ~ in her dancing> **11** : the form or pattern of something existing in reality <painted from ~> **12** : the period of usefulness of something <the expected ~ of flashlight batteries> **13** : the period of existence (as of a subatomic particle) — compare HALF-LIFE **14** : a property (as resilience or elasticity) of an inanimate substance or object resembling the animate quality of a living being **15** : living beings (as of a particular kind or environment) <forest ~> **16 a** : human activities **b** : animate activity and movement <stirrings of ~> **c** : the activities of a given sphere, area, or time <the political ~ of the country> **17** : one providing interest and vigor <~ of the party> **18** : another chance given to one likely to lose **19** *cap, Christian Science* : GOD 1b

2life *adj* **1** : of or relating to animate being **2** : LIFELONG <a ~ member> **3** : using a living model <a ~ class> **4** : of, relating to, or provided by life insurance <a ~ policy>

life-and-death *also* **life-or-death** *adj* : involving or culminating in life or death : having vital importance as if involving life or death

life belt *n* **1 :** a life preserver in the form of a buoyant belt **2 :** SAFETY BELT
life·blood \'līf-'bləd, -ˌbləd\ *n* **1 :** blood regarded as the seat of vitality **2 :** a vital or life-giving force <freedom of inquiry is the ~ of a university>
life·boat \-ˌbōt\ *n* **1 :** a strong buoyant boat designed for use in saving lives at sea **2 :** a boat carried by a ship for use in an emergency
life buoy *n* **:** a ring-shaped life preserver
life cycle *n* **1 :** the series of stages in form and functional activity through which an organism passes between successive recurrences of a specified primary stage **2 :** LIFE HISTORY 1a **3 :** a series of stages through which an individual, group, or culture passes during its lifetime
life expectancy *n* **:** an expected number of years of life based on statistical probability
life–force \'līf-'fō(ə)rs, -'fȯ(ə)rs\ *n* **:** ÉLAN VITAL
life form *n* **:** the body form that characterizes a kind of organism (as a species) at maturity
life·ful \'līf-fəl\ *adj, archaic* **:** full of or giving vitality
life–giv·ing \-ˌgiv-iŋ\ *adj* **:** giving or having power to give life and spirit **:** INVIGORATING
life·guard \-ˌgärd\ *n* **:** a usu. expert swimmer employed (as at a beach or a pool) to safeguard other swimmers — **lifeguard** *vi*
life history *n* **1 a :** a history of the changes through which an organism passes in its development from the primary stage to its natural death **b :** one series of the changes in a life history **2 :** the history of an individual's development in his social environment
life insurance *n* **:** insurance providing for payment of a stipulated sum to a designated beneficiary upon death of the insured
life jacket *n* **:** a life preserver in the form of a buoyant vest
life·less \'lī-fləs\ *adj* **:** having no life: **a :** DEAD **b :** INANIMATE **c :** lacking qualities expressive of life and vigor **:** DULL <~ voice> **d :** destitute of living beings — **life·less·ly** *adv* — **life·less·ness** *n*
life·like \'lī-ˌflīk\ *adj* **:** accurately representing or imitating real life <a ~ portrait> — **life·like·ness** *n*
life·line \'lī-ˌflīn\ *n* **1 a :** a line to which persons may cling to save or protect their lives; *esp* **:** one stretched along the deck or from the yards of a ship **b :** a line attached to a diver's helmet by which he is lowered and raised **c :** a rope line for lowering a person to safety **2 :** something (as a land, sea, or air route) regarded as indispensable for the maintaining or protection of life
life·long \'lī-ˌflȯŋ\ *adj* **1 :** lasting or continuing through life **2 :** LONG-STANDING
life·man·ship \'līf-mən-ˌship\ *n* **:** the skill or practice of achieving superiority or an appearance of superiority over others (as in conversation) by perplexing and demoralizing them
life net *n* **:** a strong net or sheet (as of canvas) used (as by firemen) to catch a person jumping from a burning building
life of Ri·ley \-'rī-lē\ **:** a carefree comfortable way of living
life peer *n* **:** a British peer whose title is not hereditary — **life peerage** *n* — **life peeress** *n*
life plant *n* **:** AIR PLANT
life preserver *n* **1 :** a device (as a life jacket or life buoy) designed to save a person from drowning by buoying up the body while in the water **2** *chiefly Brit* **:** BLACKJACK 3
lif·er \'lī-fər\ *n* **1 :** a person sentenced to imprisonment for life **2 :** a person who makes a career of one of the armed forces
life raft *n* **:** a raft usu. made of wood or an inflatable material and designed for use by people forced into the water
life·sav·er \'līf-ˌsā-vər\ *n* **1 :** one trained to save lives of drowning persons **2 :** something at once timely and effective in the relief of distress
[1]**life·sav·ing** \-viŋ\ *n* **:** the skill or practice of saving or protecting the lives esp. of drowning persons
[2]**lifesaving** *adj* **:** designed for or used in saving lives <~ drugs>
life science *n* **:** a branch of science (as biology, medicine, anthropology, or sociology) that deals with living organisms and life processes — usu. used in pl. — **life scientist** *n*
life–size \'līf-'sīz\ *or* **life–sized** \-'sīzd\ *adj* **:** of natural size **:** of the size of the original <a ~ statue>
life span *n* **1 :** the duration of existence of an individual **2 :** the average length of life of a kind of organism or of a material object esp. in a particular environment or under specified circumstances
life–style \'līf-'stī(ə)l\ *n* **:** an individual's typical way of life
life–support system *n* **:** a system that provides all or some of the items (as oxygen, food, water, control of temperature and pressure, disposition of carbon dioxide and body wastes) necessary for maintaining (as in a spacecraft or on the surface of the moon) the life and health of a person
life table *n* **:** MORTALITY TABLE
life·time \'līf-ˌtīm\ *n* **1 :** the duration of the existence of a living being or thing **2 :** the duration of the existence of an ion or subatomic particle
life vest *n* **:** LIFE JACKET
life·way \-ˌwā\ *n* **:** LIFE 6
life·work \-'wərk\ *n* **:** the entire or principal work of one's lifetime; *also* **:** a work extending over a lifetime
life zone *n* **:** a biogeographic zone
LIFO *abbr* last in, first out
[1]**lift** \'lift\ *n* [ME, fr. OE *lyft*] *chiefly Scot* **:** HEAVENS, SKY
[2]**lift** *vb* [ME *liften*, fr. ON *lypta*; akin to OE *lyft* air — more at LOFT] *vt* **1 a :** to raise from a lower to a higher position **:** ELEVATE **b :** to raise in rank or condition **c :** to raise in rate or amount **2 :** to put an end to (a blockade or siege) by withdrawing investing forces **3 :** REVOKE, RESCIND <~ an embargo> **4 a :** STEAL <had her purse ~*ed*> **b :** PLAGIARIZE **c :** to take out of normal setting <~ a word out of context> **5 :** to take up (as a root crop or transplants) from the ground **6 :** to pay off (an obligation) <~ a mortgage> **7 a :** to shift (artillery fire) from one area to another **b :** to withhold (artillery fire) from an area **8 :** to move from one place to another (as by aircraft) **:** TRANSPORT **9 :** to take up (a fingerprint) from a surface ~ *vi* **1 a :** ASCEND, RISE **b :** to appear elevated (as above surrounding objects) **2 a :** to disperse upward <until the fog ~*s*> **b :** to cease temporarily — used of rain — **lift·able** \'lif-tə-bəl\ *adj* — **lift·er** *n*
syn LIFT, RAISE, REAR, ELEVATE, HOIST, HEAVE, BOOST *shared meaning element* **:** to remove from a lower to a higher place or position ***ant*** lower
[3]**lift** *n* **1 :** the amount that may be lifted at one time **:** LOAD **2 a :** the action or an instance of lifting **b :** the action or an instance of rising **c :** elevated carriage (as of a part of the body) **d :** the lifting up of a dancer usu. by her partner **3 :** a device (as a handle or latch) for lifting **4 :** an act of stealing **:** THEFT **5 a :** ASSISTANCE, HELP **b :** a ride along one's way **6:** one of the layers forming the heel of a shoe **7 :** a rise or advance in position or condition **8 :** a slight rise or elevation **9 :** the distance or extent to which something rises **10 :** an apparatus or machine used for hoisting: as **a :** a set of pumps used in a mine **b** *chiefly Brit* **:** ELEVATOR 1b **c :** an apparatus for raising an automobile (as for repair) **d :** SKI LIFT **11 a :** an elevating influence **b :** an elevation of the spirit **12 :** the component of the total aerodynamic force acting on an airplane or airfoil that is perpendicular to the relative wind and that for an airplane constitutes the upward force that opposes the pull of gravity **13 :** an organized movement of men, equipment, or supplies by some form of transportation; *esp* **:** AIRLIFT
lift·man \'lift-ˌman\ *n, Brit* **:** an elevator operator
lift–off \'lif-ˌtȯf\ *n* **:** a vertical takeoff by an aircraft or a rocket vehicle or missile
lift truck *n* **:** a small truck equipped for lifting and transporting loads
lig·a·ment \'lig-ə-mənt\ *n* [ME, fr. ML & L; ML *ligamentum*, fr. L, band, tie, fr. *ligare*] **1 :** a tough band of tissue connecting the articular extremities of bones or supporting an organ in place **2 :** a connecting or unifying bond <the law of nations, the great ~ of mankind —Edmund Burke> — **lig·a·men·ta·ry** \ˌlig-ə-'ment-ə-rē, -'men-trē\ *adj* — **lig·a·men·tous** \-'ment-əs\ *adj*
li·gan \'lī-gən, 'lig-ən\ *var of* LAGAN
li·gand \'lig-ənd, 'līg-\ *n* [L *ligandus*, gerundive of *ligare*] **:** a group, ion, or molecule coordinated to a central atom in a complex
li·gase \'lī-ˌgās, -ˌgāz\ *n* [ISV *lig-* (fr. L *ligare*) + *-ase*] **:** SYNTHETASE
li·gate \'lī-ˌgāt, lī-'\ *vt* **li·gat·ed; li·gat·ing** [L *ligatus*] **:** to tie with a ligature
li·ga·tion \lī-'gā-shən\ *n* **1 :** an act of ligating **2 :** something that binds **:** LIGATURE
lig·a·ture \'lig-ə-ˌchu̇(ə)r, -chər, -ˌt(y)u̇(ə)r\ *n* [ME, fr. MF, fr. LL *ligatura*, fr. L *ligatus*, pp. of *ligare* to bind, tie; akin to MHG *geleich* joint, Alb *lith* I tie] **1 a :** something that is used to bind; *specif* **:** a filament (as a thread) used in surgery **b :** something that unites or connects **:** BOND **2 :** the action of binding or tying **3 :** a compound note in mensural notation indicating a group of musical notes to be sung to one syllable **4 :** a printed or written character (as *æ*) consisting of two or more letters or characters joined together
[1]**light** \'līt\ *n* [ME, fr. OE *lēoht*; akin to OHG *lioht* light, L *luc-*, *lux* light, *lucēre* to shine, Gk *leukos* white] **1 a :** something that makes vision possible **b :** the sensation aroused by stimulation of the visual receptors **:** BRIGHTNESS **c :** an electromagnetic radiation in the wavelength range including infrared, visible, ultraviolet, and X rays and traveling in a vacuum with a speed of about 186,281 miles per second; *specif* **:** the part of this range that is visible to the human eye **2 a :** DAYLIGHT **b :** DAWN **3 :** a source of light: as **a :** a celestial body **b :** CANDLE **c :** an electric light **4** *archaic* **:** SIGHT 4a **5 a :** spiritual illumination **b :** INNER LIGHT **c :** ENLIGHTENMENT **d :** TRUTH **6 a :** public knowledge <facts brought to ~> **b :** a particular aspect or appearance presented to view <now saw the matter in a different ~> **7 :** a particular illumination **8 :** something that enlightens or informs <he shed some ~ on the problem> **9 :** a medium (as a window or windowpane) through which light is admitted **10** *pl* **:** a set of principles, standards, or opinions <worship according to one's ~*s* —Adrienne Koch> **11 :** a noteworthy person in a particular place or field **:** LUMINARY **12 :** a particular expression of the eye **13 a :** LIGHTHOUSE, BEACON **b** (1) **:** TRAFFIC SIGNAL (2) **:** a green traffic light **14 :** the representation of light in art **15 :** a flame for lighting something — **in the light of 1 :** from the point of view of **2** *or* **in light of :** in view of
[2]**light** *adj* **1 :** having light **:** BRIGHT <a ~ airy room> **2 a :** not dark, intense, or swarthy in color or coloring **:** PALE **b** *of colors* **:** medium in saturation and high in lightness <~ blue> **3** *of coffee* **:** served with cream or milk
[3]**light** *vb* **light·ed** *or* **lit** \'lit\; **light·ing** *vi* **1 :** to become light **:** BRIGHTEN — usu. used with *up* <her face *lit up*> **2 :** to take fire **3 :** to ignite something (as a cigarette) — often used with *up* ~ *vt* **1 :** to set fire to **2 a :** to conduct with a light **:** GUIDE **b :** ILLUMINATE <rockets ~ up the sky> **c :** ANIMATE, BRIGHTEN <a smile *lit* up her face>
syn LIGHT, KINDLE, IGNITE, FIRE *shared meaning element* **:** to start something to burn
[4]**light** *adj* [ME, fr. OE *lēoht*; akin to OHG *līhti* light, L *levis*, Gk *elachys* small] **1 a :** having little weight **:** not heavy **b :** designed to carry a comparatively small load <a ~ truck> **c :** having relatively little weight in proportion to bulk <aluminum is a ~ metal> **d :** containing less than the legal, standard, or usual weight <a ~ coin> **2 a :** of little importance **:** TRIVIAL **b :** not abundant **:** SCANTY <~ rain> **3 a :** easily disturbed <a ~ sleeper> **b :** exerting a minimum of force or pressure **:** GENTLE <a ~ touch> **c :** resulting from a very slight pressure **:** FAINT <~ print> **4 a :** easily endurable <a ~ illness> **b :** requiring little effort <~ work> **5 :** capable of moving swiftly or nimbly <~ on his feet> **6 a :** FRIVOLOUS <~ conduct> **b :** lacking in stability **:** CHANGEABLE <~ opinions> **c :** sexually promiscuous **7 :** free from care **:** CHEERFUL **8 :** intended chiefly to entertain <~ verse> **9 a :** having a comparatively low alcoholic content

<~ wines> **b :** having a relatively mild flavor **10 a :** easily digested <a ~ soup> **b :** well leavened <a ~ crust> **11 :** lightly armed or equipped <~ cavalry> **12 :** coarse and sandy or easily pulverized <~ soil> **13 :** DIZZY, GIDDY <felt ~ in the head> **14 a :** carrying little or no cargo <the ship returned ~> **b :** producing goods for direct consumption by the consumer <~ industry> **15 :** not bearing a stress or accent <a ~ syllable> **16 :** having a clear soft quality <a ~ voice> **17 :** being in debt to the pot in a poker game <three chips ~> — **light·ish** \-ish\ *adj*

[5]light *adv* **1 :** LIGHTLY **2 :** with little baggage <travel ~>

[6]light *vi* **light·ed** *or* **lit** \ˈlit\; **light·ing** [ME *lighten,* fr. OE *līhtan;* akin to OE *lēoht* light in weight] **1 :** DISMOUNT **2 :** SETTLE, ALIGHT <a bird *lit* on the lawn> **3 :** to fall unexpectedly **4 :** to arrive by chance : HAPPEN <*lit* upon a solution> — **light into :** to attack forcefully <I *lit into* that food until I'd finished off the heel of the loaf —Helen Eustis>

light adaptation *n* **:** the process including contraction of the pupil and decrease in visual purple by which the eye adapts to conditions of increased illumination

light–adapt·ed \ˈlīt-ə-ˌdap-təd\ *adj* **:** adjusted for vision in bright light : having undergone light adaptation

light air *n* **:** wind having a speed of 1 to 3 miles per hour

light bread \ˈlīt-ˌbred\ *n* [[2]*light*] *chiefly South & Midland* **:** bread in loaves made from white flour leavened with yeast

light breeze *n* **:** wind having a speed of 4 to 7 miles per hour

light bulb *n* **:** INCANDESCENT LAMP

light chain *n* **:** either of the two smaller of the four polypeptide chains comprising antibodies — compare HEAVY CHAIN

[1]light·en \ˈlīt-ᵊn\ *vb* **light·ened; light·en·ing** \ˈlīt-niŋ, -ᵊn-iŋ\ [ME *lightenen,* fr. *light*] *vt* **1 :** to make light or clear : ILLUMINATE **2** *archaic* **:** ENLIGHTEN **3 :** to make (as a color) lighter ~ *vi* **1 a :** to shine brightly **b :** to grow lighter : BRIGHTEN **2 :** to give out flashes of lightning — **light·en·er** \ˈlīt-nər, -ᵊn-ər\ *n*

[2]lighten *vb* **light·ened; light·en·ing** \ˈlīt-niŋ, -ᵊn-iŋ\ *vt* **1 a :** to relieve of a burden in whole or in part <the news ~*ed* his mind> **b :** to reduce in weight or quantity : LESSEN <~ his duties> **c :** to make less wearisome : ALLEVIATE <~ his sorrow> **2 :** CHEER, GLADDEN ~ *vi* **1 :** to become lighter or less burdensome **2 :** to become more cheerful <his mood ~*ed*> ***syn*** see RELIEVE — **light·en·er** \ˈlīt-nər, -ᵊn-ər\ *n*

[1]light·ter \ˈlīt-ər\ *n* [ME, fr. (assumed) MD *lichter,* fr. MD *lichten* to unload; akin to OE *lēoht* light in weight] **:** a large usu. flat-bottomed barge used esp. in unloading or loading ships

[2]lighter *vt* **:** to convey by a lighter

[3]light·er \ˈlīt-ər\ *n* **1 :** one that lights or sets a fire **2 :** a device for lighting a fire; *esp* **:** a mechanical or electrical device used for lighting cigarettes, cigars, or pipes

ligh·ter·age \ˈlīt-ə-rij\ *n* **1 :** a price paid for lightering **2 :** the loading, unloading, or transportation of goods by means of a lighter **3 :** boats engaged in lightering

lighter–than–air *adj* **:** of less weight than the air displaced

light·face \ˈlīt-ˌfās\ *n* **:** a typeface having comparatively light thin lines; *also* **:** printing in lightface — **light·faced** \-ˈfāst\ *adj*

light·fast \-ˌfast\ *adj* **:** resistant to light and esp. to sunlight; *esp* **:** colorfast to light — **light·fast·ness** \-ˌfas(t)-nəs\ *n*

light–fin·gered \-ˈfiŋ-gərd\ *adj* **1 :** adroit in stealing esp. by picking pockets **2 :** having a light and dexterous touch : NIMBLE — **light–fin·gered·ness** *n*

light–foot·ed \-ˈfu̇t-əd\ *also* **light–foot** \-ˌfu̇t\ *adj* **1 :** having a light and springy step **2 :** moving gracefully and nimbly

light–hand·ed \-ˈhan-dəd\ *adj* **:** having a light or delicate touch : FACILE — **light–hand·ed·ness** *n*

light–head·ed \-ˈhed-əd\ *adj* **1 :** mentally disoriented : DIZZY **2 :** lacking in maturity or seriousness : FRIVOLOUS — **light–head·ed·ly** *adv* — **light–head·ed·ness** *n*

light·heart·ed \-ˈhärt-əd\ *adj* **1 :** free from care or anxiety : GAY **2 :** cheerfully optimistic and hopeful : EASYGOING ***syn*** see GLAD ***ant*** despondent — **light·heart·ed·ly** *adv* — **light·heart·ed·ness** *n*

light heavyweight *n* **:** a boxer weighing more than 160 but not more than 175 pounds — called also *light heavy*

light·house \ˈlīt-ˌhau̇s\ *n* **:** a structure (as a tower) with a powerful light that gives a continuous or intermittent signal to navigators

light housekeeping *n* **1 :** domestic work restricted to the less laborious duties **2 :** housekeeping in quarters with limited facilities for cooking

light·ing \ˈlīt-iŋ\ *n* **1 a :** ILLUMINATION **b :** IGNITION **2 :** an artificial supply of light or the apparatus providing it

light·less \ˈlīt-ləs\ *adj* **1 :** receiving no light : DARK **2 :** giving no light

light·ly \ˈlīt-lē\ *adv* **1 :** with little weight or force : GENTLY **2 :** in a small degree or amount <~ salted food> **3 :** with little difficulty : EASILY **4 :** in an agile manner : NIMBLY, SWIFTLY **5 :** with indifference or carelessness : UNCONCERNEDLY <the problem should not be passed over ~ —Shelly Halpern> **6 :** GAILY, CHEERFULLY <offenses not ~ forgiven>

light machine gun *n* **:** an air-cooled machine gun of not more than .30 caliber

light meter *n* **:** a small and often portable device for measuring illumination; *esp* **:** EXPOSURE METER

light–mind·ed \ˈlīt-ˈmīn-dəd\ *adj* **:** lacking in seriousness : FRIVOLOUS — **light–mind·ed·ly** *adv* — **light–mind·ed·ness** *n*

[1]light·ness \-nəs\ *n* **1 :** the quality or state of being illuminated : ILLUMINATION **2 :** the attribute of object colors by which the object appears to reflect or transmit more or less of the incident light

[2]lightness *n* **1 :** the quality or state of being light in weight **2 :** lack of seriousness and stability of character often accompanied by casual heedlessness **3 a :** the quality or state of being nimble **b :** an ease and gaiety of style or manner **4 :** a lack of weightiness or force : DELICACY

syn LIGHTNESS, LEVITY, FRIVOLITY, FLIPPANCY, VOLATILITY *shared meaning element* **:** gaiety or indifference where seriousness and attention are called for ***ant*** seriousness

[1]light·ning \ˈlīt-niŋ\ *n* [ME, fr. gerund of *lightenen* to lighten] **1 :** the flashing of light produced by a discharge of atmospheric electricity from one cloud to another or between a cloud and the earth; *also* **:** the discharge itself **2 :** a sudden stroke of fortune

[2]lightning *adj* **:** having or moving with or as if with the speed and suddenness of lightning

[3]lightning *vi* **light·ninged; lightning :** to discharge a flash of lightning

lightning arrester *n* **:** a device for protecting an electrical apparatus or a radio set from injury by lightning

lightning bug *n* **:** FIREFLY

lightning rod *n* **:** a metallic rod set up on a building or mast and connected with the moist earth or water below to diminish the chances of destructive effect by lightning

light–o'–love \ˌlīt-ᵊl-ˈəv\ *n, pl* **light–o'–loves 1 :** PROSTITUTE **2 :** LOVER, PARAMOUR

light opera *n* **:** OPERETTA

light out *vi* [[6]*light*] **:** to leave in a hurry <*lit out* for home as soon as he could>

light pen *n* **:** a pen-shaped device for direct interaction with a computer through a cathode-ray tube display — called also *light pencil*

light·plane \ˈlīt-ˈplān\ *n* **:** a small and comparatively lightweight airplane; *esp* **:** a privately owned passenger airplane

light·proof \ˈlīt-ˈprüf\ *adj* **:** impenetrable by light

light quantum *n* **:** PHOTON; *esp* **:** one of luminous radiation

light red *n* **:** any of various pale red or reddish orange pigments; *esp* **:** a calcined yellow ocher

lights \ˈlīts\ *n pl* [ME *lightes,* fr. *light* light in weight] **:** the lungs esp. of a slaughtered animal

light·ship \ˈlīt-ˌship\ *n* **:** a ship equipped with a brilliant light and moored at a place dangerous to navigation

light show *n* **:** a kaleidoscopic display of colored lights, slides, and film loops designed to imitate the effects of psychedelic drugs

[1]light·some \ˈlīt-səm\ *adj* **1 :** AIRY, NIMBLE <walked with a ~, buoyant step —O. E. Rölvaag> **2 :** free from care : LIGHTHEARTED — **light·some·ly** *adv* — **light·some·ness** *n*

[2]lightsome *adj* **1 :** giving light : LUMINOUS **2 :** well lighted : BRIGHT

lights–out \ˈlīt-ˈsau̇t\ *n* **1 :** a command or signal for putting out lights **2 :** a prescribed bedtime for persons living under discipline

light–struck \ˈlīt-ˌstrək\ *adj* **:** fogged by accidental exposure to light — used of a photographic material

light·tight \ˈlīt-ˌtīt\ *adj* **:** LIGHTPROOF

light trap *n* **1 :** a device that allows movement of a sliding part or passage of a person (as into a darkroom) but excludes light **2 :** a device for collecting or destroying insects that consists of a bright light in association with a trapping or killing medium

[1]light·weight \ˈlīt-ˌwāt\ *n* **1 :** one of less than average weight; *specif* **:** a boxer who weighs more than 126 but not more than 135 pounds **2 :** one of little consequence <shows up its author as a ~ —C. J. Rolo>

[2]lightweight *adj* **1 :** of, relating to, or characteristic of a lightweight <the ~ championship> **2 :** having less than average weight **3 :** lacking in earnestness or profundity : INCONSEQUENTIAL

light·wood \ˈlīt-ˌwu̇d, ˈlīt-əd\ *n, chiefly South* **:** wood used for kindling; *esp* **:** coniferous wood abounding in pitch

light–year \ˈlīt-ˌyi(ə)r\ *n* **:** a unit of length in interstellar astronomy equal to the distance that light travels in one year in a vacuum or about 5,878,000,000,000 miles

lign- *or* **ligni-** *or* **ligno-** *comb form* [L *lign-, ligni-,* fr. *lignum*] **:** wood <*lign*in> <*ligno*cellulose>

lig·ne·ous \ˈlig-nē-əs\ *adj* [L *ligneus,* fr. *lignum* wood, fr. *legere* to gather — more at LEGEND] **:** of or resembling wood : WOODY

lig·ni·fy \ˈlig-nə-ˌfī\ *vb* **-fied; -fy·ing** [F *lignifier,* fr. L *lignum*] *vt* **:** to convert into wood or woody tissue ~ *vi* **:** to become wood or woody — **lig·ni·fi·ca·tion** \ˌlig-nə-fə-ˈkā-shən\ *n*

lig·nin \ˈlig-nən\ *n* **:** an amorphous polymeric substance related to cellulose that together with cellulose forms the woody cell walls of plants and the cementing material between them

lig·nite \ˈlig-ˌnīt\ *n* [F, fr. L *lignum*] **:** a usu. brownish black coal intermediate between peat and bituminous coal; *esp* **:** one in which the texture of the original wood is distinct — called also *brown coal* — **lig·nit·ic** \lig-ˈnit-ik\ *adj*

lig·no·cel·lu·lose \ˌlig-nō-ˈsel-yə-ˌlōs, -ˌlōz\ *n* [ISV] **:** any of several closely related substances constituting the essential part of woody cell walls and consisting of cellulose intimately associated with lignin — **lig·no·cel·lu·los·ic** \-ˌsel-yə-ˈlō-sik, -zik\ *adj*

lig·no·sul·fo·nate \-ˈsəl-fə-ˌnāt\ *n* **:** any of various compounds that are produced from the spent sulfite liquor in the pulping of softwood in papermaking and that are used variously (as for binders or dispersing agents or as raw materials for manufacturing other products)

lig·num vi·tae \ˌlig-nəm-ˈvīt-ē\ *n, pl* **lignum vitaes** [NL, lit., wood of life] **1 :** any of several tropical American trees (genus *Guaiacum* of the family Zygophyllaceae) with very hard heavy wood **2 :** the wood of a lignum vitae

lig·ro·in \ˈlig-rə-wən\ *n* [origin unknown] **:** any of several petroleum naphtha fractions that boil usu. in the range 20° to 135°C and are used esp. as solvents

lig·u·la \ˈlig-yə-lə\ *n, pl* **-lae** \-ˌlē, -ˌlī\ *also* **-las** [NL] **1 :** LIGULE **2 :** the distal lobed part of the labium of an insect

lig·u·late \ˈlig-yə-lət, -ˌlāt\ *adj* **1** [L *ligula*] : shaped like a strap <~ corolla of a ray flower> **2** : furnished with ligules, ligulae, or ligulate corollas

lig·ule \ˈlig-(ˌ)yü(ə)l\ *n* [NL *ligula*, fr. L, small tongue, strap; akin to L *lingere* to lick — more at LICK] : a scalelike projection esp. on a plant: as **a** : a thin appendage of a foliage leaf and esp. of the sheath of a blade of grass **b** : a ligulate corolla of a ray floret in a composite head

lig·ure \ˈlig-ˌyu̇(ə)r, -yər\ *n* [LL *ligurius*, fr. Gk *ligyrion*] : a traditional precious stone that is prob. the jacinth

lik·able *also* **like·able** \ˈlī-kə-bəl\ *adj* : having qualities that bring about a favorable regard : PLEASANT, AGREEABLE — **lik·abil·i·ty** \ˌlī-kə-ˈbil-ət-ē\ *n* — **lik·able·ness** *n*

1like \ˈlīk\ *vb* **liked; lik·ing** [ME *liken*, fr. OE *līcian*; akin to OE *gelīc* alike] *vt* **1** *chiefly dial* : to be suitable or agreeable to **2 a** : to feel attraction toward or take pleasure in : ENJOY <~*s* baseball> **b** : to feel toward : REGARD <how would you ~ a change> **3** : to wish to have : WANT <would ~ a drink> ~ *vi* **1** *dial* : APPROVE **2** : to feel inclined : CHOOSE <you can leave any time you ~> **3** : to find oneself attracted

2like *n* **1** : a feeling of attraction : PREFERENCE **2** : something that one likes

3like *adj* [ME, alter. of *ilich*, fr. OE *gelīc* like, alike; akin to OHG *gilīh* like, alike; both fr. a prehistoric Gmc compound whose first constituent is represented by OE *ge-* (associative prefix) and whose second constituent is represented by OE *līc* body; akin to Lith *lygus* like — more at CO-] **1** : the same or nearly the same (as in appearance, character, or quantity) <suits of ~ design> **2** : LIKELY <the importance of statistics as the one discipline ~ to give accuracy of mind —H. J. Laski>

4like *prep* **1 a** : having the characteristics of : similar to <his house is ~ a barn> **b** : typical of <was ~ him to do that> **2** : in the manner of : similarly to <acts ~ a fool> **3** : inclined to <looks ~ rain> **4** : such as <a subject ~ physics>

5like *n* : one that is like another : COUNTERPART, EQUAL <have . . . never seen the ~ before —Sir Winston Churchill> <had no use for the ~*s* of him>

6like *adv* **1** *archaic* : EQUALLY **2** : LIKELY, PROBABLY <you'll try it, some day, ~ enough —Mark Twain> **3** : to some extent : RATHER <saunter over nonchalantly ~ —Walter Karig> **4** : NEARLY <the actual interest is more ~ 18 percent>

7like *conj* **1** : in the same way that : AS <they raven down scenery ~ children do sweetmeats —John Keats> **2** : as if <middle-aged men who looked ~ they might be out for their one night of the year —Norman Mailer>

8like *or* **liked** \ˈlīkt\ *verbal auxiliary, chiefly substand* : came near : was near <so loud I ~ to fell out of bed —Helen Eustis>

-like \ˌlīk\ *adj comb form* : resembling or characteristic of <bell-*like*> <lady*like*>

like·li·hood \ˈlī-klē-ˌhu̇d\ *n* : PROBABILITY <a strong ~ that he is correct —T. D. Anderson>

1like·ly \ˈlī-klē\ *adj* **like·li·er; -est** [ME, fr. ON *glīkligr*, fr. *glīkr* like; akin to OE *gelīc*] **1** : of such a nature or circumstance as to make something probable <~ of success> **2 a** : RELIABLE, CREDIBLE <a ~ enough story> **b** : having a high probability of occurring or being true : very probable **3** : apparently qualified : SUITABLE <a ~ place> **4** : PROMISING <a ~ subject> **5** : ATTRACTIVE <a ~ child> *syn* see PROBABLE *ant* unlikely

2likely *adv* : in all probability : PROBABLY <those who seek power will most ~ wind up exercising it —Halton Arp>

like–mind·ed \ˈlīk-ˈmīn-dəd\ *adj* : having a like disposition or purpose : of the same mind or habit of thought — **like–mind·ed·ly** *adv* — **like–mind·ed·ness**

lik·en \ˈlī-kən\ *vt* **lik·ened; lik·en·ing** \ˈlīk-(ə-)niŋ\ : COMPARE

like·ness \ˈlīk-nəs\ *n* **1** : the quality or state of being like : RESEMBLANCE **2** : APPEARANCE, SEMBLANCE **3** : COPY, PORTRAIT

syn LIKENESS, SIMILARITY, RESEMBLANCE, SIMILITUDE, ANALOGY, AFFINITY *shared meaning element* : agreement or correspondence in details (as of appearance, structure, or quality) *ant* unlikeness

like·wise \ˈlī-ˌkwīz\ *adv* **1** : in like manner : SIMILARLY <go and do ~> **2** : in addition **3** : similarly so with me <answered "~" to "Pleased to meet you">

lik·ing \ˈlī-kiŋ\ *n* : favorable regard : FONDNESS, TASTE <had a greater ~ for law —E. M. Coulter> <took a ~ to the newcomer> <things were not to his ~>

li·ku·ta \li-ˈküt-ə\ *n, pl* **ma·ku·ta** \mä-\ [of Niger-Congo origin; prob. akin to obs. Nupe *kuta* stone] — see *zaire* at MONEY table

li·lac \ˈlī-lək, -ˌlak, -ˌläk\ *n* [obs. F (now *lilas*), fr. Ar *līlak*, fr. Per *nīlak* bluish, fr. *nīl* blue, fr. Skt *nīla* dark blue] **1 a** : a European shrub (*Syringa vulgaris*) of the olive family that is often an escape in No. America and has cordate ovate leaves and large panicles of fragrant pink-purple flowers **b** : a tree or shrub congeneric with the lilac **2** : a variable color averaging a moderate purple

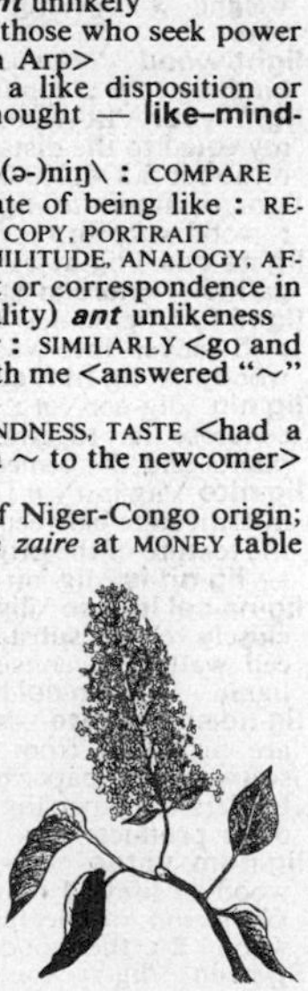

lilac 1a

lil·i·a·ceous \ˌlil-ē-ˈā-shəs\ *adj* : of or relating to lilies or the lily family

lil·ied \ˈlil-ēd\ *adj* **1** *archaic* : resembling a lily in fairness **2** : full of or covered with lilies

Lil·ith \ˈlil-əth\ *n* [LHeb *līlīth*, fr. Heb, a female demon] **1** : a female figure who in rabbinic legend is Adam's first wife, is supplanted by Eve, and becomes an evil spirit **2** : a famous witch in medieval demonology

lil·li·put \ˈlil-i-(ˌ)pət\ *n, often cap* : LILLIPUTIAN

1lil·li·pu·tian \ˌlil-ə-ˈpyü-shən\ *adj, often cap* **1** : of, relating to, or characteristic of the Lilliputians or the island of Lilliput **2 a** : SMALL, MINIATURE **b** : PETTY

2Lilliputian *n* **1** : an inhabitant of an island in Swift's *Gulliver's Travels* who is six inches tall **2** *often not cap* : one resembling a Lilliputian; *esp* : an undersized individual

1lilt \ˈlilt\ *vb* [ME *lulten*] *vt* : to sing or play in a lively cheerful manner ~ *vi* **1** : to sing or speak rhythmically and with fluctuating pitch **2** : to move in a lively springy manner

2lilt *n* **1** : a spirited and usu. gay song or tune **2** : a rhythmical swing, flow, or cadence <the ~ of the questioner's voice —Elizabeth Hardwick> **3** : a springy buoyant movement

lilt·ing \ˈlil-tiŋ\ *adj* **1** : characterized by a rhythmical swing or cadence <a ~ stride> **2** : CHEERFUL, BUOYANT <a ~ comedy> — **lilt·ing·ly** \-tiŋ-lē\ *adv* — **lilt·ing·ness** *n*

1lily \ˈlil-ē\ *n, pl* **lil·ies** [ME *lilie*, fr. OE, fr. L *lilium*] **1** : any of a genus (*Lilium* of the family Liliaceae, the lily family) of erect perennial leafy-stemmed bulbous herbs that are native to the northern hemisphere and are widely cultivated for their showy flowers; *broadly* : any of various plants of the lily family or of the related amaryllis or iris families **2** : any of various plants with showy flowers: as **a** : a scarlet anemone (*Anemone coronaria*) that grows wild in Palestine **b** : WATER LILY **c** : CALLA **3** : FLEUR-DE-LIS 2

2lily *adj* : resembling a lily in fairness, purity, or fragility <my lady's ~ hand —John Keats>

lily–liv·ered \ˌlil-ē-ˈliv-ərd\ *adj* : lacking courage : COWARDLY

lily of the valley : a low perennial herb (*Convallaria majalis*) of the lily family that has usu. two large oblong lanceolate leaves and a raceme of fragrant nodding bell-shaped white flowers

lily of the valley

lily pad *n* : a floating leaf of a water lily

1lily–white \ˌlil-ē-ˈhwīt, -ˈwīt\ *adj* **1** : white as a lily **2** : characterized by or favoring the exclusion of Negroes esp. from politics **3** : IRREPROACHABLE, PURE

2lily–white *n* : a member of a lily-white political organization

Lim *abbr* Limerick

Li·ma \ˈlē-mə\ — a communications code word for the letter *l*

li·ma bean \ˌlī-mə-\ *n* [*Lima*, Peru] **1 a** : any of various bushy or tall-growing beans derived from a perennial tropical American bean (*Phaseolus limensis*) and widely cultivated for their flat edible usu. pale green or whitish seeds **b** : SIEVA BEAN **2** : the seed of a lima bean

li·mac·i·form \lī-ˈmas-ə-ˌfȯrm, -ˈmās-\ *adj* [prob. fr. (assumed) NL *limaciformis*, fr. L *limac-*, *limax* slug + *-iformis* -iform] : resembling a slug <~ insect larvae>

li·ma·çon \ˌlē-mə-ˈsōⁿ\ *n* [F, lit., snail, fr. OF, dim. of *limaz* slug, snail, fr. L *limax*] : a curve that consists of the collection of points obtained by measuring a fixed distance in both directions from the second and variable point of intersection with a circle of a half line that extends from a fixed point on the circle

li·man \li-ˈmän, -ˈman\ *n* [Russ] : a shallow coastal bay or estuary usu. at the mouth of a river : LAGOON

1limb \ˈlim\ *n* [ME *lim*, fr. OE; akin to ON *limr* limb, L *limes* limit, *limen* threshold, Gk *leimōn* meadow] **1** : one of the projecting paired appendages (as wings) of an animal body used esp. for movement and grasping but sometimes modified into sensory or sexual organs; *esp* : a leg or arm of a human being **2** : a large primary branch of a tree **3** : an active member or agent **4** : EXTENSION, BRANCH **5** : a mischievous child — **limb·less** \ˈlim-ləs\ *adj* — **limby** \ˈlim-ē\ *adj* — **out on a limb** : in an exposed or dangerous position with little chance of retreat

2limb *vt* : DISMEMBER; *esp* : to cut off the limbs of (a felled tree)

3limb *n* [L *limbus* border — more at LIMP] **1** : the graduated margin of an arc or circle in an instrument for measuring angles **2** : the outer edge of the apparent disk of a celestial body **3** : the expanded portion of an organ or structure; *esp* : the spreading upper portion of a gamosepalous calyx or a gamopetalous corolla as distinguished from the lower tubular portion

lim·ba \ˈlim-bə\ *n* [prob. native name in West Africa] **1** : a tall whitish-trunked West African tree (*Terminalia superba*) with straight-grained wood **2** : the wood of a limba

lim·beck \ˈlim-ˌbek\ *n* [ME *lembike*, fr. ML *alembicum*] : ALEMBIC

limbed \ˈlimd\ *adj* : having limbs esp. of a specified kind or number — usu. used in combination <strong-*limbed*>

1lim·ber \ˈlim-bər\ *n* [ME *lymour*] : a two-wheeled vehicle to which a gun or caisson may be attached

2limber *adj* [origin unknown] **1** : capable of being shaped : FLEXIBLE **2** : having a supple and resilient quality (as of mind or body) : AGILE, NIMBLE — **lim·ber·ly** *adv* — **lim·ber·ness** *n*

3limber *vb* **lim·bered; lim·ber·ing** \-b(ə-)riŋ\ *vt* : to cause to become limber <~ up his fingers> ~ *vi* : to become limber <~ up by running>

lim·bers \ˈlim-bərz\ *n pl* [modif. of F *lumière*, fr. OF, light, opening, fr. L *luminare* window — more at LUMINARY] : gutters or conduits on each side of the keelson of a ship that provide a passage for water to the pump well

lim·bic \ˈlim-bik\ *adj* [NL *limbicus* of a border or margin, fr. L *limbus*] : of, relating to, or being the limbic system of the brain

limbic system *n* : a group of subcortical structures (as the hypothalamus, the hippocampus, and the amygdala) of the brain that are concerned esp. with emotion and motivation

1lim·bo \ˈlim-(ˌ)bō\ *n, pl* **limbos** [ME, fr. ML, abl. of *limbus* limbo, fr. L, border — more at LIMP] **1** *often cap* : an abode of souls that are according to Roman Catholic theology barred from heaven because of not having received Christian baptism **2 a** : a place or state of restraint or confinement **b** : a place or state of neglect or oblivion <proposals kept in ~> **c** : an intermediate or transitional place or state

2limbo *n, pl* **limbos** [native name in West Indies] : a West Indian acrobatic dance orig. for men that involves bending over backwards and passing under a horizontal pole lowered slightly for each successive pass

linear perspective *n* : representation in a drawing or painting of parallel lines as converging in order to give the illusion of depth and distance

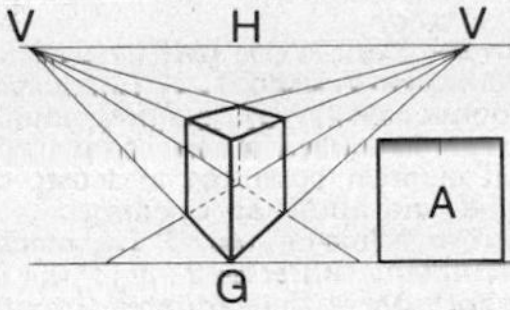

cube *A* drawn in linear perspective: *G* ground plane, *H* horizon, *V* vanishing points

linear programming *n* : a mathematical method of solving practical problems (as the allocation of resources) by means of linear functions where the variables involved are subject to constraints
linear transformation *n* **1** : a transformation in which the new variables are linear functions of the old variables **2** : a function that maps the vectors of one vector space onto the vectors of another vector space with the same field of scalars in such a way that the image of the sum of two vectors equals the sum of their images and the image of a scalar product equals the product of the scalar and the image of the vector
lin·ea·tion \ˌlin-ē-ˈā-shən\ *n* [ME *lineacion* outline, fr. L *lineation-, lineatio,* fr. *lineatus,* pp. of *lineare* to make straight, fr. *linea*] **1 a** : the action of marking with lines : DELINEATION **b** : OUTLINE **2** : an arrangement of lines
line·back·er \ˈlīn-ˌbak-ər\ *n* : a defensive football player who lines up immediately behind the line of scrimmage to make tackles on running plays through the line or defend against short passes
line·back·ing \-ˌbak-iŋ\ *n* : the action or art of playing linebacker
line·breed \ˈlīn-ˈbrēd\ *vb* **-bred** \-ˈbred\; **-breed·ing** *vi* : to interbreed individuals within a particular line of descent usu. to perpetuate desirable characters ~ *vt* : to interbreed (animals) in linebreeding; *also* : to produce by linebreeding
line·cast·er \-ˌkas-tər\ *n* : a machine that casts metal type in lines — **line·cast·ing** \-tiŋ\ *n*
line chief *n* : an air force noncommissioned officer who supervises flight-line upkeep
line·cut \ˈlīn-ˌkət\ *n* : a letterpress printing plate photoengraved from a line drawing — called also *line block, line engraving*
line drawing *n* : a drawing made in solid lines esp. as copy for a linecut
line drive *n* : a batted baseball hit in a nearly straight line usu. not far above the ground
line engraving *n* **1 a** : a metal plate for use in intaglio printing made by hand-engraving lines of different widths and closeness **b** : a process involving such plates or a print made with them **2** : LINECUT — **line engraver** *n*
line gauge *n* : a printer's ruler showing point sizes
line–haul \ˈlīn-ˌhȯl\ *n* : the transporting of items or persons between terminals
line judge *n* : a football linesman whose duties include keeping track of the official time for the game
line·man \ˈlīn-mən\ *n* **1** : one who sets up or repairs electric wire communication or power lines — called also *linesman* **2** : a player in the forward line of a team; *specif* : a football player in the line
¹lin·en \ˈlin-ən\ *adj* [ME, fr. OE *līnen,* fr. *līn* flax; akin to OHG *līn* flax; both fr. a prehistoric Gmc word borrowed fr. L *linum* flax] **1** : made of flax **2** : made of or resembling linen
²linen *n* **1 a** : cloth made of flax and noted for its strength, coolness, and luster **b** : thread or yarn spun from flax **2** : clothing or household articles made of linen cloth or similar fabric **3** : paper made from linen fibers or with a linen finish
line of credit : CREDIT LINE 2
line of duty : all that is authorized, required, or normally associated with some field of responsibility
line officer *n* : a commissioned officer assigned to the line of the army or navy — compare STAFF OFFICER
line of force : a line in a field of force (as a magnetic or electric field) whose tangent at any point gives the direction of the field at that point
line of scrimmage : an imaginary line in football that is parallel to the goal lines and tangent to the nose of the ball laid on the ground and that marks the position of the ball at the start of each down
line of sight **1** : a line from an observer's eye to a distant point toward which he is looking **2** : LINE OF VISION **3** : the straight path between a radio or television transmitting antenna and receiving antenna when unobstructed by the horizon
line of vision : a straight line joining the fovea of the eye with the fixation point
lin·eo·late \ˈlin-ē-ə-ˌlāt\ *or* **lin·eo·lat·ed** \-ˌlāt-əd\ *adj* [NL *lineolatus,* fr. *lineola,* dim. of *linea* line — more at LINE] : marked with fine lines
line out *vt* **1 a** : to mark with lines indicating material to be removed **b** : to indicate with or as if with lines : OUTLINE <*line out* a route> **2 a** : to plant (young nursery stock) in rows **b** : to arrange in an extended line **3** : BELT <*line out* a song> ~ *vi* **1** : to move rapidly <*lined out* for home> **2** : to make an out by hitting a baseball in a line drive that is caught
line printer *n* : a high-speed printing device (as for a computer) that prints each line as a unit rather than character by character — **line printing** *n*
¹lin·er \ˈlī-nər\ *n* **1** : one that makes, draws, or uses lines **2** : something with which lines are made **3 a** : a ship belonging to a regular line of ships **b** : an airplane belonging to an airline **4** : LINE DRIVE
²liner *n* **1** : one that lines or is used to line or back something **2** : explanatory notes accompanying a recording; *also* : the jacket or insert bearing the notes — **lin·er·less** \-ləs\ *adj*
line score *n* : a printed score of a baseball game giving the runs, hits, and errors made by each team — compare BOX SCORE
lines·man \ˈlīnz-mən\ *n* **1** : LINEMAN 1 **2** : an official who assists a referee in various games esp. in determining if a ball or player is out-of-bounds; *esp* : a football official whose duties include marking the distances gained or lost and the points where the ball goes out-of-bounds and noting violations of the scrimmage formation
line squall *n* : a squall or thunderstorm occurring along a cold front
line storm *n* : an equinoctial storm
line-up \ˈlī-ˌnəp\ *n* **1** : a line of persons arranged esp. for inspection or for identification by police **2 a** : a list of players taking part in a game (as of baseball) **b** : the players on such a list **3 a** : an alignment of persons or things having a common purpose or interest **b** : LINE 11
line up \(ˈ)lī-ˈnəp\ *vi* : to assume an orderly linear arrangement <*line up* for inspection> ~ *vt* **1** : to put into alignment **2** : to assemble or organize and make available <*line up* support for a candidate>
¹ling \ˈliŋ\ *n* [ME; akin to D *leng* ling, OE *lang* long] **1** : any of various fishes (as a hake or burbot) of the cod family (Gadidae) **2** : LINGCOD
²ling *n* [ME, fr. ON *lyng;* akin to Lith *lenkti* to bend — more at -LING] : a heath plant; *esp* : a common Old World heather (*Calluna vulgaris*)
³ling *abbr* linguistics
¹-ling \liŋ\ *n suffix* [ME, fr. OE; akin to OE *-ing*] **1** : one connected with or having the quality of <hire*ling*> **2** : young, small, or inferior one <duck*ling*>
²-ling \liŋ\ *or* **-lings** \liŋz\ *adv suffix* [ME *-ling* (fr. OE), *-linges* (fr. *-ling* + *-es* -s); akin to OHG *-lingūn* -ling, Lith *lenkti* to bend] : in (such) a direction or manner <side*ling*> <flat*lings*>
Lin·ga·la \liŋ-ˈgäl-ə\ *n* : a Bantu language widely used in trade and public affairs in the Congo
lin·gam \ˈliŋ-gəm\ *or* **lin·ga** \-gə\ *n* [Skt *liṅga* (nom. *liṅgam*), lit., characteristic] : a stylized phallic symbol of the masculine cosmic principle and of the Hindu god Siva — compare YONI
Lin·ga·yat \liŋ-ˈgä-yət\ *n* [Kannada *lingāyata*] : a member of a Saiva sect of southern India marked by wearing of the lingam and characterized by denial of caste distinctions
ling·cod \ˈliŋ-ˌkäd\ *n* : a large greenish-fleshed fish (*Ophiodon elongatus*) of the Pacific coast of No. America that is an important food fish closely related to the typical greenlings
lin·ger \ˈliŋ-gər\ *vb* **lin·gered; lin·ger·ing** \-g(ə-)riŋ\ [ME (northern dial.) *lengeren* to dwell, freq. of *lengen* to prolong, fr. OE *lengan;* akin to OE *lang* long] *vi* **1** : to be slow in parting or in quitting something : TARRY **2** : to remain alive although waning or gradually dying **3** : to be slow to act : PROCRASTINATE **4** : to move slowly : SAUNTER ~ *vt* **1** *obs* : DELAY **2** : to pass (as a period of time) slowly ***syn*** see STAY — **lin·ger·er** \-gər-ər\ *n* — **lin·ger·ing·ly** \-g(ə-)riŋ-lē\ *adv*
lin·ge·rie \ˌlän-jə-ˈrā, ˌlaⁿ-zhə-, -ˈrē\ *n* [F, fr. MF, fr. *linge* linen, fr. L *lineus* made of linen — more at LINE] **1** *archaic* : linen articles or garments **2** : women's intimate apparel — **lingerie** *adj*
lin·go \ˈliŋ-(ˌ)gō\ *n, pl* **lingoes** [prob. fr. Prov, tongue, fr. L *lingua* — more at TONGUE] : strange or incomprehensible language or speech: as **a** : a foreign language **b** : the special vocabulary of a particular field of interest **c** : language characteristic of an individual ***syn*** see DIALECT
ling·on·ber·ry \ˈliŋ-ən-ˌber-ē\ *n* [Sw *lingon* mountain cranberry; akin to ON *lyng* ling] : the fruit of the mountain cranberry; *also* : MOUNTAIN CRANBERRY
lingu- *or* **lingui-** *or* **linguo-** *comb form* [L *lingu-,* fr. *lingua*] **1** : language <*lingu*ist> **2** : tongue <*lingui*form>
lin·gua \ˈliŋ-gwə\ *n, pl* **lin·guae** \-ˌgwē, -ˌgwī\ [L] : a tongue or an organ resembling a tongue
lin·gua fran·ca \ˌliŋ-gwə-ˈfraŋ-kə\ *n, pl* **lingua francas** *or* **lin·guae fran·cae** \-gwē-ˈfraŋ-(ˌ)kē\ [It, lit., Frankish language] **1** : a common language that consists of Italian mixed with French, Spanish, Greek, and Arabic and is spoken in Mediterranean ports **2** : any of various languages (as Swahili) used as common or commercial tongues among peoples of diverse speech **3** : something resembling a common language
lin·gual \ˈliŋ-g(yə-)wəl\ *adj* **1 a** : of, relating to, or resembling the tongue **b** : lying near or next to the tongue **c** : produced by the tongue **2** : LINGUISTIC — **lin·gual·ly** \-ē\ *adv*
lin·gui·ne \liŋ-ˈgwē-nē\ *n pl* [It, pl. of *linguina,* dim. of *lingua* tongue, fr. L] : thin flat pasta
lin·guist \ˈliŋ-gwəst\ *n* **1** : a person accomplished in languages; *esp* : one who speaks several languages **2** : one who specializes in linguistics
lin·guis·tic \liŋ-ˈgwis-tik\ *also* **lin·guis·ti·cal** \-ti-kəl\ *adj* : of or relating to language or linguistics — **lin·guis·ti·cal·ly** \-ti-k(ə-)lē\ *adv*
linguistic analysis *n* : PHILOSOPHICAL ANALYSIS
linguistic atlas *n* : a publication containing a set of maps on which speech variations are recorded — called also *dialect atlas*
linguistic form *n* : a meaningful unit of speech (as a morpheme, word, or sentence) — called also *speech form*
linguistic geographer *n* : a specialist in linguistic geography
linguistic geography *n* : local or regional variations of a language or dialect studied as a field of knowledge — called also *dialect geography*
lin·guis·ti·cian \ˌliŋ-gwə-ˈstish-ən\ *n* : LINGUIST 2
lin·guis·tics \liŋ-ˈgwis-tiks\ *n pl but sing in constr* : the study of human speech including the units, nature, structure, and modification of language — compare PHILOLOGY
lin·gu·late \ˈliŋ-gyə-lət, -ˌlāt\ *adj* [L *lingulatus,* fr. *lingula,* dim. of *lingua*] : shaped like a tongue or strap : LIGULATE <a ~ leaf>

lin·i·ment \'lin-ə-mənt\ *n* [ME, fr. LL *linimentum*, fr. L *linere* to smear — more at LIME] **:** a liquid or semiliquid preparation that is applied to the skin as an anodyne or a counterirritant
li·nin \'lī-nən\ *n* [ISV, fr. L *linum* flax] **:** the feebly-staining portion of the reticulum of the nucleus of a resting cell in which chromatin granules appear to be embedded
lin·ing \'lī-niŋ\ *n* **1 :** material used to line esp. the inner surface of something (as a garment) **2 :** the act or process of providing something with a lining
[1]**link** \'liŋk\ *n* [ME, of Scand origin; akin to ON *hlekkr* chain; akin to OE *hlanc* lank] **1 :** a connecting structure: as **a** (1) **:** a single ring or division of a chain (2) **:** one of the standardized divisions of a surveyor's chain that is 7.92 inches long and serves as a measure of length **b :** a usu. ornamental device for fastening a cuff **c :** BOND 3c **d :** an intermediate rod or piece for transmitting force or motion; *esp* **:** a short connecting rod with a hole or pin at each end **e :** the fusible member of an electrical fuse **2 :** something analogous to a link of chain: as **a :** a segment of sausage in a chain **b :** a connecting element <sought a ~ between smoking and cancer> **c :** a unit in a communication system **d :** an identifier attached to an element (as an index term) in a system in order to indicate or permit connection with other similarly identified elements — **link·er** *n*
[2]**link** *vt* **:** to couple or connect by a link ~ *vi* **:** to become connected by a link *syn* see JOIN *ant* sunder
[3]**link** *n* [perh. modif. of ML *linchinus* candle, alter. of L *lychnus*, fr. Gk *lychnos*; akin to Gk *leukos* white — more at LIGHT] **:** a torch formerly used to light a person's way through the streets
[4]**link** *vi* [origin unknown] *Scot* **:** to skip smartly along
link·age \'liŋ-kij\ *n* **1 :** the manner or style of being united: as **a :** the manner in which atoms or radicals are linked in a molecule **b :** BOND 3c **2 :** the quality or state of being linked; *esp* **:** the relationship between genes on the same chromosome that causes them to be inherited together **3 a :** a system of links; *esp* **:** a system of links or bars which are jointed together and more or less constrained by having a link or links fixed and by means of which straight or nearly straight lines or other point paths may be traced **b :** the product of the magnetic flux through an electrical coil by its number of turns with the magnetic flux and the coil being connected like two links of a chain
linkage group *n* **:** a set of genes at different loci on the same chromosome that except for crossing-over tend to act as a single pair of genes in meiosis instead of undergoing independent assortment
link·boy \'liŋk-ˌbȯi\ *n* **:** an attendant formerly employed to bear a light for a person on the streets at night
linked \'liŋ(k)t\ *adj* **1 :** marked by linkage and esp. genetic linkage <~ genes> **2 :** having or provided with links <a ~ list>
linking verb *n* **:** COPULA b
link·man \'liŋk-mən\ *n* **:** LINKBOY
links \'liŋ(k)s\ *n pl* [ME, fr. OE *hlincas*, pl. of *hlinc* ridge; akin to OE *hlanc*] **1** *Scot* **:** sand hills esp. along the seashore **2 :** GOLF COURSE
links·man \'liŋ(k)-smən\ *n* **:** GOLFER
link·up \'liŋ-ˌkəp\ *n* **1 :** establishment of contact **:** MEETING <the ~ of two spacecraft> **2 a :** something that serves as a linking device or factor **b :** a functional whole resulting from the linking up of separate elements <an instructional TV ~>
linn \'lin\ *n* [ScGael *linne* pool] **1** *chiefly Scot* **:** WATERFALL **2** *chiefly Scot* **:** PRECIPICE
Lin·nae·an *or* **Lin·ne·an** \lə-'nē-ən, -'nā-; 'lin-ē-\ *adj* [NL Carolus *Linnaeus* (Carl von Linné)] **:** of, relating to, or following the systematic methods of the Swedish botanist Linné who established the system of binomial nomenclature
lin·net \'lin-ət\ *n* [MF *linette*, fr. *lin* flax, fr. L *linum*] **:** a common small Old World finch (*Carduelis cannabina*) having plumage that varies greatly according to age, sex, and season
li·no \'lī-(ˌ)nō\ *n, pl* **linos** *chiefly Brit* **:** LINOLEUM
li·no·cut \'lī-nō-ˌkət\ *n* **:** a print made from a design cut into a mounted piece of linoleum
li·no·le·ate \lə-'nō-lē-ˌāt\ *n* **:** a salt or ester of linoleic acid
lin·ole·ic acid \ˌlin-ə-ˌlē-ik-, -ˌlā-\ *n* [Gk *lin*on flax + ISV *oleic* (*acid*)] **:** a liquid unsaturated fatty acid $C_{18}H_{32}O_2$ found in drying and semidrying oils and held to be essential in animal nutrition
lin·ole·nate \ˌlin-ə-'lē-ˌnāt, -'lā-ˌnāt\ *n* **:** a salt or ester of linolenic acid
lin·ole·nic acid \-ˌlē-nik-, -ˌlā-\ *n* [ISV, irreg. fr. *linoleic*] **:** a liquid unsaturated fatty acid $C_{18}H_{30}O_2$ found esp. in drying oils and considered an essential animal nutrient
li·no·leum \lə-'nō-lē-əm, -'nōl-yəm\ *n, often attrib* [L *lin*um flax + *oleum* oil — more at OIL] **1 :** a floor covering made by laying on a burlap or canvas backing a mixture of solidified linseed oil with gums, cork dust or wood flour or both, and usu. pigments **2 :** a material similar to linoleum
Li·no·type \'lī-nə-ˌtīp\ *trademark* — used for a keyboard-operated typesetting machine that uses circulating matrices and produces each line of type in the form of a solid metal slug
lin·sang \'lin-ˌsaŋ\ *n* [Malay] **:** any of various Asiatic mammals (*Prionodon* and related genera) that resemble long-tailed cats and are related to the civets and genets
lin·seed \'lin-ˌsēd\ *n* [ME, fr. OE *līnsǣd*, fr. *līn* flax + *sǣd* seed — more at LINEN] **:** FLAXSEED
linseed oil *n* **:** a yellowish drying oil obtained from flaxseed and used esp. in paint, varnish, printing ink, and linoleum
lin·sey–wool·sey \ˌlin-zē-'wu̇l-zē\ *n* [ME *lynsy wolsye*] **:** a coarse sturdy fabric of wool and linen or cotton
lin·stock \'lin-ˌstäk\ *n* [D *lontstok*, fr. *lont* match + *stok* stick] **:** a staff having a pointed foot (as for sticking into the ground) and a forked tip and formerly used to hold a lighted match for firing cannon
lint \'lint\ *n* [ME] **1 a :** a soft fleecy material made from linen usu. by scraping **b :** fuzz consisting esp. of fine ravelings and short fibers of yarn and fabric **2 :** a fibrous coat of thick convoluted hairs borne by cotton seeds that yields the cotton staple — **linty** \-ē\ *adj*
lin·tel \'lint-ᵊl\ *n* [ME, fr. MF, fr. LL *limitaris* threshold, fr. L, constituting a boundary, fr. *limit-, limes* boundary — more at LIMB] **:** a horizontal architectural member spanning and usu. carrying the load above an opening

1 lintel

lint·er \'lint-ər\ *n* **1 :** a machine for removing linters **2** *pl* **:** the fuzz of short fibers that adheres to cottonseed after ginning
lint·white \'lint-ˌhwīt, -ˌwīt\ *n* [ME *lynkwhyt*, by folk etymology fr. OE *linetwige*] **:** LINNET
li·num \'lī-nəm\ *n* [NL, genus name, fr. L, flax] **:** any of a genus (*Linum*) of herbaceous small-leaved plants of the flax family; *esp* **:** one growing wild or cultivated for ornament
li·on \'lī-ən\ *n, pl* **lions** [ME, fr. OF, fr. L *leon-, leo*, fr. Gk *leōn*] **1 a** *or pl* **lion :** a large carnivorous chiefly nocturnal cat (*Felis leo*) of open or rocky areas of Africa and esp. formerly southern Asia that has a tawny body with a tufted tail and a shaggy blackish or dark brown mane in the male **b :** any of several large wildcats; *esp* **:** COUGAR **c** *cap* **:** LEO **2 a :** a person felt to resemble a lion (as in courage or ferocity) **b :** a person of outstanding interest or importance **3** *cap* [*Lions* (*club*)] **:** a member of a major national and international service club — **li·on·ess** \'lī-ə-nəs\ *n* — **li·on·like** \-ən-ˌlīk\ *adj*
li·on·fish \'lī-ən-ˌfish\ *n* **:** any of several scorpion fishes (genus *Pterois*) of the tropical Pacific that are brilliantly striped and barred with elongated fins and venomous dorsal spines
li·on·heart·ed \ˌlī-ən-'härt-əd\ *adj* **:** COURAGEOUS, BRAVE
li·on·ize \'lī-ə-ˌnīz\ *vt* **-ized; -iz·ing 1 :** to treat as an object of great interest or importance **2** *Brit* **:** to show the sights of a place to — **li·on·iza·tion** \ˌlī-ə-nə-'zā-shən\ *n* — **li·on·iz·er** \'lī-ə-ˌnī-zər\ *n*
lion's mouth *n* **:** a place of great danger
lion's share *n* **:** the largest portion <received the *lion's share* of the research money>
[1]**lip** \'lip\ *n* [ME, fr. OE *lippa*; akin to OHG *leffur* lip and prob. to L *labium, labrum* lip] **1 :** either of two fleshy folds that surround the mouth in man and many other vertebrates and in man are organs of speech **2** *slang* **:** BACK TALK **3 a :** a fleshy edge or margin (as of a wound) **b :** LABIUM **c :** LABELLUM 1 **d :** a limb of a labiate corolla **4 a :** the edge of a hollow vessel or cavity **b :** a projecting edge: as (1) **:** the slanted upper edge of the mouth of an organ flue pipe (2) **:** the sharp cutting edge on the end of an auger or similar tool (3) **:** a short spout (as on a pitcher) **5 :** EMBOUCHURE — **lip·less** \-ləs\ *adj* — **lip·like** \-ˌlīk\ *adj*
[2]**lip** *adj* **1 :** spoken with the lips only **:** INSINCERE <~ praise> **2 :** produced with the participation of the lips **:** LABIAL <~ consonants>
[3]**lip** *vt* **lipped; lip·ping 1 :** to touch with the lips; *esp* **:** KISS **2 :** UTTER **3 :** to lap against **:** LICK **4 :** to strike a golf ball so that it hits the edge of (the cup) but fails to drop in
lip- *or* **lipo-** *comb form* [NL, fr. Gk, fr. *lipos* — more at LEAVE] **:** fat **:** fatty tissue **:** fatty <*lip*oid> <*lipo*protein>
li·pase \'lī-ˌpās, -ˌpāz\ *n* [ISV] **:** an enzyme that accelerates the hydrolysis or synthesis of fats or the breakdown of lipoproteins
lip·id \'lip-əd\ *also* **lip·ide** \-ˌīd\ *n* [ISV] **:** any of various substances that are soluble in nonpolar organic solvents (as chloroform and ether), that with proteins and carbohydrates constitute the principal structural components of living cells, and that include fats, waxes, phosphatides, cerebrosides, and related and derived compounds — **li·pid·ic** \lip-'id-ik\ *adj*
li·po·gen·e·sis \ˌlī-pə-'jen-ə-səs\ *n* [NL] **:** the formation of fatty acids from acetyl coenzyme A in the living body
li·po·ic acid \lī-ˌpō-ik-, lip-ˌō-\ *n* [*lip-, lipo-*] **:** any of several microbial growth factors; *esp* **:** a crystalline compound $C_8H_{14}O_2S_2$ that is essential for the oxidation of alpha-keto acids (as pyruric acid) in metabolism
[1]**li·poid** \'lī-ˌpȯid, 'lip-ˌȯid\ *or* **li·poi·dal** \lī-'pȯid-ᵊl, lip-'ȯid-\ *adj* [ISV] **:** resembling fat
[2]**lipoid** *n* [ISV] **:** LIPID
li·pol·y·sis \lī-'päl-ə-səs, lip-'äl-\ *n* [NL] **:** the hydrolysis of fat — **li·po·lyt·ic** \ˌlī-pə-'lit-ik, ˌlip-ə-\ *adj*
li·po·ma \lī-'pō-mə, lip-'ō-\ *n, pl* **-mas** *or* **-ma·ta** \-mət-ə\ [NL] **:** a tumor of fatty tissue — **li·po·ma·tous** \-mət-əs\ *adj*
li·po·phil·ic \ˌlī-pə-'fil-ik, ˌlip-ə-\ *adj* **:** having an affinity for lipids (as fats) <a ~ metabolite>
li·po·poly·sac·cha·ride \'lī-pō-ˌpäl-i-'sak-ə-ˌrīd, ˌlip-ō-\ *n* **:** a large molecule consisting of lipids and sugars joined by chemical bonds
li·po·pro·tein \-'prō-ˌtēn, -'prōt-ē-ən\ *n* **:** a conjugated protein that is a complex of protein and lipid
li·po·tro·pic \-'trō-pik, -'träp-ik\ *adj* [ISV] **:** promoting the physiologic utilization of fat — **li·pot·ro·pism** \lī-'pä-trə-ˌpiz-əm, lip-'ä-\ *n*
lipped \'lipt\ *adj* **:** having a lip or lips esp. of a specified kind or number — often used in combination <tight-*lipped*>
lip·pen \'lip-ən\ *vb* [ME *lipnien*] *vi, chiefly Scot* **:** TRUST, RELY ~ *vt, chiefly Scot* **:** ENTRUST
Lippes loop \ˌlip-əs-, 'lips-\ *n* [Jack *Lippes*, 20th cent. Am physician] **:** an S-shaped plastic intrauterine device
lip·ping \'lip-iŋ\ *n* **1 :** outgrowth of bone in liplike form at a joint margin **2 :** a piece of wood set in an archer's bow where a flaw has been cut out **3 :** EMBOUCHURE 1
lip·py \'lip-ē\ *adj* **lip·pi·er; -est :** given to back talk **:** IMPUDENT
lip–read \'lip-ˌrēd\ *vb* **-read** \-ˌred\; **-read·ing** \-ˌrēd-iŋ\ *vt* **:** to understand by lipreading ~ *vi* **:** to use lipreading — **lip–read·er** \-ˌrēd-\ *n*
lip·read·ing \-ˌrēd-iŋ\ *n* **:** the interpreting of a speaker's words without hearing his voice by watching his lip and facial movements

lip service *n* **:** avowal of allegiance that goes no further than expression in words
lip·stick \ˈlip-ˌstik\ *n* **:** a waxy solid usu. colored cosmetic in stick form for the lips; *also* **:** a stick of such cosmetic with its case
liq *abbr* **1** liquid **2** liquor
li·quate \ˈlī-ˌkwāt\ *vt* **li·quat·ed; li·quat·ing** [L *liquatus,* pp. of *liquare;* akin to L *liquēre*] **:** to cause (a more fusible substance) to separate out of a combination or mixture by the application of heat <~ metallic lead from its ore> — **li·qua·tion** \lī-ˈkwā-shən\ *n*
liq·ue·fac·tion \ˌlik-wə-ˈfak-shən\ *n* [ME, fr. LL *liquefaction-, liquefactio,* fr. L *liquefactus,* pp. of *liquefacere,* fr. *liquēre* to be fluid + *facere* to make — more at DO] **1 :** the process of making or becoming liquid **2 :** the state of being liquid
liquefied petroleum gas *n* **:** a compressed gas that consists of flammable hydrocarbons (as propane and butane) and is used esp. as fuel or as raw material for chemical synthesis
liq·ue·fy *also* **liq·ui·fy** \ˈlik-wə-ˌfī\ *vb* **-fied; -fy·ing** [MF *liquefier,* fr. L *liquefacere*] *vt* **:** to reduce to a liquid state ~ *vi* **:** to become liquid — **liq·ue·fi·abil·i·ty** \ˌlik-wə-ˌfī-ə-ˈbil-ət-ē\ *n* — **liq·ue·fi·able** \-ˌfī-ə-bəl\ *adj* — **liq·ue·fi·er** \-ˌfī(-ə)r\ *n*
li·ques·cent \lik-ˈwes-ᵊnt\ *adj* [L *liquescent-, liquescens,* prp. of *liquescere* to become fluid, incho. of *liquēre*] **:** being or tending to become liquid **:** MELTING
li·queur \li-ˈkər, -ˈk(y)u̇(ə)r\ *n* [F, fr. OF *licour* liquid — more at LIQUOR] **:** a usu. sweetened alcoholic beverage variously flavored (as with fruit or aromatics)
1**liq·uid** \ˈlik-wəd\ *adj* [ME, fr. MF *liquide,* fr. L *liquidus,* fr. *liquēre* to be fluid; akin to L *lixa* water, lye, OIr *fliuch* damp] **1 :** flowing freely like water **2 :** neither solid nor gaseous **:** characterized by free movement of the constituent molecules among themselves but without the tendency to separate <~ mercury> **3 a :** shining and clear <large ~ eyes> **b :** being musical and free of harshness in sound **c :** smooth and unconstrained in movement **d :** articulated without friction and capable of being prolonged like a vowel <a ~ consonant> **4 :** consisting of or capable of ready conversion into cash <~ assets> — **li·quid·i·ty** \lik-ˈwid-ət-ē\ *n* — **liq·uid·ly** \ˈlik-wəd-lē\ *adv* — **liq·uid·ness** *n*
2**liquid** *n* **1 :** a liquid substance **2 :** a liquid consonant
liquid air *n* **:** air in the liquid state that can be prepared by subjecting it to great pressure and then cooling it by its own expansion to a temperature below the boiling point of its chief constituents and that is used chiefly as a refrigerant
liq·uid·am·bar \ˌlik-wə-ˈdam-bər\ *n* [NL, genus name, fr. L *liquidus* + ML *ambar, ambra* amber] **1 :** any of a genus (*Liquidambar*) of trees of the witch hazel family with monoecious flowers and a globose fruit of many woody carpels **2 :** an American storax from the sweet gum (*Liquidambar styraciflua*)
liq·ui·date \ˈlik-wə-ˌdāt\ *vb* **-dat·ed; -dat·ing** [LL *liquidatus,* pp. of *liquidare* to melt, fr. L *liquidus*] *vt* **1 a** (1) **:** to determine by agreement or by litigation the precise amount of (indebtedness, damages, or accounts) (2) **:** to determine the liabilities and apportion assets toward discharging the indebtedness of **b :** to settle (a debt) by payment or other settlement **2 :** to get rid of; *specif* **:** KILL **3** *archaic* **:** to make clear **4 :** to convert (assets) into cash ~ *vi* **1 :** to liquidate debts or damages or accounts **2 :** to determine liabilities and apportion assets toward discharging indebtedness — **liq·ui·da·tion** \ˌlik-wə-ˈdā-shən\ *n*
liq·ui·da·tor \ˈlik-wə-ˌdāt-ər\ *n* **:** one that liquidates; *esp* **:** an individual appointed by law to liquidate assets
liquid crystal *n* **:** a liquid having certain physical and esp. optical properties shown by crystalline solids but not by ordinary liquids
liq·uid·ize \ˈlik-wə-ˌdīz\ *vt* **-ized; -iz·ing :** to cause to be liquid
liquid measure *n* **:** a unit or series of units for measuring liquid capacity — see METRIC SYSTEM table, WEIGHT table
1**li·quor** \ˈlik-ər\ *n* [ME *licour,* fr. OF, fr. L *liquor,* fr. *liquēre*] **:** a liquid substance: as **a :** a usu. distilled rather than fermented alcoholic beverage **b :** a watery solution of a drug **c :** BATH 2b(1)
2**liquor** *vb* **li·quored; li·quor·ing** \ˈlik-(ə-)riŋ\ *vt* **1 :** to dress (as leather) with oil or grease **2 :** to make drunk with alcoholic liquor — usu. used with *up* ~ *vi* **:** to drink alcoholic liquor esp. to excess — usu. used with *up*
li·quo·rice *chiefly Brit var of* LICORICE
li·ra \ˈlir-ə, ˈlē-rə\ *n* [It, fr. L *libra,* a unit of weight] **1** *pl* **li·re** \ˈlē-(ˌ)rā\ *also* **liras** — see MONEY table **2** [Turk, fr. It] *pl* **liras** *also* **lire :** a Turkish or Syrian pound **3** *pl* **li·roth** *or* **li·rot** \ˈlē-ˌrōt(h)\ [NHeb, fr. It] **:** the Israeli pound
lir·i·pipe \ˈlir-ə-ˌpīp\ *n* [ML *liripipium*] **:** a pendent part of a tippet; *also* **:** TIPPET, SCARF
lisle \ˈlī(ə)l\ *n* [*Lisle* Lille, France] **:** a smooth tightly twisted thread usu. made of long-staple cotton
1**lisp** \ˈlisp\ *vb* [ME *lispen,* fr. OE *-wlyspian;* akin to OHG *lispen* to lisp] *vi* **1 :** to pronounce the sibilants *s* and *z* imperfectly esp. by giving them the sound of *th* **2 :** to speak falteringly, childishly, or with a lisp ~ *vt* **:** to utter falteringly or with a lisp — **lisp·er** *n*
2**lisp** *n* **1 :** a speech defect or affectation characterized by lisping **2 :** a sound resembling a lisp
lis·some *also* **lis·som** \ˈlis-əm\ *adj* [alter. of *lithesome*] **1 :** easily flexed **:** LITHE **2 :** NIMBLE — **lis·some·ly** *adv* — **lis·some·ness** *n*
1**list** \ˈlist\ *vb* [ME *lysten,* fr. OE *lystan;* akin to OE *lust*] *vt, archaic* **:** PLEASE, SUIT ~ *vi, archaic* **:** WISH, CHOOSE
2**list** *n* [ME, prob. fr. *lysten*] *archaic* **:** INCLINATION, CRAVING
3**list** *vb* [ME *listen,* fr. OE *hlystan,* fr. *hlyst* hearing, fr. *hlysnan* to listen] *vi, archaic* **:** LISTEN ~ *vt, archaic* **:** to listen to **:** HEAR
4**list** *n* [ME, fr. OE *līste;* akin to OHG *līsta* edge, Alb *leth*] **1 :** a band or strip of material: as **a :** LISTEL **b :** SELVAGE **c :** a narrow strip of wood cut from the edge of a plank or board **2** *pl but sing or pl in constr* **a :** an arena for jousting **b :** an arena for combat **c :** a field of competition or controversy **3** *obs* **:** LIMIT, BOUNDARY **4 :** STRIPE
5**list** *vt* **1 :** to cut away a narrow strip (as sapwood) from the edge of **2 :** to prepare or plant (land) in ridges and furrows with a lister
6**list** *n* [F *liste,* fr. It *lista,* of Gmc origin; akin to OHG *līsta*] **1 a :** a simple series of words or numerals (as the names of persons or objects) <a guest ~> <a grocery ~> **b :** an official roster **:** ROLL **2 :** INDEX, CATALOG
7**list** *vt* **1 a :** to make a list of **:** ENUMERATE **b :** to include on a list **:** REGISTER **2 :** to place (oneself) in a specified category <~*s* himself as a political liberal> **3** *archaic* **:** RECRUIT ~ *vi* **1** *archaic* **:** ENLIST **2 :** to become entered in a catalog with a selling price <a car that ~*s* for $3000>
8**list** *vb* [origin unknown] *vi* **:** to lean to one side **:** TILT ~ *vt* **:** to cause to list
9**list** *n* **:** a deviation from the vertical **:** TILT
lis·tel \ˈlis-tᵊl, lis-ˈtel\ *n* [F, fr. It *listello,* dim. of *lista* fillet, roster] **:** a narrow band in architecture **:** FILLET
1**lis·ten** \ˈlis-ᵊn\ *vb* **lis·tened; lis·ten·ing** \ˈlis-niŋ, -ᵊn-iŋ\ [ME *listnen,* fr. OE *hlysnan;* akin to Skt *śroṣati* he hears, OE *hlūd* loud] *vt, archaic* **:** to give ear to **:** HEAR ~ *vi* **1 :** to pay attention to sound <~ to music> **2 :** to hear with thoughtful attention **:** HEED <~ to a plea> **3 :** to be alert to catch an expected sound <~ for his step> — **lis·ten·er** \ˈlis-nər, -ᵊn-ər\ *n*
2**listen** *n* **:** an act of listening
lis·ten·able \ˈlis-nə-bəl, -ᵊn-ə-\ *adj* **:** agreeable to listen to
listen in *vi* **1 :** to tune in to or monitor a broadcast **2 :** to listen to a conversation without participating in it; *esp* **:** EAVESDROP — **lis·ten·er–in** \ˌlis-nə-ˈrin, ˌlis-ᵊn-ə-\ *n*
1**list·er** \ˈlis-tər\ *n* **:** one that lists or catalogs
2**lister** *n* [5*list*] **1 :** a double-moldboard plow often equipped with a subsoiling attachment and used mainly where rainfall is limited **2 :** a lister plow with an attachment for dropping seeds into the furrow
lis·te·ri·osis \lis-ˌtir-ē-ˈō-səs\ *n, pl* **-oses** \-ˌsēz\ [NL, fr. *Listeria,* genus of bacteria, fr. Joseph *Lister*] **:** a serious commonly fatal encephalitic disease of a great variety of wild and domestic mammals and birds and occas. man that is caused by a bacterium (*Listeria monocytogenes*)
list·ing *n* **1 :** an act or instance of making or including in a list **2 :** something that is listed
list·less \ˈlist-ləs\ *adj* **:** characterized by lack of inclination or impetus to exertion **:** LANGUID — **list·less·ly** *adv* — **list·less·ness** *n*
list price *n* **:** the basic price of an item as published in a catalog, price list, or advertisement but subject to discounts (as trade or quantity discounts)
1**lit** \ˈlit\ *past of* LIGHT
2**lit** *adj* [pp. of 3*light*] **:** affected by alcohol **:** DRUNK
3**lit** *abbr* **1** liter **2** literal; literally **3** literary **4** literature
lit·a·ny \ˈlit-ᵊn-ē, ˈlit-nē\ *n, pl* **-nies** [ME *letanie,* fr. OF, fr. LL *litania,* fr. LGk *litaneia,* fr. Gk, entreaty, fr. *litanos* entreating; akin to OE *līm* lime] **1 :** a prayer consisting of a series of invocations and supplications by the leader with alternate responses by the congregation **2 :** a resonant or repetitive recital or chant <a ~ of cheering phrases —Herman Wouk>
Lit B *abbr* — see LITT B
li·tchi \ˈlī-(ˌ)chē, ˈlē-\ *n* [Chin (Pek) *li*[4] *chih*[1]] **1 :** the oval fruit of a tree (*Litchi chinensis*) of the soapberry family having a hard scaly outer covering, small hard seed, and edible flesh that surrounds the seed and is firm, sweetish, and black when dried — called also *litchi nut* **2 :** a tree bearing litchis

litchi: *1* fruit and leaves, *2* cross section of fruit

Lit D *abbr* — see LITT D
-lite \ˌlīt\ *n comb form* [F, alter. of *-lithe,* fr. Gk *lithos* stone] **:** mineral <rhodo*lite*> **:** rock <aero*lite*> **:** fossil <ichno*lite*>
li·ter \ˈlēt-ər\ *n* [F *litre,* fr. ML *litra,* a measure, fr. Gk, a weight] **:** a metric unit of capacity equal to the volume of one kilogram of water at 4°C and at standard atmospheric pressure of 760 millimeters of mercury — see METRIC SYSTEM table
lit·er·a·cy \ˈlit-ə-rə-sē, ˈli-trə-\ *n* **:** the quality or state of being literate
1**lit·er·al** \ˈlit-ə-rəl, ˈli-trəl\ *adj* [ME, fr. MF, fr. ML *litteralis,* fr. L, of a letter, fr. *littera* letter] **1 a :** according with the letter of the scriptures **b :** adhering to fact or to the ordinary construction or primary meaning of a term or expression **:** ACTUAL, OBVIOUS <liberty in the ~ sense is impossible —B. N. Cardozo> **c :** free from exaggeration or embellishment <the ~ truth> **d :** characterized by a concern mainly with facts **:** PROSAIC <a very ~ man> **2 :** of, relating to, or expressed in letters **3 :** reproduced word for word **:** EXACT, VERBATIM <a ~ translation> — **lit·er·al·i·ty** \ˌlit-ə-ˈral-ət-ē\ *n* — **lit·er·al·ly** \ˈlit-ər-(ə-)lē, ˈli-trə-lē\ *adv* — **lit·er·al·ness** \ˈlit-ə-rəl-nəs, ˈli-trəl-\ *n*
2**literal** *n* **:** a small error usu. of a single letter in writing or printing
lit·er·al·ism \ˈlit-ə-rə-ˌliz-əm, ˈli-trə-\ *n* **1 :** adherence to the explicit substance of an idea or expression <biblical ~> **2 :** fidelity to observable fact **:** REALISM — **lit·er·al·ist** \-ləst\ *n* — **lit·er·al·is·tic** \ˌlit-ə-rə-ˈlis-tik, ˌli-trə-\ *adj*
lit·er·al·ize \ˈlit-ə-rə-ˌlīz, ˈli-trə-\ *vt* **-ized; -iz·ing :** to make literal
lit·er·ary \ˈlit-ə-ˌrer-ē\ *adj* **1 a :** of, relating to, or having the characteristics of letters, humane learning, or literature **b :** BOOKISH 2

c : of or relating to books **2 a :** WELL-READ **b :** of or relating to men of letters or writing as a profession <~ journals> — **lit·er·ari·ly** \ˌlit-ə-'rer-ə-lē\ *adv* — **lit·er·ari·ness** \'lit-ə-ˌrer-ē-nəs\ *n*

literary executor *n* : a person entrusted with the management of the papers and unpublished works of a deceased author

¹lit·er·ate \'lit-ə-rət, 'li-trət\ *adj* [ME *literat,* fr. L *litteratus* marked with letters, literate, fr. *litterae* letters, literature, fr. pl. of *littera*] **1 a :** EDUCATED, CULTURED **b :** able to read and write **2 a :** versed in literature or creative writing : LITERARY **b :** LUCID, POLISHED <assembling doctoral findings into a ~ thesis —J. P. Elder> — **lit·er·ate·ly** *adv* — **lit·er·ate·ness** *n*

²literate *n* **1 :** an educated person **2 :** one who can read and write

li·te·ra·ti \ˌlit-ə-'rät-(ˌ)ē\ *n pl* [obs. It *litterati,* fr. L, pl. of *litteratus*] **1 :** the educated class : INTELLIGENTSIA **2 :** men of letters

lit·er·a·tim \ˌlit-ə-'rāt-əm, -'rät-\ *adv or adj* [ML, fr. L *littera*] : letter for letter <usually printed ~ from the manuscript —I. A. Gordon>

lit·er·a·tion \ˌlit-ə-'rā-shən\ *n* [L *littera* + E *-ation*] : the representation of sound or words by letters

lit·er·a·tor \'lit-ə-ˌrāt-ər, ˌlit-ə-'rä-ˌtȯ(ə)r\ *n* : LITTERATEUR

lit·er·a·ture \'lit-ə-rə-ˌchu̇(ə)r, 'li-trə-ˌchu̇(ə)r, 'lit-ə(r)-ˌchu̇(ə)r, -chər, -ˌt(y)u̇(ə)r\ *n* **1** *archaic* : literary culture **2 :** the production of literary work esp. as an occupation **3 a :** writings in prose or verse; *esp* : writings having excellence of form or expression and expressing ideas of permanent or universal interest **b :** the body of writings on a particular subject <scientific ~> **c :** printed matter (as leaflets or circulars) <campaign ~> **4 :** the aggregate of musical compositions <Brahms' piano ~>

lit·er·a·tus \ˌlit-ə-'rät-əs\ *n* [NL, back-formation fr. *literati* (taken as L)] : a member of the literati

lith *or* **litho** *abbr* lithographic; lithography

lith- *or* **litho-** *comb form* [L, fr. Gk, fr. *lithos*] **1 :** stone <*litho*logy> **2** [NL *lithium*] : lithium <*lith*ic>

-lith \ˌlith\ *n comb form* [NL *-lithus* & F *-lithe,* fr. Gk *lithos*] **1 a :** structure or implement of stone <mega*lith*> <eo*lith*> **b :** artificial stone <grano*lith*> **2 :** calculus <uro*lith*> **3 :** -LITE <lacco*lith*>

li·tharge \'lith-ˌärj, lith-'\ *n* [ME, fr. MF, fr. L *lithargyrus,* fr. Gk *lithargyros,* fr. *lithos* + *argyros* silver — more at ARGENT] : a fused lead monoxide; *broadly* : LEAD MONOXIDE

lithe \'lī*th*, 'līth\ *adj* [ME, fr. OE *līthe* gentle; akin to OHG *lindi* gentle, L *lentus* slow] **1 :** easily bent or flexed <~ steel> <a ~ vine> **2 :** characterized by easy flexibility and grace <a ~ dancer> <treading with a ~ silent step> — **lithe·ly** *adv* — **lithe·ness** *n*

lithe·some \'lī*th*-səm, 'līth-\ *adj* : LISSOME

lith·ia \'lith-ē-ə\ *n* [NL, fr. Gk *lithos*] : a white crystalline oxide of lithium Li_2O

li·thi·a·sis \lith-'ī-ə-səs\ *n, pl* **-a·ses** \-ˌsēz\ [NL, fr. Gk, fr. *lithos*] : the formation of stony concretions in the body (as in the gall bladder)

lithia water *n* : a mineral water containing lithium salts

lith·ic \'lith-ik\ *adj* [Gk *lithikos,* fr. *lithos*] **1 :** of, relating to, or made of stone **2 :** of or relating to lithium — **lith·i·cal·ly** \-i-k(ə-)lē\ *adv*

-lith·ic \'lith-ik\ *adj comb form* [*lithic*] : relating to or characteristic of a (specified) stage in man's use of stone as a cultural tool <Neo*lithic*>

lith·i·um \'lith-ē-əm\ *n* [NL, fr. *lithia*] : a soft silver-white element of the alkali metal group that is the lightest metal known and that is used esp. in nuclear reactions and metallurgy — see ELEMENT table

lithium carbonate *n* : a crystalline salt Li_2CO_3 used in the glass and ceramic industries and in medicine in the treatment of manic-depressive psychosis

lithium fluoride *n* : a white compound LiF used esp. in making prisms and ceramics and as a flux

litho \'līth-(ˌ)ō\ *n, pl* **lith·os** **1 :** LITHOGRAPH **2 :** LITHOGRAPHY

¹litho·graph \'lith-ə-ˌgraf\ *vt* : to produce, copy, or portray by lithography — **li·thog·ra·pher** \lith-'äg-rə-fər, 'lith-ə-ˌgraf-ər\ *n*

²lithograph *n* : a print made by lithography — **litho·graph·ic** \ˌlith-ə-'graf-ik\ *adj* — **litho·graph·i·cal·ly** \-i-k(ə-)lē\ *adv*

li·thog·ra·phy \lith-'äg-rə-fē\ *n* [G *lithographie,* fr. *lith-* + *-graphie* -graphy] **1 :** the process of printing from a plane surface (as a smooth stone or metal plate) on which the image to be printed is ink-receptive and the blank area ink-repellent **2 :** PLANOGRAPHY

li·thol·o·gy \lith-'äl-ə-jē\ *n, pl* **-gies** **1 :** the study of rocks **2 :** the character of a rock formation — **lith·o·log·ic** \ˌlith-ə-'läj-ik\ *also* **lith·o·log·i·cal** \-i-kəl\ *adj* — **lith·o·log·i·cal·ly** \-i-k(ə-)lē\ *adv*

lith·o·phane \'lith-ə-ˌfān\ *n* [prob. fr. G *lithophan,* fr. Gk *lithos* + G *diaphan* diaphanous] : porcelain impressed with figures that are made distinct by transmitted light; *also* : an object (as an ornamental panel) of this material

litho·phyte \'lith-ə-ˌfīt\ *n* [F, fr. *lith-* + *-phyte*] **1 :** an organism (as a coral) having a hard stony structure or skeleton **2 :** a plant that grows on rock — **litho·phyt·ic** \ˌlith-ə-'fit-ik\ *adj*

lith·o·pone \'lith-ə-ˌpōn\ *n* [ISV *lith-* + Gk *ponos* work] : a white pigment consisting essentially of zinc sulfide and barium sulfate

litho·sol \'lith-ə-ˌsäl, -ˌsȯl\ *n* [*lith-* + L *solum* soil] : an azonal shallow soil consisting of imperfectly weathered rock fragments

litho·sphere \'lith-ə-ˌsfi(ə)r\ *n* [ISV] : the solid part of a celestial body (as the earth); *specif* : the outer part of the solid earth composed of rock essentially like that exposed at the surface and usu. considered to be about 50 miles in thickness

li·thot·o·my \lith-'ät-ə-mē\ *n, pl* **-mies** [LL *lithotomia,* fr. Gk, fr. *lithotomein* to perform a lithotomy, fr. *lith-* + *temnein* to cut — more at TOME] : surgical incision of the urinary bladder for removal of a stone

Lith·u·a·nian \ˌlith-(y)ə-'wā-nē-ən, -nyən\ *n* **1 :** a native or inhabitant of Lithuania **2 :** the Baltic language of the Lithuanian people — **Lithuanian** *adj*

lit·i·gant \'lit-i-gənt\ *n* : one engaged in a lawsuit — **litigant** *adj*

lit·i·gate \'lit-ə-ˌgāt\ *vb* **-gat·ed; -gat·ing** [L *litigatus,* pp. of *litigare,* fr. *lit-, lis* lawsuit + *agere* to drive — more at AGENT] *vi* : to carry on a legal contest by judicial process ~ *vt* **1** *archaic* : DISPUTE **2 :** to contest in law — **lit·i·ga·ble** \'lit-i-gə-bəl\ *adj* — **lit·i·ga·tion** \ˌlit-ə-'gā-shən\ *n*

li·ti·gious \lə-'tij-əs, li-\ *adj* [ME, fr. MF *litigieux,* fr. L *litigiosus,* fr. *litigium* dispute, fr. *litigare*] **1 a :** DISPUTATIOUS, CONTENTIOUS **b :** prone to engage in lawsuits **2 :** subject to litigation **3 :** of, relating to, or marked by litigation — **li·ti·gious·ly** *adv* — **li·ti·gious·ness** *n*

lit·mus \'lit-məs\ *n* [of Scand origin; akin to ON *litmosi* herbs used in dyeing, fr. *litr* color + *mosi* moss; akin to OHG ant*lizzi* face, L *vultus,* and to OE *mōs* moss] : a coloring matter from lichens that turns red in acid solutions and blue in alkaline solutions and is used as an acid-base indicator

litmus paper *n* : unsized paper colored with litmus and used as an indicator

li·to·tes \'līt-ə-ˌtēz, 'lit-\ *n, pl* **litotes** [Gk *litotēs,* fr. *litos* simple; akin to Gk *leios* smooth — more at LIME] : understatement in which an affirmative is expressed by the negative of the contrary (as in "not a bad singer")

li·tre \'lēt-ər\ *var of* LITER

Litt B *or* **Lit B** *abbr* [ML *litterarum baccalaureus*] bachelor of letters; bachelor of literature

Litt D *or* **Lit D** *abbr* [ML *litterarum doctor*] doctor of letters; doctor of literature

lit·ten \'lit-ᵊn\ *adj* [alter. of *lit,* pp. of *light*] *archaic* : being lighted

¹lit·ter \'lit-ər\ *n* [ME, fr. OF *litiere,* fr. *lit* bed, fr. L *lectus* — more at LIE] **1 a :** a covered and curtained couch provided with shafts and used for carrying a single passenger **b :** a device (as a stretcher) for carrying a sick or injured person **2 a :** material used as bedding for animals **b :** the uppermost slightly decayed layer of organic matter on the forest floor **3 :** the offspring at one birth of a multiparous animal **4 a :** trash, wastepaper, or garbage lying scattered about <trying to clean up the roadside ~> **b :** an untidy accumulation of objects <a shabby writing-desk covered with a ~ of yellowish dusty documents —Joseph Conrad> — **lit·tery** \-ə-rē\ *adj*

²litter *vt* **1 :** BED 1a **2 :** to give birth to (young) **3 a :** to strew with scattered articles **b :** to scatter about in disorder ~ *vi* **1 :** to give birth to a litter **2 :** to strew litter

lit·te·rae hu·ma·ni·o·res \'lit-ə-ˌrī-hü-ˌmän-ē-'ō(ə)r-ˌās, -'ȯ(ə)r-\ *n pl* [ML, lit., more humane letters] : HUMANITIES

lit·ter·a·teur \ˌlit-ə-rə-'tər, ˌli-trə-, -'tu̇(ə)r\ *n* [F *littérateur,* fr. L *litterator* critic, fr. *litteratus* literate] : a literary man; *esp* : a professional writer

lit·ter·bag \'lit-ər-ˌbag\ *n* : a bag used (as in an automobile) for temporary refuse disposal

lit·ter·bug \-ˌbəg\ *n* : one who litters a public area

lit·ter·er \'lit-ər-ər\ *n* : LITTERBUG

lit·ter·mate \'lit-ər-ˌmāt\ *n* : one of the offspring in a litter in relation to the others

¹lit·tle \'lit-ᵊl\ *adj* **lit·tler** \'lit-ᵊl-ər, 'lit-lər\ *or* **less** \'les\ *or* **les·ser** \'les-ər\; **lit·tlest** \'lit-ᵊl-əst, 'lit-ləst\ *or* **least** \'lēst\ [ME *littel,* fr. OE *lȳtel;* akin to OHG *luzzil* little, Lith *liusti* to be sad] **1 :** not big: as **a :** small in size or extent : TINY <has ~ feet> **b** *of a plant or animal* : small in comparison with related forms — used in vernacular names **c :** small in number **d :** small in condition, distinction, or scope <~ men temporarily inflated by big jobs —S. K. Padover> **e :** NARROW, MEAN <the pettiness of ~ minds> **f :** pleasingly small <she's a cute ~ thing> **2 :** not much: as **a :** existing only in a small amount or to a slight degree <unfortunately he has ~ money> **b :** short in duration : BRIEF **c :** existing to an appreciable though not extensive degree or amount —used with *a* <fortunately he had a ~ money in the bank> **3 :** small in importance or interest : TRIVIAL — **lit·tle·ness** \'lit-ᵊl-nəs\ *n*

²little *adv* **less** \'les\; **least** \'lēst\ **1 a :** in only a small quantity or degree : SLIGHTLY <facts that were ~ known at the time> **b :** not at all <cared ~ for his neighbors> **2 :** RARELY, INFREQUENTLY

³little *n* **1 :** a small amount, quantity, or degree **2 a :** a short time **b :** a short distance — **a little :** SOMEWHAT, RATHER <found the play *a little* dull> — **in little :** on a small scale; *esp* : in miniature

Little Bear *n* : URSA MINOR

lit·tle bit·ty \ˌlit-ᵊl-'bit-ē\ *adj* : SMALL, TINY

little bluestem *n* : a forage grass (*Andropogon scoparius*) of central No. America

little by little *adv* : by small degrees or amounts : GRADUALLY

Little Dipper *n* : DIPPER 2b

little finger *n* : the fourth and smallest finger of the hand counting the index finger as the first

Little Hours *n pl* : the offices of prime, terce, sext, and none forming part of the canonical hours

little leaf \'lit-ᵊl-ˌ(l)ēf\ *n* : a plant disorder characterized by small and often chlorotic and distorted foliage: as **a :** a zinc-deficiency disease of deciduous woody plants (as grape, peach, and pecan) **b :** a destructive disease of southern pines (as *Pinus echinata*) of unknown cause

little-leaf disease *n* : LITTLE LEAF

Little League *n* : a commercially sponsored baseball league for boys from 8 to 12 years old — **Little Leaguer** *n*

little magazine *n* : a literary usu. noncommercial magazine typically small in format that esp. features experimental writing appealing to a relatively limited number of readers

lit·tle·neck \'lit-ᵊl-ˌnek\ *n* [*Littleneck* Bay, Long Island, N.Y.] : a young quahog suitable to be eaten raw — called also *littleneck clam*

Little Office *n* : an office in honor of the Virgin Mary like but shorter than the Divine Office

little people *n pl* **1 :** tiny imaginary beings (as fairies, elves, and leprechauns) of folklore **2 :** CHILDREN **3 :** MIDGETS

little slam *n* **:** the winning of all tricks except one in bridge
little theater *n* **:** a small theater for low-cost dramatic productions designed for a relatively limited audience
little toe *n* **:** the outermost and smallest digit of the foot
little woman *n* **:** WIFE
[1]lit·to·ral \'lit-ə-rəl; ˌlit-ə-'ral, -'räl\ *adj* [L *litoralis,* fr. *litor-, litus* seashore] **:** of, relating to, or situated or growing on or near a shore esp. of the sea
[2]littoral *n* **:** a coastal region; *esp* **:** the shore zone between high and low watermarks
lit up *adj, slang* **:** DRUNK
li·tur·gi·cal \lə-'tər-ji-kəl, li-\ *adj* **1 :** of, relating to, or having the characteristics of liturgy **2 :** using or favoring the use of liturgy <~ churches> — **li·tur·gi·cal·ly** \-k(ə-)lē\ *adv*
li·tur·gics \-jiks\ *n pl but sing or pl in constr* **:** the practice or study of formal public worship
li·tur·gi·ol·o·gist \-ˌtər-jē-'äl-ə-jəst\ *n* **:** LITURGIST 2
li·tur·gi·ol·o·gy \-jē\ *n* **:** LITURGICS
lit·ur·gist \'lit-ər-jəst\ *n* **1 :** one who adheres to, compiles, or leads a liturgy **2 :** a specialist in liturgics
lit·ur·gy \'lit-ər-jē\ *n, pl* **-gies** [LL *liturgia,* fr. Gk *leitourgia,* fr. (assumed) Gk (Attic) *leïtos* public (fr. Gk *laos* — Attic *leōs* — people) + *-ourgia* -urgy] **1** *often cap* **:** a eucharistic rite **2 :** a rite or body of rites prescribed for public worship
liv·abil·i·ty *also* **live·abil·i·ty** \ˌliv-ə-'bil-ət-ē\ *n* **1 :** survival expectancy **:** VIABILITY — used esp. of poultry and livestock **2 :** suitability for human living
liv·able *also* **live·able** \'liv-ə-bəl\ *adj* **1 :** suitable for living in or with **2 :** ENDURABLE — **liv·able·ness** *n*
[1]live \'liv\ *vb* **lived; liv·ing** [ME *liven,* fr. OE *libban;* akin to OHG *lebēn* to live, L *caelebs* unmarried] *vi* **1 :** to be alive **:** have the life of an animal or plant **2 :** to continue alive **3 :** to maintain oneself **:** SUBSIST **4 :** to conduct or pass one's life <*lived* only for his work> **5 :** to occupy a home **:** DWELL <*living* in a shabby room> <they had always *lived* in the country> **6 :** to attain eternal life <though he die, yet shall he ~ —Jn 11:25 (RSV)> **7 :** to remain in human memory or record <the past ~*s* in us all —W. R. Inge> **8 :** to have a life rich in experience **9 :** COHABIT ~ *vt* **1 :** to pass through or spend the duration of **2 :** ENACT, PRACTICE **3 :** to exhibit vigor, gusto, or enthusiasm in <*lived* life to the fullest> ***syn*** see RESIDE — **live it up :** to live with gusto and usu. fast and loose <*lived it up* with wine and song —*Newsweek*> — **live up to :** to act or be in accordance with <had no intention of *living up to* his promise>
[2]live \'līv\ *adj* [short for *alive*] **1 :** having life **:** LIVING **2 :** abounding with life **:** VIVID **3 :** exerting force or containing energy: as **a :** AFIRE, GLOWING <a ~ cigar> **b :** connected to electric power **c :** charged with explosives and containing shot or a bullet <~ ammunition>; *also* **:** not exploded <a ~ bomb> **d :** imparting or driven by power **e :** charged with fissionable material **4 :** of continuing or current interest **:** UNCLOSED <~ issues> **5 :** being in a pure native state **6 :** of bright vivid color **7 :** being in play <a ~ ball> **8 a :** not yet printed from or plated <~ type> **b :** not yet typeset <~ copy> **9 a :** of or involving the actual presence of real people <a ~ audience> **b :** broadcast directly at the time of production instead of from recorded or filmed material <a ~ radio program>
[3]live \'līv\ *adv* **:** during, from, or at a live production <the programming originated ~ from New York City —*Current Biog.*>
live–bear·er \'līv-ˌbar-ər, -ˌber-\ *n* **:** a fish that brings forth living young rather than eggs
live–bear·ing \'līv-ˌba(ə)r-iŋ, -ˌbe(ə)r-\ *adj* **:** VIVIPAROUS
live–born \'līv-'bō(ə)rn\ *adj* **:** born alive — compare STILLBORN
live–box \-ˌbäks\ *n* **:** a box or pen suspended in water to keep aquatic animals alive
-lived \'līvd, 'livd\ *comb form* [ME, fr. *lif* life] **:** having a life of a specified kind or length <long-*lived*>
live down *vt* **:** to live so as to wipe out the memory or effects of <made a mistake and couldn't *live it down*>
live–for·ev·er \'liv-fə-ˌrev-ər\ *n* **:** SEDUM
live–in \ˌliv-ˌin\ *adj* **:** living in one's place of employment <a ~ maid>
live in \(')liv-'in\ *vi* **:** to live in one's place of employment — used of a servant
live·li·hood \'līv-lē-ˌhu̇d\ *n* [ME *livelode* course of life, fr. OE *līflād,* fr. *līf* + *lād* course — more at LODE] **1 :** means of support or subsistence **2** *obs* **:** the quality or state of being lively
live·long \ˌliv-ˌlȯŋ\ *adj* [ME *lef long,* fr. *lef* dear + *long* — more at LIEF] **:** WHOLE, ENTIRE <the ~ day>
live·ly \'līv-lē\ *adj* **live·li·er; -est** [ME, fr. OE *līflīc,* fr. *līf* life] **1** *obs* **:** LIVING **2 :** briskly alert and energetic **:** VIGOROUS, ANIMATED <a ~ discussion> <~ children racing home from school> **3 :** ACTIVE, INTENSE <takes a ~ interest in the people around her> **4 :** BRILLIANT, FRESH <a ~ flashing wit> **5 :** imparting spirit or vivacity **:** STIMULATING <many a peer of England brews *livelier* liquor than the Muse —A. E. Housman> **6 :** quick to rebound **:** RESILIENT **7 :** responding readily to the helm <a ~ boat> **8 :** full of life, movement, or incident <river . . . was ~ with craft of all descriptions —*Amer. Guide Series: Mich.*> — **live·li·ly** \'līv-lə-lē\ *adv* — **live·li·ness** \'līv-lē-nəs\ *n* — **lively** *adv*
syn LIVELY, ANIMATED, VIVACIOUS, SPRIGHTLY, GAY *shared meaning element* **:** keenly alive and spirited ***ant*** dull
liv·en \'lī-vən\ *vb* **liv·ened; liv·en·ing** \'līv-(ə-)niŋ\ *vt* **:** ENLIVEN — often used with *up* <he . . . ~*ed* up the editorial page —*Current Biog.*> ~ *vi* **:** to become lively
live oak \'lī-ˌvōk\ *n* **:** any of several American evergreen oaks: as **a :** a medium-sized oak (*Quercus virginiana*) of southeastern No. America often cultivated as a shelter and shade tree and noted for its extremely hard tough durable wood **b :** any of various western No. American oaks with evergreen foliage and hard durable wood
live out *vi* **:** to live outside one's place of employment — used of a servant
live parking *n* **:** the parking of a vehicle with a driver or operator in attendance
[1]liv·er \'liv-ər\ *n* [ME, fr. OE *lifer;* akin to OHG *lebra* liver] **1 a :** a large very vascular glandular organ of vertebrates that secretes bile and causes important changes in many of the substances contained in the blood (as by converting sugars into glycogen which it stores up until required and in forming urea) **b :** any of various large compound glands associated with the digestive tract of invertebrate animals and prob. concerned with the secretion of digestive enzymes **2** *archaic* **:** a determinant of the quality or temper of a man **3 :** the tissue of the liver (as of a calf or pig) eaten as food **4 :** a grayish reddish brown — called also *liver brown, liver maroon*
[2]liv·er \'liv-ər\ *n* **1 :** one that lives esp. in a specified way <a fast ~> **2 :** RESIDENT
-liv·ered \'liv-ərd\ *comb form* **:** expressing vigor or courage considered suggestive of one with (such) a liver <chicken-*livered*> <lily-*livered*>
liver fluke *n* **:** any of various trematode worms (as *Fasciola hepatica*) that invade the mammalian liver
liv·er·ied \'liv-(ə-)rēd\ *adj* **:** wearing a livery <a ~ chauffeur>
liv·er·ish \'liv-(ə-)rish\ *adj* **1 :** resembling liver esp. in color **2 a :** suffering from liver disorder **:** BILIOUS **b :** PEEVISH, IRASCIBLE — **liv·er·ish·ness** *n*
liver sausage *n* **:** a sausage containing cooked ground liver and pork trimmings — called also *liver pudding*
liv·er·wort \'liv-ər-ˌwərt, -ˌwȯ(ə)rt\ *n* **1 :** a bryophyte of a class (Hepaticae) related to and resembling the mosses but differing in reproduction, development, and in the structure of the gametophyte **2 :** HEPATICA

liverwort 1

liv·er·wurst \'liv-ə(r)-ˌwərst, -ˌwu̇(ə)rst; 'liv-ər-ˌwu̇s(h)t\ *n* [part trans. of G *leberwurst,* fr. *leber* liver + *wurst* sausage] **:** LIVER SAUSAGE
[1]liv·ery \'liv-(ə-)rē\ *n, pl* **-er·ies** [ME, fr. OF *livree,* lit., delivery, fr. *livrer* to deliver, fr. L *liberare* to free — more at LIBERATE] **1** *archaic* **:** the apportioning of provisions esp. to servants **:** ALLOWANCE **2 a :** the distinctive clothing or badge formerly worn by the retainers of a person of rank **b :** a servant's uniform **c :** distinctive dress **:** GARB **3** *archaic* **a :** one's retainers or retinue **b :** the members of a British livery company **4 a :** the feeding, stabling, and care of horses for pay **b :** LIVERY STABLE **c :** a concern offering vehicles (as boats) for rent **5 :** the act of delivering legal possession of property
[2]livery *adj* **1 :** resembling liver **2 :** suggesting liver disorder **:** LIVERISH
livery company *n* **:** any of various London craft or trade associations that are descended from medieval guilds
liv·ery·man \'liv-(ə-)rē-mən\ *n* **1** *archaic* **:** a liveried retainer **2 :** a freeman of the city of London entitled to wear the livery of the company to which he belongs **3 :** the keeper of a vehicle-rental service
livery stable *n* **:** a stable where horses and vehicles are kept for hire and where stabling is provided — called also *livery barn*
lives *pl of* LIFE
live steam *n* **:** steam direct from a boiler and under full pressure
live·stock \'līv-ˌstäk\ *n* **:** animals kept or raised for use or pleasure; *esp* **:** farm animals kept for use and profit
live·trap \'līv-ˌtrap\ *vt* **:** to capture (an animal) in a live trap
live trap *n* **:** a trap for catching an animal alive and uninjured
live wire *n* **:** an alert, active, or aggressive person
liv·id \'liv-əd\ *adj* [F *livide,* fr. L *lividus,* fr. *livēre* to be blue; akin to OE *slāh* sloe, Russ *sliva* plum] **1 :** discolored by bruising **:** BLACK-AND-BLUE <the ~ traces of the sharp scourges —Abraham Cowley> **2 :** ASHEN, PALLID <this cross, thy ~ face, thy pierced hands and feet —Walt Whitman> **3 :** REDDISH <a fan of gladiolas blushed ~ under the electric letters —Truman Capote> **4 :** very angry **:** ENRAGED <was ~ at his son's disobedience> — **li·vid·i·ty** \liv-'id-ət-ē\ *n* — **liv·id·ness** \'liv-əd-nəs\ *n*
[1]liv·ing \'liv-iŋ\ *adj* **1 a :** having life **b :** ACTIVE, FUNCTIONING <~ languages> **2 a :** exhibiting the life or motion of nature **:** NATURAL <the wilderness is a ~ museum . . . of natural history —*NEA Jour.*> **b :** [2]LIVE 3a **3 a :** full of life or vigor <made mathematics a ~ subject> **b :** true to life **:** VIVID <the program was televised in ~ color> **c :** suited for living <the ~ area> **4 :** involving living persons **5 :** VERY — used as an intensive <scared the ~ daylights out of him> — **liv·ing·ness** *n*
syn LIVING, ALIVE, ANIMATE, ANIMATED, VITAL *shared meaning element* **:** having or showing life ***ant*** lifeless
[2]living *n* **1 :** the condition of being alive **2 :** conduct or manner of life <the collegiate way of ~ —J. B. Conant> **3 a :** means of subsistence **:** LIVELIHOOD <earning a ~> **b** *archaic* **:** ESTATE, PROPERTY **c** *Brit* **:** BENEFICE 1
living death *n* **:** life emptied of joys and satisfactions <the *living death* of a concentration camp>
living fossil *n* **:** an organism (as a horseshoe crab or a ginkgo tree) that has remained essentially unchanged from earlier geologic times and whose close relatives are usu. extinct
liv·ing·ly \'liv-iŋ-lē\ *adv* **:** in a vital manner **:** REALISTICALLY
living room *n* **1 :** a room in a residence used for the common social activities of the occupants **2 :** LEBENSRAUM — called also *living space*
living standard *n* **:** STANDARD OF LIVING
living unit *n* **:** an apartment or house for use by one family

living wage *n* **1 :** a subsistence wage **2 :** a wage sufficient to provide the necessities and comforts essential to an acceptable standard of living

liv·re \ˈlēvrᵊ\ *n* [F, fr. L *libra,* a unit of weight] **1 :** an old French monetary unit equal to 20 sols **2 :** a coin representing one livre

lix·iv·i·ate \lik-ˈsiv-ē-ˌāt\ *vt* **-at·ed; -at·ing** [LL *lixivium* lye, fr. L *lixivius* made of lye, fr. *lixa* lye — more at LIQUID] **:** to extract a soluble constituent from (a solid mixture) by washing or percolation — **lix·iv·i·a·tion** \(ˌ)lik-ˌsiv-ē-ˈā-shən\ *n*

liz·ard \ˈliz-ərd\ *n* [ME *liserd,* fr. MF *laisarde,* fr. L *lacerta;* akin to L *lacertus* muscle — more at LEG] **:** any of a suborder (Lacertilia) of reptiles distinguished from the snakes by a fused inseparable lower jaw, a single temporal opening, two pairs of well differentiated functional limbs which may be lacking in burrowing forms, external ears, and eyes with movable lids; *broadly* **:** any relatively long-bodied reptile (as a crocodile or dinosaur) with legs and tapering tail

lizard's tail *n* **:** a No. American herbaceous perennial plant (*Saururus cernuus*) with small white apetalous flowers

LJ *abbr* lord justice

Lk *abbr* Luke

ll *abbr* lines

LL *abbr* **1** lending library **2** limited liability **3** lower left

ˈll \l, əl, ᵊl\ *vb* **:** WILL <you*'ll* be late>

lla·ma \ˈläm-ə\ *n* [Sp, fr. Quechua] **:** any of several wild and domesticated So. American ruminants (genus *Lama*) related to the camels but smaller and without a hump; *esp* **:** the domesticated guanaco used in the Andes as a beast of burden and a source of wool

llama

lla·no \ˈlän-(ˌ)ō, ˈlan-\ *n, pl* **llanos** [Sp, plain, fr. L *planum* — more at PLAIN] **:** an open grassy plain in Spanish America or the southwestern U.S.

LLB *abbr* [NL *legum baccalaureus*] bachelor of laws

LLD *abbr* [NL *legum doctor*] doctor of laws

LLM *abbr* [NL *legum magister*] master of laws

Lloyd's \ˈlȯidz\ *n* **:** an association of individual underwriters in London specializing in marine insurance and shipping news and insuring for losses of almost every conceivable kind

LM *abbr* **1** Legion of Merit **2** long meter **3** lunar module

LMG *abbr* light machine gun

LMT *abbr* local mean time

ln *symbol* natural logarithm

Indg *abbr* landing

LNG *abbr* liquefied natural gas

lo \ˈlō\ *interj* [ME, fr. OE *lā*] — used to call attention or to express wonder or surprise

loach \ˈlōch\ *n* [ME *loche,* fr. MF] **:** any of a family (Cobitidae) of small Old World freshwater fishes related to the carps

¹load \ˈlōd\ *n* [ME *lod,* fr. OE *lād* support, carrying — more at LODE] **1 a :** whatever is put on a man or pack animal to be carried **:** PACK **b :** whatever is put in a ship or vehicle or airplane for conveyance **:** CARGO; *esp* **:** a quantity of material assembled or packed as a shipping unit **c :** the quantity that can be carried at one time by a specified means; *esp* **:** a measured quantity of a commodity fixed for each type of carrier — often used in combination <a boat*load* of tourists> **2 a :** a mass or weight supported by something <branches bent low by their ~ of fruit> **b :** the forces to which a structure is subjected due to superposed weight or to wind pressure on the vertical surfaces **3 a :** something that weighs down the mind or spirits <took a ~ off her mind> **b :** a burdensome or laborious responsibility <always carried his share of the ~> **4** *slang* **:** an intoxicating amount of liquor drunk **5 :** a large quantity **:** LOT — usu. used in pl. **6 a :** a charge for a firearm **b :** the quantity of material loaded into a device at one time **7 :** external resistance overcome by a machine or prime mover **8 a :** power output (as of a power plant) **b :** a device to which power is delivered **9 a (1) :** the amount of work that a person carries or is expected to carry **(2) :** the amount of authorized work to be performed by a machine, a group, a department, or a factory **b :** the demand on the operating resources of a system (as a telephone exchange or a refrigerating apparatus) **10** *slang* **:** EYEFUL — used in the phrase *get a load of* **11 :** the decrease in capacity for survival of the average individual in a population due to the presence of deleterious genes in the gene pool <genetic ~> <mutational ~>

²load *vt* **1 a :** to put a load in or on <~ a truck> **b :** to place in or on a means of conveyance <~ freight> **2 a :** to encumber or oppress with something heavy, laborious, or disheartening **:** BURDEN <a company ~*ed* down with debts> **b :** to place as a burden or obligation <~ more work on him> **3 a :** to increase the weight of by adding something heavy **b :** to add a conditioning substance (as a mineral salt) to for body **c :** to add filler to (paper) **d :** to weight or shape (dice) to fall unfairly **e :** to pack with one-sided or prejudicial influences **:** BIAS **f :** to charge with emotional associations **g :** to weight (as a test) with factors influencing validity or outcome **4 a :** to supply in abundance or excess **:** HEAP **b :** to put runners on (first, second, and third bases) in baseball **5 a :** to put a load or charge in (a device or piece of equipment) <~ a gun> **b :** to place or insert as a load in a device or piece of equipment <~ film in a camera> **6 :** to alter (as an alcoholic drink) by adding an adulterant or drug **7 a :** to add loading to (an insurance premium) **b :** to add a sum to after profits and expenses are accounted for <~*ed* prices> ~ *vi* **1 :** to receive a load **2 :** to put a load on or in a carrier, device, or container; *esp* **:** to insert the charge or cartridge in the chamber of a firearm — **load·er** *n*

load·ed *adj* **1** *slang* **:** DRUNK **2 :** having a large amount of money

load·ing *n* **1 :** a cargo, weight, or stress placed on something **2 :** an amount added (as to the net premium in insurance) to represent business expenses, future contingencies, or profit **3 :** material used to load something **:** FILLER

load line *n* **:** the line on a ship indicating the depth to which it sinks in the water when properly loaded

load·star *var of* LODESTAR

load·stone *var of* LODESTONE

¹loaf \ˈlōf\ *n, pl* **loaves** \ˈlōvz\ [ME *lof,* fr. OE *hlāf;* akin to OHG *hleib* loaf] **1 :** a shaped or molded mass of bread **2 :** a regularly molded often rectangular mass: as **a :** a conical mass of sugar **b :** a dish (as of seasoned meat or fish) baked in the form of a loaf

²loaf *vi* [prob. back-formation fr. *loafer*] **:** to spend time in idleness

loaf·er \ˈlō-fər\ *n* [perh. short for *landloafer,* fr. G *landläufer* tramp, fr. *land* + *läufer* runner] **:** one that loafs **:** IDLER

Loafer *trademark* — used for a low leather step-in shoe with an upper resembling the moccasin but with a broad flat heel

loam \ˈlōm, ˈlüm\ *n* [ME *lom,* fr. OE *lām;* akin to OE *līm* lime] **1 a :** a mixture (as for plastering) composed chiefly of moistened clay **b :** a coarse molding sand used in founding **2 :** SOIL; *specif* **:** a soil consisting of a friable mixture of varying proportions of clay, silt, and sand — **loamy** \ˈlō-mē, ˈlü-\ *adj*

¹loan \ˈlōn\ *n* [ME *lon,* fr. ON *lān;* akin to OE *lǣn* loan, *lēon* to lend, L *linquere* to leave, Gk *leipein*] **1 a :** money lent at interest **b :** something lent usu. for the borrower's temporary use **2 a :** the grant of temporary use **b :** the temporary duty of a person transferred to another job for a limited time **3 :** LOANWORD

²loan *vt* **:** LEND <books . . . ~*ed* to children for home use — Phyllis A. Lewis> — **loan·able** \ˈlō-nə-bəl\ *adj*

lo and behold *interj* — used to express wonder or surprise

loan·er \ˈlō-nər\ *n* **:** one (as a car or a watch) that is lent esp. as a replacement for something being repaired

loan·ing \ˈlō-niŋ\ *n* [ME *loning,* fr. *lone,* alter. of *lane*] **1** *dial Brit* **:** LANE **2** *dial Brit* **:** a milking yard

loan shark *n* **:** one who lends money to individuals at exorbitant rates of interest

loan·shark·ing \-ˌshär-kiŋ\ *n* **:** the practice of lending money at exorbitant rates of interest

loan translation *n* **:** a compound, derivative, or phrase that is introduced into a language through translation of the constituents of a term in another language (as *superman* from German *Übermensch*)

loan·word \ˈlōn-ˌwərd\ *n* **:** a word taken from another language and at least partly naturalized

loath \ˈlōth, ˈlōth\ *also* **loathe** \ˈlōth, ˈlōth\ *adj* [ME *loth* loathsome, fr. OE *lāth;* akin to OHG *leid* loathsome, OIr *liuss* aversion] **:** unwilling to do something contrary to one's likes, sympathies, or ways of thinking **:** RELUCTANT ***syn*** see DISINCLINED ***ant*** anxious — **loath·ness** *n*

loathe \ˈlōth\ *vt* **loathed; loath·ing** [ME *lothen,* fr. OE *lāthian,* fr. *lāth*] **:** to dislike greatly and often with disgust or intolerance **:** DETEST ***syn*** see HATE ***ant*** dote (*on*) — **loath·er** *n*

loath·ing \ˈlō-thiŋ\ *n* **:** extreme disgust **:** DETESTATION

¹loath·ly \ˈlōth-lē, ˈlōth-\ *adj* **:** LOATHSOME, REPULSIVE

²loath·ly \ˈlōth-lē, ˈlōth-\ *adv* **:** not willingly **:** RELUCTANTLY

loath·some \ˈlōth-səm, ˈlōth-\ *adj* [ME *lothsum,* fr. *loth* evil, fr. OE *lāth,* fr. *lāth,* adj.] **:** giving rise to loathing **:** DISGUSTING — **loath·some·ly** *adv* — **loath·some·ness** *n*

¹lob \ˈläb\ *n* [prob. of LG origin; akin to LG *lubbe* coarse person] *dial Brit* **:** a dull heavy person **:** LOUT

²lob *vb* **lobbed; lob·bing** [*lob* (a loosely hanging object)] *vt* **1 :** to let hang heavily **:** DROOP **2 :** to throw, hit, or propel easily or in a high arc ~ *vi* **1 a :** to move slowly and heavily **b :** to move in an arc **2 :** to hit a tennis ball easily in a high arc

³lob *n* **:** a ball that is lobbed

lob- *or* **lobo-** *comb form* [*lobe*] **:** lobe <*lob*ar> <*lobo*tomy>

lo·bar \ˈlō-bər, -ˌbär\ *adj* **:** of or relating to a lobe

lo·bate \ˈlō-ˌbāt\ *also* **lo·bat·ed** \-ˌbāt-əd\ *adj* [NL *lobatus,* fr. LL *lobus*] **1 :** having lobes **2 :** resembling a lobe — **lo·bate·ly** *adv*

lo·ba·tion \lō-ˈbā-shən\ *n* **1 a :** the quality or state of being lobed **b :** the formation of lobes or lobules **2 a :** LOBE **b :** LOBULE

lobation of leaves: *1* lobed, *2* cleft, *3* parted, *4* divided

¹lob·by \ˈläb-ē\ *n, pl* **lobbies** [ML *lobium* gallery, of Gmc origin; akin to OHG *louba* porch] **1 :** a corridor or hall connected with a larger room or series of rooms and used as a passageway or waiting room: as **a :** an anteroom of a legislative chamber; *esp* **:** one of two anterooms of a British parliamentary chamber to which members go to vote during a division **b :** a large hall serving as a foyer (as of a hotel or theater) **2 :** a group of persons engaged in lobbying esp. as representatives of a particular interest group

²lobby *vb* **lob·bied; lob·by·ing** *vi* **:** to conduct activities aimed at influencing public officials and esp. members of a legislative body on legislation ~ *vt* **1 :** to promote (as a project) or secure the passage of (as legislation) by influencing public officials **2 :** to attempt to influence or sway (as a public official) toward a desired action — **lob·by·er** *n* — **lob·by·ism** \-ē-ˌiz-əm\ *n* — **lob·by·ist** \-ē-əst\ *n*

lob·by·gow \ˈläb-ē-ˌgau̇\ *n* [origin unknown] **:** an errand boy

lobe \ˈlōb\ *n* [MF, fr. LL *lobus,* fr. Gk *lobos* — more at SLEEP] **:** a curved or rounded projection or division; *specif* **:** a usu. somewhat rounded projection or division of a bodily organ or part

lo·bec·to·my \lō-ˈbek-tə-mē\ *n, pl* **-mies** [ISV] **:** surgical removal of a lobe of an organ (as a lung) or gland

lobed \ˈlōbd\ *adj* **:** LOBATE 1

lobe–fin \ˈlōb-ˌfin\ *n* **:** any of a large group (Crossopterygii) of fishes (as a latimeria) that have paired fins suggesting limbs, that may be ancestral to the terrestrial vertebrates, and that are mostly extinct — **lobe–finned** \-'find\ *adj*

lobe–finned fish *n* : LOBE-FIN

lo·be·lia \lō-'bēl-yə, -'bē-lē-ə\ *n* [NL, genus name, fr. Matthias de *Lobel* †1616 Flem botanist] **1** : any of a genus (*Lobelia* of the family Lobeliaceae, the lobelia family) of widely distributed herbaceous plants cultivated for their terminal clusters of showy lipped flowers **2** : the leaves and tops of Indian tobacco

lo·be·line \'lō-bə-ˌlēn\ *n* [NL *Lobelia* + E *-ine*] : a crystalline alkaloid $C_{22}H_{27}NO_2$ that is obtained from Indian tobacco and is used chiefly as a respiratory stimulant and as a smoking deterrent

lob·lol·ly \'läb-ˌläl-ē\ *n, pl* **-lies** [prob. fr. E dial. *lob* (to boil) + obs. E dial. *lolly* broth] **1** *dial* **a** : a thick gruel **b** : MIRE, MUDHOLE **2** *dial* : LOUT

loblolly pine *n* : a pine (*Pinus taeda*) of the southern U.S. with flaky bark, long needles in groups of three, and spiny tipped cones; *also* : its coarse-grained wood

lo·bo \'lō-(ˌ)bō\ *n, pl* **lobos** [Sp, wolf, fr. L *lupus* — more at WOLF] : TIMBER WOLF

lo·bot·o·my \lō-'bät-ə-mē\ *n, pl* **-mies** [ISV] : severance of nerve fibers (as of the frontal lobes) by incision into the brain for the relief of some mental disorders and tensions

lob·scouse \'läb-ˌskau̇s\ *n* [origin unknown] : a sailor's dish prepared by stewing or baking bits of meat with vegetables and hardtack

lob·ster \'läb-stər\ *n* [ME, fr. OE *loppestre*, fr. *loppe* spider; akin to ME *sloberen* to slobber] **1** : any of a family (Homaridae and esp. genus *Homarus*) of large edible marine decapod crustaceans that have stalked eyes, a pair of large claws, and a long abdomen and that include species from coasts on both sides of the North Atlantic and from the Cape of Good Hope **2** : SPINY LOBSTER

lobster 1

lob·ster·man \-mən\ *n* : one whose business is catching lobsters

lobster pot *n* : an oblong case with slat sides and a funnel-shaped net used as a trap for catching lobsters

lobster shift *n* : a work shift (as on a newspaper) that covers the late evening and early morning hours — called also *lobster trick*

lobster ther·mi·dor \-'thər-mə-ˌdȯ(ə)r\ *n* [*thermidor* fr. F, fr. *Thermidor*, drama (1891) by Victorien Sardou] : cooked lobster meat in a rich wine sauce stuffed into a lobster shell and browned

lobster trap *n* : LOBSTER POT

lob·u·lar \'läb-yə-lər\ *adj* : of, relating to, or resembling a lobule — **lob·u·lar·ly** *adv*

lob·u·late \'läb-yə-ˌlāt\ *also* **lob·u·lat·ed** \-ˌlāt-əd\ *adj* : made up of or provided with lobules <the pancreas is a ~ organ> — **lob·u·la·tion** \ˌläb-yə-'lā-shən\ *n*

lob·ule \'läb-(ˌ)yü(ə)l\ *n* : a small lobe; *also* : a subdivision of a lobe — **lob·u·lose** \-yə-ˌlōs\ *adj*

LOC *abbr* lines of communication

1lo·cal \'lō-kəl\ *adj* [ME *localle*, fr. MF *local*, fr. LL *localis*, fr. L *locus* place — more at STALL] **1** : characterized by or relating to position in space : having a definite spatial form or location **2** : of or relating to a particular place : characteristic of a particular place : not general or widespread **3 a** : primarily serving the needs of a particular limited district **b** *of a public conveyance* : making all the stops on a route **4** : involving or affecting only a restricted part of the organism : TOPICAL **5** : of or relating to telephone communication within a specified area — **lo·cal·ly** \-kə-lē\ *adv*

2local *n* : a local person or thing: as **a** : a local public conveyance (as a train or an elevator) **b** : a local or particular branch, lodge, or chapter of an organization

local color *n* : color in writing derived from the presentation of the features and peculiarities of a particular locality and its inhabitants

lo·cale \lō-'kal\ *n* [modif. of F *local*, fr. *local*, adj.] **1** : a place or locality esp. when viewed in relation to a particular event or characteristic **2** : SITE, SCENE <the ~ of a story>

local government *n* : the government of a specific local area constituting a subdivision of a major political unit (as a nation or state); *also* : the body of persons constituting such a government

lo·cal·ism \'lō-kə-ˌliz-əm\ *n* **1** : affection or partiality for a particular place : SECTIONALISM **2 a** : a local idiom **b** : a local peculiarity of speaking or acting

lo·cal·ite \'lō-kə-ˌlīt\ *n* : a native or resident of the locality under consideration : LOCAL

lo·cal·i·ty \lō-'kal-ət-ē\ *n, pl* **-ties** **1** : the fact or condition of having a location in space or time **2** : a particular place, situation, or location

lo·cal·ize \'lō-kə-ˌlīz\ *vb* **-ized; -iz·ing** *vt* **1** : to make local : orient locally **2** : to assign to or keep within a definite locality ~ *vi* : to collect in a specific or limited area — **lo·cal·iza·tion** \ˌlō-kə-lə-'zā-shən\ *n*

local option *n* : the power granted by a legislature to a political subdivision to determine by popular vote the local applicability of a law on a controversial issue (as the sale of liquor)

local time *n* : time based on the meridian through a particular place as contrasted with that of a time zone

lo·cate \'lō-ˌkāt, lō-'\ *vb* **lo·cat·ed; lo·cat·ing** [L *locatus*, pp. of *locare* to place, fr. *locus*] *vi* : to establish oneself or one's business : SETTLE ~ *vt* **1** : to determine or indicate the place, site, or limits of **2** : to set or establish in a particular spot : STATION **3** : to seek out and determine the location of **4** : to find or fix the place of esp. in a sequence : CLASSIFY — **lo·cat·able** \-ˌkāt-ə-bəl, -'kāt-\ *adj* — **lo·cat·er** *n*

lo·ca·tion \lō-'kā-shən\ *n* **1** : the act or process of locating **2 a** : a position or site occupied or available for occupancy or marked by some distinguishing feature : SITUATION **b** (1) : a tract of land designated for a purpose (2) *Austral* : FARM, STATION **c** : a place outside a motion-picture studio where a picture or part of it is filmed — usu. used in the phrase *on location* — **lo·ca·tion·al** \-shnəl, -shən-ᵊl\ *adj* — **lo·ca·tion·al·ly** \-ē\ *adv*

1loc·a·tive \'läk-ət-iv\ *n* [L *locus* + E *-ative* (as in *vocative*)] : the locative case; *also* : a word in that case

2locative *adj* : of or being a grammatical case that denotes place or the place where or wherein

lo·ca·tor \'lō-ˌkāt-ər, lō-'\ *n* : one that locates something (as a mining claim or the course of a road)

loc cit *abbr* [L *loco citato*] in the place cited

loch \'läk, 'läk\ *n* [ME (Sc) *louch*, fr. ScGael *loch*; akin to L *lacus* lake] **1** *Scot* : LAKE **2** *Scot* : a bay or arm of the sea esp. when nearly landlocked

loci *pl of* LOCUS

1lock \'läk\ *n* [ME *lok*, fr. OE *locc*; akin to OHG *loc* lock, L *luctari* to struggle, *luxus* dislocated] **1 a** : a tuft, tress, or ringlet of hair **b** *pl* : the hair of the head **2** : a cohering bunch (as of wool, cotton, or flax) : TUFT

2lock *n* [ME *lok*, fr. OE *loc*; akin to OHG *loh* enclosure, OE *locc* lock of hair] **1 a** : a fastening (as for a door) operated by a key or a combination **b** : the mechanism for exploding the charge or cartridge of a firearm **2 a** : an enclosure (as in a canal) with gates at each end used in raising or lowering boats as they pass from level to level **b** : AIR LOCK **3 a** : a locking or fastening together **b** : an intricate mass of objects impeding each other (as in a traffic jam) **c** : a hold in wrestling secured on one part of the body; *broadly* : a controlling hold <his paper . . . had a ~ on a large part of the state —John Corry>

3lock *vt* **1 a** : to fasten the lock of **b** : to make fast with or as if with a lock <~ up the house> **2 a** : to fasten in or out or to make secure or inaccessible by or as if by means of locks <~*ed* himself away from the curious world> <~*ed* her husband out> **b** : to hold fast or inactive : fix in a particular situation or method of operation <a team firmly ~*ed* in last place> <afraid of being ~*ed* into the system> **3 a** : to make fast by the interlacing or interlocking of parts **b** : to hold in a close embrace **c** : to grapple in combat; *also* : to bind closely <administration and students were ~*ed* in conflict> **d** : to fasten (imposed letterpress matter) securely in a chase or on the bed of a press by tightening the quoins; *also* : to attach (a curved plate) to the plate cylinder of a rotary press **4** : to invest (capital) without assurance of easy convertibility into money **5 a** : to move or permit to pass (as a ship) by raising or lowering in a lock **b** : to provide (as a canal) with locks ~ *vi* **1 a** : to become locked **b** : to be capable of being locked **2** : INTERLACE, INTERLOCK **3 a** : to build locks to facilitate navigation **b** : to go or pass by means of a lock (as in a canal) — **lock·able** \'läk-ə-bəl\ *adj* — **lock horns** : to come into conflict

lock·age \'läk-ij\ *n* **1** : an act or the process of passing a ship through a lock **2** : a system of locks **3** : toll paid for passing through a lock

lock·box \'läk-ˌbäks\ *n* : a box (as a post-office box, strongbox, or safety-deposit box) that locks

locked–in \'läk-'tin\ *adj* **1** : unalterably fixed **2** : unable or unwilling to shift invested funds because of the tax effect of realizing capital gains

lock·er \'läk-ər\ *n* **1 a** : a drawer, cupboard, or compartment that may be closed with a lock; *esp* : one for individual storage use **b** : a chest or compartment on shipboard for compact stowage of articles **c** : a compartment for storing quick-frozen foods for long periods usu. at or below 0° F and at 80% relative humidity **2** : one that locks

locker paper *n* : a flexible protective paper for wrapping food for quick-freezing and storage

locker room *n* : a room for changing clothes and for storing clothing and equipment in lockers; *esp* : one for use by sports participants

lock·et \'läk-ət\ *n* [MF *loquet* latch, fr. MD *loke*; akin to OE *loc*] : a small case usu. of precious metal that has space for a memento and that is worn typically suspended from a chain or necklace

lock·jaw \'läk-ˌjȯ\ *n* : an early symptom of tetanus characterized by spasm of the jaw muscles and inability to open the jaws; *also* : TETANUS

lock·nut \-ˌnət, -'nət\ *n* **1** : a nut screwed down hard on another to prevent it from slacking back **2** : a nut so constructed that it locks itself when screwed up tight

lock on *vt* : to sight and follow (a target) automatically by means of a radar beam or sensor

lock·out \'läk-ˌau̇t\ *n* : the withholding of employment by an employer and the whole or partial closing of his business establishment in order to gain concessions from or resist demands of employees

lock out \(ˈ)läk-'au̇t\ *vt* : to subject (a body of employees) to a lockout

lock·ram \'läk-rəm\ *n* [ME *lokerham*, fr. *Locronan*, town in Brittany] : a coarse plain-woven linen formerly used in England

lock·smith \'läk-ˌsmith\ *n* : one who makes or repairs locks

lock·smith·ing \-iŋ\ *n* : the work or business of a locksmith

lock·step \'läk-ˌstep\ *n* **1** : a mode of marching in step by a body of men going one after another as closely as possible **2** : a standard method or procedure that is mindlessly adhered to or that minimizes individuality

lock·stitch \-ˌstich\ *n* : a sewing machine stitch formed by the looping together of two threads one on each side of the material being sewn — **lockstitch** *vb*

lock, stock, and barrel *adv* [fr. the principal parts of a flintlock] : WHOLLY, COMPLETELY <the only thing which had not been sold

lock, stock, and barrel with the . . . house was this piano —Marcia Davenport>
lock·up \ˈläk-ˌəp\ *n* **1 :** an act of locking : the state of being locked **2 :** JAIL; *esp* : a local jail where persons are detained prior to court hearing
¹lo·co \ˈlō-(ˌ)kō\ *n, pl* **locos** *or* **locoes** [MexSp, fr. Sp, crazy] **1** : LOCOWEED **2 :** LOCOISM
²loco *vt* **1 :** to poison with locoweed **2 :** to make frenzied or crazy
³loco *adj* [Sp] *slang* : out of one's mind : CRAZY, FRENZIED <most of the resident foreigners . . . take to drink, driven ~ by the Portuguese peculiarities —Mary McCarthy>
⁴loco *adv or adj* [It dial, there, fr. L *in loco* in the place] : in the register as written — used as a direction in music
lo·co·fo·co \ˌlō-kə-ˈfō-(ˌ)kō\ *n, pl* **-focos** [prob. fr. ¹*loco*motive + It *fuoco, foco* fire, fr. L *focus* hearth] **1 a :** a match capable of being ignited by friction on a hard dry rough surface **b :** a cigar with an end that is ignitable by friction **2** *cap* **a :** a member of a radical group of New York Democrats organized in 1835 in opposition to the regular party organization **b :** DEMOCRAT 2
lo·co·ism \ˈlō-(ˌ)kō-ˌiz-əm\ *n* : a disease of horses, cattle, and sheep caused by chronic poisoning with locoweeds
lo·co·mote \ˈlō-kə-ˌmōt\ *vi* **-mot·ed; -mot·ing** [back-formation fr. *locomotion*] : to move about
lo·co·mo·tion \ˌlō-kə-ˈmō-shən\ *n* [L *locus* + E *motion*] **1 :** an act or the power of moving from place to place **2 :** TRAVEL
¹lo·co·mo·tive \ˌlō-kə-ˈmōt-iv\ *adj* **1 a :** of, relating to, or functioning in locomotion **b :** having the ability to move independently from place to place **2 :** of or relating to travel **3 :** of, relating to, or being a machine that moves about by operation of its own mechanism
²locomotive *n* **1 :** a self-propelled vehicle that runs on rails, utilizes any of several forms of energy for producing motion, and is used for moving railroad cars **2 :** a school or college cheer characterized by a slow beginning and a progressive increase in speed
lo·co·mo·tor \ˌlō-kə-ˈmōt-ər\ *adj* **1 :** LOCOMOTIVE 1 **2 :** affecting or involving the locomotive organs
locomotor ataxia *n* : a syphilitic disorder of the nervous system marked esp. by disturbances of gait and difficulty in coordinating voluntary movements
lo·co·mo·to·ry \ˌlō-kə-ˈmōt-ə-rē\ *adj* : LOCOMOTOR
lo·co·weed \ˈlō-(ˌ)kō-ˌwēd\ *n* : any of several leguminous plants (genera *Astragalus* and *Oxytropis*) of western No. America that cause locoism in livestock
loc·u·lar \ˈläk-yə-lər\ *adj* : having or composed of loculi — often used in combination <multi*locular*>
loc·u·late \ˈläk-yə-lət, -ˌlāt\ *or* **loc·u·lat·ed** \-ˌlāt-əd\ *adj* : having or divided into loculi — **loc·u·la·tion** \ˌläk-yə-ˈlā-shən\ *n*
loc·ule \ˈläk-(ˌ)yü(ə)l\ *n* [F, fr. L *loculus*] : LOCULUS; *esp* : any of the cells of a compound ovary of a plant — **loc·uled** \-(ˌ)yü(ə)ld\ *adj*
loc·u·li·ci·dal \ˌläk-yə-lə-ˈsīd-ᵊl\ *adj* [NL *loculus* + L *-cidere* to cut, fr. *caedere* — more at CONCISE] : dehiscing longitudinally so as to bisect each loculus <~ fruit> — **loc·u·li·ci·dal·ly** \-ᵊl-ē\ *adv*

locoweed

loc·u·lus \ˈläk-yə-ləs\ *n, pl* **-li** \-ˌlī, -ˌlē\ [NL, fr. L, dim. of *locus*] : a small chamber or cavity esp. in a plant or animal body
lo·cum te·nens \ˌlō-kəm-ˈtē-ˌnenz, -nənz\ *n, pl* **locum te·nen·tes** \-ti-ˈnen-ˌtēz\ [ML, lit., one holding a place] : one filling an office for a time or temporarily taking the place of another — used esp. of a doctor or clergyman
lo·cus \ˈlō-kəs\ *n, pl* **lo·ci** \ˈlō-ˌsī, -ˌkī, -ˌkē\ [L — more at STALL] **1 a :** PLACE, LOCALITY <was the culture of medicine in the beginning dispersed from a single focus or did it arise in several *loci?* —S. C. Harvey> **b :** a center of activity or concentration <in democracy the ~ of power is in the people —H. G. Rickover> **2 :** the set of all points whose location is determined by stated conditions **3** : the position in a chromosome of a particular gene or allele
lo·cus clas·si·cus \ˌlō-kəs-ˈklas-i-kəs\ *n, pl* **lo·ci clas·si·ci** \-ˌsī-ˈklas-ə-ˌsī, -ˌkī-ˈklas-ə-ˌkī, -ˌkē-ˈklas-ə-ˌkē\ [NL] : a passage that has become a standard for the elucidation of a word or subject
lo·cust \ˈlō-kəst\ *n* [ME, fr. L *locusta*] **1 :** SHORT-HORNED GRASSHOPPER; *esp* : a migratory grasshopper often traveling in vast swarms and stripping the areas passed of all vegetation **2 :** CICADA **3 a :** any of various hard-wooded leguminous trees: as (1) : CAROB 1 (2) : BLACK LOCUST (3) : HONEY LOCUST **b :** the wood of a locust tree
locust bean *n* : CAROB
lo·cu·tion \lō-ˈkyü-shən\ *n* [ME *locucioun,* fr. L *locution-, locutio,* fr. *locutus,* pp. of *loqui* to speak] **1 :** a particular form of expression or a peculiarity of phrasing; *esp* : a word or expression characteristic of a region, group, or cultural level **2 :** style of discourse : PHRASEOLOGY
lode \ˈlōd\ *n* [ME, fr. OE *lād* course, support; akin to OE *līthan* to go — more at LEAD] **1** *dial Eng* : WATERWAY **2 :** an ore deposit **3 :** something that resembles a lode : an abundant store
lo·den \ˈlōd-ᵊn\ *n* [G, fr. OHG *lodo* coarse cloth] **1 :** a thick woolen cloth used for outer clothing **2 :** a variable color averaging a dull grayish green
lode·star \ˈlōd-ˌstär\ *n* [ME *lode sterre,* fr. *lode* course, fr. OE *lād*] **1 :** a star that leads or guides; *esp* : NORTH STAR **2 :** something that serves as a guiding star
lode·stone \-ˌstōn\ *n* [obs. *lode* course, fr. ME] **1 :** magnetite possessing polarity **2 :** something that strongly attracts : MAGNET
¹lodge \ˈläj\ *vb* **lodged; lodg·ing** *vt* **1 a** (1) **:** to provide temporary quarters for (2) **:** to rent lodgings to **b :** to establish or settle in a place **2 :** to serve as a receptacle for : CONTAIN **3** : to beat (as a crop) flat to the ground **4 :** to bring to an intended or a fixed position (as by throwing or thrusting) **5 :** to deposit for safeguard or preservation **6 :** to place or vest esp. in a source, means, or agent **7 :** to lay (as a complaint) before a proper authority : FILE ~ *vi* **1 a :** to occupy a place temporarily : SLEEP **b** (1) **:** to have a residence : DWELL (2) **:** to be a lodger **2 :** to come to a rest **3 :** to fall or lie down — used esp. of hay or grain crops
²lodge *n* [ME *loge,* fr. OF, of Gmc origin; akin to OHG *louba* porch] **1** *chiefly dial* : a rude shelter or abode **2 a :** the meeting place of a branch of an organization and esp. a fraternal organization **b :** the body of members of such a branch **3 a** : a house set apart for residence in a particular season (as the hunting season) **b :** an inn or resort hotel **4 a :** a house on an estate orig. for the use of a gamekeeper, caretaker, or porter **b** : a shelter for an employee (as a gatekeeper) **5 :** a den or lair esp. of gregarious animals **6 a :** WIGWAM **b :** a family of No. American Indians
lodge·pole pine \ˌläj-ˌpōl-\ *n* : either of two pines of western No. America with needles in pairs and short ovoid usu. asymmetric cones: **a :** a scrubby coastal pine (*Pinus contorta*) with thick deeply furrowed bark and hard strong coarse-grained medium-light wood **b :** a tall straight pine (*P. contorta* var. *latifolia* syn. *P. murrayana*) with thin and little furrowed bark and soft weak fine-grained lightweight wood
lodg·er \ˈläj-ər\ *n* : one that lodges; *esp* : one who occupies a rented room in another's house
lodg·ing *n* **1 a :** a place to live : DWELLING **b :** LODGMENT 3b **2 a** (1) **:** sleeping accommodations <found ~ in the barn> (2) : a temporary place to stay <a ~ for the night> **b :** a room in the house of another used as a place of residence — usu. used in pl. **3 :** the act of lodging
lodging house *n* : a house where lodgings are provided and let
lodg·ment *or* **lodge·ment** \ˈläj-mənt\ *n* **1 a :** a lodging place : SHELTER <a hut for temporary ~ of cattlemen> **b :** ACCOMMODATIONS, LODGINGS <found ~ in the city> **2 a :** the act, fact, or manner of lodging **b :** a placing, depositing, or coming to rest **3 a :** an accumulation or collection deposited in a place or remaining at rest **b :** a place of rest or deposit
lod·i·cule \ˈläd-i-ˌkyü(ə)l\ *n* [L *lodicula,* dim. of *lodic-, lodix* cover] : one of usu. two delicate membranous hyaline scales at the base of the ovary of a grass that by their swelling assist in anthesis
loess \ˈles, ˈlə(r)s, ˈlō-əs\ *n* [G *löss*] : an unstratified usu. buff to yellowish brown loamy deposit found in No. America, Europe, and Asia and believed to be chiefly deposited by the wind — **loess·ial** \ˈles-ē-əl, ˈlə(r)s-, lō-ˈes-\ *adj*
¹loft \ˈlȯft\ *n* [ME, fr. OE, fr. ON *lopt* air; akin to OHG *luft* air] **1 :** an upper room or floor : ATTIC **2 a :** a gallery in a church or hall **b :** one of the upper floors of a warehouse or business building esp. when not partitioned **c :** HAYLOFT **3 a :** the backward slant of the face of a golf-club head **b :** the act of lofting
²loft *vt* **1 :** to place, house, or store in a loft **2 :** to propel through the air or into space <~*ed* a long hit to center> <instruments ~*ed* by a powerful rocket> **3 :** to lay out a full sized working drawing of the lines and contours of (as a ship's hull) ~ *vi* **1 :** to propel a ball high into the air **2 :** to rise high <a huge building ~*ing* into the sky>
lofty \ˈlȯf-tē\ *adj* **loft·i·er; -est** **1 :** having a haughty overbearing manner : SUPERCILIOUS **2 a :** elevated in character and spirit : NOBLE **b :** elevated in position : SUPERIOR **3 a :** rising to a great height : impressively high <~ mountains> **b :** REMOTE, ESOTERIC ***syn*** see HIGH — **loft·i·ly** \-tə-lē\ *adv* — **loft·i·ness** \-tē-nəs\ *n*
¹log \ˈlȯg, ˈläg\ *n, often attrib* [ME *logge,* prob. of Scand origin; akin to ON *lāg* fallen tree; akin to OE *licgan* to lie — more at LIE] **1** : a usu. bulky piece or length of unshaped timber; *esp* : a length of a tree trunk ready for sawing and over six feet long **2 :** an apparatus for measuring the rate of a ship's motion through the water that consists of a block fastened to a line and run out from a reel **3 a :** the record of the rate of a ship's speed or of her daily progress; *also* : the full nautical record of a ship's voyage **b** : the full record of a flight by an aircraft **4 :** any of various records of performance <a computer ~>
²log *vb* **logged; log·ging** *vt* **1 a :** to cut (trees) for lumber **b** : to clear (land) of trees in lumbering **2 :** to enter details of or about in a log **3 a :** to move (an indicated distance) or attain (an indicated speed) as noted in a log **b** (1) **:** to sail a ship or fly an airplane for (an indicated distance or period of time) (2) **:** to have (an indicated record) to one's credit : ACHIEVE <*logged* about 30,000 miles a year in his car> <racing drivers *logging* record speeds> ~ *vi* : ³LUMBER 1
³log *n* : LOGARITHM
⁴log *abbr* logic
log- *or* **logo-** *comb form* [Gk, fr. *logos* — more at LEGEND] : word : thought : speech : discourse <*logo*gram> <*logo*rrhea>
lo·gan·ber·ry \ˈlō-gən-ˌber-ē\ *n* [James H. *Logan* †1928 Am lawyer + E *berry*] : a red-fruited upright-growing dewberry regarded as a variety (*Rubus ursinus loganobaccus*) of the western dewberry or as a hybrid of the western dewberry and the red raspberry; *also* : its berry
log·a·oe·dic \ˌläg-ə-ˈēd-ik\ *adj* [LL *logaoedicus,* fr. LGk *logaoidikos,* fr. Gk *log-* + *aeidein* to sing; fr. the resemblance of such rhythm to prose — more at ODE] : marked by the mixture of several meters; *specif* : having a rhythm that uses both dactyls and trochees or anapests and iambs — **logaoedic** *n*
log·a·rithm \ˈlȯg-ə-ˌrith-əm, ˈläg-\ *n* [NL *logarithmus,* fr. *log-* + Gk *arithmos* number — more at ARITHMETIC] : the exponent that indicates the power to which a number is raised to produce a given number <the ~ of 100 to the base 10 is 2> — **log·a·rith·mic** \ˌlȯg-ə-ˈrith-mik, ˌläg-\ *adj* — **log·a·rith·mi·cal·ly** \-mi-k(ə-)lē\ *adv*
logarithmic function *n* : a function (as $y = \log x$) that is the inverse of an exponential function (as $e^x = y$) so that the independent variable appears in a logarithm
log·book \ˈlȯg-ˌbu̇k, ˈläg-\ *n* : LOG 3, 4

loge \'lōzh\ *n* [F — more at LODGE] **1 a :** a small compartment : BOOTH **b :** a box in a theater **2 a :** a small partitioned area **b :** a separate forward section of a theater mezzanine or balcony
logged \'lȯgd, 'lägd\ *adj* **1 :** HEAVY, SLUGGISH **2 :** sodden esp. with water
log·ger \'lȯg-ər, 'läg-\ *n* **:** one engaged in logging
log·ger·head \'lȯg-ər-,hed, 'läg-\ *n* [prob. fr. E dial. *logger* (block of wood) + *head*] **1** *chiefly dial* **a :** BLOCKHEAD **b :** HEAD; *esp* **:** a disproportionately large head **2 a :** any of various very large marine turtles (family Cheloniidae); *esp* **:** a carnivorous turtle (*Caretta caretta*) of the warmer parts of the western Atlantic **b :** ALLIGATOR SNAPPER **3 :** an iron tool consisting of a long handle terminating in a ball or bulb that is heated and used to melt tar or to heat liquids — **at loggerheads :** in or into a state of quarrelsome disagreement
log·gets *or* **log·gats** \'lȯ-gəts, 'läg-\ *n pl but sing or pl in constr* [prob. fr. [1]*log* + *-et*] **:** a game formerly played in England in which participants throw pieces of wood at a stake
log·gia \'lō-jē-ə, 'lȯ-(,)jä\ *n, pl* **loggias** \'lō-jē-əz, 'lȯ-(,)jäz\ *also* **log·gie** \'lō-(,)jā\ [It, fr. F *loge*] **:** a roofed open gallery esp. at an upper story overlooking an open court

1 loggias

log·ic \'läj-ik\ *n* [ME *logik*, fr. MF *logique*, fr. L *logica*, fr. Gk *logikē*, fr. fem. of *logikos* of reason, fr. *logos* reason — more at LEGEND] **1 a (1) :** a science that deals with the canons and criteria of validity of inference and demonstration **:** the science of the normative formal principles of reasoning **(2) :** a branch or variety of logic <modal ~> <Boolean ~> **(3) :** a branch of semiotic; *esp* **:** SYNTACTICS **(4) :** the formal principles of a branch of knowledge **b (1) :** a particular mode of reasoning viewed as valid or faulty **(2) :** RELEVANCE, PROPRIETY **c :** interrelation or sequence of facts or events when seen as inevitable or predictable **d :** the fundamental principles and the connection of circuit elements for arithmetical computation in a computer; *also* **:** the circuits themselves **2 :** something that forces a decision apart from or in opposition to reason <the ~ of war> — **lo·gi·cian** \lō-'jish-ən\ *n*
log·i·cal \'läj-i-kəl\ *adj* **1 a (1) :** of, relating to, involving, or being in accordance with logic **(2) :** skilled in logic **b :** formally true or valid **:** ANALYTIC, DEDUCTIVE **2 :** capable of reasoning or of using reason in an orderly cogent fashion <a ~ thinker> — **log·i·cal·i·ty** \,läj-ə-'kal-ət-ē\ *n* — **log·i·cal·ly** \'läj-i-k(ə-)lē\ *adv* — **log·i·cal·ness** \-kəl-nəs\ *n*
syn LOGICAL, ANALYTIC, SUBTLE *shared meaning element* **:** having or showing skill in thinking or reasoning ***ant*** illogical
logical positivism *n* **:** a 20th century philosophical movement that holds characteristically that all meaningful statements are either analytic or conclusively verifiable or at least confirmable by observation and experiment and that metaphysical theories are therefore strictly meaningless — called also *logical empiricism* — **logical positivist** *n*
log·i·co- \,läj-i-kō\ *comb form* **:** logical **:** logical and <*logico*-mathematical>
lo·gi·on \'lō-gē-,än\ *n, pl* **lo·gia** \-gē-,ä\ *or* **logions** [Gk, dim. of *logos*] **:** SAYING; *esp* **:** a saying attributed to Jesus
[1]**lo·gis·tic** \lō-'jis-tik, lə-\ *or* **lo·gis·ti·cal** \-ti-kəl\ *adj* **1 a :** of or relating to symbolic logic **b :** of or relating to the philosophical attempt to reduce mathematics to logic **2 :** of or relating to logistics — **lo·gis·ti·cal·ly** \-ti-k(ə-)lē\ *adv*
[2]**logistic** *n* **:** SYMBOLIC LOGIC
logistic curve *n* **:** an S-shaped curve that represents an exponential function and is used in mathematical models of growth processes
lo·gis·ti·cian \(,)lō-,jis-'tish-ən, ,lō-jəs-\ *n* **:** a specialist in logistics
lo·gis·tics \lō-'jis-tiks, lə-\ *n pl but sing or pl in constr* [F *logistique* art of calculating, logistics, fr. Gk *logistikē* art of calculating, fr. fem. of *logistikos* of calculation, fr. *logizein* to calculate, fr. *logos* reason] **1 :** the aspect of military science dealing with the procurement, maintenance, and transportation of military matériel, facilities, and personnel **2 :** the handling of the details of an operation ***syn*** see STRATEGY
log·jam \'lȯg-,jam, 'läg-\ *n* **1 :** a jumble of logs jammed together in a watercourse **2 :** DEADLOCK, IMPASSE
log·nor·mal \(')lȯg-'nȯr-məl, (')läg-\ *adj* **:** of, relating to, or being a logarithmic function (as the logarithm of a random variable) that has a normal distribution — **log·nor·mal·i·ty** \,lȯg-nȯr-'mal-ət-ē, ,läg-\ *n* — **log·nor·mal·ly** \(')lȯg-'nȯr-mə-lē, (')läg-\ *adv*
logo \'lȯg-(,)ō, 'läg-\ *n, pl* **log·os** \-(,)ōz\ **1 :** LOGOTYPE **2 :** an identifying statement **:** MOTTO
logo·gram \'lȯg-ə-,gram, 'läg-\ *n* **:** a letter, symbol, or sign used to represent an entire word — **logo·gram·mat·ic** \,lȯg-ə-grə-'mat-ik, ,läg-\ *adj*
logo·graph \'lȯg-ə-,graf, 'läg-\ *n* **:** LOGOGRAM
logo·graph·ic \,lȯg-ə-'graf-ik, ,läg-\ *adj* **:** of, relating to, or marked by the use of logographs **:** consisting of logographs — **logo·graph·i·cal·ly** \-i-k(ə-)lē\ *adv*
logo·griph \'lȯg-ə-,grif, 'läg-\ *n* [*log-* + Gk *griphos* reed basket, riddle — more at CRIB] **:** a word puzzle (as an anagram)
lo·gom·a·chy \lō-'gäm-ə-kē\ *n, pl* **-chies** [Gk *logomachia*, fr. *log-* + *machesthai* to fight] **1 :** a dispute over or about words **2 :** a controversy marked by verbiage
log·or·rhea \,lȯg-ə-'rē-ə, ,läg-\ *n* [NL] **:** excessive and often incoherent talkativeness or wordiness — **log·or·rhe·ic** \-'rē-ik\ *adj*
Lo·gos \'lō-,gäs, -,gōs\ *n, pl* **Lo·goi** \-,gȯi\ [Gk, speech, word, reason — more at LEGEND] **1 :** reason that in ancient Greek philosophy is the controlling principle in the universe **2 :** the divine wisdom manifest in the creation, government, and redemption of the world and often identified with the second person of the Trinity
logo·type \'lȯg-ə-,tīp, 'läg-\ *n* **1 :** a single piece of type or a single plate faced with a term (as the name of a newspaper or a trademark) **2 :** an identifying symbol (as for advertising)
log·roll \'lȯg-,rōl, 'läg-\ *vb* [back-formation fr. *logrolling*] *vi* **:** to take part in logrolling ~ *vt* **:** to promote passage of by logrolling — **log·roll·er** *n*
log·roll·ing \-,rō-liŋ\ *n* **1 :** the rolling of logs in water by treading; *also* **:** a sport in which men treading logs try to dislodge one another **2** [fr. a former American custom of neighbors assisting one another in rolling logs into a pile for burning] **:** the exchanging of assistance or favors; *specif* **:** the trading of votes by legislators to secure favorable action on projects of interest to each one
-logue *or* **-log** \,lȯg, ,läg\ *n comb form* [ME *-logue*, fr. OF, fr. L *-logus*, fr. Gk *-logos*, fr. *legein* to speak — more at LEGEND] **1 :** discourse **:** talk <duo*logue*> **2 :** student **:** specialist <sino*logue*>
log·wood \'lȯg-,wu̇d, 'läg-\ *n* **1 a :** a Central American and West Indian leguminous tree (*Haematoxylon campechianum*) **b :** the very hard brown or brownish red heartwood of logwood **2 :** a dye extracted from the heartwood of logwood — compare HEMATOXYLIN
lo·gy \'lō-gē\ *also* **log·gy** \'lȯg-ē, 'läg-\ *adj* **lo·gi·er; -est** [perh. fr. D *log* heavy; akin to MLG *luggish* lazy] **:** marked by sluggishness and lack of vitality **:** GROGGY
-l·o·gy \l-ə-jē\ *n comb form* [ME *-logie*, fr. OF, fr. L *-logia*, fr. Gk, fr. *logos* word] **1 :** oral or written expression <phraseo*logy*> **2 :** doctrine **:** theory **:** science <ethno*logy*>
Lo·hen·grin \'lō-ən-,grin\ *n* [G] **:** a son of Parsifal and knight of the Holy Grail in Germanic legend
LOI *abbr* lunar orbit insertion
loin \'lȯin\ *n* [ME *loyne*, fr. MF *loigne*, fr. (assumed) VL *lumbea*, fr. L *lumbus*; akin to OE *lendenu* loins, OSlav *lędviję*] **1 a :** the part of a human being or quadruped on each side of the spinal column between the hipbone and the false ribs **b :** a cut of meat comprising this part of one or both sides of a carcass with the adjoining half of the vertebrae included but without the flank — see BEEF illustration **2** *pl* **a :** the upper and lower abdominal regions and the region about the hips **b (1) :** the pubic region **(2) :** the generative organs
loin·cloth \-,klȯth\ *n* **:** a cloth worn about the loins often as the sole article of clothing in warm climates
loi·ter \'lȯit-ər\ *vi* [ME *loiteren*] **1 :** to delay an activity with aimless idle stops and pauses **:** DAWDLE **2 a :** to remain in an area for no obvious reason **:** hang around **b :** to lag behind — **loi·ter·er** \-ər-ər\ *n*
Lo·ki \'lō-kē\ *n* [ON] **:** a Norse god who contrives evil and mischief for his fellow gods
[1]**loll** \'läl\ *vb* [ME *lollen*] *vi* **1 :** to hang loosely or laxly **:** DROOP **2 :** to act or move in a lax, lazy, or indolent manner **:** LOUNGE ~ *vt* **:** to let droop or dangle — **loll·er** *n*
[2]**loll** *n, archaic* **:** the act of lolling **:** a relaxed posture
Lol·lard \'läl-ərd\ *n* [ME, fr. MD *lollaert*] **:** one of the followers of Wycliffe who traveled in the 14th and 15th centuries as lay preachers throughout England and Scotland — **Lol·lard·ism** \-ər-,diz-əm\ *n* — **Lol·lardy** \-ərd-ē\ *n*
lol·li·pop *or* **lol·ly·pop** \'läl-i-,päp\ *n* [prob. fr. [1]*loll* + *-i-* + *pop*] **:** a lump of hard candy on the end of a stick
lol·lop \'läl-əp\ *vi* [[1]*loll* + *-op* (as in *gallop*)] **1** *dial Eng* **:** LOLL **2 :** to proceed with a bounding or bobbing motion
lol·ly \'läl-ē\ *n, pl* **lollies** [short for *lollipop*] **1** *Brit* **:** a piece of candy; *esp* **:** hard candy **2** *Brit* **:** MONEY
lol·ly·gag \'läl-ē-,gag\ *vi* [origin unknown] **:** to fool around **:** DAWDLE
Lom·bard \'läm-,bärd, -bərd\ *n* [ME *Lumbarde*, fr. MF *lombard*, fr. OIt *lombardo*, fr. L *Langobardus*] **1 a :** a member of a Teutonic people that invaded Italy in A.D. 568, settled in the Po valley, and established a kingdom **b :** a native or inhabitant of Lombardy **2** [fr. the prominence of Lombards as moneylenders] **:** BANKER, MONEYLENDER — **Lom·bar·di·an** \läm-'bärd-ē-ən\ *adj* — **Lom·bar·dic** \läm-'bärd-ik\ *adj*
Lom·bar·dy poplar \,läm-,bärd-ē-, -bərd-\ *n* [*Lombardy*, Italy] **:** a poplar of a staminate variety (*Populus nigra italica*) of a European poplar that is distinguished by its columnar fastigiate shape and strongly ascending branches
lo·ment \'lō-,ment, -mənt\ *n* [NL *lomentum*, fr. L, wash made fr. bean meal, fr. *lotus*, pp. of *lavare* to wash — more at LYE] **:** a dry indehiscent one-celled fruit that is produced from a single superior ovary and breaks transversely into numerous segments at maturity
Lond *abbr* **1** London **2** Londonderry
Lon·don broil \,lən-dən-\ *n* **:** a boneless cut of meat (as from the shoulder or flank) usu. marinated and broiled and served sliced diagonally across the grain
lone \'lōn\ *adj* [ME, short for *alone*] **1 a :** having no company **:** SOLITARY **b :** preferring solitude **2 :** ONLY, SOLE **3 :** situated by itself **:** ISOLATED ***syn*** see ALONE — **lone·ness** \'lōn-nəs\ *n*
lone·li·ness \'lōn-lē-nəs\ *n* **:** the quality or state of being lonely
lone·ly \'lōn-lē\ *adj* **lone·li·er; -est** **1 a :** being without company **:** LONE **b :** cut off from others **:** SOLITARY **2 :** not frequented by human beings **:** DESOLATE **3 :** sad from being alone **:** LONESOME **4 :** producing a feeling of bleakness or desolation ***syn*** see ALONE — **lone·li·ly** \-lə-lē\ *adv*
lonely hearts *adj* **:** of or relating to lonely persons who are seeking companions or spouses <was convicted of mail fraud for fleecing men attracted to her through ads in a *lonely hearts* column —*Consumer Reports*>
lon·er \'lō-nər\ *n* **:** one that avoids others; *esp* **:** INDIVIDUALIST

1lone·some \ˈlōn(t)-səm\ *adj* **1 a :** sad or dejected as a result of lack of companionship or separation from others <don't be ~ while we are gone> **b :** causing a feeling of loneliness <the empty house seemed so ~> **2 a :** REMOTE, UNFREQUENTED <look down, look down that ~ road —Gene Austin> **b :** LONE ***syn*** see ALONE — **lone·some·ly** *adv* — **lone·some·ness** *n*

2lonesome *n* **:** SELF <sat all by his ~>

lone wolf *n* **:** a person who prefers to work, act, or live alone

1long \ˈlȯŋ\ *adj* **lon·ger** \ˈlȯŋ-gər\; **lon·gest** \ˈlȯŋ-gəst\ [ME *long, lang,* fr. OE; akin to OHG *lang* long, L *longus,* Gk *dolichos*] **1 a :** extending for a considerable distance **b :** having greater length than usual **c :** having greater height than usual **:** TALL **d :** having a greater length than breadth **:** ELONGATED **e :** having a greater length than desirable or necessary **2 a :** having a specified length <six feet ~> **b :** forming the chief linear dimension <the ~ side of the room> **3 a :** extending over a considerable time <a ~ friendship> **b :** having a specified duration <two hours ~> **c :** prolonged beyond the usual time <a ~ look> **4 a :** containing many items in a series <a ~ list> **b :** having a specified number of units <300 pages ~> **c :** consisting of a greater number or amount than usual **:** LARGE **5 a** *of a speech sound* **:** having a relatively long duration **b :** being the member of a pair of similarly spelled vowel or vowel-containing sounds that is descended from a vowel long in duration <~ *a* in *fate*> <~ *i* in *sign*> **c** *of a syllable in prosody* (1) **:** of relatively extended duration (2) **:** bearing a stress or accent **6 a :** having the capacity to reach or extend a considerable distance <a ~ left jab> **b :** hit for a considerable distance <a batter trying for the ~ ball> **7 :** larger or longer than the standard <a ~ dozen> **8 a :** extending far into the future <the thoughts of youth are ~, ~ thoughts —H. W. Longfellow> **b :** extending beyond what is known <a ~ guess> **c :** payable after a considerable period <a ~ note> **9 :** possessing a high degree or a great deal of something specified **:** STRONG <~ on common sense> **10 a :** of an unusual degree of difference between the amounts wagered on each side <~ odds> **b :** of or relating to the larger amount wagered <take the ~ end of the bet> **11 :** subject to great odds **12 :** owning or accumulating securities or goods esp. in anticipation of an advance in prices <they are now ~ on wheat> <take a ~ position in steel> — **long·ness** \ˈlȯŋ-nəs\ *n* — **before long :** in a short time **:** SOON — **long in the tooth :** past one's best days **:** OLD — **not long for :** having little time left to do or enjoy something

2long *adv* **1 :** for or during a long time <~ a popular hangout> **2 :** at or to a long distance **:** FAR <*long*-traveled> **3 :** for the duration of a specified period **4 :** at a point of time far before or after a specified moment or event <was excited ~ before the big day> **5 :** after or beyond a specified time <didn't stay ~*er* than midnight> <said it was no ~*er* possible> **6 :** for a considerable distance <faded back and threw the ball ~> **7 :** in or into a long position (as on a market) <went ~ 500 shares> — **so long :** GOODBYE

3long *n* **1 :** a long period of time **2 :** a long syllable **3 :** one taking a long position esp. in a security or commodity market **4 a** *pl* **:** long trousers **b :** a size in clothing for tall men — **the long and short** *or* **the long and the short :** GIST

4long *vi* **longed; long·ing** \ˈlȯŋ-iŋ\ [ME *longen,* fr. OE *langian;* akin to OHG *langēn* to long, OE *lang* long] **:** to feel a strong desire or craving esp. for something not likely to be attained <they ~ for peace but are driven to war> — **long·er** \ˈlȯŋ-ər\ *n* ***syn*** LONG, YEARN, HANKER, PINE, HUNGER, THIRST *shared meaning element* **:** to desire something strongly

5long *vi* [ME *longen,* fr. *along* (*on*) because (of)] *archaic* **:** to be suitable or fitting

6long *abbr* longitude

Long *abbr* Longford

long-ago \ˌlȯŋ-ə-ˌgō\ *adj* **:** of or relating to the past <~ leaders>

long ago *n* **:** the distant past

lon·gan \ˈlȯŋ-(g)ən\ *n* [Chin (Pek) *lung*² *yen*³, lit., dragon's eye] **1 :** a pulpy fruit related to the litchi and produced by an East Indian tree (*Euphoria longana*) **2 :** a tree that bears the longan

lon·ga·nim·i·ty \ˌlȯŋ-gə-ˈnim-ət-ē\ *n* [LL *longanimitas,* fr. *longanimis* patient, fr. L *longus* long + *animus* soul — more at ANIMATE] **:** a disposition to bear injuries patiently **:** FORBEARANCE

long·boat \ˈlȯŋ-ˌbōt\ *n* **:** the largest boat carried by a merchant sailing ship

long bone *n* **:** one of the elongated bones supporting a vertebrate limb and consisting of an essentially cylindrical shaft that contains marrow and ends in enlarged heads for articulation with other bones

long·bow \ˈlȯŋ-ˌbō\ *n* **1 :** a wooden bow drawn by hand that is usu. 5½ to 6 feet long **2 :** the medieval English bow sometimes up to 6 feet, 7 inches long

long·bow·man \-ˈbō-mən\ *n* **:** an archer who uses a longbow

long-case clock *n* **:** GRANDFATHER CLOCK

long-chain *adj* **:** having a relatively long chain of atoms and esp. carbon atoms in the molecule <~ hydrocarbons>

long-day *adj* **:** responding to a long photoperiod — used of a plant; compare DAY-NEUTRAL, SHORT-DAY

1long-distance *adj* **1 a :** situated a long distance away **b :** covering a long distance **c :** effective over long distance <~ listening devices> **2 :** of or relating to telephone communication with a distant point

2long-distance *adv* **:** by long-distance telephone

long distance *n* **1 :** communication by long-distance telephone **2 :** a telephone operator or exchange that gives long-distance connections

long division *n* **:** arithmetical division in which the several steps involved in the division of parts of the dividend by the divisor are indicated in detail

long dozen *n* **:** one more than a dozen **:** THIRTEEN

long-drawn-out *adj* **:** extended to a great length **:** PROTRACTED

lon·ge·ron \ˈlän-jə-ˌrän\ *n* [F] **:** a fore-and-aft framing member of an airplane fuselage

lon·gev·i·ty \län-ˈjev-ət-ē, lȯn-\ *n* [LL *longaevitas,* fr. L *longaevus* long-lived, fr. *longus* long + *aevum* age — more at AYE] **1 a :** a long duration of individual life **b :** length of life <a study of ~> **2 :** long continuance; *esp* **:** SENIORITY

lon·ge·vous \-ˈjē-vəs\ *adj* **:** LONG-LIVED

long face *n* **:** a facial expression of sadness or melancholy

long green *n, slang* **:** paper money **:** CASH

long·hair \ˈlȯŋ-ˌha(ə)r, -ˌhe(ə)r\ *n* [back-formation fr. *long-haired*] **1 :** a person of artistic gifts or interests; *esp* **:** a lover of classical music **2 :** an impractical intellectual **3 :** a person with long hair; *specif* **:** HIPPIE — **long-hair** *or* **long-haired** \-ˈha(ə)rd, -ˈhe(ə)rd\ *adj*

long·hand \-ˌhand\ *n* **:** the characters used in ordinary writing **:** HANDWRITING

long haul *n* **:** a considerable period of time; *esp* **:** LONG RUN — **long-haul** *adj*

long·head \ˈlȯŋ-ˌhed\ *n* **:** a dolichocephalic person

long·head·ed \-ˈhed-əd\ *adj* **1 :** having unusual foresight or wisdom **2 :** DOLICHOCEPHALIC — **long·head·ed·ness** *n*

long·horn \-ˌhȯ(ə)rn\ *n* **1 :** any of the long-horned cattle of Spanish derivation formerly common in southwestern U.S. **2 :** a firm-textured cheddar ranging from white to orange in color and from mild to sharp in flavor

long-horned beetle \ˌlȯŋ-ˌhȯrn(d)-\ *n* **:** any of various beetles (family Cerambycidae) usu. distinguished by their very long antennae — called also *longhorn beetle*

long-horned grasshopper *n* **:** any of various grasshoppers (family Tettigoniidae) distinguished by their very long antennae

long horse *n* **1 :** a vaulting apparatus resembling a side horse without pommels that is used for vaulting feats in gymnastics **2 :** an event in gymnastics competition in which the long horse is used

long·house \ˈlȯŋ-ˌhau̇s, -ˈhau̇s\ *n* **:** a long communal dwelling esp. of the Iroquois

longhouse

long hundredweight *n, Brit* **:** HUNDREDWEIGHT 1b

longi- *comb form* [ME, fr. L, fr. *longus*] **:** long <*longi*pennate>

lon·gi·corn \ˈlän-jə-ˌkȯ(ə)rn\ *adj* [deriv. of *longi-* + L *cornu* horn — more at HORN] **1 :** of, relating to, or being long-horned beetles **2 :** having long antennae — **longicorn** *n*

long·ing \ˈlȯŋ-iŋ\ *n* **:** a strong desire esp. for something unattainable **:** CRAVING — **long·ing·ly** \-iŋ-lē\ *adv*

long·ish \ˈlȯŋ-ish\ *adj* **:** somewhat long **:** moderately long

lon·gi·tude \ˈlän-jə-ˌt(y)üd\ *n* [ME, fr. L *longitudin-, longitudo,* fr. *longus*] **1 a :** LENGTH **b** *archaic* **:** long duration **2 a :** angular distance measured on a great circle of reference from the intersection of the adopted zero meridian with this reference circle to the similar intersection of the meridian passing through the object **b :** the arc or portion of the earth's equator intersected between the meridian of a given place and the prime meridian (as from Greenwich, England) and expressed either in degrees or in time

longitude 2a: hemisphere marked with meridians of longitude

lon·gi·tu·di·nal \ˌlän-jə-ˈt(y)üd-nəl, -ᵊn-əl\ *adj* **1 :** of or relating to length or the lengthwise dimension **2 :** placed or running lengthwise **3 :** dealing with the growth and change of an individual or group over a period of years <~ studies> — **lon·gi·tu·di·nal·ly** \-ē\ *adv*

longitudinal wave *n* **:** a wave (as a sound wave) in which the particles of the medium vibrate in the direction of the line of advance of the wave

long johns \ˈlȯŋ-ˌjänz\ *n pl* **:** long underwear

long jump *n* **:** a jump for distance in track-and-field athletics usu. from a running start — **long jumper** *n*

long·leaf pine \ˌlȯŋ-ˌlēf-\ *n* **:** a large pine (*Pinus palustris*) of the southern U.S. with green leaves and long cones that is a major timber tree; *also* **:** its tough coarse-grained reddish orange wood

long-leaved pine \-ˌlēv(d)-\ *n* **:** LONGLEAF PINE

long·line \ˈlȯŋ-ˌlīn, -ˈlīn\ *n* **:** a heavy fishing line that may be several miles long and that has baited hooks in series

long-lin·er \-ˈlī-nər\ *n* **:** one that fishes with a longline; *also* **:** a fishing vessel used in long-lining

long-lin·ing \-ˈlī-niŋ\ *n* **:** fishing with a longline

long-lived \ˈlȯŋ-ˈlīvd, -ˈlivd\ *adj* **1 :** having a long life **:** characterized by long life <a ~ family> **2 :** lasting a long time **:** ENDURING — **long-lived·ness** \-ˈlīv(d)-nəs, -ˈliv(d)-\ *n*

long meter *n* **:** a quatrain in iambic tetrameter in which the second and fourth lines and often the first and third lines rhyme — called also *long measure*

Lon·go·bard \ˈlȯŋ-gə-ˌbärd, ˈläŋ-\ *n, pl* **Longobards** *or* **Lon·go·bar·di** \ˌlȯŋ-gə-ˈbär-ˌdī, ˌläŋ-, -ˈbärd-ē\ [L *Langobardus, Longobardus*] **:** LOMBARD 1a — **Lon·go·bar·dic** \-ˈbärd-ik, ˌläŋ-\ *adj*

long pig *n* **:** a human victim of a cannibal feast

long play *n* **:** a long-playing record

long-play·ing \ˈlȯŋ-ˈplā-iŋ\ *adj* **:** designed to be played at 33⅓ revolutions per minute — used of a microgroove record

long–range \-'rānj\ *adj* **1 :** involving or taking into account a long period of time <~ planning> **2 :** relating to or fit for long distances <~ rockets>
long run *n* **:** a relatively long period of time — usu. used in the phrase *in the long run*
long·shore·man \'lòŋ-'shōr-mən, -'shȯr-\ *n* [*longshore,* short for *alongshore*] **:** one who loads and unloads ships at a seaport
long·shor·ing \'lòŋ-'shōr-iŋ, -'shȯr-, 'lòŋ-ˌ\ *n* **:** the act or occupation of working as a longshoreman
long shot \'lòŋ-ˌshät\ *n* **1 :** an entry (as in a horse race) given little chance of winning **2 :** a bet in which the chances of winning are slight but the possible winnings great **3 :** a venture involving great risk but promising a great reward if successful; *also* **:** a venture with little chance of success — **by a long shot :** by a great deal
long·sight·ed \-'sīt-əd\ *adj* **:** FARSIGHTED — **long·sight·ed·ness** *n*
long since *adv* **1 :** long ago <programs which have *long since* ceased to be useful> **2 :** for a long time <has *long since* been recognized as a great writer>
long·some \'lòŋ(k)-səm\ *adj* **:** tediously long — **long·some·ly** *adv* — **long·some·ness** *n*
long·spur \'lòŋ-ˌspər\ *n* **:** any of several long-clawed finches (esp. genus *Calcarius*) of the arctic regions and the Great Plains of No. America
long–stand·ing \-'stan-diŋ\ *adj* **:** of long duration
long–suf·fer·ing \-'səf(-ə)-riŋ\ *n* **:** long and patient endurance of offense — **long–suffering** *adj* — **long–suf·fer·ing·ly** \-riŋ-lē\ *adv*
long suit *n* **1 :** a holding of more than the average number of cards in a suit **2 :** the activity or quality in which a person excels
long–term \'lòŋ-'tərm\ *adj* **1 :** occurring over or involving a relatively long period of time **2 a :** of, relating to, or constituting a financial operation or obligation based on a considerable term and esp. one of more than 10 years <~ bonds> **b :** generated by assets held for longer than six months <a ~ capital gain>
long·time \ˌlòŋ-ˌtīm\ *adj* **:** LONG-STANDING
Long Tom \'lòŋ-'täm\ *n* [fr. the name *Tom*] **1 a :** a long pivot gun formerly carried on the deck of a warship **b :** a large land gun having a long range **2 :** a trough for washing gold-bearing earth
long ton *n* — see WEIGHT table
lon·gueur \lōⁿ-gœr\ *n, pl* **longueurs** \-gœr(z)\ [F, lit., length] **:** a dull and tedious passage or section (as of a book)
long view *n* **:** an approach to a problem or situation that emphasizes long-range factors
long–wind·ed \'lòŋ-'win-dəd\ *adj* **1 :** not easily subject to loss of breath **2 :** tediously long in speaking or writing — **long–wind·ed·ly** *adv* — **long–wind·ed·ness** *n*
[1]**loo** \'lü\ *n* [short for obs. E *lanterloo,* fr. F *lanturelu* piffle] **1 :** an old card game in which the winner of each trick or a majority of tricks takes a portion of the pool while losing players are obligated to contribute to the next pool **2 :** money staked at loo
[2]**loo** *vt* **:** to obligate to contribute to a new pool at loo for failing to win a trick
[3]**loo** *n* [perh. modif. of F *lieux d'aisance*] *chiefly Brit* **:** TOILET 3
loo·by \'lü-bē\ *n, pl* **loobies** [ME *loby*] **:** an awkward clumsy fellow **:** LUBBER
[1]**look** \'lu̇k\ *vb* [ME *looken,* fr. OE *lōcian;* akin to OS *lōcōn* to look] *vt* **1 :** to make sure or take care (that something is done) **2 :** to ascertain by the use of one's eyes **3 a :** to exercise the power of vision upon **:** EXAMINE **b** *archaic* **:** to search for **4 :** to await expectantly or watchfully <we cannot ~ for immediate success> **5** *archaic* **:** to bring into a place or condition by the exercise of the power of vision **6 :** to express by the eyes or facial expression **7 :** to have an appearance that befits or accords with ~ *vi* **1 a :** to exercise the power of vision **:** SEE **b :** to direct one's attention <~ upon the future with hope> **c :** to direct the eyes **2 :** to have the appearance of being **:** SEEM **3 :** to have a specified outlook <the house ~*ed* east> **4 :** to gaze in wonder or surprise **:** STARE **5 :** to show a tendency <the evidence ~*s* to acquittal> *syn* see SEE, SEEM, EXPECT — **look after :** to take care of — **look down one's nose :** to view with arrogance, disdain, or disapproval — **look for 1 :** to await with hope or anticipation **2 :** to search for
[2]**look** *n* **1 a :** the act of looking **b :** GLANCE **2 a :** the expression of the countenance **b :** physical appearance; *esp* **:** attractive physical appearance — usu. used in pl. **c :** a combination of design features giving a unified appearance <a new ~ in women's fashions> **3 :** the state or form in which something appears **:** ASPECT
look–alike \'lu̇k-ə-ˌlīk\ *n* **:** one that looks like another **:** DOUBLE
look·down \'lu̇k-ˌdau̇n\ *n* **:** any of several fishes (genus *Selene* and esp. *S. vomer*) that are widely distributed in warm seas and have high truncated foreheads
look down \(ˈ)lu̇k-'dau̇n\ *vi* **:** to regard with contempt **:** DESPISE — used with *on* or *upon* <snobbishly *looks down* on the poor>
look·er \'lu̇k-ər\ *n* **1 :** one that looks **2 a :** one having an appearance of a specified kind **b :** one that has an attractive appearance **:** BEAUTY
look·er–on \ˌlu̇k-ə-'rȯn, -'rän\ *n, pl* **lookers–on :** ONLOOKER
look–in \'lu̇k-ˌin\ *n* **1 :** a chance of success **2 :** a quick pass in football to a receiver running diagonally toward the center of the field
looking glass *n* **:** MIRROR
look·out \'lu̇k-ˌau̇t\ *n* **1 :** one engaged in keeping watch **:** WATCHMAN **2 :** an elevated place or structure affording a wide view for observation **3 :** a careful looking or watching **4 :** VIEW, OUTLOOK **5 :** a matter of care or concern
look·up \'lu̇k-ˌəp\ *n* **:** the process or an instance of looking something up; *esp* **:** the process of matching by computer the words of a text with material stored in memory
look up \(ˈ)lu̇k-'əp\ *vi* **1 :** to cheer up <*look up* — things are not all bad> **2 :** to improve in prospects or conditions <business conditions are *looking up*> ~ *vt* **1 :** to search for in or as if in a reference work <*look up* a phone number in the directory> **2 :** to seek out esp. for a brief visit
[1]**loom** \'lüm\ *n* [ME *lome* tool, loom, fr. OE *gelōma* tool; akin to MD al*lame* tool] **:** a frame or machine for interlacing at right angles two or more sets of threads or yarns to form a cloth
[2]**loom** *vi* [origin unknown] **1 :** to come into sight in enlarged or distorted and indistinct form often as a result of atmospheric conditions **2 a :** to appear in an impressively great or exaggerated form **b :** to take shape as an impending occurrence
[3]**loom** *n* **:** the indistinct and exaggerated appearance of something seen on the horizon or through fog or darkness; *also* **:** a looming shadow or reflection
LOOM *abbr* Loyal Order of Moose
[1]**loon** \'lün\ *n* [ME *loun*] **1 :** LOUT, IDLER **2** *chiefly Scot* **:** BOY **3 a :** a crazy person **b :** SIMPLETON
[2]**loon** *n* [of Scand origin; akin to ON *lōmr* loon — more at LAMENT] **:** any of several large fish-eating diving birds (genus *Gavia*) of the northern part of the northern hemisphere that have the legs placed far back under the body and as a result have a clumsy floundering gait on land
loo·ny *or* **loo·ney** \'lü-nē\ *adj* **loo·ni·er; -est** [by shortening & alter. fr. *lunatic*] **:** CRAZY, FOOLISH — **loo·ni·ness** *n* — **loony** *n*
loony bin *n* **:** an insane asylum **:** MADHOUSE
[1]**loop** \'lüp\ *n* [ME *loupe;* perh. akin to MD *lupen* to watch, peer] *archaic* **:** LOOPHOLE 1a
[2]**loop** *n* [ME *loupe,* of unknown origin] **1 a :** a curving or doubling of a line so as to form a closed or partly open curve within itself through which another line can be passed or into which a hook may be hooked **b :** such a fold of cord or ribbon serving as an ornament **2 a :** something shaped like a loop **b :** a maneuver in which an airplane starting from straight and level flight passes successively through a climb, inverted flight, a dive, and then returns to normal flight **3 :** a ring or curved piece used to form a fastening or a handle **4 a :** the portion of a vibrating body between two nodes **b :** the middle point of such a portion **5 :** a closed electric circuit **6 :** a piece of film or magnetic tape whose ends are spliced together so as to project or play back the same material continuously **7 :** a series of instructions (as for a computer) that is repeated until a terminating condition is reached **8 :** a sports league — **loopy** \'lü-pē\ *adj* — **for a loop :** into a state of amazement, confusion, or distress
[3]**loop** *vi* **1 :** to make or form a loop **2 :** to execute a loop in an airplane **3 :** to move in loops or in an arc ~ *vt* **1 a :** to make a loop in, on, or about **b :** to fasten with a loop **2 :** to join (two courses of loops) in knitting **3 :** to connect (electric conductors) so as to complete a loop **4 :** to cause to move in an arc
loop·er \'lü-pər\ *n* **1 :** any of the usu. rather small hairless caterpillars that are mostly larvae of moths (families Geometridae and Noctuidae) and move with a looping movement in which the anterior and posterior prolegs are alternately made fast and released **2 :** one that loops

looper 1

[1]**loop·hole** \'lüp-ˌhōl\ *n* [[1]*loop*] **1 a :** a small opening through which small firearms may be discharged **b :** a similar opening to admit light and air or to permit observation **2 :** a means of escape; *esp* **:** an ambiguity or omission in the text through which the intent of a statute, contract, or obligation may be evaded
[2]**loophole** *vt* **:** to make loopholes in
loop of Hen·le \-'hen-lē\ [F. G. J. *Henle* †1885 G pathologist] **:** a part of the vertebrate nephron that lies between the proximal and distal convoluted tubules and plays a part in water resorption
[1]**loose** \'lüs\ *adj* **loos·er; loos·est** [ME *lous,* fr. ON *lauss;* akin to OHG *lōs* loose — more at -LESS] **1 a :** not rigidly fastened or securely attached **b (1) :** having worked partly free from attachments <the masonry is ~ at the base of the wall> **(2) :** having relative freedom of movement **c :** produced freely and accompanied by raising of mucus <a ~ cough> **d :** not tight-fitting **2 a :** free from a state of confinement, restraint, or obligation <a lion ~ in the streets> <spend ~ funds wisely> **b :** not brought together in a bundle, container, or binding **c** *archaic* **:** DISCONNECTED, DETACHED **3 :** not dense, close, or compact in structure or arrangement **4 a :** lacking in restraint or power of restraint <a ~ tongue> <~ bowels> **b :** lacking moral restraint **:** UNCHASTE **5 a :** not tightly drawn or stretched **:** SLACK **b :** having a flexible or relaxed character **6 a :** lacking in precision, exactness, or care **b :** permitting freedom of interpretation — **loose·ly** *adv* — **loose·ness** *n*

syn LOOSE, RELAXED, SLACK, LAX *shared meaning element* **:** not tightly bound, held, restrained, or stretched. LOOSE is widely referable to persons or things freed from a usual or former material or immaterial restraint < a book with a *loose* page> <a person of *loose* morals> or to something not tight between points of contact <wore a *loose* belt> or to something not close or compact in arrangement or texture <a *loose* easily-worked soil> <a *loose*-woven woolen> RELAXED implies a loosening of prior tightness, tension, strictness, or rigidity; in comparison with *loose* it is likely to imply an easing of rather than a freeing from what restrains; thus, *relaxed* discipline is discipline made as easy as circumstances allow; *loose* discipline is essentially no discipline at all <a *relaxed* painting style> SLACK is likely to add the idea of a lack of firmness and steadiness; thus, *relaxed* control is control deliberately eased for a usually sound reason; *slack* control is irregular control, lacking in sureness and steadiness <shorebirds are notoriously *slack* in regard to the roles of the sexes . . . in nesting —Peter Mathiessen> LAX stresses lack of steadiness, firmness, and tone <the *lax* droop of his mouth> or, in respect to immaterial things, lack of needed or proper steadiness or firmness <a *lax* administration> <*lax* supervision> ***ant*** tight, strict

[2]**loose** *vb* **loosed; loos·ing** *vt* **1 a :** to let loose : RELEASE **b :** to free from restraint **2 :** to make loose : UNTIE <~ a knot> **3 :** to cast loose : DETACH **4 :** to let fly : DISCHARGE **5 :** to make less rigid, tight, or strict : RELAX ~ *vi* **:** to let fly a missile (as an arrow) : FIRE

[3]**loose** *adv* **:** LOOSELY

loose end *n* **1 :** something left hanging loose **2 :** a fragment of unfinished business

loose–joint·ed \ˈlüs-ˈjȯint-əd\ *adj* **1 :** having joints apparently not closely articulated **2 :** characterized by unusually free movements — **loose–joint·ed·ness** *n*

loose–leaf \ˈlü-ˈslēf\ *adj* **1 :** having leaves secured in book form in a cover whose backbone may be opened for the removal, rearrangement, or replacement of leaves <~ notebook> **2 :** of, relating to, or used with a loose-leaf binding <~ paper>

loos·en \ˈlüs-ᵊn\ *vb* **loos·ened; loos·en·ing** \ˈlüs-niŋ, -ᵊn-iŋ\ *vt* **1 :** to release from restraint **2 :** to make looser **3 :** to relieve (the bowels) of constipation **4 :** to cause or permit to become less strict ~ *vi* **:** to become loose or looser

loose sentence *n* **:** a sentence in which the principal clause comes first and the latter part contains subordinate modifiers or trailing elements

loose smut *n* **:** a smut disease of grains in which the entire head is transformed into a dusty mass of spores

loose·strife \ˈlü(s)-ˌstrīf\ *n* [intended as trans. of Gk *lysimacheios* loosestrife (as if fr. *lysis* act of loosing + *machesthai* to fight) — more at LYS-] **1 :** any of a genus (*Lysimachia*) of plants of the primrose family with leafy stems and yellow or white flowers **2 :** any of a genus (*Lythrum*, family Lythraceae, the loosestrife family) of herbs including some with showy spikes of purple flowers; *esp* **:** PURPLE LOOSESTRIFE

[1]**loot** \ˈlüt\ *n* [Hindi *lūṭ*, fr. Skt *luṇṭati* he robs] **1 :** goods usu. of considerable value taken in war : SPOILS **2 :** something held to resemble goods of value seized in war: as **a :** something taken by force or violence **b :** illicit gains by public officials **c :** MONEY **3 :** the action of looting ***syn*** see SPOIL

[2]**loot** *vt* **1 a :** to plunder or sack in war **b :** to rob esp. on a large scale and usu. by violence or corruption **2 :** to seize and carry away by force esp. in war ~ *vi* **:** to engage in robbing or plundering esp. in war — **loot·er** *n*

[1]**lop** \ˈläp\ *n* [ME *loppe*] **:** material cut away from a tree; *esp* **:** parts discarded in lumbering

[2]**lop** *vt* **lopped; lop·ping 1 a** (1) **:** to cut off branches or twigs from (2) **:** to sever from a woody plant **b** (1) *archaic* **:** to cut off the head or limbs of (2) **:** to cut from a person **2 a :** to remove superfluous parts from **b :** to eliminate as unnecessary or undesirable — usu. used with *off* — **lop·per** *n*

[3]**lop** *vi* **lopped; lop·ping** [perh. imit.] **:** to hang downward : DROOP

[1]**lope** \ˈlōp\ *n* [ME *loup, lope* leap, fr. ON *hlaup;* akin to OE *hlēapan* to leap — more at LEAP] **1 :** an easy natural gait of a horse resembling a canter **2 :** an easy bounding gait capable of being sustained for a long time

[2]**lope** *vi* **loped; lop·ing :** to go, move, or ride at a lope — **lop·er** *n*

lop–eared \ˈläp-ˈi(ə)rd\ *adj* **:** having ears that droop

loph·o·phore \ˈläf-ə-ˌfō(ə)r, -ˌfȯ(ə)r\ *n* [Gk *lophos* crest + E *-phore*] **:** a circular or horseshoe-shaped organ about the mouth esp. of a brachiopod or bryozoan that bears tentacles and functions esp. in food-getting

lop·py \ˈläp-ē\ *adj* **lop·pi·er; -est :** hanging loose : LIMP

lop·sid·ed \ˈläp-ˈsīd-əd\ *adj* **1 :** leaning to one side **2 :** lacking in balance, symmetry, or proportion — **lop·sid·ed·ly** *adv* — **lop·sid·ed·ness** *n*

loq *abbr* [L *loquitur*] he speaks

lo·qua·cious \lō-ˈkwā-shəs\ *adj* [L *loquac-, loquax*, fr. *loqui* to speak] **:** given to excessive talking : GARRULOUS ***syn*** see TALKATIVE — **lo·qua·cious·ly** *adv* — **lo·qua·cious·ness** *n*

lo·quac·i·ty \-ˈkwas-ət-ē\ *n* **:** the quality or state of being very talkative

lo·quat \ˈlō-ˌkwät\ *n* [Chin (Cant) *lō-kwat*] **:** an Asiatic evergreen tree (*Eriobotrya japonica*) of the rose family often cultivated for its fruit; *also* **:** its yellow edible fruit used esp. for preserves

lor·al \ˈlōr-əl, ˈlȯr-\ *adj* **:** of or relating to a lore (as of a bird or reptile)

lo·ran \ˈlō(ə)r-ˌan, ˈlȯ(ə)r-\ *n* [*long-range navigation*] **:** a system of long-range navigation in which pulsed signals sent out by two pairs of radio stations are used by a navigator to determine the geographical position of a ship or an airplane

[1]**lord** \ˈlȯ(ə)rd\ *n* [ME *loverd, lord*, fr. OE *hlāford*, fr. *hlāf* loaf + *weard* keeper — more at LOAF, WARD] **1 :** one having power and authority over others: **a :** a ruler by hereditary right or preeminence to whom service and obedience are due **b :** one of whom a fee or estate is held in feudal tenure **c :** an owner of land or other real property **d** *obs* **:** the male head of a household **e :** HUSBAND **f :** one who has achieved mastery or who exercises leadership or great power in some area <vice ~*s*> **2** *cap* **a :** GOD 1 **b :** CHRIST **3 :** a man of rank or high position: as **a :** a feudal tenant holding directly of the king **b :** a British nobleman: as (1) **:** BARON 2a (2) **:** an hereditary peer of the rank of marquess, earl, or viscount (3) **:** the son of a duke or a marquess or the eldest son of an earl (4) **:** a bishop of the Church of England **c** *pl, cap* **:** HOUSE OF LORDS **4** — used as a British title: as **a** — used as part of an official title <*Lord* Advocate> **b** — used informally in place of the full title for a marquess, earl, or viscount **c** — used for a baron **d** — used by courtesy before the name and surname of a younger son of a duke or a marquess **5 :** a person chosen to preside over a festival

[2]**lord** *vi* **:** to act like a lord; *esp* **:** to put on airs — usu. used with *it* <~*s* it over his friends>

lord chancellor *n, pl* **lords chancellor :** a British officer of state who presides over the House of Lords in both its legislative and judicial capacities, serves as the head of the British judiciary, and is usu. a leading member of the cabinet

lord·ing \ˈlȯrd-iŋ\ *n* **1** *archaic* **:** LORD **2** *obs* **:** LORDLING

lord·ling \ˈlȯ(ə)rd-liŋ\ *n* **:** a little or insignificant lord

lord·ly \-lē\ *adj* **lord·li·er; -est 1 a :** of, relating to, or having the characteristics of a lord : DIGNIFIED **b :** GRAND, NOBLE **2 :** exhibiting such pride and assurance as could only be felt as appropriate to one of the highest birth or rank ***syn*** see PROUD — **lord·li·ness** *n* — **lordly** *adv*

lord of misrule : a master of Christmas revels in England esp. in the 15th and 16th centuries

lor·do·sis \lȯr-ˈdō-səs\ *n* [NL, fr. Gk *lordōsis*, fr. *lordos* curving forward; akin to OE *belyrtan* to deceive] **:** abnormal curvature of the spine forward — **lor·dot·ic** \-ˈdät-ik\ *adj*

Lord's day *n, often cap D* [fr. the Christian belief that Christ arose from the dead on Sunday] **:** SUNDAY

lord·ship \ˈlȯ(ə)rd-ˌship\ *n* **1 a :** the rank or dignity of a lord — used as a title <his *Lordship* is not at home> **b :** the authority or power of a lord : DOMINION **2 :** the territory under the jurisdiction of a lord : SEIGNIORY

Lord's Prayer *n* **:** the prayer with variant versions in Matthew and Luke that according to the Lucan account Christ taught his disciples

Lord's Supper *n* [ME *Lordis sopere*, trans. of LL *dominica cena*, trans. of Gk *kyriakon deipnon*] **:** COMMUNION 2a

Lord's table *n, often cap T* **:** ALTAR 2

[1]**lore** \ˈlō(ə)r, ˈlȯ(ə)r\ *n* [ME, fr. OE *lār;* akin to OHG *lēra* doctrine, OE *leornian* to learn] **1** *archaic* **:** something that is taught : LESSON **2 :** something that is learned: **a :** knowledge gained through study or experience **b :** traditional knowledge or belief **3 :** a particular body of knowledge or tradition

[2]**lore** *n* [NL *lorum*, fr. L, thong, rein; akin to Gk *eulēra* reins] **:** the space between the eye and bill in a bird or the corresponding region in a reptile or fish — **lo·re·al** \ˈlōr-ē-əl, ˈlȯr-\ *adj*

Lo·re·lei \ˈlōr-ə-ˌlī, ˈlȯr-\ *n* [G] **:** a siren of Germanic legend who by her song lures Rhine river boatmen to destruction on a reef

lor·gnette \lȯrn-ˈyet\ *n* [F, fr. *lorgner* to take a sidelong look at, fr. MF, fr. *lorgne* cross-eyed] **:** a pair of eyeglasses or opera glasses with a handle

lor·gnon \lȯrn-ˈyōⁿ\ *n* [F, fr. *lorgner*] **:** LORGNETTE

lo·ri·ca \lə-ˈrī-kə\ *n, pl* **-cae** \-kē, -ˌsē\ [L, fr. *lorum*] **1 :** a Roman cuirass of leather or metal **2** [NL, fr. L] **:** a hard protective case or shell (as of a rotifer)

[1]**lor·i·cate** \ˈlȯr-i-kət, ˈlȯr-ə-, ˈlär-\ *or* **lor·i·cat·ed** \-ə-ˌkāt-əd\ *adj* **1 :** having a lorica **2 :** of or relating to a loricate animal

[2]**loricate** *n* **:** a loricate animal (as a chiton or a crocodilian)

lor·i·keet \ˈlȯr-ə-ˌkēt, ˈlär-\ *n* [*lory* + *-keet* (as in *parakeet*)] **:** any of numerous small arboreal parrots mostly of Australasia that usu. have the tongue papillae long and slender forming an organ resembling a brush

lo·ris \ˈlōr-əs, ˈlȯr-\ *n* [F] **:** either of two small nocturnal slow-moving lemurs: **a :** a slim-bodied lemur (*Loris gracilis*) of southern India and Ceylon **b :** a stocky relatively heavy-limbed lemur (*Bradicebus tardigradus*) of India and the East Indies — **lo·ris·i·form** \lō-ˈris-ə-ˌfȯrm, lə-\ *adj*

lorn \ˈlȯ(ə)rn\ *adj* [ME, fr. *loren*, pp. of *lesen* to lose, fr. OE *lēosan* — more at LOSE] **:** DESOLATE, FORSAKEN ***syn*** see ALONE — **lorn·ness** \ˈlȯ(ə)rn-nəs\ *n*

Lor·raine cross \lə-ˌrān-, lō-\ *n* **:** CROSS OF LORRAINE

lor·ry \ˈlȯr-ē, ˈlär-\ *n, pl* **lorries** [origin unknown] **1 a :** a large low horse-drawn wagon without sides **b** *Brit* **:** a motortruck esp. if open **2 :** any of various trucks running on rails

lo·ry \ˈlōr-ē, ˈlȯr-\ *n, pl* **lories** [Malay *nuri, luri*] **:** any of numerous parrots (esp. of the genera *Domicella, Trichoglossus, Chalcopsitta*, and *Eos*) of Australia, New Guinea, and adjacent islands usu. having the tongue papillose at the tip and the mandibles less toothed than other parrots

LOS *abbr* **1** line of scrimmage **2** line of sight

lose \ˈlüz\ *vb* **lost** \ˈlȯst\; **los·ing** \ˈlü-ziŋ\ [ME *losen*, fr. OE *losian* to perish, lose, fr. *los* destruction; akin to OE *lēosan* to lose; akin to ON *losa* to loosen, L *luere* to release, atone for, Gk *lyein* to loosen, dissolve, destroy] *vt* **1 a :** to bring to destruction — used chiefly in passive construction <the ship was *lost* on the reef> **b :** DAMN <if he shall gain the whole world and ~ his own soul —Mt 16:26 (AV)> **2 :** to miss from one's possession or from a customary or supposed place **3 :** to suffer deprivation of : part with esp. in an unforeseen or accidental manner **4 a :** to suffer loss through the death or removal of or final separation from (a person) **b :** to fail to keep control of or allegiance of <~ votes> **5 a :** to fail to use : let slip by : WASTE <~ the tide> **b** (1) **:** to fail to win, gain, or obtain <~ a prize> <~ a contest> (2) **:** to undergo defeat in <*lost* every battle> **c :** to fail to catch with the senses or the mind <*lost* part of what he said> **6 :** to cause the loss of <one careless statement *lost* him the election> **7 :** to fail to keep, sustain, or maintain <*lost* his balance> **8 a :** to cause to miss one's way or bearings <*lost* himself in the maze of streets> **b :** to make (oneself) withdrawn from immediate reality <*lost* himself in daydreaming> **9 a :** to wander or go astray from <*lost* his way> **b :** to draw away from : OUTSTRIP <*lost* his pursuers> **10 :** to fail to keep in sight or in mind **11 :** to free oneself from : get rid of <dieting to ~ some weight> ~ *vi* **1 :** to undergo deprivation of something of value **2 :** to undergo defeat <~ with good grace> **3** *of a timepiece* **:** to run slow — **los·able** \ˈlü-zə-bəl\ *adj* — **los·able·ness** *n* — **lose ground :** to suffer loss or disadvantage : fail to advance or improve — **lose one's heart :** to fall in love

lo·sel \ˈlō-zəl\ *n* [ME, fr. *losen* (pp. of *lesen* to lose), alter. of *loren* — more at LORN] **:** a worthless person

lose out *vi* **:** to fail to win in competition : fail to receive an expected reward or gain

los·er \'lü-zər\ *n* **1 :** one that loses esp. consistently **2 :** one that does poorly : FAILURE

loss \'lȯs\ *n* [ME *los,* prob. back-formation fr. *lost,* pp. of *losen* to lose] **1 a :** the act of losing possession **b :** the harm or privation resulting from loss or separation **c :** an instance of losing **2 :** a person or thing or an amount that is lost: as **a** *pl* : killed, wounded, or captured soldiers **b :** the power diminution of a circuit element corresponding to conversion of electric power into heat by resistance **3 a :** failure to gain, win, obtain, or utilize **b :** an amount by which the cost of an article or service exceeds the selling price **4 :** decrease in amount, magnitude, or degree **5 :** DESTRUCTION, RUIN **6:** the amount of an insured's financial detriment by death or damage that the insurer becomes liable for — **at a loss :** UNCERTAIN, PUZZLED — **for a loss :** into a state of distress

loss leader *n* **:** an article sold at a loss in order to draw customers

loss ratio *n* **:** the ratio between insurance losses incurred and premiums earned during a given period

lossy \'lȯ-sē\ *adj* **:** causing attenuation or dissipation of electrical energy <a ~ transmission line> <a ~ dielectric>

lost \'lȯst\ *adj* [pp. of *lose*] **1 :** not made use of, won, or claimed **2 a :** unable to find the way **b :** no longer visible **c :** lacking assurance or self-confidence : HELPLESS **3 :** ruined or destroyed physically or morally : DESPERATE **4 a :** no longer possessed **b :** no longer known **5 a :** taken away or beyond reach or attainment : DENIED <regions ~ to the faith> **b :** INSENSIBLE, HARDENED <~ to shame> **6 :** RAPT, ABSORBED <~ in reverie> — **lost·ness** \'lȯs(t)-nəs\ *n*

[1]**lot** \'lät\ *n* [ME, fr. OE *hlot;* akin to OHG *hlōz,* Lith *kliudyti* to hook on] **1 :** an object used as a counter in determining a question by chance **2 a :** the use of lots as a means of deciding something **b :** the resulting choice **3 a :** something that comes to one upon whom a lot has fallen : SHARE **b :** one's way of life or worldly fate : FORTUNE **4 a :** a portion of land **b :** a measured parcel of land having fixed boundaries and designated on a plot or survey **c :** a motion-picture studio and its adjoining property **5 :** a number of units of an article or a parcel of articles offered as one item (as in an auction sale) **6 a :** a number of associated persons : SET **b :** KIND, SORT **7 :** a considerable quantity or extent <a ~ of money> <~*s* of friends> <this is a ~ nicer> ***syn*** see FATE, GROUP

[2]**lot** *vt* **lot·ted; lot·ting 1 :** to form or divide into lots **2 :** ALLOT, APPORTION

Lot \'lät\ *n* [Heb *Lōṭ*] **:** a nephew of Abraham who according to the account in Genesis escaped from the doomed city of Sodom with his wife who turned into a pillar of salt when she looked back

lo·ta *or* **lo·tah** \'lōt-ə\ *n* [Hindi *loṭā*] **:** a small usu. spherical water vessel of brass or copper used in India

loth \'lōth, 'lōth\ *var of* LOATH

lo·thar·io \lō-'thar-ē-,ō, -'ther-, -'thär-\ *n, pl* **-ios** *often cap* [*Lothario,* seducer in the play *The Fair Penitent* (1703) by Nicholas Rowe] **:** a man whose chief interest is seducing women

lo·tic \'lōt-ik\ *adj* [L *lotus,* pp.] **:** of, relating to, or living in actively moving water <~ biology> — compare LENTIC

lo·tion \'lō-shən\ *n* [L *lotion-, lotio* act of washing, fr. *lotus,* pp. of *lavere* to wash — more at LYE] **:** a liquid preparation for cosmetic or external medicinal use

lots \'läts\ *adv* [pl. of [1]*lot*] **:** MUCH <feeling ~ better>

lot·tery \'lät-ə-rē, 'lä-trē\ *n, pl* **-ter·ies** *often attrib* [MF *loterie,* fr. MD, fr. *lot* lot; akin to OE *hlot* lot] **1 :** a drawing of lots in which prizes are distributed to the winners among persons buying a chance **2 :** an event or affair whose outcome is or seems to be determined by chance

lot·to \'lät-(,)ō\ *n* [It, lottery, lotto, fr. F. *lot* lot, of Gmc origin; akin to OE *hlot* lot] **:** a game of chance resembling bingo

lo·tus \'lōt-əs\ *n* [L & Gk; L *lotus,* fr. Gk *lōtos,* fr. Heb *lōṭ* myrrh] **1** *also* **lo·tos** \'lōt-əs**:** a fruit eaten by the lotus-eaters and considered to cause indolence and dreamy contentment; *also* **:** a tree (as *Zizyphus lotus* of the buckthorn family) reputed to bear this fruit **2 :** any of various water lilies including several represented in ancient Egyptian and Hindu art and religious symbolism **3** [NL, genus name, fr. L] **a :** any of a genus (*Lotus*) of widely distributed upright leguminous herbs or subshrubs **b :** SWEET CLOVER

lotus 2

lo·tus–eat·er \'lōt-ə-,sēt-ər\ *n* **:** one of a people represented in the Odyssey of Homer as subsisting on lotus fruit in Libya and living in the dreamy indolence it induced

Lou *abbr* Louth

loud \'lau̇d\ *adj* [ME, fr. OE *hlūd;* akin to OHG *hlūt* loud, L *inclutus* famous, Gk *klytos,* Skt *śṛnoti* he hears] **1 a :** marked by intensity or volume of sound **b :** producing a loud sound **2 :** CLAMOROUS, NOISY **3 :** obtrusive or offensive in appearance or smell : OBNOXIOUS — **loud** *adv* — **loud·ly** *adv*

loud·en \'lau̇d-ᵊn\ *vb* **loud·ened; loud·en·ing** \'lau̇d-niŋ, -ᵊn-iŋ\ *vi* **:** to become loud ~ *vt* **:** to make loud

loud·mouth \'lau̇d-,mau̇th\ *n* **:** a person given to loud offensive talk — **loud·mouthed** \-'mau̇thd, -'mau̇tht\ *adj*

loud·ness *n* **:** the attribute of a sound that determines the magnitude of the auditory sensation produced and that primarily depends on the amplitude of the sound wave involved

loud·speak·er \'lau̇d-'spē-kər\ *n* **:** a device similar to a telephone receiver in operation but amplifying sound

lough \'läk, 'läk\ *n* [ME, of Celt origin; akin to OIr *loch* lake; akin to L *lacus* lake] **1** *chiefly Irish* **:** LAKE **2** *chiefly Irish* **:** a bay or inlet of the sea

lou·is d'or \,lü-ē-'dȯ(ə)r\ *n, pl* **louis d'or** [F, fr. *Louis* XIII of France + *d'or* of gold] **1 :** a French gold coin first struck in 1640 and issued up to the Revolution **2 :** the French 20-franc gold piece issued after the Revolution

Lou·is Qua·torze \,lü-ē-kə-'tȯ(ə)rz\ *adj* [F, Louis XIV] **:** of, relating to, or characteristic of the architecture or furniture of the reign of Louis XIV of France

Louis Quinze \-'kaⁿz\ *adj* [F, Louis XV] **:** of, relating to, or characteristic of the architecture or furniture of the reign of Louis XV of France

Louis Seize \-'sāz, -'sez\ *adj* [F, Louis XVI] **:** of, relating to, or characteristic of the architecture or furniture of the reign of Louis XVI of France

Louis Treize \-'trāz, -'trez\ *adj* [F, Louis XIII] **:** of, relating to, or characteristic of the furniture or architecture of the reign of Louis XIII of France

[1]**lounge** \'lau̇nj\ *vb* **lounged; loung·ing** [origin unknown] *vi* **:** to act or move idly or lazily : LOAF ~ *vt* **:** to pass (time) idly <~ away the afternoon> — **loung·er** *n*

[2]**lounge** *n* **1 :** a place for lounging: as **a :** a room in a private home or public building for leisure occupations : LIVING ROOM; *also* **:** LOBBY **b :** a room in a public building or vehicle often combining lounging, smoking, and toilet facilities **2 :** a long couch

lounge car *n* **:** a railroad passenger car with seats for lounging and facilities for serving refreshments — called also *club car*

lounge lizard *n* **1** LADIES' MAN **2 :** FOP **3 :** a social parasite : NE'ER-DO-WELL

loup \'lau̇p, 'lōp\ *vb* [ME *loupen,* fr. ON *hlaupa;* akin to OE *hlēapan* to leap — more at LEAP] *chiefly Scot* **:** LEAP — **loup** *n*

loupe \'lüp\ *n* [F, gem of imperfect brilliancy, loupe] **:** a small magnifier used esp. by jewelers and watchmakers

loup–ga·rou \,lü-gə-'rü\ *n, pl* **loups–garous** \,lü-gə-'rü(z)\ [MF] **:** WEREWOLF

lour \'lau̇(-ə)r\, **loury** \'lau̇(ə)r-ē\ *var of* LOWER, LOWERY

[1]**louse** \'lau̇s\ *n* [ME *lous,* fr. OE *lūs;* akin to OHG *lūs* louse, W *llau* lice] **1** *pl* **lice** \'līs\ **a :** any of various small wingless usu. flattened insects (orders Anoplura and Mallophaga) parasitic on warm-blooded animals **b :** a small usu. sluggish arthropod that lives on other animals or on plants and sucks their blood or juices — usu. used in combination <plant ~> **c :** any of several small arthropods that are not parasitic — usu. used in combination <book ~> <wood ~> **2** *pl* **lous·es** \'lau̇-səz\ **:** a contemptible person : HEEL

louse 1a

[2]**louse** \'lau̇s, 'lau̇z\ *vt* **loused; lous·ing :** to pick lice from : DELOUSE

louse up \(')lau̇-'səp\ *vt* **:** to foul up : SNARL ~ *vi* **:** to make a mess

louse·wort \'lau̇-,swərt, -,swȯ(ə)rt\ *n* **:** any of a genus (*Pedicularis*) of plants of the figwort family with pinnate or pinnatifid leaves and variously colored bilabiate flowers in terminal spikes

lousy \'lau̇-zē\ *adj* **lous·i·er; -est 1 :** infested with lice **2 a :** totally repulsive : CONTEMPTIBLE **b :** miserably poor or inferior **c :** amply supplied : REPLETE <~ with money> **3** *of silk* **:** fuzzy and specked because of splitting of the fiber — **lous·i·ly** \-zə-lē\ *adv* — **lous·i·ness** \-zē-nəs\ *n*

[1]**lout** \'lau̇t\ *vi* [ME *louten,* fr. OE *lūtan;* akin to ON *lūta* to bow down, OE *lӯtel* little] **1 :** to bow in respect **2 :** SUBMIT, YIELD

[2]**lout** *n* [perh. fr. ON *lūtr* bent down, fr. *lūta*] **:** an awkward clownish fellow : OAF

[3]**lout** *vt* **:** to treat as a lout : SCORN

lout·ish \'lau̇t-ish\ *adj* **:** resembling or befitting a lout (as in clumsiness and stupidity) ***syn*** see BOORISH — **lout·ish·ly** *adv* — **lout·ish·ness** *n*

lou·ver *or* **lou·vre** \'lü-vər\ *n* [ME *lover,* fr. MF *lovier*] **1 :** a roof lantern or turret often with slatted apertures for escape of smoke or admission of light in a medieval building **2 a :** an opening (as in a wall or at the front of an automobile) provided with one or more slanted fixed or movable fins to allow flow of air but to exclude rain or sun or to provide privacy **b :** a finned or vaned device for controlling a flow of air or the radiation of light **c :** a fin or shutter of a louver — **lou·vered** \-vərd\ *adj*

lov·able *also* **love·able** \'ləv-ə-bəl\ *adj* **:** having qualities that attract affection — **lov·able·ness** *n* — **lov·ably** \-blē\ *adv*

lov·age \'ləv-ij\ *n* [ME *lovache,* fr. AF, fr. LL *levisticum,* alter. of L *ligusticum,* fr. neut. of *ligusticus* Ligurian, fr. *Ligur-, Ligus,* n., Ligurian] **:** any of several aromatic perennial herbs of the carrot family; *esp* **:** a European herb (*Levisticum officinale*) sometimes cultivated as a domestic remedy, flavoring agent, or potherb

[1]**love** \'ləv\ *n* [ME, fr. OE *lufu;* akin to OHG *lupa* love, OE *lēof* dear, L *lubēre, libēre* to please] **1 a (1) :** strong affection for another arising out of kinship or personal ties <maternal ~ for a child> **(2) :** attraction based on sexual desire : affection and tenderness felt by lovers **(3) :** affection based on admiration, benevolence, or common interests <~ for his old schoolmates> **b :** an assurance of love <give her my ~> **2 :** warm attachment, enthusiasm, or devotion <~ of the sea> **3 a :** the object of attachment, devotion, or admiration <baseball was his first ~> **b :** a beloved person : DARLING **4 a :** unselfish loyal and benevolent concern for the good of another: **(1) :** the fatherly concern of God for man **(2) :** brotherly concern for others **b :** a person's adoration of God **5 :** a god or personification of love **6 :** an amorous episode : LOVE AFFAIR **7 :** the sexual embrace : COPULATION **8 :** a score of zero in tennis **9** *cap, Christian Science* **:** GOD — **at love :** holding one's opponent scoreless in tennis <won three games *at love*>

[2]**love** *vb* **loved; lov·ing** *vt* **1 :** to hold dear : CHERISH **2 a :** to feel a lover's passion, devotion, or tenderness for **b (1) :** CARESS

(2) : to fondle amorously (3) : to copulate with **3** : to like or desire actively : take pleasure in <*loved* to play the violin> **4** : to thrive in <the rose ~*s* sunlight> ~ *vi* : to feel affection or experience desire
love affair *n* **1** : a romantic attachment or episode between lovers **2** : a lively enthusiasm
love apple *n* [prob. trans. of F *pomme d'amour*] : TOMATO
love beads *n pl* : beads worn as a symbol of love and peace
love·bird \'ləv-,bərd\ *n* : any of various small usu. gray or green parrots (as of the genera *Agapornis* of Africa, *Loriculus* of Asia, and *Psittacula* of So. America) that show great affection for their mates
love child *n* : an illegitimate child
love feast *n* **1** : a meal eaten in common by a Christian congregation in token of brotherly love **2** : a banquet or celebration held to reconcile differences and promote good feeling or show someone affectionate honor
love grass *n* : any of a genus (*Eragrostis*) of grasses that resemble the bluegrasses but have flattened spikelets and deciduous lemmas
love–in \'ləv-,in\ *n* [*love* + 2*-in*] : a gathering esp. of young people for the expression of their mutual love
love–in–a–mist \'ləv-ə-nə-,mist\ *n* : a European garden plant (*Nigella damascena*) of the buttercup family having the flowers enveloped in numerous finely dissected bracts
love knot *n* : a stylized knot sometimes used as an emblem of love
love·less \'ləv-ləs\ *adj* **1** : not giving love **2** : not loved — **love·less·ly** *adv* — **love·less·ness** *n*
love·lock \-,läk\ *n* : a long lock of hair worn over the shoulder by men in the 17th and 18th centuries
love·lorn \-,lȯ(ə)rn\ *adj* : bereft of love or of a lover — **love·lorn·ness** \-,lȯrn-nəs\ *n*
1love·ly \'ləv-lē\ *adj* **love·li·er; -est** **1** *obs* : LOVABLE **2** : eliciting love by moral or ideal worth **3** : delightful for beauty, harmony, or grace : ATTRACTIVE **4** : GRAND, SWELL ***syn*** see BEAUTIFUL ***ant*** unlovely — **love·li·ly** \'ləv-lə-lē\ *adv* — **love·li·ness** \'ləv-lē-nəs\ *n* — **lovely** *adv*
2lovely *n, pl* **lovelies** **1** : a beautiful woman **2** : a lovely object
love·mak·ing \'ləv-,mā-kiŋ\ *n* **1** : COURTSHIP **2** : sexual activity; *esp* : COPULATION
lov·er \'ləv-ər\ *n* **1 a** : a person in love; *esp* : a man in love with a woman **b** *pl* : two persons in love with each other **2** : an affectionate or benevolent friend **3** : DEVOTEE **4** : PARAMOUR
lov·er·ly \-lē\ *adj* : resembling or befitting a lover
love seat *n* : a double chair, sofa, or settee for two persons
love·sick \'ləv-,sik\ *adj* **1** : languishing with love : YEARNING **2** : expressing a lover's longing — **love·sick·ness** *n*
love·some \-səm\ *adj* **1** : WINSOME, LOVELY **2** : AFFECTIONATE, AMOROUS
lov·ing \'ləv-iŋ\ *adj* : AFFECTIONATE — **lov·ing·ly** \-iŋ-lē\ *adv* — **lov·ing·ness** *n*
loving cup *n* [fr. its former use in ceremonial drinking] **1** : a large ornamental drinking vessel with two or more handles **2** : a loving cup given as a token or trophy
lov·ing–kind·ness \,ləv-iŋ-'kīn(d)-nəs\ *n* : tender and benevolent affection
1low \'lō\ *vi* [ME *loowen*, vb., fr. OE *hlōwan;* akin to OHG *hluoen* to moo, L *calare* to call, summon, Gk *kalein*] : MOO
2low *n* : the deep sustained sound characteristic esp. of a cow
3low *adj* **low·er** \'lō(-ə)r\; **low·est** \'lō-əst\ [ME *lah, low,* fr. ON *lāgr;* akin to MHG *læge* low, flat] **1 a** : having a small upward extension or elevation <a ~ wall> **b** : situated or passing little above a reference line, point, or plane <~ bridges> **c** (1) : having a low-cut neckline (2) : not extending as high as the ankle <~ oxfords> **2 a** : situated or passing below the normal level, surface, or base of measurement, or the mean elevation <~ ground> **b** : marking a nadir or bottom <the ~ point of his career> **3** : DEAD — used as a predicate adjective **4 a** : not loud : SOFT; *also* : FLAT **b** : depressed in pitch <a ~ tone> **5 a** : being near the equator <~ northern latitudes> **b** : being near the horizon **6** : humble in character or status <~ birth> **7 a** : lacking strength, health, or vitality : WEAK, PROSTRATE <very ~ with pneumonia> **b** : lacking spirit or vivacity : DEPRESSED <a ~ frame of mind> **8 a** : of lesser degree, size, or amount than average or ordinary <~ pressure> **b** (1) : small in number or amount (2) : SUBSTANDARD, INADEQUATE <a ~ level of employment> <a ~ income group> (3) : CHEAP <~ prices> (4) : SHORT, DEPLETED <oil is in ~ supply> **9** : falling short of some standard: as **a** : lacking dignity or elevation <a ~ style of writing> **b** : morally reprehensible : BASE <a ~ trick> **c** : COARSE, VULGAR <~ language> **10 a** : not advanced in complexity, development, or elaboration <~ organisms> **b** *often cap* : Low Church **11** : UNFAVORABLE, DISPARAGING <had a ~ opinion of him> **12** : designed for slow and usu. the slowest speed <~ gear> **13** : articulated with a wide opening between the relatively flat tongue and the palate : OPEN <the sounds \ä\, \ȧ\, \a\ are ~> ***syn*** see BASE — **low** *adv* — **low·ness** *n*
4low *n* **1** : something that is low: as **a** : DEPTH **b** : a region of low barometric pressure **2** : the transmission gear of an automotive vehicle giving the lowest ratio of propeller-shaft to engine-shaft speed and the highest amplification of torque
5low *or* **lowe** \'lō\ *n* [ME, fr. ON *logi, log;* akin to OE *lēoht* light — more at LIGHT] *chiefly Scot* : FLAME, BLAZE
6low *or* **lowe** *vb* **lowed; low·ing** *Scot* : FLAME, BLAZE
low beam *n* : the short-range focus of a vehicle headlight
low blood pressure *n* : HYPOTENSION
low·born \'lō-'bȯ(ə)rn\ *adj* : born in a low condition or rank
low·boy \-,bȯi\ *n* : a chest or side table about three feet high with drawers and usu. with cabriole legs
low·bred \-'bred\ *adj* : RUDE, VULGAR
low·brow \-,braủ\ *n* : an uncultivated person — **lowbrow** *adj*
Low Church *adj* : tending esp. in Anglican worship to minimize emphasis on the priesthood, sacraments, and ceremonial in worship and often to emphasize evangelical principles — **Low Churchman** *n*
low comedy *n* : comedy bordering on farce and employing burlesque, horseplay, or the representation of low life — compare HIGH COMEDY

lowboy

low·down \'lō-,daủn\ *n* : the inside facts : DOPE
low–down \'lō-daủn\ *adj* **1** : CONTEMPTIBLE, BASE **2** : deeply emotional <~ blues>
1low·er \'laủ(-ə)r\ *vi* [ME *louren;* akin to MHG *lūren* to lie in wait] **1** : to look sullen : FROWN **2** : to become dark, gloomy, and threatening ***syn*** see FROWN
2lower *n* **1** : a lowering look : FROWN **2** : a gloomy sky or aspect of weather
3low·er \'lō(-ə)r\ *adj* **1** : relatively low in position, rank, or order **2** : less advanced in the scale of evolutionary development **3** : constituting the popular and often the larger and more representative branch of a bicameral legislative body **4 a** : situated or held to be situated beneath the earth's surface **b** *cap* : of, relating to, or constituting an earlier geologic period or formation **5** : SOUTHERN <~ New York State>
4low·er \'lō(-ə)r\ *vi* : to move down : DROP; *also* : DIMINISH ~ *vt* **1 a** : to let descend : let down **b** : to depress as to direction <~ your aim> **c** : to reduce the height of **2 a** : to reduce in value or amount <~ the price> **b** (1) : to bring down : DEGRADE (2) : ABASE, HUMBLE **c** : to reduce the objective of
1low·er·case \,lō(-ə)r-'kās\ *adj* [fr. the compositor's practice of keeping such types in the lower of a pair of type cases] *of a letter* : having as its typical form a f g or *b n i* rather than A F G or *B N I* — **lowercase** *n*
2lowercase *vt* **-cased; -cas·ing** : to print or set in lowercase letters
low·er–class \,lō(-ə)r-'klas\ *adj* **1** : of, relating to, or characteristic of the lower class **2** : being an inferior or low-ranking specimen of its kind
lower class *n* : a social class occupying a position below the middle class and having the lowest status in a society by virtue of a low material standard of living, social instability, and a low level of personal ambition and aspiration esp. toward education
lower criticism *n* : criticism concerned with the recovery of original texts esp. of Scripture through collation of extant manuscripts — compare HIGHER CRITICISM
lower fungus *n* : a fungus with hyphae absent or rudimentary and nonseptate
low·er·ing \'laủ-(ə-)riŋ\ *adj* : dark and threatening : GLOOMY
low·er·most \'lō(-ə)r-,mōst\ *adj* : LOWEST
low·ery \'laủ-(ə-)rē\ *adj, NewEng* : GLOOMY, LOWERING
lowest common denominator *n* : LEAST COMMON DENOMINATOR
lowest common multiple *n* : LEAST COMMON MULTIPLE
lowest terms *n pl* : the numerator and denominator of a fraction that have no factor in common <reduce a fraction to *lowest terms*>
low frequency *n* : a radio frequency between medium frequency and very low frequency — see RADIO FREQUENCY table
Low German *n* **1** : the German dialects of northern Germany esp. as used since the end of the medieval period : PLATTDEUTSCH **2** : the West Germanic languages other than High German
low–grade \'lō-'grād\ *adj* **1** : of inferior grade or quality <~ bonds> **2** : being near the lower or least favorable extreme of a specified range <a ~ fever> <a ~ imbecile>
low–key \-'kē\ *also* **low–keyed** \-'kēd\ *adj* **1** : of low intensity **2** : having or producing dark tones only with little contrast
1low·land \'lō-lənd, -,land\ *n* : low or level country
2lowland *adj* **1** : of or relating to a lowland **2** *cap* : of or relating to the Lowlands of Scotland
low·land·er \-lən-dər, -,lan-\ *n* **1** : a native or inhabitant of a lowland region **2** *cap* : an inhabitant of the Lowlands of Scotland
Low Latin *n* : postclassical Latin in its later stages
low–lev·el \'lō-'lev-əl\ *adj* **1** : being of low importance or rank **2** : occurring, done, or placed at a low level
low·li·head \'lō-lē-,hed\ *n* [ME *lowliheed,* fr. *lowly* + *-hed* -hood; akin to ME *-hod* -hood] *archaic* : lowly state
1low·ly \'lō-lē\ *adv* **1** : in a humble or meek manner **2** : in a low position, manner, or degree **3** : not loudly
2lowly *adj* **low·li·er; -est** **1** : humble in manner or spirit : free from self-assertive pride **2** : of or relating to a low social or economic rank **3** : low in the scale of biological or cultural evolution **4** : ranking low in some hierarchy **5** : not lofty or sublime : PROSAIC ***syn*** see HUMBLE ***ant*** pompous — **low·li·ness** *n*
low–ly·ing \'lō-'lī-iŋ\ *adj* **1** : rising relatively little above the base of measurement <~ hills> **2** : lying below the normal level, surface, or the base of measurement or mean elevation <~ clouds>
low mass *n, often cap L&M* : a mass that is recited without singing by the celebrant, without a deacon, subdeacon, or choir assisting the celebrant, and without the use of incense
low–mind·ed \'lō-'mīn-dəd\ *adj* : inclined to low or unworthy things — **low–mind·ed·ly** *adv* — **low–mind·ed·ness** *n*
lown \'laủn, 'lün\ *adj* [ME (Sc) *lowne*] *dial* : CALM, QUIET
low–necked \'lō-'nekt\ *or* **low–neck** \-'nek\ *adj* : DÉCOLLETÉ 2
low–pres·sure \'lō-'presh-ər\ *adj* **1** : having, exerting, or operating under a relatively small pressure **2** : EASYGOING
low–profile \'lō-'prō-,fīl\ *adj* **1** : having little height : LOW **2** : intended to attract little attention
low profile *n* : an inconspicuous life style or posture
low relief *n* : BAS-RELIEF
low–rise \'lō-'rīz\ *adj* : being one or two stories and not equipped with elevators <a ~ classroom building>
low–spir·it·ed \'lō-'spir-ət-əd\ *adj* : DEJECTED, DEPRESSED — **low–spir·it·ed·ly** *adv* — **low–spir·it·ed·ness** *n*
Low Sunday *n* : the Sunday following Easter
low–ten·sion \'lō-'ten-chən\ *adj* **1** : having a low potential or voltage **2** : constructed to be used at low voltage
low–test \-'test\ *adj* : having a low volatility <~ gasoline>
low tide *n* : the farthest ebb of the tide
low water *n* : a low stage of the water in a river or lake; *also* : LOW TIDE

[1]lox \ˈläks\ *n* [*l*iquid *ox*ygen] **:** liquid oxygen

[2]lox *n, pl* **lox** *or* **lox·es** [Yiddish *laks,* fr. MHG *lahs* salmon] **:** smoked salmon

loxo·drome \ˈläk-sə-ˌdrōm\ *n* [ISV, back-formation fr. *loxodromic*] **:** RHUMB LINE

loxo·drom·ic \ˌläk-sə-ˈdräm-ik\ *adj* [prob. fr. (assumed) NL *loxodromicus,* fr. Gk *loxos* oblique + *dromos* course; akin to L *ulna* elbow] **:** relating to a rhumb line or to sailing on rhumb lines — **loxo·drom·i·cal·ly** \-i-k(ə-)lē\ *adv*

loy·al \ˈlȯi(-ə)l\ *adj* [MF, fr. OF *leial, leel,* fr. L *legalis* legal] **1 :** unswerving in allegiance: as **a :** faithful in allegiance to one's lawful sovereign or government **b :** faithful to a private person to whom fidelity is due **c :** faithful to a cause, ideal, or custom **2 :** showing loyalty <her ~ determination to help the party> **3** *obs* **:** LAWFUL, LEGITIMATE ***syn*** see FAITHFUL ***ant*** disloyal — **loy·al·ly** \ˈlȯi-ə-lē\ *adv*

loy·al·ist \ˈlȯi-ə-ləst\ *n* **:** one who is or remains loyal to a political cause, party, government, or sovereign; *esp* **:** TORY 4

loy·al·ty \ˈlȯi(-ə)l-tē\ *n, pl* **-ties** [ME *loyaltee,* fr. MF *loialté,* fr. OF *leialté,* fr. *leial*] **1 :** the quality or state of being loyal **2 :** the tie binding a person to something to which he is loyal ***syn*** see FIDELITY ***ant*** disloyalty

loz·enge \ˈläz-ᵊnj\ *n* [ME *losenge,* fr. MF *losange*] **1 :** a figure with four equal sides and two acute and two obtuse angles **:** DIAMOND **2 :** something shaped like a lozenge **3 :** a small often medicated candy

[1]LP \ˈel-ˈpē\ *trademark* — used for a microgroove phonograph record designed to be played at 33⅓ revolutions per minute

[2]LP *abbr* low pressure

LPG *abbr* liquefied petroleum gas

LPN *abbr* licensed practical nurse

Lr *symbol* lawrencium

LR *abbr* **1** living room **2** log run **3** lower right

LRL *abbr* lunar receiving laboratory

LS *abbr* **1** left side **2** letter signed **3** library science **4** [L *locus sigilli*] place of the seal **5** long shot

LSA *abbr* Linguistic Society of America

LSAT *abbr* Law School Admissions Test

LSD \ˌel-ˌes-ˈdē\ *n* [*lys*ergic acid *d*iethylamide] **:** an organic compound $C_{20}H_{25}N_3O$ that induces psychotic symptoms similar to those of schizophrenia — called also *lysergic acid diethylamide*

LSS *abbr* **1** lifesaving service; lifesaving station **2** life-support system

LST *abbr* landing ship, tank

LSV *abbr* lunar surface vehicle

lt *abbr* light

Lt *abbr* lieutenant

LT *abbr* **1** long ton **2** low-tension

LTC *or* **Lt Col** *abbr* lieutenant colonel

Lt Comdr *abbr* lieutenant commander

ltd *abbr* limited

LTG *or* **Lt Gen** *abbr* lieutenant general

lt gov *abbr* lieutenant governor

LTh *abbr* licentiate in theology

LTJG *abbr* lieutenant, junior grade

LTL *abbr* less-than-truckload lot

ltr *abbr* **1** letter **2** lighter

LTS *abbr* **1** launch telemetry station **2** launch tracking system

Lu *symbol* lutetium

lu·au \ˈlü-ˌau̇\ *n* [Hawaiian *lu'au*] **:** an Hawaiian feast

lub *abbr* lubricant; lubricating

lub·ber \ˈləb-ər\ *n* [ME *lobre, lobur*] **1 :** a big clumsy fellow **2 :** a clumsy seaman — **lub·ber·li·ness** \-lē-nəs\ *n* — **lub·ber·ly** \-lē\ *adj or adv*

lubber line *n* **:** a fixed line on the compass of a ship or airplane that is aligned with the longitudinal axis of the vehicle

lubber's hole *n* **:** a hole in a ship's top near the mast through which one may go farther aloft without going over the rim by the futtock shrouds

lube \ˈlüb\ *n* [short for *lubricating oil*] **:** LUBRICANT

lu·bric \ˈlü-brik\ *adj* [MF *lubrique,* fr. ML *lubricus*] *archaic* **:** LUBRICIOUS — **lu·bri·cal** \-bri-kəl\ *adj*

lu·bri·cant \ˈlü-bri-kənt\ *n* **1 :** a substance (as grease) capable of reducing friction, heat, and wear when introduced as a film between solid surfaces **2 :** something that lessens or prevents friction or difficulty — **lubricant** *adj*

lu·bri·cate \ˈlü-brə-ˌkāt\ *vb* **-cat·ed; -cat·ing** [L *lubricatus,* pp. of *lubricare* fr. *lubricus* slippery — more at SLEEVE] *vt* **1 :** to make smooth or slippery **2 :** to apply a lubricant to ~ *vi* **:** to act as a lubricant — **lu·bri·ca·tion** \ˌlü-brə-ˈkā-shən\ *n* — **lu·bri·ca·tive** \ˈlü-brə-ˌkāt-iv\ *adj* — **lu·bri·ca·tor** \-ˌkāt-ər\ *n*

lu·bri·cious \lü-ˈbrish-əs\ *or* **lu·bri·cous** \ˈlü-bri-kəs\ *adj* [ML *lubricus,* fr. L, slippery, easily led astray] **1 :** marked by wantonness **:** LECHEROUS; *also* **:** SALACIOUS **2** [L *lubricus*] **:** having a smooth or slippery quality <a ~ skin> — **lu·bri·cious·ly** *adv*

lu·bric·i·ty \lü-ˈbris-ət-ē\ *n, pl* **-ties :** the property or state of being lubricious; *also* **:** the capacity for reducing friction

lu·bri·to·ri·um \ˌlü-brə-ˈtōr-ē-əm, -ˈtȯr-\ *n* [*lubricate* + *-torium* (as in *sanatorium*)] **:** a station for lubricating motor vehicles

Lu·can \ˈlü-kən\ *adj* [LL *lucanus,* fr. *Lucas* Luke, fr. Gk *Loukas*] **:** of or relating to Luke or the Gospel ascribed to him

lu·carne \lü-ˈkärn\ *n* [F] **:** DORMER

Lu·ca·yo \lü-ˈkī-(ˌ)ō\ *n* **1 :** an extinct aboriginal Arawakan tribe of the Bahamas **2 :** the language of the Lucayo people

lu·cen·cy \-ᵊn-sē\ *n* **:** the quality or state of being lucent

lu·cent \ˈlüs-ᵊnt\ *adj* [L *lucent-, lucens,* prp. of *lucēre* to shine — more at LIGHT] **1 :** glowing with light **:** LUMINOUS **2 :** marked by clarity or translucence **:** CLEAR — **lu·cent·ly** *adv*

lu·cern *n* [prob. modif. of G *lüchsern* of a lynx, fr. *luchs* lynx] *obs* **:** LYNX

lu·cerne *also* **lu·cern** \lü-ˈsərn\ *n* [F *luzerne,* fr. Prov *luserno*] *chiefly Brit* **:** ALFALFA

lu·cid \ˈlü-səd\ *adj* [L *lucidus;* akin to L *lucēre*] **1 a :** suffused with light **:** LUMINOUS **b :** TRANSLUCENT **2 :** having full use of one's faculties **:** SANE **3 :** clear to the understanding **:** INTELLIGIBLE ***syn*** see CLEAR ***ant*** obscure, vague, dark — **lu·cid·ly** *adv* — **lu·cid·ness** *n*

lu·cid·i·ty \lü-ˈsid-ət-ē\ *n* **1 :** clearness of thought or style **2 :** a presumed capacity to perceive the truth directly and instantaneously **:** CLAIRVOYANCE

Lu·ci·fer \ˈlü-sə-fər\ *n* [ME, the morning star, a fallen rebel archangel, the Devil, fr. OE, fr. L, the morning star, fr. *lucifer* light-bearing, fr. *luc-, lux* light + *-fer* -ferous — more at LIGHT] **1** — used as a name of the devil **2 :** the planet Venus when appearing as the morning star **3** *not cap* **:** a friction match having as active substances antimony sulfide and potassium chlorate

lu·cif·er·ase \lü-ˈsif-ə-ˌrās, -ˌrāz\ *n* [ISV, fr. *luciferin*] **:** an enzyme that catalyzes the oxidation of luciferin

lu·cif·er·in \-(ə-)rən\ *n* [ISV, fr. L *lucifer* light-bearing] **:** a pigment in luminescent organisms that furnishes practically heatless light in undergoing oxidation

lu·cif·er·ous \lü-ˈsif-(ə-)rəs\ *adj* [L *lucifer*] *archaic* **:** bringing light or insight **:** ILLUMINATING

Lu·ci·na \lü-ˈsī-nə\ *n* [L, Roman goddess of childbirth] *archaic* **:** MIDWIFE

Lu·cite \ˈlü-ˌsīt\ *trademark* — used for an acrylic resin or plastic consisting essentially of polymerized methyl methacrylate

[1]luck \ˈlək\ *n* [ME *lucke,* fr. MD *luc;* akin to MHG *gelücke* luck] **1 a :** a force that brings good fortune or adversity **b :** the events or circumstances that operate for or against an individual **2 :** favoring chance; *also* **:** SUCCESS — **luck·less** \-ləs\ *adj*

[2]luck *vi* **1 :** to prosper or succeed esp. through chance or good fortune <things were going bad and then he ~*ed* out> **2 :** to come upon something desirable by chance — usu. used with *out, on, onto,* or *into* <~ onto a vein of gold>

lucky \ˈlək-ē\ *adj* **luck·i·er; -est 1 :** having good luck **2 :** happening by chance **:** FORTUITOUS **3 :** producing or resulting in good by chance **:** FAVORABLE **4 :** seeming to bring good luck <a ~ rabbit's foot> — **luck·i·ly** \ˈlək-ə-lē\ *adv* — **luck·i·ness** \ˈlək-ē-nəs\ *n*

syn LUCKY, FORTUNATE, HAPPY, PROVIDENTIAL *shared meaning element* **:** meeting with or producing unforeseen success ***ant*** unlucky

lu·cra·tive \ˈlü-krət-iv\ *adj* [ME *lucratif,* fr. MF, fr. L *lucrativus,* fr. *lucratus* pp. of *lucrari* to gain, fr. *lucrum*] **:** producing wealth **:** PROFITABLE — **lu·cra·tive·ly** *adv* — **lu·cra·tive·ness** *n*

lu·cre \ˈlü-kər\ *n* [ME, fr. L *lucrum;* akin to OE *lēan* reward, OHG *lōn,* Gk *leia* booty] **:** monetary gain **:** PROFIT; *also* **:** MONEY

lu·cu·bra·tion \ˌlü-k(y)ə-ˈbrā-shən\ *n* [L *lucubration-, lucubratio* study by night, work produced at night, fr. *lucubratus,* pp. of *lucubrare* to work by lamplight; akin to L *luc-, lux*] **1 :** laborious study **:** MEDITATION **2 :** studied or pretentious expression in speech or writing

lu·cu·lent \ˈlü-kyə-lənt\ *adj* [ME, fr. L *luculentus,* fr. *luc-, lux* light] **:** clear in thought or expression **:** LUCID — **lu·cu·lent·ly** *adv*

Lu·cul·lan \lü-ˈkəl-ən\ *or* **Lu·cul·li·an** \-ˈkəl-ē-ən\ *adj* [L *lucullanus* of Lucullus, fr. L. Licinius *Lucullus*] **:** LAVISH, LUXURIOUS <a ~ feast>

Ludd·ite \ˈləd-ˌīt\ *n* [Ned *Ludd fl* 1779 half-witted Leicestershire workman] **:** one of a group of early 19th century English workmen destroying laborsaving machinery as a protest

lu·di·crous \ˈlüd-ə-krəs\ *adj* [L *ludicrus,* fr. *ludus* play, sport; akin to L *ludere* to play, Gk *loidoros* abusive] **1 :** amusing or laughable through obvious absurdity, incongruity, exaggeration, or eccentricity **2 :** meriting derisive laughter or scorn as absurdly inept, false, or foolish ***syn*** see LAUGHABLE — **lu·di·crous·ly** *adv* — **lu·di·crous·ness** *n*

lu·es \ˈlü-(ˌ)ēz\ *n, pl* **lues** [NL, fr. L, plague; akin to Gk *lyein* to loosen, destroy — more at LOSE] **:** SYPHILIS — **lu·et·ic** \lü-ˈet-ik\ *adj* — **lu·et·i·cal·ly** \-i-k(ə-)lē\ *adv*

[1]luff \ˈləf\ *n* [ME, weather side of a ship, luff, fr. MF *lof* weather side of ship] **1 :** the act of sailing a ship nearer the wind **2 :** the forward edge of a fore-and-aft sail

[2]luff *vi* **:** to sail nearer the wind

[1]lug \ˈləg\ *vb* **lugged; lug·ging** [ME *luggen* to pull by the hair or ear, drag, prob. of Scand origin; akin to Norw *lugga* to pull by the hair] *vt* **1 :** DRAG, PULL **2 :** to carry laboriously **3 :** to introduce in a forced manner <~ his name into the talk> ~ *vi* **1 :** to pull with effort **:** TUG **2 :** to move heavily or by jerks <the car ~*s* on hills>

[2]lug *n* **1** *archaic* **a :** an act of lugging **b :** something that is lugged **c :** a shipping container for fruits or vegetables **2** *pl* **:** superior airs or affectations <put on ~*s*> **3 :** LUGSAIL **4** *slang* **:** an exaction of money — used in the phrase *put the lug on*

[3]lug *n* [ME (Sc) *lugge,* perh. fr. ME *luggen*] **1** *chiefly dial* **:** EAR **2 :** something (as a handle) that projects like an ear: as **a :** a leather loop on a harness saddle through which the shaft passes **b :** a fitting of copper or brass to which electrical wires are soldered or connected **3 :** BLOCKHEAD, LOUT

luge \ˈlüzh\ *n* [F] **:** a small sled that is ridden in a supine position and used esp. in competition

lug·gage \ˈləg-ij\ *n* **:** something that is lugged; *esp* **:** suitcases or traveling bags for a traveler's belongings **:** BAGGAGE

lug·ger \ˈləg-ər\ *n* [*lugsail*] **:** a small fishing or coasting boat that carries one or more lugsails

lug·gie \ˈləg-ē\ *n* [[3]*lug*] *chiefly Scot* **:** a small wooden pail or dish with a handle

lug·sail \ˈləg-ˌsāl, -səl\ *n* [perh. fr. [3]*lug*] **:** a 4-sided sail bent to an obliquely hanging yard that is hoisted and lowered with the sail

lu·gu·bri·ous \lu̇-'gü-brē-əs *also* -'gyü-\ *adj* [L *lugubris,* fr. *lugēre* to mourn; akin to Gk *lygros* mournful] : MOURNFUL; *esp* : exaggeratedly or affectedly mournful — **lu·gu·bri·ous·ly** *adv* — **lu·gu·bri·ous·ness** *n*

lug·worm \'ləg-ˌwərm\ *n* [origin unknown] : any of a genus (*Arenicola*) of marine polychaete worms that have a row of tufted gills along each side of the back and are used for bait

Luk·an \'lü-kən\ *var of* LUCAN

Luke \'lük\ *n* [L *Lucas,* fr. Gk *Loukas*] **1 :** a Gentile physician and companion of the apostle Paul traditionally identified as the author of the third Gospel in the New Testament and of the Book of Acts **2 :** the third Gospel in the New Testament — see BIBLE table

luke·warm \'lü-'kwȯ(ə)rm\ *adj* [ME, fr. *luke* lukewarm + *warm;* akin to OHG *lāo* lukewarm — more at LEE] **1 :** moderately warm : TEPID **2 :** lacking conviction : HALFHEARTED — **luke·warm·ly** *adv* — **luke·warm·ness** *n*

1lull \'ləl\ *vt* [ME *lullen;* prob. of imit. origin] **1 :** to cause to sleep or rest : SOOTHE **2 :** to cause to relax vigilance

2lull *n* **1** *archaic* : something that lulls; *esp* : LULLABY **2 :** a temporary pause or decline in activity <the early morning ~ in urban noise>: as **a :** a temporary calm before or during a storm **b :** a temporary drop in business activity ***syn*** see PAUSE

1lul·la·by \'ləl-ə-ˌbī\ *n, pl* **-bies** [obs. E *lulla,* interj. used to lull a child (fr. ME) + *bye,* interj. used to lull a child, fr. ME *by*] : a song to quiet children or lull them to sleep

2lullaby *vt* **-bied; -by·ing :** to quiet with a lullaby

lu·lu \'lü-(ˌ)lü\ *n* [prob. fr. *Lulu,* nickname fr. *Louise*] *slang* : one that is remarkable or wonderful

lum \'ləm\ *n* [origin unknown] *chiefly Scot* : CHIMNEY

lumb- *or* **lumbo-** *comb form* [L *lumbus* loin — more at LOIN] : lumbar and <*lumbo*sacral>

lum·ba·go \ˌləm-'bā-(ˌ)gō\ *n* [L, fr. *lumbus*] : usu. painful muscular rheumatism involving the lumbar region

lum·bar \'ləm-bər, -ˌbär\ *adj* [NL *lumbaris,* fr. L *lumbus*] : of, relating to, or constituting the loins or the vertebrae between the thoracic vertebrae and sacrum <~ region>

1lum·ber \'ləm-bər\ *vi* **lum·bered; lum·ber·ing** \-b(ə-)riŋ\ [ME *lomeren*] : to move heavily or clumsily; *also* : RUMBLE

2lumber *n* [perh. fr. *Lombard;* fr. the use of pawnshops as storehouses of disused property] **1 :** surplus or disused articles (as furniture) that are stored away **2 a :** timber or logs esp. when dressed for use **b :** any of various structural materials prepared in a form similar to lumber — **lumber** *adj*

3lumber *vb* **lum·bered; lum·ber·ing** \-b(ə-)riŋ\ *vt* **1 :** to clutter with or as if with lumber : ENCUMBER **2 :** to heap together in disorder **3 :** to log and saw the timber of ~ *vi* **1 :** to cut logs for lumber **2 :** to saw logs into lumber for the market — **lum·ber·er** \-bər-ər\ *n*

lum·ber·jack \'ləm-bər-ˌjak\ *n* : LOGGER

lum·ber·man \-mən\ *n* : one who is engaged in the business of cutting, processing, and marketing lumber esp. in a supervisory or managerial capacity

lum·ber·yard \-ˌyärd\ *n* : a yard where a stock of lumber is kept for sale

lum·bo·sa·cral \ˌləm-bō-'sak-rəl, -'sā-krəl\ *adj* : relating to the lumbar and sacral regions or parts

lu·men \'lü-mən\ *n, pl* **lu·mi·na** \-mə-nə\ *or* **lumens** [NL *lumin-, lumen,* fr. L, light, air shaft, opening] **1 :** the cavity of a tubular organ <the ~ of a blood vessel> **2 :** the bore of a tube (as of a hollow needle or catheter) **3 :** a unit of luminous flux equal to the light emitted in a unit solid angle by a uniform point source of one candle intensity — **lu·mi·nal** *also* **lu·men·al** \-mən-ᵊl\ *adj*

lumin- *or* **lumini-** *or* **lumino-** *comb form* [ME *lumin-,* fr. L *lumin-, lumen*] : light <*lumini*ferous>

lu·mi·naire \ˌlü-mə-'na(ə)r, -'ne(ə)r\ *n* [F, lamp, lighting] : a complete lighting unit

Lu·mi·nal \'lü-mə-ˌnal, -ˌnȯl\ *trademark* — used for phenobarbital

lu·mi·nance \'lü-mə-nən(t)s\ *n* **1 :** the quality or state of being luminous **2 :** the luminous intensity of a surface in a given direction per unit of projected area

lu·mi·nary \'lü-mə-ˌner-ē\ *n, pl* **-nar·ies** [ME *luminarye,* fr. MF & LL; MF *luminaire* lamp, fr. LL *luminaria,* pl. of *luminare* lamp, heavenly body, fr. L, window, fr. *lumin-, lumen* light; akin to L *lucēre* to shine — more at LIGHT] : a source of light or illumination: as **a :** a body that gives light; *esp* : one of the celestial bodies **b :** a person brilliantly outstanding in some respect <the most brilliant intellectual ~ of the departing generation —H. O. Taylor> — **luminary** *adj*

lu·mi·nesce \ˌlü-mə-'nes\ *vi* **-nesced; -nesc·ing** [back-formation fr. *luminescent*] : to exhibit luminescence

lu·mi·nes·cence \-'nes-ᵊn(t)s\ *n* **1 :** an emission of light that is not ascribable directly to incandescence and therefore occurs at low temperatures and that is produced by physiological processes (as in the firefly), by chemical action, by friction, or by electrical action **2 :** the light produced by luminescence

lu·mi·nes·cent \-ᵊnt\ *adj* : relating to, exhibiting, or adapted for the production of luminescence

lu·mi·nif·er·ous \ˌlü-mə-'nif-(ə-)rəs\ *adj* : transmitting, producing, or yielding light

lu·mi·nist \'lü-mə-nəst\ *n* [F *luministe,* fr. L *lumin-, lumen*] : a painter who makes a specialty of the effects of light on colored objects

lu·mi·nos·i·ty \ˌlü-mə-'näs-ət-ē\ *n, pl* **-ties** **1 a :** the quality or state of being luminous **b :** something luminous **2 a :** the relative quantity of light **b :** relative brightness of something **3 :** the luminous efficiency of radiant energy

lu·mi·nous \'lü-mə-nəs\ *adj* [ME, fr. L *luminosus,* fr. *lumin-, lumen*] **1 a :** emitting or reflecting usu. steady, suffused, or glowing light **b :** of or relating to light or to luminous flux **2 :** bathed in or exposed to steady light <a public square ~ with sunlight> **3 :** INTELLIGENT, ENLIGHTENED; *also* : CLEAR, INTELLIGIBLE ***syn*** see BRIGHT — **lu·mi·nous·ly** *adv* — **lu·mi·nous·ness** *n*

luminous energy *n* : energy transferred in the form of visible radiation

luminous flux *n* : radiant flux in the visible-wavelength range usu. expressed in lumens instead of watts

luminous paint *n* : a paint containing a phosphor (as zinc sulfide activated with copper) and so able to glow in the dark

lum·mox \'ləm-əks, -iks\ *n* [origin unknown] : a clumsy person

1lump \'ləmp\ *n* [ME] **1 :** a piece or mass of indefinite size and shape **2 a :** AGGREGATE, TOTALITY <taken in the ~> **b :** MAJORITY **3 :** PROTUBERANCE; *esp* : an abnormal swelling **4 :** a thickset heavy person; *specif* : one who is stupid or dull **5** *pl* **a :** BEATINGS <had taken a lot of ~*s* growing up in the city> <on the back waterways the single small craft takes its ~*s* —A. W. Baum> **b :** COMEUPPANCE <self-appointed specialists on women are given their ~*s* —Brendan Gill>

2lump *vt* **1 :** to group without discrimination **2 :** to make into lumps; *also* : to make lumps on or in **3 :** to move noisily and clumsily ~ *vi* **1 :** to become formed into lumps **2 :** to move oneself noisily and clumsily

3lump *adj* : not divided into parts : ENTIRE <a ~ payment>

4lump *vt* [origin unknown] : to put up with <like it or ~ it>

lum·pen \'lu̇m-pən\ *adj* [G *lumpenproletariat* degraded and contemptible section of the proletariat, fr. *lump* contemptible person (fr. *lumpen* rags) + *proletariat*] : of or relating to dispossessed and uprooted individuals cut off from the economic and social class with which they might normally be identified <~ proletariat> <~ intellectuals>

lump·er \'ləm-pər\ *n* : a laborer employed to handle freight or cargo

lump·ish \'ləm-pish\ *adj* **1 :** DULL, SLUGGISH **2** *obs* : low in spirits : DEJECTED **3 :** HEAVY, AWKWARD **4 :** LUMPY 1a **5 :** tediously slow or dull : BORING — **lump·ish·ly** *adv* — **lump·ish·ness** *n*

lumpy \'ləm-pē\ *adj* **lump·i·er; -est** **1 a :** filled or covered with lumps **b :** characterized by choppy waves **2 :** having a thickset clumsy appearance **3 :** uneven and often crude in style — **lump·i·ly** \-pə-lē\ *adv* — **lump·i·ness** \-pē-nəs\ *n*

lumpy jaw *n* : ACTINOMYCOSIS; *esp* : actinomycosis of the head in cattle

lu·na·cy \'lü-nə-sē\ *n, pl* **-cies** [*lunatic*] **1 a :** insanity interrupted by lucid intervals **b :** any of various forms of insanity **c :** insanity amounting to lack of capacity or of responsibility in the eyes of the law **2 :** wild foolishness : extravagant folly **3 :** a foolish act

lu·na moth \ˌlü-nə-\ *n* [NL *luna* (specific epithet of *Actias luna*), fr. L, moon] : a large mostly pale green American saturniid moth (*Actias luna*) with long tails on the hind wings

lu·nar \'lü-nər *also* -ˌnär\ *adj* [L *lunaris,* fr. *luna* moon; akin to L *lucēre* to shine — more at LIGHT] **1 a :** of or relating to the moon **b :** designed for use on the moon <~ vehicles> **2 :** CRESCENT, LUNATE **3 :** measured by the moon's revolution <~ month>

lunar caustic *n* [obs. *luna* silver, fr. ML, fr. L, moon] : silver nitrate esp. when fused and molded into sticks for use as a caustic

lunar eclipse *n* : an eclipse in which the moon near the full phase passes partially or wholly through the umbra of the earth's shadow

lunar excursion module *n* : a space vehicle module designed to carry astronauts from the command module to the surface of the moon and back — called also *lunar module*

lu·nate \'lü-ˌnāt\ *adj* [L *lunatus,* pp. of *lunare* to bend in a crescent, fr. *luna*] : shaped like a crescent — **lu·nate·ly** *adv*

lu·na·tic \'lü-nə-ˌtik\ *adj* [ME *lunatik,* fr. OF or LL; OF *lunatique,* fr. LL *lunaticus,* fr. L *luna;* fr. the belief that lunacy fluctuated with the phases of the moon] **1 a :** affected with lunacy : INSANE **b :** designed for the care of insane persons <~ asylum> **2 :** wildly foolish : GIDDY — **lunatic** *n*

lunatic fringe *n* : an extreme or wild group on the periphery of a larger group; *esp* : the members of a political or social movement espousing extreme, eccentric, or fanatical views

lu·na·tion \lü-'nā-shən\ *n* [ME *lunacioun,* fr. ML *lunation-, lunatio,* fr. L *luna*] : the period of time averaging 29 days, 12 hours, 44 minutes, and 2.8 seconds elapsing between two successive new moons

1lunch \'lənch\ *n* [prob. short for *luncheon*] **1 :** a light meal; *esp* : one taken in the middle of the day **2 :** the food prepared for a lunch <eat your ~>

2lunch *vi* : to eat lunch ~ *vt* : to provide lunch for — **lunch·er** *n*

lunch counter *n* **1 :** a long counter at which lunches are sold **2 :** LUNCHEONETTE

lun·cheon \'lən-chən\ *n* [perh. alter. of *nuncheon* (light snack)] : LUNCH; *esp* : a light meal eaten in company

lun·cheon·ette \ˌlən-chə-'net\ *n* : a place where light lunches are sold to be eaten on the premises

lunch·room \'lənch-ˌrüm, -ˌru̇m\ *n* **1 :** LUNCHEONETTE **2 :** a room (as in a school) where lunches supplied on the premises or brought from home may be eaten

lunch·time \-ˌtīm\ *n* : the time at which lunches are usually served : NOON

lune \'lün\ *n* [L *luna* moon — more at LUNAR] : the part of a plane surface bounded by two intersecting arcs or of a spherical surface bounded by two great circles

lunes \'lünz\ *n pl* [F, pl. of *lune* crazy whim, fr. MF, moon, crazy whim, fr. L *luna*] : fits of lunacy

lu·nette \lü-'net\ *n* [F, fr. OF *lunete* small object shaped like the moon, fr. *lune* moon] **1 a :** an opening in a vault esp. for a window **b :** the surface at the upper part of a wall that is partly surrounded by a vault which the wall intersects and that is often filled by windows or by mural painting **2 :** a temporary fortification consisting of two faces forming a salient angle and two parallel flanks **3 :** the figure or shape of a crescent moon

lung \'ləŋ\ *n* [ME *lunge,* fr. OE *lungen;* akin to OHG *lungun* lung, *līhti* light in weight — more at LIGHT] **1 a :** one of the usu. paired compound saccular thoracic organs that constitute the basic respiratory organ of air-breathing vertebrates **b :** any of various respiratory organs of invertebrates **2 a :** a device enabling individuals abandoning a submarine to rise to the surface **b :** a mechanical device for regularly introducing fresh air into and withdrawing stale air from the lung : RESPIRATOR

lun·gan \ˈlən-gən, ˈlŋ-\ *var of* LONGAN

[1]**lunge** \ˈlənj\ *vb* **lunged; lung·ing** [by shortening & alter. fr. obs. *allonge* (to make a thrust with a sword)] *vt* : to thrust or push with a lunge ~ *vi* **:** to make a thrust or a forceful forward movement

[2]**lunge** *n* **1 :** a sudden thrust or pass (as with a sword or foil) **2 :** the act of plunging forward

lunged \ˈləŋd\ *adj* **1 :** having lungs : PULMONATE **2 :** having a lung or lungs of a specified kind or number — used in combination <one-*lunged*>

[1]**lung·er** \ˈlən-jər\ *n* **:** one that lunges

[2]**lung·er** \ˈləŋ-ər\ *n* **:** one suffering from a chronic disease of the lungs; *esp* **:** one that is tubercular

lung·fish \ˈləŋ-ˌfish\ *n* **:** any of various fishes (order Dipneusti or Cladistia) that breathe by a modified air bladder as well as gills

lung·worm \-ˌwərm\ *n* **:** any of various nematodes that infest the lungs and air passages of mammals

lung·wort \-ˌwərt, -ˌwȯ(ə)rt\ *n* **:** any of several plants (as a mullein) formerly used in the treatment of respiratory disorders; *esp* **:** a European herb (*Pulmonaria officinalis*) of the borage family with hispid leaves and bluish flowers

lu·ni·so·lar \ˌlü-ni-ˈsō-lər *also* -ˌlär\ *adj* [L *luna* moon + E *-i-* + *solar*] **:** relating or attributed to the moon and the sun

lu·ni·tid·al \-ˈtīd-ᵊl\ *adj* [L *luna* + E *-i-* + *tidal*] **:** relating to or being tidal movements dependent on the moon

lun·ker \ˈləŋ-kər\ *n* [origin unknown] **:** something large of its kind — used esp. of a fish

lunk·head \ˈləŋk-ˌhed\ *n* [prob. alter. of *lump* + *head*] **:** a dull-witted person : DOLT — **lunk·head·ed** \-ˈhed-əd\ *adj*

lunt \ˈlənt\ *n* [D *lont*] **1** *chiefly Scot* **:** SLOW MATCH **2** *chiefly Scot* **:** SMOKE

lu·nule \ˈlü-(ˌ)nyü(ə)l\ *n* [NL *lunula,* fr. L, crescent-shaped ornament, fr. dim. of *luna* moon] **:** a crescent-shaped body part or marking (as the whitish mark at the base of a fingernail)

lu·ny \ˈlü-nē\ *var of* LOONY

lu·pa·nar \lü-ˈpā-nər, -ˈpän-ər\ *n* [L, fr. *lupa* prostitute, lit., she-wolf, fem. of *lupus*] **:** BROTHEL

Lu·per·ca·lia \ˌlü-pər-ˈkā-lē-ə, -ˈkāl-yə\ *n* [L, pl., fr. *Lupercus,* god of flocks] **:** an ancient Roman festival celebrated February 15 to ensure fertility for the people, fields, and flocks — **Lu·per·ca·lian** \-ˈkā-lē-ən, -ˈkāl-yən\ *adj*

[1]**lu·pine** \ˈlü-pən\ *n* [ME, fr. L *lupinus, lupinum,* fr. *lupinus,* adj.] **:** any of a genus (*Lupinus*) of leguminous herbs some of which are poisonous and others cultivated for green manure, fodder, or their edible seeds; *also* **:** an edible lupine seed (as of the European *L. albus*)

[2]**lu·pine** \-ˌpīn\ *adj* [L *lupinus,* fr. *lupus* wolf — more at WOLF] **:** WOLFISH

lu·pu·lin \ˈlü-pyə-lən\ *n* [NL *lupulus* (specific epithet of the hop plant *Humulus lupulus*), fr. dim. of L *lupus* wolf, hop] **:** a fine yellow resinous powder on the strobiles of hops having the characteristic hop flavor and odor

lu·pus \ˈlü-pəs\ *n* [ML, fr. L, wolf] **:** any of several diseases characterized by skin lesions; *esp* **:** LUPUS VULGARIS

lupus er·y·the·ma·to·sus \-ˌer-ə-ˌthē-mə-ˈtō-səs\ *n* [NL, lit., erythematous lupus] **:** a slowly progressive systemic disease that is marked by degenerative changes of collagenous tissues with erythematous skin lesions, arthritic changes, lesions of internal organs, and wasting and by fever, leukemia, and endocarditis

lupus vul·gar·is \-ˌvəl-ˈgar-əs, -ˈger-\ *n* [NL, lit., common lupus] **:** a tuberculous disease of the skin marked by formation of soft brownish nodules with ulceration and scarring

[1]**lurch** \ˈlərch\ *vb* [ME *lorchen,* prob. alter. of *lurken* to lurk] *vi, dial chiefly Eng* **:** to loiter about a place furtively : PROWL ~ *vt* **1** *obs* **:** STEAL **2** *archaic* **:** CHEAT

[2]**lurch** *n* [MF *lourche,* adj., defeated by a lurch, deceived] **:** a decisive defeat in which an opponent wins a game by more than double the defeated player's score esp. in cribbage — **in the lurch :** in a vulnerable and unsupported position

[3]**lurch** *vt* **1 :** to defeat by a lurch (as in cribbage) **2** *archaic* **:** to leave in the lurch

[4]**lurch** *n* [origin unknown] **1 :** a sudden roll of a ship to one side **2 :** an act or instance of swaying or tipping; *esp* **:** a staggering gait

[5]**lurch** *vi* **:** to roll or tip abruptly : PITCH; *also* **:** STAGGER

lurch·er \ˈlər-chər\ *n* [[1]*lurch*] **1** *archaic* **:** a petty thief : PILFERER **2 :** SPY, LURKER **3** *Brit* **:** a mongrel dog; *esp* **:** one used by poachers

lur·dane \ˈlərd-ᵊn\ *n* [ME *lurdan,* fr. MF *lourdin* dullard, fr. *lourd* dull, stupid, fr. L *luridus* lurid] *archaic* **:** a lazy stupid person — **lurdane** *adj*

[1]**lure** \ˈlu̇(ə)r\ *n* [ME, fr. MF *loire,* of Gmc origin; akin to MHG *luoder* bait; akin to OE *lathian* to invite, OHG *ladōn*] **1 :** a bunch of feathers attached to a long cord and used by a falconer to recall a hawk **2 a :** an inducement to pleasure or gain : ENTICEMENT **b :** APPEAL, ATTRACTION **3 :** a decoy for attracting animals to capture: as **a :** artificial bait used for catching fish **b :** an often luminous structure on the head of pediculate fishes that is used to attract prey

[2]**lure** *vt* **lured; lur·ing 1 :** to recall (a hawk) by means of a lure **2 :** to draw with a hint of pleasure or gain : attract actively and strongly <*lured* from his work by the bright spring day> — **lur·er** *n*

syn LURE, ENTICE, INVEIGLE, DECOY, TEMPT, SEDUCE *shared meaning element* **:** to draw from a usual, desirable, or proper course or situation into one felt as unusual, undesirable, or wrong ***ant*** revolt, repel

lu·rid \ˈlu̇r-əd\ *adj* [L *luridus* pale yellow, sallow] **1 a :** wan and ghastly pale in appearance **b :** of any of several light or medium grayish colors ranging in hue from yellow to orange **2 :** shining with the red glow of fire seen through smoke or cloud **3 a :** causing horror or revulsion : GRUESOME **b :** highly colored : SENSATIONAL — **lu·rid·ly** *adv* — **lu·rid·ness** *n*

lurk \ˈlərk\ *vi* [ME *lurken;* akin to MHG *lūren* to lie in wait — more at LOWER] **1 a :** to lie in wait in a place of concealment esp. for an evil purpose **b :** to move furtively or inconspicuously : SNEAK **c :** to persist in staying **2 a :** to be concealed but capable of being discovered; *specif* **:** to constitute a latent threat **b :** to lie hidden — **lurk·er** *n*

syn LURK, SKULK, SLINK, SNEAK *shared meaning element* **:** to behave furtively

lus·cious \ˈləsh-əs\ *adj* [ME *lucius,* perh. alter. of *licius,* short for *delicious*] **1 a :** having a delicious taste or smell : SWEET **b** *archaic* **:** excessively sweet : CLOYING **2 :** having sensual appeal : SEDUCTIVE **3 :** richly luxurious or appealing to the senses; *also* **:** excessively ornate — **lus·cious·ly** *adv* — **lus·cious·ness** *n*

[1]**lush** \ˈləsh\ *adj* [ME *lusch* soft, tender] **1 a :** producing luxuriant foliage <~ grass> **b :** lavishly productive: as (1) **:** FERTILE (2) **:** THRIVING (3) **:** characterized by abundance : PLENTIFUL (4) **:** PROSPEROUS, PROFITABLE **2 a :** SAVORY, DELICIOUS **b :** SENSUOUS, VOLUPTUOUS **c :** OPULENT, SUMPTUOUS ***syn*** see PROFUSE — **lush·ly** *adv* — **lush·ness** *n*

[2]**lush** *n* [origin unknown] **1** *slang* **:** intoxicating liquor : DRINK **2 :** an habitual heavy drinker : DRUNKARD

[3]**lush** *vb, slang* **:** DRINK

Lu·so- *comb form* [Pg, fr. *lusitano* Portuguese, fr. L *lusitanus* of Lusitania (ancient region corresponding approximately to modern Portugal)] **1** \ˌlü-(ˌ)sō\ **:** Portuguese and <*Luso*-Brazilian> **2 :** of Portugal

[1]**lust** \ˈləst\ *n* [ME, fr. OE; akin to OHG *lust* pleasure, L *lascivus* wanton] **1** *obs* **a :** PLEASURE, DELIGHT **b :** personal inclination : WISH **2 :** usu. intense sexual desire : LASCIVIOUSNESS **3 a :** an intense longing : CRAVING **b :** ENTHUSIASM, EAGERNESS

[2]**lust** *vi* **:** to have an intense desire or need : CRAVE; *specif* **:** to have a sexual urge

[1]**lus·ter** *or* **lus·tre** \ˈləs-tər\ *n* [ME *lustre,* fr. L *lustrum*] **:** a period of five years : LUSTRUM 2

[2]**luster** *or* **lustre** *n* [MF *lustre,* fr. OIt *lustro,* fr. *lustrare* to brighten, fr. L; akin to L *lucēre* to shine — more at LIGHT] **1 :** a glow of reflected light : SHEEN; *specif* **:** the appearance of the surface of a mineral as to its reflecting qualities **2 a :** a glow of light from within : LUMINOSITY **b :** an inner beauty : RADIANCE **3 :** BRILLIANCE, DISTINCTION **4 a :** a glass pendant used esp. to ornament a candlestick or chandelier **b :** a decorative object (as a chandelier) hung with glass pendants **5** *chiefly Brit* **:** a fabric with cotton warp and a filling of wool, mohair, or alpaca **6 :** LUSTERWARE — **lus·ter·less** \-tər-ləs\ *adj*

[3]**luster** *or* **lustre** *vb* **lus·tered** *or* **lus·tred; lus·ter·ing** *or* **lus·tring** \-t(ə-)riŋ\ *vi* **:** to have luster : GLEAM ~ *vt* **1 :** to give luster or distinction to **2 :** to coat or treat with a substance that imparts luster

lus·ter·ware \ˈləs-tər-ˌwa(ə)r, -ˌwe(ə)r\ *n* **:** pottery decorated by applying to the glaze metallic compounds which become iridescent metallic films in the process of firing

lust·ful \ˈləst-fəl\ *adj* **:** excited by lust : LECHEROUS — **lust·ful·ly** \-fə-lē\ *adv* — **lust·ful·ness** *n*

lust·i·hood \ˈləs-tē-ˌhu̇d\ *n* **1 :** vigor of body or spirit : ROBUSTNESS **2 :** sexual inclination or capacity

lus·tral \ˈləs-trəl\ *adj* [L *lustralis,* fr. *lustrum*] **:** PURIFICATORY

lus·trate \ˈləs-ˌtrāt\ *vt* **lus·trat·ed; lus·trat·ing** [L *lustratus,* pp. of *lustrare* to brighten, purify] **:** to purify ceremonially — **lus·tra·tion** \ˌləs-ˈtrā-shən\ *n*

[1]**lus·tring** \ˈləs-triŋ\ *n* [modif. of It *lustrino*] **:** LUTESTRING

[2]**lus·tring** \-t(ə-)riŋ\ *n* [*lustring,* gerund of [3]*luster*] **:** a finishing process (as calendering) for giving a gloss to yarns and cloth

lus·trous \ˈləs-trəs\ *adj* **1 :** reflecting light evenly and efficiently without glitter or sparkle <a ~ satin> <the ~ glow of an opal> **2 :** radiant in character or reputation : ILLUSTRIOUS ***syn*** see BRIGHT — **lus·trous·ly** *adv* — **lus·trous·ness** *n*

lus·trum \ˈləs-trəm\ *n, pl* **lustrums** *or* **lus·tra** \-trə\ [L; akin to L *lustrare* to brighten, purify] **1 a :** a purification of the whole Roman people made in ancient times after the census every five years **b :** the Roman census **2 :** a period of five years : QUINQUENNIUM

lusty \ˈləs-tē\ *adj* **lust·i·er; -est 1** *archaic* **:** MERRY, JOYOUS **2 :** LUSTFUL <~ passion> **3 a :** full of vitality : ROBUST **b :** full of strength : POWERFUL — **lust·i·ly** \-tə-lē\ *adv* — **lust·i·ness** \-tē-nəs\ *n*

lu·sus na·tu·rae \ˌlü-səs-nə-ˈt(y)u̇(ə)r-(ˌ)ē, -ˈtu̇(ə)r-ˌī\ *n* [NL, lit., play of nature] **:** a sport or freak of nature

[1]**lute** \ˈlüt\ *n* [ME, fr. MF *lut,* fr. OProv *laut,* fr. Ar *al-ʽūd,* lit., the wood] **:** a stringed instrument with a large pear-shaped body, a neck with a fretted fingerboard, and a head with pegs for tuning

lute

[2]**lute** *n* [ME, fr. L *lutum* mud — more at POLLUTE] **:** a substance (as cement or clay) for packing a joint or coating a porous surface to make it impervious to gas or liquid

[3]**lute** *vt* **lut·ed; lut·ing :** to seal or cover with lute

lute- *or* **luteo-** *comb form* [NL (*corpus*) *luteum*] **:** corpus luteum <*lute*al>

lu·te·al \ˈlüt-ē-əl\ *adj* **:** of, relating to, or involving the corpus luteum

lu·tein \ˈlüt-ē-ən, ˈlü-ˌtēn\ *n* [fr. its occurrence in corpus luteum] **:** an orange xanthophyll $C_{40}H_{56}O_2$ occurring in plants usu. with

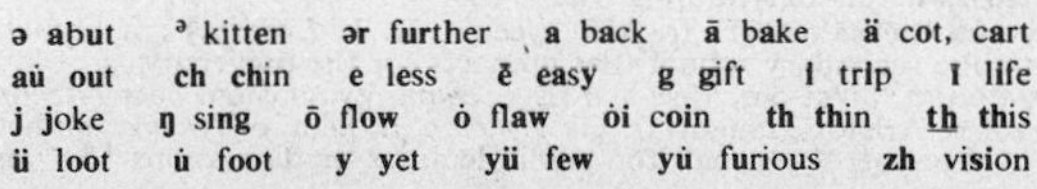

ə abut ᵊ kitten ər further a back ā bake ä cot, cart
au̇ out ch chin e less ē easy g gift i trip ī life
j joke ŋ sing ō flow ȯ flaw ȯi coin th thin th this
ü loot u̇ foot y yet yü few yu̇ furious zh vision

carotenes and chlorophylls and in animal fat, egg yolk, and corpus luteum

lu·tein·ize \-ˌīz\ *vb* **-ized; -iz·ing** *vt* **:** to cause the production of corpora lutea in ~ *vi* **:** to undergo transformation into corpus luteum — **lu·tein·iza·tion** \ˌlüt-ē-ən-ə-ˈzā-shən, ˌlü-ˌtēn-\ *n*

luteinizing hormone *n* **:** a hormone from the anterior lobe of the pituitary body that in the female stimulates esp. the development of corpora lutea and in the male the development of interstitial tissue

lu·te·nist *or* **lu·ta·nist** \ˈlüt-ᵊn-əst, ˈlüt-nəst\ *n* [ML *lutanista,* fr. *lutana* lute, prob. fr. MF *lut*] **:** a lute player

lu·teo·tro·phic \ˌlüt-ē-ə-ˈtrō-fik, -ˈträf-ik\ *adj* **:** acting on the corpora lutea

luteotrophic hormone *n* **:** PROLACTIN

lu·teo·tro·phin \ˌlüt-ē-ə-ˈtrō-fən\ *or* **lu·teo·tro·pin** \-pən\ *n* [*luteotrophic* + *-in*] **:** PROLACTIN

lu·te·ous \ˈlüt-ē-əs\ *adj* [L *luteus* yellowish, fr. *lutum,* a plant used for dyeing yellow] **:** yellow tinged with green or brown

lute·string \ˈlüt-(ˌ)striŋ\ *n* [by folk etymology fr. It *lustrino* glossy fabric, fr. *lustro* luster] **:** a plain glossy silk formerly much used for women's dresses and ribbons

lu·te·tium *also* **lu·te·cium** \lü-ˈtē-sh(ē-)əm\ *n* [NL, fr. L *Lutetia,* ancient name of Paris] **:** a metallic element of the rare-earth group — see ELEMENT table

Luth *abbr* Lutheran

[1]**Lu·ther·an** \ˈlü-th(ə-)rən\ *n* **:** a member of a Lutheran church

[2]**Lutheran** *adj* **1 :** of or relating to religious doctrines (as justification by faith alone) developed by Martin Luther or his followers **2 :** of or relating to the Protestant churches adhering to Lutheran doctrines, liturgy, and polity — **Lu·ther·an·ism** \-ˌiz-əm\ *n*

lut·ing \ˈlüt-iŋ\ *n* **:** [2]LUTE

Lu·wi·an \ˈlü-(w)ē-ən\ *n* [*Luwi* (an ancient people of the southern coast of Asia Minor)] **:** an Anatolian language of the Indo-European language family — see INDO-EUROPEAN LANGUAGES table — **Luwian** *adj*

lux \ˈləks\ *n, pl* **lux** *or* **lux·es** [L, light — more at LIGHT] **:** a unit of illumination equal to the direct illumination on a surface that is everywhere one meter from a uniform point source of one candle intensity or equal to one lumen per square meter

lux·ate \ˈlək-ˌsāt\ *vt* **lux·at·ed; lux·at·ing** [L *luxatus,* pp. of *luxare,* fr. *luxus* dislocated — more at LOCK] **:** to throw out of place or out of joint **:** DISLOCATE — **lux·a·tion** \ˌlək-ˈsā-shən\ *n*

luxe \ˈlu̇ks, ˈləks, ˈlüks\ *n* [F, fr. L *luxus* — more at LUXURY] **:** LUXURY — **luxe** *adj*

lux·u·ri·ance \(ˌ)ləg-ˈzhu̇r-ē-ən(t)s, (ˌ)lək-ˈshu̇r-\ *n* **:** the quality or state of being luxuriant

lux·u·ri·ant \-ē-ənt\ *adj* **1 a :** yielding abundantly **:** PRODUCTIVE **b :** characterized by abundant growth **:** LUSH **2 a :** exuberantly rich and varied **:** PROLIFIC **b :** excessively elaborate **:** FLORID **3 :** characterized by luxury **:** LUXURIOUS *syn* see PROFUSE — **lux·u·ri·ant·ly** *adv*

lux·u·ri·ate \-ē-ˌāt\ *vi* **-at·ed; -at·ing** [L *luxuriatus,* pp. of *luxuriare,* fr. *luxuria*] **1 a :** to grow profusely **:** THRIVE **b :** to develop extensively **2 :** to indulge oneself luxuriously **:** REVEL

lux·u·ri·ous \(ˌ)ləg-ˈzhu̇r-ē-əs, (ˌ)lək-ˈshu̇r-\ *adj* **1 :** of or relating to unrestrained gratification of the senses **:** VOLUPTUOUS **2 :** fond of luxury or self-indulgence **3 a :** exceedingly choice and costly **:** of the finest and richest kind <~ wines> <a ~ estate> **b :** excessively ornate <a style marred by too ~ descriptions> — **lux·u·ri·ous·ly** *adv* — **lux·u·ri·ous·ness** *n*

syn LUXURIOUS, SUMPTUOUS, OPULENT *shared meaning element* **:** ostentatiously rich or magnificent

lux·u·ry \ˈləksh-(ə-)rē, ˈləgzh-\ *n, pl* **-ries** [ME *luxurie,* fr. MF, fr. L *luxuria* rankness, luxury, excess; akin to L *luxus* luxury, excess] **1** *archaic* **:** LECHERY, LUST **2 :** sumptuous living or equipment **:** great ease or comfort **:** rich surroundings <lived in ~> **3 a :** something desirable but costly or hard to get <a ~ few can afford> **b :** something adding to pleasure or comfort but not absolutely necessary — **luxury** *adj*

lv *abbr* leave

LVT *abbr* landing vehicle, tracked

LW *abbr* low water

LWM *abbr* low-water mark

LWV *abbr* League of Women Voters

[1]**-ly** \lē\ *adj suffix* [ME, fr. OE *-līc, -lic;* akin to OHG *-līh;* both fr. a prehistoric Gmc noun represented by OE *līc* body — more at LIKE] **1 :** like in appearance, manner, or nature **:** having the characteristics of <queen*ly*> <father*ly*> **2 :** characterized by regular recurrence in (specified) units of time **:** every <hour*ly*>

[2]**-ly** *adv suffix* [ME, fr. OE *-līce, -lice,* fr. *-līc,* adj. suffix] **1 :** in a (specified) manner <slow*ly*> **:** in the manner of a <soldier*ly*> **2 :** from a (specified) point of view <eschatological*ly*> **3 :** with respect to <part*ly*>

ly·am–hound \ˈlī-əm-ˌhau̇nd\ *or* **lyme–hound** \ˈlīm-ˌhau̇nd\ *n* [obs. *lyam* (leash)] *archaic* **:** BLOODHOUND

ly·art \ˈlī-ərt\ *adj* [ME, fr. MF *liart*] *chiefly Scot* **:** streaked with gray **:** GRAY

ly·ase \ˈlī-ˌās, -ˌāz\ *n* [Gk *lyein* to loosen, release + E *-ase* — more at LOSE] **:** an enzyme (as a decarboxylase) that forms double bonds by removing groups from a substrate other than by hydrolysis or that adds groups to double bonds

ly·can·thrope \ˈlī-kən-ˌthrōp, lī-ˈkan-\ *n* [NL *lycanthropus,* fr. Gk *lykanthrōpos* werewolf, fr. *lykos* wolf + *anthrōpos* man — more at WOLF] **1 :** a person displaying lycanthropy **2 :** WEREWOLF

ly·can·thro·py \lī-ˈkan(t)-thrə-pē\ *n* **1 :** a delusion that one has become a wolf **2 :** the assumption of the form and characteristics of a wolf held to be possible by witchcraft or magic — **ly·can·throp·ic** \ˌlī-kən-ˈthräp-ik\ *adj*

ly·cée \lē-ˈsā\ *n* [F, fr. MF, lyceum, fr. L *Lyceum*] **:** a French public secondary school that prepares for the university

ly·ce·um \lī-ˈsē-əm, ˈlī-sē-\ *n* [L *Lyceum,* gymnasium near Athens where Aristotle taught, fr. Gk *Lykeion,* fr. neut. of *lykeios,* epithet of Apollo] **1 :** a hall for public lectures or discussions **2 :** an association providing public lectures, concerts, and entertainments **3 :** LYCÉE

ly·chee *var of* LITCHI

lych–gate \ˈlich-ˌgāt\ *n* [ME *lycheyate,* fr. *lich* body, corpse, (fr. OE *līc*) + *gate, yate* gate] **:** a roofed gate in a churchyard under which a bier rests during the initial part of the burial service

lych·nis \ˈlik-nəs\ *n* [NL, genus name, fr. L, a red flower, fr. Gk; akin to Gk *lychnos* lamp, L *lux* light — more at LIGHT] **:** any of a genus (*Lychnis*) of herbs of the pink family with terminal cymes of showy mostly red or white flowers having 5 or rarely 4 styles

Ly·cian \ˈlish-(ē-)ən\ *n* **1 :** a native or inhabitant of Lycia **2 :** an Anatolian language of the Indo-European language family — see INDO-EUROPEAN LANGUAGES table — **Lycian** *adj*

ly·co·pene \ˈlī-kə-ˌpēn\ *n* [ISV *lycop-* (fr. NL *Lycopersicon,* genus of herbs) + *-ene*] **:** a carotenoid pigment $C_{40}H_{56}$ that is the red coloring matter of the tomato

ly·co·pod \ˈlī-kə-ˌpäd\ *n* [NL *Lycopodium*] **:** LYCOPODIUM 1; *broadly* **:** CLUB MOSS

ly·co·po·di·um \ˌlī-kə-ˈpōd-ē-əm\ *n* [NL, genus name, fr. Gk *lykos* wolf + *podion,* dim. of *pod-, pous* foot — more at FOOT] **1 :** any of a large genus (*Lycopodium*) of erect or creeping club mosses with evergreen one-nerved leaves in four to many ranks **2 :** a fine yellowish flammable powder composed of lycopodium spores and used in pharmacy and as a component of fireworks and flashlight powders

lydd·ite \ˈlid-ˌīt\ *n* [*Lydd,* England] **:** a high explosive composed chiefly of picric acid

Lyd·i·an \ˈlid-ē-ən\ *n* **1 :** a native or inhabitant of Lydia **2 :** an Anatolian language of the Indo-European language family — see INDO-EUROPEAN LANGUAGES table — **Lydian** *adj*

lye \ˈlī\ *n* [ME, fr. OE *lēag,* akin to OHG *louga* lye, L *lavare, lavere* to wash, Gk *louein*] **1 :** a strong alkaline liquor rich in potassium carbonate leached from wood ashes and used esp. in making soap and washing; *broadly* **:** a strong alkaline solution (as of sodium hydroxide or potassium hydroxide) **2 :** a solid caustic (as sodium hydroxide)

ly·gus bug \ˈlī-gəs-\ *n* [NL *Lygus,* genus name] **:** any of various small sucking bugs (genus *Lygus*) including some vectors of virus diseases of plants

ly·ing \ˈlī-iŋ\ *adj* [prp. of [3]*lie*] **1 :** marked by or given to falsehood <a ~ account of the accident> <~ children> **2 :** likely or calculated to mislead <~ advertisements> *syn* see DISHONEST

ly·ing–in \ˌlī-iŋ-ˈin\ *n, pl* **lyings–in** *or* **lying–ins :** the state attending and consequent to childbirth **:** CONFINEMENT

lymph \ˈlim(p)f\ *n* [L *lympha,* water goddess, water, fr. Gk *nymphē* nymph — more at NUPTIAL] **1** *archaic* **:** a spring or stream of water; *also* **:** WATER **2** *archaic* **:** the sap of plants **3** [NL *lympha,* fr. L, water] **:** a pale coagulable fluid that bathes the tissues, passes into lymphatic channels and ducts, and is discharged into the blood by way of the thoracic duct and that consists of a liquid portion resembling blood plasma and containing white blood cells but normally no red blood cells

lymph- *or* **lympho-** *comb form* [NL *lympha*] **:** lymph **:** lymphatic tissue <*lympho*granuloma>

lymph·ad·e·ni·tis \ˌlim-ˌfad-ᵊn-ˈīt-əs\ *n* [NL, fr. *lymphaden* lymph gland, fr. *lymph-* + Gk *adēn* gland — more at ADEN-] **:** inflammation of lymph glands

[1]**lym·phat·ic** \lim-ˈfat-ik\ *adj* **1 a :** of, relating to, or produced by lymph, lymphoid tissue, or lymphocytes **b :** conveying lymph **2 :** lacking physical or mental energy **:** SLUGGISH — **lym·phat·i·cal·ly** \-i-k(ə-)lē\ *adv*

[2]**lymphatic** *n* **:** a vessel that contains or conveys lymph

lymph cell *n* **:** a cell in lymph; *specif* **:** LYMPHOCYTE

lymph follicle *n* **:** LYMPH NODE, LYMPH NODULE

lymph gland *n* **:** LYMPH NODE

lymph node *n* **:** one of the rounded masses of lymphoid tissue surrounded by a capsule of connective tissue that occur in association with the lymphatic vessels and that consist of a reticulum of connective tissue fibers in the meshes of which are contained numerous small round cells each having a large round deeply staining nucleus and when carried off by the flow of lymph through the node become a lymphocyte

lymph nodule *n* **:** a small simple lymph node

lym·pho·blast \ˈlim(p)-fə-ˌblast\ *n* [ISV] **:** a cell giving rise to lymphocytes — **lym·pho·blas·tic** \ˌlim(p)-fə-ˈblas-tik\ *adj*

lym·pho·cyte \ˈlim(p)-fə-ˌsīt\ *n* [ISV] **:** a colorless weakly motile cell produced in lymphoid tissue that is the typical cellular element of lymph and constitutes 20 to 30 percent of the leukocytes of normal human blood — **lym·pho·cyt·ic** \ˌlim(p)-fə-ˈsit-ik\ *adj*

lymphocytic cho·rio·men·in·gi·tis \-ˌmen-ən-ˈjīt-əs\ *n* [NL *choriomeningitis* cerebral meningitis, fr. *chorio-* of a membrane resembling the chorion] **:** an acute virus disease that is characterized by fever, nausea and vomiting, headache, stiff neck, and slow pulse, is marked by the presence of numerous lymphocytes in the cerebrospinal fluid, and is transmitted esp. by rodents and bloodsucking insects

lym·pho·cy·to·sis \ˌlim(p)-fə-ˌsī-ˈtō-səs, -fə-sə-\ *n* [NL, fr. ISV *lymphocyte*] **:** an increase in the number of lymphocytes in the blood usu. associated with chronic infections or inflammations — **lym·pho·cy·tot·ic** \-ˈtät-ik\ *adj*

lym·pho·gran·u·lo·ma \ˈlim(p)-fō-ˌgran-yə-ˈlō-mə\ *n, pl* **-mas** *or* **-ma·ta** \-mət-ə\ [NL] **1 :** a nodular swelling of a lymph node **2 :** a contagious venereal virus disease marked by swelling and ulceration of lymphatic tissues in the iliac and inguinal regions — **lym·pho·gran·u·lo·ma·tous** \-ˈlō-mət-əs\ *adj*

lymphogranuloma in·gui·na·le \-ˌiŋ-gwə-ˈnal-ē, -ˈnal-, -ˈnāl-\ *n* [NL, inguinal lymphogranuloma] **:** LYMPHOGRANULOMA 2

lym·pho·gran·u·lo·ma·to·sis \-ˌlō-mə-ˈtō-səs\ *n, pl* **-to·ses** \-ˌsēz\ [NL *lymphogranulomat-, lymphogranuloma* + *-osis*] **:** the development of benign or malignant lymphogranulomas in various parts of the body; *also* **:** a condition characterized by lymphogranulomas

lymphogranuloma ve·ne·re·um \-və-ˈnir-ē-əm\ *n* [NL, venereal lymphogranuloma] **:** LYMPHOGRANULOMA 2

lym·phog·ra·phy \lim-ˈfäg-rə-fē\ *n* **:** X-ray depiction of lymph vessels and nodes after use of a radiopaque material — **lym·pho·graph·ic** \ˌlim-fə-ˈgraf-ik\ *adj*

lym·phoid \ˈlim-ˌfȯid\ *adj* **1 :** of, relating to, or resembling lymph **2 :** of, relating to, or constituting the tissue characteristic of the lymph nodes

lym·pho·ma \lim-ˈfō-mə\ *n, pl* **-mas** *or* **-ma·ta** \-mət-ə\ [NL] **:** a tumor of lymphoid tissue — **lym·pho·ma·toid** \-mə-ˌtȯid\ *adj* — **lym·pho·ma·tous** \-mət-əs\ *adj*

lym·pho·ma·to·sis \(ˌ)lim-ˌfō-mə-ˈtō-səs\ *n, pl* **-to·ses** \-ˌsēz\ [NL *lymphomat-, lymphoma* + *-osis*] **:** the presence of multiple lymphomas in the body

lym·pho·poi·e·sis \ˌlim(p)-fə-pȯi-ˈē-səs\ *n, pl* **-e·ses** \-ˌsēz\ [NL] **:** the formation of lymphocytes or lymphatic tissue — **lym·pho·poi·et·ic** \-pȯi-ˈet-ik\ *adj*

lym·pho·sar·co·ma \-sär-ˈkō-mə\ *n, pl* **-mas** *or* **-ma·ta** \mət-ə\ [NL] **:** a malignant lymphoma that tends to metastasize freely esp. along the regional lymphatic drainage — **lym·pho·sar·co·ma·tous** \-mət-əs\ *adj*

lyn·ce·an \lin-ˈsē-ən, ˈlin(t)-sē-\ *adj* [L *lynceus,* fr. Gk *lynkeios,* lit., of Lynceus, Argonaut famous for his sharpness of sight, fr. *Lynkeus* Lynceus] **:** SHARP-SIGHTED

lynch \ˈlinch\ *vt* [*lynch law*] **:** to put to death by mob action without legal sanction — **lynch·er** *n*

lynch law *n* [prob. fr. Charles *Lynch* †1796 Am justice of the peace; fr. his presiding over an extralegal court to suppress Tory activity] **:** the punishment of presumed crimes or offenses usu. by death without due process of law

lynx \ˈliŋ(k)s\ *n, pl* **lynx** *or* **lynx·es** [L, fr. Gk; akin to OE *lox* lynx, Gk *leukos* white — more at LIGHT] **:** any of various wildcats with relatively long legs, a short stubby tail, mottled coat, and often tufted ears: as **a :** the common lynx (*Lynx lynx*) of northern Europe and Asia **b :** BOBCAT **c :** a No. American lynx (*L. canadensis*) distinguished from the bobcat by its larger size, longer tufted ears, large padded claws, and wholly black tail tip — called also *Canada lynx*

lynx *c*

lynx–eyed \ˈliŋ(k)-ˈsīd\ *adj* **:** SHARP-SIGHTED

lyo- *comb form* [prob. fr. NL, fr. Gk *lyein* to loosen, dissolve — more at LOSE] **:** dispersed state **:** dispersion <*lyo*philic>

ly·on·naise \ˌlī-ə-ˈnāz\ *adj* [F (*à la*) *lyonnaise* in the manner of Lyons, fr. fem. of *lyonnais* of Lyons, fr. *Lyon* Lyons, France] **:** prepared with onions <~ potatoes>

Ly·on·nesse \ˌlī-ə-ˈnes\ *n* **:** a country that according to Arthurian legend was contiguous to Cornwall before sinking beneath the sea

lyo·phile \ˈlī-ə-ˌfīl\ *adj* [ISV] **1 :** LYOPHILIC **2 a :** of or relating to lyophilization **b** *or* **lyo·philed** \-ˌfīld\ **:** obtained by lyophilization

lyo·phil·ic \ˌlī-ə-ˈfil-ik\ *adj* **:** marked by strong affinity between a dispersed phase and the liquid in which it is dispersed <a ~ colloid>

ly·oph·i·lize \lī-ˈäf-ə-ˌlīz\ *vt* **-lized; -liz·ing :** FREEZE-DRY — **ly·oph·i·li·za·tion** \-ˌäf-ə-lə-ˈzā-shən\ *n* — **ly·oph·i·liz·er** \-ˈäf-ə-ˌlī-zər\ *n*

lyo·pho·bic \ˌlī-ə-ˈfō-bik\ *adj* **:** marked by lack of strong affinity between a dispersed phase and the liquid in which it is dispersed <a ~ colloid>

Ly·ra \ˈlī-rə\ *n* [L (gen. *Lyrae*), lit., lyre] **:** a northern constellation representing the lyre of Orpheus or Mercury and containing Vega

ly·rate \ˈlī-ˌrāt\ *or* **ly·rat·ed** \-ˌrāt-əd\ *adj* **:** having or suggesting the shape of a lyre <the ~ horns of the impala> — **ly·rate·ly** *adv*

lyre \ˈlī(ə)r\ *n* [ME *lire,* fr. OF, fr. L *lyra,* fr. Gk] **1 :** a stringed instrument of the harp class used by the ancient Greeks esp. to accompany song and recitation **2** *cap* **:** LYRA

lyre·bird \-ˌbərd\ *n* **:** either of two Australian passerine birds (genus *Menura*) distinguished in the male by very long tail feathers displayed during courtship in the shape of a lyre

[1]lyr·ic \ˈlir-ik\ *adj* **1 :** suitable for singing to the lyre or for being set to music and sung **2 a :** expressing direct usu. intense personal emotion <~ poetry> **b :** EXUBERANT, RHAPSODIC **3** *of an opera singer* **:** having a light voice and a melodic style — compare DRAMATIC

[2]lyric *n* **1 :** a lyric composition; *specif* **:** a lyric poem **2** *pl* **:** the words of a popular song or musical-comedy number

lyr·i·cal \ˈlir-i-kəl\ *adj* **:** LYRIC — **lyr·i·cal·ly** \-i-k(ə-)lē\ *adv* — **lyr·i·cal·ness** \-kəl-nəs\ *n*

youth playing lyre, from a Greek vase painting

lyr·i·cism \ˈlir-ə-ˌsiz-əm\ *n* **1 a :** the quality or state of being lyric **:** SONGFULNESS **b :** a personal direct intense style or quality in an art (as poetry or music) **2 :** exuberance of style or feeling

lyr·i·cist \-səst\ *n* **:** a writer of lyrics

lyr·ism \ˈli(ə)r-ˌiz-əm\ *n* **:** LYRICISM

lyr·ist *n* **1** \ˈlī(ə)r-əst\ **:** a player on the lyre **2** \ˈlir-əst\ **:** LYRICIST

lys- *or* **lysi-** *or* **lyso-** *comb form* [NL, fr. Gk *lys-, lysi-* loosening, fr. *lysis*] **:** lysis <*lys*in>

ly·sate \ˈlī-ˌsāt\ *n* **:** a product of lysis

lyse \ˈlīs, ˈlīz\ *vb* **lysed; lys·ing** [back-formation fr. NL *lysis*] *vt* **:** to cause to undergo lysis ~ *vi* **:** to undergo lysis

Ly·sen·ko·ism \lə-ˈseŋ-kō-ˌiz-əm\ *n* [Trofim *Lysenko*] **:** a biological doctrine asserting the fundamental influence of somatic and environmental factors on heredity in contradiction of orthodox genetics

ly·ser·gic acid \lə-ˌsər-jik-, (ˌ)lī-\ *n* [*lys-* + *ergot*] **:** a crystalline acid $C_{16}H_{16}N_2O_2$ from ergotic alkaloids

lysergic acid di·eth·yl·am·ide \-ˌdī-ˌeth-ə-ˈlam-ˌīd\ *n* **:** LSD

ly·sim·e·ter \lī-ˈsim-ət-ər\ *n* **:** a device for measuring the percolation of water through soils and for determining the soluble constituents removed in the drainage — **ly·si·met·ric** \ˌlī-sə-ˈme-trik\ *adj*

ly·sin \ˈlīs-ᵊn\ *n* **:** a substance capable of causing lysis; *esp* **:** an antibody capable of causing disintegration of red blood cells or microorganisms

ly·sine \ˈlī-ˌsēn\ *n* **:** a crystalline basic amino acid $C_6H_{14}N_2O_2$ that is essential to animal nutrition

ly·sis \ˈlī-səs\ *n, pl* **ly·ses** \-ˌsēz\ [NL, fr. Gk, act of loosening, dissolution, remission of fever, fr. *lyein* to loosen — more at LOSE] **1 :** the gradual decline of a disease process (as fever) **2 :** a process of disintegration or dissolution (as of cells)

-ly·sis \l-ə-səs, -ˈlī-səs\ *n comb form, pl* **-l·y·ses** \l-ə-ˌsēz\ [NL, fr. L & Gk; L, loosening, fr. Gk, fr. *lysis*] **1 :** decomposition <electro*lysis*> **2 :** disintegration **:** breaking down <auto*lysis*>

ly·so·gen \ˈlī-sə-jən\ *n* **:** a lysogenic bacterium or bacterial strain

ly·so·gen·ic \ˌlī-sə-ˈjen-ik\ *adj* [fr. the capacity of the prophage to lyse other bacteria] **1 :** harboring a prophage as hereditary material <~ bacteria> **2 :** TEMPERATE 3 <~ viruses> — **ly·so·ge·nic·i·ty** \-jə-ˈnis-ət-ē\ *n*

ly·sog·e·nize \lī-ˈsäj-ə-ˌnīz\ *vt* **-nized; -niz·ing :** to render lysogenic — **ly·sog·e·ni·za·tion** \-ˌsäj-ə-nə-ˈzā-shən\ *n*

ly·sog·e·ny \lī-ˈsäj-ə-nē\ *n* **:** the state of being lysogenic

ly·so·lec·i·thin \ˌlī-sə-ˈles-ə-thən\ *n* **:** a hydrolytic substance formed by the enzymatic hydrolysis (as by some snake venoms) of a lecithin

ly·so·some \ˈlī-sə-ˌsōm\ *n* [ISV *lys-* + [3]*-some*] **:** a saclike cellular organelle that contains various hydrolytic enzymes — see CELL illustration — **ly·so·som·al** \ˌlī-sə-ˈsō-məl\ *adj* — **ly·so·so·mal·ly** \-mə-lē\ *adv*

ly·so·zyme \ˈlī-sə-ˌzīm\ *n* **:** a basic bacteriolytic protein that is present in egg white and in human tears and saliva and that functions as a mucolytic enzyme

-lyte \ˌlīt\ *n comb form* [Gk *lytos* that may be untied, soluble, fr. *lyein*] **:** substance capable of undergoing (such) decomposition <hydro*lyte*>

lyt·ic \ˈlit-ik\ *adj* [Gk *lytikos* able to loose, fr. *lyein*] **:** of or relating to lysis or a lysin; *also* **:** productive of or effecting lysis (as of cells) — **ly·ti·cal·ly** \-i-k(ə-)lē\ *adv*

-lyt·ic \ˈlit-ik\ *adj suffix* [Gk *lytikos*] **:** of, relating to, or effecting (such) decomposition <hydro*lytic*>

-lyze \ˌlīz\ *vb comb form* [ISV, prob. irreg. fr. NL *-lysis*] **:** produce or undergo lytic disintegration or dissolution <electro*lyze*>

LZ *abbr* landing zone

ə abut ᵊ kitten ər further a back ā bake ä cot, cart
au̇ out ch chin e less ē easy g gift i trip ī life
j joke ŋ sing ō flow ȯ flaw ȯi coin th thin t͟h this
ü loot u̇ foot y yet yü few yu̇ furious zh vision

¹m \ˈem\ *n, pl* **m's** *or* **ms** \ˈemz\ *often cap, often attrib* **1 a :** the 13th letter of the English alphabet **b:** a graphic representation of this letter **c :** a speech counterpart of orthographic *m* **2 :** one thousand — see NUMBER table **3 :** a graphic device for reproducing the letter *m* **4 :** one designated *m* esp. as the 13th in order or class **5 :** something shaped like the letter M **6 a :** EM 2 **b :** PICA

²m *abbr, often cap* **1** mach **2** male **3** manual **4** March **5** martyr **6** masculine **7** mass **8** May **9** mega- **10** [L *meridies*] noon **11** meter **12** middle **13** mile **14** [L *mille*] thousand **15** milli- **16** million **17** molal; molality **18** molar; molarity **19** mole **20** month **21** moon **22** morning **23** muscle

m- \ˌem, ˈem\ *abbr* meta-

'm \m\ *vb* **:** AM <I'*m* going>

¹ma \ˈmä, ˈmȯ\ *n* [short for *mama*] **:** MOTHER

²ma *abbr* milliampere

MA *abbr* **1** Massachusetts **2** [ML *magister artium*] master of arts **3** mental age **4** Middle Ages

MAA *abbr* master of applied arts

ma'am \ˈmam, *after "yes" often* əm\ *n* **:** MADAM

MA and A *abbr* master of aeronautics and astronautics

MAArch *abbr* master of arts in architecture

Mab \ˈmab\ *n* **:** a queen of fairies in English literature

MABE *abbr* master of agricultural business and economics

mac \ˈmak\ *n, Brit* **:** MACKINTOSH

¹Mac \ˈmak\ *n* [*Mac-, Mc-,* common patronymic prefix in Scotch and Irish surnames] **:** FELLOW — used informally to address a man whose name is not known

²Mac *or* **Macc** *abbr* Maccabees

MAc *abbr* master of accounting

MAC *abbr* **1** master of arts in communications **2** military airlift command

ma·ca·bre \mə-ˈkäb(-rə), -ˈkäb-ər, -ˈkäbrᵊ\ *adj* [F, fr. (*danse*) *macabre* dance of death, fr. MF (*danse de*) *Macabré*] **1 :** having death as a subject **:** comprising or including a personalized representation of death **2:** dwelling on the gruesome **3:** tending to produce horror in a beholder

mac·ad·am \mə-ˈkad-əm\ *n* [John L. *McAdam* †1836 Brit engineer] **:** macadamized roadway or pavement esp. with a bituminous binder

mac·a·da·mia nut \ˌmak-ə-ˈdā-mē-ə-\ *n* [NL *Macadamia,* genus of evergreens, fr. John *Macadam* †1865 Australian chemist] **:** a hard-shelled nut somewhat resembling a filbert and produced by an Australian evergreen tree (*Macadamia ternifolia*) of the protea family that is cultivated extensively in Hawaii

mac·ad·am·ize \mə-ˈkad-ə-ˌmīz\ *vt* **-ized; -iz·ing :** to construct or finish (a road) by compacting into a solid mass a layer of small broken stone on a convex well-drained roadbed and using a binder (as cement or asphalt) for the mass

ma·caque \mə-ˈkak, -ˈkäk\ *n* [F, fr. Pg *macaco*]**:** any of numerous short-tailed Old World monkeys (*Macaca* and related genera) chiefly of southern Asia and the East Indies; *esp* **:** RHESUS MONKEY

mac·a·ro·ni \ˌmak-ə-ˈrō-nē\ *n* [It *maccheroni,* pl. of *maccherone,* fr. It dial. *maccarone* dumpling, macaroni] **1 :** a paste composed chiefly of semolina dried in the form of slender tubes for use as food **2** *pl* **macaronis** *or* **macaronies a :** a member of a class of traveled young Englishmen of the late 18th and early 19th centuries who affected foreign ways **b :** an affected young man **:** FOP

mac·a·ron·ic \-ˈrän-ik\ *adj* [NL *macaronicus,* fr. It dial. *maccarone* macaroni] **1 :** characterized by a mixture of vernacular words with Latin words or with non-Latin words having Latin endings **2 :** characterized by a mixture of two languages — **macaronic** *n* — **mac·a·ron·i·cal·ly** \-i-k(ə-)lē\ *adv*

mac·a·roon \ˌmak-ə-ˈrün\ *n* [F *macaron,* fr. It dial. *maccarone*] **:** a small cookie composed chiefly of egg whites, sugar, and ground almonds or coconut

ma·caw \mə-ˈkȯ\ *n* [Pg *macau*] **:** any of numerous parrots (esp. genus *Ara*) of South and Central America including some of the largest and showiest of parrots

macaw

Mac·beth \mək-ˈbeth, mak-\ *n* **:** a Scottish general who is the protagonist of Shakespeare's tragedy *Macbeth*

Mac·ca·bees \ˈmak-ə-(ˌ)bēz\ *n pl* [Gk *Makkabaioi,* fr. pl. of *Makkabaios,* surname of Judas Maccabaeus 2d cent. B.C. Jewish patriot] **1 :** a priestly family leading a Jewish revolt begun in 168 B.C. against Hellenism and Syrian rule and reigning over Palestine from 142 B.C. to 63 B.C. **2** *sing in constr* **:** either of two narrative and historical books included in the Roman Catholic canon of the Old Testament and in the Protestant Apocrypha — see BIBLE table — **Mac·ca·be·an** \ˌmak-ə-ˈbē-ən\ *adj*

mac·ca·boy \ˈmak-ə-ˌbȯi\ *n* [F *macouba,* fr. *Macouba,* district in Martinique] **:** a snuff from Martinique

Mc·Car·thy·ism \mə-ˈkär-thē-ˌiz-əm *also* -ˈkärt-ē-\ *n* [Joseph R. *McCarthy*] **:** a mid-twentieth-century political attitude characterized chiefly by opposition to elements held to be subversive and by the use of tactics involving personal attacks on individuals by means of widely publicized indiscriminate allegations esp. on the basis of unsubstantiated charges — **Mc·Car·thy·ite** \-ˌīt\ *n*

Mc·Coy \mə-ˈkȯi\ *n* [alter. of *Mackay* (in the phrase *the real Mackay* the true chief of the Mackay clan, a position often disputed)] **:** something that is neither imitation nor substitute — often used in the phrase *the real McCoy*

¹mace \ˈmās\ *n* [ME, fr. MF, fr. (assumed) VL *mattia;* akin to OHG *medela* plow, L *mateola* mallet] **1 a :** a heavy often spiked staff or club used esp. in the Middle Ages for breaking armor **b :** a club used as a weapon **2 a :** an ornamental staff borne as a symbol of authority before a public official or a legislative body **b :** one who carries a mace

²mace *n* [ME, fr. MF *macis,* fr. L *macir,* an East Indian spice, fr. Gk *makir*] **:** an aromatic spice consisting of the dried external fibrous covering of a nutmeg

³mace *vt* **maced; mac·ing :** to attack with the liquid Mace

Mace \ˈmās\ *trademark* — used for a temporarily disabling liquid that when sprayed in the face of a person (as a rioter) causes tears, dizziness, immobilization, and sometimes nausea

ma·cé·doine \ˌmas-ə-ˈdwän\ *n* [F, fr. *Macédoine* Macedonia; perh. fr. the mixture of races in Macedonia] **1 :** a mixture of fruits or vegetables served as a salad or cocktail or in a jellied dessert or used in a sauce or as a garnish **2 :** a confused mixture **:** MEDLEY

Mac·e·do·nian \ˌmas-ə-ˈdō-nyən, -nē-ən\ *n* **1 :** a native or inhabitant of Macedonia **2 :** the Slavic language of modern Macedonia **3 :** the language of ancient Macedonia of uncertain affinity but generally assumed to be Indo-European

mac·er·ate \ˈmas-ə-ˌrāt\ *vb* **-at·ed; -at·ing** [L *maceratus,* pp. of *macerare* to soften, steep] *vt* **1 :** to cause to waste away by or as if by excessive fasting **2 :** to cause to become soft or separated into constituent elements by or as if by steeping in fluid ~ *vi* **:** to soften and wear away esp. as a result of being wetted or steeped — **mac·er·a·tion** \ˌmas-ə-ˈrā-shən\ *n* — **mac·er·a·tor** \ˈmas-ə-ˌrāt-ər\ *n*

mach *abbr* machine; machining; machinist

Mach \ˈmäk\ *n* **:** a usu. high speed expressed by a Mach number <an airplane flying at ~ 2>

Mach·a·bees \ˈmak-ə-(ˌ)bēz\ *n pl but sing in constr* [LL *Machabaei,* modif. of Gk *Makkabaioi*] **:** MACCABEES

ma·chete \mə-ˈshet-ē, -ˈchet-; -ˈshet\ *n* [Sp] **:** a large heavy knife used for cutting sugarcane and underbrush and as a weapon

Ma·chi·a·vel·lian \ˌmak-ē-ə-ˈvel-ē-ən, -ˈvel-yən\ *adj* **1 :** of or relating to Machiavelli or Machiavellianism **2 :** suggesting the principles of conduct laid down by Machiavelli; *specif* **:** characterized by cunning, duplicity, or bad faith — **Machiavellian** *n*

Ma·chi·a·vel·lian·ism \-ˌiz-əm\ *n* **:** the political theory of Machiavelli; *esp* **:** the view that politics is amoral and that any means however unscrupulous can justifiably be used in achieving political power

ma·chic·o·late \mə-ˈchik-ə-ˌlāt\ *vt* **-lat·ed; -lat·ing** [ML *machicolatus,* pp. of *machicolare,* fr. OF *machicoller,* fr. *machicoleis* machicolation, fr. *macher* to crush + *col* neck, fr. L *collum* — more at COLLAR] **:** to furnish with machicolations

ma·chic·o·la·tion \mə-ˌchik-ə-ˈlā-shən\ *n* **1 a :** an opening between the corbels of a projecting parapet or in the floor of a gallery or roof of a portal for discharging missiles upon assailants below — see BATTLEMENT illustration **b :** a gallery or parapet containing such openings **2 :** construction imitating medieval machicolation

mach·i·nate \ˈmak-ə-ˌnāt, ˈmash-ə-\ *vb* **-nat·ed; -nat·ing** [L *machinatus,* pp. of *machinari,* fr. *machina* machine, contrivance] *vi* **:** to plan or plot esp. to do harm ~ *vt* **:** to scheme or contrive to bring about **:** PLOT — **mach·i·na·tor** \-ˌnāt-ər\ *n*

mach·i·na·tion \ˌmak-ə-ˈnā-shən, ˌmash-ə-\ *n* **1 :** an act of machinating **2 :** a scheming or crafty action or artful design intended to accomplish some usu. evil end

¹ma·chine \mə-ˈshēn\ *n, often attrib* [MF, fr. L *machina,* fr. Gk *mēchanē* (Dor dial. *machana*), fr. *mēchos* means, expedient — more at MAY] **1 a** *archaic* **:** a constructed thing whether material or immaterial **b :** CONVEYANCE, VEHICLE; *specif* **:** AUTOMOBILE **c** *archaic* **:** a military engine **d :** any of various apparatus formerly used to produce stage effects **e (1) :** an assemblage of parts that transmit forces, motion, and energy one to another in a predetermined manner **(2):** an instrument (as a lever) designed to transmit or modify the application of power, force, or motion **f :** a mechanically, electrically, or electronically operated device for performing a task <a calculating ~> <a card-sorting ~> **g :** a coin-operated device <a cigarette ~> **h :** MACHINERY — used with *the* or in pl. <man must not become the servant of the ~> **2 a :** a living organism or one of its functional systems **b :** a person or organization that acts like a machine **c (1) :** a combination of persons acting together for a common end along with the agencies they use **(2) :** a highly organized political group under the leadership of a boss or small clique **3 :** a literary device or contrivance introduced for dramatic effect

²machine *vt* **ma·chined; ma·chin·ing :** to process by machine; *specif* **:** to reduce or finish as by turning, shaping, planing, or milling by machine-operated tools — **ma·chin·abil·i·ty** \-ˌshē-nə-ˈbil-ət-ē\ *n* — **ma·chin·able** *also* **ma·chine·able** \-ˈshē-nə-bəl\ *adj*

machine gun *n* **:** an automatic gun using small-arms ammunition for rapid continuous firing — **machine–gun** *vb* — **machine gunner** *n*

machine language *n* **1 :** information recorded in a form usable by a machine (as a computer) **2 :** numbers or instructions expressed in a form directly usable by a computer

ma·chine·like \mə-ˈshēn-ˌlīk\ *adj* **:** resembling a machine esp. in regularity of action or stereotyped uniformity of product

machine–readable *adj* **:** directly usable by a computer <~ text>

ma·chin·ery \mə-ˈshēn-(ə-)rē\ *n, pl* **-er·ies 1 a :** machines in general or as a functioning unit: as **(1) :** apparatus for producing stage effects **(2) :** literary devices used esp. for dramatic effect **b :** the working parts of a machine **2 :** the means by which something is kept in action or a desired result is obtained

machine shop *n* **:** a workshop in which work is machined to size and assembled

machine tool *n* **:** a usu. power-driven machine designed for shaping solid work

ma·chin·ist \mə-ˈshē-nəst\ *n* **1 a :** a worker who fabricates, assembles, or repairs machinery **b :** a craftsman skilled in the use of machine tools **c :** one who operates a machine **2** *archaic* **:** a person in charge of the mechanical aspects of a theatrical production **3 :** a warrant officer who supervises machinery and engine operation

ma·chis·mo \mä-ˈchēz-(ˌ)mō, -ˈchiz-\ *n* [MexSp, fr. Sp *macho* male] **:** a strong sense of masculine pride **:** an exaggerated awareness and assertion of masculinity

Mach number \ˈmäk-\ *n* [Ernst *Mach* †1916 Austrian physicist] **:** a number representing the ratio of the speed of a body to the speed of sound in the surrounding atmosphere <a *Mach number* of 2 indicates a speed that is twice that of sound and a *Mach number* of 0.5 a speed that is one half that of sound>

¹ma·cho \ˈmä-ˌchō\ *adj* [Sp, male, fr. L *masculus* — more at MALE] **:** aggressively virile

²macho *n* **1 :** MACHISMO **2 :** one who exhibits machismo

mack *var of* MAC

mack·er·el \ˈmak-(ə-)rəl\ *n, pl* **mackerel** *or* **mackerels** [ME *makerel,* fr. OF] **1 :** a fish (*Scomber scombrus*) of the No. Atlantic that is green above with dark blue bars and silvery below, reaches a length of about 18 inches, and is one of the most important food fishes **2 :** a fish of the suborder (Scombroidea) to which the common mackerel belongs; *esp* **:** a comparatively small member of this group as distinguished from a bonito or tuna

mackerel shark *n* **:** any of a family (Lamnidae) of large fierce pelagic sharks; *esp* **:** PORBEAGLE

mackerel sky *n* **:** a sky covered with rows of altocumulus or cirrocumulus clouds resembling the patterns on a mackerel's back

mack·i·naw \ˈmak-ə-ˌnȯ\ *n* [*Mackinaw* City, Michigan, formerly an Indian trading post] **1 :** a flat-bottomed boat with pointed prow and square stern formerly much used on the upper Great Lakes **2 :** a heavy woolen blanket formerly distributed by the U.S. government to the Indians **3 a :** a heavy cloth of wool or wool and other fibers often with a plaid design and usu. heavily napped and felted **b :** a short coat of mackinaw or similar heavy fabric

mack·in·tosh *also* **mac·in·tosh** \ˈmak-ən-ˌtäsh\ *n* [Charles *Macintosh* †1843 Sc chemist & inventor] **1** *chiefly Brit* **:** RAINCOAT **2 :** a lightweight waterproof fabric orig. of rubberized cotton

¹mack·le \ˈmak-əl\ *n* [F *macule* spot, mackle, fr. L *macula* spot, stain] **:** a blur or a double impression on a printed sheet

²mackle *vb* **mack·led; mack·ling** \-(ə-)liŋ\ **:** BLUR

Mac·lau·rin's series \mə-ˌklȯr-ən(z)-\ *n* [Colin *Maclaurin* †1746 Sc physician] **:** a Taylor's series of the form

$$f(x) = f(0) + \frac{f'(0)}{1!}x + \frac{f''(0)}{2!}x^2 + \ldots + \frac{f^{[n]}(0)}{n!}x^n + \ldots$$

in which the expansion is about the reference point zero — called also *Maclaurin series*

ma·cle \ˈmak-əl\ *n* [F, wide-meshed net, lozenge voided, macle, fr. OF, mesh, lozenge voided, of Gmc origin; akin to OHG *masca* mesh — more at MESH] **1 a :** a twin crystal **b :** a flat often triangular diamond that is usu. a twin crystal **2 :** a dark or discolored spot (as in a mineral) — **ma·cled** \ˈmak-əld\ *adj*

macr- *or* **macro-** *comb form* [F & L, fr. Gk *makr-, makro-* long, fr. *makros* — more at MEAGER] **1 :** long <*macro*diagonal> **2 :** large <*macro*spore>

mac·ra·me \ˌmak-rə-ˈmā\ *n* [F or It; F *macramé,* fr. It *macramè,* fr. Turk *makrama* napkin, towel, fr. Ar *migramah* embroidered veil] **:** a coarse lace or fringe made by knotting threads or cords in a geometrical pattern; *also* **:** the art of tying knots in patterns

macrame knot *n* **:** an ornate knot used in making macrame

macrame knot

¹mac·ro \ˈmak-(ˌ)rō\ *adj* [*macr-*] **1 :** being large, thick, or exceptionally prominent <the book as the ~ unit of thought —Eugene Garfield> **2 :** of, involving, or intended for use with relatively large quantities or on a large scale **3 :** GROSS 1c

²macro *n, pl* **macros** [short for *macroinstruction*] **:** a single computer instruction that stands for a sequence of operations — called also *macroinstruction*

mac·ro·ag·gre·gate \ˌmak-rō-ˈag-ri-gət\ *n* **:** a relatively large particle (as of soil or a protein) — **mac·ro·ag·gre·gat·ed** \-ˌgāt-əd\ *adj*

mac·ro·bi·ot·ic \-bī-ˈät-ik, -bē-\ *adj* **:** of, relating to, or being an extremely restricted diet (as one containing chiefly whole grains) that is usu. undertaken by its advocates to promote health and well-being although it may actually be deficient in essential nutrients (as fats)

mac·ro·ceph·a·lous \-ˈsef-ə-ləs\ *or* **mac·ro·ce·phal·ic** \-sə-ˈfal-ik\ *adj* [F *macrocéphale,* fr. Gk *makrokephalos* having a long head, fr. *makr-* + *kephalē* head — more at CEPHALIC] **:** having or being an exceptionally large head or cranium <a ~ idiot> — **mac·ro·ceph·a·ly** \-ˈsef-ə-lē\ *n*

mac·ro·cosm \ˈmak-rə-ˌkäz-əm\ *n* [F *macrocosme,* fr. ML *macrocosmos,* fr. L *macr-* + Gk *kosmos* order, universe] **1 :** the great world **:** UNIVERSE **2 :** a complex that is a large-scale reproduction of one of its constituents — **mac·ro·cos·mic** \ˌmak-rə-ˈkäz-mik\ *adj* — **mac·ro·cos·mi·cal·ly** \-mi-k(ə-)lē\ *adv*

mac·ro·cyte \ˈmak-rə-ˌsīt\ *n* [ISV] **:** an exceptionally large red blood cell occurring chiefly in anemias — **mac·ro·cyt·ic** \ˌmak-rə-ˈsit-ik\ *adj*

mac·ro·cy·to·sis \ˌmak-rə-sī-ˈtō-səs, -rə-sə-\ *n, pl* **-to·ses** \-ˌsēz\ [NL] **:** the occurrence of macrocytes in the blood

mac·ro·eco·nom·ics \ˈmak-rō-ˌek-ə-ˈnäm-iks, -ˌē-kə-\ *n pl but usu sing in constr* **:** a study of economics in terms of whole systems esp. with reference to general levels of output and income and to the interrelations among sectors of the economy — compare MICROECONOMICS — **mac·ro·eco·nom·ic** \-ik\ *adj*

mac·ro·evo·lu·tion \ˈmak-rō-ˌev-ə-ˈlü-shən *also* -ˌē-və-\ *n* **:** evolutionary change involving relatively large and complex steps — **mac·ro·evo·lu·tion·ary** \-shə-ˌner-ē\ *adj*

mac·ro·fos·sil \ˈmak-rō-ˌfäs-əl\ *n* **:** a fossil large enough to be observed by direct inspection

mac·ro·ga·mete \ˌmak-rō-gə-ˈmēt, -ˈgam-ˌēt\ *n* [ISV] **:** the larger and usu. female gamete of a heterogamous organism

mac·ro·glob·u·lin \-ˈgläb-yə-lən\ *n* [ISV] **:** a highly polymerized globulin of high molecular weight

mac·ro·glob·u·lin·emia \-ˌgläb-yə-lə-ˈnē-mē-ə\ *n* [NL] **:** a disorder characterized by increased blood serum viscosity and the presence of macroglobulins in the serum — **mac·ro·glob·u·lin·emic** \-mik\ *adj*

mac·ro·in·struc·tion \ˌmak-rō-in-ˈstrək-shən\ *n* **:** MACRO

mac·ro·lep·i·dop·tera \ˈmak-rō-ˌlep-ə-ˈdäp-tə-rə\ *n pl* [NL] **:** lepidoptera (as butterflies, skippers, saturniids, noctuids, and geometrids) that include most of the large forms and none of the minute ones

mac·ro·mere \ˈmak-rə-ˌmi(ə)r\ *n* **:** a large blastomere — see BLASTULA illustration

mac·ro·mol·e·cule \ˌmak-rō-ˈmäl-i-ˌkyü(ə)l\ *n* [ISV] **:** a large molecule (as of a protein or rubber) built up from smaller chemical structures — **mac·ro·mo·lec·u·lar** \-mə-ˈlek-yə-lər\ *adj*

ma·cron \ˈmā-ˌkrän, ˈmak-, -rən\ *n* [Gk *makron,* neut. of *makros* long] **:** a mark ¯ placed over a vowel to indicate that the vowel is long or placed over a syllable or used alone to indicate a stressed or long syllable in a metrical foot

mac·ro·nu·cle·us \ˌmak-rō-ˈn(y)ü-klē-əs\ *n* [NL] **:** a relatively large densely staining nucleus that is believed to exert a controlling influence over the trophic activities of most ciliated protozoans

mac·ro·nu·tri·ent \-ˈn(y)ü-trē-ənt\ *n* **:** a chemical element of which relatively large quantities are essential to the growth and welfare of a plant

mac·ro·phage \ˈmak-rə-ˌfāj, -ˌfäzh\ *n* [F, fr. *macr-* + *-phage*] **:** a large phagocyte; *specif* **:** HISTIOCYTE — **mac·ro·phag·ic** \ˌmak-rə-ˈfaj-ik\ *adj*

mac·ro·phyte \ˈmak-rə-ˌfīt\ *n* **:** a member of the macroscopic plant life esp. of a body of water — **mac·ro·phyt·ic** \ˌmak-rə-ˈfit-ik\ *adj*

mac·rop·ter·ous \ma-ˈkräp-tə-rəs\ *adj* [Gk *makropteros,* fr. *makr-* + *pteron* wing — more at FEATHER] **:** having long or large wings or fins

mac·ro·scale \ˈmak-rō-ˌskāl\ *n* **:** a large often macroscopic scale <study of atmospheric motions on a ~>

mac·ro·scop·ic \ˌmak-rə-ˈskäp-ik\ *also* **mac·ro·scop·i·cal** \-i-kəl\ *adj* [ISV *macr-* + *-scopic* (as in *microscopic*)] **1 :** large enough to be observed by the naked eye **2 :** considered in terms of large units or elements — **mac·ro·scop·i·cal·ly** \-i-k(ə-)lē\ *adv*

mac·ro·struc·ture \ˈmak-rō-ˌstrək-chər\ *n* **:** the structure (as of metal, a body part, or the soil) revealed by visual examination with little or no magnification — **mac·ro·struc·tur·al** \ˌmak-rō-ˈstrək-chə-rəl, -ˈstrək-shə-rəl\ *adj*

MACT *abbr* master of arts in college teaching

mac·u·la \ˈmak-yə-lə\ *n, pl* **-lae** \-ˌlē, -ˌlī\ *also* **-las** [L] **1 :** BLOTCH, SPOT; *esp* **:** MACULE **2 :** an anatomical structure (as the macula lutea) having the form of a spot differentiated from surrounding tissues — **mac·u·lar** \-lər\ *adj*

macula lu·tea \-ˈlüt-ē-ə\ *n, pl* **maculae lu·te·ae** \-ē-ˌē, -ē-ˌī\ [NL, lit., yellow spot] **:** a small yellowish area lying slightly lateral to the center of the retina that constitutes the region of maximum visual acuity — called also *yellow spot*

mac·u·late \ˈmak-yə-lət\ *or* **mac·u·lat·ed** \-ˌlāt-əd\ *adj* **1 :** marked with spots **:** BLOTCHED **2 :** BESMIRCHED, IMPURE

mac·u·la·tion \ˌmak-yə-ˈlā-shən\ *n* **1** *archaic* **:** the state of being spotted **2 a :** a blemish in the form of a discrete spot <acne scars and ~*s*> **b :** the arrangement of spots and markings on an animal or plant

mac·ule \ˈmak-(ˌ)yü(ə)l\ *n* [F, fr. L *macula*] **:** a patch of skin that is altered in color but usu. not elevated and that is a characteristic feature of various diseases (as smallpox)

¹mad \ˈmad\ *adj* **mad·der; mad·dest** [ME *medd, madd,* fr. OE *gemǣd,* pp. of (assumed) *gemǣdan* to madden, fr. *gemād* silly, mad; akin to OHG *gimeit* foolish, crazy, Skt *methati* he hurts] **1 :** disordered in mind **:** INSANE **2 a :** completely unrestrained by reason and judgment **:** SENSELESS **b :** incapable of being explained or accounted for **:** ILLOGICAL **3 a :** carried away by intense anger **:** FURIOUS **b :** keenly displeased **:** ANGRY **4 :** carried away by enthusiasm or desire **5 :** affected with rabies **:** RABID **6 :** marked by wild gaiety and merriment **:** HILARIOUS **7 :** intensely excited **:** FRANTIC **8 :** marked by intense and often chaotic activity **:** WILD

²mad *vb* **mad·ded; mad·ding :** MADDEN

³mad *n* **1 :** ANGER, FURY **2 :** a fit or mood of bad temper

Mad·a·gas·car periwinkle \ˌmad-ə-ˈgas-kər-\ *n* [*Madagascar,* Africa] **:** ¹PERIWINKLE b

mad·am \ˈmad-əm\ *n, pl* **madams** [ME, fr. OF *ma dame,* lit., my lady] **1** *pl* **mes·dames** \mā-ˈdäm, -ˈdam\ **:** LADY — used without a name as a form of respectful or polite address to a woman **2 :** MISTRESS 1 — used as a title formerly with the given name but now with the surname or esp. with a designation of rank or office <*Madam* Chairman> <*Madam* President> **3 :** the female head of a house of prostitution **4 :** the female head of a household **:** WIFE

ma·dame \mə-'dam, ma-', *before a surname also* ˌmad-əm\ *n* [F, fr. OF *ma dame*] **1** *pl* **mes·dames** \mā-'däm, -'dam\ — used as a title equivalent to *Mrs.* for a married woman not of English-speaking nationality **2** *pl* **madames** : MADAM 3
mad–brained \'mad-'brānd\ *adj* : HOTHEADED, RASH
mad·cap \'mad-ˌkap\ *adj* : marked by impulsiveness, recklessness, or foolishness — **madcap** *n*
mad·den \'mad-ᵊn\ *vb* **mad·dened; mad·den·ing** \'mad-niŋ, -ᵊn-iŋ\ *vi* : to become or act as if mad ~ *vt* **1** : to drive mad : CRAZE **2** : to make intensely angry : ENRAGE
mad·den·ing *adj* **1** : tending to craze **2 a** : tending to infuriate **b** : tending to vex : IRRITATING — **mad·den·ing·ly** \'mad-niŋ-lē, -ᵊn-iŋ-\ *adv*
mad·der \'mad-ər\ *n* [ME, fr. OE *mædere;* akin to OHG *matara* madder] **1** : a Eurasian herb (*Rubia tinctorum* of the family Rubiaceae, the madder family) with verticillate leaves and small yellowish panicled flowers succeeded by berries; *broadly* : any of several related herbs (genus *Rubia*) **2 a** : the root of the Eurasian madder used formerly in dyeing; *also* : an alizarin dye prepared from it **b** : a moderate to strong red
mad·ding \'mad-iŋ\ *adj* **1** : acting as if mad : FRENZIED **2** : MADDENING
mad·dish \'mad-ish\ *adj* : somewhat mad
made \'mād\ *adj* [ME, fr. pp. of *maken* to make] **1 a** : artificially produced **b** : FICTITIOUS, INVENTED <a ~ excuse> **c** : put together of various ingredients **2** : assured of success <a ~ man>
Ma·dei·ra \mə-'dir-ə, -'der-\ *n* [Pg, fr. *Madeira* islands] : an amber-colored dessert wine of Madeira; *also* : a similar wine made elsewhere
ma·de·moi·selle \ˌmad-(ə-)m(w)ə-'zel, mam-'zel\ *n, pl* **ma·de·moi·selles** \-'zelz\ *or* **mes·de·moi·selles** \ˌmād-(ə-)m(w)ə-'zel\ [F, fr. OF *ma damoisele,* lit., my (young) lady] **1** : an unmarried French girl or woman — used as a title equivalent to *Miss* for an unmarried woman not of English-speaking nationality **2** : a French governess **3** : SILVER PERCH a
made–up \'mā-'dəp\ *adj* **1** : marked by the use of makeup **2** : fancifully conceived or falsely devised **3** : fully manufactured
mad·house \'mad-ˌhau̇s\ *n* **1** : a place where insane persons are detained and treated **2** : a place of bewildering uproar or confusion
Mad·i·son Avenue \ˌmad-ə-sən-\ *n* [*Madison Avenue,* New York City, center of the American advertising business] : the American advertising industry
mad·ly \'mad-lē\ *adv* : in a mad manner or to a degree suggestive of madness
mad·man \'mad-ˌman, -mən\ *n* : a man who is or acts as if insane
mad·ness \'mad-nəs\ *n* **1** : the quality or state of being mad: as **a** : INSANITY **b** : extreme folly **c** : RAGE **d** : ECSTASY, ENTHUSIASM **2** : any of several ailments of animals marked by frenzied behavior; *specif* : RABIES
Ma·don·na \mə-'dän-ə\ *n* [It, fr. OIt *ma donna,* lit., my lady] **1** *archaic* : LADY — used as a form of respectful address **2** *obs* : an Italian lady **3** : VIRGIN MARY
Madonna lily *n* : a white lily (*Lilium candidum*) with bell-shaped to broad funnel-shaped flowers formerly extensively forced for spring blooming
ma·dras \'mad-rəs; mə-'dras, -'dräs\ *n* [*Madras,* India] **1 a** : a fine plain-woven shirting and dress fabric usu. of cotton with varied designs (as plaid) in bright colors or in white **b** : a light open usu. cotton fabric with a heavy design used for curtains **2** : a large silk or cotton kerchief usu. of bright colors that is often worn as a turban
mad·re·pore \'mad-rə-ˌpō(ə)r, -ˌpȯ(ə)r\ *n* [F *madrépore,* fr. It *madrepora,* fr. *madre* mother (fr. L *mater*) + *poro* pore (fr. L *porus*) — more at MOTHER] : any of various stony reef-building corals (order Madreporaria) of tropical seas that assume a variety of branching, encrusting, or massive forms — **mad·re·po·ri·an** \ˌmad-rə-'pōr-ē-ən, -'pȯr-\ *adj or n* — **mad·re·por·ic** \-'pōr-ik, -'pȯr-\ *adj*
mad·re·por·ite \'mad-rə-ˌpōr-ˌit, -ˌpȯr-\ *n* [ISV *madrepore* + [1]-*ite* (segment); fr. the resemblances of the perforations to those of a madrepore] : a perforated or porous body that is situated at the distal end of the stone canal in echinoderms
mad·ri·gal \'mad-ri-gəl\ *n* [It *madrigale,* fr. ML *matricale,* fr. neut. of (assumed) *matricalis* simple, fr. LL, of the womb, fr. L *matric-, matrix* womb] **1** : a medieval short lyrical poem in a strict poetic form **2 a** : a complex polyphonic unaccompanied vocal piece on a secular text developed esp. in the 16th and 17th centuries **b** : PART-SONG; *esp* : GLEE — **mad·ri·gal·ian** \ˌmad-rə-'gal-ē-ən, -'gāl-\ *adj* — **mad·ri·gal·ist** \'mad-ri-gə-ləst\ *n*
ma·dri·lene \ˌmad-rə-'len, -'lān\ *n* [F (*consommé*) *madrilène,* lit., Madrid consommé] : a consommé flavored with tomato
ma·dro·na *or* **ma·dro·ne** *or* **ma·dro·no** \mə-'drō-nə\ *n* [Sp *madroño*] : an evergreen tree or shrub (*Arbutus menziesii*) of the heath family of the Pacific coast of No. America with smooth bark, thick shining leaves, and edible red berries
ma·du·ro \mə-'du̇(ə)r-(ˌ)ō\ *n, pl* **-ros** [Sp, fr. *maduro* ripe, fr. L *maturus* — more at MATURE] : a dark-colored relatively strong cigar
mad·wom·an \'mad-ˌwu̇m-ən\ *n* : a woman who is or acts as if insane
mad·wort \-ˌwərt, -ˌwȯ(ə)rt\ *n* **1** : ALYSSUM 1 **2** : a low hairy annual herb (*Asperugo procumbens*) of the borage family with blue flowers and a root used as a substitute for madder
MAE *abbr* **1** master of aeronautical engineering **2** master of aerospace engineering **3** master of art education **4** master of arts in education
Mae·ce·nas \mi-'sē-nəs\ *n* [L, fr. Gaius *Maecenas* †8 B.C. Roman statesman & patron of literature] : a generous patron esp. of literature or art
MA Ed *abbr* master of arts in education
mael·strom \'māl(ə)l-strəm, -ˌsträm\ *n* [obs. D (now *maalstroom*), fr. *malen* to grind + *strom* stream; akin to OHG *malan* to grind and to OHG *stroum* stream — more at MEAL, STREAM] **1** : a powerful often violent whirlpool sucking in objects within a given radius **2** : something resembling a maelstrom in turbulence : TURMOIL
mae·nad \'mē-ˌnad\ *n* [L *maenad-, maenas,* fr. Gk *mainad-, mainas,* fr. *mainesthai* to be mad; akin to Gk *menos* spirit — more at MIND] **1** : a woman participant in orgiastic Dionysian rites : BACCHANTE **2** : an unnaturally excited or distraught woman — **mae·nad·ic** \mē-'nad-ik\ *adj*
MAeroE *abbr* master of aeronautical engineering
mae·sto·so \mī-'stō-(ˌ)sō, -(ˌ)zō\ *adj or adv* [It, fr. L *majestosus,* fr. *majestas* majesty] : majestic and stately — used as a direction in music
mae·stro \'mī-(ˌ)strō\ *n, pl* **maestros** *or* **mae·stri** \-ˌstrē\ [It, lit., master, fr. L *magister* — more at MASTER] : a master in an art; *esp* : an eminent composer, conductor, or teacher of music
Mae West \'mā-'west\ *n* [*Mae West* *b* 1892 Am actress noted for her full figure] : an inflatable life jacket
maf·fick \'maf-ik\ *vi* [back-formation fr. *Mafeking night,* English celebration of the lifting of the siege of Mafeking, So. Africa, May 17, 1900] : to celebrate with boisterous rejoicing and hilarious behavior
Ma·fia \'mäf-ē-ə, 'maf-\ *n* [*Mafia, Maffia,* a Sicilian secret criminal society, fr. It] **1** : a secret society of political terrorists **2** : a secret organization composed chiefly of criminal elements and usu. held to control racketeering, peddling of narcotics, gambling, and other illicit activities throughout the world
maf·ic \'maf-ik\ *adj* [NL *ma*gnesium + L *f*errum iron + E *-ic*] : of, relating to, or being a group of usu. dark-colored minerals rich in magnesium and iron
ma·fi·o·so \ˌmäf-ē-'ō-(ˌ)sō, ˌmaf-, -(ˌ)zō\ *n, pl* **-si** \-(ˌ)sē, -(ˌ)zē\ [It, fr. *Mafia*] : a member of the Mafia
[1]**mag** *abbr* **1** magnesium **2** magnetism **3** magneto **4** magnitude
[2]**mag** \'mag\ *n, slang* : MAGAZINE
mag·a·zine \'mag-ə-ˌzēn, ˌmag-ə-'\ *n* [MF *magazin,* fr. OProv, fr. Ar *makhāzin,* pl. of *makhzan* storehouse] **1** : a place where goods or supplies are stored : WAREHOUSE **2** : a room in which powder and other explosives are kept in a fort or a ship **3** : the contents of a magazine: as **a** : an accumulation of munitions of war **b** : a stock of provisions or goods **4 a** : a periodical containing miscellaneous pieces (as articles, stories, poems) often illustrated **b** : a similar section of a newspaper usu. appearing on Sunday **5** : a supply chamber: as **a** : a holder in or on a gun for cartridges to be fed into the gun chamber automatically **b** : a lightproof chamber for films or plates on a camera or for film on a motion-picture projector
mag·a·zin·ist \-ˌzē-nəst, -'zē-\ *n* : one who writes for or edits a magazine
mag·da·len \'mag-də-lən\ *or* **mag·da·lene** \-ˌlēn\ *n, often cap* [Mary *Magdalen* or *Magdalene* woman healed by Jesus of evil spirits (Lk 8:2), considered identical with a reformed prostitute (Lk 7:36–50)] **1** : a reformed prostitute **2** : a house of refuge or reformatory for prostitutes
Mag·da·le·ni·an \ˌmag-də-'lē-nē-ən\ *adj* [F *magdalénien,* fr. *La Madeleine,* rock shelter in southwest France] : of or relating to an Upper Paleolithic culture characterized by flint, bone, and ivory implements, carving, and paintings
Mag·el·lan·ic Cloud \ˌmaj-ə-ˌlan-ik-, *chiefly Brit* ˌmag-\ *n* [Ferdinand *Magellan*] : either of the two nearest galaxies to the Milky Way system located within 25 degrees of the south celestial pole and appearing as conspicuous patches of light
Ma·gen Da·vid \ˌmō-gən-'dō-vəd\ *n* [Heb *māghēn Dāwīdh,* lit., shield of David] : a hexagram used as a symbol of Judaism
ma·gen·ta \mə-'jent-ə\ *n* [*Magenta,* Italy] **1** : FUCHSINE **2** : a deep purplish red
mag·got \'mag-ət\ *n* [ME *mathek, magotte,* of Scand origin; akin to ON *mathkr* maggot; akin to OE *matha* maggot] **1** : a soft-bodied legless grub that is the larva of a dipterous insect (as the housefly) **2** : a fantastic or eccentric idea : WHIM — **mag·goty** \-ē\ *adj*
Magh \'mäg\ *n* [Skt *māgha*] : a month of the Hindu year — see MONTH table
magi *pl of* MAGUS
[1]**Ma·gi·an** \'mā-jē-ən\ *n* : MAGUS
[2]**Ma·gi·an** \-jē-ən, -jən\ *adj* : of or relating to the Magi — **Ma·gi·an·ism** \-ə-ˌniz-əm\ *n*
[1]**mag·ic** \'maj-ik\ *n* [ME *magik,* fr. MF *magique,* fr. L *magice,* fr. Gk *magikē,* fem. of *magikos* Magian, magical, fr. *magos* magus, sorcerer, of Iranian origin; akin to OPer *magush* sorcerer] **1 a** : the use of means (as charms or spells) believed to have supernatural power over natural forces **b** : magic rites or incantations **2 a** : an extraordinary power or influence seemingly from a supernatural source **b** : something that seems to cast a spell **3** : the art of producing illusions by sleight of hand
[2]**magic** *adj* **1** : of or relating to magic **2 a** : having seemingly supernatural qualities or powers **b** : giving a feeling of enchantment — **mag·i·cal** \'maj-i-kəl\ *adj* — **mag·i·cal·ly** \-i-k(ə-)lē\ *adv*
[3]**magic** *vt* **mag·icked; mag·ick·ing** : to affect or influence by magic : BEWITCH
ma·gi·cian \mə-'jish-ən\ *n* **1** : one skilled in magic; *esp* : SORCERER **2** : one who performs tricks of illusion and sleight of hand
magic lantern *n* : an early form of optical projector of still pictures using a transparent slide
magic realism *n* [trans. of G *magischer realismus*] : painting in a meticulously realistic style of imaginary or fantastic scenes or images — **magic realist** *n*
Ma·gi·not Line \ˌmazh-ə-ˌnō-, ˌmaj-\ *n* [André *Maginot* †1932 Fr minister of war] : a line of defensive fortifications built before World War II to protect the eastern border of France but easily outflanked by German invaders
mag·is·te·ri·al \ˌmaj-ə-'stir-ē-əl\ *adj* [LL *magisterialis* of authority, fr. *magisterium* office of a master, fr. *magister*] **1 a** (1) : of, relating to, or having the characteristics of a master or teacher : AUTHORITATIVE (2) : marked by a sedately dignified or pompously assured or overbearing manner or aspect <writing marred by a tone of ~ condescension> **b** : of, relating to, or required for

a master's degree **2 :** of or relating to a magistrate, his office, or his duties *syn* see DICTATORIAL — **mag·is·te·ri·al·ly** \-ē-ə-lē\ *adv*

mag·is·te·ri·um \ˌmaj-ə-ˈstir-ē-əm\ *n* [L] **:** teaching authority esp. of the Roman Catholic Church

mag·is·tra·cy \ˈmaj-ə-strə-sē\ *n, pl* **-cies 1 :** the state of being a magistrate **2 :** the office, power, or dignity of a magistrate **3 :** a body of magistrates **4 :** the district under a magistrate

ma·gis·tral \ˈmaj-ə-strəl, mə-ˈjis-trəl\ *adj* [LL *magistralis,* fr. L *magistr-, magister*] **:** of, relating to, or characteristic of a master **:** MAGISTERIAL 1a — **ma·gis·tral·ly** \-ē\ *adv*

mag·is·trate \ˈmaj-ə-ˌstrāt, -strət\ *n* [ME *magistrat,* fr. L *magistratus* magistracy, magistrate, fr. *magistr-, magister* master, political superior — more at MASTER] **:** an official entrusted with administration of the laws: as **a :** a principal official exercising governmental powers over a major political unit (as a nation) **b :** a local official exercising administrative and often judicial functions **c :** a local judiciary official having limited original jurisdiction esp. in criminal cases — **mag·is·trat·i·cal** \ˌmaj-ə-ˈstrat-i-kəl\ *adj* — **mag·is·trat·i·cal·ly** \-k(ə-)lē\ *adv*

magistrate's court *n* **1 :** POLICE COURT **2 :** a court that has minor civil and criminal jurisdiction

mag·is·tra·ture \ˈmaj-ə-ˌstrā-chər, -strə-ˌchu̇(ə)r\ *n* **:** MAGISTRACY

mag·ma \ˈmag-mə\ *n* [L *magmat-, magma,* fr. Gk, thick unguent, fr. *massein* to knead — more at MINGLE] **1** *archaic* **:** DREGS, SEDIMENT **2 :** a thin pasty suspension (as of a precipitate in water) **3 :** molten rock material within the earth from which an igneous rock results by cooling — **mag·mat·ic** \mag-ˈmat-ik\ *adj*

Mag·na Char·ta *or* **Mag·na Car·ta** \ˌmag-nə-ˈkärt-ə\ *n* [ML, lit., great charter] **1 :** a charter of liberties to which the English barons forced King John to give his assent in June 1215 at Runnymede **2 :** a document constituting a fundamental guarantee of rights and privileges

mag·na cum lau·de \ˌmäg-nə-(ˌ)ku̇m-ˈlau̇d-ə, -ˈlau̇d-ē; ˌmag-nə-ˌkəm-ˈlȯd-ē\ *adv* [L] **:** with great distinction <graduated *magna cum laude*> — compare CUM LAUDE, SUMMA CUM LAUDE

mag·na·nim·i·ty \ˌmag-nə-ˈnim-ət-ē\ *n, pl* **-ties 1 :** the quality of being magnanimous **:** loftiness of spirit enabling one to bear trouble calmly, to disdain meanness and revenge, and to make sacrifices for worthy ends **2 :** a magnanimous act

mag·nan·i·mous \mag-ˈnan-ə-məs\ *adj* [L *magnanimus,* fr. *magnus* great + *animus* spirit — more at MUCH, ANIMATE] **1 :** showing or suggesting a lofty and courageous spirit <the irreproachable lives and ~ sufferings of their followers —Joseph Addison> **2 :** showing or suggesting nobility of feeling and generosity of mind **:** FORGIVING <even his enemies considered him ~> — **mag·nan·i·mous·ly** *adv* — **mag·nan·i·mous·ness** *n*

mag·nate \ˈmag-ˌnāt, -nət\ *n* [ME *magnates,* pl., fr. LL, fr. L *magnus*] **:** a person of rank, power, influence, or distinction often in a specified area

mag·ne·sia \mag-ˈnē-shə, -ˈnē-zhə\ *n* [NL, fr. *magnes carneus,* a white earth, lit., flesh magnet] **1 :** a white highly infusible oxide of magnesium MgO used esp. in refractories, in cements, insulation, fertilizers, and rubber, and in medicine as an antacid and mild laxative **2 :** MAGNESIUM — **mag·ne·sian** \-shən, -zhən\ *adj*

mag·ne·site \ˈmag-nə-ˌsīt\ *n* **:** native magnesium carbonate used esp. in making refractories and magnesia

mag·ne·sium \mag-ˈnē-zē-əm, -zhəm\ *n* [NL, fr. *magnesia*] **:** a silver-white light malleable ductile metallic element that occurs abundantly in nature and is used in metallurgical and chemical processes, in photography, in signaling, and in the manufacture of pyrotechnics because of the intense white light it produces on burning, and in construction esp. in the form of light alloys — see ELEMENT table

magnesium carbonate *n* **:** a carbonate of magnesium; *esp* **:** a white crystalline salt $MgCO_3$ that occurs naturally as dolomite and magnesite

magnesium chloride *n* **:** a bitter deliquescent salt $MgCl_2$ used esp. as a source of magnesium metal

magnesium hydroxide *n* **:** a slightly alkaline crystalline compound $Mg(OH)_2$ used esp. as a laxative and gastric antacid

magnesium oxide *n* **:** MAGNESIA 1

magnesium sulfate *n* **:** a sulfate of magnesium: as **a :** a white salt $MgSO_4$ used in medicine and in industry **b :** EPSOM SALTS

mag·net \ˈmag-nət\ *n* [ME *magnete,* fr. MF, fr. L *magnet-, magnes,* fr. Gk *magnēs* (*lithos*), lit., stone of Magnesia, ancient city in Asia Minor] **1 a :** LODESTONE **b :** a body having the property of attracting iron and producing a magnetic field external to itself; *specif* **:** a mass of iron, steel, or alloy that has this property artificially imparted **2 :** something that attracts

magnet- *or* **magneto-** *comb form* [L *magnet-, magnes*] **1 :** magnetic force <*magneto*meter> **2 :** magnetism **:** magnetic <*magneto*electric> <*magne*ton> **3 :** magnetoelectric <*magneto*-generator>

[1]**mag·net·ic** \mag-ˈnet-ik\ *adj* **1 a :** of or relating to a magnet or to magnetism **b :** of, relating to, or characterized by the earth's magnetism **c :** magnetized or capable of being magnetized **d :** actuated by magnetic attraction **2 :** possessing an extraordinary power or ability to attract <a ~ personality> — **mag·net·i·cal·ly** \-i-k(ə-)lē\ *adv*

[2]**magnetic** *n* **:** a magnetic substance

magnetic core *n* **:** CORE 1e(2)

magnetic equator *n* **:** ACLINIC LINE

magnetic field *n* **:** the portion of space near a magnetic body or a current carrying body in which the forces due to the body or current can be detected

magnetic flux *n* **:** lines of force used to represent magnetic induction

magnetic head *n* **:** an electromagnet used in magnetic recording for converting electrical signals into a magnetic record (as on tape), converting a magnetic recording into electrical signals, or erasing a magnetic recording

magnetic moment *n* **:** a vector quantity that is a measure of the torque exerted on a magnetic system (as a bar magnet or dipole) when placed in a magnetic field **:** the product of the distance between the poles of a magnet and the strength of either pole

magnetic needle *n* **:** a slender bar of magnetized steel that when suspended so as to be free to turn indicates the direction of a magnetic field in which it is placed and that constitutes the essential part of a compass

magnetic north *n* **:** the northerly direction in the earth's magnetic field indicated by the north-seeking pole of the horizontal magnetic needle

magnetic pole *n* **1 :** either of the poles of a magnet **2 :** either of two small nonstationary regions which are located respectively in the polar areas of the northern and southern hemispheres and toward which the compass needle points from any direction throughout adjacent regions; *also* **:** either of two comparable regions on a celestial body

magnetic quantum number *n* **:** an integer that expresses the component of the quantized angular momentum of an electron, atom, or molecule in the direction of an externally applied magnetic field

magnetic recording *n* **:** the process of recording sound, data (as for a computer), or a television program by producing varying local magnetization of a moving tape, wire, or disc — **magnetic recorder** *n*

magnetic resonance *n* **:** the response of electrons, atoms, molecules, or nuclei to various discrete radiation frequencies as a result of space quantization in a magnetic field

magnetic storm *n* **:** a marked temporary disturbance of the earth's magnetic field held to be related to sunspots

magnetic tape *n* **:** a ribbon of thin paper or plastic coated for use in magnetic recording

magnetic wire *n* **:** a thin wire used in magnetic recording

mag·ne·tism \ˈmag-nə-ˌtiz-əm\ *n* **1 a :** a class of physical phenomena that include the attraction for iron observed in lodestone and a magnet, are believed to be inseparably associated with moving electricity, are exhibited by both magnets and electric currents, and are characterized by fields of force **b :** a science that deals with magnetic phenomena **2 :** an ability to attract or charm

mag·ne·tite \ˈmag-nə-ˌtīt\ *n* **:** a black isometric mineral (Fe_3O_4) of the spinel group that is an oxide of iron and an important iron ore — **mag·ne·tit·ic** \ˌmag-nə-ˈtit-ik\ *adj*

mag·ne·ti·za·tion \ˌmag-nət-ə-ˈzā-shən\ *n* **:** a magnetizing or state of being magnetized; *also* **:** degree to which a body is magnetized

mag·ne·tize \ˈmag-nə-ˌtīz\ *vt* **-tized; -tiz·ing 1 :** to attract like a magnet **:** CHARM **2 :** to communicate magnetic properties to — **mag·ne·tiz·able** \-ˌtī-zə-bəl\ *adj* — **mag·ne·tiz·er** *n*

mag·ne·to \mag-ˈnēt-(ˌ)ō\ *n, pl* **-tos :** a magnetoelectric machine; *esp* **:** an alternator with permanent magnets used to generate current for the ignition in an internal-combustion engine

mag·ne·to·elec·tric \-ˌnēt-ō-ə-ˈlek-trik\ *adj* **:** relating to or characterized by electromotive forces developed by magnetic means <~ induction>

mag·ne·to·flu·id·dy·nam·ic \mag-ˈnēt-ō-ˌflü-əd-dī-ˈnam-ik, -ˈnet-, -də-\ *adj* **:** MAGNETOHYDRODYNAMIC — **mag·ne·to·flu·id·dy·nam·ics** \-iks\ *n pl but sing or pl in constr*

mag·ne·to·flu·id·me·chan·ic \-ˌflü-əd-mə-ˈkan-ik\ *adj* **:** MAGNETOHYDRODYNAMIC — **mag·ne·to·flu·id·me·chan·ics** \-iks\ *n pl but sing or pl in constr*

mag·ne·to·gas·dy·nam·ic \-ˌgas-dī-ˈnam-ik, -də-\ *adj* **:** MAGNETOHYDRODYNAMIC — **mag·ne·to·gas·dy·nam·ics** \-iks\ *n pl but sing or pl in constr*

mag·ne·to·graph \-ˌgraf\ *n* **:** an automatic instrument for recording measurements of a magnetic field (as of the earth or the sun)

mag·ne·to·hy·dro·dy·nam·ic \mag-ˈnēt-ō-ˌhī-drə-dī-ˈnam-ik, -ˈnet-, -də-\ *adj* **:** of or relating to phenomena arising from the motion of electrically conducting fluids in the presence of electric and magnetic fields — **mag·ne·to·hy·dro·dy·nam·ics** \-iks\ *n pl but sing or pl in constr*

mag·ne·tom·e·ter \ˌmag-nə-ˈtäm-ət-ər\ *n* **:** an instrument for measuring magnetic intensity esp. of the earth's magnetic field — **mag·ne·to·met·ric** \mag-ˌnēt-ə-ˈme-trik, -ˌnet-\ *adj* — **mag·ne·tom·e·try** \ˌmag-nə-ˈtäm-ə-trē\ *n*

mag·ne·to·mo·tive force \mag-ˌnēt-ə-ˌmōt-iv-, -ˌnet-\ *n* **:** a force that is the cause of a flux of magnetic induction

mag·ne·ton \ˈmag-nə-ˌtän\ *n* [ISV *magnet-* + [2]*-on*] **:** a unit of the quantized magnetic moment of a particle (as an atom)

mag·ne·to–op·tic \mag-ˌnēt-ō-ˈäp-tik, -ˌnet-\ *also* **mag·ne·to–op·ti·cal** \-ti-kəl\ *adj* **:** of or relating to the influence of a magnetic field upon light — **mag·ne·to–op·tics** \-tiks\ *n pl but sing or pl in constr*

mag·ne·to·pause \mag-ˈnēt-ə-ˌpȯz, -ˈnet-\ *n* [*magneto*sphere + L *pausa* stop — more at PAUSE] **:** the outer boundary of a magnetosphere

mag·ne·to·plas·ma·dy·nam·ic \mag-ˈnēt-ō-ˌplaz-mə-dī-ˈnam-ik, -ˈnet-, -də-\ *adj* [*magnet-* + *plasma* + *dynamic*] **:** MAGNETOHYDRODYNAMIC — **mag·ne·to·plas·ma·dy·nam·ics** \-iks\ *n pl but sing or pl in constr*

mag·ne·to·re·sis·tance \-ˌnēt-ō-ri-ˈzis-tən(t)s, -ˌnet-\ *n* **:** a change in electrical resistance due to the presence of a magnetic field

mag·ne·to·sphere \mag-ˈnēt-ə-ˌsfi(ə)r, -ˈnet-\ *n* **1 :** a region of the upper atmosphere that surrounds the earth, extends out for thousands of miles, and is dominated by the earth's magnetic field so that charged particles are trapped in it **2 :** a region that surrounds a celestial body (as a planet) and is comparable to the earth's magnetosphere in trapping charged particles — **mag·ne·to·spher·ic** \-ˌnēt-ə-ˈsfi(ə)r-ik, -ˈsfer-\ *adj*

mag·ne·to·stat·ic \mag-ˌnēt-ō-ˈstat-ik, -ˌnet-\ *adj* **:** of, relating to, or being a stationary magnetic field

mag·ne·to·stric·tion \-'strik-shən\ *n* [ISV *magnet-* + *-striction* (as in *constriction*)] : the change in the dimensions of a ferromagnetic body caused by a change in its state of magnetization — **mag·ne·to·stric·tive** \-'strik-tiv\ *adj* — **mag·ne·to·stric·tive·ly** *adv*

mag·ne·tron \'mag-nə-,trän\ *n* [blend of *magnet* and *-tron*] : a diode vacuum tube in which the flow of electrons is controlled by an externally applied magnetic field to generate power at microwave frequencies

mag·nif·ic \mag-'nif-ik\ *adj* [MF *magnifique,* fr. L *magnificus*] **1** : MAGNIFICENT 2 **2** : imposing in size or dignity **3 a** : SUBLIME, EXALTED **b** : characterized by grandiloquence : POMPOUS — **mag·nif·i·cal** \-i-kəl\ *adj* — **mag·nif·i·cal·ly** \-k(ə-)lē\ *adv*

mag·nif·i·cat \mag-'nif-i-,kat, män-'yif-i-,kät\ *n* [ME, fr. L, magnifies, fr. *magnificare* to magnify; fr. the first word of the canticle] **1** *cap* **a** : the canticle of the Virgin Mary in Luke 1:46–55 **b** : a musical setting for the Magnificat **2** : an utterance of praise

mag·ni·fi·ca·tion \,mag-nə-fə-'kā-shən\ *n* **1** : the act of magnifying **2 a** : the state of being magnified **b** : the apparent enlargement of an object by an optical instrument

mag·nif·i·cence \mag-'nif-ə-sən(t)s, məg-\ *n* [ME, fr. MF, fr. L *magnificentia,* fr. *magnificus* noble in character, magnificent, fr. *magnus* great — more at MUCH] **1** : the quality or state of being magnificent **2** : splendor of surroundings

mag·nif·i·cent \-sent\ *adj* **1** : great in deed or exalted in place — used only of former famous rulers <Lorenzo the *Magnificent*> **2** : marked by stately grandeur and lavishness <a ~ way of life> **3** : sumptuous in structure and adornment <a ~ cathedral>; *broadly* : strikingly beautiful or impressive <a ~ physique> **4** : impressive to the mind or spirit : SUBLIME <~ prose> **5** : exceptionally fine <a ~ day> ***syn*** see GRAND ***ant*** modest — **mag·nif·i·cent·ly** *adv*

mag·nif·i·co \mag-'nif-i-,kō\ *n, pl* **-coes** *or* **-cos** [It, fr. *magnifico,* adj., magnificent, fr. L *magnificus*] **1** : a nobleman of Venice **2** : a person of high position or distinguished appearance and manner

mag·ni·fi·er \'mag-nə-,fī(-ə)r\ *n* : one that magnifies; *esp* : a lens or combination of lenses that makes something appear larger

mag·ni·fy \'mag-nə-,fī\ *vb* **-fied; -fy·ing** [ME *magnifien,* fr. MF *magnifier,* fr. L *magnificare,* fr. *magnificus*] *vt* **1 a** : EXTOL, LAUD **b** : to cause to be held in greater esteem or respect **2 a** : to increase in significance : INTENSIFY **b** : EXAGGERATE **3** : to enlarge in fact or in appearance ~ *vi* : to have the power of causing objects to appear larger than they are

mag·nil·o·quence \mag-'nil-ə-kwən(t)s\ *n* [L *magniloquentia,* fr. *magniloquus* magniloquent, fr. *magnus* + *loqui* to speak] : the quality or state of being magniloquent

mag·nil·o·quent \-kwənt\ *adj* [back-formation fr. *magniloquence*] : speaking in or characterized by a high-flown often bombastic style or manner : GRANDILOQUENT — **mag·nil·o·quent·ly** *adv*

mag·ni·tude \'mag-nə-,t(y)üd\ *n* [ME, fr. L *magnitudo,* fr. *magnus*] **1 a** : great size or extent **b** (1) : spatial quality : SIZE (2) : QUANTITY, NUMBER (3) : volume of sound : LOUDNESS **2** : the importance, quality, or caliber of something **3** : a number representing the intrinsic or apparent brightness of a celestial body on a logarithmic scale in which a difference of one unit corresponds to the multiplication or division of the brightness of light by 2.512 **4** : a numerical quantitative measure expressed usu. as a multiple of a standard unit

mag·no·lia \mag-'nōl-yə\ *n* [NL, genus name, fr. Pierre *Magnol* †1715 Fr. botanist] : any of a genus (*Magnolia* of the family Magnoliaceae, the magnolia family) of No. American and Asian shrubs and trees with entire evergreen or deciduous leaves and usu. showy white, yellow, rose, or purple flowers appearing in early spring

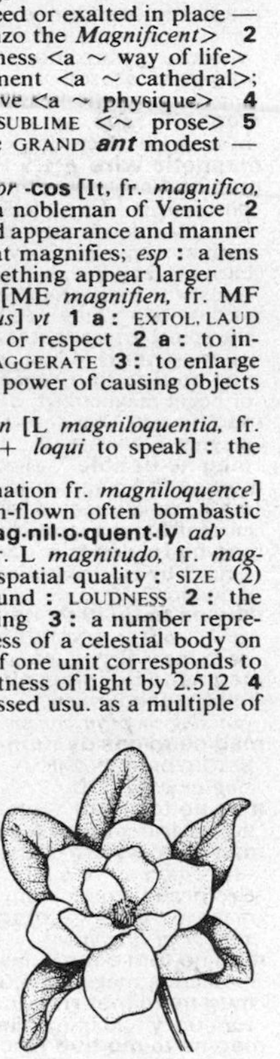

magnolia

mag·num \'mag-nəm\ *n* [L, neut. of *magnus* great] : a large wine bottle holding about ⅖ of a gallon

mag·num opus \,mag-nə-'mō-pəs\ *n* [L] : a great work; *esp* : the greatest achievement of an artist or writer

mag·pie \'mag-,pī\ *n* [*Mag* (nickname for *Margaret*) + *pie*] **1** : any of numerous birds (esp. of the genus *Pica*) related to the jays but having a long graduated tail and black-and-white plumage **2** : a person who chatters noisily

MAgr *abbr* master of agriculture

ma·guey \mə-'gā\ *n* [Sp, fr. Taino] **1** : any of various fleshy-leaved agaves; *also* : a plant (genus *Furcraea*) related to the agaves **2** : any of several hard fibers derived from magueys; *esp* : CANTALA

ma·gus \'mā-gəs\ *n, pl* **ma·gi** \'mā-,jī\ [ME, fr. L, fr. Gk *magos* — more at MAGIC] **1 a** : a member of a hereditary priestly class among the ancient Medes and Persians **b** *often cap* : one of the traditionally three wise men from the East paying homage to the infant Jesus **2** : MAGICIAN, SORCERER

Mag·yar \'mag-,yär, 'mäg-; 'mäj-,är\ *n* [Hung] **1** : a member of the dominant people of Hungary **2** : the Finno-Ugric language of the Magyars — **Magyar** *adj*

ma·ha·ra·ja *or* **ma·ha·ra·jah** \,mä-hə-'räj-ə, -'räzh-ə\ *n* [Skt *mahārāja,* fr. *mahat* great + *rājan* raja; akin to Gk *megas* great — more at MUCH] : a Hindu prince ranking above a raja

ma·ha·ra·ni *or* **ma·ha·ra·nee** \-'rän-ē\ *n* [Hindi *mahārānī,* fr. *mahā* great (fr. Skt *mahat*) + *rānī* rani] **1** : the wife of a maharaja **2** : a Hindu princess ranking above a rani

ma·ha·ri·shi \mə-'här-ə-shē\ *n* [Skt *mahārṣi,* fr. *mahat* + *ṛṣi* sage and poet] : a Hindu teacher of mystical knowledge

ma·hat·ma \mə-'hät-mə, -'hat-\ *n* [Skt *mahātman,* fr. *mahātman* great-souled, fr. *mahat* + *ātman* soul — more at ATMAN] **1** : a person to be revered for high-mindedness, wisdom, and selflessness **2** : a person of great prestige in a field of endeavor

Ma·ha·ya·na \,mä-hə-'yän-ə\ *n* [Skt *mahāyāna,* lit., great vehicle] : a liberal and theistic branch of Buddhism comprising sects chiefly in Tibet, China, and Japan, recognizing a large body of scripture in addition to the Pali canon, and teaching social concern and universal salvation — compare THERAVADA — **Ma·ha·ya·nist** \-'yan-əst\ *n* — **Ma·ha·ya·nis·tic** \-yä-'nis-tik\ *adj*

Mah·di \'mäd-ē\ *n* [Ar *mahdīy,* lit., one rightly guided] **1** : the expected messiah of Muslim tradition **2** : a Muslim leader who assumes a messianic role — **Mah·dism** \'mäd-,iz-əm\ *n* — **Mah·dist** \'mäd-əst\ *n*

Ma·hi·can \mə-'hē-kən\ *n, pl* **Mahican** *or* **Mahicans** [Mahican] **1** : a member of an Amerindian people of the upper Hudson river valley **2** : the language of the Mahican people

Mah–Jongg \(')mäzh-'äŋ, (')mäj-, -'ȯŋ, 'mäzh-,, 'mäj-,\ *trademark* — used for a game of Chinese origin usu. played by 4 persons with 144 tiles that are drawn and discarded until one player secures a winning hand

mahl·stick \'mȯl-\ *var of* MAULSTICK

ma·hoe \mə-'hō, 'mä-,\ *n* [F *maho,* fr. Taino] : any of various tropical trees with strong bast fibers: as **a** : MAJAGUA **b** : a West Indian tree (*Daphnopsis caribaea* of the family Thymelacaceae)

ma·hog·a·ny \mə-'häg-ə-nē\ *n, pl* **-nies** [origin unknown] **1** : the wood of any of various chiefly tropical trees (family Meliaceae, the mahogany family): **a** (1) : the durable yellowish brown to reddish brown usu. moderately hard and heavy wood of a West Indian tree (*Swietenia mahogani*) that is widely used for cabinetwork and fine finish work (2) : a wood similar to mahogany from a congeneric tree **b** (1) : the rather hard heavy usu. odorless wood of any of several African trees (genus *Khaya*) (2) : the rather lightweight cedar-scented wood of any of several African trees (genus *Entandrophragma*) that varies in color from pinkish to deep reddish brown **2** : any of various woods resembling or substituted for mahogany obtained from trees of the mahogany family **3** : a tree that yields mahogany **4** : a moderate reddish brown

ma·ho·nia \mə-'hō-nē-ə\ *n* [NL, genus name, fr. Bernard McMahon †1816 Am botanist] : any of a genus (*Mahonia*) of No. American and Asiatic shrubs of the barberry family

Ma·hound *n* [ME *Mahun, Mahoun,* fr. OF *Mahom, Mahun,* short for *Mahomet*] **1** \mə-'hünd, -'hau̇nd\ *archaic* : Muhammad **2** \-'hün\ *Scot* : DEVIL

ma·hout \mə-'hau̇t\ *n* [Hindi *mahāwat, mahāut*] : a keeper and driver of an elephant

mah·rat·ta *var of* MARATHA

maid \'mād\ *n* [ME *maide,* short for *maiden*] **1** : an unmarried girl or woman esp. when young : VIRGIN **2** : a female servant

¹maid·en \'mād-ᵊn\ *n* [ME, fr. OE *mægden, mæden,* dim. of *mægeth;* akin to OHG *magad* maiden, OIr *mug* serf, *macc* son] **1** : an unmarried girl or woman : MAID **2** : a former Scottish beheading device resembling the guillotine **3** : a horse that has never won a race

²maiden *adj* **1 a** (1) : not married <~ aunt> (2) : VIRGIN **b** *of a female animal* (1) : never yet mated (2) : never having borne young **2** : of, relating to, or befitting a maiden **3** : FIRST, EARLIEST <the ship's ~ voyage> **4** : INTACT, FRESH

maid·en·hair \-,ha(ə)r, -,he(ə)r\ *n* : any of a genus (*Adiantum*) of ferns with delicate palmately branched fronds — called also *maidenhair fern*

maidenhair tree *n* : GINKGO

maid·en·head \'mād-ᵊn-,hed\ *n* [ME *maidenhed,* fr. *maiden* + *-hed* -hood; akin to ME *-hod* -hood] **1** : the quality or state of being a maiden : VIRGINITY **2** : HYMEN

maid·en·hood \-,hu̇d\ *n* : the quality, state, or time of being a maiden

maid·en·li·ness \-lē-nəs\ *n* : conduct or traits befitting a maiden

maid·en·ly \-lē\ *adj* : of, resembling, or suitable to a maiden

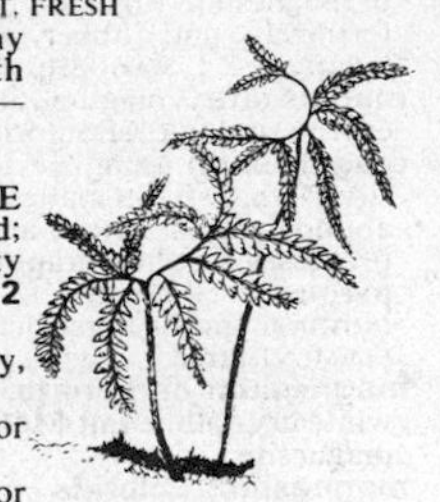
maidenhair

maiden name *n* : the surname of a woman before she married

maid·hood \'mād-,hu̇d\ *n* : MAIDENHOOD

maid–in–wait·ing \,mād-ᵊn-'wāt-iŋ\ *n, pl* **maids–in–wait·ing** \,mād-zən-\ : a young woman of a queen's or princess's household appointed to attend her

Maid Mar·i·an \-'mer-ē-ən, -'mar-\ *n* : a companion of Robin Hood in some forms of his legend

maid of honor **1** : an unmarried lady usu. of noble birth whose duty it is to attend a queen or a princess **2** : a bride's principal unmarried wedding attendant

maid·ser·vant \'mād-,sər-vənt\ *n* : a female servant

ma·ieu·tic \mā-'yüt-ik, mī-\ *adj* [Gk *maieutikos* of midwifery] : relating to or resembling the Socratic method of eliciting new ideas from another

¹mail \'mā(ə)l\ *n* [ME *male, maille,* fr. OE *māl* agreement, pay, fr. ON *māl* speech, agreement; akin to OE *mǣl* speech, *mōt* meeting — more at MEET] *chiefly Scot* : PAYMENT, RENT

²mail *n, often attrib* [ME *male,* fr. OF, of Gmc origin; akin to OHG *malaha* bag] **1** *chiefly Scot* : BAG, WALLET **2 a** : the bags of letters and the other postal matter conveyed under public authority from one post office to another **b** : the postal matter consigned at one time to or from one person or one post office or conveyed by a particular train, airplane, or ship **c** : a conveyance that transports mail **3 a** : a nation's postal system — often used in pl. **b** : postal matter

³mail *vt* : to send by mail : POST

⁴mail *n* [ME *maille,* fr. MF, fr. L *macula* spot, mesh] **1** : armor made of metal links or sometimes plates **2** : a hard enclosing covering of an animal (as a tortoise) — **mailed** \'mā(ə)ld\ *adj*

⁵mail *vt* : to arm with mail

mail·able \'mā-lə-bəl\ *adj* : adapted for mailing : legally admissible as mail — **mail·abil·i·ty** \,mā-lə-'bil-ət-ē\ *n*

mail·bag \'mā(ə)l-,bag\ *n* **1** : a letter carrier's shoulder bag **2** : a pouch used in the shipment of mail

mail·box \-ˌbäks\ *n* **1 :** a public box for deposit of outgoing mail **2 :** a box at or near a dwelling for the occupant's mail
mail drop *n* **1 :** a receptacle or a slot for deposit of mail **2 :** an address used in transmitting secret communications
mai·le \ˈmī-lē\ *n* [Hawaiian] **:** a Pacific island vine (*Alyxia olivaeformis* of the family Apocynaceae) with fragrant leaves and bark that are used for decoration and in Hawaii for leis
mailed fist *n* **:** a threat of armed force
mail·er \ˈmā-lər\ *n* **1 :** one that mails **2 :** a machine for addressing mail matter **3 :** a container for mailing something
¹mail·ing \ˈmā-liŋ\ *n* [ME *mailling,* fr. *maille* rent] **1** *Scot* **:** a rented farm **2** *Scot* **:** the rent paid for a farm
²mailing *n* **:** the mail dispatched at one time by a sender
mail·lot \mī-ˈō, mä-ˈyō\ *n* [F] **1 :** tights for dancers or gymnasts **2 :** JERSEY 2 **3 :** a woman's one-piece bathing suit
mail·man \ˈmā(ə)l-ˌman\ *n* **:** a man who delivers mail — called also *postman*
mail order *n* **:** an order for goods that is received and filled by mail
mail-order house *n* **:** a retail establishment whose business is conducted by mail
¹maim \ˈmām\ *vt* [ME *maynhen, maymen,* fr. OF *maynier*] **1 :** to commit the felony of mayhem upon **2 :** to mutilate, disfigure, or wound seriously **:** CRIPPLE — **maim·er** *n*
syn MAIM, CRIPPLE, MUTILATE, BATTER, MANGLE *shared meaning element* **:** to injure so severely as to cause lasting damage
²maim *n* **1** *obs* **:** serious physical injury; *esp* **:** loss of a member of the body **2** *obs* **:** a serious loss
¹main \ˈmān\ *n* [in sense 1, fr. ME, fr. OE *maegen;* akin to OHG *magan* strength, OE *magan* to be able; in other senses, fr. ²*main* or by shortening — more at MAY] **1 :** physical strength **:** FORCE — used in the phrase *with might and main* **2 a :** MAINLAND **b :** HIGH SEA **3 :** the chief part **:** essential point <men who are in the ~ well-trained> **4 :** a pipe, duct, or circuit to or from which lead tributary branches of a utility system and which carries their combined flow **5 a :** MAINMAST **b :** MAINSAIL
²main *adj* [ME, fr. OE *maegen-,* fr. *maegen* strength] **1 :** CHIEF, PRINCIPAL **2 :** fully exerted **:** SHEER <~ force> <by ~ strength> **3** *obs* **:** of or relating to a broad expanse (as of sea) **4 :** connected with or located near the mainmast or mainsail **5 :** expressing the chief predication in a complex sentence <the ~ clause>
³main *n* [prob. fr. ²*main*] **1 :** a number exceeding four and not exceeding nine called by the caster in the game of hazard before throwing **2 :** a cockfight series consisting of an odd number of matches
main·frame \ˈmān-ˌfrām\ *n* **:** COMPUTER; *esp* **:** the computer itself and its cabinet as distinguished from peripheral devices connected with it
main·land \ˈmān-ˌland, -lənd\ *n* **:** a continent or the main part of a continent as distinguished from an offshore island or sometimes from a cape or peninsula — **main·land·er** \-ər\ *n*
main·line \ˈmān-ˈlīn\ *vi, slang* **:** to inject a narcotic drug (as heroin) into a principal vein
main line *n* **1 :** a principal highway or railroad line **2** *slang* **a :** a principal vein <a shot of heroin in the *main line*> **b :** injection of a narcotic into a principal vein
main·lin·er \-ˈlī-nər\ *n, slang* **:** one that mainlines
main·ly \ˈmān-lē\ *adv* **1** *obs* **:** in a forceful manner **2 :** for the most part **:** CHIEFLY
main·mast \ˈmān-ˌmast, -məst\ *n* **:** a sailing ship's principal mast usu. second from the bow
mains \ˈmānz\ *n pl but sing in constr* [short for *domains*] *dial Brit* **:** the home farm of a manor
main·sail \ˈmān-ˌsāl, ˈmān(t)-səl\ *n* **:** the principal sail on the mainmast — see SAIL illustration
main·sheet \ˈmān-ˌshēt\ *n* **:** a rope by which the mainsail is trimmed and secured
main·spring \ˈmān-ˌspriŋ\ *n* **1 :** the chief spring in a mechanism esp. of a watch or clock **2 :** the chief or most powerful motive, agent, or cause
main·stay \-ˌstā\ *n* **1 :** a ship's stay extending from the maintop forward usu. to the foot of the foremast **2 :** a chief support
main stem *n* **:** a main trunk or channel: as **a :** the main course of a stream **b :** the main line of a railroad **c :** the main street of a city or town
main·stream \ˈmān-ˌstrēm\ *n* **:** a prevailing current or direction of activity or influence — **mainstream** *adj*
Main Street *n* **1 :** the principal street of a small town **2 a :** the sections of a country centering about its small towns **b :** a place or environment characterized by materialistic self-complacent provincialism — **Main Street·er** \ˈmān-ˌstrēt-ər\ *n*
main·tain \mān-ˈtān, mən-\ *vt* [ME *mainteinen,* fr. OF *maintenir,* fr. ML *manutenēre,* fr. L *manu tenēre* to hold in the hand] **1 :** to keep in an existing state (as of repair, efficiency, or validity) **:** preserve from failure or decline <~ one's health> <~ machinery> **2 :** to sustain against opposition or danger **:** uphold and defend <~ a position> **3 :** to continue or preserve in **:** carry on **:** keep up <couldn't ~ his composure> **4 a :** to support or provide for **:** bear the expense of <has a family to ~> **b :** SUSTAIN <enough food to ~ life> **5 :** to affirm in or as if in argument **:** ASSERT <~*ed* that all men are not equal> — **main·tain·abil·i·ty** \-ˌtā-nə-ˈbil-ət-ē\ *n* — **main·tain·able** \-ˈtā-nə-bəl\ *adj* — **main·tain·er** *n*
syn MAINTAIN, ASSERT, DEFEND, VINDICATE, JUSTIFY *shared meaning element* **:** to uphold as true, right, just, or reasonable
main·te·nance \ˈmānt-nən(t)s, -ᵊn-ən(t)s\ *n* [ME, fr. MF, fr. OF, fr. *maintenir*] **1 :** the act of maintaining **:** the state of being maintained **:** SUPPORT **2 :** something that maintains **3 :** the upkeep of property or equipment **4 :** an officious or unlawful intermeddling in a legal suit by assisting either party with means to carry it on
main·top \ˈmān-ˌtäp\ *n* **:** a platform about the head of the mainmast of a square-rigged ship
main-top·mast \mān-ˈtäp-ˌmast, -məst\ *n* **:** a mast next above the mainmast
main yard *n* **:** the yard of a mainsail
maiolica *var of* MAJOLICA
mair \ˈmār\ *chiefly Scot var of* MORE
mai·son·ette \ˌmāz-ᵊn-ˈet, ˌmās-\ *n* [F *maisonnette,* fr. OF, dim. of *maison* house, fr. L *mansion-, mansio* dwelling place — more at MANSION] **1 :** a small house **2 :** an apartment often on two floors
mai·tre d' \ˌmā-trə-ˈdē, ˌme-; ˌmāt-ər-ˈdē, ˌmet-\ *n, pl* **maitre d's** \-ˈdēz\ **:** MAÎTRE D'HÔTEL
mai·tre d'hô·tel \ˌmā-trə-(ˌ)dō-ˈtel, ˌme-; ˌmāt-dō-, ˌmet-\ *n, pl* **maitres d'hôtel** *same*\ [F, lit., master of house] **1 a :** MAJORDOMO **b :** HEADWAITER **2 :** a sauce of butter, parsley, salt, pepper, and lemon juice
maize \ˈmāz\ *n* [Sp *maíz,* fr. Taino *mahiz*] **:** INDIAN CORN
Maj *abbr* major
ma·ja·gua \mə-ˈhäg-wə\ *n* [AmerSp, fr. Taino] **:** either of two tropical trees of the mallow family that are often considered variant forms of a single species: **a :** an irregularly spreading or shrubby tree (*Hibiscus tilaceus*) that yields a light tough wood and a fibrous bast **b :** an erect forest tree (*H. elatus*) of the West Indian uplands that yields a moderately dense timber with variegated heartwood that is used esp. for cabinetwork and the stocks of guns
ma·jes·tic \mə-ˈjes-tik\ *adj* **:** having or exhibiting majesty **:** STATELY *syn* see GRAND — **ma·jes·ti·cal** \-ti-kəl\ *adj* — **ma·jes·ti·cal·ly** \-ti-k(ə-)lē\ *adv*
maj·es·ty \ˈmaj-ə-stē\ *n, pl* **-ties** [ME *maieste,* fr. OF *majesté,* fr. L *majestat-, majestas;* akin to L *major* greater] **1 :** sovereign power, authority, or dignity **2 —** used in addressing or referring to reigning sovereigns and their consorts <Your *Majesty*> <Her *Majesty's* Government> **3 a :** royal bearing or aspect **:** GRANDEUR **b :** greatness or splendor of quality or character
Maj Gen *abbr* major general
ma·jol·i·ca \mə-ˈjäl-i-kə\ *also* **ma·iol·i·ca** \-ˈyäl-\ *n* [It *maiolica,* fr. ML *Majolica* Majorca, fr. LL *Majorca*] **1 :** earthenware covered with an opaque tin glaze and decorated on the glaze before firing; *esp* **:** an Italian ware of this kind **2 :** a 19th century earthenware modeled in naturalistic shapes and glazed in lively colors
¹ma·jor \ˈmā-jər\ *adj* [ME *maiour,* fr. L *major,* compar. of *magnus* great, large — more at MUCH] **1 :** greater in dignity, rank, importance, or interest <one of the ~ poets> **2 :** greater in number, quantity, or extent <the ~ part of his work> **3 :** having attained majority **4 :** notable or conspicuous in effect or scope **:** CONSIDERABLE <a ~ improvement> **5 :** involving grave risk **:** SERIOUS <a ~ illness> **6 a :** of or relating to a subject of academic study chosen as a field of specialization **b :** of or relating to a secondary-school course requiring a maximum of classroom hours **7 a :** having half steps between the third and fourth and the seventh and eighth degrees <~ scale> **b :** based on a major scale <~ key> **c :** equivalent to the distance between the keynote and another tone (except the fourth and fifth) of a major scale <~ third> **d :** containing a major third <~ triad>
²major *n* **1 :** a person having attained majority **2 a :** one that is superior in rank, importance, station, or performance **b :** a major musical interval, scale, key, or mode **3 :** a commissioned officer in the army, air force, or marine corps ranking above a captain and below a lieutenant colonel **4 a :** a subject of academic study chosen as a field of specialization **b :** a student specializing in such a field <he is a history ~> **5** *pl* **:** major league baseball
³major *vi* **ma·jored; ma·jor·ing** \ˈmāj-(ə-)riŋ\ **:** to pursue an academic major
major axis *n* **:** the axis passing through the foci of an ellipse
ma·jor·do·mo \ˌmā-jər-ˈdō-(ˌ)mō\ *n, pl* **-mos** [Sp *mayordomo* or obs. It *maiordomo,* fr. ML *major domus,* lit., chief of the house] **1 :** a man having charge of a large household (as a palace) **:** a head steward **2 :** BUTLER, STEWARD
majorette *n* **:** DRUM MAJORETTE 2
major form class *n* **:** one of the parts of speech of traditional grammar (as noun, verb, or preposition)
major general *n* [F *major général,* fr. *major,* n. + *général,* adj., general] **:** a commissioned officer in the army, air force, or marine corps who ranks above a brigadier general and whose insignia is two stars
ma·jor·i·tar·i·an \mə-ˌjór-ə-ˈter-ē-ən, -ˌjär-\ *n* **:** one that believes in or advocates majoritarianism — **majoritarian** *adj*
ma·jor·i·tar·i·an·ism \-ē-ə-ˌniz-əm\ *n* **:** the philosophy or practice according to which decisions of an organized group should be made by a numerical majority of its members
ma·jor·i·ty \mə-ˈjór-ət-ē, -ˈjär-\ *n, pl* **-ties** **1** *obs* **:** the quality or state of being greater **:** SUPERIORITY **2 a :** the age at which full civil rights are accorded; *esp* **:** the age of 21 **b :** the status of one who has attained this age **3 a :** a number greater than half of a total **b :** the excess of a majority over the remainder of the total **:** MARGIN **c :** the preponderant quantity or share **4 :** the group or political party whose votes preponderate **5 :** the military office, rank, or commission of a major
majority leader *n* **:** a leader of the majority party in a legislative body (as the U.S. Senate)
majority rule *n* **:** a political principle providing that a majority usu. constituted by fifty percent plus one of an organized group will have the power to make decisions binding upon the whole
major league *n* **:** a league of highest classification in U.S. professional baseball; *broadly* **:** a league of major importance in any of various sports
major order *n* **:** one of the Roman Catholic or Eastern clerical orders that are sacramentally conferred and have a sacred character that implies major religious obligations (as clerical celibacy) — usu. used in pl.; compare MINOR ORDER

major party *n* **:** a political party having electoral strength sufficient to permit it to win control of a government usu. with comparative regularity and when defeated to constitute the principal opposition to the party in power
major penalty *n* **:** a 5-minute suspension of a player in ice hockey
major premise *n* **:** the premise of a syllogism containing the major term
major seminary *n* **:** a Roman Catholic seminary giving usu. the entire six years of senior college and theological training required for major orders
major suit *n* **:** either of two bridge suits of superior scoring value: **a :** SPADES **b :** HEARTS
major term *n* **:** the term of a syllogism constituting the predicate of the conclusion
ma·jus·cule \ˈmaj-əs-ˌkyü(ə)l, mə-ˈjəs-\ *n* [F, fr. L *majusculus* rather large, dim. of *major*] **:** a large letter (as a capital) — **ma·jus·cu·lar** \mə-ˈjəs-kyə-lər\ *adj* — **majuscule** *adj*
mak·able *or* **make·able** \ˈmā-kə-bəl\ *adj* **:** capable of being made
mak·ar \ˈmäk-ər, ˈmāk-\ *n* [ME *maker*] *chiefly Scot* **:** POET
[1]**make** \ˈmāk\ *vb* **made** \ˈmād\; **mak·ing** [ME *maken*, fr. OE *macian*; akin to OHG *mahhōn* to prepare, make, OSlav *mazati* to anoint] *vt* **1 a** *obs* **:** BEHAVE, ACT **b :** to seem to begin (an action) <he *made* to go> **2 a :** to cause to happen to or be experienced by someone <*made* trouble for him> **b :** to cause to exist, occur, or appear **:** CREATE <~ a disturbance> **c :** to favor the growth or occurrence of <haste ~*s* waste> **d :** to fit, intend, or destine by or as if by creating <was *made* to be an actor> **3 a :** to bring into being by forming, shaping, or altering material **:** FASHION <~ a dress> **b :** COMPOSE, WRITE <~ verses> **c :** to lay out and construct <~ a road> **4 :** to frame or formulate in the mind <~ plans> **5 :** to put together from components **:** CONSTITUTE <houses *made* of stone> **6 a :** to compute or estimate to be **b :** to form and hold in the mind <~ no doubt of it> **7 a :** to assemble and set alight the materials for (a fire) **b :** to set in order <~ beds> **c :** PREPARE, FIX <~ dinner> **d :** to shuffle (a deck of cards) in preparation for dealing **8 :** to prepare (hay) by cutting, drying, and storing **9 a :** to cause to be or become <*made* himself useful> **b :** APPOINT <*made* him bishop> **10 a :** ENACT, ESTABLISH <~ laws> **b :** to execute in an appropriate manner <~ a will> **c :** SET, NAME <~ a price> **11 a** *chiefly dial* **:** to make fast **:** SHUT **b:** to cause (an electric circuit) to be completed **12 a:** to conclude as to the nature or meaning of <didn't know what to ~ of his actions> **b :** to regard as being <not the fool some ~ him> **13 a :** to carry out (an action indicated or implied by the object) <~ war> <~ a speech> <*made* his lunch on bread and cheese> **b :** to perform with a bodily movement <~ a sweeping gesture> **c :** to achieve by traversing <~ a detour> <a mailman *making* his rounds> **14 a :** to produce as a result of action, effort, or behavior with respect to something <~ a mess of the job> <tried to ~ a thorough job of it> **b** *archaic* **:** to turn into another language by translation **15 :** to cause to act in a certain way **:** COMPEL <~ him return> **16 :** to cause or assure the success or prosperity of <anyone he takes a liking to is *made*> **17 a :** to amount to in significance <~*s* a great difference> **b :** to form the essential being of <clothes ~ the man> **c :** to form by an assembling of individuals <~ a quorum> **d :** to count as <that ~*s* the third time he's said it> **18 a :** to be or be capable of being changed or fashioned into <rags ~ the best paper> **b :** to develop into <she will ~ a fine wife> **c :** FORM 5b **19 a :** REACH, ATTAIN — often used with *it* <you'll never ~ it that far> **b :** to gain the rank of <~ major> **c :** to gain a place on or in <~ the team> <the story *made* the papers> **20 :** to gain (as money) by working, trading, or dealing **21 a :** to act so as to win or acquire <~*s* friends easily> **b :** to score (points) in a game or sport **c :** to convert (a split) into a spare in bowling **22 a :** to fulfill (a contract) in a card game **b :** to win a trick with (a card) **23 a :** to include in a route or itinerary <~ New York on the return trip> **b :** CATCH <*made* the bus just in time> **24 :** to persuade to consent to sexual intercourse ~ *vi* **1** *archaic* **:** to compose poetry **2 a :** BEHAVE, ACT **b :** to begin or seem to begin a certain action <*made* as though to hand it to me> **c :** to act so as to be or to seem to be <~ merry> **d** *slang* **:** to play a part — usu. used with *like* **3 :** to set out **:** HEAD <*made* after the fox> **4 :** to increase in height or size <the tide is *making* now> **5 :** to reach or extend in a certain direction **6 :** to have weight or effect **:** TELL <courtesy ~*s* for safer driving> **7 :** to undergo manufacture or processing <the silk ~*s* up beautifully>
syn MAKE, FORM, SHAPE, FASHION, FABRICATE, MANUFACTURE *shared meaning element* **:** to cause to come into being
— **make a face :** to distort one's features **:** GRIMACE — **make a mountain out of a molehill :** to treat a trifling matter as of great importance — **make away with 1 :** to carry off **2 :** SPEND, DISSIPATE **3 :** DESTROY, KILL **4 :** CONSUME, EAT — **make believe :** PRETEND, FEIGN — **make bold :** VENTURE, DARE — **make book :** to accept bets at calculated odds on all the entrants in a race or contest — **make do :** to get along or manage with the means at hand — **make ends meet :** to make one's means adequate to one's needs — **make eyes :** OGLE — **make fun of :** to make an object of amusement or laughter **:** RIDICULE, MOCK — **make good 1 :** to make valid or complete as: **a :** to make up for (a deficiency) **b :** INDEMNIFY <*make good* the loss> **c :** to carry out (a promise or prediction) **:** FULFILL **d :** PROVE <*make good* a charge> **2 :** to prove to be capable; *also* **:** SUCCEED — **make hay :** to make use of offered opportunity esp. in gaining an early advantage — **make head 1 :** to make progress esp. against resistance **2 :** to rise in armed revolt **3 :** to build up pressure (as in a steam boiler) — **make it 1 :** to be successful <trying to *make it* in the big time as a fashion photographer —Joe Kane> **2 :** to have sexual intercourse — **make light of :** to treat as of little account — **make love 1 :** WOO, COURT **2 a :** NECK, PET **b :** to engage in sexual intercourse — **make much of 1 :** to treat as of importance **2 :** to treat with obvious affection or special consideration — **make no bones :** to be straightforward, unhesitating, or sure <*makes no bones* about giving his opinion on the matter> — **make public :** DISCLOSE — **make sail 1 :** to raise or spread sail **2 :** to set out on a voyage — **make time 1 :** to travel fast **2 :** to gain time **3 :** to make progress toward winning favor <trying to *make time* with the waitress> — **make tracks 1 :** to proceed at a walk or run **2 :** to go in a hurry **:** run away **:** FLEE — **make water 1** *of a boat* **:** LEAK **2 :** URINATE — **make waves :** to create a stir or disturbance — **make way 1 :** to give room for passing, entering, or occupying <the crowd *made way* for the ambulance> <tore down the building to *make way* for a new parking lot> **2 :** to make progress <the ship could not *make way* against the winds> — **make with** *slang* **:** PRODUCE, PERFORM — usu. used with *the*
[2]**make** *n* **1 a :** the manner or style in which a thing is constructed **b :** BRAND 4 **2 :** the physical, mental, or moral constitution of a person <men of his ~ are rare> **3 a :** the action of producing or manufacturing **b :** the actual yield or amount produced over a specified period **:** OUTPUT **4 :** the declaration of trumps in an early form of bridge **5 :** the closing or completing of an electric circuit **6 :** the act of shuffling cards; *also* **:** turn to shuffle — **on the make 1 :** in the process of forming, growing, or improving **2 :** in quest of a higher social or financial status **3 :** in search of sexual adventure
make·bate \ˈmāk-ˌbāt\ *n* [[1]*make* + obs. *bate* (strife)] *archaic* **:** one that excites contention and quarrels
[1]**make–be·lieve** \ˈmāk-bə-ˌlēv\ *n* **:** a pretending to believe ***syn*** see PRETENSE
[2]**make–believe** *adj* **:** IMAGINARY, PRETENDED <the child wrote about ~ characters and situations>
make–do \ˈmāk-ˌdü\ *adj* **:** MAKESHIFT — **make–do** *n*
make·fast \-ˌfast\ *n* **:** something (as a post or buoy) to which a boat can be fastened
make off *vi* **:** to leave in haste — **make off with :** to take away **:** GRAB, STEAL
make out *vt* **1 :** to fill in (as a printed form) <*make out* a check> **2 :** to find or grasp the meaning of <tried to *make out* what had really happened> **3 :** to form an opinion or idea about **:** CONCLUDE <how do you *make* that *out*> **4 :** to pretend to be true <*made out* that he had never heard of me> **5 :** to represent or delineate in detail <every detail of the landscape was faithfully *made out*> **6 :** to see and identify with difficulty or effort **:** DISCERN <*make out* a ship through the fog> ~ *vi* **1 :** to get along **:** FARE <how is he *making out* with his new job> **2 :** to engage in sexual intercourse **3 :** NECK
make over *vt* **1 :** to transfer the title of (property) **2 :** REMAKE, REMODEL <*made* the whole house *over*>
mak·er \ˈmā-kər\ *n* **:** one that makes: as **a** *cap* **:** GOD 1 **b** *archaic* **:** POET **c :** a person who borrows money on a promissory note **d :** a declarer in bridge **e :** MANUFACTURER
syn MAKER, CREATOR, AUTHOR *shared meaning element* **:** one who brings something new into being or existence. Written with an initial capital letter all three terms designate God or the Supreme Being; without the capital they ascribe comparable but not equivalent effects and powers to a person. MAKER is likely to imply a close and immediate relationship between the one who makes and the thing that is made and an ensuing responsibility or concern for what is turned out; hence, God is often called one's Maker (as in hymns and prayers). In many of its human applications (as in king*maker*, a *maker* of men, a *maker* of phrases) *maker* suggests the use of appropriate material as an instrument through which one gives form to one's own ideas. CREATOR stresses a bringing into existence of what the mind conceives; in application to God it is likely to emphasize omnipotence and the greatness of his works <touched their golden harps, and hymning praised God and his works; *Creator* him they sung —John Milton> In relation to human endeavor *creator* is likely to suggest originality and delving into the unknown <they are genuine *creators:* they do not describe nor interpret reality as much as construct it —Howard Moss> AUTHOR applies to one who originates and is the source of something's being and is, therefore, wholly responsible for its existence. It is applied to God chiefly in the phrase "Author of one's being" when the reference is to the gift of life and its attending circumstances. In application to persons it is aptly applicable to a writer <the *author* of several books> or to one who (as a founder, an initiator, or an inventor) brings something new into existence <the policy of which he was principally the *author* —Hilaire Belloc>
make·ready \ˈmā-ˌkred-ē\ *n* **:** final preparation (as of a form on a printing press) for running; *also* **:** material used in this preparation
make·shift \ˈmāk-ˌshift\ *n* **:** a usu. crude and temporary expedient **:** SUBSTITUTE ***syn*** see RESOURCE — **makeshift** *adj*
make·up \ˈmā-ˌkəp\ *n* **1 a :** the way in which the parts or ingredients of something are put together **:** COMPOSITION **b :** physical, mental, and moral constitution **2 :** the operation of making up (as of matter for printing); *also* **:** the arrangement of such matter **3 a :** cosmetics used to color and beautify the face; *also* **:** a cosmetic applied to other parts of the body **b :** materials (as wigs and cosmetics) used in making up or in special costuming (as for a play)
make up \(ˈ)mā-ˈkəp\ *vt* **1 a :** INVENT, IMPROVISE <*make up* a story> **b :** to set (an account) in order **:** BALANCE **2 a :** to form by fitting together or assembling <*make up* a train of cars> **b :** to arrange type matter into (columns or pages) for printing **3 :** to wrap or fasten up <*make* the books *up* into a parcel> **4 :** to make good (a deficiency) **5 :** SETTLE, DECIDE <*made up* his mind to depart> **6 a :** to prepare in physical appearance for a role **b :** to apply cosmetics to ~ *vi* **1 :** to become reconciled <quarreled but later *made up*> **2 a :** to act ingratiatingly and flatteringly <*made up* to his aunt for a new bicycle> **b :** to make advances **:** COURT **3 :** COMPENSATE <*make up* for lost time> **4 a :** to put on costumes or makeup (as for a play) **b :** to apply cosmetics
make·weight \ˈmā-ˌkwāt\ *n* **1 a :** something thrown into a scale to bring the weight to a desired value **b :** something of little in-

dependent value thrown in to fill a gap **2** : COUNTERWEIGHT, COUNTERPOISE

make–work \'mā-ˌkwərk\ *n* : work assigned chiefly to keep one busy

ma·ki·mo·no \ˌmäk-i-'mō-(ˌ)nō\ *n, pl* **-nos** [Jap, scroll, fr. *maki* roll + *mono* thing] : a horizontal Japanese ornamental pictorial or calligraphic scroll

mak·ing \'mā-kiŋ\ *n* **1** : the act or process of forming, causing, doing, or coming into being <spots problems in the ~> **2** : a process or means of advancement or success **3** : something made; *esp* : a quantity produced at one time : BATCH **4 a** : POTENTIALITY — often used in pl. <had the ~*s* of a great artist> **b** *pl* : the material from which something is to be made; *esp* *usu* 'mā-kənz\ : paper and tobacco used by one who rolls his own cigarettes

ma·ko \'mäk-(ˌ)ō\ *n, pl* **makos** [Maori] : either of two mackerel sharks (*Isurus glaucus* and *I. oxyrhynchus*) that are notable sport fish and are considered dangerous to man — called also *mako shark*

makuta *pl of* LIKUTA

Mal *abbr* Malachi

mal- *comb form* [ME, fr. MF, fr. OF, fr. *mal* bad (fr. L *malus*) & *mal* badly, fr. L *male*, fr. *malus* — more at SMALL] **1 a** : bad <*mal*practice> **b** : badly <*mal*odorous> **2 a** : abnormal <*mal*formation> **b** : abnormally <*mal*formed> **3 a** : inadequate <*mal*adjustment> **b** : inadequately <*mal*nourished>

mal·ab·sorp·tion \ˌmal-əb-'sȯrp-shən, -'zȯrp-\ *n* : faulty absorption of nutrient materials from the alimentary canal

malac- *or* **malaco-** *comb form* [L, fr. Gk *malak-*, *malako-*, fr. *malakos*; akin to L *molere* to grind] : soft <*malac*oid> <*malaco*phyllous>

ma·lac·ca cane \mə-ˌlak-ə-\ *n* [*Malacca*, Malaya] : an often mottled cane from an Asiatic rattan palm (*Calamus rotang*)

Mal·a·chi \'mal-ə-ˌkī\ *n* [Heb *Mal'ākhī*] **1** — used as the conventional name for the unidentified 5th century B.C. writer of the book of Malachi **2** : a prophetic book of canonical Jewish and Christian Scripture — see BIBLE table

Mal·a·chi·as \ˌmal-ə-'kī-əs\ *n* [LL, fr. Gk, fr. Heb *Mal'ākhī*] : MALACHI

mal·a·chite \'mal-ə-ˌkīt\ *n* [ME *melochites*, fr. L *molochites*, fr. Gk *molochitēs*, fr. *molochē* mallow] : a mineral $Cu_2CO_3(OH)_2$ that is a green basic carbonate of copper used as an ore and for making ornamental objects

mal·a·col·o·gy \ˌmal-ə-'käl-ə-jē\ *n* [F *malacologie*, contr. of *malacozoologie*, fr. NL *Malacozoa*, zoological group including soft-bodied animals (fr. *malac-* + *-zoa*) + F *-logie* -logy] : a branch of zoology dealing with mollusks — **mal·a·co·log·i·cal** \ˌmal-ə-kə-'läj-i-kəl\ *also* **mal·a·co·log·ic** \-ik\ *adj* — **mal·a·col·o·gist** \ˌmal-ə-'käl-ə-jəst\ *n*

mal·a·cos·tra·can \ˌmal-ə-'käs-tri-kən\ *n* [deriv. of Gk *malakostrakos* soft-shelled, fr. *malak-* + *ostrakon* shell — more at OYSTER] : any of a major subclass (Malacostraca) of crustaceans including most of the well-known marine, freshwater, and terrestrial members of the group (as crabs and sow bugs) — **malacostracan** *adj*

mal·ad·ap·ta·tion \ˌmal-ˌad-ˌap-'tā-shən\ *n* : poor or inadequate adaptation

mal·adapt·ed \ˌmal-ə-'dap-təd\ *adj* : unsuited or poorly suited (as to a particular use, purpose, or situation)

mal·adap·tive \-tiv\ *adj* **1** : marked by poor or inadequate adaptation **2** : not conducive to adaptation

mal·ad·just·ed \ˌmal-ə-'jəs-təd\ *adj* : poorly or inadequately adjusted; *specif* : lacking harmony with one's environment from failure to adjust one's desires to the conditions of one's life

mal·ad·jus·tive \-'jəs-tiv\ *adj* : not conducive to adjustment

mal·ad·just·ment \-'jəs(t)-mənt\ *n* : poor, faulty, or inadequate adjustment

mal·ad·min·is·ter \ˌmal-əd-'min-ə-stər\ *vt* : to administer improperly or inefficiently — **mal·ad·min·is·tra·tion** \-ˌmin-ə-'strā-shən\ *n*

mal·adroit \ˌmal-ə-'drȯit\ *adj* [F, fr. MF, fr. *mal-* + *adroit*] : lacking adroitness : INEPT ***syn*** see AWKWARD ***ant*** adroit — **mal·adroit·ly** *adv* — **mal·adroit·ness** *n*

mal·a·dy \'mal-əd-ē\ *n, pl* **-dies** [ME *maladie*, fr. OF, fr. *malade* sick, fr. L *male habitus* in bad condition] **1** : a disease or disorder of the animal body **2** : an unwholesome condition

ma·la fi·de \ˌmal-ə-'fīd-ē, -'fīd-ə\ *adv or adj* [LL] : with or in bad faith

Ma·la·ga \'mal-ə-gə\ *n* : any of several usu. sweet dessert wines of Málaga, Spain; *also* : a similar wine made elsewhere

Mal·a·gasy \ˌmal-ə-'gas-ē\ *n, pl* **Malagasy** *also* **Mal·a·gas·ies** **1** : a native or inhabitant of Madagascar or of the Malagasy Republic **2** : the Austronesian language of the Malagasy people — **Malagasy** *adj*

ma·la·gue·na \ˌmal-ə-'gān-yə, ˌmäl-\ *n* [Sp *malagueña*, fr. fem. of *malagueño* of Málaga, fr. *Málaga*] **1** : a folk tune native to Málaga that is similar to a fandango **2** : a Spanish dance for couples that is similar to a fandango

mal·aise \mə-'lāz, ma-; ma-'lez\ *n* [F *malaise*, fr. OF, fr. *mal-* + *aise* comfort — more at EASE] **1** : an indefinite feeling of debility or lack of health often indicative of or accompanying the onset of an illness **2** : a vague sense of mental or moral ill-being

mal·a·mute \'mal-ə-ˌmyüt\ *n* [*Malemute*, an Alaskan Eskimo people] : a sled dog of northern No. America; *esp* : ALASKAN MALAMUTE

mal·apert \ˌmal-ə-'pərt\ *adj* [ME, fr. MF unskillful, fr. *mal-* + *apert* skillful, modif. of L *expertus* expert] : impudently bold : SAUCY — **mal·apert·ly** *adv* — **mal·apert·ness** *n*

mal·ap·por·tioned \ˌmal-ə-'pōr-shənd, -'pȯr-\ *adj* : characterized by an inequitable or unsuitable apportioning of representatives to a legislative body <one of the country's most ~ legislatures. Eight percent of the population controlled a majority of the Senate seats —*N.Y. Times*>

mal·ap·por·tion·ment \-shən-mənt\ *n* : the state of being malapportioned

¹mal·a·prop \'mal-ə-ˌpräp\ *n* [Mrs. *Malaprop*] : an example of malapropism <was famed for ~*s*: he always said "polo bears" and "Remember Pearl Island" and "neon stockings" —*Time*>

²malaprop *or* **mal·a·prop·ian** \ˌmal-ə-'präp-ē-ən\ *adj* [Mrs. *Malaprop*] : using or marked by the use of malapropisms

mal·a·prop·ism \'mal-ə-ˌpräp-ˌiz-əm\ *n* [Mrs. *Malaprop*, character noted for her misuse of words in R. B. Sheridan's comedy *The Rivals* (1775)] **1** : a usu. humorous misapplication of a word; *specif* : the use of a word sounding somewhat like the one intended but ludicrously wrong in the context **2** : MALAPROP

mal·ap·ro·pos \ˌmal-ˌap-rə-'pō, (ˌ)mal-'ap-rə-ˌ\ *adv* [F *mal à propos*] : in an inappropriate or inopportune way — **malapropos** *adj*

¹ma·lar \'mā-lər, -ˌlär\ *adj* [NL *malaris*, fr. L *mala* jawbone, cheek] : of or relating to the cheek or the side of the head

²malar *n* : ZYGOMATIC BONE — called also *malar bone*

ma·lar·ia \mə-'ler-ē-ə\ *n* [It, fr. *mala aria* bad air] **1** *archaic* : air infected with a noxious substance capable of causing disease; *esp* : MIASMA **2 a** : a human disease that is caused by sporozoan parasites (genus *Plasmodium*) in the red blood cells, is transmitted by the bite of anopheline mosquitoes, and is characterized by periodic attacks of chills and fever **b** : any of various diseases of birds and mammals caused by blood protozoans — **ma·lar·i·al** \-əl\ *also* **ma·lar·i·an** \-ən\ *adj* — **ma·lar·i·ous** \-əs\ *adj*

ma·lar·i·ol·o·gy \-ˌler-ē-'äl-ə-jē\ *n* : the scientific study of malaria — **ma·lar·i·ol·o·gist** \-jəst\ *n*

ma·lar·key \mə-'lär-kē\ *n* [origin unknown] : insincere or foolish talk : BUNKUM

ma·late \'mal-ˌāt, 'mā-ˌlāt\ *n* : a salt or ester of malic acid

mal·a·thi·on \ˌmal-ə-'thī-ən, -ˌän\ *n* [fr. *Malathion*, a trademark] : a thiophosphate insecticide $C_{10}H_{19}O_6PS_2$ with a lower mammalian toxicity than parathion

Ma·lay \mə-'lā, 'mā-(ˌ)lā\ *n* [obs. D *Malayo* (now *Maleier*), fr. Malay *Mĕlayu*] **1** : a member of a people of the Malay peninsula, eastern Sumatra, parts of Borneo, and some adjacent islands **2** : the Austronesian language of the Malays — **Malay** *adj* — **Ma·lay·an** \mə-'lā-ən, 'mā-ˌlā-\ *n or adj*

Mal·a·ya·lam \ˌmal-ə-'yäl-əm\ *n* : the Dravidian language of Kerala, southwest India, closely related to Tamil

Ma·layo- \mə-ˌlā-(ˌ)ō-, mā-\ *comb form* : Malayan and <*Malayo*-Indonesian>

¹mal·con·tent \ˌmal-kən-'tent\ *n* : a discontented person: **a** : one who bears a grudge from a sense of grievance or thwarted ambition **b** : one who is in active opposition to an established order or government : REBEL

²malcontent *adj* [MF, fr. OF, fr. *mal-* + *content*] : dissatisfied with the existing state of affairs : DISCONTENTED; *esp* : disaffected with an established order or government

mal·con·tent·ed \-əd\ *adj* : MALCONTENT — **mal·con·tent·ed·ly** *adv* — **mal·con·tent·ed·ness** *n*

mal de mer \ˌmal-də-'me(ə)r\ *n* [F] : SEASICKNESS

mal·dis·tri·bu·tion \ˌmal-ˌdis-trə-'byü-shən\ *n* : bad or faulty distribution : undesirable inequality or unevenness of placement or apportionment (as of population, resources, or wealth) over an area or among members of a group

¹male \'mā(ə)l\ *adj* [ME, fr. MF *masle*, *male*, adj. & n., fr. L *masculus*, dim. of *mar-*, *mas* male] **1 a (1)** : of, relating to, or being the sex that begets young by performing the fertilizing function in generation and produces relatively small usu. motile gametes (as sperms, spermatozoids, or spermatozoa) by which the eggs of a female are made fertile <~ organs> **(2)** : STAMINATE; *esp* : having only staminate flowers and not producing fruit or seeds <a ~ holly> **b (1)** : of, relating to, or characteristic of the male sex <a deep ~ voice> **(2)** : made up of male individuals and esp. men <a ~ choir> **2** : MASCULINE 3a **3** : designed for fitting into a corresponding hollow part — **male·ness** \-nəs\ *n*

²male *n* : a plant or animal that is male

male alto *n* : COUNTERTENOR

ma·le·ate \'mal-lē-ˌāt, -lē-ət\ *n* : a salt or ester of maleic acid

¹male·dict \ˌmal-ə-'dikt\ *adj* [LL *maledictus*] *archaic* : ACCURSED

²maledict *vt* : CURSE, EXECRATE

male·dic·tion \ˌmal-ə-'dik-shən\ *n* [ME *malediccioun*, fr. LL *malediction-*, *maledictio*, fr. *maledictus*, pp. of *maledicere* to curse, fr. L, to speak evil of, fr. *male* badly + *dicere* to speak, say — more at MAL-, DICTION] : CURSE, EXECRATION — **male·dic·to·ry** \-'dik-t(ə-)rē\ *adj*

male·fac·tion \ˌmal-ə-'fak-shən\ *n* : an evil deed : CRIME

male·fac·tor \'mal-ə-ˌfak-tər\ *n* [ME, fr. L, fr. *malefactus*, pp. of *malefacere* to do evil, fr. *male* + *facere* to do — more at DO] **1** : one who commits an offense against the law; *esp* : FELON **2** : one who does ill toward another

male fern *n* : a fern (*Dryopteris filix-mas*) producing an oleoresin used in expelling tapeworms

ma·lef·ic \mə-'lef-ik\ *adj* [L *maleficus* wicked, mischievous, fr. *male*] **1** : having malignant influence : BALEFUL **2** : MALICIOUS

ma·lef·i·cence \mə-'lef-ə-sən(t)s\ *n* **1 a** : the act of committing harm or evil **b** : a harmful or evil act **2** : the quality or state of being maleficent

ma·lef·i·cent \-sənt\ *adj* [back-formation fr. *maleficence*] : working or productive of harm or evil : BALEFUL

ma·le·ic acid \mə-ˌlē-ik-, -ˌlā-\ *n* [F *acide maléique*, alter. of *acide malique* malic acid; fr. its formation by dehydration of malic acid] : a crystalline dicarboxylic acid $C_4H_4O_4$ that is isomeric with fumaric acid and used esp. in making resins

maleic anhydride *n* : a caustic crystalline cyclic anhydride $C_4H_2O_3$ used esp. in making resins

maleic hydrazide *n* : a crystalline cyclic hydrazide $C_4H_4N_2O_2$ used to retard plant growth
mal·e·mute *var of* MALAMUTE
mal·en·ten·du \mä-läⁿ-täⁿ-dᵫ\ *n* [F, fr. *mal entendu* misunderstood] : MISUNDERSTANDING <through some stupid ~ he arrived an hour late>
male–ster·ile \'mā(ə)l-'ster-əl\ *adj* : having male gametes lacking or nonfunctional
ma·lev·o·lence \mə-'lev-ə-lən(t)s\ *n* **1** : the quality or state of being malevolent **2** : malevolent behavior ***syn*** see MALICE ***ant*** benevolence
ma·lev·o·lent \-lənt\ *adj* [L *malevolent-, malevolens,* fr. *male* badly + *volent-, volens,* prp. of *velle* to wish — more at MAL-, WILL] : having, showing, or arising from intense often vicious ill will, spite, or hatred — **ma·lev·o·lent·ly** *adv*
mal·fea·sance \(')mal-'fēz-ᵊn(t)s\ *n* [*mal-* + obs. *feasance* (doing, execution)] : wrongdoing or misconduct esp. by a public official
mal·for·ma·tion \ˌmal-fȯr-'mā-shən, -fər-\ *n* : irregular, anomalous, abnormal, or faulty formation or structure
mal·formed \(')mal-'fȯ(ə)rmd\ *adj* : characterized by malformation : badly or imperfectly formed : MISSHAPEN
mal·func·tion \(')mal-'fəŋ(k)-shən\ *vi* : to function imperfectly or badly : fail to operate in the normal or usual manner — **malfunction** *n*
mal·gré \mal-'grā, 'mal-ˌ\ *prep* [F, fr. OF *maugré* — more at MAUGRE] : DESPITE
ma·lic \'mal-ik, 'mā-lik\ *adj* : involved in and esp. catalyzing a reaction in which malic acid participates <~ dehydrogenase> <~ enzyme>
malic acid *n* [F *acide malique,* fr. L *malum* apple, fr. Gk *mēlon, malon*] : a crystalline dicarboxylic acid $C_4H_6O_5$; *esp* : the one of three optical isomers of malic acid that is found in various plant juices and is formed as an intermediate in the Krebs cycle
mal·ice \'mal-əs\ *n* [ME, fr. OF, fr. L *malitia,* fr. *malus* bad — more at SMALL] : desire to see another suffer that may be fixed and unreasonable or no more than a passing mischievous impulse; *also* : intent to commit an unlawful act or cause harm without legal justification or excuse
syn MALICE, ILL WILL, MALEVOLENCE, SPITE, MALIGNITY, MALIGNANCY, SPLEEN, GRUDGE *shared meaning element* : a desiring or wishing pain, injury, or distress to another ***ant*** charity
ma·li·cious \mə-'lish-əs\ *adj* : given to, marked by, or arising from malice — **ma·li·cious·ly** *adv* — **ma·li·cious·ness** *n*
malicious mischief *n* : willful, wanton, or reckless damage to or destruction of another's property
1**ma·lign** \mə-'līn\ *adj* [ME *maligne,* fr. MF, fr. L *malignus,* fr. *male* badly + *gignere* to beget — more at MAL-, KIN] **1 a** : evil in nature, influence, or effect : INJURIOUS **b** : MALIGNANT, VIRULENT **2** : having or showing intense often vicious ill will : MALEVOLENT ***syn*** see SINISTER — **ma·lign·ly** *adv*
2**malign** *vt* [ME *malignen,* fr. MF *maligner* to act maliciously, fr. LL *malignari,* fr. L *malignus*] : to utter injuriously misleading or false reports about : speak evil of
syn MALIGN, TRADUCE, ASPERSE, VILIFY, CALUMNIATE, DEFAME, SLANDER *shared meaning element* : to injure by speaking ill of ***ant*** defend
ma·lig·nance \mə-'lig-nən(t)s\ *n* : MALIGNANCY
ma·lig·nan·cy \-nən-sē\ *n, pl* **-cies** **1** : the quality or state of being malignant **2 a** : exhibition (as by a tumor) of malignant qualities : VIRULENCE **b** : a malignant tumor ***syn*** see MALICE ***ant*** benignancy
ma·lig·nant \mə-'lig-nənt\ *adj* [LL *malignant-, malignans,* prp. of *malignari*] **1 a** *obs* : MALCONTENT, DISAFFECTED **b** : evil in nature, influence, or effect : INJURIOUS **c** : passionately and relentlessly malevolent : aggressively malicious **2** : tending to produce death or deterioration <~ malaria>; *esp* : tending to infiltrate, metastasize, and terminate fatally <~ tumor> — **ma·lig·nant·ly** *adv*
ma·lig·ni·ty \mə-'lig-nət-ē\ *n* **1** : MALIGNANCY, MALEVOLENCE **2** : an instance of malignant or malicious behavior or nature ***syn*** see MALICE ***ant*** benignity
ma·li·hi·ni \ˌmäl-i-'hē-nē\ *n* [Hawaiian] : a newcomer or stranger among the people of Hawaii
ma·lines \mə-'lēn\ *n, pl* **ma·lines** \-'lēn(z)\ [F, fr. *Malines* (Mechelen), Belgium] **1** : MECHLIN **2** *also* **ma·line** : a fine stiff net with a hexagonal mesh that is usu. made of silk or rayon and that is often used for veils
ma·lin·ger \mə-'liŋ-gər\ *vi* **ma·lin·gered; ma·lin·ger·ing** \-g(ə-)riŋ\ [F *malingre* sickly] : to pretend incapacity (as illness) so as to avoid duty or work — **ma·lin·ger·er** \-gər-ər\ *n*
Ma·lin·ke \mə-'liŋ-kē\ *n, pl* **Malinke** *or* **Malinkes** **1** : a member of a people of Mandingo affiliation widespread in the western part of Africa **2** : the language of the Malinke people
Malinois *n* [F, one from Malines, fr. *Malines* (Mechelen), Belgium] : BELGIAN MALINOIS
mal·i·son \'mal-ə-sən, -zən\ *n* [ME, fr. OF *maleïçon,* fr. LL *malediction-, maledictio*] : CURSE, MALEDICTION
mal·kin \'mȯ(l)-kən, 'mal-\ *n* [ME *malkyn,* fr. *Malkyn,* fem. name] **1** *dial chiefly Brit* : an untidy woman : SLATTERN **2** *dial chiefly Brit* **a** : CAT **b** : HARE
1**mall** \'mȯl\ *var of* MAUL
2**mall** \'mȯl, *esp Brit & for 1* 'mal\ *n* [short for obs. *pall-mall* (mallet used in pall-mall)] **1** : an alley used for pall-mall **2** [The *Mall,* promenade in London, orig. a pall-mall alley] **a** : a usu. public area often set with shade trees and designed as a promenade or as a pedestrian walk **b** : a usu. paved or grassy strip between two roadways **3** : an open or covered passageway or concourse providing access to rows of stores and closed permanently or at stated times to motor vehicles; *also* : a complex of shops with associated passageways and parking space
mal·lard \'mal-ərd\ *n, pl* **mallard** *or* **mallards** [ME, fr. MF *mallart*] : a common and widely distributed wild duck (*Anas platyrhynchos*) of the northern hemisphere that is the source of the domestic ducks

mallard

mal·lea·ble \'mal-ē-ə-bəl, 'mal-(y)ə-bəl\ *adj* [ME *malliable,* fr. MF or ML; MF *malleable,* fr. ML *malleabilis,* fr. *malleare* to hammer, fr. L *malleus* hammer — more at MAUL] **1** : capable of being extended or shaped by beating with a hammer or by the pressure of rollers **2** : plastically open to outside forces or influences : having a capacity for adaptive change ***syn*** see PLASTIC ***ant*** refractory — **mal·lea·bil·i·ty** \ˌmal-ē-ə-'bil-ət-ē, ˌmal-(y)ə-\ *n* — **mal·lea·ble·ness** \'mal-ē-ə-bəl-nəs, 'mal-(y)ə-\ *n*
mal·lee \'mal-ē\ *n* [native name in Australia] **1** : any of several low-growing shrubby Australian eucalypts (as *Eucalyptus dumosa* and *E. oleosa*) **2** : a dense thicket or growth of mallees; *also* : land covered by such growth
mal·le·muck \'mal-i-ˌmək\ *n* [D *mallemuk,* fr. *mal* silly + *mok* gull] : any of several large oceanic birds (as the fulmar or petrel)
mal·let \'mal-ət\ *n* [ME *maillet,* fr. MF, fr. OF, dim. of *mail* maul — more at MAUL] : a hammer with typically a barrel-shaped head of wood: as **a** : a tool with a large head for driving another tool or for striking a surface without marring it **b** : an implement for striking a ball (as in polo or croquet) **c** : a light hammer with a small rounded or spherical usu. padded head used in playing certain musical instruments (as a vibraphone)
mal·le·us \'mal-ē-əs\ *n, pl* **mal·lei** \-ē-ˌī, -ē-ˌē\ [NL, fr. L, hammer] : the outermost of the three small bones of the mammalian ear — see EAR illustration
mal·low \'mal-(ˌ)ō, -ə(-w)\ *n* [ME *malwe,* fr. OE *mealwe,* fr. L *malva*] : any of a genus (*Malva* of the family Malvaceae, the mallow family) of herbs with palmately lobed or dissected leaves, usu. showy flowers, and a disk-shaped fruit
malm \'mäm, 'mälm\ *n* [ME *malme,* fr. OE *mealm-;* akin to OE *melu* meal — more at MEAL] **1** : a soft friable chalky limestone; *also* : a fertile friable loam rich in lime **2** : an artificial mixture of clay and chalk used in the manufacture of bricks
malm·sey \'mäm-zē, 'mälm-\ *n, often cap* [ME *malmesey,* fr. ML *Malmasia* Monemvasia, village in Greece where it was orig. produced] : the sweetest variety of Madeira wine
mal·nour·ished \(')mal-'nər-isht, -'nə-risht\ *adj* : UNDERNOURISHED
mal·nu·tri·tion \ˌmal-n(y)ü-'trish-ən\ *n* : faulty or inadequate nutrition
mal·oc·clu·sion \ˌmal-ə-'klü-zhən\ *n* : improper occlusion; *esp* : abnormality in the coming together of teeth
mal·odor \(')mal-'ōd-ər\ *n* : an offensive odor
mal·odor·ous \-'ōd-ə-rəs\ *adj* **1** : ill-smelling **2** : highly improper <~ practices and chicanery in high financial places —*New Republic*> — **mal·odor·ous·ly** *adv* — **mal·odor·ous·ness** *n*
syn MALODOROUS, STINKING, FETID, NOISOME, PUTRID, RANCID, RANK, FUSTY, MUSTY *shared meaning element* : having an unpleasant smell
ma·lo·lac·tic \ˌmal-ō-'lak-tik, ˌmā-lō-\ *adj* : relating to or involved in the bacterial conversion of malic acid to lactic acid in wine <~ fermentation>
Mal·pi·ghi·an \mal-'pig-ē-ən, -'pē-gē-\ *adj* : of, relating to, or discovered by Marcello Malpighi
Malpighian corpuscle *n* : the part of a nephron that consists of a glomerulus and its membrane — called also *Malpighian body*
Malpighian layer *n* : the deeper part of the epidermis consisting of cells whose protoplasm has not yet changed into horny material
Malpighian tubule *n* : any of a group of long blind vessels opening into the posterior part of the alimentary canal in most insects and some other arthropods and functioning primarily as excretory organs — called also *Malpighian tube*
mal·po·si·tion \ˌmal-pə-'zish-ən\ *n* : wrong or faulty position
mal·prac·tice \(') mal-'prak-təs\ *n* **1** : a dereliction from professional duty or a failure to exercise an accepted degree of professional skill or learning by one (as a physician) rendering professional services which results in injury, loss, or damage **2** : an injurious, negligent, or improper practice : MALFEASANCE
mal·prac·ti·tio·ner \ˌmal-prak-'tish-(ə-)nər\ *n* : one who engages in or commits malpractice
1**malt** \'mȯlt\ *n* [ME, fr. OE *mealt;* akin to OHG *malz* malt, OE *meltan* to melt] **1** : grain softened by steeping in water, allowed to germinate, and used esp. in brewing and distilling **2** : MALT LIQUOR **3** : MALTED MILK — **malty** \'mȯl-tē\ *adj*
2**malt** *vt* **1** : to convert into malt **2** : to make or treat with malt or malt extract ~ *vi* **1** : to become malt **2** : to make grain into malt
MALT *abbr* master of arts in language teaching
Mal·ta fever \ˌmȯl-tə-\ *n* [*Malta,* island in the Mediterranean] : typical human brucellosis
malt·ase \'mȯl-ˌtās, -ˌtāz\ *n* : an enzyme that accelerates the hydrolysis of maltose to glucose
malted milk *n* **1** : a soluble powder prepared from dried milk and malted cereals **2** : a beverage made by dissolving malted milk in milk often with ice cream and flavoring added — called also *malted*
Mal·tese \mȯl-'tēz, -'tēs\ *n, pl* **Maltese** **1** : a native or inhabitant of Malta **2** : the Semitic language of the Maltese people **3** : any of a breed of toy dogs with a long white coat, a black nose, and very dark eyes — **Maltese** *adj*
Maltese cat *n* : a bluish gray domestic short-haired cat
Maltese cross *n* **1 a** : a cross formée **b** : a cross that resembles the cross formée but has the outer face of each arm indented in a V — see CROSS illustration **2** : a Eurasian perennial (*Lychnis chalcedonica*) having scarlet or rarely white flowers in dense terminal heads
Mal·thu·sian \mal-'th(y)ü-zhən, mȯl-\ *adj* [Thomas R. *Malthus*] : of or relating to Malthus or to his theory that population tends to increase at a faster rate than its means of subsistence and that

unless it is checked by moral restraint or by disease, famine, war, or other disaster widespread poverty and degradation inevitably result — **Malthusian** *n* — **Mal·thu·sian·ism** \-zhə-ˌniz-əm\ *n*

malt liquor *n* : a fermented liquor (as beer) made with malt

malt·ose \ˈmȯl-ˌtōs, -ˌtōz\ *n* [F, fr. E ¹*malt*] : a crystalline dextrorotatory fermentable sugar $C_{12}H_{22}O_{11}$ formed esp. from starch by amylase

mal·treat \(ˈ)mal-ˈtrēt\ *vt* [F *maltraiter,* fr. MF, fr. *mal-* + *traiter* to treat, fr. OF *traitier* — more at TREAT] : to treat cruelly or roughly : ABUSE — **mal·treat·ment** \-mənt\ *n*

malt·ster \ˈmȯlt-stər\ *n* : a maker of malt

malt sugar *n* : MALTOSE

mal·va·sia \ˌmal-və-ˈzē-ə\ *n* [It, fr. *Monemvasia,* Greece] : MALMSEY — **mal·va·si·an** \-ən\ *adj*

mal·ver·sa·tion \ˌmal-vər-ˈsā-shən\ *n* [MF, fr. *malverser* to be corrupt, fr. *mal* + *verser* to turn, handle, fr. L *versare,* fr. *versus,* pp. of *vertere* to turn — more at WORTH] **1** : misbehavior and esp. corruption in an office, trust, or commission **2** : corrupt administration

mal·voi·sie \ˌmalv-wə-ˈzē\ *n* [F, fr. MF *malvesie,* fr. *Malvesie* Monemvasia] : MALMSEY

ma·ma *or* **mam·ma** \ˈmäm-ə, *chiefly Brit* mə-ˈmä\ *n* [baby talk] **1** : MOTHER **2** *slang* : WIFE, WOMAN

mam·ba \ˈmäm-bə, ˈmam-\ *n* [Zulu *im-amba*] : any of several tropical and southern African venomous snakes (genus *Dendraspis*) related to the cobras but with no hood; *esp* : an aggressive southern African snake (*D. angusticeps*) that grows to a length of 12 feet, has a light or olive green phase and a black phase, and readily inflicts its often fatal bite

mam·bo \ˈmäm-(ˌ)bō\ *n, pl* **mambos** [AmerSp] : a ballroom dance of Haitian origin that resembles the rumba and the cha-cha; *also* : the music for this dance — **mambo** *vi*

Mam·luk \ˈmam-ˌlük\ *or* **Mam·e·luke** \ˈmam-ə-ˌlük\ *n* [Ar *mamlūk,* lit., slave] **1** : a member of a politically powerful Egyptian military class occupying the sultanate from 1250 to 1517 **2** *usu Mameluke, often not cap* : a Caucasian or oriental slave in Muslim countries

mam·ma \ˈmam-ə\ *n, pl* **mam·mae** \ˈmam-ˌē, -ˌī\ [L, mother, breast, of baby-talk origin] : a mammary gland and its accessory parts — **mam·mate** \ˈmam-ˌāt\ *adj*

mam·mal \ˈmam-əl\ *n* [deriv. of LL *mammalis* of the breast, fr. L *mamma* breast] : any of a class (Mammalia) of higher vertebrates comprising man and all other animals that nourish their young with milk secreted by mammary glands and have the skin usu. more or less covered with hair — **mam·ma·li·an** \mə-ˈmā-lē-ən, ma-\ *adj or n*

mam·mal·o·gy \mə-ˈmal-ə-jē, ma-ˈmal-, -ˈmäl-\ *n* [ISV, blend of *mammal* and *-logy*] : a branch of zoology dealing with mammals — **mam·mal·o·gist** \-jəst\ *n*

mam·ma·ry \ˈmam-ə-rē\ *adj* : of, relating to, lying near, or affecting the mammae

mammary gland *n* : one of the large compound modified sebaceous glands that in female mammals are modified to secrete milk, are situated ventrally in pairs, and usu. terminate in a nipple

mam·ma·to·cu·mu·lus \ma-ˌmāt-ō-ˈkyü-myə-ləs\ *n* [NL, fr. L *mammatus* having breasts, (fr. *mamma*) + NL *cumulus*] : a cumulus or cumulostratus storm cloud having breast-shaped protuberances below

mammer *vi* [ME *mameren* to stammer, of imit. origin] *obs* : WAVER, HESITATE

mam·mil·la·ry \ˈmam-ə-ˌler-ē, ma-ˈmil-ə-rē\ *adj* [L *mammilla* breast, nipple, dim. of *mamma*] **1** : of, relating to, or resembling the breasts **2** : studded with breast-shaped protuberances

mam·mil·lat·ed \ˈmam-ə-ˌlāt-əd\ *adj* [LL *mammillatus,* fr. L *mammilla*] **1** : having nipples or small protuberances **2** : having the form of a bluntly rounded protuberance

¹**mam·mock** \ˈmam-ək\ *n* [origin unknown] *chiefly dial* : a broken piece : SCRAP

²**mammock** *vt, chiefly dial* : to tear into fragments : MANGLE

mam·mo·gram \ˈmam-ə-ˌgram\ *n* [L *mamma* + *-o-* + *-gram*] : a photograph of the breasts made by X rays

mam·mog·ra·phy \ma-ˈmäg-rə-fē\ *n* : X-ray examination of the breasts (as for early detection of cancer)

mam·mon \ˈmam-ən\ *n, often cap* [LL *mammona,* fr. Gk *mamōna,* fr. Aram *māmōnā* riches] : material wealth or possessions esp. as having a debasing influence <you cannot serve God and ~ —Mt 6:24 (RSV)> — **mam·mon·ism** \-ə-ˌniz-əm\ *n*

mam·mon·ist \-ə-nəst\ *n, archaic* : one devoted to the ideal or pursuit of wealth

mam·mon·ite \-ə-ˌnīt\ *n, archaic* : MAMMONIST

¹**mam·moth** \ˈmam-əth\ *n* [Russ *mamont, mamot*] **1** : any of numerous extinct Pleistocene elephants distinguished from recent elephants by molars with cementum filling the spaces between the ridges of enamel and by large size, very long tusks that curve upward, and well-developed body hair **2** : something immense of its kind : GIANT <a company that is a ~ of the industry>

mammoth 1

²**mammoth** *adj* : of very great size : GIGANTIC ***syn*** see HUGE

mam·my \ˈmam-ē\ *n, pl* **mammies** [alter. of *mamma*] **1** : MAMA **2** : a Negro woman serving as a nurse to white children esp. formerly in the southern U.S.

mammy wagon *n* : a small open-sided bus or light truck used to transport passengers or goods in West Africa

¹**man** \ˈman, *in compounds* ˌman *or* mən\ *n, pl* **men** \ˈmen, *in compounds* ˌmen *or* mən\ [ME, fr. OE; akin to OHG *man* man, Skt *manu*] **1 a** (1) : a human being; *esp* : an adult male human (2) : a man belonging to a particular category (as by birth, residence, membership, or occupation) — usu. used in combination <council*man*> (3) : HUSBAND **b** : the human race : MANKIND **c** : a bipedal primate mammal (*Homo sapiens*) that is anatomically related to the great apes but distinguished esp. by notable development of the brain with a resultant capacity for articulate speech and abstract reasoning, is usu. considered to form a variable number of freely interbreeding races, and is the sole representative of a natural family (Hominidae); *broadly* : any living or extinct member of this family **d** (1) : one possessing in high degree the qualities considered distinctive of manhood (2) *obs* : the quality or state of being manly : MANLINESS **e** : FELLOW, CHAP <come, come, my good ~> **f** — used interjectionally to express intensity of feeling <~, what a game> **2 a** : a feudal tenant : VASSAL **b** : an adult male servant **c** *pl* : the working force as distinguished from the employer and usu. the management **3** : INDIVIDUAL, PERSON <a ~ could get killed there> **4** : one of the distinctive objects moved by each player in various board games **5** *Christian Science* : the compound idea of infinite Spirit : the spiritual image and likeness of God : the full representation of Mind **6** *often cap* : POLICE <when I heard the siren, I knew it was the *Man* —*Amer. Speech*> **7** *often cap* : the white establishment : white society <surprise that any black . . . should take on so about The *Man* —Peter Goldman> — **man·less** \ˈman-ləs\ *adj* — **man·like** \-ˌlīk\ *adj* — **as one man** : with the agreement and consent of all : UNANIMOUSLY — **one's own man** : free from interference or control : INDEPENDENT — **to a man** : without exception

²**man** *vt* **manned; man·ning** **1 a** : to supply with men <~ a fleet> **b** : to station members of a ship's crew at <~ the capstan> **c** : to serve in the force or complement of <workers who ~ the production lines> **2** : to furnish with strength or powers of resistance : BRACE

³**man** *abbr* manual

Man *abbr* Manitoba

ma·na \ˈmän-ə\ *n* [of Melanesian & Polynesian origin; akin to Hawaiian & Maori *mana*] **1** : the power of the elemental forces of nature embodied in an object or person **2** : moral authority : PRESTIGE

man–about–town \ˌman-ə-ˌbaůt-ˈtaůn\ *n, pl* **men–about–town** \ˌmen-\ : a worldly and socially active man

¹**man·a·cle** \ˈman-i-kəl\ *n* [ME *manicle,* fr. MF, fr. L *manicula,* dim. of *manus* hand — more at MANUAL] **1** : a shackle for the hand or wrist : HANDCUFF **2** : something used as a restraint

²**manacle** *vt* **man·a·cled; man·a·cling** \-k(ə-)liŋ\ **1** : to confine (the hands) with manacles **2** : to make fast or secure : BIND; *broadly* : to restrain from movement, progress, or action ***syn*** see HAMPER

¹**man·age** \ˈman-ij\ *vb* **man·aged; man·ag·ing** [It *maneggiare,* fr. *mano* hand, fr. L *manus*] *vt* **1** : to handle or direct with a degree of skill or address: as **a** : to make and keep submissive <my mother . . . was the only one that ever could ~ him —George Macdonald †1905> **b** : to treat with care : HUSBAND <*managed* his resources carefully> **2** : to alter by manipulation **3** : to succeed in accomplishing : CONTRIVE ~ *vi* **1 a** : to direct or carry on business or affairs **b** : to admit of being carried on **2** : to achieve one's purpose ***syn*** see CONDUCT

²**manage** *n* [It *maneggio* management, training of a horse, fr. *maneggiare*] **1 a** *archaic* : the action and paces of a trained riding horse **b** : the schooling or handling of a horse **c** : a riding school : MANEGE **2** *obs* : MANAGEMENT

man·age·able \ˈman-ij-ə-bəl\ *adj* : capable of being managed : TRACTABLE — **man·age·abil·i·ty** \ˌman-ij-ə-ˈbil-ət-ē\ *n* — **man·age·able·ness** \ˈman-ij-ə-bəl-nəs\ *n* — **man·age·ably** \-blē\ *adv*

man·age·ment \ˈman-ij-mənt\ *n* **1** : the act or art of managing : the conducting or supervising of something (as a business) **2** : judicious use of means to accomplish an end **3** : capacity for managing : executive skill **4** : the collective body of those who manage or direct an enterprise — **man·age·men·tal** \ˌman-ij-ˈment-ᵊl\ *adj*

man·ag·er \ˈman-ij-ər\ *n* : one that manages: as **a** : one who conducts business or household affairs **b** : a person whose work or profession is management **c** (1) : a person who directs a team or athlete (2) : a student who in scholastic or collegiate sports supervises equipment and records under the direction of a coach — **man·ag·er·ess** \-ə-rəs\ *n* — **man·a·ge·ri·al** \ˌman-ə-ˈjir-ē-əl\ *adj* — **man·a·ge·ri·al·ly** \-ē-ə-lē\ *adv* — **man·ag·er·ship** \ˈman-ij-ər-ˌship\ *n*

managing editor *n* : an editor in executive and supervisory charge of all editorial activities of a publication (as a newspaper)

¹**ma·ña·na** \mən-ˈyän-ə\ *adv* [Sp, lit., tomorrow, fr. earlier *cras mañana* early tomorrow, fr. *cras* tomorrow (fr. L) + *mañana* early, fr. L *mane* early in the morning] : at an indefinite time in the future

²**mañana** *n* : an indefinite time in the future

man ape *n* **1** : GREAT APE **2** : any of various fossil primates intermediate in characters between recent man and the great apes

Ma·nas·seh \mə-ˈnas-ə\ *n* [Heb *Mĕnashsheh*] **1** : a son of Joseph and the traditional eponymous ancestor of one of the tribes of Israel **2** : a king of Judah reigning in the 7th century B.C. and noted for his attempt to establish polytheism

man–at–arms \ˌman-ət-ˈärmz\ *n, pl* **men–at–arms** \ˌmen\ : SOLDIER; *esp* : a heavily armed and usu. mounted soldier

---

ə abut	ᵊ kitten	ər further	a back	ā bake	ä cot, cart
aů out	ch chin	e less	ē easy	g gift	i trip ī life
j joke	ŋ sing	ō flow	ȯ flaw	ȯi coin	th thin <u>th</u> this
ü loot	ů foot	y yet	yü few	yů furious	zh vision

man·a·tee \'man-ə-ˌtē\ *n* [Sp *manatí*] **:** any of several chiefly tropical aquatic herbivorous mammals (genus *Trichechus*) that differ from the related dugong esp. in having the tail broad and rounded

manatee

Man·ches·ter terrier \ˌman-ˌches-tər-, -chə-stər-\ *n* [*Manchester*, England] **:** any of a breed of small slightly built short-haired black-and-tan terriers developed in England by interbreeding local rat-catching dogs with whippets

man·chet \'man-chət\ *n* [ME] *archaic* **:** a loaf or roll of fine wheat bread

man·chi·neel \ˌman-chə-'nē(ə)l\ *n* [F *mancenille*, fr. Sp *manzanilla*, fr. dim. of *manzana* apple] **:** a poisonous tropical American tree (*Hippomane mancinella*) of the spurge family having a blistering milky juice and apple-shaped fruit

Man·chu \'man-(ˌ)chü, man-'\ *n, pl* **Manchu** *or* **Manchus** **1 :** a member of the native Mongolian race of Manchuria that is related to the Tungus, was orig. nomadic but conquered China and established a dynasty there in 1644, and has largely assimilated Chinese culture **2 :** the Tungusic language of the Manchu people — **Manchu** *adj*

man·ci·ple \'man(t)-sə-pəl\ *n* [ME, fr. ML *mancipium* office of steward, fr. L, act of purchase, fr. *mancip-*, *manceps* purchaser — more at EMANCIPATE] **:** a steward or purveyor esp. for a college or monastery

-man·cy \ˌman(t)-sē\ *n comb form* [ME *-mancie*, fr. OF, fr. L *-mantia*, fr. Gk *-manteia*, fr. *manteia*, fr. *mantis* diviner, prophet — more at MANTIS] **:** divination <oneiro*mancy*>

Man·dae·an \man-'dē-ən\ *n* [Mandaean *mandayyā* having knowledge] **1 :** a member of a Gnostic sect of the lower Tigris and Euphrates **2 :** a form of Aramaic found in documents written by Mandaeans — **Mandaean** *adj*

man·da·la \'mən-də-lə\ *n* [Skt *maṇḍala* circle] **1 :** a Hindu or Buddhist graphic symbol of the universe; *specif* **:** a circle enclosing a square with a deity on each side **2 :** a graphic and often symbolic pattern usu. in the form of a circle divided into four separate sections or bearing a multiple projection of an image — **man·dal·ic** \ˌmən-'dal-ik\ *adj*

man·da·mus \man-'dā-məs\ *n* [L, we enjoin, fr. *mandare*] **:** a writ issued by a superior court commanding the performance of a specified official act or duty

[1]man·da·rin \'man-d(ə-)rən\ *n* [Pg *mandarim*, fr. Malay *mĕntĕri*, fr. Skt *mantrin* counselor, fr. *mantra* counsel — more at MANTRA] **1 a :** a public official in the Chinese Empire of any of nine superior grades **b (1) :** a pedantic official **(2) :** BUREAUCRAT **c :** a person of position and influence esp. in intellectual or literary circles; *esp* **:** an elder and often traditionalist or reactionary member of such a circle **2** *cap* **a :** the primarily northern dialect of Chinese used by the court and the official classes of the Empire **b :** the chief dialect of China that is spoken in about four fifths of the country and has a standard variety centering about Peking **3** [F *mandarine*, fr. Sp *mandarina*, prob. fr. *mandarín* mandarin, fr. Pg *mandarim*; prob. fr. the color of a mandarin's robes] **a :** a small spiny Chinese orange tree (*Citrus reticulata*) with yellow to reddish orange loose-skinned fruits; *also* **:** a derivative of the Chinese mandarin developed in cultivation by artificial selection or hybridization **b :** the fruit of a mandarin — **man·da·rin·ic** \ˌman-də-'rin-ik\ *adj* — **man·da·rin·ism** \'man-d(ə-)rə-ˌniz-əm\ *n*

[2]mandarin *adj* **1 :** of, relating to, or typical of a mandarin <~ graces> **2 :** marked by polished ornate complexity of language <~ prose>

man·da·rin·ate \'man-d(ə-)rə-ˌnāt\ *n* **1 :** a body of mandarins **2 :** rule by mandarins

mandarin collar *n* **:** a narrow stand-up collar usu. open in front

mandarin orange *n* **:** MANDARIN 3

man·da·tary \'man-də-ˌter-ē\ *n, pl* **-tar·ies :** MANDATORY

[1]man·date \'man-ˌdāt\ *n* [MF & L; MF *mandat*, fr. L *mandatum*, fr. neut. of *mandatus*, pp. of *mandare* to entrust, enjoin, prob. irreg. fr. *manus* band + *-dere* to put — more at MANUAL, DO] **1 :** an authoritative command; *esp* **:** a formal order from a superior court or official to an inferior one **2 :** an authorization to act given to a representative <accepted the ~ of the people> **3 a :** an order or commission granted by the League of Nations to a member nation for the establishment of a responsible government over a former German colony or other conquered territory **b :** a mandated territory

[2]mandate *vt* **man·dat·ed; man·dat·ing :** to administer or assign (as a territory) under a mandate

man·da·tor \'man-ˌdāt-ər\ *n* **:** one that gives a mandate

[1]man·da·to·ry \'man-də-ˌtōr-ē, -ˌtȯr-\ *adj* **1 :** containing or constituting a command **:** OBLIGATORY <~ reexamination of drivers' eyes —*Springfield (Mass.) Daily News*> **2 :** of, relating to, or holding a League of Nations mandate

[2]mandatory *n, pl* **-ries :** one given a mandate; *esp* **:** a nation holding a mandate from the League of Nations

man–day \'man-'dā\ *n* **1 :** the labor of one man in one normal working day **2 :** a unit consisting of a hypothetical average man-day

Man·de \'män-ˌdā, män-'\ *n* **1 :** MANDINGO **2 :** a branch of the Niger-Congo language family spoken in French West Africa, Sierra Leone, and Liberia

man·di·ble \'man-də-bəl\ *n* [MF, fr. LL *mandibula*, fr. L *mandere* to chew — more at MOUTH] **1 a :** JAW 1a; *esp* **:** a lower jaw consisting of a single bone or of completely fused bones **b :** the lower jaw with its investing soft parts **c :** either the upper or lower segment of the bill of a bird **2 :** any of various invertebrate mouthparts serving to hold or bite food materials; *esp* **:** either member of the anterior pair of mouth appendages of an arthropod often forming strong biting jaws — **man·dib·u·lar** \man-'dib-yə-lər\ *adj* — **man·dib·u·late** \-lət\ *adj or n*

Man·din·go \man-'diŋ-(ˌ)gō\ *n, pl* **Mandingo** *or* **Mandingoes** *or* **Mandingos 1 :** a member of a people of western Africa centering in the upper Niger valley **2 :** the language of the Mandingo people

man·di·o·ca \ˌman-dē-'ō-kə\ *var of* MANIOC

man·do·la \man-'dō-lə\ *n* [It, fr. F *mandore*, modif. of LL *pandura* 3-stringed lute — more at BANDORE] **:** a 16th and 17th century lute that is the ancestor of the smaller mandolin

man·do·lin \ˌman-də-'lin, 'man-dᵊl-ən\ *also* **man·do·line** \ˌman-də-'lēn, 'man-dᵊl-ən\ *n* [It *mandolino*, dim. of *mandola*] **:** a musical instrument of the lute family that has a pear-shaped body and fretted neck and four to six pairs of strings — **man·do·lin·ist** \ˌman-də-'lin-əst\ *n*

man·drag·o·ra \man-'drag-ə-rə\ *n* [ME] **:** MANDRAKE 1

man·drake \'man-ˌdrāk\ *n* [ME, prob. alter. of *mandragora*, fr. OE, fr. L *mandragoras*, fr. Gk] **1 a :** a Mediterranean herb (*Mandragora officinarum*) of the nightshade family with ovate leaves, whitish or purple flowers, and a large forked root traditionally credited with human attributes **b :** the root of a mandrake formerly used esp. to promote conception, as a cathartic, or as a narcotic and soporific **2 :** MAYAPPLE

mandrake 1a

man·drel *also* **man·dril** \'man-drəl\ *n* [prob. modif. of F *mandrin*] **1 a :** a usu. tapered or cylindrical axle, spindle, or arbor inserted into a hole in a piece of work to support it during machining **b :** a metal bar that serves as a core around which material (as metal) may be cast, molded, forged, bent, or otherwise shaped **2 :** the shaft and bearings on which a tool (as a circular saw) is mounted

man·drill \'man-drəl\ *n* [prob. fr. [1]*man* + *drill*] **:** a large fierce gregarious baboon (*Mandrillus mormon*) of western Africa

mane \'mān\ *n* [ME, fr. OE *manu*; akin to OHG *mana* mane, L *monile* necklace] **1 :** long and heavy hair growing about the neck of some mammals (as a horse or lion) **2 :** long heavy hair on a person's head — **maned** \'mānd\ *adj*

man–eat·er \'man-ˌēt-ər\ *n* **:** one that has or is thought to have an appetite for human flesh: as **a :** CANNIBAL 1 **b :** MACKEREL SHARK; *esp* **:** WHITE SHARK **c :** a large feline (as a lion or tiger) that has acquired the habit of feeding on human flesh — **man–eat·ing** \-ˌēt-iŋ\ *adj*

man–eater shark *n* **:** MACKEREL SHARK; *esp* **:** WHITE SHARK

man–eating shark *n* **:** MAN-EATER SHARK

ma·nege *also* **ma·nège** \ma-'nezh, mə-, -'nāzh\ *n* [F *manège*, fr. It *maneggio* training of a horse — more at MANAGE] **1 :** a school for teaching horsemanship and for training horses **2 :** the art of horsemanship or of training horses **3 :** the movements or paces of a trained horse

ma·nes \'män-ˌās, 'mā-ˌnēz\ *n pl* [L] **1** *often cap* **:** the deified spirits of the ancient Roman dead honored with graveside sacrifices **2 :** the venerated or appeased spirit of a dead person

[1]ma·neu·ver \mə-'n(y)ü-vər\ *n* [F *manœuvre*, fr. OF *maneuvre* work done by hand, fr. ML *manuopera*, fr. L *manu operare* to work by hand] **1 a :** a military or naval movement **b :** an armed forces training exercise; *esp* **:** an extended and large-scale training exercise involving military and naval units separately or in combination — often used in pl. **2 :** a procedure or method of working usu. involving expert physical movement **3 a :** evasive movement or shift of tactics **b :** an intended and controlled variation from a straight and level flight path in the operation of an airplane **4 a :** an action taken to gain a tactical end **b :** an adroit and clever management of affairs often using trickery and deception ***syn*** see TRICK

[2]maneuver *vb* **ma·neu·vered; ma·neu·ver·ing** \-'n(y)üv-(ə-)riŋ\ *vi* **1 a :** to perform a movement in military or naval tactics in order to secure an advantage **b :** to make a series of changes in direction and position for a specific purpose **2 :** to use stratagems **:** SCHEME ~ *vt* **1 :** to cause to execute tactical movements **2 :** to manage into or out of a position or condition **:** MANIPULATE **3 a :** to guide with adroitness and design **b :** to bring about or secure as a result of skillful management — **ma·neu·ver·abil·i·ty** \-ˌn(y)üv-(ə-)rə-'bil-ət-ē\ *n* — **ma·neu·ver·able** \-'n(y)üv-(ə-)rə-bəl\ *adj* — **ma·neu·ver·er** \-'n(y)ü-vər-ər\ *n*

man–for–man \ˌman-fər-'man\ *adj* **:** MAN-TO-MAN 2

man Fri·day \'man-'frīd-ē\ *n* [*Friday*, native servant in *Robinson Crusoe* (1719), novel by Daniel Defoe] **:** an efficient and devoted aide or employee **:** a right-hand man

man·ful \'man-fəl\ *adj* **:** having or showing courage and resolution — **man·ful·ly** \-fə-lē\ *adv* — **man·ful·ness** *n*

mangan- *or* **mangano-** *comb form* [G *mangan*, fr. F *manganèse*] **:** manganese <*mangan*ous>

man·ga·nate \'maŋ-gə-ˌnāt\ *n* **1 :** a salt containing manganese in the anion MnO_4 **2 :** MANGANITE

man·ga·nese \'maŋ-gə-ˌnēz, -ˌnēs\ *n* [F *manganèse*, fr. It *manganese* magnesia, manganese, fr. ML *magnesia*] **:** a grayish white usu. hard and brittle metallic element that resembles iron but is not magnetic — see ELEMENT table — **man·ga·ne·sian** \ˌmaŋ-gə-'nē-zhən, -shən\ *adj*

manganese dioxide *n* **:** a dark insoluble compound MnO_2 used esp. as an oxidizing agent, as a depolarizer of dry cells, and in making glass and ceramics

manganese spar *n* **:** RHODONITE

man·gan·ic \man-'gan-ik, maŋ-\ *adj* **:** of, relating to, or derived from manganese; *esp* **:** containing this element with a valence of three or six

man·ga·nite \'maŋ-gə-ˌnīt\ *n* **1 :** an ore of manganese MnO(OH) that is a hydroxide of manganese usu. in brilliant gray crystals **2 :** any of various unstable salts made by reaction of manganese dioxide with a base

man·ga·nous \-nəs\ *adj* **:** of, relating to, or derived from manganese; *esp* **:** containing this element with a valence of two

mange \'mānj\ *n* [ME *manjewe,* fr. MF *mangene* itching, fr. *mangier* to eat] **:** any of various persistent contagious skin diseases marked esp. by eczematous inflammation and loss of hair that affect domestic animals or sometimes man; *esp* **:** one caused by a minute parasitic mite

man·gel \'maŋ-gəl\ *n* [short for *mangel-wurzel*] **:** MANGEL-WURZEL

man·gel–wur·zel \-ˌwər-zəl\ *n* [G *mangoldwurzel, mangelwurzel,* fr. *mangold* beet + *wurzel* root] **:** a large coarse yellow to reddish orange beet extensively grown as food for cattle

man·ger \'mān-jər\ *n* [ME *mangeour, manger,* fr. MF *maingeure,* fr. *mangier* to eat, fr. L *manducare* to chew, devour, fr. *manducus* glutton, fr. *mandere* to chew — more at MOUTH] **:** a trough or open box in a stable designed to hold feed or fodder for livestock

¹man·gle \'maŋ-gəl\ *vt* **man·gled; man·gling** \-g(ə-)liŋ\ [ME *manglen,* fr. AF *mangler,* freq. of OF *maynier* to maim] **1 :** to injure with deep disorganizing wounds by cutting, tearing, or crushing <people . . . *mangled* by sharks —V. G. Heiser> **2 :** to spoil or injure in making or performing ***syn*** see MAIM — **man·gler** \-g(ə-)lər\ *n*

²mangle *n* [D *mangel,* fr. G, fr. MHG, dim. of *mange* mangonel, mangle, fr. L *manganum*] **:** a machine for ironing laundry by passing it between heated rollers

³mangle *vt* **man·gled; man·gling** \-g(ə-)liŋ\ **:** to press or smooth (as damp linen) with a mangle — **man·gler** \-g(ə-)lər\ *n*

man·go \'maŋ-(ˌ)gō\ *n, pl* **mangoes** *or* **mangos** [Pg *manga,* fr. Tamil *mān-kāy*] **1 :** a yellowish red tropical fruit with a firm skin, hard central stone, and juicy aromatic subacid pulp; *also* **:** the evergreen tree (*Mangifera indica*) of the sumac family that bears this fruit **2 :** SWEET PEPPER

man·go·nel \'maŋ-gə-ˌnel\ *n* [ME, fr. MF, prob. fr. ML *manganellus,* dim. of LL *manganum* philter, mangonel, fr. Gk *manganon;* akin to MIr *meng* deception] **:** a military engine formerly used to throw missiles

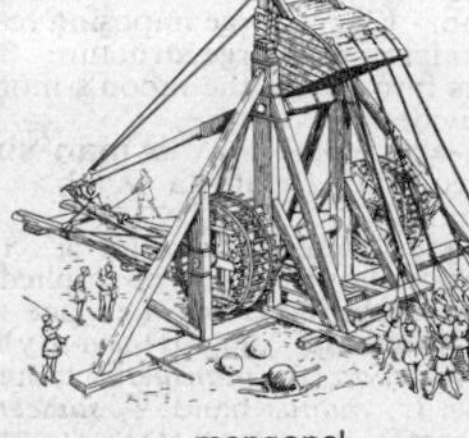
mangonel

man·go·steen \'maŋ-gə-ˌstēn\ *n* [Malay *mangustan*] **:** a dark reddish brown East Indian fruit with thick rind and juicy flesh having a flavor suggestive of both peach and pineapple; *also* **:** a tree (*Garcinia mangostana,* family Guttiferae) that bears this fruit

man·grove \'man-ˌgrōv, 'maŋ-\ *n* [prob. fr. Pg *mangue* mangrove (fr. Sp *mangle,* fr. Taino) + E *grove*] **1 :** any of a genus (*Rhizophora,* esp. *R. mangle*) of tropical maritime trees or shrubs that throw out many prop roots and form dense masses important in coastal land building **2 :** a tree (genus *Avicennia*) of the verbena family with growth habits like those of the true mangroves

mangy \'mān-jē\ *adj* **mang·i·er; -est 1 :** affected with or resulting from mange **2 :** having many worn or bare spots **:** SEEDY, SHABBY — **man·gi·ly** \-jə-lē\ *adv* — **man·gi·ness** \-jē-nəs\ *n*

man·han·dle \'man-ˌhan-dᵊl\ *vt* **1 :** to move or manage by human force <~ their car out of a ditch —*Scots Mag.*> **2 :** to handle roughly

man·hat·tan \man-'hat-ᵊn, mən-\ *n, often cap* [*Manhattan,* borough of New York city] **:** a cocktail consisting of sweet vermouth, rye or bourbon whiskey, and sometimes a dash of bitters

man·hole \'man-ˌhōl\ *n* **:** a hole through which a man may go esp. to gain access to an underground or enclosed structure

man·hood \'man-ˌhu̇d\ *n* **1 :** the condition of being a human being **2 :** manly qualities **:** COURAGE **3 :** the condition of being an adult male as distinguished from a child or female **4 :** adult males **:** MEN

man–hour \'man-'au̇(-ə)r\ *n* **:** a unit of one hour's work by one man that is used esp. as a basis for cost accounting and wages

man·hunt \'man-ˌhənt\ *n* **:** an organized and usu. intensive hunt for a person and esp. for one charged with a crime

ma·nia \'mā-nē-ə, -nyə\ *n* [ME, fr. LL, fr. Gk, fr. *mainesthai* to be mad; akin to Gk *menos* spirit — more at MIND] **1 :** excitement manifested by mental and physical hyperactivity, disorganization of behavior, and elevation of mood; *specif* **:** the manic phase of manic-depressive psychosis **2 :** excessive or unreasonable enthusiasm **:** CRAZE <had a ~ for saving things>

ma·ni·ac \'mā-nē-ˌak\ *n* [LL *maniacus* maniacal, fr. Gk *maniakos,* fr. *mania*] **1 :** LUNATIC, MADMAN **2 :** a person characterized by an inordinate or ungovernable enthusiasm for something

ma·ni·a·cal \mə-'nī-ə-kəl\ *also* **ma·ni·ac** \'mā-nē-ak\ *adj* **1 :** affected with or suggestive of madness **2 :** characterized by ungovernable excitement or frenzy **:** FRANTIC — **ma·ni·a·cal·ly** \mə-'nī-ə-k(ə-)lē\ *adv*

man·ic \'man-ik\ *adj* **:** affected with, relating to, or resembling mania — **manic** *n* — **man·i·cal·ly** \-i-k(ə-)lē\ *adv*

man·ic–de·pres·sive \ˌman-ik-di-'pres-iv\ *adj* **:** characterized either by mania or psychotic depression or by alternating mania and depression — **manic–depressive** *n*

Man·i·chae·an *or* **Man·i·che·an** \ˌman-ə-'kē-ən\ *or* **Man·i·chee** \'man-ə-ˌkē\ *n* [LL *manichaeus,* fr. LGk *manichaios,* fr. *Manichaios* Manes †*ab* 276 A.D. Pers founder of the sect] **1 :** a believer in a syncretistic religious dualism originating in Persia in the 3d century A.D. and teaching the release of the spirit from matter through asceticism **2 :** a believer in religious or philosophical dualism — **Manichaean** *adj* — **Man·i·chae·an·ism** \ˌman-ə-'kē-ə-ˌniz-əm\ *n* — **Man·i·chae·ism** \'man-ə-(ˌ)kē-ˌiz-əm\ *n*

ma·ni·cot·ti \ˌman-ə-'kät-ē\ *n, pl* **manicotti** [It, pl. of *manicotto* muff, fr. *manica* sleeve, fr. L, fr. *manus* hand] **:** tubular pasta shells that may be stuffed with ricotta or a meat mixture; **:** a dish of stuffed manicotti usu. with tomato sauce

¹man·i·cure \'man-ə-ˌkyu̇(ə)r\ *n* [F, fr. L *manus* hand + F *-icure* (as in *pédicure* pedicure) — more at MANUAL] **1 :** MANICURIST **2 :** a treatment for the care of the hands and fingernails

²manicure *vt* **-cured; -cur·ing 1 :** to do manicure work on; *esp* **:** to trim and polish the fingernails of **2 :** to trim closely and evenly <*manicured* lawns>

man·i·cur·ist \-ˌkyu̇r-əst\ *n* **:** a person who gives manicure treatments

¹man·i·fest \'man-ə-ˌfest\ *adj* [ME, fr. MF or L; MF *manifeste,* fr. L *manifestus,* lit., hit by the hand, fr. *manus* + *-festus* (akin to L *infestus* hostile) — more at DARE] **1 :** readily perceived by the senses and esp. by the sight **2 :** easily understood or recognized by the mind **:** OBVIOUS ***syn*** see EVIDENT ***ant*** latent, constructive — **man·i·fest·ly** *adv*

²manifest *vt* **:** to make evident or certain by showing or displaying ***syn*** see SHOW — **man·i·fest·er** *n*

³manifest *n* **1 :** MANIFESTATION, INDICATION **2 :** MANIFESTO **3 :** a list of passengers or an invoice of cargo for a ship or plane

man·i·fes·tant \ˌman-ə-'fes-tənt\ *n* **:** one who makes or participates in a manifestation

man·i·fes·ta·tion \ˌman-ə-fə-'stā-shən, -ˌfes-'tā-\ *n* **1 a :** the act, process, or an instance of manifesting **b :** something that manifests **c :** one of the forms in which an individual is manifested **d :** an occult phenomenon; *specif* **:** MATERIALIZATION **2 :** a public demonstration of power and purpose

manifest destiny *n, often cap M&D* **:** a future event accepted as inevitable <in the mid-19th century expansion to the Pacific was regarded as the *Manifest Destiny* of the United States>; *broadly* **:** an ostensibly benevolent or necessary policy of imperialistic expansion

¹man·i·fes·to \ˌman-ə-'fes-(ˌ)tō\ *n, pl* **-tos** *or* **-toes** [It, denunciation, manifest, fr. *manifestare* to manifest, fr. L, fr. *manifestus*] **:** a public declaration of intentions, motives, or views

²manifesto *vi* **:** to issue a manifesto

¹man·i·fold \'man-ə-ˌfōld\ *adj* [ME, fr. OE *manigfeald,* fr. *manig* many + *-feald* -fold] **1 :** marked by diversity or variety **:** VARIOUS **2 :** comprehending or uniting various features **:** MULTIFARIOUS **3 :** rightfully so-called for many reasons <a ~ liar> **4 :** consisting of or operating many of one kind combined <a ~ bellpull> — **man·i·fold·ly** \-ˌfōl-(d)lē\ *adv* — **man·i·fold·ness** \-ˌfōl(d)-nəs\ *n*

²manifold *adv* **:** many times **:** a great deal <will increase your blessings ~>

³manifold *n* **:** something that is manifold: as **a :** a whole that unites or consists of many diverse elements <the ~ of aspirations, passions, frustrations —Harry Slochower> **b :** a pipe fitting with several lateral outlets for connecting one pipe with others; *also* **:** a fitting on an internal-combustion engine that receives the exhaust gases from several cylinders **c :** SET 19 **d :** a topological space such that every point has a neighborhood which is homeomorphic to the interior of a sphere in Euclidean space of the same number of dimensions

⁴manifold *vt* **1 :** to make several or many copies of **2 :** to make manifold **:** MULTIPLY ~ *vi* **:** to make several or many copies

man·i·kin *or* **man·ni·kin** \'man-i-kən\ *n* [D *mannekijn* little man, fr. MD, dim. of *man;* akin to OE *man*] **1 :** MANNEQUIN **2 :** a little man **:** DWARF, PYGMY

ma·nila *also* **ma·nil·la** \mə-'nil-ə\ *adj* **1 :** made of manila paper **2** *cap* **:** made from Manila hemp — **manila** *n*

Manila hemp *n* [*Manila,* Philippine islands] **:** ABACA

manila paper *n, often cap M* **:** a strong and durable paper of a brownish or buff color and smooth finish made orig. from Manila hemp

ma·nille \mə-'nil\ *n* [modif. of Sp *malilla*] **:** the second highest trump in various card games (as ombre)

man in the street : an average or ordinary man

man·i·oc \'man-ē-ˌäk\ *or* **man·i·o·ca** \ˌman-ē-'ō-kə\ *n* [F *manioc* & Sp & Pg *mandioca,* of Tupian origin; akin to Tupi *manioca* cassava] **:** CASSAVA

man·i·ple \'man-ə-pəl\ *n* [ML *manipulus,* fr. L, handful, fr. *manus* hand + *-pulus* (akin to L *plēre* to fill); fr. its having been originally held in the hand — more at MANUAL, FULL] **1 :** a long narrow strip of silk worn at mass over the left arm by clerics of or above the order of subdeacon — see VESTMENT illustration **2** [L *manipulus,* fr. *manipulus* handful; fr. the custom of using a handful of hay on the end of a pole as a military standard] **:** a subdivision of the Roman legion consisting of either 120 or 60 men

ma·nip·u·la·ble \mə-'nip-yə-lə-bəl\ *adj* **:** MANIPULATABLE — **ma·nip·u·la·bil·i·ty** \-ˌnip-yə-lə-'bil-ət-ē\ *n*

ma·nip·u·lar \mə-'nip-yə-lər\ *adj* **1 :** of or relating to the ancient Roman maniple **2 :** of, relating to, or performed by manipulation **:** MANIPULATIVE

ma·nip·u·late \mə-'nip-yə-ˌlāt\ *vt* **-lat·ed; -lat·ing** [back-formation fr. *manipulation,* fr. F, fr. *manipule* handful, fr. L *manipulus*] **1 :** to treat or operate with the hands or by mechanical means esp. in a skillful manner **2 a :** to manage or utilize skillfully **b :** to control or play upon by artful, unfair, or insidious means esp. to one's own advantage **3 :** to change by artful or unfair means so as to serve one's purpose **:** DOCTOR ***syn*** see HANDLE — **ma·nip·u·lat·able** \-ˌlāt-ə-bəl\ *adj* — **ma·nip·u·la·tion** \-ˌnip-yə-'lā-shən\ *n* — **ma·nip·u·la·tive** \-'nip-yə-ˌlāt-iv\ *adj* — **ma·nip·u·la·tive·ly** *adv* — **ma·nip·u·la·tor** \-ˌlāt-ər\ *n* — **ma·nip·u·la·to·ry** \-lə-ˌtōr-ē, -ˌtȯr-\ *adj*

man·i·tou *or* **man·i·tu** \'man-ə-ˌtü\ *also* **man·i·to** \-ˌtō\ *n* [of Algonquian origin; akin to Ojibwa *manito* spirit, god] **:** a supernatural force that according to an Algonquian conception pervades the natural world

man jack \'man-ˌjak, -'jak\ *n* : individual man <every *man jack*>

man·kind *n sing but sing or pl in constr* **1** \'man-'kīnd, -ˌkīnd\ : the human race : the totality of human beings **2** \-ˌkīnd\ : men as distinguished from women

[1]**man·ly** \'man-lē\ *adj* **man·li·er; -est** **1** : having qualities generally associated with a man : STRONG, VIRILE **2** : appropriate in character to a man <~ sports> — **man·li·ness** *n*

[2]**manly** *adv* : in a manly manner

man–made \'man-'mād\ *adj* : manufactured, created, or constructed by man; *specif* : SYNTHETIC <~ fibers>

mann- *or* **manno-** *comb form* [ISV, fr. *manna*] : manna <*mannose*>

man·na \'man-ə\ *n* [ME, fr. OE, fr. LL, fr. Gk, fr. Heb *mān*] **1 a** : food miraculously supplied to the Israelites in their journey through the wilderness **b** : divinely supplied spiritual nourishment **c** : a usu. sudden and unexpected source of gratification, pleasure, or gain **2** : sweetish dried exudate esp. of a European ash that contains mannitol and has been used as a laxative and demulcent

manna grass *n* : any of a genus (*Glyceria*) of chiefly No. American perennial paludal or aquatic grasses with 5- to 9-nerved lemmas

man·nan \'man-ˌan, -ən\ *n* [ISV *mann*ose + [3]*-an*] : any of several polysaccharides that are polymers of mannose and occur esp. in plant cell walls

manned \'mand\ *adj* : carrying or performed by a man <~ space flight>

man·ne·quin \'man-i-kən\ *n* [F, fr. D *mannekijn* little man — more at MANIKIN] **1** : an artist's, tailor's, or dressmaker's lay figure; *also* : a form representing the human figure used esp. for displaying clothes **2** : a woman who models clothing : MODEL

man·ner \'man-ər\ *n* [ME *manere*, fr. OF *maniere* way of acting, fr. (assumed) VL *manuaria*, fr. L, fem. of *manuarius* of the hand, fr. *manus* hand — more at MANUAL] **1** : KIND, SORT <what ~ of man is he> **2 a** (1) : a characteristic or customary mode of acting : CUSTOM (2) : a mode of procedure or way of acting : FASHION (3) : method of artistic execution or mode of presentation : STYLE **b** *pl* : social conduct or rules of conduct as shown in the prevalent customs <Victorian ~*s*> **c** : characteristic or distinctive bearing, air, or deportment <his poised gracious ~> **d** *pl* (1) : habitual conduct or deportment : BEHAVIOR <mind your ~*s*> (2) : good manners **e** : a distinguished or stylish air ***syn*** see BEARING, METHOD — **man·ner·less** \-ləs\ *adj*

man·nered \'man-ərd\ *adj* **1** : having manners of a specified kind <well-*mannered*> **2 a** : having or displaying a particular manner **b** : having an artificial or stilted character <passages . . . so ~ as to be unintelligible —R. G. G. Price>

man·ner·ism \'man-ə-ˌriz-əm\ *n* **1 a** : exaggerated or affected adherence to a particular style or manner : ARTIFICIALITY, PRECIOSITY <refined almost to the point of ~ —Winthrop Sargeant> **b** *often cap* : an art style in late 16th century Europe characterized by spatial incongruity and excessive elongation of the human figures **2** : a characteristic and often unconscious mode or peculiarity of action, bearing, or treatment ***syn*** see POSE — **man·ner·ist** \-rəst\ *n* — **man·ner·is·tic** \ˌman-ə-'ris-tik\ *adj*

man·ner·ly \'man-ər-lē\ *adj* : showing good manners — **man·ner·li·ness** *n* — **mannerly** *adv*

man·nish \'man-ish\ *adj* **1** : resembling or suggesting a man rather than a woman **2** : generally associated with or characteristic of a man rather than a woman <her ~ clothes> — **man·nish·ly** *adv* — **man·nish·ness** *n*

man·nite \'man-ˌīt\ *n* [F, fr. *manna*, fr. LL] : MANNITOL — **man·nit·ic** \ma-'nit-ik\ *adj*

man·ni·tol \'man-ə-ˌtȯl, -ˌtōl\ *n* [ISV] : a slightly sweet crystalline alcohol $C_6H_{14}O_6$ found in many plants and used esp. in testing kidney function

man·nose \'man-ˌōs, -ˌōz\ *n* [ISV] : an aldose sugar $C_6H_{12}O_6$ obtained by oxidation of mannitol

ma·no \'män-(ˌ)ō\ *n, pl* **manos** [Sp, lit., hand, fr. L *manus* — more at MANUAL] : a stone used as the upper millstone for grinding foods (as Indian Corn) by hand in a metate

ma·noeu·vre \mə-'n(y)ü-vər\ *chiefly Brit var of* MANEUVER

man of God : CLERGYMAN

man of letters **1** : SCHOLAR **2** : AUTHOR

man of straw : STRAW MAN

man of the cloth : CLERGYMAN

man of the house : the chief male in a household

man of the world : a practical or worldly-wise man of wide experience

man–of–war \ˌman-ə(v)-'wȯ(ə)r\ *n, pl* **men–of–war** \ˌmen-\ : a combatant warship of a recognized navy

ma·nom·e·ter \mə-'näm-ət-ər\ *n* [F *manomètre*, fr. Gk *manos* sparse, loose, rare + F *-mètre* — more at MONK] **1** : an instrument (as a pressure gauge) for measuring the pressure of gases and vapors **2** : SPHYGMOMANOMETER — **mano·met·ric** \ˌman-ə-'me-trik\ *or* **mano·met·ri·cal** \-tri-kəl\ *adj* — **mano·met·ri·cal·ly** \-tri-k(ə-)lē\ *adv* — **ma·nom·e·try** \mə-'näm-ə-trē\ *n*

man on horseback [*Man on Horseback*, epithet applied to Georges E. J. M. Boulanger, who frequently appeared in public on horseback] **1** : a usu. military figure whose ambitions and popularity mark him as a potential dictator **2** : DICTATOR

man·or \'man-ər\ *n* [ME *maner*, fr. OF *manoir*, fr. *manoir* to sojourn, dwell, fr. L *manēre* — more at MANSION] **1 a** : the house or hall of an estate : MANSION **b** : a landed estate **2 a** : a unit of English rural territorial organization; *esp* : such a unit in the Middle Ages consisting of an estate under a lord enjoying a variety of rights over land and tenants including the right to hold court **b** : a tract of land in No. America occupied by tenants who pay a fixed rent in money or kind to the proprietor — **ma·no·ri·al** \mə-'nōr-ē-əl, -'nȯr-\ *adj* — **ma·no·ri·al·ism** \-ə-ˌliz-əm\ *n*

manor house *n* : the house of the lord of a manor

man–o'–war bird \ˌman-ə-'wȯr-\ *n* : FRIGATE BIRD

man·pack \'man-ˌpak\ *adj* : designed to be carried by one person <the silver-zinc battery is widely used as a power source for . . . ~ radios —*The Sciences*>

man power *n* **1** : power available from or supplied by the physical effort of man **2** *usu* **manpower** : the total supply of persons available and fitted for service (as in the armed forces or industry)

man·qué \mäⁿ-'kā\ *adj* [F, fr. pp. of *manquer* to lack, fail] : short of or frustrated in the fulfillment of one's aspirations or talents <a poet ~>

man·rope \'man-ˌrōp\ *n* : a side rope (as to a ship's gangway or ladder) used as a handrail

man·sard \'man-ˌsärd\ *n* [F *mansarde*, fr. François *Mansart* †1666 F architect] : a roof having two slopes on all sides with the lower slope steeper than the upper one — **man·sard·ed** \-əd\ *adj*

mansard roof

manse \'man(t)s\ *n* [ME *manss*, fr. ML *mansa, mansus, mansum*, fr. L *mansus*, pp. of *manēre*] **1** *archaic* : the dwelling of a householder **2** : the residence of a clergyman; *esp* : the house of a Presbyterian clergyman

man·ser·vant \'man-ˌsər-vənt\ *n, pl* **men·ser·vants** \'men-ˌsər-vən(t)s\ : a male servant

-man·ship \-mən-ˌship\ *n suffix* [*sportsmanship*] : the art or practice of maneuvering to gain a tactical advantage <games*manship*>

man·sion \'man-chən\ *n* [ME, fr. MF, fr. L *mansion-, mansio*, fr. *mansus*, pp. of *manēre* to remain, dwell; akin to Gk *menein* to remain] **1 a** *obs* : the act of remaining or dwelling : STAY **b** *archaic* : DWELLING, ABODE **2 a** (1) : the house of the lord of a manor (2) : a large imposing residence **b** : a separate apartment or lodging in a large structure **3 a** : HOUSE 3b **b** : one of the 28 parts into which the moon's monthly course through the heavens is divided

man–size \'man-ˌsīz\ *or* **man–sized** \-ˌsīzd\ *adj* **1** : suitable for or requiring a man <a ~ job> **2** : LARGE-SCALE <constructed a ~ model>

man·slaugh·ter \'man-ˌslȯt-ər\ *n* : the unlawful killing of a human being without express or implied malice

man·slay·er \-ˌslā-ər\ *n* : one who slays a man

man·sue·tude \'man(t)-swi-ˌt(y)üd, man-'sü-ə-\ *n* [ME, fr. L *mansuetudo*, fr. *mansuetus* tame, mild, fr. pp. of *mansuescere* to tame, fr. *manus* hand + *suescere* to accustom; akin to Gk *ēthos* custom — more at MANUAL, ETHICAL] : the quality or state of being gentle : MEEKNESS, TAMENESS

man·ta \'mant-ə\ *n* [Sp] **1** : a square piece of cloth or blanket used in southwestern U.S. and Latin America usu. as a cloak or shawl **2** [AmerSp, fr. Sp; fr. its being caught in traps resembling huge blankets] : DEVILFISH 1

manta ray *n* : DEVILFISH 1

man·teau \man-'tō, 'man-ˌ\ *n* [F, fr. OF *mantel*] : a loose cloak, coat, or robe

man·tel \'mant-ᵊl\ *n* [MF, fr. OF, mantle] **1 a** : a beam, stone, or arch serving as a lintel to support the masonry above a fireplace **b** : the finish around a fireplace **2** : a shelf above a fireplace

man·te·let \'mant-lət, -ᵊl-ət, ˌmant-ᵊl-'et\ *n* **1** : a very short cape or cloak **2** *or* **mant·let** \'mant-lət\ : a movable shelter formerly used by besiegers as a protection when attacking

man·tel·let·ta \ˌmant-ᵊl-'et-ə\ *n* [It] : a knee-length mantle formerly worn by a high prelate (as a cardinal) of the Roman Catholic Church

man·tel·piece \'mant-ᵊl-ˌpēs\ *n* **1** : a mantel with its side elements **2** : MANTEL 2

man·tel·shelf \-ˌshelf\ *n* : MANTEL 2

man·tic \'mant-ik\ *adj* [Gk *mantikos*, fr. *mantis*] : of or relating to the faculty of divination : PROPHETIC

man·ti·core \'mant-i-ˌkō(ə)r, -ˌkȯ(ə)r\ *n* [ME, fr. L *mantichora*, fr. Gk *mantichōras*] : a legendary animal with the head of a man, the body of a lion, and the tail of a dragon or scorpion

man·tid \'mant-əd\ *n* [NL *Mantidae*, group name, fr. *Mantis*, genus name] : MANTIS — **mantid** *adj*

man·til·la \man-'tē-(y)ə, -'til-ə\ *n* [Sp, dim. of *manta*] **1** : a light scarf worn over the head and shoulders esp. by Spanish and Latin-American women **2** : a short light cape or cloak

man·tis \'mant-əs\ *n, pl* **man·tis·es** *or* **man·tes** \'man-ˌtēz\ [NL, fr. Gk, lit., diviner, prophet; akin to Gk *mainesthai* to be mad — more at MANIA] : an insect (order Manteodea and esp. genus *Mantis*) that feeds on other insects and clasps its prey in forelimbs held up as if in prayer

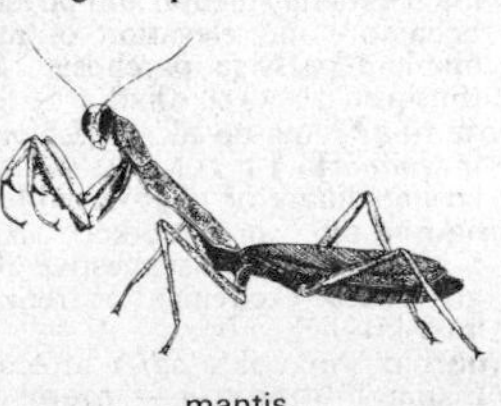

mantis

man·tis·sa \man-'tis-ə\ *n* [L *mantisa, mantissa* makeweight, fr. Etruscan] : the decimal part of a logarithm

[1]**man·tle** \'mant-ᵊl\ *n* [ME *mantel*, fr. OF, fr. L *mantellum*] **1 a** : a loose sleeveless garment worn over other clothes : CLOAK **b** : a mantle regarded as a symbol of preeminence or authority <invested his people with the ~ of universal champions of justice —Denis Goulet> **2 a** : something that covers, enfolds, or envelops **b** (1) : a fold or lobe or pair of lobes of the body wall of a mollusk or brachiopod that lines the shell in shell-bearing forms and bears shell-secreting glands (2) : the soft external body wall that lines the test or shell of a tunicate or barnacle **c** : the outer wall and casing of a blast furnace above the hearth; *broadly* : an insulated support or casing in which something is heated **3** : the back, scapulars, and wings of a bird **4** : a lacy hood or sheath of some refractory material that gives light by incandescence when placed over a flame **5 a** : MANTLEROCK **b** : the part of the interior of a terrestrial planet and esp. the earth

that lies beneath the lithosphere and above the central core 6 : MANTEL

[2]**mantle** *vb* **man·tled; man·tling** \'mant-liŋ, -ᵊl-iŋ\ *vt* : to cover with or as if with a mantle : CLOAK ~ *vi* **1** : to become covered with a coating **2** : to spread over a surface **3** : BLUSH <her rich face *mantling* with emotion —Benjamin Disraeli>

man·tle·rock \'mant-ᵊl-ˌräk\ *n* : unconsolidated residual or transported material that overlies the earth's solid rock

man-to-man \ˌman-tə-'man\ *adj* **1** : characterized by frankness and honesty <a ~ talk> **2** : of, relating to, or being a system of defense (as in football or basketball) in which each defensive player guards a specified opponent

Man·toux test \ˌman-ˌtü-, ˌmäⁿ-\ *n* [Charles *Mantoux* †1947 F physician] : an intracutaneous test for hypersensitivity to tuberculin that indicates past or present infection with tubercle bacilli

man·tra \'man-trə\ *n* [Skt, sacred counsel, formula, fr. *manyate* he thinks; akin to L *mens* mind — more at MIND] : a mystical formula of invocation or incantation (as in Hinduism)

man·trap \'man-ˌtrap\ *n* : a trap for catching men : SNARE

man·tua \'manch-(ə-)wə, 'mant-ə-wə\ *n* [modif. of F *manteau*] : a usu. loose-fitting gown worn esp. in the 17th and 18th centuries

Manu \'man-(ˌ)ü\ *n* [Skt] : the progenitor of the human race and giver of the religious laws of Manu according to Hindu mythology

[1]**man·u·al** \'man-yə(-wə)l\ *adj* [ME *manuel*, fr. MF, fr. L *manualis*, fr. *manus* hand; akin to OE *mund* hand, Gk *marē*] **1 a** : of, relating to, or involving the hands <~ dexterity> **b** : worked or done by hand and not by machine <a ~ choke> <~ computation> <~ indexing> **2** : requiring or using physical skill and energy <~ labor> <~ workers> — **man·u·al·ly** \-ē\ *adv*

[2]**manual** *n* **1** : a book that is conveniently handled; *esp* : HANDBOOK **2** : the prescribed movements in the handling of a weapon or other military item during a drill or ceremony <the ~ of arms> **3 a** : a keyboard for the hands; *specif* : one of the several keyboards of a pipe-organ console that controls a separate division of the instrument **b** : a device or apparatus intended for manual operation

manual alphabet *n* : an alphabet for deaf-mutes in which the letters are represented by finger positions

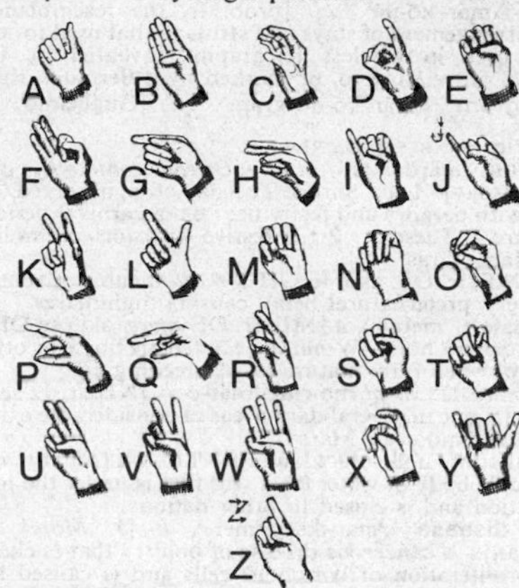

manual alphabet

manual training *n* : a course of training to develop skill in using the hands and to teach practical arts (as woodworking and metalworking)

ma·nu·bri·um \mə-'n(y)ü-brē-əm\ *n, pl* **-bria** \-brē-ə\ *also* **-bri·ums** [NL, fr. L, handle, fr. *manus*] : an anatomical process or part shaped like a handle: as **a** : the cephalic segment of the sternum of man and many other mammals **b** : the process that bears the mouth of a hydrozoan : HYPOSTOME

manuf *abbr* manufacture; manufacturing

man·u·fac·to·ry \ˌman-(y)ə-'fak-t(ə-)rē\ *n* : FACTORY 2a

[1]**man·u·fac·ture** \ˌman-(y)ə-'fak-chər\ *n* [MF, fr. L *manu factus* made by hand] **1** : something made from raw materials **2 a** : the process of making wares by hand or by machinery esp. when carried on systematically with division of labor **b** : a productive industry using mechanical power and machinery **3** : the act or process of producing something

[2]**manufacture** *vb* **man·u·fac·tured; man·u·fac·tur·ing** \-'fak-chə-riŋ, -'fak-shriŋ\ *vt* **1** : to make into a product suitable for use **2 a** : to make from raw materials by hand or by machinery **b** : to produce according to an organized plan and with division of labor **3** : INVENT, FABRICATE **4** : to produce as if by manufacturing : CREATE <writers who ~ stories for television> ~ *vi* : to engage in manufacture *syn* see MAKE — **manufacturing** *n*

manufactured gas *n* : a combustible gaseous mixture made from coal, coke, or petroleum products

man·u·fac·tur·er \ˌman-(y)ə-'fak-chər-ər, -'fak-shrər\ *n* : one that manufactures; *esp* : an employer of workers in manufacturing

man·u·mis·sion \ˌman-yə-'mish-ən\ *n* [ME, fr. MF, fr. L *manumission-, manumissio*, fr. *manumissus*, pp. of *manumittere*] : the act or process of manumitting; *esp* : formal emancipation from slavery

man·u·mit \ˌman-yə-'mit\ *vt* **-mit·ted; -mit·ting** [ME *manumitten*, fr. MF *manumitter*, fr. L *manumittere*, fr. *manus* hand + *mittere* to let go, send — more at SMITE] : to release from slavery *syn* see FREE *ant* enslave

[1]**ma·nure** \mə-'n(y)u̇(ə)r\ *vt* **ma·nured; ma·nur·ing** [ME *manouren*, fr. MF *manouvrer*, lit., to do work by hand, fr. L *manu operare*] **1** *obs* : CULTIVATE **2** : to enrich (land) by the application of manure — **ma·nur·er** *n*

[2]**manure** *n* : material that fertilizes land; *esp* : refuse of stables and barnyards consisting of livestock excreta with or without litter — **ma·nu·ri·al** \-'n(y)u̇r-ē-əl\ *adj*

ma·nus \'mā-nəs, 'mä-\ *n, pl* **ma·nus** \-nəs, -ˌnüs\ [NL, fr. L, hand] : the distal segment of the vertebrate forelimb including the carpus and forefoot or hand

[1]**manu·script** \'man-yə-ˌskript\ *adj* [L *manu scriptus*] : written by hand or typed <~ letters>

[2]**manuscript** *n* **1** : a written or typewritten composition or document as distinguished from a printed copy **2** : writing as opposed to print

[1]**man·ward** \'man-wərd\ *adv* : toward man

[2]**manward** *adj* : directed toward man

man·wise \'man-ˌwīz\ *adv* : in the manner of men

[1]**Manx** \'maŋ(k)s\ *adj* [alter. of earlier *Maniske*, fr. (assumed) ON *manskr*, fr. *Mana* Isle of Man] : of, relating to, or characteristic of the Isle of Man, its people, or the Manx language

[2]**Manx** *n* **1** *pl in constr* : the people of the Isle of Man **2** : the Celtic language of the Manx people almost completely displaced by English

Manx cat *n* : a short-haired domestic cat with no external tail

[1]**many** \'men-ē\ *adj* **more** \'mō(ə)r, 'mȯ(ə)r\; **most** \'mōst\ [ME, fr. OE *manig*; akin to OHG *manag* many, OSlav *mŭnogŭ* much] **1** : consisting of or amounting to a large but indefinite number <worked for ~ years> **2** : being one of a large but indefinite number <~ a man> <~ another student> — **as many** : the same in number <saw three plays in *as many* days>

[2]**many** *pron, pl in constr* : a large number of persons or things <~ of them>

[3]**many** *n, pl in constr* **1** : a large but indefinite number <a good ~ of them> **2** : the great majority of people <the ~>

many·fold \ˌmen-ē-'fōld\ *adv* : by many times <aid to education has increased ~>

many-sid·ed \ˌmen-ē-'sīd-əd\ *adj* **1** : having many sides or aspects **2** : having many interests or aptitudes *syn* see VERSATILE — **many-sid·ed·ness** *n*

many-val·ued \ˌmen-ē-'val-(ˌ)yüd, -yəd\ *adj* **1** : possessing more than the customary two truth-values of truth and falsehood **2** : MULTIPLE-VALUED

Man·za·nil·la \ˌman-zə-'nē-(y)ə, -'nil-ə\ *n* [Sp, dim. of *manzana* apple] : a pale dry Spanish sherry

man·za·ni·ta \ˌman-zə-'nēt-ə\ *n* [AmerSp, dim. of Sp *manzana* apple] : any of various western No. American evergreen shrubs (genus *Arctostaphylos*) of the heath family

MAO *abbr* monoamine oxidase

Mao·ism \'mau̇-ˌiz-əm\ *n* : the theory and practice of Marxism-Leninism developed in China chiefly by Mao Tse-tung — **Mao·ist** \'mau̇-əst\ *n or adj*

Mao·ri \'mau̇(ə)r-ē\ *n, pl* **Maori** *or* **Maoris** **1** : a member of a Polynesian people native to New Zealand **2** : the Austronesian language of the Maori

[1]**map** \'map\ *n* [ML *mappa*, fr. L, napkin, towel] **1 a** : a representation usu. on a flat surface of the whole or a part of an area **b** : a representation of the celestial sphere or a part of it **2** : something that represents with a clarity suggestive of a map **3** : the arrangement of genes on a chromosome — called also *genetic map* **4** : FUNCTION 5a

[2]**map** *vb* **mapped; map·ping** *vt* **1 a** : to make a map of <~ the surface of the moon> **b** : to delineate as if on a map <sorrow was *mapped* on her face> **c** : to make a survey of for the purpose of making a map **d** : to assign to every element of (a mathematical set) an element of the same or another set **2** : to plan in detail — often used with *out* <~ out a program> ~ *vi, of a gene* : to be located <a repressor ~*s* near the corresponding structural gene> — **map·pa·ble** \'map-ə-bəl\ *adj* — **map·per** *n*

MApL *abbr* master of applied linguistics

ma·ple \'mā-pəl\ *n* [ME, fr. OE *mapul-*; akin to ON *möpurr* maple] : any of a genus (*Acer* of the family Aceraceae, the maple family) of trees or shrubs with opposite leaves and a fruit of two united samaras; *also* : the hard light-colored close-grained wood of a maple used esp. for flooring and furniture

maple sugar *n* : sugar made by boiling maple syrup

maple syrup *n* : syrup made by concentrating the sap of maple trees and esp. the sugar maple

map·mak·er \'map-ˌmā-kər\ *n* : one who makes maps : CARTOGRAPHER — **map·mak·ing** \-kiŋ\ *n*

map·ping \'map-iŋ\ *n* **1** : the act or process of making a map **2** : FUNCTION 5a <a one-to-one continuous ~>

maple tree with *1* fruit and *2* leaf

ma·quette \ma-'ket\ *n* [F] : a usu. small preliminary model (as of a sculpture or a building)

ma·quil·lage \ˌmak-ē-'(y)äzh\ *n* [F] : MAKEUP 3

ma·quis \ma-'kē, mä-\ *n, pl* **ma·quis** \-'kē(z)\ [F] **1** : thick scrubby underbrush of Mediterranean shores and esp. of the island of Corsica; *also* : an area of such underbrush **2** *often cap* **a**

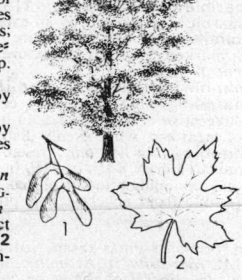

ə abut ᵊ kitten ər further a back ā bake ä cot, cart
au̇ out ch chin e less ē easy g gift i trip ī life
j joke ŋ sing ō flow ȯ flaw ȯi coin th thin t͟h this
ü loot u̇ foot y yet yü few yu̇ furious zh vision

: a guerrilla fighter in the French underground during World War II **b :** a band of maquis

1mar \'mär\ *vt* **marred; mar·ring** [ME *marren,* fr. OE *mierran* to obstruct, waste; akin to OHG *merren* to obstruct] **1 :** to detract from the perfection or wholeness of : SPOIL **2** *archaic* **a :** to inflict serious bodily harm on **b :** DESTROY ***syn*** see INJURE

2mar *n* **:** something that mars : BLEMISH

3mar *abbr* maritime

Mar *abbr* March

MAR *abbr* master of arts in religion

mar·a·bou *or* **mar·a·bout** \'mar-ə-,bü\ *n* [F *marabout,* lit., marabout] **1 a :** a large African stork (*Leptoptilos crumeniferus*) that has a distensible pouch of pink skin at the front of the neck and feeds esp. on refuse and carrion **b :** a soft feathery fluffy material prepared from the long coverts of marabous or usu. from turkey feathers and used esp. for trimming women's hats or clothes **2 a :** a thrown silk usu. dyed in the gum **b :** a fabric made of this silk

mar·a·bout \'mar-ə-bü\ *n, often cap* [F, fr. Pg *marabuto,* fr. Ar *murābiṭ*] **:** a dervish in Muslim Africa believed to have supernatural power

ma·ra·ca \mə-'räk-ə, -'rak-\ *n* [Pg *maracá*] **:** a dried gourd or a rattle like a gourd that contains dried seeds or pebbles and is used as a percussion instrument

mar·ag·ing steel \,mär-,ā-jiŋ-\ *n* [*mar*tensite + *aging*] **:** a strong tough low-carbon martensitic steel which contains up to 25 percent nickel and in which hardening precipitates are formed by aging

mar·a·schi·no \,mar-ə-'skē-(,)nō, -'shē-\ *n, pl* **-nos** *often cap* [It, fr. *marasca* bitter wild cherry] **1 :** a sweet liqueur distilled from the fermented juice of a bitter wild cherry **2 :** a usu. large cherry preserved in true or imitation maraschino

ma·ras·mus \mə-'raz-məs\ *n* [LL, fr. Gk *marasmos,* fr. *marainein* to waste away — more at SMART] **:** progressive emaciation esp. in the young associated usu. with faulty assimilation and utilization of food — **ma·ras·mic** \-'raz-mik\ *adj*

Ma·ra·tha \mə-'rät-ə\ *n* [Marathi *Marāṭhā* & Hindi *Marhaṭṭā,* fr. Skt *Mahārāṣṭra* Maharashtra] **:** a member of a people of the south central part of the subcontinent of India

Ma·ra·thi \mə-'rät-ē\ *n* [Marathi *marāṭhī*] **:** the chief Indic language of the state of Maharashtra in India

mar·a·thon \'mar-ə-,thän\ *n* [*Marathon,* Greece, site of a victory of Greeks over Persians in 490 B.C. the news of which was carried to Athens by a long-distance runner] **1 :** a long-distance race: **a :** a footrace run on an open course usu. of 26 miles 385 yards **b :** a race other than a footrace marked esp. by great length **2 a :** an endurance contest <a dance ~> **b :** something (as an event or activity) characterized by great length or concentrated effort

ma·raud \mə-'rȯd\ *vb* [F *marauder*] *vi* **:** to roam about and raid in search of plunder ~ *vt* **:** RAID, PILLAGE — **ma·raud·er** *n*

mar·a·ve·di \,mar-ə-və-'dē\ *n* [Sp *maravedí,* fr. Ar *Murābiṭīn* 11th & 12th cent. Muslim dynasty in No. Africa & Spain] **:** a medieval Spanish copper coin unit worth 1/34 real

1mar·ble \'mär-bəl\ *n* [ME, fr. OF *marbre,* fr. L *marmor,* fr. Gk *marmaros*] **1 a :** limestone that is more or less crystallized by metamorphism, that ranges from granular to compact in texture, that is capable of taking a high polish, and that is used esp. in architecture and sculpture **b :** something (as a piece of sculpture) composed of or made from marble **c :** something suggesting marble (as in hardness, coldness, or smoothness) <she has a heart of ~> **2 a :** a little ball made of a hard substance (as glass) and used in various games **b** *pl but sing in constr* **:** any of several games played with these little balls with the object being to hit a mark or hole, hit another player's marble, or knock as many marbles as possible out of a ring **3 :** MARBLING **4** *pl, slang* **:** elements of common sense; *esp* **:** SANITY <persons who are born without all their ~*s* —Arthur Miller>

2marble *vt* **mar·bled; mar·bling** \-b(ə-)liŋ\ **:** to give a veined or mottled appearance to <~ the edges of a book>

3marble *adj* **:** resembling, composed of, or suggestive of marble <~ floors>

marble cake *n* **:** a cake made with light and dark batter so as to have a mottled appearance

mar·bled \'mär-bəld\ *adj* **1** [1*marble*] **a :** done in or covered with marble **b :** marked by an extensive use of marble as an architectural or decorative feature <ancient ~ cities> **2** [2*marble*] **:** marked by an intermixture of fat and lean <a well-*marbled* cut of beef>

mar·ble·ize \'mär-bə-,līz\ *vt* **-ized; -iz·ing :** MARBLE

mar·bling \-b(ə-)liŋ\ *n* **1 :** coloration or markings resembling or suggestive of marble **2 :** an intermixture of fat and lean in a cut of meat esp. when evenly distributed

mar·bly \-b(ə-)lē\ *adj* **:** resembling or suggestive of marble

marc \'märk\ *n* [F, fr. MF, fr. *marchier* to trample] **1 :** the residue remaining after a fruit has been pressed; *broadly* **:** the organic residue from an extraction process <the protein-rich cottonseed ~> **2 :** brandy made from the residue of grapes or apples after pressing

mar·ca·site \'mär-kə-,sīt, -,zīt; ,mär-kə-'zēt\ *n* [ME *marchasite,* fr. ML *marcasita,* fr. Ar *marqashīthā*] **1 a :** crystallized iron pyrites **b :** a mineral of the same composition and appearance as iron pyrites but of different crystalline organization and lower specific gravity **2 :** a piece of marcasite used for ornaments — **mar·ca·sit·i·cal** \,mär-kə-'sit-i-kəl, -'zit-\ *adj*

1mar·cel \mär-'sel\ *n* [*Marcel* Grateau †1936 F hairdresser] **:** a deep soft wave made in the hair by the use of a heated curling iron

2marcel *vb* **mar·celled; mar·cel·ling** *vt* **:** to make a marcel in ~ *vi* **:** to make a marcel

1march \'märch\ *n* [ME *marche,* fr. OF, of Gmc origin; akin to OHG *marha* boundary — more at MARK] **:** a border region : FRONTIER; *esp* **:** a district orig. set up to defend a boundary — usu. used in pl. <the Welsh ~*es*>

2march *vi* **:** to have common borders or frontiers <a region that ~*es* with Canada in the north and the Pacific in the west>

3march \'märch, *imperatively often* 'härch *in the military*\ *vb* [MF *marchier* to trample, march, fr. OF, to trample, prob. of Gmc origin; akin to OHG *marcōn* to mark] *vi* **1 :** to move along steadily usu. with a rhythmic stride and in step with others **2 a :** to move in a direct purposeful manner : PROCEED **b :** to make steady progress : ADVANCE <time ~*es* on> **3 :** to stand in orderly array suggestive of marching <pine trees ~*ing* up the mountainside> ~ *vt* **1 :** to cause to march <~*ed* the children off to bed> **2 :** to cover by marching : TRAVERSE <~*ed* 10 miles>

4march \'märch\ *n* **1 a** (1) **:** the action of marching (2) **:** the distance covered within a specific period of time by marching (3) **:** a regular measured stride or rhythmic step used in marching **b :** forward movement : PROGRESS <the ~ of a movie towards the climax> **2 :** a musical composition that is usu. in duple or quadruple time with a strongly accentuated beat and that is designed or suitable to accompany marching — **on the march :** moving steadily : ADVANCING

March \'märch\ *n* [ME, fr. OF, fr. L *martius,* fr. *martius* of Mars, fr. *Mart-, Mars*] **:** the 3d month of the Gregorian calendar

mär·chen \'me(ə)r-k̲ən\ *n, pl* **märchen** [G] **:** TALE; *esp* **:** FOLKTALE

1march·er \'mär-chər\ *n* **:** one who inhabits a border region

2marcher *n* **:** one that marches; *esp* **:** one that marches for a specific cause <a peace ~>

mar·che·sa \mär-'kā-zə\ *n, pl* **-se** \-(,)zā\ [It, fem. of *marchese*] **:** an Italian woman holding the rank of a marchese : MARCHIONESS

mar·che·se \-(,)zā\ *n, pl* **-si** \-(,)zē\ [It, fr. ML *marcensis,* fr. *marca* border region, of Gmc origin; akin to OHG *marha*] **:** an Italian nobleman next in rank above a count : MARQUIS

mar·chio·ness \'mär-sh(ə-)nəs\ *n* [ML *marchionissa,* fr. *marchion-, marchio* marquess, fr. *marca*] **1 :** the wife or widow of a marquess **2 :** a woman who holds the rank of marquess in her own right

march·pane \'märch-,pān\ *n* [It *marzapane*] **:** MARZIPAN

march-past \'märch-,past\ *n* **:** a filing by : PROCESSION

Mar·cion·ism \'mär-shə-,niz-əm, -s(h)ē-ə-\ *n* [*Marcion* 2d cent. A.D. Christian Gnostic] **:** the doctrinal system of a sect of the 2d and 3d centuries A.D. accepting some parts of the New Testament but denying Christ's corporality and humanity and condemning the Creator God of the Old Testament — **Mar·cion·ite** \-,nīt\ *n*

Mar·co·ni \mär-'kō-nē\ *adj* [prob. fr. the resemblance of the complex arrangement of stays and struts to that used to support the antennae used in wireless telegraphy, invented by Guglielmo Marconi] **:** of, relating to, or marked by a Bermuda rig

mar·co·ni·gram \mär-'kō-nē-,gram\ *n* [Guglielmo *Marconi*] **:** RADIOGRAM

Marconi rig *n* **:** BERMUDA RIG

Mar·di Gras \'märd-ē-,grä, *in New Orleans commonly* -,grō\ *n* [F, lit., fat Tuesday] **1 a :** Shrove Tuesday often observed (as in New Orleans) with parades and festivities **b :** a carnival period climaxing on Shrove Tuesday **2 :** a festive occasion resembling a pre-Lenten Mardi Gras

1mare *n* [ME, fr. OE; akin to OHG *mara* incubus, Croatian *mora*] *obs* **:** an evil preternatural being causing nightmares

2mare \'ma(ə)r, 'me(ə)r\ *n* [ME, fr. OE *mere;* akin to OHG *merha* mare, OE *mearh* horse, W *march*] **:** a female horse or other equine animal esp. when fully mature or of breeding age

3ma·re \'mär-(,)ā\ *n, pl* **ma·ria** \'mär-ē-ə\ [NL, fr. L, sea — more at MARINE] **:** one of several dark areas of considerable extent on the surface of the moon or Mars

ma·re clau·sum \,mär-(,)ā-'klaů-səm, -'klō-\ *n* [NL, lit., closed sea] **:** a navigable body of water (as a sea) that is under the jurisdiction of one nation and is closed to other nations

Mar·ek's disease \'mar-iks-, 'mer-\ *n* [J. *Marek* †1952 G veterinarian] **:** a cancerous disease of poultry that is characterized esp. by proliferation of lymphoid cells and is caused by a virus resembling a herpes virus

ma·re li·be·rum \'mär-(,)ā-'lē-bə-,rům\ *n* [NL, lit., free sea] **1 :** a navigable body of water (as a sea) that is open to all nations **2 :** FREEDOM OF THE SEAS

ma·re no·strum \,mär-(,)ā-'nō-strəm\ *n* [L, our sea] **:** a navigable body of water (as a sea) that belongs to a single nation or is mutually shared by two or more nations

mare's nest *n, pl* **mare's nests** *or* **mares' nests 1 :** a false discovery, illusion, or deliberate hoax **2 :** a place, condition, or situation of great disorder or confusion <a *mare's nest* of spurious ambiguities to bewilder the simpleminded —J. H. Sledd>

mare's tail *n, pl* **mare's tails** *or* **mares' tails 1 :** a cirrus cloud that has a long slender flowing appearance **2 a :** a common aquatic plant (*Hippuris vulgaris*) with elongated shoots clothed with dense whorls of subulate leaves **b :** HORSETAIL **c :** HORSEWEED 1

mar·gar·ic acid \mär-,gar-ik-\ *n* [F *margarique,* fr. *margarine*] **:** a crystalline synthetic fatty acid $C_{17}H_{34}O_2$ intermediate between palmitic acid and stearic acid

mar·ga·rine \'märj-(ə-)rən, -ə-,rēn\ *n* [F, fr. Gk *margaron* pearl] **:** a food product made usu. from vegetable oils churned with ripened skim milk to a plastic consistency, often fortified with vitamins A and D, and used as a spread and a cooking fat

mar·ga·ri·ta \,mär-gə-'rēt-ə\ *n* [MexSp, prob. fr. the name *Margarita* Margaret] **:** a cocktail consisting of tequila, lime or lemon juice, and an orange-flavored liqueur

mar·ga·rite \'mär-gə-,rīt\ *n* [ME, fr. MF, fr. L *margarita,* fr. Gk *margaritēs,* fr. *margaron*] *archaic* **:** PEARL

mar·gay \'mär-,gā, mär-'\ *n* [F, fr. Tupi *maracaja*] **:** a small American spotted cat (*Felis tigrina*) resembling the ocelot and ranging from southernmost Texas to Brazil

marge \'märj\ *n* [MF, fr. L *margo*] *archaic* **:** MARGIN

mar·gent \'mär-jənt\ *n, archaic* **:** MARGIN

1mar·gin \'mär-jən\ *n* [ME, fr. L *margin-, margo* border — more at MARK] **1 :** the part of a page or sheet outside the main body of printed or written matter **2 :** the outside limit and adjoining surface of something : EDGE <at the ~ of the woods> **3 a :** a spare amount or measure or degree allowed or given for contingencies or special situations <left no ~ for error in his calculations> **b** (1) **:** a bare minimum below which or an extreme limit beyond which something becomes impossible or is no longer desirable <a joke

that was on the ~ of good taste> (2) : the limit below which economic activity cannot be continued under normal conditions **4 a :** the difference which exists between net sales and the cost of merchandise sold and from which expenses are usu. met or profit derived **b :** the excess market value of collateral over the face of a loan **c** (1) **:** cash or collateral that is deposited by a client with a commodity or securities broker to protect the broker from loss on a contract (2) **:** the client's equity in securities bought with the aid of credit obtained specif. (as from a broker) for that purpose **d :** a range about a specified figure within which a purchase is to be made **5 :** measure or degree of difference <the bill passed by a one-vote ~> ***syn*** see BORDER — **mar·gined** \-jənd\ *adj*

margay

²margin *vt* **1 :** to enter or summarize in the margin of (a page or sheet) **2 a :** to provide with an edging or border **b :** to form a margin to : BORDER **3 a :** to add margin to <~ up an account in a falling market> **b** (1) **:** to use as margin <~ bonds to buy stock> (2) **:** to provide margin for <~ a transaction> **c :** to buy (securities) on margin

mar·gin·al \ˈmärj-nəl, -ən-ᵊl\ *adj* [ML *marginalis,* fr. L *margin-, margo*] **1 :** written or printed in the margin of a page or sheet <~ notes> **2 a :** of, relating to, or situated at a margin or border <regards violence as a ~ rather than a central problem> **b** (1) **:** occupying the borderland of a relatively stable territorial or cultural area <~ tribes> (2) **:** characterized by the incorporation of habits and values from two divergent cultures and by incomplete assimilation in either <the ~ cultural habits of new immigrant groups> **3 :** located at the fringe of consciousness <~ sensations> **4 a :** close to the lower limit of qualification, acceptability, or function <a semi-literate man of ~ ability> **b** (1) **:** having a character or capacity fitted to yield a supply of goods which when marketed at existing price levels will barely cover the cost of production <~ land> (2) **:** of, relating to, or derived from goods produced and marketed with such result <~ profits> **5 :** relating to or being a function of a random variable that is obtained from a function of several random variables by integrating or summing over all possible values of the other variables <a ~ probability function> — **mar·gin·al·i·ty** \ˌmär-jə-ˈnal-ət-ē\ *n* — **mar·gin·al·ly** \ˈmärj-nə-lē, -ən-ᵊl-ē\ *adv*

mar·gi·na·lia \ˌmär-jə-ˈnā-lē-ə\ *n pl* [NL, fr. ML, neut. pl. of *marginalis*] **1 :** marginal notes (as in a book) **2 :** nonessential items <the ~ of a science>

marginal utility *n* **:** the amount of additional utility provided by an additional unit of an economic good or service

¹mar·gin·ate \ˈmär-jə-ˌnāt\ *vt* **-at·ed; -at·ing :** MARGIN 1, 2a — **mar·gin·ation** \ˌmär-jə-ˈnā-shən\ *n*

²mar·gin·ate \ˈmär-jə-nət, -ˌnāt\ *or* **mar·gin·at·ed** \-ˌnāt-əd\ *adj* **:** having a margin distinct in appearance or structure

mar·gra·vate \ˈmär-grə-ˌvāt\ *or* **mar·gra·vi·ate** \mär-ˈgrā-vē-ət, -ˌāt\ *n* **:** the territory of a margrave

mar·grave \ˈmär-ˌgrāv\ *n* [D *markgraaf,* fr. MD *marcgrave;* akin to OHG *marcgrāvo;* both fr. a prehistoric D-G compound whose constituents are akin to OHG *marha* boundary and to OHG *grāvo* count — more at MARK] **1 :** the military governor esp. of a German border province **2 :** a member of the German nobility corresponding in rank to a British marquess — **mar·gra·vi·al** \mär-ˈgrā-vē-əl\ *adj*

mar·gra·vine \ˈmär-grə-ˌvēn, ˌmär-grə-ˈ\ *n* **:** the wife of a margrave

mar·gue·rite \ˌmär-g(y)ə-ˈrēt\ *n* [F, fr. MF *margarite* pearl, daisy — more at MARGARITE] **1 :** DAISY 1 **2 :** any of various single-flowered chrysanthemums; *esp* **:** a chrysanthemum (*Chrysanthemum frutescens*) of the Canary islands **3 :** any of several cultivated chamomiles (genus *Anthemis*)

ma·ri·a·chi \ˌmär-ē-ˈäch-ē\ *n* [MexSp] **1 :** a Mexican street band; *also* **:** a musician belonging to such a band **2 :** the music performed by a mariachi

Mar·i·an \ˈmer-ē-ən, ˈmar-ē-, ˈmā-rē-\ *adj* **1 :** of or relating to Mary Tudor or her reign (1553-58) **2 :** of or relating to the Virgin Mary

Mar·i·an·ist \-ə-nəst\ *n* **:** a member of the Roman Catholic Society of Mary of Paris founded by William Joseph Chaminade in France in 1817 and devoted esp. to education

Ma·ria The·re·sa dollar \mə-ˌrē-ə-tə-ˌrā-sə-, -ˌrā-zə-\ *n* **:** a silver coin with the image of Maria Theresa and the date 1780 used as a trade coin in the Middle East

mari·cul·ture \ˈmar-ə-ˌkəl-chər\ *n* [L *mare* sea + E *-culture* (as in *agriculture*)] **:** the cultivation of marine organisms by exploiting their natural environment

mari·gold \ˈmar-ə-ˌgōld, ˈmer-\ *n* [ME, fr. *Mary,* mother of Jesus + ME *gold*] **1 :** POT MARIGOLD **2 :** any of a genus (*Tagetes*) of herbaceous composite plants with showy yellow or red and yellow flower heads

mar·i·jua·na *or* **mar·i·hua·na** \ˌmar-ə-ˈwän-ə *also* -ˈhwän-\ *n* [MexSp *mariguana, marihuana*] **1 :** a wild tobacco (*Nicotiana glauca*) **2 a :** HEMP 1a, 1c **b :** the dried leaves and flowering tops of the pistillate hemp plant that yield cannabin and are sometimes smoked in cigarettes for their intoxicating effect — compare BHANG, CHARAS, HASHISH

ma·rim·ba \mə-ˈrim-bə\ *n* [of African origin; akin to Kimbundu *marimba* xylophone] **:** a primitive xylophone of southern Africa and Central America with resonators beneath each bar; *also* **:** a modern improved form of this instrument

ma·ri·na \mə-ˈrē-nə\ *n* [It & Sp, seashore, fr. fem. of *marino,* adj., marine, fr. L *marinus*] **:** a dock or basin providing secure moorings for motorboats and yachts and often offering supply, repair, and other facilities

¹mar·i·nade \ˌmar-ə-ˈnād\ *vt* **-nad·ed; -nad·ing** [by alter.] **:** MARINATE

²marinade *n* **:** a savory usu. acidic sauce in which meat, fish, or a vegetable is soaked to enrich its flavor or to tenderize it

mar·i·nate \ˈmar-ə-ˌnāt\ *vt* **-nat·ed; -nat·ing** [prob. fr. It *marinato,* pp. of *marinare* to marinate, fr. *marino*] **:** to steep (meat, fish, or vegetables) in a marinade

¹ma·rine \mə-ˈrēn\ *adj* [ME, fr. L *marinus,* fr. *mare* sea; akin to OE *mere* sea, pool, OHG *meri* sea, OSlav *morje*] **1 a :** of or relating to the sea <~ life> **b :** of or relating to the navigation of the sea : NAUTICAL <a ~ chart> **c :** of or relating to the commerce of the sea : MARITIME <~ law> **d :** depicting the sea, seashore, or ships <a ~ painter> **2 :** of or relating to marines <~ barracks>

²marine *n* **1 a :** the mercantile and naval shipping of a country **b :** seagoing ships esp. in relation to nationality or class **2 :** one of a class of soldiers serving on shipboard or in close association with a naval force; *specif* **:** a member of the U.S. Marine Corps **3 :** an executive department (as in France) having charge of naval affairs **4 :** a marine picture : SEASCAPE

marine architect *n* **:** NAVAL ARCHITECT — **marine architecture** *n*

marine glue *n* **:** a water-insoluble adhesive

mar·i·ner \ˈmar-ə-nər\ *n* **:** one who navigates or assists in navigating a ship : SEAMAN, SAILOR

mariner's compass *n* **:** a compass used in navigation that consists of parallel magnetic needles or bundles of needles permanently attached to a card marked to indicate direction and degrees of a circle

Mar·i·ol·a·try \ˌmer-ē-ˈäl-ə-trē, ˌmar-ē-, ˌmā-rē-\ *n* **:** excessive veneration of the Virgin Mary — **Mar·i·ol·a·ter** \-ˈäl-ət-ər\ *n*

Mar·i·ol·o·gy \-ˈäl-ə-jē\ *n* **:** study or doctrine relating to the Virgin Mary — **Mar·i·o·log·i·cal** \-ə-ˈläj-i-kəl\ *adj*

mar·i·o·nette \ˌmar-ē-ə-ˈnet, ˌmer-\ *n* [F *marionnette,* fr. MF *maryonete,* fr. *Marion* dim. of *Marie* Mary] **:** a small-scale usu. wooden figure (as of a person or animal) with jointed limbs that is moved from above by manipulation of the attached strings or wires — called also *puppet*

mar·i·po·sa lily \ˌmar-ə-ˌpō-zə-, -sə-\ *n* [prob. fr. AmSp *mariposa,* fr. Sp, butterfly] **:** any of a genus (*Calochortus*) of western No. American plants of the lily family usu. with showily blotched flowers — called also *mariposa tulip*

mar·ish \ˈmar-ish\ *n, archaic* **:** MARSH

Mar·ist \ˈmar-əst, ˈmer-\ *n* [F *mariste,* fr. *Marie* Mary] **:** a member of the Roman Catholic Society of Mary founded by Jean Claude Colin in France in 1816 and devoted to education

mar·i·tal \ˈmar-ət-ᵊl, *Brit also* mə-ˈrīt-\ *adj* [L *maritalis,* fr. *maritus* married] **1 :** of or relating to marriage or the married state <~ vows> **2 :** of or relating to a husband and his role in marriage ***syn*** see MATRIMONIAL — **mar·i·tal·ly** \-ᵊl-ē\ *adv*

mar·i·time \ˈmar-ə-ˌtīm\ *adj* [L *maritimus,* fr. *mare*] **1 :** of or relating to navigation or commerce on the sea **2 :** of, relating to, or bordering on the sea <a ~ province> **3 :** having the characteristics of a mariner

mar·jo·ram \ˈmärj-(ə-)rəm\ *n* [alter. of ME *majorane,* fr. MF, fr. ML *majorana*] **:** any of various usu. fragrant and aromatic mints (genera *Origanum* and *Majorana*) often used in cookery

¹mark \ˈmärk\ *n* [ME, fr. OE *mearc* boundary, march, sign; akin to OHG *marha* boundary, L *margo*] **1 :** a boundary land **2 a** (1) **:** a conspicuous object serving as a guide for travelers (2) **:** something (as a line, notch, or fixed object) designed to record position **b :** one of the bits of leather or colored bunting placed on a sounding line at intervals **c :** TARGET **d :** the starting line or position in a track event **e** (1) **:** GOAL, OBJECT (2) **:** an object of attack, ridicule, or abuse; *specif* **:** a victim of a swindle (3) **:** the point under discussion **f :** a standard of performance, quality, or condition : NORM <hadn't been feeling up to the ~ lately> **3 a** (1) **:** SIGN, INDICATION <gave her the necklace as a ~ of his esteem> (2) **:** an impression (as a scratch, scar, or stain) made on something (3) **:** a distinguishing trait or quality : CHARACTERISTIC <the ~s of an educated man> **b :** a symbol used for identification or indication of ownership **c :** a cross made in place of a signature **d** (1) **:** TRADEMARK (2) *cap* — used with a numeral to designate a particular model of a weapon or machine <*Mark* II> **e :** POSTMARK **f :** a symbol used by a teacher to represent his estimate of a student's work or conduct; *esp* **:** GRADE **g :** a figure registering a point or level reached or achieved <the halfway ~ in the first period of play>; *esp* **:** RECORD **4 a :** ATTENTION, NOTICE <nothing worthy of ~> **b :** IMPORTANCE, DISTINCTION <stands out as a man of ~> **c :** a lasting or strong impression <worked at several jobs but didn't make much of a ~> **d :** an assessment of merits : RATING <got high ~s for honesty>

²mark *vb* [ME *marken,* fr. OE *mearcian;* akin to OHG *marcōn* to determine the boundaries of, OE *mearc* boundary] *vt* **1 a** (1) **:** to fix or trace out the bounds or limits of (2) **:** to plot the course of : CHART **b :** to set apart by or as if by a line or boundary — usu. used with *off* **2 a** (1) **:** to designate as if by a mark <~*ed* for greatness> (2) **:** to make or leave a mark on (3) **:** to furnish with natural marks <wings ~*ed* with white> (4) **:** to label so as to indicate price or quality (5) **:** to make notations in or on **b** (1) **:** to make note of in writing : JOT <~*ing* the date in his journal> (2) **:** to indicate by a mark or symbol <~ an accent> (3) **:** REGISTER, RECORD (4) **:** to determine the value of by means of marks or symbols : GRADE <~ term papers> **c** (1) **:** CHARACTERIZE, DISTINGUISH <the flamboyance that ~s her stage appearance> (2) **:** SIGNALIZE <this year ~s the 50th anniversary of the

organization> **3 :** to take notice of **:** OBSERVE <~ my words> **4 :** to pick up (one's golf ball) from a putting green and substitute a marker <picking up a penalty stroke for *~ing* and cleaning her ball —Pat Ryan> ~ *vi* **:** to take careful notice — **mark time 1 :** to keep the time of a marching step by moving the feet alternately without advancing **2 :** to function or operate in a listless or unproductive manner

3mark *n* [ME, fr. OE *marc,* prob. of Scand origin; akin to ON *mörk* mark; akin to OE *mearc* sign] **1 :** any of various old European units of weight used esp. for gold and silver; *esp* **:** a unit equal to about 8 ounces **2 :** a unit of value: **a :** an old English unit equal to 13*s* 4*d* **b :** any one of various old Scandinavian or German units of value; *specif* **:** a unit and corresponding silver coin of the 16th century worth ½ taler **c** — see MONEY table **d :** MARKKA

Mark \'märk\ *n* [L *Marcus*] **1 a :** an early Jewish Christian traditionally identified as the writer of the Gospel of Mark — called also *John Mark* **b :** the second Gospel in the New Testament — see BIBLE table **2 :** a king of Cornwall, uncle of Tristram, and husband of Isolde

mark·down \'märk-ˌdau̇n\ *n* **1 :** a lowering of price **2 :** the amount by which an original selling price is reduced

mark down \(ˈ)märk-'dau̇n\ *vt* **:** to put a lower price on <*marked down* all the merchandise for the sale>

marked \'märkt\ *adj* **1 :** having an identifying mark <a ~ card> **2 :** having a distinctive or emphasized character **:** NOTICEABLE <has a ~ drawl> **3 a :** enjoying fame or notoriety **b :** being an object of attack, suspicion, or vengeance <a ~ man> **4 :** overtly signaled by a linguistic feature <with most English nouns the plural is the ~ number> — **mark·ed·ly** \'mär-kəd-lē\ *adv*

mark·er \'mär-kər\ *n* **1 :** one that marks **2 :** something used for marking **3 :** SCORE 7; *specif* **:** RUN **4 :** GENETIC MARKER

1mar·ket \'mär-kət\ *n* [ME, fr. ONF, fr. L *mercatus* trade, marketplace, fr. *mercatus,* pp. of *mercari* to trade, fr. *merc-, merx* merchandise; akin to Oscan a*miricadut* without remuneration] **1 a** (1) **:** a meeting together of people for the purpose of trade by private purchase and sale and usu. not by auction (2) **:** the people assembled at such a meeting **b** (1) **:** a public place where a market is held; *esp* **:** a place where provisions are sold at wholesale (2) **:** a retail establishment usu. of a specified kind <a fish ~> **2** *archaic* **:** the act or an instance of buying and selling **3 :** the rate or price offered for a commodity or security **4 a :** a geographical area of demand for commodities <the foreign ~> **b :** the course of commercial activity by which the exchange of commodities is effected **:** extent of demand <the ~ is dull> **c :** an opportunity for selling <a good ~ for used cars> **d :** the area of economic activity in which buyers and sellers come together and the forces of supply and demand affect prices <producing goods for ~ rather than for consumption> — **in the market :** interested in buying <*in the market* for a house> — **on the market :** available for purchase <a good selection of fresh produce *on the market*>; *also* **:** up for sale <put his house *on the market*>

2market *vi* **:** to deal in a market ~ *vt* **1 :** to expose for sale in a market **2 :** SELL

mar·ket·able \'mär-kət-ə-bəl\ *adj* **1 a :** fit to be offered for sale in a market <contaminated food that is not ~> **b :** wanted by purchasers **:** SALABLE <~ securities> **2 :** of or relating to buying or selling — **mar·ket·abil·i·ty** \ˌmär-kət-ə-'bil-ət-ē\ *n*

mar·ket·er \'mär-kət-ər\ *n* **:** one that deals in a market; *esp* **:** one that markets a specified commodity <the company is a big gasoline ~>

market garden *n* **:** a plot in which vegetables are raised for market — **market gardener** *n* — **market gardening** *n*

mar·ket·ing *n* **1 :** the act or process of selling or purchasing in a market **2 :** an aggregate of functions involved in moving goods from producer to consumer

marketing research *n* **:** research conducted to establish the extent and location of the market for a product or to analyze the cost of products and processes as compared with that of alternative or competitive products or processes

market order *n* **:** an order to buy or sell securities or commodities immediately at the best price obtainable in the market

mar·ket·place \'mär-kət-ˌplās\ *n* **1 a :** an open square or place in a town where markets or public sales are held **b :** MARKET <the ~ is the interpreter of supply and demand> **2 :** the world of trade or economic activity **:** the everyday world <a conviction that religion belongs in the ~ —*Current Biog.*> **3 :** a sphere in which intangible values compete for acceptance <the ~ of ideas>

market price *n* **:** a price actually given in current market dealings

market research *n* **:** the gathering of factual information as to consumer preferences for goods and services

market value *n* **:** a price at which both buyers and sellers are willing to do business

mark·ing *n* **1 :** the act, process, or an instance of making or giving a mark **2 a :** a mark made **b :** arrangement, pattern, or disposition of marks

mark·ka \'mär-ˌkä\ *n, pl* **mark·kaa** \'mär-ˌkä\ *or* **markkas** \-ˌkäz\ [Finn, fr. Sw *mark,* a unit of value; akin to ON *mork*] — see MONEY table

Mar·kov chain \ˌmär-ˌkȯf-, -ˌkȯv-\ *n* [A. A. *Markov* †1922 Russ mathematician] **:** a usu. discrete stochastic process (as a random walk) in which the probabilities of occurrence of various future states depend only on the present state of the system or on the immediately preceding state and not on the path by which the present state was achieved — called also *Markoff chain*

Mar·kov·ian \mär-'kō-vē-ən, -'kȯ-\ *or* **Mar·kov** \'mär-ˌkȯf, -ˌkȯv\ *also* **Mar·koff** \'mär-ˌkȯf\ *adj* **:** of, relating to, or resembling a Markov process or Markov chain esp. by having probabilities defined in terms of transition from the possible existing states to other states <~ models>

Markov process *also* **Markoff process** *n* **:** a stochastic process (as Brownian movement) that resembles a Markov chain except that the states are continuous; *also* **:** MARKOV CHAIN

marks·man \'märk-smən\ *n* **:** one that shoots at a mark; *esp* **:** a person skillful or practiced in hitting a mark or target — **marks·man·ship** \-ˌship\ *n*

marks·wom·an \'märk-ˌswu̇m-ən\ *n* **:** a female marksman

mark·up \'mär-ˌkəp\ *n* **1 :** a raise in the price of an article **2 :** an amount added to the cost price to determine the selling price

mark up \(ˈ)mär-'kəp\ *vt* **:** to set a higher price on

1marl \'mär(ə)l\ *n* [ME, fr. MF *marle,* fr. ML *margila,* dim. of L *marga* marl, fr. Gaulish] **:** a loose or crumbling earthy deposit (as of sand, silt, or clay) that contains a substantial amount of calcium carbonate and is used esp. as a fertilizer for soils deficient in lime — **marly** \'mär-lē\ *adj*

2marl *vt* **:** to dress (land) with marl

3marl *vt* [D *marlen,* back-formation fr. *marling*] **:** to cover or fasten with marline

mar·lin \'mär-lən\ *n* [short for *marlinspike;* fr. the appearance of its beak] **:** any of several large oceanic sport fishes (genera *Makaira* and *Tetrapturus*) related to sailfishes and spearfishes

mar·line *also* **mar·lin** \'mär-lən\ *n* [D *marlijn,* alter. of *marling,* fr. *meren, marren* to tie, moor, fr. MD *meren, maren* — more at MOOR] **:** a small usu. tarred line of two strands twisted loosely left-handed that is used esp. for seizing and as a covering for wire rope

mar·line·spike *also* **mar·lin·spike** \'mär-lən-ˌspīk\ *n* **:** a tool (as of wood or iron) that tapers to a point and is used to separate strands of rope or wire (as in splicing)

marl·ite \'mär(ə)l-ˌīt\ *n* **:** a marl resistant to the action of air — **mar·lit·ic** \mär-'lit-ik\ *adj*

mar·ma·lade \'mär-mə-ˌlād\ *n* [Pg *marmelada* quince conserve, fr. *marmelo* quince, fr. L *melimelum,* a sweet apple, fr. Gk *melimēlon,* fr. *meli* honey + *mēlon* apple — more at MELLIFLUOUS] **:** a clear sweetened jelly in which pieces of fruit and fruit rind are suspended

mar·mo·re·al \mär-'mōr-ē-əl, -'mȯr-\ *or* **mar·mo·re·an** \-ē-ən\ *adj* [L *marmoreus,* fr. *marmor* marble, fr. Gk *marmaros*] **:** of, relating to, or resembling marble or a marble statue — **mar·mo·re·al·ly** \-ē-ə-lē\ *adv*

mar·mo·set \'mär-mə-ˌset, -ˌzet\ *n* [ME *marmusette,* fr. MF *marmoset* grotesque figure, fr. *marmouser* to mumble, of imit. origin] **:** any of numerous soft-furred So. and Central American monkeys (family Callithricidae) with claws instead of nails on all the digits except the great toe

mar·mot \'mär-mət\ *n* [F *marmotte*] **:** a stout-bodied short-legged burrowing rodent (genus *Marmota*) with coarse fur, a short bushy tail, and very small ears — compare WOODCHUCK

Mar·o·nite \'mar-ə-ˌnīt\ *n* [ML *maronita,* fr. *Maron-, Maro* 5th cent. A.D. Syrian monk] **:** a member of a Uniate church chiefly in Lebanon having a Syriac liturgy and married clergy

1ma·roon \mə-'rün\ *n* [modif. of AmerSp *cimarrón,* fr. *cimarrón* wild, savage] **1** *cap* **:** a fugitive Negro slave of the West Indies and Guiana in the 17th and 18th centuries; *also* **:** a descendant of such a slave **2 :** a person who is marooned

2maroon *vt* **1 :** to put ashore on a desolate island or coast and leave to one's fate **2 :** to place or leave in isolation or without hope of ready escape

3maroon *n* [F *marron* Spanish chestnut] **:** a variable color averaging a dark red

mar·plot \'mär-ˌplät\ *n* **:** one who frustrates or ruins a plan or undertaking by his meddling

1marque \'märk\ *n* [ME, fr. MF, fr. OProv *marca,* fr. *marcar* to mark, seize as pledge, of Gmc origin; akin to OHG *marcōn* to mark] **1** *obs* **:** REPRISAL, RETALIATION **2 :** LETTERS OF MARQUE

2marque *n* [F, mark, brand, fr. MF, fr. *marquer* to mark, of Gmc origin; akin to OHG *marcōn* to mark] **:** a brand or make of a product (as a sports car)

mar·quee \mär-'kē\ *n* [modif. of F *marquise,* lit., marchioness] **1 :** a large tent set up for an outdoor party, reception, or exhibition **2 :** a permanent canopy usu. of metal and glass projecting over an entrance (as of a hotel or theater)

Mar·que·san \mär-'kāz-ᵊn, -'kās-\ *n* **1 :** a native or inhabitant of the Marquesas islands **2 :** the Austronesian language of the Marquesans — **Marquesan** *adj*

mar·quess \'mär-kwəs\ *or* **mar·quis** \'mär-kwəs, mär-'kē\ *n, pl* **mar·quess·es** *or* **mar·quis·es** \-kwə-səz\ *or* **mar·quis** \-'kē(z)\ [ME *marquis, markis,* fr. MF *marquis,* alter. of *marchis,* fr. *marche* march] **1 :** a nobleman of hereditary rank in Europe and Japan **2 :** a member of the British peerage ranking below a duke and above an earl — **mar·quess·ate** \'mär-kwə-sət\ *or* **mar·quis·ate** \'mär-kwə-zət, -sət\ *n*

mar·que·try *also* **mar·que·terie** \'mär-kə-trē\ *n* [MF *marqueterie,* fr. *marqueter* to checker, inlay, fr. *marque* mark] **:** decorative work in which elaborate patterns are formed by the insertion of pieces of material (as wood, shell, or ivory) into a wood veneer that is then applied to a surface (as of a piece of furniture)

1 marquetry

mar·quise \mär-'kēz\ *n, pl* **mar·quises** \-'kēz(-əz)\ [F, fem. of *marquis*] **1 :** MARCHIONESS **2 :** MARQUEE **3 :** a gem or a ring setting or bezel usu. elliptical in shape but with pointed ends — see BRILLIANT illustration

mar·qui·sette \ˌmär-k(w)ə-'zet\ *n* [*marquise* + *-ette*] **:** a sheer meshed fabric used for clothing, curtains, and mosquito nets

mar·ram grass \'mar-əm-\ *n* [of Scand origin; akin to ON *maralmr,* a beach grass] **:** any of several beach grasses (genus *Ammophila* and esp. *A. arenaria*)

Mar·ra·no \mə-'rän-(ˌ)ō\ *n, pl* **-nos** [Sp, lit., pig] **:** a Christianized Jew or Moor of medieval Spain

mar·riage \'mar-ij\ *n* **1 a :** the state of being married **b :** the mutual relation of husband and wife **:** WEDLOCK **c :** the institution whereby men and women are joined in a special kind of social and legal dependence for the purpose of founding and maintaining a family **2 :** an act of marrying or the rite by which the married status is effected; *esp* **:** the wedding ceremony and attendant festivities or formalities **3 :** an intimate or close union <the ~ of painting and poetry —J. T. Shawcross> — **mar·riage·able** \-ə-bəl\ *adj*

marriage of convenience : a marriage contracted for social, political, or economic advantage rather than for mutual affection

[1]**mar·ried** \ˈmar-ēd\ *adj* **1 a :** being in the state of matrimony **:** WEDDED **b :** of or relating to marriage **:** CONNUBIAL **2 :** UNITED, JOINED

[2]**married** *n, pl* **marrieds** *or* **married :** a married person <young ~*s* are paid undue . . . attention —Paul Goodman>

mar·ron \ma-ˈrō^{n}\ *n* [F] **1 :** a large Mediterranean chestnut (*Castanea sativa*) or its sweet edible nut — called also *Spanish chestnut* **2 mar·rons** \-ˈrō^{n}(z)\ *pl* **:** chestnuts preserved in vanilla-flavored syrup

Mar·ron \ma-ˈrō^{n}\ *n* [F, fr. AmerSp *cimarrón*] **:** MAROON 1

mar·rons gla·cés \ma-ˌrō^{n}-gla-ˈsā\ *n pl* [F, lit., glazed marrons] **:** MARRON 2

[1]**mar·row** \ˈmar-(ˌ)ō, -ə(-w)\ *n* [ME *marowe,* fr. OE *mearg;* akin to OHG *marag* marrow, Skt *majjan*] **1 a :** a soft highly vascular modified connective tissue that occupies the cavities and cancellous part of most bones **b :** the substance of the spinal cord **2 a :** the choicest of food **b :** the seat of animal vigor **c :** the inmost, best, or essential part **:** CORE <personal liberty is the ~ of the American tradition —Clinton Rossiter> **3** *chiefly Brit* **:** VEGETABLE MARROW — **mar·row·less** \-ō-ləs, -ə-ləs\ *adj* — **mar·rowy** \ˈmar-ə-wē\ *adj*

[2]**marrow** *n* [ME *marwe, marrow*] *chiefly Scot* **:** one of a pair

mar·row·bone \ˈmar-ə-ˌbōn, -ō-ˌbōn\ *n* **1 :** a bone (as a shinbone) rich in marrow **2** *pl* **:** KNEES

mar·row·fat \-ō-ˌfat, -ə-ˌfat\ *n* **:** any of several wrinkled-seeded garden peas

[1]**mar·ry** \ˈmar-ē\ *vb* **mar·ried; mar·ry·ing** [ME *marien,* fr. *marier,* fr. L *maritare,* fr. *maritus* married] *vt* **1 a :** to join as husband and wife according to law or custom <were *married* yesterday> **b :** to give in marriage <*married* his daughter to his partner's son> **c :** to take as spouse **:** WED <*married* the girl next door> **d :** to perform the ceremony of marriage for <*married* the couple> **e :** to obtain by marriage <~ wealth> **2 :** to unite in close and usu. permanent relation ~ *vi* **1 :** to take a spouse **:** WED **2 :** to enter into a close or intimate union <these wines ~ well> — **marry into :** to become a member of by marriage <*married into* a prominent family>

[2]**marry** *interj* [ME *marie,* fr. *Marie,* the Virgin Mary] *archaic* — used for emphasis and esp. to express amused or surprised agreement

Mars \ˈmärz\ *n* [L *Mart-, Mars*] **1 :** the Roman god of war — compare ARES **2 :** the planet 4th in order from the sun and conspicuous for the redness of its light — see PLANET table

MARS *abbr* manned astronautical research station

marse \ˈmärs\ *n* [by shortening and alter.] *South* **:** MASTER <was called ~, approached with fear, and addressed hat in hand —A. W. Tourgee>

Mar·seilles \mär-ˈsā(ə)lz\ *n* [*Marseilles,* France] **:** a firm cotton fabric that is similar to piqué

marsh \ˈmärsh\ *n, often attrib* [ME *mersh,* fr. OE *merisc, mersc;* akin to MD *mersch* marsh, OE *mere* sea, pool — more at MARINE] **:** a tract of soft wet land usu. characterized by monocotyledons (as grasses or cattails)

[1]**mar·shal** *also* **mar·shall** \ˈmär-shəl\ *n* [ME, fr. OF *mareschal,* of Gmc origin; akin to OHG *marahscalc* marshal, fr. *marah* horse + *scalc* servant] **1 a :** a high official in the household of a medieval king, prince, or noble orig. having charge of the cavalry but later usu. in command of the military forces **b :** a person who arranges and directs the ceremonial aspects of a gathering **2 a :** FIELD MARSHAL **b :** a general officer of the highest military rank **3 a :** an officer having charge of prisoners **b (1) :** a ministerial officer appointed for a judicial district (as of the U.S.) to execute the process of the courts and perform various duties similar to those of a sheriff **(2) :** a city law officer entrusted with particular duties **c :** the administrative head of a city police department or fire department — **mar·shal·cy** \-sē\ *n* — **mar·shal·ship** \-ˌship\ *n*

[2]**marshal** *vb* **mar·shaled** *or* **mar·shalled; mar·shal·ing** *or* **mar·shal·ling** \ˈmärsh-(ə-)liŋ\ *vt* **1 :** to place in proper rank or position <~*ing* the troops> **2 :** to bring together and order in an appropriate or effective way <~ arguments> **3 :** to lead ceremoniously or solicitously **:** USHER <~*ing* her little group of children down the street> ~ *vi* **:** to take form or order <ideas ~*ing* neatly> *syn* see ORDER

marshal of the Royal Air Force : the highest ranking officer in the British air force

marsh elder *n* **:** any of various coarse shrubby composite plants (genus *Iva*) of moist areas in eastern and central No. America

marsh gas *n* **:** METHANE

marsh hawk *n* **:** a widely distributed No. American hawk (*Circus cyaneus hudsonius*) with a conspicuous white patch on the rump

marsh hen *n* **1 :** any of various American rails **2 :** BITTERN

marsh·land \ˈmärsh-ˌland\ *n* **:** a marshy district **:** MARSH

marsh·mal·low \ˈmärsh-ˌmel-ō, -ˌmel-ə(-w), -ˌmal-\ *n* **1 :** a pink-flowered European perennial herb (*Althaea officinalis*) of the mallow family that is naturalized in the eastern U.S. and has a mucilaginous root sometimes used in confectionery and in medicine **2 :** a confection made from the root of the marshmallow or from corn syrup, sugar, albumen, and gelatin beaten to a light creamy consistency; *also* **:** a paste-like partially dried piece of marshmallow <a bag of ~*s*> — **marsh·mal·lowy** \-ˌmel-ə-wē, -ˌmal-\ *adj*

marsh marigold *n* **:** a swamp herb (*Caltha palustris*) of the buttercup family that occurs in Europe and No. America and has bright yellow flowers — called also *cowslip*

marshy \ˈmär-shē\ *adj* **marsh·i·er; -est 1 :** resembling or constituting a marsh **:** BOGGY <~ ground> **2 :** relating to or occurring in marshes <~ vegetation> — **marsh·i·ness** *n*

[1]**mar·su·pi·al** \mär-ˈsü-pē-əl\ *adj* **1 :** of, relating to, or being a marsupial **2 :** of, relating to, or forming a marsupium

[2]**marsupial** *n* [deriv. of NL *marsupium*] **:** any of an order (Marsupialia) of lowly mammals comprising kangaroos, wombats, bandicoots, opossums, and related animals that with few exceptions develop no placenta and have a pouch on the abdomen of the female containing the teats and serving to carry the young

mar·su·pi·um \mär-ˈsü-pē-əm\ *n, pl* **-pia** \-pē-ə\ [NL, fr. L, purse, pouch, fr. Gk *marsypion*] **1 :** an abdominal pouch formed by a fold of the skin and enclosing the mammary glands of most marsupials **2 :** any of several structures in various invertebrates (as a hyozoan or mollusk) for enclosing or carrying eggs or young

[1]**mart** \ˈmärt\ *n* [ME, fr. MD *marct, mart,* prob. fr. ONF *market*] **1** *archaic* **:** a coming together of people to buy and sell **:** [5]FAIR 1 **2** *obs* **:** the activity of buying and selling; *also* **:** BARGAIN **3 :** MARKET

[2]**mart** *vt, archaic* **:** to deal in **:** SELL

mar·tel·lo tower \mär-ˈtel-ō-\ *n, often cap M* [Cape *Mortella,* Corsica] **:** a circular masonry fort or blockhouse

mar·ten \ˈmärt-ᵊn\ *n, pl* **marten** *or* **martens** [ME *martryn,* fr. MF *martrine* marten fur, fr. OF, fr. *martre* marten, of Gmc origin; akin to OE *mearth* marten] **1 :** any of several semiarboreal slender-bodied carnivorous mammals (genus *Martes*) larger than the related weasels **2 :** the fur or pelt of a marten

marten 1

mar·tens·ite \ˈmärt-ᵊn-ˌzīt\ *n* [Adolf *Martens* †1914 G metallurgist] **:** the hard constituent of which quenched steel is chiefly composed — **mar·tens·it·ic** \ˌmärt-ᵊn-ˈzit-ik, -ˈsit-\ *adj* — **mar·tens·it·i·cal·ly** \-i-k(ə-)lē\ *adv*

Mar·tha \ˈmär-thə\ *n* [LL, fr. Gk] **:** a sister of Lazarus and Mary and friend of Jesus

mar·tial \ˈmär-shəl\ *adj* [ME, fr. L *martialis* of Mars, fr. *Mart-, Mars*] **1 :** of, relating to, or suited for war or a warrior **2 :** relating to an army or to military life **3 :** experienced in or inclined to war **:** WARLIKE — **mar·tial·ly** \-shə-lē\ *adv*

syn MARTIAL, WARLIKE, MILITARY *shared meaning element* **:** of or characteristic of war

martial law *n* **1 :** the law applied in occupied territory by the military authority of the occupying power **2 :** the law administered by military forces that is invoked by a government in an emergency when the civilian law enforcement agencies are unable to maintain public order and safety

mar·tian \ˈmär-shən\ *adj, often cap* **:** of or relating to the planet Mars or its hypothetical inhabitants — **martian** *n, often cap*

mar·tin \ˈmärt-ᵊn\ *n* [MF, fr. St. *Martin;* prob. fr. the migration of martins around Martinmas] **1 :** a small European swallow (*Delichon urbica*) with a forked tail, bluish black head and back, and white rump and underparts **2 :** any of various swallows and flycatchers other than the martin

mar·ti·net \ˌmärt-ᵊn-ˈet\ *n* [Jean *Martinet,* 17th cent. F army officer] **1 :** a strict disciplinarian **2 :** one who stresses a rigid adherence to the details of forms and methods

mar·tin·gale \ˈmärt-ᵊn-ˌgal, -iŋ-\ *n* [MF] **1 :** a device for steadying a horse's head or checking its upward movement that typically consists of a strap fastened to the girth, passing between the forelegs, and bifurcating to end in two rings through which the reins pass **2 a :** a lower stay of rope or chain for the jibboom or flying jibboom used to sustain the strain of the forestays and fastened to or rove through the dolphin striker **b :** DOLPHIN STRIKER **3 :** any of several systems of betting in which a player increases his stake usu. by doubling each time he loses a bet

mar·ti·ni \mär-ˈtē-nē\ *n* [prob. fr. the name *Martini*] **:** a cocktail made of gin and dry vermouth; *also* **:** one made with vodka instead of gin

Mar·tin·mas \ˈmärt-ᵊn-məs, -ˌmas\ *n* [ME *martinmasse,* fr. St. *Martin* + ME *masse* mass] **:** November 11 celebrated as the feast of Saint Martin

mart·let \ˈmärt-lət\ *n* [MF, prob. alter. of *martinet,* dim. of *martin*] **:** MARTIN 1

[1]**mar·tyr** \ˈmärt-ər\ *n* [ME, fr. OE, fr. LL, fr. Gk *martyr-, martys,* lit., witness; akin to L *memor* mindful] **1 :** one who voluntarily suffers death as the penalty of witnessing to and refusing to renounce his religion **2 :** one who sacrifices his life or something of great value for the sake of principle **3 :** VICTIM; *esp* **:** a great or constant sufferer <a ~ to asthma all his life —A. J. Cronin> — **mar·tyr·iza·tion** \ˌmärt-ə-rə-ˈzā-shən\ *n* — **mar·tyr·ize** \ˈmärt-ə-ˌrīz\ *vt*

[2]**martyr** *vt* **1 :** to put to death for adhering to a belief, faith, or profession **2 :** to inflict agonizing pain on **:** TORTURE

mar·tyr·dom \ˈmärt-ərd-əm\ *n* **1 :** the suffering of death on account of adherence to a cause and esp. to one's religious faith **2 :** AFFLICTION, TORTURE

mar·tyr·ol·o·gist \ˌmärt-ə-ˈräl-ə-jəst\ *n* **:** a writer of or a specialist in martyrology

mar·tyr·ol·o·gy \-jē\ *n* **1 :** a catalog of Roman Catholic martyrs and saints arranged by the dates of their feasts **2 :** ecclesiastical history treating the lives and sufferings of martyrs

mar·tyry \ˈmärt-ə-rē\ *n, pl* **-tyr·ies** [LL *martyrium,* fr. LGk *martyrion,* fr. Gk *martyr-, martys*] **:** a shrine erected in honor of a martyr

[1]**mar·vel** \'mär-vəl\ *n* [ME *mervel,* fr. OF *merveille,* fr. LL *mirabilia* marvels, fr. L, neut. pl. of *mirabilis* wonderful, fr. *mirari* to wonder — more at SMILE] **1 :** something that causes wonder or astonishment **2 :** intense surprise or interest : ASTONISHMENT

[2]**marvel** *vb* **mar·veled** *or* **mar·velled; mar·vel·ing** *or* **mar·vel·ling** \'märv-(ə-)liŋ\ *vi* **:** to become filled with surprise, wonder, or amazed curiosity <~*ed* at the magician's skill> ~ *vt* **:** to feel astonishment or perplexity at or about <~*ed* that they had escaped unhurt>

mar·vel·ous *or* **mar·vel·lous** \'märv-(ə-)ləs\ *adj* **1 :** causing wonder : ASTONISHING **2 :** MIRACULOUS, SUPERNATURAL <Gothic tales of the ~ and the bizarre> **3 :** of the highest kind or quality : notably superior <has a ~ way with children> — **mar·vel·ous·ly** *adv* — **mar·vel·ous·ness** *n*

Marx·ian \'märk-sē-ən *also* 'märk-shən\ *adj* [Karl *Marx*] **:** of, developed by, or influenced by the doctrines of Marx <~ socialism>

Marx·ism \'märk-ˌsiz-əm\ *n* **:** the political, economic, and social principles and policies advocated by Marx; *esp* **:** a theory and practice of socialism including the labor theory of value, dialectical materialism, the class struggle, and dictatorship of the proletariat until the establishment of a classless society — **Marx·ist** \-səst\ *n or adj*

Marx·ism–Le·nin·ism \'märk-ˌsiz-əm-'len-ə-ˌniz-əm, -'län-\ *n* **:** a theory and practice of communism developed by Lenin from the doctrines of Marx — **Marx·ist–Len·in·ist** \'märk-səst-'len-ə-nəst\ *n or adj*

Mary \'me(ə)r-ē, 'ma(ə)r-ē, 'mā-rē\ *n* [LL *Maria,* fr. Gk *Mariam, Maria,* fr. Heb *Miryām*] **1 :** the mother of Jesus **2 :** a sister of Lazarus and Martha and a friend of Jesus

Mary Jane \-'jān\ *n* [by folk etymology (influenced by Sp *Juana* Jane)] *slang* **:** MARIJUANA

Mary·knoll·er \-ˌnō-lər\ *n* **:** a member of the Catholic Foreign Mission Society of America founded by T. F. Price and J. A. Walsh at Maryknoll, N.Y. in 1911

Mary Mag·da·lene \-'mag-də-ˌlēn, -ˌmag-də-'lē-nē\ *n* [LL *Magdalene,* fr. Gk *Magdalēnē*] **:** a woman who was healed of evil spirits by Jesus and who saw the risen Christ near his sepulcher

mar·zi·pan \'märt-sə-ˌpän, -ˌpan; 'mär-zə-ˌpan\ *n* [G, fr. It *marzapane,* a medieval coin, marzipan, fr. Ar *mawthabān,* a medieval coin] **:** a confection of crushed almonds or almond paste, sugar, and egg whites that is often shaped into various forms

Ma·sai \mä-'sī, 'mä-ˌ\ *n, pl* **Masai** *or* **Masais** **1 :** a member of a pastoral and hunting people of Kenya and Tanganyika **2 :** a Nilotic language of the Masai people

masc *abbr* masculine

mas·cara \ma-'skar-ə\ *n* [It *maschera* mask] **:** a cosmetic for coloring the eyelashes and eyebrows

mas·con \'mas-ˌkän\ *n* [[2]*mass* + *con*centration] **:** one of the concentrations of large mass under the surface of the moon in the maria held to cause perturbations of the paths of spacecraft orbiting the moon

mas·cot \'mas-ˌkät *also* -kət\ *n* [F *mascotte,* fr. Prov *mascoto,* fr. *masco* witch, fr. ML *masca*] **:** a person, animal, or object adopted by a group as a symbolic figure esp. to bring them good luck <the team had a mountain lion as their ~>

[1]**mas·cu·line** \'mas-kyə-lən\ *adj* [ME *masculin,* fr. MF, fr. L *masculinus,* fr. *masculus,* n., male, dim. of *mas* male] **1 a :** MALE **b :** having qualities appropriate to a man **2 :** of, relating to, or constituting the gender that ordinarily includes most words or grammatical forms referring to males **3 a :** having or occurring in a stressed final syllable <~ rhyme> **b :** having the final chord occurring on a strong beat <~ cadence> **4 :** of or forming the formal, active, or generative principle of the cosmos — **mas·cu·line·ly** *adv* — **mas·cu·line·ness** \-lən-nəs\ *n* — **mas·cu·lin·i·ty** \ˌmas-kyə-'lin-ət-ē\ *n*

[2]**masculine** *n* **1 :** a male person **2 :** a noun, pronoun, adjective, or inflectional form or class of the masculine gender **3 :** the masculine gender

mas·cu·lin·ize \'mas-kyə-lə-ˌnīz\ *vt* **-ized; -iz·ing :** to give a preponderantly masculine character to; *esp* **:** to cause (a female) to take on male characteristics

ma·ser \'mā-zər\ *n* [*m*icrowave *a*mplification by *s*timulated *e*mission of *r*adiation] **:** a device that utilizes the natural oscillations of atoms or molecules between energy levels for generating electromagnetic radiation in the microwave region of the spectrum

[1]**mash** \'mash\ *n* [ME, fr. OE *māx-;* akin to MHG *meisch* mash] **1 :** crushed malt or grain meal steeped and stirred in hot water to ferment (as for the production of beer or whiskey) **2 :** a mixture of ground feeds for livestock **3 :** a soft pulpy mass

[2]**mash** *vt* **1 a :** to reduce to a soft pulpy state by beating or pressure **b :** CRUSH, SMASH <~ a finger> **2 :** to subject (as crushed malt) to the action of water with heating and stirring in preparing wort

[3]**mash** *vt* [prob. fr. [2]*mash*] **:** to flirt with or seek to gain the affection of

[4]**mash** *n* **:** CRUSH 3

MASH *abbr* mobile army surgical hospital

[1]**mash·er** \'mash-ər\ *n* **:** one that mashes <a potato ~>

[2]**masher** *n* **:** a man who makes passes at women

[1]**mask** \'mask\ *n* [MF *masque,* fr. OIt *maschera*] **1 a** (1) **:** a cover or partial cover for the face used for disguise (2) **:** a person wearing a mask : MASKER **b** (1) **:** a figure of a head worn on the stage in antiquity to identify the character and project the voice (2) **:** a grotesque false face worn at carnivals or in rituals **c :** an often grotesque carved head or face used as an ornament (as on a keystone) **d :** a sculptured face or a copy of a face made by means of a mold **2 a :** something that serves to conceal or disguise : PRETENSE, CLOAK <aware of the ~*s,* facades and defenses people erect to protect themselves —Kenneth Keniston> **b :** something that conceals from view **c :** a translucent or opaque screen to cover part of the sensitive surface in taking or printing a photograph **3 a :** a protective covering for the face **b :** GAS MASK **c :** a device covering the mouth and nose to facilitate inhalation **d :** a comparable device to prevent exhalation of infective material **e :** a cosmetic preparation for the skin of the face that produces a tightening effect as it dries **4 :** the head or face of an animal (as a fox or dog)

Ceylonese mask

[2]**mask** *vi* **1 :** to take part in a masquerade **2 a :** to assume a mask **b :** to disguise one's true character or intentions ~ *vt* **1 :** to provide or conceal with a mask: as **a :** to conceal from view <~ a gun battery> **b :** to make indistinct or imperceptible <~*s* undesirable flavors> **c :** to cover up <~*ed* his real purpose> **2 :** to cover for protection **3 :** to modify the size or shape of (as a photograph) by means of an opaque border ***syn*** see DISGUISE — **mask·able** \'mas-kə-bəl\ *adj*

masked \'maskt\ *adj* **1 :** marked by the use of masks <a ~ ball> **2 :** failing to present or produce the usual symptoms : LATENT <~ infection> <a ~ virus>

mask·er \'mas-kər\ *n* **:** a person who wears a mask; *esp* **:** a participant in a masquerade

mask·ing \'mas-kiŋ\ *n* **:** a piece of scenery used to conceal parts of a stage from the audience

mas·och·ism \'mas-ə-ˌkiz-əm, 'maz-\ *n* [ISV, fr. Leopold von Sacher-*Masoch* †1895 G novelist] **1 :** a sexual perversion characterized by pleasure in being abused esp. by a love object — compare SADISM **2 :** pleasure in being abused or dominated : a taste for suffering — **mas·och·ist** \-kəst\ *n* — **mas·och·is·tic** \ˌmas-ə-'kis-tik, ˌmaz-\ *adj* — **mas·och·is·ti·cal·ly** \ˌmas-ə-'kis-ti-k(ə-)lē, ˌmaz-\ *adv*

[1]**ma·son** \'mās-ᵊn\ *n* [ME, fr. OF *maçon*] **1 :** a skilled workman who builds by laying up units of substantial material (as stone or brick) **2** *cap* **:** FREEMASON

[2]**mason** *vt* **ma·soned; ma·son·ing** \'mās-niŋ, -ᵊn-iŋ\ **1 :** to construct of or repair with masonry **2 :** to build stonework or brickwork about, under, in, or over

Ma·son–Dix·on line \ˌmās-ᵊn-'dik-sən-\ *n* [Charles *Mason* and Jeremiah *Dixon*] **:** the southern boundary line of Pennsylvania; *also* **:** the boundary line between the northern and southern states — called also *Mason and Dixon's line*

Ma·son·ic \mə-'sän-ik\ *adj* **:** of, relating to, or characteristic of Freemasons or Freemasonry

Ma·son·ite \'mās-ᵊn-ˌīt\ *trademark* — used for fiberboard made from steam-exploded wood fiber

ma·son jar \ˌmās-ᵊn-\ *n* [John L. *Mason,* 19th cent. Am inventor] **:** a widemouthed jar used esp. for home canning

ma·son·ry \'mās-ᵊn-rē\ *n, pl* **-ries** **1 a :** something constructed of materials used by masons **b :** the art, trade, or occupation of a mason **c :** work done by a mason **2** *cap* **:** FREEMASONRY

mason wasp *n* **:** any of various solitary wasps that construct nests of hardened mud

Ma·so·ra *or* **Ma·so·rah** \mə-'sōr-ə, -'sȯr-\ *n* [NHeb *mĕsōrāh,* fr. LHeb *māsōreth* tradition, fr. Heb, bond] **:** a body of notes on the textual traditions of the Hebrew Old Testament compiled by scribes during the 1st millenium of the Christian era

Mas·o·rete *or* **Mas·so·rete** \'mas-ə-ˌrēt\ *n* [MF *massoreth,* fr. LHeb *masoreth*] **:** one of the scribes who compiled the Masorah — **Mas·o·ret·ic** \ˌmas-ə-'ret-ik\ *adj*

masque *also* **mask** \'mask\ *n* [MF *masque,* fr. OIt *maschera* mask] **1 :** MASQUERADE **2 :** a short allegorical dramatic entertainment of the 16th and 17th centuries performed by masked actors

masqu·er \'mas-kər\ *n* **:** MASKER

[1]**mas·quer·ade** \ˌmas-kə-'rād\ *n* [MF, fr. OIt dial. *mascarada,* fr. OIt *maschera*] **1 a :** a social gathering of persons wearing masks and often fantastic costumes **b :** a costume for wear at such a gathering **2 :** an action or appearance that is mere disguise or outward show

[2]**masquerade** *vi* **-ad·ed; -ad·ing** **1 a :** to disguise oneself; *also* **:** to go about disguised **b :** to take part in a masquerade **2 :** to assume the appearance of something that one is not — **mas·quer·ad·er** *n*

[1]**mass** \'mas\ *n* [ME, fr. OE *mæsse,* modif. of (assumed) VL *messa,* lit., dismissal at the end of a religious service, fr. LL *missa,* fr. L, fem. of *missus,* pp. of *mittere* to send — more at SMITE] **1** *cap* **:** the liturgy of the Eucharist esp. in accordance with the traditional Latin rite **2** *often cap* **:** a celebration of the Eucharist <Sunday ~*es* held at three different hours> **3 :** a musical setting for the ordinary of the Mass

[2]**mass** *n* [ME *masse,* fr. MF, fr. L *massa,* fr. Gk *maza;* akin to Gk *massein* to knead — more at MINGLE] **1 a :** a quantity or aggregate of matter usu. of considerable size **b** (1) **:** EXPANSE, BULK (2) **:** massive quality or effect <impressed me with such ~ and such vividness —F. M. Ford> (3) **:** the principal part or main body <the great ~ of the continent is buried under an ice cap —Walter Sullivan> (4) **:** AGGREGATE, WHOLE <men in the ~> **c :** the property of a body that is a measure of its inertia, that is commonly taken as a measure of the amount of material it contains and causes it to have weight in a gravitational field, and that along with length and time constitutes one of the fundamental quantities on which all physical measurements are based **2 :** a large quantity, amount, or number <a great ~ of material> **3 a :** a large body of persons in a compact group : a body of persons regarded as an aggregate **b :** the body of people as contrasted with the elite — often used in pl. <a better future for the underprivileged and disadvantaged ~*es* —C. A. Buss> ***syn*** see BULK

[3]**mass** *vi* **:** to assemble in a mass <three thousand students had ~*ed* in the plaza —A. E. Neville> ~ *vt* **:** to form or collect into a mass

[4]**mass** *adj* **1 a :** of or relating to the mass of the people <~ market> <~ education>; *also* **:** being one of or at one with the mass : AVERAGE, COMMONPLACE <~ man> **b :** participated in by or affecting a large number of individuals <~ destruction> <~ demonstrations> **c :** having a large-scale character : WHOLESALE

<~ production> **2 :** viewed as a whole : TOTAL <the ~ effect of a design>

Mass *abbr* Massachusetts

mas·sa \ˈmas-ə\ *n, South* : MASTER <this Louisiana sugar planter was called ~ by a hundred Negroes —Katharine L. Bates>

Mas·sa·chu·set \ˌmas-(ə-)ˈchü-sət, -zət\ *n, pl* **Massachuset** *or* **Massachusets** *also* **Massachusetts** [Massachuset *Massa-adchu-es-et,* a locality, lit., about the big hill] **1 :** a member of an Amerindian people of Massachusetts **2 :** the Algonquian language of the Massachuset people

¹mas·sa·cre \ˈmas-i-kər\ *vt* **mas·sa·cred; mas·sa·cring** \-k(ə-)riŋ\ **1 :** to kill by massacre : SLAUGHTER **2 :** MANGLE <words were misspelled and syntax *massacred* —Bice Clemow> — **mas·sa·crer** \-kər-ər, -krər\ *n*

²massacre *n* [MF] **1 :** the act or an instance of killing a number of usu. helpless or unresisting human beings under circumstances of atrocity or cruelty **2 :** a cruel or wanton murder **3 :** a wholesale slaughter of animals **4 :** an act of complete destruction <the author's ~ of traditional federalist presuppositions —R. G. McCloskey>

syn MASSACRE, SLAUGHTER, BUTCHERY, CARNAGE, POGROM *shared meaning element* : a great and usu. wanton or ruthless killing of human beings

¹mas·sage \mə-ˈsäzh, -ˈsäj\ *n* [F, fr. *masser* to massage, fr. Ar *massa* to stroke] : manipulation of tissues (as by rubbing, stroking, kneading, or tapping) with the hand or an instrument for remedial or hygienic purposes

²massage *vt* **mas·saged; mas·sag·ing :** to subject to massage — **mas·sag·er** *n*

mas·sa·sau·ga \ˌmas-ə-ˈsȯ-gə\ *n* [*Missisauga* river, Ontario, Canada] : any of several small rattlesnakes (genus *Sistrurus*)

mass card *n* : a card notifying the recipient (as a bereaved family) that a mass is to be offered for the repose of the soul of a specified deceased person

mass communication *n* : communication (as magazines and television) directed to or reaching the mass of the people <printed media of *mass communication* throughout the . . . world —*Brit. Book News*>

mass defect *n* : the difference between the mass of an isotope and its mass number

mas·sé \ma-ˈsā\ *n* [F, fr. pp. of *masser* to make a massé shot, fr. *masse* sledgehammer, fr. MF *mace* mace] : a shot in billiards or pool made by hitting the cue ball vertically or nearly vertically on the side to drive it around one ball in order to strike another

mass–energy equation *n* : an equation for the interconversion of mass and energy: $E = MC^2$ where E is energy in ergs, M is mass in grams, and C is the velocity of light in centimeters per second

mas·se·ter \mə-ˈsēt-ər, ma-\ *n* [NL, fr. Gk *masētēr,* fr. *masasthai* to chew] : a large muscle that raises the lower jaw and assists in mastication — **mas·se·ter·ic** \ˌmas-ə-ˈter-ik\ *adj*

mas·seur \ma-ˈsər, mə-\ *n* [F, fr. *masser*] : a man who practices massage and physiotherapy

mas·seuse \-ˈsə(r)z, -ˈsüz\ *n* [F, fem. of *masseur*] : a female masseur

mas·si·cot \ˈmas-ə-ˌkät, -ˌkō(t)\ *n* [ME *masticot,* fr. MF *massicot, masticot,* fr. OIt *massicotto* pottery glaze] : a yellow unfused lead monoxide PbO used esp. as a pigment

mas·sif \ma-ˈsēf\ *n* [F, fr. *massif,* adj.] **1 :** a principal mountain mass **2 :** a block of the earth's crust bounded by faults or flexures and displaced as a unit without internal change

mas·sive \ˈmas-iv\ *adj* [ME *massiffe,* fr. MF *massif,* fr. *masse* mass] **1 :** forming or consisting of a large mass: **a :** BULKY **b :** WEIGHTY, HEAVY <~ walls> <a ~ volume> **c :** impressively large or ponderous **d :** having no regular form but not necessarily lacking crystalline structure <~ sandstone> **2 a :** large, solid, or heavy in structure <~ jaw> **b :** large in scope or degree <the feeling of frustration, of being ineffectual, is ~ —David Halberstam> **c (1) :** large in comparison to what is typical <~ dose of penicillin> **(2) :** being extensive and severe <~ hemorrhage> <~ collapse of a lung> **(3) :** imposing in excellence or grandeur : MONUMENTAL <~ simplicity> — **mas·sive·ly** *adv* — **mas·sive·ness** *n*

mass·less \ˈmas-ləs\ *adj* : having no mass <a ~ particle>

mass medium *n, pl* **mass media :** a medium of communication (as newspapers, radio, or television) that is designed to reach the mass of the people — usu. used in pl.

mass noun *n* : a noun that characteristically denotes in many languages a homogeneous substance or a concept without subdivisions (as *sand* or *water*) and that in English is preceded in indefinite singular constructions by *some* rather than *a* or *an* — compare COUNT NOUN

mass number *n* : an integer that expresses the mass of an isotope and designates the number of nucleons in the nucleus

Mass of Resurrection : a mass for the dead in which the celebrant wears white vestments to symbolize the joyous resurrection of the soul

Mass of the Presanctified : a Roman Catholic service for Good Friday including communion with previously consecrated elements

mass–pro·duce \ˌmas-prə-ˈd(y)üs\ *vt* [back-formation fr. *mass production*] : to produce in quantity usu. by machinery — **mass production** *n*

mass spectrograph *n* : an instrument that separates a stream of charged particles into a mass spectrum usu. with photographic recording of the data and that is used for measuring atomic masses and determining the relative abundance of isotopes in an element

mass spectrometer *n* : an instrument similar to a mass spectrograph but usu. adapted for the electrical measurement of the data for use esp. in determining abundance ratios of isotopes — **mass spectrometric** *adj* — **mass spectrometry** *n*

mass spectrum *n* : the spectrum of a stream of charged particles (as electrons or nuclear particles) dispersed according to their mass

massy \ˈmas-ē\ *adj* : MASSIVE

¹mast \ˈmast\ *n* [ME, fr. OE *mæst;* akin to OHG *mast,* L *malus*] **1 :** a long pole or spar rising from the keel or deck of a ship and supporting the yards, booms, and rigging **2 :** a vertical or nearly vertical pole (as an upright post in various cranes) **3 :** a disciplinary proceeding at which the commanding officer of a naval unit hears and disposes of cases against his enlisted men — called also *captain's mast* — **mast·ed** \ˈmas-təd\ *adj* — **before the mast 1 :** forward of the foremast **2 :** as a common sailor

²mast *vt* : to furnish with a mast

³mast *n* [ME, fr. OE *mæst;* akin to OHG *mast* food, mast, OE *mete* food — more at MEAT] : nuts (as beechnuts and acorns) accumulated on the forest floor and often serving as food for animals (as hogs)

mast- *or* **masto-** *comb form* [NL, fr. Gk, fr. *mastos* — more at MEAT] : breast : nipple : mammary gland <*mast*itis>

mas·ta·ba \ˈmas-tə-bə\ *n* [Ar *maṣṭabah* stone bench] : an Egyptian tomb of the time of the Memphite dynasties that is oblong in shape with sloping sides and a flat roof

mast cell \ˈmast-\ *n* [part trans. of G *mast zelle,* fr. *mast* food, mast (fr. OHG) + *zelle* cell] : a large cell with numerous heparin-containing basophilic granules that occurs esp. in connective tissue

mas·tec·to·my \ma-ˈstek-tə-mē\ *n, pl* **-mies :** excision or amputation of the breast

¹mas·ter \ˈmas-tər\ *n* [ME, fr. OE *magister* & OF *maistre,* both fr. L *magister;* akin to L *magnus* great — more at MUCH] **1 a (1) :** a male teacher **(2) :** a person holding an academic degree higher than a bachelor's but lower than a doctor's **b** *often cap* **:** a revered religious leader **c :** a workman qualified to teach apprentices **d (1) :** an artist, performer, or player of consummate skill **(2) :** a great figure of the past (as in science or art) whose work serves as a model or ideal **2 a :** one having authority over another : RULER, GOVERNOR **b :** one that conquers or masters : VICTOR, SUPERIOR <in this young, obscure challenger the champion found his ~> **c :** a person licensed to command a merchant ship **d (1) :** one having control **(2) :** an owner esp. of a slave or animal **e :** EMPLOYER **f (1)** *dial* **:** HUSBAND **(2) :** the male head of a household **3 a (1)** *archaic* **:** MR. **(2) :** a youth or boy too young to be called *mister* — used as a title **b :** the eldest son of a Scottish viscount or baron **4 a :** a presiding officer in an institution or society (as a college) **b :** any of several officers of court appointed to assist (as by hearing and reporting) a judge **5 a :** a master mechanism or device **b :** an original from which copies can be made; *esp* : a master phonograph record

²master *vt* **mas·tered; mas·ter·ing** \-t(ə-)riŋ\ **1 :** to become master of : OVERCOME **2 a :** to become skilled or proficient in the use of <~ a foreign language> **b :** to gain a thorough understanding of <could ~ any intricate detail of pertinent information —Robert White>

³master *adj* : being or relating to a master: as **a :** having chief authority : DOMINANT **b :** SKILLED, PROFICIENT <a prosperous ~ builder —*Current Biog.*> **c :** PRINCIPAL, PREDOMINANT **d :** SUPERLATIVE — often used in combination <a *master*-liar> **e :** being a device or mechanism that controls the operation of another mechanism or that establishes a standard (as a dimension or weight) **f :** being a master from which duplicates are made

master–at–arms *n, pl* **masters–at–arms :** a petty officer charged with maintaining discipline aboard ship

master bath *n* : a principal bathroom in a house usu. attached to or associated with the master bedroom

master bedroom *n* : a principal bedroom in a house; *esp* : one that is occupied by the head of the household

master chief petty officer *n* : an enlisted man in the navy or coast guard ranking above a senior chief petty officer

master chief petty officer of the coast guard : the ranking petty officer in the coast guard serving as adviser to the commandant

master chief petty officer of the navy : the ranking petty officer in the navy serving as adviser to the chief of naval operations

mas·ter·ful \ˈmas-tər-fəl\ *adj* **1 a :** inclined and usu. competent (as by reason of vigor and insight) to play the master **b :** suggestive of a masterful nature <his eyes were dark and ~> **2 :** having or reflecting the technical, artistic, or intellectual power and skill of a master <~ drawings> — **mas·ter·ful·ly** \-fə-lē\ *adv* — **master·ful·ness** *n*

syn MASTERFUL, DOMINEERING, IMPERIOUS, PEREMPTORY, IMPERATIVE *shared meaning element* : tending to impose one's will on another. MASTERFUL implies a strong virile personality and ability to deal authoritatively with affairs <she was ever a *masterful* woman, better fitted to command than to obey —H. O. Taylor> DOMINEERING suggests an overbearing or arbitrary manner and an obstinate determination to enforce one's will <like *domineering* mothers, the states refuse cities the right to run their own lives —T. C. Desmond> IMPERIOUS applies to one who by position or nature is fitted to command or, often, to one who assumes the manner of such a person; the term is likely to suggest arrogant assurance <she is the cynical, *imperious* guide for the politician's early steps, seething with impotent and suppressed rage as she watches him grow out of her control —Alton Cook> PEREMPTORY implies an abrupt dictatorial manner coupled with an unwillingness to brook disobedience or delay or to entertain objections however valid <his *peremptory* command that she decide at once about his proposal —James Purdy> IMPERATIVE implies peremptoriness arising more from the urgency of the situation than from an inherent will to dominate <he heard her *imperative* voice at the telephone; he heard her summon the doctor —Ellen Glasgow>

master gunnery sergeant *n* : a noncommissioned officer in the marine corps ranking above a master sergeant

master key *n* : a key designed to open several different locks

---

ə abut	ᵊ kitten	ər further	a back	ā bake	ä cot, cart	
aù out	ch chin	e less	ē easy	g gift	i trip	ī life
j joke	ŋ sing	ō flow	ȯ flaw	ȯi coin	th thin	th this
ü loot	ù foot	y yet	yü few	yù furious	zh vision	

mas·ter·ly \ˈmas-tər-lē\ *adj* **:** suitable to or resembling that of a master; *esp* **:** indicating thorough knowledge or superior skill and power <~ performance> — **mas·ter·li·ness** *n* — **masterly** *adv*

¹mas·ter·mind \ˈmas-tər-ˌmīnd, ˌmas-tər-ˈ\ *n* **:** a person who supplies the directing or creative intelligence for a project

²mastermind *vt* **:** to be the mastermind of

master of arts *often cap M&A* **1 :** the recipient of a master's degree that usu. signifies that the recipient has passed an integrated course of study in one or more of the humanities and sometimes has completed a thesis involving research or a creative project and that typically requires two years of work beyond a bachelor's degree **2 :** the degree making one a master of arts — abbr. *M.A., A.M.*

master of ceremonies **1 :** a person who determines the forms to be observed on a public occasion **2 :** a person who acts as host at a formal event **3 :** a person who acts as host for a program of entertainment (as on television)

master of science *often cap M&S* **1 :** the recipient of a master's degree that usu. signifies that the recipient has passed an integrated course of study in one or more of the sciences and sometimes has completed a thesis involving research and that typically requires two years of work beyond a bachelor's degree **2 :** the degree making one a master of science — abbr. *M.S., M.Sc.*

mas·ter·piece \ˈmas-tər-ˌpēs\ *n* **1 :** a piece of work presented to a medieval guild as evidence of qualification for the rank of master **2 :** a work done with extraordinary skill; *esp* **:** a supreme intellectual or artistic achievement <the three motion pictures that most critics consider his ~*s* —*Current Biog.*>

master plan *n* **:** a plan giving overall guidance <having an architect . . . create a *master plan* for the University's future —Samuel Coleman> — **master-plan** *vb*

master point *n* **:** a point that is permanently credited to a player (as of bridge) for winning or placing high in a tournament and that forms the basis for national ranking

master race *n* **:** a people held to be racially preeminent and hence fitted to rule or enslave other peoples

master sergeant *n* **:** a noncommissioned officer ranking in the army above a sergeant first class and below a staff sergeant major, in the air force above a technical sergeant and below a senior master sergeant, and in the marine corps above a gunnery sergeant and below a master gunnery sergeant

mas·ter·ship \ˈmas-tər-ˌship\ *n* **1 :** the authority or control of a master **2 :** the status, office, or function of a master **3 :** the proficiency of a master

mas·ter·sing·er \-ˌsiŋ-ər\ *n* **:** MEISTERSINGER

mas·ter·stroke \-ˌstrōk\ *n* **:** a masterly performance or move

mas·ter·work \-ˌwərk\ *n* **:** MASTERPIECE

mas·tery \ˈmas-t(ə-)rē\ *n* [ME *maistrie*, fr. OF, fr. *maistre* master] **1 a :** the authority of a master **:** DOMINION **b :** the upper hand in a contest or competition **:** SUPERIORITY, ASCENDANCY <a violent spirit in him was struggling for the ~ —Gilbert Parker> **2 a :** possession or display of great skill or technique **b :** skill or knowledge that makes one master of a subject **:** COMMAND

mast·head \ˈmast-ˌhed\ *n* **1 :** the top of a mast **2 a :** the printed matter in a newspaper or periodical that gives the title and pertinent details of ownership, advertising rates, and subscription rates **b :** the name of a newspaper displayed on the top of the first page

mas·tic \ˈmas-tik\ *n* [ME *mastik*, fr. L *mastiche*, fr. Gk *mastichē*; akin to Gk *mastichan*] **1 :** an aromatic resinous exudate from mastic trees used chiefly in varnishes **2 :** any of various pasty materials used as protective coatings or cements

mas·ti·cate \ˈmas-tə-ˌkāt\ *vb* **-cat·ed; -cat·ing** [LL *masticatus*, pp. of *masticare*, fr. Gk *mastichan* to gnash the teeth; akin to Gk *masasthai* to chew — more at MOUTH] *vt* **1 :** to grind or crush (food) with or as if with the teeth in preparation for swallowing **:** CHEW **2 :** to soften or reduce to pulp by crushing or kneading ~ *vi* **:** CHEW — **mas·ti·ca·tion** \ˌmas-tə-ˈkā-shən\ *n* — **mas·ti·ca·tor** \ˈmas-tə-ˌkāt-ər\ *n*

¹mas·ti·ca·to·ry \ˈmas-ti-kə-ˌtōr-ē, -ˌtȯr-\ *adj* **1 :** used for or adapted to chewing <~ limbs of an arthropod> **2 :** of, relating to, or involving the organs of mastication <~ paralysis>

²masticatory *n, pl* **-ries :** a substance chewed to increase saliva

mastic tree *n* **:** a small southern European tree (*Pistacia lentiscus*) of the sumac family that yields mastic

mas·tiff \ˈmas-təf\ *n* [ME *mastif*, modif. of MF *mastin*, fr. (assumed) VL *mansuetinus*, fr. L *mansuetus* tame — more at MANSUETUDE] **:** a very large powerful deep-chested smooth-coated dog used chiefly as a watchdog and guard dog

mas·ti·goph·o·ran \ˌmas-tə-ˈgäf-ə-rən\ *n* [deriv. of Gk *mastig-*, *mastix* whip + *pherein* to carry — more at BEAR] **:** any of a class (Mastigophora) of protozoans comprising forms with flagella and including many often treated as algae — **mastigophoran** *adj*

mas·ti·tis \ma-ˈstīt-əs\ *n, pl* **-tit·i·des** \-ˈtit-ə-ˌdēz\ [NL] **:** inflammation of the breast or udder usu. caused by infection — **mas·tit·ic** \-ˈtit-ik\ *adj*

masto- — see MAST-

mast·odon \ˈmas-tə-ˌdän, -dən\ *n* [NL *mastodont-*, *mastodon*, fr. Gk *mast-* + *odont-*, *odōn*, *odous* tooth — more at TOOTH] **1 :** any of numerous extinct mammals (esp. genus *Mammut*) that differ from the related mammoths and existing elephants chiefly in the form of the molar teeth **2 :** something unusually large **:** GIANT <military vehicles from little jeeps to six-wheel armored ~*s* —Gelett Burgess> — **mast·odon·ic** \ˌmas-tə-ˈdän-ik\ *adj* — **mast·odont** \ˈmas-tə-ˌdänt\ *adj or n*

¹mas·toid \ˈmas-ˌtȯid\ *adj* [NL *mastoides* resembling a nipple, mastoid, fr. Gk *mastoeidēs*, fr. *mastos* breast — more at MEAT] **1 :** being a process of the temporal bone behind the ear; *also* **:** being any of several bony elements that occupy a similar position in the skull of lower vertebrates **2 :** of, relating to, or occurring in the region of the mastoid process

²mastoid *n* **1 :** a mastoid bone or process **2 a :** MASTOIDITIS **b :** an operation for the relief of mastoiditis

mastoid cell *n* **:** one of the small cavities in the mastoid process that develop after birth and are filled with air

mas·toid·ec·to·my \ˌmas-ˌtȯid-ˈek-tə-mē\ *n, pl* **-mies** [ISV] **:** surgical removal of the mastoid cells or of the mastoid process

mas·toid·itis \ˌmas-ˌtȯid-ˈīt-əs\ *n* [NL] **:** inflammation of the mastoid and esp. of the mastoid cells

mas·tur·bate \ˈmas-tər-ˌbāt\ *vb* **-bat·ed; -bat·ing** [L *masturbatus*, pp. of *masturbari*] *vi* **:** to practice masturbation ~ *vt* **:** to practice masturbation on

mas·tur·ba·tion \ˌmas-tər-ˈbā-shən\ *n* **:** erotic stimulation of the genital organs commonly resulting in orgasm and achieved by manual or other bodily contact exclusive of sexual intercourse, by instrumental manipulation, occasionally by sexual fantasies, or by various combinations of these agencies

mas·tur·ba·tory \ˈmas-tər-bə-ˌtōr-ē, -ˌtȯr-\ *adj* **:** of, relating to, or associated with masturbation <~ fantasies>

¹mat \ˈmat\ *n* [ME, fr. OE *meatte*, fr. LL *matta*, of Sem origin; akin to Heb *miṭṭāh* bed] **1 a** (1) **:** a piece of coarse, woven, plaited, or felted fabric used esp. as a floor covering or a support (2) **:** a piece of material placed at a door for wiping soiled shoe soles **b :** a decorative piece of material used under a small item (as a dish) esp. for support or protection **c :** a large thick pad or cushion used as a surface for wrestling, tumbling, and gymnastics **2 :** something made up of many intertwined or tangled strands **3 :** a large slab usu. of reinforced concrete used as the supporting base of a building

²mat *vb* **mat·ted; mat·ting** *vt* **1 :** to provide with a mat or matting **2 a :** to form into a tangled mass **b :** to pack down so as to form a dense mass ~ *vi* **:** to become matted

³mat *or* **matt** *or* **matte** \ˈmat\ *vt* **mat·ted; mat·ting 1 :** to make (as a metal, glass, or color) mat **2 :** to provide (a picture) with a mat

⁴mat *or* **matt** *or* **matte** *adj* [F, fr. OF, defeated, fr. L *mattus* drunk; akin to L *madēre* to be wet — more at MEAT] **:** lacking or deprived of luster or gloss: as **a :** having a usu. smooth even surface free from shine or highlights <~ metals> <a ~ white face> **b** *usu matte* **:** having a rough or granular surface <a *matte* bacterial colony>

⁵mat *or* **matt** *or* **matte** *n* [F *mat* dull color, unpolished surface, fr. *mat*, adj.] **1 :** a border going around a picture between picture and frame or serving as the frame **2 :** a dead or dull finish or a roughened surface (as of gilt or paint)

⁶mat *n* **:** MATRIX 2a

MAT *abbr* master of arts in teaching

mat·a·dor \ˈmat-ə-ˌdȯ(ə)r\ *n* [Sp, fr. *matar* to kill] **:** a bullfighter who has the principal role and who kills the bull in a bullfight

¹match \ˈmach\ *n* [ME *macche*, fr. OE *mæcca*; akin to OE *macian* to make — more at MAKE] **1 a :** a person or thing equal or similar to another **b :** one able to cope with another **c :** an exact counterpart **2 :** a pair suitably associated <carpet and curtains are a ~> **3 a :** a contest between two or more parties <a golf ~> <a soccer ~> **b :** a tennis contest completed when one player or side wins a specified number of sets **4 a :** a marriage union **b :** a prospective partner in marriage

²match *vt* **1 a :** to encounter successfully as an antagonist **b** (1) **:** to set in competition or opposition **:** PIT 2b <~*ing* his strength against his enemy's> (2) **:** to provide with a worthy competitor **c :** to set in comparison **2 :** to join or give in marriage **3 a** (1) **:** to put in a set possessing equal or harmonizing attributes (2) **:** to cause to correspond **:** SUIT **b** (1) **:** to be the counterpart of; *also* **:** to compare favorably with <no one can ~ him when it comes to working under pressure> (2) **:** to harmonize with **c :** to provide with a counterpart **d :** to provide funds complementary to <in some highway programs the federal government ~*es* state funds at a ratio of 9 to 1> **4 :** to fit together or make suitable for fitting together **5 a :** to flip or toss (coins) and compare exposed faces **b :** to toss coins with ~ *vi* **:** to be a counterpart — **match·er** *n*

syn MATCH, RIVAL, EQUAL, APPROACH, TOUCH *shared meaning element* **:** to come up to or close to the standard of something else

³match *n* [ME *macche*, fr. MF *meiche*] **1 :** a chemically prepared wick or cord formerly used in firing firearms or powder **2 :** a short slender piece of flammable material (as wood) tipped with a combustible mixture that bursts into flame when slightly heated through friction (as by being scratched against a rough surface)

match·able \ˈmach-ə-bəl\ *adj* **:** capable of being matched

match·board \ˈmach-ˌbō(ə)rd, -ˌbȯ(ə)rd\ *n* **:** a board with a groove cut along one edge and a tongue along the other so as to fit snugly with the edges of similarly cut boards — called also *matched board*

matchboards

match·book \-ˌbu̇k\ *n* **:** a small folder containing rows of paper matches

match·less \-ləs\ *adj* **:** having no equal **:** PEERLESS — **match·less·ly** *adv*

match·lock \-ˌläk\ *n* **1 :** a slow-burning cord lowered over a hole in the breech of a musket to ignite the charge **2 :** a musket equipped with a matchlock

match·mak·er \-ˌmā-kər\ *n* **:** one that arranges a match; *esp* **:** one who tries to bring two unmarried individuals together in an attempt to promote a marriage — **match·mak·ing** \-kiŋ\ *n*

match play *n* **:** a golf competition in which the winner is the person or team winning the greater number of holes — compare STROKE PLAY

match point *n* **:** a situation (as in tennis) in which one player will win the game, set, and match by winning the next point; *also* **:** the point won

match·wood \ˈmach-ˌwu̇d\ *n* **:** small pieces of wood **:** SPLINTERS

¹mate \ˈmāt\ *vt* **mated; mat·ing** [ME *maten*, fr. MF *mater*, fr. OF *mat*, n., checkmate, fr. Ar *māt* (in *shāh māt*)] **:** CHECKMATE 2

²mate *n* **:** CHECKMATE 1

³mate *n* [ME, prob. fr. MLG *māt*; akin to OE *gemetta* guest at one's table, *mete* food — more at MEAT] **1 a** (1) **:** ASSOCIATE, COMPANION (2) **:** an assistant to a more skilled workman **:** HELPER <plumber's ~> **b** *archaic* **:** MATCH, PEER **2 :** a deck officer on a merchant ship ranking below the captain **3 :** one of a pair: as **a :** either member of a married couple **b :** either member of a breeding pair of animals **c :** either of two matched objects <a ~ to this glove>

[4]**mate** *vb* **mated; mat·ing** *vt* **1** *archaic* **:** EQUAL, MATCH **2 :** to join or fit together **:** COUPLE **3 a :** to join together as mates **b :** to provide a mate for ~ *vi* **1 :** to become mated <gears that ~ well> **2 :** COPULATE

ma·té *or* **ma·te** \'mä-ˌtā\ *n* [F & AmerSp; F *maté,* fr. AmerSp *mate,* fr. Quechua] **1 :** an aromatic beverage used chiefly in So. America **2 :** a So. American holly (*Ilex paraguayensis*) whose leaves and shoots are used in making maté; *also* **:** these leaves and shoots

ma·te·lote \ˌmat-ᵊl-'ōt, mat-'lōt\ *n* [F] **:** a stew made usu. of fish in a seasoned wine sauce

ma·ter \'māt-ər\ *n* [L] *chiefly Brit* **:** MOTHER

ma·ter·fa·mil·i·as \ˌmāt-ər-fə-'mil-ē-əs, ˌmät-\ *n* [L, fr. *mater* + *familias,* archaic gen. of *familia* household — more at FAMILY] **:** a woman who is head of a household

[1]**ma·te·ri·al** \mə-'tir-ē-əl\ *adj* [ME *materiel,* fr. MF & LL; MF, fr. LL *materialis,* fr. L *materia* matter — more at MATTER] **1 a** (1) **:** relating to, derived from, or consisting of matter; *esp* **:** PHYSICAL <the ~ world> (2) **:** BODILY <~ needs> **b** (1) **:** of or relating to matter rather than form <~ cause> (2) **:** of or relating to the subject matter of reasoning; *esp* **:** EMPIRICAL <~ knowledge> **2 :** having real importance or great consequences <facts ~ to the investigation> **3 a :** being of a physical or worldly nature **b :** relating to or concerned with physical rather than spiritual or intellectual things <~ progress> **4 :** of or relating to the production and distribution of economic goods and the social relationships of owners and laborers — **ma·te·ri·al·ly** \-ē-ə-lē\ *adv* — **ma·te·ri·al·ness** *n*

syn **1** MATERIAL, PHYSICAL, CORPOREAL, PHENOMENAL, SENSIBLE, OBJECTIVE *shared meaning element* **:** of or belonging to actuality ***ant*** immaterial
2 see RELEVANT ***ant*** immaterial

[2]**material** *n* **1 a** (1) **:** the elements, constituents, or substances of which something is composed or can be made (2) **:** matter that has qualities which give it individuality and by which it may be categorized <the table was covered with a film of sticky ~> <explosive ~*s*> **b :** data that may be worked into a more finished form **c :** MATTER 3b **d :** CLOTH **2 a :** apparatus necessary for doing or making something <writing ~*s* > **b :** MATÉRIEL

ma·te·ri·al·ism \mə-'tir-ē-ə-ˌliz-əm\ *n* **1 a :** a theory that physical matter is the only or fundamental reality and that all being and processes and phenomena can be explained as manifestations or results of matter **b :** a doctrine that the only or the highest values or objectives lie in material well-being and in the furtherance of material progress **c :** a doctrine that economic or social change is materially caused — compare HISTORICAL MATERIALISM **2 :** a preoccupation with or stress upon material rather than intellectual or spiritual things — **ma·te·ri·al·ist** \-ləst\ *n or adj* — **ma·te·ri·al·is·tic** \-ˌtir-ē-ə-'lis-tik\ *adj* — **ma·te·ri·al·is·ti·cal·ly** \-ti-k(ə-)lē\ *adv*

ma·te·ri·al·i·ty \mə-ˌtir-ē-'al-ət-ē\ *n, pl* **-ties 1 :** the quality or state of being material <questioned the ~ of the evidence> **2 :** something that is material <the former believes in visions, the latter in *materialities* —*Athenaeum*>

ma·te·ri·al·iza·tion \mə-ˌtir-ē-ə-lə-'zā-shən\ *n* **1 :** the action of materializing or becoming materialized **2 :** something that has been materialized; *esp* **:** APPARITION

ma·te·ri·al·ize \mə-'tir-ē-ə-ˌlīz\ *vb* **-ized; -iz·ing** *vt* **1 a :** to make material **:** OBJECTIFY <*materializing* an idea in words> **b :** to cause to appear in bodily form <~ the spirits of the dead> **2 :** to cause to be materialistic ~ *vi* **1 :** to assume bodily form **2 a :** to come into existence **b :** to put in an appearance; *esp* **:** to appear suddenly — **ma·te·ri·al·iz·er** *n*

ma·te·ria med·i·ca \mə-ˌtir-ē-ə-'med-i-kə\ *n* [NL, lit., medical matter] **1 :** substances used in the composition of medical remedies **:** DRUGS, MEDICINE **2 a :** a branch of medical science that deals with the sources, nature, properties, and preparation of drugs **b :** a treatise on materia medica

ma·té·ri·el *or* **ma·te·ri·el** \mə-ˌtir-ē-'el\ *n* [F *matériel,* fr. *matériel,* adj.] **:** equipment, apparatus, and supplies used by an organization or institution

ma·ter·nal \mə-'tərn-ᵊl\ *adj* [ME, fr. MF *maternel,* fr. L *maternus,* fr. *mater* mother — more at MOTHER] **1 :** of, relating to, or characteristic of a mother **:** MOTHERLY **2 a :** related through a mother <his ~ aunt> **b :** inherited or derived from the female parent <~ genes> — **ma·ter·nal·ly** \-ᵊl-ē\ *adv*

[1]**ma·ter·ni·ty** \mə-'tər-nət-ē\ *n, pl* **-ties 1 a :** the quality or state of being a mother **:** MOTHERHOOD **b :** the qualities of a mother **:** MOTHERLINESS **2 :** a hospital facility designed for the care of women before and during childbirth and for the care of newborn babies

[2]**maternity** *adj* **:** designed for wear during pregnancy <a ~ dress>

mat·ey \'māt-ē\ *adj, chiefly Brit* **:** COMPANIONABLE

[1]**math** \'math\ *n* **:** MATHEMATICS

[2]**math** *abbr* mathematical; mathematician

math·e·mat·i·cal \ˌmath-ə-'mat-i-kəl\ *also* **math·e·mat·ic** \-ik\ *adj* [L *mathematicus,* fr. Gk *mathēmatikos,* fr. *mathēmat-, mathēma* mathematics, fr. *manthanein* to learn; akin to Goth *mundon* to pay attention, Skt *medhā* intelligence] **1 :** of, relating to, or according with mathematics **2 a :** rigorously exact **:** PRECISE **b :** CERTAIN **3 :** possible but highly improbable <only a ~ chance> — **math·e·mat·i·cal·ly** \-i-k(ə-)lē\ *adv*

mathematical expectation *n* **:** EXPECTED VALUE

mathematical logic *n* **:** SYMBOLIC LOGIC

math·e·ma·ti·cian \ˌmath-(ə-)mə-'tish-ən\ *n* **:** a specialist or expert in mathematics

math·e·mat·ics \ˌmath-ə-'mat-iks\ *n pl but usu sing in constr* **1 :** the science of numbers and their operations, interrelations, combinations, generalizations, and abstractions and of space configurations and their structure, measurement, transformations, and generalizations **2 :** a branch of, operation in, or use of mathematics <the ~ of physical chemistry>

math·e·ma·ti·za·tion \ˌmath-ə-mət-ə-'zā-shən\ *n* **:** reduction to mathematical form

maths \'maths\ *n pl, chiefly Brit* **:** MATHEMATICS

mat·in \'mat-ᵊn\ *adj* **:** of or relating to matins or to early morning

mat·in·al \'mat-ᵊn-əl\ *adj* **1 :** of or relating to matins **2 :** EARLY

mat·i·nee *or* **mat·i·née** \ˌmat-ᵊn-'ā\ *n* [F *matinée,* lit., morning, fr. OF, fr. *matin* morning, fr. L *matutinum,* fr. neut. of *matutinus* of the morning, fr. *Matuta,* goddess of morning; akin to L *maturus* ripe — more at MATURE] **:** a musical or dramatic performance or social or public event held in the daytime and esp. the afternoon

mat·ins \'mat-ᵊnz\ *n pl but sing or pl in constr, often cap* [ME *matines,* fr. OF, fr. LL *matutinae,* fr. L, fem. pl. of *matutinus*] **1 :** the night office forming with lauds the first of the canonical hours **2 :** MORNING PRAYER

matr- *or* **matri-** *or* **matro-** *comb form* [L *matr-, matri-,* fr. *matr-, mater*] **:** mother <*matri*arch> <*matro*nymic>

ma·tri·arch \'mā-trē-ˌärk\ *n* **:** a woman who rules a family, group, or state; *specif* **:** a mother who is head and ruler of her family and descendants — **ma·tri·ar·chal** \ˌmā-trē-'är-kəl\ *adj*

ma·tri·ar·chate \'mā-trē-ˌär-kət, -ˌkāt\ *n* **1 :** a family, group, or state governed by a matriarch **2 :** a theoretical stage or state in primitive society in which matriarchs hold the chief authority

ma·tri·ar·chy \'mā-trē-ˌär-kē\ *n, pl* **-chies 1 :** MATRIARCHATE **2 :** a system of social organization in which descent and inheritance are traced through the female line

matric *abbr* matriculated; matriculation

ma·tri·cide \'ma-trə-ˌsīd, 'mā-\ *n* **1** [L *matricidium,* fr. *matr-* + *-cidium* -cide] **:** murder of a mother by her son or daughter **2** [L *matricida,* fr. *matr-* + *-cida* -cide] **:** one that murders his mother — **ma·tri·cid·al** \ˌma-trə-'sīd-ᵊl, ˌmā-\ *adj*

ma·tric·u·late \mə-'trik-yə-ˌlāt\ *vb* **-lat·ed; -lat·ing** [ML *matriculatus,* pp. of *matriculare,* fr. LL *matricula* public roll, dim. of *matric-, matrix* list, fr. L, womb] *vt* **:** to enroll as a member of a body and esp. of a college or university ~ *vi* **:** to become matriculated — **ma·tric·u·lant** \-lənt\ *n* — **ma·tric·u·la·tion** \-ˌtrik-yə-'lā-shən\ *n*

ma·tri·lin·eal \ˌma-trə-'lin-ē-əl, ˌmā-\ *adj* **:** relating to, based on, or tracing descent through the maternal line <~ society> — **ma·tri·lin·eal·ly** \-ē-ə-lē\ *adv*

mat·ri·mo·nial \ˌma-trə-'mō-nē-əl, -nyəl\ *adj* **:** of or relating to marriage, the married state, or married persons — **mat·ri·mo·nial·ly** \-ē\ *adv*

syn MATRIMONIAL, MARITAL, CONJUGAL, CONNUBIAL, NUPTIAL *shared meaning element* **:** of, relating to, or characteristic of marriage

mat·ri·mo·ny \'ma-trə-ˌmō-nē\ *n* [ME, fr. MF *matremoine* fr. L *matrimonium,* fr. *matr-, mater* mother, matron — more at MOTHER] **:** the union of man and woman as husband and wife **:** MARRIAGE

matrimony vine *n* **:** a shrub or vine (genus *Lycium*) of the nightshade family with often showy flowers and bright berries

ma·trix \'mā-triks\ *n, pl* **ma·tri·ces** \'mā-trə-ˌsēz, 'ma-\ *or* **ma·trix·es** \'mā-trik-səz\ [L, womb, fr. *matr-, mater*] **1 :** something within which something else originates or develops **2 a :** a mold from which a relief surface (as a stereotype) is made by pouring or pressing **b :** DIE 4a(1) **c :** an engraved or inscribed die or stamp **d :** an electroformed impression of a phonograph record used for mass-producing duplicates of the original **3 a :** the natural material in which a fossil, metal, gem, crystal, or pebble is embedded **b :** material in which something is enclosed or embedded (as for protection or study) **4 a :** the intercellular substance in which tissue cells (as of connective tissue) are embedded **b :** the thickened epithelium at the base of a fingernail or toenail from which new nail substance develops **5 a :** a rectangular array of mathematical elements (as the coefficients of simultaneous linear equations) that can be combined to form sums and products with similar arrays having an appropriate number of rows and columns **b :** something resembling a mathematical matrix esp. in rectangular arrangement of elements into rows and columns

matrix sentence *n* **:** that one of a pair of transformationally joined sentences that maintains its essential external structure <in "the book that I want is gone", "the book is gone" is a *matrix sentence*>

ma·tron \'mā-trən\ *n* [ME *matrone,* fr. MF, fr. L *matrona,* fr. *matr-, mater*] **1 a :** a married woman usu. marked by dignified maturity or social distinction **b :** a woman who supervises women or children (as in a school or police station) **c :** the chief officer in a women's organization **2 :** a brood female

ma·tron·ize \-trə-ˌnīz\ *vt* **-ized; -iz·ing 1 :** to make matronly **2 :** to superintend as a matron **:** CHAPERONE

ma·tron·ly \'mā-trən-lē\ *adj* **:** having the character of or suitable to a matron

matron of honor : a bride's principal married wedding attendant

mat·ro·nym·ic \ˌma-trə-'nim-ik\ *n* [*matr-* + *-onymic* (as in *patronymic*)] **:** a name derived from that of the mother or a maternal ancestor

matt *or* **matte** \'mat\ *var of* MAT

Matt *abbr* Matthew

matte \'mat\ *n* [F] **:** a crude mixture of sulfides formed in smelting sulfide ores of metals (as copper, lead, or nickel)

[1]**mat·ter** \'mat-ər\ *n* [ME *matere,* fr. OF, fr. L *materia* matter, physical substance, fr. *mater*] **1 a :** a subject under consideration **b :** a subject of disagreement or litigation **c** *pl* **:** the events or circumstances of a particular situation **d :** the elements that constitute material for treatment in thought, discourse, or writing **e :** an element of a field of knowledge, inquiry, or specialization <~*s*

ə abut ᵊ kitten ər further a back ā bake ä cot, cart
aù out ch chin e less ē easy g gift i trip ī life
j joke ŋ sing ō flow ȯ flaw ȯi coin th thin t͟h this
ü loot ù foot y yet yü few yù furious zh vision

of faith> **f :** something to be proved in law **g** *obs* **:** sensible or serious material as distinguished from nonsense or drollery **h** (1) *obs* **:** REASON, CAUSE (2) **:** a source esp. of feeling or emotion **i :** a condition affecting a person or thing usu. unfavorably <what's the ~> **2 a :** the substance of which a physical object is composed **b :** material substance that occupies space and has weight, that constitutes the observable universe, and that together with energy forms the basis of objective phenomena **c :** a material substance of a particular kind or for a particular purpose <vegetable ~> **d** (1) **:** material (as feces or urine) discharged from the living body (2) **:** material discharged by suppuration **:** PUS **3 a :** the indeterminate subject of reality; *esp* **:** the element in the universe that undergoes formation and alteration **b :** the formless substratum of all things which exists only potentially and upon which form acts to produce realities **4 :** a more or less definite amount or quantity <a ~ of 10 years> **5 a :** something written or printed **b** (1) **:** set type (2) **:** text material esp. as distinguished from illustrations **6 :** MAIL **7** *Christian Science* **:** the illusion that the objects perceived by the physical senses have the reality of substance — **for that matter :** so far as that is concerned — **no matter :** without regard to **:** irrespective of <was calm *no matter* what the provocation>

[2]**matter** *vi* **1 :** to be of importance **:** SIGNIFY **2 :** to form or discharge pus **:** SUPPURATE <~*ing* wound>

matter of course : something that is to be expected as a natural or logical consequence

mat·ter–of–fact \ˌmat-ə-rə(v)-ˈfakt\ *adj* **1** adhering to or concerned with fact; *esp* **:** not fanciful or imaginative **:** PRACTICAL *syn* see PROSAIC — **mat·ter–of–fact·ly** \-ˈfak-(t)lē\ *adv* — **mat·ter–of–fact·ness** \-ˈfak(t)-nəs\ *n*

mat·tery \ˈmat-ə-rē\ *adj* **:** producing or containing pus or material resembling pus <eyes all ~>

Mat·the·an *or* **Mat·thae·an** \ma-ˈthē-ən, mə-\ *adj* [LL *Matthaeus*] **:** of, relating to, or characteristic of the evangelist Matthew or the gospel ascribed to him

Mat·thew \ˈmath-(ˌ)yü *also* ˈmath-(ˌ)ü\ *n* [F *Mathieu,* fr. LL *Matthaeus,* fr. Gk *Matthaios,* fr. Heb *Mattithyāh*] **1 :** an apostle traditionally identified as the author of the first Gospel in the New Testament **2 :** the first Gospel in the New Testament — see BIBLE table

[1]**mat·ting** \ˈmat-iŋ\ *n* **1 :** material for mats **2 :** MATS

[2]**matting** *n* [fr. gerund of [3]*mat*] **:** a dull lusterless surface (as on gilding, metalwork, or satin)

mat·tins *often cap, chiefly Brit var of* MATINS

mat·tock \ˈmat-ək\ *n* [ME *mattok,* fr. OE *mattuc*] **:** a digging and grubbing implement with features of an adz, ax, and pick

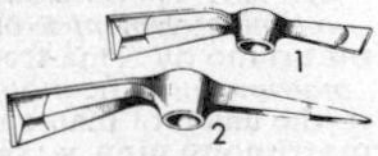

mattocks: *1* cutter, *2* pick

mat·tress \ˈma-trəs\ *n* [ME *materas,* fr. OF, fr. Ar *maṭraḥ* place where something is thrown] **1 a :** a fabric case filled with resilient material (as cotton, hair, feathers, foam rubber, or an arrangement of coiled springs) used either alone as a bed or on a bedstead **b :** an inflatable airtight sack for use as a mattress **2 :** a mass of interwoven brush and poles to protect a bank from erosion; *also* **:** a similar mass serving as a foundation in soft ground

mat·u·rate \ˈmach-ə-ˌrāt\ *vb* **-rat·ed; rat·ing :** MATURE

mat·u·ra·tion \ˌmach-ə-ˈrā-shən\ *n* **1 a :** the process of becoming mature **b :** the emergence of personal and behavioral characteristics through growth processes **c :** the final stages of differentiation of cells, tissues, or organs **2 a :** the entire process by which diploid gonocytes are transformed into haploid gametes that includes both meiosis and physiological and structural changes fitting the gamete for its future role **b :** SPERMIOGENESIS 1 — **mat·u·ra·tion·al** \-shnəl, -shən-ᵊl\ *adj* — **ma·tur·a·tive** \mə-ˈt(y)u̇r-ət-iv\ *adj*

[1]**ma·ture** \mə-ˈt(y)u̇(ə)r *also* -ˈchu̇(ə)r\ *adj* **ma·tur·er; -est** [ME, fr. L *maturus* ripe; akin to L *mane* in the morning, *manus* good] **1 :** based on slow careful consideration <a ~ judgment> **2 a** (1) **:** having completed natural growth and development **:** RIPE (2) **:** having undergone maturation **b :** having attained a final or desired state <~ wine> **3 a :** of or relating to a condition of full development **b :** characteristic of or suitable to a mature individual <~ outlook> **4 :** due for payment <a ~ loan> **5 a :** well dissected by the erosion of running water so that slopes predominate greatly over flats **b :** belonging to the middle portion of a cycle of erosion — **ma·ture·ly** *adv* — **ma·ture·ness** *n*

syn MATURE, RIPE, ADULT, GROWN-UP *shared meaning element* **:** fully developed *ant* immature

[2]**mature** *vb* **ma·tured; ma·tur·ing** *vt* **:** to bring to maturity or completion ~ *vi* **1 :** to become fully developed or ripe **2 :** to become due

ma·tu·ri·ty \mə-ˈt(y)u̇r-ət-ē *also* -ˈchu̇r\ *n* **1 :** the quality or state of being mature; *esp* **:** full development **2 :** termination of the period that an obligation has to run **3 :** the second of the three principal stages in a cycle of geologic change (as erosion)

ma·tu·ti·nal \ˌmach-ü-ˈtīn-ᵊl; mə-ˈt(y)üt-nəl, -ᵊn-əl\ *adj* [LL *matutinalis,* fr. L *matutinus* — more at MATINEE] **:** of, relating to, or occurring in the morning **:** EARLY — **ma·tu·ti·nal·ly** \-ē\ *adv*

mat·zo \ˈmät-sə, -(ˌ)sō\ *n, pl* **mat·zoth** \-ˌsōt(h), -sōs\ *or* **mat·zos** \-səz, -səs, -ˌsōz\ [Yiddish *matse,* fr. Heb *maṣṣāh*] **1 :** unleavened bread eaten at the Passover **2 :** a wafer of matzo

matzo ball *n* **:** a small ball-shaped dumpling made from matzo meal

maud·lin \ˈmȯd-lən\ *adj* [alter. of Mary *Magdalene;* fr. the practice of depicting her as a weeping, penitent sinner] **1 :** weakly and effusively sentimental **2 :** drunk enough to be emotionally silly **:** FUDDLED

mau·gre \ˈmȯ-gər\ *prep* [ME, fr. OF *maugré,* fr. *maugré* displeasure, fr. *mau, mal* evil + *gré* pleasure] *archaic* **:** in spite of

[1]**maul** \ˈmȯl\ *n* [ME *malle,* fr. OF *mail,* fr. L *malleus;* akin to L *molere* to grind — more at MEAL] **:** a heavy hammer often with a wooden head used esp. for driving wedges or piles

[2]**maul** *vt* **1 :** BEAT, BRUISE **2 :** to injure by beating **:** MANGLE **3 :** to handle roughly — **maul·er** *n*

maul·stick \ˈmȯl-stik\ *n* [part trans. of D *maalstok,* fr. obs. D *malen* to paint + D *stok* stick] **:** a stick used by painters as a rest for the hand while working

maun \(ˈ)mȯn, (ˈ)män, mən\ *verbal auxiliary* [ME *man,* fr. ON] *chiefly Scot* **:** MUST

maund \ˈmȯnd\ *n* [Hindi *man*] **:** any of various Indian units of weight; *esp* **:** a unit equal to 82.28 pounds

maun·der \ˈmȯn-dər, ˈmän-\ *vi* **maun·dered; maun·der·ing** \-d(ə-)riŋ\ [prob. imit] **1** *dial Brit* **:** GRUMBLE **2 :** to wander slowly and idly **3 :** to speak indistinctly or disconnectedly — **maun·der·er** \-dər-ər\ *n*

Maun·dy Thursday \ˌmȯn-dē-, ˌmän-\ *n* [ME *maunde* ceremony of washing the feet of the poor on Maundy Thursday, fr. OF *mandé,* fr. L *mandatum* command; fr. Jesus' words in John 13:34 — more at MANDATE] **:** the Thursday before Easter observed in commemoration of the institution of the Eucharist

mau·so·le·um \ˌmȯ-sə-ˈlē-əm, ˌmȯ-zə-\ *n, pl* **-leums** *or* **-lea** \-ˈlē-ə\ [L, fr. Gk *mausōleion,* fr. *Mausōlos* Mausolus †*ab* 353 B.C., ruler of Caria] **1 :** a large tomb; *esp* **:** a usu. stone building with places for entombment of the dead above ground **2 :** a large gloomy building or room

mauve \ˈmōv, ˈmȯv\ *n* [F, mallow, fr. L *malva*] **1 a :** a moderate purple, violet, or lilac color **b :** a strong purple **2 :** a dyestuff that produces a mauve color

ma·ven *or* **ma·vin** *or* **may·vin** \ˈmā-vən\ *n* [Yiddish, fr. LHeb *mēbhīn*] **:** one who is experienced or knowledgeable **:** EXPERT

mav·er·ick \ˈmav-(ə-)rik\ *n* [Samuel A. *Maverick* †1870 Am pioneer who did not brand his calves] **1 :** an unbranded range animal; *esp* **:** a motherless calf **2 :** an independent individual who refuses to conform with his group

ma·vis \ˈmā-vəs\ *n* [ME, fr. MF *mauvis*] **1 :** SONG THRUSH **2 :** a European thrush (*Turdus viscivorus*) with spotted underparts that feeds on mistletoe berries — called also *mistle thrush*

ma·vour·neen *also* **ma·vour·nin** \mə-ˈvu̇(ə)r-ˌnēn\ *n* [IrGael *mo muirnīn*] *Irish* **:** my darling

maw \ˈmȯ\ *n* [ME, fr. OE *maga;* akin to OHG *mago* stomach, Lith *makas* purse] **1 :** the receptacle into which food is taken by swallowing: **a :** STOMACH **b :** CROP **2 :** the throat, gullet, or jaws esp. of a voracious carnivore

mawk·ish \ˈmȯ-kish\ *adj* [ME *mawke* maggot, fr. ON *mathkr* — more at MAGGOT] **1 :** having an insipid often unpleasant taste **2 :** sickly or puerilely sentimental — **mawk·ish·ly** *adv* — **mawk·ish·ness** *n*

max *abbr* maximum

maxi \ˈmak-sē\ *n, pl* **max·is** [*maxi-*] **1 :** a long skirt that usu. extends to the ankle **2 :** a long coat that usu. extends to the ankle

maxi- *comb form* [*maximum,* after E *minimum: mini-*] **1 :** extra long <*maxi*-kilt> **2 :** extra large <*maxi*-problems>

maxi·coat \ˈmak-sē-ˌkōt\ *n* **:** MAXI 2

max·il·la \mak-ˈsil-ə\ *n, pl* **max·il·lae** \-ˈsil-(ˌ)ē, -ˌī\ *or* **maxillas** [L, dim. of *mala* jaw] **1 a :** JAW 1a **b** (1) **:** an upper jaw esp. of man or other mammals in which the bony elements are closely fused (2) **:** either of two membrane bone elements of the upper jaw lying lateral to the premaxillae and in higher vertebrates and man bearing most of the teeth **2 :** one of the first or second pair of mouthparts posterior to the mandibles in insects, myriopods, crustaceans, and closely related arthropods — **max·il·lary** \ˈmak-sə-ˌler-ē, *chiefly Brit* mak-ˈsil-ə-rē\ *adj or n*

max·il·li·ped \mak-ˈsil-ə-ˌped\ *also* **max·il·li·pede** \-ˌpēd\ *n* [ISV] **:** any of the crustacean appendages that comprise the first pair or first three pairs situated next behind the maxillae

max·il·lo- \mak-ˌsil-(ˌ)ō, ˌmak-sə-(ˌ)lō\ *comb form* [L *maxilla*] **:** maxillary and <*maxillo*facial>

max·il·lo·fa·cial \-ˈfā-shəl\ *adj* **:** of, relating to, or treating the maxilla and the face <~ surgeons>

max·im \ˈmak-səm\ *n* [ME *maxime,* fr. MF, fr. ML *maxima,* fr. L, fem. of *maximus,* superl. of *magnus* great — more at MUCH] **1 :** a general truth, fundamental principle, or rule of conduct **2 :** a saying of proverbial nature

max·i·mal \ˈmak-s(ə-)məl\ *adj* **1 :** most comprehensive **:** COMPLETE **2 :** being an upper limit **:** HIGHEST — **max·i·mal·ly** \-ē\ *adv*

max·i·mal·ist \-s(ə-)mə-ləst\ *n* **:** one who advocates immediate and direct action to secure the whole of a program; *specif* **:** a socialist advocating the immediate seizure of power by revolutionary means

maxi·min \ˈmak-sə-ˌmin\ *n* [*maxi*mum + *min*imum] **:** the maximum of a set of minima; *esp* **:** the largest of a set of minimum possible gains each of which occurs in the least advantageous outcome of a strategy followed by a participant in a situation governed by the theory of games — compare MINIMAX

max·i·mize \ˈmak-sə-ˌmīz\ *vb* **-mized; -miz·ing** *vt* **1 :** to increase to a maximum **2 :** to assign maximum importance to **3 :** to find a maximum value of ~ *vi* **:** to interpret something in the broadest sense — **max·i·mi·za·tion** \ˌmak-sə-mə-ˈzā-shən\ *n* — **max·i·miz·er** \ˈmak-sə-ˌmī-zər\ *n*

max·i·mum \ˈmak-s(ə-)məm\ *n, pl* **max·i·ma** \-sə-mə\ *or* **max·i·mums** \-s(ə-)məmz\ [L, neut. of *maximus*] **1 a :** the greatest quantity or value attainable or attained **b :** the period of highest, greatest, or utmost development **2 :** an upper limit allowed (as by a legal authority) or allowable (as by the circumstances of a particular case) **3 :** the largest of a set of numbers; *specif* **:** the largest value assumed by a real-valued continuous function defined on a closed interval — **maximum** *adj*

maximum likelihood *n* **:** a statistical method for estimating population parameters (as the mean and variance) from sample data that selects as estimates those parameter values maximizing the probability of obtaining the observed data

maxi·skirt \ˈmak-sē-ˌskərt\ *n* **:** MAXI 1

ma·xixe \mə-ˈshēsh(-ə)\ *n, pl* **ma·xi·xes** \-ˈshē-shəz\ [Pg] **:** a ballroom dance of Brazilian origin that resembles the two-step

max·well \'mak-ˌswel, -swəl\ *n* [James Clerk *Maxwell*] **:** the cgs electromagnetic unit of magnetic flux equal to the flux per square centimeter of normal cross section in a region where the magnetic induction is one gauss

1may \(ˈ)mā\ *verbal auxiliary, past* **might** \(ˈ)mīt\; *pres sing & pl* **may** [ME (1st & 3d sing. pres. indic.), fr. OE *mæg;* akin to OHG *mag* (1st & 3d sing. pres. indic.) have power, am able (infin. *magan*), Gk *mēchos* means, expedient] **1** *archaic* **:** have the ability to **:** CAN **2 a :** have permission to <you ~ go now> **:** have liberty to — used nearly interchangeably with *can* **b :** be in some degree likely to <you ~ be right> **3** — used in auxiliary function to express a wish or desire esp. in prayer, imprecation, or benediction <long ~ he reign> **4** — used in auxiliary function expressing purpose or expectation <I laugh that I ~ not weep> or contingency <he'll do his duty come what ~> or concession <he ~ be slow but he is thorough> **5 :** SHALL, MUST — used in law where the sense, purpose, or policy requires this interpretation

2may \'mā\ *n* [ME, fr. OE *mæg* kinsman, kinswoman, maiden] *archaic* **:** MAIDEN

May \'mā\ *n* [ME, fr. OF & L; OF *mai,* fr. L *Maius,* fr. *Maia,* Roman goddess] **1 :** the 5th month of the Gregorian calendar **2** *often not cap* **:** the early vigorous blooming part of human life **:** PRIME **3 :** the festivities of May Day **4** *not cap* **a :** green or flowering branches used for May Day decorations **b :** a plant that yields may: as **(1) :** HAWTHORN **(2) :** a spring-flowering spirea

ma·ya \'mä-yə, 'mī-ə\ *n* [Skt *māyā*] **:** the sense-world of manifold phenomena held in Vedanta to conceal the unity of absolute being; *broadly* **:** ILLUSION

Ma·ya \'mī-ə\ *n, pl* **Maya** *or* **Mayas** [Sp] **1 :** a member of a group of Indian peoples chiefly of Yucatán, British Honduras, Guatemala, and the state of Tabasco, Mexico whose languages are Mayan **2 a :** a Mayan language of the ancient Maya peoples recorded in inscriptions **b :** YUCATEC; *esp* **:** the older form of that language known from documents of the Spanish period

Ma·yan \'mī-ən\ *n* **1 :** an extensive language stock of Central America and Mexico **2 a :** the peoples speaking Mayan languages **b :** a member of these peoples — **Mayan** *adj*

may·ap·ple \'mā-ˌap-əl\ *n* [*May*] **:** a No. American herb (*Podophyllum peltatum*) of the barberry family with a poisonous rootstock, one or two large-lobed peltate leaves, and a single large white flower followed by a yellow egg-shaped edible but often insipid fruit; *also* **:** its fruit

mayapple

may·be \'mā-bē, 'meb-ē\ *adv* **:** PERHAPS

May·day \mā-'dā, 'mā-ˌ\ [F *m'aider* help me] — an international radio-telephone signal word used as a distress call

May Day \'mā-ˌdā\ *n* **:** May 1 celebrated as a springtime festival and in some countries as Labor Day

may·est *or* **mayst** \'mā-əst, (ˈ)māst\ *archaic pres 2d sing of* MAY

may·flow·er \'mā-ˌflau̇(-ə)r\ *n* **:** any of various spring-blooming plants; *esp* **:** ARBUTUS 2

may·fly \'mā-flī\ *n* **:** any of an order (Ephemeroptera) of insects with an aquatic nymph and a short-lived fragile adult having membranous wings and two or three long caudal styles — called also *ephemerid*

may·hap \'mā-ˌhap, mā-'\ *adv* [fr. the phrase *may hap*] **:** PERHAPS

may·hem \'mā-ˌhem, 'mā-əm\ *n* [ME *mayme,* fr. AF *mahaim,* fr. OF, loss of a limb, fr. *maynier* to maim] **1 a :** willful and permanent deprivation of a bodily member resulting in the impairment of a person's fighting ability **b :** willful and permanent crippling, mutilation, or disfigurement of any part of the body **2 :** needless or willful damage

may·ing \'mā-iŋ\ *n, often cap* **:** the celebrating of May Day

mayn't \'mā-ənt, (ˈ)mānt\ **:** may not

may·on·naise \'mā-ə-ˌnāz, ˌmā-ə-'\ *n* [F] **:** a dressing of raw eggs or egg yolks, vegetable oils, and vinegar or lemon juice

may·or \'mā-ər, 'me(-ə)r, *esp before names* (ˌ)mer\ *n* [ME *maire,* fr. OF, fr. L *major* greater — more at MAJOR] **:** an official elected or appointed to act as chief executive or nominal head of a city or borough — **may·or·al** \'mā-ə-rəl, 'me-ə-\ *adj*

may·or·al·ty \'mā-ə-rəl-tē, 'me-; 'mer-\ *n* [ME *mairaltee,* fr. MF *mairalté,* fr. OF, fr. *maire*] **:** the office or term of office of a mayor

may·or·ess \'mā-ə-rəs, 'me-\ *n* **1 :** the wife of a mayor **2 :** a woman holding the office of mayor

mayor's court *n* **:** a court in some cities that has jurisdiction over violations of city ordinances and petty criminal or civil matters and that is presided over by the mayor

may·pole \'mā-ˌpōl\ *n, often cap* **:** a tall flower-wreathed pole forming a center for May Day sports and dances

may·pop \'mā-ˌpäp\ *n* [modif. of *maracock* (in some Algonquian language of Virginia)] **:** a climbing perennial passionflower (*Passiflora incarnata*) of the southern U.S. with a large ovoid yellow edible but insipid berry; *also* **:** its fruit

May queen *n* **:** a girl chosen queen of a May Day festival

May·tide \'mā-ˌtīd\ *n* **:** the month of May

May·time \-ˌtīm\ *n* **:** MAYTIDE

ma·zae·di·um \mə-'zēd-ē-əm, ˌmaz-ə-'ēd-\ *n, pl* **-dia** [NL, fr. Gk *maza* lump, mass + L *aedes* temple, house — more at MASS, EDIFY] **:** a fruiting body (as of some lichens) consisting of a powdery mass of free ascospores interspersed with sterile elements and enclosed in a peridium

maz·ard \'maz-ərd\ *n* [obs. E *mazard* mazer, alter. of E *mazer*] *chiefly dial* **:** HEAD, FACE

1maze \'māz\ *vt* **mazed; maz·ing** [ME *mazen*] **1** *chiefly dial* **:** STUPEFY, DAZE **2 :** BEWILDER, PERPLEX

2maze *n* **1 a :** a confusing intricate network of passages **b :** something intricately or confusingly elaborate or complicated <a ~ of regulations> **2** *chiefly dial* **:** a state of bewilderment

ma·zer \'mā-zər\ *n* [ME, fr. OF *mazere,* of Gmc origin; akin to OHG *masar* gnarled excrescence on a tree] **:** a large drinking bowl orig. of a hard wood

ma·zur·ka \mə-'zər-kə, -'zu̇(ə)r-\ *also* **ma·zour·ka** \-'zu̇(ə)r-\ *n* [Russ, fr. Pol *mazurek*] **1 :** a Polish folk dance in moderate triple measure **2 :** music for the mazurka or in its rhythm usu. in moderate 3/4 or 3/8 time

mazy \'mā-zē\ *adj* **:** resembling a maze

maz·zard \'maz-ərd\ *n* [origin unknown] **:** SWEET CHERRY; *esp* **:** wild or seedling sweet cherry used as a rootstock for grafting

mb *abbr* millibar

MB *abbr* municipal borough

MBA *abbr* master of business administration

MBE *abbr* **1** master of business economics **2** master of business education **3** member of the Order of the British Empire

mbi·ra \em-'bir-ə\ *n* [of Bantu origin] **:** an African musical instrument that consists of a gourd resonator, a wooden box, and a varying number of tuned metal or wooden strips that vibrate when plucked with the thumb or fingers

MBS *abbr* Mutual Broadcasting System

mc *abbr* **1** megacycle **2** millicurie

1MC *n* **:** MASTER OF CEREMONIES

2MC *abbr* member of Congress

MCAT *abbr* Medical College Admissions Test

mcf *abbr* thousand cubic feet

mcg *abbr* microgram

MCL *abbr* **1** Marine Corps League **2** master of civil law **3** master of comparative law

MCPO *abbr* master chief petty officer

MCS *abbr* **1** master of commercial science **2** master of computer science **3** missile control system

1Md *abbr* Maryland

2Md *symbol* mendelevium

MD *abbr* **1** [NL *medicinae doctor*] doctor of medicine **2** [It *mano destra*] right hand **3** Maryland **4** medical department **5** months after date

M-day \'em-ˌdā\ *n* [*mobilization day*] **:** a day on which a military mobilization is to begin

mdnt *abbr* midnight

MDS *abbr* master of dental surgery

mdse *abbr* merchandise

me \(ˈ)mē\ *pron* [ME, fr. OE *mē;* akin to OHG *mih* me, L *me,* Gk *me,* Skt *mā*] *objective case of* I

1Me *abbr* Maine

2Me *symbol* methyl

ME *abbr* **1** Maine **2** mechanical engineer **3** medical examiner **4** Middle English

Mea *abbr* Meath

mea cul·pa \ˌmā-ä-'ku̇l-pä\ *n* [L, through my fault] **:** a formal acknowledgment of personal fault or error

1mead \'mēd\ *n* [ME *mede,* fr. OE *medu;* akin to OHG *metu* mead, Gk *methy* wine] **:** a fermented drink made of water and honey, malt, and yeast

2mead *n* [ME *mede,* fr. OE *mǣd*] *archaic* **:** MEADOW

mead·ow \'med-(ˌ)ō, -ə(-w)\ *n, often attrib* [ME *medwe,* fr. OE *mǣdwe,* oblique case form of *mǣd;* akin to OE *māwan* to mow — more at MOW] **:** land in or predominantly in grass; *esp* **:** a tract of moist low-lying usu. level grassland

meadow beauty *n* **:** any of a genus (*Rhexia*) of low perennial American herbs (family Melastomaceae, the meadow-beauty family) with showy cymose flowers

meadow fescue *n* **:** a tall vigorous perennial European fescue grass (*Festuca elatior*) with broad flat leaves widely cultivated for permanent pasture and hay

meadow grass *n* **:** any of various grasses (as of the genus *Poa*) that thrive in the presence of abundant moisture; *esp* **:** KENTUCKY BLUEGRASS

mead·ow·land \'med-ō-ˌland, -ə-\ *n* **:** land that is or is used for meadow

mead·ow·lark \'med-ō-ˌlärk, -ə-\ *n* **:** any of several No. American songbirds (genus *Sturnella*) that are largely brown and buff above and have a yellow breast marked with a black crescent

meadow mouse *n* **:** any of various voles (esp. genus *Microtus*) that frequent open fields

meadow mushroom *n* **:** a common edible agaric (*Agaricus campestris*) that occurs naturally in moist open organically rich soil and is the cultivated edible mushroom of commerce

meadow nematode *n* **:** any of numerous plant-parasitic nematode worms (esp. genus *Pratylenchus*) that were formerly classified as a single variable species (*P. pratensis*) and that destructively invade the roots of plants

meadow rue *n* **:** any of a genus (*Thalictrum*) of plants of the buttercup family with leaves resembling those of rue

meadow saffron *n* **:** COLCHICUM 1

meadow spittlebug *n* **:** a No. American spittlebug (*Philaenus spumarius*) that does severe damage esp. to grasses

mead·ow·sweet \'med-ō-ˌswēt, -ə-\ *n* **1 :** SPIREA 1; *esp* **:** a No. American native or naturalized spirea (as *Spiraea alba* or *S. tomentosa*) **2 :** a plant of a genus (*Filipendula*) closely related to the spireas

mea·ger *or* **mea·gre** \'mē-gər\ *adj* [ME *megre,* fr. MF *maigre,* fr. L *macr-, macer* lean; akin to OE *mæger* lean, Gk *makros* long] **1 :** having little flesh **:** THIN **2 a :** lacking desirable qualities (as

richness or strength) <leading a ~ life> **b :** deficient in quality and quantity <a ~ diet> — **mea·ger·ly** *adv* — **mea·ger·ness** *n*
syn MEAGER, SCANTY, SCANT, SKIMPY, EXIGUOUS, SPARE, SPARSE *shared meaning element* : falling short of what is normal, necessary, or desirable ***ant*** ample, copious

[1]meal \'mē(ə)l\ *n* [ME *meel* appointed time, meal, fr. OE *mǣl;* akin to OHG *māl* time, L *metiri* to measure — more at MEASURE] **1 :** the portion of food taken at one time to satisfy appetite **2 :** an act or the time of eating a meal

[2]meal *n* [ME *mele,* fr. OE *melu;* akin to OHG *melo* meal, L *molere* to grind, Gk *mylē* mill] **1 :** the usu. coarsely ground and unbolted seeds of a cereal grass or pulse; *esp* **:** CORNMEAL **2 :** a product resembling seed meal esp. in particle size or texture

-meal \ˌmēl, 'mē(ə)l\ *adv comb form* [ME *-mele,* fr. OE *-mǣlum,* fr. *mǣlum,* dat. pl. of *mǣl*] **:** by a (specified) portion or measure at a time <piece*meal*>

mea·lie \'mē-lē\ *n* [Afrik *mielie*] **1** *So Afr* **:** INDIAN CORN **2** *So Afr* **:** an ear of Indian corn

meal·time \'mē(ə)l-ˌtīm\ *n* **:** the usual time at which a meal is served

meal·worm \-ˌwərm\ *n* **:** the larva of various beetles (family Tenebrionidae) that infests and pollutes grain products but is often raised as food for insectivorous animals, for laboratory use, or as bait for fishing

mealy \'mē-lē\ *adj* **meal·i·er; -est** **1 :** soft, dry, and friable **2 :** containing meal **:** FARINACEOUS **3 a :** covered with meal or with fine granules **b :** flecked with another color **c :** SPOTTY, UNEVEN **d :** PALLID, BLANCHED <a ~ complexion> **4 :** MEALY-MOUTHED

mealy·bug \'mē-lē-ˌbəg\ *n* **:** any of numerous scale insects (family Pseudococcidae) that have a white powdery covering and are destructive pests esp. of fruit trees

mealy-mouthed \ˌmē-lē-'mau̇t͟hd, -'mau̇tht\ *adj* **:** not plain and straightforward **:** DEVIOUS <a ~ orator>

[1]mean \'mēn\ *adj* [ME *mene,* fr. *imene,* fr. OE *gemǣne;* akin to OHG *gimeini* common, L *communis* common, *munus* service, gift] **1 :** lacking distinction or eminence **:** HUMBLE **2 :** lacking in mental discrimination **:** DULL **3 a :** of poor shabby inferior quality or status <~*er* quarters of the city> **b :** worthy of little regard **:** CONTEMPTIBLE <living in ~ circumstances> **4 :** lacking dignity or honor **:** BASE **5 a :** PENURIOUS, STINGY **b :** characterized by petty selfishness or malice **c :** causing trouble or bother **:** VEXATIOUS **d :** EXCELLENT, EFFECTIVE <plays a ~ trumpet> **6 a :** ASHAMED 1b **b :** being in low spirits or health **:** INDISPOSED — **mean·ness** \'mēn-nəs\ *n*
syn MEAN, IGNOBLE, ABJECT, SORDID *shared meaning element* **:** so low as to be out of accord with normal standards of human decency and dignity

[2]mean \'mēn\ *vb* **meant** \'ment\; **mean·ing** \'mē-niŋ\ [ME *menen,* fr. OE *mǣnan;* akin to OHG *meinen* to have in mind, OSlav *mĕniti* to mention] *vt* **1 :** to have in the mind as a purpose **:** INTEND **2 :** to serve or intend to convey, show, or indicate **:** SIGNIFY **3 :** to direct to a particular individual ~ *vi* **1 :** to have an intended purpose <he ~*s* well> **2 :** to be of a specified degree of importance <health ~*s* everything> — **mean·er** \'mē-nər\ *n* — **mean business :** to be in earnest

[3]mean *n* [ME *mene,* fr. MF *meien,* fr. *meien,* adj.] **1 a (1) :** something intervening or intermediate **(2) :** a middle point between extremes **b :** a value that lies within a range of values and is computed according to a prescribed law: as **(1) :** ARITHMETIC MEAN **(2) :** EXPECTED VALUE **c :** the arithmetic mean of the two extremes of a range of values **d :** either of the middle two terms of a proportion **2** *pl but sing or pl in constr* **:** something useful or helpful to a desired end **3** *pl* **:** resources available for disposal; *esp* **:** material resources affording a secure life
syn **1** see AVERAGE ***ant*** extreme
2 MEAN (as MEANS), INSTRUMENT, AGENT, MEDIUM *shared meaning element* **:** something or someone necessary or useful in effecting an end

[4]mean *adj* [ME *mene,* fr. MF *meien,* fr. L *medianus* — more at MEDIAN] **1 :** occupying a middle position **:** intermediate in space, order, time, kind, or degree **2 :** occupying a position about midway between extremes: as **a :** being near the average **b :** of a moderate degree of excellence **:** MIDDLING **c :** being the mean of a set of values **:** AVERAGE <~ temperature> **3 :** serving as a means **:** INTERMEDIARY

[1]me·an·der \mē-'an-dər\ *n* [L *maeander,* fr. Gk *maiandros,* fr. *Maiandros* (now *Menderes*), river in Asia Minor] **1 :** a turn or winding of a stream **2 :** a winding path or course; *esp* **:** LABYRINTH — **me·an·drous** \-drəs\ *adj*

[2]meander *vi* **me·an·dered; me·an·der·ing** \-d(ə-)riŋ\ **1 :** to follow a winding or intricate course **2 :** to wander aimlessly or casually without urgent destination **:** RAMBLE

mean deviation *n* **:** the mean of the absolute values of the numerical differences between the numbers of a set (as statistical data) and their mean or median

mean distance *n* **:** the arithmetical mean of the maximum and minimum distances of a planet, satellite, or secondary star from its primary

mean·ing \'mē-niŋ\ *n* **1 a :** the thing one intends to convey esp. by language **:** PURPORT **b :** the thing that is conveyed esp. by language **:** IMPORT **2 :** something meant or intended **:** AIM <a mischievous ~ was apparent> **3 :** significant quality; *esp* **:** implication of a hidden or special significance <a glance full of ~> **4 a :** the logical connotation of a word or phrase **b :** the logical denotation or extension of a phrase — **meaning** *adj*
syn MEANING, SENSE, ACCEPTATION, SIGNIFICATION, SIGNIFICANCE, IMPORT *shared meaning element* **:** the idea that something conveys to the mind. MEANING is the general term, usable of anything admitting of interpretation <I don't know the *meaning* of his conduct> <a dictionary gives the *meaning* of words> SENSE denotes the or, more often, a particular meaning (as of a word or phrase) <some words have many *senses*> In more abstract use it refers to intelligibility in general <speaks things . . . that carry but half *sense* —Shak.> ACCEPTATION is used of a sense of a word or phrase as regularly understood and implies general acceptance <the term . . . will be used in its common *acceptation* —H. O. Taylor> *Signification* and *significance* are often used interchangeably, but distinctively SIGNIFICATION can apply to an established meaning of a term, symbol, or character with the implication that this meaning is uniquely the one called to mind by use of the term, symbol, or character in question <the *signification* of the cross to Christians> while SIGNIFICANCE can apply specifically to a covert as distinct from the ostensible meaning of something <the mood was . . . , I thought, indicative of chinks in the saintly armor. Of course, I tend to see *significances* in everything —John Barth> IMPORT usually imputes momentousness to the idea or impression conveyed by words <spoke words in her ear that had an awful *import* to her —George Meredith> <disturbed by the *import* of his answer>

mean·ing·ful \-fəl\ *adj* **1 a :** having a meaning or purpose **b :** full of meaning **:** SIGNIFICANT <a ~ life> **2 :** having an assigned function in a language system <~ propositions> — **mean·ing·ful·ly** \-fə-lē\ *adv* — **mean·ing·ful·ness** *n*

mean·ing·less \'mē-niŋ-ləs\ *adj* **1 :** having no meaning **2 :** having no assigned function in a language system <a ~ metaphysical statement> — **mean·ing·less·ly** *adv* — **mean·ing·less·ness** *n*

[1]mean·ly \'mēn-lē\ *adv, obs* **:** fairly well **:** MODERATELY

[2]meanly *adv* **:** in a mean manner: as **a :** in a lowly manner **:** HUMBLY **b :** in an inferior manner **:** BADLY **c :** in a base or ungenerous manner

mean proportional *n* **:** GEOMETRIC MEAN; *esp* **:** the square root (as x) of the product of two numbers (as a and b) when expressed as the means of a proportion (as $\frac{a}{x} = \frac{x}{b}$

mean square *n* **:** the mean of the squares of a set of values

mean square deviation *n* **1 :** VARIANCE 5 **2 :** STANDARD DEVIATION

means test \'mēnz-\ *n* **:** an examination into the financial state of a person to determine his eligibility for public assistance

mean sun *n* **:** a fictitious sun used for timekeeping that moves uniformly along the celestial equator and maintains a constant rate of apparent motion

[1]mean·time \'mēn-ˌtīm\ *n* **:** the intervening time

[2]meantime *adv* **:** MEANWHILE

mean time *n* **:** time that is based on the motion of the mean sun and that has the mean solar second as its unit — called also *mean solar time*

mean value theorem *n* **:** a theorem in calculus: if a function of one variable is continuous on a closed interval and differentiable on the interval minus its end points there is at least one point where the derivative of the function is equal to the slope of the line joining the end points of the curve representing the function on the interval

[1]mean·while \'mēn-ˌhwīl, -ˌwīl\ *n* **:** MEANTIME

[2]meanwhile *adv* **:** during the intervening time

meas *abbr* **measure**

mea·sle \'mē-zəl\ *n* [sing. of *measles*] **:** a tapeworm cysticercus larva; *specif* **:** one found in the muscles of a domesticated mammal — **mea·sled** \-zəld\ *adj*

mea·sles \'mē-zəlz\ *n pl but sing or pl in constr* [ME *meseles,* pl. of *mesel* measles, spot characteristic of measles; akin to MD *masel* spot characteristic of measles] **1 a :** an acute contagious viral disease marked by an eruption of distinct red circular spots **b :** any of various eruptive diseases (as German measles) **2** [ME *mesel* infested with tapeworms, lit., leprous, fr. OF, fr. ML *misellus* leper, fr. L, wretch, fr. *misellus,* dim. of *miser* miserable] **:** infestation with or disease caused by larval tapeworms in the muscles and tissues

mea·sly \'mēz-(ə-)lē\ *adj* **mea·sli·er; -est** **1 :** infected with measles **2 a :** containing larval tapeworms **b :** TRICHINIZED **3 :** contemptibly small

[1]mea·sure \'mezh-ər, 'māzh-\ *n* [ME *mesure,* fr. OF, fr. L *mensura,* fr. *mensus,* pp. of *metiri* to measure; akin to OE *mǣth* measure, Gk *metron*] **1 a (1) :** an adequate or due portion **(2) :** a moderate degree; *also* **:** MODERATION, TEMPERANCE **(3) :** a fixed or suitable limit **:** BOUNDS **b :** the dimensions, capacity, or amount of something ascertained by measuring **c (1) :** a measured quantity **(2) :** AMOUNT, DEGREE **2 a :** an instrument or utensil for measuring **b (1) :** a standard or unit of measurement — see WEIGHT table **(2) :** a system of standard units of measure <metric ~> **3 :** the act or process of measuring **4 a (1) :** MELODY, TUNE **(2) :** DANCE; *esp* **:** a slow and stately dance **b :** rhythmic structure or movement **:** CADENCE: as **(1) :** poetic rhythm measured by temporal quantity or accent; *specif* **:** METER **(2) :** musical time **c (1) :** a grouping of musical beats made by the regular recurrence of primary accents and located on the staff immediately following a vertical bar **(2) :** a metrical unit **:** FOOT **5 :** an exact divisor of a number **6 :** a basis or standard of comparison **:** CRITERION **7 :** a step planned or taken as a means to an end; *specif* **:** a proposed legislative act

[2]measure *vb* **mea·sured; mea·sur·ing** \'mezh-(ə-)riŋ, 'māzh-\ *vt* **1 a :** to choose or control with cautious restraint **:** REGULATE <~ his acts> **b :** to regulate by a standard **:** GOVERN **2 :** to allot or apportion in measured amounts <~ out 3 cups> **3 :** to lay off by making measurements **4 :** to ascertain the measurements of **5 :** to estimate or appraise by a criterion <~*s* his skill against his rival> **6** *archaic* **:** to travel over **:** TRAVERSE **7 :** to serve as a measure of <a thermometer ~*s* temperature> ~ *vi* **1 :** to take or make a measurement **2 :** to have a specified measurement — **mea·sur·abil·i·ty** \ˌmezh-(ə-)rə-'bil-ət-ē, ˌmāzh-\ *n* — **mea·sur·able** \'mezh-(ə-)rə-bəl, 'māzh-\ *adj* — **mea·sur·ably** \-blē\ *adv* — **mea·sur·er** \-ər-ər\ *n*

mea·sured \'mezh-ərd, 'māzh-\ *adj* **1 :** marked by due proportion **2 a :** marked by rhythm **:** regularly recurrent **b :** METRICAL **3 :** DELIBERATE, CALCULATED — **mea·sured·ly** *adv*

mea·sure·less \-ər-ləs\ *adj* **1 :** having no observable limit : IMMEASURABLE <the ~ universe> **2 :** very great <treated them with ~ contempt>

mea·sure·ment \'mezh-ər-mənt, 'māzh-\ *n* **1 :** the act or process of measuring **2 :** a figure, extent, or amount obtained by measuring : DIMENSION **3 :** MEASURE 2b

measurement ton *n* : TON 2c

measure up *vi* **1 :** to have necessary or fitting qualifications **2 :** to be the equal (as in ability) — used with *to*

measuring worm *n* : LOOPER 1

meat \'mēt\ *n* [ME *mete*, fr. OE; akin to OHG *maz* food, L *madēre* to be wet, Gk *madaros* wet, *mastos* breast] **1 a :** FOOD; *esp* : solid food as distinguished from drink **b :** the edible part of something as distinguished from its covering (as a husk or shell) **2 :** animal tissue used as food: **a :** FLESH 2b **b :** FLESH 1a; *specif* : flesh of domesticated animals **3** *archaic* : [1]MEAL 2; *esp* : DINNER **4 :** the core of something : SUBSTANCE **5 :** favorite pursuit or interest

meat·ball \-,bȯl\ *n* : a small ball of chopped or ground meat often mixed with bread crumbs and spices

meat by–product *n* : a usable product other than flesh obtained from slaughter animals

meat·man \'mēt-,man\ *n* : a vendor of meat : BUTCHER

meat type *n* : a type of hog esp. suitable for the production of pork without excessive early fattening — compare LARD TYPE

me·atus \mē-'āt-əs\ *n, pl* **me·atus·es** \-ə-səz\ *or* **me·atus** \-'āt-əs, -'ā-,tüs\ [LL, fr. L, going, passage, fr. *meatus*, pp. of *meare* to go — more at PERMEATE] : a natural body passage

meaty \'mēt-ē\ *adj* **meat·i·er; -est 1 :** full of meat **2 :** rich in matter for thought — **meat·i·ness** *n*

mec·a·myl·a·mine \,mek-ə-'mil-ə-,mēn\ *n* [fr. *Mecamylamine*, a trademark] : a drug that in the hydrochloride $C_{11}H_{21}N.HCl$ is used orally as a ganglionic blocking agent to effect a rapid lowering of severely elevated blood pressure

mec·ca \'mek-ə\ *n, often cap* [*Mecca*, Saudi Arabia, birthplace of Muhammad and holy city of Islam] : a place sought as a goal by numerous people

mech *abbr* mechanical; mechanics

mechan- *or* **mechano-** *comb form* [ME *mechan-*, fr. MF or L, fr. Gk *mēchan-*, fr. *mēchanē* machine — more at MACHINE] : machine <*mechano*morphic> : mechanical <*mechanize*>

[1]me·chan·ic \mi-'kan-ik\ *adj* [prob. fr. MF *mechanique*, adj. & n., fr. L *mechanicus*, fr. Gk *mēchanikos*, fr. *mēchanē* machine — more at MACHINE] **1 :** of or relating to manual work or skill **2 :** of the nature of or resembling a machine esp. in routine or automatic performance

[2]mechanic *n* **1 :** a manual worker : ARTISAN **2 :** MACHINIST; *esp* : one who repairs machines

[1]me·chan·i·cal \mi-'kan-i-kəl\ *adj* **1 a** (1) **:** of or relating to machinery or tools <~ applications of science> <a ~ genius> <~ aptitude> (2) **:** produced or operated by a machine or tool <~ power> <a ~ refrigerator> <a ~ saw> **b :** of or relating to manual operations **2 :** of or relating to artisans or machinists <the ~ trades> **3 a :** done as if by machine : seemingly uninfluenced by the mind or emotions : AUTOMATIC <her singing was cold and ~> **b :** of or relating to technicalities or petty matters **4 a :** relating to, governed by, or in accordance with the principles of mechanics <~ work> <~ energy> **b :** relating to the quantitative relations of force and matter <~ pressure of wind on a tower> **5 :** caused by, resulting from, or relating to a process that involves a purely physical as opposed to a chemical change <~ erosion of rock> ***syn*** see SPONTANEOUS — **me·chan·i·cal·ly** \-i-k(ə-)lē\ *adv*

[2]mechanical *n* : a piece of finished copy consisting typically of type proofs and artwork positioned and mounted for photomechanical reproduction

mechanical advantage *n* : the advantage gained by the use of a mechanism in transmitting force; *specif* : the ratio of the force that performs the useful work of a machine to the force that is applied to the machine

mechanical drawing *n* **1 :** drawing done with the aid of instruments **2 :** a drawing made with instruments

mech·a·ni·cian \,mek-ə-'nish-ən\ *n* : MECHANIC, MACHINIST

me·chan·ics \mi-'kan-iks\ *n pl but sing or pl in constr* **1 :** a branch of physical science that deals with energy and forces and their effect on bodies **2 :** the practical application of mechanics to the design, construction, or operation of machines or tools **3 :** mechanical or functional details

mech·a·nism \'mek-ə-,niz-əm\ *n* **1 a :** a piece of machinery **b :** a process or technique for achieving a result **2 :** mechanical operation or action **3 :** a doctrine that holds natural processes (as of life) to be mechanically determined and capable of complete explanation by the laws of physics and chemistry **4 :** the fundamental physical or chemical processes involved in or responsible for an action, reaction, or other natural phenomenon (as organic evolution)

mech·a·nist \-nəst\ *n* **1** *archaic* : MECHANIC **2 :** an adherent of the doctrine of mechanism

mech·a·nis·tic \,mek-ə-'nis-tik\ *adj* **1 :** mechanically determined <~ universe> **2 :** of or relating to the doctrine of mechanism **3 :** MECHANICAL — **mech·a·nis·ti·cal·ly** \-ti-k(ə-)lē\ *adv*

mech·a·nize \'mek-ə-,nīz\ *vt* **-nized; -niz·ing 1 :** to make mechanical; *esp* : to make automatic or routine **2 a :** to equip with machinery esp. to replace human or animal labor **b :** to equip with armed and armored motor vehicles **c :** to provide with mechanical power **3 :** to produce by or as if by machine — **mech·a·niz·able** \-,nī-zə-bəl\ *adj* — **mech·a·ni·za·tion** \,mek-ə-nə-'zā-shən\ *n* — **mech·a·niz·er** \'mek-ə-,nī-zər\ *n*

mech·a·no·chem·is·try \,mek-ə-nō-'kem-ə-strē\ *n* : chemistry that deals with the conversion of chemical energy into mechanical work (as in the contraction of a muscle) — **mech·a·no·chem·i·cal** \-'kem-i-kəl\ *adj*

mech·a·no·re·cep·tor \-ri-'sep-tər\ *n* : a neural end organ (as a tactile receptor) that responds to a mechanical stimulus (as a change in pressure or tension) — **mech·a·no·re·cep·tion** \-'sep-shən\ *n* — **mech·a·no·re·cep·tive** \-'sep-tiv\ *adj*

Mech·lin \'mek-lən\ *n* [*Mechlin*, Belgium] : a delicate bobbin lace used for dresses and millinery

me·co·ni·um \mi-'kō-nē-əm\ *n* [L, lit., poppy juice, fr. Gk *mēkōnion*, fr. *mēkōn* poppy; akin to OHG *mago* poppy] : a dark greenish mass that accumulates in the bowel during fetal life and is discharged shortly after birth

me·cop·ter·ous \mi-'käp-tə-rəs\ *adj* [NL *Mecoptera* group name, fr. *meco-* long (fr. Gk *mēkos* length) + Gk *pteron* wing; akin to Gk *makros* long — more at MEAGER, FEATHER] : of, relating to, or being any of an order (Mecoptera) of primitive carnivorous insects (as scorpion flies) usu. with membranous wings and a long beak with biting mouthparts at the tip

med *abbr* **1** medical; medicine **2** medieval **3** medium

MEd *abbr* master of education

med·al \'med-ᵊl\ *n* [MF *medaille*, fr. OIt *medaglia* coin worth half a denarius, medal, fr. (assumed) VL *medalis* half, fr. LL *medialis* middle, fr. L *medius* — more at MID] **1 :** a metal disk bearing a religious emblem or picture **2 :** a piece of metal often resembling a coin and having a stamped design that is issued to commemorate a person or event or awarded for excellence or achievement

Medal for Merit : a U.S. decoration awarded to civilians for exceptionally meritorious conduct in the performance of outstanding services

med·al·ist *or* **med·al·list** \'med-ᵊl-əst\ *n* **1 :** a designer, engraver, or maker of medals **2 :** a recipient of a medal as an award

me·dal·lic \mə-'dal-ik\ *adj* : of, relating to, or shown on a medal <a ~ sculptor>

me·dal·lion \mə-'dal-yən\ *n* [F *médaillon*, fr. It *medaglione*, aug. of *medaglia*] **1 :** a large medal **2 :** something resembling a large medal; *esp* : a tablet or panel in a wall or window bearing a figure in relief, a portrait, or an ornament

Medal of Freedom : a U.S. decoration awarded to civilians for meritorious achievement in any of various fields

Medal of Honor : a U.S. military decoration awarded in the name of the Congress for conspicuous gallantry and intrepidity at the risk of life above and beyond the call of duty in action with an enemy

medal play *n* : STROKE PLAY

med·dle \'med-ᵊl\ *vi* **med·dled; med·dling** \'med-liŋ, -ᵊl-iŋ\ [ME *medlen*, fr. OF *mesler*, *medler*, fr. (assumed) VL *misculare*, fr. L *miscēre* to mix — more at MIX] : to interest oneself in what is not one's concern : interfere without right or propriety — **med·dler** \'med-lər, -ᵊl-ər\ *n*

syn MEDDLE, INTERFERE, INTERMEDDLE, TAMPER *shared meaning element* : to concern oneself with officiously, impertinently, or indiscreetly

med·dle·some \'med-ᵊl-səm\ *adj* : given to meddling ***syn*** see IMPERTINENT — **med·dle·some·ness** *n*

Mede \'mēd\ *n* [ME, fr. L *Medus*, fr. Gk *Mēdos*] : a native or inhabitant of ancient Media in Persia

Me·dea \mə-'dē-ə\ *n* [L, fr. Gk *Medeia*] : an enchantress noted in Greek myth for helping Jason gain the Golden Fleece and notorious for repeatedly resorting to murder to gain her ends

medi- *or* **medio-** *comb form* [L, fr. *medius*] : middle <*medi*eval>

[1]me·dia \'mēd-ē-ə\ *n, pl* **me·di·ae** \-ē-,ē\ **1** [LL, fr. L, fem. of *medius*; fr. the voiced stops' being regarded as intermediate between the tenues and the aspirates] : a voiced stop **2** [NL, fr. L, fem. of *medius*] : the middle coat of the wall of a blood or lymph vessel consisting chiefly of circular muscle fibers

[2]media *n, pl* **me·di·as** [pl. of *medium*] : MEDIUM 2b

me·di·ad \'mēd-ē-,ad\ *adv* : toward the median line or plane of a body or part

me·di·al \'mēd-ē-əl\ *adj* **1 a :** being or occurring in the middle : MEDIAN **b :** extending toward the middle **2 :** situated between the extremes of initial and final in a word or morpheme **3 :** MEAN, AVERAGE — **medial** *n* — **me·di·al·ly** \-ə-lē\ *adv*

[1]me·di·an \'mēd-ē-ən\ *n* **1 :** a medial part (as a vein or nerve) **2 a :** a value in an ordered set of values below and above which there is an equal number of values or which is the arithmetic mean of the two middle values if there is no one middle number **b :** a vertical line that divides the histogram of a frequency distribution into two parts of equal area **c :** a value of a random variable for which all greater values make the distribution function greater than one half and all lesser values make it less than one half **3 a :** a line from a vertex of a triangle to the midpoint of the opposite side **b :** a line joining the midpoints of the nonparallel sides of a trapezoid ***syn*** see AVERAGE

[2]median *adj* [MF or L; MF, fr. L *medianus*, fr. *medius* middle — more at MID] **1 :** being in the middle or in an intermediate position : MEDIAL **2 :** relating to or constituting a statistical median **3 :** lying in the plane dividing a bilateral animal into right and left halves **4 :** produced without occlusion along the lengthwise middle line of the tongue — **me·di·an·ly** *adv*

median strip *n* : a paved or planted strip dividing a highway into lanes according to direction of travel

me·di·ant \'mēd-ē-ənt\ *n* [It *mediante*, fr. LL *mediant-*, *medians*, prp. of *mediare* to be in the middle] : the third tone of a diatonic scale midway between the tonic and the dominant

me·di·as·ti·num \,mēd-ē-ə-'stī-nəm\ *n, pl* **-na** \-nə\ [NL, fr. L, neut. of *mediastinus* medial, fr. *medius*] : an irregular median septum of the thoracic cavity that is formed of the opposing medial walls of the parietal pleura and encloses the thoracic viscera except the lungs — **me·di·as·ti·nal** \-'stīn-ᵊl\ *adj*

[1]me·di·ate \'mēd-ē-ət\ *adj* [ME, fr. LL *mediatus* intermediate, fr. pp. of *mediare*] **1 :** occupying a middle position **2 a :** acting through an intervening agency **b** : exhibiting indirect causation, connection, or relation — **me·di·a·cy** \-ē-ə-sē\ *n* — **me·di·ate·ly** *adv* — **me·di·ate·ness** *n*

²**me·di·ate** \ˈmēd-ē-ˌāt\ *vb* **-at·ed; -at·ing** [ML *mediatus,* pp. of *mediare,* fr. LL, to be in the middle, fr. L *medius* middle — more at MID] *vi* **1** : to interpose between parties in order to reconcile them **2** : to reconcile differences ~ *vt* **1 a** : to effect by action as an intermediary **b** : to bring accord out of by action as an intermediary **2 a** : to act as intermediary agent in bringing, effecting, or communicating : CONVEY **b** : to transmit as intermediate mechanism or agency ***syn*** see INTERPOSE — **me·di·a·tive** \-ˌāt-iv\ *adj* — **me·di·a·to·ry** \-ə-ˌtōr-ē, -ˌtȯr-\ *adj*

me·di·a·tion \ˌmēd-ē-ˈā-shən\ *n* : the act or process of mediating; *esp* : intervention between conflicting parties to promote reconciliation, settlement, or compromise — **me·di·a·tion·al** \-shnəl, -shən-ᵊl\ *adj*

me·di·a·tor \ˈmēd-ē-ˌāt-ər\ *n* **1** : one that mediates; *esp* : one that mediates between parties at variance **2** : a mediating agent in a chemical or biological process

me·di·a·tress \ˈmēd-ē-ˌā-trəs\ *n* : a female mediator

me·di·a·trice \ˈmēd-ē-ˈā-trəs\ *n* [ME, fr. MF, fr. LL *mediatric-, mediatrix,* fem. of *mediator,* fr. *mediatus,* pp.] : MEDIATRESS

me·di·a·trix \-ˈā-triks\ *n* [ME, fr. LL] : MEDIATRESS

¹**med·ic** \ˈmed-ik\ *n* [ME *medike,* fr. L *medica,* fr. Gk *mēdikē,* fr. fem. of *mēdikos* of Media, fr. *Mēdia* Media, ancient country in Asia] : any of a genus (*Medicago*) of leguminous herbs (as alfalfa)

²**medic** *n* [L *medicus*] : one engaged in medical work; *esp* : CORPSMAN

med·i·ca·ble \ˈmed-i-kə-bəl\ *adj* : CURABLE, REMEDIABLE

med·ic·aid \ˈmed-i-ˌkād\ *n* [*medical aid*] : a program of medical aid designed for those unable to afford regular medical service and financed jointly by the state and federal governments

med·i·cal \ˈmed-i-kəl\ *adj* [F or LL; F *médical,* fr. LL *medicalis,* fr. L *medicus* physician, fr. *mederi* to heal; akin to Av *vī-mad-* healer, L *meditari* to meditate] **1** : of, relating to, or concerned with physicians or the practice of medicine **2** : requiring or devoted to medical treatment — **med·i·cal·ly** \-k(ə-)lē\ *adv*

medical examiner *n* : a public officer who makes postmortem examinations of bodies to find the cause of death

me·di·ca·ment \mi-ˈdik-ə-mənt, ˈmed-i-kə-\ *n* : a substance used in therapy — **me·di·ca·men·tous** \mi-ˌdik-ə-ˈment-əs, ˌmed-i-kə-\ *adj*

medi·care \ˈmed-i-ˌke(ə)r, -ˌka(ə)r\ *n* [blend of *medical* and *care*] : a government program of medical care esp. for the aged

med·i·cate \ˈmed-ə-ˌkāt\ *vt* **-cat·ed; -cat·ing** [L *medicatus,* pp. of *medicare* to heal, fr. *medicus*] **1** : to treat medicinally **2** : to impregnate with a medicinal substance <~*ed* soap>

med·i·ca·tion \ˌmed-ə-ˈkā-shən\ *n* **1** : the act or process of medicating **2** : a medicinal substance : MEDICAMENT

me·dic·i·na·ble \mi-ˈdis-nə-bəl, -ᵊn-ə-; *archaic or Brit* ˈmed-sə-nə-\ *adj* : MEDICINAL

me·dic·i·nal \mə-ˈdis-nəl, -ᵊn-əl\ *adj* **1** : tending or used to cure disease or relieve pain **2** : SALUTARY — **medicinal** *n* — **me·dic·i·nal·ly** \-ē\ *adv*

medicinal leech *n* : a large European freshwater leech (*Hirudo medicinalis*) formerly used by physicians for bleeding patients

med·i·cine \ˈmed-ə-sən, *Brit usu* ˈmed-sən\ *n* [ME, fr. OF, fr. L *medicina,* fr. fem. of *medicinus* of a physician, fr. *medicus*] **1 a** : a substance or preparation used in treating disease **b** : something that affects well-being **2 a** : the science and art dealing with the maintenance of health and the prevention, alleviation, or cure of disease **b** : the branch of medicine concerned with the nonsurgical treatment of disease **3** : a substance (as a drug or potion) used to treat something other than disease **4** : an object held by the American Indians to give control over natural or magical forces; *also* : magical power or a magical rite — **medicine** *vt*

medicine ball *n* : a heavy stuffed leather-covered ball used for conditioning exercises

medicine dropper *n* : DROPPER 2

medicine man *n* : a priestly healer or sorcerer esp. among the American Indians : SHAMAN

medicine show *n* : a traveling show using entertainers to attract a crowd among which remedies or nostrums are sold

med·i·co \ˈmed-i-ˌkō\ *n, pl* **-cos** [It *medico* or Sp *médico,* both fr. L *medicus*] : a medical practitioner : PHYSICIAN; *also* : a medical student

medico- *comb form* [NL, fr. L *medicus*] **1** : medical <*medico*psychology> **2** : medical and <*medico*legal>

med·i·co·le·gal \ˌmed-i-kō-ˈlē-gəl\ *adj* [NL *medicolegalis,* fr. L *medicus* medical + *-o-* + *legalis* legal] : of or relating to both medicine and law

¹**me·di·eval** *or* **me·di·ae·val** \ˌmēd-ē-ˈē-vəl, ˌmed-, ˌmid-; mē-ˈdē-vəl\ *adj* [*medi-* + L *aevum* age — more at AYE] : of, relating to, or characteristic of the Middle Ages — **me·di·eval·ly** \-ē\ *adv*

²**medieval** *or* **mediaeval** *n* : a person belonging to the Middle Ages

me·di·eval·ism \-ˌiz-əm\ *n* **1** : medieval quality, character, or state **2** : devotion to the institutions, arts, and practices of the Middle Ages

me·di·eval·ist \-ˈēv-(ə-)ləst, -ˈdēv-\ *n* **1** : a specialist in medieval history and culture **2** : a connoisseur or devotee of medieval arts and culture

Medieval Latin *n* : the Latin used esp. for liturgical and literary purposes from the 7th to the 15th centuries inclusive

medio- — see MEDI-

me·di·o·cre \ˌmēd-ē-ˈō-kər\ *adj* [MF, fr. L *mediocris,* lit., halfway up a mountain, fr. *medi-* + *ocris* stony mountain; akin to L *acer* sharp — more at EDGE] : of moderate or low quality : ORDINARY

me·di·oc·ri·ty \ˌmēd-ē-ˈäk-rət-ē\ *n, pl* **-ties** **1 a** : the quality or state of being mediocre **b** : moderate ability or value **2** : a mediocre person

med·i·tate \ˈmed-ə-ˌtāt\ *vb* **-tat·ed; -tat·ing** [L *meditatus,* pp. of *meditari* — more at METE] *vt* **1** : to focus one's thoughts on : reflect on or ponder over **2** : to plan or project in the mind : INTEND, PURPOSE ~ *vi* : to engage in contemplation or reflection ***syn*** see PONDER — **med·i·ta·tor** \-ˌtāt-ər\ *n*

med·i·ta·tion \ˌmed-ə-ˈtā-shən\ *n* **1** : a discourse intended to express its author's reflections or to guide others in contemplation **2** : the act or process of meditating

med·i·ta·tive \ˈmed-ə-ˌtāt-iv\ *adj* : disposed or given to meditation — **med·i·ta·tive·ly** *adv* — **med·i·ta·tive·ness** *n*

Med·i·ter·ra·nean \ˌmed-ə-tə-ˈrā-nē-ən, -nyən\ *adj* **1** *not cap* [L *mediterraneus,* fr. *medi-* + *terra* land — more at TERRACE] : enclosed or nearly enclosed with land **2** : of or relating to the Mediterranean sea **3** : of or relating to a group or physical type of the Caucasian race characterized by medium or short stature, slender build, dolichocephaly, and dark complexion

Mediterranean flour moth *n* : a small largely gray and black nearly cosmopolitan moth (*Anagasta kuehniella*) whose larva destroys processed grain products

Mediterranean fruit fly *n* : a widely distributed two-winged fly (*Ceratitis capitata*) with black and white markings whose larva lives and feeds in ripening fruit

¹**me·di·um** \ˈmēd-ē-əm\ *n, pl* **mediums** *or* **me·dia** \-ē-ə\ [L, fr. neuter of *medius* middle — more at MID] **1 a** : something in a middle position **b** : a middle condition or degree : MEAN **2** : a means of effecting or conveying something: as **a** (1) : a substance regarded as the means of transmission of a force or effect (2) : a surrounding or enveloping substance **b** *pl usu media* (1) : a channel of communication (2) : a publication or broadcast that carries advertising (3) : a mode of artistic expression or communication **c** : GO-BETWEEN, INTERMEDIARY **d** *pl mediums* : an individual held to be a channel of communication between the earthly world and a world of spirits **e** : material or technical means of artistic expression **3 a** : a condition or environment in which something may function or flourish **b** *pl media* (1) : a nutrient system for the artificial cultivation of cells or organisms and esp. bacteria (2) : a fluid or solid in which organic structures are placed (as for preservation or mounting) **c** : a liquid with which pigment is mixed by a painter **4** : a size of paper usu. 23 x 18 inches ***syn*** see MEAN

²**medium** *adj* : intermediate in amount, quality, position, or degree

medium frequency *n* : a radio frequency between high frequency and low frequency — see RADIO FREQUENCY table

me·di·um·is·tic \ˌmēd-ē-ə-ˈmis-tik\ *adj* : of, relating to, or having the qualities of a spiritualistic medium

medium of exchange : something commonly accepted in exchange for goods and services and recognized as representing a standard of value

med·lar \ˈmed-lər\ *n* [ME *medeler,* fr. MF *medlier,* fr. *medle* medlar fruit, fr. L *mespilum,* fr. Gk *mespilon*] : a small Eurasian tree (*Mespilus germanica*) of the rose family whose fruit resembles a crab apple and is used in preserves; *also* : its fruit

¹**med·ley** \ˈmed-lē\ *n, pl* **medleys** [ME *medle,* fr. MF *medlee,* fr. fem. of *medlé,* pp. of *medler* to mix — more at MEDDLE] **1** *archaic* : MELEE **2** : MIXTURE; *esp* : HODGEPODGE **3** : a musical composition made up of a series of songs or short musical pieces

²**medley** *adj* : MIXED, MOTLEY

medley relay *n* : a relay race in swimming in which each member of a team uses a different stroke

me·dul·la \mə-ˈdəl-ə\ *n, pl* **-las** *or* **-lae** \-(ˌ)ē, -ˌī\ [L] **1** *pl medullae* **a** : MARROW 1 **b** : MEDULLA OBLONGATA **2 a** : the inner or deep part of an animal or plant structure <the adrenal ~> **b** : MEDULLARY SHEATH

medulla ob·lon·ga·ta \-ˌäb-ˌlȯŋ-ˈgät-ə\ *n, pl* **medulla oblongatas** *or* **medullae ob·lon·ga·tae** \-ˈgät-ē, -ˈgä-ˌtī\ [NL, lit., oblong medulla] : the somewhat pyramidal last part of the vertebrate brain continuous posteriorly with the spinal cord — see BRAIN illustration

med·ul·lary \ˈmed-ᵊl-ˌer-ē, ˈmej-ə-ˌler-; mə-ˈdəl-ə-rē\ *adj* **1** : of or relating to a medulla and esp. the medulla oblongata **2** : of or relating to the pith of a plant

medullary ray *n* **1** : a primary tissue composed of radiating bands of parenchyma cells extending between the vascular bundles of herbaceous dicotyledonous stems and connecting the pith with the cortex **2** : VASCULAR RAY

medullary sheath *n* : the layer of myelin surrounding a medullated nerve fiber

med·ul·lat·ed \ˈmed-ᵊl-ˌāt-əd, ˈmej-ə-ˌlāt-\ *adj* **1** *of a nerve fiber* : having a medullary sheath **2** : having a medulla — used of fibers other than nerve fibers

me·du·sa \mi-ˈd(y)ü-sə, -zə\ *n* **1** *cap* [L, fr. Gk *Medousa*] : a Gorgon who could turn a beholder into stone by her glance **2** *pl* **me·du·sae** \-ˌsē, -ˌzē, -ˌsī, -ˌzī\ [NL, fr. L] : JELLYFISH; *esp* : a small hydrozoan jellyfish — **me·du·san** \-ˈd(y)üs-ᵊn, -ˈd(y)üz-\ *adj or n* — **me·du·soid** \-ˈd(y)ü-ˌsȯid, -ˌzȯid\ *adj or n*

meed \ˈmēd\ *n* [ME, fr. OE *mēd;* akin to OHG *miata* reward, Gk *misthos*] **1** *archaic* : an earned reward or wage **2** : a fitting return or recompense

meek \ˈmēk\ *adj* [ME, of Scand origin; akin to ON *mjūkr* gentle; akin to L *mucus*] **1** : enduring injury with patience and without resentment : MILD **2** : deficient in spirit and courage : SUBMISSIVE **3** : not violent or strong : MODERATE ***syn*** see HUMBLE ***ant*** arrogant — **meek·ly** *adv* — **meek·ness** *n*

meer·schaum \ˈmi(ə)r-shəm, -ˌshȯm\ *n* [G, fr. *meer* sea + *schaum* foam] **1** : a fine light white clayey mineral that is a hydrous magnesium silicate $H_4Mg_2Si_3O_{10}$ found chiefly in Asia Minor and used esp. for tobacco pipes **2** : a tobacco pipe of meerschaum

¹**meet** \ˈmēt\ *vb* **met** \ˈmet\; **meet·ing** [ME *meten,* fr. OE *mētan;* akin to OHG *muoz* meeting, Arm *matčim* I approach] *vt* **1 a** : to come into the presence of : FIND **b** : to approach from another direction **c** : to come into contact or conjunction with : JOIN **d** : to appear to the perception of **2** : to encounter as antagonist or foe : OPPOSE **3** : to enter into conference, argument, or personal dealings with **4** : to conform to esp. with exactitude and precision <expand a concept to ~ new problems> **5** : to pay fully : SETTLE **6** : to cope with : MATCH <was able to ~ every social situation> **7** : to provide for <had enough money to ~ the

needs of the moment> **8** : to become acquainted with **9** : ENCOUNTER, EXPERIENCE **10** : to receive or greet in an official capacity ~ *vi* **1 a** : to come together from different directions **b** : to come together for a common purpose : ASSEMBLE **c** : to come together as contestants, opponents, or enemies **2** : to become joined into one : UNITE ***syn*** see SATISFY — **meet·er** *n* — **meet one halfway** : to make concessions to : compromise with

²meet *n* **1** : the act of assembling for a hunt or for competitive sports **2** : a competition in which individuals (as athletes) match skills

³meet *adj* [ME *mete,* fr. OE *gemǣte;* akin to OE *metan* to mete] : precisely adapted to a particular situation, need, or circumstance : very proper ***syn*** see FIT ***ant*** unmeet — **meet·ly** *adv*

meet·ing \ˈmēt-iŋ\ *n* **1** : an act or process of coming together: as **a** : an assembly for a common purpose (as worship) **b** : a session of horse or dog racing **2** : a permanent organizational unit of the Society of Friends **3** : INTERSECTION, JUNCTION

meet·ing·house \-ˌhau̇s\ *n* : a building used for public assembly and esp. for Protestant worship

meeting of minds : AGREEMENT, CONCORD

meg *abbr* megohm

mega- *or* **meg-** *comb form* [Gk, fr. *megas* large — more at MUCH] **1 a** : great : large <*mega*spore> **b** : having a (specified) part of large size <*mega*cephalic> **2** : million : multiplied by one million <*meg*ohm> <*mega*cycle>

mega·bar \ˈmeg-ə-ˌbär\ *n* [ISV] : a unit of pressure equal to 1,000,000 bars

mega·bit \-ˌbit\ *n* : 1,000,000 bits

mega·buck \-ˌbək\ *n* : 1,000,000 dollars

mega·cy·cle \-ˌsī-kəl\ *n* : MEGAHERTZ

mega·death \-ˌdeth\ *n* : 1,000,000 deaths — used as a unit in reference to atomic warfare

mega·ga·mete \ˌmeg-ə-gə-ˈmēt, -ˈgam-ˌēt\ *n* : MACROGAMETE

mega·ga·me·to·phyte \-gə-ˈmēt-ə-ˌfīt\ *n* : the female gametophyte produced by a megaspore

mega·hertz \ˈmeg-ə-ˌhərts, -ˌhe(ə)rts\ *n* [ISV] : a unit of frequency equal to 1,000,000 hertz — abbr. *MHz*

mega·kar·yo·cyte \ˌmeg-ə-ˈkar-ē-ō-ˌsīt\ *n* [*mega-* + *kary-* + *-cyte*] : a large cell that has a lobulate nucleus, is found esp. in the bone marrow, and is considered to be the source of blood platelets

megal- *or* **megalo-** *comb form* [NL, fr. Gk, fr. *megal-, megas* — more at MUCH] : large : of giant size <*megalo*polis> : grandiose <*megalo*mania>

mega·lith \ˈmeg-ə-ˌlith\ *n* : one of the huge undressed stones used in various prehistoric monuments — **mega·lith·ic** \ˌmeg-ə-ˈlith-ik\ *adj*

meg·a·lo·blast \ˈmeg-ə-lō-ˌblast\ *n* : a large erythroblast that appears in the blood esp. in pernicious anemia — **meg·a·lo·blas·tic** \ˌmeg-ə-lō-ˈblas-tik\ *adj*

meg·a·lo·ma·nia \ˌmeg-ə-lō-ˈmā-nē-ə, -nyə\ *n* [NL] **1** : a mania for great or grandiose performance **2** : a delusional mental disorder that is marked by infantile feelings of personal omnipotence and grandeur — **meg·a·lo·ma·ni·ac** \-ˈmā-nē-ˌak\ *adj or n* — **meg·a·lo·ma·ni·a·cal** \-mə-ˈnī-ə-kəl\ *or* **meg·a·lo·man·ic** \-ˈman-ik\ *adj* — **meg·a·lo·ma·ni·a·cal·ly** \-mə-ˈnī-ə-k(ə-)lē\ *adv*

meg·a·lop·o·lis \ˌmeg-ə-ˈläp-ə-ləs\ *n* **1** : a very large city **2** : a thickly populated region centering in a metropolis or embracing several metropolises — **meg·a·lop·o·lis·tic** \-ˌläp-ə-ˈlis-tik\ *adj* — **meg·a·lo·pol·i·tan** \-lō-ˈpäl-ət-ᵊn\ *n or adj* — **meg·a·lo·pol·i·tan·ism** \-ˌiz-əm\ *n*

meg·a·lop·ter·an \ˌmeg-ə-ˈläp-tə-rən\ *n* [NL *Megaloptera,* group name, fr. *megal-* + Gk *pteron* wing — more at FEATHER] : any of a small order (Megaloptera) of usu. large insects (as a dobsonfly) that are often classified as neuropterans, have wings with a folded anal area in the hind pair, and develop from aquatic predacious larvae (as a hellgrammite) — **meg·a·lop·ter·ous** \-tə-rəs\ *adj*

mega·par·sec \ˌmeg-ə-ˈpär-ˌsek\ *n* [ISV] : a unit of measure for distances in interstellar space equal to 1,000,000 parsecs

¹mega·phone \ˈmeg-ə-ˌfōn\ *n* : a cone-shaped device used to intensify or direct the voice — **mega·phon·ic** \ˌmeg-ə-ˈfän-ik\ *adj*

²megaphone *vt* : to transmit or address through or as if through a megaphone ~ *vi* : to speak through or as if through a megaphone

me·gap·o·lis \mə-ˈgap-ə-ləs, me-\ *n* : MEGALOPOLIS — **meg·a·pol·i·tan** \ˌmeg-ə-ˈpäl-ət-ᵊn\ *adj*

Me·gar·i·an \mə-ˈgar-ē-ən, me-\ *adj* : of or relating to a Socratic school of philosophy founded by Euclid of Megara and noted for its subtle attention to logic — **Megarian** *n*

Me·gar·ic \-ˈgar-ik\ *adj* : MEGARIAN — **Megaric** *n*

mega·scop·ic \ˌmeg-ə-ˈskäp-ik\ *adj* [*mega-* + *-scopic* (as in *microscopic*)] **1** : MACROSCOPIC 1 <~ features of leaves> **2** : based on or relating to observations made with the unaided eye — **mega·scop·i·cal·ly** \-i-k(ə-)lē\ *adv*

mega·spo·ran·gi·um \ˌmeg-ə-spə-ˈran-jē-əm\ *n* [NL] : a sporangium that develops only megaspores

mega·spore \ˈmeg-ə-ˌspō(ə)r, -ˌspȯ(ə)r\ *n* [ISV] : a spore in heterosporous plants that gives rise to female gametophytes and is generally larger than a microspore — **mega·spor·ic** \ˌmeg-ə-ˈspōr-ik, -ˈspȯr-\ *adj*

mega·spo·ro·gen·e·sis \ˌmeg-ə-ˌspōr-ə-ˈjen-ə-səs, -ˌspȯr-\ *n* [NL] : the formation and maturation of a megaspore

mega·spo·ro·phyll \ˌmeg-ə-ˈspōr-ə-ˌfil, -ˈspȯr-\ *n* : a sporophyll that develops only megasporangia

mega·ton \ˈmeg-ə-ˌtən\ *n* : an explosive force equivalent to that of 1,000,000 tons of TNT

mega·watt \-ˌwät\ *n* [ISV] : 1,000,000 watts

me·gil·lah \mə-ˈgil-ə\ *n* [Yiddish, fr. Heb *mĕgillāh* scroll, volume (used esp. of the Book of Esther, read aloud at the Purim celebration)] *slang* : a long involved story or account

me·gilp \mə-ˈgilp\ *n* [origin unknown] : a gelatinous preparation commonly of linseed oil and mastic varnish that is used by artists as a vehicle for oil colors

meg·ohm \ˈmeg-ˌōm\ *n* [ISV] : 1,000,000 ohms

¹me·grim \ˈmē-grəm\ *n* [ME *migreime,* fr. MF *migraine*] **1 a** : MIGRAINE **b** : VERTIGO, DIZZINESS **2 a** : FANCY, WHIM **b** *pl* : low spirits

²megrim *n* [origin unknown] : any of several small flatfishes; *esp* : a European flounder (*Arnoglossus laterna*)

Mei·ji \ˈmā-(ˌ)jē\ *n* [Jap, lit., enlightened rule] : the period of the reign (1868–1912) of Emperor Mutsuhito of Japan

mei·kle \ˈmē-kəl\ *var of* MICKLE

mei·ny *n, pl* **meinies** [ME *meynie* — more at MENIAL] **1** \ˈmā-nē\ *archaic* : RETINUE, COMPANY **2** \ˈmen-yē\ *chiefly Scot* : MULTITUDE

mei·o·sis \mī-ˈō-səs\ *n* [NL, fr. Gk *meiōsis* diminution, fr. *meioun* to diminish, fr. *meiōn* less — more at MINOR] **1** : the representation of a thing as less than it actually is in order to compel greater esteem for it : UNDERSTATEMENT **2** : the cellular process that results in the number of chromosomes in gamete-producing cells being reduced to one half and that involves a reduction division in which one of each pair of homologous chromosomes passes to each daughter cell and a mitotic division — compare MITOSIS — **mei·ot·ic** \mī-ˈät-ik\ *adj* — **mei·ot·i·cal·ly** \-i-k(ə-)lē\ *adv*

Meis·sen \ˈmīs-ᵊn\ *n* : a ceramic ware made at Meissen near Dresden; *esp* : a European porcelain developed under the patronage of the king of Saxony about 1715 and used for both ornamental and table wares — called also *Meissen china, Meissen ware*

Mei·ster·sing·er \ˈmī-stər-ˌsiŋ-ər, -ˌziŋ-\ *n, pl* **Meistersinger** *or* **Meistersingers** [G, fr. MHG, fr. *meister* master + *singer*] : a member of any of various German guilds formed chiefly in the 15th and 16th centuries by workingmen and craftsmen for the cultivation of poetry and music

mel·a·mine \ˈmel-ə-ˌmēn\ *n* [G *melamin*] **1** : a white crystalline organic base $C_3H_6N_6$ with a high melting point that is used esp. in melamine resins **2** : a melamine resin or a plastic made from such a resin

melamine resin *n* : a thermosetting resin made from melamine and an aldehyde and used esp. in molded or laminated products, adhesives, and coatings

melan- *or* **melano-** *comb form* [ME, fr. MF, fr. LL, fr. Gk, fr. *melan-, melas* — more at MULLET] **1** : black : dark <*melan*ic> <*melan*in> **2** : melanin <*melan*oid>

mel·an·cho·lia \ˌmel-ən-ˈkō-lē-ə\ *n* [NL, fr. LL, melancholy] : a mental condition characterized by extreme depression, bodily complaints, and often hallucinations and delusions; *esp* : a manic-depressive psychosis — **mel·an·cho·li·ac** \-lē-ˌak\ *n*

mel·an·chol·ic \ˌmel-ən-ˈkäl-ik\ *adj* **1** : of, relating to, or subject to melancholy : DEPRESSED **2** : of or relating to melancholia **3** : tending to depress the spirits : SADDENING — **melancholic** *n* — **mel·an·chol·i·cal·ly** \-i-k(ə-)lē\ *adv*

¹mel·an·choly \ˈmel-ən-ˌkäl-ē\ *n, pl* **-chol·ies** [ME *malencolie,* fr. MF *melancolie,* fr. LL *melancholia,* fr. Gk, fr. *melan-* + *cholē* bile — more at GALL] **1 a** : an abnormal state attributed to an excess of black bile and characterized by irascibility or depression **b** : BLACK BILE **c** : MELANCHOLIA **2 a** : depression of spirits : DEJECTION **b** : a pensive mood

²melancholy *adj* **1 a** : depressed in spirits : DEJECTED, SAD **b** : PENSIVE **2 a** : causing or tending to cause depression of mind or spirit : DISMAL **b** : causing sadness

Mel·a·ne·sian \ˌmel-ə-ˈnē-zhən, -shən\ *n* **1** : a member of the dominant native group of Melanesia **2** : a language group consisting of the Austronesian languages of Melanesia — **Melanesian** *adj*

mé·lange \mā-ˈläⁿzh, -ˈlänj\ *n* [F, fr. MF, fr. *mesler, meler* to mix — more at MEDDLE] : a mixture often of incongruous elements

¹me·lan·ic \mə-ˈlan-ik\ *adj* **1** : MELANOTIC **2** : affected with or characterized by melanism

²melanic *n* : a melanic individual

mel·a·nin \ˈmel-ə-nən\ *n* : a dark brown or black animal or plant pigment

mel·a·nism \ˈmel-ə-ˌniz-əm\ *n* **1** : an increased amount of black or nearly black pigmentation (as of skin, feathers, or hair) of an individual or kind of organism **2** : intense pigmentation in man in skin, eyes, and hair — **mel·a·nist** \-nəst\ *n* — **mel·a·nis·tic** \ˌmel-ə-ˈnis-tik\ *adj*

mel·a·nite \ˈmel-ə-ˌnīt\ *n* [G *melanit,* fr. *melan-*] : a black andradite garnet — **mel·a·nit·ic** \ˌmel-ə-ˈnit-ik\ *adj*

mel·a·nize \ˈmel-ə-ˌnīz\ *vt* **-nized; -niz·ing** **1** : to convert into or infiltrate with melanin **2** : to make dark or black — **mel·a·ni·za·tion** \ˌmel-ə-nə-ˈzā-shən\ *n*

me·la·no·blast \mə-ˈlan-ə-ˌblast, ˈmel-ə-nō-\ *n* [ISV] : a cell that is a precursor of a melanocyte or melanophore — **me·la·no·blas·tic** \mə-ˌlan-ə-ˈblas-tik, ˌmel-ə-nō-\ *adj*

me·la·no·blas·to·ma \mə-ˌlan-ə-blas-ˈtō-mə, ˌmel-ə-nō-\ *n, pl* **-mas** *or* **-ma·ta** \-mət-ə\ [NL] : a malignant tumor derived from melanoblasts

mel·a·noch·roi \ˌmel-ə-ˈnäk-rə-ˌwī, -ˈnäk-ˌrȯi\ *n pl* [NL, irreg. fr. *melan-* + Gk *ōchros* yellow, pale] : Caucasians having dark hair and pale complexion — **mel·a·no·chro·ic** \ˌmel-ə-nō-ˈkrō-ik\ *adj*

me·la·no·cyte \mə-ˈlan-ə-ˌsīt, ˈmel-ə-nō-\ *n* [ISV] : an epidermal cell that produces melanin

melanocyte–stimulating hormone *n* : a vertebrate hormone of the pituitary gland that lightens the skin by stimulating melanin dispersion in pigment-containing cells — called also *melanophore-stimulating hormone*

me·la·no·gen·e·sis \mə-ˌlan-ə-ˈjen-ə-səs, ˌmel-ə-nō-\ *n* [NL] : the formation of melanin

mel·a·noid \ˈmel-ə-ˌnȯid\ *n* [ISV] : a pigment (as one contributing esp. to the yellow color of the skin) that is a disintegration product of a melanin

mel·a·no·ma \ˌmel-ə-ˈnō-mə\ *n, pl* **-mas** *also* **-ma·ta** \-mət-ə\ [NL] **:** a usu. malignant tumor containing dark pigment
me·la·no·phore \mə-ˈlan-ə-ˌfō(ə)r, ˈmel-ə-nə-, -ˌfȯ(ə)r\ *n* **:** a melanin-containing cell esp. of fishes, amphibians, and reptiles
mel·a·no·sis \ˌmel-ə-ˈnō-səs\ *n* [NL] **:** a condition characterized by abnormal deposition of melanins or sometimes other pigments in the tissues of the body
mel·a·not·ic \-ˈnät-ik\ *adj* **:** having or characterized by black pigmentation
mela·phyre \ˈmel-ə-ˌfī(ə)r\ *n* [F *mélaphyre,* fr. Gk *melas* black + F *-phyre* — more at MULLET] **:** a porphyritic igneous rock with dark-colored aphanitic groundmass and phenocrysts of various kinds
mel·a·to·nin \ˌmel-ə-ˈtō-nən\ *n* [prob. fr. *mela*nocyte + sero*tonin*] **:** a vertebrate hormone of the pineal gland that produces lightening of the skin by causing concentration of melanin in pigment-containing cells
mel·ba toast \ˌmel-bə-\ *n* [Nellie *Melba*] **:** very thin bread toasted till crisp
Mel·chite *or* **Mel·kite** \ˈmel-ˌkīt\ *n* [ML *Melchita,* fr. MGk, *Melchitēs,* lit., royalist, fr. Syr *malkā* king] **1 :** an Eastern Christian chiefly of Syria and Egypt adhering to Chalcedonian orthodoxy in preference to Monophysitism **2 :** a member of a Uniate body derived from the Melchites
[1]**Mel·chiz·e·dek** \mel-ˈkiz-ə-ˌdek\ *n* [Gk *Melchisedek,* fr. Heb *Malkī-ṣedheq*] **:** a priest-king of Jerusalem who prepared a ritual meal for Abraham and received tithes from him
[2]**Melchizedek** *adj* **:** of or relating to the higher order of the Mormon priesthood
[1]**meld** \ˈmeld\ *vb* [G *melden* to announce, fr. OHG *meldōn;* akin to OE *meldian* to announce, OSlav *moliti* to ask for] *vt* **:** to declare or announce (a card or combination of cards) for a score in a card game esp. by placing face up on the table ~ *vi* **:** to declare a card or combination of cards as a meld
[2]**meld** *n* **:** a card or combination of cards that is or can be melded in a card game
[3]**meld** *vb* [blend of *melt* and *weld*] **:** MERGE
me·lee \ˈmā-ˌlā, mā-ˈ\ *n* [F *mêlée,* fr. OF *meslee,* fr. *mesler* to mix — more at MEDDLE] **:** a confused struggle; *esp* **:** a hand-to-hand fight among several people
mel·ic \ˈmel-ik\ *adj* [L *melicus,* fr. Gk *melikos,* fr. *melos* song — more at MELODY] **:** of or relating to song **:** LYRIC; *esp* **:** of or relating to Greek lyric poetry of the 7th and 6th centuries B.C.
mel·i·lot \ˈmel-ə-ˌlät\ *n* [ME *mellilot,* fr. MF *melilot,* fr. L *melilotos,* fr. Gk *melilōtos,* fr. *meli* honey + *lōtos* clover, lotus — more at MELLIFLUOUS] **:** SWEET CLOVER; *esp* **:** a yellow-flowered sweet clover (*Melilotus officinalis*)
me·lio·rate \ˈmēl-yə-ˌrāt, ˈmē-lē-ə-\ *vb* **-rat·ed; -rat·ing** [LL *melioratus,* pp. of *meliorare,* fr. L *melior* better; akin to L *multus* much, Gk *mala* very] **:** AMELIORATE — **me·lio·ra·tion** \ˌmēl-yə-ˈrā-shən, ˌmē-lē-ə-\ *n* — **me·lio·ra·tive** \ˈmēl-yə-ˌrāt-iv, ˈmē-lē-ə-\ *adj* — **me·lio·ra·tor** \-ˌrāt-ər\ *n*
me·lio·rism \ˈmēl-yə-ˌriz-əm, ˈmē-lē-ə-\ *n* **:** the belief that the world tends to become better and that man can aid its betterment — **me·lio·rist** \-rəst\ *adj or n* — **me·lio·ris·tic** \ˌmēl-yə-ˈris-tik, ˌmē-lē-ə-\ *adj*
me·lis·ma \mi-ˈliz-mə\ *n, pl* **-ma·ta** \-mət-ə\ [NL, fr. Gk, song, melody, fr. *melizein* to sing, fr. *melos* song] **1 :** a group of notes or tones sung on one syllable in plainsong **2 :** melodic embellishment or ornamentation **3 :** CADENZA — **mel·is·mat·ic** \ˌmel-əz-ˈmat-ik\ *adj*
mell \ˈmel\ *vb* [ME *mellen,* fr. MF *mesler*] *archaic* **:** MIX
mel·lif·er·ous \me-ˈlif-(ə-)rəs\ *adj* [L *mellifer,* fr. *mell-, mel* + *-fer* -ferous] **:** producing or yielding honey
mel·lif·lu·ent \me-ˈlif-lə-wənt\ *adj* [LL *mellifluent-, mellifluens,* fr. L *mell-, mel* + *fluent-, fluens,* prp. of *fluere*] **:** MELLIFLUOUS — **mel·lif·lu·ent·ly** *adv*
mel·lif·lu·ous \me-ˈlif-lə-wəs, mə-\ *adj* [LL *mellifluus,* fr. L *mell-, mel* honey + *fluere* to flow; akin to Goth *milith* honey, Gk *melit-, meli*] **1 :** filled with something (as honey) that sweetens **2 :** having a smooth rich flow <a ~ voice> — **mel·lif·lu·ous·ly** *adv* — **mel·lif·lu·ous·ness** *n*
mel·lo·phone \ˈmel-ə-ˌfōn\ *n* [[1]*mellow* + *-phone*] **:** a circular valved brass instrument having a conical tube, a cup-shaped mouthpiece, and a range similar to that of the French horn
[1]**mel·low** \ˈmel-(ˌ)ō, -ə(-w)\ *adj* [ME *melowe*] **1 a** *of a fruit* **:** tender and sweet because of ripeness **b** *of a wine* **:** well aged and pleasingly mild **2 a :** made gentle by age or experience **b :** rich and full but free from garishness or stridency **c :** warmed and relaxed by liquor **d :** PLEASING, AGREEABLE <in a ~ mood> **3** *of soil* **:** having a soft and loamy consistency — **mel·low·ly** *adv* — **mel·low·ness** *n*
[2]**mellow** *vt* **:** to make mellow ~ *vi* **:** to become mellow
me·lo·de·on \mə-ˈlōd-ē-ən\ *n* [G *melodion,* fr. *melodie* melody, fr. OF] **:** a small reed organ in which a suction bellows draws air inward through the reeds
me·lod·ic \mə-ˈläd-ik\ *adj* **:** of or relating to melody **:** MELODIOUS — **me·lod·i·cal·ly** \-i-k(ə-)lē\ *adv*
me·lo·di·ous \mə-ˈlōd-ē-əs\ *adj* **1 :** having a pleasing melody **2 :** of, relating to, or producing melody — **me·lo·di·ous·ly** *adv* — **me·lo·di·ous·ness** *n*
mel·o·dist \ˈmel-əd-əst\ *n* **1 :** SINGER **2 :** a composer of melodies
mel·o·dize \ˈmel-ə-ˌdīz\ *vb* **-dized; -diz·ing** *vt* **:** to make melodious **:** set to melody ~ *vi* **:** to compose a melody — **mel·o·diz·er** *n*
melo·dra·ma \ˈmel-ə-ˌdräm-ə, -ˌdram-\ *n* [modif. of F *mélodrame,* fr. Gk *melos* + F *drame* drama, fr. LL *drama*] **1 a :** a work (as a movie or play) characterized by extravagant theatricality and by the predominance of plot and physical action over characterization **b :** the genre of dramatic literature constituted by such works **2 :** melodramatic events or behavior — **melo·dra·ma·tist** \ˌmel-ə-ˈdram-ət-əst, -ˈdräm-\ *n*
melo·dra·mat·ic \ˌmel-ə-drə-ˈmat-ik\ *adj* **1 :** of, relating to, or characteristic of melodrama **2 :** appealing to the emotions **:** SENSATIONAL — **melo·dra·mat·i·cal·ly** \-i-k(ə-)lē\ *adv*
melo·dra·mat·ics \-iks\ *n pl but sing or pl in constr* **:** melodramatic conduct or writing
melo·dra·ma·tize \ˌmel-ə-ˈdram-ə-ˌtīz, -ˈdräm-\ *vt* **1 :** to make melodramatic <~ a situation> **2 :** to make a melodrama of (as a novel) — **melo·dra·ma·ti·za·tion** \-ˌdram-ət-ə-ˈzā-shən, -ˌdräm-\ *n*
mel·o·dy \ˈmel-əd-ē\ *n, pl* **-dies** [ME *melodie,* fr. OF, fr. LL *melodia,* fr. Gk *melōidia* chanting, music, fr. *melos* limb, musical phrase, song + *aeidein* to sing; akin to Bret *mell* joint — more at ODE] **1 :** a sweet or agreeable succession or arrangement of sounds **:** TUNEFULNESS **2 a :** a rhythmic succession of single tones organized as an aesthetic whole **b :** a musical line as it appears on the staff when viewed horizontally **c :** the chief part in a harmonic composition
mel·on \ˈmel-ən\ *n, often attrib* [ME, fr. MF, fr. LL *melon-, melo,* short for L *melopepon-, melopepo,* fr. Gk *mēlopepōn,* fr. *mēlon* apple + *pepōn,* an edible gourd — more at PUMPKIN] **1 :** any of various gourds (as a muskmelon or watermelon) usu. eaten raw as fruits **2 :** something rounded like a melon; *also* **:** a protruding abdomen **3 a :** a surplus of profits available for distribution to stockholders **b :** a financial windfall
Mel·pom·e·ne \mel-ˈpäm-ə-(ˌ)nē\ *n* [L, fr. Gk *Melpomenē*] **:** the Greek Muse of tragedy
[1]**melt** \ˈmelt\ *vb* [ME *melten,* fr. OE *meltan;* akin to L *mollis* soft, *molere* to grind — more at MEAL] *vi* **1 :** to become altered from a solid to a liquid state usu. by heat **2 a :** DISSOLVE, DISINTEGRATE <the sugar ~*ed* in the coffee> **b :** to disappear as if by dissolving <her anger ~*ed* at his kind words> **3** *obs* **:** to become subdued or crushed **4 :** to become mild, tender, or gentle **5 :** to lose distinct outline **:** BLEND ~ *vt* **1 :** to reduce from a solid to a liquid state usu. by heat **2 :** to cause to disappear or disperse **3 :** to make tender or gentle **:** SOFTEN — **melt·abil·i·ty** \ˌmel-tə-ˈbil-ət-ē\ *n* — **melt·able** \ˈmel-tə-bəl\ *adj* — **melt·er** *n*
[2]**melt** *n* **1 a :** material in the molten state **b :** the mass melted at a single operation or the quantity melted during a specified period **2 a :** the action or process of melting or the period during which it occurs <roads softened during the spring ~> **b :** the condition of being melted
[3]**melt** *n* [ME *milte,* fr. OE; akin to OHG *miltzi* spleen] **:** SPLEEN; *esp* **:** spleen of slaughtered animals for use as feed or food
melt·ing·ly \ˈmel-tiŋ-lē\ *adv* **:** in a melting manner **:** DELICATELY, TENDERLY <luscious background music, ~ played —E. T. Canby>
melting point *n* **:** the temperature at which a solid melts
melting pot *n* **1 :** a vessel for melting something **:** CRUCIBLE **2 a :** a place where racial amalgamation and social and cultural assimilation are going on <long cherished the myth of the public school as the *melting pot* —M. R. Berube> **b :** the population of such a place **3 :** a process of blending that often results in invigoration or novelty
mel·ton \ˈmelt-ᵊn\ *n* [*Melton* Mowbray, England] **:** a heavy smooth woolen fabric with short nap
melt·wa·ter \ˈmelt-ˌwȯt-ər, -ˌwät-\ *n* **:** water derived from the melting of ice and snow
[1]**mem** \ˈmem\ *n* [Heb *mēm,* lit., water] **:** the 13th letter of the Hebrew alphabet — see ALPHABET table
[2]**mem** *abbr* **1** member **2** memoir **3** memorial
mem·ber \ˈmem-bər\ *n* [ME *membre,* fr. OF, fr. L *membrum;* akin to Goth *mimz* flesh, Gk *mēros* thigh, *mēninx* membrane] **1 :** a body part or organ: as **a :** LIMB **b :** PENIS **c :** a unit of structure in a plant body **2 :** one of the individuals composing a group **3 :** a person baptized or enrolled in a church **4 :** a constituent part of a whole: as **a :** a syntactic or rhythmic unit of a sentence **:** CLAUSE **b :** one of the propositions of a syllogism **c :** one of the elements of a mathematical set **d :** one of the components of a logical class **e :** either of the equated elements in a mathematical equation ***syn*** see PART
member bank *n* **:** a bank having membership in the Federal Reserve System
mem·bered \ˈmem-bərd\ *adj* **:** consisting of or divided into members
mem·ber·ship \ˈmem-bər-ˌship\ *n* **1 :** the state or status of being a member **2 :** the body of members <an organization with a large ~> **3 :** the relation between an element of a set or class and the set or class — compare INCLUSION 3
mem·brane \ˈmem-ˌbrān\ *n* [L *membrana* skin, parchment, fr. *membrum*] **1 :** a thin soft pliable sheet or layer esp. of animal or plant origin **2 :** a piece of parchment forming part of a roll — **mem·bran·al** \mem-ˈbrān-ᵊl\ *adj* — **mem·braned** \ˈmem-ˌbrānd\ *adj*
membrane bone *n* **:** a bone that ossifies directly in connective tissue without previous existence as cartilage
mem·bra·nous \ˈmem-brə-nəs\ *adj* **1 :** of, relating to, or resembling membrane **2 :** thin, pliable, and often somewhat transparent <~ leaves> **3 :** characterized or accompanied by the formation of a usu. abnormal membrane or membranous layer <~ croup> — **mem·bra·nous·ly** *adv*
membranous labyrinth *n* **:** the sensory structures of the inner ear
me·men·to \mi-ˈment-(ˌ)ō\ *n, pl* **-tos** *or* **-toes** [ME, fr. L, remember, imper. of *meminisse* to remember; akin to L *ment-, mens* mind] **:** something that serves to warn or remind; *also* **:** SOUVENIR
me·men·to mo·ri \mi-ˌment-ō-ˈmōr-ē, -ˈmȯr-ē\ *n, pl* **memento mori** [L, remember that you must die] **1 :** a reminder of mortality; *esp* **:** DEATH'S HEAD **2 :** a reminder of man's failures or mistakes
Mem·non \ˈmem-ˌnän\ *n* [Gk *Memnōn*] **:** an Ethiopian king slain by Achilles at a late stage of the Trojan War
memo \ˈmem-(ˌ)ō\ *n, pl* **mem·os :** MEMORANDUM
mem·oir \ˈmem-ˌwär, -ˌwȯ(ə)r\ *n* [F *mémoire,* lit., memory, fr. L *memoria*] **1 :** an official note or report **:** MEMORANDUM **2 a :** a narrative composed from personal experience **b :** AUTOBIOGRAPHY — usu. used in pl. **c :** BIOGRAPHY **3 a :** an account of some-

thing noteworthy : REPORT **b** *pl* : the record of the proceedings of a learned society

mem·o·ra·bil·ia \ˌmem-ə-rə-ˈbil-ē-ə, -ˈbil-yə\ *n pl* [L, fr. neut. pl. of *memorabilis*] : things that are remarkable and worthy of remembrance; *also* : records of such things

mem·o·ra·bil·i·ty \-ˈbil-ət-ē\ *n* **1** : the quality or state of being memorable **2** : the quality or state of being rememberable

mem·o·ra·ble \ˈmem-(ə-)rə-bəl, ˈmem-ər-bəl\ *adj* [ME, fr. L *memorabilis*, fr. *memorare* to remind, mention, fr. *memor* mindful] : worth remembering : NOTABLE ***syn*** see NOTEWORTHY — **mem·o·ra·ble·ness** *n* — **mem·o·ra·bly** \-blē\ *adv*

mem·o·ran·dum \ˌmem-ə-ˈran-dəm\ *n, pl* **-dums** *or* **-da** \-də\ [ME, fr. L, neut. of *memorandus* to be remembered, gerundive of *memorare*] **1** : an informal record; *also* : a written reminder **2** : an informal written note of a transaction or proposed instrument **3 a** : an informal diplomatic communication **b** : a usu. brief communication written for interoffice circulation **c** : a communication that contains directive, advisory, or informative matter

1**me·mo·ri·al** \mə-ˈmōr-ē-əl, -ˈmȯr-\ *adj* **1** : serving to preserve remembrance : COMMEMORATIVE **2** : of or relating to memory — **me·mo·ri·al·ly** \-ə-lē\ *adv*

2**memorial** *n* **1** : something that keeps remembrance alive: as **a** : MONUMENT **b** : something (as a speech or ceremony) that commemorates **c** : KEEPSAKE, MEMENTO **2 a** : RECORD, MEMOIR <language and literature . . . the ~*s* of another age —J. H. Fisher> **b** : MEMORANDUM, NOTE; *specif* : a legal abstract **c** : a statement of facts addressed to a government and often accompanied with a petition or remonstrance

Memorial Day *n* **1** : May 30 formerly observed as a legal holiday in most states of the U.S. in remembrance of war dead **2** : the last Monday in May observed as a legal holiday in most states of the U.S. **3** : CONFEDERATE MEMORIAL DAY

me·mo·ri·al·ist \mə-ˈmōr-ē-ə-ləst, -ˈmȯr-\ *n* **1** : a person who writes or signs a memorial **2** : a person who writes a memoir

me·mo·ri·al·ize \-ˌlīz\ *vt* **-ized; -iz·ing 1** : to address or petition by a memorial **2** : COMMEMORATE

memorial park *n* : CEMETERY

me·mo·ri·ter \mə-ˈmȯr-ə-ˌte(ə)r, -ˈmär-\ *adj* [L, fr. *memor*] : marked by emphasis on memorization

mem·o·rize \ˈmem-ə-ˌrīz\ *vt* **-rized; -riz·ing** : to commit to memory : learn by heart — **mem·o·riz·able** \-ˌrī-zə-bəl\ *adj* — **mem·o·ri·za·tion** \ˌmem-(ə-)rə-ˈzā-shən\ *n* — **mem·o·riz·er** *n*

mem·o·ry \ˈmem-(ə-)rē\ *n, pl* **-ries** [ME *memorie*, fr. MF *memoire*, fr. L *memoria*, fr. *memor* mindful; akin to OE *mimorian* to remember, L *mora* delay, Gk *mermēra* care, Skt *smarati* he remembers] **1 a** : the power or process of reproducing or recalling what has been learned and retained esp. through associative mechanisms **b** : the store of things learned and retained from an organism's activity or experience as evidenced by modification of structure or behavior or by recall and recognition **2 a** : commemorative remembrance <erected a statue in ~ of the hero> **b** : the fact or condition of being remembered <days of recent ~> **3 a** : a particular act of recall or recollection **b** : an image or impression of one that is remembered **c** : the time within which past events can be or are remembered <within the ~ of living men> **4 a** : a device in which information esp. for a computer can be inserted and stored and from which it may be extracted when wanted **b** : capacity for storing information <a computer with 16K words of ~> **5** : a capacity for showing effects as the result of past treatment or for returning to a former condition — used esp. of a material (as metal or plastic)

syn MEMORY, REMEMBRANCE, RECOLLECTION, REMINISCENCE *shared meaning element* : the capacity for or act or action of remembering or something remembered ***ant*** oblivion

memory trace *n* : an alteration that is held to take place within the central nervous system and to constitute the physical basis of learning — called also *engram*

mem·sa·hib \ˈmem-ˌsä-(h)ib, -ˌsäb\ *n* [Hindi *memsāhib*, fr. E *ma'am* + Hindi *ṣāhib* sahib] : a white foreign woman of high social status living in India; *esp* : the wife of a British official

men *pl of* MAN

men- *or* **meno-** *comb form* [NL, fr. Gk *mēn* month — more at MOON] : menstruation <*meno*rrhagia>

1**men·ace** \ˈmen-əs\ *n* [ME, fr. MF, fr. L *minacia*, fr. *minac-*, *minax* threatening, fr. *minari* to threaten — more at MOUNT] **1** : a show of intention to inflict harm : THREAT **2 a** : one that represents a threat : DANGER **b** : a person who causes annoyance

2**menace** *vb* **men·aced; men·ac·ing** *vt* **1** : to make a show of intention to harm **2** : to represent or pose a threat to : ENDANGER ~ *vi* : to act in a threatening manner ***syn*** see THREATEN — **men·ac·ing·ly** \-ə-siŋ-lē\ *adv*

me·nad *var of* MAENAD

men·a·di·one \ˌmen-ə-ˈdī-ˌōn, -dī-ˈ\ *n* [*me*thyl + *na*phthoquinone + *di-* + ket*one*] : a yellow crystalline compound $C_{11}H_8O_2$ with the biological activity of natural vitamin K

mé·nage \mā-ˈnäzh\ *n* [F, fr. OF *mesnage* dwelling, fr. (assumed) VL *mansionaticum*, fr. L *mansion-*, *mansio* mansion] : a domestic establishment : HOUSEHOLD; *also* : HOUSEKEEPING

mé·nage à trois \-ä-ˈtrwä\ *n* [F, lit., household for three] : a relationship in which three persons (as a married pair and the lover of one of the pair) live together

me·nag·er·ie \mə-ˈnaj-(ə-)rē *also* -ˈnazh-\ *n* [F *ménagerie*, fr. MF, management of a household or farm, fr. *menage*] **1 a** : a place where animals are kept and trained esp. for exhibition **b** : a collection of wild or foreign animals kept esp. for exhibition **2** : a varied mixture <a wonderful ~ of royal hangers-on —V. S. Pritchett>

men·ar·che \ˈmen-ˌär-kē\ *n* [NL, fr. *men-* + Gk *archē* beginning] : the beginning of the menstrual function; *esp* : the first menstrual period of an individual — **men·ar·che·al** \ˌmen-är-kē-əl\ *adj*

1**mend** \ˈmend\ *vb* [ME *menden*, short for *amenden* — more at AMEND] *vt* **1** : to free from faults or defects: as **a** : to improve in manners or morals : REFORM **b** : to set right : CORRECT **c** : to put into good shape or working order again : patch up : REPAIR **d** : to restore to health : CURE **2** : to make amends or atonement for <least said, soonest ~*ed*> ~ *vi* **1** : to improve morally : REFORM **2** : to become corrected or improved **3** : to improve in health; *also* : HEAL — **mend·able** \ˈmen-də-bəl\ *adj* — **mend·er** *n*

syn MEND, REPAIR, PATCH, REBUILD *shared meaning element* : to put into good order something that is injured, damaged, or defective

2**mend** *n* **1** : an act of mending : REPAIR **2** : a mended place — **on the mend** : getting better : IMPROVING

men·da·cious \men-ˈdā-shəs\ *adj* [L *mendac-*, *mendax* — more at AMEND] : given to or characterized by deception or falsehood which often is not intended to genuinely mislead or delude <spinning ~ tales of his adventures> ***syn*** see DISHONEST ***ant*** veracious — **men·da·cious·ly** *adv* — **men·da·cious·ness** *n*

men·dac·i·ty \men-ˈdas-ət-ē\ *n, pl* **-ties 1** : the quality or state of being mendacious **2** : LIE

men·de·le·vi·um \ˌmen-də-ˈlē-vē-əm, -ˈlā-\ *n* [NL, fr. Dmitri *Mendeleev*] : a radioactive element that is artificially produced — see ELEMENT table

Men·de·lian \men-ˈdē-lē-ən, -ˈdēl-yən\ *adj* : of, relating to, or according with Mendel's laws or Mendelism — **Mendelian** *n* — **Men·de·lian·ist** \-əst\ *n*

Mendelian factor *n* : GENE

Mendelian inheritance *n* : PARTICULATE INHERITANCE

Men·del·ism \ˈmen-dᵊl-ˌiz-əm\ *n* : the principles or the operations of Mendel's laws; *also* : PARTICULATE INHERITANCE — **Men·del·ist** \-dᵊl-əst\ *adj or n*

Men·del's law \ˌmen-dᵊlz-\ *n* [Gregor *Mendel*] **1** : a principle in genetics: hereditary units occur in pairs that separate during gamete formation so that every gamete receives but one member of a pair — called also *law of segregation* **2** : a principle in genetics limited and modified by the subsequent discovery of the phenomenon of linkage: the different pairs of hereditary units are distributed to the gametes independently of each other, the gametes combine at random, and the various combinations of hereditary pairs occur in the zygotes according to the laws of chance — called also *law of independent assortment* **3** : a principle in genetics proved subsequently to be subject to many limitations: because one of each pair of hereditary units dominates the other in expression, characters are inherited alternatively on an all or nothing basis — called also *law of dominance*

men·di·can·cy \ˈmen-di-kən-sē\ *n* **1** : the condition of being a beggar **2** : the practice of begging

men·di·cant \ˈmen-di-kənt\ *n* [L *mendicant-*, *mendicans*, prp. of *mendicare* to beg, fr. *mendicus* beggar — more at AMEND] **1** : BEGGAR 1 **2** *often cap* : a member of a religious order (as the Franciscans) combining monastic life and outside religious activity and orig. owning neither personal nor community property : FRIAR — **mendicant** *adj*

men·dic·i·ty \men-ˈdis-ət-ē\ *n* [ME *mendicite*, fr. MF *mendicité*, fr. L *mendicitat-*, *mendicitas*, fr. *mendicus*] : MENDICANCY

Men·e·la·us \ˌmen-ᵊl-ˈā-əs\ *n* [L, fr. Gk *Menelaos*] : a king of Sparta, brother of Agamemnon, and husband of the abducted Helen of Troy

men·folk \ˈmen-ˌfōk\ *or* **men·folks** \-ˌfōks\ *n pl* **1** : men in general **2** : the men of a family or community

men·ha·den \men-ˈhād-ᵊn, mən-\ *n, pl* **-den** *also* **-dens** [of Algonquian origin; prob. akin to Narraganset *munnawhatteaûg* menhaden] : a marine fish (*Brevoortia tyrannus*) of the herring family abundant along the Atlantic coast of the U.S. where it is used for bait or converted into oil and fertilizer

men·hir \ˈmen-ˌhi(ə)r\ *n* [F, fr. Bret, fr. *men* stone + *hir* long] : a single upright rude monolith usu. of prehistoric origin

1**me·nial** \ˈmē-nē-əl, -nyəl\ *adj* [ME *meynial*, fr. *meynie* household, retinue, fr. OF *mesnie*, fr. (assumed) VL *mansionata*, fr. L *mansion-*, *mansio* dwelling] **1** : of or relating to servants : LOWLY **2 a** : appropriate to a servant : HUMBLE, SERVILE <answered in ~ tones> **b** : lacking interest or dignity <a ~ task> ***syn*** see SUBSERVIENT — **me·nial·ly** \-ē\ *adv*

2**menial** *n* : a domestic servant or retainer

Mé·nière's disease \mən-ˈye(ə)rz-\ *n* [Émile A. *Ménière* †1905 F physician] : a disorder of the membranous labyrinth of the inner ear that is marked by recurrent attacks of dizziness, tinnitus, and deafness — called also *Ménière's syndrome*

mening- *or* **meningo-** *also* **meningi-** *comb form* [NL, fr. *mening-*, *meninx*] **1** : meninges <*meningo*coccus> <*mening*itis> **2** : meninges and <*meningo*encephalitis>

men·in·ge·al \ˌmen-ən-ˈjē-əl\ *adj* : of, relating to, or affecting the meninges

meninges *pl of* MENINX

me·nin·gi·o·ma \mə-ˌnin-jē-ˈō-mə\ *n, pl* **-o·mas** *or* **-o·ma·ta** \-ˈō-mət-ə\ [NL] : a slow-growing encapsulated tumor arising from the meninges and often causing damage by pressing upon the brain and adjacent parts

men·in·gi·tis \ˌmen-ən-ˈjīt-əs\ *n, pl* **-git·i·des** \-ˈjit-ə-ˌdēz\ [NL] **1** : inflammation of the meninges and esp. of the pia mater and the arachnoid **2** : a usu. bacterial disease in which inflammation of the meninges occurs — **men·in·git·ic** \-ˈjit-ik\ *adj*

me·nin·go·coc·cus \mə-ˌniŋ-gə-ˈkäk-əs, -ˌnin-jə-\ *n, pl* **-coc·ci** \-ˈkäk-ˌ(s)ī, -(ˌ)(s)ē\ [NL] : the bacterium (*Neisseria meningitidis*) that causes cerebrospinal meningitis — **me·nin·go·coc·cal** \-ˈkäk-əl\ *also* **me·nin·go·coc·cic** \-ˈkäk-(s)ik\ *adj*

me·nin·go·en·ceph·a·li·tis \-gō-ən-ˌsef-ə-ˈlīt-əs\ *n, pl* **-lit·i·des** \-ˈlit-ə-ˌdēz\ [NL] : inflammation of the brain and meninges — **me·nin·go·en·ceph·a·lit·ic** \-ˈlit-ik\ *adj*

me·ninx \'mē-niŋ(k)s, 'men-iŋ(k)s\ *n, pl* **me·nin·ges** \mə-'nin-(,)jēz\ [NL, fr. Gk *mēning-, mēninx* membrane; akin to L *membrana* membrane] **:** any of the three membranes that envelop the brain and spinal cord

me·nis·cus \mə-'nis-kəs\ *n, pl* **me·nis·ci** \-'nis-,(k)ī, -,kē\ *also* **me·nis·cus·es** [NL, fr. Gk *mēniskos,* fr. dim. of *mēn* moon, crescent — more at MOON] **1 :** a crescent or crescent-shaped body **2 :** a fibrous cartilage within a joint esp. of the knee **3 :** a concavo-convex lens — see LENS illustration **4 :** the curved upper surface of a liquid column that is concave when the containing walls are wetted by the liquid and convex when not

A B

meniscus 4: *A* concave meniscus of water, *B* convex meniscus of mercury

Men·no·nite \'men-ə-,nīt\ *n* [G *Mennonit,* fr. *Menno* Simons †1561 Frisian religious reformer] **:** a member of any of various Protestant groups derived from the Anabaptist movement in Holland and characterized by congregational autonomy and rejection of military service

me·no mos·so \,mā-nō-'mō(s)-(,)sō\ *adv* [It] **:** less rapid — used as a direction in music

meno·pause \'men-ə-,pȯz\ *n* [F *ménopause,* fr. *méno-* men- + *pause*] **:** the period of natural cessation of menstruation occurring usu. between the ages of 45 and 50 — **meno·paus·al** \,men-ə-'pȯ-zəl\ *adj*

me·no·rah \mə-'nōr-ə, -'nȯr-\ *n* [Heb *mĕnōrāh* candlestick] **:** a candelabrum used in Jewish worship

men·or·rha·gia \,men-ə-'rā-j(ē-)ə, -'rā-zhə; -'räj-ə, -'räzh-\ *n* [NL] **:** abnormally profuse menstrual flow — **men·or·rhag·ic** \-'raj-ik\ *adj*

men·sal \'men(t)-səl\ *adj* [LL *mensalis,* fr. L *mensa* table] **:** of, relating to, or done at the table

1**mense** \'men(t)s\ *n* [ME *menske,* fr. ON *mennska* humanity] *chiefly Scot* **:** PROPRIETY — **mense·ful** \-fəl\ *adj* — **mense·less** \-ləs\ *adj*

2**mense** *vt* **mensed; mens·ing** *chiefly Scot* **:** to do honor to **:** GRACE

men·ses \'men-,sēz\ *n pl but sing or pl in constr* [L, lit., months, pl. of *mensis* month — more at MOON] **:** the menstruous flow

Men·she·vik \'men-chə-,vik, -,vēk\ *n, pl* **Mensheviks** *or* **Men·she·vi·ki** \,men-chə-'vik-ē, -'vē-kē\ [Russ *men'shevik,* fr. *men'she* less; fr. their forming the minority group of the party] **:** a member of a wing of the Russian Social Democratic party before and during the Russian Revolution believing in the gradual achievement of socialism by parliamentary methods in opposition to the Bolsheviks — **Men·she·vism** \'men-chə-,viz-əm\ *n* — **Men·she·vist** \-vəst\ *n or adj*

mens rea \(')menz-'rē-ə\ *n* [NL, lit., guilty mind] **:** criminal intent

men's room *n* **:** a room equipped with lavatories, toilets, and usu. urinals for the use of men

men·stru·al \'men(t)-strə(-wə)l\ *adj* **:** of or relating to menstruation

men·stru·ate \'men(t)-strə-,wāt, 'men-,strāt\ *vi* **-at·ed; -at·ing** [LL *menstruatus,* pp. of *menstruari,* fr. L *menstrua* menses, fr. neut. pl. of *menstruus* monthly, fr. *mensis*] **:** to undergo menstruation

men·stru·a·tion \,men(t)-strə-'wā-shən, men-'strā-\ *n* **:** a discharging of blood, secretions, and tissue debris from the uterus that recurs in nonpregnant breeding-age primate females at approximately monthly intervals and that is considered to represent a readjustment of the uterus to the nonpregnant state following proliferative changes accompanying the preceding ovulation; *also* **:** PERIOD 6c

men·stru·ous \'men(t)-strə(-wə)s\ *adj* [L *menstruus*] **:** of, relating to, or undergoing menstruation

men·stru·um \'men(t)-strə(-wə)m\ *n, pl* **-stru·ums** *or* **-strua** \-str(ə-w)ə\ [ML, lit., menses, alter. of L *menstrua*] **:** a substance that dissolves a solid or holds it in suspension **:** SOLVENT

men·su·ra·ble \'men(t)s-(ə-)rə-bəl, 'mench-(ə-)rə-\ *adj* [LL *mensurabilis,* fr. *mensurare* to measure, fr. *mensura* measure — more at MEASURE] **1 :** capable of being measured **:** MEASURABLE **2 :** MENSURAL 1 — **men·su·ra·bil·i·ty** \,men(t)s-(ə-)rə-'bil-ət-ē, ,mench-(ə-)rə-\ *n* — **men·su·ra·ble·ness** \'men(t)s-(ə-)rə-bəl-nəs, 'mench-(ə-)rə-\ *n*

men·su·ral \'men(t)s-(ə-)rəl, 'mench-(ə-)rəl\ *adj* [LL *mensuralis* measurable, fr. L *mensura*] **1 :** of, relating to, or being polyphonic music originating in the 13th century with each note having a definite and exact time value **2 :** of or relating to measure

men·su·ra·tion \,men(t)-sə-'rā-shən; ,men-chə-\ *n* **1 :** the act of measuring **:** MEASUREMENT **2 :** geometry applied to the computation of lengths, areas, or volumes from given dimensions or angles

mens·wear \'menz-,wa(ə)r, -,we(ə)r\ *n* **:** clothing for men

-ment \mənt; *homographic verbs are* ,ment *also* mənt, *the latter less often before a syllable-increasing suffix*\ *n suffix* [ME, fr. OF, fr. L *-mentum;* akin to L *-men,* suffix denoting concrete result, Gk *-mat-, -ma*] **1 a :** concrete result, object, or agent of a (specified) action <embank*ment*> <entangle*ment*> **b :** concrete means or instrument of a (specified) action <entertain*ment*> **2 a :** action **:** process <encircle*ment*> <develop*ment*> **b :** place of a (specified) action <encamp*ment*> **3 :** state or condition resulting from (a specified action)

1**men·tal** \'ment-ᵊl\ *adj* [ME, fr. MF, fr. LL *mentalis,* fr. L *ment-, mens* mind — more at MIND] **1 a :** of or relating to the mind; *specif* **:** of or relating to the total emotional and intellectual response of an individual to his environment <~ health> **b :** of or relating to intellectual as contrasted with emotional activity **c :** of, relating to, or being intellectual as contrasted with overt physical activity **d :** occurring or experienced in the mind **:** INNER <~ anguish> **e :** relating to the mind, its activity, or its products as an object of study **:** IDEOLOGICAL **f :** relating to spirit or idea as opposed to matter **2 a :** of, relating to, or affected by a psychiatric disorder <a ~ patient> <~ illness> **b :** intended for the care or treatment of persons affected by psychiatric disorders <~ hospitals> **3 :** of or relating to telepathic or mind-reading powers <a ~ medium> — **men·tal·ly** \-ᵊl-ē\ *adv*

2**mental** *adj* [L *mentum* chin; akin to L *mont-, mons* mountain — more at MOUNT] **:** of or relating to the chin **:** GENIAL

mental age *n* **:** a measure used in psychological testing that expresses an individual's mental attainment in terms of the number of years it takes an average child to reach the same level

mental deficiency *n* **:** failure in intellectual development that results in social incompetence and is considered to be the result of a defective central nervous system and to be incurable **:** FEEBLEMINDEDNESS

men·tal·ist \'ment-ᵊl-əst\ *n* **:** MIND READER

men·tal·i·ty \men-'tal-ət-ē\ *n, pl* **-ties 1 :** mental power or capacity **:** INTELLIGENCE <a man of high ~> **2 :** mode or way of thought **:** OUTLOOK <a provincial ~>

men·ta·tion \men-'tā-shən\ *n* [L *ment-, mens* + E *-ation*] **:** mental activity

men·thol \'men-,thȯl, -,thōl\ *n* [G, deriv. of L *mentha* mint] **:** a crystalline alcohol $C_{10}H_{20}O$ that occurs esp. in mint oils and has the odor and cooling properties of peppermint

men·tho·lat·ed \'men(t)-thə-,lāt-əd\ *adj* **:** containing or impregnated with menthol <a ~ salve>

1**men·tion** \'men-chən\ *n* [ME *mencioun,* fr. OF *mention,* fr. L *mention-, mentio,* fr. *ment-, mens*] **1 :** the act or an instance of citing or calling attention to someone or something esp. in a casual or incidental manner **2 :** formal citation for outstanding achievement

2**mention** *vt* **men·tioned; men·tion·ing** \'mench-(ə-)niŋ\ **:** to make mention of **:** refer to; *also* **:** to cite for outstanding achievement — **men·tion·able** \'mench-(ə-)nə-bəl\ *adj* — **men·tion·er** \-(ə-)nər\ *n*

syn MENTION, NAME, INSTANCE, SPECIFY *shared meaning element* **:** to refer to someone or something in a clear unmistakable manner

men·tor \'men-,tȯ(ə)r, 'ment-ər\ *n* [L, fr. Gk *Mentōr*] **1** *cap* **:** a friend of Odysseus entrusted with the education of Odysseus' son Telemachus **2 a :** a trusted counselor or guide **b :** TUTOR, COACH — **men·tor·ship** \-,ship\ *n*

men·tum \'ment-əm\ *n, pl* **men·ta** \-ə\ [L — more at MENTAL] **1 :** CHIN **2 :** a median plate of the labium of an insect

menu \'men-(,)yü, 'mān-\ *n, pl* **menus** [F, fr. *menu* small, detailed, fr. L *minutus* minute (adj.)] **1 a :** a list of the dishes that may be ordered (as in a restaurant) **b :** a list of the dishes that are to be served (as at a banquet) **2 :** the dishes available for or served at a meal; *also* **:** the meal itself

me·ow \mē-'aü\ *n* [imit.] **1 :** the cry of a cat **2 :** a spiteful or malicious remark — **meow** *vi*

me·per·i·dine \mə-'per-ə-,dēn\ *n* [*me*thyl + pi*peridine*] **:** a synthetic narcotic drug $C_{15}H_{21}NO_2$ used in the form of its hydrochloride as an analgesic, sedative, and antispasmodic

Meph·is·toph·e·les \,mef-ə-'stäf-ə-,lēz\ *n* [G] **:** a chief devil in the Faust legend — **Me·phis·to·phe·lian** \,mef-ə-stə-'fēl-yən, mə-,fis-tə-\ *or* **Me·phis·to·phe·lean** *same, or* ,mef-ə-,stäf-ə-'lē-ən\ *adj*

me·phit·ic \mə-'fit-ik\ *adj* **:** of, relating to, or resembling mephitis **:** foul-smelling

me·phi·tis \mə-'fīt-əs\ *n* [L, fr. Oscan] **:** a noxious, pestilential, or foul exhalation from the earth; *also* **:** STENCH

mep·ro·bam·ate \,mep-rō-'bam-,āt\ *n* [*me*thyl + *pro*pyl + dicar*bamate*] **:** a bitter carbamate $C_9H_{18}N_2O_4$ used as a tranquilizer

mer *abbr* meridian

mer- *comb form* [ME, fr. *mere,* fr. OE] **:** sea <*mer*maid>

mer·bro·min \,mər-'brō-mən\ *n* [*mer*curic acetate + di*brom-* + fluoresce*in*] **:** a green crystalline mercurial compound $C_{20}H_8Br_2HgNa_2O_6$ used as a local antiseptic and germicide in the form of its red solution

mer·can·tile \'mər-kən-,tēl, -,tīl\ *adj* [F, fr. It, fr. *mercante* merchant, fr. L *mercant-, mercans,* fr. prp. of *mercari* to trade — more at MERCHANT] **1 :** of or relating to merchants or trading **2 :** of, relating to, or having the characteristics of mercantilism <~ system>

mer·can·til·ism \-,tē-,liz-əm, -,tī-\ *n* **1 :** the theory or practice of mercantile pursuits **:** COMMERCIALISM **2 :** an economic system developing during the decay of feudalism to unify and increase the power and esp. the monetary wealth of a nation by a strict governmental regulation of the entire national economy usu. through policies designed to secure an accumulation of bullion, a favorable balance of trade, the development of agriculture and manufactures, and the establishment of foreign trading monopolies — **mer·can·til·ist** \-ləst\ *n or adj* — **mer·can·til·is·tic** \,mər-kən-,tē-'lis-tik, -,tī-\ *adj*

mercapt- *or* **mercapto-** *comb form* **:** derived from or related to a mercaptan <*mercapto*purine>

mer·cap·tan \(,)mər-'kap-,tan\ *n* [G, fr. Dan, fr. ML *mercurium captans,* lit., seizing mercury] **:** any of various compounds with the general formula RSH that are analogous to the alcohols and phenols but contain sulfur in place of oxygen and often have disagreeable odors

mer·cap·to·pu·rine \(,)mər-,kap-tə-'pyu̇(ə)r-,ēn\ *n* **:** an antimetabolite $C_5H_4N_4S$ that interferes esp. with the metabolism of purine bases and the biosynthesis of nucleic acids and that is sometimes useful in the treatment of acute leukemia

Mer·ca·tor projection \(,)mər-,kāt-ər-\ *n* [Gerhardus *Mercator*] **:** a map projection in which the meridians are drawn parallel to each other and the parallels of latitudes are straight lines whose distance from each other increases with their distance from the equator

1**mer·ce·nary** \'mərs-ᵊn-,er-ē\ *n, pl* **-nar·ies** [ME, fr. L *mercenarius,* fr. *merced-, merces* wages — more at MERCY] **:** one that serves merely for wages; *esp* **:** a soldier hired into foreign service

2**mercenary** *adj* **1 :** serving merely for pay or sordid advantage **:** VENAL; *also* **:** GREEDY **2 :** hired for service in the army of a foreign country — **mer·ce·nari·ly** \,mərs-ᵊn-'er-ə-lē\ *adv* — **mer·ce·nari·ness** \'mərs-ᵊn-,er-ē-nəs\ *n*

mer·cer \'mər-sər\ *n* [ME, fr. OF *mercier* merchant, fr. *mers* merchandise, fr. L *merc-, merx* — more at MARKET] *Brit* : one who deals in textile fabrics
mer·cer·ize \'mər-sə-ˌrīz\ *vt* **-ized; -iz·ing** [John *Mercer* †1866 E calico printer] : to give (as cotton yarn) luster, strength, and receptiveness to dyes by treatment under tension with caustic soda — **mer·cer·iza·tion** \ˌmərs-(ə-)rə-'zā-shən\ *n*
mer·cery \'mərs-(ə-)rē\ *n, pl* **-cer·ies** *Brit* : a mercer's wares, shop, or occupation
[1]**mer·chan·dise** \'mər-chən-ˌdīz, -ˌdīs\ *n* [ME *marchaundise,* fr. OF *marcheandise,* fr. *marcheant*] **1** : the commodities or goods that are bought and sold in business : WARES **2** *archaic* : the occupation of a merchant : TRADE
[2]**mer·chan·dise** \-ˌdīz\ *vb* **-dised; -dis·ing** *vi, archaic* : to carry on commerce : TRADE ~ *vt* **1** : to buy and sell in business **2** : to promote the sale of — **mer·chan·dis·er** *n*
mer·chan·dis·ing \-ˌdī-ziŋ\ *n* : sales promotion as a comprehensive function including market research, development of new products, coordination of manufacture and marketing, and effective advertising and selling
[1]**mer·chant** \'mər-chənt\ *n* [ME *marchant,* fr. OF *marcheant,* fr. (assumed) VL *mercatant-, mercatans,* fr. prp. of *mercatare* to trade, fr. L *mercatus,* pp. of *mercari* — more at MARKET] **1** : a buyer and seller of commodities for profit : TRADER **2** : the operator of a retail business : STOREKEEPER — **merchant** *adj*
[2]**merchant** *vi, archaic* : to deal or trade as a merchant ~ *vt* : to deal or trade in
mer·chant·able \'mər-chənt-ə-bəl\ *adj* : of commercially acceptable quality : SALABLE — **mer·chant·abil·i·ty** \ˌmər-chənt-ə-'bil-ət-ē\ *n*
mer·chant·man \'mər-chənt-mən\ *n* **1** *archaic* : MERCHANT **2** : a ship used in commerce
merchant marine *n* **1** : the privately or publicly owned commercial ships of a nation **2** : the personnel of a merchant marine
merchant ship *n* : MERCHANTMAN 2
Mer·cian \'mər-sh(ē-)ən\ *n* **1** : a native or inhabitant of Mercia **2** : the Old English dialect of Mercia — **Mercian** *adj*
mer·ci·ful \'mər-si-fəl\ *adj* : full of mercy : COMPASSIONATE — **mer·ci·ful·ly** \-f(ə-)lē\ *adv* — **mer·ci·ful·ness** \-fəl-nəs\ *n*
mer·ci·less \'mər-si-ləs\ *adj* : having no mercy : PITILESS — **mer·ci·less·ly** *adv* — **mer·ci·less·ness** *n*
mercur- *or* **mercuro-** *comb form* [ISV, fr. *mercury*] : mercury <*mercurous*>
mer·cu·rate \'mər-kyə-ˌrāt\ *vt* **-rat·ed; -rat·ing** : to combine or treat with mercury or a mercury salt — **mer·cu·ra·tion** \ˌmər-kyə-'rā-shən\ *n*
[1]**mer·cu·ri·al** \(ˌ)mər-'kyu̇r-ē-əl\ *adj* **1** : of, relating to, or born under the planet Mercury **2** : having qualities of eloquence, ingenuity, or thievishness attributed to the god Mercury or to the influence of the planet Mercury **3** : characterized by rapid and unpredictable changeableness of mood **4** : of, relating to, containing, or caused by mercury ***syn*** see INCONSTANT ***ant*** saturnine — **mer·cu·ri·al·ly** \-ē-ə-lē\ *adv* — **mer·cu·ri·al·ness** *n*
[2]**mercurial** *n* : a pharmaceutical or chemical containing mercury
mer·cu·ric \(ˌ)mər-'kyu̇(ə)r-ik\ *adj* : of, relating to, or containing mercury; *esp* : containing mercury with a valence of two
mercuric chloride *n* : a heavy crystalline poisonous compound $HgCl_2$ used as a disinfectant and fungicide and in photography — called also *corrosive sublimate*
Mer·cu·ro·chrome \(ˌ)mər-'kyu̇r-ə-ˌkrōm\ *trademark* — used for merbromin
mer·cu·rous \(ˌ)mər-'kyu̇r-əs, 'mər-kyə-rəs\ *adj* : of, relating to, or containing mercury; *esp* : containing mercury with a valence of one
mercurous chloride *n* : CALOMEL
mer·cu·ry \'mər-kyə-rē, -k(ə-)rē\ *n, pl* **-ries** [L *Mercurius,* Roman god and the planet] **1 a** *cap* : the Roman god of trade, commerce, gain, luck, travel, and good gifts and the messenger of the gods — compare HERMES **b** *often cap, archaic* : a bearer of messages or news or a conductor of travelers **2** [ME *mercurie,* fr. ML *mercurius,* fr. L, the god] **a** : a heavy silver-white poisonous metallic element that is liquid at ordinary temperatures and used esp. in scientific instruments — called also *quicksilver;* see ELEMENT table **b** : the mercury in a thermometer or barometer **3** *cap* : the planet nearest the sun — see PLANET table **4** : a poisonous European plant (*Mercurialis perennis*) of the spurge family
mercury chloride *n* : a chloride of mercury: as **a** : CALOMEL **b** : MERCURIC CHLORIDE
mercury–vapor lamp *n* : an electric lamp in which the discharge takes place through mercury vapor — called also *mercury lamp*
mer·cy \'mər-sē\ *n, pl* **mercies** [ME, fr. OF *merci,* fr. ML *merced-, merces,* fr. L, price paid, wages, fr. *merc-, merx* merchandise — more at MARKET] **1 a** : compassion or forbearance shown esp. to an offender or to one subject to one's power <as God shows ~ to a sinner> **b** : imprisonment rather than death imposed as penalty for first-degree murder **2 a** : a blessing that is an act of divine favor or compassion **b** : a fortunate circumstance <it was a ~ they found her before she froze> **3** : compassionate treatment of those in distress <deaconesses who do works of ~ among the poor> — **mercy** *adj*
syn MERCY, CHARITY, GRACE, CLEMENCY, LENITY *shared meaning element* : a showing or a disposition to show kindness or compassion. MERCY implies compassion that forbears punishing even when justice demands it or that extends help even to the lowliest or most undeserving <earthly power doth then show likest God's when *mercy* seasons justice —Shak.> CHARITY stresses benevolence and goodwill <with malice toward none, with *charity* for all —Abraham Lincoln> GRACE implies a benign attitude, especially toward dependents or inferiors, and a willingness to grant favors or make concessions <God's *grace* was not an efficacious infusion of a power moving toward the perfection of man; it was the forgiveness of sins, needed newly in each moment —J. M. Gustafson> CLEMENCY imputes mildness and mercy to one called upon to judge and punish <saved from prison by executive *clemency*> LENITY adds to *clemency* the notion of extreme, often undue lack of severity and may suggest weak softness more than manly compassion <what makes robbers bold but too much *lenity?* —Shak.>
— **at the mercy of** : wholly in the power of : with no way to protect oneself against
mercy seat *n* **1** : the gold plate resting on the ancient Jewish ark according to the account in Exodus **2** : the throne of God
[1]**mere** \'mi(ə)r\ *n* [ME, fr. OE — more at MARINE] : a sheet of standing water : POOL
[2]**mere** *n* [ME, fr. OE *mǣre* — more at MUNITION] *archaic* : BOUNDARY, LANDMARK
[3]**mere** \'mi(ə)r\ *adj* **mer·est** [ME, fr. L *merus* pure, unmixed — more at MORN] **1** *obs* : ABSOLUTE, UNDIMINISHED **2** : exclusive of or considered apart from anything else : nothing more than : BARE **3** : having no admixture : PURE — **mere·ly** *adv*
-mere \ˌmi(ə)r\ *n comb form* [F *-mère,* fr. Gk *meros* part — more at MERIT] : part : segment <arthro*mere*>
mer·e·tri·cious \ˌmer-ə-'trish-əs\ *adj* [L *meretricius,* fr. *meretric-, meretrix* prostitute, fr. *merēre* to earn — more at MERIT] **1** : of or relating to a prostitute **2 a** : tawdrily and falsely attractive <~ glamour> **b** : based on pretense or insincerity : SPECIOUS <~ argument> ***syn*** see GAUDY — **mer·e·tri·cious·ly** *adv* — **mer·e·tri·cious·ness** *n*
mer·gan·ser \(ˌ)mər-'gan(t)-sər\ *n* [NL, fr. L *mergus,* a waterfowl (fr. *mergere*) + *anser* goose — more at GOOSE] : any of various fish-eating diving ducks (esp. genus *Mergus*) with a slender bill hooked at the end and serrated along the margins and usu. a crested head

merganser

merge \'mərj\ *vb* **merged; merg·ing** [L *mergere;* akin to Skt *majjati* he dives] *vt* **1** *archaic* : to plunge or engulf in something : IMMERSE **2** : to cause to combine, unite, or coalesce **3** : to blend gradually by stages that blur the distinctness of <as cultures are *merged* and traditions lost> ~ *vi* **1** : to become combined into one **2** : to blend or come together without abrupt change <*merging* traffic> ***syn*** see MIX — **mer·gence** \'mər-jən(t)s\ *n*
merg·er \'mər-jər\ *n* [*merge* + *-er* (as in *waiver*)] **1** *law* : the absorption of an estate, a contract, or an interest in another, of a minor offense in a greater, or of an obligation into a judgment **2** : absorption by a corporation of one or more others; *also* : any of various methods of combining two or more organizations (as business concerns)
me·rid·i·an \mə-'rid-ē-ən\ *n* [ME, fr. MF *meridien,* fr. *meridien* of noon, fr. L *meridianus,* fr. *meridies* noon, south, irreg. fr. *medius* mid + *dies* day — more at MID, DEITY] **1** *archaic* : the hour of noon : MIDDAY **2** : a great circle of the celestial sphere passing through its poles and the zenith of a given place **3** : a high point **4 a** (1) : a great circle on the surface of the earth passing through the poles (2) : the half of such a circle included between the poles **b** : a representation of such a circle or half circle numbered for longitude on a map or globe — see LONGITUDE illustration **5** : a line or circle (as on a projection of a planet or a lens) comparable to a meridian of longitude — **meridian** *adj*
[1]**me·rid·i·o·nal** \mə-'rid-ē-ən-ᵊl\ *adj* [ME, fr. MF *meridionel,* fr. LL *meridionalis,* irreg. fr. L *meridies* noon, south] **1** : of, relating to, or situated in the south : SOUTHERN **2** : of, relating to, or characteristic of people living in the south esp. of France **3** : of or relating to a meridian — **me·rid·i·o·nal·ly** \-ᵊl-ē\ *adv*
[2]**meridional** *n* : a native or inhabitant of southern Europe and esp. southern France
me·ringue \mə-'raŋ\ *n* [F] **1** : a dessert topping baked from a mixture of stiffly beaten egg whites and sugar **2** : a shell made of meringue and filled with fruit or ice cream
me·ri·no \mə-'rē-(ˌ)nō\ *n, pl* **-nos** [Sp] **1** : any of a breed of fine-wooled white sheep originating in Spain and producing a heavy fleece of exceptional quality **2** : a soft wool or wool and cotton clothing fabric resembling cashmere **3** : a fine wool and cotton yarn used for hosiery and knitwear — **merino** *adj*
Merion *abbr* Merionethshire
-m·er·ism \m-ə-ˌriz-əm\ *n comb form* [ISV, fr. Gk *meros* part — more at MERIT] **1** : possession of (such) an arrangement of or relation among constituent chemical units <tauto*merism*> **2** : possession of (such or so many) parts <penta*merism*>
mer·i·stem \'mer-ə-ˌstem\ *n* [Gk *meristos* divided (fr. *merizein* to divide, fr. *meros*) + E *-em* (as in *system*)] : a formative plant tissue usu. made up of small cells capable of dividing indefinitely and giving rise to similar cells or to cells that differentiate to produce the definitive tissues and organs — **mer·i·ste·mat·ic** \ˌmer-ə-stə-'mat-ik\ *adj* — **mer·i·ste·mat·i·cal·ly** \-i-k(ə-)lē\ *adv*
me·ris·tic \mə-'ris-tik\ *adj* [Gk *meristos*] **1** : SEGMENTAL **2** : involving modification in number or in geometrical relation of body parts <~ variation in flower petals> — **me·ris·ti·cal·ly** \-ti-k(ə-)lē\ *adv*
[1]**mer·it** \'mer-ət\ *n* [ME, fr. OF *merite,* fr. L *meritum,* fr. neut. of *meritus,* pp. of *merēre* to deserve, earn; akin to Gk *meros* part, L *memor* mindful — more at MEMORY] **1 a** *obs* : reward or punishment due **b** : the qualities or actions that constitute the basis of one's deserts **c** : a praiseworthy quality : VIRTUE **d** : character or conduct deserving reward, honor, or esteem **2** : spiritual credit held to be earned by performance of righteous acts and to ensure future benefits **3 a** *pl* : the intrinsic rights and wrongs of a legal

case as determined by substance rather than form **b :** legal significance, standing, or importance

²merit *vt* **:** to be worthy of or entitled or liable to **:** EARN ~ *vi* **1** *obs* **:** to be entitled to reward or honor **2 :** DESERVE

mer·i·toc·ra·cy \ˌmer-ə-ˈtäk-rə-sē\ *n, pl* **-cies** [¹*merit* + *-o-* + *-cracy*] **1 :** an educational system whereby the talented are chosen and moved ahead on the basis of their achievement (as in competitive examinations) **2 :** leadership by the talented — **mer·it·ocrat·ic** \ˌmer-ət-ə-ˈkrat-ik\ *adj*

mer·i·to·ri·ous \ˌmer-ə-ˈtōr-ē-əs, -ˈtȯr-\ *adj* **:** deserving of reward or honor — **mer·i·to·ri·ous·ly** *adv* — **mer·i·to·ri·ous·ness** *n*

merit system *n* **:** a system by which appointments and promotions in the civil service are based on competence rather than political favoritism

merl *or* **merle** \ˈmər(-ə)l\ *n* [MF *merle,* fr. L *merulus;* akin to OE *ōsle* blackbird, OHG *amsla*] **:** BLACKBIRD 1a

mer·lin \ˈmər-lən\ *n* [ME *meriloun,* fr. AF *merilun,* fr. OF *esmerillon,* aug. of *esmeril,* of Gmc origin; akin to OHG *smiril* merlin] **1 :** a small European falcon (*Falco aesalon*) with pointed wings and prominently streaked underparts **2 :** PIGEON HAWK 1

Mer·lin \ˈmər-lən\ *n* [ML *Merlinus,* fr. W *Myrddin*] **:** a wise man and sorcerer in Arthurian legend

mer·lon \ˈmər-lən\ *n* [F, fr. It *merlone,* aug. of *merlo* battlement, fr. ML *merulus,* fr. L, merl] **:** one of the solid intervals between crenels of a battlemented parapet — see BATTLEMENT illustration

mer·maid \ˈmər-ˌmād\ *n* **:** a fabled marine creature usu. represented with a woman's body to the hips and a fish's tail instead of legs

mer·man \-ˌman, -mən\ *n* **:** a fabled marine male creature usu. represented with a man's body to the hips and a fish's tail instead of legs

mero·blas·tic \ˌmer-ə-ˈblas-tik\ *adj* [Gk *meros* part + ISV *-blastic*] *of an egg* **:** undergoing incomplete cleavage as a result of the presence of an impeding mass of yolk material — compare HOLOBLASTIC — **mero·blas·ti·cal·ly** \-ti-k(ə-)lē\ *adv*

mero·crine \ˈmer-ə-krən, -ˌkrīn, -ˌkrēn\ *adj* [ISV fr. Gk *meros* + *krinein* to separate — more at CERTAIN] **:** producing a secretion that is discharged without major damage to the secreting cells; *also* **:** produced by a merocrine gland

mero·mor·phic \ˌmer-ə-ˈmȯr-fik\ *adj* [Gk *meros* + E *-morphic*] **:** relating to or being functions of complex variables that are analytic in a region except for a finite number of points at which infinity is the limit

mero·my·o·sin \ˌmer-ə-ˈmī-ə-sən\ *n* [Gk *meros* + E *myosin*] **:** either of two structural subunits of myosin that are obtained esp. by tryptic digestion

-m·er·ous \m-ə-rəs\ *adj comb form* [NL *-merus,* fr. Gk *-merēs,* fr. *meros* — more at MERIT] **:** having (such or so many) parts <di*merous*> <poly*merous*>

Mer·o·vin·gian \ˌmer-ə-ˈvin-j(ē-)ən\ *adj* [F *mérovingien,* fr. ML *Merovingi* Merovingians, fr. *Merovaeus* Merowig †458 Frankish founder of the dynasty] **:** of or relating to the first Frankish dynasty reigning from about A.D. 500 to 751 — **Merovingian** *n*

mer·ri·ment \ˈmer-i-mənt\ *n* **1 :** lighthearted gaiety or fun-making **:** HILARITY **2 :** a gay celebration or party **:** FESTIVITY

mer·ry \ˈmer-ē\ *adj* **mer·ri·er; -est** [ME *mery,* fr. OE *myrge, merge;* akin to OHG *murg* short — more at BRIEF] **1** *archaic* **:** giving pleasure **:** DELIGHTFUL **2 :** full of gaiety or high spirits **:** MIRTHFUL **3 :** marked by festivity or gaiety **4 :** BRISK, INTENSE <a ~ pace> — **mer·ri·ly** \ˈmer-ə-lē\ *adv* — **mer·ri·ness** \ˈmer-ē-nəs\ *n*

syn MERRY, BLITHE, JOCUND, JOVIAL, JOLLY *shared meaning element* **:** showing high spirits or lightheartedness

mer·ry-an·drew \ˌmer-ē-ˈan-(ˌ)drü\ *n, often cap M&A* [*merry* + *Andrew,* proper name] **:** one that clowns publicly **:** BUFFOON

merry-go-round \ˈmer-ē-gō-ˌraůnd, -gə-\ *n* **1 :** an amusement park ride with seats often in the form of animals (as horses) revolving about a fixed center **2 :** a busy rapid round **:** WHIRL

mer·ry·mak·er \ˈmer-ē-ˌmā-kər\ *n* **:** one that shares in festivity or gaiety **:** REVELER

mer·ry·mak·ing \-kiŋ\ *n* **1 :** gay or festive activity **:** CONVIVIALITY **2 :** a convivial occasion **:** FESTIVITY

mer·ry·thought \ˈmer-ē-ˌthȯt\ *n, chiefly Brit* **:** WISHBONE

Mer·thi·o·late \(ˌ)mər-ˈthī-ə-ˌlāt, -lət\ *trademark* — used for thimerosal

mes- *or* **meso-** *comb form* [L, fr. Gk, fr. *mesos* — more at MID] **1 :** mid **:** in the middle <*meso*carp> **2 :** intermediate (as in size or type) <*meso*morph> <*meson*>

me·sa \ˈmā-sə\ *n* [Sp, lit., table, fr. L *mensa*] **:** a usu. isolated hill having steeply sloping sides and a level top; *also* **:** a broad terrace with an abrupt slope on one side **:** BENCH

mes·al·liance \ˌmā-ˌzal-ˈyäⁿs, ˌmā-zə-ˈlī-ən(t)s\ *n, pl* **mes·al·li·ances** \-ˈyäⁿs(-əz), -ˈlī-ən-səz\ [F, fr. *mes-* mis- + *alliance*] **:** a marriage with a person of inferior social position

mes·arch \ˈmez-ˌärk, ˈmēz-, ˈmēs-, ˈmes-\ *adj* **1 :** having metaxylem developed both internal and external to the protoxylem **2 :** originating in a mesic habitat — used of an ecological succession

mes·cal \me-ˈskal, mə-\ *n* [Sp *mezcal, mescal,* fr. Nahuatl *mexcalli* mescal liquor] **1 :** a small cactus (*Lophophora williamsii*) with rounded stems covered with jointed tubercles that are used as a stimulant and antispasmodic esp. among the Mexican Indians **2 a :** a usu. colorless Mexican liquor distilled esp. from the central leaves of maguey plants **b :** a plant from which mescal is produced; *esp* **:** MAGUEY

mescal button *n* **:** one of the dried discoid tops of the mescal

Mes·ca·le·ro \ˌmes-kə-ˈle(ə)r-(ˌ)ō\ *n, pl* **Mescalero** *or* **Mescaleros** [AmerSp, fr. *mezcal, mescal*] **:** a member of an Apache people of Texas and New Mexico

mes·ca·line \ˈmes-kə-lən, -ˌlēn\ *n* **:** a hallucinatory crystalline alkaloid $C_{11}H_{17}NO_3$ that is the chief active principle in mescal buttons

mesdames *pl of* MADAM *or of* MADAME *or of* MRS.

mesdemoiselles *pl of* MADEMOISELLE

me·seems \mi-ˈsēmz\ *vb impersonal, past* **me·seemed** \-ˈsēmd\ *archaic* **:** it seems to me

mescal 1

me·sem·bry·an·the·mum \mə-ˌzem-brē-ˈan(t)-thə-məm\ *n* [NL, genus name, fr. Gk *mesēmbria* midday (fr. *mes-* + *hēmera* day) + *anthemon* flower, fr. *anthos* — more at HEMERA, ANTHOLOGY] **:** any of a genus (*Mesembryanthemum*) of chiefly southern African fleshy-leaved herbs or subshrubs of the carpetweed family

mes·en·ceph·a·lon \ˌmez-ˌen-ˈsef-ə-ˌlän, ˌmez-ᵊn-, ˌmēz-, ˌmēs-, ˌmes-, -lən\ *n* [NL] **:** the middle division of the brain **:** MIDBRAIN — **mes·en·ce·phal·ic** \-ˌen(t)-sə-ˈfal-ik, -ᵊn-sə-\ *adj*

mes·en·chy·mal \mə-ˈzeŋ-kə-məl, -ˈseŋ-; ˌmez-ᵊn-ˈkī-məl, ˌmēz-, ˌmēs-, ˌmes-\ *adj* [ISV] **:** of, resembling, or being mesenchyme

mes·en·chy·ma·tous \ˌmez-ᵊn-ˈkim-ət-əs, ˌmēz-, ˌmēs-, ˌmes-, -ˈkī-mət-\ *adj* [NL *mesenchymat-, mesenchyma* mesenchyme] **:** MESENCHYMAL

mes·en·chyme \ˈmez-ᵊn-ˌkīm, ˈmēz-, ˈmes-, ˈmes-\ *n* [G *mesenchym,* fr. *mes-* + NL *-enchyma*] **:** a loosely organized mesodermal connective tissue comprising all the mesoblast except the mesothelium and giving rise to such structures as connective tissues, blood, lymphatics, bone, and cartilage

mes·en·ter·on \(ˈ)mez-ˈent-ə-ˌrän, (ˈ)mēz-, (ˈ)mēs-, (ˈ)mes-, -rən\ *n, pl* **-tera** \-ə-rə\ [NL] **:** the part of the alimentary canal that is developed from the archenteron and is lined with hypoblast

mes·en·tery \ˈmez-ᵊn-ˌter-ē, ˈmes-\ *n, pl* **-ter·ies** [NL *mesenterium,* fr. MF & Gk; MF *mesentere,* fr. Gk *mesenterion,* fr. *mes-* + *enteron* intestine — more at INTER-] **1 a :** one or more vertebrate membranes that consist of a double fold of the peritoneum and invest the intestines and their appendages and connect them with the dorsal wall of the abdominal cavity **b :** a fold of membrane comparable to a mesentery and supporting a viscus (as the heart) that is not a part of the digestive tract **2 :** a support or partition in an invertebrate like the vertebrate mesentery — **mes·en·ter·ic** \ˌmez-ᵊn-ˈter-ik, ˌmes-\ *adj*

¹mesh \ˈmesh\ *n* [prob. fr. obs. D *maesche;* akin to OHG *masca* mesh, Lith *mazgos* knot] **1 :** one of the openings between the threads or cords of a net; *also* **:** one of the similar spaces in a network — often used to designate screen size as the number of openings per linear inch **2 a :** the fabric of a net **b :** a woven, knit, or knotted fabric of open texture with evenly spaced small holes **c :** an arrangement of interlocking metal links used esp. for jewelry **3 a :** an interlocking or intertwining arrangement or construction **:** NETWORK **b :** WEB, SNARE — usu. used in pl. **4 :** working contact (as of the teeth of gears) <in ~> — **meshed** \ˈmesht\ *adj*

²mesh *vt* **1 a :** to catch in the openings of a net **b :** ENMESH, ENTANGLE **2 a :** to provide with a mesh **b :** to cause to resemble network **3 a :** to cause to engage **b :** to coordinate closely **:** INTERLOCK ~ *vi* **1 :** to become entangled in or as if in meshes **2 :** to be in or come into mesh — used esp. of gears **3 :** to fit together properly **:** COORDINATE

mesh·work \ˈmesh-ˌwərk\ *n* **:** a system of meshes **:** NETWORK <a vascular ~>

me·si·al \ˈmē-zē-əl, -sē-\ *adj* [*mes-* + *-ial*] **:** MIDDLE; *esp* **:** dividing an animal into right and left halves — **me·si·al·ly** \-ə-lē\ *adv*

¹me·sic \ˈmez-ik, ˈmēz-, ˈmēs-, ˈmes-\ *adj* [*mes-* + *-ic*] **:** characterized by, relating to, or requiring a moderate amount of moisture <a ~ habitat> <a ~ plant> — compare HYDRIC, XERIC — **me·si·cal·ly** \-i-k(ə-)lē\ *adv*

²mesic *adj* [*meson* + *-ic*] **:** of or relating to a meson

me·sio- \ˌmē-zē-ō, -sē-\ *comb form* **:** mesial and <*mesio*distal> <*mesio*buccal>

me·sit·y·lene \mə-ˈsit-ᵊl-ˌēn\ *n* [*mesityl* (the radical C_3H_5)] **:** an oily hydrocarbon C_9H_{12} that is found in coal tar and petroleum or made synthetically and is a powerful solvent

mes·i·tyl oxide \ˌmes-ə-ˌtil-, -ət-ᵊl-\ *n* [*mesityl* (the radical C_3H_5)] **:** a fragrant liquid ketone $C_6H_{10}O$ used esp. as a solvent

mes·mer·ic \mez-ˈmer-ik *also* mes-\ *adj* **1 :** of, relating to, or induced by mesmerism **2 :** IRRESISTIBLE, FASCINATING — **mes·mer·i·cal·ly** \-i-k(ə-)lē\ *adv*

mes·mer·ism \ˈmez-mə-ˌriz-əm *also* ˈmes-\ *n* [F. A. *Mesmer*] **1 :** hypnotic induction held to involve animal magnetism; *broadly* **:** HYPNOTISM **2 :** hypnotic appeal — **mes·mer·ist** \-rəst\ *n*

mes·mer·ize \-mə-ˌrīz\ *vt* **-ized; -iz·ing** **1 :** to subject to mesmerism **:** HYPNOTIZE **2 :** SPELLBIND, FASCINATE — **mes·mer·iz·er** *n*

mesne \ˈmēn\ *adj* [AF, alter. of MF *meien* — more at MEAN] **:** MIDDLE, INTERVENING; *specif* **:** intermediate in time of occurrence or performance

mesne lord *n* **:** a feudal lord who holds land as tenant of a superior but is lord to his own tenant

me·so·blast \ˈmez-ə-ˌblast, ˈmēz-, ˈmēs-, ˈmes-\ *n* **:** the embryonic cells that give rise to mesoderm; *broadly* **:** MESODERM — **me·so·blas·tic** \ˌmez-ə-ˈblas-tik, ˌmēz-, ˌmēs-, ˌmes-\ *adj*

me·so·carp \ˈmez-ə-ˌkärp, ˈmēz-, ˈmēs-, ˈmes-\ *n* **:** the middle layer of a pericarp — see ENDOCARP illustration

me·so·derm \-ˌdərm\ *n* [ISV] **:** the middle of the three primary germ layers of an embryo that is the source of bone, muscle, connective tissue, inner layer of the skin, and other adult structures; *broadly* **:** tissue derived from this germ layer — **me·so·der·mal** \ˌmez-ə-ˈdər-məl, ˌmēz-, ˌmēs-, ˌmes-\ *or* **me·so·der·mic** \-mik\ *adj*

me·so·glea *or* **me·so·gloea** \ˌmez-ə-ˈglē-ə, ˌmēz-, ˌmēs-, ˌmes-\ *n* [NL, fr. *mes-* + LGk *gloia, glia* glue — more at CLAY] **:** a gelatinous substance between the endoderm and ectoderm of sponges or coelenterates — **me·so·gloe·al** \-ˈglē-əl\ *adj*

Me·so·lith·ic \-ˈlith-ik\ *adj* [ISV] **:** of or relating to a transitional period of the Stone Age between the Paleolithic and the Neolithic

me·so·mere \ˈmez-ə-ˌmi(ə)r, ˈmēz-, ˈmēs-, ˈmes-\ *n* **1 :** a primitive segment of an embryo **2 :** a blastomere of medium size

me·som·er·ism \mə-ˈsäm-ə-ˌriz-əm, -ˈzäm-\ *n* [*mes-* + *-merism*] **:** RESONANCE 4

me·so·morph \ˈmez-ə-ˌmȯrf, ˈmēz-, ˈmēs-, ˈmes-\ *n* [*meso*derm + *-morph*] **:** an intermediate or average type of human body; *also* **:** a mesomorphic body or person

me·so·mor·phic \ˌmez-ə-ˈmȯr-fik, ˌmēz-, ˌmēs-, ˌmes-\ *adj* [*meso*derm + *-morphic;* fr. the predominance in such types of structures developed from the mesoderm] **1 :** of or relating to the component in W. H. Sheldon's classification of body types that measures esp. the degree of muscularity and bone development **2 :** having a husky muscular body build — **me·so·mor·phism** \-ˌfiz-əm\ *n* — **me·so·mor·phy** \ˈmez-ə-ˌmȯr-fē, ˈmes-\ *n*

me·son \ˈmez-ˌän, ˈmēz-, ˈmēs-, ˈmes-\ *n* [ISV *mes-* + [2]*-on*] **:** any of a group of unstable, strongly interacting nuclear particles that has a mass between that of an electron and a proton and that occurs in more than one variety — **me·son·ic** \me-ˈzän-ik, mē-, -ˈsän-\ *adj*

me·so·neph·ros \ˌmez-ə-ˈnef-rəs, ˌmēz-, ˌmēs-, ˌmes-, -ˌräs\ *n, pl* **-neph·roi** \-ˌrȯi\ [NL, fr. *mes-* + Gk *nephros* kidney — more at NEPHRITIS] **:** a member of the middle pair of the three pairs of embryonic renal organs of higher vertebrates — **me·so·neph·ric** \-rik\ *adj*

me·so·pause \ˈmez-ə-ˌpȯz, ˈmēz-, ˈmēs-, ˈmes-\ *n* [*meso*sphere + *pause*] **:** the transition zone between the mesosphere and the exosphere

me·so·pe·lag·ic \ˌmez-ə-pə-ˈlaj-ik, ˌmēz-, ˌmēs-, ˌmes-\ *adj* **:** of or relating to oceanic depths from about 600 feet to 3000 feet

me·so·phyll \ˈmez-ə-ˌfil, ˈmēz-, ˈmēs-, ˈmes-\ *n* [NL *mesophyllum,* fr. *mes-* + Gk *phyllon* leaf — more at BLADE] **:** the parenchyma between the epidermal layers of a foliage leaf — **me·so·phyl·lic** \ˌmez-ə-ˈfil-ik, ˌmes-\ *adj* — **me·so·phyl·lous** \ˌmez-ə-ˈfil-əs, ˌmēz-, ˌmēs-, ˌmes-\ *adj*

me·so·phyte \ˈmez-ə-ˌfīt, ˈmēz-, ˈmēs-, ˈmes-\ *n* [ISV] **:** a plant that grows under medium conditions of moisture — **me·so·phyt·ic** \ˌmez-ə-ˈfit-ik, ˌmēz-, ˌmēs-, ˌmes-\ *adj*

me·so·scale \ˈmez-ə-ˌskāl, ˈmēz-, ˈmēs-, ˈmes-\ *adj* **:** of or relating to a meteorological phenomenon approximately 1 to 100 kilometers in horizontal extent <~ cloud pattern> <~ wind circulation>

me·so·some \-ˌsōm\ *n* [*mes-* + [3]*-some*] **:** a cell organelle that appears in electron micrographs as an invagination of the plasma membrane and is a site of localization of respiratory enzymes

me·so·sphere \-ˌsfi(ə)r\ *n* **:** a layer of the atmosphere extending from the top of the stratosphere to an altitude of about 50 miles — **me·so·spher·ic** \ˌmez-ə-ˈsfi(ə)r-ik, ˌmēz-, ˌmēs-, ˌmes-, -ˈsfer-\ *adj*

me·so·the·li·o·ma \ˌmez-ə-ˌthē-lē-ˈō-mə, ˌmēz-, ˌmēs-, ˌmes-\ *n, pl* **-mas** *or* **-ma·ta** \-mət-ə\ [NL] **:** a tumor derived from mesothelial tissue (as that lining the peritoneum or pleura)

me·so·the·li·um \-ˈthē-lē-əm\ *n, pl* **-lia** \-lē-ə\ [NL, fr. *mes-* + epi*thelium*] **:** epithelium derived from mesoderm that lines the body cavity of a vertebrate embryo and gives rise to epithelia (as of the peritoneum, pericardium, and pleurae), striated and heart muscle, and several minor structures — **me·so·the·li·al** \-lē-əl\ *adj*

me·so·tho·rac·ic \-thə-ˈras-ik\ *adj* **:** of or relating to the mesothorax

me·so·tho·rax \-ˈthō(ə)r-ˌaks, -ˈthȯ(ə)r-\ *n* [NL] **:** the middle of the three segments of the thorax of an insect — see INSECT illustration

me·so·tho·ri·um \-ˈthōr-ē-əm, -ˈthȯr-\ *n* [NL] **:** either of two radioactive products intermediate between thorium and radiothorium: **a :** an isotope of radium — called also *mesothorium 1* **b :** an isotope of actinium — called also *mesothorium 2*

me·so·tron \ˈmez-ə-ˌträn, ˈmēz-, ˈmēs-, ˈmes-\ *n* [*mes-* + elec*tron*] **:** MESON — **me·so·tron·ic** \ˌmez-ə-ˈträn-ik, ˌmēz-, ˌmēs-, ˌmes-\ *adj*

me·so·tro·phic \ˌmez-ə-ˈtrō-fik, ˌmēz-, ˌmēs-, ˌmes-, -ˈträf-ik\ *adj, of a body of water* **:** having a moderate amount of dissolved nutrients — compare EUTROPHIC, OLIGOTROPHIC

Me·so·zo·ic \-ˈzō-ik\ *adj* **:** of, relating to, or being an era of geological history including the interval between the Permian and the Tertiary and marked by the dinosaurs, marine and flying reptiles, ganoid fishes, cycads, and evergreen trees; *also* **:** relating to the system of rocks formed in this era — see GEOLOGIC TIME table — **Mesozoic** *n*

mes·quite \mə-ˈskēt, me-\ *n* [Sp, fr. Nahuatl *mizquitl*] **:** a spiny deep-rooted leguminous tree or shrub (*Prosopis fuliflora*) that forms extensive thickets in the southwestern U.S. and Mexico, bears pods rich in sugar, and is important as a livestock feed

[1]**mess** \ˈmes\ *n* [ME *mes,* fr. OF, fr. LL *missus* course at a meal, fr. *missus,* pp. of *mittere* to put, fr. L, to send — more at SMITE] **1 :** a quantity of food: **a** *archaic* **:** food set on a table at one time **b :** a prepared dish of soft food; *also* **:** a mixture of ingredients cooked or eaten together **c :** enough food of a specified kind for a dish or a meal <picked a ~ of peas for dinner> **2 a :** a group of persons who regularly take their meals together; *also* **:** a meal so taken **b :** a place where meals are regularly served to a group **:** MESS HALL **3 a :** a confused, dirty, or offensive state or condition **:** JUMBLE <the whole house is a ~> **b :** a disordered situation, state, or condition resulting from misunderstanding, blundering, or misconduct <got himself into a real ~>

[2]**mess** *vt* **1 a :** to assign to a mess **b :** to supply with meals **2 a :** to make dirty or untidy **:** DISARRANGE <warned not to ~ up his room> **b :** to mix up **:** BUNGLE <she really *~ed* up her life> **3 :** to interfere with <magnetic storms that ~ up communications —*Time*> **4 :** to rough up **:** MANHANDLE <~ him up good so he won't double-cross us again> ~ *vi* **1 :** to prepare food for and serve messes **2 :** to take meals with a mess **3 :** to make a mess **4 a :** PUTTER, TRIFLE <small boys and girls who like to ~ around with paints> **b :** to handle or play with something esp. carelessly <told the child not to ~ with his father's camera> **c :** INTERFERE, MEDDLE <*~ing* in other people's affairs> **5 :** to become confused or make an error <got another chance and didn't want to ~ up again>

[1]**mes·sage** \ˈmes-ij\ *n* [ME, fr. OF, fr. ML *missaticum,* fr. L *missus,* pp. of *mittere*] **1 :** a communication in writing, in speech, or by signals **2 :** a messenger's errand or function **3 :** an underlying theme or idea

[2]**message** *vt* **mes·saged; mes·sag·ing 1 :** to send as a message or by messenger **2 :** to order or instruct by message ~ *vi* **:** to communicate by message

mes·sa·line \ˌmes-ə-ˈlēn\ *n* [F] **:** a soft lightweight silk dress fabric with a satin weave

mes·san \ˈmes-ᵊn\ *n* [ScGael *measan*] *chiefly Scot* **:** LAPDOG

mess around *vi* **1 :** to waste time **:** DAWDLE, IDLE **2 a :** ASSOCIATE <don't *mess around* with admirals much —K. M. Dodson> **b :** FLIRT <caught him *messing around* with my wife>

messeigneurs *pl of* MONSEIGNEUR

mes·sen·ger \ˈmes-ᵊn-jər\ *n* [ME *messangere,* fr. OF *messagier,* fr. *message*] **1 :** one who bears a message or does an errand: as **a** *archaic* **:** FORERUNNER, HERALD **b :** a dispatch bearer in government or military service **c :** an employee who carries messages **2 :** a light line used in hauling a heavier line (as between ships)

messenger RNA *n* **:** an RNA that carries the code for a particular protein from the nuclear DNA to the ribosome and acts as a template for the formation of that protein — compare TRANSFER RNA

mess hall *n* **1 :** a dining hall in which mess is served **2 :** a building (as in an army camp) that serves chiefly as a dining hall

mes·si·ah \mə-ˈsī-ə\ *n* [Heb *māshīaḥ* & Aram *mĕshīḥā,* lit., anointed] **1** *cap* **a :** the expected king and deliverer of the Jews **b :** JESUS 1 **2 :** a professed or accepted leader of some hope or cause — **mes·si·ah·ship** \-ˌship\ *n*

mes·si·an·ic \ˌmes-ē-ˈan-ik\ *adj* [(assumed) NL *messianicus,* fr. LL *Messias* + L *-anicus* (as in *romanicus* Romanic)] **1 :** of or relating to a messiah **2 :** marked by mystical idealism in behalf of a cherished cause <a ~ sense of historic mission —Edmond Taylor>

mes·si·a·nism \ˈmes-ē-ə-ˌniz-əm; mə-ˈsī-ə-, me-\ *n* **1 :** belief in a messiah **2 :** belief in the absolute rightness of a cause

Mes·si·as \mə-ˈsī-əs\ *n* [ME, fr. LL, fr. Gk, fr. Aram *mĕshīḥā*] **:** MESSIAH 1

messieurs *pl of* MONSIEUR

mess jacket *n* **:** a short fitted man's jacket reaching to the waist and worn esp. as part of a dress uniform

mess kit *n* **:** a compact kit of nested cooking and eating utensils for use by soldiers and campers

mess·mate \ˈmes-ˌmāt\ *n* **:** a member of a mess (as on a ship)

Messrs. \ˌmes-ərz\ *pl of* MR. <~ Jones, Brown, and Robinson>

mes·suage \ˈmes-wij\ *n* [ME, fr. AF, prob. alter. of OF *mesnage* — more at MENAGE] **:** a dwelling house with the adjacent buildings and curtilage and the adjoining lands used in connection with the household

messy \ˈmes-ē\ *adj* **mess·i·er; -est 1 :** marked by confusion, disorder, or dirt **:** UNTIDY <a ~ room> **2 :** lacking neatness or precision **:** CARELESS, SLOVENLY <~ thinking> **3 :** unpleasantly or tryingly difficult of execution or settlement <~ lawsuits> — **mess·i·ly** \ˈmes-ə-lē\ *adv* — **mess·i·ness** \ˈmes-ē-nəs\ *n*

mes·ti·za \me-ˈstē-zə\ *n* [Sp, fem. of *mestizo*] **:** a female mestizo

mes·ti·zo \-(ˌ)zō\ *n, pl* **-zos** [Sp, fr. *mestizo* mixed, fr. LL *mixticius,* fr. L *mixtus,* pp. of *miscēre* to mix — more at MIX] **:** a person of mixed blood; *specif* **:** a person of mixed European and American Indian ancestry

mes·tra·nol \ˈmes-trə-ˌnȯl, -ˌnōl\ *n* [*meth-* + *estr*ogen + pregn*ane* ($C_{21}H_{36}$) + *-ol*] **:** a synthetic estrogen $C_{21}H_{26}O_2$ used in oral contraceptives

[1]**met** *past of* MEET

[2]**met** *abbr* **1** meteorological; meteorology **2** metropolitan

meta- *or* **met-** *prefix* [NL & ML, fr. L or Gk; L, change, fr. Gk, among, with, after, change, fr. *meta* among, with, after; akin to OE *mid, mith* with, OHG *mit*] **1 a :** occurring later than or in succession to **:** after <*met*estrus> **b :** situated behind or beyond <*met*encephalon> <*meta*carpus> **c :** later or more highly organized or specialized form of <*meta*xylem> **2 :** change **:** transformation **3 :** more comprehensive **:** transcending <*meta*psychology> — used with the name of a discipline to designate a new but related discipline designed to deal critically with the original one <*meta*mathematics> **4 a :** isomeric with or otherwise closely related to <*met*aldehyde> **b :** involving substitution at or characterized by two positions in the benzene ring that are separated by one carbon atom **c :** derived from by loss of water <*meta*phosphoric acid>

met·a·bol·ic \ˌmet-ə-ˈbäl-ik\ *adj* **:** of, relating to, or based on metabolism — **met·a·bol·i·cal·ly** \-i-k(ə-)lē\ *adv*

me·tab·o·lism \mə-ˈtab-ə-ˌliz-əm\ *n* [ISV, fr. Gk *metabolē* change, fr. *metaballein* to change, fr. *meta-* + *ballein* to throw — more at DEVIL] **1 a :** the sum of the processes in the building up and destruction of protoplasm; *specif* **:** the chemical changes in living cells by which energy is provided for vital processes and activities and new material is assimilated to repair the waste **b :** the sum of the processes by which a particular substance is handled in the living body **c :** the sum of the metabolic activities taking place in a particular environment <the ~ of a lake> **2 :** METAMORPHOSIS 2 — usu used in combination <holo*metabolism*>

me·tab·o·lite \-ˌlīt\ *n* **1 :** a product of metabolism **2 :** a substance essential to the metabolism of a particular organism or to a particular metabolic process

me·tab·o·lize \-ˌlīz\ *vb* **-lized; -liz·ing** *vt* **:** to subject to metabolism ~ *vi* **:** to perform metabolism

[1]**meta·car·pal** \ˌmet-ə-ˈkär-pəl\ *adj* **:** of or relating to the metacarpus

[2]**metacarpal** *n* **:** a metacarpal bone

meta·car·pus \ˌmet-ə-ˈkär-pəs\ *n* [NL] **:** the part of the hand or forefoot between the carpus and the phalanges that typically contains five more or less elongated bones when all the digits are present

meta·cen·ter \ˈmet-ə-ˌsent-ər\ *n* [F *métacentre,* fr. *méta-* meta- + *centre* center] **:** the point of intersection of the vertical through the center of buoyancy of a floating body with the vertical through the new center of buoyancy when the body is displaced

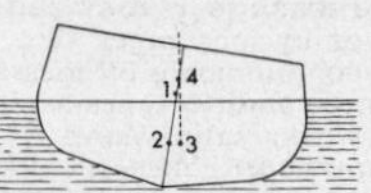

metacenter: *1* center of gravity, *2* center of buoyancy, *3* new center of buoyancy when floating body is displaced, *4* point of intersection

meta·cen·tric \ˌmet-ə-ˈsen-trik\ *adj* **1 :** of or relating to a metacenter **2 :** having two equal arms because of the median position of the centromere <a ~ chromosome> — **metacentric** *n*

meta·cer·car·ia \ˌmet-ə-(ˌ)sər-ˈkar-ē-ə, -ˈker-\ *n* [NL] **:** a tailless encysted late larva of a digenetic trematode that is usu. the form which is infective for the definitive host — **meta·cer·car·i·al** \-ē-əl\ *adj*

meta·chro·mat·ic \-krō-ˈmat-ik\ *adj* **1 :** staining or characterized by staining in a different color or shade from what is typical <~ granules in a bacterium> **2 :** having the capacity to stain different elements of a cell or tissue in different colors or shades <~ stains>

meta·eth·ics \ˌmet-ə-ˈeth-iks\ *n pl but usu sing in constr* **:** the study of the meanings of ethical terms, the nature of ethical judgments, and the types of ethical arguments — **meta·eth·i·cal** \-i-kəl\ *adj*

meta·gal·axy \-ˈgal-ək-sē\ *n* [ISV] **:** the entire system of galaxies **:** UNIVERSE — **meta·ga·lac·tic** \-gə-ˈlak-tik\ *adj*

meta·gen·e·sis \-ˈjen-ə-səs\ *n* [NL] **:** ALTERNATION OF GENERATIONS; *esp* **:** regular alternation of a sexual and an asexual generation — **meta·ge·net·ic** \-jə-ˈnet-ik\ *adj* — **meta·ge·net·i·cal·ly** \-i-k(ə-)lē\ *adv*

[1]**met·al** \ˈmet-ᵊl\ *n, often attrib* [ME, fr. OF, fr. L *metallum* mine, metal, fr. Gk *metallon*] **1 :** any of various opaque, fusible, ductile, and typically lustrous substances that are good conductors of electricity and heat, form cations by loss of electrons, and yield basic oxides and hydroxides; *esp* **:** one that is a chemical element as distinguished from an alloy **2 a :** METTLE 2a **b :** the material or substance out of which a person or thing is made **3 :** glass in its molten state **4 a :** printing type metal **b :** set type matter

[2]**metal** *vt* **-aled** *or* **-alled; -al·ing** *or* **-al·ling :** to cover or furnish with metal

[3]**metal** *or* **metall** *abbr* metallurgical; metallurgy

meta·lan·guage \ˈmet-ə-ˌlaŋ-gwij\ *n* **:** a language used to talk about another language

me·tal·lic \mə-ˈtal-ik\ *adj* **1 a :** of, relating to, or being a metal **b :** made of or containing a metal **c :** having properties of a metal **2 :** yielding metal **3 :** resembling metal: as **a :** having iridescent and reflective properties <~ blond hair> **b :** having an acrid quality <the tea has a ~ taste> **4 :** having a harsh resonance **:** GRATING <a ~ voice> — **me·tal·li·cal·ly** \-i-k(ə-)lē\ *adv*

met·al·lif·er·ous \ˌmet-ᵊl-ˈif-(ə-)rəs\ *adj* [L *metallifer,* fr. *metallum* + *-fer* -ferous] **:** yielding or containing metal

met·al·lize *also* **met·al·ize** \ˈmet-ᵊl-ˌīz\ *vt* **met·al·lized** *also* **met·al·ized; met·al·liz·ing** *also* **met·al·iz·ing :** to treat or combine with a metal — **met·al·li·za·tion** \ˌmet-ᵊl-ə-ˈzā-shən\ *n*

met·al·log·ra·phy \ˌmet-ᵊl-ˈäg-rə-fē\ *n* [F *métallographie,* fr. L *metallum* + F *-graphie* -graphy] **:** a study of the structure of metals esp. with the microscope — **met·al·log·ra·pher** \ˌmet-ᵊl-ˈäg-rə-fər\ *n* — **me·tal·lo·graph·ic** \mə-ˌtal-ə-ˈgraf-ik\ *adj* — **me·tal·lo·graph·i·cal·ly** \-graf-i-k(ə-)lē\ *adv*

[1]**met·al·loid** \ˈmet-ᵊl-ˌȯid\ *n* [L *metallum*] **1 :** a nonmetal that can combine with a metal to form an alloy **2 :** an element intermediate in properties between the typical metals and nonmetals

[2]**metalloid** *also* **met·al·loi·dal** \ˌmet-ᵊl-ˈȯid-ᵊl\ *adj* **1 :** resembling a metal **2 :** of, relating to, or being a metalloid

met·al·lur·gy \ˈmet-ᵊl-ˌər-jē, *esp Brit* mə-ˈtal-ər-\ *n* [NL *metallurgia,* fr. Gk *metallon* + NL *-urgia* -urgy] **:** the science and technology of metals — **met·al·lur·gi·cal** \ˌmet-ᵊl-ˈər-ji-kəl\ *adj* — **met·al·lur·gi·cal·ly** \-k(ə-)lē\ *adv* — **met·al·lur·gist** \ˈmet-ᵊl-ˌər-jəst, *esp Brit* mə-ˈtal-ər-\ *n*

met·al·mark \ˈmet-ᵊl-ˌmärk\ *n* **:** any of a family (Riodinidae) of small or medium-sized usu. brightly colored butterflies that have metallic coloration on the wings

met·al·ware \-ˌwa(ə)r, -ˌwe(ə)r\ *n* **:** ware made of metal; *esp* **:** metal utensils for household use

met·al·work \-ˌwərk\ *n* **:** the product of metalworking — **met·al·work·er** \-ˌwər-kər\ *n*

met·al·work·ing \-ˌwər-kiŋ\ *n* **:** the act or process of shaping things out of metal

meta·math·e·mat·ics \ˈmet-ə-ˌmath-ə-ˈmat-iks\ *n pl but usu sing in constr* **:** the philosophy of mathematics; *esp* **:** the logical syntax of mathematics — **meta·math·e·mat·i·cal** \-i-kəl\ *adj*

meta·mere \ˈmet-ə-ˌmi(ə)r\ *n* [ISV] **:** any of a linear series of primitively similar segments into which the body of a higher invertebrate or vertebrate is divisible — **meta·mer·ic** \ˌmet-ə-ˈmer-ik, -ˈmi(ə)r-\ *adj* — **meta·mer·i·cal·ly** \-i-k(ə-)lē\ *adv*

me·tam·er·ism \mə-ˈtam-ə-ˌriz-əm\ *n* **:** the condition of having or the stage of evolutionary development characterized by a body made up of metameres

meta·mor·phic \ˌmet-ə-ˈmȯr-fik\ *adj* **1 :** of or relating to metamorphosis **2** *of a rock* **:** of, relating to, or produced by metamorphism — **meta·mor·phi·cal·ly** \-fi-k(ə-)lē\ *adv*

meta·mor·phism \-ˈmȯr-ˌfiz-əm\ *n* **:** a change in the constitution of rock; *specif* **:** a pronounced change effected by pressure, heat, and water that results in a more compact and more highly crystalline condition

meta·mor·phose \-ˌfōz, -ˌfōs\ *vb* **-phosed; -phos·ing** [prob. fr. MF *metamorphoser,* fr. *metamorphose* metamorphosis, fr. L *metamorphosis*] *vt* **1 a :** to change into a different physical form esp. by supernatural means **b :** to change strikingly the appearance or character of **:** TRANSFORM <you are so *metamorphosed* I can hardly think you my master —Shak.> **2 :** to cause (rock) to undergo metamorphism ~ *vi* **:** to undergo metamorphosis ***syn*** see TRANSFORM

meta·mor·pho·sis \ˌmet-ə-ˈmȯr-fə-səs\ *n, pl* **-pho·ses** \-ˌsēz\ [L, fr. Gk *metamorphōsis,* fr. *metamorphoun* to transform, fr. *meta-* + *morphē* form] **1 a :** change of physical form, structure, or substance esp. by supernatural means **b :** a striking alteration in appearance, character, or circumstances **2 :** a marked and more or less abrupt change in the form or structure of an animal (as a butterfly or a frog) occurring subsequent to birth or hatching

meta·neph·ros \-ˈnef-rəs, -ˌräs\ *n, pl* **-roi** \-ˌrȯi\ [NL, fr. *meta-* + Gk *nephros* kidney — more at NEPHRITIS] **:** a member of the posterior pair of the three pairs of embryonic renal organs of higher vertebrates that persists as a definitive kidney — **meta·neph·ric** \-rik\ *adj*

metaph *abbr* metaphysics

meta·phase \ˈmet-ə-ˌfāz\ *n* [ISV] **:** the stage of mitosis and meiosis in which the chromosomes become arranged in the equatorial plane of the spindle

metaphase plate *n* **:** the equatorial plane of the spindle with the chromosomes as oriented therein during metaphase

met·a·phor \ˈmet-ə-ˌfȯ(ə)r *also* -fər\ *n* [MF or L; MF, *metaphore,* fr. L *metaphora,* fr. Gk, fr. *metapherein* to transfer, fr. *meta-* + *pherein* to bear — more at BEAR] **1 :** a figure of speech in which a word or phrase literally denoting one kind of object or idea is used in place of another to suggest a likeness or analogy between them (as in *the ship plows the sea*) <using ~, we say that computers have senses and a memory —William Jovanovich>; *broadly* **:** figurative language — compare SIMILE **2 :** an object, activity, or idea treated as a metaphor — **met·a·phor·ic** \ˌmet-ə-ˈfȯr-ik, -ˈfär-\ *or* **met·a·phor·i·cal** \-i-kəl\ *adj* — **met·a·phor·i·cal·ly** \-i-k(ə-)lē\ *adv*

meta·phos·phate \ˌmet-ə-ˈfäs-ˌfāt\ *n* [ISV] **:** a salt or ester of a metaphosphoric acid

meta·phos·pho·ric acid \-ˌfäs-ˌfȯr-ik-, -ˌfär-; -ˌfäs-f(ə-)rik-\ *n* **:** a glassy solid acid HPO_3 or $(HPO_3)_n$ formed by heating orthophosphoric acid

meta·phys·ic \ˌmet-ə-ˈfiz-ik\ *n* [ME *metaphesyk,* fr. ML *Metaphysica*] **1 a :** METAPHYSICS **b :** a particular system of metaphysics **2 :** the system of principles underlying a particular study or subject — **metaphysic** *adj*

meta·phys·i·cal \ˌmet-ə-ˈfiz-i-kəl\ *adj* **1 :** of or relating to metaphysics **2 a :** of or relating to the transcendent or supersensible **b :** SUPERNATURAL **3 :** highly abstract or abstruse **4** *often cap* **:** of or relating to poetry esp. of the early 17th century that is marked by elaborate subtleties of thought and expression — **meta·phys·i·cal·ly** \-i-k(ə-)lē\ *adv*

Metaphysical *n* **:** a metaphysical poet of the 17th century

meta·phy·si·cian \ˌmet-ə-fə-ˈzish-ən\ *n* **:** a student of or specialist in metaphysics

meta·phys·ics \ˌmet-ə-ˈfiz-iks\ *n pl but sing in constr* [ML *Metaphysica,* title of Aristotle's treatise on the subject, fr. Gk (*ta*) *meta* (*ta*) *physika,* lit., the (works) after the physical (works); fr. its position in his collected works] **1 a (1) :** a division of philosophy that includes ontology and cosmology **(2) :** philosophy made up of ontology and epistemology **(3) :** ONTOLOGY **b :** the more abstruse philosophical sciences **2 :** METAPHYSIC 2

meta·pla·sia \ˌmet-ə-ˈplā-zh(ē-)ə\ *n* [NL] **1 :** transformation of one tissue into another **2 :** abnormal replacement of cells of one type by cells of another — **meta·plas·tic** \-ˈplas-tik\ *adj*

meta·plasm \ˈmet-ə-ˌplaz-əm\ *n* **1** [L *metaplasmus,* lit., transformation, fr. Gk *metaplasmos,* fr. *metaplassein* to remold, fr. *meta-* + *plassein* to mold — more at PLASTER] **:** alteration of regular structure usu. by transposition of the letters or syllables of a word or of the words in a sentence **2** [ISV] **:** material consisting of lifeless derivatives of protoplasm — **meta·plas·mic** \ˌmet-ə-ˈplaz-mik\ *adj*

meta·pro·tein \ˌmet-ə-ˈprō-ˌtēn, -ˈprōt-ē-ən\ *n* **:** any of various products derived from proteins through the action of acids or alkalies by which the solubility and sometimes the composition of the proteins is changed

meta·psy·chol·o·gy \-sī-ˈkäl-ə-jē\ *n* [ISV] **:** a theory that aims to supplement the facts and empirical laws of psychology by speculations on the connection of mental and physical processes or on the place of mind in the universe — **meta·psy·cho·log·i·cal** \-ˌsī-kə-ˈläj-i-kəl\ *adj*

meta·se·quoia \-si-ˈkwȯi-ə\ *n* [NL, genus name, fr. *meta-* + *Sequoia*] **:** any of a genus (*Metasequoia*) of fossil and living deciduous coniferous trees of the pine family that have leaves, buds, and branches arranged oppositely and flat leaves resembling needles

meta·so·ma·tism \ˌmet-ə-ˈsō-mə-ˌtiz-əm\ *n* [*meta-* + Gk *sōmat-, sōma* body — more at SOMAT-] **:** metamorphism that involves changes in the chemical composition as well as in the texture of rock — **meta·so·mat·ic** \-sō-ˈmat-ik\ *adj* — **meta·so·mat·i·cal·ly** \-i-k(ə-)lē\ *adv*

meta·sta·ble \ˌmet-ə-ˈstā-bəl\ *adj* [ISV] **:** having or characterized by only a slight margin of stability <a ~ compound> — **meta·sta·bil·i·ty** \-stə-ˈbil-ət-ē\ *n* — **meta·sta·bly** \-ˈstā-b(ə-)lē\ *adv*

me·tas·ta·sis \mə-ˈtas-tə-səs\ *n, pl* **-ta·ses** \-ˌsēz\ [NL, fr. LL, transition, fr. Gk, fr. *methistanai* to change, fr. *meta-* + *histanai* to set — more at STAND] **:** change of position, state, or form: as **a :** transfer of a disease-producing agency from the site of disease to another part of the body **b :** a secondary metastatic growth of a malignant tumor — **met·a·stat·ic** \ˌmet-ə-ˈstat-ik\ *adj* — **met·a·stat·i·cal·ly** \-i-k(ə-)lē\ *adv*

me·tas·ta·size \mə-ˈtas-tə-ˌsīz\ *vi* **-sized; -siz·ing :** to spread by metastasis

[1]**meta·tar·sal** \ˌmet-ə-ˈtär-səl\ *adj* **:** of or relating to the metatarsus — **meta·tar·sal·ly** \-sə-lē\ *adv*

[2]**metatarsal** *n* **:** a metatarsal bone

meta·tar·sus \ˌmet-ə-ˈtär-səs\ *n* [NL] **:** the part of the foot in man or of the hind foot in quadrupeds between the tarsus and phalanges

me·ta·te \mə-ˈtät-ē\ *n* [Sp, fr. Nahuatl *metatl*] **:** a stone with a concave upper surface used as the nether millstone for grinding grains and esp. maize

me·tath·e·sis \mə-ˈtath-ə-səs\ *n, pl* **-e·ses** \-ˌsēz\ [Gk, fr. *metatithenai* to transpose, fr. *meta-* + *tithenai* to place — more at DO] **:** a change of place or condition: as **a :** transposition of two phonemes in a word (as in Old English *bridd,* Modern English *bird*) **b :** a chemical reaction in which different kinds of molecules exchange parts to form other kinds of molecules — called also *double decomposition* — **met·a·thet·i·cal** \ˌmet-ə-ˈthet-i-kəl\ *or* **met·a·thet·ic** \-ik\ *adj* — **met·a·thet·i·cal·ly** \-i-k(ə-)lē\ *adv*

meta·tho·rac·ic \ˌmet-ə-thə-ˈras-ik\ *adj* **:** of or relating to the metathorax

meta·tho·rax \-ˈthō(ə)r-ˌaks, -ˈthȯ(ə)r-\ *n* [NL] **:** the posterior segment of the thorax of an insect — see INSECT illustration

meta·xy·lem \-ˈzī-ləm, -ˌlem\ *n* **:** the part of the primary xylem that differentiates after the protoxylem and that is distinguished typically by broader tracheids and vessels with pitted or reticulate walls

meta·zo·al \ˌmet-ə-ˈzō-əl\ *adj* [NL *Metazoa*] **:** of or relating to the metazoans

meta·zo·an \-ˈzō-ən\ *n* [NL *Metazoa,* group name, fr. *meta-* + *-zoa*] **:** any of a group (*Metazoa*) that comprises all animals having the body composed of cells differentiated into tissues and organs and usu. a digestive cavity lined with specialized cells — **metazoan** *adj*

1mete \ˈmēt\ *vt* **met·ed; met·ing** [ME *meten,* fr. OE *metan;* akin to OHG *mezzan* to measure, L *modus* measure, *meditari* to meditate] **1** *archaic* **:** MEASURE **2 :** to assign by measure **:** ALLOT — usu. used with *out* <~ out punishment>

2mete *n* [AF, fr. L *meta*] **:** BOUNDARY <~*s* and bounds>

me·tem·psy·cho·sis \mə-ˌtem(p)-si-ˈkō-səs, ˌmet-əm-ˌsī-\ *n* [LL, fr. Gk *metempsychōsis,* fr. *metempsychousthai* to undergo metempsychosis, fr. *meta-* + *empsychos* animate, fr. *en-* + *psychē* soul — more at PSYCHE] **:** the passing of the soul at death into another body either human or animal

met·en·ceph·a·lon \ˌmet-ˌen-ˈsef-ə-ˌlän, -lən\ *n* [NL] **1 :** the anterior segment of the rhombencephalon **2 :** the cerebellum and pons that evolve from this segment — **met·en·ce·phal·ic** \-ˌen(t)-sə-ˈfal-ik\ *adj*

me·te·or \ˈmēt-ē-ər, -ē-ˌȯ(ə)r\ *n* [ME, fr. MF *meteore,* fr. ML *meteorum,* fr. Gk *meteōron* phenomenon in the sky, fr. neut. of *meteōros* high in air, fr. *meta-* + *-eōros* (akin to Gk *aeirein* to lift)] **1 :** a phenomenon or appearance in the atmosphere (as lightning, a rainbow, or a snowfall) **2 a :** one of the small particles of matter in the solar system observable directly only when it falls into the earth's atmosphere where friction may cause its temporary incandescence **b :** the streak of light produced by the passage of a meteor

me·te·or·ic \ˌmēt-ē-ˈȯr-ik, -ˈär-\ *adj* **1 :** of, relating to, or derived from the earth's atmosphere **2 a :** of or relating to a meteor **b :** resembling a meteor in speed or in sudden and temporary brilliance <a ~ rise to fame> — **me·te·or·i·cal·ly** \-i-k(ə-)lē\ *adv*

me·te·or·ite \ˈmēt-ē-ə-ˌrīt\ *n* **:** a meteor that reaches the surface of the earth without being completely vaporized — **me·te·or·it·ic** \ˌmēt-ē-ə-ˈrit-ik\ *or* **me·te·or·it·i·cal** \-i-kəl\ *adj*

me·te·or·it·ics \ˌmēt-ē-ə-ˈrit-iks\ *n pl but sing in constr* **:** a science that deals with meteors

me·te·or·o·graph \-ˈȯr-ə-ˌgraf, -ˈär-\ *n* **:** an apparatus for recording automatically and simultaneously several meteorologic elements — **me·te·or·o·graph·ic** \-ˌȯr-ə-ˈgraf-ik, -ˌär-\ *adj*

me·te·or·oid \ˈmēt-ē-ə-ˌrȯid\ *n* **1 :** a meteor revolving around the sun **2 :** a meteor particle itself without relation to the phenomena it produces when entering the earth's atmosphere — **me·te·or·oi·dal** \ˌmēt-ē-ə-ˈrȯid-ᵊl\ *adj*

meteorol *abbr* meteorological; meteorology

me·te·o·rol·o·gy \ˌmēt-ē-ə-ˈräl-ə-jē\ *n* [F or Gk; F *météorologie,* fr. MF, fr. Gk *meteōrologia,* fr. *meteōron* + *-logia* -logy] **1 :** a science that deals with the atmosphere and its phenomena and esp. with weather and weather forecasting **2 :** the atmospheric phenomena and weather of a region — **me·te·o·ro·log·ic** \-rə-ˈläj-ik\ *or* **me·te·o·ro·log·i·cal** \-i-kəl\ *adj* — **me·te·o·ro·log·i·cal·ly** \-i-k(ə-)lē\ *adv* — **me·te·o·rol·o·gist** \-ˈräl-ə-jəst\ *n*

meteor shower *n* **:** the phenomenon observed when members of a group of meteors encounter the earth's atmosphere and their luminous paths appear to diverge from a single point

me·te·pa \mə-ˈtē-pə, me-\ *n* [*me*thyl + *tepa*] **:** an insect chemosterilant that is a methyl derivative of tepa

1me·ter \ˈmēt-ər\ *n* [ME, fr. OE & MF; OE *mēter,* fr. L *metrum,* fr. Gk *metron* measure, meter; MF *metre,* fr. OF, fr. L *metrum* — more at MEASURE] **1 a :** systematically arranged and measured rhythm in verse: (1) **:** rhythm that continuously repeats a single basic pattern <iambic ~> (2) **:** rhythm characterized by regular recurrence of a systematic arrangement of basic patterns in larger figures <ballad ~> **b :** a measure or unit of metrical verse — usu. used in combination and pronounced \m-ət-ər\ <penta*meter*>; compare FOOT 4 **c :** a fixed metrical pattern **:** verse form **2 :** the basic recurrent rhythmical pattern of note values, accents, and beats per measure in music

2me·ter \ˈmēt-ər\ *n* [ME, fr. *meten* to mete] **:** one that measures; *esp* **:** an official measurer of commodities

3me·ter \ˈmēt-ər\ *n* [F *mètre,* fr. Gk *metron* measure] **:** the basic metric unit of length — see METRIC SYSTEM table

4me·ter \ˈmēt-ər\ *n* [*-meter*] **1 :** an instrument for measuring and sometimes recording the amount of something <a gas ~> **2 :** a philatelic cover bearing an impression of a postage meter

5me·ter *vt* **1 :** to measure by means of a meter **2 :** to supply in a measured or regulated amount **3 :** to print postal indicia on by means of a postage meter

-me·ter \m-ət-ər, *in some words* ˌmēt-\ *n comb form* [F *-mètre,* fr. Gk *metron* measure] **:** instrument or means for measuring <baro*meter*>

meter–kilogram–second *adj* **:** of, relating to, or being a system of units based on the meter as the unit of length, the kilogram as the unit of mass, and the mean solar second as the unit of time — abbr. *mks*

meter maid *n* **:** a female member of a police department who is assigned to write tickets for parking violations

met·es·trus \(ˈ)met-ˈes-trəs\ *n* [NL] **:** the period of regression that follows estrus

meth- *or* **metho-** *comb form* [ISV, fr. *methyl*] **:** methyl <*meth*acrylic>

meth·ac·ry·late \(ˈ)meth-ˈak-rə-ˌlāt\ *n* [ISV] **1 :** a salt or ester of methacrylic acid **2 :** an acrylic resin or plastic made from a derivative of methacrylic acid

meth·acryl·ic acid \ˌmeth-ə-ˌkril-ik-\ *n* [ISV] **:** an acid $C_4H_6O_2$ used esp. in making acrylic resins or plastics

meth·a·done \ˈmeth-ə-ˌdōn\ *or* **meth·a·don** \-ˌdän\ *n* [6-di-*meth*-yl*a*mino-4, 4-*d*iphenyl-3-heptan*one*] **:** a synthetic addictive narcotic drug $C_{21}H_{27}NO$ used esp. in the form of its hydrochloride for the relief of pain and as a substitute narcotic in the treatment of heroin addiction

meth·am·phet·amine \ˌmeth-am-ˈfet-ə-ˌmēn, ˌmeth-əm-, -mən\ *n* [*meth-* + *amphetamine*] **:** an amine $C_{10}H_{15}N$ used in the form of its crystalline hydrochloride as a stimulant for the central nervous system and in the treatment of obesity

meth·ane \ˈmeth -ˌān\ *n* [ISV] **:** a colorless odorless flammable gaseous hydrocarbon CH_4 that is a product of decomposition of organic matter in marshes and mines or of the carbonization of coal and is used as a fuel and as a raw material in chemical synthesis

methane series *n* **:** a homologous series of saturated open-chain hydrocarbons C_nH_{2n+2} of which methane is the first and lowest member

meth·a·nol \ˈmeth-ə-ˌnȯl, -ˌnōl\ *n* [ISV] **:** a light volatile flammable poisonous liquid alcohol CH_4O formed in the destructive distillation of wood or made synthetically and used esp. as a solvent, antifreeze, or denaturant for ethyl alcohol and in the synthesis of other chemicals

Meth·e·drine \ˈmeth-ə-ˌdrēn, -drən\ *trademark* — used for methamphetamine

me·theg·lin \mə-ˈtheg-lən\ *n* [W *meddyglyn*] **:** a beverage usu. made of fermented honey and water **:** MEAD

met·he·mo·glo·bin \(ˈ)met-ˈhē-mə-ˌglō-bən\ *n* [ISV] **:** a soluble brown crystalline basic blood pigment that differs from hemoglobin in containing ferric iron and in being unable to combine reversibly with molecular oxygen

me·the·na·mine \mə-ˈthē-nə-ˌmēn, -mən\ *n* [*methene* (methylene) + *amine*] **:** HEXAMETHYLENETETRAMINE

meth·i·cil·lin \ˌmeth-ə-ˈsil-ən\ *n* [*meth-* + pen*icillin*] **:** a synthetic penicillin that is esp. effective against penicillinase-producing staphylococci

me·thinks \mi-ˈthiŋ(k)s\ *vb impersonal, past* **me·thought** \-ˈthȯt\ [ME *me thinketh,* fr. OE *mē thincth,* fr. *mē* (dat. of *ic* I) + *thincth* seems, fr. *thyncan* to seem — more at I, THINK] *archaic* **:** it seems to me

me·thi·o·nine \mə-ˈthī-ə-ˌnēn\ *n* [ISV, fr. *methyl* + *thion-* + *-ine*] **:** a crystalline sulfur-containing essential amino acid $C_5H_{11}NO_2S$

meth·od \ˈmeth-əd\ *n* [MF or L; MF *methode,* fr. L *methodus,* fr. Gk *methodos,* fr. *meta-* + *hodos* way — more at CEDE] **1 :** a procedure or process for attaining an object: as **a** (1) **:** a systematic procedure, technique, or mode of inquiry employed by or proper to a particular discipline or art (2) **:** a systematic plan followed in presenting material for instruction **b** (1) **:** a way, technique, or process of or for doing something (2) **:** a body of skills or techniques **2 :** a discipline that deals with the principles and techniques of scientific inquiry **3 a :** orderly arrangement, development, or classification **:** PLAN **b :** the habitual practice of orderliness and regularity **4** *cap* **:** a dramatic technique by which an actor seeks to gain complete identification with the inner personality of the character being portrayed — usu. used with *the*

syn METHOD, MODE, MANNER, WAY, FASHION, SYSTEM *shared meaning element* **:** the means or procedures used in attaining an end

me·thod·i·cal \mə-ˈthäd-i-kəl\ *or* **me·thod·ic** \-ik\ *adj* **1 :** arranged, characterized by, or performed with method or order <a ~ treatment of the subject> **2 :** habitually proceeding according to method **:** SYSTEMATIC <~ in his daily routine> — **me·thod·i·cal·ly** \-i-k(ə-)lē\ *adv* — **me·thod·i·cal·ness** \-i-kəl-nəs\ *n*

meth·od·ism \ˈmeth-ə-ˌdiz-əm\ *n* **1** *cap* **a :** the doctrines and practice of Methodists **b :** the Methodist churches **2 :** methodical procedure

meth·od·ist \-əd-əst\ *n* **1 :** a person devoted to or laying great stress on method **2** *cap* **:** a member of one of the denominations deriving from the Wesleyan revival in the Church of England, having Arminian doctrine and in the U.S. modified episcopal polity, and stressing personal and social morality — **methodist** *adj* — **meth·od·is·tic** \ˌmeth-ə-ˈdis-tik\ *adj*

meth·od·ize \ˈmeth-ə-ˌdīz\ *vt* **-ized; -iz·ing :** to reduce to method **:** SYSTEMATIZE *syn* see ORDER

meth·od·olog·i·cal \ˌmeth-əd-ᵊl-ˈäj-i-kəl\ *adj* **:** of or relating to method or methodology — **meth·od·olog·i·cal·ly** \-k(ə-)lē\ *adv*

meth·od·ol·o·gist \-ə-ˈdäl-ə-jəst\ *n* **:** a student of methodology

meth·od·ol·o·gy \ˌmeth-ə-ˈdäl-ə-jē\ *n, pl* **-gies** [NL *methodologia,* fr. L *methodus* + *-logia* -logy] **1 :** a body of methods, rules, and postulates employed by a discipline **:** a particular procedure or set of procedures **2 :** the analysis of the principles or procedures of inquiry in a particular field

meth·o·trex·ate \ˌmeth-ə-ˈtrek-ˌsāt\ *n* [*meth-* + *-trexate,* of unknown origin] **:** a toxic anticancer drug $C_{20}H_{22}N_8O_5$ that is an analogue of folic acid and an antimetabolite

me·thoxy·chlor \me-ˈthäk-si-ˌklō(ə)r, -ˌklȯ(ə)r\ *n* [*meth-* + *oxy-* + tri*chlor*ethane] **:** a chlorinated hydrocarbon insecticide $C_{16}Cl_3H_{15}O_2$

me·thoxy·flu·rane \me-ˌthäk-sē-ˈflu̇(ə)r-ˌān\ *n* [*meth-* + *oxy-* + *fluor* + eth*ane*] **:** a nonexplosive gaseous general anesthetic $C_3H_4Cl_2F_2O$ related to chloroform

ə abut	ᵊ kitten	ər further	a back	ā bake	ä cot, cart
au̇ out	ch chin	e less	ē easy	g gift	i trip	ī life
j joke	ŋ sing	ō flow	ȯ flaw	ȯi coin	th thin	th this
ü loot	u̇ foot	y yet	yü few	yu̇ furious	zh vision

Me·thu·se·lah \mə-ˈth(y)üz-(ə-)lə\ *n* [Heb *Mĕthūshāʼēl*] **1 :** an ancestor of Noah held to have lived 969 years **2 :** an oversize wine bottle holding about 208 ounces

meth·yl \ˈmeth-əl\ *n* [ISV, back-formation fr. *methylene*] **:** an alkyl radical CH_3 derived from methane by removal of one hydrogen atom — **me·thyl·ic** \mə-ˈthil-ik\ *adj*

methyl acetate *n* **:** a flammable fragrant liquid $C_3H_6O_2$ used esp. as a solvent and paint remover

meth·yl·al \ˈmeth-ə-ˌlal\ *n* [ISV] **:** a volatile flammable liquid $C_3H_8O_2$ of pleasant ethereal odor used esp. as a solvent, in perfumery, and in making adhesives

methyl alcohol *n* **:** METHANOL

me·thyl·amine \ˌmeth-ə-lə-ˈmēn, -ˈlam-ən; mə-ˈthil-ə-ˌmēn\ *n* [ISV] **:** a flammable explosive gas CH_5N with a strong ammoniacal odor used esp. in organic synthesis (as of dyes and insecticides)

meth·yl·ase \ˈmeth-ə-ˌlās, -ˌlāz\ *n* **:** an enzyme that catalyzes methylation (as of RNA or DNA)

meth·yl·ate \ˈmeth-ə-ˌlāt\ *vt* **-at·ed; -at·ing 1 :** to impregnate or mix with methanol **2 :** to introduce the methyl group into — **meth·yl·ation** \ˌmeth-ə-ˈlā-shən\ *n* — **meth·yl·ator** \ˈmeth-ə-ˌlāt-ər\ *n*

methyl bromide *n* **:** a poisonous gaseous compound CH_3Br used chiefly as a fumigant against rodents, worms, and insects

meth·yl·cho·lan·threne \ˌmeth-əl-kə-ˈlan-ˌthrēn\ *n* [*methyl* + *chol*ic acid + *anthracene*] **:** a potent carcinogenic hydrocarbon $C_{21}H_{16}$

meth·yl·do·pa \ˌmeth-əl-ˈdō-pə\ *n* **:** a drug $C_{10}H_{13}NO_4$ used to lower blood pressure

meth·y·lene \ˈmeth-ə-ˌlēn, -lən\ *n* [F *méthylène,* fr. Gk *methy* wine + *hylē* wood — more at MEAD] **:** a bivalent hydrocarbon radical CH_2 derived from methane by removal of two hydrogen atoms

methylene blue *n* **:** a basic thiazine dye $C_{16}H_{18}ClN_3S·3H_2O$ used esp. as a biological stain, an antidote in cyanide poisoning, and an oxidation-reduction indicator

methylene chloride *n* **:** a nonflammable liquid CH_2Cl_2 used esp. as a solvent, paint remover, and refrigerant

methyl methacrylate *n* **:** a volatile flammable liquid $C_5H_8O_2$ that polymerizes readily and is used esp. as a monomer for resins

meth·yl·naph·tha·lene \ˌmeth-əl-ˈnaf-thə-ˌlēn, -ˈnap-\ *n* **:** either of two isomeric hydrocarbons $C_{11}H_{10}$; *esp* **:** an oily liquid used in determining cetane numbers

methyl parathion *n* **:** a potent synthetic organophosphate insecticide $C_8H_{10}NO_5PS$ that is more toxic than parathion

meth·yl·phe·ni·date \ˌmeth-əl-ˈfen-ə-ˌdāt, -ˈfē-nə-\ *n* [*methyl* + *phen*yl + piper*id*ine + acet*ate*] **:** a mild stimulant $C_{14}H_{19}NO_2$ of the central nervous system used in the form of the hydrochloride to treat narcolepsy and hyperkinetic behavior disorders in children

meth·y·ser·gide \ˌmeth-ə-ˈsər-ˌjīd\ *n* [*methy*l + ly*serg*ic acid + am*ide*] **:** a drug $C_{21}H_{27}N_3O_2$ used in the form of its maleate in the treatment and prevention of vascular headache

me·tic·u·lous \mə-ˈtik-yə-ləs\ *adj* [L *meticulosus* timid, fr. *metus* fear] **:** marked by extreme or excessive care in the consideration or treatment of details *syn* see CAREFUL — **me·tic·u·los·i·ty** \-ˌtik-yə-ˈläs-ət-ē\ *n* — **me·tic·u·lous·ly** \-ˈtik-yə-lə-slē\ *adv* — **me·tic·u·lous·ness** \-lə-snəs\ *n*

mé·tier \ˈme-ˌtyā, me-ˈ\ *n* [F, fr. (assumed) VL *misterium,* alter. of L *ministerium* work, ministry] **1 :** VOCATION, TRADE **2 :** an area of activity in which one is expert or successful **:** FORTE

mé·tis \mā-ˈtē(s)\ *n, pl* **mé·tis** \-ˈtē(s), -ˈtēz\ [F, fr. LL *mixticius* mixed — more at MESTIZO] **:** one of mixed blood: **a :** HALF-BREED **b :** a crossbred animal

METO *abbr* Middle East Treaty Organization

Me·tol \ˈmē-ˌtȯl, -ˌtōl\ *trademark* — used for a photographic developer

met·onym \ˈmet-ə-ˌnim\ *n* [back-formation fr. *metonymy*] **:** a word used in metonymy

met·onym·ic \ˌmet-ə-ˈnim-ik\ *or* **met·onym·i·cal** \-i-kəl\ *adj* **:** of, relating to, or used in metonymy — **met·onym·i·cal·ly** \-i-k(ə-)lē\ *adv*

me·ton·y·my \mə-ˈtän-ə-mē\ *n, pl* **-mies** [L *metonymia,* fr. Gk *metōnymia,* fr. *meta-* + *-ōnymia* -onymy] **:** a figure of speech consisting of the use of the name of one thing for that of another of which it is an attribute or with which it is associated (as in "lands belonging to the *crown*")

me–too \ˈmē-ˈtü\ *adj* **:** marked by similarity to or acceptance of the successful or persuasive policies or practices of a rival or opponent — **me–too·er** \-ər\ *n* — **me–too·ism** \-ˌiz-əm\ *n*

met·o·pe \ˈmet-ə-(ˌ)pē\ *n* [Gk *metopē,* fr. *meta-* + *opē* opening; akin to Gk *ōps* eye, face — more at EYE] **:** the space between two triglyphs of a Doric frieze often adorned with carved work

met·o·pon \ˈmet-ə-ˌpän\ *n* [*met*hyldihydr*o*mor*p*hin*on*e] **:** a narcotic drug $C_{18}H_{21}NO_3$ that is derived from morphine and is used in the form of the hydrochloride to relieve pain

metr- *or* **metro-** *comb form* [NL, fr. Gk *mētr-,* fr. *mētra,* fr. *mētēr* mother — more at MOTHER] **:** uterus <*metr*itis> <*metror*rhagia>

me·tre \ˈmēt-ər\ *chiefly Brit var of* METER

¹met·ric \ˈme-trik\ *n* **1** *pl* **:** a part of prosody that deals with metrical structure **2 :** a standard of measurement <no ~ exists that can be applied directly to happiness —*Scientific Monthly*> **3 :** a mathematical function that associates with each pair of elements of a set a real nonnegative number constituting their distance and satisfying the conditions that the number is zero only if the two elements are identical, the number is the same regardless of the order in which the two elements are taken, and the number associated with one pair of elements plus that associated with one member of the pair and a third element is equal to or greater than the number associated with the other member of the pair and the

METRIC SYSTEM[1]

LENGTH

unit	*abbreviation*	*number of meters*	*approximate U.S. equivalent*
myriameter	mym	10,000	6.2 miles
kilometer	km	1,000	0.62 mile
hectometer	hm	100	109.36 yards
dekameter	dam	10	32.81 feet
meter	m	1	39.37 inches
decimeter	dm	0.1	3.94 inches
centimeter	cm	0.01	0.39 inch
millimeter	mm	0.001	0.04 inch

AREA

unit	*abbreviation*	*number of square meters*	*approximate U.S. equivalent*
square kilometer	sq km *or* km²	1,000,000	0.3861 square mile
hectare	ha	10,000	2.47 acres
are	a	100	119.60 square yards
centare	ca	1	10.76 square feet
square centimeter	sq cm *or* cm²	0.0001	0.155 square inch

VOLUME

unit	*abbreviation*	*number of cubic meters*	*approximate U.S. equivalent*
dekastere	das	10	13.10 cubic yards
stere	s	1	1.31 cubic yards
decistere	ds	0.10	3.53 cubic feet
cubic centimeter	cu cm *or* cm³ *also* cc	0.000001	0.061 cubic inch

CAPACITY

unit	*abbreviation*	*number of liters*	*approximate U.S. equivalent*		
			cubic	*dry*	*liquid*
kiloliter	kl	1,000	1.31 cubic yards		
hectoliter	hl	100	3.53 cubic feet	2.84 bushels	
dekaliter	dal	10	0.35 cubic foot	1.14 pecks	2.64 gallons
liter	l	1	61.02 cubic inches	0.908 quart	1.057 quarts
deciliter	dl	0.10	6.1 cubic inches	0.18 pint	0.21 pint
centiliter	cl	0.01	0.6 cubic inch		0.338 fluidounce
milliliter	ml	0.001	0.06 cubic inch		0.27 fluidram

MASS AND WEIGHT

unit	*abbreviation*	*number of grams*	*approximate U.S. equivalent*
metric ton	MT *or* t	1,000,000	1.1 tons
quintal	q	100,000	220.46 pounds
kilogram	kg	1,000	2.2046 pounds
hectogram	hg	100	3.527 ounces
dekagram	dag	10	0.353 ounce
gram	g *or* gm	1	0.035 ounce
decigram	dg	0.10	1.543 grains
centigram	cg	0.01	0.154 grain
milligram	mg	0.001	0.015 grain

[1] For metric equivalents of U.S. units see Weights and Measures table.

third element

[2]**metric** *or* **met·ri·cal** \'me-tri-kəl\ *adj* **1 :** based on the meter as a standard of measurement <the ~ system> **2 :** of or relating to the metric system <a ~ study> — **met·ri·cal·ly** \-tri-k(ə-)lē\ *adv*

-met·ric \'me-trik\ *or* **-met·ri·cal** \-tri-kəl\ *adj comb form* **1 :** of, employing, or obtained by (such) a meter <galvano*metric*> **2 :** of or relating to (such) an art, process, or science of measuring <chrono*metric*> <gravi*metrical*>

met·ri·cal \'me-tri-kəl\ *or* **met·ric** \-trik\ *adj* **1 :** of, relating to, or composed in meter **2 :** of or relating to measurement — **met·ri·cal·ly** \-tri-k(ə-)lē\ *adv*

met·ri·ca·tion \,me-tri-'kā-shən\ *n* **:** the act or process of metricizing; *specif* **:** conversion of an existent system of units into the metric system

metric hundredweight *n* **:** a unit of weight equal to 50 kilograms

met·ri·cize \'me-trə-,sīz\ *vt* **-cized; -ciz·ing:** to change into or express in the metric system

metric space *n* **:** a mathematical set for which a metric is defined for any pair of elements

metric system *n* **:** a decimal system of weights and measures based on the meter and on the kilogram

metric ton *n* — see METRIC SYSTEM table

me·trist \'me-trəst, 'mē-\ *n* **1 :** a maker of verses **2 :** one skillful in handling meter **3 :** a student of meter or metrics

met·ro \'me-(,)trō, mā-'\ *n, pl* **metros** [F *métro,* short for (*chemin de fer*) *métropolitain* metropolitan railroad] **:** a subway system in a French-speaking city

me·trol·o·gy \me-'träl-ə-jē\ *n* [F *métrologie,* fr. Gk *metrologia* theory of ratios, fr. *metron* measure — more at MEASURE] **1 :** the science of weights and measures or of measurement **2 :** a system of weights and measures — **met·ro·log·i·cal** \,me-trə-'läj-i-kəl\ *adj* — **met·ro·log·i·cal·ly** \-k(ə-)lē\ *adv* — **me·trol·o·gist** \me-'träl-ə-jəst\ *n*

met·ro·ni·da·zole \,me-trə-'nīd-ə-,zōl\ *n* [*methyl* + *-tron-* (prob. fr. *nitro*) + im*ide* + *azole*] **:** a drug $C_6H_9N_3O_3$ used in treating vaginal trichomoniasis

met·ro·nome \'me-trə-,nōm\ *n* [Gk *metron* + *-nomos* controlling, fr. *nomos* law — more at NIMBLE] **:** an instrument designed to mark exact time by a regularly repeated tick

met·ro·nom·ic \,me-trə-'näm-ik\ *also* **met·ro·nom·i·cal** \-i-kəl\ *adj* **:** mechanically regular in action or tempo — **met·ro·nom·i·cal·ly** \-i-k(ə-)lē\ *adv*

me·trop·o·lis \mə-'träp-(ə-)ləs\ *n* [LL, fr. Gk *mētropolis,* fr. *mētr-, mētēr* mother + *polis* city — more at MOTHER, POLICE] **1 :** the mother city or state of a colony esp. in ancient Greece **2 :** the chief or capital city of a country, state, or region **3 a :** a city regarded as a center of a specified activity <a great business ~> **b :** a large important city <the world's great ~*es* —P. E. James>

metronome

[1]**met·ro·pol·i·tan** \,me-trə-'päl-ət-ᵊn\ *n* **1 :** the primate of an ecclesiastical province **2 :** one who lives in a metropolis or displays metropolitan manners or customs

[2]**metropolitan** *adj* [LL *metropolitanus* of the see of a metropolitan, fr. *metropolita,* n., metropolitan, fr. LGk *mētropolitēs,* fr. *mētropolis* see of a metropolitan, fr. Gk, capital] **1 :** of or constituting a metropolitan or his see **2 :** of, relating to, or characteristic of a metropolis **3 :** of, relating to, or constituting a mother country

me·tror·rha·gia \,mē-trə-'rā-j(ē-)ə, -'rā-zhə; -'räj-ə, -'räzh-\ *n* [NL] **:** profuse bleeding from the uterus esp. between menstrual periods — **me·tror·rhag·ic** \-'raj-ik\ *adj*

-me·try \m-ə-trē\ *n comb form* [ME *-metrie,* fr. MF, fr. L *-metria,* fr. Gk, fr. *metrein* to measure, fr. *metron* — more at MEASURE] **:** art, process, or science of measuring (something specified) <chrono*metry*> <photo*metry*>

met·tle \'met-ᵊl\ *n* [alter. of *metal*] **1 :** quality of temperament or disposition <gentlemen of brave ~ —Shak.> **2 a :** vigor and strength of spirit or temperament **:** ARDOR <suspected to have more tongue in his head than ~ in his bosom —Sir Walter Scott> **b :** staying quality **:** STAMINA <trucks had proved their ~ in army transport —*Pioneer & Pacemaker*> *syn* see COURAGE — **met·tled** \-ᵊld\ *adj* — **on one's mettle :** aroused to do one's best

met·tle·some \'met-ᵊl-səm\ *adj* **:** full of mettle **:** SPIRITED

MEV *abbr* million electron volts

[1]**mew** \'myü\ *n* [ME, fr. OE *mǣw;* akin to ON *mār* gull] **:** GULL; *esp* **:** the common European gull (*Larus canus*)

[2]**mew** *vb* [ME *mewen,* of imit. origin] *vi* **:** to utter a mew or similar sound <gulls ~*ed* over the bay> ~ *vt* **:** to utter by mewing **:** MEOW

[3]**mew** *n* **:** MEOW

[4]**mew** *n* [ME *mewe,* fr. MF *mue,* fr. *muer* to molt, fr. L *mutare* to change — more at MISS] **1** *archaic* **:** a cage for hawks esp. while molting **2 :** a place for hiding or retirement **3** *pl but sing or pl in constr, chiefly Brit* **a** (1) **:** stables usu. with living quarters built around a court (2) **:** living quarters adapted from such stables **b :** back street **:** ALLEY

[5]**mew** *vt* **:** to shut up **:** CONFINE — often used with *up*

mewl \'myü(ə)l\ *vi* [imit.] **:** to cry weakly **:** WHIMPER

Mex *abbr* Mexican; Mexico

Mex·i·can \'mek-si-kən\ *n* **1 a :** a native or inhabitant of Mexico **b :** a person of Mexican descent **c** *Southwest* **:** a person of mixed Spanish and Indian descent **2 :** NAHUATL 2 — **Mexican** *adj*

Mexican bean beetle *n* **:** a spotted ladybug (*Epilachna varivestis*) that feeds on the leaves of beans

Mexican fruit fly *n* **:** a small fly (*Anastrepha ludens,* family Trypetidae) whose maggot feeds in and damages various fruits (as citruses and mangoes)

Mexican hairless *n* **:** any of a breed of small nearly hairless dogs

Mexican Spanish *n* **:** the Spanish used in Mexico

me·ze·re·on \mə-'zir-ē-ən\ *n* [ME *mizerion,* fr. ML *mezereon,* fr. Ar *māzariyūn,* fr. Per] **:** a small European shrub (*Daphne mezereum* of the family Thymelaeaceae, the mezereon family) with fragrant lilac purple flowers and an acrid bark used in medicine

me·zu·zah *or* **me·zu·za** \mə-'zu̇z-ə\ *n* [Heb *mĕzūzāh* doorpost] **:** a small parchment scroll inscribed with Deut 6:4–9 and 11:13–21 and the name Shaddai and placed in a case fixed to the doorpost by some Jewish families as a sign and reminder of their faith

mez·za·nine \'mez-ᵊn-,ēn, ,mez-ᵊn-'\ *n* [F, fr. It *mezzanino,* fr. *mezzano* middle, fr. L *medianus* middle, median] **1 :** a low-ceilinged story between two main stories of a building; *esp* **:** an intermediate story that projects in the form of a balcony **2 a :** the lowest balcony in a theater **b :** the first few rows of such a balcony

mez·za vo·ce \,met-sä-'vō-(,)chā, ,med-zä-\ *adv or adj* [It, half voice] **:** with medium or half volume of tone — used as a direction in music

mez·zo \'met-(,)sō, 'med-(,)zō\ *n, pl* **mezzos :** MEZZO-SOPRANO

mez·zo for·te \,met-(,)sō-'fȯr-,tā, ,med-(,)zō-, -'fȯrt-ē\ *adj or adv* [It] **:** moderately loud — used as a direction in music

mez·zo pia·no \-pē-'än-(,)ō\ *adj or adv* [It] **:** moderately soft — used as a direction in music

mez·zo–re·lie·vo \-ri-'lē-(,)vō, -rēl-'yā-(,)vō\ *n, pl* **mezzo–relievos** [It *mezzorilievo,* fr. *mezzo* middle, moderate, half + *rilievo* relief] **:** sculptural relief intermediate between bas-relief and high relief

mez·zo–so·pra·no \-sə-'pran-(,)ō, -'prän-\ *n* [It *mezzosoprano,* fr. *mezzo* + *soprano*] **1 :** a woman's voice of a full deep quality between that of the soprano and contralto **2 :** a singer having a mezzo-soprano voice

mez·zo·tint \'met-sō-,tint, 'med-zō-\ *n* [modif. of It *mezzatinta,* fr. *mezza* (fem. of *mezzo*) + *tinta* tint] **1 :** a manner of engraving on copper or steel by scraping or burnishing a roughened surface to produce light and shade **2 :** an engraving produced by mezzotint

mf *abbr* millifarad

MF *abbr* **1** master of forestry **2** medium frequency **3** mezzo forte **4** microfiche

MFA *abbr* master of fine arts

mfd *abbr* manufactured

mfg *abbr* manufacturing

MFH *abbr* master of foxhounds

MFN *abbr* most favored nation

mfr *abbr* manufacture; manufacturer

MFS *abbr* master of foreign study

mg *abbr* milligram

Mg *symbol* magnesium

MG *abbr* **1** machine gun **2** major general **3** military government

mgal *abbr* milligal

MGB *abbr* [Russ *Ministerstvo Gosudarstvennoi Bezopasnosti*] Ministry of State Security

mgd *abbr* million gallons per day

mgr *abbr* **1** manager **2** monseigneur **3** monsignor

mgt *abbr* management

MGy Sgt *abbr* master gunnery sergeant

mh *abbr* millihenry

MH *abbr* **1** master of humanities **2** medal of honor **3** mobile home

MHD *abbr* magnetohydrodynamic; magnetohydrodynamics

mhg *abbr* mahogany

MHL *abbr* master of Hebrew literature

mho \'mō\ *n, pl* **mhos** [backward spelling of *ohm*] **:** the practical unit of conductance equal to the reciprocal of the ohm

MHW *abbr* mean high water

MHz *abbr* megahertz

[1]**mi** \'mē\ *n* [ML, fr. the syllable sung to this note in a medieval hymn to St. John the Baptist] **:** the 3d tone of the diatonic scale in solmization

[2]**mi** *abbr* **1** mile; mileage **2** mill

MI *abbr* **1** Michigan **2** military intelligence

mi- *or* **mio-** *comb form* [prob. fr. NL *meio-,* fr. Gk, fr. *meiōn* — more at MINOR] **:** less <*Mio*cene>

MIA *abbr* missing in action

Mi·ami \mī-'am-ē, -'am-ə\ *n, pl* **Mi·ami** *or* **Mi·am·is :** a member of an Amerindian people orig. of Wisconsin and Indiana

mi·aow \mē-'au̇\ *var of* MEOW

mi·as·ma \mī-'az-mə, mē-\ *n, pl* **-mas** *also* **-ma·ta** \-mət-ə\ [NL, fr. Gk, defilement, fr. *miainein* to pollute] **1 :** a vaporous exhalation formerly believed to cause disease; *broadly* **:** a heavy vaporous emanation or atmosphere <a ~ of tobacco smoke> **2 :** a pervasive influence or atmosphere that tends to deplete or corrupt <freed from the ~ of poverty —Sir Arthur Bryant> — **mi·as·mal** \-məl\ *adj* — **mi·as·mat·ic** \,mī-əz-'mat-ik\ *adj* — **mi·as·mic** \mī-'az-mik, mē-\ *adj*

Mic *abbr* Micah

mi·ca \'mī-kə\ *n* [NL, fr. L, grain, crumb; akin to Gk *mikros* small] **:** any of various colored or transparent mineral silicates crystallizing in monoclinic forms that readily separate into very thin leaves — **mi·ca·ceous** \mī-'kā-shəs\ *adj*

Mi·cah \'mī-kə\ *n* [Heb *Mīkhāh,* short for *Mīkhāyāh*] **1 :** a Hebrew prophet of the 8th century B.C. **2 :** a prophetic book of canonical Jewish and Christian Scripture — see BIBLE table

mice *pl of* MOUSE

mi·celle \mī-'sel\ *n* [NL *micella,* fr. L *mica*] **:** a unit of structure built up from polymeric molecules or ions: as **a :** an ordered region in a fiber (as of cellulose or rayon) **b :** a molecular aggregate that constitutes a colloidal particle — **mi·cel·lar** \-'sel-ər\ *adj*

Mich *abbr* Michigan

Mi·chael \'mī-kəl\ *n* [Heb *Mīkhā'ēl*] **:** one of the four archangels named in Hebrew tradition

Mi·chae·lis constant \mī-ˈkā-ləs-, mə-\ *n* [Leonor *Michaelis* †1949 Am biochemist] : a constant that is a measure of the kinetics of an enzyme reaction and that is equivalent to the concentration of substrate at which the reaction takes place at one half its maximum velocity

Mich·ael·mas \ˈmik-əl-məs\ *n* [ME *mychelmesse,* fr. OE *Michaeles mæsse* Michael's mass] : September 29 celebrated as the feast of St. Michael the Archangel

Michaelmas daisy *n* : a wild aster; *esp* : one blooming about Michaelmas

Mi·che·as \ˈmī-kē-əs, mī-ˈ\ *n* [LL *Michaeas,* fr. Gk *Michaias,* fr. Heb *Mīkhāyāh*] : MICAH

mick \ˈmik\ *n* [*Mick,* nickname for *Michael,* common Irish given name] : IRISHMAN — often taken to be offensive

Mick·ey Finn \ˌmik-ē-ˈfin\ *n* [prob. fr. the name *Mickey Finn*] : a drink of liquor doctored with a purgative or a drug

Mickey Mouse \-ˈmau̇s\ *adj* [*Mickey Mouse,* cartoon character created by Walt Disney] : lacking importance : INSIGNIFICANT, PETTY <*Mickey Mouse* courses, where you don't work too hard —Willie Cager>

mick·le \ˈmik-əl\ *adj* [ME *mikel,* fr. OE *micel* — more at MUCH] *chiefly Scot* : GREAT, MUCH — **mickle** *adv, chiefly Scot*

Mic·mac \ˈmik-ˌmak\ *n, pl* **Micmac** *or* **Micmacs** [Micmac *Migmac,* lit., allies] **1** : a member of an Amerindian people of eastern Canada **2** : the Algonquian language of the Micmac people

MICR *abbr* magnetic ink character recognition

micr- *or* **micro-** *comb form* [ME *micro-,* fr. L, fr. Gk *mikr-, mikro-,* fr. *mikros, smikros* small, short; akin to OE *smēalīc* careful, exquisite] **1 a** : small : minute <*micro*film> **b** : used for or involving minute quantities or variations <*micro*barograph> **c** : minutely <*micro*level> **2** : one millionth part of a (specified) unit <*micro*gram> <*micro*hm> **3 a** : using microscopy <*micro*dissection> : used in microscopy **b** : revealed by or having its structure discernible only by microscopical examination <*micro*organism> **4** : abnormally small <*micro*cyte> **5** : of or relating to a small area <*micro*climate> **6** : employed in or connected with microphotographing or microfilming <*micro*copy>

mi·cro \ˈmī-(ˌ)krō\ *adj* [*micr-*] : very small; *esp* : MICROSCOPIC

mi·cro·anal·y·sis \ˌmī-krō-ə-ˈnal-ə-səs\ *n* : chemical analysis on a small or minute scale that usu. requires special, very sensitive, or small-scale apparatus — **mi·cro·an·a·lyst** \-ˈan-ᵊl-əst\ *n* — **mi·cro·an·a·lyt·ic** \-ˌan-ᵊl-ˈit-ik\ *or* **mi·cro·an·a·lyt·i·cal** \-ˈit-i-kəl\ *adj*

mi·cro·anat·o·my \-ə-ˈnat-ə-mē\ *n* : HISTOLOGY — **mi·cro·an·a·tom·i·cal** \-ˌan-ə-ˈtäm-i-kəl\ *adj*

mi·cro·baro·graph \ˌmī-krō-ˈbar-ə-ˌgraf\ *n* [ISV] : a barograph for recording small and rapid changes

mi·crobe \ˈmī-ˌkrōb\ *n* [ISV *micr-* + Gk *bios* life — more at QUICK] : MICROORGANISM, GERM — **mi·cro·bi·al** \mī-ˈkrō-bē-əl\ *also* **mi·cro·bic** \-bik\ *adj*

mi·cro·beam \ˈmī-krō-ˌbēm\ *n* : a beam of radiation of small cross section <a focused laser ~> <a ~ of electrons>

mi·cro·bi·ol·o·gy \ˌmī-krō-bī-ˈäl-ə-jē\ *n* [ISV] : a branch of biology dealing esp. with microscopic forms of life — **mi·cro·bi·o·log·i·cal** \ˈmī-krō-ˌbī-ə-ˈläj-i-kəl\ *also* **mi·cro·bi·o·log·ic** \-ˈläj-ik\ *adj* — **mi·cro·bi·o·log·i·cal·ly** \-i-k(ə-)lē\ *adv* — **mi·cro·bi·ol·o·gist** \ˌmī-krō-bī-ˈäl-ə-jəst\ *n*

mi·cro·bus \ˈmī-krō-ˌbəs\ *n* : a station wagon shaped like a bus

mi·cro·cap·sule \-ˌkap-səl, -(ˌ)sül\ *n* : a tiny capsule containing material (as an adhesive or a medicine) that is released when the capsule is broken, melted, or dissolved

Mi·cro·card \-ˌkärd\ *trademark* — used for a sensitized card approximately 3 in. x 5 in. on which printed matter is reproduced photographically in greatly reduced form

¹mi·cro·ce·phal·ic \ˌmī-krō-sə-ˈfal-ik\ *adj* : having a small head; *specif* : having an abnormally small head

²microcephalic *n* : an individual with an abnormally small head

mi·cro·ceph·a·ly \-ˈsef-ə-lē\ *n* [NL *microcephalia,* fr. *microcephalus* microcephalic, fr. *micr-* + Gk *kephalē* head — more at CEPHALIC] : a condition of abnormal smallness of the head usu. associated with mental defects

mi·cro·cir·cuit \ˈmī-krō-ˌsər-kət\ *n* : a compact electronic circuit consisting of elements of small size — **mi·cro·cir·cuit·ry** \-kə-trē\ *n*

mi·cro·cir·cu·la·tion \ˈmī-krō-ˌsər-kyə-ˈlā-shən\ *n* : the part of the circulatory system made up of very fine channels (as capillaries and venules) — **mi·cro·cir·cu·la·to·ry** \ˌmī-krō-ˈsər-kyə-lə-ˌtōr-ē, -ˌtȯr-\ *adj*

mi·cro·cli·mate \ˈmī-krō-ˌklī-mət\ *n* [ISV] : the essentially uniform local climate of a usu. small site or habitat — **mi·cro·cli·mat·ic** \ˌmī-krō-klī-ˈmat-ik\ *adj*

mi·cro·cli·ma·tol·o·gy \ˈmī-krō-ˌklī-mə-ˈtäl-ə-jē\ *n* : the study of microclimates : climatology of restricted areas — **mi·cro·cli·ma·to·log·i·cal** \-mət-ᵊl-ˈäj-i-kəl\ *adj* — **mi·cro·cli·ma·tol·o·gist** \-mə-ˈtäl-ə-jəst\ *n*

mi·cro·cline \ˈmī-krō-ˌklīn\ *n* [G *mikroklin,* fr. *mikr-* micr- + Gk *klinein* to lean — more at LEAN] : a triclinic white to pale yellow, red, or green mineral $KAlSi_3O_8$ of the feldspar group that is like orthoclase in composition

mi·cro·coc·cus \ˌmī-krō-ˈkäk-əs\ *n, pl* **-coc·ci** \-ˈkäk-ˌ(s)ī, -ˈkäk-(ˌ)(s)ē\ [NL, genus name] : a small spherical bacterium; *esp* : one of a genus (*Micrococcus*) in which growth forms irregular groups — **mi·cro·coc·cal** \-ˈkäk-əl\ *adj*

mi·cro·code \ˈmī-krə-ˌkōd\ *n* : code used in microprogramming

¹mi·cro·copy \ˈmī-krō-ˌkäp-ē\ *n* [ISV] : a photographic copy in which graphic matter is reduced in size

²microcopy *vt* : to prepare a microcopy of ~ *vi* : to make microcopies

mi·cro·cosm \ˈmī-krə-ˌkäz-əm\ *n* [ME, fr. ML *microcosmus,* modif. of Gk *mikros kosmos*] **1** : a little world; *esp* : man or human nature that is an epitome of the world or the universe **2** : a community or other unity that is an epitome of a larger unity <the boardinghouse was a ~ of a larger world —Van Wyck Brooks> — **mi·cro·cos·mic** \ˌmī-krə-ˈkäz-mik\ *adj* — **mi·cro·cos·mi·cal·ly** \-mi-k(ə-)lē\ *adv*

microcosmic salt *n* : a white crystalline salt $NaNH_5PO_4 \cdot 4H_2O$ used as a flux in testing for metallic oxides and salts

mi·cro·crys·tal \ˈmī-krō-ˌkris-tᵊl\ *n* : a crystal visible only under the microscope — **mi·cro·crys·tal·line** \ˌmī-krō-ˈkris-tə-lən *also* -ˌlīn *or* -ˌlēn\ *adj* — **mi·cro·crys·tal·lin·i·ty** \-ˌkris-tə-ˈlin-ət-ē\ *n*

mi·cro·cul·ture \ˈmī-krō-ˌkəl-chər\ *n* **1** : the culture of a small group of human beings with limited perspective **2** : a microscopic culture of cells or organisms — **mi·cro·cul·tur·al** \ˌmī-krō-ˈkəlch-(ə-)rəl\ *adj*

mi·cro·cyte \ˈmī-krə-ˌsīt\ *n* [ISV] : a small red blood cell present esp. in some anemias — **mi·cro·cyt·ic** \ˌmī-krə-ˈsit-ik\ *adj*

mi·cro·den·si·tom·e·ter \ˈmī-krō-ˌden(t)-sə-ˈtäm-ət-ər\ *n* : a densitometer for measuring the densities of very small areas of a photographic film or plate (as for detecting invisible spectrographic lines) — **mi·cro·den·si·to·met·ric** \-sət-ə-ˈme-trik\ *adj* — **mi·cro·den·si·tom·e·try** \-sə-ˈtäm-ə-trē\ *n*

mi·cro·dis·sec·tion \ˌmī-krō-dis-ˈek-shən, -dī-ˈsek-\ *n* : dissection under the microscope; *specif* : dissection of cells and tissues by means of fine needles that are precisely manipulated by a series of levers

mi·cro·eco·nom·ics \-ˌek-ə-ˈnäm-iks, -ˌē-kə-\ *n pl but usu sing in constr* : a study of economics in terms of individual areas of activity (as a firm, household, or prices) — compare MACROECONOMICS — **mi·cro·eco·nom·ic** \-ˈnäm-ik\ *adj*

mi·cro·elec·trode \ˌmī-krō-i-ˈlek-ˌtrōd\ *n* : a minute electrode; *esp* : one that is inserted in a living biological cell or tissue in studying its electrical characteristics

mi·cro·elec·tron·ics \ˈmī-krō-i-ˌlek-ˈträn-iks\ *n pl but sing in constr* : a branch of electronics that deals with the miniaturization of electronic circuits and components — **mi·cro·elec·tron·ic** \-ik\ *adj* — **mi·cro·elec·tron·i·cal·ly** \-i-k(ə-)lē\ *adv*

mi·cro·elec·tro·pho·re·sis \-ˌlek-trə-fə-ˈrē-səs\ *n* [NL] : electrophoresis in which the movement of single particles is observed in a microscope; *also* : electrophoresis in which micromethods are used — **mi·cro·elec·tro·pho·ret·ic** \-ˈret-ik\ *or* **mi·cro·elec·tro·pho·ret·i·cal** \-i-kəl\ *adj* — **mi·cro·elec·tro·pho·ret·i·cal·ly** \-i-k(ə-)lē\ *adv*

mi·cro·el·e·ment \ˌmī-krō-ˈel-ə-mənt\ *n* : TRACE ELEMENT

mi·cro·en·cap·sulate \-in-ˈkap-sə-ˌlāt\ *vt* : to enclose in a microcapsule <*microencapsulated* aspirin> — **mi·cro·en·cap·su·la·tion** \-in-ˌkap-sə-ˈlā-shən\ *n*

mi·cro·en·vi·ron·ment \-in-ˈvī-rən-mənt, -ˈvī(-ə)rn-\ *n* : MICROHABITAT — **mi·cro·en·vi·ron·men·tal** \-ˌvī-rən-ˈment-ᵊl\ *adj*

mi·cro·evo·lu·tion \ˈmī-krō-ˌev-ə-ˈlü-shən *also* -ˌē-və-\ *n* : evolutionary change resulting from selective accumulation of minute variations — **mi·cro·evo·lu·tion·ary** \-shə-ˌner-ē\ *adj*

mi·cro·fau·na \ˌmī-krō-ˈfȯn-ə, -ˈfän-\ *n* [NL] **1** : a small or strictly localized fauna (as of a microhabitat) **2** : minute animals; *esp* : those invisible to the naked eye <the soil ~> — **mi·cro·fau·nal** \-ˈfȯn-ᵊl, -ˈfän-\ *adj*

mi·cro·fi·bril \-ˈfīb-rəl, -ˈfib-\ *n* : a fine fibril; *esp* : one of the submicroscopic elongated bundles of cellulose of a plant cell wall — **mi·cro·fi·bril·lar** \-rə-lər\ *adj*

mi·cro·fiche \ˈmī-krō-ˈfēsh, -ˌfish\ *n, pl* **-fiche** *or* **-fiches** \-ˌfēsh(-əz), -ˌfish(-əz)\ [F, fr. *micr-* + *fiche* peg, tag, slide, fr. OF, fr. *ficher* to stick in — more at FICHU] : a sheet of microfilm containing rows of microimages of pages of printed matter

mi·cro·fi·lar·ia \ˌmī-krō-fə-ˈlar-ē-ə, -ˈler-\ *n* [NL] : a minute larval filaria — **mi·cro·fi·lar·i·al** \-ē-əl\ *adj*

¹mi·cro·film \ˈmī-krə-ˌfilm\ *n* [ISV] : a film bearing a photographic record on a reduced scale of printed or other graphic matter

²microfilm *vt* : to reproduce on microfilm <~ a report> ~ *vi* : to make microfilms — **mi·cro·film·able** \-fil-mə-bəl\ *adj* — **mi·cro·film·er** *n*

mi·cro·flo·ra \ˌmī-krə-ˈflōr-ə, -ˈflȯr-\ *n* [NL] **1** : a small or strictly localized flora (as of a microhabitat) **2** : minute plants; *esp* : those invisible to the naked eye <aquatic ~> — **mi·cro·flo·ral** \-əl\ *adj*

mi·cro·form \ˈmī-krə-ˌfȯrm\ *n* [*micr-* + *form*] **1** : a process for reproducing printed matter in a much reduced size <documents in ~> **2 a** : matter reproduced by microform **b** : MICROCOPY

mi·cro·fos·sil \ˌmī-krō-ˈfäs-əl\ *n* : a fossil that can be studied only microscopically and that may be either a fragment of a larger organism or an entire minute organism

mi·cro·fun·gus \-ˈfəŋ-gəs\ *n* [NL] : a fungus (as a mold) with a microscopic fruiting body — **mi·cro·fun·gal** \-gəl\ *adj*

mi·cro·ga·mete \ˌmī-krō-gə-ˈmēt, -ˈgam-ˌēt\ *n* [ISV] : the smaller and usu. male gamete of a heterogamous organism

mi·cro·ga·me·to·cyte \-gə-ˈmēt-ə-ˌsīt\ *n* [ISV] : a gametocyte producing microgametes

mi·cro·gauss \ˈmī-krō-ˌgau̇s\ *n* [ISV] : one millionth of a gauss

mi·cro·gram \ˈmī-krə-ˌgram\ *n* [ISV] : one millionth of a gram

mi·cro·graph \-ˌgraf\ *n* [ISV] : a graphic reproduction of the image of an object formed by a microscope — **micrograph** *vt*

mi·cro·groove \ˈmī-krō-ˌgrüv\ *n* : a narrow continuous V-shaped spiral track that has closely spaced turns and that is used on long-playing records

mi·cro·hab·i·tat \ˌmī-krō-ˈhab-ə-ˌtat\ *n* : a small usu. distinctly specialized and effectively isolated habitat (as a decaying stump or a pat of dung)

mi·cro·im·age \-ˈim-ij\ *n* : an image (as on a microfilm) that is greatly reduced in size

mi·cro·inch \-ˈinch\ *n* : one millionth of an inch

mi·cro·in·jec·tion \ˌmī-krō-in-ˈjek-shən\ *n* : injection under the microscope; *specif* : injection into tissues by means of a fine mechanically controlled capillary tube

mi·cro·in·struc·tion \-ˈstrək-shən\ *n* : a computer instruction corresponding to a single machine operation

mi·cro·lep·i·dop·tera \ˈmī-krō-ˌlep-ə-ˈdäp-tə-rə\ *n pl* [NL] : lepidopterous insects (as tortricids) that belong to families of minute or medium-sized moths — **mi·cro·lep·i·dop·ter·ous** \-tə-rəs\ *adj*

mi·cro·li·ter \ˌmī-krō-ˈlēt-ər\ *n* [ISV] : a unit of capacity equal to one millionth of a liter

mi·cro·lith \'mī-krə-ˌlith\ *n* [ISV] **:** a tiny blade tool esp. of the late Paleolithic usu. in the form of a geometrical figure (as a triangle) and often set in a bone or wooden haft

mi·cro·lith·ic \ˌmī-krə-'lith-ik\ *adj* **1 :** being or resembling a microlith **2 :** of or relating to the people who produced microliths

mi·cro·ma·nip·u·la·tion \'mī-krō-mə-ˌnip-yə-'lā-shən\ *n* **:** the technique or practice of microdissection and microinjection

mi·cro·ma·nip·u·la·tor \-'nip-yə-ˌlāt-ər\ *n* **:** an instrument for micromanipulation

mi·cro·mere \'mī-krō-ˌmi(ə)r\ *n* [ISV] **:** a small blastomere — see BLASTULA illustration

mi·cro·me·te·or·ite \ˌmī-krō-'mēt-ē-ə-ˌrīt\ *n* **1 :** a meteorite so small that it can pass through the earth's atmosphere without becoming intensely heated **2 :** a very small particle in interplanetary space — **mi·cro·me·te·or·it·ic** \-ˌmēt-ē-ə-'rit-ik\ *adj*

mi·cro·me·te·or·oid \-'mēt-ē-ə-ˌrȯid\ *n* **:** MICROMETEORITE 2

mi·cro·me·te·o·rol·o·gy \-ˌmēt-ē-ə-'räl-ə-jē\ *n* **:** meteorology that deals with small-scale weather systems ranging up to several kilometers in diameter and confined to the lower troposphere — **mi·cro·me·te·o·ro·log·i·cal** \-ˌmēt-ē-ˌȯr-ə-'läj-i-kəl, -ˌär-ə-, -ə-rə-\ *adj* — **mi·cro·me·te·o·rol·o·gist** \-ˌmēt-ē-ə-'räl-ə-jəst\ *n*

[1]**mi·crom·e·ter** \mī-'kräm-ət-ər\ *n* [F *micromètre*, fr. *micr-* + *-mètre* -meter] **:** an instrument used with a telescope or microscope for measuring minute distances

[2]**mi·cro·me·ter** \'mī-krō-ˌmēt-ər\ *n* [ISV *micr-* + [3]*meter*] **:** a unit of length equal to one millionth of a meter — called also *micron*

mi·crom·e·ter caliper \mī-ˌkräm-ət-ər-\ *n* **:** a caliper having a spindle moved by a finely threaded screw for making precise measurements

mi·cro·meth·od \'mī-krō-ˌmeth-əd\ *n* **:** a method (as of microanalysis) that requires only very small quantities of material or that involves the use of the microscope

mi·crom·e·try \mī-'kräm-ə-trē\ *n* [ISV] **:** measurement with a micrometer

mi·cro·mi·cron \ˌmī-krō-'mī-ˌkrän\ *n* **:** one millionth of a micrometer

mi·cro·min·ia·ture \-'min-ē-ə-ˌchu̇(ə)r, -'min-i-ˌchu̇(ə)r, -'min-yə-, -chər, -ˌt(y)u̇(ə)r\ *adj* **1 :** MICROMINIATURIZED **2 :** suitable for use with microminiaturized parts

mi·cro·min·ia·tur·iza·tion \-ˌmin-ē-ə-ˌchu̇r-ə-'zā-shən, -ˌmin-i-ˌchu̇r-, -ˌmin-yə-ˌchu̇r-, -chər-, -ˌt(y)u̇r-\ *n* **:** the process of producing microminiaturized things

mi·cro·min·ia·tur·ized *adj* **:** reduced to or produced in a very small size and esp. in a size smaller than one considered miniature <a ~ electronic circuit>

mi·cro·mole \'mī-krə-ˌmōl\ *n* [ISV] **:** one millionth of a mole — **mi·cro·mo·lar** \ˌmī-krə-'mō-lər\ *adj*

mi·cro·mor·phol·o·gy \ˌmī-krə-mȯr-'fäl-ə-jē\ *n* **1 :** MICROSTRUCTURE — used esp. with reference to soils **2 :** the study of minute morphological detail esp. by electron microscopy — **mi·cro·mor·pho·log·ic** \-ˌmȯr-fə-'läj-ik\ *or* **mi·cro·mor·pho·log·i·cal** \-i-kəl\ *adj* — **mi·cro·mor·pho·log·i·cal·ly** \-i-k(ə-)lē\ *adv*

mi·cron \'mī-ˌkrän\ *n, pl* **microns** *also* **mi·cra** \-krə\ [NL, fr. Gk *mikron*, neut. of *mikros* small — more at MICR-] **:** [2]MICROMETER

Mi·cro·ne·sian \ˌmī-krə-'nē-zhən, -shən\ *n* **1 :** a native or inhabitant of Micronesia **2 :** a group of Austronesian languages spoken in the Micronesian islands — **Micronesian** *adj*

mi·cron·ize \'mī-krə-ˌnīz\ *vt* **-ized; -iz·ing** [*micron*] **:** to pulverize esp. into particles a few micrometers in diameter

mi·cro·nu·cle·us \ˌmī-krō-'n(y)ü-klē-əs\ *n* [NL] **:** a minute nucleus; *specif* **:** one regarded as primarily concerned with reproductive and genetic functions in most ciliated protozoans

mi·cro·nu·tri·ent \-'n(y)ü-trē-ənt\ *n* **1 :** TRACE ELEMENT **2 :** an organic compound (as a vitamin) essential in minute amounts to the growth and welfare of an animal

mi·cro·or·gan·ism \-'ȯr-gə-ˌniz-əm\ *n* [ISV] **:** an organism of microscopic or ultramicroscopic size

mi·cro·pa·le·on·tol·o·gy \-ˌpā-lē-ˌän-'täl-ə-jē, -ən-, *esp Brit* -ˌpal-ē-\ *n* [ISV] **:** the study of microscopic fossils — **mi·cro·pa·le·on·to·log·i·cal** \-ˌänt-ᵊl-'äj-i-kəl\ *also* **mi·cro·pa·le·on·to·log·ic** \-ik\ *adj* — **mi·cro·pa·le·on·tol·o·gist** \-ˌän-'täl-ə-jəst, -ən-\ *n*

mi·cro·par·a·site \ˌmī-krō-'par-ə-ˌsīt\ *n* **:** a parasitic microorganism — **mi·cro·par·a·sit·ic** \-ˌpar-ə-'sit-ik\ *adj*

mi·cro·phage \'mī-krə-ˌfāj, -ˌfäzh\ *n* [ISV] **:** a small phagocyte

mi·cro·phone \'mī-krə-ˌfōn\ *n* [ISV] **:** an instrument whereby sound waves are caused to generate or modulate an electric current usu. for the purpose of transmitting or recording sound (as speech or music) — **mi·cro·phon·ic** \ˌmī-krə-'fän-ik\ *adj*

mi·cro·phon·ics \ˌmī-krə-'fän-iks\ *n pl* **:** noises in a loudspeaker resulting from mechanical movement of tubes or other parts

mi·cro·pho·to·graph \-'fōt-ə-ˌgraf\ *n* [ISV] **1 :** a small photograph that is normally magnified for viewing **:** MICROCOPY **2 :** PHOTOMICROGRAPH — **microphotograph** *vt* — **mi·cro·pho·tog·ra·pher** \-fə-'täg-rə-fər\ *n* — **mi·cro·pho·to·graph·ic** \-ˌfōt-ə-'graf-ik\ *adj* — **mi·cro·pho·tog·ra·phy** \-fə-'täg-rə-fē\ *n*

mi·cro·pho·tom·e·ter \-fō-'täm-ət-ər\ *n* [ISV] **:** an instrument for measuring the amount of light transmitted or reflected by small areas or for measuring the relative densities of spectral lines on a photographic film or plate — **mi·cro·pho·to·met·ric** \-ˌfōt-ə-'me-trik\ *adj* — **mi·cro·pho·to·met·ri·cal·ly** \-tri-k(ə-)lē\ *adv* — **mi·cro·pho·tom·e·try** \-fō-'täm-ə-trē\ *n*

mi·cro·phyll \'mī-krə-ˌfil\ *n* [ISV] **1 :** a small leaf **2 :** a leaf (as of a club moss) that has single unbranched veins and no demonstrable leaf gap — **mi·cro·phyl·lous** \ˌmī-krə-'fil-əs\ *adj*

mi·cro·phys·ics \ˌmī-krō-'fiz-iks\ *n* **:** the physics of molecules, atoms, and elementary particles — **mi·cro·phys·i·cal** \-'fiz-i-kəl\ *adj* — **mi·cro·phys·i·cal·ly** \-k(ə-)lē\ *adv*

mi·cro·pi·pette *or* **mi·cro·pi·pet** \-pī-'pet\ *n* **1 :** a pipette for the measurement of minute volumes **2 :** a small and extremely fine-pointed pipette used in making microinjections

mi·cro·plank·ton \-'plaŋ(k)-tən, -ˌtän\ *n* [ISV] **:** microscopic plankton

mi·cro·pop·u·la·tion \'mī-krō-ˌpäp-yə-'lā-shən\ *n* **1 :** a population of microorganisms **2 :** a population of organisms within a small area

mi·cro·pore \'mī-krə-ˌpō(ə)r, -ˌpȯ(ə)r\ *n* [ISV] **:** a very fine pore — **mi·cro·po·ros·i·ty** \-pə-'räs-ət-ē, -pōr-'äs-, -pȯ-'räs-\ *n* — **mi·cro·po·rous** \ˌmī-krə-'pōr-əs, -'pȯr-\ *adj*

mi·cro·print \'mī-krə-ˌprint\ *n* **:** a photographic or photomechanical copy of graphic matter in reduced size — **microprint** *vt*

mi·cro·probe \-ˌprōb\ *n* **:** a device for microanalysis that operates by exciting radiation in a minute area of material so that the composition may be determined from the emission spectrum

mi·cro·pro·gram \ˌmī-krə-'prō-ˌgram, -grəm\ *n* **:** a routine used in microprogramming

mi·cro·pro·gram·ming \-ˌgram-iŋ\ *n* **:** the use of routines stored in memory rather than specialized circuits to control a device (as a computer)

mi·cro·pro·jec·tor \ˌmī-krō-prə-'jek-tər\ *n* **:** a projector utilizing a compound microscope for projecting on a screen a greatly enlarged image of a microscopic object — **mi·cro·pro·jec·tion** \-'jek-shən\ *n*

mi·cro·pub·lish·ing \-'pəb-lish-iŋ\ *n* **:** publishing in microform — **mi·cro·pub·lish·er** \-lish-ər\ *n*

mi·cro·pul·sa·tion \-ˌpəl-'sā-shən\ *n* **:** a pulsation having a short period <a ~ of the earth's magnetic field with a period in the range from a fraction of a second to several hundred seconds>

mi·cro·punc·ture \-'pəŋ(k)-chər\ *n* **:** an extremely small puncture <a ~ of the nephron>

mi·cro·pyle \'mī-krə-ˌpīl\ *n* [ISV *micr-* + Gk *pylē* gate] **1 :** a differentiated area of surface in an egg through which a sperm enters **2 :** a minute opening in the integument of an ovule of a seed plant through which the pollen tube penetrates to the embryo sac — **mi·cro·py·lar** \ˌmī-krə-'pī-lər\ *adj*

mi·cro·ra·dio·graph \ˌmī-krə-'rād-ē-ə-ˌgraf\ *n* **:** an X-ray photograph showing minute internal structure — **mi·cro·ra·dio·graph·ic** \-ˌrād-ē-ə-'graf-ik\ *adj* — **mi·cro·ra·di·og·ra·phy** \-ē-'äg-rə-fē\ *n*

mi·cro·read·er \'mī-krə-ˌrēd-ər\ *n* **:** an apparatus that gives an enlarged image of a microphotograph esp. for reading

mi·cro·re·pro·duc·tion \'mī-krō-ˌrē-prə-'dək-shən\ *n* **:** the reproduction of written or printed matter in microform; *also* **:** an item so reproduced

mi·cro·scale \'mī-krō-ˌskāl\ *n* **:** a very small scale <a chemical produced on a ~>

mi·cro·scope \'mī-krə-ˌskōp\ *n* [NL *microscopium*, fr. *micr-* + *-scopium* -scope] **1 :** an optical instrument consisting of a lens or combination of lenses for making enlarged images of minute objects; *esp* **:** COMPOUND MICROSCOPE **2 :** an instrument using radiations other than light for making enlarged images of minute objects

mi·cro·scop·ic \ˌmī-krə-'skäp-ik\ *or* **mi·cro·scop·i·cal** \-i-kəl\ *adj* **1 :** of, relating to, or conducted with the microscope or microscopy **2 :** resembling a microscope esp. in perception **3 a :** invisible or indistinguishable without the use of a microscope **b :** very small or fine or precise — **mi·cro·scop·i·cal·ly** \-i-k(ə-)lē\ *adv*

mi·cros·co·py \mī-'kräs-kə-pē\ *n* **:** the use of or investigation with the microscope — **mi·cros·co·pist** \-pəst\ *n*

mi·cro·sec·ond \ˌmī-krō-'sek-ənd, -ənt\ *n* [ISV] **:** one millionth of a second

mi·cro·seism \'mī-krə-ˌsī-zəm\ *n* [ISV] **:** a feeble rhythmically and persistently recurring earth tremor — **mi·cro·seis·mic** \ˌmī-krə-'sīz-mik, -'sīs-\ *adj* — **mi·cro·seis·mic·i·ty** \-sīz-'mis-ət-ē, -sīs-\ *n*

mi·cro·some \'mī-krə-ˌsōm\ *n* [G *mikrosom*, fr. *mikr-* micr- + *-som* -some] **1 :** any of various minute structures of the cell esp. as observed at the limit of resolution of the light microscope **2 :** a particle in a particulate fraction that is obtained by heavy centrifugation of broken cells and consists of various amounts of ribosomes, fragmented endoplasmic reticulum, and mitochondrial cristae — **mi·cro·som·al** \ˌmī-krə-'sō-məl\ *adj*

mi·cro·spec·tro·pho·tom·e·ter \ˌmī-krə-ˌspek-trə-fō-'täm-ət-ər\ *n* **:** a spectrophotometer adapted to the examination of light transmitted by a very small specimen (as a single organic cell) — **mi·cro·spec·tro·pho·to·met·ric** \-ˌfōt-ə-'me-trik\ *also* **mi·cro·spec·tro·pho·to·met·ri·cal** \-tri-kəl\ *adv* — **mi·cro·spec·tro·pho·to·met·ri·cal·ly** \-tri-k(ə-)lē\ *adv* — **mi·cro·spec·tro·pho·tom·e·try** \-fō-'täm-ə-trē\ *n*

mi·cro·sphere \'mī-krə-ˌsfi(ə)r\ *n* **:** a minute sphere <a glass ~ 30 microns in diameter> — **mi·cro·spher·i·cal** \ˌmī-krə-'sfir-i-kəl, -'sfer-\ *adj*

mi·cro·spo·ran·gi·um \ˌmī-krō-spə-'ran-jē-əm\ *n* [NL] **:** a sporangium that develops only microspores — **mi·cro·spo·ran·gi·ate** \-jē-ət\ *adj*

mi·cro·spore \'mī-krə-ˌspō(ə)r, -ˌspȯ(ə)r\ *n* [ISV] **:** one of the spores in heterosporous plants that give rise to male gametophytes and are generally smaller than the megaspore — **mi·cro·spo·rous** \ˌmī-krə-'spōr-əs, -'spȯr-; mī-'kräs-pə-rəs\ *adj*

mi·cro·spo·rid·i·an \-spə-'rid-ē-ən\ *n* [NL, fr. *Microsporidia*, group name, fr. *micr-* + *sporidium* small spore, fr. *spor-* + *-idium*] **:** any of an order (Microsporidia) of sporozoan parasites of arthropods and fishes that typically invade and destroy host cells — **microsporidian** *adj*

mi·cro·spo·ro·cyte \-'spōr-ə-ˌsīt, -'spȯr-\ *n* **:** a microspore mother cell

mi·cro·spo·ro·gen·e·sis \ˌmī-krə-ˌspōr-ə-'jen-ə-səs, -ˌspȯr-\ *n* [NL] **:** the formation and maturation of microspores

mi·cro·spo·ro·phyll \-ˌfil\ *n* **:** a sporophyll that develops only microsporangia

mi·cro·state \'mī-krō-ˌstāt\ *n* **:** a nation that is extremely small in area and population and poor in resources

mi·cro·struc·ture \'mī-krō-ˌstrək-chər\ *n* [ISV] **:** the microscopic structure of a material (as a mineral or a biological cell) — **mi·cro·struc·tur·al** \ˌmī-krō-'strək-chə-rəl, -'strək-shrəl\ *adj*

mi·cro·sur·gery \ˌmī-krō-'sərj-(ə-)rē\ *n* **:** minute dissection or manipulation (as by a micromanipulator or laser beam) of living structures (as cells) for surgical or experimental purposes — **mi·cro·sur·gi·cal** \-'sər-ji-kəl\ *adj*

mi·cro·tech·nic \'mī-krō-ˌtek-nik, ˌmī-krō-tek-'nēk\ *or* **mi·cro·tech·nique** \ˌmī-krō-tek-'nēk\ *n* [ISV] **:** the art of handling and preparing material for microscopic observation and study

mi·cro·tome \'mī-krə-ˌtōm\ *n* [ISV] **:** an instrument for cutting sections (as of organic tissues) for microscopic examination

mi·cro·tone \'mī-krə-ˌtōn\ *n* **:** a musical interval smaller than a halftone — **mi·cro·ton·al** \ˌmī-krə-'tōn-ᵊl\ *adj* — **mi·cro·to·nal·i·ty** \-tō-'nal-ət-ē\ *n* — **mi·cro·ton·al·ly** \-'tōn-ᵊl-ē\ *adv*

mi·cro·tu·bule \ˌmī-krō-'t(y)ü-(ˌ)byü(ə)l\ *n* **:** any of the minute cylindrical structures that are widely distributed in protoplasm and are made up of longitudinal fibrils — **mi·cro·tu·bu·lar** \-byə-lər\ *adj*

mi·cro·vil·lus \-'vil-əs\ *n* [NL] **:** a microscopic projection of a tissue, a cell, or a cell organelle; *esp* **:** one of the fingerlike outward projections of some cell surfaces — **mi·cro·vil·lar** \-'vil-ər\ *adj* — **mi·cro·vil·lous** \-'vil-əs\ *adj*

mi·cro·wave \'mī-krə-ˌwāv\ *n* **:** a comparatively short electromagnetic wave; *esp* **:** one between 100 centimeters and 1 centimeter in wavelength

microwave oven *n* **:** an oven in which food is cooked by the heat produced as a result of microwave penetration of the food

mic·tu·rate \'mik-chə-ˌrāt, 'mik-tə-\ *vi* **-rat·ed; -rat·ing** [L *micturire,* fr. *mictus,* pp. of *mingere;* akin to OE *mīgan* to urinate, Gk *omeichein*] **:** URINATE — **mic·tu·ri·tion** \ˌmik-chə-'rish-ən, ˌmik-tə-\ *n*

[1]mid \'mid\ *adj* [ME, fr. OE *midde;* akin to OHG *mitti* middle, L *medius,* Gk *mesos*] **1 :** being the part in the middle or midst <in ~ ocean> — often used in combination <*mid*-August> **2 :** occupying a middle position <the ~ finger> **3** *of a vowel* **:** articulated with the arch of the tongue midway between its highest and its lowest elevation — **mid** *adv*

[2]mid \(ˌ)mid\ *prep* **:** AMID

[3]mid *abbr* middle

mid·air \'mid-'a(ə)r, -'e(ə)r\ *n* **:** a point or region in the air not immediately adjacent to the ground <planes collided in ~>

Mi·das \'mīd-əs\ *n* [L, fr. Gk] **:** a legendary Phrygian king who for a time was given the power of turning to gold everything he touched

mid·brain \'mid-ˌbrān\ *n* **:** the middle division of the embryonic vertebrate brain; *also* **:** the parts of the definitive brain developed from this region — see BRAIN illustration

mid·day \'mid-ˌdā, -'dā\ *n* **:** the middle part of the day **:** NOON

mid·den \'mid-ᵊn\ *n* [ME *midding,* of Scand origin; akin to ON *myki* dung & ON *dyngja* manure pile — more at MUCUS, DUNG] **1 :** DUNGHILL **2 :** a refuse heap; *esp* **:** KITCHEN MIDDEN

[1]mid·dle \'mid-ᵊl\ *adj* [ME *middel,* fr. OE; akin to L *medius*] **1 :** equally distant from the extremes **:** MEDIAL, CENTRAL <the ~ house in the row> **2 :** being at neither extreme **:** INTERMEDIATE **3** *cap* **a :** constituting a division intermediate between those prior and later or upper and lower <*Middle* Paleozoic> **b :** constituting a period of a language or literature intermediate between one called *Old* and one called *New* or *Modern* <*Middle* Dutch> **4** *of a verb form or voice* **:** typically asserting that a person or thing both performs and is affected by the action represented

[2]middle *n* **1 :** a middle part, point, or position **2 :** the central portion of the human body **:** WAIST **3 :** the position of being among or in the midst of something **4 :** something intermediate between extremes **:** MEAN **5 :** the center of an offensive or defensive formation; *esp* **:** the area between the second baseman and the shortstop

middle age *n* **:** the period of life from about 40 to 60 — **mid·dle–aged** \ˌmid-ᵊl-'ājd\ *adj*

Middle Ages *n pl* **:** the period of European history from about A.D. 500 to about 1500

Middle America *n* **1 :** the region of the western hemisphere including Mexico, Central America, often the West Indies, and sometimes Colombia and Venezuela **2 :** the midwestern section of the U.S. **3 :** the middle-class segment of the U.S. population — **Middle American** *n*

mid·dle·brow \'mid-ᵊl-ˌbrau̇\ *n* **:** a person who is moderately but not highly cultivated — **middlebrow** *adj*

mid·dle·bust·er \-ˌbəs-tər\ *n* **:** LISTER 1

middle C *n* **:** the note designated by the first ledger line below the treble staff and the first above the bass staff

middle–class *adj* **:** of or relating to the middle class; *esp* **:** characterized by a high material standard of living, sexual morality, and respect for property

middle class *n* **:** a class occupying a position between the upper class and the lower class; *esp* **:** a fluid heterogeneous socioeconomic grouping composed principally of business and professional people, bureaucrats, and some farmers and skilled workers sharing common social characteristics and values

middle distance *n* **1 :** a part of a pictorial representation or scene between the foreground and the background **2 :** any footrace distance from 400 meters or 440 yards to 1500 meters or one mile

middle ear *n* **:** a small membrane-lined cavity that is separated from the outer ear by the eardrum and that transmits sound waves from the eardrum to the partition between the middle and inner ears through a chain of tiny bones

Middle English *n* **:** the English in manuscripts of the 12th to 15th centuries — see INDO-EUROPEAN LANGUAGES table

middle finger *n* **:** the midmost of the five digits of the hand

Middle French *n* **:** the French in manuscripts of the 14th to 16th centuries — see INDO-EUROPEAN LANGUAGES table

middle game *n* **:** the middle phase of a board game; *specif* **:** the part of a chess game after the pieces have been developed when players attempt to gain and exploit positional and material superiority — compare END GAME, OPENING

Middle Greek *n* **:** the Greek language used in the 7th to 15th centuries

middle ground *n* **1 :** MIDDLE DISTANCE 1 **2 :** a standpoint midway between extremes

Middle High German *n* **:** the High German in use from about 1100 to 1500 — see INDO-EUROPEAN LANGUAGES table

Middle Irish *n* **:** the Irish in use between the 11th and 15th centuries — see INDO-EUROPEAN LANGUAGES table

middle lamella *n* **:** a layer of pectinous intercellular material that as seen by conventional staining and microscopic techniques lies between the walls of adjacent plant cells

Middle Low German *n* **:** the Low German in use from about 1100 to 1500 — see INDO-EUROPEAN LANGUAGES table

mid·dle·man \'mid-ᵊl-ˌman\ *n* **:** an intermediary or agent between two parties; *esp* **:** a dealer or agent intermediate between the producer of goods and the retailer or consumer

middle name *n* **:** a name between one's first name and surname

middle–of–the–road *adj* **:** standing for or following a course of action midway between extremes; *esp* **:** being neither liberal nor conservative in politics — **mid·dle–of–the–road·er** \-'rōd-ər\ *n* — **mid·dle–of–the–road·ism** \-'rōd-ˌiz-əm\ *n*

middle of the road : a course of action or a standpoint midway between extremes

mid·dler \'mid-lər, -ᵊl-ər\ *n* **:** one belonging to an intermediate group, division, or class: as **a :** a student in the second year class of a theological seminary having a three-year program **b :** a student in the second or third year class in some private secondary schools having a four-year course **c :** a student in a division in some private schools that corresponds approximately to junior high school

middle school *n* **:** a school usu. including grades 5–8

Middle Scots *n* **:** the Scots language in use between the latter half of the 15th and the early decades of the 17th centuries

middle term *n* **:** the term of a syllogism that occurs in both premises

mid·dle·weight \'mid-ᵊl-ˌwāt\ *n* **:** one of average weight; *specif* **:** a boxer who weighs more than 147 but not more than 160 pounds

Middle Welsh *n* **:** the Welsh in use from about 1150 to 1500 — see INDO-EUROPEAN LANGUAGES table

[1]mid·dling \'mid-liŋ, -lən\ *adj* **1 :** of middle, medium, or moderate size, degree, or quality **2 :** MEDIOCRE, SECOND-RATE — **middling** *adv* — **mid·dling·ly** \-liŋ-lē, -lən-\ *adv*

[2]middling *n* **1 :** any of various commodities of intermediate size, quality, or position **2** *pl but sing or pl in constr* **:** a granular product of grain milling; *esp* **:** a wheat milling by-product used in animal feeds

mid·dor·sal \(ˈ)mid-'dȯr-səl\ *adj* **:** situated in the middle part or median line of the back

Middx *abbr* Middlesex

mid·dy \'mid-ē\ *n, pl* **middies** [by shortening & alter.] **1 :** MIDSHIPMAN **2 :** a loosely fitting blouse with a sailor collar worn by women and children

mid·field \'mid-ˌfēld, (ˈ)mid-'\ *n* **1 :** the middle portion of a field; *esp* **:** the portion of a playing field (as in football) that is midway between goals **2 :** the players on a team (as in lacrosse) that normally play in midfield

mid·field·er \-ər\ *n* **:** a member of a midfield (as in lacrosse)

Mid·gard \'mid-ˌgärd\ *n* [ON *mithgarthr*] **:** the abode of human beings in Norse mythology

midge \'mij\ *n* [ME *migge,* fr. OE *mycg;* akin to OHG *mucka* midge, Gk *myia* fly, L *musca*] **:** a tiny two-winged fly (as a chironomid)

midg·et \'mij-ət\ *n* [*midge*] **1 :** a very small person **:** DWARF **2 :** something (as an animal) much smaller than usual **3 :** a front-engine, single-seat, open-wheel racing car smaller and of less engine displacement than standard cars of the type — **midget** *adj*

mid·gut \'mid-ˌgət\ *n* **:** the middle part of an alimentary canal

midi \'mid-ē\ *n* [[1]*mid* + *-i* (as in *mini*)] **:** a dress, skirt, or coat that usu. extends to the mid-calf

Mid·i·an·ite \'mid-ē-ə-ˌnīt\ *n* [*Midian,* son of Abraham] **:** a member of an ancient northern Arabian people

MidL *abbr* Midlothian

mid·land \'mid-lənd, -ˌland\ *n* **1 :** the interior or central region of a country **2** *cap* **a :** the dialect of English spoken in the midland counties of England **b :** the dialect of English spoken in parts of New Jersey and Delaware, northern Maryland, central and southern Pennsylvania, Ohio, Indiana, Illinois, the Appalachian Mountain area, West Virginia, Kentucky, and most of Tennessee — **midland** *adj, often cap*

mid·line \-ˌlīn, -'līn\ *n* **:** a median line; *esp* **:** the median line or median plane of the body or some part of the body

mid·most \-ˌmōst\ *adj* **1 :** being in or near the exact middle **2 :** most intimate **:** INNERMOST — **midmost** *adv or n*

midn *abbr* midshipman

mid·night \'mid-ˌnīt\ *n* **1 :** the middle of the night; *specif* **:** 12 o'clock at night **2 :** deep or extended darkness or gloom — **midnight** *adj* — **mid·night·ly** *adv or adj*

midnight sun *n* **:** the sun above the horizon at midnight in the arctic or antarctic summer

mid·point \'mid-ˌpȯint, -'pȯint\ *n* **:** a point at or near the center or middle

mid·rash \'mid-ˌräsh\ *n, pl* **mid·rash·im** \mid-'räsh-əm\ [Heb *midhrāsh* exposition, explanation] **1 :** a haggadic or halakic exposition of the underlying significance of a Bible text **2 :** a collection of midrashim **3** *cap* **:** the midrashic literature written during the first Christian millenium — **mid·rash·ic** \mid-'räsh-ik\ *adj, often cap*

mid·rib \'mid-ˌrib\ *n* **:** the central vein of a leaf

mid·riff \'mid-ˌrif\ *n* [ME *midrif,* fr. OE *midhrif,* fr. *midde* mid + *hrif* belly; akin to OHG *href* body, L *corpus*] **1 :** DIAPHRAGM 1 **2 :** the mid-region of the human torso **3 a :** a section of a woman's garment that covers the midriff **b :** a woman's garment that exposes the midriff

mid·sec·tion \ˈmid-ˌsek-shən\ *n* **:** a section midway between the extremes; *esp* **:** MIDRIFF 2

mid·ship·man \ˈmid-ˌship-mən, (ˈ)mid-ˈ\ *n* **:** one in training for a naval commission; *esp* **:** a student in a naval academy

mid·ships \ˈmid-ˌships\ *adv* **:** AMIDSHIPS

midst \ˈmidst, ˈmitst\ *n* [ME *middest,* alter. of *middes,* back-formation, fr. *amiddes* amid] **1 :** the interior or central part or point **:** MIDDLE, INTERIOR <in the ~ of the forest> **2 :** a position of proximity to the members of a group or company <a visitor in our ~> **3 :** the condition of being surrounded or beset <in the ~ of his troubles> **4 :** a period of time about the middle of a continuing act or condition <in the ~ of a long reign> — **midst** *prep*

mid·stream \ˈmid-ˈstrēm, -ˌstrēm\ *n* **1 :** the portion of a stream away from both sides <keep the boat in ~> **2 :** the portion of a course away from both the beginning and the end <in the ~ of his career —Arthur Berger>

mid·sum·mer \ˈmid-ˈsəm-ər, -ˌsəm-\ *n* **1 :** the middle of summer **2 :** the summer solstice

Midsummer Day *n* **:** June 24 celebrated as the feast of the nativity of John the Baptist

mid·town \ˈmid-ˌtau̇n, -ˈtau̇n\ *n* **:** a central section of a city; *esp* **:** one situated between sections conventionally called *downtown* and *uptown* — **midtown** *adj*

1**mid·way** \ˈmid-ˌwā, -ˈwā\ *adv* **:** in the middle of the way or distance **:** HALFWAY

2**mid·way** \-ˌwā\ *n* [*Midway* (*Plaisance*), Chicago, site of the amusement section of the Columbian Exposition 1893] **:** an avenue at a fair, carnival, or amusement park for concessions and amusements (as rides and games of chance)

mid·week \-ˌwēk\ *n* **:** the middle of the week — **midweek** *adj* — **mid·week·ly** \-ˌwē-klē, -ˈwē-\ *adj or adv*

1**mid·wife** \ˈmid-ˌwīf\ *n* [ME *midwif,* fr. *mid* with (fr. OE) + *wif* woman] **1 :** a woman who assists other women in childbirth **2 :** one that helps to produce or bring forth something

2**midwife** *vt* **mid·wifed** \-ˌwīft\ *or* **mid·wived** \-ˌwīvd\; **mid·wif·ing** *or* **mid·wiv·ing :** to assist in producing, bringing forth, or bringing about

mid·wife·ry \ˈmid-ˌwī-f(ə-)rē\ *n* **1 :** the art or act of assisting at childbirth; *also* **:** OBSTETRICS **2 :** the art, act, or process of producing, bringing forth, or bringing about

mid·win·ter \ˈmid-ˈwint-ər, -ˌwint-\ *n* **1 :** the middle of winter **2 :** the winter solstice

mid·year \-ˌyi(ə)r\ *n* **1 a :** the middle or middle portion of a calendar year **b :** the middle of an academic year **2 a :** a midyear examination **b** *pl* **:** the set of examinations at midyear; *also* **:** the period of midyear examinations — **midyear** *adj*

mien \ˈmēn\ *n* [by shortening & alter. fr. 2*demean*] **1 :** air or bearing esp. as expressive of mood or personality **:** DEMEANOR <beneath that ~ of a commercial traveller who has been everywhere . . . he was very nervous —Arnold Bennett> **2 :** APPEARANCE, ASPECT <the inherent dangers of government encroachment . . . presented such a distasteful ~ —H. W. Baldwin> ***syn*** see BEARING

1**miff** \ˈmif\ *n* [origin unknown] **1 :** a fit of ill humor **2 :** a trivial quarrel

2**miff** *vt* **:** to put into an ill humor **:** OFFEND

1**might** \(ˈ)mīt\ [ME, fr. OE *meahte, mihte;* akin to OHG *mahta, mohta* could] *past of* MAY — used in auxiliary function to express permission, liberty, probability, possibility in the past <the king ~ do nothing without parliament's consent> or a present condition contrary to fact <if he were older he ~ understand> or less probability or possibility than *may* <~ get there before it rains> or as a polite alternative to *may* <~ I ask who is calling> or to *ought* or *should* <you ~ at least apologize>

2**might** \ˈmīt\ *n* [ME, fr. OE *miht;* akin to OHG *maht* might, *magan* to be able — more at MAY] **1 a :** the power, authority, or resources wielded (as by an individual or group) <the growing ~ of the middle class> **b (1) :** bodily strength **(2) :** the power, energy, or intensity of which one is capable <striving with ~ and main> **2** *dial* **:** a great deal

might·i·ly \ˈmīt-ᵊl-ē\ *adv* **1 :** in a mighty manner **:** VIGOROUSLY **2 :** very much

might·i·ness \ˈmīt-ē-nəs\ *n* **:** the quality or state of being mighty **:** POWER

mightn't \ˈmīt-ᵊnt\ **:** might not

1**mighty** \ˈmīt-ē\ *adj* **might·i·er; -est 1 :** possessing might **:** POWERFUL **2 :** accomplished or characterized by might <a ~ thrust> **3 :** great or imposing in size or extent **:** EXTRAORDINARY

2**mighty** *adv* **:** to a great degree **:** EXTREMELY, VERY <a ~ big man>

mignon *n* **:** FILET MIGNON

mi·gnon·ette \ˌmin-yə-ˈnet\ *n* [F *mignonnette,* fr. obs. F, fem. of *mignonnet* dainty, fr. MF, fr. *mignon* darling] **:** any of a genus (*Reseda* of the family Resedaceae, the mignonette family) of herbs; *esp* **:** a garden annual (*R. odorata*) bearing racemes of fragrant greenish yellow flowers

mi·graine \ˈmī-ˌgrān\ *n* [F, fr. LL *hemicrania* pain in one side of the head, fr. Gk *hēmikrania,* fr. *hēmi-* hemi- + *kranion* cranium] **:** a condition marked by recurrent severe headache often with nausea and vomiting — **mi·grain·ous** \-ˌgrā-nəs\ *adj*

mi·grant \ˈmī-grənt\ *n* **:** one that migrates: as **a :** a person who moves regularly in order to find work esp. in harvesting crops **b :** an animal that shifts from one habitat to another — **migrant** *adj*

mi·grate \ˈmī-ˌgrāt, mī-ˈ\ *vi* **mi·grat·ed; mi·grat·ing** [L *migratus,* pp. of *migrare;* akin to Gk *ameibein* to change] **1 :** to move from one country, place, or locality to another **2 :** to pass usu. periodically from one region or climate to another for feeding or breeding **3 :** to change position in an organism or substance <filarial worms ~ within the human body> — **mi·gra·tion** \mī-ˈgrā-shən\ *n* — **mi·gra·tion·al** \-shnəl, -shən-ᵊl\ *adj* — **mi·gra·tor** \ˈmī-ˌgrāt-ər, mī-ˈ\ *n*

mi·gra·to·ry \ˈmī-grə-ˌtōr-ē, -ˌtȯr-\ *adj* **1 :** of, relating to, or characterized by migration **2 :** WANDERING, ROVING

mi·ka·do \mə-ˈkäd-(ˌ)ō\ *n, pl* **-dos** [Jap] **:** an emperor of Japan

mike \ˈmīk\ *n* [by shortening & alter.] **:** MICROPHONE

Mike \ˈmīk\ — a communications code word for the letter *m*

1**mil** \ˈmil\ *n* [L *mille* thousand — more at MILE] **1 :** a unit of length equal to 1/1000 inch used esp. for the diameter of wire **2 :** a unit of angular measurement equal to 1/6400 of 360 degrees and used esp. in artillery **3 :** THOUSAND <found a salinity of 38.4 per ~> **4** — see *pound* at MONEY table

2**mil** *abbr* military

mi·la·dy \mil-ˈād-ē, *US also* mī-ˈlād-\ *n* [F, fr. E *my lady*] **1 :** an Englishwoman of noble or gentle birth **2 :** a woman of fashion

milch \ˈmilk, ˈmilch, ˈmilks\ *adj* [ME *milche,* fr. OE *-milce;* akin to OE *melcan* to milk — more at EMULSION] **:** giving milk; *specif* **:** bred or suitable primarily for milk production <~ cows>

mil·chig \ˈmilk-ik\ *adj* [Yiddish, fr. *milch* milk, fr. MHG, fr. OHG *miluh* — more at MILK] **:** made of or derived from milk or dairy products

mild \ˈmī(ə)ld\ *adj* [ME, fr. OE *milde;* akin to Gk *malthakos* soft, OE *melu* meal — more at MEAL] **1 :** gentle in nature or behavior **2 a :** moderate in action or effect <a ~ cigar> **b :** not being or involving what is extreme <an analysis under ~ conditions> <a ~ slope> **3 :** not severe **:** TEMPERATE <a ~ climate> <~ symptoms of disease> **4 :** comparatively soft and easily worked **:** MALLEABLE <~ steel> ***syn*** see SOFT ***ant*** harsh, fierce — **mild·ly** \ˈmī(ə)l-(d)lē\ *adv* — **mild·ness** \ˈmī(ə)l(d)-nəs\ *n*

1**mil·dew** \ˈmil-ˌd(y)ü\ *n* [ME, fr. OE *meledēaw;* akin to OHG *militou* honeydew] **1 a :** a superficial usu. whitish growth produced on organic matter or living plants by fungi (as of the families Erysiphaceae and Peronosporaceae) **b :** a fungus producing mildew **2 :** a discoloration caused by fungi — **mil·dewy** \-ē\ *adj*

2**mildew** *vt* **:** to affect with or as if with mildew ~ *vi* **:** to become affected with mildew

mile \ˈmī(ə)l\ *n* [ME, fr. OE *mīl;* akin to OHG *mīla* mile; both fr. a prehistoric WGmc word borrowed fr. L *milia* miles, fr. *milia passuum,* lit., thousands of paces, fr. *milia,* pl. of *mille* thousand, perh. fr. a prehistoric compound whose constituents are akin to Gk *mia* (fem. of *heis* one) and to Gk *chilioi* thousand, Skt *sahasra* — more at SAME] **1 :** any of various units of distance: as **a :** a unit equal to 5280 feet — see WEIGHT table **b :** NAUTICAL MILE **2 :** a race of a mile **3 :** a relatively great distance

mile·age \ˈmī-lij\ *n* **1 :** an allowance for traveling expenses at a certain rate per mile **2 :** aggregate length or distance in miles: as **a :** the total miles traveled in a day or other period of time **b :** the amount of service that something will yield esp. as expressed in terms of miles of travel **c :** the average number of miles a car will travel on a gallon of gas <gets good ~> **3 :** USEFULNESS, PROFIT

mile·post \ˈmī(ə)l-ˌpōst\ *n* **:** a post indicating the distance in miles from or to a given point; *also* **:** a post placed a mile from a similar post

mil·er \ˈmī-lər\ *n* **:** a man or a horse that competes in mile races

-mil·er \ˈmī-lər\ *comb form* **1 :** one that competes in a race of a specified number of miles <he was the best quarter-*miler* in our school> **2 :** one that is a specified number of miles in length <the ski run was a two-*miler*>

mi·les glo·ri·o·sus \ˈmē-ˌlās-ˌglōr-ē-ˈō-səs, -ˌglȯr-\ *n, pl* **mi·li·tes glo·ri·o·si** \ˈmē-lə-ˌtās-ˌglōr-ē-ˈō-(ˌ)sē, -ˌglȯr-\ [L] **:** a boastful soldier; *esp* **:** a stock character of this type in comedy

mi·le·si·mo \mi-ˈles-ə-ˌmō, -ˈlās-\ *n, pl* **-mos** [Sp, fr. *milésimo* one thousandth] — see *escudo* at MONEY table

mile·stone \ˈmī(ə)l-ˌstōn\ *n* **1 :** a stone serving as a milepost **2 :** a significant point in development

mil·foil \ˈmil-ˌfȯil\ *n* [ME, fr. OF, fr. L *millefolium,* fr. *mille* + *folium* leaf — more at BLADE] **1 :** YARROW **2 :** WATER MILFOIL

mil·i·ar·ia \ˌmil-ē-ˈar-ē-ə, -ˈer-\ *n* [NL, fr. L, fem. of *miliarius*] **:** an inflammatory disorder of the skin characterized by redness, eruption, burning or itching, and excessive sweating; *esp* **:** PRICKLY HEAT — **mil·i·ar·i·al** \-əl\ *adj*

mil·i·ary \ˈmil-ē-ˌer-ē\ *adj* [L *miliarius* of millet, fr. *milium* millet — more at MILLET] **:** having or made up of many small projections or lesions <~ tubercles>

mi·lieu \mēl-ˈyə(r), -ˈyü; mē-lyœ̄\ *n, pl* **milieus** *or* **mi·lieux** \-ˈyə(r)(z), -ˈyüz, -lyœ̄(z)\ [F, fr. OF, midst, fr. *mi* middle (fr. L *medius*) + *lieu* place, fr. L *locus*] **:** ENVIRONMENT, SETTING <three studies of women, each from a different ~ —Edmund Wilson>

mil·i·tan·cy \ˈmil-ə-tən-sē\ *n* **:** the quality or state of being militant

mil·i·tant \-tənt\ *adj* **1 :** engaged in warfare or combat **:** FIGHTING **2 :** aggressively active (as in a cause) **:** COMBATIVE <~ conservationists> <a ~ attitude> ***syn*** see AGGRESSIVE — **militant** *n* — **mil·i·tant·ly** *adv* — **mil·i·tant·ness** *n*

mil·i·tari·ly \ˌmil-ə-ˈter-ə-lē\ *adv* **1 :** in a military manner **2 :** from a military standpoint

mil·i·ta·rism \ˈmil-ə-tə-ˌriz-əm\ *n* **1 a :** predominance of the military class or its ideals **b :** exaltation of military virtues and ideals **2 :** a policy of aggressive military preparedness — **mil·i·ta·rist** \-rəst\ *n* — **mil·i·ta·ris·tic** \ˌmil-ə-tə-ˈris-tik\ *adj* — **mil·i·ta·ris·ti·cal·ly** \-ti-k(ə-)lē\ *adv*

mil·i·ta·rize \ˈmil-ə-tə-ˌrīz\ *vt* **-rized; -riz·ing 1 :** to equip with military forces and defenses **2 :** to give a military character to **3 :** to adapt for military use — **mil·i·ta·ri·za·tion** \ˌmil-ə-t(ə-)rə-ˈzā-shən\ *n*

1**mil·i·tary** \ˈmil-ə-ˌter-ē\ *adj* [MF *militaire,* fr. L *militaris,* fr. *milit-, miles*] **1 a :** of or relating to soldiers, arms, or war **b :** of or relating to armed forces; *esp* : of or relating to ground or sometimes ground and air forces as opposed to naval forces **2 a** : performed or made by armed forces **b** : supported by armed force **3** : of or relating to the army ***syn*** see MARTIAL

²**military** *n, pl* **military** *also* **mil·i·tar·ies** **1** : ARMED FORCES **2** : military persons; *esp* : army officers

military police *n* : a branch of an army that exercises guard and police functions

military science *n* : the principles of military conflict

mil·i·tate \ˈmil-ə-ˌtāt\ *vi* **-tat·ed; -tat·ing** [L *militatus,* pp. of *militare* to engage in warfare, fr. *milit-, miles* soldier] : to have weight or effect <his boyish appearance *militated* against his getting an early promotion>

mi·li·tia \mə-ˈlish-ə\ *n* [L, military service, fr. *milit-, miles*] **1** : a part of the organized armed forces of a country liable to call only in emergency **2** : the whole body of able-bodied male citizens declared by law as being subject to call to military service — **mi·li·tia·man** \-mən\ *n*

mil·i·um \ˈmil-ē-əm\ *n, pl* **mil·ia** \-ē-ə\ [NL, fr. L, millet — more at MILLET] : a small whitish lump in the skin due to retention of secretion in an oil gland duct

¹**milk** \ˈmilk\ *n* [ME, fr. OE *meolc, milc;* akin to OHG *miluh* milk] **1** : a fluid secreted by the mammary glands of females for the nourishment of their young; *esp* : cow's milk used as a food by humans **2** : a liquid resembling milk in appearance: as **a** : the latex of a plant **b** : the juice of a coconut **c** : the contents of an unripe kernel of grain

²**milk** *vt* **1 a** (1) : to draw milk from the breasts or udder of (2) *obs* : SUCKLE 2 **b** : to draw (milk) from the breast or udder **c** : SUCKLE 1 — used of lower mammals **2** : to draw something from as if by milking: as **a** : to draw venom from (a snake) by inducing to bite **b** : to compel or persuade to yield profit or advantage illicitly or to an unreasonable degree : EXPLOIT ~ *vi* : to draw or yield milk — **milk·er** *n*

milk–and–wa·ter \ˌmil-kən-ˈ(d)wȯt-ər, -ˈ(d)wät-\ *adj* : WEAK, INSIPID

milk fever *n* **1** : a febrile disorder following parturition **2 a** : a disease of recently calved cows or occas. sheep or goats that is caused by excessive drain on the body mineral reserves during the establishment of the milk flow **b** : ketosis of domestic animals

milk·fish \ˈmilk-ˌfish\ *n* : a large active silvery herbivorous food fish (*Chanos chanos*) that is widely distributed in the warm parts of the Pacific and Indian oceans and is the sole living representative of its family (Chanidae)

milk glass *n* : an opaque and typically milk white glass used esp. for novelty and ornamental objects

milk leg *n* : a painful swelling of the leg at childbirth caused by inflammation and clotting in the veins

milk–liv·ered \ˈmil-ˈkliv-ərd\ *adj* : COWARDLY, TIMOROUS

milk·maid \ˈmilk-ˌmād\ *n* : DAIRYMAID

milk·man \-ˌman, -mən\ *n* : a man who sells or delivers milk

milk of magnesia : a milk-white suspension of magnesium hydroxide in water used as an antacid and laxative

milk punch *n* : a mixed drink of alcoholic liquor, milk, and sugar

milk shake *n* : a thoroughly shaken or blended drink made of milk, a flavoring syrup, and often ice cream

milk sickness *n* **1** : an acute disease characterized by weakness, vomiting, and constipation and caused by eating dairy products or meat from cattle poisoned by various plants **2** : TREMBLE 2

milk snake *n* : a common harmless grayish or tan snake (*Lampropeltis triangulum*) with black-bordered brown blotches and an arrow-shaped occipital spot; *broadly* : KING SNAKE

milk snake

milk·sop \ˈmilk-ˌsäp\ *n* : an unmanly man : MOLLYCODDLE

milk sugar *n* : LACTOSE

milk tooth *n* : a temporary deciduous tooth of a mammal; *esp* : one of man's set consisting of four incisors, two canines, and four molars in each jaw

milk vetch *n* [fr. the popular belief that it increases the milk yield of goats] : a perennial Old World leguminous herb (*Astragalus glycyphyllos*) that has sulfur yellow flowers in dense spikes; *also* : any of various related plants

milk·weed \ˈmil-ˌkwēd\ *n* : any of various plants that secrete latex; *esp* : any of a genus (*Asclepias* of the family Asclepiadaceae, the milkweed family) of erect perennial herbs with milky juice and umbellate flowers

milkweed bug *n* : a large black red-marked bug (*Oncopeltus fasciatus*) now cultured widely as a research organism

milk·wort \ˈmil-ˌkwərt, -ˌkwȯ(ə)rt\ *n* : any of a genus (*Polygala* of the family Polygalaceae, the milkwort family) of herbs and shrubs that have many-colored often showy flowers with the three sometimes crested petals united below into a tube and an irregular calyx with two petaloid sepals

milky \ˈmil-kē\ *adj* **milk·i·er; -est** **1** : resembling milk in color or consistency **2** : MILD, TIMOROUS **3 a** : consisting of, containing, or abounding in milk **b** : yielding milk; *specif* : having the characteristics of a good milk producer — **milk·i·ness** *n*

milky disease *n* : a destructive bacterial disease of Japanese beetle larvae and other scarabaeid grubs

Milky Way *n* **1** : a broad luminous irregular band of light that stretches completely around the celestial sphere and is caused by the light of myriads of faint stars **2** : MILKY WAY GALAXY **3** *not cap* : GALAXY

Milky Way galaxy *n* : the galaxy of which the sun and the solar system are a part and which contains the myriads of stars that comprise the Milky Way together with all the individual stars, clusters, and bright and dark nebulosities in the sky

¹**mill** \ˈmil\ *n* [ME *mille,* fr. OE *mylen;* akin to OHG *muli* mill; both fr. a prehistoric NGmc-WGmc word borrowed fr. LL *molina, molinum,* fr. fem. and neut. of *molinus* of a mill, of a millstone, fr. L *mola* mill, millstone; akin to L *molere* to grind — more at MEAL] **1** : a building provided with machinery for grinding grain into flour **2 a** : a machine or apparatus (as a quern) for grinding grain **b** : a machine for crushing or comminuting **3** : a machine that manufactures by the continuous repetition of some simple action **4** : a building or collection of buildings with machinery for manufacturing **5 a** : a machine for stamping coins **b** : a machine for expelling juice from vegetable tissues by pressure or grinding **c** : a machine for polishing **6** : MILLING MACHINE, MILLING CUTTER **7 a** : a slow, laborious, or mechanical process or routine **b** : a place that processes people or things mechanically <a diploma ~> **8** *slang* : the engine of an automobile or boat

²**mill** *vt* **1** : to subject to an operation or process in a mill: as **a** : to grind into flour, meal, or powder **b** : to shape or dress by means of a rotary cutter **c** : to mix and condition (as rubber) by passing between rotating rolls **2** : to give a raised rim or a ridged or corrugated edge to (a coin) **3** : to cut grooves in the metal surface of (as a knob) ~ *vi* **1** : to hit out with the fists **2** : to move in a circle or in an eddying mass **3** : to undergo milling

³**mill** *n* [L *mille* thousand — more at MILE] : a money of account equal to $^{1}/_{10}$ cent

mill·age \ˈmil-ij\ *n* : a rate (as of taxation) expressed in mills per dollar

mill·board \ˈmil-ˌbō(ə)rd, -ˌbȯ(ə)rd\ *n* [alter. of *milled board*] : strong heavy firm paperboard suitable for lining book covers and for paneling in furniture

mill·dam \-ˌdam\ *n* : a dam to make a millpond; *also* : MILLPOND

mille \ˈmil\ *n* [L] : MIL 3

¹**mil·le·nar·i·an** \ˌmil-ə-ˈner-ē-ən\ *adj* **1** : of or relating to 1000 years **2** : of or relating to belief in the millennium

²**millenarian** *n* : one that believes in a millennium

mil·le·nar·i·an·ism \-ē-ə-ˌniz-əm\ *n* **1** : belief in the millennium of Christian prophecy **2** : belief in a coming ideal society and esp. one created by revolutionary action

¹**mil·le·na·ry** \ˈmil-ə-ˌner-ē, mə-ˈlen-ə-rē\ *n, pl* **-ries** [LL *millenarium,* fr. neut. of *millenarius* of a thousand, fr. L *milleni* one thousand each, fr. *mille*] **1 a** : a group of 1000 units or things **b** : 1000 years : MILLENNIUM **2** : MILLENARIAN

²**millenary** *adj* [L *millenarius*] **1** : relating to or consisting of 1000 **2** : suggesting a millennium

mil·len·ni·al \mə-ˈlen-ē-əl\ *adj, archaic* : of or relating to a millennium

mil·len·ni·al·ism \-ē-ə-ˌliz-əm\ *n* : MILLENARIANISM

mil·len·ni·um \mə-ˈlen-ē-əm\ *n, pl* **-nia** \-ē-ə\ *or* **-niums** [NL, fr. L *mille* thousand + NL *-ennium* (as in *biennium*)] **1 a** : a period of 1000 years **b** : a 1000th anniversary or its celebration **2 a** : the thousand years mentioned in Revelation 20 during which holiness is to prevail and Christ is to reign on earth **b** : a period of great happiness or human perfection

mil·le·pore \ˈmil-ə-ˌpō(ə)r, -ˌpȯ(ə)r\ *n* [deriv. of L *mille* thousand + *porus* pore] : any of an order (Milleporina) of often large stony hydrozoan reef-building corals of encrusting, branching, or massive form that differ from the madrepores in passing through a free-swimming medusoid stage

mill·er \ˈmil-ər\ *n* **1** : one that operates a mill; *specif* : one that grinds grain into flour **2** : any of various moths having powdery wings **3 a** : MILLING MACHINE **b** : a tool for use in a milling machine

mil·ler·ite \ˈmil-ə-ˌrīt\ *n* [G *millerit,* fr. William H. *Miller* †1880 E mineralogist] : sulfide of nickel NiS usu. occurring as a mineral in capillary yellow crystals

mill·er's–thumb \ˌmil-ərz-ˈthəm\ *n* : any of several small freshwater spiny-finned sculpins (genus *Cottus*) of Europe and No. America

mil·les·i·mal \mə-ˈles-ə-məl\ *n* [L *millesimus,* adj., thousandth, fr. *mille*] : the quotient of a unit divided by 1000 : one of 1000 equal parts of anything — **millesimal** *adj* — **mil·les·i·mal·ly** \-ə-mə-lē\ *adv*

mil·let \ˈmil-ət\ *n* [ME *milet,* fr. MF, dim. of *mil,* fr. L *milium;* akin to Gk *melinē* millet] **1** : any of various small-seeded annual cereal and forage grasses: **a** : a grass (*Panicum miliaceum*) cultivated for its grain which is used for food **b** : any of several grasses related to common millet **2** : the seed of a millet

Mill Hill Father \ˌmil-ˌhil-\ *n* [*Mill Hill,* site of its college in Barnet, England] : a member of a Roman Catholic missionary order founded by Herbert Vaughan in 1866

milli- *comb form* [F, fr. L *milli-* thousand, fr. *mille* — more at MILE] : thousandth <*milli*ampere>

mil·li·am·pere \ˌmil-ē-ˈam-ˌpi(ə)r\ *n* [ISV] : one thousandth of an ampere

mil·liard \ˈmil-ˌyärd, ˈmil-ē-ˌärd\ *n* [F, fr. MF *miliart,* fr. *mili-,* (fr. *milion* million)] *Brit* : a thousand millions — see NUMBER table

mil·li·ary \ˈmil-ē-ˌer-ē\ *adj* [L *milliarius, miliarius* consisting of a thousand, one mile long, fr. *mille* thousand, mile] : marking the distance of a Roman mile

mil·li·bar \ˈmil-ə-ˌbär\ *n* [ISV] : a unit of atmospheric pressure equal to $^{1}/_{1000}$ bar or 1000 dynes per square centimeter

mil·li·cu·rie \ˌmil-ə-ˈkyu̇(ə)r-(ˌ)ē, -kyu̇-ˈrē\ *n* [ISV] : one thousandth of a curie

mil·li·de·gree \-di-ˈgrē\ *n* : one thousandth of a degree

mil·lieme \mē(l)-ˈyem\ *n, pl* **milliemes** \-ˈyem(z)\ [F *millième* thousandth, fr. MF, fr. *mille* thousand, fr. L] — see *pound* at MONEY table

mil·li·far·ad \ˌmil-ə-ˈfar-ˌad, -əd\ *n* [ISV] : one thousandth of a farad

mil·li·gal \ˈmil-ə-ˌgal\ *n* [ISV] : a unit of acceleration equivalent to $^{1}/_{1000}$ gal

mil·li·gram \-ˌgram\ *n* [F *milligramme,* fr. *milli-* + *gramme* gram] — see METRIC SYSTEM table

mil·li·hen·ry \-ˌhen-rē\ *n* [ISV] : one thousandth of a henry

mil·li·lam·bert \-ˈlam-bərt\ *n* : one thousandth of a lambert

mil·li·li·ter \ˈmil-ə-ˌlēt-ər\ *n* [F *millilitre,* fr. *milli-* + *litre* liter] — see METRIC SYSTEM table

mil·lime \mə-'lēm\ *n* [modif. of Ar *mallim,* fr. F *millième*] — see *dinar* at MONEY table

mil·li·me·ter \'mil-ə-ˌmēt-ər\ *n* [F *millimètre,* fr. *milli-* + *mètre* meter] — see METRIC SYSTEM table

mil·li·mi·cro- \ˌmil-ə-'mī-krə, -krō\ *comb form* : billionth <*millimicro*second>

mil·li·mi·cron \ˌmil-ə-'mī-ˌkrän\ *n* [ISV] : a unit of length equal to one thousandth of a micrometer

mil·li·mole \'mil-ə-ˌmōl\ *n* [ISV *milli-* + [5]*mole*] : one thousandth of a gram molecule

mil·line \'mil-'līn\ *n* [blend of *million* and *line*] : a unit of space and circulation equivalent to one agate line appearing in one million copies of a publication

mil·li·ner \'mil-ə-nər\ *n* [irreg. fr. *Milan,* Italy; fr. the importation of women's finery from Italy in the 16th century] : one who designs, makes, trims, or sells women's hats

mil·li·nery \'mil-ə-ˌner-ē\ *n* **1** : women's apparel for the head **2** : the business or work of a milliner

mill·ing \'mil-iŋ\ *n* : a corrugated edge on a coin

milling cutter *n* : a rotary tool-steel cutter used in a milling machine for shaping and dressing metal surfaces

milling machine *n* : a machine tool on which work usu. of metal secured to a carriage is shaped by being fed against rotating milling cutters

mil·lion \'mil-yən\ *n, pl* **millions** *or* **million** [ME *milioun,* fr. MF *milion,* fr. OIt *milione,* aug. of *mille* thousand, fr. L — more at MILE] **1** — see NUMBER table **2** : a very large number <~*s* of cars on the road> **3** : the mass of common people <someone who writes for the ~*s* —Bergen Evans> — **million** *adj* — **mil·lionth** \-yən(t)th\ *adj or n*

mil·lion·aire \ˌmil-yə-'na(ə)r, -'ne(ə)r, 'mil-yə-ˌ\ *n* [F *millionnaire,* fr. *million,* fr. MF *milion*] : one whose wealth is estimated at a million or more (as of dollars or pounds)

mil·lion·air·ess \-'ar-əs, -'er-, -ˌar-, -ˌer-\ *n* : a woman who is a millionaire or the wife of a millionaire

mil·li·pede \'mil-ə-ˌpēd\ *n* [L *millepeda* a small crawling animal, fr. *mille* thousand + *ped-, pes* foot — more at FOOT] : any of numerous myriopods (class Diplopoda) having usu. a cylindrical segmented body covered with hard integument, two pairs of legs on most apparent segments, and no poison fangs

mil·li·ra·di·an \ˌmil-ə-'rād-ē-ən\ *n* [ISV] : one thousandth of a radian

mil·li·rem \'mil-ə-ˌrem\ *n* : one thousandth of a rem

mil·li·roent·gen \ˌmil-ə-'rent-gən, -'rənt-, -jən; -'ren-chən, -'rən-\ *n* [ISV] : one thousandth of a roentgen

mil·li·sec·ond \'mil-ə-ˌsek-ənd, -ənt\ *n* [ISV] : one thousandth of a second

mil·li·volt \-ˌvōlt\ *n* [ISV] : one thousandth of a volt

mil·li·watt \-ˌwät\ *n* [ISV] : one thousandth of a watt

mill·pond \'mil-ˌpänd\ *n* : a pond produced by damming a stream to produce a head of water for operating a mill

mill·race \-ˌrās\ *n* : a canal in which water flows to and from a mill wheel; *also* : the current that drives the wheel

mill run *n* **1** : the salable lumber output of a sawmill **2** : the common run of an article passing through a mill

mill·stone \'mil-ˌstōn\ *n* **1** : either of two circular stones used for grinding (as grain) **2 a** : something that grinds or crushes **b** : a heavy burden

mill·stream \-ˌstrēm\ *n* **1** : a stream whose flow is utilized to run a mill **2** : MILLRACE

mill wheel *n* : a waterwheel that drives a mill

mill·wright \'mil-ˌrīt\ *n* **1** : one whose occupation is planning and building mills or setting up their machinery **2** : one who maintains and cares for mechanical equipment (as of a mill or factory)

mi·lo \'mī-(ˌ)lō\ *n, pl* **milos** [Sotho *maili*] : a small usu. early and drought-resistant grain sorghum with compact bearded heads of large yellow or whitish seeds

mi·lord \mil-'ȯ(ə)r(d)\ *n* [F, fr. E *my lord*] : an Englishman of noble or gentle birth

mil·pa \'mil-pə\ *n* [MexSp, fr. Nahuatl] **1 a** : a small field in Mexico or Central America that is cleared from the jungle, cropped for a few seasons, and abandoned for a fresh clearing **b** : a maize field in Mexico or Central America **2** : the maize plant

Milque·toast \'milk-ˌtōst\ *n* [Caspar *Milquetoast,* comic strip character created by H. T. Webster †1952 Am cartoonist] : a timid, meek, or unassertive person

mil·reis \mil-'rās(h)\ *n, pl* **mil·reis** \-'rās(h), -'rāz(h)\ [Pg *milréis*] **1** : a Portuguese unit of value equal before 1911 to 1000 reis **2** : the basic monetary unit of Brazil until 1942 **3** : a coin representing one milreis

milt \'milt\ *n* [prob. fr. MD *milte* milt of fish, spleen; akin to OE *milte* spleen — more at MELT] : the male reproductive glands of fishes when filled with secretion; *also* : the secretion itself — **milty** \-tē\ *adj*

milt·er \'mil-tər\ *n* : a male fish in breeding condition

mim \'mim\ *adj* [imit. of the act of pursing the lips] *dial* : affectedly shy or modest

[1]**mime** \'mīm, 'mēm\ *n* [L *mimus,* fr. Gk *mimos;* akin to Gk *mimeisthai* to imitate] **1 a** : an actor in a mime **b** : one that practices mime **2** : MIMIC **3** : an ancient dramatic entertainment representing scenes from life usu. in a ridiculous manner **4 a** : the art of portraying a character or of narration by body movement **b** : a performance of mime

[2]**mime** *vb* **mimed; mim·ing** *vi* : to act a part with mimic gesture and action usu. without words ~ *vt* **1** : MIMIC **2** : to act out in the manner of a mime — **mim·er** *n*

mim·eo·graph \'mim-ē-ə-ˌgraf\ *n* [fr. *Mimeograph,* a trademark] : a duplicator for making many copies that utilizes a stencil through which ink is pressed — **mimeograph** *vt*

mi·me·sis \mə-'mē-səs, mī-\ *n* [LL, fr. Gk *mimēsis,* fr. *mimeisthai*] : IMITATION, MIMICRY

mi·met·ic \-'met-ik\ *adj* [LL *mimeticus,* fr. Gk *mimētikos,* fr. *mimeisthai*] **1** : IMITATIVE **2** : relating to, characterized by, or exhibiting mimicry <~ coloring of a butterfly> —**mi·met·i·cal·ly** \-i-k(ə-)lē\ *adv*

[1]**mim·ic** \'mim-ik\ *n* **1** : MIME 1 **2** : one that mimics

[2]**mimic** *adj* [L *mimicus,* fr. Gk *mimikos,* fr. *mimos* mime] **1 a** : IMITATIVE **b** : IMITATION, MOCK <a ~ battle> **2** : of or relating to mime or mimicry — **mim·i·cal** \-i-kəl\ *adj*

[3]**mimic** *vt* **mim·icked** \-ikt\; **mim·ick·ing 1** : to imitate closely : APE **2** : to ridicule by imitation **3** : SIMULATE **4** : to resemble by biological mimicry *syn* see COPY

mim·ic·ry \'mim-i-krē\ *n, pl* **-ries 1 a** : an instance of mimicking **b** : the action, practice, or art of mimicking **2** : a superficial resemblance of one organism to another or to natural objects among which it lives that secures it a selective advantage (as protection from predation)

mi·mo·sa \mə-'mō-sə, mī-, -zə\ *n* [NL, genus name, fr. L *mimus* mime] : any of a genus (*Mimosa*) of leguminous trees, shrubs, and herbs of tropical and warm regions with usu. bipinnate often prickly leaves and globular heads of small white or pink flowers

min *abbr* **1** minim **2** minimum **3** mining **4** minister **5** minor **6** minute

mi·na \'mī-nə\ *n* [L, fr. Gk *mna,* of Sem origin; akin to Heb *māneh* mina] : an ancient unit of weight and value equal to 1/60 talent

min·able *or* **mine·able** \'mī-nə-bəl\ *adj* : capable of being mined

min·a·ret \ˌmin-ə-'ret, 'min-ə-ˌ\ *n* [F, fr. Turk *minare,* fr. Ar *manārah* lighthouse] : a slender lofty tower attached to a mosque and surrounded by one or more projecting balconies from which the summons to prayer is cried by the muezzin

1 minaret

mi·na·to·ry \'min-ə-ˌtōr-ē, 'mī-nə-, -ˌtȯr-\ *adj* [LL *minatorius,* fr. L *minatus,* pp. of *minari* to threaten — more at MOUNT] : having a menacing quality : THREATENING

[1]**mince** \'min(t)s\ *vb* **minced; minc·ing** [ME *mincen,* fr. MF *mincer,* fr. (assumed) VL *minutiare,* fr. L *minutia* smallness — more at MINUTIA] *vt* **1 a** : to cut or chop into very small pieces **b** : to subdivide minutely; *esp* : to damage by cutting up **2** : to utter or pronounce with affectation **3 a** *archaic* : to diminish the force of : MINIMIZE **b** : to restrain (words) within the bounds of decorum ~ *vi* : to walk with short steps in a prim affected manner — **minc·er** *n*

[2]**mince** *n* : small chopped bits (as of food); *specif* : MINCEMEAT

mince·meat \'min(t)-ˌsmēt\ *n* **1** : minced meat **2** : a finely chopped mixture (as of raisins, apples, and spices) with or without meat

mince pie *n* : a pie filled with mincemeat

minc·ing \'min(t)-siŋ\ *adj* : affectedly dainty or delicate — **minc·ing·ly** \-siŋ-lē\ *adv*

[1]**mind** \'mīnd\ *n* [ME, fr. OE *gemynd;* akin to OHG *gimunt* memory; both fr. a prehistoric EGmc-WGmc compound whose first constituent is represented by OE *ge-* (perfective prefix) and whose second constituent is akin to L *ment-, mens* mind, *monēre* to remind, warn, Gk *menos* spirit, *mnasthai, mimnēskesthai* to remember — more at CO-] **1** : RECOLLECTION, MEMORY <keep that in ~> <time out of ~> **2 a** : the element or complex of elements in an individual that feels, perceives, thinks, wills, and esp. reasons **b** : the conscious mental events and capabilities in an organism **c** : the organized conscious and unconscious adaptive mental activity of an organism **3** : INTENTION, DESIRE <she changed her ~> **4** : the normal or healthy condition of the mental faculties **5** : OPINION, VIEW **6** : DISPOSITION, MOOD **7 a** : a person or group embodying mental qualities <the public ~> **b** : intellectual ability **8** *cap, Christian Science* : GOD 1b **9** : a conscious substratum or factor in the universe

[2]**mind** *vt* **1** *chiefly dial* : REMIND **2** *chiefly dial* : REMEMBER **3** : to attend to closely **4 a** : to become aware of : NOTICE **b** *chiefly dial* : INTEND, PURPOSE **5 a** : to give heed to attentively in order to obey **b** : to follow the orders or instructions of **6 a** : to be concerned about **b** : DISLIKE <I don't ~ going> **7 a** : to be careful : SEE <~ you finish it> **b** : to be cautious about <~ the broken rung> **8** : to give protective care to : TEND ~ *vi* **1** : to be attentive or wary **2** : to become concerned : CARE **3** : to pay obedient heed or attention *syn* see OBEY, TEND — **mind·er** *n*

mind–blow·ing \'mīn(d)-ˌblō-iŋ\ *adj* **1** : PSYCHEDELIC; *also* : of, relating to, or causing a psychic state similar to that produced by a psychedelic drug **2** : mentally or emotionally stimulating : OVERWHELMING — **mind·blow·er** \-ˌblō(-ə)r\ *n*

mind·ed \'mīn-dəd\ *adj* **1** : having a mind esp. of a specified kind — usu. used in combination <narrow-*minded*> **2** : INCLINED, DISPOSED — **mind·ed·ness** \-dəd-nəs\ *n*

mind–ex·pand·ing \'mīn-dik-ˌspan-diŋ\ *adj* : PSYCHEDELIC 1a

mind·ful \'mīn(d)-fəl\ *adj* **1** : bearing in mind : AWARE **2** : inclined to be aware — **mind·ful·ly** \-fə-lē\ *adv* — **mind·ful·ness** *n*

mind·less \'mīn-(d)ləs\ *adj* **1** : destitute of mind or consciousness; *esp* : UNINTELLIGENT **2** : INATTENTIVE, HEEDLESS — **mind·less·ly** *adv* — **mind·less·ness** *n*

mind reader *n* : one that professes or is held to be able to perceive another's thought without normal means of communication — **mind reading** *n*

mind's eye *n* **:** the mental faculty of conceiving imaginary or recollected scenes

¹mine \(ˈ)mīn\ *adj* [ME *min* — more at MY] *archaic* **:** MY — used before a word beginning with a vowel or *h* <this treasure in ~ arms —Shak.> or sometimes as a modifier of a preceding noun

²mine \ˈmīn\ *pron, sing or pl in constr* **:** that which belongs to me — used without a following noun as a pronoun equivalent in meaning to the adjective *my*

³mine \ˈmīn\ *n* [ME, fr. MF] **1 a :** a pit or excavation in the earth from which mineral substances are taken **b :** an ore deposit **2 :** a subterranean passage under an enemy position **3 :** an encased explosive designed to destroy enemy personnel, vehicles, or ships **4 :** a rich source of supply **5 :** a pyrotechnic piece comprising various small fireworks that are scattered into the air with a loud report

⁴mine \ˈmīn\ *vb* **mined; min·ing** *vi* **:** to dig a mine ~ *vt* **1 a :** to dig under to gain access or cause the collapse of (an enemy position) **b :** UNDERMINE **2 :** to get (as ore) from the earth **3 :** to burrow beneath the surface of <larva that ~*s* leaves> **4 :** to place military mines in, on, or under <~ a harbor> **5 a :** to dig into for ore or metal **b :** to process for obtaining a natural constituent <~ the air for nitrogen> **c :** to seek valuable material in — **min·er** *n*

mine·lay·er \ˈmīn-ˌlā-ər, -ˌle(-ə)r\ *n* **:** a naval vessel for laying underwater mines

¹min·er·al \ˈmin(-ə)-rəl\ *n* [ME, fr. ML *minerale,* fr. neut. of *mineralis*] **1 a :** a solid homogeneous crystalline chemical element or compound that results from the inorganic processes of nature; *broadly* **:** any of various naturally occurring homogeneous substances (as stone, coal, salt, sulfur, sand, petroleum, water, or natural gas) obtained for man's use usu. from the ground **b :** a synthetic substance having the chemical composition and crystalline form and properties of a naturally occurring mineral **2** *obs* **:** MINE **3 :** something neither animal nor vegetable **4 :** ORE **5 :** an inorganic substance (as in the ash of calcined tissue) **6** *pl, Brit* **:** MINERAL WATER

²mineral *adj* [ME, fr. ML *mineralis,* fr. *minera* mine, ore, fr. OF *miniere,* fr. *mine*] **1 :** of or relating to minerals; *also* **:** INORGANIC **2 :** impregnated with mineral substances

min·er·al·ize \ˈmin-(ə-)rə-ˌlīz\ *vt* **-ized; -iz·ing 1 :** to transform (a metal) into an ore **2 a :** to impregnate or supply with minerals or an inorganic compound **b :** to convert into mineral or inorganic form **3 :** PETRIFY — **min·er·al·iz·able** \-rə-ˌlī-zə-bəl\ *adj* — **min·er·al·iza·tion** \ˌmin(-ə)-rə-lə-ˈzā-shən\ *n* — **min·er·al·iz·er** \ˈmin(-ə)-rə-ˌlī-zər\ *n*

mineral kingdom *n* **:** the one of the three basic groups of natural objects that includes inorganic objects — compare ANIMAL KINGDOM, PLANT KINGDOM

min·er·al·o·gy \ˌmin-ə-ˈräl-ə-jē, -ˈral-\ *n* [prob. fr. (assumed) NL *mineralogia,* irreg. fr. ML *minerale* + L- *-logia* -logy] **1 :** a science dealing with minerals, their crystallography, physical and chemical properties, classification, and the ways of distinguishing them **2 :** the materials of mineralogy **3 :** a treatise on mineralogy — **min·er·al·og·i·cal** \ˌmin(-ə)-rə-ˈläj-i-kəl\ *adj* — **min·er·al·o·gist** \ˌmin-ə-ˈräl-ə-jəst, -ˈral-\ *n*

mineral oil *n* **:** an oil of mineral origin; *esp* **:** a refined petroleum oil used as a laxative

mineral spirits *n pl but sing or pl in constr* **:** a petroleum distillate that is used esp. as a paint or varnish thinner

mineral water *n* **:** water naturally or artificially impregnated with mineral salts or gases (as carbon dioxide)

mineral wax *n* **:** a wax of mineral origin; *esp* **:** OZOKERITE

mineral wool *n* **:** any of various lightweight vitreous fibrous materials used esp. in heat and sound insulation

Mi·ner·va \mə-ˈnər-və\ *n* [L] **:** the Roman goddess of wisdom — compare ATHENE

min·e·stro·ne \ˌmin-ə-ˈstrō-nē, -ˈstrōn\ *n* [It, aug. of *minestra,* fr. *minestrare* to serve, dish up, fr. L *ministrare,* fr. *minister* servant — more at MINISTER] **:** a rich thick vegetable soup usu. with dried beans and pasta (as macaroni or vermicelli)

mine·sweep·er \ˈmīn-ˌswē-pər\ *n* **:** a warship designed for removing or neutralizing mines by dragging — **mine·sweep·ing** \-piŋ\ *n*

Ming \ˈmiŋ\ *n* [Chin (Pek) *ming²* luminous] **:** a Chinese dynasty dated 1368–1644 and marked by restoration of earlier traditions and in the arts by perfection of established techniques

min·gle \ˈmiŋ-gəl\ *vb* **min·gled; min·gling** \-g(ə-)liŋ\ [ME *menglen,* freq. of *mengen* to mix, fr. OE *mengan;* akin to MHG *mengen* to mix, Gk *massein* to knead] *vt* **1 :** to bring or mix together or with something else usu. without fundamental loss of identity **:** INTERMIX **2 :** to prepare by mixing **:** CONCOCT ~ *vi* **:** to become mingled *syn* see MIX

ming tree \ˈmiŋ-\ *n* [perh. fr. *Ming*] **1 a :** a dwarfed evergreen conifer grown in a container or pot **b :** BONSAI **2 :** an artificial plant made by attaching flattened pads of alpine buckwheat (*Eriogonum ovalifolium*) left natural gray or colored to one or more twiggy branches usu. of manzanita

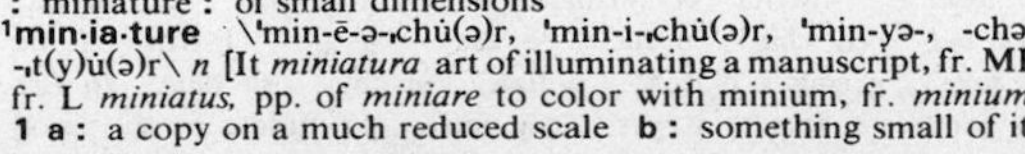

ming tree 1a

min·gy \ˈmin-jē\ *adj* **min·gi·er; -est** [perh. blend of ¹*mean* and *stingy*] **:** MEAN, STINGY

mini \ˈmin-ē\ *n, pl* **min·is** [*mini-*] **:** something small of its kind: as **a :** MINICAR **b :** MINISKIRT — **mini** *adj*

mini- *comb form* [*miniature*] **:** miniature **:** of small dimensions

¹min·ia·ture \ˈmin-ē-ə-ˌchü(ə)r, ˈmin-i-ˌchü(ə)r, ˈmin-yə-, -chər, -ˌt(y)ü(ə)r\ *n* [It *miniatura* art of illuminating a manuscript, fr. ML, fr. L *miniatus,* pp. of *miniare* to color with minium, fr. *minium*] **1 a :** a copy on a much reduced scale **b :** something small of its kind **2 :** a painting in an illuminated book or manuscript **3 :** the art of painting miniatures **4 :** a very small portrait or other painting (as on ivory or metal) — **min·ia·tur·ist** \-ˌchür-əst, -chər-, -ˌt(y)ür-\ *n* — **min·ia·tur·is·tic** \ˌmin-ē-ə-chə-ˈris-tik, ˌmin-i-, ˌmin-yə-, -ˌtyü-\ *adj*

²miniature *adj* **1 :** being or represented on a small scale **2 :** of or relating to still photography using film 35 mm. wide or smaller *syn* see SMALL

miniature golf *n* **:** a novelty golf game played with a putter on a miniature course having tunnels, bridges, sharp corners, and obstacles

miniature pinscher *n* **:** a toy dog that suggests a small Doberman pinscher and measures 10 to 12½ inches in height at the withers

miniature schnauzer *n* **:** a schnauzer of a breed that is 12 to 14 inches in height and is classified as a terrier

min·ia·tur·ize \ˈmin-ē-ə-ˌchə-ˌrīz, ˈmin-i-, ˈmin-yə-, -ˌtyü-\ *vt* **-ized; -iz·ing :** to design or construct in small size — **min·ia·tur·iza·tion** \ˌmin-ē-ə-ˌchür-ə-ˈzā-shən, ˌmin-i-, ˌmin-yə-, -chər-, -ˌtyür-\ *n*

mini·bike \ˈmin-i-ˌbīk\ *n* **:** a small one-passenger motorcycle having a low frame and elevated handlebars

mini·bus \-ˌbəs\ *n* **:** a small bus for comparatively short trips

mini·car \-ˌkär\ *n* **:** a very small automobile; *esp* **:** SUBCOMPACT

mini·com·put·er \ˌmin-i-kəm-ˈpyüt-ər\ *n* **:** a small and relatively inexpensive computer

min·ié ball \ˈmin-ē-ˌbōl, ˌmin-ē-ˌā-ˈbōl\ *n* [Claude Étienne *Minié* †1879 F army officer] **:** a rifle bullet with a conical head used in the middle of the 19th century

min·i·fy \ˈmin-ə-ˌfī\ *vt* **-fied; -fy·ing** [L *mini*mus smallest + E *-fy*] **:** LESSEN

min·i·kin \ˈmin-i-kən\ *n* [obs. D *minneken* darling] *archaic* **:** a small or dainty creature — **minikin** *adj*

min·im \ˈmin-əm\ *n* [L *minimus* least] **1 :** HALF NOTE **2 :** something very minute **3** — see WEIGHT table — **minim** *adj*

min·i·mal \ˈmin-ə-məl\ *adj* **1 :** relating to or being a minimum **:** constituting the least possible **2** *often cap* **:** of, relating to, or being minimal art — **min·i·mal·ly** \-mə-lē\ *adv*

minimal art *n* **:** abstract art and esp. sculpture consisting primarily of simple geometric forms executed in an impersonal style

min·i·mal·ism \ˈmin-ə-mə-ˌliz-əm\ *n* **:** MINIMAL ART

min·i·mal·ist \-ləst\ *n* **1 :** one who favors restricting the functions and powers of a political organization or the achievement of a set of goals to a minimum **2 :** a minimal artist

mini·max \ˈmin-i-ˌmaks\ *n* [*mini*mum + *max*imum] **:** the minimum of a set of maxima; *esp* **:** the smallest of a set of maximum possible losses each of which occurs in the most unfavorable outcome of a strategy followed by a participant in a situation governed by the theory of games — compare MAXIMIN

min·i·mize \ˈmin-ə-ˌmīz\ *vt* **-mized; -miz·ing 1 :** to reduce to a minimum **2 :** to estimate at a minimum often as a measure of disparagement or self-defense <the habit of *minimizing* losses in our own forces while maximizing those of the enemy> *syn* see DECRY *ant* maximize — **min·i·mi·za·tion** \ˌmin-ə-mə-ˈzā-shən\ *n* — **min·i·miz·er** \ˈmin-ə-ˌmī-zər\ *n*

min·i·mum \ˈmin-ə-məm\ *n, pl* **-i·ma** \-ə-mə\ *or* **-i·mums** [L, neuter of *minimus* smallest; akin to L *minor* smaller] **1 :** the least quantity assignable, admissible, or possible **2 :** the least of a set of numbers; *specif* **:** the smallest value assumed by a continuous function defined on a closed interval **3 a :** the lowest degree or amount of variation reached or recorded **b :** the lowest speed allowed on a highway **4 :** the time of least brightness or the magnitude at this time — used of a variable star — **mini·mum** *adj*

minimum wage *n* **1 :** LIVING WAGE **2 :** the lowest wage paid or permitted to be paid; *specif* **:** a wage fixed by legal authority or by contract as the least that may be paid either to employed persons generally or to a particular category of employed persons

min·ing \ˈmī-niŋ\ *n* **:** the process or business of working mines

min·ion \ˈmin-yən\ *n* [MF *mignon* darling] **1 :** a servile dependent **2 :** one highly favored **:** IDOL **3 :** a subordinate official

min·is·cule \ˈmin-əs-ˌkyü(ə)l\ *var of* MINUSCULE

mini·skirt \ˈmin-i-ˌskərt\ *n* **:** a woman's short skirt with the hemline several inches above the knee

mini·state \-ˌstāt\ *n* **:** a small independent nation

¹min·is·ter \ˈmin-ə-stər\ *n* [ME *ministre,* fr. OF, fr. L *minister* servant; akin to L *minor*] **1 :** AGENT **2 a :** one officiating or assisting the officiant in church worship **b :** a clergyman esp. of a Protestant communion **3 a :** the superior of one of several religious orders — called also *minister-general* **b :** the assistant to the rector or the bursar of a Jesuit house **4 :** a high officer of state entrusted with the management of a division of governmental activities **5 a :** a diplomatic representative (as an ambassador) accredited to the court or seat of government of a foreign state **b :** a diplomatic representative ranking below an ambassador

²minister *vi* **min·is·tered; min·is·ter·ing** \-st(ə-)riŋ\ **1 :** to perform the functions of a minister of religion **2 :** to give aid or service <~ to the sick>

min·is·te·ri·al \ˌmin-ə-ˈstir-ē-əl\ *adj* **1 :** of or relating to a minister or the ministry **2 a :** being or having the characteristics of an act or duty prescribed by law as part of the duties of an administrative office **b :** relating to or being an act done after ascertaining the existence of a specified state of facts in obedience to a legal order without exercise of personal judgment or discretion **3 :** acting or active as an agent **:** INSTRUMENTAL — **min·is·te·ri·al·ly** \-ē-ə-lē\ *adv*

minister plenipotentiary *n, pl* **ministers plenipotentiary :** a diplomatic agent ranking below an ambassador but possessing full power and authority

minister resident *n, pl* **ministers resident :** a diplomatic agent resident at a foreign court or seat of government and ranking below a minister plenipotentiary

¹min·is·trant \ˈmin-ə-strənt\ *adj, archaic* **:** performing service in attendance on someone

²ministrant *n* **:** one that ministers

min·is·tra·tion \ˌmin-ə-ˈstrā-shən\ *n* **:** the act or process of ministering

min·is·try \ˈmin-ə-strē\ *n, pl* **-tries** **1 :** MINISTRATION **2 :** the office, duties, or functions of a minister **3 :** the body of ministers of religion : CLERGY **4 :** AGENCY 2, INSTRUMENTALITY **5 :** the period of service or office of a minister or ministry **6** *often cap* **a :** the body of ministers governing a nation or state from which a smaller cabinet is sometimes selected **b :** the group of ministers constituting a cabinet **7 a :** a government department presided over by a minister **b :** the building in which the business of a ministry is transacted
mini·track \ˈmin-i-ˌtrak\ *n* **:** an electronic system for tracking an earth satellite by radio waves transmitted from it to a chain of ground stations
min·i·um \ˈmin-ē-əm\ *n* [ME, fr. L, cinnabar, red lead, of Iberian origin; akin to Basque *arminéa* cinnabar] **:** RED LEAD
min·i·ver \ˈmin-ə-vər\ *n* [ME *meniver,* fr. OF *menu vair* small vair] **:** a white fur worn orig. by medieval nobles and used chiefly for robes of state
mink \ˈmiŋk\ *n, pl* **mink** *or* **minks** [ME] **1 :** soft fur or pelt of the mink varying in color from white to dark brown **2 :** any of several slender-bodied semiaquatic carnivorous mammals (genus *Mustela*) that resemble and are closely related to the weasels and have partially webbed feet, a rather short bushy tail, and a soft thick coat

mink 2

Minn *abbr* Minnesota
min·ne·sing·er \ˈmin-i-ˌsiŋ-ər, ˈmin-ə-ˌziŋ-\ *n* [G, fr. MHG, fr. *minne* love + *singer*] **:** one of a class of German lyric poets and musicians of the 12th to the 14th centuries
Min·ne·so·ta Multiphasic Personality Inventory \ˌmin-ə-ˈsōt-ə-ˌməl-ti-ˈfā-zik-, -ˌməl-ˌtī-\ *n* [University of *Minnesota*] **:** a test of personal and social adjustment based on a complex scaling of the answers to an elaborate true or false test
min·now \ˈmin-(ˌ)ō, -ə(-w)\ *n, pl* **minnows** *also* **minnow** [ME *menawe;* akin to OE *myne* minnow, Russ *men'* eelpout] **1 a :** a small cyprinid, killifish, or topminnow **b :** any of various small fish that are less than a designated size and are not game fish **2 :** a live or artificial minnow used as bait
¹Mi·no·an \mə-ˈnō-ən, mī-\ *adj* [L *minous* of Minos, fr. Gk *minōios,* fr. *Minōs* Minos] **:** of or relating to a Bronze Age culture of Crete (3000 B.C.–1100 B.C.)
²Minoan *n* **:** a native or inhabitant of ancient Crete
¹mi·nor \ˈmī-nər\ *adj* [ME, fr. L, smaller, inferior; akin to OHG *minniro* smaller, L *minuere* to lessen, Gk *meiōn* less] **1 :** inferior in importance, size, or degree **:** comparatively unimportant **2 :** not having reached majority **3 a :** having the third, sixth, and sometimes the seventh degrees lowered a semitone <~ scale> **b :** based on a minor scale <~ key> **c :** less by a semitone than the corresponding major interval <~ third> **d :** containing a minor third <~ triad> **4 :** not serious or involving risk to life <~ illness> **5 :** of or relating to an academic subject requiring fewer courses than a major
²minor *n* **1 :** a person who has not attained majority **2 :** a minor musical interval, scale, key, or mode **3 a :** a minor academic subject **b :** a student taking a specified minor **4 :** a determinant or matrix obtained from a given determinant or matrix by eliminating the row and column in which a given element lies **5** *pl* **:** minor league baseball
³minor *vi* **:** to take courses in a minor subject
minor axis *n* **:** the chord of an ellipse passing through the center and perpendicular to the major axis
mi·nor·ca \mə-ˈnȯr-kə\ *n* [*Minorca,* one of the Balearic islands] **:** any of a breed of domestic fowls that resemble leghorns but are larger
minor element *n* **:** TRACE ELEMENT
Mi·nor·ite \ˈmī-nə-ˌrīt\ *n* [fr. *Friar Minor* (Franciscan)] **:** FRANCISCAN
mi·nor·i·ty \mə-ˈnȯr-ət-ē, mī-, -ˈnär-\ *n, pl* **-ties** *often attrib* **1 a :** the period before attainment of majority **b :** the state of being a legal minor **2 :** the smaller in number of two groups constituting a whole; *specif* **:** a group having less than the number of votes necessary for control **3 :** a part of a population differing from others in some characteristics and often subjected to differential treatment
minority leader *n* **:** the leader of the minority party in a legislative body
minor league *n* **:** a league of professional clubs in a sport other than the recognized major leagues
minor order *n* **:** one of the Roman Catholic or Eastern clerical orders that are lower in rank and less sacred in character than major orders — usu. used in pl.
minor party *n* **:** a political party whose electoral strength is so small as to prevent its gaining control of a government except in rare and exceptional circumstances
minor penalty *n* **:** a two-minute suspension of a player in ice hockey with no substitute allowed
minor planet *n* **:** ASTEROID
minor premise *n* **:** the premise of a syllogism that contains the minor term
minor seminary *n* **:** a Roman Catholic seminary giving all or part of high school and junior college training with emphasis on preparing candidates for a major seminary
minor suit *n* **:** either of two bridge suits of inferior scoring value: **a :** DIAMONDS **b :** CLUBS
minor term *n* **:** the term of a syllogism that forms the subject of the conclusion
Mi·nos \ˈmī-nəs\ *n* [L, fr. Gk *Minōs*] **:** a son of Zeus and Europa and king of Crete who for his just rule was made supreme judge in the underworld after his death
Mi·no·taur \ˈmin-ə-ˌtȯ(ə)r, ˈmī-nə-\ *n* [ME, fr. MF, fr. L *Minotaurus,* fr. Gk *Minōtauros,* fr. *Minōs* + *tauros* a bull] **:** a monster shaped half like a man and half like a bull, confined in the labyrinth built by Daedalus for Minos, and given a periodical tribute of youths and maidens as food until slain by Theseus
min·ster \ˈmin(t)-stər\ *n* [ME, monastery, church attached to a monastery, fr. OE *mynster,* fr. LL *monasterium* monastery] **:** a large or important church often having cathedral status
min·strel \ˈmin(t)-strəl\ *n* [ME *menestrel,* fr. OF, official, servant, minstrel, fr. LL *ministerialis* imperial household officer, fr. L *ministerium* service, fr. *minister* servant — more at MINISTER] **1 :** one of a class of medieval musical entertainers; *esp* **:** a singer of verses to the accompaniment of a harp **2 a :** MUSICIAN **b :** POET **3 a :** one of a troupe of performers typically giving a program of Negro melodies, jokes, and impersonations and usu. blacked in imitation of Negroes **b :** a performance by a troupe of minstrels
min·strel·sy \-sē\ *n* [ME *minstralcie,* fr. MF *menestralsie,* fr. *menestrel*] **1 :** the singing and playing of a minstrel **2 :** a body of minstrels **3 :** a group of songs or verse
¹mint \ˈmint\ *n* [ME *mynt* coin, money, fr. OE *mynet;* akin to OHG *munizza* coin; both fr. a prehistoric WGmc word borrowed fr. L *moneta* mint, coin, fr. *Moneta,* epithet of Juno; fr. the fact that the Romans coined money in the temple of Juno Moneta] **1 :** a place where coins, medals, or tokens are made **2 :** a place where something is manufactured **3 :** a vast sum or amount
²mint *vt* **1 :** to make (as coins) out of metal **:** COIN **2 :** FABRICATE, INVENT — **mint·er** *n*
³mint *adj* **:** unmarred as if fresh from a mint <~ coins>
⁴mint *n* [ME *minte,* fr. OE; akin to OHG *minza;* both fr. a prehistoric WGmc compound borrowed fr. L *mentha* mint] **1 :** any of a family (Labiatae, the mint family) of aromatic plants with a 4-lobed ovary which produces four 1-seeded nutlets in fruit; *esp* **:** any of a genus (*Mentha*) of mints which have white or pink verticillate flowers with a nearly regular corolla and four equal stamens and some of which are used in flavoring and cookery **2 :** a confection flavored with mint
mint·age \ˈmint-ij\ *n* **1 :** the action or process of minting coins **2 :** an impression placed upon a coin **3 :** coins produced by minting or in a single period of minting **4 :** the cost of minting coins
mint julep *n* **:** JULEP 2
min·u·end \ˈmin-yə-ˌwend\ *n* [L *minuendum,* neut. of *minuendus,* gerundive of *minuere* to lessen — more at MINOR] **:** a number from which the subtrahend is to be subtracted
min·u·et \ˌmin-yə-ˈwet\ *n* [F *menuet,* fr. obs. F, tiny, fr. OF, fr. *menu* small, fr. L *minutus*] **1 :** a slow graceful dance in ¾ time characterized by forward balancing, bowing, and toe pointing **2 :** music for or in the rhythm of a minuet
¹mi·nus \ˈmī-nəs\ *prep* [ME, fr. L *minus,* adv., less, fr. neut. of *minor* smaller — more at MINOR] **1 :** diminished by **:** LESS <seven ~ four is three> **2 :** deprived of **:** WITHOUT <~ his hat>
²minus *n* **1 :** a negative quantity **2 :** DEFICIENCY, DEFECT
³minus *adj* **1 :** algebraically negative <a ~ quantity> **2 :** having negative qualities **3 :** relating to or being a particular one of the two mating types that are required for successful fertilization in sexual reproduction in some lower plants (as a fungus)
¹mi·nus·cule \ˈmin-əs-ˌkyü(ə)l, min-ˈəs-, ˈmin-yəs-, mī-ˈnəs-\ *n* [F, fr. L *minusculus* rather small, dim. of *minor* smaller] **1 a :** one of several ancient and medieval writing styles developed from cursive and having simplified and small forms **b :** a letter in this style **2 :** a lowercase letter
²minuscule *adj* **1 :** written in or in the size or style of minuscules **2 :** very small
minus sign *n* **:** a sign — used in mathematics to indicate subtraction (as in 8−6=2) or a negative quantity (as in −10°)
¹min·ute \ˈmin-ət\ *n* [ME, fr. MF, fr. LL *minuta,* fr. L *minutus* small, fr. pp. of *minuere* to lessen — more at MINOR] **1 :** the 60th part of an hour of time or of a degree **2 :** the distance one can traverse in a minute **3 :** a short space of time **:** MOMENT **4 a :** MEMORANDUM, DRAFT **b** *pl* **:** the official record of the proceedings of a meeting
²minute *vt* **min·ut·ed; min·ut·ing :** to make notes or a brief summary of
³mi·nute \mī-ˈn(y)üt, mə-\ *adj* **mi·nut·er; -est** [L *minutus*] **1 :** very small **:** INFINITESIMAL **2 :** of small importance **:** TRIFLING **3 :** marked by close attention to details ***syn*** see SMALL, CIRCUMSTANTIAL — **mi·nute·ness** *n*
minute hand *n* **:** the long hand that marks the minutes on the face of a watch or clock
¹mi·nute·ly \mī-ˈn(y)üt-lē, mə-\ *adv* **1 :** into very small pieces **2 :** in a minute manner or degree
²min·ute·ly \ˈmin-ət-lē\ *adj, archaic* **:** minute by minute
min·ute·man \ˈmin-ət-ˌman\ *n* **:** a member of a group of armed men pledged to take the field at a minute's notice during and immediately before the American Revolution
min·ute steak \ˌmin-ət-\ *n* **:** a small thin steak that can be quickly cooked
mi·nu·tia \mə-ˈn(y)ü-sh(ē-)ə, mī-\ *n, pl* **-ti·ae** \-shē-ˌē, -ˌī\ [L *minutiae* trifles, details, fr. pl. of *minutia* smallness, fr. *minutus*] **:** a minute or minor detail — usu. used in pl.
minx \ˈmiŋ(k)s\ *n* [origin unknown] **1 :** a pert girl **2** *obs* **:** a wanton woman
MIO *abbr* minimum identifiable odor
mio- — see MI-
Mio·cene \ˈmī-ə-ˌsēn\ *adj* **:** of, relating to, or being an epoch of the Tertiary between the Pliocene and the Oligocene or the corresponding system of rocks — **Miocene** *n*

mi·o·sis \mī-'ō-səs, mē-\ *n, pl* **mi·o·ses** \-ˌsēz\ [NL, fr. Gk *myein* to be closed (of the eyes) + NL *-osis*] : excessive smallness or contraction of the pupil of the eye

1mi·ot·ic \-'ät-ik\ *adj* : relating to or characterized by miosis

2miotic *n* : an agent that causes miosis

mi·que·let \ˌmik-ə-'let, ˌmēk-\ *n* [Sp *miquelete*] : a Spanish or French irregular soldier during the Peninsular War

mir \'mi(ə)r\ *n* [Russ] : a village community in czarist Russia characterized by joint ownership of the land and cultivation by individual families

mi·ra·bi·le dic·tu \mə-ˌräb-ə-lē-'dik-(ˌ)tü\ [L] : wonderful to relate

mi·ra·cid·i·um \ˌmir-ə-'sid-ē-əm, ˌmī-rə-\ *n, pl* **-cid·ia** \-ē-ə\ [NL, fr. Gk *meirak-, meirax* youth, stripling + NL *-idium*] : the free-swimming ciliated first larva of a digenetic trematode that seeks out and penetrates a suitable snail intermediate host in which it develops into a sporocyst — **mi·ra·cid·i·al** \-ē-əl\ *adj*

mir·a·cle \'mir-i-kəl\ *n* [ME, fr. OF, fr. L *miraculum*, fr. *mirari* to wonder at — more at SMILE] **1** : an extraordinary event manifesting divine intervention in human affairs **2** : an extremely outstanding or unusual event, thing, or accomplishment **3** *Christian Science* : a divinely natural occurrence that must be learned humanly

miracle fruit *n* : a small shrubby tropical African tree (*Synsepalum dulcificum* of the family Sapotaceae) whose fruit contains a glycoprotein that when applied to the tongue causes sour substances to taste sweet; *also* : its fruit

miracle play *n* : a medieval dramatic representation of episodes from the life of a miracle-working saint or martyr

mi·rac·u·lous \mə-'rak-yə-ləs\ *adj* [MF *miraculeux*, fr. ML *miraculosus*, fr. L *miraculum*] **1** : of the nature of a miracle : SUPERNATURAL <a ~ event> **2** : suggesting a miracle : MARVELOUS <gave proof of a ~ memory —*Time*> **3** : working or able to work miracles <~ power> — **mi·rac·u·lous·ly** *adv* — **mi·rac·u·lous·ness** *n*

mir·a·dor \'mir-ə-ˌdȯ(ə)r, ˌmir-ə-'\ *n* [Sp, fr. Catal, fr. *mirar* to look at, fr. L *mirari*] : a turret, window, or balcony designed to command an extensive outlook

mi·rage \mə-'räzh\ *n* [F, fr. *mirer* to look at, fr. L *mirari*] **1** : an optical effect that is sometimes seen at sea, in the desert, or over a hot pavement, that may have the appearance of a pool of water or a mirror in which distant objects are seen inverted, and that is caused by the bending or reflection of rays of light by a layer of heated air of varying density **2** : something illusory and unattainable like a mirage ***syn*** see DELUSION

1mire \'mī(ə)r\ *n* [ME, fr. ON *mȳrr*; akin to OE *mōs* marsh — more at MOSS] **1** : wet spongy earth : MARSH, BOG **2** : heavy often deep mud or slush — **miry** \'mī(ə)r-ē\ *adj*

2mire *vb* **mired; mir·ing** *vt* **1 a** : to cause to stick fast in or as if in mire **b** : to hamper or hold back as if by mire : ENTANGLE **2** : to cover or soil with mire ~ *vi* : to stick or sink in mire

mi·rex \'mī-ˌreks\ *n* [origin unknown] : a chlorinated-hydrocarbon insecticide $C_{10}Cl_{12}$ used esp. against ants

mirk, mirky *var of* MURK, MURKY

1mir·ror \'mir-ər\ *n* [ME *mirour*, fr. OF, fr. *mirer* to look at, fr. L *mirari* to wonder at — more at SMILE] **1** : a polished or smooth surface (as of glass) that forms images by reflection **2 a** : something that gives a true representation **b** : an exemplary model — **mir·ror·like** \-ˌlīk\ *adj*

2mirror *vt* : to reflect in or as if in a mirror

mirror image *n* : something that has its parts reversely arranged in comparison with another similar thing or that is reversed with reference to an intervening axis or plane

mirth \'mərth\ *n* [ME, fr. OE *myrgth*, fr. *myrge* merry — more at MERRY] : gladness or gaiety as shown by or accompanied with laughter — **mirth·ful** \-fəl\ *adj* — **mirth·ful·ly** \-fə-lē\ *adv* — **mirth·ful·ness** *n* — **mirth·less** \-ləs\ *adj*

syn MIRTH, GLEE, JOLLITY, HILARITY *shared meaning element* : a mood or temper characterized by joy and high spirits and usually manifested in laughter and merrymaking

MIRV *n* [*m*ultiple *i*ndependently targeted *r*eentry *v*ehicle] : a missile with two or more warheads designed to reenter the atmosphere on the way to separate enemy targets; *also* : any of the warheads of such a missile

1mis- *prefix* [partly fr. ME, fr. OE; partly fr. ME *mes-, mis-*, fr. OF *mes-*, of Gmc origin; akin to OE *mis-*; akin to OE *missan* to miss] **1 a** : badly : wrongly <*mis*judge> **b** : unfavorably <*mis*esteem> **c** : in a suspicious manner <*mis*doubt> **2** : bad : wrong <*mis*deed> **3** : opposite or lack of <*mis*trust> **4** : not <*mis*know>

2mis- *or* **miso-** *comb form* [Gk, fr. *misein* to hate] : hatred <*mi*sogamy>

mis·ad·ven·ture \ˌmis-əd-'ven-chər\ *n* [ME *mesaventure*, fr. OF, fr. *mesavenir* to chance badly, fr. *mis-* + *avenir* to chance, happen, fr. L *advenire* — more at ADVENTURE] : MISFORTUNE, MISHAP

mis·aligned \ˌmis-ə-'līnd\ *adj* : not properly aligned — **mis·align·ment** \-'līn-mənt\ *n*

mis·al·li·ance \ˌmis-ə-'lī-ən(t)s\ *n* [modif. of F *mésalliance*] **1** : an improper alliance **2 a** : MÉSALLIANCE **b** : a marriage between persons unsuited to each other

mis·al·lo·ca·tion \(ˌ)mis-ˌal-ə-'kā-shən\ *n* : faulty or improper allocation <dangerous ~ of our intellectual resources —K. E. Boulding>

mis·an·thrope \'mis-ᵊn-ˌthrōp\ *n* [Gk *misanthrōpos* hating mankind, fr. *mis-* + *anthrōpos* man] : one who hates or distrusts mankind

mis·an·throp·ic \ˌmis-ᵊn-'thräp-ik\ *adj* **1** : of, relating to, or characteristic of a misanthrope **2** : marked by a hatred or contempt for mankind ***syn*** see CYNICAL ***ant*** philanthropic — **mis·an·throp·i·cal·ly** \-i-k(ə-)lē\ *adv*

mis·an·thro·py \mis-'an(t)-thrə-pē\ *n* : a hatred or distrust of mankind

mis·ap·pli·ca·tion \(ˌ)mis-ˌap-lə-'kā-shən\ *n* : the act or an instance of misapplying

mis·ap·ply \ˌmis-ə-'plī\ *vt* : to apply wrongly

mis·ap·pre·hend \(ˌ)mis-ˌap-ri-'hend\ *vt* : to apprehend wrongly : MISUNDERSTAND — **mis·ap·pre·hen·sion** \-'hen-chən\ *n*

mis·ap·pro·pri·ate \ˌmis-ə-'prō-prē-ˌāt\ *vt* : to appropriate wrongly (as by theft or embezzlement) — **mis·ap·pro·pri·a·tion** \-ˌprō-prē-'ā-shən\ *n*

mis·be·come \ˌmis-bi-'kəm\ *vt* : to be inappropriate or unbecoming to

mis·be·got·ten \-'gät-ᵊn\ *adj* **1** : unlawfully conceived : ILLEGITIMATE <a ~ child> **2 a** : having a disreputable or improper origin : ill-conceived <antiquated and ~ tax laws —R. M. Blough> **b** : CONTEMPTIBLE, DEFORMED <a ~ scoundrel>

mis·be·have \ˌmis-bi-'hāv\ *vi* : to behave improperly — **mis·be·hav·er** *n* — **mis·be·hav·ior** \-'hā-vyər\ *n*

mis·be·lief \ˌmis-bə-'lēf\ *n* : erroneous or false belief

mis·be·lieve \-'lēv\ *vi, obs* : to hold a false or unorthodox belief

mis·be·liev·er \-'lē-vər\ *n* : HERETIC, INFIDEL

mis·brand \(')mis-'brand\ *vt* : to brand falsely or in a misleading way; *also* : to label in violation of statutory requirements

misc *abbr* miscellaneous

mis·cal·cu·late \(')mis-'kal-kyə-ˌlāt\ *vt* : to calculate wrongly ~ *vi* : to make a mistake in calculation — **mis·cal·cu·la·tion** \(ˌ)mis-ˌkal-kyə-'lā-shən\ *n*

mis·call \(')mis-'kȯl\ *vt* : to call by a wrong name : MISNAME

mis·car·riage \mis-'kar-ij\ *n* **1** : corrupt or incompetent management; *esp* : a failure in the administration of justice **2** : expulsion of a human fetus before it is viable and esp. between the 12th and 28th weeks of gestation

mis·car·ry \(')mis-'kar-ē\ *vi* **1** *obs* : to come to harm **2** : to suffer miscarriage of a fetus **3** : to fail of the intended purpose : go wrong or amiss <the plan *miscarried*>

mis·cast \(')mis-'kast\ *vt* **-cast; -cast·ing** : to cast in an unsuitable role <life had ~ her in the role of wife and mother —Edna Ferber>

mis·ce·ge·na·tion \(ˌ)mis-ˌej-ə-'nā-shən, ˌmis-i-jə-'nā-\ *n* [L *miscēre* to mix + *genus* race — more at MIX, KIN] : a mixture of races; *esp* : marriage or cohabitation between a white person and a member of another race — **mis·ce·ge·na·tion·al** \-shnəl, -shən-ᵊl\ *adj*

mis·cel·la·nea \ˌmis-ə-'lā-nē-ə, -nyə\ *n pl* [L, fr. neut. pl. of *miscellaneus*] : a collection of miscellaneous objects or writings

mis·cel·la·neous \ˌmis-ə-'lā-nē-əs, -nyəs\ *adj* [L *miscellaneus*, fr. *miscellus* mixed, prob. fr. *miscēre*] **1** : consisting of diverse things or members : HETEROGENEOUS **2 a** : having various traits **b** : dealing with or interested in diverse subjects <as a writer I was too ~ —George Santayana> — **mis·cel·la·neous·ly** *adv* — **mis·cel·la·neous·ness** *n*

mis·cel·la·nist \'mis-ə-ˌlā-nəst, *chiefly Brit* mis-'el-ə-nist\ *n* : a writer of miscellanies

mis·cel·la·ny \-nē\ *n, pl* **-nies** [prob. modif. of F *miscellanées*, pl., fr. L *miscellanea*] **1** : a mixture of various things **2 a** *pl* : separate writings collected in one volume **b** : a collection of writings on various subjects

mis·chance \(')mis(h)-'chan(t)s\ *n* [ME *mischaunce*, fr. OF *meschance*, fr. *mis-* + *chance*] **1** : bad luck **2** : a piece of bad luck : MISHAP ***syn*** see MISFORTUNE

mis·chief \'mis(h)-chəf\ *n* [ME *meschief*, fr. OF, calamity, fr. *mes-* + *chief* head, end — more at CHIEF] **1** : a specific injury or damage attributed to a particular agent **2** : a cause or source of harm, evil, or irritation; *esp* : a person who causes mischief **3 a** : action that annoys or irritates **b** : the quality or state of being mischievous : MISCHIEVOUSNESS <had ~ in his eyes>

mis·chie·vous \'mis(h)-chə-vəs\ *adj* **1** : HARMFUL, INJURIOUS <~ gossip> **2 a** : able or tending to cause annoyance, trouble, or minor injury **b** : irresponsibly playful <~ behavior> — **mis·chie·vous·ly** *adv* — **mis·chie·vous·ness** *n*

misch metal \'mish-\ *n* [G *mischmetall*, fr. *mischen* to mix + *metall* metal] : a complex alloy of rare earth metals used esp. in tracer bullets and as a flint in lighters

mis·ci·ble \'mis-ə-bəl\ *adj* [ML *miscibilis*, fr. L *miscēre* to mix — more at MIX] : capable of being mixed; *specif* : capable of mixing in any ratio without separation of two phases <~ liquids> — **mis·ci·bil·i·ty** \ˌmis-ə-'bil-ət-ē\ *n*

mis·clas·si·fy \(')mis-'klas-ə-ˌfī\ *vt* : to classify wrongly — **mis·clas·si·fi·ca·tion** \(ˌ)mis-ˌklas-ə-fə-'kā-shən\ *n*

mis·com·mu·ni·ca·tion \ˌmis-kə-ˌmyü-nə-'kā-shən\ *n* : failure to communicate clearly

mis·con·ceive \ˌmis-kən-'sēv\ *vt* : to interpret incorrectly : MISUNDERSTAND — **mis·con·ceiv·er** *n* — **mis·con·cep·tion** \-'sep-shən\ *n*

mis·con·duct \(')mis-'kän-(ˌ)dəkt\ *n* **1** : mismanagement esp. of governmental or military responsibilities **2** : intentional wrongdoing; *specif* : deliberate violation of a law or standard esp. by a government official : MALFEASANCE **3 a** : improper behavior **b** : ADULTERY — **mis·con·duct** \ˌmis-kən-'dəkt\ *vt*

mis·con·struc·tion \ˌmis-kən-'strək-shən\ *n* : the act, the process, or an instance of misconstruing

mis·con·strue \ˌmis-kən-'strü\ *vt* : to construe wrongly : MISINTERPRET

mis·count \(')mis-'kau̇nt\ *vb* [ME *misconten*, fr. MF *mesconter*, fr. *mes-* + *conter* to count] *vt* : to count wrongly : MISCALCULATE ~ *vi* : to make a wrong count — **miscount** \(')mis-'kau̇nt, 'mis-ˌ\ *n*

1mis·cre·ant \'mis-krē-ənt\ *adj* [ME *miscreaunt*, fr. MF *mescreant*, prp. of *mescroire* to disbelieve, fr. *mes-* 1mis- + *croire* to believe, fr. L *credere* — more at CREED] **1** : UNBELIEVING, HERETICAL **2** : DEPRAVED, VILLAINOUS

2miscreant *n* **1** : INFIDEL, HERETIC **2** : one who behaves criminally or viciously

mis·cre·ate \ˌmis-krē-'āt\ *vt* : to create badly or wrongly — **mis·cre·ate** \'mis-krē-ət, ˌmis-krē-'āt\ *adj* — **mis·cre·ation** \ˌmis-krē-'ā-shən\ *n*

1mis·cue \(')mis-'kyü\ *n* **1** : a faulty stroke in billiards in which the cue slips **2** : MISTAKE, SLIP

2miscue *vi* **1** : to make a miscue **2 a** : to miss a stage cue **b** : to answer a wrong cue

mis·deal \(')mis-'dē(ə)l\ *vi* : to deal cards incorrectly ~ *vt* : to deal incorrectly — **misdeal** *n*

mis·deed \(ˌ)mis-ˈdēd\ *n* : a wrong deed : OFFENSE
mis·deem \-ˈdēm\ *vt* : MISJUDGE
mis·de·mean·ant \ˌmis-di-ˈmē-nənt\ *n* : a person convicted of a misdemeanor
mis·de·mean·or \ˌmis-di-ˈmē-nər\ *n* **1** : a crime less serious than a felony **2** : MISDEED
mis·de·scribe \ˌmis-di-ˈskrīb\ *vt* : to describe wrongly — **mis·de·scrip·tion** \-ˈskrip-shən\ *n*
mis·di·ag·nose \(ˌ)mis-ˈdī-ig-ˌnōs, -ˌnōz\ *vt* : to diagnose incorrectly
mis·di·ag·no·sis \(ˌ)mis-ˌdī-ig-ˈnō-səs\ *n* : an incorrect diagnosis
mis·di·rect \ˌmis-də-ˈrekt, -(ˌ)dī-\ *vt* : to give a wrong direction to
mis·di·rec·tion \-ˈrek-shən\ *n* **1 a** : the act or an instance of misdirecting **b** : the state of being misdirected **2** : a wrong direction
mis·do \(ˌ)mis-ˈdü\ *vt* **-did** \-ˈdid\; **-done** \-ˈdən\; **-do·ing** \-ˈdü-iŋ\; **-does** \-ˈdəz\ : to do wrongly or improperly — **mis·do·er** *n* — **mis·do·ing** *n*
mis·doubt \(ˌ)mis-ˈdau̇t\ *vt* **1** : to doubt the reality or truth of **2** : SUSPECT, FEAR — **misdoubt** *n*
mis·ed·u·cate \(ˌ)mis-ˈej-ə-ˌkāt\ *vt* : to educate wrongly — **mis·ed·u·ca·tion** \(ˌ)mis-ˌej-ə-ˈkā-shən\ *n*
mise–en–scène \ˌmē-ˌzäⁿ-ˈsen, -ˈsän\ *n, pl* **mise–en–scènes** \-ˈsen(z), -ˈsän(z)\ [F *mise en scène*] **1 a** : the arrangement of actors and scenery on a stage for a theatrical production **b** : stage setting **2 a** : the physical setting of an action **b** : ENVIRONMENT, MILIEU
mi·ser \ˈmī-zər\ *n* [L *miser* miserable] : a mean grasping person; *esp* : one who lives miserably in order to hoard his wealth
mis·er·a·ble \ˈmiz-ər-bəl, ˈmiz-(ə-)rə-bəl\ *adj* [ME, fr. MF, fr. L *miserabilis* wretched, pitiable, fr. *miserari* to pity, fr. *miser*] **1 a** : wretchedly inadequate or meager <a ~ hovel> **b** : causing extreme discomfort or unhappiness <a ~ situation> **2** : being in a pitiable state of distress or unhappiness (as from want or shame) <~ refugees> **3** : being likely to discredit or shame <his ~ neglect of his wife> <it was ~ of you to make fun of him> — **miserable** *n* — **mis·er·a·ble·ness** *n* — **mis·er·a·bly** \-blē\ *adv*
syn MISERABLE, WRETCHED *shared meaning element* : deplorably or distressingly bad or mean. MISERABLE implies a state of suffering that may arise from extreme distress of body or mind or in pitiable poverty or degradation <a *miserable* creature of a crazed aspect . . . shattered and made drunk by horror —Charles Dickens> In reference to things, *miserable,* often used hyperbolically, suggests such meanness or inferiority or unpleasantness as must inflict misery on a person affected or arouse utter dislike or disgust in an observer <worked for a *miserable* wage> <the squalor of mean and *miserable* streets —Laurence Binyon> WRETCHED is likely to stress the unhappiness of a person exposed to a grave distress (as want, grief, oppression, pain, or anxiety) <the *wretched* wife of the innocent man thus doomed to die —Charles Dickens> Applied to things, *wretched* stresses extreme or deplorable badness <a *wretched* French cabaret, smelling vilely —George Meredith> ***ant*** comfortable
mi·se·re·re \ˌmiz-ə-ˈri(ə)r-ē, -ˈre(ə)r-; ˌmē-zə-ˈrā-(ˌ)rā\ *n* [L, be merciful, fr. *misereri* to be merciful, fr. *miser* wretched; fr. the first word of the Psalm] **1** *cap* : the 50th Psalm in the Vulgate **2** : MISERICORD **3** : a vocal complaint or lament
mi·seri·cord *or* **mi·seri·corde** \mə-ˈzer-ə-ˌkȯ(ə)rd, -ˈser-\ *n* [ML *misercordia* seat in church, fr. L, mercy, fr. *misericord-, misericors* merciful, fr. *misereri* + *cord-, cor* heart — more at HEART] : a small projection on the bottom of a hinged church seat that gives support to a standing worshiper when the seat is turned up
mi·ser·ly \ˈmī-zər-lē\ *adj* : of, relating to, or characteristic of a miser; *esp* : marked by sordid grasping meanness and penuriousness ***syn*** see STINGY — **mi·ser·li·ness** *n*
mis·ery \ˈmiz-(ə-)rē\ *n, pl* **-er·ies** **1** : a state of suffering and want that is the result of poverty or affliction **2** : a circumstance, thing, or place that causes suffering or discomfort **3** : a state of great unhappiness and emotional distress ***syn*** see DISTRESS
mis·es·teem \ˌmis-ə-ˈstēm\ *vt* : to esteem wrongly; *esp* : to hold in too little regard
mis·es·ti·mate \(ˌ)mis-ˈes-tə-ˌmāt\ *vt* : to estimate wrongly — **mis·es·ti·ma·tion** \(ˌ)mis-ˌes-tə-ˈmā-shən\ *n*
mis·fea·sance \mis-ˈfēz-ᵊn(t)s\ *n* [MF *mesfaisance,* fr. *mesfaire* to do wrong, fr. *mes-* ¹mis- + *faire* to make, do, fr. L *facere* — more at DO] : TRESPASS; *specif* : the performance of a lawful action in an illegal or improper manner — **mis·fea·sor** \-ˈfē-zər, -ˌzȯ(ə)r\ *n*
mis·file \(ˌ)mis-ˈfī(ə)l\ *vt* : to file in an inappropriate place
¹**mis·fire** \(ˌ)mis-ˈfī(ə)r\ *vi* **1** : to have the explosive or propulsive charge fail to ignite at the proper time <the engine *misfired*> **2** : to fail to fire <the gun *misfired*> **3** : to miss an intended effect or objective
²**mis·fire** \(ˌ)mis-ˈfī(ə)r, ˈmis-ˌ\ *n* **1** : a failure to fire **2** : something that misfires
mis·fit \ˈmis-ˌfit, (ˌ)mis-ˈfit\ *n* **1** : something that fits badly **2** : a person poorly adjusted to his environment <social ~*s*>
mis·for·tune \(ˌ)mis-ˈfȯr-chən\ *n* **1 a** : an event or conjunction of events that causes an unfortunate or distressing result : bad fortune <by ~ he fell into bad company> <had the ~ to break his leg> **b** : the ensuing unhappy situation <always ready to help people in ~> **2** : a distressing or unfortunate incident or event <~*s* never come singly>
syn MISFORTUNE, MISCHANCE, MISHAP, ADVERSITY *shared meaning element* : adverse fortune or an instance of this ***ant*** happiness, prosperity
mis·give \(ˌ)mis-ˈgiv\ *vb* **-gave** \-ˈgāv\; **-giv·en** \-ˈgiv-ən\; **-giv·ing** *vt* : to suggest doubt or fear to ~ *vi* : to be fearful or apprehensive
mis·giv·ing \-ˈgiv-iŋ\ *n* : a feeling of doubt or suspicion esp. concerning a future event
mis·gov·ern \(ˌ)mis-ˈgəv-ərn\ *vt* : to govern badly — **mis·gov·ern·ment** \-ˈgəv-ər(n)-mənt, -ˈgəv-ᵊm-ənt\ *n*
mis·guid·ance \(ˌ)mis-ˈgīd-ᵊn(t)s\ *n* : MISDIRECTION
mis·guide \-ˈgīd\ *vt* : to lead astray : MISDIRECT <well-meaning but *misguided* benefactors> — **mis·guid·ed·ly** *adv* — **mis·guid·ed·ness** *n* — **mis·guid·er** *n*
mis·han·dle \-ˈhan-dᵊl\ *vt* **1** : to treat roughly : MALTREAT **2** : to manage wrongly or ignorantly
mi·shan·ter \mish-ˈänt-ər\ *n* [ME *misaunter,* alter. of *mesaventure*] *chiefly Scot* : MISADVENTURE
mis·hap \ˈmis-ˌhap, mis-ˈ\ *n* **1** : bad luck : MISFORTUNE **2** : an unfortunate accident ***syn*** see MISFORTUNE
mis·hear \(ˌ)mis-ˈhi(ə)r\ *vt* : to hear wrongly ~ *vi* : to misunderstand what is heard
mis·hit \(ˌ)mis-ˈhit\ *vt* **-hit; -hit·ting** : to hit in a faulty manner — **mis·hit** \(ˌ)mis-ˈhit, ˈmis-ˌ\ *n*
mish·mash \ˈmish-ˌmäsh, -ˌmash\ *n* [partly fr. MHG *misch-masch,* redupl. of *mischen* to mix; partly fr. Yiddish *mishmash,* fr. MHG *mischmasch*] : HODGEPODGE, JUMBLE <a ~ of proprietaries, toiletries, cosmetics, and confections —*Forbes*>
Mish·mi \ˈmish-mē\ *n* : a Tibeto-Burman language of northeastern India
Mish·nah *or* **Mish·na** \ˈmish-nə\ *n* [Heb *mishnāh* instruction, oral law] : the collection of mostly halakic Jewish traditions compiled about A.D. 200 and made the basic part of the Talmud — **Mish·na·ic** \mish-ˈnā-ik\ *adj*
mis·iden·ti·fy \ˌmis-ī-ˈdent-ə-ˌfī, ˌmis-ə-\ *vt* : to identify wrongly — **mis·iden·ti·fi·ca·tion** \-ˌdent-ə-fə-ˈkā-shən\ *n*
mis·im·pres·sion \ˌmis-im-ˈpresh-ən\ *n* : a mistaken impression
mis·in·form \ˌmis-ᵊn-ˈfȯ(ə)rm\ *vt* : to give untrue or misleading information to — **mis·in·for·ma·tion** \(ˌ)mis-ˌin-fər-ˈmā-shən\ *n*
mis·in·ter·pret \ˌmis-ᵊn-ˈtər-prət, *rapid* -pət\ *vt* **1** : to understand wrongly **2** : to explain wrongly — **mis·in·ter·pre·ta·tion** \-ˌtər-prə-ˈtā-shən, *rapid* -pə-\ *n*
mis·join·der \(ˌ)mis-ˈjȯin-dər\ *n* : an improper union of parties or of causes of action in a single legal proceeding
mis·judge \(ˌ)mis-ˈjəj\ *vt* **1** : to estimate wrongly **2** : to have an unjust opinion of ~ *vi* : to be mistaken in judgment — **mis·judg·ment** \-ˈjəj-mənt\ *n*
Mi·ski·to \mis-ˈkēt-(ˌ)ō\ *n, pl* **Miskito** *or* **Miskitos** **1** : a member of a people of the Atlantic coast of Nicaragua and Honduras **2** : a language of the Miskito people
mis·know \-ˈnō\ *vt* : MISUNDERSTAND — **mis·knowl·edge** \-ˈnäl-ij\ *n*
mis·la·bel \-ˈlā-bəl\ *vt* : to label incorrectly or falsely
mis·lay \(ˌ)mis-ˈlā\ *vt* **-laid** \-ˈlād\; **-lay·ing** : to put in an unremembered place : LOSE
mis·lead \(ˌ)mis-ˈlēd\ *vt* **-led** \-ˈled\; **-lead·ing** : to lead in a wrong direction or into a mistaken action or belief often by deliberate deceit ***syn*** see DECEIVE — **mis·lead·er** *n* — **mis·lead·ing·ly** \-iŋ-lē\ *adv*
mis·leared \-ˈli(ə)rd, -ˈle(ə)rd\ *adj* [¹*mis-* + *lear* (to learn)] *chiefly Scot* : UNMANNERLY, ILL-BRED
mis·like \-ˈlīk\ *vt* **1** *archaic* : DISPLEASE **2** : DISLIKE — **mislike** *n*
mis·man·age \(ˌ)mis-ˈman-ij\ *vt* : to manage wrongly or incompetently — **mis·man·age·ment** \-mənt\ *n*
mis·mar·riage \-ˈmar-ij\ *n* : an unsuitable marriage
mis·match \(ˌ)mis-ˈmach\ *vt* : to match wrongly or unsuitably — **mis·match** \(ˌ)mis-ˈmach, ˈmis-ˌ\ *n*
mis·mate \(ˌ)mis-ˈmāt\ *vt* : to mate unsuitably
mis·name \-ˈnām\ *vt* : to name incorrectly : MISCALL
mis·no·mer \(ˌ)mis-ˈnō-mər\ *n* [ME *misnoumer,* fr. MF *mesnommer* to misname, fr. *mes-* ¹mis- + *nommer* to name, fr. L *nominare* — more at NOMINATE] **1** : the misnaming of a person in a legal instrument **2 a** : a use of a wrong name **b** : a wrong name or designation — **mis·no·mered** \-mərd\ *adj*
mi·so \ˈmē-(ˌ)sō\ *n* [Jap] : a food paste that is used esp. in preparing soups and that is made by grinding a mixture of steamed rice, cooked soybeans, and salt and fermenting it in brine
miso- — see MIS-
mi·sog·a·mist \mə-ˈsäg-ə-məst\ *n* [*misogamy*] : one who hates marriage — **mi·sog·a·my** \-ə-mē\ *n*
miso·gy·nic \ˌmis-ə-ˈjin-ik, -ˈgin-\ *adj* [*misogyny,* fr. Gk *misogynia,* fr. *mis-* + *gynē* woman — more at QUEEN] : having or showing a hatred and distrust of women ***syn*** see CYNICAL — **mi·sog·y·nist** \mə-ˈsäj-ə-nəst\ *n* — **mi·sog·y·nis·tic** \mə-ˌsäj-ə-ˈnis-tik\ *adj* — **mi·sog·y·ny** \mə-ˈsäj-ə-nē\ *n*
mi·sol·o·gy \mə-ˈsäl-ə-jē\ *n* [Gk *misologia,* fr. *mis-* + *-logia* -logy] : a hatred of argument, reasoning, or enlightenment
miso·ne·ism \ˌmis-ə-ˈnē-ˌiz-əm\ *n* [It *misoneismo,* fr. *mis-* + Gk *neos* new + It *-ismo* -ism — more at NEW] : a hatred, fear, or intolerance of innovation or change
mis·ori·ent \(ˌ)mis-ˈōr-ē-ˌent, -ˈȯr-\ *vt* : to orient improperly or incorrectly — **mis·ori·en·ta·tion** \(ˌ)mis-ˌōr-ē-ən-ˈtā-shən, -ˌȯr-, -ˌen-\ *n*
mis·per·ceive \ˌmis-pər-ˈsēv\ *vt* : to perceive incorrectly or falsely : MISUNDERSTAND — **mis·per·cep·tion** \-ˈsep-shən\ *n*
mis·place \(ˌ)mis-ˈplās\ *vt* **1 a** : to put in a wrong place <~ a comma> **b** : MISLAY <*misplaced* his keys> **2** : to set on a wrong object or eventuality <his trust had been *misplaced*> — **mis·place·ment** \-ˈplā-smənt\ *n*
mis·play \(ˌ)mis-ˈplā\ *n* : a wrong or unskillful play : ERROR <one ~ caused them to lose the game> — **mis·play** \(ˌ)mis-ˈplā, ˈmis-ˌ\ *vt*
mis·print \(ˌ)mis-ˈprint\ *vt* : to print incorrectly — **mis·print** \ˈmis-ˌprint, (ˌ)mis-ˈ\ *n*
¹**mis·pri·sion** \mis-ˈprizh-ən\ *n* [ME, fr. MF *mesprison* error, wrongdoing, fr. OF, fr. *mespris,* pp. of *mesprendre* to make a mistake, fr. *mes-* mis- + *prendre* to take, fr. L *prehendere* to seize — more at PREHENSILE] **1 a** : neglect or wrong performance of official duty **b** : concealment of treason or felony by one who is not a participant in the treason or felony **c** : seditious conduct

against the government or the courts **2 :** MISUNDERSTANDING, MISTAKE
[2]misprision *n* [*misprize*] **:** CONTEMPT, SCORN
mis·prize \(ˈ)mis-ˈprīz\ *vt* [MF *mesprisier*, fr. *mes-* mis- + *prisier* to appraise — more at PRIZE] **1 :** to hold in contempt **:** DESPISE **2 :** UNDERVALUE
mis·pro·nounce \ˌmis-prə-ˈnau̇n(t)s\ *vt* **:** to pronounce incorrectly or in a way regarded as incorrect
mis·pro·nun·ci·a·tion \-ˌnən(t)-sē-ˈā-shən\ *n* **:** the act or an instance of mispronouncing
mis·quote \(ˈ)mis-ˈkwōt *also* -ˈkōt\ *vt* **:** to quote incorrectly — **mis·quo·ta·tion** \ˈmis-kwō-ˈtā-shən *also* -kō-\ *n*
mis·read \(ˈ)mis-ˈrēd\ *vt* **-read** \-ˈred\; **-read·ing** \-ˈrēd-iŋ\ **1 :** to read incorrectly **2 :** to misinterpret in or as if in reading <totally ~ the lesson of history —Christopher Hollis>
mis·reck·on \-ˈrek-ən\ *vb* **:** MISCALCULATE, MISCOUNT
mis·re·mem·ber \ˌmis-ri-ˈmem-bər\ *vt* **:** to remember incorrectly or inadequately
mis·re·port \-ˈpō(ə)rt, -ˈpȯ(ə)rt\ *vt* **:** to report falsely — **misreport** *n*
mis·rep·re·sent \(ˌ)mis-ˌrep-ri-ˈzent\ *vt* **1 :** to give a false or misleading representation of usu. with an intent to deceive or be unfair <~*ed* the facts to suit his purpose> **2 :** to serve badly or improperly as a representative of — **mis·rep·re·sen·ta·tion** \(ˌ)mis-ˌrep-ri-ˌzen-ˈtā-shən, -zən-\ *n* — **mis·rep·re·sen·ta·tive** \-ˈzent-ət-iv\ *adj*
syn MISREPRESENT, FALSIFY, BELIE, GARBLE *shared meaning element* **:** to present or represent in a manner at odds with the truth
[1]mis·rule \(ˈ)mis-ˈrül\ *vt* **:** to rule incompetently **:** MISGOVERN
[2]misrule *n* **1 :** the action of misruling **:** the condition of being misruled **2 :** DISORDER, ANARCHY
[1]miss \ˈmis\ *vb* [ME *missen*, fr. OE *missan*; akin to OHG *missan* to miss, L *mutare* to change] *vt* **1 :** to fail to hit, reach, or contact **2 :** to discover or feel the absence of **3 :** to fail to obtain **4 :** ESCAPE, AVOID <just ~*ed* hitting the other car> **5 :** to leave out **:** OMIT **6 :** to fail to comprehend, sense, or experience <he ~*ed* the point of the speech> **7 :** to fail to perform or attend <had to ~ school for a week> ~ *vi* **1** *archaic* **:** to fail to get, reach, or do something **2 :** to fail to hit something **3 a :** to be unsuccessful **b :** MISFIRE <the engine ~*ed*> — **miss out on :** to lose a good opportunity <people who *missed out on* a college education —*Atlantic*> — **miss the boat :** to fail to take advantage of an opportunity
[2]miss *n* **1** *chiefly dial* **:** disadvantage or regret resulting from loss <we know the ~ of you, and even hunger . . . to see you —Samuel Richardson> **2 a :** a failure to hit **b :** a failure to attain a desired result **3 :** MISFIRE
[3]miss *n* [short for *mistress*] **1 a** — used as a title prefixed to the name of an unmarried woman or girl **b** — used before the name of a place or of a line of activity or before some epithet to form a title for a usu. young unmarried female who is representative of the thing indicated <*Miss* America> **2 :** young lady — used without a name as a conventional term of address to a young woman **3 :** a young unmarried woman or girl
Miss *abbr* Mississippi
mis·sa can·ta·ta \ˌmis-ə-kən-ˈtät-ə\ *n* [NL, sung mass] **:** HIGH MASS
mis·sal \ˈmis-əl\ *n* [ME *messel*, fr. MF & ML; MF, fr. ML *missale*, fr. neut. of *missalis* of the mass, fr. LL *missa* mass — more at MASS] **:** a book containing all that is said or sung at mass during the entire year
mis·send \(ˈ)mis-ˈsend\ *vt* **:** to send incorrectly <*missent* mail>
mis·sense \ˈmis-ˌsen(t)s\ *n* [*mis-* + *-sense* (as in *nonsense*)] **:** genetic mutation involving alteration of one or more codons so that different amino acids are determined
mis·shape \(ˈ)mis(h)-ˈshāp\ *vt* **:** to shape badly **:** DEFORM — **mis·shap·en** \-ˈshā-pən\ *adj* — **mis·shap·en·ly** *adv*
[1]mis·sile \ˈmis-əl, *chiefly Brit* -ˌīl\ *adj* [L *missilis*, fr. *missus*, pp. of *mittere* to throw, send — more at SMITE] **1 :** capable of being thrown or projected to strike a distant object **2 :** adapted for throwing or hurling missiles **3 :** of or relating to missiles <a ~ crisis>
[2]missile *n* **:** an object (as a weapon) thrown or projected usu. so as to strike something at a distance <stones, artillery shells, bullets, and rockets are ~*s*>: as **a :** GUIDED MISSILE **b :** BALLISTIC MISSILE
mis·sil·eer \ˌmis-ə-ˈli(ə)r\ *n* **:** MISSILEMAN
mis·sile·man \ˈmis-əl-mən\ *n* **:** one engaged in designing, building, or operating guided missiles
mis·sile·ry *also* **mis·sil·ry** \ˈmis-əl-rē\ *n* **1 :** MISSILES; *esp* **:** GUIDED MISSILES **2 :** the science dealing with the design, manufacture, and use of guided missiles
miss·ing \ˈmis-iŋ\ *adj* **:** ABSENT; *also* **:** LOST <~ in action>
missing link *n* **1 :** an absent member needed to complete a series **2 :** a hypothetical intermediate form between man and his presumed simian progenitors
mis·si·ol·o·gy \ˌmis-ē-ˈäl-ə-jē\ *n* [*mission* + *-logy*] **:** the study of the church's mission esp. with respect to missionary activity
[1]mis·sion \ˈmish-ən\ *n* [NL, ML, & L; NL *mission-*, *missio* religious mission, fr. ML, task assigned, fr. L, act of sending, fr. *missus*, pp. of *mittere*] **1** *obs* **:** the act or an instance of sending **2 a :** a ministry commissioned by a religious organization to propagate its faith or carry on humanitarian work **b :** assignment to or work in a field of missionary enterprise **c** (1) **:** a mission establishment (2) **:** a local church or parish dependent on a larger religious organization for direction or financial support **d** *pl* **:** organized missionary work **e :** a course of sermons and services given to convert the unchurched or quicken Christian faith **3 :** a body of persons sent to perform a service or carry on an activity: as **a :** a group sent to a foreign country to conduct diplomatic or political negotiations **b :** a permanent embassy or legation **c :** a team of specialists or cultural leaders sent to a foreign country **4 a :** a specific task with which a person or a group is charged **b** (1) **:** a definite military, naval, or aerospace task <a bombing ~> <a space ~> (2) **:** a flight operation of an aircraft or spacecraft in the performance of a mission <a ~ to Mars> **5 :** CALLING, VOCATION
[2]mission *vt* **mis·sioned; mis·sion·ing** \ˈmish-(ə-)niŋ\ **1 :** to send on or entrust with a mission **2 :** to carry on a religious mission among or in
[3]mission *adj* **:** of or relating to a style used in the early Spanish missions of the southwestern U.S. <~ architecture>
[1]mis·sion·ary \ˈmish-ə-ˌner-ē\ *adj* **1 :** relating to, engaged in, or devoted to missions **2 :** characteristic of a missionary
[2]missionary *n, pl* **-ar·ies :** a person undertaking a mission and esp. a religious mission
mis·sion·er \ˈmish-(ə-)nər\ *n* **:** MISSIONARY
mis·sion·ize \ˈmish-ə-ˌnīz\ *vb* **-ized; -iz·ing** *vi* **:** to carry on missionary work ~ *vt* **:** to do missionary work among — **mis·sion·iza·tion** \ˌmish-ə-nə-ˈzā-shən\ *n* — **mis·sion·iz·er** \ˈmish-ə-ˌnī-zər\ *n*
Mis·sis·sip·pi·an \ˌmis-(ə-)ˈsip-ē-ən\ *adj* [*Mississippi* river] **1 :** of or relating to Mississippi, its people, or the Mississippi river **2 :** of, relating to, or being the period of the Paleozoic era in No. America following the Devonian and preceding the Pennsylvanian or the corresponding system of rocks — **Mississippian** *n*
mis·sive \ˈmis-iv\ *n* [MF *lettre missive*, lit., letter intended to be sent] **:** a written communication **:** LETTER
miss·out \ˈmis-ˌau̇t\ *n* **:** a throw of dice that loses the main bet
mis·spell \(ˈ)mis-ˈspel\ *vt* **:** to spell incorrectly
mis·spell·ing \-iŋ\ *n* **:** an incorrect spelling
mis·spend \(ˈ)mis-ˈspend\ *vt* **-spent** \-ˈspent\; **-spend·ing :** to spend wrongly **:** SQUANDER <a *misspent* life>
mis·state \(ˈ)mis-ˈstāt\ *vt* **:** to state incorrectly **:** give a false account of — **mis·state·ment** \-mənt\ *n*
mis·step \-ˈstep\ *n* **1 :** a wrong step **2 :** a mistake in judgment or action **:** BLUNDER
mis·sus *or* **mis·sis** \ˈmis-əz, -əs, *esp South* ˈmiz-\ *n* [alter. of *mistress*] **1 :** WIFE <men spend money on themselves, but argue over every dime the ~ wants —W. A. Lydgate> **2** *dial* **:** MISTRESS 1a
missy \ˈmis-ē\ *n* **:** a young girl **:** MISS
[1]mist \ˈmist\ *n* [ME, fr. OE; akin to MD *mist* mist, Gk *omichlē*] **1 :** water in the form of particles floating or falling in the atmosphere at or near the surface of the earth and approaching the form of rain **2 :** something that dims or obscures **3 :** a film before the eyes **4 a :** a cloud of small particles or objects suggestive of a mist **b :** a suspension of a finely divided liquid in a gas **c :** a fine spray **5 :** a drink of alcoholic liquor (as Scotch) served over cracked ice and garnished with a twist of lemon peel ***syn*** see HAZE
[2]mist *vi* **1 :** to be or become misty **2 :** to become dim or blurred ~ *vt* **:** to cover with or convert to mist
mis·tak·able \mə-ˈstā-kə-bəl\ *adj* **:** capable of being misunderstood or mistaken
[1]mis·take \mə-ˈstāk\ *vb* **mis·took** \-ˈstu̇k\; **mis·tak·en** \-ˈstā-kən\; **mis·tak·ing** [ME *mistaken*, fr. ON *mistaka* to take by mistake, fr. *mis-* + *taka* to take — more at TAKE] *vt* **1 :** to blunder in the choice of <*mistook* her way in the dark> **2 a :** to misunderstand the meaning or intention of **:** MISINTERPRET <don't ~ me, I mean exactly what I said> **b :** to make a wrong judgment of the character or ability of **3 :** to identify wrongly **:** confuse with another <I *mistook* him for his brother> ~ *vi* **:** to be wrong <you *mistook* when you thought I laughed at you —Thomas Hardy> — **mis·tak·en·ly** *adv* — **mis·tak·er** *n*
syn MISTAKE, CONFUSE, CONFOUND *shared meaning element* **:** to take one thing to be another. One MISTAKES one thing *for* another when (as by error of perception or thought) one fails to recognize the thing or grasp its nature and therefore identifies it with something not itself <*mistake* gush for vigor and substitute rhetoric for imagination —C. D. Lewis> <he often was *mistaken* for a preacher> One CONFUSES one thing usually *with* another when one fails to differentiate two things that have similarities <far too intellectually keen to *confuse* moral problems with purely aesthetic problems —Havelock Ellis> One CONFOUNDS things, or one thing *with* another, when one mixes them up so hopelessly as to be unable to detect or grasp their differences; the term usually carries a strong suggestion of mental bewilderment or a muddled mind <the temptation to *confound* accumulated knowledge and experience with intrinsic progress is almost irresistible —W. R. Inge> ***ant*** recognize
[2]mistake *n* **1 :** a misunderstanding of the meaning or implication of something **2 :** a wrong action or statement proceeding from faulty judgment, inadequate knowledge, or inattention ***syn*** see ERROR
mis·ter \ˈmis-tər, *for 1* ˌmis-\ *n* [alter. of [1]*master*] **1** — used sometimes in writing instead of the usual *Mr.* **2 :** SIR — used without a name as a generalized term of direct address of a man who is a stranger <hey, ~, do you want to buy a paper> **3 :** a man not entitled to a title of rank or an honorific or professional title <though he was only a ~, he was a greater scholar in his field than any Ph.D.> **4 :** HUSBAND <maybe your *Mister* likes herbs, but then again, he mayn't —Alice Ross>
mis·think \(ˈ)mis-ˈthiŋk\ *vb* **-thought** \-ˈthȯt\; **-think·ing** *vi, archaic* **:** to think mistakenly or unfavorably ~ *vt, archaic* **:** to think badly or unfavorably of
mis·time \-ˈtīm\ *vt* **:** to time wrongly <*mistimed* his swing and struck out>
mis·tle thrush \ˈmis-əl-\ *n* [obs. E *mistle* mistletoe, fr. ME *mistel*, fr. OE] **:** MAVIS 2
mis·tle·toe \ˈmis-əl-ˌtō, *chiefly Brit* ˈmiz-\ *n* [ME *mistilto* basil, fr. OE *misteltān*, fr. *mistel* mistletoe, basil + *tān* twig; akin to OHG & OS *mistil* mistletoe and to OHG *zein* twig] **:** a European semiparasitic green shrub (*Viscum album* of the family Loranthaceae, the mistletoe family) with thick leaves, small yellowish flowers, and waxy-white glutinous berries; *broadly* **:** any of various plants of the mistletoe family (as of an American genus *Phoradendron*) resembling the true mistletoe
mis·tral \ˈmis-trəl, mi-ˈsträl\ *n* [F, fr. Prov, fr. *mistral* masterful, fr. L *magistralis* — more at MAGISTRAL] **:** a strong cold dry northerly wind of southern France

mis·trans·late \ˌmis-tran(t)s-ˈlāt, -tranz-\ *vt* : to translate incorrectly

mis·trans·la·tion \-ˈlā-shən\ *n* : the act or an instance of mistranslating

mis·treat \(ˈ)mis-ˈtrēt\ *vt* [ME *mistreten*, prob. fr. MF *mestraitier*, fr. OF, fr. *mis-* + *traitier* to treat — more at TREAT] : to treat badly : ABUSE — **mis·treat·ment** \-mənt\ *n*

mistletoe

mis·tress \ˈmis-trəs\ *n* [ME *maistresse*, fr. MF, fr. OF, fem. of *maistre* master — more at MASTER] **1 :** a woman who has power, authority, or ownership: as **a :** the female head of a household **b :** a woman who employs or supervises servants **c :** a woman who possesses or controls something **d :** a woman who is in charge of a school or other establishment **e :** a woman of the Scottish nobility having a status comparable to that of a master **2 a** *chiefly Brit* : a female teacher or tutor **b :** a woman who has achieved mastery in some field **3 :** a country or state have supremacy over others **4 :** something personified as female that rules or directs **5 a :** a woman with whom a man habitually fornicates **b** *archaic* : SWEETHEART **6 a** — used archaically as a title prefixed to the name of a married or unmarried woman and now superseded by *Mrs.* and *Miss* **b** \ˈmiz-əz, ˈmis-, -əs\ *chiefly South & Midland* : MRS. 1a

mistress of ceremonies : a woman who presides at a public ceremony or who acts as hostess of a stage, radio, or television show

mis·tri·al \(ˈ)mis-ˈtrī(-ə)l\ *n* : a trial that has no legal effect by reason of some error or serious prejudicial misconduct in the proceedings

[1]**mis·trust** \(ˈ)mis-ˈtrəst\ *n* : a lack of confidence : DISTRUST ***syn*** see UNCERTAINTY ***ant*** trust, assurance — **mis·trust·ful** \-fəl\ *adj* — **mis·trust·ful·ly** \-fə-lē\ *adv* — **mis·trust·ful·ness** *n*

[2]**mistrust** *vt* **1 :** to have no trust or confidence in : SUSPECT <~*ed* his neighbors> **2 :** to doubt the truth, validity, or effectiveness of <~*ed* his own judgment> **3 :** SURMISE <your mind ~*ed* there was something wrong —Robert Frost> ~ *vi* : to be suspicious

misty \ˈmis-tē\ *adj* **mist·i·er; -est 1 a :** obscured by mist **b :** consisting of or marked by mist **2 a :** INDISTINCT <a ~ recollection of the event> **b :** VAGUE, CONFUSED <avoided the large, vague, ~ issues —Reuben Abel> — **mist·i·ly** \-tə-lē\ *adv* — **mist·i·ness** \-tē-nəs\ *n*

misty-eyed \ˌmis-tē-ˈīd\ *adj* **1 :** having eyes covered with mist **2 :** DREAMY, SENTIMENTAL <~ recollections>

mis·un·der·stand \(ˌ)mis-ˌən-dər-ˈstand\ *vt* **1 :** to fail to understand **2 :** to interpret incorrectly

mis·un·der·stand·ing \-ˈstan-diŋ\ *n* **1 :** a failure to understand : MISINTERPRETATION **2 :** QUARREL, DISAGREEMENT

mis·us·age \mish-ˈü-sij, (ˈ)mis(h)-ˈyü-, -zij\ *n* [MF *mesusage*, fr. *mis-* + *usage*] **1 :** bad treatment : ABUSE **2 :** wrong or improper use (as of words)

[1]**mis·use** \mish-ˈüz, (ˈ)mis(h)-ˈyüz\ *vt* [ME *misusen*, partly fr. *mis-* + *usen* to use; partly fr. MF *mesuser* to abuse, fr. OF, fr. *mis-* + *user* to use] **1 :** to use incorrectly : MISAPPLY <*misused* his talents> **2 :** ABUSE, MISTREAT <*misused* his servants>

[2]**mis·use** \mish-ˈüs, (ˈ)mis(h)-ˈyüs\ *n* : incorrect or improper use : MISAPPLICATION

mis·val·ue \(ˈ)mis-ˈval-(ˌ)yü, -yə(-w)\ *vt* : UNDERVALUE

mis·ven·ture \(ˈ)mis-ˈven-chər\ *n* : MISADVENTURE

mis·write \(ˈ)mis-ˈrīt\ *vt* **-wrote** \-ˈrōt\; **-writ·ten** \-ˈrit-ᵊn\; **-writ·ing** \-ˈrīt-iŋ\ : to write incorrectly

mite \ˈmīt\ *n* [ME, fr. OE *mīte*; akin to MD *mite* mite, small copper coin, OHG *meizan* to cut, OE *gemād* silly — more at MAD] **1 :** any of numerous small to very minute arachnids (order Acarina) that often infest animals, plants, and stored foods and include important disease vectors **2** [ME, fr. MF or MD; MF, small Flemish copper coin, fr. MD] : a small coin or sum of money **3 a :** a very little : BIT <could be that I am a ~ prejudiced —John Fischer> **b :** a very small object or creature

[1]**mi·ter** *or* **mi·tre** \ˈmīt-ər\ *n* [ME *mitre*, fr. MF, fr. L *mitra* headband, turban, fr. Gk; akin to Skt *mitra* friend] **1 :** a liturgical headdress worn by bishops and abbots — see VESTMENT illustration **2 a :** a surface forming the beveled end or edge of a piece where a joint is made by cutting two pieces at an angle and fitting them together **b :** MITER SQUARE

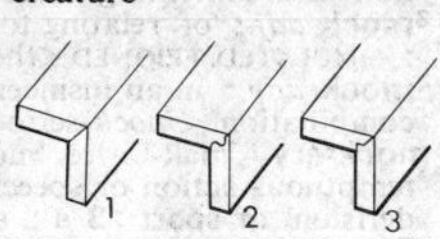

miter joints: *1* plain, *2* milled, *3* rabbeted

[2]**miter** *or* **mitre** *vt* **mi·tered** *or* **mi·tred; mi·ter·ing** *or* **mi·tring** \ˈmīt-ə-riŋ\ **1 :** to confer a miter on **2 a :** to match or fit together in a miter joint **b :** to bevel the ends of for making a miter joint — **mi·ter·er** \ˈmīt-ər-ər\ *n*

miter box *n* : a device for guiding a handsaw at the proper angle in making a miter joint in wood

miter gear *n* : one of a pair of interchangeable bevel gears with axes at right angles

miter square *n* : a bevel with an immovable arm at an angle of 45 degrees for striking miter lines; *also* : a square with an arm adjustable to any angle

mi·ter·wort *or* **mi·tre·wort** \ˈmīt-ər-ˌwərt, -ˌwȯ(ə)rt\ *n*: any of a genus (*Mitella*) of rhizomatous perennial herbs of the saxifrage family that bear a capsule resembling a bishop's miter

Mith·ra·ic \mith-ˈrā-ik\ *adj* [LGk *mithraikos* of Mithras, ancient Per god of light, fr. Gk *Mithras*, fr. OPer *Mithra*] : of or relating to an oriental mystery cult for men flourishing in the late Roman empire — **Mith·ra·ism** \ˈmith-rə-ˌiz-əm, -(ˌ)rā-\ *n* — **Mith·ra·ist** \mith-ˈrā-əst\ *n or adj*

mith·ri·date \ˈmith-rə-ˌdāt\ *n* [ML *mithridatum*, fr. LL *mithridatium*, fr. L, dogtooth violet (used as an antidote), fr. Gk *mithridation*, fr. *Mithridatēs*] : an antidote against poison; *esp* : an electuary held to be effective against poison

mith·ri·da·tism \ˌmith-rə-ˈdāt-ˌiz-əm\ *n* [*Mithridates* VI †63 B.C. king of Pontus, fr. L *Mithridates*, fr. Gk *Mithridatēs*; fr. the fact that he reputedly produced this condition in himself] : tolerance to a poison acquired by taking gradually increased doses of it

mi·ti·cide \ˈmīt-ə-ˌsīd\ *n* [*mite*] : an agent used to kill mites — **mi·ti·cid·al** \ˌmīt-ə-ˈsīd-ᵊl\ *adj*

mit·i·gate \ˈmit-ə-ˌgāt\ *vt* **-gat·ed; -gat·ing** [ME *mitigaten*, fr. L *mitigatus*, pp. of *mitigare* to soften, fr. *mitis* soft + *-igare* (akin to L *agere* to drive); akin to OIr *mōith* soft — more at AGENT] **1 :** to cause to become less harsh or hostile : MOLLIFY <aggressiveness may be *mitigated* or . . . channeled —Ashley Montagu> **2 a :** to make less severe or painful : ALLEVIATE **b :** EXTENUATE ***syn*** see RELIEVE ***ant*** intensify — **mit·i·ga·tion** \ˌmit-ə-ˈgā-shən\ *n* — **mit·i·ga·tive** \ˈmit-ə-ˌgat-iv\ *adj* — **mit·i·ga·tor** \-ˌgāt-ər\ *n* — **mit·i·ga·to·ry** \ˈmit-i-gə-ˌtōr-ē, -ˌtȯr-\ *adj*

mi·to·chon·dri·on \ˌmīt-ə-ˈkän-drē-ən\ *n, pl* **-dria** \-drē-ə\ [NL, fr. Gk *mitos* thread + *chondrion*, dim. of *chondros* grain — more at GRIND] : any of various round or long cellular organelles that are found outside the nucleus, produce energy for the cell through cellular respiration, and are rich in fats, proteins, and enzymes — see CELL illustration — **mi·to·chon·dri·al** \-drē-əl\ *adj*

mi·to·gen \ˈmīt-ə-jən\ *n* [*mitosis* + *-gen*] : a substance that induces mitosis — **mi·to·gen·ic** \ˌmīt-ə-ˈjen-ik\ *adj* — **mi·to·ge·nic·i·ty** \-jə-ˈnis-ət-ē\ *n*

mi·to·my·cin \ˌmīt-ə-ˈmīs-ᵊn\ *n* [ISV *mito-* (prob. fr. NL *mitosis*) + *-mycin*] : a complex of antibiotic substances which is produced by a Japanese streptomyces and one form of which acts directly on DNA and shows promise as an anticancer agent

mi·to·sis \mī-ˈtō-səs\ *n, pl* **-to·ses** \-ˌsēz\ [NL, fr. Gk *mitos* thread] **1 :** a process that takes place in the nucleus of a dividing cell, involves typically a series of steps consisting of prophase, metaphase, anaphase, and telophase, and results in the formation of two new nuclei each having the same number of chromosomes as the parent nucleus — compare MEIOSIS **2 :** cell division in which mitosis occurs — **mi·tot·ic** \-ˈtät-ik\ *adj* — **mi·tot·i·cal·ly** \-i-k(ə-)lē\ *adv*

mi·trail·leuse \ˌmē-trə-ˈyə(r)z\ *n* [F] **1 :** a breech-loading machine gun with a number of barrels **2 :** MACHINE GUN

mi·tral \ˈmī-trəl\ *adj* **1 :** resembling a miter **2 :** relating to, being, or adjoining a mitral valve or orifice

mitral valve *n* : BICUSPID VALVE

mitt \ˈmit\ *n* [short for *mitten*] **1 a :** a woman's glove that leaves the fingers uncovered **b :** MITTEN 1 **c :** a baseball catcher's or first baseman's glove made in the style of a mitten **2** *slang* : HAND

mit·ten \ˈmit-ᵊn\ *n* [ME *mitain*, fr. MF *mitaine*, fr. OF, fr. *mite* mitten] **1 :** a covering for the hand and wrist having a separate section for the thumb only **2 :** MITT 1a

mit·ti·mus \ˈmit-ə-məs\ *n* [L, we send, fr. *mittere* to send — more at SMITE] : a warrant of commitment to prison

mitz·vah \ˈmits-və\ *n, pl* **mitz·voth** \-ˌvōt(h), -ˌvōs\ *or* **mitz·vahs** [Heb *miṣwāh*] **1 :** a commandment of the Jewish law **2 :** a meritorious or charitable act

[1]**mix** \ˈmiks\ *vb* [ME *mixen*, back-formation fr. *mixte* mixed, fr. MF, fr. L *mixtus*, pp. of *miscēre* to mix; akin to Gk *mignynai* to mix] *vt* **1 a** (1) : to combine or blend into one mass (2) : to combine with another **b :** to bring into close association <~ business with pleasure> **2 :** to form by mixing components <~ a drink at the bar> **3 :** CONFUSE — often used with *up* <~*es* things up in his eagerness to speak out —Irving Howe> ~ *vi* **1 a :** to become mixed **b :** to be capable of mixing **2 :** to enter into relations : ASSOCIATE **3 :** CROSSBREED **4 :** to become involved : PARTICIPATE <decided not to ~ in politics> — **mix·able** \ˈmik-sə-bəl\ *adj*

syn MIX, MINGLE, COMMINGLE, BLEND, MERGE, COALESCE, AMALGAMATE, FUSE *shared meaning element* : to combine or be combined into a more or less uniform whole

[2]**mix** *n* **1 :** an act or process of mixing **2 :** a product of mixing; *specif* : a commercially prepared mixture of food ingredients <a cake ~> **3 :** MIXER 2b

mixed \ˈmikst\ *adj* [ME *mixte*] **1 :** combining characteristics of more than one kind; *specif* : combining features of two or more systems of government <a ~ constitution> **2 :** made up of or involving individuals or items of more than one kind: as **a :** made up of or involving persons differing in race, national origin, religion, or class **b :** made up of or involving individuals of both sexes <~ company> **3 :** including or accompanied by inconsistent or incompatible elements <~ emotions> **4 :** deriving from two or more races or breeds <a person of ~ blood>

mixed alphabet *n* : an alphabet (as in a cryptographic system) that has been rearranged or disordered systematically or randomly

mixed bag *n* : a miscellaneous collection : ASSORTMENT

mixed bud *n* : a bud that produces a branch and leaves as well as flowers

mixed drink *n* : an alcoholic beverage prepared from a recipe calling for two or more ingredients stirred or shaken before serving

mixed farming *n* : the growing of food or cash crops, feed crops, and livestock on the same farm

mixed grill *n* : meats (as lamb chop, kidney, and bacon) and vegetables broiled together and served on one plate

mixed marriage *n* : a marriage between persons of different races or religions

mixed-media *adj* : MULTIMEDIA

mixed nerve *n* : a nerve containing both sensory and motor fibers

mixed number *n* : a number (as $5\frac{2}{3}$) composed of an integer and a fraction

mixed–up \ˈmik-ˈstəp\ *adj* **:** marked by bewilderment, perplexity, or disorder **:** CONFUSED <an abandoner of husband and child, and a totally ~ kid —Hollis Alpert>

mix·er \ˈmik-sər\ *n* **1 :** one that mixes: as **a** (1) **:** one whose work is mixing the ingredients of a product (2) **:** one who balances and controls the dialogue, music, and sound effects to be recorded for or with a motion picture or television **b :** a container, device, or machine for mixing **c :** a game, stunt, or dance used at a get-together to give members of the group an opportunity to meet one another in a friendly and informal atmosphere — called also *icebreaker* **2 :** one that mixes with others: as **a :** a person considered as to his casual sociability <was shy and a poor ~> **b :** a nonalcoholic beverage (as ginger ale) used in a mixed drink

mix·ol·o·gy \mik-ˈsäl-ə-jē\ *n* **:** the art or skill of preparing mixed drinks — **mix·ol·o·gist** \-jəst\ *n*

mixt *abbr* mixture

Mix·tec \mēs(h)-ˈtek, mis(h)-\ *n, pl* **Mixtec** *or* **Mixtecs** [AmerSp *mixteco*] **1 :** a member of an American Indian people of Mexico **2 :** the language of the Mixtec people

mix·ture \ˈmiks-chər\ *n* [MF, fr. OF *misture,* fr. L *mixtura,* fr. *mixtus*] **1 a :** the act, the process, or an instance of mixing **b** (1) **:** the state of being mixed (2) **:** the relative proportions of constituents; *specif* **:** the proportion of fuel to air produced in a carburetor **2 :** a product of mixing **:** COMBINATION: as **a :** a portion of matter consisting of two or more components in varying proportions that retain their own properties **b :** a fabric woven of variously colored threads **c :** a combination of several different kinds

mix–up \ˈmik-ˌsəp\ *n* **1 :** a state or instance of confusion <a ~ about who was to meet the train> **2 :** MIXTURE **3 :** CONFLICT, FIGHT

Mi·zar \ˈmī-ˌzär\ *n* [Ar *Mi'zar,* lit., veil, cloak] **:** a star of the second magnitude in the handle of the Big Dipper

[1]**miz·zen** *or* **miz·en** \ˈmiz-ᵊn\ *n* [ME *meson,* prob. fr. MF *misaine,* deriv. of Ar *mazzān* mast] **1 :** a fore-and-aft sail set on the mizzenmast **2 :** MIZZENMAST

[2]**mizzen** *or* **mizen** *adj* **:** of or relating to the mizzenmast <~ shrouds>

miz·zen·mast \-ˌmast, -məst\ *n* **:** the mast aft or next aft of the mainmast in a ship

[1]**miz·zle** \ˈmiz-əl\ *vi* **miz·zled; miz·zling** \-(ə-)liŋ\ [ME *misellen;* akin to Flem *mizzelen* to drizzle, MD *mist* fog, mist] **:** to rain in very fine drops **:** DRIZZLE <standing up hatless in the *mizzling* rain —Helen Eustis> — **mizzle** *n* — **miz·zly** \-(ə-)lē\ *adj*

[2]**mizzle** *vi* **miz·zled; miz·zling** \-(ə-)liŋ\ [origin unknown] *chiefly Brit* **:** to depart suddenly

mk *abbr* **1** mark **2** markka

Mk *abbr* Mark

mks *abbr* meter-kilogram-second

mktg *abbr* marketing

ml *abbr* milliliter

mL *abbr* millilambert

MLA *abbr* **1** Member of the Legislative Assembly **2** Modern Language Association

MLD *abbr* **1** median lethal dose **2** minimum lethal dose

MLF *abbr* multilateral force

Mlle *abbr* [F] mademoiselle

Mlles *abbr* [F] mesdemoiselles

MLS *abbr* master of library science

MLW *abbr* mean low water

mm *abbr* millimeter

MM *abbr* **1** Maryknoll Missioners **2** [F] messieurs **3** mutatis mutandis

Mme *abbr* [F] madame

mmf *abbr* magnetomotive force

MMPI *abbr* Minnesota Multiphasic Personality Inventory

MMus *abbr* master of music

Mn *symbol* manganese

MN *abbr* **1** magnetic north **2** Minnesota

[1]**mne·mon·ic** \ni-ˈmän-ik\ *adj* [Gk *mnēmonikos,* fr. *mnēmōn* mindful, fr. *mimnēskesthai* to remember — more at MIND] **1 :** assisting or intended to assist memory; *also* **:** of or relating to mnemonics **2 :** of or relating to memory — **mne·mon·i·cal·ly** \-i-k(ə-)lē\ *adv*

[2]**mnemonic** *n* **:** a mnemonic device or code

mne·mon·ics \ni-ˈmän-iks\ *n pl but sing in constr* **:** a technique of improving the memory

Mne·mos·y·ne \ni-ˈmäs-ᵊn-ē, -ˈmäz-\ *n* [L, fr. Gk *Mnēmosynē*] **:** the Greek goddess of memory and the mother of the Muses by Zeus

mo *abbr* month

[1]**Mo** *abbr* Missouri

[2]**Mo** *symbol* molybdenum

MO *abbr* **1** mail order **2** medical officer **3** Missouri **4** modus operandi **5** money order

-mo \(ˌ)mō\ *n suffix* [duodeci*mo*] — after numerals or their names to indicate the number of leaves made by folding a sheet of paper <sixteen*mo*> <16*mo*>

moa \ˈmō-ə\ *n* [Maori] **:** any of various usu. very large extinct flightless ratite birds of New Zealand (family Dinornithidae) including one (*Dinornis giganteus*) about 12 feet in height

Mo·ab·ite \ˈmō-ə-ˌbīt\ *n* [ME, fr. LL *Moabita, Moabites,* fr. Gk *Mōabitēs,* fr. *Mōab* Moab, ancient kingdom in Syria] **:** a member of an ancient Semitic people related to the Hebrews — **Moabite** *or* **Mo·ab·it·ish** \-ˌbīt-ish\ *adj* — **Mo·ab·it·ess** \-ˌbīt-əs\ *n*

[1]**moan** \ˈmōn\ *n* [ME *mone,* fr. (assumed) OE *mān*] **1 :** LAMENTATION, COMPLAINT **2 :** a low prolonged sound of pain or of grief

[2]**moan** *vt* **1 :** to bewail audibly **:** LAMENT **2 :** to utter with moans ~ *vi* **1 :** LAMENT, COMPLAIN **2 a :** to make a moan **:** GROAN **b :** to emit a sound resembling a moan <the wind ~*ed* in the trees>

[1]**moat** \ˈmōt\ *n* [ME *mote*] **1 :** a deep and wide trench around the rampart of a fortified place (as a castle) that is usu. filled with water **2 :** a channel resembling a moat (as about a seamount or for confinement of animals in a zoo) — **moat·like** \-ˌlīk\ *adj*

[2]**moat** *vt* **:** to surround with or as if with a moat

[1]**mob** \ˈmäb\ *n* [L *mobile vulgus* vacillating crowd] **1 :** the lower classes of a community **:** MASSES, RABBLE **2 :** a large or disorderly crowd; *esp* **:** one bent on riotous or destructive action **3** *chiefly Austral* **:** a flock, drove, or herd of animals **4 :** a criminal set **:** GANG *syn* see CROWD — **mob·bish** \ˈmäb-ish\ *adj*

[2]**mob** *vt* **mobbed; mob·bing 1 :** to crowd about and attack or annoy <*mobbed* by autograph hunters before he could enter the theater> **2 :** to crowd into or around <customers ~ the stores on sale days>

mob·cap \ˈmäb-ˌkap\ *n* [*mob* (woman's cap) + *cap*] **:** a woman's fancy indoor cap made with a high full crown and often tied under the chin

[1]**mo·bile** \ˈmō-bəl, -ˌbēl, -ˌbīl\ *adj* [MF, fr. L *mobilis,* fr. *movēre* to move] **1 :** capable of moving or being moved **:** MOVABLE <a ~ missile launcher> **2 a :** changeable in appearance, mood, or purpose **b :** ADAPTABLE, VERSATILE **3 :** MIGRATORY **4 a :** characterized by the mixing of social groups **b :** having the opportunity for or undergoing a shift in status within the hierarchical social levels of a society <upward ~ middle-class workers> **5 :** marked by the use of vehicles for transportation <~ warfare> **6 :** of or relating to a mobile — **mo·bil·i·ty** \mō-ˈbil-ət-ē\ *n*

[2]**mo·bile** \ˈmō-ˌbēl\ *n* **:** a construction or sculpture frequently of wire and sheet metal shapes with parts that can be set in motion by air currents; *also* **:** a similar structure (as of paper or plastic) suspended so that it moves in a current of air

mobile home *n* **:** a trailer that is used as a permanent dwelling, is usu. connected to utilities, and is designed without a permanent foundation — compare MOTOR HOME

mo·bi·li·za·tion \ˌmō-bə-lə-ˈzā-shən\ *n* **1 :** the act of mobilizing **2 :** the state of being mobilized

mo·bi·lize \ˈmō-bə-ˌlīz\ *vb* **-lized; -liz·ing** *vt* **1 a :** to put into movement or circulation <~ financial assets> **b :** to release (something stored in the organism) for bodily use **2 a :** to assemble and make ready for war duty **b :** to marshal (as resources) for action <~ support for a proposal> ~ *vi* **:** to undergo mobilization

Mö·bi·us strip \ˌmə(r)b-ē-əs-, ˌmäb-\ *n* [August F. *Möbius* †1868 G mathematician] **:** a one-sided surface that is constructed from a rectangle by holding one end fixed, rotating the opposite end through 180 degrees, and applying it to the first end

mob·oc·ra·cy \mä-ˈbäk-rə-sē\ *n* **1 :** rule by the mob **2 :** the mob as a ruling class — **mob·o·crat** \ˈmäb-ə-ˌkrat\ *n* — **mob·o·crat·ic** \ˌmäb-ə-ˈkrat-ik\ *adj*

mob·ster \ˈmäb-stər\ *n* **:** a member of a criminal gang

moc·ca·sin \ˈmäk-ə-sən\ *n* [of Algonquian origin; akin to Natick *mokkussin* shoe] **1 a :** a soft leather heelless shoe or boot with the sole brought up the sides of the foot and over the toes where it is joined with a puckered seam to a U-shaped piece lying on top of the foot **b :** a regular shoe having a seam on the forepart of the vamp imitating the seam of a true moccasin **2 a :** WATER MOCCASIN **b :** a snake (as of the genus *Natrix*) resembling a water moccasin

moccasin flower *n* **:** any of several lady's slippers (genus *Cypripedium*); *esp* **:** a once common woodland orchid (*C. acaule*) of eastern No. America with pink or white moccasin-shaped flowers

mo·cha \ˈmō-kə\ *n* [*Mocha,* Arabia] **1 a** (1) **:** superior Arabian coffee with small green or yellowish beans grown in Arabia (2) **:** a coffee of superior quality **b :** a flavoring made of a strong coffee infusion or of a mixture of cocoa or chocolate with coffee **2 :** a pliable suede-finished glove leather from African sheepskins

[1]**mock** \ˈmäk, ˈmȯk\ *vb* [ME *mocken,* fr. MF *mocquer*] *vt* **1 :** to treat with contempt or ridicule **:** DERIDE **2 :** to disappoint the hopes of **:** DELUDE **3 :** DEFY, CHALLENGE **4 a :** to imitate (as a sound or mannerism) closely **:** MIMIC **b :** to mimic in sport or derision ~ *vi* **:** JEER, SCOFF *syn* see RIDICULE, COPY — **mock·er** *n* — **mock·ing·ly** \-iŋ-lē\ *adv*

[2]**mock** *n* **1 :** an act of ridicule or derision **:** JEER **2 :** one that is an object of derision or scorn **3 :** MOCKERY **4 a :** an act of imitation **b :** something made as an imitation

[3]**mock** *adj* **:** of, relating to, or having the character of an imitation **:** SIMULATED, FEIGNED <the ~ solemnity of the parody>

[4]**mock** *adv* **:** in an insincere or counterfeit manner — usu. used in combination <*mock*-serious>

mock·ery \ˈmäk-(ə-)rē, ˈmȯk-\ *n, pl* **-er·ies 1 :** insulting or contemptuous action or speech **:** DERISION **2 :** a subject of laughter, derision, or sport **3 a :** a counterfeit appearance **:** IMITATION **b :** an insincere, contemptible, or impertinent imitation <arbitrary methods that make a ~ of justice> **4 :** something ridiculously or impudently unsuitable

[1]**mock–he·ro·ic** \ˌmäk-hi-ˈrō-ik, ˌmȯk-\ *adj* **:** ridiculing or burlesquing heroic style, character, or action <a ~ poem> — **mock–he·ro·ical·ly** \-i-k(ə-)lē\ *adv*

[2]**mock–heroic** *n* **:** a mock-heroic composition — called also *mock-epic*

mock·ing·bird \ˈmäk-iŋ-ˌbərd, ˈmȯk-\ *n* **:** a common bird (*Mimus polyglottos*) esp. of the southern U.S. that is remarkable for its exact imitations of the notes of other birds

mock orange *n* **:** any of various usu. shrubby plants considered to resemble the orange; *esp* **:** PHILADELPHUS

mock turtle soup *n* **:** a soup made of meat (as calf's head or veal), wine, and spices in imitation of green turtle soup

mock–up \ˈmäk-ˌəp, ˈmȯk-\ *n* **:** a full-sized structural model built accurately to scale chiefly for study, testing, or display <a ~ of lunar terrain —R. N. Watts, Jr.>

[1]**mod** \ˈmäd\ *adj* **:** MODERN; *esp* **:** bold and free in style, behavior, or dress

[2]**mod** *n* **:** one who wears mod clothes

[3]**mod** *abbr* **1** moderate **2** modern **3** modification; modified **4** modulo; modulus

mod·acryl·ic fiber \ˌmäd-ə-ˌkril-ik-\ *n* [*mod*ified *acrylic*] **:** any of various synthetic textile fibers that are long-chain polymers composed of 35 to 85 percent by weight of acrylonitrile units

mod·al \ˈmōd-ᵊl\ *adj* [ML *modalis,* fr. L *modus*] **1 :** of or relating to modality in logic **2 :** containing provisions as to the mode of procedure or the manner of taking effect — used of a contract or legacy **3 :** of or relating to a musical mode **4 :** of or relating to structure as opposed to substance **5 :** of, relating to, or constituting a grammatical form or category characteristically indicating predication of an action or state in some manner other than as a simple fact **6 :** of or relating to a statistical mode — **mod·al·ly** \-ᵊl-ē\ *adv*

modal auxiliary *n* **:** an auxiliary verb (as *can, must, might, may*) that is characteristically used with a verb of predication and expresses a modal modification and that in English differs formally from other verbs in lacking *-s* and *-ing* forms

mo·dal·i·ty \mō-ˈdal-ət-ē\ *n, pl* **-ties** **1 a :** the quality or state of being modal **b :** a modal quality or attribute **:** FORM **2 :** the classification of logical propositions according to their asserting or denying the possibility, impossibility, contingency, or necessity of their content **3 :** one of the main avenues of sensation (as vision) **4 :** a therapeutic agency used esp. in physical therapy

¹mode \ˈmōd\ *n* [ME *moede,* fr. L *modus* measure, manner, musical mode — more at METE] **1 a :** an arrangement of the eight diatonic notes or tones of an octave according to one of several fixed schemes of their intervals **b :** a rhythmical scheme (as in 13th and 14th century music) **2 :** ²MOOD 2 **3** [LL *modus,* fr. L] **a :** ²MOOD 1 **b :** the modal form of the assertion or denial of a logical proposition **4 a :** a particular form or variety of something **b :** a form or manner of expression **:** STYLE **5 :** a possible, customary, or preferred way of doing something <explained in the usual solemn ~> **6 a :** a manifestation, form, or arrangement of being; *specif* **:** a particular form or manifestation of an underlying substance **b :** a particular functioning arrangement or condition **:** STATUS <a spacecraft in reentry ~> <a computer operating in parallel ~> **7 a :** the most frequent value of a set of data **b :** a value of a random variable for which a function of probabilities defined on it achieves a relative maximum **8 :** any of various stationary vibration patterns of which an elastic body or oscillatory system is capable <the vibration ~ of an airplane propeller blade> <the ~*s* of electromagnetic radiation in a waveguide> **9 :** the actual mineral composition of a rock ***syn*** see METHOD

²mode *n* [F, fr. L *modus*] **:** a prevailing fashion or style (as of dress or behavior) ***syn*** see FASHION

¹mod·el \ˈmäd-ᵊl\ *n* [MF *modelle,* fr. OIt *modello,* fr. (assumed) VL *modellus,* fr. L *modulus* small measure, fr. *modus*] **1** *obs* **:** a set of plans for a building **2** *dial Brit* **:** COPY, IMAGE **3 :** structural design <built his home on the ~ of an old farmhouse> **4 :** a miniature representation of something; *also* **:** a pattern of something to be made **5 :** an example for imitation or emulation **6 :** a person or thing that serves as a pattern for an artist; *esp* **:** one who poses for an artist **7 :** ARCHETYPE **8 :** an organism whose appearance a mimic imitates **9 :** one who is employed to display clothes or other merchandise **:** MANNEQUIN **10 a :** a type or design of clothing **b :** a type or design of product (as a car or airplane) **11 :** a description or analogy used to help visualize something (as an atom) that cannot be directly observed **12 :** a system of postulates, data, and inferences presented as a mathematical description of an entity or state of affairs

syn MODEL, EXAMPLE, PATTERN, EXEMPLAR, IDEAL *shared meaning element* **:** something set or held before one for guidance or imitation

²model *vb* **mod·eled** *or* **mod·elled; mod·el·ing** *or* **mod·el·ling** \ˈmäd-liŋ, -ᵊl-iŋ\ *vt* **1 :** to plan or form after a pattern **:** SHAPE **2** *archaic* **:** to make into an organization (as an army, government, or parish) **3 :** to shape or fashion in a plastic material; *broadly* **:** to produce a representation or simulation of <using a computer to ~ a problem> **4 :** to construct or fashion in imitation of a particular model <~*ed* its constitution on that of the U.S.> **5 :** to display by wearing, using, or posing with <~*ed* gowns> ~ *vi* **1 :** to design or imitate forms **:** make a pattern <enjoys ~*ing* in clay> **2 :** to work or act as a fashion model — **mod·el·er** \ˈmäd-lər, -ᵊl-ər\ *n*

³model *adj* **1 :** serving as or capable of serving as a pattern <a ~ student> **2 :** being a miniature representation of something <a ~ airplane>

¹mod·er·ate \ˈmäd-(ə-)rət\ *adj* [ME, fr. L *moderatus,* fr. pp. of *moderare* to moderate; akin to L *modus* measure] **1 a :** avoiding extremes of behavior or expression **:** observing reasonable limits <a ~ drinker> **b :** CALM, TEMPERATE **2 a :** tending toward the mean or average amount or dimension **b :** having average or less than average quality **:** MEDIOCRE **3 :** avoiding extreme political or social measures <a ~ candidate> **4 :** limited in scope or effect **5 :** not expensive **:** reasonable or low in price **6** *of a color* **:** of medium lightness and medium chroma — **mod·er·ate·ly** *adv* — **mod·er·ate·ness** *n*

²mod·er·ate \ˈmäd-ə-ˌrāt\ *vb* **-at·ed; -at·ing** *vt* **1 :** to lessen the intensity or extremeness of <the sun *moderated* the chill> **2 :** to preside over or act as chairman of ~ *vi* **1 :** to act as a moderator **2 :** to become less violent, severe, or intense — **mod·er·a·tion** \ˌmäd-ə-ˈrā-shən\ *n*

syn MODERATE, QUALIFY, TEMPER *shared meaning element* **:** to modify so as to avoid an extreme or keep within bounds

³mod·er·ate \ˈmäd-(ə-)rət\ *n* [¹*moderate*] **:** one who holds moderate views or who belongs to a group favoring a moderate course or program (as in politics or religion)

moderate breeze *n* **:** wind having a speed of 13 to 18 miles per hour

moderate gale *n* **:** wind having a speed of 32 to 38 miles per hour

mo·der·a·to \ˌmäd-ə-ˈrät-(ˌ)ō\ *adv or adj* [It, fr. L *moderatus*] **:** MODERATE — used as a direction in music to indicate tempo

mod·er·a·tor \ˈmäd-ə-ˌrāt-ər\ *n* **1 :** one who arbitrates **:** MEDIATOR **2 :** one who presides over an assembly, meeting, or discussion: as **a :** the presiding officer of a Presbyterian governing body **b :** the nonpartisan presiding officer of a town meeting **c :** the chairman of a discussion group **3 :** a substance (as graphite) used for slowing down neutrons in a nuclear reactor — **mod·er·a·tor·ship** \-ˌship\ *n*

¹mod·ern \ˈmäd-ərn, *nonstand* ˈmäd-(ə-)rən\ *adj* [LL *modernus,* fr. L *modo* just now, fr. *modus* measure — more at METE] **1 a :** of, relating to, or characteristic of a period extending from a relevant remote past to the present time **b :** of, relating to, or characteristic of the present or the immediate past **:** CONTEMPORARY **2 :** involving recent techniques, methods, or ideas **:** UP-TO-DATE **3** *cap* **:** of, relating to, or having the characteristics of the present or most recent period of development of a language — **mo·der·ni·ty** \mə-ˈdər-nət-ē, mä-\ *n* — **mod·ern·ly** \ˈmäd-ərn-lē\ *adv* — **mod·ern·ness** \-ərn-nəs\ *n*

syn **1** MODERN, RECENT, LATE *shared meaning element* **:** having taken place, existed, or developed in times close to the present. In spite of the common element of meaning these words are seldom freely interchangeable without loss of precision. MODERN may date anything that is not ancient or medieval <wrecks of ancient galleys, medieval ships, and *modern* dreadnoughts —William Beebe> or anything that bears the marks of a period nearer in time than another <ornate mansions of a bygone era mingle with more *modern* concepts of architecture —*N. Y. Times*> or, less clearly, may apply to whatever is felt as new, fresh, or up-to-date <what is *modern* today and up-to-date . . . becomes obsolete and outworn tomorrow —F. D. Roosevelt> In all these uses a change or contrast in character or quality is implicit. RECENT usually lacks such implications and applies to a date that approximates the immediate past more or less precisely according to the nature of the thing qualified; thus, "the *Recent* geological epoch" dates back thousands of years but extends to the present time; "Shakespeare is a more *recent* author than Chaucer" implies only a comparative relation; "we have all the *recent* books on the subject" implies an absolute relation to the near or immediate past <*recent* news> <a *recent* change of plans> LATE usually implies a series or succession of which the one described is the most recent in time <the *late* war>

2 see NEW ***ant*** antique, ancient

²modern *n* **1 :** a person of modern times or views **2 :** a style of printing type distinguished by regularity of shape, precise curves, straight hairline serifs, and heavy downstrokes

modern

Modern Hebrew *n* **:** Hebrew as used in present-day Israel

mod·ern·ism \ˈmäd-ər-ˌniz-əm\ *n* **1 :** a practice, usage, or expression peculiar to modern times **2** *often cap* **:** a tendency in theology to accommodate traditional religious teaching to contemporary thought and esp. to devalue traditional supernatural elements **3 :** the philosophy and practices of modern art; *esp* **:** a self-conscious break with the past and a search for new forms of expression — **mod·ern·ist** \-nəst\ *n or adj* — **mod·ern·is·tic** \ˌmäd-ər-ˈnis-tik\ *adj*

mod·ern·iza·tion \ˌmäd-ər-nə-ˈzā-shən\ *n* **1 :** the act of modernizing **:** the state of being modernized **2 :** something modernized **:** a modernized version

mod·ern·ize \ˈmäd-ər-ˌnīz\ *vb* **-ized; -iz·ing** *vt* **:** to make modern in taste, style, or usage ~ *vi* **:** to adopt modern ways — **mod·ern·iz·er** *n*

modern pentathlon *n* **:** a composite contest in which all contestants compete in a 300-meter freestyle swim, a 4000-meter cross-country run, a 5000-meter 30-jump equestrian steeplechase, épée fencing, and target shooting at 25 meters

mod·est \ˈmäd-əst\ *adj* [L *modestus* moderate; akin to L *modus* measure] **1 a :** placing a moderate estimate on one's abilities or worth **b :** neither bold nor self-assertive **:** tending toward diffidence **2 :** arising from or characteristic of a modest nature **3 :** observing the proprieties of dress and behavior **:** DECENT **4 :** limited in size, amount, or aim **:** UNPRETENTIOUS <a ~ cottage> ***syn*** **1** see HUMBLE ***ant*** ambitious **2** see SHY **3** see CHASTE ***ant*** immodest — **mod·est·ly** *adv*

mod·es·ty \ˈmäd-ə-stē\ *n* **1 :** freedom from conceit or vanity **2 :** propriety in dress, speech, or conduct

mod·i·cum \ˈmäd-i-kəm, ˈmōd-\ *n* [ME, fr. L, neut. of *modicus* moderate, fr. *modus* measure] **:** a small portion **:** a limited quantity

modif *abbr* modification

mod·i·fi·ca·tion \ˌmäd-ə-fə-ˈkā-shən\ *n* **1 :** the limiting of a statement **:** QUALIFICATION **2 :** ¹MODE 6a **3 a :** the making of a limited change in something <a ~ of plans> **b :** a change in an organism caused by environmental factors

mod·i·fi·er \ˈmäd-ə-ˌfī(-ə)r\ *n* **1 :** one that modifies **2 :** a grammatical qualifier **3 :** a gene that modifies the effect of another

mod·i·fy \ˈmäd-ə-ˌfī\ *vb* **-fied; -fy·ing** [ME *modifien,* fr. MF *modifier,* fr. L *modificare* to measure, moderate, fr. *modus*] *vt* **1 :** to make less extreme **:** MODERATE **2 a :** to limit or restrict the meaning of esp. in a grammatical construction **:** QUALIFY **b :** to change (a vowel) by umlaut **3 a :** to make minor changes in **b :** to make basic or fundamental changes in often to give a new orientation to or to serve a new end <the wing of a bird is an arm *modified* for flying> ~ *vi* **:** to undergo change ***syn*** see CHANGE — **mod·i·fi·abil·i·ty** \ˌmäd-ə-ˌfī-ə-ˈbil-ət-ē\ *n* — **mod·i·fi·able** \ˈmäd-ə-ˌfī-ə-bəl\ *adj* **mod·i·fi·able·ness** *n*

mo·dil·lion \mō-ˈdil-yən\ *n* [It *modiglione*] **:** an ornamental block or bracket under the corona of the cornice (as in the Corinthian order)

mod·ish \ˈmōd-ish\ *adj* **:** FASHIONABLE, STYLISH <a ~ hat> <a ~ writer> — **mod·ish·ly** *adv* — **mod·ish·ness** *n*

mo·diste \mō-ˈdēst\ *n* [F, fr. *mode* style, mode] : one who makes and sells fashionable dresses and hats for women

mod·u·la·bil·i·ty \ˌmäj-ə-lə-ˈbil-ət-ē\ *n* : the capability of being modulated

mod·u·lar \ˈmäj-ə-lər\ *adj* **1 :** of, relating to, or based on a module or a modulus **2 :** constructed with standardized units or dimensions for flexibility and variety in use — **mod·u·lar·i·ty** \ˌmäj-ə-ˈlar-ət-ē\ *n* — **mod·u·lar·ly** \ˈmäj-ə-lər-lē\ *adv*

modular arithmetic *n* : arithmetic that deals with whole numbers where the numbers are replaced by their remainders after division by a fixed number <in a *modular arithmetic* with modulus 5, 3 multiplied by 4 would be 2> <5 hours after 10 o'clock is 3 o'clock because clocks follow a *modular arithmetic* with modulus 12>

mod·u·lar·ized \ˈmäj-ə-lə-ˌrīzd\ *adj* **1 :** containing or consisting of modules <~ electronic equipment> **2 :** produced in the form of modules

mod·u·late \ˈmäj-ə-ˌlāt\ *vb* **-lat·ed; -lat·ing** [L *modulatus,* pp. of *modulari* to play, sing, fr. *modulus* small measure, rhythm, dim. of *modus* measure — more at METE] *vt* **1 :** to tune to a key or pitch **2 :** to adjust to or keep in proper measure or proportion : TEMPER **3 :** to vary the amplitude, frequency, or phase of (a carrier wave or signal) in telephony, telegraphy, radio, or television ~ *vi* **1 :** to play or sing with modulation **2 :** to pass by regular chord or melodic progression from one musical key or tonality into another — **mod·u·la·tor** \-ˌlāt-ər\ *n* — **mod·u·la·to·ry** \-lə-ˌtōr-ē, -ˌtȯr-\ *adj*

mod·u·la·tion \ˌmäj-ə-ˈlā-shən\ *n* **1 :** a regulating according to measure or proportion : TEMPERING **2 :** an inflection of the tone or pitch of the voice; *specif* : the use of stress or pitch to convey meaning **3 :** a changing from one tonality to another by regular melodic or chord succession **4 :** the process of varying the amplitude, frequency, or phase of a carrier or signal in telegraphy, telephony, radio, or television; *also* : the resultant variation

mod·ule \ˈmäj-(ˌ)ü(ə)l\ *n* [L *modulus*] **1 :** a standard or unit of measurement **2 :** the size of some one part taken as a unit of measure by which the proportions of an architectural composition are regulated **3 a :** any in a series of standardized units for use together **b :** a usu. packaged functional assembly of electronic components for use with other such assemblies **4 :** an independent unit that is a part of the total structure of a space vehicle **5 a :** a subset of an additive group that is also a group under addition **b :** a mathematical set that is a commutative group under addition and that is closed under multiplication which is distributive from the left or right or both by elements of a ring and for which $a(bx) = (ab)x$ or $(xb)a = x(ba)$ or both where a and b are elements of the ring and x belongs to the set

mod·u·lo \ˈmäj-ə-ˌlō\ *prep* [NL, abl. of *modulus*] : with respect to a modulus of <19 and 54 are congruent ~ 7>

mod·u·lus \ˈmäj-ə-ləs\ *n, pl* **-li** \-ˌlī, -ˌlē\ [NL, fr. L, small measure] **1 :** a constant or coefficient that expresses usu. numerically the degree in which a property is possessed by a substance or body **2 a :** ABSOLUTE VALUE 2 **b (1) :** the number (as a positive integer) or other mathematical entity (as a polynomial) in a congruence that divides the difference of the two congruent members without leaving a remainder — compare RESIDUE b **(2) :** the number of different numbers used in a system of modular arithmetic **c :** the factor by which a logarithm of a number to one base is multiplied to obtain the logarithm of the number to a new base

mo·dus ope·ran·di \ˌmōd-ə-ˌsäp-ə-ˈran-dē, -ˌdī\ *n, pl* **mo·di ope·randi** \ˈmō-ˌdē-ˌäp-, ˈmō-ˌdī-\ [NL] : a method of procedure

mo·dus vi·ven·di \ˌmōd-əs-vi-ˈven-dē, -ˌdī\ *n, pl* **mo·di vivendi** \ˈmō-ˌdē-vi-, ˈmō-ˌdī-\ [NL, manner of living] **1 :** a feasible arrangement or practical compromise; *esp* : one that bypasses difficulties **2 :** a manner of living : a way of life

mo·fette *or* **mof·fette** \mō-ˈfet, mä-\ *n* [F *mofette* gaseous exhalation] : a vent in the earth from which carbon dioxide and some nitrogen and oxygen issue

mog \ˈmäg, ˈmȯg\ *vi* **mogged; mog·ging** [origin unknown] *dial* : to move away; *also* : JOG

1**mo·gul** \ˈmō-(ˌ)gəl, mō-ˈ\ *n* [Per *Mughul,* fr. Mongolian *Mongol*] **1** *or* **mo·ghul** *cap* : an Indian Muslim of or descended from one of several conquering groups of Mongol, Turkish, and Persian origin **2 :** a great personage : MAGNATE — **mogul** *adj, often cap*

2**mogul** \ˈmo-gəl\ *n* [prob. of Scand origin; akin to Norw dial. *muge* heap, fr. ON *mugi* — more at MOW] : a bump in a ski run

mo·hair \ˈmō-ˌha(ə)r, -ˌhe(ə)r\ *n* [modif. of obs. It *mocaiarro,* fr. Ar *mukhayyar,* lit., choice] : a fabric or yarn made wholly or in part of the long silky hair of the Angora goat; *also* : this hair

Mo·ham·med·an *var of* MUHAMMADAN

Mo·hawk \ˈmō-ˌhȯk\ *n, pl* **Mohawk** *or* **Mohawks** [of Algonquian origin; akin to Narraganset *Mohowaùuck*] **1 a :** an Amerindian people of the Mohawk river valley, New York **b :** a member of this people **2 :** the language of the Mohawk people

Mo·he·gan \mō-ˈhē-gən, mə-\ *or* **Mo·hi·can** \-ˈhē-kən\ *n, pl* **Mohegan** *or* **Mohegans** *or* **Mohican** *or* **Mohicans** : a member of an Amerindian people of southeastern Connecticut

Mo·hi·can \mō-ˈhē-kən, mə-\ *var of* MAHICAN

Moh·ism \ˈmō-ˌiz-əm\ *n* [*Mo Ti fl* 400 B.C. Chin philosopher] : the teachings of Mo Ti characterized by an emphasis on egalitarian universal love and opposition to traditionalism and Confucianism — **Moh·ist** \ˈmō-əst\ *n or adj*

Mo·ho \ˈmō-ˌhō\ *n* [short for *Mohorovicic discontinuity,* fr. Andrija *Mohorovičic* †1936 Yugoslav geologist] : a point ranging from about three miles beneath the ocean basin floor to about 25 miles beneath the continental surface at which seismological studies indicate a transition in earth materials from those of the earth's crust to those of the subjacent mantle

Mo·hock \ˈmō-ˌhäk\ *n* [alter. of *Mohawk*] : one of a gang of aristocratic ruffians who assaulted and otherwise maltreated people in London streets in the early 18th century — **Mo·hock·ism** \-ˌiz-əm\ *n*

Mo·ho·ro·vi·cic discontinuity \ˌmō-hə-ˈrō-və-ˌchich-\ *n* : MOHO

Mohs' scale \ˈmōz-, ˈmōs-, ˌmō-səz-\ *n* [Friedrich *Mohs* †1839 G mineralogist] **1 :** a scale of hardness for minerals in which 1 represents the hardness of talc; 2, gypsum; 3, calcite; 4, fluorite; 5, apatite; 6, orthoclase; 7, quartz; 8, topaz; 9, corundum; and 10, diamond **2 :** a revised and expanded version of the original Mohs' scale in which 1 represents the hardness of talc; 2, gypsum; 3, calcite; 4, fluorite; 5, apatite; 6, orthoclase; 7, vitreous pure silica; 8, quartz; 9, topaz; 10, garnet; 11, fused zirconium oxide; 12, fused alumina; 13, silicon carbide; 14, boron carbide; and 15, diamond

mo·hur \ˈmō(-ə)r, mə-ˈhu̇(ə)r\ *n* [Hindi *muhr* gold coin, seal, fr. Per; akin to Skt *mudrā* seal] : a former gold coin of India and Persia equal to 15 rupees

moi·dore \mȯi-dō(ə)r, -ˈdȯ(ə)r\ *n* [modif. of Pg *moeda de ouro,* lit., coin of gold] : a former Portuguese gold coin

moi·ety \ˈmȯi-ət-ē\ *n, pl* **-eties** [ME *moite,* fr. MF *moitié,* fr. LL *medietat-, medietas,* fr. L *medius* middle — more at MID] **1 a :** one of two equal parts : HALF **b :** one of two approximately equal parts **2 :** one of the portions into which something is divided : COMPONENT, PART **3 :** one of two basic complementary tribal subdivisions

1**moil** \ˈmȯi(ə)l\ *vb* [ME *moillen,* fr. MF *moillier,* fr. (assumed) VL *molliare,* fr. L *mollis* soft — more at MELT] *vt, chiefly dial* : to make wet or dirty ~ *vi* **1 :** to work hard : DRUDGE **2 :** to be in continuous agitation : CHURN, SWIRL — **moil·er** *n*

2**moil** *n* **1 :** hard work : DRUDGERY **2 :** CONFUSION, TURMOIL

moil·ing \ˈmȯi-liŋ\ *adj* **1 a :** requiring hard work **b :** INDUSTRIOUS **2 :** violently agitated : TURBULENT — **moil·ing·ly** \-liŋ-lē\ *adv*

Moi·rai \ˈmȯi-ˌrī\ *n pl* [Gk, fr. pl. of *moira* lot, fate; akin to Gk *meros* part — more at MERIT] : FATE 4

moire \ˈmȯi(-ə)r, ˈmȯ(ə)r, ˈmwär\ *n* [F, fr. E *mohair*] *archaic* : a watered mohair

moi·ré \mȯ-ˈrā, mwä-\ *or* **moire** *same, or* ˈmȯi(-ə)r, ˈmȯ(ə)r, ˈmwär\ *n* [F *moiré,* fr. *moiré* like moire, fr. *moire*] **1 a :** an irregular wavy finish on a fabric **b :** a ripple pattern on a stamp **2 :** a fabric having a wavy watered appearance **3 :** an independent usu. shimmering pattern seen when two geometrically regular patterns (as two sets of parallel lines or two halftone screens) are superimposed esp. at an acute angle — **moiré** *adj*

moist \ˈmȯist\ *adj* [ME *moiste,* fr. MF, fr. (assumed) VL *muscidus,* alter. of L *mucidus* slimy, fr. *mucus*] **1 :** slightly or moderately wet : DAMP **2 :** TEARFUL **3 :** characterized by high humidity ***syn*** see WET — **moist·ly** *adv* — **moist·ness** \ˈmȯis(t)-nəs\ *n*

moist·en \ˈmȯis-ᵊn\ *vb* **moist·ened; moist·en·ing** \ˈmȯis-niŋ, -ᵊn-iŋ\ *vt* : to make moist ~ *vi* : to become moist — **moist·en·er** \ˈmȯis-nər, -ᵊn-ər\ *n*

mois·ture \ˈmȯis(h)-chər\ *n* [ME, modif. of MF *moistour,* fr. *moiste*] : liquid diffused or condensed in relatively small quantity

mois·tur·ize \-chə-ˌrīz\ *vt* **-ized; -iz·ing** : to add moisture to <~ the air> — **mois·tur·iz·er** *n*

moke \ˈmōk\ *n* [origin unknown] **1** *slang Brit* : DONKEY **2** *slang Austral* : NAG

mol *abbr* molecular; molecule

MOL *abbr* manned orbiting laboratory

mo·la \ˈmō-lə\ *n, pl* **mola** *or* **molas** [NL, fr. L, millstone] : OCEAN SUNFISH

mol·al \ˈmō-ləl\ *adj* [5*mole*] : of, relating to, or containing a gram molecule esp. of solute per 1000 grams of solvent — **mo·lal·i·ty** \mō-ˈlal-ət-ē\ *n*

1**mo·lar** \ˈmō-lər\ *n* [L *molaris,* fr. *molaris* of a mill, fr. *mola* millstone — more at MILL] : a tooth with a rounded or flattened surface adapted for grinding; *specif* : one of the cheek teeth in mammals behind the incisors and canines — see TOOTH illustration

2**molar** *adj* **1 :** pulverizing by friction : GRINDING **2 :** of, relating to, or located near the molar teeth

3**molar** *adj* **1** [L *moles* mass — more at MOLE] : of or relating to a mass of matter as distinguished from the properties or motions of molecules or atoms **2** [5*mole*] : of, relating to, or containing a gram molecule esp. of solute in 1000 milliliters of solution — **mo·lar·i·ty** \mō-ˈlar-ət-ē\ *n*

mo·las·ses \mə-ˈlas-əz\ *n* [Pg *melaço,* fr. LL *mellaceum* grape juice, fr. L *mell-, mel* honey — more at MELLIFLUOUS] **1 :** the thick dark to light brown syrup that is separated from raw sugar in sugar manufacture **2 :** a syrup made from boiling down sweet vegetable or fruit juice <citrus ~>

1**mold** \ˈmōld\ *n* [ME, fr. OE *molde;* akin to OHG *molta* soil, L *molere* to grind — more at MEAL] **1 :** crumbling soft friable earth suited to plant growth : SOIL; *esp* : soil rich in humus — compare LEAF MOLD **2** *dial Brit* **a :** the surface of the earth : GROUND **b :** the earth of the burying ground **3** *archaic* : earth that is the substance of the human body <be merciful great Duke to men of ~ —Shak.>

2**mold** *n* [ME, fr. OF *modle,* fr. L *modulus,* dim. of *modus* measure — more at METE] **1 :** distinctive nature or character : TYPE **2 :** the frame on or around which an object is constructed **3 a :** a cavity in which a substance is shaped: as **(1) :** a matrix for casting metal **(2) :** a form for a jelly or other food **b :** a molded object **4 :** MOLDING **5 a** *obs* : an example to be followed **b :** PROTOTYPE **c :** a fixed pattern or contour

3**mold** *vt* **1** *archaic* : to knead (dough) into a desired consistency or shape **2 :** to give shape to <the wind ~*s* the waves> **3 :** to form in a mold <~ candles> **4 :** to exert influence on <~ public opinion> **5 :** to fit the contours of **6 :** to ornament with molding or carving <~*ed* picture frames> — **mold·able** \ˈmōl-də-bəl\ *adj* — **mold·er** *n*

4**mold** *n* [ME *mowlde*] **1 :** a superficial often woolly growth produced on damp or decaying organic matter or on living organisms **2 :** a fungus (as of the order Mucorales) that produces mold

5**mold** *vi* : to become moldy

mold·board \ˈmōl(d)-ˌbō(ə)rd, -ˌbȯ(ə)rd\ *n* **1 a :** a curved iron plate attached above a plowshare to lift and turn the soil **b :** the flat or curved blade (as of a bulldozer) that pushes material to one side as the machine advances **2 :** one of the boards forming a mold for concrete

mold·er \ˈmōl-dər\ *vi* **mold·ered; mold·er·ing** \-d(ə-)riŋ\ [freq. of 5*mold*] : to crumble into particles : DISINTEGRATE, DECAY

mold·ing \ˈmōl-diŋ\ *n* **1 a :** an act or process of molding **b :** an object produced by molding **c :** the art or occupation of a molder **2 a :** a decorative recessed or relieved surface **b :** a decorative plane or curved strip used for ornamentation or finishing

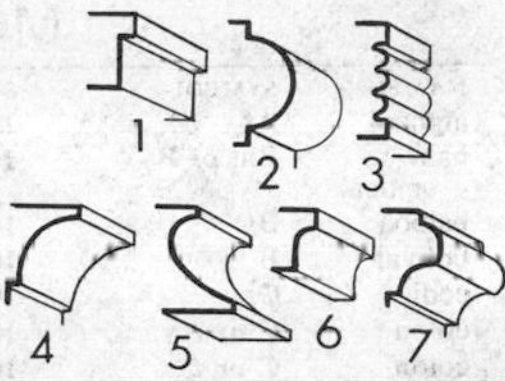

moldings 2a: *1* fillet and fascia, *2* torus, *3* reeding, *4* cavetto, *5* scotia, *6* congé, *7* beak

moldy \ˈmōl-dē\ *adj* **mold·i·er; -est 1 :** of, resembling, or covered with a mold-producing fungus <~ bread> **2 a :** being old and moldering : CRUMBLING **b :** ANTIQUATED, FUSTY <~ tradition> — **mold·i·ness** *n*

[1]mole \ˈmōl\ *n* [ME, fr. OE *māl;* akin to OHG *meil* spot] **:** a pigmented spot, mark, or small permanent protuberance on the human body; *esp* **:** NEVUS

[2]mole *n* [ME; akin to MLG *mol*] **1 :** any of numerous burrowing insectivores (esp. family Talpidae) with minute eyes, concealed ears, and soft fur **2 :** one who works in the dark **3 :** a machine for tunneling

[3]mole *n* [MF, fr. OIt *molo,* fr. LGk *mōlos,* fr. L *moles,* lit., mass, exertion; akin to OHG *muodi* weary, Gk *mōlos* exertion] **1 :** a massive work formed of masonry and large stones or earth laid in the sea as a pier or breakwater **2 :** the harbor formed by a mole

[4]mole *n* [F *môle,* fr. L *mola* mole, lit., mill, millstone — more at MILL] **:** an abnormal mass in the uterus esp. when containing fetal tissues

[5]mole *also* **mol** \ˈmōl\ *n* [G *mol,* short for *molekulargewicht* molecular weight, fr. *molekular* molecular + *gewicht* weight] **:** GRAM MOLECULE

mo·lec·u·lar \mə-ˈlek-yə-lər\ *adj* **1 :** of, relating to, or produced by molecules <~ oxygen> **2 :** of or relating to simple or elementary organization — **mo·lec·u·lar·i·ty** \-ˌlek-yə-ˈlar-ət-ē\ *n* — **mo·lec·u·lar·ly** \mə-ˈlek-yə-lər-lē\ *adv*

molecular biology *n* **:** a branch of biology dealing with the ultimate physicochemical organization of living matter and esp. with the molecular basis of inheritance and protein synthesis — **molecular biological** *adj* — **molecular biologist** *n*

molecular formula *n* **:** a chemical formula that is based on both analysis and molecular weight and gives the total number of atoms of each element in a molecule — compare STRUCTURAL FORMULA

molecular weight *n* **:** the weight of a molecule that may be calculated as the sum of the atomic weights of its constituent atoms — compare FORMULA WEIGHT

mol·e·cule \ˈmäl-i-ˌkyü(ə)l\ *n* [F *molécule,* fr. NL *molecula,* dim. of L *moles* mass] **1 :** the smallest particle of a substance that retains the properties of the substance and is composed of one or more atoms **2 :** a tiny bit : PARTICLE

mole·hill \ˈmōl-ˌhil\ *n* **:** a little ridge of earth thrown up by a mole

mole·skin \-ˌskin\ *n* **1 :** the skin of the mole used as fur **2 a :** a heavy durable cotton fabric with a short thick velvety nap on one side **b :** a garment made of moleskin — usu. used in pl.

mo·lest \mə-ˈlest\ *vt* [ME *molesten,* fr. MF *molester,* fr. L *molestare,* fr. *molestus* burdensome, annoying, fr. *moles* mass] **1 :** to annoy, disturb, or persecute esp. with hostile intent or injurious effect **2 :** to make annoying sexual advances to — **mo·les·ta·tion** \ˌmōl-ˌes-ˈtā-shən, ˌmōl-əs-, ˌmäl-\ *n* — **mo·lest·er** \mə-ˈles-tər\ *n*

mo·line \mə-ˈlēn, -ˈlīn\ *adj* [(assumed) AF *moliné,* fr. OF *molin* mill, fr. LL *molinum* — more at MILL] *of a heraldic cross* **:** having the end of each arm forked and recurved — see CROSS illustration

moll \ˈmäl, ˈmȯl\ *n* [prob. fr. *Moll,* nickname for Mary] **1 :** PROSTITUTE **2 a :** DOLL 2 **b :** a gangster's girl friend

mol·lie *also* **mol·ly** \ˈmäl-ē\ *n* **:** MOLLIENISIA

mol·lie·ni·sia \ˌmäl-i-ˈnizh-(ē-)ə\ *n* [NL, genus name, fr. Comte François N. *Mollien* †1850 F statesman] **:** any of a genus (*Mollienisia*) of brightly colored topminnows (family Poeciliidae) highly valued as aquarium fishes

mol·li·fy \ˈmäl-ə-ˌfī\ *vb* **-fied; -fy·ing** [ME *mollifien,* fr. MF *mollifier,* fr. LL *mollificare,* fr. L *mollis* soft — more at MELT] *vt* **1 :** to soothe in temper or disposition : APPEASE <*mollified* her by flattery> **2 :** to reduce the rigidity of : SOFTEN **3 :** to reduce in intensity : ASSUAGE, TEMPER ~ *vi, archaic* **:** SOFTEN, RELENT — **mol·li·fi·ca·tion** \ˌmäl-ə-fə-ˈkā-shən\ *n*

mol·lus·ci·cide \mə-ˈləs-(k)ə-ˌsīd\ *n* [NL *Mollusca* + E *-i-* + *-cide*] **:** an agent for destroying mollusks (as snails) — **mol·lus·ci·cid·al** \-ˌləs-(k)ə-ˈsīd-ᵊl\ *adj*

mol·lusk *or* **mol·lusc** \ˈmäl-əsk\ *n* [F *mollusque,* fr. NL *Mollusca,* phylum name, fr. L, neut. pl. of *molluscus* soft, fr. *mollis*] **:** any of a large phylum (Mollusca) of invertebrate animals (as snails or clams) with a soft unsegmented body usu. enclosed in a calcareous shell; *broadly* **:** SHELLFISH — **mol·lus·can** *also* **mol·lus·kan** \mə-ˈləs-kən, mä-\ *adj*

Moll·wei·de projection \ˌmȯl-ˌvīd-ə-, mōl-ˌwīd-ə-\ *n* [Karl B. *Mollweide* †1825 G mathematician and astronomer] **:** an equal-area map projection capable of showing the entire surface of the earth in the form of an ellipse with all parallels as straight lines more widely spaced at the equator than at the poles, with the central meridian as one half the length of the equator, and with all other meridians as ellipses equally spaced

[1]mol·ly·cod·dle \ˈmäl-ē-ˌkäd-ᵊl\ *n* [*Molly,* nickname for Mary] **1 :** a pampered or effeminate man or boy **2 :** GOODY-GOODY

[2]mollycoddle *vt* **mol·ly·cod·dled; mol·ly·cod·dling** \-ˌkäd-liŋ, -ᵊl-iŋ\ **:** to surround with an excessive or absurd degree of indulgence and attention : CODDLE ***syn*** see INDULGE — **mol·ly·cod·dler** \-ˌkäd-lər, -ᵊl-ər\ *n*

mol·ly·mawk \ˈmäl-i-ˌmȯk\ *var of* MALLEMUCK

Mo·loch \ˈmäl-ək, ˈmō-ˌläk\ *n* [LL, fr. Gk, fr. Heb *Mōlekh*] **:** a Semitic god to whom children were sacrificed

Mo·lo·tov cocktail \ˌmäl-ə-ˌtȯf-, ˌmȯl-, ˌmōl, -ˌtȯv\ *n* [Vyacheslav M. *Molotov*] **:** a crude hand grenade made of a bottle filled with a flammable liquid (as gasoline), fitted with a device (as a wick or saturated rag) capable of touching off the liquid and ignited at the moment of hurling

[1]molt \ˈmōlt\ *vb* [alter. of ME *mouten,* fr. OE *-mūtian* to change, fr. L *mutare* — more at MISS] *vi* **:** to shed hair, feathers, shell, horns, or an outer layer periodically ~ *vt* **:** to cast off (an outer covering) periodically; *specif* **:** to throw off (the old cuticle) — used of arthropods — **molt·er** *n*

[2]molt *n* **:** the act or process of molting; *specif* **:** ECDYSIS

mol·ten \ˈmōlt-ᵊn\ *adj* [ME, fr. pp. of *melten* to melt] **1** *obs* **:** made by melting and casting **2 :** fused or liquefied by heat : MELTED <~ lava> **3 :** having warmth or brilliance : GLOWING <the ~ sunlight of warm skies —T. B. Costain>

mol·to \ˈmōl-(ˌ)tō, ˈmȯl-\ *adv* [It, fr. L *multum,* fr. neut. of *multus* much] **:** MUCH, VERY — used in music directions <~ sostenuto>

mol wt *abbr* molecular weight

mo·ly \ˈmō-lē\ *n* [L, fr. Gk *mōly;* akin to Skt *mūla* root] **:** a mythical herb with a black root, milk-white blossoms, and magical powers

mo·lyb·date \mə-ˈlib-ˌdāt\ *n* **:** a salt of molybdenum containing the group MoO_4 or Mo_2O_7

molybdate orange *n* **:** a brilliant orange pigment consisting of the chromate, molybdate, and usu. sulfate of lead

mo·lyb·de·nite \mə-ˈlib-də-ˌnīt\ *n* [NL *molybdena*] **:** a blue usu. foliated mineral MoS_2 that is molybdenum disulfide and a source of molybdenum

mo·lyb·de·num \-nəm\ *n* [NL, fr. *molybdena,* a lead ore, molybdenite, molybdenum, fr. L *molybdaena* galena, fr. Gk *molybdaina,* fr. *molybdos* lead] **:** a metallic element that resembles chromium and tungsten in many properties, is used esp. in strengthening and hardening steel, and is a trace element in plant and animal metabolism — see ELEMENT table

molybdenum disulfide *n* **:** a compound MoS_2 used esp. as a lubricant in grease

mo·lyb·dic \mə-ˈlib-dik\ *adj* [NL *molybdenum*] **:** of, relating to, or containing molybdenum esp. with one of its higher valences

mo·lyb·dous \-dəs\ *adj* [NL *molybdenum*] **:** of, relating to, or containing molybdenum esp. with one of its lower valences

mom \ˈmäm, ˈməm\ *n* [short for *momma*] **:** MOTHER

MOM *abbr* middle of month

mome \ˈmōm\ *n, archaic* [origin unknown] **:** BLOCKHEAD, FOOL

mo·ment \ˈmō-mənt\ *n* [ME, fr. MF, fr. L *momentum* movement, particle sufficient to turn the scales, moment, fr. *movēre* to move] **1 :** a minute portion or point of time : INSTANT **2 a :** present time <at the ~ he is working on a novel> **b :** a time of excellence or conspicuousness <he has his ~*s*> **3 :** importance in influence or effect : notable or conspicuous consequence **4** *obs* **:** a cause or motive of action **5 :** a stage in historical or logical development **6 a :** tendency or measure of tendency to produce motion esp. about a point or axis **b :** the product of quantity (as a force) and the distance to a particular axis or point **7 a :** the mean of the *n*th powers of the deviations of the observed values in a set of statistical data from a fixed value **b :** the expected value of a power of the deviation of a random variable from a fixed value ***syn*** see IMPORTANCE

mo·men·tar·i·ly \ˌmō-mən-ˈter-ə-lē\ *adv* **1 :** for a moment **2 :** INSTANTLY **3 :** at any moment

mo·men·tary \ˈmō-mən-ˌter-ē\ *adj* **1 a :** continuing only a moment : TRANSITORY **b :** having a very brief life : EPHEMERAL **2 :** operative or recurring at every moment ***syn*** see TRANSIENT ***ant*** agelong — **mo·men·tari·ness** *n*

mo·ment·ly \ˈmō-mənt-lē\ *adv* **1 :** from moment to moment **2 :** at any moment **3 :** for a moment

mo·men·to \mə-ˈment-(ˌ)ō\ *var of* MEMENTO

moment of inertia : the ratio of the torque applied to a rigid body free to rotate about a given axis to the angular acceleration thus produced about that axis

moment of truth 1 : the final sword thrust in a bullfight **2 :** a moment of crisis on whose outcome much or everything depends

mo·men·tous \mō-ˈment-əs, mə-ˈment-\ *adj* **:** IMPORTANT, CONSEQUENTIAL — **mo·men·tous·ly** *adv* — **mo·men·tous·ness** *n*

mo·men·tum \mō-ˈment-əm, mə-ˈment-\ *n, pl* **mo·men·ta** \-ˈment-ə\ *or* **momentums** [NL, fr. L, movement] **:** a property of a moving body that determines the length of time required to bring it to rest when under the action of a constant force or moment; *broadly* **:** IMPETUS

mom·ma \ˈmäm-ə, ˈməm-\ *var of* MAMMA

Mo·mus \ˈmō-məs\ *n* [L, fr. Gk *Mōmos*] **:** the Greek god of blame and mockery

[1]mon \ˈmän\ *dial chiefly Brit var of* MAN

[2]mon *abbr* **1** monastery **2** monetary

[1]Mon \ˈmōn\ *n, pl* **Mon** *or* **Mons 1 :** a member of the dominant native people of Pegu in Burma **2 :** the Mon-Khmer language of the Mon people

[2]Mon *abbr* **1** Monaghan **2** Monday **3** Monmouthshire

mon- *or* **mono-** *under stress the (1st) "o" is sometimes* ō *although not shown at individual entries*\ *comb form* [ME, fr. MF & L; MF, fr. L, fr. Gk, fr. *monos* alone, single — more at MONK] **1 :** one : single : alone <*mono*plane> <*mono*drama> <*mono*phobia> **2 a :** containing one (usu. specified) atom, radical, or group <*mono*hydrate> <*mon*oxide> **b :** monomolecular <*mono*film> <*mono*layer>

ə abut	ᵊ kitten	ər further	a back	ā bake	ä cot, cart
aü out	ch chin	e less	ē easy	g gift	i trip	ī life
j joke	ŋ sing	ō flow	ȯ flaw	ȯi coin	th thin	t͟h this
ü loot	u̇ foot	y yet	yü few	yu̇ furious	zh vision

mon·a·chal \'män-i-kəl\ *adj* [MF or LL; MF, fr. LL *monachalis,* fr. *monachus* monk — more at MONK] : MONASTIC

mon·a·chism \'män-ə-,kiz-əm\ *n* : MONASTICISM

mo·nad \'mō-,nad\ *n* [LL *monad-, monas,* fr. Gk, fr. *monos*] **1 a** : UNIT, ONE **b** : ATOM 1 **c** : an elementary unextended individual spiritual substance from which material properties are derived **2** : a flagellated protozoan (as of the genus *Monas*) — **mo·nad·ic** \mō-'nad-ik, mə-\ *adj* — **mo·nad·ism** \'mō-,nad-,iz-əm\ *n*

mon·adel·phous \,män-ə-'del-fəs\ *adj, of stamens* : united by the filaments into one group usu. forming a tube around the gynoecium

mo·nad·nock \mə-'nad-,näk\ *n* [Mt. *Monadnock,* N.H.] : a hill or mountain of resistant rock surmounting a peneplain

mon·an·drous \mə-'nan-drəs, (')mä-\ *adj* **1** : having a single stamen or flowers with a single stamen **2** [Gk *monandros,* fr. *mon-* + *-andros* having (so many) men — more at -ANDROUS] : of, relating to, or characterized by monandry

mon·an·dry \'män-,an-drē\ *n, pl* **-dries** **1** [*monandrous*] : a marriage form or custom in which a woman has only one husband at a time **2** : a monandrous condition of a plant or flower

mon·arch \'män-ərk, -,ärk\ *n* [LL *monarcha,* fr. Gk *monarchos,* fr. *mon-* + *-archos* -arch] **1** : a person who reigns over a kingdom or empire: as **a** : a sovereign ruler **b** : a constitutional king or queen **2** : someone or something holding preeminent position or power **3** : a large migratory American butterfly (*Danaus plexippus*) that has orange-brown wings with black veins and borders and a larva that feeds on milkweed — **mo·nar·chal** \mə-'när-kəl, mä-\ *or* **mo·nar·chi·al** \-kē-əl\ *adj*

monarch 3

Mo·nar·chi·an \mə-'när-kē-ən, mä-\ *n* : an adherent of one of two anti-Trinitarian groups of the 2d and 3d centuries A.D. teaching that God is one person as well as one being — **Mo·nar·chi·an·ism** \-,iz-əm\ *n*

mo·nar·chi·cal \mə-'när-ki-kəl, mä-\ *or* **mo·nar·chic** \-kik\ *adj* : of, relating to, or characteristic of a monarch or monarchy — **mo·nar·chi·cal·ly** \-ki-k(ə-)lē\ *adv*

mon·ar·chism \'män-ər-,kiz-əm, -,är-\ *n* : monarchical government or principles — **mon·ar·chist** \-kəst\ *n or adj* — **mon·ar·chis·tic** \,män-ər-'kis-tik, -,är-\ *adj*

mon·ar·chy \'män-ər-kē *also* -,är-\ *n, pl* **-chies** **1** : undivided rule or absolute sovereignty by a single person **2** : a nation or state having a monarchical government **3** : a government having an hereditary chief of state with life tenure and powers varying from nominal to absolute

mo·nar·da \mə-'närd-ə\ *n* [NL, genus name, fr. Nicolas *Monardes* †1588 Sp botanist] : any of a genus (*Monarda*) of coarse No. American mints with a tubular many-nerved calyx and whorls of showy flowers

mon·as·te·ri·al \,män-ə-'stir-ē-əl, -'ster-\ *adj, archaic* : of or relating to monasteries or monastic life

mon·as·tery \'män-ə-,ster-ē\ *n, pl* **-ter·ies** [ME *monasterie,* fr. LL *monasterium,* fr. LGk *monastērion,* fr. Gk, hermit's cell, fr. *monazein* to live alone, fr. *monos* single — more at MONK] : a house for persons under religious vows; *esp* : an establishment for monks

mo·nas·tic \mə-'nas-tik\ *adj* **1** : of or relating to monasteries or to monks or nuns **2** : resembling (as in seclusion or ascetic simplicity) life in a monastery — **monastic** *n* — **mo·nas·ti·cal·ly** \-ti-k(ə-)lē\ *adv* — **mo·nas·ti·cism** \-tə-,siz-əm\ *n*

mon·atom·ic \,män-ə-'täm-ik\ *adj* **1 a** : consisting of one atom; *esp* : having but one atom in the molecule **b** : having a thickness equal to the diameter of a constituent atom **2** : UNIVALENT 1 **3** : having one replaceable atom or radical <~ alcohols> — **mon·a·tom·i·cal·ly** \-i-k(ə-)lē\ *adv*

mon·au·ral \(')mä-'nȯr-əl\ *adj* : MONOPHONIC 2 — **mon·au·ral·ly** \-ə-lē\ *adv*

mon·ax·i·al \(')mä-'nak-sē-əl\ *adj* : having or based on a single axis : UNIAXIAL; *specif* : having flowers developing on a single axis

mon·a·zite \'män-ə-,zīt\ *n* [G *monazit,* fr. Gk *monazein*] : a mineral (Ce,La,Md,Pr,Th)PO_4 that is a yellow, red, or brown phosphate of the cerium metals and thorium found often in sand and gravel deposits

Mon·day \'mən-dē\ *n* [ME, fr. OE *mōnandæg;* akin to OHG *mānatag* Monday; both fr. a prehistoric WGmc compound whose components are represented by OE *mōna* moon and by OE *dæg* day] : the second day of the week — **Mon·days** \-dēz\ *adv*

mon·ecious *var of* MONOECIOUS

M1 rifle \'em-,wən-\ *n* : a .30 caliber gas-operated clip-fed semiautomatic rifle used by U.S. troops in World War II

mon·es·trous \(')mä-'nes-trəs\ *adj* : experiencing estrus once each year : having a single annual breeding period

mon·e·tary \'män-ə-,ter-ē, 'mən-\ *adj* [LL *monetarius* of a mint, of money, fr. L *moneta*] : of or relating to money or to the mechanisms by which it is supplied to and circulates in the economy ***syn*** see FINANCIAL — **mon·e·tari·ly** \,män-ə-'ter-ə-lē, ,mən-\ *adv*

monetary unit *n* : the standard unit of value of a currency

mon·e·tize \'män-ə-,tīz, 'mən-\ *vt* **-tized; -tiz·ing** [L *moneta*] : to coin into money; *also* : to establish as legal tender — **mon·e·ti·za·tion** \,män-ət-ə-'zā-shən, ,mən-\ *n*

mon·ey \'mən-ē\ *n, pl* **moneys** *or* **mon·ies** \'mən-ēz\ [ME *moneye,* fr. MF *moneie,* fr. L *moneta* mint, money — more at MINT] **1** : something generally accepted as a medium of exchange, a measure of value, or a means of payment: as **a** : officially coined or stamped metal currency **b** : MONEY OF ACCOUNT **c** : PAPER MONEY **2** : wealth reckoned in terms of money **3** : a form or denomination of coin or paper money **4 a** : the first, second, and third place winners in a horse or dog race — usu. used in the phrases *in the money* or *out of the money* **b** : prize money <his horse took third ~> **5** : persons or interests possessing or controlling great wealth

MONEY

NAME	SYMBOL	SUBDIVISIONS	COUNTRY
afghani	Af	100 puls	Afghánistan
baht *or* tical	Bht *or* B	100 satang	Thailand
balboa	B/	100 centesimos	Panama
bolivar	B	100 centimos	Venezuela
cedi	₵	100 pesewas	Ghana
colon	₵ *or* ¢	100 centimos	Costa Rica
colon	₵ *or* ¢	100 centavos	El Salvador
cordoba	C$	100 centavos	Nicaragua
cruzeiro	$ *or* Cr$	100 centavos	Brazil
dalasi	D	100 bututs	Gambia
deutsche mark	DM	100 pfennigs	West Germany
dinar	DA	100 centimes	Algeria
dinar	BD	1000 fils	Bahrain
dinar	ID	5 riyals 20 dirhams 1000 fils	Iraq
dinar	JD	1000 fils	Jordan
dinar	KD	1000 fils	Kuwait
dinar	LD	1000 dirhams	Libya
dinar	£SY	1000 fils	Southern Yemen
dinar	D	1000 millimes	Tunisia
dinar	Din	100 paras	Yugoslavia
dirham	DH	100 francs	Morocco
dollar	$A	100 cents	Australia
dollar	B$	100 cents	Bahamas
dollar	$	100 cents	Barbados
dollar	$	100 cents	Belize (British Honduras)
dollar	$	100 cents	Bermuda
dollar	$	100 sen	Brunei
dollar	$	100 cents	Canada
dollar	Eth$ *or* E$	100 cents	Ethiopia
dollar	$F	100 cents	Fiji
dollar	G$	100 cents	Guyana
dollar	HK$	100 cents	Hong Kong
dollar	$	100 cents	Jamaica
dollar	$	100 cents	Liberia
dollar	M$	100 cents	Malaysia
dollar	NZ$	100 cents	New Zealand
dollar	S$	100 cents	Singapore
dollar	TT$	100 cents	Trinidad and Tobago
dollar	$	100 cents	United States
dollar — see YUAN, below			
dong	D	100 xu	North Vietnam
drachma	Dr	100 lepta	Greece
escudo	E *or* E°	100 centesimos 1000 milesimos	Chile
escudo	$ *or* Esc	100 centavos	Portugal
florin — see GULDEN, below			
forint	F *or* Ft	100 filler	Hungary
franc	Fr *or* F	100 centimes	Belgium
franc	FBu	100 centimes	Burundi
franc	Fr *or* F	100 centimes	Cameroon
franc	Fr *or* F	100 centimes	Central African Republic
franc	Fr *or* F	100 centimes	Chad
franc	Fr *or* F	100 centimes	Congo (Brazzaville)
franc	Fr *or* F	100 centimes	Dahomey
franc	Fr *or* F	100 centimes	France
franc	Fr *or* F	100 centimes	Gabon
franc	Fr *or* F	100 centimes	Guinea
franc	Fr *or* F	100 centimes	Ivory Coast
franc	Fr *or* F	100 centimes	Luxembourg
franc	Fr *or* F *or* FMG	100 centimes	Malagasy Republic
franc	Fr *or* F	100 centimes	Mali
franc	Fr *or* F	100 centimes	Mauritania
franc	Fr *or* F	100 centimes	Niger
franc	Fr *or* F	100 centimes	Rwanda
franc	Fr *or* F	100 centimes	Senegal
franc	Fr *or* F	100 centimes *or* rappen	Switzerland
franc	Fr *or* F	100 centimes	Togo
franc	Fr *or* F	100 centimes	Upper Volta
gourde	G *or* G *or* Gde	100 centimes	Haiti
guarani	G *or* G	100 centimos	Paraguay
gulden *or* guilder *or* florin	f *or* fl *or* g	100 cents	Netherlands
kip	K	100 at	Laos
koruna	Kčs	100 halers	Czechoslovakia
krona	Kr	100 aurar	Iceland
krona	Kr	100 öre	Sweden
krone	Kr	100 öre	Denmark
krone	Kr	100 öre	Norway
kwacha	K	100 tambala	Malawi
kwacha	K	100 ngwee	Zambia
kyat	K	100 pyas	Burma

NAME	SYMBOL	SUBDIVISIONS	COUNTRY
lek	L	100 qintar	Albania
lempira	L	100 centavos	Honduras
leone	Le	100 cents	Sierra Leone
leu	L	100 bani	Rumania
lev	Lv	100 stotinki	Bulgaria
lira	L *or* Lit	100 centesimi	Italy
lira *or* pound	£T *or* LT *or* TL	100 kurus *or* piasters	Turkey
mark *or* ostmark	M *or* OM	100 pfennigs	East Germany
mark — see DEUTSCHE MARK, above			
markka	M *or* Mk	100 pennia	Finland
naira	₦	100 kobo	Nigeria
ostmark — see MARK, above			
pa'anga	T$	100 seniti	Tonga
pataca	P *or* $	100 avos	Macao
peseta	Pta *or* P (*pl* Pts)	100 centimos	Equatorial Guinea
peseta	Pta *or* P (*pl* Pts)	100 centimos	Spain
peso	$	100 centavos	Argentina
peso	$B	100 centavos	Bolivia
peso	$ *or* P	100 centavos	Colombia
peso	$	100 centavos	Cuba
peso	RD$	100 centavos	Dominican Republic
peso	$	100 centavos	Mexico
peso	₱ *or* P	100 sentimos *or* centavos	Philippines
peso	$	100 centesimos	Uruguay
piaster	VN$ *or* Pr	100 cents	South Vietnam
pound	£	1000 mils	Cyprus
pound	£E	100 piasters 1000 milliemes	Egypt
pound	£	100 pence	Ireland
pound *or* lira	I£ *or* IL	100 agorot	Israel
pound	L£ *or* LL	100 piasters	Lebanon
pound	£	100 pence	Malta
pound	£	20 shillings 240 pence	Rhodesia
pound	£S *or* LSd	100 piasters 1000 milliemes	Sudan
pound *or* lira	£S *or* LS	100 piasters	Syria
pound	£	100 pence	United Kingdom
pound — see LIRA, above			
quetzal	Q *or* Q	100 centavos	Guatemala
rand	R	100 cents	Botswana
rand	R	100 cents	Lesotho
rand	R	100 cents	South Africa
rand	R	100 cents	Swaziland
rial	R *or* Rl	100 dinars	Iran
rial	R	1000 baizas	Oman
rial	YR	40 buqshas	Yemen
riel	៛ *or* CR	100 sen	Cambodia
riyal	R *or* SR	20 qursh 100 halala	Saudi Arabia
ruble	R *or* Rub	100 kopecks	U.S.S.R.
rupee	Re (*pl* Rs)	100 paise	Bhutan
rupee	Re (*pl* Rs)	100 paise	India
rupee	Re (*pl* Rs)	100 cents	Mauritius
rupee	Re (*pl* Rs)	100 paise	Nepal
rupee	Re (*pl* Rs)	100 paisa	Pakistan
rupee	Re (*pl* Rs)	100 cents	Seychelles
rupee	Re (*pl* Rs)	100 cents	Sri Lanka
rupiah	Rp	100 sen	Indonesia
schilling	S *or* Sch	100 groschen	Austria
shilingi *or* shilling	Sh	100 senti	Tanzania
shilling	Sh	100 cents	Kenya
shilling	Sh *or* So Sh	100 cents	Somalia
shilling	Sh	100 cents	Uganda
sol	S/ *or* $	100 centavos	Peru
sucre	S/	100 centavos	Ecuador
taka		100 paisa	Bangladesh
tala	WS$	100 senes	Western Samoa
tical — see BAHT, above			
tugrik		100 mongo	Outer Mongolia
won	W	100 jun	North Korea
won	W	100 chon	South Korea
yen	¥ *or* Y	100 sen	Japan
yuan	$	10 chiao 100 fen	China (mainland)
yuan *or* dollar	NT$	10 chiao	China (Taiwan)
zaire	Z	100 makuta (*sing:* likuta) 10,000 sengi	Zaire
zloty	Zl *or* Z	100 groszy	Poland

mon·ey·bags \ˈmən-ē-ˌbagz\ *n pl but sing or pl in constr* **1** : WEALTH **2** : a wealthy person

money changer *n* **1** : one whose occupation is the exchanging of kinds or denominations of currency **2** : a device for holding and dispensing sorted change

mon·eyed \ˈmən-ēd\ *adj* **1** : having money : WEALTHY **2** : consisting in or derived from money

mon·ey·er \ˈmən-ē-ər\ *n* [ME, fr. OF *monier*, fr. LL *monetarius* master of a mint, coiner, fr. *monetarius* of a mint] : an authorized coiner of money : MINTER

mon·ey·lend·er \ˈmən-ē-ˌlen-dər\ *n* : one whose business is lending money; *specif* : PAWNBROKER

mon·ey–mak·er \ˈmən-ē-ˌmā-kər\ *n* **1** : one that accumulates wealth **2** : a plan or product that produces profit — **mon·ey·mak·ing** \-kiŋ\ *adj or n*

money of account : a denominator of value or basis of exchange which is used in keeping accounts and for which there may or may not be an equivalent coin or denomination of paper money

money order *n* : an order issued by a post office, bank, or telegraph office for payment of a specified sum of money usu. at another office

mon·ey·wort \ˈmən-ē-ˌwərt, -ˌwȯ(ə)rt\ *n* : a trailing perennial herb (*Lysimachia nummularia*) with rounded opposite leaves and solitary yellow flowers in their axils

¹mon·ger \ˈməŋ-gər, ˈmäŋ-\ *n* [ME *mongere*, fr. OE *mangere*, fr. L *mangon-, mango*, of Gk origin; akin to Gk *manganon* charm, philter — more at MANGONEL] **1** : BROKER, DEALER — usu. used in combination <ale*monger*> **2** : one who attempts to stir up or spread something that is usu. petty or discreditable — usu. used in combination <gossip*monger*> <war*monger*>

²monger *vt* **mon·gered; mon·ger·ing** \-g(ə-)riŋ\ : to deal in : PEDDLE

mon·go \ˈmäŋ-(ˌ)gō\ *n, pl* **mongo** [Mongolian] — see *tugrik* at MONEY table

Mon·gol \ˈmäŋ-gəl; ˈmän-ˌgōl, ˈmäŋ-\ *n* [Mongolian *Mongol*] **1** : a member of one of the chiefly pastoral Mongoloid peoples of Mongolia **2** : MONGOLIAN 2 **3** : a person of Mongoloid racial stock **4** *often not cap* : one affected with mongolism — **Mongol** *adj*

¹Mon·go·lian \män-ˈgōl-yən, mäŋ-, -ˈgō-lē-ən\ *adj* **1** : of, relating to, or constituting Mongolia, the Mongolian People's Republic, the Mongols, or Mongolian **2** : MONGOLOID

²Mongolian *n* **1 a** : MONGOL 1 **b** : a person of Mongoloid racial stock **c** : a native or inhabitant of the Mongolian People's Republic **2** : the Mongolic language of the Mongol people **3** *often not cap* : MONGOL 4

Mongolian fold *n* [fr. its being characteristic of Mongoloid peoples] : EPICANTHIC FOLD

Mongolian gerbil *n* : a gerbil (*Meriones unguiculatus*) of Mongolia and northern China that has an external resemblance to a rat, has a high capacity for temperature regulation, and is used as an experimental laboratory animal

mon·go·lian·ism \män-ˈgōl-yə-ˌniz-əm, mäŋ-, -ˈgō-lē-ə-\ *n* : MONGOLISM

¹Mon·gol·ic \män-ˈgäl-ik, mäŋ-\ *adj* : MONGOLOID 1

²Mongolic *n* : a group of Altaic languages including Mongolian and Kalmuck

mon·gol·ism \ˈmäŋ-gə-ˌliz-əm\ *n* : a congenital idiocy in which a child is born with slanting eyes, a broad short skull, and broad hands with short fingers and which is associated with trisomy of the chromosome numbered 21 in man — called also *Down's syndrome*

Mon·gol·oid \ˈmäŋ-gə-ˌlȯid\ *adj* **1** : of, constituting, or characteristic of a major racial stock native to Asia including peoples of northern and eastern Asia, Malaysians, Eskimos, and often American Indians **2** *not cap* : of, relating to, or affected with mongolism — **Mongoloid** *n*

mon·goose \ˈmän-ˌgüs, ˈmäŋ-\ *n, pl* **mon·goos·es** *also* **mon·geese** \-ˌgēs\ [Hindi *magūs*, fr. Prakrit *maṅguso*] : an agile grizzled ferret-sized mammal (*Herpestes nyula*) of India that feeds on snakes and rodents and that is related to the civets and genets; *broadly* : any of various related Asian and African mammals

mongoose

mon·grel \ˈməŋ-grəl, ˈmäŋ-\ *n* [prob. fr. ME *mong* mixture, short for *ymong*, fr. OE *gemong* crowd — more at AMONG] **1** : an individual resulting from the interbreeding of diverse breeds or strains; *esp* : one of unknown ancestry **2** : a cross between types of persons or things — **mongrel** *or* **mon·grel·ly** \-grə-lē\ *adj* — **mon·grel·ism** \-grə-ˌliz-əm\ *n* — **mon·grel·iza·tion** \ˌməŋ-grə-lə-ˈzā-shən, ˌmäŋ-\ *n* — **mon·grel·ize** \ˈməŋ-grə-ˌlīz, ˈmäŋ-\ *vt*

mon·ied \ˈmən-ēd\ *var of* MONEYED

monies *pl of* MONEY

mon·i·ker *or* **mon·ick·er** \ˈmän-i-kər\ *n* [origin unknown] *slang* : NAME, NICKNAME

mo·ni·li·a·sis \ˌmō-nə-ˈlī-ə-səs, ˌmän-ə-\ *n, pl* **-a·ses** \-ˌsēz\ [NL, fr. *Monilia*, genus of fungi, fr. L *monile* necklace] : CANDIDIASIS; *specif* : THRUSH

mo·nil·i·form \mə-ˈnil-ə-ˌfȯrm\ *adj* [L *monile* necklace — more at MANE] : jointed or constricted at regular intervals so as to resemble a string of beads <a ~ root> <~ insect antennae> — **mo·nil·i·form·ly** *adv*

mon·ish \ˈmän-ish\ *vt* [ME *monesen*, alter. of *monesten*, fr. OF *monester*, fr. (assumed) VL *monestare*, fr. L *monēre* to warn] : WARN

mo·nism \ˈmō-ˌniz-əm, ˈmän-ˌiz-\ *n* [G *monismus*, fr. *mon-* + *-ismus* -ism] **1 a** : a view that there is only one kind of ultimate substance **b** : the view that reality is one unitary organic whole with no independent parts **2 :** MONOGENESIS — **mo·nist** \ˈmō-nəst, ˈmän-əst\ *n* — **mo·nis·tic** \mō-ˈnis-tik, mä-\ *or* **mo·nis·ti·cal** \-ti-kəl\ *adj*

mo·ni·tion \mō-ˈnish-ən, mə-\ *n* [ME *monicioun,* fr. MF *monition,* fr. L *monition-, monitio,* fr. *monitus,* pp. of *monēre*] **1 :** WARNING, CAUTION **2 :** an intimation of danger

1**mon·i·tor** \ˈmän-ət-ər\ *n* [L, one that warns, overseer, fr. *monitus,* pp. of *monēre* to warn — more at MIND] **1 a :** a student appointed to assist a teacher **b :** a person or thing that warns or instructs **c :** one that monitors or is used in monitoring: as (1) **:** a receiver used to view the picture being picked up by a television camera (2) **:** a device for observing a biological condition or function <a heart ~> (3) **:** software or hardware that monitors the operation of a system and esp. a computer system **2 :** any of various large tropical Old World pleurodont lizards (genus *Varanus* and family Varanidae) closely related to the iguanas **3** [*Monitor,* first ship of the type] **a :** a heavily armored warship formerly used in coastal operations having a very low freeboard and one or more revolving gun turrets **b :** a small modern warship with shallow draft for coastal bombardment **4 :** a raised central portion of a roof having low windows or louvers for providing light and air — **mon·i·to·ri·al** \ˌmän-ə-ˈtōr-ē-əl, -ˈtȯr-\ *adj* — **mon·i·tor·ship** \ˈmän-ət-ər-ˌship\ *n* — **mon·i·tress** \ˈmän-ə-trəs\ *n*

2**monitor** *vt* **mon·i·tored; mon·i·tor·ing** \ˈmän-ət-ə-riŋ, ˈmän-ə-triŋ\ **1 :** to check (as a radio or television signal or program) by means of a receiver for quality or fidelity to a band or for military, political, or criminal significance **2 :** to test for intensity of radiations esp. if due to radioactivity **3 :** to watch, observe, or check esp. for a special purpose **4 :** to keep track of, regulate, or control the operation of (as a machine or process) **5 :** to check or regulate the volume or quality of (sound) in recording

1**mon·i·to·ry** \ˈmän-ə-ˌtōr-ē, -ˌtȯr-\ *adj* [L *monitorius,* fr. *monitus*] **:** giving admonition **:** WARNING

2**monitory** *n, pl* **-ries :** a letter containing an admonition or warning

1**monk** \ˈməŋk\ *n* [ME, fr. OE *munuc,* fr. LL *monachus,* fr. LGk *monachos,* fr. Gk, adj., single, fr. *monos* single, alone; akin to OHG *mengen* to lack, Gk *manos* sparse] **:** a man who is a member of a religious order and lives in a monastery; *also* **:** FRIAR

2**monk** *n* **:** MONKEY

monk·ery \ˈməŋ-kə-rē\ *n, pl* **-er·ies 1 :** monastic life or practice **:** MONASTICISM **2 :** a monastic house **:** MONASTERY

1**mon·key** \ˈməŋ-kē\ *n, pl* **monkeys** [prob. fr. LG origin; akin to *Moneke,* name of an ape, prob. of Romance origin; akin to OSp *mona* monkey] **1 :** a primate mammal with the exception of man and usu. the lemurs and tarsiers; *esp* **:** any of the smaller longer-tailed primates as contrasted with the apes **2 a :** a person resembling a monkey **b :** a ludicrous figure **:** DUPE **3 :** any of various machines, implements, or vessels; *esp* **:** the falling weight of a pile driver **4 :** a desperate desire for or addiction to drugs — often used in the phrase *monkey on one's back*

2**monkey** *vb* **mon·keyed; mon·key·ing** *vi* **1 :** to act in a grotesque or mischievous manner **2 a :** FOOL, TRIFLE **b :** TAMPER ~ *vt* **:** MIMIC, MOCK

monkey jacket *n* **:** MESS JACKET

mon·key·pod \ˈməŋ-kē-ˌpäd\ *n* **1 :** an ornamental tropical tree (*Pithecolobium saman*) that has bipinnate leaves, globose clusters of flowers with crimson stamens, sweet-pulp pods eaten by cattle, and wood used in carving — called also *rain tree* **2 :** the wood of a monkeypod

mon·key·shine \-ˌshīn\ *n* **:** PRANK — usu. used in pl.

monkey wrench *n* **1 :** a wrench with one fixed and one adjustable jaw at right angles to a straight handle **2 :** something that disrupts <threw a *monkey wrench* into the peace negotiations>

Mon-Khmer \ˌmōn-kə-ˈme(ə)r\ *n* **:** a language family containing Mon, Khmer, and several other languages of southeast Asia

monk·hood \ˈməŋk-ˌhu̇d\ *n* **1 :** the character, condition, or profession of a monk **:** MONASTICISM **2 :** monks as a class

monk·ish \ˈməŋ-kish\ *adj* **1 :** of or relating to monks **2 :** inclined to disciplinary self-denial

monk's cloth *n* **:** a coarse heavy fabric in basket weave made orig. of worsted and used for monk's habits but now chiefly of cotton or linen and used for draperies

monks·hood \ˈməŋ(k)s-ˌhu̇d\ *n* **:** ACONITUM 1; *esp* **:** a poisonous Eurasian herb (*Aconitum napellus*) often cultivated for its showy terminal racemes of white or purplish flowers

1**mono** \ˈmän-(ˌ)ō\ *adj* [by shortening] **:** MONOPHONIC 2

2**mono** *n, pl* **monos 1 :** a monophonic phonograph record **2 :** monophonic reproduction

3**mono** *n* **:** INFECTIOUS MONONUCLEOSIS

mono- — see MON-

mono·ac·id \ˌmän-ō-ˈas-əd\ *n* **:** an acid having only one acid hydrogen atom

mono·acid·ic \-ə-ˈsid-ik\ *adj* **:** having a single hydroxyl group and able to react with only one molecule of a monobasic acid to form a salt or ester — used of bases and alcohols

mono·al·pha·bet·ic substitution \ˈmän-ō-ˌal-fə-ˌbet-ik-\ *n* **:** substitution in cryptography that uses a single cipher alphabet so that each plaintext letter always has the same cipher equivalent — compare POLYALPHABETIC SUBSTITUTION

mono·amine \ˌmän-ō-ə-ˈmēn\ *n* [ISV] **:** an amine RNH_2 that has one organic substituent attached to the nitrogen atom; *esp* **:** one (as serotonin) that is functionally important in neural transmission

monoamine oxidase *n* **:** an enzyme that deaminates monoamines oxidatively and that affects the nervous system by breaking down monoamine neurotransmitters

mono·am·in·er·gic \ˌmän-ō-ˌam-ə-ˈnər-jik\ *adj* [*monoamine* + Gk *ergon* work — more at WORK] **:** liberating or involving monoamines (as serotonin or norepinephrine) in neural transmission <~ neurons> <~ mechanisms>

mono·ba·sic \ˌmän-ə-ˈbā-sik\ *adj* [ISV] **:** having only one acid and replaceable hydrogen atom

mono·car·box·yl·ic \-ˌkär-(ˌ)bäk-ˈsil-ik\ *adj* **:** containing one carboxyl group <acetic acid is a ~ acid>

mono·car·pic \-ˈkär-pik\ *adj* [prob. fr. (assumed) NL *monocarpicus,* fr. NL *mon-* + *-carpicus* -carpic] **:** bearing fruit but once and then dying

mono·cha·si·um \-ˈkä-z(h)ē-əm\ *n, pl* **-sia** \-z(h)ē-ə\ [NL, fr. *mon-* + *-chasium* (as in *dichasium*)] **:** a cymose inflorescence that produces only one main axis — **mono·cha·sial** \-zh(ē-)əl, -zē-əl\ *adj*

mono·chord \ˈmän-ə-ˌkȯ(ə)rd\ *n* [ME *monocorde,* fr. MF, fr. ML *monochordum,* fr. Gk *monochordon,* fr. *mon-* + *chordē* string — more at YARN] **:** an instrument of ancient origin for measuring and demonstrating the mathematical relations of musical tones and that consists of a single string stretched over a sounding board and a movable bridge set on a graduated scale

mono·chro·mat \ˈmän-ə-krō-ˌmat, ˌmän-ə-ˈ\ *n* [*mon-* + Gk *chrōmat-, chrōma*] **:** a completely color-blind individual

mono·chro·mat·ic \ˌmän-ə-krō-ˈmat-ik\ *adj* [L *monochromatos,* fr. Gk *monochrōmatos,* fr. *mon-* + *chrōmat-, chrōma* color — more at CHROMATIC] **1 a :** having or consisting of one color or hue **b :** MONOCHROME 2 **2 :** consisting of radiation of a single wavelength or of a very small range of wavelengths **3 :** of, relating to, or exhibiting monochromatism — **mono·chro·mat·i·cal·ly** \-i-k(ə-)lē\ *adv* — **mono·chro·ma·tic·i·ty** \-ˌkrō-mə-ˈtis-ət-ē\ *n*

mono·chro·ma·tism \-ˈkrō-mə-ˌtiz-əm\ *n* **:** complete color blindness in which all colors appear as shades of gray

mono·chro·ma·tor \ˌmän-ə-ˈkrō-ˌmāt-ər\ *n* [*monochrom*atic + illumin*ator*] **:** a device for isolating a narrow portion of a spectrum

1**mono·chrome** \ˈmän-ə-ˌkrōm\ *n* [ML *monochroma,* fr. L, fem. of *monochromos* of one color, fr. Gk *monochrōmos,* fr. *mon-* + *-chrōmos* -chrome] **:** a painting, drawing, or photograph in a single hue — **mono·chro·mic** \ˌmän-ə-ˈkrō-mik\ *adj* — **mono·chrom·ist** \ˈmän-ə-ˌkrō-məst\ *n*

2**monochrome** *adj* **1 :** of, relating to, or made with a single color or hue **2 :** characterized by the reproduction of visual images in tones of gray <~ television>

mon·o·cle \ˈmän-i-kəl\ *n* [F, fr. LL *monoculus* having one eye, fr. L *mon-* + *oculus* eye — more at EYE] **:** an eyeglass for one eye — **mon·o·cled** \-kəld\ *adj*

mono·cli·nal \ˌmän-ə-ˈklīn-ᵊl\ *adj* **:** having or relating to a single oblique inclination <~ folding of rock layers> — **monoclinal** *n*

mono·cline \ˈmän-ə-ˌklīn\ *n* **:** a monoclinal geologic fold

mono·clin·ic \ˌmän-ə-ˈklin-ik\ *adj* [ISV] **:** having one oblique intersection of the crystallographic axes

monoclinic system *n* **:** a crystal system characterized by three unequal axes with one oblique intersection

mono·cli·nous \-ˈklī-nəs\ *adj* [NL *monoclinus,* fr. *mon-* + *-clinus* -clinous] **:** having both stamens and pistils in the same flower

mono·coque \ˈmän-ə-ˌkōk, -ˌkäk\ *n* [F, fr. *mon-* + *coque* shell, fr. L *coccum* excrescence on a tree, fr. Gk *kokkos* berry] **1 :** a type of construction (as of a fuselage or a rocket body) in which the outer skin carries all or a major part of the stresses **2 :** a type of vehicle construction (as of a motortruck or railroad car) in which the body is integral with the chassis

mono·cot \-ˌkät\ *n* **:** MONOCOTYLEDON

mono·cot·yl \-ˌkät-ᵊl\ *n* **:** MONOCOTYLEDON

mono·cot·y·le·don \ˌmän-ə-ˌkät-ᵊl-ˈēd-ᵊn\ *n* [deriv. of NL *mon-* + *cotyledon*] **:** any of a subclass (Monocotyledoneae) of seed plants having an embryo with a single cotyledon and usu. parallel-veined leaves — **mono·cot·y·le·don·ous** \-ᵊn-əs\ *adj*

mo·noc·ra·cy \mä-ˈnäk-rə-sē, mə-\ *n* **:** government by a single person — **mono·crat** \ˈmän-ə-ˌkrat\ *n* — **mono·crat·ic** \ˌmän-ə-ˈkrat-ik\ *adj*

mon·oc·u·lar \mä-ˈnäk-yə-lər, mə-\ *adj* [LL *monoculus* having one eye] **1 :** of, involving, or affecting a single eye **2 :** suitable for use with only one eye — **mon·oc·u·lar·ly** *adv*

mono·cul·ture \ˈmän-ə-ˌkəl-chər\ *n* **:** the cultivation of a single product to the exclusion of other uses of land — **mono·cul·tur·al** \ˌmän-ə-ˈkəlch-(ə-)rəl\ *adj*

mono·cy·clic \ˌmän-ə-ˈsī-klik, ˈsik-lik\ *adj* [ISV *mon-* + *cyclic*] **1 :** arranged in or consisting of one whorl or circle **2 :** containing one ring in the molecular structure — **mono·cy·cly** \ˈmän-ə-ˌsī-klē\ *n*

mono·cyte \ˈmän-ə-ˌsīt\ *n* [ISV] **:** a large phagocytic leukocyte with basophlic cytoplasm containing faint eosinophilic granulations — **mono·cyt·ic** \ˌmän-ə-ˈsit-ik\ *adj* — **mono·cyt·oid** \-ˈsīt-ˌȯid\ *adj*

mon·o·dist \ˈmän-əd-əst\ *n* **:** a writer, singer, or composer of monody

mono·dra·ma \ˈmän-ə-ˌdräm-ə, -ˌdram-\ *n* **:** a drama acted or designed to be acted by a single person — **mono·dra·mat·ic** \ˌmän-ə-drə-ˈmat-ik\ *adj*

mon·o·dy \ˈmän-əd-ē\ *n, pl* **-dies** [ML *monodia,* fr. Gk *monōidia,* fr. *monōidos* singing alone, fr. *mon-* + *aidein* to sing — more at ODE] **1 :** an ode sung by one voice (as in a Greek tragedy) **2 :** an elegy or dirge performed by one person **3 a :** a monophonic vocal piece **b :** the monophonic style of 17th century opera — **mo·nod·ic** \mə-ˈnäd-ik\ *or* **mo·nod·i·cal** \-i-kəl\ *adj* — **mo·nod·i·cal·ly** \-i-k(ə-)lē\ *adv*

mon·oe·cious \mə-ˈnē-shəs, (ˈ)mä-,\ *adj* [deriv. of Gk *mon-* + *oikos* house — more at VICINITY] **1 :** having male and female sex organs in the same individual **:** HERMAPHRODITIC **2 :** having pistillate and staminate flowers on the same plant — **mon·oe·cious·ly** *adv*

mon·oe·cism \-ˈnē-ˌsiz-əm\ *n* **:** the condition of being monoecious

mono·es·ter \ˈmän-ō-ˌes-tər\ *n* **:** an ester (as of a dibasic acid) that contains only one ester group

mono·fil·a·ment \ˌmän-ə-ˈfil-ə-mənt\ *n* **:** a single untwisted synthetic filament (as of nylon)

mo·nog·a·mist \mə-ˈnäg-ə-məst\ *n* **:** one who practices or upholds monogamy

mo·nog·a·my \-mē\ *n* [F *monogamie,* fr. LL *monogamia,* fr. Gk, fr. *monogamos* monogamous, fr. *mon-* + *gamos* marriage — more at BIGAMY] **1** *archaic* **:** the practice of marrying only once during a lifetime **2 :** the state or custom of being married to one person at a time — **mono·gam·ic** \ˌmän-ə-ˈgam-ik\ *adj* — **mo·nog·a-**

mous \mə-ˈnäg-ə-məs\ *adj* — **mo·nog·a·mous·ly** *adv* — **mo·nog·a·mous·ness** *n*

mono·gas·tric \ˌmän-ə-ˈgas-trik\ *adj* : having one digestive cavity <swine, chicks, and men are ~>

mono·ge·ne·an \-ˈjē-nē-ən\ *n* [NL *Monogenea*, group name] : any of a subclass (Monogenea) of trematode worms that ordinarily live as ectoparasites on a single fish host throughout the entire life cycle — **monogenean** *adj*

mono·gen·e·sis \-ˈjen-ə-səs\ *n* [NL] : unity of origin; *specif* : the presumed origin of all life from one original entity or cell

mono·ge·net·ic \-jə-ˈnet-ik\ *adj* **1** : relating to or involving monogenesis **2** : of, relating to, or being a monogenean trematode worm

mono·gen·ic \-ˈjen-ik\ *adj* [ISV] : of, relating to, or controlled by a single gene and esp. by either of an allelic pair — **mono·gen·i·cal·ly** \-i-k(ə-)lē\ *adv*

mono·germ \ˈmän-ə-ˌjərm\ *adj* [*mon-* + *germ*inate] : producing or being a fruit that gives rise to a single plant <a ~ variety of sugar beet>

[1]**mono·gram** \ˈmän-ə-ˌgram\ *n* [LL *monogramma*, fr. Gk *mon-* + *gramma* letter — more at GRAM] : a sign of identity usu. formed of the combined initials of a name — **mono·gram·mat·ic** \ˌmän-ə-grə-ˈmat-ik\ *adj*

[2]**monogram** *vt* **-grammed; -gram·ming** : to mark with a monogram

[1]**mono·graph** \ˈmän-ə-ˌgraf\ *n* : a learned treatise on a small area of learning; *also* : a written account of a single thing — **mono·graph·ic** \ˌmän-ə-ˈgraf-ik\ *adj*

[2]**monograph** *vt* : to write a monograph on

mo·nog·y·nous \mə-ˈnäj-ə-nəs, mä-\ *adj* : of, relating to, or living in monogyny

mo·nog·y·ny \-nē\ *n* [ISV] : the state or custom of having only one wife at a time

mono·hy·brid \ˌmän-ō-ˈhī-brəd\ *n* : an individual or strain heterozygous for one specified factor or gene — **monohybrid** *adj*

mono·hy·dric \-ˈhī-drik\ *adj* **1** : containing one atom of acid hydrogen **2** : MONOHYDROXY

mono·hy·droxy \-(ˌ)hī-ˈdräk-sē\ *adj* [ISV *monohydroxy-*, fr. *mon-* + *hydroxy-*] : containing one hydroxyl group in the molecule

mono·lay·er \ˈmän-ō-ˌlā-ər, -ˌle(-ə)r\ *n* : a single continuous layer or film that is one cell or molecule in thickness

mono·lin·gual \ˌmän-ə-ˈliŋ-g(yə-)wəl, ˌmō-nə-\ *adj* : knowing or using only one language — **monolingual** *n*

mono·lith \ˈmän-ᵊl-ˌith\ *n* [F *monolithe*, fr. *monolithe* consisting of a single stone, fr. L *monolithus*, fr. Gk *monolithos*, fr. *mon-* + *lithos* stone] **1** : a single great stone often in the form of an obelisk or column **2** : a massive structure **3** : an organized whole that acts as a single powerful force

mono·lith·ic \ˌmän-ᵊl-ˈith-ik\ *adj* **1 a** : of or relating to a monolith **b (1)** : formed from a single crystal <a ~ silicon chip> **(2)** : produced in or on a monolithic chip <a ~ circuit> **2 a** : cast as a single piece <a ~ concrete wall> **b** : formed or composed of material without joints or seams <a ~ floor covering> <a ~ furnace lining> **c** : consisting of or constituting a single unit **3 a** : constituting a massive undifferentiated and often rigid whole <a ~ society> **b** : exhibiting or characterized by often rigidly fixed uniformity <~ party unity> — **mono·lith·i·cal·ly** \-i-k(ə-)lē\ *adv*

mono·logue *also* **mono·log** \ˈmän-ᵊl-ˌȯg, -ˌäg\ *n* [F *monologue*, fr. *mon-* + *-logue* (as in *dialogue*)] **1** : a dramatic soliloquy; *also* : a dramatic sketch performed by one actor **2** : a literary soliloquy **3** : a long speech monopolizing conversation — **mono·logu·ist** \-ˌȯg-əst, -ˌäg-\ *or* **mo·no·lo·gist** \mə-ˈnäl-ə-jəst; ˈmän-ᵊl-ˌȯg-əst, -ˌäg-\ *n*

mono·ma·nia \ˌmän-ə-ˈmā-nē-ə, -nyə\ *n* [NL] **1** : mental illness esp. when limited in expression to one idea or area of thought **2** : excessive concentration on a single object or idea — **mono·ma·ni·ac** \-nē-ˌak\ *n or adj*

mono·mer \ˈmän-ə-mər\ *n* [ISV *mon-* + *-mer* (as in *polymer*)] : a chemical compound that can undergo polymerization — **mo·no·mer·ic** \ˌmän-ə-ˈmer-ik, ˌmō-nə-\ *adj*

mono·me·tal·lic \ˌmän-ō-mə-ˈtal-ik\ *adj* **1** : consisting of or employing one metal **2** : of or relating to monometallism

mono·met·al·lism \-ˈmet-ᵊl-ˌiz-əm\ *n* [ISV *mon-* + *-metallism* (as in *bimetallism*)] : the adoption of one metal only in a currency — **mono·met·al·list** \-ᵊl-əst\ *n*

mo·nom·e·ter \mə-ˈnäm-ət-ər, mä-\ *n* [LL, fr. Gk *monometros*, fr. *mon-* + *metron* measure — more at MEASURE] : a line of verse consisting of a single metrical foot or dipody

mo·no·mi·al \mä-ˈnō-mē-əl, mə-\ *n* [blend of *mon-* + *-nomial* (as in *binomial*)] **1** : a mathematical expression consisting of a single term **2** : a taxonomic name consisting of a single word or term — **monomial** *adj*

mono·mo·lec·u·lar \ˌmän-ō-mə-ˈlek-yə-lər\ *adj* : being only one molecule thick <a ~ film> — **mono·mo·lec·u·lar·ly** *adv*

mono·mor·phe·mic \-mȯr-ˈfē-mik\ *adj* : consisting of only one morpheme <*talk* is ~ but *talked* is not>

mono·mor·phic \-ˈmȯr-fik\ *adj* : having but a single form or structural pattern <a ~ species of insect> — **mono·mor·phism** \-ˌfiz-əm\ *n*

mono·mor·phous \-fəs\ *adj* : MONOMORPHIC

mono·nu·cle·ar \ˌmän-ō-ˈn(y)ü-klē-ər\ *adj* [ISV] **1** : having only one nucleus <a ~ cell> **2** : MONOCYCLIC 2 — **mononuclear** *n*

mono·nu·cle·o·sis \-ˌn(y)ü-klē-ˈō-səs\ *n* [NL, fr. ISV *mononuclear* + NL *-osis*] : an abnormal increase of agranulocytes in the blood; *specif* : INFECTIOUS MONONUCLEOSIS

mono·nu·cle·o·tide \-ˈn(y)ü-klē-ə-ˌtīd\ *n* : a nucleotide that is derived from one molecule each of a nitrogenous base, a sugar, and a phosphoric acid

mo·noph·a·gous \mə-ˈnäf-ə-gəs, mä-\ *adj* : feeding on or utilizing a single kind of food; *esp* : feeding on a single kind of plant or animal — **mo·noph·a·gy** \-ə-jē\ *n*

mono·pho·nic \ˌmän-ə-ˈfän-ik, -ˈfō-nik\ *adj* **1** : having a single melodic line with little or no accompaniment **2** : of or relating to sound transmission, recording, or reproduction involving a single transmission path — **mono·pho·ni·cal·ly** \-i-k(ə-)lē, -ni-\ *adv*

mo·noph·o·ny \mə-ˈnäf-ə-nē, mä-\ *n* : monophonic music

mon·oph·thong \ˈmän-ə(f)-ˌthȯŋ\ *n* [LGk *monophthongos* single vowel, fr. Gk *mon-* + *phthongos* sound] : a vowel sound that throughout its duration has a single constant articulatory position — **mon·oph·thon·gal** \ˌmän-ə(f)-ˈthȯŋ-(g)əl\ *adj*

mono·phy·let·ic \ˌmän-ō-fī-ˈlet-ik\ *adj* [ISV] : of or relating to a single stock; *specif* : developed from a single common ancestral form — **mono·phy·le·tism** \-ˈfī-lə-ˌtiz-əm\ *n* — **mono·phy·le·ty** \-lət-ē\ *n*

Mo·noph·y·site \mə-ˈnäf-ə-ˌsīt\ *n* [ML *Monophysita*, fr. MGk *Monophysitēs*, fr. Gk *mon-* + *physis* nature — more at PHYSICS] : one holding the anti-Chalcedonian doctrine that Christ's nature remains altogether divine and not human even though he has taken on an earthly and human body with its cycle of birth, life, and death — **Monophysite** *or* **Mo·noph·y·sit·ic** \-ˌnäf-ə-ˈsit-ik\ *adj* — **Mo·noph·y·sit·ism** \-ˈnäf-ə-ˌsīt-ˌiz-əm\ *n*

mono·plane \ˈmän-ə-ˌplān\ *n* : an airplane with only one main supporting surface

[1]**mono·ploid** \ˈmän-ə-ˌplȯid\ *adj* [ISV] **1** : having or being a haploid chromosome set **2** : having or being the basic haploid number of chromosomes in a polyploid series of organisms

[2]**monoploid** *n* : a monoploid individual or organism

mono·po·di·al \ˌmän-ə-ˈpōd-ē-əl\ *adj* [NL *monopodium*, fr. *mon-* + *-podium*] : having or involving the formation of offshoots from a main axis — **mono·po·di·al·ly** \-ē-ə-lē\ *adv*

mono·pole \ˈmän-ə-ˌpōl\ *n* **1** : a hypothetical single concentrated electric charge or magnetic pole; *also* : a hypothetical unpolarized particle having such a pole **2** : a radio antenna consisting of a single often straight radiating element

mo·nop·o·list \mə-ˈnäp-ə-ləst\ *n* : one who monopolizes — **mo·nop·o·lis·tic** \-ˌnäp-ə-ˈlis-tik\ *adj* — **mo·nop·o·lis·ti·cal·ly** \-ti-k(ə-)lē\ *adv*

mo·nop·o·lize \mə-ˈnäp-ə-ˌlīz\ *vt* **-lized; -liz·ing** : to get a monopoly of : assume complete possession or control of <~ a conversation> — **mo·nop·o·li·za·tion** \-ˌnäp-ə-lə-ˈzā-shən\ *n* — **mo·nop·o·liz·er** \-ˈnäp-ə-ˌlī-zər\ *n*

syn MONOPOLIZE, ENGROSS, ABSORB, CONSUME *shared meaning element* : to take up completely

mo·nop·o·ly \mə-ˈnäp-(ə-)lē\ *n, pl* **-lies** [L *monopolium*, fr. Gk *monopōlion*, fr. *mon-* + *pōlein* to sell] **1** : exclusive ownership through legal privilege, command of supply, or concerted action **2** : exclusive possession **3** : a commodity controlled by one party **4** : a person or group having a monopoly

mono·pro·pel·lant \ˌmän-ō-prə-ˈpel-ənt\ *n* : a rocket propellant containing both the fuel and the oxidizer in a single substance

mo·nop·so·ny \mə-ˈnäp-sə-nē\ *n, pl* **-nies** [*mon-* + *-opsony* (as in *oligopsony*)] : an oligopsony limited to one buyer

mono·rail \ˈmän-ə-ˌrāl\ *n* : a single rail serving as a track for a wheeled vehicle; *also* : a vehicle traveling on such a track

mon·or·chid \mä-ˈnȯr-kəd\ *n* [irreg. fr Gk *monorchis*, fr. *mon-* + *orchis* testicle — more at ORCHIS] : an individual who has only one testis or only one descended into the scrotum — **monorchid** *adj* — **mon·or·chi·dism** \-kə-ˌdiz-əm\ *n*

mono·rhyme \ˈmän-ə-ˌrīm\ *n* : a strophe or poem in which all the lines have the same end rhyme — **mono·rhymed** \-ˌrīmd\ *adj*

mono·sac·cha·ride \ˌmän-ə-ˈsak-ə-ˌrīd\ *n* [ISV] : a sugar not decomposable to simpler sugars by hydrolysis

mono·so·di·um glu·ta·mate \ˌmän-ə-ˌsōd-ē-əm-ˈglüt-ə-ˌmāt\ *n* : a crystalline salt $C_5H_8O_4NaN$ used for seasoning foods — abbr. *MSG*

mono·some \ˈmän-ə-ˌsōm\ *n* **1** : a chromosome lacking a synaptic mate; *esp* : an unpaired X chromosome **2** : a single ribosome

mono·so·mic \ˌmän-ə-ˈsō-mik\ *adj* : having one less than the diploid number of chromosomes — **monosomic** *n*

mono·stele \ˈmän-ə-ˌstēl, ˌmän-ə-ˈstē-lē\ *n* : PROTOSTELE — **mono·ste·lic** \ˌmän-ə-ˈstē-lik\ *adj* — **mono·ste·ly** \ˈmän-ə-ˌstē-lē, ˈmō-nə-\ *n*

mono·syl·lab·ic \ˌmän-ə-sə-ˈlab-ik\ *adj* [prob. fr. F *monosyllabique*, fr. *monosyllabe*] **1** : consisting of one syllable or of monosyllables **2** : using or speaking only monosyllables **3** : conspicuously brief in answering or commenting : TERSE — **mono·syl·lab·i·cal·ly** \-i-k(ə-)lē\ *adv* — **mono·syl·la·bic·i·ty** \-ˌsil-ə-ˌbis-ət-ē\ *n*

mono·syl·la·ble \ˈmän-ə-ˌsil-ə-bəl, ˌmän-ə-ˈ\ *n* [modif. of MF or LL; MF *monosyllabe*, fr. LL *monosyllabon*, fr. Gk, fr. neut. of *monosyllabos* having one syllable, fr. *mon-* + *syllabē* syllable] : a word of one syllable

mono·sym·met·ric \ˌmän-ə-sə-ˈme-trik\ *adj* : MONOCLINIC

mono·syn·ap·tic \ˌmän-ō-sə-ˈnap-tik\ *adj* : having or involving a single neural synapse — **mono·syn·ap·ti·cal·ly** \-ti-k(ə-)lē\ *adv*

mono·the·ism \ˈmän-ə-(ˌ)thē-ˌiz-əm\ *n* : the doctrine or belief that there is but one God — **mono·the·ist** \-ˌthē-əst\ *n* — **mono·the·is·tic** \ˌmän-ə-thē-ˈis-tik\ *also* **mono·the·is·ti·cal** \-ti-kəl\ *adj* — **mono·the·is·ti·cal·ly** \-ti-k(ə-)lē\ *adv*

mono·tint \ˈmän-ə-ˌtint\ *n* : MONOCHROME

[1]**mono·tone** \ˈmän-ə-ˌtōn\ *n* [Gk *monotonos* monotonous] **1** : a succession of syllables, words, or sentences in one unvaried key or pitch **2** : a single unvaried musical tone **3** : a tedious sameness or reiteration **4** : a person unable to produce or to distinguish between musical intervals

[2]**monotone** *adj* **1** : having a uniform color **2** : MONOTONIC 2

mono·ton·ic \ˌmän-ə-ˈtän-ik\ *adj* **1** : of, relating to, or uttered in a monotone **2** : having the property of never increasing or never decreasing as the independent variable increases <~ functions> <a ~ sequence> — **mono·ton·i·cal·ly** \-i-k(ə-)lē\ *adv*

ə abut	ᵊ kitten	ər further	a back	ā bake	ä cot, cart
au̇ out	ch chin	e less	ē easy	g gift	i trip	ī life
j joke	ŋ sing	ō flow	ȯ flaw	ȯi coin	th thin	t͟h this
ü loot	u̇ foot	y yet	yü few	yu̇ furious	zh vision

mo·not·o·nous \mə-ˈnät-^{ə}n-əs, -ˈnät-nəs\ *adj* [Gk *monotonos,* fr. *mon-* + *tonos* tone] **1 :** uttered or sounded in one unvarying tone **2 :** tediously uniform or unvarying — **mo·not·o·nous·ly** *adv* — **mo·not·o·nous·ness** *n*

mo·not·o·ny \mə-ˈnät-^{ə}n-ē, -ˈnät-nē\ *n* **1 :** tedious sameness **2 :** sameness of tone or sound

mono·tre·ma·tous \ˌmän-ə-ˈtrem-ət-əs, -ˈtrē-mət-\ *n* [NL *Monotremata* + E *-ous*] **:** of, relating to, or being a monotreme

mono·treme \ˈmän-ə-ˌtrēm\ *n* [NL *Monotremata,* group name, fr. Gk *mon-* + *trēmat-, trēma* hole — more at TREMATODE] **:** any of an order (Monotremata) of lower mammals comprising the duckbills and echidnas

mo·not·ri·chous \mə-ˈnä-tri-kəs\ *adj* **:** having a single flagellum at one pole — used of bacteria

mono·type \ˈmän-ə-ˌtīp\ *n* **:** an impression on paper of a design painted usu. with the finger or a brush on a surface (as glass)

Monotype *trademark* — used for a keyboard typesetting machine that casts and sets type in separate characters

mono·typ·ic \ˌmän-ə-ˈtip-ik\ *adj* [*mon-* + *type*] **:** including a single representative — used esp. of a genus with only one species

mono·va·lent \ˌmän-ə-ˈvā-lənt\ *adj* [ISV] **1 :** UNIVALENT 1 **2 :** containing antibodies specific for or antigens of a single strain of an organism

mon·ovu·lar \(ˈ)mä-ˈnäv-yə-lər, -ˈnōv-\ *adj* **:** MONOZYGOTIC <~ twins>

mon·ox·ide \mə-ˈnäk-ˌsīd\ *n* [ISV] **:** an oxide containing one atom of oxygen in the molecule

mono·zy·got·ic \ˌmän-ə-zī-ˈgät-ik\ *adj* **:** derived from a single egg <~ twins>

Mon·roe Doctrine \mən-ˌrō- *also* ˌmən- *or* ˌmän-\ *n* [James *Monroe*] **:** a statement of U.S. foreign policy expressing opposition to extension of European control or influence in the western hemisphere

mon·sei·gneur \ˌmō^{n}-ˌsān-ˈyər\ *n, pl* **mes·sei·gneurs** \ˌmā-ˌsān-ˈyər(z)\ [F, lit., my lord] **:** a French dignitary (as a prince or prelate) — used as a title preceding a title of office or rank

mon·sieur \məs(h)-(ˈ)yə(r), mə-ˈsi(ə)r\ *n, pl* **mes·sieurs** \məs(h)-(ˈ)yə(r)(z), mās-; mə-ˈsi(ə)r(z)\ [MF, lit., my lord] **:** a Frenchman of high rank or station — used as a title equivalent to *Mister* and prefixed to the name of a Frenchman

mon·si·gnor \män-ˈsē-nyər, mən-\ *n, pl* **monsignors** *or* **mon·si·gno·ri** \ˌmän-ˌsēn-ˈyōr-ē, -ˈyȯr-\ [It *monsignore,* fr. F *monseigneur*] **:** a Roman Catholic prelate having a dignity or titular distinction (as of chamberlain, domestic prelate, or protonotary apostolic) usu. conferred by the pope — used as a title prefixed to the surname or to the given name and surname — **mon·si·gno·ri·al** \ˌmän-ˌsēn-ˈyōr-ē-əl, -ˈyȯr-\ *adj*

mon·soon \män-ˈsün\ *n* [obs. D *monssoen,* fr. Pg *monção,* fr. Ar *mawsim* time, season] **:** a periodic wind esp. in the Indian ocean and southern Asia; *also* **:** the season of the southwest monsoon in India and adjacent countries — **mon·soon·al** \-^{ə}l\ *adj*

mon·ster \ˈmän(t)-stər\ *n* [ME *monstre,* fr. MF, fr. L *monstrum* omen, monster] **1 a :** an animal or plant of abnormal form or structure **b :** one who deviates from normal behavior or character **2 :** a threatening force **3 a :** an animal of strange or terrifying shape **b :** one unusually large for its kind **4 :** something monstrous; *esp* **:** a person of unnatural or extreme ugliness, deformity, wickedness, or cruelty **5 :** a football linebacker who plays in no set position — called also *monster back, monster man*

mon·strance \ˈmän(t)-strən(t)s\ *n* [MF, fr. ML *monstrantia,* fr. L *monstrant-, monstrans,* prp. of *monstrare* to show — more at MUSTER] **:** a vessel in which the consecrated Host is exposed for the veneration of the faithful

monstrance

mon·stros·i·ty \män-ˈsträs-ət-ē\ *n, pl* **-ties** **1 a :** a malformation of a plant or animal **b :** something deviating from the normal **:** FREAK **2 :** the quality or state of being monstrous **3 a :** an object of terrifying size or force or complexity **b :** an excessively bad or shocking example

mon·strous \ˈmän(t)-strəs\ *adj* **1** *obs* **:** STRANGE, UNNATURAL **2 :** having extraordinary often overwhelming size **:** GIGANTIC **3 a :** having the qualities or appearance of a monster **b** *obs* **:** teeming with monsters **4 a :** extraordinarily ugly or vicious **:** HORRIBLE **b :** shockingly wrong or ridiculous **5 :** deviating greatly from the natural form or character **:** ABNORMAL **6 :** very great — used as an intensive — **mon·strous·ly** *adv* — **mon·strous·ness** *n*

syn **1** MONSTROUS, PRODIGIOUS, TREMENDOUS, STUPENDOUS *shared meaning element* **:** extremely impressive. MONSTROUS implies a departure from the normal (as in size, form, or character) and often carries suggestions of deformity, ugliness, or fabulousness <the imagination turbid with *monstrous* fancies and misshapen dreams —Oscar Wilde> <a *monstrous* cliff reared from the plain> PRODIGIOUS suggests a marvelousness exceeding belief, usually in something felt as going far beyond a previous maximum (as of goodness, greatness, intensity, or size) <made a *prodigious* effort and rolled the stone aside> <men have always reverenced *prodigious* inborn gifts —C. W. Eliot> TREMENDOUS may imply a power to terrify or inspire awe <the spell and *tremendous* incantation of the thought of death —L. P. Smith> but in more general and much weakened use it means little more than very large or great or intense <a *tremendous* noise> <success gave him *tremendous* satisfaction> STUPENDOUS implies a power to stun or astound, usually because of size, numbers, complexity, or greatness beyond one's power to describe <all are but parts of one *stupendous* whole, whose body Nature is, and God the soul —Alexander Pope>
2 see OUTRAGEOUS

mons ve·ne·ris \ˈmänz-ˈven-ə-rəs\ *n, pl* **mon·tes veneris** \ˌmän-ˌtēz-ˈven-\ [NL, lit., eminence of Venus or of venery] **:** a rounded eminence of fatty tissue upon the pubic symphysis of the human female

Mont *abbr* Montana

mon·ta·dale \ˈmänt-ə-ˌdāl\ *n* [*Montana* state + *dale*] **:** any of an American breed of white-faced hornless sheep noted for heavy fleece and good meat conformation

[1]**mon·tage** \män-ˈtäzh, mō^{n}(n)-, -ˈtȧzh\ *n* [F, fr. *monter* to mount] **1 a :** a composite picture made by combining several separate pictures **b :** a literary, musical, or artistic composite of juxtaposed more or less heterogeneous elements **2 :** a heterogeneous mixture **:** JUMBLE **3 :** the production of a rapid succession of images in a motion picture to illustrate an association of ideas

[2]**montage** *vt* **mon·taged; mon·tag·ing :** to combine into or depict in a montage

mon·ta·gnard \ˌmō^{n}-ˌtän-ˈyär(d)\ *n, often cap* [F, mountaineer, fr. *montagne* mountain] **:** a member of a people inhabiting a highland region chiefly in southern Vietnam bordering on Cambodia — **montagnard** *adj, often cap*

Mon·ta·gue \ˈmänt-ə-ˌgyü\ *n* **:** the family of Romeo in Shakespeare's *Romeo and Juliet*

mon·tane \(ˈ)män-ˈtān, ˈmän-ˌ\ *adj* [L *montanus* of a mountain —

MONTHS OF THE PRINCIPAL CALENDARS

GREGORIAN[1] name	days	JEWISH name	days	MUHAMMADAN name	days	HINDU[5] name
January begins 10 days after the winter solstice	31	Tishri the seventh month in the Hebrew calendar	30	Muharram[4] in A.H. 1392 began Feb. 16, 1972	30	Chait[6] (March-April)
February in leap years	28 29	Heshvan	29 or 30	Safar	29	Baisakh (April-May)
March	31	Kislev	29 or 30	Rabi I	30	Jeth (May-June)
April	30	Tebet	29	Rabi II	29	Asarh (June-July)
May	31	Shebat	30	Jumada I	30	Sawan (July-August)
June	30	Adar[2]	29 or 30	Jumada II	29	Bhadon (August-September)
July	31	Nisan[3]	30	Rajab	30	Asin (September-October)
August	31	Iyar	29	Sha'ban	29	Kartik (October-November)
September	30	Sivan	30	Ramadan	30	Aghan (November-December)
October	31	Tammuz	29	Shawwal	29	Pus (December-January)
November	30	Ab	30	Dhu'l-Qa'dah	30	Magh (January-February)
December	31	Elul	29	Dhu'l-Hijja in leap years	29 30	Phagun (February-March)

[1] The equinoxes occur on March 21 and September 23, the solstices on June 22 and December 22.

[2] In leap years Adar is followed by Veadar or Adar Sheni, an intercalary month of 29 days.

[3] Anciently called Abib; the first month of the postexilic calendar; sometimes called the first month of the ecclesiastical year.

[4] Retrogresses through the seasons; the Muhammadan year is lunar and each month begins at the approximate new moon; the year 1 A.H. began on Friday, July 16, A.D. 622.

[5] An extra month is inserted after every month in which two new moons occur (once in three years). The intercalary month has the name of the one that precedes it.

[6] Baisakh is sometimes considered the first month of the Hindu year.

more at MOUNTAIN] **1 :** of, relating to, growing in, or being the biogeographic zone that is made up of relatively moist cool upland slopes below timberline and that is characterized by large evergreen trees as a dominant life form **2 :** of, relating to, or made up of montane plants or animals

Mon·ta·nist \ˈmänt-ᵊn-əst\ *n* [*Montanus,* 2d cent. A.D. Phrygian schismatic] **:** an adherent of a Christian sect arising in the late second century and stressing apocalyptic expectations, the continuing prophetic gifts of the Spirit, and strict ascetic discipline — **Mon·ta·nism** \-ᵊn-ˌiz-əm\ *n*

mon·tan wax \ˈmänt-ᵊn-\ *n* [L *montanus* of a mountain] **:** a hard brittle mineral wax obtained usu. from lignites by extraction and used esp. in polishes, carbon paper, and insulating compositions

mon·te \ˈmänt-ē\ *n* [Sp, lit., bank, fr. It, mountain, heap, bank, fr. L *mont-, mons* mountain] **1 :** a card game in which players select any two of four cards faced in a layout and bet that one of them will be matched before the other as cards are dealt one at a time from the pack — called also *monte bank* **2 :** THREE-CARD MONTE

Mon·te Car·lo \ˌmänt-i-ˈkär-(ˌ)lō\ *adj* [*Monte Carlo,* Monaco, famous for its gambling casino] **:** of, relating to, or involving the use of random sampling techniques and often the use of computer simulation to obtain approximate solutions to mathematical or physical problems esp. in terms of a range of values each of which has a calculated probability of being the solution <*Monte Carlo* methods> <*Monte Carlo* calculations>

mon·teith \män-ˈtēth\ *n* [*Monteith,* 17th cent. Sc eccentric who wore a cloak with a scalloped hem] **:** a large silver punch bowl with scalloped rim

mon·te·ro \män-ˈte(ə)r-(ˌ)ō\ *n, pl* **-ros** [Sp, hunter, fr. *monte* mountain] **:** a round cap with a flap worn by huntsmen

Mon·tes·so·ri·an \ˌmänt-ə-ˈsōr-ē-ən, -ˈsȯr-\ *adj* [Maria *Montessori*] **:** of or relating to a system of teaching young children by individual guidance rather than strict control

Montg *abbr* Montgomeryshire

month \ˈmən(t)th\ *n, pl* **months** \ˈmən(t)s, ˈmən(t)ths\ [ME, fr. OE *mōnath;* akin to OHG *mānōd* month, OE *mōna* moon] **1 :** a measure of time corresponding nearly to the period of the moon's revolution and amounting to approximately 4 weeks or 30 days or 1/12 of a year **2** *pl* **:** an indefinite usu. extended period of time <he has been gone for ~*s*> **3 :** one ninth of the typical duration of human pregnancy <she was in her 8th ~>

1**month·ly** \ˈmən(t)th-lē\ *adv* **:** once a month **:** by the month

2**monthly** *adj* **1 a :** of or relating to a month **b :** payable or reckoned by the month **2 :** lasting a month **3 :** occurring every month

3**monthly** *n, pl* **monthlies** **1 :** a monthly periodical **2** *pl* **:** a menstrual period

Monthly Meeting *n* **:** a district unit of an organization of Friends

month's mind *n* **:** a Roman Catholic requiem mass for a person a month after his death

mon·ti·cule \ˈmänt-i-ˌkyü(ə)l\ *n* [F, fr. LL *monticulus,* dim. of L *mont-, mons* mountain — more at MOUNT] **:** a small elevation or prominence; *esp* **:** a subordinate cone of a volcano

Mont·mo·ren·cy \ˌmänt-mə-ˈren(t)-sē\ *n* [F, fr. *Montmorency,* France] **:** a cherry that is grown commercially for its bright red sour fruit

mont·mo·ril·lon·ite \ˌmänt-mə-ˈril-ə-ˌnīt, -ˈrē-ə-\ *n* [F, fr. *Montmorillon,* commune in western France] **:** a soft clayey mineral that is a hydrous aluminum silicate with considerable capacity for exchanging part of the aluminum for magnesium and bases — **mont·mo·ril·lon·it·ic** \-ˌril-ə-ˈnit-ik, -ˌrē-ə-\ *adj*

mon·u·ment \ˈmän-yə-mənt\ *n* [ME, fr. L *monumentum,* lit., memorial, fr. *monēre* to remind — more at MIND] **1** *obs* **:** a burial vault **:** SEPULCHER **2 :** a written legal document or record **:** TREATISE **3 a :** a lasting evidence or reminder of someone or something notable **b :** a memorial stone or a building erected in remembrance of a person or event **4** *archaic* **:** an identifying mark **:** EVIDENCE; *also* **:** PORTENT, SIGN **5** *obs* **:** a carved statue **:** EFFIGY **6 :** a boundary or position marker (as a stone) **7 :** NATIONAL MONUMENT **8 :** a written tribute

mon·u·men·tal \ˌmän-yə-ˈment-ᵊl\ *adj* **1 :** serving as or resembling a monument **:** MASSIVE; *also* **:** OUTSTANDING **2 :** of or relating to a monument **3 :** very great — **mon·u·men·tal·i·ty** \-mən-ˈtal-ət-ē, -ˌmen-\ *n* — **mon·u·men·tal·ly** \-ᵊl-ē\ *adv*

mon·u·men·tal·ize \-ˈment-ᵊl-ˌīz\ *vt* **-ized; -iz·ing** **:** to record or memorialize lastingly by a monument

mon·u·ron \ˈmän-yə-ˌrän\ *n* [*mon-* + *urea* + 1*-on*] **:** a persistent herbicide $C_9H_{11}ClN_2O$ used esp. to control mixed broad-leaved weeds

mon·zo·nite \män-ˈzō-ˌnīt, ˈmän-zə-\ *n* [F, fr. Mt. *Monzoni,* Italy] **:** a granular igneous rock composed of plagioclase and orthoclase in about equal quantities together with augite and a little biotite — **mon·zo·nit·ic** \ˌmän-zə-ˈnit-ik\ *adj*

moo \ˈmü\ *vi* [imit.] **:** to make the throat noise of a cow — **moo** *n*

mooch \ˈmüch\ *vb* [prob. fr. F dial. *muchier* to hide, lurk] *vi* **1 :** to wander aimlessly **:** AMBLE; *also* **:** SNEAK **2 :** SPONGE, CADGE ~ *vt* **1 :** to take surreptitiously **:** STEAL **2 :** CADGE, BEG — **mooch·er** *n*

1**mood** \ˈmüd\ *n* [ME, fr. OE *mōd;* akin to OHG *muot* mood, L *mos* will, custom] **1 :** a conscious state of mind or predominant emotion **:** FEELING; *also* **:** the expression of mood esp. in art or literature <the language, the stresses . . . are imposed upon the writer by the special ~ of the piece —Willa Cather> **2** *archaic* **:** a fit of anger **:** RAGE **3 :** a prevailing attitude **:** DISPOSITION

syn MOOD, HUMOR, TEMPER, VEIN *shared meaning element* **:** a state of mind in which an emotion or set of emotions gains ascendancy

2**mood** *n* [alter. of 1*mode*] **1 :** the form of a syllogism as determined by the quantity and quality of its constituent propositions **2 :** distinction of form or a particular set of inflectional forms of a verb to express whether the action or state it denotes is conceived as fact or in some other manner (as command, possibility, or wish) **3 :** MODE 1b

moody \ˈmüd-ē\ *adj* **mood·i·er; -est** **1 :** subject to depression **:** GLOOMY **2 :** subject to moods **:** TEMPERAMENTAL — **mood·i·ly** \ˈmüd-ᵊl-ē\ *adv* — **mood·i·ness** \ˈmüd-ē-nəs\ *n*

mool \ˈmül\ *n* **1** *dial Brit* **:** 1MOLD 1 **2** *dial Brit* **:** 1MOLD 2b

moo·la *or* **moo·lah** \ˈmü-lə\ *n* [origin unknown] *slang* **:** MONEY

1**moon** \ˈmün\ *n* [ME *mone,* fr. OE *mōna;* akin to OHG *māno* moon, L *mensis* month, Gk *mēn* month, *mēnē* moon] **1 a :** the earth's only known natural satellite shining by the sun's reflected light, revolving about the earth from west to east in about 29 1/2 days with reference to the sun or about 27 1/3 days with reference to the stars and having a diameter of 2160 miles and a mean distance from the earth of about 238,857 miles, a mass about one eightieth that of the earth, and a volume about one forty-ninth **b :** one complete moon cycle consisting of four phases **c :** SATELLITE **2 :** SYNODIC MONTH **3 :** MOONLIGHT **4 :** something that resembles a moon: as **a :** a highly translucent spot on old porcelain **b :** LUNULE — **moon·like** \-ˌlīk\ *adj*

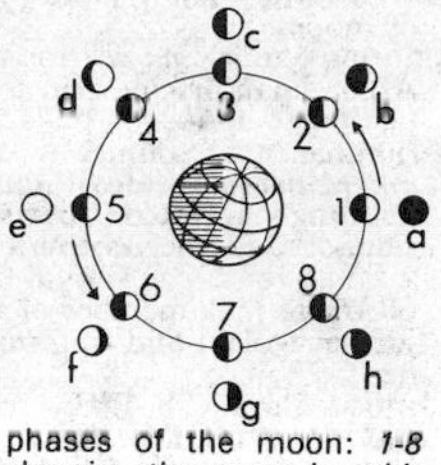

phases of the moon: *1-8* showing the moon in orbit around the earth; *a-h* corresponding phases as seen from the earth; *1* new moon, *3* first quarter, *5* full moon, *7* last quarter; *a* new moon, *b* waxing crescent, *c* half-moon, *d* gibbous, *e* full moon, *f* gibbous, *g* half-moon, *h* waning crescent

2**moon** *vt* **:** to spend in idle reverie **:** DREAM — used with *away* ~ *vi* **:** to spend time in idle reverie

moon·beam \ˈmün-ˌbēm\ *n* **:** a ray of light from the moon

moon–blind \-ˌblīnd\ *adj* **:** afflicted with moon blindness

moon blindness *n* **:** a recurrent inflammation of the eye of the horse

moon·calf \ˈmün-ˌkaf, -ˌkȧf\ *n* **1 :** MONSTER 1a **2 :** a foolish or absentminded person **:** SIMPLETON

moon·eye \ˈmü-ˌnī\ *n* **:** any of a genus (*Hiodon*) of silvery No. American freshwater fishes that resemble shad

moon–eyed \ˈmü-ˈnīd\ *adj* **:** having the eyes wide open

moon·fish \ˈmün-ˌfish\ *n, pl* **moonfish** *or* **moon·fish·es** **:** any of various compressed often short deep-bodied silvery or yellowish marine fishes: as **a :** OPAH **b :** PLATY

moon·flow·er \-ˌflau̇(-ə)r\ *n* **:** a tropical American morning glory (*Calonyction aculeatum*) with fragrant flowers; *also* **:** any of several related plants

moon·ish \ˈmü-nish\ *adj* **:** influenced by the moon; *also* **:** CAPRICIOUS — **moon·ish·ly** *adv*

moon·less \ˈmün-ləs\ *adj* **:** lacking the light of the moon <a dark ~ night>

moon·let \ˈmün-lət\ *n* **:** a small natural or artificial satellite

1**moon·light** \-ˌlīt\ *n* **:** the light of the moon

2**moonlight** *vi* **moon·light·ed; moon·light·ing** [back-formation fr. *moonlighter*] **:** to hold a second job in addition to a regular one — **moon·light·er** *n*

moon·lit \ˈmün-ˌlit\ *adj* **:** lighted by the moon

moon·quake \-ˌkwāk\ *n* **:** a seismic event on the moon

moon·rise \-ˌrīz\ *n* **1 :** the rising of the moon above the horizon **2 :** the time of the moon's rising

moon·scape \-ˌskāp\ *n* **:** the surface of the moon as seen or as depicted

moon·seed \-ˌsēd\ *n* **:** any of a genus (*Menispermum* of the family Menispermaceae, the moonseed family) of twining plants with crescent-shaped seeds and black fruits

moon·set \-ˌset\ *n* **1 :** the descent of the moon below the horizon **2 :** the time of the moon's setting

moon shell *n* **:** any of a family (Naticidae) of globose smooth-shelled carnivorous marine snails

moon·shine \ˈmün-ˌshīn\ *n* **1 :** MOONLIGHT **2 :** empty talk **:** NONSENSE **3 :** intoxicating liquor; *esp* **:** illegally distilled corn whiskey

moon·shin·er \-ˌshī-nər\ *n* **:** a maker or seller of illicit whiskey

moon shot *also* **moon shoot** *n* **:** the launching of a spacecraft to the moon or its vicinity

moon·stone \ˈmün-ˌstōn\ *n* **:** a transparent or translucent feldspar of pearly or opaline luster used as a gem

moon·struck \-ˌstrək\ *adj* **:** affected by or as if by the moon: as **a :** mentally unbalanced **b :** romantically sentimental **c :** BEMUSED

moon·ward \ˈmün-wərd\ *adv* **:** toward the moon

moony \ˈmü-nē\ *adj* **1 :** of or relating to the moon **2 a :** crescent shaped **b :** resembling the full moon **:** ROUND **3 :** MOONLIT **4 :** DREAMY, MOONSTRUCK

1**moor** \ˈmu̇(ə)r\ *n* [ME *mor,* fr. OE *mōr;* akin to OHG *meri* sea — more at MARINE] **1** *chiefly Brit* **:** an expanse of open rolling infertile land **2 :** a boggy area of wasteland usu. peaty and dominated by grasses and sedges

2**moor** *vb* [ME *moren;* akin to MD *meren, maren* to tie, moor] *vt* **:** to make fast with cables, lines, or anchors ~ *vi* **1 :** to secure a boat by mooring **:** ANCHOR **2 :** to be made fast

Moor \ˈmu̇(ə)r\ *n* [ME *More,* fr. MF, fr. L *Maurus* inhabitant of Mauretania] **1 :** one of the mixed Arab and Berber conquerors of Spain in the 8th century A.D. **2 :** BERBER — **Moor·ish** \-ish\ *adj*

moor·age \ˈmu̇(ə)r-ij\ *n* **1 :** an act of mooring **2 :** a place to moor

moor·hen \-ˌhen\ *n* **:** GALLINULE

moor·ing \ˈmu̇r-iŋ\ *n* **1 :** an act of making fast a boat or aircraft with lines or anchors **2 a :** a place where or an object to which a craft can be made fast **b :** a device (as a line or chain) by which an object is secured in place **3 :** moral or spiritual resources : ANCHORAGE 2 — usu. used in pl.

moor·land \-lənd, -ˌland\ *n* **:** land consisting of moors **:** a stretch of moor

moose \ˈmüs\ *n, pl* **moose** [of Algonquian origin; akin to Natick *moos* moose] **1 :** a large ruminant mammal (*Alces americana*) of the deer family inhabiting forested parts of Canada and the northern U.S. **2 :** ELK 1a **3** *cap* [Loyal Order of *Moose*] **:** a member of a major benevolent and fraternal order

moose 1

1moot \ˈmüt\ *n* [ME, fr. OE *mōt;* akin to OE *mētan* to meet — more at MEET] **1 :** a deliberative assembly primarily for the administration of justice; *esp* **:** one held by the freemen of an Anglo-Saxon community **2** *obs* **:** ARGUMENT, DISCUSSION

2moot *vt* **1** *archaic* **:** to discuss from a legal standpoint **:** ARGUE **2 a :** to bring up for discussion **:** BROACH **b :** DEBATE

3moot *adj* **1 a :** open to question **:** DEBATABLE **b :** subjected to discussion **:** DISPUTED **2 :** deprived of practical significance **:** made abstract or purely academic

moot court *n* **:** a mock court in which law students argue hypothetical cases for practice

1mop \ˈmäp\ *n* [ME *mappe*] **1 :** an implement made of absorbent material fastened to a handle and used esp. for cleaning floors **2 :** something that resembles a mop; *esp* **:** a thick mass of hair

2mop *vb* **mopped; mopping** *vt* **1 :** to use a mop on: as **a :** to clean by mopping <~ the floors> — often used with *up* <~ up the spillage from the water tank> **b :** to wipe as if with a mop <*mopped* his brow with a handkerchief> **2** *Brit* **:** to consume eagerly — usu. used with *up* **3 :** to overcome decisively **:** TROUNCE — often used with *up* ~ *vi* **:** to clean a surface (as a floor) with a mop — **mop·per** *n*

mop·board \ˈmäp-ˌbō(ə)rd, -ˌbȯ(ə)rd\ *n* **:** BASEBOARD

1mope \ˈmōp\ *vb* **moped; mop·ing** [prob. fr. obs. *mop, mope* fool] *vi* **1** *archaic* **:** to act in a dazed or stupid manner **2 :** to give oneself up to brooding **:** become listless or dejected **3 :** to move slowly or aimlessly **:** DAWDLE ~ *vt* **:** to make dull, dejected, or listless — **mop·er** *n*

2mope *n* **1 :** one that mopes **2** *pl* **:** BLUES 1

mop·pet \ˈmäp-ət\ *n* [obs. E *mop* fool, child] **1** *archaic* **:** BABY, DARLING **2 :** CHILD

mop–up \ˈmäp-ˌəp\ *n* **:** a concluding action

mop up \(ˈ)mäp-ˈəp\ *vt* **1 :** to follow in the wake of an attacking military force and clear (an area) of remaining pockets of resistance **2 :** to take up **:** GARNER, ABSORB <*mopped up* 18 of the 20 first= prize awards> ~ *vi* **:** to complete a project or transaction

mo·quette \mō-ˈket\ *n* [F] **:** a carpet or upholstery fabric having a velvety pile

1mor \ˈmȯ(ə)r\ *n* [Dan] **:** forest humus that forms a layer of largely organic matter abruptly distinct from the mineral soil beneath

2mor *abbr* morocco

mo·ra \ˈmōr-ə, ˈmȯr-\ *n, pl* **mo·rae** \ˈmō(ə)r-(ˌ)ē, ˈmȯ(ə)r-, -ˌī\ *or* **moras** [L, delay — more at MEMORY] **:** the minimal unit of measure in quantitative verse equivalent to the time of an average short syllable

mo·raine \mə-ˈrān\ *n* [F] **:** an accumulation of earth and stones carried and finally deposited by a glacier — **mo·rain·al** \-ˈrān-ᵊl\ *adj* — **mo·rain·ic** \-ˈrā-nik\ *adj*

1mor·al \ˈmȯr-əl, ˈmär-\ *adj* [ME, fr. MF, fr. L *moralis,* fr. *mor-, mos* custom — more at MOOD] **1 a :** of or relating to principles of right and wrong in behavior **:** ETHICAL <~ judgments> **b :** expressing or teaching a conception of right behavior <a ~ poem> **c :** conforming to a standard of right behavior **d :** sanctioned by or operative on one's conscience or ethical judgment <a ~ obligation> **e :** capable of right and wrong action <a ~ agent> **2 :** probable though not proved **:** VIRTUAL <a ~ certainty> **3 :** of, relating to, or acting on the mind, character, or will <a ~ victory> — **mor·al·ly** \-ə-lē\ *adv*

syn MORAL, ETHICAL, VIRTUOUS, RIGHTEOUS, NOBLE *shared meaning element* **:** conforming to a standard of what is right and good

2moral \ˈmȯr-əl, ˈmär-; *3 is* mə-ˈral\ *n* **1 a :** the moral significance or practical lesson (as of a story) **b :** a passage pointing out usu. in conclusion the lesson to be drawn from a story **2** *pl* **a :** moral practices or teachings **:** modes of conduct **b :** ETHICS **3 :** MORALE

mo·rale \mə-ˈral\ *n* [in sense 1, fr. F, fr. fem. of *moral,* adj.; in other senses, modif. of F *moral* morale, fr. *moral,* adj.] **1 :** moral principles, teachings, or conduct **2 a :** the mental and emotional condition (as of enthusiasm, confidence, or loyalty) of an individual or group with regard to the function or tasks at hand **b :** a sense of common purpose with respect to a group **:** ESPRIT DE CORPS **3 :** the level of individual psychological well-being based on such factors as a sense of purpose and confidence in the future

moral hazard *n* **:** the possibility of loss to an insurance company arising from the character or circumstances of the insured

mor·al·ism \ˈmȯr-ə-ˌliz-əm, ˈmär-\ *n* **1 a :** the habit or practice of moralizing **b :** a moral reflection **2 :** an often exaggerated emphasis on morality (as in religion or politics)

mor·al·ist \-ləst\ *n* **1 :** one who leads a moral life **2 :** a teacher or student of morals **:** a philosopher or writer concerned with moral principles and problems **3 :** one concerned with regulating the morals of others

mor·al·is·tic \ˌmȯr-ə-ˈlis-tik, ˌmär-\ *adj* **1 :** characterized by or expressive of a concern with morality **2 :** characterized by or expressive of a narrow and conventional moral attitude — **mor·al·is·ti·cal·ly** \-ti-k(ə-)lē\ *adv*

mo·ral·i·ty \mə-ˈral-ət-ē, mȯ-\ *n, pl* **-ties** **1 a :** a moral discourse, statement, or lesson **b :** a literary or other imaginative work teaching a moral lesson **2 a :** a doctrine or system of moral conduct **b** *pl* **:** particular moral principles or rules of conduct **3 :** conformity to ideals of right human conduct **4 :** moral conduct **:** VIRTUE

morality play *n* **:** an allegorical play popular esp. in the 15th and 16th centuries in which the characters personify moral qualities or abstractions (as death or youth)

mor·al·ize \ˈmȯr-ə-ˌlīz, ˈmär-\ *vb* **-ized; -iz·ing** *vt* **1 :** to explain or interpret morally **2 a :** to give a moral quality or direction to **b :** to improve the morals of ~ *vi* **:** to make moral reflections — **mor·al·iza·tion** \ˌmȯr-ə-lə-ˈzā-shən, ˌmär-\ *n* — **mor·al·iz·er** \ˈmȯr-ə-ˌlī-zər, ˈmär-\ *n*

moral philosophy *n* **:** ETHICS; *also* **:** the study of human conduct and values

mo·rass \mə-ˈras, mȯ-\ *n* [D *moeras,* modif. of OF *maresc,* of Gmc origin; akin to OE *mersc* marsh — more at MARSH] **1 :** MARSH, SWAMP **2 :** something that traps, confuses, or impedes — **morassy** \-ˈras-ē\ *adj*

mor·a·to·ri·um \ˌmȯr-ə-ˈtōr-ē-əm, ˌmär-, -ˈtȯr-\ *n, pl* **-ri·ums** *or* **-ria** \-ē-ə\ [NL, fr. LL, neut. of *moratorius* dilatory, fr. L *moratus,* pp. of *morari* to delay, fr. *mora* delay] **1 a :** a legally authorized period of delay in the performance of a legal obligation or the payment of a debt **b :** a waiting period set by an authority **2 :** a suspension of activity

Mo·ra·vi·an \mə-ˈrā-vē-ən\ *n* **1 :** a member of a Protestant denomination arising from a 15th century religious reform movement in Bohemia and Moravia **2 a :** a native or inhabitant of Moravia **b :** the group of Czech dialects spoken by the Moravian people and transitional between Slovak and Bohemian — **Moravian** *adj*

mo·ray \mə-ˈrā, ˈmȯr-(ˌ)ā\ *n* [Pg *moréia,* fr. L *muraena,* fr. Gk *myraina*] **:** any of numerous often brightly colored eels (family Muraenidae) that have sharp teeth capable of inflicting a savage bite, that occur in warm seas, and that include a Mediterranean eel (*Muraena helena*) valued for food

mor·bid \ˈmȯr-bəd\ *adj* [L *morbidus* diseased, fr. *morbus* disease; akin to Gk *marainein* to waste away — more at SMART] **1 a :** of, relating to, or characteristic of disease <~ anatomy> **b :** affected with or induced by disease <a ~ condition> **c:** productive of disease <~ substances> **2 :** abnormally susceptible to or characterized by gloomy or unwholesome feelings **3 :** GRISLY, GRUESOME <~ details> <~ curiosity> — **mor·bid·ly** *adv* — **mor·bid·ness** *n*

mor·bid·i·ty \mȯr-ˈbid-ət-ē\ *n* **1 :** the quality or state of being morbid **2 :** the relative incidence of disease

mor·da·cious \mȯr-ˈdā-shəs\ *adj* [L *mordac-, mordax* biting, fr. *mordēre* to bite — more at SMART] **1 :** biting in style or manner **:** CAUSTIC **2 :** given to biting — **mor·dac·i·ty** \-ˈdas-ət-ē\ *n*

mor·dan·cy \ˈmȯrd-ᵊn-sē\ *n* **1 :** a biting and caustic quality of style **:** INCISIVENESS **2 :** a sharply critical or bitter quality of thought or feeling **:** HARSHNESS

1mor·dant \ˈmȯrd-ᵊnt\ *adj* [MF, prp. of *mordre* to bite, fr. L *mordēre*] **1 :** biting and caustic in thought, manner, or style **:** INCISIVE **2 :** acting as a mordant **3 :** BURNING, PUNGENT — **mor·dant·ly** *adv*

2mordant *n* **1 :** a chemical that fixes a dye in or on a substance by combining with the dye to form an insoluble compound **2 :** a corroding substance used in etching

3mordant *vt* **:** to treat with a mordant

Mor·de·cai \ˈmȯrd-i-ˌkī\ *n* [Heb *Mordĕkhai*] **:** a relative of Esther who gives advice on saving the Jews from the destruction planned by Haman

mor·dent \ˈmȯrd-ᵊnt, mȯr-ˈdent\ *n* [It *mordente,* fr. L *mordent-, mordens,* prp. of *mordēre*] **:** a musical ornament made by a quick alternation of a principal tone with the tone usu. a half step lower

mordents: *1* as written, *2* as played

1more \ˈmō(ə)r, ˈmȯ(ə)r\ *adj* [ME, fr. OE *māra;* akin to OE *mā,* adv., more, OHG *mēr,* OIr *mōr* large] **1 :** GREATER <something ~ than she expected> **2 :** ADDITIONAL, FURTHER <~ guests arrived>

2more *adv* **1 a :** in addition <not much ~ to do> **b :** MOREOVER **2 :** to a greater or higher degree — often used with an adjective or adverb to form the comparative <~ evenly matched>

3more *n* **1 :** a greater quantity, number, or amount <the ~ the merrier> **2 :** something additional **:** an additional amount **3** *obs* **:** persons of higher rank

4more *pron, pl in constr* **:** additional persons or things <~ were found as the search continued>

more and more *adv* **:** to a progressively increasing extent

mo·reen \mə-ˈrēn, mō-\ *n* [prob. irregular fr. ¹*moire*] **:** a strong fabric of wool, wool and cotton, or cotton with a plain glossy or moiré finish

mo·rel \mə-ˈrel, mȯ-\ *n* [F *morille,* of Gmc origin; akin to OHG *morhila* morel] **:** any of several large pitted edible fungi (genus *Morchella,* esp. *M. esculenta*)

mo·rel·lo \mə-ˈrel-(ˌ)ō\ *n, pl* **-los** [prob. modif. of Flem *amarelle, marelle,* fr. ML *amarellum* amarelle] **:** a cultivated sour cherry (as the Montmorency) that is distinguished from an amarelle by the darker-colored skin and juice

more or less *adv* **1 :** to a varying or undetermined extent or degree **:** SOMEWHAT <they were *more or less* willing to help> **2 :** with small variations **:** APPROXIMATELY <contains 16 acres *more or less*>

more·over \mōr-ˈō-vər, mȯr-, ˈmōr-ˌ, ˈmȯr-ˌ\ *adv* **:** in addition to what has been said **:** BESIDES

mo·res \ˈmȯ(ə)r-ˌāz, ˈmō(ə)r- *also* -(ˌ)ēz\ *n pl* [L, pl. of *mor-, mos* custom — more at MOOD] **1 :** the fixed morally binding customs of a particular group **2 :** moral attitudes **3 :** HABITS, MANNERS

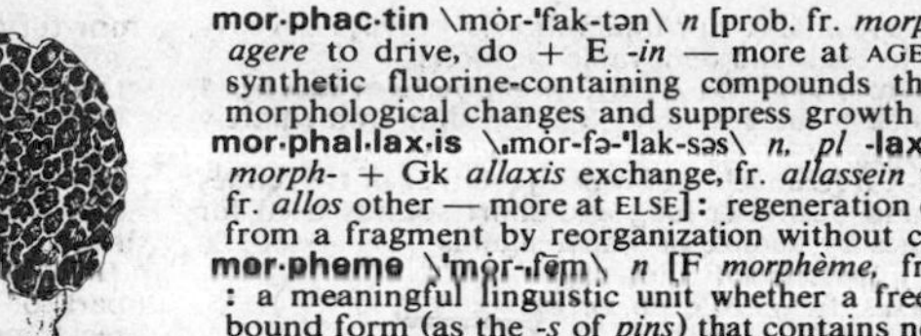
morel

¹mo·resque \mȯ-ˈresk, mə-\ *adj, often cap* [F, fr. Sp *morisco,* fr. *moro* Moor, fr. L *Maurus*] **:** having the characteristics of Moorish art or architecture

²moresque *n, often cap* **:** an ornament or decorative motif in Moorish style

Mor·gan \ˈmȯr-gən\ *n* [Justin *Morgan* †1798 Am teacher] **:** any of an American breed of lightly-built horses originated in Vermont from the progeny of one prepotent stallion of uncertain ancestry

mor·ga·nat·ic \ˌmȯr-gə-ˈnat-ik\ *adj* [NL *matrimonium ad morganaticam,* lit., marriage with morning gift] **:** of or relating to a marriage between a member of a royal or noble family and a person of inferior rank in which the rank of the inferior partner remains unchanged and the children of the marriage do not succeed to the titles, fiefs, or entailed property of the parent of higher rank — **mor·ga·nat·i·cal·ly** \-i-k(ə-)lē\ *adv*

mor·gan·ite \ˈmȯr-gə-ˌnīt\ *n* [J. P. *Morgan* †1913] **:** a rose-colored gem variety of beryl

Morgan le Fay \-lə-ˈfā\ *n* [OF *Morgain la fee* Morgan the fairy] **:** a sorceress and sister of King Arthur in Arthurian legend

mor·gen \ˈmȯr-gə(n)\ *n, pl* **morgen** [D, lit., morning] **:** a Dutch and southern African unit of land area equal to 2.116 acres

morgue \ˈmȯ(ə)rg\ *n* [F] **1 :** a place where the bodies of persons found dead are kept until identified and claimed by relatives or are released for burial **2 :** a collection of reference works and files of reference material in a newspaper or news periodical office

mor·i·bund \ˈmȯr-ə-(ˌ)bənd, ˈmär-\ *adj* [L *moribundus,* fr. *mori* to die — more at MURDER] **:** being in the state of dying **:** approaching death — **mor·i·bun·di·ty** \ˌmȯr-ə-ˈbən-dət-ē, ˌmär-\ *n*

¹mo·ri·on \ˈmōr-ē-ˌän, ˈmȯr-\ *n* [MF] **:** a high-crested helmet with no visor

²morion *n* [modif. of L *mormorion*] **:** a nearly black variety of smoky quartz

Mo·ris·co \mə-ˈris-(ˌ)kō, mȯ-\ *n, pl* **-cos** *or* **-coes** [Sp, fr. *morisco,* adj., fr. *moro* Moor] **:** MOOR; *esp* **:** a Spanish Moor — **Morisco** *adj*

Mor·mon \ˈmȯr-mən\ *n* **1 :** the ancient redactor and compiler of the Book of Mormon presented as divine revelation by Joseph Smith **2 :** LATTER-DAY SAINT; *esp* **:** a member of the Church of Jesus Christ of Latter-Day Saints — **Mor·mon·ism** \-mə-ˌniz-əm\ *n*

Mormon cricket *n* **:** a large dark wingless katydid (*Anabrus simplex*) that resembles a cricket and is found in the arid parts of the western U.S. where it is occas. an abundant pest of crops

morn \ˈmȯ(ə)rn\ *n* [ME, fr. OE *morgen;* akin to OHG *morgan* morning, L *merus* pure, unmixed] **1 :** DAWN **2 :** MORNING

morn·ing \ˈmȯr-niŋ\ *n* [ME, fr. *morn* + *-ing* (as in *evening*)] **1 a :** DAWN **b :** the time from sunrise to noon **c :** the time from midnight to noon **2 :** a period of first development **:** BEGINNING

morning glory *n* **:** any of various usu. twining plants (genus *Ipomoea* of the family Convolvulaceae, the morning-glory family) with showy trumpet-shaped flowers; *broadly* **:** a plant of the morning-glory family including herbs, vines, shrubs, or trees with alternate leaves and regular pentamerous flowers

morning line *n* **:** a bookmaker's list of entries for a race meet and the probable odds on each that is printed or posted before the betting begins

Morning Prayer *n* **:** a service of liturgical prayer used for regular morning worship in churches of the Anglican communion

morn·ings \ˈmȯr-niŋz\ *adv* **:** in the morning repeatedly **:** on any morning

morning sickness *n* **:** nausea and vomiting that occurs on rising in the morning esp. during the earlier months of pregnancy

morning star *n* **:** a bright planet (as Venus) seen in the eastern sky before or at sunrise

Mo·ro \ˈmō(ə)r-(ˌ)ō, ˈmȯ(ə)r-\ *n, pl* **Moro** *or* **Moros** [Sp, lit., Moor, fr. L *Maurus*] **1 :** a member of any of several Muslim peoples of the southern Philippines **2 :** any of the Austronesian languages of the Moro peoples

mo·roc·co \mə-ˈräk-(ˌ)ō\ *n* [*Morocco,* Africa] **:** a fine leather from goatskin tanned with sumac

mo·ron \ˈmō(ə)r-ˌän, ˈmȯ(ə)r-\ *n* [irreg. fr. Gk *mōros* foolish, stupid; akin to Skt *mūra* foolish] **1 :** a feebleminded person or mental defective who has a potential mental age of between 8 and 12 years and is capable of doing routine work under supervision **2 :** a very stupid person ***syn*** see FOOL — **mo·ron·ic** \mə-ˈrän-ik, mȯ-\ *adj* — **mo·ron·i·cal·ly** \-i-k(ə-)lē\ *adv* — **mo·ron·ism** \ˈmōr-ˌän-ˌiz-əm, ˈmȯr-\ *n* — **mo·ron·i·ty** \mə-ˈrän-ət-ē, mȯ-\ *n*

mo·rose \mə-ˈrōs, mȯ-\ *adj* [L *morosus,* lit., capricious, fr. *mor-, mos* will — more at MOOD] **1 :** having a sullen and gloomy disposition **2 :** marked by or expressive of gloom ***syn*** see SULLEN — **mo·rose·ly** *adv* — **mo·rose·ness** *n* — **mo·ros·i·ty** \-ˈräs-ət-ē\ *n*

¹morph \ˈmȯrf\ *n* [back-formation fr. *morpheme*] **1 :** ²ALLOMORPH **2 :** a phoneme or sequence of phonemes that is presumably an allomorph but that is not considered as assigned to any particular morpheme **3 a :** a local population of a species that consists of interbreeding organisms and is distinguishable from other populations by morphology or behavior though capable of interbreeding with them **b :** a phenotypic variant of a species

²morph *abbr* morphology

morph- *or* **morpho-** *comb form* [G, fr. Gk, fr. *morphē*] **1 :** form <*morpho*genesis> **2 :** relating to form and <*morpho*functional>

-morph \ˌmȯrf\ *n comb form* [ISV, fr. *-morphous*] **:** one having (such) a form <iso*morph*>

mor·phac·tin \mȯr-ˈfak-tən\ *n* [prob. fr. *morph-* + L *actus,* pp. of *agere* to drive, do + E *-in* — more at AGENT] **:** any of several synthetic fluorine-containing compounds that tend to produce morphological changes and suppress growth in plants

mor·phal·lax·is \ˌmȯr-fə-ˈlak-səs\ *n, pl* **-lax·es** \-ˌsēz\ [NL, fr. *morph-* + Gk *allaxis* exchange, fr. *allassein* to change, exchange, fr. *allos* other — more at ELSE] **:** regeneration of a part or organism from a fragment by reorganization without cell proliferation

mor·pheme \ˈmȯr-ˌfēm\ *n* [F *morphème,* fr. Gk *morphē* form] **:** a meaningful linguistic unit whether a free form (as *pin*) or a bound form (as the *-s* of *pins*) that contains no smaller meaningful parts — **mor·phe·mic** \mȯr-ˈfē-mik\ *adj* — **mor·phe·mi·cal·ly** \-mi-k(ə-)lē\ *adv*

mor·phe·mics \mȯr-ˈfē-miks\ *n pl but sing in constr* **1 :** a branch of linguistic analysis that consists of the study of morphemes **2 :** the structure of a language in terms of morphemes

Mor·pheus \ˈmȯr-fē-əs, -ˌf(y)üs\ *n* [L, fr. Gk] **:** the Greek god of dreams

mor·phia \ˈmȯr-fē-ə\ *n* [NL, fr. *Morpheus*] **:** MORPHINE

-mor·phic \ˈmȯr-fik\ *adj comb form* [prob. fr. F *-morphique,* fr. Gk *morphē*] **:** having (such) a form <dolicho*morphic*>

mor·phine \ˈmȯr-ˌfēn\ *n* [F, fr. *Morpheus*] **:** a bitter crystalline addictive narcotic base $C_{17}H_{19}NO_3$ that is the principal alkaloid of opium and is used in the form of a soluble salt (as a hydrochloride or a sulfate) as an analgesic and sedative — **mor·phin·ic** \mȯr-ˈfē-nik, -ˈfin-ik\ *adj*

mor·phin·ism \ˈmȯr-ˌfē-ˌniz-əm, -fə-\ *n* **:** a disordered condition of health produced by habitual use of morphine

-mor·phism \ˈmȯr-ˌfiz-əm\ *n comb form* [LL *-morphus* -morphous fr. Gk *-morphos*] **1 :** quality or state of having (such) a form <hetero*morphism*> **2 :** conceptualization in (such) a form <zoo*morphism*>

mor·pho \ˈmȯr-(ˌ)fō\ *n, pl* **morphos** [NL, genus name, fr. Gk *Morphō,* epithet of Aphrodite] **:** any of a genus (*Morpho*) of large showy tropical American butterflies that typically have a brilliant blue metallic luster on the upper surface of the wings

mor·pho·gen·e·sis \ˌmȯr-fə-ˈjen-ə-səs\ *n* [NL] **:** the formation and differentiation of tissues and organs — compare ORGANOGENESIS

mor·pho·ge·net·ic \-jə-ˈnet-ik\ *adj* **:** relating to or concerned with the development of normal organic form <~ movements of early embryonic cells> — **mor·pho·ge·net·i·cal·ly** \-i-k(ə-)lē\ *adv*

mor·pho·gen·ic \-ˈjen-ik\ *adj* **:** MORPHOGENETIC

mor·phol·o·gy \mȯr-ˈfäl-ə-jē\ *n* [G *morphologie,* fr. *morph-* + *logie* -logy] **1 a :** a branch of biology that deals with the form and structure of animals and plants **b :** the form and structure of an organism or any of its parts **2 a :** a study and description of word formation in a language including inflection, derivation, and compounding **b :** the system of word-forming elements and processes in a language **3 a :** a study of structure or form **b :** STRUCTURE, FORM **4 :** the external structure of rocks in relation to the development of erosional forms or topographic features — **mor·pho·log·i·cal** \ˌmȯr-fə-ˈläj-i-kəl\ *adj* — **mor·pho·log·i·cal·ly** \-k(ə-)lē\ *adv* — **mor·phol·o·gist** \mȯr-ˈfäl-ə-jəst\ *n*

mor·phom·e·try \mȯr-ˈfäm-ə-trē\ *n* **1 :** measurement of external form **2 :** a branch of limnology that deals with the morphological measurements of a lake and its basin — **mor·pho·met·ric** \ˌmȯr-fə-ˈme-trik\ *also* **mor·pho·met·ri·cal** \-tri-kəl\ *adj* — **mor·pho·met·ri·cal·ly** \-tri-k(ə-)lē\ *adv*

mor·pho·pho·ne·mics \ˌmȯr-fō-fə-ˈnē-miks\ *n pl but sing in constr* [*morph*eme + *-o-* + *phonemics*] **1 :** a study of the phonemic differences between allomorphs of the same morpheme **2 :** the distribution of allomorphs in one morpheme **3 :** the structure of a language in terms of morphophonemics

-mor·pho·sis \ˈmȯr-fə-səs *also* mȯr-ˈfō-\ *n comb form, pl* **-mor·pho·ses** \-ˌsēz\ [L, fr. Gk *morphōsis* process of forming, fr. *morphoun* to form, fr. *morphē* form] **:** development or change of form of a (specified) thing or in a (specified) manner <geronto*morphosis*>

-mor·phous \ˈmȯr-fəs\ *adj comb form* [Gk *-morphos,* fr. *morphē* form] **:** having (such) a form <iso*morphous*>

-mor·phy \ˌmȯr-fē\ *n comb form* [ISV, fr. *-morphous*] **:** quality or state of having (such) a form <homo*morphy*>

mor·ris \ˈmȯr-əs, ˈmär-\ *n* [ME *moreys daunce,* fr. *moreys* Moorish (fr. *More* Moor) + *daunce* dance] **:** a vigorous English dance performed by men wearing costumes and bells

INTERNATIONAL MORSE CODE

A ·–	N –·	Á ·––·–	8 –––··
B –···	O –––	Ä ·–·–	9 ––––·
C –·–·	P ·––·	É ··–··	0 –––––
D –··	Q ––·–	Ñ ––·––	, (comma) ––··––
E ·	R ·–·	Ö –––·	. ·–·–·–
F ··–·	S ···	Ü ··––	? ··––··
G ––·	T –	1 ·––––	; –·–·–·
H ····	U ··–	2 ··–––	: –––···
I ··	V ···–	3 ···––	' (apostrophe) ·––––·
J ·–––	W ·––	4 ····–	- (hyphen) –····–
K –·–	X –··–	5 ·····	/ –··–·
L ·–··	Y –·––	6 –····	parenthesis –·––·–
M ––	Z ––··	7 ––···	underline ··––·–

[1] Often called the continental code; a modification of this code, with dots only, is used on ocean cables

ə abut	ᵊ kitten	ər further	a back	ā bake	ä cot, cart	
aů out	ch chin	e less	ē easy	g gift	i trip	ī life
j joke	ŋ sing	ō flow	ȯ flaw	ȯi coin	th thin	t͟h this
ü loot	u̇ foot	y yet	yü few	yu̇ furious	zh vision	

mor·ris chair \ˌmȯr-əs-, ˌmär-\ *n* [William *Morris* †1896] **:** an easy chair with adjustable back and removable cushions

mor·row \ˈmär-(ˌ)ō, ˈmȯr-, -ə(-w)\ *n* [ME *morn, morwen* morn] **1** *archaic* **:** MORNING **2 :** the next day **3 :** the time immediately after a specified event

Morse code \ˈmȯrs-\ *n* [Samuel F. B. *Morse*] **:** either of two codes consisting of dots and dashes or long and short sounds used for transmitting messages by audible or visual signals

[1]**mor·sel** \ˈmȯr-səl\ *n* [ME, fr. OF, dim. of *mors* bite, fr. L *morsus,* fr. *morsus,* pp. of *mordēre* to bite — more at SMART] **1 :** a small piece of food **:** BITE **2 :** a small quantity **:** FRAGMENT **3 a :** a tasty dish **b :** something delectable and pleasing <the girl . . . is young and very pretty . . . a ~ worth a little lordly condescension —Eric Blom> **4 :** a negligible person

[2]**morsel** *vt* **-seled** *or* **-selled; -sel·ing** *or* **-sel·ling :** to divide into or distribute in small pieces

[1]**mort** \ˈmȯ(ə)rt\ *n* [prob. alter. of ME *mot* horn note, fr. MF word, horn note — more at MOT] **1 :** a note sounded on a hunting horn when a deer is killed **2 :** KILLING

[2]**mort** *n* [prob. back-formation fr. [1]*mortal*] **:** a great quantity or number

morris chair

[1]**mor·tal** \ˈmȯrt-ᵊl\ *adj* [ME, fr. MF, fr. L *mortalis,* fr. *mort-, mors* death — more at MURDER] **1 :** having caused or being about to cause death **:** FATAL <a ~ injury> **2 a :** subject to death <~ man> **b :** EARTHLY, CONCEIVABLE <every ~ thing> **c :** very tedious or prolonged <waited three ~ hours> **3 :** marked by unrelenting hostility **:** IMPLACABLE <a ~ enemy> **4 a :** marked by great intensity or severity **:** EXTREME <~ fear> **b :** very great **:** AWFUL <a ~ shame> **5 :** HUMAN <~ limitations> **6 :** of, relating to, or connected with death <~ agony> ***syn*** see DEADLY

[2]**mortal** *adv, chiefly dial* **:** MORTALLY

[3]**mortal** *n* **:** a human being

mor·tal·i·ty \mȯr-ˈtal-ət-ē\ *n* **1 :** the quality or state of being mortal **2 :** the death of large numbers (as of people or animals) **3** *archaic* **:** DEATH **4 :** the human race **:** MANKIND **5 a :** the number of deaths in a given time or place **b :** the proportion of deaths to population **c :** the number lost or the rate of loss or failure

mortality table *n* **:** an actuarial table based on mortality statistics over a number of years

mor·tal·ly \ˈmȯrt-ᵊl-ē\ *adv* **1 :** in a deadly or fatal manner **:** to death <~ wounded> **2 :** to an extreme degree **:** INTENSELY <~ afraid>

mortal mind *n, Christian Science* **:** a belief that life, substance, and intelligence are in and of matter **:** ILLUSION

mortal sin *n* **:** a sin (as murder) that is deliberately committed and is of such serious consequence according to Thomist theology that it deprives the soul of sanctifying grace — compare VENIAL SIN

[1]**mor·tar** \ˈmȯrt-ər\ *n* [ME *morter,* fr. OE *mortere* & MF *mortier,* fr. L *mortarium;* akin to Gk *marainein* to waste away — more at SMART] **1 a :** a strong vessel in which material is pounded or rubbed with a pestle **b :** a large cast-iron receptacle in which ore is crushed in a stamp mill **2** [MF *mortier*] **a :** a muzzle-loading cannon having a tube short in relation to its caliber that is used to throw projectiles with low muzzle velocities at high angles **b :** any of several similar firing devices

[2]**mortar** *n* [ME *morter,* fr. OF *mortier,* fr. L *mortarium*] **:** a plastic building material (as a mixture of cement, lime, or gypsum plaster with sand and water) that hardens and is used in masonry or plastering

[3]**mortar** *vt* **:** to plaster or make fast with mortar

mor·tar·board \ˈmȯrt-ər-ˌbō(ə)rd, -ˌbȯ(ə)rd\ *n* **1 a :** HAWK 2 **b :** a board or platform about 3 feet square for holding mortar **2 :** an academic cap consisting of a closely fitting headpiece with a broad flat projecting square top

mortarboard 2

[1]**mort·gage** \ˈmȯr-gij\ *n* [ME *morgage,* fr. MF, fr. OF, fr. *mort* dead (fr. L *mortuus,* fr. pp. of *mori* to die) + *gage* — more at MURDER] **1 :** a conveyance of property (as for security on a loan) on condition that the conveyance becomes void on payment or performance according to stipulated terms **2 a :** the instrument by which a mortgage conveyance is made **b :** the state of the property so conveyed **c :** the interest of the mortgagee in such property

[2]**mortgage** *vt* **mort·gaged; mort·gag·ing 1 :** to grant or convey by a mortgage **2 :** to subject to a claim or obligation **:** PLEDGE

mort·gag·ee \ˌmȯr-gi-ˈjē\ *n* **:** a person to whom property is mortgaged

mort·gag·or \ˌmȯr-gi-ˈjȯ(ə)r\ *also* **mort·gag·er** \ˈmȯr-gi-jər\ *n* **:** a person who mortgages his property

mor·ti·cian \mȯr-ˈtish-ən\ *n* [L *mort-, mors* death] **:** UNDERTAKER 2

mor·ti·fi·ca·tion \ˌmȯrt-ə-fə-ˈkā-shən\ *n* **1 :** the subjection and denial of bodily passions and appetites by abstinence or self-inflicted pain or discomfort **2 :** NECROSIS, GANGRENE **3 a :** a sense of humiliation and shame caused by something that wounds one's pride or self-respect **b :** the cause of such humiliation or shame

mor·ti·fy \ˈmȯrt-ə-ˌfī\ *vb* **-fied; -fy·ing** [ME *mortifien,* fr. MF *mortifier,* fr. LL *mortificare,* fr. L *mort-, mors*] *vt* **1** *obs* **:** to destroy the strength, vitality, or functioning of **2 :** to subdue or deaden (as the body or bodily appetites) esp. by abstinence or self-inflicted pain or discomfort **3 :** to subject to severe and vexing embarrassment **:** SHAME ~ *vi* **1 :** to practice mortification **2 :** to become necrotic or gangrenous

[1]**mor·tise** *also* **mor·tice** \ˈmȯrt-əs\ *n* [ME *mortays,* fr. MF *mortaise*] **:** a hole, groove, or slot into or through which some other part of an arrangement of parts fits or passes; *esp* **:** a usu. rectangular cavity cut into a piece of timber or other material to receive a tenon — see DOVETAIL illustration

[2]**mortise** *also* **mortice** *vt* **mor·tised; mor·tis·ing 1 :** to join or fasten securely; *specif* **:** to join or fasten by a tenon and mortise **2 :** to cut or make a mortise in

mort·main \ˈmȯrt-ˌmān\ *n* [ME *morte-mayne,* fr. MF *mortemain,* fr. OF, fr. *morte* (fem. of *mort* dead) + *main* hand, fr. L *manus* — more at MANUAL] **1 a :** an inalienable possession of lands or buildings by an ecclesiastical or other corporation **b :** the condition of property or other gifts left to a corporation in perpetuity esp. for religious, charitable, or public purposes **2 :** the influence of the past regarded as controlling the present

[1]**mor·tu·ary** \ˈmȯr-chə-ˌwer-ē\ *n, pl* **-ar·ies** [ME *mortuarie,* fr. ML *mortuarium,* fr. L, neut. of *mortuarius* of the dead, fr. *mortuus,* pp.] **:** a place in which dead bodies are kept until burial; *esp* **:** FUNERAL HOME

[2]**mortuary** *adj* **1 :** of or relating to the burial of the dead **2 :** of, relating to, or characteristic of death

mor·u·la \ˈmȯr-(y)ə-lə, ˈmär-\ *n, pl* **-lae** \-ˌlē, -ˌlī\ [NL, fr. L *morum* mulberry] **:** a globular solid mass of blastomeres formed by cleavage of a zygote that typically precedes the blastula — **mor·u·lar** \-lər\ *adj* — **mor·u·la·tion** \ˌmȯr-(y)ə-ˈlā-shən, ˌmär-\ *n*

[1]**mo·sa·ic** \mō-ˈzā-ik\ *n* [ME *musycke,* fr. MF *mosaique,* fr. OIt *mosaico,* fr. ML *musaicum,* alter. of LL *musivum,* fr. neut. of *musivus* of a muse, artistic, fr. L *Musa* muse] **1 :** a surface decoration made by inlaying small pieces of variously colored material to form pictures or patterns; *also* **:** the process of making it **2 a :** a picture or design made in mosaic **3 :** something resembling a mosaic <a ~ of visions and daydreams and memories —Lawrence Shainberg> **4 a :** an organism or one of its parts composed of cells of more than one genotype **:** CHIMERA 3 **b :** a virus disease of plants characterized by diffuse light and dark green or yellow and green mottling of the foliage **5 :** a composite map made of aerial photographs **6 :** the part of a television camera tube consisting of many minute photoelectric particles that convert light to an electric charge — **mosaic** *adj* — **mo·sa·ical·ly** \-ˈzā-ə-k(ə-)lē\ *adv*

[2]**mosaic** *vt* **-icked; -ick·ing 1 :** to decorate with mosaics **2 :** to form into a mosaic

Mo·sa·ic \mō-ˈzā-ik\ *adj* [NL *Mosaicus,* fr. *Moses*] **:** of or relating to Moses or the institutions or writings attributed to him

mosaic gold *n* **:** a yellow scaly crystalline substance that is essentially a yellow sulfide SnS_2 of tin and is used as a pigment and in gilding and bronzing

mo·sa·icism \mō-ˈzā-ə-ˌsiz-əm\ *n* **:** a condition in which patches of tissue of unlike genetic constitution are mingled in an organism

mo·sa·icist \-səst\ *n* **1 a :** a designer of mosaics **b :** a workman who makes mosaics **2 :** a dealer in mosaics

Mos·an \ˈmōs-ᵊn\ *n* [*mōs* four (in various Mosan languages)] **:** an American Indian language phylum of British Columbia and Washington including the Salishan, Wakashan, and Chemakuan stocks

Mo·selle \mō-ˈzel\ *n* [G *moselwein,* fr. *Mosel,* Moselle, river in Germany + G *wein* wine] **:** a white table wine made in the valley of the Moselle; *also* **:** a similar wine made elsewhere

Mo·ses \ˈmō-zəz *also* -zəs\ *n* [L, fr. Gk *Mōsēs,* fr. Heb *Mōsheh*] **:** a Hebrew prophet who led the Israelites out of Egyptian slavery and at Mt. Sinai delivered to them the Law establishing God's covenant with them

mo·sey \ˈmō-zē\ *vi* **mo·seyed; mo·sey·ing** [origin unknown] **1 :** to hurry away **2 :** to move in a leisurely or aimless manner **:** SAUNTER <~*ed* around the general store, testing the cheese straight off the round —Eric Sevareid>

mo·shav \mō-ˈshäv\ *n, pl* **mo·sha·vim** \ˌmō-shə-ˈvēm\ [NHeb *mōshābh,* fr. Heb, dwelling] **:** a cooperative settlement of small individual farms in Israel — compare KIBBUTZ

Mos·lem \ˈmäz-ləm *also* ˈmäs-\ *var of* MUSLIM

mosque \ˈmäsk\ *n* [MF *mosquee,* fr. OIt *moschea,* fr. OSp *mezquita,* fr. Ar *masjid* temple, fr. *sajada* to prostrate oneself] **:** a building used for public worship by Muslims

mos·qui·to \mə-ˈskēt-(ˌ)ō, -ə(-w)\ *n, pl* **-toes** *also* **-tos** [Sp, fr. *mosca* fly, fr. L *musca* — more at MIDGE] **:** any of numerous two-winged flies (family Culicidae) with females that have a set of slender organs in the proboscis adapted to puncture the skin of animals and to suck their blood and that are in some cases vectors of serious diseases — **mos·qui·to·ey** \-ˈskēt-ə-wē\ *adj*

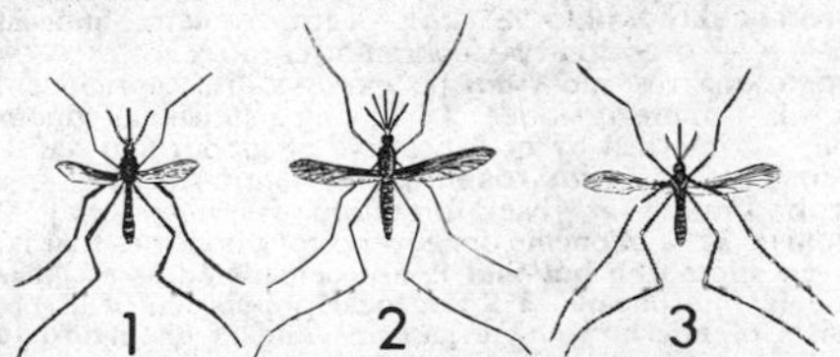

mosquito: *1* culex, *2* anopheles, *3* aëdes

mosquito boat *n* **:** PT BOAT

mosquito fish *n* **:** any of numerous small fishes used to exterminate mosquito larvae; *esp* **:** either of two No. American live-bearers (*Gambusia affinis* and *Heterandria formosa*)

mosquito hawk *n* : DRAGONFLY

mosquito net *n* : a net or screen for keeping out mosquitoes

1moss \'mȯs\ *n* [ME, fr. OE *mōs;* akin to OHG *mos* moss, L *muscus*] **1** *chiefly Scot* : BOG, SWAMP; *esp* : a peat bog **2 a** : any of a class (Musci) of bryophytic plants having a small leafy often tufted stem bearing sex organs at its tip; *also* : a clump or sward of these plants **b** : any of various plants resembling moss in appearance or habit of growth **3** : a mossy covering — **moss·like** \-ˌlīk\ *adj*

2moss *vt* : to cover or overgrow with moss

moss agate *n* : an agate mineral containing brown, black, or green mosslike or dendritic markings

moss animal *n* : BRYOZOAN

moss·back \'mȯs-ˌbak\ *n* **1 a** : a large sluggish fish **b** : a wild old range steer or cow **2** : an extremely reactionary person : FOGY — **moss·backed** \-ˌbakt\ *adj*

moss·er \'mȯ-sər\ *n* : one that gathers and prepares Irish moss for market

moss green *n* : a variable color averaging a moderate yellow-green

moss–grown \'mȯs-ˌgrōn\ *adj* **1** : overgrown with moss **2** : ANTIQUATED

moss pink *n* : a low tufted perennial phlox (*Phlox subulata*) widely cultivated for its abundant usu. pink or white flowers

moss rose *n* : an old-fashioned garden rose that has a glandular mossy calyx and flower stalk

moss–troop·er \'mȯ-'strü-pər\ *n* **1** : one of a class of 17th century raiders in the marshy border country between England and Scotland **2** : FREEBOOTER — **moss–troop·ing** \-piŋ\ *adj*

mossy \'mȯ-sē\ *adj* **moss·i·er; -est** **1** : covered with moss or something like moss **2** : resembling moss **3** : ANTIQUATED <the ~ precepts of the . . . prescriptive grammarians —Thomas Pyles>

1most \'mōst\ *adj* [ME, fr. OE *mǣst;* akin to OHG *meist* most, OE *māra* more — more at MORE] **1** : the majority of <~ men> **2** : greatest in quantity, extent, or degree <the ~ ability> — **for the most part** : as a general rule : in most cases : MAINLY

2most *adv* **1** : to the greatest or highest degree — often used with an adjective or adverb to form the superlative <the ~ challenging job he ever had> **2** : to a very great degree <her argument was ~ persuasive>

3most *n* : the greatest amount <it's the ~ I can do> — **at most** *or* **at the most** : as an extreme limit <took him an hour *at most* to finish the job>

4most *pron, sing or pl in constr* : the greatest number or part <~ become discouraged and quit>

5most *adv* : ALMOST <we'll be crossing the river ~ any time now —Hamilton Basso>

-most \ˌmōst, *Brit also* məst\ *adj suffix* [ME, alter. of *-mest* (as in *formest* foremost)] : most <inner*most*> : most toward <head*most*>

most·ly \'mōst-lē\ *adv* : for the greatest part : MAINLY

Most Reverend — used as a title for an archbishop or a Roman Catholic bishop

mot \'mō\ *n, pl* **mots** \'mō(z)\ [F, word, saying, fr. L *muttum* grunt — more at MOTTO] : a pithy or witty saying

1mote \(')mōt\ *verbal auxiliary* [ME *moten,* fr. OE *mōtan* to be allowed to — more at MUST] *archaic* : MAY, MIGHT

2mote \'mōt\ *n* [ME *mot,* fr. OE; akin to MD & Fris *mot* sand] : a small particle : SPECK

mo·tel \mō-'tel\ *n* [blend of *motor* and *hotel*] : an establishment which provides lodging and parking and in which the rooms are usu. accessible from an outdoor parking area

mo·tet \mō-'tet\ *n* [ME, fr. MF, dim. of *mot*] : a polyphonic choral composition on a sacred text usu. without instrumental accompaniment

moth \'mȯth\ *n, pl* **moths** \'mȯt͟hz, 'mȯths\ [ME *mothe,* fr. OE *moththe;* akin to MHG *motte* moth] **1** : CLOTHES MOTH **2** : a usu. nocturnal insect (order Lepidoptera) with antennae that are often feathery, with a stouter body, duller coloring, and proportionately smaller wings than the butterflies, and with larvae that are plant-eating caterpillars

1moth·ball \'mȯth-ˌbȯl\ *n* **1** : a ball made formerly of camphor but now often of naphthalene and used to keep moths from clothing **2** *pl* : a condition of protective storage <put the ships in ~*s* after the war>; *also* : a state of having been rejected for further use or dismissed from further consideration <put that idea in ~*s*>

2mothball *vt* : to deactivate (as a ship) and prevent deterioration chiefly by dehumidification

moth bean \'mȯth-\ *n* [prob. by folk etymology fr. Marathi *maṭh* moth bean] : a bean (*Phaseolus aconitifolius*) that is cultivated esp. in India for forage and soil conditioning, for its cylindrical pods, and for its small yellowish brown seeds; *also* : its seed

moth–eat·en \'mȯ-ˌthēt-ᵊn\ *adj* **1** : eaten into by moth larvae <~ clothes> **2 a** : DILAPIDATED **b** : ANTIQUATED, OUTMODED

1moth·er \'mət͟h-ər\ *n* [ME *moder,* fr. OE *mōdor;* akin to OHG *muoter* mother, L *mater,* Gk *mētēr,* Skt *mātṛ*] **1 a** : a female parent **b** (1) : a woman in authority; *specif* : the superior of a religious community of women (2) : an old or elderly woman **2** : SOURCE, ORIGIN <necessity is the ~ of invention> **3** : maternal tenderness or affection — **moth·er·less** \-ləs\ *adj* — **moth·er·less·ness** *n*

2mother *adj* **1 a** : of, relating to, or being a mother **b** : bearing the relation of a mother **2** : derived from or as if from one's mother **3** : acting as or providing parental stock — used without reference to sex

3mother *vt* **moth·ered; moth·er·ing** \'mət͟h-(ə-)riŋ\ **1 a** : to give birth to **b** : to give rise to : PRODUCE **2** : to care for or protect like a mother

4mother *n* [akin to MD *modder* mud, lees, dregs, MLG *mudde* mud] : a slimy membrane composed of yeast and bacterial cells that develops on the surface of alcoholic liquids undergoing acetous fermentation and is added to wine or cider to produce vinegar — called also *mother of vinegar*

Mother Car·ey's chicken \-ˌkar-ēz-, -ˌker-\ *n* [origin unknown] : any of several small petrels; *esp* : STORM PETREL

mother cell *n* : a cell that gives rise to other cells usu. of a different sort

Mother Goose *n* : the legendary author of a collection of nursery rhymes first published in London about 1760

moth·er·hood \'mət͟h-ər-ˌhu̇d\ *n* : the state of being a mother

moth·er·house \-ˌhau̇s\ *n* **1** : the convent in which the superior of a religious community resides **2** : the original convent of a religious community

Mother Hub·bard \ˌmət͟h-ər-'həb-ərd\ *n* [prob. fr. *Mother Hubbard,* character in a nursery rhyme] : a loose usu. shapeless dress

moth·er–in–law \'mət͟h-(ə-)rən-ˌlȯ, 'mət͟h-ərn-ˌlȯ\ *n, pl* **mothers–in–law** \'mət͟h-ər-zən-\ **1** : the mother of one's spouse **2** : STEPMOTHER

moth·er·land \'mət͟h-ər-ˌland\ *n* **1** : a country regarded as a place of origin (as of an idea or a movement) **2** : FATHERLAND

moth·er·ly \-lē\ *adj* **1** : of, proper to, or characteristic of a mother <~ advice> **2** : resembling a mother : MATERNAL <a kind ~ sort of woman> — **moth·er·li·ness** *n*

moth·er–na·ked \ˌmət͟h-ər-'nā-kəd, *esp South* -'nek-əd\ *adj* : stark naked

moth·er–of–pearl \ˌmət͟h-ə-rə(v)-'pər(-ə)l\ *n* : the hard pearly iridescent substance forming the inner layer of a mollusk shell

Mother's Day *n* : the 2d Sunday in May appointed for the honoring of mothers

mother tongue *n* **1** : one's native language **2** : a language from which another language derives

mother wit *n* : natural wit or intelligence

1moth·proof \'mȯth-'prüf\ *adj* : impervious to penetration by moths <~ wool>

2mothproof *vt* : to make mothproof — **moth·proof·er** *n*

mo·tif \mō-'tēf\ *n* [F, motive, motif] **1 a** : a usu. recurring salient thematic element in a work of art; *esp* : a dominant idea or central theme **b** : a single or repeated design or color **2** : an influence or stimulus prompting to action

1mo·tile \'mōt-ᵊl, 'mō-ˌtīl\ *adj* [L *motus,* pp.] : exhibiting or capable of movement — **mo·til·i·ty** \mō-'til-ət-ē\ *n*

2motile *n* : a person whose prevailing mental imagery takes the form of inner feelings of action

1mo·tion \'mō-shən\ *n* [ME *mocioun,* fr. MF *motion,* fr. L *motion-, motio* movement, fr. *motus,* pp. of *movēre* to move] **1 a** : a proposal for action; *esp* : a formal proposal made in a deliberative assembly **b** : an application made to a court or judge to obtain an order, ruling, or direction **2 a** : an act, process, or instance of changing place : MOVEMENT **b** : an active or functioning state or condition <set the divorce proceedings in ~> **3** : an impulse or inclination of the mind or will **4** *obs* **a** : a puppet show **b** : PUPPET **5** : MECHANISM <a straight-line ~> **6 a** : an act or instance of moving the body or its parts : GESTURE **b** *pl* : ACTIVITIES, MOVEMENTS **7** : melodic change of pitch — **mo·tion·al** \'mō-shnəl, -shən-ᵊl\ *adj* — **mo·tion·less** \'mō-shən-ləs\ *adj* — **mo·tion·less·ly** *adv* — **mo·tion·less·ness** *n* — **in motion** *of an offensive football player* : running parallel to the line of scrimmage before the snap

2motion *vb* **mo·tioned; mo·tion·ing** \'mō-sh(ə-)niŋ\ *vt* : to direct by a motion <~*ed* me to the seat> ~ *vi* : to signal by a movement or gesture <the pitcher ~*ed* to the catcher>

motion picture *n* **1** : a series of pictures projected on a screen in rapid succession with objects shown in successive positions slightly changed so as to produce the optical effect of a continuous picture in which the objects move **2** : a representation (as of a story) by means of motion pictures : MOVIE

motion sickness *n* : sickness induced by motion (as in travel by air, car, or ship) and characterized by nausea

mo·ti·vate \'mōt-ə-ˌvāt\ *vt* **-vat·ed; -vat·ing** : to provide with a motive : IMPEL <questions that excite and ~ youth> — **mo·ti·va·tive** \-ˌvāt-iv\ *adj* — **mo·ti·va·tor** \-ˌvāt-ər\ *n*

mo·ti·va·tion \ˌmōt-ə-'vā-shən\ *n* **1 a** : the act or process of motivating **b** : the condition of being motivated **2** : a motivating force or influence : INCENTIVE, DRIVE — **mo·ti·va·tion·al** \-shnəl, -shən-ᵊl\ *adj* — **mo·ti·va·tion·al·ly** \-ē\ *adv*

1mo·tive \'mōt-iv, *2 is also* mō-'tēv\ *n* [ME, fr. MF *motif,* fr. *motif,* adj., moving] **1** : something (as a need or desire) that causes a person to act **2** : a recurrent phrase or figure that is developed through the course of a musical composition **3** : MOTIF 1 — **mo·tive·less** \-ləs\ *adj* — **mo·ti·vic** \mō-'tē-vik\ *adj*

syn MOTIVE, SPRING, IMPULSE, INCENTIVE, INDUCEMENT, SPUR, GOAD *shared meaning element* : a stimulus to action

2mo·tive \'mōt-iv\ *adj* [MF or ML; MF *motif,* fr. ML *motivus,* fr. L *motus,* pp.] **1** : moving or tending to move to action **2** : of or relating to motion or the causing of motion <~ energy>

3mo·tive \'mōt-iv\ *vt* **mo·tived; mo·tiv·ing** : MOTIVATE

motive power *n* **1** : an agency (as water or steam) used to impart motion to machinery **2** : something (as a locomotive or a motor) that provides motive power to a system

mo·tiv·i·ty \mō-'tiv-ət-ē\ *n* : the power of moving or producing motion

mot juste \mō-zhü̅st\ *n, pl* **mots justes** *same*\ [F] : the exactly right word or phrasing

1mot·ley \'mät-lē\ *adj* [ME, perh. fr. *mot* mote, speck] **1** : variegated in color <a ~ coat> **2** : composed of diverse often incongruous elements <a ~ crowd>

2motley *n* [ME, prob. fr. [1]*motley*] **1** : a woolen fabric of mixed colors made in England between the 14th and 17th centuries **2** : a garment made of motley; *esp* : the characteristic dress of the professional fool **3** : JESTER, FOOL **4** : a mixture esp. of incongruous elements

mot·mot \ˈmät-ˌmät\ *n* [AmerSp *mot-mot,* of imit. origin] **:** any of numerous long-tailed mostly green nonpasserine birds (family Momotidae) of tropical forests from Mexico to Brazil
mo·to·cross \ˈmōt-ō-ˌkrós\ *n* [*motor* + *cross*-country] **:** a motorcycle race on a tight closed course over natural terrain that includes steep hills, sharp turns, and often mud
mo·to·neu·ron \ˌmōt-ə-ˈn(y)ü-ˌrän, -ˈn(y)u̇(ə)r-ˌän\ *n* [*motor* + *neuron*] **:** a motor nerve cell with its processes
[1]**mo·tor** \ˈmōt-ər\ *n* [L, fr. *motus,* pp. of *movēre* to move] **1 :** one that imparts motion; *specif* **:** PRIME MOVER **2 :** any of various power units that develop energy or impart motion: as **a :** a small compact engine **b :** INTERNAL-COMBUSTION ENGINE; *esp* **:** a gasoline engine **c :** a rotating machine that transforms electrical energy into mechanical energy **3 :** MOTOR VEHICLE; *esp* **:** AUTOMOBILE — **mo·tor·less** \-ləs\ *adj*
[2]**motor** *adj* **1 a :** causing or imparting motion **b :** of, relating to, or being a nerve or nerve fiber that passes from the central nervous system or a ganglion to a muscle and conducts an impulse that causes movement <~ end plate> **c :** of, relating to, or involving muscular movement **2 a :** equipped with or driven by a motor **b :** of, relating to, or involving an automobile **c :** designed for motor vehicles or motorists
[3]**motor** *vi* **:** to travel by automobile **:** DRIVE ~ *vt* **:** to transport by automobile
mo·tor·bike \ˈmōt-ər-ˌbīk\ *n* **:** a small usu. lightweight motorcycle
mo·tor·boat \-ˌbōt\ *n* **:** a boat propelled by an internal-combustion engine or an electric motor — **mo·tor·boat·er** \-ər\ *n* — **mo·tor·boat·ing** \-iŋ\ *n*
motor bus *n* **:** BUS 1a — called also *motor coach*
mo·tor·cade \ˈmōt-ər-ˌkād\ *n* **:** a procession of motor vehicles
mo·tor·car \-ˌkär\ *n* **1 :** AUTOMOBILE **2** *usu* **motor car :** a railroad car containing motors for propulsion
motor court *n* **:** MOTEL
mo·tor·cy·cle \ˈmōt-ər-ˌsī-kəl\ *n* [*motor* bi*cycle*] **:** a 2-wheeled automotive vehicle having 1 or 2 saddles and sometimes a sidecar with a third supporting wheel — **motorcycle** *vi* — **mo·tor·cy·clist** \-k(ə-)ləst\ *n*
mo·tor·drome \ˈmōt-ər-ˌdrōm\ *n* **:** a track or course with seats for spectators that is used for races or tests of automobiles or motorcycles
motor home *n* **:** an automotive vehicle built on a truck or bus chassis and equipped as a self-contained traveling home — compare MOBILE HOME
mo·tor·ic \mō-ˈtȯr-ik, -ˈtär-\ *adj* **:** MOTOR 1c — **mo·tor·i·cal·ly** \-i-k(ə-)lē\ *adv*
motor inn *n* **:** a usu. multistory urban motel — called also *motor hotel*
mo·tor·ist \ˈmōt-ə-rəst\ *n* **:** a person who travels by automobile
mo·tor·ize \ˈmōt-ə-ˌrīz\ *vt* **-ized; -iz·ing :** to equip with a motor: as **a :** to provide with motor-driven equipment (as for transportation) **b :** to equip with automobiles — **mo·tor·iza·tion** \ˌmōt-ə-rə-ˈzā-shən\ *n*
motor lodge *n* **:** MOTEL
mo·tor·man \ˈmōt-ər-mən\ *n* **:** an operator of a motor-driven vehicle (as a streetcar or subway train)
motor pool *n* **:** a group of motor vehicles centrally controlled (as by a governmental agency) and dispatched for use as needed
motor scooter *n* **:** a low 2- or 3-wheeled automotive vehicle resembling a child's scooter and having a seat so that the rider does not straddle the engine
motor torpedo boat *n* **:** PT BOAT
mo·tor·truck \ˈmōt-ər-ˌtrək\ *n* **:** an automotive truck for transporting freight
motor unit *n* **:** a motoneuron together with the muscle fibers on which it acts
motor vehicle *n* **:** an automotive vehicle not operated on rails; *esp* **:** one with rubber tires for use on highways
mo·tor·way \ˈmōt-ər-ˌwā\ *n, Brit* **:** a motor highway; *esp* **:** SUPERHIGHWAY
[1]**mot·tle** \ˈmät-əl\ *n* [prob. back-formation fr. *motley*] **1 :** a colored spot **2 a :** a surface having colored spots or blotches **b :** the arrangement of such spots or blotches on a surface **3 :** MOSAIC 4b — **mot·tled** \-əld\ *adj*
[2]**mottle** *vt* **mot·tled; mot·tling** \ˈmät-liŋ, -əl-iŋ\ **:** to mark with spots or blotches of different color or shades of color as if stained — **mot·tler** \ˈmät-lər, -əl-ər\ *n*
mottled enamel *n* **:** spotted tooth enamel caused by drinking water containing excessive fluorides during the time the teeth are calcifying
mot·to \ˈmät-(ˌ)ō\ *n, pl* **mottoes** *also* **mottos** [It, fr. L *muttum* grunt, fr. *muttire* to mutter] **1 :** a sentence, phrase, or word inscribed on something as appropriate to or indicative of its character or use **2 :** a short expression of a guiding principle
moue \ˈmü\ *n* [F — more at MOW] **:** a little grimace **:** POUT
mou·flon *or* **mouf·flon** \mü-ˈflōn\ *n* [F *mouflon,* fr. It dial. *movrone,* fr. LL *mufron-, mufro*] **:** a wild sheep (*Ovis musimon*) of the mountains of Sardinia and Corsica with large curling horns in the male; *broadly* **:** a wild sheep with large horns
mouil·lé \mü-ˈyā\ *adj* [F, lit., moistened] **:** pronounced palatally
mou·jik \mü-ˈzhēk, -ˈzhik\ *var of* MUZHIK
mou·lage \mü-ˈläzh\ *n* [F, molding, fr. MF, fr. *mouler* to mold, fr. OF *modle* mold — more at MOLD] **1 :** the taking of an impression for use as evidence in a criminal investigation **2 :** an impression or cast made for use esp. as evidence in a criminal investigation
mould \ˈmōld\ *var of* MOLD
mou·lin \mü-ˈlan\ *n* [F, lit., mill, fr. LL *molinum* — more at MILL] **:** a nearly cylindrical vertical shaft in a glacier scoured out by water from melting snow and ice and by rock debris
moult \ˈmōlt\ *var of* MOLT
[1]**mound** \ˈmau̇nd\ *vt* [origin unknown] **1** *archaic* **:** to enclose or fortify with a fence or a ridge of earth **2 :** to form into a mound
[2]**mound** *n, often attrib* [origin unknown] **1** *archaic* **:** HEDGE, FENCE **2 a (1) :** an artificial bank or hill of earth or stones **(2) :** the slightly elevated ground on which a baseball pitcher stands **b :** KNOLL, HILL **3 :** HEAP, PILE
Mound Builder *n* **:** a member of a prehistoric Amerindian people whose extensive earthworks are found from the Great Lakes down the Mississippi valley to the Gulf of Mexico
[1]**mount** \ˈmau̇nt\ *n* [ME, fr. OE *munt* & OF *mont,* fr. L *mont-, mons;* akin to ON *mœna* to project, L *minari* to project, threaten] **1 :** a high hill **:** MOUNTAIN — used esp. before an identifying name <*Mount* Everest> **2** *archaic* **:** a protective earthwork **3 :** MOUND 2a(1) **4** *cap* **:** a small area of raised flesh on the palm of the hand esp. at the base of a finger that is held by palmists to indicate temperament or traits of character — see PALMISTRY illustration
[2]**mount** *vb* [ME *mounten,* fr. MF *monter,* fr. (assumed) VL *montare,* fr. L *mont-, mons*] *vi* **1 :** to increase in amount or extent <expenses began to ~> **2 :** RISE, ASCEND **3 :** to get up on something above the level of the ground; *esp* **:** to seat oneself (as on a horse) for riding ~ *vt* **1 a :** to go up **:** CLIMB **b (1) :** to seat or place oneself on **(2) :** COVER 6a **2 a :** to lift up **:** RAISE **b (1) :** to put or have (as artillery) in position **(2) :** to have as equipment **c (1) :** to organize and equip (an attacking force) <~ an army> **(2) :** to launch and carry out (as an assault or a campaign) **3 :** to set on something that elevates **4 a :** to cause to get on a means of conveyance **b :** to furnish with animals for riding **5 :** to post or set up for defense or observation <~*ed* some guards> **6 a :** to attach to a support **b :** to arrange or assemble for use or display **7 a :** to prepare (as a specimen) for examination or display **b :** to prepare and supply with the materials necessary for performance or execution **:** PRODUCE <~*ed* a sumptuous opera> ***syn*** see ASCEND ***ant*** dismount — **mount·able** \-ə-bəl\ *adj* — **mount·er** *n*
[3]**mount** *n* **1 :** an act or instance of mounting; *specif* **:** an opportunity to ride a horse in a race **2 :** FRAME, SUPPORT: as **a :** the material (as cardboard) on which a picture is mounted **b :** a jewelry setting **c (1) :** an undercarriage or part on which a device (as a motor or an artillery piece) rests in service **(2) :** an attachment for an accessory **d :** a hinge, card, or acetate envelope for mounting a stamp **e :** a glass slide with its accessories on which objects are placed for examination with a microscope **3 :** a means of conveyance; *esp* **:** SADDLE HORSE
moun·tain \ˈmau̇nt-ən\ *n, often attrib* [ME, fr. OF *montaigne,* fr. (assumed) VL *montanea,* fr. fem. of *montaneus* of a mountain, alter. of L *montanus,* fr. *mont-, mons*] **1 :** a landmass that projects conspicuously above its surroundings and is higher than a hill **2 a :** a great mass **b :** a vast number or quantity <had ~*s* of work to do>
mountain ash *n* **:** any of various trees (genus *Sorbus*) of the rose family with pinnate leaves and red or orange-red fruits
mountain cranberry *n* **:** a low evergreen shrub (*Vaccinium vitis-idaea*) of north temperate uplands with red edible berries — called also *lingonberry*
mountain dew *n* **:** MOONSHINE 3
moun·tain·eer \ˌmau̇nt-ən-ˈi(ə)r\ *n* **1 :** a native or inhabitant of a mountainous region **2 :** one who climbs mountains for sport
moun·tain·eer·ing *n* **:** the sport or technique of scaling mountains
mountain goat *n* **:** an antelope (*Oreamnos montanus*) of mountainous northwestern No. America that has a thick white coat and slightly curved black horns and resembles a goat

mountain goat

mountain laurel *n* **:** a No. American evergreen shrub (*Kalmia latifolia*) of the heath family with glossy leaves and umbels of rose-colored or white flowers
mountain lion *n* **:** COUGAR
mountain mahogany *n* **:** any of several western No. American shrubs or small shrubby trees (genus *Cercocarpus*) of the rose family that are often important as browse or forage plants
moun·tain·ous \ˈmau̇nt-ən-əs, ˈmau̇nt-nəs\ *adj* **1 :** containing many mountains **2 :** resembling a mountain **:** HUGE — **moun·tain·ous·ly** *adv* — **moun·tain·ous·ness** *n*
mountain sickness *n* **:** altitude sickness experienced esp. above 10,000 feet and caused by insufficient oxygen in the air
moun·tain·side \ˈmau̇nt-ən-ˌsīd\ *n* **:** the side of a mountain
mountain time *n, often cap M* **:** the time of the 7th time zone west of Greenwich that includes the Rocky mountain states of the U.S. — see TIME ZONE illustration
moun·tain·top \ˈmau̇nt-ən-ˌtäp\ *n* **:** the summit of a mountain
moun·tainy \ˈmau̇nt-ən-ē, ˈmau̇nt-nē\ *adj* **1 :** MOUNTAINOUS **2 :** of, relating to, or living in mountains
[1]**moun·te·bank** \ˈmau̇nt-i-ˌbaŋk\ *n* [It *montimbanco,* fr. *montare* to mount (fr.—assumed—VL) + *in* in, on (fr. L) + *banco, banca* bench — more at BANK] **1 :** a person who sells quack medicines from a platform **2 :** a boastful unscrupulous pretender **:** CHARLATAN — **moun·te·bank·ery** \-ˌbaŋ-k(ə-)rē\ *n*
[2]**mountebank** *vt, obs* **:** to beguile or transform by trickery <I'll ~ their loves —Shak.> ~ *vi* **:** to play the mountebank
Mount·ie \ˈmau̇nt-ē\ *n* [*mounted* policeman] **:** a member of the Royal Canadian Mounted Police
mount·ing \ˈmau̇nt-iŋ\ *n* **:** [3]MOUNT 2
mourn \ˈmō(ə)rn, ˈmȯ(ə)rn\ *vb* [ME *mournen,* fr. OE *murnan;* akin to OHG *mornēn* to mourn, Gk *mermēra* care — more at MEMORY] *vi* **1 :** to feel or express grief or sorrow **2 :** to show the customary signs of grief for a death; *esp* **:** to wear mourning **3 :** to murmur mournfully — used esp. of doves ~ *vt* **1 :** to feel or express grief or sorrow for **2 :** to utter mournfully ***syn*** see GRIEVE — **mourn·er** *n* — **mourn·ing·ly** \ˈmōr-niŋ-lē, ˈmȯr-\ *adv*

mourn·ful \'mō(ə)rn-fəl, 'mȯ(ə)rn-\ *adj* **1 :** expressing sorrow **:** SORROWFUL **2 :** full of sorrow **:** SAD **3 :** causing sorrow **:** SADDENING — **mourn·ful·ly** \-fə-lē\ *adv* — **mourn·ful·ness** *n*

mourn·ing \'mōr-niŋ, 'mȯr-\ *n* **1 :** the act of sorrowing **2 a :** an outward sign (as black clothes or an armband) of grief for a person's death <is wearing ~> **b :** a period of time during which signs of grief are shown

mourning cloak *n* **:** a blackish brown butterfly (*Nymphalis antiopa*) with a broad yellow border on the wings found in temperate parts of Europe, Asia, and No. America

mourning dove *n* **:** a wild dove (*Zenaidura macroura carolinensis*) of the U.S. with a plaintive call

[1]**mouse** \'mau̇s\ *n, pl* **mice** \'mīs\ [ME, fr. OE *mūs;* akin to OHG *mūs* mouse, L *mus,* Gk *mys* mouse, muscle] **1 :** any of numerous small rodents (as of the genus *Mus*) with pointed snout, rather small ears, elongated body, and slender tail **2 a** *slang* **:** WOMAN **b :** a timid person **3 :** a dark-colored swelling caused by a blow; *specif* **:** BLACK EYE

[2]**mouse** \'mau̇z\ *vb* **moused; mous·ing** *vi* **1 :** to hunt for mice **2 :** to search or move stealthily or slowly ~ *vt* **1** *obs* **a :** BITE, GNAW **b :** to toy with roughly **2 :** to search for carefully — usu. used with *out*

mouse–ear \'mau̇-ˌsi(ə)r\ *n* **1 :** a European hawkweed (*Hieracium pilosella*) that has soft hairy leaves and has been introduced into No. America **2 :** any of several plants other than mouse-ear that have soft hairy leaves

mouse–ear chickweed *n* **:** any of several hairy chickweeds (esp. *Cerastium vulgatum* and *C. viscosum*)

mous·er \'mau̇-zər\ *n* **:** a catcher of mice and rats; *esp* **:** a cat proficient at mousing

[1]**mouse·trap** \'mau̇-ˌstrap\ *n* **1 :** a trap for mice **2 :** a stratagem that lures one to defeat or destruction **3 :** TRAP 2b

[2]**mousetrap** *vt* **:** to snare in or as if in a mousetrap

Mous·que·taire \ˌmü-skə-'ta(ə)r, -'te(ə)r\ *n* [F — more at MUSKETEER] **:** a French musketeer; *esp* **:** one of the royal musketeers of the 17th and 18th centuries conspicuous for their daring and their dandified dress

mous·sa·ka \ˌmü-sə-'kä\ *n* [NGk *mousakas*] **:** a spiced Middle Eastern dish made of ground meat (as lamb or beef) and eggplant often with a cheese topping

mousse \'müs\ *n* [F, lit., froth, fr. LL *mulsa* hydromel; akin to L *mel* honey — more at MELLIFLUOUS] **:** a light spongy food usu. containing cream or gelatin; *esp* **:** a molded chilled dessert made with sweetened and flavored whipped cream or egg whites and gelatin <chocolate ~>

mous·se·line \ˌmüs-(ə-)'lēn\ *n* [F, lit., muslin — more at MUSLIN] **:** a fine sheer fabric (as of rayon) that resembles muslin

mousseline de soie \-də-'swä\ *n, pl* **mousselines de soie** *same*\ [F, lit., silk muslin] **:** a silk muslin resembling chiffon but having a crisp finish

mous·tache \'məs-ˌtash, (ˌ)məs-'\ *var of* MUSTACHE

mous·ta·chio \(ˌ)məs-\ *var of* MUSTACHIO

Mous·te·ri·an \mü-'stir-ē-ən\ *adj* [F *moustérien,* fr. Le *Moustier,* cave in Dordogne, France] **:** of or relating to a lower Paleolithic culture that is characterized by well-made flake tools often considered the work of Neanderthal man

mousy *or* **mous·ey** \'mau̇-sē, -zē\ *adj* **mous·i·er; -est :** of, relating to, or resembling a mouse: as **a :** QUIET, STEALTHY **b :** TIMID, COLORLESS — **mous·i·ly** \-sə-lē, -zə-\ *adv* — **mous·i·ness** \-sē-nəs, -zē-\ *n*

[1]**mouth** \'mau̇th\ *n, pl* **mouths** \'mau̇t͟hz, 'mau̇ths; *in synecdochic compounds like "blabbermouths"* ths *more frequently*\ *often attrib* [ME, fr. OE *mūth;* akin to OHG *mund* mouth, L *mandere* to chew, Gk *masasthai* to chew, *mastax* mouth, jaws] **1 a (1) :** the opening through which food passes into the body of an animal **(2) :** the cavity bounded externally by the lips and internally by the pharynx that encloses in the typical vertebrate the tongue, gums, and teeth **b :** GRIMACE <made a ~> **c :** an individual requiring food <had too many ~*s* to feed> **2 a :** VOICE, SPEECH <finally gave ~ to her feelings> **b :** MOUTHPIECE 3a **c (1) :** a tendency to excessive talk **(2) :** saucy or disrespectful language **:** IMPUDENCE **3 :** something that resembles a mouth esp. in affording entrance or exit: as **a :** the place where a stream enters a larger body of water **b :** the surface opening of an underground cavity **c :** the opening of a container **d :** an opening in the side of an organ flue pipe — **mouth·like** \'mau̇th-ˌlīk\ *adj* — **down in the mouth :** DEJECTED, SULKY

[2]**mouth** \'mau̇t͟h\ *vt* **1 a :** SPEAK, PRONOUNCE **b :** to utter bombastically **:** DECLAIM **c :** to repeat without comprehension or sincerity <always ~*ing* platitudes> **d :** to form soundlessly with the lips <the librarian ~*ed* the word "quiet"> **e :** to utter indistinctly **:** MUMBLE <~*ed* his words> **2 :** to take into the mouth; *esp* **:** EAT ~ *vi* **1 :** to talk pompously **:** RANT **2 :** to move the mouth esp. so as to make faces — **mouth·er** *n*

mouth·breed·er \'mau̇th-ˌbrēd-ər\ *n* **:** any of several fishes that carry their eggs and young in the mouth; *esp* **:** a No. African percoid fish (*Haplochromes multicolor*) often kept in aquariums

mouthed \'mau̇t͟hd, 'mau̇tht\ *adj* **:** having a mouth esp. of a specified kind — often used in combination <a large-*mouthed* bass>

mouth·ful \'mau̇th-ˌfu̇l\ *n* **1 a :** as much as a mouth will hold **b :** the quantity usu. taken into the mouth at one time **2 :** a small quantity **3 a :** a very long word or phrase **b :** a comment or a statement rich in meaning or substance

mouth hook *n* **:** one of a pair of hooked larval mouthparts of some two-winged flies that function as jaws

mouth organ *n* **1 :** PANPIPE **2 :** HARMONICA 2

mouth·part \'mau̇th-ˌpärt\ *n* **:** a structure or appendage near the mouth

mouth·piece \-ˌpēs\ *n* **1 :** something placed at or forming a mouth **2 :** a part (as of an instrument) that goes in the mouth or to which the mouth is applied **3 a :** one that expresses or interprets another's views **:** SPOKESMAN **b** *slang* **:** a criminal lawyer

mouth–to–mouth *adj* **:** of, relating to, or being a method of artificial respiration in which the rescuer's mouth is placed tightly over the victim's mouth in order to force air into his lungs by blowing forcefully enough every few seconds to inflate them

mouthy \'mau̇-t͟hē, -thē\ *adj* **mouth·i·er; -est 1 :** excessively talkative **:** GARRULOUS **2 :** marked by or given to bombast

mou·ton \'mü-ˌtän, mü-'\ *n* [F, sheep, sheepskin, fr. MF, ram — more at MUTTON] **:** processed sheepskin that has been sheared and dyed to resemble beaver or seal

[1]**mov·able** *or* **move·able** \'mü-və-bəl\ *adj* **1 :** capable of being moved **2 :** changing date from year to year <~ holidays> — **mov·abil·i·ty** \ˌmü-və-'bil-ət-ē\ *n* — **mov·able·ness** \'mü-və-bəl-nəs\ *n* — **mov·ably** \-blē\ *adv*

[2]**movable** *or* **moveable** *n* **:** something (as an article of furniture) that can be removed or displaced

[1]**move** \'müv\ *vb* **moved; mov·ing** [ME *moven,* fr. MF *movoir,* fr. L *movēre*] *vi* **1 a (1) :** to go or pass from one place to another with a continuous motion <*moved* into the shade> **(2) :** to proceed in a certain direction or toward a certain state or condition <*moving* up the executive ladder> <*moved* into second place in the tournament> **(3) :** to keep pace <*moving* with the times> **b :** to start away from some point or place **:** DEPART **c :** to change one's residence or location **2 :** to live one's life in a specified environment <~*s* in the best circles> **3 :** to change position or posture **:** STIR <told him to be quiet and not to ~> **4 :** to take action **:** ACT **5 a :** to begin operating or functioning or working in a usual way **b :** to show marked activity <after a brief lull things really began to ~> **6 :** to make a formal request, application, or appeal **7 :** to change hands by being sold or rented <goods that were *moving* slowly> **8** *of the bowels* **:** EVACUATE ~ *vt* **1 a (1) :** to change the place or position of **(2) :** to dislodge or displace from a fixed position **:** BUDGE **b :** to transfer (as a piece in chess) from one position to another **2 a (1) :** to cause to go or pass from one place to another with a continuous motion <*moved* the flag slowly up and down> **(2) :** to cause to advance **b :** to cause to operate or function **:** ACTUATE <this button ~*s* the whole machine> **c :** to put into activity or rouse up from inactivity **3 :** to cause to change position or posture **4 :** to prompt or rouse to the doing of something **:** PERSUADE <the report *moved* the faculty to take action> **5 a :** to stir the emotions, feelings, or passions of <was deeply *moved* by such kindness> **b :** to affect in such a way as to lead to an indicated show of emotion <the story *moved* her to tears> **6 a** *obs* **:** BEG **b :** to make a formal application to **7 :** to propose formally in a deliberative assembly <*moved* that the meeting adjourn> **8 :** to cause (the bowels) to void **9 :** to cause to change hands through sale or rent

syn MOVE, ACTUATE, DRIVE, IMPEL *shared meaning element* **:** to set or keep in motion or action

[2]**move** *n* **1 a :** the act of moving a piece (as in chess) **b :** the turn of a player to move **2 a :** a step taken so as to gain an objective **:** MANEUVER <a ~ to end the dispute> **b :** the action of moving from a motionless position **c :** a change of residence or location — **on the move 1 :** in a state of moving about from place to place <a salesman is constantly *on the move*> **2 :** in a state of moving ahead or making progress <said that civilization is always *on the move*>

move in *vi* **:** to occupy a dwelling or place of work — **move in on :** to make advances or aggressive movements toward

move·less \'müv-ləs\ *adj* **:** being without motion **:** FIXED — **move·less·ly** *adv* — **move·less·ness** *n*

move·ment \'müv-mənt\ *n* **1 a (1) :** the act or process of moving; *esp* **:** change of place or position or posture **(2) :** a particular instance or manner of moving **b (1) :** a tactical or strategic shifting of a military unit **:** MANEUVER **(2) :** the advance of a military unit **c :** ACTION, ACTIVITY — usu. used in pl. **2 a (1) :** TENDENCY, TREND <detected a ~ toward fairer pricing> **(2) :** a trend in prices (as of a security or on an exchange) <a downward ~ was apparent from the opening> **b :** a series of organized activities working toward an objective; *also* **:** an organized effort to promote or attain an end <the civil rights ~> **3 :** the moving parts of a mechanism that transmit a definite motion **4 a :** MOTION 7 **b :** the rhythmic character or quality of a musical composition **c :** a distinct structural unit or division having its own key, rhythmic structure, and themes and forming part of an extended musical composition **d :** particular rhythmic flow of language **:** CADENCE **5 a :** the quality (as in a painting or sculpture) of representing or suggesting motion **b :** the quality in literature of having a quickly moving plot or an abundance of incident **6 a :** an act of voiding the bowels **b :** matter expelled from the bowels at one passage **:** STOOL

move over *vi* **:** to make room <asked him to *move over* so she could sit down>

mov·er \'mü-vər\ *n* **:** one that moves or sets something in motion; *esp* **:** one whose business or occupation is the moving of household goods from one residence to another

mov·ie \'mü-vē\ *n* [*moving picture*] **1 :** MOTION PICTURE **2** *pl* **:** a showing of a motion picture **3** *pl* **:** the motion-picture industry

mov·ie·dom \'mü-vēd-əm\ *n* **:** FILMDOM

mov·ie·go·er \'mü-vē-ˌgō(-ə)r\ *n* **:** one who frequently attends the movies

mov·ie·mak·er \-ˌmā-kər\ *n* **:** one who makes movies

mov·ing *adj* **1 a :** marked by or capable of movement **b :** of or relating to a change of residence <~ expenses> <a ~ van> **2 a :** producing or transferring motion or action **b :** stirring deeply in

ə abut	ə kitten	ər further	a back	ā bake	ä cot, cart
au̇ out	ch chin	e less	ē easy	g gift	i trip	ī life
j joke	ŋ sing	ō flow	ȯ flaw	ȯi coin	th thin	t͟h this
ü loot	u̇ foot	y yet	yü few	yu̇ furious	zh vision

a way that evokes a strong emotional response <a ~ story of a faithful dog> — **mov·ing·ly** \'mü-viŋ-lē\ *adv*
syn MOVING, IMPRESSIVE, POIGNANT, AFFECTING, TOUCHING, PATHETIC *shared meaning element* : having the power to excite deep and usu. somber emotion
moving picture *n* : MOTION PICTURE
[1]**mow** \'mau̇\ *n* [ME, heap, stack fr. OE *mūga;* akin to ON *mūgi* heap, Gk *mykōn*] **1** : a piled-up stack (as of hay or fodder); *also* : a pile of hay or grain in a barn **2** : the part of a barn where hay or straw is stored
[2]**mow** \'mō\ *vb* **mowed; mowed** *or* **mown** \'mōn\; **mow·ing** [ME *mowen,* fr. OE *māwan;* akin to OHG *māen* to mow, L *metere* to reap, mow, Gk *aman*] *vt* **1 a** : to cut down with a scythe or sickle or machine **b** : to cut the standing herbage (as grass) of **2 a** (1) : to kill or destroy in great numbers or mercilessly <machine guns ~*ed* down the unarmed civilians> (2) : to cause to fall : knock down **b** : to overcome swiftly and decisively : ROUT <~*ed* down the opposing team> ~ *vi* : to cut down standing herbage (as grass) — **mow·er** \'mō(-ə)r\ *n*
[3]**mow** \'mau̇, 'mō\ *n* [ME *mowe,* fr. MF *moue,* of Gmc origin; akin to MD *mouwe* protruding lip] : GRIMACE
[4]**mow** \'mau̇, 'mō\ *vi* : to make grimaces
mox·ie \'mäk-sē\ *n* [fr. *Moxie,* a trademark for a soft drink] **1** : ENERGY, PEP <streetcars with so much ~ they can run out from under you —G. S. Perry> **2** : COURAGE <there is, as he knows, no excess of backbone or ~ in himself —Frederic Morton>
moyen-âge \mwȧ-ye-näzh\ *adj* [F *moyen âge* middle ages] : of or relating to medieval times
moz·za·rel·la \ˌmät-sə-'rel-ə\ *n* [It] : a moist white unsalted unripened cheese of mild flavor and a smooth rubbery texture
moz·zet·ta \mōt-'set-ə\ *n* [It] : a short cape with a small ornamental hood worn over the rochet by Roman Catholic prelates
MP *abbr* **1** melting point **2** member of parliament **3** metropolitan police **4** military police; military policeman
MPA *abbr* master of public administration
MPG *abbr* miles per gallon
MPH *abbr* **1** master of public health **2** miles per hour
MPM *abbr* meters per minute
MPS *abbr* meters per second
MPX *abbr* multiplex
mr *abbr* milliroentgen
Mr. \ˌmis-tər\ *n, pl* **Messrs.** \ˌmes-ərz\ [*Mr.* fr. ME, abbr. of *maister* master; *Messrs.* abbr. of *Messieurs,* fr. F, pl. of *Monsieur*] **1** — used as a conventional title of courtesy except when usage requires the substitution of a title of rank or an honorific or professional title before a man's surname <spoke to *Mr.* Doe> **2** — used in direct address as a conventional title of respect before a man's title of office <may I ask one more question, *Mr.* President> **3** — used before the name of a place (as a country or city) or of a profession or activity (as a sport) or before some epithet (as *clever*) to form a title applied to a male viewed or recognized as representative of the thing indicated <*Mr.* Baseball>
MR *abbr* **1** map reference **2** mill run
mri·dan·ga \mri-'däŋ-gə, ˌmər-i-\ *or* **mri·dan·gam** \-gəm\ *n* [Skt *mṛdaṅga*] : a drum of India that is shaped like an elongated barrel and has tuned heads of different diameters
mRNA *abbr* messenger RNA
Mrs. \ˌmis-əz, -əs, *esp South* ˌmiz-əz, -əs, *or* (*for sense 1*) (ˌ)miz, *or before given names* (ˌ)mis\ *n, pl* **Mes·dames** \mā-'däm, -'dam\ [*Mrs.* abbr. of [1]*mistress; Mesdames* fr. F, pl. of *Madame*] **1 a** — used as a conventional title of courtesy except when usage requires the substitution of a title of rank or an honorific or professional title before a married woman's surname <spoke to *Mrs.* Doe> **b** — used before the name of a place (as a country or city) or of a profession or activity (as a sport) or before some epithet (as *clever*) to form a title applied to a married female viewed or recognized as representative of the thing indicated <*Mrs.* Homemaker> **2** : WIFE <pick up the *Mrs.* at the five-and-dime —Alan Kapelner>
Mrs. Grun·dy \-'grən-dē\ *n* [fr. a character alluded to in Thomas Morton's *Speed the Plough* (1798)] : one marked by prudish conventionality in personal conduct
ms *abbr* millisecond
Ms. \(ˈ)miz\ *n* — used instead of *Miss* or *Mrs.* (as when the marital status of a woman is unknown) <*Ms.* Mary Smith>
MS *abbr* **1** [It *mano sinistra*] left hand **2** manuscript **3** master of science **4** military science **5** Mississippi **6** motor ship **7** multiple sclerosis
MSAT *abbr* Minnesota Scholastic Aptitude Test
MSc *abbr* master of science
msec *abbr* millisecond
msg *abbr* message
MSG *abbr* **1** master sergeant **2** monosodium glutamate
msgr *abbr* monseigneur; monsignor
MSgt *abbr* master sergeant
M16 rifle \ˌem-ˌsik-ˌstēn-\ *n* [*model 16*] : a .22 caliber gas-operated magazine-fed semiautomatic or automatic rifle used by U.S. troops since 1967
M60 machine gun \em-'sik-stē-\ *n* [*model 60*] : a .30 caliber gas-operated air-cooled machine gun fed by a cartridge belt and currently used by U.S. and NATO troops
MSL *abbr* mean sea level
MSS *abbr* manuscripts
MST *abbr* mountain standard time
MSTS *abbr* Military Sea Transportation Service
MSW *abbr* **1** master of social welfare **2** master of social work
mt *abbr* mount; mountain
Mt *abbr* Matthew
MT *abbr* **1** metric ton **2** Montana **3** mountain time
mtg *abbr* **1** meeting **2** mortgage
mtge *abbr* mortgage
MTO *abbr* Mediterranean theater of operations
mu \'myü, 'mü\ *n* [Gk *my*] **1** : the 12th letter of the Greek alphabet — see ALPHABET table **2** [μ (*mu*), symbol for *micron*] : [2]MICROMETER
muc- *or* **muci-** *or* **muco-** *comb form* [L *muc-,* fr. *mucus*] **1** : mucus <*muco*protein> **2** : mucous and <*muco*purulent>
[1]**much** \'məch\ *adj* **more** \'mō(ə)r, 'mȯ(ə)r\; **most** \'mōst\ [ME *muche* large, much, fr. *michel, muchel,* fr. OE *micel, mycel;* akin to OHG *mihhil* great, large, L *magnus,* Gk *megas*] **1 a** : great in quantity, amount, extent, or degree **b** : existing or present in a relative quantity or amount or to a relative extent or degree <taken too ~ time> **2** *obs* : many in number — **too much 1** : WONDERFUL, EXCITING **2** : TERRIBLE, AWFUL
[2]**much** *adv* **more; most 1 a** (1) : to a great degree or extent : CONSIDERABLY <~ happier> (2) : VERY **b** (1) : FREQUENTLY, OFTEN (2) : LONG **c** : by far <was ~ the brightest student> **2** : NEARLY, APPROXIMATELY <looks ~ the way his father did> — **as much** : the same in quantity — **much less** : and certainly not <can't hit .200, *much less* .300>
[3]**much** *n* **1** : a great quantity, amount, extent, or degree <gave away ~> **2** : something considerable or impressive <was not ~ to look at>
much as *conj* : however much : even though
much·ness \'məch-nəs\ *n* : the quality or state of being great : GREATNESS — **much of a muchness** : very much the same
mu·cic acid \ˌmyü-sik-\ *n* [ISV *muc-*] : an optically inactive crystalline acid $C_6H_{10}O_8$ obtained from galactose or lactose by oxidation with nitric acid
mu·cif·er·ous \myü-'sif-(ə-)rəs\ *adj* : producing or filled with mucus <~ ducts>
mu·ci·lage \'myü-s(ə-)lij\ *n* [ME *muscilage,* fr. LL *mucilago* mucus, musty juice, fr. L *mucus*] **1** : a gelatinous substance esp. from seaweeds that contains protein and polysaccharides and is similar to plant gums **2** : an aqueous usu. viscid solution (as of a gum) used esp. as an adhesive
mu·ci·lag·i·nous \ˌmyü-sə-'laj-ə-nəs\ *adj* [LL *mucilaginosus,* fr. *mucilagin-, mucilago*] **1** : STICKY, VISCID **2** : of, relating to, full of, or secreting mucilage — **mu·ci·lag·i·nous·ly** *adv*
mu·cin \'myüs-ᵊn\ *n* [ISV *muc-*] : any of various mucoproteins that occur esp. in secretions of mucous membranes — **mu·cin·ous** \-ᵊn-əs, 'myü-snəs\ *adj*
[1]**muck** \'mək\ *n* [ME *muk,* perh. fr. OE *-moc;* akin to ON *myki* dung — more at MUCUS] **1** : soft moist farmyard manure **2** : slimy dirt or filth **3** : defamatory remarks or writings **4 a** (1) : dark highly organic soil (2) : MIRE, MUD **b** : something resembling muck : GUNK **5** : material removed in the process of excavating or mining — **mucky** \'mək-ē\ *adj*
[2]**muck** *vt* **1 a** : to clean up; *esp* : to clear of manure or filth **b** : to clear of muck **2** : to dress (as soil) with muck **3** : to dirty with or as if with muck : SOIL ~ *vi* **1** : to move or load muck (as in a mine) **2** *chiefly Brit* : to engage in aimless activity — **muck·er** *n*
muck·luck *var of* MUKLUK
muck·rake \'mək-ˌrāk\ *vi* [obs. *muckrake,* n. (rake for dung)] : to search out and expose publicly real or apparent misconduct of prominent individuals — **muck·rak·er** *n*
muck up *vb, chiefly Brit* : BUNGLE
mu·co·cu·ta·ne·ous \ˌmyü-kō-kyü-'tā-nē-əs\ *adj* : made up of or involving both typical skin and mucous membrane
[1]**mu·coid** \'myü-ˌkȯid\ *adj* [ISV *muc-*] : resembling mucus
[2]**mucoid** *n* [ISV] : MUCOPROTEIN
mu·coi·tin·sul·fu·ric acid \myü-'kō-ət-ᵊn-ˌsəl-ˌfyu̇r-ik-, -'kȯit-ᵊn-\ *n* [ISV *mucoitin* (a mucopolysaccharide acid)] : an acidic mucopolysaccharide found esp. in the cornea of the eye and in gastric mucosa
mu·co·lyt·ic \ˌmyü-kə-'lit-ik\ *adj* : hydrolyzing mucopolysaccharides : tending to break down or lower the viscosity of mucin-containing body secretions or components <~ enzymes>
mu·co·poly·sac·cha·ride \'myü-kō-ˌpäl-i-'sak-ə-ˌrīd\ *n* [ISV] : any of various polysaccharides derived from a hexosamine that are constituents of mucoproteins, glycoproteins, and blood-group substances
mu·co·pro·tein \ˌmyü-kə-'prō-ˌtēn, -'prōt-ē-ən\ *n* : any of various complex conjugated proteins (as mucins) that contain polysaccharides and occur in body fluids and tissues
mu·cor \'myü-ˌkȯ(ə)r\ *n* [NL, genus name, fr. L, mold, moldiness; akin to L *mucus*] : any of a genus (*Mucor*) of molds with round usu. cylindrical or pear-shaped sporangia that are not clustered and are not limited in location to the points where rhizoids develop
mu·co·sa \myü-'kō-zə\ *n, pl* **-sae** \-(ˌ)zē, -ˌzī\ *or* **-sas** [NL, fr. L, fem. of *mucosus* mucous] : MUCOUS MEMBRANE — **mu·co·sal** \-zəl\ *adj*
mu·cous \'myü-kəs\ *adj* [L *mucosus,* fr. *mucus*] **1** : covered with or as if with mucus : SLIMY **2** : of, relating to, or resembling mucus **3** : secreting or containing mucus
mucous membrane *n* : a membrane rich in mucous glands; *specif* : one that lines body passages and cavities which communicate directly or indirectly with the exterior
mu·cro \'myü-ˌkrō\ *n, pl* **mu·cro·nes** \myü-'krō-(ˌ)nēz\ [NL *mucron-, mucro,* fr. L, point, edge; akin to Gk *amyssein* to scratch, sting] : an abrupt sharp terminal point or tip or process (as of a leaf) — **mu·cro·nate** \'myü-krə-ˌnāt\ *adj* — **mu·cro·na·tion** \ˌmyü-krə-'nā-shən\ *n*
mu·cus \'myü-kəs\ *n* [L, nasal mucus; akin to ON *myki* dung, Gk *myxa* mucus] : a viscid slippery secretion that is usu. rich in mucins and is produced by mucous membranes which it moistens and protects
[1]**mud** \'məd\ *n* [ME *mudde,* prob. fr. MLG; akin to OE *mōs* bog — more at MOSS] **1** : a slimy sticky mixture of solid material with a liquid and esp. water; *esp* : soft wet earth **2** : abusive and malicious remarks or charges
[2]**mud** *vt* **mud·ded; mud·ding 1** : to make muddy or turbid **2** : to treat or plaster with mud
mud dauber *n* : any of various wasps (esp. family Sphecidae) that construct mud cells in which the female places an egg with spiders or insects paralyzed by a sting to serve as food for the larva
[1]**mud·dle** \'məd-ᵊl\ *vb* **mud·dled; mud·dling** \'məd-liŋ, -ᵊl-iŋ\ [prob. fr. obs. D *moddelen,* fr. MD, fr. *modde* mud; akin to MLG *mudde*] *vt* **1** : to make turbid or muddy **2** : to befog or stupefy

esp. with liquor **3 :** to mix confusedly **4 :** to make a mess of **:** BUNGLE ~ *vi* **:** to think or act in a confused aimless way — **mud·dler** \ˈməd-lər, -ᵊl-ər\ *n*

[2]**muddle** *n* **1 :** a state of esp. mental confusion **2 :** a confused mess

mud·dle·head·ed \ˌməd-ᵊl-ˈhed-əd\ *adj* **1 :** mentally confused **2 :** INEPT, BUNGLING — **mud·dle·head·ed·ness** *n*

[1]**mud·dy** \ˈməd-ē\ *adj* **mud·di·er; -est 1 :** morally impure **:** BASE **2 a :** full of or covered with mud **b :** characteristic or suggestive of mud <a ~ flavor> <~ colors> **c :** turbid with sediment **3 a :** lacking in clarity or brightness **:** CLOUDY, DULL <retained only a distorted ~ image of the event> <eyes ~ with sleep> **b :** obscure in meaning **:** MUDDLED, CONFUSED <~ thinking> <a ~ style> ***syn*** see TURBID — **mud·di·ly** \ˈməd-ᵊl-ē\ *adv* — **mud·di·ness** \ˈməd-ē-nəs\ *n*

[2]**muddy** *vt* **mud·died; mud·dy·ing 1 :** to soil or stain with or as if with mud **2 :** to make turbid **3 :** to make cloudy or dull **4 :** CONFUSE

mud eel *n* **:** a siren (*Siren lacertina*) that is lead gray in color, attains a length of about two feet, and inhabits the swamps and ditches of the southern U.S.

mud·guard \ˈməd-ˌgärd\ *n* **1 a :** FENDER d **b :** SPLASH GUARD **2 :** a strip of material applied to a shoe upper just above the sole for protection against dampness or as an ornament

mud puppy *n* **:** any of several large American salamanders; *esp* **:** one (*Necturus maculosus*) that has external gills and is gray to rusty brown usu. with bluish black spots

mud·room \ˈməd-ˌrüm, -ˌrům\ *n* **:** a room in a house designed for the shedding of dirty or wet footwear and clothing and located typically off the kitchen or in the basement

mud·sill \ˈməd-ˌsil\ *n* **1 :** a supporting sill (as of a building or bridge) resting directly on a base and esp. the earth **2 :** a person of the lowest social level

mud·sling·er \-ˌsliŋ-ər\ *n* **:** one that uses offensive epithets and invective esp. against a political opponent — **mud·sling·ing** \-ˌsliŋ-iŋ\ *n*

mud·stone \ˈməd-ˌstōn\ *n* **:** an indurated shale produced by the consolidation of mud

mud turtle *n* **:** a bottom-dwelling freshwater turtle: as **a :** any of a genus (*Kinosternon*) of musk turtles with two transverse hinges on the plastron **b :** SOFT-SHELLED TURTLE

Muen·ster \ˈmən(t)-stər, ˈm(y)ün(t)-, ˈmůn(t)-\ *n* [*Münster, Munster,* France] **:** a semisoft cheese that may be bland or sharp in flavor

mu·ez·zin \m(y)ü-ˈez-ᵊn, ˈmwez-ᵊn\ *n* [Ar *mu'adhdhin*] **:** a Muslim crier who calls the hour of daily prayers

[1]**muff** \ˈməf\ *n* [D *mof,* fr. MF *moufle* mitten, fr. ML *muffula*] **1 :** a warm tubular covering for the hands **2 :** a cluster of feathers on the side of the face of some domestic fowls

[2]**muff** *n* **1 :** a bungling performance **2 :** a failure to hold a ball in attempting a catch

[3]**muff** *vt* **1 :** to handle awkwardly **:** BUNGLE **2 :** to fail to hold (a ball) when attempting a catch ~ *vi* **1 :** to act or do something stupidly or clumsily **2 :** to muff a ball — compare FUMBLE

muf·fin \ˈməf-ən\ *n* [prob. fr. LG *muffen,* pl. of *muffe* cake] **:** a quick bread made of batter containing egg and baked in a muffin pan

muffin pan *n* **:** a baking pan formed of a group of connected cups and used esp. for baking muffins or cupcakes

[1]**muf·fle** \ˈməf-əl\ *vt* **muf·fled; muf·fling** \ˈməf-(ə-)liŋ\ [ME *muflen*] **1 :** to wrap up so as to conceal or protect **:** ENVELOP **2** *obs* **:** BLINDFOLD **3 a :** to wrap or pad with something to dull the sound <~ the oarlocks> **b :** to deaden the sound of <the sands . . . have *muffled* the tread of countless armies —Rex Keating> **4 :** to keep down **:** SUPPRESS

[2]**muffle** *n* [F *mufle*] **:** the tip of the mammalian muzzle

muf·fler \ˈməf-lər\ *n* **1 a :** a scarf worn around the neck **b :** something that hides or disguises **2 :** a device to deaden noise; *esp* **:** one forming part of the exhaust system of an automotive vehicle

[1]**muf·ti** \ˈməf-tē, ˈmůf-\ *n* [Ar *mufti*] **:** a professional jurist who interprets Muslim law

[2]**muf·ti** \ˈməf-tē\ *n* [prob. fr. [1]*mufti*] **:** civilian clothes

[1]**mug** \ˈməg\ *n* [origin unknown] **1 :** a cylindrical drinking cup **2 a :** the face or mouth of a person **b :** GRIMACE **c :** a photograph of a suspect's face **3 a** *Brit* **:** a person easily deceived **b :** PUNK, THUG

[2]**mug** *vb* **mugged; mug·ging** *vi* **:** to make faces esp. to attract attention ~ *vt* **:** PHOTOGRAPH

[3]**mug** *vb* **mugged; mug·ging** [back-formation fr. [2]*mugger*] **:** to assault usu. with intent to rob

[1]**mug·ger** \ˈməg-ər\ *n* [Hindi *magar,* fr. Skt *makara* water monster] **:** a common usu. harmless freshwater crocodile (*Crocodylus palustris*) of southeastern Asia

[2]**mugger** *n* [prob. fr. obs. *mug* (to punch in the face)] **:** one who attacks with intent to rob

[3]**mugger** *n* [[2]*mug*] **:** one that grimaces esp. before an audience

mug·gy \ˈməg-ē\ *adj* **mug·gi·er; -est** [E dial. *mug* (drizzle)] **:** being warm, damp, and close — **mug·gi·ly** \ˈməg-ə-lē\ *adv* — **mug·gi·ness** \ˈməg-ē-nəs\ *n*

mu·gho pine \ˌm(y)ü-(ˌ)gō-\ *n* [prob. fr. F *mugho* mugho pine, fr. It *mugo*] **:** a shrubby spreading pine (*Pinus mugo mughus*) widely cultivated as an ornamental

mug·wump \ˈməg-ˌwəmp\ *n* [obs. slang *mugwump* (kingpin), fr. Natick *mugwomp* captain] **1 :** a bolter from the Republican party in 1884 **2 :** an independent in politics

Mu·ham·mad·an \mō-ˈham-əd-ən, -ˈhäm- *also* mü-\ *adj* **:** of or relating to Muhammed or Islam — **Muhammadan** *n* — **Mu·ham·mad·an·ism** \-ˌiz-əm\ *n*

Muhammadan calendar *n* **:** a lunar calendar reckoned from the Hegira in A.D. 622 and organized in cycles of 30 years — see MONTH table

Muhammadan era *n* **:** the era used in Muhammadan countries for numbering Muhammadan calendar years since the Hegira — called also *Muslim era*

Mu·har·ram \mü-ˈhar-əm\ *n* [Ar *Muharram*] **1 :** the 1st month of the Muhammadan year — see MONTH table **2 :** a Muslim festival held during Muharram

mu·jik \mü-ˈzhēk, -ˈzhik\ *var of* MUZHIK

muk·luk \ˈmək-ˌlək\ *n* [Esk *muklok* large seal] **1 :** a sealskin or reindeer-skin boot worn by Eskimos **2 :** a boot often of duck with a soft leather sole and worn over several pairs of socks

mu·lat·to \m(y)ů-ˈlat-(ˌ)ō, -ə(-w)\ *n, pl* **-toes** *or* **-tos** [Sp *mulato,* fr. *mulo* mule, fr. L *mulus*] **1 :** the first-generation offspring of a Negro and a white **2 :** a person of mixed Caucasian and Negro ancestry

mul·ber·ry \ˈməl-ˌber-ē, -b(ə-)rē\ *n* [ME *murberie, mulberie,* fr. OF *moure* mulberry (fr. L *morum,* fr. Gk *moron*) + ME *berie* berry] **1 :** any of a genus (*Morus* of the family Moraceae, the mulberry family) of trees with an edible usu. purple multiple fruit that is an aggregate of juicy one-seeded drupes; *also* **:** the fruit **2 :** a dark purple or purplish black

mulch \ˈməlch\ *n* [perh. irreg. fr. E dial. *melch* (soft, mild)] **:** a protective covering (as of sawdust, compost, or paper) spread or left on the ground esp. to reduce evaporation, maintain even soil temperature, prevent erosion, control weeds, or enrich the soil — **mulch** *vt*

[1]**mulct** \ˈməlkt\ *n* [L *multa, mulcta*] **:** FINE, PENALTY

[2]**mulct** *vt* **1 :** to punish by a fine **2 a :** to defraud esp. of money **:** SWINDLE **b :** to obtain by fraud, duress, or theft

[1]**mule** \ˈmyü(ə)l\ *n* [ME, fr. OF *mul,* fr. L *mulus*] **1 a :** a hybrid between a horse and an ass; *esp* **:** the offspring of a male ass and a mare **b :** a self-sterile plant whether hybrid or not **c :** a usu. sterile hybrid **2 :** a very stubborn person **3 :** a machine for simultaneously drawing and twisting fiber into yarn or thread and winding it into cops **4 :** a coin or token struck from dies belonging to two different issues

[2]**mule** *vt* **muled; mul·ing 1 :** to combine (dies that do not match) to make a mule **2 :** to strike (a coin or token) with nonmatching dies making a mule

[3]**mule** *n* [MF, a kind of slipper, fr. L *mulleus* shoe worn by magistrates] **:** a shoe or slipper without quarter or heel strap — compare SCUFF

mule deer *n* **:** a long-eared deer (*Odocoileus hemionus* syn. *Cariacus macrotis*) of western No. America that is larger and more heavily built than the common whitetail — see DEER illustration

mule–foot \ˈmyü(ə)l-ˌfůt\ *or* **mule–foot·ed** \-ˈfůt-əd\ *adj* **:** having a solid rather than a cleft hoof <~ swine>

mule skinner *n* **:** MULETEER

mu·le·ta \m(y)ü-ˈlāt-ə\ *n* [Sp, crutch, muleta, dim. of *mula* she-mule, fr. L, fem. of *mulus* mule] **:** a small cloth attached to a short tapered stick and used by a matador in place of the large cape during the final stage of a bullfight

mu·le·teer \ˌmyü-lə-ˈti(ə)r\ *n* [F *muletier,* fr. *mulet,* fr. OF, dim. of *mul* mule] **:** one who drives mules

mu·ley *also* **mul·ley** \ˈmyü-lē, ˈmůl-ē, ˈmü-lē\ *adj* [of Celtic origin; akin to IrGael & ScGael *maol* bald, hornless, W *moel*] **:** POLLED, HORNLESS; *esp* **:** naturally hornless

mu·li·eb·ri·ty \ˌmyü-lē-ˈeb-rət-ē\ *n* [LL *muliebritat-, muliebritas,* fr. L *muliebris* of a woman, fr. *mulier* woman] **:** FEMININITY

mul·ish \ˈmyü-lish\ *adj* [[1]*mule*] **:** unreasonably and inflexibly obstinate **:** RECALCITRANT ***syn*** see OBSTINATE — **mul·ish·ly** *adv* — **mul·ish·ness** *n*

[1]**mull** \ˈməl\ *vb* [ME *mullen,* fr. *mul, mol* dust, prob. fr. MD; akin to OE *melu* meal — more at MEAL] *vt* **1 :** to grind or mix thoroughly **:** PULVERIZE **2 :** to consider at length **:** PONDER ~ *vi* **:** MEDITATE, PONDER

[2]**mull** *vt* [origin unknown] **:** to heat, sweeten, and flavor (as wine or cider) with spices

[3]**mull** *n* [by shortening & alter. fr. *mulmul* (muslin)] **:** a soft fine sheer fabric of cotton, silk, or rayon

[4]**mull** *n* [G, fr. Dan *muld,* fr. ON *mold* dust, soil; akin to OHG *molta* dust, soil — more at MOLD] **1 :** granular forest humus that forms a layer of mixed organic matter and mineral soil and merges gradually into the mineral soil beneath **2 :** a finely powdered solid esp. in a suspension

mul·lah \ˈməl-ə, ˈmůl-ə\ *n* [Turk *molla* & Per & Hindi *mulla,* fr. Ar *mawlā*] **1 :** a Muslim of a quasi-clerical class trained in traditional law and doctrine **2 :** a religious teacher — usu. used disparagingly — **mul·lah·ism** \-ə-ˌiz-əm\ *n*

mul·lein *also* **mul·len** \ˈməl-ən\ *n* [ME *moleyne,* fr. AF *moleine*] **:** any of a genus (*Verbascum*) of usu. woolly-leaved herbs of the figwort family

mullein pink *n* **:** a European herb (*Lychnis coronaria*) cultivated for its white woolly herbage and showy crimson flowers

mull·er \ˈməl-ər\ *n* [alter. of ME *molour,* prob. fr. *mullen* to grind] **:** a stone or piece of wood, metal, or glass used as a pestle

Mül·le·ri·an \myül-ˈir-ē-ən, mil-, ˌməl-\ *adj* [Fritz *Müller* †1897 G zoologist] **:** of, relating to, or being mimicry that exists between two or more inedible or dangerous species (as of butterflies) and that is considered in evolutionary theory to be a mechanism reducing loss to predation by simplification of the recognition process

mul·let \ˈməl-ət\ *n, pl* **mullet** *or* **mullets** [ME *molet,* fr. MF *mulet,* fr. L *mullus* red mullet, fr. Gk *myllos;* akin to Gk *melas* black, Skt *malina* dirty, black] **1 :** any of a family (Mugilidae) of valuable food fishes with an elongate rather stout body — called also *gray mullet* **2 :** any of a family (Mullidae) of moderate-sized

---

usu. red or golden fishes with two barbels on the chin — called also *red mullet*

mul·li·gan stew \ˌməl-i-gən-\ *n* [prob. fr. the name *Mulligan*] : a stew made basically of vegetables and meat or fish — called also *mulligan*

mul·li·ga·taw·ny \ˌməl-i-gə-ˈtȯ-nē, -ˈtän-ē\ *n* [Tamil *milakutaṇṇi*, a strongly seasoned soup, fr. *milaku* pepper + *taṇṇi* water] : a rich soup usu. of chicken stock seasoned with curry

mul·lion \ˈməl-yən\ *n* [prob. alter. of *monial* (mullion)] : a slender vertical member placed between lights (as of windows or doors) or used decoratively (as on the surface of a building) — **mullion** *vt*

mull·ite \ˈməl-ˌīt\ *n* [*Mull*, island of the Inner Hebrides] : a mineral $Al_6Si_2O_{13}$ or $3Al_2O_3.2SiO_2$ that is an orthorhombic silicate of aluminum resistant to corrosion and heat and used as a refractory

multi- *comb form* [ME, fr. MF or L; MF, fr. L, fr. *multus* much, many — more at MELIORATE] **1 a** : many : multiple : much <*multi*valent> **b** : more than two <*multi*lateral> **c** : more than one <*multi*para> **2** : many times over <*multi*millionaire>

mul·ti·cel·lu·lar \ˌməl-ti-ˈsel-yə-lər, -ˌtī-\ *adj* [ISV] : having or consisting of many cells — **mul·ti·cel·lu·lar·i·ty** \-ˌsel-yə-ˈlar-ət-ē\ *n*

mul·ti·col·ored \ˌməl-ti-ˈkəl-ərd\ *also* **mul·ti·col·or** \-ər\ *adj* : of various colors : PARTI-COLORED <a ~ carpet>

mul·ti·cul·tur·al \ˌməl-ti-ˈkəlch-(ə-)rəl, -ˌtī-\ *adj* : of, relating to, or designed for a combination of several distinct cultures <a ~ urban environment> <a ~ curriculum>

mul·ti·di·men·sion·al \-ti-də-ˈmench-nəl, -dī-; -ˌtī-də-\ *adj* : of, relating to, or marked by several dimensions <a ~ problem> <~ calculus> — **mul·ti·di·men·sion·al·i·ty** \-ˌmen-chə-ˈnal-ət-ē\ *n*

mul·ti·di·rec·tion·al \-ˈrek-shnəl, -shən-ᵊl\ *adj* : extending in many directions <~ efforts to win the election>

mul·ti·dis·ci·plin·ary \ˌməl-ti-ˈdis-ə-plə-ˌner-ē, -ˌtī-\ *adj* : of, relating to, or using a combination of several disciplines for a common purpose <a ~ approach to child guidance>

mul·ti·eth·nic \-ˈeth-nik\ *adj* : of, relating to, or designed for a combination of several distinct ethnic groups <~ textbooks>

mul·ti·fac·et·ed \-ˈfas-ət-əd\ *adj* : having several distinct facets <the ~ problems of foreign policy>

mul·ti·fac·to·ri·al \-fak-ˈtōr-ē-əl, -ˈtȯr-\ *adj* **1** : having characters or a mode of inheritance dependent on a number of genes at different loci **2** *or* **mul·ti·fac·tor** \-ˈfak-tər\ : having or involving a variety of elements <a ~ study> — **mul·ti·fac·to·ri·al·ly** \-ē-ə-lē\ *adv*

mul·ti·fam·i·ly \-ˈfam-(ə-)lē\ *adj* : of, relating to, or designed for use by several distinct families <~ dwellings>

mul·ti·far·i·ous \ˌməl-tə-ˈfar-ē-əs, -ˈfer-\ *adj* [L *multifarius*, fr. *multi-* + *-farius* (akin to *facere* to make, do)] : having or occurring in great variety : DIVERSE <the ~ duties of a farmer> — **mul·ti·far·i·ous·ly** *adv* — **mul·ti·far·i·ous·ness** *n*

mul·ti·flo·ra rose \ˌməl-tə-ˌflōr-ə-, -ˌflȯr-\ *n* [NL *multiflora*, specific epithet, lit., having many flowers] : a vigorous thorny rose (*Rosa multiflora*) with clusters of small flowers

mul·ti·fold \ˈməl-ti-ˌfōld\ *adj* : MANIFOLD, NUMEROUS

mul·ti·font \ˌməl-ti-ˈfänt, -ˌtī-\ *adj* : of, involving, or capable of reading several fonts of type <a ~ OCR machine> <~ composition>

mul·ti·form \ˈməl-ti-ˌfȯrm\ *adj* [F *multiforme*, fr. L *multiformis*, fr. *multi-* + *-formis* -form] : having many forms or appearances — **mul·ti·for·mi·ty** \ˌməl-ti-ˈfȯr-mət-ē\ *n*

mul·ti·germ \ˌməl-ti-ˈjərm, -ˌtī-\ *adj* [prob. fr. *multi-* + *germinate*] : producing or being a fruit cluster capable of giving rise to several plants <a ~ variety of sugar beet>

mul·ti·lane \-ˈlān\ *also* **mul·ti·laned** \-ˈlānd\ *adj* : having several lanes <~ highways>

mul·ti·lat·er·al \ˌməl-ti-ˈlat-ə-rəl, -ˌtī-, -ˈla-trəl\ *adj* **1** : having many sides **2** : participated in by more than two nations or parties <~ agreements> — **mul·ti·lat·er·al·ly** \-ē\ *adv*

mul·ti·lay·ered \-ˈlā-ərd, -ˈle(-ə)rd\ *or* **mul·ti·lay·er** \-ˈlā-ər, -ˈle(-ə)r\ *adj* : having or involving several distinct layers, strata, or levels <~ epidermis> <~ tropical rain forest> <~ insights>

mul·ti·lev·el \-ˈlev-əl\ *also* **mul·ti·lev·eled** \-əld\ *adj* : having several levels <freeways with ~ interchanges —*Lamp*>

mul·ti·lin·gual \-ˈliŋ-g(yə-)wəl\ *adj* **1** : of, containing, or expressed in several languages <a ~ sign> <~ dictionaries> **2** : using or able to use several languages <a ~ stewardess> — **mul·ti·lin·qual·ly** \-ē\ *adv*

mul·ti·lin·gual·ism \-g(yə-)wə-ˌliz-əm\ *n* : the use of or the ability to use several languages

mul·ti·me·dia \-ˈmēd-ē-ə\ *adj* : using, involving, or encompassing several media <a ~ approach to learning> <a ~ exhibition>

mul·ti·mil·lion·aire \ˌməl-ti-ˌmil-yə-ˈna(ə)r, -ˌtī-, -ˈne(ə)r, -ˈmil-yə-ˌ\ *n* : one whose wealth is estimated at many millions

mul·ti·na·tion·al \-ˈnash-nəl, -ən-ᵊl\ *adj* **1 a** : of, relating to, or involving more than two nations <a ~ alliance> **b** : having divisions in more than two countries <a ~ corporation> **2** : of or relating to more than two nationalities <a ~ society> — **multinational** *n*

mul·ti·no·mi·al \-ˈnō-mē-əl\ *n* [*multi-* + *-nomial* (as in *binomial*)] : a mathematical expression that consists of the sum of several terms : POLYNOMIAL — **multinomial** *adj*

mul·ti·nu·cle·ar \ˌməl-ti-ˈnyü-klē-ər, -ˌtī-\ *adj* : MULTINUCLEATE

mul·ti·nu·cle·ate \-klē-ət\ *also* **mul·ti·nu·cle·at·ed** \-klē-ˌāt-əd\ *adj* [ISV] : having more than two nuclei

mul·tip·a·rous \ˌməl-ˈtip-ə-rəs\ *adj* [NL *multiparus*, fr. *multi-* + L *-parus* -parous] **1** : producing many or more than one at a birth **2** : having experienced one or more previous parturitions

mul·ti·par·tite \ˌməl-ti-ˈpär-ˌtīt\ *adj* [L *multipartitus*, fr. *multi-* + *partitus*, pp. of *partire* to divide, fr. *part-*, *pars* part] **1** : divided into several or many parts **2** : having numerous members or signatories <a ~ treaty>

mul·ti·par·ty \ˌməl-ti-ˈpärt-ē, -ˌtī-\ *adj* : of, relating to, or involving more than two parties <our two-party system cloaks a ~ reality —Dean Acheson>

mul·ti·phase \-ˌfāz\ *adj* : having various phases; *esp* : POLYPHASE

mul·ti·pha·sic \ˌməl-ti-ˈfā-zik, -ˌtī-\ *adj* : having various phases or elements <a ~ test>

[1]**mul·ti·ple** \ˈməl-tə-pəl\ *adj* [F, fr. L *multiplex*, fr. *multi-* + *-plex* -fold — more at SIMPLE] **1** : consisting of, including, or involving more than one <~ births> **2** : MANY, MANIFOLD <~ achievements> **3** : shared by many <~ ownership> **4** : having numerous aspects or functions : VARIOUS **5 a** : being a circuit with a number of conductors in parallel **b** : being a group of terminals which make a circuit available at a number of points **6** : formed by coalescence of the ripening ovaries of several flowers <a ~ fruit>

[2]**multiple** *n* **1 a** : the product of a quantity by an integer <35 is a ~ of 7> **b** : an assemblage with respect to any of its divisions or parts <lay mines in ~> **2** : PARALLEL 4b

multiple allele *n* : any of more than two allelic factors located at one chromosomal locus

multiple–choice *adj* **1** : having several answers from which one is to be chosen <a ~ question> **2** : composed of multiple-choice questions <a ~ test>

multiple factor *n* : one of a group of nonallelic genes that according to the multiple-factor hypothesis control various quantitative hereditary characters

multiple myeloma *n* : a disease of bone marrow that is characterized by the presence of numerous myelomas in various bones of the body

multiple regression *n* : regression in which one variable is estimated by the use of more than one other variable

multiple sclerosis *n* : a diseased condition marked by patches of hardened tissue in the brain or the spinal cord and associated esp. with partial or complete paralysis and jerking muscle tremor

multiple star *n* : several stars in close proximity that appear to form a single system

multiple store *n, chiefly Brit* : CHAIN STORE

mul·ti·plet \ˈməl-tə-plət\ *n* **1** : a spectrum line having several components **2** : a group of elementary particles that are different in charge but similar in other properties (as mass)

mul·ti·ple–val·ued \ˌməl-tə-pəl-ˈval-(ˌ)yüd\ *adj* : having at least one and sometimes more of the values of the range associated with each value of the domain <a ~ function> — compare SINGLE-VALUED

multiple voting *n* : illegal voting by one person in two or more constituencies

[1]**mul·ti·plex** \ˈməl-tə-ˌpleks\ *adj* [L] **1** : MANIFOLD, MULTIPLE <the ~ moods of our human nature —Herbert Read> **2** : being or relating to a system of transmitting several messages simultaneously on the same circuit or channel

[2]**multiplex** *vt* : to send (messages or signals) by a multiplex system ~ *vi* : to multiplex messages or signals — **mul·ti·plex·er** *or* **mul·ti·plex·or** \-ər\ *n*

mul·ti·pli·able \ˈməl-tə-ˌplī-ə-bəl\ *adj* : capable of being multiplied

mul·ti·plic·a·ble \ˌməl-tə-ˈplik-ə-bəl\ *adj* : MULTIPLIABLE

mul·ti·pli·cand \ˌməl-tə-pli-ˈkand\ *n* [L *multiplicandus*, gerundive of *multiplicare*] : the number that is to be multiplied by another

mul·tip·li·cate \ˌməl-ˈtip-li-kət\ *adj* [ME, fr. L *multiplicatus*, pp.] : MULTIPLE

mul·ti·pli·ca·tion \ˌməl-tə-plə-ˈkā-shən\ *n* [ME *multiplicacioun*, fr. MF *multiplication*, fr. L *multiplication-*, *multiplicatio*, fr. *multiplicatus*, pp. of *multiplicare* to multiply] **1** : the act or process of multiplying : the state of being multiplied **2** : a mathematical operation that at its simplest is an abbreviated process of adding an integer to itself a specified number of times and that is extended to other numbers in accordance with laws that are valid for integers

multiplication sign *n* : a symbol used to indicate multiplication: **a** : TIMES SIGN **b** : DOT 2b

mul·ti·pli·ca·tive \ˌməl-tə-ˈplik-ət-iv, ˈməl-tə-plə-ˌkāt-\ *adj* : tending or having the power to multiply numbers — **mul·ti·pli·ca·tive·ly** *adv*

multiplicative identity *n* : an identity element (as 1 in the group of rational numbers without 0) that in a given mathematical system leaves unchanged any element by which it is multiplied

multiplicative inverse *n* : an element of a mathematical set that when multiplied by a given element yields the identity element — called also *reciprocal*

mul·ti·plic·i·ty \ˌməl-tə-ˈplis-ət-ē\ *n, pl* **-ties** [MF *multiplicité*, fr. LL *multiplicitat-*, *multiplicitas*, fr. L *multiplic-*, *multiplex*] **1** : the quality or state of being multiple or various <the vast ~ of the visible world —Howard Nemerov> **2** : a great number <a ~ of errors> **3** : the number of components in a system (as a multiplet or a group of energy states)

mul·ti·pli·er \ˈməl-tə-ˌplī(-ə)r\ *n* : one that multiplies: as **a** : a number by which another number is multiplied **b** : an instrument or device for multiplying or intensifying some effect **c** : a key-operated machine or mechanism or circuit on a machine that multiplies figures and records the products **d** : the ratio between the ultimate increase of income arising from an increment of investment and the initial new investment itself

[1]**mul·ti·ply** \ˈməl-tə-ˌplī\ *vb* **-plied; -ply·ing** [ME *multiplien*, fr. OF *multiplier*, fr. L *multiplicare*, fr. *multiplic-*, *multiplex* multiple] *vt* **1** : to increase in number esp. greatly or in multiples : AUGMENT **2 a** : to combine by multiplication <~ 7 and 8> **b** : to combine with (another number) by multiplication <7 *multiplied* by 8 is 56> ~ *vi* **1 a** : to become greater in number : SPREAD **b** : BREED, PROPAGATE **2** : to perform multiplication ***syn*** see INCREASE

[2]**mul·ti·ply** \-plē\ *adv* : in a multiple manner : in several ways <the use of ~ applicable names —A. I. Melden>

mul·ti–ply \ˌməl-ti-ˈplī\ *adj* : composed of several plies

mul·ti·po·lar \ˌməl-ti-ˈpō-lər, -ˌtī-\ *adj* [ISV] **1** : having several poles <a ~ generator> **2** : having several dendrites <~ nerve cells> — **mul·ti·po·lar·i·ty** \-pō-ˈlar-ət-ē\ *n*

mul·ti·pro·cess·ing \-ˈpräs-ˌes-iŋ, -ˈpräs-əs-, -ˈprōs-\ *n* : the processing of several computer programs at the same time esp. by a computer system with several processors sharing a single memory — **mul·ti·pro·ces·sor** \-ˌes-ər, -əs-\ *n*

mul·ti·pro·gram·ming \-'prō-ˌgram-iŋ, -grəm-\ *n* **:** the technique of utilizing several interleaved programs concurrently in a single computer system

mul·ti·pronged \-'prọŋd\ *adj* **1 :** having several prongs <~ fishing spears> **2 :** having several distinct aspects or elements <a ~ attack on the problem>

mul·ti·pur·pose \-'pər-pəs\ *adj* **:** having or serving several purposes <a ~ fabric>

mul·ti·ra·cial \ˌməl-ti-'rā-shəl, -ˌtī-\ *adj* **:** composed of, involving, or representing various races <~ organizations> — **mul·ti·ra·cial·ism** \-shə-ˌliz-əm\ *n*

mul·ti·sense \-ˌsen(t)s\ *adj* **:** having several meanings <~ words>

mul·ti·sen·so·ry \-'sen(t)s-(ə-)rē\ *adj* **:** relating to or involving several physiological senses <~ teaching methods> <~ experience>

mul·ti·stage \-ˌstāj\ *adj* **1 :** having successive operating stages; *esp* **:** having propulsion units that operate in turn <~ rockets> **2 :** conducted by stages <a ~ investigation>

mul·ti·state \-'stāt\ *adj* **1 :** of, relating to, or involving several states <a ~ attack on environmental pollution> **2 :** having divisions in several states <~ enterprises>

mul·ti·sto·ry \-ˌstōr-ē, -ˌstȯr-\ *also* **mul·ti·sto·ried** \-ēd\ *adj* **:** having several stories <~ buildings>

mul·ti·syl·lab·ic \-sə-'lab-ik\ *adj* **:** POLYSYLLABIC

mul·ti·tude \'məl-tə-ˌt(y)üd\ *n* [ME, fr. MF or L; MF, fr. L *multitudin-, multitudo,* fr. *multus* much — more at MELIORATE] **1 :** the state of being many **2 :** a great number **:** HOST <a ~ of voices> **3 :** CROWD <buses disgorged their ~*s* —Mollie Panter-Downes> **4 :** POPULACE, PUBLIC <seeks the . . . approbation of the ~ —Arthur Knight>

mul·ti·tu·di·nous \ˌməl-tə-'t(y)üd-nəs, -ᵊn-əs\ *adj* **1 :** including a multitude of individuals **:** POPULOUS **2 :** existing in a great multitude **3 :** existing in or consisting of innumerable elements or aspects — **mul·ti·tu·di·nous·ly** *adv* — **mul·ti·tu·di·nous·ness** *n*

mul·tiv·a·lence \ˌməl-'tiv-ə-lən(t)s\ *n* **:** the quality or state of having many values, meanings, or appeals

mul·ti·va·lent \ˌməl-ti-'vā-lənt, -ˌtī-, *esp in sense 3* ˌməl-'tiv-ə-\ *adj* [ISV] **1 :** POLYVALENT **2 :** represented more than twice in the somatic chromosome number <~ chromosomes> **3 :** having many values, meanings, or appeals — **multivalent** *n*

mul·ti·val·ued \ˌməl-ti-'val-(ˌ)yüd, -yəd\ *adj* **:** having several or many values

mul·ti·var·i·ate \-'ver-ē-ət, -ē-ˌāt\ *adj* [*multi-* + *variable* + [3]*-ate*] **:** having or involving a number of independent mathematical variables — used esp. in statistical analysis

mul·ti·ver·si·ty \-'vər-sət-ē, -stē\ *n, pl* **-ties** [*multi-* + *-versity* (as in *university*)] **:** a very large university with many component schools, colleges, or divisions, with widely diverse functions (as the teaching of freshmen and the carrying on of advanced research), and with a large staff engaged in activities other than instruction

mul·ti·vol·tine \-'vōl-ˌtēn, -'vȯl-\ *adj* **:** having several broods in a season <~ insects>

mul·ti·vol·ume \ˌməl-ti-'väl-yəm, -ˌtī-, -(ˌ)yüm\ *or* **mul·ti·vol·umed** \-yəmd, -(ˌ)yümd\ *adj* **:** comprising several volumes

mul·ture \'məl-chər, *Scot usu* 'müt-ər\ *n* [ME *multyr,* fr. OF *molture,* lit., grinding, fr. (assumed) VL *molitura,* fr. L *molitus,* pp. of *molere* to grind — more at MEAL] *chiefly Scot* **:** a fee for grinding grain at a mill

[1]**mum** \'məm\ *adj* [prob. imit. of a sound made with closed lips] **:** SILENT <keep ~> — often used interjectionally

[2]**mum** *vi* **mummed; mum·ming** [ME *mommen,* fr. MF *momer* to go masked] **1 :** to perform in a pantomime **2 :** to go about merrymaking in disguise during festivals

[3]**mum** *n* [G *mumme*] **:** a strong ale or beer

[4]**mum** *chiefly Brit var of* MOM

[5]**mum** *n* **:** CHRYSANTHEMUM

mum·ble \'məm-bəl\ *vb* **mum·bled; mum·bling** \-b(ə-)liŋ\ [ME *momelen,* of imit. origin] *vi* **:** to utter words in a low confused indistinct manner **:** MUTTER ~ *vt* **1 :** to utter with a low inarticulate voice **2 :** to chew or bite with or as if with toothless gums — **mumble** *n* — **mum·bler** \-b(ə-)lər\ *n*

mum·ble·ty–peg *or* **mum·ble–the–peg** \'məm-bəl-ˌpeg, -(b)lē-ˌpeg, -(b)əl-tē-, -(b)əl-t͟hə-\ *n* [fr. the phrase *mumble the peg;* fr. the loser's originally having to pull out with his teeth a peg driven into the ground] **:** a game in which the players try to flip a knife from various positions so that the blade will stick into the ground

mum·bo jum·bo \ˌməm-bō-'jəm-(ˌ)bō\ *n* [*Mumbo Jumbo,* an idol or deity held to have been worshiped in Africa] **1 :** an object of superstitious homage and fear **2 a :** a complicated often ritualistic observance with elaborate trappings **b :** complicated activity intended to obscure and confuse **3 :** unnecessarily involved and incomprehensible language **:** GIBBERISH

mum·mer \'məm-ər\ *n* [MF *momeur,* fr. *momer* to go masked] **1 :** a performer in a pantomime; *broadly* **:** ACTOR **2 :** one who goes merrymaking in disguise during festivals

mum·mery \'məm-ə-rē\ *n, pl* **-mer·ies** **1 :** a performance by mummers **2 :** a ridiculous, hypocritical, or pretentious ceremony or performance

mum·mi·chog \'məm-i-ˌchȯg, -ˌchäg\ *n* [Narraganset *moamitteaúg,* lit., they go in great numbers] **:** any of various killifishes; *esp* **:** a common American killifish (*Fundulus heteroclitus*)

mum·mi·fy \'məm-i-ˌfī\ *vb* **-fied; -fy·ing** *vt* **1 :** to embalm and dry as or as if a mummy **2 a :** to make into or like a mummy **b :** to cause to dry up and shrivel ~ *vi* **:** to dry up and shrivel like a mummy — **mum·mi·fi·ca·tion** \ˌməm-i-fə-'kā-shən\ *n*

mum·my \'məm-ē\ *n, pl* **mummies** [ME *mummie* powdered parts of a mummified body used as a drug, fr. MF *momie,* fr. ML *mumia* mummy, powdered mummy, fr. Ar *mūmiyah* bitumen, mummy, fr. Per *mūm* wax] **1 a :** a body embalmed or treated for burial with preservatives in the manner of the ancient Egyptians **b :** a body unusually well preserved **2 :** one resembling a mummy

mump *vi* [obs. D *mompen*] *archaic* **:** BEG, SPONGE — **mump·er** *n*

mumps \'məm(p)s\ *n pl but sing or pl in constr* [fr. pl. of obs. *mump* (grimace)] **:** an acute contagious viral disease marked by fever and by swelling esp. of the parotid gland

mun *or* **munic** *abbr* municipal

munch \'mənch\ *vb* [ME *monchen,* prob. of imit. origin] *vt* **:** to chew with a crunching sound **:** eat with relish ~ *vi* **:** to chew food with a crunching sound **:** eat food with relish — **munch·er** *n*

mun·dane \ˌmən-'dān, 'mən-ˌ\ *adj* [ME *mondeyne,* fr. MF *mondain,* fr. LL *mundanus,* fr. L *mundus* world] **1 :** of, relating to, or characteristic of the world **2 :** characterized by the practical, transitory, and ordinary ***syn*** see EARTHLY ***ant*** eternal — **mun·dane·ly** *adv* — **mun·dane·ness** \-'dān-nəs, -ˌdān-\ *n*

mun·dun·gus \ˌmən-'dəŋ-(g)əs\ *n* [modif. of Sp *mondongo* tripe] *archaic* **:** foul-smelling tobacco

mung bean \'məŋ-\ *n* [Hindi *mūg,* fr. Skt *mudga*]**:** an erect bushy annual bean (*Phaseolus aureus*) that is widely cultivated in warm regions for its edible usu. green or yellow seeds, for forage, and as the chief source of bean sprouts

mun·go \'məŋ-(ˌ)gō\ *n, pl* **mungos** [origin unknown] **:** reclaimed wool of poor quality and very short staple

[1]**mu·nic·i·pal** \myu̇-'nis-(ə-)pəl, *nonstand* ˌmyü-nə-'sip-əl\ *adj* [L *municipalis* of a municipality, fr. *municip-, municeps* inhabitant of a municipality, lit., undertaker of duties, fr. *munus* duty, service + *capere* to take — more at MEAN, HEAVE] **1 :** of or relating to the internal affairs of a major political unit (as a nation) **2 a :** of, relating to, or characteristic of a municipality **b :** having local self-government **3 :** restricted to one locality

[2]**municipal** *n* **:** a security issued by a state or local government or by an authority set up by such a government — usu. used in pl.

municipal court *n* **1 :** POLICE COURT **2 :** a court that sits in some cities and larger towns and that usu. has civil and criminal jurisdiction over cases arising within the municipality

mu·nic·i·pal·i·ty \myu̇-ˌnis-ə-'pal-ət-ē\ *n, pl* **-ties** **1 :** a primarily urban political unit having corporate status and usu. powers of self-government **2 :** the governing body of a municipality

mu·nic·i·pal·ize \myu̇-'nis-ə-pə-ˌlīz\ *vt* **-ized; -iz·ing :** to bring under municipal ownership or supervision — **mu·nic·i·pal·iza·tion** \-ˌnis-(ə-)pə-lə-'zā-shən\ *n*

mu·nic·i·pal·ly \myu̇-'nis-ə-p(ə-)lē\ *adv* **:** by or in terms of a municipality

mu·nif·i·cent \myu̇-'nif-ə-sənt\ *adj* [back-formation fr. *munificence,* fr. L *munificentia,* fr. *munificus* generous, fr. *munus* service, gift] **1 :** very liberal in giving or bestowing **:** LAVISH **2 :** characterized by great liberality or generosity ***syn*** see LIBERAL — **mu·nif·i·cence** \-sən(t)s\ *n* — **mu·nif·i·cent·ly** *adv*

mu·ni·ment \'myü-nə-mənt\ *n* [AF, fr. MF, defense, fr. L *munimentum,* fr. *munire* to fortify] **1** *pl* **:** the evidences or writings that enable one to defend the title to an estate or a claim to rights and privileges **2** *archaic* **:** a means of defense

mu·ni·tion \myu̇-'nish-ən\ *n* [MF, fr. L *munition-, munitio,* fr. *munitus,* pp. of *munire* to fortify, fr. *moenia* walls; akin to OE *mǣre* boundary, L *murus* wall] **1** *archaic* **:** RAMPART, DEFENSE **2 :** ARMAMENT, AMMUNITION — **munition** *vt*

mun·tin \'mənt-ᵊn\ *also* **mun·ting** \-ᵊn, -iŋ\ *n* [alter. of *montant* vertical dividing bar, fr. F, fr. prp. of *monter* to rise — more at MOUNT] **:** a strip separating panes of glass in a sash

munt·jac *also* **munt·jak** \'mən(t)-ˌjak, 'mən-ˌchak\ *n* [prob. modif. of Jav *mindjangan* deer] **:** any of several small deer (genus *Muntiacus*) of southeastern Asia and the East Indies

mu·on \'myü-ˌän\ *n* [contr. of earlier *mu-meson,* fr. *mu* (taken as a symbol for *meson,* and used to distinguish it from the short-lived pi-meson)] **:** an unstable elementary particle that belongs to the lepton family, is common in the cosmic radiation near the earth's surface, has a mass about 207 times the mass of the electron, and exists in negative and positive forms — **mu·on·ic** \myü-'än-ik\ *adj*

[1]**mu·ral** \'myu̇r-əl\ *adj* [L *muralis,* fr. *murus* wall — more at MUNITION] **1 :** of, relating to, or resembling a wall **2 :** applied to and made integral with a wall or ceiling surface

[2]**mural** *n* **:** a mural work of art (as a painting) — **mu·ral·ist** \-ə-ləst\ *n*

mu·ram·ic acid \myu̇-ˌram-ik-\ *n* [*mur-* (fr. L *murus* wall) + glucos*amide* + *-ic*] **:** an amino sugar $C_9H_{17}NO_7$ that is a lactic acid derivative of glucosamine and is found esp. in bacterial cell walls and in blue-green algae

[1]**mur·der** \'mərd-ər\ *n* [partly fr. ME *murther,* fr. OE *morthor;* partly fr. ME *murdre,* fr. OF, of Gmc origin; akin to OE *morthor;* akin to OHG *mord* murder, L *mort-, mors* death, *mori* to die, Gk *brotos* mortal] **1 :** the crime of unlawfully killing a person esp. with malice aforethought **2 :** something very difficult or dangerous

[2]**murder** *vb* **mur·dered; mur·der·ing** \'mərd-(ə-)riŋ\ *vt* **1 :** to kill (a human being) unlawfully and with premeditated malice **2 :** to slaughter wantonly **:** SLAY **3 a :** to put an end to **b :** TEASE, TORMENT **c :** MUTILATE, MANGLE <~*s* French> ~ *vi* **:** to commit murder ***syn*** see KILL — **mur·der·ess** \-ə-rəs\ *n*

mur·der·ee \ˌmər-də-'rē\ *n* **:** an actual or potential victim of a murder

murderer *n* **:** one who murders; *esp* **:** one who commits the crime of murder

mur·der·ous \'mərd-(ə-)rəs\ *adj* **1 a :** having the purpose or capability of murder **b :** characterized by or causing murder or bloodshed **2 :** having the ability or power to overwhelm **:** DEVASTATING <~ heat> — **mur·der·ous·ly** *adv* — **mur·der·ous·ness** *n*

mure \'myu̇(ə)r\ *vt* **mured; mur·ing** [ME *muren,* fr. MF *murer,* fr. LL *murare,* fr. L *murus* wall] **:** IMMURE

mu·rein \'myu̇r-ē-ən, 'myu̇(ə)r-ˌēn\ *n* [*mur*amic acid + *-ein*] **:** a polymer that is composed of alternating units of muramic acid and glucosamine bearing an acetyl group and that is characteristic of the cell walls of procaryotic cells

mu·rex \'myu̇(ə)r-ˌeks\ *n, pl* **mu·ri·ces** \'myu̇r-ə-ˌsēz\ *or* **mu·rex·es** [NL, genus name, fr. L, purple shell; akin to Gk *myak-, myax* sea-mussel] **:** any of a genus (*Murex*) of marine gastropod mollusks having a rough and often spinose shell, abounding in tropical seas, and yielding a purple dye

mu·ri·ate \'myu̇r-ē-ˌāt\ *n* [F, back-formation fr. (*acide*) *muriatique* muriatic acid] **:** CHLORIDE

mu·ri·at·ic acid \ˌmyu̇r-ē-ˌat-ik-\ *n* [F *muriatique,* fr. L *muriaticus* pickled in brine, fr. *muria* brine; akin to OHG *mos* moss] **:** HYDROCHLORIC ACID

mu·rid \'myu̇r-əd\ *adj* [deriv. of L *mur-, mus* mouse — more at MOUSE] **:** of or relating to a family (Muridae) comprising the typical mice and rats — **murid** *n*

mu·rine \'myu̇(ə)r-ˌīn\ *adj* [deriv. of L *mur-, mus*] **:** of or relating to a genus (*Mus*) or the subfamily to which it belongs and which includes the common household rats and mice; *also* **:** of, relating to, or involving these rodents and esp. the house mouse — **murine** *n*

murine typhus *n* **:** a mild febrile disease that is marked by headache and rash, is caused by a rickettsia (*Rickettsia mooseri*), is widespread in nature in rodents, and is transmitted to man by a flea

murk \'mərk\ *n* [ME *mirke*] **:** GLOOM, DARKNESS; *also* **:** FOG — **murk** *adj, archaic*

murky \'mər-kē\ *adj* **murk·i·er; -est** **1 :** characterized by a heavy dimness or obscurity caused by or like that caused by overhanging fog or smoke **2 :** characterized by thickness and heaviness of air **:** FOGGY, MISTY **3 :** darkly vague or obscure <~ official rhetoric> ***syn*** see DARK — **murk·i·ly** \-kə-lē\ *adv* — **murk·i·ness** \-kē-nəs\ *n*

1mur·mur \'mər-mər\ *n* [ME *murmure,* fr. MF, fr. L *murmur* murmur, roar, of imit. origin] **1 :** a half-suppressed or muttered complaint **:** GRUMBLING **2 a :** a low indistinct but often continuous sound **b :** a soft or gentle utterance **3 :** an atypical sound of the heart indicating a functional or structural abnormality

2murmur *vi* **1 :** to make a murmur <the breeze ~*ed* in the pines> **2 :** COMPLAIN, GRUMBLE ~ *vt* **:** to say in a murmur — **mur·mur·er** *n*

mur·mur·ous \'mərm-(ə-)rəs\ *adj* **:** filled with or characterized by murmurs **:** low and indistinct — **mur·mur·ous·ly** *adv*

mur·phy \'mər-fē\ *n, pl* **murphies** [*Murphy,* a common Irish surname] **:** POTATO

Mur·phy bed \ˌmər-fē-\ *n* [William L. *Murphy,* 20th cent. Am inventor] **:** a bed that may be folded or swung into a closet

mur·rain \'mər-ən, 'mə-rən\ *n* [ME *moreyne,* fr. MF *morine,* fr. *morir* to die, fr. L *mori* — more at MURDER] **:** a pestilence or plague affecting domestic animals or plants

murre \'mər\ *n* [origin unknown] **:** any of several guillemots (genus *Uria*); *esp* **:** a common bird (*U. aalge*) of southern seas

mur·rey \'mər-ē, 'mə-rē\ *n* [ME, fr. MF *moré,* fr. ML *moratum,* fr. neut. of *moratus* mulberry colored, fr. L *morum* mulberry — more at MULBERRY] **:** a purplish black **:** MULBERRY

mur·ther \'mər-t͟hər\ *chiefly dial var of* MURDER

mus *abbr* **1** museum **2** music; musical; musician

mus·ca·dine \'məs-kə-ˌdīn\ *n* [prob. alter. of *muscatel*] **:** a grape (*Vitis rotundifolia*) of the southern U.S. with musky fruits borne in small clusters

mus·cae vo·li·tan·tes \'məs-ˌ(k)ē-ˌväl-ə-'tan-ˌtēz\ *n pl* [NL, lit., flying flies] **:** spots before the eyes due to cells and cell fragments in the vitreous humor and lens

mus·ca·rine \'məs-kə-ˌrēn\ *n* [G *muskarin,* fr. NL *muscaria,* specific epithet of *Amanita muscaria* fly agaric] **:** an ammonium base $C_8H_{19}NO_3$ that is chemically related to choline, was first found in the fly agaric, and acts directly on smooth muscle — **mus·ca·rin·ic** \ˌməs-kə-'rin-ik\ *adj*

mus·cat \'məs-ˌkat, -kət\ *n* [F, fr. Prov, fr. *muscat* musky, fr. *musc* musk, fr. LL *muscus*] **1 :** any of several cultivated grapes used in making wine and raisins **2 :** MUSCATEL

mus·ca·tel \ˌməs-kə-'tel\ *n* [ME *muskadelle,* fr. MF *muscadel,* fr. OProv, fr. *muscadel* resembling musk, fr. *muscat*] **1 :** a sweet dessert wine from muscat grapes **2 :** a raisin from muscat grapes

1mus·cle \'məs-əl\ *n, often attrib* [MF, fr. L *musculus,* fr. dim. of *mus* mouse — more at MOUSE] **1 a :** a body tissue consisting of long cells that contract when stimulated and produce motion **b :** an organ that is essentially a mass of muscle tissue attached at either end to a fixed point and that by contracting moves or checks the movement of a body part **2 a :** muscular strength **:** BRAWN **b :** effective strength **:** POWER

2muscle *vi* **mus·cled; mus·cling** \'məs-(ə-)liŋ\ **:** to make one's way by brute strength or by force

mus·cle–bound \'məs-əl-ˌbau̇nd\ *adj* **1 :** having some of the muscles tense and enlarged and of impaired elasticity sometimes as a result of excessive exercise **2 :** lacking in flexibility **:** RIGID

mus·cled \'məs-əld\ *adj* **:** having muscles esp. of a specified kind — often used in combination <hard-*muscled* arms>

muscle spindle *n* **:** a sensory end organ in a muscle that is sensitive to stretch in the muscle, consists of small striated muscle fibers richly supplied with nerve fibers, and is enclosed in a connective tissue sheath — called also *stretch receptor*

mus·co·vite \'məs-kə-ˌvīt\ *n* [ML or NL *Muscovia, Moscovia* Moscow] **1** *cap* **a :** a native or resident of the ancient principality of Moscow or of the city of Moscow **b :** RUSSIAN **2** [*muscovy* (*glass*)] **:** a mineral essentially $KAl_3Si_3O_{10}(OH)_2$ that is a colorless to pale brown potassium mica — **Muscovite** *adj*

Mus·co·vy duck \ˌməs-ˌkō-vē-\ *n* [*Muscovy,* principality of Moscow, Russia] **:** a large crested duck (*Cairina moschata*) native from Mexico to southern Brazil but widely kept in domestication

muscul- *or* **musculo-** *comb form* [LL *muscul-,* fr. L *musculus*] **1 :** muscle <*muscul*ar> **2 :** muscular and <*musculo*skeletal>

mus·cu·lar \'məs-kyə-lər\ *adj* **1 a :** of, relating to, or constituting muscle **b :** of, relating to, or performed by the muscles **2 :** having well-developed musculature **3 a :** of or relating to physical strength **:** BRAWNY **b :** having strength of expression or character **:** VIGOROUS — **mus·cu·lar·i·ty** \ˌməs-kyə-'lar-ət-ē\ *n* — **mus·cu·lar·ly** \'məs-kyə-lər-lē\ *adv*

muscular dystrophy *n* **:** a hereditary disease characterized by progressive wasting of muscles

mus·cu·la·ture \'məs-kyə-lə-ˌchu̇(ə)r, -chər, -ˌt(y)u̇(ə)r\ *n* [F, fr. L *musculus*] **:** the muscles of all or a part of the animal body

mus·cu·lo·skel·e·tal \ˌməs-kyə-lō-'skel-ət-ᵊl\ *adj* **:** of, relating to, or involving both musculature and skeleton

1muse \'myüz\ *vb* **mused; mus·ing** [ME *musen,* fr. MF *muser* to gape, idle, muse, fr. *muse* mouth of an animal, fr. ML *musus*] *vi* **1 :** to become absorbed in thought; *esp* **:** to turn something over in the mind meditatively and often inconclusively **2** *archaic* **:** WONDER, MARVEL ~ *vt* **:** to think or say reflectively ***syn*** see PONDER — **mus·er** *n*

2muse *n* **:** a state of deep thought or dreamy abstraction **:** BROWN STUDY

3muse *n* [ME, fr. MF, fr. L *Musa,* fr. Gk *Mousa*] **1** *cap* **:** any of the nine sister goddesses in Greek mythology presiding over song and poetry and the arts and sciences **2 :** a source of inspiration; *esp* **:** a guiding genius **3 :** POET

mu·sette \myü-'zet\ *n* [F, fr. MF, dim. of *muse* bagpipe, fr. *muser* to muse, play the bagpipe] **1 :** a small bagpipe having a soft sweet tone **2 :** a small knapsack; *also* **:** a similar bag with one shoulder strap — called also *musette bag*

mu·se·um \myü-'zē-əm\ *n* [L *Museum* place for learned occupation, fr. Gk *Mouseion,* fr. neut. of *Mouseios* of the Muses, fr. *Mousa*] **:** an institution devoted to the procurement, care, study, and display of objects of lasting interest or value; *also* **:** a place where objects are exhibited

1mush \'məsh\ *n* [prob. alter. of *mash*] **1 :** a thick porridge made with cornmeal boiled in water or milk **2 :** something soft and spongy or shapeless **3 a :** weak sentimentality **:** DRIVEL **b :** mawkish amorousness

2mush *vt, chiefly dial* **:** to reduce to a crumbly mass ~ *vi, of an airplane* **:** to fly in a partly stalled condition with controls ineffective; *also* **:** to fail to gain altitude — **mush·er** *n*

3mush *vi* [prob. fr. AmerF *moucher* to go fast, fr. F *mouche* fly, fr. L *musca* — more at MIDGE] **:** to travel esp. over snow with a sled drawn by dogs — often used as a command to a dog team

4mush *n* **:** a trip esp. across snow with a dog team

1mush·room \'məsh-ˌrüm, -ˌru̇m\ *n* [ME *musseroun,* fr. MF *mousseron,* fr. LL *mussirion-, mussirio*] **1 a :** an enlarged complex aerial fleshy fruiting body of a fungus (as of the class Basidiomycetes) that consists typically of a stem bearing a flattened cap; *esp* **:** one that is edible **b :** FUNGUS 1 **2 :** UPSTART **3 :** something resembling a mushroom

2mushroom *vi* **1 :** to spring up suddenly or multiply rapidly **2 a** *of a bullet* **:** to flatten at the end at impact **b :** to well up and spread out laterally from a central source

mushy \'məsh-ē\ *adj* **mush·i·er; -est** **1 :** having the consistency of mush **:** SOFT **2 :** excessively tender or emotional; *esp* **:** mawkishly amorous — **mush·i·ly** \'məsh-ə-lē\ *adv* — **mush·i·ness** \'məsh-ē-nəs\ *n*

mu·sic \'myü-zik\ *n, often attrib* [ME *musik,* fr. OF *musique,* fr. L *musica,* fr. Gk *mousikē* any art presided over by the Muses, esp. music, fr. fem. of *mousikos* of the Muses, fr. *Mousa* Muse] **1 a :** the science or art of ordering tones or sounds in succession, in combination, and in temporal relationships to produce a composition having unity and continuity **b :** vocal, instrumental, or mechanical sounds having rhythm, melody, or harmony **2 :** an agreeable sound **:** EUPHONY <the gentle sound was ~ to my ears> **3 :** a musical accompaniment <a play set to ~> **4 :** the score of a musical composition set down on paper **5 :** a distinctive type or category of music <there is a ~ for everybody —Eric Salzman> <come up with some special collections of jazz, Latin, country, rock and other ~*s* —Hal Levy>

1mu·si·cal \'myü-zi-kəl\ *adj* **1 a :** of or relating to music **b :** having the pleasing harmonious qualities of music **:** MELODIOUS **2 :** having an interest in or talent for music **3 :** set to or accompanied by music **4 :** of or relating to musicians or music lovers <~ organizations> — **mu·si·cal·ly** \-k(ə-)lē\ *adv*

2musical *n* **1** *archaic* **:** MUSICALE **2 :** a film or theatrical production typically of a sentimental or humorous nature that consists of musical numbers and dialogue based upon a unifying plot — called also *musical comedy*

musical box *n, chiefly Brit* **:** MUSIC BOX

musical chairs *n pl but sing in constr* **1 :** a game in which players march to music around a row of chairs numbering one less than the players and scramble for seats when the music stops **2 :** a change from one position, situation, or arrangement to another esp. without significant effect

mu·si·cale \ˌmyü-zi-'kal\ *n* [F *soirée musicale,* lit., musical evening] **:** a social entertainment with music as the leading feature

mu·si·cal·i·ty \ˌmyü-zi-'kal-ət-ē\ *n* **1 :** the quality or state of being musical **:** MELODIOUSNESS **2 :** sensitivity to, knowledge of, or talent for music

mu·si·cal·ize \'myü-zi-kə-ˌlīz\ *vt* **-ized; -iz·ing** **:** to set to music — **mu·si·cal·iza·tion** \ˌmyü-zi-kə-lə-'zā-shən\ *n*

musical saw *n* **:** a handsaw made to produce melody by bending the blade with varying tension while sounding it with a hammer or violin bow

music box *n* **:** a container enclosing an apparatus that reproduces music mechanically when activated by a clockwork

music drama *n* **:** an opera in which the action is not interrupted by formal song divisions (as recitatives or arias) and the music is determined solely by dramatic appropriateness

music hall *n* **:** a vaudeville theater; *also* **:** VAUDEVILLE

mu·si·cian \myü-'zish-ən\ *n* **:** a composer, conductor, or performer of music; *esp* **:** INSTRUMENTALIST — **mu·si·cian·ly** \-lē\ *adj* — **mu·si·cian·ship** \-ˌship\ *n*

music of the spheres : an ethereal harmony thought by the Pythagoreans to be produced by the vibration of the celestial spheres

mu·si·col·o·gy \ˌmyü-zi-ˈkäl-ə-jē\ *n* [It *musicologia*, fr. L *musica* music + *-logia* -logy] : a study of music as a branch of knowledge or field of research; *esp* : the historical and theoretical investigation and analysis of specific types of music — **mu·si·co·log·i·cal** \-kə-ˈläj-i-kəl\ *adj* — **mu·si·col·o·gist** \-ˈkäl-ə-jəst\ *n*

1**mus·ing** \ˈmyü-ziŋ\ *n* : MEDITATION

2**musing** *adj* : thoughtfully abstracted : MEDITATIVE — **mus·ing·ly** \-ziŋ-lē\ *adv*

mu·sique con·crète \myü-ˌzēk-kōⁿ-ˈkret, mue-\ *n* [F, lit., concrete music] : a montage of recorded natural sounds (as voices, traffic noise, and bird calls) arbitrarily modified and arranged

musk \ˈməsk\ *n* [ME *muske*, fr. MF *musc*, fr. LL *muscus*, fr. Gk *moschos*, fr. Per *mushk*, fr. Skt *muṣka* testicle, fr. dim. of *mūṣ* mouse; akin to OE *mūs* mouse] **1 a** : a substance with a penetrating persistent odor obtained from a sac beneath the abdominal skin of the male musk deer and used as a perfume fixative; *also* : a similar substance from another animal or a synthetic substitute **b** : the odor of musk; *also* : an odor resembling musk esp. in heaviness or persistence **2** : any of various plants with musky odors; *esp* : MUSK PLANT

musk deer *n* : a small heavy-limbed hornless deer (*Moschus moschiferus*) of central Asiatic uplands that produces musk in the male

mus·keg \ˈməs-ˌkeg, -ˌkāg\ *n* [of Algonquian origin; akin to Ojibwa *mŭskeg* grassy bog] **1** : BOG; *esp* : a sphagnum bog of northern No. America often with tussocks **2** : a usu. thick deposit of partially decayed vegetable matter of wet boreal regions

mus·kel·lunge \ˈməs-kə-ˌlənj\ *n, pl* **muskellunge** [of Algonquian origin; akin to Cree *maskinonge* muskellunge] : a large No. American pike (*Esox masquinongy*) that may weigh 60 to 80 pounds and is a valuable sport fish

mus·ket \ˈməs-kət\ *n* [MF *mousquet*, fr. OIt *moschetto* arrow for a crossbow, musket, fr. dim. of *mosca* fly, fr. L *musca* — more at MIDGE] : a heavy large-caliber shoulder firearm (as a flintlock or matchlock); *broadly* : a shoulder gun carried by infantry

mus·ke·teer \ˌməs-kə-ˈti(ə)r\ *n* [modif. of MF *mousquetaire*, fr. *mousquet*] : a soldier armed with a musket

mus·ket·ry \ˈməs-kə-trē\ *n* **1** : MUSKETS **2** : MUSKETEERS **3 a** : musket fire **b** : the art or science of using small arms esp. in battle

mus·kie *or* **mus·ky** \ˈməs-kē\ *n, pl* **muskies** : MUSKELLUNGE

musk·mel·on \ˈməsk-ˌmel-ən\ *n* : a usu. sweet musky-odored edible melon that is the fruit of a trailing or climbing Asiatic herbaceous vine (*Cucumis melo*): as **a** : any of various melons of small or moderate size with netted skin that include most of the muskmelons cultivated in No. America **b** : CANTALOUPE 1 **c** : WINTER MELON

Mus·ko·ge·an *or* **Mus·kho·ge·an** \(ˌ)məs-ˈkō-gē-ən\ *n* : a language family of southeastern U.S. that includes Muskogee

Mus·ko·gee *n, pl* **Muskogee** *or* **Muskogees** **1** : a member of an Amerindian people of Georgia and eastern Alabama constituting the nucleus of the Creek confederacy **2** : the language of the Muskogees and of some of the Seminoles

musk–ox \ˈməs-ˌkäks\ *n* : a heavy-set shaggy-coated wild ox (*Ovibos moschatus*) now confined to Greenland and the barren northern lands of No. America

musk-ox

musk plant *n* : a yellow-flowered No. American herb (*Mimulus moschatus*) of the figwort family that has hairy foliage and sometimes a musky odor

musk·rat \ˈməs-ˌkrat\ *n, pl* **muskrat** *or* **muskrats** [prob. by folk etymology fr. a word of Algonquian origin; akin to Natick *musquash* muskrat] : an aquatic rodent (*Ondatra zibethica*) of the U.S. and Canada with a long scaly laterally compressed tail, webbed hind feet, and dark glossy brown fur; *also* : its fur or pelt

musk rose *n* : a rose (*Rosa moschata*) of the Mediterranean region with flowers having a musky odor

musk thistle *n* : a Eurasian thistle (*Carduus nutans*) that has nodding musky flower heads and is naturalized in eastern No. America

musk turtle *n* : a small American freshwater turtle (genera *Sternotherus* and *Kinosternon*); *esp* : a turtle (*S. odoratus*) having a strong musky odor

musky \ˈməs-kē\ *adj* **musk·i·er; -est** : having an odor of or resembling musk — **musk·i·ness** *n*

Mus·lim \ˈməz-ləm, ˈmüs-, ˈmüz-\ *n* [Ar *muslim*, lit., one who surrenders (to God)] **1** : an adherent of Islam **2** : BLACK MUSLIM — **Muslim** *adj*

Muslim era *n* : MUHAMMADAN ERA

mus·lin \ˈməz-lən\ *n* [F *mousseline*, fr. It *mussolina*, fr. Ar *mawṣilīy* of Mosul, fr. al-*Mawṣil* Mosul, Iraq] : a plain-woven sheer to coarse cotton fabric

mus·quash \ˈməs-ˌkwäsh, -ˌkwȯsh\ *n* [of Algonquian origin; akin to Natick *musquash* muskrat] : MUSKRAT

1**muss** \ˈməs\ *n* [origin unknown] **1** *obs* **a** : a game in which players scramble for small objects thrown to the ground **b** : SCRAMBLE **2** *slang* : a confused conflict : ROW **3** : a state of disorder

2**muss** *vt* : to make untidy : DISARRANGE

mus·sel \ˈməs-əl\ *n* [ME *muscle*, fr. OE *muscelle*; akin to OHG *muscula* mussel; both fr. a prehistoric WGmc word borrowed fr. (assumed) VL *muscula*, fr. L *musculus* muscle, mussel] **1** : a marine bivalve mollusk (esp. genus *Mytilus*) usu. having a dark elongated shell **2** : a freshwater bivalve mollusk (as of *Unio*, *Anodonta*, or related genera) that is esp. abundant in rivers of the central U.S. and has a shell with a lustrous nacreous lining

Mus·sul·man *also* **Mus·sal·man** \ˈməs-əl-mən\ *n, pl* **Mus·sul·men** \-mən\ *or* **Mussulmans** [Turk *müslüman* & Per *musulmān*, modif. of Ar *muslim*] : MUSLIM

mussy \ˈməs-ē\ *adj* **muss·i·er; -est** : characterized by clutter or muss : MESSY — **muss·i·ly** \ˈməs-ə-lē\ *adv* — **muss·i·ness** \ˈməs-ē-nəs\ *n*

1**must** \məs(t), ˈməst\ *vb, pres & past all persons* **must** [ME *moste*, fr. OE *mōste*, past indic. & subj. of *mōtan* to be allowed to, have to; akin to OHG *muozan* to be allowed to, have to, OE *metan* to measure — more at METE] *verbal auxiliary* **1 a** : be commanded or requested to <you ~ stop> **b** : be urged to : ought by all means to <you ~ read that book> **2** : be compelled by physical necessity to <man ~ eat to live> : be required by immediate or future need or purpose to <we ~ hurry if we want to catch the bus> **3 a** : be obliged to : be compelled by social considerations to <I ~ say you're looking much better> **b** : be required by law, custom, or moral conscience to <we ~ obey the rules> **c** : be determined to <if you ~ go at least wait till the storm is over> **d** : be unreasonably or perversely compelled to <why ~ you be so stubborn> **4** : be logically inferred or supposed to <it ~ be time> **5** : be compelled by fate or by natural law to <what ~ be will be> **6** : was or were presumably certain to : was or were bound to <if he had really been there I ~ have seen him> **7** *dial* : MAY, SHALL — used chiefly in questions ~ *vi, archaic* : to be obliged to go <I ~ to Coventry —Shak.>

2**must** \ˈməst\ *n* **1** : an imperative need or duty : REQUIREMENT **2** : an indispensable item : ESSENTIAL

3**must** \ˈməst\ *n* [ME, fr. OE, fr. L *mustum*] : the expressed juice of fruit and esp. grapes before and during fermentation

4**must** \ˈməst\ *n* [MF, alter. of *musc* musk] **1** : MUSK **2** : MOLD, MUSTINESS

mus·tache \ˈməs-ˌtash, (ˌ)məs-ˈ\ *n* [MF *moustache*, fr. OIt *mustaccio*, fr. MGk *moustaki*, dim. of Gk *mystak-*, *mystax* upper lip, mustache] **1** : the hair growing on the human upper lip **2** : hair or bristles about the mouth of a mammal

mus·ta·chio \(ˌ)məs-ˈtash-(ē-ˌ)ō, -ˈtäsh-\ *n, pl* **-chios** [Sp & It; Sp *mostacho*, fr. It *mustaccio*] : MUSTACHE; *esp* : a large mustache — **mus·ta·chioed** \-(ē-ˌ)ōd\ *adj*

mus·tang \ˈməs-ˌtaŋ\ *n* [MexSp *mestengo*, fr. Sp, stray, fr. *mesteño* strayed, fr. *mesta* annual roundup of cattle that disposed of strays, fr. ML (*animalia*) *mixta* mixed animals] : the small hardy naturalized horse of the western plains directly descended from horses brought in by the Spaniards; *also* : BRONCO

mus·tard \ˈməs-tərd\ *n* [ME, fr. OF *mostarde*, fr. *moust* must, fr. L *mustum*] **1 a** : a pungent yellow powder of the seeds of a common mustard used as a condiment or in medicine as a stimulant and diuretic, an emetic, or a counterirritant **b** *slang* : ZEST **2** : any of several herbs (genus *Brassica* of the family Cruciferae, the mustard family) with lyrately lobed leaves, yellow flowers, and linear beaked pods

mustard gas *n* : an irritant vesicant oily liquid $(ClCH_2CH_2)_2S$ used as a war gas

mustard plaster *n* : a counterirritant and rubefacient plaster containing powdered mustard

1**mus·ter** \ˈməs-tər\ *vb* **mus·tered; mus·ter·ing** \-t(ə-)riŋ\ [ME *mustren* to show, muster, fr. OF *monstrer*, fr. L *monstrare* to show, fr. *monstrum* evil omen, monster — more at MONSTER] *vt* **1 a** : to enroll formally — usu. used with *in* or *into* <~ *ed* into the army> **b** : to cause to gather : CONVENE **c** : to call the roll of **2 a** : to bring together : COLLECT **b** : to call forth : ROUSE **3** : to amount to : COMPRISE ~ *vi* : to come together : CONGREGATE **syn** see SUMMON

2**muster** *n* **1** : a representative specimen : SAMPLE **2 a** : an act of assembling; *specif* : formal military inspection **b** : critical examination **c** : an assembled group : COLLECTION **d** : INVENTORY

muster out *vt* : to discharge from service

muster roll *n* : INVENTORY, ROSTER; *specif* : a register of the officers and men in a military unit or ship's company

musth *or* **must** \ˈməst\ *n* [Hindi *mast* intoxicated, fr. Per; akin to OE *mete* meat] : a periodic state of frenzy of the bull elephant usu. connected with the rutting season

mustn't \ˈməs-ᵊnt\ : must not

musty \ˈməs-tē\ *adj* **mus·ti·er; -est** **1 a** : impaired by damp or mildew : MOLDY **b** : tasting of mold **c** : smelling of damp and decay : FUSTY **2 a** : TRITE, STALE **b** (1) : ANTIQUATED (2) : SUPERANNUATED **syn** see MALODOROUS — **must·i·ly** \ˈməs-tə-lē\ *adv* — **must·i·ness** \-tē-nəs\ *n*

mu·ta·ble \ˈmyüt-ə-bəl\ *adj* [L *mutabilis*, fr. *mutare* to change — more at MISS] **1** : prone to change : INCONSTANT **2 a** : capable of change or of being changed in form, quality, or nature **b** : capable of or liable to mutation — **mu·ta·bil·i·ty** \ˌmyüt-ə-ˈbil-ət-ē\ *n* — **mu·ta·ble·ness** \ˈmyüt-ə-bəl-nəs\ *n* — **mu·ta·bly** \-blē\ *adv*

mu·ta·fa·cient \ˌmyüt-ə-ˈfā-shənt\ *adj* [*muta*tion + *-facient*] : capable of inducing biological mutation

mu·ta·gen \ˈmyüt-ə-jən\ *n* [ISV *muta*tion + *-gen*] : a substance (as mustard gas or various radiations) that tends to increase the frequency or extent of mutation — **mu·ta·gen·ic** \ˌmyüt-ə-ˈjen-ik\ *adj* — **mu·ta·gen·i·cal·ly** \-i-k(ə-)lē\ *adv*

mu·ta·gen·e·sis \ˌmyüt-ə-ˈjen-ə-səs\ *n* [NL] : the occurrence or induction of mutation

mu·ta·ge·nic·i·ty \-jə-ˈnis-ət-ē\ *n* : the capacity to induce mutations

mu·tant \ˈmyüt-ᵊnt\ *adj* [L *mutant-*, *mutans*, prp. of *mutare*] : of, relating to, or produced by mutation — **mutant** *n*

mu·tase \ˈmyü-ˌtās, -ˌtāz\ *n* [ISV *mut-* (fr. L *mutare*) + *-ase*] **1** : an enzyme considered capable of catalyzing a process involving simultaneous oxidation and reduction **2 :** any of various enzymes that catalyze molecular rearrangements

mu·tate \ˈmyü-ˌtāt, myü-ˈ\ *vb* **mu·tat·ed; mu·tat·ing** [L *mutatus,* pp. of *mutare*] *vt* **:** to cause to undergo mutation ~ *vi* **:** to undergo mutation — **mu·ta·tive** \ˈmyü-ˌtāt-iv, ˈmyüt-ət-\ *adj*

mu·ta·tion \myü-ˈtā-shən\ *n* **1 :** a significant and basic alteration **:** CHANGE **2 :** UMLAUT **3 a :** a relatively permanent change in hereditary material involving either a physical change in chromosome relations or a biochemical change in the codons that make up genes **b** (1) **:** an individual or strain resulting from mutation (2) **:** an animal of a domesticated strain that differs esp. in coat color from the wild type ***syn*** see CHANGE — **mu·ta·tion·al** \-shnəl, -shən-ᵊl\ *adj* — **mu·ta·tion·al·ly** \-ē\ *adv*

mu·ta·tis mu·tan·dis \mü-ˌtät-ə-smü-ˈtän-dəs\ *adv* [NL] **1 :** with the necessary changes having been made **2 :** with the respective differences having been considered

mutch·kin \ˈməch-kən\ *n* [ME (Sc) *muchekyn*] **:** a Scotch unit of liquid capacity equal to 0.90 pint

[1]mute \ˈmyüt\ *adj* **mut·er; mut·est** [ME *muet,* fr. MF, fr. OF *mu,* fr. L *mutus;* akin to OHG *māwen* to cry out, Gk *mytēs* mute] **1 :** unable to speak **:** DUMB **2 :** characterized by absence of speech: as **a :** felt or experienced but not expressed <touched her hand in ~ sympathy> **b :** refusing to plead directly or stand trial <the prisoner stands ~> **3 a :** contributing nothing to the pronunciation of a word <the *b* in *plumb* is ~> **b :** contributing to the pronunciation of a word but not representing the nucleus of a syllable <the *e* in *mate* is ~> — **mute·ly** *adv* — **mute·ness** *n*

[2]mute *n* **1 :** a person who cannot or does not speak **2 :** STOP 9 **3 :** a device attached to a musical instrument to reduce, soften, or muffle its tone

[3]mute *vt* **mut·ed; mut·ing 1 :** to muffle or reduce the sound of **2 :** to tone down (a color)

[4]mute *vi* **mut·ed; mut·ing** [ME *muten,* fr. MF *meutir*] *of a bird* **:** to evacuate the cloaca

mutes 3: *1* for violin, *2* for trumpet

mut·ed \ˈmyüt-əd\ *adj* **1 :** being mute **:** SILENT, SUBDUED **2 :** provided with or produced or modified by the use of a mute — **mut·ed·ly** *adv*

mute swan *n* **:** the common white swan (*Cygnus olor*) of Europe and western Asia that produces no loud notes

mu·ti·cous \ˈmyüt-i-kəs\ *adj* [L *muticus*] **:** lacking an awn or point

mu·ti·late \ˈmyüt-ᵊl-ˌāt\ *vt* **-lat·ed; -lat·ing** [L *mutilatus,* pp. of *mutilare,* fr. *mutilus* mutilated; akin to L *muticus* muticous, OIr *mut* short] **1 :** to cut off or permanently destroy a limb or essential part of **:** CRIPPLE **2 :** to cut up or alter radically so as to make imperfect ***syn*** see MAIM — **mu·ti·la·tion** \ˌmyüt-ᵊl-ˈā-shən\ *n* — **mu·ti·la·tor** \ˈmyüt-ᵊl-ˌāt-ər\ *n*

mu·tine \ˈmyüt-ᵊn\ *vi* **mu·tined; mu·tin·ing** [MF (*se*) *mutiner*] *obs* **:** REBEL, MUTINY

mu·ti·neer \ˌmyüt-ᵊn-ˈi(ə)r\ *n* **:** one that mutinies

mu·ti·nous \ˈmyüt-ᵊn-əs, ˈmyüt-nəs\ *adj* **1 a :** disposed to or in a state of mutiny **:** REBELLIOUS **b :** TURBULENT, UNRULY **2 :** of, relating to, or constituting mutiny — **mu·ti·nous·ly** *adv* — **mu·ti·nous·ness** *n*

mu·ti·ny \ˈmyüt-ᵊn-ē, ˈmyüt-nē\ *n, pl* **-nies** [*mutine* to rebel, fr. MF (*se*) *mutiner,* fr. *mutin* mutinous, fr. *meute* revolt, fr. (assumed) VL *movita,* fr. fem. of *movitus,* alter. of L *motus,* pp. of *movēre* to move] **1** *obs* **:** TUMULT **2 :** forcible or passive resistance to lawful authority; *esp* **:** concerted revolt (as of a naval crew) against discipline or a superior officer ***syn*** see REBELLION — **mutiny** *vi*

mutt \ˈmət\ *n* [short for *muttonhead* (dull-witted person)] **1 :** a stupid or insignificant person **:** FOOL **2 :** a mongrel dog **:** CUR

mut·ter \ˈmət-ər\ *vb* [ME *muteren;* akin to L *muttire* to mutter, *mutus* mute] *vi* **1 :** to utter sounds or words indistinctly or with a low voice and with the lips partly closed **2 :** to murmur complainingly or angrily **:** GRUMBLE ~ *vt* **:** to utter esp. in a low or imperfectly articulated manner — **mutter** *n* — **mut·ter·er** \-ər-ər\ *n*

mut·ton \ˈmət-ᵊn\ *n* [ME *motoun,* fr. OF *moton* ram, wether, of Celt origin; akin to MBret *mout* wether] **:** the flesh of a mature sheep used for food — **mut·tony** \ˈmət-ᵊn-ē, -nē\ *adj*

mut·ton·chops \ˈmət-ᵊn-ˌchäps\ *n pl* **:** side-whiskers that are narrow at the temple and broad and round by the lower jaws — called also *muttonchop whiskers*

muttonchops

mut·ton·fish \-ˌfish\ *n* [fr. its flavor] **:** a common snapper (*Lutjanus analis*) of the warmer parts of the western Atlantic that is usu. olive green and sometimes nearly white or tinged with rosy red and that is a commercially important food and sport fish — called also *mutton snapper*

mu·tu·al \ˈmyüch-(ə-)wəl, ˈmyü-chəl\ *adj* [ME, fr. MF *mutuel,* fr. L *mutuus* lent, borrowed, mutual; akin to L *mutare* to change — more at MISS] **1 a :** directed by each toward the other or the others <~ affection> **b :** having the same feelings one for the other <they had long been ~ enemies> **c :** shared in common <enjoying their ~ hobby> **d :** JOINT **2 :** characterized by intimacy **3 :** of or relating to a plan whereby the members of an organization share in the profits and expenses; *specif* **:** of, relating to, or taking the form of an insurance method in which the policyholders constitute the members of the insuring company ***syn*** see RECIPROCAL — **mu·tu·al·ly** \-ē\ *adv*

mutual fund *n* **:** an open-end investment company that invests money of its shareholders in a usu. diversified group of securities of other corporations

mu·tu·al·ism \ˈmyüch-(ə-)wə-ˌliz-əm, ˈmyü-chə-ˌliz-\ *n* **1 :** the doctrine or practice of mutual dependence as the condition of individual and social welfare **2 :** mutually beneficial association between different kinds of organisms — **mu·tu·al·ist** \-ləst\ *n* — **mu·tu·al·is·tic** \ˌmyüch-(ə-)wə-ˈlis-tik, ˌmyü-chə-ˈlis-\ *adj*

mu·tu·al·i·ty \ˌmyü-chə-ˈwal-ət-ē\ *n* **1 :** the quality or state of being mutual **2 :** a sharing of sentiments **:** INTIMACY

mu·tu·al·ize \ˈmyüch-(ə-)wə-ˌlīz, ˈmyü-chə-ˌlīz\ *vt* **-ized; -iz·ing :** to make mutual — **mu·tu·al·iza·tion** \ˌmyüch-(ə-)wə-lə-ˈzā-shən, ˌmyü-chə-lə-\ *n*

mutuel *n* **:** PARI-MUTUEL

muu·muu \ˈmü-ˌmü\ *n* [Hawaiian *mu'umu'u,* fr. *mu'umu'u* cut off] **:** a loose often long dress having bright colors and patterns and adapted from the dresses orig. distributed by missionaries to the native women of Hawaii

mu·zhik \mü-ˈzhēk, -ˈzhik\ *n* [Russ] **:** a Russian peasant

[1]muz·zle \ˈməz-əl\ *n* [ME *musell,* fr. MF *musel,* fr. dim. of *muse* mouth of an animal, fr. ML *musus*] **1 :** the projecting jaws and nose of an animal **:** SNOUT — see DOG illustration **2 a :** a fastening or covering for the mouth of an animal used to prevent eating or biting **b :** something (as censorship) that restrains normal expression **3 :** the open end or mouth of an implement; *esp* **:** the discharging end of a weapon

[2]muzzle *vt* **muz·zled; muz·zling** \-(ə-)liŋ\ **1 :** to fit with a muzzle **2 :** to restrain from expression **:** GAG — **muz·zler** \-(ə-)lər\ *n*

muz·zy \ˈməz-ē\ *adj* **muz·zi·er; -est** [perh. blend of *muddled* and *fuzzy*] **1 :** muddled or confused in mind <poets gone ~ with economics —*Saturday Rev.*> **2 a :** lacking in clarity and precision <his conclusions can be ~ and naive —*Times Lit. Supp.*> **b :** deficient in brightness **:** DULL, GLOOMY <a ~ day> — **muz·zi·ly** \ˈməz-ə-lē\ *adv* — **muz·zi·ness** \ˈməz-ē-nəs\ *n*

mv *abbr* millivolt

Mv *symbol* mendelevium

MV *abbr* **1** main verb **2** mean variation **3** motor vessel

MVA *abbr* Missouri Valley Authority

MVD *abbr* [Russ *Ministerstvo Vnutrennikh Del*] Ministry of Internal Affairs

MVP *abbr* most valuable player

Mw *abbr* megawatt

MWA *abbr* Modern Woodmen of America

mxd *abbr* mixed

[1]my \(ˈ)mī, mə\ *adj* [ME, fr. OE *mīn,* fr. *mīn,* suppletive gen. of *ic* I; akin to OE *mē* me] **1 :** of or relating to me or myself esp. as possessor, agent, or object of an action <~ car> <~ promise> <~ injuries> **2** — used interjectionally to express surprise and sometimes reduplicated <~ oh ~>; used also interjectionally with names of various parts of the body to express doubt or disapproval <~ foot>

[2]my *abbr* million years

my- *or* **myo-** *comb form* [NL, fr. Gk, fr. *mys* mouse, muscle — more at MOUSE] **:** muscle <*myo*graph> **:** muscle and <*myo*neural>

my·al·gia \mī-ˈal-j(ē-)ə\ *n* [NL] **:** pain in one or more muscles — **my·al·gic** \-jik\ *adj*

my·as·the·nia \ˌmī-əs-ˈthē-nē-ə\ *n* [NL] **:** muscular debility — **my·as·then·ic** \-ˈthen-ik\ *adj*

myasthenia gra·vis \-ˈgrav-əs, -ˈgräv-\ *n* [NL, lit., grave myasthenia] **:** a disease characterized by progressive weakness and exhaustibility of voluntary muscles without atrophy or sensory disturbance

myc *or* **mycol** *abbr* mycology

myc- *or* **myco-** *comb form* [NL, fr. Gk *mykēt-, mykēs* fungus; akin to Gk *myxa* nasal mucus] **:** fungus <*myco*logy> <*myc*osis>

my·ce·li·um \mī-ˈsē-lē-əm\ *n, pl* **-lia** \-lē-ə\ [NL, fr. *myc-* + Gk *hēlos* nail, wart, callus] **:** the mass of interwoven filamentous hyphae that forms esp. the vegetative portion of the thallus of a fungus and is often submerged in another body (as of soil or organic matter or the tissues of a host); *also* **:** a similar mass of filaments formed by a higher bacterium — **my·ce·li·al** \-əl\ *adj*

My·ce·nae·an \ˌmī-sə-ˈnē-ən\ *also* **My·ce·ni·an** \mī-ˈsē-nē-ən\ *adj* **:** of, relating to, or characteristic of Mycenae, its people, the period (1400 to 1100 B.C.) of Mycenae's political ascendancy, or the Bronze Age Mycenaean culture of the eastern Mediterranean area — **Mycenaean** *n*

my·ce·to·ma \ˌmī-sə-ˈtō-mə\ *n, pl* **-mas** *or* **-ma·ta** \-mət-ə\ [NL, fr. Gk *mykēt-, mykēs*] **:** a condition marked by invasion of the deep subcutaneous tissues with fungi or actinomycetes; *also* **:** a tumorous mass occurring in such a condition — **my·ce·to·ma·tous** \-mət-əs\ *adj*

my·ce·toph·a·gous \ˌmī-sə-ˈtäf-ə-gəs\ *adj* [Gk *mykēt-, mykēs* + E *-phagous*] **:** feeding on fungi

my·ce·to·zo·an \mī-ˌsēt-ə-ˈzō-ən\ *n* [NL *Mycetozoa,* order of protozoans, fr. Gk *mykēt-, mykēs* + NL *-zoa*] **:** SLIME MOLD — **mycetozoan** *adj*

-my·cin \ˈmīs-ᵊn\ *n comb form* [*streptomycin*] **:** substance obtained from a fungus <erythro*mycin*>

my·co·bac·te·ri·um \ˌmī-kō-bak-ˈtir-ē-əm\ *n* [NL, genus name, fr. *myc-* + *Bacterium*] **:** any of a genus (*Mycobacterium*) of nonmotile aerobic bacteria that are difficult to stain and include numerous saprophytes and the organisms causing tuberculosis and leprosy — **my·co·bac·te·ri·al** \-ē-əl\ *adj*

my·co·flo·ra \ˌmī-kə-ˈflōr-ə, -ˈflȯr-\ *n* [NL] **:** the fungi characteristic of a region or special environment

my·col·o·gy \mī-ˈkäl-ə-jē\ *n* [NL *mycologia,* fr. *myc-* + L *-logia* -logy] **1 :** a branch of botany dealing with fungi **2 :** fungal life — **my·co·log·i·cal** \ˌmī-kə-ˈläj-i-kəl\ *also* **my·co·log·ic** \-ˈläj-ik\ *adj* — **my·co·log·i·cal·ly** \ˌmī-kə-ˈläj-i-k(ə-)lē\ *adv* — **my·col·o·gist** \mī-ˈkäl-ə-jəst\ *n*

my·coph·a·gist \mī-ˈkäf-ə-jəst\ *n* [*mycophagy,* fr. *myc-* + *-phagy*] **:** one that eats fungi (as mushrooms) — **my·coph·a·gy** \-jē\ *n*

my·coph·a·gous \-ə-gəs\ *adj* **:** feeding on fungi <~ nematodes>

my·co·plas·ma \mī-kō-'plaz-mə\ *n, pl* **-mas** *or* **-ma·ta** \-mət-ə\ [NL, genus name, fr. *myc-* + *plasma*] **:** any of a genus (*Mycoplasma*) of minute pleomorphic gram-negative nonmotile microorganisms without cell walls that are intermediate in some respects between viruses and bacteria and are mostly parasitic usu. in mammals — called also *pleuropneumonia-like organism* — **my·co·plas·mal** \-məl\ *adj*

my·cor·rhi·za \,mī-kə-'rī-zə\ *n, pl* **-zae** \-,zē\ *or* **-zas** [NL, fr. *myc-* + Gk *rhiza* root — more at ROOT] **:** the symbiotic association of the mycelium of a fungus with the roots of a seed plant — **my·cor·rhi·zal** \-zəl\ *adj*

my·co·sis \mī-'kō-səs\ *n, pl* **my·co·ses** \-,sēz\ [NL] **:** infection with or disease caused by a fungus — **my·cot·ic** \-'kät-ik\ *adj*

my·co·tox·in \,mī-kə-'täk-sən\ *n* **:** a toxic substance produced by a fungus and esp. a mold

my·dri·a·sis \mə-'drī-ə-səs\ *n* [L, fr. Gk] **:** a long-continued or excessive dilatation of the pupil of the eye — **myd·ri·at·ic** \,mid-rē-'at-ik\ *adj or n*

myel- *or* **myelo-** *comb form* [NL, fr. Gk, fr. *myelos*, fr. *mys* mouse, muscle — more at MOUSE] **:** marrow **:** spinal cord <*myel*encephalon>

my·el·en·ceph·a·lon \,mī-ə-len-'sef-ə-,län, -lən\ *n* [NL] **:** the posterior portion of the rhombencephalon: **a :** MEDULLA OBLONGATA **b :** the posterior part of the medulla oblongata that is continuous with the spinal cord — **my·el·en·ce·phal·ic** \-,len(t)-sə-'fal-ik\ *adj*

my·elin \'mī-ə-lən\ *n* [ISV] **:** a soft white somewhat fatty material that forms a thick medullary sheath about the protoplasmic core of a medullated nerve fiber — **my·elin·ic** \,mī-ə-'lin-ik\ *adj*

my·elin·at·ed \'mī-ə-lə-,nāt-əd\ *adj* **:** having a medullary sheath <~ nerve fibers>

myelin sheath *n* **:** MEDULLARY SHEATH

my·eli·tis \,mī-ə-'līt-əs\ *n* [NL] **:** inflammation of the spinal cord or of the bone marrow

my·elo·blast \'mī-ə-lə-,blast\ *n* [ISV] **:** a large mononuclear nongranular bone-marrow cell; *esp* **:** one that is a precursor of a myelocyte — **my·elo·blas·tic** \,mī-ə-lə-'blas-tik\ *adj*

my·elo·cyte \'mī-ə-lə-,sīt\ *n* [ISV] **:** a bone-marrow cell; *esp* **:** a motile cell with cytoplasmic granules that gives rise to the granulocytes of the blood but is not present in normal blood — **my·elo·cyt·ic** \,mī-ə-lə-'sit-ik\ *adj*

my·elo·fi·bro·sis \,mī-ə-lō-fī-'brō-səs\ *n* [NL] **:** an anemic condition in which bone marrow becomes fibrotic and the liver and spleen usu. exhibit a development of blood-cell precursors — **my·elo·fi·brot·ic** \-'brät-ik\ *adj*

my·elo·gen·ic \,mī-ə-lō-'jen-ik\ *adj* **:** MYELOGENOUS

my·elog·e·nous \,mī-ə-'läj-ə-nəs\ *adj* [ISV] **:** of, relating to, originating in, or produced by the bone marrow <~ sarcoma>

myelogenous leukemia *n* **:** leukemia characterized by proliferation of myeloid tissue (as of the bone marrow and spleen) and an abnormal increase in the number of granulocytes, myelocytes, and myeloblasts in the circulating blood

my·eloid \'mī-ə-,lȯid\ *adj* [ISV] **1 :** of or relating to the spinal cord **2 :** of, relating to, or resembling bone marrow

my·elo·ma \,mī-ə-'lō-mə\ *n* [NL] **:** a primary tumor of the bone marrow — **my·elo·ma·tous** \-mət-əs\ *adj*

my·elop·a·thy \-'läp-ə-thē\ *n* [ISV] **:** a disease or disorder of the spinal cord or bone marrow — **my·elo·path·ic** \,mī-ə-lō-'path-ik\ *adj*

my·elo·pro·lif·er·a·tive \'mī-ə-lō-prə-'lif-ə-,rāt-iv, -rət-\ *adj* **:** of, relating to, or being a disorder (as leukemia) marked by excessive proliferation of blood-cell precursors

my·ia·sis \mī-'ī-ə-səs, mē-\ *n, pl* **my·ia·ses** \-,sēz\ [NL, fr. Gk *myia* fly — more at MIDGE] **:** infestation with fly maggots

mym *abbr* myriameter

my·na *or* **my·nah** \'mī-nə\ *n* [Hindi *mainā*, fr. Skt *madana*] **:** any of various Asiatic starlings (esp. genera *Acridotheres, Gracula*, and *Sturnus*); *esp* **:** a dark brown slightly crested bird (*A. tristis*) of southeastern Asia with a white tail tip and wing markings and bright yellow bill and feet

myn·heer \mə-'ne(ə)r\ *n* [D *mijnheer*, fr. *mijn* my + *heer* master, sir] **:** a male Netherlander — used as a title equivalent to *Mr.*

myo- — see MY-

myo·blast \'mī-ə-,blast\ *n* [ISV] **:** an undifferentiated cell capable of giving rise to muscle cells

myo·car·dio·graph \,mī-ə-'kärd-ē-ə-,graf\ *n* **:** a recording instrument for making a tracing of the action of the heart muscles

myo·car·di·tis \,mī-ə-(,)kär-'dīt-əs\ *n* [NL] **:** inflammation of the myocardium

myo·car·di·um \,mī-ə-'kärd-ē-əm\ *n* [NL, fr. *my-* + Gk *kardia* heart — more at HEART] **:** the middle muscular layer of the heart wall — **myo·car·di·al** \-ē-əl\ *adj*

myo·fi·bril \,mī-ō-'fīb-rəl, -'fib-\ *n* [NL *myofibrilla*, fr. *my-* + *fibrilla* fibril] **:** one of the longitudinal parallel contractile elements of a muscle cell that are composed of myosin and actin — **myo·fi·bril·lar** \-rə-lər\ *adj*

myo·fil·a·ment \-'fil-ə-mənt\ *n* **:** one of the individual filaments of actin or myosin that make up a myofibril

myo·gen·ic \,mī-ə-'jen-ik\ *adj* [ISV] **1 :** originating in muscle <~ pain> **2 :** taking place or functioning in ordered rhythmic fashion because of inherent properties of cardiac muscle rather than by reason of specific neural stimuli <a ~ heart beat>

myo·glo·bin \-'glō-bən, 'mī-ə-,\ *n* [ISV] **:** a red iron-containing protein pigment in muscles that is similar to hemoglobin

myo·ino·si·tol \,mī-ō-in-'ō-sə-,tȯl, -,tōl\ *n* **:** an optically inactive inositol that is a component of the vitamin B complex and a lipotropic agent and that occurs widely in plants, microorganisms, and higher animals including man

my·ol·o·gy \mī-'äl-ə-jē\ *n* [F or NL; F *myologie*, fr. NL *myologia*, fr. *my-* + L *-logia* -logy] **:** a scientific study of muscles — **my·o·log·ic** \,mī-ə-'läj-ik\ *or* **my·o·log·i·cal** \-i-kəl\ *adj*

my·o·ma \mī-'ō-mə\ *n, pl* **-mas** *or* **-ma·ta** \-mət-ə\ [NL] **:** a tumor consisting of muscle tissue — **my·o·ma·tous** \-mət-əs\ *adj*

myo·neu·ral \,mī-ə-'n(y)u̇r-əl\ *adj* **:** of or relating to both muscle and nerve

my·op·a·thy \mī-'äp-ə-thē\ *n* [ISV] **:** a disorder of muscle tissue or muscles — **myo·path·ic** \,mī-ə-'path-ik\ *adj*

my·ope \'mī-,ōp\ *n* [F, fr. LL *myops* myopic, fr. Gk *myōps*, fr. *myein* to be closed + *ōps* eye, face — more at MYSTERY, EYE] **:** a myopic person

my·o·pia \mī-'ō-pē-ə\ *n* [NL, fr. Gk *myōpia*, fr. *myōp-*, *myōps*] **1 :** a condition in which the visual images come to a focus in front of the retina of the eye resulting esp. in defective vision of distant objects **2 :** deficiency of foresight or discernment — **my·o·pic** \-'ō-pik, -'äp-ik\ *adj* — **my·o·pi·cal·ly** \-(ə-)lē\ *adv*

my·o·sin \'mī-ə-sən\ *n* [ISV *myos-* (fr. Gk *myos*, gen. of *mys* mouse, muscle)] **1 :** ACTOMYOSIN **2 :** a fibrous globulin of muscle that can split ATP and that reacts with actin to form actomyosin

my·o·sis, my·ot·ic *var of* MIOSIS, MIOTIC

my·os·otis \,mī-ə-'sōt-əs\ *n* [NL, genus name, fr. L, mouse-ear, fr. Gk *myosōtis*, fr. *myos* (gen. of *mys* mouse) + *ōt-*, *ous* ear — more at MOUSE, EAR] **:** FORGET-ME-NOT

myo·tome \'mī-ə-,tōm\ *n* [ISV] **1 :** the portion of an embryonic somite from which skeletal musculature is produced **2 :** the muscles of a metamere esp. in a segmented invertebrate

myo·to·nia \,mī-ə-'tō-nē-ə\ *n* [NL] **:** tonic spasm of one or more muscles; *also* **:** a condition characterized by such spasms — **myo·ton·ic** \-'tän-ik\ *adj*

[1]myr·i·ad \'mir-ē-əd\ *n* [Gk *myriad-*, *myrias*, fr. *myrioi* countless, ten thousand] **1 :** ten thousand **2 :** an immense number

[2]myriad *adj* **1 :** INNUMERABLE, MULTITUDINOUS **2 :** having innumerable aspects or elements <the ~ activity of the new land —Meridel Le Sueur>

myr·ia·me·ter \'mir-ē-ə-,mēt-ər\ *n* [F *myriamètre*, fr. Gk *myrioi* + F *-mètre* -meter] — see METRIC SYSTEM table

myr·io·pod *or* **myr·ia·pod** \'mir-ē-ə-,päd\ *n* [deriv. of Gk *myrioi* + *pod-*, *pous* foot — more at FOOT] **:** any of a group (Myriopoda) of arthropods having the body made up of numerous similar segments nearly all of which bear true jointed legs and including the millipedes and centipedes — **myriopod** *or* **myriapod** *adj*

my·ris·tate \mə-'ris-,tāt, mī-; 'mir-əs-, 'mī-rəs-\ *n* [ISV] **:** a salt or ester of myristic acid

my·ris·tic acid \mə-,ris-tik-, mī-\ *n* [ISV, fr. NL *Myristica*, genus of trees] **:** a crystalline fatty acid $C_{14}H_{28}O_2$ occurring esp. in the form of glycerides in most fats

myrmec- *or* **myrmeco-** *comb form* [Gk *myrmēk-*, *myrmēko-*, fr. *myrmēk-*, *myrmēx* — more at PISMIRE] **:** ant <*myrmeco*phagous>

myr·me·col·o·gy \,mər-mə-'käl-ə-jē\ *n* [ISV] **:** the scientific study of ants — **myr·me·co·log·i·cal** \-kə-'läj-i-kəl\ *adj* — **myr·me·col·o·gist** \-'käl-ə-jəst\ *n*

myr·me·coph·a·gous \-'käf-ə-gəs\ *adj* **:** feeding on ants

myr·meco·phile \'mər-mi-kə-,fīl\ *n* [ISV] **:** an organism that habitually shares an ant nest — **myr·me·coph·i·lous** \,mər-mə-'käf-ə-ləs\ *adj* — **myr·me·coph·i·ly** \-lē\ *n*

myr·mi·don \'mər-mə-,dän, -məd-ən\ *n* [L *Myrmidon-*, *Myrmido*, fr. Gk *Myrmidōn*] **1** *cap* **:** a member of a legendary Thessalian people who took part with Achilles their king in the Trojan War **2 :** a loyal follower; *esp* **:** a subordinate who executes orders unquestioningly or pitilessly

my·rob·a·lan \mī-'räb-ə-lən, mə-\ *n* [MF *mirobolan*, fr. L *myrobalanus*, fr. Gk *myrobalanos*, fr. *myron* unguent + *balanos* acorn — more at SMEAR, GLAND] **1 :** the dried astringent fruit of an East Indian tree (genus *Terminalia*) used chiefly in tanning and in inks **2 :** CHERRY PLUM

myrrh \'mər\ *n* [ME *myrre*, fr. OE, fr. L *myrrha*, fr. Gk, of Sem origin; akin to Ar *murr* myrrh] **:** a yellowish brown to reddish brown aromatic gum resin with a bitter slightly pungent taste obtained from a tree (esp. *Commiphora abyssinica*) of east Africa and Arabia; *also* **:** a mixture of myrrh and labdanum

myr·tle \'mərt-ᵊl\ *n, often attrib* [ME *mirtille*, fr. MF, fr. ML *myrtillus*, fr. L *myrtus*, fr. Gk *myrtos*] **1 a :** a common evergreen bushy shrub (*Myrtus communis*) of southern Europe with oval to lance-shaped shiny leaves, fragrant white or rosy flowers, and black berries **b :** any of a family (Myrtaceae, the myrtle family) of chiefly tropical shrubs or trees to which the common myrtle belongs **2 a :** [1]PERIWINKLE a **b :** CALIFORNIA LAUREL

my·self \mī-'self, mə-\ *pron* **1 :** that identical one that is I — used reflexively <I'm going to get ~ a new suit>, for emphasis <I ~ will go>, or in absolute constructions <~ a tourist, I nevertheless avoided other tourists> **2 :** my normal, healthy, or sane condition <didn't feel ~ yesterday>

mys·ost \'mē-,sȯst\ *n* [Norw, fr. *myse* whey + *ost* cheese] **:** a brown Norwegian whey cheese of hard buttery consistency and mild sweetish taste

mys·ta·gogue \'mis-tə-,gäg\ *n* [L *mystagogus*, fr. Gk *mystagōgos*, fr. *mystēs* initiate + *agein* to lead — more at AGENT] **1 :** one who initiates another into a mystery cult **2 :** one who disseminates mystical doctrines — **mys·ta·go·gy** \-,gäj-ē, -,gō-jē\ *n*

mys·te·ri·ous \mis-'tir-ē-əs\ *adj* **1 a :** of, relating to, or constituting mystery <the ~ ways of God> **b :** exciting wonder, curiosity, or surprise while baffling efforts to comprehend or identify **:** MYSTIFYING <heard a ~ noise each night> <a ~ stranger> **2 :** stirred by or attracted to the inexplicable — **mys·te·ri·ous·ly** *adv* — **mys·te·ri·ous·ness** *n*

syn MYSTERIOUS, INSCRUTABLE, ARCANE *shared meaning element* **:** being beyond one's powers to discover, understand, or explain

[1]mys·tery \'mis-t(ə-)rē\ *n, pl* **-ter·ies** [ME *mysterie*, fr. L *mysterium*, fr. Gk *mystērion*, fr. (assumed) *mystos* keeping silence, fr. Gk *myein* to be closed (of the eyes or lips)] **1 a :** a religious truth that man can know by revelation alone and cannot fully understand **b (1) :** any of the 15 events (as the Nativity, the Crucifixion, or the

Assumption) serving as a subject for meditation during the saying of the rosary (2) *cap* : a Christian sacrament; *specif* : EUCHARIST **c** (1) : a secret religious rite believed (as in Eleusinian and Mithraic cults) to impart enduring bliss to the initiate (2) : a cult devoted to such rites **2 a** : something not understood or beyond understanding : ENIGMA **b** *obs* : a private secret **c** : the secret or specialized practices or ritual peculiar to an occupation or a body of people <the *mysteries* of the tailor's craft> **d** : a piece of fiction dealing usu. with the solution of a mysterious crime **3** : profound, inexplicable, or secretive quality or character <the ~ of her smile> ***syn*** MYSTERY, PROBLEM, ENIGMA, RIDDLE, PUZZLE, CONUNDRUM *shared meaning element* : something which baffles or perplexes

[2]**mystery** *n, pl* **-ter·ies** [LL *misterium, mysterium,* alter. of *ministerium* service, occupation, fr. *minister* servant — more at MINISTER] **1** *archaic* : TRADE, CRAFT **2** *archaic* : a body of persons engaged in a particular trade, business, or profession : GUILD **3** : MYSTERY PLAY

mystery play *n* [[2]*mystery*] : a medieval drama based on scriptural incidents and usu. centering on the life, death, and resurrection of Christ

[1]**mys·tic** \ˈmis-tik\ *adj* [ME *mistik,* fr. L *mysticus* of mysteries, fr. Gk *mystikos,* fr. (assumed) *mystos*] **1** : MYSTICAL 1 **2** : of or relating to mysteries or esoteric rites : OCCULT **3** : of or relating to mysticism or mystics **4 a** : MYSTERIOUS **b** : OBSCURE, ENIGMATIC **c** : inducing a feeling of awe or wonder **d** : having magical properties

[2]**mystic** *n* **1** : a follower of a mystical way of life **2** : an advocate of a theory of mysticism

mys·ti·cal \ˈmis-ti-kəl\ *adj* **1** : having a spiritual meaning or reality that is neither apparent to the senses nor obvious to the intelligence <the ~ food of the sacrament> **2 a** : of, relating to, or resulting from an individual's direct communion with God or ultimate reality <the ~ experience of the Inner Light> **b** : based on subjective experience (as intuition or insight) <the ~ religions of the East> **3** : CRYPTIC, UNINTELLIGIBLE **4** : MYSTIC 2 — **mys·ti·cal·ly** \-k(ə-)lē\ *adv*

mys·ti·cism \ˈmis-tə-ˌsiz-əm\ *n* **1** : the experience of mystical union or direct communion with ultimate reality reported by mystics **2** : the belief that direct knowledge of God, spiritual truth, or ultimate reality can be attained through subjective experience (as intuition or insight) **3 a** : vague speculation : a belief without sound basis **b** : a theory postulating the possibility of direct and intuitive acquisition of ineffable knowledge or power

mys·ti·fi·ca·tion \ˌmis-tə-fə-ˈkā-shən\ *n* **1** : an act or instance of mystifying **2** : the quality or state of being mystified **3** : something designed to mystify

mys·ti·fy \ˈmis-tə-ˌfī\ *vt* **-fied; -fy·ing** [F *mistifier,* fr. *mystère* mystery, fr. L *mysterium*] **1** : to perplex the mind of : BEWILDER **2** : to make mysterious or obscure <~ an interpretation of a prophecy> — **mys·ti·fi·er** \-ˌfī(-ə)r\ *n* — **mys·ti·fy·ing·ly** \-ˌfī-iŋ-lē\ *adv*

mys·tique \mis-ˈtēk\ *n* [F, fr. *mystique,* adj., mystic, fr. L *mysticus*] **1** : a complex of transcendental or somewhat mystical beliefs and attitudes developing around something (as an idea) <the ~ of progress> **2** : the special esoteric skill essential in a calling or activity <the ~ of confrontation politics>

myth \ˈmith\ *n* [Gk *mythos*] **1** : a usu. traditional story of ostensibly historical events that serves to unfold part of the world view of a people or explain a practice, belief, or natural phenomenon **2** : PARABLE, ALLEGORY **3 a** : a person or thing having only an imaginary or unverifiable existence **b** : an ill-founded belief held uncritically esp. by an interested group **4** : the whole body of myths ***syn*** MYTH, LEGEND, SAGA *shared meaning element* : a traditional story of ostensibly historical content whose origin has been lost

myth·i·cal \ˈmith-i-kəl\ *also* **myth·ic** \-ik\ *adj* **1** : based on or described in a myth esp. as contrasted with factual history : IMAGINARY **2 a** : fabricated, invented, or imagined in an arbitrary way or in defiance of facts **b** : having qualities suitable to myth ***syn*** see FICTITIOUS — **myth·i·cal·ly** \-i-k(ə-)lē\ *adv*

myth·i·cize \ˈmith-ə-ˌsīz\ *vt* **-cized; -ciz·ing** **1** : to turn into or envelop in myth **2** : to treat as myth — **myth·i·ciz·er** *n*

myth·mak·er \ˈmith-ˌmā-kər\ *n* : a creator of myths or of mythical situations or lore — **myth·mak·ing** \-kiŋ\ *n*

my·thog·ra·phy \mith-ˈäg-rə-fē\ *n* [Gk *mythographia,* fr. *mythos* + *-graphia* -graphy] **1** : the representation of mythical subjects in art **2** : a critical compilation of myths — **my·thog·ra·pher** \-fər\ *n*

myth·o·log·i·cal \ˌmith-ə-ˈläj-i-kəl\ *also* **myth·o·log·ic** \-ik\ *adj* **1** : of or relating to mythology or myths : dealt with in mythology **2** : lacking factual basis or historical validity : MYTHICAL, FABULOUS — **myth·o·log·i·cal·ly** \-i-k(ə-)lē\ *adv*

my·thol·o·gize \mith-ˈäl-ə-ˌjīz\ *vb* **-gized; -giz·ing** *vt* **1** *obs* : to explain the mythological significance of **2** : to build a myth around : MYTHICIZE ~ *vi* : to relate, classify, and explain myths — **my·thol·o·giz·er** *n*

my·thol·o·gy \mith-ˈäl-ə-jē\ *n, pl* **-gies** [F or LL; F *mythologie,* fr. LL *mythologia* interpretation of myths, fr. Gk, legend, myth, fr. *mythologein* to relate myths, fr. *mythos* + *logos* speech — more at LEGEND] **1 a** : an allegorical narrative **b** : a body of myths; *esp* : the myths dealing with the gods, demigods, and legendary heroes of a particular people and usu. involving supernatural elements **2** : a branch of knowledge that deals with myth — **my·thol·o·ger** \-jər\ *n* — **my·thol·o·gist** \-jəst\ *n*

mytho·ma·nia \ˌmith-ə-ˈmā-nē-ə, -nyə\ *n* [NL, fr. Gk *mythos* + LL *mania*] : an excessive or abnormal propensity for lying and exaggerating — **mytho·ma·ni·ac** \-nē-ˌak\ *n or adj*

mytho·poe·ia \ˌmith-ə-ˈpē-(y)ə\ *n* [LL, fr. Gk *mythopoiia,* fr. *mythopoiein* to make a myth, fr. *mythos* + *poiein* to make — more at POEM] : a creating of myth : a giving rise to myths — **mytho·poe·ic** \-ˈpē-ik\ *or* **mytho·po·et·ic** \-pō-ˈet-ik\ *or* **mytho·po·et·i·cal** \-i-kəl\ *adj*

my·thos \ˈmī-ˌthäs, ˈmith-ˌäs\ *n, pl* **my·thoi** \-ˌthȯi, -ˌȯi\ [Gk] **1 a** : MYTH 1 **b** : MYTHOLOGY 1b **2** : a pattern of beliefs expressing often symbolically the characteristic or prevalent attitudes in a group or culture **3** : THEME, PLOT

my word *interj* — used to express surprise or astonishment

myx·ede·ma \ˌmik-sə-ˈdē-mə\ *n* [NL, fr. Gk *myxa* lamp wick, nasal mucus + NL *edema* — more at MUCUS] : severe hypothyroidism characterized by firm inelastic edema, dry skin and hair, and loss of mental and physical vigor — **myx·ede·ma·tous** \-ˈdem-ət-əs, -ˈdē-mət-\ *adj*

myx·o·ma \mik-ˈsō-mə\ *n, pl* **-mas** *or* **-ma·ta** \-mət-ə\ [NL, fr. Gk *myxa*] : a soft tumor made up of gelatinous connective tissue resembling that found in the umbilical cord — **myx·o·ma·tous** \-mət-əs\ *adj*

myx·o·ma·to·sis \mik-ˌsō-mə-ˈtō-səs\ *n* [NL, fr. *myxomat-, myxoma*] : a condition characterized by the presence of myxomas in the body; *specif* : a severe virus disease of rabbits that is transmitted by mosquitoes and has been used in the biological control of rabbits in plague areas

myxo·my·cete \ˌmik-sō-ˈmī-ˌsēt, ˌmik-sō-(ˌ)mī-ˈ\ *n* [deriv. of Gk *myxa* + *mykēt-, mykēs* fungus — more at MYC-] : SLIME MOLD — **myxo·my·ce·tous** \-(ˌ)mī-ˈsēt-əs\ *adj*

myxo·vi·rus \ˈmik-sə-ˌvī-rəs\ *n* [NL, fr. Gk *myxa* mucus + NL *virus;* fr. its affinity for certain mucins] : any of a group of rather large RNA-containing viruses that includes influenza and mumps viruses — **myxo·vi·ral** \ˌmik-sə-ˈvī-rəl\ *adj*

[1]**n** \ˈen\ *n, pl* **n's** *or* **ns** \ˈenz\ *often cap, often attrib* **1 a** : the 14th letter of the English alphabet **b** : a graphic representation of this letter **c** : a speech counterpart of orthographic *n* **2** : a graphic device for reproducing the letter *n* **3 a** : one designated *n* esp. as the 14th in order or class **b** : an indefinite number; *esp* : a constant integer or a variable taking on integral values **4** : something shaped like the letter N **5** : the haploid or gametic number of chromosomes **6** : EN 2

[2]**n** *abbr, often cap* **1** name **2** nano- **3** navy **4** net **5** neuter **6** noon **7** normal **8** north **9** note **10** noun **11** number

[3]**n** *symbol* **1** exponent denoting an unspecified degree, order, or power **2** *usu ital* neutron **3** *usu ital* index of refraction

N *symbol* nitrogen

-n — see -EN

'n' *also* **'n** \ən, ᵊn\ *conj* : AND <fish *'n'* chips>

Na *symbol* [NL *natrium*] sodium

NA *abbr* **1** national academician **2** no account **3** North America **4** not applicable **5** not available

NAACP \ˌen-ˌdəb-ə-ˌlā-ˌsē-ˈpē, ˌen-ˌā-ˌā-ˌsē-\ *abbr* National Association for the Advancement of Colored People

nab \ˈnab\ *vt* **nabbed; nab·bing** [perh. alter. of E dial. *nap*] **1** : to catch or seize in arrest : APPREHEND **2** : to seize suddenly

NAB *abbr* New American Bible

na·bob \ˈnā-ˌbäb\ *n* [Hindi & Urdu *nawwāb,* fr. Ar *nuwwāb,* pl. of *nā'ib* governor] **1** : a provincial governor of the Mogul empire in India **2** : a man of great wealth or prominence — **na·bob·ess** \-əs\ *n*

Na·both \ˈnā-ˌbäth\ *n* [Heb *Nābhōth*] : the owner of a vineyard coveted and seized by Ahab king of Israel

na·celle \nə-ˈsel\ *n* [F, lit., small boat, fr. LL *navicella,* dim. of L *navis* ship — more at NAVE] : an enclosed shelter on an aircraft for an engine or sometimes for the crew

na·ore \ˈnā-kər\ *n* [MF, fr. OIt *naccara* drum, nacre, fr. Ar *naqqarah* drum] : MOTHER-OF-PEARL — **na·cred** \-kərd\ *adj* — **na·cre·ous** \-krē-əs, -k(ə-)rəs\ *adj*

NACS *abbr* National Association of College Stores

NACU *abbr* National Association of Colleges and Universities

[1]**NAD** \ˌen-ˌā-ˈdē\ *n* [*n*icotinamide-*a*denine *d*inucleotide] : a coenzyme $C_{21}H_{27}N_7O_{14}P_2$ of numerous dehydrogenases that occurs in most cells and plays an important role in all phases of intermediary metabolism as an oxidizing agent or when in the reduced form as

a reducing agent for various metabolites — called also *nicotinamide-adenine dinucleotide, diphosphopyridine nucleotide, DPN*

²NAD *abbr* **1** National Academy of Design **2** no appreciable disease

Na-dene *also* **Na-dé-né** \nä-'den-ē\ *n* [*na-* (fr. an Athapaskan word stem akin to Haida *na* to dwell) + *Déné*] **:** a group of related American Indian languages spoken in parts of western No. America from Alaska to northern Mexico

na·dir \'nā-,di(ə)r, 'nād-ər\ *n* [ME, fr. MF, fr. Ar *nazīr* opposite] **1 :** the point of the celestial sphere that is directly opposite the zenith and vertically downward from the observer **2 :** the lowest point

NADP \en-,ā-,dē-'pē\ *n* [*n*icotinamide-*a*denine *d*inucleotide *p*hosphate] **:** a coenzyme $C_{21}H_{28}N_7O_{17}P_3$ of numerous dehydrogenases (as that acting on glucose-6-phosphate) that occurs esp. in red blood cells and plays a role in intermediary metabolism similar to NAD but acting often on different metabolites — called also *nicotinamide-adenine dinucleotide phosphate, TPN, triphosphopyridine nucleotide*

NAEB *abbr* National Association of Educational Broadcasters

¹nag \'nag\ *n* [ME *nagge;* akin to D *negge* small horse] **:** HORSE; *esp* **:** one that is old or in poor condition

²nag *vb* **nagged; nag·ging** [prob. of Scand origin; akin to ON *gnaga* to gnaw; akin to OE *gnagan* to gnaw] *vi* **1 :** to find fault incessantly **:** COMPLAIN **2 :** to be a continuing source of annoyance ~ *vt* **1 :** to irritate by constant scolding or urging **2 :** BADGER, WORRY — **nag·ger** *n* — **nagging** *adj* — **nag·ging·ly** \-iŋ-lē\ *adv*

³nag *n* **:** one who nags habitually

Nah *abbr* Nahum

Na·huatl \'nä-,wät-ᵊl\ *n, pl* **Nahuatl** *or* **Nahuatls** [Sp, fr. Nahuatl] **1 :** a group of Amerindian peoples of southern Mexico and Central America **2 :** the Uto-Aztecan language of the Nahuatl people — **Na·huat·lan** \nä-'wät-lən\ *adj or n*

Na·hum \'nā-(h)əm\ *n* [Heb *Naḥūm*] **1 :** a Hebrew prophet of the 7th century B.C. **2 :** a prophetic book of canonical Jewish and Christian Scripture — see BIBLE table

NAIA *abbr* National Association of Intercollegiate Athletes

na·iad \'nā-əd, 'nī-, -,ad\ *n, pl* **na·iads** *or* **na·ia·des** \-ə-,dēz\ [F or L; F *naïade,* fr. L *naiad-, naias,* fr. Gk, fr. *nan* to flow — more at NOURISH] **1 :** one of the nymphs in ancient mythology living in and giving life to lakes, rivers, springs, and fountains **2 :** the aquatic young of a mayfly, dragonfly, damselfly, or stone fly **3 :** any of a genus (*Naias*) of submerged aquatic plants

na·if \nä-'ēf\ *adj* [F] **:** NAIVE — **naif** *n*

¹nail \'nā(ə)l\ *n* [ME, fr. OE *nægl;* akin to OHG *nagal* nail, fingernail, L *unguis* fingernail, toenail, claw, Gk *onyx*] **1 a :** a horny sheath protecting the upper end of each finger and toe of man and most other primates **b :** a structure (as a claw) that terminates a digit and corresponds to a nail **2 :** a slender usu. pointed and headed fastener designed to be pounded in **3 :** an English unit of length equal to $^1/_{16}$ yard

²nail *vt* **1 :** to fasten with or as if with a nail **2 :** to fix in steady attention <~*ed* his eye on the crack> **3 :** CATCH, TRAP; *esp* **:** to detect and expose so as to discredit **4 a :** STRIKE, HIT **b :** to put out (a runner) in baseball — **nail·er** *n*

nail·brush \'nā(ə)l-,brəsh\ *n* **:** a small firm-bristled brush for cleaning the hands and esp. the fingernails

nail down *vt* **1 :** to settle or establish clearly and unmistakably **2 :** to gain or win decisively <~ down his consent>

nail file *n* **:** a small narrow instrument (as of metal or cardboard) with a rough or emery surface that is used for shaping fingernails

nain·sook \'nān-,sùk\ *n* [Hindi *nainsukh,* fr. *nain* eye + *sukh* delight] **:** a soft lightweight muslin

nai·ra \'nī-rə\ *n* [native name in Nigeria] — see MONEY table

na·ive *or* **na·ïve** \nä-'ēv\ *adj* **na·iv·er; -est** [F *naïve,* fem. of *naïf,* fr. OF, inborn, natural, fr. L *nativus* native] **1 :** marked by unaffected simplicity **:** ARTLESS, INGENUOUS **2 a :** deficient in worldly wisdom or informed judgment; *esp* **:** CREDULOUS **b :** not previously subjected to experimentation or a particular experimental situation <made the test with ~ rats> ***syn*** see NATURAL — **na·ive·ly** *adv* — **na·ive·ness** *n*

na·ive·té *or* **na·ïve·té** *or* **na·ive·te** \(,)nä-,ē-və-'tā, nä-'ē-və-,; ,nä-,ēv-'tā\ *n* [F *naïveté,* fr. OF, inborn character, fr. *naif*] **1 :** the quality or state of being naive **2 :** a naive remark or action

na·ive·ty *also* **na·ïve·ty** \nä-'ē-vət-ē, -'ēv-tē\ *n, pl* **-ties :** NAIVETÉ

na·ked \'nā-kəd, *esp South* 'nek-əd\ *adj* [ME, fr. OE *nacod;* akin to OHG *nackot* naked, L *nudus,* Gk *gymnos*] **1 :** not covered by clothing **:** NUDE **2 :** devoid of customary or natural covering **:** BARE: as **a :** not enclosed in a sheath or scabbard **b :** not provided with a shade **c** *of a plant or one of its parts* **:** lacking pubescence or enveloping or subtending parts **d :** lacking foliage or vegetation **e** *of an animal or one of its parts* **:** lacking an external covering (as of hair, feathers, or shell) **3 a :** scantily supplied or furnished **b :** lacking embellishment **:** UNADORNED **4 :** UNARMED, DEFENSELESS **5 :** lacking confirmation or support **6 :** devoid of concealment or disguise **7 :** unaided by any optical device or instrument <visible to the ~ eye> ***syn*** see BARE — **na·ked·ly** *adv* — **na·ked·ness** *n*

na·led \'nā-,led\ *n* [origin unknown] **:** a short-lived insecticide of relatively low toxicity to warm-blooded animals that is used esp. to control crop pests and mosquitoes

na·li·dix·ic acid \,nā-lə-,dik-sik-\ *n* [origin unknown] **:** an antibacterial agent $C_{12}H_{12}N_2O_3$ that is used esp. in the treatment of genitourinary infections

na·lor·phine \nal-'ȯr-,fēn\ *n* [*N-al*lyl + m*orphine*] **:** a white crystalline compound $C_{19}H_{21}NO_3$ that is derived from morphine and is used in the form of its hydrochloride as a respiratory stimulant to counteract poisoning by morphine and similar narcotic drugs

nal·ox·one \'nal-ək-,sōn\ *n* [*N-al*lyl + hydr*oxy-* + *-one*] **:** a potent antagonist $C_{19}H_{21}NO_4$ of narcotic drugs and esp. morphine

NAM *abbr* National Association of Manufacturers

nam·by–pam·by \,nam-bē-'pam-bē\ *adj* [*Namby Pamby,* nickname given to Ambrose Philips] **1 :** lacking in character or substance **:** INSIPID **2 :** WEAK, INDECISIVE — **namby–pamby** *n*

¹name \'nām\ *n* [ME, fr. OE *nama;* akin to OHG *namo* name, L *nomen,* Gk *onoma, onyma*] **1 a :** a word or phrase that constitutes the distinctive designation of a person or thing **b :** a word or symbol used in logic to designate **2 :** a descriptive often disparaging epithet <called him ~*s*> **3 a :** REPUTATION <gave the town a bad ~> **b :** an illustrious record **:** FAME <made a ~ for himself in golf> **c :** a person or thing with a reputation **4 :** FAMILY, CLAN **5 :** appearance as opposed to reality <a friend in ~ only> **6 :** one referred to by a name <praise his holy ~> — **in the name of :** by authority of <open *in the name of* the law>

²name *vt* **named; nam·ing 1 :** to give a name to **:** CALL **2 a :** to mention or identify by name **b :** to accuse by name **3 :** to nominate for office **:** APPOINT **4 :** to decide upon **:** CHOOSE <~ the day for the wedding> **5 :** to mention explicitly **:** SPECIFY <unwilling to ~ a price> ***syn*** see MENTION — **nam·er** *n*

³name *adj* **1 :** of, relating to, or bearing a name <~ tags> **2 :** appearing in the name of a literary or theatrical production **3 a :** having an established reputation **b :** featuring celebrities

name·able *also* **nam·able** \'nā-mə-bəl\ *adj* **1 :** capable of being named **:** IDENTIFIABLE **2 :** worthy of being named **:** MEMORABLE

name–call·ing \'nām-,kȯ-liŋ\ *n* **:** the use of offensive names esp. to win an argument or to induce rejection or condemnation (as of a person or project) without objective consideration of the facts

name day *n* **:** the day of a church feast (as a saint's day) whose name corresponds to one's given name

name·less \'nām-ləs\ *adj* **1 :** OBSCURE, UNDISTINGUISHED **2 :** not known by name **:** ANONYMOUS **3 :** having no legal right to a name **:** ILLEGITIMATE **4 :** not having been given a name **:** UNNAMED **5 :** not marked with a name <a ~ grave> **6 a :** incapable of precise description **:** INDEFINABLE **b :** too repulsive or distressing to describe — **name·less·ly** *adv* — **name·less·ness** *n*

name·ly \'nām-lē\ *adv* **:** that is to say **:** to wit

name of the game : the essential quality or matter <patience is the *name of the game* in coastal duck hunting —Dick Beals>

name·plate \-,plāt\ *n* **1 :** a plate or plaque bearing a name (as of a resident) **2 :** a line of merchandise **:** BRAND

name·sake \-,sāk\ *n* [prob. fr. *name's sake*] **:** one that has the same name as another; *esp* **:** one named after another

NAMH *abbr* National Association for Mental Health

nance \'nan(t)s\ *n* [short for *nancy,* fr. the name *Nancy*] **1 :** an effeminate male **2 :** HOMOSEXUAL

NAND \'nand\ *n* [*not AND*] **:** a computer logic circuit that produces an output which is the inverse of that of an AND circuit

nan·keen \(')nan-'kēn\ *n* [*Nanking,* China] **1 :** a durable brownish yellow cotton fabric orig. loomed by hand in China **2** *pl* **:** trousers made of nankeen

Nan·kin \'nan-'kin, 'nän-\ *or* **Nan·king** \-'kiŋ\ *n* [*Nanking,* China] **:** Chinese porcelain decorated in blue on a white ground

nan·no·plank·ton *also* **nano·plank·ton** \,nan-ō-'plaŋ(k)-tən, -,tän\ *n* [NL, fr. Gk *nanos, nannos* dwarf + NL *plankton*] **:** the smallest plankton that consists of those organisms (as bacteria) passing through nets of very fine mesh silk bolting cloth — **nan·no·plank·ton·ic** \-plaŋ(k)-'tän-ik\ *adj*

nan·ny *also* **nan·nie** \'nan-ē\ *n, pl* **nannies** [prob. of baby-talk origin] *chiefly Brit* **:** a child's nurse **:** NURSEMAID

nan·ny goat \'nan-ē-\ *n* [*Nanny,* nickname for *Anne*] **:** a female domestic goat

nano- \'nan-(,)ō, -ə\ *comb form* [ISV, fr. Gk *nanos* dwarf] **:** one billionth (10^{-9}) part of <*nano*second>

nano·gram \'nan-ə-,gram\ *n* [ISV] **:** one billionth of a gram

nano·me·ter \'nan-ə-,mēt-ər\ *n* [ISV] **:** one billionth of a meter

nano·sec·ond \-,sek-ənd, -ənt\ *n* [ISV] **:** one billionth of a second

Na·o·mi \nā-'ō-mē\ *n* [Heb *Nā'ŏmī*] **:** the mother-in-law of the Old Testament heroine Ruth

¹nap \'nap\ *vi* **napped; nap·ping** [ME *nappen,* fr. OE *hnappian;* akin to OHG *hnaffezen* to doze] **1 :** to sleep briefly esp. during the day **:** DOZE **2 :** to be off guard

²nap *n* **:** a short sleep esp. during the day **:** SNOOZE

³nap *n* [ME *noppe,* fr. MD, flock of wool, nap; akin to OE *hnoppian* to pluck, Gk *konis* ashes — more at INCINERATE] **:** a hairy or downy surface (as on a woven fabric) — **nap·less** \-ləs\ *adj* — **napped** \'napt\ *adj*

⁴nap *vt* **napped; nap·ping :** to raise a nap on (fabric or leather)

NAPA *abbr* **1** National Association of Performing Artists **2** National Automotive Parts Association

¹na·palm \'nā-,päm, -,pälm\ *n* [*na*phthene + *palm*itate] **1 :** a thickener consisting of a mixture of aluminum soaps used in jelling gasoline (as for incendiary bombs) **2 :** fuel jelled with napalm

²napalm *vt* **:** to assault with napalm

nape \'nāp, 'nap\ *n* [ME] **:** the back of the neck

na·pery \'nā-p(ə-)rē\ *n* [ME, fr. MF *naperie,* fr. *nappe, nape* tablecloth — more at NAPKIN] **:** household linen; *esp* **:** TABLE LINEN

Naph·ta·li \'naf-tə-,lī\ *n* [Heb *Naphtālī*] **:** a son of Jacob and the traditional eponymous ancestor of one of the tribes of Israel

naphth- *or* **naphtho-** *comb form* [ISV, fr. *naphtha & naphthalene*] **1 :** naphtha <*naphth*ene> **2 :** naphthalene <*naphtho*quinone>

naph·tha \'naf-thə, 'nap-\ *n* [L, fr. Gk, of Iranian origin; akin to Per *neft* naphtha] **1 :** PETROLEUM **2 :** any of various volatile often flammable liquid hydrocarbon mixtures used chiefly as solvents and diluents

naph·tha·lene \-,lēn\ *n* [alter. of earlier *naphthaline,* irreg. fr. *naphtha*] **:** a crystalline aromatic hydrocarbon $C_{10}H_8$ usu. obtained by distillation of coal tar and used esp. in organic synthesis — **naph·tha·len·ic** \ˌnaf-thə-ˈlen-ik, ˌnap-, -ˈlēn-\ *adj*

naph·thene \ˈnaf-ˌthēn, ˈnap-\ *n* [ISV] **:** CYCLOPARAFFIN; *esp* **:** one that occurs in shale or tar oil and yields aromatic hydrocarbons on dehydrogenation — **naph·then·ic** \naf-ˈthē-nik, nap-, -ˈthen-\ *adj*

naph·thol \ˈnaf-ˌthȯl, ˈnap-, -ˌthōl\ *n* [ISV] **1 :** either of two isomeric derivatives $C_{10}H_8O$ of naphthalene found in coal tar or made synthetically and used as antiseptics and in manufacture of dyes **2 :** any of various hydroxy derivatives of naphthalene that resemble the simpler phenols

naph·thyl·amine \naf-ˈthil-ə-ˌmēn, nap-\ *n* [ISV] **:** either of two isomeric crystalline bases $C_{10}H_9N$ that are used esp. as dye intermediates

na·pi·er grass \ˈnā-pē-ər-\ *n* [*Napier*, town in So. Africa] **:** a tall stout perennial grass (*Pennisetum purpureum*) that resembles sugarcane and is widely grown for forage — called also *elephant grass*

Na·pier·ian logarithm \nə-ˌpir-ē-ən, nā-\ *n* [John *Napier*] **:** NATURAL LOGARITHM

Na·pi·er's bones \ˌnā-pē-ərz-\ *n* [fr. the short rods by which it was operated] **:** a pocket calculator for multiplication and division that was invented by John Napier

na·pi·form \ˈnā-pə-ˌfȯrm\ *adj* [L *napus* turnip (fr. Gk *napy* mustard) + ISV *-iform;* akin to Gk *sinapy* mustard] **:** globular at the top and tapering off abruptly — used esp. of roots

nap·kin \ˈnap-kən\ *n* [ME *nappekin*, fr. *nappe* tablecloth, fr. MF, fr. L *mappa* napkin] **1 :** a piece of material (as cloth or paper) used at table to wipe the lips or fingers and protect the clothes **2 :** a small cloth or towel: as **a** *dial Brit* **:** HANDKERCHIEF **b** *chiefly Scot* **:** KERCHIEF **c** *chiefly Brit* **:** DIAPER 2 **3 :** SANITARY NAPKIN

na·po·leon \nə-ˈpōl-yən, -ˈpō-lē-ən\ *n* [F *napoléon*, fr. *Napoléon* Napoleon I] **1 :** a French 20-franc gold coin **2 :** an oblong pastry with a filling of cream, custard, or jelly

nappe \ˈnap\ *n* [F, tablecloth, sheet, nappe — more at NAPKIN] **1 :** a large mass thrust over other rocks **2 :** SHEET 6 **3 :** one of the two sheets that lie on opposite sides of the vertex and together make up a cone

[1]nap·per \ˈnap-ər\ *n* **:** one that takes naps

[2]napper *n* **:** one that naps cloth

[1]nap·py \ˈnap-ē\ *n* [obs. *nappy*, adj. (foaming)] *chiefly Scot* **:** LIQUOR; *specif* **:** ALE

[2]nappy *n, pl* **nappies** [E dial. *nap* bowl, fr. ME, fr. OE *hnæpp;* akin to OHG *hnapf* bowl] **:** a rimless shallow open serving dish

[3]nappy *n, pl* **nappies** [*nap*kin + *-y*] *chiefly Brit* **:** DIAPER 2

[4]nappy *adj* **nap·pi·er; -est** [[3]*nap*] **:** KINKY 1

nap·ra·path \ˈnap-rə-ˌpath\ *n* **:** a practitioner of naprapathy

na·prap·a·thy \nə-ˈprap-ə-thē\ *n* [Czech *naprava* correction + E *-pathy*] **:** a therapeutic system of treatment by manipulation and without use of drugs that is based on a theory that disease symptoms result from disorder in the ligaments and connective tissue

narc *or* **nark** \ˈnärk\ *n* [short for *narcotic agent*] *slang* **:** one (as a government agent) who investigates narcotics violations

nar·cism \ˈnär-ˌsiz-əm\ *n* [G *narcismus*, fr. L *Narcissus*] **:** NARCISSISM — **nar·cist** \-səst\ *n*

nar·cis·sism \ˈnär-sə-ˌsiz-əm\ *n* [G *narzissismus*, fr. *Narziss* Narcissus, fr. L *Narcissus*] **1 :** EGOISM, EGOCENTRISM **2 :** love of or sexual desire for one's own body — **nar·cis·sist** \ˈnär-sə-səst\ *n or adj* — **nar·cis·sis·tic** \ˌnär-sə-ˈsis-tik\ *adj*

nar·cis·sus \när-ˈsis-əs\ *n* [L, fr. Gk *Narkissos*] **1** *cap* **:** a youth of Greek myth caused to pine away for love of his own reflection and transformed into a narcissus **2** *pl* **narcissus** *or* **nar·cis·sus·es** \-ˈsis-ə-səz\ *or* **nar·cis·si** \-ˈsis-ˌī, -(ˌ)ē\ [NL, genus name, fr. L, narcissus, fr. Gk *narkissos*] **:** DAFFODIL; *esp* **:** one whose flowers have a short corona and are usu. borne separately

nar·co \ˈnär-(ˌ)kō\ *n, pl* **narcos** [short for *narcotic agent*] *slang* **:** NARC

nar·co·lep·sy \ˈnär-kə-ˌlep-sē\ *n* [ISV, fr. Gk *narkē*] **:** a condition characterized by brief attacks of deep sleep

[1]nar·co·lep·tic \ˌnär-kə-ˈlep-tik\ *adj* [fr. *narcolepsy*, after such pairs as E *epilepsy: epileptic*] **:** of, relating to, or affected with narcolepsy

[2]narcoleptic *n* **:** one who is subject to attacks of narcolepsy

nar·co·sis \när-ˈkō-səs\ *n, pl* **-co·ses** \-ˌsēz\ [NL, fr. Gk *narkōsis*, action of benumbing, fr. *narkoun*] **:** a state of stupor, unconsciousness, or arrested activity produced by the influence of narcotics or other chemicals

[1]nar·cot·ic \när-ˈkät-ik\ *n* [ME *narkotik*, fr. MF *narcotique*, fr. *narcotique*, adj., fr. ML *narcoticus*, fr. Gk *narkōtikos*, fr. *narkoun* to benumb, fr. *narkē* numbness — more at SNARE] **1 a :** a drug (as opium) that in moderate doses dulls the senses, relieves pain, and induces profound sleep but in excessive doses causes stupor, coma, or convulsions **b :** a drug (as marijuana or LSD) subject to restriction similar to that of addictive narcotics whether in fact physiologically addictive and narcotic or not **2 :** something that soothes, relieves, or lulls

[2]narcotic *adj* **1 a :** having the properties of or yielding a narcotic **b :** inducing mental lethargy **:** SOPORIFEROUS **2 :** of, induced by, or concerned with narcotics **3 :** of, involving, or intended for narcotic addicts — **nar·cot·i·cal·ly** \-i-k(ə-)lē\ *adv*

nar·co·tize \ˈnär-kə-ˌtīz\ *vb* **-tized; -tiz·ing** [ISV] *vt* **1 a :** to treat with or subject to a narcotic **b :** to put into a state of narcosis **2 :** to soothe to unconsciousness or unawareness ~ *vi* **:** to act as a narcotizing agent

nard \ˈnärd\ *n* [ME *narde*, fr. MF or L; MF, fr. L *nardus*, fr. Gk *nardos*, of Sem origin; akin to Heb *nērd* nard] **:** SPIKENARD 1b

na·ris \ˈnar-əs, ˈner-\ *n, pl* **na·res** \ˈna(ə)r-(ˌ)ēz, ˈne(ə)r-\ [L; akin to L *nasus* nose — more at NOSE] **:** the opening of the nose or nasal cavity of a vertebrate

nark \ˈnärk\ *n* [perh. fr. Romany *nak* nose] *Brit* **:** STOOL PIGEON

Nar·ra·gan·set \ˌnar-ə-ˈgan(t)-sət\ *n, pl* **Narraganset** *or* **Narra·gansets 1 :** a member of an Amerindian people of Rhode Island **2 :** an Algonquian language of the Narraganset people

nar·rate \ˈna(ə)r-ˌāt, na-ˈrāt\ *vt* **nar·rat·ed; nar·rat·ing** [L *narratus*, pp. of *narrare*, fr. L *gnarus* knowing; akin to L *gnoscere*, *noscere* to know — more at KNOW] **:** to recite the details of (a story) **:** RELATE — **nar·ra·tor** \ˈna(ə)r-ˌāt-ər; na-ˈrāt-, nə-; ˈnar-ət-\ *n*

nar·ra·tion \na-ˈrā-shən, nə-\ *n* **1 :** the act or process or an instance of narrating **2 :** STORY, NARRATIVE — **nar·ra·tion·al** \-shnəl, -shən-ᵊl\ *adj*

nar·ra·tive \ˈnar-ət-iv\ *n* **1 :** something that is narrated **:** STORY **2 :** the art or practice of narration — **narrative** *adj* — **nar·ra·tive·ly** *adv*

[1]nar·row \ˈnar-(ˌ)ō, -ə(-w)\ *adj* [ME *narowe*, fr. OE *nearu;* akin to OHG *narwa* scar, *snuor* cord, Gk *narnax* box] **1 a :** of slender width **b :** of less than standard width **c** *of a textile* **:** woven in widths less than 18 inches **2 :** limited in size or scope **:** RESTRICTED **3 a :** illiberal in views or disposition **:** PREJUDICED **b** *chiefly dial* **:** STINGY, NIGGARDLY **4 a :** barely sufficient **:** CLOSE **b :** barely successful **5 :** minutely precise **:** METICULOUS **6** *of a ration* **:** relatively rich in protein as compared with carbohydrate and fat **7 :** TENSE 3 — **nar·row·ly** *adv* — **nar·row·ness** *n*

[2]narrow *n* **:** a narrow part or passage; *specif* **:** a strait connecting two bodies of water — usu. used in pl. but sing. or pl. in constr.

[3]narrow *vt* **1 :** to decrease the breadth or extent of **:** CONTRACT **2 :** to decrease the scope or sphere of **:** LIMIT ~ *vi* **:** to lessen in width or extent **:** CONTRACT

nar·row–mind·ed \ˌnar-ō-ˈmīn-dəd, ˌnar-ə-\ *adj* **:** lacking in tolerance or breadth of vision **:** PETTY — **nar·row–mind·ed·ly** *adv* — **nar·row–mind·ed·ness** *n*

nar·thex \ˈnär-ˌtheks\ *n* [LGk *narthēx*, fr. Gk, giant fennel, cane, casket] **1 :** the portico of an ancient church **2 :** a vestibule leading to the nave of a church — see BASILICA illustration

nar·whal *also* **nar·wal** \ˈnär-ˌ(h)wäl, -wəl\ *or* **nar·whale** \-ˌ(h)wāl\ *n* [Norw & Dan *narhval* & Sw *narval*, prob. modif. of Icel *nárhvalur*, fr. ON *nāhvalr*, fr. *nār* corpse + *hvalr* whale; fr. its color] **:** an arctic cetacean (*Monodon monoceros*) about 20 feet long with the male having a long twisted ivory tusk of commercial value

narwhal

nary \ˈna(ə)r-ē, ˈne(ə)r-\ *adj* [alter. of *ne'er a*] *chiefly dial* **:** not one

NAS *abbr* **1** National Academy of Sciences **2** naval air station

nas- *or* **naso-** *also* **nasi-** *comb form* [L *nasus* nose — more at NOSE] **1 :** nose **:** nasal <*naso*scope> <*naso*sinusitis> **2 :** nasal and <*naso*labial>

NASA \ˈnas-ə\ *abbr* National Aeronautics and Space Administration

[1]na·sal \ˈnā-zəl\ *n* [MF, fr. OF, fr. *nes* nose, fr. L *nasus*] **1 :** the nosepiece of a helmet **2 :** a nasal part **3 :** a nasal consonant or vowel

[2]nasal *adj* **1 :** of or relating to the nose **2 a :** uttered through the nose with the mouth passage occluded (as with English *m, n, ng*) **b :** uttered with the mouth open, the soft palate lowered, and the nose passage producing a phonemically essential resonance (as of a vowel in French) or a phonemically nonessential resonance (as of a vowel in English) **c :** characterized by resonance produced through the nose **3** *of a musical tone* **:** SHARP, PENETRATING — **na·sal·i·ty** \nā-ˈzal-ət-ē\ *n* — **na·sal·ly** \ˈnāz-(ə-)lē\ *adv*

na·sal·ize \ˈnā-zə-ˌlīz\ *vb* **-ized; -iz·ing** *vt* **:** to make nasal ~ *vi* **:** to speak in a nasal manner — **na·sal·iza·tion** \ˌnā-zə-lə-ˈzā-shən\ *n*

NASCAR *abbr* National Association of Stock Car Auto Racing

na·scence \ˈnas-ᵊn(t)s, ˈnās-\ *n* **:** NASCENCY

na·scen·cy \-ᵊn-sē\ *n, pl* **-cies :** BIRTH, ORIGIN

na·scent \ˈnas-ᵊnt, ˈnās-\ *adj* [L *nascent-*, *nascens*, prp. of *nasci* to be born — more at NATION] **:** coming or having recently come into existence **:** beginning to develop

NASD *abbr* National Association of Security Dealers

na·so·pha·ryn·geal \ˌnā-zō-fə-ˈrin-j(ē-)əl, -ˌfar-ən-ˈjē-əl\ *adj* **:** of or relating to the nose and pharynx or the nasopharynx

na·so·phar·ynx \-ˈfar-iŋ(k)s\ *n* [NL] **:** the upper part of the pharynx continuous with the nasal passages

nas·tic \ˈnas-tik\ *adj* [Gk *nastos* close-pressed, fr. *nassein* to press] **:** of, relating to, or constituting a movement of a plant part caused by disproportionate growth or increase of turgor in one surface

na·stur·tium \nə-ˈstər-shəm, na-\ *n* [L, a cress] **:** any of a genus (*Tropaeolum* of the family Tropaeolaceae, the nasturtium family) of herbs with showy spurred flowers and pungent seeds; *esp* **:** either of two widely cultivated ornamentals (*T. majus* and *T. minus*)

nas·ty \ˈnas-tē\ *adj* **nastier; -est** [ME] **1 a :** disgustingly filthy **b :** physically repugnant **2 :** INDECENT, OBSCENE **3 :** MEAN, TAWDRY **4 a :** extremely hazardous or harmful <had a ~ climb to reach the summit> **b :** sharply unpleasant **:** DISAGREEABLE <~ weather> **5 a :** difficult to understand or deal with **:** VEXATIOUS <a ~ problem> **b :** psychologically unsettling **:** TRYING <faced with a ~ fear that she was lost> **6 :** lacking in courtesy or sportsmanship **:** SPITEFUL ***syn*** see DIRTY — **nas·ti·ly** \-tə-lē\ *adv* — **nas·ti·ness** \-tē-nəs\ *n*

-nas·ty \ˌnas-tē\ *n comb form* [G *-nastie*, fr. Gk *nastos*] **:** nastic movement of a plant part <epi*nasty*>

nat *abbr* **1** national **2** native **3** natural

na·tal \ˈnāt-ᵊl\ *adj* [ME, fr. L *natalis*, fr. *natus*, pp. of *nasci* to be born — more at NATION] **1 :** NATIVE **2 :** of, relating to, or present at birth; *esp* **:** associated with one's birth <a ~ star>

na·tal·i·ty \nā-ˈtal-ət-ē, nə-\ *n, pl* **-ties :** BIRTHRATE

na·tant \ˈnāt-ᵊnt\ *adj* [L *natant-*, *natans*, prp. of *natare* to swim; akin to L *nare* to swim — more at NOURISH] **:** swimming or floating in water <~ decapods>

na·ta·tion \nā-ˈtā-shən, na-\ *n* **:** the action or art of swimming

na·ta·to·ri·al \ˌnāt-ə-ˈtōr-ē-əl, ˌnat-, -ˈtȯr-\ *or* **na·ta·to·ry** \ˈnāt-ə-ˌtōr-ē, ˈnat-, -ˌtȯr-\ *adj* **1 :** of or relating to swimming **2 :** adapted to or characterized by swimming <a ~ leg of an aquatic insect>

na·ta·to·ri·um \ˌnāt-ə-ˈtōr-ē-əm, ˌnat-, -ˈtȯr-\ *n* [LL, fr. L *natatus*, pp. of *natare*] **:** an indoor swimming pool

NATE *abbr* National Association of Teachers of English
na·tes \'nā-ˌtēz\ *n pl* [L, pl. of *natis* buttock; akin to Gk *nōtos, nōton* back] **:** BUTTOCKS
nathe·less \'nāth-ləs\ *or* **nath·less** \'nath-\ *adv* [ME, fr. OE *nā thē lǣs* not the less] *archaic* **:** NEVERTHELESS, NOTWITHSTANDING
Na·tick \'nāt-ik\ *n* **:** a dialect of Massachuset
na·tion \'nā-shən\ *n* [ME *nacioun,* fr. MF *nation,* fr. L *nation-, natio* birth, race, nation, fr. *natus,* pp. of *nasci* to be born; akin to L *gignere* to beget — more at KIN] **1 a (1) :** NATIONALITY 5a **(2) :** a politically organized nationality **(3) :** a non-Jewish nationality <why do the ~*s* conspire —Ps 2:1 (RSV)> **b :** a community of people composed of one or more nationalities and possessing a more or less defined territory and government **c :** a territorial division containing a body of people of one or more nationalities and usu. characterized by relatively large size and independent status **2** *archaic* **:** GROUP, AGGREGATION **3 :** a tribe or federation of tribes (as of American Indians)
[1]**na·tion·al** \'nash-nəl, -ən-ᵊl\ *adj* **1 :** of or relating to a nation **2 :** NATIONALIST **3 :** comprising or characteristic of a nationality **4 :** belonging to or maintained by the federal government **5 :** of, relating to, or being a coalition government formed by most or all major political parties usu. in a crisis — **na·tion·al·ly** \-ē\ *adv*
[2]**national** *n* **1 :** one that owes allegiance to or is under the protection of a nation without regard to the more formal status of citizen or subject **2 :** a competition that is national in scope — usu. used in pl. ***syn*** see CITIZEN
national bank *n* **1 :** a bank associated with the finances of a nation **2 :** a bank operating under federal charter and supervision
national forest *n* **:** a usu. forested area of considerable extent that is preserved by government decree from private exploitation and is harvested only under supervision
National Guard *n* **:** a militia force recruited by each state, equipped by the federal government, and jointly maintained subject to the call of either
national income *n* **:** the aggregate of earnings from a nation's current production including compensation of employees, interest, rental income, and profits of business after taxes
na·tion·al·ism \'nash-nəl-ˌiz-əm, -ən-ᵊl-\ *n* **:** loyalty and devotion to a nation; *esp* **:** a sense of national consciousness exalting one nation above all others and placing primary emphasis on promotion of its culture and interests as opposed to those of other nations or supranational groups
[1]**na·tion·al·ist** \-əst\ *n* **1 :** an advocate of or believer in nationalism **2** *cap* **:** a member of a political party or group advocating national independence or strong national government
[2]**nationalist** *adj* **1 :** of, relating to, or advocating nationalism **2** *cap* **:** of, relating to, or being a political group advocating or associated with nationalism
na·tion·al·is·tic \ˌnash-nəl-'is-tik, -ən-ᵊl-\ *adj* **1 :** of, favoring, or characterized by nationalism <~ election speeches> **2 :** NATIONAL 1 — **na·tion·al·is·ti·cal·ly** \-ti-k(ə-)lē\ *adv*
na·tion·al·i·ty \ˌnash-(ə-)'nal-ət-ē\ *n, pl* **-ties 1 :** national character **2 :** NATIONALISM **3 a :** national status; *specif* **:** a legal relationship involving allegiance on the part of an individual and usu. protection on the part of the state **b :** membership in a particular nation **4 :** political independence or existence as a separate nation **5 a :** a people having a common origin, tradition, and language and capable of forming or actually constituting a nation-state **b :** an ethnic group constituting one element of a larger unit (as a nation)
na·tion·al·ize \'nash-nəl-ˌīz, -ən-ᵊl-\ *vt* **-ized; -iz·ing 1 :** to give a national character to **2 :** to invest control or ownership of in the national government — **na·tion·al·iza·tion** \ˌnash-nəl-ə-'zā-shən, -ən-ᵊl-\ *n* — **na·tion·al·iz·er** \'nash-nəl-ˌī-zər, -ən-ᵊl-\ *n*
national monument *n* **:** a place of historic, scenic, or scientific interest set aside for preservation usu. by presidential proclamation
national park *n* **:** an area of special scenic, historical, or scientific importance set aside and maintained by a national government and in the U.S. by an act of Congress
national product *n* **:** the value of the goods and services produced in a nation during a year
national seashore *n* **:** a recreational area adjacent to a seacoast and maintained by the federal government
national socialism *n* **:** NAZISM — **national socialist** *adj*
na·tion·hood \'nā-shən-ˌhu̇d\ *n* **:** NATIONALITY 1, 3a, 4
na·tion–state \'nā-shən-'stāt, -ˌstāt\ *n* **:** a form of political organization under which a relatively homogeneous people inhabits a sovereign state; *esp* **:** a state containing one as opposed to several nationalities
na·tion·wide \ˌnā-shən-'wīd\ *adj* **:** extending throughout a nation
[1]**na·tive** \'nāt-iv\ *adj* [ME *natif,* fr. MF, fr. L *nativus,* fr. *natus,* pp. of *nasci* to be born — more at NATION] **1 :** INBORN, INNATE <~ talents> **2 :** belonging to a particular place by birth <~ to Wisconsin> **3** *archaic* **:** closely related **4 :** belonging to or associated with one by birth **5 :** NATURAL, NORMAL **6 a :** grown, produced, or originating in a particular place or in the vicinity **:** LOCAL **b :** living or growing naturally in a particular region **:** INDIGENOUS **7 :** SIMPLE, UNAFFECTED **8 a :** constituting the original substance or source **b :** found in nature esp. in an unadulterated form <mining ~ silver> **9** *chiefly Austral* **:** having a usu. superficial resemblance to a specified English plant or animal — **na·tive·ly** *adv* — **na·tive·ness** *n*
syn NATIVE, INDIGENOUS, ENDEMIC, ABORIGINAL *shared meaning element* **:** belonging to a locality ***ant*** alien, foreign
[2]**native** *n* **1 :** one born or reared in a particular place **2 a :** an original or indigenous inhabitant **b :** something indigenous to a particular locality **3 :** a local resident; *esp* **:** a person who has lived all his life in a place as distinguished from a visitor or a temporary resident
na·tiv·ism \'nāt-iv-ˌiz-əm\ *n* **1 :** a policy of favoring native inhabitants as opposed to immigrants **2 :** the revival or perpetuation of an indigenous culture esp. in opposition to acculturation — **na·tiv·ist** \-əst\ *n or adj* — **na·tiv·is·tic** \ˌnāt-iv-'is-tik\ *adj*
na·tiv·i·ty \nə-'tiv-ət-ē, nā-\ *n, pl* **-ties** [ME *nativite,* fr. MF *nativité,* fr. ML *nativitat-, nativitas,* fr. LL, birth, fr. L *nativus*] **1 :** the process or circumstances of being born **:** BIRTH; *specif, cap* **:** the birth of Jesus **2 :** a horoscope at or of the time of one's birth **3 :** the place of origin
natl *abbr* national
NATO \'nāt-(ˌ)ō\ *abbr* North Atlantic Treaty Organization
na·tri·ure·sis \ˌnā-trē-yu̇-'rē-səs\ *n* [NL, fr. *natrium* sodium (fr. ISV *natron*) + *uresis* urination, fr. Gk *ourēsis,* fr. *ourein* to urinate — more at URINE] **:** excessive loss of cations and esp. sodium in the urine — **na·tri·uret·ic** \-'ret-ik\ *adj*
na·tro·lite \'nā-trə-ˌlīt\ *n* [G *natrolith,* fr. *natron* (fr. F) + *-lith* -lite] **:** a hydrous sodium aluminum silicate $Na_2Al_2Si_3O_{10}.2H_2O$ related to zeolite
na·tron \'nā-ˌträn, -trən\ *n* [F, fr. Sp *natrón,* fr. Ar *natrūn,* fr. Gk *nitron*] **:** a hydrated native sodium carbonate $Na_2CO_3.10H_2O$ used in ancient times in embalming, in ceramic pastes, and as a cleansing agent
nat·ter \'nat-ər\ *vi* [prob. imit.] *chiefly Brit* **:** CHATTER
nat·ty \'nat-ē\ *adj* **nat·ti·er; -est** [perh. alter. of earlier *netty,* fr. obs. *net* neat, clean] **:** trimly neat and tidy **:** SMART — **nat·ti·ly** \'nat-ᵊl-ē\ *adv* — **nat·ti·ness** \'nat-ē-nəs\ *n*
[1]**nat·u·ral** \'nach-(ə-)rəl\ *adj* [ME, fr. MF, fr. L *naturalis* of nature, fr. *natura* nature] **1 :** based on an inherent sense of right and wrong <~ justice> **2 a :** being in accordance with or determined by nature **b :** having or constituting a classification based on features existing in nature **3 a (1) :** begotten as distinguished from adopted; *also* **:** LEGITIMATE **(2) :** being a relation by actual consanguinity as distinguished from adoption <~ parents> **b :** ILLEGITIMATE <a ~ child> **4 :** having an essential relation with someone or something **:** following from the nature of the one in question <his guilt is a ~ deduction from the evidence> **5 :** implanted or being as if implanted by nature **:** seemingly inborn <a ~ talent for art> **6 :** of or relating to nature as an object of study and research **7 :** having a specified character by nature <a ~ athlete> **8 a :** occurring in conformity with the ordinary course of nature **:** not marvelous or supernatural <~ causes> **b :** developed by human reason alone rather than revelation <~ religion> **c :** having a normal or usual character <events followed their ~ course> **9 :** possessing or exhibiting the higher qualities (as kindliness and affection) of human nature <a noble . . . brother . . . ever most kind and ~ —Shak.> **10 a :** growing without human care; *also* **:** not cultivated <~ prairie unbroken by the plow> **b :** existing in or produced by nature <~ scenery> <~ curiosities> **11 a :** being in a state of nature without spiritual enlightenment **:** UNREGENERATE <~ man> **b :** living in or as if in a state of nature untouched by the influences of civilization and society **12 a :** having a physical or real existence as contrasted with one that is spiritual, intellectual, or fictitious <a corporation is a legal but not a ~ person> **b :** of, relating to, or operating in the physical as opposed to the spiritual world <~ laws describe phenomena of the physical universe> **13 a :** closely resembling an original **:** true to nature **b :** marked by easy simplicity and freedom from artificiality, affectation, or constraint **c :** having a form or appearance found in nature **14 a :** having neither flats nor sharps <the ~ scale of C major> **b :** being neither sharp nor flat **c :** having the pitch modified by the natural sign — **nat·u·ral·ness** \-(ə-)rəl-nəs\ *n*
syn* 1** see REGULAR ***ant unnatural, artificial
2 NATURAL, INGENUOUS, NAIVE, UNSOPHISTICATED, ARTLESS *shared meaning element* **:** free from pretension or calculation. NATURAL at once implies freedom from all artificiality and constraint and an easy spontaneity that suggests nature rather than art <set him to write poetry, he is limited, artificial, and impotent; set him to write prose, he is free, *natural,* and effective — Matthew Arnold> INGENUOUS stresses inability to hide one's thoughts and feelings and usually suggests candidness and lack of reserve, often with a hint of childlike simplicity <how deliciously *ingenuous* she was, both in her confidences and in her reservations —Victoria Sackville-West> NAIVE is likely to stress lack of worldly wisdom <he claimed to himself to be innocent or *naive,* but his pretense was the thinnest —John Cheever> and may further suggest incapacity for enlightenment <that *naive* patriotism which leads every race to regard itself as evidently superior to every other —J. W. Krutch> UNSOPHISTICATED also stresses lack of worldly wisdom but tends to suggest lack of experience and training as its source <she's not the type of the moment, not elegant or artificial, too much the *unsophisticated* child of nature —Rose Macaulay> ARTLESS lays stress on the absence of design and suggests a naturalness resulting from unawareness of the effect one is producing <moving with *artless* grace>
[2]**natural** *n* **1 :** one born without the usual powers of reason and understanding **2 a :** a sign placed on any degree of the musical staff to nullify the effect of a preceding sharp or flat **b :** a note or tone affected by the natural sign **3 :** a result or combination that immediately wins the stake in a game; *specif* **:** a throw of 7 or 11 on the first cast in craps **4 a :** one having natural skills, talents, or abilities **b :** something that is likely to become an immediate success **c :** one that is obviously suitable for a specific purpose **5 :** AFRO ***syn*** see FOOL

natural 2a

natural gas *n* **:** gas issuing from the earth's crust through natural openings or bored wells; *esp* **:** a combustible mixture of methane and higher hydrocarbons used chiefly as a fuel and raw material
natural history *n* **1 :** a treatise on some aspect of nature **2**

ə abut ᵊ kitten ər further a back ā bake ä cot, cart
au̇ out ch chin e less ē easy g gift i trip ī life
j joke ŋ sing ō flow ȯ flaw ȯi coin th thin t͟h this
ü loot u̇ foot y yet yü few yu̇ furious zh vision

: the natural development of something (as an organism or disease) over a period of time **3 :** the study of natural objects esp. in the field from an amateur or popular point of view

nat·u·ral·ism \ˈnach-(ə-)rə-ˌliz-əm\ *n* **1 :** action, inclination, or thought based only on natural desires and instincts **2 :** a theory denying that an event or object has a supernatural significance; *specif* **:** the doctrine that scientific laws are adequate to account for all phenomena **3 :** realism in art or literature; *specif* **:** a theory in literature emphasizing scientific observation of life without idealization or the avoidance of the ugly

[1]**nat·u·ral·ist** \-ləst\ *n* **1 :** one that advocates or practices naturalism **2 :** a student of natural history; *esp* **:** a field biologist

[2]**naturalist** *or* **nat·u·ral·is·tic** \ˌnach-(ə-)rə-ˈlis-tik\ *adj* **:** of, characterized by, or according with naturalism — **nat·u·ral·is·ti·cal·ly** \-ti-k(ə-)lē\ *adv*

nat·u·ral·ize \ˈnach-(ə-)rə-ˌlīz\ *vb* **-ized; -iz·ing** *vt* **1 a :** to introduce into common use or into the vernacular **b :** to cause (as a plant) to become established as if native **2 :** to bring into conformity with nature **3 :** to confer the rights of a national on; *esp* **:** to admit to citizenship ~ *vi* **:** to become established as if native — **nat·u·ral·iza·tion** \ˌnach-(ə-)rə-lə-ˈzā-shən\ *n*

natural law *n* **:** a body of law or a specific principle held to be derived from nature and binding upon human society in the absence of or in addition to positive law

natural logarithm *n* **:** a logarithm with *e* as a base

nat·u·ral·ly \ˈnach-(ə-)rə-lē, ˈnach-ər-lē\ *adv* **1 :** by nature **:** by natural character or ability <~ timid> **2 :** according to the usual course of things **:** as might be expected <we ~ dislike being hurt> **3 a :** without artificial aid <hair that curls ~> **b :** without affectation <speak ~> **4 :** with truth to nature **:** REALISTICALLY

natural number *n* **:** the number 1 or any number (as 3, 12, 432) obtained by repeatedly adding 1 to this number

natural philosophy *n* **:** NATURAL SCIENCE; *esp* **:** PHYSICAL SCIENCE — **natural philosopher** *n*

natural resources *n pl* **:** industrial materials and capacities (as mineral deposits and waterpower) supplied by nature

natural right *n* **:** a right based upon natural law

natural science *n* **:** any of the sciences (as physics, chemistry, or biology) that deal with matter, energy, and their interrelations and transformations or with objectively measurable phenomena — **natural scientist** *n*

natural selection *n* **:** a natural process that tends to cause the survival of individuals or groups best adjusted to the conditions under which they live and that is equally important for the perpetuation of desirable genetic qualities and for the elimination of undesirable ones as these are produced by genic recombination or mutation

natural theology *n* **:** theology deriving its knowledge of God from the study of nature independent of special revelation

na·ture \ˈnā-chər\ *n* [ME, fr. MF, fr. L *natura,* fr. *natus,* pp. of *nasci* to be born — more at NATION] **1 a :** the inherent character or basic constitution of a person or thing **:** ESSENCE **b :** DISPOSITION, TEMPERAMENT **2 a :** a creative and controlling force in the universe **b :** an inner force or the sum of such forces in an individual **3 :** a kind or class usu. distinguished by fundamental or essential characteristics <documents of a confidential ~> <acts of a ceremonial ~> **4 :** the physical constitution or drives of an organism; *esp* **:** an excretory organ or function — usu. used in the phrase *call of nature* **5 :** a spontaneous attitude (as of generosity) **6 :** the external world in its entirety **7 a :** a man's original or natural condition **b :** a simplified mode of life resembling this condition **8 :** natural scenery ***syn*** see TYPE

na·tu·ro·path \ˈnā-chə-rə-ˌpath, nə-ˈt(y)u̇r-ə-\ *n* [back-formation fr. *naturopathy*] **:** a practitioner of naturopathy

na·tu·rop·a·thy \ˌnā-chə-ˈräp-ə-thē\ *n* [*nature* + *-o-* + *-pathy*] **:** a system of treatment of disease emphasizing assistance to nature and including the use of natural medicinal substances and physical means (as manipulation and electrical treatment) — **na·tu·ro·path·ic** \ˌnā-chə-rə-ˈpath-ik, nə-ˌt(y)ür-ə-\ *adj*

[1]**naught** \ˈnȯt, ˈnät\ *pron* [ME, fr. OE *nāwiht,* fr. *nā* no + *wiht* creature, thing — more at NO, WIGHT] **:** NOTHING

[2]**naught** *n* **1 a :** NOTHING <his efforts had gone for ~> **b :** NOTHINGNESS, NONEXISTENCE **2 :** the arithmetical symbol 0 **:** ZERO, CIPHER

[3]**naught** *adj* **:** of no importance **:** INSIGNIFICANT

naugh·ty \ˈnȯt-ē, ˈnät-\ *adj* **naugh·ti·er; -est** [[2]*naught*] **1 a** *archaic* **:** vicious in moral character **:** WICKED **b :** guilty of disobedience or misbehavior **2 :** lacking in taste or propriety ***syn*** see BAD — **naugh·ti·ly** \ˈnȯt-ᵊl-ē, ˈnät-\ *adv* — **naugh·ti·ness** \ˈnȯt-ē-nəs, ˈnät-\ *n*

nau·ma·chia \nȯ-ˈmāk-ē-ə, -ˈmak-\ *n, pl* **-chi·ae** \-ē-ˌē, -ē-ˌī\ *or* **-chi·as** [L, fr. Gk, naval battle, fr. *naus* ship + *machesthai* to fight — more at NAVE] **1 :** an ancient Roman spectacle representing a naval battle **2 :** a place for naumachiae

nau·pli·us \ˈnȯ-plē-əs\ *n, pl* **-plii** \-plē-ˌī, -ˌē\ [NL, fr. L, a shellfish, fr. Gk *nauplios*] **:** a crustacean larva in usu. the first stage after leaving the egg and with three pairs of appendages, a median eye, and little or no segmentation

nau·sea \ˈnȯ-zē-ə, -shə, -sē-ə, -zhə\ *n* [L, seasickness, nausea, fr. Gk *nautia, nausia,* fr. *nautēs* sailor] **1 :** a stomach distress with distaste for food and an urge to vomit **2 :** extreme disgust — **nau·se·ant** \-z(h)ē-ənt, -s(h)ē-\ *n or adj*

nau·se·ate \ˈnȯ-z(h)ē-ˌāt, -s(h)ē-\ *vb* **-at·ed; -at·ing** *vi* **1 :** to become affected with nausea **2 :** to feel disgust ~ *vt* **:** to affect with nausea or disgust — **nau·se·at·ing·ly** \-iŋ-lē\ *adv*

nau·seous \ˈnȯ-shəs, ˈnȯ-zē-əs\ *adj* **1 :** causing nausea **:** SICKENING **2 :** affected with nausea or disgust — **nau·seous·ly** *adv* — **nau·seous·ness** *n*

naut *abbr* nautical

nautch \ˈnȯch\ *n* [Hindi *nāc,* fr. Skt *nṛtya,* fr. *nṛtyati* he dances] **:** an entertainment in India consisting chiefly of dancing by professional dancing girls

nau·ti·cal \ˈnȯt-i-kəl, ˈnät-\ *adj* [L *nauticus,* fr. Gk *nautikos,* fr. *nautēs* sailor, fr. *naus* ship — more at NAVE] **:** of, relating to, or associated with seamen, navigation, or ships — **nau·ti·cal·ly** \-k(ə-)lē\ *adv*

nautical mile *n* **:** any of various units of distance used for sea and air navigation based on the length of a minute of arc of a great circle of the earth and differing because the earth is not a perfect sphere: as **a :** a British unit equal to 6080 feet or 1853.2 meters — called also *Admiralty mile* **b :** a U.S. unit no longer in official use equal to 6080.20 feet or 1853.248 meters **c :** an international unit equal to 6076.115 feet or 1852 meters used officially in the U.S. since July 1, 1959

nau·ti·loid \ˈnȯt-ᵊl-ˌȯid, ˈnät-\ *n* **:** any of a group (Nautiloidea) of cephalopods that were important in the Ordovician and esp. the Silurian but are represented in the recent fauna only by the nautiluses — **nautiloid** *adj*

nau·ti·lus \ˈnȯt-ᵊl-əs, ˈnät-\ *n, pl* **-lus·es** *or* **-li** \-ᵊl-ˌī, -ˌē\ [NL, genus name, fr. L, paper nautilus, fr. Gk *nautilos,* lit., sailor, fr. *naus* ship] **1 :** any of a genus (*Nautilus*) of cephalopod mollusks of the So. Pacific and Indian oceans with a spiral chambered shell that is pearly on the inside **2 :** PAPER NAUTILUS

nautilus 1

nav *abbr* **1** naval **2** navigable; navigation

Na·va·ho *or* **Na·va·jo** \ˈnav-ə-ˌhō, ˈnäv-\ *n, pl* **Navaho** *or* **Navahos** *or* **Navajo** *or* **Navajos** [Sp (*Apache de*) *Navajó,* lit., Apache of Navajó, fr. *Navajó,* a pueblo] **1 :** a member of an Amerindian people of northern New Mexico and Arizona **2 :** the language of the Navaho people

nav·aid \ˈnav-ˌād\ *n* [*navigation aid*] **:** a device or system (as a radar beacon) that provides a navigator with navigational data

na·val \ˈnā-vəl\ *adj* [L *navalis,* fr. *navis* ship] **1** *obs* **:** of or relating to ships or shipping **2 a :** of or relating to a navy **b :** consisting of or involving warships

naval architect *n* **:** one whose profession is the designing of ships

naval stores *n pl* [fr. their former use in the construction and maintenance of wooden sailing vessels] **:** products (as turpentine, pitch, and rosin) obtained from resinous conifers and esp. pines

[1]**nave** \ˈnāv\ *n* [ME, fr. OE *nafu;* akin to OE *nafela* navel] **:** the hub of a wheel

[2]**nave** *n* [ML *navis,* fr. L, ship; akin to OE *nōwend* sailor, Gk *naus* ship, Skt *nau*] **:** the main part of the interior of a church; *esp* **:** the long narrow central hall in a cruciform church that rises higher than the aisles flanking it to form a clerestory — see BASILICA illustration

na·vel \ˈnā-vəl\ *n* [ME, fr. OE *nafela;* akin to OHG *nabalo* navel, L *umbilicus,* Gk *omphalos*] **1 :** a depression in the middle of the abdomen that marks the point of former attachment of the umbilical cord or yolk stalk **2 :** the central point **:** MIDDLE

navel orange *n* **:** a seedless orange having a pit at the apex where the fruit encloses a small secondary fruit — called also *navel*

[1]**na·vic·u·lar** \nə-ˈvik-yə-lər\ *adj* [L *navicula* boat, dim. of *navis*] **:** shaped like a boat <a ~ bone>

[2]**navicular** *n* [NL *(os) naviculare* navicular bone] **:** a navicular bone; *esp* **:** one situated at the medial side of the tarsus

nav·i·ga·ble \ˈnav-i-gə-bəl\ *adj* **1 :** deep enough and wide enough to afford passage to ships **2 :** capable of being steered — **nav·i·ga·bil·i·ty** \ˌnav-i-gə-ˈbil-ət-ē\ *n* — **nav·i·ga·ble·ness** \ˈnav-i-gə-bəl-nəs\ *n* — **nav·i·ga·bly** \-blē\ *adv*

nav·i·gate \ˈnav-ə-ˌgāt\ *vb* **-gat·ed; -gat·ing** [L *navigatus,* pp. of *navigare,* fr. *navis* ship + *-igare* (fr. *agere* to drive) — more at AGENT] *vi* **1 :** to travel by water **:** SAIL **2 :** to steer a course through a medium; *specif* **:** to operate an airplane **3 :** to get about **:** WALK <well enough to ~ under his own power> ~ *vt* **1 a :** to sail over, on, or through **b :** to make one's way over or through **:** TRAVERSE **2 a :** to steer or manage (a boat) in sailing **b :** to operate or control the course of (as an airplane)

nav·i·ga·tion \ˌnav-ə-ˈgā-shən\ *n* **1 :** the act or practice of navigating **2 :** the science of getting ships, aircraft, or spacecraft from place to place; *esp* **:** the method of determining position, course, and distance traveled **3 :** ship traffic or commerce — **nav·i·ga·tion·al** \-shnəl, -shən-ᵊl\ *adj* — **nav·i·ga·tion·al·ly** \-ē\ *adv*

nav·i·ga·tor \ˈnav-ə-ˌgāt-ər\ *n* **:** one that navigates or is qualified to navigate

nav·vy \ˈnav-ē\ *n, pl* **navvies** [by shortening & alter. fr. *navigator* (construction worker on a canal, navvy)] *Brit* **:** an unskilled laborer

na·vy \ˈnā-vē\ *n, pl* **navies** [ME *navie,* fr. MF, fr. L *navigia* ships, fr. *navigare*] **1 :** a group of ships **:** FLEET **2 :** a nation's ships of war and of logistic support **3** *often cap* **:** the complete naval establishment of a nation including yards, stations, ships, and personnel **4 :** a variable color averaging a grayish purplish blue

navy bean *n* **:** a white-seeded kidney bean grown esp. for its nutritious seeds

Navy Cross *n* **:** a U.S. Navy decoration awarded for extraordinary heroism in operations against an armed enemy

navy exchange *n* **:** a post exchange at a naval installation

navy yard *n* **:** a yard where naval vessels are built or repaired

na·wab \nə-ˈwäb\ *n* [Hindi & Urdu *nawwāb*] **:** NABOB 1

[1]**nay** \ˈnā\ *adv* [ME, fr. ON *nei,* fr. *ne* not + *ei* ever — more at AYE] **1 :** NO **2 :** not merely this but also **:** not only so but <the letter made him happy, ~, ecstatic>

[2]**nay** *n* **1 :** DENIAL, REFUSAL **2 a :** a negative reply or vote **b :** one who votes no

Naz·a·rene \ˌnaz-ə-ˈrēn\ *n* [ME *Nazaren,* fr. LL *Nazarenus,* fr. Gk *Nazarēnos,* fr. *Nazareth*] **1 :** a native or resident of Nazareth **2 a :** CHRISTIAN 1a **b :** a member of the Church of the Nazarene that is a Protestant denomination deriving from the merging of three holiness groups, stressing sanctification, and following Methodist polity

na·zi \ˈnät-sē, ˈnat-\ *n* [G, by shortening & alter. fr. *nationalsozialist,* fr. *national* + *sozialist* socialist] **1** *cap* **:** a member of a German fascist party controlling Germany from 1933 to 1945 under Adolf Hitler **2** *often cap* **:** one held to resemble a German Nazi — **nazi**

adj, often cap — **na·zi·fi·ca·tion** \ˌnät-si-fə-ˈkā-shən, ˌnat-\ n, often cap — **na·zi·fy** \ˈnät-si-ˌfī, ˈnat-\ vt, often cap

Naz·i·rite or **Naz·a·rite** \ˈnaz-ə-ˌrīt\ n [LL *nazaraeus,* fr. Gk *naziraios, nazaraios,* fr. Heb *nāzīr,* lit., consecrated] : a Jew of biblical times consecrated to God by a vow to avoid drinking wine, cutting the hair, and being defiled by the presence of a corpse — **Naz·i·rit·ism** \-ˌrīt-ˌiz-əm\ n

Na·zism \ˈnät-ˌsiz-əm, ˈnat-\ or **Na·zi·ism** \-sē-ˌiz-əm\ n [*Nazi* + *-ism*] : the body of political and economic doctrines held and put into effect by the National Socialist German Workers' party in the Third German Reich including the totalitarian principle of government, state control of all industry, predominance of groups assumed to be racially superior, and supremacy of the führer

Nb *symbol* niobium

NB *abbr* 1 New Brunswick 2 northbound 3 nota bene

NBA *abbr* 1 National Basketball Association 2 National Boxing Association

NBC *abbr* National Broadcasting Company

NBS *abbr* National Bureau of Standards

NC *abbr* 1 no charge 2 no credit 3 North Carolina 4 nurse corps

NCAA *abbr* National Collegiate Athletic Association

NCC *abbr* National Council of Churches

NCCJ *abbr* National Conference of Christians and Jews

NCCM *abbr* National Council of Catholic Men

NCCW *abbr* National Council of Catholic Women

NCE *abbr* New Catholic Edition

NCO \ˌen-ˌsē-ˈō\ n : NONCOMMISSIONED OFFICER

NCTE *abbr* National Council of Teachers of English

NCTM *abbr* National Council of Teachers of Mathematics

NCV *abbr* no commercial value

Nd *symbol* neodymium

ND *abbr* 1 no date 2 North Dakota

N Dak *abbr* North Dakota

NDEA *abbr* National Defense Education Act

Ne *symbol* neon

NE *abbr* 1 Nebraska 2 New England 3 no effects 4 northeast

ne- or **neo-** *comb form* [Gk, fr. *neos* new — more at NEW] **1 a** : new : recent <*Neo*cene> **b** : new and different period or form of <*Neo*platonism> : in a new and different form or manner <*Neo*platonic> **c** : New World <*Neo*tropical> **d** : new and abnormal <*neo*plasm> **2** : new chemical compound isomeric with or otherwise related to (such) a compound <*neo*arsphenamine>

NEA *abbr* National Education Association

Ne·an·der·thal \nē-ˈan-dər-ˌt(h)ȯl, nā-ˈän-dər-ˌtäl\ adj **1** : being, relating to, or resembling Neanderthal man **2** : suggesting a caveman in appearance or behavior — **Neanderthal** n

Neanderthal man n [*Neanderthal,* valley in western Germany] : a Middle Paleolithic man (*Homo neanderthalensis*) known from skeletal remains in Europe, northern Africa, and western Asia — **Ne·an·der·thal·oid** \-ˌȯid\ adj or n

[1]**neap** \ˈnēp\ adj [ME *neep,* fr. OE *nēp* being at the stage of neap tide] : of, relating to, or constituting a neap tide

[2]**neap** n : NEAP TIDE

Ne·a·pol·i·tan \ˌnē-ə-ˈpäl-ət-ᵊn\ n [L *neapolitanus* of Naples, fr. Gk *neapolitēs* citizen of Naples, fr. *Neapolis* Naples] : a native or inhabitant of Naples, Italy — **Neapolitan** adj

Neapolitan ice cream n : a brick of from two to four layers of ice cream of different flavors

neap tide n : a tide of minimum range occurring at the first and the third quarters of the moon

[1]**near** \ˈni(ə)r\ adv [ME *ner,* partly fr. *ner* nearer, fr. OE *nēar,* comparative of *nēah* nigh; partly fr. ON *nær* nearer, compar. of *nā-nigh* — more at NIGH] **1** : at, within, or to a short distance or time **2** : ALMOST, NEARLY <~ dead> **3** : in a close or intimate manner <~ related> **4** *archaic* : in a frugal manner

[2]**near** \(ˈ)ni(ə)r\ prep : close to

[3]**near** \ˈni(ə)r\ adj **1** : closely related or intimately associated **2 a** : not far distant in time, place, or degree <in the ~ future> **b** : barely avoided **c** : CLOSE, NARROW <a ~ miss> **3 a** : being the closer of two <the ~ side> **b** : being the left-hand one of a pair <the ~ wheel of a cart> **4** : DIRECT, SHORT <the ~*est* road> **5** : CLOSEFISTED, STINGY **6 a** : closely resembling a prototype **b** : approximating the genuine <~ silk> — **near·ness** n

[4]**near** \ˈni(ə)r\ vb : APPROACH

near beer n : any of various malt liquors that are considered non-alcoholic because they contain less than a specified percentage of alcohol

near·by \ni(ə)r-ˈbī, ˈni(ə)r-ˌ\ adv or adj : close at hand

Ne·arc·tic \(ˈ)nē-ˈärk-tik, -ˈärt-ik\ adj : of, relating to, or being the biogeographic subregion that includes Greenland, arctic America, and the parts of No. America north of tropical Mexico

near gale n : MODERATE GALE — see BEAUFORT SCALE table

nearly adv **1** : in a close manner or relationship <~ related> **2** : almost but not quite <~ identical> <~ a year later>

near point n : the point nearest the eye at which an object is accurately focused on the retina at full accommodation

near·sight·ed \ˈni(ə)r-ˈsīt-əd\ adj : able to see near things more clearly than distant ones : MYOPIC — **near·sight·ed·ly** adv — **near·sight·ed·ness** n

[1]**neat** \ˈnēt\ n, pl **neat** or **neats** [ME *neet,* fr. OE *nēat;* akin to OHG *nōz* head of cattle, OE *nēotan* to make use of] : the common domestic bovine (*Bos taurus*)

[2]**neat** adj [MF *net,* fr. L *nitidus* bright, neat, fr. *nitēre* to shine; akin to OPer *naiba-* beautiful] **1 a** : free from admixture or dilution : STRAIGHT <~ brandy> <~ cement> **b** : free from irregularity : SMOOTH <~ silk> **2** : marked by tasteful simplicity <a ~ outfit> **3 a** : PRECISE, SYSTEMATIC **b** : marked by skill or ingenuity : ADROIT **4** : free from dirt and disorder : habitually clean and orderly <the room was ~ and ready for company> <a ~ careful little man> **5** : CLEAR, NET <~ profit> **6** *slang* : FINE, ADMIRABLE — **neat·ly** adv — **neat·ness** n

syn NEAT, TIDY, TRIM, TRIG *shared meaning element* : manifesting care and orderliness

[3]**neat** adv : without admixture or dilution : STRAIGHT <drinks his whiskey ~>

neath \(ˈ)nēth\ prep, dial : BENEATH

neat·herd \ˈnēt-ˌhərd\ n : HERDSMAN

neat's-foot oil \ˈnēts-ˌfu̇t-\ n : a pale yellow fatty oil made esp. from the bones of cattle and used chiefly as a leather dressing

neb \ˈneb\ n [ME, fr. OE; akin to ON *nef* beak] **1 a** : the beak of a bird or tortoise : BILL **b** *chiefly dial* : a person's mouth **c** : NOSE 1, SNOUT **2** : NIB, TIP

Neb *abbr* Nebraska

NEB *abbr* New English Bible

neb·bish \ˈneb-ik, -ish\ n [Yiddish *nebach, nebech* poor thing (used interjectionally), of Slav origin; akin to Polish *nieboże* poor thing] : a timid, meek, or ineffectual person

ne·ben·kern \ˈnā-bən-ˌkərn, -ˌke(ə)rn\ n [G, lit., subsidiary nucleus] : a two-stranded helical structure of the proximal tail region of spermatozoa that is derived from mitochondria

Nebr *abbr* Nebraska

Neb·u·chad·nez·zar \ˌneb-(y)ə-kəd-ˈnez-ər, -ˌkad-\ also **Neb·u·chad·rez·zar** \-ˈrez-\ n [Heb *Nĕbhūkhadhnĕssar,* modif. of Bab *Nabû-kudurri-uṣur*] : king of Babylon from 605 to 562 B.C. and conqueror of Jerusalem

neb·u·la \ˈneb-yə-lə\ n, pl **-las** or **-lae** \-ˌlē, -ˌlī\ [NL, fr. L, mist, cloud; akin to OHG *nebul* fog, Gk *nephelē, nephos* cloud] **1** : a slight cloudy opacity of the cornea **2 a** : any of many immense bodies of highly rarefied gas or dust in interstellar space **b** : GALAXY; *esp* : a galaxy other than the Milky Way galaxy — **neb·u·lar** \-lər\ adj

nebular hypothesis n : a hypothesis in astronomy: the solar system has evolved from a hot gaseous nebula

neb·u·lize \ˈneb-yə-ˌlīz\ vt **-lized; -liz·ing** [L *nebula*] : to reduce to a fine spray — **neb·u·li·za·tion** \ˌneb-yə-lə-ˈzā-shən\ n — **neb·u·liz·er** \ˈneb-yə-ˌlī-zər\ n

neb·u·los·i·ty \ˌneb-yə-ˈläs-ət-ē\ n, pl **-ties** **1** : the quality or state of being nebulous **2** : nebulous matter; *also* : NEBULA 2

neb·u·lous \ˈneb-yə-ləs\ adj [L *nebulosus* misty, fr. *nebula*] **1** : INDISTINCT, VAGUE **2** : of, relating to, or resembling a nebula : NEBULAR — **neb·u·lous·ly** adv — **neb·u·lous·ness** n

nec·es·sar·i·ly \ˌnes-ə-ˈser-ə-lē\ adv : of necessity : UNAVOIDABLY

[1]**nec·es·sary** \ˈnes-ə-ˌser-ē\ n, pl **-saries** : an indispensable item : ESSENTIAL; *esp* : an item needed to maintain a reasonable or accustomed standard of living

[2]**necessary** adj [ME *necessarie,* fr. L *necessarius,* fr. *necesse* necessary, fr. *ne-* not + *cedere* to withdraw — more at NO, CEDE] **1 a** : of an inevitable nature : INESCAPABLE **b (1)** : logically unavoidable **(2)** : that cannot be denied without contradiction **c** : determined or produced by the previous condition of things **d** : COMPULSORY **2** : absolutely needed : REQUIRED

necessary condition n **1** : a proposition whose falsity assures the falsity of another **2** : a state of affairs that must prevail if another is to occur : PREREQUISITE

ne·ces·si·tar·i·an·ism \ni-ˌses-ə-ˈter-ē-ə-ˌniz-əm, -ˌiz-əm\ n : the theory that results follow by invariable sequence from causes — **ne·ces·si·tar·i·an** \-ē-ən\ adj or n

ne·ces·si·tate \ni-ˈses-ə-ˌtāt\ vt **-tat·ed; -tat·ing** **1** : to cause to be a necessary concomitant, result, or consequence **2** : FORCE, COMPEL — **ne·ces·si·ta·tion** \-ˌses-ə-ˈtā-shən\ n

ne·ces·si·tous \ni-ˈses-ət-əs\ adj **1** : NEEDY, IMPOVERISHED **2** : URGENT, PRESSING **3** : NECESSARY — **ne·ces·si·tous·ly** adv — **ne·ces·si·tous·ness** n

ne·ces·si·ty \ni-ˈses-ət-ē, -ˈses-tē\ n, pl **-ties** [ME *necessite,* fr. MF *necessité,* fr. L *necessitat-, necessitas,* fr. *necesse*] **1** : the quality or state of being necessary : INDISPENSABILITY **2 a** : pressure of circumstance **b** : natural compulsion <physical ~> **c** : impossibility of a contrary order or condition **3** : the quality or state of being in need; *esp* : POVERTY **4 a** : something that is necessary : REQUIREMENT **b** : an urgent need or desire ***syn*** see NEED

[1]**neck** \ˈnek\ n [ME *nekke,* fr. OE *hnecca;* akin to OHG *hnac* nape, OE *hnutu* nut — more at NUT] **1 a** : the part of an animal that connects the head with the body **b** : the part of a garment that covers or is next to the neck **2** : a relatively narrow part suggestive of a neck: as **a (1)** : the constricted end of a bottle **(2)** : the slender proximal end of a fruit **b** : CERVIX 2 **c** : the part of a stringed musical instrument extending from the body and supporting the fingerboard and strings **d** : a narrow stretch of land **e** : STRAIT 1b **f** : a column of solidified magma of a volcanic pipe or laccolith **3** : a narrow margin <won by a ~> **4** : REGION, PART <my ~ of the woods>

[2]**neck** vt **1** : to reduce in diameter **2** : to kiss and caress amorously ~ vi **1** : to engage in amorous kissing and caressing **2** : to become constricted : NARROW

necked \ˈnekt\ adj : having a neck esp. of a specified kind — often used in combination <long-*necked*>

neck·er·chief \ˈnek-ər-chəf, -(ˌ)chif, -ˌchēf\ n, pl **-chiefs** also **-chieves** *see* HANDKERCHIEF *pl*\ [ME *nekkerchef,* fr. *nekke* + *kerchef* kerchief] : a kerchief for the neck

neck·ing \ˈnek-iŋ\ n **1** : a small molding near the top of a column or pilaster **2** : the act or practice of kissing and caressing amorously

neck·lace \ˈnek-ləs\ n : an ornament (as a string of beads) worn around the neck

neck·line \-ˌlīn\ n : the line formed by the neck opening of a garment

neck–rein \-ˌrān\ *vi, of a saddle horse* : to respond to the pressure of a rein on one side of the neck by turning in the opposite direction ~ *vt* : to direct (a horse) by pressures of the rein on the neck

neck·tie \-ˌtī\ *n* : a narrow length of material worn about the neck and tied in front; *esp* : FOUR-IN-HAND

necr- *or* **necro-** *comb form* [LL, fr. Gk *nekr-, nekro-,* fr. *nekros* dead body — more at NOXIOUS] **1 a** : those that are dead <*necro*philia> **b** : one that is dead <*necro*psy> **2** : conversion to dead tissue <*necro*biosis>

ne·crol·o·gist \nə-ˈkräl-ə-jəst, ne-\ *n* : one that writes or compiles a necrology

ne·crol·o·gy \-jē\ *n, pl* **-gies** [NL *necrologium,* fr. *necr-* + *-logium* (as in ML *eulogium* eulogy)] **1** : a list of the recently dead **2** : OBITUARY — **nec·ro·log·i·cal** \ˌnek-rə-ˈläj-i-kəl\ *adj*

nec·ro·man·cy \ˈnek-rə-ˌman(t)-sē\ *n* [alter. of ME *nigromancie,* fr. MF, fr. ML *nigromantia,* by folk etymology fr. LL *necromantia,* fr. LGk *nekromanteia,* fr. Gk *nekr-* + *-manteia* -mancy] **1** : conjuration of the spirits of the dead for purposes of magically revealing the future or influencing the course of events **2** : MAGIC, SORCERY — **nec·ro·man·cer** \-sər\ *n* — **nec·ro·man·tic** \ˌnek-rə-ˈmant-ik\ *adj* — **nec·ro·man·ti·cal·ly** \-i-k(ə-)lē\ *adv*

nec·ro·pha·gia \ˌnek-rə-ˈfā-j(ē-)ə\ *n* [NL] : the act or practice of eating corpses or carrion

ne·croph·a·gous \nə-ˈkräf-ə-gəs, ne-\ *adj* : feeding on corpses or carrion <~ insects> <~ savages>

ne·croph·a·gy \-jē\ *n* : NECROPHAGIA

nec·ro·phil·ia \ˌnek-rə-ˈfil-ē-ə\ *n* [NL] : obsession with and usu. erotic interest in or stimulation by corpses — **nec·ro·phil·ic** \-ˈfil-ik\ *adj*

ne·croph·i·lism \nə-ˈkräf-ə-ˌliz-əm, ne-\ *n* : NECROPHILIA

ne·crop·o·lis \nə-ˈkräp-ə-ləs, ne-\ *n, pl* **-lis·es** *or* **-les** \-ˌlēz\ *or* **-leis** \-ˌlās\ *or* **-li** \-ˌlī, -ˌlē\ [LL, city of the dead, fr. Gk *nekropolis,* fr. *nekr-* + *-polis*] : CEMETERY; *esp* : a large elaborate cemetery of an ancient city

[1]nec·rop·sy \ˈnek-ˌräp-sē\ *n, pl* **-sies** : POSTMORTEM EXAMINATION

[2]necropsy *vt* **-sied; -sy·ing** : to perform a postmortem examination upon

ne·cro·sis \nə-ˈkrō-səs, ne-\ *n, pl* **ne·cro·ses** \-ˌsēz\ [LL, fr. Gk *nekrōsis,* fr. *nekroun* to make dead, fr. *nekros* — more at NOXIOUS] : usu. localized death of living tissue — **ne·crot·ic** \-ˈkrät-ik\ *adj*

nec·ro·tize \ˈnek-rə-ˌtīz\ *vb* **-tized; -tiz·ing** [Gk *nekrōtikos* necrotic, fr. *nekroun*] *vi* : to undergo necrosis ~ *vt* : to cause necrosis

nec·tar \ˈnek-tər\ *n* [L, fr. Gk *nektar*] **1** : the drink of the Greek and Roman gods; *broadly* : a delicious drink **2** : a sweet liquid that is secreted by the nectaries of a plant and is the chief raw material of honey — **nec·tar·ous** \-t(ə-)rəs\ *adj*

nec·tar·ine \ˌnek-tə-ˈrēn\ *n* [obs. *nectarine,* adj. (like nectar)] : a peach with a smooth-skinned fruit that is a frequent somatic mutation of the normal peach; *also* : its fruit

nec·tary \ˈnek-t(ə-)rē\ *n, pl* **-tar·ies** [NL *nectarium,* irreg. fr. L *nectar* + *-arium* -ary] : a plant gland that secretes nectar

NED *abbr* New English Dictionary

née *or* **nee** \ˈnā\ *adj* [F *née,* fem. of *né,* lit., born, pp. of *naître* to be born, fr. L *nasci* — more at NATION] **1** — used to identify a woman by her maiden family name **2** : originally or formerly called <Cape Kennedy (~ Canaveral) in Florida —John Lear>

[1]need \ˈnēd\ *n* [ME *ned,* fr. OE *nied, nēd;* akin to OHG *nōt* distress, need] **1** : necessary duty : OBLIGATION **2 a** : a lack of something requisite, desirable, or useful **b** : a physiological or psychological requirement for the well-being of an organism **3** : a condition requiring supply or relief : EXIGENCY **4** : lack of the means of subsistence : POVERTY

syn NEED, NECESSITY, EXIGENCY *shared meaning element* : a pressing lack of something essential

[2]need *vi* **1** : to be in want **2** : to be needful or necessary ~ *vt* : to be in need of : REQUIRE ~ *verbal auxiliary* : be under necessity or obligation to <he ~ not answer> ***syn*** see LACK

[1]need·ful \ˈnēd-fəl\ *adj* : NECESSARY, REQUISITE — **need·ful·ly** \-fə-lē\ *adv* — **need·ful·ness** *n*

[2]needful *n* **1** : something needed or requisite **2** : MONEY

[1]nee·dle \ˈnēd-ᵊl\ *n* [ME *nedle,* fr. OE *nǣdl;* akin to OHG *nādala* needle, *nājan* to sew, L *nēre* to spin, Gk *nēn*] **1 a** : a small slender usu. steel instrument that has an eye for thread at one end and that is used for sewing **b** : any of various devices for carrying thread and making stitches (as in crocheting or knitting) **c** (1) : a needle designed to carry sutures when sewing tissues in surgery (2) : a slender hollow instrument for introducing material into or removing material from the body parenterally (3) : a hollow device designed to contain radioactive material **2** : a slender usu. sharp-pointed indicator on a dial; *esp* : MAGNETIC NEEDLE **3 a** : a slender pointed object resembling a needle: as (1) : a pointed crystal (2) : a sharp rock (3) : OBELISK **b** : a needle-shaped leaf (as of a conifer) **c** : a slender piece of jewel, steel, wood, or fiber with a rounded tip used in a phonograph to transmit vibrations from the record : STYLUS **d** : a slender pointed rod controlling a fine inlet or outlet (as in a valve) — **nee·dle·like** \ˈnēd-ᵊl-ˌ(l)īk\ *adj*

[2]needle *vb* **nee·dled; nee·dling** \ˈnēd-liŋ, -ᵊl-iŋ\ *vt* **1** : to sew or pierce with or as if with a needle **2 a** : TEASE, TORMENT **b** : to incite to action by repeated gibes <*needled* the boy into a fight> **3** : to strengthen (a beverage) by adding raw alcohol ~ *vi* : SEW, EMBROIDER — **nee·dler** \ˈnēd-lər, -ᵊl-ər\ *n* — **nee·dling** *n*

nee·dle·fish \ˈnēd-ᵊl-ˌfish\ *n* **1** : any of a family (Belonidae) of voracious elongate teleost fishes resembling but not related to the freshwater gars **2** : PIPEFISH

nee·dle·point \-ˌpȯint\ *n* **1** : lace worked with a needle in buttonhole stitch over a paper pattern **2** : embroidery done on canvas usu. in simple even stitches across counted threads — **needlepoint** *adj*

need·less \ˈnēd-ləs\ *adj* : not needed : UNNECESSARY <~ waste> — **need·less·ly** *adv* — **need·less·ness** *n*

nee·dle·wom·an \ˈnēd-ᵊl-ˌwu̇m-ən\ *n* : a woman who does needlework; *esp* : SEAMSTRESS

nee·dle·work \-ˌwərk\ *n* **1** : work done with a needle; *esp* : work (as embroidery) other than plain sewing **2** : the occupation of one who does needlework — **nee·dle·work·er** \-ˌwər-kər\ *n*

needn't \ˈnēd-ᵊnt\ : need not

needs \ˈnēdz\ *adv* [ME *nedes,* fr. OE *nēdes,* fr. gen. of *nēd* need] : of necessity : NECESSARILY <must ~ be recognized>

needy \ˈnēd-ē\ *adj* **need·i·er; -est** : being in want : POVERTY-STRICKEN <~ families> — **need·i·ness** *n*

neem \ˈnēm\ *n* [Hindi *nīm,* fr. Skt *nimba*] : a large East Indian tree (*Azadirachta indica*) whose trunk exudes a tenacious gum and has a bitter bark used as a tonic and whose fruit and seeds yield a medicinal aromatic oil

ne'er \(ˈ)ne(ə)r, (ˈ)na(ə)r\ *adv* : NEVER

ne'er–do–well \ˈne(ə)r-du̇-ˌwel, ˈna(ə)r-\ *n* : an idle worthless person — **ne'er–do–well** *adj*

ne·far·i·ous \ni-ˈfar-ē-əs, -ˈfer-\ *adj* [L *nefarius,* fr. *nefas* crime, fr. *ne-* not + *fas* right, divine law; akin to L *fari* to speak] : flagrantly wicked or impious : EVIL ***syn*** see VICIOUS — **ne·far·i·ous·ly** *adv* — **ne·far·i·ous·ness** *n*

neg *abbr* negative

ne·gate \ni-ˈgāt\ *vt* **ne·gat·ed; ne·gat·ing** [L *negatus,* pp. of *negare* to say no, deny, fr. *neg-* no, not (akin to *ne-* not) — more at NO] **1** : to deny the existence or truth of **2** : to cause to be ineffective or invalid ***syn*** see NULLIFY — **negate** *n* — **ne·ga·tor** *or* **ne·gat·er** \-ˈgāt-ər\ *n*

ne·ga·tion \ni-ˈgā-shən\ *n* **1 a** : the action of negating : DENIAL **b** : a negative doctrine or statement **2 a** : something that is the absence of something actual : NONENTITY **b** : something that is the negative opposite of something positive; *esp* : a logical proposition formed by asserting the falsity of a given proposition — **ne·ga·tion·al** \-shnəl, -shən-ᵊl\ *adj*

[1]neg·a·tive \ˈneg-ət-iv\ *adj* **1 a** : marked by denial, prohibition, or refusal **b** (1) : denying a predicate of a subject or a part of a subject <"no A is B" is a ~ proposition> (2) : denoting the absence or the contradictory of something <*nonwhite* is a ~ term> (3) : expressing negation <~ particles such as *no* and *not*> **2 a** : lacking positive qualities; *esp* : DISAGREEABLE **b** : marked by features (as hostility or withdrawal) opposing constructive treatment or development <had a ~ pessimistic outlook on life> **3 a** : less than zero and opposite in sign to a positive number that when added to the given number yields zero <−2 is a ~ number> **b** : extending or generated in a direction opposite to an arbitrarily chosen regular direction or position <~ angle> **4 a** : being, relating to, or charged with electricity of which the electron is the elementary unit **b** : gaining electrons **c** (1) : having lower electric potential and constituting the part toward which the current flows from the external circuit <the ~ pole> (2) : constituting an electrode through which a stream of electrons enters the space between electrodes in an electron tube **5 a** : not affirming the presence of the organism or condition in question <a ~ TB test> **b** : directed or moving away from a source of stimulation <~ tropism> **c** : less than the pressure of the atmosphere <~ pressure> **6** : having the light and dark parts in approximately inverse order to those of the original photographic subject **7** *of a lens* : diverging light rays and forming a virtual inverted image — **neg·a·tive·ly** *adv* — **neg·a·tive·ness** *n* — **neg·a·tiv·i·ty** \ˌneg-ə-ˈtiv-ət-ē\ *n*

[2]negative *n* **1 a** : a proposition which denies or contradicts another; *esp* : the one of a pair of propositions in which negation is expressed **b** (1) : a reply that indicates the withholding of assent : REFUSAL (2) *archaic* : a right of veto (3) *obs* : an adverse vote : VETO **2** : something that is the opposite or negation of something else **3 a** : an expression (as the word *no*) of negation or denial **b** : a negative number **4** : the side that upholds the contradictory proposition in a debate **5** : the plate of a voltaic or electrolytic cell that is at the lower potential **6** : a negative photographic image on transparent material used for printing positive pictures; *also* : the material that carries such an image **7** : a reverse impression taken from a piece of sculpture or ceramics

[3]negative *vt* **-tived; -tiv·ing** **1 a** : to refuse assent to **b** (1) : to reject by or as if by a vote (2) : VETO **2** : to demonstrate the falsity of : DISPROVE **3** : to deny the truth, reality, or validity of : CONTRADICT **4** : NEUTRALIZE, COUNTERACT ***syn*** see DENY

negative income tax *n* : a system of federal subsidy payments to families with incomes below a stipulated level proposed as a substitute for or supplement to welfare payments

negative staining *n* : a method of demonstrating the form of small objects (as bacteria) by surrounding them with a stain that they do not take up so that they appear as sharply outlined unstained bright bodies on a colored ground

negative transfer *n* : the impeding of learning or performance in a situation by the carry-over of learned responses from another situation — called also *negative transfer effect*

neg·a·tiv·ism \ˈneg-ət-iv-ˌiz-əm\ *n* **1** : an attitude of mind marked by skepticism about nearly everything affirmed by others **2** : a tendency to refuse to do, to do the opposite of, or to do something at variance with what is asked — **neg·a·tiv·ist** \-əst\ *n* — **neg·a·tiv·is·tic** \ˌneg-ət-iv-ˈis-tik\ *adj*

neg·a·tron \ˈneg-ə-ˌträn\ *also* **neg·a·ton** \-ˌtän\ *n* [*negatron* fr. *nega*tive + elec*tron; negaton* fr. *negative* + [2]*-on*] : ELECTRON

[1]ne·glect \ni-ˈglekt\ *vt* [L *neglectus,* pp. of *neglegere, neclegere,* fr. *nec-* not (akin to *ne-* not) + *legere* to gather — more at NO, LEGEND] **1** : to give little attention or respect to : DISREGARD **2** : to leave undone or unattended to esp. through carelessness — **ne·glect·er** *n*

syn NEGLECT, OMIT, DISREGARD, IGNORE, OVERLOOK, SLIGHT, FORGET *shared meaning element* : to pass over without giving due attention ***ant*** cherish

[2]neglect *n* **1** : an act or instance of neglecting something **2** : the condition of being neglected

ne·glect·ful \ni-ˈglek(t)-fəl\ *adj* : given to neglecting : CARELESS, HEEDLESS ***syn*** see NEGLIGENT ***ant*** attentive — **ne·glect·ful·ly** \-fə-lē\ *adv* — **ne·glect·ful·ness** *n*

neg·li·gee *or* **neg·li·gé** \ˌneg-lə-ˈzhā\ *n* [F *négligé*, fr. pp. of *négliger* to neglect, fr. L *neglegere*] **1 :** a woman's long flowing usu. sheer dressing gown **2 :** carelessly informal or incomplete attire

neg·li·gence \ˈneg-li-jən(t)s\ *n* **1 a :** the quality or state of being negligent **b :** failure to exercise the care that a prudent person usu. exercises **2 :** an act or instance of negligence

neg·li·gent \-jənt\ *adj* [ME, fr. MF & L; MF, fr. L *neglegent-, neglegens*, prp. of *neglegere*] **1 :** marked by or given to neglect esp. habitually or culpably **2 :** marked by a carelessly easy manner — **neg·li·gent·ly** *adv*
syn NEGLIGENT, NEGLECTFUL, LAX, SLACK, REMISS *shared meaning element* **:** culpably careless or indicative of such carelessness

neg·li·gi·ble \ˈneg-li-jə-bəl\ *adj* [L *neglegere, negligere*] **:** so small or unimportant or of so little consequence as to warrant little or no attention **:** TRIFLING — **neg·li·gi·bil·i·ty** \ˌneg-li-jə-ˈbil-ət-ē\ *n* — **neg·li·gi·bly** \ˈneg-li-jə-blē\ *adv*

ne·go·tia·ble \ni-ˈgō-sh(ē-)ə-bəl\ *adj* **:** capable of being negotiated: as **a :** transferable from one person to another by being delivered with or without endorsement so that the title passes to the transferee <~ securities> **b :** capable of being traversed, dealt with, or accomplished <a difficult but ~ road> <~ demands> — **ne·go·tia·bil·i·ty** \-ˌgō-sh(ē-)ə-ˈbil-ət-ē\ *n*

ne·go·tiant \-ˈgō-sh(ē-)ənt\ *n* **:** one that negotiates

ne·go·ti·ate \ni-ˈgō-shē-ˌāt\ *vb* **-at·ed; -at·ing** [L *negotiatus*, pp. of *negotiari* to carry on business, fr. *negotium* business, fr. *neg-* not + *otium* leisure — more at NEGATE] *vi* **:** to confer with another so as to arrive at the settlement of some matter ~ *vt* **1 a :** to deal with (some matter or affair that requires ability for its successful handling) **:** MANAGE **b :** to arrange for or bring about through conference, discussion, and compromise <~ a treaty> **2 a :** to transfer (as a bill of exchange) to another by delivery or endorsement **b :** to convert into cash or the equivalent value <~ a check> **3 a :** to successfully travel along or over <~ the turn> **b :** COMPLETE, ACCOMPLISH <~ the trip in two hours> — **ne·go·ti·a·tor** \-ˌāt-ər\ *n* — **ne·go·tia·to·ry** \-sh(ē-)ə-ˌtōr-ē, -ˌtȯr-\ *adj*
syn NEGOTIATE, ARRANGE, CONCERT *shared meaning element* **:** to bring about by mutual agreement

ne·go·ti·a·tion \ni-ˌgō-s(h)ē-ˈā-shən\ *n* **:** the action or process of negotiating or being negotiated; *esp* **:** PARLEY 1 — often used in pl.

Ne·gress \ˈnē-grəs\ *n* **:** a female Negro

Ne·gril·lo \ni-ˈgril-(ˌ)ō, -ˈgrē-(ˌ)(y)ō\ *n, pl* **Negrillos** *or* **Negrilloes** [Sp, dim. of *negro*] **:** a member of a people (as Pygmies) belonging to a group of Negroid peoples of small stature that live in Africa

Ne·gri·to \nə-ˈgrēt-(ˌ)ō\ *n, pl* **Negritos** *or* **Negritoes** [Sp, dim. of *negro*] **:** a member of a people (as the Andamanese) belonging to a group of Negroid peoples of small stature that live in Oceania and the southeastern part of Asia

ne·gri·tude \ˈneg-rə-ˌtüd, ˈnē-grə-, -ˌtyüd\ *n* [F *négritude*, fr. *nègre* Negro + *-i-* + *-tude*] **:** a consciousness of and pride in the cultural and physical aspects of the African heritage

Ne·gro \ˈnē-(ˌ)grō\ *n, pl* **Negroes** [Sp or Pg, fr. *negro* black, fr. L *nigr-, niger*] **1 :** a member of the black race of mankind distinguished from members of other races by physical features without regard to language or culture; *esp* **:** a member of a people belonging to the African branch of the black race **2 :** a person of Negro descent — **Negro** *adj* — **Ne·groid** \ˈnē-ˌgrȯid\ *n or adj, often not cap* — **Ne·gro·ness** \-grō-nəs\ *n*

ne·gro·phile \ˈnē-grō-ˌfīl\ *n, often cap* **:** one who is esp. friendly to Negroes and their interests — **ne·gro·phi·lism** \-ˌfī-ˌliz-əm, ni-ˈgräf-ə-ˌliz-\ *n, often cap*

ne·gro·phobe \ˈnē-grə-ˌfōb\ *n, often cap* **:** one who strongly dislikes or fears Negroes — **ne·gro·pho·bia** \ˌnē-grə-ˈfō-bē-ə\ *n, often cap*

[1]**ne·gus** \ˈnē-gəs, ni-ˈgüs\ *n* [Amharic *negūs*, fr. Eth *nĕgūš̂a nagaŝt* king of kings] **:** KING — used as a title of the sovereign of Ethiopia

[2]**ne·gus** \ˈnē-gəs\ *n* [Francis *Negus* †1732 E colonel] **:** a beverage of wine, hot water, sugar, lemon juice, and nutmeg

Neh *abbr* Nehemiah

Ne·he·mi·ah \ˌnē-(h)ə-ˈmī-ə\ *n* [Heb *Nĕḥemyāh*] **1 :** a Jewish leader of the 5th century B.C. who supervised the rebuilding of the Jerusalem city walls and instituted religious reforms in the city **2 :** a narrative and historical book of canonical Jewish and Christian Scripture — see BIBLE table

Ne·he·mi·as \-ˈmī-əs\ *n* [LL, fr. Heb *Nĕḥemyāh*] **:** NEHEMIAH

NEI *abbr* not elsewhere included

neigh \ˈnā\ *vi* [ME *neyen*, fr. OE *hnǣgan*; akin to MHG *nēgen* to neigh] **:** to make the loud prolonged cry of a horse — **neigh** *n*

[1]**neigh·bor** \ˈnā-bər\ *n* [ME, fr. OE *nēahgebūr*; akin to OHG *nāhgibūr* neighbor; both fr. a prehistoric WGmc compound represented by OE *nēah* near and by OE *gebūr* dweller — more at NIGH, BOOR] **1 :** one living or located near another **2 :** FELLOWMAN

[2]**neighbor** *adj* **:** being immediately adjoining or relatively near

[3]**neighbor** *vb* **neigh·bored; neigh·bor·ing** \-b(ə-)riŋ\ *vt* **:** to adjoin immediately or lie relatively near to ~ *vi* **1 :** to live or be located as a neighbor **2 :** to associate in a neighborly way

neigh·bor·hood \ˈnā-bər-ˌhu̇d\ *n* **1 :** neighborly relationship **2 :** the quality or state of being neighbors **:** PROXIMITY **3 a :** a place or region near **:** VICINITY **b :** an approximate amount, extent, or degree <cost in the ~ of $10> **4 a :** the people living near one another **b :** a section lived in by neighbors and usu. having distinguishing characteristics **5 :** the set of all points whose distances from a given point are not greater than a given positive number

neigh·bor·ly \-lē\ *adj* **:** of, relating to, or characteristic of congenial neighbors; *esp* **:** FRIENDLY *syn* see AMICABLE *ant* unneighborly, ill-disposed — **neigh·bor·li·ness** *n*

neigh·bour \-bər\ *chiefly Brit var of* NEIGHBOR

[1]**nei·ther** \ˈnē-t͟hər *also* ˈnī-\ *pron* [ME, alter. of *nauther, nother*, fr. OE *nāhwæther, nōther*, fr. *nā, nō* not + *hwæther* which of two, whether] **:** not the one or the other of two or more

[2]**neither** *conj* **1 :** not either <~ black nor white> **2 :** also not <~ did I>

[3]**neither** *adj* **:** not either <~ hand>

[4]**neither** *adv* **1** *chiefly dial* **:** EITHER <are not to be understood ~ —Earl of Chesterfield> **2 :** similarly not **:** also not <just as the serf was not permitted to leave the land, so ~ was his offspring —G. G. Coulton>

nek·ton \ˈnek-tən, -ˌtän\ *n* [G *nekton*, fr. Gk *nēkton*, neut. of *nēktos* swimming, fr. *nēchein* to swim; akin to L *nare* to swim — more at NOURISH] **:** free-swimming aquatic animals (as whales or squid) essentially independent of wave and current action — **nek·ton·ic** \nek-ˈtän-ik\ *adj*

nel·son \ˈnel-sən\ *n* [prob. fr. the name *Nelson*] **:** a wrestling hold marked by the application of leverage against an opponent's arm, neck, and head — compare FULL NELSON, HALF NELSON

ne·ma \ˈnē-mə, ˈnem-ə\ *n* [by shortening] **:** NEMATODE

nemat- *or* **nemato-** *comb form* [NL, fr. Gk *nēmat-*, fr. *nēmat-, nēma*, fr. *nēn* to spin — more at NEEDLE] **1 :** thread <*nemato*cyst> **2 :** nematode <*nemato*logy>

ne·ma·thel·minth \ˌnem-ə-ˈthel-ˌmin(t)th, ˌnē-mə-\ *n* [deriv. of Gk *nēma* + *helmis* worm — more at HELMINTH] **:** any of a phylum (Nemathelminthes) of wormlike animals with a cylindrical unsegmented body covered by an unciliated ectoderm that secretes an external cuticle

ne·mat·ic \ni-ˈmat-ik\ *adj* [ISV *nemat-* + *-ic*] **:** of, relating to, or being the phase of a liquid crystal characterized by having the long axes of the molecules in parallel lines but not layers — compare SMECTIC

ne·ma·to·cid·al *also* **ne·ma·ti·cid·al** \ˌnem-ət-ə-ˈsīd-ᵊl, ni-ˌmat-ə-\ *adj* **:** capable of destroying nematodes

ne·ma·to·cide *also* **ne·ma·ti·cide** \ˈnem-ət-ə-ˌsīd, ni-ˈmat-ə-\ *n* **:** a substance or preparation used to destroy nematodes

ne·ma·to·cyst \ˈnem-ət-ə-ˌsist, ni-ˈmat-ə-\ *n* [ISV] **:** one of the minute stinging organs of various coelenterates

nem·a·tode \ˈnem-ə-ˌtōd\ *n, often attrib* [deriv. of Gk *nēmat-, nēma*] **:** any of a class or phylum (Nematoda) of elongated cylindrical worms parasitic in animals or plants or free-living in soil or water

nem·a·tol·o·gy \ˌnem-ə-ˈtäl-ə-jē\ *n* **:** a branch of zoology that deals with nematodes — **nem·a·to·log·i·cal** \ˌnem-ət-ᵊl-ˈäj-i-kəl\ *adj* — **nem·a·tol·o·gist** \ˌnem-ə-ˈtäl-ə-jəst\ *n*

Nem·bu·tal \ˈnem-byə-ˌtȯl\ *trademark* — used for the sodium salt of pentobarbital

nem con *abbr* [NL *nemine contradicente*] no one contradicting

nem diss *abbr* [NL *nemine dissentiente*] no one dissenting

ne·mer·te·an \ni-ˈmərt-ē-ən\ *n* [deriv. of Gk *Nēmertēs* Nemertes, one of the Nereids] **:** any of a class (Nemertea) of often vividly colored marine worms most of which burrow in the mud or sand along seacoasts — called also *ribbon worm* — **nemertean** *adj* — **nem·er·tine** \ˈnem-ər-ˌtīn\ *or* **nem·er·tin·e·an** \ˌnem-ər-ˈtin-ē-ən\ *adj or n*

nem·e·sis \ˈnem-ə-səs\ *n* [L, fr. Gk] **1** *cap* **:** the Greek goddess of fate and punisher of extravagant pride **2** *pl* **nem·e·ses** \-ˌsēz\ **a :** one that inflicts retribution or vengeance **b :** a formidable and usu. victorious rival or opponent **3** *pl* **nemeses a :** an act or effect of retribution **b :** BANE 2

ne·moph·i·la \ni-ˈmäf-ə-lə\ *n* [NL, genus name, fr. Gk *nemos* wooded pasture + *philos* loving] **:** any of a genus (*Nemophila*) of American annual herbs of the waterleaf family cultivated for their showy blue usu. spotted flowers

ne·ne \ˈnā-(ˌ)nā\ *n* [Hawaiian *nēnē*] **:** a nearly extinct goose (*Nesochen sandvicensis*) of the Hawaiian islands that inhabits waterless uplands and feeds on berries and vegetation

neo- — see NE-

neo·an·throp·ic \ˌnē-ō-an-ˈthräp-ik\ *adj* **:** belonging to the same species (*Homo sapiens*) as recent man **:** modern in anatomy or type

neo·ars·phen·a·mine \ˌnē-ō-ärs-ˈfen-ə-ˌmēn\ *n* **:** a yellow powder $C_{13}H_{13}As_2N_2NaO_4S$ similar to arsphenamine in structure and use

Neo·cene \ˈnē-ə-ˌsēn\ *adj* **:** relating to or being the later portion of the Tertiary including the Miocene and Pliocene — **Neocene** *n*

neo·clas·sic \ˌnē-ō-ˈklas-ik\ *adj* **:** of, relating to, or constituting a revival or adaptation of the classical esp. in literature, music, art, or architecture — **neo·clas·si·cal** \-i-kəl\ *adj* — **neo·clas·si·cism** \-ˈklas-ə-ˌsiz-əm\ *n* — **neo·clas·si·cist** \-səst\ *n or adj*

neo·co·lo·nial \ˌnē-ō-kə-ˈlō-nyəl, -ˈlō-nē-əl\ *adj* **:** of or relating to neocolonialism

neo·co·lo·nial·ism \-ˌiz-əm\ *n* **:** the economic and political policies by which a great power indirectly maintains or extends its influence over other areas or people — **neo·co·lo·nial·ist** \-əst\ *n or adj*

neo·cor·tex \ˌnē-ō-ˈkȯr-ˌteks\ *n* [NL; fr. its being the cortex of the phylogenetically most recently developed part of the brain] **:** the dorsal region of the cerebral cortex that is unique to mammals — **neo·cor·ti·cal** \-ˈkȯrt-i-kəl\ *adj* **:** of or relating to the neocortex

neo–Dar·win·ian \-där-ˈwin-ē-ən\ *adj, often cap N* **:** of or relating to neo-Darwinism

neo–Dar·win·ism \-ˈdär-wə-ˌniz-əm\ *n, often cap N* **:** a theory that explains evolution in terms of natural selection and population genetics and specif. denies the possibility of inheriting acquired characters — **neo–Dar·win·ist** \-nəst\ *n, often cap N*

neo·dym·i·um \ˌnē-ō-ˈdim-ē-əm\ *n* [NL, fr. *ne-* + *-dymium* (fr. *didymium*)] **:** a yellow metallic element of the rare-earth group — see ELEMENT table

neo–Freud·ian \-ˈfrȯid-ē-ən\ *adj, often cap N* **:** of or relating to a school of psychoanalysis that differs from Freudian orthodoxy in emphasizing the importance of social and cultural factors in the development of an individual's personality — **neo–Freudian** *n, often cap N*

neo·gen·e·sis \ˌnē-ō-ˈjen-ə-səs\ *n* [NL] **:** new formation **:** REGENERATION <~ in rat skin> — **neo·ge·net·ic** \ˌnē-ō-jə-ˈnet-ik\ *adj*

ə abut	ᵊ kitten	ər further	a back	ā bake	ä cot, cart
au̇ out	ch chin	e less	ē easy	g gift	i trip	ī life
j joke	ŋ sing	ō flow	ȯ flaw	ȯi coin	th thin	t͟h this
ü loot	u̇ foot	y yet	yü few	yu̇ furious	zh vision

neo–im·pres·sion·ism \ˌnē-ō-im-ˈpresh-ə-ˌniz-əm\ *n, often cap N&I* [F *néo-impressionisme,* fr. *né-* ne- + *impressionisme* impressionism] : a late 19th century French art theory and practice characterized by an attempt to make impressionism more precise in form and the use of a pointillist painting technique — **neo–im·pres·sion·ist** \-ˈpresh-(ə-)nəst\ *adj or n, often cap N&I*

Neo–Lat·in \-ˈlat-ᵊn\ *n* [ISV] **1 :** NEW LATIN **2 :** ROMANCE

neo·lith \ˈnē-ə-ˌlith\ *n* [back-formation fr. *neolithic*] : a Neolithic stone implement

neo·lith·ic \ˌnē-ə-ˈlith-ik\ *adj* **1** *cap* : of or relating to the latest period of the Stone Age characterized by polished stone implements **2 :** belonging to an earlier age and now outmoded

ne·ol·o·gism \nē-ˈäl-ə-ˌjiz-əm\ *n* **1 :** a word, usage, or expression that is often disapproved because of its newness or barbarousness **2 :** a meaningless word coined by a psychotic — **ne·ol·o·gis·tic** \-ˌäl-ə-ˈjis-tik\ *adj*

ne·ol·o·gy \nē-ˈäl-ə-jē\ *n, pl* **-gies** [F *néologie,* fr. *né-* ne- + *-logie* -logy] **1 :** the use of a new word or expression or of an established word in a new or different sense **2 :** NEOLOGISM 1 — **neo·log·i·cal** \ˌnē-ə-ˈläj-i-kəl\ *adj*

neo·my·cin \ˌnē-ə-ˈmīs-ᵊn\ *n* [*ne-* + *myc-* + *-in*] : a broad-spectrum antibiotic or mixture of antibiotics produced by a soil actinomycete (*Streptomyces fradiae*)

ne·on \ˈnē-ˌän\ *n* [Gk, neut. of *neos* new — more at NEW] **1 :** a colorless odorless primarily inert gaseous element found in minute amounts in air and used in electric lamps — see ELEMENT table **2 a :** a discharge lamp in which the gas contains a large proportion of neon **b :** a sign composed of such lamps **c :** the illumination provided by such lamps or signs — **neon** *adj* — **ne·oned** \-ˌänd\ *adj*

neo·na·tal \ˌnē-ō-ˈnāt-ᵊl\ *adj* : of, relating to, or affecting the newborn and esp. the human infant during the first month after birth — **neo·na·tal·ly** \-ᵊl-ē\ *adv*

ne·o·nate \ˈnē-ə-ˌnāt\ *n* [NL *neonatus,* fr. *ne-* + *natus,* pp. of *nasci* to be born — more at NATION] : a newborn child; *esp* : a child less than a month old

neo·or·tho·dox \ˌnē-ō-ˈȯr-thə-ˌdäks\ *adj* : of or relating to a 20th century movement in Protestant theology characterized by a reaction against liberalism and emphasis on various scripturally based Reformation doctrines — **neo·or·tho·doxy** \-ˌdäk-sē\ *n*

neo·phyte \ˈnē-ə-ˌfīt\ *n* [LL *neophytus,* fr. Gk *neophytos,* fr. *neophytos* newly planted, newly converted, fr. *ne-* + *phyein* to bring forth — more at BE] **1 :** a new convert : PROSELYTE **2 :** NOVICE 1 **3 :** TYRO, BEGINNER

neo·pla·sia \ˌnē-ə-ˈplā-zh(ē-)ə\ *n* [NL] **1 :** the formation of tumors **2 :** a tumorous condition

neo·plasm \ˈnē-ə-ˌplaz-əm\ *n* [ISV] : a new growth of tissue serving no physiologic function : TUMOR

neo·plas·tic \ˌnē-ə-ˈplas-tik\ *adj* [ISV] **1 :** of, relating to, or constituting a neoplasm or neoplasia **2 :** of or relating to neoplasticism

neo·plas·ti·cism \-tə-ˌsiz-əm\ *n* [*ne-* + *plastic* + *-ism*] : the de Stijl art principle in painting — **neo·plas·ti·cist** \-səst\ *n*

Neo·pla·to·nism \ˌnē-ō-ˈplāt-ᵊn-ˌiz-əm\ *n* [ISV] **1 :** Platonism modified in later antiquity to accord with Aristotelian, post-Aristotelian, and oriental conceptions that conceives of the world as an emanation from the One with whom the soul is capable of being reunited in trance or ecstasy **2 :** doctrines similar to ancient Neoplatonism — **Neo·pla·ton·ic** \-plə-ˈtän-ik, -plā-\ *adj* — **Neo·pla·to·nist** \-ˈplāt-ᵊn-əst\ *n*

neo·prene \ˈnē-ə-ˌprēn\ *n* [*ne-* + chlor*oprene*] : a synthetic rubber made by the polymerization of chloroprene and characterized by superior resistance (as to oils)

Ne·op·tol·e·mus \ˌnē-ˌäp-ˈtäl-ə-məs\ *n* [L, fr. Gk *Neoptolemos*] : a son of Achilles and slayer of Priam at the taking of Troy

neo–scho·las·ti·cism \ˌnē-ō-skə-ˈlas-tə-ˌsiz-əm\ *n* : a contemporary movement among Catholic scholars aiming to restate the methods and teachings of medieval Scholasticism in a manner suited to the intellectual needs of the present

neo·stig·mine \ˌnē-ə-ˈstig-ˌmēn\ *n* [*ne-* + *-stigmine* (as in *physostigmine*)] : a cholinergic drug used in the form of its bromide $C_{12}H_{19}BrN_2O_2$ or a methyl sulfate derivative $C_{13}H_{22}N_2O_6S$ esp. in the treatment of some ophthalmic conditions and in the diagnosis and treatment of myasthenia gravis

ne·o·te·ny \ˈnē-ə-ˌtē-nē, nē-ˈät-ᵊn-ē\ *n* [NL *neotenia,* fr. *ne-* + Gk *teinein* to stretch — more at THIN] **1 :** attainment of sexual maturity during the larval stage **2 :** retention of some larval or immature characters in adulthood — **ne·o·ten·ic** \ˌnē-ə-ˈten-ik\ *adj*

ne·o·ter·ic \ˌnē-ə-ˈter-ik\ *adj* [LL *neotericus,* fr. LGk *neōterikos,* fr. Gk, youthful, fr. *neōterios* compar. of *neos* new, young — more at NEW] : recent in origin : MODERN

Neo·trop·i·cal \ˌnē-ō-ˈträp-i-kəl\ *also* **Neo·trop·ic** \-ik\ *adj* [ISV] : of, relating to, or constituting the biogeographic region that includes So. America, the West Indies, and tropical No. America

neo·type \ˈnē-ə-ˌtīp\ *n* : a type specimen that is selected subsequent to the description of a species to replace a preexisting type that has been lost or destroyed

Neo·zo·ic \ˌnē-ə-ˈzō-ik\ *adj* : of, relating to, or constituting the entire period from the end of the Mesozoic to the present time

Ne·pali \nə-ˈpȯl-ē, -ˈpäl-, -ˈpal-\ *n, pl* **Nepali** *also* **Nepal·is** [Hindi *naipālī* of Nepal, fr. Skt *naipālīya,* fr. *Nepāla* Nepal] **1 :** the Indic language of Nepal **2 :** a native or inhabitant of Nepal — **Nepali** *adj*

ne·pen·the \nə-ˈpen(t)-thē\ *n* [L *nepenthes,* fr. Gk *nēpenthes,* neut. of *nēpenthēs* banishing pain and sorrow, fr. *nē-* not + *penthos* grief, sorrow; akin to Gk *pathos* suffering — more at NO, PATHOS] **1 :** a potion used by the ancients to induce forgetfulness of pain or sorrow **2 :** something capable of causing oblivion of grief or suffering — **ne·pen·the·an** \-thē-ən\ *adj*

neph·anal·y·sis \ˌnef-ə-ˈnal-ə-səs\ *n* [NL, fr. Gk *nephos* cloud + *analysis* — more at NEBULA] : the analysis of the clouds and related phenomena over a large area of the earth on a chart used esp. in weather forecasting; *also* : the chart itself

neph·e·line \ˈnef-ə-ˌlēn\ *also* **neph·e·lite** \-ˌlīt\ *n* [F *néphéline,* fr. Gk *nephelē* cloud — more at NEBULA] : a hexagonal mineral $KNa_3Al_4Si_4O_{16}$ that is a usu. glassy crystalline silicate of sodium, potassium, and aluminum common in igneous rocks — **neph·e·lin·ic** \ˌnef-ə-ˈlin-ik\ *adj*

neph·e·lin·ite \ˈnef-ə-lə-ˌnīt\ *n* [ISV] : a silica-deficient igneous rock having nepheline as the predominant mineral — **neph·e·lin·it·ic** \ˌnef-ə-lə-ˈnit-ik\ *adj*

neph·e·lom·e·ter \ˌnef-ə-ˈläm-ət-ər\ *n* [Gk *nephelē* cloud + ISV *-meter*] **1 :** an instrument for measuring the extent or degree of cloudiness **2 :** an instrument for determining the concentration or particle size of suspensions by means of transmitted or reflected light — **neph·e·lo·met·ric** \ˌnef-ə-lō-ˈme-trik\ *adj* — **neph·e·lom·e·try** \-ˈläm-ə-trē\ *n*

neph·ew \ˈnef-(ˌ)yü, *chiefly Brit* ˈnev-\ *n* [ME *nevew,* fr. OF *neveu,* fr. L *nepot-, nepos* grandson, nephew; akin to OE *nefa* grandson, nephew, Skt *napāt* grandson] **1 a :** a son of one's brother or sister or of one's brother-in-law or sister-in-law **b :** an illegitimate son of an ecclesiastic **2** *obs* : a lineal descendant; *esp* : GRANDSON

ne·phom·e·ter \ne-ˈfäm-ət-ər\ *n* [Gk *nephos* cloud] : NEPHELOMETER 1

nepho·scope \ˈnef-ə-ˌskōp\ *n* [Gk *nephos* cloud + ISV *-scope* — more at NEBULA] : an instrument for observing the direction and velocity of clouds

nephr- *or* **nephro-** *comb form* [NL, fr. Gk, fr. *nephros* — more at NEPHRITIS] : kidney <*nephr*ic> <*nephro*logy>

ne·phrec·to·my \ni-ˈfrek-tə-mē\ *n, pl* **-mies** [ISV] : the surgical removal of a kidney — **ne·phrec·to·mized** \-ˌmīzd\ *adj*

neph·ric \ˈnef-rik\ *adj* [*nephr-* + *-ic*] : RENAL

ne·phrid·i·um \ni-ˈfrid-ē-əm\ *n, pl* **-ia** \-ē-ə\ [NL] **1 :** a tubular glandular excretory organ characteristic of various coelomate invertebrates **2 :** a primarily excretory structure; *esp* : NEPHRON — **ne·phrid·i·al** \-ē-əl\ *adj*

neph·rite \ˈnef-ˌrīt\ *n* [G *nephrit,* fr. Gk *nephros;* fr. its formerly being worn as a remedy for kidney diseases] : a compact tremolite or actinolite that is the commoner and less valuable kind of jade and that varies in color from white to dark green or black

ne·phrit·ic \ni-ˈfrit-ik\ *adj* **1 :** RENAL **2 :** of, relating to, or affected with nephritis

ne·phri·tis \ni-ˈfrīt-əs\ *n, pl* **ne·phrit·i·des** \-ˈfrit-ə-ˌdēz\ [LL, fr. Gk, fr. *nephros* kidney; akin to ME *nere* kidney] : acute or chronic inflammation of the kidney caused by infection, degenerative process, or vascular disease

neph·ro·gen·ic \ˌnef-rə-ˈjen-ik\ *adj* **1 :** originating in the kidney **2 :** developing into or producing kidney tissue

neph·ron \ˈnef-ˌrän\ *n* [G, fr. Gk *nephros*] : a single excretory unit esp. of the vertebrate kidney

ne·phrop·a·thy \ni-ˈfräp-ə-thē\ *n* [ISV] : an abnormal state of the kidney; *esp* : one associated with or secondary to some other pathological process

ne·phro·sis \ni-ˈfrō-səs\ *n* [NL] : noninflammatory degeneration of the kidneys chiefly affecting the renal tubules — **ne·phrot·ic** \-ˈfrät-ik\ *adj or n*

neph·ro·stome \ˈnef-rə-ˌstōm\ *n* [NL *nephrostoma,* fr. *nephr-* + *stoma*] : the ciliated funnel-shaped coelomic opening of a typical nephridium

ne plus ul·tra \ˌnē-ˌpləs-ˈəl-trə\ *n* [NL, (go) no more beyond] **1 :** the highest point capable of being attained : ACME **2 :** the most profound degree of a quality or state

nep·o·tism \ˈnep-ə-ˌtiz-əm\ *n* [F *népotisme,* fr. It *nepotismo,* fr. *nepote* nephew, fr. L *nepot-, nepos* grandson, nephew — more at NEPHEW] : favoritism shown to a relative (as by giving an appointive job) on a basis of relationship

Nep·tune \ˈnep-ˌt(y)ün\ *n* [L *Neptunus*] **1 a :** the Roman god of the sea — compare POSEIDON **b :** OCEAN **2 :** the planet 8th in order from the sun — see PLANET table — **Nep·tu·ni·an** \nep-ˈt(y)ü-nē-ən\ *adj*

nep·tu·ni·um \nep-ˈt(y)ü-nē-əm\ *n* [NL, fr. ISV *Neptune*] : a radioactive metallic element that is chemically similar to uranium and is obtained in nuclear reactors as a by-product in the production of plutonium — see ELEMENT table

Ne·re·id \ˈnir-ē-əd\ *n* [L *Nereid-, Nereis,* fr. Gk *Nēreid-, Nēreis,* fr. *Nēreus* Nereus] : any of the sea nymphs fathered by the sea-god Nereus according to Greek myth

ne·re·is \ˈnir-ē-əs\ *n, pl* **ne·re·ides** \nə-ˈrē-ə-ˌdēz\ [NL, genus name, fr. L, Nereid] : any of a genus (*Nereis*) of usu. large often dimorphic and greenish marine polychaete worms — see ANNELID illustration

ne·rit·ic \nə-ˈrit-ik\ *adj* [perh. fr. NL *Nerita,* genus of marine snails] : of, relating to, or constituting the belt or region of shallow water adjoining the seacoast

ne·rol \ˈne(ə)r-ˌȯl, ˈni(ə)r-\ *n* [ISV *ner-* (fr. *neroli oil*) + *-ol*] : a liquid alcohol $C_{10}H_{18}O$ that has a rose scent and is used esp. in perfumery

ner·o·li oil \ˈner-ə-lē-\ *n* [F *néroli,* fr. It *neroli,* fr. Anna Maria de La Trémoille, princess of *Nerole fl* 1670] : a fragrant pale yellow essential oil obtained from orange flowers and used esp. in cologne and as a flavoring

nerts \ˈnərts\ *n pl* [alter. of *nuts*] *slang* : NONSENSE, NUTS

nerv- *or* **nervi-** *or* **nervo-** *comb form* [ME *nerv-,* fr. L, fr. *nervus*] : NEUR- <*nerv*ine>

ner·va·tion \ˌnər-ˈvā-shən\ *n* : an arrangement or system of nerves; *also* : VENATION

[1]**nerve** \ˈnərv\ *n* [L *nervus* sinew, nerve; akin to Gk *neuron* sinew, nerve, *nēn* to spin — more at NEEDLE] **1 :** SINEW, TENDON <strain every ~> **2 :** one of the filamentous bands of nervous tissue that connect parts of the nervous system with the other organs, conduct nervous impulses, and are made up of axons and dendrites together with protective and supportive structures **3 a :** NERVE CENTER 2 **b :** power of endurance or control : FORTITUDE, STRENGTH **c :** ASSURANCE, BOLDNESS; *also* : presumptuous audacity : GALL **4 a :** a sore or sensitive point **b** *pl* : nervous disorganization or collapse : HYSTERIA **5 :** VEIN 3 **6 :** the sensitive pulp of a tooth *syn* see TEMERITY

[2]**nerve** *vt* **nerved; nerv·ing** : to give strength or courage to : supply with physical or moral force

nerve cell *n* : NEURON; *also* : a nerve cell body exclusive of its processes

nerve center *n* **1** : CENTER 2c **2** : a source of leadership, control, or energy <the financial *nerve center* of the nation>

nerve cord *n* : the pair of closely united ventral longitudinal nerves with their segmental ganglia that is characteristic of many elongate invertebrates (as earthworms)

nerved \'nərvd\ *adj* **1 a** : VEINED <a ~ wing> **b** : having veins or nerves esp. of a specified kind or number — used in combination <fan-*nerved* leaves> **2** : showing courage or strength

nerve fiber *n* : AXON, DENDRITE

nerve gas *n* : an organophosphate war gas that interferes with normal nerve transmission and induces intense bronchial spasm with resulting inhibition of respiration

nerve impulse *n* : the progressive alteration in the protoplasm of a nerve fiber that follows stimulation and serves to transmit a record of sensation from a receptor or an instruction to act to an effector — called also *nervous impulse*

nerve·less \'nərv-ləs\ *adj* **1** : lacking strength or courage : FEEBLE **2** : exhibiting control or balance : POISED, COOL — **nerve·less·ly** *adv* — **nerve·less·ness** *n*

nerve net *n* : a network of nerve cells apparently continuous with one another and conducting impulses in all directions; *also* : a primitive nervous system (as in a jellyfish) consisting of such a network

nerve–rack·ing *or* **nerve–wrack·ing** \'nərv-ˌrak-iŋ\ *adj* : extremely trying on the nerves <a ~ ordeal>

nerve trunk *n* : a bundle of nerve fibers enclosed in a connective tissue sheath

ner·vos·i·ty \ˌnər-'väs-ət-ē\ *n* : the quality or state of being nervous

ner·vous \'nər-vəs\ *adj* **1** *archaic* : SINEWY, STRONG **2** : marked by strength of thought, feeling, or style : SPIRITED <a vibrant tight-packed ~ style of writing> **3** : of, relating to, or composed of neurons **4 a** : of or relating to the nerves; *also* : originating in or affected by the nerves **b** : easily excited or irritated : JUMPY **c** : TIMID, APPREHENSIVE <a ~ smile> **5 a** : tending to produce nervousness or agitation : UNEASY <a ~ situation> **b** : appearing or acting unsteady, erratic, or irregular — used of inanimate things — **ner·vous·ly** *adv* — **ner·vous·ness** *n*

nervous breakdown *n* **1** : NEURASTHENIA **2** : a case of neurasthenia

nervous Nel·lie *or* **nervous Nel·ly** \-'nel-ē\ *n, pl* **nervous Nellies** *often cap 1st N* [fr. the name *Nellie*] **1** : a timid or ineffectual person **2** : a person who is given to often unwarranted worrying

nervous system *n* : the bodily system that in vertebrates is made up of brain and spinal cord, nerves, ganglia, and parts of the receptor organs and that receives and interprets stimuli and transmits impulses to the effector organs

ner·vure \'nər-vyər\ *n* [F, fr. *nerf* sinew, fr. L *nervus*] : VEIN 3

nervy \'nər-vē\ *adj* **nerv·i·er; -est** **1** *archaic* : SINEWY, STRONG **2 a** : showing calm courage : BOLD **b** : marked by effrontery or presumption : BRASH **3** : EXCITABLE, NERVOUS — **nerv·i·ness** *n*

NES *abbr* not elsewhere specified

ne·science \'nesh-(ē-)ən(t)s, 'nēsh-; 'nes-ē-ən(t)s, 'nēs-\ *n* [LL *nescientia*, fr. L *nescient-, nesciens*, prp. of *nescire* not to know, fr. *ne-* not + *scire* to know — more at NO, SCIENCE] : lack of knowledge or awareness : IGNORANCE — **ne·scient** \-(ē-)ənt, -ē-ənt\ *adj*

ness \'nes\ *n* [ME *nasse*, fr. OE *næss*; akin to OE *nasu* nose — more at NOSE] : CAPE, PROMONTORY

-ness \nəs\ *n suffix* [ME *-nes*, fr. OE; akin to OHG *-nissa* -ness] : state : condition : quality : degree <good*ness*>

Nes·sel·rode \'nes-əl-ˌrōd\ *n* [Count Karl R. *Nesselrode* †1862 Russ statesman] : a mixture of candied fruits, nuts, and maraschino used in puddings, pies, and ice cream

Nes·sus \'nes-əs\ *n* [L, fr. Gk *Nessos*] : a centaur slain by Hercules but avenged by means of a poisoned garment that caused Hercules to die in torment

[1]**nest** \'nest\ *n* [ME, fr. OE; akin to OHG *nest* nest, L *nidus*] **1 a** : a bed or receptacle prepared by a bird for its eggs and young **b** : a place or specially modified structure serving as an abode of animals and esp. of their immature stages <an ants' ~> **c** : a receptacle resembling a bird's nest **2 a** : a place of rest, retreat, or lodging **b** : DEN, HANGOUT **3** : the occupants or frequenters of a nest **4 a** : a group of similar things : AGGREGATION <a ~ of giant mountains —Helen MacInnes> **b** : HOTBED 2 <a ~ of rebellion> **5** : a group of objects made to fit close together or one within another **6** : an emplaced group of weapons

[2]**nest** *vi* **1** : to build or occupy a nest **2** : to fit compactly together or within one another : EMBED ~ *vt* **1** : to form a nest for **2** : to pack compactly together

nest egg *n* **1** : a natural or artificial egg left in a nest to induce a fowl to continue to lay there **2** : a fund of money accumulated as a reserve

nest·er \'nes-tər\ *n* **1** : one that nests **2** *West* : a homesteader or squatter who takes up land on open range for a farm

nes·tle \'nes-əl\ *vb* **nes·tled; nes·tling** \-(ə-)liŋ\ [ME *nestlen*, fr. OE *nestlian*, fr. *nest*] *vi* **1** *archaic* : NEST 1 **2** : to settle snugly or comfortably <the children were *nestled* all snug in their beds —Clement Moore> **3** : to lie in an inconspicuous or sheltered manner ~ *vt* **1** : to settle, shelter, or house in or as if in a nest **2** : to press closely and affectionately <~*s* a kitten in her arms> — **nes·tler** \-(ə-)lər\ *n*

nest·ling \'nest-liŋ\ *n* : a young bird that has not abandoned the nest

Nes·tor \'nes-tər, -ˌtȯ(ə)r\ *n* [L, fr. Gk *Nestōr*] **1** : a king of Pylos who served in his old age as a counselor to the Greeks at Troy **2** *often not cap* : one who is a patriarch or leader in his field

Nes·to·ri·an \ne-'stōr-ē-ən, -'stȯr-\ *adj* **1** : of or relating to the doctrine ascribed to Nestorius and ecclesiastically condemned in 431 that divine and human persons remained separate in the incarnate Christ **2** : of or relating to a church separating from Byzantine Christianity after 431, centering in Persia, and surviving chiefly in Asia Minor — **Nestorian** *n* — **Nes·to·ri·an·ism** \-ˌiz-əm\ *n*

[1]**net** \'net\ *n* [ME *nett*, fr. OE; akin to OHG *nezzi* net, L *nodus* knot] **1 a** : an open meshed fabric twisted, knotted, or woven together at regular intervals **b** : something made of net: as (1) : a device for catching fish, birds, or insects (2) : a fabric barricade which divides a court in half (as in tennis or volleyball) and over which a ball or shuttlecock must be hit to be in play (3) : the fabric that encloses the sides and back of the goal in various games (as soccer or hockey) **2** : an entrapping situation <caught in the ~ of suspicious circumstances> **3** : something resembling a net in reticulation (as of lines, fibers, or figures) **4** : a ball hit into the net in a racket game **5 a** : a group of communications stations operating under unified control **b** : NETWORK 4 — **net·less** \-ləs\ *adj* — **net·like** \-ˌlīk\ *adj* — **net·ty** \'net-ē\ *adj*

[2]**net** *vt* **net·ted; net·ting** **1** : to cover or enclose with or as if with a net **2** : to catch in or as if in a net **3** : to cover with a network **4 a** : to hit (a ball) into the net for the loss of a point in a racket game **b** : to hit (a ball) into the goal for a score (as in hockey or soccer) — **net·ter** *n*

[3]**net** *adj* [ME, clean, bright, fr. MF] **1** : free from all charges or deductions: as **a** : remaining after the deduction of all charges, outlay, or loss <~ earnings> — compare GROSS **b** : excluding all tare <~ weight> **2** : FINAL <the ~ result>

[4]**net** *vt* **net·ted; net·ting** **1 a** : to make by way of profit : CLEAR **b** : to produce by way of profit **2** : to get possession : GAIN

[5]**net** *n* **1** : a net amount, profit, weight, or price **2** : the score of a golfer in a handicap match after deducting his handicap from his gross **3** : ESSENCE, GIST

NET *abbr* National Educational Television

NETFS *abbr* National Educational Television Film Service

Neth *abbr* Netherlands

neth·er \'neth-ər\ *adj* [ME, fr. OE *nithera*, fr. *nither* down; akin to OHG *nidar* down, Skt *ni*, Gk *en, eni* in — more at IN] **1** : situated down or below : LOWER <the ~ side> **2** : situated or believed to be situated beneath the earth's surface <the ~ regions>

neth·er·most \-ˌmōst\ *adj* : farthest down : LOWEST

neth·er·world \-ˌwərld\ *n* **1** : the world of the dead **2** : UNDERWORLD 4 <the ~ of deceit, subversion, and espionage —R. M. Nixon>

net·keep·er \'net-ˌkē-pər\ *n* : GOALKEEPER

net·mind·er \-ˌmīn-dər\ *n* : GOALKEEPER

net·su·ke \'net-s(ə-)kē\ *n, pl* **netsuke** *or* **netsukes** [Jap] : a small and often intricately carved toggle (as of wood, ivory, or metal) used to fasten a small pouch or purse to a kimono sash

nett *Brit var of* NET

net·ting \'net-iŋ\ *n* **1** : NETWORK **2** : the act or process of making a net or network **3** : the act, process, or right of fishing with a net

[1]**net·tle** \'net-ᵊl\ *n* [ME, fr. OE *netel*; akin to OHG *nazza* nettle, Gk *adikē*] **1** : any of a genus (*Urtica* of the family Urticaceae, the nettle family) of chiefly coarse herbs armed with stinging hairs **2** : any of various prickly or stinging plants other than the nettle

nettle 1

[2]**nettle** *vt* **net·tled; net·tling** \'net-liŋ, -ᵊl-iŋ\ **1** : to strike or sting with or as if with nettles **2** : to arouse to sharp but transitory annoyance or anger ***syn*** see IRRITATE

nettle rash *n* : URTICARIA

net·tle·some \'net-ᵊl-səm\ *adj* : causing vexation : IRRITATING

net–veined \-'vānd\ *adj* : having veins arranged in a fine network <a ~ leaf> <a ~ wing> — compare PARALLEL-VEINED

net–winged \'net-'wiŋd\ *adj* : having wings with a fine network of veins

[1]**net·work** \'net-ˌwərk\ *n* **1** : a fabric or structure of cords or wires that cross at regular intervals and are knotted or secured at the crossings **2** : a system of lines or channels resembling a network **3** : an interconnected or interrelated chain, group, or system <a ~ of hotels> **4 a** : a group of radio or television stations linked by wire or radio relay **b** : a radio or television company that produces programs for broadcast over such a network

[2]**network** *vt* **1** : to cover with or as if with a network <a continent . . . so ~*ed* with navigable rivers and canals —*Lamp*> **2** : to present on or integrate into a radio or television network <~*ed* programs>

Neuf·cha·tel \ˌn(y)ü-shə-ˌtel, ˌnə(r)sh-ə-\ *n* [F, fr. *Neufchâtel*, France] : a soft unripened cheese similar to cream cheese but containing less fat and more moisture

neume \'n(y)üm\ *n* [F, fr. ML *pneuma, neuma*, fr. Gk *pneuma* breath — more at PNEUMATIC] : any of various symbols used in the notation of Gregorian chant — **neu·mat·ic** \n(y)ü-'mat-ik\ *adj*

neur- *or* **neuro-** *comb form* [NL, fr. Gk, nerve, sinew, fr. *neuron* — more at NERVE] **1** : nerve <*neur*al> <*neuro*logy> **2** : neural and <*neuro*muscular>

neu·ral \'n(y)ůr-əl\ *adj* **1** : of, relating to, or affecting a nerve or the nervous system **2** : situated in the region of or on the same side of the body as the brain and spinal cord : DORSAL — **neu·ral·ly** \-ə-lē\ *adv*

neural arch *n* **:** the cartilaginous or bony arch enclosing the spinal cord on the dorsal side of a vertebra — see VERTEBRA illustration

neu·ral·gia \n(y)u̇-'ral-jə\ *n* [NL] **:** acute paroxysmal pain radiating along the course of one or more nerves usu. without demonstrable changes in the nerve structure — **neu·ral·gic** \-jik\ *adj*

neural tube *n* **:** the hollow longitudinal tube formed by infolding and subsequent fusion of the opposite ectodermal folds in the vertebrate embryo

neur·amin·i·dase \ˌn(y)u̇r-ə-'min-ə-ˌdās, -ˌdāz\ *n* [*neuraminic* acid (an amino acid) + *-ide* + *-ase*] **:** a hydrolytic enzyme that is found esp. in microorganisms of the respiratory or intestinal tract and that splits mucoproteins by breaking a glucoside link

neur·as·the·nia \ˌn(y)u̇r-əs-'thē-nē-ə\ *n* [NL] **:** an emotional and psychic disorder that is characterized by impaired functioning in interpersonal relationships and often by fatigue, depression, feelings of inadequacy, headaches, hypersensitivity to sensory stimulation (as by light or noise), and psychosomatic symptoms (as disturbances of digestion and circulation) — **neur·as·then·ic** \-'thenik\ *adj* — **neur·as·then·i·cal·ly** \-i-k(ə-)lē\ *adv*

neu·ri·lem·ma \ˌn(y)u̇r-ə-'lem-ə\ *n* [NL, fr. *neur-* + Gk *eilēma* covering, coil, fr. *eilein* to wind; akin to Gk *eilyein* to wrap — more at VOLUBLE] **1 :** the delicate nucleated outer sheath of a nerve fiber **2 :** PERINEURIUM — **neu·ri·lem·mal** \-'lem-əl\ *adj*

neu·ris·tor \n(y)u̇-'ris-tər\ *n* [*neuron* + *transistor;* fr. its functioning like a neuron and not requiring the use of transistors] **:** a usu. electronic device along which a signal propagates with uniform velocity and without attenuation

neu·ri·tis \n(y)u̇-'rīt-əs\ *n, pl* **-rit·i·des** \-'rit-ə-ˌdēz\ *or* **-ri·tis·es** [NL] **:** an inflammatory or degenerative lesion of a nerve marked esp. by pain, sensory disturbances, and impaired or lost reflexes — **neu·rit·ic** \-'rit-ik\ *adj or n*

neu·ro·ac·tive \ˌn(y)u̇r-ō-'ak-tiv\ *adj* **:** stimulating neural tissue

neu·ro·bi·ol·o·gy \-bī-'äl-ə-jē\ *n* **:** a branch of the life sciences that deals with the anatomy, physiology, and pathology of the nervous system from a holistic viewpoint — **neu·ro·bi·o·log·i·cal** \-ˌbī-ə-'läj-i-kəl\ *adj* — **neu·ro·bi·ol·o·gist** \-bī-'äl-ə-jəst\ *n*

neu·ro·blas·to·ma \-blas-'tō-mə\ *n, pl* **-mas** *or* **-ma·ta** \-mət-ə\ [NL, fr. ISV *neuroblast* (embryonic ganglion cell), fr. *neur-* + *-blast*] **:** a malignant tumor formed of embryonic ganglion cells

neu·ro·chem·is·try \'kem-ə-strē\ *n* **:** the study of the chemical makeup and activitie of nervous tissue — **neu·ro·chem·i·cal** \-'kem-i-kəl\ *adj* — **neu·ro·chem·ist** \-'kem-əst\ *n*

neu·ro·cir·cu·la·to·ry \ˌn(y)u̇r-ō-'sər-kyə-lə-ˌtōr-ē, -ˌtȯr-\ *adj* **:** of or relating to the nervous and circulatory systems

neu·ro·en·do·crine \-'en-də-krən, -ˌkrīn, -ˌkrēn\ *adj* **1 :** of, relating to, or being a hormonal substance that influences the activity of nerves **2 :** of, relating to, or being neurosecretion or a neurosecretion

neu·ro·ep·i·the·li·al \ˌn(y)u̇r-ō-ˌep-ə-'thē-lē-əl\ *adj* **:** having qualities of both neural and epithelial cells

neu·ro·fi·bril \ˌn(y)u̇r-ō-'fīb-rəl, -'fib-\ *n* [NL *neurofibrilla,* fr. *neur-* + *fibrilla* fibril] **:** a fine proteinaceous fibril that is found in conductile protoplasm (as in a neuron or a paramecium) — **neu·ro·fi·bril·lary** \-rə-ˌler-ē\ *adj*

neu·ro·gen·ic \ˌn(y)u̇r-ə-'jen-ik\ *adj* **1 :** originating in or controlled by nervous tissue <~ heartbeat> **2 :** induced or modified by nervous factors; *esp* **:** disordered because of abnormally altered neural relations — **neu·ro·gen·i·cal·ly** \-i-k(ə-)lē\ *adv*

neu·ro·glia \n(y)u̇-'räg-lē-ə; ˌn(y)u̇r-ə-'glē-ə, -'glī-\ *n* [NL, fr. *neur-* + MGk *glia* glue] **:** supporting tissue intermingled with the essential elements of nervous tissue esp. in the brain, spinal cord, and ganglia — **neu·ro·gli·al** \-əl\ *adj*

neu·ro·hor·mon·al \ˌn(y)u̇r-ō-hȯr-'mōn-ᵊl\ *adj* **1 :** involving both neural and hormonal mechanisms **2 :** of, relating to, or being a neurohormone

neu·ro·hor·mone \-'hȯr-ˌmōn\ *n* [ISV] **:** a hormone (as acetylcholine or norepinephrine) produced by or acting on nervous tissue

neu·ro·hu·mor \ˌn(y)u̇r-ō-'hyü-mər, -'yü-\ *n* **:** a substance liberated at a nerve ending that participates in the transmission of a nerve impulse — **neu·ro·hu·mor·al** \-mə-rəl\ *adj*

neu·ro·hy·poph·y·sis \-hī-'päf-ə-səs\ *n* [NL] **:** the portion of the pituitary body that is composed of the infundibulum and posterior lobe and is concerned with the secretion of various hormones — **neu·ro·hy·poph·y·se·al** \-(ˌ)hī-ˌpäf-ə-'sē-əl\ *or* **neu·ro·hy·po·phys·i·al** \-ˌhī-pə-'fiz-ē-əl\ *adj*

neurol *abbr* neurological; neurology

neu·ro·lept·an·al·ge·sia \'n(y)u̇r-ə-ˌlep-ˌtan-ᵊl-'jē-zhə, -z(h)ē-ə\ *or* **neu·ro·lep·to·an·al·ge·sia** \ˌn(y)u̇r-ə-'lep-tō-ˌan-\ *n* [NL, fr. ISV *neuroleptic* + *analgesic* + NL *-ia* (as in *analgesia*)] **:** joint administration of a tranquilizing drug and an analgesic esp. for relief of surgical pain — **neu·ro·lept·an·al·ge·sic** \-'jē-zik, -sik\ *adj*

neu·ro·lep·tic \ˌn(y)u̇r-ə-'lep-tik\ *n* [F *neuroleptique,* fr. *neur-* + *-leptique* affecting, fr. Gk *lēptikos* seizing, fr. *lambanein* to take, seize — more at LATCH] **:** TRANQUILIZER 2 — **neuroleptic** *adj*

neu·rol·o·gist \n(y)u̇-'räl-ə-jəst\ *n* **:** one specializing in neurology; *esp* **:** a physician skilled in the diagnosis and treatment of disease of the nervous system

neu·rol·o·gy \-jē\ *n* [NL *neurologia,* fr. *neur-* + *-logia* -logy] **:** the scientific study of the nervous system — **neu·ro·log·i·cal** \ˌn(y)u̇r-ə-'läj-i-kəl\ *or* **neu·ro·log·ic** \-ik\ *adj* — **neu·ro·log·i·cal·ly** \-i-k(ə-)lē\ *adv*

neu·ro·ma \n(y)u̇-'rō-mə\ *n, pl* **-mas** *or* **-ma·ta** \-mət-ə\ [NL] **:** a tumor or mass growing from a nerve and usu. consisting of nerve fibers

neu·ro·mo·tor \ˌn(y)u̇r-ə-'mōt-ər\ *adj* **:** relating to efferent nervous impulses

neu·ro·mus·cu·lar \ˌn(y)u̇r-ō-'məs-kyə-lər\ *adj* [ISV] **:** of or relating to nerves and muscles; *esp* **:** jointly involving nervous and muscular elements <a ~ junction>

neu·ron \'n(y)ü-ˌrän, 'n(y)u̇(ə)r-ˌän\ *also* **neu·rone** \-ˌrōn, -ˌōn\ *n* [NL *neuron,* fr. Gk, nerve, sinew — more at NERVE] **:** a grayish or reddish granular cell with specialized processes that is the fundamental functional unit of nervous tissue — **neu·ro·nal** \'n(y)u̇r-ən-ᵊl, n(y)u̇-'rōn-ᵊl\ *also* **neu·ron·ic** \n(y)u̇-'rän-ik\ *adj*

1
2
3
4

neuron: *1* cell body, *2* dendrite, *3* axon, *4* nerve ending

neu·rop·a·thy \n(y)u̇-'räp-ə-thē\ *n, pl* **-thies** [ISV] **:** an abnormal and usu. degenerative state of the nervous system or nerves; *also* **:** a systemic condition that stems from a neuropathy — **neu·ro·path·ic** \ˌn(y)u̇r-ə-'path-ik\ *adj* — **neu·ro·path·i·cal·ly** \-i-k(ə-)lē\ *adv*

neu·ro·phar·ma·col·o·gy \'n(y)u̇r-ō-ˌfär-mə-'käl-ə-jē\ *n* **:** a branch of medical science dealing with the action of drugs on and in the nervous system — **neu·ro·phar·ma·co·log·ic** \-kə-'läj-ik\ *or* **neu·ro·phar·ma·co·log·i·cal** \-i-kəl\ *adj* — **neu·ro·phar·ma·col·o·gist** \-'käl-ə-jəst\ *n*

neu·ro·phys·i·ol·o·gy \ˌn(y)u̇r-ō-ˌfiz-ē-'äl-ə-jē\ *n* **:** physiology of the nervous system — **neu·ro·phys·i·o·log·i·cal** \-ē-ə-'läj-i-kəl\ *also* **neu·ro·phys·i·o·log·ic** \-ik\ *adj* — **neu·ro·phys·i·o·log·i·cal·ly** \-i-k(ə-)lē\ *adv* — **neu·ro·phys·i·ol·o·gist** \-ē-'äl-ə-jəst\ *n*

neu·ro·psy·chi·a·try \-sə-'kī-ə-trē, -sī-\ *n* **:** a branch of medicine concerned with both the psychic and organic aspects of mental disorder — **neu·ro·psy·chi·at·ric** \-ˌsī-kē-'a-trik\ *adj* — **neu·ro·psy·chi·at·ri·cal·ly** \-tri-k(ə-)lē\ *adv* — **neu·ro·psy·chi·a·trist** \-sə-'kī-ə-trəst, -sī-\ *n*

neu·ro·psy·chic \ˌn(y)u̇r-ə-'sī-kik\ *also* **neu·ro·psy·chi·cal** \-ki-kəl\ *adj* **:** of or relating to both the mind and the nervous system as affecting mental processes

neu·rop·ter·an \n(y)u̇-'räp-tə-rən\ *n* [deriv. of Gk *neur-* + *pteron* wing — more at FEATHER] **:** any of an order (Neuroptera) of usu. net-winged insects that include the lacewings and ant lions — **neuropteran** *adj* — **neu·rop·ter·ous** \-rəs\ *adj*

neu·ro·sci·ence \ˌn(y)u̇r-ō-'sī-ən(t)s\ *n* **:** a branch (as neurophysiology) of the life sciences that deals with the anatomy, physiology, biochemistry, or molecular biology of nerves and nervous tissue and esp. with their relation to behavior and learning — **neu·ro·sci·en·tist** \-ənt-əst\ *n*

neu·ro·se·cre·tion \-si-'krē-shən\ *n* **1 :** a secretion produced by nerve cells **2 :** the act or process of producing a neurosecretion — **neu·ro·se·cre·to·ry** \-'krēt-ə-rē\ *adj*

neu·ro·sen·so·ry \-'sen(t)s-(ə-)rē\ *adj* **:** of or relating to afferent nerves

neu·ro·sis \n(y)u̇-'rō-səs\ *n, pl* **-ro·ses** \-ˌsēz\ [NL] **:** a functional nervous disorder without demonstrable physical lesion

neu·ros·po·ra \n(y)u̇-'räs-pə-rə\ *n* [NL, genus name, fr. *neur-* + *spora* spore] **:** any of a genus (*Neurospora* of the family Sphaeriaceae) of ascomycetous fungi which are used extensively in genetic research and have black perithecia and persistent asci and some of which have salmon pink or orange spore masses and are severe pests in bakeries

neu·ro·sur·geon \ˌn(y)u̇r-ō-'sər-jən\ *n* **:** a surgeon specializing in neurosurgery

neu·ro·sur·gery \-'sərj-(ə-)rē\ *n* **:** surgery of nervous structures (as nerves, the brain, or the spinal cord) — **neu·ro·sur·gi·cal** \-'sər-ji-kəl\ *adj*

[1]**neu·rot·ic** \n(y)u̇-'rät-ik\ *adj* **:** of, relating to, constituting, or affected with neurosis — **neu·rot·i·cal·ly** \-i-k(ə-)lē\ *adv*

[2]**neurotic** *n* **1 :** an emotionally unstable individual **2 :** one affected with a neurosis

neu·rot·i·cism \n(y)u̇-'rät-ə-ˌsiz-əm\ *n* **:** a neurotic character, condition, or trait

neu·ro·tox·ic \ˌn(y)u̇r-ə-'täk-sik\ *adj* **:** toxic to the nerves or nervous tissue — **neu·ro·tox·ic·i·ty** \-ˌtäk-'sis-ət-ē\ *n*

neu·ro·tox·in \-'täk-sən\ *n* [ISV] **:** a poisonous protein complex that acts on the nervous system

neu·ro·trans·mit·ter \ˌn(y)u̇r-ō-tran(t)s-'mit-ər, -tranz-\ *n* **:** a substance (as norepinephrine) that transmits nerve impulses across a synapse

neu·ro·trop·ic \ˌn(y)u̇r-ə-'träp-ik\ *adj* [ISV] **:** having an affinity for or localizing selectively in nerve tissue

neus·ton \'n(y)ü-ˌstän\ *n* [G, fr. Gk, neut. of *neustos* swimming, fr. *nein* to swim — more at NOURISH] **:** minute organisms that float in the surface film of water

neut *abbr* neuter

[1]**neu·ter** \'n(y)üt-ər\ *adj* [ME *neutre,* fr. MF & L; MF *neutre,* fr. L *neuter,* lit., neither, fr. *ne-* not + *uter* which of two — more at NO, WHETHER] **1 a :** of, relating to, or constituting the gender that ordinarily includes most words or grammatical forms referring to things classed as neither masculine nor feminine **b :** neither active nor passive **:** INTRANSITIVE **2 :** taking no side **:** NEUTRAL **3 :** lacking or having imperfectly developed or nonfunctional generative organs <the worker bee is ~>

[2]**neuter** *n* **1 a :** a noun, pronoun, adjective, or inflectional form or class of the neuter gender **b :** the neuter gender **2 :** one that is neutral **3 a :** WORKER 2 **b :** a spayed or castrated animal

[3]**neuter** *vt* **:** CASTRATE, ALTER

neu·ter·cane \-ˌkān\ *n* [L *neuter* neither + E *-cane* (as in hurricane); from the difficulty of classifying it as either hurricane or frontal storm] **:** a subtropical cyclone that is usu. less than 100 miles in diameter and that draws energy from sources common to both the hurricane and the frontal cyclone

[1]**neu·tral** \'n(y)ü-trəl\ *adj* [MF, fr. (assumed) ML *neutralis,* fr. L, of neuter gender, fr. *neutr-, neuter*] **1 :** not engaged on either side; *specif* **:** not aligned with a political or ideological grouping <a ~ nation> **2 :** of or relating to a neutral state or power <~ territory> **3 a :** neither one thing nor the other **:** INDIFFERENT **b (1) :** ACHROMATIC **(2) :** nearly achromatic **c (1) :** NEUTER 3 **(2) :** lacking stamens or pistils **d :** neither acid nor basic **e :** not electrically charged **4 :** produced with the tongue in the

position it has when at rest <the ~ vowels of \ə-ˈbəv\ *above*> — **neu·tral·ly** \-trə-lē\ *adv* — **neu·tral·ness** *n*

²**neutral** *n* **1** : one that is neutral **2** : a neutral color **3** : a position of disengagement (as of gears)

neu·tral·ism \ˈn(y)ü-trə-ˌliz-əm\ *n* **1** : NEUTRALITY **2** : a policy or the advocacy of neutrality esp. in international affairs — **neu·tral·ist** \-ləst\ *n* — **neu·tral·is·tic** \ˌn(y)ü-trə-ˈlis-tik\ *adj*

neu·tral·i·ty \n(y)ü-ˈtral-ət-ē\ *n* : the quality or state of being neutral; *esp* : immunity from invasion or use by belligerents

neu·tral·iza·tion \ˌn(y)ü-trə-lə-ˈzā-shən\ *n* **1** : an act or process of neutralizing **2** : the quality or state of being neutralized

neu·tral·ize \ˈn(y)ü-trə-ˌlīz\ *vb* **-ized; -iz·ing** *vt* **1** : to make chemically neutral **2** : to counteract the activity or effect of : make ineffective <propaganda that is difficult to ~> **3** : to make electrically inert by combining equal positive and negative quantities **4** : to invest (as a territory or a nation) with conventional or obligatory neutrality conferring inviolability during a war **5** : to make neutral by blending with the complementary color ~ *vi* : to undergo neutralization — **neu·tral·iz·er** *n*

neutral red *n* : a basic phenazine dye used chiefly as a biological stain and acid-base indicator

neutral spirits *n pl but sing or pl in constr* : ethyl alcohol of 190 or higher proof used esp. for blending other alcoholic liquors

neu·tri·no \n(y)ü-ˈtrē-(ˌ)nō\ *n, pl* **-nos** [It, dim. of *neutrone* neutron] : an uncharged elementary particle that has two forms associated respectively with the electron and the muon, that is believed to be massless, and that interacts very weakly with matter after being created in the process of particle decay

neu·tron \ˈn(y)ü-ˌträn\ *n* [prob. fr. *neutral*] : an uncharged elementary particle that has a mass nearly equal to that of the proton and is present in all known atomic nuclei except the hydrogen nucleus

neutron star *n* [fr. the hypothesis that the cores of such stars are composed entirely of neutrons] : any of various hypothetical dense celestial objects that consist of closely packed nuclear particles resulting from the collapse of a much larger stellar body and that may be detectable through their emission of X rays

¹**neu·tro·phil** \ˈn(y)ü-trə-ˌfil\ *or* **neu·tro·phil·ic** \ˌn(y)ü-trə-ˈfil-ik\ *also* **neu·tro·phile** \ˈn(y)ü-trə-ˌfīl\ *adj* [ISV *neutro-* (fr. L *neutr-*, *neuter* neither) + *-phil*] : staining to the same degree with acid or basic dyes <~ granulocytes>

²**neutrophil** *also* **neutrophile** *n* : a finely granular cell that is the chief phagocytic leukocyte of the blood

Nev *abbr* Nevada

né·vé \nā-ˈvā\ *n* [F (Swiss dial.), fr. L *niv-*, *nix* snow — more at SNOW] : the partially compacted granular snow that forms the surface part of the upper end of a glacier; *broadly* : a field of granular snow

nev·er \ˈnev-ər\ *adv* [ME, fr. OE *nǣfre*, fr. *ne* not + *ǣfre* ever — more at NO] **1** : not ever : at no time <~ saw him before> **2** : not in any degree : not under any condition <~ the wiser for his experience>

nev·er·more \ˌnev-ər-ˈmō(ə)r, -ˈmȯ(ə)r\ *adv* : never again

nev·er–nev·er land \ˌnev-ər-ˈnev-ər-\ *n* : an ideal or imaginary place

nev·er·the·less \ˌnev-ər-thə-ˈles\ *adv* : in spite of that : HOWEVER <her childish but ~ real delight —Richard Corbin>

ne·vus \ˈnē-vəs\ *n, pl* **ne·vi** \-ˌvī\ [NL, fr. L *naevus*] : a congenital pigmented area on the skin : BIRTHMARK

¹**new** \ˈn(y)ü, *before a stress in geographical names also* n(y)ü *or* n(y)ə(-w)\ *adj* [ME, fr. OE *nīwe*; akin to OHG *niuwi* new, L *novus*, Gk *neos*] **1** : having existed or having been made but a short time : RECENT **2 a** (1) : having been seen, used, or known for a short time : NOVEL <rice was a ~ crop for the area> (2) : UNFAMILIAR <visit ~ places> **b** : being other than the former or old <a ~ model> **3** : having been in a relationship or condition but a short time <~ to the job> **4 a** : beginning as the resumption or repetition of a previous act or thing <a ~ day> <the ~ edition> **b** : made or become fresh <awoke a ~ man> **5** : different from one of the same category that has existed previously <~ realism> **6** : of dissimilar origin and usu. of superior quality <introducing ~ blood> **7** *cap* : MODERN 3; *esp* : having been in use after medieval times — **new·ish** \ˈn(y)ü-ish\ *adj* — **new·ness** *n*

syn NEW, NOVEL, MODERN, ORIGINAL, FRESH *shared meaning element* : having recently come into existence or use or into a particular state or relationship. NEW may apply to what is freshly made and unused <*new* bricks> <a *new* dress> or to what has not been known or experienced before <a *new* design> <love was a *new* experience to her> or to a person just taken into a group or association <met *new* boys at school> <her *new* roommate> NOVEL applies to what is both new and strange or unfamiliar <a single courageous state may . . . try *novel* social and economic experiments without risk to the rest of the country —L. D. Brandeis> MODERN applies to what belongs to or is characteristic of the present time or era <*modern* manners> <*modern* as opposed to classical physics> ORIGINAL applies to what is or produces something at once new or novel and the first of its kind <the Aztec character was perfectly *original* and unique —W. H. Prescott> <an *original* thinker> FRESH applies to what is or seems new or has not lost its qualities of newness (as liveliness, purity, or energy) <put out *fresh* towels for guests> <make a *fresh* start> *ant* old

²**new** \ˈn(y)ü\ *adv* : NEWLY, RECENTLY — usu. used in combination

¹**new·born** \-ˈbȯ(ə)rn\ *adj* **1** : recently born **2** : born anew

²**newborn** *n, pl* **newborn** *or* **newborns** : a newborn individual : NEONATE

New·burg *or* **New·burgh** \ˈn(y)ü-ˌbərg\ *adj* [origin unknown] : served with a sauce made of cream, butter, wine, and egg yolks <lobster ~> <shrimp ~>

new candle *n* : CANDLE 3

New·cas·tle disease \ˈn(y)ü-ˌkas-əl-, n(y)ü-ˈ\ *n* [*Newcastle* upon Tyne, England] : a destructive virus disease of birds and esp. domestic fowl that involves respiratory and nervous symptoms

new·com·er \ˈn(y)ü-ˌkəm-ər\ *n* **1** : one recently arrived **2** : BEGINNER

New Criticism *n* : an analytic literary criticism that regards the events of an author's life as having no bearing on his work and that is marked by concentration on the language, imagery, and emotional or intellectual tensions in the work — **New Critic** *n*

new deal *n* [fr. the supposed resemblance to the situation of freshness and equality of opportunity afforded by a fresh deal in a card game] **1** *cap N&D* **a** : the legislative and administrative program of President F. D. Roosevelt designed to promote economic recovery and social reform during the 1930s **b** : the period of this program **2** : a governmental program resembling the Roosevelt New Deal in objectives or techniques — **new deal·er** \-ˈdē-lər\ *n, often cap N&D* — **new deal·ish** \-ˈdē-lish\ *adj, often cap N&D* — **new deal·ism** \-ˈdē(ə)l-ˌiz-əm\ *n, often cap N&D*

new drug *n* : a drug that has not been declared safe and effective by qualified experts under the conditions prescribed, recommended, or suggested in the label and that may be a new chemical formula or an established drug prescribed for use in a new way

new economics *n pl but usu sing in constr* : an economic concept that is a logical extension of Keynesianism and that holds that appropriate fiscal and monetary maneuvering can maintain healthy economic growth and prosperity indefinitely

new·el \ˈn(y)ü-əl\ *n* [ME *nowell*, fr. MF *nouel* stone of a fruit, fr. LL *nucalis* like a nut, fr. L *nuc-*, *nux* nut — more at NUT] **1** : an upright post about which the steps of a circular staircase wind **2** : a post at the foot of a straight stairway or one at a landing

newel 2

New Eng *abbr* New England

New English Bible *n* : a translation of the Bible by a British interdenominational committee first published in its entirety in 1970

new·fan·gled \ˈn(y)ü-ˈfaŋ-gəld\ *adj* [ME, fr. *newefangel*, fr. *new* + OE *fangen*, pp. of *fōn* to take, seize — more at PACT] **1** : attracted to novelty **2** : of the newest style — **new·fan·gled·ness** *n*

new–fash·ioned \-ˈfash-ənd\ *adj* **1** : made in a new fashion or form **2** : UP-TO-DATE

new·found \-ˈfau̇nd\ *adj* : newly found <a ~ friend>

New·found·land \ˈn(y)ü-fən-(d)lənd, -ˌ(d)land, n(y)ü-ˈfau̇n-(d)lənd\ *n* [*Newfoundland*, Canada] : any of a breed of very large heavy highly intelligent usu. black dogs developed in Newfoundland

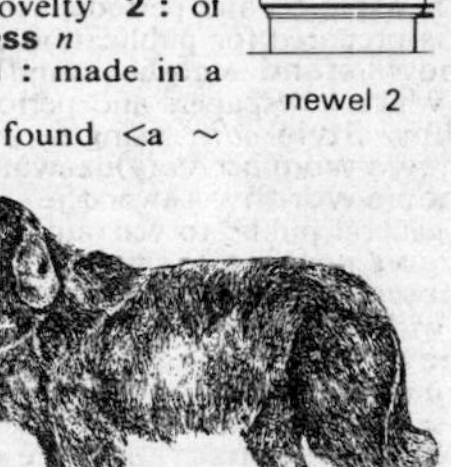

Newfoundland

New·gate \ˈn(y)ü-ˌgāt, -gət\ *n* : a London prison razed in 1902

New Greek *n* : Greek as used by the Greeks since the end of the medieval period

New Hamp·shire \n(y)ü-ˈham(p)-shər, -ˌshi(ə)r\ *n* [*New Hampshire*, U.S.A.] : any of a breed of single-combed general purpose domestic fowls developed chiefly in New Hampshire and noted for heavy winter egg production

New Hebrew *n* : the Hebrew language in use in present-day Israel

New Jer·sey tea \n(y)ü-ˌjər-zē-\ *n* [*New Jersey*, U.S.A.; fr. the use of its leaves as a substitute for tea during the American Revolution] : a low deciduous shrub (*Ceanothus americanus*) of the eastern U.S. with dull green leaves and small white flowers borne in large terminal panicles

New Je·ru·sa·lem \-jə-ˈrü-s(ə-)ləm, -ˈrüz-(ə-)ləm\ *n* [fr. the phrase "the holy city, *New Jerusalem*" (Rev. 21:2)] **1** : the final abode of souls redeemed by Christ **2** : an ideal earthly community

New Latin *n* : Latin as used since the end of the medieval period esp. in scientific description and classification

New Left *n* : a political movement originating in the U.S. in the 1960s that is composed chiefly of students and various extremist groups and that actively advocates (as by demonstrations) radical changes in prevailing political, social, and educational practices — **new leftist** *n, often cap N&L*

new·ly \ˈn(y)ü-lē\ *adv* **1** : LATELY, RECENTLY <a ~ married couple> **2** : ANEW, AFRESH

new·ly·wed \-ˌwed\ *n* : one recently married

new·mar·ket \ˈn(y)ü-ˌmär-kət\ *n* [*Newmarket*, England] : a long close-fitting coat worn in the 19th century

new math *n* : mathematics that is based on set theory esp. as taught in elementary and secondary school — called also *new mathematics*

new moon *n* **1** : the moon's phase when it is in conjunction with the sun so that its dark side is toward the earth; *also* : the thin crescent moon seen shortly after sunset a few days after the actual occurrence of the new moon phase **2** : the first day of the Jewish month

news \ˈn(y)üz\ *n pl but sing in constr, often attrib* **1** : a report of recent events **2 a** : material reported in a newspaper or news periodical or on a newscast **b** : matter that is newsworthy **3** : NEWSCAST — **news·less** \-ləs\ *adj*

news agency *n* : an organization that supplies news to subscribing newspapers, periodicals, and newscasters

news·agent \ˈn(y)ü-ˌzā-jənt\ *n, chiefly Brit* : NEWS DEALER

news·boy \'n(y)üz-ˌbȯi\ *n* : a person who delivers or sells newspapers
news·break \-ˌbrāk\ *n* : a newsworthy event
news·cast \-ˌkast\ *n* [*news* + broad*cast*] : a radio or television broadcast of news — **news·cast·er** \-ˌkas-tər\ *n* — **news·cast·ing** \-tiŋ\ *n*
news conference *n* : PRESS CONFERENCE
news dealer *n* : a dealer in newspapers and magazines
news·let·ter \'n(y)üz-ˌlet-ər\ *n* : a printed sheet, pamphlet, or small newspaper containing news or information of interest chiefly to a special group
news·mag·a·zine \'n(y)üz-ˌmag-ə-ˌzēn, -'zēn\ *n* : a usu. weekly magazine devoted chiefly to summarizing and analyzing news
news·man \-mən, -ˌman\ *n* : one who gathers, reports, or comments on the news : REPORTER, CORRESPONDENT
news·mon·ger \-ˌməŋ-gər, -ˌmäŋ-\ *n* : one who is active in gathering and repeating news; *esp* : GOSSIP
[1]**news·pa·per** \-ˌpā-pər\ *n* **1** : a paper that is printed and distributed usu. daily or weekly and that contains news, articles of opinion, features, and advertising **2** : an organization that publishes a newspaper **3** : the paper making up a newspaper
[2]**newspaper** *vi* : to do newspaper work
news·pa·per·man \'n(y)üz-ˌpā-pər-ˌman\ *n* : one who owns or is employed by a newspaper; *esp* : one who writes or edits news or prepares advertising copy for a newspaper
new·speak \'n(y)ü-ˌspēk\ *n*, *often cap* [*Newspeak*, a language "designed to diminish the range of thought," in the novel *Nineteen Eighty-Four* (1949) by George Orwell] : propagandistic language marked by ambiguity and contradictions : DOUBLE-TALK 2
news·print \'n(y)üz-ˌprint\ *n* : cheap machine-finished paper made chiefly from wood pulp and used mostly for newspapers
news·reel \-ˌrēl\ *n* : a short movie dealing with current events
news release *n* : HANDOUT 3
news·room \'n(y)üz-ˌrüm, -ˌru̇m\ *n* **1** : a room or place where newspapers and periodicals are sold **2** : a reading room having newspapers and periodicals **3** : a place (as an office) where news is prepared for publication or broadcast
news·stand \'n(y)üz-ˌstand\ *n* : a place (as an outdoor stall) where newspapers and periodicals are sold
New Style *adj* : using or according to the Gregorian calendar
news·wom·an \'n(y)üz-ˌwu̇m-ən\ *n* : a female newsman
news·wor·thy \-ˌwər-thē\ *adj* : sufficiently interesting to the general public to warrant reporting (as in a newspaper)
news·writ·ing \-ˌrīt-iŋ\ *n* : JOURNALISM 1a
newsy \'n(y)ü-zē\ *adj* **news·i·er**; **-est** **1** : containing or filled with news <~ letters> **2** : NEWSWORTHY — **news·i·ness** *n*
newt \'n(y)üt\ *n* [ME, alter. (resulting from incorrect division of *an ewte*) of *ewte* — more at EFT] : any of various small semiaquatic salamanders (as of the genus *Triturus*)
New Testament *n* : the second part of the Christian Bible comprising the canonical Gospels and Epistles and also the book of Acts and book of Revelation — see BIBLE table
new thing *n*, *often cap N&T* : freely improvised jazz that has no particular tempo and that is often based on no particular tune
New Thought *n* : a mental healing movement embracing small groups devoted to spiritual healing and the creative power of constructive thinking
new·ton \'n(y)üt-ᵊn\ *n* [Sir Isaac *Newton*] : the unit of force in the mks system of physical units that is of such size that under its influence a body whose mass is one kilogram would experience an acceleration of one meter per second per second
New·to·ni·an \n(y)ü-'tō-nē-ən\ *adj* : of, relating to, or following Sir Isaac Newton, his discoveries, or his doctrines <~ dynamics>
new town *n* : an urban development comprising a small to medium-sized city with a broad range of housing and planned industrial, commercial, and recreational facilities
new wave *n*, *often cap N&W* [trans. of F *nouvelle vague*] : a cinematic movement that is characterized by improvisation, abstraction, and subjective symbolism and that often makes use of experimental photographic techniques
New World *n* : the western hemisphere; *esp* : the continental landmass of No. and So. America
New Year *n* **1** : NEW YEAR'S DAY; *also* : New Year's Day and the first days of the year **2** : ROSH HASHANAH
New Year's Day *n* : January 1 observed as a legal holiday in many countries
[1]**next** \'nekst\ *adj* [ME, fr. OE *nīehst*, superl. of *nēah* nigh — more at NIGH] : immediately preceding or following (as in place, rank, or time)
[2]**next** *adv* **1** : in the time, place, or order nearest or immediately succeeding <~ we drove home> <the ~ closest school> **2** : on the first occasion to come <when ~ we meet>
[3]**next** \(')nekst\ *prep* : nearest or adjacent to
next–door *adj* : located or living in the next building, house, apartment, or room <~ neighbors>
next door *adv* : in or to the next building, house, apartment, or room <lives *next door*> — **next door to** : next to
next friend *n* : a person admitted to or appointed by a court to act for the benefit of a person (as an infant) lacking full legal capacity to act for himself
next of kin : one or more persons in the nearest degree of relationship to another person
[1]**next to** *prep* : immediately following or adjacent to
[2]**next to** *adv* : very nearly : ALMOST <it was *next to* impossible to see in the fog>
nex·us \'nek-səs\ *n*, *pl* **nex·us·es** \-sə-səz\ *or* **nex·us** \-səs, -ˌsüs\ [L, fr. *nexus*, pp. of *nectere* to bind] **1** : CONNECTION, LINK <this traditional ~ between work and income —Elizabeth Wickenden> **2** : a connected group or series
Nez Percé \'nez-'pərs, 'nes-'pe(ə)rs, *F* nā-per-sā\ *n* [F, lit., pierced nose] **1** : a member of an Amerindian people of Idaho, Washington, and Oregon **2** : a language of the Nez Percé people
NF *abbr* **1** national formulary **2** no funds
NFC *abbr* National Football Conference
NFL *abbr* National Football League
Nfld *abbr* Newfoundland
NFS *abbr* not for sale
NG *abbr* **1** national guard **2** no good
N gauge *n* [prob. fr. *nine*] : a gauge of track in model railroading in which the rails are approximately 9 millimeters apart
ngwee \en-'gwē\ *n*, *pl* **ngwee** [native name in Zambia, lit., bright] — see *kwacha* at MONEY table
NH *abbr* **1** never hinged **2** New Hampshire
NHI *abbr* national health insurance
NHL *abbr* National Hockey League
NHP *abbr* nominal horsepower
NHRA *abbr* National Hot Rod Association
Ni *symbol* nickel
ni·a·cin \'nī-ə-sən\ *n* [*ni*cotinic *ac*id + *-in*] : NICOTINIC ACID
Ni·ag·a·ra \nī-'ag-(ə-)rə\ *n* [*Niagara* Falls] : an overwhelming flood : TORRENT <a ~ of protests>
ni·al·amide \nī-'al-ə-ˌmīd\ *n* [*ni*cotinic acid + *amyl* + *amide*] : an antidepressant drug $C_{16}H_{18}N_4O_2$ that is an inhibitor of monoamine oxidase
nib \'nib\ *n* [prob. alter. of *neb*] **1** : BILL, BEAK **2 a** : the sharpened point of a quill pen **b** : PEN POINT; *also* : each of the two divisions of a pen point **3** : a small pointed or projecting part
[1]**nib·ble** \'nib-əl\ *vb* **nib·bled**; **nib·bling** \-(ə-)liŋ\ [origin unknown] *vt* **1 a** : to bite gently **b** : to eat or chew in small bits **2** : to take away bit by bit <waves *nibbling* the shore> ~ *vi* **1** : to take gentle, small, or cautious bites **2** : to deal with something cautiously — **nib·bler** \-(ə-)lər\ *n*
[2]**nibble** *n* **1** : an act of nibbling **2** : a very small quantity (as of food)
Ni·be·lung \'nē-bə-ˌlu̇ŋ\ *n* [G] **1** : a member of a race of dwarfs in Germanic legend **2** : any of the followers of Siegfried **3** : any of the Burgundian kings in the medieval German *Nibelungenlied*
nibs \'nibz\ *n pl but sing in constr* [origin unknown] : an important or self-important person — usu. used in the phrase *his nibs*
nic·co·lite \'nik-ə-ˌlīt\ *n* [NL *niccolum* nickel, prob. fr. Sw *nickel*] : a pale copper-red usu. massive mineral NiAs of metallic luster that is essentially a nickel arsenide
nice \'nīs\ *adj* **nic·er**; **nic·est** [ME, foolish, wanton, fr. OF, fr. L *nescius* ignorant, fr. *nescire* not to know — more at NESCIENCE] **1** *obs* **a** : WANTON, DISSOLUTE **b** : COY, RETICENT **2 a** : showing fastidious even finicky tastes : PARTICULAR **b** : exacting in requirements or standards : PUNCTILIOUS **3** : possessing, marked by, or demanding great, sometimes excessive, precision and delicacy (as in doing, discriminating, or stating) <the ~ and subtle ramifications of meaning —Samuel Johnson> **4** *obs* : TRIVIAL **5 a** : PLEASING, AGREEABLE <a ~ time> <a ~ person> **b** : well-executed <~ shot> **6** : most inappropriate : BAD <a ~ one to talk> **7 a** : socially acceptable : WELL-BRED **b** : VIRTUOUS, RESPECTABLE — **nice** *adv* — **nice·ly** *adv* — **nice·ness** *n*
syn **1** NICE, DAINTY, FASTIDIOUS, FINICKY, FINICAL, PARTICULAR, FUSSY, SQUEAMISH *shared meaning element* : having or displaying exacting standards
2 see CORRECT
Ni·cene \'nī-ˌsēn, nī-'\ *adj* [ME, fr. LL *nicaenus*, fr. L *Nicaea* Nicaea] **1** : of or relating to Nicaea or the Nicaeans **2** : of or relating to a church council held in Nicaea in A.D. 325 or to the Nicene Creed
Nicene Creed *n* : a Christian creed expanded from a creed issued by the first Nicene Council, beginning "I believe in one God", and used in liturgical worship
nice–nel·ly \'nī-'snel-ē\ *adj*, *often cap 2d N* [fr. the name *Nelly*] **1** : PRUDISH **2** : marked by euphemism — **nice nelly** *n*, *often cap 2d N* — **nice–nel·ly·ism** \-ˌiz-əm\ *n*, *often cap 2d N*
nice·ty \'nī-sət-ē, -stē\ *n*, *pl* **-ties** [ME *nicete*, fr. MF *niceté* foolishness, fr. *nice*, adj.] **1** : the quality or state of being nice **2** : an elegant, delicate, or civilized feature <enjoy the *niceties* of life> **3** : a fine point or distinction : SUBTLETY <the *niceties* of table manners> **4** : careful attention to details : delicate exactness : PRECISION **5** : delicacy of taste or feeling : FASTIDIOUSNESS
[1]**niche** \'nich\ *n* [F, fr. MF, fr. *nicher* to nest, fr. (assumed) VL *nidicare*, fr. L *nidus* nest — more at NEST] **1 a** : a recess in a wall esp. for a statue **b** : something that resembles a niche **2 a** : a place, employment, or activity for which a person is best fitted **b** : a habitat supplying the factors necessary for the existence of an organism or species **c** : the ecological role of an organism in a community esp. in regard to food consumption

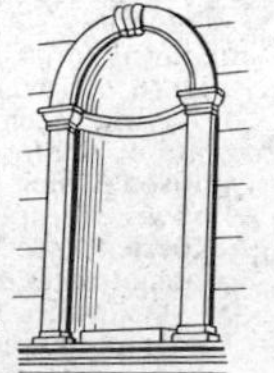
niche 1a

[2]**niche** *vt* **niched**; **nich·ing** : to place in or as if in a niche
[1]**nick** \'nik\ *n* [ME *nyke*, prob. alter. of *nocke* nock] **1** : a small notch or groove **2** : a final critical moment <in the ~ of time>
[2]**nick** *vt* **1 a** : to make a nick in : NOTCH, CHIP **b** : to cut into or wound slightly <a bullet ~*ed* his leg> **2** : to jot down : RECORD **3** : to cut short <cold weather, which ~*ed* steel and automobile output —*Time*> **4** : to catch at the right point or time **5** : CHEAT, OVERCHARGE ~ *vi* **1** : to make petty attacks : SNIPE **2** : to complement one another genetically and produce superior offspring
[1]**nick·el** *also* **nick·le** \'nik-əl\ *n* [prob. fr. Sw, fr. G *kupfernickel* niccolite, prob. fr. *kupfer* copper + *nickel* goblin; fr. the deceptive copper color of niccolite] **1** : a silver-white hard malleable ductile metallic element capable of a high polish and resistant to corrosion that is used chiefly in alloys and as a catalyst — see ELEMENT table **2 a** (1) : the U.S. 5-cent piece regularly containing 25 percent nickel and 75 percent copper (2) : the Canadian 5-cent piece **b** : five cents
[2]**nick·el** *vt* **nick·eled** *or* **nick·elled**; **nick·el·ing** *or* **nick·el·ling** \'nik-(ə-)liŋ\ : to plate with nickel
nick·el·ic \nik-'el-ik\ *adj* : of, relating to, or containing nickel esp. with a higher valence than two
nick·el·if·er·ous \ˌnik-ə-'lif-(ə-)rəs\ *adj* : containing nickel

nick·el·ode·on \ˌnik-ə-ˈlōd-ē-ən\ *n* [prob. fr. ¹*nickel* + *-odeon* (as in archaic *melodeon* music hall)] **1 :** an early movie theater presenting entertainment for an admission price of usu. five cents **2 :** JUKEBOX
nick·el·ous \ˈnik-ə-ləs\ *adj* **:** of, relating to, or containing nickel esp. when bivalent
nickel silver *n* **:** a silver-white alloy of copper, zinc, and nickel
nick·er \ˈnik-ər\ *vi* **nick·ered; nick·er·ing** \-(ə-)riŋ\ [perh. alter. of *neigh*] **:** NEIGH, WHINNY — **nicker** *n*
nick·nack *var of* KNICKKNACK
¹**nick·name** \ˈnik-ˌnām\ *n* [ME *nekename* additional name, alter. (resulting from incorrect division of *an ekename*) of *ekename*, fr. *eke* + *name*] **1 :** a usu. descriptive name given instead of or in addition to the one belonging to an individual **2 :** a familiar form of a proper name (as of a person or a city)
²**nickname** *vt* **1 :** MISNAME, MISCALL **2 :** to give a nickname to — **nick·nam·er** *n*
ni·co·ti·a·na \nik-ˌō-shē-ˈan-ə, -ˈän-ə, -ˈā-nə\ *n* [NL, fr. *herba nicotiana*, lit., Nicot's herb, fr. Jean *Nicot* †1600 F diplomat and scholar] **:** any of several tobaccos (as *Nicotiana alata*) grown for their showy flowers
nic·o·tin·amide \ˌnik-ə-ˈtē-nə-ˌmīd, -ˈtin-ə-\ *n* [ISV] **:** a compound $C_6H_6N_2O$ of the vitamin B complex found esp. as a constituent of coenzymes and used similarly to nicotinic acid
nicotinamide–adenine dinucleotide *n* **:** NAD
nicotinamide–adenine dinucleotide phosphate *n* **:** NADP
nic·o·tine \ˈnik-ə-ˌtēn\ *n* [F, fr. NL *nicotiana*] **:** a poisonous alkaloid $C_{10}H_{14}N_2$ that is the chief active principle of tobacco and is used as an insecticide
nic·o·tin·ic \ˌnik-ə-ˈtē-nik, -ˈtin-ik\ *adj* [ISV] **:** of or relating to nicotine or nicotinic acid
nicotinic acid *n* **:** an acid $C_6H_5NO_2$ of the vitamin B complex found widely in animals and plants and used esp. against pellagra — called also *niacin*
nic·ti·tate \ˈnik-tə-ˌtāt\ *vi* **-tat·ed; -tat·ing** [alter. of *nictate* (to wink), fr. L *nictatus*, pp. of *nictare* — more at CONNIVE] **:** WINK
nictitating membrane *n* **:** a thin membrane found in many animals at the inner angle or beneath the lower lid of the eye and capable of extending across the eyeball
nid·get \ˈnij-ət\ *n* [alter. of earlier *nidiot*, alter. (resulting from incorrect division of *an idiot*) of *idiot*] *archaic* **:** IDIOT, FOOL
ni·dic·o·lous \nī-ˈdik-ə-ləs\ *adj* [L *nidus* nest + E *-colous*] **1 :** reared for a time in a nest **2 :** sharing the nest of another kind of animal
ni·di·fi·ca·tion \ˌnid-ə-fə-ˈkā-shən, ˌnīd-\ *n* [ML *nidification-, nidificatio*, fr. L *nidificatus*, pp. of *nidificare* to build a nest, fr. *nidus* nest] **:** the act, process, or technique of building a nest
ni·dif·u·gous \nī-ˈdif-yə-gəs\ *adj* [L *nidus* nest + *fugere* to flee — more at FUGITIVE] **:** leaving the nest soon after hatching
ni·dus \ˈnīd-əs\ *n, pl* **ni·di** \ˈnī-ˌdī\ *or* **ni·dus·es** [NL, fr. L] **1 :** a nest or breeding place; *esp* **:** a place or substance in an animal or plant where bacteria or other organisms lodge and multiply **2 :** a place where something originates, develops, or is located
niece \ˈnēs\ *n* [ME *nece*, granddaughter, niece, fr. OF *niece*, fr. LL *neptia*, fr. L *neptis*; akin to L *nepot-, nepos* grandson, nephew — more at NEPHEW] **1 :** a daughter of one's brother, sister, brother-in-law, or sister-in-law **2 :** an illegitimate daughter of an ecclesiastic
¹**ni·el·lo** \nē-ˈel-(ˌ)ō\ *n, pl* **ni·el·li** \-ˈel-(ˌ)ē\ *or* **niellos** [It, fr. ML *nigellum*, fr. neut. of L *nigellus* blackish, dim. of *niger* black] **1 :** any of several enamel-like alloys usu. of sulfur with silver, copper, and lead and a deep black color **2 :** the art or process of decorating metal with incised designs filled with niello **3 :** a piece of metal or an object decorated with niello
²**niello** *vt* **:** to inlay or ornament with niello
Nif·lheim \ˈniv-əl-ˌhām\ *n* [ON *Niflheimr*] **:** the abode of the dead in Norse mythology
¹**nif·ty** \ˈnif-tē\ *adj* **nif·ti·er; -est** [origin unknown] **:** very good **:** very attractive **:** FINE <~ clothes>
²**nifty** *n, pl* **nifties :** something that is nifty; *esp* **:** a clever or neatly turned phrase or joke
Ni·ger–Con·go \ˌnī-jər-ˈkäŋ-(ˌ)gō\ *n* [*Niger* (river) + *Congo* (river)] **:** a language family that includes the Mande and Kwa branches and that is spoken by most of the indigenous peoples of west, central, and south Africa
¹**nig·gard** \ˈnig-ərd\ *n* [ME, of Scand origin; akin to ON *hnøggr* niggardly; akin to L *cinis* ashes — more at INCINERATE] **:** a meanly covetous and stingy person **:** MISER — **niggard** *adj*
²**niggard** *vi, obs* **:** to act niggardly ~ *vt, obs* **:** to treat in a niggardly manner
nig·gard·ly \-lē\ *adj* **1 :** grudgingly mean about spending or granting **2 :** provided in meanly limited supply *syn* see STINGY *ant* bountiful — **nig·gard·li·ness** *n* — **niggardly** *adv*
nig·ger \ˈnig-ər\ *n* [alter. of earlier *neger*, fr. MF *negre*, fr. Sp or Pg *negro*, fr. *negro* black, fr. L *niger*] **1 :** NEGRO — usu. taken to be offensive **2 :** a member of any dark-skinned race — usu. taken to be offensive
nig·gle \ˈnig-əl\ *vb* **nig·gled; nig·gling** \-(ə-)liŋ\ [origin unknown] *vi* **1 a :** TRIFLE **b :** to spend too much effort on minor details **2 :** to find fault constantly in a petty way **:** CARP <she haggles, she ~*s*, she wears out our patience —Virginia Woolf> **3 :** GNAW ~ *vt* **:** to give stingily or in tiny portions — **nig·gler** \-(ə-)lər\ *n*
nig·gling \ˈnig-(ə-)liŋ\ *adj* **1 :** PETTY **2 a :** demanding meticulous care **b :** overly elaborate in execution — **niggling** *n* — **nig·gling·ly** \-(ə-)liŋ-lē\ *adv*
¹**nigh** \ˈnī\ *adv* [ME, fr. OE *nēah*; akin to OHG *nāh*, adv., nigh, prep., nigh, after, ON *nā-* nigh] **1 :** near in place, time, or relationship — often used with *on, onto*, or *unto* **2 :** NEARLY, ALMOST
²**nigh** *adj* **1 :** CLOSE, NEAR **2** *chiefly dial* **:** DIRECT, SHORT **3 :** being on the left side <the ~ horse>
³**nigh** \(ˌ)nī\ *prep* **:** NEAR
⁴**nigh** \ˈnī\ *vt* **:** to draw or come near to **:** APPROACH ~ *vi* **:** to draw near

¹**night** \ˈnīt\ *n* [ME, fr. OE *niht*; akin to OHG *naht* night, L *noct-, nox*, Gk *nykt-, nyx*] **1 :** the time from dusk to dawn when no light of the sun is visible **2 a :** an evening or night taken as an occasion or point of time <the opening ~> **b :** an evening set aside for a particular purpose **3 a :** the quality or state of being dark **b :** a condition or period felt to resemble the darkness of night: as (1) **:** a period of dreary inactivity or affliction (2) **:** absence of moral values **c :** the beginning of darkness **:** NIGHTFALL
²**night** *adj* **1 :** of, relating to, or associated with the night <~ air> **2 :** intended for use at night <a ~ lamp> **3 :** existing, occurring, or functioning at night <~ baseball> <a ~ nurse>
night and day *adv* **:** all the time **:** CONTINUALLY
night–blind \ˈnīt-ˌblīnd\ *adj* [back-formation fr. *night blindness*] **:** afflicted with night blindness
night blindness *n* **:** reduced visual capacity in faint light (as at night)
night–blooming cereus *n* **:** any of several night-blooming cacti; *esp* **:** a slender sprawling or climbing cactus (*Selenicereus grandiflorus*) often cultivated for its large showy fragrant white flowers
night·cap \ˈnīt-ˌkap\ *n* **1 :** a cloth cap worn with nightclothes **2 :** a usu. alcoholic drink taken at bedtime **3 :** the final race or contest of a day's sports; *esp* **:** the final game of a baseball doubleheader
night·clothes \-ˌklō(th)z\ *n pl* **:** garments worn in bed
¹**night·club** \-ˌkləb\ *n* **:** a place of entertainment open at night usu. serving food and liquor, having a floor show, and providing music and space for dancing
²**nightclub** *vi* **:** to patronize nightclubs — **night·club·ber** *n*
night court *n* **:** a criminal court in a large city that sits at night (as for the summary disposition of criminal charges and the granting of bail)
night crawler *n* **:** EARTHWORM; *esp* **:** a large earthworm found on the soil surface at night
night·dress \ˈnīt-ˌdres\ *n* **1 :** NIGHTGOWN **2 :** NIGHTCLOTHES
night editor *n* **:** an editor in charge of the final makeup of a morning newspaper
night·fall \ˈnīt-ˌfȯl\ *n* **:** the close of the day **:** DUSK
night·glow \-ˌglō\ *n* **:** airglow seen during the night
night·gown \-ˌgau̇n\ *n* **1** *archaic* **:** DRESSING GOWN **2 :** a loose garment worn in bed
night·hawk \-ˌhȯk\ *n* **1 a :** any of several No. American goatsuckers (genus *Chordeiles*) related to the whippoorwill **b :** the European nightjar **2 :** a person who habitually stays up or goes about late at night
night heron *n* **:** any of various widely distributed nocturnal or crepuscular herons (as of the genus *Nycticorax*)
night·ie \ˈnīt-ē\ *or* **nighty** *n, pl* **night·ies** [*night*gown + *-ie* or *-y*] **:** a nightgown for a woman or child
night·in·gale \ˈnīt-ᵊn-ˌgāl, -iŋ-\ *n* [ME, fr. OE *nihtegale*, fr. *niht* + *galan* to sing — more at YELL] **:** any of several Old World thrushes (genus *Luscinia*) noted for the sweet usu. nocturnal song of the male; *also* **:** any of various other birds that sing at night
night·jar \ˈnīt-ˌjär\ *n* [fr. its harsh sound] **:** a common grayish brown European goatsucker (*Caprimulgus europaeus*); *broadly* **:** GOATSUCKER
night latch *n* **:** a door lock having a spring bolt operated from the outside by a key and from the inside by a knob
night letter *n* **:** a telegram sent at night at a reduced rate per word for delivery the following morning
night·life \ˈnīt-ˌlīf\ *n* **:** the activity of pleasure-seekers at night (as in nightclubs)
night–light \-ˌlīt\ *n* **:** a light kept burning throughout the night
¹**night·long** \-ˌlȯŋ\ *adj* **:** lasting the whole night <~ festivities>
²**night·long** \-ˈlȯŋ\ *adv* **:** through the whole night
¹**night·ly** \ˈnīt-lē\ *adj* **1 :** of or relating to the night or every night **2 :** happening, done, or used by night or every night
²**nightly** *adv* **:** every night; *also* **:** at or by night
night·mare \ˈnīt-ˌma(ə)r, -ˌme(ə)r\ *n* [¹*night* + ¹*mare*] **1 :** an evil spirit formerly thought to oppress people during sleep **2 :** a frightening dream accompanied by a sense of oppression or suffocation that usu. awakens the sleeper **3 :** an experience, situation, or object having the monstrous character of a nightmare or producing a feeling of anxiety or terror — **nightmare** *adj* — **night·mar·ish** \-ˌma(ə)r-ish, -ˌme(ə)r-\ *adj* — **night·mar·ish·ly** *adv*
night owl *n* **:** a person who keeps late hours at night **:** NIGHTHAWK
night rail \-ˌrāl\ *n* [*night* + *rail* (garment)] *archaic* **:** NIGHTGOWN
night raven *n* **:** a bird that cries at night
night rider *n* **:** a member of a secret band who ride masked at night doing acts of violence for the purpose of punishing or terrorizing

nightshade 1

nights \ˈnīts\ *adv* **:** in the nighttime repeatedly **:** on any night <works ~>
night·shade \ˈnīt-ˌshād\ *n* **1 :** any of a genus (*Solanum* of the family Solanaceae, the nightshade family) which comprises herbs, shrubs, and trees with alternate leaves, cymose flowers, and fruits that are berries and includes some poisonous weeds, various ornamentals, and important crop plants (as the potato and eggplant) **2 :** BELLADONNA 1
night·shirt \-ˌshərt\ *n* **:** a nightgown resembling a shirt

night·side \-ˌsīd\ *n* **:** the side of a body (as the earth, the moon, or a planet) not in daylight
night soil *n* **:** human excrement collected for fertilizing the soil
night·stand \ˈnīt-ˌstand\ *n* **:** NIGHT TABLE
night·stick \-ˌstik\ *n* **:** a policeman's club
night table *n* **:** a small bedside table or stand
night·tide \ˈnīt-ˌtīd\ *n* **:** NIGHTTIME
night·time \-ˌtīm\ *n* **:** the time from dusk to dawn — **nighttime** *adj*
night·walk·er \-ˌwȯ-kər\ *n* **:** a person who roves about at night esp. with criminal or immoral intent
ni·gri·tude \ˈnī-grə-ˌt(y)üd, ˈnig-rə-\ *n* [L *nigritudo,* fr. *nigr-, niger* black] **:** intense darkness **:** BLACKNESS
ni·gro·sine \ˈnī-grə-ˌsēn\ *also* **ni·gro·sin** \-sən\ *n, often cap* [L *nigr-, niger*] **:** any of several azine dyes closely related to the indulines
ni·hil·ism \ˈnī-(h)ə-ˌliz-əm, ˈnē-\ *n* [G *nihilismus,* fr. L *nihil* nothing — more at NIL] **1 a :** a viewpoint that traditional values and beliefs are unfounded and that existence is senseless and useless **b :** a doctrine that denies any objective ground of truth and esp. of moral truths **2 a** (1) **:** a doctrine or belief that conditions in the social organization are so bad as to make destruction desirable for its own sake independent of any constructive program or possibility (2) *cap* **:** the program of a 19th century Russian party advocating revolutionary reform and using terrorism and assassination **b :** TERRORISM — **ni·hil·ist** \-ləst\ *n or adj* — **ni·hil·is·tic** \ˌnī-(h)ə-ˈlis-tik, ˌnē-\ *adj*
ni·hil·i·ty \nī-ˈhil-ət-ē, nē-\ *n* **:** absence of existence **:** NULLITY
ni·hil ob·stat \ˌnī-ˌhil-ˈäb-ˌstät, ˌnē-ˌhil-, ˌnik-ˌil-, -ˌstat\ *n* [L, nothing hinders] **:** authoritative or official approval
-nik \nik\ *n suffix* [Yiddish, fr. Russ & Pol] **:** one connected with or characterized by being <beat*nik*>
Ni·ke \ˈnī-kē\ *n* [Gk *Nikē*] **:** the Greek goddess of victory
nil \ˈnil\ *n* [L, nothing, contr. of *nihil,* fr. OL *nihilum,* fr. *ne-* not + *hilum* trifle — more at NO] **:** NOTHING, ZERO — **nil** *adj*
nile green *n, often cap N* [*Nile* (river)] **:** a variable color averaging a pale yellow green
nill \ˈnil\ *vb* [ME *nilen,* fr. OE *nyllan,* fr. *ne* not + *wyllan* to wish — more at NO, WILL] *vi, archaic* **:** to be unwilling <will you ~ you, I will marry you —Shak.> ~ *vt, archaic* **:** not to will **:** REFUSE
Ni·lot·ic \nī-ˈlät-ik\ *adj* [L *Niloticus,* fr. Gk *Neilōtēs,* fr. *Neilos* Nile] **:** of or relating to the Nile or the peoples of the Nile basin
nil·po·tent \ˈnil-ˌpōt-ᵊnt\ *adj* [L *nil* nothing + *potent-, potens* having power — more at POTENT] **:** equal to zero when raised to some power <~ matrices>
[1]**nim** \ˈnim\ *vb* **nimmed; nim·ming** [earlier *nim* to take, fr. ME *nimen,* fr. OE *niman*] *vt, archaic* **:** STEAL, FILCH ~ *vi, archaic* **:** THIEVE
[2]**nim** *n* [prob. fr. [1]*nim*] **:** any of various games in which counters are laid out in one or more piles and each player in turn draws one or more counters with the object of taking the last counter, forcing the opponent to take it, or taking the most or fewest counters
nim·ble \ˈnim-bəl\ *adj* **nim·bler** \-b(ə-)lər\; **nim·blest** \-b(ə-)ləst\ [ME *nimel,* fr. OE *numol* holding much, fr. *niman* to take; akin to OHG *neman* to take, L *numerus* number, Gk *nemein* to distribute, manage, *nomos* pasture, *nomos* usage, custom, law] **1 :** marked by quick light movement **:** LIVELY <~ fingers> **2 a :** marked by quick, alert, clever conception, comprehension, or resourcefulness <a ~ mind> **b :** SENSITIVE, RESPONSIVE <a ~ listener> ***syn*** see AGILE — **nim·ble·ness** \-bəl-nəs\ *n* — **nim·bly** \-blē\ *adv*
nim·bo·stra·tus \ˌnim-bō-ˈstrāt-əs, -ˈstrat-\ *n* [NL, fr. L *nimbus* + NL *stratus*] **:** a low dark gray rainy cloud layer — see CLOUD illustration
nim·bus \ˈnim-bəs\ *n, pl* **nim·bi** \-ˌbī, -ˌbē\ *or* **nim·bus·es** [L, rainstorm, cloud; akin to Pahlavi *namb* mist] **1 a :** a luminous vapor, cloud, or atmosphere about a god or goddess when on earth **b :** a cloud or atmosphere (as of romance) about a person or thing **2 :** an indication (as a circle) of radiant light or glory about the head of a drawn or sculptured divinity, saint, or sovereign **3 a :** the rain cloud that is of uniform grayness and extends over the entire sky **b :** a cloud from which rain is falling

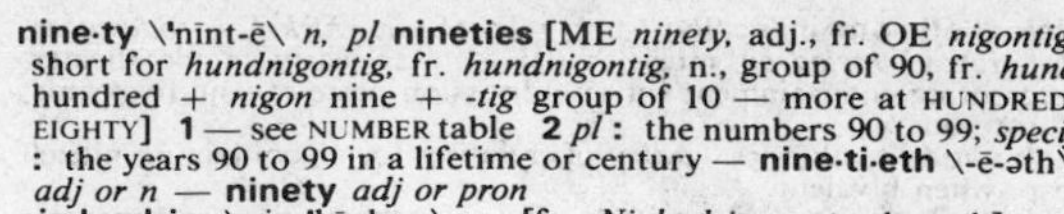

nimbus 2

nim·bused \-bəst\ *adj* **:** furnished with or surrounded by a nimbus
ni·mi·ety \nim-ˈī-ət-ē\ *n, pl* **-eties** [LL *nimietas,* fr. L *nimius* too much, adj., fr. *nimis,* adv.] **:** EXCESS, REDUNDANCY
nim·i·ny–pim·i·ny \ˌnim-ə-nē-ˈpim-ə-nē\ *adj* [prob. alter. of *namby-pamby*] **:** affectedly refined **:** FINICKY
Nim·rod \ˈnim-ˌräd\ *n* [Heb *Nimrōdh*] **1 :** a descendant of Ham represented in Genesis as a mighty hunter and a king of Shinar **2** *not cap* **:** HUNTER
nin·com·poop \ˈnin-kəm-ˌpüp, ˈniŋ-\ *n* [origin unknown] **:** FOOL, SIMPLETON — **nin·com·poop·ery** \-ə-rē\ *n*
nine \ˈnīn\ *n* [ME, fr. *nyne,* adj., fr. OE *nigon;* akin to OHG *niun* nine, L *novem,* Gk *ennea*] **1** — see NUMBER table **2 :** the ninth in a set or series <wears a ~> **3 :** something having nine units or members: as **a** *cap* **:** the nine Muses **b :** a baseball team **c :** the first or last nine holes of an 18-hole golf course — **nine** *adj or pron* — **to the nines :** to the highest degree
nine days' wonder *n* **:** something that creates a short-lived sensation
nine·fold \ˈnīn-ˌfōld, -ˈfōld\ *adj* **1 :** having nine units or members **2 :** being nine times as great or as many — **nine·fold** \-ˈfōld\ *adv*
nine·pin \-ˌpin\ *n* **1 :** a pin used in ninepins **2** *pl but sing in constr* **:** a bowling game resembling tenpins played without the headpin
nine·teen \(ˈ)nīn(t)-ˈtēn\ *n* [ME *nynetene,* adj., fr. OE *nigontēne;* akin to OE *tien* ten] — see NUMBER table — **nineteen** *adj or pron* — **nine·teenth** \-ˈtēn(t)th\ *adj or n*
nine·ty \ˈnīnt-ē\ *n, pl* **nineties** [ME *ninety,* adj., fr. OE *nigontig,* short for *hundnigontig,* fr. *hundnigontig,* n., group of 90, fr. *hund* hundred + *nigon* nine + *-tig* group of 10 — more at HUNDRED, EIGHTY] **1** — see NUMBER table **2** *pl* **:** the numbers 90 to 99; *specif* **:** the years 90 to 99 in a lifetime or century — **nine·ti·eth** \-ē-əth\ *adj or n* — **ninety** *adj or pron*
nin·hy·drin \nin-ˈhī-drən\ *n* [fr. *Ninhydrin,* a trademark] **:** a poisonous crystalline oxidizing agent $C_9H_6O_4$ used esp. as an analytical reagent
ninhydrin reaction *n* **:** a reaction of ninhydrin with amino acids or related amino compounds that is used esp. for the colorimetric determination of amino acids, peptides, or proteins
nin·ny \ˈnin-ē\ *n, pl* **ninnies** [perh. by shortening and alter. fr. *an innocent*] **:** FOOL, SIMPLETON
nin·ny·ham·mer \ˈnin-ē-ˌham-ər\ *n* **:** NINNY
ni·non \ˈnē-ˌnän\ *n* [prob. fr. F *Ninon,* nickname for *Anne*] **:** a smooth sheer fabric
ninth \ˈnīn(t)th\ *n* **1** — see NUMBER table **2 a :** a musical interval embracing an octave and a second **b :** the tone at this interval **c :** a chord containing a ninth — **ninth** *adj or adv*
ninth cranial nerve *n* **:** GLOSSOPHARYNGEAL NERVE
Ni·o·be \ˈnī-ə-bē\ *n* [L, fr. Gk *Niobē*] **:** a daughter of Tantalus and the wife of Amphion who after losing her children was turned to stone and became a mountain whose streams are her tears
ni·o·bi·um \nī-ˈō-bē-əm\ *n* [NL, fr. L *Niobe;* fr. its occurrence in tantalite] **:** a lustrous platinum-gray ductile metallic element that resembles tantalum chemically and is used in alloys — see ELEMENT table
[1]**nip** \ˈnip\ *vb* **nipped; nip·ping** [ME *nippen;* akin to ON *hnippa* to prod, Gk *konis* ashes — more at INCINERATE] *vt* **1 :** to catch hold of and squeeze tightly between two surfaces, edges, or points **:** PINCH <the dog *nipped* his ankle> **2 a :** to sever by or as if by pinching sharply **b :** to destroy the growth, progress, maturing, or fulfillment of <*nipped* in the bud> **3 :** to injure or make numb with cold **:** CHILL **4 :** SNATCH, STEAL ~ *vi, chiefly Brit* **:** to move briskly, nimbly, or quickly
[2]**nip** *n* **1 :** something that nips: as **a :** a sharp biting comment **b :** a sharp stinging cold <the ~ of the winter air> **c :** a biting or pungent flavor **:** TANG <cheese with a ~> **2 :** the act of nipping **:** PINCH, BITE **3 :** the region of a squeezing or crushing device (as a calender) where the rolls or jaws are closest together **4 :** a small portion **:** BIT
[3]**nip** *n* [prob. fr. *nipperkin* (a liquor container)] **:** a small quantity of liquor **:** SIP
[4]**nip** *vi* **nipped; nip·ping :** to take liquor in nips **:** TIPPLE
ni·pa \ˈnē-pə\ *n* [prob. fr. It, fr. Malay *nipah* nipa palm] **1 :** an alcoholic drink made from the juice of an Australasian creeping palm (*Nipa fruticans*); *also* **:** this palm **2 :** thatch made of nipa leaves
nip and tuck \ˌnip-ən-ˈtək\ *adj or adv* **:** being so close that the lead or advantage shifts rapidly from one contestant to another
nip·per \ˈnip-ər\ *n* **1 :** any of various devices (as pincers) for nipping — usu. used in pl. **2** *chiefly Brit* **a :** a boy employed as a helper (as of a carter or hawker) **b :** CHILD; *esp* **:** a small boy
nip·ping \ˈnip-iŋ\ *adj* **:** SHARP, CHILLING — **nip·ping·ly** \-iŋ-lē\ *adv*
nip·ple \ˈnip-əl\ *n* [earlier *neble, nible,* prob. dim. of *neb, nib*] **1 :** the protuberance of a mammary gland upon which the ducts open and from which milk is drawn **2 a :** an artificial teat through which a bottle-fed infant nurses **b :** a device with an orifice through which the discharge of a liquid can be regulated **3 a :** a protuberance resembling or suggesting the nipple of a breast **b :** a small projection through which oil or grease is injected into machinery **4 :** a pipe coupling consisting of a short piece of threaded tubing
Nip·pon·ese \ˌnip-ə-ˈnēz, -ˈnēs\ *adj* [*Nippon* (Japan)] **:** JAPANESE — **Nipponese** *n*
nip·py \ˈnip-ē\ *adj* **nip·pi·er; -est 1 :** marked by a tendency to nip <a ~ dog> **2 :** brisk, quick, or nimble in movement **:** SNAPPY **3 :** PUNGENT, SHARP **4 :** CHILLY, CHILLING <a ~ day> — **nip·pi·ly** \ˈnip-ə-lē\ *adv* — **nip·pi·ness** \ˈnip-ē-nəs\ *n*
nip–up \ˈnip-ˌəp\ *n* **:** a spring from a supine position to a standing position
nir·va·na \ni(ə)r-ˈvän-ə, (ˌ)nər-\ *n, often cap* [Skt *nirvāṇa,* lit., act of extinguishing, fr. *nis-* out + *vāti* it blows — more at WIND] **1 :** the final beatitude that transcends suffering, karma, and samsara and is sought esp. in Buddhism through the extinction of desire and individual consciousness **2 a :** a place or state of oblivion to care, pain, or external reality **b :** a goal hoped for but apparently unattainable **:** DREAM
Ni·san \ˈnis-ᵊn, nē-ˈsän\ *n* [Heb *Nisān*] **:** the 7th month of the civil year or the 1st month of the ecclesiastical year in the Jewish calendar — see MONTH table
ni·sei \(ˈ)nē-ˈsā, ˈnē-ˌ\ *n, pl* **nisei** *also* **niseis** [Jap, lit., second generation, fr. *ni* second + *sei* generation] **:** a son or daughter of immigrant Japanese parents who is born and educated in America and esp. in the U.S.
ni·si \ˈnī-ˌsī\ *adj* [L, unless, fr. *ne-* not + *si* if] **:** taking effect at a specified time unless previously modified or avoided by cause shown, further proceedings, or a condition fulfilled <decree ~>
Nis·roch \ˈnis-ˌräk, -ˌrōk\ *n* [Heb *Nisrōkh*] **:** an Assyrian deity honored with a temple at Nineveh
Nis·sen hut \ˌnis-ᵊn-\ *n* [Peter N. *Nissen* †1930 Brit. mining engineer] **:** a prefabricated shelter built of a semicircular arching roof of corrugated iron with a cement floor
ni·sus \ˈnī-səs\ *n, pl* **ni·sus** \-səs, -ˌsüs\ [L, fr. *nisus,* pp. of *niti* to bear down, strive; akin to L con*nivēre* to close the eyes — more at CONNIVE] **:** a mental or physical effort to attain an end **:** a perfective urge or endeavor
[1]**nit** \ˈnit\ *n* [ME *nite,* fr. OE *hnitu;* akin to OHG *hniz* nit, Gk *konid-, konis*] **:** the egg of a louse or other parasitic insect; *also* **:** the insect itself when young
[2]**nit** *n, chiefly Brit* **:** NITWIT

NIT *abbr* 1 National Intelligence Test 2 National Invitational Tournament
ni·ter *also* **ni·tre** \ˈnīt-ər\ *n* [ME *nitre* natron, fr. MF, fr. L *nitrum*, fr. Gk *nitron*, fr. Egypt *ntry*] 1 : POTASSIUM NITRATE 2 : SODIUM NITRATE; *esp* : CHILE SALTPETER
nit·id \ˈnit-əd\ *adj* [L *nitidus* — more at NEAT] : BRIGHT, LUSTROUS
nit·pick \ˈnit-ˌpik\ *vi* [back-formation fr. *nitpicking*] : to engage in nit-picking — **nit·pick·er** *n*
nit–pick·ing \ˈnit-ˌpik-iŋ\ *n* [[1]*nit*] : minute and usu. unjustified criticism
nitr- *or* **nitro-** *comb form* [*niter*] 1 : niter : nitrate <*nitro*bacteria> 2 a : nitrogen <*nitr*ide> <*nitro*meter> b *usu* *nitro-* : containing the univalent group NO_2 composed of one nitrogen and two oxygen atoms <*nitro*benzene>
[1]**ni·trate** \ˈnī-ˌtrāt, -trət\ *n* [F, fr. *nitrique*] 1 : a salt or ester of nitric acid 2 : sodium nitrate or potassium nitrate used as a fertilizer
[2]**ni·trate** \-ˌtrāt\ *vt* **ni·trat·ed; ni·trat·ing** : to treat or combine with nitric acid or a nitrate; *esp* : to convert (an organic compound) into a nitro compound or a nitrate — **ni·tra·tion** \nī-ˈtrā-shən\ *n* — **ni·tra·tor** \ˈnī-ˌtrāt-ər\ *n*
nitrate bacterium *n* : a bacterium that converts nitrites to nitrates in the nitrogen cycle
ni·tric \ˈnī-trik\ *adj* [F *nitrique*, fr. *nitr-*] : of, relating to, or containing nitrogen esp. with a higher valence than in corresponding nitrous compounds
nitric acid *n* : a corrosive liquid inorganic acid HNO_3 used esp. as an oxidizing agent, in nitrations, and in making organic compounds (as fertilizers, explosives, and dyes)
nitric oxide *n* : a colorless poisonous gas NO obtained by oxidation of nitrogen or ammonia
ni·tride \ˈnī-ˌtrīd\ *n* [ISV] : a binary compound of nitrogen with a more electropositive element
ni·tri·fi·ca·tion \ˌnī-trə-fə-ˈkā-shən\ *n* : the process of nitrifying; *specif* : the oxidation (as by bacteria) of ammonium salts to nitrites and the further oxidation of nitrites to nitrates
ni·tri·fy \ˈnī-trə-ˌfī\ *vt* **-fied; -fy·ing** [F *nitrifier*, fr. *nitr-*] 1 : to combine or impregnate with nitrogen or a nitrogen compound 2 : to subject to or produce by nitrification
ni·trile \ˈnī-trəl, -ˌtrēl\ *n* [ISV *nitr-* + *-il*, *-ile* (fr. L *-ilis* [1]-ile)] : an organic cyanide containing the group CN which on hydrolysis yields an acid with elimination of ammonia
ni·trite \ˈnī-ˌtrīt\ *n* : a salt or ester of nitrous acid
nitrite bacterium *n* : a bacterium that oxidizes ammonium to nitrites — called also *nitrosobacterium, nitrous bacterium*
[1]**ni·tro** \ˈnī-(ˌ)trō\ *adj* [*nitr-*] : containing or being the univalent group NO_2 united through nitrogen
[2]**nitro** *n, pl* **nitros** : any of various nitrated products; *esp* : NITROGLYCERIN
ni·tro·ben·zene \ˌnī-trō-ˈben-ˌzēn, -ben-ˈ\ *n* [ISV] : a poisonous yellow insoluble oil $C_6H_5NO_2$ with an almond odor that is used esp. as a solvent, mild oxidizing agent, and starting material in making aniline
ni·tro·cel·lu·lose \-ˈsel-yə-ˌlōs, -ˌlōz\ *n* [ISV] : nitrated cellulose : CELLULOSE NITRATE — **ni·tro·cel·lu·los·ic** \-ˌsel-yə-ˈlō-sik, -zik\ *adj*
ni·tro·fu·ran \ˌnī-trō-ˈfyu̇(ə)r-ˌan, -fyu̇-ˈran\ *n* : any of several derivatives of furan that contain a nitro group and are used as bacteria-inhibiting agents
ni·tro·gen \ˈnī-trə-jən\ *n, often attrib* [F *nitrogène*, fr. *nitr-* + *-gène* -gen] : a colorless tasteless odorless gaseous element that constitutes 78 percent of the atmosphere by volume and occurs as a constituent of all living tissues in combined form — see ELEMENT table — **ni·trog·e·nous** \nī-ˈträj-ə-nəs\ *adj*
nitrogen balance *n* : the difference between nitrogen intake and nitrogen loss in the body or the soil
nitrogen cycle *n* : a continuous series of natural processes by which nitrogen passes through successive stations in air, soil, and organisms involving principally nitrogen fixation, nitrification, decay, and denitrification
nitrogen fixation *n* 1 : the industrial conversion of free nitrogen into combined forms useful esp. as starting materials for fertilizers or explosives 2 : the metabolic assimilation of atmospheric nitrogen by soil microorganisms and esp. rhizobia and its release for plant use by nitrification in the soil on the death of the microorganisms
nitrogen–fixer *n* : any of various soil organisms that are involved in nitrogen fixation
nitrogen–fixing *adj* : capable of nitrogen fixation <~ bacteria>
nitrogen mustard *n* : any of various toxic blistering compounds analogous to mustard gas but containing nitrogen instead of sulfur
nitrogen narcosis *n* : a state of euphoria and exhilaration that occurs when nitrogen in normal air enters the bloodstream at approximately seven times atmospheric pressure (as in deep-water diving) — called also *rapture of the deep*
ni·tro·glyc·er·in *or* **ni·tro·glyc·er·ine** \ˌnī-trə-ˈglis-(ə-)rən\ *n* [ISV] : a heavy oily explosive poisonous liquid $C_3H_5(NO_3)_3$ used chiefly in making dynamites and in medicine as a vasodilator
ni·tro·par·af·fin \ˌnī-trō-ˈpar-ə-fən\ *n* [ISV] : a nitro derivative of any member of the methane series
nitros- *or* **nitroso-** *comb form* [NL *nitrosus* nitrous] : containing the group NO composed of one nitrogen and one oxygen atom <*nitroso*benzene C_6H_5NO> <*nitros*amines>
ni·tro·sa·mine \nī-ˈtrō-sə-ˌmēn\ *also* **ni·tro·so·amine** \-sō-ə-ˌmēn\ *n* : any of various neutral compounds which are characterized by the grouping NNO and some of which are powerful carcinogens
ni·tro·so·bac·te·ri·um \nī-ˌtrō-sō-bak-ˈtir-ē-əm\ *n* [NL, fr. *nitrosus* + *-o-* + *bacterium*] : NITRITE BACTERIUM
ni·trous \ˈnī-trəs\ *adj* [NL *nitrosus*, fr. L, full of natron, fr. *nitrum* natron — more at NITER] 1 : of, relating to, or containing niter 2 : of, relating to, or containing nitrogen esp. with a lower valence than in corresponding nitric compounds
nitrous acid *n* : an unstable acid HNO_2 known only in solution or in the form of its salts
nitrous bacterium *n* : NITRITE BACTERIUM
nitrous oxide *n* : a colorless gas N_2O that when inhaled produces loss of sensibility to pain preceded by exhilaration and sometimes laughter and is used esp. as an anesthetic in dentistry — called also *laughing gas*
nit·ty–grit·ty \ˈnit-ē-ˌgrit-ē, ˌnit-ē-ˈ\ *n* [origin unknown] : the actual state of things : what is ultimately essential and true <immersed himself in getting to the ~ of the problems —Ronald Martinetti> — **nitty–gritty** *adj*
nit·wit \ˈnit-ˌwit\ *n* [prob. fr. G dial. *nit* not + E *wit*] : a scatterbrained or stupid person
[1]**nix** \ˈniks\ *n* [G, fr. OHG *nihhus*; akin to OE *nicor* water monster, Gk *nizein* to wash] : a water sprite of Germanic folklore
[2]**nix** *n* [G *nichts* nothing] : NOTHING : no one
[3]**nix** *adv* : NO — used to express disagreement or the withholding of permission; often used with *on* <father said ~ on our plan>
[4]**nix** *vt* : VETO, FORBID <the court ~*ed* the merger>
[1]**nix·ie** \ˈnik-sē\ *n* [G *nixe* female nix, fr. OHG *nichessa*, fem. of *nihhus* nix] : [1]NIX
[2]**nix·ie** *also* **nixy** \ˈnik-sē\ *n, pl* **nix·ies** [[2]*nix* + *-ie* or *-y*] : a piece of mail that is undeliverable because illegibly or incorrectly addressed
ni·zam \ni-ˈzäm, ˈnī-ˌzam, nī-ˈ\ *n* [Hindi *nizām* order, governor, fr. Ar *niẓām*] : one of a line of sovereigns of Hyderabad, India, reigning from 1713 to 1950 — **ni·zam·ate** \ni-ˈzäm-ˌāt, nī-ˈzam-\ *n*
NJ *abbr* New Jersey
NL *abbr* 1 National League 2 new line 3 night letter 4 [L *non licet*] it is not permitted 5 north latitude
NLAA *abbr* National Legal Aid Association
NLF *abbr* National Liberation Front
NLRB *abbr* National Labor Relations Board
NLT *abbr* night letter
nm *abbr* nanometer
NM *abbr* 1 nautical mile 2 New Mexico 3 night message 4 no mark; not marked
N Mex *abbr* New Mexico
NMR *abbr* nuclear magnetic resonance
NNE *abbr* north-northeast
NNW *abbr* north-northwest
[1]**no** \(ˈ)nō\ *adv* [ME, fr. OE *nā*, fr. *ne* not + *ā* always; akin to ON & OHG *ne* not, L *ne-*, Gk *nē-* — more at AYE] 1 a *chiefly Scot* : NOT b — used as a function word to express the negative of an alternative choice or possibility 2 : in no respect or degree — used in comparisons 3 : not so — used to express negation, dissent, denial, or refusal <~, I'm not going> 4 — used with a following adjective to imply a meaning expressed by the opposite positive statement <~ uncertain terms> 5 — used as a function word to emphasize a following negative or to introduce a more emphatic, explicit, or comprehensive statement 6 — used as an interjection to express surprise, doubt, or incredulity
[2]**no** *adj* 1 a : not any <~ parking> b : hardly any : very little <finished in ~ time> 2 : not a : quite other than a <he's ~ expert>
[3]**no** \ˈnō\ *n, pl* **noes** *or* **nos** \ˈnōz\ 1 : an act or instance of refusing or denying by the use of the word *no* : DENIAL 2 a : a negative vote or decision b *pl* : persons voting in the negative
[4]**no** *abbr* 1 north 2 [L *numero*, abl. of *numerus*] number
[1]**No** *or* **Noh** \ˈnō\ *n, pl* **No** *or* **Noh** [Jap *nō*, lit., talent] : classic Japanese dance-drama having a heroic theme, a chorus, and highly stylized action, costuming, and scenery
[2]**No** *symbol* nobelium
no–account *adj* : of no account : TRIFLING <his ~ relatives>
No·a·chi·an \nō-ˈā-kē-ən\ *adj* [Heb *Nōaḥ* Noah] 1 : of or relating to the patriarch Noah or his time 2 : ANCIENT, ANTIQUATED
No·ah \ˈnō-ə\ *n* [Heb *Nōaḥ*] : the builder of the Ark by means of which he and his family escaped the Flood
[1]**nob** \ˈnäb\ *n* [prob. alter. of *knob*] 1 : HEAD 1 2 : a jack of the same suit as the starter in cribbage that scores one point for the holder — usu. used in the phrases *his nob* or *his nobs*
[2]**nob** *n* [perh. fr. [1]*nob*] *chiefly Brit* : one in a superior position in life
nob·ble \ˈnäb-əl\ *vt* **nob·bled; nob·bling** \-(ə-)liŋ\ [perh. irreg. freq. of *nab*] 1 *Brit* : to incapacitate (a racehorse) esp. by drugging 2 *slang Brit* a : to win over to one's side b : STEAL c : SWINDLE, CHEAT — **nob·bler** \-(ə-)lər\ *n*
nob·by \ˈnäb-ē\ *adj* **nob·bi·er; -est** : CHIC, SMART <the ~ nightclub atop a skyscraper —*Holiday*>
No·bel·ist \nō-ˈbel-əst\ *n* : a winner of a Nobel prize
no·bel·i·um \nō-ˈbel-ē-əm\ *n* [NL, fr. Alfred B. *Nobel*] : a radioactive element produced artificially — see ELEMENT table
No·bel prize \(ˌ)nō-ˌbel-\ *n* : any of various annual prizes (as in peace, literature, medicine) established by the will of Alfred Nobel for the encouragement of persons who work for the interests of humanity
no·bil·i·ty \nō-ˈbil-ət-ē\ *n* [ME *nobilite*, fr. MF *nobilité*, fr. L *nobilitat-, nobilitas*, fr. *nobilis*] 1 : the quality or state of being noble in character, quality, or rank 2 : the body of persons forming the noble class in a country or state : ARISTOCRACY
[1]**no·ble** \ˈnō-bəl\ *adj* **no·bler** \-b(ə-)lər\; **no·blest** \-b(ə-)ləst\ [ME, fr. OF, fr. L *nobilis* knowable, well known, noble, fr. *noscere* to come to know — more at KNOW] 1 a : possessing outstanding qualities : ILLUSTRIOUS b : FAMOUS, NOTABLE <~ deed> 2 : of high birth or exalted rank : ARISTOCRATIC 3 a : possessing very high or excellent qualities or properties <~ hawk> b : very good or excellent 4 : grand or impressive esp. in appearance <~

edifice> **5 :** possessing, characterized by, or arising from superiority of mind or character or of ideals or morals : LOFTY <a ~ aim, faithfully kept, is as a ~ deed —William Wordsworth> **6 :** chemically inert or inactive esp. toward oxygen <~ metal> ***syn*** see MORAL ***ant*** base (*of actions*), atrocious (*of deeds*) — **no·ble·ness** \-bəl-nəs\ *n* — **no·bly** \-blē *also* -bə-lē\ *adv*

2**no·ble** *n* **1 :** a person of noble rank or birth **2 :** an old English gold coin equivalent to 6*s* 8*d*

noble gas *n* : any of a group of rare gases that include helium, neon, argon, krypton, xenon, and sometimes radon and exhibit great stability and extremely low reaction rates — called also *inert gas*

no·ble·man \ˈnō-bəl-mən\ *n* : a man of noble rank : PEER

no·blesse \nō-ˈbles\ *n* [ME, fr. OF *noblesce*, fr. *noble*] **1 :** noble birth or condition : NOBILITY **2 :** the members esp. of the French nobility

no·blesse oblige \nō-ˌbles-ə-ˈblēzh\ *n* [F, lit., nobility obligates] : the obligation of honorable, generous, and responsible behavior associated with high rank or birth

no·ble·wom·an \ˈnō-bəl-ˌwu̇m-ən\ *n* : a woman of noble rank : PEERESS

1**no·body** \ˈnō-ˌbäd-ē, -bəd-ē\ *pron* : no person : not anybody

2**nobody** *n, pl* **no·bod·ies :** a person of no influence or consequence

no·cent \ˈnōs-ᵊnt\ *adj* [ME, fr. L *nocent-, nocens*, fr. prp. of *nocēre* to harm, hurt — more at NOXIOUS] : HARMFUL <a ~ dose>

no·ci·cep·tive \ˌnō-si-ˈsep-tiv\ *adj* [L *nocēre* + E *-i-* + *receptive*] **1** *of a stimulus* : PAINFUL, INJURIOUS **2 :** of, induced by, or responding to a nociceptive stimulus — used esp. of receptors or protective reflexes

1**nock** \ˈnäk\ *n* [ME *nocke* notched tip on the end of a bow; akin to MD *nocke* summit, tip, L *nux* nut — more at NUT] **1 :** one of the notches cut in either of two tips of horn fastened on the ends of a bow or in the bow itself for holding the string **2 a :** the part of an arrow having a notch for the bowstring **b :** the notch itself

2**nock** *vt* : to make a notch in or fit into or by means of a notch

noct- *or* **nocti-** *or* **nocto-** *comb form* [L *noct-, nocti-*, fr. *noct-, nox* — more at NIGHT] : night <*noct*ambulation>

noct·am·bu·la·tion \(ˌ)näk-ˌtam-byə-ˈlā-shən\ *n* [*noct-* + *-ambulation* (as in *somnambulation*)] : SOMNAMBULISM

noct·am·bu·lism \näk-ˈtam-byə-ˌliz-əm\ *n* : NOCTAMBULATION — **noct·am·bu·list** \-ləst\ *n*

noc·ti·lu·ca \ˌnäk-tə-ˈlü-kə\ *n* [NL, genus name, fr. L, something that shines by night, fr. *noct-* + *lucēre* to shine — more at LIGHT] : any of a genus (*Noctiluca*) of marine bioluminescent flagellates (order Dinoflagellata) that often cause phosphorescence of the sea

noc·ti·lu·cent cloud \-ˌlüs-ᵊnt-\ *n* [*noctilucent* deriv. of L *noct-* & *lucent-, lucens* lucent] : a luminous thin usu. colored cloud seen at night at a height of about 50 miles

noc·tu·id \ˈnäk-chə-wəd, ˈnäk-tə-\ *n* [NL *Noctuidae*, group name, fr. *Noctua*, genus of moths, fr. L, night owl; akin to L *nox* night] : any of a large family (Noctuidae) of medium-sized often dull-colored moths with larvae (as cutworms and armyworms) that are often destructive agricultural pests — **noctuid** *adj*

noc·turn \ˈnäk-ˌtərn\ *n* [ME *nocturne*, fr. MF, fr. ML *nocturna*, fr. L, fem. of *nocturnus*] : a principal division of the office of matins

noc·tur·nal \näk-ˈtərn-ᵊl\ *adj* [MF or LL; MF fr. LL *nocturnalis*, fr. L *nocturnus* of night, nocturnal, fr. *noct-, nox* night] **1 :** of, relating to, or occurring in the night <a ~ journey> **2 :** active at night <a ~ predator> — **noc·tur·nal·ly** \-ᵊl-ē\ *adv*

noc·turne \ˈnäk-ˌtərn\ *n* [F, adj., nocturnal, fr. L *nocturnus*] : a work of art dealing with evening or night; *esp* : a dreamy pensive composition for the piano — compare AUBADE 3

noc·u·ous \ˈnäk-yə-wəs\ *adj* [L *nocuus*, fr. *nocēre* to harm — more at NOXIOUS] : HARMFUL — **noc·u·ous·ly** *adv*

1**nod** \ˈnäd\ *vb* **nod·ded; nod·ding** [ME *nodden*; akin to OHG *hnotōn* to shake, L *cinis* ashes — more at INCINERATE] *vi* **1 :** to make a quick downward motion of the head whether deliberately (as in expressing assent, salutation, or command) or involuntarily (as from drowsiness) **2 :** to incline or sway from the vertical as though ready to fall **3 :** to bend or sway the upper part gently downward or forward : bob gently **4 :** to make a slip or error in a moment of abstraction <there are lapses; even Homer ~*s* —Emerson Tuttle> ~ *vt* **1 :** to incline (as the head) downward or forward **2 :** to bring, invite, or send by a nod <*nodded* them into the room> **3 :** to signify by a nod <*nodded* their approval> — **nod·der** *n*

2**nod** *n* **1 :** the act or an instance of nodding <gave a ~ of greeting> **2 :** an indication of something (as agreement or approval) <received the party's ~ as candidate for governor>

nod·al \ˈnōd-ᵊl\ *adj* : being, relating to, or located at or near a node — **no·dal·i·ty** \nō-ˈdal-ət-ē\ *n* — **nod·al·ly** \ˈnōd-ᵊl-ē\ *adv*

nod·ding *adj* : bending downward or forward : PENDULOUS, DROOPING <a plant with ~ flowers>

nod·dle \ˈnäd-ᵊl\ *n* [ME *nodle* back of the head or neck] : HEAD, PATE

nod·dy \ˈnäd-ē\ *n, pl* **noddies** [prob. short for obs. *noddypoll*, alter. of *hoddypoll* (fumbling inept person)] **1 :** a stupid person **2 :** any of several stout-bodied terns (genera *Anous* and *Micranous*) of warm seas

node \ˈnōd\ *n* [L *nodus* knot, node — more at NET] **1 :** an entangling complication (as in a drama) : PREDICAMENT **2 a :** a thickened or swollen enlargement (as of a rheumatic joint) **b :** a discrete mass of one kind of tissue enclosed in tissue of a different kind **3 :** either of the two points where the orbit of a planet or comet intersects the ecliptic; *also* : either of the points at which the orbit of an earth satellite crosses the plane of the equator **4 a :** a point at which subsidiary parts originate or center **b :** a point on a stem at which a leaf or leaves are inserted **c :** a point at which a curve intersects itself in such a manner that the branches have different tangents **d :** VERTEX 1a(2) **5 :** a point, line, or surface of a vibrating body that is free or relatively free from vibratory motion

node of Ran·vier \-ˈrän-vē-ˌā\ [Louis A. *Ranvier* †1922 F histologist] : a constriction in the medullary sheath of a medullated nerve fiber

no·di·cal \ˈnōd-i-kəl, ˈnäd-\ *adj* : of or relating to astronomical nodes

no·dose \ˈnō-ˌdōs\ *adj* [L *nodosus*, fr. *nodus*] : having numerous or conspicuous protuberances <~ antennae> — **no·dos·i·ty** \nō-ˈdäs-ət-ē\ *n*

nod·u·lar \ˈnäj-ə-lər\ *adj* : of, relating to, characterized by, or occurring in the form of nodules <~ lesions>

nod·u·la·tion \ˌnäj-ə-ˈlā-shən\ *n* **1 :** the process of forming nodules and esp. root nodules containing symbiotic bacteria **2 :** NODULE

nod·ule \ˈnäj-(ˌ)ü(ə)l\ *n* [L *nodulus*, dim. of *nodus*] : a small mass of rounded or irregular shape: as **a :** a small rounded lump of a mineral or mineral aggregate **b :** a swelling on a leguminous root that contains symbiotic bacteria

no·dus \ˈnōd-əs\ *n, pl* **no·di** \ˈnō-ˌdī, -ˌdē\ [L, knot, node] : COMPLICATION, DIFFICULTY

no·el \nō-ˈel\ *n* [F *noël* Christmas, carol, fr. L *natalis* birthday, fr. *natalis* natal] **1 :** a Christmas carol **2** *cap* : the Christmas season

noes *pl of* NO

no·et·ic \nō-ˈet-ik\ *adj* [Gk *noētikos* intellectual, fr. *noein* to think, fr. *nous* mind] : of, relating to, or based on the intellect

no–fault *adj* : of, relating to, or being a motor vehicle insurance plan under which an accident victim is compensated usu. up to a stipulated limit for actual losses (as medical bills and lost wages) but not for nuisance claims (as of pain and suffering) by his own insurance company regardless of who is responsible for the accident

1**nog** \ˈnäg\ *n* [origin unknown] : a wooden peg, pin, or block of the size of a brick; *esp* : one built into a wall as a hold for nails

2**nog** *n* [origin unknown] **1 :** a strong ale formerly brewed in Norfolk, England **2** [by shortening] : EGGNOG **3 :** an often alcoholic drink containing beaten egg, milk, or both

nog·gin \ˈnäg-ən\ *n* [origin unknown] **1 :** a small mug or cup **2 :** a small quantity (as a gill) of drink **3 :** a person's head

nog·ging \ˈnäg-ən, -iŋ\ *n* [1*nog*] : rough brick masonry used to fill in the open spaces of a wooden frame

1**no–good** \ˌnō-ˌgu̇d\ *adj* : having no worth, use, or chance of success

2**no–good** \ˈnō-ˌgu̇d\ *n* : a no-good person or thing

Noh *var of* NO

no–hit *adj* : of, relating to, or being a baseball game or a part of a game in which a pitcher allows the opposition no base hits

no–hit·ter \(ˈ)nō-ˈhit-ər\ *n* : a no-hit game in baseball

no·how \ˈnō-ˌhau̇\ *adv* **1 :** in no manner or way : not at all <was ~ equal to the task> **2** *dial* : ANYHOW

noil \ˈnȯi(ə)l\ *n* [origin unknown] : short fiber removed during the combing of a textile fiber and often separately spun into yarn

1**noise** \ˈnȯiz\ *n* [ME, fr. OF, strife, quarrel, noise, fr. L *nausea* nausea] **1 :** loud, confused, or senseless shouting or outcry **2 a :** SOUND; *esp* : one that lacks agreeable musical quality or is noticeably unpleasant **b :** any sound that is undesired or interferes with one's hearing of something **c :** an unwanted signal or a disturbance (as static or a variation of voltage) in an electronic communication system (as radio or television); *broadly* : a disturbance interfering with the operation of a mechanical device or system **d :** electromagnetic radiation (as light or radio waves) that is composed of several frequencies and that involves random changes in frequency or amplitude **e :** irrelevant or meaningless bits or words occurring along with desired information (as in a computer output) **3 :** common talk : RUMOR; *esp* : SLANDER ***syn*** see SOUND — **noise·less** \-ləs\ *adj* — **noise·less·ly** *adv*

2**noise** *vb* **noised; nois·ing** *vt* : to spread by rumor or report — usu. used with *about* or *abroad* <the scandal was quickly *noised* about> ~ *vi* **1 :** to talk much or loudly **2 :** to make a noise

noise·mak·er \ˈnȯiz-ˌmā-kər\ *n* : one that makes noise; *esp* : a device (as a horn or rattle) used to make noise at parties — **noise·mak·ing** \-kiŋ\ *n or adj*

noise pollution *n* : environmental pollution consisting of annoying or harmful noise (as of automobiles or jet airplanes)

noi·some \ˈnȯi-səm\ *adj* [ME *noysome*, fr. *noy* annoyance, fr. OF *enui, anoi* — more at ENNUI] **1 :** NOXIOUS, UNWHOLESOME **2 :** offensive to the senses and esp. to the sense of smell ***syn*** see MALODOROUS — **noi·some·ly** *adv* — **noi·some·ness** *n*

noisy \ˈnȯi-zē\ *adj* **nois·i·er; -est** **1 :** making noise **2 :** full of or characterized by noise — **nois·i·ly** \ˈnȯi-zə-lē\ *adv* — **nois·i·ness** \-zē-nəs\ *n*

no·li me tan·ge·re \ˌnō-lē-(ˌ)mē-ˈtan-jə-rē, -ˌlī-mē-\ *n* [L, do not touch me] : a warning against touching or interference

nol·le pro·se·qui \ˌnäl-ē-ˈpräs-ə-ˌkwī\ *n* [L, to be unwilling to pursue] : an entry on the record of a legal action denoting that the prosecutor or plaintiff will proceed no further in his action or suit either as a whole or as to some count or as to one or more of several defendants

no·lo \ˈnō-(ˌ)lō\ *n* : NOLO CONTENDERE

no–load \ˌnō-ˌlōd\ *adj* : sold at net asset value <a ~ mutual fund>

no·lo con·ten·de·re \ˌnō-(ˌ)lō-kən-ˈten-də-rē\ *n* [L, I do not wish to contend] : a plea by the defendant in a criminal prosecution that without admitting guilt subjects him to conviction but does not preclude him from denying the truth of the charges in a collateral proceeding

nol–pros \ˈnäl-ˈpräs\ *vt* **nol–prossed; nol–pros·sing** [*nol*le *prosequi*] : to discontinue by entering a nolle prosequi

nom *abbr* nominative

no·ma \ˈnō-mə\ *n* [NL, fr. Gk *nomē*, fr. *nemein* to spread (of an ulcer), lit., to graze, pasture — more at NIMBLE] : a spreading gangrene of the lining of cheek and lips that occurs usu. in severely debilitated persons

no·mad \ˈnō-ˌmad, *Brit also* ˈnäm-ˌad\ *n* [L *nomad-, nomas* member of a wandering pastoral people, fr. Gk, fr. *nemein* to pasture — more at NIMBLE] **1 :** a member of a people that has no fixed residence but wanders from place to place usu. seasonally and within a well-defined territory in order to secure its food supply

2 : an individual who roams about aimlessly — **nomad** *adj* — **no·mad·ism** \'nō-ˌmad-ˌiz-əm\ *n*

no·mad·ic \nō-'mad-ik\ *adj* **1 :** of, relating to, or characteristic of nomads <a ~ tribe> **2 :** roaming about from place to place aimlessly or without a fixed pattern of movement <lived ~ lives, moving from . . . house to . . . house —Frank Conroy>

no–man's–land \'nō-ˌmanz-ˌland\ *n* **1 a :** an area of unowned, unclaimed, or uninhabited land **b :** an unoccupied area between opposing armies **2 :** an area of anomalous, ambiguous, or indefinite character <the ~ of the generation gap —*Psychology Today*>

nom·bril \'näm-brəl\ *n* [MF, lit., navel, deriv. of L *umbilicus*] **:** the center point of the lower half of an armorial escutcheon — see ESCUTCHEON illustration

nom de guerre \ˌnäm-di-'ge(ə)r\ *n, pl* **noms de guerre** \ˌnäm(z)-di-\ [F, lit., war name] **:** PSEUDONYM

nom de plume \-'plüm\ *n, pl* **noms de plume** \ˌnäm(z)-di-\ [F *nom* name + *de* of + *plume* pen] **:** PSEUDONYM, PEN NAME

nome \'nōm\ *n* [Gk *nomos* district — more at NIMBLE] **:** a province of ancient Egypt

no·men \'nō-mən\ *n, pl* **no·mi·na** \'näm-ə-nə, 'nō-mə-\ [L *nomin-, nomen* name — more at NAME] **:** the second of the three usual names of an ancient Roman

no·men·cla·tor \'nō-mən-ˌklāt-ər\ *n* [L, slave whose duty was to tell his master the names of persons he met when campaigning for office, fr. *nomen* + *calatus*, pp. of *calare* to call — more at LOW] **1 :** a book containing collections or lists of words **2** *archaic* **:** one who announces the names of guests or of persons generally **3 :** one who gives names to or invents names for things

no·men·cla·to·ri·al \ˌnō-mən-klə-'tōr-ē-əl, -'tȯr-\ *adj* **:** relating to or connected with nomenclature

no·men·cla·ture \'nō-mən-ˌklā-chər *also* nō-'men-klə-ˌchu̇(ə)r, -'meŋ-, -klə-chər, -klə-ˌt(y)u̇(ə)r\ *n* [L *nomenclatura* calling by name, list of names, fr. *nomen* + *calatus*, pp.] **1 :** NAME, DESIGNATION **2 :** the act or process or an instance of naming **3 a :** a system or set of terms or symbols **b :** a system of terms used in a particular science, discipline, or art; *esp* **:** an international system of standardized New Latin names used in biology for kinds and groups of kinds of animals and plants — **no·men·cla·tur·al** \ˌnō-mən-'klāch-(ə-)rəl\ *adj*

no·men con·ser·van·dum \'nō-mən-ˌkän(t)-sər-'van-dəm\ *n, pl* **no·mi·na con·ser·van·da** \'näm-ə-nə-ˌkän(t)-sər-'van-də, 'nō-mə-\ [NL, name to be kept] **:** a biological taxonomic name (as of a genus) that is preserved by special sanction in exception to the usual rules (as of priority)

nomen du·bi·um \-'d(y)ü-bē-əm\ *n, pl* **nomina du·bia** \-bē-ə\ [NL, doubtful name] **:** a taxonomic name that cannot be assigned with certainty to any taxonomic group because the description is insufficient for identification and the original specimens are lost or destroyed

no·men nu·dum \-'n(y)üd-əm\ *n, pl* **nomina nu·da** \-ə\ [NL, bare name] **:** a proposed taxonomic name that is invalid because the group designated is not described or illustrated sufficiently for recognition, that has no nomenclatural status, and that consequently can be used as though never previously proposed

¹nom·i·nal \'näm-ən-ᵊl, 'näm-nəl\ *adj* [ME *nominalle*, fr. ML *nominalis*, fr. L, of a name, fr. *nomin-, nomen* name] **1 :** of, relating to, or being a noun or a word or expression taking a noun construction **2 a :** of, relating to, or constituting a name **b :** bearing the name of a person **3 a :** existing or being something in name or form only <~ head of his party> **b :** of, being, or relating to a designated or theoretical size that may vary from the actual **:** APPROXIMATE **c :** TRIFLING, INSIGNIFICANT **4 :** being according to plan **:** SATISFACTORY <everything was ~ during the spacecraft launch> — **nom·i·nal·ly** \-ē\ *adv*

²nominal *n* **:** a word or word group functioning as a noun

nom·i·nal·ism \-ˌiz-əm\ *n* **1 :** a theory that there are no universal essences in reality and that the mind can frame no single concept or image corresponding to any universal or general term **2 :** the theory that only individuals and no abstract entities (as essences, classes, or propositions) exist — **nom·i·nal·ist** \-əst\ *n* — **nominalist** *or* **nom·i·nal·is·tic** \ˌnäm-ən-ᵊl-'is-tik, ˌnäm-nəl-\ *adj*

nominal value *n* **:** PAR 1b

nominal wages *n pl* **:** wages measured in money as distinct from actual purchasing power

nom·i·nate \'näm-ə-ˌnāt\ *vt* **-nat·ed; -nat·ing** [L *nominatus*, pp. of *nominare*, fr. *nomin-, nomen* name] **1 :** DESIGNATE, NAME **2 a :** to appoint or propose for appointment to an office or place **b :** to propose as a candidate for election to office **c :** to propose for an honor <~ him for player of the year> **3 :** to enter (a horse) in a race — **nom·i·na·tor** \-ˌnāt-ər\ *n*

nom·i·na·tion \ˌnäm-ə-'nā-shən\ *n* **1 :** the act, process, or an instance of nominating **2 :** the state of being nominated

nom·i·na·tive \'näm-(ə-)nət-iv; *2 & 3 are also* 'näm-ə-ˌnāt-\ *adj* [fr. the traditional use of the nominative form in naming a noun] **1 a :** marking typically the subject of a verb esp. in languages that have relatively full inflection <~ case> **b :** of or relating to the nominative case <a ~ ending> **2 :** nominated or appointed by nomination **3 :** bearing a person's name — **nominative** *n*

nom·i·nee \ˌnäm-ə-'nē\ *n* [*nominate*] **:** a person who has been nominated

no·mo·gram \'näm-ə-ˌgram, 'nō-mə-\ *n* [Gk *nomos* law + ISV *-gram* — more at NIMBLE] **:** a graphic representation that consists of several lines marked off to scale and arranged in such a way that by using a straightedge to connect known values on two lines an unknown value can be read at the point of intersection with another line

no·mo·graph \-ˌgraf\ *n* **:** NOMOGRAM — **no·mo·graph·ic** \ˌnäm-ə-'graf-ik, ˌnō-mə-\ *adj* — **no·mog·ra·phy** \nō-'mäg-rə-fē\ *n*

no·mo·log·i·cal \ˌnäm-ə-'läj-i-kəl, ˌnō-mə-\ *adj* [*nomology* (science of physical and logical laws)] **:** relating to or expressing basic physical laws or rules of reasoning <~ universals>

no·mo·thet·ic \-'thet-ik\ *adj* [Gk *nomothetikos* of legislation, fr. *nomothetēs* lawgiver, fr. *nomos* law + *-thetēs* one who establishes, fr. *tithenai* to put — more at DO] **:** relating to, involving, or dealing with abstract, general, or universal statements or laws

-n·o·my \n-ə-mē\ *n comb form* [ME *-nomie*, fr. OF, fr. L *-nomia*, fr. Gk, fr. *nemein* to distribute] **:** system of laws governing or sum of knowledge regarding a (specified) field <agro*nomy*>

non- \(ˈ)nän *also* ˌnən *or* 'nən *before* '*-stressed syllable*, ˌnän *also* ˌnən *before* ˌ*-stressed or unstressed syllable; the variant with* ə *is also to be understood at pronounced entries, where it is not shown* \ *prefix* [ME, fr. MF, fr. L *non* not, fr. OL *noenum*, fr. *ne-* not + *oinom*, neut. of *oinos* one — more at NO, ONE] **1 :** not **:** reverse of **:** absence of **2 :** of little or no consequence **:** unimportant **:** worthless <*non*issues> <*non*system> **3 :** lacking the usual characteristics of the thing specified <*non*celebration> <*non*theater>

nonabrasive
nonabsorbable
nonabsorbent
nonabstainer
nonacademic
nonacceptance
nonaccredited
nonacid
nonacidic
nonactinic
nonaction
nonactive
nonadaptive
nonaddicted
nonaddicting
nonaddictive
nonadherence
nonadhesion
nonadhesive
nonadiabatic
nonadjacent
nonadjustable
nonadministrative
nonadmission
nonaffluent
nonaggression
nonaggressive
nonagreement
nonagricultural
nonalcoholic
nonallergenic
nonallergic
nonalphabetic
nonanalytic
nonanthropological
nonantigenic
nonappearance
nonaquatic
nonaqueous
nonarbitrary
nonascetic
nonaspirated
nonassessable
nonassimilable
nonassociative
nonathlete
nonathletic
nonattendance
nonattributive
nonauditory
nonauthoritative
nonautomatic
nonautomotive
nonbacterial
nonbasic
nonbearing
nonbeing
nonbeliever
nonbelieving
nonbelligerency
nonbelligerent
nonbetting
nonbinding
nonbiodegradable
nonbiological
nonbiting
nonbonded
nonbonding
nonbreakable
nonbureaucratic
noncaking
noncancerous
noncanonical
noncarbohydrate
noncarbonaceous
noncarbonated
noncarnivorous
noncash
noncatalytic
noncellular
noncertified
nonchargeable
nonchurchgoer
noncircadian
noncitizen
nonclassical
nonclassified
nonclerical
nonclinical
nonclotting
noncoagulable
noncoercive
noncognitive
noncoherent
noncohesive
noncoital
noncollapsible
noncollectible
noncollegiate
noncolloid
noncombat
noncombining
noncombustible
noncommerical
noncommunicable
noncommunicant
noncommunication
noncommutative
noncommutativity
noncompensating
noncompetent
noncompeting
noncompetition
noncompetitive
noncomplementary
noncompliance
noncomplying
noncompound
noncomprehension
noncompressible
nonconclusive
nonconcurrent
noncondensable
noncondensing
nonconditioned
nonconductibility
nonconducting
nonconduction
nonconductive
nonconfidence
nonconfidential
nonconflicting
noncongenital
nonconjugated
nonconscious
nonconservation
nonconserved
nonconsolidated
nonconstitutional
nonconstructive
nonconsumable
noncontact
noncontagious
noncontemporary
noncontentious
noncontiguous
noncontinuous
noncontraband
noncontradiction
noncontradictory
noncontributing
noncontributory
noncontrollable
noncontrolled
noncontrolling
noncontroversial
nonconventional
nonconvertible
noncorporate
noncorrodible
noncorroding
noncorrosive
noncovalent
noncovered
noncreative
noncriminal
noncritical
noncryogenic
noncrystalline
noncultivated
noncultivation
noncumulative
noncurrent
noncyclic
noncyclical
nondecreasing
nondeferrable
nondefining
nondegenerate
nondegenerated
nondegradable
nondelegable
nondelinquent
nondelivery
nondemocratic
nondenominational
nondenominationalism
nondepartmental
nondeposition
nonderivative
nondeteriorative
nondetonating
nondevelopable
nondevelopment
nondiabetic
nondialyzable
nondifferentiation
nondiffusible
nondigestible
nondipolar
nondipole
nondirectional
nondisclosure
nondiscrimination
nondiscriminatory
nondiscursive
nondisqualifying
nondisruptive
nondistribution
nondivided
nondoctrinaire
nondocumentary
nondogmatic
nondollar
nondomesticated
nondramatic
nondurable
nondynastic
nonecclesiastical
noneffective
noneffervescent
nonelastic
nonelect
nonelection
nonelective
nonelectric
nonelectrical
nonelectronic
noneligible
nonemergency
nonemotional
nonempirical
nonempty
nonencapsulated
nonenforcement
nonentanglement
nonenzymatic
nonenzymic
nonepiscopal
nonequilibrium
nonequivalence
nonequivalent
noneruptive
nonessential
nonesterified
nonexchangeable
nonexclusive
nonexempt
nonexistence

ə abut ᵊ kitten ər further a back ā bake ä cot, cart
au̇ out ch chin e less ē easy g gift i trip ī life
j joke ŋ sing ō flow ȯ flaw ȯi coin th thin t͟h this
ü loot u̇ foot y yet yü few yu̇ furious zh vision

nonexistent
nonexpendable
nonexperimental
nonexplosive
nonexportation
nonextant
nonfarmer
nonfatal
nonfattening
nonfebrile
nonfederal
nonfederated
nonfeeding
nonferromagnetic
nonfilamentous
nonfilterable
nonfinancial
nonfissionable
nonflagellated
nonfluorescent
nonflying
nonforfeiture
nonfossiliferous
nonfraternal
nonfreezing
nonfulfillment
nonfunctional
nongame
nongaseous
nongeneric
nongenetic
nongonococcal
nongraded
nongranular
nongregarious
nongrowing
nonhandicapped
nonhardy
nonharmonic
nonhazardous
nonhelical
nonhereditary
nonheritable
nonhistorical
nonhomogeneous
nonhomologous
nonhormonal
nonhostile
nonhuman
nonhypergolic
nonideal
nonidentity
nonideological
nonimmigrant
nonimmune
nonimportation
nonincreasing
nonindustrial
nonindustrialized
noninfectious
noninfective
noninfested
noninflammable
noninflammatory
noninflationary
noninflectional
noninjurious
noninjury
noninsecticidal
noninstitutional
noninstitutionalized
noninstructional
nonintegrated
nonintellectual
nonintercourse
noninterference
nonintersecting
nonintoxicant
nonintoxicating
nonirradiated
nonirrigated
nonirritating
nonisothermal
nonleaded
nonlegal
nonlegume
nonleguminous
nonlethal
nonlexical
nonlife
nonlinear
nonliquid
nonliterary
nonliturgical
nonliving
nonlocal
nonlogical
nonluminous
nonlysogenic
nonmagnetic
nonmailable
nonmalignant
nonmalleable
nonman
nonmanufacturing
nonmarine
nonmarketable
nonmaterial
nonmaterialistic
nonmathematical
nonmechanical
nonmechanistic
nonmember
nonmembership
nonmetameric
nonmetered
nonmetrical
nonmetropolitan
nonmigratory
nonmilitary
nonmimetic
nonmolecular
nonmoney
nonmotile
nonmotility
nonmoving
nonmusical
nonmutant
nonmyelinated
nonnarcotic
nonnational
nonnative
nonnatural
nonnaturalism
nonnaturalist
nonnecessity
nonnegotiable
nonneoplastic
nonnitrogenous
nonnormative
nonnumeric
nonnumerical
nonnutritive
nonobese
nonobligatory
nonobservance
nonobvious
nonoccurrence
nonofficial
nonopaque
nonoperating
nonoperational
nonorganic
nonoriented
nonorthodox
nonorthogonal
nonoscillatory
nonoverlapping
nonpalatal
nonpalatalization
nonparallel
nonparalytic
nonparasitic
nonparticipant
nonparticipating
nonparticipation
nonparty
nonpaternity
nonpaying
nonpayment
nonpecuniary
nonpenetrating
nonperformance
nonperishable
nonpermanent
nonpersonal
nonphonemic
nonphonetic
nonphosphatic
nonphotosynthetic
nonphysical
nonphytotoxic
nonpigmented
nonplastic
nonplaying
nonpoisonous
nonpolarizable
nonpolitical
nonpolluting
nonporosity
nonporous
nonpossession
nonpractical
nonpredicative
nonpregnant
nonprinting
nonproducer
nonprogressive
nonpropositional
nonproprietary
nonproven
nonpsychedelic
nonpublic
nonpungent
nonpunitive
nonquota
nonrabbinic
nonracial
nonracialism
nonradiative
nonradical
nonradioactive
nonrandom
nonrandomness
nonrated
nonrational
nonreactive
nonreactivity
nonreactor
nonrealistic
nonreciprocal
nonrecognition
nonrecourse
nonrecoverable
nonrecurrent
nonrecurring
nonreducing
nonrefillable
nonregistered
nonregulation
nonreligious
nonremovable
nonrenewable
nonrepayable
nonrepresentative
nonresidential
nonresonant
nonrestraint
nonrestricted
nonretractile
nonretroactive
nonrevenue
nonreversible
nonrhetorical
nonrotating
nonruminant
nonsalable
nonsaline
nonsaponifiable
nonscientific
nonscientist
nonseasonal
nonsecret
nonsecretory
nonsegregated
nonsegregation
nonselected
nonselective
non-self-governing
nonsensitive
nonsensuous
nonseptate
nonserious
nonsexual
nonshrinkable
nonsingular
nonsinkable
nonskier
nonslaveholding
nonsmoker
nonsmoking
nonsolar
nonsolid
nonspatial
nonspeaking
nonspecialist
nonspecialized
nonspecific
nonspecifically
nonspectacular
nonspectral
nonspeculative
nonspherical
nonspontaneous
nonstaining
nonstationary
nonstatistical
nonstellar
nonstrategic
nonstriated
nonstriker
nonstriking
nonstructural
nonstructured
nonstudent
nonsubscriber
nonsuccess
nonsugar
nonsurfer
nonsurgical
nonsymbiotic
nonsymbolic
nonsymmetric
nonsymmetrical
nonsynchronous
nonsyntactical
nonsystemic
nontarnishable
nontaxable
nontechnical
nontechnological
nonteleological
nontemporal
nonterritorial
nontheatrical
nontheistic
nonthermal
nonthreatening
nontidal
nontoxic
nontoxicity
nontraditional
nontransferable
nontransparency
nontransparent
nontransposing
nontreated
nontropical
nontrump
nontuberculous
nontypical
nonunderstandable
nonuniform
nonuniformity
nonurban
nonutilitarian
nonvariable
nonvariant
nonvascular
nonvegetative
nonvenomous
nonvibratory
nonvintage
nonviolation
nonviral
nonvirulent
nonviscous
nonvisual
nonvocal
nonvocational
nonvoluntary
nonvoter
nonvoting
nonwoody
nonworker
nonworking
nonyellowing

non·ad·di·tive \(ˌ)nän-ˈad-ət-iv\ *adj* **1 :** not having a numerical value equal to the sum of values for the component parts **2 :** of, relating to, or being a genic effect that is not additive — **non·ad·di·tiv·i·ty** \ˌnän-ˌad-ə-ˈtiv-ət-ē\ *n*

non·age \ˈnän-ij, ˈnō-nij\ *n* [ME, fr. MF, fr. *non-* + *age*] **1 :** MINORITY 1 **2 a :** a period of youth **b :** lack of maturity

no·na·ge·nar·i·an \ˌnō-nə-jə-ˈner-ē-ən, ˌnän-ə-\ *n* [L *nonagenarius* containing ninety, fr. *nonageni* ninety each, fr. *nonaginta* ninety, fr. *nona-* (akin to *novem* nine) + *-ginta* (akin to *viginti* twenty) — more at NINE, VIGESIMAL] **:** a person who is in his nineties — **nonagenarian** *adj*

no·na·gon \ˈnō-nə-ˌgän\ *n* [L *nonus* ninth + E *-gon* — more at NOON] **:** a polygon of nine angles and nine sides

non·aligned \ˌnän-əl-ˈīnd\ *adj* **:** not allied with other nations and esp. with one of the great powers — **non·align·ment** \-ˈīn-mənt\ *n*

non·al·le·lic \ˌnän-ə-ˈlē-lik, -ˈlel-ik\ *adj* **:** not behaving as alleles toward one another <~ genes>

non·bank \ˈnän-ˈbaŋk\ *adj* **:** done by or being something other than a bank

[1]**non·book** \ˈnän-ˈbu̇k\ *adj* **:** being something other than a book; *esp* **:** being a library holding (as a microfilm) that is not a book

[2]**non·book** \-ˌbu̇k\ *n* **:** a book of little literary merit which is often a compilation (as of pictures, press clippings, or speeches)

non·busi·ness \-ˈbiz-nəs, -nəz\ *adj* **:** not related to business; *esp* **:** not related to one's primary business

non·cal·car·e·ous \ˌnän-kal-ˈkar-ē-əs, -ˈker-\ *adj* **:** lacking or deficient in lime <~ soils>

non·ca·lo·ric \ˌnän-kə-ˈlȯr-ik, -ˈlōr-, -ˈlär-; (ˌ)nän-ˈkal-ə-rik\ *adj* **:** free from or very low in calories

non·can·di·date \(ˌ)nän-ˈkan-(d)ə-ˌdāt, -(d)əd-ət\ *n* **:** one who is not a candidate; *esp* **:** one who has declared himself not a candidate for a particular political office

[1]**nonce** \ˈnän(t)s\ *n* [ME *nanes*, alter. (fr. incorrect division of *then anes* in such phrases as *to then anes* for the one purpose) of *anes* one purpose, irreg. fr. *an* one, fr. OE *ān*] **:** the one, particular, or present occasion, purpose, or use <for the ~>

[2]**nonce** *adj* **:** occurring, used, or made only once or for a special occasion <~ word>

non·cha·lance \ˌnän-shə-ˈlän(t)s; ˈnän-shə-ˌlän(t)s, -lən(t)s\ *n* **:** the state of being nonchalant

non·cha·lant \-ˈlänt, -ˌlänt, -lənt\ *adj* [F, fr. OF, fr. prp. of *nonchaloir* to disregard, fr. *non-* + *chaloir* to concern, fr. L *calēre* to be warm — more at LEE] **:** giving an effect of easy unconcern or indifference *syn* see COOL — **non·cha·lant·ly** *adv*

non·chro·mo·som·al \ˌnän-ˌkrō-mə-ˈsō-məl\ *adj* **1 :** not situated on a chromosome **2 :** not involving chromosomes

non·com \ˈnän-ˌkäm\ *n* **:** NONCOMMISSIONED OFFICER

non·com·ba·tant \ˌnän-kəm-ˈbat-ənt, (ˌ)nän-ˈkäm-bət-ənt\ *n* **:** one that does not engage in combat: as **a :** a member (as a chaplain) of the armed forces whose duties do not include fighting **b :** CIVILIAN — **noncombatant** *adj*

non·com·mis·sioned officer \ˌnän-kə-ˌmish-ənd-\ *n* **:** a subordinate officer (as a sergeant) in the army, air force, or marine corps appointed from among the enlisted men

non·com·mit·tal \ˌnän-kə-ˈmit-əl\ *adj* **1 :** giving no clear indication of attitude or feeling **2 :** having no clear or distinctive character — **non·com·mit·tal·ly** \-əl-ē\ *adv*

non–Com·mu·nist \(ˌ)nän-ˈkäm-yə-nəst\ *adj* **:** not Communist **:** being other than Communist

non com·pos men·tis \ˌnän-ˌkäm-pə-ˈsment-əs, ˌnōn-\ *adj* [L, lit., not having mastery of one's mind] **:** not of sound mind

non·con·cur·rence \ˌnän-kən-ˈkər-ən(t)s, -ˈkə-rən(t)s\ *n* **:** the act or an instance of refusing to concur

non·con·duc·tor \ˌnän-kən-ˈdək-tər\ *n* **:** a substance that conducts heat, electricity, or sound only in very small degree

non·con·form \-ˈfȯ(ə)rm\ *vi* [back-formation fr. *nonconformist*] **:** to fail to conform — **non·con·form·er** *n*

non·con·for·mance \-ˈfȯr-mən(t)s\ *n* **:** failure to conform

non·con·form·ism \-ˈfȯr-ˌmiz-əm\ *n* **:** NONCONFORMITY

non·con·form·ist \-ˈfȯr-məst\ *n* **1** *often cap* **:** a person who does not conform to an established church; *esp* **:** one who does not conform to the Church of England **2 :** a person who does not conform to a generally accepted pattern of thought or action — **nonconformist** *adj, often cap*

non·con·for·mi·ty \-ˈfȯr-mət-ē\ *n* **1 a :** failure or refusal to conform to an established church **b** *often cap* **:** the movement or principles of English Protestant dissent **c** *often cap* **:** the body of English Nonconformists **2 :** refusal to conform to an established or conventional creed, rule, or practice **3 :** absence of agreement or correspondence

non·co·op·er·a·tion \ˌnän-kō-ˌäp-ə-ˈrā-shən\ *n* **:** failure or refusal to cooperate with the government of a country — **non·co·op·er·a·tion·ist** \-sh(ə-)nəst\ *n* — **non·co·op·er·a·tor** \-ˈäp-ə-ˌrāt-ər\ *n*

non·co·op·er·a·tive \-ˈäp-(ə-)rət-iv, -ə-ˌrāt-\ *adj* **:** of, relating to, or characterized by noncooperation

non·cred·it \(ˌ)nän-ˈkred-ət\ *adj* **:** not offering credit toward a degree <~ courses>

non·cross·over \(ˌ)nän-ˈkrȯ-ˌsō-vər\ *adj* : having or being chromosomes that have not participated in genetic crossing-over <~ offspring>

non·dairy \ˈnän-ˈde(ə)r-ē\ *adj* : containing no milk or milk products <~ whipped topping>

non·de·duct·ible \ˌnän-di-ˈdək-tə-bəl\ *adj* : not deductible; *esp* : not deductible for income tax purposes — **non·de·duct·ibil·i·ty** \-ˌdək-tə-ˈbil-ət-ē\ *n*

non·de·fense \ˌnän-di-ˈfen(t)s\ *adj* : not used or intended for or associated with the military <~ spending>

non·de·script \ˌnän-di-ˈskript\ *adj* [*non-* + L *descriptus*, pp. of *describere* to describe] : belonging or appearing to belong to no particular class or kind : not easily described — **nondescript** *n*

non·de·struc·tive \-ˈstrək-tiv\ *adj* : not destructive; *specif* : involving no alteration of physical state or arrangement or of chemical constitution <~ analysis> — **non·de·struc·tive·ly** *adv* — **non·de·struc·tive·ness** *n*

non·dia·paus·ing \ˌnän-ˌdī-ə-ˈpȯ-ziŋ\ *adj* **1** : not having a diapause **2** : not being in a state of diapause

non·di·rec·tive \ˌnän-də-ˈrek-tiv, -(ˌ)dī-\ *adj* : of, relating to, or being psychotherapy, counseling, or interviewing in which the counselor refrains from interpretation or explanation but encourages the client (as by repeating phrases) to express himself freely

non·dis·junc·tion \ˌnän-dis-ˈjəŋ(k)-shən\ *n* [ISV] : failure of two chromosomes to separate subsequent to metaphase in meiosis or mitosis so that one daughter cell has both and the other neither of the chromosomes — **non·dis·junc·tion·al** \-shnəl, -shən-ᵊl\ *adj*

non·dis·tinc·tive \-ˈtiŋ(k)-tiv\ *adj, of a speech sound* : having no signaling value

non·di·vid·ing \ˌnän-də-ˈvīd-iŋ\ *adj* : not undergoing cell division

non·dor·mant \(ˌ)nän-ˈdȯr-mənt\ *adj* **1** : being in such a condition that germination is possible <~ seeds> **2** : being in active vegetative growth <~ plants>

non·drink·er \-ˈdriŋ-kər\ *n* : one who abstains from alcoholic beverages

non·drink·ing \-kiŋ\ *n* : abstinence from alcoholic beverages

nondrying oil \ˌnän-ˌdrī-iŋ-\ *n* : a highly saturated oil (as olive oil) that is unable to solidify when exposed in a thin film to air

¹none \ˈnən\ *pron, sing or pl in constr* [ME, fr. OE *nān*, fr. *ne* not + *ān* one — more at NO, ONE] **1** : not any : NOTHING **2** : not one : NOBODY **3** : not any such thing or person

²none *adj, archaic* : not any : NO

³none *adv* **1** : by no means : not at all <~ too soon to begin> **2** : in no way : to no extent < ~ the worse for wear>

⁴none \ˈnōn\ *n, often cap* [LL *nona*, fr. L, 9th hour of the day from sunrise — more at NOON] : the fifth of the canonical hours

non·eco·nom·ic \ˌnän-ˌek-ə-ˈnäm-ik, -ˌē-kə-\ *adj* : not economic; *esp* : having no economic importance or implication

non·elec·tro·lyte \ˌnän-ə-ˈlek-trə-ˌlīt\ *n* : a substance (as sugar or benzene) that is not appreciably ionized

non·en·force·able \ˌnän-in-ˈfōr-sə-bəl, -ˈfȯr-\ *adj* : not enforceable — **non·en·force·abil·i·ty** \-ˌfōr-sə-ˈbil-ət-ē, -ˌfȯr-\ *n*

non·en·ti·ty \nä-ˈnen(t)-ət-ē\ *n* **1** : something that does not exist or exists only in the imagination **2** : NONEXISTENCE **3** : one of no consequence or significance

nones \ˈnōnz\ *n pl but sing or pl in constr* [ME *nonys*, fr. L *nonae*, fr. fem. pl. of *nonus* ninth] **1** : the ninth day before the ides according to ancient Roman reckoning **2** *often cap* : ⁴NONE

none·such \ˈnən-ˌsəch\ *n* : a person or thing without an equal — **nonesuch** *adj*

none·the·less \ˌnən-t͟hə-ˈles\ *adv* : NEVERTHELESS

non–eu·clid·e·an \ˌnän-yu̇-ˈklid-ē-ən\ *adj, often cap E* : not assuming or in accordance with all the postulates of Euclid's *Elements* <~ geometry>

non·event \ˈnän-i-ˌvent, ˌnän-i-ˈ\ *n* : an expected event that fails to take place or to satisfy expectations

non·ex·is·tence \ˌnän-ig-ˈzis-tən(t)s\ *n* : absence of existence : the negation of being

non·ex·pert \(ˌ)nän-ˈek-ˌspərt\ *n* : one who is not an expert

non·farm \ˈnän-ˈfärm\ *adj* : not of or related to the farm

non·fat \ˈnän-ˈfat\ *adj* : lacking fat solids : having fat solids removed <~ milk>

non·fea·sance \(ˌ)nän-ˈfēz-ᵊn(t)s\ *n* [*non-* + obs. E *feasance* (doing, execution)] : failure to act; *esp* : failure to do what ought to be done

non·fer·rous \(ˌ)nän-ˈfer-əs\ *adj* **1** : not containing, including, or relating to iron **2** : of or relating to metals other than iron

non·fic·tion \ˈnän-ˈfik-shən\ *n* : literature that is not fictional — **non·fic·tion·al** \(ˌ)nän-ˈfik-shnəl, -shən-ᵊl\ *adj*

non·fig·u·ra·tive \(ˌ)nän-ˈfig-(y)ə-rət-iv\ *adj* : NONOBJECTIVE 2

non·flam·ma·ble \-ˈflam-ə-bəl\ *n* : not flammable; *specif* : not easily ignited and not burning rapidly if ignited — **non·flam·ma·bil·i·ty** \ˌnän-ˌflam-ə-ˈbil-ət-ē\ *n*

non·flow·er·ing \-ˈflau̇-(ə-)riŋ\ *adj* : producing no flowers; *specif* : lacking a flowering stage in the life cycle

non·flu·en·cy \-ˈflü-ən-sē\ *n, pl* **-cies** **1** : lack of fluency **2** : an instance of nonfluency

non·food \ˈnän-ˈfüd\ *adj* : of, relating to, or being something other than food <~ items sold in supermarkets>

non·gov·ern·men·tal \ˌnän-ˌgəv-ər(n)-ˈment-ᵊl\ *or* **non·gov·ern·ment** \ˈnän-ˈgəv-ər(n)-mənt, -ˈgəv-ᵊm-ənt\ *adj* : not governmental

non·grad·u·ate \ˈnän-ˈgraj-(ə-)wət, -ə-ˌwāt\ *n* : one who is not a graduate

non·green \ˈnän-ˈgrēn\ *adj* : not green; *specif* : containing no chlorophyll <~ saprophytes>

non·he·ro \ˈnän-ˈhē-(ˌ)rō, -ˈhi(ə)r-(ˌ)ō\ *n* : ANTI-HERO

non·his·tone \(ˌ)nän-ˈhis-ˌtōn\ *adj* : rich in aromatic amino acids and esp. tryptophan <~ proteins>

non·iden·ti·cal \ˌnän-(ˌ)ī-ˈdent-i-kəl, ˌnän-ə-ˈdent-\ *adj* **1** : DIFFERENT **2** : FRATERNAL 2

no·nil·lion \nō-ˈnil-yən\ *n, often attrib* [F, fr. L *nonus* ninth + F *-illion* (as in *million*) — more at NOON] — see NUMBER table

non·in·duc·tive \ˌnän-in-ˈdək-tiv\ *adj* : not inductive; *esp* : having negligible inductance

non·in·fect·ed \-ˈfek-təd\ *adj* : not having been subjected to infection

non·in·ter·ven·tion \ˌnän-ˌint-ər-ˈven-chən\ *n* : the state or policy of not intervening <~ in the affairs of other countries> — **non·in·ter·ven·tion·ist** \-ˈvench-(ə-)nəst\ *n or adj*

non·in·volve·ment \ˌnän-in-ˈväl-vmənt\ *n* : absence of emotional involvement or attachment

non·ion·ic \ˌnän-(ˌ)ī-ˈän-ik\ *adj* : not ionic; *esp* : not dependent on a surface-active anion for effect <~ surfactants>

nonionic detergent *n* : a synthetic detergent that produces electrically neutral colloidal particles in solution

non·join·der \(ˌ)nän-ˈjȯin-dər\ *n* : failure to include a necessary party to a suit at law

non·judg·men·tal \ˌnän-ˌjəj-ˈment-ᵊl\ *adj* : avoiding judgments based on one's personal and esp. moral standards

non·jur·ing \(ˌ)nän-ˈju̇(ə)r-iŋ\ *adj* [*non-* + L *jurare* to swear — more at JURY] : not swearing allegiance — used esp. of a member of a party in Great Britain that would not swear allegiance to William and Mary or to their successors

non·ju·ror \(ˌ)nän-ˈju̇r-ər, -ˈju̇(ə)r-ˌȯ(ə)r\ *n* : a person refusing to take an oath esp. of allegiance, supremacy, or abjuration; *specif* : one of the beneficed clergy in England and Scotland refusing to take an oath of allegiance to William and Mary or to their successors after the revolution of 1688

non·lin·guis·tic \ˌnän-liŋ-ˈgwis-tik\ *adj* : not consisting of or relating to language

non·lit·er·ate \(ˌ)nän-ˈlit-ə-rət, -ˈli-trət\ *adj* : having no written language — **nonliterate** *n*

non·match·ing \-ˈmach-iŋ\ *adj* **1** : not matching **2** : not requiring a matching contribution <~ grants>

non·met·al \(ˌ)nän-ˈmet-ᵊl\ *n* : a chemical element (as boron, carbon, or nitrogen) that lacks typical metallic properties and is able to form anions, acidic oxides and acids, and stable compounds with hydrogen

non·me·tal·lic \ˌnän-mə-ˈtal-ik\ *adj* **1** : not metallic **2** : of, relating to, or being a nonmetal

non·mon·e·tary \(ˌ)nän-ˈmän-ə-ˌter-ē, -ˈmən-\ *adj* : not monetary : not involving money

non·mor·al \-ˈmȯr-əl, -ˈmär-\ *adj* : not falling into or existing in the sphere of morals or ethics ***syn*** see IMMORAL

non·neg·a·tive \-ˈneg-ət-iv\ *adj* : not negative : being either positive or zero

non·nu·cle·ar \(ˌ)nän-ˈn(y)ü-klē-ər\ *adj* **1** : not producing or involving a nuclear explosion <a ~ bomb> **2** : not operated by or involving atomic energy <a ~ propulsion system> **3** : not having the atom bomb <a ~ country> **4** : not involving the use of atom bombs <a ~ war>

non·ob·jec·tive \ˌnän-əb-ˈjek-tiv\ *adj* **1** : not objective **2** : representing or intended to represent no natural or actual object, figure, or scene <~ art> — **non·ob·jec·tiv·ism** \-tiv-ˌiz-əm\ *n* — **non·ob·jec·tiv·ist** \-əst\ *n* — **non·ob·jec·tiv·i·ty** \ˌnän-ˌäb-ˌjek-ˈtiv-ət-ē, ˌnän-əb-\ *n*

non obst *or* **non obs** *abbr* non obstante

non ob·stan·te \ˌnän-əb-ˈstant-ē, ˌnōn-\ *prep* [L] : NOTWITHSTANDING

no–nonsense *adj* : tolerating no nonsense : SERIOUS, BUSINESSLIKE

non·para·met·ric \ˌnän-ˌpar-ə-ˈme-trik\ *adj* : not involving the estimation of parameters of a statistical function <~ statistical tests>

¹non·pa·reil \ˌnän-pə-ˈrel\ *adj* [MF, fr. *non-* + *pareil* equal, fr. (assumed) VL *pariculus*, fr. L *par* equal] : having no equal

²nonpareil *n* **1** : an individual of unequaled excellence : PARAGON **2 a** : a small flat disk of chocolate covered with white sugar pellets **b** : small sugar pellets of various colors

non·par·ti·san \(ˌ)nän-ˈpärt-ə-zən, -sən\ *adj* : not partisan; *esp* : free from party affiliation, bias, or designation <~ ballot> <a ~ board> — **non·par·ti·san·ship** \-ˌship\ *n*

non·pas·ser·ine \(ˌ)nän-ˈpas-ə-ˌrīn\ *adj* : not passerine; *esp* : CORACIIFORM

non·patho·gen·ic \ˌnän-ˌpath-ə-ˈjen-ik\ *adj* : not capable of inducing disease — compare AVIRULENT

non·per·sis·tent \ˌnän-pər-ˈsis-tənt, -ˈzis-\ *adj* : not persistent: as **a** : decomposed rapidly by environmental action <~ insecticides> **b** : capable of being transmitted by a vector for only a relatively short time <~ viruses>

non·per·son \ˈnän-ˈpərs-ᵊn, -ˌpərs-\ *n* **1** : a person who is regarded as nonexistent or as never having existed **2** : UNPERSON

non pla·cet \ˈnän-ˈplā-sət, ˈnōn-\ *n* [L, it does not please] : a negative vote

¹non·plus \ˈnän-ˈpləs\ *n* [L *non plus* no more] : a state of bafflement or perplexity : QUANDARY

²nonplus *vt* **-plussed** *also* **-plused** \-ˈpləst\; **-plus·sing** *also* **-plus·ing** : to cause to be at a loss as to what to say, think, or do : PERPLEX ***syn*** see PUZZLE

non·po·lar \(ˌ)nän-ˈpō-lər\ *adj* : not polar; *esp* : not having or requiring the presence of electrical poles <a ~ solvent>

non pos·su·mus \ˈnän-ˈpäs-ə-məs, ˈnōn-\ *n* [L, we cannot] : a statement expressing inability to do something

non·pre·scrip·tion \ˌnän-pri-ˈskrip-shən\ *adj* : capable of being bought without a doctor's prescription

non·pro·duc·tive \ˌnän-prə-ˈdək-tiv\ *adj* : not productive: as **a** : failing to produce or yield : UNPRODUCTIVE <a ~ oil well> **b** : not directly concerned with production <the ~ labor of clerks and inspectors> **c** *of a cough* : DRY — **non·pro·duc·tive·ness** *n*

non·pro·fes·sion·al \-ˈfesh-nəl, -ən-ᵊl\ *adj* : not professional — **nonprofessional** *n* — **non·pro·fes·sion·al·ly** \-ē\ *adv*

ə abut	ᵊ kitten	ər further	a back	ā bake	ä cot, cart
au̇ out	ch chin	e less	ē easy	g gift	i trip ī life
j joke	ŋ sing	ō flow	ȯ flaw	ȯi coin	th thin t͟h this
ü loot	u̇ foot	y yet	yü few	yu̇ furious	zh vision

non·prof·it \ˈnän-ˈpräf-ət\ *adj* : not conducted or maintained for the purpose of making a profit
non·pro·lif·er·a·tion \ˌnän-prə-ˌlif-ə-ˈrā-shən\ *adj* : providing for the stoppage of proliferation (as of nuclear arms) <~ treaty> — **nonproliferation** *n*
non·pros \ˈnän-ˈpräs\ *vt* **non·prossed; non·pros·sing** [*non prosequitur*] : to enter a non prosequitur against
non pro·se·qui·tur \ˌnän-prə-ˈsek-wət-ər, ˌnōn-\ *n* [LL, he does not prosecute] : a judgment entered against the plaintiff in a suit in which he does not appear to prosecute
non·pro·tein \ˈnän-ˈprō-ˌtēn, -ˈprōt-ē-ən\ *adj* : not being or derived from protein <the ~ part of an enzyme> <~ nitrogen> — **non·pro·tein·aceous** \ˌnän-ˌprō-ˌtē-ˈnā-shəs, -ˌprōt-ē-ə-ˈnā-\ *adj*
non·read·er \ˈnän-ˈrēd-ər\ *n* : one who does not or cannot read; *esp* : a child who is very slow in learning to read
non·re·com·bi·nant \ˌnän-(ˌ)rē-ˈkäm-bə-nənt\ *adj* : not exhibiting the results of genetic recombination <~ progeny> — **nonrecombinant** *n*
non·re·fund·able \ˌnän-ri-ˈfən-də-bəl\ *adj* : not subject to refunding <a ~ bond>
non·rel·a·tiv·is·tic \ˌnän-ˌrel-ət-iv-ˈis-tik\ *adj* **1** : not based on or involving the theory of relativity <~ equations> <~ kinematics> **2 a** : moving at less than a relativistic velocity **b** : of or relating to a body moving at such a velocity — **non·rel·a·tiv·is·ti·cal·ly** \-ˈis-ti-k(ə-)lē\ *adv*
non·rep·re·sen·ta·tion·al \ˌnän-ˌrep-ri-ˌzen-ˈtā-shnəl, -zən-, -shən-ᵊl\ *adj* : NONOBJECTIVE 2 — **non·rep·re·sen·ta·tion·al·ism** \-ˌiz-əm\ *n*
non·res·i·dence \(ˈ)nän-ˈrez-əd-ən(t)s, -ˈrez-dən(t)s, -ˈrez-ə-ˌden(t)s\ *n* : the state or fact of being nonresident
non·res·i·den·cy \-ˈrez-əd-ən-sē, -ˈrez-dən-, -ˈrez-ə-ˌden-\ *n* : NONRESIDENCE
non·res·i·dent \-ˈrez-əd-ənt, -ˈrez-dənt, -ˈrez-ə-ˌdent\ *adj* : not residing in a particular place — **nonresident** *n*
non·re·sis·tance \ˌnän-ri-ˈzis-tən(t)s\ *n* : the principles or practice of passive submission to constituted authority even when unjust or oppressive; *also* : the principle or practice of not resisting violence by force
non·re·sis·tant \-tənt\ *adj* : not resistant; *specif* : susceptible to the effects of a deleterious agent (as an insecticide, a pathogen, or an extreme environmental condition) — **nonresistant** *n*
non·re·stric·tive \ˌnän-ri-ˈstrik-tiv\ *adj* : not restrictive; *specif* : not limiting the reference of a modified word or phrase
nonrestrictive clause *n* : a descriptive clause that is not essential to the definiteness of the meaning of its antecedent (as in "the aldermen, *who were present,* assented")
non·re·turn·able \ˌnän-ri-ˈtər-nə-bəl\ *adj* : not returnable; *specif* : not returnable to a dealer in exchange for a deposit <~ bottles>
non·rig·id \(ˈ)nän-ˈrij-əd\ *adj* : not rigid; *esp* : maintaining form by pressure of contained gas <a ~ airship> — **non·ri·gid·i·ty** \ˌnän-rə-ˈjid-ət-ē\ *n*
non·sched·uled \(ˈ)nän-ˈskej-(ˌ)ü(ə)ld, -ˈskej-əld\ *adj* : licensed to carry passengers or freight by air without a regular schedule <~ airlines>
[1]**non·sci·ence** \(ˈ)nän-ˈsī-ən(t)s\ *n* : one (as a discipline) that is not a science
[2]**nonscience** *adj* : of or relating to fields other than science
non·se·cre·tor \ˌnän(t)-si-ˈkrēt-ər\ *n* : an individual of blood group A, B, or AB who does not secrete the antigens characteristic of these blood groups in bodily fluids (as saliva)
non·sec·tar·i·an \ˌnän-(ˌ)sek-ˈter-ē-ən\ *adj* : not having a sectarian character : not affiliated with or restricted to a particular religious group
non·sed·i·ment·able \ˌnän-ˌsed-ə-ˈment-ə-bəl\ *adj* : not capable of being sedimented under specified conditions (as of centrifugation)
[1]**non·sense** \ˈnän-ˌsen(t)s, ˈnän(t)-sən(t)s\ *n* **1 a** : words or language having no meaning or conveying no intelligible ideas **b** (1) : language, conduct, or an idea that is absurd or contrary to good sense (2) : an instance of absurd action **2 a** : things of no importance or value : TRIFLES **b** : affected or impudent conduct <took no ~ from his subordinates> **3** : nonsense genetic material — **non·sen·si·cal** \(ˈ)nän-ˈsen(t)-si-kəl\ *adj* — **non·sen·si·cal·ly** \-k(ə-)lē\ *adv* — **non·sen·si·cal·ness** \-kəl-nəs\ *n*
[2]**nonsense** *adj* **1** : consisting of an arbitrary grouping of speech sounds or symbols <\ˈshrȯg-ˌthī-əmpth\ is a ~ word> <a ~ syllable> **2** : consisting of one or more codons that do not code for any amino acid and usu. cause termination of the molecular chain in protein synthesis <~ mutation>
nonsense verse *n* : humorous or whimsical verse that features unique characters and actions and often contains evocative but meaningless nonce words
non seq *abbr* non sequitur
non se·qui·tur \(ˈ)nän-ˈsek-wət-ər *also* -ˌtu̇(ə)r\ *n* [L, it does not follow] **1** : an inference that does not follow from the premises; *specif* : a fallacy resulting from a simple conversion of a universal affirmative proposition or from the transposition of a condition and its consequent **2** : a statement (as a response) that does not follow logically from anything previously said
non·sig·nif·i·cant \ˌnän(t)-sig-ˈnif-i-kənt\ *adj* : not significant: as **a** : INSIGNIFICANT **b** : MEANINGLESS **c** : having or yielding a value lying within limits between which variation is attributed to chance <a ~ statistical test> — **non·sig·nif·i·cant·ly** *adv*
non·sked \ˈnän-ˈsked\ *n* [by shortening & alter. fr. *nonscheduled*] : a nonscheduled airline or transport plane
non·skid \-ˈskid\ *adj* : designed or equipped to prevent skidding
non·slip \-ˈslip\ *adj* : designed to reduce or prevent slipping
non·so·cial \(ˈ)nän-ˈsō-shəl\ *adj* : not socially oriented : lacking a social component <~ speech continues . . . in the stream of consciousness —Joseph Church> ***syn*** see UNSOCIAL ***ant*** social
non·sport·ing \-ˈspōrt-iŋ, -ˈspȯrt-\ *adj* : lacking the qualities characteristic of a hunting dog
non·stan·dard \-ˈstan-dərd\ *adj* **1** : not standard **2** : not conforming in pronunciation, grammatical construction, idiom, or word choice to the usage generally characteristic of educated native speakers of a language — compare SUBSTANDARD
non·start·er \-ˈstärt-ər\ *n* **1** : one that does not start **2** : one that gets off to a poor start
non·ste·roid \-ˈsti(ə)r-ˌȯid *also* -ˈste(ə)r-\ *n* : a compound and esp. a drug that is not a steroid — **nonsteroid** *or* **non·ste·roi·dal** \ˌnän-stə-ˈrȯid-ᵊl\ *adj*
non·stick \ˈnän-ˈstik\ *adj* [[3]*stick*] : allowing of easy removal of cooked food particles <a ~ coating in a frying pan>
non·stop \ˈnän-ˈstäp\ *adj* : done, made, or held without a stop : not easing or letting up — **nonstop** *adv*
non·such \ˈnən-ˌsəch *also* ˈnän-\ *var of* NONESUCH
non·suit \ˈnän-ˈsüt\ *n* [ME, fr. AF *nounsuyte,* fr. *noun-* non- + OF *siute* following, pursuit — more at SUIT] : a judgment against a plaintiff for his failure to prosecute his case or inability to establish a prima facie case — **nonsuit** *vt*
non·sup·port \ˌnän(t)-sə-ˈpō(ə)rt, -ˈpȯ(ə)rt\ *n* : failure to support; *specif* : failure (as of a parent) to honor a statutory or contractual obligation to provide maintenance
non·swim·mer \ˈnän-ˈswim-ər\ *n* : one who is unable to swim
non·syl·lab·ic \ˌnän(t)-sə-ˈlab-ik\ *adj* : not constituting a syllable or the nucleus of a syllable <\n\ is syllabic in \ˈbät-ᵊn-ē\ *botany,* ~ in \ˈbät-nē\> <the second vowel of a falling diphthong is ~ (as \i\ in \ȯi\)>
non·sys·tem \ˈnän-ˈsis-təm\ *n* : a system that lacks effective organization
non·tar·get \-ˈtär-gət\ *adj* : not being the intended object of action by a particular agent <effect of insecticides on ~ organisms>
non·teach·ing \-ˈtē-chiŋ\ *adj* : not concerned with or involving teaching
non·ten·ured \-ˈten-yərd\ *adj* : not having tenure
non·ti·tle \-ˈtīt-ᵊl\ *adj* : of, relating to, or being an athletic contest in which a title is not at stake
non·triv·i·al \(ˈ)nän-ˈtriv-ē-əl\ *adj* **1** : not trivial **2** : having the value of at least one variable not equal to zero <~ solutions to linear equations>
non trop·po \(ˈ)nän-ˈtrȯ-(ˌ)pō, ˈnōn-\ *adv or adj* [It, lit., not too much] : without excess — used to qualify a direction in music
non–U \(ˈ)nän-ˈyü\ *adj* : not characteristic of the upper classes
non·union \(ˈ)nän-ˈyü-nyən\ *adj* **1** : not belonging to or connected with a trade union <~ carpenters> <a ~ job> **2** : not recognizing or favoring trade unions or their members
non·use \ˈnän-ˈyüs\ *n* **1** : failure to use <~ of available material> **2** : the fact or condition of not being used
non·us·er \-ˈyü-zər\ *n* : one who does not make use of something (as an available public facility or a harmful drug)
non·vec·tor \(ˈ)nän-ˈvek-tər\ *n* : an organism (as an insect) that does not transmit a particular pathogen (as a virus)
non·ver·bal \-ˈvər-bəl\ *adj* : not verbal: as **a** : being other than verbal <~ factors> **b** : involving minimal use of language <~ tests> **c** : ranking low in verbal skill — **non·ver·bal·ly** \-bə-lē\ *adv*
non·vi·a·ble \-ˈvī-ə-bəl\ *adj* : not capable of living, growing, or developing and functioning successfully
non·vi·o·lence \-ˈvī-ə-lən(t)s\ *n* **1** : abstention from violence as a matter of principle; *also* : the principle of such abstention **2 a** : the quality or state of being nonviolent : avoidance of violence **b** : nonviolent demonstrations for the purpose of securing political ends <studied the history and techniques of ~>
non·vi·o·lent \-lənt\ *adj* : abstaining or free from violence — **non·vi·o·lent·ly** *adv*
non·vol·a·tile \-ˈväl-ət-ᵊl\ *adj* : not volatile; *esp* : not volatilizing readily
non–West·ern \(ˈ)nän-ˈwes-tərn\ *adj* **1** : not being part of the western tradition <~ countries> **2** : of or relating to non-Western societies <~ values>
non·white \-ˈhwīt, -ˈwīt\ *n* : a person whose features and esp. whose skin color are distinctively different than those of Caucasians of northwestern Europe; *esp* : one who has African ancestors of the black race — **nonwhite** *adj*
non·ze·ro \-ˈzē-(ˌ)rō, -ˈzi(ə)r-(ˌ)ō\ *adj* : being, having, or involving a value other than zero
[1]**noo·dle** \ˈnüd-ᵊl\ *n* [perh. alter. of *noddle*] **1** : a stupid person : SIMPLETON **2** : HEAD
[2]**noodle** *n* [G *nudel*] : a food paste made with egg and shaped typically in ribbon form
[3]**noodle** *vi* **noo·dled; noo·dling** \ˈnüd-liŋ, -ᵊl-iŋ\ [imit.] : to improvise on an instrument in an informal or desultory manner
nook \ˈnu̇k\ *n* [ME *noke, nok*] **1** *chiefly Scot* : a right-angled corner **2 a** : an interior angle formed by two meeting walls : RECESS **b** : a secluded or sheltered place or part
nooky \ˈnu̇k-ē\ *n* [prob. fr. *nook* + *-y,* n. suffix forming diminutives] : SEXUAL INTERCOURSE — usu. considered vulgar
noon \ˈnün\ *n* [ME, fr. OE *nōn* ninth hour from sunrise, fr. L *nona,* fr. fem. of *nonus* ninth; akin to L *novem* nine — more at NINE] **1** : the middle of the day : MIDDAY **2** *archaic* : MIDNIGHT — used chiefly in the phrase *noon of night* **3** : the highest point
noon·day \-ˌdā\ *n* : MIDDAY
no one *pron* : no person : NOBODY
noon·ing \ˈnü-niŋ, -nən\ *n* **1** *chiefly dial* : a meal eaten at noon **2** *chiefly dial* : a period at noon for eating or resting
noon·tide \ˈnün-ˌtīd\ *n* **1** : the time of noon : MIDDAY **2** : the highest or culminating point
noon·time \-ˌtīm\ *n* : NOONTIDE
[1]**noose** \ˈnüs, *Brit also* ˈnüz\ *n* [prob. fr. Prov. *nous* knot, fr. L *nodus* — more at NET] **1** : a loop with a running knot that binds closer the more it is drawn **2** : something that snares like a noose
[2]**noose** *vt* **noosed; noos·ing** **1** : to secure by a noose **2** : to make a noose in or of
noo·sphere \ˈnō-ə-ˌsfi(ə)r\ *n* [ISV *noo-* mind (fr. Gk *noos, nous*) + *sphere*] : the biosphere as altered consciously or unconsciously by human activities
Noot·ka \ˈnu̇t-kə\ *n, pl* **Nootka** *or* **Nootkas** **1** : a member of a Wakashan people of Vancouver Island and the Cape Flattery region

in northwestern Washington **2 :** the language of the Nootka people

NOP *abbr* not otherwise provided for

no·pal \nō-ˈpäl, -ˈpal; ˈnō-pəl\ *n* [Sp, fr. Nahuatl *nopalli*] **:** any of a genus (*Nopalea*) of cacti that differ from the prickly pears in having erect petals and scarlet flowers with the stamens much longer than the petals; *broadly* **:** PRICKLY PEAR

no–par *or* **no–par–val·ue** *adj* **:** having no nominal value <~ stocks>

nope \ˈnōp, *or with glottal stop instead of* p\ *adv* [by alter.] **:** NO

[1]**nor** \nər, (ˈ)nȯ(ə)r\ *conj* [ME, contr. of *nother* neither, nor, fr. *nother,* pron. & adj., neither — more at NEITHER] **1** — used as a function word to introduce the second or last member or the second and each following member of a series of items each of which is negated <neither here ~ there> <not done by you ~ me ~ anyone> **2** — used as a function word to introduce and negate a following clause or phrase **3** *archaic* **:** NEITHER

[2]**nor** \nər\ *conj* [ME, perh. fr. [1]*nor*] *dial* **:** THAN

Nor *abbr* Norway, Norwegian

NOR \ˈnȯ(ə)r\ *n* [*not or*]**:** a computer logic circuit that produces an output that is the inverse of that of an OR circuit

nor·adren·a·line *also* **nor·adren·a·lin** \ˌnȯr-ə-ˈdren-ᵊl-ən\ *n* [*nor*mal + *adrenaline*] **:** NOREPINEPHRINE

[1]**Nor·dic** \ˈnȯrd-ik\ *adj* [F *nordique,* fr. *nord* north, fr. OE *north*] **1 :** of or relating to the Germanic peoples of northern Europe and esp. of Scandinavia **2 :** of or relating to a physical type characterized by tall stature, long head, light skin and hair, and blue eyes **3 :** of or relating to competitive ski events consisting of ski jumping and cross-country racing — compare ALPINE

[2]**Nordic** *n* **1 :** a native of northern Europe **2 :** a person of Nordic physical type or of a hypothetical Nordic division of the Caucasian race **3 :** a member of the peoples of Scandinavia

Nordic combined *n* **:** a competitive ski event consisting of cross-country skiing and ski jumping

nor·epi·neph·rine \ˈnȯ(ə)r-ˌep-ə-ˈnef-rən\ *n* [*nor*mal + *epinephrine*] **:** a crystalline compound $C_8H_{11}NO_3$ that occurs with epinephrine, has a strong vasoconstrictor action, and mediates transmission of sympathetic nerve impulses

Norf *abbr* Norfolk

Nor·folk jacket \ˌnȯr-fək, -ˌfōk-\ *n* [*Norfolk,* England]**:** a loose-fitting belted single-breasted jacket with box pleats

no·ria \ˈnōr-ē-ə, ˈnȯr-\ *n* [Sp, fr. Ar *nāʽūrah*] **:** an undershot waterwheel of the bucket type used esp. in primitive irrigation systems

nor·land \ˈnȯ(ə)r-lənd\ *n, chiefly dial* **:** NORTHLAND

[1]**norm** \ˈnȯ(ə)rm\ *n* [L *norma,* lit., carpenter's square] **1 :** an authoritative standard **:** MODEL **2 :** a principle of right action binding upon the members of a group and serving to guide, control or regulate proper and acceptable behavior **3 :** AVERAGE: as **a :** a set standard of development or achievment usu. derived from the average or median achievement of a large group **b :** a pattern or trait taken to be typical in the behavior of a social group **4 a :** a real-valued nonnegative function defined on a vector space and satisfying the conditions that the function is zero if and only if the vector is zero, the function of the product of a scalar and a vector is equal to the product of the absolute value of the scalar and the function of the vector, and the function of the sum of two vectors is less than or equal to the sum of the functions of the two vectors; *specif* **:** the square root of the sum of the squares of the absolute values of the elements of a matrix or of the components of a vector **b :** the greatest distance between two successive points of a set of points that partition an interval into smaller intervals ***syn*** see AVERAGE

[2]**norm** *abbr* normal

[1]**nor·mal** \ˈnȯr-məl\ *adj* [L *normalis,* fr. *norma* carpenter's square] **1 :** PERPENDICULAR: *esp* **:** perpendicular to a tangent at a point of tangency **2 :** according with, constituting, or not deviating from a norm, rule, or principle **:** REGULAR **3 :** occurring naturally <~ immunity> **4 a :** of, relating to, or characterized by average intelligence or development **b :** free from mental disorder **:** SANE **5 a** *of a solution* **:** having a concentration of one gram equivalent of solute per liter **b :** containing neither basic hydroxyl nor acid hydrogen <~ silver phosphate> **c :** not associated <~ molecules> **d :** having a straight-chain structure <~ pentane> <~ butyl alcohol> **6** *of a subgroup* **:** having the property that every coset produced by operating on the left by a given element is equal to the coset produced by operating on the right by the same element **7 :** relating to, involving, or being a normal curve or normal distribution <~ approximation to the binomial distribution> **8** *of a matrix* **:** having the property of commutativity under multiplication by the transpose of the matrix each of whose elements is a conjugate complex number with respect to the corresponding element of the given matrix ***syn*** see REGULAR ***ant*** abnormal — **nor·mal·i·ty** \nȯr-ˈmal-ət-ē\ *n* — **nor·mal·ly** \ˈnȯr-mə-lē\ *adv*

[2]**normal** *n* **1 a :** a normal line **b :** the portion of a normal line to a plane curve between the curve and the x-axis **2 :** one that is normal **3 :** a form or state regarded as the norm **:** STANDARD

normal curve *n* **:** the symmetrical bell-shaped curve of a normal distribution

nor·mal·cy \ˈnȯr-məl-sē\ *n* **:** the state or fact of being normal

normal distribution *n* **:** a probability density function that approximates the distribution of many random variables (as the proportion of outcomes of a particular sort in a large number of independent repetitions of an experiment in which the probabilities remain constant from trial to trial) and that has the form

$$f(x) = \frac{1}{\sigma\sqrt{2\pi}}\, e^{-\frac{1}{2}\left(\frac{x-\mu}{\sigma}\right)^2}$$

where μ is the mean and σ is the standard deviation — compare NORMAL CURVE

normal divisor *n* **:** a normal subgroup

nor·mal·ize \ˈnȯr-mə-ˌlīz\ *vt* **ized; -iz·ing 1 :** to make conform to or reduce to a norm or standard **2 :** to make normal (as by a transformation of variables) — **nor·mal·iz·able** \-ˌlī-zə-bəl\ *adj* — **nor·mal·iza·tion** \ˌnȯr-mə-lə-ˈzā-shən\ *n*

nor·mal·iz·er \ˈnȯr-mə-ˌlī-zər\ *n* **1 :** one that normalizes **2 a :** a subgroup consisting of those elements of a group for which the group operation with regard to a given element is commutative **b :** the set of elements of a group for which the group operation with regard to every element of a given subgroup is commutative

normal orthogonal *adj* **:** ORTHONORMAL

normal school *n* [trans. of F *école normale;* fr. the fact that the first French school so named was intended to serve as a model]**:** a usu. two-year school for training chiefly elementary teachers

Nor·man \ˈnȯr-mən\ *n* [ME, fr. OF *Normant,* fr. ON *Northmann-, Northmathr* Norseman, fr. *northr* north + *mann-, mathr* man; akin to OE *north* and to OE *man*] **1 :** a native or inhabitant of Normandy: **a :** one of the Scandinavian conquerors of Normandy in the 10th century **b :** one of the Norman-French conquerors of England in 1066 **2 :** NORMAN-FRENCH — **Norman** *adj*

Norman architecture *n* **:** a Romanesque style first appearing in and near Normandy about A.D. 950; *also* **:** architecture resembling or imitating this style

Norman–French *n* **1 :** the French language of the medieval Normans **2 :** the modern dialect of Normandy

nor·ma·tive \ˈnȯr-mət-iv\ *adj* [F *normatif,* fr. *norme* norm, fr. L *norma*] **:** of, relating or conforming to, or prescribing norms — **nor·ma·tive·ly** *adv* — **nor·ma·tive·ness** *n*

normed \ˈnȯ(ə)rmd\ *adj* **:** being a mathematical entity upon which a norm is defined <a ~ vector space>

nor·mo·ten·sive \ˌnȯr-mō-ˈten(t)-siv\ *adj* [*normal* + *-o-* + *tens*ion + *-ive*] **:** having blood pressure typical of the age group and community to which one belongs — **normotensive** *n*

nor·mo·ther·mia \-ˈthər-mē-ə\ *n* [NL, fr. *normalis* normal + *-o-* + *-thermia* -thermy] **:** normal body temperature — **nor·mo·ther·mic** \-mik\ *adj*

Norn \ˈnȯ(ə)rn\ *n* [ON]**:** any of the three Norse goddesses of fate

[1]**Norse** \ˈnȯ(ə)rs\ *n, pl* **Norse** [prob. fr. obs. D *noorsch,* adj., Norwegian, Scandinavian, alter. of obs. D *noordsch* northern, fr. D *noord* north; akin to OE *north*] **1** *pl* **a :** SCANDINAVIANS **b :** NORWEGIANS **2 a :** NORWEGIAN 2 **b :** any of the western Scandinavian dialects or languages **c :** the Scandinavian group of Germanic languages

[2]**Norse** *adj* **1 :** of or relating to ancient Scandinavia or the language of its inhabitants **2 :** NORWEGIAN

Norse·man \ˈnȯrs-mən\ *n* **:** one of the ancient Scandinavians

[1]**north** \ˈnȯ(ə)rth\ *adv* [ME, fr. OE; akin to OHG *nord* north, Gk *nerteros* lower, infernal] **:** to, toward, or in the north

[2]**north** *adj* **1 :** situated toward or at the north <the ~ entrance> **2 :** coming from the north <a ~ wind>

[3]**north** *n* **1 a :** the direction of the north terrestrial pole **:** the direction to the left of one facing east **b :** the compass point directly opposite to south **2** *cap* **:** regions or countries lying to the north of a specified or implied point of orientation **3** *often cap* **a :** the one of four positions at 90-degree intervals that lies to the north or opposite south **b :** a person (as a bridge player) occupying this position in the course of a specified activity

Northants *or* **Nthptn** *abbr* Northamptonshire

north·bound \ˈnȯrth-ˌbau̇nd\ *adj* **:** traveling or heading north

north by east : a compass point that is one point east of due north **:** N11°15′E

north by west : a compass point that is one point west of due north **:** N11°15′W

[1]**north·east** \nȯr-ˈthēst, *naut* nȯ-ˈrēst\ *adv* **:** to, toward, or in the northeast

[2]**northeast** *n* **1 a :** the general direction between north and east **b :** the point midway between the north and east compass points **2** *cap* **:** regions or countries lying to the northeast of a specified or implied point of orientation

[3]**northeast** *adj* **1 :** coming from the northeast <a ~ wind> **2 :** situated toward or at the northeast <the ~ corner>

northeast by east : a compass point that is one point east of due northeast **:** N56°15′E

northeast by north : a compass point that is one point north of due northeast **:** N33°45′E

north·east·er \nȯr-ˈthē-stər, nȯ-ˈrē-\ *n* **1 :** a strong northeast wind **2 :** a storm with northeast winds

north·east·er·ly \-stər-lē\ *adv or adj* [[2]*northeast* + *-erly* (as in *easterly*)] **1 :** from the northeast **2 :** toward the northeast

north·east·ern \-stərn\ *adj* [[2]*northeast* + *-ern* (as in *eastern*)] **1** *often cap* **:** of, relating to, or characteristic of a region conventionally designated Northeast **2 :** lying toward or coming from the northeast — **north·east·ern·most** \-stərn-ˌmōst\ *adj*

North·east·ern·er \-stə(r)-nər\ *n* **:** a native or inhabitant of a northeastern region (as of the U.S.)

[1]**north·east·ward** \nȯr-ˈthēs-twərd, nȯ-ˈrēs-\ *adv or adj* **:** toward the northeast — **north·east·wards** \-wərdz\ *adv*

[2]**northeastward** *n* **:** NORTHEAST

north·er \ˈnȯr-t͟hər\ *n* **1 :** a strong north wind **2 :** a storm with north winds

[1]**north·er·ly** \-lē\ *adj or adv* [[3]*north* + *-erly* (as in *easterly*)] **1 :** situated toward or belonging to the north <the ~ border> **2 :** coming from the north <a ~ wind>

[2]**northerly** *n, pl* **-lies :** a wind from the north

[1]**north·ern** \ˈnȯr-t͟hə(r)n\ *adj* [ME *northerne,* fr. OE; akin to OHG *nordrōni* northern, OE *north* north] **1** *cap* **a :** of, relating to, or characteristic of a region conventionally designated North **b**

ə abut ᵊ kitten ər further a back ā bake ä cot, cart
au̇ out ch chin e less ē easy g gift i trip ī life
j joke ŋ sing ō flow ȯ flaw ȯi coin th thin t͟h this
ü loot u̇ foot y yet yü few yu̇ furious zh vision

: of, relating to, or constituting the northern dialect **2 a :** lying toward the north **b :** coming from the north <a ~ storm> — **north·ern·most** \-ˌmōst\ *adj*

²**northern** *n* : the dialect of English spoken in the part of the U.S. north of a line running northwest from central New Jersey across the northern tier of counties in Pennsylvania and through northern Ohio, Indiana, and Illinois

northern corn rootworm *n* : a corn rootworm (*Diabrotica longicornis*) often destructive to maize in the northern parts of the central and eastern U.S.

Northern Cross *n* : a cross formed by six stars in Cygnus

Northern Crown *n* : CORONA BOREALIS

North·ern·er \ˈnȯr-th̲ə(r)-nər\ *n* : a native or inhabitant of the North; *esp* : a native or resident of the northern part of the U.S.

northern lights *n pl* : AURORA BOREALIS

northern white cedar *n* : an arborvitae (*Thuja occidentalis*) of eastern No. America that has branchlets in horizontal planes; *also* : its wood — called also *white cedar*

North Germanic *n* : a subdivision of the Germanic languages including Icelandic, Norwegian, Swedish, and Danish — see INDO-EUROPEAN LANGUAGES table

north·ing \ˈnȯr-thiŋ, -th̲iŋ\ *n* **1 :** difference in latitude to the north from the last preceding point of reckoning **2 :** northerly progress

north·land \ˈnȯrth-ˌland, -lənd\ *n, often cap* : land in the north : the north of a country

North·man \ˈnȯrth-mən\ *n* : NORSEMAN

north–north·east \ˈnȯrth-ˌnȯr-ˈthēst, -ˌnō-ˈrēst\ *n* : a compass point that is two points east of due north : N22°30′E

north–north·west \ˈnȯrth-ˌnȯr(th)-ˈwest\ *n* : a compass point that is two points west of due north : N22°30′W

north pole *n* **1 a** *often cap N&P* : the northernmost point of the earth; *broadly* : the corresponding point of a celestial body (as a planet) **b :** the zenith of the heavens as viewed from the north terrestrial pole **2** *of a magnet* : the pole that points toward the north

North Star *n* : the star of the northern hemisphere toward which the axis of the earth points — called also *polestar*

¹**North·um·bri·an** \nȯr-ˈthəm-brē-ən\ *adj* **1 :** of, relating to, or characteristic of ancient Northumbria, its people, or its language **2 :** of, relating to, or characteristic of Northumberland, its people, or its language

²**Northumbrian** *n* **1 :** a native or inhabitant of ancient Northumbria **2 :** a native or inhabitant of Northumberland **3 a :** the Old English dialect of Northumbria **b :** the Modern English dialect of Northumberland

¹**north·ward** \ˈnȯrth-wərd\ *adv or adj* : toward the north — **north·wards** \-wərdz\ *adv*

²**northward** *n* : northward direction or part

¹**north·west** \nȯrth-ˈwest, *naut* nȯr-ˈwest\ *adv* : to, toward, or in the northwest

²**northwest** *n* **1 a :** the general direction between north and west **b :** the point midway between the north and west compass points **2** *cap* : regions or countries lying to the northwest of a specified or implied point of orientation

³**northwest** *adj* **1 :** coming from the northwest **2 :** situated toward or at the northwest

northwest by north : a compass point that is one point north of due northwest : N33°45′W

northwest by west : a compass point that is one point west of due northwest : N56°15′W

north·west·er \nȯr(th)-ˈwes-tər\ *n* : a strong northwest wind

north·west·er·ly \-lē\ *adv or adj* [²*northwest* + *-erly* (as in *westerly*)] **1 :** from the northwest **2 :** toward the northwest

north·west·ern \-ˈwes-tərn\ *adj* [²*northwest* + *-ern* (as in *western*)] **1** *often cap* : of, relating to, or characteristic of a region conventionally designated Northwest **2 :** lying toward or coming from the northwest

North·west·ern·er \-tə(r)-nər\ *n* : a native or inhabitant of the Northwest and esp. of the northwestern part of the U.S.

¹**north·west·ward** \-ˈwes-twərd\ *adv or adj* : toward the northwest — **north·west·wards** \-twərdz\ *adv*

²**northwestward** *n* : NORTHWEST

nor·trip·ty·line \nȯr-ˈtrip-tə-ˌlēn\ *n* [*normal* + *-triptylene* (of unknown origin)] : a tricyclic drug $C_{19}H_{21}N$ that is used as an antidepressant

Norw *abbr* Norway; Norwegian

Nor·way maple \ˌnȯ(ə)r-ˌwā-\ *n* : a European maple (*Acer platanoides*) with dark green or often reddish or red veined leaves that is much planted for shade in the U.S.

Norway spruce *n* : a widely cultivated spruce (*Picea abies*) that is native to northern Europe and has a pyramidal shape, spreading branches and pendulous branchlets, dark foliage, and long pendulous cones

Nor·we·gian \nȯr-ˈwē-jən\ *n* [ML *Norwegia* Norway] **1 a :** a native or inhabitant of Norway **b :** a person of Norwegian descent **2 :** the Germanic language of the Norwegian people — **Norwegian** *adj*

Norwegian elkhound *n* : any of a Norwegian breed of medium-sized compact short-bodied dogs with a very heavy gray coat tipped with black

Nor·wich terrier \ˌnȯr(ˌ)wich-, *Brit* ˌnär-ich- *or* ˌnär-ij-\ *n* [*Norwich*, England] : any of an English breed of small active low-set terriers that have a rather long straight wiry coat of red, black and tan, or grizzle

nos *abbr* numbers

NOS *abbr* not otherwise specified

nos- *or* **noso-** *comb form* [Gk, fr. *nosos*] : disease <*noso*logy>

¹**nose** \ˈnōz\ *n* [ME, fr. OE *nosu;* akin to OHG *nasa* nose, L *nasus*] **1 a :** the part of the face that bears the nostrils and covers the anterior part of the nasal cavity; *broadly* : this part together with the nasal cavity **b :** the anterior part of the head above or projecting beyond the muzzle : SNOUT, PROBOSCIS, MUZZLE **2 a :** the sense of smell : OLFACTION **b :** AROMA, BOUQUET **3 :** the vertebrate olfactory organ **4 a :** the forward end or projection of something **b :** the projecting or working end of a tool **5 :** the stem of a boat or its protective metal covering **6 a :** the nose as a symbol of prying or meddling curiosity or interference **b :** a knack for discovery or understanding : FLAIR <a keen ~ for absurdity> — **on the nose 1 :** at or to a target point <the bombs landed right *on the nose*> **2 :** to win — used of horse or dog racing bets

²**nose** *vb* **nosed; nos·ing** *vt* **1 :** to detect by or as if by smell : SCENT **2 a :** to push or move with the nose **b :** to advance the nose into **3 :** to touch or rub with the nose : NUZZLE **4 :** to defeat by a narrow margin in a sport or contest ~ *vi* **1 :** to use the nose in examining, smelling, or showing affection **2 :** to search impertinently : PRY **3 :** to move ahead slowly or cautiously <the car *nosed* out into traffic>

nose·band \ˈnōz-ˌband\ *n* : the part of a headstall that passes over a horse's nose

nose·bleed \-ˌblēd\ *n* : an attack of bleeding from the nose

nose cone *n* : a protective cone constituting the forward end of a rocket or missile

nosed \ˈnōzd\ *adj* : having a nose esp. of a specified kind — usu. used in combination <snub-*nosed*>

nose dive *n* **1 :** the downward nose-first plunge of a flying object (as an airplane) **2 :** a sudden extreme drop — **nose–dive** *vi*

no–see–um \nō-ˈsē-əm\ *n* [E dial. (American Indian) *no see um* you don't see them] : BITING MIDGE

nose·gay \ˈnōz-ˌgā\ *n* [¹*nose* + E dial. *gay* (ornament)] : a small bunch of flowers : POSY

nose·piece \-ˌpēs\ *n* **1 :** a piece of armor for protecting the nose **2 :** the end piece of a microscope body to which an objective is attached **3 :** the bridge of a pair of eyeglasses

¹**nosh** \ˈnäsh\ *vb* [Yiddish *nashn*, fr. MHG *naschen* to eat on the sly] *vi* : to eat a snack ~ *vt* : CHEW, MUNCH — **nosh·er** *n*

²**nosh** *n* : TIDBIT, SNACK

no–show \(ˈ)nō-ˈshō\ *n* [¹*no* + *show*, v. (as in *show up*)] : a person who reserves space on a train, ship, or airplane but neither uses nor cancels the reservation

nos·ing \ˈnō-ziŋ\ *n* : the usu. rounded edge of a stair tread that projects over the riser; *also* : any of various similar rounded projections

no·sol·o·gy \nō-ˈsäl-ə-jē, -ˈzäl-\ *n* [prob. fr. NL *nosologia*, fr. *nos-* + *-logia* -logy] **1 :** a branch of medical science that deals with classification of diseases **2 :** a classification or list of diseases — **no·so·log·i·cal** \ˌnō-sə-ˈläj-i-kəl\ *or* **no·so·log·ic** \-ik\ *adj* — **no·so·log·i·cal·ly** \-i-k(ə-)lē\ *adv*

nos·tal·gia \nä-ˈstal-jə, nə- *also* nō- *&* -ˈstäl-\ *n* [NL, fr. Gk *nostos* return home + NL *-algia;* akin to OE ge*nesan* to survive, Skt *nasate* he approaches] **1 :** the state of being homesick : HOMESICKNESS **2 :** a wistful or excessively sentimental sometimes abnormal yearning for return to or of some past period or irrecoverable condition — **nos·tal·gic** \-jik\ *adj* — **nos·tal·gi·cal·ly** \-ji-k(ə-)lē\ *adv*

nos·toc \ˈnäs-ˌtäk\ *n* [NL, genus name] : any of a genus (*Nostoc*) of blue-green algae that are able to use atmospheric nitrogen

nos·tril \ˈnäs-trəl\ *n* [ME *nosethirl*, fr. OE *nosthyrl*, fr. *nosu* nose + *thyrel* hole; akin to OE *thurh* through] **1 :** an external naris; *broadly* : a naris with the adjoining passage on the same side of the nasal septum **2 :** either fleshy lateral wall of the nose

nos·trum \ˈnäs-trəm\ *n* [L, neut. of *noster* our, ours, fr. *nos* we — more at US] **1 :** a medicine of secret composition recommended by its preparer but usu. without scientific proof of its effectiveness **2 :** a questionable remedy or scheme : PANACEA

nosy *or* **nos·ey** \ˈnō-zē\ *adj* **nos·i·er; -est** [¹*nose*] : of prying or inquisitive disposition or quality : INTRUSIVE — **nos·i·ly** \ˈnō-zə-lē\ *adv* — **nos·i·ness** \-zē-nəs\ *n*

not \(ˈ)nät\ *adv* [ME, alter. of *nought*, fr. *nought*, pron. — more at NAUGHT] **1** — used as a function word to make negative a group of words or a word **2** — used as a function word to stand for the negative of a preceding group of words <is sometimes hard to see and sometimes ~>

NOT \ˈnät\ *n* [*not*] : a logical operator that produces a statement that is the inverse of an input statement

not- *or* **noto-** *comb form* [NL, fr. Gk *nōt-*, *nōto-*, fr. *nōton*, *nōtos* back — more at NATES] : back : back part <*noto*chord>

nota *pl of* NOTUM

no·ta be·ne \ˌnōt-ə-ˈbē-nē, -ˈben-ē\ [L, mark well] — used to call attention to something important

no·ta·bil·i·ty \ˌnōt-ə-ˈbil-ət-ē\ *n, pl* **-ties :** a notable or prominent person

¹**no·ta·ble** \ˈnōt-ə-bəl, *for 2 also* ˈnät-\ *adj* **1 a :** worthy of note : REMARKABLE **b :** DISTINGUISHED, PROMINENT **2** *archaic* : efficient or capable in performance of housewifely duties ***syn*** see NOTEWORTHY — **no·ta·ble·ness** *n* — **no·ta·bly** \-blē\ *adv*

²**no·ta·ble** \ˈnōt-ə-bəl\ *n* **1 :** a person of note : NOTABILITY **2** *pl, often cap* : a group of persons summoned esp. in monarchical France to act as a deliberative body

no·tar·i·al \nō-ˈter-ē-əl\ *adj* **1 :** of, relating to, or characteristic of a notary **2 :** done or executed by a notary — **no·tar·i·al·ly** \-ə-lē\ *adv*

no·ta·ri·za·tion \ˌnōt-ə-rə-ˈzā-shən\ *n* **1 :** the act, process, or an instance of notarizing **2 :** the notarial certificate appended to a document

no·ta·rize \ˈnōt-ə-ˌrīz\ *vt* **-rized; -riz·ing :** to acknowledge or attest as a notary public

no·ta·ry public \ˌnōt-ə-rē-\ *n, pl* **notaries public** *or* **notary publics** [ME *notary* clerk, notary public, fr. L *notarius* clerk, secretary, fr. *notarius* of shorthand, fr. *nota* note, shorthand character] : a public officer who attests or certifies writings (as a deed) to make them authentic and takes affidavits, depositions, and protests of negotiable paper

no·tate \ˈnō-ˌtāt\ *vt* **no·tat·ed; no·tat·ing** [back-formation fr. *notation*] : to put into notation

no·ta·tion \nō-ˈtā-shən\ *n* [L *notation-*, *notatio*, fr. *notatus*, pp. of *notare* to note] **1 :** ANNOTATION, NOTE **2 a :** the act, process, method, or an instance of representing by a system or set of marks, signs, figures, or characters **b :** a system of characters, symbols, or abbreviated expressions used in an art or science to express technical facts or quantities — **no·ta·tion·al** \-shnəl, -shən-ᵊl\ *adj*

¹notch \ˈnäch\ *n* [perh. alter. (fr. incorrect division of *an otch*) of (assumed) *otch*, fr. MF *oche*] **1 a :** a V-shaped indentation **b :** a slit made to serve as a record **c :** a rounded indentation cut on the fore edge of a book **2 :** a deep close pass **:** GAP **3 :** DEGREE, STEP — **notched** \ˈnächt\ *adj*

²notch *vt* **1 :** to cut or make a notch in **2 a :** to mark or record by a notch **b :** SCORE, ACHIEVE

notch·back \ˈnäch-ˌbak\ *n* **1 :** a back on a closed passenger automobile having a distinct deck as opposed to a fastback **2 :** an automobile having a notchback

¹note \ˈnōt\ *vt* **not·ed; not·ing** [ME *noten*, fr. OF *noter*, fr. L *notare* to mark, note, fr. *nota*] **1 a :** to notice or observe with care **b :** to record or preserve in writing **2 a :** to make special mention of **:** REMARK **b :** INDICATE, SHOW — **not·er** *n*

²note *n* [L *nota* mark, character, written note] **1 a (1)** *obs* **:** MELODY, SONG **(2) :** TONE 2a **(3) :** CALL, SOUND; *esp* **:** the musical call of a bird **b :** a written symbol used to indicate duration and pitch of a tone by its shape and position on the staff **2 a :** a characteristic feature (as of odor or flavor) **b :** MOOD, QUALITY **c :** an element which reveals an emotion <a ~ of sadness in her voice> **3 a (1) :** MEMORANDUM **(2) :** a condensed or informal record **b (1) :** a brief comment or explanation **(2) :** a printed comment or reference set apart from the text **c (1) :** a written promise to pay a debt **(2) :** a piece of paper money **d (1) :** a short informal letter **(2) :** a formal diplomatic communication **e :** a scholarly or technical essay shorter than an article and restricted in scope **f :** a sheet of notepaper **4 a :** DISTINCTION, REPUTATION <a figure of international ~> **b :** OBSERVATION, NOTICE <took full ~ of the proceedings> **c :** KNOWLEDGE, INFORMATION

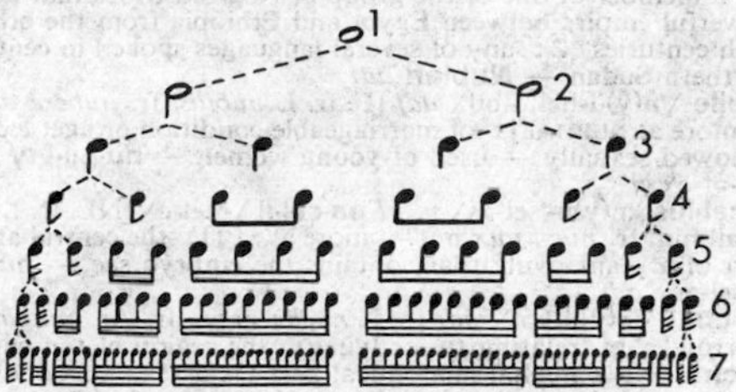

relative duration of notes 1b: *1* whole, *2* half, *3* quarter, *4* eighth, *5* sixteenth, *6* thirty-second, *7* sixty-fourth

note·book \ˈnōt-ˌbu̇k\ *n* **:** a book for notes or memoranda

note·case \-ˌkās\ *n, Brit* **:** BILLFOLD

not·ed \ˈnōt-əd\ *adj* **:** widely and favorably known by reputation ***syn*** see FAMOUS — **not·ed·ly** *adv* — **not·ed·ness** *n*

note·less \ˈnōt-ləs\ *adj* **:** not noticed **:** UNDISTINGUISHED

note of hand : PROMISSORY NOTE

note·pa·per \ˈnōt-ˌpā-pər\ *n* **:** writing paper suitable for notes

note·wor·thy \-ˌwər-t͟hē\ *adj* **:** worthy of or attracting attention esp. because of some special excellence — **note·wor·thi·ly** \-t͟hə-lē\ *adv* — **note·wor·thi·ness** \-t͟hē-nəs\ *n*

syn NOTEWORTHY, NOTABLE, MEMORABLE *shared meaning element* **:** having a quality that demands attention

¹noth·ing \ˈnəth-iŋ\ *pron* [ME, fr. OE *nān thing, nāthing*, fr. *nān* no + *thing* — more at NONE] **1 :** not any thing **:** no thing <leaves ~ to the imagination> **2 :** no part **3 :** one of no interest, value, or consequence <she means ~ to me> — **nothing doing :** by no means **:** definitely no — **nothing short of :** nothing less than **:** something which is <the plan is *nothing short of* revolutionary>

²nothing *adv* **:** not at all **:** in no degree

³nothing *n* **1 a :** something that does not exist **b :** NOTHINGNESS 3b **2 :** someone or something of no or slight value or size

⁴nothing *adj* **:** of no account **:** WORTHLESS

noth·ing·ness \-nəs\ *n* **1 :** the quality or state of being nothing: as **a :** NONEXISTENCE **b :** utter insignificance **c :** DEATH **2 :** something insignificant or valueless **3 a :** VOID, EMPTINESS **b :** a metaphysical entity opposed to and devoid of being and regarded by some existentialists as the ground of anxiety

¹no·tice \ˈnōt-əs\ *n* [ME, fr. MF, acquaintance, fr. L *notitia* knowledge, acquaintance, fr. *notus* known, fr. pp. of *noscere* to come to know — more at KNOW] **1 a (1) :** warning or intimation of something **:** ANNOUNCEMENT **(2) :** notification by one of the parties to an agreement or relation of intention of terminating it at a specified time **(3) :** the condition of being warned or notified — usu. used in the phrase *on notice* **b :** INFORMATION, INTELLIGENCE **2 a :** ATTENTION, HEED **b :** polite or favorable attention **:** CIVILITY **3 :** a written or printed announcement **4 :** a short critical account or examination

²notice *vt* **no·ticed; no·tic·ing 1 :** to give notice of **2 a :** to comment upon **:** NOTE **b :** REVIEW **3 a :** to treat with attention or civility **b :** to take notice of **:** MARK **4 :** to give a formal notice to

no·tice·able \ˈnōt-ə-sə-bəl\ *adj* **1 :** worthy of notice **2 :** capable of being noticed — **no·tice·ably** \-blē\ *adv*

syn NOTICEABLE, REMARKABLE, PROMINENT, OUTSTANDING, CONSPICUOUS, SALIENT, SIGNAL, STRIKING *shared meaning element* **:** attracting notice or attention

no·ti·fi·ca·tion \ˌnōt-ə-fə-ˈkā-shən\ *n* **1 :** the act or an instance of notifying **2 :** a written or printed matter that gives notice

no·ti·fy \ˈnōt-ə-ˌfī\ *vt* **-fied; -fy·ing** [ME *notifien*, fr. MF *notifier* to make known, fr. LL *notificare*, fr. L *notus* known] **1** *obs* **:** to point out **2 :** to give notice of or report the occurrence of <he *notified* his intention to sue> **3 :** to give formal notice to <~ a family of the death of a relation> ***syn*** see INFORM — **no·ti·fi·er** \-ˌfī(-ə)r\ *n*

no–till \(ˈ)nō-ˈtil\ *n* **:** NO-TILLAGE

no–till·age \-ij\ *n* **:** a system of farming that consists of planting a narrow slit trench without tillage and with the use of herbicides to suppress weeds

no·tion \ˈnō-shən\ *n* [L *notion-, notio*, fr. *notus*, pp. of *noscere*] **1 a (1) :** an inclusive general concept **(2) :** an individual's conception or impression of something known, experienced, or imagined **(3) :** a theory or belief held by a person or group **b :** a personal inclination **:** WHIM **2** *obs* **:** MIND, INTELLECT **3** *pl* **:** small useful items **:** SUNDRIES ***syn*** see IDEA

no·tion·al \ˈnō-shnəl, -shən-ᵊl\ *adj* **1 :** THEORETICAL, SPECULATIVE **2 :** existing in the mind only **:** IMAGINARY **3 :** given to foolish or fanciful moods or ideas **4 a :** of, relating to, or being a notion or idea **:** CONCEPTUAL **b (1) :** presenting an idea of a thing, action, or quality <*has* is ~ in *he has luck*, relational in *he has gone*> **(2) :** of or representing what exists or occurs in the world of things — **no·tion·al·i·ty** \ˌnō-shə-ˈnal-ət-ē\ *n* — **no·tion·al·ly** \ˈnō-shnə-lē, -shən-ᵊl-ē\ *adv*

noto- — see NOT-

no·to·chord \ˈnōt-ə-ˌkȯ(ə)rd\ *n* [*not-* + L *chorda* cord — more at CORD] **:** a longitudinal flexible rod of cells that in the lowest chordates (as a lancelet or a lamprey) and in the embryos of the higher vertebrates forms the supporting axis of the body — **no·to·chord·al** \ˌnōt-ə-ˈkȯrd-ᵊl\ *adj*

no·to·ri·ety \ˌnōt-ə-ˈrī-ət-ē\ *n, pl* **-eties** [MF or ML; MF *notorieté*, fr. ML *notorietat-, notorietas*, fr. *notorius*] **1 :** the quality or state of being notorious **2 :** a notorious person

no·to·ri·ous \nō-ˈtōr-ē-əs, nə-, -ˈtȯr-\ *adj* [ML *notorius*, fr. LL *notorium* information, indictment, fr. neut. of (assumed) LL *notorius* making known, fr. L *notus*, pp. of *noscere* to come to know — more at KNOW] **:** generally known and talked of; *esp* **:** widely and unfavorably known — **no·to·ri·ous·ly** *adv* — **no·to·ri·ous·ness** *n*

not·or·nis \nō-ˈtȯr-nəs\ *n, pl* **notornis** [NL, genus name, fr. Gk *notos* south + *ornis* bird; akin to Gk *noteros* damp — more at NOURISH, ERNE] **:** any of a genus (*Notornis*) of flightless New Zealand birds that are related to the gallinules

no–trump \(ˈ)nō-ˈtrəmp\ *adj* **:** being a bid, contract, or hand suitable to play without any suit being trumps — **no–trump** *n*

Notts *abbr* Nottinghamshire

no·tum \ˈnōt-əm\ *n, pl* **no·ta** \ˈnōt-ə\ [NL, fr. Gk *nōton* back — more at NATES] **:** the dorsal surface of a thoracic segment of an insect

¹not·with·stand·ing \ˌnät-with-ˈstan-diŋ, -wit͟h-\ *prep* [ME *notwithstonding*, fr. *not* + *withstonding*, prp. of *withstonden* to withstand] **:** in spite of

²notwithstanding *adv* **:** NEVERTHELESS, HOWEVER

³notwithstanding *conj* **:** ALTHOUGH

nou·gat \ˈnü-gət, *esp Brit* -ˌgä\ *n* [F, fr. Prov, fr. OProv *nogat*, fr. *noga* nut, fr. L *nuc-, nux* — more at NUT] **:** a confection of nuts or fruit pieces in a sugar paste

nought \ˈnȯt, ˈnät\ *var of* NAUGHT

nou·me·non \ˈnü-mə-ˌnän\ *n, pl* **-na** \-nə, -ˌnä\ [G, fr. Gk *nooumenon* that which is apprehended by thought, fr. neut. of pres. pass. part. of *noein* to think, conceive, fr. *nous* mind] **:** a ground of phenomena that according to Kant cannot be experienced, can be known to exist, but to which no properties can be intelligibly ascribed — **nou·men·al** \-mən-ᵊl\ *adj*

noun \ˈnau̇n\ *n* [ME *nowne*, fr. AF *noun* name, noun, fr. OF *nom*, fr. L *nomen* — more at NAME] **1 :** a word that is the name of a subject of discourse (as a person, animal, plant, place, thing, substance, quality, idea, action, or state) and that in languages with grammatical number, case, and gender is inflected for number and case but has inherent gender **2 :** a word except a pronoun used in a sentence as subject or object of a verb, as object of a preposition, as the predicate after a copula, or as a name in an absolute construction

nour·ish \ˈnər-ish, ˈnə-rish\ *vt* [ME *nurishen*, fr. OF *noriss-*, stem of *norrir*, fr. L *nutrire* to suckle, nourish; akin to Gk *nan* to flow, *noteros* damp, L *nare* to swim, Gk *nein*] **1 :** NURTURE, REAR **2 :** to promote the growth of <no occasions to exercise the feelings nor ~ passion —L. O. Coxe> **3 a :** to furnish or sustain with nutriment **:** FEED **b :** MAINTAIN, SUPPORT <their profits flow into the underworld and ~ other criminal activities —Beverly Smith> — **nour·ish·er** *n*

nour·ish·ing *adj* **:** giving nourishment **:** NUTRITIOUS

nour·ish·ment \ˈnər-ish-mənt, ˈnə-rish-\ *n* **1 :** FOOD, NUTRIMENT **2 :** the act of nourishing or the state of being nourished

nous \ˈnüs\ *n* [Gk *noos, nous* mind] **:** MIND, REASON: as **a :** an intelligent purposive principle of the world **b :** the divine reason regarded in Neoplatonism as the first emanation of God

nou·veau riche \ˌnü-ˌvō-ˈrēsh\ *n, pl* **nou·veaux riches** *same*\ [F, lit., new rich] **:** a person newly rich **:** PARVENU

nou·velle vague \ˌnü-ˌvel-ˈväg, -ˈvåg\ *n* [F] **:** NEW WAVE

nov *abbr* novelist

Nov *abbr* November

no·va \ˈnō-və\ *n, pl* **novas** *or* **no·vae** \-(ˌ)vē, -ˌvī\ [NL, fem. of L *novus* new] **:** a star that suddenly increases its light output tremendously and then fades away to its former obscurity in a few months or years — **no·va·like** \-və-ˌlīk\ *adj*

no·vac·u·lite \nō-ˈvak-yə-ˌlīt\ *n* [L *novacula* razor] **:** a very hard fine-grained siliceous rock used for whetstones and possibly of sedimentary origin

---

no·va·tion \nō-ˈvā-shən\ *n* [LL *novation-, novatio* renewal, legal novation, fr. L *novatus,* pp. of *novare* to make new, fr. *novus*] **:** the substitution of a new legal obligation for an old one

1**nov·el** \ˈnäv-əl\ *adj* [ME, fr. MF, new, fr. L *novellus,* fr. dim. of *novus* new — more at NEW] **1 :** new and not resembling something formerly known or used **2 :** original or striking esp. in conception or style <a ~ scheme to collect money> ***syn*** see NEW

2**novel** *n* [It *novella*] **1 :** an invented prose narrative that is usu. long and complex and deals esp. with human experience through a usu. connected sequence of events **2 :** the literary type constituted by novels — **nov·el·is·tic** \ˌnäv-ə-ˈlis-tik\ *adj*

nov·el·ette \ˌnäv-ə-ˈlet\ *n* **1 :** a brief novel **2 :** a long short story

nov·el·ett·ish \-ˈet-ish\ *adj* **:** of, relating to, or characteristic of a novelette; *esp* **:** SENTIMENTAL

nov·el·ist \ˈnäv-(ə-)ləst\ *n* **:** a writer of novels

nov·el·ize \ˈnäv-ə-ˌlīz\ *vt* **-ized; -iz·ing :** to convert into the form of a novel <~ a play> — **nov·el·iza·tion** \ˌnäv-ə-lə-ˈzā-shən\ *n*

no·vel·la \nō-ˈvel-ə\ *n, pl* **novellas** *or* **no·vel·le** \-ˈvel-ē\ [It, fr. fem. of *novello* new, fr. L *novellus*] **1** *pl novelle* **:** a story with a compact and pointed plot **2** *pl usu novellas* **:** a short novel

nov·el·ty \ˈnäv-əl-tē\ *n, pl* **-ties** [ME *novelte,* fr. MF *noveleté,* fr. *novel*] **1 :** something new or unusual **2 :** the quality or state of being novel **:** NEWNESS **3 :** a small manufactured article intended mainly for personal or household adornment — usu. used in pl.

1**No·vem·ber** \nō-ˈvem-bər, nə-\ *n* [ME *Novembre,* fr. OF, fr. L *November* (ninth month), fr. *novem* nine — more at NINE] **:** the 11th month of the Gregorian calendar

2**November** — a communications code word for the letter *n*

no·vem·de·cil·lion \ˌnō-ˌvem-di-ˈsil-yən\ *n, often attrib* [L *novemdecim* nineteen (fr. *novem* + *decem* ten) + E *-illion* (as in *million*) — more at TEN] — see NUMBER table

no·ve·na \nō-ˈvē-nə\ *n* [ML, fr. L, fem. of *novenus* nine each, fr. *novem*] **:** a Roman Catholic nine days' devotion

nov·ice \ˈnäv-əs\ *n* [ME, fr. MF, fr. ML *novicius,* fr. L, new, inexperienced, fr. *novus* — more at NEW] **1 :** a person admitted to probationary membership in a religious community **2 :** BEGINNER, TYRO

no·vi·lle·ro \ˌnō-vē-ˈe(ə)r-(ˌ)ō, -vəl-ˈye(ə)r-\ *n, pl* **-ros** [Sp, fr. *novillo* young bull, fr. L *novellus* new — more at NOVEL] **:** an aspiring bullfighter who has not yet attained the rank of matador

no·vi·tiate \nō-ˈvish-ət, nə-\ *n* [F *noviciat,* fr. ML *noviciatus,* fr. *novicius*] **1 :** the period or state of being a novice **2 :** NOVICE **3 :** a house where novices are trained

no·vo·bi·o·cin \ˌnō-və-ˈbī-ə-sən\ *n* [prob. fr. *novo-* (fr. L *novus* new) + E anti*biotic* + streptomy*cin*] **:** a weak dibasic acid $C_{31}H_{36}N_2O_{11}$ that is highly toxic to man and is used as an antimicrobial drug in some serious cases of staphylococcic and urinary tract infection

No·vo·cain \ˈnō-və-ˌkān\ *trademark* — used for a preparation containing procaine hydrochloride

no·vo·caine \-ˌkān\ *n* [ISV *novo-* (fr. L *novus* new) + co*caine*] **:** PROCAINE; *also* **:** its hydrochloride

1**now** \(ˈ)nau̇\ *adv* [ME, fr. OE *nū;* akin to OHG *nū* now, L *nunc,* Gk *nyn*] **1 a :** at the present time or moment **b :** in the time immediately before the present <thought of him just ~> **c :** in the time immediately to follow **:** FORTHWITH <come in ~> **2** — used with the sense of present time weakened or lost to express command, request, or admonition <~ hear this> **3** — used with the sense of present time weakened or lost to introduce an important point or indicate a transition **4 :** SOMETIMES <~ one and ~ another> **5 :** under the present circumstances **6 :** at the time referred to <~ the trouble began>

2**now** *conj* **:** in view of the fact that **:** SINCE — often followed by *that* <~ that we are here>

3**now** \ˈnau̇\ *n* **:** the present time or moment <been ill up to ~>

4**now** \ˈnau̇\ *adj* **1 :** of or relating to the present time **:** EXISTING <the ~ president> **2 a :** excitingly new <~ clothes> **b :** constantly aware of what is new <~ people>

now·a·days \ˈnau̇-(ə-)ˌdāz\ *adv* [ME *now a dayes,* fr. 1*now* + *a dayes* during the day] **:** at the present time

no·way \ˈnō-ˌwā\ *or* **no·ways** \-ˌwāz\ *adv* **:** NOWISE

1**no·where** \ˈnō-ˌ(h)we(ə)r, -ˌ(h)wa(ə)r, -(h)wər\ *adv* **1 :** not in or at any place **2 :** to no place

2**nowhere** *n* **1 :** a nonexistent place **2 :** an unknown, distant, or obscure place or state <rose to fame out of ~> — **miles from nowhere :** in an extremely remote place

nowhere near *adv* **:** not nearly

no·wheres \ˈnō-ˌ(h)we(ə)rz, -ˌ(h)wa(ə)rz, -(ˌ)(h)wərz\ *adv, chiefly dial* **:** NOWHERE

no·whith·er \nō-ˈ(h)wit͟h-ər, ˈnō-ˌ\ *adv* **:** to or toward no place

no·wise \ˈnō-ˌwīz\ *adv* **:** not at all

nox·ious \ˈnäk-shəs\ *adj* [L *noxius,* fr. *noxa* harm; akin to L *nocēre* to harm, *nec-, nex* violent death, Gk *nekros* dead body] **1 a :** physically harmful or destructive to living beings <~ wastes that turn our streams into sewers> **b :** constituting a harmful influence on mind or behavior **:** morally corrupting <~ doctrines> **2 :** DISTASTEFUL, OBNOXIOUS ***syn*** see PERNICIOUS ***ant*** wholesome — **nox·ious·ly** *adv* — **nox·ious·ness** *n*

noz·zle \ˈnäz-əl\ *n* [dim. of *nose*] **1 a :** a projecting vent of something **b :** a short tube with a taper or constriction used (as on a hose) to speed up or direct a flow of fluid **c :** a part in a rocket engine that accelerates the exhaust gases from the combustion chamber to a high velocity **2** *slang* **:** NOSE

np *abbr* **1** no pagination **2** no place (of publication)

Np *symbol* neptunium

NP *abbr* **1** neuropsychiatric; neuropsychiatry **2** no protest **3** notary public **4** noun phrase

NPCF *abbr* National Pollution Control Foundation

NPF *abbr* not provided for

NPN *abbr* nonprotein nitrogen

NRA *abbr* **1** National Recovery Administration **2** National Rifle Association

NRC *abbr* National Research Council

Ns *abbr* nimbostratus

NS *abbr* **1** national special **2** new series **3** new style **4** not specified **5** not sufficient **6** Nova Scotia **7** nuclear ship

NSA *abbr* **1** National Security Agency **2** National Shipping Authority **3** National Students Association

NSC *abbr* National Security Council

NSE *abbr* National Stock Exchange

nsec *also* **ns** *abbr* nanosecond

NSF *abbr* **1** National Science Foundation **2** not sufficient funds

NSW *abbr* New South Wales

NT *abbr* **1** New Testament **2** Northern Territory

-n't \(ᵊ)nt\ *adv comb form* **:** not <is*n't*>

NTE *abbr* National Teacher Examination

nth \ˈen(t)th\ *adj* [*n* + *-th*] **1 :** numbered with an unspecified or indefinitely large ordinal number **2 :** EXTREME, UTMOST <to the ~ degree>

Nthmb *abbr* Northumberland

NTP *abbr* normal temperature and pressure

nt wt *or* **n wt** *abbr* net weight

nu \ˈn(y)ü\ *n* [Gk *ny,* of Sem origin; akin to Heb *nūn* nun] **:** the 13th letter of the Greek alphabet — see ALPHABET table

NU *abbr* name unknown

nu·ance \ˈn(y)ü-ˌän(t)s, -ˌäⁿs, n(y)u̇-ˈ\ *n* [F, fr. MF, shade of color, fr. *nuer* to make shades of color, fr. *nue* cloud, fr. L *nubes;* akin to Gk *nythos* dark] **1 :** a subtle distinction or variation **2 :** a subtle quality **:** NICETY — **nu·anced** \-ˌän(t)st, -ˈän(t)st\ *adj*

nub \ˈnəb\ *n* [alter. of E dial. *knub,* prob. fr. LG *knubbe*] **1 :** KNOB, LUMP **2 :** NUBBIN **3 :** GIST, POINT

nub·bin \ˈnəb-ən\ *n* [perh. dim. of *nub*] **1 :** something (as an ear of Indian corn) that is small for its kind, stunted, undeveloped, or imperfect **2 :** a small usu. projecting part or bit **3 :** NUB 3

nub·ble \ˈnəb-əl\ *n* [dim. of *nub*] **:** a small knob or lump — **nub·bly** \-(ə-)lē\ *adj*

Nu·bi·an \ˈn(y)ü-bē-ən\ *n* **1 a :** a native or inhabitant of Nubia **b :** a member of one of the group of Negroid tribes that formed a powerful empire between Egypt and Ethiopia from the 6th to the 14th centuries **2 :** any of several languages spoken in central and northern Sudan — **Nubian** *adj*

nu·bile \ˈn(y)ü-bəl, -ˌbīl\ *adj* [F, fr. L *nubilis,* fr. *nubere* to marry — more at NUPTIAL] **:** of marriageable condition or age; *esp* **:** well endowed sexually — used of young women — **nu·bil·i·ty** \n(y)ü-ˈbil-ət-ē\ *n*

nu·cel·lus \n(y)ü-ˈsel-əs\ *n, pl* **nu·cel·li** \-ˈsel-ˌī\ [NL, fr. L *nucella* small nut, fr. *nuc-, nux* nut — more at NUT] **:** the central and chief part of a plant ovule that contains the embryo sac — **nu·cel·lar** \-ˈsel-ər\ *adj*

1**nu·chal** \ˈn(y)ü-kəl\ *adj* [ML *nucha* nape, fr. Ar *nukhāʿ* spinal marrow] **:** of, relating to, or lying in the region of the nape

2**nuchal** *n* **:** a nuchal anatomical part (as a scale or bone)

nucle- *or* **nucleo-** *comb form* [F *nuclé-, nucléo-,* fr. NL *nucleus*] **1 :** nucleus <*nucle*on> **2 :** nucleic acid <*nucleo*protein>

nu·cle·ar \ˈn(y)ü-klē-ər, *nonstand* -kyə-lər\ *adj* **1 :** of, relating to, or constituting a nucleus <~ civilizations of the New World —R. W. Ehrich> **2 :** of, relating to, or utilizing the atomic nucleus, atomic energy, the atom bomb, or atomic power

nuclear family *n* **:** a family group that consists only of father, mother, and children

nuclear magnetic resonance *n* **:** the magnetic resonance of an atomic nucleus

nuclear membrane *n* **:** the boundary of a cell nucleus

nuclear resonance *n* **:** the resonance absorption of a gamma ray by a nucleus identical to the nucleus that emitted the gamma ray

nuclear sap *n* **:** the clear homogeneous ground substance of a cell nucleus — called also *karyolymph*

nu·cle·ase \ˈn(y)ü-klē-ˌās, -ˌāz\ *n* **:** any of various enzymes that promote hydrolysis of nucleic acids

nu·cle·ate \ˈn(y)ü-klē-ˌāt\ *vb* **-at·ed; -at·ing** [LL *nucleatus,* pp. of *nucleare* to become stony, fr. L *nucleus*] *vt* **1 :** to form into a nucleus **:** CLUSTER **2 :** to act as a nucleus for **3 :** to supply nuclei to ~ *vi* **1 :** to form a nucleus **:** CLUSTER **2 :** to act as a nucleus **3 :** to begin to form — **nu·cle·ation** \ˌn(y)ü-klē-ˈā-shən\ *n* — **nu·cle·a·tor** \ˈn(y)ü-klē-ˌāt-ər\ *n*

nu·cle·at·ed \ˈn(y)ü-klē-ˌāt-əd\ *or* **nu·cle·ate** \-klē-ət\ *adj* [L *nucleatus,* fr. *nucleus* kernel] **1 :** having a nucleus or nuclei <~ cells> **2** *usu nucleate* **:** originating or occurring at nuclei <*nucleate* boiling>

nu·cle·ic acid \n(y)u̇-ˌklē-ik-, -ˌklā-\ *n* **:** any of various acids (as an RNA or a DNA) composed of a sugar or derivative of a sugar, phosphoric acid, and a base and found esp. in cell nuclei

nu·cle·in \ˈn(y)ü-klē-ən\ *n* **1 :** NUCLEOPROTEIN **2 :** NUCLEIC ACID

nu·cleo·cap·sid \ˌn(y)ü-klē-ō-ˈkap-səd\ *n* **:** the nucleic acid and surrounding protein coat in a virus

nu·cle·o·lus \n(y)ü-ˈklē-ə-ləs\ *n, pl* **-li** \-ˌlī\ [NL, fr. L, dim. of *nucleus*] **:** a spherical body of the metabolic nucleus that is associated with a specific part of a chromosome and contains much ribosomal RNA — see CELL illustration — **nu·cle·o·lar** \-lər\ *adj*

nucleolus organizer *n* **:** the specific part of a chromosome with which a nucleolus is associated esp. during its reorganization after nuclear division — called also *nucleolar organizer*

nu·cle·on \ˈn(y)ü-klē-ˌän\ *n* [ISV] **:** a proton or neutron esp. in the atomic nucleus — **nu·cle·on·ic** \ˌn(y)ü-klē-ˈän-ik\ *adj*

nu·cle·on·ics \ˌn(y)ü-klē-ˈän-iks\ *n pl but sing or pl in constr* **:** a branch of physical science that deals with nucleons or with all phenomena of the atomic nucleus

nu·cleo·phile \ˈn(y)ü-klē-ə-ˌfīl\ *n* **:** a nucleophilic substance (as an electron-donating reagent)

nu·cleo·phil·ic \ˌn(y)ü-klē-ə-ˈfil-ik\ *adj* **:** having an affinity for atomic nuclei **:** electron-donating — **nu·cleo·phil·i·cal·ly** \-i-k(ə-)lē\ *adv* — **nu·cleo·phi·lic·i·ty** \-klē-ō-fil-ˈis-ət-ē\ *n*

nu·cleo·plasm \ˈn(y)ü-klē-ə-ˌplaz-əm\ *n* [ISV] **:** the protoplasm of a nucleus; *esp* **:** NUCLEAR SAP — **nu·cleo·plas·mat·ic** \ˌn(y)ü-klē-ō-ˌplaz-ˈmat-ik\ *or* **nu·cleo·plas·mic** \-klē-ə-ˈplaz-mik\ *adj*

nu·cleo·pro·tein \ˌn(y)ü-klē-ō-ˈprō-ˌtēn, -ˈprōt-ē-ən\ *n* [ISV] **:** a compound that consists of a protein (as a histone) conjugated with a nucleic acid (as a DNA) and that is the principal constituent of the hereditary material in chromosomes

nu·cle·o·side \'n(y)ü-klē-ə-ˌsīd\ *n* [ISV *nucle-* + *-ose* + *-ide*] **:** a compound (as guanosine or adenosine) that consists of a purine or pyrimidine base combined with deoxyribose or ribose and is found esp. in DNA or RNA

nu·cleo·syn·the·sis \ˌn(y)ü-klē-ō-'sin(t)-thə-səs\ *n* [NL] **:** the production of a chemical element from hydrogen nuclei or protons (as in stellar evolution)

nu·cle·o·tid·ase \ˌn(y)ü-klē-ə-'tīd-ˌās, -ˌāz\ *n* **:** a phosphatase that promotes hydrolysis of a nucleotide (as into a nucleoside and phosphoric acid)

nu·cle·o·tide \'n(y)ü-klē-ə-ˌtīd\ *n* [ISV, irreg. fr. *nucle-* + *-ide*] **:** any of several compounds that consist of a ribose or deoxyribose sugar joined to a purine or pyrimidine base and to a phosphate group and that are the basic structural units of RNA and DNA — compare NUCLEOSIDE

nu·cle·us \'n(y)ü-klē-əs\ *n, pl* **nu·clei** \-klē-ˌī\ *also* **nu·cle·us·es** [NL, fr. L, kernel, dim. of *nuc-, nux* nut — more at NUT] **1 :** the small, brighter, and denser portion of a galaxy or of the head of a comet **2 :** a central point, group, or mass about which gathering, concentration, or accretion takes place: as **a :** a cellular organelle that is essential to cell functions (as reproduction and protein synthesis), is composed of nuclear sap and a nucleoprotein-rich network from which chromosomes and nucleoli arise, and is enclosed in a definite membrane — see CELL illustration **b :** a mass of gray matter or group of nerve cells in the central nervous system **c :** a characteristic and stable complex of atoms or groups in a molecule; *esp* **:** RING <the napthalene ~> **d :** the positively charged central portion of an atom that comprises nearly all of the atomic mass and that consists of protons and neutrons except in hydrogen which consists of one proton only **3 :** the peak of energy in the utterance of a syllable

nu·clide \'n(y)ü-ˌklīd\ *n* [*nucl*eus + Gk *eidos* form, species — more at IDOL] **:** a species of atom characterized by the constitution of its nucleus and hence by the number of protons, the number of neutrons, and the energy content — **nu·clid·ic** \n(y)ü-'klid-ik\ *adj*

1**nude** \'n(y)üd\ *adj* **nud·er; nud·est** [L *nudus* naked — more at NAKED] **1 :** lacking something essential esp. to legal validity <a ~ contract> **2 a :** devoid of covering **:** NAKED; *esp* **:** UNCLOTHED **b** (1) **:** of the color of Caucasian flesh (2) **:** giving the appearance of nudity <a ~ dress> **c :** featuring nudes <a ~ movie> ***syn*** see BARE ***ant*** clothed — **nude** *adv* — **nude·ly** *adv* — **nude·ness** *n* — **nu·di·ty** \'n(y)üd-ət-ē\ *n*

2**nude** *n* **1 a :** a representation of a nude human figure **b :** a nude person **2 :** the condition of being nude <in the ~>

nudge \'nəj\ *vt* **nudged; nudg·ing** [perh. of Scand origin; akin to ON *gnaga* to gnaw; akin to OE *gnagan* to gnaw] **1 :** to touch or push gently; *esp* **:** to seek the attention of by a push of the elbow **2 :** APPROACH <its circulation is *nudging* the four million mark —Bennett Cerf> — **nudge** *n* — **nudg·er** *n*

nu·di·branch \'n(y)üd-ə-ˌbraŋk\ *n, pl* **-branchs** [deriv. of L *nudus* + *branchia* gill — more at BRANCHIA] **:** any of a suborder (Nudibranchia) of marine gastropod mollusks without a shell in the adult state and without true gills — **nudibranch** *adj* — **nu·di·bran·chi·ate** \ˌn(y)üd-ə-'braŋ-kē-ət\ *adj or n*

nud·ism \'n(y)üd-ˌiz-əm\ *n* **:** the practice of going nude esp. in sexually mixed groups and during periods of time spent at specially secluded places — **nud·ist** \'n(y)üd-əst\ *adj or n*

nu·ga·to·ry \'n(y)ü-gə-ˌtōr-ē, -ˌtȯr-\ *adj* [L *nugatorius,* fr. *nugatus,* pp. of *nugari* to trifle, fr. *nugae* trifles] **1 :** of little or no consequence **:** TRIFLING, INCONSEQUENTIAL **2 :** having no force **:** INOPERATIVE ***syn*** see VAIN

nug·get \'nəg-ət\ *n* [origin unknown] **:** a solid lump; *esp* **:** a native lump of precious metal

nui·sance \'n(y)üs-ᵊn(t)s\ *n* [ME *nusaunce,* fr. AF, fr. OF *nuisir* to harm, fr. L *nocēre* — more at NOXIOUS] **1 :** HARM, INJURY **2 :** one that is annoying, unpleasant, or obnoxious

nuisance tax *n* **:** an excise tax collected in small amounts directly from the consumer

1**null** \'nəl\ *adj* [MF *nul,* lit., not any, fr. L *nullus,* fr. *ne-* not + *ullus* any; akin to L *unus* one — more at NO, ONE] **1 :** having no legal or binding force **:** INVALID **2 :** amounting to nothing **:** NIL **3 :** having no value **:** INSIGNIFICANT **4 a :** having no elements <~ set> **b :** having zero as a limit <~ sequence> **c** *of a matrix* **:** having all elements equal to zero **5 a :** indicating usu. by a zero reading on a scale when current or voltage is zero — used of an instrument **b :** being or relating to a method of measurement in which an unknown quantity (as of electric current) is compared with a known quantity of the same kind and found equal by a null detector **6 :** of, being, or relating to zero

2**null** *n* **1 :** ZERO 3a(1) **2 a :** a condition of a radio receiver when minimum or zero signal is received **b :** a minimum or zero value of an electric current or of a radio signal **3 :** a meaningless letter or code group included in a cryptogram to impede cryptanalysis by interceptors

3**null** *vt* **:** to make null

nul·lah \'nəl-ə\ *n* [Hindi *nālā*] **:** GULLY, RAVINE

null and void *adj* **:** having no force, binding power, or validity

null hypothesis *n* **:** a statistical hypothesis to be tested and accepted or rejected in favor of an alternative; *specif* **:** the hypothesis that an observed difference (as between the means of two samples) is due to chance alone and not due to a systematic cause

nul·li·fi·ca·tion \ˌnəl-ə-fə-'kā-shən\ *n* **1 :** the act of nullifying **:** the state of being nullified **2 :** the action of a state impeding or attempting to prevent the operation and enforcement within its territory of a law of the U.S. — **nul·li·fi·ca·tion·ist** \-sh(ə-)nəst\ *n*

nul·li·fi·er \'nəl-ə-ˌfī(-ə)r\ *n* **:** one that nullifies; *specif* **:** one maintaining the right of nullification against the U.S. government

nul·li·fy \'nəl-ə-ˌfī\ *vt* **-fied; -fy·ing** [LL *nullificare,* fr. L *nullus*] **1 :** to make null; *esp* **:** to make legally null and void **2 :** to make of no value or consequence ***syn*** NULLIFY, NEGATE, ANNUL, ABROGATE, INVALIDATE *shared meaning element* **:** to deprive of effective or continued existence

nul·lip·a·rous \ˌnə-'lip-ə-rəs\ *adj* [NL *nullipara* one who has never borne an offspring, fr. L *nullus* not any + *-para*] **:** of, relating to, or being a female that has not borne offspring

nul·li·ty \'nəl-ət-ē\ *n, pl* **-ties 1 :** the quality or state of being null; *esp* **:** legal invalidity **2 :** something that is null; *specif* **:** an act void of legal effect **3 :** the number of elements in a basis of a null-space

null–space \'nəl-ˌspās\ *n* **:** a subspace of a vector space consisting of vectors that under a given linear transformation are equal to zero

num *abbr* numeral

Num *or* **Numb** *abbr* Numbers

numb \'nəm\ *adj* [ME *nomen,* fr. pp. of *nimen* to take — more at NIM] **1 :** devoid of sensation esp. as a result of cold or anesthesia **2 :** devoid of emotion **:** INDIFFERENT — **numb** *vt* — **numb·ing·ly** \'nəm-iŋ-lē\ *adv* — **numb·ly** \'nəm-lē\ *adv* — **numb·ness** *n*

1**num·ber** \'nəm-bər\ *n* [ME *nombre,* fr. OF, fr. L *numerus* — more at NIMBLE] **1 a** (1) **:** a sum of units **:** TOTAL (2) **:** COMPLEMENT 1b (3) **:** an indefinite usu. large total <a ~ of members were absent> (4) *pl* **:** a numerous group **:** MANY; *also* **:** a numerical preponderance **b :** the characteristic of an individual by which it is treated as a unit or of a collection by which it is treated in terms of a determinate unit of units **c** (1) **:** a unit belonging to an abstract mathematical system and subject to specified laws of succession, addition, and multiplication; *esp* **:** NATURAL NUMBER (2) **:** an element (as π) of any of many mathematical systems obtained by extension of or analogy with the natural number system (3) *pl* **:** ARITHMETIC **2 :** a distinction of word form to denote reference to one or more than one; *also* **:** a form or group of forms so distinguished **3** *pl* **a** (1) **:** metrical structure **:** METER (2) **:** metrical lines **:** VERSES **b** *archaic* **:** musical sounds **:** NOTES **4 a :** a word, symbol, letter, or combination of symbols representing a number **b :** a numeral or combination of numerals or other symbols used to identify or designate **c** (1) **:** a member of a sequence or collection designated by esp. consecutive numbers; *also* **:** an individual or item (as a single act in a variety show or an issue of a periodical) singled out from a group (2) **:** a position in a numbered sequence **d :** a group of one kind <not of their ~> **5 :** insight into a person's ability or character <had his ~> **6** *pl but sing or pl in constr* **a :** a form of lottery in which an individual bets that a certain 3-digit combination will appear in numbers regularly published in newspapers (as for stock market receipts or pari-mutuel payoffs) — called also *numbers game* **b :** 2POLICY 2a — **by the numbers 1 :** in unison to a specific count or cadence **2 :** in a systematic, routine, or mechanical manner

2**number** *vb* **num·bered; num·ber·ing** \-b(ə-)riŋ\ *vt* **1 :** COUNT, ENUMERATE **2 :** to claim as part of a total **:** INCLUDE **3 :** to restrict to a definite number **4 :** to assign a number to **5 :** to comprise in number **:** TOTAL ~ *vi* **1 :** to comprise a total number **2 :** to call off numbers in sequence — **num·ber·able** \-b(ə-)rə-bəl\ *adj* — **num·ber·er** \-bər-ər\ *n*

num·ber·less \'nəm-bər-ləs\ *adj* **:** INNUMERABLE, COUNTLESS

number line *n* **:** a line of infinite extent whose points correspond to the real numbers according to their distance in a positive or negative direction from a point arbitrarily taken as zero

Num·bers \'nəm-bərz\ *n pl but sing in constr* **:** the mainly narrative fourth book of canonical Jewish and Christian Scripture — see BIBLE table

number theory *n* **:** the study of the properties of integers

numb·fish \'nəm-ˌfish\ *n* **:** ELECTRIC RAY

numb·skull \'nəm-ˌskəl\ *var of* NUMSKULL

nu·men \'n(y)ü-mən\ *n, pl* **nu·mi·na** \-mə-nə\ [L, nod, divine will, numen; akin to L *nuere* to nod, Gk *neuein*] **:** a spiritual force or influence often identified with a natural object, phenomenon, or locality

nu·mer·a·ble \'n(y)üm-(ə-)rə-bəl\ *adj* **:** capable of being counted

1**nu·mer·al** \'n(y)üm-(ə-)rəl\ *adj* [MF, fr. LL *numeralis,* fr. L *numerus*] **1 :** of, relating to, or expressing numbers **2 :** consisting of numbers or numerals — **nu·mer·al·ly** \-ē\ *adv*

2**numeral** *n* **1 :** a conventional symbol that represents a number **2** *pl* **:** numbers that designate by year a school or college class and that are awarded for distinction in an extracurricular activity

1**nu·mer·ate** \'n(y)ü-mə-ˌrāt\ *vt* **-at·ed; -at·ing** [L *numeratus,* pp. of *numerare* to count, fr. *numerus*] **:** ENUMERATE

2**nu·mer·ate** \'n(y)üm-(ə-)rət\ *adj* [L *numerus* number + E *-ate* (as in *literate*)] *Brit* **:** marked by an understanding of the scientific approach and by the ability to think quantitatively

nu·mer·a·tion \ˌn(y)ü-mə-'rā-shən\ *n* **1 a :** the act or process or an instance of enumeration **:** a system of enumeration **b :** an act or instance of designating by a number **2 :** the art of reading in words numbers expressed by numerals

nu·mer·a·tor \'n(y)ü-mə-ˌrāt-ər\ *n* **1 :** the part of a fraction that is above the line and signifies the number of parts of the denominator taken **2 :** one that numbers

1**nu·mer·ic** \n(y)ù-'mer-ik\ *adj* **:** NUMERICAL; *esp* **:** denoting a number or a system of numbers <~ code> <a ~ sign>

2**numeric** *n* **:** NUMBER, NUMERAL

nu·mer·i·cal \n(y)ù-'mer-i-kəl\ *adj* [L *numerus*] **1 :** of or relating to numbers <the ~ superiority of the enemy> **2 :** expressed in or involving numbers or a number system <~ standing in a class> <a ~ code> — **nu·mer·i·cal·ly** \-k(ə-)lē\ *adv*

numerical analysis *n* **:** the study of quantitative approximations to the solutions of mathematical problems including consideration of the errors and bounds to the errors involved

TABLE OF NUMBERS

CARDINAL NUMBERS[1] ORDINAL NUMBERS[4]

NAME[2]	SYMBOL Arabic	SYMBOL Roman[3]	NAME[5]	SYMBOL[6]
zero *or* naught *or* cipher	0		first	1st
one	1	I	second	2d *or* 2nd
two	2	II	third	3d *or* 3rd
three	3	III	fourth	4th
four	4	IV	fifth	5th
five	5	V	sixth	6th
six	6	VI	seventh	7th
seven	7	VII	eighth	8th
eight	8	VIII	ninth	9th
nine	9	IX	tenth	10th
ten	10	X	eleventh	11th
eleven	11	XI	twelfth	12th
twelve	12	XII	thirteenth	13th
thirteen	13	XIII	fourteenth	14th
fourteen	14	XIV	fifteenth	15th
fifteen	15	XV	sixteenth	16th
sixteen	16	XVI	seventeenth	17th
seventeen	17	XVII	eighteenth	18th
eighteen	18	XVIII	nineteenth	19th
nineteen	19	XIX	twentieth	20th
twenty	20	XX	twenty-first	21st
twenty-one	21	XXI	twenty-second	22d *or* 22nd
twenty-two	22	XXII	twenty-third	23d *or* 23rd
twenty-three	23	XXIII	twenty-fourth	24th
twenty-four	24	XXIV	twenty-fifth	25th
twenty-five	25	XXV	twenty-sixth	26th
twenty-six	26	XXVI	twenty-seventh	27th
twenty-seven	27	XXVII	twenty-eighth	28th
twenty-eight	28	XXVIII	twenty-ninth	29th
twenty-nine	29	XXIX	thirtieth	30th
thirty	30	XXX	thirty-first	31st
thirty-one	31	XXXI	thirty-second *etc*	32d *or* 32nd
thirty-two *etc*	32	XXXII	fortieth	40th
forty	40	XL	forty-first	41st
forty-one *etc*	41	XLI	forty-second *etc*	42d *or* 42nd
fifty	50	L	fiftieth	50th
sixty	60	LX	sixtieth	60th
seventy	70	LXX	seventieth	70th
eighty	80	LXXX	eightieth	80th
ninety	90	XC	ninetieth	90th
one hundred	100	C	hundredth *or* one hundredth	100th
one hundred and one *or* one hundred one	101	CI	hundred and first *or* one hundred and first	101st
one hundred and two *etc*	102	CII	hundred and second *etc*	102d *or* 102nd
two hundred	200	CC	two hundredth	200th
three hundred	300	CCC	three hundredth	300th
four hundred	400	CD	four hundredth	400th
five hundred	500	D	five hundredth	500th
six hundred	600	DC	six hundredth	600th
seven hundred	700	DCC	seven hundredth	700th
eight hundred	800	DCCC	eight hundredth	800th
nine hundred	900	CM	nine hundredth	900th
one thousand *or* ten hundred *etc*	1,000	M	thousandth *or* one thousandth	1,000th
two thousand *etc*	2,000	MM	two thousandth *etc*	2,000th
five thousand	5,000	$\overline{V}$	ten thousandth	10,000th
ten thousand	10,000	$\overline{X}$	hundred thousandth *or* one hundred thousandth	100,000th
one hundred thousand	100,000	$\overline{C}$		
one million	1,000,000	$\overline{M}$	millionth *or* one millionth	1,000,000th

[1] The cardinal numbers are used in simple counting or in answer to "how many?" The words for these numbers may be used as nouns (he counted to *twelve*), as pronouns (*twelve* were found), or as adjectives (*twelve* boys).
[2] In formal contexts the numbers one to one hundred and in less formal contexts the numbers one to nine are commonly written out, while larger numbers are given in numerals. In nearly all contexts a number occurring at the beginning of a sentence is usually written out. Except in very formal contexts numerals are invariably used for dates. Arabic numerals from 1,000 to 9,999 are often written without commas (1000, 9999). Year numbers are always written without commas (1783).
[3] The Roman numerals are written either in capitals or in lowercase letters.
[4] The ordinal numbers are used to show the order or succession in which such items as names, objects, and periods of time are considered (the *twelfth* month; the *fourth* row of seats; the *18th* century).
[5] Each of the terms for the ordinal numbers excepting *first* and *second* is used in designating one of a number of parts into which a whole may be divided (a *fourth*; a *sixth*; a *tenth*) and as the denominator in fractions designating the number of such parts constituting a certain portion of a whole (*one fourth*; *three fifths*). When used as nouns the fractions are usually written as two words, although they are regularly hyphenated as adjectives (a *two-thirds* majority). When fractions are written in numerals, the cardinal symbols are used ($^1/_4$, $^3/_5$, $^5/_6$).
[6] The Arabic symbols for the cardinal numbers may be read as ordinals in certain contexts (January 1 = January first; 2 Samuel = Second Samuel). The Roman numerals are sometimes read as ordinals (Henry IV = Henry the Fourth); sometimes they are written with the ordinal suffixes (XIXth Dynasty).

DENOMINATIONS ABOVE ONE MILLION

American system[1]

NAME	VALUE IN POWERS OF TEN	NUMBER OF ZEROS[2]	NUMBER OF GROUPS OF THREE 0's AFTER 1,000
billion	10^{9}	9	2
trillion	10^{12}	12	3
quadrillion	10^{15}	15	4
quintillion	10^{18}	18	5
sextillion	10^{21}	21	6
septillion	10^{24}	24	7
octillion	10^{27}	27	8
nonillion	10^{30}	30	9
decillion	10^{33}	33	10
undecillion	10^{36}	36	11
duodecillion	10^{39}	39	12
tredecillion	10^{42}	42	13
quattuordecillion	10^{45}	45	14
quindecillion	10^{48}	48	15
sexdecillion	10^{51}	51	16
septendecillion	10^{54}	54	17
octodecillion	10^{57}	57	18
novemdecillion	10^{60}	60	19
vigintillion	10^{63}	63	20
centillion	10^{303}	303	100

British system[1]

NAME	VALUE IN POWERS OF TEN	NUMBER OF ZEROS[2]	POWERS OF 1,000,000
milliard	10^{9}	9	—
billion	10^{12}	12	2
trillion	10^{18}	18	3
quadrillion	10^{24}	24	4
quintillion	10^{30}	30	5
sextillion	10^{36}	36	6
septillion	10^{42}	42	7
octillion	10^{48}	48	8
nonillion	10^{54}	54	9
decillion	10^{60}	60	10
undecillion	10^{66}	66	11
duodecillion	10^{72}	72	12
tredecillion	10^{78}	78	13
quattuordecillion	10^{84}	84	14
quindecillion	10^{90}	90	15
sexdecillion	10^{96}	96	16
septendecillion	10^{102}	102	17
octodecillion	10^{108}	108	18
novemdecillion	10^{114}	114	19
vigintillion	10^{120}	120	20
centillion	10^{600}	600	100

[1] The American system of numeration for denominations above one million was modeled on the French system but more recently the French system has been changed to correspond to the German and British systems. In the American system each of the denominations above 1,000 millions (the American *billion*) is 1,000 times the one preceding (one trillion=1,000 billions; one quadrillion=1,000 trillions). In the British system the first denomination above 1,000 millions (the British *milliard*) is 1,000 times the preceding one, but each of the denominations above 1,000 milliards (the British *billion*) is 1,000,000 times the preceding one (one trillion=1,000,000 billions; one quadrillion=1,000,000 trillions).
[2] For convenience in reading large numerals the thousands, millions, etc., are usually separated by commas (21,530; 1,155,465) or by half spaces (1 155 465). Serial numbers (as a social security number or the engine number of a car) are often written with hyphens (583-695-20).

numerical taxonomy *n* : taxonomy that applies the quantitative measurement of many characters to the determination of taxa and to the construction of diagrams indicating systematic relationships — **numerical taxonomic** *adj* — **numerical taxonomist** *n*
nu·mer·ol·o·gy \ˌn(y)ü-mə-ˈräl-ə-jē\ *n* [L *numerus* + E *-o-* + *-logy*] : the study of the occult significance of numbers — **nu·mer·o·log·i·cal** \-mə-rə-ˈläj-i-kəl\ *adj* — **nu·mer·ol·o·gist** \-mə-ˈräl-ə-jəst\ *n*
nu·mer·ous \ˈn(y)üm-(ə-)rəs\ *adj* [MF *numereux*, fr. L *numerosus*, fr. *numerus*] : consisting of great numbers of units or individuals — **nu·mer·ous·ly** *adv* — **nu·mer·ous·ness** *n*
nu·mi·nous \ˈn(y)ü-mə-nəs\ *adj* [L *numin-*, *numen* numen] **1** : SUPERNATURAL, MYSTERIOUS **2** : filled with a sense of the presence of divinity : HOLY **3** : appealing to the higher emotions or to the aesthetic sense : SPIRITUAL
numis *abbr* numismatic; numismatical; numismatics
nu·mis·mat·ic \ˌn(y)ü-məz-ˈmat-ik, -məs-\ *adj* [F *numismatique*, fr. L *nomismat-*, *nomisma* coin, fr. Gk, custom, coin; akin to Gk *nomos* custom, law — more at NIMBLE] **1** : of or relating to numismatics **2** : of or relating to currency : MONETARY — **nu·mis·mat·i·cal·ly** \-i-k(ə-)lē\ *adv*
nu·mis·mat·ics \-iks\ *n pl but sing in constr* : the study or collection of coins, tokens, and paper money and sometimes related objects (as medals) — **nu·mis·ma·tist** \n(y)ü-ˈmiz-mət-əst\ *n*
num·mu·lar \ˈnəm-yə-lər\ *adj* [F *nummulaire*, fr. L *nummulus*, dim. of *nummus* coin, fr. Gk *nomimos* customary; akin to Gk *nomos*] **1** : circular or oval in shape <~ lesions> **2** : characterized by circular or oval lesions or drops <~ dermatitis> <~ sputum>
num·mu·lit·ic limestone \ˌnəm-yə-ˌlit-ik-\ *n* [NL *Nummulites*, genus of foraminifers, fr. L *nummulus*] : the most widely distributed and distinctive formation of the Eocene in Europe, Asia, and northern Africa
num·skull \ˈnəm-ˌskəl\ *n* [*numb* + *skull*] **1** : a dull or stupid person : DUNCE **2** : a thick or muddled head
¹nun \ˈnən\ *n* [ME, fr. OE *nunne*, fr. LL *nonna*] : a woman belonging to a religious order; *esp* : one under solemn vows of poverty, chastity, and obedience
²nun \ˈnün\ *n* [Heb *nūn*] : the 14th letter of the Hebrew alphabet — see ALPHABET table
Nunc Di·mit·tis \ˌnəŋk-də-ˈmit-əs, ˌnu̇ŋk-\ *n* [L, now lettest thou depart; fr. the first words of the canticle] : the prayer of Simeon in Luke 2:29–32 used as a canticle
nun·ci·a·ture \ˈnən(t)-sē-ə-ˌchu̇(ə)r, ˈnu̇n(t)-, -chər, -ˌt(y)u̇(ə)r\ *n* [It *nunciatura*, fr. *nuncio*] **1** : the office or period of office of a nuncio **2** : a papal diplomatic mission headed by a nuncio
nun·cio \ˈnən(t)-sē-ˌō, ˈnu̇n(t)-\ *n, pl* **-ci·os** [It, fr. L *nuntius* messenger, message] : a papal legate of the highest rank permanently accredited to a civil government
nun·cle \ˈnəŋ-kəl\ *n* [by alter. (resulting fr. incorrect division of *an uncle*] *chiefly dial* : UNCLE
nun·cu·pa·tive \ˈnən-kyu̇-ˌpāt-iv, ˈnəŋ-; ˌnən-ˈkyü-pət-\ *adj* [ML *nuncupativus*, fr. LL, so-called, fr. L *nuncupatus*, pp. of *nuncupare* to name, contr. of *nomen capere*, fr. *nomen* name + *capere* to take — more at NAME, HEAVE] : not written : ORAL <a ~ will>
nun·nery \ˈnən-(ə-)rē\ *n, pl* **-ner·ies** : a convent of nuns
Nu·pe \ˈnü-(ˌ)pā\ *n, pl* **Nupe** *or* **Nupes** **1** : a member of a Negro people of west central Nigeria **2** : a Kwa language of the Nupe people
¹nup·tial \ˈnəp-shəl, -chəl, *nonstand* -chə-wəl\ *adj* [L *nuptialis*, fr. *nuptiae*, pl., wedding, fr. *nuptus*, pp. of *nubere* to marry; akin to Gk *nymphē* bride, nymph] **1** : of or relating to marriage or the marriage ceremony **2** : characteristic of or occurring in the breeding season <~ flight> *syn* see MATRIMONIAL
²nuptial *n* : MARRIAGE, WEDDING — usu. used in pl.
nuptial plumage *n* : the brilliantly colored plumage assumed by the males of many birds prior to the start of the annual breeding period — compare ECLIPSE PLUMAGE
¹nurse \ˈnərs\ *n* [ME, fr. OF *nurice*, fr. LL *nutricia*, fr. L, fem. of *nutricius* nourishing — more at NUTRITIOUS] **1 a** : a woman who suckles an infant not her own **b** : a woman who takes care of a young child **2** : one that looks after, fosters, or advises **3** : a person who is skilled or trained in caring for the sick or infirm esp. under the supervision of a physician **4 a** : a worker of a social insect that cares for the young **b** : a female mammal used to suckle the young of another
²nurse *vb* **nursed; nurs·ing** [ME *nurshen* to nourish, contr. of *nurishen*] *vt* **1 a** : to nourish at the breast : SUCKLE **b** : to take nourishment from the breast of **2** : REAR, EDUCATE **3 a** : to promote the development or progress of **b** : to manage with care or economy **c** : to take charge of and watch over **4 a** : to care for and wait on (as a sick person) **b** : to attempt to cure by care and treatment **5** : to hold in one's memory or consideration <~ a grievance> **6 a** : to use, handle, or operate carefully so as to conserve energy or avoid injury or pain <~ a sprained ankle> **b** : to use sparingly ~ *vi* **1 a** : to feed an offspring from the breast **b** : to feed at the breast : SUCK **2** : to act or serve as a nurse — **nurs·er** *n*
nurse·maid \ˈnər-ˌsmād\ *n* : a girl or woman who is regularly employed to look after children
nurs·ery \ˈnərs-(ə-)rē\ *n, pl* **-er·ies** **1** *obs* : attentive care : FOSTERAGE **2 a** : a child's bedroom **b** : a place where children are temporarily cared for in their parents' absence **c** : DAY NURSERY **3 a** : something that fosters, develops, or promotes **b** : a place in which persons are trained or educated **4** : an area where plants (as trees and shrubs) are grown for transplanting, for use as stocks for budding and grafting, or for sale **5** : a place where young animals (as fish) grow or are cared for
nurs·ery·maid \-(ə-)rē-ˌmād\ *n* : NURSEMAID
nurs·ery·man \-mən\ *n* : one whose occupation is the cultivation of plants (as trees and shrubs) esp. for sale
nursery rhyme *n* : a short rhyme for children that often tells a story
nursery school *n* : a school for children usu. under five years
nurse's aide *n* : a worker who assists trained nurses in a hospital by performing nonspecialized services (as giving baths)
nurse shark *n* [alter. of ME *nusse*] : any of various sharks of a widely distributed family (Orectolobidae); *esp* : a shark (*Ginglymostoma cirratum*) of the warmer parts of the Atlantic ocean
nurs·ing *n* **1** : the profession of a nurse <schools of ~> **2** : the duties of a nurse <proper ~ is difficult work>
nursing bottle *n* : a bottle with a rubber nipple used in supplying food to infants
nursing home *n* : a privately operated establishment where maintenance and personal or nursing care are provided for persons (as the aged or the chronically ill) who are unable to care for themselves properly
nurs·ling \ˈnər-sliŋ\ *n* **1** : one that is solicitously cared for **2** : a nursing child
nur·tur·ance \ˈnər-chə-rən(t)s\ *n* [²*nurture* + *-ance*] : affectionate care and attention — **nur·tur·ant** \-rənt\ *adj*
¹nur·ture \ˈnər-chər\ *n* [ME, fr. MF *norriture*, fr. LL *nutritura* act of nursing, fr. L *nutritus*, pp. of *nutrire* to suckle, nourish — more at NOURISH] **1** : TRAINING, UPBRINGING **2** : something that nourishes : FOOD **3** : the sum of the influences modifying the expression of the genetic potentialities of an organism
²nurture *vt* **nur·tured; nur·tur·ing** \ˈnərch-(ə-)riŋ\ **1** : to supply with nourishment **2** : EDUCATE **3** : to further the development of : FOSTER — **nur·tur·er** \ˈnər-chər-ər\ *n*
¹nut \ˈnət\ *n* [ME *nute*, *note*, fr. OE *hnutu*; akin to OHG *nuz* nut, L *nux*] **1 a** (1) : a hard-shelled dry fruit or seed with a separable rind or shell and interior kernel (2) : the kernel of a nut **b** : a dry indehiscent one-seeded fruit with a woody pericarp **2** : a hard problem or undertaking **3** : a perforated block usu. of metal that has an internal screw thread and is used on a bolt or screw for tightening or holding something **4** : the ridge in a stringed instrument (as a violin) over which the strings pass on the upper end of the fingerboard **5** *pl* : NONSENSE — often used interjectionally **6** *pl* : TESTES — usu. considered vulgar **7** *slang* : a person's head **8 a** : a foolish, eccentric, or crazy person **b** : ENTHUSIAST **9** : EN 2 — **nut·like** \-ˌlīk\ *adj*

nuts 3

²nut *vi* **nut·ted; nut·ting** : to gather or seek nuts
nu·tate \ˈn(y)ü-ˌtāt\ *vi* **nu·tat·ed; nu·tat·ing** : to exhibit or undergo nutation
nu·ta·tion \n(y)ü-ˈtā-shən\ *n* [L *nutation-*, *nutatio*, fr. *nutatus*, pp. of *nutare* to nod, rock, freq. of *nuere* to nod — more at NUMEN] **1** : the act of nodding the head **2 a** : a libratory motion of the earth's axis like the nodding of a top **b** : oscillatory movement of the axis of a rotating body : WOBBLE **3** : a spontaneous usu. spiral movement of a growing plant part — **nu·ta·tion·al** \-shnəl, -shən-ᵊl\ *adj*
nut–brown \ˈnət-ˈbrau̇n\ *adj* : of the color of a brown nut
nut·crack·er \-ˌkrak-ər\ *n* : an implement for cracking nuts
nut·gall \-ˌgȯl\ *n* : a gall that resembles a nut; *esp* : a gall produced on oak
nut grass *n* : a perennial sedge (*Cyperus rotundus*) of wide distribution that has slender rootstocks bearing small edible tubers resembling nuts; *also* : a related sedge (*C. esculentus*)

nutcracker

nut·hatch \ˈnət-ˌhach\ *n* [ME *notehache*, fr. *note* nut + *hache* ax, fr. OF, battle-ax — more at HASH] : any of various small tree-climbing birds (family Sittidae) that have a compact body, a long bill, a short tail, and sometimes a black cap and a ring around the eye

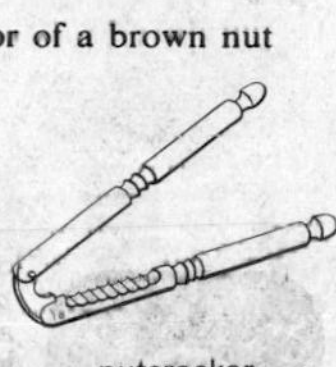

nut·house \ˈnət-ˌhau̇s\ *n, slang* : an insane asylum
nut·let \ˈnət-lət\ *n* **1 a** : a small nut **b** : a small fruit similar to a nut **2** : the stone of a drupelet

nuthatch

nut·meg \ˈnət-ˌmeg, -ˌmāg\ *n* [ME *notemuge*, deriv. of OProv. *noz muscada*, fr. *noz* nut (fr. L *nuc-*, *nux*) + *muscada*, fem. of *muscat* musky — more at MUSCAT] : an aromatic seed that is used as a spice and is produced by a tree (*Myristica fragrans* of the family Myristicaceae, the nutmeg family) native to the Moluccas; *also* : this tree
nut·pick \ˈnət-ˌpik\ *n* : a small sharp-pointed implement for extracting the kernels from nuts
nu·tria \ˈn(y)ü-trē-ə\ *n* [Sp, modif. of L *lutra* otter; akin to OE *oter* otter] **1** : COYPU 1 **2** : the durable usu. light brown fur of the coypu
¹nu·tri·ent \ˈn(y)ü-trē-ənt\ *adj* [L *nutrient-*, *nutriens*, prp. of *nutrire* to nourish — more at NOURISH] : furnishing nourishment
²nutrient *n* : a nutritive substance or ingredient
nu·tri·ment \ˈn(y)ü-trə-mənt\ *n* [L *nutrimentum*, fr. *nutrire*] : something that nourishes or promotes growth and repairs the natural wastage of organic life
nu·tri·tion \n(y)u̇-ˈtrish-ən\ *n* [MF, fr. LL *nutrition-*, *nutritio*, fr. L *nutritus*, pp. of *nutrire*] : the act or process of nourishing or being nourished; *specif* : the sum of the processes by which an animal or plant takes in and utilizes food substances — **nu·tri·tion·al** \-ˈtrish-nəl, -ən-ᵊl\ *adj* — **nu·tri·tion·al·ly** \-ē\ *adv*
nu·tri·tion·ist \-ˈtrish-(ə-)nəst\ *n* : a specialist in the study of nutrition

nu·tri·tious \n(y)ü-'trish-əs\ *adj* [L *nutricius*, fr. *nutric-*, *nutrix* nurse; akin to L *nutrire* to nourish — more at NOURISH] : NOURISHING — **nu·tri·tious·ly** *adv* — **nu·tri·tious·ness** *n*

nu·tri·tive \'n(y)ü-trət-iv\ *adj* **1 :** of or relating to nutrition **2** : NOURISHING — **nu·tri·tive·ly** *adv*

nutritive ratio *n* **:** the ratio of digestible protein to other nutrients in a foodstuff or ration

nuts \'nəts\ *adj* **1 :** ENTHUSIASTIC, KEEN <everyone seems ~ about it —Lois Long> **2 :** CRAZY, DEMENTED <thought I would go ~ waiting around —Polly Adler>

nuts and bolts *n* **1 :** the working parts or elements **2 :** the practical workings of a machine or enterprise as opposed to theoretical considerations or speculative possibilities

nut·sedge \'nət-,sej\ *n* **:** NUT GRASS

nut·shell \'nət-,shel\ *n* **1 :** the hard external covering in which the kernel of a nut is enclosed **2 :** something of small size, amount, or scope — **in a nutshell :** in a very brief statement

nut·ty \'nət-ē\ *adj* **nut·ti·er; -est 1 :** having or producing nuts **2 :** ECCENTRIC, SILLY; *also* **:** mentally unbalanced **3 :** having a flavor like that of nuts — **nut·ti·ness** *n*

nux vom·i·ca \'nəks-'väm-i-kə\ *n, pl* **nux vomica** [NL, lit., emetic nut] **:** the poisonous seed of an Asiatic tree (*Strychnos nux-vomica* of the family Longaniaceae) that contains several alkaloids and esp. strychnine and brucine; *also* **:** the tree yielding nux vomica

nuz·zle \'nəz-əl\ *vb* **nuz·zled; nuz·zling** \-(ə-)liŋ\ [ME *noselen*, to bring the nose toward the ground, fr. *nose*] *vi* **1 :** to work with or as if with the nose; *esp* **:** to root, rub, or snuff something **2 :** to lie close or snug **:** NESTLE ~ *vt* **:** to root, rub, or touch with or as if with the nose **:** NUDGE

NV *abbr* **1** Nevada **2** nonvoting

NW *abbr* northwest

NWT *abbr* Northwest Territories

NY *abbr* New York

NYA *abbr* National Youth Administration

ny·a·la \nē-'äl-ə\ *n, pl* **nyalas** *or* **nyala** [of Bantu origin; akin to Venda *nyala* nyala, Zulu *inxala*] **:** an antelope (*Tragelaphus angasi*) of southeastern Africa with vertical white stripes on the sides of the body and with shaggy black hair along the male underside; *also* **:** a related antelope (*T. buxtoni*)

NYC *abbr* New York City

nyc·ta·lo·pia \,nik-tə-'lō-pē-ə\ *n* [LL] **:** NIGHT BLINDNESS

ny·lon \'nī-,län\ *n* [coined word] **1 :** any of numerous strong tough elastic synthetic polyamide materials that are fashioned into fibers, filaments, bristles, or sheets, and used esp. in textiles and plastics **2** *pl* **:** stockings made of nylon

nymph \'nim(p)f\ *n* [ME *nimphe*, fr. MF, fr. L *nympha* bride, nymph, fr. Gk *nymphē* — more at NUPTIAL] **1 :** one of the minor divinities of nature in ancient mythology represented as beautiful maidens dwelling in the mountains, forests, trees, and waters **2 :** GIRL **3 :** any of various immature insects; *esp* **:** a larva of an insect (as a dragonfly or mayfly) with incomplete metamorphosis that differs from the imago esp. in size and in its incompletely developed wings and genitalia — **nymph·al** \'nim(p)-fəl\ *adj*

nym·pha·lid \nim-'fal-əd, 'nim-fə-ləd\ *n* [NL *Nymphalidae*, group name, deriv. of L *nympha* nymph] **:** any of a family (Nymphalidae) of butterflies (as a mourning cloak or fritillary) with the first pair of legs reduced in size in both sexes and useless for walking — **nymphalid** *adj*

nym·phet *also* **nym·phette** \nim-'fet, 'nim(p)-fət\ *n* [obs. *nymphet* young nymph, fr. MF *nymphette*, dim. of *nymphe* nymph] **:** a sexually precocious girl barely in her teens

nym·pho·lep·sy \'nim(p)-fə-,lep-sē\ *n* [*nympholept*, fr. Gk *nympholēptos* frenzied, lit., caught by nymphs, fr. *nymphē* + *lambanein* to seize — more at CATCH] **1 :** a demoniac enthusiasm held by the ancients to seize one bewitched by a nymph **2 :** a frenzy of emotion — **nym·pho·lept** \-,lept\ *n* — **nym·pho·lep·tic** \,nim(p)-fə-'lep-tik\ *adj*

nym·pho·ma·nia \,nim(p)-fə-'mā-nē-ə, -nyə\ *n* [NL, fr. *nymphae* inner lips of the vulva (fr. L, pl. of *nympha*) + LL *mania*] **:** excessive sexual desire by a female — **nym·pho·ma·ni·ac** \-nē-,ak\ *n or adj* — **nym·pho·ma·ni·a·cal** \-mə-'nī-ə-kəl\ *adj*

Ny·norsk \n(y)ü-'nȯ(ə)rsk, nüē-\ *n* [Norw, lit., new Norwegian] **:** a literary form of Norwegian based on the spoken dialects of Norway — compare BOKMÅL

NYSE *abbr* New York Stock Exchange

nys·tag·mus \nis-'tag-məs\ *n* [NL, fr. Gk *nystagmos* drowsiness, fr. *nystazein* to doze; akin to Lith *snusti* to doze] **:** a rapid involuntary oscillation of the eyeballs (as from dizziness) — **nys·tag·mic** \-mik\ *adj*

NZ *abbr* New Zealand

[1]**o** \'ō\ *n, pl* **o's** *or* **os** \'ōz\ *often cap, often attrib* **1 a :** the 15th letter of the English alphabet **b :** a graphic representation of this letter **c :** a speech counterpart of orthographic *o* **2 :** a graphic device for reproducing the letter *o* **3 :** one designated *o* esp. as the 15th in order or class **4 :** something shaped like the letter O; *esp* **:** ZERO

[2]**o** *abbr, often cap* **1** ocean **2** Ohio **3** ohm **4** old **5** order **6** oriental **7** over

[1]**O** \'ō\ *var of* OH

[2]**O** *symbol* **1** oxygen **2** [NL *octarius*] pint

[1]**o-** *or* **oo-** *comb form* [Gk *ōi-*, *ōio-*, fr. *ōion* — more at EGG] **:** egg <*oology*>; *specif* **:** ovum <*oogonium*>

[2]**o-** *abbr* ortho-

-o- [ME, fr. OF, fr. L, fr. Gk, thematic vowel of many nouns and adjectives in combination] — used as a connective vowel orig. to join word elements of Greek origin and now also to join word elements of Latin or other origin <drunk*o*meter> <elast*o*mer>

[1]**-o** \(,)ō\ *n suffix* [perh. fr. [1]*oh*] **:** one that is, has the qualities of, or is associated with <buck*o*>

[2]**-o** \(,)ō, 'ō\ *interj suffix* [prob. fr. [1]*oh*] — in interjections formed from other parts of speech <cheeri*o*> <right*o*>

o' *also* **o** \ə\ *prep* [ME *o*, *o-*, contr. of *on & of*] **1** *chiefly dial* **:** ON **2 :** OF <one *o'*clock>

o/a *abbr* on or about

oaf \'ōf\ *n* [of Scand origin; akin to ON *alfr* elf — more at ELF] **1 :** a stupid person **:** BOOB **2 :** a big clumsy slow-witted person — **oaf·ish** \'ō-fish\ *adj* — **oaf·ish·ly** *adv* — **oaf·ish·ness** *n*

oak \'ōk\ *n, pl* **oaks** *or* **oak** *often attrib* [ME *ook*, fr. OE *āc*; akin to OHG *eih* oak, Gk *aigilōps*, a kind of oak] **1 a :** a tree or shrub (genera *Quercus* or *Lithocarpus*) of the beech family that produces a rounded one-seeded thin-shelled nut surrounded at the base by an indurated cup **b :** the tough hard durable wood of an oak tree **2 :** the leaves of an oak used as decoration — **oak·en** \'ō-kən\ *adj*

oak apple *n* **:** a large round gall produced on oak leaves by a gall wasp (esp. *Amphibolips concluentus* or *Andricus californicus*)

oak–leaf cluster *n* **:** a bronze or silver cluster of oak leaves and acorns added to various military decorations to signify a second or subsequent award of the basic decoration

oak·moss \'ōk-,mȯs\ *n* **:** any of several lichens that grow on oak trees and yield a resin used in perfumery

oa·kum \'ō-kəm\ *n* [ME *okum*, fr. OE *ācumba* tow, fr. *ā-* (separative & perfective prefix) + *-cumba* (akin to OE *camb* comb) — more at ABIDE] **:** loosely twisted hemp or jute fiber impregnated with tar or a tar derivative and used in caulking seams (as of wooden ships) and packing joints (as of pipes)

oak wilt *n* **:** a destructive disease of oak trees that is caused by a fungus (*Chalara quercina*) and is characterized by wilting, discoloration, and defoliation

[1]**oar** \'ō(ə)r, 'ȯ(ə)r\ *n* [ME *oor*, fr. OE *ār*; akin to ON *ār* oar] **1 :** a long pole with a broad blade at one end used for propelling or steering a boat **2 :** OARSMAN — **oared** \'ō(ə)rd, 'ȯ(ə)rd\ *adj*

[2]**oar** *vt* **:** to propel with or as if with oars **:** ROW ~ *vi* **:** to progress by or as if by using oars

oar·fish \'ō(ə)r-,fish, 'ȯ(ə)r-\ *n* **:** any of several sea fishes (genus *Regalecus*) with narrow soft bodies from 20 to 30 feet long, a dorsal fin running the entire length of the body, and red-tipped anterior rays rising above the head

oar·lock \-,läk\ *n* **:** a U-shaped device for holding an oar in place

oars·man \'ō(ə)rz-mən, 'ȯ(ə)rz-\ *n* **:** one who rows esp. in a racing crew — **oars·man·ship** \-,ship\ *n*

oak tree with *1* leaf and *2* acorns

OAS *abbr* Organization of American States

oa·sis \ō-'ā-səs\ *n, pl* **oa·ses** \-,sēz\ [LL, fr. Gk] **1 :** a fertile or green area in an arid region **2 :** something providing relief from boring or dreary routine **:** REFUGE

oat \'ōt\ *n, often attrib* [ME *ote*, fr. OE *āte*] **1 a :** any of several grasses (genus *Avena*); *esp* **:** a widely cultivated cereal grass (*Avena sativa*) **b :** a crop or plot of the oat; *also* **:** oat seed — usu. used in pl. but sing. or pl. in constr. **2** *archaic* **:** a reed instrument made of an oat straw

oat·cake \'ōt-,kāk\ *n* **:** a thin flat oatmeal cake

oat·en \'ōt-ᵊn\ *adj* **:** of or relating to oats, oat straw, or oatmeal

oat·er \'ōt-ər\ *n* **:** WESTERN 2

oat grass *n* **:** WILD OAT 1a; *broadly* **:** one of several grasses resembling the oat

oath \'ōth\ *n, pl* **oaths** \'ōthz, 'ōths\ [ME *ooth*, fr. OE *āth*; akin to OHG *eid* oath] **1 a** (1) **:** a solemn usu. formal calling upon God or a god to witness to the truth of what one says or to witness that one sincerely intends to do what one says (2) **:** a solemn attestation of the truth or inviolability of one's words **b :** something (as a promise) corroborated by an oath **c :** a form of expression used in taking an oath **2 :** an irreverent or careless use of a sacred name; *broadly* **:** SWEARWORD

oat·meal \'ōt-,mēl, ōt-'mē(ə)l\ *n* **1 a :** meal made from oats **b :** rolled oats **2 :** porridge made from ground or rolled oats

ob *abbr* **1** [L *obiit*] he died **2** observation **3** obstetrical; obstetrician

Ob *or* **Obad** *abbr* Obadiah

ob- *prefix* [NL, fr. L, in the way, against, toward, fr. *ob* in the way of, on account of — more at EPI-] **:** inversely <*ob*ovate>

Oba·di·ah \,ō-bə-'dī-ə\ *n* [Heb *'Ōbhadhyāh*] **1 :** a minor Hebrew prophet **2 :** a prophetic book of canonical Jewish and Christian Scripture — see BIBLE table

oat 1a

[1]ob·bli·ga·to \,äb-lə-'gät-(,)ō\ *adj* [It, obligatory, fr. pp. of *obbligare* to oblige, fr. L *obligare*] **:** not to be omitted **:** OBLIGATORY — used as a direction in music

[2]obbligato *n, pl* **-tos** *also* **-ti** \-'gät-ē\ **1 :** an elaborate esp. melodic part accompanying a solo or principal melody and usu. played by a single instrument <a song with violin ~> **2 :** a persistent background sound

ob·cor·date \(')äb-'kȯ(ə)r-,dāt\ *adj* **:** heart-shaped with the notch apical <~ leaf>

ob·du·ra·cy \'äb-d(y)ə-rə-sē; äb-'d(y)u̇r-ə-, əb-\ *n, pl* **-cies :** the quality or state of being obdurate

ob·du·rate \'äb-d(y)ə-rət; äb-'d(y)u̇r-ət, əb-\ *adj* [ME, fr. L *obduratus*, pp. of *obdurare* to harden, fr. *ob-* against + *durus* hard — more at DURING] **1 a :** hardened in feelings **b :** stubbornly persistent in wrongdoing **2 :** resistant to persuasion or softening influences **:** UNYIELDING ***syn*** see INFLEXIBLE — **ob·du·rate·ly** *adv* — **ob·du·rate·ness** *n*

OBE *abbr* Officer of the Order of the British Empire

obe·ah \'ō-bē-ə\ *also* **obi** \'ō-bē\ *n, often cap* [of African origin; akin to Twi *a*¹*bi*²*a*³, a creeper used in making charms] **:** a system of belief among Negroes chiefly of the British West Indies, the Guianas, and the southeastern U.S. that is characterized by the use of sorcery and magic ritual

obe·di·ence \ō-'bēd-ē-ən(t)s, ə-\ *n* **1 a :** an act or instance of obeying **b :** the quality or state of being obedient **2 :** a sphere of jurisdiction; *esp* **:** an ecclesiastical or sometimes secular dominion

obe·di·ent \-ənt\ *adj* [ME, fr. OF, fr. L *oboedient-, oboediens*, fr. prp. of *oboedire* to obey — more at OBEY] **:** submissive to the restraint or command of authority — **obe·di·ent·ly** *adv*

syn OBEDIENT, DOCILE, TRACTABLE, AMENABLE *shared meaning element* **:** submissive to the control of another ***ant*** disobedient, contumacious

obei·sance \ō-'bās-ᵊn(t)s, ə-, -'bēs-\ *n* [ME *obeisaunce* obedience, obeisance, fr. MF *obeissance*, fr. *obeissant*, prp. of *obeir* to obey] **1 :** a movement of the body made in token of respect or submission **:** BOW **2 :** DEFERENCE, HOMAGE — **obei·sant** \-ᵊnt\ *adj* — **obei·sant·ly** *adv*

obe·lia \ō-'bēl-yə\ *n* [NL, genus name] **:** any of a genus (*Obelia*) of small colonial marine hydroids with colonies branched like trees

obe·lisk \'äb-ə-,lisk *also* 'ō-bə-\ *n* [MF *obelisque*, fr. L *obeliscus*, fr. Gk *obeliskos*, fr. dim. of *obelos*] **1 :** an upright 4-sided usu. monolithic pillar that gradually tapers as it rises and terminates in a pyramid **2 a :** OBELUS **b :** DAGGER 2b

obe·lize \-,līz\ *vt* **-lized; -liz·ing :** to designate or annotate with an obelus

obe·lus \-ləs\ *n, pl* **ob·e·li** \-,lī, -,lē\ [LL, fr. Gk *obelos* spit, pointed pillar, obelus] **:** a symbol — or ÷ used in ancient manuscripts to mark a questionable passage

Ober·on \'ō-bə-,rän, -rən\ *n* [F, fr. OF *Auberon*] **:** king of the fairies in medieval folklore

obese \ō-'bēs\ *adj* [L *obesus*, fr. pp. of *obedere* to eat up, fr. *ob-* against + *edere* to eat — more at OB-, EAT] **:** excessively fat

obe·si·ty \ō-'bē-sət-ē\ *n* **:** a condition characterized by excessive bodily fat

obelisk 1

obey \ō-'bā, ə-\ *vb* **obeyed; obey·ing** [ME *obeien*, fr. OF *obeir*, fr. L *oboedire*, fr. *ob-* toward + *-oedire* (akin to *audire* to hear) — more at OB-, AUDIBLE] *vt* **1 :** to follow the commands or guidance of **2 :** to comply with **:** EXECUTE <~ an order> ~ *vi* **:** to behave obediently — **obey·er** *n*

syn OBEY, COMPLY, MIND *shared meaning element* **:** to follow the direction of another

ob·fus·cate \'äb-fə-,skāt; äb-'fəs-,kāt, əb-\ *vt* **-cat·ed; -cat·ing** [LL *obfuscatus*, pp. of *obfuscare*, fr. L *ob-* in the way + *fuscus* dark brown — more at OB-, DUSK] **1 a :** DARKEN **b :** to make obscure **2 :** CONFUSE — **ob·fus·ca·tion** \,äb-(,)fəs-'kā-shən\ *n* — **ob·fus·ca·to·ry** \äb-'fəs-kə-,tōr-ē, əb-, -,tȯr-\ *adj*

obi \'ō-bē\ *n* [Jap] **:** a broad sash worn with a Japanese kimono

Obie \'ō-bē\ *n* [*O.B.*, abbr. for *off Broadway*] **:** an award presented annually by a professional organization for notable achievement in plays performed off Broadway

obit \ō-'bit, 'ō-bət, *esp Brit* 'äb-it\ *n* [ME, fr. MF, fr. L *obitus* decease, fr. *obitus*, pp. of *obire* to go to meet, die, fr. *ob-* in the way + *ire* to go — more at ISSUE] **:** OBITUARY

obi·ter dic·tum \,ō-bət-ər-'dik-təm, ,äb-ət-\ *n, pl* **obiter dic·ta** \-tə\ [LL, lit., something said in passing] **1 :** an incidental and collateral opinion that is uttered by a judge but is not binding **2 :** an incidental remark or observation

obit·u·ary \ə-'bich-ə-,wer-ē, ō-, -'bich-ə-rē\ *n, pl* **-ar·ies** [ML *obituarium*, fr. L *obitus* decease] **:** a notice of a person's death usu. with a short biographical account — **obituary** *adj*

obj *abbr* object; objective

[1]ob·ject \'äb-jikt\ *n* [ME, fr. ML *objectum*, fr. L, neut. of *obicere* to throw in the way, present, hinder, fr. *ob-* in the way + *jacere* to throw — more at OB-, JET] **1 a :** something that is or is capable of being seen, touched, or otherwise sensed **b :** something physical or mental of which a subject is cognitively aware **2 :** something that arouses an emotion in an observer **3 a :** an end toward which effort or action or emotion is directed **:** GOAL **b :** MOTIVE **4 :** a thing that forms an element of or constitutes the subject matter of an investigation or science **5 a :** a noun or noun equivalent denoting in verb constructions that on or toward which the action of a verb is directed **b :** a noun or noun equivalent in a prepositional phrase ***syn*** see INTENTION — **ob·ject·less** \-jik-tləs\ *adj* — **ob·ject·less·ness** *n*

[2]ob·ject \əb-'jekt\ *vb* [ME *objecten*, fr. L *objectus*, pp. of *obicere* to throw in the way, object] *vt* **:** to offer in opposition **:** cite as an objection ~ *vi* **1 :** to oppose something firmly and usu. with words or arguments **2 :** to feel distaste for something **:** DISAPPROVE — **ob·jec·tor** \-'jek-tər\ *n*

syn OBJECT, PROTEST, REMONSTRATE, EXPOSTULATE, KICK *shared meaning element* **:** to oppose by arguing against. OBJECT stresses dislike or aversion <*object* vociferously to a new zoning ordinance> PROTEST suggests an orderly presentation of objections in speech or in writing <professors . . . who signed an open letter . . . *protesting* the construction of fallout shelters —*Current Biog.*> or, sometimes, activity designed to focus attention on what is felt as wrong <marched with the pickets, *protesting* atmospheric testing —Dick Kleiner> REMONSTRATE implies protestation but stresses so strongly an intent to persuade or convince that it is more appropriate in intimate than in official or impersonal situations <*remonstrated* with her son over his untruthfulness> EXPOSTULATE carries a strong implication of firm, earnest, but usually friendly reasoning or insistence on the merits of one's stand <reporters at his press conference *expostulated* against playing favorites —*New Republic*> KICK implies strenuous protestation and, usually, an exhibition of recalcitrancy <wherefore *kick* ye, at my sacrifice and at mine offering —1 Sam 2:29 (AV)> ***ant*** acquiesce

object ball \'äb-jik(t)-\ *n* **:** the ball first struck by the cue ball in pool or billiards; *also* **:** a ball hit by the cue ball

ob·jec·ti·fy \əb-'jek-tə-,fī\ *vt* **-fied; -fy·ing 1 a :** to cause to become an object **b :** to make objective **2 :** EXTERNALIZE 2 — **ob·ject·ti·fi·ca·tion** \-,jek-tə-fə-'kā-shən\ *n*

ob·jec·tion \əb-'jek-shən\ *n* **1 :** an act of objecting **2 a :** a reason or argument presented in opposition **b :** a feeling of disapproval

ob·jec·tion·able \-sh(ə-)nə-bəl\ *adj* **:** arousing objection **:** OFFENSIVE — **ob·jec·tion·able·ness** *n* — **ob·jec·tion·ably** \-blē\ *adv*

[1]ob·jec·tive \əb-'jek-tiv, äb-\ *adj* **1 a :** of or relating to an object of action or feeling **b :** having the status of or constituting an object: as **(1) :** existing only in relation to a knowing subject or willing agent **(2) :** existing independent of mind **(3) :** belonging to the sensible world and being observable or verifiable esp. by scientific methods **(4)** *of a symptom of disease* **:** perceptible to persons other than an affected individual **c :** emphasizing or expressing the nature of reality as it is apart from personal reflections or feelings **d (1) :** expressing or involving the use of facts without distortion by personal feelings or prejudices **(2) :** relating to or being methods that eliminate the subjective by limiting choices to fixed alternatives requiring a minimum of creative interpretation <~ tests of personality> **2 :** derived from sense perception **3 :** belonging or relating to an object to be delineated **4 :** relating to, characteristic of, or constituting the case that follows a preposition or a transitive verb ***syn* 1** see MATERIAL ***ant*** subjective **2** see FAIR ***ant*** subjective — **ob·jec·tive·ly** *adv* — **ob·jec·tive·ness** *n* — **ob·jec·tiv·i·ty** \(')äb-,jek-'tiv-ət-ē, əb-\ *n*

[2]objective *n* **1 :** something toward which effort is directed **:** an aim or end of action **:** GOAL, OBJECT **2 :** something that is objective; *specif* **:** something external to the mind **3 a :** the objective case **b :** a word in the objective case **4 :** a strategic position to be attained or purpose to be achieved by a military operation **5 :** a lens or system of lenses that forms an image of an object ***syn*** see INTENTION

objective complement *n* **:** a noun, adjective, or pronoun used in the predicate as complement to a verb and as qualifier of its direct object <*chairman* in "we elected him chairman" is an *objective complement*>

objective correlative *n* **:** a situation or chain of events that symbolizes or objectifies a particular emotion and that may be used in creative writing to evoke a desired emotional response in the reader

objective test *n* [fr. the fact that subjective judgment by the grader is eliminated] **:** a test made up of factual questions to be answered in a word or two or by a check mark — compare ESSAY TEST

ob·jec·tiv·ism \əb-'jek-tiv-,iz-əm, äb-\ *n* **1 :** any of various theories stressing objective reality esp. as distinguished from subjective experience or appearance **2 :** an ethical theory that moral good is objectively real or that moral precepts are objectively valid **3 :** the theory or practice of objective art or literature — **ob·jec·tiv·ist** \-əst\ *n* — **ob·jec·tiv·is·tic** \-,jek-tiv-'is-tik\ *adj*

object language \'äb-jikt-\ *n* **:** TARGET LANGUAGE

object lesson \'äb-jikt-\ *n* **1 :** a lesson having a material object as the basis of instruction **2 :** something that teaches by exemplifying a principle in concrete form

ob·jet d'art \,ȯb-,zhā-'där\ *n, pl* **ob·jets d'art** *same*\ [F, lit., art object] **1 :** an article of some artistic value **2 :** CURIO

ob·jet trou·vé \'ȯb-,zhā-trü-'vā\ *n* [F, lit., found object] **:** a natural object (as a piece of driftwood) found by chance and held to have aesthetic value esp. through the working of natural forces on it; *also*

ə abut ᵊ kitten ər further a back ā bake ä cot, cart
au̇ out ch chin e less ē easy g gift i trip ī life
j joke ŋ sing ō flow ȯ flaw ȯi coin th thin t͟h this
ü loot u̇ foot y yet yü few yu̇ furious zh vision

: an artifact not orig. intended as art but held to have aesthetic value esp. when displayed as a work of art

ob·jur·gate \ˈäb-jər-ˌgāt\ *vt* **-gat·ed; -gat·ing** [L *objurgatus*, pp. of *objurgare*, fr. *ob-* against + *jurgare* to quarrel, lit., to take to law, fr. *jur-*, *jus* law + *-igare* (fr. *agere* to lead) — more at OB-, JUST, AGENT] : to denounce harshly : CASTIGATE — **ob·jur·ga·tion** \ˌäb-jər-ˈgā-shən\ *n* — **ob·jur·ga·to·ry** \əb-ˈjər-gə-ˌtōr-ē, -ˌtȯr-\ *adj*

obl *abbr* **1** oblique **2** oblong

ob·lan·ceo·late \(ˈ)äb-ˈlan(t)-sē-ə-ˌlāt\ *adj* : inversely lanceolate <an ~ leaf>

ob·last \ˈäb-ˌlast, ˈȯb-ləst\ *n, pl* **oblasts** *also* **ob·las·ti** \-ˌlas-tē, -ləs-\ [Russ *oblast'*] : a political subdivision of a republic in the U.S.S.R.

[1]**ob·late** \äb-ˈlāt, ˈäb-ˌ\ *adj* [prob. fr. NL *oblatus*, fr. *ob-* + *-latus* (as in *prolatus* prolate)] : flattened or depressed at the poles <an ~ spheroid> — **ob·late·ness** *n*

[2]**ob·late** \ˈäb-ˌlāt\ *n* [ML *oblatus*, lit., one offered up, fr. L, pp. of *offerre*] **1** : a layman living in a monastery under a modified rule and without vows **2** : a member of one of several Roman Catholic communities of men or women

ob·la·tion \ə-ˈblā-shən, ō-\ *n* [ME *oblacioun*, fr. MF *oblation*, fr. LL *oblation-*, *oblatio*, fr. L *oblatus*, pp. of *offerre* to offer] **1** : the act of making a religious offering; *specif*, *cap* : the act of offering the eucharistic elements to God **2** : something offered in worship or devotion : a holy gift offered usu. at an altar or shrine

[1]**ob·li·gate** \ˈäb-li-gət, -lə-ˌgāt\ *adj* **1** : restricted to one particularly characteristic mode of life <an ~ parasite> **2** : ESSENTIAL, NECESSARY <~ parasitism> — **ob·li·gate·ly** *adv*

[2]**ob·li·gate** \ˈäb-lə-ˌgāt\ *vt* **-gat·ed; -gat·ing** [L *obligatus*, pp. of *obligare*] **1 a** : to bind legally or morally : CONSTRAIN **b** : OBLIGE 2a **2** : to commit (as funds) to meet an obligation

ob·li·ga·tion \ˌäb-lə-ˈgā-shən\ *n* **1** : the action of obligating oneself to a course of action **2 a** : something (as a formal contract, a promise, or the demands of conscience or custom) that obligates one to a course of action **b** : a debt security (as a mortgage or corporate bond) **c** : a commitment (as by a government) to pay a particular sum of money; *also* : an amount owed under such an obligation : LIABILITY <unable to meet its ~*s* the company went into bankruptcy> **3** : something that one is bound to do or forbear (as by law, conscience, or social pressure) : DUTY **4** : a condition or feeling of being indebted esp. legally, ethically, or socially <felt her ~ to these kind friends very deeply>

oblig·a·to·ry \ə-ˈblig-ə-ˌtōr-ē, ä-, -ˌtȯr- *also* ˈäb-li-gə-\ *adj* **1** : binding in law or conscience **2** : relating to or enforcing an obligation <a writ ~> **3** : MANDATORY, REQUIRED **4** : OBLIGATE 1 — **oblig·a·to·ri·ly** \ə-ˌblig-ə-ˈtōr-ə-lē, ä-, -ˈtȯr- *also* ˌäb-li-gə-\ *adv*

oblige \ə-ˈblīj\ *vb* **obliged; oblig·ing** [ME *obligen*, fr. OF *obliger*, fr. L *obligare*, lit., to bind to, fr. *ob-* toward + *ligare* to bind — more at LIGATURE] *vt* **1** : to constrain by physical, moral, or legal force or by the exigencies of circumstance <*obliged* to find money for his taxes> **2 a** : to put in one's debt by a favor or service <you will ~ us if you get there early> **b** : to do a favor for <always ready to ~ a friend> ~ *vi* : to do something as a favor — **oblig·er** *n*

syn **1** see FORCE
2 OBLIGE, ACCOMMODATE, FAVOR *shared meaning element* : to do a service or courtesy ***ant*** disoblige

ob·li·gee \ˌäb-lə-ˈjē\ *n* **1** : one to whom another is obligated **2** : one who is obliged

oblig·ing \ə-ˈblī-jiŋ\ *adj* : willing to do favors : ACCOMMODATING ***syn*** see AMIABLE ***ant*** disobliging, inconsiderate — **oblig·ing·ly** \-jiŋ-lē\ *adv* — **oblig·ing·ness** *n*

ob·li·gor \ˌäb-lə-ˈgȯ(ə)r, -ˈjȯ(ə)r\ *n* : one that places himself under a legal obligation

[1]**oblique** \ō-ˈblēk, ə-, -ˈblīk; *military usu* ī\ *adj* [ME *oblike*, fr. L *obliquus*, fr. *ob-* toward + *-liquus* (akin to *ulna* elbow) — more at ELL] **1 a** : neither perpendicular nor parallel : INCLINED **b** : having the axis not perpendicular to the base <an ~ cone> **c** : having no right angle <an ~ triangle> **2 a** : not straightforward : INDIRECT **b** : DEVIOUS, UNDERHAND **3** : situated obliquely and having one end not inserted on bone <~ muscles> **4** : taken from an airplane with the camera directed horizontally or diagonally downward <an ~ photograph> ***syn*** see CROOKED — **oblique·ly** *adv* — **oblique·ness** *n*

[2]**oblique** *n* **1** : something (as a line) that is oblique **2** : any of several oblique muscles; *esp* : one of the thin flat muscles forming the middle and outer layers of the lateral walls of the abdomen

[3]**oblique** *adv* : at a 45 degree angle <to the right ~, march>

oblique angle *n* : an acute or obtuse angle

oblique case *n* : a grammatical case other than the nominative or vocative

obliq·ui·ty \ō-ˈblik-wət-ē, ə-\ *n, pl* **-ties** **1** : deviation from moral rectitude or sound thinking **2 a** : deviation from parallelism or perpendicularity; *also* : the amount of such deviation : DIVERGENCE **b** : the angle between the planes of the earth's equator and orbit having a mean value of 23°26′34″.52 in 1972 and diminishing 0″.47 per year <~ of the ecliptic> **3 a** : indirectness or deliberate obscurity of speech or conduct **b** : an obscure or confusing statement

oblit·er·ate \ə-ˈblit-ə-ˌrāt, ō-\ *vt* **-at·ed; -at·ing** [L *oblitteratus*, pp. of *oblitterare*, fr. *ob* in the way of + *littera* letter — more at EPI-] **1** : to make undecipherable or imperceptible by obscuring or wearing away **2 a** : to remove utterly from recognition or memory **b** : to destroy utterly all trace, indication, or significance of **c** : to cause to disappear (as a bodily part or a scar) or collapse (as the lumen of a duct) : REMOVE <a blood vessel *obliterated* by inflammation> **3** : CANCEL 4 ***syn*** see ERASE — **oblit·er·a·tion** \-ˌblit-ə-ˈrā-shən\ *n* — **oblit·er·a·tor** \-ˈblit-ə-ˌrāt-ər\ *n*

oblit·er·a·tive \ə-ˈblit-ə-ˌrāt-iv, ō-, -ə-rət-\ *adj* : inducing or characterized by obliteration: as **a** : causing or accompanied by closure or collapse of a lumen <~ arterial disease> **b** : tending to make inconspicuous <~ behavior>

obliv·i·on \ə-ˈbliv-ē-ən, ō-, ä-\ *n* [ME, fr. MF, fr. L *oblivion-*, *oblivio*, fr. *oblivisci* to forget, perh. fr. *ob-* in the way + *levis* smooth — more at OB-, LIME] **1** : an act or instance of forgetting : FORGETFULNESS **2** : the quality or state of being forgotten <contentedly accepted his own political ~> **3** : official ignoring of offenses

obliv·i·ous \-ē-əs\ *adj* **1** : lacking remembrance, memory, or mindful attention **2** : lacking active conscious knowledge : UNAWARE — usu. used with *of* or *to* ***syn*** see FORGETFUL — **obliv·i·ous·ly** *adv* — **obliv·i·ous·ness** *n*

ob·long \ˈäb-ˌlȯŋ\ *adj* [ME, fr. L *oblongus*, fr. *ob-* toward + *longus* long] : deviating from a square or circular form through elongation <the ~ fruit of a lemon tree>: **a** : rectangular with adjacent sides unequal **b** : rectangular with the normally horizontal dimension the greater — **oblong** *n*

ob·lo·quy \ˈäb-lə-kwē\ *n, pl* **-quies** [LL *obloquium*, fr. *obloqui* to speak against, fr. *ob-* against + *loqui* to speak — more at OB-] **1** : a strongly condemnatory utterance : abusive language **2** : the condition of one that is discredited : bad repute ***syn*** see ABUSE

ob·nox·ious \äb-ˈnäk-shəs, əb-\ *adj* [L *obnoxius*, fr. *ob* in the way of, exposed to + *noxa* harm — more at EPI-, NOXIOUS] **1** : liable esp. to a hurtful influence — used with *to* **2** *archaic* : deserving of censure **3** : odiously or disgustingly objectionable : highly offensive ***syn*** see REPUGNANT ***ant*** grateful — **ob·nox·ious·ly** *adv* — **ob·nox·ious·ness** *n*

ob·nu·bi·late \äb-ˈn(y)ü-bə-ˌlāt\ *vt* **-lat·ed; -lat·ing** [L *obnubilatus*, pp. of *obnubilare*, fr. *ob-* in the way + *nubilare* to be cloudy, fr. *nubilus* cloudy, fr. *nubes* cloud — more at OB-, NUANCE] : BECLOUD — **ob·nu·bi·la·tion** \-ˌn(y)ü-bə-ˈlā-shən\ *n*

oboe \ˈō-(ˌ)bō\ *n* [It, fr. F *hautbois* — more at HAUTBOIS] : a double-reed woodwind instrument having a conical tube, a nasal tone, and a usual range from B flat below middle C upward for $3\frac{1}{2}$ octaves — **obo·ist** \ˈō-ˌbō-əst\ *n*

oboe

obol \ˈäb-əl, ˈō-bəl\ *n* [L *obolus*, fr. Gk *obolos*; akin to Gk *obelos* spit] : an ancient Greek coin or weight equal to $\frac{1}{6}$ drachma

ob·ovate \(ˈ)äb-ˈō-ˌvāt\ *adj* : ovate with the narrower end basal <~ leaves>

ob·ovoid \-ˌvȯid\ *adj* : ovoid with the broad end toward the apex <an ~ fruit>

ob·scene \äb-ˈsēn, əb-\ *adj* [MF, fr. L *obscenus*, *obscaenus*] **1** : disgusting to the senses : REPULSIVE **2** : abhorrent to morality or virtue; *specif* : designed to incite to lust or depravity ***syn*** see COARSE ***ant*** decent — **ob·scene·ly** *adv*

ob·scen·i·ty \-ˈsen-ət-ē *also* -ˈsēn-\ *n, pl* **-ties** **1** : the quality or state of being obscene **2** : something (as an utterance or act) that is obscene

ob·scur·ant \äb-ˈskyu̇r-ənt, əb-\ *or* **ob·scu·ran·tic** \ˌäb-skyə-ˈrant-ik\ *adj* : tending to make obscure — **obscurant** *n*

ob·scu·ran·tism \äb-ˈskyu̇r-ən-ˌtiz-əm, əb-; ˌäb-skyu̇-ˈran-\ *n* **1** : opposition to the spread of knowledge : a policy of withholding knowledge from the general public **2 a** : a style (as in literature or art) characterized by deliberate vagueness or abstruseness **b** : an act or instance of obscurantism — **ob·scu·ran·tist** \-ən-təst, -ˈrant-əst\ *n or adj*

[1]**ob·scure** \äb-ˈskyu̇(ə)r, əb-\ *adj* [ME, fr. MF *obscur*, fr. L *obscurus*, fr. *ob-* in the way + *-scurus* (akin to Gk *keuthein* to conceal) — more at HIDE] **1** : lacking or inadequately supplied with light : DARK, DUSKY **2 a** : withdrawn from the centers of human activity : REMOTE <an ~ country village> **b** : not readily understood or not clearly expressed : ABSTRUSE **c** : lacking showiness or prominence : INCONSPICUOUS, HUMBLE <an ~ Roman poet> **d** : not distinct : FAINT <an ~ stain> **3** : constituting the unstressed vowel \ə\ or having unstressed \ə\ as its value — **ob·scure·ly** *adv* — **ob·scure·ness** *n*

syn OBSCURE, DARK, VAGUE, ENIGMATIC, CRYPTIC, AMBIGUOUS, EQUIVOCAL *shared meaning element* : not clearly understandable ***ant*** distinct, obvious

[2]**obscure** *vt* **ob·scured; ob·scur·ing** **1** : to make dark, dim, or indistinct **2** : to conceal or hide by or as if by covering **3** : to reduce (a vowel) to the value \ə\ — **ob·scu·ra·tion** \ˌäb-skyu̇-ˈrā-shən\ *n*

[3]**obscure** *n* : OBSCURITY

ob·scu·ri·ty \äb-ˈskyu̇r-ət-ē, əb-\ *n, pl* **-ties** **1** : the quality or state of being obscure **2** : one that is obscure

ob·se·qui·ous \əb-ˈsē-kwē-əs, äb-\ *adj* [ME, fr. L *obsequiosus* compliant, fr. *obsequium* compliance, fr. *obsequi* to comply, fr. *ob-* toward + *sequi* to follow — more at OB-, SUE] : exhibiting a servile attentiveness or complaisance ***syn*** see SUBSERVIENT ***ant*** contumelious — **ob·se·qui·ous·ly** *adv* — **ob·se·qui·ous·ness** *n*

ob·se·quy \ˈäb-sə-kwē\ *n, pl* **-quies** [ME *obsequie*, fr. MF, fr. ML *obsequiae* (pl.), alter. of L *exsequiae* — more at EXEQUY] : a funeral or burial rite — usu. used in pl.

ob·serv·able \əb-ˈzər-və-bəl\ *adj* **1** : NOTEWORTHY **2** : capable of being observed : DISCERNIBLE — **observable** *n* — **ob·serv·ably** \-blē\ *adv*

ob·ser·vance \əb-ˈzər-vən(t)s\ *n* **1 a** : a customary practice, rite, or ceremony <Sabbath ~*s*> **b** : a rule governing members of a religious order **2** : an act or instance of following a custom, rule, or law <~ of the speed limits> **3** : an act or instance of watching

[1]**ob·ser·vant** \-vənt\ *n, obs* : an assiduous or obsequious servant or attendant

[2]**observant** *adj* **1** : paying strict attention : WATCHFUL <~ spectators> **2** : careful in observing : MINDFUL <always ~ of the amenities> **3** : quick to observe : KEEN — **ob·ser·vant·ly** *adv*

ob·ser·va·tion \ˌäb-sər-ˈvā-shən, -zər-\ *n* [MF, fr. L *observation-*, *observatio*, fr. *observatus*, pp. of *observare*] **1** : an act or the faculty of observing **2 a** : an act of recognizing and noting a fact or occurrence often involving measurement with instruments <weather ~*s*> **b** : a record so obtained **3** : a judgment on or inference from what one has observed; *broadly* : REMARK, STATEMENT **4** *obs* : HEED **5** : the condition of one that is observed <under ~ at the hospital> — **ob·ser·va·tion·al** \-shnəl, -shən-ᵊl\ *adj*

ob·ser·va·to·ry \əb-ˈzər-və-ˌtōr-ē, -ˌtȯr-\ *n, pl* **-ries** [prob. fr. NL *observatorium,* fr. L *observatus*] **1 :** a building or place given over to or equipped for observation of natural phenomena (as in astronomy); *also* **:** an institution whose primary purpose is making such observations **2 :** a situation or structure commanding a wide view **:** LOOKOUT

ob·serve \əb-ˈzərv\ *vb* **ob·served; ob·serv·ing** [ME *observen,* fr. MF *observer,* fr. L *observare* to guard, watch, observe, fr. *ob-* in the way, toward + *servare* to keep — more at CONSERVE] *vt* **1 :** to conform one's action or practice to <~ rules> **2 :** to inspect or take note of as an augury, omen, or presage **3 :** to celebrate or solemnize (as a ceremony or festival) after a customary or accepted form **4 :** to see or sense esp. through directed careful analytic attention **5 :** to come to realize or know esp. through consideration of noted facts **6 :** to utter as a remark **7 :** to make a scientific observation on or of ~ *vi* **1 a :** to take notice **b :** to make observations **:** WATCH **2 :** REMARK, COMMENT ***syn*** see KEEP ***ant*** violate — **ob·serv·ing·ly** \-ˈzər-viŋ-lē\ *adv*

ob·serv·er \əb-ˈzər-vər\ *n* **:** one that observes: as **a :** a representative sent to observe but not participate officially in a gathering **b :** one who accompanies the pilot of an airplane to make observations

ob·sess \əb-ˈses, äb-\ *vt* [L *obsessus,* pp. of *obsidēre* to besiege, beset, fr. *ob-* against + *sedēre* to sit — more at OB-, SIT] **1** *archaic* **:** HARASS, BESET **2 :** to preoccupy intensely or abnormally

ob·ses·sion \äb-ˈsesh-ən, əb-\ *n* **1 :** a persistent disturbing preoccupation with an often unreasonable idea or feeling **2 :** an emotion or idea causing an obsession — **ob·ses·sion·al** \-ˈsesh-nəl, -ən-ᵊl\ *adj* — **ob·ses·sion·al·ly** \-ē\ *adv*

ob·ses·sive \äb-ˈses-iv, əb-\ *adj* **1 a :** tending to cause obsession **b :** excessive often to an abnormal degree <our ~ need for quick solutions —A. E. Stevenson †1965> **2 :** of, relating to, or characterized by obsession — **obsessive** *n* — **ob·ses·sive·ly** *adv* — **ob·ses·sive·ness** *n*

ob·sid·i·an \əb-ˈsid-ē-ən\ *n* [NL *obsidianus,* fr. L *obsidianus lapis,* false MS reading for *obsianus lapis,* lit., stone of Obsius, fr. *Obsius,* its supposed discoverer] **:** volcanic glass that is generally black, banded, or spherulitic and has a marked conchoidal fracture and a composition similar to rhyolite

ob·so·lesce \ˌäb-sə-ˈles\ *vi* **-lesced; -lesc·ing** [L *obsolescere*] **:** to be or become obsolescent

ob·so·les·cence \-ˈles-ᵊn(t)s\ *n* **:** the process of becoming obsolete or the condition of being nearly obsolete <the gradual ~ of machinery> <reduced to ~>

ob·so·les·cent \-ᵊnt\ *adj* **:** going out of use **:** becoming obsolete — **ob·so·les·cent·ly** *adv*

[1]**ob·so·lete** \ˌäb-sə-ˈlēt, ˈäb-sə-ˌ\ *adj* [L *obsoletus,* fr. pp. of *obsolescere* to grow old, become disused] **1 a :** no longer in use **:** DISUSED **b :** of a kind or style no longer current **:** OUTMODED **2** *of a plant or animal part* **:** indistinct or imperfect as compared with a corresponding part in related organisms **:** VESTIGIAL ***syn*** see OLD ***ant*** current — **ob·so·lete·ly** *adv* — **ob·so·lete·ness** *n*

[2]**obsolete** *vt* **-let·ed; -let·ing :** to make obsolete <newer media are *obsoleting* the book —Daniel Melcher>

ob·sta·cle \ˈäb-sti-kəl, -ˌstik-əl\ *n* [ME, fr. MF, fr. L *obstaculum,* fr. *obstare* to stand in the way, fr. *ob-* in the way + *stare* to stand — more at OB-, STAND] **:** something that stands in the way or opposes **:** OBSTRUCTION

obstacle course *n* **:** a military training course filled with obstacles (as hurdles, fences, walls, and ditches) that must be negotiated; *broadly* **:** a series of obstacles that must be negotiated

obstet *abbr* obstetrical; obstetrics

ob·stet·ric \əb-ˈste-trik, äb-\ *or* **ob·stet·ri·cal** \-tri-kəl\ *adj* [prob. fr. (assumed) NL *obstetricus,* fr. L *obstetric-, obstetrix* midwife, fr. *obstare* to stand in the way, stand in front of] **:** of, relating to, or associated with childbirth or obstetrics — **ob·stet·ri·cal·ly** \-tri-k(ə-)lē\ *adv*

ob·ste·tri·cian \ˌäb-stə-ˈtrish-ən\ *n* **:** a physician specializing in obstetrics

ob·stet·rics \əb-ˈste-triks, äb-\ *n pl but sing or pl in constr* **:** a branch of medical science that deals with birth and with its antecedents and sequels

ob·sti·na·cy \ˈäb-stə-nə-sē\ *n* **1 a :** the quality or state of being obstinate **:** STUBBORNNESS **b :** the quality or state of being difficult to remedy, relieve, or subdue <the ~ of tuberculosis> **2 :** an instance of being obstinate

ob·sti·nate \ˈäb-stə-nət\ *adj* [ME, fr. L *obstinatus,* pp. of *obstinare* to be resolved, fr. *ob-* in the way + *-stinare* (akin to *stare* to stand)] **1 :** perversely adhering to an opinion, purpose, or course in spite of reason, arguments, or persuasion **2 :** not easily subdued, remedied, or removed <~ fever> — **ob·sti·nate·ly** *adv* — **ob·sti·nate·ness** *n*

syn OBSTINATE, DOGGED, STUBBORN, PERTINACIOUS, MULISH *shared meaning element* **:** fixed and unyielding in course or purpose ***ant*** pliant, pliable

ob·strep·er·ous \əb-ˈstrep-(ə-)rəs, äb-\ *adj* [L *obstreperus,* fr. *obstrepere* to clamor against, fr. *ob-* against + *strepere* to make a noise; akin to OE *thrǣft* discord — more at OB-] **1 :** marked by unruly or aggressive noisiness **:** CLAMOROUS <~ merriment> **2 :** stubbornly defiant **:** UNRULY ***syn*** see VOCIFEROUS — **ob·strep·er·ous·ly** *adv* — **ob·strep·er·ous·ness** *n*

ob·struct \əb-ˈstrəkt, äb-\ *vt* [L *obstructus,* pp. of *obstruere,* fr. *ob-* in the way + *struere* to build — more at OB-, STRUCTURE] **1 :** to block or close up by an obstacle **2 :** to hinder from passage, action, or operation **:** IMPEDE **3 :** to cut off from sight <a wall ~*s* the view> ***syn*** see HINDER — **ob·struc·tive** \-ˈstrək-tiv\ *adj or n* — **ob·struc·tive·ness** *n* — **ob·struc·tor** \-tər\ *n*

ob·struc·tion \əb-ˈstrək-shən, äb-\ *n* **1 :** an act of obstructing **:** the state of being obstructed: as **a :** a condition of being clogged or blocked **b :** a delay or attempted delay of business in a deliberative body (as a legislature) **2 :** something that obstructs

ob·struc·tion·ism \-shə-ˌniz-əm\ *n* **:** deliberate interference with the progress or business esp. of a legislative body — **ob·struc·tion·ist** \-sh(ə-)nəst\ *n* — **ob·struc·tion·is·tic** \-ˌstrək-shə-ˈnis-tik\ *adj*

ob·tain \əb-ˈtān, äb-\ *vb* [ME *obteinen,* fr. MF & L; MF *obtenir,* fr. L *obtinēre* to hold on to, possess, obtain, fr. *ob-* in the way + *tenēre* to hold — more at THIN] *vt* **:** to gain or attain usu. by planned action or effort ~ *vi* **1** *archaic* **:** SUCCEED **2 :** to be generally recognized or established **:** PREVAIL ***syn*** see GET — **ob·tain·abil·i·ty** \-ˌtā-nə-ˈbil-ət-ē\ *n* — **ob·tain·able** \-ˈtā-nə-bəl\ *adj* — **ob·tain·er** *n* — **ob·tain·ment** \-ˈtān-mənt\ *n*

ob·tect \əb-ˈtekt, äb-\ *also* **ob·tect·ed** \-ˈtek-təd\ *adj* [L *obtectus,* pp. of *obtegere* to cover over, fr. *ob-* in the way + *tegere* to cover — more at THATCH] **:** enclosed in or characterized by enclosure in a firm chitinous case or covering <an ~ pupa>

ob·test \äb-ˈtest\ *vb* [MF *obtester,* fr. L *obtestari* to call to witness, beseech, fr. *ob-* toward + *testis* witness — more at OB-, TESTAMENT] **:** BESEECH, SUPPLICATE — **ob·tes·ta·tion** \ˌäb-ˌtes-ˈtā-shən\ *n*

ob·trude \əb-ˈtrüd, äb-\ *vb* **ob·trud·ed; ob·trud·ing** [L *obtrudere* to thrust at, fr. *ob-* in the way + *trudere* to thrust — more at OB-, THREAT] *vt* **1 :** to thrust out **:** EXTRUDE **2 :** to thrust forward or call to notice without warrant or request <not a man to ~ his beliefs casually> ~ *vi* **:** to thrust oneself forward so as to call attention to oneself <do what we may, our childhood background will ~> — **ob·trud·er** *n* — **ob·tru·sion** \-ˈtrü-zhən\ *n*

ob·tru·sive \-ˈtrü-siv, -ziv\ *adj* [L *obtrusus,* pp. of *obtrudere*] **1 :** thrust out **:** PROTRUDING **2 a :** forward in manner or conduct **:** PUSHING <~ behavior> **b :** undesirably noticeable or showy ***syn*** see IMPERTINENT ***ant*** unobtrusive, shy — **ob·tru·sive·ly** *adv* — **ob·tru·sive·ness** *n*

ob·tund \äb-ˈtənd\ *vt* [ME *obtunden,* fr. L *obtundere* — more at OBTUSE] **:** to reduce the edge or violence of **:** DULL <~*ed* reflexes>

ob·tu·rate \ˈäb-t(y)ə-ˌrāt\ *vt* **-rat·ed; -rat·ing** [L *obturatus,* pp. of *obturare,* fr. *ob-* in the way + *-turare* (akin to *tumēre* to swell) — more at THUMB] **:** OBSTRUCT, CLOSE — **ob·tu·ra·tion** \ˌäb-t(y)ə-ˈrā-shən\ *n*

ob·tu·ra·tor \ˈäb-t(y)ə-ˌrāt-ər\ *n* [NL, fr. L *obturatus,* pp.] **:** one that closes: as **a :** either of two muscles that cover part of the interior or exterior wall of the pelvis **b :** one (as a prosthetic device) that closes or blocks up an opening (as a fissure in the palate) **c :** a hooded swelling of the placenta that fits over the nucellus in some plants

ob·tuse \äb-ˈt(y)üs, əb-\ *adj* **ob·tus·er; -est** [L *obtusus* blunt, dull, fr. pp. of *obtundere* to beat against, blunt, fr. *ob-* against + *tundere* to beat — more at OB-, STUTTER] **1 :** lacking sharpness or quickness of sensibility **:** INSENSITIVE **2 a** (1) *of an angle* **:** exceeding 90 degrees but less than 180 degrees (2) **:** having an obtuse angle **b :** not pointed or acute **:** BLUNT **c** *of a leaf* **:** rounded at the free end ***syn*** see DULL ***ant*** acute — **ob·tuse·ly** *adv* — **ob·tuse·ness** *n*

obv *abbr* obverse

[1]**ob·verse** \äb-ˈvərs, əb-, ˈäb-ˌ\ *adj* [L *obversus,* fr. pp. of *obvertere* to turn toward, fr. *ob-* toward + *vertere* to turn — more at OB-, WORTH] **1 :** facing the observer or opponent **2 :** having the base narrower than the top <an ~ leaf> **3 :** constituting a counterpart or complement — **ob·verse·ly** *adv*

[2]**ob·verse** \ˈäb-ˌvərs, äb-ˈ, əb-ˈ\ *n* **1 a :** the side of a coin or currency note that bears the principal device and lettering; *broadly* **:** a front or principal surface **b :** the more conspicuous of two possible sides, things, or cases <the ~ of this situation> **2 a :** a counterpart necessarily involved in or answering to a fact or truth **b :** a proposition inferred immediately from another by denying the opposite of that which the given proposition affirms <the ~ of "all *A* is *B*" is "no *A* is not *B*">

ob·vert \äb-ˈvərt, əb-\ *vt* [L *obvertere* to turn toward] **1 :** to turn so as to present a different surface to view **2 :** to change the appearance of

ob·vi·ate \ˈäb-vē-ˌāt\ *vt* **-at·ed; -at·ing** [LL *obviatus,* pp. of *obviare* to meet, withstand, fr. L *obviam* in the way] **:** to see beforehand and dispose of **:** make unnecessary ***syn*** see PREVENT — **ob·vi·a·tion** \ˌäb-vē-ˈā-shən\ *n*

ob·vi·ous \ˈäb-vē-əs\ *adj* [L *obvius,* fr. *obviam* in the way, fr. *ob* in the way of + *viam,* acc. of *via* way — more at EPI-, VIA] **1** *archaic* **:** being in the way or in front **:** OPPOSITE **2 :** easily discovered, seen, or understood ***syn*** see EVIDENT ***ant*** obscure, abstruse — **ob·vi·ous·ly** *adv* — **ob·vi·ous·ness** *n*

oc *abbr* ocean

OC *abbr* **1** off center **2** officer candidate **3** on center **4** on course

oca \ˈō-kə\ *n* [Sp, fr. Quechua *ókka*] **:** either of two So. American wood sorrels (*Oxalis crenata* and *O. tuberosa*) cultivated for their edible tubers

oc·a·ri·na \ˌäk-ə-ˈrē-nə\ *n* [It, fr. *oca* goose, fr. LL *auca,* deriv. of L *avis* bird — more at AVIARY] **:** a simple wind instrument having an oval body with finger holes and a projecting mouthpiece

ocarina

Oc·cam's razor \ˌäk-əmz-\ *n* [William of *Ockham*] **:** a scientific and philosophic rule that entities should not be multiplied unnecessarily which is interpreted as requiring that the simplest of competing theories be preferred to the more complex or that explanations of unknown phenomena be sought first in terms of known quantities

occas *abbr* occasionally

[1]**oc·ca·sion** \ə-ˈkā-zhən\ *n* [ME, fr. MF or L; MF, fr. L *occasion-, occasio,* fr. *occasus,* pp. of *occidere* to fall, fall down, fr. *ob-* toward + *cadere* to fall — more at OB-, CHANCE] **1 :** a favorable opportunity or circumstance **2 :** a state of affairs that provides a ground or reason <the ~ of the discord was their mutual intolerance> **3**

: an occurrence or condition that brings something about; *esp* : the immediate inciting circumstance as distinguished from the fundamental cause <his insulting remark was the ~ of a bitter quarrel> **4 a** : HAPPENING, INCIDENT **b** : a time at which something happens **5 a** : a need arising from a particular circumstance **b** *archaic* : a personal want or need — usu. used in pl. **6** *pl* : AFFAIRS, BUSINESS **7** : a special event or ceremony : CELEBRATION *syn* see CAUSE — **on occasion** : from time to time

[2]**occasion** *vt* **oc·ca·sioned; oc·ca·sion·ing** \-ˈkāzh-(ə-)niŋ\ : to bring about : CAUSE

oc·ca·sion·al \-ˈkāzh-nəl, -ən-ᵊl\ *adj* **1** : of or relating to a particular occasion <a budget able to meet ~ demands as well as regular ones> **2** : acting as the occasion or contributing cause of something **3** : composed for a particular occasion <~ verse> **4** : met with, appearing, or occurring at irregular or infrequent intervals <~ visitors> <takes an ~ vacation> **5** : acting in a specified capacity from time to time **6** : designed or constructed to be used as the occasion demands <~ furniture>

oc·ca·sion·al·ly \-ē\ *adv* : now and then : SOMETIMES

Oc·ci·dent \ˈäk-səd-ənt, -sə-ˌdent\ *n* [ME, fr. MF, fr. L *occident-, occidens,* fr. prp. of *occidere* to fall, set (of the sun)] : WEST 2a

oc·ci·den·tal \ˌäk-sə-ˈdent-ᵊl\ *adj, often cap* **1** : of, relating to, or situated in the Occident : WESTERN **2** : of or relating to Occidentals — **oc·ci·den·tal·ly** \-ᵊl-ē\ *adv*

Occidental *n* : a member of one of the occidental peoples; *esp* : a person of European ancestry

Oc·ci·den·tal·ism \ˌäk-sə-ˈdent-ᵊl-ˌiz-əm\ *n* : the characteristic features of occidental peoples or culture

oc·ci·den·tal·ize \-ᵊl-ˌīz\ *vt* **-ized; -iz·ing** *often cap* : to make occidental (as in culture)

oc·cip·i·tal \äk-ˈsip-ət-ᵊl\ *adj* : of or relating to the occiput or the occipital bone — **occipital** *n* — **oc·cip·i·tal·ly** \-ᵊl-ē\ *adv*

occipital bone *n* : a compound bone that forms the posterior part of the skull and bears a condyle by which the skull articulates with the atlas

occipital condyle *n* : an articular surface on the occipital bone by which the skull articulates with the atlas

occipital lobe *n* : the posterior lobe of the cerebral hemisphere that bears the visual areas and has the form of a 3-sided pyramid

oc·ci·put \ˈäk-sə-(ˌ)pət\ *n, pl* **occiputs** *or* **oc·cip·i·ta** \äk-ˈsip-ət-ə\ [L *occipit-, occiput,* fr. *ob-* against + *capit-, caput* head — more at OB-, HEAD] : the back part of the head or skull

oc·clude \ə-ˈklüd, ä-\ *vb* **oc·clud·ed; oc·clud·ing** [L *occludere,* fr. *ob-* in the way + *claudere* to shut, close — more at CLOSE] *vt* **1** : to stop up : OBSTRUCT <a thrombus *occluding* a coronary artery> **2** : PREVENT, HINDER **3** : SORB **4** : to cut off from contact with the surface of the earth and force aloft by the convergence of a cold front on a warm front <*occluded* warm air> ~ *vi* **1** : to close with the cusps fitting together <his teeth do not ~ properly> **2** : to become occluded — **oc·clud·ent** \-ˈklüd-ᵊnt\ *adj* — **oc·clu·sive** \-ˈklü-siv, -ziv\ *adj*

occluded front *n* : OCCLUSION 2

oc·clu·sal \ə-ˈklü-səl, ä-, -zəl\ *adj* : of or relating to the grinding or biting surface of a tooth or to occlusion of the teeth

oc·clu·sion \ə-ˈklü-zhən\ *n* [prob. fr. (assumed) NL *occlusion-, occlusio,* fr. L *occlusus,* pp. of *occludere*] **1** : the act of occluding : the state of being occluded: as **a** : the complete obstruction of the breath passage in the articulation of a speech sound **b** : the bringing of the opposing surfaces of the teeth of the two jaws into contact; *also* : the relation between the surfaces when in contact **c** : the inclusion or sorption of gas trapped during solidification of a material **2** : the front formed by a cold front overtaking a warm front and lifting the warm air above the earth's surface

[1]**oc·cult** \ə-ˈkəlt, ä-\ *vb* [L *occultare,* fr. *occultus,* pp.] *vt* **1** : to hide from sight : CONCEAL **2** : to conceal by occultation ~ *vi* : to become concealed or extinguished — **oc·cult·er** *n*

[2]**oc·cult** \ə-ˈkəlt, ä-; ˈäk-ˌəlt\ *adj* [L *occultus,* fr. pp. of *occulere* to cover up, fr. *ob-* in the way + *-culere* (akin to *celare* to conceal) — more at OB-, HELL] **1** : not revealed : SECRET **2** : not easily apprehended or understood : ABSTRUSE **3** : not able to be seen or detected : CONCEALED **4** : of or relating to the occult **5** : not manifest or detectable by clinical methods alone <~ carcinoma>; *esp* : not present in macroscopic amounts — **oc·cult·ly** *adv*

[3]**occult** *like*[2]\ *n* : matters regarded as involving the action or influence of supernatural agencies or some secret knowledge of them — used with *the*

oc·cul·ta·tion \ˌäk-(ˌ)əl-ˈtā-shən\ *n* **1** : the state of being hidden from view or lost to notice : ECLIPSE **2** : the shutting off of the light of one celestial body by the intervention of another; *esp* : an eclipse of a star or planet by the moon

oc·cult·ism \ə-ˈkəl-ˌtiz-əm, ä-; ˈäk-ˌəl-\ *n* : occult theory or practice : belief in or study of the action or influence of supernatural powers — **oc·cult·ist** \-təst\ *n*

oc·cu·pan·cy \ˈäk-yə-pən-sē\ *n, pl* **-cies** **1** : the act of taking and holding possession **2 a** : the act of becoming an occupant : the state of being an occupant **b** : the condition of being occupied **3** : the use to which property is put <industrial ~> **4** : an occupied building or part of a building (as an apartment or office)

oc·cu·pant \-pənt\ *n* **1** : one who acquires title by occupancy **2** : one who occupies a particular place; *esp* : RESIDENT

oc·cu·pa·tion \ˌäk-yə-ˈpā-shən\ *n* [ME *occupacioun,* fr. MF *occupation,* fr. L *occupation-, occupatio,* fr. *occupatus,* pp. of *occupare*] **1 a** : an activity in which one engages <in the first three grades learning to read is perhaps the major ~ of the pupil —J. B. Conant> **b** : the principal business of one's life : VOCATION **2 a** : the possession, use, or settlement of land : OCCUPANCY **b** : the holding of an office or position **3 a** : the act or process of taking possession of a place or area : SEIZURE **b** : the holding and control of an area by a foreign military force **c** : the military force occupying a country or the policies carried out by it

oc·cu·pa·tion·al \-shnəl, -shən-ᵊl\ *adj* **1** : of, relating to, or resulting from a particular occupation <~ hazards> **2** : of or relating to a military occupation — **oc·cu·pa·tion·al·ly** \-ē\ *adv*

occupational therapy *n* : therapy by means of activity; *esp* : creative activity prescribed for its effect in promoting recovery or rehabilitation — **occupational therapist** *n*

oc·cu·py \ˈäk-yə-ˌpī\ *vt* **-pied; -py·ing** [ME *occupien* to take possession of, occupy, modif. of MF *occuper,* fr. L *occupare,* fr. *ob-* toward + *-cupare* (akin to *capere* to seize) — more at OB-, HEAVE] **1** : to engage the attention or energies of **2** : to fill up (an extent in space or time) **3** : to take or hold possession of **4** : to reside in as an owner or tenant — **oc·cu·pi·er** \-ˌpī(-ə)r\ *n*

oc·cur \ə-ˈkər\ *vi* **oc·curred; oc·cur·ring** \-ˈkər-iŋ\ [L *occurrere,* fr. *ob-* in the way + *currere* to run — more at OB-, CURRENT] **1** : to be found or met with : APPEAR **2** : to take place **3** : to come to mind *syn* see HAPPEN

oc·cur·rence \ə-ˈkər-ən(t)s, -ˈkə-rən(t)s\ *n* **1** : something that takes place usu. unexpectedly and without design <a startling ~> **2** : the action or process of happening <the repeated ~ of petty theft in the locker room>

syn OCCURRENCE, EVENT, INCIDENT, EPISODE, CIRCUMSTANCE, HAPPENING *shared meaning element* : something that happens or takes place

[1]**oc·cur·rent** \ə-ˈkər-ənt, -ˈkə-rənt\ *adj* [MF, fr. L *occurrent-, occurrens,* prp. of *occurrere*] **1** : occurring at present : CURRENT **2** : INCIDENTAL

[2]**occurrent** *n* : something that occurs as distinguished from something that continues to exist

OCDM *abbr* Office of Civil and Defense Mobilization

ocean \ˈō-shən\ *n* [ME *occean,* fr. L *oceanus,* fr. Gk *Ōkeanos,* a river thought of as encircling the earth, ocean] **1** : the whole body of salt water that covers nearly three fourths of the surface of the globe **2** : one of the large bodies of water into which the great ocean is divided **3** : an unlimited space or quantity

ocean·ar·i·um \ˌō-shə-ˈnar-ē-əm, -ˈner-\ *n, pl* **-iums** *or* **-ia** : a large marine aquarium

ocean·front \ˈō-shən-ˌfrənt\ *n* : an area that fronts on the ocean

ocean·go·ing \-ˌgō-iŋ\ *adj* : of, relating to, or designed for travel on the ocean

oce·an·ic \ˌō-shē-ˈan-ik\ *adj* **1** : of, relating to, produced by, or frequenting the ocean and esp. the open sea as distinguished from littoral or neritic waters **2** : VAST, GREAT

Oce·anid \ō-ˈsē-ə-nəd\ *n* [Gk *ōkeanid-, ōkeanis,* fr. *Ōkeanos* Oceanus] : any of the ocean nymphs that are daughters of Oceanus and Tethys according to Greek myth

oceanog *abbr* oceanography

ocean·og·ra·phy \ˌō-shə-ˈnäg-rə-fē\ *n* [ISV] : a science that deals with the oceans and includes the delimitation of their extent and depth, the physics and chemistry of their waters, marine biology, and the exploitation of their resources — **ocean·og·ra·pher** \-fər\ *n* — **ocean·o·graph·ic** \-nə-ˈgraf-ik\ *also* **ocean·o·graph·i·cal** \-i-kəl\ *adj* — **ocean·o·graph·i·cal·ly** \-i-k(ə-)lē\ *adv*

ocean·ol·o·gy \ˌō-shə-ˈnäl-ə-jē\ *n* : OCEANOGRAPHY; *specif* : the science of marine resources and technology — **ocean·o·log·ic** \-nə-ˈläj-ik\ *or* **ocean·o·log·i·cal** \-i-kəl\ *adj* — **ocean·o·log·i·cal·ly** \-i-k(ə-)lē\ *adv* — **ocean·ol·o·gist** \-ˈnäl-ə-jəst\ *n*

ocean sunfish *n* : a large deep-bodied truncated marine fish (*Mola mola*) of warm and temperate seas

Oce·anus \ō-ˈsē-ə-nəs\ *n* [L, fr. Gk *Ōkeanos*] : a river in Greek mythology that encircles the earth and is personified as a Titan who is the progenitor with Tethys of the gods

ocel·lat·ed \ˈō-sə-ˌlāt-əd, ō-ˈsel-ˌāt-\ *or* **ocel·late** \ˈō-sə-ˌlāt, ō-ˈsel-ət\ *adj* **1** : having ocelli **2** : resembling an ocellus — **ocel·la·tion** \ˌō-sə-ˈlā-shən\ *n*

ocel·lus \ō-ˈsel-əs\ *n, pl* **ocel·li** \-ˈsel-ˌī, -(ˌ)ē\ [NL, fr. L, dim. of *oculus* eye — more at EYE] **1** : a minute simple eye or eyespot of an invertebrate **2** : a spot of color encircled by a band of another color — **ocel·lar** \ō-ˈsel-ər\ *adj*

oce·lot \ˈäs-ə-ˌlät, ˈō-sə-\ *n* [F, fr. Nahuatl *ocelotl* jaguar] : a medium-sized American wildcat (*Felis pardalis*) that ranges from Texas to Patagonia and has a tawny yellow or grayish coat dotted and striped with black

ocher *or* **ochre** \ˈō-kər\ *n* [ME *oker,* fr. MF *ocre,* fr. L *ochra,* fr. Gk *ōchra,* fr. fem. of *ōchros* yellow] **1** : an earthy usu. red or yellow and often impure iron ore used as a pigment **2** : the color of ocher; *esp* : the color of yellow ocher — **ocher·ous** \ˈō-k(ə-)rəs\ *or* **ochre·ous** \ˈō-k(ə-)rəs, -krē-əs\ *adj*

och·loc·ra·cy \äk-ˈläk-rə-sē\ *n* [Gk & MF; MF *ochlocratie,* fr. Gk *ochlokratia,* fr. *ochlos* mob + *-kratia* -cracy] : government by the mob : mob rule — **och·lo·crat** \ˈäk-lə-ˌkrat\ *n* — **och·lo·crat·ic** \ˌäk-lə-ˈkrat-ik\ *or* **och·lo·crat·i·cal** \-i-kəl\ *adj*

-ock \ək, ik, ˌäk\ *n suffix* [ME *-oc,* fr. OE] : small one <hill*ock*>

Ock·ham's razor \ˌäk-əmz-\ *n* : OCCAM'S RAZOR

o'clock \ə-ˈkläk\ *adv* [contr. of *of the clock*] **1** : according to the clock <the time is three ~> **2** — used for indicating position or direction as if on a clock dial that is oriented vertically or horizontally <an airplane approaching at six ~>

oco·ti·llo \ˌō-kə-ˈtē-(ˌ)(y)ō\ *n, pl* **-llos** [MexSp] : a thorny scarlet-flowered candlewood (*Fouquieria splendens*) of the southwestern U.S. and Mexico

OCR *abbr* optical character reader; optical character recognition

OCS *abbr* officer candidate school

oct *abbr* octavo

Oct *abbr* October

octa- *or* **octo-** *also* **oct-** *comb form* [Gk *okta-, oktō-, okt-* (fr. *oktō*) & L *octo-, oct-,* fr. *octo* — more at EIGHT] : eight <*octa*merous> <*oct*ane> <*octo*roon>

oc·ta·gon \ˈäk-tə-ˌgän\ *n* [L *octagonum,* fr. Gk *oktagōnon,* fr. *okta-* + *-gōnon* -gon] : a polygon of eight angles and eight sides — **oc·tag·o·nal** \äk-ˈtag-ən-ᵊl\ *adj* — **oc·tag·o·nal·ly** \-ᵊl-ē\ *adv*

oc·ta·he·dral \ˌäk-tə-ˈhē-drəl\ *adj* **1** : having eight plane faces **2** : of, relating to, or formed in octahedrons — **oc·ta·he·dral·ly** \-drə-lē\ *adv*

oc·ta·he·dron \-drən\ *n, pl* **-drons** *or* **-dra** \-drə\ [Gk *oktaedron,* fr. *okta-* + *-edron* -hedron] : a solid bounded by eight plane faces

oc·tal \ˈäk-tᵊl\ *adj* : of, relating to, or being a number system with a base of eight

oc·tam·e·ter \äk-ˈtam-ət-ər\ *n* [LL, having eight feet, fr. LGk *oktametros,* fr. *okta-* + *metron* measure — more at MEASURE] : a line of verse consisting of eight metrical feet

octagons: *1* regular, *2* irregular

oct·an·dri·ous \äk-ˈtan-drē-əs\ *adj* [deriv. of NL *octa-* + *andr-*] : having eight stamens or flowers with eight stamens

oc·tane \ˈäk-ˌtān\ *n* [ISV] **1** : any of several isomeric liquid paraffin hydrocarbons C_8H_{18} **2** : OCTANE NUMBER

octane number *n* : a number that is used to measure the antiknock properties of a liquid motor fuel and that represents the percentage by volume of isooctane in a reference fuel consisting of a mixture of isooctane and normal heptane and matching in knocking properties the fuel being tested — called also *octane rating;* compare CETANE NUMBER

octahedron

oc·tant \ˈäk-tənt\ *n* [L *octant-, octans* eighth of a circle, fr. *octo*] **1 a** : the position or aspect of a celestial body when distant from another body by 45 degrees **b** : an instrument for observing altitudes of a celestial body from a moving ship or aircraft **2** : any of the eight parts into which a space is divided by three coordinate planes

oc·ta·pep·tide \ˌäk-tə-ˈpep-ˌtīd\ *n* : a protein fragment or molecule (as oxytocin or vasopressin) that consists of eight amino acids linked in a polypeptide chain

oc·tave \ˈäk-tiv, -təv, -ˌtāv\ *n* [ME, fr. ML *octava,* fr. L, fem. of *octavus* eighth, fr. *octo* eight — more at EIGHT] **1** : an eight-day period of observances beginning with a festival day **2 a** : a stanza of eight lines : OTTAVA RIMA **b** : the first eight lines of an Italian sonnet **3 a** : a musical interval embracing eight diatonic degrees **b** : a tone or note at this interval **c** : the harmonic combination of two tones an octave apart **d** : the whole series of notes, tones, or digitals comprised within this interval and forming the unit of the modern scale **e** : an organ stop giving tones an octave above those corresponding to the digitals **4** : a group of eight

octave 3a

oc·ta·vo \äk-ˈtā-(ˌ)vō, -ˈtäv-(ˌ)ō\ *n, pl* **-vos** [L, abl. of *octavus* eighth] : the size of a piece of paper cut eight from a sheet; *also* : a book, a page, or paper of this size

oc·tet \äk-ˈtet\ *n* **1** : a musical composition for eight instruments or voices **2** : a group or set of eight: as **a** : the performers of an octet **b** : OCTAVE 2b

oc·til·lion \äk-ˈtil-yən\ *n* [F, fr. MF, fr. *oct-* octa- + *-illion* (as in *million*)] — see NUMBER table

Oc·to·ber \äk-ˈtō-bər\ *n* [ME *Octobre,* fr. OF, fr. L *October* (eighth month), fr. *octo*] **1** : the 10th month of the Gregorian calendar **2** *Brit* : ale brewed in October

oc·to·de·cil·lion \ˌäk-tō-di-ˈsil-yən\ *n* [L *octodecim* eighteen + E *-illion* (as in *million*)] — see NUMBER table

oc·to·dec·i·mo \ˌäk-tə-ˈdes-ə-ˌmō\ *n* [L, abl. of *octodecimus* eighteenth, fr. *octodecim* eighteen, fr. *octo* eight + *decem* ten — more at TEN] : EIGHTEENMO

oc·to·ge·nar·i·an \ˌäk-tə-jə-ˈner-ē-ən\ *n* [L *octogenarius* containing eighty, fr. *octogeni* eighty each, fr. *octoginta* eighty, fr. *octo* eight + *-ginta* (akin to *viginti* twenty) — more at VIGESIMAL] : a person who is in his eighties — **octogenarian** *adj*

oc·to·ploid *also* **oc·ta·ploid** \ˈäk-tə-ˌplȯid\ *adj* [ISV] : having a chromosome number eight times the basic haploid chromosome number — **octoploid** *n* — **oc·to·ploi·dy** \-ˌplȯid-ē\ *n*

oc·to·pod \ˈäk-tə-ˌpäd\ *n* [deriv. of Gk *oktōpod-, oktōpous* scorpion, fr. *oktō* octa- + *pod-, pous* foot — more at FOOT] : any of an order (Octopoda) of cephalopod mollusks (as an octopus or argonaut) that have eight arms bearing sessile suckers — **octopod** *adj* — **oc·top·o·dan** \äk-ˈtäp-əd-ən\ *adj or n* — **oc·top·o·dous** \-əd-əs\ *adj*

oc·to·pus \ˈäk-tə-pəs *also* -ˌpu̇s\ *n, pl* **-pus·es** *or* **-pi** \-ˌpī\ [NL *Octopod-, Octopus,* genus name, fr. Gk *oktōpous*] **1** : any of a genus (*Octopus*) of cephalopod mollusks that have eight muscular arms equipped with two rows of suckers; *broadly* : any octopod excepting the paper nautilus **2** : something that resembles an octopus esp. in having many centrally directed branches

oc·to·roon \ˌäk-tə-ˈrün\ *n* [*octa-* + *-roon* (as in *quadroon*)] : a person of one-eighth Negro ancestry

oc·to·syl·lab·ic \ˌäk-tə-sə-ˈlab-ik\ *adj* [LL *octosyllabus,* fr. Gk *oktasyllabos,* fr. *okta-* + *-syllabē* syllable] **1** : consisting of eight syllables **2** : composed of verses of eight syllables — **octosyllabic** *n*

oc·to·syl·la·ble \ˈäk-tə-ˌsil-ə-bəl, ˌäk-tə-ˈ\ *n* : a word or line of eight syllables

oc·troi \ˌäk-trə-ˈwä, äk-ˈtrwä, ˈäk-ˌtrȯi\ *n* [F] : a tax on commodities brought into a town esp. in certain European countries

OCTV *abbr* open-circuit television

ocul- *or* **oculo-** *comb form* [L *ocul-,* fr. *oculus* — more at EYE] **1** : eye <*oculo*motor> **2** : ocular and <*oculo*cardiac>

¹oc·u·lar \ˈäk-yə-lər\ *adj* [LL *ocularis* of eyes, fr. L *oculus* eye] **1 a** : done or perceived by the eye <~ inspection> **b** : based on what has been seen <~ testimony> **2 a** : of or relating to the eye <~ muscles> **b** : resembling an eye in form or function

²ocular *n* : EYEPIECE

oc·u·list \ˈäk-yə-ləst\ *n* [F *oculiste,* fr. L *oculus*] **1** : OPHTHALMOLOGIST **2** : OPTOMETRIST

oc·u·lo·mo·tor \ˌäk-yə-lə-ˈmōt-ər\ *adj* **1** : moving or tending to move the eyeball **2** : of or relating to the oculomotor nerve

oculomotor nerve *n* : either of the pair of chiefly motor nerves that comprise the 3d pair of cranial nerves, arise from the midbrain, and supply most muscles of the eye

od *or* **odd** \ˈäd\ *interj, often cap* [euphemism for *God*] *archaic* — used as a mild oath

¹OD \(ˈ)ō-ˈdē\ *n* [*over*dose] : an overdose of a narcotic

²OD *abbr* **1** doctor of optometry **2** [L *oculus dexter*] right eye **3** officer of the day **4** olive drab **5** on demand **6** outside diameter **7** outside dimension **8** overdraft **9** overdrawn

oda·lisque \ˈōd-ᵊl-ˌisk\ *n* [F, fr. Turk *odalık*] : a female slave or concubine in a harem

odd \ˈäd\ *adj* [ME *odde,* fr. ON *oddi* point of land, triangle, odd number; akin to OE *ord* point of a weapon] **1 a** : being without a corresponding mate <an ~ shoe> **b** (1) : left over after others are paired or grouped (2) : separated from a set or series **2 a** : somewhat more than the indicated approximate quantity, extent, or degree — usu. used in combination <300-*odd* pages> **b** (1) : left over as a remainder <had a few ~ dollars for entertainment after paying his bills> (2) : constituting a small amount <had some ~ change in her pocket> **3 a** : being one of the sequence of natural numbers beginning with one and counting by twos that are not divisible by two **b** : marked by an odd number of units **4** : not regular, expected, or planned <worked at ~ jobs> **5** : having an out-of-the-way location : REMOTE **6** : differing markedly from the usual or ordinary or accepted : PECULIAR — **odd·ness** *n*

odd·ball \ˈäd-ˌbȯl\ *n* : one whose behavior is eccentric — **oddball** *adj*

Odd Fellow *n* [Independent Order of *Odd Fellows*] : a member of a major benevolent and fraternal order

odd function *n* : a function whose value is changed by reversing the sign of its independent variable <the function $f(-x) = -f(x)$ is an *odd function*>

odd·i·ty \ˈäd-ət-ē\ *n, pl* **-ties** **1** : an odd person, thing, event, or trait **2** : the quality or state of being odd

odd lot *n* : a number or quantity other than the usual unit in transactions; *esp* : a quantity of less than 100 shares of stock

odd·ly \ˈäd-lē\ *adv* : in an odd manner <behaved ~>

odd man out *n* : a person who is eccentric or unorthodox

odd·ment \ˈäd-mənt\ *n* **1 a** : something left over : REMNANT **b** *pl* : ODDS AND ENDS **2** : something odd : ODDITY

odd permutation *n* : a permutation that is produced by the successive application of an odd number of interchanges of pairs of elements

odd–pin·nate \ˈäd-ˈpin-ˌāt\ *adj* : having leaflets on each side of the petiole and having a single leaflet at the tip of the petiole — **odd–pin·nate·ly** *adv*

odds \ˈädz\ *n pl but sing or pl in constr* **1 a** *archaic* : INEQUALITIES **b** *obs* : degree of unlikeness **2 a** : an amount by which one thing exceeds or falls short of another <won the election by considerable ~> **b** (1) : a difference favoring one of two opposed things <the overwhelming ~ it affords the sportsman over bird and animal — Richard Jefferies> (2) : a difference in terms of advantage or disadvantage <what's the ~, if thinking so makes them happy —Flora Thompson> **c** (1) : the probability that one thing is so or will happen rather than another : CHANCES <the ~ are against it> (2) : the ratio of the probability of one event to that of an alternative event <it is even ~ which makes the more noise —Claudia Cassidy> **3** : DISAGREEMENT, VARIANCE — usu. used with *at* <faculty and administration often are at ~ on everything —W. E. Brock *b*1930> **4 a** : special favor : PARTIALITY **b** : an allowance granted by one making a bet to one accepting the bet and designed to equalize the chances favoring one of the bettors **c** : the ratio between the amount to be paid off for a winning bet and the amount of the bet — **by all odds** : in every way : without question <*by all odds* the best book of the year>

odds and ends *n pl* **1 a** : miscellaneous articles **b** : miscellaneous small matters (as of business) to be attended to **2** : miscellaneous remnants or leftovers <*odds and ends* of food>

odds–on \(ˈ)äd-ˈzȯn, -ˈzän\ *adj* **1** : having or viewed as having a better than even chance to win <the ~ favorite> **2** : not involving much risk : pretty sure <an ~ bet>

odd trick *n* : each trick in excess of six won by declarer's side at bridge — compare BOOK 9

ode \ˈōd\ *n* [MF or LL; MF, fr. LL, fr. Gk *ōidē,* lit., song, fr. *aeidein, aidein* to sing; akin to Gk *audē* voice, OHG far*wāzan* to deny] : a lyric poem usu. marked by exaltation of feeling and style, varying length of line, and complexity of stanza forms

-ode \ˌōd\ *n comb form* [Gk *-odos,* fr. *hodos* — more at CEDE] **1** : way : path <electr*ode*> **2** : electrode <di*ode*>

ode·um \ō-ˈdē-əm, ˈōd-ē-\ *n, pl* **odea** \-ə\ [L & Gk; L, fr. Gk *ōideion,* fr. *ōidē* song] **1** : a small roofed theater of ancient Greece and Rome used chiefly for competitions in music and poetry **2** : a theater or concert hall

od·ic \ˈōd-ik\ *adj* : of, relating to, or forming an ode

Odin \ˈōd-ᵊn\ *n* [Dan, fr. ON *Óthinn;* akin to OE *Wōden* Odin] : the supreme god and creator in Norse mythology who reigned in Asgard with his wife Frigga

odi·ous \ˈōd-ē-əs\ *adj* [ME, fr. MF *odieus,* fr. L *odiosus,* fr. *odium*] : exciting or deserving hatred or repugnance <~ associates> <an ~ business> — **odi·ous·ly** *adv* — **odi·ous·ness** *n*

odi·um \ˈōd-ē-əm\ *n* [L, hatred, fr. *odisse* to hate; akin to OE *atol* terrible, Gk *odyssasthai* to be angry] **1** : the state or fact of being subjected to hatred and contempt as a result of a despicable act or blameworthy situation **2** : hatred and condemnation accompanied by loathing or contempt : DETESTATION **3** : something (as a despicable act) that excites hatred or condemnation **4** : disrepute or infamy attached to something : OPPROBRIUM

odo·graph \ˈōd-ə-ˌgraf, ˈäd-\ *n* [*odo-* (as in *odometer*) + *-graph*] : an instrument for automatically plotting (as on a map) the course and distance traveled by a vehicle
odom·e·ter \ō-ˈdäm-ət-ər\ *n* [F *odomètre,* fr. Gk *hodometron,* fr. *hodos* way, road + *metron* measure — more at CEDE, MEASURE] : an instrument for measuring the distance traveled (as by a vehicle)
odo·nate \ˈōd-ᵊn-ˌāt, ō-ˈdän-\ *n* [irreg. deriv. of Gk *odous, odōn* tooth] : any of an order (Odonata) of predacious insects comprising the dragonflies and damselflies — **odonate** *adj*
odont- *or* **odonto-** *comb form* [F, fr. Gk, *odont-, odous* — more at TOOTH] : tooth <*odont*itis> <*odonto*blast>
-odont \ə-ˌdänt\ *adj comb form* [Gk *odont-, odous* tooth] : having teeth of a (specified) nature <mes*odont*>
-odon·tia \ə-ˈdän-ch(ē-)ə\ *n comb form* [NL, fr. Gk *odont-, odous*] : form, condition, or mode of treatment of the teeth <orth*odontia*>
odon·to·blast \ō-ˈdänt-ə-ˌblast\ *n* [ISV] : one of the elongated radially arranged outer cells of the dental pulp that secrete dentin — **odon·to·blas·tic** \-ˌdänt-ə-ˈblas-tik\ *adj*
odon·to·glos·sum \ō-ˌdänt-ə-ˈgläs-əm\ *n* [NL, genus name, fr. *odont-* + Gk *glōssa* tongue — more at GLOSS] : any of a genus (*Odontoglossum*) of widely cultivated tropical American epiphytic orchids
odon·toid process \ō-ˌdän-ˌtȯid-\ *n* : a toothlike process projecting from the anterior end of the centrum of the axis vertebra on which the atlas vertebra rotates
odon·tol·o·gy \(ˌ)ō-ˌdän-ˈtäl-ə-jē\ *n* [F *odontologie,* fr. *odont-* + *-logie* -logy] : a science dealing with the teeth, their structure and development, and their diseases — **odon·to·log·i·cal** \-ˌdänt-ᵊl-ˈäj-i-kəl\ *adj* — **odon·tol·o·gist** \-ˌdän-ˈtäl-ə-jəst\ *n*
odor \ˈōd-ər\ *n* [ME *odour,* fr. OF, fr. L *odor;* akin to L *olēre* to smell, Gk *ozein* to smell, *osmē* smell, odor] **1 a :** a quality of something that stimulates the olfactory organ **b :** a sensation resulting from adequate stimulation of the olfactory organ : SMELL **2 a :** a characteristic or predominant quality : FLAVOR <the ~ of sanctity> **b :** REPUTE, ESTIMATION <in bad ~> **3** *archaic* : something that emits a sweet or pleasing scent : PERFUME *syn* see SMELL — **odored** \ˈōd-ərd\ *adj*
odor·ant \ˈōd-ə-rənt\ *n* : an odorous substance; *esp* : one added to a dangerous odorless substance to warn of its presence
odor·if·er·ous \ˌōd-ə-ˈrif-(ə-)rəs\ *adj* **1 :** yielding an odor : ODOROUS **2 :** morally offensive — **odor·if·er·ous·ly** *adv* — **odor·if·er·ous·ness** *n*
odor·ize \ˈōd-ə-ˌrīz\ *vt* **-ized; -iz·ing :** to make odorous : SCENT
odor·less \ˈōd-ər-ləs\ *adj* : free of odor
odor·ous \ˈōd-ə-rəs\ *adj* : having an odor: as **a :** FRAGRANT **b :** MALODOROUS — **odor·ous·ly** *adv* — **odor·ous·ness** *n*
odour *chiefly Brit var of* ODOR
Odys·se·an \ō-ˈdis-ē-ən ("*Odysseus*"), ˌäd-ə-ˈsē-ən ("*journey*")\ *adj* : of, relating to, or characteristic of Odysseus or his journey
Odys·seus \ō-ˈdish-ˌüs, -ˈdis-ˌyüs, -ˈdis-ē-əs\ *n* [Gk] : a king of Ithaca and Greek leader in the Trojan War who after the war wandered 10 years before reaching home
od·ys·sey \ˈäd-ə-sē\ *n, pl* **-seys** [the *Odyssey,* epic poem attributed to Homer recounting the long wanderings of Odysseus] **1 :** a long wandering or voyage usu. marked by many changes of fortune **2 :** an intellectual or spiritual wandering or quest
Oe *abbr* oersted
OE *abbr* Old English
OECD *abbr* Organization for Economic Cooperation and Development
oe·cu·men·i·cal *esp Brit* ˌēk-\ *var of* ECUMENICAL
OED *abbr* Oxford English Dictionary
oe·de·ma *var of* EDEMA
oe·di·pal \ˈed-ə-pəl, ˈēd-\ *adj, often cap* : of or relating to the Oedipus complex — **oe·di·pal·ly** \-pə-lē\ *adv, often cap*
1Oe·di·pus \-pəs\ *n* [L, fr. Gk *Oidipous*] : a son of Laius and Jocasta who in fulfillment of an oracle kills his father and marries his mother
2Oedipus *adj* : OEDIPAL
Oedipus complex *n* : the positive libidinal feelings that a child develops toward the parent of the opposite sex and that may be a source of adult personality disorder when unresolved
oeil–de–boeuf \ˌə(r)d-ə-ˈbəf, ˌəid-\ *n, pl* **oeils–de–boeuf** *same*\ [F, lit., ox's eye] : a circular or oval window
oeil·lade \ˌə(r)-ˈyäd, œ-yäd\ *n* [F, fr. MF, fr. *oeil* eye, fr. L *oculus* — more at EYE] : a glance of the eye; *esp* : OGLE
oe·nol·o·gy *var of* ENOLOGY
oe·no·mel \ˈē-nə-ˌmel\ *n* [LL *oenomeli,* fr. Gk *oinomeli,* fr. *oinos* wine + *meli* honey — more at WINE, MELLIFLUOUS] : an ancient Greek beverage of wine and honey
Oe·no·ne \ē-ˈnō-nē\ *n* [L, fr. Gk *Oinōnē*] : a nymph who loves Paris and is deserted by him for Helen
OEO *abbr* Office of Economic Opportunity
1o'er \ˈō(ə)r, ˈȯ(ə)r\ *adv* : OVER
2o'er \(ˈ)ō(ə)r, (ˈ)ȯ(ə)r\ *prep* : OVER
Oer·li·kon \ˈər-li-ˌkän\ *n* [*Oerlikon,* Switzerland] : any of several 20 mm. automatic aircraft and antiaircraft cannon
oer·sted \ˈər-stəd\ *n* [Hans Christian *Oersted* †1851 Dan physicist] : the cgs electromagnetic unit of magnetic intensity equal to the intensity of a magnetic field in a vacuum in which a unit magnetic pole experiences a mechanical force of one dyne in the direction of the field
OES *abbr* Order of the Eastern Star
oe·soph·a·gus *var of* ESOPHAGUS
oestr- *or* **oestro-** — see ESTR-
oeu·vre \œvrᵊ\ *n, pl* **oeuvres** *same*\ [F *œuvre,* lit., work, fr. L *opera* — more at OPERA] : a substantial body of work constituting the lifework of a writer, an artist, or a composer
of \əv, *before consonants also* ə; ˈəv, ˈäv\ *prep* [ME, off, of, fr. OE, adv. & prep.; akin to OHG *aba* off, away, L *ab* from, away, Gk *apo*] **1** — used as a function word to indicate a point of reckoning <north ~ the lake> **2 a** — used as a function word to indicate origin or derivation <a man ~ noble birth> **b** — used as a function word to indicate the cause, motive, or reason <died ~ flu> **c :** BY <plays ~ Shakespeare> **d :** on the part of <very kind ~ him> **3** — used as a function word to indicate the component material, parts, or elements or the contents <throne ~ gold> <cup ~ water> **4 a** — used as a function word to indicate the whole that includes the part denoted by the preceding word <most ~ the army> **b** — used as a function word to indicate a whole or quantity from which a part is removed or expended <gave ~ his time> **5 a :** relating to : ABOUT <stories ~ his travels> **b :** in respect to <slow ~ speech> **6** — used as a function word to indicate belonging or a possessive relationship <king ~ England> **7** — used as a function word to indicate separation <eased ~ pain> **8 a** — used as a function word to indicate a particular example belonging to the class denoted by the preceding noun <the city ~ Rome> **b** — used as a function word to indicate apposition <that fool ~ a husband> **9 a** — used as a function word to indicate the object of an action denoted or implied by the preceding noun <love ~ nature> **b** — used as a function word to indicate the application of a verb <cheats him ~ a dollar> or of an adjective <fond ~ candy> **10** — used as a function word to indicate a characteristic or distinctive quality or possession <a man ~ courage> **11 a** — used as a function word to indicate the position in time of an action or occurrence <died ~ a Monday> **b :** BEFORE <quarter ~ ten> **12** *archaic* : ON <a plague ~ all cowards —Shak.>
OF *abbr* outfield
ofay \ˈō-ˌfā, ō-ˈ\ *n* [origin unknown] : a white person — usu. used disparagingly
1off \ˈȯf\ *adv* [ME *of,* fr. OE — more at OF] **1 a (1) :** from a place or position <march ~>; *specif* : away from land <ship stood ~ to sea> **(2) :** at a distance in space or time <stood 10 paces ~> <a long way ~> **b :** from a course : ASIDE <turned ~ into a bypath>; *specif* : away from the wind **c :** into an unconscious state <dozed ~> **2 a :** so as to be separated from support <rolled to the edge of the table and ~> or close contact <blew the lid ~> <the handle came ~> **b :** so as to be divided <surface marked ~ into squares> **3 a :** to a state of discontinuance or suspension <shut ~ an engine> **b** — used as an intensifier <drink ~ a glass> <finish it ~> **4 :** in absence from or suspension of regular work or service <take time ~ for lunch> **5 :** OFFSTAGE **6 :** to a state of relief resulting from or as if from orgasm
2off \(ˈ)ȯf\ *prep* **1 a** — used as a function word to indicate physical separation or distance from a position of rest, attachment, or union <take it ~ the table> <a path ~ the main walk> <a shop just ~ the main street> **b :** to seaward of <two miles ~ shore> **2 a** — used as a function word to indicate the object of an action <borrowed a dollar ~ him> <dined ~ oysters> **3 a** — used as a function word to indicate the suspension of an occupation or activity <~ duty> <~ liquor> **b :** below the usual standard or level of <~ his game>
3off \(ˈ)ȯf\ *adj* **1 a :** more removed or distant <the ~ side of the building> **b :** SEAWARD **c :** RIGHT **2 a :** started on the way <~ on a spree> **b :** not taking place or staying in effect : CANCELED **c :** not operating **d :** not placed so as to permit operation **3 a :** not corresponding to fact : INCORRECT <~ in his reckoning> **b :** POOR, SUBNORMAL **c :** not entirely sane : ECCENTRIC **d :** REMOTE, SLIGHT <an ~ chance> **4 a :** spent off duty <reading on his ~ days> **b :** SLACK <~ season> **5 a :** OFF-COLOR **b :** INFERIOR <~ grade of oil>; *also* : affected with putrefaction **c :** DOWN <stocks were ~> **6 :** CIRCUMSTANCED <well ~>
4off \ˈȯf\ *vi* : to go away : DEPART — used chiefly as an imperative <~, or I'll shoot>
5off *abbr* office; officer; official
of·fal \ˈȯ-fəl, ˈäf-əl\ *n* [ME, fr. *of* off + *fall*] **1 :** the waste or by-product of a process: as **a :** trimmings of a hide **b :** the by-products of milling used esp. for stock feeds **c :** the viscera and trimmings of a butchered animal removed in dressing **2 :** RUBBISH
off and on *adv* : with periodic cessation : INTERMITTENTLY <rained *off and on* all day>
1off·beat \ˈȯf-ˌbēt\ *n* : the unaccented beat of a musical measure
2offbeat *adj* : ECCENTRIC, UNCONVENTIONAL
off Broadway *n, often cap O* [fr. its usu. being produced in smaller theaters outside of the Broadway theatrical district] : a part of the New York professional theater stressing fundamental and artistic values and formerly engaging in experimentation
off·cast \ˈȯf-ˌkast\ *adj* : cast off : DISCARDED — **offcast** *n*
off–col·or \ˈȯf-ˈkəl-ər\ *or* **off–col·ored** \-ərd\ *adj* **1 a :** not having the right or standard color **b :** being out of sorts **2 a :** of doubtful propriety : DUBIOUS **b :** verging on the indecent
of·fend \ə-ˈfend\ *vb* [ME *offenden,* fr. MF *offendre,* fr. L *offendere* to strike against, offend, fr. *ob-* against + *-fendere* to strike — more at OB-, DEFEND] *vi* **1 a :** to transgress the moral or divine law : SIN <if it be a sin to covet honor, I am the most ~*ing* soul alive —Shak.> **b :** to violate a law or rule : do wrong <~ against the law> **2 a :** to cause difficulty, discomfort, or injury <took off his shoe and removed the ~*ing* pebble> **b :** to cause dislike, anger, or vexation <thoughtless words that ~ needlessly> ~ *vt* **1 a :** VIOLATE, TRANSGRESS **b :** to cause pain to : HURT **2** *obs* : to cause to sin or fall **3 :** to cause to feel vexation or resentment usu. by violation of what is proper or fitting <she was ~*ed* by their failure to introduce her to their new friend> — **of·fend·er** *n*
syn OFFEND, OUTRAGE, AFFRONT, INSULT *shared meaning element* : to cause hurt feelings or deep resentment
of·fense *or* **of·fence** \ə-ˈfen(t)s, *esp for 3* ˈäf-ˌen(t)s\ *n* [ME, fr. MF, fr. L *offensa,* fr. *offensus,* pp. of *offendere*] **1 a** *obs* : an act of stumbling **b** *archaic* : a cause or occasion of sin : STUMBLING BLOCK **2 :** something that outrages the moral or physical senses <corruption in high places that was an ~ to the public conscience> **3 a :** the act of attacking : ASSAULT **b :** the means or method of attacking or of attempting to score **c :** the offensive team or members of a team playing offensive positions **d :** scoring ability **4 a :** the act of displeasing or affronting **b :** the state of being insulted or morally outraged <he takes ~ at the slightest criticism>

5 a : a breach of a moral or social code **:** SIN, MISDEED **b :** an infraction of law; *esp* **:** MISDEMEANOR — **of·fense·less** \-ləs\ *adj*
***syn* 1** OFFENSE, RESENTMENT, UMBRAGE, PIQUE, DUDGEON, HUFF *shared meaning element* **:** an emotional response to a slight or indignity
2 OFFENSE, SIN, VICE, CRIME, SCANDAL *shared meaning element* **:** a transgression of law or custom

[1]of·fen·sive \ə-ˈfen(t)-siv *esp for 1* ˈäf-ˌen(t)-\ *adj* **1 a :** making attack **:** AGGRESSIVE **b :** of, relating to, or designed for attack <~ weapons> **c :** of or relating to an attempt to score in a game or contest; *also* **:** of or relating to a team in possession of the ball or puck **2 :** giving painful or unpleasant sensations **:** NAUSEOUS, OBNOXIOUS <~ odor of garbage> **3 :** causing displeasure or resentment — **of·fen·sive·ly** *adv* — **of·fen·sive·ness** *n*

[2]offensive *n* **1 :** the act of an attacking party **2 :** ATTACK

[1]of·fer \ˈȯf-ər, ˈäf-\ *vb* **of·fered; of·fer·ing** \-(ə-)riŋ\ [ME *offren*, in sense 1, fr. OE *offrian*, fr. LL *offerre*, fr. L, to present, tender, fr. *ob-* toward + *ferre* to carry; in other senses, fr. OF *offrir*, fr. L *offerre* — more at OB-, BEAR] *vt* **1 a :** to present as an act of worship or devotion **:** SACRIFICE **b :** to utter (as a prayer) in devotion **2 a :** to present for acceptance or rejection **:** TENDER <was ~*ed* a job> **b :** to present in order to satisfy a requirement <candidates for degrees may ~ French as one of their foreign languages> **3 a :** PROPOSE, SUGGEST <~ a solution to a problem> **b :** to declare one's readiness or willingness <~*ed* to help me> **4 a :** to put up <~*ed* stubborn resistance> **b :** THREATEN <~*ed* to strike him with his cane> **5 :** to make available **:** AFFORD; *esp* **:** to place (merchandise) on sale **6 :** to present in performance or exhibition **7 :** to propose as payment **:** BID ~ *vi* **1 :** to present something as an act of worship or devotion **:** SACRIFICE **2** *archaic* **:** to make an attempt **3 :** to present itself **4 :** to make a proposal (as of marriage)

[2]offer *n* **1 a :** PROPOSAL <considering job ~*s* from several firms>; *specif* **:** a proposal of marriage **b :** an undertaking to do an act or give something on condition that the party to whom the proposal is made do some specified act or make a return promise **2** *obs* **:** OFFERING **3 :** a price named by one proposing to buy **:** BID **4 a :** ATTEMPT, TRY **b :** an action or movement indicating a purpose or intention

of·fer·ing \ˈȯf-(ə-)riŋ, ˈäf-\ *n* **1 a :** the act of one who offers **b :** something offered; *esp* **:** a sacrifice ceremonially offered as a part of worship **c :** a contribution to the support of a church **2 :** something offered for sale or patronage <latest ~*s* of the leading novelists> **3 :** a course of instruction or study

of·fer·to·ry \ˈȯf-ə(r)-ˌtōr-ē, ˈäf-, -ˌtȯr-\ *n, pl* **-ries** [ML *offertorium*, fr. *offertus*, pp. of LL *offerre*] **1** *often cap* **a :** the eucharistic offering of bread and wine to God before they are consecrated at Communion **b :** a verse from a Psalm said or sung at the beginning of the offertory **2 a :** the period of collection and presentation of the offerings of the congregation at public worship **b :** a musical composition played or sung during an offertory

off·hand \ˈȯf-ˈhand\ *adv or adj* **1 :** without premeditation or preparation **:** EXTEMPORE <couldn't give the figures ~> **2 :** from a standing position without a support or rest <~ shooting>

off·hand·ed \-ˈhan-dəd\ *adj* **:** OFFHAND — **off·hand·ed·ly** *adv* — **off·hand·ed·ness** *n*

off-hour \ˈȯf-ˌau̇(-ə)r\ *n* **1 :** a period of time other than a rush hour **2 :** a period of time other than regular business hours

offic *abbr* official

of·fice \ˈȯf-əs, ˈäf-\ *n* [ME, fr. OF, fr. L *officium* service, duty, office, fr. *opus* work + *facere* to make, do — more at OPERATE, DO] **1 a :** a special duty, charge, or position conferred by an exercise of governmental authority and for a public purpose **:** a position of authority to exercise a public function and to receive whatever emoluments may belong to it <hold public ~> **b :** a position of responsibility or some degree of executive authority **2** [ME, fr. OF, fr. LL *officium*, fr. L] **:** a prescribed form or service of worship; *specif, cap* **:** DIVINE OFFICE **3 :** a religious or social ceremonial observance **:** RITE **4 a :** something that one ought to do or must do **:** an assigned or assumed duty, task, or role **b :** the proper or customary action of something **:** FUNCTION **5 :** a place where a particular kind of business is transacted or a service is supplied: as **a :** a place in which the functions (as consulting, record keeping, clerical work) of a public officer are performed **b :** the directing headquarters of an enterprise or organization **c :** the place in which a professional man (as a physician or lawyer) conducts his professional business **6** *pl, chiefly Brit* **:** the apartments, attached buildings, or outhouses in which the activities attached to the service of a house are carried on **7 a :** a major administrative unit in some governments <British Foreign *Office*> **b :** a subdivision of some government departments <Patent *Office*> ***syn*** see FUNCTION

office boy *n* **:** a boy employed for odd jobs in a business office

of·fice·hold·er \-ˌhōl-dər\ *n* **:** one holding a public office esp. in the civil service

[1]of·fi·cer \ˈȯf-ə-sər, ˈäf-\ *n* [ME, fr. MF *officier*, fr. ML *officiarius*, fr. L *officium*] **1 a** *obs* **:** AGENT **b :** one charged with police duties **2 :** one who holds an office of trust, authority, or command <the ~*s* of the bank> **3 a :** one who holds a position of authority or command in the armed forces; *specif* **:** COMMISSIONED OFFICER **b :** the master or any of the mates of a merchant or passenger ship

[2]officer *vt* **1 :** to furnish with officers **2 :** to command or direct as an officer

officer of arms : any of the officers (as king of arms, herald, or pursuivant) of a monarch or government responsible for devising and granting armorial bearings

[1]of·fi·cial \ə-ˈfish-əl\ *n* **1 :** one who holds or is invested with an office **:** OFFICER <government ~*s*> **2 :** one who administers the rules of a game or sport esp. as a referee or umpire

[2]official *adj* **1 :** of or relating to an office, position, or trust <~ duties> **2 :** holding an office **3 a :** AUTHORITATIVE, AUTHORIZED <~ statement> **b :** prescribed or recognized as authorized; *specif* **:** described by the U.S. Pharmacopeia or the National Formulary **4 :** befitting or characteristic of a person in office **:** FORMAL <was extended an ~ greeting> — **of·fi·cial·ly** \-ˈfish-(ə-)lē\ *adv*

of·fi·cial·dom \ə-ˈfish-əl-dəm\ *n* **:** officials as a class

of·fi·cial·ese \ə-ˌfish-ə-ˈlēz, -ˈlēs\ *n* **:** the characteristic language of official statements **:** wordy, pompous, or obscure language

official family *n* **:** a group of top officials (as a cabinet) in an organization or government **:** STAFF

of·fi·cial·ism \ə-ˈfish-ə-ˌliz-əm\ *n* **:** lack of flexibility and initiative combined with excessive adherence to regulations in the behavior of usu. government officials

of·fi·ci·ant \ə-ˈfish-ē-ənt\ *n* **:** one (as a priest) that officiates at a religious rite

[1]of·fi·ci·ary \ə-ˈfish-ē-ˌer-ē, ȯ-, ä-\ *n, pl* **-ar·ies** [ML *officiarius*] **1 :** OFFICER, OFFICIAL **2 :** a body of officers or officials

[2]officiary *adj* **:** connected with, derived from, or having a title or rank by virtue of holding an office <~ earl>

of·fi·ci·ate \ə-ˈfish-ē-ˌāt\ *vb* **-at·ed; -at·ing** *vi* **1 :** to perform a ceremony, function, or duty <~ at a wedding> **2 :** to act in an official capacity **:** act as an official (as at a sports contest) ~ *vt* **1 :** to carry out (an official duty or function) **2 :** to serve as a leader or celebrant of (a ceremony) **3 :** to administer the rules of (a game or sport) esp. as a referee or umpire — **of·fi·ci·a·tion** \-ˌfish-ē-ˈā-shən\ *n*

of·fi·ci·nal \ə-ˈfis-ᵊn-əl, ȯ-, ä-; ˌȯf-ə-ˈsīn-ᵊl, ˌäf-\ *adj* [ML *officinalis* of a storeroom, fr. *officina* storeroom, fr. L, workshop, fr. *opific-, opifex* workman, fr. *opus* work + *facere* to do] **1 :** available without special preparation or compounding <~ medicine>; *also* **:** OFFICIAL 3b **2 :** MEDICINAL <~ herbs> — **officinal** *n* — **of·fi·ci·nal·ly** \-ē\ *adv*

of·fi·cious \ə-ˈfish-əs\ *adj* [L *officiosus*, fr. *officium* service, office] **1** *archaic* **a :** KIND, OBLIGING **b :** DUTIFUL **2 :** volunteering one's services where they are neither asked nor needed **:** MEDDLESOME **3 :** INFORMAL, UNOFFICIAL ***syn*** see IMPERTINENT — **of·fi·cious·ly** *adv* — **of·fi·cious·ness** *n*

off·ing \ˈȯf-iŋ, ˈäf-\ *n* [[1]*off*] **1 :** the part of the deep sea seen from the shore **2 :** the near or foreseeable future

off·ish \ˈȯf-ish\ *adj* [[1]*off*] **:** inclined to stand aloof — **off·ish·ly** *adv* — **off·ish·ness** *n*

off-key \ˈȯf-ˈkē\ *adj* **1 :** varying in pitch from the proper tone of a melody **2 :** IRREGULAR, ANOMALOUS

off limits *adj* **:** not to be entered or patronized by a designated class (as military personnel, students, or athletes in training)

off-line \ˈȯ-ˈflīn\ *adj* **1 :** not controlled directly by a computer <~ equipment> **2 :** of, relating to, or being a cryptographic system in which encryption and decryption are accomplished independently of telecommunication machines — compare ON-LINE

off-load \ȯ-ˈflōd\ *vb* **:** UNLOAD

off of *prep* **:** OFF

off-off-Broadway *n, often cap both Os* [fr. its relation to off Broadway being analogous to the relation of off Broadway to Broadway] **:** an avant-garde theatrical movement in New York that stresses untraditional techniques and radical experimentation — called also *OOB*

off·print \ˈȯf-ˌprint\ *n* **:** a separately printed excerpt (as a magazine article) — **offprint** *vt*

off·scour·ing \-ˌskau̇(-ə)r-iŋ\ *n* **1 :** something that is scoured off **:** REFUSE **2 :** someone rejected by society **:** OUTCAST

off·screen \ˈȯf-ˈskrēn\ *adv or adj* **1 :** out of sight of the motion-picture or television viewer **2 :** in private life

off-sea·son \ˈȯf-ˌsēz-ᵊn\ *n* **:** a time of suspended or reduced activity

[1]off·set \ˈȯf-ˌset\ *n* **1 a** *archaic* **:** OUTSET, START **b :** CESSATION **2 a (1) :** a short prostrate lateral shoot arising from the base of a plant **(2) :** a small bulb arising from the base of another bulb **b :** a lateral or collateral branch (as of a family or race) **:** OFFSHOOT **c :** a spur from a range of hills **3 a :** a horizontal ledge on the face of a wall formed by a diminution of its thickness above **b :** DISPLACEMENT **c :** an abrupt change in the dimension or profile of an object or the part set off by such change **4 :** something that sets off to advantage or embellishes something else **:** FOIL **5 :** an abrupt bend in an object by which one part is turned aside out of line **6 :** something that serves to counterbalance or to compensate for something else; *specif* **:** either of two balancing ledger items **7 a :** unintentional transfer of ink (as from a freshly printed sheet) **b :** a printing process in which an inked impression from a plate is first made on a rubber-blanketed cylinder and then transferred to the paper being printed — **offset** *adj or adv*

[2]off·set \ˈȯf-ˌset, *vt senses are also* ȯf-ˈ\ *vb* **-set; -set·ting** *vt* **1 a :** to place over against **:** BALANCE <credits ~ debits> **b :** to serve as a counterbalance for **:** COMPENSATE <his speed ~ his opponent's greater weight> **2 :** to form an offset in <~ a wall> ~ *vi* **:** to become marked by offset ***syn*** see COMPENSATE

off·shoot \ˈȯf-ˌshüt\ *n* **1 :** a branch of a main stem esp. of a plant **2 a :** a lateral branch (as of a mountain range) **b :** a collateral or derived branch, descendant, or member **:** OUTGROWTH

[1]off·shore \ˈȯf-ˈshō(ə)r, -ˈshȯ(ə)r\ *adv* **:** from the shore **:** at a distance from the shore

[2]off·shore \ˈȯf-ˌ\ *adj* **1 :** coming or moving away from the shore <an ~ breeze> **2 a :** situated off the shore within a zone extending three miles from low-water line <~ fisheries> **b :** distant from the shore

off·side \ˈȯf-ˈsīd\ *adv or adj* **:** illegally in advance of the ball or puck

off-speed \-ˈspēd\ *adj* **:** being slower than usual or expected <throwing ~ pitches>

off·spring \ˈȯf-ˌspriŋ\ *n, pl* **offspring** *also* **offsprings** [ME *ofspring,* fr. OE, fr. *of* off + *springan* to spring] **1 :** the progeny of an animal or plant : YOUNG **2 :** PRODUCT, RESULT
off·stage \ˈȯf-ˈstāj, -ˌstāj\ *adv or adj* **1 :** on a part of the stage not visible to the audience **2 :** in private life <known ~ as a kindly man> **3 :** behind the scenes : out of the public view <much of the important work of the conference was done ~>
off–the–record *adj* : given or made in confidence and not for publication <~ comments>
off–the–shelf *adj* : available as a stock item : not specially designed or custom-made
off–white \ˈȯf-ˈhwīt, -ˈwīt\ *n* : a yellowish or grayish white
off year *n* **1 :** a year in which no major election is held **2 :** a year of diminished activity or production <an *off year* for auto sales>
OFM *abbr* Order of Friars Minor
OFS *abbr* Orange Free State
oft \ˈȯft\ *adv* [ME, fr. OE; akin to OHG *ofto* often] : OFTEN
of·ten \ˈȯf-(t)ən\ *adv* [ME, alter. of *oft*] : many times
of·ten·times \-ˌtīmz\ *or* **oft·times** \ˈȯf(t)-ˌtīmz\ *adv* : time and again : OFTEN
OG *abbr* **1** officer of the guard **2** original gum
O gauge \ˈō-\ *n* [²*oh*] : a gauge of track in model railroading in which the rails are approximately 1¼ inches apart
ogee *also* **OG** \ˈō-ˌjē\ *n* [obs. E *ogee* (ogive); fr. the use of such moldings in ogives] **1 :** a molding with an S-shaped profile **2 :** a pointed arch having on each side a reversed curve near the apex — see ARCH illustration
ogham *or* **ogam** \ˈō(-ə)m; ˈäg-əm, ˈōg-\ *n* [IrGael *ogham,* fr. MIr *ogom, ogum*] : the alphabetic system of 5th and 6th century Old Irish in which an alphabet of 20 letters is represented by notches for vowels and lines for consonants and which is known principally from inscriptions cut on the edges of rough standing tombstones — **ogham·ic** \ˈō-(ə-)mik; ä-ˈgäm-ik, ō-\ *adj* — **ogham·ist** \ˈō-(ə-)məst; ˈäg-ə-məst, ˈōg-\ *n*

n q r i s c z e f t ng u l d g o b h m a
ogham

ogi·val \ō-ˈjī-vəl\ *adj* : of, relating to, or having the form of an ogive or an ogee
ogive \ˈō-ˌjīv\ *n* [F] **1 a :** a diagonal arch or rib across a Gothic vault **b :** a pointed arch **2 :** a graph each of whose ordinates represents the sum of all the frequencies up to and including a corresponding frequency in a frequency distribution **3 :** OGEE 1
¹ogle \ˈōg-əl *also* ˈäg-\ *vb* **ogled; ogling** \-(ə-)liŋ\ [prob. fr. LG *oegeln,* fr. *oog* eye; akin to OHG *ouga* eye — more at EYE] *vi* : to glance with amorous invitation or challenge ~ *vt* : to eye amorously or provocatively — **ogler** \-(ə-)lər\ *n*
²ogle *n* : an amorous or coquettish glance
ogre \ˈō-gər\ *n* [F] **1 :** a hideous giant of fairy tales and folklore that feeds on human beings : MONSTER **2 :** a dreaded person or object — **ogre·ish** \ˈō-g(ə-)rish\ *adj* — **ogress** \ˈō-g(ə-)rəs\ *n*
¹oh \(ˈ)ō\ *interj* [ME *o*] **1** — used to express an emotion (as astonishment, pain, or desire) **2** — used in direct address <*Oh,* porter! Will you come here, please?> **3** — used to express acknowledgment or understanding of a statement
²oh \ˈō\ *n* [*o;* fr. the similarity of the symbol for zero (0) to the letter *O*] : ZERO
OH *abbr* Ohio
ohia \ō-ˈhē-ə\ *n* [Hawaiian *ʻōhiʻa*] : LEHUA
ohia lehua *n* [Hawaiian *ʻōhiʻa-lehua*] : LEHUA
ohm \ˈōm\ *n* [Georg Simon *Ohm*] : the practical mks unit of electric resistance equal to the resistance of a circuit in which a potential difference of one volt produces a current of one ampere — **ohm·ic** \ˈō-mik\ *adj* — **ohm·i·cal·ly** \-mi-k(ə-)lē\ *adv*
ohm·age \ˈō-mij\ *n* : the ohmic resistance of a conductor
ohm·me·ter \ˈō(m)-ˌmēt-ər\ *n* [ISV] : an instrument for indicating resistance in ohms directly
OHMS *abbr* on her majesty's service; on his majesty's service
-o·ic \ˈō-ik\ *adj suffix* [*-o-* + *-ic*] : containing carboxyl or a derivative <decan*oic* acid>
¹-oid \ˌȯid\ *n suffix* : something resembling a (specified) object or having a (specified) quality <glob*oid*>
²-oid *adj suffix* [MF & L; MF *-oïde,* fr. L *-oides,* fr. Gk *-oeidēs,* fr. *-o-* + *eidos* appearance, form — more at WISE] : resembling : having the form or appearance of <petal*oid*>
oid·i·um \ō-ˈid-ē-əm\ *n, pl* **-ia** \-ē-ə\ [NL, fr. *o-* + *-idium*] **1 a :** any of a genus (*Oidium* of the family Moniliaceae) of imperfect fungi many of which are now considered to be conidial stages of various powdery mildews **b :** one of the small conidia borne in chains by various fungi (as an oidium) — called also *arthrospore* **2 :** a powdery mildew caused by an oidium esp. in the grape
¹oil \ˈȯi(ə)l\ *n* [ME *oile,* fr. OF, fr. L *oleum* olive oil, fr. Gk *elaion,* fr. *elaia* olive] **1 a :** any of numerous unctuous combustible substances that are liquid or at least easily liquefiable on warming, are soluble in ether but not in water, and leave a greasy stain on paper or cloth **b :** PETROLEUM **2 :** a substance (as a cosmetic preparation) of oily consistency <bath ~> **3 a :** an oil color used by an artist **b :** a painting done in oil colors **4 :** unctuous or flattering speech — **oil** *adj*
²oil *vt* : to smear, rub over, furnish, or lubricate with oil ~ *vi* : to take on fuel oil — **oil the hand** *or* **oil the palm :** BRIBE, TIP
oil beetle *n* : a blister beetle (*Meloe* or a related genus) that emits a yellowish liquid from the leg joints when disturbed
oil·bird \ˈȯi(ə)l-ˌbərd\ *n* : a nocturnal bird (*Steatornis caripensis*) of northern So. America and Trinidad that is related to the goatsuckers, feeds chiefly on the fatty fruits of various palms, and has fatty young from which oil is extracted for use instead of butter — called also *guacharo*
oil cake *n* : the solid residue after extracting the oil from seeds (as of cotton)
oil·can \ˈȯi(ə)l-ˌkan\ *n* : a can for oil; *esp* : a spouted can designed to release oil drop by drop (as for lubricating machinery)
oil·cloth \-ˌklȯth\ *n* : cloth treated with oil or paint and used for table and shelf coverings
oil color *n* **1 :** a pigment used for oil paint **2 :** OIL PAINT
oiled \ˈȯi(ə)ld\ *adj* **1 :** lubricated or treated with or as if with oil <~ paper> **2** *slang* : DRUNK
oil·er \ˈȯi-lər\ *n* **1 :** one (as a workman) that oils something **2 :** a receptacle or device for applying oil **3 :** a producing oil well **4 a :** a ship using oil as fuel **b :** an oil-cargo ship : TANKER **5** *pl* : OILSKINS
oil field *n* : a region rich in petroleum deposits; *esp* : one that has been brought into production
oil gland *n* : a gland (as of the skin) that produces an oily secretion; *specif* : UROPYGIAL GLAND
oil of turpentine : TURPENTINE 2a
oil of vitriol : concentrated sulfuric acid
oil of wintergreen : the methyl ester of salicylic acid that is used as a flavoring and as a counterirritant
oil paint *n* : paint in which a drying oil is the vehicle
oil painting *n* **1 a :** the act or art of painting in oil colors **b :** a picture painted in oils **2 :** painting that uses pigments orig. ground in oil
oil palm *n* : an African pinnate-leaved palm (*Elaeis guineensis*) that is cultivated for its clustered fruit whose flesh and seeds yield palm oil
oil pan *n* : the lower section of the crankcase used as a lubricating oil reservoir on an internal-combustion engine
oil·seed \ˈȯi(ə)l-ˌsēd\ *n* : a seed or crop (as linseed) grown largely for oil
oil shale *n* : shale from which oil can be recovered by distillation
oil·skin \ˈȯi(ə)l-ˌskin\ *n* **1 :** an oiled waterproof cloth used for coverings and garments **2 :** an oilskin raincoat **3** *pl* : an oilskin suit of coat and trousers
oil slick *n* : a film of oil floating on water
oil·stone \ˈȯi(ə)l-ˌstōn\ *n* : a whetstone for use with oil
oil well *n* : a well from which petroleum is obtained
oily \ˈȯi-lē\ *adj* **oil·i·er; -est 1 :** of, relating to, or consisting of oil **2 :** covered or impregnated with oil : GREASY <~ rags> **3 :** excessively smooth or suave in manner : UNCTUOUS, INGRATIATING — **oil·i·ly** \ˈȯi-lə-lē\ *adv* — **oil·i·ness** \-lē-nəs\ *n*
oink \ˈȯiŋk\ *n* [imit.] : the natural noise of a hog — **oink** *vi*
oint·ment \ˈȯint-mənt\ *n* [ME, alter. of *oignement,* fr. OF, modif. of L *unguentum,* fr. *unguere* to anoint; akin to OHG *ancho* butter, Skt *añjati* he salves] : a salve or unguent for application to the skin
OIT *abbr* Office of International Trade
oi·ti·ci·ca \ˌȯit-ə-ˈsē-kə\ *n* [Pg, fr. Tupi] : any of several So. American trees; *esp* : a Brazilian tree (*Licania rigida*) with seeds that yield a drying oil similar to tung oil
Ojib·wa *or* **Ojib·way** \ō-ˈjib-(ˌ)wā\ *n, pl* **Ojibwa** *or* **Ojibwas** *or* **Ojibway** *or* **Ojibways** [Ojibwa *ojib-ubway,* a kind of moccasin worn by the Ojibwa] **1 :** a member of an Amerindian people orig. of Michigan **2 :** an Algonquian language of the Ojibwa people
OJT *abbr* on-the-job training
¹OK *or* **okay** \ō-ˈkā, *in assenting or agreeing also* ˈō-ˌkā *or* ˈō-ˌkā\ *adv or adj* [abbr. of *oll korrect,* alter. of *all correct*] : all right
²OK *or* **okay** \ō-ˈkā\ *vt* **OK'd** *or* **okayed; OK'·ing** *or* **okay·ing** : APPROVE, AUTHORIZE
³OK *or* **okay** \ō-ˈkā\ *n* : APPROVAL, ENDORSEMENT
⁴OK *abbr* **1** Oklahoma **2** outer keel
oka *var of* OCA
oka·pi \ō-ˈkäp-ē\ *n* [native name in Africa] : an African mammal (*Okapia johnstoni*) that is closely related to the giraffe but has a relatively short neck, a coat of solid reddish chestnut on the trunk, yellowish white on the cheeks, and purplish black and cream rings on the upper parts of the legs

okapis

oke \ˈōk, ˈȯk\ *or* **oka** \ō-ˈkä\ *n* [F, NGk & Turk; F *ocque,* fr. NGk & Turk; NGk *oka,* fr. Turk *okka,* fr. Ar *ūqīyah*] : any of three units of weight varying around 2.8 pounds and used respectively in Greece, Turkey, and Egypt
okey·doke \ˌō-kē-ˈdōk\ *or* **okey·do·key** \-ˈdō-kē\ *adv* [redupl. of *OK*] — used as a function word to express assent
Okie \ˈō-kē\ *n* [*Ok*lahoma + *-ie*] : a migrant agricultural worker; *esp* : one from Oklahoma in the 1930s
Okla *abbr* Oklahoma
okra \ˈō-krə, *South also* -krē\ *n* [of African origin; akin to Twi ŋ¹ku¹ru¹ma³ okra] **1 :** a tall annual (*Hibiscus esculentus*) of the mallow family that is cultivated for its mucilaginous green pods used esp. in soups or stews; *also* : the pods of this plant **2 :** GUMBO 2
¹-ol \ˌȯl, ˌōl\ *n suffix* [ISV, fr. *alcohol*] : chemical compound (as an alcohol or phenol) containing hydroxyl <glycer*ol*> <creos*ol*>
²-ol — see -OLE
³-ol *n comb form* [ISV, fr. L *oleum* oil — more at OIL] : hydrocarbon chemically related to benzene <xyl*ol*>
¹old \ˈōld\ *adj* [ME, fr. OE *eald;* akin to OHG *alt* old, L *alere* to nourish, *alescere* to grow, *altus* high, deep] **1 a :** dating from the remote past : ANCIENT <~ traditions> **b :** persisting from an earlier time <an ~ ailment> <they brought up the same ~ argument> **c :** of long standing <an ~ friend> **2 a :** distinguished from an object of the same kind by being of an earlier date <many still used the ~ name> **b** *cap* : belonging to an early period in the development of a language or literature <*Old* Irish> **3 :** having existed for a specified period of time <a girl three years ~> **4 :** of, relating to, or originating in a past era <~ chronicles record the event> **5 a :** advanced in years or age <an ~ man> **b :** showing the characteristics of age <looked ~ at 20> **6**

: EXPERIENCED <an ~ trooper speaking of the last war> **7** : FORMER <his ~ students> **8 a** : showing the effects of time or use : WORN, AGED <~ shoes> **b** : well advanced toward reduction to baselevel — used of topographic features **c** : no longer in use : DISCARDED <~ rags> **d** : of a grayish or dusty color <~ mauve> **9 a** : long familiar <same ~ story> <good ~ Joe> **b** — used as an intensive <a high ~ time> <any ~ time>
syn OLD, ANCIENT, VENERABLE, ANTIQUE, ANTIQUATED, ARCHAIC, OBSOLETE *shared meaning element* : having come into existence or use in the more or less distant past ***ant*** new

2old *n* **1** : old or earlier time — used in the phrase *of old* <mighty men of ~> **2** : one of a specified age — usu. used in combination <a 3-year-*old*>

Old Bulgarian *n* : OLD CHURCH SLAVONIC

Old Catholic *n* : a member of one of various hierarchical and liturgical churches separating from the Roman Catholic Church at various times since the 18th century

Old Christmas *n, chiefly Midland* : EPIPHANY 1

Old Church Slavonic *n* : the Slavic language used in the Bible translation of Cyril and Methodius and as the liturgical language of several Eastern churches — called also *Old Church Slavic;* see INDO-EUROPEAN LANGUAGES table

old country *n* : an emigrant's country of origin; *esp* : EUROPE

old·en \ˈōl-dən\ *adj* : of or relating to a bygone era

Old English *n* **1 a** : the language of the English people from the time of the earliest documents in the 7th century to about 1100 — see INDO-EUROPEAN LANGUAGES table **b** : English of any period before Modern English **2** : BLACK LETTER

Old English sheepdog *n* : any of an English breed of medium-sized sheep and cattle dogs with a profuse, shaggy, blue-gray and white coat that hangs almost to the ground

Old English sheepdog

old·fan·gled \ˈōl(d)-ˈfaŋ-gəld\ *adj* [*old* + *-fangled* (as in *newfangled*)] : OLD-FASHIONED

1old–fash·ioned \-ˈfash-ənd\ *adj* **1 a** : of, relating to, or characteristic of a past era <wears an ~ black bow tie —Green Peyton> **b** : adhering to customs of a past era **2** : out of date — **old–fash·ioned·ly** \-ən-dlē\ *adv*

2old–fashioned *n* : a cocktail usu. made with whiskey, bitters, sugar, a twist of lemon peel, and a small amount of water or soda

Old French *n* : the French language from the 9th to the 16th century; *esp* : French from the 9th to the 13th century — see INDO-EUROPEAN LANGUAGES table

Old Glory *n* : the flag of the U.S.

old gold *n* : a variable color averaging a dark yellow

old guard *n, often cap O & G* : the conservative members (as of a political party) who are unwilling to accept new ideas, practices, or conditions

old hand *n* : VETERAN

old hat *adj* **1** : OLD-FASHIONED **2** : lacking in freshness : TRITE

Old High German *n* : High German exemplified in documents prior to the 12th century — see INDO-EUROPEAN LANGUAGES table

old·ie \ˈōl-dē\ *n* : something that is old; *esp* : a popular song of an earlier day

Old Ionic *n* : the Greek dialect of the Homeric epics

old·ish \ˈōl-dish\ *adj* : somewhat old or elderly

old lady *n* **1** : WIFE **2** : MOTHER

Old Latin *n* : Latin used in the early inscriptions and in literature prior to the classical period

old–line \ˈōl-ˈ(d)līn\ *adj* **1** : having a reputation or authority based on seniority : ESTABLISHED **2** : adhering to traditional policies or practices : CONSERVATIVE

old maid *n* **1** : SPINSTER 3 **2** : a prim fussy person <he was a real *old maid* about burning rubbish —R. C. Ruark> **3** : a simple card game in which the player holding a designated card (as an odd queen) at the end is an "old maid"— **old–maid·ish** \(ˈ)ōl(d)-ˈmād-ish\ *adj*

old man *n* **1 a** : HUSBAND **b** : FATHER **2** *cap* : one in authority; *esp* : COMMANDING OFFICER

old–man's beard \ˌōl(d)-ˌmanz-\ *n* **1** : any of several clematises (esp. *Clematis vitalba* in England and *C. virginiana* in the U.S.) having plumose styles **2** : a greenish gray pendulous lichen (*Usnea barbata*) growing on trees

old master *n* **1** : a superior artist or craftsman of established reputation; *esp* : a distinguished painter of the 16th, 17th, or early 18th century **2** : a work by an old master

Old Nick \(ˈ)ōl(d)-ˈnik\ *n* — used as a name of the devil

Old Norse *n* : the North Germanic language of the Scandinavian peoples prior to about 1350 — see INDO-EUROPEAN LANGUAGES table

Old North French *n* : the northern dialects of Old French including esp. those of Normandy and Picardy

Old Prussian *n* : a Baltic language used in East Prussia until the 17th century — see INDO-EUROPEAN LANGUAGES table

old rose *n* : a variable color averaging a grayish red

Old Saxon *n* : the language of the Saxons of northwest Germany until about the 12th century — see INDO-EUROPEAN LANGUAGES table

old school *n* : adherents of traditional policies and practices of the past

old school tie *n* **1 a** : a necktie displaying the colors of an English public school **b** : an attitude of conservatism, aplomb, and upper-class solidarity associated with English public school graduates **2** : clannishness among members of an established clique

old sledge *n* : SEVEN-UP

old–squaw \ˈōl(d)-ˈskwȯ\ *n* : a common sea duck (*Clangula hyemalis*) of the more northern parts of the northern hemisphere

old·ster \ˈōl(d)-stər\ *n* : an old or elderly person

old style *n* **1** *cap O&S* : a style of reckoning time used before the adoption of the Gregorian calendar **2** : a style of type distinguished by graceful irregularity among individual letters, bracketed serifs, and but slight contrast between light and heavy strokes

old style

Old Style *adj* : using or according to the Julian calendar

Old Testament *n* : the first part of the Christian Bible containing the books of the Jewish canon of Scripture — see BIBLE table

old–time \ˌōl(d)-ˌtīm\ *adj* **1** : of, relating to, or characteristic of an earlier period **2** : of long standing

old–tim·er \ōl(d)-ˈtī-mər\ *n* **1 a** : VETERAN **b** : OLDSTER **2** : something that is old-fashioned : ANTIQUE

Old Welsh *n* : the Welsh language exemplified in documents prior to about 1150 — see INDO-EUROPEAN LANGUAGES table

old·wife \ˈōl-ˌ(d)wīf\ *n* **1** : any of several marine fishes (as an alewife, menhaden, or triggerfish) **2** : OLD-SQUAW

old wives' tale *n* : a traditional tale or bit of lore; *esp* : a traditional superstitious notion

old–world \ˈōl-ˈ(d)wər(-ə)ld\ *adj* : of, relating to, or characteristic of the Old World; *esp* : having the charm or picturesque qualities of the Old World <narrow ~ streets>

Old World *n* : EASTERN HEMISPHERE; *specif* : Europe

ole- *or* **oleo-** *comb form* [F *olé-, oléo-,* fr. L *ole-,* fr. *oleum* — more at OIL] : oil <*oleic*> <*oleograph*>

-ole \ˌōl\ *also* **-ol** \ˌōl, ˌōl\ *n comb form* [ISV, fr. L *oleum*] **1** : chemical compound containing a five-membered usu. heterocyclic ring <diaz*ole*> <pyrr*ole*> **2** : chemical compound not containing hydroxyl <eucalypt*ol*> — esp. in names of ethers <phenet*ole*>

olé \ō-ˈlā\ *n* : 2BRAVO

ole·ag·i·nous \ˌō-lē-ˈaj-ə-nəs\ *adj* [MF *oleagineux,* fr. L *oleagineus* of an olive tree, fr. *olea* olive tree, fr. Gk *elaia*] **1** : resembling or having the properties of oil; *also* : containing or producing oil : OILY <~ seeds> **2** : UNCTUOUS — **ole·ag·i·nous·ly** *adv* — **ole·ag·i·nous·ness** *n*

ole·an·der \ˈō-lē-ˌan-dər, ˌō-lē-ˈ\ *n* [ML] : a poisonous evergreen shrub (*Nerium oleander*) of the dogbane family with fragrant white to red flowers

ole·an·do·my·cin \ˌō-lē-ˌan-də-ˈmīs-ᵊn\ *n* [prob. fr. *oleander* + *-o-* + *-mycin*] : an antibiotic $C_{35}H_{61}NO_{12}$ produced by a streptomyces (*Streptomyces antibioticus*)

ole·as·ter \ˈō-lē-ˌas-tər, ˌō-lē-ˈ\ *n* [L, fr. *olea*] : any of several plants (genus *Elaeagnus* of the family Elaeagnaceae, the oleaster family) having alternate leaves and perfect flowers with four stamens; *esp* : RUSSIAN OLIVE

ole·ate \ˈō-lē-ˌāt\ *n* : a salt or ester of oleic acid

olec·ra·non \ō-ˈlek-rə-ˌnän\ *n* [NL, fr. Gk *ōlekranon,* fr. *ōlenē* elbow + *kranion* skull — more at ELL, CRANIUM] : the process of the ulna projecting behind the elbow joint

ole·fin \ˈō-lə-fən\ *n* [ISV, fr. F (*gaz*) *oléfiant* ethylene, fr. L *oleum*] : an unsaturated open-chain hydrocarbon containing at least one double bond; *esp* : any of various long-chain synthetic polymers (as of ethylene or propylene) used esp. as textile fibers and in cordage — **ole·fin·ic** \ˌō-lə-ˈfin-ik\ *adj*

ole·ic \ō-ˈlē-ik, -ˈlā-\ *adj* **1** : relating to, derived from, or contained in oil **2** : of or relating to oleic acid

oleic acid *n* : an unsaturated fatty acid $C_{18}H_{34}O_2$ found as glycerides in natural fats and oils

ole·in \ˈō-lē-ən\ *n* [F *oléine,* fr. L *oleum*] **1** : an ester of glycerol and oleic acid **2** *also* **ole·ine** \-ən, -ˌēn\ : the liquid portion of a fat

oleo \ˈō-lē-ˌō\ *n, pl* **ole·os** **1** [short for *oleomargarine*] : MARGARINE **2** : OLEOGRAPH

oleo·graph \ˈō-lē-ə-ˌgraf\ *n* [ISV *ole-* + *-graph*] : a chromolithograph printed on cloth to imitate an oil painting — **oleo·graph·ic** \ˌō-lē-ə-ˈgraf-ik\ *adj* — **ole·og·ra·phy** \ˌō-lē-ˈäg-rə-fē\ *n*

oleo·mar·ga·rine \ˌō-lē-ō-ˈmärj-(ə-)rən, -ˈmärj-ə-ˌrēn\ *n* [F *oléomargarine,* fr. *olé-* + *margarine*] : MARGARINE

oleo·res·in \ˌō-lē-ō-ˈrez-ᵊn\ *n* [ISV] **1** : a plant product (as copaiba) containing chiefly essential oil and resin; *esp* : TURPENTINE 1b **2** : a preparation consisting essentially of oil holding resin in solution — **oleo·res·in·ous** \-ˈrez-ᵊn-əs, -ˈrez-nəs\ *adj*

oleri·cul·ture \ə-ˈler-ə-ˌkəl-chər, ä-; ˈäl-ə-ri-\ *n* [L *holer-, holus* vegetables + E *-i-* + *culture;* akin to L *helvus* light bay — more at YELLOW] : a branch of horticulture that deals with the production, storage, processing, and marketing of vegetables — **oleri·cul·tur·ist** \ə-ˌler-ə-ˈkəlch-(ə-)rəst, ä-; ˌäl-ə-ri-\ *n*

ole·um \ˈō-lē-əm\ *n* [L — more at OIL] **1** *pl* **olea** \-lē-ə\ : OIL **2** *pl* **oleums** : a heavy oily strongly corrosive solution of sulfur trioxide in anhydrous sulfuric acid

ol·fac·tion \äl-ˈfak-shən, ōl-\ *n* **1** : the sense of smell **2** : the act or process of smelling

ol·fac·tive \-ˈfak-tiv\ *adj* : OLFACTORY

ol·fac·tom·e·ter \ˌäl-ˌfak-ˈtäm-ət-ər, ˌōl-\ *n* : an instrument for measuring the sensitivity of the sense of smell

ol·fac·to·ry \äl-ˈfak-t(ə-)rē, ōl-\ *adj* [L *olfactorius,* fr. *olfactus,* pp. of *olfacere* to smell, fr. *olēre* to smell + *facere* to do — more at ODOR, DO] : of, relating to, or connected with the sense of smell

olfactory bulb *n* : a bulbous anterior projection of the olfactory lobe that is the place of termination of the olfactory nerves and is esp. well developed in lower vertebrates (as fishes)

olfactory lobe *n* : an anterior projection of each cerebral hemisphere that is continuous anteriorly with the olfactory nerve

olfactory nerve *n* **:** either of the pair of nerves that are the first cranial nerves and that arise in the olfactory organ, pass to the anterior part of the cerebrum, and conduct stimuli from the olfactory organ to the brain

olfactory organ *n* **:** a membranous organ of chemical sense in the nasal cavity that receives stimuli interpreted as odors from volatile and soluble substances in low dilution

olig- *or* **oligo-** *comb form* [ML, fr. Gk, fr. *oligos;* akin to Arm *alkat* scant] **:** few <*oligo*phagous>

oli·garch \ˈäl-ə-ˌgärk, ˈō-lə-\ *n* [Gk *oligarchēs,* fr. *olig-* + *-archēs* -arch] **:** a member or supporter of an oligarchy

oli·gar·chic \ˌäl-ə-ˈgär-kik, ˌō-lə-\ *or* **oli·gar·chi·cal** \-ki-kəl\ *adj* **:** of, relating to, or based on an oligarchy

oli·gar·chy \ˈäl-ə-ˌgär-kē, ˈō-lə-\ *n, pl* **-chies** **1 :** government by the few **2 :** a government in which a small group exercises control esp. for corrupt and selfish purposes; *also* **:** a group exercising such control **3 :** an organization under oligarchic control

Oli·go·cene \ˈäl-i-gō-ˌsēn, ˈō-li-; ə-ˈlig-ə-\ *adj* [ISV] **:** of, relating to, or being an epoch of the Tertiary between the Eocene and Miocene or the corresponding system of rocks — **Oligocene** *n*

oli·go·chaete \-ˌkēt\ *n* [deriv. of Gk *olig-* + *chaitē* long hair — more at CHAETA] **:** any of a class or order (Oligochaeta) of hermaphroditic terrestrial or aquatic annelids (as an earthworm) that lack a specialized head — **oligochaete** *or* **oli·go·chae·tous** \ˌäl-i-gō-ˈkēt-əs, ˌō-li-\ *adj*

oli·go·clase \ˈäl-i-gō-ˌklās, ˈō-li-, -ˌklāz; ə-ˈlig-ə-\ *n* [G *oligoklas,* fr. *olig-* + Gk *klasis* breaking, fr. *klan* to break — more at HALT] **:** a mineral of the plagioclase series

oligo·mer \ə-ˈlig-ə-mər\ *n* [*olig-* + *-mer* (as in *polymer*)] **:** a polymer or polymer intermediate containing relatively few structural units — **oligo·mer·ic** \-ˌlig-ə-ˈmer-ik\ *adj* — **oligo·mer·iza·tion** \-mə-rə-ˈzā-shən\ *n*

oli·go·my·cin \ˌäl-i-gō-ˈmīs-ᵊn, ˌō-li-\ *n* **:** any of several antibiotic substances produced by an actinomycete

oli·go·nu·cle·o·tide \-ˈn(y)ü-klē-ə-ˌtīd\ *n* **:** a chain of usu. from 2 to 10 nucleotides

oli·goph·a·gous \ˌäl-ə-ˈgäf-ə-gəs, ˌō-lə-\ *adj* **:** eating only a few specific kinds of food — **oli·goph·a·gy** \-ˈgäf-ə-jē\ *n*

oli·gop·o·ly \-ˈgäp-ə-lē\ *n* [*olig-* + mono*poly*] **:** a market situation in which each of a few producers affects but does not control the market — **oli·gop·o·lis·tic** \-ˌgäp-ə-ˈlis-tik\ *adj*

oli·gop·so·ny \-ˈgäp-sə-nē\ *n* [*olig-* + Gk *opsōnia* purchase of victuals, fr. *opsōnein* to purchase victuals, fr. *opson* food + *ōneisthai* to buy — more at VENAL] **:** a market situation in which each of a few buyers exerts a disproportionate influence on the market

oli·go·sac·cha·ride \ˌäl-i-gō-ˈsak-ə-ˌrīd, ˌō-li-\ *n* [ISV] **:** a saccharide (as a disaccharide) that contains a known small number of monosaccharide units

oli·go·tro·phic \-ˈtrō-fik\ *adj* [ISV] **:** deficient in plant nutrients <~ boggy acid soils>; *esp* **:** having abundant dissolved oxygen with no marked stratification <an ~ body of water> — compare EUTROPHIC

olio \ˈō-lē-ˌō\ *n, pl* **oli·os** [modif. of Sp *olla*] **1 :** OLLA PODRIDA 1 **2 a :** a miscellaneous mixture **:** HODGEPODGE **b :** a miscellaneous collection (as of literary or musical selections)

ol·i·va·ceous \ˌäl-ə-ˈvā-shəs\ *adj* **:** OLIVE 1

[1]**ol·ive** \ˈäl-iv, -əv\ *n* [ME, fr. OF, fr. L *oliva,* fr. Gk *elaia*] **1 a :** an Old World evergreen tree (*Olea europaea* of the family Oleaceae, the olive family) cultivated for its drupaceous fruit that is an important food and source of oil; *also* **:** the fruit **b :** any of various shrubs and trees resembling the olive **2 :** any of several colors resembling that of the unripe fruit of the olive tree that are yellow to yellow green in hue, of medium to low lightness, and of moderate to low saturation

olive 1a: *1* fruit, *2* flowering branch

[2]**olive** *adj* **1 :** of the color olive or olive green **2 :** approaching olive in color or complexion

olive branch *n* **1 :** a branch of the olive tree esp. when used as a symbol of peace **2 :** an offer or gesture of conciliation or goodwill

olive drab *n* **1 :** a variable color averaging a grayish olive **2 a :** a wool or cotton fabric of an olive drab color **b :** a uniform of this fabric

olive green *n* **:** a variable color that is greener, lighter, and stronger than average olive color

oliv·enite \ō-ˈliv-ə-ˌnīt\ *n* [G *olivenit,* fr. *oliven-, olive* olive] **:** a mineral $Cu_2(AsO_4)(OH)$ that is a basic olive green, dull brown, or yellowish arsenate of copper

Ol·i·ver \ˈäl-ə-vər\ *n* [F *Olivier*] **:** the close friend of Roland in the Charlemagne legends

ol·iv·ine \ˈäl-ə-ˌvēn\ *n* [G *olivin,* fr. L *oliva*] **:** a usu. greenish mineral $(Mg,Fe)_2SiO_4$ that is a complex silicate of magnesium and iron used esp. in refractories — compare PERIDOT — **ol·iv·in·ic** \ˌäl-ə-ˈvin-ik\ *or* **ol·iv·in·it·ic** \-və-ˈnit-ik\ *adj*

ol·la \ˈäl-ə, ˈòi-ə\ *n* [Sp, fr. L, pot — more at OVEN] **:** a large bulging widemouthed earthenware vessel often with looped handles used (as in Latin America) esp. as a pot for stewing or as a container for water

ol·la po·dri·da \ˌäl-ə-pə-ˈdrēd-ə, ˌòi-ə-\ *n, pl* **olla podridas** \-ˈdrēd-əz\ *also* **ollas podridas** \ˌäl-ə(z)-, ˌòi-ə(z)-pə\ [Sp, lit., rotten pot] **1 :** a rich highly seasoned stew of meat and vegetables usu. including sausage and chick-peas that is slowly simmered and is a traditional Spanish and Latin American dish **2 :** HODGEPODGE

olo·li·u·qui \ˌō-ˌlō-lē-ˈü-kē\ *n* [Sp *ololiuque,* fr. Nahuatl *ololiuhqui,* lit., one that covers] **:** a woody stemmed Mexican vine (*Rivea corymbosa*) of the morning glory family having small fleshy fruits with single seeds that are used esp. by the Indians for medicinal, narcotic, and religious purposes

olym·pi·ad \ə-ˈlim-pē-ˌad, ō-\ *n, often cap* [MF *Olympiade,* fr. L *Olympiad-, Olympias,* fr. Gk, fr. *Olympia,* site of ancient Olympian games] **1 :** one of the four-year intervals between Olympian games by which time was reckoned in ancient Greece **2 :** a quadrennial celebration of the modern Olympic Games

[1]**Olym·pi·an** \-pē-ən\ *adj* **1 :** of or relating to the ancient Greek region of Olympia **2 :** of, relating to, or constituting the Olympian games

[2]**Olympian** *n* **:** a participant in Olympic Games

[3]**Olympian** *adj* **1 :** of or relating to Mount Olympus in Thessaly **2 :** befitting or characteristic of an Olympian; *esp* **:** LOFTY <his . . . formula of glib simplicity and ~ arrogance —Richard Pollak>

[4]**Olympian** *n* **1 :** one of the ancient Greek deities dwelling on Olympus **2 :** a being of lofty detachment or superior attainments

Olympian Games *n pl* **:** an ancient Panhellenic festival held every 4th year and made up of contests of sports, music, and literature with the victor's prize a crown of wild olive

Olym·pic \ə-ˈlim-pik, ō-\ *adj* **1 :** [3]OLYMPIAN **2 :** of or relating to the Olympic Games

Olympic Games *n pl* **1 :** OLYMPIAN GAMES **2 :** a modified revival of the Olympian games held once every four years and made up of international athletic contests — called also *Olympics*

Olym·pus \ə-ˈlim-pəs, ō-\ *n* [L, fr. Gk *Olympos*] **:** a mountain in Thessaly that is the abode of the gods in Greek mythical narratives

om \ˈōm\ *n* [Skt] **:** a mantra consisting of the sound "om" and used in contemplation of ultimate reality

OM *abbr* order of merit

-o·ma \ˈō-mə\ *n suffix, pl* **-o·mas** \-məz\ *or* **-o·ma·ta** \-mət-ə\ [L *-omat-, -oma,* fr. Gk *-ōmat-, -ōma,* fr. *-ō-* (stem of causative verbs in *-oun*) + *-mat-, -ma,* suffix denoting result — more at -MENT] **:** tumor <aden*oma*> <fibr*oma*>

Oma·ha \ˈō-mə-ˌhò, -ˌhä\ *n, pl* **Omaha** *or* **Omahas** [Omaha, lit., those going upstream or against the wind] **:** a member of an Amerindian people of northeastern Nebraska

Omar stanza \ˌō-ˌmär-\ *n* **:** RUBAIYAT STANZA

oma·sum \ō-ˈmā-səm\ *n, pl* **oma·sa** \-sə\ [NL, fr. L, tripe of a bullock] **:** the division between the reticulum and the abomasum in the stomach of a ruminant

om·bre \ˈäm-bər; ˈäm-brē, ˈəm-, -ˌbrā\ *n* [F or Sp; F *hombre,* fr. Sp, lit., man] **:** an old three-handed card game popular in Europe esp. in the 17th and 18th centuries

om·bré \ˈäm-ˌbrā\ *adj* [F, pp. of *ombrer* to shade, fr. It *ombrare,* fr. *ombra* shade, fr. L *umbra* — more at UMBRAGE] **:** having colors or tones that shade into each other — used esp. of fabrics in which the color is graduated from light to dark — **ombré** *n*

om·buds·man \ˈäm-ˌbu̇dz-mən, ˈòm-, -bədz-; äm-ˈbu̇dz-, òm-\ *n, pl* **-men** \-mən\ [Sw, lit., representative, fr. ON *umbothsmathr,* fr. *umboth* commission + *mathr* man] **1 :** a government official (as in Sweden or New Zealand) appointed to receive and investigate complaints made by individuals against abuses or capricious acts of public officials **2 :** one that investigates reported complaints (as from students or consumers), reports findings, and helps to achieve equitable settlements

-ome \ˌōm\ *n suffix* [NL *-oma,* fr. L, -oma] **:** mass <phyll*ome*>

ome·ga \ō-ˈmeg-ə, -ˈmē-gə, -ˈmā-gə\ *n* [Gk *ō mega,* lit., large o] **1 :** the 24th and last letter of the Greek alphabet — see ALPHABET table **2 :** LAST, ENDING **3 a :** a negatively charged elementary particle that has a mass 3280 times the mass of an electron and that decays into a xi and a pion — called also *omega particle* **b :** a very short-lived unstable meson with mass 1532 times the mass of an electron — called also *omega meson*

om·elet *or* **om·elette** \ˈäm-(ə-)lət\ *n* [F *omelette,* alter. of MF *alumelle,* lit., knife blade, modif. of L *lamella,* dim. of *lamina* thin plate] **:** beaten eggs cooked without stirring until set and served folded in half

omen \ˈō-mən\ *n* [L *omin-, omen*] **:** an occurrence or phenomenon believed to portend a future event **:** AUGURY

omen·tum \ō-ˈment-əm\ *n, pl* **-ta** \-ə\ *or* **-tums** [L, fr. *o-* (akin to *-uere* to put on) — more at EXUVIAE] **:** a free fold of peritoneum or one connecting or supporting abdominal structures (as the viscera) — **omen·tal** \-ˈment-ᵊl\ *adj*

omer \ˈō-mər\ *n* [Heb *ʿōmer*] **1 :** an ancient Hebrew unit of dry capacity equal to $^1/_{10}$ ephah **2** *often cap* **:** the sheaf of barley traditionally offered in Jewish Temple worship on a day that marks the start of a 7-week liturgical period of expectancy between Passover and Shabuoth

om·i·cron \ˈäm-ə-ˌkrän, *Brit* ō-ˈmī-krən\ *n* [Gk *o mikron,* lit., small o] **:** the 15th letter of the Greek alphabet — see ALPHABET table

om·i·nous \ˈäm-ə-nəs\ *adj* **:** being or exhibiting an omen **:** PORTENTOUS; *esp* **:** foreboding or foreshowing evil **:** INAUSPICIOUS — **om·i·nous·ly** *adv* — **om·i·nous·ness** *n*

syn OMINOUS, PORTENTOUS, FATEFUL *shared meaning element* **:** having a menacing or threatening aspect

omis·si·ble \ō-ˈmis-ə-bəl\ *adj* **:** that may be omitted

omis·sion \ō-ˈmish-ən, ə-\ *n* [ME *omissioun,* fr. LL *omission-, omissio,* fr. L *omissus,* pp. of *omittere*] **1 a :** apathy toward or neglect of duty **b :** something neglected or left undone **2 :** the act of omitting **:** the state of being omitted

omit \ō-ˈmit, ə-\ *vt* **omit·ted; omit·ting** [ME *omitten,* fr. L *omittere,* fr. *ob-* toward + *mittere* to let go, send — more at OB-, SMITE] **1 :** to leave out or leave unmentioned **2 :** to fail to perform or make use of **:** FORBEAR **3** *obs* **:** DISREGARD **4** *obs* **:** to give up ***syn*** see NEGLECT

om·ma·tid·i·um \ˌäm-ə-ˈtid-ē-əm\ *n, pl* **-tid·ia** \-ē-ə\ [NL, fr. Gk *ommat-, omma* eye] **:** one of the elements corresponding to a small simple eye that make up the compound eye of an arthropod — **om·ma·tid·i·al** \-ē-əl\ *adj*

omni- *comb form* [L, fr. *omnis*] **:** all **:** universally <*omni*directional>

[1]**om·ni·bus** \ˈäm-ni-(ˌ)bəs\ *n* [F, fr. L, for all, dat. pl. of *omnis*] **1 :** a usu. automotive public vehicle designed to carry a comparative-

ly large number of passengers : BUS **2** : a book containing reprints of a number of works

[2]**omnibus** *adj* **1** : of, relating to, or providing for many things at once **2** : containing or including many items

om·ni·di·rec·tion·al \ˌäm-ni-də-ˈrek-shnəl, -ˌnī-də-, -ni-(ˌ)dī-, -shən-ᵊl\ *adj* : being in or involving all directions; *esp* : receiving or sending radio waves equally well in all directions <~ antenna>

om·ni·far·i·ous \ˌäm-nə-ˈfar-ē-əs, -ˈfer-\ *adj* [LL *omnifarius*, fr. L *omni-* + *-farius* (as in *multifarius* having great diversity) — more at MULTIFARIOUS] : of all varieties, forms, or kinds

om·nif·i·cent \äm-ˈnif-ə-sənt\ *adj* [L *omni-* + E *-ficent* (as in *magnificent*)] : unlimited in creative power

om·nip·o·tence \äm-ˈnip-ət-ən(t)s\ *n* **1** : the quality or state of being omnipotent **2** : an agency or force of unlimited power

[1]**om·nip·o·tent** \-ət-ənt\ *adj* [ME, fr. MF, fr. L *omnipotent-*, *omnipotens*, fr. *omni-* + *potent-*, *potens* potent] **1** *often cap* : ALMIGHTY 1 **2** : having virtually unlimited authority or influence **3** *obs* : ARRANT — **om·nip·o·tent·ly** *adv*

[2]**omnipotent** *n* **1** : one who is omnipotent **2** *cap* : GOD 1

om·ni·pres·ence \ˌäm-ni-ˈprez-ᵊn(t)s\ *n* : the quality or state of being omnipresent : UBIQUITY

om·ni·pres·ent \-ᵊnt\ *adj* : present in all places at all times

om·ni·range \ˈäm-ni-ˌrānj\ *n* : a system of radio navigation in which any bearing relative to a special radio transmitter on the ground may be chosen and flown by an airplane pilot — called also *omnidirectional range*

om·ni·science \äm-ˈnish-ən(t)s\ *n* [ML *omniscientia*, fr. L *omni-* + *scientia* science] : the quality or state of being omniscient

om·ni·scient \-ənt\ *adj* [NL *omniscient-*, *omnisciens*, back-formation fr. ML *omniscientia*] **1** : having infinite awareness, understanding, and insight **2** : possessed of universal or complete knowledge — **om·ni·scient·ly** *adv*

om·ni·um–gath·er·um \ˌäm-nē-əm-ˈgath-ə-rəm\ *n*, *pl* **omnium–gatherums** [L *omnium* (gen. pl. of *omnis*) + E *gather* + L *-um*, noun ending] : a miscellaneous collection (as of things or persons)

om·niv·o·ra \äm-ˈniv-ə-rə\ *n pl* [NL, fr. L, neut. pl. of *omnivorus*] : omnivorous animals

om·ni·vore \ˈäm-ni-ˌvō(ə)r, -ˌvo̊(ə)r\ *n* [NL *omnivora*] : one that is omnivorous

om·niv·o·rous \äm-ˈniv-(ə-)rəs\ *adj* [L *omnivorus*, fr. *omni-* + *-vorus* -vorous] **1** : feeding on both animal and vegetable substances **2** : avidly taking in everything as if devouring or consuming — **om·niv·o·rous·ly** *adv* — **om·niv·o·rous·ness** *n*

[1]**on** \(ˈ)ȯn, (ˈ)än\ *prep* [ME *an*, *on*, prep. & adv., fr. OE; akin to OHG *ana* on, Gk *ana* up, on] **1 a** (1) — used as a function word to indicate a position over and in contact with <the book is ~ the table> (2) — used as a function word to indicate a position in contact or juxtaposition with <a fly ~ the ceiling> (3) — used as a function word to indicate a means of conveyance <left ~ the early train> (4) — used as a function word to indicate a part (as of the body) that supports and is in contact with something underneath <stand ~ one foot> (5) — used as a function word to indicate movement in the direction or area of <~ the right> **b** (1) — used as a function word to indicate movement to a position over and in contact with <jumped ~ the horse> (2) — used as a function word to indicate movement to a position in contact with <put the notice ~ the bulletin board> **2 a** — used as a function word to indicate the object of actual or implied action of a preceding noun, verb, or adjective directed against or toward the object <crept up ~ him> <a satire ~ society> <keen ~ sports> **b** : to the disadvantage of <have some evidence ~ him> **3** — used as a function word to indicate the basis or source (as of an action, opinion, or computation) <know it ~ good authority> <ten cents ~ the dollar> **4** *archaic* : OF **5 a** — used as a function word to indicate connection, association, or activity with or with regard to <~ a committee> <~ tour> **b** — used as a function word to indicate a state or process of <~ fire> <~ the increase> **6** — used as a function word to indicate occurrence within the limits of a specified day, at a set time, or under specified circumstances <came ~ Monday> <every hour ~ the hour> <cash ~ delivery> **7** — used as a function word to indicate means or agency <cut ~ a knife> <talking ~ the telephone> **8** — used as a function word to indicate reduplication or succession in a series <loss ~ loss>

[2]**on** \ˈȯn, ˈän\ *adv* **1 a** : in or into a position of contact with an upper surface <put the plates ~> **b** : in or into a position of being attached to or covering a surface <has new shoes ~> **2 a** : forward in space, time, or action : ONWARD <went ~ home> **b** : in continuance or succession <and so ~> **3** : into operation or a position permitting operation <turn the light ~>

[3]**on** \ˈȯn, ˈän\ *adj* **1** : engaged in an activity or function (as a dramatic role) **2 a** (1) : being in operation <the radio is ~> (2) : placed so as to permit operation <the switch is ~> **b** : taking place <the game is ~> **3** : INTENDED, PLANNED <has nothing ~ for tonight>

[1]**-on** \ˌän, ən\ *n suffix* [ISV, alter. of *-one*] : chemical compound not a ketone or other oxo compound <parathi*on*>

[2]**-on** \ˌän\ *n suffix* [fr. *-on* (in *ion*)] **1** : elementary particle <nucle*on*> **2 a** : unit : quantum <phot*on*> <magnet*on*> **b** : basic hereditary component <cistr*on*> <oper*on*>

[3]**-on** \ˌän\ *n suffix* [NL, fr. *-on* (in *argon*)] : noble gas <rad*on*>

on–again, off–again *adj* : existing briefly and then disappearing in an intermittent unpredictable way <*on-again, off-again* fads>

on·a·ger \ˈän-i-jər\ *n* [ME, wild ass, fr. L, fr. Gk *onagros*, fr. *onos* ass + *agros* field — more at ACRE] **1** : a small pale-colored kiang with a broad dorsal stripe **2** [LL, fr. L] : a heavy catapult used in ancient and medieval times

on and off *adv* : off and on

onan·ism \ˈō-nə-ˌniz-əm\ *n* [prob. fr. NL *onanismus*, fr. *Onan*, son of Judah (Gen 38:9)] **1** : coitus deliberately interrupted to prevent insemination **2** : MASTURBATION **3** : SELF-GRATIFICATION — **onan·is·tic** \ˌō-nə-ˈnis-tik\ *adj*

[1]**once** \ˈwən(t)s\ *adv* [ME *ones*, fr. gen. of *on* one] **1** : one time and no more **2** : at any one time : under any circumstances : EVER **3** : at some indefinite time in the past : FORMERLY **4** : by one degree of relationship

[2]**once** *adj* : that once was : FORMER

[3]**once** *n* : one single time : one time at least — **at once** **1** : at the same time : SIMULTANEOUSLY **2** : IMMEDIATELY **3** : [3]BOTH

[4]**once** *conj* : at the moment when : as soon as

once–over \ˈwən(t)-ˌsō-vər\ *n* : a swift examination or survey; *esp* : a swift comprehensive appraising glance

once that *conj* : ONCE

on·cho·cer·ci·a·sis \ˌäŋ-kō-ˌsər-ˈkī-ə-səs\ *n*, *pl* **-a·ses** \-ˌsēz\ [NL, fr. *Onchocerca*, genus of worms] : infestation with or disease caused by filarial worms (genus *Onchocerca*); *esp* : a disease of man caused by a worm (*O. volvulus*) that is native to Africa but now present in parts of tropical America and is transmitted by several biting flies

on·cho·cer·co·sis \-ˈkō-səs\ *n*, *pl* **-co·ses** \-ˌsēz\ [NL, fr. *Onchocerca*] : ONCHOCERCIASIS

on·cid·i·um \än-ˈsid-ē-əm, äŋ-ˈkid-\ *n* [NL, genus name, fr. Gk *onkos* barbed hook — more at ANGLE] : any of a genus (*Oncidium*) of showy tropical American epiphytic or terrestrial orchids

on·co·gen·e·sis \ˌäŋ-kō-ˈjen-ə-səs\ *n* [NL, fr. Gk *onkos* mass] : the induction or formation of tumors

on·co·gen·ic \-ˈjen-ik\ *adj* **1** : relating to tumor formation **2** : tending to cause tumors

on·co·ge·nic·i·ty \-jə-ˈnis-ət-ē\ *n* : the capacity to induce or form tumors

on·col·o·gy \än-ˈkäl-ə-jē, äŋ-\ *n* [Gk *onkos* mass + ISV *-logy*; akin to Gk *enenkein* to carry — more at ENOUGH] : the study of tumors — **on·co·log·i·cal** \ˌäŋ-kə-ˈläj-i-kəl\ *also* **on·co·log·ic** \-ik\ *adj* — **on·col·o·gist** \än-ˈkäl-ə-jəst, äŋ-\ *n*

on·com·ing \ˈȯn-ˌkəm-iŋ, ˈän-\ *adj* **1 a** : coming nearer in time or space <the ~ year> <an ~ car> **b** : FUTURE <looked forward to his ~ visit> **2** : EMERGENT, RISING <schools needed for the ~ generation of students>

[1]**one** \ˈwən, ˌwən\ *adj* [ME *on*, fr. OE *ān*; akin to OHG *ein* one, L *unus* (OL *oinos*), Skt *eka*] **1** : being a single unit or thing <~ day at a time> **2 a** : being one in particular <early ~ morning> **b** : being preeminently what is indicated <~ fine person> **3 a** : being the same in kind or quality <both of ~ species> **b** (1) : constituting a unified entity of two or more components <the combined elements form ~ substance> (2) : UNITED **4** : existing or occurring as something not definitely fixed or placed <will see you again ~ day> **5** : being the only individual of an indicated or implied kind <the ~ person she wanted to marry> — **at one** : at harmony : in a state of agreement

[2]**one** *pron* **1** : a certain indefinitely indicated person or thing **2** — sometimes used as a third person substitute for a first person pronoun <I'd like to read more but ~ doesn't have the time>

[3]**one** \ˈwən\ *n* **1** — see NUMBER table **2** : the number denoting unity **3** : the first in a set or series <wears a ~> **4** : a single person or thing <has the ~ but needs the other> **5** : a one-dollar bill

-one \ˌōn\ *n suffix* [ISV, alter. of *-ene*] : ketone or related or analogous compound or class of compounds <lact*one*> <quin*one*>

one another *pron* : EACH OTHER

one–armed bandit \ˌwən-ˌärm(d)-\ *also* **one–arm bandit** *n* : SLOT MACHINE 2

one–bagger \ˈwən-ˈbag-ər\ *n* : SINGLE 2

one–dimensional *adj* : lacking depth : SUPERFICIAL <~ stereotype characters> — **one–dimensionality** *n*

one–egg *adj* : MONOZYGOTIC

one·fold \ˈwən-ˌfōld, -ˈfōld\ *adj* : constituting a single undivided whole

one–hand·ed \-ˈhan-dəd\ *adj* **1** : having or using only one hand <could beat him up ~> **2 a** : designed for or requiring the use of only one hand **b** : effected by the use of only one hand

one–horse *adj* **1** : drawn or operated by one horse **2** : of little real importance or consequence <a ~ town>

Onei·da \ō-ˈnīd-ə\ *n*, *pl* **Oneida** *or* **Oneidas** [Iroquois *Onē̃yóde'*, lit., standing rock] **1 a** : an Amerindian people orig. of New York **b** : a member of this people **2** : the language of the Oneida people

onei·ric \ō-ˈnī-rik\ *adj* [Gk *oneiros* dream; akin to Arm *anurj* dream] : of or relating to dreams : DREAMY

onei·ro·crit·i·cal \ō-ˌnī-rō-ˈkrit-i-kəl\ *adj* [Gk *oneirokritikos*, fr. *oneiros* + *kritikos* able to discern — more at CRITIC] : of, relating to, or specializing in the interpretation of dreams — **onei·ro·crit·i·cal·ly** \-k(ə-)lē\ *adv*

onei·ro·man·cy \ō-ˈnī-rə-ˌman(t)-sē\ *n* [Gk *oneiros* + E *-mancy*] : divination by means of dreams

one–line octave *n* : the musical octave that begins on middle C — see PITCH illustration

one–man *adj* : of or relating to just one individual: as **a** : consisting of only one individual <a ~ committee> **b** (1) : done, presented, or produced by only one individual <a ~ stage play> (2) : featuring the work of a single artist (as a painter) <a ~ show of oils> **c** : designed for or limited to one individual

one·ness \ˈwən-nəs\ *n* : the quality or state or fact of being one: as **a** : SINGLENESS **b** : INTEGRITY, WHOLENESS **c** : HARMONY **d** : SAMENESS, IDENTITY **e** : UNITY, UNION

one–night stand *n* **1** : a performance (as of a play or concert) given (as by a traveling group of actors or musicians) only once in each of a series of localities **2 a** : a locality used for one-night stands **b** : a stopover for a one-night stand

one–on–one \ˌwən-ȯn-ˈwən, ˌwən-än-\ *adj* : MAN-TO-MAN 2

one–piece *adj* : consisting of or made in a single undivided piece <a ~ bathing suit> — **one–piec·er** \ˈwən-ˈpē-sər\ *n*

on·er·ous \ˈän-ə-rəs, ˈō-nə-\ *adj* [ME, fr. MF *onereus,* fr. L *onerosus,* fr. *oner-, onus* burden; akin to Skt *anas* cart] **1 :** involving, imposing, or constituting a burden : TROUBLESOME <an ~ task> **2 :** having legal obligations that outweigh the advantages <~ contract> — **oner·ous·ly** *adv* — **oner·ous·ness** *n*
syn ONEROUS, BURDENSOME, OPPRESSIVE, EXACTING *shared meaning element* : imposing hardship

one·self \(ˌ)wən-ˈself\ *also* **one's self** \(ˌ)wən-, ˌwənz-\ *pron* **1 :** a person's self : one's own self — used reflexively as object of a preposition or verb or for emphasis in various constructions **2 :** one's normal, healthy, or sane condition or self — **be oneself :** to conduct oneself in a usual or fitting manner

one–shot \ˈwən-ˌshät\ *adj* **1 :** that is complete or effective through being done or used or applied only once <there is no easy ~ answer to the problem> **2 :** that is not followed by something else of the same kind <an intensive ~ drive for funds was made>

one–sid·ed \ˈwən-ˈsīd-əd\ *adj* **1 a (1) :** having or occurring on one side only **(2) :** having one side prominent or more developed **b :** limited to one side : PARTIAL <a ~ interpretation> **2 :** UNILATERAL <a ~ decision> — **one–sid·ed·ly** *adv* — **one–sid·ed·ness** *n*

one–step \ˈwən-ˌstep\ *n* **1 :** a ballroom dance in 2/4 time marked by quick walking steps backward and forward **2 :** music used for the one-step — **one–step** *vi*

one–suit·er \ˈwən-ˈsüt-ər\ *n* **:** a man's traveling bag designed to hold one suit and accessories

one–tailed test \ˌwən-ˌtāl(d)-\ *n* **:** a statistical test for which the critical region consists of all values of the test statistic greater than a given value or less than a given value but not both — called also *one-sided test, one-tail test;* compare TWO-TAILED TEST

[1]**one·time** \ˌwən-ˌtīm\ *adj* **:** FORMER, SOMETIME

[2]**onetime** *adv* **:** FORMERLY

one–to–one \ˌwən-tə-ˈwən, -də-\ *adj* **:** pairing each element of a set uniquely with an element of another set

one–track *adj* **:** marked by often narrowly restricted attention to or absorption in just one thing <a ~ mind>

one–two \ˈwən-ˈtü, -ˌtü\ *n* **:** a combination of two quick blows in rapid succession in boxing; *esp* **:** a left jab followed at once by a hard blow with the right hand

one–up \ˌwən-ˈəp, ˈwən-\ *vt* [back-formation fr. *one-upmanship*] **:** to practice one-upmanship on

one up *adj* **:** being in a position of advantage — usu. used with *on*

one–up·man·ship \ˌwən-ˈəp-mən-ˌship\ *n* **:** the art or practice of going a friend or competitor one better or keeping one jump ahead of him

one–way *adj* **1 :** that moves in or allows movement in only one direction <~ traffic> **2 :** ONE-SIDED, UNILATERAL <a ~ conversation> **3 :** that functions in only one of two or more ways

on·go·ing \ˈȯn-ˌgō-iŋ, ˈän-, -ˌgō(-)iŋ\ *adj* **1 :** being actually in process **2 :** continuously moving forward : GROWING

ONI *abbr* Office of Naval Intelligence

on·ion \ˈən-yən\ *n* [ME, fr. MF *oignon,* fr. L *union-, unio*] **1 :** a widely cultivated Asiatic herb (*Allium cepa*) of the lily family with pungent edible bulbs; *also* **:** its bulb **2 :** any of various plants of the same genus as the onion

on·ion·skin \-ˌskin\ *n* **:** a thin strong translucent paper of very light weight

oni·um \ˈō-nē-əm\ *adj* [*-onium*] **:** being or characterized by a usu. complex cation

-o·ni·um \ˈō-nē-əm\ *n suffix* [NL, fr. *ammonium*] **:** an ion having a positive charge <ox*onium*> — compare -IUM 1b

on–line *adj* **1 :** located at a point served directly by a particular railroad <~ industry> **2 :** being controlled directly by or in direct communication with a computer <~ equipment> **3 :** of, relating to, or being a cryptographic system whose telecommunication machines automatically encipher, transmit, receive, and decipher messages in a single instantaneous operation — compare OFF-LINE — **on–line** *adv*

on·look·er \ˈȯn-ˌlu̇k-ər, ˈän-\ *n* **:** one that looks on; *esp* **:** a passive spectator — **on·look·ing** \-iŋ\ *adj*

[1]**on·ly** \ˈōn-lē\ *adj* [ME, fr. OE *ānlīc,* fr. *ān* one — more at ONE] **1 :** unquestionably the best : PEERLESS **2 :** alone in its class or kind : SOLE <an ~ child>

[2]**only** *adv* **1 a :** as a single fact or instance and nothing more or different : MERELY <has ~ lost one election —George Orwell> **b :** SOLELY, EXCLUSIVELY <known ~ to him> **2 :** at the very least <it was ~ too true> **3 a :** in the final outcome <will ~ make you sick> **b :** with nevertheless the final result <won the battles, ~ to lose the war> **4 a :** as recently as <~ last week> **b :** in the immediate past <~ just talked to her>

[3]**only** *conj* **1 a :** with the restriction that : BUT <you may go, ~ come back early> **b :** and yet : HOWEVER <they look very nice, ~ we can't use them> **2 :** were it not that : EXCEPT

on·o·mas·tic \ˌän-ə-ˈmas-tik\ *adj* [Gk *onomastikos,* fr. *onomazein* to name, fr. *onoma* name — more at NAME] **1 :** of, relating to, or consisting of a name or names **2** *of a signature* **:** written in the handwriting of the author of a letter or document the body of which is in the handwriting of another person

on·o·mas·tics \-tiks\ *n pl but sing or pl in constr* **1 a :** the science or study of the origins and forms of words esp. as used in a specialized field **b :** the science or study of the origin and forms of proper names of persons or places **2 :** the system underlying the formation and use of words esp. for proper names or of words used in a specialized field

on·o·ma·tol·o·gy \ˌän-ə-mə-ˈtäl-ə-jē\ *n* [F *onomatologie,* fr. Gk *onomat-, onoma* name + F *-logie* -logy] **:** ONOMASTICS

on·o·mato·poe·ia \ˌän-ə-ˌmat-ə-ˈpē-(y)ə\ *n* [LL, fr. Gk *onomatopoiia,* fr. *onomat-, onoma* name + *poiein* to make — more at POET] **1 :** the naming of a thing or action by a vocal imitation of the sound associated with it (as *buzz, hiss*) **2 :** the use of words whose sound suggests the sense — **on·o·mato·poe·ic** \-ˈpē-ik\ *or* **on·o·mato·po·et·ic** \-pō-ˈet-ik\ *adj* — **on·o·mato·poe·i·cal·ly** \-ˈpē-ə-k(ə-)lē\ *or* **on·o·mato·po·et·i·cal·ly** \-pō-ˈet-i-k(ə-)lē\ *adv*

On·on·da·ga \ˌän-ə(n)-ˈdȯ-gə\ *n, pl* **Onondaga** *or* **Onondagas** [Iroquois *Onōtáge,* village of the Onondaga people] **1 a :** an Amerindian people of New York and Canada **b :** a member of this people **2 :** the language of the Onondaga people

ONR *abbr* Office of Naval Research

on·rush \ˈȯn-ˌrəsh, ˈän-\ *n* **1 :** a rushing forward or onward **2 :** ONSET — **on·rush·ing** \-iŋ\ *adj*

on·set \-ˌset\ *n* **1 :** ATTACK, ASSAULT <withstand the ~ of the army> **2 :** BEGINNING, COMMENCEMENT <the ~ of winter> — **on·set·ting** \-ˌset-iŋ\ *adj*

on·shore \ˈȯn-ˌshō(ə)r, ˈän-, -ˌshȯ(ə)r\ *adj* **1 :** coming or moving toward or onto the shore <an ~ wind> **2 a :** situated on or near the shore **b :** DOMESTIC <~ oil production> <~ purchases> — **on·shore** \ˈȯn-ˈ, ˈän-ˈ\ *adv*

on·side \-ˈsīd\ *adv or adj* **:** not off side : in a position legally to play or receive the ball or puck

onside kick *n* **:** a kickoff in football in which the ball travels just far enough to be legally recoverable by the kicking team

on·slaught \ˈän-ˌslȯt, ˈȯn-\ *n* [modif. of D *aanslag* act of striking; akin to OE *an* on and to OE *slēan* to strike — more at SLAY] **:** an esp. fierce attack

on·stage \ˈȯn-ˈstāj, ˈän-, -ˌstāj\ *adv or adj* **:** on a part of the stage visible to the audience

Ont *abbr* Ontario

ont- *or* **onto-** *comb form* [NL, fr. LGk, fr. Gk *ont-, ōn,* prp. of *einai* to be — more at IS] **1 :** being : existence <*onto*logy> **2 :** organism <*onto*geny>

-ont \ˌänt\ *n comb form* [Gk *ont-, ōn,* prp.] **:** cell : organism <dipl*ont*>

on–the–job *adj* **:** of or relating to something (as training or experience) learned, gained, or done while working at a job and often under supervision

on–the–scene *adj* **:** being at the place of an action or occurrence <an ~ witness>

on·tic \ˈänt-ik\ *adj* **:** of, relating to, or having real being — **on·ti·cal·ly** \-i-k(ə-)lē\ *adv*

[1]**on·to** \ˌȯn-tə(-w), ˌän-; ˈȯn-(ˌ)tü, ˈän-\ *prep* **1 :** to a position on **2 :** in or into a state of awareness about <put me ~ your methods> **3** — used as a function word to indicate a set each element of which is the image of at least one element of another set <a function mapping the set *S* ~ the set *T*>

[2]**on·to** \ˈȯn-(ˌ)tü, ˈän-\ *adj* **:** mapping in such a way that every element in one set is the image of at least one element in another set <a function that is one-to-one and ~>

on·to·gen·e·sis \ˌänt-ə-ˈjen-ə-səs\ *n* [NL] **:** ONTOGENY

on·to·ge·net·ic \-jə-ˈnet-ik\ *adj* [ISV] **1 :** of, relating to, or appearing in the course of ontogeny **2 :** based on visible morphological characters — **on·to·ge·net·i·cal·ly** \-i-k(ə-)lē\ *adv*

on·tog·e·ny \än-ˈtäj-ə-nē\ *n* [ISV] **:** the development or course of development of an individual organism

on·to·log·i·cal \ˌänt-ᵊl-ˈäj-i-kəl\ *adj* **1 :** of or relating to ontology **2 :** relating to or based upon being or existence — **on·to·log·i·cal·ly** \-k(ə-)lē\ *adv*

ontological argument *n* **:** an argument for the existence of God based upon the meaning of the term *God*

on·tol·o·gy \än-ˈtäl-ə-jē\ *n* [NL *ontologia,* fr. *ont-* + *-logia* -logy] **1 :** a branch of metaphysics concerned with the nature and relations of being **2 :** a particular theory about the nature of being or the kinds of existents — **on·tol·o·gist** \-jəst\ *n*

onus \ˈō-nəs\ *n* **1** [L — more at ONEROUS] **a :** BURDEN **b :** a disagreeable necessity : OBLIGATION **c :** BLAME **d :** STIGMA **2** [NL] **:** BURDEN OF PROOF

[1]**on·ward** \ˈȯn-wərd, ˈän-\ *also* **on·wards** \-wərdz\ *adv* **:** toward or at a point lying ahead in space or time : FORWARD

[2]**onward** *adj* **:** directed or moving onward : FORWARD

on·y·choph·o·ran \ˌän-i-ˈkäf-ə-rən\ *n* [NL *Onychophora,* group name, fr. Gk *onych-, onyx* claw + *-phoros* -phore] **:** PERIPATUS — **onychophoran** *adj*

-onym \ə-ˌnim\ *n comb form* [ME, fr. L *-onymum,* fr. Gk *-ōnymon,* fr. *onyma* — more at NAME] **:** name : word <ant*onym*>

on·yx \ˈän-iks\ *n* [ME *onix,* fr. OF & L; OF, fr. L *onych-, onyx,* fr. Gk, lit., claw, nail — more at NAIL] **:** a translucent chalcedony in parallel layers of different colors

oo- — see O-

OOB \ˌō-ˌō-ˈbē\ *n* **:** OFF-OFF-BROADWAY

oo·cyst \ˈō-ə-ˌsist\ *n* [ISV] **:** ZYGOTE; *specif* **:** a sporozoan zygote undergoing sporogenous development

oo·cyte \ˈō-ə-ˌsīt\ *n* [ISV] **:** an egg before maturation : a female gametocyte

oo·dles \ˈüd-ᵊlz\ *also* **ood·lins** \ˈüd-lənz\ *n pl but sing or pl in constr* [perh. alter. of [2]*huddle*] **:** a great quantity : LOT

oo·ga·mete \ˌō-ə-gə-ˈmēt, -ˈgam-ˌēt\ *n* **:** a female gamete; *specif* **:** a relatively large nonmotile gamete containing reserve material

oog·a·mous \ō-ˈäg-ə-məs\ *adj* **:** having or involving a small motile male gamete and a large immobile female gamete — **oog·a·my** \-mē\ *n*

O O gauge \ˌdəb-ə-ˈlō-\ *n* **:** a gauge of track in model railroading in which the rails are approximately 3/4 inch apart

oo·gen·e·sis \ˌō-ə-ˈjen-ə-səs\ *n* [NL] **:** formation and maturation of the egg — **oo·ge·net·ic** \-jə-ˈnet-ik\ *adj*

oo·go·ni·um \ˌō-ə-ˈgō-nē-əm\ *n* [NL] **1 :** a female sexual organ in various algae and fungi that corresponds to the archegonium of ferns and mosses **2 :** a descendant of a primordial germ cell that gives rise to oocytes — **oo·go·ni·al** \-nē-əl\ *adj*

[1]**ooh** \ˈü\ *interj* — used to express amazement, joy, or surprise

[2]**ooh** *vi* **:** to exclaim in amazement, joy, or surprise <one finds oneself ~*ing* and aahing over the exciting new TV commercials —Walter Goodman> — **ooh** *n*

oo·lite \ˈō-ə-ˌlīt\ *n* [prob. fr. F *oolithe,* fr. *o-* + *-lithe* -lite] **:** a rock consisting of small round grains usu. of calcium carbonate cemented together — **oo·lit·ic** \ˌō-ə-ˈlit-ik\ *adj*

ool·o·gist \ō-ˈäl-ə-jəst\ *n* **1 :** one specializing in oology **2 :** a collector of birds' eggs

ool·o·gy \-jē\ *n* : a branch of ornithology dealing with birds' eggs — **oo·log·i·cal** \ˌō-ə-ˈläj-i-kəl\ *also* **oo·log·ic** \-ik\ *adj* — **oo·log·i·cal·ly** \-i-k(ə-)lē\ *adv*

oo·long \ˈü-ˌlȯŋ\ *n* [Chin (Pek) *wu*[1] *lung*[2], lit., black dragon] : a tea that combines the characteristics of black and green teas due to the leaf's being partially fermented before drying

oo·mi·ak *also* **oo·mi·ack** *var of* UMIAK

oomph \ˈùm(p)f\ *n* [prob. imit. of an appreciative *mm* uttered by a man at the sight of an attractive woman] **1** : personal charm or magnetism : GLAMOUR **2** : SEX APPEAL **3** : VITALITY, ENTHUSIASM

oops \ˈ(w)ù(ə)ps\ *interj* — used typically to express mild apology, surprise, or dismay

oo·sperm \ˈō-ə-ˌspərm\ *n* : ZYGOTE, OOSPORE

oo·sphere \-ˌsfi(ə)r\ *n* [ISV] : OVUM — used esp. of lower plants

oo·spore \-ˌspō(ə)r, -ˌspȯ(ə)r\ *n* [ISV] : ZYGOTE; *esp* : a spore produced by heterogamous fertilization that yields a sporophyte

oo·the·ca \ˌō-ə-ˈthē-kə\ *n, pl* **oo·the·cae** \-ˈthē-(ˌ)kē, -(ˌ)sē\ [NL] : a firm-walled and distinctive egg case (as of a cockroach) — **oo·the·cal** \-ˈthē-kəl\ *adj*

oo·tid \ˈō-ə-ˌtid\ *n* [irreg. fr. *o-* + *-id*] : an egg cell after meiosis

[1]**ooze** \ˈüz\ *n* [ME *wose,* fr. OE *wāse* mire; akin to L *virus* slime — more at VIRUS] **1** : a soft deposit (as of mud, slime, or shells) on the bottom of a body of water **2** : a piece of soft wet plastic ground (as a marsh or bog)

[2]**ooze** *n* [ME *wose* sap, juice, fr. OE *wōs;* akin to OHG *waso* damp, Gk *hearon* ewer] **1** : a decoction of vegetable material used for tanning leather **2** : the act of oozing **3** : something that oozes

[3]**ooze** *vb* **oozed; ooz·ing** *vi* **1** : to pass or flow slowly through or as if through small openings or interstices **2** : to move slowly or imperceptibly <the crowd began to ~ forward —Bruce Marshall> **3 a** : to exude moisture **b** : to exude something in a way suggestive of the emitting of moisture <a woman *oozing* with charm> ~ *vt* **1** : to emit or give out slowly **2** : to exude or give off in a way suggestive of the emitting of moisture

ooze leather *n* : leather that is usu. made from calfskins by a vegetable tanning process and has a soft suede finish on the flesh side

oozy \ˈü-zē\ *adj* **ooz·i·er; -est** **1** : containing or composed of ooze : resembling ooze **2** : exuding moisture : SLIMY

[1]**op** \ˈäp\ *n* : OPTICAL ART

[2]**op** *abbr* opus

OP *abbr* **1** observation post **2** Order of Preachers **3** out of print

OPA *abbr* Office of Price Administration

opac·i·ty \ō-ˈpas-ət-ē\ *n, pl* **-ties** [F *opacité* shadiness, fr. L *opacitat-, opacitas,* fr. *opacus* shaded, dark] **1** : the quality or state of a body that makes it impervious to the rays of light; *broadly* : the relative capacity of matter to obstruct the transmission of radiant energy **2 a** : obscurity of sense : UNINTELLIGIBLENESS <obscurity which on a third reading deepens to ~ —Ellery Sedgwick> **b** : the quality or state of being mentally obtuse : DULLNESS **3** : an opaque spot on a normally transparent structure (as the lens of the eye)

opah \ˈō-pə, -ˌpä\ *n* [Ibo *úbà*] : a large elliptical marine fish (*Lampris regius*) with brilliant colors and rich oily red flesh

opal \ˈō-pəl\ *n* [L *opalus,* fr. Skt *upala* stone, jewel] : a mineral $SiO_2.nH_2O$ that is a hydrated amorphous silica softer and less dense than quartz and typically with definite and often marked iridescent play of colors

opal·es·cent \ˌō-pə-ˈles-ᵊnt\ *adj* : reflecting an iridescent light — **opal·es·cence** \-ᵊn(t)s\ *n*

opal·ine \ˈō-pə-ˌlīn, -ˌlēn\ *adj* : resembling opal esp. in appearance

[1]**opaque** \ō-ˈpāk\ *adj* [L *opacus*] **1** : exhibiting opacity : not pervious to radiant energy and esp. light **2 a** : hard to understand or explain : UNINTELLIGIBLE **b** : OBTUSE, STUPID — **opaque·ly** *adv* — **opaque·ness** *n*

[2]**opaque** *n* : something that is opaque; *esp* : an opaque paint for blocking out portions of a photographic negative or print

opaque projector *n* : a projector using reflected light for projecting an image of an opaque object or matter on an opaque support (as a photograph)

op art \ˈäp-\ *n* : OPTICAL ART — **op artist** *n*

op cit *abbr* [L *opere citato*] in the work cited

ope \ˈōp\ *vb* **oped; op·ing** *archaic* : OPEN

op ed \ˈäp-ˈed\ *n* [short for *opposite editorial*] : a page of special features usu. opposite the editorial page of a newspaper

[1]**open** \ˈō-pən, ˈōp-ᵊm\ *adj* **open·er** \ˈōp-(ə-)nər\; **open·est** \ˈōp-(ə-)nəst\ [ME, fr. OE; akin to OHG *offan* open; both fr. a prehistoric NGmc-WGmc word akin to OE *ūp* up] **1** : having no enclosing or confining barrier : accessible on all or nearly all sides <cattle grazing on an ~ range> **2 a (1)** : being in a position or adjustment to permit passage : not shut or locked <an ~ door> **(2)** : having a barrier (as a door) so adjusted as to allow passage <the house was ~> **b** : having the lips parted <stood there with his mouth wide ~> **3 a** : completely free from concealment : exposed to general view or knowledge <their hostilities eventually erupted with ~ war> **b** : exposed or vulnerable to attack or question : SUBJECT <~ to doubt> **4 a** : not covered with a top, roof, or lid <an ~ car> <her eyes were ~> **b** : having no protective covering <~ wiring> <an ~ wound> **5** : not restricted to a particular group or category of participants <~ to the public> <~ housing>: as **a** : enterable by both amateur and professional contestants **b** : enterable by a registered voter regardless of political affiliation <in the ~ primary a Democrat could nominate Republican candidates —H. U. Faulkner & Tyler Kepner> **6** : fit to be traveled over : presenting no obstacle to passage or view <the ~ road> <~ country> **7** : having the parts or surfaces laid out in an expanded position : spread out : UNFOLDED <an ~ book> **8 a (1)** : LOW 13 **(2)** : formed with the tongue in a lower position <Italian has an ~ and a close *e*> **b (1)** : having clarity and resonance unimpaired by undue tension or constriction of the throat <an ~ vocal tone> **(2)** *of a tone* : produced by an open string or on a wind instrument by the lip without the use of slides, valves, or keys **9 a** : available to follow or make use of <the only course ~ to us> **b** : not taken up with duties or engagements <keep an hour ~ on Friday> c finally decided : subject to further consideration <leave the ~> <an ~ question> **d** : available for a qualified app : VACANT <the job is still ~> **e** : remaining available for us filling until canceled <an ~ order for more items> **f** : availa for future purchase <these items are in ~ stock> <an ~ patter **10 a** : characterized by ready accessibility and usu. genero attitude: as **(1)** : generous in giving **(2)** : willing to hear an consider or to accept and deal with : RESPONSIVE **(3)** : free from reserve or pretense : candidly and often artlessly frank **b** : accessible to the influx of new factors (as foreign goods) <an ~ market> **11 a** : having openings, interruptions, or spaces: as **(1)** : being porous and friable <~ soil> **(2)** : sparsely distributed : SCATTERED <~ population> **(3)** : having relatively wide spacing between words or lines <~ type> **(4)** *of a compound* : having components separated by a space in writing or printing <*Spanish mackerel* is an ~ compound> **b** : not made up of a continuous closed circuit of channels <the insect circulatory system is ~> **12 a** *of an organ pipe* : not stopped at the top **b** *of a string on a musical instrument* : not stopped by the finger **13** : being in operation <the microphone is ~>; *esp* : ready for business, patronage, or use <the store is ~ from 9 to 5> <the new highway will be ~ next week> **14 a (1)** : characterized by lack of effective regulation of various commercial enterprises <notorious as an ~ town> **(2)** : not repressed by legal controls <~ gambling> **b** : free from checking or hampering restraints <an ~ economy> <faced with ~ inflation> **c** : relatively unguarded by opponents <passed to an ~ teammate> **15** : having been opened by a first ante, bet, or bid <the bidding is ~> **16** *of punctuation* : characterized by sparing use esp. of the comma **17 a** : containing none of its endpoints <an ~ interval> **b** : being a set each point of which has a neighborhood all of whose points are contained in the set <the interior of a sphere is an ~ set> ***syn*** see FRANK ***ant*** close, closemouthed — **open** *adv* — **open·ly** \ˈō-pən-lē\ *adv* — **open·ness** \-pən-nəs\ *n*

[2]**open** \ˈō-pən, ˈōp-ᵊm\ *vb* **opened** \ˈō-pənd, ˈōp-ᵊmd\; **open·ing** \ˈōp-(ə-)niŋ\; **opens** \ˈō-pənz, ˈōp-ᵊmz\ *vt* **1 a** : to move (as a door) from closed position **b** : to make available for entry or passage by turning back (as a barrier), removing (as a cover), or clearing away (as an obstruction) **2 a** : to make available for or active in a regular function <~ a new store> **b** : to make accessible for a particular purpose <~*ed* new land for settlement> **3 a** : to disclose or expose to view : REVEAL **b** : to make more discerning or responsive : ENLIGHTEN <must ~ our minds to the needs of minorities> **c** : to bring into view or come in sight of by changing position **4 a** : to make one or more openings in <~*ed* the boil> **b** : to loosen and make less compact <~ the soil> **5** : to spread out : UNFOLD <~*ed* the book> **6 a** : to enter upon : BEGIN <~*ed* the meeting> **b** : to commence action in a card game by making (a first bid), putting a first bet in (the pot), or playing (a card or suit) as first lead **7** : to restore or recall (as an order) from a finally determined state to a state in which the parties are free to prosecute or oppose ~ *vi* **1** : to become open <the office ~*ed* early> **2 a** : to spread out : EXPAND <the wound ~*ed* under the strain> **b** : to become disclosed <his grief ~*ed* then and he wept on his daughter's shoulder —Lorene Forshee> **3** : to become enlightened or responsive **4** : to give access <the rooms ~ onto a hall> **5** : to speak out <finally he ~*ed* freely on the subject> **6 a** : to begin a course or activity <the play ~*s* on Tuesday> **b** : to make a bet, bid, or lead in commencing a round or hand of a card game — **open·abil·i·ty** \ˌōp-(ə-)nə-ˈbil-ət-ē\ *n* — **open·able** \ˈōp-(ə-)nə-bəl\ *adj*

[3]**open** *n* **1** : OPENING **2** : open and unobstructed space: as **a** : OPEN AIR **b** : open water **3** : an open contest, competition, or tournament

open-air *adj* : OUTDOOR

open air *n* : the space where air is unconfined; *esp* : OUT-OF-DOORS

open-and-shut \ˌōp-(ə-)nən-ˈshət\ *adj* **1** : perfectly simple : OBVIOUS **2** : easily settled <an ~ case>

open chain *n* : an arrangement of atoms represented in a structural formula by a chain whose ends are not joined so as to form a ring

open-circuit *adj* : of or relating to an open circuit; *esp* : being or relating to television in which programs are broadcast so that they are available to all receivers within range

open city *n* : a city that is not occupied or defended by military forces and that is immune from enemy bombardment under international law

open couplet *n* : a rhymed couplet in which the sense is incomplete

open door *n* **1** : a recognized right of admittance : freedom of access **2** : a policy giving opportunity for commercial relations with a country to all nations on equal terms — **open-door** *adj*

open-end *adj* : organized to allow for contingencies: as **a** : permitting additional debt to be incurred under the original indenture subject to specified conditions <an ~ mortgage> **b** : having a fluctuating capitalization of shares that are issued or redeemed at the current net asset value or at a figure in fixed ratio to this <an ~ investment company> — compare CLOSED-END

open-end·ed \ˌō-pə-ˈnen-dəd\ *adj* : not rigorously fixed: as **a** : adaptable to the developing needs of a situation **b** : permitting or designed to permit spontaneous and unguided responses

open·er \ˈōp-(ə-)nər\ *n* : one that opens <a bottle ~>: as **a** *archaic* : an aperient substance **b** *pl* : cards of sufficient value for a player to open the betting in a poker game **c** : the first item, contest, or event of a series **d** *pl* : START, BEGINNING

eyed \ˌō-pə-ˈnīd\ *adj* **1** : having the eyes open **2** TCHFUL, DISCERNING

-hand·ed \ˌō-pən-ˈhan-dəd\ *adj* : generous in giving UNIFICENT — **open·hand·ed·ly** *adv* — **open·hand·ed·ness** *n*

en–heart *adj* : of, relating to, or performed on a heart emporarily relieved of circulatory function and surgically opened or inspection and treatment <~ surgery>

open·heart·ed \ˌō-pən-ˈhärt-əd\ *adj* : candidly straightforward : FRANK — **open·heart·ed·ly** *adv* — **open·heart·ed·ness** *n*

open–hearth *adj* : of, relating to, involving, or produced by an open hearth <~ steel>

open–hearth process *n* : a process of making steel from pig iron in a furnace of the regenerative reverberatory type

open house *n* : ready and usu. informal hospitality or entertainment for all comers

open·ing \ˈōp-(ə-)niŋ\ *n* **1 a** : an act or instance of making or becoming open **b** : an act or instance of beginning : COMMENCEMENT; *esp* : a formal and usu. public event by which something new is put officially into operation **2** : something that is open: as **a (1)** : BREACH, APERTURE **(2)** : an open width : SPAN **b** : an area without trees or with scattered usu. mature trees that occurs as a break in a forest **c** : two pages that face one another in a book **3** : something that constitutes a beginning: as **a** : a planned series of moves made at the beginning of a game of chess or checkers — compare END GAME, MIDDLE GAME **b** : a first performance **4 a** : OCCASION, CHANCE **b** : an opportunity for employment

open letter *n* : a letter of protest or appeal usu. addressed to an individual but intended for the general public and printed in a newspaper or periodical

open loop *n* : a control system for an operation or process in which there is no self-correcting action as there is in a closed loop

open–mind·ed \ˌō-pən-ˈmīn-dəd\ *adj* : receptive to arguments or ideas : UNPREJUDICED — **open–mind·ed·ly** *adv* — **open–mind·ed·ness** *n*

open·mouthed \ˌō-pən-ˈmau̇t͟hd, -ˈmau̇tht\ *adj* **1** : having the mouth widely open **2** : struck with amazement or wonder **3** : CLAMOROUS, VOCIFEROUS — **open·mouth·ed·ly** \-ˈmau̇-t͟həd-lē, -thəd-\ *adv* — **open·mouth·ed·ness** \-ˈmau̇-t͟həd-nəs, -thəd-\ *n*

open order *n* : a military formation in which the units are separated by considerable intervals

open–pol·li·nat·ed \ˌō-pən-ˈpäl-ə-ˌnāt-əd\ *adj* : pollinated by natural agencies without human intervention

open season *n* : a period during which it is legal to kill or catch game or fish protected at other times by law

open secret *n* : an ostensibly secret but generally known matter

open sentence *n* : a statement (as in mathematics) that contains at least one blank or unknown and that becomes true or false when the blank is filled or a quantity is substituted for the unknown

open ses·a·me \-ˈses-ə-mē\ *n* [fr. *open sesame*, the magical command used by Ali Baba to open the door of the robbers' den in *Ali Baba and the Forty Thieves*] : something that unfailingly brings about a desired end

open shop *n* : an establishment in which eligibility for employment and retention on the payroll are not determined by membership or nonmembership in a labor union though there may be an agreement by which a union is recognized as sole bargaining agent

open sight *n* : a firearm rear sight having an open notch instead of a peephole or a telescope

open stance *n* : a preparatory position (as in baseball batting or golf) in which the forward foot (as the left foot of a right-handed person) is farther from the line of play than the back foot — compare CLOSED STANCE

open syllable *n* : a syllable ended by a vowel or diphthong

open up *vi* **1** : to commence firing **2** : to become communicative <*open up* and tell these guys what they want to know —*Sat. Eve. Post*> **3** : to spread out or come into view <the road *opens up* ahead> **4** : to turn toward an audience or a camera ~ *vt* **1** : to open by cutting into **2** : to make plain or visible : DISCLOSE **3** : to make available

open·work \ˈō-pən-ˌwərk\ *n* : work constructed so as to show openings through its substance : work that is perforated or pierced <wrought-iron ~> — **open–worked** \-ˌwərkt\ *adj*

¹opera *pl of* OPUS

²op·era \ˈäp-(ə-)rə\ *n* [It, work, opera, fr. L, work, pains; akin to L *oper-, opus*] **1** : a drama set to music and made up of vocal pieces with orchestral accompaniment and orchestral overtures and interludes; *specif* : GRAND OPERA **2** : the score of a musical drama **3** : the performance of an opera; *also* : a house where operas are performed — **op·er·at·ic** \ˌäp-ə-ˈrat-ik\ *adj* — **op·er·at·i·cal·ly** \-i-k(ə-)lē\ *adv*

op·er·a·ble \ˈäp-(ə-)rə-bəl\ *adj* **1** : fit, possible, or desirable to use : PRACTICABLE **2** : suitable for surgical treatment <an ~ cancer> — **op·er·a·bil·i·ty** \ˌäp-(ə-)rə-ˈbil-ət-ē\ *n* — **op·er·a·bly** \ˈäp-ə-rə-blē\ *adv*

opé·ra bouffe \ˌäp-(ə-)rə-ˈbüf\ *n* [F, fr. It *opera buffa*] : satirical comic opera

op·era buf·fa \ˌäp-(ə-)rə-ˈbü-fə\ *n* [It, lit., comic opera] : an 18th century farcical comic opera with dialogue in recitative

opé·ra co·mique \ˌäp-(ə-)rə-käm-ˈēk, -kō-ˈmēk\ *n* [F] : COMIC OPERA

opera glass *n* : a small binocular optical instrument that is similar to the field glass and suitable for use at the opera or theater — often used in pl.

op·era·go·er \ˈäp-(ə-)rə-ˌgō(-ə)r\ *n* : a person who frequently goes to operas

opera hat *n* : a man's collapsible top hat consisting usu. of a dull silky fabric stretched over a steel frame

opera house *n* : a theater devoted principally to the performance of operas; *broadly* : THEATER

op·er·and \ˌäp-ə-ˈrand\ *n* [L *operandum*, neut. of gerundive of *operari*] : something (as a quantity or data) that is operated on (as in a mathematical operation); *also* : the address in a computer instruction of data to be operated on

¹op·er·ant \ˈäp-ə-rənt\ *adj* **1** : functioning or tending to produce effects : EFFECTIVE <an ~ conscience> **2** : of or relating to the observable or measurable **3** : of, relating to, or being an operant <~ conditioning> <~ behavior> — **op·er·ant·ly** *adv*

²operant *n* : behavior or responses (as bar pressing by a rat to obtain food) that operate on the environment to produce rewarding and reinforcing effects

op·era se·ria \ˌäp-ə-rə-ˈser-ē-ə, -ˈsir-\ *n* [It, lit., serious opera] : an 18th century opera with a heroic or legendary subject

op·er·ate \ˈäp-(ə-)ˌrāt\ *vb* **-at·ed; -at·ing** [L *operatus*, pp. of *operari* to work, fr. *oper-, opus* work; akin to OE *efnan* to perform, Skt *apas* work] *vi* **1** : to perform a function : exert power or influence <factors *operating* against our success> **2** : to produce an appropriate effect <the drug *operated* quickly> **3 a** : to perform an operation or a series of operations **b** : to perform surgery **c** : to carry on a military or naval action or mission **4** : to follow a course of conduct that is often irregular <crooked gamblers *operating* in the club> ~ *vt* **1** : to bring about : EFFECT **2 a** : to cause to function : WORK **b** : to put or keep in operation **3** : to perform an operation on; *esp* : to perform surgery on

op·er·at·ing \ˈäp-(ə-)ˌrāt-iŋ\ *adj* : of, relating to, or used for or in operations <~ expenses> <a hospital ~ room>

operating system *n* : software that supports or complements the hardware of a computer system (as by keeping track of the different programs in multiprogramming)

op·er·a·tion \ˌäp-ə-ˈrā-shən\ *n* **1** : performance of a practical work or of something involving the practical application of principles or processes **2 a** : an exertion of power or influence <the ~ of a drug> **b** : the quality or state of being functional or operative <the plant is now in ~> **c** : a method or manner of functioning <a machine of very simple ~> **3** : EFFICACY, POTENCY — archaic except in legal usage **4** : a procedure carried out on a living body usu. with instruments esp. for the repair of damage or the restoration of health **5** : any of various mathematical or logical processes (as addition) of deriving one expression from others according to a rule **6 a** : a usu. military action, mission, or maneuver including its planning and execution **b** *pl* : the office on the flight line of an airfield where pilots file clearance for flights and where flying from the field is controlled **c** *pl* : the agency of an organization charged with carrying on the principal planning and operating functions of a headquarters and its subordinate units **7** : a business transaction esp. when speculative **8** : a single step performed by a computer in the execution of a program

op·er·a·tion·al \-shnəl, -shən-ᵊl\ *adj* **1** : of or relating to operation or to an operation <the ~ gap between planning and production> **2** : of, relating to, or based on operations <~ definitions> **3 a** : of, engaged in, or connected with execution of military or naval operations in campaign or battle **b** : ready for or in condition to undertake a destined function — **op·er·a·tion·al·ly** \-ē\ *adv*

op·er·a·tion·al·ism \-ˌiz-əm\ *n* : a view that the concepts or terms used in nonanalytic scientific statements must be definable in terms of identifiable and repeatable operations — **op·er·a·tion·al·ist** \-əst\ *n* — **op·er·a·tion·al·is·tic** \-ˌrā-shnəl-ˈis-tik, -shən-ᵊl-\ *adj*

op·er·a·tion·ism \ˌäp-ə-ˈrā-shə-ˌniz-əm\ *n* : OPERATIONALISM — **op·er·a·tion·ist** \-sh(ə-)nəst\ *n*

operations research *n* : the application of scientific and esp. mathematical methods to the study and analysis of complex overall problems

¹op·er·a·tive \ˈäp-(ə-)rət-iv, ˈäp-ə-ˌrāt-\ *adj* **1** : producing an appropriate effect : EFFICACIOUS **2** : exerting force or influence : OPERATING **3 a** : having to do with physical operations (as of machines) **b** : WORKING <an ~ craftsman> **4** : based upon or consisting of an operation <~ dentistry> — **op·er·a·tive·ly** *adv* — **op·er·a·tive·ness** *n*

²operative *n* : OPERATOR: as **a** : ARTISAN, MECHANIC **b** : a secret agent **c** : PRIVATE DETECTIVE

op·er·a·tor \ˈäp-(ə-)ˌrāt-ər\ *n* **1** : one that operates: as **a** : one that operates a machine or device **b** : one that operates a business **c** : one that performs surgical operations **d** : one that deals in stocks or commodities **2 a** : MOUNTEBANK, FRAUD **b** : a shrewd and skillful person who knows how to circumvent restrictions or difficulties **3 a** : a mathematical or logical symbol denoting an operation to be performed **b** : a mathematical function **4** : a chromosomal region that triggers formation of messenger RNA by one or more nearby structural genes and is itself subject to inhibition by a genetic repressor — called also *operator gene;* compare OPERON

¹oper·cu·lar \ō-ˈpər-kyə-lər\ *adj* : of, relating to, or constituting an operculum

²opercular *n* : an opercular part (as a bone or scale)

oper·cu·late \ō-ˈpər-kyə-lət\ *also* **oper·cu·lat·ed** \-ˌlāt-əd\ *adj* : having an operculum

oper·cu·lum \ō-ˈpər-kyə-ləm\ *n, pl* **-la** \-lə\ *also* **-lums** [NL, fr. L, cover, fr. *operire* to shut, cover — more at WEIR] **1** : a lid or covering flat (as of a moss capsule or a pyxidium in a seed plant) **2** : a body process or part that suggests a lid: as **a** : a horny or shelly plate on the posterior dorsal surface of the foot in many gastropod mollusks that closes the shell when the animal is retracted **b** : the covering of the gills of a fish — see FISH illustration

op·er·et·ta \ˌäp-ə-ˈret-ə\ *n* [It, dim. of *opera*] : a usu. romantic comic opera that includes songs and dancing — **op·er·et·tist** \-ˈret-əst\ *n*

op·er·on \ˈäp-ə-ˌrän\ *n* [*operator* + ²*-on*] : the closely linked combination of an operator and the structural genes it regulates

op·er·ose \ˈäp-ə-ˌrōs\ *adj* [L *operosus*, fr. *oper-, opus* work — more at OPERATE] : TEDIOUS, WEARISOME — **op·er·ose·ly** *adv* — **op·er·ose·ness** *n*

Ophe·lia \ō-ˈfēl-yə\ *n* : the daughter of Polonius in Shakespeare's *Hamlet*

ophid·i·an \ō-ˈfid-ē-ən\ *adj* [deriv. of Gk *ophis*] : of, relating to, or resembling snakes — **ophidian** *n*

ophi·ol·o·gy \ˌō-fē-ˈäl-ə-jē, ˌäf-ē-\ *n* [Gk *ophis* + E *-logy*] **:** a branch of herpetology dealing with snakes
ophi·oph·a·gous \ˌō-fē-ˈäf-ə-gəs, ˌäf-ē-\ *adj* [Gk *ophiophagos,* fr. *ophis* + *-phagos* -phagous] **:** feeding on snakes
Ophir \ˈō-fər\ *n* [Heb *Ōphīr*] **:** a biblical land of uncertain location but reputedly rich in gold
ophite \ˈäf-ˌīt, ˈō-ˌfīt\ *n* [L, fr. Gk *ophitēs* (*lithos*), lit., serpentine (stone), fr. *ophitēs* snakelike, fr. *ophis* snake; akin to L *anguis* snake, *anguilla* eel, Gk *enchelys* eel, *echidna* viper, *echinos* hedgehog, OE *igil*] **:** any of various usu. green and often mottled or blotched rocks
ophit·ic \ä-ˈfit-ik, ō-\ *adj* **:** having or being a rock fabric in which lath-shaped plagioclase crystals are enclosed in later formed augite
ophi·u·roid \ˌō-fē-ˈyu̇(ə)r-ˌȯid, ˌäf-ē-\ *n* [NL *Ophiuroidea,* group name, fr. *Ophiura,* genus name, fr. Gk *ophis* + *oura* tail — more at SQUIRREL] **:** BRITTLE STAR — **ophiuroid** *adj*
ophthalm- *or* **ophthalmo-** *comb form* [Gk, fr. *ophthalmos*] **:** eye <*ophthalmo*logy> **:** eyeball <*ophthalm*itis>
oph·thal·mia \äf-ˈthal-mē-ə, äp-\ *n* [ME *obtalmia,* fr. LL *ophthalmia,* fr. Gk, fr. *ophthalmos* eye; akin to Gk *ōps* eye — more at EYE] **:** inflammation of the conjunctiva or the eyeball
oph·thal·mic \-mik\ *adj* **:** of, relating to, or situated near the eye
oph·thal·mol·o·gist \ˌäf-ˌthal-ˈmäl-ə-jəst, ˌäp-, -thə(l)-ˈmäl-\ *n* **:** a physician that specializes in ophthalmology — compare OPTICIAN, OPTOMETRIST
oph·thal·mol·o·gy \-ˈmäl-ə-jē\ *n* **:** a branch of medical science dealing with the structure, functions, and diseases of the eye — **oph·thal·mo·log·ic** \-mə-ˈläj-ik\ *adj* — **oph·thal·mo·log·i·cal·ly** \-i-k(ə-)lē\ *adv*
oph·thal·mo·scope \äf-ˈthal-mə-ˌskōp, äp-\ *n* [ISV] **:** an instrument with a mirror centrally perforated for use in viewing the interior of the eye and esp. the retina — **oph·thal·mo·scop·ic** \(ˌ)äf-ˌthal-mə-ˈskäp-ik, (ˌ)äp-\ *or* **oph·thal·mo·scop·i·cal** \-i-kəl\ *adj* — **oph·thal·mos·co·py** \ˌäf-ˌthal-ˈmäs-kə-pē, ˌäp-\ *n*
-opia \ˈō-pē-ə\ *n comb form* [NL, fr. Gk *-ōpia,* fr. *ōps*] **1 :** condition of having (such) vision <dipl*opia*> **2 :** condition of having (such) a visual defect <hyper*opia*>
¹opi·ate \ˈō-pē-ət, -ˌāt\ *adj* **1 :** containing or mixed with opium **2 a :** inducing sleep **:** NARCOTIC **b :** causing dullness or inaction
²opiate *n* **1 :** a preparation or derivative of opium; *broadly* **:** NARCOTIC 1a **2 :** something that induces rest or inaction or quiets uneasiness
opine \ō-ˈpīn\ *vb* **opined; opin·ing** [MF *opiner,* fr. L *opinari* to have an opinion] *vt* **:** to state as an opinion ~ *vi* **:** to express opinions
opin·ion \ə-ˈpin-yən\ *n* [ME, fr. MF, fr. L *opinion-, opinio;* akin to L *opinari*] **1 a :** a view, judgment, or appraisal formed in the mind about a particular matter **b :** APPROVAL, ESTEEM **2 a :** belief stronger than impression and less strong than positive knowledge **b :** a generally held view **3 a :** a formal expression by an expert of his judgment or advice **b :** the formal expression (as by a judge, court, or referee) of the legal reasons and principles upon which a legal decision is based
syn OPINION, VIEW, BELIEF, CONVICTION, PERSUASION, SENTIMENT *shared meaning element* **:** a judgment one holds to be true
opin·ion·at·ed \-yə-ˌnāt-əd\ *adj* **:** unduly adhering to one's own opinion or to preconceived notions — **opin·ion·at·ed·ly** *adv* — **opin·ion·at·ed·ness** *n*
opin·ion·ative \-ˌnāt-iv\ *adj* **1 :** of, relating to, or consisting of opinion **:** DOCTRINAL **2 :** OPINIONATED — **opin·ion·ative·ly** *adv* — **opin·ion·ative·ness** *n*
opis·tho·branch \ə-ˈpis-thə-ˌbraŋk\ *n, pl* **-branchs** [NL *Opisthobranchia,* group name, fr. Gk *opisthen* behind + *branchion* gill — more at BRANCHIA] **:** any of a large order (*Opisthobranchia*) of marine gastropod mollusks that have the gills when present posterior to the heart and have no operculum — **opisthobranch** *adj*
op·is·thog·na·thous \ˌäp-əs-ˈthäg-nə-thəs\ *adj* [Gk *opisthen* behind + E *-gnathous;* akin to Gk *epi-* on — more at EPI-] **1 :** having retreating jaws **2 :** having the mouthparts ventral and posterior to the cranium — used esp. of insects
opi·um \ˈō-pē-əm\ *n* [ME, fr. L, fr. Gk *opion,* fr. dim. of *opos* sap] **1 :** a bitter brownish addictive narcotic drug that consists of the dried juice of the opium poppy **2 :** something having an effect like that of opium **:** STUPEFIER
opium poppy *n* **:** an annual Eurasian poppy (*Papaver somniferum*) cultivated since antiquity as the source of opium, for its edible oily seeds, or for its showy flowers
opos·sum \(ə-)ˈpäs-əm\ *n, pl* **opossums** *also* **opossum** [fr. *âpäsûm,* lit., white animal (in some Algonquian language of Virginia)] **1 :** any of various American marsupials (family Didelphidae); *esp* **:** a common omnivorous largely nocturnal and arboreal mammal (*Didelphis virginiana*) of the eastern U.S. **2 :** any of several Australian phalangers

opossum 1

opp *abbr* opposite
¹op·po·nent \ə-ˈpō-nənt\ *n* [L *opponent-, opponens,* prp. of *opponere*] **1 :** one that takes an opposite position (as in a debate, contest, or conflict) **2 :** a muscle that opposes or counteracts and limits the action of another
syn OPPONENT, ANTAGONIST, ADVERSARY *shared meaning element* **:** one who expresses or manifests opposition
²opponent *adj* **1 :** ANTAGONISTIC, OPPOSING **2 :** situated in front
op·por·tune \ˌäp-ər-ˈt(y)ün\ *adj* [ME, fr. MF *opportun,* fr. L *opportunus,* fr. *ob-* toward + *portus* port, harbor — more at OB-] **1 :** suitable or convenient for a particular occurrence <an ~ moment> **2 :** occurring at an appropriate time <an ~ offer of assistance> *syn* see SEASONABLE *ant* inopportune — **op**[…]**tune·ly** *adv* — **op·por·tune·ness** \-ˈt(y)ün-nəs\ *n*
op·por·tun·ism \-ˈt(y)ü-ˌniz-əm\ *n* **:** the art, policy, or practic[e of] taking advantage of opportunities or circumstances esp. with li[ttle] regard for principles or consequences — **op·por·tun·ist** \-nəst\ *n or adj* — **op·por·tu·nis·tic** \-t(y)ü-ˈnis-tik\ *adj* — **op·por·tu·ni**[s]**ti·cal·ly** \-ti-k(ə-)lē\ *adv*
op·por·tu·ni·ty \ˌäp-ər-ˈt(y)ü-nət-ē\ *n, pl* **-ties** **1 :** a favorable juncture of circumstances <the halt provided an ~ for rest and refreshment> **2 :** a good chance for advancement or progress
op·pos·able \ə-ˈpō-zə-bəl\ *adj* **1 :** capable of being opposed or resisted **2 :** capable of being placed against one or more of the remaining digits <man's ~ thumb> — **op·pos·abil·i·ty** \-ˌpō-zə-ˈbil-ət-ē\ *n*
op·pose \ə-ˈpōz\ *vt* **op·posed; op·pos·ing** [F *opposer,* fr. L *opponere* (perf. indic. *opposui*), fr. *ob-* against + *ponere* to place — more at OB-, POSITION] **1 :** to place opposite or against something **2 :** to place over against something for resistance, counterbalance, or contrast **3 :** to offer resistance to — **op·pos·er** *n*
syn OPPOSE, COMBAT, RESIST, WITHSTAND, ANTAGONIZE *shared meaning element* **:** to set oneself against someone or something
op·posed \-ˈpōzd\ *adj* **:** set or placed in opposition **:** CONTRARY
op·pose·less \ə-ˈpōz-ləs\ *adj* **:** IRRESISTIBLE
¹op·po·site \ˈäp-ə-zət, ˈäp-sət\ *n* **1 :** something that is opposed or contrary **2 :** ANTONYM
²opposite *adj* [ME, fr. MF, fr. L *oppositus,* pp. of *opponere*] **1 a :** set over against something that is at the other end or side of an intervening line or space <~ interior angles> <~ ends of a diameter> **b :** situated in pairs on an axis each being separated from the other by half the circumference of the axis <~ leaves> — compare ALTERNATE **2 a :** occupying an opposing and often antagonistic position <~ sides of the question> **b :** diametrically different (as in nature or character) <~ meanings> **3 :** contrary to one another or to a thing specified **:** REVERSE <gave them ~ directions> **4 :** being the other of a matching or contrasting pair **:** COMPLEMENTARY <members of the ~ sex> **5 :** of, relating to, or being the side of a baseball field that is near the first base line for a right-handed batter and near the third base line for a left-handed batter <hit a single to the ~ field> — **op·po·site·ly** *adv* — **op·po·site·ness** *n*
syn OPPOSITE, CONTRADICTORY, CONTRARY, ANTITHETICAL *shared meaning element* **:** being so far apart as to be or seem irreconcilable. OPPOSITE, the inclusive term, may replace any of the others but finds its typical application in description of abstract things that stand in sharp contrast or complete antagonism <held *opposite* views on the solution of the problem> <the boys went in *opposite* directions> CONTRADICTORY applies to things that so completely negate each other that if one is true or valid the other must be false or invalid <the suspects made *contradictory* statements to the police> CONTRARY can imply extreme divergence (as of opinions or motives) or, especially as used in formal logic, diametrical opposition <his conclusion was *contrary* to mine> <they drifted off in a *contrary* direction> ANTITHETICAL stresses clear and unequivocal diametric opposition <the essential interests of men and women are eternally *antithetical* —H. L. Mencken>
³opposite *adv* **:** on or to an opposite side
⁴opposite *prep* **1 :** across from and usu. facing or on the same level with <sat ~ each other> **2 :** in a role complementary to <played ~ the leading man in the comedy>
opposite number *n* **:** a member of a system or class who holds relatively the same position as a particular member in a corresponding system or class <union executives met with their *opposite numbers* in industry>
op·po·si·tion \ˌäp-ə-ˈzish-ən\ *n* **1 :** a configuration in which one celestial body is opposite another in the sky or in which the elongation is near or equal to 180 degrees **2 :** the relation between two propositions having the same subject and predicate but differing in quantity or quality or both **3 :** an act of setting opposite or over against **:** the condition of being so set **4 :** hostile or contrary action or condition **5 a :** something that opposes; *specif* **:** a body of persons opposing something **b** *often cap* **:** a political party opposing and prepared to replace the party in power — **op·po·si·tion·al** \-ˈzish-nəl, -ən-ᵊl\ *adj*
op·press \ə-ˈpres\ *vt* [ME *oppressen,* fr. MF *oppresser,* fr. L *oppressus,* pp. of *opprimere,* fr. *ob-* against + *premere* to press — more at OB-, PRESS] **1 a** *archaic* **:** SUPPRESS **b :** to crush or burden by abuse of power or authority **2 :** to burden spiritually or mentally **:** weigh heavily upon — **op·pres·sor** \-ˈpres-ər\ *n*
op·pres·sion \ə-ˈpresh-ən\ *n* **1 a :** unjust or cruel exercise of authority or power **b :** something that oppresses esp. in being an unjust or excessive exercise of power **2 :** a sense of being weighed down in body or mind **:** DEPRESSION
op·pres·sive \ə-ˈpres-iv\ *adj* **1 :** unreasonably burdensome or severe <~ legislation> **2 :** TYRANNICAL **3 :** overwhelming or depressing to the spirit or senses <an ~ climate> *syn* see ONEROUS — **op·pres·sive·ly** *adv* — **op·pres·sive·ness** *n*
op·pro·bri·ous \ə-ˈprō-brē-əs\ *adj* **1 :** expressive of opprobrium **:** SCURRILOUS <~ language> **2 :** deserving of opprobrium **:** INFAMOUS — **op·pro·bri·ous·ly** *adv* — **op·pro·bri·ous·ness** *n*
op·pro·bri·um \-brē-əm\ *n* [L, fr. *opprobrare* to reproach, fr. *ob* in the way of + *probrum* reproach; akin to L *pro* forward and to L *ferre* to carry, bring — more at EPI-, FOR, BEAR] **1 :** something that brings disgrace **2 a :** public disgrace or ill fame that follows from conduct considered grossly wrong or vicious **:** INFAMY **b :** CONTEMPT, REPROACH *syn* see DISGRACE

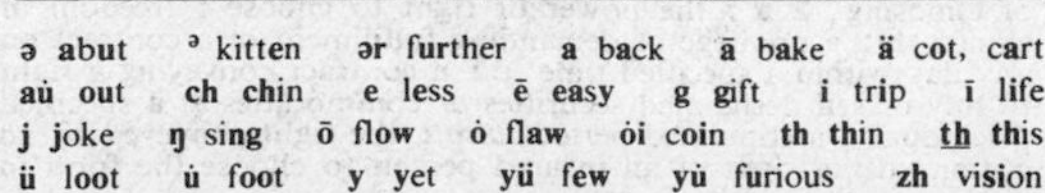
ə abut ᵊ kitten ər further a back ā bake ä cot, cart
au̇ out ch chin e less ē easy g gift i trip ī life
j joke ŋ sing ō flow ȯ flaw ȯi coin th thin th this
ü loot u̇ foot y yet yü few yu̇ furious zh vision

ugn \ə-ˈpyün, ä-\ *vt* [ME *oppugnen,* fr. L *oppugnare,* fr. *ob-* ainst + *pugnare* to fight — more at OB-, PUNGENT] **1 :** to fight ainst : ASSAIL **2 :** to call in question — **op·pugn·er** *n*

s \ˈäps\ *n* [L] **:** the Roman goddess of fertility and plenty and he wife of Saturn

p·sin \ˈäp-sən\ *n* [prob. back-formation fr. *rhodopsin*] **:** any of various colorless proteins that are formed with retinal by the action of light on a visual pigment (as rhodopsin)

-op·sis \ˈäp-səs\ *n comb form, pl* **-op·ses** \-ˌsēz\ *or* **-op·si·des** \-sə-ˌdēz\ [NL, fr. Gk, fr. *opsis* appearance, vision] **:** structure resembling a (specified) thing <cary*opsis*>

op·son·ic \äp-ˈsän-ik\ *adj* **:** of, relating to, or involving opsonin

op·so·nin \ˈäp-sə-nən\ *n* [L *opsonium* relish (fr. Gk *opsōnion* victuals, fr. *opsōnein* to purchase victuals) + E *-in* — more at OLIGOPSONY] **:** an antibody of blood serum that makes foreign cells more susceptible to the action of the phagocytes

-op·sy \ˌäp-sē, əp-\ *n comb form* [Gk *-opsia,* fr. *opsis*] **:** examination <necr*opsy*>

[1]**opt** \ˈäpt\ *vi* [F *opter,* fr. L *optare* — more at OPTION] **:** to make a choice; *esp* **:** to decide in favor of something <~*ed* for a tax increase —Tom Wicker>

[2]**opt** *abbr* **1** optical; optician; optics **2** optional

op·ta·tive \ˈäp-tət-iv\ *adj* **1 a :** of, relating to, or constituting a verbal mood that is expressive of wish or desire **b :** of, relating to, or constituting a sentence that is expressive of wish or hope **2 :** expressing desire or wish — **optative** *n* — **op·ta·tive·ly** *adv*

[1]**op·tic** \ˈäp-tik\ *adj* [MF *optique,* fr. ML *opticus,* fr. Gk *optikos,* fr. *opsesthai* to be going to see; akin to Gk *opsis* appearance, *ōps* eye — more at EYE] **1 :** of or relating to vision or the eye **2 :** dependent chiefly on vision for orientation

[2]**optic** *n* **1 :** EYE **2 :** any of the lenses, prisms, or mirrors of an optical instrument; *also* **:** an optical instrument

op·ti·cal \ˈäp-ti-kəl\ *adj* **1 :** of or relating to the science of optics **2 a :** of or relating to vision : VISUAL <an ~ illusion> **b :** VISIBLE <an ~ galaxy> **c :** designed to aid vision <an ~ instrument> **3 a :** of, relating to, or utilizing light <an ~ emission> <an ~ telescope> <~ microscopy> **b :** involving the use of light-sensitive devices to acquire information for a computer <~ character recognition> **4 :** of or relating to optical art — **op·ti·cal·ly** \-k(ə-)lē\ *adv*

optical activity *n* **:** ability to rotate the plane of vibration of polarized light to the right or left

optical art *n* **:** nonobjective art characterized by the use of straight or curved lines or geometric patterns often for an illusory effect (as of motion)

optical bench *n* **:** an apparatus that is fitted for the convenient location and adjustment of light sources and optical devices and that is used for the observation and measurement of optical phenomena

optical glass *n* **:** flint or crown glass of well-defined characteristics used esp. for making lenses

optical illusion *n* **:** ILLUSION 2a(1)

optical rotation *n* **:** the angle through which the plane of vibration of polarized light that traverses an optically active substance is rotated

optic axis *n* **:** a line in a doubly refracting medium that is parallel to the direction in which all components of plane-polarized light travel with the same speed

optic chiasma *n* [NL *chiasma* X-shaped configuration — more at CHIASMA] **:** the X-shaped partial decussation on the undersurface of the hypothalamus through which the optic nerves are continuous with the brain — called also *optic chiasm*

optic disk *n* **:** the nearly circular light-colored area at the back of the retina where the optic nerve enters the eyeball

op·ti·cian \äp-ˈtish-ən\ *n* **1 :** a maker of or dealer in optical items and instruments **2 :** one that grinds spectacle lenses to prescription and dispenses spectacles — compare OPHTHALMOLOGIST, OPTOMETRIST

optic nerve *n* **:** either of the pair of nerves that comprise the second pair of cranial nerves, arise from the ventral part of the diencephalon, supply the retina, and conduct visual stimuli to the brain — see EYE illustration

op·tics \ˈäp-tiks\ *n pl but sing or pl in constr* **1 :** a science that deals with the genesis and propagation of light, the changes that it undergoes and produces, and other phenomena closely associated with it **2 :** optical properties

op·ti·mal \ˈäp-tə-məl\ *adj* **:** most desirable or satisfactory : OPTIMUM — **op·ti·mal·i·ty** \ˌäp-tə-ˈmal-ət-ē\ *n* — **op·ti·mal·ly** \-mə-lē\ *adv*

op·ti·mism \ˈäp-tə-ˌmiz-əm\ *n* [F *optimisme,* fr. L *optimum,* n., best, fr. neut. of *optimus* best; akin to L *ops* power — more at OPULENT] **1 :** a doctrine that this world is the best possible world **2 :** an inclination to put the most favorable construction upon actions and events or to anticipate the best possible outcome — **op·ti·mist** \-məst\ *n* — **optimist** *or* **op·ti·mis·tic** \ˌäp-tə-ˈmis-tik\ *or* **op·ti·mis·ti·cal** \-ti-kəl\ *adj* — **op·ti·mis·ti·cal·ly** \-ti-k(ə-)lē\ *adv*

Op·ti·mist \ˈäp-tə-məst\ *n* [*Optimist* (*club*)] **:** a member of a major international service club

op·ti·mize \ˈäp-tə-ˌmīz\ *vt* **-mized; -miz·ing :** to make as perfect, effective, or functional as possible — **op·ti·mi·za·tion** \ˌäp-tə-mə-ˈzā-shən\ *n* — **op·ti·miz·er** \ˈäp-tə-ˌmī-zər\ *n*

op·ti·mum \ˈäp-tə-məm\ *n, pl* **-ma** \-mə\ *also* **-mums** [L] **1 :** the amount or degree of something that is most favorable to some end; *esp* **:** the most favorable condition for the growth and reproduction of an organism **2 :** greatest degree attained or attainable under implied or specified conditions — **optimum** *adj*

[1]**op·tion** \ˈäp-shən\ *n* [F, fr. L *option-, optio* free choice; akin to L *optare* to choose, Gk epi*opsesthai* to be going to choose] **1 :** an act of choosing **2 a :** the power or right to choose : freedom of choice **b :** a privilege of demanding fulfillment of a contract on any day within a specified time **c :** a contract conveying a right to buy or sell designated securities or commodities at a specified price during a stipulated period; *also* **:** the right conveyed by an option **d :** a right of an insured person to choose the form in which payments due him on a policy shall be made or applied **3 :** something that may be chosen: as **a :** an alternative course of action <didn't have many ~*s* open to him in choosing a career> **b :** an item that is offered in addition to or in place of standard equipment <a car that includes air-conditioning and a V-8 engine among its ~*s*> **4 :** an offensive football play in which a back may choose whether to pass or run with the ball — called also *option pass, option play* **syn** see CHOICE

[2]**option** *vt* **:** to grant or take an option on

op·tion·al \ˈäp-shnəl, -shən-ᵊl\ *adj* **:** involving an option : not compulsory — **op·tion·al·ly** \-ē\ *adv*

op·to·ki·net·ic \ˌäp-tō-kə-ˈnet-ik, -kī-\ *adj* [Gk *optos* + *kinetic*] **:** of, relating to, or involving movements of the eyes

op·tom·e·trist \äp-ˈtäm-ə-trəst\ *n* **:** a specialist in optometry — compare OPHTHALMOLOGIST, OPTICIAN

op·tom·e·try \-trē\ *n* [Gk *optos* (verbal of *opsesthai* to be going to see) + ISV *-metry* — more at OPTIC] **:** the art or profession of examining the eye for defects and faults of refraction and prescribing correctional lenses or exercises but not drugs or surgery — **op·to·met·ric** \ˌäp-tə-ˈme-trik\ *also* **op·to·met·ri·cal** \-tri-kəl\ *adj*

opt out *vi* **:** to choose not to participate in something — often used with *of* <impossible for anybody to *opt out* of politics —Brian Crozier>

op·u·lence \ˈäp-yə-lən(t)s\ *n* **1 :** WEALTH, AFFLUENCE **2 :** ABUNDANCE, PROFUSION

op·u·lent \-lənt\ *adj* [L *opulentus,* fr. *ops* power, help; akin to L *opus* work] **:** exhibiting or characterized by opulence: as **a :** having a large estate or property : WEALTHY <hoping to marry an ~ widow> **b :** amply or plentifully provided or fashioned often to the point of ostentation <living in ~ comfort> **syn 1** see RICH **ant** destitute, indigent **2** see LUXURIOUS — **op·u·lent·ly** *adv*

opun·tia \ō-ˈpən-ch(ē-)ə\ *n* [L, a plant, fr. fem. of *opuntius* of Opus, fr. *Opunt-, Opus* Opus, ancient city in Greece] **:** PRICKLY PEAR

opus \ˈō-pəs\ *n, pl* **opera** \ˈō-pə-rə, ˈäp-ə-\ *also* **opus·es** \ˈō-pə-səz\ [L *oper-, opus* — more at OPERATE] **:** WORK; *esp* **:** a musical composition or set of compositions usu. numbered in the order of its issue — abbr. *op*

opus·cule \ō-ˈpəs-(ˌ)kyü(ə)l\ *n* [F, fr. L *opusculum,* dim. of *opus*] **:** a small or petty work : OPUSCULUM

opus·cu·lum \ō-ˈpəs-kyə-ləm\ *n, pl* **-la** \-lə\ [L] **:** a minor work (as of literature) — usu. used in pl.

[1]**or** \ər, (ˌ)ȯ(ə)r\ *conj* [ME *other, or,* fr. OE *oththe;* akin to OHG *eddo* or] **1** — used as a function word to indicate an alternative <coffee ~ tea> <sink ~ swim>, the equivalent or substitutive character of two words or phrases <lessen ~ abate>, or approximation or uncertainty <in five ~ six days> **2** *archaic* **:** EITHER **3** *archaic* **:** WHETHER **4** — used in logic as a sentential connective that forms a complex sentence which is true when at least one of its constituent sentences is true — compare DISJUNCTION

[2]**or** *prep* [ME, fr. *or,* adv., early, before, fr. ON *ār;* akin to OE *ǣr* early — more at ERE] *archaic* **:** BEFORE

[3]**or** *conj, archaic* **:** BEFORE

[4]**or** \ˈȯ(ə)r\ *n* [MF, gold, fr. L *aurum* — more at ORIOLE] **:** the heraldic color gold or yellow

[1]**OR** \ˈȯ(ə)r\ *n* [[1]*or*] **:** a logical operator equivalent to the sentential connective *or* <~ gate in a computer>

[2]**OR** *abbr* **1** operating room **2** Oregon **3** owner's risk

[1]**-or** \ər, ˌȯ(ə)r, ˈȯ(ə)r\ *n suffix* [ME, fr. OF *-eur, -eor* & L *-or;* OF *-eur,* fr. L *-or;* OF *-eor,* fr. L *-ator* -or, fr. *-atus,* pp. suffix + *-or* — more at -ATE] **:** one that does a (specified) thing <grant*or*>

[2]**-or** \ər\ *n suffix* [ME, fr. OF *-eur,* fr. L *-or*] **:** condition : activity <demean*or*>

ora *pl of* OS

or·ache *or* **or·ach** \ˈȯr-ich, ˈär-\ *n* [ME *orage,* fr. MF *arrache,* fr. (assumed) VL *atrapic-, atrapex,* fr. Gk *atraphaxys*] **:** any of a genus (*Atriplex*) of herbs of the goosefoot family that have small diclinous flowers and a utricular fruit enclosed in two bracts

or·a·cle \ˈȯr-ə-kəl, ˈär-\ *n* [ME, fr. MF, fr. L *oraculum,* fr. *orare* to speak — more at ORATION] **1 a :** a person (as a priestess of ancient Greece) through whom a deity is believed to speak **b :** a shrine in which a deity reveals hidden knowledge or the divine purpose through such a person **c :** an answer or decision given by an oracle **2 a :** a person giving wise or authoritative decisions or opinions **b :** an authoritative or wise expression or answer

orac·u·lar \ȯ-ˈrak-yə-lər, ə-\ *adj* [L *oraculum*] **1 :** of, relating to, or being an oracle **2 :** resembling an oracle (as in solemnity of delivery) **syn** see DICTATORIAL — **orac·u·lar·i·ty** \-ˌrak-yə-ˈlar-ət-ē\ *n* — **orac·u·lar·ly** \-ˈrak-yə-lər-lē\ *adv*

[1]**oral** \ˈōr-əl, ˈȯr-, ˈär-\ *adj* [L *or-, os* mouth; akin to OE *ōra* border, L *ora*] **1 a :** uttered by the mouth or in words : SPOKEN **b :** using speech or the lips esp. in teaching the deaf **2 a :** of, given through, or affecting the mouth **b :** being on or relating to the same surface as the mouth **3 a :** of, relating to, or characterized by the first stage of psychosexual development in which libidinal gratification is derived from intake (as of food), by sucking, and later by biting **b :** of, relating to, or characterized by personality traits of passive dependency and aggressiveness — **oral·i·ty** \ō-ˈral-ət-ē, ȯ-\ *n* — **oral·ly** \ˈōr-ə-lē, ˈȯr-, ˈär-\ *adv*

[2]**oral** *n* **:** an oral examination — usu. used in pl. <passed his ~*s* and was awarded the doctorate>

oral history *n* **:** historical information that is obtained in interviews with persons who have led significant lives and that is usu. tape-recorded — **oral historian** *n*

[1]**or·ange** \ˈȯr-inj, ˈär-, -ənj\ *n* [ME, fr. MF, fr. OProv *auranja,* fr. Ar *nāranj,* fr. Per *nārang,* fr. Skt *nāraṅga* orange tree, of Dravidian origin; akin to Tamil *naṟu* fragrant] **1 a :** a globose berry with a reddish yellow rind and a sweet edible pulp **b :** any of various rather small evergreen trees (genus *Citrus*) with ovate unifoliolate leaves, hard yellow wood, fragrant white flowers, and fruits that are oranges **2 :** any of several trees or fruits resembling the orange **3 :** any of a group of colors that lie midway between red and yellow in hue and are of medium lightness and moderate to high saturation

[2]**orange** *adj* **1 :** of or relating to the orange **2 :** of the color orange

Orange *adj* **:** of, relating to, or sympathizing with Orangemen — **Or·ange·ism** \-ˌiz-əm\ *n*

or·ange·ade \ˌȯr-in-ˈjād, ˌär-, -ən-\ *n* [F, fr. *orange* + *-ade*] **:** a beverage of sweetened orange juice mixed with plain or carbonated water

orange chromide *n* **:** a brilliant orange or yellow red-spotted fish (*Etroplus maculatus*) often kept in tropical aquariums

orange hawkweed *n* **:** a European hawkweed (*Hieracium aurantiacum*) that has flower heads with bright orange-red rays and is a troublesome weed esp. in northeastern No. America — called also *Indian paintbrush*

Or·ange·man \ˈȯr-inj-mən, ˈär-, -ənj-\ *n* [William III of England, prince of *Orange*] **1 :** a member of a secret society organized in the north of Ireland in 1795 to defend the British sovereign and to support the Protestant religion **2 :** a Protestant Irishman esp. of Ulster

orange peel *n* **:** a rough surface (as on porcelain) like that of an orange

orange pekoe *n* **:** a tea formerly made from the tiny leaf and end bud of the spray; *broadly* **:** India or Ceylon tea of good quality

or·ange·ry \ˈȯr-inj-(ə-)rē, ˈär-, -ənj-\ *n, pl* **-ries :** a greenhouse or other protected place for raising oranges in cool climates

or·ange·wood \ˈȯr-inj-ˌwu̇d, ˈär-, -ənj-\ *n* **:** the wood of the orange tree used esp. in turnery and carving

or·ang·ish \-in-jish, -ən-\ *adj* **:** somewhat orange

orang·utan *or* **orang·ou·tan** \ə-ˈraŋ-ə-ˌtaŋ, -ˌtan\ *n* [Malay *orang hutan,* fr. *orang* man + *hutan* forest] **:** a largely herbivorous arboreal anthropoid ape (*Pongo pygmaeus*) of Borneo and Sumatra that is about two thirds as large as the gorilla and has brown skin, long sparse reddish brown hair, and very long arms

orangutan

or·angy *or* **or·ang·ey** \ˈȯr-in-jē, ˈär-, -ən-\ *adj* **:** having an orange color or tinge

orate \ȯ-ˈrāt\ *vi* **orat·ed; orat·ing** [back-formation fr. *oration*] **:** to speak in an elevated and often pompous manner

ora·tion \ə-ˈrā-shən, ȯ-\ *n* [L *oration-, oratio* speech, oration, fr. *oratus,* pp. of *orare* to plead, speak, pray; akin to Russ *orat'* to yell] **:** an elaborate discourse delivered in a formal and dignified manner

or·a·tor \ˈȯr-ət-ər, ˈär-\ *n* **1 :** one who delivers an oration **2 :** one distinguished for his skill and power as a public speaker

Or·a·to·ri·an \ˌȯr-ə-ˈtȯr-ē-ən, ˌär-, -ˈtȯr-\ *n* **:** a member of the Congregation of the Oratory of St. Philip Neri founded in Rome in 1575 and comprising independent communities of secular priests under obedience but without vows — **Oratorian** *adj*

or·a·tor·i·cal \ˌȯr-ə-ˈtȯr-i-kəl, ˌär-ə-ˈtär-\ *adj* **:** of, relating to, or characteristic of an orator or oratory — **or·a·tor·i·cal·ly** \-k(ə-)lē\ *adv*

or·a·to·rio \ˌȯr-ə-ˈtōr-ē-ˌō, ˌär-, -ˈtȯr-\ *n, pl* **-ri·os** [It, fr. the *Oratorio* di San Filippo Neri (Oratory of St. Philip Neri) in Rome] **:** a choral work usu. on a scriptural subject consisting chiefly of recitatives, arias, and choruses without action or scenery

[1]**or·a·to·ry** \ˈȯr-ə-ˌtōr-ē, ˈär-, -ˌtȯr-\ *n, pl* **-ries** [ME *oratorie,* fr. LL *oratorium,* fr. L *oratus,* pp.] **1 :** a place of prayer; *esp* **:** a private or institutional chapel **2** *cap* **:** an Oratorian congregation, house, or church

[2]**oratory** *n* [L *oratoria,* fr. fem. of *oratorius* oratorical, fr. *oratus,* pp.] **1 :** the art of speaking in public eloquently or effectively <a student of ~> **2 a :** public speaking that employs oratory **b :** public speaking that is characterized by the use of stock phrases and that appeals chiefly to the emotions

[1]**orb** \ˈȯ(ə)rb\ *n* [MF *orbe,* fr. L *orbis* circle, disk, orb; akin to L *orbita* track, rut] **1 :** any of the concentric spheres in old astronomy surrounding the earth and carrying the celestial bodies in their revolutions **2** *archaic* **:** something circular **:** CIRCLE, ORBIT **3 :** a spherical body; *esp* **:** a celestial sphere **4 :** EYE **5 :** a sphere surmounted by a cross symbolizing kingly power and justice

[2]**orb** *vt* **1 :** to form into a disk or circle **2** *archaic* **:** ENCIRCLE, SURROUND, ENCLOSE ~ *vi, archaic* **:** to move in an orbit

or·bic·u·lar \ȯr-ˈbik-yə-lər\ *adj* [ME *orbiculer,* fr. MF or LL; MF *orbiculaire,* fr. LL *orbicularis,* fr. L *orbiculus,* dim. of *orbis*] **:** SPHERICAL, CIRCULAR — **or·bic·u·lar·i·ty** \-ˌbik-yə-ˈlar-ət-ē\ *n* — **or·bic·u·lar·ly** \-ˈbik-yə-lər-lē\ *adv*

or·bic·u·late \ȯr-ˈbik-yə-lət\ *adj* **:** circular or nearly circular in outline <an ~ leaf>

[1]**or·bit** \ˈȯr-bət\ *n* [L *orbita*] **1** [ML *orbita,* fr. L] **:** the bony socket of the eye **2 :** a path described by one body in its revolution about another (as by the earth about the sun or by an electron about an atomic nucleus); *also* **:** one complete revolution of a body describing such a path **3 :** a range or sphere of activity or influence <countries that are in the communist ~> — **or·bit·al** \-ᵊl\ *adj*

[2]**orbit** *vt* **1 :** to revolve in an orbit around **:** CIRCLE **2 :** to send up and make revolve in an orbit <~ a satellite> ~ *vi* **:** to travel in circles

or·bit·al \ˈȯr-bət-ᵊl\ *n* [*orbital,* adj.] **:** a subdivision of a nuclear shell containing one or two electrons or none

or·bit·er \-bət-ər\ *n* **:** one that orbits; *esp* **:** a spacecraft designed to orbit a celestial body without landing on its surface

ORC *abbr* Organized Reserve Corps

Or·ca·di·an \ȯr-ˈkād-ē-ən\ *n* [L *Orcades* Orkney islands] **:** a native or inhabitant of the Orkney islands — **Orcadian** *adj*

orch *abbr* orchestra

or·chard \ˈȯr-chərd\ *n* [ME, fr. OE *ortgeard,* fr. L *hortus* garden + OE *geard* yard — more at YARD] **:** a planting of fruit trees or nut trees; *also* **:** the trees of such a planting

orchard grass *n* **:** a widely grown tall stout hay and pasture grass (*Dactylis glomerata*) that grows in tufts with loose open panicles

or·chard·ist \ˈȯr-chərd-əst\ *n* **:** an owner or supervisor of orchards

or·chard·man \-mən, -ˌman\ *n* **:** ORCHARDIST

or·ches·tra \ˈȯr-kə-strə, -ˌkes-trə\ *n* [L, fr. Gk *orchēstra,* fr. *orcheisthai* to dance; akin to Skt *ṛghāyati* he raves] **1 a :** the circular space used by the chorus in front of the proscenium in an ancient Greek theater **b :** a corresponding semicircular space in a Roman theater used for seating important persons **2 a :** the space in front of the stage in a modern theater that is used by an orchestra **b :** the forward section of seats on the main floor of a theater **c :** the main floor of a theater **3 :** a group of musicians including esp. string players organized to perform ensemble music — compare BAND

or·ches·tral \ȯr-ˈkes-trəl\ *adj* **1 :** of, relating to, or composed for an orchestra **2 :** suggestive of an orchestra or its musical qualities — **or·ches·tral·ly** \-trə-lē\ *adv*

or·ches·trate \ˈȯr-kə-ˌstrāt\ *vt* **-trat·ed; -trat·ing 1 a :** to compose or arrange (music) for an orchestra **b :** to provide with orchestration <~ a ballet> **2 :** to arrange or combine so as to achieve a maximum effect <~*s* the elements of his art> — **or·ches·tra·tor** *also* **or·ches·trat·er** \-ˌstrāt-ər\ *n*

or·ches·tra·tion \ˌȯr-kə-ˈstrā-shən\ *n* **1 :** the arrangement of a musical composition for performance by an orchestra; *also* **:** orchestral treatment of a musical composition **2 :** harmonious organization <develop a world community through ~ of cultural diversities —L. K. Frank> — **or·ches·tra·tion·al** \-shnəl, -shən-ᵊl\ *adj*

or·chid \ˈȯr-kəd\ *n* [irreg. fr. NL *Orchis*] **1 :** a plant or flower of a large family (Orchidaceae, the orchid family) of perennial epiphytic or terrestrial plants that usu. have showy 3-petaled flowers with the middle petal enlarged into a lip and differing from the others in shape and color **2 :** a variable color averaging a light purple

or·chis \ˈȯr-kəs\ *n* [NL, genus name, fr. L, orchid, fr. Gk, testicle, orchid; akin to MIr *uirgge* testicle] **:** ORCHID; *esp* **:** one of a genus (*Orchis*) with fleshy roots and a spurred lip

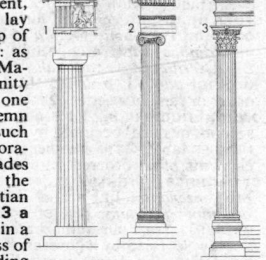

ord *abbr* **1** order **2** ordnance

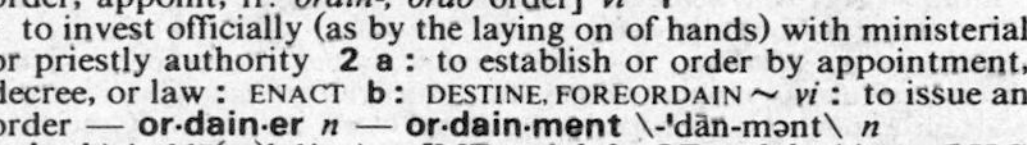

orchid 1

or·dain \ȯr-ˈdān\ *vb* [ME *ordeinen,* fr. OF *ordener,* fr. LL *ordinare,* fr. L, to put in order, appoint, fr. *ordin-, ordo* order] *vt* **1 :** to invest officially (as by the laying on of hands) with ministerial or priestly authority **2 a :** to establish or order by appointment, decree, or law **:** ENACT **b :** DESTINE, FOREORDAIN ~ *vi* **:** to issue an order — **or·dain·er** *n* — **or·dain·ment** \-ˈdān-mənt\ *n*

or·deal \ȯr-ˈdē(-ə)l, ˈȯr-ˌ\ *n* [ME *ordal,* fr. OE *ordāl;* akin to OHG *urteil* judgment; both from a prehistoric WGmc compound derived fr. a compound verb represented by OHG *irteilen* to judge, distribute, fr. *ir-,* perfective prefix + *teilen* to divide, render a verdict; akin to OHG *teil* part — more at ABIDE, DEAL] **1 :** a primitive means used to determine guilt or innocence by submitting the accused to dangerous or painful tests believed to be under supernatural control <~ by fire> **2 :** a severe trial or experience

[1]**or·der** \ˈȯrd-ər\ *n* [MF *ordre,* fr. ML & L; ML *ordin-, ordo* ecclesiastical order, fr. L, arrangement, group, class; akin to L *ordiri* to lay the warp, begin] **1 a :** a group of people united in a formal way: as (1) **:** a fraternal society <the Masonic *Order*> (2) **:** a community under a religious rule; *esp* **:** one requiring members to take solemn vows **b :** a badge or medal of such a society; *also* **:** a military decoration **2 a :** any of the several grades of the Christian ministry **b** *pl* **:** the office of a person in the Christian ministry **c** *pl* **:** ORDINATION **3 a :** a rank, class, or special group in a community or society **b :** a class of persons or things grouped according to quality, value, or natural characteristics: as (1) **:** a category of taxonomic classification ranking above the family and below the class (2) **:** the broadest category in soil classification **4 a** (1) **:** RANK, LEVEL <a statesman of the first ~> (2) **:** CATEGORY, CLASS <in emergencies of this ~ —R. B. Westerfield> **b** (1) **:** the arrangement or sequence of objects or of events in time <listed the items in ~ of importance> (2) **:** a sequential arrangement of mathematical elements **c :** DEGREE 11a, 11b **d** (1) **:** the number of times differentiation is applied successively <derivatives of higher ~> (2) **:** the order of the highest order derivative in a differential equation **e :** the number of columns or rows in a square matrix **f :** the number of elements in a finite mathematical group **5 a** (1) **:** a sociopolitical system <was opposed to changes in the established ~> (2) **:** a particular sphere or aspect of a sociopolitical system <the present economic ~> **b :** a regular or harmonious arrangement <the ~ of nature> **6 a :** the customary mode of procedure esp. in debate <point of ~> **b :** a prescribed form of a religious service **:** RITE **7 a :** the rule of law or proper authority <promised to restore law and

orders 8b: *1* Doric, *2* Ionic, *3* Corinthian

ə abut ᵊ kitten ər further a back ā bake ä cot, cart
au̇ out ch chin e less ē easy g gift i trip ī life
j joke ŋ sing ō flow ȯ flaw ȯi coin th thin t͟h this
ü loot u̇ foot y yet yü few yu̇ furious zh vision

~> **b** : a specific rule, regulation, or authoritative direction : COMMAND **8 a** : a style of building **b** : a type of column and entablature forming the unit of a style **9 a** : state or condition esp. with regard to functioning or repair <things were in terrible ~> **b** : a proper or orderly condition <their passports were in ~> **10 a** : a written direction to pay money to someone **b** : a commission to purchase, sell, or supply goods or to perform work **c** : goods or items bought or sold **d** : an assigned or requested undertaking <landing men on the moon was a large ~> **11** : order of the day <flat roofs were the ~ in the small villages> — **or·der·less** \-ləs\ *n* — **in order** : APPROPRIATE, DESIRABLE <an apology is *in order*> — **in order that** : so that — **in order to** : for the purpose of — **on order** : in the process of being ordered — **on the order of** **1** : after the fashion of : LIKE <much *on the order of* Great Lakes bulk carriers —*Ships and the Sea*> **2** : ABOUT, APPROXIMATELY <spent *on the order of* two million dollars> — **to order** : according to the specifications of an order <shoes made *to order*>

²order *vb* **or·dered; or·der·ing** \ˈȯrd-(ə-)riŋ\ *vt* **1** : to put in order : ARRANGE **2 a** : to give an order to : COMMAND **b** : DESTINE, ORDAIN **c** : to command to go or come to a specified place **d** : to give an order for <~ a meal> ~ *vi* **1** : to bring about order : REGULATE **2 a** : to issue orders : COMMAND **b** : to give or place an order — **or·der·er** \-ər-ər\ *n*
syn* 1** ORDER, ARRANGE, MARSHAL, ORGANIZE, SYSTEMATIZE, METHODIZE *shared meaning element* : to put persons or things into their proper places in relation to each other ***ant disorder
2 see COMMAND

order arms *n* [fr. the command *order arms!*] **1** : a position in the manual of arms in which the rifle is held vertically beside the right leg with the butt resting on the ground **2** : a command to return the rifle to order arms from present arms or to drop the hand from a hand salute

or·dered \ˈȯrd-ərd\ *adj* : characterized by order: as **a** : marked by regularity or discipline <led an ~ life> **b** : marked by regular or harmonious arrangement or disposition <an ~ landscape> **c** (1) : having elements succeeding according to rule; *specif* : having the property that every pair of different elements is related by a transitive relationship that is not symmetric (2) : having a specified first element <a set of ~ pairs>

¹or·der·ly \ˈȯrd-ər-lē\ *adj* **1 a** (1) : arranged or disposed in some order or pattern : REGULAR <~ rows of houses> (2) : not marked by disorder : TIDY <keeps an ~ desk> **b** : governed by law : REGULATED <an ~ universe> **c** : METHODICAL <an ~ mind> **2** : well behaved : PEACEFUL <an ~ crowd> — **or·der·li·ness** *n* — **orderly** *adv*

²orderly *n, pl* **-lies** **1** : a soldier assigned to perform various services (as carrying messages) for a superior officer **2** : a hospital attendant who does routine or heavy work (as cleaning, carrying supplies, or moving patients)

order of business [*order of business* (predetermined sequence of matters to be dealt with by an assembly)] : a matter which must be dealt with : TASK <the discipline problem was the first *order of business* at the meeting of the school board>

order of magnitude : a range of magnitude extending from some value to ten times that value

order of the day **1** : the business or tasks appointed for an assembly for a given day **2** : the characteristic or dominant feature or activity <growth and change are the *order of the day* in every field —Ruth G. Strickland>

order up *vt* : to summon for active military duty

¹or·di·nal \ˈȯrd-nəl, -ᵊn-əl\ *n* **1** [ME, fr. ML *ordinale,* fr. LL, neut. of *ordinalis*] *cap* : a collection of forms to be used in ordination **2** [LL *ordinalis,* fr. *ordinalis,* adj.] : ORDINAL NUMBER

²ordinal *adj* [LL *ordinalis,* fr. L *ordin-, ordo*] **1** : of a specified order or rank in a series **2** : of or relating to an order (as of fishes)

ordinal number *n* **1** : a number designating the place (as first, second, or third) occupied by an item in an ordered sequence — see NUMBER table **2** : a number that designates both the order of the elements of an ordered set and the cardinal number of the set

or·di·nance \ˈȯrd-nən(t)s, ˈȯrd-ᵊn-ən(t)s\ *n* [ME, fr. MF & ML; MF *ordenance,* lit., art of arranging, fr. ML *ordinantia,* fr. L *ordinant-, ordinans,* prp. of *ordinare* to put in order — more at ORDAIN] **1 a** : an authoritative decree or direction : ORDER **b** : a law set forth by a governmental authority; *specif* : a municipal regulation **2** : something ordained or decreed by fate or a deity **3** : a prescribed usage, practice, or ceremony

or·di·nand \ˌȯrd-ᵊn-ˈand\ *n* [LL *ordinandus,* gerundive of *ordinare* to ordain] : a candidate for ordination

¹or·di·nary \ˈȯrd-ᵊn-ˌer-ē\ *n, pl* **-nar·ies** [ME *ordinarie,* fr. AF & ML; AF, fr. ML *ordinarius,* fr. L *ordinarius,* adj.] **1 a** (1) : a prelate exercising original jurisdiction over a specified territory or group (2) : a clergyman appointed formerly in England to attend condemned criminals **b** : a judge of probate in some states of the U.S. **2** *often cap* : the parts of the Mass that do not vary from day to day **3** : the regular or customary condition or course of things — usu. used in the phrase *out of the ordinary* **4 a** *Brit* : a meal served to all comers at a fixed price **b** *chiefly Brit* : a tavern or eating house serving regular meals **5** : a common heraldic charge (as the bend or chevron) of simple form

²ordinary *adj* [ME *ordinarie,* fr. L *ordinarius,* fr. *ordin-, ordo* order] **1** : of a kind to be expected in the normal order of events : ROUTINE, USUAL **2** : having or constituting immediate or original jurisdiction; *also* : belonging to such jurisdiction **3 a** : of common quality, rank, or ability **b** : deficient in quality : POOR, INFERIOR **c** : lacking in refinement ***syn*** see COMMON ***ant*** extraordinary — **or·di·nari·ly** \ˌȯrd-ᵊn-ˈer-ə-lē\ *adv* — **or·di·nari·ness** \ˈȯrd-ᵊn-ˌer-ē-nəs\ *n*

ordinary–language philosophy *n* : a trend in philosophical analysis that seeks to resolve philosophical perplexity by revealing sources of puzzlement in the misunderstanding of ordinary language

ordinary seaman *n* : a seaman of some experience but not as skilled as an able seaman

or·di·nate \ˈȯrd-nət, -ᵊn-ət, -ᵊn-ˌāt\ *n* [NL (*linea*) *ordinate* (*applicata*), lit., line applied in an orderly manner] : the Cartesian coordinate obtained by measuring parallel to the y-axis — compare ABSCISSA

or·di·na·tion \ˌȯrd-ᵊn-ˈā-shən\ *n* : the act or an instance of ordaining : the state of being ordained

ord·nance \ˈȯrd-nən(t)s\ *n* [ME *ordinaunce,* fr. MF *ordenance,* lit., act of arranging] **1 a** : military supplies including weapons, ammunition, combat vehicles, and maintenance tools and equipment **b** : a service of the army charged with the procuring, distributing, and safekeeping of ordnance **2** : CANNON, ARTILLERY

or·do \ˈȯ(ə)rd-(ˌ)ō\ *n, pl* **ordos** *or* **or·di·nes** \ˈȯrd-ᵊn-ˌēz\ [ML, fr. L, order] : a list of offices and feasts of the Roman Catholic Church for each day of the year

or·don·nance \ˌȯrd-ᵊn-ˈäⁿs\ *n* [F, alter. of MF *ordenance*] : disposition of the parts (as of a literary composition) with regard to one another and the whole : ARRANGEMENT

Or·do·vi·cian \ˌȯrd-ə-ˈvish-ən\ *adj* [L *Ordovices,* ancient people in northern Wales] : of, relating to, or being the period between the Cambrian and the Silurian or the corresponding system of rocks — **Ordovician** *n*

or·dure \ˈȯr-jər\ *n* [ME, fr. MF, fr. *ord* filthy, fr. L *horridus* horrid] **1** : EXCREMENT **2** : something that is morally degrading

ore \ˈō(ə)r, ˈȯ(ə)r\ *n, often attrib* [ME *or,* fr. OE *ār;* akin to OHG *ēr* bronze, L *aes* copper, bronze] **1** : a mineral containing a valuable constituent (as metal) for which it is mined and worked **2** : a source from which valuable matter is extracted

öre \ˈər-ə\ *n, pl* **öre** [Sw *öre* & Dan & Norw *øre*] — see *krona, krone* at MONEY table

ore·ad \ˈōr-ē-ˌad, ˈȯr-, -ē-əd\ *n* [L *oread-, oreas,* fr. Gk *oreiad-, oreias,* fr. *oreios* of a mountain, fr. *oros* mountain — more at RISE] : one of the nymphs of mountains and hills in Greek mythology

ore dressing *n* : mechanical preparation (as by crushing) and concentration (as by flotation) of ore

Oreg *or* **Ore** *abbr* Oregon

oreg·a·no \ə-ˈreg-ə-ˌnō\ *n* [AmerSp *orégano,* fr. Sp, wild marjoram, fr. L *origanum* — more at ORIGANUM] **1** : a bushy perennial mint (*Origanum vulgare*) that is used as a seasoning and a source of aromatic oil — called also *origanum, wild marjoram* **2** : any of several plants (genera *Lippia* and *Coleus*) other than oregano of the vervain or mint families

Or·e·gon grape \ˌȯr-i-gən-, ˌär-, -ˌgän-\ *n* [*Oregon,* U.S.A.] : an evergreen shrub (*Mahonia aquifolia*) of the barberry family that has yellow flowers, bears bluish black berries, and is native to the Pacific coast — called also *hollygrape*

Ores·tes \ə-ˈres-(ˌ)tēz, ō-\ *n* [L, fr. Gk *Orestēs*] : the son of Agamemnon and Clytemnestra who with his sister Electra avenges his father by killing his mother and her lover Aegisthus

org *abbr* **1** organic **2** organization; organized

or·gan \ˈȯr-gən\ *n* [ME, partly fr. OE *organa,* fr. L *organum,* fr. Gk *organon,* lit., tool, instrument; partly fr. OF *organe,* fr. L *organum;* akin to Gk *ergon* work — more at WORK] **1 a** *archaic* : any of various musical instruments; *esp* : WIND INSTRUMENT **b** (1) : a wind instrument consisting of sets of pipes made to sound by compressed air and controlled by keyboards and producing a variety of musical effects — called also *pipe organ* (2) : REED ORGAN (3) : an instrument in which the sound and resources of the pipe organ are approximated by means of electronic devices (4) : any of various similar cruder instruments **2 a** : a differentiated structure (as a heart, kidney, leaf, or stem) consisting of cells and tissues and performing some specific function in an organism **b** : bodily parts performing a function or cooperating in an activity <the eyes and related structures that make up the visual ~*s*> **3** : a subordinate group or organization that performs specialized functions <the various ~*s* of government> **4** : PERIODICAL

organ- *or* **organo-** *comb form* [ME, fr. ML, fr. L *organum*] **1** : organ <*organo*genesis> **2** : organic <*organo*mercurial>

or·gan·dy *also* **or·gan·die** \ˈȯr-gən-dē\ *n, pl* **-dies** [F *organdi*] : a very fine transparent muslin with a stiff finish

or·gan·elle \ˌȯr-gə-ˈnel\ *n* [NL *organella,* fr. L *organum*] : a specialized cellular part (as a mitochondrion) that is analogous to an organ

or·gan–grind·er \ˈȯr-gən-ˌgrīn-dər\ *n* : one that cranks a hand organ; *esp* : an itinerant street musician who operates a barrel organ

¹or·gan·ic \ȯr-ˈgan-ik\ *adj* **1** *archaic* : INSTRUMENTAL **2 a** : of, relating to, or arising in a bodily organ **b** : affecting the structure of the organism **3 a** (1) : of, relating to, or derived from living organisms (2) : relating to, produced with, or based on the use of fertilizer of plant or animal origin without employment of chemically formulated fertilizers or pesticides <~ farming> <~ foods> **b** (1) : of, relating to, or containing carbon compounds (2) : of, relating to, or dealt with by a branch of chemistry concerned with the carbon compounds of living beings and most other carbon compounds **4 a** : forming an integral element of a whole : FUNDAMENTAL <incidental music rather than ~ parts of the action —Francis Fergusson> **b** : having systematic coordination of parts : ORGANIZED <an ~ whole> **c** : having the characteristics of an organism : developing in the manner of a living plant or animal <society is ~> **5** : of, relating to, or constituting the law by which a government or organization exists — **or·gan·i·cal·ly** \-i-k(ə-)lē\ *adv*

²organic *n* : an organic substance: as **a** : a fertilizer of plant or animal origin **b** : a pesticide whose active component is an organic compound or a mixture of organic compounds

or·gan·i·cism \ȯr-ˈgan-ə-ˌsiz-əm\ *n* [ISV] **1 a** : a doctrine that the independent organization of a living system rather than its components separately constitutes life and living processes **b** : VITALISM **2** : any of various theories that society or the universe as a whole is organic — **or·gan·i·cist** \-səst\ *n*

or·gan·ism \ˈȯr-gə-ˌniz-əm\ *n* **1** : a complex structure of interdependent and subordinate elements whose relations and properties are largely determined by their function in the whole **2** : an individual constituted to carry on the activites of life by means of organs separate in function but mutually dependent : a living being — **or·gan·is·mic** \ˌȯr-gə-ˈniz-mik\ *also* **or·gan·is·mal** \-məl\ *adj* — **or·gan·is·mi·cal·ly** \-mi-k(ə-)lē\ *adv*

or·gan·ist \ˈȯr-gə-nəst\ *n* : one who plays the organ

¹or·ga·ni·za·tion \ˌȯrg-(ə-)nə-ˈzā-shən\ *n* **1 a** : the act or process of organizing or of being organized <~ was his one talent> **b** : the condition or manner of being organized <a high degree of ~> **2 a** : ASSOCIATION, SOCIETY <tax exemptions for charitable ~*s*> **b** : an administrative and functional structure (as a business or a political party); *also* : the personnel of such a structure

²organization *adj* : characterized by complete conformity to the standards and requirements of an organization <an ~ man>

or·ga·ni·za·tion·al \-shnəl, -shən-ᵊl\ *adj* **1** : of or relating to an organization : involving organization <the ~ state of a crystal> **2** : ORGANIZATION — **or·ga·ni·za·tion·al·ly** \-ē\ *adv*

or·ga·nize \ˈȯr-gə-ˌnīz\ *vb* **-nized; -niz·ing** *vt* **1** : to cause to develop an organic structure **2** : to arrange or form into a coherent unity or functioning whole : INTEGRATE <trying to ~ her thoughts> **3 a** : to set up an administrative structure for **b** : to persuade to associate in an organization; *esp* : UNIONIZE **4** : to arrange by systematic planning and united effort <*organized* a field trip> ~ *vi* **1** : to undergo physical or organic organization **2** : to arrange elements into a whole of interdependent parts **3** : to form an organization; *specif* : to form or persuade workers to join a union ***syn*** see ORDER ***ant*** disorganize — **or·gan·iz·able** \-ˌnī-zə-bəl\ *adj*

or·ga·nized *adj* **1** : having a formal organization to coordinate and carry out activities <~ baseball> <~ crime> **2** : affiliated by membership in an organization <~ steelworkers>

or·ga·niz·er \-ˌnī-zər\ *n* **1** : one that organizes **2** : a substance capable of inducing a specific type of development in undifferentiated tissue — called also *inductor*

or·gano·chlo·rine \ȯr-ˌgan-ə-ˈklō(ə)r-ˌēn, -ˈklȯ(ə)r-, -ən\ *adj* : of, relating to, or belonging to the chlorinated hydrocarbon pesticides (as aldrin, DDT, or dieldrin) — **organochlorine** *n*

organ of Cor·ti \-ˈkȯrt-ē\ [Alfonso *Corti* †1876 It anatomist] : a complex epithelial structure in the cochlea that rests on the internal surface of the basilar membrane and in mammals is the chief part of the ear by which sound is directly perceived

or·gan·o·gen·e·sis \ˌȯr-gə-nō-ˈjen-ə-səs, ȯr-ˌgan-ə-\ *n* [NL] : the origin and development of bodily organs — compare MORPHOGENESIS — **or·gan·o·ge·net·ic** \-jə-ˈnet-ik\ *adj* — **or·gan·o·ge·net·i·cal·ly** \-i-k(ə-)lē\ *adv*

or·gan·og·ra·phy \ˌȯr-gə-ˈnäg-rə-fē\ *n* : a descriptive study of the organs of plants or animals

or·gan·o·lep·tic \ˌȯr-gə-nō-ˈlep-tik, ȯr-ˌgan-ə-\ *adj* [F *organoleptique,* fr. *organ-* + Gk *lēptikos* disposed to take, fr. *lambanein* to take — more at LATCH] **1** : affecting or employing one or more of the organs of special sense **2** : determined by organoleptic examination <~ evaluation of foods> — **or·gan·o·lep·ti·cal·ly** \-ti-k(ə-)lē\ *adv*

or·gan·ol·o·gy \ˌȯr-gə-ˈnäl-ə-jē\ *n* [ISV] : the study of the organs of plants and animals — **or·gan·o·log·ic** \ˌȯr-gən-ᵊl-ˈäj-ik, ȯr-ˌgan-\ *or* **or·gan·o·log·i·cal** \-i-kəl\ *adj*

or·gano·mer·cu·ri·al \ȯr-ˌgan-ō-(ˌ)mər-ˈkyu̇r-ē-əl\ *n* : an organic compound or a pharmaceutical preparation containing mercury

or·gano·me·tal·lic \-mə-ˈtal-ik\ *adj* [ISV] : of, relating to, or being an organic compound that usu. contains a metal or metalloid bonded directly to carbon — **organometallic** *n*

or·ga·non \ˈȯr-gə-ˌnän\ *n* [Gk, lit., tool — more at ORGAN] : an instrument for acquiring knowledge; *specif* : a body of principles of scientific or philosophic investigation

or·gano·phos·phate \ȯr-ˌgan-ə-ˈfäs-ˌfāt\ *n* : an organophosphorus pesticide — **organophosphate** *adj*

or·gano·phos·pho·rus \-ˈfäs-f(ə-)rəs\ *also* **or·gano·phos·pho·rous** \-fäs-ˈfōr-əs, -ˈfȯr-\ *adj* : of, relating to, or being a phosphorus-containing organic pesticide (as malathion) that acts by inhibiting cholinesterase — **organophosphorus** *n*

or·gan·o·ther·a·py \ˌȯr-gə-nō-ˈther-ə-pē, ȯr-ˌgan-ə-\ *n* [ISV] : treatment of disease by the use of animal organs or their extracts

or·gan·o·trop·ic \ˌȯr-gə-nō-ˈträp-ik, ȯr-ˌgan-ə-\ *adj* : having an affinity for particular bodily tissues or organs (as the viscera) — **or·gan·o·trop·i·cal·ly** \-i-k(ə-)lē\ *adv* **or·gan·ot·ro·pism** \ˌȯr-gə-ˈnä-trə-ˌpiz-əm\ *n*

organ–pipe cactus *n* : any of several tall upright cacti of the southwestern U.S. and adjacent Mexico: as **a** : SAGUARO **b** : a cactus (*Lemnaireocereus marginatus* or *Pachycereus marginatus*) that branches at the base to form several ridged upright stems and bears 2-inch red and greenish white flowers

or·ga·num \ˈȯr-gə-nəm\ *n* [ML, fr. L, organ] **1** : ORGANON **2** : early polyphony of the late Middle Ages that consists of one or more voice parts accompanying the cantus firmus in parallel motion usu. at a fourth, fifth, or octave above or below; *also* : a composition in this style

or·gan·za \ȯr-ˈgan-zə\ *n* [prob. alter. of *Lorganza,* a trademark] : a sheer dress fabric resembling organdy and usu. made of silk, rayon, or nylon

or·gan·zine \ˈȯr-gən-ˌzēn\ *n* [F or It; F *organsin,* fr. It *organzino*] : a raw silk yarn used for warp threads in fine fabrics

or·gasm \ˈȯr-ˌgaz-əm\ *n* [NL *orgasmus,* fr. Gk *orgasmos,* fr. *organ* to grow ripe, be lustful; akin to Skt *ūrjā* sap, strength] **1** : intense or paroxysmal emotional excitement; *esp* : the climax of sexual excitement typically occurring toward the end of coitus **2** : an instance of orgasm — **or·gas·mic** \ȯr-ˈgaz-mik\ *or* **or·gas·tic** \-ˈgas-tik\ *adj*

or·geat \ˈȯ(ə)r-ˌzhä(t)\ *n* [F, fr. MF, fr. *orge* barley, fr. L *hordeum;* akin to OHG *gersta* barley, Gk *kri*] : a sweet almond-flavored nonalcoholic syrup used as a cocktail ingredient or food flavoring

or·gi·as·tic \ˌȯr-jē-ˈas-tik\ *adj* [Gk *orgiastikos,* fr. *orgiazein* to celebrate orgies, fr. *orgia*] **1** : of, relating to, or marked by orgies **2** : characterized by unrestrained emotion — **or·gi·as·ti·cal·ly** \-ti-k(ə-)lē\ *adv*

or·gu·lous \ˈȯr-g(y)ə-ləs\ *adj* [ME, fr. OF *orgueilleus,* fr. *orgueil* pride, of Gmc origin; akin to OHG *urguol* distinguished] : PROUD

or·gy \ˈȯr-jē\ *n, pl* **orgies** [MF *orgie,* fr. L *orgia,* pl., fr. Gk; akin to Gk *ergon* work — more at WORK] **1** : secret ceremonial rites held in honor of an ancient Greek or Roman deity and usu. characterized by ecstatic singing and dancing **2 a** : drunken revelry **b** : an excessive sexual indulgence (as at a wild party) **3** : something that resembles an orgy in lack of control or moderation <soldiers engaging in an ~ of destruction>

-oria *pl of* -ORIUM

-o·ri·al \ˈōr-ē-əl, ˈȯr-\ *adj suffix* [ME, fr. L *-orius* -ory + ME *-al*] : of, belonging to, or connected with <insess*orial*>

orib·a·tid \ȯ-ˈrib-ət-əd, ˌȯr-ə-ˈbat-əd\ *n* [NL *Oribatidae,* group name (coextensive with *Oribatoidea*), fr. *Oribata,* genus name, fr. Gk *oribatēs* walking the mountains] : any of a superfamily (Oribatoidea) of small oval eyeless nonparasitic mites having a heavily sclerotized integument with a leathery appearance — **oribatid** *adj*

ori·el \ˈōr-ē-əl, ˈȯr-\ *n* [ME, porch, oriel, fr. MF *oriol* porch] : a large bay window projecting from a wall and supported by a corbel or bracket

oriel

¹ori·ent \ˈōr-ē-ənt, ˈȯr-, -ē-ˌent\ *n* [ME, fr. MF, fr. L *orient-, oriens,* fr. prp. of *oriri* to rise — more at RISE] **1** *archaic* : EAST 1b **2** *cap* : EAST 2 **3 a** : a pearl of great luster **b** : the luster or sheen of a pearl

²orient *adj* **1** *archaic* : ORIENTAL 1 **2 a** : LUSTROUS, SPARKLING <~ gems> **b** *archaic* : RADIANT, GLOWING **3** *archaic* : rising in the sky

³ori·ent \ˈōr-ē-ˌent, ˈȯr-\ *vt* [F *orienter,* fr. MF, fr. *orient*] **1 a** : to cause to face or point toward the east; *specif* : to build (a church or temple) with the longitudinal axis pointing eastward and the chief altar at the eastern end **b** : to set or arrange in any determinate position esp. in relation to the points of the compass **c** : to ascertain the bearings of **2 a** : to set right by adjusting to facts or principles **b** : to acquaint with the existing situation or environment **3** : to cause the axes of the molecules of to assume the same direction

ori·en·tal \ˌōr-ē-ˈent-ᵊl, ˌȯr-\ *adj* **1** *often cap* : of, relating to, or situated in the Orient **2 a** : of superior grade, luster, or value **b** : being corundum or sapphire but simulating another gem in color **3** *often cap* : of, relating to, or having the characteristics of Orientals **4** *cap* : of, relating to, or constituting the biogeographic region that includes Asia south and southeast of the Himalayas and the Malay archipelago west of Wallace's line — **ori·en·tal·ly** \-ᵊl-ē\ *adv*

Oriental *n* : a member of one of the indigenous peoples of the Orient

oriental fruit moth *n* : a small nearly cosmopolitan moth (*Grapolitha molesta*) prob. of Japanese origin whose larva is injurious to the twigs and fruit of orchard trees and esp. the peach — called also *oriental peach moth*

ori·en·tal·ism \ˌōr-ē-ˈent-ᵊl-ˌiz-əm\ *n, often cap* **1** : a trait, custom, or habit of expression characteristic of oriental peoples **2** : scholarship or learning in oriental subjects — **ori·en·tal·ist** \-ᵊl-əst\ *n, often cap*

ori·en·tal·ize \-ᵊl-ˌīz\ *vb* **-ized; -iz·ing** *vt, often cap* : to make oriental ~ *vi, often cap* : to become oriental

Oriental poppy *n* : an Asiatic perennial poppy (*Papaver orientale*) that is commonly cultivated for its large showy flowers

Oriental rug *n* : a handwoven or hand-knotted one-piece rug or carpet made in the Orient — called also *Oriental carpet*

ori·en·tate \ˈōr-ē-ən-ˌtāt, ˈȯr-, -ˌen-\ *vb* **-tat·ed; -tat·ing** *vt* : ORIENT ~ *vi* : to face or turn to the east

ori·en·ta·tion \ˌōr-ē-ən-ˈtā-shən, ˌȯr-, -ˌen-\ *n* **1 a** : the act or process of orienting or of being oriented **b** : the state of being oriented; *broadly* : ARRANGEMENT, ALIGNMENT **2** : a usu. general or lasting direction of thought, inclination, or interest **3** : change of position by organs, organelles, or organisms in response to external stimulus — **ori·en·ta·tion·al** \-shnəl, -shən-ᵊl\ *adj* — **ori·en·ta·tion·al·ly** \-ē\ *adv*

ori·ent·ed \ˈōr-ē-ˌent-əd, ˈȯr-\ *adj* : intellectually or emotionally directed <humanistically ~ scholars>

ori·en·teer·ing \ˌōr-ē-ən-ˈti(ə)r-iŋ, ˌȯr-, -ˌen-\ *n* [modif. (influenced by *-eer*) of Sw *orientering,* fr. *orientera* to orient] : a cross-country race in which each participant uses a map and compass to navigate his way between checkpoints along an unfamiliar course

or·i·fice \ˈȯr-ə-fəs, ˈär-\ *n* [MF, fr. LL *orificium,* fr. L *or-, os* mouth — more at ORAL] : an opening (as a vent, mouth, or hole) through which something may pass ***syn*** see APERTURE — **or·i·fi·cial** \ˌȯr-ə-ˈfish-əl, ˌär-\ *adj*

ori·flamme \ˈȯr-ə-ˌflam, ˈär-\ *n* [ME *oriflamble,* fr. MF, fr. ML *aurea flamma,* lit., golden flame] : a banner, symbol, or ideal inspiring devotion or courage

orig *abbr* original; originally; originator

ori·ga·mi \ˌȯr-ə-ˈgäm-ē\ *n* [Jap] : the art or process of Japanese paper folding

orig·a·num \ə-ˈrig-ə-nəm\ *n* [ME, fr. L, wild marjoram, fr. Gk *origanon*] : any of various fragrant aromatic plants of the mint or vervain families used as seasonings; *esp* : OREGANO 1

or·i·gin \ˈȯr-ə-jən, ˈär-\ *n* [ME *origine,* prob. fr. MF, fr. L *origin-, origo,* fr. *oriri* to rise — more at RISE] **1** : ANCESTRY, PARENTAGE **2 a** : rise, beginning, or derivation from a source **b** : the point at which something begins or rises or from which it derives <the ~ of the custom is lost in the mist of time> <this spring is the ~ of

the brook> **3 :** the more fixed, central, or larger attachment of a muscle **4 :** the intersection of coordinate axes
syn ORIGIN, SOURCE, INCEPTION, ROOT *shared meaning element* **:** the point at which something begins its course or existence

[1]**orig·i·nal** \ə-ˈrij-ən-ᵊl, -ˈrij-nəl\ *n* **1** *archaic* **:** the source or cause from which something arises; *specif* **:** ORIGINATOR **2 a :** that from which a copy, reproduction, or translation is made **b :** a work composed firsthand **3 a :** a person of fresh initiative or inventive capacity **b :** an eccentric person

[2]**original** *adj* **1 :** of, relating to, or constituting an origin or beginning **:** INITIAL <the ~ part of the house> **2 a :** not secondary, derivative, or imitative **b :** being the first instance or source from which a copy, reproduction, or translation is or can be made **3 :** independent and creative in thought or action **:** INVENTIVE *syn* see NEW *ant* banal, trite — **orig·i·nal·ly** \-ē\ *adv*

orig·i·nal·i·ty \ə-ˌrij-ə-ˈnal-ət-ē\ *n* **1 :** the quality or state of being original **2 :** freshness of aspect, design, or style **3 :** the power of independent thought or constructive imagination

original sin *n* **:** the state of sin that according to Christian theology characterizes all human beings as a result of Adam's fall

orig·i·nate \ə-ˈrij-ə-ˌnāt\ *vb* **-nat·ed; -nat·ing** *vt* **:** to give rise to **:** INITIATE ~ *vi* **:** to take or have origin **:** BEGIN *syn* see SPRING — **orig·i·na·tion** \-ˌrij-ə-ˈnā-shən\ *n* — **orig·i·na·tor** \-ˈrij-ə-ˌnāt-ər\ *n*

orig·i·na·tive \ə-ˈrij-ə-ˌnāt-iv, -nət-\ *adj* **:** having ability to originate **:** CREATIVE — **orig·i·na·tive·ly** *adv*

O–ring \ˈō-ˌriŋ\ *n* **:** a ring (as of synthetic rubber) used as a gasket

ori·ole \ˈōr-ē-ˌōl, ˈȯr-, -ē-əl\ *n* [F *oriol,* fr. L *aureolus,* dim. of *aureus* golden, fr. *aurum* gold; akin to Lith *auksas* gold] **1 :** any of a family (Oriolidae) of usu. brightly colored Old World passerine birds related to the crows **2 :** any of a family (Icteridae) of New World passerine birds of which the males are usu. bright black and yellow or orange and the females are chiefly greenish or yellowish

Ori·on \ə-ˈrī-ən, ō-\ *n* [L, fr. Gk *Ōriōn*] **1 :** a giant and hunter of Boeotia who was placed after his death among the stars **2** [L (gen. *Orionis*)] **:** a constellation on the equator east of Taurus represented on charts by the figure of a hunter with belt and sword

or·is·mol·o·gy \ˌȯr-əz-ˈmäl-ə-jē, ˌär-\ *n* [Gk *horismos* definition (fr. *horizein* to define) + E *-logy* — more at HORIZON] **:** the science of defining technical terms **:** TERMINOLOGY — **or·is·mo·log·i·cal** \ˌȯr-əz-mə-ˈläj-i-kəl, ˌär-; ō-ˌriz-\ *adj*

or·i·son \ˈȯr-ə-sən, ˈär-, -zən\ *n* [ME, fr. OF, fr. LL *oration-, oratio,* fr. L, oration] **:** PRAYER

-o·ri·um \ˈōr-ē-əm, ˈȯr-\ *n suffix, pl* **-oriums** *or* **-o·ria** \-ē-ə\ [L, fr. neut. of *-orius* -ory] **:** [1]-ORY <haust*orium*>

Ori·ya \ō-ˈrē-(y)ə\ *n* **:** the Indic language of Orissa, India

Ork *abbr* Orkney

Or·lean·ist \ˈȯr-lē-ə-nəst, ȯr-ˈlē-(ə-)nəst\ *n* **:** a supporter of the Orleans family in its claim to the throne of France by descent from a younger brother of Louis XIV

Or·lon \ˈȯ(ə)r-ˌlän\ *trademark* — used for an acrylic fiber

or·lop deck \ˌȯr-ˌläp-\ *n* [ME *overlop* deck of a single decker, fr. MLG *overlōp,* lit., something that overleaps] **:** the lowest deck in a ship having four or more decks

Or·mazd \ˈȯ(ə)r-(ˌ)məzd, -ˌmazd\ *n* [Per *Urmazd,* fr. OPer *Auramazdāh-,* fr. Av *Ahuramazdāh-*] **:** AHURA MAZDA

or·mo·lu \ˈȯr-mə-ˌlü\ *n, often attrib* [F *or moulu,* lit., ground gold] **:** golden or gilded brass or bronze used for decorative purposes (as in mounts for furniture)

[1]**or·na·ment** \ˈȯr-nə-mənt\ *n* [ME, fr. OF *ornement,* fr. L *ornamentum,* fr. *ornare*] **1** *archaic* **:** a useful accessory **2 a :** something that lends grace or beauty **b :** a manner or quality that adorns **3 :** one whose virtues or graces add luster to his place or society **4 :** the act of adorning or being adorned **5 :** an embellishing note not belonging to the essential harmony or melody — called also *embellishment, fioritura*

[2]**or·na·ment** \-ˌment\ *vt* **:** to provide with ornament **:** EMBELLISH *syn* see ADORN

[1]**or·na·men·tal** \ˌȯr-nə-ˈment-ᵊl\ *adj* **:** of, relating to, or serving as ornament; *specif* **:** grown as an ornamental — **or·na·men·tal·ly** \-ᵊl-ē\ *adv*

[2]**ornamental** *n* **:** a decorative object; *esp* **:** a plant cultivated for its beauty rather than for use

or·na·men·ta·tion \ˌȯr-nə-mən-ˈtā-shən, -ˌmen-\ *n* **1 :** the act or process of ornamenting **:** the state of being ornamented **2 :** something that ornaments **:** EMBELLISHMENT

or·nate \ȯr-ˈnāt\ *adj* [ME *ornat,* fr. L *ornatus,* pp. of *ornare* to furnish, embellish; akin to L *ordinare* to order — more at ORDAIN] **1 :** marked by elaborate rhetoric or florid style **2 :** elaborately or excessively decorated — **or·nate·ly** *adv* — **or·nate·ness** *n*

or·nery \ˈȯrn-(ə-)rē, ˈän-\ *adj* [alter. of *ordinary*] **:** having an irritable disposition **:** CANTANKEROUS — **or·neri·ness** *n*

ornith *abbr* ornithology

ornith- *or* **ornitho-** *comb form* [L, fr. Gk, fr. *ornith-, ornis* — more at ERNE] **:** bird <*ornith*ology>

or·nith·ic \ȯr-ˈnith-ik\ *adj* [Gk *ornithikos,* fr. *ornith-, ornis*] **:** of, relating to, or characteristic of birds

or·ni·thine \ˈȯr-nə-ˌthēn\ *n* [ISV *ornith*uric acid (an acid of which it is a component, found in the urine of birds) + *-ine*] **:** a crystalline amino acid $C_5H_{12}N_2O_2$ that functions esp. in urea production as a carrier by undergoing conversion to citrulline and then arginine in reaction with ammonia and carbon dioxide followed by recovery along with urea by enzymatic hydrolysis of arginine

or·nith·is·chi·an \ˌȯr-nə-ˈthis-kē-ən\ *n* [NL *Ornithischia,* group name, fr. *ornith-* + *ischium*] **:** any of an order (Ornithischia) of herbivorous dinosaurs (as a stegosaurus) that have a pelvis with four axes of symmetry — **ornithischian** *adj*

or·ni·thol·o·gy \ˌȯr-nə-ˈthäl-ə-jē\ *n, pl* **-gies** [NL *ornithologia,* fr. *ornith-* + *-logia* -logy] **1 :** a branch of zoology dealing with birds **2 :** a treatise on ornithology — **or·ni·tho·log·i·cal** \-thə-ˈläj-i-kəl\ *also* **or·ni·tho·log·ic** \-ik\ *adj* — **or·ni·tho·log·i·cal·ly** \-i-k(ə-)lē\ *adv* — **or·ni·thol·o·gist** \-ˈthäl-ə-jəst\ *n*

or·ni·thop·ter \ˈȯr-nə-ˌthäp-tər\ *n* [ISV *ornith-* + *-pter* (as in *helicopter*)] **:** an aircraft designed to derive its chief support and propulsion from flapping wings

or·ni·tho·sis \ˌȯr-nə-ˈthō-səs\ *n, pl* **-tho·ses** \-ˌsēz\ [NL] **:** PSITTACOSIS — **or·ni·thot·ic** \-ˈthät-ik\ *adj*

[1]**oro-** *comb form* [Gk *oros* — more at RISE] **:** mountain <*oro*logy>

[2]**oro-** *comb form* [L *or-, os* — more at ORAL] **:** mouth <*oro*pharynx> **:** oral and <*oro*facial>

oro·gen·e·sis \ˌōr-ə-ˈjen-ə-səs, ˌȯr-\ *n* [NL] **:** OROGENY — **oro·ge·net·ic** \-jə-ˈnet-ik\ *adj*

orog·e·ny \ō-ˈräj-ə-nē\ *n* [ISV] **:** the process of mountain formation esp. by folding of the earth's crust — **oro·gen·ic** \ˌōr-ə-ˈjen-ik, ˌȯr-\ *adj*

oro·graph·ic \ˌōr-ə-ˈgraf-ik, ˌȯr-\ *also* **oro·graph·i·cal** \-i-kəl\ *adj* **:** of or relating to mountains; *esp* **:** associated with or induced by the presence of mountains <~ rainfall> — **oro·graph·i·cal·ly** \-k(ə-)lē\ *adv*

orog·ra·phy \ō-ˈräg-rə-fē\ *n* [ISV [1]*oro-* + geo*graphy*] **:** a branch of physical geography that deals with mountains

oro·tund \ˈōr-ə-ˌtənd, ˈär-, ˈōr-\ *adj* [modif. of L *ore rotundo,* lit., with round mouth] **1 :** marked by fullness, strength, and clarity of sound **:** SONOROUS **2 :** POMPOUS, BOMBASTIC — **oro·tun·di·ty** \ˌōr-ə-ˈtən-dət-ē, ˌär-, ˌōr-\ *n*

[1]**or·phan** \ˈȯr-fən\ *n* [LL *orphanus,* fr. Gk *orphanos;* akin to OHG *erbi* inheritance, L *orbus* orphaned] **1 :** a child deprived by death of one or usu. both parents **2 :** a young animal that has lost its mother — **orphan** *adj* — **or·phan·hood** \-ˌhu̇d\ *n*

[2]**orphan** *vt* **or·phaned; or·phan·ing** \ˈȯrf-(ə-)niŋ\ **:** to cause to become an orphan

or·phan·age \ˈȯrf-(ə-)nij\ *n* **1 :** the state of being an orphan **2 :** an institution for the care of orphans

orphan's court *n* **:** a probate court which in some states has jurisdiction over the affairs of minors and the administration of estates

Or·pheus \ˈȯr-ˌfyüs, -fē-əs\ *n* [L, fr. Gk] **:** a poet and musician of Greek myth who almost rescued his wife Eurydice from Hades by charming Pluto and Persephone with his lyre

or·phic \ˈȯr-fik\ *adj* **1** *cap* **:** of or relating to Orpheus or the rites or doctrines ascribed to him **2 :** MYSTIC, ORACULAR **3 :** FASCINATING, ENTRANCING — **or·phi·cal·ly** \-fi-k(ə-)lē\ *adv*

Or·phism \ˈȯr-ˌfiz-əm\ *n* [*Orpheus,* its reputed founder] **:** a mystic Greek religion offering initiates purification of the soul from innate evil and release from the cycle of reincarnation

or·phrey \ˈȯr-frē\ *n, pl* **orphreys** [ME *orfrey,* fr. MF *orfreis,* fr. ML *aurifrigium,* fr. L *aurum* gold + *Phrygius* Phrygian — more at ORIOLE] **1 a :** elaborate embroidery **b :** a piece of such embroidery **2 :** an ornamental border or band esp. on an ecclesiastical vestment

or·pi·ment \ˈȯr-pə-mənt\ *n* [ME, fr. MF, fr. L *auripigmentum,* fr. *aurum* + *pigmentum* pigment] **:** native orange to lemon yellow arsenic trisulfide

or·pine \ˈȯr-pən\ *n* [ME *orpin,* fr. MF, fr. *orpiment*] **:** an herb (*Sedum telephium* of the family Crassulaceae, the orpine family) that has fleshy leaves and pink or purple flowers and was formerly used in folk medicine; *broadly* **:** SEDUM

Or·ping·ton \ˈȯr-piŋ-tən\ *n* [*Orpington,* England] **:** any of an English breed of large deep-chested domestic fowls

or·rery \ˈȯr-ər-ē, ˈär-\ *n, pl* **or·rer·ies** [Charles Boyle †1731 4th Earl of *Orrery*] **:** an apparatus showing the relative positions and motions of bodies in the solar system by balls moved by wheelwork

or·ris \ˈȯr-əs, ˈär-\ *n* [prob. alter. of ME *ireos,* fr. ML, alter. of L *iris*] **:** a European iris (*Iris florentina*) with a fragrant rootstock that is used esp. in perfume and sachet powder; *also* **:** its rootstock

or·ris·root \-ˌrüt, -ˌru̇t\ *n* **:** the fragrant rootstock of any of several European irises used esp. in perfumery

ort \ˈȯ(ə)rt\ *n* [ME] **:** a morsel left at a meal **:** SCRAP

orth- *or* **ortho-** *comb form* [ME, fr. MF, straight, right, true, fr. L, fr. Gk, fr. *orthos* — more at ARDUOUS] **1 :** straight **:** upright **:** vertical <*ortho*tropic> **2 :** perpendicular <*ortho*rhombic> **3 :** correct **:** corrective <*ortho*dontia> **4 a :** hydrated or hydroxylated to the highest degree <*ortho*phosphoric acid> **b :** involving substitution at or characterized by or having the relationship of two neighboring positions in the benzene ring <*ortho*-xylene>

or·thi·con \ˈȯr-thi-ˌkän\ *n* [ISV *orth-* + *icono*scope] **:** a camera tube similar to but more sensitive than an iconoscope in which the charges are scanned by a low-velocity beam

or·tho \ˈȯr-(ˌ)thō\ *adj* **:** ORTHOCHROMATIC

or·tho·cen·ter \ˈȯr-thə-ˌsent-ər\ *n* [ISV] **:** the common intersection of the three altitudes of a triangle or their extensions or of the several altitudes of a polyhedron provided these latter exist and meet in a point

or·tho·ce·phal·ic \ˌȯr-thō-sə-ˈfal-ik\ *or* **or·tho·ceph·a·lous** \-thə-ˈsef-ə-ləs\ *adj* [NL *orthocephalus* orthocephalic person, fr. *orth-* + Gk *kephalē* head — more at CEPHALIC] **:** having a medium ratio of the height to the length or breadth of the skull — **or·tho·ceph·a·ly** \-thə-ˈsef-ə-lē\ *n*

or·tho·chro·mat·ic \ˌȯr-thə-krō-ˈmat-ik\ *adj* [ISV] **1 :** of, relating to, or producing tone values of light and shade in a photograph that correspond to the tones in nature **2 :** sensitive to all colors except red

or·tho·clase \ˈȯr-thə-ˌklās, -ˌklāz\ *n* [G *orthoklas,* fr. *orth-* + Gk *klasis* breaking, fr. *klan* to break — more at HALT] **:** a mineral $KAlSi_3O_8$ consisting of a monoclinic polymorph of common potassic feldspar often with sodium in place of some of the potassium

or·tho·clas·tic \ˌȯr-thə-ˈklas-tik\ *adj* [G *orthoklastisch,* fr. *orth-* + Gk *klastos* broken — more at CLASTIC] **:** cleaving in directions at right angles to each other <an ~ feldspar>

orth·odon·tia \ˌȯr-thə-ˈdän-ch(ē-)ə\ *n* [NL] **:** ORTHODONTICS

orth·odon·tics \-ˈdänt-iks\ *n pl but sing in constr* **:** a branch of dentistry dealing with irregularities of the teeth and their correction (as by means of braces) — **orth·odon·tic** \-ik\ *adj* — **orth·odon·tist** \-ˈdänt-əst\ *n*

[1]**or·tho·dox** \ˈȯr-thə-ˌdäks\ *adj* [MF or LL; MF *orthodoxe,* fr. LL *orthodoxus,* fr. LGk *orthodoxos,* fr. Gk *orth-* + *doxa* opinion — more at DOXOLOGY] **1 a :** conforming to established doctrine esp. in religion **b :** CONVENTIONAL **2** *cap* **:** of, relating to, or constituting any of various conservative religious or political groups: as **a :** Eastern Orthodox **b :** of or relating to Orthodox Judaism — **or·tho·dox·ly** *adv*

[2]**orthodox** *n, pl* **orthodox** *also* **or·tho·dox·es 1 :** one that is orthodox **2** *cap* **:** a member of an Eastern Orthodox church

Orthodox Judaism *n* **:** Judaism that adheres to the Torah and Talmud as interpreted in an authoritative rabbinic law code and applies their principles and regulations to modern living — compare CONSERVATIVE JUDAISM

or·tho·doxy \ˈȯr-thə-ˌdäk-sē\ *n, pl* **-dox·ies 1 :** the quality or state of being orthodox **2 :** an orthodox belief or practice **3** *cap* **a :** Eastern Orthodox Christianity **b :** ORTHODOX JUDAISM

or·tho·epist \ˈȯr-thə-ˌwep-əst, ȯr-ˈthō-ə-pəst\ *n* **:** a person who is skilled in orthoepy

or·tho·epy \ˈȯr-thə-ˌwep-ē, ȯr-ˈthō-ə-pē\ *n* [NL *orthoepia,* fr. Gk *orthoepeia,* fr. *orth-* + *epos* word — more at VOICE] **1 :** the customary pronunciation of a language **2 :** the study of the pronunciation of a language — **or·tho·ep·ic** \ˌȯr-thə-ˈwep-ik\ *also* **or·tho·ep·i·cal** \-i-kəl\ *adj* — **or·tho·ep·i·cal·ly** \-i-k(ə-)lē\ *adv*

or·tho·gen·e·sis \ˌȯr-thə-ˈjen-ə-səs\ *n* [NL] **1 :** variation of organisms in successive generations that in some evolutionary theories takes place in some predestined direction and results in progressive evolutionary trends independent of external factors **2 :** the theory that social evolution takes place in the same direction and through the same stages in every culture despite differing external conditions — **or·tho·ge·net·ic** \-jə-ˈnet-ik\ *adj* — **or·tho·ge·net·i·cal·ly** \-i-k(ə-)lē\ *adv*

or·tho·gen·ic \-ˈjen-ik\ *adj* [*orth-* + *-genic*] **:** of, relating to, or devoted to the rehabilitation of emotionally disturbed or mentally retarded children

or·thog·na·thous \ȯr-ˈthäg-nə-thəs\ *adj* [ISV] **:** having straight jaws **:** not having the lower parts of the face projecting — **or·thog·na·thy** \-thē\ *or* **or·thog·na·thism** \-ˌthiz-əm\ *n*

or·thog·o·nal \ȯr-ˈthäg-ən-ᵊl\ *adj* [MF, fr. L *orthogonius,* fr. Gk *orthogōnios,* fr. *orth-* + *gōnia* angle — more at -GON] **1 :** mutually perpendicular **2 :** having a sum of products or an integral that is zero or sometimes one under specified conditions: as **a** *of real-valued functions* **:** having the integral of the product over a specific interval equal to zero **b** *of vectors* **:** having the scalar product equal to zero **c** *of a square matrix* **:** having the sum of products of corresponding elements in any two rows or any two columns equal to one if the rows or columns are the same and equal to zero otherwise **:** having a transpose with which the product equals the identity matrix **3** *of a linear transformation* **:** having a matrix that is orthogonal **:** preserving length and distance **4 :** composed of mutually orthogonal elements <an ~ basis of a vector space> **5 :** statistically independent — **or·thog·o·nal·i·ty** \-ˌthäg-ə-ˈnal-ət-ē\ *n* — **or·thog·o·nal·ly** \-ˈthäg-ən-ᵊl-ē\ *adv*

or·thog·o·nal·ize \ȯr-ˈthäg-ən-ᵊl-ˌīz\ *vt* **-ized; -iz·ing :** to make orthogonal — **or·thog·o·nal·iza·tion** \-ˌthäg-ən-ᵊl-ə-ˈzā-shən\ *n*

or·tho·grade \ˈȯr-thə-ˌgrād\ *adj* **:** walking with the body upright or vertical

or·tho·graph·ic \ˌȯr-thə-ˈgraf-ik\ *also* **or·tho·graph·i·cal** \-i-kəl\ *adj* **1 :** characterized by perpendicular lines or right angles **2 a :** of or relating to orthography **b :** correct in spelling — **or·tho·graph·i·cal·ly** \-i-k(ə-)lē\ *adv*

orthographic projection *n* **1 :** projection of a single view of an object in which the view is projected along lines perpendicular to both the view and the drawing surface **2 :** the representation of related views of an object as if they were all in the same plane and projected by orthographic projection

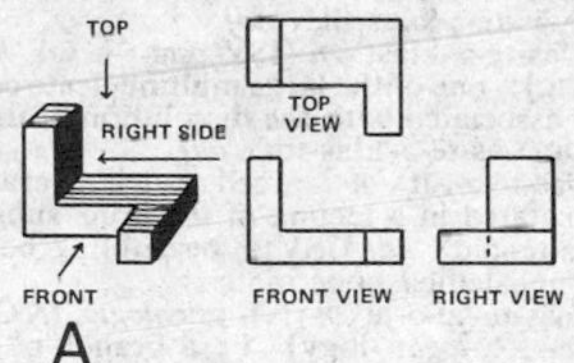

object *A* with top view, front view, and right view in orthographic projection

or·thog·ra·phy \ȯr-ˈthäg-rə-fē\ *n* [ME *ortografie,* fr. MF, fr. L *orthographia,* fr. Gk, fr. *orth-* + *graphein* to write — more at CARVE] **1 a :** the art of writing words with the proper letters according to standard usage **b :** the representation of the sounds of a language by written or printed symbols **2 :** a part of language study that deals with letters and spelling

or·tho·nor·mal \ˌȯr-thə-ˈnȯr-məl\ *adj* **1 :** being normal and orthogonal <~ functions> **2 :** being or composed of orthogonal elements of unit length <~ basis of a vector space>

or·tho·pe·dic *also* **or·tho·pae·dic** \ˌȯr-thə-ˈpēd-ik\ *adj* [F *orthopédique,* fr. *orthopédie* orthopedics, fr. *orth-* + Gk *paid-, pais* child — more at FEW] **1 :** of, relating to, or employed in orthopedics **2 :** marked by deformities or crippling

or·tho·pe·di·cal·ly \-ˈpēd-i-k(ə-)lē\ *adv* **:** by reason or means of or in respect to an orthopedic state or orthopedics

or·tho·pe·dics *also* **or·tho·pae·dics** \-ˈpēd-iks\ *n pl but sing or pl in constr* **:** the correction or prevention of skeletal deformities — **or·tho·pe·dist** \-ˈpēd-əst\ *n*

or·tho·phos·phate \ˌȯr-thə-ˈfäs-ˌfāt\ *n* **:** a salt or ester of orthophosphoric acid

or·tho·phos·pho·ric acid \ˌȯr-thə-ˌfäs-ˌfȯr-ik-, -ˌfär-; -ˌfäs-f(ə-)rik-\ *n* [ISV] **:** phosphoric acid in its unhydrated form

or·tho·psy·chi·a·try \-sə-ˈkī-ə-trē, -(ˌ)sī-\ *n* **:** prophylactic psychiatry concerned esp. with incipient mental and behavioral disorders in youth — **or·tho·psy·chi·at·ric** \-ˌsī-kē-ˈa-trik\ *adj* — **or·tho·psy·chi·a·trist** \-sə-ˈkī-ə-trəst, -(ˌ)sī-\ *n*

or·thop·ter·an \ȯr-ˈthäp-tə-rən\ *n* [NL *Orthoptera,* group name] **:** any of an order (Orthoptera) of insects (as crickets, grasshoppers, and sometimes mantises) that are characterized by biting mouthparts, two pairs of wings or none, and an incomplete metamorphosis — **orthopteran** *adj* — **or·thop·ter·ist** \-rəst\ *n* — **or·thop·ter·oid** \-ˌrȯid\ *n or adj*

or·thop·ter·on \ȯr-ˈthäp-tə-rən, -ˌrän\ *n, pl* **-tera** \-tə-rə\ [NL, sing. of *Orthoptera,* group name, fr. *orth-* + Gk *pteron* wing — more at FEATHER] **:** ORTHOPTERAN

or·tho·rhom·bic \ˌȯr-thə-ˈräm-bik\ *adj* [ISV] **:** of, relating to, or constituting a system of crystallization characterized by three unequal axes at right angles to each other

or·tho·scop·ic \-ˈskäp-ik\ *adj* [ISV *orth-* + *-scopic* (as in *microscopic*)] **1 :** giving an image in correct and normal proportions **2 :** giving a flat field of view

or·thot·ics \ȯr-ˈthät-iks\ *n pl but sing in constr* [NL *orthosis* straightening (fr. Gk *orthōsis,* fr. *orthoun* to straighten, fr. *orthos*), after such pairs as NL *prosthesis:* E *prosthetics*] **:** a branch of mechanical and medical science that deals with the support and bracing of weak or ineffective joints or muscles — **or·thot·ic** \-ik\ *adj* — **or·tho·tist** \ˈȯr-thət-əst\ *n*

or·tho·tro·pic \ˌȯr-thə-ˈtrōp-ik, -ˈträp-\ *adj* **:** having the longer axis more or less vertical <~ plant stems> — **or·tho·tro·pi·cal·ly** \-i-k(ə-)lē\ *adv* — **or·thot·ro·pism** \ȯr-ˈthä-trə-ˌpiz-əm\ *n*

or·thot·ro·pous \ȯr-ˈthä-trə-pəs\ *adj* [ISV] **:** having the ovule straight so that the chalaza, hilum, and micropyle are in the same axial line

or·to·lan \ˈȯrt-ᵊl-ən\ *n* [F or It; F, fr. It *ortolano,* lit., gardener, fr. L *hortulanus,* fr. *hortulus,* dim. of *hortus* garden — more at YARD] **:** a European bunting (*Emberiza hortulana*) that is about six inches long and is valued as a table delicacy

[1]**-o·ry** \ˌȯr-ē, ˌȯr-ē, (ə-)rē\ *n suffix* [ME *-orie,* fr. L *-orium,* fr. neut. of *-orius,* adj. suffix] **1 :** place of or for <observat*ory*> **2 :** something that serves for <cremat*ory*>

[2]**-ory** *adj suffix* [ME *-orie,* fr. MF & L; MF, fr. L *-orius*] **1 :** of, relating to, or characterized by <gustat*ory*> **2 :** serving for, producing, or maintaining <justificat*ory*>

oryx \ˈȯr-iks, ˈōr-, ˈär-\ *n, pl* **oryx** *or* **oryx·es** [NL, genus name, fr. L, a gazelle, fr. Gk, pickax, antelope, fr. *oryssein* to dig — more at ROUGH] **:** any of a genus (*Oryx*) of large straight-horned African antelopes

oryx

[1]**os** \ˈäs\ *n, pl* **os·sa** \ˈäs-ə\ [L *oss-, os* — more at OSSEOUS] **:** BONE

[2]**os** \ˈōs\ *n, pl* **ora** \ˈōr-ə, ˈȯr-ə\ [L *or-, os* — more at ORAL] **:** MOUTH, ORIFICE

[3]**os** \ˈōs\ *n, pl* **osar** \ˈō-ˌsär\ [Sw *ås* mountain ridge, fr. ON *āss;* akin to Gk *ōmos* shoulder — more at HUMERUS] **:** ESKER

Os *symbol* osmium

OS *abbr* **1** [L *oculus sinister*] left eye **2** old series **3** old style **4** ordinary seaman **5** out of stock

OSA *abbr* Order of St. Augustine

Osage \ō-ˈsāj\ *n, pl* **Osag·es** *or* **Osage 1 :** a member of an Amerindian people orig. of Missouri **2 :** the language of the Osage people

Osage orange *n* **:** an ornamental American tree (*Maclura pomifera*) of the mulberry family with shiny ovate leaves and hard bright orange wood; *also* **:** its yellowish fruit

OSB *abbr* Order of St. Benedict

Os·can \ˈäs-kən\ *n* [L *Oscus*] **1 :** a member of a people of ancient Italy occupying Campania **2 :** the language of the Oscan people — see INDO-EUROPEAN LANGUAGES table

[1]**Os·car** \ˈäs-kər\ *n* [*Oscar* Pierce, 20th cent. Am wheat and fruit grower] **:** a statuette awarded annually by a professional organization for notable achievement in motion pictures

[2]**Oscar** — a communications code word for the letter *o*

os·cil·late \ˈäs-ə-ˌlāt\ *vi* **-lat·ed; -lat·ing** [L *oscillatus,* pp. of *oscillare* to swing, fr. *oscillum* swing] **1 a :** to swing backward and forward like a pendulum **:** VIBRATE **b :** to move or travel back and forth between two points **2 :** to vary between opposing beliefs, feelings, or theories **3 :** to vary above and below a mean value *syn* see SWING — **os·cil·la·to·ry** \ˈäs-ə-lə-ˌtōr-ē, -ˌtȯr-\ *adj*

os·cil·la·tion \ˌäs-ə-ˈlā-shən\ *n* **1 :** the action or fact of oscillating **:** VIBRATION **2 :** VARIATION, FLUCTUATION **3 :** a flow of electricity changing periodically from a maximum to a minimum; *esp* **:** a flow periodically changing direction **4 :** a single swing (as of an oscillating body) from one extreme limit to the other — **os·cil·la·tion·al** \-shnəl, -shən-ᵊl\ *adj*

os·cil·la·tor \ˈäs-ə-ˌlāt-ər\ *n* **1 :** one that oscillates **2 :** a device for producing alternating current; *esp* **:** a radio-frequency or audio-frequency generator

os·cil·lo·gram \ä-ˈsil-ə-ˌgram, ə-\ *n* [L *oscillare* + ISV *-gram*] **:** a record made by an oscillograph or oscilloscope

os·cil·lo·graph \-ˌgraf\ *n* [F *oscillographe,* fr. L *oscillare* + F *-graphe* -graph] **:** an instrument for recording alternating current wave forms or other electrical oscillations — **os·cil·lo·graph·ic**

ə abut   ᵊ kitten   ər further   a back   ā bake   ä cot, cart
au̇ out   ch chin   e less   ē easy   g gift   i trip   ī life
j joke   ŋ sing   ō flow   ȯ flaw   ȯi coin   th thin   t͟h this
ü loot   u̇ foot   y yet   yü few   yu̇ furious   zh vision

\ä-ˌsil-ə-ˈgraf-ik, ˌäs-ə-lə-\ *adj* — **os·cil·lo·graph·i·cal·ly** \-i-k(ə-)lē\ *adv* — **os·cil·log·ra·phy** \ˌäs-ə-ˈläg-rə-fē\ *n*

os·cil·lo·scope \ä-ˈsil-ə-ˌskōp, ə-\ *n* [L *oscillare* + ISV *-scope*] : an instrument in which the variations in a fluctuating electrical quantity appear temporarily as a visible wave form on the fluorescent screen of a cathode-ray tube; *broadly* : OSCILLOGRAPH — **os·cil·lo·scop·ic** \ä-ˌsil-ə-ˈskäp-ik, ˌäs-ə-lə-\ *adj* — **os·cil·lo·scop·i·cal·ly** \-i-k(ə-)lē\ *adv*

os·cine \ˈäs-ˌīn\ *adj* [deriv. of L *oscin-, oscen* bird used in divination, fr. *obs-* in front of + *canere* to sing — more at OSTENSIBLE, CHANT] : PASSERINE 2 — **oscine** *n*

Os·co–Um·bri·an \ˌäs-kō-ˈəm-brē-ən\ *n* [L *Oscus* + E *Umbrian*] : a subdivision of the Italic branch of the Indo-European language family containing Oscan and Umbrian — see INDO-EUROPEAN LANGUAGES table

os·cu·late \ˈäs-kyə-ˌlāt\ *vt* **-lat·ed; -lat·ing** [L *osculatus,* pp. of *osculari,* fr. *osculum* kiss, fr. dim. of *os* mouth — more at ORAL] : KISS

osculating circle *n* : a circle whose center lies on the concave side of a curve on the normal to a given point of the curve and whose radius is equal to the radius of curvature at that point

os·cu·la·tion \ˌäs-kyə-ˈlā-shən\ *n* : the act of kissing; *also* : KISS — **os·cu·la·to·ry** \ˈäs-kyə-lə-ˌtōr-ē, -ˌtȯr-\ *adj*

os·cu·lum \ˈäs-kyə-ləm\ *n* [NL, fr. L, dim. of *os* mouth] : an excurrent opening of a sponge

¹-ose \ˌōs, ˈōs *sometimes* ˌōz, ˈōz\ *adj suffix* [ME, fr. L *-osus*] : full of : having : possessing the qualities of <cym*ose*>

²-ose \ˌōs, ˌōz\ *n suffix* [F, fr. *glucose*] **1** : carbohydrate <amyl*ose*>; *esp* : sugar <pent*ose*> **2** : primary hydrolysis product <prote*ose*>

Osee \ˈō-ˌzē, ō-ˈzā-ə\ *n* [LL, fr. Heb *Hōshēaʻ*] : HOSEA

OSF *abbr* Order of St. Francis

osier \ˈō-zhər\ *n* [ME, fr. MF, fr. ML *auseria* osier bed] **1** : any of various willows (esp. *Salix viminalis*) whose pliable twigs are used for furniture and basketry **2** : a willow rod used in basketry **3** : any of several American dogwoods

Osi·ris \ō-ˈsī-rəs\ *n* [L, fr. Gk, fr. Egypt *Wsʼr*] : a mythical Egyptian hero who was king and educator of his people and was regarded as god of the dead

-o·sis \ˈō-səs\ *n suffix, pl* **-o·ses** \-ˌsēz\ *or* **-o·sis·es** [ME, fr. L, fr. Gk *-ōsis,* fr. *-ō-* (stem of causative verbs in *-oun*) + *-sis*] **1 a** : action : process : condition <hypn*osis*> **b** : abnormal or diseased condition <leuk*osis*> **2** : increase : formation <leukocyt*osis*>

Os·man·li \äz-ˈman-lē\ *n* [Turk *osmanli,* fr. *Osman,* founder of the Ottoman Empire] **1** : a Turk of the western branch of the Turkish peoples **2** : TURKISH

os·mat·ic \äz-ˈmat-ik\ *or* **os·mic** \ˈäz-mik\ *adj* [Gk *osmē* odor + E *-atic* (as in *aquatic*) — more at ODOR] : depending chiefly on the sense of smell for orientation <the dog is a highly ~ animal>

os·me·te·ri·um \ˌäz-mə-ˈtir-ē-əm\ *n, pl* **-ria** \-ē-ə\ [NL, fr. Gk *osmē* odor + *-tērion,* suffix denoting an instrument] : a protrusible forked process that emits a disagreeable odor, is borne on the first thoracic segment of the larvae of many swallowtail butterflies and their relatives, and is prob. a defensive organ

os·mic \ˈäz-mik\ *adj* [ISV] : of, relating to, or derived from osmium esp. with a relatively high valence

osmic acid *n* : OSMIUM TETROXIDE

os·mi·rid·i·um \ˌäz-mə-ˈrid-ē-əm\ *n* [Gk *osmē* + NL *iridium*] : IRIDOSMINE

os·mi·um \ˈäz-mē-əm\ *n* [NL, fr. Gk *osmē* odor] : a hard brittle blue-gray or blue-black polyvalent metallic element of the platinum group with a high melting point that is the heaviest metal known and that is used esp. as a catalyst and in hard alloys — see ELEMENT table

osmium tetroxide *n* : a crystalline compound OsO_4 that is an oxide of osmium, has a poisonous irritating vapor, and is used as a catalyst, oxidizing agent, and biological stain

os·mol \ˈäz-ˌmōl, ˈäs-\ *n* [blend of *osmosis* and *mol*] : a standard unit of osmotic pressure based on the concentration of an ion in a solution — **os·mol·al** \äz-ˈmō-ləl, äs-\ *adj* — **os·mo·lal·i·ty** \ˌäz-mō-ˈlal-ət-ē, ˌäs-\ *n*

os·mo·lar \äz-ˈmō-lər, äs-\ *adj* [*osmol*] : OSMOTIC — used chiefly of biological fluids — **os·mo·lar·i·ty** \ˌäz-mō-ˈlar-ət-ē, ˌäs-\ *n*

os·mom·e·ter \äz-ˈmäm-ət-ər, äs-\ *n* [*osmosis* + *-meter*] : an apparatus for measuring osmotic pressure — **os·mo·met·ric** \ˌäz-mə-ˈme-trik, ˌäs-\ *adj* — **os·mom·e·try** \äz-ˈmäm-ə-trē\ *n*

os·mo·reg·u·la·tion \ˈäz-mō-ˌreg-yə-ˈlā-shən, ˈäs-\ *n* [*osmosis* + *regulation*] : regulation of osmotic pressure esp. in the body of a living organism

os·mo·reg·u·la·to·ry \-ˈreg-yə-lə-ˌtōr-ē, -ˌtȯr-\ *adj* : of, relating to, or concerned with the maintenance of constant osmotic pressure

os·mose \ˈäz-ˌmōs, ˈäs-, äz-ˈ, äs-ˈ\ *vi* **os·mosed; os·mos·ing** [back-formation fr. *osmosis*] : to diffuse by osmosis

os·mo·sis \äz-ˈmō-səs, äs-\ *n* [NL, short for *endosmosis*] **1** : diffusion through a semipermeable membrane (as of a living cell) typically separating a solvent and a solution that tends to equalize their concentrations; *esp* : the passage of solvent in distinction from the passage of solute **2** : a process of absorption or diffusion suggestive of the flow of osmotic action

os·mot·ic \-ˈmät-ik\ *adj* : of, relating to, or having the properties of osmosis — **os·mot·i·cal·ly** \-i-k(ə-)lē\ *adv*

osmotic pressure *n* : the pressure produced by or associated with osmosis and dependent on molar concentration and absolute temperature: as **a** : the maximum pressure that develops in a solution separated from a solvent by a membrane premeable only to the solvent **b** : the pressure that must be applied to a solution to just prevent osmosis

osmotic shock *n* : a rapid change in the osmotic pressure (as by transfer to a medium of different concentration) affecting a living system

os·mous \ˈäz-məs\ *adj* : of, relating to, or derived from osmium esp. with a relatively low valence

os·mun·da \äz-ˈmən-də\ *n* [NL, genus name, fr. ML, osmunda, fr. OF *osmonde*] : any of a genus (*Osmunda*) of rather large ferns with fibrous creeping rhizomes

os·prey \ˈäs-prē, -ˌprā\ *n, pl* **ospreys** [ME *ospray,* fr. (assumed) MF *osfraie,* fr. L *ossifraga*] **1** : a large fish-eating hawk (*Pandion haliaetus*) that is a dark brown color above and mostly pure white below **2** : a feather trimming used for millinery

ossa *pl of* OS

os·se·in \ˈäs-ē-ən\ *n* [ISV, fr. L *oss-, os*] : the collagen of bones

os·se·ous \ˈäs-ē-əs\ *adj* [L *osseus,* fr. *oss-, os* bone; akin to Gk *osteon* bone] : BONY 1 — **os·se·ous·ly** *adv*

Os·set \ˈäs-ət, -ˌet\ *or* **Os·sete** \ˈäs-ˌēt\ *n* [Russ *Osetin*] : a member of an Aryan people of central Caucasia — **Os·se·tian** \ä-ˈsē-shən\ *adj or n*

Os·set·ic \ä-ˈset-ik\ *n* : the Iranian language of the Ossets

Os·si·an·ic \ˌäs(h)-ē-ˈan-ik\ *adj* : of, relating to, or resembling the legendary Irish bard Ossian, the poems ascribed to him, or the rhythmic prose style used by James Macpherson in his alleged translations

os·si·cle \ˈäs-i-kəl\ *n* [L *ossiculum,* dim. of *oss-, os*] : a small bone or bony structure (as the malleus, incus, or stapes) — **os·sic·u·lar** \ä-ˈsik-yə-lər\ *adj* — **os·sic·u·late** \-lət\ *adj*

os·si·fi·ca·tion \ˌäs-ə-fə-ˈkā-shən\ *n* **1 a** : the natural process of bone formation **b** : the hardening (as of muscular tissue) into a bony substance **2** : a mass or particle of ossified tissue **3** : a tendency toward or state of being molded into a rigid, conventional, sterile, or unimaginative condition <a revolt against the ~*s* of institutions —Amos Vogel> — **os·sif·i·ca·to·ry** \ä-ˈsif-i-kə-ˌtōr-ē, -ˌtȯr-\ *adj*

os·si·frage \ˈäs-ə-frij, -ˌfrāj\ *n* [L *ossifraga* sea eagle, fr. fem. of *ossifragus* bone-breaking, fr. *oss-, os* + *frangere* to break — more at BREAK] : LAMMERGEIER

os·si·fy \ˈäs-ə-ˌfī\ *vb* **-fied; -fy·ing** [prob. fr. (assumed) NL *ossificare,* fr. L *oss-, os*] *vi* **1** : to change into bone **2** : to become callous or conventional ~ *vt* **1** : to change (as cartilage) into bone **2** : to make rigidly conventional and opposed to change

os·su·ary \ˈäsh-ə-ˌwer-ē, ˈäs-(y)ə-\ *n, pl* **-ar·ies** [LL *ossuarium,* fr. L, neut. of *ossuarius* of bones, fr. OL *ossua,* pl. of *oss-, os*] : a depository for the bones of the dead

oste- *or* **osteo-** *comb form* [NL, fr. Gk, fr. *osteon* — more at OSSEOUS] : bone <*oste*al> <*osteo*myelitis>

os·te·al \ˈäs-tē-əl\ *adj* [ISV] : of, relating to, or resembling bone; *also* : affecting or involving bone or the skeleton

os·te·itis \ˌäs-tē-ˈīt-əs\ *n* [NL] : inflammation of bone

os·ten·si·ble \ä-ˈsten(t)-sə-bəl, ə-\ *adj* [F, fr. L *ostensus,* pp. of *ostendere* to show, fr. *obs-* in front of (akin to *ob-* in the way) + *tendere* to stretch — more at OB-, THIN] **1** : intended for display : open to view **2** : being such in appearance : plausible rather than demonstrably true or real <his ~ frankness covered a devious scheme> ***syn*** see APPARENT — **os·ten·si·bly** \-blē\ *adv*

os·ten·sive \ä-ˈsten(t)-siv\ *adj* **1** : OSTENSIBLE 2 **2** : of, relating to, or constituting definition by exhibiting the thing or quality being defined — **os·ten·sive·ly** *adv*

os·ten·so·ri·um \ˌäs-tən-ˈsōr-ē-əm, -ˌten-, -ˈsȯr-\ *n* [ML, fr. L *ostensus*] : MONSTRANCE

os·ten·ta·tion \ˌäs-tən-ˈtā-shən\ *n* [ME *ostentacion,* fr. MF *ostentation,* fr. L *ostentation-, ostentatio,* fr. *ostentatus,* pp. of *ostentare* to display ostentatiously, fr. *ostentus,* pp. of *ostendere*] **1** : excessive display : PRETENTIOUSNESS **2** *archaic* : an act of displaying

os·ten·ta·tious \-shəs\ *adj* : marked by or indulging in conspicuous or vainglorious and sometimes pretentious display ***syn*** see SHOWY — **os·ten·ta·tious·ly** *adv* — **os·ten·ta·tious·ness** *n*

os·teo·ar·thri·tis \ˌäs-tē-ō-är-ˈthrīt-əs\ *n* [NL] : degenerative arthritis — **os·teo·ar·thrit·ic** \-ˈthrit-ik\ *adj*

os·teo·blast \ˈäs-tē-ə-ˌblast\ *n* [ISV] : a bone-forming cell — **os·teo·blas·tic** \ˌäs-tē-ə-ˈblas-tik\ *adj*

os·teo·clast \ˈäs-tē-ə-ˌklast\ *n* [ISV *oste-* + Gk *klastos* broken — more at CLASTIC] : one of the large multinucleate cells in developing bone that are associated with the dissolution of unwanted bone — **os·teo·clas·tic** \ˌäs-tē-ə-ˈklas-tik\ *adj*

os·teo·cyte \ˈäs-tē-ə-ˌsīt\ *n* : a cell that is characteristic of adult bone and is isolated in a lacuna of the bone substance

¹os·te·oid \ˈäs-tē-ˌȯid\ *adj* [ISV] : resembling bone

²osteoid *n* : uncalcified bone matrix

os·te·ol·o·gy \ˌäs-tē-ˈäl-ə-jē\ *n* [NL *osteologia,* fr. Gk, description of bones, fr. *oste-* + *-logia* -logy] **1** : a branch of anatomy dealing with the bones **2** : the bony structure of an organism — **os·te·o·log·i·cal** \-tē-ə-ˈläj-i-kəl\ *adj* — **os·te·o·log·i·cal·ly** \-k(ə-)lē\ *adv* — **os·te·ol·o·gist** \-tē-ˈäl-ə-jəst\ *n*

os·te·o·ma \ˌäs-tē-ˈō-mə\ *n, pl* **-mas** *or* **-ma·ta** \-mət-ə\ [NL] : a benign tumor composed of bone tissue

os·teo·ma·la·cia \ˌäs-tē-ō-mə-ˈlā-sh(ē-)ə\ *n* [NL, fr. *oste-* + Gk *malakia* softness, fr. *malakos* soft — more at MALAC-] : a disease characterized by softening of the bones in the adult and equivalent to rickets in the immature

os·teo·my·eli·tis \-ˌmī-ə-ˈlīt-əs\ *n* [NL] : an infectious inflammatory disease of bone marked by local death and separation of tissue

os·teo·path \ˈäs-tē-ə-ˌpath\ *n* : a practitioner of osteopathy

os·te·op·a·thy \ˌäs-tē-ˈäp-ə-thē\ *n* [NL *osteopathia,* fr. *oste-* + L *-pathia* -pathy] : a system of medical practice based on a theory that diseases are due chiefly to loss of structural integrity which can be restored by manipulation of the parts supplemented by therapeutic measures (as use of medicine or surgery) — **os·teo·path·ic** \ˌäs-tē-ə-ˈpath-ik\ *adj* — **os·teo·path·i·cal·ly** \-i-k(ə-)lē\ *adv*

os·teo·phyte \ˈäs-tē-ə-ˌfīt\ *n* [ISV] : a pathological bony outgrowth — **os·teo·phyt·ic** \ˌäs-tē-ə-ˈfit-ik\ *adj*

os·teo·plas·tic \ˌäs-tē-ə-ˈplas-tik\ *adj* : of or relating to the surgical replacement of bone — **os·teo·plas·ty** \ˈäs-tē-ə-ˌplas-tē\ *n*

osti·na·to \ˌäs-tə-ˈnät-(ˌ)ō, ˌō-stə-\ *n, pl* **-tos** [It, obstinate, fr. L *obstinatus*] : a musical figure repeated persistently at the same pitch throughout a composition — compare IMITATION, SEQUENCE

os·ti·ole \ˈäs-tē-ˌōl\ *n* [NL *ostiolum,* fr. L, dim. of *ostium*] : a small bodily aperture, orifice, or pore

os·ti·um \'äs-tē-əm\ *n, pl* **os·tia** \-tē-ə\ [NL, fr. L, door, mouth of a river; akin to L *os* mouth — more at ORAL] **:** a mouthlike opening in a bodily organ

ostler *var of* HOSTLER

ost·mark \'ōst-ˌmärk, 'ȯst-\ *n* [G, lit., East mark] — see MONEY table

os·to·my \'äs-tə-mē\ *n, pl* **-mies** [*colostomy*] **:** an operation (as a colostomy) to create an artificial anus

-os·to·sis \äs-'tō-səs\ *n comb form, pl* **-os·to·ses** \-ˌsēz\ *or* **-os·to·sis·es** \-'tō-sə-səz\ [NL, fr. GK *-ostōsis,* fr. *osteon* bone — more at OSSEOUS] **:** ossification of a (specified) part or to a (specified) degree <hyper*ostosis*> <ect*ostosis*>

os·tra·cism \'äs-trə-ˌsiz-əm\ *n* **1 :** a method of temporary banishment by popular vote without trial or special accusation practiced in ancient Greece **2 :** exclusion by general consent from common privileges or social acceptance

os·tra·cize \-ˌsīz\ *vt* **-cized; -ciz·ing** [Gk *ostrakizein* to banish by voting with potsherds, fr. *ostrakon* shell, potsherd — more at OYSTER] **1 :** to exile by ostracism **2 :** to exclude from a group by common consent

os·tra·cod \'äs-trə-ˌkäd\ *also* **os·tra·code** \-ˌkōd\ *n* [deriv. of Gk *ostrakon*] **:** any of a subclass (Ostracoda) of small active mostly freshwater crustaceans that have the body enclosed in a bivalve shell, the body segmentation obscured, the abdomen rudimentary, and only seven pairs of appendages

os·tra·co·derm \'äs-trə-kō-ˌdərm, äs-'trak-ə-\ *n* [deriv. of Gk *ostrakon* + *derma* skin — more at DERM-] **:** any of an order (Ostracodermi) of primitive fossil armored fishes — **ostracoderm** *adj*

os·trich \'äs-trich, 'ȯs- *also* -trij\ *n* [ME, fr. OF *ostrusce,* fr. (assumed) VL *avis struthio,* fr. L *avis* bird + LL *struthio* ostrich — more at STRUTHIOUS] **1 a :** a swift-footed 2-toed flightless ratite bird (genus *Struthio,* esp. *S. camelus* of northern Africa) that has valuable wing and tail plumes, is the largest of existing birds, and often weighs 300 pounds **b :** RHEA **2** [fr. the belief that the ostrich when pursued hides his head in the sand and believes himself to be unseen] **:** one who attempts to avoid danger by refusing to face it

ostrich 1a

Os·tro·goth \'äs-trə-ˌgäth\ *n* [LL *Ostrogothi,* pl.] **:** a member of the eastern division of the Goths — **Os·tro·goth·ic** \ˌäs-trə-'gäth-ik\ *adj*

Os·we·go tea \ä-ˌswē-gō-\ *n* [*Oswego* river, N. Y.] **:** a No. American mint (*Monarda didyma*) with showy scarlet irregular flowers

OT *abbr* **1** occupational therapy **2** Old Testament **3** overtime

ot- *or* **oto-** *comb form* [Gk *ōt-, ōto-,* fr. *ōt-, ous* — more at EAR] **:** ear <*otitis*> **:** ear and <*oto*laryngology>

Othel·lo \ə-'thel-(ˌ)ō, ō-\ *n* **:** a Moor in the military service of Venice, husband of Desdemona, and protagonist of Shakespeare's tragedy *Othello*

1**oth·er** \'əth-ər\ *adj* [ME, fr. OE *ōther;* akin to OHG *andar* other, Skt *antara*] **1 a :** being the one (as of two or more) left <held on with one hand and waved with the ~ one> **b :** being the ones distinct from those first mentioned <taller than the ~ boys> **c :** SECOND <every ~ day> **2 :** not the same **:** DIFFERENT <schools ~ than his own> **3 :** ADDITIONAL **4 a :** recently past <the ~ evening> **b :** FORMER <in ~ times>

2**other** *n* **1 a :** one that remains of two or more **b :** a thing opposite to or excluded by something else <went from one side to the ~> **2 :** a different or additional one <the ~*s* came later>

3**other** *pron, sometimes pl in constr* **1** *obs* **a :** one of two that remains **b :** each preceding one **2 :** a different or additional one <something or ~> <some left, but many ~*s* stayed>

4**other** *adv* **:** OTHERWISE — used with *than*

oth·er–di·rect·ed \ˌəth-ər-də-'rek-təd, -dī-\ *adj* **:** directed in thought and action primarily by external norms as opposed to one's own scale of values — **oth·er–di·rect·ed·ness** *n*

oth·er·guess \'əth-ər-ˌges\ *adj* [alter. of E dial. *othergates*] *archaic* **:** DIFFERENT

oth·er·ness \'əth-ər-nəs\ *n* **1 :** the quality or state of being other or different **2 :** something that is other or different

oth·er·where \-ˌ(h)we(ə)r, -ˌ(h)wa(ə)r\ *adv* **:** ELSEWHERE

oth·er·while \-ˌhwīl, -ˌwīl\ *also* **oth·er·whiles** \-ˌhwīlz, -ˌwīlz\ *adv, chiefly dial* **:** at another time

1**oth·er·wise** \-ˌwīz\ *adv* [ME, fr. OE (*on*) *ōthre wīsan* in another manner] **1 :** in a different way or manner <glossed over or ~ handled —*Playboy*> **2 :** in different circumstances <might ~ have left> **3 :** in other respects <an ~ flimsy farce —*Current Biog.*> **4 :** if not <do what I tell you, ~ you'll be sorry>

2**otherwise** *adj* **:** DIFFERENT

oth·er·world \'əth-ər-ˌwərld\ *n* **:** a world beyond death or beyond present reality

oth·er·world·ly \-ˌwərl-(d)lē\ *adj* **1 a :** of or relating to a world other than the actual world **:** TRANSCENDENTAL **b :** devoted to preparing for a world to come **2 :** devoted to intellectual or imaginative pursuits — **oth·er·world·li·ness** *n*

otic \'ōt-ik\ *adj* [Gk *ōtikos,* fr. *ōt-, ous* ear — more at EAR] **:** of, relating to, or located in the region of the ear

1**-ot·ic** \'ät-ik\ *adj suffix* [Gk *-ōtikos,* fr. *-ōtos,* ending of verbals, fr. *-o-* (stem of causative verbs in *-oun*) + *-tos,* suffix forming verbals — more at -ED] **1 a :** of, relating to, or characterized by a (specified) action, process, or condition <symbi*otic*> **b :** having an abnormal or diseased condition of a (specified) kind <epizo*otic*> **2 :** showing an increase or a formation of <leukocyt*otic*>

2**-otic** \'ōt-ik\ *adj comb form* [Gk *ōtikos*] **:** having (such) a relationship to the ear <peri*otic*>

oti·ose \'ō-shē-ˌōs, 'ōt-ē-\ *adj* [L *otiosus,* fr. *otium* leisure] **1 :** being at leisure **:** IDLE **2 :** producing no useful result **:** FUTILE **3 :** lacking use or effect **:** FUNCTIONLESS *syn* see VAIN — **oti·ose·ly** *adv* — **oti·ose·ness** *n* — **oti·os·i·ty** \ˌō-shē-'äs-ət-ē, ˌōt-ē-\ *n*

oti·tis \ō-'tīt-əs\ *n* [NL] **:** inflammation of the ear

oto·cyst \'ōt-ə-ˌsist\ *n* [ISV, fr. its probable auditory function] **:** a fluid-containing organ of many invertebrates that contains an otolith **:** STATOCYST — **oto·cys·tic** \ˌōt-ə-'sis-tik\ *adj*

oto·lar·yn·gol·o·gy \'ōt-ō-ˌlar-ən-'gäl-ə-jē\ *n* [*ot-* + *laryng-* + *-logy*] **:** a branch of medicine dealing with the ear, nose, and throat — **oto·lar·yn·go·log·i·cal** \-ˌlar-ən-gə-'läj-i-kəl\ *adj* — **oto·lar·yn·gol·o·gist** \-'gäl-ə-jəst\ *n*

oto·lith \'ōt-ᵊl-ˌith\ *n* [F *otolithe,* fr. *ot-* + *-lithe* -lith] **:** a calcareous concretion in the internal ear of a vertebrate or in the otocyst of an invertebrate — **oto·lith·ic** \ˌōt-ᵊl-ith-ik\ *adj*

Oto·mac \ˌōt-ə-'mäk, -'mak\ *n* **1 :** a member of an extinct aboriginal people of southern Venezuela **2 :** the language of the Otomac people

OTS *abbr* officers' training school

ot·ta·va \ō-'täv-ə\ *adv or adj* [It, octave, fr. ML *octava*] **:** at an octave higher or lower than written — used as a direction in music

ot·ta·va ri·ma \ō-ˌtäv-ə-'rē-mə\ *n, pl* **ottava rimas** [It, lit., eighth rhyme] **:** a stanza of eight lines of heroic verse with a rhyme scheme of *abababcc*

Ot·ta·wa \'ät-ə-wə, -ˌwä, -ˌwȯ\ *n, pl* **Ottawas** *or* **Ottawa :** a member of an Amerindian people of Michigan and southern Ontario

ot·ter \'ät-ər\ *n, pl* **otters** *also* **otter** [ME *oter,* fr. OE *otor;* akin to OHG *ottar* otter, Gk *hydōr* water — more at WATER] **1 :** any of several aquatic fish-eating mammals (genus *Lutra*) that are related to the weasels and minks and have webbed and clawed feet and dark brown fur **2 :** the fur or pelt of an otter

otter 1

otter hound *n* [fr. its use in hunting otters] **:** a British hound of complex ancestry that in many respects resembles the bloodhound, that has a wiry shaggy coat, long pendulous ears, and a scowling expression, and that is a good but slow water dog with a keen scent

ot·to \'ät-(ˌ)ō\ *var of* ATTAR

ot·to·man \'ät-ə-mən\ *n* **1** *cap* **:** TURK **2** [F *ottomane,* fr. fem. of *ottoman,* adj.] **a :** an upholstered often overstuffed seat or couch usu. without a back **b :** an overstuffed footstool

Ot·to·man \'ät-ə-mən\ *adj* [F, adj. & n., prob. fr. It *ottomano,* fr. Ar *'othmānī,* fr. *'Othmān* Othman, founder of the Ottoman Empire] **:** of or relating to the Turks or Turkey **:** TURKISH

oua·bain \wä-'bā-ən, 'wä-ˌbän\ *n* [ISV, fr. F *ouabaïo,* an African tree, fr. Somali *waba yo*] **:** a poisonous glycoside $C_{29}H_{44}O_{12}$ obtained from several African shrubs or trees of the dogbane family and used medically like digitalis and in Africa as an arrow poison

ou·bli·ette \ˌü-blē-'et\ *n* [F, fr. MF, fr. *oublier* to forget, fr. L *oblitus,* pp. of *oblivisci* — more at OBLIVION] **:** a dungeon with an opening only at the top

1**ouch** \'au̇ch\ *n* [ME, alter. (resulting fr. incorrect division of *a nouche*) of *nouche,* fr. MF, of Gmc origin; akin to OHG *nusca* clasp; akin to OE *nett* net] **1** *obs* **:** CLASP, BROOCH **2 a :** a setting for a precious stone **b :** JEWEL, ORNAMENT; *esp* **:** a buckle or brooch set with precious stones

2**ouch** *interj* [origin unknown] — used esp. to express sudden pain

oud \'üd\ *n* [Ar *'ūd,* lit., wood] **:** a musical instrument of the lute family used in southwest Asia and northern Africa

1**ought** \'ȯt\ *verbal auxiliary* [ME *oughte* (1st & 3d sing. pres. indic.), fr. *oughte,* 1st & 3d sing. past indic. & subj. of *owen* to own, owe — more at OWE] — used to express obligation <~ to pay our debts>, advisability <~ to take care of yourself>, natural expectation <~ to be here by now>, or logical consequence <the result ~ to be infinity>

2**ought** \'ȯ(k)t\ *vt* [ME *oughte,* 1st & 3d sing. past indic. of *owen*] **1** *chiefly Scot* **:** OWE **2** *chiefly Scot* **:** POSSESS

3**ought** \'ȯt\ *n* **:** moral obligation **:** DUTY

4**ought** \'ȯt, 'ät\ *var of* AUGHT

oughtn't \'ȯt-ᵊnt\ **:** ought not

Oui·ja \'wē-jə, -jē\ *trademark* — used for a board with the alphabet and other signs on it that is used with a planchette to seek spiritualistic or telepathic messages

1**ounce** \'au̇n(t)s\ *n* [ME, fr. MF *unce,* fr. L *uncia* twelfth part, ounce, fr. *unus* one — more at ONE] **1 a :** any of various units of weight based on the ancient Roman unit equal to $^1/_{12}$ Roman pound — see WEIGHT table **b :** a small portion <an ~ of common sense> **2 :** FLUIDOUNCE

2**ounce** *n* [ME *once,* fr. OF, alter. (by incorrect division, as if *l'once* the ounce) of *lonce,* fr. (assumed) VL *lyncea,* fr. L *lync-, lynx* lynx] **:** SNOW LEOPARD

ouph *or* **ouphe** \'au̇f\ *n* [prob. alter. of earlier *auf,* prob. fr. ON *alfr*] **:** ELF

our \'är, (')au̇(ə)r\ *adj* [ME *oure,* fr. OE *ūre;* akin to OHG *unsēr* our, OE *ūs* us] **:** of or relating to us or ourselves or ourself esp. as possessors or possessor, agents or agent, or objects or object of an action <~ throne> <~ actions> <~ being chosen>

Our Father *n* **:** LORD'S PRAYER

ours \(ˈ)au̇(ə)rz, ärz\ *pron, sing or pl in constr* **:** that which belongs to us — used without a following noun as a pronoun equivalent in meaning to the adjective *our*
our·self \är-ˈself, au̇(ə)r-\ *pron* **:** MYSELF — used to refer to the single-person subject when *we* is used instead of *I* (as by a sovereign) <will keep ~ till supper time alone —Shak.>
our·selves \-ˈselvz\ *pron pl* **1 :** those identical ones that are we — compare WE 1; used reflexively <we're doing it solely for ~>, for emphasis <we ~ will never go >, or in absolute constructions <~ no longer young, we can sympathize with those who are old> **2 :** our normal, healthy, or sane condition
-ous \əs\ *adj suffix* [ME, partly fr. OF *-ous, -eus, -eux,* fr. L *-osus;* partly fr. L *-us,* nom. sing. masc. ending of many adjectives] **1 :** full of **:** abounding in **:** having **:** possessing the qualities of <clamor*ous*> <poison*ous*> **2 :** having a valence lower than in compounds or ions named with an adjective ending in *-ic* <mercur*ous*>
ou·sel \ˈü-zəl\ *var of* OUZEL
oust \ˈau̇st\ *vt* [AF *ouster,* fr. OF *oster,* fr. LL *obstare* to ward off, fr. L, to stand against, fr. *ob-* against + *stare* to stand — more at OB-, STAND] **1 a :** to remove from or dispossess of property or position by legal action, by force, or by the compulsion of necessity **b :** to take away (as a right or authority) **:** BAR, REMOVE **2 :** to take the place of **:** SUPPLANT ***syn*** see EJECT
oust·er \ˈau̇s-tər\ *n* [AF, to oust] **1 a :** a wrongful dispossession **b :** a judgment removing an officer or depriving a corporation of a franchise **2 :** EXPULSION
[1]**out** \ˈau̇t\ *adv* [ME, fr. OE *ūt;* akin to OHG *ūz* out, Gk *hysteros* later, *hybris* arrogance, Skt *ud* up, out] **1 a :** in a direction away from the inside or center <went ~ into the garden> **b :** from among others **c :** away from the shore **d :** away from home or business <~ to lunch> **2 a :** out of the usual or proper place <left a word ~> <threw his shoulder ~> **b :** beyond possession, control, or occupation <lent ~ money> **c :** into a state of loss or deprivation <voted him ~> **d :** into a state of vexation or disagreement <they do not mark me, and that brings me ~ —Shak.> **e :** into portions, shares, or allotments <parceled ~ the farm> **3 a :** beyond the limits of existence, continuance, or supply <the food ran ~> **b :** to extinction, exhaustion, or completion <burn ~> <hear me ~> <before the year runs ~> **c :** to the fullest extent or degree <all decked ~> **d :** in or into competition or determined effort <went ~ for the football team> **4 a :** in or into the open <the sun came ~> **b :** ALOUD <cried ~> **c :** in or into public circulation <the evening paper came ~ late> **5 a :** so as to put out a batter, batsman, or base runner **b :** so as to be put out **6 —** used on a two-way radio circuit to indicate that a message is complete and no reply is expected
[2]**out** *vt* **:** to put out **:** EJECT <did their best to ~ him —F. T. Wood> ~ *vi* **:** to become publicly known <the truth will ~>
[3]**out** *adj* **1 :** situated outside **:** EXTERNAL **2 :** situated at a distance **:** OUTLYING <the ~ islands> **3 :** not being in power **4 :** ABSENT **5 a :** not allowed to continue batting, to occupy a base, or to score — used of a player in baseball **b :** not allowed to continue as a batsman — used of a player in cricket **6 :** directed outward or serving to direct something outward **:** OUTGOING <put the letter in the ~ basket> **7 :** not being in vogue or fashion **:** not up-to-date **8 :** out of the question **:** IMPOSSIBLE <these last two proposals seem definitely ~ —Tom Fitzsimmons>
[4]**out** \(ˌ)au̇t\ *prep* — used as a function word to indicate an outward movement <ran ~ the door> <looked ~ the window>
[5]**out** \ˈau̇t\ *n* **1 :** OUTSIDE <the width of the building from ~ to ~> **2 :** one who is out of office or power or on the outside <a matter of ~*s* versus ins> **3 :** copy matter inadvertently omitted in typesetting **4 a :** an act or instance of putting out a player in baseball **b :** an act or instance of being put out **c :** a player that is put out **d :** a situation in which a player has been put out **5 :** a ball hit out-of-bounds in tennis or squash **6 :** an item that is out of stock **7 :** a way of escaping from an embarrassing or difficult situation — **on the outs :** on unfriendly terms **:** at variance
out- *prefix* [[1]*out*] **:** in a manner that goes beyond, surpasses, or excels <*out*maneuver>
out·age \ˈau̇t-ij\ *n* **1 :** a quantity or bulk of something lost in transportation or storage **2 a :** a failure or interruption in use or functioning **b :** a period of interruption esp. of electric current
out-and-out \ˌau̇t-ᵊn-ˈ(d)au̇t\ *adj* **:** being completely as described at all times, in every part, or from every point of view <this is an ~ fraud> ***syn*** see OUTRIGHT
out-and-out·er \-ər\ *n* **:** one who goes to extremes <~*s* for devotion to the Truth —W. W. Comfort †1955>
out·back \ˈau̇t-ˈbak\ *n* **:** isolated rural country esp. of Australia
out·bal·ance \(ˈ)au̇t-ˈbal-ən(t)s\ *vt* **:** OUTWEIGH
out·bid \-ˈbid\ *vt* **:** to make a higher bid than
[1]**out·board** \ˈau̇t-ˌbō(ə)rd, -ˌbȯ(ə)rd\ *adj* **1 :** situated outboard **2 :** being a machine bearing, center, or other support used in conjunction with and outside of a main bearing **3 :** having, using, or limited to the use of an outboard motor
[2]**outboard** *adv* **1 :** outside a ship's bulwarks **:** in a lateral direction from the hull **2 :** in a position closer or closest to either of the wing tips of an airplane or of the sides of an automobile
[3]**outboard** *n* **1 :** OUTBOARD MOTOR **2 :** a boat with an outboard motor
outboard motor *n* **:** a small internal-combustion engine with propeller integrally attached for mounting at the stern of a small boat
out·bound \ˈau̇t-ˌbau̇nd\ *adj* **:** outward bound <~ traffic>
out·brave \(ˈ)au̇t-ˈbrāv\ *vt* **1 :** to face or resist defiantly **2 :** to exceed in courage
out·break \ˈau̇t-ˌbrāk\ *n* **1 a :** a sudden or violent increase in activity or currency <the ~ of war> **b :** a sudden rise in the incidence of a disease <an ~ of measles> **c :** a sudden increase in numbers of a harmful organism and esp. an insect within a particular area <an ~ of locusts> **2 :** INSURRECTION, REVOLT
out·breed *vt* **-bred** \-ˌbred, -ˈbred\; **-breed·ing 1** \ˈau̇t-ˌbrēd\ **:** to subject to outbreeding **2** \(ˈ)au̇t-ˈ\ **:** to breed faster than
out·breed·ing \ˈau̇t-ˌbrēd-iŋ\ *n* **:** the interbreeding of individuals or stocks that are relatively unrelated
out·build·ing \ˈau̇t-ˌbil-diŋ\ *n* **:** a building (as a stable or a woodshed) separate from but accessory to a main house
out·burst \-ˌbərst\ *n* **1 :** a violent expression of feeling <an ~ of anger> **2 :** a surge of activity or growth <new ~*s* of creative power —C. E. Montague> **3 :** ERUPTION <volcanic ~*s*>
out·bye *or* **out·by** \üt-ˈbī\ *adv* [ME (Sc) *out-by,* fr. *out* + *by*] *chiefly Scot* **1 :** a short distance away **2 :** OUTDOORS
out·cast \ˈau̇t-ˌkast\ *n* **1 :** one who is cast out by society **:** PARIAH **2** [Sc *cast out* to quarrel] *Scot* **:** QUARREL — **outcast** *adj*
out·caste \-ˌkast\ *n* **1 :** a Hindu who has been ejected from his caste for violation of its customs or rules **2 :** one who has no caste
out·class \(ˈ)au̇t-ˈklas\ *vt* **:** to excel or surpass so decisively as to appear of a higher class
out·come \ˈau̇t-ˌkəm\ *n* **:** something that follows as a result or consequence
[1]**out·crop** \ˈau̇t-ˌkräp\ *n* **1 a :** a coming out of bedrock or of an unconsolidated deposit to the surface of the ground **b :** the part of a rock formation that appears at the surface of the ground **2 :** OUTBREAK <the recent ~ of unofficial strikes —*Economist*>
[2]**out·crop** \ˈau̇t-ˌkräp, (ˈ)au̇t-ˈ\ *vi* **1 :** to project from the surrounding soil <ledges *outcropping* from the eroded slope> **2 :** to come to the surface **:** APPEAR <originality ~*s* in the course of planning —*Psychiatry*>
[1]**out·cross** \ˈau̇t-ˌkrȯs\ *n* **1 :** a cross between relatively unrelated individuals **2 :** the progeny of an outcross
[2]**outcross** *vt* **:** to cross with a relatively unrelated individual or strain
out·cry \ˈau̇t-ˌkrī\ *n* **1 a :** a loud cry **:** CLAMOR **b :** a vehement protest **2 :** AUCTION <sold it at public ~ —W. M. Thackeray>
out·dat·ed \(ˈ)au̇t-ˈdāt-əd\ *adj* **:** OUTMODED — **out·dat·ed·ness** *n*
out·dis·tance \(ˈ)au̇t-ˈdis-tən(t)s\ *vt* **:** to go far ahead of (as in a race) **:** OUTSTRIP
out·do \-ˈdü\ *vt* **-did** \-ˈdid\; **-done** \-ˈdən\; **-do·ing** \-ˈdü-iŋ\; **-does** \-ˈdəz\ **1 :** to go beyond in action or performance **2 :** DEFEAT, OVERCOME ***syn*** see EXCEED
out·door \ˌau̇t-ˌdō(ə)r, -ˌdȯ(ə)r\ *also* **out·doors** \-ˌdō(ə)rz, -ˌdȯ(ə)rz\ *adj* [*out* (*of*) *door, out* (*of*) *doors*] **1 :** of or relating to the outdoors **2 :** performed outdoors <~ sports> **3 :** not enclosed **:** having no roof <an ~ restaurant>
[1]**out·doors** \(ˈ)au̇t-ˈdō(ə)rz, -ˈdȯ(ə)rz\ *adv* **:** outside a building **:** in or into the open air
[2]**outdoors** *n pl but sing in constr* **1 :** the open air **2 :** the world away from human habitations
out·doors·man \-mən\ *n* **1 :** one who lives or spends much time in the outdoors **2 :** one who frequently engages in outdoor activities (as hunting or fishing) — **out·doors·man·ship** \-ˌship\ *n*
out·doorsy \(ˈ)au̇t-ˈdōr-zē, -ˈdȯr-\ *adj* **1 :** of, relating to, or characteristic of the outdoors <an ~ dress> **2 :** fond of outdoor activities <sounded rugged and ~ —*N.Y. Times*>
out·draw \(ˈ)au̇t-ˈdrȯ\ *vt* **-drew** \-ˈdrü\; **-drawn** \-ˈdrȯn\; **-draw·ing 1 :** to surpass in drawing power **:** attract a larger audience or following than <basketball ~*s* football here> **2 :** to draw a handgun more quickly than
out·er \ˈau̇t-ər\ *adj* [ME, fr. [3]*out* + *-er,* compar. suffix] **1 :** existing independent of mind **:** OBJECTIVE **2 a :** situated farther out <the ~ limits> **b :** being away from a center **c :** situated or belonging on the outside <the ~ covering>
out·er·coat \ˈau̇t-ər-ˌkōt\ *n* **:** COAT 1a
outer ear *n* **:** the outer visible portion of the ear that collects and directs sound waves toward the eardrum by way of a canal which extends inward through the temporal bone
out·er·most \ˈau̇t-ər-ˌmōst\ *adj* **:** farthest out
outer planet *n* **:** any of the planets Jupiter, Saturn, Uranus, Neptune, and Pluto that as a group have orbits farther from the sun than the inner planets
outer space *n* **:** space immediately outside the earth's atmosphere; *broadly* **:** interplanetary or interstellar space
out·face \(ˈ)au̇t-ˈfās\ *vt* **1 :** to cause to waver or submit by or as if by staring **2 :** to confront unflinchingly **:** DEFY <people who have *outfaced* the terrors of a total war —H. V. Gregory>
out·fall \ˈau̇t-ˌfȯl\ *n* **:** the outlet of a body of water (as a river or lake); *esp* **:** the mouth of a drain or sewer
out·field \-ˌfēld\ *n* **1 :** the part of a baseball field beyond the infield and between the foul lines **2 :** the baseball defensive positions comprising right field, center field, and left field; *also* **:** the players who occupy these positions — **out·field·er** \-ˌfēl-dər\ *n*
out·fight \(ˈ)au̇t-ˈfīt\ *vt* **:** to surpass in fighting **:** DEFEAT
out·fight·ing \ˈau̇t-ˌfīt-iŋ\ *n* **:** fighting at long range
[1]**out·fit** \ˈau̇t-ˌfit\ *n* **1 :** the act of fitting out or equipping (as for a voyage or expedition) **2 a :** the tools or equipment for the practice of a trade **b :** wearing apparel with accessories usu. for a special occasion or activity **c :** physical, mental, or moral endowments or resources <perception is only part of our mental ~ —A. S. Eddington> **3 :** a group that works as a team **:** ORGANIZATION; *esp* **:** a military unit
[2]**outfit** *vb* **out·fit·ted; out·fit·ting** *vt* **1 :** to furnish with an outfit **2 :** SUPPLY <*outfitting* every family with shoes —*Amer. Guide Series: Vt.*> ~ *vi* **:** to acquire an outfit ***syn*** see FURNISH
out·fit·ter \-ˌfit-ər\ *n* **:** one who outfits: as **a :** HABERDASHER **b :** a dealer in equipment and supplies (as for camping trips)
out·flank \(ˈ)au̇t-ˈflaŋk\ *vt* **1 :** to get around the flank of (an opposing force) **2 :** to get around **:** CIRCUMVENT — **out·flank·er** *n*
[1]**out·flow** \ˈau̇t-ˌflō, (ˈ)au̇t-ˈ\ *vi* **:** to flow out
[2]**out·flow** \ˈau̇t-ˌflō\ *n* **1 :** a flowing out <the ~ of gold from the country —E. W. Kemmerer> **2 :** something that flows out
out·foot \(ˈ)au̇t-ˈfu̇t\ *vt* **:** to outdo in speed **:** OUTSTRIP
out·fox \-ˈfäks\ *vt* **:** OUTSMART

out·gas \ˈau̇t-ˌgas, (ˈ)au̇t-ˈ\ *vt* **1 :** to remove occluded gases from usu. by heating; *broadly* **;** to remove gases from **2 :** to remove (gases) from a material or a space ~ *vi* **:** to lose gases

out·gen·er·al \(ˈ)au̇t-ˈjen-(ə-)rəl\ *vt* **;** to surpass in generalship **:** OUTMANEUVER

[1]**out·giv·ing** \ˈau̇t-ˌgiv-iŋ\ *n* **:** something that is given out; *esp* **:** a public statement or utterance

[2]**outgiving** *adj* **:** socially responsive and demonstrative

[1]**out·go** \(ˈ)au̇t-ˈgō\ *vt* **:** to go beyond **:** OUTDO

[2]**out·go** \ˈau̇t-ˌgō\ *n, pl* **outgoes 1 :** something that goes out; *specif* **:** EXPENDITURE **2 a :** the act of going out **b :** DEPARTURE **3 :** OUTLET

out·go·ing \ˈau̇t-ˌgō-iŋ, -ˌgō(-)iŋ\ *adj* **1 a :** going away **:** DEPARTING <an ~ ship> **b :** retiring or withdrawing from a place or position <the ~ president> **c :** directed to an intended recipient <~ mail> **2 :** FRIENDLY, RESPONSIVE <an ~ person> — **out·go·ing·ness** *n*

out–group \ˈau̇t-ˌgrüp\ *n* **:** a group that is distinct from one's own and so usu. an object of hostility or dislike — compare IN-GROUP

out·grow \(ˈ)au̇t-ˈgrō\ *vt* **-grew** \-ˈgrü\; **-grown** \-ˈgrōn\; **-grow·ing 1 :** to grow or increase faster than <mankind is ~*ing* food supplies —R. C. Murphy> **2 :** to grow too large or too mature for <*outgrew* his clothes>

out·growth \ˈau̇t-ˌgrōth\ *n* **1 :** a process or product of growing out <an ~ of hair> **2 :** CONSEQUENCE, BY-PRODUCT <crime is often an ~ of poverty>

out·guess \(ˈ)au̇t-ˈges\ *vt* **:** to anticipate the expectations, intentions, or actions of **:** OUTWIT

out·gun \-ˈgən\ *vt* **:** to surpass in firepower; *broadly* **:** DEFEAT

out·haul \ˈau̇t-ˌhȯl\ *n* **:** a rope used to haul a sail taut along a spar

out–Her·od \(ˈ)au̇t-ˈher-əd\ *vt* [*out-* + *Herod* Antipas, depicted in medieval mystery plays as a blustering tyrant] **:** to exceed in violence or extravagance — usu. used in the phrase *out-Herod Herod*

out·house \ˈau̇t-ˌhau̇s\ *n* **:** OUTBUILDING; *esp* **:** PRIVY 2a

out·ing \ˈau̇t-iŋ\ *n* **:** a brief usu. outdoor pleasure trip

outing flannel *n* **:** a flannelette sometimes having an admixture of wool

out·land \ˈau̇t-ˌland, -lənd\ *n* **1 :** a foreign land **2** *pl* **:** the outlying regions of a country **:** PROVINCES — **outland** *adj*

out·land·er \-ˌlan-dər, -lən-\ *n* **:** FOREIGNER, STRANGER

out·land·ish \(ˈ)au̇t-ˈlan-dish\ *adj* **1 :** of or relating to another country **:** FOREIGN **2 :** strikingly out of the ordinary **:** BIZARRE <an ~ costume> **3 :** remote from civilization — **out·land·ish·ly** *adv* — **out·land·ish·ness** *n*

out·last \(ˈ)au̇t-ˈlast\ *vt* **:** to last longer than <customs that have long ~*ed* their usefulness —W. R. Inge>

[1]**out·law** \ˈau̇t-ˌlȯ\ *n* [ME *outlawe*, fr. OE *ūtlaga*, fr. ON *ūtlagi*, fr. *ūt* out (akin to OE *ūt* out) + *lag-, lög* law — more at OUT, LAW] **1 :** a person excluded from the benefit or protection of the law **2 a :** a lawless person or a fugitive from the law **b :** a person or organization under a ban or restriction **3 :** an animal (as a horse) that is wild and unmanageable — **outlaw** *adj*

[2]**outlaw** *vt* **1 a :** to deprive of the benefit and protection of law **:** declare to be an outlaw **b :** to make illegal <the type of legislation which ~*ed* dueling —Margaret Mead> **2 :** to place under a ban or restriction **3 :** to remove from legal jurisdiction or enforcement — **out·law·ry** \ˈau̇t-ˌlȯ(ə)r-ē\ *n*

[1]**out·lay** \ˈau̇t-ˌlā, (ˈ)au̇t-ˈ\ *vt* **-laid** \-ˌlād, -ˈlād\; **-lay·ing :** to lay out (money) **:** EXPEND

[2]**out·lay** \ˈau̇t-ˌlā\ *n* **1 :** the act of expending **2 :** EXPENDITURE, PAYMENT <~*s* for national defense>

out·let \ˈau̇t-ˌlet, -lət\ *n* [[1]*out* + *let*, v.] **1 a :** a place or opening through which something is let out **:** EXIT, VENT **b :** a means of release or satisfaction for an emotion or impulse <sexual ~*s*> **2 :** a stream flowing out of a lake or pond **3 a :** a market for a commodity **b :** an agency (as a store or dealer) through which a product is marketed <retail ~*s*> **4 :** a set of mounted and insulated electric-service terminals (as in a receptacle or an electric socket) to which electric appliances may be connected

out·li·er \-ˌlī(-ə)r\ *n* **1 :** one that does not live where his office, business, or estate is **2 :** something (as a geological feature) that lies or is situated or classed away from a main or related body

[1]**out·line** \ˈau̇t-ˌlīn\ *n* **1 a :** a line that marks the outer limits of an object or figure **:** BOUNDARY **b :** SHAPE **2 a :** a style of drawing in which contours are marked without shading **b :** a sketch in outline **3 a :** a condensed treatment of a particular subject <an ~ of world history> **b :** a summary of a written work **:** SYNOPSIS **4 :** a preliminary account of a project **:** PLAN **5 :** a fishing line set out overnight **:** TROTLINE
syn OUTLINE, CONTOUR, PROFILE, SILHOUETTE *shared meaning element* **:** the line that bounds and gives form to something

[2]**outline** *vt* **1 :** to draw the outline of **2 :** to indicate the principal features or different parts of <*outlined* their responsibilities>

out·live \(ˈ)au̇t-ˈliv\ *vt* **1 :** to live longer than <*outlived* most of his friends> **2 :** to survive the effects of <universities . . . ~ many political and social changes —J. B. Conant>

out·look \ˈau̇t-ˌlu̇k\ *n* **1 a :** a place offering a view **b :** a view from a particular place **2 :** POINT OF VIEW <his ~ on life> **3 :** the act of looking out **4 :** the prospect for the future <the ~ for steel demand in the U.S. —*Wall Street Jour.*> ***syn*** see PROSPECT

out loud *adv* **:** ALOUD

out·ly·ing \ˈau̇t-ˌlī-iŋ\ *adj* **:** remote from a center or main body <~ areas>

out·ma·neu·ver \ˌau̇t-mə-ˈn(y)ü-vər\ *vt* **1 :** to defeat by more skillful maneuvering **2 :** to surpass in maneuverability

out·match \(ˈ)au̇t-ˈmach\ *vt* **:** to prove superior to **:** OUTDO

out–mi·grant \ˈau̇t-ˌmī-grənt\ *n* **:** one that out-migrates

out–mi·grate \-ˌgrāt\ *vi* **:** to leave one region or community in order to settle in another esp. as part of a large-scale and continuing movement of population — compare IN-MIGRATE — **out–mi·gra·tion** \ˌau̇t-mī-ˈgrā-shən\ *n*

out·mode \(ˈ)au̇t-ˈmōd\ *vt* **out·mod·ed; out·mod·ing** [*out* (*of*) *mode*] **:** to make unfashionable or obsolete

out·mod·ed \-ˈmōd-əd\ *adj* **1 :** not being in style **2 :** no longer acceptable or usable <~ beliefs>

out·most \ˈau̇t-ˌmōst\ *adj* **:** farthest out **:** OUTERMOST

out·num·ber \(ˈ)au̇t-ˈnəm-bər\ *vt* **:** to exceed in number

out of *prep* **1 a** (1) — used as a function word to indicate direction or movement from within to the outside of <walked *out of* the room> (2) — used as a function word to indicate a change in quality, state, or form <woke up *out of* a deep sleep> **b** (1) — used as a function word to indicate a position or situation beyond the range, limits, or sphere of <*out of* sight> (2) — used as a function word to indicate a position or state away from the usual or expected <*out of* practice> **2** — used as a function word to indicate origin, source, or cause <a colt *out of* an ordinary mare> <built *out of* old lumber> <came *out of* fear> **3** — used as a function word to indicate exclusion from or deprivation of <cheated him *out of* his savings> **4** — used as a function word to indicate choice or selection from a group <one *out of* four survived> — **out of it :** not part of a group, activity, or fashion

out–of–bounds \ˌau̇t-ə(v)-ˈbau̇n(d)z\ *adv or adj* **:** outside the prescribed boundaries or limits

out–of–date \-ˈdāt\ *adj* **:** OUTMODED, OBSOLETE — **out–of–date·ness** *n*

out–of–door \-ˈdō(ə)r, -ˈdȯ(ə)r\ *or* **out–of–doors** \-ˈdō(ə)rz, -ˈdȯ(ə)rz\ *adj* **:** OUTDOOR

out–of–doors *n pl but sing in constr* **:** OUTDOORS

out–of–pock·et \-ˈpäk-ət\ *adj* **:** requiring an outlay of cash <~ expenses>

out–of–the–way \-t͟hə-ˈwā\ *adj* **1 :** being off the beaten track <an ~ restaurant> **2 :** UNUSUAL <~ information . . . not found in any other book —John Morris>

out·pace \(ˈ)au̇t-ˈpās\ *vt* **1 :** to surpass in speed **2 :** OUTDO

out·pa·tient \ˈau̇t-ˌpā-shənt\ *n* **:** a patient who is not an inmate of a hospital but who visits a clinic or dispensary connected with it for diagnosis or treatment — compare INPATIENT

out·per·form \ˌau̇t-pər-ˈfȯ(ə)rm\ *vt* **:** to do better than <a sports car that ~*s* them all>

out·play \(ˈ)au̇t-ˈplā\ *vt* **:** to excel or defeat in a game

out·point \-ˈpȯint\ *vt* **1 :** to sail closer to the wind than **2 :** to win more points than

out·port \ˈau̇t-ˌpō(ə)rt, -ˌpȯ(ə)rt\ *n* **1 :** a port other than the main port of a country **2 :** a port of export or departure **3 :** a small fishing village in Newfoundland

out·post \ˈau̇t-ˌpōst\ *n* **1 a :** a security detachment thrown out by a main body of troops to protect it from enemy surprise **b :** a military base established by treaty or agreement in another country **2 a :** an outlying or frontier settlement **b :** an outlying branch or position of a main organization or group

[1]**out·pour** \au̇t-ˈpō(ə)r, -ˈpȯ(ə)r, ˈau̇t-ˌ\ *vt* **:** to pour out

[2]**out·pour** \ˈau̇t-ˌpō(ə)r, -ˈpȯ(ə)r\ *n* **:** OUTPOURING

out·pour·ing \ˈau̇t-ˌpōr-iŋ, -ˌpȯr-\ *n* **1 :** the act of pouring out **2 :** something that pours out or is poured out **:** OUTFLOW

out·pull \(ˈ)au̇t-ˈpu̇l\ *vt* **:** OUTDRAW 1

[1]**out·put** \ˈau̇t-ˌpu̇t\ *n* **1 :** something produced: as **a :** mineral, agricultural, or industrial production <steel ~> **b :** mental or artistic production <literary ~> **c :** the amount produced by a person in a given time **d :** power or energy produced or delivered by a machine or system (as for storage or for conversion in kind or in characteristics) <solar X-ray ~> **e :** the terminal for the output on an electrical device **f :** the information fed out by a computer or accounting machine **2 :** the act, process, or an instance of producing

[2]**output** *vt* **out·put·ted** *or* **output; out·put·ting :** to produce as output

out·race \(ˈ)au̇t-ˈrās\ *vt* **:** OUTPACE

[1]**out·rage** \ˈau̇t-ˌrāj\ *n* [ME, fr. OF, excess, outrage, fr. *outre* beyond, in excess, fr. L *ultra* — more at ULTRA-] **1 :** an act of violence or brutality **2 a :** INJURY, INSULT <do no ~*s* on silly women or poor passengers —Shak.> **b :** an act that violates accepted standards of behavior or taste <an ~ alike against decency and dignity —John Buchan> **3 :** the anger and resentment aroused by injury or insult

[2]**outrage** *vt* **out·raged; out·rag·ing 1 a :** RAPE **b :** to violate the standards or principles of <he has *outraged* respectability past endurance —John Braine> **2 :** to arouse anger or resentment in usu. by some grave offense ***syn*** see OFFEND

out·ra·geous \au̇t-ˈrā-jəs\ *adj* **1 a :** exceeding the limits of what is usual **b :** not conventional or matter-of-fact **:** FANTASTIC **2 :** VIOLENT, UNRESTRAINED **3 a :** going beyond all standards of what is right or decent <an ~ disregard of human rights> **b :** deficient in propriety or good taste <~ language> <~ manners> — **out·ra·geous·ly** *adv* — **out·ra·geous·ness** *n*
syn OUTRAGEOUS, MONSTROUS, HEINOUS, ATROCIOUS *shared meaning element* **:** exceedingly bad or horrible

ou·trance \ü-ˈträⁿs\ *n* [ME, fr. MF, fr. *outrer* to pass beyond, carry to excess, fr. *outre*] **:** the last extremity

out·range \(ˈ)au̇t-ˈrānj\ *vt* **:** to surpass in range

out·rank \-ˈraŋk\ *vt* **1 :** to rank higher than **2 :** to exceed in importance

ou·tré \ü-ˈtrā\ *adj* [F, fr. pp. of *outrer* to carry to excess] **:** violating convention or propriety **:** BIZARRE

[1]**out·reach** \(ˈ)au̇t-ˈrēch\ *vt* **1 a :** to surpass in reach **b :** EXCEED <the demand ~*es* the supply> **2 :** to get the better of by trickery ~ *vi* **1 :** to go too far **2 :** to reach out

[2]**out·reach** \ˈau̇t-ˌrēch\ *n* **1 :** the act of reaching out **2 :** the extent or limit of reach <the ~ of the Ohio floods —Clifton Johnson>

1out·ride \(ˈ)au̇t-ˈrīd\ *vt* **-rode** \-ˈrōd\; **-rid·den** \-ˈrid-ᵊn\; **-rid·ing** \-ˈrīd-iŋ\ **1 :** to ride better, faster, or farther than : OUTSTRIP **2 :** to ride out (a storm)

2out·ride \ˈau̇t-ˌrīd\ *n* **:** an unstressed syllable or group of syllables added to a foot in sprung rhythm but not counted in the scansion

out·rid·er \-ˌrīd-ər\ *n* **1 :** a mounted attendant **2 :** FORERUNNER, HARBINGER

out·rig·ger \ˈau̇t-ˌrig-ər\ *n* **1 a :** a projecting spar with a shaped log at the end attached to a canoe to prevent upsetting **b :** a spar or projecting beam run out from a ship's side to help secure the masts or from a mast to extend a rope or sail **c :** a projecting support for an oarlock; *also* **:** a boat so equipped **2 :** a projecting member run out from a main structure to provide additional stability or to support something; *esp* **:** a projecting frame to support the elevator or tail planes of an airplane or the rotor of a helicopter

outrigger 1a

1out·right \(ˈ)au̇t-ˈrīt\ *adv* **1** *archaic* **:** straight ahead : DIRECTLY **2 :** in entirety : COMPLETELY <rejected the proposal ~> **3 :** on the spot : INSTANTANEOUSLY <was killed ~> **4 :** without lien or encumbrance <purchased the property ~ for cash>

2out·right \ˈau̇t-ˌrīt\ *adj* **1 a :** being completely or exactly what is stated <an ~ lie> **b :** given without reservation <~ grants for research> **c :** made without encumbrance or lien <~ purchases> **2** *archaic* **:** proceeding directly onward **3 :** COMPLETE, ENTIRE — **out·right·ly** *adv*

syn OUTRIGHT, OUT-AND-OUT, UNMITIGATED, ARRANT ***shared meaning element*** **:** being what is stated without limit or qualification

out·ri·val \(ˈ)au̇t-ˈrī-vəl\ *vt* **:** to outdo in a competition or rivalry

out·run \(ˈ)au̇t-ˈrən\ *vt* **-ran** \-ˈran\; **-run; -run·ning 1 :** to run faster than **2 :** EXCEED, SURPASS <his ambitions ~ his abilities>

out·sell \-ˈsel\ *vt* **-sold** \-ˈsōld\; **-sell·ing 1** *archaic* **:** to exceed in value **2 :** to exceed in number of items sold **3 :** to surpass in selling or salesmanship

out·sert \ˈau̇t-ˌsərt\ *n* [³*out* + *-sert* (as in *insert*)] **:** a usu. 4-page section (as of a magazine) so imposed and printed that it can be placed outside another signature

out·set \ˈau̇t-ˌset\ *n* **:** BEGINNING, START

out·shine \(ˈ)au̇t-ˈshīn\ *vb* **-shone** \-ˈshōn, *esp Brit* -ˈshän\ *or* **-shined; -shin·ing** *vt* **1 a :** to shine brighter than **b :** to excel in splendor or showiness **2 :** OUTDO, SURPASS <*outshone* most of the other films in quality —Kathleen Karr> ~ *vi* **:** to shine out

1out·shoot \(ˈ)au̇t-ˈshüt\ *vt* **-shot** \-ˈshät\; **-shoot·ing 1 :** to surpass in shooting or making shots **2 :** to shoot or go beyond

2out·shoot \ˈau̇t-ˌshüt\ *n* **:** something that shoots out

out·shout \(ˈ)au̇t-ˈshau̇t\ *vt* **:** to shout louder than

1out·side \(ˈ)au̇t-ˈsīd, ˈau̇t-ˌ\ *n* **1 a :** a place or region beyond an enclosure or boundary **b :** the area farthest from a specified point of reference: as **(1) :** the side of home plate farthest from the batter **(2) :** the section of a playing area toward the sidelines; *also* **:** CORNER **2 :** an outer side or surface **3 :** an outer manifestation **:** APPEARANCE **4 :** the extreme limit of a guess : MAXIMUM <the crowd numbered 10,000 at the ~>

2outside *adj* **1 a :** of, relating to, or being on or toward the outer side or surface <the ~ edge> **b :** of, relating to, or being on or toward the outer side of a curve or turn **c :** of, relating to, or being on or near the outside <an ~ pitch> **2 a :** situated or performed outside a particular place **b :** connected with or giving access to the outside <~ telephone line> **3 :** MAXIMUM **4 a :** not included or originating in a particular group or organization <blamed the riot on ~ agitators> **b :** not belonging to one's regular occupation or duties <~ interests> **5 :** barely possible : REMOTE <an ~ chance> **6 :** made or done from the outside or from a distance <borrowed a basketball and practiced his ~ shot>

3outside *adv* **1 :** on or to the outside **2 :** OUTDOORS

4outside *prep* **1** — used as a function word to indicate movement to or position on the outer side of **2 :** beyond the limits of <~ the law> **3 :** EXCEPT

outside of *prep* **:** OUTSIDE

out·sid·er \(ˈ)au̇t-ˈsīd-ər\ *n* **1 :** a person who does not belong to a particular group **2 :** a contender not expected to win — **out·sid·er·ness** *n*

out·sight \ˈau̇t-ˌsīt\ *n* **:** the power or act of perceiving external things <the clear-eyed insight and ~ of the born writer —*New Yorker*>

out·sit \(ˈ)au̇t-ˈsit\ *vt* **-sat** \-ˈsat\; **-sit·ting :** to remain sitting or in session longer than or beyond the duration of <caverns, wherein one or two might . . . ~ a shower —C. F. Saunders>

1out·size \ˈau̇t-ˌsīz\ *n* **:** an unusual size; *esp* **:** a size larger than the standard

2outsize *also* **out·sized** \-ˌsīzd\ *adj* **:** unusually large or heavy

out·skirt \ˈau̇t-ˌskərt\ *n* **:** a part remote from the center : BORDER — usu. used in pl. <on the ~*s* of town>

out·smart \(ˈ)au̇t-ˈsmärt\ *vt* **:** to get the better of; *esp* **:** OUTWIT

out·soar \-ˈsō(ə)r, -ˈsȯ(ə)r\ *vt* **:** to soar beyond or above

out·sole \ˈau̇t-ˌsōl\ *n* **:** the outside sole of a boot or shoe

out·speak \(ˈ)au̇t-ˈspēk\ *vt* **-spoke** \-ˈspōk\; **-spo·ken** \-ˈspō-kən\; **-speak·ing 1 :** to excel in speaking **2 :** to declare openly or boldly

out·spend \-ˈspend\ *vt* **1 :** to exceed the limits of in spending <~*s* his income> **2 :** to outdo in spending <he *outspent* the other candidates>

out·spent \-ˈspent\ *adj* **:** completely worn out : EXHAUSTED <spurred him, like an ~ horse, to death —P. B. Shelley>

out·spo·ken \au̇t-ˈspō-kən\ *adj* **1 :** direct and open in speech or expression : FRANK <candidly ~ in his criticism —*Current Biog.*> **2 :** spoken or expressed without reserve <his ~ advocacy of population control> — **out·spo·ken·ly** *adv* — **out·spo·ken·ness** \-kən-nəs\ *n*

out·spread \au̇t-ˈspred\ *vt* **-spread; -spread·ing :** to spread out : EXTEND

out·stand \(ˈ)au̇t-ˈstand\ *vb* **-stood; -stand·ing** *vt* **:** to endure beyond <I have *outstood* my time —Shak.> ~ *vi* **:** to stand out

out·stand·ing \au̇t-ˈstan-diŋ, ˈau̇t-ˌ\ *adj* **1 :** standing out : PROJECTING **2 a :** UNPAID <left several bills ~> **b :** CONTINUING, UNRESOLVED <a long ~ problem> **c** *of stocks and bonds* **:** publicly issued and sold **3 a :** standing out from a group : CONSPICUOUS **b :** marked by eminence and distinction ***syn*** see NOTICEABLE ***ant*** commonplace — **out·stand·ing·ly** \-diŋ-lē\ *adv*

out·stare \(ˈ)au̇t-ˈsta(ə)r, -ˈste(ə)r\ *vt* **:** OUTFACE 1

out·sta·tion \ˈau̇t-ˌstā-shən\ *n* **:** a remote or outlying station

out·stay \(ˈ)au̇t-ˈstā\ *vt* **1 :** OVERSTAY 1 <~*ed* his welcome> **2 :** to surpass in staying power <~*ed* his competitors>

out·stretch \au̇t-ˈstrech\ *vt* **:** to stretch out : EXTEND

out·strip \au̇t-ˈstrip\ *vt* [*out-* + obs. *strip* (to move fast)] **1 :** to go faster or farther than **2 :** to get ahead of : leave behind <has civilization *outstripped* the ability of its users to use it? —Margaret Mead> ***syn*** see EXCEED

out·take \ˈau̇t-ˌtāk\ *n* **1 :** a passage outwards : FLUE, VENT **2 :** an unused film take **3 :** something that is taken out

out·talk \(ˈ)au̇t-ˈtȯk\ *vt* **1 :** to surpass in talking **2 :** to get the better of by talking

out·think \-ˈthiŋk\ *vt* **-thought** \-ˈthȯt\; **-think·ing 1 :** to surpass in thinking **2 :** to get the better of by thinking

out·turn \ˈau̇t-ˌtərn\ *n* **:** a quantity produced : OUTPUT

out·vote \(ˈ)au̇t-ˈvōt\ *vt* **:** to cast more votes than : defeat by a majority of votes <the conservatives can ~ the radicals>

1out·ward \ˈau̇t-wərd\ *adj* **1 :** moving, directed, or turned toward the outside or away from a center <an ~ flow> **2 :** situated on the outside : EXTERIOR **3 :** of or relating to the body or to appearances rather than to the mind or the inner life <~ beauty> **4 :** EXTERNAL

2outward *or* **out·wards** \-wərdz\ *adv* **1 :** toward the outside **2** *obs* **:** on the outside : EXTERNALLY

3outward *n* **:** external form, appearance, or reality

out·ward–bound \ˌau̇t-wərd-ˈbau̇nd\ *adj* **:** bound in an outward direction or to foreign parts <an ~ ship>

out·ward·ly \ˈau̇t-wərd-lē\ *adv* **1 a :** on the outside : EXTERNALLY **b :** toward the outside **2 :** in outward state, behavior, or appearance <was ~ friendly>

out·ward·ness \-nəs\ *n* **1 :** the quality or state of being external **2 :** concern with or responsiveness to outward things

out·wear \(ˈ)au̇t-ˈwa(ə)r, -ˈwe(ə)r\ *vt* **-wore** \-ˈwō(ə)r, -ˈwȯ(ə)r\; **-worn** \-ˈwō(ə)rn, -ˈwȯ(ə)rn\; **-wear·ing 1 :** to wear out : EXHAUST **2 :** to last longer than <a fabric that ~*s* others>

out·weigh \-ˈwā\ *vt* **:** to exceed in weight, value, or importance <the advantages ~ the disadvantages>

out·wit \au̇t-ˈwit\ *vt* **1 :** to get the better of by superior cleverness : OUTSMART **2** *archaic* **:** to surpass in wisdom ***syn*** see FRUSTRATE

1out·work *vt* **1** \au̇t-ˈwərk\ **:** to work out : COMPLETE **2** \(ˈ)au̇t-\ **:** to work harder, faster, or better than

2out·work \ˈau̇t-ˌwərk\ *n* **:** a minor defensive position constructed outside a fortified area

out·worn \au̇t-ˈwō(ə)rn, -ˈwȯ(ə)rn\ *adj* **:** no longer useful or acceptable : OUTMODED <an ~ social system>

ou·zel \ˈü-zəl\ *n* [ME *ousel,* fr. OE *ōsle* — more at MERL] **1 :** BLACKBIRD 1a; *also* **:** a related bird **2 :** WATER OUZEL

ou·zo \ˈü-(ˌ)zō, -(ˌ)zō\ *n* [NGk *ouzon, ouzo*] **:** a colorless anise-flavored unsweetened Greek liqueur

ov- *or* **ovi-** *or* **ovo-** *comb form* [L *ov-, ovi-,* fr. *ovum* — more at EGG] **:** egg <*oviform*> : ovum <*oviduct*> <*ovocyte*> <*ovogenesis*>

ova *pl of* OVUM

1oval \ˈō-vəl\ *adj* [ML *ovalis,* fr. LL, of an egg, fr. L *ovum*] **:** having the shape of an egg; *also* **:** broadly elliptical — **oval·ly** \-və-lē\ *adv* — **oval·ness** *n*

2oval *n* **1 :** an oval figure or object **2 :** a racetrack in the shape of an oval or a rectangle having rounded corners

ov·al·bu·min \ˌäv-al-ˈbyü-mən, ˌōv-\ *n* **1 :** the principal albumin of white of egg; *esp* **:** the crystalline part of egg albumins **2 :** dried whites of eggs

ovals of Cas·si·ni \-kə-ˈsē-nē\ [G. D. *Cassini* †1712 F astronomer] **:** a curve that is the locus of points of the vertex of a triangle whose opposite side is fixed and the product of whose adjacent sides is a constant and that has the equation $[(x + a)^2 + y^2][(x - a)^2 + y^2] - k^4 = 0$ where k is the constant and a is one half the length of the fixed side

oval window *n* **:** the oval fenestra of the ear

ovar·i·an \ō-ˈvar-ē-ən, -ˈver-\ *also* **ovar·i·al** \-ē-əl\ *adj* **:** of, relating to, or involving an ovary

ovari·ec·to·my \ō-ˌvar-ē-ˈek-tə-mē, -ˌver-\ *n, pl* **-mies :** the surgical removal of an ovary — **ovari·ec·to·mized** \-ˌmīzd\ *adj*

ovar·i·ole \ō-ˈvar-ē-ˌōl, -ˈver-\ *n* [(assumed) NL *ovariolum,* dim. of *ovarium*] **:** one of the tubes of which the ovaries of most insects are composed

ovar·i·ot·o·my \ō-ˌvar-ē-ˈät-ə-mē, -ˌver-\ *n, pl* **-mies 1 :** surgical incision of an ovary **2 :** OVARIECTOMY

ova·ri·tis \ˌō-və-ˈrīt-əs\ *n* [NL, fr. *ovarium*] **:** inflammation of an ovary

ova·ry \ˈōv-(ə-)rē\ *n, pl* **-ries** [NL *ovarium,* fr. L *ovum* egg] **1 :** the typically paired essential female reproductive organ that produces eggs and in vertebrates female sex hormones **2 :** the enlarged rounded usu. basal portion of the pistil or gynoecium of an angiospermous plant that bears the ovules and consists of one or more carpels — see FLOWER illustration

ovate \ˈō-ˌvāt\ *adj* **1 :** shaped like an egg **2 :** having an outline like a longitudinal section of an egg with the basal end broader <~ leaves>

ova·tion \ō-ˈvā-shən\ *n* [L *ovation-, ovatio,* fr. *ovatus,* pp. of *ovare* to exult; akin to Gk *euoi,* interjection used in bacchic revels] **1 :** a ceremony attending the entering of Rome by a general who had won a victory of less importance than that for which a triumph was granted **2 :** an expression or demonstration of popular acclain <received a standing ~>

ov·en \ˈəv-ən\ *n* [ME, fr. OE *ofen;* akin to OHG *ofan* oven, Gk *ipnos,* L *aulla, olla* pot] : a chamber used for baking, heating, or drying

oven·bird \-ˌbərd\ *n* [fr. the shape of its nest] **1** : any of various So. American small brown passerine birds (genus *Furnarius*) **2** : an American warbler (*Seiurus aurocapillus*) that builds a dome-shaped nest on the ground

ovenbird 1

[1]**over** \ˈō-vər\ *adv* [ME, adv. & prep., fr. OE *ofer;* akin to OHG *ubar* (prep.) above, beyond, over, L *super,* Gk *hyper*] **1 a** : across a barrier or intervening space; *esp* : across the goal line in football **b** : down or forward and down <fell ~> **c** : across the brim <soup boiled ~> **d** : so as to bring the underside up <turned his cards ~> **e** : from a vertical to a prone or inclined position <knocked him ~> **f** : from one person or side to another <hand it ~> **g** : ACROSS <got his point ~> **h** : to agreement or concord <won them ~> **2 a** (1) : beyond some quantity, limit, or norm often by a specified amount or to a specified degree <show ran a minute ~> (2) : in an excessive manner : INORDINATELY — often used in combination <an *over*-optimistic view> **b** : till a later time **3 a** : ABOVE **b** : so as to cover the whole surface <windows boarded ~> **4 a** : at an end <the day is ~> **b** — used on a two-way radio circuit to indicate that a message is complete and a reply is expected **5 a** : THROUGH <read it ~>; *also* : in an intensive or comprehensive manner **b** : once more <do it ~>

[2]**over** \ˌō-vər, ˈō-\ *prep* **1** — used as a function word to indicate motion or situation in a position higher than or above another <towered ~ his mother> <flew ~ the lake> <rode ~ the old Roman road> **2 a** — used as a function word to indicate the possession of authority, power, or jurisdiction in regard to some thing or person <respected those ~ him> **b** — used as a function word to indicate superiority, advantage, or preference <a big lead ~ the others> **3** : more than <cost ~ $5> **4 a** — used as a function word to indicate position upon or movement down upon <laid a blanket ~ the child> <hit him ~ the head> **b** : all through or throughout <showed me ~ the house> <went ~ his notes> **c** — used as a function word to indicate a particular medium or channel of communication <~ the radio> **5** — used as a function word to indicate position on the other side or beyond <lives ~ the way> **6 a** : THROUGHOUT, DURING <~ the past 25 years> **b** : until the end of <stay ~ Sunday> **7 a** — used as a function word to indicate an object of solicitude, interest, consideration, or reference <the Lord watches ~ his own> **b** — used as a function word to indicate the object of an expressed or implied occupation, activity, or concern <spent an hour ~ cards> <trouble ~ money> — **over one's head** : beyond one's comprehension

[3]**over** \ˈō-vər, ˌō-\ *adj* **1 a** : UPPER, HIGHER **b** : OUTER, COVERING **c** : EXCESSIVE <~ imagination> **2 a** : not used up : REMAINING <something ~ to provide for unusual requirements —J. A. Todd> **b** : having or showing an excess or surplus

[4]**over** \ˈō-vər\ *vt* **overed; over·ing** \ˈōv-(ə-)riŋ\ : to leap over

over- *prefix* **1** : so as to exceed or surpass **2** : EXCESSIVE **3** : EXCESSIVELY

over·abun·dance \ˌō-və-rə-ˈbən-dən(t)s\ *n* : EXCESS, SURFEIT — **over·abun·dant** \-dənt\ *adj*

over·achiev·er \ˌō-və-rə-ˈchē-vər\ *n* : one who achieves success over and above the standard or expected level

over·act \ˌō-və-ˈrakt\ *vt* : to exaggerate in acting ~ *vi* **1** : to act more than is necessary **2** : to overact a part — **over·ac·tion** \-ˈrak-shən\ *n*

over·ac·tive \-ˈrak-tiv\ *adj* : excessively or abnormally active

over against *prep* : as opposed to : in contrast with

[1]**over·age** \ˌō-və-ˈrāj\ *adj* [[2]*over* + *age*] **1** : too old to be useful **2** : older than is normal for one's position, function, or grade

[2]**over·age** \ˈōv-(ə-)rij\ *n* [[3]*over* + *-age*] : SURPLUS, EXCESS

over·ag·gres·sive \ˌō-və-rə-ˈgres-iv\ *adj* : excessively aggressive

[1]**over·all** \ˌō-və-ˈrȯl\ *adv* **1** : as a whole : GENERALLY <~, prices are still rising —*Forbes*> **2** : from the extreme forward point to the extreme after point of a ship's deck including overhangs

[2]**over·all** \ˈō-və-ˌrȯl\ *n* **1** *pl* **a** *archaic* : loose protective trousers worn over regular clothes **b** : trousers of strong material usu. with a bib and shoulder straps **2** *chiefly Brit* : a loose-fitting protective smock worn over regular clothing

[3]**over·all** \ˌō-və-ˈrȯl, ˈō-və-ˌ\ *adj* : including everything

over and above *prep* : BESIDES

over and over *adv* : REPEATEDLY

over·arch·ing \ˌō-və-ˈrär-chiŋ\ *adj* **1** : forming an arch overhead **2** : dominating or embracing all else

over·arm \ˈō-və-ˌrärm\ *adj* **1** : OVERHAND **2** *of a swimming stroke* : made with the arm lifted out of the water and stretched forward over the shoulder to begin the stroke

over·awe \ˌō-və-ˈrȯ\ *vt* : to restrain or subdue by awe

[1]**over·bal·ance** \ˌō-vər-ˈbal-ən(t)s\ *vt* **1** : OUTWEIGH **2** : to cause to lose balance

[2]**over·bal·ance** \ˈō-vər-ˌ\ *n* : something more than an equivalent

over·bear \ˌō-vər-ˈba(ə)r, -ˈbe(ə)r\ *vb* **-bore** \-ˈbō(ə)r, -ˈbȯ(ə)r\; **-borne** \-ˈbō(ə)rn, -ˈbȯ(ə)rn\ *also* **-born** \-ˈbȯ(ə)rn\; **-bear·ing** *vt* **1** : to bring down by superior weight or force : OVERWHELM **2 a** : to domineer over **b** : to surpass in importance or cogency : OUTWEIGH ~ *vi* : to bear fruit or offspring to excess

over·bear·ing *adj* **1 a** : tending to overwhelm : OVERPOWERING **b** : decisively important : DOMINANT **2** : harshly and haughtily arrogant ***syn*** see PROUD ***ant*** subservient — **over·bear·ing·ly** \-iŋ-lē\ *adv*

over·bid \ˌō-vər-ˈbid\ *vb* **-bid; -bid·ding** *vi* **1** : to bid in excess of value **2 a** : to bid more than the scoring capacity of a hand at cards **b** *Brit* : to make a higher bid than the preceding one ~ *vt* : to bid beyond or in excess of; *esp* : to bid more than the value of (one's hand at cards) — **over·bid** \ˈō-vər-ˌbid\ *n*

over·bite \ˈō-vər-ˌbīt\ *n* : the projection of the upper anterior teeth over the lower in the normal occlusal position of the jaws

[1]**over·blown** \ˌō-vər-ˈblōn\ *adj* [[1]*blow*] **1** : excessively large of girth : PORTLY **2** : INFLATED, PRETENTIOUS

[2]**overblown** *adj* [[3]*blow*] : past the prime of bloom <~ roses>

over·board \ˈō-vər-ˌbō(ə)rd, -ˌbȯ(ə)rd\ *adv* **1** : over the side of a ship or boat into the water **2** : to extremes of enthusiasm **3** : into discard : ASIDE

over·book \ˌō-vər-ˈbu̇k\ *vt* : to issue reservations for (as an airplane flight) in excess of the space available ~ *vi* : to issue reservations in excess of the space available

over·bought \-ˈbȯt\ *adj* : not likely to show an immediate rise in price because of prior heavy buying and accompanying price rises <an ~ market>

over·build \-ˈbild\ *vb* **-built** \-ˈbilt\; **-build·ing** *vt* : to build beyond the actual demand of ~ *vi* : to build houses in excess of demand

[1]**over·bur·den** \-ˈbərd-ᵊn\ *vt* : to place an excessive burden on

[2]**over·bur·den** \ˈō-vər-ˌbərd-ᵊn\ *n* : material overlying a deposit of useful geological materials

over·buy \ˌō-vər-ˈbī\ *vb* **-bought** \-ˈbȯt\; **-buy·ing** *vt* : to buy in excess of needs or demand ~ *vi* : to make purchases beyond one's needs or in excess of one's ability to pay

over·call \-ˈkȯl\ *vt* : to make a higher bid than (the previous bid or player) in a card game ~ *vi* : to bid over an opponent's bid in bridge when one's partner has not bid or doubled — **over·call** \ˈō-vər-ˌkȯl\ *n*

over·ca·pac·i·ty \ˌō-vər-kə-ˈpas-ət-ē, -ˈpas-tē\ *n* : excessive capacity for production or services in relation to demand

over·cap·i·tal·ize \-ˈkap-ət-ᵊl-ˌīz, -ˈkap-tᵊl-\ *vt* **1** : to put a nominal value on the capital of (a corporation) higher than actual cost or fair market value **2** : to capitalize beyond what the business or the profit-making prospects warrant — **over·cap·i·tal·iza·tion** \-ˌkap-ət-ᵊl-ə-ˈzā-shən, -ˌkap-tᵊl-\ *n*

[1]**over·cast** *vt* **-cast; -cast·ing** **1** \ˌō-vər-ˈkast, ˈō-vər-ˌ\ : DARKEN, OVERSHADOW **2** \ˈō-vər-ˌ\ : to sew (raw edges of a seam) with long slanting widely spaced stitches to prevent raveling

[2]**over·cast** \ˈō-vər-ˌkast, ˌō-vər-ˈ\ *adj* : clouded over <an ~ day>

[3]**over·cast** \ˈō-vər-ˌkast\ *n* : COVERING; *esp* : a covering of clouds over the sky

over·cast·ing \ˈō-vər-ˌkas-tiŋ\ *n* : the act of stitching raw edges of fabric to prevent raveling; *also* : the stitching so done

overcast stitch *n* : a small close embroidery stitch sometimes done over a foundation thread and used to form outlines

over·cau·tious \ˌō-vər-ˈkȯ-shəs\ *adj* : too cautious

over·charge \-ˈchärj\ *vt* **1** : to charge too much or too fully **2** : to fill too full **3** : EXAGGERATE, OVERDRAW ~ *vi* : to make an excessive charge — **over·charge** \ˈō-vər-ˌ\ *n*

over·cloud \ˌō-vər-ˈklau̇d\ *vt* : to overspread with clouds

over·coat \ˈō-vər-ˌkōt\ *n* **1** : a warm coat worn over indoor clothing **2** : a protective coating (as of paint)

over·coat·ing \-iŋ\ *n* : OVERCOAT 2

over·come \ˌō-vər-ˈkəm\ *vb* **-came** \-ˈkām\; **-come; -com·ing** [ME *overcomen,* fr. OE *ofercuman,* fr. *ofer* over + *cuman* to come] *vt* **1** : to get the better of : SURMOUNT <~ difficulties> **2** : OVERPOWER, OVERWHELM ~ *vi* : to gain the superiority : WIN — **over·com·er** *n*

over·com·mit \-kə-ˈmit\ *vt* : to commit excessively: as **a** : to obligate (as oneself) beyond the ability for fulfilment **b** : to allocate (resources) in excess of the capacity for replenishment — **over·com·mit·ment** \-mənt\ *n*

over·com·pen·sa·tion \-ˌkäm-pən-ˈsā-shən, -ˌpen-\ *n* : excessive compensation; *specif* : excessive reaction to a feeling of inferiority, guilt, or inadequacy leading to an exaggerated attempt to overcome the feeling — **over·com·pen·sa·to·ry** \-kəm-ˈpen(t)-sə-ˌtōr-ē, -ˌtȯr-\ *adj*

over·con·fi·dence \-ˈkän-fəd-ən(t)s, -fə-ˌden(t)s\ *n* : excess of confidence — **over·con·fi·dent** \-fəd-ənt, -fə-ˌdent\ *adj* — **over·con·fi·dent·ly** *adv*

over·crowd \ˌō-vər-ˈkrau̇d\ *vt* : to cause to be too crowded ~ *vi* : to crowd together too much

over·de·ter·mined \-di-ˈtər-mənd\ *adj* **1** : excessively determined **2** : having more than one determining psychological factor

over·de·vel·op \-di-ˈvel-əp\ *vt* : to develop excessively; *esp* : to subject (exposed photographic material) to a developing solution for excessive time or at excessive temperature, agitation, or concentration — **over·de·vel·op·ment** \-mənt\ *n*

over·do \ˌō-vər-ˈdü\ *vb* **-did** \-ˈdid\; **-done** \-ˈdən\; **-do·ing** \-ˈdü-iŋ\; **-does** \-ˈdəz\ *vt* **1 a** : to do in excess **b** : to use to excess **c** : EXAGGERATE **2** : to cook too long **3** : EXHAUST ~ *vi* : to go to extremes

over·dom·i·nance \-ˈdäm(-ə)-nən(t)s\ *n* : the property of having a heterozygote that produces a phenotype more extreme or better adapted than that of the homozygote — **over·dom·i·nant** \-nənt\ *adj*

[1]**over·dose** \ˈō-vər-ˌdōs\ *n* : too great a dose

2over·dose \ˌō-vər-ˈdōs\ *vt* **:** to give an overdose or too many doses to

over·draft \ˈō-vər-ˌdraft\ *n* **1 :** an act of overdrawing at a bank **:** the state of being overdrawn; *also* **:** the sum overdrawn **2 :** a draft or current of air passing over a fire in a furnace

over·draw \ˌō-vər-ˈdrȯ\ *vb* **-drew** \-ˈdrü\; **-drawn** \-ˈdrȯn\; **-draw·ing** *vt* **1 :** to draw checks on (a bank account) for more than the balance <his account was *overdrawn*> **2 :** EXAGGERATE, OVERSTATE ~ *vi* **:** to make an overdraft

over·drawn *adj* **:** having an overdrawn account <the bank informed him that he was ~>

1over·dress \ˌō-vər-ˈdres\ *vt* **:** to dress or adorn to excess ~ *vi* **:** to dress oneself to excess

2over·dress \ˈō-vər-ˌdres\ *n* **:** a dress worn over another

over·drive \ˈō-vər-ˌdrīv\ *n* **:** an automotive transmission gear that transmits to the drive shaft a speed greater than engine speed

over·due \ˌō-vər-ˈd(y)ü\ *adj* **1 a :** unpaid when due **b :** delayed beyond an appointed time **2 :** too great **:** EXCESSIVE **3 :** more than ready ***syn*** see TARDY

over·eat \ˌō-və-ˈrēt\ *vi* **over·ate** \-ˈrāt\; **over·eat·en** \-ˈrēt-ᵊn\; **over·eat·ing :** to eat to excess — **over·eat·er** *n*

over·em·pha·sis \ˌō-və-ˈrem(p)-fə-səs\ *n* **:** excessive emphasis

over·em·pha·size \-ˌsīz\ *vt* **:** to give excessive emphasis to ~ *vi* **:** to use too much emphasis

over·es·ti·mate \ˌō-və-ˈres-tə-ˌmāt\ *vt* **:** to estimate too highly — **over·es·ti·mate** \-mət\ *n* — **over·es·ti·ma·tion** \-ˌres-tə-ˈmā-shən\ *n*

over·ex·pose \ˌō-və-rik-ˈspōz\ *vt* **:** to expose excessively; *esp* **:** to expose (as film) to excessive radiation (as light) — **over·ex·po·sure** \-ˈspō-zhər\ *n*

over·ex·tend \ˌō-və-rik-ˈstend\ *vt* **:** to extend or expand beyond a safe or reasonable point; *esp* **:** to commit (oneself) financially beyond what can be paid

over·fa·tigue \ˌō-vər-fə-ˈtēg\ *n* **:** excessive fatigue esp. when carried beyond the recuperative capacity of the individual — **over·fa·tigued** \-ˈtēgd\ *adj*

over·fill \ˌō-vər-ˈfil\ *vt* **:** to fill to overflowing ~ *vi* **:** to become full to overflowing

over·fish \-ˈfish\ *vt* **:** to fish to the detriment of (a fishing ground) or to the depletion of (a kind of organism)

over·flight \ˈō-vər-ˌflīt\ *n* **:** a passage over an area in an airplane

1over·flow \ˌō-vər-ˈflō\ *vt* **1 :** to cover with or as if with water **:** INUNDATE **2 :** to flow over the brim of **3 :** to cause to overflow ~ *vi* **:** to flow over bounds

2over·flow \ˈō-vər-ˌflō\ *n* **1 :** a flowing over **:** INUNDATION **2 :** something that flows over **:** SURPLUS **3 :** an outlet or receptacle for surplus liquid

over·fly \ˌō-vər-ˈflī\ *vt* **-flew** \-ˈflü\; **-flown** \-ˈflōn\; **-fly·ing :** to fly over; *esp* **:** to pass over in an airplane

over·gar·ment \ˈō-vər-ˌgär-mənt\ *n* **:** an outer garment

over·glaze \-ˌglāz\ *adj* **:** applied or suitable for applying on top of a fired glaze <~ enamels> — **overglaze** *n*

over·graze \ˌō-vər-ˈgrāz\ *vt* **:** to allow animals to graze to the point of damaging vegetational cover

over·grow \ˌō-vər-ˈgrō\ *vb* **-grew** \-ˈgrü\; **-grown** \-ˈgrōn\; **-grow·ing** *vt* **1 :** to grow over so as to cover with herbage **2:** to grow beyond or rise above **:** OUTGROW ~ *vi* **1 :** to grow excessively **2:** to become grown over — **over·growth** \ˈō-vər-ˌgrōth\ *n*

1over·hand \ˈō-vər-ˌhand\ *adj* **:** made with the hand brought forward and down from above shoulder level — **overhand** *adv* — **over·hand·ed** \ˌō-vər-ˈhan-dəd\ *adv*

2over·hand \ˈō-vər-ˌhand\ *n* **:** an overhand stroke (as in tennis)

3over·hand \ˈō-vər-ˌ\ *vt* **:** to sew with short vertical stitches

overhand knot \ˌō-vər-ˌhan(d)-\ *n* **:** a small knot often used to prevent the end of a cord from fraying — see KNOT illustration

1over·hang \ˈō-vər-ˌhaŋ, ˌō-vər-ˈ\ *vb* **-hung** \-ˌhəŋ, -ˈhəŋ\; **-hang·ing** *vt* **1 :** to project over **2 :** to impend over **:** THREATEN ~ *vi* **:** to project so as to be over something

2over·hang \ˈō-vər-ˌhaŋ\ *n* **1 :** something that overhangs; *also* **:** the extent of the overhanging **2 :** the part of the bow or stern of a ship that projects over the water above the waterline **3 :** a projection of the roof or upper story of a building beyond the wall of the lower part

over·haul \ˌō-vər-ˈhȯl\ *vt* **1 :** to haul or drag over **2 a :** to examine thoroughly **b (1) :** REPAIR **(2) :** to renovate, revise, or renew thoroughly **3 :** OVERTAKE — **over·haul** \ˈō-vər-ˌhȯl\ *n*

1over·head \ˌō-vər-ˈhed\ *adv* **:** above one's head **:** ALOFT

2over·head \ˈō-vər-ˌhed\ *adj* **1 :** operating, lying, or coming from above **2 :** of or relating to overhead expense

3over·head \ˈō-vər-ˌhed\ *n* **1 :** business expenses (as rent, insurance, or heating) not chargeable to a particular part of the work or product **2 :** CEILING; *esp* **:** the ceiling of a ship's compartment **3 :** a stroke in a racket game made above head height **:** SMASH

overhead projector *n* **:** a projector for projecting onto a vertical screen magnified images of graphic material on a horizontal transparency illuminated from below — called also *overhead*

over·hear \ˌō-vər-ˈhi(ə)r\ *vb* **-heard** \-ˈhərd\; **-hear·ing** \-ˈhi(ə)r-iŋ\ *vt* **:** to hear without the speaker's knowledge or intention ~ *vi* **:** to overhear something

over·heat \-ˈhēt\ *vt* **1 :** to heat to excess **2 :** to stimulate unduly <~*ing* the economy> ~ *vi* **:** to become overheated

over·in·dulge \ˌō-və-rin-ˈdəlj\ *vt* **1 :** to indulge in to an excessive degree **2 :** to indulge (someone) to an excessive degree ~ *vi* **:** to indulge in something to an excessive degree — **over·in·dul·gence** \-ˈdəl-jən(t)s\ *n* — **over·in·dul·gent** \-jənt\ *adj*

over·is·sue \ˌō-və-ˈrish-(ˌ)ü, -ˈrish-ə(-w)\ *n* **:** an issue exceeding the limit of capital, credit, or authority — **overissue** *vt*

over·joy \ˌō-vər-ˈjȯi\ *vt* **:** to fill with great joy

1over·kill \ˌō-vər-ˈkil\ *vt* **:** to obliterate (a target) with more nuclear force than required

2over·kill \ˈō-vər-ˌkil\ *n* **1 :** the capability of destroying an enemy or target with a nuclear force larger than is required **2 :** an excess of something (as a quantity or an action) beyond what is required or suitable for a particular purpose <a propaganda ~> <an ~ in weaponry> **3 :** killing in excess of what is intended or required

1over·land \ˈō-vər-ˌland, -lənd\ *adv* **:** by, upon, or across land

2overland *adj* **:** going or accomplished over the land instead of by sea <an ~ route>

over·lap \ˌō-vər-ˈlap\ *vt* **1 :** to extend over and cover a part of **2 :** to have something in common with ~ *vi* **1 :** to lap over **2 :** to have something in common — **over·lap** \ˈō-vər-ˌlap\ *n*

1over·lay \ˌō-vər-ˈlā\ *vt* **-laid** \-ˈlād\; **-lay·ing 1 a :** to lay or spread over or across **:** SUPERIMPOSE **b :** to prepare an overlay for **2 :** OVERLIE 2

2over·lay \ˈō-vər-ˌlā\ *n* **:** a covering either permanent or temporary: as **a :** an ornamental veneer **b :** paper patches added to the packing on a printing press to make a stronger impression **c :** a decorative and contrasting design or article placed on top of a plain one **d :** a transparent sheet containing graphic matter to be superimposed on another sheet

over·leap \ˌō-vər-ˈlēp\ *vt* **-leaped** *or* **-leapt** \-ˈlēpt *also* -ˈlept\; **-leap·ing** \-ˈlē-piŋ\ **1 :** to leap over or across **2 :** to defeat (oneself) by going too far

over·learn \-ˈlərn\ *vt* **:** to continue to study or practice after attaining proficiency

over·lie \-ˈlī\ *vt* **-lay** \-ˈlā\; **-lain** \-ˈlān\; **-ly·ing** \-ˈlī-iŋ\ **1 :** to lie over or upon **2 :** to cause the death of by lying upon

over·load \-ˈlōd\ *vt* **:** to load to excess — **over·load** \ˈō-vər-ˌlōd\ *n*

1over·long \ˌō-vər-ˈlȯŋ\ *adj* **:** too long

2overlong *adv* **:** for too long a time

1over·look \-ˈlu̇k\ *vt* **1 :** to look over **:** INSPECT **2 a :** to look down upon from above **b :** to rise above or afford a view of **3 a :** to look past **:** MISS **b :** IGNORE **c :** EXCUSE **4 :** SUPERVISE **5 :** to look on with the evil eye **:** BEWITCH ***syn*** see NEGLECT

2over·look \ˈō-vər-ˌlu̇k\ *n* **:** a place from which one may look down upon a scene below <plenty of ~*s* and trails —Thelma H. Bell>

over·lord \ˈō-vər-ˌlȯ(ə)rd\ *n* **1 :** a lord who is lord over other lords **:** a lord paramount **2 :** an absolute or supreme ruler — **over·lord·ship** \-ˌship, ˌō-vər-ˈ\ *n*

over·ly \ˈō-vər-lē\ *adv* **:** to an excessive degree

1over·man \-mən, -ˌman\ *n* **1 :** a man in authority over others; *specif* **:** FOREMAN **2** \-ˌman\ [trans. of G *übermensch*] **:** SUPERMAN 1

2over·man \ˌō-vər-ˈman\ *vt* **:** to have or get too many men for the needs of <~ a ship>

over·mas·ter \-ˈmas-tər\ *vt* **:** OVERPOWER, SUBDUE

over·match \-ˈmach\ *vt* **1 :** to be more than a match for **:** DEFEAT **2 :** to match with a superior opponent

1over·much \-ˈməch\ *adj* **:** too much

2overmuch *adv* **:** in too great a degree

3over·much \ˈō-vər-ˌməch, ˌō-vər-ˈ\ *n* **:** too great an amount

1over·night \ˌō-vər-ˈnīt\ *adv* **1:** on or during the evening or night <stayed away ~> **2 :** SUDDENLY <became famous ~>

2overnight *adj* **1 :** of or lasting the night **2 :** SUDDEN, RAPID

overnight bag *n* **:** a traveling bag of a size to carry clothing and personal articles for an overnight trip — called also *overnight case, overnighter*

over·op·ti·mism \ˌō-və-ˈräp-tə-ˌmiz-əm\ *n* **:** excessive optimism — **over·op·ti·mist** \-məst\ *n* — **over·op·ti·mis·tic** \-ˌräp-tə-ˈmis-tik\ *adj* — **over·op·ti·mis·ti·cal·ly** \-ti-k(ə-)lē\ *adv*

1over·pass \ˌō-vər-ˈpas\ *vt* **1 :** to pass across, over, or beyond **:** CROSS; *also* **:** SURPASS **2 :** TRANSGRESS **3 :** DISREGARD, IGNORE

2over·pass \ˈō-vər-ˌpas\ *n* **:** a crossing of two highways or of a highway and pedestrian path or railroad at different levels where clearance to traffic on the lower level is obtained by elevating the higher level; *also* **:** the upper level of such a crossing

over·per·suade \ˌō-vər-pər-ˈswād\ *vt* **:** to persuade to act contrary to one's conviction or preference — **over·per·sua·sion** \-ˈswā-zhən\ *n*

over·play \ˌō-vər-ˈplā\ *vt* **1 a :** to present (as a dramatic role) extravagantly **:** EXAGGERATE **b :** OVEREMPHASIZE **2 :** to rely too much upon the strength of — usu. used in the phrase *overplay one's hand* **3 :** to strike a golf ball beyond (a putting green)

over·plus \ˈō-vər-ˌpləs\ *n* [ME, part trans. of MF *surplus*] **:** SURPLUS

over·pop·u·la·tion \ˌō-vər-ˌpäp-yə-ˈlā-shən\ *n* **:** the condition of having a population so dense as to cause environmental deterioration, a reduced quality of life, or a population crash — **over·pop·u·lat·ed** \-ˈpäp-yə-ˌlāt-əd\ *adj*

over·pow·er \ˌō-vər-ˈpau̇(-ə)r\ *vt* **1 :** to overcome by superior force **:** DEFEAT **2 :** OVERWHELM **3 :** to provide with more power than is needed or desirable <a dangerously ~*ed* car> — **over·pow·er·ing·ly** \-ˈpau̇r-iŋ-lē\ *adv*

over·praise \-ˈprāz\ *vt* **:** to praise excessively

over·pres·sure \ˈō-vər-ˌpresh-ər\ *n* **:** pressure significantly above what is usual or normal

over·price \ˌō-vər-ˈprīs\ *vt* **:** to price too high

1over·print \-ˈprint\ *vt* **:** to print over with something additional

2over·print \ˈō-vər-ˌprint\ *n* **:** something added by or as if by overprinting; *esp* **:** a printed marking added to a postage or revenue stamp esp. to alter the original or to commemorate a special event

over·prize \ˌō-vər-ˈprīz\ *vt* **:** to prize excessively

over·pro·duce \-prə-ˈd(y)üs\ *vt* **:** to produce beyond demand, need, or allotment — **over·pro·duc·tion** \-prə-ˈdək-shən\ *n*

over·proof \ˌō-vər-ˈprüf\ *adj* **:** containing more alcohol than proof spirit

over·pro·por·tion \-prə-ˈpōr-shən, -ˈpȯr-\ *vt* **:** to make disproportionately large — **overproportion** *n* — **over·pro·por·tion·ate** \-sh(ə-)nət\ *adj* — **over·pro·por·tion·ate·ly** *adv*

over·pro·tect \-prə-ˈtekt\ *vt* **:** to protect unduly — **over·pro·tec·tion** \-ˈtek-shən\ *n* — **over·pro·tec·tive** \-ˈtek-tiv\ *adj*

over·qual·i·fied \-ˈkwäl-ə-ˌfīd\ *adj* **:** having more education, training, or experience than a job calls for

over·rate \ˌō-və(r)-ˈrāt\ *vt* **:** to rate too highly

over·reach \-ˈrēch\ *vt* **1 :** to reach above or beyond **:** OVERTOP **2 :** to defeat (oneself) by seeking to do or gain too much **3 :** to get the better of esp. in dealing and bargaining and typically by unscrupulous or crafty methods ~ *vi* **1** *of a horse* **:** to strike the toe of the hind foot against the heel or quarter of the forefoot **2 a :** to go to excess **b :** EXAGGERATE **3 :** to overreach oneself *syn* see CHEAT — **over·reach·er** *n*

over·re·act \-rē-ˈakt\ *vi* **:** to react excessively — **over·re·ac·tion** \-ˈak-shən\ *n*

over·re·fine·ment \-ri-ˈfīn-mənt\ *n* **:** excessive refinement

over·rep·re·sent·ed \ˈō-və(r)-ˌrep-ri-ˈzent-əd\ *adj* **:** represented excessively; *esp* **:** having representatives in a proportion higher than the average

1over·ride \-ˈrīd\ *vt* **-rode** \-ˈrōd\; **-rid·den** \-ˈrid-ᵊn\; **-rid·ing** \-ˈrīd-iŋ\ **1 :** to ride over or across **:** TRAMPLE **2 :** to ride (as a horse) too much or too hard **3 a :** to prevail over **:** DOMINATE **b :** to set aside **:** ANNUL; *esp* **:** to neutralize the action of (as an automatic control) **4 :** to extend or pass over; *esp* **:** OVERLAP

2over·ride \ˈo-və(r)-ˌrīd\ *n* **1 :** a commission paid to managerial personnel on sales made by subordinates **2 :** a device or system used to override a control

over·ripe \ˌō-və(r)-ˈrīp\ *adj* **1 :** passed beyond maturity or ripeness toward decay **2 :** DECADENT

over·rule \-ˈrül\ *vt* **1 :** to rule over **:** GOVERN **2 :** to prevail over **:** OVERCOME **3 a :** to rule against **b :** to set aside **:** REVERSE

1over·run \-ˈrən\ *vt* **-ran** \-ˈran\; **-run·ning** **1 a :** to defeat decisively and occupy the positions of **b :** to swarm over **:** INFEST **2 a :** to run or go beyond or past <the plane *overran* the runway> **b :** EXCEED **c** (1) **:** to readjust (set type) by shifting letters or words from one line into another (2) **:** OVERSET **3 :** to flow over

2over·run \ˈō-və(r)-ˌrən\ *n* **1 :** an act or instance of overrunning; *esp* **:** an exceeding of the costs estimated in a contract for development and manufacture of new equipment **2 :** the amount by which something overruns

over·sea \ˌo-vər-ˈsē, ˈō-vər-ˌ\ *adj or adv* **:** OVERSEAS

over·seas \-ˈsēz, -ˌsēz\ *adv or adj* **:** beyond or across the sea

over·see \ˌō-vər-ˈsē\ *vt* **-saw** \-ˈsȯ\; **-seen** \-ˈsēn\; **-see·ing** **1 :** SURVEY, WATCH **2 a :** INSPECT, EXAMINE **b :** SUPERVISE

over·seer \ˈō-və(r)-ˌsi(ə)r, -ˌsē-ər, ˌō-və(r)-ˈ\ *n* **:** SUPERINTENDENT, SUPERVISOR

over·sell \ˌō-vər-ˈsel\ *vt* **-sold** \-ˈsōld\; **-sell·ing** **1 a :** to sell too much to **b :** to sell too much of **2 :** to make excessive claims for **:** OVERPRAISE — **over·sell** \ˈō-vər-ˌsel\ *n*

over·sen·si·tive \ˌō-vər-ˈsen(t)-sət-iv, -stiv\ *adj* **:** unduly or extremely sensitive — **over·sen·si·tive·ness** *n*

over·set \-ˈset\ *vt* **-set; -set·ting** **1 a :** to disturb mentally or physically **:** UPSET **b :** to turn or tip over **:** OVERTURN **2 :** to set too much type matter for — **over·set** \ˈō-vər-ˌset\ *n*

over·sexed \ˌō-vər-ˈsekst\ *adj* **:** exhibiting an excessive sexual drive or interest

over·shad·ow \-ˈshad-(ˌ)ō, -ə(-w)\ *vt* **1 :** to cast a shadow over **:** DARKEN **2 :** to exceed in importance **:** OUTWEIGH

over·shoe \ˈō-vər-ˌshü\ *n* **:** an outer shoe; *esp* **:** GALOSH

over·shoot \ˌō-vər-ˈshüt\ *vt* **-shot** \-ˈshät\; **-shoot·ing** **1 :** to pass swiftly beyond **2 :** to shoot or pass over or beyond so as to miss **3 :** to excel in shooting — **over·shoot** \ˈō-vər-ˌshüt\ *n*

1over·shot \ˈō-vər-ˌshät\ *adj* **1 a :** having the upper jaw extending beyond the lower **b :** projecting beyond the lower jaw **2 :** actuated by the weight of water passing over and flowing from above <an ~ waterwheel>

2overshot *n* **:** a pattern or weave featuring filling threads which pass two or more warp yarns before reentering the fabric

over·sight \ˈō-vər-ˌsīt\ *n* **1 :** watchful and responsible care **2 :** an inadvertent omission or error
syn OVERSIGHT, SUPERVISION, SURVEILLANCE *shared meaning element* **:** a careful watching

over·sim·ple \ˌō-vər-ˈsim-pəl\ *adj* **:** too simple **:** not thoroughgoing or exhaustive <~ theories of personality>

over·sim·pli·fy \-ˈsim-plə-ˌfī\ *vt* **:** to simplify to such an extent as to bring about distortion, misunderstanding, or error ~ *vi* **:** to engage in undue or extreme simplification — **over·sim·pli·fi·ca·tion** \-ˌsim-plə-fə-ˈkā-shən\ *n*

over·size \ˌō-vər-ˈsīz\ *or* **over·sized** \-ˈsīzd\ *adj* **:** being of more than ordinary size

over·skirt \ˈō-vər-ˌskərt\ *n* **:** a skirt worn over another skirt

over·slaugh \ˌō-vər-ˈslȯ\ *vt* [D *overslaan* to pass over, omit] **:** to pass over for appointment or promotion in favor of another

over·sleep \ˌō-vər-ˈslēp\ *vi* **-slept** \-ˈslept\; **-sleep·ing** **:** to sleep beyond the time for waking

over·slip \ˌō-vər-ˈslip\ *vt* **1** *archaic* **:** to let pass by unawares **:** MISS **2** *obs* **:** ESCAPE

over·sold \ˌō-vər-ˈsōld\ *adj* **:** likely to show a rise in price because of prior heavy selling and accompanying decline in price <an ~ stock>

over·soul \ˈō-vər-ˌsōl\ *n* **:** the absolute reality and ground of existences conceived as a spiritual being in which the ideal nature manifested in human beings is perfectly realized

over·spe·cial·iza·tion \ˌō-vər-ˌspesh-(ə-)lə-ˈzā-shən\ *n* **:** excessive specialization

over·spec·u·late \-ˈspek-yə-ˌlāt\ *vi* **:** to speculate to excess and esp. beyond one's means — **over·spec·u·la·tion** \-ˌspek-yə-ˈlā-shən\ *n*

over·spend \-ˈspend\ *vb* **-spent** \-ˈspent\; **-spend·ing** *vt* **1 :** to spend or use to excess **:** EXHAUST **2 :** to exceed in expenditure ~ *vi* **:** to spend beyond one's means — **over·spend·er** *n*

over·spill \ˈō-vər-ˌspil\ *n, chiefly Brit* **:** the movement of excess urban population into less crowded areas

over·spread \ˌō-vər-ˈspred\ *vt* **-spread; -spread·ing** **:** to spread over or above — **over·spread** \ˈō-vər-ˌspred\ *n*

over·state \-ˈstāt\ *vt* **:** to state in too strong terms **:** EXAGGERATE — **over·state·ment** \-mənt\ *n*

over·stay \-ˈstā\ *vt* **:** to stay beyond the time or the limits of

over·steer \ˈō-vər-ˌsti(ə)r\ *n* **:** the tendency of an automobile to steer into a sharper turn than the driver intends sometimes with a thrusting of the rear to the outside

over·step \ˌō-vər-ˈstep\ *vt* **:** EXCEED, TRANSGRESS

over·stock \-ˈstäk\ *vt* **:** to stock beyond requirements or facilities

over·sto·ry \ˈō-vər-ˌstōr-ē, -ˌstȯr-\ *n* **1 :** the layer of foliage in a forest canopy **2 :** the trees contributing to an overstory

over·strew \ˌō-vər-ˈstrü\ *vt* **-strewed; -strewed** *or* **-strewn** \-ˈstrün\; **-strew·ing** **1 :** to strew or scatter about **2 :** to cover here and there

over·stride \-ˈstrīd\ *vt* **-strode** \-ˈstrōd\; **-strid·den** \-ˈstrid-ᵊn\; **-strid·ing** \-ˈstrīd-iŋ\ **1 a :** to stride over, across, or beyond **b :** BESTRIDE **2 :** to stride faster than or beyond

over·strung \-ˈstrəŋ\ *adj* **:** too highly strung **:** too sensitive

over·stuff \-ˈstəf\ *vt* **1 :** to stuff too full **2 :** to cover (as a chair or sofa) completely and deeply with upholstery

over·sub·scribe \-səb-ˈskrīb\ *vt* **:** to subscribe for more of than is offered for sale — **over·sub·scrip·tion** \-ˈskrip-shən\ *n*

over·sub·tle \-ˈsət-ᵊl\ *adj* **:** excessively or impracticably subtle

over·sup·ply \-sə-ˈplī\ *n* **:** an excessive supply — **oversupply** *vt*

overt \ō-ˈvərt, ˈō-ˌvərt *also* ˈō-vərt\ *adj* [ME, fr. MF *ouvert, overt,* fr. pp. of *ouvrir* to open, fr. (assumed) VL *operire,* alter. of L *aperire* — more at WEIR] **:** open to view **:** MANIFEST — **overt·ly** *adv* — **overt·ness** *n*

over·take \ˌō-vər-ˈtāk\ *vt* **-took** \-ˈtu̇k\; **-tak·en** \-ˈtā-kən\; **-tak·ing** [ME *overtaken,* fr [1]*over* + *taken* to take] **1 a :** to catch up with **b :** to catch up with and pass by **2 :** to come upon suddenly

over·tax \ˌō-vər-ˈtaks\ *vt* **1 :** to tax too heavily **2 :** to put too great a burden or strain on

over–the–count·er *adj* **1 :** not traded or effected on an organized securities exchange <~ transactions>; *esp* **:** traded by negotiation between buyers and sellers or their representatives <~ securities> **2 :** sold lawfully without prescription

over·throw \ˌō-vər-ˈthrō\ *vt* **-threw** \-ˈthrü\; **-thrown** \-ˈthrōn\; **-throw·ing** **1 :** OVERTURN, UPSET **2 :** to bring down **:** DEFEAT **3 :** to throw a baseball over or past (as a base) — **over·throw** \ˈō-vər-ˌthrō\ *n*

over·time \ˈō-vər-ˌtīm\ *n* **1 :** time in excess of a set limit; *esp* **:** working time in excess of a standard day or week **2 :** the wage paid for overtime — **overtime** *adv*

over·tone \-ˌtōn\ *n* **1 a :** one of the higher tones produced simultaneously with the fundamental and that with the fundamental comprise a complex musical tone **:** HARMONIC 1a **b :** HARMONIC 2 **2 :** the color of the light reflected (as by a paint) **3 :** a secondary effect, quality, or meaning **:** SUGGESTION

over·top \ˌō-vər-ˈtäp\ *vt* **1 :** to rise above the top of **2 :** to be superior to **3 :** SURPASS

over·trade \-ˈtrād\ *vi* **1 :** to trade beyond one's capital **2 :** CHURN 3

over·train \-ˈtrān\ *vt* **:** to train more than is necessary or desirable ~ *vi* **:** to engage in training to an excessive degree

over·trick \ˈō-vər-ˌtrik\ *n* **:** a card trick won in excess of the number bid

over·trump \ˌō-vər-ˈtrəmp\ *vt* **:** to trump with a higher trump card than the highest previously played on the same trick ~ *vi* **:** to play a higher trump card than the highest previously played on the same trick

1over·ture \ˈō-və(r)-ˌchu̇(ə)r, -chər, -ˌt(y)u̇(ə)r\ *n* [ME, lit., opening, fr. MF, fr. (assumed) VL *opertura,* alter. of L *apertura* — more at APERTURE] **1 a :** an initiative toward agreement or action **:** PROPOSAL **b :** something introductory **:** PRELUDE **2 a :** the orchestral introduction to a musical dramatic work **b :** an orchestral concert piece written esp. as a single movement in sonata form

2overture *vt* **-tured; -tur·ing** **1 :** to put forward as an overture **2 :** to make or present an overture to

1over·turn \ˌō-vər-ˈtərn\ *vt* **1 :** to cause to turn over **:** UPSET **2 :** OVERTHROW, DESTROY ~ *vi* **:** to turn over

2over·turn \ˈō-vər-ˌtərn\ *n* **1 :** the act of overturning **:** the state of being overturned **2 :** the sinking of surface water and rise of bottom water in a lake or sea that results from changes in temperature that commonly occur in spring and fall wherever lakes are icebound in winter

over·use \ˌō-vər-ˈyüs\ *n* **:** excessive use — **over·use** \-ˈyüz\ *vt*

over·val·ue \-ˈval-(ˌ)yü, -yə(-w)\ *vt* **:** to assign an excessive or fictitious value to — **over·valu·ation** \-ˌval-yə-ˈwā-shən\ *n*

over·view \ˈō-vər-ˌvyü\ *n* **:** a usu. brief general survey **:** SUMMARY

over·volt·age \ˌō-vər-ˈvōl-tij\ *n* **1 :** voltage in excess of the normal operating voltage of a device or circuit **2 :** the excess potential required for the discharge of an ion at an electrode over and above the equilibrium potential of the electrode

over·watch \-ˈwäch\ *vt* **1** *archaic* **:** to weary or exhaust by keeping awake **2 :** to watch over

over·wear \-ˈwa(ə)r, -ˈwe(ə)r\ *vt* **-wore** \-ˈwō(ə)r, -ˈwȯ(ə)r\; **-worn** \-ˈwō(ə)rn, -ˈwȯ(ə)rn\; **-wear·ing** **:** to wear out **:** EXHAUST

1over·wea·ry \-ˈwi(ə)r-ē\ *vt* **:** to tire out

2overweary *adj* **:** wearied to excess

over·ween·ing \-ˈwē-niŋ\ *adj* [ME *overwening,* prp. of *overwenen* to be arrogant, fr. *over* + *wenen* to ween] **1 :** ARROGANT, PRESUMPTUOUS **2 :** IMMODERATE, EXAGGERATED

over·weigh \-ˈwā\ *vt* **1 :** OVERWEIGHT 3 **2 :** OPPRESS

1over·weight \ˈō-vər-ˌwāt, *2 is usu* ˌō-vər-ˈ\ *n* **1 :** weight over and above what is required or allowed **2 :** excessive or burdensome weight

2over·weight \ˌō-vər-ˈwāt\ *vt* **1 :** to give too much weight or consideration to **2 :** to weight excessively **3 :** to exceed in weight

3over·weight \ˌō-vər-ˈwāt\ *adj* **:** exceeding expected, normal, or proper weight; *esp* **:** exceeding the bodily weight normal for one's age, height, and build

over·whelm \ˌō-vər-ˈhwelm, -ˈwelm\ *vt* [ME *overwhelmen,* fr. [1]*over* + *whelmen* to turn over, cover up] **1 :** OVERTHROW, UPSET **2 a :** to cover over completely **:** SUBMERGE **b :** to overcome by

superior force or numbers : CRUSH — **over·whelm·ing·ly** \-ˈhwel-miŋ-lē, -ˈwel-\ *adv*
over·wind \-ˈwīnd\ *vt* **-wound** \-ˈwau̇nd\; **-wind·ing** : to wind too much
1over·win·ter \-ˈwint-ər\ *vi* : to survive the winter
2overwinter *adj* : occurring during the period spanning the winter
over with *adj* : FINISHED, COMPLETED
over·word \ˈō-vər-ˌwərd\ *n* : the refrain of a song
over·work \ˌō-vər-ˈwərk\ *vt* **1** : to cause to work too hard, too long, or to exhaustion **2** : to decorate all over **3 a** : to work too much on : OVERDO **b** : to make excessive use of ~ *vi* : to work too much or too long : OVERDO — **overwork** *n*
over·write \ˌō-və(r)-ˈrīt\ *vb* **-wrote** \-ˈrōt\; **-writ·ten** \-ˈrit-ᵊn\; **-writ·ing** \-ˈrīt-iŋ\ *vt* **1** : to write over the surface of **2** : to write in inflated or pretentious style ~ *vi* : to write too much
over·wrought \-ˈrȯt\ *adj* [pp. of *overwork*] **1** : extremely excited : AGITATED **2** : elaborated to excess : OVERDONE
ovi- *or* **ovo-** — see OV-
ovi·cid·al \ˌō-və-ˈsīd-ᵊl\ *adj* : capable of killing eggs
ovi·cide \ˈō-və-ˌsīd\ *n* [ISV] : an agent that kills eggs; *esp* : an insecticide effective against the egg stage
ovi·duct \ˈō-və-ˌdəkt\ *n* [NL *oviductus,* fr. *ov-* + *ductus* duct] : a tube that serves exclusively or esp. for the passage of eggs from an ovary — **ovi·duc·tal** \ˌō-və-ˈdək-tᵊl\ *adj*
ovine \ˈō-ˌvīn\ *adj* [LL *ovinus,* fr. L *ovis* sheep — more at EWE] : of, relating to, or resembling sheep — **ovine** *n*
ovip·a·rous \ō-ˈvip-(ə-)rəs\ *adj* [L *oviparus,* fr. *ov-* + *-parus* -parous] : producing eggs that develop and hatch outside the maternal body; *also* : involving the production of such eggs — **ovip·a·rous·ly** *adv* — **ovip·a·rous·ness** *n*
ovi·pos·it \ˈō-və-ˌpäz-ət, ˌō-və-ˈ\ *vi* [prob. back-formation fr. *ovipositor*] : to lay eggs — used esp. of insects — **ovi·po·si·tion** \ˌō-və-pə-ˈzish-ən\ *n* — **ovi·po·si·tion·al** \-ˈzish-nəl, -ən-ᵊl\ *adj*
ovi·pos·i·tor \ˈō-və-ˌpäz-ət-ər, ˌō-və-ˈ\ *n* [NL, fr. L *ov-* + *positor* one that places, fr. *positus,* pp. of *ponere* to place — more at POSITION] : a specialized organ (as of an insect) for depositing eggs — see INSECT illustration
ovoid \ˈō-ˌvȯid\ *or* **ovoi·dal** \ō-ˈvȯid-ᵊl\ *adj* [F *ovoïde,* fr. L *ovum* egg — more at EGG] : shaped like an egg : OVATE — **ovoid** *n*
ovo·lo \ˈō-və-ˌlō\ *n, pl* **-los** [It, dim. of *uovo, ovo* egg, fr. L *ovum*] : a rounded convex molding
Ovon·ics \ō-ˈvän-iks\ *n pl but usu sing in constr* [Stanford R. *Ov*shinsky *b*1923 Am inventor + electr*onics*] : a branch of electronics that deals with applications of the change from an electrically nonconducting state to a semiconducting state shown by glasses of special composition upon application of a certain minimum voltage — **ovon·ic** \-ik\ *adj*
ovo·tes·tis \ˌō-vō-ˈtes-təs\ *n* [NL] : a hermaphrodite gonad (as in some scale insects)
ovo·vi·vip·a·rous \ˈō-vō-ˌvī-ˈvip-(ə-)rəs\ *adj* [prob. fr. (assumed) NL *ovoviviparus,* fr. L *ov-* + *viviparus* viviparous] : producing eggs that develop within the maternal body and hatch within or immediately after extrusion from the parent — **ovo·vi·vip·a·rous·ly** *adv* — **ovo·vi·vip·a·rous·ness** *n*
1ovu·late \ˈäv-yə-ˌlāt, ˈōv-, -lət\ *adj* : bearing an ovule
2ovu·late \-ˌlāt\ *vi* **-lat·ed; -lat·ing** : to produce eggs or discharge them from an ovary — **ovu·la·tion** \ˌäv-yə-ˈlā-shən, ˌōv-\ *n*
ovu·la·to·ry \ˈäv-yə-lə-ˌtōr-ē, ˈōv-, -ˌtȯr-\ *adj* : of, relating to, or involving ovulation
ovule \ˈäv-(ˌ)yü(ə)l, ˈōv-\ *n* [NL *ovulum,* dim. of L *ovum*] **1** : an outgrowth of the ovary of a seed plant that is a megasporangium and encloses an embryo sac within a nucellus **2** : a small egg; *esp* : one in an early stage of growth — **ovu·lar** \-yə-lər\ *adj*
ovum \ˈō-vəm\ *n, pl* **ova** \-və\ [NL, fr. L, egg — more at EGG] : a female gamete : MACROGAMETE
owe \ˈō\ *vb* **owed; ow·ing** [ME *owen* to possess, own, owe, fr. OE *āgan;* akin to OHG *eigun* (1st & 3d pl. pres. indic.) possess, Skt *īśe* he possesses] *vt* **1 a** *archaic* : POSSESS, OWN **b** : to have or bear (an emotion or attitude) to someone or something <~*s* the boss a grudge> **2 a** (1) : to be under obligation to pay or repay in return for something received : be indebted in the sum of <~*s* me five dollars> (2) : to be under obligation to render (as duty or service) **b** : to be indebted to <~*s* the grocer for supplies> **3** : to be indebted for <*owed* his wealth to his father> ~ *vi* : to be in debt <~*s* for his house>
owing to *prep* : because of <delayed *owing to* a crash>
owl \ˈau̇(ə)l\ *n* [ME *owle,* fr. OE *ūle;* akin to OHG *uwila* owl] : any of an order (Strigiformes) of birds of prey with large head and eyes, short hooked bill, strong talons, and more or less nocturnal habits
owl·et \ˈau̇-lət\ *n* : a small or young owl
owl·ish \ˈau̇-lish\ *adj* : resembling or suggesting an owl — **owl·ish·ly** *adv* — **owl·ish·ness** *n*
1own \ˈōn\ *adj* [ME *owen,* fr. OE *āgen;* akin to OHG *eigan* own, ON *eiginn,* OE *āgan* to possess — more at OWE] : belonging to oneself or itself — usu. used following a possessive case or pronoun <cooked his ~ dinner>
2own *vt* **1** : to have or hold as property : POSSESS **2** : to acknowledge to be true, valid, or as claimed : ADMIT <~ a debt> ~ *vi* : to acknowledge something to be true, valid, or as claimed — used with *to* or *up* **syn 1** see HAVE **2** see ACKNOWLEDGE **ant** disown, repudiate — **own·er** \ˈō-nər\ *n* — **own·er·ship** \-ˌship\ *n*
3own *pron, sing or pl in constr* : one or ones belonging to oneself — used after a possessive and without a following noun as a pronoun equivalent in meaning to the adjective *own* <gave out books so that each student had his ~> — **on one's own** : for or by oneself : independently of assistance or control
ox \ˈäks\ *n, pl* **ox·en** \ˈäk-sən\ *also* **ox** [ME, fr. OE *oxa;* akin to OHG *ohso* ox, Gk *hygros* wet — more at HUMOR] **1** : a domestic bovine mammal (*Bos taurus*); *broadly* : a bovine mammal **2** : an adult castrated male domestic ox
ox- *or* **oxo-** *comb form* [F, fr. *oxygène*] : oxygen <*ox*azine>
ox·a·cil·lin \ˌäk-sə-ˈsil-ən\ *n* [*ox-* + *a*zole + peni*cillin*] : a semisynthetic penicillin that is esp. effective in the control of infections caused by penicillin-resistant staphylococci
ox·al·ac·e·tate \ˌäk-sə-ˈlas-ə-ˌtāt\ *or* **ox·a·lo·ac·e·tate** \ˌäk-sə-lō-ˈas-\ *n* : a salt or ester of oxalacetic acid
ox·al·ace·tic \ˌäk-sə-lə-ˈsēt-ik\ *or* **ox·a·lo·ace·tic** \ˌäk-sə-lō-ə-ˈsēt-\ *adj* : involving oxalacetic acid or its production
oxalacetic acid *n* [*oxal*ic + *acetic acid*] : a crystalline acid $C_4H_4O_5$ that is formed by reversible oxidation of malic acid (as in carbohydrate metabolism via the citric acid cycle) and in reversible transamination reactions (as from aspartic acid) — called also *oxaloacetic acid*
ox·a·late \ˈäk-sə-ˌlāt\ *n* : a salt or ester of oxalic acid
ox·al·ic acid \(ˌ)äk-ˌsal-ik-\ *n* [F (*acide*) *oxalique,* fr. L *oxalis* wood sorrel] : a poisonous strong acid $(COOH)_2$ or $H_2C_2O_4$ that occurs in various plants as oxalates and is used esp. as a bleaching or cleaning agent and in making dyes
ox·al·is \äk-ˈsal-əs\ *n* [NL, genus name, fr. L, wood sorrel, fr. Gk, fr. *oxys* sharp — more at OXYGEN] : WOOD SORREL 1
ox·a·lo·suc·cin·ic acid \ˈäk-sə-lō-sək-ˌsin-ik-, äk-ˈsal-ō-\ *n* [*oxal*ic + *succinic acid*] : a tricarboxylic acid $C_6H_6O_7$ that is formed as an intermediate in the metabolism of fats and carbohydrates
ox·a·zine \ˈäk-sə-ˌzēn\ *n* [ISV *ox-* + *azine*] : any of several parent compounds C_4H_5NO containing a ring composed of four carbon atoms, one oxygen atom, and one nitrogen atom
ox·blood \ˈäks-ˌbləd\ *n* : a moderate reddish brown
ox·bow \ˈäks-ˌbō\ *n* **1** : a U-shaped frame forming a collar about an ox's neck and supporting the yoke **2** : something (as a bend in a river) resembling an oxbow — **oxbow** *adj*
ox·eye \ˈäk-ˌsī\ *n* : any of several composite plants (as of the genera *Chrysanthemum, Heliopsis,* or *Buphthalmum*) having heads with both disk and ray flowers; *esp* : DAISY 1b
oxeye daisy *n* : DAISY 1b
ox·ford \ˈäks-fərd\ *n* [*Oxford,* England] : a low shoe laced or tied over the instep
Oxford down *n, often cap D* [*Oxfordshire,* England] : any of a Down breed of large hornless sheep developed by crossing Cotswolds and Hampshires
Oxford movement *n* : a High Church movement within the Church of England begun at Oxford in 1833
ox·heart \ˈäks-ˌhärt\ *n* : any of various large sweet cherries
ox·i·dant \ˈäk-səd-ənt\ *n* : OXIDIZING AGENT — **oxidant** *adj*
ox·i·dase \ˈäk-sə-ˌdās, -ˌdāz\ *n* [ISV] : any of various enzymes that catalyze oxidations; *esp* : one able to react directly with molecular oxygen — **ox·i·da·sic** \ˌäk-sə-ˈdā-sik, -zik\ *adj*
ox·i·da·tion \ˌäk-sə-ˈdā-shən\ *n* [F, fr. *oxider, oxyder* to oxidize, fr. *oxide*] **1** : the act or process of oxidizing **2** : the state or result of being oxidized — **ox·i·da·tive** \ˈäk-sə-ˌdāt-iv\ *adj* — **ox·i·da·tive·ly** *adv*
oxidation number *n* : the degree of or potential for oxidation of an element or atom which is usu. expressed as a positive or negative number representing the ionic or effective charge : VALENCE — called also *oxidation state*
oxidation–reduction *n* : a chemical reaction in which one or more electrons are transferred from one atom or molecule to another
oxidative phosphorylation *n* : the synthesis of ATP by phosphorylation of ADP for which energy is obtained by electron transfer from reduced carbon compounds to oxygen
ox·ide \ˈäk-ˌsīd\ *n* [F *oxide, oxyde,* fr. *ox-* (fr. *oxygène* oxygen) + *-ide* (fr. *acide* acid)] : a binary compound of oxygen with an element or radical — **ox·id·ic** \äk-ˈsid-ik\ *adj*
ox·i·dize \ˈäk-sə-ˌdīz\ *vb* **-dized; -diz·ing** [*oxide* + *-ize*] *vt* **1** : to combine with oxygen **2** : to dehydrogenate esp. by the action of oxygen **3** : to change (a compound) by increasing the proportion of the electronegative part or change (an element or ion) from a lower to a higher positive valence : remove one or more electrons from (an atom, ion, or molecule) ~ *vi* : to become oxidized — **ox·i·diz·able** \-ˌdī-zə-bəl\ *adj*
ox·i·diz·er \-ˌdī-zər\ *n* : OXIDIZING AGENT; *esp* : one used to support the combustion of a rocket propellant
oxidizing agent *n* : a substance that oxidizes something esp. chemically (as by accepting electrons)
ox·i·do·re·duc·tase \ˈäk-səd-ō-ri-ˈdək-ˌtās, -ˌtāz\ *n* [*oxid*ation + *-o-* + *reduct*ion + *-ase*] : an enzyme that catalyzes an oxidation-reduction reaction
ox·ime \ˈäk-ˌsēm\ *n* [ISV *ox-* + *-ime* (fr. *imide*)] : any of various compounds obtained chiefly by the action of hydroxylamine on aldehydes and ketones and characterized by the bivalent grouping $C{=}NOH$
ox·lip \ˈäk-ˌslip\ *n* [(assumed) ME *oxeslippe,* fr. OE *oxanslyppe,* lit., ox dung, fr. *oxa* ox + *slypa, slyppe* paste — more at SLIP] : a Eurasian primula (*Primula elatior*) differing from the cowslip chiefly in the flat corolla limb
Ox·on \ˈäk-ˌsän, -sən\ *abbr* [L *Oxonia*] **1** Oxford **2** Oxfordshire **3** [L *Oxoniensis*] of Oxford
Ox·o·ni·an \äk-ˈsō-nē-ən\ *n* [ML *Oxonia* Oxford] : a student or graduate of Oxford University — **Oxonian** *adj*
ox·tail \ˈäk-ˌstāl\ *n* : the tail of cattle; *esp* : the skinned tail used for food (as in soup)
ox·ter \ˈäk-stər\ *n* [(assumed) ME, alter. of OE *ōxta;* akin to L *axilla* armpit — more at AXIS] **1** *chiefly Scot & Irish* : ARMPIT **2** *chiefly Scot & Irish* : ARM
ox·tongue \ˈäk-ˌstəŋ\ *n* : any of several plants having rough tongue-shaped leaves: as **a** : a bugloss (genus *Anchusa*) **b** : a European hawkweed (*Picris echioides*) that has yellow flowers and is now naturalized in the eastern U.S.
oxy \ˈäk-sē\ *adj* [F, fr. *oxygène* oxygen] : OXYGENIC; *esp* : containing oxygen or additional oxygen — often used in combination <*oxy*hemoglobin> <*oxy*hydrogen>
oxy·acet·y·lene \ˌäk-sē-ə-ˈset-ᵊl-ən, -ᵊl-ˌēn\ *adj* [ISV] : of, relating to, or utilizing a mixture of oxygen and acetylene <an ~ torch>
oxy·ac·id \ˈäk-sē-ˌas-əd\ *n* : an acid (as sulfuric acid) that contains oxygen — called also *oxygen acid*

ox·y·gen \'äk-si-jən\ *n, often attrib* [F *oxygène,* fr. Gk *oxys,* adj., acid, lit., sharp + F *-gène* -gen; akin to L *acer* sharp — more at EDGE] : an element that is found free as a colorless tasteless odorless gas in the atmosphere of which it forms about 21 percent or combined in water, in most rocks and minerals, and in numerous organic compounds, that is capable of combining with all elements except the inert gases, is active in physiological processes, and is involved esp. in combustion processes — see ELEMENT table — **ox·y·gen·ic** \ˌäk-si-'jen-ik\ *adj* — **ox·y·gen·ic·i·ty** \-jə-'nis-ət-ē\ *n* — **ox·y·gen·less** \'äk-si-jən-ləs\ *adj*

ox·y·gen·ate \'äk-si-jə-ˌnāt, äk-'sij-ə-\ *vt* **-at·ed; -at·ing** : to impregnate, combine, or supply (as blood) with oxygen — **ox·y·gen·ation** \ˌäk-si-jə-'nā-shən, äk-ˌsij-ə-\ *n*

ox·y·gen·ator \'äk-si-jə-ˌnāt-ər, äk-'sij-ə-\ *n* : one (as an apparatus for perfusing an organ or tissue) that oxygenates

oxygen cycle *n* : the cycle whereby atmospheric oxygen is converted to carbon dioxide in animal respiration and regenerated by green plants in photosynthesis

oxygen debt *n* : a cumulative oxygen deficit that develops during periods of intense bodily activity and must be made good when the body returns to rest

oxygen mask *n* : a device worn over the nose and mouth (as by airmen at high altitudes) through which oxygen is supplied from a storage tank

oxygen tent *n* : a canopy which can be placed over a bedridden person and within which a flow of oxygen can be maintained

oxy·he·mo·glo·bin \ˌäk-si-'hē-mə-ˌglō-bən\ *n* [ISV] : hemoglobin loosely combined with oxygen that it releases to the tissues

oxy·hy·dro·gen \-'hī-drə-jən\ *adj* : of, relating to, or utilizing a mixture of oxygen and hydrogen <~ torch>

oxy·mo·ron \ˌäk-si-'mō(ə)r-ˌän, -'mò(ə)r-\ *n, pl* **-mo·ra** \-'mōr-ə, -'mòr-\ [LGk *oxymōron,* fr. neut. of *oxymōros* pointedly foolish, fr. Gk *oxys* sharp, keen + *mōros* foolish — more at MORON] : a combination of contradictory or incongruous words (as *cruel kindness*)

oxygen mask

oxy·phil·ic \ˌäk-si-'fil-ik\ *also* **oxy·phile** \'äk-si-ˌfīl\ *or* **oxy·phil** \-ˌfil\ *adj* [Gk *oxys* acid + E *-phil* — more at OXYGEN] : ACIDOPHILIC — **oxyphile** *also* **oxyphil** *n*

oxy·some \'äk-si-ˌsōm\ *n* : one of the structural units of mitochondrial cristae that are observable by the electron microscope usu. as spheres or stalked spheres and are prob. the seat of fundamental energy-producing reactions

oxy·sul·fide \ˌäk-si-'səl-ˌfīd\ *n* [ISV] : a compound of oxygen and sulfur with an element or radical that may be regarded as a sulfide in which part of the sulfur is replaced by oxygen

oxy·tet·ra·cy·cline \-ˌte-trə-'sī-ˌklēn\ *n* : a yellow crystalline broad-spectrum antibiotic $C_{22}H_{24}N_2O_9$ produced by a soil actinomycete (*Streptomyces rimosus*)

oxy·to·cic \ˌäk-si-'tō-sik\ *adj* [ISV, fr. Gk *oxys* sharp, quick + *tokos* childbirth, fr. *tiktein* to bear — more at THANE] : hastening parturition; *also* : inducing contraction of uterine smooth muscle — **oxytocic** *n*

oxy·to·cin \-'tōs-ᵊn\ *n* [ISV, fr. *oxytocic*] : a postpituitary octapeptide hormone $C_{43}H_{66}N_{12}O_{12}S_2$ that stimulates esp. the contraction of uterine muscle and the ejection of milk

oxy·tone \'äk-si-ˌtōn\ *adj* [F *oxyton,* fr. Gk *oxytonos,* fr. *oxys* sharp, acute in pitch + *tonos* tone] **1** *of a Greek word* : having an acute accent on the last syllable **2** : having heavy stress on the last syllable — **oxytone** *n*

oxy·uri·a·sis \ˌäk-si-yù-'rī-ə-səs\ *n* [NL, fr. *Oxyuris,* genus of worms + *-iasis*] : infestation with or disease caused by pinworms (family Oxyuridae)

oy·er and ter·mi·ner \ˌòi-ə-rən-'tər-mə-nər\ *n* [ME, part trans. of AF *oyer et terminer,* lit., to hear and determine] **1** : a commission authorizing a British judge to hear and determine a criminal case at the assizes **2** : a high criminal court in some U.S. states

[1]**oyez** \ō-'yā, -'yes\ *vb imper* [ME, fr. AF, hear ye, imper. pl. of *oir* to hear, fr. L *audire* — more at AUDIBLE] — used by a court or public crier to gain attention before a proclamation

[2]**oyez** *n, pl* **oyes·ses** \-'yes-əz\ : a cry of oyez

oys·ter \'òi-stər\ *n, often attrib* [ME, *oistre,* fr. MF, fr. L *ostrea,* fr. Gk *ostreon;* akin to Gk *ostrakon* shell, *osteon* bone — more at OSSEOUS] **1 a** : any of various marine bivalve mollusks (family Ostreidae) that have a rough irregular shell closed by a single adductor muscle and include important shellfish **b** : any of various mollusks resembling or related to the oysters **2** : something valuable or deserved and won by skill **3** : a small mass of muscle contained in a concavity of the pelvic bone on each side of the back of a fowl **4** : an extremely taciturn person

oyster bed *n* : a place where oysters grow or are cultivated

oyster catcher *n* : any of a genus (*Haematopus*) of wading birds that have stout legs, a heavy wedge-shaped bill, and often black and white plumage

oyster crab *n* : a crab (*Pinnotheres ostreum*) that lives as a commensal in the gill cavity of the oyster

oyster cracker *n* : a small salted usu. round cracker

oyster drill *n* : DRILL 4a

oys·ter·ing \'òi-st(ə-)riŋ\ *n* : the act or business of taking oysters for the market or for food

oys·ter·man \'òi-stər-mən\ *n* : one who gathers, opens, breeds, or sells oysters

oyster plant *n* : SALSIFY

oz *abbr* [It *onza*] ounce; ounces

ozo·ke·rite \ˌō-zō-'ki(ə)r-ˌīt\ *also* **ozo·ce·rite** \-'si(ə)r-\ *n* [G *ozokerit,* fr. Gk *ozein* to smell + *kēros* wax — more at CERUMEN] : a waxy mineral mixture of hydrocarbons that is colorless or white when pure and often of unpleasant odor and is used esp. in making candles and in electrotyping

ozon- *or* **ozono-** *comb form* [ISV, fr. *ozone*] : ozone <*ozonize*>

ozone \'ō-ˌzōn\ *n* [G *ozon,* fr. Gk *ozōn,* prp. of *ozein* to smell — more at ODOR] **1** : a triatomic form of oxygen that is a bluish irritating gas of pungent odor, is formed naturally in the upper atmosphere by a photochemical reaction with solar ultraviolet radiation or generated commercially by a silent electric discharge in ordinary oxygen or air, is a major agent in the formation of smogs, and is used esp. in disinfection and deodorization and in oxidation and bleaching **2** : pure and refreshing air — **ozo·nic** \ō-'zō-nik, -'zän-ik\ *adj* — **ozo·nif·er·ous** \ˌō-zō-'nif-(ə-)rəs\ *adj* — **ozon·ous** \'ō-ˌzō-nəs, ō-'\ *adj*

ozon·ide \'ō-(ˌ)zō-ˌnīd\ *n* : a compound of ozone; *specif* : a compound formed by the addition of ozone to the double or triple bond of an unsaturated organic compound

ozon·ize \-ˌnīz\ *vt* **-ized; -iz·ing 1** : to convert (oxygen) into ozone **2** : to treat, impregnate, or combine with ozone — **ozon·iza·tion** \ˌō-(ˌ)zō-nə-'zā-shən\ *n* — **ozon·iz·er** \'ō-(ˌ)zō-ˌnī-zər\ *n*

ozo·no·sphere \ō-'zō-nə-ˌsfi(ə)r\ *n* : an atmospheric layer at heights of approximately 20 to 30 miles characterized by high ozone content

P

[1]**p** \'pē\ *n, pl* **p's** *or* **ps** \'pēz\ *often cap, often attrib* **1 a** : the 16th letter of the English alphabet **b** : a graphic representation of this letter **c** : a speech counterpart of orthographic *p* **2** : a graphic device for reproducing the letter *p* **3** : one designated *p* esp. as the 16th in order or class **4** [abbr. for *pass*] **a** : a grade rating a student's work as passing **b** : one graded or rated with a P **5** : something shaped like the letter P

[2]**p** *abbr, often cap* **1** page **2** parental generation **3** part **4** participle **5** past **6** pater **7** pawn **8** pence; penny **9** per **10** peseta **11** peso **12** piano **13** pico- **14** pint **15** pipe **16** pitch **17** pole **18** port **19** power **20** pressure **21** pro **22** purl

[3]**p** *symbol* **1** momentum of a particle **2** proton **3** *often cap* the probability of obtaining a result as great as or greater than the observed result in a statistical test if the null hypothesis is true

P *symbol* **1** phosphorus **2** [F *poids*] weight

p- *abbr* para-

pa \'pä, 'pò\ *n* [short for *papa*] : FATHER

[1]**Pa** *abbr* Pennsylvania

[2]**Pa** *symbol* protactinium

PA *abbr* **1** particular average **2** passenger agent **3** Pennsylvania **4** per annum **5** personal appearance **6** power amplifier **7** power of attorney **8** press agent **9** private account **10** protonotary apostolic **11** public address **12** purchasing agent

pa·'an·ga \pä-'äŋ-(g)ə\ *n* [Tongan, lit., seed] — see MONEY table

PABA \'pab-ə, ˌpē-ˌā-'bē-ˌā\ *n* [*para-a*mino-*b*enzoic *a*cid] : PARA-AMINOBENZOIC ACID

pab·u·lum \'pab-yə-ləm\ *n* [L, food, fodder; akin to L *pascere* to feed — more at FOOD] **1** : FOOD; *esp* : a suspension or solution of nutrients in a state suitable for absorption **2** : intellectual sustenance **3** : an insipid piece of writing

Pac *abbr* Pacific

PAC *abbr* Political Action Committee

pa·ca \'päk-ə, 'pak-\ *n* [Pg & Sp, fr. Tupi *páca*] : any of a genus (*Cuniculus*) of large So. and Central American rodents; *esp* : a common edible rodent (*C. paca*) of northern So. America that has a brown coat spotted with white and a head used locally for leather

[1]**pace** \'pās\ *n* [ME *pas,* fr. OF, step, fr. L *passus,* fr. *passus,* pp. of *pandere* to spread — more at FATHOM] **1 a** : rate of movement; *esp* : an established rate of locomotion **b** : rate of progress; *specif*

: parallel rate of growth or development **c** : an example to be emulated; *specif* : first place in a competition <three strokes off the ~ —*Time*> **d** (1) : rate of performance or delivery : TEMPO (2) : rhythmic animation : FLUENCY <writes with color, with zest, and with ~ —Amy Loveman> **e** : ROUTINE <the circus is change of ~ — beauty against our daily ugliness —John Steinbeck> **2** : a manner of walking : TREAD **3 a** : STEP 2a(1) **b** : any of various units of distance based on the length of a human step **4 a** *pl* : an exhibition of skills or capacities <the trainer put the tiger through its ~*s*> **b** : GAIT; *esp* : a fast 2-beat gait (as of the horse) in which the legs move in lateral pairs and support the animal alternately on the right and left legs

[2]**pace** *vb* **paced; pac·ing** *vi* **1 a** : to walk with slow or measured tread **b** : to move along : PROCEED **2** : to go at a pace — used esp. of a horse ~ *vt* **1 a** : to measure by pacing — often used with *off* <*paced* off a 10-yard penalty> **b** : to cover at a walk <could hear him *pacing* the floor> **2** : to cover (a course) by pacing — used of a horse **3 a** : to set or regulate the pace of <~*s* his teaching to his students' abilities> **b** (1) : to go before : PRECEDE (2) : to set an example for : LEAD **c** : to keep pace with

[3]**pace** \'pā-(,)sē\ *prep* [L, abl. of *pac-, pax* peace, permission] : with due respect to <I do not, ~ . . . the correspondents, claim to have made any "discovery" —E. M. Almedingen>

pace car *n* : an automobile that leads the field of competitors through a pace lap but does not participate in the race

pace lap *n* : a lap of an auto racecourse by the entire field of competitors before the start of a race to allow the engines to warm up and to permit a flying start

pace·mak·er \'pā-,smā-kər\ *n* **1 a** : one that sets the pace for another **b** : one that takes the lead or sets an example **2 a** : a body part (as the sinoatrial node of the heart) that serves to establish and maintain a rhythmic activity **b** : an electrical device for stimulating or steadying the heartbeat or reestablishing the rhythm of an arrested heart — **pace·mak·ing** \-kiŋ\ *n*

pac·er \'pā-sər\ *n* **1** : one that paces; *specif* : a horse whose gait is the pace **2** : PACEMAKER

pace·set·ter \'pās-,set-ər\ *n* : PACEMAKER 1a

pa·chi·si \pə-'chē-zē\ *n* [Hindi *pacīsī*] : an ancient board game played with dice and counters on a cruciform board in which players attempt to be the first to reach the home square

pa·chu·co \pə-'chü-(,)kō\ *n, pl* **-cos** [MexSp] : a young usu. underprivileged Mexican-American having a taste for flashy clothes and a special jargon, usu. belonging to a neighborhood gang, and often identified by a small tattoo

pachy·derm \'pak-i-,dərm\ *n* [F *pachyderme*, fr. Gk *pachydermos* thick-skinned, fr. *pachys* thick + *derma* skin; akin to ON *bingr* heap, Skt *bahu* dense, much — more at DERM-] : any of various nonruminant hoofed mammals (as an elephant, a rhinoceros, or a pig) most of which have a thick skin — **pachy·der·mal** \,pak-i-'dər-məl\ *adj*

pachy·der·ma·tous \,pak-i-'dər-mət-əs\ *adj* [deriv. of Gk *pachys* + *dermat-, derma* skin] **1** : of or relating to the pachyderms **2 a** : THICK, THICKENED <~ skin> **b** : CALLOUS, INSENSITIVE — **pachy·der·ma·tous·ly** *adv*

pach·ys·an·dra \,pak-i-'san-drə\ *n* [NL, genus name, fr. Gk *pachys* + NL *-andrus* -androus] : any of a genus (*Pachysandra*) of the box family of evergreen woody trailing plants often used as a ground cover

pachy·tene \'pak-i-,tēn\ *n* [ISV *pachy-* (fr. Gk *pachys*) + *-tene*] : the stage of meiotic prophase which immediately follows the zygotene and in which the paired chromosomes are thickened and visibly divided into chromatids

pa·cif·ic \pə-'sif-ik\ *adj* [ME *pacifique*, fr. L *pacificus*, fr. *pac-, pax* peace + *-i-* + *-ficus* -fic — more at PEACE] **1 a** : tending to lessen conflict : CONCILIATORY **b** : rejecting the use of force as an instrument of policy **2 a** : having a soothing appearance or effect <mild ~ breezes> **b** : mild of temper : PEACEABLE **3** *cap* : of or relating to the Pacific ocean — **pa·cif·i·cal·ly** \-i-k(ə-)lē\ *adv*

syn PACIFIC, PEACEABLE, PEACEFUL, IRENIC, PACIFIST, PACIFISTIC *shared meaning element* : affording or promoting peace. PACIFIC applies chiefly to persons or to utterances, acts, influences, or ideas that tend to maintain peace or to conciliate strife <a naturally *pacific*, sociable man —Glenway Wescott> <a *pacific* policy> PEACEABLE stresses enjoyment of peace as a way of life and often implies absence of all aggressive intent <the police descended on the *peaceable* . . . middle-class assemblage as if they were invading a black ghetto in revolt —Nat Hentoff> PEACEFUL implies freedom not only from strife or contention but from all disturbing influences <and may at last my weary age find out the *peaceful* hermitage —John Milton> IRENIC may describe attitudes and measures likely to allay dispute <the book . . . is written in an *irenic* rather than polemic style —*Times Lit. Supp.*> PACIFIST and PACIFISTIC both stress opposition, and especially active opposition, to war or violence, usually on moral or conscientious grounds. The former is more general in application, being equally applicable to persons or organizations or things (as attitudes, writings, or arguments), while the latter is ordinarily restricted to things <a *pacifist* group on the campus> <*pacifist* critics of the State Department> <a *pacifist* philosophy> <a determinedly *pacifistic* outlook> *ant* bellicose

pac·i·fi·ca·tion \,pas-ə-fə-'kā-shən\ *n* **1** : the act or process of pacifying : the state of being pacified **2** : a treaty of peace

pa·cif·i·ca·tor \pə-'sif-ə-,kāt-ər\ *n* : PACIFIER 1

pa·cif·i·ca·to·ry \pə-'sif-i-kə-,tōr-ē, -,tȯr-\ *adj* : tending to promote peace : CONCILIATORY

pa·cif·i·cism \pə-'sif-ə-,siz-əm\ *n* : PACIFISM — **pa·cif·i·cist** \-səst\ *n*

Pacific time \pə-'sif-ik-\ *n* [*Pacific* ocean] : the time of the 8th time zone west of Greenwich that includes the Pacific coastal region of the U.S. — see TIME ZONE illustration

pac·i·fi·er \'pas-ə-,fī(-ə)r\ *n* **1** : one that pacifies **2** : a usu. nipple-shaped device for babies to suck or bite upon

pac·i·fism \'pas-ə-,fiz-əm\ *n* [F *pacifisme*, fr. *pacifique* pacific] **1** : opposition to war or violence as a means of settling disputes; *specif* : refusal to bear arms on moral or religious grounds **2** : an attitude or policy of nonresistance — **pac·i·fist** \-fəst\ *n*

pac·i·fist \'pas-ə-fəst\ *or* **pac·i·fis·tic** \,pas-ə-'fis-tik\ *adj* **1** : of, relating to, or characteristic of pacifism or pacifists **2** : strongly and actively opposed to conflict and esp. war *syn* see PACIFIC — **pac·i·fis·ti·cal·ly** \,pas-ə-'fis-ti-k(ə-)lē\ *adv*

pac·i·fy \'pas-ə-,fī\ *vt* **-fied; -fy·ing** [ME *pacifien*, fr. L *pacificare*, fr. *pac-, pax* peace] **1 a** : to allay the anger or agitation of : SOOTHE <~ a crying child> **b** : APPEASE, PROPITIATE **2 a** : to restore to a tranquil state : SETTLE <made an attempt to ~ the commotion> **b** : to reduce to a submissive state : SUBDUE <forces moved in to ~ the country> — **pac·i·fi·able** \-,fī-ə-bəl\ *adj*

Pa·cin·i·an corpuscle \pə-,sin-ē-ən-\ *n* [Filippo *Pacini* †1883 It anatomist] : an oval capsule that terminates some sensory nerve fibers esp. in the skin of the hands and feet

[1]**pack** \'pak\ *n, often attrib* [ME, of LG or D origin; akin to MLG & MD *pak* pack, MFlem *pac*] **1 a** : a bundle arranged for convenience in carrying esp. on the back **b** : a group or pile of related objects: as (1) : a number of separate photographic films packed so as to be inserted together into a camera (2) : a set of two or three color films or plates for simultaneous exposure (3) : a stack of theatrical flats arranged in sequence **c** (1) : PACKET (2) : CONTAINER (3) : a compact unitized assembly to perform a specific function **2 a** : the contents of a bundle **b** : a large amount or number : HEAP **c** : a full set of playing cards **3 a** : an act or instance of packing **b** : a method of packing **4 a** : a set of persons with a common interest : CLIQUE **b** : an organized troop (as of cub scouts) **5 a** (1) : a group of domesticated animals trained to hunt or run together (2) : a group of often predatory animals of the same kind <a wolf ~> **b** : an organized group of combat craft <a submarine ~> **6** : a concentrated mass (as of snow) **7** : wet absorbent material for therapeutic application to the body **8 a** : a cosmetic paste for the face **b** : an application or treatment of oils or creams for conditioning the scalp and hair **9** : material used in packing

[2]**pack** *vt* **1 a** : to make into a compact bundle **b** : to fill completely **c** : to fill with packing <~ a joint in a pipe> **d** : to load with a pack <~ a mule> **e** : to put in a protective container <goods ~*ed* for shipment> **2 a** : to crowd together **b** : to increase the density of : COMPRESS **3 a** : to cause or command to go without ceremony <~*ed* him off to school> **b** : to bring to an end : FINISH — used with *up* or *in* <~ up the assignment> <he's ~*ing* it all in — to lead a life of his own —Peter Oakes> **4** : to gather into tight formation : make a pack of (as hounds) **5** : to cover or surround with a pack **6 a** : to transport on foot or on the back of an animal <~ a canoe overland> **b** : to wear or carry as equipment <~ a gun> **c** : to be supplied or equipped with : POSSESS <a storm ~*ing* hurricane winds> **d** : to cause or be capable of making (an impact) <a book that ~*s* a man-sized punch —C. J. Rolo> ~ *vi* **1 a** : to go away without ceremony : DEPART <simply ~*ed* up and left> **b** : QUIT, STOP — used with *up* or *in* <why don't you ~ in, before you kill yourself —Millard Lampell> **2 a** : to stow goods and equipment for transportation **b** : to be suitable for packing <a knit dress ~*s* well> **3 a** : to assemble in a group : CONGREGATE **b** : to crowd together **4** : to become built up or compacted in a layer or mass <the ore ~*ed* into a stony mass> **5 a** : to carry goods or equipment **b** : to travel with one's baggage (as by horse) — **pack·abil·i·ty** \,pak-ə-'bil-ət-ē\ *n* — **pack·able** \'pak-ə-bəl\ *adj*

[3]**pack** *vt* [obs. *pack* (to make a secret agreement)] **1** : to influence the composition of (as a political agency) so as to bring about a desired result <~ a jury> **2** *archaic* : to arrange (the cards in a pack) so as to cheat **3** : to add a pack to (as an automobile) <try to ~ the final price with phony or unordered extras —*Consumer Reports*>

[4]**pack** *n* [perh. fr. obs. *pack* (secret compact)] : an unjustified surcharge or markup added to a price by a dealer

[5]**pack** *adj* [perh. fr. obs. *pack* (to make a secret agreement)] *chiefly Scot* : INTIMATE

[1]**pack·age** \'pak-ij\ *n* **1** *archaic* : the act or process of packing **2 a** : a small or moderate-sized pack : PARCEL **b** : a commodity or a unit of a product uniformly wrapped or sealed **c** : a preassembled unit **3** : a covering wrapper or container **4** : something that suggests a package: as **a** : PACKAGE DEAL **b** : a radio or television series offered for sale at a lump sum **c** : contract benefits gained through collective bargaining **d** (1) : a ready-made computer program (2) : an assembly or apparatus essentially complete and ready for installation or use

[2]**package** *vt* **pack·aged; pack·ag·ing** **1** : to make into a package **2** : to enclose in a package or covering — **pack·ag·er** *n*

package deal *n* **1** : an offer or agreement involving a number of related items or one making acceptance of one item dependent on the acceptance of another **2** : the items offered in a package deal

package store *n* : a store that sells alcoholic beverages only in sealed containers whose contents may not lawfully be drunk on the premises

pack animal *n* : an animal (as a donkey) used for carrying packs

pack·board \'pak-,bō(ə)rd, -,bȯ(ə)rd\ *n* : a usu. canvas-covered light wood or metal frame with shoulder straps used for carrying goods and equipment

packed \'pakt\ *adj* **1 a** : that is crowded or stuffed — often used in combination <an action-*packed* story> **b** : COMPRESSED <hard-*packed* snow> **2** : filled to capacity <played to a ~ house>

pack·er \'pak-ər\ *n* **1** : one that packs: as **a** : a wholesale dealer **b** : an automotive vehicle with a closed body and a compressing device (as for compacting rubbish) in the rear **2 a** : [2]PORTER 1 **b** : one who conveys goods on pack animals

pack·et \'pak-ət\ *n* [MF *pacquet*, of Gmc origin; akin to MD *pak* pack] **1 a** : a number of letters dispatched at one time **b** : a small group, cluster, or mass **2** : a passenger boat carrying mail and cargo on a regular schedule **3 a** : a small bundle or parcel **b** : a small thin package **c** *Brit* : PAY ENVELOPE

pack·horse \'pak-,hȯrs\ *n* : a horse used as a pack animal

pack ice *n* **:** sea ice formed into a mass by the crushing together of pans, floes, and brash

pack·ing \ˈpak-iŋ\ *n* **1 a :** the action or process of packing something; *also* **:** a method of packing **b :** the processing of food and esp. meat for future sale **2 :** material used to pack

pack·ing·house \-ˌhau̇s\ *n* **:** an establishment for slaughtering, processing, and packing livestock into meat, meat products, and by-products; *also* **:** one for processing and packing other foodstuffs — called also *packing plant*

pack·man \ˈpak-mən\ *n* **:** PEDDLER

pack rat *n* **1 :** WOOD RAT; *esp* **:** a large bushy-tailed rodent (*Neotoma cinerea*) of the Rocky Mountain area that has well-developed cheek pouches and hoards food and miscellaneous objects **2 :** one who collects or hoards esp. unneeded items

pack rat 1

pack·sack \ˈpak-ˌsak\ *n* **:** a canvas or leather case held on the back by shoulder straps and used to carry gear when traveling on foot

pack·sad·dle \-ˌsad-ᵊl\ *n* **:** a saddle designed to support loads on the backs of pack animals

pack·thread \-ˌthred\ *n* **:** strong thread or small twine used for sewing or tying packs or parcels

pact \ˈpakt\ *n* [ME, fr. MF, fr. L *pactum*, fr. neut. of *pactus*, pp. of *pacisci* to agree, contract; akin to OE *fōn* to seize, L *pangere* to fix, fasten, Gk *pēgnynai*] **:** [4]COMPACT; *esp* **:** an international treaty

[1]pad \ˈpad\ *n* [origin unknown] **1 a :** a thin flat mat or cushion: as (1) **:** a piece of soft stuffed material used as or under a saddle (2) **:** padding used to shape an article of clothing (3) **:** a guard worn to shield body parts against impact (4) **:** a piece of usu. folded absorbent material (as gauze) used as a surgical dressing or protective covering **b :** a piece of material saturated with ink for inking the surface of a rubber stamp **2 a :** the foot of an animal **b :** the cushioned thickening of the underside of the toes of an animal **3 :** a floating leaf of a water plant **4 :** TABLET **5 a :** a section of an airstrip used for warm-ups, takeoffs, or landings **b :** LAUNCHING PAD **6 a :** living quarters **b :** BED

[2]pad *vt* **pad·ded; pad·ding 1 a :** to furnish with a pad or padding **b :** MUTE, MUFFLE **2 :** to expand or increase with needless or fraudulent matter <~ a short speech> <~ an expense account>

[3]pad *vb* **pad·ded; pad·ding** [perh. fr. MD *paden* to follow a path, fr. *pad* path — more at PATH] *vt* **:** to traverse on foot ~ *vi* **1 :** to go on foot **:** WALK **2 :** to move along with a muffled step

[4]pad *n* [MD *pad*] **1** *dial Brit* **:** PATH **2 :** a horse that moves along at an easy pace **3** *archaic* **:** FOOTPAD

[5]pad *n* [imit.] **:** a soft muffled or slapping sound

pad·ding \ˈpad-iŋ\ *n* **:** material with which something is padded

[1]pad·dle \ˈpad-ᵊl\ *n* [ME *padell*] **1 a :** a usu. wooden implement that has a long handle and a broad flattened blade and that is used to propel and steer a small craft (as a canoe) **b :** an implement that often has a short handle and a broad flat blade and that is used for stirring, mixing, or hitting; *esp* **:** a small wooden or plastic implement used to hit a ball in any of various games (as table tennis) **2 a :** one of the broad boards at the circumference of a paddle wheel or waterwheel **b :** one of a series of broad blades attached to a shaft (as in an ice cream machine) and used for stirring

[2]paddle *vb* **pad·dled; pad·dling** \ˈpad-liŋ, -ᵊl-iŋ\ *vi* **:** to go on or through water by or as if by means of a paddle or paddle wheel ~ *vt* **1 a :** to propel by a paddle **b :** to transport in a paddled craft <*paddled* us to shore in his canoe> **2 a :** to beat or stir with or as if with a paddle (as in washing or dyeing) **b :** to punish with or as if with a paddle — **pad·dler** \ˈpad-lər, -ᵊl-ər\ *n*

[3]paddle *vi* **pad·dled; pad·dling** \ˈpad-liŋ, -ᵊl-iŋ\ [origin unknown] **1 :** to move the hands or feet about in shallow water **2** *archaic* **:** to use the hands or fingers in toying or caressing **3 :** TODDLE — **pad·dler** \ˈpad-lər, -ᵊl-ər\ *n*

pad·dle·ball \ˈpad-ᵊl-ˌbȯl\ *n* **:** a game for 2, 3, or 4 players played on a 1-, 3-, or 4-walled court with a wood or plastic paddle and a ball similar to a tennis ball; *also* **:** the ball used in this game

pad·dle·board \-ˌbō(ə)rd, -ˌbȯ(ə)rd\ *n* **:** a long narrow buoyant board used for riding the surf or in rescuing swimmers

pad·dle·boat \-ˌbōt\ *n* **:** a boat propelled by a paddle wheel

pad·dle·fish \-ˌfish\ *n* **:** any of a family (Polyodontidae) of ganoid fishes; *esp* **:** one (*Polyodon spathula*) of the Mississippi valley that is about four feet long and has a spatula-shaped snout

paddle tennis *n* **:** a game that resembles tennis and is played with a wooden paddle and sponge rubber ball over a low net on a court one half the size of a tennis court

paddle wheel *n* **:** a wheel with paddles, floats, or boards around its circumference used to propel a boat

pad·dock \ˈpad-ək, -ik\ *n* [alter. of ME *parrok*, fr. OE *pearroc;* akin to OHG *pfarrih* enclosure; both fr. a prehistoric Gmc word borrowed fr. (assumed) VL *parricus*] **1 :** a usu. enclosed area used esp. for pasturing or exercising animals; *esp* **:** an enclosure where racehorses are saddled and paraded before a race **2 :** an area at an automobile racecourse where racing cars are parked and often worked on before a race

pad·dy \ˈpad-ē\ *n, pl* **paddies** [Malay *padi*] **1 :** RICE; *esp* **:** threshed unmilled rice **2 :** wet land in which rice is grown

pad·dy wagon \ˈpad-ē-\ *n* [prob. fr. E slang *Paddy* (Irishman, policeman)] **:** PATROL WAGON

padi·shah \ˈpäd-(i-)ˌshä, -(i-)ˌshȯ\ *n* [Per *pādshāh*] **:** a chief ruler **:** SOVEREIGN; *esp* **:** the shah of Iran

pad·lock \ˈpad-ˌläk\ *n* [ME *padlok*, fr. *pad-* (of unknown origin) + *lok* lock] **:** a removable lock with a shackle that can be passed through a staple or link and then secured — **padlock** *vt*

pa·dre \ˈpäd-(ˌ)rā, -rē\ *n* [Sp or It or Pg, lit., father, fr. L *pater* — more at FATHER] **1 :** a Christian clergyman; *esp* **:** PRIEST **2 :** a military chaplain

pa·dro·ne \pə-ˈdrō-nē\ *n, pl* **-nes** *or* **-ni** \-nē\ [It, protector, owner, fr. L *patronus* patron] **1 :** an Italian innkeeper **2 :** one that secures employment for immigrants esp. of Italian extraction

pad·u·a·soy \ˈpaj-(ə-)wə-ˌsȯi\ *n* [alter. of earlier *poudesoy*, fr. F *pou-de-soie*] **:** a corded silk fabric; *also* **:** a garment made of it

pae·an \ˈpē-ən\ *n* [L, hymn of thanksgiving esp. addressed to Apollo, fr. Gk *paian, paiōn*, fr. *Paian, Paiōn*, epithet of Apollo in the hymn] **:** a joyously exultant song or hymn of praise, tribute, thanksgiving, or triumph

paed- *or* **paedo-** *or* **ped-** *or* **pedo-** *comb form* [Gk *paid-, paido-*, fr. *paid-, pais* child, boy — more at FEW] **:** child <*ped*iatric> **:** childhood <*paedo*genesis>

pae·do·gen·e·sis \ˌpēd-ō-ˈjen-ə-səs\ *n* [NL] **:** reproduction by young or larval animals **:** NEOTENY — **pae·do·ge·net·ic** \-jə-ˈnet-ik\ *or* **pae·do·gen·ic** \-ˈjen-ik\ *adj*

pae·do·mor·phic \ˌpēd-ə-ˈmȯr-fik\ *adj* **:** of, relating to, or involving paedomorphosis or paedomorphism

pae·do·mor·phism \-ˌfiz-əm\ *n* **:** retention in the adult of infantile or juvenile characters

pae·do·mor·pho·sis \-ˈmȯr-fə-səs\ *n* [NL] **:** phylogenetic change that involves retention of juvenile characters by the adult

pa·el·la \pä-ˈel-ə, -ˈā(l)-yə\ *n* [Catal, lit., pot, pan, fr. MF *paelle*, fr. L *patella* small pan — more at PATELLA] **:** a saffron-flavored dish containing rice, meat, seafood, and vegetables

pae·on \ˈpē-ən, -ˌän\ *n* [L, fr. Gk *paiōn*, fr. *paian, paiōn* paean] **:** a metrical foot of four syllables with one long and three short syllables (as in classical prosody) or with one stressed and three unstressed syllables (as in English prosody)

pa·gan \ˈpā-gən\ *n* [ME, fr. LL *paganus*, fr. L, country dweller, fr. *pagus* country district; akin to L *pangere* to fix — more at PACT] **1 :** HEATHEN 1; *esp* **:** a follower of a polytheistic religion (as in ancient Rome) **2 :** one who has little or no religion and who delights in sensual pleasures and material goods **:** an irreligious or hedonistic person — **pagan** *adj* — **pa·gan·ish** \-gə-nish\ *adj*

pa·gan·ism \ˈpā-gə-ˌniz-əm\ *n* **1 a :** pagan beliefs or practices **b :** a pagan religion **2 :** the quality or state of being a pagan

pa·gan·ize \-ˌnīz\ *vb* **-ized; -iz·ing** *vt* **:** to make pagan ~ *vi* **:** to become pagan — **pa·gan·iz·er** *n*

[1]page \ˈpāj\ *n* [ME, fr. OF, fr. It *paggio*] **1 a** (1) **:** a youth being trained for the medieval rank of knight and in the personal service of a knight (2) **:** a youth attendant on a person of rank esp. in the medieval period **b :** a boy serving as an honorary attendant at a formal function (as a wedding) **2 :** one employed to deliver messages, assist patrons, serve as a guide, or attend to similar duties

[2]page *vt* **paged; pag·ing 1 :** to wait on or serve in the capacity of a page **2 :** to summon by repeatedly calling out the name of

[3]page *n* [MF, fr. L *pagina;* akin to L *pangere* to fix, fasten] **1 :** one of the leaves of a book, magazine, letter, or manuscript; *also* **:** a single side of one of these leaves **2 a :** a written record **b :** something (as an event) worth being recorded in writing <one of the brightest ~*s* of his life> **3 :** a sizable subdivision of computer memory used chiefly for convenience of reference in programming

[4]page *vb* **paged; pag·ing** *vt* **:** to number or mark the pages of ~ *vi* **:** to turn the pages (as of a book or magazine) esp. in a steady or haphazard manner — usu. used with *through*

pag·eant \ˈpaj-ənt\ *n* [ME *pagyn, padgeant*, lit., scene of a play, fr. ML *pagina*, fr. L, page] **1 a :** a mere show **:** PRETENSE **b :** an ostentatious display **2 :** SHOW, EXHIBITION; *esp* **:** an elaborate colorful exhibition or spectacle often with music that consists of a series of tableaux, of a loosely unified drama, or of a procession usu. with floats **3 :** PAGEANTRY 1

pag·eant·ry \ˈpaj-ən-trē\ *n* **1 :** pageants and the presentation of pageants **2 :** colorful, rich, or splendid display **:** SPECTACLE **3 :** mere show **:** empty display

page boy *n* [[1]*page*] **1 :** a boy serving as a page **2** *usu* **page·boy :** an often shoulder-length hair-do with the ends of the hair turned under in a smooth roll

pag·i·nal \ˈpaj-ən-ᵊl\ *adj* [LL *paginalis*, fr. L *pagina* page] **:** of, relating to, or consisting of pages

pag·i·nate \ˈpaj-ə-ˌnāt\ *vt* **-nat·ed; -nat·ing** [L *pagina* page] **:** [4]PAGE

pag·i·na·tion \ˌpaj-ə-ˈnā-shən\ *n* **1 :** the action of paging **:** the condition of being paged **2 a :** the numbers or marks used to indicate the sequence of pages (as of a book) **b :** the number and arrangement of pages or an indication of these

pa·go·da \pə-ˈgōd-ə\ *n* [Pg *pagode* oriental idol, temple] **:** a Far Eastern tower usu. with roofs curving upward at the division of each of several stories and erected as a temple or memorial

pagoda

pah·la·vi \ˈpal-ə-(ˌ)vē, ˈpäl-\ *n, pl* **pahlavi** *or* **pahlavis** [Per *pahlawī*, fr. Riza Shah *Pahlawī* †1944 Shah of Iran] **1 :** a monetary unit of Iran equal to 100 rials **2 :** a coin representing one pahlavi

Pah·la·vi \ˈpal-ə-(ˌ)vē, ˈpäl-\ *n* [Per *pahlawī*, fr. *Pahlav* Parthia, fr. OPer *Parthava-*] **1 :** the Iranian language of Sassanian Persia — see INDO-EUROPEAN LANGUAGES table **2 :** a script used for writing Pahlavi

paid *past of* PAY

pai–hua \ˈbī-ˈhwä\ *n* [Chin (Pek) *pai*[2] *hua*[4], lit., plain speech] **:** a form of written Chinese based on modern colloquial

pail \ˈpā(ə)l\ *n* [ME *payle, paille*] **1 :** a usu. cylindrical container with a handle **:** BUCKET **2 :** the quantity that a pail contains — **pail·ful** \-ˌfu̇l\ *n*

pail·lette \pī-'(y)et, pā-'yet, pə-'let\ *n* [F, fr. *paille* straw — more at PALLET] **1 :** a small shiny object (as a spangle) applied in clusters as a decorative trimming (as on women's clothing) **2 :** a trimming made of paillettes

[1]**pain** \'pān\ *n* [ME, fr. OF *peine,* fr. L *poena,* fr. Gk *poinē* payment, penalty; akin to Gk *tinein* to pay, *tinesthai* to punish, *timē* price, value, honor] **1 :** PUNISHMENT **2 a :** usu. localized physical suffering associated with bodily disorder (as a disease or an injury) <the ~ of a boil>; *also* **:** a basic bodily sensation induced by a noxious stimulus, received by naked nerve endings, characterized by physical discomfort (as pricking, throbbing, or aching), and typically leading to evasive action **b :** acute mental or emotional distress or suffering **:** GRIEF **3** *pl* **:** the throes of childbirth **4** *pl* **:** trouble, care, or effort taken for the accomplishment of something **5 :** one that irks or annoys or is otherwise troublesome <she's a real ~> ***syn*** see EFFORT — **pain·less** \-ləs\ *adj* — **pain·less·ly** *adv* — **pain·less·ness** *n* — **on pain of** *or* **under pain of :** subject to penalty or punishment of <ordered not to leave the country *on pain of* death> — **pain in the neck :** a source of annoyance **:** NUISANCE

[2]**pain** *vt* **1 :** to make suffer or cause distress to **:** HURT **2** *archaic* **:** to put (oneself) to trouble or exertion ~ *vi* **1** *archaic* **:** SUFFER **2 :** to give or have a sensation of pain

pain·ful \'pān-fəl\ *adj* **pain·ful·ler** \-fə-lər\; **pain·ful·lest** **1 a :** feeling or giving pain **b :** IRKSOME, ANNOYING **2 :** requiring effort or exertion <a long ~ trip> **3** *archaic* **:** CAREFUL, DILIGENT — **pain·ful·ly** \-f(ə-)lē\ *adv* — **pain·ful·ness** \-fəl-nəs\ *n*

pain·kill·er \-ˌkil-ər\ *n* **:** something (as a drug) that relieves pain — **pain·kill·ing** \-iŋ\ *adj*

[1]**pains·tak·ing** \'pān-ˌstā-kiŋ\ *n* **:** the action of taking pains **:** diligent care and effort

[2]**painstaking** *adj* **:** taking pains **:** expending or showing diligent care and effort — **pains·tak·ing·ly** \-kiŋ-lē\ *adv*

[1]**paint** \'pānt\ *vb* [ME *painten,* fr. OF *peint,* pp. of *peindre,* fr. L *pingere* to tattoo, embroider, paint; akin to OE *fāh* variegated, Gk *poikilos* variegated, *pikros* sharp, bitter] *vt* **1 a (1) :** to apply color, pigment, or paint to **(2) :** to color with a cosmetic **b (1) :** to apply with a movement resembling that used in painting **(2) :** to treat with a liquid by brushing or swabbing <~ the wound with iodine> **2 a (1) :** to produce in lines and colors on a surface by applying pigments **(2) :** to depict by such lines and colors **b :** to decorate, adorn, or variegate by applying lines and colors **c :** to produce or evoke as if by painting <~*s* glowing pictures of the farm> **3 :** to touch up or cover over by or as if by painting **4 :** to depict as having specified or implied characteristics <~*s* them whiter than the evidence justifies —Oliver La Farge> ~ *vi* **1 :** to practice the art of painting **2 :** to use cosmetics

[2]**paint** *n* **1 :** the action of painting **:** something produced by painting **2 :** MAKEUP; *esp* **:** a cosmetic to add color **3 a (1) :** a mixture of a pigment and a suitable liquid to form a closely adherent coating when spread on a surface in a thin coat **(2) :** the pigment used in this mixture esp. when in the form of a cake <a box of ~*s*> **b :** an applied coating of paint

paint·brush \'pānt-ˌbrəsh\ *n* **1 :** a brush for applying paint **2 a :** INDIAN PAINTBRUSH 1 **b :** ORANGE HAWKWEED

painted bunting *n* **:** a brightly colored finch (*Passerina ciris*) of the southern U.S.

painted cup *n* **:** INDIAN PAINTBRUSH 1

painted lady *n* **:** a migratory nymphalid butterfly (*Vanessa cardui*) with wings mottled in brown, orange, red, and white

painted trillium *n* **:** a trillium (*Trillium undulatum*) of northeastern No. America that has a solitary flower with white petals streaked with purple

[1]**paint·er** \'pānt-ər\ *n* **:** one that paints: as **a :** an artist who paints **b :** one who applies paint (as to a building) esp. as an occupation

[2]**paint·er** \'pānt-ər\ *n* [ME *paynter,* prob. fr. MF *pendoir, pentoir* clothesline, fr. *pendre* to hang — more at PENDANT] **:** a line used for securing or towing a boat

[3]**pain·ter** *n* [alter. of *panther*] *chiefly South & Midland* **:** COUGAR

paint·er·ly \'pānt-ər-lē\ *adj* **:** of, relating to, or typical of a painter **:** ARTISTIC — **paint·er·li·ness** *n*

painter's colic *n* **:** LEAD COLIC

paint·ing *n* **1 :** a product of painting; *esp* **:** a work produced through the art of painting **2 :** the art or occupation of painting

[1]**pair** \'pa(ə)r, 'pe(ə)r\ *n, pl* **pairs** *also* **pair** [ME *paire,* fr. OF, fr. L *paria* equal things, fr. neut. pl. of *par* equal] **1 a (1) :** two corresponding things designed for use together <a ~ of shoes> **(2) :** two corresponding bodily parts or members <a ~ of hands> **b :** something made up of two corresponding pieces <a ~ of trousers> **2 a :** two similar or associated things: as **(1) :** two mated animals **(2) :** a couple in love, engaged, or married <were a devoted ~> **(3) :** two playing cards of the same value or denomination <held a ~> **(4) :** two horses harnessed side by side **(5) :** two members of a deliberative body that agree not to vote on a specific issue during a time agreed on; *also* **:** an agreement not to vote made by the two members **b :** a partnership esp. of two players in a contest against another partnership **3** *chiefly dial* **:** a set or series of small objects (as beads)

[2]**pair** *vt* **1 a :** to make a pair of — often used with *off* or *up* <~*ed* off the animals> **b :** to arrange a voting pair between **2 :** to arrange in pairs ~ *vi* **1 :** to constitute a member of a pair <a sock that didn't ~> **2 a :** to become associated with another — often used with *off* or *up* <~*ed* up with an old friend> **b :** to become grouped or separated into pairs — often used with *off* <~*ed* off for the next dance>

paired-associate learning *n* **:** the learning of syllables, digits, or words in pairs (as in the study of a foreign language) so that one member of the pair evokes recall of the other

pair of compasses : COMPASS 3c

pair of virginals : VIRGINAL

pair production *n* **:** the simultaneous and complete transformation of a quantum of radiant energy into an electron and a positron when the quantum interacts with the intense electric field near a nucleus

pai·sa \pī-'sä\ *n, pl* **pai·se** \-'sā\ *or* **paisa** *or* **paisas** [Hindi *paisā*] — see *rupee, taka* at MONEY table

pais·ley \'pāz-lē\ *adj, often cap* [*Paisley,* Scotland] **1 :** made typically of soft wool and woven or printed with colorful curved abstract figures **2 :** marked by designs, patterns, or figures typically used in paisley fabrics <a ~ print> — **paisley** *n*

Pai·ute \'pī-ˌ(y)üt\ *n* **1 :** a member of an Amerindian people orig. of Utah, Arizona, Nevada, and California **2 :** the language of the Paiute people

pa·ja·ma \pə-'jäm-ə, -'jam-\ *n* [Hindi *pājāma,* fr. Per *pā* leg + *jāma* garment] **:** PAJAMAS

pa·ja·mas \pə-'jäm-əz, -'jam-\ *n pl* [pl. of *pajama*] **1 :** loose lightweight trousers formerly much worn in the Near East **2 :** a loose usu. two-piece lightweight suit designed for sleeping or lounging

[1]**pal** \'pal\ *n* [Romany *phral, phal* brother, friend, fr. Skt *bhrātṛ* brother; akin to OE *brōthor* brother] **:** a close friend

[2]**pal** *vi* **palled; pal·ling :** to be or become pals **:** associate as pals

[1]**pal·ace** \'pal-əs\ *n* [ME *palais,* fr. OF, fr. L *palatium,* fr. *Palatium,* the Palatine Hill in Rome where the emperors' residences were built] **1 a :** the official residence of a sovereign **b** *chiefly Brit* **:** the official residence of an archbishop or bishop **2 a :** a large stately house **b :** a large public building **c :** a gaudy place for public amusement or refreshment <a movie ~>

[2]**palace** *adj* **1 :** of or relating to a palace **2 :** of, relating to, or involving the intimates of a chief executive <a ~ revolution> <~ politics> **3 :** LUXURIOUS, DELUXE

pal·a·din \'pal-əd-ən\ *n* [F, fr. It *paladino,* fr. ML *palatinus* courtier, fr. L, palace official — more at PALATINE] **1 :** a champion of a medieval prince **2 :** an outstanding protagonist of a cause

Pa·lae·arc·tic *or* **Pa·le·arc·tic** \ˌpā-lē-'ärk-tik, -'ärt-ik, *esp Brit* ˌpal-ē-\ *adj* [*pale-*] **:** of, relating to, or being a biogeographic region or subregion that includes Europe, Asia north of the Himalayas, northern Arabia, and Africa north of the Sahara

pa·laeo·an·throp·ic \ˌpā-lē-(ˌ)ō-an-'thräp-ik, *esp Brit* ˌpal-ē-\ *adj* [*pale-* + Gk *anthrōpos* man] **:** of or relating to hominids more primitive than those included in the species (*Homo sapiens*) that includes recent man

pa·laes·tra \pə-'les-trə\ *n, pl* **-trae** \-(ˌ)trē\ [L, fr. Gk *palaistra,* fr. *palaiein* to wrestle; akin to Gk *pallein* to brandish — more at POLEMIC] **1 :** a school in ancient Greece or Rome for sports (as wrestling) **2 :** GYMNASIUM

pa·lan·quin \ˌpal-ən-'kēn, -'k(w)in; pə-'laŋ-kwən\ *n* [Pg *palanquim,* fr. Jav *pĕlaṅki*] **:** a conveyance formerly used in eastern Asia esp. for one person that consists of an enclosed litter borne on the shoulders of men by means of poles

pal·at·able \'pal-ət-ə-bəl\ *adj* **1 :** agreeable to the palate or taste **2 :** agreeable to the mind — **pal·at·abil·i·ty** \ˌpal-ət-ə-'bil-ət-ē\ *n* — **pal·at·able·ness** *n* — **pal·at·ably** \-blē\ *adv*

syn PALATABLE, APPETIZING, SAVORY, TASTY, TOOTHSOME *shared meaning element* **:** agreeable or pleasant esp. to the sense of taste ***ant*** unpalatable, distasteful

pal·a·tal \'pal-ət-ᵊl\ *adj* **1 :** of or relating to the palate **2 a :** formed with the front of the tongue behind the tip near or touching the hard palate <the \k̲\ in German \ik̲\ *ich* and the \y\ in English *yeast* are ~ sounds> **b (1) :** formed with the blade of the tongue near the hard palate <the ~ sounds represented by *sh* in *she* and *si* in *vision*> **(2)** *of a vowel* **:** FRONT 2 — **palatal** *n* — **pal·a·tal·ly** \-ᵊl-ē\ *adv*

pal·a·tal·iza·tion \ˌpal-ət-ᵊl-ə-'zā-shən\ *n* **1 :** the quality or state of being palatalized **2 :** an act or instance of palatalizing an utterance

pal·a·tal·ize \'pal-ət-ᵊl-ˌīz\ *vt* **-ized; -iz·ing :** to pronounce as or change into a palatal sound

pal·ate \'pal-ət\ *n* [ME, fr. L *palatum*] **1 :** the roof of the mouth separating the mouth from the nasal cavity **2 a :** a usu. intellectual relish **b :** the seat of the sense of taste **3 :** a projection from the base of the lower lip into the throat of a personate corolla ***syn*** see TASTE

pa·la·tial \pə-'lā-shəl\ *adj* [L *palatium* palace] **1 :** of, relating to, or being a palace **2 :** suitable to a palace **:** MAGNIFICENT — **pa·la·tial·ly** \-shə-lē\ *adv* — **pa·la·tial·ness** *n*

pa·lat·i·nate \pə-'lat-ᵊn-ət\ *n* **:** the territory of a palatine

[1]**pal·a·tine** \'pal-ə-ˌtīn\ *adj* [L *palatinus,* fr. *palatium*] **1 a :** of or relating to a palace esp. of a Roman or Holy Roman emperor **b :** PALATIAL **2 a :** possessing royal privileges **b :** of or relating to a palatine or a palatinate

[2]**palatine** \-ˌtīn, *3 is also* -ˌtēn\ *n* [L *palatinus,* fr. *palatinus,* adj.] **1 a :** a high officer of an imperial palace **b :** a feudal lord having sovereign power within his domains **2** *cap* **:** a native or inhabitant of the Palatinate **3** [F, fr. Elisabeth Charlotte of Bavaria †1722 Princess *Palatine*] **:** a fur cape or stole covering the neck and shoulders

[3]**palatine** \-ˌtīn\ *adj* **:** of, relating to, or lying near the palate

[4]**palatine** \-ˌtīn\ *n* **:** either of a pair of bones that are situated behind and between the maxillae and in man are of extremely irregular form

[1]**pa·la·ver** \pə-'lav-ər, -'läv-\ *n* [Pg *palavra* word, speech, fr. LL *parabola* parable, speech] **1 a :** a long parley usu. between persons of different levels of culture or sophistication **b :** CONFERENCE, DISCUSSION **2 a :** idle talk **b :** misleading or beguiling speech

[2]**palaver** *vb* **pa·la·vered; pa·la·ver·ing** \-(ə-)riŋ\ *vi* **1 :** to talk profusely or idly **2 :** PARLEY ~ *vt* **:** to use palaver to **:** CAJOLE

pa·laz·zo \pə-'lät-(ˌ)sō\ *n, pl* **pa·laz·zi** \-(ˌ)sē\ [It, fr. L *palatium* palace] **:** a large imposing building (as a museum or a place of residence) esp. in Italy

[1]**pale** \'pā(ə)l\ *adj* **pal·er; pal·est** [ME, fr. MF, fr. L *pallidus,* fr. *pallēre* to be pale — more at FALLOW] **1 :** deficient in color or intensity of color **:** PALLID <a ~ face> **2 :** not bright or brilliant **:** DIM <a ~ sun shining through the fog> **3 :** FEEBLE, FAINT <a ~

imitation> **4** : deficient in chroma <a ~ pink> — **pale·ly** \'pā(l)-lē\ *adv* — **pale·ness** \-nəs\ *n*

[2]**pale** *vb* **paled; pal·ing** *vi* : to become pale ~ *vt* : to make pale

[3]**pale** *vt* **paled; pal·ing** [ME *palen*, fr. MF *paler*, fr. *pal*] : to enclose with pales : FENCE

[4]**pale** *n* [ME, fr. MF *pal* stake, fr. L *palus* — more at POLE] **1** *archaic* : PALISADE, PALING **2 a** : one of the stakes of a palisade **b** : PICKET **3 a** : a space or field having bounds : ENCLOSURE **b** : a territory or district within certain bounds or under a particular jurisdiction **4** : an area or the limits within which one is privileged or protected (as from censure) <conduct that was beyond the ~> **5** : a perpendicular stripe on a heraldic shield

pale- *or* **paleo-** *or* **palae-** *or* **palaeo-** *comb form* [Gk *palai-*, *palaio-* ancient, fr. *palaios*, fr. *palai* long ago; akin to Gk *tēle* far off, Skt *carama* last] **1** : involving or dealing with ancient forms or conditions <*paleo*botany> **2** : early : primitive : archaic <*Paleo*lithic>

pa·lea \'pā-lē-ə\ *n, pl* **pa·le·ae** \-lē-ˌē\ [NL, fr. L, chaff — more at PALLET] **1** : one of the chaffy scales on the receptacle of many composite plants **2** : the upper bract that with the lemma encloses the flower in grasses — **pa·le·al** \-lē-əl\ *adj*

pale dry *adj* : dry and light colored <*pale dry* ginger ale>

pale·face \'pā(ə)l-ˌfās\ *n* : a white person : CAUCASIAN

pa·leo·bot·a·ny \ˌpā-lē-ō-'bät-ᵊn-ē, -'bät-nē, *esp Brit* ˌpal-ē-\ *n* [ISV] : a branch of botany dealing with fossil plants — **pa·leo·bo·tan·i·cal** \-bə-'tan-i-kəl\ *or* **pa·leo·bo·tan·ic** \-'tan-ik\ *adj* — **pa·leo·bo·tan·i·cal·ly** \-i-k(ə-)lē\ *adv*

Pa·leo·cene \'pā-lē-ə-ˌsēn, *esp Brit* 'pal-ē-\ *adj* [ISV *pale-* + *-cene*] : of, relating to, or being the earliest epoch of the Tertiary or the corresponding system of rocks — **Paleocene** *n*

pa·leo·cli·ma·tol·o·gy \'pā-lē-ō-ˌklī-mə-'täl-ə-jē, *esp Brit* 'pal-ē-\ *n* [ISV] : a science dealing with the climate of past ages

pa·leo·ecol·o·gy \-i-'käl-ə-jē, -e-\ *n* : a branch of ecology that is concerned with the characteristics of ancient environments and with their relationships to ancient plants and animals — **paleo·eco·log·i·cal** \-ˌē-kə-'läj-i-kəl, -ˌek-ə-\ *or* **paleo·eco·log·ic** \-ik\ *adj* — **paleo·ecol·o·gist** \-i-'käl-ə-jəst, -e-\ *n*

pa·leo·ge·og·ra·phy \-jē-'äg-rə-fē\ *n* [ISV] : the geography of ancient times or of a particular past geological epoch — **pa·leo·geo·graph·ic** \-ˌjē-ə-'graf-ik\ *or* **pa·leo·geo·graph·i·cal** \-i-kəl\ *adj* — **pa·leo·geo·graph·i·cal·ly** \-i-k(ə-)lē\ *adv*

pa·le·og·ra·pher \ˌpā-lē-'äg-rə-fər, *esp Brit* ˌpal-ē-\ *n* : a specialist in paleography

pa·le·og·ra·phy \-'äg-rə-fē\ *n* [NL *palaeographia*, fr. Gk *palai-* pale + *-graphia* -graphy] **1 a** : an ancient manner of writing **b** : ancient writings **2** : the study of ancient writings and inscriptions — **pa·leo·graph·ic** \-ə-'graf-ik\ *or* **pa·leo·graph·i·cal** \-i-kəl\ *adj* — **pa·leo·graph·i·cal·ly** \-i-k(ə-)lē\ *adv*

pa·leo·lith \'pā-lē-ə-ˌlith, *esp Brit* 'pal-ē-\ *n* : a Paleolithic stone implement

Pa·leo·lith·ic \ˌpā-lē-ə-'lith-ik, *esp Brit* ˌpal-ē-\ *adj* [ISV] : of or relating to the second period of the Stone Age characterized by rough or chipped stone implements

pa·leo·mag·ne·tism \ˌpā-lē-ō-'mag-nə-ˌtiz-əm, *chiefly Brit* ˌpal-ē-\ *n* **1** : the intensity and direction of residual magnetization in ancient rocks **2** : a study that deals with paleomagnetism — **pa·leo·mag·net·ic** \-mag-'net-ik\ *adj* — **pa·leo·mag·net·i·cal·ly** \-i-k(ə-)lē\ *adv* — **pa·leo·mag·ne·tist** \-nət-əst\ *n*

paleon *abbr* paleontology

pa·le·on·tol·o·gy \ˌpā-lē-ˌän-'täl-ə-jē, -ən-, *esp Brit* ˌpal-ē-\ *n* [F *paléontologie*, fr. *palé-* pale- + Gk *onta* existing things (fr. neut. pl. of *ont-*, *ōn*, prp. of *einai* to be) + F *-logie* -logy — more at IS] : a science dealing with the life of past geological periods as known from fossil remains — **pa·le·on·to·log·i·cal** \-ˌänt-ᵊl-'äj-i-kəl\ *or* **pa·le·on·to·log·ic** \-ik\ *adj* — **pa·le·on·tol·o·gist** \-ˌän-'täl-ə-jəst, -ən-\ *n*

Pa·leo·zo·ic \ˌpā-lē-ə-'zō-ik, *esp Brit* ˌpal-ē-\ *adj* : of, relating to, or being an era of geological history which extends from the beginning of the Cambrian to the close of the Permian and is marked by the culmination of nearly all classes of invertebrates except the insects and in the later epochs of which seed-bearing plants, amphibians, and reptiles first appeared; *also* : relating to the system of rocks formed in this era — see GEOLOGIC TIME table — **Paleozoic** *n*

pa·leo·zo·ol·o·gy \-zō-'äl-ə-jē, -zə-'wäl-\ *n* [F *paléozoologie*, fr. *palé-* pale- + *zoologie* zoology, fr. NL *zoologia*] : a branch of paleontology dealing with ancient and fossil animals — **pa·leo·zoo·log·i·cal** \-ˌzō-ə-'läj-i-kəl\ *adj*

pal·et \pā-'let, 'pā-lət\ *n* [*pale* (palea) + *-et*] : PALEA

pal·ette \'pal-ət\ *n* [F, fr. MF, dim. of *pale* spade, shovel, fr. L *pala*] **1** : a thin oval or rectangular board or tablet which a painter holds and on which he mixes pigments **2 a** : the set of colors put on the palette **b** (1) : a particular range, quality, or use of color (2) : a comparable range, quality, or use of available elements esp. in another art (as music)

palette knife *n* : a knife with a flexible steel blade and no cutting edge used to mix colors or to apply colors (as to a painting)

pale western cutworm *n* : a noctuid moth (*Agrotis orthogonia*) whose larva is a serious pest on grains in the central U.S.

pal·frey \'pȯl-frē\ *n, pl* **palfreys** [ME, fr. OF *palefrei*, fr. ML *palafredus*, fr. LL *paraveredus* post-horse for secondary roads, fr. Gk *para-* beside, subsidiary + L *veredus* post-horse, fr. a Gaulish word akin to W *gorwydd* horse; akin to OIr *rīadaim* I ride — more at PARA-, RIDE] *archaic* : a saddle horse other than a war-horse; *esp* : a light easy-gaited horse suitable for a woman

Pa·li \'päl-ē\ *n* [Skt *pāli* row, series of Buddhist sacred texts] : an Indic language used as the liturgical and scholarly language of Theravada Buddhism — see INDO-EUROPEAN LANGUAGES table

pa·limp·sest \'pal-əm(p)-ˌsest, pə-'lim(p)-\ *n* [L *palimpsestus*, fr. Gk *palimpsēstos* scraped again, fr. *palin* + *psēn* to rub, scrape — more at SAND] : writing material (as a parchment or tablet) used one or more times after earlier writing has been erased

pal·in·drome \'pal-ən-ˌdrōm\ *n* [Gk *palindromos* running back again, fr. *palin* back, again + *dramein* to run; akin to Gk *polos* axis, pole — more at POLE, DROMEDARY] : a word, verse, or sentence (as "Able was I ere I saw Elba") or a number (as 1881) that reads the same backward or forward — **pal·in·drom·ic** \ˌpal-ən-'drō-mik\ *adj*

pal·ing \'pā-liŋ\ *n* **1** : a fence of pales or pickets **2** : wood for making pales **3** : a pale or picket for a fence

pal·in·gen·e·sis \ˌpal-ən-'jen-ə-səs\ *n* [NL, fr. Gk *palin* again + L *genesis*] : METEMPSYCHOSIS

pal·in·ge·net·ic \-jə-'net-ik\ *adj* **1** : of or relating to palingenesis **2** : of, relating to, or being biological characters (as the gill slits in a human embryo) that are derivations from distant ancestral forms rather than adaptations of recent origin

pal·in·ode \'pal-ə-ˌnōd\ *n* [Gk *palinōidia*, fr. *palin* back + *aeidein* to sing — more at ODE] **1** : an ode or song recanting or retracting something in an earlier poem **2** : a formal retraction

[1]**pal·i·sade** \ˌpal-ə-'sād\ *n* [F *palissade*, deriv. of L *palus* stake — more at POLE] **1 a** : a fence of stakes esp. for defense **b** : a long strong stake pointed at the top and set close with others as a defense **2** : a line of bold cliffs

[2]**palisade** *vt* **-sad·ed; -sad·ing** : to surround or fortify with palisades

palisade cell *n* : a cell of palisade parenchyma

palisade parenchyma *n* : a layer of columnar cells rich in chloroplasts found beneath the upper epidermis of foliage leaves — called also *palisade layer, palisade mesophyll, palisade tissue;* compare SPONGY PARENCHYMA

pal·ish \'pā-lish\ *adj* : somewhat pale

[1]**pall** \'pȯl\ *n* [ME, cloak, mantle, fr. OE *pæll*, fr. L *pallium*] **1** : PALLIUM 1b **2 a** : a square of linen usu. stiffened with cardboard that is used to cover the chalice **b** (1) : a heavy cloth draped over a coffin (2) : a coffin esp. when holding a body **3** : something that covers or conceals; *esp* : an overspreading element that produces an effect of gloom <a ~ of thick black smoke>

[2]**pall** *vt* : to cover with a pall : DRAPE

[3]**pall** *vb* [ME *pallen*, short for *appallen* to become pale — more at APPALL] *vi* **1** : to lose strength or effectiveness **2** : to lose in interest or attraction **3** : to become tired of something ~ *vt* **1** : to cause to become insipid **2** : to deprive of pleasure in something by satiating ***syn*** see SATIATE

Pal·la·di·an \pə-'lād-ē-ən, -'läd-\ *adj* : of or relating to a revived classic style in architecture based on the works of Andrea Palladio — **Pal·la·di·an·ism** \-ˌiz-əm\ *n*

[1]**pal·la·di·um** \pə-'lād-ē-əm\ *n* [L, fr. Gk *palladion*, fr. *Pallad-*, *Pallas*] **1** *cap* : a statue of Pallas Athena whose preservation was believed to ensure the safety of Troy **2** *pl* **pal·la·dia** \-ē-ə\ : SAFEGUARD

[2]**palladium** *n* [NL, fr. *Pallad-*, *Pallas*, an asteroid] : a silver-white ductile malleable metallic element of the platinum group that is used esp. in electrical contacts, as a catalyst, and in alloys — see ELEMENT table — **pal·la·dous** \pə-'lād-əs\ *adj*

Pal·las \'pal-əs\ *n* [L *Pallad-*, *Pallas*, fr. Gk] : ATHENE

pall·bear·er \'pȯl-ˌbar-ər, -ˌber-\ *n* [[1]*pall*] **1** : a person who helps to carry the coffin at a funeral **2** : a member of the immediate escort or honor guard of the coffin who does not actually help to carry it

[1]**pal·let** \'pal-ət\ *n* [ME *pailet*, fr. (assumed) MF *paillet*, fr. *paille* straw, fr. L *palea* chaff, straw; akin to Skt *palāva* chaff] **1** : a straw-filled tick or mattress **2** : a small, hard, or temporary bed

[2]**pallet** *n* [ME *palette*, lit., small shovel — more at PALETTE] **1** : a wooden flat-bladed instrument **2** : a lever or surface in a timepiece that receives an impulse from the escapement wheel and imparts motion to a balance or pendulum **3** : a portable platform for handling, storing, or moving materials and packages (as in warehouses, factories, or vehicles)

pal·let·ize \'pal-ət-ˌīz\ *vt* **-ized; -iz·ing** : to place on, transport, or store by means of pallets — **pal·let·iza·tion** \ˌpal-ət-ə-'zā-shən\ *n* — **pal·let·iz·er** \'pal-ət-ˌī-zər\ *n*

pal·lette \pa-'let\ *n* [alter. of *palette*] : one of the plates at the armpits of a suit of armor — see ARMOR illustration

pal·li·al \'pal-ē-əl\ *adj* [NL *pallium*] **1** : of or relating to the cerebral cortex **2** : of, relating to, or produced by a mantle of a mollusk

pal·liasse \pal-'yas\ *n* [modif. of F *paillasse*, fr. *paille* straw] : a thin straw mattress used as a pallet

pal·li·ate \'pal-ē-ˌāt\ *vt* **-at·ed; -at·ing** [LL *palliatus*, pp. of *palliare* to cloak, conceal, fr. *pallium* cloak] **1** : to reduce the violence of (a disease) : ABATE **2** : to cover by excuses and apologies **3** : to moderate the intensity of <trying to ~ the boredom> — **pal·li·a·tion** \ˌpal-ē-'ā-shən\ *n* — **pal·li·a·tor** \'pal-ē-ˌāt-ər\ *n*

[1]**pal·lia·tive** \'pal-ē-ˌāt-iv, 'pal-yət-\ *adj* : serving to palliate <~ surgery> — **pal·lia·tive·ly** *adv*

[2]**palliative** *n* : something that palliates

pal·lid \'pal-əd\ *adj* [L *pallidus* — more at PALE] **1** : deficient in color : WAN <a ~ countenance> **2** : lacking sparkle or liveliness : DULL <a ~ entertainment> — **pal·lid·ly** *adv* — **pal·lid·ness** *n*

pal·li·um \'pal-ē-əm\ *n, pl* **-lia** \-ē-ə\ *or* **-li·ums** [L] **1 a** : a draped rectangular cloth worn as a cloak by men of ancient Greece and Rome **b** : a white woolen band with pendants in front and back worn over the chasuble by a pope or archbishop as a symbol of full episcopal authority — see VESTMENT illustration **2** [NL, fr. L, cloak] **a** : CEREBRAL CORTEX **b** : the mantle of a mollusk, brachiopod, or bird

pall–mall \'pel-'mel, 'pal-'mal, *US often* 'pȯl-'mȯl\ *n* [MF *pallemaille*, fr. It *pallamaglio*, fr. *palla* ball (of Gmc origin; akin to OHG *balla* ball) + *maglio* mallet, fr. L *malleus* — more at BALL, MAUL] : a 17th century game in which each player attempts to drive

---

ə abut	ᵊ kitten	ər further	a back	ā bake	ä cot, cart
au̇ out	ch chin	e less	ē easy	g gift	i trip	ī life
j joke	ŋ sing	ō flow	ȯ flaw	ȯi coin	th thin	th this
ü loot	u̇ foot	y yet	yü few	yu̇ furious	zh vision

a wooden ball with a mallet down an alley and through a raised ring in as few strokes as possible; *also* : the alley in which it is played
pal·lor \'pal-ər\ *n* [L, fr. *pallēre* to be pale — more at FALLOW] : deficiency of color esp. of the face : PALENESS
pal·ly \'pal-ē\ *adj* : sharing the relationship of pals : INTIMATE
1palm \'päm, 'pälm\ *n* [ME, fr. OE; akin to OHG *palma* palm tree; both fr. a prehistoric NGmc-WGmc word borrowed fr. L *palma* palm of the hand, palm tree; fr. the resemblance of the tree's leaves to the outstretched hand] **1** : any of a family (Palmae, the palm family) of mostly tropical or subtropical monocotyledonous trees, shrubs, or vines with usu. a simple stem and a terminal crown of large pinnate or fan-shaped leaves **2** : a leaf of the palm as a symbol of victory or rejoicing; *also* : a branch (as of laurel) similarly used **3** : a symbol of triumph; *also* : VICTORY, TRIUMPH **4** : an addition to a military decoration in the form of a palm frond esp. to indicate a second award of the basic decoration — **pal·ma·ceous** \pal-'mā-shəs, pä(l)-'mā-\ *adj* — **palm·like** \'pä(l)m-,līk\ *adj*
2palm *n* [ME *paume*, fr. MF, fr. L *palma;* akin to OE *flōr* floor] **1** : the somewhat concave part of the human hand between the bases of the fingers and the wrist or the corresponding part of the forefoot of a lower mammal **2** : a flat expanded part esp. at the end of a base or stalk: as **a** : the blade of an oar or paddle **b** (1) : the flat inner face of an anchor fluke (2) : 2FLUKE 1 **3** [L *palmus*, fr. *palma*] : a unit of length based on the breadth or length of the hand **4** : something (as a part of a glove) that covers the palm of the hand **5** : an act of palming (as of cards)
3palm \'päm, 'pälm\ *vt* **1** : to touch with the palm: as **a** : to stroke with the palm or hand **b** : to shake hands with **c** : to allow (a basketball) to come to rest momentarily in the hand while dribbling thus committing a violation **2 a** : to conceal in or with the hand <~ a card> **b** : to pick up stealthily <likely to ~ small merchandise in a store> **3** : to impose by fraud <a second imposter to be ~*ed* upon you —Sir Walter Scott>
pal·mar \'pal-mər, 'pä(l)m-ər\ *adj* : of, relating to, or involving the palm of the hand
pal·ma·ry \'pal-mə-rē, 'pä(l)m-ə-\ *adj* [L *palmarius* deserving the palm, fr. *palma*] : OUTSTANDING, BEST
pal·mate \'pal-,māt, 'pä(l)m-,āt\ *also* **pal·mat·ed** \-,māt-əd, -,āt-\ *adj* : resembling a hand with the fingers spread: **a** : having lobes radiating from a common point <a ~ leaf> **b** (1) *of an aquatic bird* : having the anterior toes united by a web (2) : having the distal portion broad, flat, and lobed <a ~ antler> — **pal·mate·ly** *adv* — **pal·ma·tion** \pal-'mā-shən, pä(l)-'mā-\ *n*
pal·mat·i·fid \pal-'mat-ə-fəd, pä(l)-'mat-, -,fid\ *adj* [ISV] : cleft in a palmate manner <a ~ leaf>
-palmed \'pämd, 'pälmd\ *adj comb form* : having (such) a palm or palms <leather-*palmed* gloves>
palm·er \'päm-ər, 'päl-mər\ *n* : a person wearing two crossed palm leaves as a sign of his pilgrimage to the Holy Land
palm·er·worm \-,wərm\ *n* : a caterpillar that suddenly appears in great numbers devouring herbage; *esp* : a No. American moth (*Dichomeris lingulella*) whose larva is destructive to fruit trees
pal·met·to \pal-'met-(,)ō *also* pä(l)-\ *n, pl* **-tos** *or* **-toes** [modif. of Sp. *palmito*, fr. *palma* palm, fr. L] **1** : any of several usu. low-growing fan-leaved palms; *esp* : CABBAGE PALMETTO **2** : strips of the leaf blade of a palmetto used in weaving
palm·ist \'päm-əst, 'päl-məst\ *n* [prob. back-formation fr. *palmistry*] : one who practices palmistry
palm·ist·ry \'päm-ə-strē, 'päl-mə-\ *n* [ME *pawmestry*, prob. fr. *paume* palm + *maistrie* mastery] : the art or practice of reading a person's character or future from the markings on his palms

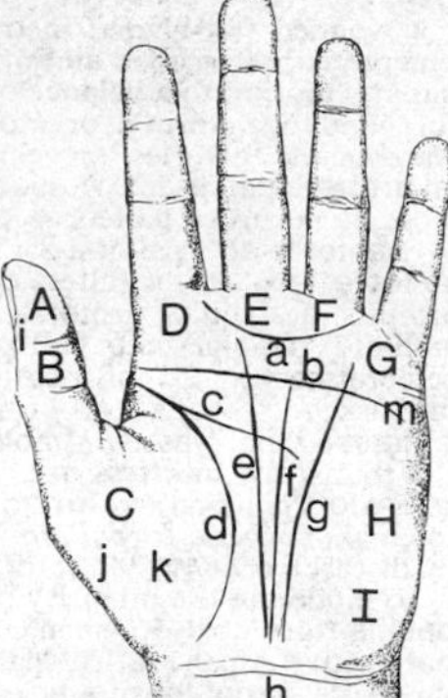

features examined in palmistry: *A* first phalanx, *B* second phalanx, *C* Mount of Venus, *D* Mount of Jupiter, *E* Mount of Saturn, *F* Mount of Apollo, *G* Mount of Mercury, *H* Mount of Mars, *I* Mount of the Moon, *a* ring of Venus, *b* line of the heart, *c* line of the head, *d* line of life, *e* line of fate, *f* line of fortune, *g* line of health, *h* bracelets, *i* will, *j* reason, *k* love, *m* line of marriage

pal·mi·tate \'pal-mə-,tāt, 'pä(l)m-ə-\ *n* : a salt or ester of palmitic acid
pal·mit·ic acid \(,)pal-,mit-ik-, (,)pä(l)-\ *n* [ISV, fr. *palmitin*] : a waxy crystalline fatty acid $C_{16}H_{32}O_2$ occurring free or in the form of esters (as glycerides) in most fats and fatty oils and in several essential oils and waxes
pal·mi·tin \'pal-mət-ən, 'pä(l)m-ət-\ *n* [F *palmitine*, prob. fr. *palmite* pith of the palm tree, fr. Sp *palmito*, fr. *palma* palm, fr. L] : an ester of glycerol and palmitic acid; *esp* : a solid ester found with stearin and olein in animal fats
palm off *vt* : to pass off
palm oil *n* : an edible fat obtained from the flesh of the fruit of several palms and used esp. in soap, candles, and lubricating greases
Palm Sunday *n* [fr. the palm branches strewn in Christ's way] : the Sunday before Easter celebrated in commemoration of Christ's triumphal entry into Jerusalem
palmy \'päm-ē, 'päl-mē\ *adj* **palm·i·er; -est 1** : abounding in or bearing palms **2** : marked by prosperity : FLOURISHING
pal·my·ra \pal-'mī-rə\ *n* [Pg *palmeira*, fr. *palma* palm, fr. L] : a tall African fan-leaved palm (*Borassus flabellifer*) cultivated for its hard resistant wood, fiber, and sugar-rich sap
pal·o·mi·no \,pal-ə-'mē-(,)nō, -nə(-w)\ *n, pl* **-nos** [AmerSp, fr. Sp, like a dove, fr. L *palumbinus*, fr. *palumbes* ringdove; akin to Gk *peleia* dove, L *pallēre* to be pale — more at FALLOW] : a slender-legged horse of largely Arabian ancestry and of a light tan or cream color with a short coupling and a flaxen or white mane and tail
palp \'palp\ *n* [NL *palpus*] : PALPUS
pal·pa·ble \'pal-pə-bəl\ *adj* [ME, fr. LL *palpabilis*, fr. L *palpare* to stroke, caress — more at FEEL] **1** : capable of being touched or felt : TANGIBLE **2** : easily perceptible : NOTICEABLE **3** : easily perceptible by the mind : MANIFEST ***syn*** see PERCEPTIBLE ***ant*** impalpable — **pal·pa·bil·i·ty** \,pal-pə-'bil-ət-ē\ *n* — **pal·pa·bly** \'pal-pə-blē\ *adv*
pal·pal \'pal-pəl\ *adj* : of, relating to, or functioning as a palpus
1pal·pate \'pal-,pāt\ *vt* **pal·pat·ed; pal·pat·ing** [prob. back-formation fr. *palpation*, fr. L *palpation- palpatio*, fr. *palpatus*, pp. of *palpare*] : to examine by touch esp. medically ***syn*** see TOUCH — **pal·pa·tion** \pal-'pā-shən\ *n*
2palpate *adj* [NL *palpatus*, fr. *palpus*] : having a palpus
pal·pe·bral \pal-'pē-brəl\ *adj* [LL *palpebralis*, fr. L *palpebra* eyelid; akin to L *palpare*] : of, relating to, or located on or near the eyelids
pal·pi·tant \'pal-pət-ənt\ *adj* : marked by trembling or throbbing
pal·pi·tate \'pal-pə-,tāt\ *vi* **-tat·ed; -tat·ing** [L *palpitatus*, pp. of *palpitare*, freq. of *palpare* to stroke] : to beat rapidly and strongly : THROB — **pal·pi·ta·tion** \,pal-pə-'tā-shən\ *n*
pal·pus \'pal-pəs\ *n, pl* **pal·pi** \-,pī, -(,)pē\ [NL, fr. L, caress, soft palm of the hand; akin to L *palpare*] : a segmented usu. tactile or gustatory process on an arthropod mouthpart
pals·grave \'pȯlz-,grāv\ *n* [D *paltsgrave*] : COUNT PALATINE 1b
pal·sied \'pȯl-zēd\ *adj* : affected with palsy
1pal·sy \'pȯl-zē\ *n, pl* **palsies** [ME *parlesie*, fr. MF *paralisie*, fr. L *paralysis*] **1** : PARALYSIS **2** : a condition marked by uncontrollable tremor of the body or a part
2palsy *vt* **pal·sied; pal·sy·ing** : to affect with or as if with palsy
palsy–walsy \,pal-zē-'wal-zē\ *adj* [redupl. of *palsy* (pally), fr. *pals*, pl. of *pal*] *slang* : appearing to be very intimate with another
pal·ter \'pȯl-tər\ *vi* **pal·tered; pal·ter·ing** \-t(ə-)riŋ\ [origin unknown] **1** : to act insincerely or deceitfully : EQUIVOCATE **2** : HAGGLE, CHAFFER ***syn*** see LIE — **pal·ter·er** \-tər-ər\ *n*
pal·try \'pȯl-trē\ *adj* **pal·tri·er; -est** [obs. *paltry* (trash)] **1** : INFERIOR, TRASHY **2** : MEAN, DESPICABLE **3** : TRIVIAL — **pal·tri·ness** *n*
pa·lu·dal \pə-'lüd-ᵊl, 'pal-yəd-ᵊl\ *adj* [L *palud-*, *palus* marsh; akin to Skt *palvala* pond] : of or relating to marshes or fens : MARSHY
pal·u·dism \'pal-yə-,diz-əm\ *n* [ISV, fr. L *palud-*, *palus*] : MALARIA
paly \'pā-lē\ *adj* : somewhat pale : PALLID
pal·y·nol·o·gy \,pal-ə-'näl-ə-jē\ *n* [Gk *palynein* to sprinkle, fr. *palē* fine meal — more at POLLEN] : a branch of science dealing with pollen and spores — **pal·y·no·log·i·cal** \-nə-'läj-i-kəl\ *or* **pal·y·no·log·ic** \-ik\ *adj* — **pal·y·no·log·i·cal·ly** \-i-k(ə-)lē\ *adv* — **pal·y·nol·o·gist** \-'näl-ə-jəst\ *n*
pam *abbr* pamphlet
pam·pa \'pam-pə\ *n, pl* **pam·pas** \-pəz, -pəs\ [AmerSp, fr. Quechua & Aymara, plain] : an extensive generally grass-covered plain of temperate So. America east of the Andes : PRAIRIE
pam·pe·an \'pam-pē-ən, pam-'\ *adj* : of or relating to the pampas of So. America or their Indian inhabitants
pam·per \'pam-pər\ *vt* **pam·pered; pam·per·ing** \-p(ə-)riŋ\ [ME *pamperen*, prob. of D origin; akin to Flem *pamperen* to pamper] **1** *archaic* : to cram with rich food : GLUT **2 a** : to treat with extreme or excessive care and attention <~*ed* their guests> **b** : GRATIFY, HUMOR <enabled him to ~ his wanderlust —*New Yorker*> ***syn*** see INDULGE ***ant*** chasten — **pam·per·er** \-pər-ər\ *n*
pam·pe·ro \pam-'pe(ə)r-(,)ō, päm-\ *n, pl* **-ros** [AmerSp, fr. *pampa*] : a strong cold wind from the west or southwest that sweeps over the pampas
pam·phlet \'pam(p)-flət\ *n* [ME *pamflet* unbound booklet, fr. *Pamphilus seu De Amore* Pamphilus or On Love, popular Latin love poem of the 12th cent.] : an unbound printed publication with no cover or with a paper cover
1pam·phle·teer \,pam(p)-flə-'ti(ə)r\ *n* : a writer of pamphlets attacking something or urging a cause
2pamphleteer *vi* **1** : to write and publish pamphlets **2** : to engage in partisan arguments indirectly in writings
1pan \'pan\ *n* [ME *panne*, fr. OE; akin to OHG *phanna* pan; both fr. a prehistoric WGmc-NGmc word borrowed fr. L *patina*, fr. Gk *patanē*; akin to L *patēre* to be open — more at FATHOM] **1 a** : a usu. broad, shallow, and open container for domestic use (as for warming, baking, or frying) **b** : any of various similar usu. metal receptacles: as (1) : the hollow part of the lock in old guns or pistols that receives the priming (2) : either of the receptacles in a pair of scales (3) : a round shallow metal container for separating metal (as gold) from waste by washing **2 a** (1) : a natural basin or depression in land (2) : a similar artificial basin (as for evaporating brine) **b** : a drifting fragment of the flat thin ice that forms in bays or along the shore **3** : HARDPAN 1 **4** *slang* : FACE **5** : a harsh criticism
2pan *vb* **panned; pan·ning** *vi* **1** : to wash earth, gravel, or other materials in a pan in search of metal (as gold) **2** : to yield precious metal in the process of panning ~ *vt* **1 a** : to wash in a pan for the purpose of separating heavy particles **b** : to separate (as gold) by panning **c** : to place in a pan **2** : to criticize severely
3pan \'pän\ *n* [Hindi *pān*, fr. Skt *parna* wing, leaf — more at FERN] **1** : a betel leaf **2** : a masticatory of betel nut, lime, and pan
4pan \'pan\ *vb* **panned; pan·ning** [*panorama*] *vi* **1** : to rotate a motion-picture or television camera so as to keep an object in the picture or secure a panoramic effect **2** *of a camera* : to undergo panning ~ *vt* : to cause to pan
5pan \'pan\ *n* : the process of panning a motion-picture or television camera
1Pan \'pan\ *n* [L, fr. Gk] : a Greek god of shepherds and hunters and the traditional inventor of the panpipe
2Pan *abbr* Panama
pan- *comb form* [Gk, fr. *pan*, neut. of *pant-*, *pas* all, every; akin to Skt *śaśvat* all, every, *śvayati* he swells] **1** : all : completely <*pan*chromatic> **2 a** : involving all of a (specified) group <*Pan*-

American> **b :** advocating or involving the union of a (specified) group <*Pan-Asian*> **3 :** whole : general <*pan*leucopenia>

pan·a·cea \ˌpan-ə-ˈsē-ə\ *n* [L, fr. Gk *panakeia,* fr. *pan-* + *akeisthai* to heal, fr. *akos* remedy — more at AUTACOID] **:** a remedy for all ills or difficulties **:** CURE-ALL — **pan·a·ce·an** \-ˈsē-ən\ *adj*

pa·nache \pə-ˈnash, -ˈnäsh\ *n* [MF *pennache,* fr. OIt *pennacchio,* fr. LL *pinnaculum* small wing — more at PINNACLE] **1 :** an ornamental tuft (as of feathers) esp. on a helmet **2 :** dash or flamboyance in style and action **:** VERVE

pa·na·da \pə-ˈnäd-ə\ *n* [Sp, fr. *pan* bread, fr. L *panis* — more at FOOD] **:** a paste of flour or bread crumbs and water or stock used as a base for sauce or a binder for forcemeat or stuffing

pan·a·ma \ˈpan-ə-ˌmä, -ˌmȯ\ *n, often cap* [AmerSp *panamá,* fr. *Panama,* Central America] **:** a lightweight hat of natural-colored straw hand-plaited of narrow strips from the young leaves of the jipijapa; *also* **:** a machine-made imitation of this

Pan–Amer·i·can \ˌpan-ə-ˈmer-ə-kən\ *adj* **:** of, relating to, or involving the independent republics of No. and So. America

Pan American Day *n* **:** April 14 observed as the anniversary of the founding of the Pan American Union in 1890

Pan–Amer·i·can·ism \-kə-ˌniz-əm\ *n* **:** a movement for greater cooperation among the Pan-American nations esp. in defense, commerce, and cultural relations

pan·a·tela \ˌpan-ə-ˈtel-ə\ *n* [Sp, fr. AmerSp, a long thin biscuit, deriv. of L *panis* bread] **:** a long slender straight-sided cigar rounded off at the sealed end

[1]**pan·cake** \ˈpan-ˌkāk\ *n* **:** a flat cake made of thin batter and cooked (as on a griddle) on both sides

[2]**pancake** *vb* **pan·caked; pan·cak·ing** *vi* **:** to make a pancake landing ~ *vt* **:** to cause to pancake

Pan–Cake \ˈpan-ˌkāk\ *trademark* — used for a cosmetic in semimoist cake form

pancake landing *n* **:** a landing in which the airplane is leveled off higher than for a normal landing causing it to stall and drop in an approximately horizontal position with little forward motion

pan·chax \ˈpan-ˌkaks\ *n* [NL] **:** any of numerous small brilliantly colored Old World killifishes (genus *Aplocheilus*) often kept in the tropical aquarium

Pan·chen Lama \ˌpän-chən-\ *n* [*Panchen* fr. Chin (Pek) *pan*[1] *ch'an*[2]] **:** the lama next in rank to the Dalai Lama

pan·chro·mat·ic \ˌpan-krō-ˈmat-ik\ *adj* [ISV] **:** sensitive to light of all colors in the visible spectrum <~ film>

pan·cra·ti·um \pan-ˈkrā-shē-əm\ *n* [L, fr. Gk *pankration,* fr. *pan-* + *kratos* strength — more at HARD] **:** an ancient Greek athletic contest involving both boxing and wrestling

pan·cre·as \ˈpaŋ-krē-əs, ˈpan-\ *n* [NL, fr. Gk *pankreas,* fr. *pan-* + *kreas* flesh, meat — more at RAW] **:** a large compound racemose gland of vertebrates that secretes digestive enzymes and the hormone insulin — **pan·cre·at·ic** \ˌpaŋ-krē-ˈat-ik, ˌpan-\ *adj*

pancreat- *or* **pancreato-** *comb form* [NL, fr. Gk *pankreat-, pancreas*] **:** pancreas <*pancreat*ic>

pan·cre·atec·to·my \ˌpaŋ-krē-ə-ˈtek-tə-mē, ˌpan-\ *n* **:** surgical removal of all or part of the pancreas — **pan·cre·atec·to·mized** \-ˌmīzd\ *adj*

pancreatic juice *n* **:** a clear alkaline secretion of pancreatic enzymes that is poured into the duodenum and acts on food already acted on by the gastric juice and saliva

pan·cre·atin \pan-ˈkrē-ət-ən; ˈpaŋ-krē-, ˈpan-\ *n* **:** a mixture of enzymes from the pancreatic juice; *also* **:** a preparation containing such a mixture

pan·cre·ati·tis \ˌpaŋ-krē-ə-ˈtīt-əs, ˌpan-\ *n, pl* **-atit·i·des** \-ˈtit-ə-ˌdēz\ [NL] **:** inflammation of the pancreas

pan·creo·zy·min \-krē-ō-ˈzī-mən\ *n* [*pancre*as + *-o-* + *zym-* + *-in*] **:** a hormonal product of the duodenal mucosa that stimulates pancreatic enzyme production

pan·da \ˈpan-də\ *n* [F, fr. native name in Nepal] **1 :** a long-tailed Himalayan carnivore (*Ailurus fulgens*) that is related to and closely resembles the American raccoon, has long fur, and is basically rusty or chestnut in color with mottling and barring of black **2 :** a large black-and-white mammal (*Ailuropoda melanoleuca*) of western China that suggests a bear but is related to the raccoons

panda 2

pan·da·nus \pan-ˈdān-əs, -ˈdan-əs\ *n, pl* **-ni** \-ˌī\ [NL, genus name, fr. Malay *pandan* screw pine] **:** SCREW PINE

Pan·da·rus \ˈpan-də-rəs\ *n* [L, fr. Gk *Pandaros*] **:** a Lycian archer in the Trojan War who in medieval legend procures Cressida for Troilus

pan·dect \ˈpan-ˌdekt\ *n* [LL *Pandectae,* the Pandects, digest of Roman civil law (6th cent. A.D.), fr. L, pl. of *pandectes* encyclopedic work, fr. Gk *pandektēs* all-receiving, fr. *pan-* + *dechesthai* to receive; akin to Gk *dokein* to seem, seem good — more at DECENT] **1 :** a complete code of the laws of a country or system of law **2 :** a treatise covering an entire subject

[1]**pan·dem·ic** \pan-ˈdem-ik\ *adj* [LL *pandemus,* fr. Gk *pandēmos* of all the people, fr. *pan-* + *dēmos* people — more at DEMAGOGUE] **:** occurring over a wide geographic area and affecting an exceptionally high proportion of the population <~ malaria>

[2]**pandemic** *n* **:** a pandemic outbreak of a disease

Pan·de·mo·ni·um \ˌpan-də-ˈmō-nē-əm\ *n* [NL, fr. Gk *pan-* + *daimōn* evil spirit — more at DEMON] **1 :** the capital of Hell in Milton's *Paradise Lost* **2 :** the infernal regions **:** HELL **3** *not cap* **:** a wild uproar **:** TUMULT

[1]**pan·der** \ˈpan-dər\ *n* [ME *Pandare* Pandarus, fr. L *Pandarus*] **1 a :** a go-between in love intrigues **b :** PIMP **2 :** someone who caters to or exploits the weaknesses of others

[2]**pander** *vi* **pan·dered; pan·der·ing** \-d(ə-)riŋ\ **:** to act as a pander; *esp* **:** to provide gratification for others' desires <the audience is vulgar and stupid, you've got to ~ to them —Herman Wouk> — **pan·der·er** \-dər-ər\ *n*

pan·dit \ˈpan-dət, ˈpən-\ *n* [Hindi *pandit,* fr. Skt *pandita*] **:** a wise or learned man in India — often used as an honorary title

P and L *abbr* profit and loss

pan·do·ra \pan-ˈdōr-ə, -ˈdȯr-\ *n* [It, fr. LL *pandura* 3-stringed lute] **:** BANDORE

Pan·do·ra's box \pan-ˌdōr-əz-, -ˌdȯr-\ *n* [fr. the box, sent by the gods with Pandora as a gift to Epimetheus, which she was forbidden to open and which loosed a swarm of evils upon mankind when she opened it out of curiosity] **:** a prolific source of troubles

pan·dow·dy \pan-ˈdau̇d-ē\ *n, pl* **-dies** [origin unknown] **:** a deep-dish spiced apple dessert sweetened with sugar, molasses, or maple syrup and covered with a rich crust

pan·dy \ˈpan-dē\ *vt* **pan·died; pan·dy·ing** [prob. fr. L *pande,* imper. sing. of *pandere* to spread out (the hand); command of the schoolmaster to the boy — more at FATHOM] *Brit* **:** to punish (a schoolboy) with a blow on the palm of the hand <came in . . . and *pandied* me because I was not writing my theme —James Joyce>

pane \ˈpān\ *n* [ME *pan, pane* strip of cloth, pane, fr. MF *pan,* fr. L *pannus* cloth, rag — more at VANE] **1 :** a piece, section, or side of something: as **a :** a framed sheet of glass in a window or door **b :** one of the sides of a nut or bolt head **2 :** one of the sections into which a sheet of postage stamps is cut for distribution

pan·e·gy·ric \ˌpan-ə-ˈjir-ik, -ˈjī-rik\ *n* [L *panegyricus,* fr. Gk *panēgyrikos,* fr. *panēgyrikos* of or for a festival assembly, fr. *panēgyris* festival assembly, fr. *pan-* + *agyris* assembly; akin to Gk *ageirein* to gather — more at GREGARIOUS] **:** a eulogistic oration or writing; *also* **:** formal or elaborate praise *syn* see ENCOMIUM — **pan·e·gy·ri·cal** \-ˈjir-i-kəl, -ˈjī-ri-\ *adj* — **pan·e·gy·ri·cal·ly** \-k(ə-)lē\ *adv*

pan·e·gy·rist \ˌpan-ə-ˈjir-əst, -ˈjī-rəst\ *n* **:** EULOGIST

[1]**pan·el** \ˈpan-ᵊl\ *n* [ME, piece of cloth, slip of parchment, jury schedule, fr. MF, piece of cloth, piece, prob. fr. (assumed) VL *pannellus,* dim. of L *pannus* cloth] **1 a (1) :** a schedule containing names of persons summoned as jurors **(2) :** the group of persons so summoned **(3) :** JURY 1 **b (1) :** a group of persons selected for some service (as investigation or arbitration) <a ~ of experts> **(2) :** a group of persons who discuss before an audience a topic of usu. political or social interest; *also* **:** PANEL DISCUSSION **(3) :** a group of entertainers or guests engaged as players in a quiz or guessing game on a radio or television program **2 :** a separate or distinct part of a surface: as **a :** a fence section **:** HURDLE **b (1) :** a thin usu. rectangular board set in a frame (as in a door) **(2) :** a usu. sunken or raised section of a surface set off by a margin **(3) :** a flat usu. rectangular piece of construction material (as plywood or precast masonry) made to form part of a surface **c :** a vertical section of fabric (as a gore) **d :** any of several units of construction of an airplane wing surface **3 :** a thin flat piece of wood on which a picture is painted; *also* **:** a painting on such a surface **4 a :** a section of a switchboard **b :** a flat often insulating support (as for computer hardware or parts of an electrical device) usu. with control handles on one face **c :** a usu. vertical mount for controls or dials (as of instruments of measurement)

[2]**panel** *vt* **-eled** *or* **-elled; -el·ing** *or* **-el·ling :** to furnish or decorate with panels <*paneled* the living room>

panel discussion *n* **:** a formal discussion by a panel of a topic of public interest

panel heating *n* **:** space heating by means of wall, floor, baseboard, or ceiling panels with embedded electric conductors or hot-air or hot-water pipes

pan·el·ing *n* **:** panels joined in a continuous surface; *esp* **:** decorative wood panels so joined

pan·el·ist \ˈpan-ᵊl-əst\ *n* **:** a member of a discussion or advisory panel or of a radio or television panel

panel truck *n* **:** a small light motortruck with a fully enclosed body

pan·e·tela *or* **pan·e·tel·la** *var of* PANATELA

pan·fish \ˈpan-ˌfish\ *n* **:** a small food fish (as a sunfish) usu. taken with hook and line and not available on the market

pan·ful \ˈpan-ˌfu̇l\ *n* **:** as much or as many as a pan will hold

[1]**pang** \ˈpaŋ\ *n* [origin unknown] **1 :** a brief piercing spasm of pain **2 :** a sharp attack of mental anguish <~*s* of remorse>

[2]**pang** *vt* **:** to cause to have pangs **:** TORMENT

pan·gen·e·sis \(ˈ)pan-ˈjen-ə-səs\ *n* [NL] **:** a hypothetical mechanism of heredity in which the cells throw off particles that circulate freely throughout the system, multiply by subdivision, and collect in the reproductive products or in buds so that the egg or bud contains particles from all parts of the parent — **pan·ge·net·ic** \ˌpan-jə-ˈnet-ik\ *adj*

Pan·gloss·ian \pan-ˈgläs-ē-ən, paŋ-, -ˈglȯs-\ *adj* [*Pangloss,* optimistic tutor in Voltaire's *Candide* (1759)] **:** marked by the view that all is for the best in this best of possible worlds

pan·go·la grass \pan-ˈgō-lə-, paŋ-\ *n* [*pangola,* fr. native name in So. Africa] **:** a rapid-growing perennial grass (*Digitaria decumbens*) of southern Africa that has been introduced into the southern U.S. as a pasture grass

pan·go·lin \ˈpaŋ-gə-lən; pan-ˈgō-lən, paŋ-\ *n* [Malay *pĕngguling*] **:** any of several Asiatic and African edentate mammals (*Manis* or related genera of the order Pholidota) having the body covered with large imbricated horny scales

[1]pan·han·dle \'pan-ˌhan-dᵊl\ *n* **:** a narrow projection of a larger territory (as a state) <the Texas ~>

pangolin

[2]panhandle *vb* **pan·han·dled; pan·han·dling** \-ˌhan-(d)liŋ, dᵊl-iŋ\ [back-formation fr. *panhandler,* prob. fr. *panhandle,* n.; fr. the extended forearm] *vi* **:** to stop people on the street and ask for food or money **:** BEG ~ *vt* **1 :** to accost on the street and beg from **2 :** to get by panhandling — **pan·han·dler** \-(d)lər, -dᵊl-ər\ *n*

Pan·hel·len·ic \ˌpan-hə-'len-ik\ *adj* **1 :** of or relating to all Greece or all the Greeks **2 :** of or relating to the Greek-letter sororities or fraternities in American colleges and universities or to an association representing them

pan·hu·man \(ˈ)pan-'hyü-mən, -'yü-\ *adj* **:** of or relating to all humanity <the ~ problem of evil —R. K. Merton>

[1]pan·ic \'pan-ik\ *adj* [F *panique,* fr. Gk *panikos,* lit., of Pan, fr. *Pan*] **1 :** of, relating to, or resembling the mental or emotional state believed induced by the god Pan <~ fear> **2 :** of, relating to, or arising from a panic <a wave of ~ buying> **3 :** of or relating to the god Pan

[2]panic *n* **1 :** a sudden overpowering fright; *esp* **:** a sudden unreasoning terror often accompanied by mass flight **2 :** a sudden widespread fright concerning financial affairs and resulting in a depression in values caused by violent measures for protection of property (as securities) **3** *slang* **:** something very funny **4 :** a shortage of narcotics on the market ***syn*** see FEAR — **pan·icky** \'pan-i-kē\ *adj*

[3]panic *vb* **pan·icked** \-ikt\; **pan·ick·ing** *vt* **1 :** to affect with panic **2 :** to produce demonstrative appreciation on the part of <~ an audience with a gag> ~ *vi* **:** to be affected with panic

panic button *n* **:** something setting off a precipitous emergency response <there was no pushing of *panic buttons* at the White House, no rushing of troops —J. C. Harsch>

pan·ic grass \'pan-ik-\ *n* [ME *panik,* fr. MF or L; MF *panic* foxtail millet, fr. L *panicum,* fr. *panus* swelling, ear of millet] **:** any of various grasses (*Panicum* or related genera) of which some are important forage and cereal grasses

pan·i·cle \'pan-i-kəl\ *n* [L *panicula,* fr. dim. of *panus* swelling] **1 :** a compound racemose inflorescence — see INFLORESCENCE illustration **2 :** a pyramidal loosely branched flower cluster — **pan·i·cled** \-kəld\ *adj* — **pa·nic·u·late** \pa-'nik-yə-lət, pə-\ *adj*

pan·ic–strick·en \'pan-ik-ˌstrik-ən\ *adj* **:** overcome with panic

pan·i·cum \'pan-i-kəm\ *n* [NL, genus name, fr. L, panic grass] **:** any of a large and widely distributed genus (*Panicum*) of grasses that have a very diverse habit and 1- to 2-flowered spikelets disposed in a panicle

Pan·ja·bi \ˌpən-'jäb-ē, -'jab-\ *n* [Hindi *pañjābī,* fr. *pañjābī* of Punjab] **1 :** an Indic language of the Punjab **2 :** PUNJABI 1

pan·jan·drum \pan-'jan-drəm\ *n, pl* **-drums** *also* **-dra** \-drə\ [Grand *Panjandrum,* burlesque title of an imaginary personage in some nonsense lines by Samuel Foote] **:** a powerful personage or pretentious official

pan·leu·co·pe·nia \ˌpan-ˌlü-kə-'pē-nē-ə\ *n* [NL] **:** an acute usu. fatal viral epizootic disease of cats characterized by fever, diarrhea and dehydration, and extensive destruction of white blood cells

pan·mic·tic \(ˈ)pan-'mik-tik\ *adj* [*pan-* + Gk *miktos,* verbal of *mignynai* to mix] **:** of, relating to, or exhibiting panmixia

pan·mix·ia \-'mik-sē-ə\ *n* [NL, fr. *pan-* + Gk *mixis* act of mingling, mating, fr. *mignynai* to mix — more at MIX] **:** random mating within a breeding population

panne \'pan\ *n* [F, fr. OF *penne, panne* fur used for lining, fr. L *pinna* feather, wing — more at PEN] **1 :** a silk or rayon velvet with lustrous pile flattened in one direction **2 :** a heavy silk or rayon satin with high luster and waxy smoothness

pan·nier *or* **pan·ier** \'pan-yər, 'pan-ē-ər\ *n* [ME *panier,* fr. MF, fr. L *panarium,* fr. *panis* bread — more at FOOD] **1 :** a large basket; *esp* **:** one often carried on the back of an animal or the shoulders of a person **2 a :** one of a pair of hoops formerly used to expand women's skirts at the sides **b :** an overskirt draped at the sides of a skirt for an effect of fullness

pan·ni·kin \'pan-i-kən\ *n* [[1]*pan* + *-nikin* (as in *cannikin*)] *Brit* **:** a small pan or cup

pa·no·cha \pə-'nō-chə\ *or* **pa·no·che** \-chē\ *var of* PENUCHE

pan·o·plied \'pan-ə-plēd\ *adj* **:** dressed in or having a panoply

pan·o·ply \'pan-ə-plē\ *n, pl* **-plies** [Gk *panoplia,* fr. *pan-* + *hopla* arms, armor, pl. of *hoplon* tool, weapon — more at HOPLITE] **1 a :** a full suit of armor **b :** ceremonial attire **2 :** something forming a protective covering **3 a :** a magnificent or impressive array <the full ~ of a military funeral> **b :** a display of all appropriate appurtenances <has the ~ of science fiction . . . but it is not true science fiction —Isaac Asimov>

pan·ora·ma \ˌpan-ə-'ram-ə, -'räm-\ *n* [*pan-* + Gk *horama* sight, fr. *horan* to see — more at WARY] **1 a :** CYCLORAMA 1 **b :** a picture exhibited a part at a time by being unrolled before the spectator **2 a :** an unobstructed or complete view of a region in every direction **b :** a comprehensive presentation of a subject <a ~ of American history> **c :** RANGE **3 :** a mental picture of a series of images or events — **pan·oram·ic** \-'ram-ik\ *adj* — **pan·oram·i·cal·ly** \-i-k(ə-)lē\ *adv*

pan out *vi* [[2]*pan*] **:** to turn out; *esp* **:** SUCCEED <the signs revealed that the experiment wasn't *panning out* — Ronald Reagan>

pan·pipe \'pan-ˌpīp\ *n* [*Pan,* its traditional inventor] **:** a primitive wind instrument consisting of a graduated series of short vertical pipes bound together with the mouthpieces in an even row — often used in pl.

Pan–Slav·ism \(ˈ)pan-'släv-ˌiz-əm, -'slav-\ *n* **:** a political and cultural movement orig. emphasizing the cultural ties between the Slavic peoples but later associated with Russian expansionist policies — **Pan–Slav·ic** \-'slav-ik, -'släv-\ *adj* — **Pan–Slav·ist** \-'släv-əst, -'slav-\ *n*

pan·sy \'pan-zē\ *n, pl* **pansies** [MF *pensée,* fr. *pensée* thought, fr. fem. of *pensé,* pp. of *penser* to think, fr. L *pensare* to ponder — more at PENSIVE] **1 :** a garden plant (*Viola tricolor hortensis*) derived chiefly from the wild pansy of Europe by hybridizing the latter with other wild violets; *also* **:** its flower **2 a :** an effeminate youth **b :** a male homosexual

panpipe

[1]pant \'pant\ *vb* [ME *panten,* fr. MF *pantaisier,* fr. (assumed) VL *phantasiare* to have hallucinations, fr. Gk *phantasioun,* fr. *phantasia* appearance, imagination — more at FANCY] *vi* **1 a :** to breathe quickly, spasmodically, or in a labored manner **b :** to run panting <~*ing* along beside the bicycle> **c :** to move with or make a throbbing or puffing sound **2 :** to long eagerly **:** YEARN **3 :** THROB, PULSATE ~ *vt* **:** to utter with panting **:** GASP

[2]pant *n* **1 a :** a panting breath **b :** the visible movement of the chest accompanying such a breath **2 :** a throbbing or puffing sound

[3]pant *adj* **:** of or relating to pants <a ~ leg>

pant- *or* **panto-** *comb form* [MF, fr. L, fr. Gk, fr. *pant-, pas* — more at PAN-] **:** all <*panto*logy>

Pan·ta·gru·el \ˌpant-ə-'grü-əl; pan-'tag-rə-wəl, -ˌwel\ *n* [F] **:** the huge son of Gargantua in Rabelais's *Pantagruel* — **Pan·ta·gru·el·ian** \ˌpant-ə-grü-'el-ē-ən, (ˌ)pan-ˌtag-rə-'wel-\ *adj* — **Pan·ta·gru·el·ism** \ˌpant-ə-'grü-əl-ˌiz-əm; pan-'tag-rə-wəl-ˌiz-əm, -ˌwel-\ *n* — **Pan·ta·gru·el·ist** \-əst\ *n*

pan·ta·lets *or* **pan·ta·lettes** \ˌpant-ᵊl-'ets\ *n pl* [*pantaloons*] **:** long drawers with a ruffle at the bottom of each leg worn by women and children in the first half of the 19th century

pan·ta·loon \ˌpant-ᵊl-'ün\ *n* [MF & OIt; MF *Pantalon,* fr. OIt *Pantaleone, Pantalone*] **1 a** *or* **pan·ta·lo·ne** \-ᵊl-'ō-nē\ *cap* **:** a character in the commedia dell'arte that is usu. a skinny old dotard who wears spectacles, slippers, and a tight-fitting combination of trousers and stockings **b :** a buffoon in pantomimes **2** *pl* **a :** wide breeches worn in England during the reign of Charles II **b :** close-fitting trousers usu. having straps passing under the instep and worn esp. in the 19th century

pant·dress \'pant-ˌdres\ *n* **:** a dress having a divided skirt

pan·tech·ni·con \pan-'tek-ni-kən\ *n* [short for *pantechnicon van,* fr. *pantechnicon* (storage warehouse)] *Brit* **:** [3]VAN 1

pan·the·ism \'pan(t)-thē-ˌiz-əm\ *n* [F *panthéisme,* fr. *panthéiste* pantheist, fr. E *pantheist,* fr. *pan-* + *-theist*] **1 :** a doctrine that equates God with the forces and laws of the universe **2 :** the worship of all gods of different creeds, cults, or peoples indifferently; *also* **:** toleration of worship of all gods (as at certain periods of the Roman empire) — **pan·the·ist** \-thē-əst\ *n* — **pan·the·is·tic** \ˌpan(t)-thē-'is-tik\ *or* **pan·the·is·ti·cal** \-ti-kəl\ *adj* — **pan·the·is·ti·cal·ly** \-ti-k(ə-)lē\ *adv*

pan·the·on \'pan(t)-thē-ˌän, -ən\ *n* [ME *Panteon,* a temple at Rome, fr. L *Pantheon,* fr. Gk *pantheion* temple of all the gods, fr. neut. of *pantheios* of all gods, fr. *pan-* + *theos* god] **1 :** a temple dedicated to all the gods **2 :** a building serving as the burial place of or containing memorials to famous dead **3 :** the gods of a people; *esp* **:** the officially recognized gods **4 :** a group of illustrious persons

pan·ther \'pan(t)-thər\ *n, pl* **panthers** *also* **panther** [ME *pantere,* fr. OF, fr. L *panthera,* fr. Gk *panthēr*] **1 :** LEOPARD: as **a :** a leopard of a hypothetical exceptionally large fierce variety **b :** a leopard of the black color phase **2 :** COUGAR **3 :** JAGUAR

pant·ie *or* **panty** \'pant-ē\ *n, pl* **pant·ies** [*pants*] **:** a woman's or child's undergarment covering the lower trunk and made with closed crotch and very short legs — usu. used in pl.

pantie girdle *n* **:** a woman's girdle with a sewed-in or detachable crotch made with or without garters and bones

pan·tile \'pan-ˌtīl\ *n* [[1]*pan*] **1 :** a roofing tile whose cross section is an ogee curve **2 :** a roofing tile of which the cross section is an arc of a circle and which is laid with alternate convex and concave surfaces uppermost — **pan·tiled** \-ˌtīld\ *adj*

pantiles 1

pant·isoc·ra·cy \ˌpant-ə-'säk-rə-sē, ˌpant-ˌī-\ *n, pl* **-cies** [*pant-* + *isocracy* (equal rule), fr. Gk *isokratia,* fr. *is-* + *-kratia* -cracy] **:** a utopian community in which all rule equally — **pant·iso·crat·ic** \ˌpant-ˌī-sə-'krat-ik\ *or* **pant·iso·crat·i·cal** \-'krat-i-kəl\ *adj* — **pant·isoc·ra·tist** \ˌpant-ə-'säk-rət-əst, ˌpant-ˌī-\ *n*

pan·to·fle \pan-'tōf-əl, -'täf-, -'tüf-; 'pant-ə-fəl\ *n* [ME *pantufle,* fr. MF *pantoufle*] **:** SLIPPER

pan·to·graph \'pant-ə-ˌgraf\ *n* [F *pantographe,* fr. *pant-* + *-graphe* -graph] **1 :** an instrument for copying (as a map) on a predetermined scale consisting of four light rigid bars jointed in parallelogram form; *also* **:** any of various extensible devices of similar construction (as for use as brackets or gates) **2 :** an electrical trolley carried by a collapsible and adjustable frame — **pan·to·graph·ic** \ˌpant-ə-'graf-ik\ *adj*

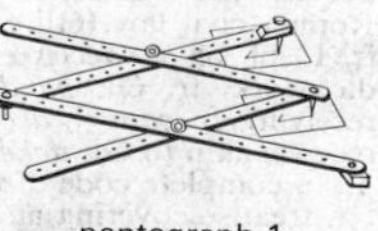
pantograph 1

[1]pan·to·mime \'pant-ə-ˌmīm\ *n* [L *pantomimus,* fr. *pant-* + *mimus* mime] **1 :** PANTOMIMIST **2 a :** an ancient Roman dramatic performance featuring a solo dancer and a narrative chorus **b :** any of various dramatic or dancing performances in which a story is told by expressive bodily or facial movements of the performers **3 :** conveyance of a story by bodily or facial movements esp. in drama or dance **4 :** the art or genre of conveying a story by bodily movements only — **pan·to·mim·ic** \ˌpant-ə-ˈmim-ik\ *adj*

2pantomime *vb* **-mimed; -mim·ing** *vt* **:** to represent by pantomime ~ *vi* **:** to engage in pantomime

pan·to·mim·ist \ˈpant-ə-ˌmīm-əst, -ˌmim-\ *n* **1 :** an actor or dancer in pantomimes **2 :** a composer of pantomimes

pan·to·the·nate \ˌpant-ə-ˈthen-ˌāt, pan-ˈtäth-ə-ˌnāt\ *n* **:** a salt or ester of pantothenic acid

pan·to·then·ic acid \ˌpant-ə-ˌthen-ik-\ *n* [Gk *pantothen* from all sides, fr. *pant-, pas* all — more at PAN-] **:** a viscous oily acid $C_9H_{17}NO_5$ of the vitamin B complex found in all living tissues

pan·trop·ic \(ˈ)pan-ˈträp-ik\ *adj* **:** occurring or distributed throughout the tropical regions of the earth

pan·try \ˈpan-trē\ *n, pl* **pantries** [ME *panetrie,* fr. MF *paneterie,* fr. OF, fr. *panetier* servant in charge of the pantry, irreg. fr. *pan* bread, fr. L *panis* — more at FOOD] **1 :** a room or closet used for storing provisions or glassware and china or from which food is brought to the table **2 :** a room (as in a hotel or hospital) for preparation of cold foods on order

pan·try·man \-trē-mən\ *n* **:** a man in charge of or working in a pantry (as in a hotel or hospital)

pants \ˈpan(t)s\ *n pl* [short for *pantaloons*] **1 :** TROUSERS **2** *chiefly Brit* **:** men's short underpants **3 :** PANTIE — **with one's pants down :** in an embarrassing position (as of being unprepared to act)

pant·suit \ˈpant-ˌsüt\ *n* **:** a woman's ensemble consisting usu. of a long jacket and tailored pants of the same material

pants suit \ˈpan(t)s-ˌsüt, ˈpant-ˌ\ *n* **:** PANTSUIT

panty hose *n pl* **:** a one-piece undergarment for women consisting of hosiery combined with a panty

panty raid *n* **:** a raid on a women's dormitory by college boys usu. to obtain panties as trophies

panty·waist \ˈpant-ē-ˌwāst\ *n* **1 :** a child's garment consisting of short pants buttoned to a waist **2 :** SISSY — **pantywaist** *adj*

Pan·urge \ˈpan-ˌərj, pa-ˈnu̇(ə)rzh\ *n* [F] **:** a witty rascal and companion of Pantagruel in Rabelais's *Pantagruel*

1pan·zer \ˈpan-zər, ˈpän(t)-sər\ *adj* [G *panzer-,* fr. *panzer* coat of mail, armor, fr. OF *pancière,* fr. *pance* belly, paunch — more at PAUNCH] **:** of or relating to an armored unit and esp. a panzer division

2panzer *n* **:** TANK 3

panzer division *n* **:** a German armored division

1pap \ˈpap\ *n* [ME *pappe*] **1** *chiefly dial* **:** NIPPLE, TEAT **2 :** something shaped like a nipple

2pap *n* [ME] **1 :** a soft food for infants or invalids **2 :** political patronage **3 :** something lacking solid value or substance

pa·pa \ˈpäp-ə, *chiefly Brit* pə-ˈpä\ *n* [F (baby talk)] **:** FATHER

Papa — a communications code word for the letter *p*

pa·pa·cy \ˈpā-pə-sē\ *n, pl* **-cies** [ME *papacie,* fr. ML *papatia,* fr. LL *papa* pope — more at POPE] **1 :** the office of pope **2 :** a succession or line of popes **3 :** the term of a pope's reign **4** *cap* **:** the system of government of the Roman Catholic Church of which the pope is the supreme head

pa·pa·in \pə-ˈpā-ən, -ˈpī-ən\ *n* [ISV, fr. *papaya*] **:** a proteinase in the juice of unripe papaya that is used esp. as a tenderizer for meat and in medicine

pa·pal \ˈpā-pəl\ *adj* [ME, fr. MF, fr. ML *papalis,* fr. LL *papa*] **:** of or relating to a pope or to the Roman Catholic Church — **pa·pal·ly** \-pə-lē\ *adv*

papal cross *n* **:** a figure of a cross having a long upright shaft and three crossbars with the longest at or somewhat above its middle and the two other successively shorter crossbars above the longest one — see CROSS illustration

Pa·pa·ni·co·laou test \ˌpäp-ə-ˈnē-kə-ˌlau̇-, ˌpap-ə-ˈnik-ə-\ *n* [George N. *Papanicolaou* †1962 Am medical scientist] **:** PAP SMEAR

pa·pa·raz·zo \ˌpäp-ə-ˈrät-(ˌ)sō\ *n, pl* **-raz·zi** \-(ˌ)sē\ **:** a news reporter or photographer who doggedly searches for a story that can be sensationalized

pa·pav·er·ine \pə-ˈpav-ə-ˌrēn, -(ə-)rən\ *n* [ISV, fr. L *papaver* poppy] **:** a crystalline alkaloid $C_{20}H_{21}NO_4$ that is found in opium and is used chiefly as an antispasmodic because of its ability to relax smooth muscle

pa·paw *n* [prob. modif. of Sp *papaya*] **1** \pə-ˈpȯ\ **:** PAPAYA **2** \ˈpäp-(ˌ)ȯ, ˈpȯp-\ **:** a No. American tree (*Asimina triloba*) of the custard-apple family with purple flowers and a yellow edible fruit; *also* **:** its fruit

pa·pa·ya \pə-ˈpī-ə\ *n* [Sp, of AmerInd origin; akin to Otomac *papai*] **:** a tropical American tree (*Carica papaya* of the family Caricaceae, the papaya family) with large oblong yellow edible fruit; *also* **:** its fruit

1pa·per \ˈpā-pər\ *n* [ME *papir,* fr. MF *papier,* fr. L *papyrus* papyrus, paper, fr. Gk *papyros* papyrus] **1 a** (1) **:** a felted sheet of usu. vegetable fibers laid down on a fine screen from a water suspension (2) **:** a similar sheet of other material (as plastic) **b :** a piece of paper **2 a :** a piece of paper containing a written or printed statement **:** DOCUMENT <pedigree ~*s*> **b :** a piece of paper containing writing or print **c :** a formal written composition often designed for publication and often intended to be read aloud <presented a scholarly ~ at the meeting> **d :** a piece of written schoolwork <had to write a ~ a week in English class> **3 :** a paper container or wrapper **4 :** NEWSPAPER **5 :** the negotiable notes or instruments of commerce **6 :** WALLPAPER **7 :** TICKETS; *esp* **:** free passes — **on paper 1 :** in theory <the plan looks good *on paper*> **2 :** figured at face value <*on paper* he was worth nearly a million dollars>

2paper *vb* **pa·pered; pa·per·ing** \ˈpā-p(ə-)riŋ\ *vt* **1** *archaic* **:** to put down or describe in writing **2 :** to fold or enclose in paper **3 :** to cover or line with paper; *esp* **:** to apply wallpaper to **4 :** to fill by giving out free passes <~ the theater for opening night> **5 :** to cover (an area) with advertising bills, circulars, or posters ~ *vi* **:** to hang wallpaper — **pa·per·er** \-pər-ər\ *n*

3paper *adj* **1 a :** made of paper, paperboard, or papier-mâché <a ~ bag> **b :** PAPERY **2 :** of or relating to clerical work or written communication **3 :** existing only in theory **:** NOMINAL <a ~ blockade> **4 :** admitted by free passes <a ~ audience> **5 :** issued as paper money **6 :** finished with a crisp smooth surface similar to that of paper <~ taffeta>

pa·per·back \ˈpā-pər-ˌbak\ *n* **:** a book with a flexible paper binding — **paperback** *adj*

paper birch *n* **:** an American birch (*Betula papyrifera*) with peeling white bark that is often worked into fancy articles

pa·per·board \ˈpā-pər-ˌbō(ə)rd, -ˌbȯ(ə)rd\ *n* **:** a composition board **:** CARDBOARD — **paperboard** *adj*

pa·per·bound \-ˌbau̇nd\ *n* **:** PAPERBACK — **paperbound** *adj*

pa·per·boy \-ˌbȯi\ *n* **:** NEWSBOY

paper chase *n* **:** HARE AND HOUNDS

paper cutter *n* **1 :** PAPER KNIFE **2 :** a machine or device for cutting or trimming sheets of paper to required dimensions

pa·per·hang·er \ˈpā-pər-ˌhaŋ-ər\ *n* **1 :** one that applies wallpaper **2** *slang* **:** one who passes worthless checks

pa·per·hang·ing \-ˌhaŋ-iŋ\ *n* **:** the act of applying wallpaper

paper knife *n* **1 :** a knife for slitting envelopes or uncut pages **2 :** the knife of a paper cutter

pa·per·mak·er \ˈpā-pər-ˌmā-kər\ *n* **:** one that makes paper

pa·per·mak·ing \-kiŋ\ *n* **:** the making of paper

paper money *n* **1 :** money consisting of government notes and bank notes **2 :** BANK MONEY

paper mulberry *n* **:** an Asiatic tree (*Broussonetia papyrifera*) of the mulberry family that is widely grown as a shade tree

paper nautilus *n* **:** a cephalopod (genus *Argonauta*) whose female has a delicate papery shell

paper over *vt* **1 :** to gloss over, explain away, or patch up (as major differences or disparities) esp. in order to maintain a semblance of unity or agreement **2 :** HIDE, CONCEAL

paper profit *n* **:** a profit that can be realized only by selling something (as a security) that has appreciated in market value

paper–thin *adj* **:** very thin or narrow <~ partitions>

paper tiger *n* **:** one that is outwardly powerful or dangerous but inwardly weak or ineffectual <necessary to show that the . . . military presence was not a *paper tiger* —Kaye Whiteman>

pa·per·weight \ˈpā-pər-ˌwāt\ *n* **:** a usu. small heavy object used to hold down loose papers (as on a desk)

pa·per·work \-ˌwərk\ *n* **:** routine clerical or record-keeping work often incidental to a more important task

pa·pery \ˈpā-p(ə-)rē\ *adj* **:** resembling paper in thinness or consistency <~ leaves> <~ silk> — **pa·per·i·ness** *n*

pa·pe·terie \ˈpap-ə-trē, ˌpap-ə-ˈ\ *n* [F] **:** packaged fancy stationery

1Pa·phi·an \ˈpā-fē-ən\ *adj* [L *paphius,* fr. Gk *paphios,* fr. *Paphos,* ancient city of Cyprus that was the center of worship of Aphrodite] **1 :** of or relating to Paphos or its people **2 :** of or relating to illicit love **:** WANTON

2Paphian *n* **1 :** a native or inhabitant of Paphos **2** *often not cap* **:** PROSTITUTE

pa·pier col·lé \ˌpäp-ˌyā-(ˌ)kō-ˈlā, ˌpap-\ *n, pl* **papiers collés** \-ˌyā-(ˌ)kō-ˈlā(z)\ [F, glued paper] **:** COLLAGE

pa·pier–mâ·ché \ˌpā-pər-mə-ˈshā, ˌpap-ˌyā-mə-, -(ˌ)ma-\ *n* [F, lit., chewed paper] **:** a light strong molding material of wastepaper pulped with glue and other additives — **papier–mâché** *adj*

pa·pil·i·o·na·ceous \pə-ˌpil-ē-ə-ˈnā-shəs\ *adj* [L *papilion-, papilio* butterfly — more at PAVILION] **:** having a corolla (as in the bean or pea) with usu. five petals that include a large standard enclosing two lateral wings and a lower carina

pa·pil·la \pə-ˈpil-ə\ *n, pl* **pa·pil·lae** \-ˈpil-(ˌ)ē, -ˌī\ [L, nipple; akin to L *papula* pimple, Lith *papas* nipple] **:** a small projecting body part similar to a nipple in form: **a :** a vascular process of connective tissue extending into and nourishing the root of a hair, feather, or developing tooth — see HAIR illustration **b :** one of the vascular protuberances of the dermal layer of the skin extending into the epidermal layer and often containing tactile corpuscles **c :** one of the small protuberances on the upper surface of the tongue — **pap·il·lary** \ˈpap-ə-ˌler-ē, *esp Brit* pə-ˈpil-ə-rē\ *adj* — **pa·pil·late** \ˈpap-ə-ˌlāt, pə-ˈpil-ət\ *adj* — **pa·pil·lose** \ˈpap-ə-ˌlōs, pə-ˈpil-ˌōs\ *adj*

pap·il·lo·ma \ˌpap-ə-ˈlō-mə\ *n, pl* **-mas** *or* **-ma·ta** \-mət-ə\ **1 :** a benign tumor (as a wart) due to overgrowth of epithelial tissue on papillae of vascular connective tissue (as of the skin) **2 :** an epithelial tumor caused by a virus — **pap·il·lo·ma·tous** \-ˈlō-mət-əs\ *adj*

pa·pil·lon \ˌpäp-ē-ˈ(y)ōⁿ, ˌpap-\ *n* [F, lit., butterfly, fr. L *papilion-, papilio*] **:** any of a breed of small slender toy spaniels resembling long-haired Chihuahuas

pa·pil·lote \ˌpäp-ē-ˈ(y)ōt, ˌpap-\ *n* [F, fr. *papillon* butterfly] **:** a greased paper wrapper in which food (as meat or fish) is cooked

pa·pist \ˈpā-pəst\ *n, often cap* [MF or NL; MF *papiste,* fr. *pape* pope; NL *papista,* fr. LL *papa* pope] **:** ROMAN CATHOLIC — usu. used disparagingly — **papist** *adj*

pa·pist·ry \ˈpā-pə-strē\ *n* **:** the Roman Catholic religion — usu. used disparagingly

pa·poose \pa-ˈpüs, pə-\ *n* [Narraganset *papoòs*] **:** a young child of American Indian parents

pa·po·va·vi·rus \pə-ˈpō-və-ˌvī-rəs\ *n* [*pa*pilloma + *po*lyoma + *va*cuolation + *virus*] **:** any of a group of viruses that have a capsid with 42 protuberances resembling knobs and that are associated with or responsible for various neoplasms (as some warts) of mammals

pap·pose \ˈpap-ˌōs\ *adj* **:** having or being a pappus

pap·pus \ˈpap-əs\ *n, pl* **pap·pi** \ˈpap-ˌī, -ˌē\ [L, fr. Gk *pappos*] **:** an appendage or tuft of appendages that crowns the ovary or fruit in various seed plants and functions in dispersal of the fruit

pap·py \ˈpap-ē\ *n, chiefly South & Midland* **:** PAPA

pa·pri·ka \pə-ˈprē-kə, pa-\ *n* [Hung, fr. Serb, fr. *papar* pepper, fr. Gk *peperi*] **:** a mild red condiment consisting of the dried finely ground pods of various cultivated sweet peppers; *also* **:** a sweet pepper used for making paprika

Pap smear \ˈpap-\ *n* [George N. *Papanicolaou* †1962 Am medical scientist] **:** a method for the early detection of cancer employing exfoliated cells and a special staining technique that differentiates diseased tissue — called also *Papanicolaou test, Pap test*

Pap·u·an \ˈpap-yə-wən\ *n* **1 :** a native or inhabitant of Papua **2 :** a member of any of the Negroid native peoples of New Guinea and adjacent areas of Melanesia **3 :** any of a heterogeneous group of languages spoken in New Guinea, New Britain, and the Solomon islands — **Papuan** *adj*

pap·u·lar \ˈpap-yə-lər\ *adj* **:** consisting of or characterized by papules

pap·ule \ˈpap-(ˌ)yü(ə)l\ *n* [L *papula*] **:** a small solid usu. conical elevation of the skin

pap·y·rol·o·gy \ˌpap-ə-ˈräl-ə-jē\ *n* [ISV] **:** the study of papyrus manuscripts — **pap·y·rol·o·gist** \-jəst\ *n*

pa·py·rus \pə-ˈpī-rəs\ *n, pl* **pa·py·rus·es** *or* **pa·py·ri** \-ˈpī(ə)r-(ˌ)ē, -ˌī\ [ME, fr. L — more at PAPER] **1 :** a tall sedge (*Cyperus papyrus*) of the Nile valley **2 :** the pith of the papyrus plant esp. when cut in strips and pressed into a writing material **3 a :** a writing on papyrus **b :** a written scroll made of papyrus

papyrus 1

1par \ˈpär\ *n* [L, one that is equal, fr. *par* equal] **1 a :** the established value of the monetary unit of one country expressed in terms of the monetary unit of another country using the same metal as the standard of value **b :** the face amount of an instrument of value (as a check or note): as (1) **:** the monetary value assigned to each share of stock in the charter of a corporation (2) **:** the principal of a bond **2 :** common level **:** EQUALITY **3 a :** an amount taken as an average or norm **b :** an accepted standard; *specif* **:** a usual standard of physical condition or health **4 :** the score standard for each hole of a golf course; *also* **:** a score equal to par — **par** *adj*

2par *vt* **parred; par·ring :** to score par on (a hole)

3par *abbr* **1** paragraph **2** parallel **3** parish

pa·ra \ˈpär-ə\ *n, pl* **paras** *or* **para** [Turk, fr. Per *pārah,* lit., piece] **1 a :** any of several monetary units of the Turkish Empire **b :** a coin representing one para **2** — see *dinar* at MONEY table

1para- \ˌpar-ə, ˈpar-ə\ *or* **par-** *prefix* [ME, fr. MF, fr. L, fr. Gk, fr. *para;* akin to Gk *pro* before — more at FOR] **1 :** beside **:** alongside of **:** beyond **:** aside from <*para*thyroid> <*par*enteral> **2 a :** closely related to <*par*aldehyde> **b :** involving substitution at or characterized by two opposite positions in the benzene ring that are separated by two carbon atoms <*para*dichlorobenzene> **3 a :** faulty **:** abnormal <*par*esthesia> **b :** associated in a subsidiary or accessory capacity <*para*medical> **c :** closely resembling **:** almost <*para*typhoid>

2para- \ˈpar-ə\ *comb form* [*parachute*] **1 :** parachute <*para*trooper> **2 :** parachutist <*para*spotter>

-p·a·ra \p-ə-rə\ *n comb form, pl* **-p·a·ras** \-ə-rəz\ *or* **-p·a·rae** \-ə-ˌrē, -ˌrī\ [L, fr. *parere* to give birth to — more at PARE] **:** woman delivered of (so many) children <tri*para*>

para–ami·no·ben·zo·ic acid \ˈpar-ə-ə-ˌmē-ˌnō-ˌben-ˌzō-ik-, ˈpar-ə-ˌam-ə-(ˌ)nō-\ *n* [ISV] **:** a colorless para-substituted aminobenzoic acid that is a growth factor of the vitamin B complex — abbr. *PABA*

para–ami·no·sal·i·cyl·ic acid \-ˌsal-ə-ˌsil-ik-\ *n* **:** the white crystalline para-substituted isomer of aminosalicylic acid that is made synthetically and is used in the treatment of tuberculosis

para·bi·o·sis \ˌpar-ə-(ˌ)bī-ˈō-səs, -bē-\ *n* [NL] **1 :** reversible suspension of obvious vital activities **2 :** anatomical and physiological union of two organisms — **para·bi·ot·ic** \-ˈät-ik\ *adj* — **para·bi·ot·i·cal·ly** \-i-k(ə-)lē\ *adv*

par·a·ble \ˈpar-ə-bəl\ *n* [ME, fr. MF, fr. LL *parabola,* fr. Gk *parabolē,* fr. *paraballein* to compare, fr. *para-* + *ballein* to throw — more at DEVIL] **:** COMPARISON; *specif* **:** a usu. short fictitious story that illustrates a moral attitude or a religious principle

pa·rab·o·la \pə-ˈrab-ə-lə\ *n* [NL, fr. Gk *parabolē,* lit., comparison] **1 :** a plane curve generated by a point moving so that its distance from a fixed point is equal to its distance from a fixed line **:** the intersection of a right circular cone with a plane parallel to an element of the cone **2 :** something bowl-shaped (as a microphone)

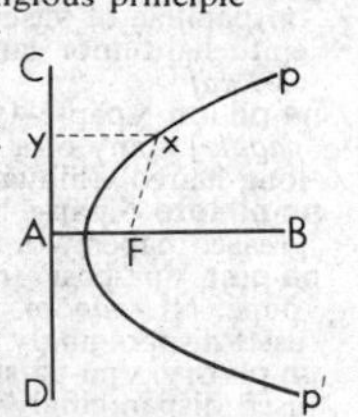

parabola 1: *F* fixed point; *CD* fixed line; *x* moving point; *AB* axis; *xy* distance from *x* to *CD*; *pp'* parabola

par·a·bol·ic \ˌpar-ə-ˈbäl-ik\ *adj* [in sense 1, fr. LL *parabola* parable; in sense 2, fr. NL *parabola*] **1 :** expressed by or being a parable **:** ALLEGORICAL **2 :** of, having the form of, or relating to a parabola <motion in a ~ curve> — **par·a·bol·i·cal·ly** \-i-k(ə-)lē\ *adv*

pa·rab·o·loid \pə-ˈrab-ə-ˌlȯid\ *n* **:** a surface all of whose intersections by planes are either parabolas and ellipses or parabolas and hyperbolas — **pa·rab·o·loi·dal** \-ˌrab-ə-ˈlȯid-ᵊl\ *adj*

1para·chute \ˈpar-ə-ˌshüt\ *n* [F, fr. *para-* (as in *parasol*) + *chute* fall — more at CHUTE] **1 :** a folding umbrella-shaped device of light fabric used esp. for making a safe descent from an airplane **2 :** PATAGIUM **3 :** a device suggestive of a parachute in form, use, or operation — **para·chut·ic** \ˌpar-ə-ˈshüt-ik\ *adj*

2parachute *vb* **-chut·ed; -chut·ing** *vt* **:** to convey by means of a parachute ~ *vi* **:** to descend by means of a parachute

parachute spinnaker *n* **:** an exceptionally large spinnaker used esp. on racing yachts

para·chut·ist \ˈpar-ə-ˌshüt-əst\ *n* **:** one that parachutes: as **a :** PARATROOPER **b :** a person who parachutes as a sport

Par·a·clete \ˈpar-ə-ˌklēt\ *n* [ME *Paraclit,* fr. MF *Paraclet,* fr. LL *Paracletus,* fr. Gk *Paraklētos,* lit., advocate, intercessor, fr. *parakalein* to invoke, fr. *para-* + *kalein* call — more at LOW] **:** HOLY SPIRIT

1pa·rade \pə-ˈrād\ *n* [F, fr. MF, fr. *parer* to prepare — more at PARE] **1 :** a pompous show **:** EXHIBITION **2 a :** the ceremonial formation of a body of troops before a superior officer **b :** a place where troops assemble regularly for parade **3 :** a public procession **4 a :** a place for strolling **b :** those who promenade

2parade *vb* **pa·rad·ed; pa·rad·ing** *vt* **1 :** to cause to maneuver or march **:** MARSHAL **2 :** PROMENADE **3 :** to exhibit ostentatiously ~ *vi* **1 :** to march in a procession **2 :** PROMENADE **3 a :** to show off **b :** MASQUERADE <myths which ~ as modern science —M. R. Cohen> — **pa·rad·er** *n*

para·di·chlo·ro·ben·zene \ˌpar-ə-ˌdī-ˌklōr-ə-ˈben-ˌzēn, -ˌklȯr-, -ˌben-ˈ\ *n* [ISV] **:** a white crystalline compound $C_6H_4Cl_2$ made by chlorinating benzene and used chiefly as a fumigant against clothes moths

par·a·digm \ˈpar-ə-ˌdīm, -ˌdim\ *n* [LL *paradigma,* fr. Gk *paradeigma,* fr. *paradeiknynai* to show side by side, fr. *para-* + *deiknynai* to show — more at DICTION] **1 :** EXAMPLE, PATTERN; *esp* **:** an outstandingly clear or typical example or archetype **2 :** an example of a conjugation or declension showing a word in all its inflectional forms — **par·a·dig·mat·ic** \ˌpar-ə-dig-ˈmat-ik\ *adj*

par·a·di·sa·ic \ˌpar-ə-ˌdī-ˈsā-ik, -ˈzā-\ *adj* [*paradise* + *-aic* (as in *Hebraic*)] **:** PARADISIACAL — **par·a·di·sa·ical** \-ˈsā-ə-kəl, -ˈzā-\ *adj* — **par·a·di·sa·ical·ly** \-ə-k(ə-)lē\ *adv*

par·a·dis·al \ˌpar-ə-ˈdī-səl, -ˈdī-zəl\ *adj* **:** PARADISIACAL

par·a·dise \ˈpar-ə-ˌdīs, -ˌdīz\ *n* [ME *paradis,* fr. OF, fr. LL *paradisus,* fr. Gk *paradeisos,* lit., enclosed park, of Iranian origin; akin to Av *pairi-daēza-* enclosure; akin to Gk *peri* around and to Gk *teichos* wall — more at PERI-, DOUGH] **1 a :** the garden of Eden **b :** an intermediate place or state where the righteous departed await resurrection and judgment **c :** HEAVEN **2 :** a place of bliss, felicity, or delight

par·a·di·si·a·cal \ˌpar-ə-də-ˈsī-ə-kəl, -ˌdī-, -ˈzī-\ *or* **par·a·dis·i·ac** \-ˈdiz-ē-ˌak, -ˈdis-\ *adj* [LL *paradisiacus,* fr. *paradisus*] **:** of, relating to, or resembling paradise — **par·a·di·si·a·cal·ly** \-də-ˈsī-ə-k(ə-)lē, -ˌdī-, -ˈzī-\ *adv*

par·a·dox \ˈpar-ə-ˌdäks\ *n* [L *paradoxum,* fr. Gk *paradoxon,* fr. neut. of *paradoxos* contrary to expectation, fr. *para-* + *dokein* to think — more at DECENT] **1 :** a tenet contrary to received opinion **2 a :** a statement that is seemingly contradictory or opposed to common sense and yet is perhaps true **b :** a self-contradictory statement that at first seems true **c :** an argument that apparently derives self-contradictory conclusions by valid deduction from acceptable premises **3 :** something (as a person, condition, or act) with seemingly contradictory qualities or phases

syn PARADOX, ANTINOMY, ANOMALY *shared meaning element* **:** something involving an inherent contradiction

par·a·dox·i·cal \ˌpar-ə-ˈdäk-si-kəl\ *adj* **1 a :** of the nature of a paradox **b :** inclined to paradoxes **2 :** not being the normal or usual kind <~ pulse> — **par·a·dox·i·cal·ly** \-k(ə-)lē\ *adv* — **par·a·dox·i·cal·ness** \-kəl-nəs\ *n*

paradoxical sleep *n* **:** a state of sleep that is characterized by increased neuronal activity of the forebrain and midbrain, by depressed muscle tone, and esp. in man by dreaming, rapid eye movements, and vascular congestion of the sex organs — called also *REM sleep*

par·aes·the·sia *var of* PARESTHESIA

1par·af·fin \ˈpar-ə-fən\ *n* [G, fr. L *parum* too little + *affinis* bordering on; akin to L *paucus* few — more at FEW, AFFINITY] **1 a :** a waxy crystalline flammable substance obtained esp. from distillates of wood, coal, petroleum, or shale oil that is a complex mixture of hydrocarbons and is used chiefly in coating and sealing, in candles, in rubber compounding, and in pharmaceuticals and cosmetics **b :** any of various mixtures of similar hydrocarbons including mixtures that are semisolid or oily **2 :** a hydrocarbon of the methane series **3** *chiefly Brit* **:** KEROSINE — **par·af·fin·ic** \ˌpar-ə-ˈfin-ik\ *adj*

2paraffin *vt* **:** to coat or saturate with paraffin

para·gen·e·sis \ˌpar-ə-ˈjen-ə-səs\ *n* [NL] **:** the formation of minerals in contact in such a manner as to affect one another's development — **para·ge·net·ic** \-jə-ˈnet-ik\ *adj* — **para·ge·net·i·cal·ly** \-i-k(ə-)lē\ *adv*

1par·a·gon \ˈpar-ə-ˌgän, -gən\ *n* [MF, fr. OIt *paragone,* lit., touchstone, fr. *paragonare* to test on a touchstone, fr. Gk *parakonan* to sharpen, fr. *para-* + *akonē* whetstone, fr. *akē* point; akin to Gk *akmē* point — more at EDGE] **:** a model of excellence or perfection

2paragon *vt* **1 :** to compare with **:** PARALLEL **2 :** to put in rivalry **:** MATCH **3** *obs* **:** SURPASS

1para·graph \ˈpar-ə-ˌgraf\ *n* [MF & ML; MF *paragraphe,* fr. ML *paragraphus* sign marking a paragraph, fr. Gk *paragraphos* line used to mark change of persons in a dialogue, fr. *paragraphein* to write alongside, fr. *para-* + *graphein* to write — more at CARVE] **1 a :** a subdivision of a written composition that consists of one or more sentences, deals with one point or gives the words of one speaker, and begins on a new usu. indented line **b :** a short composition or note that is complete in one paragraph **2 :** a character (as ¶) used to indicate the beginning of a paragraph and in printing as the sixth in series of the reference marks — **para·graph·ic** \ˌpar-ə-ˈgraf-ik\ *adj*

2paragraph *vt* **1 :** to write paragraphs about **2 :** to divide into paragraphs ~ *vi* **:** to write paragraphs

para·graph·er \ˈpar-ə-ˌgraf-ər\ *n* **:** a writer of paragraphs esp. for the editorial page of a newspaper

para·in·flu·en·za virus \ˈpar-ə-ˌin-flü-ˌen-zə-\ *n* **:** any of several myxoviruses that are associated with or responsible for some respiratory infections in children — called also *parainfluenza*

par·a·keet \ˈpar-ə-ˌkēt\ *n* [Sp & MF; Sp *periquito,* fr. MF *perroquet* parrot] **:** any of numerous usu. small slender parrots with a long graduated tail

para·lan·guage \ˈpar-ə-ˌlaŋ-gwij\ *n* **:** optional vocal effects (as tone of voice) that accompany or modify the phonemes of an utterance and that may communicate meaning

par·al·de·hyde \pa-ˈral-də-ˌhīd, pə-\ *n* **:** a colorless liquid polymeric modification $C_6H_{12}O_3$ of acetaldehyde used as a hypnotic
para·lim·ni·on \ˌpar-ə-ˈlim-nē-ˌän, -nē-ən\ *n* [NL, fr. *para-* + Gk *limnion,* dim. of *limnē* marshy lake; akin to Gk *limēn* harbor — more at LIMB] **:** the littoral portion of a lake extending to the limit of rooted vegetation
para·lin·guis·tics \ˌpar-ə-liŋ-ˈgwis-tiks\ *n* **:** the study of paralanguage — **para·lin·guis·tic** \-tik\ *adj*
Par·a·li·pom·e·non \ˌpar-ə-lə-ˈpäm-ə-ˌnän, -lī-\ *n* [LL, fr. Gk *Paraleipomenōn,* gen. of *Paraleipomena,* lit., things left out, fr. neut. pl. of prp. passive of *paraleipein* to leave out, fr. *para-* + *leipein* to leave; fr. its forming a supplement to Samuel and Kings — more at LOAN] **:** CHRONICLES
par·al·lac·tic \ˌpar-ə-ˈlak-tik\ *adj* [NL *parallacticus,* fr. Gk *parallaktikos,* fr. *parallaxis*] **:** of, relating to, or due to parallax
par·al·lax \ˈpar-ə-ˌlaks\ *n* [MF *parallaxe,* fr. Gk *parallaxis,* fr. *parallassein* to change, fr. *para-* + *allassein* to change, fr. *allos* other — more at ELSE] **:** the apparent displacement or the difference in apparent direction of an object as seen from two different points not on a straight line with the object; *specif* **:** the difference in direction of a celestial body as measured from two points on the earth
[1]**par·al·lel** \ˈpar-ə-ˌlel, -ləl\ *adj* [L *parallelus,* fr. Gk *parallēlos,* fr. *para* beside + *allēlōn* of one another, fr. *allos . . . allos* one . . . another, fr. *allos* other — more at PARA-, ELSE] **1 a :** extending in the same direction, everywhere equidistant, and not meeting <~ rows of trees> **b :** everywhere equally distant <concentric spheres are ~> **2 a :** having parallel sides <a ~ reamer> **b :** being or relating to an electrical circuit having a number of conductors in parallel **c :** arranged in parallel <a ~ computer> **3 a :** similar, analogous, or interdependent in tendency or development **b :** readily compared **:** COMPANION **c :** having identical syntactical elements in corresponding positions **d** (1) **:** having the same tonic — used of major and minor keys and scales (2) **:** keeping the same distance apart in musical pitch **4 :** performed while keeping one's skis parallel <~ turns> ***syn*** see SIMILAR
[2]**parallel** *n* **1 a :** a parallel line, curve, or surface **b :** one of the imaginary circles on the surface of the earth paralleling the equator and marking the latitude; *also* **:** the corresponding line on a globe or map — see LATITUDE illustration **c :** a character ‖ used in printing as the fifth in series of the reference marks **2 a :** something equal or similar in all essential particulars **:** COUNTERPART **b :** SIMILARITY, ANALOGUE **3 :** a comparison to show resemblance **:** a tracing of similarity **4 a :** the state of being physically parallel **:** PARALLELISM **b :** the arrangement of electrical devices in which all positive poles, electrodes, and terminals are joined to one conductor and all negative ones to another conductor so that each unit is in effect on a parallel branch **c :** an arrangement or state that permits several operations or tasks to be performed simultaneously rather than consecutively
syn PARALLEL, COUNTERPART, ANALOGUE, CORRELATE *shared meaning element* **:** one that corresponds to or closely resembles another
[3]**parallel** *vt* **1 :** to indicate analogy of **:** COMPARE **2 a :** to show something equal to **:** MATCH **b :** to correspond to **3 :** to place so as to be parallel in direction with something **4 :** to extend, run, or move in a direction parallel to
[4]**parallel** *adv* **:** in a parallel manner
parallel bars *n pl* **1 :** a pair of wooden bars supported horizontally above the floor at the same height or at different heights usu. by a common base and used in gymnastics **2 :** an event in gymnastics competition in which even or uneven parallel bars are used
par·al·lel·epi·ped \ˌpar-ə-ˌlel-ə-ˈpī-pəd, -ˈpip-əd; -ˌlel-ˈep-ə-ˌped\ *n* [Gk *parallēlepipedon,* fr. *parallēlos* + *epipedon* plane surface, fr. neut. of *epipedos* flat, fr. *epi-* + *pedon* ground; akin to L *ped-, pes* foot — more at FOOT] **:** a prism whose bases are parallelograms
par·al·lel·ism \ˈpar-ə-ˌlel-ˌiz-əm, -ləl-\ *n* **1 :** the quality or state of being parallel **2 :** RESEMBLANCE, CORRESPONDENCE **3 :** recurrent syntactical similarities introduced for rhetorical effect **4 :** a theory that mind and matter accompany one another but are not causally related **5 :** the development of similar new characters by two or more related organisms in response to similarity of environment — called also *parallel evolution*
par·al·lel·o·gram \ˌpar-ə-ˈlel-ə-ˌgram\ *n* [LL or Gk; LL *parallelogrammum,* fr. Gk *parallēlogrammon,* fr. neut. of *parallēlogrammos* bounded by parallel lines, fr. *parallēlos* + *grammē* line, fr. *graphein* to write — more at CARVE] **:** a quadrilateral with opposite sides parallel and equal

parallelograms

par·al·lel–veined \ˌpar-ə-ˌlel-ˈvānd, -ləl-\ *adj, of a leaf* **:** having veins nearly parallel to one another — compare NET-VEINED
pa·ral·o·gism \pə-ˈral-ə-ˌjiz-əm\ *n* [MF *paralogisme,* fr. LL *paralogismus,* fr. Gk *paralogismos,* fr. *paralogos* unreasonable, fr. *para-* + *logos* speech, reason — more at LEGEND] **:** a fallacious argument
par·a·lyse *Brit var of* PARALYZE
pa·ral·y·sis \pə-ˈral-ə-səs\ *n, pl* **-y·ses** \-ˌsēz\ [L, fr. Gk, fr. *paralyein* to loosen, disable, fr. *para-* + *lyein* to loosen — more at LOSE] **1 :** complete or partial loss of function esp. when involving the motion or sensation in a part of the body **2 :** loss of the ability to move **3 :** a state of powerlessness or incapacity to act
paralysis agi·tans \-ˈaj-ə-ˌtanz\ *n* [NL, lit., shaking palsy] **:** PARKINSON'S DISEASE
[1]**par·a·lyt·ic** \ˌpar-ə-ˈlit-ik\ *adj* **1 :** affected with or characterized by paralysis **2 :** of, relating to, or resembling paralysis
[2]**paralytic** *n* **:** one affected with paralysis
par·a·lyze \ˈpar-ə-ˌlīz\ *vt* **-lyzed; -lyz·ing** [F *paralyser,* back-formation fr. *paralysie* paralysis, fr. L *paralysis*] **1 :** to affect with paralysis **2 :** to make powerless or ineffective **3 :** UNNERVE **4 :** STUN, STUPEFY **5 :** to bring to an end **:** PREVENT, DESTROY — **par·a·ly·za·tion** \ˌpar-ə-lə-ˈzā-shən\ *n* — **par·a·lyz·er** \ˈpar-ə-ˌlī-zər\ *n* — **par·a·lyz·ing·ly** \-ˌlī-ziŋ-lē\ *adv*
para·mag·net \ˈpar-ə-ˌmag-nət\ *n* [back-formation fr. *paramagnetic*] **:** a paramagnetic substance
para·mag·net·ic \ˌpar-ə-mag-ˈnet-ik\ *adj* [ISV] **:** being or relating to a magnetizable substance that like aluminum and platinum has small but positive susceptibility varying but little with magnetizing force — **para·mag·net·i·cal·ly** \-i-k(ə-)lē\ *adv* — **para·mag·ne·tism** \-ˈmag-nə-ˌtiz-əm\ *n*
par·a·mat·ta \ˌpar-ə-ˈmat-ə\ *n* [*Parramatta,* Australia] **:** a fine lightweight dress fabric of silk and wool or cotton and wool
par·a·me·cium \ˌpar-ə-ˈmē-sh(ē-)əm, -sē-əm\ *n, pl* **-cia** \-sh(ē-)ə, -sē-ə\ *also* **-ci·ums** [NL, genus name, fr. Gk *paramēkēs* oblong, fr. *para-* + *mēkos* length; akin to Gk *makros* long — more at MEAGER] **:** any of a genus (*Paramecium*) of ciliate protozoans that have an elongate body rounded at the anterior end and an oblique funnel-shaped buccal groove bearing the mouth at the extremity

paramecium

para·med·ic \ˈpar-ə-ˌmed-ik\ *n* **:** one who assists a physician (as by giving injections and taking X rays)
para·med·i·cal \ˌpar-ə-ˈmed-i-kəl\ *also* **para·med·ic** \-ik\ *adj* **:** concerned with supplementing the work of highly trained medical professionals <~ aides and technicians>
par·a·ment \ˈpar-ə-mənt\ *n* [ME, fr. ML *paramentum,* fr. *parare* to adorn, fr. L, to prepare — more at PARE] **:** an ornamental ecclesiastical hanging or vestment
pa·ram·e·ter \pə-ˈram-ət-ər\ *n* [NL, fr. *para-* + Gk *metron* measure — more at MEASURE] **1 :** an arbitrary constant whose value characterizes a member of a system (as a family of curves); *specif* **:** a quantity (as a mean or variance) that describes a statistical population **2 :** any of a set of physical properties whose values determine the characteristics or behavior of something <~*s* of the atmosphere such as temperature, pressure, and density> **3 :** something represented by a parameter **:** a characteristic element; *broadly* **:** CHARACTERISTIC, ELEMENT, FACTOR <political dissent as a ~ of modern life> — **para·met·ric** \ˌpar-ə-ˈme-trik\ *also* **para·met·ri·cal** \-tri-kəl\ *adj* — **para·met·ri·cal·ly** \-tri-k(ə-)lē\ *adv*
pa·ram·e·ter·ize \pə-ˈram-ət-ə-ˌrīz\ *or* **pa·ram·e·trize** \-ˈram-ə-ˌtrīz\ *vt* **-ter·ized** *or* **-trized; -ter·iz·ing** *or* **-triz·ing :** to express in terms of parameters — **pa·ram·e·ter·iza·tion** \-ˌram-ət-ə-rə-ˈzā-shən, -ə-trə-ˈzā-\ *or* **pa·ram·e·tri·za·tion** \-ə-trə-ˈzā-\ *n*
parametric amplifier *n* **:** a high-frequency amplifier whose operation is based on time variations in a parameter (as reactance) and which converts the energy at the frequency of an alternating current into energy at the input signal frequency in such a way as to amplify the signal
parametric equation *n* **:** any of a set of equations that express the coordinates of the points of a curve as functions of one parameter or that express the coordinates of the points of a surface as functions of two parameters
para·mil·i·tary \ˌpar-ə-ˈmil-ə-ˌter-ē\ *adj* **1 :** formed on a military pattern esp. as a potential auxiliary military force <a ~ border patrol> **2 :** of or relating to a paramilitary force <~ training>
par·am·ne·sia \ˌpar-ˌam-ˈnē-zhə, -əm-\ *n* [NL, fr. *para-* + *-mnesia* (as in *amnesia*)] **:** a disorder of memory: as **a :** a condition in which the proper meaning of words cannot be remembered **b :** the illusion of remembering scenes and events when experienced for the first time
[1]**par·a·mount** \ˈpar-ə-ˌmau̇nt\ *adj* [AF *paramont,* fr. OF *par* by (fr. L *per*) + *amont* above, fr. *a* to (fr. L *ad*) + *mont* mountain — more at FOR, AT, MOUNT] **:** superior to all others **:** SUPREME ***syn*** see DOMINANT — **par·a·mount·cy** \-ˌmau̇n(t)-sē\ *n*
[2]**paramount** *n* **:** a supreme ruler
par·amour \ˈpar-ə-ˌmu̇(ə)r\ *n* [ME, fr. *par amour* by way of love, fr. OF] **:** an illicit lover; *esp* **:** MISTRESS
par·am·y·lum \(ˈ)pa(ə)r-ˈam-ə-ləm\ *n* [NL, fr. *para-* + L *amylum* starch — more at AMYL-] **:** a reserve carbohydrate of various protozoans and algae that resembles starch
pa·rang \ˈpär-ˌaŋ\ *n* [Malay] **:** a short sword, cleaver, or machete common in Malaysia and Indonesia
para·noia \ˌpar-ə-ˈnȯi-ə\ *n* [NL, fr. Gk, madness, fr. *paranous* demented, fr. *para-* + *nous* mind] **1 :** a psychosis characterized by systematized delusions of persecution or grandeur usu. without hallucinations **2 :** a tendency on the part of an individual or group toward excessive or irrational suspiciousness and distrustfulness of others — **para·noi·ac** \-ˈnȯi-ˌak, -ˈnȯi-ik\ *adj or n*
para·noid \ˈpar-ə-ˌnȯid\ *adj* **1 :** characterized by or resembling paranoia **2 :** characterized by suspiciousness, persecutory trends, or megalomania — **paranoid** *n*
paranoid schizophrenia *n* **:** a psychosis resembling paranoia but commonly displaying hallucinations and marked behavioral deterioration
para·nor·mal \ˌpar-ə-ˈnȯr-məl\ *adj* **:** not scientifically explainable **:** SUPERNATURAL — **para·nor·mal·i·ty** \-ˌnȯr-ˈmal-ət-ē\ *n* — **para·nor·mal·ly** \-ˈnȯr-mə-lē\ *adv*
para·nymph \ˈpar-ə-ˌnim(p)f\ *n* [LL *paranymphus,* fr. Gk *paranymphos,* fr. *para-* + *nymphē* bride — more at NUPTIAL] **1 :** a friend going with a bridegroom to fetch home the bride in ancient Greece; *also* **:** the bridesmaid conducting the bride to the bridegroom **2 a :** BEST MAN **b :** BRIDESMAID
par·a·pet \ˈpar-ə-pət, -ˌpet\ *n* [It *parapetto,* fr. *parare* to shield (fr. L, to prepare) + *petto* chest, fr. L *pectus* — more at PARE, PECTORAL] **1 :** a wall, rampart, or elevation of earth or stone to protect soldiers **:** BREASTWORK **2 :** a low wall or railing to protect

the edge of a platform, roof, or bridge — called also *parapet wall* — **par·a·pet·ed** \-ˌpet-əd\ *adj*

pa·raph \'par-əf, pə-'raf\ *n* [MF, fr. L *paragraphus* paragraph] : a flourish at the end of a signature

par·a·pher·na·lia \ˌpar-ə-fə(r)-'nāl-yə\ *n pl but sing or pl in constr* [ML, deriv. of Gk *parapherna* goods a bride brings over and above the dowry, fr. *para-* + *phernē* dowry, fr. *pherein* to bear — more at BEAR] **1 :** the separate real or personal property of a married woman that she can dispose of by will and sometimes according to common law during her life **2 :** personal belongings **3 a :** articles of equipment : FURNISHINGS **b :** accessory items

¹para·phrase \'par-ə-ˌfrāz\ *n* [MF, fr. L *paraphrasis,* fr. Gk, fr. *paraphrazein* to paraphrase, fr. *para-* + *phrazein* to point out] **1 :** a restatement of a text, passage, or work giving the meaning in another form **2 :** the use or process of paraphrasing in studying or teaching composition

²paraphrase *vb* **-phrased; -phras·ing** *vt* **:** to make a paraphrase of ~ *vi* **:** to make a paraphrase — **para·phras·able** \-ˌfrā-zə-bəl\ *adj* — **para·phras·er** *n*

para·phras·tic \ˌpar-ə-'fras-tik\ *adj* [F *paraphrastique,* fr. Gk *paraphrastikos,* fr. *paraphrazein*] **:** explaining or translating more clearly and amply **:** having the nature of a paraphrase — **para·phras·ti·cal·ly** \-ti-k(ə-)lē\ *adv*

pa·raph·y·sis \pə-'raf-ə-səs\ *n, pl* **-y·ses** \-ˌsēz\ [NL, fr. Gk, sucker, offshoot, fr. *paraphyein* to produce at the side, fr. *para-* + *phyein* to bring forth — more at PHYSICS] **:** one of the slender sterile filaments borne among the sporogenous or gametogenous organs in cryptogamic plants

para·ple·gia \ˌpar-ə-'plē-j(ē-)ə\ *n* [NL, fr. Gk *paraplēgiē* hemiplegia, fr. *para-* + *-plēgia* -plegia] **:** paralysis of the lower half of the body with involvement of both legs — **para·ple·gic** \-jik\ *adj or n*

para·po·di·um \-'pōd-ē-əm\ *n, pl* **-dia** \-ē-ə\ [NL] **:** either of a pair of fleshy lateral processes borne by most segments of a polychaete worm — **parapodial** *adj*

para·pro·fes·sion·al \-prə-'fesh-nəl, -ən-ᵊl\ *n* **:** a trained aide who assists a professional person; *esp* **:** a teacher's aide

para·pro·tein \-'prō-ˌtēn, -'prōt-ē-ən\ *n* **:** any of various abnormal serum globulins with unique physical and electrophoretic characteristics

para·psy·chol·o·gy \ˌpar-ə-(ˌ)sī-'käl-ə-jē\ *n* [ISV] **:** a field of study concerned with the investigation of evidence for telepathy, clairvoyance, and psychokinesis — **para·psy·cho·log·i·cal** \-ˌsī-kə-'läj-i-kəl\ *adj* — **para·psy·chol·o·gist** \-(ˌ)sī-'käl-ə-jəst\ *n*

par·a·quat \'par-ə-ˌkwät\ *n* [*para-* + *quat*ernary] **:** an herbicide $C_{12}H_{14}N_2Cl_2$ used esp. as a weed killer

para·ros·an·i·line \ˌpar-ə-ˌrō-'zan-ᵊl-ən\ *n* [ISV] **:** a white crystalline base $C_{19}H_{19}N_3O$ that is the parent compound of many dyes; *also* **:** its red chloride used esp. in coloring paper and as a biological stain

Pa·ra rubber \ˌpar-ə-, pə-ˌrä-\ *n* [*Pará,* Brazil] **:** native rubber from So. American rubber trees (genus *Hevea* and esp. *H. brasiliensis*)

Para rubber tree *n* **:** a So. American rubber tree (*Hevea brasiliensis*)

par·a·sang \'par-ə-ˌsaŋ\ *n* [L *parasanga,* fr. Gk *parasangēs,* of Iranian origin; akin to Per *farsung* parasang] **:** any of various Persian units of distance; *esp* **:** an ancient unit of about four miles

para·se·le·ne \ˌpar-ə-sə-'lē-nē\ *n, pl* **-nae** \-(ˌ)nē, -ˌnī\ [NL, fr. *para-* + Gk *selēnē* moon — more at SELENIUM] **:** a bright spot comparable to a parhelion seen in connection with lunar halos — **para·se·le·nic** \-'lēn-ik, -'len-\ *adj*

para·sex·u·al \-'seksh-(ə-)wəl, -'sek-shəl\ *adj* **:** relating to or being reproduction that results in recombination of genes from different individuals but does not involve meiosis and formation of a zygote by fertilization as in sexual reproduction <the ~ cycle in some fungi> — **para·sex·u·al·i·ty** \-ˌsek-shə-'wal-ət-ē\ *n*

pa·ra·shah \'pär-ə-ˌshä\ *n* [Heb *pārāshāh,* lit., explanation] **:** a passage in Jewish Scripture dealing with a single topic; *specif* **:** a section of the Torah assigned for weekly reading in synagogue worship

par·a·site \'par-ə-ˌsīt\ *n* [MF, fr. L *parasitus,* fr. Gk *parasitos,* fr. *para-* + *sitos* grain, food] **1 :** one frequenting the tables of the rich and earning welcome by flattery **:** SYCOPHANT **2 :** an organism living in or on another organism in parasitism **3 :** something that resembles a biological parasite in dependence on something else for existence or support without making a useful or adequate return — **par·a·sit·ic** \ˌpar-ə-'sit-ik\ *also* **par·a·sit·i·cal** \-i-kəl\ *adj* — **par·a·sit·i·cal·ly** \-i-k(ə-)lē\ *adv*

par·a·sit·i·cid·al \ˌpar-ə-ˌsit-ə-'sīd-ᵊl\ *adj* **:** destructive to parasites

par·a·sit·i·cide \-'sit-ə-ˌsīd\ *n* [L *parasitus* + E *-cide*] **:** a parasiticidal agent

par·a·sit·ism \'par-ə-sə-ˌtiz-əm, -ˌsīt-ˌiz-\ *n* **1 :** the behavior of a parasite **2 :** an intimate association between organisms of two or more kinds; *esp* **:** one in which a parasite obtains benefits from a host which it usu. injures **3 :** PARASITOSIS

par·a·sit·ize \-sə-ˌtīz, -ˌsīt-ˌīz\ *vt* **-ized; -iz·ing :** to infest or live on or with as a parasite — **par·a·sit·iza·tion** \ˌpar-ə-sət-ə-'zā-shən, -ˌsīt-\ *n*

par·a·sit·oid \'par-ə-sə-ˌtȯid, -ˌsīt-ˌȯid\ *n* **:** an insect and esp. a wasp that develops within the body usu. of another insect and eventually kills it — **parasitoid** *adj*

par·a·si·tol·o·gy \ˌpar-ə-sə-'täl-ə-jē, -ˌsīt-'äl-\ *n* [L *parasitus* + ISV *-logy*] **:** a branch of biology dealing with parasites and parasitism esp. among animals — **par·a·si·to·log·i·cal** \-ˌsit-ᵊl-'äj-i-kəl, -ˌsīt-\ *also* **par·a·si·to·log·ic** \-ik\ *adj* — **par·a·si·tol·o·gist** \-sə-'täl-ə-jəst, -ˌsīt-'äl-\ *n*

par·a·sit·osis \-sə-'tō-səs, -ˌsīt-'ō-\ *n, pl* **-o·ses** \-ˌsēz\ [NL] **:** infestation with or disease caused by parasites

para·sol \'par-ə-ˌsȯl, -ˌsäl\ *n* [F, fr. OIt *parasole,* fr. *parare* to shield + *sole* sun, fr. L *sol* — more at PARAPET, SOLAR] **:** a lightweight umbrella used as a sunshade esp. by women

¹para·sym·pa·thet·ic \ˌpar-ə-ˌsim-pə-'thet-ik\ *adj* [ISV] **:** of, relating to, being, or acting on the parasympathetic nervous system

²parasympathetic *n* **1 :** a parasympathetic nerve **2 :** PARASYMPATHETIC NERVOUS SYSTEM

parasympathetic nervous system *n* **:** the part of the autonomic nervous system that contains chiefly cholinergic fibers, that tends to induce secretion, to increase the tone and contractility of smooth muscle, and to cause the dilatation of blood vessels, and that consists of a cranial and a sacral part — compare SYMPATHETIC NERVOUS SYSTEM

para·sym·pa·tho·mi·met·ic \ˌpar-ə-ˌsim-pə-(ˌ)thō-mī-'met-ik, -mə-\ *adj* [ISV] **:** simulating parasympathetic nervous action in physiological effect

para·syn·the·sis \ˌpar-ə-'sin(t)-thə-səs\ *n* [NL] **:** the formation of words by adding a derivative ending and prefixing a particle (as in *denationalize*) — **para·syn·thet·ic** \-sin-'thet-ik\ *adj*

para·tac·tic \ˌpar-ə-'tak-tik\ *adj* **:** of or relating to parataxis — **para·tac·ti·cal** \-ti-kəl\ *adj* — **para·tac·ti·cal·ly** \-ti-k(ə-)lē\ *adv*

para·tax·is \ˌpar-ə-'tak-səs\ *n* [NL, fr. Gk, act of placing side by side, fr. *paratassein* to place side by side, fr. *para-* + *tassein* to arrange — more at TACTICS] **:** the placing of clauses or phrases one after another without coordinating or subordinating connectives

para·thi·on \ˌpar-ə-'thī-ən, -ˌän\ *n* [*para-* + *thio*phosphate + *-on*] **:** an extremely toxic thiophosphate insecticide $C_{10}H_{14}NO_5PS$

¹para·thy·roid \-'thī-ˌrȯid\ *n* **:** PARATHYROID GLAND

²parathyroid *adj* [ISV] **:** of, relating to, or produced by the parathyroid glands

para·thy·roid·ec·to·my \-ˌrȯid-'ek-tə-mē\ *n, pl* **-mies :** excision of the parathyroid glands — **para·thy·roid·ec·to·mized** \-ˌmīzd\ *adj*

parathyroid gland *n* [ISV] **:** any of usu. four small endocrine glands that are adjacent to or embedded in the thyroid gland and produce a hormone concerned with calcium metabolism

para·troop·er \'par-ə-ˌtrü-pər\ *n* **:** a member of the paratroops

para·troops \-ˌtrüps\ *n pl* [²*-para*] **:** troops trained and equipped to parachute from an airplane — **para·troop** \-ˌtrüp\ *adj*

¹para·ty·phoid \ˌpar-ə-'tī-ˌfȯid, -(ˌ)tī-'\ *adj* [ISV] **1 :** resembling typhoid fever **2 :** of or relating to paratyphoid or its causative organisms <~ infection>

²paratyphoid *n* **:** a salmonellosis that resembles typhoid fever and is commonly contracted by eating contaminated food — called also *paratyphoid fever*

para·vane \'par-ə-ˌvān\ *n* **:** a torpedo-shaped underwater protective device with serrate teeth in its forward end towed from the bow of a ship in mined areas to sever the moorings of mines

par·boil \'pär-ˌbȯil\ *vt* [ME *parboilen,* fr. *parboilen* to boil thoroughly, fr. MF *parboillir,* fr. LL *perbullire,* fr. L *per-* thoroughly (fr. *per* through) + *bullire* to boil, fr. *bulla* bubble — more at FOR] **:** to boil briefly as a preliminary or incomplete cooking procedure

¹par·buck·le \'pär-ˌbək-əl\ *n* [origin unknown] **1 :** a purchase for hoisting or lowering a cylindrical object by making fast the middle of a long rope aloft and looping both ends around the object which rests in the loops and rolls in them as the ends are hauled up or paid out **2 :** a double sling made of a single rope (as for slinging a cask)

²parbuckle *vb* **par·buck·led; par·buck·ling** \-ˌbək-(ə-)liŋ\ **:** to hoist or lower by means of a parbuckle

Par·cae \'pär-ˌkī, -ˌsē\ *n pl* [L] **:** FATE 4

¹par·cel \'pär-səl\ *n* [ME, fr. MF, fr. (assumed) VL *particella,* fr. L *particula* small part — more at PARTICLE] **1 :** FRAGMENT, PORTION **2 :** a tract or plot of land **3 :** a company, collection, or group of persons, animals, or things **:** LOT <the whole story was a ~ of lies> **4 a :** a wrapped bundle **:** PACKAGE **b :** a unit of salable merchandise **5 :** PARCELING 2 ***syn*** see GROUP

²parcel *adv, archaic* **:** PARTLY

³parcel *vt* **par·celed** *or* **par·celled; par·cel·ing** *or* **par·cel·ling** \'pär-s(ə-)liŋ\ **1 :** to divide into parts **:** DISTRIBUTE — often used with *out* **2 :** to make up into a parcel **:** WRAP **3 :** to cover (as a rope) with strips of canvas

⁴parcel *adj* **:** PART-TIME, PARTIAL

par·cel·ing *or* **par·cel·ling** *n* **1 a :** the act of dividing and distributing in portions **b :** the act of wrapping into bundles **2 a :** the covering of a caulked seam with canvas and then tarring it **b :** long narrow tarred slips of canvas wound about a rope to exclude moisture

parcel post *n* **1 :** a mail service handling parcels **2 :** packages handled by parcel post

parcel post zone *n* **:** ZONE 5b

par·ce·nary \'pärs-ᵊn-ˌer-ē\ *n* [AF *parcenarie,* fr. OF *parçonerie,* fr. *parçon* portion, fr. L *partition-, partitio* partition] **:** COPARCENARY 1

par·ce·ner \'pärs-nər, -ᵊn-ər\ *n* [AF, fr. OF *parçonier,* fr. *parçon*] **:** COPARCENER

parch \'pärch\ *vb* [ME *parchen*] *vt* **1 :** to toast under dry heat **2 :** to shrivel with heat **3 :** to dry or shrivel with cold ~ *vi* **:** to become dry or scorched

Par·chee·si \pär-'chē-zē, pər-, *esp Brit* -sē\ *trademark* — used for a board game adapted from pachisi

parch·ment \'pärch-mənt\ *n* [ME *parchemin,* fr. OF, modif. of L *pergamena,* fr. Gk *pergamēnē,* fr. fem. of *Pergamēnos* of Pergamum, fr. *Pergamon* Pergamum] **1 :** the skin of a sheep or goat prepared for writing on **2 :** strong, tough, and often somewhat translucent paper made to resemble parchment **3 :** a parchment manuscript; *also* **:** an academic diploma

¹pard \'pärd\ *n* [ME *parde,* fr. OF, fr. L *pardus,* fr. Gk *pardos*] **:** LEOPARD

²pard *n* [short for *pardner*] *chiefly dial* **:** PARTNER, CHUM

par·die *or* **par·di** *or* **par·dy** \pər-'dē, pär-\ *interj* [ME *pardee,* fr. OF *par Dé* by God] *archaic* — used as a mild oath

pard·ner \'pärd-nər\ *n, chiefly dial* **:** PARTNER, CHUM

¹par·don \'pärd-ᵊn\ *n* **1 :** the excusing of an offense without exacting a penalty **2 :** INDULGENCE 1 **3 a :** a release from the legal penalties of an offense **b :** an official warrant of remission of penalty **4 :** excuse or forgiveness for a fault, offense, or discourtesy

²pardon *vt* **par·doned; par·don·ing** \'pärd-niŋ, -ᵊn-iŋ\ [ME *pardonen,* fr. MF *pardoner,* fr. LL *perdonare* to grant freely, fr. L *per-*

thoroughly + *donare* to give — more at PARBOIL, DONATION] **1 a** : to absolve from the consequences of a fault or crime **b** : to allow (an offense) to pass without punishment : FORGIVE **c** : to relieve of a penalty improperly assessed **2** : TOLERATE ***syn*** see EXCUSE ***ant*** punish

par·don·able \ˈpärd-nə-bəl, -ᵊn-ə-bəl\ *adj* : admitting of being pardoned : EXCUSABLE <~ offenses> — **par·don·able·ness** *n* — **par·don·ably** \-blē\ *adv*

par·don·er \ˈpärd-nər, -ᵊn-ər\ *n* **1** : a medieval preacher delegated to raise money for religious works by soliciting offerings and granting indulgences **2** : one that pardons

pare \ˈpa(ə)r, ˈpe(ə)r\ *vt* **pared; par·ing** [ME *paren*, fr. MF *parer* to prepare, trim, fr. L *parare* to prepare, acquire; akin to OE *fearr* bull, ox, L *parere* to give birth to, produce] **1** : to trim or shave off <~ the skin from an apple> **2** : to diminish gradually by or as if by paring <~ expenses> — **par·er** *n*

par·e·go·ric \ˌpar-ə-ˈgȯr-ik, -ˈgōr-, -ˈgär-\ *n* [F *parégorique* mitigating pain, fr. LL *paregoricus*, fr. Gk *parēgorikos*, fr. *parēgorein* to talk over, soothe, fr. *para-* + *agora* assembly — more at GREGARIOUS] : camphorated tincture of opium used esp. to relieve pain

pa·ren·chy·ma \pə-ˈreŋ-kə-mə\ *n* [NL, fr. Gk, visceral flesh, fr. *parenchein* to pour in beside, fr. *para-* + *en-* + *chein* to pour — more at FOUND] **1** : a tissue of higher plants that consists of thin-walled living photosynthetic or storage cells capable of division even when mature and that makes up much of the substance of leaves and roots, the pulp of fruits, and parts of stems and supporting structures **2** : the essential and distinctive tissue of an organ or an abnormal growth as distinguished from its supportive framework — **par·en·chy·ma·tous** \ˌpar-ən-ˈkim-ət-əs, -ˈkīm-\ *also* **pa·ren·chy·mal** \pə-ˈreŋ-kə-məl, ˌpar-ən-ˈkī-\ *adj* — **par·en·chy·ma·tous·ly** *adv*

¹par·ent \ˈpar-ənt, ˈper-\ *n* [ME, fr. MF, fr. L *parent-, parens*, fr. prp. of *parere* to give birth to] **1** : one that begets or brings forth offspring **2 a** : an animal or plant that is regarded in relation to its offspring **b** : the material or source from which something is derived — **parent** *adj* — **pa·ren·tal** \pə-ˈrent-ᵊl\ *adj* — **pa·ren·tal·ly** \-ᵊl-ē\ *adv*

²parent *vt* : to be or act as the parent of : ORIGINATE, PRODUCE

par·ent·age \ˈpar-ənt-ij, ˈper-\ *n* **1 a** : descent from parents or ancestors : LINEAGE <a man of noble ~> **b** : DERIVATION, ORIGIN <the ballads about them are of common ~ —G. B. Johnson> **2** : the standing or position of a parent : PARENTHOOD

parental generation *n* : a generation of individuals of distinctively different genotypes that are crossed to produce hybrids

par·en·ter·al \pə-ˈrent-ə-rəl\ *adj* [ISV *para-* + *enteral*] : situated or occurring outside the intestine; *esp* : introduced otherwise than by way of the intestines — **par·en·ter·al·ly** \-rə-lē\ *adv*

pa·ren·the·sis \pə-ˈren(t)-thə-səs\ *n, pl* **-the·ses** \-ˌsēz\ [LL, fr. Gk, lit., act of inserting, fr. *parentithenai* to insert, fr. *para-* + *en-* + *tithenai* to place — more at DO] **1 a** : an amplifying or explanatory word, phrase, or sentence inserted in a passage from which it is usu. set off by punctuation **b** : a remark or passage that departs from the theme of a discourse : DIGRESSION **2** : INTERLUDE, INTERVAL **3** : one or both of the curved marks ( ) used in writing and printing to enclose a parenthetic expression or to group a symbolic unit in a logical or mathematical expression — **par·en·thet·ic** \ˌpar-ən-ˈthet-ik\ *or* **par·en·thet·i·cal** \-i-kəl\ *adj* — **par·en·thet·i·cal·ly** \-k(ə-)lē\ *adv*

pa·ren·the·size \pə-ˈren(t)-thə-ˌsīz\ *vt* **-sized; -siz·ing** : to make a parenthesis of

par·ent·hood \ˈpar-ənt-ˌhu̇d, ˈper-\ *n* : the position, function, or standing of a parent

parent-teacher association *n* : an organization of local groups of teachers and the parents of their pupils that works for the improvement of the schools and the benefit of the pupils

pa·re·sis \pə-ˈrē-səs, ˈpar-ə-\ *n, pl* **pa·re·ses** \-ˌsēz\ [NL, fr. Gk, fr. *parienai* to let fall, fr. *para-* + *hienai* to let go, send — more at JET] **1** : slight or partial paralysis **2** : GENERAL PARESIS — **pa·ret·ic** \pə-ˈret-ik\ *adj or n*

par·es·the·sia \ˌpar-əs-ˈthē-zhə\ *n* [NL] : a sensation of pricking, tingling, or creeping on the skin that has no objective cause — **par·es·thet·ic** \-ˈthet-ik\ *adj*

pa·reu \ˈpär-ē-ˌü\ *n* [Tahitian] : a wraparound skirt or loincloth of Polynesia

pa·re·ve \ˈpär-(ə-)və\ *adj* [Yiddish *parev*] : made without milk, meat, or their derivatives <~ margarine> — compare FLEISHIG, MILCHIG

par ex·cel·lence \ˌpär-ˌek-sə-ˈläⁿs\ *adj* [F, lit., by excellence] : being the best of a kind : PREEMINENT

par·fait \pär-ˈfā\ *n* [F, lit., something perfect, fr. *parfait* perfect, fr. L *perfectus*] **1** : a flavored custard containing whipped cream and syrup frozen without stirring **2** : a cold dessert made of layers of fruit, syrup, ice cream, and whipped cream

parfait glass *n* : a tall narrow glass with a short stem used for serving a parfait

par·fleche \ˈpär-ˌflesh\ *n* [CanF *parflèche*] **1** : a raw hide soaked in lye to remove the hair and dried **2** : an article (as a bag or case) made of parfleche

par·fo·cal \(ˈ)pär-ˈfō-kəl\ *adj* [L *par* equal + E *focal*] : being or having lenses or lens sets (as eyepieces) with the corresponding focal points all in the same plane — **par·fo·cal·i·ty** \ˌpär-fō-ˈkal-ət-ē\ *n* — **par·fo·cal·ize** \(ˈ)pär-ˈfō-kə-ˌlīz\ *vt*

parge \ˈpärj\ *vt* **parged; parg·ing** : PARGET

¹par·get \ˈpär-jət\ *vt* **-get·ed** *or* **-get·ted; -get·ing** *or* **-get·ting** [ME *pargetten*, fr. MF *parjeter* to throw on top of, fr. *par-* thoroughly (fr. L *per-*) + *jeter* to throw — more at JET] : to coat with plaster; *esp* : to apply ornamental or waterproofing plaster to

²parget *n* **1** : plaster, whitewash, or roughcast for coating a wall **2** : plasterwork esp. in raised ornamental figures on walls

par·gy·line \ˈpär-jə-ˌlēn\ *n* [pro*pargyl* (an alcohol) + *-ine*] : a monoamine oxidase inhibitor $C_{11}H_{13}N$ that is used as an antihypertensive and antidepressant agent

parhelic circle *n* : a luminous circle or halo parallel to the horizon at the altitude of the sun — called also *parhelic ring*

par·he·lion \pär-ˈhēl-yən\ *n, pl* **-lia** \-yə\ [L *parelion*, fr. Gk *parēlion*, fr. *para-* + *hēlios* sun — more at SOLAR] : any one of several bright spots often tinged with color that often appear on the parhelic circle — **par·he·lic** \-ˈhē-lik\ *adj*

pa·ri·ah \pə-ˈrī-ə\ *n* [Tamil *paraiyan*, lit., drummer] **1** : a member of a low caste of southern India and Burma **2** : OUTCAST

par·i·an \ˈpar-ē-ən, ˈper-\ *n* [*Parian*; fr. its suitability for making statuettes] : a porcelaneous ceramic ware composed essentially of kaolin and feldspar and usu. used unglazed in ornamental articles

Par·i·an \ˈpar-ē-ən, ˈper-\ *adj* : of or relating to the island of Paros noted for its marble used extensively for sculpture in ancient times

Parian ware *n* **1** : PARIAN **2** : articles made of parian

par·i·es \ˈpar-ē-ˌēz, ˈper-\ *n, pl* **pa·ri·etes** \pə-ˈrī-ə-ˌtēz\ [NL *pariet-, paries*, fr. L, wall; akin to L *sparus* spear — more at SPEAR] : the wall of a cavity or hollow organ — usu. used in pl.

¹pa·ri·etal \pə-ˈrī-ət-ᵊl\ *adj* **1 a** : of or relating to the walls of a part or cavity **b** : of, relating to, or forming the upper posterior wall of the head **2** : attached to the main wall rather than the axis or a cross wall of a plant ovary — used of an ovule or a placenta **3** : of or relating to college living or its regulation; *esp* : of or relating to parietals

²parietal *n* **1** : a parietal part (as a bone, scale, or plate) **2** *pl* : the regulations governing the visiting privileges of members of the opposite sex in campus dormitories

parietal bone *n* : either of a pair of membrane bones of the roof of the skull between the frontal bones and the occipital bones

parietal cell *n* : any of the large oval acid-secreting cells of the gastric mucous membrane

parietal lobe *n* : the middle division of each cerebral hemisphere that contains an area concerned with bodily sensations

pari-mu·tu·el \ˌpar-i-ˈmyüch-(ə-)wəl, -ˈmyü-chəl\ *n* [F *pari mutuel*, lit., mutual stake] **1** : a betting pool in which those who bet on the winners of the first three places share the total amount bet minus a percentage for the management **2** : a machine for registering the bets and computing the payoffs in pari-mutuel betting

par·ing \ˈpa(ə)r-iŋ, ˈpe(ə)r-\ *n* **1** : the act of cutting away an edge or surface **2** : something pared off <apple ~*s*>

paring knife *n* : a small short-bladed knife (as for paring fruit)

pa·ri pas·su \ˌpar-i-ˈpas-(ˌ)ü\ *adv or adj* [L, with equal step] : at an equal rate or pace

Par·is \ˈpar-əs\ *n* [L, fr. Gk] : a son of Priam whose abduction of Helen leads to the Trojan War according to Homer's *Iliad*

Par·is green \ˌpar-əs-\ *n* [*Paris*, France] **1** : a very poisonous bright green powder that is used as an insecticide and pigment **2** : a variable color averaging a brilliant yellowish green

par·ish \ˈpar-ish\ *n* [ME *parisshe*, fr. MF *parroche*, fr. LL *parochia*, fr. LGk *paroikia*, fr. *paroikos* Christian, fr. Gk, stranger, fr. *para-* + *oikos* house — more at VICINITY] **1 a** (1) : the ecclesiastical unit of area committed to one pastor (2) : the residents of such an area **b** *Brit* : a subdivision of a county often coinciding with an original ecclesiastical parish and constituting the unit of local government **2** : a local church community composed of the members or constituents of a Protestant church **3** : a civil division of the state of Louisiana corresponding to a county in other states

pa·rish·io·ner \pə-ˈrish-(ə-)nər\ *n* [ME *parisshoner*, prob. modif. of MF *parrochien*, fr. *parroche*] : a member or inhabitant of a parish

¹par·i·ty \ˈpar-ət-ē\ *n, pl* **-ties** [L *paritas*, fr. *par* equal] **1** : the quality or state of being equal or equivalent **2 a** : equivalence of a commodity price expressed in one currency to its price expressed in another **b** : equality of purchasing power established by law between different kinds of money at a given ratio **3** : an equivalence between farmers' current purchasing power and their purchasing power at a selected base period maintained by government support of agricultural commodity prices **4 a** : the property of an integer with respect to being odd or even <3 and 7 have the same ~> **b** : the property of oddness or evenness of an odd or even function (as certain functions in quantum mechanics) **c** (1) : the state of being odd or even used as the basis of a method of detecting errors in binary-coded data (2) : PARITY BIT **5** : the property of an elementary particle or physical system that indicates whether or not its mirror image occurs in nature

²parity *n* [*-parous*] : the state or fact of having borne offspring; *also* : the number of children previously borne

parity bit *n* : a bit added to an array of bits (as on magnetic tape) to provide parity

¹park \ˈpärk\ *n* [ME, fr. OF *parc* enclosure, fr. (assumed) VL *parricus*] **1 a** : an enclosed piece of ground stocked with game and held by royal prescription or grant **b** : a tract of land that often includes lawns, woodland, and pasture attached to a country house and is used as a game preserve and for recreation **2 a** : a piece of ground in or near a city or town kept for ornament and recreation **b** : an area maintained in its natural state as a public property **3 a** : a level valley between mountain ranges **b** : an open space and esp. a grassland that is often all or partly surrounded by woodland and is suitable for cultivation or grazing **4 a** : a space occupied by military animals, vehicles, or materials **b** : PARKING LOT **5** : an enclosed arena or stadium used esp. for ball games — **park·like** \ˈpär-ˌklīk\ *adj*

²park *vt* **1** : to enclose in a park **2 a** (1) : to bring to a stop and keep standing at the edge of a public way (2) : to leave temporarily on a public way or in a parking lot or garage **b** : to land or leave (as an airplane) **c** : to establish (as a satellite) in orbit **3** : to set and leave temporarily **4** : to assemble (as

equipment or stores) in a military dump or park ~ *vi* : to park a vehicle — **park·er** *n*
par·ka \'pär-kə\ *n* [Aleut, skin, outer garment, fr. Russ, pelt, fr. Yurak] **1** : a hooded fur pullover garment for arctic wear **2** : a fabric pullover or jacket for sports or military wear
parking lot *n* : an area used for the parking of motor vehicles
parking meter *n* : a coin-operated device which registers the purchase of parking time for a motor vehicle
par·kin·so·nian \,pär-kən-'sō-nē-ən, -nyən\ *adj* **1** : of or similar to that of parkinsonism **2** : affected with parkinsonism and esp. Parkinson's disease
par·kin·son·ism \'pär-kən-sə-,niz-əm\ *n* **1** : PARKINSON'S DISEASE **2** : a chronic nervous disorder that is marked by muscle rigidity but without tremor of resting muscles
Par·kin·son's disease \'pär-kən-sənz-\ *n* [James *Parkinson* †1824 E physician] : a chronic progressive nervous disease of later life that is marked by tremor and weakness of resting muscles and by a peculiar gait — called also *paralysis agitans, parkinsonism, Parkinson's syndrome*
Par·kin·son's Law \,pär-\ *n* [C. Northcote *Parkinson* b1909 E historian] **1** : an observation in office organization: the number of subordinates increases at a fixed rate regardless of the amount of work produced **2** : an observation in office organization: work expands so as to fill the time available for its completion
park·land \'pär-,kland\ *n* : land with clumps of trees and shrubs in cultivated condition used as or felt to be suitable for use as a park
park·way \'pär-,kwā\ *n* : a broad landscaped thoroughfare
par·lance \'pär-lən(t)s\ *n* [MF, fr. OF, fr. *parler*] **1** : SPEECH; *esp* : formal debate or parley **2** : manner or mode of speech : IDIOM
par·lan·do \pär-'län-(,)dō\ *or* **par·lan·te** \-(,)tā\ *adj* [*parlando* fr. It. verbal of *parlare* to speak, fr. ML *parabolare; parlante* fr. It, prp. of *parlare*] : delivered or performed in an unsustained style suggestive of speech — used as a direction in music
¹par·lay \'pär-,lā, -lē\ *vt* [F *paroli,* n., parlay, fr. It dial., pl. of *parolo,* fr. *paro* equal, fr. L *par*] **1** : to bet in a parlay **2 a** : to exploit successfully **b** : to increase or otherwise transform into something of much greater value
²parlay *n* : a series of two or more bets so set up in advance that the original stake plus its winnings are risked on the successive wagers; *broadly* : the fresh risking of an original stake together with its winnings
parle \'pär(ə)l\ *vi* **parled; parl·ing** [ME *parlen* to parley, fr. MF *parler*] *archaic* : PARLEY — **parle** *n, archaic*
¹par·ley \'pär-lē\ *vi* [MF *parler* to speak, fr. ML *parabolare,* fr. LL *parabola* speech, parable — more at PARABLE] : to speak with another : CONFER; *specif* : to discuss terms with an enemy
²parley *n, pl* **parleys** **1 a** : a conference for discussion of points in dispute **b** : a conference with an enemy **2** : DISCUSSION
par·lia·ment \'pär-lə-mənt *also* 'pärl-yə-\ *n* [ME, fr. OF *parlement,* fr. *parler*] **1** : a formal conference for the discussion of public affairs; *specif* : a council of state in early medieval England **2 a** : an assemblage of the nobility, clergy, and commons called together by the British sovereign as the supreme legislative body in the United Kingdom **b** : a similar assemblage in another nation or state **3 a** : the supreme legislative body of a usu. major political unit that is a continuing institution comprising a series of individual parliaments **b** : the British House of Commons **4** : one of several principal courts of justice existing in France before the revolution of 1789
par·lia·men·tar·i·an \,pär-lə-,men-'ter-ē-ən, -mən- *also* ,pärl-yə-\ *n* **1** *often cap* : an adherent of the parliament in opposition to the king during the English Civil War **2** : an expert in the rules and usages of a deliberative assembly (as a parliament)
par·lia·men·ta·ry \-'ment-ə-rē, -'men-trē\ *adj* **1 a** : of or relating to a parliament **b** : enacted, done, or ratified by a parliament **2** : of or adhering to the parliament as opposed to the king during the English Civil War **3** : of, based on, or having the characteristics of parliamentary government **4** : of or relating to members of a parliament **5** : of or according to parliamentary law <~ procedure>
parliamentary government *n* : a system of government having the real executive power vested in a cabinet composed of members of the legislature who are individually and collectively responsible to the legislature
parliamentary law *n* : the rules and precedents governing the proceedings of deliberative assemblies and other organizations
¹par·lor \'pär-lər\ *n* [ME *parlour,* fr. OF, fr. *parler*] **1** : a room used primarily for conversation or the reception of guests: as **a** : a room in a private dwelling for the entertainment of guests **b** : a conference chamber or private reception room **c** : a room in an inn, hotel, or club for conversation or semiprivate uses **2** : any of various business places <a funeral ~> <a beauty ~>
²parlor *adj* **1** : used in or suitable for a parlor <~ furniture> **2 a** : fostered or advocated in comfortable seclusion without consequent action or application to affairs <~ bolshevism> **b** : given to or characterized by fostering or advocating something (as a doctrine) in such a manner <~ socialist>
parlor car *n* : an extra-fare railroad passenger car for day travel equipped with individual chairs
parlor game *n* : a game suitable for playing indoors (as in a parlor)
parlor grand *n* : a grand piano intermediate in length between a concert grand and a baby grand
par·lour \'pär-lər\ *chiefly Brit var of* PARLOR
¹par·lous \'pär-ləs\ *adj* [ME, alter. of *perilous*] **1** : full of danger or risk : HAZARDOUS **2** *obs* : dangerously shrewd or cunning — **par·lous·ly** *adv*
²parlous *adv* : to a very great extent : EXCEEDINGLY
Par·me·san \'pär-mə-,zän, -,zan, -zən\ *n* [*Parmesan* (of Parma)] : a very hard dry sharply flavored cheese that is sold grated or in wedges
par·mi·gia·na \,pär-mi-'jän-ə\ *or* **par·mi·gia·no** \-'jän-(,)ō\ *adj* [It *Parmigiana,* fem. of *Parmigiano* of Parma, fr. *Parma*] : made or covered with Parmesan cheese <veal ~>

Par·nas·si·an \pär-'nas-ē-ən\ *adj* **1** [L *parnassius* of Parnassus, fr. Gk *parnasios,* fr. *Parnasos* Parnassus, mountain in Greece sacred to Apollo and the Muses] : of or relating to poetry **2** [F *parnassien,* fr. *Parnasse* Parnassus; fr. *Le Parnasse contemporain* (1866) an anthology of poetry] : of or relating to a school of French poets of the second half of the 19th century emphasizing metrical form rather than emotion — **Parnassian** *n*
pa·ro·chi·al \pə-'rō-kē-əl\ *adj* [ME *parochiall,* fr. MF *parochial,* fr. LL *parochialis,* fr. *parochia* parish — more at PARISH] **1** : of or relating to a church parish **2** : of or relating to a parish as a unit of local government **3** : confined or restricted as if within the borders of a parish : limited in range or scope (as to a narrow area or region) : PROVINCIAL, NARROW — **pa·ro·chi·al·ly** \-kē-ə-lē\ *adv*
pa·ro·chi·al·ism \-kē-ə-,liz-əm\ *n* : the quality or state of being parochial; *esp* : selfish pettiness or narrowness (as of interests, opinions, or views)
parochial school *n* : a private school maintained by a religious body usu. for elementary and secondary instruction
par·o·dist \'par-əd-əst\ *n* : a writer of parodies
¹par·o·dy \'par-əd-ē\ *n, pl* **-dies** [L *parodia,* fr. Gk *parōidia,* fr. *para-* + *aidein* to sing — more at ODE] **1** : a literary or musical work in which the style of an author or work is closely imitated for comic effect or in ridicule **2** : a feeble or ridiculous imitation ***syn*** see CARICATURE — **pa·rod·ic** \pə-'räd-ik, pa-\ *adj* — **par·o·dis·tic** \,par-ə-'dis-tik\ *adj*
²parody *vt* **-died; -dy·ing** **1** : to compose a parody on <~ a poem> **2** : to imitate in the manner of a parody
par·ol \'par-əl\ *n* [MF *parole*] : WORD OF MOUTH — **parol** *adj*
¹pa·role \pə-'rōl\ *n* [F, speech, parole, fr. MF, fr. LL *parabola* speech — more at PARABLE] **1** : a promise made with or confirmed by a pledge of one's honor; *esp* : the promise of a prisoner of war to fulfill stated conditions in consideration of his release **2** : a watchword given only to officers of the guard and of the day **3** : a conditional release of a prisoner serving an indeterminate or unexpired sentence **4** : a linguistic act : linguistic behavior — compare LANGUE — **parole** *adj*
²parole *vt* **pa·roled; pa·rol·ing** : to release (a prisoner) on parole
pa·rol·ee \pə-,rō-'lē, -'rō-(,); ,par-ə-'lē\ *n* : one released on parole
par·ono·ma·sia \,par-ə-nō-'mā-zh(ē-)ə, ,par-,än-ə-'mā-\ *n* [L, fr. Gk, fr. *paronomazein* to call with a slight change of name, fr. *para-* + *onoma* name — more at NAME] : a play on words : PUN — **par·ono·mas·tic** \-'mas-tik\ *adj*
par·onym \'par-ə-,nim\ *n* [LL *paronymon,* fr. Gk *parōnymon,* neut. of *parōnymos*] : a paronymous word
par·on·y·mous \pə-'rän-ə-məs, pa-\ *adj* [Gk *parōnymos,* fr. *para-* + *-ōnymos* (as in *homōnymos* homonymous)] **1** : CONJUGATE **4** **2 a** : formed from a word in another language **b** : having a form similar to that of a cognate foreign word
par·ot·id \pə-'rät-əd\ *adj* [NL *parotid-, parotis* parotid gland, fr. L, tumor near the ear, fr. Gk *parōtid-, parōtis,* fr. *para-* + *ōt-, ous* ear — more at EAR] : of or relating to the parotid gland
parotid gland *n* : either of a pair of large serous salivary glands situated below and in front of the ear
par·oti·tis \,par-ō-'tīt-əs\ *n* : inflammation of the parotid glands; *also* : MUMPS
par·ous \'par-əs, 'per-\ *adj* [*-parous*] : having produced offspring
-p·a·rous \p-(ə-)rəs\ *adj comb form* [L *-parus,* fr. *parere* to give birth to, produce] : giving birth to : producing <bi*parous*>
Par·ou·sia \,pär-ü-'sē-ə, pə-'rü-zē-ə\ *n* [Gk, lit., presence, fr. *paront-, parōn,* prp. of *pareinai* to be present, fr. *para-* + *einai* to be — more at IS] : SECOND COMING
par·ox·ysm \'par-ək-,siz-əm *also* pə-'räk-\ *n* [F & ML; F *paroxysme,* fr. ML *paroxysmus,* fr. Gk *paroxysmos,* fr. *paroxynein* to stimulate, fr. *para-* + *oxynein* to provoke, fr. *oxys* sharp — more at OXYGEN] **1** : a fit, attack, or sudden increase or recurrence of symptoms (as of a disease) : CONVULSION <a ~ of coughing> **2** : a sudden violent emotion or action <a ~ of rage> — **par·ox·ys·mal** \,par-ək-'siz-məl *also* pə-,räk-\ *adj*
par·oxy·tone \(')pa(ə)r-'äk-si-,tōn\ *adj* [NL *paroxytonus,* fr. Gk *paroxytonos,* fr. *para-* + *oxytonos* oxytone] : having or characterized by an acute accent on the penult — **paroxytone** *n*
¹par·quet \pär-'kā\ *vt* **par·queted** \-'kād\; **par·quet·ing** \-'kā-iŋ\ **1** : to furnish with a floor of parquet **2** : to make of parquetry
²par·quet \'pär-,kā, pär-'\ *n* [F, fr. MF, small enclosure, fr. *parc* park] **1 a** : a patterned flooring; *esp* : one made of parquetry **b** : PARQUETRY **2** : the main floor of a theater; *specif* : the part from the front of the stage to the parquet circle
parquet circle *n* : the part of the main floor of a theater that is beneath the galleries
par·que·try \'pär-kə-trē\ *n, pl* **-tries** : work in the form of usu. geometrically patterned wood laid or inlaid esp. for floors

parquetry

parr \'pär\ *n, pl* **parr** *also* **parrs** [origin unknown] : a young salmon actively feeding in fresh water; *also* : the young of any of several other fishes
par·ra·keet *var of* PARAKEET
par·rel *or* **par·ral** \'par-əl\ *n* [ME *perell,* fr. alter. of *parail* apparel, short for *apparail,* fr. MF *apareil,* fr. *apareillier* to prepare — more at APPAREL] : a rope loop or sliding collar by which a yard or spar is held to a mast in such a way that it may be hoisted or lowered
par·ri·cid·al \,par-ə-'sīd-ᵊl\ *adj* : of, relating to, or guilty of parricide
par·ri·cide \'par-ə-,sīd\ *n* **1** [L *parricida* killer of a close relative, fr. *parri-* (akin to Gk *pēos* kinsman by marriage) + *-cida* -cide] : one that murders his father, mother, or a close relative **2** [L *parricidium* murder of a close relative, fr. *parri-* + *-cidium* -cide] : the act of a parricide
¹par·rot \'par-ət\ *n* [prob. irreg. fr. MF *perroquet*] **1** : any of numerous widely distributed tropical zygodactyl birds (order Psittaciformes) that have a distinctive stout curved hooked bill, are often crested and brightly variegated, and are excellent mimics **2**

: a person who sedulously echoes another's words — **parrot** *adj*

²parrot *vt* : to repeat by rote

parrot fever *n* : PSITTACOSIS

parrot fish *n* : any of numerous marine percoid fishes (as of the families Scaridae and Labridae) that have the teeth in each jaw fused into a cutting plate like a beak

par·ry \'par-ē\ *vb* **par·ried; par·ry·ing** [prob. fr. F *parez*, imper. of *parer* to parry, fr. OProv *parar*, fr. L *parare* to prepare — more at PARE] *vi* **1** : to ward off a weapon or blow **2** : to evade or turn aside something ~ *vt* **1** : to ward off (as a blow) **2** : to evade esp. by an adroit answer <~ an embarrassing question> — **parry** *n*

parse \'pärs, 'pärz\ *vb* **parsed; pars·ing** [L *pars orationis* part of speech] *vt* **1** : to resolve (as a sentence) into component parts of speech and describe them grammatically **2** : to describe grammatically by stating the part of speech and explaining the inflection and syntactical relationships ~ *vi* **1** : to give a grammatical description of a word or a group of words **2** : to admit of being parsed

par·sec \'pär-ˌsek\ *n* [*par*allax + *sec*ond] : a unit of measure for interstellar space equal to a distance having a heliocentric parallax of one second or to 206,265 times the radius of the earth's orbit or to 3.26 light-years or to 19.2 trillion miles

Par·si *also* **Par·see** \'pär-(ˌ)sē\ *n* [Per *pārsī*, fr. *Pārs* Persia] **1** : a Zoroastrian descended from Persian refugees settled principally at Bombay **2** : the Iranian dialect of the Parsi religious literature — **Par·si·ism** \-ˌiz-əm\ *n*

Par·si·fal \'pär-zi-ˌfäl, -sə-ˌfȯl\ *n* [G] : a knight of the Holy Grail in Wagner's *Parsifal*

par·si·mo·ni·ous \ˌpär-sə-'mō-nē-əs\ *adj* : frugal to the point of stinginess : NIGGARDLY ***syn*** see STINGY ***ant*** prodigal — **par·si·mo·ni·ous·ly** *adv*

par·si·mo·ny \'pär-sə-ˌmō-nē\ *n* [ME *parcimony*, fr. L *parsimonia*, fr. *parsus*, pp. of *parcere* to spare] **1 a** : the quality of being careful with money or resources : THRIFT **b** : the quality or state of being niggardly : STINGINESS **2** : economy in the use of a means to an end

pars·ley \'pär-slē\ *n* [ME *persely*, fr. OE *petersilie*, fr. (assumed) VL *petrosilium*, alter. of L *petroselinum*, fr. Gk *petroselinon*, fr. *petros* stone + *selinon* celery] : a southern European annual or biennial herb (*Petroselinum crispum*) of the carrot family widely cultivated for its leaves which are used as a culinary herb or garnish

pars·nip \'pär-snəp\ *n* [ME *pasnepe*, modif. of MF *pasnaie*, fr. L *pastinaca*, fr. *pastinum* 2-pronged dibble] : a European biennial herb (*Pastinaca sativa*) of the carrot family with large pinnate leaves and yellow flowers; *also* : its long tapered root of which some cultivated varieties are used as a vegetable

par·son \'pärs-ᵊn\ *n* [ME *persone*, fr. OF, fr. ML *persona*, lit., person, fr. L] **1** : RECTOR **2** : CLERGYMAN; *esp* : a Protestant pastor

par·son·age \'pär-snij, 'pärs-ᵊn-ij\ *n* : the house provided by a church for its pastor

¹part \'pärt\ *n* [ME, fr. OF & OE, both fr. L *part-, pars*; akin to L *parare* to prepare — more at PARE] **1 a** (1) : one of the often indefinite or unequal subdivisions into which something is or is regarded as divided and which together constitute the whole (2) : an essential portion or integral element **b** : one of several or many equal units of which something is composed or into which it is divisible : an amount equal to another amount <mix one ~ of the powder with three ~*s* of water> **c** (1) : an exact divisor of a quantity : ALIQUOT (2) : PARTIAL FRACTION **d** : one of the constituent elements of a plant or animal body: as (1) : ORGAN, MEMBER (2) *pl* : PRIVATE PARTS **e** : a division of a literary work **f** (1) : a vocal or instrumental line or melody in concerted music or in harmony (2) : a particular voice or instrument in concerted music; *also* : the score for it **g** : a constituent member of a machine or other apparatus; *also* : a spare part **2** : something falling to one in a division or apportionment : SHARE **3** : one's share or allotted task (as in an action) <each must do his ~> **4** : one of the opposing sides in a conflict or dispute **5** : a portion of an unspecified territorial area <took off for ~*s* unknown> **6** : a function or course of action performed **7 a** : an actor's lines in a play **b** : the role of a character in a play **8** : a constituent of character or capacity : TALENT <a man of many ~*s*> **9** : the line where the hair is parted

syn PART, PORTION, PIECE, MEMBER, DIVISION, SECTION, SEGMENT, FRAGMENT *shared meaning element* : something less than the whole to which it belongs. PART is a general and neutral term capable of replacing any of the others and especially appropriate when a notion of indefiniteness is prominent <give me *part* of the paper> <they walked *part* of the way> PORTION is likely to imply an assigned or allotted part <cut the pie into six *portions*> PIECE stresses separateness and applies to a part or portion in some way set apart from an expressed or implied whole; thus, one cuts a *piece* of bread from a loaf; one works a *piece* of iron at the forge with the implication that a larger mass exists; one tells a *piece* of news out of a budget of news one possesses <bought a big *piece* of land> MEMBER applies to any of the functional units comprising a whole <the club has 500 *members*> <the saddle seat is a distinctive *member* of a Windsor chair> *Division* and *section* apply to a part set off by or as if by cutting, DIVISION usually suggesting a larger or more diversified and SECTION a smaller or more uniform part; thus, one would speak of the graduate *division* of the university but of the several *sections* of the freshman English class. SEGMENT applies to a part separated or marked off by or as if by natural lines of cleavage <the *segments* of an orange> <the small Jewish *segment* of this gentile community —Bernard Malamud> FRAGMENT applies to a random bit and especially one remaining after the rest has been used, eaten, worn away, or lost <they took up of the *fragments* . . . twelve baskets full —Mt 14:20 (AV)> <a remembered *fragment* of verse> ***ant*** whole

— **for the most part** : in general : on the whole <*for the most part* the crowd was orderly> — **in part** : in some degree : PARTIALLY — **on the part of** : with regard to the one specified

²part *vb* [ME *parten*, fr. OF *partir*, fr. L *partire* to divide, fr. *part-, pars*] *vi* **1 a** : to separate from or take leave of someone **b** : to take leave of one another **2** : to become separated into parts **3 a** : to go away : DEPART **b** : DIE **4** : to become separated, detached, or broken **5** : to relinquish possession or control <hated to ~ with his money> ~ *vt* **1 a** : to divide into parts **b** : to separate by combing on each side of a line **c** : to break or suffer the breaking of (as a rope or anchor chain) **2** : to divide into shares and distribute : APPORTION **3 a** : to remove from contact or association <if aught but death ~ thee and me —Ruth 1:17(AV)> **b** : to keep separate <the narrow channel that ~*s* England from France> **c** : to hold (as brawlers) apart **d** : to separate by a process of extraction, elimination, or secretion **4 a** *archaic* : LEAVE, QUIT **b** *dial Brit* : to give up : RELINQUISH ***syn*** see SEPARATE ***ant*** cleave

³part *adv* : PARTLY

⁴part *adj* : PARTIAL 3

⁵part *abbr* **1** participial; participle **2** particular

par·take \pär-'tāk, pər-\ *vb* **-took** \-'tu̇k\; **-tak·en** \-'tā-kən\; **-tak·ing** [back-formation fr. *partaker*, alter. of *part taker*] *vi* **1** : to take a part or share : PARTICIPATE **2** : to have some of the qualities or attributes of something ~ *vt* : to take part in ***syn*** see SHARE — **par·tak·er** *n*

par·tan \'pärt-ᵊn\ *n* [ME (Sc), of Celt origin; akin to ScGael *partan* crab] : a European edible crab (*Cancer pagurus*)

part·ed \'pärt-əd\ *adj* **1 a** : divided into parts **b** : cleft so that the divisions reach nearly but not quite to the base — usu. used in combination <a 3-*parted* corolla> **2** *archaic* : DEAD

par·terre \pär-'te(ə)r\ *n* [F, fr. MF, fr. *par terre* on the ground] **1** : an ornamental garden with paths between the beds **2** : the part of the main floor of a theater that is behind the orchestra; *esp* : PARQUET CIRCLE

par·the·no·car·py \'pär-thə-nō-ˌkär-pē\ *n* [ISV, fr. Gk *parthenos* virgin + *karpos* fruit — more at HARVEST] : the production of fruits without fertilization <bananas set fruit by ~ and without pollination> — **par·the·no·car·pic** \ˌpär-thə-nō-'kär-pik\ *adj* — **par·the·no·car·pi·cal·ly** \-pi-k(ə-)lē\ *adv*

par·the·no·gen·e·sis \ˌpär-thə-nō-'jen-ə-səs\ *n* [NL, fr. Gk *parthenos* + L *genesis*] : reproduction by development of an unfertilized gamete that occurs esp. among lower plants and invertebrate animals

par·the·no·ge·net·ic \-jə-'net-ik\ *adj* : of, characterized by, or produced by parthenogenesis — **par·the·no·ge·net·i·cal·ly** \-i-k(ə-)lē\ *adv*

Par·the·non \'pär-thə-ˌnän\ *n* [L, fr. Gk *Parthenōn*] : a celebrated Doric temple of Athena built on the acropolis at Athens in the 5th century B.C.

Par·thi·an \'pär-thē-ən\ *adj* **1** : of, relating to, or characteristic of ancient Parthia or its people **2** : of or relating to a shot fired while in real or feigned retreat — **Parthian** *n*

¹par·tial \'pär-shəl\ *adj* [ME *parcial*, fr. MF *partial*, fr. ML *partialis*, fr. LL, of a part, fr. L *part-, pars* part] **1** : inclined to favor one party more than the other : BIASED **2** : markedly fond of someone or something — used with *to* <~ to beans> **3** : of or relating to a part rather than the whole : not general or total <found a ~ solution to the problem> — **par·tial·ly** \'pärsh-(ə-)lē\ *adv*

²partial *n* : OVERTONE 1a

partial denture *n* : an often removable artificial replacement of one or more teeth

partial derivative *n* : the derivative of a function of several variables with respect to one of them and with the remaining variables treated as constants

partial differential equation *n* : a differential equation containing at least one partial derivative

partial differentiation *n* : the process of finding a partial derivative

partial fraction *n* : one of the simpler fractions into the sum of which the quotient of two polynomials may be decomposed

par·tial·i·ty \ˌpär-shē-'al-ət-ē, pär-'shal-\ *n, pl* **-ties** **1** : the quality or state of being partial : BIAS **2** : a special taste or liking

partially ordered *adj* : having some but not all elements connected by a relation that is transitive and not symmetric

partial pressure *n* : the pressure exerted by a (specified) component in a mixture of gases

partial product *n* : a product obtained by multiplying a multiplicand by one digit of a multiplier with more than one digit

par·ti·ble \'pärt-ə-bəl\ *adj* : capable of being parted : DIVISIBLE

par·tic·i·pant \pər-'tis-ə-pənt, pär-\ *n* : one that participates — **participant** *adj*

par·tic·i·pate \pər-'tis-ə-ˌpāt, pär-\ *vb* **-pat·ed; -pat·ing** [L *participatus*, pp. of *participare*, fr. *particip-, particeps* participant, fr. *part-, pars* part + *capere* to take — more at HEAVE] *vt, archaic* : PARTAKE ~ *vi* **1** : to possess something of the nature of a person, thing, or quality **2 a** : to take part <always tried to ~ in class discussions> **b** : to have a part or share in something ***syn*** see SHARE — **par·tic·i·pa·tive** \-ˌpāt-iv\ *adj* — **par·tic·i·pa·tor** \-ˌpāt-ər\ *n*

par·tic·i·pa·tion \pər-ˌtis-ə-'pā-shən, (ˌ)pär-\ *n* **1** : the act of participating **2** : the state of being related to a larger whole

par·tic·i·pa·to·ry \pər-'tis-ə-pə-ˌtōr-ē, pär-, -ˌtȯr-\ *adj* : characterized by or involving participation; *esp* : providing the opportunity for individual participation <~ democracy>

par·ti·cip·i·al \ˌpärt-ə-'sip-ē-əl\ *adj* [L *participialis*, fr. *participium*] : of, relating to, or formed with or from a participle — **par·ti·cip·i·al·ly** \-ē-ə-lē\ *adv*

par·ti·ci·ple \'pärt-ə-ˌsip-əl\ *n* [ME, fr. MF, modif. of L *participium*, fr. *particip-, particeps*] : a word having the characteristics of both verb and adjective; *esp* : an English verbal form that has the function of an adjective and at the same time shows such verbal features as tense and voice and capacity to take an object

par·ti·cle \'pärt-i-kəl\ *n* [ME, fr. L *particula*, fr. dim. of *part-, pars*] **1** *archaic* : a clause or article of a composition or document **2** : one of the minute subdivisions of matter (as an atom or molecule); *also* : ELEMENTARY PARTICLE **3 a** : a minute quantity or fragment **b** : a relatively small or the smallest possible discrete portion or amount of something **4 a** : a unit of speech expressing some general aspect of meaning or some connective or limiting relation and including the articles, most prepositions and conjunctions, and some interjections and adverbs **b** : an element that resembles a word but that is used only in composition (as *un-* in *unfair* and *-ward* in *backward*) **5** : a small eucharistic wafer distributed to a Roman Catholic layman at Communion

particle board *n* : a composition board made of very small pieces of wood bonded together (as with a synthetic resin)

particle physics *n* : HIGH-ENERGY PHYSICS

par·ti–col·ored \ˌpärt-ē-'kəl-ərd\ *adj* [obs. E *party* (parti-colored) + E *colored*] : showing different colors or tints <~ threads>

[1]**par·tic·u·lar** \pə(r)-'tik-yə-lər\ *adj* [ME *particuler*, fr. MF, fr. LL *particularis*, fr. L *particula* small part] **1** : of, relating to, or being a single person or thing <the ~ person I had in mind> **2** *obs* : PARTIAL **3** : of, relating to, or concerned with details <gave us a very ~ account of her day> **4 a** : distinctive among others of the same general category <suffered from measles of ~ severity> **b** : being one unit or element among others <~ incidents in the account seem contrived> **5 a** : being a particular in logic **b** : affirming or denying a predicate to a part of the subject — used of a proposition in logic <"some men are wise" is a ~ affirmative> **6 a** : concerned over or attentive to details : METICULOUS <a very ~ housekeeper> **b** : nice in taste : FASTIDIOUS **c** : hard to please : EXACTING ***syn* 1** see SINGLE ***ant*** general **2** see SPECIAL **3** see CIRCUMSTANTIAL **4** see NICE

[2]**particular** *n* **1** *archaic* : a separate part of a whole **2 a** : an individual fact, point, circumstance, or detail **b** : a specific item or detail of information or news <bill of ~*s*> **3 a** : an individual or a specific subclass in logic falling under some general concept or term **b** : a particular proposition in logic ***syn*** see ITEM — **in particular** : in distinction from others : SPECIFICALLY

par·tic·u·lar·ism \pə(r)-'tik-yə-lə-ˌriz-əm, pär-\ *n* **1** : exclusive or special devotion to a particular interest **2** : a political theory that each political group has a right to promote its own interests and esp. independence without regard to the interests of larger groups **3** : a tendency to explain complex social phenomena in terms of a single causative factor — **par·tic·u·lar·ist** \-rəst\ *n* — **par·tic·u·lar·is·tic** \-ˌtik-yə-lə-'ris-tik\ *adj*

par·tic·u·lar·i·ty \pə(r)-ˌtik-yə-'lar-ət-ē, (ˌ)pär-\ *n*, *pl* **-ties 1 a** : a minute detail : PARTICULAR **b** : an individual characteristic : PECULIARITY; *also* : SINGULARITY **2 a** : the quality or state of being particular as opposed to universal **b** : attentiveness to detail : EXACTNESS **c** : the quality or state of being fastidious in behavior or expression

par·tic·u·lar·iza·tion \-yə-lə-rə-'zā-shən\ *n* : the act of particularizing : the condition of being particularized

par·tic·u·lar·ize \pə(r)-'tik-yə-lə-ˌrīz, pär-\ *vb* **-ized; -iz·ing** *vt* : to state in detail : SPECIFY ~ *vi* : to go into details

par·tic·u·lar·ly \pə(r)-'tik-yə-(lər-)lē, pär-'tik-yə-lər-lē\ *adv* **1** : in a particular manner : in detail **2** : to an unusual degree

[1]**par·tic·u·late** \pər-'tik-yə-lət, pär-, -ˌlāt\ *adj* [L *particula*] : of or relating to minute separate particles

[2]**particulate** *n* : a particulate substance

particulate inheritance *n* : inheritance of characters specif. transmitted by genes in accord with Mendel's laws

[1]**part·ing** \'pärt-iŋ\ *n* : a place or point where a division or separation occurs — **parting of the ways 1** : a point of separation or divergence **2** : a place or time at which a choice must be made

[2]**parting** *adj* : given, taken, or performed at parting <a ~ kiss>

par·ti pris \ˌpär-ˌtē-'prē\ *n*, *pl* **par·tis pris** \-ˌtē-'prē(z)\ [F, lit., side taken] : a preconceived opinion : PREJUDICE, BIAS — **parti pris** *adj*

[1]**par·ti·san** *or* **par·ti·zan** \'pärt-ə-zən, -sən\ *n* [MF *partisan*, fr. OIt *partigiano*, fr. *parte* part, party, fr. L *part-, pars* part] **1** : a firm adherent to a party, faction, cause, or person; *esp* : one exhibiting blind, prejudiced, and unreasoning allegiance **2 a** : a member of a body of detached light troops making forays and harassing an enemy **b** : a member of a guerrilla band operating within enemy lines ***syn*** see FOLLOWER — **partisan** *adj* — **par·ti·san·ship** \-ˌship\ *n*

[2]**partisan** *or* **partizan** *n* [MF *partisane*, fr. OIt *partigiana*, fem. of *partigiano*] : a weapon of the 16th and 17th centuries with long shaft and broad blade

par·ti·ta \pär-'tēt-ə\ *n* [It. fr. *partire*, to divide, fr. L — more at PART] **1** : VARIATION 5 **2** : SUITE 2b(1)

par·tite \'pär-ˌtīt\ *adj* [L *partitus*, fr. pp. of *partire*] **1** : divided into a usu. specified number of parts **2** : PARTED 1b <a ~ leaf>

[1]**par·ti·tion** \pər-'tish-ən, pär-\ *n* **1 a** : the action of parting : the state of being parted : DIVISION **b** (1) : separation of a class or whole into constituent elements (2) : the separation of a set (as the points of a line) into subsets such that every element belongs to one set and no two subsets have an element in common **2** : something that divides; *esp* : an interior dividing wall **3** : one of the parts or sections of a whole — **par·ti·tion·ist** \-'tish-(ə-)nəst\ *n*

[2]**partition** *vt* **1 a** : to divide into parts or shares **b** : to divide (as a country) into two or more territorial units having separate political status **2** : to separate or divide by a partition (as a wall) — often used with *off* <~*ed* off a closet from the storage area> — **par·ti·tion·er** \-'tish-(ə-)nər\ *n*

par·ti·tion·ist \-'tish-(ə-)nəst\ *n* : an advocate of political partition

par·ti·tive \'pärt-ət-iv\ *adj* **1** : serving to part or divide into parts **2 a** : of, relating to, or denoting a part <a ~ construction> **b** : serving to indicate the whole of which a part is specified <~ genitive> — **par·ti·tive·ly** *adv*

part·let \'pärt-lət\ *n* [ME (Sc) *patelet*, fr. MF *patelette*, fr. dim. of *patte* paw] : a 16th century chemisette with a band or collar

part·ly \'pärt-lē\ *adv* : in some measure or degree : PARTIALLY

[1]**part·ner** \'pärt-nər, *as a term of address often* 'pärd-\ *n* [ME *partener*, alter. of *parcener*, fr. AF, coparcener — more at PARCENER] **1** *archaic* : one that shares : PARTAKER **2 a** : ASSOCIATE, COLLEAGUE **b** : either of a couple who dance together **c** : one of two or more persons who play together in a game against an opposing side **d** : HUSBAND, WIFE **3** : a member of a partnership **4** : one of the heavy timbers that strengthen a ship's deck to support a mast — usu. used in pl.

[2]**partner** *vt* **1** : to join as partner **2** : to provide with a partner ~ *vi* : to act as a partner

part·ner·ship \-ˌship\ *n* **1** : the state of being a partner : PARTICIPATION **2 a** : a legal relation existing between two or more persons contractually associated as joint principals in a business **b** : the persons joined together in a partnership **3** : a relationship resembling a legal partnership and usu. involving close cooperation between parties having specified and joint rights and responsibilities (as in a common enterprise)

part of speech : a traditional class of words distinguished according to the kind of idea denoted and the function performed in a sentence : MAJOR FORM CLASS

par·ton \'pär-ˌtän\ *n* [[1]*part* + [2]*-on*] : a hypothetical particle that is held to be a constituent of nucleons

par·tridge \'pär-trij, *dial or archaic* 'pa-trij\ *n*, *pl* **partridge** *or* **par·tridg·es** [ME *partrich*, modif. of OF *perdris*, modif. of L *perdic-, perdix*, fr. Gk *perdik-, perdix*] **1** : any of various typically medium-sized stout-bodied Old World gallinaceous game birds (*Perdix*, *Alectoris*, and related genera) with variegated plumage **2** : any of numerous gallinaceous birds (as the American ruffed grouse or bobwhite) somewhat like the Old World partridges in size, habits, or value as game

partridge 1

par·tridge·ber·ry \-ˌber-ē\ *n* : an American trailing evergreen plant (*Mitchella repens*) of the madder family with insipid scarlet berries; *also* : its fruit

part–song \'pärt-ˌsóŋ\ *n* : a usu. unaccompanied song consisting of two or more voice parts with one part carrying the melody

part–time \'pärt-'tīm\ *adj* : involving or working less than customary or standard hours <a ~ job> <~ students> — **part–time** *adv*

[1]**par·tu·ri·ent** \pär-'t(y)u̇r-ē-ənt\ *adj* [L *parturient-, parturiens*, prp. of *parturire* to be in labor, fr. *parere* to produce — more at PARE] **1 a** : bringing forth or about to bring forth young **b** : of or relating to parturition **2** : being at the point of producing something (as an idea, discovery, or literary work)

[2]**parturient** *n* : a parturient individual

par·tu·ri·tion \ˌpärt-ə-'rish-ən, ˌpär-chə-, ˌpär-tyu̇-\ *n* [LL *parturition-, parturitio*, fr. L *parturitus*, pp. of *parturire*] : the action or process of giving birth to offspring

part·way \'pärt-'wā\ *adv* : to some extent : PARTIALLY, PARTLY

[1]**par·ty** \'pärt-ē\ *n*, *pl* **parties** [ME *partie* part, party, fr. OF, fr. *partir* to divide — more at PART] **1** : a person or group taking one side of a question, dispute, or contest **2** : a group of persons organized for the purpose of directing the policies of a government **3** : a person or group participating in an action or affair : PARTICIPANT <a ~ to the transaction> **4** : a particular individual : PERSON <a coquettish little ~> **5** : a detail of soldiers **6** : a social gathering; *also* : the entertainment provided for it **7 a** : an act of sexual intercourse **b** : ORGY — **party** *adj*

[2]**party** *vi* **par·tied; par·ty·ing** : to attend or give parties

party line *n* **1** : the policy or practice of a political party <elections fought on *party lines*> **2** : a single telephone circuit connecting two or more subscribers with the exchange — called also *party wire* **3** : the principles or policies of an individual or organization; *esp* : the official policies of the Communist party — **par·ty–lin·er** \ˌpärt-ē-'lī-nər\ *n*

party wall *n* : a wall which divides two adjoining properties and in which each of the owners of the adjoining properties has rights of enjoyment

pa·rure \pə-'ru̇(ə)r\ *n* [F, lit., adornment, fr. OF *pareure*, fr. *parer* to prepare, adorn — more at PARE] : a matched set of ornaments (as jewelry)

par value *n* : PAR 1b(1)

par·ve \'pär-və\ *var of* PAREVE

par·ve·nu \'pär-və-ˌn(y)ü\ *n* [F, fr. pp. of *parvenir* to arrive, fr. L *pervenire*, fr. *per* through + *venire* to come — more at FOR, COME] : one who has recently or suddenly attained to wealth or power and has not yet secured the social position appropriate to it : UPSTART — **parvenu** *or* **par·ve·nue** \-ˌn(y)ü\ *adj*

par·vis *also* **par·vise** \'pär-vəs\ *n* [ME *parvis*, fr. MF, modif. of LL *paradisus* enclosed park — more at PARADISE] **1** : a court or enclosed space before a building (as a church) **2** : a single portico or colonnade before a church

pas \'pä\ *n*, *pl* **pas** \'pä(z)\ [F, fr. L *passus* step — more at PACE] **1** : the right of precedence **2** : a dance step or combination of steps

PAS \ˌpē-ˌā-'es\ *abbr* para-aminosalicylic acid

Pas·cal's triangle \pas-'kalz-, pȧs-'kȧlz-\ *n* [Blaise *Pascal*] : a system of numbers triangularly arranged in rows that consist of the coefficients in the expansion of $(a + b)^n$ for $n = 0, 1, 2, 3, \ldots$

Pasch \'pask\ *n* [ME *pasche* Passover, Easter, fr. OF, fr. LL *pascha*, fr. LGk, fr. Gk, Passover, fr. Heb *pesaḥ*] **1** : PASSOVER **2** : EASTER — **pas·chal** \'pas-kəl\ *adj*

Paschal Lamb *n* : AGNUS DEI 2

pas de bour·rée \ˌpäd-ə-bu̇-ˈrā\ *n, pl* **pas de bourrée** *same*\ [F, lit., bourrée step] **:** a walking or running ballet step usu. executed on the points of the toes

pas de deux \ˌpäd-ə-ˈdə(r), -ˈdü\ *n, pl* **pas de deux** \-ˈdər(z), -ˈdə(z), -ˈdü(z)\ [F, lit., step for two] **:** a dance or figure for two performers

pas de trois \-ˈtrwä, -trə-ˈwä\ *n, pl* **pas de trois** \-ˈtrwä(z), -trə-ˈwä(z)\ [F, lit., step for three] **:** a dance or figure for three performers

pa·se \ˈpäs-(ˌ)ā\ *n* [Sp, lit., feint, fr. *pase* let him pass, fr. *pasar* to pass, fr. (assumed) VL *passare*] **:** a movement of a cape by a matador in drawing a bull and taking his charge

pa·seo \pə-ˈsā-(ˌ)ō, pä-\ *n, pl* **paseos** [Sp] **1 a :** a leisurely stroll **:** PROMENADE **b :** a public walk or boulevard **2 :** a formal entrance march of bullfighters into an arena

¹pash \ˈpash\ *vt* [ME *passhen*] *dial Eng* **:** SMASH

²pash *n* [origin unknown] *dial Eng* **:** HEAD

pa·sha \ˈpäsh-ə, ˈpash-; pə-ˈshä, -ˈshȯ\ *n* [Turk *paşa*] **:** a man of high rank or office (as in Turkey or northern Africa)

Pash·to \ˈpəsh-(ˌ)tō\ *n* [Per *pashtū*, fr. Pashto] **:** the Iranian language of the Pathan people which is the chief vernacular of eastern Afghanistan and adjacent parts of West Pakistan

Pa·siph·aë \pə-ˈsif-ə-ˌē\ *n* [L, fr. Gk *Pasiphaē*] **:** the wife of Minos and mother of the Minotaur by a white bull

pasque·flow·er \ˈpask-ˌflau̇(-ə)r\ *n* [MF *passefleur*, fr. *passer* to pass + *fleur* flower, fr. L *flor-*, *flos* — more at BLOW] **:** any of several low perennial herbs (genus *Anemone*) of the buttercup family with palmately compound leaves and large usu. white or purple early spring flowers

pas·qui·nade \ˌpas-kwə-ˈnād\ *n* [MF, fr. It *pasquinata*, fr. *Pasquino*, name given to a statue in Rome on which lampoons were posted] **1 :** a lampoon posted in a public place **2 :** satirical writing **:** SATIRE — **pasquinade** *vt*

¹pass \ˈpas\ *vb* [ME *passen*, fr. OF *passer*, fr. (assumed) VL *passare*, fr. L *passus* step — more at PACE] *vi* **1 :** MOVE, PROCEED **2 a :** to go away **:** DEPART **b :** DIE — often used with *on* **3 a :** to go by **:** move past **b :** to glide by <time ~*es* swiftly> **c :** to move past another vehicle going in the same direction **4 a :** to go or make one's way through <allow no one to ~> **b :** to go uncensured or unchallenged <let his remark ~> **5 :** to go from one quality, state, or form to another <~*es* from a liquid to a gaseous state> **6 a :** to sit in inquest or judgment **b (1) :** to render a judgment, verdict, or opinion <the court ~*ed* on the legality of wiretapping> **(2) :** to become legally rendered <judgment ~*ed* for the plaintiff> **7 a :** to become legally transferred <title ~*es* from the buyer to the seller upon payment in full> **b :** to go from the control or possession of one person or group to that of another <the throne ~*ed* to the king's son> **8 a :** HAPPEN, OCCUR **b :** to take place as a mutual exchange or transaction <words ~*ed*> **9 a :** to become approved by a legislature or other body empowered to sanction or reject <the proposal ~*ed*> **b :** to undergo an inspection, test, or course of study successfully **10 a :** to serve as a medium of exchange **b :** to be held or regarded <~ for an honest man> **c :** to identify oneself or accept identification as a white person though having some Negro ancestry **11 a** *obs* **:** to make a pass in fencing **b :** to throw or hit a ball or puck to a teammate — often used with *off* **12 a :** to decline to bid, double, or redouble in a card game **b :** to withdraw from the current poker pot ~ *vt* **1 :** to go beyond: as **a :** SURPASS, EXCEED <~*es* all expectations> **b :** to advance or develop beyond **c :** to go past (one moving in the same direction) **2 a :** to omit a regularly scheduled declaration and payment of (a dividend) **b :** to leave out in an account or narration **3 a :** to go across, over, or through **:** CROSS **b :** to live through **:** UNDERGO **c :** to cause or permit to elapse **:** SPEND <~ time> **4 a :** to secure the approval of <the bill ~*ed* the Senate> **b :** to go through successfully **:** satisfy the requirements of <~ an exam> **5 a :** to cause or permit to win approval or legal or official sanction <~ a law> **b :** to let go unnoticed **:** OVERLOOK **c :** to cause or allow to pass an examination or course of study **6 a :** PLEDGE **b :** to transfer the right to or property in <~ title to a house> **7 a :** to put in circulation <~ bad checks> **b :** to transfer from one person to another <please ~ the salt> **c :** to cause or enable to go **:** TRANSPORT **d :** to take a turn with (as a rope) around something **e :** to throw or hit (a ball or puck) esp. to a teammate **8 a :** to pronounce judicially <~ sentence> **b :** UTTER **9 a :** to cause or permit to go past or through a barrier **b :** to cause to march or go by in order <~ the troops in review> **10 :** to emit or discharge from a bodily part and esp. the bowels **11 a :** to give a base on balls to **b :** to hit a ball past (an opponent) in a game (as tennis) — **pass·er** *n* — **in passing :** by the way **:** PARENTHETICALLY — **pass muster :** to pass an inspection or examination — **pass the buck :** to shift a responsibility to someone else — **pass the hat :** to take up a collection for money

²pass *n* **1 :** a means (as an opening, road, or channel) by which a barrier may be passed or access to a place may be gained; *esp* **:** a low place in a mountain range **2 :** a position to be maintained usu. against odds

³pass *n* **1 :** the act or an instance of passing **:** PASSAGE **2 :** REALIZATION <brought his dream to ~> **3 :** a usu. distressing or bad state of affairs <what has brought you to such a ~?> **4 a :** a written permission to move about freely in a place or to leave or enter it **b :** a written leave of absence from a military post or station for a brief period **c :** a permit or ticket allowing one free transportation or free admission **5** *archaic* **:** a thrust or lunge in fencing **6 a :** a transference of objects by sleight of hand or other deceptive means **b :** a moving of the hands over or along something **7** *archaic* **:** an ingenious sally (as of wit) **8 :** the passing of an examination or course of study; *also* **:** the mark or certification of such passing **9 :** a single complete mechanical operation; *also* **:** a single complete cycle of operations (as for processing, manufacturing, or printing) **10 a (1) :** a transfer of a ball or a puck from one player to another on the same team **(2) :** an instance of such a transfer **(3) :** a ball or puck so transferred **b :** a ball hit to the side and out of reach of an opponent in a game (as tennis or paddleball) **11 :** BASE ON BALLS **12 a :** an election not to bid, bet, or draw an additional card in a card game **b :** an election not to bid, double, or redouble in bridge **13 :** a throw of dice in the game of craps that wins the shooter his bet — compare CRAP, MISSOUT **14 :** a single passage or movement of an airplane or other man-made object over a place or toward a target **15 a :** EFFORT, TRY **b :** a sexually inviting gesture or approach **16 :** PASE *syn* see JUNCTURE

⁴pass *abbr* **1** passenger **2** passive

pass·able \ˈpas-ə-bəl\ *adj* **1 a :** capable of being passed, crossed, or traveled on <~ roads> **b :** capable of being freely circulated **2 :** barely good enough **:** TOLERABLE — **pass·ably** \-blē\ *adv*

pas·sa·ca·glia \ˌpäs-ə-ˈkäl-yə, ˌpas-ə-ˈkal-yə\ *n* [modif. of Sp *pasacalle*] **1 a :** an old Italian or Spanish dance tune **b :** an instrumental musical composition consisting of variations usu. on a ground bass in moderately slow triple time **2 :** an old dance performed to a passacaglia

pas·sa·do \pə-ˈsäd-(ˌ)ō\ *n, pl* **-dos** *or* **-does** [modif. of F *passade* (fr. It *passata*) or It *passata*, fr. *passare* to pass, fr. (assumed) VL] *archaic* **:** a thrust in fencing with one foot advanced

¹pas·sage \ˈpas-ij\ *n* **1 a :** the action or process of passing from one place or condition to another **b** *obs* **:** DEATH **2 a :** a way of exit or entrance **:** a road, path, channel, or course by which something passes **b :** a corridor or lobby giving access to the different rooms or parts of a building or apartment **3 a (1) :** a specific act of traveling or passing esp. by sea or air **(2) :** a privilege of conveyance as a passenger **:** ACCOMMODATIONS **b :** the passing of a legislative measure or law **:** ENACTMENT **4 :** a right, liberty, or permission to pass **5 a :** something that happens or is done **:** INCIDENT **b :** something that takes place between two persons mutually **6 a :** a usu. brief portion of a written work or speech that is relevant to a point under discussion or noteworthy for content or style **b :** a phrase or short section of a musical composition **c :** a detail of a work of art (as a painting) **7 :** the act or action of passing something or undergoing a passing **8 :** incubation of a pathogen (as a virus) in culture, a living organism, or a developing egg

²passage *vb* **pas·saged; pas·sag·ing** *vi* **:** to go past or across **:** CROSS ~ *vt* **:** to subject to passage <*passaged* a virus>

pas·sage·way \-ij-ˌwā\ *n* **:** a way that allows passage

pas·sant \ˈpas-ᵊnt\ *adj* [MF, fr. prp. of *passer* to pass] **:** walking with the farther forepaw raised — used of a heraldic animal

pass away *vi* **1 :** to go out of existence **2 :** DIE

pass·band \ˈpas-ˌband\ *n* **:** a band of frequencies (as in a radio circuit or a light filter) that is transmitted with maximum efficiency

pass·book \-ˌbu̇k\ *n* **:** BANKBOOK

pass degree *n* **:** a bachelor's degree without honors that is taken at a British university

pas·sé \pa-ˈsā\ *adj* [F, fr. pp. of *passer*] **1 :** past one's prime **2 a :** OUTMODED **b :** behind the times

passed ball *n* **:** a pitched baseball not hit by the batter that passes the catcher when he should have stopped it and allows a base runner to advance a base — compare WILD PITCH

passed pawn *n* **:** a chess pawn that has no enemy pawn in front of it on its own or an adjacent file

pas·sel \ˈpas-əl\ *n* [alter. of *parcel*] **:** a large number **:** GROUP

passe·men·terie \pas-ˈmen-trē, -ˈment-ə-rē\ *n* [F, fr. *passement* ornamental braid, fr. *passer*] **:** a fancy edging or trimming made of braid, cord, gimp, beading, or metallic thread

pas·sen·ger \ˈpas-ᵊn-jər\ *n* [ME *passager*, fr. MF, fr. *passager*, adj., passing, fr. *passage* act of passing, fr. OF, fr. *passer*] **1 :** WAYFARER **2 :** a traveler in a public or private conveyance

passenger pigeon *n* **:** an extinct but formerly abundant No. American migratory pigeon (*Ectopistes migratorius*)

passe–par·tout \ˌpas-pər-ˈtü, -ˌpär-\ *n* [F, fr. *passe partout* pass everywhere] **1 :** MASTER KEY **2 a :** ⁵MAT 1 **b :** a method of framing in which a picture, a mat, a glass, and a back (as of cardboard) are held together by strips of paper or cloth pasted over the edges **3 :** a strong paper gummed on one side and used esp. for mounting pictures

pass·er·by \ˌpas-ər-ˈbī, ˈpas-ər-ˌ\ *n, pl* **pass·ers·by** \-ərz-\ **:** one who passes by

pas·ser·ine \ˈpas-ə-ˌrīn\ *adj* [L *passerinus* of sparrows, fr. *passer* sparrow] **1 :** of or relating to the largest order (Passeriformes) of birds which includes more than half of all living birds and consists chiefly of altricial songbirds of perching habits **2 :** of or relating to a suborder (Passeres) of passerine birds comprising the true songbirds with specialized vocal apparatus — **passerine** *n*

pas seul \pä-ˈsər(-ə)l, -ˈsəl\ *n* [F, lit., solo step] **:** a solo dance or dance figure

pass–fail \ˈpas-ˈfā(ə)l\ *n* **:** a system of recording whether a student has passed or failed a course rather than assigning a letter grade

pas·si·ble \ˈpas-ə-bəl\ *adj* [ME, fr. MF, fr. LL *passibilis*, fr. L *passus*, pp. of *pati* to suffer — more at PATIENT] **:** capable of feeling or suffering

pas·sim \ˈpas-əm; ˈpas-ˌim, ˈpäs-\ *adv* [L, fr. *passus* scattered, fr. pp. of *pandere* to spread — more at FATHOM] **:** here and there

¹pass·ing *adj* **1 :** going by or past <a ~ pedestrian> **2 :** having a brief duration <a ~ whim> **3** *obs* **:** SURPASSING **4 :** SUPERFICIAL **5 a :** of, relating to, or used in or for the act or process of passing <~ lanes> **b :** given on satisfactory completion of an examination or course of study <a ~ grade>

²passing *adv* **:** to a surpassing degree **:** EXCEEDINGLY <~ fair>

passing note *n* : a nonharmonic tone interposed between essential harmonic tones of adjacent chords — called also *passing tone*
passing shot *n* : a stroke in tennis that drives the ball to one side and beyond the reach of an opponent who is at or coming toward the net
pas·sion \ˈpash-ən\ *n* [ME, fr. OF, fr. LL *passion-, passio* suffering, being acted upon, fr. L *passus,* pp. of *pati* to suffer — more at PATIENT] **1** *often cap* **a** : the sufferings of Christ between the night of the Last Supper and his death **b** : an oratorio based on a gospel narrative of the Passion **2** *obs* : SUFFERING **3** : the state or capacity of being acted on by external agents or forces **4 a** (1) : EMOTION <his ruling ~ is greed> (2) *pl* : the emotions as distinguished from reason **b** : intense, driving, or overmastering feeling <driven to paint by a ~ beyond his control> **c** : an outbreak of anger **5 a** : ardent affection : LOVE **b** : a strong liking for or devotion to some activity, object, or concept **c** : sexual desire **d** : an object of desire or deep interest — **pas·sion·less** \-ləs\ *adj*
syn **1** see FEELING
2 PASSION, FERVOR, ARDOR, ENTHUSIASM, ZEAL *shared meaning element* : intense emotion compelling action
pas·sion·al \ˈpash-ən-ᵊl, ˈpash-nəl\ *adj* : of, relating to, or marked by passion
pas·sion·ate \ˈpash-(ə-)nət\ *adj* **1 a** : easily aroused to anger **b** : filled with anger : ANGRY **2 a** : capable of, affected by, or expressing intense feeling **b** : ENTHUSIASTIC **3** : swayed by or affected with sexual desire ***syn*** see IMPASSIONED — **pas·sion·ate·ly** *adv* — **pas·sion·ate·ness** *n*
pas·sion·flow·er \ˈpash-ən-ˌflau̇(-ə)r\ *n* [fr. the fancied resemblance of parts of the flower to the instruments of Christ's crucifixion] : any of a genus (*Passiflora* of the family Passifloraceae, the passionflower family) of chiefly tropical woody tendriled climbing vines or erect herbs with usu. showy flowers and pulpy often edible berries

passionflower

Pas·sion·ist \ˈpash-(ə-)nəst\ *n* [It *passionista,* fr. *passione* passion, fr. LL *passion-, passio*] : a member of a Roman Catholic mendicant order founded by St. Paul of the Cross in Italy in 1720 and devoted chiefly to missionary work and retreats
passion play *n, often cap 1st P* : a dramatic representation of the scenes connected with the passion and crucifixion of Christ
Passion Sunday *n* : the fifth Sunday in Lent
Pas·sion·tide \ˈpash-ən-ˌtīd\ *n* : the last two weeks of Lent
Passion Week *n* **1** : HOLY WEEK **2** : the second week before Easter
pas·siv·ate \ˈpas-iv-ˌāt\ *vt* **-at·ed; -at·ing** **1** : to make inactive or less reactive <~ the surface of steel by chemical treatment> **2** : to protect (as a semiconductor device) against failure by coating (as with silicon nitride) — **pas·siv·ation** \ˌpas-iv-ˈā-shən\ *n*
1**pas·sive** \ˈpas-iv\ *adj* [ME, fr. L *passivus,* fr. *passus,* pp.] **1 a** (1) : acted upon by an external agency (2) : receptive to outside impressions or influences **b** (1) : asserting that the grammatical subject of a verb is subjected to or affected by the action represented by that verb (2) : containing a passive verb form **c** : lacking in energy or will : LETHARGIC **d** : induced by an outside agency <~ exercise> **2 a** : not active or operating : INERT **b** : LATENT **c** (1) : of, relating to, or characterized by a state of chemical inactivity; *esp* : resistant to corrosion (2) : not involving expenditure of chemical energy <~ transport across a cell membrane> **d** : exhibiting no gain or control — used of an electronic device (as a capacitor or resistor) **e** : operating solely by means of the power of an input signal <a ~ communication satellite that reflects television signals> **f** : relating to the detection of or orientation by means of an object through its emission of energy **3 a** : receiving or enduring without resistance : SUBMISSIVE **b** : existing without being active or open <~ support> ***syn*** see INACTIVE ***ant*** active — **pas·sive·ly** *adv* — **pas·sive·ness** *n* — **pas·siv·i·ty** \pa-ˈsiv-ət-ē\ *n*
2**passive** *n* **1** : a passive verb form **2** : the passive voice of a language
passive immunity *n* : immunity acquired by transfer of antibodies (as by injection of serum from an individual with active immunity)
passive resistance *n* : resistance esp. to a government or an occupying power characterized mainly by techniques and acts of noncooperation
passive transfer *n* : a local transfer of skin sensitivity from an allergic to a normal person by injection of serum from the former that is used esp. for identifying specific allergens when a high degree of allergic sensitivity is suspected
pas·siv·ism \ˈpas-iv-ˌiz-əm\ *n* : a passive attitude, behavior, or way of life — **pas·siv·ist** \-əst\ *n*
pass·key \ˈpas-ˌkē\ *n* **1** : MASTER KEY **2** : SKELETON KEY
pass off *vt* **1** : to make public or offer for sale with intent to deceive **2** : to give a false identity or character to
pass out *vi* **1** : to lose consciousness **2** : DIE ~ *vt* : to reject (a deal in bridge) as unplayable because everyone has passed on the first round of bidding
Pass·over \ˈpas-ˌō-vər\ *n* [fr. the exemption of the Israelites from the slaughter of the first-born in Egypt (Exod 12:23-27)] : a Jewish holiday beginning on the 14th of Nisan and commemorating the Hebrews' liberation from slavery in Egypt
pass over \(ˈ)pas-ˈō-vər\ *vt* **1** : to ignore in passing **2** : to pay no attention to the claims of : DISREGARD
pass·port \ˈpas-ˌpō(ə)rt, -ˌpȯ(ə)rt\ *n* [MF *passeport,* fr. *passer* to pass + *port* port, fr. L *portus* — more at FORD] **1 a** : a formal document that is issued by an authorized official of a country to one of its citizens and usu. necessary for exit from and reentry into the country, that allows him to travel in a foreign country in accordance with visa requirements, and that requests protection for him while abroad **b** : a license issued by a country permitting a foreign citizen to pass or take goods through its territory : SAFE-CONDUCT **c** : a document of identification required by law to be carried by persons residing or traveling within a country **2 a** : a permission or authorization to go somewhere **b** : something that secures admission or acceptance <education as a ~ to success>
pass up *vt* : DECLINE, REJECT
pass·word \ˈpas-ˌwərd\ *n* **1** : a word or phrase that must be spoken by a person before he is allowed to pass a guard **2** : WATCHWORD 1
1**past** \ˈpast\ *adj* [ME, fr. pp. of *passen* to pass] **1 a** : AGO <ten years ~> **b** : just gone or elapsed <for the ~ few months> **2** : having existed or taken place in a period before the present : BYGONE **3** : of, relating to, or constituting a verb tense that in English is usu. formed by internal vowel change (as in *sang*) or by the addition of a suffix (as in *laughed*) and that is expressive of elapsed time **4** : having served as a specified officer in an organization <~ president>
2**past** *prep* **1 a** : beyond the age for or of <~ playing with dolls> **b** : AFTER <half ~ two> **2 a** : at the farther side of : BEYOND **b** : in a course or direction going close to and then beyond <drove ~ the house> **3** *obs* : more than **4** : beyond the capacity, range, or sphere of <~ belief>
3**past** *n* **1 a** : time gone by **b** : something that happened or was done in the past <regret the ~> **2 a** : the past tense of a language **b** : a verb form in the past tense **3** : a past life, history, or course of action; *esp* : one that is kept secret
4**past** *adv* : so as to reach and go beyond a point near at hand
pas·ta \ˈpäs-tə\ *n* [It, fr. LL] **1** : a paste in processed form (as spaghetti) or in the form of fresh dough (as ravioli) **2** : a dish of cooked pasta
1**paste** \ˈpāst\ *n* [ME, fr. MF, fr. LL *pasta* dough, paste] **1 a** : a dough that contains a considerable proportion of fat and is used for pastry crust or fancy rolls **b** : a confection made by evaporating fruit with sugar or by flavoring a gelatin, starch, or gum arabic preparation **c** : a smooth food product made by evaporation or grinding <tomato ~> <almond ~> **d** : a shaped dough (as spaghetti or ravioli) prepared from semolina, farina, or wheat flour **2** : a soft plastic mixture or composition: as **a** : a preparation usu. of flour or starch and water used as an adhesive or a vehicle for mordant or color **b** : clay or a clay mixture used in making pottery or porcelain **3** : a brilliant glass of high lead content used for the manufacture of artificial gems
2**paste** *vt* **past·ed; past·ing** **1** : to cause to adhere by paste : STICK **2** : to cover with something pasted on
3**paste** *vt* **past·ed; past·ing** [alter. of *baste*] : to strike hard at
1**paste·board** \ˈpās(t)-ˌbō(ə)rd, -ˌbȯ(ə)rd\ *n* **1** : paperboard made by pasting together two or more sheets of paper; *broadly* : PAPERBOARD **2 a** : VISITING CARD **b** : PLAYING CARD **c** : TICKET
2**pasteboard** *adj* **1** : made of pasteboard **2** : SHAM, UNSUBSTANTIAL
paste·down \-ˌdau̇n\ *n* : the outer leaf of an endpaper that is pasted down to the inside of the front or back cover of a book
1**pas·tel** \pas-ˈtel\ *n* [F, fr. It *pastello,* fr. LL *pastellus* woad, fr. dim. of *pasta*] **1** : a paste made of ground color and used for making crayons; *also* : a crayon made of such paste **2 a** : a drawing in pastel **b** : the process or art of drawing with pastels **3** : a light literary sketch **4** : any of various pale or light colors
2**pastel** *adj* **1 a** : of or relating to a pastel **b** : made with pastels **2** : pale and light in color **3** : lacking in body or vigor
pas·tel·ist *or* **pas·tel·list** \-ˈtel-əst\ *n* : an artist who works with pastels
pas·tern \ˈpas-tərn\ *n* [MF *pasturon,* fr. *pasture* pasture, tether attached to a horse's foot] **1** : a part of the foot of an equine extending from the fetlock to the coffin bone — see HORSE illustration **2** : a part of the leg of an animal other than an equine that corresponds to the pastern
pas·teur·iza·tion \ˌpas-chə-rə-ˈzā-shən, ˌpas-tə-\ *n* **1** : partial sterilization of a substance and esp. a liquid (as milk) at a temperature and for a period of exposure that destroys objectionable organisms without major chemical alteration of the substance **2** : partial sterilization of perishable food products (as fruit or fish) with radiation (as gamma rays)
pas·teur·ize \ˈpas-chə-ˌrīz, ˈpas-tə-\ *vt* **-ized; -iz·ing** [Louis *Pasteur*] : to subject to pasteurization — **pas·teur·iz·er** *n*
Pasteur treatment *n* : a method of aborting rabies by stimulating production of antibodies through successive inoculations with attenuated virus of gradually increasing strength
pas·tic·cio \pas-ˈtē-ch(ē-ˌ)ō, päs-\ *n, pl* **-ci** \-(ˌ)chē\ *or* **-cios** [It, lit., pasty, fr. ML *pasticius,* fr. LL *pasta*] : PASTICHE
pas·tiche \pas-ˈtēsh, päs-\ *n* [F, fr. It *pasticcio*] **1** : a literary, artistic, or musical work that imitates the style of previous work **2 a** : a musical, literary, or artistic composition made up of selections from different works : POTPOURRI **b** : HODGEPODGE
past·ies \ˈpā-stēz\ *n pl* [2*paste*] : small round coverings for a woman's nipples worn esp. by a stripteaser
pas·tille \pas-ˈtē(ə)l\ *also* **pas·til** \ˈpas-tᵊl\ *n* [F *pastille,* fr. L *pastillus* small loaf, lozenge; akin to L *panis* bread — more at FOOD] **1** : a small mass of aromatic paste for fumigating or scenting the air of a room **2** : an aromatic or medicated lozenge : TROCHE
pas·time \ˈpas-ˌtīm\ *n* : something that amuses and serves to make time pass agreeably : DIVERSION
past·i·ness \ˈpā-stē-nəs\ *n* : the quality or state of being pasty
past master *n* **1** : one who has held the office of worshipful master in a lodge of Freemasons or of master in a guild, club, or society **2** [alter. of *passed master*] : one who is expert : ADEPT — **past mistress** *n*
past·ness \ˈpas(t)-nəs\ *n* **1** : the quality or state of being past **2** : the subjective quality of something being remembered rather than immediately experienced
1**pas·tor** \ˈpas-tər, *for 2* päs-ˈtȯ(ə)r\ *n* [ME *pastour,* fr. OF, fr. L *pastor,* herdsman, fr. *pastus,* pp. of *pascere* to feed — more at FOOD] **1** : a spiritual overseer; *esp* : a clergyman serving a local church

or parish **2** *chiefly Southwest* [Sp, fr. L] **:** HERDSMAN — **pas·tor·ship** \-ˌship\ *n*

2pas·tor \ˈpas-tər\ **-tored; -tor·ing** \-t(ə-)riŋ\ *vt* **:** to serve as pastor of (as a church)

1pas·to·ral \ˈpas-t(ə-)rəl\ *adj* [ME, fr. L *pastoralis*, fr. *pastor* herdsman] **1 a** (1) **:** of, relating to, or composed of shepherds or herdsmen (2) **:** devoted to or based on livestock raising **b :** of or relating to the countryside **:** not urban **c :** portraying or expressive of the life of shepherds or country people esp. in an idealized and conventionalized manner <~ poetry> **d :** pleasingly peaceful and innocent **:** IDYLLIC **2 a :** of or relating to spiritual care or guidance esp. of a congregation **b :** of or relating to the pastor of a church ***syn*** see RURAL — **pas·to·ral·ly** \-t(ə-)rə-lē\ *adv* — **pas·to·ral·ness** *n*

2pastoral \ˈpas-t(ə-)rəl, *2d is often* ˌpas-tə-ˈräl, -ˈral\ *n* **1 :** a letter of a pastor to his charge: as **a :** a letter addressed by a bishop to his diocese **b :** a letter of the house of bishops of the Protestant Episcopal Church to be read in each parish **2 a :** a literary work (as a poem or play) dealing with shepherds or rural life in a usu. artificial manner and typically drawing a contrast between the innocence and serenity of the simple life and the misery and corruption of city and esp. court life **b :** pastoral poetry or drama **c :** a rural picture or scene **d :** PASTORALE 1b **3 :** CROSIER

pas·to·rale \ˌpas-tə-ˈräl, -ˈral *also* -ˈräl-ē\ *n* [It, fr. *pastorale* of herdsmen, fr. L *pastoralis*, fr. *pastor*] **1 a :** an opera of the 16th or 17th centuries having a pastoral plot **b :** an instrumental or vocal composition having a pastoral theme **2 :** PASTORAL 2a

Pastoral Epistle *n* **:** one of three New Testament letters including two addressed to Timothy and one to Titus that give advice on matters of church government and discipline

pas·to·ral·ism \ˈpas-t(ə-)rə-ˌliz-əm\ *n* **1 :** the quality or style characteristic of pastoral writing **2 a :** livestock raising **b :** social organization based on livestock raising as the primary economic activity — **pas·tor·al·ist** \-ləst\ *n*

pas·tor·ate \ˈpas-t(ə-)rət\ *n* **1 :** the office, state, jurisdiction, or tenure of office of a pastor **2 :** a body of pastors

pas·to·ri·um \pas-ˈtōr-ē-əm, -ˈtȯr-\ *n* [irreg. fr. *pastor* + *-orium*] *chiefly South* **:** a Protestant parsonage

past participle *n* **:** a participle that typically expresses completed action, that is traditionally one of the principal parts of the verb, and that is traditionally used in English in the formation of perfect tenses in the active voice and of all tenses in the passive voice

past perfect *adj* **:** of, relating to, or constituting a verb tense that is traditionally formed in English with *had* and denotes an action or state as completed at or before a past time spoken of — **past perfect** *n*

pas·tra·mi \pə-ˈsträm-ē\ *also* **pas·tromi** *n* [Yiddish, fr. Rum *pastramă*] **:** a highly seasoned smoked beef prepared esp. from shoulder cuts

pas·try \ˈpā-strē\ *n, pl* **pastries** [*1paste*] **1 a :** PASTE 1a **b :** sweet baked goods made of dough or having a crust made of enriched dough **2 :** a piece of pastry

past tense *n* **:** a verb tense expressing action or state in or as if in the past: **a :** a verb tense expressive of elapsed time (as *wrote* in "on arriving I wrote a letter") **b :** a verb tense expressing action or state in progress or continuance or habitually done or customarily occurring at a past time (as *was writing* in "I was writing while he dictated" or *loved* in "their sons loved fishing")

pas·tur·age \ˈpas-chə-rij\ *n* **:** PASTURE

1pas·ture \ˈpas-chər\ *n* [ME, fr. MF, fr. LL *pastura*, fr. L *pastus*, pp. of *pascere* to feed — more at FOOD] **1 :** plants (as grass) grown for the feeding esp. of grazing animals **2 :** land or a plot of land used for grazing **3 :** the feeding of livestock **:** GRAZING

2pasture *vb* **pas·tured; pas·tur·ing** *vi* **:** GRAZE, BROWSE ~ *vt* **1 :** to feed (as cattle) on pasture **2 :** to use as pasture — **pas·tur·er** *n*

pas·ture·land \ˈpas-chər-ˌland\ *n* **:** PASTURE 2

1pas·ty \ˈpas-tē\ *n, pl* **pasties** [ME *pastee*, fr. MF *pasté*, fr. *paste* dough, paste] **1 :** 2PIE 1, 2; *esp* **:** a meat pie **2 :** TURNOVER 5

2pasty \ˈpā-stē\ *adj* **past·i·er; -est :** resembling paste; *esp* **:** pallid and unhealthy in appearance

PA system \pē-ˈā-\ *n* **:** PUBLIC-ADDRESS SYSTEM

1pat \ˈpat\ *n* [ME *patte*] **1 :** a light blow esp. with the hand or a flat instrument **2 :** a light tapping often rhythmical sound **3 :** something (as butter) shaped into a small flat usu. square individual portion

2pat *vb* **pat·ted; pat·ting** *vt* **1 :** to strike lightly with a flat instrument **2 :** to flatten, smooth, or put into place or shape with light blows **3 :** to tap or stroke gently with the hand to soothe, caress, or show approval ~ *vi* **1 :** to strike or beat gently **2 :** to walk or run with a light beating sound

3pat *adv* **:** in a pat manner **:** APTLY, PROMPTLY

4pat *adj* **1 a :** exactly suited to the purpose or occasion **:** APT **b :** suspiciously appropriate **:** CONTRIVED **2 :** learned, mastered, or memorized exactly **3 :** FIRM, UNYIELDING ***syn*** see SEASONABLE

5pat *abbr* patent

pa·ta·ca \pə-ˈtäk-ə\ *n* [Pg] — see MONEY table

pa·ta·gi·um \pə-ˈtā-jē-əm\ *n, pl* **-gia** \-jē-ə\ [NL, fr. L, gold edging on a tunic] **:** a wing membrane: as **a :** the fold of skin connecting the forelimbs and hind limbs of a flying squirrel or dragon lizard **b :** the fold of skin in front of the main segments of a bird's wing

1patch \ˈpach\ *n* [ME *pacche*] **1 :** a piece of material used to mend or cover a hole or a weak spot **2 :** a tiny piece of black silk or court plaster worn on the face or neck esp. by women to hide a blemish or to heighten beauty **3 a :** a piece of adhesive plaster or other cover applied to a wound **b :** a shield worn over the socket of an injured or missing eye **4 a :** a small piece **:** SCRAP **b :** a small area distinct from that about it <cabbage ~> **5 :** a piece of cloth sewed on a garment as an ornament or insignia; *esp* **:** SHOULDER PATCH **6 :** a temporary connection in a communication system (as a telephone hookup) **7 :** a temporary correction in a faulty computer program

2patch *vt* **1 :** to mend, cover, or fill up a hole or weak spot in **2 :** to provide with a patch **3 a :** to make of patches or fragments **b :** to mend or put together esp. in hasty or shabby fashion — usu. used with *up* **c :** to make a patch in (a computer program) **4 :** to connect (as circuits) by a patch cord ***syn*** see MEND

3patch *n* [perh. by folk etymology fr. It dial. *paccio*] **:** FOOL, DOLT

patch·board \ˈpach-ˌbō(ə)rd, -ˌbȯ(ə)rd\ *n* **:** a plugboard in which circuits are interconnected by patch cords

patch cord *n* **:** a wire with a plug at each end that is used to effect a communication patch

pa·tchou·li *or* **pa·tchou·ly** \ˈpach-ə-lē, pə-ˈchü-lē\ *n* [Tamil *pacculi*] **1 :** an East Indian shrubby mint (*Pogostemon cablin*) that yields a fragrant essential oil **2 :** a heavy perfume made from patchouli

patch pocket *n* **:** a flat pocket applied to the outside of a garment

patch test *n* **:** a test for determining allergic sensitivity that is made by applying to the unbroken skin small pads soaked with the allergen to be tested

patch·work \ˈpach-ˌwərk\ *n* **1 :** something composed of miscellaneous or incongruous parts **:** HODGEPODGE **2 :** pieces of cloth of various colors and shapes sewed together to form a covering

patchy \ˈpach-ē\ *adj* **patch·i·er; -est :** marked by, consisting of, or diversified with patches — **patch·i·ly** \ˈpach-ə-lē\ *adv* — **patch·i·ness** \ˈpach-ē-nəs\ *n*

pate \ˈpāt\ *n* [ME] **1 :** HEAD **2 :** the crown of the head **3 :** BRAIN — used chiefly disparagingly — **pat·ed** \ˈpāt-əd\ *adj*

pâte \ˈpät\ *n* [F, lit., paste, fr. OF *paste*] **:** PASTE 2b

pâ·té \pä-ˈtā, pa-\ *n* [F, fr. OF *pasté*, fr. *paste*] **1 :** a meat or fish pie or patty **2 :** a spread of finely mashed seasoned and spiced meat <chicken liver ~>

pâ·té de foie gras \(ˌ)pä-ˌtād-ə-ˌfwä-ˈgrä, (ˌ)pa-ˌtād-\ *n, pl* **pâ·tés de foie gras** \-ˌtā(z)d-ə-\ [F] **:** a rich pâté of fat goose liver and truffles sometimes with added fat pork

pa·tel·la \pə-ˈtel-ə\ *n, pl* **pa·tel·lae** \-ˈtel-(ˌ)ē, -ˌī\ *or* **patellas** [L, fr. dim. of *patina* shallow dish] **:** a thick flat triangular movable bone that forms the anterior point of the knee and protects the front of the joint — called also *kneecap* — **pa·tel·lar** \-ˈtel-ər\ *adj*

pa·tel·li·form \pə-ˈtel-ə-ˌfȯrm\ *adj* [NL *Patella* genus including the limpet, fr. L, small shallow dish] **1 :** resembling a limpet or limpet shell **2 :** disk-shaped with a narrow rim

pat·en \ˈpat-ᵊn\ *n* [ME, fr. OF *patene*, fr. ML & L; ML *patina*, fr. L, shallow dish, fr. Gk *patanē*; akin to L *patēre*] **1 :** a plate usu. made of precious metal and used to carry the bread at the Eucharist **2 a :** PLATE **b :** something (as a metal disk) resembling a plate

pa·ten·cy \ˈpat-ᵊn-sē, ˈpāt-\ *n* **:** the quality or state of being patent

1pa·tent *4-7 are* ˈpat-ᵊnt, ˈpāt-; *1-3 are* ˈpat-, *Brit* ˈpat- *or* ˈpāt-\ *adj* [ME, fr. MF, fr. L *patent-, patens*, fr. prp. of *patēre* to be open — more at FATHOM] **1 a :** open to public inspection — used chiefly in the phrase *letters patent* **b** (1) **:** secured by letters patent or by a patent to the exclusive control and possession of a particular individual or party (2) **:** protected by a patent **:** made under a patent <~ locks> **c :** protected by a trademark or a trade name so as to establish proprietary rights analogous to those conveyed by letters patent or a patent **:** PROPRIETARY <~ drugs> **2 :** of, relating to, or concerned with the granting of patents esp. for inventions <a ~ lawyer> **3 :** making exclusive or proprietary claims or pretensions **4 :** affording free passage **:** UNOBSTRUCTED <a ~ opening> **5 :** PATULOUS, SPREADING <a ~ calyx> **6** *archaic* **:** ACCESSIBLE, EXPOSED **7 :** readily visible or intelligible **:** not hidden or obscure ***syn*** see EVIDENT ***ant*** latent — **pa·tent·ly** *adv*

2pat·ent \ˈpat-ᵊnt, *Brit also* ˈpāt-\ *n* **1 :** an official document conferring a right or privilege **:** LETTERS PATENT **2 a :** a writing securing to an inventor for a term of years the exclusive right to make, use, or sell his invention **b :** the monopoly or right so granted **c :** a patented invention **3 :** PRIVILEGE, LICENSE **4 :** an instrument making a conveyance of public lands; *also* **:** the land so conveyed

3pat·ent *vt* **1 :** to grant a privilege, right, or license to by patent **2 :** to obtain or secure by patent; *esp* **:** to secure by letters patent exclusive right to make, use, or sell **3 :** to obtain a patent right or grant one to — **pat·ent·abil·i·ty** \ˌpat-ᵊn-tə-ˈbil-ət-ē, *Brit also* ˌpāt-\ *n* — **pat·ent·able** \ˈpat-ᵊn-tə-bəl, *Brit also* ˈpāt-\ *adj*

pat·en·tee \ˌpat-ᵊn-ˈtē, *Brit also* ˌpāt-\ *n* **:** one to whom a grant is made or a privilege secured by patent

pat·ent flour \ˌpat-ᵊn(t)-, *Brit also* ˌpāt-\ *n* **:** a high-grade wheat flour that consists solely of endosperm

pat·ent leather \ˌpat-ᵊn(t)-, *Brit usu* ˌpāt-\ *n* **:** a leather with a hard smooth glossy surface

patent medicine *n* **:** PROPRIETARY 3

patent office *n* **:** a government office for examining claims to patents and granting patents

pat·en·tor \ˈpat-ᵊn-tər, ˌpat-ᵊn-ˈtȯ(ə)r, *Brit also* ˈpāt-, ˌpāt-\ *n* **:** one that grants a patent

patent right *n* **:** a right granted by letters patent; *esp* **:** the exclusive right to an invention

pa·ter *n* **1** *often cap* \ˈpä-ˌte(ə)r\ **:** PATERNOSTER **2** \ˈpāt-ər\ [L] *chiefly Brit* **:** FATHER

pa·ter·fa·mil·i·as \ˌpāt-ər-fə-ˈmil-ē-əs, ˌpät-\ *n, pl* **pa·tres·fa·mil·i·as** \ˌpä-ˌtrēz-, ˌpä-ˌtrās-\ [L, fr. *pater* father + *familias*, archaic gen. of *familia* household — more at FATHER, FAMILY] **1 :** the male head of a household **2 :** the father of a family

pa·ter·nal \pə-ˈtərn-ᵊl\ *adj* [L *paternus*, fr. *pater*] **1 a :** of or relating to a father **b :** like that of a father <~ benevolence> **2 :** received or inherited from one's male parent **3 :** related through one's father <~ grandfather> — **pa·ter·nal·ly** \-ᵊl-ē\ *adv*

pa·ter·nal·ism \pə-ˈtərn-ᵊl-ˌiz-əm\ *n* **1 :** a system under which an authority undertakes to supply needs or regulate conduct of those under its control in matters affecting them as individuals as well as in their relations to authority and to each other **2 :** a policy or practice based on or characteristic of paternalism — **pa·ter·nal·ist** \-ᵊl-əst\ *n or adj* — **pa·ter·nal·is·tic** \-ˌtərn-ᵊl-ˈis-tik\ *adj*

pa·ter·ni·ty \pə-ˈtər-nət-ē\ *n* **1 :** the quality or state of being a father **2 :** origin or descent from a father

paternity test *n* **:** a test to determine whether a given man could be the biological father of a given child that is made by comparison of genetic traits (as blood groups) of the mother, child, and suspected man

pa·ter·nos·ter \ˈpat-ər-ˌnäs-tər; ˌpät-ər-ˈnäs-tər, -ˌte(ə)r\ *n* [ME, fr. ML, fr. L *pater noster* our father] **1** *often cap* **:** LORD'S PRAYER **2 :** a word formula repeated as a prayer or magical charm

[1]path \ˈpath, ˈpȧth\ *n, pl* **paths** \ˈpat͟hz, ˈpaths, ˈpȧt͟hz, ˈpȧths\ [ME, fr. OE *pæth;* akin to OHG *pfad* path] **1 :** a trodden way **2 :** a track specially constructed for a particular use **3 a :** COURSE, ROUTE **b :** a way of life, conduct, or thought **4 a :** the continuous series of positions or configurations that can be assumed in any motion or process of change by a moving or varying system **b :** a sequence of arcs in a network that can be traced continuously without retracing any arc **5 :** a line of communication over interconnecting neurons extending from one organ or center to another

[2]path *or* **pathol** *abbr* pathological; pathology

path- *or* **patho-** *comb form* [NL, fr. Gk, fr. *pathos,* lit., suffering — more at PATHOS] **:** pathological state **:** DISEASE <*patho*gen>

-path \ˌpath\ *n comb form* [G, back-formation fr. *-pathie* -pathy] **1 :** practitioner of a (specified) system of medicine that emphasizes one aspect of disease or its treatment <naturo*path*> **2** [ISV, fr. Gk *-pathēs,* adj., suffering, fr. *pathos*] **:** one suffering from a disorder (of such a part or system) <psycho*path*>

Pa·than \pə-ˈtän *also* ˈpā-thən\ *n* [Hindi *Paṭhān*] **:** a member of the principal ethnic group of Afghanistan

pa·thet·ic \pə-ˈthet-ik\ *adj* [MF or LL; MF *pathetique,* fr. LL *patheticus,* fr. Gk *pathētikos* capable of feeling, pathetic, fr. *paschein* to experience, suffer — more at PATHOS] **1 :** having a capacity to move one to either compassionate or contemptuous pity **2 :** marked by sorrow or melancholy **:** SAD ***syn*** see MOVING — **pa·thet·i·cal** \-i-kəl\ *adj* — **pa·thet·i·cal·ly** \-i-k(ə-)lē\ *adv*

pathetic fallacy *n* **:** the ascription of human traits or feelings to inanimate nature (as in *cruel sea*)

path·find·er \ˈpath-ˌfīn-dər, ˈpȧth-\ *n* **:** one that discovers a way; *esp* **:** one that explores untraversed regions to mark out a new route — **path·find·ing** \-diŋ\ *n or adj*

path·less \-ləs\ *adj* **:** UNTRODDEN, TRACKLESS — **path·less·ness** *n*

patho·gen \ˈpath-ə-jən\ *n* [ISV] **:** a specific causative agent (as a bacterium or virus) of disease

patho·gen·e·sis \ˌpath-ə-ˈjen-ə-səs\ *n* [NL] **:** the origination and development of a disease

patho·ge·net·ic \-jə-ˈnet-ik\ *adj* [ISV] **1 :** of or relating to pathogenesis **2 :** PATHOGENIC 2

patho·gen·ic \-ˈjen-ik\ *adj* [ISV] **1 :** PATHOGENETIC 1 **2 :** causing or capable of causing disease — **patho·gen·i·cal·ly** \-i-k(ə-)lē\ *adv* — **patho·ge·nic·i·ty** \-jə-ˈnis-ət-ē\ *n*

pa·tho·gno·mon·ic \ˌpath-ə(g)-nō-ˈmän-ik\ *adj* [Gk *pathognōmonikos,* fr. *path-* + *gnōmonikos* fit to judge, fr. *gnōmon* interpreter] **:** distinctively characteristic of a particular disease

patho·log·i·cal \ˌpath-ə-ˈläj-i-kəl\ *or* **patho·log·ic** \-ik\ *adj* **1 :** of or relating to pathology **2 :** altered or caused by disease — **patho·log·i·cal·ly** \-i-k(ə-)lē\ *adv*

pa·thol·o·gist \pə-ˈthäl-ə-jəst, pa-\ *n* **:** a specialist in pathology; *specif* **:** one who interprets and diagnoses the changes caused by disease in tissues

pa·thol·o·gy \-jē\ *n, pl* **-gies** [NL *pathologia* & MF *pathologie,* fr. Gk *pathologia* study of the emotions, fr. *path-* + *-logia* -logy] **1 :** the study of the essential nature of diseases and esp. of the structural and functional changes produced by them **2 :** something abnormal: **a :** the anatomic and physiologic deviations from the normal that constitute disease or characterize a particular disease **b :** deviation from propriety or from an assumed normal state of something nonliving or nonmaterial

pa·thom·e·ter \pə-ˈthäm-ət-ər, pa-\ *n* **:** an instrument that measures changes in bodily electrical conductivity and is used as a lie detector

patho·mor·phol·o·gy \ˈpath-ō-mȯr-ˈfäl-ə-jē\ *n* **:** morphology of abnormal conditions — **patho·mor·pho·log·i·cal** \-ˌmȯr-fə-ˈläj-i-kəl\ *or* **patho·mor·pho·log·ic** \-ik\ *adj*

patho·phys·i·ol·o·gy \-ˌfiz-ē-ˈäl-ə-jē\ *n* **:** the physiology of abnormal states; *specif* **:** the functional changes that accompany a particular syndrome or disease — **patho·phys·i·o·log·i·cal** \-ē-ə-ˈläj-i-kəl\ *or* **patho·phys·i·o·log·ic** \-ik\ *adj*

pa·thos \ˈpā-ˌthäs\ *n* [Gk, suffering, experience, emotion, fr. *paschein* to experience, suffer; akin to Lith *kesti* to suffer] **1 :** an element in experience or in artistic representation evoking pity or compassion **2 :** an emotion of sympathetic pity

syn PATHOS, POIGNANCY, BATHOS *shared meaning element* **:** a quality that moves one to pity or sorrow

path·way \ˈpath-ˌwā, ˈpȧth-\ *n* **1 :** PATH, COURSE **2 :** the sequence of enzyme catalyzed reactions by which an energy-yielding substance is utilized by protoplasm <metabolic *~s*>

-p·a·thy \p-ə-thē\ *n comb form* [L *-pathia,* fr. Gk *-patheia,* fr. *-pathēs* suffering — more at -PATH] **1 :** feeling **:** suffering <em*pathy*> **:** being acted upon <tele*pathy*> **2 :** disorder of (such) a part or kind <neuro*pathy*> **3 :** system of medicine based on (such) a factor <osteo*pathy*>

pa·tience \ˈpā-shən(t)s\ *n* **1 :** the capacity, habit, or fact of being patient **2** *chiefly Brit* **:** SOLITAIRE 2

[1]pa·tient \ˈpā-shənt\ *adj* [ME *pacient,* fr. MF, fr. L *patient-, patiens,* fr. prp. of *pati* to suffer; akin to L *paene* almost, *penuria* need, Gk *pēma* suffering] **1 :** bearing pains or trials calmly or without complaint **2 :** manifesting forbearance under provocation or strain **3 :** not hasty or impetuous **4 :** steadfast despite opposition, difficulty, or adversity **5 a :** able or willing to bear — used with *of* **b :** SUSCEPTIBLE, ADMITTING <~ of one interpretation> — **pa·tient·ly** *adv*

[2]patient *n* **1 a :** an individual awaiting or under medical care and treatment **b :** the recipient of any of various personal services **2 :** one that is acted upon

pa·ti·na \ˈpat-ə-nə, pə-ˈtē-nə\ *n, pl* **pa·ti·nas** \-nəz\ *or* **pa·ti·nae** \ˈpat-ə-ˌnē, -ˌnī\ [NL, fr. L, shallow dish — more at PATEN] **1 a :** a usu. green film formed naturally on copper and bronze by long exposure or artificially (as by acids) and often valued aesthetically for its color **b :** a surface appearance of something grown beautiful esp. with age or use **2 :** an appearance or aura that is derived from association, habit, or established character

[1]pa·tine \pa-ˈtēn\ *n* [F, fr. NL *patina*] **:** PATINA

[2]patine *vt* **pa·tined; pa·tin·ing :** to cover with a patina

pa·tio \ˈpat-ē-ˌō *also* ˈpät-\ *n, pl* **pa·ti·os** [Sp] **1 :** COURTYARD; *esp* **:** an inner court open to the sky **2 :** a recreation area that adjoins a dwelling, is often paved, and is adapted esp. to outdoor dining

pa·tois \ˈpa-ˌtwä, ˈpä-\ *n, pl* **pa·tois** \-ˌtwäz\ [F] **1 a :** a dialect other than the standard or literary dialect **b :** illiterate or provincial speech **2 :** the characteristic special language of an occupational or social group **:** JARGON

patr- *or* **patri-** *or* **patro-** *comb form* [*patr-, patri-* fr. L, fr. *patr-, pater; patr-, patro-* fr. Gk, fr. *patr-, patēr* — more at FATHER] **:** father <*patri*stic>

pa·tri·arch \ˈpā-trē-ˌärk\ *n* [ME *patriarche,* fr. OF, fr. LL *patriarcha,* fr. Gk *patriarchēs,* fr. *patria* lineage (fr. *patr-, patēr* father) + *-archēs* -arch — more at FATHER] **1 a :** one of the scriptural fathers of the human race or of the Hebrew people **b :** a man who is father or founder **c (1) :** the oldest member or representative of a group **(2) :** a venerable old man **d :** a man who is head of a patriarchy **2 a :** any of the bishops of the ancient or Eastern Orthodox sees of Constantinople, Alexandria, Antioch, and Jerusalem or the ancient and Western see of Rome with authority over other bishops **b :** the head of any of various Eastern churches **c :** a Roman Catholic bishop next in rank to the pope with purely titular or with metropolitan jurisdiction **3 :** a Mormon of the Melchizedek priesthood empowered to perform the ordinances of the church and pronounce blessings within a stake or other prescribed jurisdiction — **pa·tri·ar·chal** \ˌpā-trē-ˈär-kəl\ *adj*

patriarchal cross *n* **:** a chiefly heraldic cross denoting a cardinal's or archbishop's rank and having two crossbars of which the lower is the longer and intersects the upright above or at its center — see CROSS illustration

pa·tri·arch·ate \ˈpā-trē-ˌär-kət, -ˌkāt\ *n* **1 a :** the office, jurisdiction, or time in office of a patriarch **b :** the residence or headquarters of a patriarch **2 :** PATRIARCHY

pa·tri·ar·chy \-ˌär-kē\ *n, pl* **-chies 1 :** social organization marked by the supremacy of the father in the clan or family, the legal dependence of wives and children, and the reckoning of descent and inheritance in the male line **2 :** a society organized according to the principles of patriarchy

pa·tri·cian \pə-ˈtrish-ən\ *n* [ME *patricion,* fr. MF *patricien,* fr. L *patricius,* fr. *patres* senators, fr. pl. of *pater* father — more at FATHER] **1 :** a member of one of the original citizen families of ancient Rome **2 a :** a person of high birth **:** ARISTOCRAT **b :** a person of breeding and cultivation — **patrician** *adj*

pa·tri·ci·ate \-ˈtrish-ē-ət, -ē-ˌāt\ *n* **1 :** the position or dignity of a patrician **2 :** a patrician class

pat·ri·cide \ˈpa-trə-ˌsīd\ *n* **1** [L *patricida,* fr. *patr-* + *-cida* -cide] **:** one who murders his own father **2** [LL *patricidium,* fr. L *patr-* + *-cidium* -cide] **:** the murder of one's own father — **pat·ri·cid·al** \ˌpa-trə-ˈsīd-ᵊl\ *adj*

pat·ri·lin·eal \ˌpa-trə-ˈlin-ē-əl\ *adj* **:** relating to, based on, or tracing descent through the paternal line <~ society>

pat·ri·mo·ny \ˈpa-trə-ˌmō-nē\ *n* [ME *patrimonie,* fr. MF, fr. L *patrimonium,* fr. *patr-, pater* father] **1 a :** an estate inherited from one's father or ancestor **b :** anything derived from one's father or ancestors **:** HERITAGE **2 :** an estate or endowment belonging by ancient right to a church ***syn*** see HERITAGE — **pat·ri·mo·ni·al** \ˌpa-trə-ˈmō-nē-əl\ *adj*

pa·tri·ot \ˈpā-trē-ət, -trē-ˌät, *also chiefly Brit* ˈpa-\ *n* [MF *patriote,* fr. LL *patriota,* fr. Gk *patriōtēs,* fr. *patrios* of one's father, fr. *patr-, patēr* father] **:** one who loves his country and zealously supports its authority and interests

pa·tri·ot·ic \ˌpā-trē-ˈät-ik, *also chiefly Brit* ˌpa-\ *adj* **1 :** inspired by patriotism **2 :** befitting or characteristic of a patriot — **pa·tri·ot·i·cal·ly** \-i-k(ə-)lē\ *adv*

pa·tri·o·tism \ˈpā-trē-ə-ˌtiz-əm, *also chiefly Brit* ˈpa-\ *n* **:** love for or devotion to one's country

Patriots' Day *n* **:** the third Monday in April observed as a legal holiday in Maine and Massachusetts in commemoration of the battles of Lexington and Concord in 1775

pa·tris·tic \pə-ˈtris-tik\ *adj* **:** of or relating to the church fathers or their writings — **pa·tris·ti·cal** \-ti-kəl\ *adj*

pa·tris·tics \-tiks\ *n pl but sing in constr* **:** the study of the writings and background of the church fathers

Pa·tro·clus \pə-ˈtrō-kləs, -ˈträk-ləs\ *n* [L, fr. Gk *Patroklos*] **:** a Greek hero and friend of Achilles slain by Hector at Troy

[1]pa·trol \pə-ˈtrōl\ *n* **1 a :** the action of traversing a district or beat or of going the rounds along a chain of guards for observation or the maintenance of security **b :** the person performing such an action **c :** a detachment of men employed for reconnaissance, security, or combat **2 a :** a subdivision of a boy scout troop made up of two or more boys **b :** a subdivision of a girl scout troop usu. composed of from six to eight girls

[2]patrol *vb* **pa·trolled; pa·trol·ling** [F *patrouiller,* fr. MF, to tramp around in the mud, fr. *patte* paw — more at PATTEN] *vi* **:** to carry out a patrol **~** *vt* **:** to carry out a patrol of — **pa·trol·ler** *n*

pa·trol·man \pə-ˈtrōl-mən\ *n* **:** one who patrols; *esp* **:** a policeman assigned to a beat

patrol wagon *n* **:** an enclosed motortruck used by police to carry prisoners

pa·tron \ˈpā-trən, *for 6 also* pa-ˈtrōⁿ\ *n* [ME, fr. MF, fr. ML & L; ML *patronus* patron saint, patron of a benefice, pattern, fr. L, defender, fr. *patr-, pater*] **1 a :** a person chosen, named, or honored as a special guardian, protector, or supporter **b :** a wealthy or influential supporter of an artist or writer **c :** a social or financial sponsor of a social function (as a ball or concert) **2 :** one who uses his wealth or influence to help an individual, an institution, or a cause **3 a :** CUSTOMER **b :** one who uses the services of a library and esp. a public library **4 :** the holder of the right of presentation to an English ecclesiastical benefice **5 :** a master in ancient times who freed his slave but retained some rights over him **6** [F, fr. MF] **:** the proprietor of an establishment (as an inn) esp. in France **7 :** the chief male officer in some fraternal lodges having both men and women members — **pa·tron·al** \ˈpā-trən-ᵊl\ *adj*

pa·tron·age \ˈpa-trə-nij, ˈpā-\ *n* **1 :** ADVOWSON **2 :** the support or influence of a patron **3 :** kindness done with an air of superiority **4 :** business or activity provided by patrons <the new branch library is expected to have a heavy ~> **5 a :** the power to make appointments to government jobs on a basis other than merit alone **b :** the distribution of jobs on the basis of patronage **c :** jobs distributed by patronage

pa·tron·ess \ˈpā-trə-nəs\ *n* **:** a female patron

pa·tron·ize \ˈpā-trə-ˌnīz, ˈpa-\ *vt* **-ized; -iz·ing** **1 :** to act as patron of **2 :** to adopt an air of condescension toward **3 :** to be a patron of — **pa·tron·iza·tion** \ˌpā-trə-nə-ˈzā-shən, pa-\ *n* — **pa·tron·iz·ing·ly** \ˈpā-trə-ˌnī-ziŋ-lē, ˈpa-\ *adv*

patron saint *n* **1 :** a saint to whose protection and intercession a person, a society, a church, or a place is dedicated **2 :** an original leader or prime exemplar

pat·ro·nym·ic \ˌpa-trə-ˈnim-ik\ *n* [LL *patronymicum*, fr. neut. of *patronymicus* of a patronymic, fr. Gk *patronymikos*, fr. *patronymia* patronymic, fr. *patr-* + *onyma* name — more at NAME] **:** a name derived from that of the father or a paternal ancestor usu. by the addition of an affix — **patronymic** *adj*

pa·troon \pə-ˈtrün\ *n* [F *patron* & Sp *patrón*, fr. ML *patronus*, fr. L, patron] **1** *archaic* **:** the captain or officer commanding a ship **2** [D, fr. F *patron*] **:** the proprietor of a manorial estate esp. in New York originally granted under Dutch rule but in some cases existing until the mid-19th century

pat·sy \ˈpat-sē\ *n, pl* **pat·sies** [perh. fr. It *pazzo* fool] **:** one who is duped or victimized **:** SUCKER

pat·ten \ˈpat-ᵊn\ *n* [ME *patin*, fr. MF, fr. *patte* paw, hoof, fr. (assumed) VL *patta*, of imit. origin] **:** a clog, sandal, or overshoe often with a wooden sole or metal device to elevate the foot and increase the wearer's height or aid in walking in mud

[1]**pat·ter** \ˈpat-ər\ *vb* [ME *patren*, fr. *paternoster*] *vt* **:** to say or speak in a rapid or mechanical manner ~ *vi* **1 :** to recite prayers (as paternosters) rapidly or mechanically **2 :** to talk glibly and volubly **3 :** to speak or sing rapid-fire words in a theatrical performance — **pat·ter·er** \-ər-ər\ *n*

[2]**patter** *n* **1 :** a specialized lingo **:** CANT; *esp* **:** the jargon of criminals (as thieves) **2 :** the spiel of a street hawker or of a circus barker **3 :** empty chattering talk **4 a** (1) **:** the rapid-fire talk of a comedian (2) **:** the talk with which an entertainer accompanies his routine **b :** the words of a comic song or of a rapidly spoken usu. humorous monologue introduced into such a song

[3]**patter** *vb* [freq. of [2]*pat*] *vi* **1 :** to strike or pat rapidly and repeatedly **2 :** to run with quick light-sounding steps ~ *vt* **:** to cause to patter

[4]**patter** *n* **:** a quick succession of slight sounds or pats

[1]**pat·tern** \ˈpat-ərn\ *n* [ME *patron*, fr. MF, fr. ML *patronus*] **1 :** a form or model proposed for imitation **:** EXEMPLAR **2:** something designed or used as a model for making things <a dressmaker's ~> **3 :** a model for making a mold into which molten metal is poured to form a casting **4 :** SPECIMEN, SAMPLE **5 a :** an artistic or mechanical design **b :** form or style in literary or musical composition **6 :** a natural or chance configuration <frost ~> <the ~ of events> **7 :** a length of fabric sufficient for an article **8 a :** the distribution of the shot from a shotgun or the bullets from an exploded shrapnel **b :** the grouping made on a target by bullets **9 :** a reliable sample of traits, acts, or other observable features characterizing an individual <behavior ~> **10 :** the flight path prescribed for an airplane that is coming in for a landing **11 :** a standard diagram transmitted for testing television circuits **12 :** a prescribed route to be followed by a pass receiver in football ***syn*** see MODEL — **pat·terned** \-ərnd\ *adj*

[2]**pattern** *vt* **1 :** to make or fashion according to a pattern **2** *dial chiefly Eng* **a :** MATCH **b :** IMITATE **3 :** to furnish, adorn, or mark with a design ~ *vi* **:** to form a pattern

pat·tern·ing *n* **1 :** decoration, composition, or configuration according to a pattern **2 :** physiotherapy that is designed to improve malfunctioning nervous control by means of feedback from muscular activity imposed by an outside source or induced by other muscles

pat·ty *also* **pat·tie** \ˈpat-ē\ *n, pl* **patties** [F *pâté*] **1 :** a little pie **2 a :** a small flat cake of chopped food <a hamburger ~> **b :** a small flat candy <a peppermint ~> **3 :** PATTY SHELL

patty shell *n* **:** a shell of puff paste made to hold a creamed meat, fish, or vegetable filling

pat·u·lous \ˈpach-ə-ləs\ *adj* [L *patulus*, fr. *patēre* to be open — more at FATHOM] **:** spreading widely from a center <a tree with ~ branches> — **pat·u·lous·ly** *adv* — **pat·u·lous·ness** *n*

PAU *abbr* Pan American Union

pau·ci·ty \ˈpȯ-sət-ē\ *n* [ME *paucite*, fr. MF or L; MF *paucité*, fr. L *paucitat-, paucitas*, fr. *paucus* little — more at FEW] **1 :** smallness of number **:** FEWNESS **2 :** smallness of quantity **:** DEARTH

Paul \ˈpȯl\ *n* [L *Paulus*, fr. Gk *Paulos*] **:** an early Christian apostle and missionary and author of several New Testament epistles

Paul Bun·yan \-ˈbən-yən\ *n* **:** a giant lumberjack of American mythology

Pau·li exclusion principle \ˈpau̇-lē-\ *n* [Wolfgang *Pauli*] **:** EXCLUSION PRINCIPLE — called also *Pauli principle*

Pau·line \ˈpȯ-ˌlīn\ *adj* **:** of or relating to the apostle Paul, his epistles, or the doctrine or theology implicit in his epistles

Paul·ist \ˈpȯ-ləst\ *n* **:** a member of the Roman Catholic Congregation of the Missionary Priests of St. Paul the Apostle founded by I. T. Hecker in the U.S. in 1858

pau·low·nia \pȯ-ˈlō-nē-ə\ *n* [NL, genus name, fr. Anna *Paulovna* †1865 Russ princess] **:** any of a genus (*Paulownia*) of Chinese trees of the figwort family; *esp* **:** one (*P. tomentosa*) widely cultivated for its panicles of fragrant violet flowers

paunch \ˈpȯnch, ˈpänch\ *n* [ME, fr. MF *panche*, fr. L *pantic-, pantex*] **1 a :** the belly and its contents **b :** POTBELLY **2 :** RUMEN

paunchy \ˈpȯn-chē, ˈpän-\ *adj* **paunch·i·er; -est :** having a potbelly — **paunch·i·ness** *n*

pau·per \ˈpȯ-pər\ *n* [L, poor] **1 :** a person destitute of means except such as are derived from charity; *specif* **:** one who receives aid from public poor funds **2 :** a very poor person — **pau·per·ism** \-pə-ˌriz-əm\ *n*

pau·per·ize \ˈpȯ-pə-ˌrīz\ *vt* **-ized; -iz·ing :** to reduce to poverty

[1]**pause** \ˈpȯz\ *n* [ME, fr. L *pausa*, fr. Gk *pausis*, fr. *pauein* to stop; akin to Gk *paula* rest] **1 :** a temporary stop **2 a :** a break in a verse **b :** a brief suspension of the voice to indicate the limits and relations of sentences and their parts **3 :** temporary inaction esp. as caused by uncertainty **:** HESITATION **4 a :** the sign denoting a fermata **b :** a mark (as a period or comma) used in writing or printing to indicate or correspond to a pause of voice **5 :** a reason or cause for pausing <a thought that should give one ~>
syn PAUSE, RECESS, RESPITE, LULL, INTERMISSION *shared meaning element* **:** a temporary cessation of activity or an activity

[2]**pause** *vb* **paused; paus·ing** *vi* **1 :** to stop temporarily **2 :** to linger for a time ~ *vt* **:** to cause to pause **:** STOP

pa·vane \pə-ˈvän, -ˈvan\ *also* **pa·van** *same or* ˈpav-ən\ *n* [MF *pavane*, fr. OSp *pavana*, fr. OIt] **1 :** a stately court dance by couples that was introduced from southern Europe into England in the 16th century **2 :** music for the pavane; *also* **:** music having the slow duple rhythm of a pavane

pave \ˈpāv\ *vt* **paved; pav·ing** [ME *paven*, fr. MF *paver*, fr. L *pavire* to strike, stamp; akin to OHG *arfūrian* to castrate, L *putare* to prune, reckon, think, Gk *paiein* to strike] **1 :** to lay or cover with material (as stone or concrete) that forms a firm level surface for travel **2 :** to cover firmly and solidly as if with paving material **3 :** to serve as a covering or pavement of — **pav·er** *n* — **pave the way :** to prepare a smooth easy way **:** facilitate development

paved \ˈpāvd\ *adj* **1 :** covered with a pavement **2** *or* **pa·vé** \pa-ˈvā\ [*pavé* fr. F, fr. pp. of *paver* to pave] *of jewels* **:** set as close together as possible to conceal a metal base

pave·ment \ˈpāv-mənt\ *n* [ME, fr. OF, fr. L *pavimentum*, fr. *pavire*] **1 :** a paved surface: as **a :** the artificially covered surface of a public thoroughfare **b** *chiefly Brit* **:** SIDEWALK **2 :** the material with which something is paved **3 :** something that suggests a pavement (as in flatness, hardness, and extent of surface)

pav·id \ˈpav-əd\ *adj* [L *pavidus*, fr. *pavēre* to be frightened; akin to L *pavire*] **:** TIMID

[1]**pa·vil·ion** \pə-ˈvil-yən\ *n* [ME *pavilon*, fr. OF *paveillon*, fr. L *papilion-, papilio* butterfly; akin to OHG *fīfaltra* butterfly, Lith *peteliske* flighty] **1 a :** a large often sumptuous tent **b :** something resembling a canopy or tent <tree ferns spread their delicate ~s —Blanche E. Baughan> **2 a :** a part of a building projecting from the rest **b :** one of several detached or semidetached units into which a building is sometimes divided **3 a :** a light sometimes ornamental structure in a garden, park, or place of recreation that is used for entertainment or shelter **b :** a temporary structure erected at an exposition by an individual exhibitor **4 :** the lower faceted part of a brilliant between the girdle and the culet — see BRILLIANT illustration

[2]**pavilion** *vt* **:** to furnish or cover with or put in a pavilion

pav·ing \ˈpā-viŋ\ *n* **:** PAVEMENT

pav·ior *or* **pav·iour** \ˈpāv-yər\ *n* [ME *pavier*, fr. *paven* to pave] *Brit* **:** one that paves

Pav·lov·ian \pav-ˈlō-vē-ən, -ˈlō-; -ˈlȯ-fē-\ *adj* **:** of or relating to Ivan Pavlov or to his work and theories <~ conditioning>

[1]**paw** \ˈpȯ\ *n* [ME, fr. MF *poue*] **1 :** the foot of a quadruped (as a lion or dog) that has claws; *broadly* **:** the foot of an animal **2 :** a human hand esp. when large or clumsy

[2]**paw** *vt* **1 :** to feel of or touch clumsily, amorously, or rudely **2 :** to touch or strike at with a paw **3 :** to scrape or beat with or as if with a hoof **4 :** to flail at or grab for wildly ~ *vi* **1 :** to beat or scrape something with or as if with a hoof **2 :** to touch or strike with a paw **3 :** to feel or touch clumsily, amorously, or rudely **4 :** to flail or grab wildly ***syn*** see TOUCH

paw·ky \ˈpȯ-kē\ *adj* [obs. E dial. *pawk* (trick)] *chiefly Brit* **:** artfully shrewd **:** CANNY

pawl \ˈpȯl\ *n* [perh. modif. of D *pal* pawl] **:** a pivoted tongue or sliding bolt on one part of a machine that is adapted to fall into notches or interdental spaces on another part (as a ratchet wheel) so as to permit motion in only one direction

[1]**pawn** \ˈpȯn, ˈpän\ *n* [ME *paun*, modif. of MF *pan*] **1 a :** something delivered to or deposited with another as security for a loan **b :** HOSTAGE **2 :** the state of being pledged **3 :** something used as a pledge **:** GUARANTY **4 :** the act of pawning

[2]**pawn** *vt* **:** to deposit in pledge or as security — **pawn·er** \ˈpȯ-nər, ˈpän-ər\ *or* **paw·nor** *same or* pȯ-nȯ(ə)r, pä-\ *n*

[3]**pawn** *n* [ME *pown*, fr. MF *poon*, fr. ML *pedon-, pedo* foot soldier, fr. LL, one with broad feet, fr. L *ped-, pes* foot — more at FOOT] **1 :** one of the chessmen of least value having the power to move only forward ordinarily one square at a time, to capture only diagonally forward, and be promoted to any piece except a king

ə abut	ᵊ kitten	ər further	a back	ā bake	ä cot, cart
au̇ out	ch chin	e less	ē easy	g gift	i trip	ī life
j joke	ŋ sing	ō flow	ȯ flaw	ȯi coin	th thin	t͟h this
ü loot	u̇ foot	y yet	yü few	yu̇ furious	zh vision

upon reaching the eighth rank **2 :** one that can be used to further the purposes of another
pawn·bro·ker \ˈpȯn-ˌbrō-kər, ˈpän-\ *n* **:** one who loans money on the security of personal property pledged in his keeping — **pawn·bro·king** \-kiŋ\ *n*
Paw·nee \pȯ-ˈnē, pä-\ *n, pl* **Pawnee** *or* **Pawnees :** a member of an Amerindian people orig. of Kansas and Nebraska
pawn·shop \ˈpȯn-ˌshäp, ˈpän-\ *n* **:** a pawnbroker's shop
paw·paw *var of* PAPAW
pax \ˈpaks, ˈpäks\ *n* [ME, fr. ML, fr. L, peace — more at PEACE] **1 :** a tablet decorated with a sacred figure (as of Christ) and sometimes ceremonially kissed by participants at mass **2 :** the kiss of peace in the Mass **3 :** PEACE
[1]**pay** \ˈpā\ *vb* **paid** \ˈpād\ *also in sense 7* **payed; pay·ing** [ME *payen,* fr. OF *paier,* fr. L *pacare* to pacify, fr. *pac-, pax* peace] *vt* **1 a :** to make due return to for services rendered or property delivered **b :** to engage for money **:** HIRE <you couldn't ~ me to do that> **2 a :** to give in return for goods or service <~ wages> **b :** to discharge indebtedness for **:** SETTLE <~ a bill> **c :** to make a disposal or transfer of (money) **3 :** to give or forfeit in expiation or retribution <~ the penalty> **4 a :** to make compensation for **b :** to requite according to what is deserved <~ him back> **5 :** to give, offer, or make freely or as fitting <~ attention> **6 a :** to return value or profit to <it ~*s* you to stay open> **b :** to bring in as a return <an investment ~*ing* five percent> **7 :** to slacken (as a rope) and allow to run out — used with *out* ~ *vi* **1 :** to discharge a debt or obligation **2 :** to be worth the expense or effort <it ~*s* to advertise>
syn PAY, COMPENSATE, REMUNERATE, SATISFY, REIMBURSE, INDEMNIFY, REPAY, RECOMPENSE *shared meaning element* **:** to give money or an equivalent in return for something
[2]**pay** *n* **1 a :** the act or fact of paying or being paid **b :** the status of being paid by an employer **:** EMPLOY **2 :** something paid for a purpose and esp. as a salary or wage **:** REMUNERATION **3 :** a person viewed with respect to reliability or promptness in paying debts or bills **4 a :** ore or a natural situation that yields metal and esp. gold in profitable amounts **b :** an oil-yielding stratum or zone ***syn*** see WAGE
[3]**pay** *adj* **1 :** containing or leading to something precious or valuable **2 :** equipped with a coin slot for receiving a fee for use **3 :** requiring payment
[4]**pay** *vt* **payed** *also* **paid; pay·ing** [obs. F *peier,* fr. L *picare,* fr. *pic-, pix* pitch] **:** to coat with a waterproof composition
pay·able \ˈpā-ə-bəl\ *adj* **1 :** that may, can, or must be paid **2 :** PROFITABLE
pay–as–you–go *adj* **:** of or relating to a system or policy of paying bills when due or of paying for goods and services when purchased
pay·check \ˈpā-ˌchek\ *n* **1 :** a check in payment of wages or salary **2 :** WAGES, SALARY
pay·day \-ˌdā\ *n* **:** a regular day on which wages are paid
pay dirt *n* **1 :** earth or ore that yields a profit to a miner **2 :** a useful or remunerative discovery or object
PAYE *abbr* **1** pay as you earn **2** pay as you enter
pay·ee \pā-ˈē\ *n* **:** one to whom money is or is to be paid
pay·er \ˈpā-ər\ *also* **pay·or** \ˈpā-ər, pā-ˈȯ(ə)r\ *n* **:** one that pays; *esp* **:** the person by whom a bill or note has been or should be paid
pay·load \ˈpā-ˌlōd\ *n* **1 :** the revenue-producing or useful load that a vehicle of transport can carry **2 :** the explosive charge carried in the warhead of a missile **3 :** the load that is carried by a spacecraft and that consists of things (as passengers or instruments) that relate directly to the purpose of the flight as opposed to things (as fuel) that are necessary for operation; *also* **:** the weight of such a load
pay·mas·ter \-ˌmas-tər\ *n* **:** an officer or agent whose duty it is to pay salaries or wages
pay·ment \ˈpā-mənt\ *n* **1 :** the act of paying **2 :** something that is paid **:** PAY **3 :** REQUITAL
pay·nim \ˈpā-nəm\ *n* [ME *painim,* fr. OF *paienime* heathendom, fr. LL *paganismus,* fr. *paganus* pagan] *archaic* **:** PAGAN; *esp* **:** MUSLIM
[1]**pay·off** \ˈpā-ˌȯf\ *n* **1 :** the act or occasion of paying employees' wages or distributing gains (as profits or bribe money) **2 a :** PROFIT, REWARD; *esp* **:** an amount received by a player in a game **b :** RETRIBUTION **3 :** the climax of an incident or enterprise; *specif* **:** the denouement of a narrative **4 :** a decisive fact or factor resolving a situation or bringing about a definitive conclusion
[2]**payoff** *adj* **:** yielding results in the final test **:** DECISIVE
pay off \(ˈ)pā-ˈȯf\ *vt* **1 a :** to give all due wages to; *esp* **:** to pay in full and discharge (an employee) **b :** to pay (a debt or a creditor) in full **2 :** to inflict retribution on **3 :** to allow (a thread or rope) to run off a spool or drum ~ *vi* **:** to yield returns
pay·ola \pā-ˈō-lə\ *n* [prob. alter. of [1]*payoff*] **:** undercover or indirect payment (as to a disc jockey) for a commercial favor (as plugging a record)
pay·roll \ˈpā-ˌrōl\ *n* **1 :** a paymaster's or employer's list of those entitled to pay and of the amounts due to each **2 :** the sum necessary for distribution to those on a payroll; *also* **:** the money to be distributed
pay station *n* **:** a public telephone usu. equipped with a slot-machine device for payment of toll
payt *abbr* payment
pay up *vt* **:** to pay in full ~ *vi* **:** to pay what is due
Pb *symbol* [L *plumbum*] lead
PBX *abbr* private branch exchange
PC *abbr* **1** Peace Corps **2** percent; percentage **3** postcard **4** [L *post cibum*] after meals
PCB \ˌpē-ˌsē-ˈbē\ *n* **:** POLYCHLORINATED BIPHENYL
pct *abbr* percent
PCV *abbr* positive crankcase ventilation
pd *abbr* paid
Pd *symbol* palladium
PD *abbr* **1** per diem **2** police department **3** postal district **4** potential difference
PDA *abbr* **1** predicted drift angle **2** public display of affection
PDD *abbr* past due date
PDQ \ˌpē-ˌdē-ˈkyü\ *adv, often not cap* [abbr. of *pretty damned quick*] **:** IMMEDIATELY
PDT *abbr* Pacific daylight time
pe \ˈpā\ *n* [Heb *pē*] **:** the 17th letter of the Hebrew alphabet — see ALPHABET table
PE *abbr* **1** physical education **2** printer's error **3** probable error **4** professional engineer
pea \ˈpē\ *n, pl* **peas** *also* **pease** \ˈpēz\ *often attrib* [back-formation fr. ME *pease* (taken as a pl.), fr. OE *pise,* fr. L *pisa,* pl. of *pisum,* fr. Gk *pison*] **1 a :** a variable annual leguminous vine (*Pisum sativum*) that is cultivated for its rounded smooth or wrinkled edible protein-rich seeds **b :** the seed of the pea **c** *pl* **:** the immature pods of the pea with their included seeds **2 :** any of various leguminous plants related to or resembling the pea — usu. used with a qualifying term <chick-*pea*> <black-eyed ~>; *also* **:** the seed of such a plant **3 :** something resembling a pea

pea 1a

pea aphid *n* **:** a widely distributed aphid (*Acyrthosiphon pisum*) that is a serious pest on legumes (as alfalfa, pea, and clover)
pea bean *n* **:** any of various kidney beans cultivated for their small white seeds which are used dried (as for baking)
[1]**peace** \ˈpēs\ *n* [ME *pees,* fr. OF *pais,* fr. L *pac-, pax;* akin to L *pacisci* to agree — more at PACT] **1 :** a state of tranquillity or quiet: as **a :** freedom from civil disturbance **b :** a state of security or order within a community provided for by law or custom <a breach of the ~> **2 :** freedom from disquieting or oppressive thoughts or emotions **3 :** harmony in personal relations **4 a :** a state or period of mutual concord between governments **b :** a pact or agreement to end hostilities between those who have been at war or in a state of enmity **5** — used interjectionally as a command or request for silence or calm or as a greeting or farewell — **at peace :** in a state of concord or tranquillity
[2]**peace** *vi, obs* **:** to be, become, or keep silent or quiet
peace·able \ˈpē-sə-bəl\ *adj* **1 a :** disposed to peace **:** not contentious or quarrelsome **b :** quietly behaved **2 :** marked by freedom from strife or disorder ***syn*** see PACIFIC ***ant*** contentious — **peace·able·ness** *n* — **peace·ably** \-blē\ *adv*
peace corps *n* **:** a body of trained personnel sent as volunteers esp. to assist underdeveloped nations
peace·ful \ˈpēs-fəl\ *adj* **1 :** PEACEABLE 1 **2 :** untroubled by conflict, agitation, or commotion **:** QUIET, TRANQUIL **3 :** of or relating to a state or time of peace **4 :** devoid of violence or force ***syn*** **1** see CALM ***ant*** turbulent **2** see PACIFIC — **peace·ful·ly** \-fə-lē\ *adv* — **peace·ful·ness** *n*
peaceful coexistence *n* **:** a living together in peace rather than in constant hostility
peace·keep·ing \ˈpē-ˌskē-piŋ\ *n* **:** the preserving of peace; *esp* **:** international enforcement and supervision of a truce between hostile states or communities — **peace·keep·er** \-pər\ *n*
peace·mak·er \ˈpē-ˌsmā-kər\ *n* **:** one who makes peace esp. by reconciling parties at variance — **peace·mak·ing** \-kiŋ\ *n or adj*
peace offering *n* **:** a gift or service for the purpose of procuring peace or reconciliation
peace officer *n* **:** a civil officer (as a policeman) whose duty it is to preserve the public peace
peace pipe *n* **:** CALUMET
peace sign *n* **:** a sign made by holding the palm outward and forming a V with the index and middle fingers and used to indicate the desire for peace
peace·time \ˈpē-ˌstim\ *n* **:** a time when a nation is not at war
[1]**peach** \ˈpēch\ *n* [ME *peche,* fr. MF (the fruit), fr. LL *persica,* fr. L *persicum,* fr. neut. of *persicus* Persian, fr. *Persia*] **1 a :** a low spreading freely branching Chinese tree (*Prunus persica*) of the rose family that is cosmopolitan in cultivation in temperate areas and has lanceolate leaves, sessile usu. pink flowers borne on the naked twigs in early spring, and a fruit which is a single-seeded drupe with a hard endocarp, a pulpy white or yellow mesocarp, and a thin downy epicarp **b :** the edible fruit of the peach **2 :** a variable color averaging a moderate yellowish pink
[2]**peach** *vb* [ME *pechen,* short for *apechen* to accuse, fr. (assumed) AF *apecher,* fr. LL *impedicare* to entangle — more at IMPEACH] *vt* **:** to inform against **:** BETRAY ~ *vi* **:** to turn informer **:** BLAB
peach leaf curl *n* **:** leaf curl of the peach that is caused by a fungus (*Tephrina deformans*)
peach tree borer *n* **:** a blue-black orange-marked clearwing moth (*Sanninoidea exitiosa*) whose white brown-headed larva bores in the wood of stone fruit trees (as the peach) in eastern No. America
peachy \ˈpē-chē\ *adj* **peach·i·er; -est 1 :** resembling a peach **2 :** unusually fine **:** DANDY
[1]**pea·cock** \ˈpē-ˌkäk\ *n* [ME *pecok,* fr. *pe-* (fr. OE *pēa* peafowl) + *cok* cock; akin to OHG *pfāwo* peacock; both fr. a prehistoric WGmc-NGmc word borrowed fr. L *pavon-, pavo* peacock] **1 :** a male peafowl distinguished by a crest of upright plumules and by greatly elongated loosely webbed upper tail coverts which are mostly tipped with ocellated spots and can be erected and spread at will in a fan shimmering with iridescent color; *broadly* **:** PEAFOWL **2 :** one making a proud display of himself **:** SHOW-OFF — **pea·cock·ish** \-ish\ *adj* — **pea·cocky** \-ē\ *adj*
[2]**peacock** *vi* **:** to show off
peacock blue *n* **:** a variable color averaging a moderate greenish blue
peacock flower *n* **:** ROYAL POINCIANA
pea·fowl \ˈpē-ˌfau̇l\ *n* [*pea-* (as in *peacock*) + *fowl*] **:** a very large terrestrial pheasant (genus *Pavo*) of southeastern Asia and the East Indies that is often reared as an ornamental fowl

pea green *n* : a variable color averaging a moderate yellow-green
pea·hen \'pē-ˌhen, -'hen\ *n* [ME *pehenne,* fr. *pe-* + *henne* hen] : a female peafowl
pea jacket \'pē-\ *n* [by folk etymology fr. D *pijjekker,* fr. *pij,* a kind of cloth + *jekker* jacket] : a heavy woolen double-breasted jacket worn by sailors; *also* : a similar jacket worn by civilians
[1]**peak** \'pēk\ *vi* [origin unknown] **1** : to grow thin or sickly **2** : to dwindle away
[2]**peak** *n* [perh. alter. of *pike*] **1** : a pointed or projecting part of a garment; *esp* : the visor of a cap or hat **2** : PROMONTORY **3** : a sharp or pointed end **4 a** (1) : the top of a hill or mountain ending in a point (2) : a prominent mountain usu. having a well-defined summit **b** : something resembling a mountain peak **5 a** : the upper aftermost corner of a fore-and-aft sail **b** : the narrow part of a ship's bow or stern or the part of the hold in it **6 a** : the highest level or greatest degree **b** : a high point in a course of development esp. as represented on a graph **7** : a point formed by the hair on the forehead ***syn*** see SUMMIT
[3]**peak** *vi* : to reach a maximum ~ *vt* : to cause to come to a peak, point, or maximum
[4]**peak** *adj* : being at or reaching the maximum
[5]**peak** *vt* [fr. *apeak* (held vertically)] **1** : to set (as a gaff) nearer the perpendicular **2** : to hold (oars) with blades well raised
[1]**peaked** \'pēkt *also* 'pē-kəd\ *adj* : having a peak : POINTED — **peaked·ness** \'pēk(t)-nəs, 'pē-kəd-nəs\ *n*
[2]**peak·ed** \'pē-kəd *also* 'pik-əd\ *adj* : looking pale and wan
[1]**peal** \'pē(ə)l\ *n* [ME, appeal, summons to church, short for *appel* appeal, fr. *appelen* to appeal] **1 a** : the loud ringing of bells **b** : a complete set of changes on a given number of bells **c** : a set of bells tuned to the tones of the major scale for change ringing **2** : a loud sound or succession of sounds <heard ~*s* of laughter>
[2]**peal** *vi* : to give out peals ~ *vt* : to utter or give forth loudly
pea·like \'pē-ˌlīk\ *adj* **1** : resembling a garden pea esp. in size, firmness, and shape <a ~ lump under the skin> **2** *of a flower* : being showy and papilionaceous
[1]**pea·nut** \'pē-(ˌ)nət\ *n* **1 a** : a low-branching widely cultivated leguminous annual herb (*Arachis hypogaea*) with showy yellow flowers having a peduncle which elongates and bends into the soil where the ovary ripens into a pod containing one to three oily edible seeds **b** : the seed or seed-containing pod of the peanut **2** : an insignificant or tiny person **3** *pl* : a trifling amount
[2]**peanut** *adj* : INSIGNIFICANT, PETTY <~ politics>
peanut butter *n* : a paste made by grinding roasted skinned peanuts
peanut oil *n* : a colorless to yellow nondrying fatty oil that is obtained from peanuts and is used chiefly as a salad oil, in margarine, in soap, and as a vehicle in pharmaceutical preparations and cosmetics
pear \'pa(ə)r, 'pe(ə)r\ *n* [ME *pere,* fr. OE *peru,* fr. L *pirum*] **1** : a fleshy pome fruit that is borne by a tree (genus *Pyrus,* esp. *P. communis*) of the rose family and is usu. larger at the apical end **2** : a tree bearing pears
[1]**pearl** \'pər(-ə)l\ *n* [ME *perle,* fr. MF, fr. (assumed) VL *pernula,* dim. of L *perna* haunch, sea mussel; akin to OE *fiersn* heel, Gk *pternē*] **1 a** : a dense variously colored and usu. lustrous concretion formed of concentric layers of nacre as an abnormal growth within the shell of some mollusks and used as a gem **b** : MOTHER-OF-PEARL **2** : one that is very choice or precious **3** : something resembling a pearl intrinsically or physically **4** : a nearly neutral slightly bluish medium gray
[2]**pearl** *vt* **1** : to set or adorn with pearls **2** : to sprinkle or bead with pearly drops **3** : to form into small round grains **4** : to give a pearly color or luster to ~ *vi* **1** : to form drops or beads like pearls **2** : to fish or search for pearls — **pearl·er** \'pər-lər\ *n*
[3]**pearl** *adj* **1 a** : of, relating to, or resembling pearl **b** : made of or adorned with pearls **2** : having medium-sized grains
[4]**pearl** *n or vt* [alter. of *purl*] *Brit* : PICOT
pearl danio *n* : a small lustrous cyprinid fish (*Brachydanio albolineatus*) that is often kept in tropical aquariums
pearl·es·cent \ˌpər-'les-ᵊnt\ *adj* : having a pearly luster <a ~ lacquer> — **pearl·es·cence** \-ᵊn(t)s\ *n*
pearl essence *n* : a translucent substance that occurs in the silvery scales of various fish (as herring) and is used in making artificial pearls, lacquers, and plastics
pearl gray *n* **1** : a yellowish to light gray **2** : a variable color averaging a pale blue
Pearl Harbor *n* [*Pearl Harbor,* Oahu, Hawaii, Am naval station attacked without warning by the Japanese] : a sneak attack usu. with devastating effect
pearl·ite \'pər(-ə)l-ˌīt\ *n* [F *perlite,* fr. *perle* pearl] **1** : the lamellar mixture of ferrite and cementite in slowly cooled iron-carbon alloys occurring normally as a principal constituent of both steel and cast iron **2** : PERLITE — **pearl·it·ic** \ˌpər-'lit-ik\ *adj*
pearl·ized \'pər(-ə)l-ˌīzd\ *adj* : given a pearlescent surface or finish
pearl millet *n* : a tall cereal grass (*Pennisetum glaucum*) that has large leaves and dense round spikes and is widely grown for its seeds and for forage
pearl onion *n* : a very small usu. pickled onion used esp. in appetizers and as a garnish
pearly \'pər-lē\ *adj* **pearl·i·er; -est** **1** : resembling, containing, or adorned with pearls or mother-of-pearl **2** : highly precious
pearly everlasting *n* : an American everlasting (*Anaphalis margaritacea*) that has herbage covered with white woolly hairs and corymbose heads with white scarious involucres
pearly nautilus *n* : NAUTILUS 1
pear psylla *n* : a yellowish or greenish jumping plant louse (*Psylla pyricola*) that is often destructive to the pear
pear-shaped \'pa(ə)r-ˌshāpt, 'pe(ə)r-\ *adj* **1** : having an oval shape markedly tapering at one end **2** *of a vocal tone* : free from harshness, thinness, or nasality
peart \'pi(ə)rt\ *adj* [alter. of *pert*] *chiefly South & Midland* : being in good spirits : LIVELY — **peart·ly** *adv*
peas·ant \'pez-ᵊnt\ *n* [ME *paissaunt,* fr. MF *paisant,* fr. OF, fr. *païs* country, fr. LL *pagensis* inhabitant of a district, fr. L *pagus* district] **1** : a member of a European class of persons tilling the soil as small landowners or as laborers; *also* : a member of a similar class elsewhere **2** : a usu. uneducated person of low social status
peas·ant·ry \-ᵊn-trē\ *n* **1** : PEASANTS **2** : the position, rank, or behavior of a peasant
[1]**pease** \'pēz\ *n* [ME *pese*] *chiefly Brit* : PEA
[2]**pease** *pl of* PEA
pease·cod *or* **peas·cod** \'pēz-ˌkäd\ *n* [ME *pesecod,* fr. *pese* + *cod* bag, husk — more at CODPIECE] : a pea pod
pea·shoot·er \'pē-'shüt-ər, -ˌshüt-\ *n* : a toy blowgun for shooting peas
pea soup *n* **1** : a thick purée made of dried peas **2** : a heavy fog
[1]**peat** \'pēt\ *n, often attrib* [ME *pete,* fr. ML *peta*] **1** : TURF 2b **2** : partially carbonized vegetable tissue formed by partial decomposition in water of various plants (as mosses of the genus *Sphagnum*) — **peaty** \-ē\ *adj*
[2]**peat** *n* [origin unknown] : a bold gay woman
peat moss *n* : SPHAGNUM
pea·vey *or* **pea·vy** \'pē-vē\ *n, pl* **peaveys** *or* **peavies** [prob. fr. the name *Peavey*] : a stout lever like a cant hook but with the end armed with a strong sharp spike used esp. in handling logs

peavey

[1]**peb·ble** \'peb-əl\ *n* [ME *pobble,* fr. OE *papolstān,* fr. *papol-* (prob. imit.) + *stān* stone] **1** : a small usu. rounded stone esp. when worn by the action of water **2** : transparent and colorless quartz : ROCK CRYSTAL **3** : an irregular, crinkled, or grainy surface — **peb·bly** \-(ə-)lē\ *adj*
[2]**pebble** *vt* **peb·bled; peb·bling** \-(ə-)liŋ\ **1** : to pelt with pebbles **2** : to pave or cover with pebbles or something resembling pebbles **3** : to grain (as leather) so as to produce a rough and irregularly indented surface
pe·can \pi-'kän, -'kan; 'pē-ˌkan\ *n* [of Algonquian origin; akin to Ojibwa *pagân,* a hard-shelled nut] **1** : a large hickory (*Carya illinoensis*) that has roughish bark and hard but brittle wood and is widely grown in the warmer parts of the U.S. and in Mexico for its edible nut **2** : the wood of the pecan tree **3** : the smooth oblong thin-shelled nut of the pecan tree
pec·ca·ble \'pek-ə-bəl\ *adj* [MF, fr. L *peccare*] : prone to sin
pec·ca·dil·lo \ˌpek-ə-'dil-(ˌ)ō\ *n, pl* **-loes** *or* **-los** [Sp *pecadillo,* dim. of *pecado* sin, fr. L *peccatum,* fr. neut. of *peccatus,* pp. of *peccare*] : a slight offense
pec·can·cy \'pek-ən-sē\ *n, pl* **-cies** **1** : the quality or state of being peccant **2** : OFFENSE
pec·cant \'pek-ənt\ *adj* [L *peccant-, peccans,* prp. of *peccare* to stumble, sin] **1** : guilty of a moral offense : SINNING **2** : violating a principle or rule — **pec·cant·ly** *adv*
pec·ca·ry \'pek-ə-rē\ *n, pl* **-ries** [of Cariban origin; akin to Chaima *paquera* peccary] : either of two largely nocturnal gregarious American mammals resembling the related pigs: **a** : a grizzled animal (*Tayassu angulatus*) with an indistinct white collar **b** : a blackish animal (*Tayassu pecari*) with whitish cheeks

peccary a

pec·ca·vi \pe-'kä-(ˌ)wē, -(ˌ)vē; -'kā-ˌvī\ *n* [L, I have sinned, fr. *peccare*] : an acknowledgement of sin
[1]**peck** \'pek\ *n* [ME *pek,* fr. OF] **1** — see WEIGHT table **2** : a large quantity or number
[2]**peck** *vb* [ME *pecken,* alter. of *piken* to pierce — more at PICK] *vt* **1 a** : to strike or pierce esp. repeatedly with the bill or a pointed tool **b** : to make by pecking <~ a hole> **2** : to pick up with the bill ~ *vi* **1 a** : to strike, pierce, or pick up something with or as if with the bill **b** : CARP, NAG **2** : to eat reluctantly and in small bites <~ at food>
[3]**peck** *n* **1** : an impression or hole made by pecking **2** : a quick sharp stroke
peck·er \'pek-ər\ *n* **1** : one that pecks **2** *chiefly Brit* : COURAGE **3** : PENIS — often considered vulgar
pecking order *or* **peck order** *n* **1** : the basic pattern of social organization within a flock of poultry in which each bird pecks another lower in the scale without fear of retaliation and submits to pecking by one of higher rank **2** : a social hierarchy
peck·sniff·ian \pek-'snif-ē-ən\ *adj* [Seth *Pecksniff,* character in *Martin Chuzzlewit* (1843-44) by Charles Dickens] : selfish and corrupt behind a display of seeming benevolence : SANCTIMONIOUS
pecky \'pek-ē\ *adj* [[3]*peck*] **1** : marked by lenticular or finger-shaped pockets of decay caused by fungi <~ cypress> **2** : containing discolored or shriveled grains <~ rice>
pec·tate \'pek-ˌtāt\ *n* : a salt or ester of a pectic acid
pec·ten \'pek-tən\ *n, pl* **pectens** [NL *pectin-, pecten,* fr. L, comb, scallop] **1** *pl usu* **pec·ti·nes** \-tə-ˌnēz\ : a body part that resembles a comb; *esp* : a folded vascular pigmented membrane projecting into the vitreous humor in the eye of a bird or reptile **2** : [1]SCALLOP 1a

---

ə abut ᵊ kitten ər further a back ā bake ä cot, cart
au̇ out ch chin e less ē easy g gift i trip ī life
j joke ŋ sing ō flow ȯ flaw ȯi coin th thin t͟h this
ü loot u̇ foot y yet yü few yu̇ furious zh vision

pec·tic \ˈpek-tik\ *adj* [F *pectique,* fr. Gk *pēktikos* coagulating, fr. *pēgnynai* to fix, coagulate — more at PACT] : of, relating to, or derived from pectin

pectic acid *n* : any of various water-insoluble substances formed by hydrolyzing the methyl ester groups of pectins

pec·tin \ˈpek-tən\ *n* [F *pectine,* fr. *pectique*] : any of various water-soluble substances that bind adjacent cell walls in plant tissues and yield a gel which is the basis of fruit jellies; *also* : a commercial product rich in pectins

pec·tin·aceous \ˌpek-tə-ˈnā-shəs\ *adj* : of, relating to, or containing pectin

pec·ti·nate \ˈpek-tə-ˌnāt\ *also* **pec·ti·nat·ed** \-ˌnāt-əd\ *adj* [L *pectinatus,* fr. *pectin-, pecten* comb; akin to Gk *kten-, kteis* comb, L *pectere* to comb — more at FEE] : having narrow parallel projections or divisions suggestive of the teeth of a comb <~ antennae> — **pec·ti·na·tion** \ˌpek-tə-ˈnā-shən\ *n*

pec·tin·es·ter·ase \ˌpek-tə-ˈnes-tə-ˌrās, -ˌrāz\ *n* : an enzyme that catalyzes the hydrolysis of pectins into pectic acids and methanol

¹pec·to·ral \ˈpek-t(ə-)rəl\ *n* : something worn on the breast

²pectoral *adj* [MF or L; MF, fr. L *pectoralis,* fr. *pector-, pectus* breast; akin to Toch A *päśśäm* the two breasts] **1** : of, situated in or on, or worn on the chest **2** : coming from the breast or heart as the seat of emotion

pectoral cross *n* : a cross worn on the breast esp. by a prelate

pectoral fin *n* : either of the fins of a fish that correspond to the forelimbs of a quadruped

pectoral girdle *n* : the bony or cartilaginous arch that supports the forelimbs of a vertebrate

pectoral muscle *n* : one of the muscles which connect the ventral walls of the chest with the bones of the upper arm and shoulder and of which there are two on each side in man

pec·u·late \ˈpek-yə-ˌlāt\ *vt* **-lat·ed; -lat·ing** [L *peculatus,* pp. of *peculari,* fr. *peculium*] : EMBEZZLE — **pec·u·la·tion** \ˌpek-yə-ˈlā-shən\ *n* — **pec·u·la·tor** \ˈpek-yə-ˌlāt-ər\ *n*

¹pe·cu·liar \pi-ˈkyül-yər\ *adj* [ME *peculier,* fr. L *peculiaris* of private property, special, fr. *peculium* private property, fr. *pecu* cattle; akin to L *pecus* cattle — more at FEE] **1** : belonging exclusively to one person or group **2** : felt to be characteristic of one only : DISTINCTIVE **3** : different from the usual or normal: **a** : SPECIAL, PARTICULAR **b** : CURIOUS **c** : ECCENTRIC, QUEER ***syn*** see CHARACTERISTIC, STRANGE — **pe·cu·liar·ly** *adv*

²peculiar *n* : something exempt from ordinary jurisdiction; *esp* : a church or parish exempt from the jurisdiction of the ordinary in whose territory it lies

pe·cu·liar·i·ty \pi-ˌkyül-ˈyar-ət-ē, -ˌkyü-lē-ˈar-\ *n, pl* **-ties** **1** : the quality or state of being peculiar **2** : a distinguishing characteristic **3** : ODDITY, QUIRK

pe·cu·ni·ary \pi-ˈkyü-nē-ˌer-ē\ *adj* [L *pecuniarius,* fr. *pecunia* money — more at FEE] **1** : consisting of or measured in money **2** : of or relating to money : MONETARY ***syn*** see FINANCIAL — **pe·cu·ni·ari·ly** \-ˌkyü-nē-ˈer-ə-lē\ *adv*

ped \ˈped\ *n* [Gk *pedon* ground; akin to L *ped-, pes* foot — more at FOOT] : a natural soil aggregate

PED *abbr* doctor of physical education

ped- — see PAED-

-ped \ˌped *also* pəd\ *or* **-pede** \ˌpēd\ *n comb form* [L *ped-, pes*] : foot <maxilli*ped*> <maxilli*pede*>

ped·a·gog·ic \ˌped-ə-ˈgäj-ik, -ˈgōj-\ *adj* : of, relating to, or befitting a teacher or education — **ped·a·gog·i·cal** \-i-kəl\ *adj* — **ped·a·gog·i·cal·ly** \-i-k(ə-)lē\ *adv*

ped·a·gog·ics \-iks\ *n pl but sing in constr* : PEDAGOGY

ped·a·gogue *also* **ped·a·gog** \ˈped-ə-ˌgäg\ *n* [ME *pedagoge,* fr. MF, fr. L *paedagogus,* fr. Gk *paidagōgos,* slave who escorted children to school, fr. *paid-* paed- + *agōgos* leader, fr. *agein* to lead — more at AGENT] : TEACHER, SCHOOLMASTER

ped·a·go·gy \ˈped-ə-ˌgōj-ē *also* -ˌgäj-, *esp Brit* -ˌgäg-\ *n* : the art, science, or profession of teaching; *esp* : EDUCATION 2

¹ped·al \ˈped-ᵊl\ *n* [MF *pedale,* fr. It, fr. L *pedalis,* adj.] **1** : a lever pressed by the foot in the playing of a musical instrument (as an organ or piano) **2** : a foot lever or treadle by which a part is activated in a mechanism

²ped·al *adj* [L *pedalis,* fr. *ped-, pes*] **1** \ˈped-ᵊl *also* ˈpēd-\ : of or relating to the foot **2** \ˈped-\ : of, relating to, or involving a pedal

³ped·al \ˈped-ᵊl\ *vb* **ped·aled** *also* **ped·alled; ped·al·ing** *also* **ped·al·ling** \ˈped-ᵊl-iŋ, ˈped-liŋ\ *vi* **1** : to use or work a pedal **2** : to ride a bicycle ~ *vt* : to work the pedals of

pedal disk *n* : the base by which a coelenterate polyp (as a sea anemone) is attached to the substrate

pe·dal·fer \pə-ˈdal-fər, -ˌfe(ə)r\ *n* [Gk *ped*on ground + E *al*umen + L *fer*rum iron] : a soil that lacks a hardened layer of accumulated carbonates — **ped·al·fer·ic** \ˌped-(ˌ)al-ˈfer-ik\ *adj*

ped·al–note \ˈped-ᵊl-ˌnōt\ *n* [fr. the playing of the lowest notes on the organ by means of pedals] **1** : PEDAL POINT **2** : one of the lowest tones that can be sounded on a brass instrument being an octave below the normal usable range and representing the fundamental of the harmonic series

pedal point *n* : a single tone usu. the tonic or dominant that is normally sustained in the bass and sounds against changing harmonies in the other parts

pedal pushers *n pl* : women's and girls' calf-length trousers

ped·ant \ˈped-ᵊnt\ *n* [MF, fr. It *pedante*] **1** *obs* : a male schoolteacher **2 a** : one who parades his learning **b** : one who is unimaginative or who unduly emphasizes minutiae in the presentation or use of knowledge **c** : a formalist or precisionist in teaching

pe·dan·tic \pi-ˈdant-ik\ *adj* **1** : of, relating to, or being a pedant **2** : narrowly, stodgily, and often ostentatiously learned <~ concern with detail> — **pe·dan·ti·cal·ly** \-ˈdant-i-k(ə-)lē\ *adv*
syn PEDANTIC, ACADEMIC, SCHOLASTIC, BOOKISH *shared meaning element* : too narrowly concerned with learned matters

ped·ant·ry \ˈped-ᵊn-trē\ *n, pl* **-ries** **1** : pedantic presentation or application of knowledge or learning **2** : an instance of pedantry

ped·dle \ˈped-ᵊl\ *vb* **ped·dled; ped·dling** \ˈped-liŋ, -ᵊl-iŋ\ [back-formation fr. *peddler,* fr. ME *pedlere*] *vi* **1** : to travel about with wares for sale; *broadly* : SELL **2** : to be busy with trifles : PIDDLE ~ *vt* **1** : to sell or offer for sale from place to place : HAWK **2** : to deal out or seek to disseminate

ped·dler *or* **ped·lar** \ˈped-lər\ *n* : one who peddles: as **a** : one who offers merchandise (as fresh produce) for sale along the street or from door to door **b** : one who deals in or promotes something intangible (as a personal asset or an idea) <influence ~*s*>

ped·dling \ˈped-lən, -ᵊl-ən, -liŋ, -ᵊl-iŋ\ *adj* [alter. of *piddling*] : PETTY

ped·er·ast \ˈped-ə-ˌrast\ *n* [Gk *paiderastēs,* lit., lover of boys, fr. *paid-* paed- + *erastēs* lover, fr. *erasthai* to love — more at EROS] : one that practices anal intercourse esp. with a boy — **ped·er·as·tic** \ˌped-ə-ˈras-tik\ *adj* — **ped·er·as·ty** \ˈped-ə-ˌras-tē\ *n*

pedes *pl of* PES

¹ped·es·tal \ˈped-əs-tᵊl\ *n* [MF *piedestal,* fr. OIt *piedestallo,* fr. *pie di stallo* foot of a stall] **1 a** : the support or foot of a late classic or neoclassic column — see COLUMN illustration **b** : the base of an upright structure **2** : BASE, FOUNDATION **3** : a position of esteem

²pedestal *vt* **-taled** *or* **-talled; -tal·ing** *or* **-tal·ling** : to place on or furnish with a pedestal

¹pe·des·tri·an \pə-ˈdes-trē-ən\ *adj* [L *pedestr-, pedester,* lit., going on foot, fr. *pedes* one going on foot, fr. *ped-, pes* foot — more at FOOT] **1** : COMMONPLACE, UNIMAGINATIVE **2 a** : going or performed on foot **b** : of, relating to, or designed for walking <a ~ mall>

²pedestrian *n* : a person going on foot : WALKER

pe·des·tri·an·ism \-ˌiz-əm\ *n* **1 a** : the practice of walking **b** : fondness for walking for exercise or recreation **2** : the quality or state of being unimaginative or commonplace

pe·di·at·ric \ˌpēd-ē-ˈa-trik\ *adj* : of or relating to pediatrics

pe·di·a·tri·cian \ˌpēd-ē-ə-ˈtrish-ən\ *or* **pe·di·a·trist** \ˌpēd-ē-ˈa-trəst, pē-ˈdī-ə-\ *n* : a specialist in pediatrics

pe·di·at·rics \ˌpēd-ē-ˈa-triks\ *n pl but sing or pl in constr* : a branch of medicine dealing with the development, care, and diseases of children

pedi·cab \ˈped-i-ˌkab\ *n* [L *ped-, pes* + E *cab*] : a small 3-wheeled hooded passenger vehicle that is pedaled

ped·i·cel \ˈped-ə-ˌsel\ *n* [NL *pedicellus,* dim. of L *pediculus*] **1** : a slender basal part of an organism or one of its parts: as **a** : a plant stalk that supports a fruiting or spore-bearing organ — see CORYMB illustration **b** : a narrow basal attachment (as of the abdomen of an ant) of an animal organ or part **2** : a small foot or footlike organ — **ped·i·cel·late** \ˌped-ə-ˈsel-ət\ *adj*

ped·i·cle \ˈped-i-kəl\ *n* [L *pediculus,* fr. dim. of *ped-, pes*] : PEDICEL — **ped·i·cled** \-kəld\ *adj*

pe·dic·u·late \pi-ˈdik-yə-lət\ *adj* [deriv. of L *pediculus* footstalk] : of or relating to an order (Pediculati) of marine teleost fishes with jugular ventral fins, pectoral fins at the end of an armlike process, and part of the dorsal fin modified into a lure — **pediculate** *n*

pe·dic·u·lo·sis \pi-ˌdik-yə-ˈlō-səs\ *n* [NL, fr. L *pediculus* louse] : infestation with lice

pe·dic·u·lous \pi-ˈdik-yə-ləs\ *adj* [L *pediculosus,* fr. *pediculus*] : infested with lice : LOUSY

pedi·cure \ˈped-i-ˌkyu̇(ə)r\ *n* [F *pédicure,* fr. L *ped-, pes* foot + *curare* to take care, fr. *cura* care — more at CURE] **1** : one who practices chiropody **2 a** : care of the feet, toes, and nails **b** : a single treatment of these parts — **pedi·cur·ist** \-ˌkyu̇r-əst\ *n*

ped·i·gree \ˈped-ə-ˌgrē\ *n* [ME *pedegru,* fr. MF *pie de grue* crane's foot; fr. the shape made by the lines of a genealogical chart] **1** : a register recording a line of ancestors **2 a** : an ancestral line : LINEAGE **b** : the origin and the history of something **3 a** : a distinguished ancestry **b** : the recorded purity of breed of an individual or strain — **ped·i·greed** \-ˌgrēd\ *adj*

ped·i·ment \ˈped-ə-mənt\ *n* [obs. E *periment,* prob. alter. of E *pyramid*] **1** : a triangular space forming the gable of a 2-pitched roof in classic architecture; *also* : a similar form used as a decoration **2** : a broad gently sloping bedrock surface with low relief that is situated at the base of a steeper slope and is usu. thinly covered with alluvial gravel and sand — **ped·i·men·tal** \ˌped-ə-ˈment-ᵊl\ *adj*

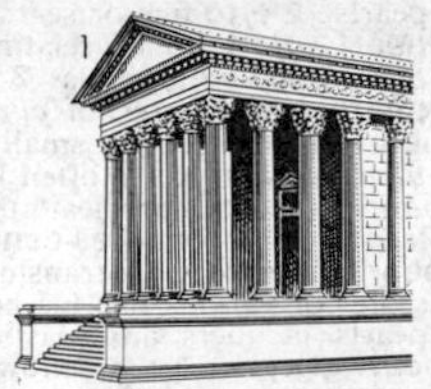

1, pediment 1

pedi·palp \ˈped-ə-ˌpalp\ *n* [NL *pedipalpus,* fr. *ped-, pes* foot + *palpus*] : either of the second pair of appendages of an arachnid (as a spider) that are borne near the mouth and are often modified for a special (as sensory) function

ped·lary *or* **ped·dlery** \ˈped-lə-rē\ *n* **1** *archaic* : peddlers' merchandise **2** *archaic* : the trade of a peddler

pedo- — see PAED-

ped·o·cal \ˈped-ə-ˌkal\ *n* [Gk *pedon* earth + L *calc-, calx* lime — more at PED, CHALK] : a soil that includes a definite hardened layer of accumulated carbonates — **ped·o·cal·ic** \ˌped-ə-ˈkal-ik\ *adj*

¹pe·do·gen·e·sis \ˌpēd-ə-ˈjen-ə-səs\ *var of* PAEDOGENESIS

²pedo·gen·e·sis \ˌped-ə-ˈjen-ə-səs\ *n* [NL, fr. Gk *pedon* + L *genesis*] : the formation and development of soil — **pedo·gen·ic** \-ˈjen-ik\ *or* **pedo·ge·net·ic** \-jə̇-ˈnet-ik\ *adj*

¹ped·o·log·ic \ˌped-ᵊl-ˈäj-ik\ *or* **ped·o·log·i·cal** \-i-kəl\ *adj* : of or relating to soil science

²pe·do·log·ic \ˌpēd-ᵊl-ˈäj-ik\ *or* **pe·do·log·i·cal** \-i-kəl\ *adj* : of or relating to child study

¹pe·dol·o·gist \pē-ˈdäl-ə-jəst\ *n* : a specialist in child study

²pe·dol·o·gist \pi-ˈdäl-ə-jəst, pe-\ *n* : a soil scientist

¹pe·dol·o·gy \pē-ˈdäl-ə-jē\ *n* [*paed-* + *-logy*] : the scientific study of the life and development of children

²pe·dol·o·gy \pi-ˈdäl-ə-jē, pe-\ *n* [Gk *pedon* + ISV *-logy*] : a science dealing with soils

pe·dom·e·ter \pi-ˈdäm-ət-ər\ *n* [F *pédomètre,* fr. L *ped-, pes* foot + F *-mètre* -meter — more at FOOT] : an instrument usu. in watch form that records the distance a walker covers by responding to his body motion at each step

pe·do·phile \ˈpēd-ə-ˌfīl\ *n* **:** one affected with pedophilia

pe·do·phil·ia \ˌpēd-ə-ˈfil-ē-ə\ *n* [NL] **:** sexual perversion in which children are the preferred sexual object — **pe·do·phil·i·ac** \-ˈfil-ē-ˌak\ *or* **pe·do·phil·ic** \-ˈfil-ik\ *adj*

pe·dun·cle \ˈpē-ˌdəŋ-kəl, pi-ˈ\ *n* [NL *pedunculus,* dim. of L *ped-, pes*] **1 :** a stalk bearing a flower or flower cluster or a fructification — see CORYMB illustration **2 :** a narrow part by which some larger part or the whole body of an organism is attached **:** STALK, PEDICEL **3 :** a narrow stalk by which a tumor or polyp is attached — **pe·dun·cled** \-kəld\ *adj* — **pe·dun·cu·lar** \pi-ˈdəŋ-kyə-lər\ *adj*

pe·dun·cu·late \pi-ˈdəŋ-kyə-lət\ *or* **pe·dun·cu·lat·ed** \-ˌlāt-əd\ *adj* [NL *pedunculus*] **:** having, growing on, or being attached by a peduncle <a ~ tumor>

1pee \ˈpē\ *n* **:** the letter *p*

2pee *vi* **peed; pee·ing** [euphemism fr. the initial letter of *piss*] **:** URINATE —sometimes considered vulgar

Peeb *abbr* Peeblesshire

1peek \ˈpēk\ *vi* [ME *piken*] **1 a :** to look furtively **b :** to peer through a crack or hole or from a place of concealment — often used with *in* or *out* **2 :** to take a brief look **:** GLANCE

2peek *n* **1 :** a surreptitious look **2 :** a brief look **:** GLANCE

1peek·a·boo \ˌpē-kə-ˈbü\ *n* [1*peek* + 1*boo*] **:** a game for amusing a baby in which one repeatedly hides his face or body and pops back into view exclaiming "Peekaboo!"

2peek·a·boo \-ˌbü\ *adj* **1 :** trimmed with eyelet embroidery <a ~ blouse> **2 :** made of a sheer or transparent fabric

1peel \ˈpē(ə)l\ *vb* [ME *pelen,* fr. MF *peler,* fr. L *pilare* to remove the hair from, fr. *pilus* hair — more at PILE] *vt* **1 :** to strip off an outer layer of <~ an orange> **2 :** to remove by stripping <~ the label off the can> ~ *vi* **1 a :** to come off in sheets or scales **b :** to lose an outer layer (as of skin) <his face is ~*ing*> **2 :** to take off one's clothes — **peel·able** \ˈpē-lə-bəl\ *adj*

2peel *n* **1 :** the skin or rind of a fruit **2 :** a thin layer of organic material that is embedded in a film of collodion and stripped from the surface of an object (as a plant fossil) for microscopic study

3peel *also* **pele** \ˈpē(ə)l\ *n* [ME *pel* stockade, stake, fr. AF, stockade & MF, stake, fr. L *palus* stake — more at POLE] **:** a medieval small massive fortified tower along the Scottish-English border

4peel *n* [ME *pele,* fr. MF, fr. L *pala*] **:** a usu. long-handled spade-shaped instrument that is used chiefly by bakers for getting something (as bread or pies) into or out of the oven

1peel·er \ˈpē-lər\ *n* **1 :** one that peels **2 :** a log of wood (as Douglas fir) suitable for cutting into rotary veneer — called also *peeler log*

2peeler *n* [Sir Robert *Peel*] *Brit* **:** POLICEMAN

peel·ing \ˈpē-liŋ\ *n* **:** a peeled-off piece or strip (as of skin or rind)

peel off *vi* **1 :** to veer away from an airplane formation esp. for diving or landing **2 :** DEPART, LEAVE

1peen \ˈpēn\ *vt* **:** to draw, bend, or flatten by or as if by hammering with a peen

2peen *or* **pein** \ˈpēn\ *n* [prob. of Scand origin; akin to Norw *penn* peen] **:** a usu. hemispherical or wedge-shaped end of the head of a hammer that is opposite the face and is used esp. for bending, shaping, or cutting the material struck

1peep \ˈpēp\ *vi* [ME *pepen,* of imit. origin] **1 :** to utter a feeble shrill sound as of a bird newly hatched **:** CHEEP **2 :** to utter the slightest sound

2peep *n* **1 :** a feeble shrill sound **:** CHEEP **2 :** a slight utterance esp. of complaint or protest <don't let me hear another ~ out of you> **3 :** any of several small sandpipers

3peep *vb* [ME *pepen,* perh. alter. of *piken* to peek] *vi* **1 a :** to peer through or as if through a crevice **b :** to look cautiously or slyly **2 :** to begin to emerge from or as if from concealment **:** show slightly ~ *vt* **:** to put forth or cause to protrude slightly

4peep *n* **1 :** the first glimpse or faint appearance <at the ~ of dawn> **2 a :** a brief look **:** GLANCE **b :** a furtive look

1peep·er \ˈpē-pər\ *n* **1 :** one that makes a peeping sound **2 :** any of various tailless amphibians (as a tree frog or a spring peeper) that peep shrilly

2peeper *n* **1 :** one that peeps; *specif* **:** VOYEUR **2 :** EYE

peep·hole \ˈpēp-ˌhōl\ *n* **:** a hole or crevice to peep through

Peeping Tom \-ˈtäm\ *n* **1 :** a legendary man who looked at Lady Godiva riding naked through Coventry and was struck blind **2** *often not cap P* **:** a pruriently prying person — **Peeping Tom·ism** \-ˈtäm-ˌiz-əm\ *n*

peep show *n* **:** an entertainment (as a film) or object (as a small painting) viewed through a small opening or a magnifying glass

peep sight *n* **:** a rear sight for a gun having an adjustable metal piece pierced with a small hole to peep through in aiming

1peer \ˈpi(ə)r\ *n* [ME, fr. OF *per,* fr. *per,* adj., equal, fr. L *par*] **1 :** one that is of equal standing with another **:** EQUAL **2** *archaic* **:** COMPANION **3 a :** a member of one of the five ranks (as duke, marquess, earl, viscount, or baron) of the British peerage **b :** NOBLE 1

2peer *vt, archaic* **:** RIVAL, MATCH

3peer *adj* **:** belonging to the same group in society esp. when membership is determined by age, grade, or status <a ~ group of adolescents>

4peer *vi* [perh. by shortening & alter. fr. *appear*] **1 :** to look narrowly or curiously; *esp* **:** to look searchingly at something difficult to discern **2 :** to come slightly into view **:** emerge partly *syn* see GAZE

peer·age \ˈpi(ə)r-ij\ *n* **1 :** the body of peers **2 :** the rank or dignity of a peer **3 :** a book containing a list of peers with their genealogy, history, and titles

peer·ess \ˈpir-əs\ *n* **1 :** the wife or widow of a peer **2 :** a woman who holds in her own right the rank of a peer

peer·less \ˈpi(ə)r-ləs\ *adj* **:** MATCHLESS, INCOMPARABLE — **peer·less·ly** *adv* — **peer·less·ness** *n*

1peeve \ˈpēv\ *vt* **peeved; peev·ing** [back-formation fr. *peevish*] **:** to make peevish or resentful **:** ANNOY *syn* see IRRITATE

2peeve *n* **1 :** a feeling or mood of resentment **2 :** a particular grievance **:** GRUDGE

pee·vish \ˈpē-vish\ *adj* [ME *pevish* spiteful] **1 :** querulous in temperament or mood **:** FRETFUL **2 :** perversely obstinate **3 :** marked by ill temper — **pee·vish·ly** *adv* — **pee·vish·ness** *n*

pee·wee \ˈpē-(ˌ)wē\ *n* [imit.] **1 :** PEWEE **2 :** one that is diminutive or small; *esp* **:** a small child — **peewee** *adj*

pee·wit \ˈpē-ˌwit, ˈpyü-ət\ *n* [imit.] **:** any of several birds: as **a :** LAPWING **b :** a small black-headed European gull (*Larus ridibundus*) **c :** PEWEE

1peg \ˈpeg\ *n* [ME *pegge*] **1 a :** a small usu. cylindrical pointed or tapered piece (as of wood) used to pin down or fasten things or to fit into or close holes **:** PIN, PLUG **b** *Brit* **:** CLOTHESPIN **c :** a predetermined level at which something (as a price) is fixed **2 a :** a projecting piece used as a support or boundary marker **b :** something (as a fact or opinion) used as a support, pretext, or reason **3 a :** one of the movable wooden pegs set in the head of a stringed instrument (as a violin) and that are turned to regulate the pitch of the strings — see VIOLIN illustration **b :** a step or degree esp. in estimation **4 :** a pointed prong or claw for catching or tearing **5** *Brit* **:** DRINK <poured himself out a stiff ~ — Dorothy Sayers> **6 :** something (as a leg) resembling a peg **7 :** THROW; *esp* **:** a hard throw in baseball made in an attempt to put out a base runner

2peg *vb* **pegged; peg·ging** *vt* **1 a :** to put a peg into **b** *Brit* **:** to pin (laundry) on a clothesline **c :** to pin down **:** RESTRICT **d :** to fix or hold (as prices) at a predetermined level **e :** to place in a definite category **:** IDENTIFY **2 :** to mark by pegs **3 :** THROW ~ *vi* **1 :** to work steadily and diligently — often used with *away* **2 :** to move along vigorously or hastily **:** HUSTLE

3peg \ˈpeg\ *or* **pegged** \ˈpegd\ *adj* **:** wide at the top and narrow at the bottom <~ pants>

Peg·a·sus \ˈpeg-ə-səs\ *n* [L (gen. *Pegasi*), fr. Gk *Pēgasos*] **1 :** a winged horse that caused the stream Hippocrene to spring from Mount Helicon with a blow of his hoof **2 :** poetic inspiration **3 :** a northern constellation near the vernal equinoctial point

peg·board \ˈpeg-ˌbō(ə)rd, -ˌbȯ(ə)rd\ *n* **1 :** a small board perforated with a pattern of holes into which pegs are stuck in playing certain games (as solitaire) **2 :** material (as fiberboard) pierced at regular intervals with holes into which hooks or pegs may be inserted for the storage or display of articles

peg leg *n* [1*peg*] **:** an artificial leg; *esp* **:** one fitted at the knee

peg·ma·tite \ˈpeg-mə-ˌtīt\ *n* [F, fr. Gk *pēgmat-, pēgma* something fastened together, fr. *pēgnynai* to fasten together — more at PACT] **1 :** a coarse variety of granite occurring in dikes or veins **2 :** a formation similar to pegmatite in other rocks <syenite ~> — **peg·ma·tit·ic** \ˌpeg-mə-ˈtit-ik\ *adj*

peg–top \ˈpeg-ˈtäp\ *or* **peg–topped** \-ˈtäpt\ *adj* **:** PEG

peg top *n* **1** \ˈpeg-ˈtäp\ **:** a pear-shaped top that is made to spin on the sharp metal peg in its base by the unwinding of a string wound round its center **2** *pl* \-ˌtäps\ **:** peg-top trousers

Peh·le·vi \ˈpel-ə-(ˌ)vē\ *var of* PAHLAVI

PEI *abbr* Prince Edward Island

pei·gnoir \pān-ˈwär, pen-\ *n* [F, lit., garment worn while combing the hair, fr. MF, fr. *peigner* to comb the hair, fr. L *pectinare,* fr. *pectin-, pecten* comb — more at PECTINATE] **:** a woman's loose negligee or dressing gown

pe·jo·ra·tive \pi-ˈjȯr-ət-iv, -ˈjär-; ˈpej-(ə-)rət-, ˈpej-ə-ˌrāt-, ˈpē-j-\ *adj* [LL *pejoratus,* pp. of *pejorare* to make or become worse, fr. L *pejor* worse; akin to L *pessimus* worst, Gk *pedon* ground — more at PARALLELEPIPED] **:** having a tendency to make or become worse **:** DEPRECIATORY, DISPARAGING — **pe·jo·ra·tive·ly** *adv*

peke \ˈpēk\ *n, often cap* **:** PEKINGESE 2

Pe·kin \pi-ˈkin, ˈpē-ˌ\ *n* [*Peking, Pekin,* China] **:** any of a breed of large white ducks of Chinese origin used for meat production

Pe·king·ese *or* **Pe·kin·ese** \ˌpē-kən-ˈēz, -kiŋ-, -ˈēs\ *n, pl* **Pekingese** *or* **Pekinese 1 a :** a native or resident of Peking **b :** the Chinese dialect of Peking **2 :** any of a Chinese breed of small short-legged dogs with a broad flat face and a profuse long soft coat

Pe·king man \ˌpē-ˌkiŋ-\ *n* **:** an extinct Pleistocene man that is known from skeletal and cultural remains in cave deposits at Choukoutien, China and that is more advanced in some details than Java man but nearer to him than to other fossil hominids or to recent man

pe·koe \ˈpē-(ˌ)kō\ *n* [Chin (Amoy) *pek-ho*] **1 :** a black tea made from the first three leaves on the spray **2 :** a black tea of India or Ceylon made from leaves of approximately the same size obtained by screening fired tea

pel·age \ˈpel-ij\ *n* [F, fr. MF, fr. *poil* hair, fr. L *pilus* — more at PILE] **:** the hairy covering of a mammal

1Pe·la·gian \pə-ˈlā-j(ē-)ən\ *n* **:** one agreeing with Pelagius in denying original sin and consequently in holding that man has perfect freedom to do either right or wrong

2Pelagian *adj* **:** of or relating to Pelagians or Pelagianism

Pe·la·gian·ism \-ˌiz-əm\ *n* **:** the teaching of Pelagius or Pelagians

pe·lag·ic \pə-ˈlaj-ik\ *adj* [L *pelagicus,* fr. Gk *pelagikos,* fr. *pelagos* sea — more at FLAKE] **:** of, relating to, or living or occurring in the open sea **:** OCEANIC

pel·ar·go·ni·um \ˌpel-är-ˈgō-nē-əm, ˌpel-ər-\ *n* [NL, genus name, irreg. fr. Gk *pelargos* stork] **:** any of a genus (*Pelargonium*) of southern African herbs (as a garden geranium) of the geranium family with showy flowers of various shades of red, pink, or white distinguished by a spurred calyx and irregular corolla

Pe·las·gian \pə-ˈlaz-j(ē-)ən, -ˈlaz-gē-ən\ *n* [Gk *pelasgios,* adj., Pelasgian, fr. *Pelasgoi* Pelasgians] **:** a member of an ancient people mentioned by classical writers as early inhabitants of Greece and the eastern islands of the Mediterranean — **Pelasgian** *adj* — **Pe·las·gic** \-jik, -gik\ *adj*

pele *var of* PEEL
pe·lecy·pod \pə-ˈles-ə-ˌpäd\ *n* [NL *Pelecypoda,* group name, fr. Gk *pelekys* ax + *pod-, pous* foot — more at FOOT]**:** LAMELLIBRANCH
pel·er·ine \ˌpel-ə-ˈrēn, ˈpel-ə-rən\ *n* [obs. F, neckerchief, fr. F *pèlerine,* fem. of *pèlerin* pilgrim, fr. LL *pelegrinus* — more at PILGRIM]**:** a woman's narrow cape made of fabric or fur and usu. with long ends hanging down in front
Pe·leus \ˈpēl-ˌyüs, ˈpē-lē-əs\ *n* [L, fr. Gk *Pēleus*]**:** a son of Aeacus who became by the goddess Thetis the father of Achilles
pelf \ˈpelf\ *n* [ME, fr. MF *pelfre* booty]**:** MONEY, RICHES
pel·i·can \ˈpel-i-kən\ *n* [ME, fr. OE *pellican,* fr. LL *pelecanus,* fr. Gk *pelekan*]**:** any of a genus (*Pelecanus*) of large web-footed birds with a very large bill and distensible gular pouch in which fish are caught
pe·lisse \pə-ˈlēs, pe-\ *n* [F, fr. LL *pellicia,* fr. fem. of *pellicius* made of skin, fr. L *pellis* skin — more at FELL] **1 :** a long cloak or coat made of fur or lined or trimmed with fur **2 :** a woman's loose lightweight cloak with wide collar and fur trimming
pel·la·gra \pə-ˈlag-rə, -ˈlāg-, -ˈläg-\ *n* [It, fr. *pelle* skin (fr. L *pellis*) + *-agra* (as in *podagra,* fr. L)]**:** a disease marked by dermatitis, gastrointestinal disorders, and central nervous symptoms and associated with a diet deficient in niacin and protein — **pel·la·grous** \-rəs\ *adj*
pel·la·grin \-rən\ *n* [irreg. fr. *pellagra*]**:** one that is affected with pellagra
¹pel·let \ˈpel-ət\ *n* [ME *pelote,* fr. MF, fr. (assumed) VL *pilota,* dim. of L *pila* ball — more at PILE] **1 :** a usu. small rounded or spherical body (as of food, medicine, debris, or snow) **2 a :** a usu. stone ball used as a missile in medieval times **b :** CANNONBALL **c :** BULLET **d :** a piece of small shot **e :** an imitation bullet — **pel·let·al** \-ət-ᵊl\ *adj*
²pellet *vt* **1 :** PELLETIZE **2 :** to strike with pellets
pel·let·ize \ˈpel-ət-ˌīz\ *vt* **-ized; -iz·ing :** to form or compact into pellets <~ ore> — **pel·let·iza·tion** \ˌpel-ət-ə-ˈzā-shən\ *n* — **pel·let·iz·er** \ˈpel-ət-ˌī-zər\ *n*
pel·li·cle \ˈpel-i-kəl\ *n* [MF *pellicule,* fr. ML *pellicula,* fr. L, dim. of *pellis*]**:** a thin skin or film; *esp* **:** one that reflects a part of the light falling upon it and transmits the rest of the light through it and that is used for dividing a beam of light (as in a photographic device)
¹pel·li·to·ry \ˈpel-ə-ˌtōr-ē, -ˌtȯr-\ *n, pl* **-ries** [ME *peletre,* fr. MF *piretre,* fr. L *pyrethrum*] **1 :** a southern European composite plant (*Anacyclus pyrethrum*) resembling yarrow — called also *pellitory-of-Spain* **2 :** any of several plants (as the feverfew or yarrow) that resemble the pellitory
²pellitory *n* [ME *paritorie,* fr. MF *paritaire,* fr. LL *parietaria,* fr. fem. of *parietarius* of a wall, fr. L *pariet-, paries* wall — more at PARIES]**:** any of a genus (*Parietaria*) of herbs of the nettle family with alternate leaves and inconspicuous flowers — called also *pellitory-of-the-wall*
pell–mell \ˈpel-ˈmel\ *adv* [MF *pelemele*] **1 :** in mingled confusion or disorder **2 :** in confused haste — **pell–mell** *adj or n*
pel·lu·cid \pə-ˈlü-səd\ *adj* [L *pellucidus,* fr. *per* through + *lucidus* lucid — more at FOR] **1 :** admitting maximum passage of light without diffusion or distortion **2 :** reflecting light evenly from all surfaces **3 :** easy to understand — **pel·lu·cid·i·ty** \ˌpel-yü-ˈsid-ət-ē\ *n* — **pel·lu·cid·ly** \pə-ˈlü-səd-lē\ *adv* — **pel·lu·cid·ness** *n*
Pe·lops \ˈpē-ˌläps, ˈpel-ˌäps\ *n* [L, fr. Gk]**:** a son of Tantalus cut up by his father and served to the gods but restored to life by Hermes
pe·lo·ria \pə-ˈlōr-ē-ə, -ˈlȯr-\ *n* [NL, fr. Gk *pelōros* monstrous, fr. *pelōr* monster; akin to Gk *teras* marvel — more at TERATOLOGY]**:** an abnormal regularity of structure occurring in normally irregular flowers — **pe·lor·ic** \-ˈlȯr-ik, -ˈlär-\ *adj*
pe·lo·rus \pə-ˈlōr-əs, -ˈlȯr-\ *n* [origin unknown]**:** a navigational instrument resembling a mariner's compass without magnetic needles and having two sight vanes by which bearings are taken
pe·lo·ta \pə-ˈlōt-ə\ *n* [Sp, fr. OF *pelote* little ball — more at PELLET] **1 :** a court game related to jai alai **2 :** the ball used in jai alai
¹pelt \ˈpelt\ *n* [ME] **1 :** a usu. undressed skin with its hair, wool, or fur **2 :** a skin stripped of hair or wool for tanning
²pelt *vt* **:** to strip off the skin or pelt of (an animal)
³pelt *vb* [ME *pelten*] *vt* **1 :** to strike with a succession of blows or missiles <~*ed* him with stones> **2 :** HURL, THROW <hand me anything hard . . . to ~ at her —Charles Dickens> **3 :** to beat or dash repeatedly against <hailstones ~*ing* the roof> ~ *vi* **1 :** to deliver a succession of blows or missiles **2 :** to beat incessantly **3 :** to move rapidly and vigorously **:** HURRY — **pelt·er** *n*
⁴pelt *n* **:** BLOW, WHACK
pel·tate \ˈpel-ˌtāt\ *adj* [prob. fr. (assumed) NL *peltatus,* fr. L *pelta* small shield, fr. Gk *peltē*]**:** shaped like a shield; *specif* **:** having the stem or support attached to the lower surface instead of at the base or margin <a ~ leaf> — **pel·tate·ly** *adv*
pelt·ing \ˈpel-tiŋ\ *adj* [prob. fr. E dial. *pelt* piece of trash] *archaic* **:** PALTRY, INSIGNIFICANT
pelt·ry \ˈpel-trē\ *n, pl* **peltries** [ME, fr. AF *pelterie*]**:** PELTS, FURS; *esp* **:** raw undressed skins
pel·vic \ˈpel-vik\ *adj* **:** of, relating to, or located in or near the pelvis — **pelvic** *n*
pelvic fin *n* **:** one of the paired fins of a fish that are homologous with the hind limbs of a quadruped — called also *ventral fin*
pelvic girdle *n* **:** a bony or cartilaginous arch that supports the hind limbs of a vertebrate
pel·vis \ˈpel-vəs\ *n, pl* **pel·vis·es** \-və-səz\ *or* **pel·ves** \-ˌvēz\ [NL, fr. L, basin; akin to OE & ON *full* cup, Gk *pella* wooden bowl] **1 :** a basin-shaped structure in the skeleton of many vertebrates that is formed by the pelvic girdle and adjoining bones of the spine **2 :** the cavity of the pelvis **3 :** the funnel-shaped cavity of the kidney into which urine is discharged
pel·y·co·saur \ˈpel-i-kə-ˌsȯ(ə)r\ *n* [deriv. of Gk *pelyc-, pelyx* wooden bowl + *sauros* lizard]**:** any of an order (Pelycosauria) of primitive Permian reptiles that resemble mammals and often have extreme development of the dorsal vertebral processes
Pemb *abbr* Pembrokeshire
Pem·broke Welsh corgi \ˈpem-ˌbrōk-, -ˌbrůk-\ *n* [*Pembroke,* Wales]**:** a Welsh corgi of a variety characterized by pointed erect ears, straight legs, and short tail — called also *Pembroke*
pem·mi·can *also* **pem·i·can** \ˈpem-i-kən\ *n* [Cree *pimikân*]**:** a concentrated food used by No. American Indians and consisting of lean meat dried, pounded fine, and mixed with melted fat; *also* **:** a similar preparation (as of dried beef, flour, molasses, suet) used for emergency rations
pem·o·line \ˈpem-ə-ˌlēn\ *n* [origin unknown]**:** a synthetic organic drug $C_9H_8N_2O_2$ that is usu. mixed with magnesium hydroxide; is a mild stimulant of the central nervous system, and is used experimentally to improve memory
pem·phi·gus \ˈpem(p)-fi-gəs, pem-ˈfī-\ *n* [NL, fr. Gk *pemphig-, pemphix* breath, pustule]**:** a disease characterized by large blisters on skin and mucous membranes and often by itching or burning
¹pen \ˈpen\ *n* [ME, fr. OE *penn*] **1 a :** a small enclosure for animals **b :** the animals in a pen <a ~ of sheep> **2 :** a small place of confinement or storage **3 :** a dock or slip for reconditioning submarines
²pen *vt* **penned; pen·ning :** to shut in a pen
³pen *n* [ME *penne,* fr. MF, feather, pen, fr. L *penna, pinna* feather; akin to Gk *pteron* wing — more at FEATHER] **1 :** an implement for writing or drawing with ink or a similar fluid: as **a :** QUILL **b :** PEN POINT **c :** a penholder containing a pen point **d :** FOUNTAIN PEN **e :** BALL-POINT PEN **2 a :** a writing instrument that is a means of expression <enlisted the ~*s* of the best writers —F. H. Chase> **b :** WRITER **3 :** the internal horny feather-shaped shell of a squid
⁴pen *vt* **penned; pen·ning :** WRITE, INDITE <~ a letter>
⁵pen *n* [origin unknown]**:** a female swan
⁶pen *n* **:** PENITENTIARY
⁷pen *abbr* peninsula
PEN *abbr* International Association of Poets, Playwrights, Editors, Essayists and Novelists
pe·nal \ˈpēn-ᵊl\ *adj* [ME, fr. MF, fr. L *poenalis,* fr. *poena* punishment — more at PAIN] **1 :** of, relating to, or involving punishment, penalties, or punitive institutions **2 :** liable to punishment <a ~ offense> **3 :** used as a place of confinement and punishment <a ~ colony> — **pe·nal·ly** \-ᵊl-ē\ *adv*
penal code *n* **:** a code of laws concerning crimes and offenses and their punishment
pe·nal·iza·tion \ˌpēn-ᵊl-ə-ˈzā-shən, ˌpen-\ *n* **:** the act of penalizing **:** the state of being penalized
pe·nal·ize \ˈpēn-ᵊl-ˌīz, ˈpen-\ *vt* **-ized; -iz·ing 1 :** to inflict a penalty on **2 :** to put at a serious disadvantage
pen·al·ty \ˈpen-ᵊl-tē\ *n, pl* **-ties** [ML *poenalitas,* fr. L *poenalis*] **1 :** the suffering in person, rights, or property that is annexed by law or judicial decision to the commission of a crime or public offense **2 :** the suffering or the sum to be forfeited to which a person subjects himself by agreement in case of nonfulfillment of stipulations **3 a :** disadvantage, loss, or hardship due to some action **b :** a disadvantage (as loss of yardage, time, or possession of the ball or an addition to or subtraction from the score) imposed on a team or competitor for violation of the rules of a sport **4 :** points scored in bridge by the side that defeats the opposing contract — usu. used in pl. — **penalty** *adj*
penalty box *n* **:** an area alongside an ice-hockey rink to which penalized players are confined for the duration of their penalty
penalty kick 1 : a free kick in rugby **2 :** a free kick at the goal in soccer made from a point 12 yards in front of the goal and allowed for certain violations within a designated area around the goal
penalty shot *n* **:** an unhindered shot at the goal in ice hockey awarded to an individual for certain violations by an opponent
¹pen·ance \ˈpen-ən(t)s\ *n* [ME, fr. OF, fr. ML *poenitentia* penitence] **1 :** an act of self-abasement, mortification, or devotion performed to show sorrow or repentance for sin **2 :** a sacramental rite that is practiced in Roman, Eastern, and some Anglican churches and that consists of private confession, absolution, and a penance directed by the confessor
²penance *vt* **pen·anced; pen·anc·ing :** to impose penance on
Pe·na·tes \pə-ˈnāt-ēz, -ˈnät-\ *n pl* [L — more at PENETRATE]**:** the Roman gods of the household worshiped in close connection with Vesta and with the Lares
pence \ˈpen(t)s\ *pl of* PENNY
pen·cel *or* **pen·cil** \ˈpen(t)-səl\ *n* [ME *pencel,* modif. of OF *penoncel*]**:** PENNONCEL
pen·chant \ˈpen-chənt, *esp Brit* ˈpän-ˌshän\ *n* [F, fr. prp. of *pencher* to incline, fr. (assumed) VL *pendicare,* fr. L *pendere* to weigh] **:** a strong leaning **:** LIKING ***syn*** see LEANING
¹pen·cil \ˈpen(t)-səl\ *n* [ME *pensel,* fr. MF *pincel,* fr. (assumed) VL *penicellus,* fr. L *penicillus,* lit., little tail, fr. dim. of *penis* tail, penis] **1 :** an artist's brush **2 :** an artist's individual skill or style **3 a :** an implement for writing, drawing, or marking consisting of or containing a slender cylinder or strip of a solid marking substance **b :** a small medicated or cosmetic roll or stick for local applications **4 a :** an aggregate of rays of radiation (as light) esp. when diverging from or converging to a point **b :** a set of geometric objects each pair of which has a common property <the lines in a plane through a point comprise a ~ of lines> **5 :** something long and thin like a pencil
²pencil *vt* **-ciled** *or* **-cilled; -cil·ing** *or* **-cil·ling** \-s(ə-)liŋ\ **:** to paint, draw, write, or mark with a pencil — **pen·cil·er** \-s(ə-)lər\ *n*
pen·cil·ing *or* **pen·cil·ling** *n* **:** the work of the pencil or brush; *also* **:** a product of this
pencil pusher *n* **:** a person whose work involves writing
pen·dant *also* **pen·dent** \ˈpen-dənt; *3 & 4 are also* ˈpen-ˌant, *6 is also* pän-dän\ *n* [ME *pendaunt,* fr. MF *pendant,* fr. prp. of *pendre* to hang, fr. (assumed) VL *pendere,* fr. L *pendēre;* akin to L *pendere* to weigh, estimate, pay, *pondus* weight — more at SPAN] **1 :** something suspended: as **a :** an ornament allowed to hang free **b :** an electrical fixture suspended from the ceiling **2 :** a hanging ornament of roofs or ceilings much used in the later styles of Gothic architecture **3 :** a short rope hanging from a spar and having at its free end a block or spliced thimble **4** *chiefly Brit* **:** PENNANT 1a

5 : the shank on a pocket watch stem to which the bow attaches **6** : a companion piece or supplement

pen·den·cy \ˈpen-dən-sē\ *n* : the state of being pending

pen·dent *or* **pen·dant** \ˈpen-dənt\ *adj* [ME *pendaunt*] **1** : supported from above : SUSPENDED <icicles ~ from the eaves> **2** : jutting or leaning over : OVERHANGING <a ~ cliff> **3** : remaining undetermined : PENDING — **pen·dent·ly** *adv*

pen·den·tive \pen-ˈdent-iv\ *n* [F *pendentif*, fr. L *pendent-, pendens*, prp. of *pendēre*] : the part of a groined vault that springs from a single pier or corbel

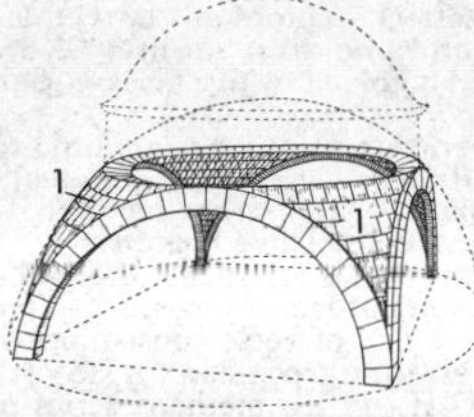

1 pendentives

¹pend·ing \ˈpen-diŋ\ *prep* [F *pendant*, fr. prp. of *pendre*] **1** : DURING **2** : while awaiting

²pending *adj* **1** : not yet decided : being in continuance **2** : IMMINENT, IMPENDING

pen·drag·on \pen-ˈdrag-ən\ *n* [ME, fr. W, fr. *pen* chief + *dragon* leader] : the chief leader among the ancient British chiefs

pen·du·lar \ˈpen-jə-lər, ˈpen-d(y)ə-\ *adj* : being or resembling the movement of a pendulum

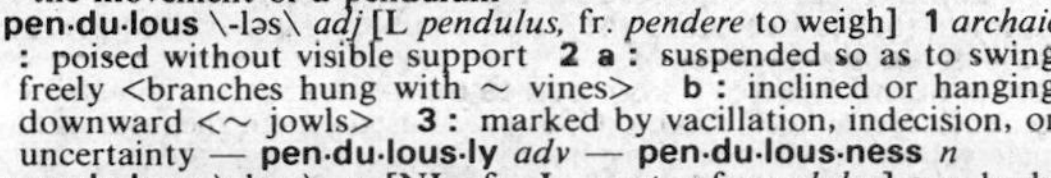

pen·du·lous \-ləs\ *adj* [L *pendulus*, fr. *pendere* to weigh] **1** *archaic* : poised without visible support **2 a** : suspended so as to swing freely <branches hung with ~ vines> **b** : inclined or hanging downward <~ jowls> **3** : marked by vacillation, indecision, or uncertainty — **pen·du·lous·ly** *adv* — **pen·du·lous·ness** *n*

pen·du·lum \-ləm\ *n* [NL, fr. L, neut. of *pendulus*] : a body suspended from a fixed point so as to swing freely to and fro under the action of gravity and commonly used to regulate movements (as of clockwork)

Pe·nel·o·pe \pə-ˈnel-ə-pē\ *n* [L, fr. Gk *Pēnelopē*] : the wife of Odysseus who waited faithfully for him during his 20 years' absence

pe·ne·plain *also* **pe·ne·plane** \ˈpēn-i-ˌplān, ˈpen-\ *n* [L *paene, pene* almost + E *plain* or *plane* — more at PATIENT] : a land surface of considerable area and slight relief shaped by erosion

pen·e·tra·ble \ˈpen-ə-trə-bəl\ *adj* : capable of being penetrated — **pen·e·tra·bil·i·ty** \ˌpen-ə-trə-ˈbil-ət-ē\ *n* — **pen·e·tra·ble·ness** \ˈpen-ə-trə-bəl-nəs\ *n* — **pen·e·tra·bly** \-blē\ *adv*

pen·e·tra·lia \ˌpen-ə-ˈtrā-lē-ə\ *n pl* [L, neut. pl. of *penetralis* inner, fr. *penetrare* to penetrate] : the innermost or most private parts

pen·e·trance \ˈpen-ə-trən(t)s\ *n* : the proportion of individuals of a particular genotype that express its phenotypic effect in a given environment

¹pen·e·trant \-trənt\ *adj* : PENETRATING

²penetrant *n* : one that penetrates or is capable of penetrating

pen·e·trate \ˈpen-ə-ˌtrāt\ *vb* **-trat·ed; -trat·ing** [L *penetratus*, pp. of *penetrare*; akin to L *penitus* inward, *Penates* household gods, Lith *peneti* to nourish] *vt* **1 a** : to pass into or through **b** : to enter by overcoming resistance : PIERCE **2 a** : to see into or through **b** : to discover the inner contents or meaning of **3** : to affect profoundly with feeling **4** : to diffuse through or into ~ *vi* **1 a** : to pass, extend, pierce, or diffuse into or through something **b** : to pierce something with the eye or mind **2** : to affect deeply the senses or feelings ***syn*** see ENTER

pen·e·trat·ing *adj* **1** : having the power of entering, piercing, or pervading <a ~ shriek> **2** : ACUTE, DISCERNING <~ insights into life> — **pen·e·trat·ing·ly** \-ˌtrāt-iŋ-lē\ *adv*

pen·e·tra·tion \ˌpen-ə-ˈtrā-shən\ *n* **1** : the act or process of penetrating: as **a** : the act of entering a country so that actual establishment of influence is accomplished **b** : an attack that penetrates the enemy's front or territory **2 a** : the depth to which something penetrates **b** : the power to penetrate; *esp* : the ability to discern deeply and acutely ***syn*** see DISCERNMENT

pen·e·tra·tive \ˈpen-ə-ˌtrāt-iv\ *adj* **1** : tending to penetrate : PIERCING **2** : ACUTE <~ observations> **3** : IMPRESSIVE <a ~ speaker> — **pen·e·tra·tive·ly** *adv* — **pen·e·tra·tive·ness** *n*

pen·e·trom·e·ter \ˌpen-ə-ˈträm-ət-ər\ *n* [L *penetrare* + ISV *-meter*] : an instrument for measuring firmness or consistency (as of soil)

pen·gö \ˈpeŋ-ˌgə(r), -ˌgœ\ *n, pl* **pengö** *or* **pengös** [Hung *pengo*, lit., jingling] : the basic monetary unit of Hungary from 1925 to 1946

pen·guin \ˈpen-gwən, ˈpeŋ-\ *n* [perh. fr. W *pen gwyn* white head] : any of various erect short-legged flightless aquatic birds (family Spheniscidae) of the southern hemisphere

penguins

pen·hold·er \ˈpen-ˌhōl-dər\ *n* : a holder or handle for a pen point

pen·i·cil·la·mine \ˌpen-ə-ˈsil-ə-ˌmēn\ *n* : an amino acid $C_5H_{11}NO_2S$ that is obtained from penicillins and is used esp. in the treatment of poisoning by metals (as copper or lead) and of cystinuria

pen·i·cil·late \ˌpen-ə-ˈsil-ət, -ˌāt\ *adj* [prob. fr. (assumed) NL *penicillatus*, fr. L *penicillus* brush — more at PENCIL] : furnished with a tuft of fine filaments <a ~ stigma> — **pen·i·cil·late·ly** *adv* — **pen·i·cil·la·tion** \-sə-ˈlā-shən\ *n*

pen·i·cil·lin \ˌpen-ə-ˈsil-ən\ *n* **1** : any of several relatively nontoxic antibiotic acids of the general constitution $C_9H_{11}N_2O_4SR$ that are produced by molds (genus *Penicillium* and esp. *P. notatum* or *P. chrysogenum*) or synthetically and are used esp. against cocci; *also* : a mixture of such acids **2** : a salt or ester of a penicillin or a mixture of such salts or acids

pen·i·cil·lin·ase \-ˈsil-ə-ˌnās, -ˌnāz\ *n* : an enzyme that inactivates the penicillins by hydrolyzing them and that is found esp. in bacteria

pen·i·cil·li·um \-ˈsil-ē-əm\ *n, pl* **-lia** \-ē-ə\ [NL, genus name, fr. L *penicillus*] : any of a genus (*Penicillium* of the family Moniliaceae) of fungi (as a blue mold) that are found chiefly on moist nonliving organic matter

pe·nile \ˈpē-ˌnīl\ *adj* : of, relating to, or affecting the penis

pen·in·su·la \pə-ˈnin(t)-s(ə-)lə, -ˈnin-chə-lə\ *n* [L *paeninsula*, fr. *paene* almost + *insula* island — more at PATIENT] : a portion of land nearly surrounded by water and connected with a larger body by an isthmus; *also* : a piece of land jutting out into the water whether with or without a well-defined isthmus — **pen·in·su·lar** \-s(ə-)lər, -chə-lər\ *adj*

pe·nis \ˈpē-nəs\ *n, pl* **pe·nes** \ˈpē-(ˌ)nēz\ *or* **pe·nis·es** [L, penis, tail; akin to OHG *faselt* penis, Gk *peos*] : a male organ of copulation

penis envy *n* : an unverbalized longing that in psychoanalytic theory is attributed to the female and is based on a desire to be a male

pen·i·tence \ˈpen-ə-tən(t)s\ *n* [ME, fr. OF, fr. ML *poenitentia*, alter. of L *paenitentia* regret, fr. *paenitent-, paenitens*, prp.] : the quality or state of being penitent : sorrow for sins or faults

syn PENITENCE, REPENTANCE, CONTRITION, COMPUNCTION, REMORSE *shared meaning element* : regret for sin or wrongdoing. PENITENCE implies sad and humble realization of and regret for one's misdeeds <the attitude that no sin is beyond forgiveness if it is followed by true *penitence* —K. S. Latourette> REPENTANCE adds a suggestion of awareness of one's general moral shortcomings and a resolve to change <I came not to call the righteous, but sinners to *repentance* —Lk 5:32 (AV)> CONTRITION stresses the sorrowful regret that accompanies true penitence <the tears of my *contrition* . . . repentance for things past —Edmund Spenser> COMPUNCTION implies a painful sting of conscience especially for planned sin or wrong not yet performed <they no longer felt *compunctions* about replacing men with machines —J. S. Vandiver> REMORSE suggests prolonged and insistent self-reproach and mental anguish for past wrongs and especially for those whose consequences cannot be remedied <*remorse* that makes one walk on thorns —Oscar Wilde>

¹pen·i·tent \-tənt\ *adj* [ME, fr. MF, fr. L *paenitent-, paenitens*, fr. prp. of *paenitēre* to be sorry; akin to L *paene* almost — more at PATIENT] : feeling or expressing humble or regretful pain or sorrow for sins or offenses : REPENTANT — **pen·i·tent·ly** *adv*

²penitent *n* **1** : a person who repents of sin **2** : a person under church censure but admitted to penance esp. under the direction of a confessor

pen·i·ten·tial \ˌpen-ə-ˈten-chəl\ *adj* : of or relating to penitence or penance — **pen·i·ten·tial·ly** \-ˈtench-(ə-)lē\ *adv*

¹pen·i·ten·tia·ry \ˌpen-ə-ˈtench-(ə-)rē\ *n, pl* **-ries** [ME *penitenciary*, fr. ML *poenitentiarius*, fr. *poenitentia*] **1 a** : an officer in some Roman Catholic dioceses vested with power from the bishop to absolve in cases reserved to him **b** *cap* : a cardinal presiding over a tribunal of the Roman curia concerned with dispensations and indulgences — called also *Grand Penitentiary* **2** : a public institution in which offenders against the law are confined for detention or punishment; *specif* : a state or federal prison in the U.S.

²pen·i·ten·tia·ry \ˌpen-ə-ˈtench-(ə-)rē, *1 also* -ˈtench-ē-ˌer-ē\ *adj* **1** : PENITENTIAL **2** : of, relating to, or incurring confinement in a penitentiary

pen·knife \ˈpen-ˌnīf\ *n* [fr. its original use for mending quill pens] : a small pocketknife usu. with only one blade

pen·light *or* **pen·lite** \ˈpen-ˌlīt\ *n* : a small flashlight resembling a fountain pen in size or shape

pen·man \ˈpen-mən\ *n* **1 a** : COPYIST, SCRIBE **b** : a person with a specified quality or kind of handwriting <a poor ~> **c** : CALLIGRAPHER **2** : AUTHOR

pen·man·ship \-ˌship\ *n* **1** : the art or practice of writing with the pen **2** : quality or style of handwriting

Penn *or* **Penna** *abbr* Pennsylvania

pen·na \ˈpen-ə\ *n, pl* **pen·nae** \ˈpen-ˌē, -ˌī\ [L, feather, wing — more at PEN] : a contour feather esp. as distinguished from a down feather or plume — **pen·na·ceous** \pe-ˈnā-shəs\ *adj*

pen name *n* : an author's pseudonym

pen·nant \ˈpen-ənt\ *n* [alter. of *pendant*] **1 a** : any of various nautical flags tapering usu. to a point or swallowtail and used for identification or signaling **b** : a flag or banner longer in the fly than in the hoist; *esp* : one that tapers to a point **2** : a flag emblematic of championship (as in a professional baseball league)

pen·nate \ˈpen-ˌāt\ *adj* [irreg. fr. NL *Pennales*, group name] : of, relating to, or being diatoms of an order (Pennales) characterized by a raphe or a structure resembling a raphe and by ornamentation of the valves that is always bilaterally arranged in relation to a line rather than to a point

pen·ni \ˈpen-ē\ *n, pl* **pen·nia** \-ē-ə\ *or* **pen·nis** \-ēz\ [Finn] — see *markka* at MONEY table

pen·ni·less \ˈpen-i-ləs, ˈpen-ᵊl-əs\ *adj* : destitute of money : POOR

pen·non \ˈpen-ən\ *n* [ME, fr. MF *penon*, aug. of *penne* feather — more at PEN] **1 a** : a long usu. triangular or swallow-tailed streamer typically attached to the head of a lance as an ensign **b** : PENNANT 1a **2** : WING, PINION

pen·non·cel *or* **pen·on·cel** \ˈpen-ən-ˌsel\ *n* [ME *penoncell*, fr. MF *penoncel*, dim. of *penon*] : a small pennon borne esp. at the head of a lance in late medieval or Renaissance times

Penn·syl·va·nia Dutch \ˌpen(t)-səl-ˌvā-nyə-, -nē-ə-\ *n* **1** : a people living mostly in eastern Pennsylvania whose characteristic cultural traditions go back to the German migrations of the 18th century **2** : a dialect of High German spoken in parts of Pennsylvania and Maryland — **Pennsylvania Dutchman** *n*

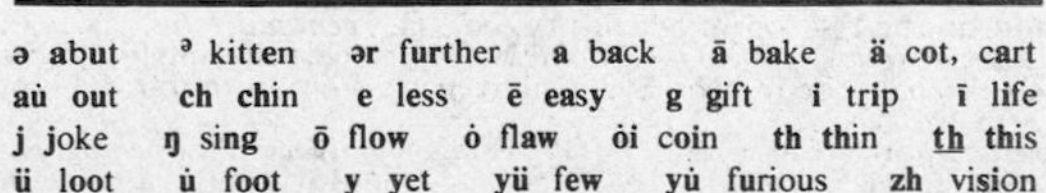

ə abut ᵊ kitten ər further a back ā bake ä cot, cart
aù out ch chin e less ē easy g gift i trip ī life
j joke ŋ sing ō flow ȯ flaw ȯi coin th thin t͟h this
ü loot u̇ foot y yet yü few yu̇ furious zh vision

Pennsylvania German *n* : PENNSYLVANIA DUTCH 2

Penn·syl·va·nian \-ˈvā-nyən, -nē-ən\ *adj* **1** : of or relating to Pennsylvania or its people **2** : of, relating to, or being the period of the Paleozoic era in No. America between the Mississippian and Permian or the corresponding system of rocks — **Pennsylvanian** *n*

pen·ny \ˈpen-ē\ *n, pl* **pennies** \-ēz\ *or* **pence** \ˈpen(t)s\ [ME, fr. OE *penning, penig;* akin to OHG *pfenning,* a coin] **1 a** : a monetary unit of the United Kingdom formerly equal to $^1/_{240}$ pound but now equal to $^1/_{100}$ pound **b** : a similar monetary unit of any of various other countries in or formerly in the British Commonwealth — see *pound* at MONEY table **c** : a coin representing one penny **2** : DENARIUS **3** *pl pennies* : CENT **4** : a trivial amount **5** : a piece or sum of money

-pen·ny \ˌpen-ē\ *adj comb form* [*penny;* fr. the original price per hundred] : being a (specified) nail length — compare EIGHTPENNY NAIL, FOURPENNY NAIL, SIXPENNY NAIL, TENPENNY NAIL

penny ante *n* : poker played for very low stakes

penny arcade *n* : an amusement center having coin-operated devices for entertainment

pen·ny·cress \ˈpen-ē-ˌkres\ *n* : a Eurasian herb (*Thlaspi arvense*) with round flat pods that is widely naturalized in the New World

penny dreadful *n* : a novel of violent adventure or crime orig. costing one penny

pen·ny–pinch \ˈpen-ē-ˌpinch\ *vt* [back-formation fr. *penny pincher*] : to give money to in a niggardly manner — **penny pincher** *n*

pen·ny·roy·al \ˌpen-ē-ˈrȯi(-ə)l, ˈpen-i-ˌrīl\ *n* [prob. by folk etymology fr. MF *poullieul,* modif. of L *pulegium*] **1** : a European perennial mint (*Mentha pulegium*) with small aromatic leaves **2** : an aromatic American mint (*Hedeoma pulegioides*) that has blue or violet flowers borne in axillary tufts and yields an oil used in folk medicine or to drive away mosquitoes

pen·ny·weight \ˈpen-ē-ˌwāt\ *n* — see WEIGHT table

pen·ny–wise \ˈpen-ē-ˌwīz\ *adj* [fr. the phrase *penny-wise and pound-foolish*] : wise or prudent only in dealing with small sums or matters

pen·ny·wort \-ˌwərt, -ˌwȯ(ə)rt\ *n* : any of several round-leaved plants: as **a** : any of several low creeping plants (genus *Hydrocotyle*) of the carrot family with crenate peltate leaves and umbellate flowers **b** : a leafless perennial (*Obolaria virginica*) of the gentian family with white or purplish flowers

pen·ny·worth \ˈpen-ē-ˌwərth, *Brit often* ˈpen-ərth\ *n, pl* **pennyworth** *or* **pennyworths** **1** : a penny's worth **2** : value for the money spent : BARGAIN **3** : a small quantity : MODICUM

Pe·nob·scot \pə-ˈnäb-skət, -ˌskät\ *n, pl* **Penobscot** *or* **Penobscots** : a member of an Amerindian people of the Penobscot river valley and Penobscot Bay region of Maine

pe·no·che \pə-ˈnō-chē\ *var of* PENUCHE

pe·nol·o·gy \pi-ˈnäl-ə-jē\ *n* [Gk *poinē* penalty + E *-logy* — more at PAIN] : a branch of criminology dealing with prison management and the treatment of offenders — **pe·no·log·i·cal** \ˌpē-nə-ˈläj-i-kəl\ *adj* — **pe·nol·o·gist** \pi-ˈnäl-ə-jəst\ *n*

pen pal *n* : a friend made and kept through correspondence

pen point *n* : a small thin convex metal device that tapers to a split point, fits into a holder, and is used for writing or drawing

pen pusher *n* : PENCIL PUSHER

pen·sile \ˈpen-ˌsīl\ *adj* [L *pensilis,* fr. *pensus,* pp. of *pendēre* to hang] **1** : PENDENT, HANGING <~ nests> **2** : having or building a hanging nest <~ birds>

[1]**pen·sion** *n* [ME, fr. MF, fr. L *pension-, pensio,* fr. *pensus,* pp. of *pendere* to pay — more at PENDANT] **1** \ˈpen-chən\ : a fixed sum paid regularly to a person: **a** *archaic* : WAGE **b** : a gratuity granted (as by a government) as a favor or reward **c** : one paid under given conditions to a person following his retirement from service or to his surviving dependents **2** \päⁿs-yōⁿ\ [F, fr. MF] **a** : accommodations esp. at a continental European hotel or boardinghouse : ROOM AND BOARD **b** *also* **pen·si·o·ne** \ˌpen-sē-ˈō-(ˌ)nā\ [*pensione,* It] : a hotel or boardinghouse esp. in continental Europe — **pen·sion·less** \ˈpen-chən-ləs\ *adj*

[2]**pen·sion** \ˈpen-chən\ *vt* **pen·sioned; pen·sion·ing** \ˈpench-(ə-)niŋ\ **1** : to grant or pay a pension to **2** : to dismiss or retire from service with a pension <~*ed* off his faithful old servant> — **pen·sion·able** \ˈpench-(ə-)nə-bəl\ *adj*

pen·sion·ary \ˈpen-chə-ˌner-ē\ *n, pl* **-ar·ies** : PENSIONER; *esp* : HIRELING — **pensionary** *adj*

pen·sion·er \ˈpench-(ə-)nər\ *n* **1** : a person who receives or lives on a pension **2** *obs* **a** : GENTLEMAN-AT-ARMS **b** : RETAINER **c** : MERCENARY, HIRELING

pen·sive \ˈpen(t)-siv\ *adj* [ME *pensif,* fr. MF, fr. *penser* to think, fr. L *pensare* to ponder, fr. *pensus,* pp. of *pendere* to weigh — more at PENDANT] **1** : musingly or dreamily thoughtful **2** : suggestive of sad thoughtfulness — **pen·sive·ly** *adv* — **pen·sive·ness** *n*

pen·ster \ˈpen(t)-stər\ *n* [[3]*pen* + *-ster*] : a hack writer

pen·stock \ˈpen-ˌstäk\ *n* **1** : a sluice or gate for regulating a flow (as of water) **2** : a conduit or pipe for conducting water

pent \ˈpent\ *adj* [prob. fr. pp. of obs. E *pend* (to confine)] : shut up : CONFINED <a ~ crowd> <*pent*-up feelings>

penta- *or* **pent-** *comb form* [ME, fr. Gk, fr. *pente* — more at FIVE] **1** : five <*penta*hedron> **2** : containing five atoms, groups, or equivalents <*pent*ane>

pen·ta·chlo·ro·phe·nol \ˌpent-ə-ˌklōr-ə-ˈfē-ˌnōl, -ˌklȯr-, -fi-ˈ\ *n* : a crystalline compound C_6Cl_5OH used esp. as a wood preservative and fungicide and a disinfectant

pen·ta·cle \ˈpent-i-kəl\ *n* [(assumed) ML *pentaculum,* prob. fr. Gk *pente*] **1** : a 5-pointed star used as a magical symbol **2** : HEXAGRAM

pen·tad \ˈpen-ˌtad\ *n* [Gk *pentad-, pentas,* fr. *pente*] : a group of five

pen·ta·dac·tyl \ˌpent-ə-ˈdak-tᵊl\ *adj* [L *pentadactylus,* fr. Gk *pentadaktylos,* fr. *penta-* + *daktylos* finger, toe] : having five digits to the hand or foot or five digitate parts — **pen·ta·dac·tyl·ism** \-tə-ˌliz-əm\ *n*

pen·ta·gon \ˈpent-ə-ˌgän\ *n* [Gk *pentagōnon,* fr. neut. of *pentagōnos* pentagonal, fr. *penta-* + *gōnia* angle — more at -GON] : a polygon of five angles and five sides — **pen·tag·o·nal** \pen-ˈtag-ən-ᵊl\ *adj* — **pen·tag·o·nal·ly** \-ᵊl-ē\ *adv*

Pentagon *n* [the *Pentagon* building, headquarters of the Department of Defense] : the U.S. military establishment

pen·ta·gram \ˈpent-ə-ˌgram\ *n* [Gk *pentagrammon,* fr. *penta-* + *-grammon* (akin to *gramma* letter) — more at GRAM] : PENTACLE 1

pentacle 1

pen·ta·he·dron \ˌpent-ə-ˈhē-drən\ *n* [NL] : a solid bounded by five faces — **pen·ta·he·dral** \-drəl\ *adj*

pen·tam·er·ous \pen-ˈtam-ə-rəs\ *adj* [NL *pentamerus,* fr. *penta-* (fr. Gk) + *-merus* -merous] : divided into or consisting of five parts; *specif* : having each floral whorl consisting of five or a multiple of five members

pen·tam·e·ter \pen-ˈtam-ət-ər\ *n* [L, fr. Gk *pentametros* having five metrical feet, fr. *penta-* + *metron* measure — more at MEASURE] : a line of verse consisting of five metrical feet

pen·tane \ˈpen-ˌtān\ *n* [ISV] : any of three isomeric hydrocarbons C_5H_{12} of the methane series occurring in petroleum

pent·an·gle \ˈpent-ˌaŋ-gəl\ *n* : PENTACLE

pen·ta·pep·tide \ˌpent-ə-ˈpep-ˌtīd\ *n* : a polypeptide that contains five amino acid residues

pen·ta·ploid \ˈpent-ə-ˌplȯid\ *adj* : having or being a chromosome number that is five times the basic number — **pentaploid** *n* — **pen·ta·ploi·dy** \-ˌplȯid-ē\ *n*

pen·ta·quine \-ˌkwēn\ *also* **pen·ta·quin** \-kwən\ *n* [*penta-* + *quin*oline] : an antimalarial $C_{18}H_{27}N_3O$ used esp. in the form of its pale yellow crystalline phosphate

pen·tar·chy \ˈpen-ˌtär-kē\ *n* [Gk *pentarchia,* fr. *penta-* + *-archia* -archy] : a group of five countries or districts each under its own ruler or government

Pen·ta·teuch \ˈpent-ə-ˌt(y)ük\ *n* [LL *Pentateuchus,* fr. Gk *Pentateuchos,* fr. *penta-* + *teuchos* tool, vessel, book; akin to Gk *teuchein* to make — more at DOUGHTY] : the first five books of Jewish and Christian Scriptures

pen·tath·lete \pen-ˈtath-ˌlēt\ *n* : an athlete participating in a pentathlon

pen·tath·lon \pen-ˈtath-lən, -ˌlän\ *n* [Gk, fr. *penta-* + *athlon* contest — more at ATHLETE] : an athletic contest involving participation by each contestant in five different events; *esp* : MODERN PENTATHLON

pen·ta·ton·ic scale \ˌpent-ə-ˌtän-ik-\ *n* : a musical scale of five tones; *specif* : one in which the tones are arranged like a major scale with the fourth and seventh tones omitted

pen·ta·va·lent \ˌpent-ə-ˈvā-lənt\ *adj* : having a valence of five

pen·taz·o·cine \pen-ˈtaz-ə-ˌsēn\ *n* [*penta-* + *azo* + *-cine* (of unknown origin)] : an analgesic drug $C_{19}H_{27}NO$ that does not have the strong addictive properties of morphine

Pen·te·cost \ˈpent-i-ˌkȯst, -ˌkäst\ *n* [ME, fr. OE *pentecosten,* fr. LL *pentecoste,* fr. Gk *pentēkostē,* lit., fiftieth day, fr. *pentēkostos* fiftieth, fr. *pentēkonta* fifty, fr. *penta-* + *-konta* (akin to L *viginti* twenty) — more at VIGESIMAL] **1** : SHABUOTH **2** : a Christian feast on the seventh Sunday after Easter commemorating the descent of the Holy Spirit on the apostles

[1]**Pen·te·cos·tal** \ˌpent-i-ˈkäs-tᵊl, -ˈkȯs-\ *adj* **1** : of, relating to, or suggesting Pentecost **2** : of, relating to, or constituting any of various Christian religious bodies that emphasize revivalistic worship, baptism conferring the gift of tongues, faith healing, and premillennial teaching — **Pen·te·cos·tal·ism** \-tə-ˌliz-əm\ *n* — **Pen·te·cos·tal·ist** \-tə-ləst\ *n*

[2]**Pentecostal** *n* : a member of a Pentecostal religious body

pent·house \ˈpent-ˌhau̇s\ *n* [ME *pentis,* fr. MF *appentis,* prob. fr. ML *appenticium* appendage, fr. L *appendic-, appendix* — more at APPENDIX] **1 a** : a shed or roof attached to and sloping from a wall or building **b** : a smaller structure joined to a building : ANNEX **2** : a structure or dwelling built on the roof of a building

pent·land·ite \ˈpent-lən-ˌdīt\ *n* [F, fr. Joseph *Pentland* †1873 Irish scientist] : a bronzy yellow mineral $(Fe,Ni)_9S_8$ that is an isometric nickel iron sulfide and the principal ore of nickel

pen·to·bar·bi·tal \ˌpent-ə-ˈbär-bə-ˌtȯl\ *n* [*penta-* + *-o-* + *barbital*] : a granular barbiturate $C_{11}H_{18}N_2O_3$ used esp. in the form of its sodium or calcium salt as a sedative, hypnotic, and antispasmodic

pen·to·bar·bi·tone \-ˌtōn\ *n* [*penta-* + *-o-* + *barbitone* (barbital)] *Brit* : PENTOBARBITAL

pen·tom·ic \pen-ˈtäm-ik\ *adj* [blend of *penta-* and *atomic*] **1** : made up of five battle groups <a ~ division> **2** : organized into pentomic divisions <a ~ army>

pen·to·san \ˈpent-ə-ˌsan\ *n* : any of various polysaccharides that yield only pentoses on hydrolysis and are widely distributed in plants

pen·tose \ˈpen-ˌtōs, -ˌtōz\ *n* [ISV] : any of various monosaccharides $C_5H_{10}O_5$ (as ribose) that contain five carbon atoms in the molecule

pen·to·side \ˈpent-ə-ˌsīd\ *n* : a glycoside that yields a pentose on hydrolysis

Pen·to·thal \ˈpent-ə-ˌthȯl\ *trademark* — used for thiopental

pent·ox·ide \pent-ˈäk-ˌsīd\ *n* [ISV] : an oxide containing five atoms of oxygen in the molecule

pent·ste·mon *or* **pen·ste·mon** \pent-ˈstē-mən, ˈpen(t)-stə-\ *n* [NL *pentstemon,* alter. of *Penstemon,* genus name, fr. Gk *penta-* + *stēmōn* thread — more at STAMEN] : any of a genus (*Penstemon*) of chiefly American herbs of the figwort family with showy blue, purple, red, yellow, or white flowers

pen·tyl \ˈpent-ᵊl\ *n* [*pent*ane + *-yl*] : AMYL

pen·tyl·ene·tet·ra·zol \ˌpent-ᵊl-ˌēn-ˈte-trə-ˌzȯl, -ˌzōl\ *n* [*pent*amethy*lene-tetrazole*] : a compound $C_6H_{10}N_4$ used as a respiratory and circulatory stimulant and for producing a state of convulsion in treating mental disorders

pe·nu·che \pə-ˈnü-chē\ *n* [MexSp *panocha* raw sugar, fr. dim. of Sp *pan* bread, fr. L *panis* — more at FOOD] : fudge made usu. of brown sugar, butter, cream or milk, and nuts

pe·nult \ˈpē-ˌnəlt, pi-ˈ\ *n* [L *paenultima* penult, fr. fem. of *paenultimus* almost last, fr. *paene* almost + *ultimus* last] **:** the next to the last member of a series; *esp* **:** the next to the last syllable of a word

pen·ul·ti·ma \pi-ˈnəl-tə-mə\ *n* [L] **:** PENULT

pen·ul·ti·mate \pi-ˈnəl-tə-mət\ *adj* **1 :** next to the last <the ~ chapter of a book> **2 :** of or relating to a penult <a ~ accent> — **pen·ul·ti·mate·ly** *adv*

pen·um·bra \pə-ˈnəm-brə\ *n, pl* **-brae** \-(ˌ)brē, -ˌbrī\ *or* **-bras** [NL, fr. L *paene* almost + *umbra* shadow — more at PATIENT, UMBRAGE] **1 :** a space of partial illumination (as in an eclipse) between the perfect shadow on all sides and the full light **2 :** a shaded region surrounding the dark central portion of a sunspot **3 :** a surrounding or adjoining region in which something exists in a lesser degree **:** FRINGE — **pen·um·bral** \-brəl\ *adj*

pe·nu·ri·ous \pə-ˈn(y)u̇r-ē-əs\ *adj* **1 :** marked by or suffering from penury **2 :** given to or marked by extreme stinting frugality ***syn*** see STINGY — **pe·nu·ri·ous·ly** *adv* — **pe·nu·ri·ous·ness** *n*

pen·u·ry \ˈpen-yə-rē\ *n* [ME, fr. L *penuria* want — more at PATIENT] **1 :** a cramping and oppressive lack of resources (as money); *esp* **:** severe poverty **2 :** extreme and often niggardly frugality ***syn*** see POVERTY

pe·on \ˈpē-ˌän, -ən *also* pā-ˈōn *for 2, Brit also* ˈpyün *for 1*\ *n, pl* **peons** *or* **pe·o·nes** \pā-ˈō-nēz\ [Pg *peão* & F *pion,* fr. ML *pedon-, pedo* foot soldier — more at PAWN] **1 :** any of various Indian or Ceylonese workers: as **a :** INFANTRYMAN **b :** ORDERLY **2** [Sp *peón,* fr. L *pedon-, pedo*] **:** a member of the landless laboring class in Spanish America **3** *pl peons* **a :** a person held in compulsory servitude to a master for the working out of an indebtedness **b :** DRUDGE, MENIAL

pe·on·age \ˈpē-ə-nij\ *n* **1 :** the condition of a peon **2 a :** the use of laborers bound in servitude because of debt **b :** a system of convict labor by which convicts are leased to contractors

pe·o·ny \ˈpē-ə-nē\ *n, pl* **-nies** [ME *piony,* fr. MF *pioine,* fr. L *paeonia,* fr. Gk *paiōnia,* fr. *Paiōn* Paeon, physician of the gods] **:** any of a genus (*Paeonia*) of plants of the buttercup family with large usu. double flowers of red, pink, or white

¹peo·ple \ˈpē-pəl\ *n, pl* **people** [ME *peple,* fr. OF *peuple,* fr. L *populus*] **1** *pl* **a :** persons who form part of the aggregate of human beings **b :** human beings as distinguished from the lower animals **2** *pl* **:** human beings making up a group or assembly or linked by a common interest **3** *pl* **:** the members of a family or kinship **4** *pl* **:** the mass of a community as distinguished from a special class <disputes between the ~ and the nobles> — often used by Communists to distinguish Communists or those under Communist control from other people <the *People's* Court> <Bulgarian *People's* Republic> **5** *pl* **peoples :** a body of persons that are united by a common culture, tradition, or sense of kinship, that typically have common language, institutions, and beliefs, and that often constitute a politically organized group **6 :** lower animals usu. of a specified kind or situation <squirrels and chipmunks: the little furry ~> **7 :** the body of enfranchised citizens of a state

²people *vt* **peo·pled; peo·pling** \-p(ə-)liŋ\ [MF *peupler,* fr. OF, fr. *peuple*] **1 :** to supply or fill with people **2 :** to dwell in **:** INHABIT

peo·ple·hood \ˈpē-pəl-ˌhu̇d\ *n* **1 :** the quality or state of constituting a people **2 :** the awareness of the underlying unity that makes the individual a part of a people

peo·ple·less \ˈpē-pəl-(l)əs\ *adj* **:** void of people

¹pep \ˈpep\ [short for *pepper*] **:** brisk energy or initiative and high spirits

²pep *vt* **pepped; pep·ping :** to inject pep into <~ him up>

pep·los \ˈpep-ləs, -ˌläs\ *also* **pep·lus** \-ləs\ *n* [L *peplus,* fr. Gk *peplos*] **:** a garment like a shawl worn by women of ancient Greece

pep·lum \-ləm\ *n* [L, fr. Gk *peplon* peplos] **:** a short section attached to the waistline of a blouse, jacket, or dress — **pep·lumed** \-ləmd\ *adj*

pe·po \ˈpē-(ˌ)pō\ *n, pl* **pepos** [L, a melon — more at PUMPKIN] **:** an indehiscent fleshy 1-celled or falsely 3-celled many-seeded berry (as a pumpkin, squash, melon, or cucumber) that has a hard rind and is the characteristic fruit of the gourd family

¹pep·per \ˈpep-ər\ *n* [ME *peper,* fr. OE *pipor;* akin to OHG *pfeffar* pepper; both fr. a prehistoric WGmc-NGmc word borrowed fr. L *piper* pepper, fr. Gk *peperi*] **1 a :** either of two pungent products from the fruit of an East Indian plant that are used as a condiment, carminative, or stimulant: (1) **:** BLACK PEPPER (2) **:** WHITE PEPPER **b :** any of a genus (*Piper* of the family Piperaceae, the pepper family) of tropical mostly jointed climbing shrubs with aromatic leaves; *esp* **:** a woody vine (*P. nigrum*) with ovate leaves and spicate flowers that is widely cultivated in the tropics for its red berries from which black pepper and white pepper are prepared **2 a :** any of several products similar to pepper that are obtained from close relatives of the pepper plant **b :** any of various pungent condiments obtained from plants of other genera than that of the pepper — used with a qualifying term <cayenne ~> **3 a :** CAPSICUM 1; *esp* **:** a New World capsicum (*Capsicum frutescens*) whose fruits are hot peppers or sweet peppers **b :** the usu. red or yellow fruit of a pepper — **pepper** *adj*

pepper 1b

²pepper *vt* **pep·pered; pep·per·ing** \ˈpep-(ə-)riŋ\ **1 a :** to sprinkle, season, or cover with or as if with pepper **b :** to shower with shot or other missiles **2 :** to hit with rapid repeated blows **3 :** to sprinkle as pepper is sprinkled <~*ed* his report with statistics> — **pep·per·er** \-ər-ər\ *n*

pepper–and–salt \ˌpep-ər(-ə)n-ˈsȯlt\ *adj* **:** having black and white or dark and light color intermingled in small flecks <a ~ overcoat>

pep·per·box \ˈpep-ər-ˌbäks\ *n* **1 :** a small usu. cylindrical box or bottle with a perforated top used for sprinkling ground pepper on food **2 :** a small cylindrical tower or turret **3 :** a late 18th century pistol with five or six revolving barrels

pep·per·corn \-ˌkȯ(ə)rn\ *n* **:** a dried berry of the black pepper

peppered moth *n* **:** a European geometrid moth (*Biston betularia*) that typically has white wings with small black specks but also occurs as a solid black form esp. in areas where the air is heavily polluted by industry

pep·per·grass \ˈpep-ər-ˌgras\ *n* **:** any of a genus (*Lepidium*) of cresses; *esp* **:** GARDEN CRESS

pepper mill *n* **:** a hand mill for grinding peppercorns

pep·per·mint \-ˌmint, -mənt, *rapid* ˈpep-mənt *or* -ᵊm-ənt\ *n* **1 a :** a pungent and aromatic mint (*Mentha piperita*) with dark green lanceolate leaves and whorls of small pink flowers in spikes **b :** any of several mints (as *M. arvensis*) that are related to the peppermint **2 :** candy flavored with peppermint — **pep·per·minty** \ˈpep-ər-ˌmint-ē\ *adj*

pepper pot *n* **1** *Brit* **:** PEPPERBOX **2 a :** a highly seasoned West Indian stew of vegetables and meat or fish **b :** a thick soup of tripe, meat, dumplings, and vegetables highly seasoned esp. with crushed peppercorns — called also *Philadelphia pepper pot*

pep·per·tree \ˈpep-ər-ˌtrē\ *n* **:** a Peruvian evergreen tree (*Schinus molle*) of the sumac family grown as a shade tree in mild regions

pep·pery \ˈpep-(ə-)rē\ *adj* **1 :** of, relating to, or having the qualities of pepper **:** HOT, PUNGENT <a ~ taste> **2 :** having a hot temper **:** TOUCHY <a ~ boss> **3 :** FIERY, STINGING <a ~ satire>

pep pill *n* **:** any of various stimulant drugs in pill or tablet form

pep·py \ˈpep-ē\ *adj* **pep·pi·er; -est :** full of pep — **pep·pi·ness** *n*

pep·sin \ˈpep-sən\ *n* [G, fr. Gk *pepsis* digestion, fr. *pessein*] **1 :** a proteinase of the stomach that breaks down most proteins to polypeptides **2 :** a preparation containing pepsin that is obtained from the stomach esp. of the hog and is used esp. as a digestive

pep·sin·o·gen \pep-ˈsin-ə-jən\ *n* [ISV *pepsin* + *-o-* + *-gen*] **:** a granular zymogen of the gastric glands that is readily converted into pepsin in a slightly acid medium

pep talk *n* **:** a usu. brief, high-pressure, and emotional talk designed to influence or encourage an audience

pep·tic \ˈpep-tik\ *adj* [L *pepticus,* fr. Gk *peptikos,* fr. *peptos* cooked, fr. *peptein, pessein* to cook, digest — more at COOK] **1 :** relating to or promoting digestion **:** DIGESTIVE **2 :** of, relating to, producing, or caused by pepsin <~ digestion> **3 :** connected with or resulting from the action of digestive juices <a ~ ulcer>

pep·ti·dase \ˈpep-tə-ˌdās, -ˌdāz\ *n* **:** an enzyme that hydrolyzes simple peptides or their derivatives

pep·tide \ˈpep-ˌtīd\ *n* [ISV, fr. *peptone*] **:** any of various amides that are derived from two or more amino acids by combination of the amino group of one acid with the carboxyl group of another and are usu. obtained by partial hydrolysis of proteins — **pep·tid·ic** \pep-ˈtid-ik\ *adj* — **pep·tid·i·cal·ly** \-i-k(ə-)lē\ *adv*

peptide bond *n* **:** the chemical bond between carbon and nitrogen in a peptide linkage

peptide linkage *n* **:** the bivalent group CO–NH that unites the amino acid residues in a peptide

pep·ti·do·gly·can \ˌpep-təd-ō-ˈglī-ˌkan\ *n* [*peptide* + *-o-* + *glycan* (polysaccharide)] **:** a polymer that is composed of polysaccharide and peptide chains and is found esp. in bacterial cell walls

pep·tize \ˈpep-ˌtīz\ *vt* **pep·tized; pep·tiz·ing** [prob. fr. Gk *peptein*] **:** to cause to disperse in a medium; *specif* **:** to bring into colloidal solution — **pep·ti·za·tion** \ˌpep-tə-ˈzā-shən\ *n* — **pep·tiz·er** \ˈpep-ˌtī-zər\ *n*

pep·tone \ˈpep-ˌtōn\ *n* [G *pepton,* fr. Gk, neut. of *peptos*] **:** any of various water-soluble products of partial hydrolysis of proteins

pep·to·nize \ˈpep-tə-ˌnīz\ *vt* **-nized; -niz·ing 1 :** to convert into peptone; *esp* **:** to digest or dissolve by a proteolytic enzyme **2 :** to combine with peptone

Pe·quot \ˈpē-ˌkwät\ *n* [prob. modif. of Narraganset *paquatanog* destroyers] **:** a member of an Amerindian people of eastern Connecticut

¹per \(ˈ)pər\ *prep* [L, through, by means of, by — more at FOR] **1 :** by the means or agency of **:** THROUGH <~ bearer> **2 :** with respect to every member of a specified group **:** for each **3 :** according to <~ list price>

²per *abbr* **1** period **2** person

per- *prefix* [L, through, throughout, thoroughly, to destruction, fr. *per*] **1 :** throughout **:** thoroughly <*per*chlorinate> **2 a :** containing the largest possible or a relatively large proportion of a (specified) chemical element (*per*chloride> **b :** containing an element in its highest or a high oxidation state <*per*chloric acid>

¹per·ad·ven·ture \ˈpər-əd-ˌven-chər, ˈper-; ˌpər-əd-ˈ, ˌper-\ *adv* [ME *per aventure,* fr. OF, by chance] *archaic* **:** PERHAPS, POSSIBLY

²peradventure *n* **:** DOUBT, CHANCE

per·am·bu·late \pə-ˈram-byə-ˌlāt\ *vb* **-lat·ed; -lat·ing** [L *perambulatus,* pp. of *perambulare,* fr. *per-* through + *ambulare* to walk — more at AMBLE] *vt* **1 :** to travel over or through esp. on foot **:** TRAVERSE **2 :** to make an official inspection of (a boundary) on foot ~ *vi* **:** STROLL — **per·am·bu·la·tion** \-ˌram-byə-ˈlā-shən\ *n*

per·am·bu·la·tor \pə-ˈram-byə-ˌlāt-ər, *for 2 also* ˈpram-\ *n* **1 :** one that perambulates **2** *chiefly Brit* **:** a baby carriage — **per·am·bu·la·to·ry** \-lə-ˌtōr-ē, -ˌtȯr-\ *adj*

per an·num \(ˌ)pər-ˈan-əm\ *adv* [ML] **:** in or for each year

per·bo·rate \(ˈ)pər-ˈbō(ə)r-ˌāt, -ˈbȯ(ə)r-\ *n* [ISV] **:** a salt that is a compound of a borate with hydrogen peroxide

per·cale \(ˌ)pər-ˈkā(ə)l, ˈpər-ˌ; (ˌ)pər-ˈkal\ *n* [Per *pargālah*] **:** a fine closely woven cotton cloth variously finished for clothing, sheeting, and industrial uses

per·ca·line \ˌpər-kə-ˈlēn\ *n* [F, fr. *percale*] **:** a lightweight cotton fabric; *esp* **:** a glossy fabric used for bookbindings
per cap·i·ta \(ˌ)pər-ˈkap-ət-ə\ *adv or adj* [ML, by heads] **1 :** per unit of population **:** by or for each person <the highest income *per capita* of any state in the union> **2 :** equally to each individual
per·ceiv·able \pər-ˈsē-və-bəl\ *adj* **:** PERCEPTIBLE, INTELLIGIBLE — **per·ceiv·ably** \-blē\ *adv*
per·ceive \pər-ˈsēv\ *vt* **per·ceived; per·ceiv·ing** [ME *perceiven*, fr. OF *perceivre*, fr. L *percipere*, fr. *per-* thoroughly + *capere* to take — more at PER-, HEAVE] **1 :** to attain awareness or understanding of **2 :** to become aware of through the senses; *esp* **:** SEE, OBSERVE — **per·ceiv·er** *n*
[1]**per·cent** \pər-ˈsent\ *adv* [earlier *per cent*, fr. *per* + L *centum* hundred — more at HUNDRED] **:** in the hundred **:** of each hundred
[2]**percent** *n, pl* **percent** *or* **percents** **1** *pl percent* **a :** one part in a hundred **b :** PERCENTAGE <a large ~ of his income> **2** *percents pl, Brit* **:** securities bearing a specified rate of interest
[3]**percent** *adj* **1 :** reckoned on the basis of a whole divided into one hundred parts **2 :** paying interest at a specified percent
per·cent·age \pər-ˈsent-ij\ *n* **1 :** a part of a whole expressed in hundredths **2 a :** a share of winnings or profits **b :** ADVANTAGE, PROFIT <no ~ in going around looking like an old sack of laundry —Wallace Stegner> **3 :** an indeterminate part **:** PROPORTION **4 a :** PROBABILITY **b :** favorable odds
per·cen·tile \pər-ˈsen-ˌtīl\ *n* [prob. fr. *percent* + *-ile* (as in *quartile*, n.)] **:** a value on a scale of one hundred that indicates the percent of a distribution that is equal to or below it <a ~ score of 95 is a score equal to or better than 95 percent of the scores>
per cen·tum \pər-ˈsent-əm\ *n* [*per* + L *centum*] **:** PERCENT
per·cept \ˈpər-ˌsept\ *n* [back-formation fr. *perception*] **:** an impression of an object obtained by use of the senses **:** SENSE-DATUM
per·cep·ti·bil·i·ty \pər-ˌsep-tə-ˈbil-ət-ē\ *n* **:** capability of being perceived
per·cep·ti·ble \-ˈsep-tə-bəl\ *adj* **:** capable of being perceived esp. by the senses <a ~ change in her tone> <the light became increasingly ~> — **per·cep·ti·bly** \-blē\ *adv*
syn PERCEPTIBLE, SENSIBLE, PALPABLE, TANGIBLE, APPRECIABLE, PONDERABLE *shared meaning element* **:** apprehensible as real or existent ***ant*** imperceptible
per·cep·tion \pər-ˈsep-shən\ *n* [L *perception-*, *perceptio* act of perceiving, fr. *perceptus*, pp. of *percipere*] **1** *obs* **:** CONSCIOUSNESS **2 a :** a result of perceiving **:** OBSERVATION **b :** a mental image **:** CONCEPT **3 a :** awareness of the elements of environment through physical sensation <color ~> **b :** physical sensation interpreted in the light of experience **4 a :** quick, acute, and intuitive cognition **:** APPRECIATION **b :** a capacity for comprehension ***syn*** see DISCERNMENT — **per·cep·tion·al** \-shnəl, -shən-ᵊl\ *adj*
per·cep·tive \pər-ˈsep-tiv\ *adj* **1 :** responsive to sensory stimulus **:** DISCERNING <a ~ eye> **2 a :** capable of or exhibiting keen perception **:** OBSERVANT <a ~ scholar> **b :** characterized by sympathetic understanding or insight — **per·cep·tive·ly** *adv* — **per·cep·tive·ness** *n* — **per·cep·tiv·i·ty** \(ˌ)pər-ˌsep-ˈtiv-ət-ē\ *n*
per·cep·tu·al \(ˌ)pər-ˈsep-chə(-wə)l, -ˈsepsh-wəl\ *adj* [L *perceptus*] **:** of, relating to, or involving perception esp. in relation to immediate sensory experience — **per·cep·tu·al·ly** \-ē\ *adv*
Per·ce·val \ˈpər-sə-vəl\ *n* [OF] **:** a knight of King Arthur who in Arthurian legend wins a sight of the Holy Grail
[1]**perch** \ˈpərch\ *n* [ME *perche*, fr. OF, fr. L *pertica* pole] **1 :** a bar or peg on which something is hung **2 a :** a roost for a bird **b :** a resting place or vantage point **:** SEAT **c :** a prominent position <his new ~ as president> **3 a** *chiefly Brit* **:** ROD 2 **b :** any of various units of measure for stonework
[2]**perch** *vt* **:** to place on a perch, a height, or a precarious spot ~ *vi* **:** to alight, settle, or rest uneasily or precariously on a perch
[3]**perch** *n, pl* **perch** *or* **perch·es** [ME *perche*, fr. MF, fr. L *perca*, fr. Gk *perkē*; akin to OHG *faro* colored, L *porcus*, a spiny fish] **1 a :** a small European freshwater spiny-finned fish (*Perca fluviatilis*) **b :** an American fish (*P. flavescens*) that is closely related to the perch **2 :** any of numerous teleost fishes (as of the families Percidae, Centrarchidae, Serranidae)
per·chance \pər-ˈchan(t)s\ *adv* [ME *per chance*, fr. MF, by chance] **:** PERHAPS, POSSIBLY
Per·che·ron \ˈpər-chə-ˌrän, -shə-\ *n* [F] **:** any of a breed of powerful rugged draft horses that originated in the Perche region of France
per·chlo·rate \(ˈ)pər-ˈklō(ə)r-ˌāt, -ˈklȯ(ə)r-, -ət\ *n* [ISV] **:** a salt or ester of perchloric acid
per·chlo·ric acid \(ˌ)pər-ˌklōr-ik-, -ˌklȯr-\ *n* **:** a fuming corrosive strong acid $HClO_4$ that is the highest oxygen acid of chlorine and a powerful oxidizing agent when heated
per·cip·i·ence \pər-ˈsip-ē-ən(t)s\ *n* **:** PERCEPTION
per·cip·i·ent \-ənt\ *adj* [L *percipient-*, *percipiens*, prp. of *percipere* to perceive] **:** capable of or characterized by perception **:** DISCERNING — **percipient** *n*
per·coid \ˈpər-ˌkȯid\ *also* **per·coi·de·an** \ˌpər-ˈkȯid-ē-ən\ *adj* [deriv. of L *perca* perch] **:** of or relating to a very large suborder (Percoidea) of spiny-finned fishes including the true perches, sunfishes, sea basses, and sea breams — **percoid** *n*
per·co·late \ˈpər-kə-ˌlāt, *nonstand* -kyə-\ *vb* **-lat·ed; -lat·ing** [L *percolatus*, pp. of *percolare*, fr. *per-* through + *colare* to sieve — more at PER-, COLANDER] *vt* **1 a :** to cause (a solvent) to pass through a permeable substance (as a powdered drug) esp. for extracting a soluble constituent **b :** to prepare (coffee) in a percolator **2 :** to be diffused through **:** PENETRATE ~ *vi* **1 :** to ooze or trickle through a permeable substance **:** SEEP **2 a :** to become percolated **b :** to become lively or effervescent **3 :** to become diffused <allow the sunlight to ~ into our rooms —Norman Douglas> — **per·co·la·tion** \ˌpər-kə-ˈlā-shən\ *n*
per·co·la·tor \ˈpər-kə-ˌlāt-ər, *nonstand* -kyə-\ *n* **:** one that percolates; *specif* **:** a coffeepot in which boiling water rising through a tube is repeatedly deflected downward through a perforated basket containing ground coffee beans to extract their essence
per con·tra \(ˌ)pər-ˈkän-trə\ *adv* [It, by the opposite side (of the ledger)] **1 a :** on the contrary **b :** by way of contrast **2 :** as an offset
per·cuss \pər-ˈkəs\ *vt* [L *percussus*] **:** to tap sharply; *esp* **:** to practice percussion on
per·cus·sion \pər-ˈkəsh-ən\ *n* [L *percussion-*, *percussio*, fr. *percussus*, pp. of *percutere* to beat, fr. *per-* thoroughly + *quatere* to shake — more at PER-, QUASH] **1 :** the act of percussing: as **a :** the striking of a percussion cap so as to set off the charge in a firearm **b :** the beating or striking of a musical instrument **c :** the act or technique of tapping the surface of a body part to learn the condition of the parts beneath by the resultant sound **2 :** the striking of sound on the ear **3 :** percussion instruments that form a section of a band or orchestra — **percussion** *adj*
percussion cap *n* **:** CAP 6
percussion instrument *n* **:** a musical instrument (as a drum, xylophone, or maraca) sounded by striking, shaking, or scraping
per·cus·sion·ist \pər-ˈkəsh-(ə-)nəst\ *n* **:** one skilled in the playing of percussion instruments
per·cus·sive \pər-ˈkəs-iv\ *adj* **:** of or relating to percussion; *esp* **:** operative or operated by striking — **per·cus·sive·ly** *adv* — **per·cus·sive·ness** *n*
per·cu·ta·ne·ous \ˌpər-kyu̇-ˈtā-nē-əs\ *adj* **:** effected or performed through the skin — **per·cu·ta·ne·ous·ly** *adv*
per·die \(ˌ)pər-ˈdē, per-\ *var of* PARDIE
[1]**per di·em** \(ˌ)pər-ˈdē-əm, -ˈdī-\ *adv* [ML] **:** by the day **:** for each day
[2]**per diem** *adj* **1 :** based on use or service by the day **:** DAILY **2 :** paid by the day
[3]**per diem** *n, pl* **per diems** **1 :** a daily allowance **2 :** a daily fee
per·di·tion \pər-ˈdish-ən\ *n* [ME *perdicion*, fr. LL *perdition-*, *perditio*, fr. L *perditus*, pp. of *perdere* to destroy, fr. *per-* to destruction + *dare* to give — more at PER-, DATE] **1 a** *archaic* **:** utter destruction **b** *obs* **:** LOSS **2 a :** eternal damnation **b :** HELL
[1]**per·du** *or* **per·due** \ˈpər-(ˌ)d(y)ü, (ˌ)pər-ˈ\ *n, obs* [F *sentinelle perdue*, lit., lost sentinel] **:** a soldier assigned to extremely hazardous duty
[2]**per·du** *or* **per·due** \per-dᵫ\ *adj* [F *perdu*, masc., & *perdue*, fem., fr. pp. of *perdre* to lose, fr. L *perdere*] **:** remaining out of sight
per·du·ra·bil·i·ty \(ˌ)pər-ˌd(y)u̇r-ə-ˈbil-ət-ē, *archaic* ˌpər-jə-rə-\ *n* **:** the quality or state of being perdurable **:** PERMANENCE
per·du·ra·ble \(ˌ)pər-ˈd(y)u̇r-ə-bəl, *archaic* ˈpər-jə-rə-\ *adj* [ME, fr. OF, fr. LL *perdurabilis*, fr. L *perdurare* to endure, fr. *per-* throughout + *durare* to last — more at DURING] **:** very durable — **per·du·ra·bly** \-blē\ *adv*
per·e·gri·nate \ˈper-ə-grə-ˌnāt\ *vb* **-nat·ed; -nat·ing** *vi* **:** to travel esp. on foot **:** WALK ~ *vt* **:** to walk or travel over **:** TRAVERSE — **per·e·gri·na·tion** \ˌper-ə-grə-ˈnā-shən\ *n*
[1]**per·e·grine** \ˈper-ə-grən, -ˌgrēn, -ˌgrīn\ *adj* [ML *peregrinus*, fr. L, foreign — more at PILGRIM] **:** having a tendency to wander
[2]**peregrine** *n* **:** a swift nearly cosmopolitan falcon (*Falco peregrinus*) that is much used in falconry

peregrine

pe·remp·to·ry \pə-ˈrem(p)-t(ə-)rē\ *adj* [LL & L; LL *peremptorius*, fr. L, destructive, fr. *peremptus*, pp. of *perimere* to take entirely, destroy, fr. *per-* to destruction + *emere* to take — more at REDEEM] **1 a :** putting an end to or precluding a right of action, debate, or delay <a ~ mandamus> **b :** admitting of no contradiction <a ~ conclusion based on absolute evidence> **2 :** expressive of urgency or command <a ~ call> **3 a :** characterized by often imperious or arrogant self-assurance <how insolent of late he is become, how proud, how ~ —Shak.> **b :** indicative of a peremptory attitude or nature **:** HAUGHTY <a ~ tone> <~ disregard of an objection> ***syn*** see MASTERFUL — **pe·remp·to·ri·ly** \-ˈrem(p)-t(ə-)rə-lē; -ˌrem(p)-ˈtōr-ə-lē, -ˈtȯr-\ *adv* — **pe·remp·to·ri·ness** \-ˈrem(p)-t(ə-)rē-nəs\ *n*
pe·ren·nate \ˈper-ə-ˌnāt, pə-ˈren-ˌāt\ *vi* **-nat·ed; -nat·ing** [L *perennatus*, pp. of *perennare*, fr. *perennis*] **:** to live over from season to season <a *perennating* rhizome> — **per·en·na·tion** \ˌper-ə-ˈnā-shən\ *n*
pe·ren·ni·al \pə-ˈren-ē-əl\ *adj* [L *perennis*, fr. *per-* throughout + *annus* year — more at PER-, ANNUAL] **1 :** present at all seasons of the year **2 :** persisting for several years usu. with new herbaceous growth from a perennating part <~ asters> **3 a :** PERSISTENT, ENDURING **b :** continuing without interruption **:** CONSTANT **c :** regularly repeated or renewed **:** RECURRENT ***syn*** see CONTINUOUS — **perennial** *n* — **pe·ren·ni·al·ly** \-ē-ə-lē\ *adv*
perf *abbr* **1** perfect **2** perforated **3** performance
[1]**per·fect** \ˈpər-fikt\ *adj* [ME *parfit*, fr. OF, fr. L *perfectus*, fr. pp. of *perficere* to carry out, perfect, fr. *per-* thoroughly + *facere* to make, do — more at DO] **1 :** EXPERT, PROFICIENT <practice makes ~> **2 a :** being entirely without fault or defect **:** FLAWLESS <a ~ crime> **b :** satisfying all requirements **:** ACCURATE **c :** corresponding to an ideal standard or abstract concept <a ~ gentleman> **d :** faithfully reproducing the original; *specif* **:** LETTER-PERFECT **e :** legally valid **3 a :** PURE, TOTAL **b :** lacking in no essential detail **:** COMPLETE **c** *obs* **:** SANE **d :** ABSOLUTE, UNEQUIVOCAL **e :** of an extreme kind **:** UNMITIGATED **4** *obs* **:** MATURE **5 :** of, relating to, or constituting a verb form or verbal that expresses an action or state completed at the time of speaking or at a time spoken of **6** *obs* **a :** CERTAIN, SURE **b :** CONTENT, SATISFIED **7** *of an interval* **:** belonging to the consonances unison, fourth, fifth, and octave which retain their character when inverted and when raised or lowered by a half step become augmented or

diminished **8 a** : sexually mature and fully differentiated <a ~ insect> **b** : MONOCLINOUS <a ~ flower> — **per·fect·ness** \-fik(t)-nəs\ *n*

²**per·fect** \pər-ˈfekt *also* ˈpər-fikt\ *vt* **1** : to make perfect : IMPROVE, REFINE **2** : to bring to final form — **per·fect·er** *n*

³**per·fect** \ˈpər-fikt\ *n* : the perfect tense of a language; *also* : a verb form in the perfect tense

per·fec·ta \pər-ˈfek-tə\ *n* [AmerSp *quiniela perfecta* perfect quiniela] : a system of betting (as on dog races) in which the bettor must pick the first and second place finishers in this sequence in order to win — compare QUINIELA, TRIPLE

perfect game *n* **1** : a baseball game in which a pitcher allows no hits, no runs, and no opposing batter to reach first base **2** : a game in bowling in which a bowler gets 12 consecutive strikes

per·fect·ibil·i·ty \pər-ˌfek-tə-ˈbil-ət-ē *also* ˌpər-fik-\ *n* : a capacity for improvement esp. in moral qualities

per·fect·ible \pər-ˈfek-tə-bəl *also* ˈpər-fik-\ *adj* : capable of improvement or perfection

per·fec·tion \pər-ˈfek-shən\ *n* **1** : the quality or state of being perfect: as **a** : freedom from fault or defect : FLAWLESSNESS **b** : MATURITY **c** : the quality or state of being saintly **2 a** : an exemplification of supreme excellence **b** : an unsurpassable degree of accuracy or excellence **3** : the act or process of perfecting

per·fec·tion·ism \-shə-ˌniz-əm\ *n* **1 a** : the doctrine that the perfection of moral character constitutes man's highest good **b** : the theological doctrine that a state of freedom from sin is attainable on earth **2** : a disposition to regard anything short of perfection as unacceptable — **per·fec·tion·ist** \-sh(ə-)nəst\ *n or adj*

per·fec·tive \pər-ˈfek-tiv *also* ˈpər-fik-\ *adj* **1** *archaic* **a** : tending to make perfect **b** : becoming better **2** : expressing action as complete or as implying the notion of completion, conclusion, or result <~ verb> — **perfective** *n* — **per·fec·tive·ly** *adv* — **per·fec·tive·ness** *n* — **per·fec·tiv·i·ty** \pər-ˌfek-ˈtiv-ət-ē *also* ˌpər-fik-\ *n*

per·fect·ly \ˈpər-fik-(t)lē\ *adv* **1** : in a perfect manner **2** : to an adequate extent : QUITE

perfect number *n* : an integer (as 6 or 28) the sum of whose integral factors including 1 but excluding itself is equal to itself

per·fec·to \pər-ˈfek-(ˌ)tō\ *n, pl* **-tos** [Sp, perfect, fr. L *perfectus*] : a cigar that is thick in the middle and tapers almost to a point at each end

perfect participle *n* : PAST PARTICIPLE

perfect pitch *n* : ABSOLUTE PITCH 2

perfect square *n* : an integer whose square root is an integer <9 is a *perfect square* because it is the square of 3>

perfect year *n* : a common year of 355 days or a leap year of 385 days in the Jewish calendar

per·fer·vid \(ˌ)pər-ˈfər-vəd, ˈpər-\ *adj* [NL *perfervidus*, fr. L *per-* thoroughly + *fervidus* fervid] : marked by overwrought or exaggerated emotion : excessively fervent **syn** see IMPASSIONED

per·fid·i·ous \(ˌ)pər-ˈfid-ē-əs\ *adj* : of, relating to, or characterized by perfidy **syn** see FAITHLESS — **per·fid·i·ous·ly** *adv* — **per·fid·i·ous·ness** *n*

per·fi·dy \ˈpər-fəd-ē\ *n* [L *perfidia*, fr. *perfidus* faithless, fr. *per fidem decipere* to betray, lit., to deceive by trust] : the quality or state of being faithless or disloyal : TREACHERY

per·fo·li·ate \ˌpər-ˈfō-lē-ət, ˈpər-\ *adj* [NL *perfoliata*, an herb having leaves pierced by the stem, fr. L *per* through + *foliata*, fem. of *foliatus* foliate] **1** : having the basal part naturally united around the stem <a ~ leaf> **2** : having the terminal joints expanded into flattened plates and encircling the stalk which connects them <~ antennae of a beetle> — **per·fo·li·a·tion** \ˌpər-ˌfō-lē-ˈā-shən\ *n*

per·fo·rate \ˈpər-fə-ˌrāt\ *vb* **-rat·ed; -rat·ing** [L *perforatus*, pp. of *perforare* to bore through, fr. *per-* through + *forare* to bore — more at BORE] *vt* **1** : to make a hole through <an ulcer ~*s* the duodenal wall>; *specif* : to make a line of holes in to facilitate separation **2** : to pass through or into by or as if by making a hole ~ *vi* : to penetrate a surface — **per·fo·rate** \ˈpər-f(ə-)rət, -fə-ˌrāt\ *adj* — **per·fo·ra·tor** \-fə-ˌrāt-ər\ *n*

per·fo·rat·ed \-fə-ˌrāt-əd\ *adj* **1** : having a hole or series of holes; *esp* : having a specified number of perforations in 20 millimeters <the stamps are ~ 10> **2** : characterized by perforation <a ~ ulcer>

per·fo·ra·tion \ˌpər-fə-ˈrā-shən\ *n* **1** : the act or process of perforating **2 a** : a hole or pattern made by or as if by piercing or boring **b** : one of the series of holes between rows of postage stamps in a sheet that serve as an aid in separation

per·force \pər-ˈfō(ə)rs, -ˈfȯ(ə)rs\ *adv* [ME *par force*, fr. MF, by force] **1** *obs* : by physical coercion **2** : by force of circumstances

per·form \pə(r)-ˈfȯ(ə)rm\ *vb* [ME *performen*, fr. AF *performer*, alter. of OF *perfournir*, fr. *per-* thoroughly (fr. L) + *fournir* to complete — more at FURNISH] *vt* **1** : to adhere to the terms of : FULFILL <~ a contract> **2** : to carry out : DO **3 a** : to do in a formal manner or according to prescribed ritual **b** : to give a rendition of : PRESENT ~ *vi* **1** : to carry out an action or pattern of behavior : ACT, FUNCTION **2** : to give a performance : PLAY — **per·form·able** \-ˈfȯr-mə-bəl\ *adj*

syn PERFORM, EXECUTE, DISCHARGE, ACCOMPLISH, ACHIEVE, EFFECT, FULFILL *shared meaning element* : to carry out or into effect

per·for·mance \pə(r)-ˈfȯr-mən(t)s\ *n* **1 a** : the execution of an action **b** : something accomplished : DEED, FEAT **2** : the fulfillment of a claim, promise, or request : IMPLEMENTATION **3 a** : the action of representing a character in a play **b** : a public presentation or exhibition <a benefit ~> **4 a** : the ability to perform : EFFICIENCY **b** : the manner in which a mechanism performs <engine ~> **5** : the manner of reacting to stimuli : BEHAVIOR — **per·for·ma·to·ry** \-mə-ˌtōr-ē, -ˌtȯr-\ *adj*

per·for·ma·tive \-ˈfȯr-mət-iv\ *n* : an expression that serves to effect a transaction or that constitutes the performance of the specified act by virtue of its utterance <many ~*s* are *contractual* ("I bet") or *declaratory* ("I declare war") utterances —J. L. Austin>

per·form·er \-ˈfȯr-mər\ *n* : one that performs

per·form·ing *adj* : of, relating to, or constituting an art (as drama) that involves public performance <the ~ arts>

¹**per·fume** \ˈpər-ˌfyüm, (ˌ)pər-ˈ\ *n* [MF *perfum*, prob. fr. OProv, fr. *perfumar* to perfume, fr. *per-* thoroughly (fr. L) + *fumar* to smoke, fr. L *fumare* — more at FUME] **1** : the scent of something sweet-smelling **2** : a substance that emits a pleasant odor; *esp* : a fluid preparation of floral essences or synthetics and a fixative used for scenting **syn** see FRAGRANCE

²**per·fume** \(ˌ)pər-ˈfyüm, ˈpər-ˌ\ *vt* **per·fumed; per·fum·ing** : to fill or imbue with an odor

per·fum·er \pə(r)-ˈfyü-mər, ˈpər-ˌ\ *n* : one that makes or sells perfumes

per·fum·ery \pə(r)-ˈfyüm-(ə-)rē\ *n, pl* **-er·ies** **1 a** : the art or process of making perfume **b** : the products made by a perfumer **2** : a perfume establishment

per·func·to·ry \pər-ˈfəŋ(k)-t(ə-)rē\ *adj* [LL *perfunctorius*, fr. L *perfunctus*, pp. of *perfungi* to accomplish, get through with, fr. *per-* through + *fungi* to perform — more at PER-, FUNCTION] **1** : characterized by routine or superficiality : MECHANICAL <a ~ smile> **2** : lacking in interest or enthusiasm : APATHETIC — **per·func·to·ri·ly** \-t(ə-)rə-lē\ *adv* — **per·func·to·ri·ness** \-t(ə-)rē-nəs\ *n*

per·fuse \(ˌ)pər-ˈfyüz\ *vt* **per·fused; per·fus·ing** [L *perfusus*, pp. of *perfundere* to pour over, fr. *per-* through + *fundere* to pour — more at FOUND] **1** : SUFFUSE **2 a** : to cause to flow or spread : DIFFUSE **b** : to force a fluid through (an organ or tissue) esp. by way of the blood vessels — **per·fu·sion** \-ˈfyü-zhən\ *n* — **per·fu·sive** \-ˈfyü-siv, -ziv\ *adj*

per·go·la \ˈpər-gə-lə, pər-ˈgō-\ *n* [It, fr. L *pergula* projecting roof] **1** : ARBOR, TRELLIS **2** : a structure usu. consisting of parallel colonnades supporting an open roof of girders and cross rafters

perh *abbr* perhaps

¹**per·haps** \pər-ˈ(h)aps, ˈpraps\ *adv* [*per* + *hap*] : possibly but not certainly : MAYBE

²**perhaps** *n* : something open to doubt or conjecture

pe·ri \ˈpi(ə)r-ē\ *n* [Per *perī* fairy, genius, modif. of Av *pairikā* witch; akin to L *paelex* concubine] **1** : a supernatural being in Persian folklore descended from fallen angels and excluded from paradise until penance is accomplished **2** : a beautiful and graceful girl

peri- *prefix* [L, fr. Gk, around, in excess, fr. *peri*; akin to Gk *peran* to pass through — more at FARE] **1** : all around : about <*peri*scope> **2** : near <*peri*helion> **3** : enclosing : surrounding <*peri*neurium>

peri·anth \ˈper-ē-ˌan(t)th\ *n* [NL *perianthium*, fr. *peri-* + Gk *anthos* flower — more at ANTHOLOGY] : the external envelope of a flower esp. when not differentiated into a calyx and corolla

peri·apt \ˈper-ē-ˌapt\ *n* [MF or Gk; MF *periapte*, fr. Gk *periapton*, fr. *periaptein* to fasten around (oneself), fr. *peri-* + *haptein* to fasten] : AMULET

peri·car·di·al \ˌper-ə-ˈkärd-ē-əl\ *adj* : of, relating to, or affecting the pericardium; *also* : situated around the heart

peri·car·di·tis \-ˌkär-ˈdīt-əs\ *n* [NL] : inflammation of the pericardium

peri·car·di·um \ˌper-ə-ˈkärd-ē-əm\ *n, pl* **-dia** \-ē-ə\ [NL, fr. Gk *perikardion*, neut. of *perikardios* around the heart, fr. *peri-* + *kardia* heart — more at HEART] **1** : the conical sac of serous membrane that encloses the heart and the roots of the great blood vessels of vertebrates **2** : a cavity or space that contains the heart of an invertebrate and in arthropods is a part of the hemocoel

peri·carp \ˈper-ə-ˌkärp\ *n* [NL *pericarpium*, fr. Gk *perikarpion* pod, fr. *peri-* + *-karpion* -carp] : the ripened and variously modified walls of a plant ovary — see ENDOCARP illustration

peri·chon·dri·um \ˌper-ə-ˈkän-drē-əm\ *n, pl* **-dria** \-drē-ə\ [NL, fr. *peri-* + Gk *chondros* grain, cartilage — more at GRIND] : the membrane of fibrous connective tissue that invests cartilage except at joints — **peri·chon·dri·al** \-drē-əl\ *also* **peri·chon·dral** \-drəl\ *adj*

pe·ric·o·pe \pə-ˈrik-ə-pē\ *n* [LL, fr. Gk *perikopē* section, fr. *peri-* + *kopē* act of cutting; akin to Gk *koptein* to cut — more at CAPON] : a selection from a book; *specif* : LECTION 1

peri·cra·ni·um \ˌper-ə-ˈkrā-nē-əm\ *n, pl* **-nia** \-nē-ə\ [NL, fr. Gk *perikranion*, neut. of *perikranios* around the skull, fr. *peri-* + *kranion* skull] : the external periosteum of the skull — **peri·cra·ni·al** \-nē-əl\ *adj*

peri·cy·cle \ˈper-ə-ˌsī-kəl\ *n* [F *péricycle*, fr. Gk *perikyklos* spherical, fr. *peri-* + *kyklos* circle — more at WHEEL] : a thin layer of parenchymatous or sclerenchymatous cells that surrounds the stele in most vascular plants — **peri·cy·clic** \ˌper-ə-ˈsī-klik, -ˈsik-lik\ *adj*

peri·cyn·thi·on \ˌper-ə-ˈsin(t)-thē-ən\ *n* [NL, fr. *peri-* + *Cynthia* + *-on* (as in *perihelion*)] : PERILUNE

peri·derm \ˈper-ə-ˌdərm\ *n* [NL *peridermis*, fr. *peri-* + *-dermis*] : an outer layer of tissue; *esp* : a cortical protective layer of many roots and stems that typically consists of phellem, phellogen, and phelloderm — **peri·der·mal** \ˌper-ə-ˈdər-məl\ *or* **peri·der·mic** \-mik\ *adj*

pe·rid·i·um \pə-ˈrid-ē-əm\ *n, pl* **pe·rid·ia** \-ē-ə\ [NL, fr. Gk *pēridion*, dim. of *pēra* leather bag] : the outer envelope of the sporophore of many fungi

peri·dot \ˈper-ə-ˌdōt, -ˌdät\ *n* [F *péridot*] : a deep yellowish green transparent olivine used as a gem — **per·i·dot·ic** \ˌper-ə-ˈdōt-ik, -ˈdät-\ *adj*

pe·ri·do·tite \pə-ˈrid-ə-ˌtīt; ˈper-ə-ˌdōt-ˌīt, -ˌdät-\ *n* [F *péridotite*, fr. *péridot*] : any of a group of granitoid igneous rocks composed of ferromagnesian minerals and esp. olivine — **pe·ri·do·tit·ic** \pə-ˌrid-ə-ˈtit-ik, ˌper-əd-ə-\ *adj*

peri·ge·an \ˌper-ə-ˈjē-ən\ *adj* : of or relating to perigee

per·i·gee \'per-ə-(ˌ)jē\ *n* [Gk *gē* earth] **:** the point in the orbit of a satellite of the earth or of a vehicle orbiting the earth that is nearest to the center of the earth; *also* **:** the point nearest a planet or a satellite (as the moon) reached by any object orbiting it — compare APOGEE

pe·rig·y·nous \pə-'rij-ə-nəs\ *adj* [NL *perigynus*, fr. *peri-* + *-gynus* -gynous] **:** borne on a ring or cup of the receptacle surrounding a pistil <~ petals>; *also* **:** having perigynous stamens and petals <~ flowers> — **pe·rig·y·ny** \-nē\ *n*

peri·he·lion \ˌper-ə-'hēl-yən\ *n, pl* **-he·lia** \-'hēl-yə\ [NL, fr. *peri-* + Gk *hēlios* sun — more at SOLAR] **:** the point in the path of a celestial body (as a planet) that is nearest to the sun — compare APHELION — **peri·he·lial** \-'hēl-yəl\ *adj*

peri·kary·on \-'kar-ē-ˌän, -ən\ *n, pl* **-karya** \-ē-ə\ [NL, fr. *peri-* + Gk *karyon* nut, kernel — more at CAREEN] **:** the cytoplasmic body of a nerve cell — **peri·kary·al** \-ē-əl\ *adj*

[1]**per·il** \'per-əl\ *n* [ME, fr. OF, fr. L *periculum* — more at FEAR] **1 :** exposure to the risk of being injured, destroyed, or lost **:** DANGER <fire put the city in ~> **2 :** something that imperils **:** RISK <lessen the ~*s* of the streets>

[2]**peril** *vt* **-iled** *also* **-illed; -il·ing** *also* **-il·ling :** to expose to danger

pe·ril·la \pə-'ril-ə\ *n* [NL, genus name] **:** any of a genus (*Perilla*) of Asiatic mints that have four didynamous stamens, a bilabiate fruiting calyx, and rugose nutlets

perilla oil *n* **:** a light yellow drying oil that is obtained from seeds of perillas and is used chiefly in varnish, printing ink, and linoleum and in the Orient as an edible oil

per·il·ous \'per-ə-ləs\ *adj* **:** full of or involving peril **:** HAZARDOUS *syn* see DANGEROUS — **per·il·ous·ly** *adv* — **per·il·ous·ness** *n*

peri·lune \'per-ə-ˌlün\ *n* [*peri-* + L *luna* moon — more at LUNAR] **:** the point in the path of a body orbiting the moon that is nearest to the center of the moon — compare APOLUNE

peri·lymph \-ˌlim(p)f\ *n* [ISV] **:** the fluid between the membranous and bony labyrinths of the ear

pe·rim·e·ter \pə-'rim-ət-ər\ *n* [F *périmètre*, fr. L *perimetros*, fr. Gk, fr. *peri-* + *metron* measure — more at MEASURE] **1 a :** the boundary of a closed plane figure **b :** the length of a perimeter **2 :** a line or strip bounding or protecting an area **3 :** outer limits

peri·morph \'per-ə-ˌmȯrf\ *n* [ISV] **:** a crystal of one species enclosing one of another species

peri·my·si·um \ˌper-ə-'miz(h)-ē-əm\ *n, pl* **-sia** \-ē-ə\ [NL, irreg. fr. *peri-* + Gk *mys* mouse, muscle — more at MOUSE] **:** the connective-tissue sheath that surrounds a muscle and forms sheaths for the bundles of muscle fibers

peri·na·tal \-'nāt-ᵊl\ *adj* **:** occurring at about the time of birth

per·i·ne·um \ˌper-ə-'nē-əm\ *n, pl* **-nea** \-'nē-ə\ [NL, fr. LL *perinaion*, fr. Gk, fr. *peri-* + *inein* to empty out; akin to L *ira* ire] **:** an area of tissue that marks externally the approximate boundary of the outlet of the pelvis and gives passage to the urinogenital ducts and rectum; *also* **:** the area between the anus and the posterior part of the external genitalia esp. in the female — **per·i·ne·al** \-'nē-əl\ *adj*

peri·neu·ri·um \ˌper-ə-'n(y)u̇r-ē-əm\ *n, pl* **-ria** \-ē-ə\ [NL, fr. *peri-* + Gk *neuron* nerve — more at NERVE] **:** the connective-tissue sheath that surrounds a bundle of nerve fibers

[1]**pe·ri·od** \'pir-ē-əd\ *n* [ME *pariode*, fr. MF *periode*, fr. ML, L, & Gk; ML *periodus* period of time, punctuation mark, fr. L & Gk; L, rhetorical period, fr. Gk *periodos* circuit, period of time, rhetorical period, fr. *peri-* + *hodos* way — more at CEDE] **1 a (1) :** an utterance from one full stop to another **:** SENTENCE **(2) :** a well-proportioned sentence of several clauses **(3) :** PERIODIC SENTENCE **b :** a musical structure or melodic section usu. composed of two or more contrasting or complementary phrases and ending with a cadence **2 a :** the full pause with which the utterance of a sentence closes **b :** END, STOP **3** *obs* **:** GOAL, PURPOSE **4 a :** a point . used to mark the end (as of a declarative sentence or an abbreviation) **b :** a rhythmical unit in Greek verse composed of a series of two or more cola **5 :** the completion of a cycle, a series of events, or a single action **:** CONCLUSION **6 a :** a portion of time determined by some recurring phenomenon **b (1) :** the interval of time required for a cyclic motion or phenomenon to complete a cycle and begin to repeat itself **(2) :** a number k that does not change the value of a periodic function f when added to the independent variable: $f(x + k) = f(x)$; *esp* **:** the smallest such number **c :** a single cyclic occurrence of menstruation **7 a :** a chronological division **:** STAGE **b :** a division of geologic time longer than an epoch and included in an era **c :** a stage of culture having a definable place in time and space **8 a :** one of the divisions of the academic day **b :** one of the divisions of the playing time of a game

syn PERIOD, EPOCH, ERA, AGE *shared meaning element* **:** a portion or division of time

[2]**period** *adj* **:** of, relating to, or representing a particular historical period <~ furniture>

pe·ri·od·ic \ˌpir-ē-'äd-ik\ *adj* **1 :** occurring or recurring at regular intervals **2 :** consisting of or containing a series of repeated stages **:** CYCLIC <~ decimals> <a ~ vibration> **3 :** expressed in or characterized by periodic sentences *syn* see INTERMITTENT

per·iod·ic acid \ˌpər-(ˌ)ī-ˌäd-ik-\ *n* [ISV *per-* + *iodic*] **:** any of the strongly oxidizing acids (as H_5IO_6 or HIO_4) that are the highest oxygen acids of iodine

[1]**pe·ri·od·i·cal** \ˌpir-ē-'äd-i-kəl\ *adj* **1 :** PERIODIC 1 **2 a :** published with a fixed interval between the issues or numbers **b :** published in, characteristic of, or connected with a periodical — **pe·ri·od·i·cal·ly** \-k(ə-)lē\ *adv*

[2]**periodical** *n* **:** a periodical publication

periodical cicada *n* **:** SEVENTEEN-YEAR LOCUST

periodic function *n* **:** a function any value of which recurs at regular intervals

pe·ri·od·ic·i·ty \ˌpir-ē-ə-'dis-ət-ē\ *n* **:** the quality, state, or fact of being regularly recurrent

periodic law *n* **:** a law in chemistry: the elements when arranged in the order of their atomic numbers show a periodic variation in most of their properties

periodic sentence *n* **:** a usu. complex sentence that has no subordinate or trailing elements following its principal clause (as in "yesterday while I was walking down the street, I saw him")

periodic table *n* **:** an arrangement of chemical elements based on the periodic law

pe·ri·od·iza·tion \ˌpir-ē-əd-ə-'zā-shən\ *n* **:** division (as of history) into periods

peri·odon·tal \ˌper-ē-ō-'dänt-ᵊl\ *adj* **1 :** investing or surrounding a tooth **2 :** of or affecting periodontal tissues or regions — **peri·odon·tal·ly** \-ᵊl-ē\ *adv*

peri·odon·tics \-'dänt-iks\ *n pl but sing or pl in constr* [NL *periodontium*, fr. *peri-* + Gk *odont-, odous, odōn* tooth — more at TOOTH] **:** a branch of dentistry that deals with diseases of the supporting structures of the teeth — **peri·odon·tist** \-'dänt-əst\ *n*

PERIODIC TABLE

This is a common long form of the table. Roman numerals and letters heading the vertical columns indicate the groups (there are differences of opinion regarding the letter designations, those given here being probably the most generally used). The horizontal rows represent the periods, with two series removed from the two very long periods and represented below the main table. Atomic numbers are given above the symbols for the elements. Compare ELEMENT table.

IA	IIA	IIIB	IVB	VB	VIB	VIIB	VIII	VIII	VIII	IB	IIB	IIIA	IVA	VA	VIA	VIIA	Zero
1 H																1 H	2 He
3 Li	4 Be											5 B	6 C	7 N	8 O	9 F	10 Ne
11 Na	12 Mg											13 Al	14 Si	15 P	16 S	17 Cl	18 Ar
19 K	20 Ca	21 Sc	22 Ti	23 V	24 Cr	25 Mn	26 Fe	27 Co	28 Ni	29 Cu	30 Zn	31 Ga	32 Ge	33 As	34 Se	35 Br	36 Kr
37 Rb	38 Sr	39 Y	40 Zr	41 Nb	42 Mo	43 Tc	44 Ru	45 Rh	46 Pd	47 Ag	48 Cd	49 In	50 Sn	51 Sb	52 Te	53 I	54 Xe
55 Cs	56 Ba	57 *La	72 Hf	73 Ta	74 W	75 Re	76 Os	77 Ir	78 Pt	79 Au	80 Hg	81 Tl	82 Pb	83 Bi	84 Po	85 At	86 Rn
87 Fr	88 Ra	89 #Ac															

*LANTHANIDE SERIES	58 Ce	59 Pr	60 Nd	61 Pm	62 Sm	63 Eu	64 Gd	65 Tb	66 Dy	67 Ho	68 Er	69 Tm	70 Yb	71 Lu
#ACTINIDE SERIES	90 Th	91 Pa	92 U	93 Np	94 Pu	95 Am	96 Cm	97 Bk	98 Cf	99 Es	100 Fm	101 Md	102 No	103 Lr

pe·ri·od piece *n* **:** a piece (as of fiction, art, furniture, or music) whose special value lies in its evocation of an historical period

peri·onych·i·um \ˌper-ē-ō-ˈnik-ē-əm\ *n, pl* **-ia** \-ē-ə\ [NL, fr. *peri-* + Gk *onych-, onyx* nail — more at NAIL] **:** the tissue bordering the root and sides of a fingernail or toenail

periost- *or* **perioste-** *or* **periosteo-** *comb form* [NL *periosteum*] **:** periosteum <*periosteo*myelitis> <*perioste*oma> <*periost*itis>

peri·os·te·al \ˌper-ē-ˈäs-tē-əl\ *adj* **1 :** situated around or produced external to bone **2 :** of, relating to, or involving the periosteum

peri·os·te·um \-tē-əm\ *n, pl* **-tea** \-tē-ə\ [NL, fr. LL *periosteon,* fr. Gk, neut. of *periosteos* around the bone, fr. *peri-* + *osteon* bone — more at OSSEOUS] **:** the membrane of connective tissue that closely invests all bones except at the articular surfaces

peri·os·ti·tis \-ˌäs-ˈtīt-əs\ *n* [NL] **:** inflammation of the periosteum

peri·ot·ic \ˌper-ē-ˈōt-ik\ *adj* **1 :** situated around the ear; *specif* **:** being, relating to, or composed of the bony elements that are typically three in number, surround the internal ear, and form or help to form its capsule

[1]**peri·pa·tet·ic** \ˌper-ə-pə-ˈtet-ik\ *n* **1** *cap* **:** a follower of Aristotle or adherent of Aristotelianism **2 :** PEDESTRIAN, ITINERANT **3** *pl* **:** movement or journeys hither and thither

[2]**peripatetic** *adj* [MF & L; MF *peripatetique,* fr. L *peripateticus,* fr. Gk *peripatētikos,* fr. *peripatein* to walk up and down, discourse while pacing (as did Aristotle), fr. *peri-* + *patein* to tread; akin to Skt *patha* path — more at FIND] **1** *cap* **:** ARISTOTELIAN **2 :** of or relating to walking **:** ITINERANT — **peri·pa·tet·i·cal·ly** \-i-k(ə-)lē\ *adv* — **Peri·pa·tet·i·cism** \-ˈtet-ə-ˌsiz-əm\ *n*

pe·rip·a·tus \pə-ˈrip-ət-əs\ *n* [NL, genus name, fr. Gk *peripatos* act of walking about, fr. *peri-* + *patein* to tread] **:** any of a class (Onychophora) of primitive tropical arthropods that in some respects are intermediate between annelid worms and typical arthropods

peri·pe·teia \ˌper-ə-pə-ˈtē-(y)ə, -ˈtī-ə\ *n* [Gk, fr. *peripiptein* to fall around, change suddenly, fr. *peri-* + *piptein* to fall — more at FEATHER] **:** a sudden or unexpected reversal of circumstances or situation esp. in a literary work

pe·rip·e·ty \pə-ˈrip-ət-ē\ *n, pl* **-ties :** PERIPETEIA

pe·riph·er·ad \pə-ˈrif-ə-ˌrad\ *adv* **:** toward the periphery

[1]**pe·riph·er·al** \pə-ˈrif-(ə-)rəl\ *adj* **1 :** of, relating to, or forming a periphery **2 :** located away from a center or central portion **:** EXTERNAL **3 :** of, relating to, or involving the surface of the body **4 :** of, relating to, or being the outer part of the field of vision <good ~ vision> **5 :** AUXILIARY, SUPPLEMENTARY <~ equipment> — **pe·riph·er·al·ly** \-ē\ *adv*

[2]**peripheral** *n* **:** a device connected to a computer to provide communication (as input and output) or auxiliary functions (as additional storage)

pe·riph·ery \pə-ˈrif-(ə-)rē\ *n, pl* **-er·ies** [MF *peripherie,* fr. LL *peripheria,* fr. Gk *periphereia,* fr. *peripherein* to carry around, fr. *peri-* + *pherein* to carry — more at BEAR] **1 :** the perimeter of a circle or other closed curve; *also* **:** the perimeter of a polygon **2 :** the external boundary or surface of a body **3 a :** the outward bounds of something as distinguished from its internal regions or center **:** CONFINES **b :** an area lying beyond the strict limits of a thing **4 :** the regions (as the sense organs, the muscles, or the viscera) in which nerves terminate

pe·riph·ra·sis \pə-ˈrif-rə-səs\ *n, pl* **-ra·ses** \-ˌsēz\ [L, fr. Gk, fr. *periphrazein* to express periphrastically, fr. *peri-* + *phrazein* to point out] **1 :** use of a longer phrasing in place of a possible shorter form of expression **2 :** an instance of periphrasis

peri·phras·tic \ˌper-ə-ˈfras-tik\ *adj* **1 :** of, relating to, or characterized by periphrasis **2 :** formed by the use of function words or auxiliaries instead of by inflection <*more fair* is a ~ comparative> — **peri·phras·ti·cal·ly** \-ti-k(ə-)lē\ *adv*

pe·riph·y·ton \pə-ˈrif-ə-ˌtän\ *n* [NL, fr. Gk *periphytos* (verbal of *periphyein* to grow around, fr. *peri-* + *phyein* to bring forth, grow) + *-on* (as in *plankton*) — more at BE] **:** organisms (as some algae) that live attached to underwater surfaces — **peri·phyt·ic** \ˌper-ə-ˈfit-ik\ *adj*

peri·plast \ˈper-ə-ˌplast\ *n* **:** PLASMA MEMBRANE; *also* **:** a proteinaceous subcellular layer below the plasma membrane esp. of a euglena

peri·proct \-ˌpräkt\ *n* [ISV *peri-* + Gk *prōktos* anus] **:** the well-defined area surrounding the anus of various invertebrates (as a sea urchin)

pe·rique \pə-ˈrēk\ *n* [LaF *périque*] **:** an aromatic fermented Louisiana tobacco used in smoking mixtures

peri·sarc \ˈper-ə-ˌsärk\ *n* [ISV *peri-* + Gk *sark-, sarx* flesh — more at SARCASM] **:** the outer usu. chitinous integument of a hydroid

peri·scope \-ˌskōp\ *n* [ISV] **:** a tubular optical instrument containing lenses and mirrors by which an observer obtains an otherwise obstructed field of view

peri·scop·ic \ˌper-ə-ˈskäp-ik\ *adj* **1 :** providing a view all around or on all sides <~ lens> **2 :** of or relating to a periscope

peri·se·le·ne \-sə-ˈlē-nē\ *n* [ISV *peri-* + Gk *selēnē* moon — more at SELENIUM] **:** PERILUNE

per·ish \ˈper-ish\ *vb* [ME *perisshen,* fr. OF *periss-,* stem of *perir,* fr. L *perire,* fr. *per-* to destruction + *ire* to go — more at PER-, ISSUE] *vi* **1 :** to become destroyed or ruined **:** DIE <recollection of a past already long since ~*ed* —Philip Sherrard> <guard against your mistakes or your attempts (~ the thought) to cheat —C. B. Davis> **2** *chiefly Brit* **:** DETERIORATE, SPOIL ~ *vt* **1** *chiefly Brit* **:** to cause to die **:** DESTROY **2 :** WEAKEN, BENUMB

per·ish·able \ˈper-ish-ə-bəl\ *adj* **:** liable to perish **:** liable to spoil or decay <such ~ products as fruit, vegetables, butter and eggs> — **per·ish·abil·i·ty** \ˌper-ish-ə-ˈbil-ət-ē\ *n* — **perishable** *n*

per·ish·ing \ˈper-ish-iŋ\ *adj* **:** that perishes **:** that causes extreme discomfort, pain, or hardship — **per·ish·ing·ly** \-iŋ-lē\ *adv*

pe·ris·so·dac·tyl \pə-ˈris-ə-ˌdak-tᵊl\ *n* [NL *Perissodactyla,* group name, fr. Gk *perissos* excessive, odd in number + *daktylos* finger, toe] **:** any of an order (Perissodactyla) of nonruminant ungulate mammals (as a horse, a tapir, or a rhinoceros) that usu. have an odd number of toes, molar teeth with transverse ridges on the grinding surface, and the posterior premolars resembling true molars — **perissodactyl** *adj*

peri·stal·sis \ˌper-ə-ˈstȯl-səs, -ˈstäl-, -ˈstal-\ *n* [NL, fr. Gk *peristaltikos* peristaltic] **:** successive waves of involuntary contraction passing along the walls of the intestine or other hollow muscular structure and forcing the contents onward

peri·stal·tic \-tik\ *adj* [Gk *peristaltikos,* fr. *peristellein* to wrap around, fr. *peri-* + *stellein* to place — more at STALL] **1 :** of, relating to, resulting from, or being peristalsis **2 :** having an action suggestive of peristalsis <a ~ pump> — **per·i·stal·ti·cal·ly** \-ti-k(ə-)lē\ *adv*

peri·stome \ˈper-ə-ˌstōm\ *n* [NL *peristoma,* fr. *peri-* + Gk *stoma* mouth — more at STOMACH] **1 :** the fringe of teeth surrounding the orifice of a moss capsule **2 :** the region around the mouth in various invertebrates — **peri·sto·mi·al** \ˌper-ə-ˈstō-mē-əl\ *adj*

periscope

peri·style \ˈper-ə-ˌstīl\ *n* [F *péristyle,* fr. L *peristylum,* fr. Gk *peristylon,* fr. neut. of *peristylos* surrounded by a colonnade, fr. *peri-* + *stylos* pillar — more at STEER] **1 :** a colonnade surrounding a building or court **2 :** an open space enclosed by a colonnade

peri·the·ci·um \ˌper-ə-ˈthē-s(h)ē-əm\ *n, pl* **-cia** \-s(h)ē-ə\ [NL, fr. *peri-* + Gk *thēkion,* dim. of *thēkē* case — more at TICK] **:** a spherical, cylindrical, or flask-shaped hollow fruiting body in various ascomycetous fungi that contains the asci and usu. opens by a terminal pore — **peri·the·cial** \-ˈthē-sh(ē-)əl, -sē-əl\ *adj*

periton- *or* **peritone-** *or* **peritoneo-** *comb form* [LL *peritoneum*] **:** peritoneum <*periton*itis>

peri·to·ne·um \ˌper-ət-ᵊn-ˈē-əm\ *n, pl* **-ne·ums** \-ˈē-əmz\ *or* **-nea** \-ˈē-ə\ [LL, fr. Gk *peritonaion,* neut. of *peritonaios* stretched around, fr. *peri-* + *teinein* to stretch — more at THIN] **1 :** the smooth transparent serous membrane that lines the cavity of the abdomen of a mammal and is reflected inward over the abdominal and pelvic viscera **2 :** PLEUROPERITONEUM — **peri·to·ne·al** \-ˈē-əl\ *adj* — **peri·to·ne·al·ly** \-ə-lē\ *adv*

peri·to·ni·tis \ˌper-ət-ᵊn-ˈīt-əs\ *n* [NL] **:** inflammation of the peritoneum

pe·rit·ri·chous \pə-ˈri-tri-kəs\ *adj* [*peri-* + Gk *trich-, thrix* hair — more at TRICH-] **1 :** having flagella uniformly distributed over the body <~ bacteria> **2 :** having a spiral line of modified cilia around the oral disk <~ protozoa> — **pe·rit·ri·chous·ly** *adv*

peri·wig \ˈper-i-ˌwig\ *n* [modif. of MF *perruque*] **:** PERUKE — **peri·wigged** \-ˌwigd\ *adj*

[1]**per·i·win·kle** \ˈper-i-ˌwiŋ-kəl\ *n* [ME *perwinke,* fr. OE *perwince,* fr. L *pervinca*] **:** any of several trailing or woody evergreen herbs (genus *Vinca*) of the dogbane family: as **a :** a European creeper (*V. minor*) widely cultivated as a ground cover and for its blue or white flowers — called also *myrtle* **b :** a commonly cultivated subshrub (*V. rosea*) of the Old World tropics that is the source of several antineoplastic drugs — called also *Madagascar periwinkle*

[2]**periwinkle** *n* [(assumed) ME, alter. of OE *pinewincle,* fr. L *pina,* a kind of mussel (fr. Gk) + OE *-wincle* (akin to Dan *vincle* snail shell); akin to OE *wincian* to wink] **:** any of various gastropod mollusks: as **a :** any of a genus (*Littorina*) of edible littoral marine snails; *also* **:** any of various similar or related marine snails (as various American members of *Thais*) **b :** any of several No. American freshwater snails

per·jure \ˈpər-jər\ *vt* **per·jured; per·jur·ing** \ˈpərj-(ə-)riŋ\ [MF *perjurer,* fr. L *perjurare,* fr. *per-* to destruction, to the bad + *jurare* to swear — more at PER-, JURY] **1** *obs* **:** to cause to commit perjury **2 :** to make a perjurer of (oneself)

per·jur·er \ˈpər-jər-ər\ *n* **:** a person guilty of perjury

per·ju·ri·ous \(ˌ)pər-ˈju̇r-ē-əs\ *adj* **:** marked by perjury <~ testimony> — **per·ju·ri·ous·ly** *adv*

per·ju·ry \ˈpərj-(ə-)rē\ *n* **:** the voluntary violation of an oath or vow either by swearing to what is untrue or by omission to do what has been promised under oath **:** false swearing

[1]**perk** \ˈpərk\ *vb* [ME *perken*] *vi* **1 a :** to thrust up the head, stretch out the neck, or carry the body in a bold or insolent manner **b :** to stick up or out jauntily **2 :** to gain in vigor or cheerfulness esp. after a period of weakness or depression — usu. used with *up* <he ~*ed* up noticeably when the letter arrived> ~ *vt* **1 :** to make smart or spruce in appearance **:** FRESHEN, IMPROVE **2 :** to thrust up quickly or impudently

[2]**perk** *n, chiefly Brit* **:** PERQUISITE — usu. used in pl.

[3]**perk** *vi* **:** PERCOLATE

perky \ˈpər-kē\ *adj* **perk·i·er; -est 1 :** briskly self-assured **:** COCKY <a ~ salesman> **2 :** JAUNTY <a ~ . . . waltz —*New Yorker*> — **perk·i·ly** \-kə-lē\ *adv* — **perk·i·ness** \-kē-nəs\ *n*

per·lite \ˈpər-ˌlīt\ *n* [F, fr. *perle* pearl] **:** volcanic glass that has a concentric shelly structure, appears as if composed of concretions, is usu. grayish and sometimes spherulitic, and when expanded by heat forms a lightweight aggregate used esp. in concrete and plaster — **per·lit·ic** \ˌpər-ˈlit-ik\ *adj*

[1]**perm** \ˈpərm\ *n* **:** PERMANENT

[2]**perm** *abbr* permanent

per·ma·frost \ˈpər-mə-ˌfrȯst\ *n* [*perma*nent + *frost*] **:** a permanently frozen layer at variable depth below the earth's surface in frigid regions

ə abut	ᵊ kitten	ər further	a back	ā bake	ä cot, cart
au̇ out	ch chin	e less	ē easy	g gift	i trip ī life
j joke	ŋ sing	ō flow	ȯ flaw	ȯi coin	th thin t͟h this
ü loot	u̇ foot	y yet	yü few	yu̇ furious	zh vision

per·ma·nence \ˈpərm(-ə)-nən(t)s\ *n* **:** the quality or state of being permanent **:** DURABILITY
per·ma·nen·cy \-nən-sē\ *n, pl* **-cies** **1 :** PERMANENCE **2 :** something permanent
1**per·ma·nent** \-nənt\ *adj* [ME, fr. MF, fr. L *permanent-, permanens,* prp. of *permanēre* to endure, fr. *per-* throughout + *manēre* to remain — more at PER-, MANSION] **:** continuing or enduring without fundamental or marked change **:** STABLE — **per·ma·nent·ly** *adv* — **per·ma·nent·ness** *n*
2**permanent** *n* **:** a long-lasting hair wave or straightening produced by mechanical and chemical means — called also *permanent wave*
permanent magnet *n* **:** a magnet that retains its magnetism after removal of the magnetizing force
permanent press *n* **:** DURABLE PRESS
permanent tissue *n* **:** tissue that has completed its growth and differentiation and is generally incapable of meristematic activity
permanent tooth *n* **:** one of the second set of teeth of a mammal that follow the milk teeth, typically persist into old age, and in man are 32 in number
per·man·ga·nate \(ˌ)pər-ˈmaŋ-gə-ˌnāt\ *n* **:** a dark purple crystalline compound that is a salt of permanganic acid
per·man·gan·ic acid \ˌpər-(ˌ)man-ˌgan-ik-, -(ˌ)maŋ-\ *n* [ISV] **:** an unstable strong acid $HMnO_4$ known chiefly in purple-colored strongly oxidizing aqueous solutions
per·me·abil·i·ty \ˌpər-mē-ə-ˈbil-ət-ē\ *n* **1 :** the quality or state of being permeable **2 :** the property of a magnetizable substance that determines the degree in which it modifies the magnetic flux in the region occupied by it in a magnetic field
per·me·able \ˈpər-mē-ə-bəl\ *adj* **:** capable of being permeated **:** PENETRABLE; *esp* **:** having pores or openings that permit liquids or gases to pass through <a ~ membrane> <~ limestone> — **per·me·able·ness** *n* — **per·me·ably** \-blē\ *adv*
per·me·ance \-ən(t)s\ *n* **1 :** PERMEATION **2 :** the reciprocal of magnetic reluctance
per·me·ase \-ˌās, -ˌāz\ *n* [ISV *perme-* (fr. *permeate*) + *-ase*] **:** a substance that catalyzes the transport of another substance across a cell membrane
per·me·ate \ˈpər-mē-ˌāt\ *vb* **-at·ed; -at·ing** [L *permeatus,* pp. of *permeare,* fr. *per-* through + *meare* to go, pass; akin to MW *mynet* to go, OSlav *minoti* to pass] *vi* **:** to diffuse through or penetrate something ~ *vt* **1 :** to spread or diffuse through <a room *permeated* with tobacco smoke> **2 :** to pass through the pores or interstices of — **per·me·ative** \-ˌāt-iv\ *adj*
per·me·ation \ˌpər-mē-ˈā-shən\ *n* **1 :** the quality or state of being permeated **2 :** the action or process of permeating
per men·sem \(ˌ)pər-ˈmen(t)-səm\ *adv* [ML] **:** by the month
Perm·ian \ˈpər-mē-ən, ˈper-\ *adj* [*Perm,* region in eastern Russia] **:** of, relating to, or being the last period of the Paleozoic era or the corresponding system of rocks — **Permian** *n*
per mill \(ˌ)pər-ˈmil\ *adv* [*per* + L *mille* thousand — more at MILE] **:** per thousand — **per·mil·lage** \(ˌ)pər-ˈmil-ij\ *n*
per·mis·si·ble \pər-ˈmis-ə-bəl\ *adj* [ME, fr. ML *permissibilis,* fr. L *permissus,* pp.] **:** that may be permitted **:** ALLOWABLE — **per·mis·si·bil·i·ty** \-ˌmis-ə-ˈbil-ət-ē\ *n* — **per·mis·si·ble·ness** \-ˈmis-ə-bəl-nəs\ *n* — **per·mis·si·bly** \-blē\ *adv*
per·mis·sion \pər-ˈmish-ən\ *n* [ME, fr. MF, fr. L *permission-, permissio,* fr. *permissus,* pp. of *permittere*] **1 :** the act of permitting **2 :** formal consent **:** AUTHORIZATION
syn PERMISSION, LEAVE, SUFFERANCE *shared meaning element* **:** sanction to act or to do something granted by one in authority ***ant*** prohibition
per·mis·sive \pər-ˈmis-iv\ *adj* [F *permissif,* fr. L *permissus,* pp.] **1** *archaic* **:** granted on sufferance **:** TOLERATED **2 :** granting or tending to grant permission **:** TOLERANT **3 :** allowing discretion **:** OPTIONAL <reduced the ~ retirement age from 65 to 62> — **per·mis·sive·ly** *adv* — **per·mis·sive·ness** *n*
1**per·mit** \pər-ˈmit\ *vb* **per·mit·ted; per·mit·ting** [L *permittere* to let through, permit, fr. *per-* through + *mittere* to let go, send — more at PER-, SMITE] *vt* **1 :** to consent to expressly or formally <~ access to records> **2 :** to give leave **:** AUTHORIZE **3 :** to make possible ~ *vi* **:** to give an opportunity **:** ALLOW <if time ~*s*> ***syn*** see LET ***ant*** prohibit, forbid — **per·mit·ter** *n*
2**per·mit** \ˈpər-ˌmit, pər-ˈ\ *n* **1 :** a written warrant or license granted by one having authority <a gun ~> **2 :** PERMISSION
per·mit·tiv·i·ty \ˌpər-ˌmi-ˈtiv-ət-ē, -mə-\ *n* [1*permit* + *-ive* + *-ity*] **:** the ability of a dielectric to store electrical potential energy under the influence of an electric field measured by the ratio of the capacitance of a condenser with the material as dielectric to its capacitance with vacuum as dielectric
per·mu·ta·tion \ˌpər-myu̇-ˈtā-shən\ *n* [ME *permutacioun* exchange, transformation, fr. MF *permutation,* fr. L *permutation-, permutatio,* fr. *permutatus,* pp. of *permutare*] **1 :** often major or fundamental change (as in character or condition) based primarily on rearrangement of existent elements <land-owners and peasants . . . in the ~*s* of their tortured interdependence —P. E. Mosley> **2 a :** the act or process of changing the lineal order of an ordered set of objects **b :** an ordered arrangement of a set of objects ***syn*** see CHANGE — **per·mu·ta·tion·al** \-shnəl, -shən-ᵊl\ *adj*
permutation group *n* **:** a group whose elements are permutations and in which the product of two permutations is a permutation whose effect is the same as the successive application of the first two
per·mute \pər-ˈmyüt\ *vt* **per·mut·ed; per·mut·ing** [ME *permuten,* fr. MF or L; MF *permuter,* fr. L *permutare,* fr. *per-* + *mutare* to change — more at MISS] **:** to change the order or arrangement of; *esp* **:** to arrange in all possible ways
per·ni·cious \pər-ˈnish-əs\ *adj* [MF *pernicieus,* fr. L *perniciosus,* fr. *pernicies* destruction, fr. *per-* + *nec-, nex* violent death — more at NOXIOUS] **1 :** highly injurious or destructive **:** DEADLY **2** *archaic* **:** WICKED — **per·ni·cious·ly** *adv* — **per·ni·cious·ness** *n*
syn PERNICIOUS, BANEFUL, NOXIOUS, DELETERIOUS, DETRIMENTAL *shared meaning element* **:** exceedingly harmful ***ant*** innocuous
pernicious anemia *n* **:** a severe hyperchromic anemia marked by a progressive decrease in number and increase in size of the red blood cells and by pallor, weakness, and gastrointestinal and nervous disturbances and associated with reduced ability to absorb vitamin B_{12} due to the absence of intrinsic factor
per·nick·e·ty \pər-ˈnik-ət-ē\ *var of* PERSNICKETY
Per·nod \per-ˈnō, ˌpər-\ *trademark* — used for an aromatic French liqueur
pe·ro·ne·al \ˌper-ō-ˈnē-əl, pə-ˈrō-nē-\ *adj* [NL *peroneus,* fr. *perone* fibula, fr. Gk *peronē,* lit., pin; akin to L *per* through — more at FOR] **:** of, relating to, or located near the fibula
per·oral \(ˌ)pər-ˈōr-əl, pe(ə)r-, -ˈȯr-, -ˈär-\ *adj* [ISV, fr. L *per* through + *or-, os* mouth — more at ORAL] **:** occurring through or by way of the mouth — **per·oral·ly** \-ə-lē\ *adv*
per·orate \ˈper-ər-ˌāt *also* ˈpər-\ *vi* **-orat·ed; -orat·ing** [L *peroratus,* pp. of *perorare* to declaim at length, wind up an oration, fr. *per-* through + *orare* to speak — more at PER-, ORATION] **1 :** to deliver a long or grandiloquent oration **2 :** to make a peroration
per·ora·tion \ˌper-ər-ˈā-shən, ˌpər-\ *n* **1 :** the concluding part of a discourse and esp. an oration **2 :** a highly rhetorical speech — **per·ora·tion·al** \ˌper-ər-ˈā-shnəl, pər-, -shən-ᵊl\ *adj*
per·ox·i·dase \pə-ˈräk-sə-ˌdās, -ˌdāz\ *n* **:** an enzyme that catalyzes the oxidation of various substances by peroxides
1**per·ox·ide** \pə-ˈräk-ˌsīd\ *n* [ISV] **:** an oxide containing a high proportion of oxygen; *esp* **:** a compound (as hydrogen peroxide) in which oxygen is visualized as joined to oxygen — **per·ox·id·ic** \-ˌräk-ˈsid-ik\ *adj*
2**peroxide** *vt* **-id·ed; -id·ing** **:** to treat with a peroxide; *esp* **:** to bleach (hair) with hydrogen peroxide
per·oxi·some \pə-ˈräk-sə-ˌsōm\ *n* [*peroxi*de + 3*-some*] **:** a cytoplasmic cell organelle containing enzymes for the production and decomposition of hydrogen peroxide — **per·oxi·som·al** \-ˌräk-sə-ˈsō-məl\ *adj*
per·oxy- \pə-ˈräk-si\ *comb form* [ISV *per-* + *oxy-*] **:** containing the bivalent group O–O
perp *abbr* perpendicular
per·pend \(ˌ)pər-ˈpend\ *vb* [L *perpendere,* fr. *per-* thoroughly + *pendere* to weigh — more at PER-, PENDANT] *vt* **:** to reflect on carefully **:** PONDER ~ *vi* **:** to be attentive **:** REFLECT
1**per·pen·dic·u·lar** \ˌpər-pən-ˈdik-yə-lər\ *adj* [ME *perpendiculer,* fr. MF, fr. L *perpendicularis,* fr. *perpendiculum* plumb line, fr. *per-* + *pendēre* to hang — more at PENDANT] **1 a :** standing at right angles to the plane of the horizon **:** exactly upright **b :** being at right angles to a given line or plane **2 :** extremely steep **:** PRECIPITOUS **3 :** of or relating to a medieval English Gothic style of architecture in which vertical lines predominate **4 :** relating to, uniting, or consisting of individuals of dissimilar type or on different levels ***syn*** see VERTICAL ***ant*** horizontal — **per·pen·dic·u·lar·i·ty** \-ˌdik-yə-ˈlar-ət-ē\ *n* — **per·pen·dic·u·lar·ly** \-ˈdik-yə-lər-lē\ *adv*
2**perpendicular** *n* **1 :** a line at right angles to the plane of the horizon or to another line or surface **2 :** an extremely steep face (as of a cliff)
per·pe·trate \ˈpər-pə-ˌtrāt\ *vt* **-trat·ed; -trat·ing** [L *perpetratus,* pp. of *perpetrare,* fr. *per-* through + *patrare* to accomplish] **:** to bring about or carry out (as a crime) **:** COMMIT — **per·pe·tra·tion** \ˌpər-pə-ˈtrā-shən\ *n* — **per·pe·tra·tor** \ˈpər-pə-ˌtrāt-ər\ *n*
per·pet·u·al \pər-ˈpech-(ə-)wəl, -ˈpech-əl\ *adj* [ME *perpetuel,* fr. MF, fr. L *perpetuus,* fr. *per-* through + *petere* to go to — more at FEATHER] **1 a :** continuing forever **:** EVERLASTING **b** (1) **:** valid for all time (2) **:** holding (as an office) for life or for an unlimited time **2 :** occurring continually **:** indefinitely long-continued **3 :** blooming continuously throughout the season ***syn*** see CONTINUOUS ***ant*** transitory, transient — **per·pet·u·al·ly** \-ē\ *adv*
perpetual calendar *n* **1 :** a table for finding the day of the week for any one of a wide range of dates **2 :** a calendar having the years uniform in the correspondence of days and dates
perpetual check *n* **:** an endless succession of checks to which an opponent's king may be subjected to force a draw in chess
per·pet·u·ate \pər-ˈpech-ə-ˌwāt\ *vt* **-at·ed; -at·ing** [L *perpetuatus,* pp. of *perpetuare,* fr. *perpetuus*] **:** to make perpetual or cause to last indefinitely <~ the species> — **per·pet·u·a·tion** \-ˌpech-ə-ˈwā-shən\ *n* — **per·pet·u·a·tor** \-ˈpech-ə-ˌwāt-ər\ *n*
per·pe·tu·i·ty \ˌpər-pə-ˈt(y)ü-ət-ē\ *n, pl* **-ities** [ME *perpetuite,* fr. MF *perpetuité,* fr. L *perpetuitat-, perpetuitas,* fr. *perpetuus*] **1 :** endless time **:** ETERNITY **2 :** the quality or state of being perpetual <bequeathed to them in ~> **3 a :** the condition of an estate limited so that it will not take effect or vest within the period fixed by law **b :** an estate so limited **4 :** an annuity payable forever
per·phe·na·zine \(ˌ)pər-ˈfē-nə-ˌzēn, -ˈfen-ə-\ *n* [blend of *piperazine* and *phen-*] **:** a tranquilizing drug $C_{21}H_{26}ClN_3OS$ that is used to control tension, anxiety, and agitation esp. in psychotic conditions
per·plex \pər-ˈpleks\ *vt* [obs. *perplex,* adj., involved, perplexed, fr. L *perplexus,* fr. *per-* thoroughly + *plexus* involved, fr. pp. of *plectere* to braid, twine — more at PER-, PLY] **1 :** to make unable to grasp something clearly or to think logically and decisively about something <her attitude ~*es* me> <a ~*ing* problem> **2 :** to make intricate or involved **:** COMPLICATE ***syn*** see PUZZLE
per·plexed \-ˈplekst\ *adj* **1 :** filled with uncertainty **:** PUZZLED **2 :** full of difficulty — **per·plexed·ly** \-ˈplek-səd-lē, -ˈpleks-tlē\ *adv*
per·plex·i·ty \pər-ˈplek-sət-ē\ *n, pl* **-ties** [ME *perplexite,* fr. OF *perplexité,* fr. LL *perplexitat-, perplexitas,* fr. L *perplexus*] **1 :** the state of being perplexed **:** BEWILDERMENT **2 :** something that perplexes **3 :** ENTANGLEMENT
per·qui·site \ˈpər-kwə-zət\ *n* [ME, property acquired by other means than inheritance, fr. ML *perquisitum,* fr. neut. of *perquisitus,* pp. of *perquirere* to purchase, acquire, fr. L, to search for thoroughly, fr. *per-* thoroughly + *quaerere* to seek] **1 :** a privilege, gain, or profit incidental to regular salary or wages; *esp* **:** one expected or promised **2 :** GRATUITY, TIP **3 :** something held or claimed as an exclusive right or possession <concepts . . . not the ~*s* of any particular groups —Gilbert Ryle>
per·ron \ˈper-ən, pe-rōⁿ\ *n* [F, fr. OF, aug. of *perre, pierre* rock, stone, fr. L *petra,* fr. Gk] **:** an outdoor stairway leading up to a building entrance or a platform at its top

per·ry \'per-ē\ *n* [ME *peirrie,* fr. MF *peré,* fr. (assumed) VL *piratum,* fr. L *pirum* pear] **:** the expressed juice of pears often made alcoholic by fermentation

pers *abbr* person; personal; personnel

Pers *abbr* Persia; Persian

per·salt \'pər-ˌsȯlt\ *n* **1 :** a salt containing a relatively large proportion of the acidic element or group **2 :** a salt of a peracid

perse \'pərs\ *adj* [ME *pers,* fr. MF, fr. ML *persus*] **:** dark grayish blue and resembling indigo

per se \(ˌ)pər-'sā *also* pe(ə)r-'sā *or* (ˌ)pər-'sē\ *adv* [L] **:** by, of, or in itself or oneself or themselves **:** as such **:** INTRINSICALLY

per second per second *adv* **:** per second every second — used of a rate of acceleration over an indefinite period

per·se·cute \'pər-si-ˌkyüt\ *vt* **-cut·ed; -cut·ing** [MF *persecuter,* back-formation fr. *persecuteur* persecutor, fr. LL *persecutor,* fr. *persecutus,* pp. of *persequi* to persecute, fr. L, to pursue, fr. *per-* through + *sequi* to follow — more at SUE] **1 :** to harass in a manner designed to injure, grieve, or afflict; *specif* **:** to cause to suffer because of belief **2 :** to annoy with persistent or urgent approaches (as attacks, pleas, or importunities) **:** PESTER — **per·se·cu·tive** \-ˌkyüt-iv\ *adj* — **per·se·cu·tor** \-ˌkyüt-ər\ *n* — **per·se·cu·to·ry** \-kyü-ˌtōr-ē, -ˌtȯr-; -ˌkyüt-ə-rē\ *adj*

per·se·cu·tion \ˌpər-si-'kyü-shən\ *n* **1 :** the act or practice of persecuting esp. those who differ in origin, religion, or social outlook **2 :** the condition of being persecuted, harassed, or annoyed

Per·se·id \'pər-sē-əd\ *n* [L *Perseus*; fr. their appearing to radiate from a point in Perseus] **:** any of a group of meteors that appear annually about August 11

Per·seph·o·ne \pər-'sef-ə-nē\ *n* [L, fr. Gk *Persephonē*] **:** a daughter of Zeus and Demeter abducted by Pluto to reign with him over the underworld

Per·seus \'pər-ˌsüs, -sē-əs\ *n* [L, fr. Gk] **1 :** the son of Zeus and Danaë and slayer of Medusa **2** [L (gen. *Persei*), fr. Gk] **:** a northern constellation between Taurus and Cassiopeia

per·se·ver·ance \ˌpər-sə-'vir-ən(t)s\ *n* **:** the action or condition or an instance of persevering **:** STEADFASTNESS

per·sev·er·a·tion \pər-ˌsev-ə-'rā-shən\ *n* [L *perseveration-, perseveratio,* fr. *perseveratus,* pp. of *perseverare*] **:** continuation of something (as repetition of a word) usu. to an exceptional degree or beyond a desired point

per·se·vere \ˌpər-sə-'vi(ə)r\ *vi* **-vered; -ver·ing** [ME *perseveren,* fr. MF *perseverer,* fr. L *perseverare,* fr. *per-* through + *severus* severe] **:** to persist in a state, enterprise, or undertaking in spite of counter influences, opposition, or discouragement

Per·sian \'pər-zhən, *esp Brit* -shən\ *n* **1 :** one of the people of Persia: as **a :** one of the ancient Iranian Caucasians who under Cyrus and his successors became the dominant Asian race **b :** a member of one of the peoples forming the modern Iranian nationality **2 a :** any of several Iranian languages dominant in Persia at different periods **b :** the modern language of Iran and western Afghanistan used also in Pakistan and by Indian Muslims as a literary language — see INDO-EUROPEAN LANGUAGES table **3 :** a thin soft silk formerly used esp. for linings — **Persian** *adj*

Persian cat *n* **:** a stocky round-headed domestic cat that has long and silky fur and is the long-haired cat of shows and fanciers

Persian lamb *n* **1 :** the young of the karakul sheep that furnishes skins used in furriery **2 :** a pelt that is obtained from karakul lambs older than those yielding broadtail and that is characterized by very silky tightly curled fur

per·si·flage \'pər-si-ˌfläzh, 'per-\ *n* [F, fr. *persifler* to banter, fr. *per-* thoroughly + *siffler* to whistle, hiss, boo fr. L *sibilare,* of imit. origin] **:** frivolous bantering talk **:** light raillery

per·sim·mon \pər-'sim-ən\ *n* [of Algonquian origin; akin to Cree *pasiminan* dried fruit] **1 :** any of a genus (*Diospyros*) of trees of the ebony family with hard fine wood, oblong leaves, and small bell-shaped white flowers; *esp* **:** an American tree (*D. virginiana*) or a Japanese tree (*D. kaki*) **2 :** the usu. orange several-seeded globular berry of a persimmon that is edible when fully ripe but usu. extremely astringent when unripe

per·sist \pər-'sist, -'zist\ *vi* [MF *persister,* fr. L *persistere,* fr. *per-* + *sistere* to take a stand, stand firm; akin to L *stare* to stand — more at STAND] **1 :** to go on resolutely or stubbornly in spite of opposition, importunity, or warning **2** *obs* **:** to remain unchanged or fixed in a specified character, condition, or position **3 :** to be insistent in the repetition or pressing of an utterance (as a question or an opinion) **4 :** to continue to exist esp. past a usual, expected, or normal time ***syn*** see CONTINUE — **per·sist·er** *n*

per·sis·tence \pər-'sis-tən(t)s, -'zis-\ *n* **1 :** the action or fact of persisting **2 :** the quality or state of being persistent; *esp* **:** PERSEVERANCE

per·sis·ten·cy \-tən-sē\ *n* **:** PERSISTENCE 2

per·sis·tent \-tənt\ *adj* [L *persistent-, persistens,* prp. of *persistere*] **1 a :** continuing or inclined to persist in a course **b :** continuing to exist in spite of interference or treatment <a ~ cough> **2 :** existing for a long or longer than usual time or continuously: as **a :** retained beyond the usual period <a ~ leaf> **b :** continuing without change in function or structure <~ gills> **c :** effective in the open for an appreciable time usu. through slow volatilizing <mustard gas is ~> **d :** degraded only slowly by the environment <~ pesticides> **e :** remaining infective for a relatively long time in a vector after an initial period of incubation <~ viruses> — **per·sis·tent·ly** *adv*

per·snick·e·ty \pər-'snik-ət-ē\ *adj* [alter. of *pernickety,* perh. alter. of *particular*] **1 a :** fussy about small details **:** FASTIDIOUS <a ~ teacher> **b :** having the characteristics of a snob **2 :** requiring great precision **:** EXACTING <a ~ job>

per·son \'pərs-ᵊn\ *n* [ME, fr. OF *persone,* fr. L *persona* actor's mask, character in a play, person, prob. fr. Etruscan *phersu* mask] **1 :** an individual human being; *esp* **:** a human being as distinguished from an animal or thing **2 :** a character or part in or as if in a play **:** GUISE **3 a :** one of the three modes of being in the Trinitarian Godhead as understood by Christians **b :** the unitary personality of Christ that unites the divine and human natures **4 a** *archaic* **:** bodily appearance **b :** the body of a human being <unlawful search of the ~> **5 :** the individual personality of a human being **:** SELF **6 :** one (as a human being, a partnership, or a corporation) that is recognized by law as the subject of rights and duties **7 :** reference of a segment of discourse to the speaker, to one spoken to, or to one spoken of as indicated by means of certain pronouns or in many languages by verb inflection — **per·son·hood** \-ˌhu̇d\ *n* — **in person :** in one's bodily presence

per·so·na \pər-'sō-nə, -ˌnä\ *n* [L] **1 per·so·nae** \-(ˌ)nē, -ˌnī\ *pl* **:** the characters of a fictional presentation (as a novel or play) <comic *personae*> **2** *pl* **personas** [NL, fr. L] **:** an individual's social facade or front that esp. in the analytic psychology of C. G. Jung reflects the role in life the individual is playing — compare ANIMA

per·son·able \'pərs-nə-bəl, -ᵊn-ə-bəl\ *adj* **:** pleasing in person **:** ATTRACTIVE — **per·son·able·ness** *n*

per·son·age \'pərs-nij, -ᵊn-ij\ *n* **1 :** a person of rank, note, or distinction; *esp* **:** one distinguished for presence and personal power **2 :** a dramatic, fictional, or historical character; *also* **:** IMPERSONATION **3 :** a human individual **:** PERSON

per·so·na gra·ta \pər-ˌsō-nə-'grät-ə, -'grät-\ *adj* [NL, acceptable person] **:** being personally acceptable or welcome

[1]**per·son·al** \'pərs-nəl, -ᵊn-əl\ *adj* [ME, fr. MF, fr. LL *personalis,* fr. L *persona*] **1 :** of, relating to, or affecting a person **:** PRIVATE <done purely for ~ financial gain> **2 a :** done in person without the intervention of another; *also* **:** proceeding from a single person **b :** carried on between individuals directly <a ~ interview> **3 :** relating to the person or body **4 :** relating to an individual or his character, conduct, motives, or private affairs often in an offensive manner <a ~ insult> **5 :** being rational and self-conscious <~, responsive government is still possible —John Fischer> **6 :** of, relating to, or constituting personal property <a ~ estate> **7 :** denoting grammatical person

[2]**personal** *n* **1 :** a short newspaper paragraph relating to the activities of a person or a group or to personal matters **2 :** a short personal or private communication in a special column of the classified ads section of a newspaper or periodical

personal effects *n pl* **:** privately owned items (as clothing and toilet articles) normally worn or carried on the person

personal equation *n* **:** variation (as in observation) occasioned by the personal peculiarities of an individual; *also* **:** a correction or allowance made for such variation

personal foul *n* **:** a foul in a game (as basketball) involving usu. physical contact with or deliberate roughing of an opponent — compare TECHNICAL FOUL

per·son·al·ism \'pərs-nə-ˌliz-əm, -ᵊn-ə-\ *n* **:** a doctrine emphasizing the significance, uniqueness, and inviolability of personality — **per·son·al·ist** \-ləst\ *n or adj* — **per·son·al·is·tic** \ˌpərs-nə-'lis-tik, -ᵊn-ə-\ *adj*

per·son·al·i·ty \ˌpərs-ᵊn-'al-ət-ē, ˌpər-'snal-\ *n, pl* **-ties** [ME *personalite,* fr. LL *personalitat-, personalitas,* fr. *personalis*] **1 a :** the quality or state of being a person **b :** personal existence **2 a :** the condition or fact of relating to a particular person; *specif* **:** the condition of referring directly to or being aimed disparagingly or hostilely at an individual **b :** an offensively personal remark <indulgence in *personalities*> **3 a :** the complex of characteristics that distinguishes an individual or a nation or group **b** (1) **:** the totality of an individual's behavioral and emotional tendencies (2) **:** the organization of the individual's distinguishing character traits, attitudes, or habits **4 a :** distinction or excellence of personal and social traits; *also* **:** a person having such quality **b :** a person of importance, prominence, renown, or notoriety <a well-known stage ~> ***syn*** see DISPOSITION

personality inventory *n* **:** any of several tests that attempt to characterize the personality of an individual by objective scoring of replies to a large number of questions concerning his own behavior — compare MINNESOTA MULTIPHASIC PERSONALITY INVENTORY

personality test *n* **:** any of several tests that consist of standardized tasks designed to determine various aspects of the personality or the emotional status of the individual examined

per·son·al·ize \'pərs-nə-ˌlīz, -ᵊn-ə-\ *vt* **-ized; -iz·ing 1 :** PERSONIFY **2 :** to make personal or individual; *specif* **:** to mark as the property of a particular person <*personalized* stationery> — **per·son·al·iza·tion** \ˌpərs-nə-lə-'zā-shən, -ᵊn-ə-\ *n*

per·son·al·ly \'pərs-nə-lē, -ᵊn-ə-\ *adv* **1 :** in person <attend to the matter ~> **2 :** as a person **:** in personality <~ attractive but not very trustworthy> **3 :** for oneself **:** as far as oneself is concerned

personal pronoun *n* **:** a pronoun (as *I, you,* or *they*) that expresses a distinction of person

personal property *n* **:** property other than real property consisting of things temporary or movable **:** CHATTELS

personal shopper *n* **:** a person (as a store employee) who assists shoppers in choosing their purchases or who personally selects merchandise to fill telephone or mail orders

personal tax *n* **:** DIRECT TAX

per·son·al·ty \'pərs-nəl-tē, -ᵊn-əl-\ *n, pl* **-ties** [AF *personalté,* fr. LL *personalitat-, personalitas* personality] **:** PERSONAL PROPERTY

per·so·na non gra·ta \pər-ˌsō-nə-ˌnän-'grat-ə, -'grät-\ *adj* [NL, person not acceptable] **:** being personally unacceptable or unwelcome

[1]**per·so·nate** \'pərs-nət, -ᵊn-ət\ *adj* [L *personatus* masked, fr. *persona* mask] **1** *of a bilabiate corolla* **:** having the throat nearly closed by a palate **2 :** having a personate bilabiate corolla <a ~ flower>

[2]**per·son·ate** \'pərs-ᵊn-ˌāt\ *vt* **-at·ed; -at·ing 1 a :** IMPERSONATE, REPRESENT **b :** to assume without authority some character or

capacity with fraudulent intent **2 :** to invest with personality or personal characteristics <*personating* their gods ridiculous, and themselves past shame —John Milton> — **per·son·ation** \ˌpərs-ᵊn-ˈā-shən\ *n* — **per·son·ative** \ˈpərs-ᵊn-ˌāt-iv\ *adj* — **per·son·a·tor** \-ˌāt-ər\ *n*

per·son·i·fi·ca·tion \pər-ˌsän-ə-fə-ˈkā-shən\ *n* **1 :** attribution of personal qualities; *esp* **:** representation of a thing or abstraction as a person or by the human form **2 :** a divinity or imaginary being representing a thing or abstraction **3 :** EMBODIMENT, INCARNATION

per·son·i·fy \pər-ˈsän-ə-ˌfī\ *vt* **-fied; -fy·ing** **1 :** to conceive of or represent as a person or as having human qualities or powers **2 :** to be the embodiment or personification of **:** INCARNATE <a man who *personified* kindness> — **per·son·i·fi·er** \-ˌfī(-ə)r\ *n*

per·son·nel \ˌpərs-ᵊn-ˈel\ *n* [F, fr. G *personale, personal,* fr. ML *personale,* fr. LL, neut. of *personalis* personal] **1 a :** a body of persons usu. employed (as in a factory, office, or organization) **b** **personnel** *pl* **:** PERSONS **2 :** a division of an organization concerned with personnel

[1]**per·spec·tive** \pər-ˈspek-tiv\ *n* [ML *perspectivum,* fr. neut. of *perspectivus* of sight, optical, fr. L *perspectus,* pp. of *perspicere* to look through, see clearly, fr. *per-* through + *specere* to look — more at PER-, SPY] **:** an optical glass (as a telescope)

[2]**perspective** *adj* [ME, fr. ML *perspectivus*] **1** *obs* **:** aiding the vision <his eyes should be like unto the wrong end of a ~ glass —Alexander Pope> **2 :** of, relating to, employing, or seen in perspective <~ drawing> — **per·spec·tive·ly** *adv*

[3]**perspective** *n* [MF, prob. modif. of OIt *prospettiva,* fr. *prospetto* view, prospect, fr. L *prospectus* — more at PROSPECT] **1 a :** the technique or process of representing on a plane or curved surface the spatial relation of objects as they might appear to the eye; *specif* **:** LINEAR PERSPECTIVE **b :** the technique of adjusting the apparent sources of sounds (as on a radio program) into a natural-seeming and integrated whole **2 a :** the interrelation in which a subject or its parts are mentally viewed **:** CONFIGURATION **b :** the capacity to view things in their true relations or relative importance <by failing to maintain an historical ~ . . . they . . . fail to see the solution —Herbert Ratner> **3 a** (1) **:** a visible scene; *esp* **:** one giving a distinctive impression of distance **:** VISTA (2) **:** a mental view or prospect **b :** a picture in linear perspective **4 :** the appearance to the eye of objects in respect to their relative distance and positions

per·spi·ca·cious \ˌpər-spə-ˈkā-shəs\ *adj* [L *perspicac-, perspicax,* fr. *perspicere*] **:** of acute mental vision or discernment **:** KEEN ***syn*** see SHREWD ***ant*** dull — **per·spi·ca·cious·ly** *adv* — **per·spi·ca·cious·ness** *n* — **per·spi·cac·i·ty** \-ˈkas-ət-ē\ *n*

per·spic·u·ous \pər-ˈspik-yə-wəs\ *adj* [L *perspicuus* transparent, perspicuous, fr. *perspicere*] **:** plain to the understanding esp. because of clarity and precision of presentation <a ~ argument> ***syn*** see CLEAR — **per·spi·cu·ity** \ˌpər-spə-ˈkyü-ət-ē\ *n* — **per·spic·u·ous·ly** \pər-ˈspik-yə-wə-slē\ *adv* — **per·spic·u·ous·ness** *n*

per·spi·ra·tion \ˌpər-spə-ˈrā-shən\ *n* **1 :** the action or process of perspiring **2 :** a saline fluid secreted by the sweat glands **:** SWEAT

per·spi·ra·to·ry \pər-ˈspī-rə-ˌtōr-ē, ˈpər-sp(ə-)rə-, -ˌtȯr-\ *adj* **:** of, relating to, secreting, or inducing perspiration

per·spire \pər-ˈspī(ə)r\ *vi* **per·spired; per·spir·ing** [F *perspirer,* fr. MF, fr. L *per-* through + *spirare* to blow, breathe — more at PER-, SPIRIT] **:** to emit matter through the skin; *specif* **:** to secrete and emit perspiration

per·suad·able \pər-ˈswād-ə-bəl\ *adj* **:** capable of being persuaded

per·suade \pər-ˈswād\ *vt* **per·suad·ed; per·suad·ing** [L *persuadēre,* fr. *per-* thoroughly + *suadēre* to advise, urge — more at SUASION] **1 :** to move by argument, entreaty, or expostulation to a belief, position, or course of action **2 :** to plead with **:** URGE **3 :** to get with difficulty (as by coaxing) <finally *persuaded* an answer out of him> ***syn*** see INDUCE — **per·suad·er** *n*

per·sua·si·ble \-ˈswā-zə-bəl, -ˈswā-sə-\ *adj* [MF, fr. L *persuasibilis* persuasive, fr. *persuasus*] **:** PERSUADABLE

per·sua·sion \pər-ˈswā-zhən\ *n* [ME *persuasioun,* fr. MF or L; MF *persuasion,* fr. L *persuasion-, persuasio,* fr. *persuasus,* pp. of *persuadēre*] **1 a :** the act or process or an instance of persuading **b :** a persuading argument **:** INDUCEMENT **c :** the ability to persuade **:** PERSUASIVENESS **2 :** the condition of being persuaded **3 a :** an opinion held with complete assurance <despite your arguments I remain of the same ~ as before> **b :** a system of religious beliefs; *also* **:** a group adhering to a particular system of beliefs **4 :** KIND, SORT ***syn*** see OPINION

per·sua·sive \-ˈswā-siv, -ziv\ *adj* **:** tending to persuade — **per·sua·sive·ly** *adv* — **per·sua·sive·ness** *n*

[1]**pert** \ˈpərt\ *adj* [ME, open, bold, pert, modif. of OF *apert,* fr. L *apertus* open, fr. pp. of *aperire* to open] **1 a :** saucily free and forward **:** flippantly cocky and assured **b :** being trim and chic **:** JAUNTY <a ~ little hat> **c :** piquantly stimulating <is a ~ notion and one to fascinate the attention —G. J. Nathan> **2 :** LIVELY, VIVACIOUS ***syn*** see SAUCY — **pert·ly** *adv* — **pert·ness** *n*

[2]**pert** *abbr* pertaining

per·tain \pər-ˈtān\ *vi* [ME *perteinen,* fr. MF *partenir,* fr. L *pertinēre* to reach to, belong, fr. *per-* through + *tenēre* to hold] **1 a** (1) **:** to belong as a part, member, accessory, or product (2) **:** to belong as an attribute, feature, or function <the destruction and havoc ~*ing* to war> (3) **:** to belong as a duty or right <responsibilities that ~ to fatherhood> **b :** to be appropriate to something <the criteria . . . will be different from those that ~ elsewhere —J. B. Conant> **2 :** to have reference <books ~*ing* to birds>

per·ti·na·cious \ˌpərt-ᵊn-ˈā-shəs\ *adj* [L *pertinac-, pertinax,* fr. *per-* thoroughly + *tenac-, tenax* tenacious, fr. *tenēre*] **1 a :** adhering resolutely to an opinion, purpose, or design **b :** perversely persistent **2 :** stubbornly unyielding or tenacious ***syn*** see OBSTINATE — **per·ti·na·cious·ly** *adv* — **per·ti·na·cious·ness** *n* — **per·ti·nac·i·ty** \-ˈas-ət-ē\ *n*

per·ti·nence \ˈpərt-ᵊn-ən(t)s, ˈpərt-nən(t)s\ *n* **:** the quality or state of being pertinent **:** RELEVANCE

per·ti·nen·cy \-ᵊn-ən-sē, -nən-sē\ *n* **:** PERTINENCE

per·ti·nent \ˈpərt-ᵊn-ənt, ˈpərt-nənt\ *adj* [ME, fr. MF, fr. L *pertinent-, pertinens,* prp. of *pertinēre*] **:** having a clear decisive relevance to the matter in hand **:** highly significant ***syn*** see RELEVANT ***ant*** impertinent, foreign — **per·ti·nent·ly** *adv*

per·turb \pər-ˈtərb\ *vt* [ME *perturben,* fr. MF *perturber,* fr. L *perturbare* to throw into confusion, fr. *per-* + *turbare* to disturb — more at TURBID] **1 :** to disturb greatly in mind **:** DISQUIET **2 :** to throw into confusion **:** DISORDER **3 :** to cause (a celestial body) to deviate from a theoretically regular orbital motion ***syn*** see DISCOMPOSE — **per·turb·able** \-ˈtər-bə-bəl\ *adj*

per·tur·ba·tion \ˌpərt-ər-ˈbā-shən, ˌpər-ˌtər-\ *n* **1 :** the action of perturbing **:** the state of being perturbed **2 :** a disturbance of the regular and usu. elliptic course of motion of a celestial body that is produced by some force additional to that which causes its regular motion — **per·tur·ba·tion·al** \-shnəl, -shən-ᵊl\ *adj*

per·tus·sis \pər-ˈtəs-əs\ *n* [NL, fr. L *per-* thoroughly + *tussis* cough] **:** WHOOPING COUGH

Peru balsam *n* **:** BALSAM OF PERU

pe·ruke \pə-ˈrük\ *n* [MF *perruque,* fr. OIt *parrucca, perrucca* hair, wig] **:** WIG; *specif* **:** one of a type popular from the 17th to the early 19th century

peruke

pe·ruse \pə-ˈrüz\ *vt* **pe·rused; pe·rus·ing** [ME *perusen,* prob. fr. L *per-* thoroughly + ME *usen* to use] **1 :** to examine or consider with attention and in detail **:** STUDY **2 :** READ — **pe·rus·al** \-ˈrü-zəl\ *n* — **pe·rus·er** *n*

Pe·ru·vi·an bark \pə-ˌrü-vē-ən-\ *n* [NL *Peruvia* Peru, country of So. America, fr. Sp *Perú*] **:** CINCHONA 2

per·vade \pər-ˈvād\ *vt* **per·vad·ed; per·vad·ing** [L *pervadere* to go through, pervade, fr. *per-* through + *vadere* to go — more at PER-, WADE] **:** to become diffused throughout every part of — **per·va·sion** \-ˈvā-zhən\ *n* — **per·va·sive** \-ˈvā-siv, -ziv\ *adj* — **per·va·sive·ly** *adv* — **per·va·sive·ness** *n*

per·verse \(ˌ)pər-ˈvərs, ˈpər-ˌ\ *adj* [ME, fr. L *perversus,* fr. pp. of *pervertere*] **1 a :** turned away from what is right or good **:** CORRUPT **b :** INCORRECT, IMPROPER **c :** contrary to the evidence or the direction of the judge on a point of law <~ verdict> **2 a :** obstinate in opposing what is right, reasonable, or accepted **:** WRONGHEADED **b :** arising from or indicative of stubbornness or obstinacy **3 :** marked by peevishness or petulance **:** CRANKY ***syn*** see CONTRARY — **per·verse·ly** *adv* — **per·verse·ness** *n* — **per·ver·si·ty** \pər-ˈvər-sət-ē, -stē\ *n*

per·ver·sion \pər-ˈvər-zhən, -shən\ *n* **1 :** the action of perverting **:** the condition of being perverted **2 :** a perverted form; *esp* **:** an aberrant sexual practice esp. when habitual and preferred to normal coitus

per·ver·sive \-ˈvər-siv, -ziv\ *adj* **1 :** that perverts or tends to pervert **2 :** arising from or indicative of perversion

[1]**per·vert** \pər-ˈvərt\ *vt* [ME *perverten,* fr. MF *pervertir,* fr. L *pervertere* to overturn, corrupt, pervert, fr. *per-* thoroughly + *vertere* to turn — more at PER-, WORTH] **1 a :** to cause to turn aside or away from what is good or true or morally right **:** CORRUPT **b :** to cause to turn aside or away from what is generally done or accepted **:** MISDIRECT **2 a :** to divert to a wrong end or purpose **:** MISUSE **b :** to twist the meaning or sense of **:** MISINTERPRET ***syn*** see DEBASE — **per·vert·er** *n*

[2]**per·vert** \ˈpər-ˌvərt\ *n* **:** one that has been perverted; *specif* **:** one given to some form of sexual perversion

per·vert·ed \pər-ˈvərt-əd\ *adj* **1 :** CORRUPT **2 :** marked by perversion — **per·vert·ed·ly** *adv* — **per·vert·ed·ness** *n*

per·vi·ous \ˈpər-vē-əs\ *adj* [L *pervius,* fr. *per-* through + *via* way — more at PER, VIA] **1 :** ACCESSIBLE <~ to reason> **2 :** PERMEABLE <~ soil> — **per·vi·ous·ness** *n*

pes \ˈpēz\ *n, pl* **pe·des** \ˈpēd-(ˌ)ēz, ˈped-\ [NL *ped-, pes,* fr. L, foot — more at FOOT] **:** the distal segment of the hind limb of a vertebrate including the tarsus and foot

Pe·sach \ˈpā-ˌsäk\ *n* [Heb *pesaḥ*] **:** PASSOVER

pe·se·ta \pə-ˈsāt-ə\ *n* [Sp, fr. dim. of *peso*] — see MONEY table

pe·se·wa \pə-ˈsā-wə\ *n* [native name in Ghana] — see *cedi* at MONEY table

pes·ky \ˈpes-kē\ *adj* **pes·ki·er; -est** [prob. irreg. fr. *pest* + *-y*] **:** TROUBLESOME, VEXATIOUS

pe·so \ˈpā-(ˌ)sō, ˈpes-(ˌ)ō\ *n, pl* **pesos** [Sp, lit., weight, fr. L *pensum* — more at POISE] **1 :** an old silver coin of Spain and Spanish America equal to eight reals **2** — see MONEY table **3 :** the former basic monetary unit of Chile replaced in 1960 by the escudo

pes·sa·ry \ˈpes-ə-rē\ *n, pl* **-ries** [ME *pessarie,* fr. LL *pessarium,* fr. *pessus, pessum* pessary, fr. Gk *pessos* oval stone for playing checkers, pessary] **1 :** a vaginal suppository **2 :** a device worn in the vagina to support the uterus, remedy a malposition, or prevent conception

pes·si·mism \ˈpes-ə-ˌmiz-əm *also* ˈpez-\ *n* [F *pessimisme,* fr. L *pessimus* worst — more at PEJORATIVE] **1 :** an inclination to emphasize adverse aspects, conditions, and possibilities or to expect the worst possible outcome **2 a :** the doctrine that reality is essentially evil **b :** the doctrine that evil overbalances happiness in life — **pes·si·mist** \-məst\ *n*

pes·si·mis·tic \ˌpes-ə-ˈmis-tik *also* ˌpez-\ *adj* **:** of, relating to, or characterized by pessimism **:** GLOOMY ***syn*** see CYNICAL ***ant*** optimistic — **pes·si·mis·ti·cal·ly** \-ti-k(ə-)lē\ *adv*

pest \ˈpest\ *n* [MF *peste,* fr. L *pestis*] **1 :** an epidemic disease associated with high mortality; *specif* **:** PLAGUE **2 :** something resembling a pest in destructiveness; *esp* **:** a plant or animal detrimental to man **3 :** one that pesters or annoys **:** NUISANCE

pes·ter \ˈpes-tər\ *vt* **pes·tered; pes·ter·ing** \-t(ə-)riŋ\ [modif. of MF *empestrer* to hobble, embarrass, fr. (assumed) VL *impastoriare,* fr. L *in-* + (assumed) VL *pastoria* hobble, fr. L *pastor* herdsman — more at PASTOR] **1** *obs* **:** OVERCROWD **2 :** to harass with petty irritations **:** ANNOY ***syn*** see WORRY

pest·hole \ˈpest-ˌhōl\ *n* **:** a place liable to epidemic disease

pest·house \-ˌhau̇s\ *n* **:** a shelter or hospital for those infected with a pestilential or contagious disease

pes·ti·cide \ˈpes-tə-ˌsīd\ *n* **:** an agent used to destroy pests

pes·tif·er·ous \pes-ˈtif-(ə-)rəs\ *adj* [ME, fr. L *pestifer* pestilential, noxious, fr. *pestis* + *-fer* -ferous] **1 :** dangerous to society **:** PERNICIOUS **2 a :** carrying or propagating infection **:** PESTILENTIAL **b :** infected with a pestilential disease **3 :** TROUBLESOME, ANNOYING — **pes·tif·er·ous·ly** *adv* — **pes·tif·er·ous·ness** *n*

pes·ti·lence \ˈpes-tə-lən(t)s\ *n* **1 :** a contagious or infectious epidemic disease that is virulent and devastating; *specif* **:** BUBONIC PLAGUE **2 :** something that is destructive or pernicious <I'll pour this ~ into his ear —Shak.>

pes·ti·lent \-lənt\ *adj* [ME, fr. L *pestilent-, pestilens* pestilential, fr. *pestis*] **1 :** destructive of life **:** DEADLY **2 :** injuring or endangering society **:** PERNICIOUS **3 :** causing displeasure or annoyance **4 :** INFECTIOUS, CONTAGIOUS <~ disease> — **pes·ti·lent·ly** *adv*

pes·ti·len·tial \ˌpes-tə-ˈlen-chəl\ *adj* **1 a :** causing or tending to cause pestilence **:** DEADLY **b :** of or relating to pestilence **2 :** morally harmful **:** PERNICIOUS **3 :** giving rise to vexation or annoyance **:** IRRITATING — **pes·ti·len·tial·ly** \-ˈlench-(ə-)lē\ *adv*

1**pes·tle** \ˈpes-əl *also* ˈpes-tᵊl\ *n* [ME *pestel*, fr. MF, fr. L *pistillum*; akin to MLG *vīsel* pestle, L *pilum* pestle, javelin, *pinsere* to pound, crush] **1 :** a usu. club-shaped implement for pounding or grinding substances in a mortar **2 :** any of various devices for pounding, stamping, or pressing

2**pestle** *vb* **pes·tled; pes·tling** \ˈpes-(ə-)liŋ *also* ˈpes-t(ə-)liŋ\ *vt* **:** to beat, pound, or pulverize with or as if with a pestle ~ *vi* **:** to work with a pestle **:** use a pestle

1**pet** \ˈpet\ *n* [perh. back-formation fr. ME *pety* small — more at PETTY] **1 :** a domesticated animal kept for pleasure rather than utility **2 a :** a pampered and usu. spoiled child **b :** a person who is treated with unusual kindness or consideration **:** DARLING

2**pet** *adj* **1 :** kept or treated as a pet **2 :** expressing fondness or endearment <a ~ name> **3 :** FAVORITE <his ~ project>

3**pet** *vb* **pet·ted; pet·ting** *vt* **1 a :** to treat as a pet **b :** to stroke in a gentle or loving manner **2 :** to treat with unusual kindness and consideration **:** PAMPER ~ *vi* **:** to engage in amorous embracing, caressing, and kissing **:** NECK *syn* see CARESS — **pet·ter** *n*

4**pet** *n* [origin unknown] **:** a fit of peevishness, sulkiness, or anger

5**pet** *vi* **pet·ted; pet·ting :** to take offense **:** SULK

6**pet** *abbr* petroleum

Pet *abbr* Peter

pet·al \ˈpet-ᵊl\ *n* [NL *petalum*, fr. Gk *petalon*; akin to Gk *petannynai* to spread out — more at FATHOM] **:** one of the modified leaves of a corolla of a flower — see FLOWER illustration — **pet·aled** *or* **pet·alled** \-ᵊld\ *adj* — **pet·al·like** \-ᵊl-ˌ(l)īk\ *adj*

pet·al·oid \ˈpet-ᵊl-ˌȯid\ *adj* **1 :** resembling a flower petal **2 :** consisting of petaloid elements

pet·al·ous \ˈpet-ᵊl-əs\ *adj* **1 :** having petals **2 :** having (such or so many) petals — used in combination <poly*petalous*>

pe·tard \pə-ˈtär(d)\ *n* [MF, fr. *peter* to break wind, fr. *pet* expulsion of intestinal gas, fr. L *peditum*, fr. neut. of *peditus*, pp. of *pedere* to break wind; akin to Gk *bdein* to break wind] **1 :** a case containing an explosive to break down a door or gate or breach a wall **2 :** a firework that explodes with a loud report

pet·a·sos *or* **pet·a·sus** \ˈpet-ə-səs\ *n* [L & Gk; L *petasus*, fr. Gk *petasos*; akin to Gk *petannynai* to spread out] **:** a broad-brimmed low-crowned hat worn by ancient Greeks and Romans; *esp* **:** the winged hat of Hermes

petasos

pet·cock \ˈpet-ˌkäk\ *n* [*pet-* (perh. fr. *petty*) + *cock*] **:** a small cock, faucet, or valve for letting out air, releasing compression, or draining

pe·te·chia \pə-ˈtē-kē-ə\ *n, pl* **-chi·ae** \-kē-ˌī\ [NL, fr. It *petecchia*, deriv. of L *impetigo*] **:** a minute hemorrhagic or purpuric spot that appears in skin or mucous membrane esp. in some infectious diseases — **pe·te·chi·al** \-kē-əl\ *adj* — **pe·te·chi·ate** \-kē-ət, -ˌāt\ *adj*

1**pe·ter** \ˈpēt-ər\ *n* [fr. the name *Peter*] **:** PENIS — often considered vulgar

2**peter** *vi* [origin unknown] **1 :** to diminish gradually and come to an end **:** give out — usu. used with *out* <novelists whose creative impetus seems largely to have ~*ed* out —*Times Lit. Supp.*> **2 :** to become exhausted — usu. used with *out*

Pe·ter \ˈpēt-ər\ *n* [LL *Petrus*, fr. Gk *Petros*, fr. *petra* rock] **1 :** a fisherman of Galilee and one of the twelve apostles **2 :** either of two hortatory letters written to early Christians and included as books of the New Testament — see BIBLE table

Peter Pan \-ˈpan\ *n* **:** a boy in Sir James Barrie's play *Peter Pan* who lives without growing older in a never-never land

Peter Pan collar *n* **:** a usu. small flat close-fitting collar with rounded ends that meet in front

pe·ter·sham \ˈpēt-ər-ˌsham, -shəm\ *n* [Charles Stanhope, Lord *Petersham* †1851 E colonel] **1 :** a rough nubby woolen cloth used chiefly for men's coats; *also* **:** a coat made of this material **2 :** a heavy corded ribbon used for belts and hatbands

Peter's pence *n pl but sing in constr* [fr. the tradition that St. Peter founded the papal see] **1 :** an annual tribute of a penny formerly paid by each householder in England to the papal see **2 :** a voluntary annual contribution made by Roman Catholics to the pope

pet·i·o·lar \ˌpet-ē-ˈō-lər\ *adj* **:** of, relating to, or proceeding from a petiole

pet·i·o·late \ˈpet-ē-ə-ˌlāt, ˌpet-ē-ˈō-lət\ *also* **pet·i·o·lat·ed** \ˈpet-ē-ō-ˌlāt-əd\ *adj* **:** having a stalk or petiole

pet·i·ole \ˈpet-ē-ˌōl\ *n* [NL *petiolus*, fr. L, small foot, fruit stalk, alter. of *pediculus*, dim. of *ped-, pes* foot — more at FOOT] **1 :** a slender stem that supports the blade of a foliage leaf **2 :** PEDUNCLE; *specif* **:** a slender abdominal segment joining the rest of the abdomen to the thorax in some insects — **pet·i·oled** \-ˌōld\ *adj*

pet·i·o·lule \ˈpet-ē-ō-ˌlül, ˌpet-ē-ˈōl-(ˌ)yü(ə)l\ *n* [NL *petiolulus*, dim. of *petiolus*] **:** a stalk of a leaflet of a compound leaf

pet·it \ˈpet-ē\ *adj* [ME, small, minor, fr. MF, small] **:** PETTY 1 — used chiefly in legal compounds

pe·tit bourgeois \pə-ˈtē-, ˌpet-ē-\ *n* [F, lit., small bourgeois] **1 :** a member of the petite bourgeoisie **2 :** PETITE BOURGEOISIE — **petit bourgeois** *adj*

1**pe·tite** \pə-ˈtēt\ *adj* [F, fem. of *petit*] **:** having a small trim figure — usu. used of a woman *syn* see SMALL — **pe·tite·ness** *n*

2**petite** *n* **:** a clothing size for short women

pe·tite bourgeoisie \pə-ˌtēt-\ *n* [F, lit., small bourgeoisie] **:** the lower middle class including esp. small shopkeepers and artisans

pe·tit four \ˌpet-ē-ˈfō(ə)r, pə-ˌtē-, -ˈfȯ(ə)r; -ˈfü(ə)r\ *n, pl* **petits fours** *or* **petit fours** \-ˈfō(ə)rz, -ˈfȯ(ə)rz, -ˈfü(ə)r(z)\ [F, lit., small oven] **:** a small cake cut from pound or sponge cake and frosted

1**pe·ti·tion** \pə-ˈtish-ən\ *n* [ME, fr. MF, fr. L *petition-, petitio*, fr. *petitus*, pp. of *petere* to seek, request — more at FEATHER] **1 :** an earnest request **:** ENTREATY **2 a :** a formal written request made to a superior **b :** a document embodying such a formal written request **3 :** something asked or requested — **pe·ti·tion·ary** \-ˈtish-ə-ˌner-ē\ *adj*

2**petition** *vb* **pe·ti·tioned; pe·ti·tion·ing** \-ˈtish-(ə-)niŋ\ *vt* **:** to make a request to or for **:** SOLICIT ~ *vi* **:** to make a request; *esp* **:** to make a formal written request — **pe·ti·tion·er** \-(ə-)nər\ *n*

pe·ti·tio prin·ci·pii \pə-ˈtēt-ē-ˌō-(ˌ)priŋ-ˈkip-ē-ˌē\ *n* [ML, lit., postulation of the beginning, begging the question] **:** a logical fallacy in which a premise is assumed to be true without warrant or in which what is to be proved is implicitly taken for granted

pet·it jury \ˈpet-ē-\ *n* **:** a jury of 12 persons impaneled to try and to decide finally upon the facts at issue in causes for trial in a court

petit larceny *n* **:** larceny involving property of a value below a legally established minimum

pe·tit–mai·tre \pə-ˌtē-ˈmātrᵊ\ *n, pl* **petits–maitres** *same*\ [F, lit., small master] **:** DANDY, FOP

pe·tit mal \ˈpet-ē-ˌmal, -ˌmäl\ *n* [F, lit., small illness] **:** epilepsy characterized by mild convulsive seizure with transient clouding of consciousness

pet·it point \ˈpet-ē-ˌpȯint\ *n* [F, lit., small point] **:** TENT STITCH; *also* **:** embroidery made with this stitch

pet·nap·ping \ˈpet-ˌnap-iŋ\ *n* [*pet* + *-napping* (as in *kidnapping*)] **:** the act of stealing a pet (as a cat or dog) usu. for profit

petr- *or* **petri-** *or* **petro-** *comb form* [NL, fr. Gk *petr-, petro-*, fr. *petros* stone & *petra* rock] **:** stone **:** rock <*petr*ology>

Pe·trar·chan sonnet \pi-ˌträr-kən-, ˌpē-, (ˌ)pe-\ *n* [*Petrarch* (Francesco Petrarca)] **:** ITALIAN SONNET

pe·trel \ˈpe-trəl, ˈpē-\ *n* [alter. of earlier *pitteral*] **:** any of numerous sea birds (families Procellariidae and Hydrobatidae); *esp* **:** one of the smaller long-winged birds that fly far from land — compare STORM PETREL

pe·tri dish \ˌpē-trē-\ *n* [Julius R. *Petri* †1921 G bacteriologist] **:** a small shallow dish of thin glass with a loose cover used esp. for cultures in bacteriology

pet·ri·fac·tion \ˌpe-trə-ˈfak-shən\ *n* **1 :** the process of petrifying **2 :** something petrified **3 :** the quality or state of being petrified

pet·ri·fi·ca·tion \ˌpe-trə-fə-ˈkā-shən\ *n* **:** PETRIFACTION

pet·ri·fy \ˈpe-trə-ˌfī\ *vb* **-fied; -fy·ing** [MF *petrifier*, fr. *petr-* + *-ifier* -ify] *vt* **1 :** to convert into stone or a stony substance **2 :** to make rigid or inert like stone: **a :** to make lifeless or inactive **:** DEADEN <slogans are apt to ~ a man's thinking —*Saturday Rev.*> **b :** to confound with fear, amazement, or awe **:** PARALYZE <is *petrified* of talking in public —Alan Frank> ~ *vi* **:** to become stone or of stony hardness or rigidity

Pe·trine \ˈpē-ˌtrin\ *adj* [LL *Petrus* Peter] **1 :** of, relating to, or characteristic of the apostle Peter or the doctrines associated with his name **2 :** of, relating to, or characteristic of Peter the Great or his reign

pet·ro·chem·i·cal \ˌpe-trō-ˈkem-i-kəl\ *n* [*petro*leum + *chemical*] **:** a chemical isolated or derived from petroleum or natural gas — **pet·ro·chem·is·try** \-ˈkem-ə-strē\ *n*

pet·ro·gen·e·sis \-ˈjen-ə-səs\ *n* [NL] **:** the origin or formation of rocks — **pet·ro·ge·net·ic** \-jə-ˈnet-ik\ *adj*

pet·ro·glyph \ˈpe-trə-ˌglif\ *n* [F *pétroglyphe*, fr. *pétr-* petr- + *-glyphe* (as in *hiéroglyphe* hieroglyph)] **:** a carving or inscription on a rock

pe·trog·ra·phy \pə-ˈträg-rə-fē, pe-\ *n* [NL *petrographia*, fr. *petr-* + L *-graphia* -graphy] **:** the description and systematic classification of rocks — **pe·trog·ra·pher** \-fər\ *n* — **pet·ro·graph·ic** \ˌpe-trə-ˈgraf-ik\ *or* **pet·ro·graph·i·cal** \-i-kəl\ *adj* — **pet·ro·graph·i·cal·ly** \-i-k(ə-)lē\ *adv*

pet·rol \ˈpe-trəl, -ˌträl\ *n* [F *essence de pétrole*, lit., essence of petroleum] *chiefly Brit* **:** GASOLINE

pet·ro·la·tum \ˌpe-trə-ˈlāt-əm, -ˈlät-\ *n* [NL, fr. ML *petroleum*] **:** a neutral unctuous odorless tasteless substance obtained from petroleum and used esp. in ointments and dressings

pe·tro·leum \pə-ˈtrō-lē-əm, -ˈtrōl-yəm\ *n* [ML, fr. L *petr-* + *oleum* oil — more at OIL] **:** an oily flammable bituminous liquid that may vary from almost colorless to black, occurs in many places in the upper strata of the earth, is a complex mixture of hydrocarbons with small amounts of other substances, and is prepared for use as gasoline, naphtha, or other products by various refining processes

petroleum jelly *n* **:** PETROLATUM

pe·trol·o·gy \pə-ˈträl-ə-jē, pe-\ *n* [ISV] **:** a science that deals with the origin, history, occurrence, structure, chemical composition, and classification of rocks — **pet·ro·log·ic** \ˌpe-trə-ˈläj-ik\ *or*

pet·ro·log·i·cal \ˌi-kəl\ *adj* — **pet·ro·log·i·cal·ly** \-i-k(ə-)lē\ *adv* — **pe·trol·o·gist** \pə-ˈträl-ə-jəst, pe-\ *n*

pet·ro·nel \ˌpe-trə-ˈnel\ *n* [perh. modif. of MF *poitrinal, petrinal,* fr. *poitrinal* of the chest, fr. *poitrine* chest] **:** a portable firearm resembling a carbine of large caliber

pe·tro·sal \pə-ˈtrō-səl\ *adj* [NL *petrosa* petrous portion of the temporal bone, fr. L, fem. of *petrosus*] **:** HARD, STONY; *specif* **:** of, relating to, or situated in the region of the petrous portion of the temporal bone or capsule of the internal ear

pe·trous \ˈpe-trəs, ˈpē-\ *adj* [MF *petreux,* fr. L *petrosus,* fr. *petra* rock, fr. Gk] **:** resembling stone esp. in hardness **:** ROCKY; *specif* **:** of, relating to, or constituting the exceptionally hard and dense portion of the temporal bone of man that contains the internal auditory organs

1pet·ti·coat \ˈpet-ē-ˌkōt\ *n* [ME *petycote* short tunic, petticoat, fr. *pety* small + *cote* coat] **1 :** a skirt worn by women, girls, or young children: as **a :** an outer skirt formerly worn by women and small children **b :** a fancy skirt made to show below a draped-up overskirt **c :** an underskirt usu. a little shorter than outer clothing and often made with a ruffled, pleated, or lace edge **d** *archaic* **:** the skirt of a woman's riding habit **2 a :** a garment characteristic or typical of women **b :** WOMAN <a little nervous lest ~*s* in a government office might demoralize the male staff —Langston Day> **3 :** something (as a valance) resembling a petticoat — **pet·ti·coat·ed** \-əd\ *adj*

2petticoat *adj* **:** of, relating to, or exercised by women **:** FEMALE <~ government>

pet·ti·fog \ˈpet-ē-ˌfȯg, -ˌfäg\ *vi* **-fogged; -fog·ging** [back-formation fr. *pettifogger*] **1 :** to engage in legal chicanery **2 :** to quibble over insignificant details **:** CAVIL, BICKER

pet·ti·fog·ger \-ˌfȯg-ər, -ˌfäg-\ *n* [prob. fr. *petty* + obs. E *fogger* (pettifogger)] **1 :** a lawyer whose methods are petty, underhanded, or disreputable **:** SHYSTER **2 :** one given to quibbling over insignificant details

pet·ti·fog·gery \-(ə-)rē\ *n, pl* **-ger·ies :** the practice of a pettifogger **:** CHICANERY

pet·ti·ness \ˈpet-ē-nəs\ *n* **1 :** the quality or state of being petty **2 :** something petty **:** TRIVIALITY

pet·tish \ˈpet-ish\ *adj* [prob. fr. ⁴*pet*] **:** FRETFUL, PEEVISH — **pet·tish·ly** *adv* — **pet·tish·ness** *n*

pet·ti·skirt \-ē-ˌskərt\ *n* [*petticoat* + *skirt*] **:** PETTICOAT 1c

pet·ti·toes \ˈpet-ē-ˌtōz\ *n pl* [pl. of obs. *pettytoe* (offal)] **1 :** the feet of a pig used as food **2 :** TOES, FEET

pet·ty \ˈpet-ē\ *adj* **pet·ti·er; -est** [ME *pety* small, minor, alter. of *petit*] **1 :** having secondary rank or importance **:** MINOR, SUBORDINATE **2 :** having little or no importance or significance **3 :** marked by or reflective of narrow interests and sympathies **:** SMALL-MINDED — **pet·ti·ly** \ˈpet-ᵊl-ē\ *adv*

petty cash *n* **:** cash kept on hand for payment of minor items

petty larceny *n* **:** PETIT LARCENY

petty officer *n* **:** a subordinate officer in the navy or coast guard appointed from among the enlisted men — compare NONCOMMISSIONED OFFICER

petty officer first class *n* **:** an enlisted man in the navy or coast guard ranking above a petty officer second class and below a chief petty officer

petty officer second class *n* **:** an enlisted man in the navy or coast guard ranking above a petty officer third class and below a petty officer first class

petty officer third class *n* **:** an enlisted man in the navy or coast guard ranking above a seaman and below a petty officer second class

pet·u·lance \ˈpech-ə-lən(t)s\ *n* **:** the quality or state of being petulant **:** PEEVISHNESS

pet·u·lan·cy \-lən-sē\ *n, archaic* **:** PETULANCE

pet·u·lant \-lənt\ *adj* [L or MF; MF, fr. L *petulant-, petulans;* akin to L *petere* to go to, attack, seek — more at FEATHER] **1 :** insolent or rude in speech or behavior **2 :** characterized by temporary or capricious ill humor **:** PEEVISH — **pet·u·lant·ly** *adv*

pe·tu·nia \pi-ˈt(y)ün-yə\ *n* [NL, genus name, fr. obs. F *petun* tobacco, fr. Tupi *petyn*] **:** any of a genus (*Petunia*) of tropical American herbs of the nightshade family with funnel-shaped corollas

pew \ˈpyü\ *n* [ME *pewe,* fr. MF *puie* balustrade, fr. L *podia,* pl. of *podium* parapet, podium, fr. Gk *podion* base, dim. of *pod-, pous* foot — more at FOOT] **1 :** a compartment in the auditorium of a church providing seats for several persons **2 :** one of the benches with backs and sometimes doors fixed in rows in a church

pe·wee \ˈpē-(ˌ)wē\ *n* [imit.] **:** any of various small olivaceous flycatchers

pew·hold·er \ˈpyü-ˌhōl-dər\ *n* **:** a renter or owner of a church pew

pe·wit *var of* PEEWIT

pew·ter \ˈpyüt-ər\ *n* [ME, fr. MF *peutre;* akin to It *peltro* pewter] **1 :** any of various alloys having tin as chief component; *esp* **:** a dull alloy with lead formerly used for domestic utensils **2 :** utensils of pewter — **pewter** *adj*

pew·ter·er \ˈpyüt-ər-ər\ *n* **:** one that makes pewter utensils or vessels

pey·o·te \pā-ˈōt-ē\ *or* **pey·otl** \-ˈōt-ᵊl\ *n* [MexSp *peyote,* fr. Nahuatl *peyotl*] **1 :** any of several American cacti (genus *Lophophora*); *esp* **:** MESCAL **2 :** a stimulant drug derived from mescal buttons

pf *abbr* **1** pfennig **2** picofarad **3** preferred

PF *abbr* **1** power factor **2** pianoforte **3** [It *più forte*] louder

PFC *abbr* private first class

pfd *abbr* preferred

pfen·nig \ˈfen-ig, -ik, *G* ˈ(p)fen-ik\ *n, pl* **pfen·nigs** \ˈfen-igz, -iks\ *or* **pfen·ni·ge** \ˈ(p)fen-i-gə, -i-yə\ [G, fr. OHG *pfenning* — more at PENNY] — see *deutsche mark, mark* at MONEY table

pg *abbr* page

1PG \ˈpē-ˈjē\ *adj* [abbr. for *parental guidance*] *of a motion picture* **:** of such a nature that all ages may be allowed admission but parental guidance is suggested — compare G, R, X

2PG *abbr* **1** paying guest **2** postgraduate

PGA *abbr* Professional Golfers' Association

ph *abbr* phase

pH \(ˈ)pē-ˈāch\ *n* **:** the negative logarithm of the effective hydrogen-ion concentration or hydrogen-ion activity in gram equivalents per liter used in expressing both acidity and alkalinity on a scale whose values run from 0 to 14 with 7 representing neutrality, numbers less than 7 increasing acidity, and numbers greater than 7 increasing alkalinity; *also* **:** the condition represented by such a number

PH *abbr* **1** pinch hit **2** public health **3** Purple Heart

PHA *abbr* Public Housing Administration

Phae·dra \ˈfē-drə\ *n* [L, fr. Gk *Phaidra*] **:** a daughter of Minos who marries Theseus and falls in love with her stepson Hippolytus

Pha·ë·thon \ˈfā-ə-ˌthän\ *n* [L, fr. Gk *Phaethōn*] **:** a son of Helios who drives his father's sun-chariot through the sky but loses control and is struck down by a thunderbolt of Zeus

pha·eton \ˈfā-ət-ᵊn\ *n* [*Phaëthon*] **1 :** any of various light four-wheeled horse-drawn vehicles **2 :** TOURING CAR

phaeton 1

phage \ˈfāj *also* ˈfäzh\ *n* [by shortening] **:** BACTERIOPHAGE

-phage \ˌfāj *also* ˌfäzh\ *n comb form* [Gk *-phagos,* fr. *-phagos* -phagous] **:** one that eats <bacterio*phage*>

-pha·gia \ˈfā-j(ē-)ə\ *n comb form* [NL, fr. Gk] **:** -PHAGY <dys*phagia*>

phago·cyte \ˈfag-ə-ˌsīt\ *n* [ISV, fr. Gk *phagein* + NL *-cyta* -cyte] **:** a cell (as a leukocyte) that characteristically engulfs foreign material and consumes debris and foreign bodies — **phago·cyt·ic** \ˌfag-ə-ˈsit-ik\ *adj*

phago·cy·tize \ˈfag-ə-sə-ˌtīz, -ˌsīt-ˌīz\ *vt* **-tized; -tiz·ing :** PHAGOCYTOSE

phago·cy·tose \-sə-ˌtōs, -sī-, -tōz\ *vt* **-tosed; -tos·ing** [back-formation fr. *phagocytosis*] **:** to consume by phagocytosis

phago·cy·to·sis \ˌfag-ə-sə-ˈtō-səs, -sī-\ *n, pl* **-to·ses** \-ˌsēz\ [NL] **:** the engulfing and usu. destruction of particulate matter by phagocytes — **phago·cy·tot·ic** \-ˈtäk-ik\ *adj*

phago·some \ˈfag-ə-ˌsōm\ *n* [Gk *phagein* + E *-o-* + *-some*] **:** a membrane-surrounded vesicle that encloses materials taken into the cell by endocytosis

-ph·a·gous \f-ə-gəs\ *adj comb form* [Gk *-phagos,* fr. *phagein* to eat — more at BAKSHEESH] **:** eating <sapro*phagous*>

Pha·gun \ˈpäg-ün\ *n* [Hindi *phāgun,* fr. Skt *phālguna*] **:** a month of the Hindu year — see MONTH table

-ph·a·gy \f-ə-jē\ *n comb form* [Gk *-phagia,* fr. *phagein*] **:** eating of a (specified) type or substance <geo*phagy*>

pha·lange \ˈfā-ˌlanj, fə-ˈ, fā-ˈ\ *n* [F, fr. Gk *phalang-, phalanx*] **:** PHALANX 2

pha·lan·ge·al \ˌfā-lən-ˈjē-əl, ˌfal-ən-; fə-ˈlan-jē-, fā-\ *adj* **:** of or relating to a phalanx or the phalanges

pha·lan·ger \fə-ˈlan-jər, ˈfā-ˌ\ *n* [NL, fr. Gk *phalang-, phalanx*] **:** any of various marsupial mammals (family Phalangeridae) of the Australian region ranging in size from a mouse to a large cat

phal·an·stery \ˈfal-ən-ˌster-ē\ *n, pl* **-ster·ies** [F *phalanstère* dwelling of a Fourierist community, fr. L *phalang-, phalanx* + *-stère* (as in *monastère* monastery)] **1 a :** a Fourierist cooperative community **b :** a self-contained structure housing such a community **2 :** something resembling a Fourierist phalanstery

pha·lanx \ˈfā-ˌlaŋ(k)s, *Brit usu* ˈfal-ˌaŋ(k)s\ *n, pl* **pha·lanx·es** *or* **pha·lan·ges** \fə-ˈlan-(ˌ)jēz, fā-\ [L *phalang-, phalanx,* fr. Gk, battle line, digital bone, lit., log — more at BALK] **1 :** a body of heavily armed infantry in ancient Greece formed in close deep ranks and files; *broadly* **:** a body of troops in close array **2** *pl phalanges* **:** one of the digital bones of the hand or foot of a vertebrate **3** *pl usu phalanxes* **a :** a massed arrangement of persons, animals, or things **b :** an organized body of persons

phal·a·rope \ˈfal-ə-ˌrōp\ *n, pl* **phalaropes** *also* **phalarope** [F, fr. NL *phalaropod-, phalaropus,* fr. Gk *phalaris* coot + *pod-, pous* foot; akin to Gk *phalios* having a white spot — more at BALD, FOOT] **:** any of various small shorebirds (family Phalaropodidae) that resemble sandpipers but have lobate toes and are good swimmers

phal·lic \ˈfal-ik\ *adj* **1 :** of or relating to phallicism <a ~ cult> **2 :** of, relating to, or resembling a phallus **3 :** relating to or being the stage of psychosexual development in psychoanalytic theory during which a child becomes interested in his own sexual organs — **phal·li·cal·ly** \-i-k(ə-)lē\ *adv*

phal·li·cism \ˈfal-ə-ˌsiz-əm\ *n* **:** the worship of the generative principle as symbolized by the phallus

phal·lus \ˈfal-əs\ *n, pl* **phal·li** \ˈfal-ˌī, -ˌē\ *or* **phal·lus·es** [L, fr. Gk *phallos* penis, representation of the penis — more at BLOW] **1 :** a symbol or representation of the penis **2 :** PENIS

-phane \ˌfān\ *n comb form* [Gk *phanēs* appearing, fr. *phainein* to show — more at FANCY] **:** substance having a (specified) form, quality, or appearance <hydro*phane*>

pha·nero·gam \ˈfan-ə-rə-ˌgam, fə-ˈner-ə-\ *n* [F *phanérogame,* deriv. of Gk *phaneros* visible (fr. *phainein*) + *gamos* marriage — more at BIGAMY] **:** a seed plant or flowering plant **:** SPERMATOPHYTE — **pha·nero·gam·ic** \ˌfan-ə-rə-ˈgam-ik, fə-ˌner-ə-\ *adj* — **phan·er·og·a·mous** \ˌfan-ə-ˈräg-ə-məs\ *adj*

pha·nero·phyte \ˈfan-ə-rə-ˌfīt, fə-ˈner-ə-\ *n* [Gk *phaneros* + ISV *-phyte*] **:** a perennial plant that bears its overwintering buds well above the surface of the ground

Pha·nero·zo·ic \ˌfan-ə-rə-ˈzō-ik, fə-ˌner-ə-\ *adj* [Gk *phaneros* + E ²*-zoic*] **:** of, relating to, or being a period of geologic time that comprises the Paleozoic, Mesozoic, and Cenozoic

phan·tasm \ˈfan-ˌtaz-əm\ *n* [ME *fantasme,* fr. OF, fr. L *phantasma,* fr. Gk, fr. *phantazein* to present to the mind — more at FANCY] **1 :** a product of phantasy: as **a :** delusive appearance **:** ILLUSION **b :** GHOST, SPECTER **c :** a figment of the imagination **:** FANTASY **2 :** a mental representation of a real object **3 :** a deceptive or illusory appearance of a thing — **phan·tas·mal** \fan-ˈtaz-məl\ *adj* — **phan·tas·mic** \-mik\ *adj*

phan·tas·ma \fan-ˈtaz-mə\ *n, pl* **-ma·ta** \-mət-ə\ [L *phantasmat-, phantasma*] : PHANTASM 1

phan·tas·ma·go·ria \(ˌ)fan-ˌtaz-mə-ˈgōr-ē-ə, -ˈgȯr-\ *n* [F *phantasmagorie,* fr. *phantasme* phantasm (fr. OF *fantasme*) + *-agorie* (prob. fr. Gk *ageirein* to assemble, collect) — more at GREGARIOUS] **1 :** an optical effect by which figures on a screen appear to dwindle into the distance or to rush toward the observer with enormous increase of size **2 a :** a constantly shifting complex succession of things seen or imagined <drugs that . . . can project the mind into a ~ lasting hours —John Kobler> **b :** a scene that constantly changes — **phan·tas·ma·go·ric** \-ˈgōr-ik, -ˈgȯr-, -ˈgär-\ *adj*

phantasy *var of* FANTASY

¹phan·tom \ˈfant-əm\ *n* [ME *fantosme, fantome,* fr. MF *fantosme,* modif. of L *phantasma*] **1 a :** something (as a specter) apparent to sense but with no substantial existence : APPARITION **b :** something elusive or visionary : WILL-O'-THE-WISP **c :** an object of continual dread or abhorrence : BUGBEAR <the ~ of disease and want> **2 :** something existing in appearance only <a ~ of a king> **3 :** a representation of something abstract, ideal, or incorporeal <she was a ~ of delight —William Wordsworth> — **phan·tom·like** \-ˌlīk\ *adv or adj*

²phantom *adj* **1 :** of the nature of, suggesting, or being a phantom : ILLUSORY **2 :** FICTITIOUS, DUMMY <~ voters>

phar *abbr* **1** pharmacopoeia **2** pharmacy

pha·raoh \ˈfe(ə)r-(ˌ)ō, ˈfa(ə)r-(ˌ)ō, ˈfā-(ˌ)rō\ *n, often cap* [LL *pharaon-, pharao,* fr. Gk *pharaō,* fr. Heb *par'ōh,* fr. Egypt *pr-*ʿ*3*] **1 :** a ruler of ancient Egypt **2 :** TYRANT — **phar·a·on·ic** \ˌfer-ā-ˈän-ik, ˌfar-\ *adj, often cap*

pharaoh ant *n* **:** a little red ant (*Monomorium pharaonis*) that is a common household pest

phar·i·sa·ic \ˌfar-ə-ˈsā-ik\ *adj* [LL *pharisaicus,* fr. LGk *pharisaikos,* fr. Gk *pharisaios* Pharisee] **1** *cap* **:** of or relating to the Pharisees **2 :** PHARISAICAL

phar·i·sa·ical \-ˈsā-ə-kəl\ *adj* **:** marked by hypocritical censorious self-righteousness ***syn*** see HYPOCRITICAL — **phar·i·sa·ical·ly** \-k(ə-)lē\ *adv* — **phar·i·sa·ical·ness** \-kəl-nəs\ *n*

phar·i·sa·ism \ˈfar-ə-(ˌ)sā-ˌiz-əm\ *n* [NL *pharisaismus,* fr. Gk *pharisaios*] **1** *cap* **:** the doctrines or practices of the Pharisees **2** *often cap* **:** pharisaical character, spirit, or attitude **:** HYPOCRISY

phar·i·see \ˈfar-ə-(ˌ)sē\ *n* [ME *pharise,* fr. OE *farise,* fr. LL *pharisaeus,* fr. Gk *pharisaios,* fr. Aram *pĕrīshayyā,* pl. of *pĕrīshā,* lit., separated] **1** *cap* **:** a member of a Jewish sect of the intertestamental period noted for strict observance of rites and ceremonies of the written law and for insistence on the validity of their own oral traditions concerning the law **2 :** a pharisaical person

pharm *abbr* pharmaceutical; pharmacist; pharmacy

¹phar·ma·ceu·ti·cal \ˌfär-mə-ˈsüt-i-kəl\ *also* **phar·ma·ceu·tic** \-ik\ *adj* [LL *pharmaceuticus,* fr. Gk *pharmakeutikos,* fr. *pharmakeuein* to administer drugs — more at PHARMACY] **:** of or relating to pharmacy or pharmacists — **phar·ma·ceu·ti·cal·ly** \-i-k(ə-)lē\ *adv*

²pharmaceutical *n* **:** a medicinal drug

phar·ma·ceu·tics \-iks\ *n pl but sing in constr* **:** the science of preparing, using, or dispensing medicines **:** PHARMACY

phar·ma·cist \ˈfär-mə-səst\ *n* **:** one engaged in pharmacy

pharmaco- *comb form* [Gk *pharmako-,* fr. *pharmakon*] **:** medicine **:** drug <*pharmaco*logy>

phar·ma·co·dy·nam·ic \ˌfär-mə-kō-dī-ˈnam-ik, -də-\ *adj* [back-formation fr. *pharmacodynamics*] **:** of, relating to, or used in pharmacodynamics — **phar·ma·co·dy·nam·i·cal·ly** \-i-k(ə-)lē\ *adv*

phar·ma·co·dy·nam·ics \-iks\ *n pl but sing in constr* **:** a branch of pharmacology dealing with the reactions between drugs and living structures

phar·ma·co·ge·net·ics \-jə-ˈnet-iks\ *n pl but sing in constr* **:** the study of the interrelation of hereditary constitution and response to drugs — **phar·ma·co·ge·net·ic** \-ik\ *adj*

phar·ma·cog·no·sy \ˌfär-mə-ˈkäg-nə-sē\ *n* [ISV, fr. Gk *pharmakon* + *-gnōsia* knowledge, fr. *gnōsis* — more at GNOSIS] **:** descriptive pharmacology dealing with crude drugs and simples — **phar·ma·cog·nos·tic** \-ˌkäg-ˈnäs-tik\ *or* **phar·ma·cog·nos·ti·cal** \-ti-kəl\ *adj*

phar·ma·co·ki·net·ics \-kō-kə-ˈnet-iks, -kō-ki-\ *n pl but sing in constr* **:** the study of the bodily absorption, distribution, metabolism, and excretion of drugs — **phar·ma·co·ki·net·ic** \-ik\ *adj*

phar·ma·col·o·gy \ˌfär-mə-ˈkäl-ə-jē\ *n* **1 :** the science of drugs including materia medica, toxicology, and therapeutics **2 :** the properties and reactions of drugs esp. with relation to their therapeutic value — **phar·ma·co·log·ic** \-kə-ˈläj-ik\ *or* **phar·ma·co·log·i·cal** \-i-kəl\ *adj* — **phar·ma·co·log·i·cal·ly** \-i-k(ə-)lē\ *adv* — **phar·ma·col·o·gist** \-ˈkäl-ə-jəst\ *n*

phar·ma·co·poe·ia \-kə-ˈpē-(y)ə\ *n* [NL, fr. LGk *pharmakopoiia* preparation of drugs, fr. Gk *pharmako-* + *poiein* to make — more at POET] **1 :** a book describing drugs, chemicals, and medicinal preparations; *esp* **:** one issued by an officially recognized authority and serving as a standard **2 :** a collection or stock of drugs — **phar·ma·co·poe·ial** \-(y)əl\ *adj*

phar·ma·cy \ˈfär-mə-sē\ *n, pl* **-cies** [LL *pharmacia* administration of drugs, fr. Gk *pharmakeia,* fr. *pharmakeuein* to administer drugs, fr. *pharmakon* magic charm, poison, drug; akin to Lith *burti* to practice magic] **1 :** the art or practice of preparing, preserving, compounding, and dispensing drugs **2 a :** a place where medicines are compounded or dispensed **b :** DRUGSTORE **3 :** PHARMACOPOEIA 2

phar·os \ˈfa(ə)r-ˌäs, ˈfe(ə)r-\ *n* [Gk, fr. *Pharos,* island in the bay of Alexandria, Egypt, famous for its lighthouse] **:** a lighthouse or beacon to guide seamen

pharyng- *or* **pharyngo-** *comb form* [Gk, fr. *pharyng-, pharynx*] **:** pharynx <*pharyng*itis> <*pharyngo*logy>

pha·ryn·geal \ˌfar-ən-ˈjē-əl, fə-ˈrin-j(ē-)əl\ *adj* [NL *pharyngeus,* fr. *pharyng-, pharynx*] **:** relating to or located or produced in the region of the pharynx

phar·yn·gi·tis \ˌfar-ən-ˈjīt-əs\ *n, pl* **-git·i·des** \-ˈjit-ə-ˌdēz\ **:** inflammation of the pharynx

phar·ynx \ˈfar-iŋ(k)s\ *n, pl* **pha·ryn·ges** \fə-ˈrin-(ˌ)jēz\ *also* **phar·ynx·es** [NL *pharyng-, pharynx,* fr. Gk, throat, pharynx; akin to ON *barki* throat, L *forare* to bore — more at BORE] **1 :** the part of the vertebrate alimentary canal between the cavity of the mouth and the esophagus **2 :** a differentiated part of the alimentary canal in some invertebrates that may be thickened and muscular, eversible and toothed, or adapted as a suctorial organ

¹phase \ˈfāz\ *n* [NL *phasis,* fr. Gk, appearance of a star, phase of the moon, fr. *phainein* to show (middle voice, to appear) — more at FANCY] **1 :** a particular appearance or state in a regularly recurring cycle of changes <~*s* of the moon> **2 a :** a distinguishable part in a course, development, or cycle <the early ~*s* of his career> **b :** an aspect or part (as of a problem) under consideration **3 :** the point or stage in a period of uniform circular motion, harmonic motion, or the periodic changes of any magnitude varying according to a simple harmonic law to which the rotation, oscillation, or variation has advanced considered in its relation to a standard position or assumed instant of starting **4 :** a homogeneous, physically distinct, and mechanically separable portion of matter present in a nonhomogeneous physical-chemical system **5 :** an individual or subgroup distinguishably different in appearance or behavior from the norm of the group to which it belongs; *also* **:** the distinguishing peculiarity — **pha·sic** \ˈfā-zik\ *adj*

syn PHASE, ASPECT, SIDE, FACET, ANGLE *shared meaning element* **:** one of the possible ways of viewing or being presented to view. PHASE implies a change of appearance, either literal or figurative, often without clear reference to an observer <the red fox occurs in several color *phases*> <the *phases* of development> ASPECT may stress the point of view of the observer and the limitations it imposes <the north *aspect* of the house> <the *aspects* of the poor that we resent> SIDE, sometimes interchangeable with *phase* or *aspect,* is used typically with reference to something felt as having two or more faces and not fully comprehensible unless it or its observer shifts position <see life only on its pleasant *side*> FACET implies the presence of a multiplicity of sides, usually comparable to the one singled out for attention <the different shades of green on the planes and *facets* of each clipped tree —Roald Dahl> <delighted to explore the *facets* of her complex nature> ANGLE denotes an aspect seen from a very restricted or specific point of view <examine the contemporary scene from various *angles*> — **in phase :** in a synchronized or correlated manner — **out of phase :** in an unsynchronized manner **:** not in correlation

²phase *vt* **phased; phas·ing** **1 :** to adjust so as to be in a synchronized condition **2 a :** to conduct or carry out by planned phases **b :** to schedule (as operations) or contract for (as goods or services) to be performed or supplied as required <guiding industry to ~ its development programs —Barbara Ward> **3 :** to introduce in stages — often used with *in* <~ in new models>

phase-contrast *adj* **:** of or employing the phase microscope

phase microscope *n* **:** a microscope that translates differences in phase of the light transmitted through or reflected by the object into differences of intensity in the image — called also *phase-contrast microscope*

phase modulation *n* **:** modulation of the phase of a radio carrier wave by voice or other signal

phase·out \ˈfā-ˌzau̇t\ *n* **:** a gradual stopping of operations or production **:** a closing down by phases

phase out \ˈfā-ˈzau̇t\ *vt* **:** to discontinue the practice, production, or use of by phases <*phase out* the old machinery> ~ *vi* **:** to stop production or operation by phases

-pha·sia \ˈfā-zh(ē-)ə\ *n comb form* [NL, fr. Gk, speech, fr. *phasis* utterance, fr. *phanai* to speak, say — more at BAN] **:** speech disorder of a (specified) type <dys*phasia*>

phas·mid \ˈfaz-məd\ *n* [NL *Phasmida,* group name, fr. *Phasma,* type genus, fr. Gk, apparition, fr. *phainein* to show — more at FANCY] **:** any of an order or suborder (Phasmatodea) of large cylindrical or sometimes flattened chiefly tropical insects (as a walking stick) with long strong legs, strictly phytophagous habits, and slight metamorphosis

pheasant 1

phat \ˈfat\ *adj* [alter. of ¹*fat*] *of copy or type matter* **:** susceptible of easy and rapid setting

phat·ic \ˈfat-ik\ *adj* [Gk *phatos,* verbal of *phanai* to speak] **:** revealing or sharing feelings or establishing an atmosphere of sociability rather than communicating ideas — **phat·i·cal·ly** \-i-k(ə-)lē\ *adv*

PhB *abbr* [L *philosophiae baccalaureus*] bachelor of philosophy

PhC *abbr* pharmaceutical chemist

PhD *abbr* [L *philosophiae doctor*] doctor of philosophy

pheas·ant \ˈfez-ᵊnt\ *n, pl* **pheasant** *or* **pheasants** [ME *fesaunt,* fr. AF, fr. OF *fesan,* fr. L *phasianus,* fr. Gk *phasianos,* fr. *phasianos* of the Phasis river, fr. *Phasis,* river in Colchis] **1 :** any of numerous large often long-tailed and brightly colored Old World gallinaceous birds (*Phasianus* and related genera of the family Phasianidae) many of which are reared as ornamental or game birds **2 :** any of various birds resembling a pheasant

phel·lem \ˈfel-ˌem\ *n* [Gk *phellos* cork + E *-em* (as in *phloem*)] : a layer of usu. suberized cells produced outwardly by a phellogen

phel·lo·derm \ˈfel-ə-ˌdərm\ *n* [Gk *phellos* + ISV *-derm*] : a layer of parenchyma produced inwardly by a phellogen

phel·lo·gen \ˈfel-ə-jən\ *n* [Gk *phellos* + ISV *-gen*] : a secondary meristem that initiates phellem and phelloderm in the periderm of a stem

phen- *or* **pheno-** *comb form* [obs. *phene* (benzene), fr. F *phène*, fr. Gk *phainein* to show; fr. its occurrence in illuminating gas — more at FANCY] : related to or derived from benzene <*phen*ol> : containing phenyl <*pheno*barbital>

phe·na·caine *or* **phe·no·cain** \ˈfē-nə-ˌkān, ˈfen-ə-\ *n* [*phenacaine* prob. fr. *phene*tidine + *acet-* + *-caine; phenocain* prob. irreg. fr. *phen-* + *-caine*] : a crystalline base $C_{18}H_{22}N_2O_2$ or its hydrochloride used as a local anesthetic

phen·ac·e·tin \fi-ˈnas-ət-ən\ *n* [ISV] : ACETOPHENETIDIN

phen·a·kite \ˈfen-ə-ˌkīt, ˈfēn-\ *or* **phen·a·cite** \-ˌsīt\ *n* [G *phenakit*, fr. Gk *phenak-, phenax* deceiver; fr. its being easily mistaken for quartz] : a glassy mineral Be_2SiO_4 that consists of a beryllium silicate and occurs in rhombohedral crystals

phen·an·threne \fə-ˈnan-ˌthrēn\ *n* [ISV *phen-* + *anthracene*] : a crystalline aromatic hydrocarbon $C_{14}H_{10}$ of coal tar isomeric with anthracene

phen·azine \ˈfen-ə-ˌzēn\ *n* [ISV] : a yellowish crystalline base $C_{12}H_8N_2$ that is the parent compound of many azine dyes and a few antibiotics

phen·el·zine \ˈfen-ᵊl-ˌzēn\ *n* [*phen*yl + *ethyl* + hydra*zine*] : a monoamine oxidase inhibitor $C_8H_{12}N_2$ used esp. as an antidepressant drug

phe·net·ic \fi-ˈnet-ik\ *adj* [*pheno*type + *-etic* (as in *genetic*)] : of, relating to, or being classificatory systems and procedures that are based on overall similarity usu. of many characters without regard to the evolutionary history of the organisms involved

phe·net·ics \-iks\ *n pl but sing in constr* : phenetic classification of plants and animals — **phe·net·i·cist** \-ˈnet-ə-səst\ *n*

phe·net·i·dine \fə-ˈnet-ə-ˌdēn\ *n* [*phenet*ole + *-idine*] : any of three liquid basic amino derivatives $C_8H_{11}NO$ of phenetole used esp. in manufacturing dyestuffs

phen·e·tole \ˈfen-ə-ˌtōl\ *n* [ISV *phen-* + *ethyl* + *-ole*] : the aromatic liquid ethyl ether $C_8H_{10}O$ of phenol

phen·for·min \fen-ˈfȯr-mən\ *n* [*phen*yl + *form*amide ($HCONH_2$) + *-in*] : a somewhat toxic drug $C_{10}H_{15}N_5$ that is used orally to lower blood sugar in some cases of diabetes

phen·met·ra·zine \(ˈ)fen-ˈme-trə-ˌzēn\ *n* [*phen*yl + *me*thyl + te*tra-* + oxa*zine*] : a sympathomimetic stimulant $C_{11}H_{15}NO$ that tends to cause loss of appetite

phe·no·bar·bi·tal \ˌfē-nō-ˈbär-bə-ˌtȯl\ *n* : a crystalline barbiturate $C_{12}H_{12}N_2O_3$ used as a hypnotic and sedative

phe·no·bar·bi·tone \-bə-ˌtōn\ *n, chiefly Brit* : PHENOBARBITAL

phe·no·copy \ˈfē-nə-ˌkäp-ē\ *n* [*pheno*type + *copy*] : a phenotypic variation that is caused by unusual environmental conditions and resembles the normal expression of a genotype other than its own

phe·no·cryst \-ˌkrist\ *n* [F *phénocryste*, fr. Gk *phainein* to show + *krystallos* crystal — more at FANCY] : one of the prominent embedded crystals of a porphyry — **phe·no·crys·tic** \ˌfē-nə-ˈkris-tik\ *adj*

phe·nol \ˈfē-ˌnōl, -ˌnȯl, fi-ˈ\ *n* [ISV *phen-* + *-ol*] **1** : a caustic poisonous crystalline acidic compound C_6H_5OH present in coal tar and wood tar that in dilute solution is used as a disinfectant **2** : any of various acidic compounds analogous to phenol and regarded as hydroxyl derivatives of aromatic hydrocarbons

phe·no·late \ˈfēn-ᵊl-ˌāt\ *n* : PHENOXIDE

¹phe·no·lic \fi-ˈnō-lik, -ˈnäl-ik\ *adj* **1 a** : of, relating to, or having the characteristics of a phenol **b** : containing or derived from a phenol **2** : of, relating to, or being a phenolic

²phenolic *n* : a usu. thermosetting resin or plastic made by condensation of a phenol with an aldehyde and used esp. for molding and insulating and in coatings and adhesives — called also *phenolic resin*

phe·nol·o·gy \fi-ˈnäl-ə-jē\ *n* [*pheno*mena + *-logy*] **1** : a branch of science dealing with the relations between climate and periodic biological phenomena (as bird migration or plant flowering) **2** : phenological phenomena (as of a kind of organism) — **phe·no·log·i·cal** \ˌfēn-ᵊl-ˈäj-i-kəl\ *adj* — **phe·no·log·i·cal·ly** \-k(ə-)lē\ *adv*

phe·nol·phtha·lein \ˌfēn-ᵊl-ˈthal-ē-ən, -ˈthal-ˌēn, -ˈthāl-\ *n* [ISV] : a white or yellowish white crystalline compound $C_{20}H_{14}O_4$ used in analysis as an indicator because its solution is brilliant red in alkalies and is decolorized by acids and in medicine as a laxative

phenol red *n* : a red crystalline compound $C_{19}H_{14}O_5S$ used esp. as an acid-base indicator

phe·nom \fi-ˈnäm\ *n* : PHENOMENON; *esp* : a person of phenomenal ability or promise

phe·nom·e·nal \fi-ˈnäm-ən-ᵊl\ *adj* : relating to or being a phenomenon: as **a** : known through the senses rather than through thought or intuition **b** : concerned with phenomena rather than with hypotheses **c** : EXTRAORDINARY, REMARKABLE ***syn*** see MATERIAL ***ant*** noumenal — **phe·nom·e·nal·ly** \-ᵊl-ē\ *adv*

phe·nom·e·nal·ism \-ən-ᵊl-ˌiz-əm\ *n* **1** : a theory that limits knowledge to phenomena only **2** : a theory that all knowledge is of phenomena and all existence is phenomenal — **phe·nom·e·nal·ist** \-ᵊl-əst\ *n* — **phe·nom·e·nal·is·tic** \-ˌnäm-ən-ᵊl-ˈis-tik\ *adj* — **phe·nom·e·nal·is·ti·cal·ly** \-ti-k(ə-)lē\ *adv*

phe·nom·e·no·log·i·cal \fi-ˌnäm-ən-ᵊl-ˈäj-i-kəl\ *adj* **1** : of or relating to phenomenology **2** : PHENOMENAL **3** : of or relating to phenomenalism — **phe·nom·e·no·log·i·cal·ly** \-k(ə-)lē\ *adv*

phe·nom·e·nol·o·gy \fi-ˌnäm-ə-ˈnäl-ə-jē\ *n, pl* **-gies** [G *phänomenologie*, fr. *phänomenon* phenomenon + *-logie* -logy] **1** : the study of the development of human consciousness and self-awareness as a preface to philosophy or a part of philosophy **2 a** (1) : the description of the formal structure of the objects of awareness and of awareness itself in abstraction from any claims concerning existence <the ~ of internal time-consciousness> (2) : the typological classification of a class of phenomena <the ~ of religion> **b** : an analysis produced by phenomenological investigation — **phe·nom·e·nol·o·gist** \-jəst\ *n*

phe·nom·e·non \fi-ˈnäm-ə-ˌnän, -nən\ *n, pl* **-na** \-nə, -ˌnä\ *or* **-nons** [LL *phaenomenon*, fr. Gk *phainomenon*, fr. neut. of *phainomenos*, prp. of *phainesthai* to appear, middle voice of *phainein* to show — more at FANCY] **1** *pl phenomena* : an observable fact or event **2** *pl phenomena* **a** : an object or aspect known through the senses rather than by thought or nonsensuous intuition **b** : a temporal or spatiotemporal object of sensual experience as distinguished from a noumenon **c** : a fact or event of scientific interest susceptible of scientific description and explanation **3 a** : a rare or significant fact or event **b** *pl phenomenons* : an exceptional, unusual, or abnormal person, thing, or occurrence

phe·no·thi·azine \ˌfē-nō-ˈthī-ə-ˌzēn\ *n* [ISV] **1** : a greenish yellow crystalline compound $C_{12}H_9NS$ used as an anthelmintic and insecticide esp. in veterinary practice **2** : any of various phenothiazine derivatives (as chlorpromazine) that are used as tranquilizing agents esp. in the treatment of schizophrenia

phe·no·type \ˈfē-nə-ˌtīp\ *n* [G *phänotypus*, fr. Gk *phainein* to show + *typos* type] **1** : the visible properties of an organism that are produced by the interaction of the genotype and the environment **2** : a group of organisms sharing a particular phenotype — **phe·no·typ·ic** \ˌfē-nə-ˈtip-ik\ *also* **phe·no·typ·i·cal** \-i-kəl\ *adj* — **phe·no·typ·i·cal·ly** \-i-k(ə-)lē\ *adv*

phen·ox·ide \fi-ˈnäk-ˌsīd\ *n* : a salt of a phenol esp. in its capacity as a weak acid

phen·oxy- \fi-ˈnäk-sē\ *comb form* [*phen*yl + *oxy-*] : containing the univalent radical C_6H_5O

phen·tol·amine \fen-ˈtäl-ə-ˌmēn, -mən\ *n* [*phen-* + *tol*uidine + *amine*] : an adrenergic blocking agent $C_{17}H_{19}N_3O$ that is used esp. in the diagnosis of pheochromocytoma

phe·nyl \ˈfen-ᵊl, ˈfēn-\ *n* [ISV] : a univalent radical C_6H_5 that is an aryl group derived from benzene by removal of one hydrogen atom — often used in combination — **phe·nyl·ic** \fi-ˈnil-ik\ *adj*

phen·yl·al·a·nine \ˌfen-ᵊl-ˈal-ə-ˌnēn\ *n* [ISV] : an essential amino acid $C_9H_{11}NO_2$ that is converted in the normal body to tyrosine

phen·yl·bu·ta·zone \-ˈbyüt-ə-ˌzōn\ *n* [*phenyl* + *but*yric acid + pyr*azolone* ($C_3H_4N_2O$)] : a drug $C_{19}H_{20}N_2O_2$ that is used for its analgesic and anti-inflammatory properties esp. in the treatment of arthritis, gout, and bursitis

phen·yl·ene \ˈfen-ᵊl-ˌēn\ *n* [ISV] : any of three bivalent radicals C_6H_4 derived from benzene by removal of two hydrogen atoms

phen·yl·eph·rine \-ˈef-ˌrēn, -rən\ *n* [*phenyl* + epin*ephrine*] : a sympathomimetic agent $C_9H_{13}NO_2$ that is used in the form of the hydrochloride as a vasoconstrictor, a mydriatic, and by injection to raise the blood pressure

phe·nyl·ke·ton·uria \ˌfen-ᵊl-ˌkēt-ᵊn-ˈ(y)u̇r-ē-ə, ˌfēn-\ *n* [*phenyl* + *ketone* + *-uria*] : an inherited metabolic disease in man that is characterized by inability to oxidize a metabolic product of phenylalanine and by severe mental deficiency

phe·nyl·ke·ton·uric \-ˈ(y)u̇r-ik\ *n* : one affected with phenylketonuria

phe·nyl·thio·car·ba·mide \-ˌthī-ō-ˈkär-bə-ˌmīd\ *n* : a crystalline compound $C_7H_8N_2S$ that is extremely bitter or tasteless depending on the presence or absence of a single dominant gene in the taster — called also *phenylthiourea, PTC*

phe·nyl·thio·urea \-ˌthī-ō-yu̇-ˈrē-ə\ *n* : PHENYLTHIOCARBAMIDE

pheo·chro·mo·cy·to·ma \ˌfē-ə-ˌkrō-mə-sə-ˈtō-mə, -sī-\ *n, pl* **-mas** *or* **-ma·ta** \-mət-ə\ [NL, fr. ISV *pheochromocyte* (chromaffin cell) + NL *-oma*] : a tumor that is derived from chromaffin cells and is usu. associated with paroxysmal or sustained hypertension

pher·o·mone \ˈfer-ə-ˌmōn\ *n* [ISV *phero-* (fr. Gk *pherein* to carry) + *-mone* (as in *hormone*) — more at BEAR] : a chemical substance that is produced by an animal and serves esp. as a stimulus to other individuals of the same species for one or more behavioral responses — **pher·o·mon·al** \ˌfer-ə-ˈmōn-ᵊl\ *adj*

phi \ˈfī\ *n* [MGk, fr. Gk *phei*] : the 21st letter of the Greek alphabet — see ALPHABET table

phi·al \ˈfī(-ə)l\ *n* [ME, fr. L *phiala*, fr. Gk *phialē*] : VIAL

Phi Be·ta Kap·pa \ˌfī-ˌbāt-ə-ˈkap-ə\ *n* [*Phi Beta Kappa* (*Society*), fr. *phi* + *beta* + *kappa*, initials of the society's Gk motto *philosophia biou kybernētēs* philosophy the guide of life] : a person winning high scholastic distinction in an American college or university and being elected to membership in a national honor society founded in 1776

phil *or* **philol** *abbr* philological; philology

phil- *or* **philo-** *comb form* [ME, fr. OF, fr. L, fr. Gk, fr. *philos* dear, friendly] : loving : having an affinity for <*philo*progenitive>

¹-phil \ˌfil\ *or* **-phile** \ˌfīl\ *n comb form* [F *-phile*, fr. Gk *-philos* -philous] : lover : one having an affinity for or a strong attraction to <acido*phil*> <Slavo*phile*>

²-phil *or* **-phile** *adj comb form* [NL *-philus*, fr. L, fr. Gk *-philos*] : loving : having a fondness or affinity for <hemo*phile*> <Franco*phil*>

Phil·a·del·phia lawyer \ˌfil-ə-ˌdel-fyə-, -fē-ə-\ *n* [*Philadelphia*, Pa.] : a shrewd lawyer versed in the intricacies of legal phraseology and adept at exploiting legal technicalities

Philadelphia pepper pot *n* : PEPPER POT 2b

phil·a·del·phus \ˌfil-ə-ˈdel-fəs\ *n* [NL, genus name, fr. Gk *philadelphos* brotherly, fr. *phil-* + *adelphos* brother — more at -ADELPHOUS] : any of a genus of ornamental shrubs of the saxifrage family of which several are widely grown in temperate regions for their showy white flowers — called also *mock orange, syringa*

phi·lan·der \fə-ˈlan-dər\ *vi* **phi·lan·dered; phi·lan·der·ing** \-d(ə-)riŋ\ [fr. obs. *philander* (lover, philanderer), prob. fr. the name *Philander*] **1** : to make love to someone with whom marriage is impossible (as because of an existing marriage) or with no intention of proposing marriage **2** : to have many love affairs — **phi·lan·der·er** \-dər-ər\ *n*

phil·an·throp·ic \ˌfil-ən-ˈthräp-ik\ *also* **phil·an·throp·i·cal** \-i-kəl\ *adj* **1** : of, relating to, or characterized by philanthropy : HUMANITARIAN **2** : dispensing or receiving aid from funds set aside for humanitarian purposes <a ~ foundation> — **phil·an·throp·i·cal·ly** \-i-k(ə-)lē\ *adv*

phi·lan·thro·pist \fə-ˈlan(t)-thrə-pəst\ *n* **:** one who practices philanthropy

phi·lan·thro·py \-pē\ *n, pl* **-pies** [LL *philanthropia,* fr. Gk *philanthrōpia,* fr. *philanthrōpos* loving mankind, fr. *phil-* + *anthrōpos* man] **1 :** goodwill to fellowmen; *esp* **:** active effort to promote human welfare **2 a :** a philanthropic act or gift **b :** an organization distributing or supported by philanthropic funds

phi·lat·e·list \fə-ˈlat-ᵊl-əst\ *n* **:** a specialist in philately **:** one who collects or studies stamps

phi·lat·e·ly \fə-ˈlat-ᵊl-ē\ *n* [F *philatélie,* fr. *phil-* + Gk *ateleia* tax exemption, fr. *atelēs* free from tax, fr. *a-* + *telos* tax; akin to Gk *telein* to pay, *tlēnai* to bear; fr. the fact that a stamped letter frees the recipient from paying the mailing charges — more at TOLERATE] **:** the collection and study of postage and imprinted stamps **:** stamp collecting — **phil·a·tel·ic** \ˌfil-ə-ˈtel-ik\ *adj* — **phil·a·tel·i·cal·ly** \-i-k(ə-)lē\ *adv*

Phi·le·mon \fə-ˈlē-mən, fī-\ *n* [Gk *Philēmōn*] **1 :** a friend and probable convert of the apostle Paul **2 :** a letter written by St. Paul to a Christian living in the area of Colossae and included as a book in the New Testament — see BIBLE table **3 :** a poor aged Phrygian who with his wife Baucis entertained Zeus and was rewarded with a splendid temple over which the couple presided

Phil·har·mon·ic \ˌfil-ər-ˈmän-ik, ˌfil-(ˌ)(h)är-\ *n* [F *philharmonique,* lit., loving harmony, fr. It *filarmonico,* fr. *fil-* phil- + *armonia* harmony, fr. L *harmonia*] **:** SYMPHONY ORCHESTRA

phil·hel·lene \(ˈ)fil-ˈhel-ˌēn\ *or* **phil·hel·len·ic** \ˌfil-hə-ˈlen-ik\ *adj* [Gk *philellēn,* fr. *phil-* + *Hellēn* Hellene] **:** admiring Greece or the Greeks — **philhellene** *n* — **phil·hel·le·nism** \(ˈ)fil-ˈhel-ə-ˌniz-əm\ *n* — **phil·hel·le·nist** \-nəst\ *n*

-phil·ia \ˈfil-ē-ə\ *n comb form* [NL, fr. Gk *philia* friendship, fr. *philos* dear] **1 :** tendency toward <hemo*philia*> **2 :** abnormal appetite or liking for <necro*philia*>

-phil·i·ac \ˈfil-ē-ˌak\ *n comb form* [NL *-philia* + Gk *-akos,* adj. suffix] **1 :** one having a tendency toward <hemo*philiac*> **2 :** one having an abnormal appetite or liking for <copro*philiac*>

-phil·ic \ˈfil-ik\ *adj comb form* [Gk *-philos* -philous] **:** having an affinity for **:** loving <photo*philic*>

Phi·lip·pi·ans \fə-ˈlip-ē-ənz\ *n pl but sing in constr* [short for *Epistle to the Philippians*] **:** a hortatory letter written by St. Paul to the Christians of Philippi and included as a book in the New Testament — see BIBLE table

phi·lip·pic \fə-ˈlip-ik\ *n* [MF *philippique,* fr. L & Gk; L *philippica, orationes philippicae,* speeches of Cicero against Mark Anthony, trans. of Gk *philippikoi logoi,* speeches of Demosthenes against Philip II of Macedon, lit., speeches relating to Philip] **:** a discourse or declamation full of bitter condemnation **:** TIRADE

Phil·ip·pine mahogany \ˌfil-ə-ˌpēn-\ *n* [*Philippine* islands] **:** any of several Philippine timber trees (family Dipterocarpaceae) with wood resembling that of the true mahoganies; *also* **:** its wood

phi·lis·tia \fə-ˈlis-tē-ə\ *n pl, often cap* [*Philistia,* ancient country of southwest Palestine] **:** the class or world of cultural philistines

phi·lis·tine \ˈfil-ə-ˌstēn; fə-ˈlis-tən, -ˌtēn; ˈfil-ə-stən\ *n* **1** *cap* **:** a native or inhabitant of ancient Philistia **2** *often cap* **a :** a crass prosaic often priggish individual guided by material rather than intellectual or artistic values **:** BABBITT **b :** one uninformed in a special area of knowledge — **philistine** *adj* — **phi·lis·tin·ism** \-ˌstē-ˌniz-əm, -tə-, -stə-\ *n*

phil·lu·men·ist \fi-ˈlü-mə-nəst\ *n* [*phil-* + L *lumen* light — more at LUMINARY] **:** one who collects matchbooks or matchbox labels

philo·den·dron \ˌfil-ə-ˈden-drən\ *n, pl* **-drons** *or* **-dra** \-drə\ [NL, fr. Gk, neut. of *philodendros* loving trees, fr. *phil-* + *dendron* tree — more at DENDR-] **:** any of various aroid plants (as of the genus *Philodendron*) that are cultivated for their showy foliage

philodendron

phi·log·y·ny \fə-ˈläj-ə-nē\ *n* [Gk *philogynia,* fr. *phil-* + *gynē* woman — more at QUEEN] **:** fondness for women

phi·lol·o·gist \fə-ˈläl-ə-jəst *also* fī-\ *n* **:** a specialist in philology

phi·lol·o·gy \-jē\ *n* [F *philologie,* fr. L *philologia* love of learning and literature, fr. Gk, fr. *philologos* fond of learning and literature, fr. *phil-* + *logos* word, speech — more at LEGEND] **1 :** the study of literature and of disciplines relevant to literature or to language as used in literature **2 a :** LINGUISTICS; *esp* **:** historical and comparative linguistics **b :** the study of human speech esp. as the vehicle of literature and as a field of study that sheds light on cultural history — **phil·o·log·i·cal** \ˌfil-ə-ˈläj-i-kəl\ *adj* — **phil·o·log·i·cal·ly** \-k(ə-)lē\ *adv*

Phil·o·mel \ˈfil-ə-ˌmel\ *n* [L *Philomela* Philomela, nightingale] **:** NIGHTINGALE

Phil·o·me·la \ˌfil-ə-ˈmē-lə\ *n* [L, fr. Gk *Philomēlē*] **:** an Athenian princess of Greek mythology raped and deprived of her tongue by her brother-in-law Tereus, avenged by the killing of his son, and changed into a nightingale while fleeing from him — compare PROCNE

philo·pro·gen·i·tive \ˌfil-ə-prō-ˈjen-ət-iv\ *adj* [*phil-* + L *progenitus,* pp. of *progignere* to beget — more at PROGENITOR] **1 :** tending to produce offspring **:** PROLIFIC **2 :** of, relating to, or characterized by love of offspring — **philo·pro·gen·i·tive·ness** *n*

philos *abbr* philosopher; philosophy

phi·lo·sophe \ˌfē-lə-ˈzȯf\ *n* [F, lit., philosopher] **:** one of the deistic or materialistic writers and thinkers of the 18th century French Enlightenment

phi·los·o·pher \fə-ˈläs-(ə-)fər\ *n* [ME, modif. of MF *philosophe,* fr. L *philosophus,* fr. Gk *philosophos,* fr. *phil-* + *sophia* wisdom, fr. *sophos* wise] **1 a :** one who seeks wisdom or enlightenment **:** SCHOLAR, THINKER **b :** a student of philosophy **2 a :** a person whose philosophical perspective enables him to meet trouble with equanimity **b :** the expounder of a theory in a particular area of experience **c :** one who philosophizes

philosophers' stone *n* **:** an imaginary stone, substance, or chemical preparation believed to have the power of transmuting baser metals into gold and sought for by alchemists

philo·soph·ic \ˌfil-ə-ˈsäf-ik *also* -ˈzäf-\ *or* **phil·o·soph·i·cal** \-i-kəl\ *adj* **1 a :** of or relating to philosophers or philosophy **b :** based on philosophy **2 :** characterized by the attitude of a philosopher; *specif* **:** calm in face of trouble — **philo·soph·i·cal·ly** \-i-k(ə-)lē\ *adv*

philosophical analysis *n* **:** an Anglo-American philosophical movement that seeks the solution of philosophical problems in the analysis of propositions or sentences — called also *analytic philosophy, linguistic analysis;* compare ORDINARY-LANGUAGE PHILOSOPHY

phi·los·o·phize \fə-ˈläs-ə-ˌfīz\ *vb* **-phized; -phiz·ing** *vi* **1 :** to reason in the manner of a philosopher **2 :** to expound a moralizing and often superficial philosophy ~ *vt* **:** to consider from or bring into conformity with a philosophic point of view — **phi·los·o·phiz·er** *n*

phi·los·o·phy \fə-ˈläs-(ə-)fē\ *n, pl* **-phies** [ME *philosophie,* fr. OF, fr. L *philosophia,* fr. Gk, fr. *philosophos* philosopher] **1 a :** pursuit of wisdom **b :** a search for a general understanding of values and reality by chiefly speculative rather than observational means **c :** an analysis of the grounds of and concepts expressing fundamental beliefs **2 a** (1) *archaic* **:** PHYSICAL SCIENCE (2) **:** ETHICS **b** (1) **:** all learning exclusive of technical precepts and practical arts (2) **:** the sciences and liberal arts exclusive of medicine, law, and theology <a doctor of ~> (3) **:** the 4-year college course of a major seminary **c :** a discipline comprising as its core logic, aesthetics, ethics, metaphysics, and epistemology **3 a :** a system of philosophical concepts <Kantian ~> **b :** a theory underlying or regarding a sphere of activity or thought <the ~ of cooking> <~ of science> **4 a :** the most general beliefs, concepts, and attitudes of an individual or group <the hippie ~> **b :** calmness of temper and judgment befitting a philosopher

philosophy of life **1 :** an overall vision of or attitude toward life and the purpose of life **2** [trans. of G *Lebensphilosophie*] **:** any of various philosophies that emphasize human life or life in general

-ph·i·lous \f-(ə-)ləs\ *adj comb form* [Gk *-philos,* fr. *philos* dear, friendly] **:** loving **:** having an affinity for <acido*philous*>

phil·ter *or* **phil·tre** \ˈfil-tər\ *n* [MF *philtre,* fr. L *philtrum,* fr. Gk *philtron;* akin to Gk *philos* dear] **1 :** a potion, drug, or charm held to have the power to arouse sexual passion **2 :** a potion credited with magical power

phi phenomenon \ˌfī-\ *n* **:** apparent motion resulting from an orderly sequence of stimuli (as lights flashed in rapid succession a short distance apart on a sign) without any actual motion being presented to the eye

PhL *abbr* licentiate in philosophy

phleb- *or* **phlebo-** *comb form* [ME *fleb-,* fr. MF, fr. LL *phlebo-,* fr. Gk *phleb-, phlebo-,* fr. *phleb-, phleps;* akin to L *fluere* to flow — more at FLUID] **:** vein <*phleb*itis>

phle·bi·tis \fli-ˈbīt-əs\ *n* [NL] **:** inflammation of a vein

phle·bo·gram \ˈflē-bə-ˌgram\ *n* [ISV] **:** a figure of a vein or a record of its movements (as by roentgenography following injection of a radiopaque substance)

phle·bog·ra·phy \fli-ˈbäg-rə-fē\ *n* [ISV] **:** the art of making phlebograms — **phle·bo·graph·ic** \ˌflē-bə-ˈgraf-ik\ *adj*

phle·bol·o·gy \fli-ˈbäl-ə-jē\ *n* [ISV] **:** a branch of medicine concerned with the veins

phle·bot·o·mize \fli-ˈbät-ə-ˌmīz\ *vb* **-mized; -miz·ing** *vt* **:** to draw blood from **:** BLEED ~ *vi* **:** to practice phlebotomy

phle·bo·to·mus fever \fli-ˌbät-ə-məs-\ *n* [NL *Phlebotomus,* genus of sand flies] **:** SANDFLY FEVER

phle·bot·o·my \fli-ˈbät-ə-mē\ *n, pl* **-mies** [ME *fleobotomie,* fr. MF *flebotomie,* fr. LL *phlebotomia,* fr. Gk, fr. *phleb-* + *-tomia* -tomy] **:** the letting of blood in the treatment of disease **:** VENESECTION — **phle·bot·o·mist** \-məst\ *n*

Phleg·e·thon \ˈfleg-ə-ˌthän\ *n* [L, fr. Gk *Phlegethōn*] **:** a river of fire in Hades

phlegm \ˈflem\ *n* [ME *fleume,* fr. MF, fr. LL *phlegmat-, phlegma,* fr. Gk, flame, inflammation, phlegm, fr. *phlegein* to burn — more at BLACK] **1 :** the one of the four humors in early physiology that was considered to be cold and moist and to cause sluggishness **2 :** viscid mucus secreted in abnormal quantity in the respiratory passages **3 a :** dull or apathetic coldness or indifference **b :** intrepid coolness or calm fortitude ***syn*** see EQUANIMITY — **phlegmy** \-ē\ *adj*

phleg·mat·ic \fleg-ˈmat-ik\ *adj* **1 :** resembling, consisting of, or producing the humor phlegm **2 :** having or showing a slow and stolid temperament ***syn*** see IMPASSIVE — **phleg·mat·i·cal·ly** \-i-k(ə-)lē\ *adv*

phlo·em \ˈflō-ˌem\ *n* [G, fr. Gk *phloios, phloos* bark; akin to Gk *phallos* penis — more at BLOW] **:** a complex tissue in the vascular system of higher plants that consists mainly of sieve tubes and elongated parenchyma cells usu. with fibers and that functions in translocation and in support and storage — compare XYLEM

phloem necrosis *n* **:** a pathological state in a plant characterized by brown discoloration and disintegration of the phloem; *esp* **:** a fatal virus disease of the American elm

phloem ray *n* **:** a vascular ray or part of a vascular ray that is located in phloem — called also *bast ray;* compare XYLEM RAY

phlo·gis·tic \flō-ˈjis-tik\ *adj* **1** [NL *phlogiston*] **:** of or relating to phlogiston **2** [Gk *phlogistos*] **:** of or relating to inflammations and fevers

phlo·gis·ton \-tən\ *n* [NL, fr. Gk, neut. of *phlogistos* inflammable, fr. *phlogizein* to set on fire, fr. *phlog-, phlox* flame, fr. *phlegein*] : the hypothetical principle of fire regarded formerly as a material substance

phlog·o·pite \'fläg-ə-ˌpīt\ *n* [G *phlogopit,* fr. Gk *phlogōpos* fiery-looking, fr. *phlog-, phlox* + *ōps* face — more at EYE] : a usu. brown to red form of mica

phlo·ri·zin *or* **phlo·rhi·zin** \'flōr-ə-zən, 'flȯr-; flə-'rīz-ᵊn\ *or* **phlo·rid·zin** \'flōr-əd-zən, 'flȯr-; flə-'rid-zən\ *n* [ISV *phlo-* (fr. Gk *phloos* bark) + *rhiz-* + *-in*] : a bitter crystalline glucoside $C_{21}H_{24}O_{10}$ that is extracted from root bark or bark (as of the apple, pear, or cherry), produces glycosuria if injected hypodermically, and is used chiefly in producing experimental diabetes in animals

phlox \'fläks\ *n, pl* **phlox** *or* **phlox·es** [NL, genus name, fr. L, a flower, fr. Gk, flame, wallflower] : any of a genus (*Phlox* of the family Polemoniaceae, the phlox family) of American annual or perennial herbs that have red, purple, white, or variegated flowers, a salverform corolla with the stamens on its tube, and a 3-valved capsular fruit

phlyc·te·nule \flik-'ten-(ˌ)yü(ə)l, 'flik-tə-ˌn(y)ü(ə)l\ *n* [NL *phlyctenula,* dim. of *phlyctena* pustule, fr. Gk *phlyktaina* blister, fr. *phlyzein* to boil over — more at FLUID] : a small vesicle or pustule; *esp* : one on the conjunctiva or cornea of the eye

-phobe \ˌfōb\ *n comb form* [Gk *-phobos* fearing] : one fearing or averse to (something specified) <Franco*phobe*>

pho·bia \'fō-bē-ə\ *n* [NL, fr. LL *-phobia,* fr. Gk, fr. *-phobos* fearing, fr. *phobos* fear, flight; akin to Gk *phebesthai* to flee, be frightened, Lith *begti* to flee] : an exaggerated usu. inexplicable and illogical fear of a particular object or class of objects

pho·bic \'fō-bik\ *adj* **1** : of, relating to, or constituting phobia **2** : motivated by or based on withdrawal from an unpleasant stimulus rather than movement toward a pleasant one <a ~ taxis>

-pho·bic \'fō-bik\ *or* **-ph·o·bous** \f-ə-bəs\ *adj comb form* [*-phobic* fr. F *-phobique,* fr. LL *-phobicus,* fr. Gk *-phobikos,* fr. *-phobia; -phobous* fr. LL *-phobus,* fr. Gk *-phobos*] **1** : having an aversion for <calci*phobous*> **2** : lacking affinity for <lyo*phobic*>

phobic reaction *n* : a psychoneurosis in which the principal symptom is a phobia

phoe·be \'fē-(ˌ)bē\ *n* [alter. of *pewee*] : any of several American flycatchers (genus *Sayornis*); *esp* : one (*S. phoebe*) of the eastern U.S. that has a slight crest and is plain grayish brown above and yellowish white below

Phoe·be \'fē-bē\ *n* [L, fr. Gk *Phoibē,* fr. *phoibē,* fem. of *phoibos*] : ARTEMIS

Phoe·bus \'fē-bəs\ *n* [L, fr. Gk *Phoibos,* fr. *phoibos* radiant] : APOLLO

Phoe·ni·cian \fi-'nish-ən, -'nē-shən\ *n* **1** : a native or inhabitant of ancient Phoenicia **2** : the Semitic language of ancient Phoenicia — **Phoenician** *adj*

phoe·nix \'fē-niks\ *n* [ME *fenix,* fr. OE, fr. L *phoenix,* fr. Gk *phoinix* purple, crimson, Phoenician, phoenix, date palm, fr. *phoinos* bloodred; akin to Gk *phonos* murder, *theinein* to strike — more at DEFEND] : a legendary bird which according to one account lived 500 years, burned itself to ashes on a pyre, and rose youthfully alive from the ashes to live another period — **phoe·nix·like** \-ˌlīk\ *adj*

¹phon \'fän\ *n* [ISV, fr. Gk *phōnē* voice, sound] : the unit of loudness on a scale beginning at zero for the faintest audible sound and corresponding to the decibel scale of sound intensity with the number of phons of a given sound being equal to the decibels of a pure 1000-cycle tone judged by the average listener to be equal in loudness to the given sound

²phon *abbr* phonetics

phon- *or* **phono-** *comb form* [L, fr. Gk *phōn-, phōno-,* fr. *phōnē* — more at BAN] : sound : voice : speech <*phon*ate> <*phono*graph>

pho·nate \'fō-ˌnāt\ *vi* **pho·nat·ed; pho·nat·ing** : to produce vocal sounds and esp. speech — **pho·na·tion** \fō-'nā-shən\ *n*

¹phone \'fōn\ *n* [by shortening] **1** : EARPHONE **2** : TELEPHONE

²phone *vb* **phoned; phon·ing** : TELEPHONE

³phone *n* [Gk *phōnē*] : a speech sound considered as a physical event without regard to its place in the sound system of a language

-phone \ˌfōn\ *n comb form* [Gk *-phōnos* sounding, fr. *phōnē*] : sound <homo*phone*> — often in names of musical instruments and sound-transmitting devices <radio*phone*> <xylo*phone*>

pho·ne·mat·ic \ˌfō-ni-'mat-ik\ *adj* : PHONEMIC

pho·neme \'fō-ˌnēm\ *n* [F *phonème,* fr. Gk *phōnēmat-, phōnēma* speech sound, utterance, fr. *phōnein* to sound] : a member of the set of the smallest units of speech that serve to distinguish one utterance from another in a language or dialect <the *p* of English *pat* and the *f* of English *fat* are two different *~s*>

pho·ne·mic \fə-'nē-mik, fō-\ *adj* **1** : of, relating to, or having the characteristics of a phoneme **2 a** : constituting members of different phonemes <in English \n\ and \ŋ\ are ~> **b** : DISTINCTIVE 2 — **pho·ne·mi·cal·ly** \-mi-k(ə-)lē\ *adv*

pho·ne·mics \-miks\ *n pl but sing in constr* **1** : a branch of linguistic analysis that consists of the study of phonemes **2** : the structure of a language in terms of phonemes

pho·net·ic \fə-'net-ik\ *adj* [NL *phoneticus,* fr. Gk *phōnētikos,* fr. *phōnein* to sound with the voice, fr. *phōnē* voice] **1 a** : of or relating to spoken language or speech sounds **b** : of or relating to the science of phonetics **2** : representing the sounds and other phenomena of speech: **a** : constituting an alteration of ordinary spelling that better represents the spoken language, that employs only characters of the regular alphabet, and that is used in a context of conventional spelling **b** : representing speech sounds by means of symbols that have one value only **c** : employing for speech sounds more than the minimum number of symbols necessary to represent the significant differences in a speaker's speech — **pho·net·i·cal** \-i-kəl\ *adj* — **pho·net·i·cal·ly** \-i-k(ə-)lē\ *adv*

phonetic alphabet *n* **1** : a set of symbols used for phonetic transcription **2** : any of various systems of identifying letters of the alphabet by means of code words in voice communication

pho·ne·ti·cian \ˌfō-nə-'tish-ən *also* ˌfän-ə-\ *n* : a specialist in phonetics

pho·net·ics \fə-'net-iks\ *n pl but sing in constr* **1 a** : the study and systematic classification of the sounds made in spoken utterance **b** : the practical application of this science to language study **2** : the system of speech sounds of a language or group of languages

pho·nic \'fän-ik, *except 2b also* 'fō-nik\ *adj* **1** : of, relating to, or producing sound : ACOUSTIC **2 a** : of or relating to the sounds of speech **b** : of or relating to phonics — **pho·ni·cal·ly** \-(ə-)lē\ *adv*

pho·nics \'fän-iks, *1 is also* 'fō-niks\ *n pl but sing in constr* **1** : the science of sound : ACOUSTICS **2** : a method of teaching beginners to read and pronounce words by learning the phonetic value of letters, letter groups, and esp. syllables

pho·no \'fō-(ˌ)nō\ *n, pl* **phonos** : PHONOGRAPH

pho·no·car·dio·gram \ˌfō-nə-'kärd-ē-ə-ˌgram\ *n* [ISV] : a graphic record of heart sounds made by means of a microphone, amplifier, and galvanometer

pho·no·car·dio·graph \-ˌgraf\ *n* : an instrument used for the graphic recording of the sounds of the heart by phonocardiogram — **pho·no·car·dio·graph·ic** \-ˌkärd-ē-ə-'graf-ik\ *adj* — **pho·no·car·di·og·ra·phy** \-ē-'äg-rə-fē\ *n*

pho·no·gram \'fō-nə-ˌgram\ *n* [ISV] **1** : a character or symbol used to represent a word, syllable, or phoneme **2** : a succession of orthographic letters that occurs with the same phonetic value in several words (as the *ight* of *bright, fight,* and *flight*) — **pho·no·gram·mic** *or* **pho·no·gram·ic** \ˌfō-nə-'gram-ik\ *adj* — **pho·no·gram·mi·cal·ly** *or* **pho·no·gram·i·cal·ly** \-i-k(ə-)lē\ *adv*

pho·no·graph \'fō-nə-ˌgraf\ *n* : an instrument for reproducing sounds by means of the vibration of a stylus or needle following a spiral groove on a revolving disc or cylinder

pho·nog·ra·pher \fə-'näg-rə-fər, fō-\ *n* : a specialist in phonography

pho·no·graph·ic \ˌfō-nə-'graf-ik, *1 is also* ˌfän-ə-\ *adj* **1** : of or relating to phonography **2** : of or relating to a phonograph — **pho·no·graph·i·cal·ly** \-i-k(ə-)lē\ *adv*

pho·nog·ra·phy \fə-'näg-rə-fē, fō-\ *n* **1** : spelling based on pronunciation **2** : a system of shorthand writing based on sound

pho·no·lite \'fōn-ᵊl-ˌīt\ *n* [F, fr. G *phonolith,* fr. *phon-* + *-lith;* fr. its ringing sound when struck] : a gray or green volcanic rock consisting essentially of orthoclase and nepheline — **pho·no·lit·ic** \ˌfōn-ᵊl-'it-ik\ *adj*

pho·no·log·i·cal \ˌfōn-ᵊl-'äj-i-kəl *also* ˌfän-ᵊl-\ *also* **pho·no·log·ic** \-ik\ *adj* : of or relating to phonology — **pho·no·log·i·cal·ly** \-i-k(ə-)lē\ *adv*

pho·nol·o·gist \fə-'näl-ə-jəst, fō-\ *n* : a specialist in phonology

pho·nol·o·gy \-jē\ *n* **1** : the science of speech sounds including esp. the history and theory of sound changes in a language or in two or more related languages **2** : the phonetics and phonemics of a language at a particular time

pho·non \'fō-ˌnän\ *n* [*phon-* + ²*-on*] : a quantum of vibrational energy (as in a crystal)

pho·no·re·cep·tion \ˌfō-nō-ri-'sep-shən\ *n* : the perception of vibratory motion of relatively high frequency; *specif* : HEARING

pho·no·re·cep·tor \-'sep-tər\ *n* : an animal organ for phonoreception; *esp* : OTOCYST

pho·no·rec·ord \'fō-nō-ˌrek-ərd *also* -ˌȯ(ə)rd\ *n* : a phonograph record

¹pho·ny *or* **pho·ney** \'fō-nē\ *adj* **pho·ni·er; -est** [origin unknown] : not genuine or real: as **a** (1) : intended to deceive or mislead (2) : intended to defraud : COUNTERFEIT <a ~ $10 bill> <a ~ check> **b** : arousing suspicion : probably dishonest <something ~ about his alibi> **c** : having no genuine existence : FICTITIOUS <~ publicity stories> **d** : FALSE, SHAM <a ~ name> <~ pearls> **e** : making a false show: as (1) : HYPOCRITICAL (2) : SPECIOUS <has a ~ poetic elegance — *New Republic*> — **pho·ni·ly** \'fōn-ᵊl-ē\ *adv* — **pho·ni·ness** \'fō-nē-nəs\ *n*

²phony *or* **phoney** *n, pl* **phonies** : one that is phony

-pho·ny \f-ə-nē, ˌfō-nē\ *also* **-pho·nia** \'fō-nē-ə\ *n comb form* [ME *-phonie,* fr. OF, fr. L *-phonia,* fr. Gk *-phōnia,* fr. *-phōnos* sounding — more at -PHONE] **1** : sound <tele*phony*> **2** *usu* *-phonia* : speech disorder of a (specified) type <dys*phonia*>

pho·rate \'fō(ə)r-ˌāt, 'fȯ(ə)r-\ *n* [phos*phor*us + thion*ate*] : a very toxic organophosphate systemic insecticide $C_7H_{17}O_2PS_3$ that is used esp. in seed treatments

-phore \ˌfō(ə)r, ˌfȯ(ə)r\ *n comb form* [NL *-phorus,* fr. Gk *-phoros,* fr. *-phoros* (adj. comb. form) carrying, fr. *pherein* to carry — more at BEAR] : carrier <gameto*phore*>

-pho·re·sis \fə-'rē-səs\ *n comb form, pl* **-pho·re·ses** \-ˌsēz\ [NL, fr. Gk *phorēsis* act of carrying, fr. *phorein* to carry, wear, freq. of *pherein*] : transmission <electro*phoresis*>

phos- *comb form* [Gk *phōs-,* fr. *phōs*] : light <*phos*gene>

phos·gene \'fäz-ˌjēn\ *n* [fr. its originally having been obtained by the action of sunlight] : a colorless gas $COCl_2$ of unpleasant odor that is a severe respiratory irritant

phosph- *or* **phospho-** *comb form* [*phosphorus*] **1** : phosphorus <*phosph*ide> <*phospho*protein> **2** : phosphate <*phospho*fructokinase>

phos·pham·i·don \fäs-'fam-ə-ˌdän\ *n* [*phospha*te + *amide* + *-on,* of unknown origin] : a contact and systemic organophosphorus insecticide and miticide $C_{10}H_{19}ClNO_5P$

phos·pha·tase \'fäs-fə-ˌtās, -ˌtāz\ *n* : an enzyme that accelerates the hydrolysis and synthesis of organic esters of phosphoric acid and the transfer of phosphate groups to other compounds: **a** : ALKALINE PHOSPHATASE **b** : ACID PHOSPHATASE

phos·phate \'fäs-ˌfāt\ *n* [F, fr. *acide phosphorique* phosphoric acid] **1 a** : a salt or ester of a phosphoric acid **b** : an organic compound of phosphoric acid in which the acid unit is bound to nitrogen or a carboxyl group in a way that permits useful energy to be released (as in metabolism) **2** : an effervescent drink of carbonated water with a small amount of phosphoric acid or an acid phosphate flavored with fruit syrup **3** : a phosphatic material used for fertilizers

phosphate group *n* : a group or radical derived from phosphoric acid by removal of one or more hydrogen atoms

phosphate rock *n* : a rock that consists largely of calcium phosphate usu. together with other minerals (as calcium carbonate), is used in making fertilizers, and is a source of phosphorus compounds

phos·phat·ic \fäs-ˈfat-ik, -ˈfāt-\ *adj* **:** of, relating to, or containing phosphoric acid or phosphates <~ fertilizers>

phos·pha·tide \ˈfäs-fə-ˌtīd\ *n* [ISV] **:** PHOSPHOLIPID — **phos·pha·tid·ic** \ˌfäs-fə-ˈtid-ik\ *adj*

phos·pha·ti·dyl \ˌfäs-fə-ˈtīd-ᵊl, fäs-ˈfat-əd-ᵊl\ *n* **:** any of several univalent radicals $(RCOO)_2C_3H_5OPO(OH)$ that are derived from phosphatidic acids

phos·pha·tize \ˈfäs-fə-ˌtīz\ *vt* **-tized; -tiz·ing 1 :** to change to a phosphate or phosphates **2 :** to treat with phosphoric acid or a phosphate — **phos·pha·ti·za·tion** \ˌfäs-fət-ə-ˈzā-shən, -ˌfāt-\ *n*

phos·pha·tu·ria \ˌfäs-fə-ˈt(y)u̇r-ē-ə\ *n* [NL, fr. ISV *phosphate* + NL *-uria*] **:** the excessive discharge of phosphates in the urine — **phos·pha·tu·ric** \-ˈt(y)u̇(ə)r-ik\ *adj*

phos·phene \ˈfäs-ˌfēn\ *n* [ISV *phos-* + Gk *phainein* to show — more at FANCY] **:** a luminous impression due to excitation of the retina

phos·phide \-ˌfīd\ *n* [ISV] **:** a binary compound of phosphorus usu. with a more electropositive element or radical

phos·phine \-ˌfēn\ *n* [ISV] **1 :** a colorless poisonous flammable gas PH_3 that is a weaker base than ammonia and that is used esp. to fumigate stored grain **2 :** any of various derivatives of phosphine analogous to amines but weaker as bases

phos·phite \-ˌfīt\ *n* **:** a salt or ester of phosphorous acid

phos·pho·cre·atine \ˌfäs-(ˌ)fō-ˈkrē-ə-ˌtēn\ *n* [ISV] **:** a compound $C_4H_{10}N_3O_5P$ of creatine and phosphoric acid that is found esp. in vertebrate muscle where it is an energy source for muscle contraction

phos·pho·di·es·ter·ase \-dī-ˈes-tə-ˌrās, -ˌrāz\ *n* [*phosph-* + *diester* + *-ase*] **:** a phosphatase (as from snake venom) that acts on diesters (as some nucleotides) to hydrolyze only one of the two ester groups

phos·pho·enol·pyr·uvate \ˈfäs-ˌfō-ə-ˌnōl-pī-ˈrü-ˌvāt, -ˌnȯl-, -ˌpī(ə)r-ˈyü-\ *n* **:** a salt or ester of phosphoenolpyruvic acid

phos·pho·enol·pyr·uvic acid \-ˌü-vik-, -ˈyü-\ *n* **:** the phosphate $CH_2{=}O(OPO_3H_2)COOH$ of the enol form of pyruvic acid that is formed as an intermediate in carbohydrate metabolism (as in the reversible dehydration of phosphoglyceric acid)

phos·pho·fruc·to·kinase \ˈfäs-(ˌ)fō-ˌfrək-tō-ˈkī-ˌnās, -ˌfrük-, -ˌfru̇k-, -ˌnāz\ *n* [*phospho-* + *fructose* + *kinase*] **:** an enzyme that catalyzes the transfer of a second phosphate (as from ATP) to fructose in carbohydrate metabolism

phos·pho·glu·co·mu·tase \-ˌglü-kō-ˈmyü-ˌtās, -ˌtāz\ *n* [*phosph-* + *gluc-* + *mutase*] **:** an enzyme that is found in all plant and animal cells and that catalyzes the reversible isomerization of glucose-1-phosphate to glucose-6-phosphate

phos·pho·glyc·er·al·de·hyde \-ˌglis-ə-ˈral-də-ˌhīd\ *n* **:** a phosphate of glyceraldehyde $C_3H_5O_3(H_2PO_3)$ that is formed esp. in anaerobic metabolism of carbohydrates by the splitting of a diphosphate of fructose

phos·pho·gly·cer·ic acid \-glis-ˌer-ik-\ *n* **:** either of two isomeric phosphates $HOOCC_2H_3(OH)OPO_3H_2$ of glyceric acid that are formed as intermediates in photosynthesis and in carbohydrate metabolism

phos·pho·ki·nase \ˌfäs-fō-ˈkī-ˌnās, -ˌnāz\ *n* **:** KINASE

phos·pho·li·pase \-ˈlī-ˌpās, -ˌpāz\ *n* **:** LECITHINASE

phos·pho·lip·id \-ˈlip-əd\ *n* **:** a complex phosphoric ester lipid that is found in all living cells in association with stored fats

phos·pho·mono·es·ter·ase \-ˌmän-ō-ˈes-tə-ˌrās, -ˌrāz\ *n* **:** a phosphatase that acts on monoesters

phos·pho·ni·um \fäs-ˈfō-nē-əm\ *n* [NL] **:** a univalent radical PH_4 analogous to ammonium and derived from phosphine

phos·pho·pro·tein \ˌfäs-fō-ˈprō-ˌtēn, -ˈprōt-ē-ən\ *n* **:** any of various proteins (as casein) that contain combined phosphoric acid

phos·phor \ˈfäs-fər, -ˌfō(ə)r\ *also* **phos·phore** \-ˌfō(ə)r, -ˌfȯ(ə)r, -fər\ *n* [L *phosphorus*, fr. Gk *phōsphoros*, lit., light bringer, fr. *phōsphoros* light-bearing, fr. *phōs-* + *pherein* to carry, bring — more at BEAR] **:** a phosphorescent substance; *specif* **:** a substance that emits light when excited by radiation

phosphor- *or* **phosphoro-** *comb form* **:** phosphorus <*phosphor*ism> **:** phosphoric acid <*phosphoro*lysis>

phosphor bronze *n* **:** a bronze of great hardness, elasticity, and toughness that contains a small amount of phosphorus

phos·pho·resce \ˌfäs-fə-ˈres\ *vi* **-resced; -resc·ing** [prob. back-formation fr. *phosphorescent*] **:** to exhibit phosphorescence

phos·pho·res·cence \-ˈres-ᵊn(t)s\ *n* **1 :** luminescence that is caused by the absorption of radiations and continues for a noticeable time after these radiations have stopped **2 :** an enduring luminescence without sensible heat

phos·pho·res·cent \-ᵊnt\ *adj* **:** exhibiting phosphorescence — **phos·pho·res·cent·ly** *adv*

phos·pho·ret·ed *or* **phos·pho·ret·ted** \ˈfäs-fə-ˌret-əd\ *adj* [NL *phosphoretum* phosphide, fr. *phosphorus*] **:** impregnated or combined with phosphorus

phos·pho·ric \fäs-ˈfȯr-ik, -ˈfär-; ˈfäs-f(ə-)rik\ *adj* **:** of, relating to, or containing phosphorus esp. with a valence higher than in phosphorous compounds

phosphoric acid *n* **1 :** a syrupy or deliquescent tribasic acid H_3PO_4 used esp. in preparing phosphates (as for fertilizers), in rust-proofing metals, and as a flavoring in soft drinks — called also *orthophosphoric acid* **2 :** any of several hydrated forms of phosphoric acid (as metaphosphoric acid or pyrophosphoric acid)

phos·pho·rism \ˈfäs-fə-ˌriz-əm\ *n* **:** a poisoning by phosphorus esp. when chronic

phos·pho·rite \-ˌrīt\ *n* **1 :** a fibrous concretionary apatite **2 :** PHOSPHATE ROCK — **phos·pho·rit·ic** \ˌfäs-fə-ˈrit-ik\ *adj*

phos·pho·rol·y·sis \ˌfäs-fə-ˈräl-ə-səs\ *n* [NL] **:** a reversible reaction analogous to hydrolysis in which phosphoric acid functions in a manner similar to that of water with the formation of a phosphate (as glucose-1-phosphate in the breakdown of liver glycogen) — **phos·pho·ro·lyt·ic** \-rō-ˈlit-ik\ *adj*

phos·pho·rous \ˈfäs-f(ə-)rəs; fäs-ˈfōr-əs, -ˈfȯr-\ *adj* **:** of, relating to, or containing phosphorus esp. with a valence lower than in phosphoric compounds

phosphorous acid *n* **:** a deliquescent crystalline acid H_3PO_3 used esp. as a reducing agent and in making phosphites

phos·pho·rus \ˈfäs-f(ə-)rəs\ *n, often attrib* [NL, fr. Gk *phōsphoros* light-bearing — more at PHOSPHOR] **1 :** a phosphorescent substance or body; *esp* **:** one that shines or glows in the dark **2 :** a nonmetallic multivalent element of the nitrogen family that occurs widely esp. as phosphates — see ELEMENT table

phos·pho·ryl \ˈfäs-fə-ˌril\ *n* [ISV] **:** a usu. trivalent radical PO consisting of phosphorus and oxygen

phos·phor·y·lase \fäs-ˈfȯr-ə-ˌlās, -ˌlāz\ *n* [*phosphoryl* + *-ase*] **:** any enzyme that catalyzes phosphorolysis with the formation of organic phosphates

phos·phor·y·late \-ˌlāt\ *vt* **-lat·ed; -lat·ing :** to cause (an organic compound) to take up or combine with phosphoric acid or a phosphorus-containing group — **phos·phor·y·la·tive** \-ˌlāt-iv\ *adj*

phos·phor·y·la·tion \ˌfäs-ˌfȯr-ə-ˈlā-shən\ *n* **:** the process of phosphorylating either by reaction with inorganic phosphate or by transfer of phosphate from another organic phosphate; *esp* **:** the enzymatic conversion of carbohydrates into their phosphoric esters in metabolic processes

phot \ˈfōt\ *n* [ISV, fr. Gk *phōt-*, *phōs* light] **:** the cgs unit of illumination equal to one lumen per square centimeter

phot- *or* **photo-** *comb form* [Gk *phōt-*, *phōto-*, fr. *phōt-*, *phōs* — more at FANCY] **1 :** light **:** radiant energy <*phot*on> <*photo*graphy> **2 :** photograph **:** photographic <*photo*engraving> **3 :** photoelectric <*photo*cell>

pho·tic \ˈfōt-ik\ *adj* **1 :** of, relating to, or involving light esp. in relation to organisms **2 :** penetrated by light esp. of the sun <~ zone of the ocean> — **pho·ti·cal·ly** \ˈfōt-i-k(ə-)lē\ *adv*

[1]**pho·to** \ˈfōt-(ˌ)ō\ *n, pl* **photos :** PHOTOGRAPH

[2]**photo** *vb* **:** PHOTOGRAPH

[3]**photo** *adj* **:** PHOTOGRAPHIC 1

pho·to·au·to·tro·phic \ˌfōt-ō-ˌȯt-ə-ˈtrō-fik\ *adj* **:** autotrophic and obtaining energy from light <green plants are ~> — **pho·to·au·to·tro·phi·cal·ly** \-fi-k(ə-)lē\ *adv*

pho·to·bi·ol·o·gy \ˌfōt-ō-(ˌ)bī-ˈäl-ə-jē\ *n* [ISV] **:** a branch of biology that deals with the effects on living beings of radiant energy (as light) — **pho·to·bi·o·log·ic** \-ˌbī-ə-ˈläj-ik\ *or* **pho·to·bi·o·log·i·cal** \-i-kəl\ *adj* — **pho·to·bi·ol·o·gist** \-(ˌ)bī-ˈäl-ə-jəst\ *n*

pho·to·bi·ot·ic \-(ˌ)bī-ˈät-ik\ *adj* **:** requiring light in order to live or thrive

pho·to·cath·ode \-ˈkath-ˌōd\ *n* [ISV] **:** a cathode that emits electrons when exposed to radiant energy and esp. light

pho·to·cell \ˈfōt-ə-ˌsel\ *n* [ISV] **:** PHOTOELECTRIC CELL

pho·to·chem·i·cal \ˌfōt-ō-ˈkem-i-kəl\ *adj* **1 :** of, relating to, or resulting from the chemical action of radiant energy and esp. light <~ smog> **2 :** of or relating to photochemistry <~ studies> — **pho·to·chem·i·cal·ly** \-k(ə-)lē\ *adv*

pho·to·chem·is·try \-ˈkem-ə-strē\ *n* **1 :** a branch of chemistry that deals with the effect of radiant energy in producing chemical changes **2 a :** photochemical properties <the ~ of gases> **b :** photochemical processes <the ~ of vision> — **pho·to·chem·ist** \-ˈkem-əst\ *n*

pho·to·chro·mic \ˌfōt-ə-ˈkrō-mik\ *adj* [*phot-* + *chrom-* + *-ic*] **1 :** capable of changing color on exposure to radiant energy (as light) <~ glass> **2 :** of, relating to, or utilizing the change of color shown by a photochromic substance <a ~ process> — **pho·to·chro·mism** \-ˌmiz-əm\ *n*

pho·to·co·ag·u·la·tion \-kō-ˌag-yə-ˈlā-shən\ *n* **:** a surgical process of coagulating tissue by means of a precisely oriented high-energy light source (as a light beam)

pho·to·com·pose \ˌfōt-ō-kəm-ˈpōz\ *vt* **:** to set (as reading matter) by photocomposition — **pho·to·com·pos·er** *n*

pho·to·com·po·si·tion \-ˌkäm-pə-ˈzish-ən\ *n* **:** composition of reading matter directly on film or photosensitive paper for reproduction

pho·to·con·duc·tive \-kən-ˈdək-tiv\ *adj* **:** having, involving, or operating by photoconductivity

pho·to·con·duc·tiv·i·ty \-ˌkän-ˌdək-ˈtiv-ət-ē, -kən-\ *n* **:** electrical conductivity that is affected by exposure to light or other radiation

[1]**pho·to·copy** \ˈfōt-ə-ˌkäp-ē\ *n* [ISV] **:** a photographic reproduction of graphic matter

[2]**photocopy** *vt* **:** to make a photocopy of ~ *vi* **:** to make a photocopy — **pho·to·copi·er** *n*

pho·to·cur·rent \ˈfōt-ō-ˌkər-ənt, -kə-rənt\ *n* [*photo*electric *current*] **:** a stream of electrons produced by photoelectric or photovoltaic effects

pho·to·de·com·po·si·tion \-ˌdē-ˌkäm-pə-ˈzish-ən\ *n* **:** chemical breaking down (as of a pesticide) by means of radiant energy

pho·to·de·tec·tor \ˌfōt-ō-di-ˈtek-tər\ *n* **:** any of various devices for detecting and measuring the intensity of radiant energy through photoelectric action

pho·to·dis·in·te·gra·tion \ˈfōt-ō-dis-ˌint-ə-ˈgrā-shən\ *n* **:** disintegration of the nucleus of an atom produced by absorption of radiant energy — **pho·to·dis·in·te·grate** \-ˈint-ə-ˌgrāt\ *vt*

pho·to·dis·so·ci·a·tion \-dis-ˌō-sē-ˈā-shən, -shē-\ *n* **:** dissociation (as of water) under the influence of radiant energy — **pho·to·dis·so·ci·ate** \-ˈō-s(h)ē-ˌāt\ *vt* — **pho·to·dis·so·ci·a·tive** \-s(h)ē-ˌāt-iv, -shət-iv\ *adj*

pho·to·dra·ma \ˈfōt-ə-ˌdräm-ə, -ˌdram-\ *n* **:** MOTION PICTURE

pho·to·du·pli·cate \ˌfōt-ō-ˈd(y)ü-plə-ˌkāt\ *vb* **:** PHOTOCOPY — **pho·to·du·pli·cate** \-pli-kət\ *n* — **pho·to·du·pli·ca·tion** \-ˌd(y)ü-plə-ˈkā-shən\ *n*

pho·to·dy·nam·ic \-(ˌ)dī-ˈnam-ik\ *adj* [ISV] : of, relating to, or having the property of intensifying or inducing a toxic reaction to light and esp. sunlight in living systems — **pho·to·dy·nam·i·cal·ly** \-i-k(ə-)lē\ *adv*

pho·to·elec·tric \ˌfōt-ō-i-ˈlek-trik\ *adj* [ISV] : involving, relating to, or utilizing any of various electrical effects due to the interaction of radiation (as light) with matter — **pho·to·elec·tri·cal·ly** \-tri-k(ə-)lē\ *adv*

photoelectric cell *n* : a cell whose electrical properties are modified by the action of light

pho·to·elec·tron \ˌfōt-ō-i-ˈlek-ˌträn\ *n* [ISV] : an electron released in photoemission — **pho·to·elec·tron·ic** \-ˌlek-ˈträn-ik\ *adj*

pho·to·emis·sion \-i-ˈmish-ən\ *n* : the release of electrons from a metal by means of energy supplied by incidence of radiation and esp. light — **pho·to·emis·sive** \-ˈmis-iv\ *adj*

pho·to·en·grave \-in-ˈgrāv\ *vt* [back-formation fr. *photoengraving*] : to make a photoengraving of — **pho·to·en·grav·er** *n*

pho·to·en·grav·ing *n* **1** : a photomechanical process for making linecuts and halftone cuts by photographing an image on a metal plate and then etching **2 a** : a plate made by photoengraving **b** : a print made from such a plate

photo finish *n* **1** : a race finish in which contestants are so close that a photograph of them as they cross the finish line has to be examined to determine the winner **2** : a close contest

pho·to·flash \ˈfōt-ə-ˌflash\ *n* : an electrically or mechanically operated flash lamp; *esp* : FLASHBULB

pho·to·flood \-ˌfləd\ *n* : an electric lamp using excess voltage to give intense sustained illumination for taking photographs

pho·to·flu·o·ro·gram \ˌfōt-ə-ˈflu̇r-ə-ˌgram\ *n* : a photograph made by photofluorography

pho·to·flu·o·rog·ra·phy \-(ˌ)flu̇(-ə)r-ˈäg-rə-fē\ *n* : the photography of the image produced on a fluorescent screen by X rays — **pho·to·flu·o·ro·graph·ic** \-ˌflu̇r-ə-ˈgraf-ik\ *adj*

[1]**pho·tog** \fə-ˈtäg\ *n* [short for *photographer*] : one who takes photographs : PHOTOGRAPHER

[2]**photog** *abbr* photographic; photography

pho·to·gene \ˈfōt-ə-ˌjēn\ *n* [ISV *phot-* + *-gen*] : an afterimage or retinal impression

pho·to·ge·nic \ˌfōt-ə-ˈjen-ik, -ˈjēn-\ *adj* **1** : produced or precipitated by light <~ dermatitis> **2** : producing or generating light : PHOSPHORESCENT <~ bacteria> **3** : suitable or suited for being photographed — **pho·to·ge·ni·cal·ly** \-i-k(ə-)lē\ *adv*

pho·to·ge·ol·o·gy \ˌfōt-ō-jē-ˈäl-ə-jē\ *n* : a branch of geology concerned with the identification of geological features through the study of aerial photographs — **pho·to·geo·log·ic** \-ˌjē-ə-ˈläj-ik\ *also* **pho·to·geo·log·i·cal** \-i-kəl\ *adj*

pho·to·gram \ˈfōt-ə-ˌgram\ *n* [ISV] : a shadowlike photograph made by placing objects between light-sensitive paper and a light source

pho·to·gram·met·ric \ˌfōt-ə-grə-ˈme-trik, -gra-\ *adj* : of, made by, or relating to photogrammetry

pho·to·gram·me·try \-ˈgram-ə-trē\ *n* [ISV *photogram* photograph (fr. *phot-* + *-gram*) + *-metry*] : the science of making reliable measurements by the use of photographs and esp. aerial photographs (as in surveying) — **pho·to·gram·me·trist** \-trəst\ *n*

[1]**pho·to·graph** \ˈfōt-ə-ˌgraf\ *n* : a picture or likeness obtained by photography

[2]**photograph** *vt* : to take a photograph of ~ *vi* **1** : to take a photograph **2** : to undergo being photographed — **pho·tog·ra·pher** \fə-ˈtäg-rə-fər\ *n*

pho·to·graph·ic \ˌfōt-ə-ˈgraf-ik\ *adj* **1** : relating to, obtained by, or used in photography **2** : representing nature and human beings with the exactness of a photograph **3** : capable of retaining vivid impressions <a ~ mind> — **pho·to·graph·i·cal·ly** \-i-k(ə-)lē\ *adv*

pho·tog·ra·phy \fə-ˈtäg-rə-fē\ *n* : the art or process of producing images on a sensitized surface (as a film) by the action of radiant energy and esp. light

pho·to·gra·vure \ˌfōt-ə-grə-ˈvyu̇(ə)r\ *n* [F, fr. *phot-* + *gravure*] : a process for making prints from an intaglio plate prepared by photographic methods; *also* : a print produced by photogravure

pho·to·he·lio·graph \ˌfōt-ō-ˈhē-lē-ə-ˌgraf\ *n* : a telescope adapted for photographing the sun

pho·to·in·duced \-in-ˈd(y)üst\ *adj* : induced by the action of light — **pho·to·in·duc·tion** \-ˈdək-shən\ *n* — **pho·to·in·duc·tive** \-ˈdək-tiv\ *adj*

pho·to·ion·iza·tion \-ˌī-ə-nə-ˈzā-shən\ *n* : ionization (as in the ionosphere) resulting from collision of a molecule or atom with a photon

pho·to·jour·nal·ism \ˌfōt-ō-ˈjərn-ᵊl-ˌiz-əm\ *n* : journalism in which written copy is subordinate to pictorial usu. photographic presentation of news stories or in which a high proportion of pictorial presentation is used — **pho·to·jour·nal·ist** \-ᵊl-əst\ *n* — **pho·to·jour·nal·is·tic** \-ˌjərn-ᵊl-ˈis-tik\ *adj*

pho·to·ki·ne·sis \-kə-ˈnē-səs, -kī-\ *n* [NL, fr. *phot-* + Gk *kinēsis* motion — more at KINESIOLOGY] : motion or activity induced by light — **pho·to·ki·net·ic** \-ˈnet-ik\ *adj*

pho·to·li·thog·ra·phy \-lith-ˈäg-rə-fē\ *n* [ISV] : lithography in which photographically prepared plates are used — **pho·to·litho·graph** \-ˈlith-ə-ˌgraf\ *n or vt* — **pho·to·li·thog·ra·pher** \-lith-ˈäg-rə-fər, -ˈlith-ə-ˌgraf-ər\ *n* — **pho·to·litho·graph·ic** \-ˌlith-ə-ˈgraf-ik\ *adj* — **pho·to·litho·graph·i·cal·ly** \-i-k(ə-)lē\ *adv*

pho·tol·y·sis \fō-ˈtäl-ə-səs\ *n* [NL] : chemical decomposition by the action of radiant energy — **pho·to·lyt·ic** \ˌfōt-ᵊl-ˈit-ik\ *adj* — **pho·to·lyt·i·cal·ly** \-i-k(ə-)lē\ *adv*

pho·to·lyze \ˈfōt-ᵊl-ˌīz\ *vb* **-lyzed; -lyz·ing** *vt* : to cause to undergo photolysis ~ *vi* : to undergo photolysis — **pho·to·lyz·able** \-ˌī-zə-bəl\ *adj*

[1]**pho·to·map** \ˈfōt-ō-ˌmap\ *n* : a photograph which is taken vertically from above (as from an airplane) and upon which a grid and data pertinent to maps have been added

[2]**photomap** *vt* : to make a photomap of ~ *vi* : to make a photomap

pho·to·me·chan·i·cal \ˌfōt-ō-mi-ˈkan-i-kəl\ *adj* [ISV] : relating to or involving any of various processes for producing printed matter from a photographically prepared surface — **pho·to·me·chan·i·cal·ly** \-i-k(ə-)lē\ *adv*

pho·tom·e·ter \fō-ˈtäm-ət-ər\ *n* [NL *photometrum,* fr. *phot-* + *-metrum* -meter] : an instrument for measuring luminous intensity, luminous flux, illumination, or brightness

pho·to·met·ric \ˌfōt-ə-ˈme-trik\ *adj* : of or relating to photometry or the photometer — **pho·to·met·ri·cal·ly** \-tri-k(ə-)lē\ *adv*

pho·tom·e·try \fō-ˈtäm-ə-trē\ *n* [NL *photometria,* fr. *phot-* + *-metria* -metry] : a branch of science that deals with measurement of the intensity of light; *also* : the practice of using a photometer

pho·to·mi·cro·graph \ˌfōt-ə-ˈmī-krə-ˌgraf\ *n* [*phot-* + *micr-* + *-graph*] : a photograph of a magnified image of a small object — **photomicrograph** *vt* — **pho·to·mi·cro·graph·ic** \-ˌmī-krə-ˈgraf-ik\ *also* **pho·to·mi·cro·graph·i·cal** \-i-kəl\ *adj* — **pho·to·mi·crog·ra·phy** \-mī-ˈkräg-rə-fē\ *n*

pho·to·mi·cro·scope \-ˈmī-krə-ˌskōp\ *n* : an instrument or system that combines a microscope, camera, and light source and is used for making photomicrographs — **pho·to·mi·cro·scop·ic** \-ˌmī-krə-ˈskäp-ik\ *adj*

pho·to·mon·tage \-män-ˈtäzh, mōⁿ(n)-, -ˈtȧzh\ *n* [ISV] : montage using photographic images; *also* : a picture made by photomontage

pho·to·mor·pho·gen·e·sis \ˌfōt-ə-ˌmȯr-fə-ˈjen-ə-səs\ *n* [NL] : plant morphogenesis controlled by radiant energy (as light) — **pho·to·mor·pho·gen·ic** \-ˈjen-ik\ *adj*

pho·to·mul·ti·pli·er \ˌfōt-ō-ˈməl-tə-ˌplī(-ə)r\ *n* : an electron multiplier in which electrons released by photoelectric emission are multiplied in successive stages by dynodes that produce secondary emission

pho·to·mu·ral \-ˈmyu̇r-əl\ *n* : an enlarged photograph usu. several yards long used on walls esp. as decoration

pho·ton \ˈfō-ˌtän\ *n* [*phot-* + [2]*-on*] **1** : a quantum of radiant energy **2** : a unit of intensity of light at the retina equal to the illumination received per square millimeter of a pupillary area from a surface having a brightness of one candle per square meter — **pho·ton·ic** \fō-ˈtän-ik\ *adj*

pho·to·neg·a·tive \ˌfōt-ō-ˈneg-ət-iv\ *adj* : exhibiting negative phototropism or phototaxis

pho·to·nu·cle·ar \-ˈn(y)ü-klē-ər\ *adj* : relating to or caused by the incidence or radiant energy (as gamma rays) on atomic nuclei

pho·to–off·set \-ˈȯf-ˌset\ *n* : offset printing from photolithographic plates

pho·to·ox·i·da·tion \-ˌäk-sə-ˈdā-shən\ *n* : oxidation under the influence of radiant energy (as light) — **pho·to·ox·i·da·tive** \-ˈäk-sə-ˌdāt-iv\ *adj*

pho·to·pe·ri·od \-ˈpir-ē-əd\ *n* : the relative lengths of alternating periods of lightness and darkness as they affect the growth and maturity of an organism — **pho·to·pe·ri·od·ic** \-ˌpir-ē-ˈäd-ik\ *adj* — **pho·to·pe·ri·od·i·cal·ly** \-i-k(ə-)lē\ *adv* — **pho·to·pe·ri·od·ism** \-ˈpir-ē-əd-ˌiz-əm\ *n*

pho·to·phil·ic \ˌfōt-ə-ˈfil-ik\ *or* **pho·toph·i·lous** \fō-ˈtäf-ə-ləs\ *also* **pho·to·phile** \ˈfōt-ə-ˌfīl\ *adj* : thriving in full light : requiring abundant light <~ plants> — **pho·toph·i·ly** \fō-ˈtäf-ə-lē\ *n*

pho·to·pho·bia \ˌfōt-ə-ˈfō-bē-ə\ *n* [NL] : intolerance to light; *esp* : painful sensitiveness to strong light

pho·to·pho·bic \-ˈfō-bik\ *adj* **1 a** : shunning or avoiding light **b** : growing best under reduced illumination **2** : of or relating to photophobia

pho·to·phore \ˈfōt-ə-ˌfō(ə)r, -ˌfȯ(ə)r\ *n* [ISV] : a light-emitting organ; *esp* : one of the luminous spots on various marine mostly deep-sea fishes

pho·to·phos·phor·y·la·tion \ˈfōt-ō-ˌfäs-ˌfȯr-ə-ˈlā-shən\ *n* [*phot-* + *phosphorylation*] : the conversion of ADP to ATP in photosynthesis using radiant energy

phot·opia \fōt-ˈō-pē-ə\ *n* [NL, fr. *phot-* + *-opia*] : vision in bright light with light-adapted eyes that is mediated by the cones of the retina — **phot·opic** \-ˈō-pik, -ˈäp-ik\ *adj*

pho·to·play \ˈfōt-ō-ˌplā\ *n* : MOTION PICTURE 2

pho·to·poly·mer \ˌfōt-ō-ˈpäl-ə-mər\ *n* : a photosensitive plastic used in the manufacture of printing plates

pho·to·pos·i·tive \-ˈpäz-ət-iv, -ˈpäz-tiv\ *adj* : exhibiting positive phototropism or phototaxis

pho·to·print \ˈfōt-ō-ˌprint\ *n* : a reproduction of graphic matter on photographic paper

pho·to·prod·uct \ˌfōt-ō-ˈpräd-(ˌ)əkt\ *n* : a product of a photochemical reaction

pho·to·pro·duc·tion \-prə-ˈdək-shən\ *n* : the production of mesons as a result of the action of photons on atomic nuclei; *also* : the production of a substance (as hydrogen) by a photochemical reaction (as in photosynthetic bacteria)

pho·to·re·ac·ti·va·tion \-rē-ˌak-tə-ˈvā-shən\ *n* : repair of DNA (as of a bacterium) by a light-dependent enzymatic reaction after being damaged by ultraviolet irradiation — **pho·to·re·ac·ti·vat·ing** \-ˈak-tə-ˌvāt-iŋ\ *adj*

pho·to·re·cep·tion \-ri-ˈsep-shən\ *n* : perception of waves in the range of visible light; *specif* : VISION — **pho·to·re·cep·tive** \-ˈsep-tiv\ *adj*

pho·to·re·cep·tor \-ˈsep-tər\ *n* : a receptor for light stimuli

pho·to·re·con·nais·sance \ˌfōt-ō-ri-ˈkän-ə-zən(t)s *also* -sən(t)s\ *n* : reconnaissance in which aerial photographs are taken

pho·to·re·duc·tion \-ri-ˈdək-shən\ *n* : chemical reduction under the influence of radiant energy (as light) : photochemical reduction

pho·to·res·pi·ra·tion \-ˌres-pə-ˈrā-shən\ *n* : oxidation involving production of carbon dioxide during photosynthesis

pho·to·sen·si·tive \-ˈsen(t)-sət-iv, -ˈsen(t)-stiv\ *adj* : sensitive or sensitized to the action of radiant energy — **pho·to·sen·si·tiv·i·ty** \-ˌsen(t)-sə-ˈtiv-ət-ē\ *n*

pho·to·sen·si·ti·za·tion \-ˌsen(t)-sət-ə-ˈzā-shən, -ˌsen(t)-stə-ˈzā-\ *n* **1** : the process of photosensitizing **2** : the condition of being photosensitized; *esp* : the development of an abnormal capacity to react to sunlight typically by edematous swelling and dermatitis

pho·to·sen·si·tize \-ˈsen(t)-sə-ˌtīz\ *vt* : to make sensitive to the influence of radiant energy and esp. light — **pho·to·sen·si·tiz·er** *n*

pho·to·set \ˈfōt-ō-ˌset\ *vt* : PHOTOCOMPOSE — **pho·to·set·ter** *n*

pho·to·sphere \'fōt-ə-ˌsfi(ə)r\ *n* **1 :** a sphere of light or radiance **2 :** the luminous surface layer of the sun or a star — **pho·to·spher·ic** \ˌfōt-ə-'sfi(ə)r-ik, -'sfer-\ *adj*

pho·to·stat \'fōt-ə-ˌstat\ *vt* **:** to copy by a Photostat device

Photostat *trademark* — used for a device for making a photographic copy of graphic matter

pho·to·stat·ic \ˌfōt-ə-'stat-ik\ *adj* **:** of, made by, or using a Photostat device <as ~ copy> <a ~ process>

pho·to·syn·the·sis \ˌfōt-ō-'sin(t)-thə-səs\ *n* [NL] **:** synthesis of chemical compounds with the aid of radiant energy and esp. light; *esp* **:** formation of carbohydrates in the chlorophyll-containing tissues of plants exposed to light — **pho·to·syn·the·size** \-ˌsīz\ *vi* — **pho·to·syn·thet·ic** \-sin-'thet-ik\ *adj* — **pho·to·syn·thet·i·cal·ly** \-i-k(ə-)lē\ *adv*

pho·to·tac·tic \-'tak-tik\ *adj* [ISV] **:** of, relating to, or exhibiting phototaxis — **pho·to·tac·ti·cal·ly** \-ti-kə-lē\ *adv*

pho·to·tax·is \-'tak-səs\ *n* [NL] **:** a taxis in which light is the directive factor

pho·to·te·leg·ra·phy \-tə-'leg-rə-fē\ *n* [ISV] **:** FACSIMILE 2

pho·to·tro·pic \ˌfōt-ə-'trōp-ik, -'träp-\ *adj* **:** of, relating to, or capable of phototropism — **pho·to·tro·pi·cal·ly** \-i-k(ə-)lē\ *adv*

pho·tot·ro·pism \fō-'tä-trə-ˌpiz-əm\ *n* [ISV] **:** a tropism in which light is the orienting stimulus

pho·to·tube \'fōt-ō-ˌt(y)üb\ *n* **:** an electron tube having a photoemissive cathode whose released electrons are drawn to the anode by reason of its positive potential

pho·to·type·set·ting \ˌfōt-ō-'tīp-ˌset-iŋ\ *n* **:** PHOTOCOMPOSITION; *esp* **:** photocomposition done on a keyboard or tape-operated composing machine — **pho·to·type·set·ter** *n*

pho·to·ty·pog·ra·phy \-tī-'päg-rə-fē\ *n* [ISV] **:** a photomechanical process for composing type on film or paper **:** PHOTOCOMPOSITION — **pho·to·ty·po·graph·ic** \-ˌtī-pə-'graf-ik\ *adj*

pho·to·vol·ta·ic \-väl-'tā-ik, -vōl-\ *adj* [ISV] **:** of, relating to, or utilizing the generation of an electromotive force when radiant energy falls on the boundary between dissimilar substances

phr *abbr* phrase

phrag·mo·plast \'frag-mō-ˌplast\ *n* [ISV *phragmo-* (fr. Gk *phragmos* fence, fr. *phrassein* to enclose) + *-plast* — more at FARCE] **:** the enlarged barrel-shaped spindle that is characteristic of the later stages of plant mitosis and within which the cell plate forms

phras·al \'frā-zəl\ *adj* **:** of, relating to, or consisting of a phrase <~ prepositions> — **phras·al·ly** \-zə-lē\ *adv*

¹phrase \'frāz\ *n* [L *phrasis,* fr. Gk, fr. *phrazein* to point out, explain, tell] **1 :** a characteristic manner of style or expression **:** DICTION **2 a :** a brief expression; *esp* **:** CATCHWORD **b :** WORD **3 :** a short musical thought typically two to four measures long closing with a cadence **4 :** a group of two or more grammatically related words that bear to one another the modifying relation, the coordinate relation, or the composite relation <an adverbial ~>

²phrase *vt* **phrased; phras·ing 1 a :** to express in words or in appropriate or telling terms **b :** to designate by a descriptive word or phrase **2 :** to divide into melodic phrases

phrase book *n* **:** a book containing idiomatic expressions of a foreign language and their translation

phrase·mak·er \'frāz-ˌmā-kər\ *n* **1 :** one who coins telling phrases **2 :** one given to making fine-sounding but often hollow and meaningless phrases — **phrase·mak·ing** \-kiŋ\ *n*

phrase·mon·ger \-ˌməŋ-gər, -ˌmäŋ-\ *n* **:** PHRASEMAKER 2 — **phrase·mon·ger·ing** \-g(ə-)riŋ\ *n*

phra·seo·gram \'frā-zē-ə-ˌgram\ *n* [*phraseo-* (as in *phraseology*) + *-gram*] **:** a symbol for a phrase in some shorthand systems

phra·seo·graph \-ˌgraf\ *n* **:** PHRASEOGRAM

phra·seo·log·i·cal \ˌfrā-zē-ə-'läj-i-kəl\ *adj* **1 a :** expressed in formal often sententious phrases **b :** marked by frequently insincere use of such phrases **2 :** of or relating to phraseology — **phra·seo·log·i·cal·ly** \-k(ə-)lē\ *adv*

phrase·ol·o·gist \ˌfrā-zē-'äl-ə-jəst, frā-'zäl-\ *n* **:** one who uses sententious or insincere phrases

phrase·ol·o·gy \-jē\ *n, pl* **-gies** [NL *phraseologia,* fr. Gk *phrase-, phrasis* + *-logia* -logy] **1 :** a manner of organization of words and phrases into longer elements **:** STYLE **2 :** choice of words

phras·ing \'frā-ziŋ\ *n* **1 :** style of expression **:** PHRASEOLOGY **2 :** the act, method, or result of grouping notes into musical phrases

phra·try \'frā-trē\ *n, pl* **phratries** [Gk *phratria,* fr. *phratēr* member of the same clan, member of a phratry — more at BROTHER] **1 :** a kinship group forming a subdivision of a Greek phyle **2 :** a tribal subdivision; *specif* **:** an exogamous group typically comprising several totemic clans

phre·at·ic \frē-'at-ik\ *adj* [Gk *phreat-, phrear* well] **1 :** of, relating to, or being ground water **2 :** of, relating to, or being an explosion caused by steam derived from ground water

phre·ato·phyte \frē-'at-ə-ˌfīt\ *n* [Gk *phreat-, phrear* well + E *-o-* + *-phyte*] **:** a deep-rooted plant that obtains its water from the water table or the layer of soil just above it — **phre·ato·phyt·ic** \-ˌat-ə-'fit-ik\ *adj*

phren- *or* **phreno-** *comb form* [Gk, fr. *phren-, phrēn* diaphragm, mind] **1 :** mind <*phreno*logy> **2 :** diaphragm <*phren*ic>

phre·net·ic \fri-'net-ik\ *adj* [L *phreneticus*] **:** FRENETIC

-phre·nia \'frē-nē-ə\ *n comb form* [NL, fr. Gk *phren-, phrēn*] **:** disordered condition of mental functions <hebe*phrenia*>

phren·ic \'fren-ik\ *adj* [NL *phrenicus,* fr. *phren-*] **1 :** of or relating to the diaphragm **2 :** of or relating to the mind

phre·nol·o·gy \fri-'näl-ə-jē\ *n* **:** the study of the conformation of the skull based on the belief that it is indicative of mental faculties and character — **phre·no·log·i·cal** \ˌfren-ᵊl-'äj-i-kəl, ˌfrēn-\ *adj* — **phre·no·log·i·cal·ly** \-k(ə-)lē\ *adv* — **phre·nol·o·gist** \fri-'näl-ə-jəst\ *n*

phren·sy *var of* FRENZY

Phry·gian \'frij-(ē-)ən\ *n* **1 :** a native or inhabitant of ancient Phrygia **2 :** the language of the Phrygians usu. assumed to be Indo-European — see INDO-EUROPEAN LANGUAGES table — **Phrygian** *adj*

PHS *abbr* Public Health Service

phtha·lein \'thal-ē-ən, 'thal-ˌēn, 'thāl-\ *n* [ISV, fr. *phthalic acid*] **:** any of various xanthene dyes that are intensely colored in alkaline solution

phthal·ic acid \ˌthal-ik-\ *n* [ISV, short for obs. *naphthalic acid,* fr. *naphthalene*] **:** any of three isomeric acids $C_8H_6O_4$ obtained by oxidation of various benzene derivatives

phthalic anhydride *n* **:** a crystalline cyclic acid anhydride $C_8H_4O_3$ used esp. in making alkyd resins

phtha·lo·cy·a·nine \ˌthal-ō-'sī-ə-ˌnēn, ˌthā-lō-\ *n* [ISV *phthal*ic acid + *-o-* + *cyanine*] **:** a bright greenish blue crystalline compound $C_{32}H_{18}N_8$; *also* **:** any of several metal derivatives that are brilliant fast blue to green dyes or pigments

phthi·ri·a·sis \thə-'rī-ə-səs, thī-\ *n* [L, fr. Gk *phtheiriasis,* fr. *phtheir* louse; akin to Gk *phtheirein* to destroy, Skt *kaarati* it flows, perishes] **:** PEDICULOSIS; *esp* **:** infestation with crab lice

phthis·ic \'tiz-ik\ *n* [ME *tisike,* fr. MF *tisique,* fr. *tisique* tubercular, fr. L *phthisicus,* fr. Gk *phthisikos,* fr. *phthisis*] **:** PHTHISIS — **phthisic** *or* **phthis·i·cal** \-i-kəl\ *adj*

phthi·sis \'t(h)ī-səs, 't(h)is-əs\ *n, pl* **phthi·ses** \'t(h)ī-ˌsēz, 't(h)is-ˌēz\ [L, fr. Gk, fr. *phthinein* to waste away; akin to Skt *kṣinoti* he destroys] **:** a progressively wasting or consumptive condition; *esp* **:** pulmonary tuberculosis

phy·co·cy·a·nin \ˌfī-kō-'sī-ə-nən\ *n* [ISV *phyco-* (fr. Gk *phykos*) + *cyan-* + *-in*] **:** any of various bluish green protein pigments in the cells of blue-green algae

phy·co·er·y·thrin \-'er-i-thrən\ *n* [ISV *phyco-* + *erythr-* + *-in*] **:** any of the red protein pigments in the cells of red algae

phy·col·o·gy \fī-'käl-ə-jē\ *n* [Gk *phykos* seaweed + ISV *-logy* — more at FUCUS] **:** ALGOLOGY — **phy·co·log·i·cal** \ˌfī-kə-'läj-i-kəl\ *adj* — **phy·col·o·gist** \fī-'käl-ə-jəst\ *n*

phy·co·my·cete \ˌfī-kō-'mī-ˌsēt, -ˌmī-'sēt\ *n* [deriv. of Gk *phykos* + *mykēt-, mykēs* fungus — more at MYC-] **:** any of a large class (Phycomycetes) of highly variable lower fungi in many respects similar to algae — **phy·co·my·ce·tous** \-ˌmī-'sēt-əs\ *adj*

phyl- *or* **phylo-** *comb form* [L, fr. Gk, fr. *phylē, phylon;* akin to Gk *phyein* to bring forth — more at BE] **:** tribe **:** race **:** phylum <*phylo*geny>

phy·lac·tery \fə-'lak-t(ə-)rē\ *n, pl* **-ter·ies** [ME *philaterie,* fr. ML *philaterium,* alter. of LL *phylacterium,* fr. Gk *phylaktērion* amulet, phylactery, fr. *phylassein* to guard, fr. *phylak-, phylax* guard] **1 :** one of two small square leather boxes containing slips inscribed with scriptural passages and traditionally worn on the left arm and forehead by Jewish men during morning weekday prayers **2 :** AMULET

worshiper wearing phylacteries

phy·lar \'fī-lər, -ˌlär\ *adj* **:** of or relating to a phylum

phy·le \'fī-(ˌ)lē\ *n, pl* **phy·lae** \-ˌlē\ [Gk *phylē* tribe, phyle] **:** the largest political subdivision among the ancient Athenians

phy·le·sis \fī-'lē-səs, 'fī-lə-\ *n* [NL, fr. *phyl-* + *-esis* (as in *genesis*)] **:** the course of evolutionary or phylogenetic development — **phy·let·ic** \fī-'let-ik\ *adj* — **phy·let·i·cal·ly** \-i-k(ə-)lē\ *adv*

phyll- *or* **phyllo-** *comb form* [NL, fr. Gk, fr. *phyllon* — more at BLADE] **:** leaf <*phyll*ome>

-phyll \ˌfil\ *n comb form* [NL *-phyllum,* fr. Gk *phyllon* leaf] **:** leaf <sporo*phyll*>

phyl·la·ry \'fil-ə-rē\ *n, pl* **-ries** [NL *phyllarium,* fr. Gk *phyllarion,* dim. of *phyllon* leaf] **:** one of the involucral bracts subtending the flower head of a composite plant

phyl·lo·clade \'fil-ə-ˌklād\ *n* [NL *phyllocladium,* fr. *phyll-* + Gk *klados* branch — more at GLADIATOR] **:** a flattened stem or branch (as a joint of a cactus) that functions as a leaf

phyl·lode \'fil-ˌōd\ *n* [NL *phyllodium,* fr. Gk *phyllōdēs* like a leaf, fr. *phyllon* leaf] **:** a flat expanded petiole that replaces the blade of a foliage leaf, fulfills the same functions, and is analogous to a cladophyll

phyl·lo·di·um \fil-'ōd-ē-əm\ *n, pl* **-dia** \-ē-ə\ [NL] **:** PHYLLODE

phyl·loid \'fil-ˌȯid\ *adj* **:** resembling a leaf — **phylloid** *n*

phyl·lome \'fil-ˌōm\ *n* [ISV] **:** a plant part that is a leaf or is phylogenetically derived from a leaf — **phyl·lo·mic** \fil-'ōm-ik\ *adj*

phyl·loph·a·gous \fil-'äf-ə-gəs\ *adj* [prob. fr. (assumed) NL *phyllophagus,* fr. NL *phyll-* + *-phagus* -phagous] **:** feeding on leaves

phyl·lo·pod \'fil-ə-ˌpäd\ *n* [deriv. of Gk *phyllon* leaf + *pod-, pous* foot — more at FOOT] **:** any of a group (Phyllopoda) of crustaceans (subclass Entomostraca) that typically have leaflike swimming appendages that also serve as gills — **phyllopod** *adj* — **phyl·lop·o·dan** \fil-'äp-əd-ən\ *adj or n* — **phyl·lop·o·dous** \-əd-əs\ *adj*

phyl·lo·tac·tic \ˌfil-ə-'tak-tik\ *or* **phyl·lo·tac·ti·cal** \-ti-kəl\ *adj* **:** of or relating to phyllotaxy

phyl·lo·taxy \'fil-ə-ˌtak-sē\ *also* **phyl·lo·tax·is** \ˌfil-ə-'tak-səs\ *n* [NL *phyllotaxis,* fr. *phyll-* + *-taxis*] **1 :** the arrangement of leaves on a stem and in relation to one another **2 :** the study of phyllotaxy and of the laws that govern it

-phyl·lous \'fil-əs\ *adj comb form* [NL *-phyllus,* fr. Gk *-phyllos,* fr. *phyllon* leaf — more at BLADE] **:** having (such or so many) leaves, leaflets, or leaflike parts <di*phyllous*>

ə abut	ᵊ kitten	ər further	a back	ā bake	ä cot, cart
au̇ out	ch chin	e less	ē easy	g gift	i trip
ī life	j joke	ŋ sing	ō flow	ȯ flaw	ȯi coin
th thin	t͟h this	ü loot	u̇ foot	y yet	yü few
yu̇ furious	zh vision				

phyl·lox·e·ra \ˌfil-ˌäk-ˈsir-ə, fə-ˈläk-sə-rə\ *n* [NL, genus name, fr. *phyll-* + Gk *xēros* dry — more at SERENE] : any of various plant lice (esp. genus *Phylloxera*) that differ from aphids esp. in wing structure and in being continuously oviparous — **phyl·lox·e·ran** \-ˈsir-ən, -sə-rən\ *adj or n*

phy·lo·ge·net·ic \ˌfī-lō-jə-ˈnet-ik\ *adj* [ISV, fr. NL *phylogenesis* phylogeny, fr. *phyl-* + *genesis*] **1 :** of or relating to phylogeny **2 :** based on natural evolutionary relationships **3 :** acquired in the course of phylogenetic development : RACIAL — **phy·lo·ge·net·i·cal·ly** \-i-k(ə-)lē\ *adv*

phy·log·e·ny \fī-ˈläj-ə-nē\ *n, pl* **-nies** [ISV] **1 :** the racial history of a kind of organism **2 :** the evolution of a genetically related group of organisms as distinguished from the development of the individual organism **3 :** the history or course of the development of something (as a word or custom)

phy·lum \ˈfī-ləm\ *n, pl* **phy·la** \-lə\ [NL, fr. Gk *phylon* tribe, race — more at PHYL-] **1 a :** a direct line of descent within a group **b :** a group that constitutes or has the unity of a phylum; *esp* : one of the usu. primary divisions of the animal kingdom <the ~ Arthropoda> **2 :** a group of languages related more remotely than those of a family or stock

-phyre \ˌfī(ə)r\ *n comb form* [F, fr. *porphyre* porphyry, fr. ML *porphyrium*] : porphyritic rock <grano*phyre*>

phys *abbr* **1** physical **2** physician **3** physics

physi- *or* **physio-** *comb form* [L, fr. Gk, fr. *physis* — more at PHYSICS] **1 :** nature <*physio*graphy> **2 :** physical <*physio*therapy>

phys·iat·rics \ˌfiz-ē-ˈa-triks\ *n pl but sing or pl in constr* [Gk *physis* + ISV *-iatrics*] : PHYSICAL THERAPY

phys·iat·rist \ˌfiz-ē-ˈa-trəst\ *n* : a physician who specializes in physical medicine

[1]**phys·ic** \ˈfiz-ik\ *n* [ME *physik* natural science, art of medicine — more at PHYSICS] **1 a :** the art or practice of healing disease **b :** the practice or profession of medicine **2 :** a medicinal agent or preparation; *esp* : PURGATIVE

[2]**physic** *vt* **phys·icked; phys·ick·ing** [ME *phisiken*, fr. *phisik* medicine — more at PHYSICS] **1 :** to treat with or administer medicine to; *esp* : PURGE **2 :** HEAL, CURE

[1]**phys·i·cal** \ˈfiz-i-kəl\ *adj* [ME, fr. ML *physicalis*, fr. L *physica* physics] **1 a :** having material existence : perceptible esp. through the senses and subject to the laws of nature <everything ~ is measurable by weight, motion, and resistance — Thomas DeQuincey> **b :** of or relating to material things **2 a :** of or relating to natural science **b (1) :** of or relating to physics **(2) :** characterized or produced by the forces and operations of physics **3 a :** of or relating to the body **b :** concerned or preoccupied with the body and its needs : CARNAL *syn* see BODILY, MATERIAL — **phys·i·cal·ly** \-k(ə-)lē\ *adv*

[2]**physical** *n* : PHYSICAL EXAMINATION

physical anthropology *n* : anthropology concerned with the comparative study of human evolution, variation, and classification esp. through measurement and observation — compare CULTURAL ANTHROPOLOGY — **physical anthropologist** *n*

physical education *n* : instruction in the development and care of the body ranging from simple calisthenic exercises to a course of study providing training in hygiene, gymnastics, and the performance and management of athletic games

physical examination *n* : an examination of the bodily functions and condition of an individual

physical geography *n* : geography that deals with the exterior physical features and changes of the earth

phys·i·cal·ism \ˈfiz-i-kə-ˌliz-əm\ *n* : a thesis that the descriptive terms of scientific language are reducible to terms which refer to spatiotemporal things or events or to their properties — **phys·i·cal·ist** \-ləst\ *n* — **phys·i·cal·is·tic** \ˌfiz-i-kə-ˈlis-tik\ *adj*

phys·i·cal·i·ty \ˌfiz-ə-ˈkal-ət-ē\ *n* : intensely physical orientation : predominance of the physical usu. at the expense of the mental, spiritual, or social

physical science *n* : the natural sciences (as physics, chemistry, and astronomy) that deal primarily with nonliving materials — **physical scientist** *n*

physical therapy *n* : the treatment of disease by physical and mechanical means (as massage, regulated exercise, water, light, heat, and electricity) — **physical therapist** *n*

phy·si·cian \fə-ˈzish-ən\ *n* [ME *fisicien*, fr. OF, fr. *fisique* medicine] **1 :** a person skilled in the art of healing; *specif* : a doctor of medicine **2 :** one exerting a remedial or salutary influence

phys·i·cist \ˈfiz-(ə-)səst\ *n* **1 :** a specialist in physics **2** *archaic* : a person skilled in natural science

phys·i·co·chem·i·cal \ˌfiz-i-kō-ˈkem-i-kəl\ *adj* **1 :** being physical and chemical **2 :** of or relating to chemistry that deals with the physicochemical properties of substances — **phys·i·co·chem·i·cal·ly** \-k(ə-)lē\ *adv*

phys·ics \ˈfiz-iks\ *n pl but sing or pl in constr* [*physics* fr. L *physica*, pl., natural science, fr. Gk *physika*, fr. neut. pl. of *physikos* of nature, fr. *physis* growth, nature, fr. *phyein* to bring forth; *physic* fr. ME *phisik* natural science, art of medicine, fr. OF *fisique*, fr. L *physica*, sing., natural science, fr. Gk *physikē*, fr. fem. of *physikos* — more at BE] **1** *also* **physic** *archaic* : NATURAL SCIENCE **2 :** a science that deals with matter and energy and their interactions in the fields of mechanics, acoustics, optics, heat, electricity, magnetism, radiation, atomic structure and nuclear phenomena **3 a :** the physical processes and phenomena of a particular system **b :** the physical properties and composition of something

Phys·io·crat \ˈfiz-ē-ə-ˌkrat\ *n* [F *physiocrate*, fr. *physi-* + *-crate* -crat] : a member of a school of political economists founded in 18th century France and characterized chiefly by a belief that government policy should not interfere with the operation of natural economic laws and that land is the source of all wealth — **phys·io·crat·ic** \ˌfiz-ē-ə-ˈkrat-ik\ *adj, often cap*

phys·i·og·nom·ic \ˌfiz-ē-ə(g)-ˈnäm-ik\ *adj* : of, relating to, or characteristic of physiognomy or the physiognomy — **phys·i·og·nom·i·cal** \-i-kəl\ *adj* — **phys·i·og·nom·i·cal·ly** \-i-k(ə-)lē\ *adv*

phys·i·og·no·my \ˌfiz-ē-ˈä(g)-nə-mē\ *n, pl* **-mies** [ME *phisonomie*, fr. MF, fr. LL *physiognomonia, physiognomia*, fr. Gk *physiognōmonia*, fr. *physiognōmōn* judging character by the features, fr. *physis* nature, physique, appearance + *gnōmōn* interpreter — more at GNOMON] **1 :** the art of discovering temperament and character from outward appearance **2 :** the facial features held to show qualities of mind or character by their configuration or expression **3 :** external aspect; *also* : inner character or quality revealed outwardly <the ~ of a political party>

physiographic climax *n* : an ecological climax that develops in association with a particular physiographic situation and persists only while the physiographic factors remain stable — compare EDAPHIC CLIMAX

phys·i·og·ra·phy \ˌfiz-ē-ˈäg-rə-fē\ *n* [prob. fr. (assumed) NL *physiographia*, fr. NL *physi-* + L *-graphia* -graphy] **1 :** a description of nature or natural phenomena in general **2 :** PHYSICAL GEOGRAPHY — **phys·i·og·ra·pher** \-fər\ *n* — **phys·io·graph·ic** \ˌfiz-ē-ō-ˈgraf-ik\ *also* **phys·io·graph·i·cal** \-i-kəl\ *adj*

physiol *abbr* physiologist; physiology

phys·i·o·log·i·cal \ˌfiz-ē-ə-ˈläj-i-kəl\ *or* **phys·i·o·log·ic** \-ik\ *adj* **1 :** of or relating to physiology **2 :** characteristic of or appropriate to an organism's healthy or normal functioning **3 :** differing in, involving, or affecting physiological factors <a ~ strain of bacteria> — **phys·i·o·log·i·cal·ly** \-i-k(ə-)lē\ *adv*

physiological psychology *n* : a branch of psychology that deals with the effects of normal and pathological physiological processes on mental life — called also *psychophysiology*

physiological saline *n* : a solution of a salt or salts that is essentially isotonic with tissue fluids or blood

phys·i·ol·o·gy \ˌfiz-ē-ˈäl-ə-jē\ *n* [L *physiologia* natural science, fr. Gk, fr. *physi-* + *-logia* -logy] **1 :** a branch of biology that deals with the functions and activities of life or of living matter (as organs, tissues, or cells) and of the physical and chemical phenomena involved — compare ANATOMY **2 :** the organic processes and phenomena of an organism or any of its parts or of a particular bodily process — **phys·i·ol·o·gist** \-jəst\ *n*

phys·io·pa·thol·o·gy \ˈfiz-ē-ō-pə-ˈthäl-ə-jē, -pa-\ *n* : a branch of biology or medicine that combines physiology and pathology esp. in the study of altered bodily function in disease — **phys·io·path·o·log·ic** \-ˌpath-ə-ˈläj-ik\ *or* **phys·io·path·o·log·i·cal** \-i-kəl\ *adj*

phys·io·ther·a·py \ˌfiz-ē-ō-ˈther-ə-pē\ *n* [NL *physiotherapia*, fr. *physi-* + *therapia* therapy] : PHYSICAL THERAPY — **phys·io·ther·a·pist** \-pəst\ *n*

phy·sique \fə-ˈzēk\ *n* [F, fr. *physique* physical, bodily, fr. L *physicus* of nature, fr. Gk *physikos*] : the form or structure of a person's body : bodily makeup — **phy·siqued** \-ˈzēkt\ *adj*
syn PHYSIQUE, BUILD, HABIT, CONSTITUTION *shared meaning element* : bodily makeup or type

phy·so·stig·mine \ˌfī-sə-ˈstig-ˌmēn\ *n* [ISV, fr. NL *Physostigma*, genus of vines whose fruit is the Calabar bean] : a crystalline tasteless alkaloid $C_{15}H_{21}N_3O_2$ from the Calabar bean that is used in medicine esp. in the form of its salicylate

phyt- *or* **phyto-** *comb form* [NL, fr. Gk, fr. *phyton*, fr. *phyein* to bring forth — more at BE] : plant <*phyto*phagous>

phy·tane \ˈfī-ˌtān\ *n* : an isoprenoid hydrocarbon $C_{20}H_{42}$ that is found esp. associated with fossilized plant remains from the Precambrian on and in meteorites

-phyte \ˌfīt\ *n comb form* [ISV, fr. Gk *phyton* plant] **1 :** plant having a (specified) characteristic or habitat <xero*phyte*> **2 :** pathological growth <osteo*phyte*>

-phyt·ic \ˈfit-ik\ *adj comb form* [ISV, fr. Gk *phyton* plant] : like a plant <holo*phytic*>

phy·to·alex·in \ˌfit-ō-ə-ˈlek-sən\ *n* [*phyt-* + *alexin* (substance combating infection), fr. G, fr. Gk *alexein* to ward off, protect] : a chemical substance produced by a plant to combat infection by a pathogen (as a fungus)

phy·to·chem·i·cal \-ˈkem-i-kəl\ *adj* : of, relating to, or being phytochemistry — **phy·to·chem·i·cal·ly** \-i-k(ə-)lē\ *adv*

phy·to·chem·is·try \-ˈkem-ə-strē\ *n* : the chemistry of plants, plant processes, and plant products — **phy·to·chem·ist** \-ˈkem-əst\ *n*

phy·to·chrome \ˈfīt-ə-ˌkrōm\ *n* : a chromoprotein that is present in traces in many plants and that plays a role in initiating floral and developmental processes when activated by red or far-red radiation

phy·to·fla·gel·late \ˌfīt-ō-ˈflaj-ə-lət, -ˌlāt; -flə-ˈjel-ət\ *n* : PLANTLIKE FLAGELLATE

phy·to·gen·ic \ˌfīt-ə-ˈjen-ik\ *adj* : of plant origin

phy·to·ge·og·ra·phy \ˌfit-ō-jē-ˈäg-rə-fē\ *n* [ISV] : the biogeography of plants — **phy·to·geo·graph·i·cal** \-ˌjē-ə-ˈgraf-i-kəl\ *or* **phy·to·geo·graph·ic** \-ik\ *adj* — **phy·to·geo·graph·i·cal·ly** \-i-k(ə-)lē\ *adv*

phy·tog·ra·phy \fī-ˈtäg-rə-fē\ *n* [NL *phytographia*, fr. *phyt-* + L *-graphia* -graphy] : descriptive botany sometimes including plant taxonomy

phy·to·he·mag·glu·ti·nin *also* **phy·to·hae·mag·glu·ti·nin** \ˈfit-ō-ˌhē-mə-ˈglüt-ᵊn-ən\ *n* : a protein extract of the red kidney bean that has been used to agglutinate red blood cells and to induce structural changes followed by mitosis in white blood cells in culture

phy·to·hor·mone \ˌfit-ə-ˈhȯr-ˌmōn\ *n* [ISV] : PLANT HORMONE

phy·tol·o·gy \fī-ˈtäl-ə-jē\ *n* [NL *phytologia*, fr. *phyt-* + L *-logia* -logy] : BOTANY — **phy·to·log·ic** \ˌfit-ᵊl-ˈäj-ik\ *or* **phy·to·log·i·cal** \-i-kəl\ *adj* — **phy·to·log·i·cal·ly** \-i-k(ə-)lē\ *adv*

phy·ton \ˈfī-ˌtän\ *n* [NL, fr. Gk, plant] **1 :** a structural unit of a plant consisting of a leaf and its associated portion of stem **2 :** the smallest part of a stem, root, or leaf that when severed may grow into a new plant — **phy·ton·ic** \fī-ˈtän-ik\ *adj*

phy·to·path·o·gen \ˌfit-ō-ˈpath-ə-jən\ *n* : an organism parasitic on a plant host — **phy·to·path·o·gen·ic** \-ˌpath-ə-ˈjen-ik\ *adj*

phy·to·pa·thol·o·gy \-pə-ˈthäl-ə-jē, -pa-\ *n* [ISV] : plant pathology — **phy·to·path·o·log·i·cal** \-ˌpath-ə-ˈläj-i-kəl\ *or* **phy·to·path·o·log·ic** \-ik\ *adj*

phy·toph·a·gous \fī-ˈtäf-ə-gəs\ *adj* : feeding on plants <~ insect> — **phy·toph·a·gy** \-ə-jē\ *n*

phy·to·plank·ton \ˌfīt-ō-ˈplaŋ(k)-tən, -ˌtän\ *n* [ISV] **:** planktonic plant life — **phy·to·plank·ton·ic** \-plaŋ(k)-ˈtän-ik\ *adj*

phy·to·so·ci·ol·o·gy \-ˌsō-sē-ˈäl-ə-jē, -shē-\ *n* **:** a branch of ecology that deals with the interrelations among the flora of particular areas and esp. with plant communities — **phy·to·so·cio·log·i·cal** \-sē-ə-ˈläj-i-kəl\ *adj* — **phy·to·so·cio·log·i·cal·ly** \-k(ə-)lē\ *adv* — **phy·to·so·ci·ol·o·gist** \-ˌsō-sē-ˈäl-ə-jəst, -shē-\ *n*

phy·tos·ter·ol \fī-ˈtäs-tə-ˌrōl, -ˌrōl\ *n* [ISV] **:** any of various sterols derived from plants — compare ZOOSTEROL

phy·to·tox·ic \ˌfīt-ə-ˈtäk-sik\ *adj* **:** poisonous to plants — **phy·to·tox·ic·i·ty** \-ˌtäk-ˈsis-ət-ē\ *n*

1pi \ˈpī\ *n, pl* **pis** \ˈpīz\ [MGk, fr. Gk *pei,* of Sem origin; akin to Heb *pē* pe] **1 :** the 16th letter of the Greek alphabet — see ALPHABET table **2 a :** the symbol π denoting the ratio of the circumference of a circle to its diameter **b :** the ratio itself **:** a transcendental number having a value to eight decimal places of 3.14159265

2pi *also* **pie** \ˈpī\ *n, pl* **pies** [origin unknown] **1 :** type that is spilled or mixed **2 :** a pi character or matrix

3pi *adj* **1 :** not intended to appear in final printing <~ lines> **2 :** capable of being inserted only by hand <~ characters>

4pi *also* **pie** *vb* **pied; pi·ing** *or* **pie·ing** *vt* **:** to spill or throw (type or type matter) into disorder ~ *vi* **:** to become pied

5pi *or* **pias** *abbr* piaster

PI *abbr* programmed instruction

pi·al \ˈpī-əl, ˈpē-\ *adj* **:** of or relating to the pia mater

pia ma·ter \ˈpī-ə-ˌmāt-ər, ˈpē-ə-ˌmät-\ *n* [ME, fr. ML, fr. L, tender mother] **:** the thin vascular membrane that invests the brain and spinal cord internal to the arachnoid and dura mater

pi·a·nism \ˈpē-ə-ˌniz-əm\ *n* **:** the art or technique of piano playing

1pi·a·nis·si·mo \ˌpē-ə-ˈnis-ə-ˌmō\ *adv or adj* [It, fr. *piano* softly] **:** very softly — used as a direction in music

2pianissimo *n, pl* **-mi** \-(ˌ)mē\ *or* **-mos :** a passage played, sung, or spoken very softly

pi·a·nist \pē-ˈan-əst, ˈpē-ə-nəst\ *n* **:** one who plays the piano; *esp* **:** a skilled or professional performer on the piano

pi·a·nis·tic \ˌpē-ə-ˈnis-tik\ *adj* **1 :** of, relating to, or characteristic of the piano **2 :** skilled in or well adapted to piano playing — **pi·a·nis·ti·cal·ly** \-ti-k(ə-)lē\ *adv*

1pi·a·no \pē-ˈän-(ˌ)ō\ *adv or adj* [It, fr. LL *planus* smooth, fr. L, level — more at FLOOR] **:** in a soft or quiet manner — used as a direction in music

2pi·ano \pē-ˈan-(ˌ)ō *also* -ˈän-\ *n, pl* **pianos** [It, short for *pianoforte,* fr. *piano e forte* soft and loud; fr. the fact that its tones could be varied in loudness] **:** a stringed instrument having steel wire strings that sound when struck by felt-covered hammers operated from a keyboard

piano

piano accordion *n* **:** an accordion with a keyboard for the right hand resembling and corresponding to the middle register of a piano keyboard

pi·ano·forte \pē-ˈan-ə-ˌfō(ə)rt, -ˈän-, -ˌfō(ə)rt, -ˌfȯrt-ē; -ˌan-ə-ˈfȯrt-ē, -ˌän-\ *n* [It] **:** PIANO

piano hinge *n* **:** a hinge that has a thin pin joint and extends along the full length of the part to be moved

pi·as·sa·va \ˌpē-ə-ˈsäv-ə\ *n* [Pg *piassaba,* fr. Tupi *piaçaba*] **1 :** any of several stiff coarse fibers obtained from palms and used esp. in cordage or brushes **2 :** a palm yielding piassava; *esp* **:** either of two Brazilian palms (*Attalia funifera* and *Leopoldinia piassaba*)

pi·as·ter *or* **pi·as·tre** \pē-ˈas-tər, -ˈäs-\ *n* [F *piastre*] **1 :** PIECE OF EIGHT **2 a —** see MONEY table **b —** see *pound* at MONEY table

pi·az·za \pē-ˈaz-ə, -ˈäz-ə, *1 is usu* -ˈat-sə, -ˈät-\ *n, pl* **piazzas** *or* **pi·az·ze** \-ˈat-(ˌ)sā, -ˈät-\ [It, fr. L *platea* broad street — more at PLACE] **1** *pl piazze* **:** an open square in an Italian or other European town **2 a :** an arcaded and roofed gallery **b** *chiefly North & Midland* **:** VERANDA, PORCH

pi·broch \ˈpē-ˌbräk, -ˌbräḵ\ *n* [ScGael *piobaireachd* pipe-music] **:** a set of martial or mournful variations for the Scottish Highland bagpipe

1pic \ˈpik\ *n, pl* **pics** *or* **pix** \ˈpiks\ [short for *picture*] **1 :** PHOTOGRAPH **2 :** MOTION PICTURE

2pic \ˈpik, ˈpēk\ *n* [Sp *pica,* fr. picar to prick] **:** the picador's lance

1pi·ca \ˈpī-kə\ *n* [prob. fr. ML, collection of church rules] **1 :** 12-point type **2 :** a unit of about 1/6 inch used in measuring typographical material **3 :** a typewriter type providing 10 characters to the linear inch and six lines to the vertical inch

2pica *n* [NL, fr. L, magpie — more at PIE] **:** a craving for unnatural food (as chalk or ashes)

pic·a·dor \ˈpik-ə-ˌdȯ(ə)r, ˌpik-ə-ˈ\ *n, pl* **picadors** \-ˌdȯ(ə)rz, -ˈdȯ(ə)rz\ *or* **pic·a·do·res** \ˌpik-ə-ˈdōr-ēz, -ˈdȯr-\ [Sp, fr. *picar* to prick, fr. (assumed) VL *piccare* — more at PIKE] **:** a horseman in a bullfight who prods the bull with a lance to weaken its neck and shoulder muscles

pi·ca·ra \ˈpē-kä-ˌrä\ *n* [Sp *pícara,* fem. of *pícaro*] **:** a female picaro

1pi·ca·resque \ˌpik-ə-ˈresk, ˌpē-kə-\ *adj* [Sp *picaresco,* fr. *pícaro*] **:** of or relating to rogues or rascals; *also* **:** of, relating to, or being a type of fiction of Spanish origin dealing with rogues and vagabonds

2picaresque *n* **:** one that is picaresque

pi·ca·ro \ˈpē-kä-ˌrō\ *n, pl* **-ros** [Sp *pícaro*] **:** ROGUE, BOHEMIAN

1pic·a·roon *or* **pick·a·roon** \ˌpik-ə-ˈrün\ *n* [Sp *picarón,* aug. of *pícaro*] **1 :** PICARO **2 :** PIRATE

2picaroon *vi* **:** to act as a pirate

1pic·a·yune \ˌpik-ē-ˈ(y)ün\ *n* [F *picaillon* halfpenny, fr. Prov *picaioun,* fr. *picaio* money, fr. *pica* to prick, jingle, fr. (assumed) VL *piccare* to prick — more at PIKE] **1 a :** a Spanish half real piece formerly current in Louisiana and other southern states **b :** HALF DIME **2 :** something trivial

2picayune *adj* **:** of little value **:** PALTRY; *also* **:** PETTY, SMALL-MINDED — **pic·a·yun·ish** \-ˈ(y)ü-nish\ *adj*

pic·ca·lil·li \ˌpik-ə-ˈlil-ē\ *n* [prob. alter. of *pickle*] **:** a pungent relish of chopped vegetables and spices

1pic·co·lo \ˈpik-ə-ˌlō\ *n, pl* **-los** [It, short for *piccolo flauto* small flute] **:** a small shrill flute whose range is an octave higher than that of an ordinary flute — **pic·co·lo·ist** \-ˌlō-əst\ *n*

2piccolo *adj* [It, small] **:** smaller than ordinary size <~ banjo>

pice \ˈpīs\ *n, pl* **pice** [Hindi *paisā*] **:** PAISA

pi·ce·ous \ˈpī-sē-əs\ *adj* [L *piceus,* fr. *pic-, pix* pitch — more at PITCH] **:** of, relating to, or resembling pitch; *esp* **:** glossy brownish black in color <an insect with a ~ brown abdomen>

1pick \ˈpik\ *vb* [ME *piken,* partly fr. (assumed) OE *pician* (akin to MD *picken* to prick); partly fr. MF *piquer* to prick — more at PIKE] *vt* **1 :** to pierce, penetrate, or break up with a pointed instrument <~*ed* the hard clay> **2 a :** to remove bit by bit <~ meat from bones> **b :** to remove covering or adhering matter from <~ the bones> **3 a :** to gather by plucking <~ apples> **b :** CHOOSE, SELECT <tried to ~ the shortest route> <she ~*ed* out the most expensive dress> **4 :** PILFER, ROB <~ pockets> **5 :** PROVOKE <~ a quarrel> **6 a :** to dig into **:** PROBE <~ his teeth> **b :** to pluck with a pick or with the fingers <reputed to ~ a mighty mean guitar —G. S. Perry> **c :** to loosen or pull apart with a sharp point <~ wool> **7 :** to unlock with a device (as a wire) other than the key <~ a lock> ~ *vi* **1 :** to use or work with a pick **2 :** to gather or harvest something by plucking **3 :** PILFER — used in the phrase *picking and stealing* **4 :** to eat sparingly or mincingly <~*ing* listlessly at his dinner> — **pick and choose :** to select with care and deliberation — **pick on 1 :** HARASS <*picked on* smaller boys> **2 :** to single out for a particular purpose or for special attention

2pick *n* **1 :** a blow or stroke with a pointed instrument **2 a :** the act or privilege of choosing or selecting **:** CHOICE <take your ~> **b :** the best or choicest one <the ~ of the herd> **3 :** the portion of a crop gathered at one time <the first ~ of peaches> **4 :** a screen in basketball

3pick *vt* [ME *pykken,* alter. of *picchen* to pitch] **1** *chiefly dial* **:** to throw or thrust with effort **:** HURL **2 :** to throw (a shuttle) across the loom

4pick *n* **1** *dial Eng* **a :** the act of pitching or throwing **b :** something thrown **2 a :** a throw of the shuttle **b :** one filling thread taken as a unit of fineness of fabric

5pick *n* [ME *pik*] **1 :** a heavy wooden-handled iron or steel tool pointed at one or both ends — compare MATTOCK **2 a :** TOOTHPICK **b :** PICKLOCK **c :** a small thin piece (as of plastic or metal) used to pluck the strings of a stringed instrument **3 :** one of the points of the forepart of a figure skate blade

pick·a·back \ˈpig-ē-ˌbak, ˈpik-ə-\ *var of* PIGGYBACK

pick–and–shovel *adj* **:** done with or as if with a pick and shovel **:** LABORIOUS

pick·a·nin·ny *or* **pic·a·nin·ny** \ˈpik-ə-ˌnin-ē, ˌpik-ə-ˈ\ *n, pl* **-nies** [prob. modif. of Pg *pequenino* very little] **:** a Negro child

pick·ax \ˈpik-ˌaks\ *n* [alter. of ME *pikois,* fr. OF *picois,* fr. *pic* pick, fr. L *picus* woodpecker — more at PIE] **:** 5PICK 1

1picked \ˈpikt\ *adj* **:** CHOICE, PRIME

2pick·ed \ˈpik-əd\ *adj* [ME, fr. 5*pick*] *chiefly dial* **:** POINTED, PEAKED

pick·eer \pik-ˈi(ə)r\ *vi* [prob. modif. of F *picorer* to steal sheep, maraud, fr. MF *pecore* sheep, fr. OIt *pecora,* fr. L, neut. pl. of *pecor-, pecus* cattle — more at FEE] *archaic* **:** to skirmish in advance of an army; *also* **:** SCOUT, RECONNOITER

pick·er \ˈpik-ər\ *n* **:** one that picks: as **a :** a worker who picks something (as crops) **b :** a tool, implement, or machine used in picking something

pick·er·el \ˈpik(-ə)-rəl\ *n, pl* **pickerel** *or* **pickerels** [ME *pikerel,* dim. of *pike*] **1 a** *dial chiefly Brit* **:** a young or small pike **b :** any of several comparatively small fishes (genus *Esox*) — usu. used with a qualifying term <grass ~> **2 :** WALLEYE

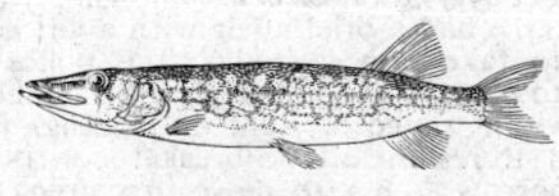

pickerel 1b

pick·er·el·weed \-rəl-ˌwēd\ *n* **:** any of various monocotyledonous aquatic plants: as **a :** any of a genus (*Pontederia*); *esp* **:** a blue-flowered American shallow-water herb (*P. cordata*) **b :** any of several still-water herbs (genus *Potamogeton*)

1pick·et \ˈpik-ət\ *n* [F *piquet,* fr. MF, fr. *piquer* to prick — more at PIKE] **1 :** a pointed or sharpened stake, post, or pale **2 a :** a detached body of soldiers serving to guard an army from surprise **b :** a detachment kept ready in camp for such duty **c :** SENTINEL **3 :** a person posted by a labor organization at a place of work affected by a strike; *also* **:** a person posted for a demonstration or protest

2picket *vt* **1 :** to enclose, fence, or fortify with pickets **2 a :** to guard with a picket **b :** to post as a picket **3 :** TETHER **4 a**

: to post pickets at **b :** to walk or stand in front of as a picket ~ *vi* : to serve as a picket — **pick·et·er** *n*

pick·et·boat \'pik-ət-ˌbōt\ *n* : a craft used (as by the coast guard) for harbor patrol

picket line *n* **1 :** a position held by a line of military pickets **2 :** a line of individuals (as workers) picketing a business, organization, or institution

picket ship *n* : a ship or airplane stationed outside a formation or geographical area as a rescue or warning unit

pick·ings \'pik-iŋz, -ənz\ *n pl* : something that is picked or picked up: as **a :** gleanable or eatable fragments : SCRAPS **b :** yield or return for effort expended

[1]pick·le \'pik-əl\ *n* [ME *pekille*] **1 :** a solution or bath for preserving or cleaning: as **a :** a brine or vinegar solution in which foods are preserved **b :** any of various baths used in industrial cleaning or processing **2 :** a difficult situation : PLIGHT <could see no way out of the ~ I was in —R. L. Stevenson> **3 :** an article of food (as a cucumber) that has been preserved in brine or in vinegar **4** *Brit* : a mischievous or troublesome person

[2]pickle *vt* **pick·led; pick·ling** \-(ə-)liŋ\ : to treat, preserve, or clean in or with a pickle

[3]pickle *n* [perh. fr. Sc *pickle* (to trifle, pilfer)] **1** *Scot* : GRAIN, KERNEL **2** *Scot* : a small quantity

pick·led *adj* **1 :** preserved in or cured with pickle <~ herring> **2 :** DRUNK <gets thoroughly ~ before dinner —*New Yorker*>

pick·lock \'pik-ˌläk\ *n* **1 :** a tool for picking locks **2 :** BURGLAR

pick–me–up \'pik-mē-ˌəp\ *n* : something that stimulates or restores : TONIC, BRACER

pick·off \'pik-ˌȯf\ *n* : a baseball play in which a base runner is picked off

pick–off *n* : a sensing device that responds to angular movement and produces a signal or effects control

pick off \(ˈ)pik-'ȯf\ *vt* **1 :** to shoot or bring down one by one **2 :** to put out (a base runner who is off base) with a quick throw (as from the pitcher or catcher) **3 :** INTERCEPT <*picked off* a pass>

pick out *vt* : to play the notes of by ear or one by one <learned to *pick out* tunes on the piano>

pick over *vt* : to examine in order to select the best or remove the unwanted

pick·pock·et \'pik-ˌpäk-ət\ *n* : one who steals from pockets

pick·proof \-'prüf\ *adj* : designed to prevent picking <a ~ lock>

pick·thank \-ˌthaŋk\ *n* [fr. *pick a thank* to seek someone's favor] *archaic* : SYCOPHANT

[1]pick·up \'pik-ˌəp\ *n* **1 :** the act or process of picking up: as **a :** a revival of business activity **b :** ACCELERATION **2 :** one that is picked up: as **a :** a hitchhiker who is given a ride **b :** a temporary chance acquaintance **3 :** the conversion of mechanical movements into electrical impulses in the reproduction of sound; *also* : a device (as on a phonograph) for making such conversion **4 a** (1) **:** the reception of sound or an image into a radio or television transmitting apparatus for conversion into electrical signals (2) **:** interference (as with such reception) from an adjacent electrical circuit or system **b :** a device (as a microphone or a television camera) for converting sound or the image of a scene into electrical signals **c :** the place where a broadcast originates **d :** the electrical system for connecting to a broadcasting station a program produced outside the studio **5 :** a light truck having an open body with low sides and tailboard — called also *pickup truck*

[2]pickup *adj* : utilizing or comprising local or available personnel esp. without formal organization <a ~ basketball game>

pick up \(ˈ)pik-'əp\ *vt* **1 a :** to take hold of and lift up **b :** to gather together : COLLECT <*picked up* all the pieces> **c :** to clean up : TIDY **2 a :** to take (passengers or freight) into a vehicle **b :** to use as a means of transportation <people waiting to *pick up* the bus> **3 a :** to acquire casually or by chance <*picked up* a valuable antique at a tag sale> **b :** to acquire by study or experience : LEARN <*picking up* a great deal of knowledge in the process —Robert Schleicher> **c :** CLAIM <*picked up* his clothes at the cleaners> **d :** to obtain esp. by payment : BUY <*picked up* some groceries on the way home> **e :** to acquire (a player) esp. from another team through a trade or by financial recompense **f :** to accept for the purpose of paying <offered to *pick up* the tab> **g :** to come down with : CATCH <*picked up* a cold> **h :** GAIN, TRAVERSE <*picked up* a few yards on the last play> **4 :** to enter informally into conversation or companionship with (a previously unknown person) <had a brief affair with a girl he *picked up* in a bar> **5 a :** to take into custody <the police *picked up* the fugitive> **b :** to come to and follow <*picked up* the outlaw's trail> **c :** to bring within range of sight or hearing **6 a :** REVIVE **b :** INCREASE **7 :** to resume after a break : CONTINUE <*pick up* the discussion tomorrow> **8 :** to move in conjunction with in an athletic contest; *also* : to move into position to guard (an opponent) ~ *vi* **1 :** to recover speed, vigor, or activity : IMPROVE <after the strike, business *picked up*> **2 :** to put things in order <was always *picking up* after her> **3 :** to pack up one's belongings <couldn't just *pick up* and leave>

Pick·wick·ian \(ˈ)pik-'wik-ē-ən\ *adj* [Samuel *Pickwick*, character in the novel *Pickwick Papers* (1836–37) by Charles Dickens] **1 :** marked by simplicity and generosity **2 :** intended or taken in a sense other than the obvious or literal one

picky \'pik-ē\ *adj* **pick·i·er; -est :** FUSSY, CHOOSY <a ~ eater>

pi·clo·ram \'pik-lə-ˌram, 'pīk-\ *n* [*pic*oline + ch*lor*- + *am*ine] : a systemic herbicide $C_6H_3Cl_3N_2O_2$ that breaks down only very slowly in the soil

[1]pic·nic \'pik-(ˌ)nik\ *n* [G or F; G *picknick*, fr. F *pique-nique*] **1 :** an excursion or outing with food usu. provided by members of the group and eaten in the open **2 a :** a pleasant or amusingly carefree experience <I don't expect being married to be a ~ like you seem to —Josephine Pinckney> **b :** an easy task or feat **3 :** a shoulder of pork with much of the butt removed — see PORK illustration — **pic·nic·ky** \-(ˌ)nik-ē\ *adj*

[2]picnic *vi* **pic·nicked; pic·nick·ing :** to go on a picnic : eat in picnic fashion — **pic·nick·er** *n*

picnometer *var of* PYCNOMETER

pi·co- \'pē-(ˌ)kō, -kə\ *comb form* [ISV, perh. fr. It *piccolo* small] **1 :** one trillionth (10^{-12}) part of <*pico*gram> **2 :** very small <*picor*navirus>

pi·co·far·ad \ˌpē-kō-'far-ˌad, -əd\ *n* [ISV] **:** one trillionth of a farad

pi·co·gram \'pē-kō-ˌgram, -kə-\ *n* [ISV] **:** one trillionth of a gram

pic·o·line \'pik-ə-ˌlēn, 'pīk-\ *n* [L *pic-*, *pix* pitch + ISV *-ol* + *-ine* — more at PITCH] **:** any of the three liquid pyridine bases C_6H_7N found esp. in coal tar, ammonia liquor, and bone oil and used chiefly as solvents and in organic synthesis

pi·cor·na·vi·rus \(ˌ)pē-ˌkȯr-nə-'vī-rəs\ *n* [*pico-* + *RNA* + *virus*] : any of a group of RNA-containing viruses that includes the enteroviruses and rhinoviruses

pi·co·sec·ond \ˌpē-kō-'sek-ənd, -ənt\ *n* [ISV] **:** one trillionth of a second

[1]pi·cot \'pē-(ˌ)kō, pē-'\ *n* [F, lit., small point, fr. MF, fr. *pic* prick, fr. *piquer* to prick — more at PIKE] **:** one of a series of small ornamental loops forming an edging on ribbon or lace

[2]picot *vt* : to finish with picots

pic·o·tee \ˌpik-ə-'tē\ *n* [F *picoté* pointed, fr. *picoter* to mark with points, fr. *picot*] **:** a flower (as some carnations or tulips) having one basic color with a margin of another color

picr- *or* **picro-** *comb form* [F, fr. Gk *pikr-*, *pikro-*, fr. *pikros* — more at PAINT] **1 :** bitter <*picr*ic acid> **2 :** picric acid <*picr*ate>

pic·rate \'pik-ˌrāt\ *n* : a salt or ester of picric acid

pic·ric acid \ˌpik-rik-\ *n* [ISV] **:** a bitter toxic explosive yellow crystalline strong acid $C_6H_3N_3O_7$ used esp. in high explosives, as a dye, or in medicine

pic·ro·tox·in \ˌpik-rō-'täk-sən\ *n* [ISV] **:** a poisonous bitter crystalline stimulant and convulsive drug $C_{30}H_{34}O_{13}$ used intravenously as an antidote for barbiturate poisoning

Pict \'pikt\ *n* [ME *Pictes*, pl., Picts, fr. LL *Picti*] **:** a member of a possibly non-Celtic people who once occupied Great Britain, carried on continual border wars with the Romans, and about the 9th century became amalgamated with the Scots — **Pict·ish** \'pik-tish\ *adj or n*

pic·to·gram \'pik-tə-ˌgram\ *n* [ISV *picto-* (fr. L *pictus*) + *-gram*] : PICTOGRAPH

pic·to·graph \-ˌgraf\ *n* [L *pictus* + E *-o-* + *-graph*] **1 :** an ancient or prehistoric drawing or painting on a rock wall **2 :** one of the symbols belonging to a pictorial graphic system **3 :** a diagram representing statistical data by pictorial forms — **pic·to·graph·ic** \ˌpik-tə-'graf-ik\ *adj*

pic·tog·ra·phy \pik-'täg-rə-fē\ *n* : use of pictographs : PICTURE WRITING 1

[1]pic·to·ri·al \pik-'tōr-ē-əl, -'tȯr-\ *adj* [LL *pictorius*, fr. L *pictor* painter] **1 :** of or relating to a painter, a painting, or the painting or drawing of pictures <~ perspective> **2 a :** consisting of pictures <~ records> **b :** illustrated by pictures <~ weekly> **c :** consisting of or displaying the characteristics of pictographs **d :** suggesting or conveying visual images <he made ~ drama out of the most commonplace intimacies of . . . life —J. T. Soby> ***syn*** see GRAPHIC — **pic·to·ri·al·ly** \-ē-ə-lē\ *adv* — **pic·to·ri·al·ness** *n*

[2]pictorial *n* : a periodical having much pictorial matter

pic·to·ri·al·ism \-ē-ə-ˌliz-əm\ *n* : the use or creation of pictures or visual images

pic·to·ri·al·iza·tion \pik-ˌtōr-ē-ə-lə-'zā-shən, -ˌtȯr-\ *n* : the act, process, or an instance of representing by a picture or illustrating with pictures <detailed ~ of the . . . coronation —*Newsweek*>

pic·to·ri·al·ize \pik-'tōr-ē-ə-ˌlīz, -'tȯr-\ *vt* **-ized; -iz·ing :** to make pictorial

[1]pic·ture \'pik-chər\ *n* [ME, fr. L *pictura*, fr. *pictus*, pp. of *pingere* to paint — more at PAINT] **1 :** a design or representation made by various means (as painting, drawing, or photography) **2 :** a description so vivid or graphic as to suggest a mental image or give an accurate idea of something <the book gives a detailed ~ of what is happening> **3 :** IMAGE, COPY <he was the ~ of his father> **4 a :** a transitory visible image or reproduction **b :** MOTION PICTURE **c** *pl, chiefly Brit* : MOVIES **5 :** TABLEAU 1, 2 <stage ~*s*> **6 :** SITUATION <took a hard look at his financial ~>

[2]picture *vt* **pic·tured; pic·tur·ing** \'pik-chə-riŋ, 'pik-shriŋ\ **1 :** to paint or draw a representation, image, or visual conception of : DEPICT; *also* : ILLUSTRATE **2 :** to describe graphically in words **3 :** to form a mental image of : IMAGINE

picture book *n* : a book that consists wholly or chiefly of pictures

pic·ture·go·er \'pik-chər-ˌgō(-ə)r\ *n, chiefly Brit* : MOVIEGOER

picture hat *n* : a woman's dressy hat with a broad brim

Pic·ture·phone \'pik-chər-ˌfōn\ *service mark* — used for a combined telephone and television apparatus

picture puzzle *n* : JIGSAW PUZZLE

pic·tur·esque \ˌpik-chə-'resk\ *adj* [F & It; F *pittoresque*, fr. It *pittoresco*, fr. *pittore* painter, fr. L *pictor*, fr. *pictus*, pp.] **1 a :** resembling a picture : suggesting a painted scene **b :** QUAINT, CHARMING **2 :** evoking mental images : VIVID ***syn*** see GRAPHIC — **pic·tur·esque·ly** *adv* — **pic·tur·esque·ness** *n*

picture tube *n* : a cathode-ray tube having at one end a screen of luminescent material on which are produced visible images

picture window *n* : an outsize usu. single-paned window designed to frame an exterior view

picture writing *n* **1 :** the recording of events or expression of messages by pictures representing actions or facts **2 :** the record or message represented by picture writing

pic·tur·ize \'pik-chə-ˌrīz\ *vt* **-ized; -iz·ing :** to make a picture of : present in pictures; *esp* : to make into a motion picture — **pic·tur·iza·tion** \ˌpik-chə-rə-'zā-shən\ *n*

pic·ul \'pik-əl\ *n* [Malay *pikul* to carry a heavy load] **:** any of various units of weight used in China and southeast Asia; *esp* : a Chinese unit equal to 133.33 pounds

pid·dle \'pid-ᵊl\ *vi* **pid·dled; pid·dling** \'pid-liŋ, -ᵊl-iŋ\ [origin unknown] **:** to behave or work in an idle manner : DAWDLE

pid·dling \'pid-lən, -liŋ, -ᵊl-ən, -ᵊl-iŋ\ *adj* : TRIVIAL, PALTRY

pid·dock \'pid-ək, -ik\ *n* [origin unknown] **:** a bivalve mollusk (genus *Pholas* or family Pholadidae) that bores holes in wood, clay, and rocks

pid·gin \'pij-ən\ *n* [*Pidgin English*] **:** a simplified speech used for communication between people with different languages — **pid·gin·ize** \-ə-ˌnīz\ *vt* — **pid·gin·iza·tion** \ˌpij-ə-nə-'zā-shən\ *n*

Pidgin English *n* [Pidgin E, modif. of E *business English*] **:** an English-based pidgin; *esp* **:** one orig. used in parts of the Orient

[1]pie \'pī\ *n* [ME, fr. OF, fr. L *pica*; akin to L *picus* woodpecker, OHG *speh*] **1 :** MAGPIE **2 :** a parti-colored animal

[2]pie *n* [ME] **1 :** a meat dish baked with biscuit or pastry crust — compare POTPIE **2 :** a dessert consisting of a filling (as of fruit or custard) baked in a dish or pan lined with pastry or topped with pastry or both **3 a :** AFFAIR, BUSINESS <she wanted her finger . . . in every possible social ~ — Mary Deasy> **b :** a whole regarded as divisible into shares <giving the less fortunate . . . a larger share of the economic ~ —R. M. Hutchins>

[3]pie *var of* PI

[4]pie *n* [Hindi *pāī*, fr. Skt *pādikā* quarter] **:** a former monetary unit of India and Pakistan equal to $^1/_{192}$ of the rupee

[1]pie·bald \'pī-ˌbȯld\ *adj* **1 :** of different colors: **a :** spotted or blotched with black and white **b :** SKEWBALD **2 :** composed of incongruous parts **:** HETEROGENEOUS

[2]piebald *n* **:** a piebald animal (as a horse)

[1]piece \'pēs\ *n* [ME, fr. OF, fr. (assumed) VL *pettia*, of Gaulish origin; akin to Bret *peg* piece] **1 :** a part of a whole **2 :** an object or individual regarded as a unit of a kind or class **:** EXAMPLE **3 :** a standard quantity (as of length, weight, or size) in which something is made or sold **4 a :** a literary composition **b :** PAINTING, SCULPTURE **c :** a theatrical production **:** PLAY **d :** a musical composition **5 :** FIREARM **6 :** COIN; *also* **:** TOKEN **7 :** a man used in playing a board game; *specif* **:** a chessman of superior rank **8 a :** an act of copulation — usu. considered vulgar **b :** the female partner in sexual intercourse — usu. considered vulgar ***syn*** see PART — **of a piece :** ALIKE, CONSISTENT — **piece of one's mind :** a severe scolding **:** TONGUE-LASHING — **piece of the action :** a share in activity or profit — **to pieces 1 :** without reserve or restraint **:** COMPLETELY **2 :** into fragments **3 :** out of control <went *to pieces* from shock>

[2]piece *vt* **pieced; piec·ing 1 :** to repair, renew, or complete by adding pieces **:** PATCH **2 :** to join into a whole — often used with *together* <his new book . . . has been *pieced* together from talks —Merle Miller> — **piec·er** *n*

piece by piece *adv* **:** by degrees **:** PIECEMEAL

pièce de ré·sis·tance \pē-ˌes-də-rə-ˌzē-'stän(t)s, -rā-, -'stäⁿs\ *n, pl* **pièces de ré·sis·tance** *same*\ [F, lit., piece of resistance] **1 :** the chief dish of a meal **2 :** an outstanding item **:** SHOWPIECE

piece–dye \'pēs-ˌdī\ *vt* **:** to dye after weaving or knitting

piece goods *n pl* **:** cloth fabrics sold from the bolt at retail in lengths specified by the customer — called also *yard goods*

[1]piece·meal \'pē-ˌsmēl, -'smē(ə)l\ *adv* **1 :** one piece at a time **:** GRADUALLY **2 :** in pieces or fragments **:** APART

[2]piecemeal *adj* **:** done, made, or accomplished piece by piece or in a fragmentary way **:** GRADUAL

piece of eight : an old Spanish peso of eight reals

piece·wise \'pē-ˌswīz\ *adv* **:** with respect to a number of discrete intervals, sets, or pieces <~ continuous functions>

piece·work \'pē-ˌswərk\ *n* **:** work done by the piece and paid for at a set rate per unit — **piece·work·er** \-ˌswər-kər\ *n*

pie chart *n* **:** a circular chart cut by radii into segments illustrating relative magnitudes or frequencies — called also *circle graph*

pie·crust \'pī-ˌkrəst\ *n* **:** the pastry shell of a pie

pied \'pīd\ *adj* **:** of two or more colors in blotches; *also* **:** wearing or having a parti-colored coat <a ~ horse>

pied–à–terre \pē-ˌād-ə-'te(ə)r, -ˌäd-ä-\ *n, pl* **pieds–à–terre** *same*\ [F, lit., foot to the ground] **:** a temporary or second lodging

pied·mont \'pēd-ˌmänt\ *adj* [*Piedmont*, region of Italy] **:** lying or formed at the base of mountains — **piedmont** *n*

pied piper *n, often cap both Ps* [*The Pied Piper of Hamelin*, title & hero of a poem (1842) by Robert Browning] **1 :** one that offers strong but delusive enticement **2 :** a leader who makes irresponsible promises

pie–eyed \'pī-'īd\ *adj* **:** INTOXICATED

pie–faced \-'fāst\ *adj* **:** having a round, smooth, or blank face

pie·fort *or* **pied·fort** \pē-ā-'fō(ə)r\ *n, often attrib* [F *pied-fort*, lit., strong-footed one] **:** a coin struck on an unusually thick flan

pie in the sky : a prospect or promise of deferred happiness or prosperity

pie·plant \'pī-ˌplant\ *n* **:** garden rhubarb

pier \'pi(ə)r\ *n* [ME *per*, fr. OE, fr. ML *pera*] **1 :** an intermediate support for the adjacent ends of two bridge spans **2 :** a structure (as a breakwater) extending into navigable water for use as a landing place or promenade or to protect or form a harbor **3 :** a vertical structural support: as **a :** the wall between two openings **b :** PILLAR, PILASTER **c :** a vertical member that supports the end of an arch or lintel **d :** an auxiliary mass of masonry used to stiffen a wall **4 :** a structural mount (as for a telescope) usu. of stonework, concrete, or steel

pierce \'pi(ə)rs\ *vb* **pierced; pierc·ing** [ME *percen*, fr. OF *percer*] *vt* **1 a :** to run into or through as a pointed weapon does **:** STAB **b :** to enter or thrust into sharply or painfully **2 :** to make a hole through **:** PERFORATE **3 :** to force or make a way into or through **4 :** to penetrate with the eye or mind **:** DISCERN **5 :** to penetrate so as to move or touch the emotions of ~ *vi* **:** to force a way into or through something ***syn*** see ENTER

pierced *adj* **1 :** having holes; *esp* **:** decorated with perforations **2 :** having the earlobe punctured for an earring <~ ears>

pierc·ing *adj* **:** PENETRATING: as **a :** LOUD, SHRILL <~ cries> **b :** PERCEPTIVE <~ eyes> **c :** penetratingly cold **:** BITING <a ~ winter wind> **d :** CUTTING, INCISIVE <~ sarcasm> — **pierc·ing·ly** \'pir-siŋ-lē\ *adv*

pier glass *n* **:** a large high mirror; *esp* **:** one designed to occupy the wall space between windows

Pi·eri·an \pī-'ir-ē-ən, -'er-\ *adj* **1 :** of or relating to the region of Pieria in ancient Macedonia or to the Muses who were early worshiped there **2 :** of or relating to learning or poetry

Pier·rot \'pē-ə-ˌrō\ *n* [F, dim. of *Pierre* Peter] **:** a stock comic character of old French pantomime usu. having a whitened face and wearing loose white clothes

pier table *n* **:** a table to be placed under a pier glass

pies *pl of* PI *or of* PIE

pie·tà \ˌpē-(ˌ)ā-'tä, pyā-\ *n, often cap* [It, lit., pity, fr. L *pietat-*, *pietas*] **:** a representation of the Virgin Mary mourning over the dead body of Christ

pi·etism \'pī-ə-ˌtiz-əm\ *n* **1** *cap* **:** a 17th century religious movement originating in Germany in reaction to formalism and intellectualism and stressing Bible study and personal religious experience **2 a :** emphasis on devotional experience and practices **b :** affectation of devotion — **pi·etist** \'pī-ət-əst\ *n, often cap*

pi·etis·tic \ˌpī-ə-'tis-tik\ *or* **pi·etis·ti·cal** \-'tis-ti-kəl\ *adj* **1 :** of or relating to Pietism **2 a :** of or relating to religious devotion or devout persons **b :** marked by overly sentimental or emotional devotion to religion **:** RELIGIOSE ***syn*** see DEVOUT — **pi·etis·ti·cal·ly** \-ti-k(ə-)lē\ *adv*

pi·ety \'pī-ət-ē\ *n, pl* **pi·eties** [F *piété* piety, pity, fr. L *pietat-*, *pietas*, fr. *pius* dutiful — more at PIOUS] **1 :** the quality or state of being pious: as **a :** fidelity to natural obligations (as to parents) **b :** dutifulness in religion **:** DEVOUTNESS **2 :** an act inspired by piety **3 :** a conventional belief or standard **:** ORTHODOXY ***syn*** see FIDELITY ***ant*** impiety

piezo- *comb form* [Gk *piezein* to press; akin to Skt *pīḍayati* he squeezes] **:** pressure <*piezo*meter>

[1]pi·ezo·elec·tric \pē-ˌā-(ˌ)zō-ə-'lek-trik, pē-ˌāt-(ˌ)sō-\ *adj* [ISV] **:** of, relating to, marked by, or functioning by means of piezoelectricity — **pi·ezo·elec·tri·cal·ly** \-tri-k(ə-)lē\ *adv*

[2]piezoelectric *n* **:** a piezoelectric substance

pi·ezo·elec·tric·i·ty \-ˌlek-'tris-ət-ē, -'tris-tē\ *n* [ISV] **:** electricity or electric polarity due to pressure esp. in a crystalline substance (as quartz)

pi·ezom·e·ter \ˌpē-ə-'zäm-ət-ər, pē-ˌāt-'säm-\ *n* **:** an instrument for measuring pressure or compressibility; *esp* **:** one for measuring the change of pressure of a material subjected to hydrostatic pressure — **pi·ezo·met·ric** \pē-ˌā-zə-'me-trik, pē-ˌāt-sə-\ *adj* — **pi·ezom·e·try** \ˌpē-ə-'zäm-ə-trē, pē-ˌāt-'säm-\ *n*

[1]pif·fle \'pif-əl\ *vi* **pif·fled; pif·fling** \-(ə-)liŋ\ [perh. blend of *piddle* and *trifle*] **:** to talk or act in a trivial, inept, or ineffective way

[2]piffle *n* **:** trivial nonsense **:** INEPTITUDE

[1]pig \'pig\ *n, often attrib* [ME *pigge*] **1 :** a young swine not yet sexually mature; *broadly* **:** a wild or domestic swine **2 a :** PORK **b :** the dressed carcass of a young swine weighing less than 130 pounds **c :** PIGSKIN **3 a :** one resembling a pig **b :** an animal related to or resembling the pig — usu. used in combination <guinea ~> **4 :** a crude casting of metal (as iron) **5 :** an immoral woman **6** *slang* **:** POLICEMAN

[2]pig *vb* **pigged; pig·ging** *vi* **1 :** FARROW **2 :** to live like a pig <~ it> ~ *vt* **:** FARROW

[3]pig *n* [ME *pygg*] *chiefly Scot* **:** an earthenware vessel **:** CROCK

pig bed *n* **:** a bed of sand in which iron is cast into pigs

pig·boat \'pig-ˌbōt\ *n* **:** SUBMARINE

pi·geon \'pij-ən\ *n* [ME, fr. MF *pijon*, fr. LL *pipion-*, *pipio* young bird, fr. L *pipire* to chirp] **1 :** any of a widely distributed family (Columbidae, order Columbiformes) of birds with a stout body, rather short legs, and smooth and compact plumage; *esp* **:** a member of one of the many domesticated varieties derived from the rock pigeon **2 :** a young woman **3 :** an easy mark **:** DUPE **4 :** CLAY PIGEON **5** [alter. of *pidgin*] **:** an object of special concern **:** BUSINESS

pigeon breast *n* **:** a rachitic deformity of the chest marked by sharp projection of the sternum — **pi·geon–breast·ed** \ˌpij-ən-'bres-təd\ *adj*

pigeon hawk *n* **1 :** a small American falcon (*Falco columbarius*) related to the European merlin **2 :** SHARP-SHINNED HAWK

pi·geon·heart·ed \ˌpij-ən-'härt-əd\ *adj* **:** TIMID, COWARDLY

[1]pi·geon·hole \'pij-ən-ˌhōl\ *n* **1 :** a hole or small recess for pigeons to nest **2 :** a small open compartment (as in a desk or cabinet) for keeping letters or documents **3 :** a neat category which usu. fails to reflect actual complexities

[2]pigeonhole *vt* **1 a :** to place in or as if in the pigeonhole of a desk **b :** to lay aside **:** SHELVE <his reports continued to be *pigeonholed* and his advice not taken —Walter Mills> **2 :** to assign to a category **:** CLASSIFY

pi·geon–liv·ered \ˌpij-ən-'liv-ərd\ *adj* **:** GENTLE, MILD

pigeon pea *n* **:** a leguminous woody herb (*Cajanus cajan*) that has trifoliate leaves, yellow flowers, and somewhat flat pods and is much cultivated esp. in the tropics; *also* **:** its small highly nutritious seed

pi·geon–toed \ˌpij-ən-'tōd\ *adj* **:** having the toes turned in

pi·geon·wing \'pij-ən-ˌwiŋ\ *n* **:** a fancy dance step executed by jumping and striking the legs together

pig·fish \'pig-ˌfish\ *n* **1 :** a saltwater grunt (*Orthopristis chrysopterus*) that is a food fish found from Long Island southward **2 :** any of several grunts other than the pigfish

pig·gery \'pig-ə-rē\ *n, pl* **-ger·ies :** a place where swine are kept

pig·gin \'pig-ən\ *n* [origin unknown] *dial* **:** a small wooden pail with one stave extended upward as a handle

pig·gish \'pig-ish\ *adj* [[1]*pig*] **1 :** GREEDY <their wishes for a somewhat ~ material happiness —Paul de Kruif> **2 :** STUBBORN — **pig·gish·ly** *adv* — **pig·gish·ness** *n*

[1]pig·gy·back \'pig-ē-ˌbak\ *adv* [alter. of earlier *a pick pack*, of unknown origin] **1 :** up on the back and shoulders **2 :** on a railroad flatcar <the trailer rode ~ from coast to coast>

2piggyback *n* **1 :** the act of carrying piggyback **2 :** the movement of loaded truck trailers on railroad flatcars or cars of special design — compare BIRDYBACK, FISHYBACK
3piggyback *adj* **1 :** marked by being up on the shoulders and back <a child needs hugging, tussling, and ~ rides —Benjamin Spock> **2 :** of or relating to the hauling of truck trailers on railroad flatcars **3 :** of or relating to radio or television advertising that includes within usu. a one minute period more than one commercial by the same company **4 :** being or relating to something carried into space as an extra load by a vehicle (as a spacecraft)
4piggyback *vt* **1 :** to carry up on the shoulders and back **2 :** to haul (as a truck trailer) by railroad car ~ *vi* **:** to haul truck trailers on railroad cars
piggy bank *n* **:** a coin bank often in the shape of a pig
pig·head·ed \ˈpig-ˈhed-əd\ *adj* **:** OBSTINATE, STUBBORN — **pig·head·ed·ness** *n*
pig in a poke : something offered in such a way as to obscure its real nature or worth <unwilling to buy a *pig in a poke*>
pig iron *n* **:** crude iron that is the direct product of the blast furnace and is refined to produce steel, wrought iron, or ingot iron
pig latin *n, often cap L* **:** a jargon that is made by systematic mutilation of English (as *ipskay the ointjay* for *skip the joint*)
pig lead *n* **:** lead cast in pigs
pig·let \ˈpig-lət\ *n* **:** a small usu. young hog
1pig·ment \ˈpig-mənt\ *n* [L *pigmentum*, fr. *pingere* to paint — more at PAINT] **1 :** a substance that imparts black or white or a color to other materials; *esp* **:** a powdered substance that is mixed with a liquid in which it is relatively insoluble and used esp. to impart color to coating materials (as paints) or to inks, plastics, and rubber **2 :** a coloring matter in animals and plants esp. in a cell or tissue; *also* **:** any of various related colorless substances — **pig·men·tary** \-mən-ˌter-ē\ *adj*
2pig·ment \-mənt, -ˌment\ *vt* **:** to color with or as if with pigment
pig·men·ta·tion \ˌpig-mən-ˈtā-shən, -ˌmen-\ *n* **:** coloration with or deposition of pigment; *esp* **:** an excessive deposition of bodily pigment
pigmy *var of* PYGMY
pig·nut \ˈpig-ˌnət\ *n* **1 :** any of several bitter-flavored hickory nuts **2 :** a hickory (as *Carya glabra, C. ovalis,* or *C. cordiformis*) bearing pignuts
pig·pen \-ˌpen\ *n* **1 :** a pen for pigs **2 :** a dirty slovenly place
pig·skin \-ˌskin\ *n* **1 :** the skin of a swine or leather made of it **2 a :** a jockey's saddle **b :** FOOTBALL 2a
pig·stick \-ˌstik\ *vi* **:** to hunt the wild boar on horseback with a spear — **pig·stick·er** *n*
pig·sty \ˈpig-ˌstī\ *n* **:** PIGPEN 1
pig·tail \-ˌtāl\ *n* **1 :** tobacco in small twisted strands or rolls **2 :** a tight braid of hair
pig·tailed \-ˌtāld\ *adj* **:** wearing a pigtail <~ little girls>
pig·weed \-ˌwēd\ *n* **:** any of various strongly growing weedy plants esp. of the goosefoot or amaranth families
pi·ka \ˈpē-kə, ˈpī-\ *n* [Tungusic *piika*] **:** any of various short-eared small lagomorph mammals (family Ochotonidae) of rocky uplands of Asia and western No. America that are related to the rabbits
pi·ka·ke \ˈpē-kə-ˌkā\ *n* [Hawaiian *pīkake*] **:** an East Indian vine (*Jasminum sambuc*) that is cultivated for its profuse fragrant white flowers
1pike \ˈpīk\ *n* [ME, fr. OE *pīc* pickax] **1 :** PIKESTAFF 1 **2 :** a sharp point or spike; *also* **:** the tip of a spear — **piked** \ˈpīkt\ *adj*
2pike *vi* **piked; pik·ing** [ME *pyken* (refl.)] **1 :** to leave abruptly <get lonely and sore, and ~ out —Sinclair Lewis> **2 :** to make one's way <~ along>
3pike *n* [ME, perh. of Scand origin; akin to Norw dial. *pīk* pointed mountain] **1** *dial Eng* **:** a mountain or hill having a peaked summit — used esp. in place names **2** [Sp *pico*, fr. *picar* to prick — more at PICADOR] *archaic* **:** PEAK
4pike *n, pl* **pike** *or* **pikes** [ME, fr. [1]*pike*] **1 a :** a large elongate long-snouted teleost fish (*Esox lucius*) valued for food and sport and widely distributed in cooler parts of the northern hemisphere **b :** any of various fishes (family Esocidae) related to the pike: as (1) **:** MUSKELLUNGE (2) **:** PICKEREL **2 :** any of various fishes resembling the pike in appearance or habits
5pike *n* [MF *pique*, fr. *piquer* to prick, fr. (assumed) VL *piccare*, fr. *piccus* woodpecker, fr. L *picus* — more at PIE] **:** a weapon formed of a long wooden shaft with a pointed steel head and used by the foot soldier until superseded by the bayonet
6pike *vt* **piked; pik·ing :** to pierce, kill, or wound with a pike
7pike *n* **1 :** TURNPIKE **2 :** a railroad or model railroad line or system <railroading on . . . backwoods ~*s* —F. P. Donovan>
8pike *n* [prob. fr. [4]*pike*] **:** a body position (as in diving) in which the hips are bent, the knees are straight, the head is pressed forward, and the hands touch the toes or clasp the legs behind or just above the knees
pike·man \ˈpīk-mən\ *n* **:** a soldier armed with a pike
pike perch *n* **:** a fish (as the walleye) of the perch group that resembles the pike
pik·er \ˈpī-kər\ *n* [*Pike* county, Missouri, thought to be the original home of many shiftless farmers] **1 :** one who gambles or speculates with small amounts of money **2 :** one who does things in a small way; *also* **:** TIGHTWAD, CHEAPSKATE
pike·staff \ˈpīk-ˌstaf\ *n* **1 :** a spiked staff for use on slippery ground **2 :** the staff of a foot soldier's pike
pil- *or* **pili-** *or* **pilo-** *comb form* [L *pilus* — more at PILE] **:** hair <*pil*eous> <*pili*ferous>
pi·laf *or* **pi·laff** \pi-ˈläf, ˈpē-ˌ\ *or* **pi·lau** \pi-ˈlō, -ˈlȯ, ˈpē-(ˌ); *South often* ˈpər-(ˌ)lü, -(ˌ)lō\ *n* [Per & Turk *pilāu*] **:** a dish made of seasoned rice and often meat
pi·las·ter \ˈpī-ˌlas-tər *also* pə-ˈlas- *or* pī-ˈ\ *n* [MF *pilastre*, fr. It *pilastro*] **:** an upright architectural member that is rectangular in plan and is structurally a pier but architecturally treated as a column and that usu. projects a third of its width or less from the wall

pil·chard \ˈpil-chərd\ *n* [origin unknown] **1 :** a fish (*Sardinia pilchardus*) of the herring family resembling the herring and occurring in great schools along the coasts of Europe **2 :** any of several sardines related to the European pilchard
1pile \ˈpī(ə)l\ *n* [ME, dart, stake, fr. OE *pīl;* akin to OHG *pfīl* dart; both fr. a prehistoric WGmc word borrowed fr. L *pilum* javelin — more at PESTLE] **1 :** a long slender column usu. of timber, steel, or reinforced concrete driven into the ground to carry a vertical load **2 :** a wedge-shaped heraldic charge usu. placed vertically with the broad end up **3 a :** a target-shooting arrowhead without cutting edges **b** [L *pilum*] **:** an ancient Roman foot soldier's heavy javelin

1 pilasters

2pile *vt* **piled; pil·ing :** to drive piles into
3pile *n* [ME, fr. MF, fr. L *pila* pillar] **1 a** (1) **:** a quantity of things heaped together (2) **:** a heap of wood for burning a corpse or a sacrifice **b :** any great number or quantity **:** LOT **2 :** a large building or group of buildings **3 :** a great amount of money **:** FORTUNE **4 a :** a vertical series of alternate disks of two dissimilar metals (as copper and zinc) with disks of cloth or paper moistened with an electrolyte between them for producing a current of electricity **b :** a battery made up of cells similarly constructed **5 :** REACTOR 3b
4pile *vb* **piled; pil·ing** *vt* **1 :** to lay or place in a pile **:** STACK **2 :** to heap in abundance **:** LOAD <*piled* potatoes on his plate> ~ *vi* **1 :** to form a pile **:** ACCUMULATE **2 :** to move or press forward in or as if in a mass **:** CROWD <*piled* into a car>
5pile *n* [ME, fr. L *pilus* hair; akin to L *pila* ball, *pilleus, pileus* felt cap, Gk *pilos*] **1 :** a coat or surface of usu. short close fine furry hairs **2 :** a velvety surface produced by an extra set of filling yarns that form raised loops which are cut and sheared
6pile *n* [ME, fr. L *pila* ball] **1 :** a single hemorrhoid **2** *pl* **piles :** HEMORRHOIDS; *also* **:** the condition of one affected with hemorrhoids
pi·le·ate \ˈpī-lē-ˌāt\ *adj* **:** having a pileus
pi·le·at·ed \-ˌāt-əd\ *adj* **:** having a crest covering the pileum <a ~ woodpecker>
piled \ˈpī(ə)ld\ *adj* **:** having a pile <a deep-*piled* rug>
pile driver *n* **1 :** a machine for driving down piles with a pile hammer or a steam or air hammer **2 :** an operator of a pile driver
pi·le·um \ˈpī-lē-əm\ *n, pl* **pi·lea** \-lē-ə\ [NL, fr. L *pileus, pileum* felt cap] **:** the top of the head of a bird from the bill to the nape
pile·up \ˈpī-ˌləp\ *n* **1 :** a collision involving usu. several motor vehicles and causing damage or injury **2 :** a jammed tangled mass or pile (as of motor vehicles or people) resulting from collision
pi·le·us \ˈpī-lē-əs\ *n, pl* **pi·lei** \-lē-ˌī\ [NL, fr. L] **1 :** the umbrella-shaped fruiting body of many fungi (as the mushrooms) **2** [L] **:** a pointed or close-fitting cap worn by ancient Romans
pile·wort \ˈpī(ə)l-ˌwərt, -ˌwȯ(ə)rt\ *n* [[6]*pile;* fr. its use in treating piles] **1 :** CELANDINE 2 **2 :** a coarse hairy perennial figwort (*Scrophularia marilandica*) of the eastern and central U.S.
pil·fer \ˈpil-fər\ *vb* **pil·fered; pil·fer·ing** \-f(ə-)riŋ\ [MF *pelfrer*, fr. *pelfre* booty] *vi* **:** to steal stealthily in small amounts or to small value and often again and again <the mouse that ~*s* from our pantry> ~ *vt* **:** to steal in small quantities *syn* see STEAL — **pil·fer·age** \-f(ə-)rij\ *n* — **pil·fer·er** \-fər-ər\ *n*
pil·gar·lic \pil-ˈgär-lik\ *n* [*pilled garlic*] **1 a :** a bald head **b :** a bald-headed man **2 :** a man looked upon with humorous contempt or mock pity
pil·grim \ˈpil-grəm\ *n* [ME, fr. OF *peligrin*, fr. LL *pelegrinus*, alter. of L *peregrinus* foreigner, fr. *peregrinus* foreign, fr. *pereger* being abroad, fr. *per* through + *agr-, ager* land — more at FOR, ACRE] **1 :** one who journeys in foreign lands **:** WAYFARER **2 :** one who travels to a shrine or holy place as a devotee **3** *cap* **:** one of the English colonists settling at Plymouth in 1620
1pil·grim·age \ˈpil-grə-mij\ *n* **1 :** a journey of a pilgrim; *esp* **:** one to a shrine or a sacred place **2 :** the course of life on earth
2pilgrimage *vi* **-aged; -ag·ing :** to go on a pilgrimage
pilgrim bottle *n* **:** COSTREL
pil·ing \ˈpī-liŋ\ *n* **:** a structure of piles; *also* **:** PILES
Pi·li·pi·no \ˌpil-ə-ˈpē-(ˌ)nō, ˌpēl-\ *n* [Pilipino, fr. Sp *Filipino* Philippine] **:** the Tagalog-based official language of the Republic of the Philippines
1pill \ˈpil\ *vb* [ME *pilen, pillen*, partly fr. OE *pilian* to peel, partly fr. MF *piller* to plunder] *vi, dial chiefly Eng* **:** to come off in flakes or scales **:** PEEL ~ *vt* **1** *archaic* **:** to subject to depredation or extortion **2** *dial* **:** to peel or strip off
2pill *n* [L *pilula*, fr. dim. of *pila* ball — more at PILE] **1 a :** medicine in a small rounded mass to be swallowed whole **b :** an oral contraceptive — usu. used with *the* **2 :** something repugnant or unpleasant that must be accepted or endured **3 :** something resembling a pill in size or shape **4 :** a disagreeable or tiresome person
3pill *vt* **1 :** to dose with pills **2 :** BLACKBALL ~ *vi* **:** to become rough with or mat into little balls <brushed woolens often ~>
1pil·lage \ˈpil-ij\ *n* [ME, fr. MF, fr. *piller* to plunder, fr. *peille* rag, fr. L *pilleum, pilleus* felt cap] **1 :** the act of looting or plundering esp. in war **2 :** something taken as booty *syn* see SPOIL
2pillage *vb* **pil·laged; pil·lag·ing** *vt* **:** to plunder ruthlessly **:** LOOT ~ *vi* **:** to take booty *syn* see RAVAGE — **pil·lag·er** *n*
1pil·lar \ˈpil-ər\ *n* [ME *piler*, fr. OF, fr. ML *pilare*, fr. L *pila*] **1 a :** a firm upright support for a superstructure **:** POST **b :** a usu. ornamental column or shaft; *esp* **:** one standing alone for a monument **2 :** a chief supporter **:** PROP **3 :** a solid mass of coal, rock, or ore left standing to support a mine roof **4 :** a body part that resembles a column — **from pillar to post :** from one place or one situation to another

²pillar *vt* : to provide or strengthen with or as if with pillars
pil·lar–box \'pil-ər-,bäks\ *n, Brit* : a pillar-shaped mailbox
pill·box \'pil-,bäks\ *n* **1** : a box for pills; *esp* : a shallow round box of pasteboard **2** : a small low concrete emplacement for machine guns and antitank weapons **3** : a small round hat without a brim; *specif* : a woman's shallow hat with a flat crown and straight sides
pill bug *n* [*²pill;* fr. its rolling into a ball when disturbed] : WOOD LOUSE 1
¹pil·lion \'pil-yən\ *n* [ScGael or IrGael; ScGael *pillean,* dim. of *peall* covering, couch; IrGael *pillín,* dim. of *peall* covering, couch] **1 a** : a light saddle for women consisting chiefly of a cushion **b** : a pad or cushion put on behind a man's saddle chiefly for a woman to ride on **2** : a motorcycle or bicycle riding saddle for a passenger
²pillion *adv* : on or as if on a pillion <ride ~>
¹pil·lo·ry \'pil-(ə-)rē\ *n, pl* **-ries** [ME, fr. OF *pilori*] **1** : a device for publicly punishing offenders consisting of a wooden frame with holes in which the head and hands can be locked **2** : a means for exposing one to public scorn or ridicule

pillory 1

²pillory *vt* **-ried; -ry·ing** **1** : to set in a pillory as punishment **2** : to expose to public contempt, ridicule, or scorn
¹pil·low \'pil-(,)ō, -ə(-w)\ *n* [ME *pilwe,* fr. OE *pyle;* akin to OHG *pfuliwi* pillow; both fr. a prehistoric WGmc word borrowed fr. L *pulvinus* pillow] **1 a** : a support for the head of a reclining person; *esp* : a cloth bag filled with feathers, down, sponge rubber, or plastic fiber **b** : something resembling a pillow esp. in form **2** : a block or support used esp. to equalize or distribute pressure **3** : a cushion or pad tightly stuffed and used as a support for the design and tools in making lace with a bobbin
²pillow *vt* **1** : to rest or lay on or as if on a pillow **2** : to serve as a pillow for ~ *vi* : to lay or rest one's head on or as if on a pillow
pillow block *n* : a block or standard to support a journal (as of a shaft) : BEARING
pil·low·case \'pil-ə-,kās, -ō-\ *n* : a removable covering for a pillow usu. of linen or cotton
pillow lace *n* [fr. its being worked over a pillow on which the pattern is marked] : lace made with a bobbin
pillow sham *n* : an ornamental covering for a bed pillow
pillow slip *n* : PILLOWCASE
pilo- — see PIL-
pi·lo·car·pine \,pī-lə-'kär-,pēn\ *n* [ISV, fr. NL *Pilocarpus jaborandi,* species of tropical shrubs] : a muscarinic alkaloid $C_{11}H_{16}N_2O_2$ that is obtained from jaborandi and is a strong sialagogue and diaphoretic
pi·lose \'pī-,lōs\ *adj* [L *pilosus,* fr. *pilus* hair — more at PILE] : covered with usu. soft hair — **pi·los·i·ty** \pī-'läs-ət-ē\ *n*
¹pi·lot \'pī-lət\ *n* [MF *pilote,* fr. It *pilota,* alter. of *pedota,* fr. (assumed) MGk *pēdōtēs,* fr. Gk *pēda* steering oars, pl. of *pēdon* oar; akin to Gk *pod-, pous* foot — more at FOOT] **1 a** : one employed to steer a ship : HELMSMAN **b** : a person who is qualified and usu. licensed to conduct a ship into and out of a port or in specified waters, often for fixed fees **2** : GUIDE, LEADER **3** : COWCATCHER **4** : one who handles or is qualified to handle the controls of an aircraft or spacecraft **5** : a piece that guides a tool or machine part **6** : a television show produced and filmed or taped as a sample of a proposed series **7** : PILOT BURNER — **pi·lot·less** \-ləs\ *adj*
²pilot *vt* **1** : to act as a guide to : lead or conduct over a usu. difficult course **2 a** : to set and conn the course of <~ a ship> **b** : to act as pilot of <~ a plane> ***syn*** see GUIDE
³pilot *adj* : serving as a guiding or tracing device, an activating or auxiliary unit, or a trial apparatus or operation
pi·lot·age \'pī-lət-ij\ *n* **1** : the action or business of piloting **2** : the compensation paid to a pilot
pilot balloon *n* : a small unmanned balloon sent up to show the direction and speed of the wind
pilot biscuit *n* : HARDTACK — called also *pilot bread*
pilot burner *n* : a small burner kept lighted to rekindle a principal burner
pilot engine *n* : a locomotive going in advance of a train to make sure that the way is clear
pilot fish *n* : a pelagic carangid fish (*Naucrates ductor*) that often swims in company with a shark
pi·lot·house \'pī-lət-,haùs\ *n* : a deckhouse for a ship's helmsman containing the steering wheel, compass, and navigating equipment
pilot light *n* **1** : an indicator light showing where a switch or circuit breaker is located or whether a motor is in operation or power is on — called also *pilot lamp* **2** : a small permanent flame used to ignite gas at a burner
pilot officer *n* : a commissioned officer in the British air force who ranks with a second lieutenant in the army
pil·sner *also* **pil·sen·er** \'pilz-(ə-)nər, 'pil-snər\ *n* [G, lit., of Pilsen, city in Czechoslovakia (now Plzen)] **1** : a light beer with a strong flavor of hops **2** : a tall slender footed glass for beer
Pilt·down man \,pilt-,daùn-\ *n* [*Piltdown,* East Sussex, England] : a supposedly very early primitive modern man based on skull fragments that were uncovered in a gravel pit at Piltdown and were used in combination with comparatively recent skeletal remains of various animals in the development of an elaborate fraud
pil·u·lar \'pil-yə-lər\ *adj* : of, relating to, or resembling a pill
pil·ule \'pil-(,)yü(ə)l\ *n* [MF, fr. L *pilula* pill — more at PILE] : a little pill
pi·lus \'pī-ləs\ *n, pl* **pi·li** \-,lī\ [L — more at PILE] : a hair or a structure (as of a bacterium) resembling a hair
pi·ma cotton \,pē-mə-, ,pim-ə-\ *n* [*Pima* county, Arizona] : a cotton that produces fiber of exceptional strength and firmness and that was developed in the southwestern U.S. by selection and breeding of Egyptian cottons
Pi·man \'pē-mən\ *adj* : of, relating to, or constituting a language family of the Uto-Aztecan phylum
pi·men·to \pə-'ment-(,)ō\ *n, pl* **pimentos** *or* **pimento** [Sp *pimienta* allspice, pepper, fr. LL *pigmenta,* pl. of *pigmentum* plant juice, fr. L, pigment] **1** : PIMIENTO 1 **2** : ALLSPICE
pimento cheese *n* : a Neufchâtel, process, cream, or occas. cheddar cheese to which ground pimientos have been added
pi–me·son \'pī-'mez-,än, -'mēz-, -'mēs-, -'mes-\ *n* [¹*pi*] : PION
pi·mien·to \pə-'ment-(,)ō, pəm-'yent-\ *n, pl* **-tos** [Sp, fr. *pimienta*] **1** : any of various bluntly conical thick-fleshed sweet peppers of European origin that have a distinctive mild sweet flavor and are used esp. as a garnish, as a stuffing for olives, and as a source of paprika **2** : a plant that bears pimientos
¹pimp \'pimp\ *n* [origin unknown] : a man who solicits clients for a prostitute
²pimp *vi* : to work as a pimp
pim·per·nel \'pim-pər-,nel, -pər-nəl\ *n* [ME *pimpernele,* fr. MF *pimprenelle,* fr. LL *pimpinella,* a medicinal herb] : any of a genus (*Anagallis*) of herbs of the primrose family; *esp* : SCARLET PIMPERNEL
pimp·ing \'pim-pən, -piŋ\ *adj* [origin unknown] **1** : PETTY, INSIGNIFICANT **2** *chiefly dial* : PUNY, SICKLY
pim·ple \'pim-pəl\ *n* [ME *pinple*] **1** : a small inflamed elevation of the skin : PAPULE; *esp* : PUSTULE **2** : a swelling or protuberance like a pimple — **pim·pled** \-pəld\ *adj* — **pim·ply** \-p(ə-)lē\ *adj*
¹pin \'pin\ *n* [ME, fr. OE *pinn;* akin to OHG *pfinn* peg] **1 a** : a piece of solid material (as wood or metal) used esp. for fastening separate articles together or as a support by which one article may be suspended from another **b** *obs* : the center peg of a target; *also* : the center itself **c** : something that resembles a pin esp. in slender elongated form **d** (1) : one of the wooden pieces constituting the target in various games (as bowling) (2) : the peg at which a quoit is pitched (3) : the staff of the flag marking a hole on a golf course **e** : a peg for regulating the tension of the strings of a musical instrument **f** : the part of a key stem that enters a lock **g** (1) : THOLE 2 (2) : a belaying pin **2 a** (1) : a small pointed piece of wire with a head used esp. for fastening cloth (2) : something of small value : TRIFLE **b** : an ornament or emblem fastened to clothing with a pin **c** (1) : BOBBY PIN (2) : HAIRPIN (3) : SAFETY PIN **3** : LEG — usu. used in pl. <wobbly on his ~*s*>
²pin *vt* **pinned; pin·ning** **1 a** : to fasten, join, or secure with a pin **b** : to hold fast or immobile **2 a** : ATTACH, HANG <*pinned* his hopes on a miracle> **b** : to assign the blame or responsibility for <~ the robbery on a night watchman> **3 a** : to make (a chess opponent's man) unable to move without exposing the king to check or a valuable piece to capture **b** *of a wrestler* : to secure a fall over (an opponent)
³pin *adj* **1** : of or relating to a pin **2** *of leather* : having a grain suggesting the heads of pins
pi·ña cloth \,pēn-yə-\ *n* [Sp *piña*] : a lustrous transparent cloth of Philippine origin that is woven of silky pineapple fibers
pin·afore \'pin-ə-,fō(ə)r, -,fò(ə)r\ *n* [²*pin* + *afore*] : a sleeveless usu. low-necked garment fastened in the back and worn as an apron or dress by girls and women
pi·nas·ter \pī-'nas-tər, 'pī-,\ *n* [L, wild pine, fr. *pinus* pine] : a pine (*Pinus pinaster*) of the Mediterranean region with reflexed bud scales and needles in pairs
pi·ña·ta *or* **pi·na·ta** \pēn-'yät-ə\ *n* [Sp *piñata,* lit., pot] : a decorated pottery jar filled with candies, fruits, and gifts and hung from the ceiling to be broken as part of Mexican festivities (as at Christmas or for a birthday party)
pin·ball machine \'pin-,bòl-\ *n* : an amusement device in which a ball propelled by a plunger scores points as it rolls down a slanting surface among pins and targets — called also *pinball game*
pin·bone \'pin-'bōn, -,bōn\ *n* : the hipbone esp. of a quadruped — see COW illustration
pince–nez \paⁿ-'snā, pan(t)-\ *n, pl* **pince–nez** \-'snā(z)\ [F, fr. *pincer* to pinch + *nez* nose, fr. L *nasus* — more at NOSE] : eyeglasses clipped to the nose by a spring
pin·cer \'pin-chər (*usual US for 1*), 'pin(t)-sər\ *n* [ME *pinceour*] **1** *pl but sing or pl in constr* **a** : an instrument having two short handles and two grasping jaws working on a pivot and used for gripping things **b** : a claw (as of a lobster) resembling a pair of pincers : CHELA **2** : one part of a double envelopment in which two military forces converge upon opposite sides of an enemy position — **pin·cer·like** \-,līk\ *adj*
¹pinch \'pinch\ *vb* [ME *pinchen,* fr. (assumed) ONF *pinchier*] *vt* **1 a** : to squeeze between the finger and thumb or between the jaws of an instrument **b** : to prune the tip of (a plant or shoot) usu. to induce branching **c** : to squeeze or compress painfully **d** : to cause physical or mental pain to **e** (1) : to cause to appear thin or shrunken (2) : to cause to shrivel or wither **2** : to subject to strict economy or want : STRAITEN **3 a** : STEAL **b** : ARREST **4** : to sail too close to the wind ~ *vi* **1** : COMPRESS, SQUEEZE **2** : to be miserly or closefisted **3** : to press painfully **4** : NARROW, TAPER

ə abut	ᵊ kitten	ər further	a back	ā bake	ä cot, cart	
aù out	ch chin	e less	ē easy	g gift	i trip	ī life
j joke	ŋ sing	ō flow	ò flaw	òi coin	th thin	t͟h this
ü loot	ù foot	y yet	yü few	yù furious	zh vision	

2pinch *n* **1 a :** a critical juncture : EMERGENCY **b** (1) : PRESSURE, STRESS (2) : HARDSHIP, PRIVATION **c :** SHORTAGE **2 a :** an act of pinching : SQUEEZE **b :** as much as may be taken between the finger and thumb <a ~ of snuff> **3 :** a marked thinning of a vein or bed **4 a :** THEFT **b :** a police raid; *also* : ARREST ***syn*** see JUNCTURE — **with a pinch of salt :** with doubts about the truth of something proposed

3pinch *adj* [2*pinch*] **1 :** SUBSTITUTE <~ runner> **2 :** made by a pinch hitter <~ homer>

pinch bar *n* **:** a bar similar in form and use to a crowbar and sometimes having an end adapted for pulling spikes or inserting under a heavy wheel that is to be rolled

pinch·beck \'pinch-ˌbek\ *n* [Christopher *Pinchbeck* †1732 E watchmaker] **1 :** an alloy of copper and zinc used esp. to imitate gold in jewelry **2 :** something counterfeit or spurious — **pinchbeck** *adj*

pinch·cock \-ˌkäk\ *n* **:** a clamp used on a flexible tube to regulate the flow of a fluid through the tube

pinch·er \'pin-chər\ *n* **1 :** one that pinches **2** *pl* : PINCERS

pinch–hit \(ˈ)pinch-'hit\ *vi* [back-formation fr. *pinch hitter*] **1 :** to bat in the place of another player esp. in an emergency when a hit is particularly needed **2 :** to act or serve in place of another

pinch hit *n* **:** a hit made by a pinch hitter

pinch hitter *n* **:** one that pinch-hits

pin curl *n* **:** a curl made usu. by dampening a strand of hair with water or lotion, coiling it, and securing it by a hairpin or clip

pin·cush·ion \'pin-ˌku̇sh-ən\ *n* **:** a small cushion in which pins may be stuck ready for use

1Pin·dar·ic \pin-'dar-ik\ *adj* **1 :** of or relating to the poet Pindar **2 :** written in the manner or style characteristic of Pindar

2Pindaric *n* **1 :** a Pindaric ode **2** *pl* **:** loose irregular verses similar to those used in Pindaric odes

pin·dling \'pin-(d)lən, -(d)liŋ, -dᵊl-ən, -dᵊl-iŋ\ *adj* [perh. alter. of *spindling*] *dial* : PUNY, FRAIL

1pine \'pīn\ *vi* **pined; pin·ing** [ME *pinen*, fr. OE *pinian*, fr. (assumed) OE *pīn* punishment, fr. L *poena* — more at PAIN] **1 :** to lose vigor, health, or flesh (as through grief) : LANGUISH **2 :** to yearn intensely and persistently esp. for something unattainable <they still *pined* for their lost wealth> ***syn*** see LONG

2pine *n, often attrib* [ME, fr. OE *pīn*, fr. L *pinus*; akin to Gk *pitys* pine, L *opimus* fat — more at FAT] **1 :** any of a genus (*Pinus* of the family Pinaceae, the pine family) of coniferous evergreen trees which have slender elongated needles and some of which are valuable timber trees or ornamentals **2 :** the straight-grained white or yellow usu. durable and resinous wood of a pine varying from extreme softness in the white pine to hardness in the longleaf pine **3 :** any of various Australian coniferous trees (as of the genera *Callitris, Araucaria*, or *Cupressus*) **4 :** PINEAPPLE — **piny** *or* **pin·ey** \'pī-nē\ *adj*

pi·ne·al \'pī-nē-əl, pī-'\ *adj* [F *pinéal*, fr. MF, fr. L *pinea* pinecone, fr. fem. of *pineus* of pine, fr. *pinus*] **:** of, relating to, or being the pineal body

pineal body *n* **:** a small usu. conical appendage of the brain of all craniate vertebrates that in a few reptiles has the essential structure of an eye, that functions in some birds as part of a time-measuring system, and that is variously postulated to be a vestigial third eye, an endocrine organ, or the seat of the soul — called also *pineal gland, pineal organ*

pine·ap·ple \'pī-ˌnap-əl\ *n* **1 a :** a tropical monocotyledonous plant (*Ananas comosus* of the family Bromeliaceae, the pineapple family) that has rigid spiny-margined recurved leaves and a short stalk with a dense oblong head of small abortive flowers **b :** the multiple fruit of the pineapple that consists of the succulent fleshy inflorescence **2 a :** a dynamite bomb **b :** a hand grenade

pine·cone \'pīn-ˌkōn\ *n* **:** a cone of a pine tree

pine·drops \'pīn-ˌdräps\ *n pl but sing or pl in constr* **1 :** a purplish brown leafless saprophytic plant (*Pterospora andromedea*) of the wintergreen family with racemose drooping white flowers **2** : BEECHDROPS

pi·nene \'pī-ˌnēn\ *n* [ISV, fr. L *pinus*] **:** either of two liquid isomeric unsaturated bicyclic terpene hydrocarbons $C_{10}H_{16}$ of which one is a major constituent of wood turpentine

pine nut *n* **:** the edible seed of any of several chiefly western No. American pines

pin·ery \'pīn-(ə-)rē\ *n, pl* **-er·ies 1 :** a hothouse or area where pineapples are grown **2 :** a grove or forest of pine

pine·sap \'pīn-ˌsap\ *n* **:** any of several yellowish or reddish parasitic or saprophytic herbs (genus *Monotropa*) of the wintergreen family resembling the Indian pipe

pine siskin *n* **:** a No. American finch (*Spinus pinus*) with streaked plumage

pine snake *n* **1 :** a large constricting snake (*Pituophis melanoleucus*) of the eastern U.S. that is typically white and black and is found esp. in coastal regions from New Jersey southward **2 :** any of various snakes related to the pine snake

pine tar *n* **:** tar obtained by destructive distillation of the wood of the pine tree and used esp. in roofing and soaps and in the treatment of skin diseases

pi·ne·tum \pī-'nēt-əm\ *n, pl* **pi·ne·ta** \-'nēt-ə\ [L, fr. *pinus*] **1 :** a plantation of pine trees; *esp* **:** a scientific collection of living coniferous trees **2 :** a treatise on pines

pine·wood \'pīn-ˌwu̇d\ *n* **1 :** a wood of pines — often used in pl. but sing. or pl. in constr. **2 :** the wood of the pine tree

pin·feath·er \'pin-ˌfet͟h-ər\ *n* **:** a feather not fully developed; *esp* **:** a feather just emerging through the skin — **pin·feath·ered** \-ərd\ *adj* — **pin·feath·ery** \-ˌfet͟h-(ə-)rē\ *adj*

pin·fish \-ˌfish\ *n* **:** a small compressed dark green grunt (*Lagodon rhomboides*) that has sharp dorsal spines and is found along the Atlantic coast

pin·fold \-ˌfōld\ *n* [ME, fr. OE *pundfald*, fr. *pund-* enclosure + *fald* fold] **1 :** 4POUND 1a **2 :** a place of restraint

ping \'piŋ\ *n* [imit.] **1 :** a sharp sound like that of a striking bullet **2 :** ignition knock — **ping** *vi*

ping·er \'piŋ-ər\ *n* **:** a device for producing pulses of sound (as for marking an underwater site or detecting an underwater object)

pin·go \'piŋ-(ˌ)gō\ *n* [Esk] **:** a low hill or mound forced up by hydrostatic pressure in an area underlain by permafrost

Ping–Pong \'piŋ-ˌpäŋ, -ˌpȯŋ\ *trademark* — used for table tennis

pin·head \'pin-ˌhed\ *n* **1 :** something very small or insignificant **2 :** a very dull or stupid person : FOOL

pin·head·ed \-'hed-əd\ *adj* **:** lacking intelligence or understanding : DULL, STUPID — **pin·head·ed·ness** *n*

pin·hole \-ˌhōl\ *n* **:** a small hole made by, for, or as if by a pin

1pin·ion \'pin-yən\ *n* [ME, fr. MF *pignon*] **1 :** the terminal section of a bird's wing including the carpus, metacarpus, and phalanges; *broadly* : WING **2 :** FEATHER, QUILL; *also* : FLIGHT FEATHERS — **pin·ioned** \-yənd\ *adj*

2pinion *vt* **1 :** to restrain (a bird) from flight esp. by cutting off the pinion of one wing **2 a :** to disable or restrain by binding the arms **b :** to bind fast : SHACKLE

3pi·nion *like* PIÑON\ *n* [AmerSp *piñón*] : PIÑON

4pin·ion \'pin-yən\ *n* [F *pignon*, fr. MF *peignon*, fr. *peigne* comb, fr. L *pecten* — more at PECTINATE] **1 :** a gear with a small number of teeth designed to mesh with a larger wheel or rack — see RACK illustration **2 :** the smaller of a pair or the smallest of a train of gear wheels

1pink \'piŋk\ *vt* [ME *pinken*] **1 a :** PIERCE, STAB **b :** to wound by irony, criticism, or ridicule **2 a :** to perforate in an ornamental pattern **b :** to cut a saw-toothed edge on

2pink *n* [ME, fr. MD *pinke*] **:** a ship with a narrow overhanging stern — called also *pinkie*

3pink *n* [origin unknown] **1 :** any of a genus (*Dianthus* of the family Caryophyllaceae, the pink family) of plants having a cylindrical many-veined calyx with bracts at its base **2 a :** the very embodiment : PARAGON **b** (1) : one dressed in the height of fashion (2) : ELITE **c :** highest degree possible : HEIGHT <keep their house in the ~ of repair —Rebecca West> — **in the pink :** in the best of health

4pink *adj* **1 :** of the color pink **2 :** holding moderately radical and usu. socialistic political or economic views **3 :** emotionally moved : EXCITED — often used as an intensive <was tickled ~ by her flattery> — **pink·ness** *n*

5pink *n* **1 :** any of a group of colors bluish red to red in hue, of medium to high lightness, and of low to moderate saturation **2 a** (1) : the scarlet color of a fox hunter's coat (2) : a fox hunter's coat of this color **b :** pink-colored clothing **c** *pl* **:** light-colored trousers formerly worn by army officers **3 :** a person who holds advanced liberal or moderately radical political or economic views

pink bollworm *n* **:** a small dark brown moth (*Pectinophora gossypiella*) whose pinkish larva bores into the flowers and bolls of cotton and is a destructive pest in most cotton-growing regions

pink elephants *n pl* **:** any of various hallucinations arising esp. from heavy drinking or use of narcotics

pink·eye \'piŋ-ˌkī\ *n* **:** an acute highly contagious conjunctivitis of man and various domestic animals

1pin·kie *or* **pin·ky** \'piŋ-kē\ *n, pl* **pinkies** [prob. fr. D *pinkje*, dim. of *pink* little finger] **:** a little finger

2pinkie *n* [prob. fr. D *pinkje* small pink, dim. of *pink*, fr. MD *pinke*] : 2PINK

pinking shears *n pl* **:** shears with a saw-toothed inner edge on the blades for making a zigzag cut

pink·ish \'piŋ-kish\ *adj* **:** somewhat pink; *esp* **:** tending to be pink in politics — **pink·ish·ness** *n*

pink lady *n* **:** a cocktail consisting of gin, brandy, lemon juice, grenadine, and white of egg shaken with ice and strained

pink·ly \'piŋ-klē\ *adv* **:** in a pink manner **:** with a pink hue

pin knot *n* **:** a sound knot in lumber not over ½ inch in diameter

pinko \'piŋ-(ˌ)kō\ *n, pl* **pink·os** *or* **pink·oes** : 5PINK 3

pink·root \'piŋ-ˌkrüt, -ˌkru̇t\ *n* **:** any of several plants (genus *Spigelia*) related to the nux vomica and used as anthelmintics; *esp* **:** an American woodland herb (*S. marilandica*) sometimes cultivated for its showy red and yellow flowers

pin money *n* **1 a :** money given by a man to his wife for her own use **b :** money set aside for the purchase of incidentals **2 :** a trivial amount of money <worked for *pin money*>

pin·na \'pin-ə\ *n, pl* **pin·nae** \'pin-ˌē, -ˌī\ *or* **pinnas** [NL, fr. L, feather, wing — more at PEN] **1 :** a leaflet or primary division of a pinnate leaf or frond **2 a :** a projecting body part (as a feather, wing, or fin) **b :** the largely cartilaginous projecting portion of the external ear — see EAR illustration — **pin·nal** \'pin-ᵊl\ *adj*

pin·nace \'pin-əs\ *n* [MF *pinace*, prob. fr. OSp *pinaza*, fr. *pino* pine, fr. L *pinus*] **1 :** a light sailing ship; *esp* **:** one used as a tender **2 :** any of various ship's boats

1pin·na·cle \'pin-i-kəl\ *n* [ME *pinacle*, fr. MF, fr. LL *pinnaculum* gable, fr. dim. of L *pinna* wing, battlement] **1 :** an upright architectural member generally ending in a small spire and used esp. in Gothic construction to give weight to a buttress or angle pier **2 :** a structure or formation suggesting a pinnacle; *specif* **:** a lofty peak **3 :** the highest point of development or achievement : ACME ***syn*** see SUMMIT

2pinnacle *vt* **pin·na·cled; pin·na·cling** \-k(ə-)liŋ\ **1 :** to surmount with a pinnacle **2 :** to raise or rear on a pinnacle

1, pinnacle 1

pin·nate \'pin-ˌāt\ *adj* [NL *pinnatus*, fr. L, feathered, fr. *pinna*] **:** resembling a feather esp. in having similar parts arranged on opposite sides of an axis like the barbs on the rachis of a feather <~ leaf> — **pin·nate·ly** *adv* — **pin·na·tion** \pin-'ā-shən\ *n*

pinnati- *comb form* [NL, fr. *pinnatus*] **:** pinnately <*pinnati*sect>

pin·nati·fid \pə-ˈnat-ə-fəd, -ˌfid\ *adj* [NL *pinnatifidus,* fr. *pinnati-* + L *-fidus* -fid] **:** cleft in a pinnate manner <a ~ leaf> — **pin·nati·fid·ly** *adv*

pin·nati·sect \-ˌsekt\ *adv* **:** cleft pinnately to or almost to the midrib

pin·ner \ˈpin-ər\ *n* **1 :** a woman's cap with long lappets worn in the 17th and 18th centuries **2 :** one that pins

pin·ni·ped \ˈpin-ə-ˌped\ *n* [deriv. of L *pinna* + *ped-, pes* foot — more at FOOT] **:** any of a suborder (Pinnipedia) of aquatic carnivorous mammals (as a seal or walrus) with all four limbs modified into flippers — **pinniped** *adj*

pin·nu·la \ˈpin-yə-lə\ *n, pl* **-lae** \-ˌlē, -ˌlī\ [NL, fr. L, dim. of *pinna*] **1 :** PINNULE **2 :** BARB 4 — **pin·nu·lar** \-lər\ *adj*

pin·nu·late \-ˌlāt\ *or* **pin·nu·lat·ed** \-ˌlāt-əd\ *adj* **:** having pinnules

pin·nule \ˈpin-(ˌ)yü(ə)l\ *n* [NL *pinnula*] **1 a :** one of the secondary branches of a plumose organ **b :** a small fish fin separated from a major fin **2 :** one of the ultimate divisions of a twice pinnate leaf

pi·noch·le \ˈpē-ˌnək-əl\ *n* [prob. modif. of G dial. *binokel,* a game resembling bezique, fr. F dial. *binocle*] **:** a card game played with a 48-card pack containing two each of A, K, Q, J, 10, 9 in each suit with the object to score points by melding certain combinations of cards or by winning tricks that contain scoring cards; *also* **:** the meld of queen of spades and jack of diamonds scoring 40 points in this game

pi·no·cy·to·sis \ˌpin-ə-sə-ˈtō-səs, ˌpīn-, -ˌsī-\ *n, pl* **-to·ses** \-ˌsēz\ [NL, fr. Gk *pinein* to drink + NL *cyt-* + *-osis* — more at POTABLE] **:** the uptake of fluid by a cell by invagination and pinching off of the cell membrane

pi·no·cy·tot·ic \-ˈtät-ik\ *adj* **:** of or relating to pinocytosis — **pi·no·cy·tot·i·cal·ly** \-i-k(ə-)lē\ *adv*

pi·no·le \pi-ˈnō-lē\ *n* [AmerSp, fr. Nahuatl *pinolli*] **1 :** a finely ground flour made from parched corn **2 :** any of various flours resembling pinole and ground from the seeds of other plants

pi·ñon *or* **pin·yon** \ˈpin-ˌyōn, -ˌyän, -yən; pin-ˈyōn\ *n, pl* **pi·ñons** *or* **pin·yons** *or* **pi·ño·nes** \pin-ˈyō-nēz\ [AmerSp *piñón,* fr. Sp, pine nut, fr. *piña* pine cone, fr. L *pinea* — more at PINEAL] **1 :** any of various low-growing nut pines (as *Pinus parryana, P. cembroides, P. edulis,* and *P. monophylla*) of western No. America **2 :** the edible seed of a piñon

[1]**pin·point** \ˈpin-ˌpȯint\ *vt* **1 :** to locate or aim with great precision or accuracy **2 a :** to fix, determine, or identify with precision **b :** to cause to stand out conspicuously **:** HIGHLIGHT

[2]**pinpoint** *adj* **1 :** extremely fine or precise **2 :** located, fixed, or directed with extreme precision

[1]**pin·prick** \ˈpin-ˌprik\ *n* **1 :** a small puncture made by or as if by a pin **2 :** a petty irritation or annoyance

[2]**pinprick** *vt* **:** to administer pinpricks to ~ *vi* **:** to administer pinpricks

pins and needles *n pl* **:** a pricking tingling sensation in a limb recovering from numbness — **on pins and needles :** in a nervous or jumpy state of anticipation

pin·set·ter \ˈpin-ˌset-ər\ *n* **:** an employee or a mechanical device that spots pins in a bowling alley

pin·spot·ter \-ˌspät-ər\ *n* **:** PINSETTER

pin·stripe \-ˌstrīp\ *n* **:** a very thin stripe esp. on a fabric; *also* **:** a suit with such stripes — **pin–striped** \-ˌstrīpt\ *adj*

pint \ˈpīnt\ *n* [ME *pinte,* fr. MF, fr. ML *pincta,* fr. (assumed) VL, fem. of *pinctus,* pp. of L *pingere* to paint — more at PAINT] **1** — see WEIGHT table **2 :** a pint pot or vessel

pin·ta \ˈpint-ə, ˈpin-ˌtä\ *n* [AmerSp, fr. Sp, spot, mark, fr. (assumed) VL *pincta*] **:** a chronic skin disease that is endemic in tropical America, that occurs successively as an initial papule, a generalized eruption, and a patchy loss of pigment, and that is caused by a spirochete (*Treponema careteum*) morphologically indistinguishable from the causative agent of syphilis

pin·tail \ˈpin-ˌtāl\ *n, pl* **pintail** *or* **pintails :** a bird having elongated central tail feathers: as **a :** a slender gray and white river duck (*Dafila acuta*) with a white line on the side of the neck and head **b :** any of several grouse

pin–tailed \-ˌtāld\ *adj* **1 :** having a tapered tail with the middle feathers longest **2 :** having the tail feathers spiny

pin·tle \ˈpint-ᵊl\ *n* [ME *pintel,* lit., penis, fr. OE; akin to MLG *pint* penis, OE *pinn* pin] **:** a usu. upright pivot pin on which another part turns

[1]**pin·to** \ˈpin-(ˌ)tō\ *n, pl* **pintos** *also* **pintoes** [AmerSp, fr. *pinto* spotted, fr. obs. Sp, fr. (assumed) VL *pinctus*] *chiefly West* **:** a spotted or calico horse or pony

[2]**pinto** *adj* **:** PIED, MOTTLED

pint–size \ˈpīnt-ˌsīz\ *or* **pint–sized** \-ˌsīzd\ *adj* **:** SMALL

[1]**pin–up** \ˈpin-ˌəp\ *n* **:** something fastened to a wall: as **a :** a photograph of a pinup girl **b :** something (as a lamp) designed for wall attachment

[2]**pinup** *adj* **1 :** of or relating to pinup girls **2 :** designed for hanging on a wall

pinup girl *n* **1 :** a girl whose glamorous qualities make her a suitable subject of a photograph pinned up on an admirer's wall **2 :** a photograph of a pinup girl

pin·wale \ˈpin-ˌwāl\ *adj, of a fabric* **:** made with narrow wales

pin·weed \-ˌwēd\ *n* **1 :** any of a genus (*Lechea*) of herbs of the rockrose family with slender stems and leaves **2 :** ALFILARIA

pin·wheel \-ˌhwēl, -ˌwēl\ *n* **1 :** a toy consisting of lightweight vanes that revolve at the end of a stick **2 :** a fireworks device in the form of a revolving wheel of colored fire

pin·work \-ˌwərk\ *n* **:** fine stitches raised from the surface of a design in needlepoint lace to add lightness to the effect

pin·worm \-ˌwərm\ *n* **1 :** any of numerous small nematode worms (family Oxyuridae) that infest the intestines and esp. the cecum of various vertebrates; *esp* **:** a worm (*Enterobius vermicularis*) parasitic in man **2 :** any of several rather slender insect larvae that burrow in plant tissue

pinx *abbr* [L *pinxit*] he painted it

pinx·ter flower \ˈpiŋ(k)-stər-\ *n* [D *pinkster* Whitsuntide] **:** a deciduous pink-flowered azalea (*Rhododendron nudiflorum*) that is native to rich moist woodlands of eastern No. America

pi·o·let \ˌpē-ə-ˈlā\ *n* [F] **:** an ice ax used in mountaineering

pi·on \ˈpī-ˌän\ *n* [contr. of *pi-meson*] **:** a short-lived meson that is primarily responsible for the nuclear force and that exists as a positive or negative particle with mass 273.2 times the electron mass or a neutral particle with mass 264.2 times the electron mass — **pi·on·ic** \pī-ˈän-ik\ *adj*

[1]**pi·o·neer** \ˌpī-ə-ˈni(ə)r\ *n* [MF *pionier,* fr. OF *peonier* foot soldier, fr. *peon* foot soldier, fr. ML *pedon-, pedo* — more at PAWN] **1 :** a member of a military unit usu. of construction engineers **2 a :** a person or group that originates or helps open up a new line of thought or activity or a new method or technical development **b :** one of the first to settle in a territory **3 :** a plant or animal capable of establishing itself in a bare or barren area and initiating an ecological cycle

[2]**pioneer** *adj* **1 :** ORIGINAL, EARLIEST **2 :** relating to or being a pioneer; *esp* **:** of, relating to, or characteristic of early settlers or their time

[3]**pioneer** *vi* **:** to act as a pioneer <~*ed* in the development of nuclear reactors> ~ *vt* **1 :** to open or prepare for others to follow; *esp* **:** SETTLE **2 :** to originate or take part in the development of

Pioneer Day *n* **:** July 24 observed as a legal holiday in Utah in commemoration of the arrival of Brigham Young at the present site of Salt Lake City in 1847

pi·ous \ˈpī-əs\ *adj* [L *pius;* akin to L *piare* to appease] **1 a :** marked by or showing reverence for deity and devotion to divine worship **b :** marked by conspicuous religiosity <a hypocrite — a thing all ~ words and uncharitable deeds —Charles Reade> **2 :** sacred or devotional as distinct from the profane or secular **:** RELIGIOUS <a ~ opinion> **3 :** showing loyal reverence for a person or thing **:** DUTIFUL **4 a :** marked by sham or hypocrisy **b :** marked by self-conscious virtue **:** VIRTUOUS **5 :** deserving commendation **:** WORTHY <a ~ effort> ***syn*** see DEVOUT ***ant*** impious — **pi·ous·ly** *adv* — **pi·ous·ness** *n*

[1]**pip** \ˈpip\ *n* [ME *pippe,* fr. MD; akin to OHG *pfiffiz* pip; both fr. a prehistoric WGmc word borrowed fr. (assumed) VL *pipita,* alter. of L *pituita* phlegm, pip; akin to L *opimus* fat — more at FAT] **1 a :** a disorder of a bird marked by formation of a scale or crust on the tongue **b :** the scale or crust of this disorder **2 :** any of various human ailments; *esp* **:** a slight nonspecific disorder

[2]**pip** *n* [origin unknown] **1 a :** one of the dots used on dice and dominoes to indicate numerical value **b :** SPOT 2c **2 a :** SPOT, SPECK **b :** an inverted V or a spot of light on a radarscope indicating the return of radar waves reflected from an object; *broadly* **:** BLIP **3 :** an individual rootstock of the lily of the valley **4 :** a diamond worn to indicate rank by a second lieutenant, lieutenant, or captain in the British army

[3]**pip** *n* [short for *pippin*] **1 :** a small fruit seed; *esp* **:** one of a several-seeded fleshy fruit **2 :** one extraordinary of its kind

[4]**pip** *vb* **pipped; pip·ping** [imit.] *vi* **1 :** [1]PEEP 1 **2 :** to break through the shell of the egg <the chick *pipped*> ~ *vt* **:** to break open (the shell of an egg) in hatching

[5]**pip** *n* [imit.] **:** a short high-pitched tone

pip·age *or* **pipe·age** \ˈpī-pij\ *n* **1 a :** transportation by means of pipes **b :** the charge for such transportation **2 :** material for pipe lines **:** PIPING

pi·pal \ˈpē-(ˌ)pəl\ *n* [Hindi *pīpal,* fr. Skt *pippala*] **:** a large long-lived fig (*Ficus religiosa*) of India that yields a product like lac and lacks prop roots

[1]**pipe** \ˈpīp\ *n* [ME, fr. OE *pīpa;* akin to OHG *pfīfa* pipe; both fr. a prehistoric WGmc word borrowed fr. (assumed) VL *pipa* pipe, fr. L *pipare* to peep, of imit. origin] **1 a :** a tubular wind instrument; *specif* **:** a small fipple flute held in and played by the left hand **b :** one of the tubes of a pipe organ: (1) **:** FLUE PIPE (2) **:** REED PIPE **c :** BAGPIPE — usu. used in pl. **d** (1) **:** VOICE, VOCAL CORD — usu. used in pl. (2) **:** PIPING 1 **2 :** a long tube or hollow body for conducting a liquid, gas, or finely divided solid or for structural purposes **3 a :** a tubular or cylindrical object, part, or passage **b :** a roughly cylindrical and vertical geological formation **c :** the eruptive channel opening into the crater of a volcano **4 a :** a large cask of varying capacity used esp. for wine and oil **b :** any of various units of liquid capacity based on the size of a pipe; *esp* **:** a unit equal to 2 hogsheads **5 :** a device for smoking usu. consisting of a tube having a bowl at one end and a mouthpiece at the other **6 :** something easy **:** SNAP <considered the course a ~>

[2]**pipe** *vb* **piped; pip·ing** *vi* **1 a :** to play on a pipe **b :** to convey orders by signals on a boatswain's pipe **2 a :** to speak in a high or shrill voice **b :** to emit a shrill sound ~ *vt* **1 a :** to play (a tune) on a pipe **b :** to utter in the shrill tone of a pipe **2 a :** to lead or cause to go with pipe music **b** (1) **:** to call or direct by the boatswain's pipe (2) **:** to receive aboard or attend the departure of by a boatswain's pipe **3 :** to trim with piping **4 :** to furnish or equip with pipes **5 :** to convey by or as if by pipes; *specif* **:** to transmit by wire or coaxial cable **6** *slang* **:** NOTICE

pipe–clay *vt* **:** to whiten or clean with pipe clay

pipe clay *n* **:** highly plastic grayish white clay used esp. in making tobacco pipes and for whitening leather

pipe cleaner *n* **:** something used to clean the inside of a pipe; *specif* **:** a piece of flexible wire in which tufted fabric is twisted and which is used to clean the stem of a tobacco pipe

pipe cutter *n* **:** a tool or machine for cutting pipe; *esp* **:** a hand tool comprising a grasping device and three sharp-edged wheels forced inward by screw pressure that cut into the pipe as the tool is rotated

pipe down *vi* [[2]*pipe*] **:** to stop talking or making noise

pipe dream *n* [fr. the fantasies brought about by the smoking of opium] : an illusory or fantastic plan, hope, or story

pipe·fish \ˈpīp-ˌfish\ *n* : any of various long slender fishes (of *Syngnathus* and related genera) that are related to the sea horses and have a tube-shaped snout and an angular body covered with bony plates

pipe fitter *n* : one who installs and repairs piping

pipe fitting *n* **1** : a piece (as a coupling or elbow) used to connect pipes or as accessory to a pipe **2** : the work of a pipe fitter

pipe·ful \ˈpīp-ˌfu̇l\ *n* : a quantity of tobacco smoked in a pipe at one time

pipe·less \ˈpī-pləs\ *adj* : having no pipe

pipe·like \ˈpī-ˌplīk\ *adj* : resembling a pipe or piping

pipe·line \ˈpī-ˌplīn\ *n* **1** : a line of pipe with pumps, valves, and control devices for conveying liquids, gases, or finely divided solids **2** : a direct channel for information **3** : the processes through which supplies pass from source to user

pipe major *n* : the principal player in a band of bagpipes

pipe of peace : CALUMET

pipe organ *n* : ORGAN 1b(1)

pip·er \ˈpī-pər\ *n* **1** : one that plays on a pipe **2 a** : a maker, layer, or repairer of pipes **b** : one that applies piping

pi·per·a·zine \pī-ˈper-ə-ˌzēn\ *n* [ISV, blend of *piperidine* and *az-*] : a crystalline heterocyclic base $C_4H_{10}N_2$ or $C_4H_{10}N_2 \cdot 6H_2O$ used esp. as an anthelmintic

pi·per·i·dine \pī-ˈper-ə-ˌdēn\ *n* [ISV, blend of *piperine* and *-ide*] : a liquid heterocyclic base $C_5H_{11}N$ that has a peppery ammoniacal odor and is obtained usu. by hydrolysis of piperine

pip·er·ine \ˈpip-ə-ˌrēn\ *n* [ISV, fr. L *piper* pepper] : a white crystalline alkaloid $C_{17}H_{19}NO_3$ that is the chief active constituent of pepper

pi·per·o·nal \pī-ˈper-ə-ˌnal\ *n* [ISV *piperine* + *-one* + *-al*] : a crystalline aldehyde $C_8H_6O_3$ with an odor of heliotrope that is used esp. in perfumery

pi·per·o·nyl bu·tox·ide \pī-ˈper-ə-ˌnil-byu̇-ˈtäk-ˌsīd, -ən-ᵊl-\ *n* [*piperone* + *-yl* + *but-* + *oxide*] : an insecticide $C_{19}H_{30}O_5$; *esp* : an oily liquid containing this compound that is used chiefly as a synergist (as for pyrethrum insecticides)

pipe·stone \ˈpīp-ˌstōn\ *n* : a pink or mottled pink-and-white argillaceous stone carved by the Indians into tobacco pipes

pipe stop *n* : an organ stop composed of flue pipes

pi·pette *or* **pi·pet** \pī-ˈpet\ *n* [F *pipette,* dim. of *pipe* pipe, cask, fr. (assumed) VL *pipa, pippa* pipe] : a small piece of apparatus which typically consists of a narrow tube into which fluid is drawn by suction (as for dispensing or measurement) and retained by closing the upper end

pipe up *vi* : to begin to play or to sing or speak

pipe wrench *n* : a wrench for gripping and turning a cylindrical object (as a pipe) usu. by use of two serrated jaws so designed as to grip the pipe when turning in one direction only

¹pip·ing \ˈpī-piŋ\ *n* **1 a** : the music of a pipe **b** : a sound, note, or call like that of a pipe **2** : a quantity or system of pipes **3** : trimming stitched in seams or along edges of clothing, slipcovers, or curtains

²piping *adj* : marked by peaceful pipe music rather than martial drum and fife music : TRANQUIL

piping hot *adj* : so hot as to sizzle or hiss : very hot

pip·it \ˈpip-ət\ *n* [imit.] : any of various small singing birds (family Motacillidae and esp. genus *Anthus*) resembling the lark

pip·kin \ˈpip-kən\ *n* [perh. fr. *pipe*] : a small earthenware or metal pot usu. with a horizontal handle

pip·pin \ˈpip-ən\ *n* [ME *pepin,* fr. OF] **1** : any of numerous apples that have usu. yellow or greenish yellow skins strongly flushed with red and are used esp. for cooking **2** : a highly admired or very admirable person or thing

pip–pip \pip-ˈip, ˈpip-ˈpip\ *interj* [origin unknown] *Brit* : GOOD-BYE

pip·sis·se·wa \pip-ˈsis-ə-ˌwȯ\ *n* [Cree *pipisisikweu*] : any of a genus (*Chimaphila,* esp. *C. corymbosa*) of evergreen herbs of the wintergreen family with astringent leaves used as a tonic and diuretic

pip–squeak \ˈpip-ˌskwēk\ *n* : a small or insignificant person

pi·quan·cy \ˈpē-kən-sē, ˈpik-wən-\ *n* : the quality or state of being piquant

pi·quant \ˈpē-kənt, -ˌkänt; ˈpik-wənt\ *adj* [MF, fr. prp. of *piquer*] **1** : agreeably stimulating to the palate : SAVORY **2** : engagingly provocative; *also* : having a lively arch charm <her ~ face> ***syn*** see PUNGENT ***ant*** bland — **pi·quant·ly** *adv* — **pi·quant·ness** *n*

¹pique \ˈpēk\ *n* : a transient feeling of wounded vanity : a fit of resentment ***syn*** see OFFENSE

²pique *vt* **piqued; piqu·ing** [F *piquer,* lit., to prick — more at PIKE] **1** : to arouse anger or resentment in : IRRITATE; *specif* : to offend by slighting **2 a** : to excite or arouse by a provocation, challenge, or rebuff **b** : to stir up the pride or interest of esp. in respect to a particular accomplishment <he ~*s* himself on his skill as a cook> ***syn*** see PROVOKE, PRIDE

pi·qué *or* **pi·que** \pi-ˈkā, ˈpē-ˌ\ *n* [F *piqué,* fr. pp. of *piquer* to prick, quilt] : a durable ribbed clothing fabric of cotton, rayon, or silk

pi·quet \pi-ˈkā, pik-ˈet\ *n* [F] : a two-handed card game played with 32 cards and in which points are scored for certain combinations of cards and for taking tricks

pi·ra·cy \ˈpī-rə-sē\ *n, pl* **-cies** [ML *piratia,* fr. LGk *peirateia,* fr. Gk *peiratēs* pirate] **1** : robbery on the high seas **2** : the unauthorized use of another's production, invention, or conception esp. in infringement of a copyright **3 a** : an act of piracy **b** : an act resembling piracy

pi·ra·gua \pə-ˈräg-wə, -ˈrag-\ *n* [Sp] **1** : DUGOUT 1 **2** : a 2-masted flat-bottomed boat

pi·ra·nha \pə-ˈran-yə, -ˈrän-(y)ə\ *n* [Pg, fr. Tupi] : a small So. American characin fish (genus *Serrasalmo*) that often attacks and inflicts dangerous wounds upon men and large animals — called also *caribe*

pi·ra·ru·cu \pi-ˌrär-ə-ˈkü\ *n* [Pg, fr. Tupi *pirá-rucú*] : a very large food fish (*Arapaima gigas,* order Isospondyli) of the rivers of northern So. America

¹pi·rate \ˈpī-rət\ *n* [ME, fr. MF or L; MF, fr. L *pirata,* fr. Gk *peiratēs,* fr. *peiran* to attempt — more at FEAR] : one who commits or practices piracy — **pi·rat·i·cal** \pə-ˈrat-i-kəl, pī-\ *adj* — **pi·rat·i·cal·ly** \-k(ə-)lē\ *adv*

²pirate *vb* **pi·rated; pi·rat·ing** *vt* **1** : to commit piracy on **2** : to take or appropriate by piracy: as **a** : to reproduce without authorization esp. in infringement of copyright **b** : to lure away from another employer by offers of betterment ~ *vi* : to commit or practice piracy

pirn \ˈpərn, *2 is also* ˈpi(ə)rn\ *n* [ME] **1** : QUILL 1a(1) **2** *chiefly Scot* : a device resembling a reel

pi·rogue \ˈpē-ˌrōg\ *n* [F, fr. Sp *piragua,* of Cariban origin; akin to Galibi *piraua* pirogue] **1** : DUGOUT 1 **2** : a boat like a canoe

piro·plasm \ˈpir-ə-ˌplaz-əm\ *or* **piro·plas·ma** \ˌpir-ə-ˈplaz-mə\ *n, pl* **piroplasms** *or* **piro·plas·ma·ta** \ˌpir-ə-ˈplaz-mət-ə\ [NL *Piroplasma,* genus of piroplasms] : any of a family (Babesiidae) of parasitic sporozoans : BABESIA

pi·rosh·ki \ˌpir-əsh-ˈkē\ *n pl* [Russ *pirozhki,* pl. of *pirozhok* small tart] : small pastry turnovers stuffed esp. with a savory meat filling

pir·ou·ette \ˌpir-ə-ˈwet\ *n* [F, lit., teetotum] : a rapid whirling about of the body; *specif* : a full turn on the toe or ball of one foot in ballet — **pirouette** *vi*

pis *pl of* PI

pis al·ler \ˌpē-za-ˈlā\ *n, pl* **pis al·lers** \-ˈlā(z)\ [F, lit., to go worst] : a last resource or device : EXPEDIENT

pis·ca·ry \ˈpis-kə-rē\ *n, pl* **-ries** **1** [ME *piscarie,* fr. ML *piscaria,* fr. L, neut. pl. of *piscarius* of fish, fr. *piscis*] : FISHERY 4; *esp* : the right of fishing in waters belonging to another **2** [ML *piscaria,* fr. L, fem. of *piscarius*] : FISHERY 2

pis·ca·to·ri·al \ˌpis-kə-ˈtōr-ē-əl, -ˈtȯr-\ *adj* : PISCATORY — **pis·ca·to·ri·al·ly** \-ē-ə-lē\ *adv*

pis·ca·to·ry \ˈpis-kə-ˌtōr-ē, -ˌtȯr-\ *adj* [L *piscatorius,* fr. *piscatus,* pp. of *piscari* to fish, fr. *piscis*] : of, relating to, or dependent on fishermen or fishing

Pi·sces \ˈpī-(ˌ)sēz, ˈpis-ˌēz, ˈpis-ˌkās\ *n pl but sing in constr* [ME, fr. L (gen. *Piscium*), fr. pl. of *piscis* fish — more at FISH] **1** : a zodiacal constellation directly south of Andromeda **2 a** : the 12th sign of the zodiac in astrology — see ZODIAC table **b** : one born under this sign

pi·sci·cul·ture \ˈpī-sə-ˌkəl-chər, ˈpis-(k)ə-\ *n* [prob. F, fr. L *piscis* + F *culture*] : fish culture — **pi·sci·cul·tur·al** \ˌpī-sə-ˈkəlch-(ə-)rəl\ *adj* — **pi·sci·cul·tur·ist** \-rəst\ *n*

pi·sci·na \pə-ˈsē-nə, -ˈsī-, *R.C. also* -ˈshē-\ *n* [ML, fr. L, fishpond, fr. *piscis*] : a basin with a drain near the altar of a church for disposing of water from liturgical ablutions

pi·scine \ˈpī-ˌsēn, ˈpis-ˌ(k)īn\ *adj* [L *piscinus,* fr. *piscis*] : of, relating to, or characteristic of fish

pi·sciv·o·rous \pə-ˈsiv-ə-rəs, pī-\ *adj* [L *piscis* + E *-vorous*] : feeding on fishes

pish \ˈpish\ *interj* — used to express disdain or contempt

¹pi·si·form \ˈpī-sə-ˌfȯrm\ *adj* [L *pisum* pea + E *-iform* — more at PEA] : resembling a pea in size or shape

²pisiform *n* : a bone on the ulnar side of the carpus in most mammals

pis·mire \ˈpis-ˌmī(ə)r, ˈpiz-\ *n* [ME *pissemire,* fr. *pisse* urine + *mire* ant, of Scand. origin; akin to ON *maurr* ant; akin to L *formica* ant, Gk *myrmēx*] : ANT

pis·mo clam \ˌpiz-(ˌ)mō-\ *n, often cap P* [*Pismo* Beach, Calif.] : a thick-shelled clam (*Tivela stultorum*) of the southwest coast of No. America used extensively for food

pi·so·lite \ˈpī-sə-ˌlīt\ *n* [NL *pisolithus,* fr. Gk *pisos* pea + *-lithos* -lith] : a limestone composed of pisiform concretions — **pi·so·lit·ic** \ˌpī-sə-ˈlit-ik\ *adj*

¹piss \ˈpis\ *vb* [ME *pissen,* fr. OF *pissier,* fr. (assumed) VL *pissiare,* of imit. origin] *vi* : URINATE — sometimes considered vulgar ~ *vt* : to urinate in or on <~ the bed> — sometimes considered vulgar

²piss *n* **1** : URINE — sometimes considered vulgar **2** : an act of urinating — often used with *take;* sometimes considered vulgar

pissed off *adj, slang* : ANGRY, DISAPPOINTED, DISGUSTED <a lot of guys . . . are *pissed off* at me 'cause I came in after them and made corporal —Norman Mailer>

pis·soir \pi-ˈswär\ *n* [F, fr. MF, fr. *pisser* to urinate, fr. OF *pissier*] : a public urinal usu. located on the street in some European countries

pis·ta·chio \pə-ˈstash-(e-ˌ)ō, -ˈstäsh-\ *n, pl* **-chios** [It *pistacchio,* fr. L *pistacium* pistachio nut, fr. Gk *pistakion,* fr. *pistakē* pistachio tree, fr. Per *pistah*] : a small tree (*Pistacia vera*) of the sumac family whose drupaceous fruit contains a greenish edible seed; *also* : its seed

pis·ta·reen \ˌpis-tə-ˈrēn\ *n* [prob. modif. of Sp *peseta* peseta] : an old Spanish 2-real silver piece circulating in Spain, the West Indies, and the U.S. at a debased rate

pis·til \ˈpis-tᵊl\ *n* [NL *pistillum,* fr. L, pestle — more at PESTLE] : the ovule-bearing organ of a seed plant that consists of the ovary with its appendages — see FLOWER illustration

pis·til·late \ˈpis-tə-ˌlāt\ *adj* : having pistils; *specif* : having pistils but no stamens

pis·tol \ˈpis-tᵊl\ *n* [MF *pistole,* fr. G, fr. MHG dial. *pischulle,* fr. Czech *pistal,* lit., pipe; akin to Russ *pischal* harquebus] : a short firearm intended to be aimed and fired with one hand; *esp* : a handgun whose chamber is integral with the barrel — **pistol** *vt*

pis·tole \pis-ˈtōl\ *n* [ME] : an old gold 2-escudo piece of Spain; *also* : any of several old gold coins of Europe of approximately the same value

pis·tol·eer \ˌpis-tə-ˈli(ə)r\ *n* : one who uses a pistol or is armed with a pistol

pistol grip *n* **1** : a grip of a shotgun or rifle shaped like a pistol stock **2** : a handle (as on a tool) shaped like a pistol stock

pistol–whip *vt* : to beat with a pistol; *broadly* : to assail violently and intemperately

pis·ton \ˈpis-tən\ *n* [F, fr. It *pistone,* fr. *pistare* to pound, fr. ML *pistare,* fr. L *pistus,* pp. of *pinsere* to crush — more at PESTLE] **1** : a sliding piece moved by or moving against fluid pressure which usu. consists of a short cylinder fitting within a cylindrical vessel

along which it moves back and forth **2 a :** a valve sliding in a cylinder in a brass instrument and serving when depressed by a finger knob to lower its pitch **b :** a button on an organ console to bring in a previously selected registration
piston pin *n* **:** WRIST PIN
piston ring *n* **:** a springy split metal ring for sealing the gap between a piston and the cylinder wall
piston rod *n* **:** a rod by which a piston is moved or by which it communicates motion
[1]**pit** \'pit\ *n* [ME, fr. OE *pytt;* akin to OHG *pfuzzi* well] **1 a** (1) **:** a hole, shaft, or cavity in the ground (2) **:** MINE **b :** an area often sunken or depressed below the adjacent floor area: as (1) **:** an enclosure in which animals are made to fight each other (2) **:** a space at the front of a theater for the orchestra (3) **:** an area in a securities or commodities exchange in which members do trading **2 :** HELL — used with *the* **3 :** a hollow or indentation esp. in the surface of an organism: as **a :** a natural hollow in the surface of the body **b :** one of the indented scars left in the skin by a pustular disease **:** POCKMARK **c :** a minute depression in the secondary wall of a plant cell functioning in the intercellular movement of water and dissolved material **4 :** any of the areas alongside an auto racecourse used for refueling and repairing the cars during a race — often used in pl. with *the* **5 :** the area comprising the middle of the offensive and defensive lines in football
[2]**pit** *vb* **pit·ted; pit·ting** *vt* **1 a :** to place, cast, bury, or store in a pit **b :** to make pits in; *esp* **:** to scar or mark with pits **2 a :** to set (as gamecocks) into or as if into a pit to fight **b :** to set into opposition or rivalry **:** OPPOSE ~ *vi* **1 :** to become marked with pits; *esp* **:** to preserve for a time an indentation made by pressure **2 :** to make a usu. brief stop at one's pit during a race for fuel or repairs
[3]**pit** *n* [D, fr. MD — more at PITH] **:** the stone of a drupaceous fruit
[4]**pit** *vt* **pit·ted; pit·ting :** to remove the pit from (a fruit)
pi·ta \'pēt-ə\ *n* [Sp & Pg] **1 :** any of several fiber-yielding plants: as **a :** CENTURY PLANT **b :** YUCCA **c :** a Central American wild pineapple (*Ananas magdalenae*) **2 :** the fiber of a pita; *also* **:** any of several fibers from other sources
pit–a–pat \,pit-i-'pat\ *n* [imit.] **:** PITTER-PATTER — **pit–a–pat** *adv or adj* — **pit–a–pat** *vi*
[1]**pitch** \'pich\ *n* [ME *pich,* fr. OE *pic,* fr. L *pic-, pix;* akin to L *opimus* fat — more at FAT] **1 :** a black or dark viscous substance obtained as a residue in the distillation of organic materials and esp. tars **2 :** any of various bituminous substances **3 :** resin obtained from various conifers and often used medicinally **4 :** any of various artificial mixtures resembling resinous or bituminous pitches
[2]**pitch** *vt* **:** to cover, smear, or treat with or as if with pitch
[3]**pitch** *vb* [ME *pichen*] *vt* **1 :** to erect and fix firmly in place <~ a tent> **2 :** to throw usu. with a particular objective or toward a particular point <~ hay onto a wagon>: as **a :** to throw (a baseball) to a batter **b :** to toss (as coins) so as to fall at or near a mark <~ pennies> **c :** to put aside or discard by throwing <~*ed* his cigarette into the fire> **3 :** to sell or advertise esp. in a high-pressure way **4 a** (1) **:** to cause to be at a particular level or of a particular quality (2) **:** to set in a particular musical key **b :** to cause to be set at a particular angle **:** SLOPE **5 :** to utter glibly and insincerely **6 a :** to use as a starting pitcher **b :** to play as pitcher **7 :** to hit (a golf ball) in a high arc with backspin so that it rolls very little after striking the green ~ *vi* **1 a :** to fall precipitately or headlong **b** (1) *of a ship* **:** to have the bow alternately plunge precipitately down and rise abruptly up (2) *of an aircraft* **:** to turn about a lateral axis so that the nose rises or falls in relation to the tail (3) *of a missile or spacecraft* **:** to turn about a lateral axis that is both perpendicular to the longitudinal axis and horizontal with respect to the earth **c :** BUCK 1 **2 :** ENCAMP **3 :** to choose something usu. in a casual way <~*ed* on a present for his wife> **4 :** to incline downward **:** SLOPE **5 a :** to throw a ball to a batter **b :** to play ball as a pitcher **c :** to pitch a golf ball *syn* see PLUNGE, THROW — **pitch into 1 :** ATTACK, ASSAIL **2 :** to set to work on energetically
[4]**pitch** *n* **1 :** the action or a manner of pitching; *esp* **:** an up-and-down movement — compare YAW **2 a :** SLOPE; *also* **:** degree of slope **:** RAKE **b** (1) **:** distance between one point on a gear tooth and the corresponding point on the next tooth (2) **:** distance from any point on the thread of a screw to the corresponding point on an adjacent thread measured parallel to the axis **c :** the distance advanced by a propeller in one revolution **d :** the number of teeth or of threads per inch **3** *archaic* **:** TOP, ZENITH **4 a :** the relative level, intensity, or extent of some quality or state **b** (1) **:** the property of a sound and esp. a musical tone that is determined by the frequency of the waves producing it **:** highness or lowness of sound (2) **:** a standard frequency for tuning instruments **c** (1) **:** the difference in the relative vibration frequency of the human voice that contributes to the total meaning of speech (2) **:** a definite relative pitch that is a significant phenomenon in speech **5 :** a steep place **:** DECLIVITY **6** *chiefly Brit* **:** a field used for playing certain games (as soccer or cricket) **7 :** an all-fours game in which the first card led is a trump **8 a :** an often high-pressure sales talk **b :** ADVERTISEMENT **9 a :** the delivery of a baseball by a pitcher to a batter **b :** a baseball so thrown **c :** PITCHOUT 2 — **pitched** \'picht\ *adj*

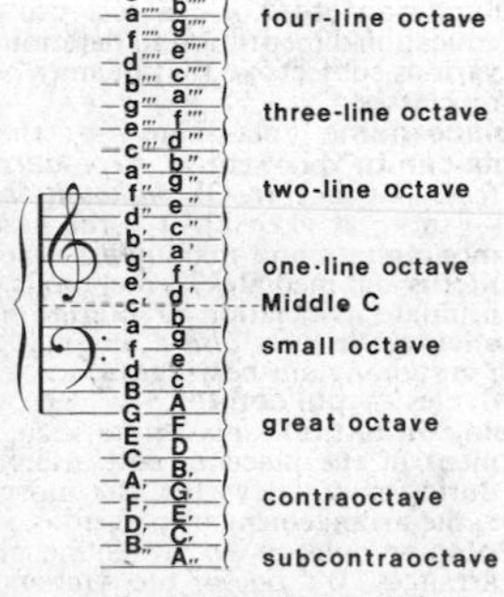

staff notation of pitch 4b(1)

pitch–and–toss \,pich-ən-'tòs, -'täs\ *n* **:** a game in which the player who pitches coins nearest to a mark has first chance at tossing the pitched coins and winning those that fall heads up
pitch–black \'pich-'blak\ *adj* **:** extremely dark or black
pitch·blende \'pich-,blend\ *n* [part trans. of G *pechblende,* fr. *pech* pitch + *blende*] **:** a brown to black mineral that consists of massive uraninite, has a distinctive luster, contains radium, and is the chief ore-mineral source of uranium
pitch–dark \'pich-'därk\ *adj* **:** extremely dark **:** PITCH-BLACK
pitched battle \'pich(t)-\ *n* **:** an intensely fought battle in which the opposing forces are locked in close combat
[1]**pitch·er** \'pich-ər\ *n* [ME *picher,* fr. OF *pichier,* fr. ML *bicarius* goblet, fr. Gk *bikos* earthen jug] **1 :** a container for holding and pouring liquids that usu. has a lip or spout and a handle **2 :** ASCIDIUM; *esp* **:** a modified leaf of a pitcher plant in which the hollowed petiole and base of the blade form an elongated receptacle
[2]**pitcher** *n* **:** one that pitches; *specif* **:** the player that pitches in a game of baseball
pitcher plant *n* **:** a plant (esp. family Sarraceniaceae, the pitcher-plant family) with leaves modified into pitchers in which insects are trapped and digested by the plant by means of liquids secreted by the leaves
pitch·fork \'pich-,fò(ə)rk\ *n* [ME *pikfork,* fr. *pik* pick + *fork*] **:** a long-handled fork that has two or three long somewhat curved prongs and is used esp. in pitching hay — **pitchfork** *vt*
pitch in *vi* **1 :** to begin to work **2 :** to contribute to a common endeavor
pitch·man \'pich-mən\ *n* **:** SALESMAN; *esp* **:** one who vends novelties or similar articles on the streets or from a concession
pitch·out \'pich-,aůt\ *n* **1 :** a pitch in baseball deliberately out of reach of the batter to enable the catcher to check or put out a base runner **2 :** a lateral pass in football between two backs behind the scrimmage line — **pitch out** *vi*
pitch pipe *n* **:** a small reed pipe or flue pipe producing one or more tones to establish the pitch in singing or in tuning an instrument
pitch·stone \'pich-,stōn\ *n* **:** a glassy rock with a resinous luster that contains more water than obsidian does
pitchy \'pich-ē\ *adj* **1 a :** full of pitch **:** TARRY **b :** of, relating to, or having the qualities of pitch **2 :** PITCH-BLACK
pit·e·ous \'pit-ē-əs\ *adj* **:** of a kind to move to pity or compassion *syn* see PITIFUL — **pit·e·ous·ly** *adv* — **pit·e·ous·ness** *n*
pit·fall \'pit-,fòl\ *n* **1 :** TRAP, SNARE; *specif* **:** a pit flimsily covered or camouflaged and used to capture and hold animals or men **2 :** a hidden or not easily recognized danger or difficulty
[1]**pith** \'pith\ *n* [ME, fr. OE *pitha;* akin to MD & MLG *pit* pith, pit] **1 a :** a usu. continuous central strand of spongy tissue in the stems of most vascular plants that prob. functions chiefly in storage **b :** any of various loose spongy plant tissues that resemble true pith **c :** the soft or spongy interior of a part of the body **2 a :** the essential part **:** CORE **b :** substantial quality (as of meaning) **3 :** IMPORTANCE, SIGNIFICANCE
[2]**pith** *vt* **1 a :** to kill (as cattle) by piercing or severing the spinal cord **b :** to destroy the spinal cord or central nervous system of (as a frog) usu. by passing a wire or needle up and down the vertebral canal **2 :** to remove the pith from (a plant stem)
pit·head \'pit-,hed\ *n* **:** the top of a mining pit or coal shaft; *also* **:** the immediately adjacent ground and buildings
pith·ec·an·thro·pine \,pith-i-'kan(t)-thrə-,pīn\ *n* **:** PITHECANTHROPUS — **pithecanthropine** *adj*
pith·ec·an·thro·poid \,pith-i-'kan(t)-thrə-,pòid\ *adj* **:** of, relating to, or resembling the pithecanthropi — **pithecanthropoid** *n*
pith·ec·an·thro·pus \-'kan(t)-thrə-pəs, -,kan-'thrō-\ *n, pl* **-pi** \-,pī, -,pē\ [NL, fr. Gk *pithēkos* ape + *anthrōpos* human being; akin to OHG *bibēn* to tremble, L *foedus* ugly] **:** any of the primitive extinct men (genus *Pithecanthropus*) known from skeletal remains from Javanese Pliocene gravels
pith ray *n* **:** MEDULLARY RAY
pithy \'pith-ē\ *adj* **pith·i·er; -est 1 :** consisting of or abounding in pith **2 :** having substance and point **:** tersely cogent *syn* see CONCISE — **pith·i·ly** \'pith-ə-lē\ *adv* — **pith·i·ness** \'pith-ē-nəs\ *n*
piti·able \'pit-ē-ə-bəl\ *adj* **1 :** deserving or exciting pity **:** LAMENTABLE **2 :** of a kind to evoke mingled pity and contempt esp. because of inadequacy <a ~ excuse> *syn* see PITIFUL, CONTEMPTIBLE — **piti·able·ness** *n* — **piti·ably** \-blē\ *adv*
piti·er \'pit-ē-ər\ *n* **:** one that pities
piti·ful \'pit-i-fəl\ *adj* **1 a :** deserving or arousing pity or commiseration **b :** exciting pitying contempt (as by meanness or inadequacy) **2** *archaic* **:** full of pity **:** COMPASSIONATE — **piti·ful·ly** \-f(ə-)lē\ *adv* — **piti·ful·ness** \-fəl-nəs\ *n*
syn PITIFUL, PITEOUS, PITIABLE *shared meaning element* **:** arousing or deserving pity *ant* cruel
piti·less \'pit-i-ləs, 'pit-ᵊl-əs\ *adj* **:** devoid of pity **:** MERCILESS — **pit·i·less·ly** *adv* — **pit·i·less·ness** *n*
pit·man \'pit-mən\ *n* **1** *pl* **pit·men** \-mən\ **:** one who works in or near a pit (as in a coal mine) **2** *pl* **pitmans :** CONNECTING ROD
pi·ton \'pē-,tän\ *n* [F] **:** a spike, wedge, or peg that is driven into a rock or ice surface as a support and often has an eye through which a rope may pass
Pi·tot–stat·ic tube \,pē-,tō-'stat-ik-\ *n* **:** a device that consists of a Pitot tube and a static tube and that measures pressures in such a way that the relative speed of a fluid can be determined
Pi·tot tube \,pē-,tō-\ *n* [F (*tube de*) *Pitot,* fr. Henri *Pitot* †1771 F physicist] **1 :** a device that consists of a tube having a short right-angled bend which is placed vertically in a moving body of

ə abut ᵊ kitten ər further a back ā bake ä cot, cart
aů out ch chin e less ē easy g gift i trip ī life
j joke ŋ sing ō flow ò flaw òi coin th thin th this
ü loot ů foot y yet yü few yů furious zh vision

fluid with the mouth of the bent part directed upstream and that is used with a manometer to measure the velocity of fluid flow **2** : PITOT-STATIC TUBE

pit saw *n* : a handsaw worked by two men one of whom stands on or above the log being sawed into planks and the other below it usu. in a pit

pit·tance \'pit-ᵊn(t)s\ *n* [ME *pitance,* fr. OF, piety, pity, fr. ML *pietantia,* fr. *pietant-, pietans,* prp. of *pietari* to be charitable, fr. L *pietas*] : a small portion, amount, or allowance; *also* : a meager wage or remuneration ***syn*** see RATION

pit·ted \'pit-əd\ *adj* : marked with pits

pit·ter–pat·ter \'pit-ər-ˌpat-ər, 'pit-ē-ˌ\ *n* [imit.] : a rapid succession of light sounds or beats : PATTER — **pitter–patter** \ˌpit-ər-', ˌpit-ē-'\ *adv or adj* — **pitter–patter** *like adv*\ *vi*

pit·ting *n* **1** : the action or process of forming pits **2** : an arrangement of pits **3** : the bringing of gamecocks together to fight

[1]pi·tu·itary \pə-'t(y)ü-ə-ˌter-ē\ *adj* [L *pituita* phlegm; fr. the former belief that the pituitary gland secreted phlegm — more at PIP] **1** : of or relating to the pituitary gland **2** : of, relating to, or being a physique with a symptom complex characteristic of secretory disturbances of the pituitary gland

[2]pituitary *n, pl* **-itar·ies** : PITUITARY GLAND

pituitary gland *n* : a small oval endocrine organ that is attached to the infundibulum of the brain, consists of an epithelial anterior lobe joined by an intermediate part to a posterior lobe of nervous origin, and produces various internal secretions directly or indirectly impinging on most basic body functions — called also *pituitary body;* see BRAIN illustration

Pi·tu·itrin \pə-'t(y)ü-ə-trən\ *trademark* — used for an aqueous extract of the fresh pituitary gland of cattle

pit viper *n* : any of various mostly New World specialized venomous snakes (family Crotalidae) with a sensory pit on each side of the head and hollow perforated fangs

[1]pity \'pit-ē\ *n, pl* **pi·ties** [ME *pite,* fr. OF *pité,* fr. L *pietat-, pietas* piety, pity, fr. *pius* pious] **1 a** : sympathetic sorrow for one suffering, distressed, or unhappy **b** : capacity to feel pity **2** : something to be regretted <it's a ~ you can't go> ***syn*** see SYMPATHY

[2]pity *vb* **pit·ied; pity·ing** *vt* : to feel pity for ~ *vi* : to feel pity

pity·ing *adj* : expressing or feeling pity — **pity·ing·ly** \-iŋ-lē\ *adv*

pit·y·ri·a·sis \ˌpit-i-'rī-ə-səs\ *n* [NL, fr. Gk, fr. *pityron* scurf] : a condition of man or domestic animals marked by dry scaling or scurfy patches of skin

più \(ˌ)pyü, pē-ˌü\ *adv* [It, fr. L *plus*] : MORE — used to qualify an adverb or adjective used as a direction in music

Pi·ute *var of* PAIUTE

[1]piv·ot \'piv-ət\ *n* [F] **1** : a shaft or pin on which something turns **2 a** : a person, thing, or factor having a major or central role, function, or effect **b** : a key player or position; *specif* : an offensive player position in basketball that is occupied by a player (as a center) who stands usu. with his back to his own basket to relay passes, shoot, or provide a screen for teammates **3** : the action of pivoting

[2]pivot *vi* : to turn on or as if on a pivot ~ *vt* **1** : to provide with, mount on, or attach by a pivot **2** : to cause to pivot — **pivot·able** \-ə-bəl\ *adj*

[3]pivot *adj* **1** : turning on or as if on a pivot **2** : PIVOTAL

piv·ot·al \'piv-ət-ᵊl\ *adj* **1** : of, relating to, or constituting a pivot **2** : vitally important : CRUCIAL — **piv·ot·al·ly** \-ᵊl-ē\ *adv*

piv·ot·man \'piv-ət-ˌman\ *n* : one who plays the pivot; *specif* : a center on a basketball team

pivot tooth *n* : an artificial crown attached to the root of a tooth by a usu. metallic pin — called also *pivot crown*

pix *pl of* PIC

[1]pix·ie *or* **pixy** \'pik-sē\ *n, pl* **pix·ies** [origin unknown] : FAIRY; *specif* : a cheerful mischievous sprite — **pix·ie·ish** \-sē-ish\ *adj*

[2]pixie *or* **pixy** *adj* : playfully mischievous — **pixi·ness** *n*

pix·i·lat·ed \'pik-sə-ˌlāt-əd\ *adj* [irreg. fr. *pixie*] **1** : somewhat unbalanced mentally; *also* : BEMUSED **2** : WHIMSICAL — **pix·i·la·tion** \ˌpik-sə-'lā-shən\ *n*

pizz *abbr* pizzicato

piz·za \'pēt-sə\ *n* [It, fr. (assumed) VL *picea,* fr. L, fem. of *piceus* of pitch, fr. *pic-, pix* pitch — more at PITCH] : an open pie made typically of thinly rolled bread dough spread with a spiced mixture (as of tomatoes, cheese, and ground meat) and baked — called also *pizza pie*

piz·zazz *or* **pi·zazz** \pə-'zaz\ *n* [origin unknown] : the quality of being exciting or attractive: as **a** : GLAMOUR **b** : VITALITY

piz·ze·ria \ˌpēt-sə-'rē-ə\ *n* [It, fr. *pizza*] : an establishment where pizzas are made or sold

[1]piz·zi·ca·to \ˌpit-si-'kät-(ˌ)ō\ *adv or adj* [It] : by means of plucking instead of bowing — used as a direction in music; compare ARCO

[2]pizzicato *n, pl* **-ca·ti** \-'kät-(ˌ)ē\ : a note or passage played by plucking strings

piz·zle \'piz-əl\ *n* [prob. fr. Flem *pezel;* akin to LG *pesel* pizzle] **1** : the penis of an animal **2** : a whip made of a bull's pizzle

pj's \(')pē-'jāz\ *n pl* [*pa*jama*s*] : PAJAMAS

pk *abbr* **1** park **2** peak **3** peck **4** pike

PK \'pē-'kā\ *n* : PSYCHOKINESIS

pkg *abbr* package

pkt *abbr* **1** packet **2** pocket

PKU \ˌpē-ˌkā-'yü\ *abbr* phenylketonuria

pkwy *abbr* parkway

pl *abbr* **1** place **2** plate **3** plural

PL *abbr* **1** partial loss **2** private line

pla·ca·ble \'plak-ə-bəl, 'plā-kə-\ *adj* : easily placated : TOLERANT, TRACTABLE — **pla·ca·bil·i·ty** \ˌplak-ə-'bil-ət-ē, ˌplā-kə-\ *n* — **pla·ca·bly** \'plak-ə-blē, 'plā-\ *adv*

[1]plac·ard \'plak-ərd, -ˌärd\ *n* [ME *placquart,* a formal document, fr. MF, fr. *plaquier* to plate — more at PLAQUE] **1** : a notice posted in a public place : POSTER **2** : a small card or metal plaque

[2]plac·ard \-ˌärd, -ərd\ *vt* **1 a** : to cover with or as if with posters **b** : to post in a public place **2** : to announce by or as if by posting

pla·cate \'plā-ˌkāt, 'plak-ˌāt\ *vt* **pla·cat·ed; pla·cat·ing** [L *placatus,* pp. of *placare* — more at PLEASE] : to soothe or mollify esp. by concessions : APPEASE — **pla·ca·tion** \plā-'kā-shən, pla-\ *n* — **pla·ca·tive** \'plā-ˌkāt-iv, 'plak-\ *adj* — **pla·ca·to·ry** \'plāk-ə-ˌtōr-ē, 'plak-, -ˌtȯr-\ *adj*

pla·cat·er \'plāk-ˌāt-ər, 'plak-\ *n* : one that placates; *esp* : MEDIATOR

[1]place \'plās\ *n* [ME, fr. MF, open space, fr. L *platea* broad street, fr. Gk *plateia (hodos),* fr. fem. of *platys* broad, flat; akin to Skt *pṛthu* broad, L *planta* sole of the foot] **1 a** : a way for admission or transit **b** : physical environment : SPACE **c** : physical surroundings : ATMOSPHERE **2 a** : an indefinite region or expanse : AREA **b** : a building or locality used for a special purpose <a ~ of amusement> **c** *archaic* : the three-dimensional compass of a material object **3 a** : a particular region or center of population **b** : HOUSE, DWELLING <invited them to his ~ for the evening> **4** : a particular part of a surface or body : SPOT **5** : relative position in a scale or series: as **a** : degree of prestige <put her in her ~> **b** : a step in a sequence <in the first ~, you're wrong> **c** : one of the leading positions at the conclusion of a competition **6 a** : a proper or designated niche <thought that a woman's ~ is in the home> **b** : an appropriate moment or point <this is not the ~ to discuss compensation —Robert Moses> **7 a** : an available seat or accommodation **b** : an empty or vacated position **8** : the position of a figure in relation to others of a row or series; *esp* : the position of a digit within a numeral <12 is a two ~ number> <in 316 the figure 1 is in the tens ~> **9 a** : remunerative employment : JOB; *esp* : public office **b** : prestige accorded to one of high rank : STATUS <an endless quest for preferment and ~ —*Time*> **10** : a public square : PLAZA **11** : second place at the finish of a horse race

[2]place *vb* **placed; plac·ing** *vt* **1** : to distribute in an orderly manner : ARRANGE **2 a** : to put in a particular place : SET **b** : to present for consideration <a question *placed* before the group> **c** : to put in a particular state <~ a performer under contract> **d** : to direct to a desired spot **e** : to cause (the voice) to produce free and well resonated singing or speaking tones **3** : to appoint to a position **4** : to find employment or a home for **5 a** : to assign to a position in a series or category : RANK **b** : ESTIMATE <*placed* the value of the estate too high> **c** : to identify by connecting with an associated context <couldn't quite ~ her face> **6 a** : to give (an order) to a supplier **b** : to give an order for <~ a bet> ~ *vi* : to earn a top spot in a competition; *specif* : to come in second in a horse race — **place·able** \'plā-sə-bəl\ *adj*

pla·ce·bo *n, pl* **-bos** **1** \plä-'chā-(ˌ)bō\ [ME, fr. L, I shall please, fr. *placēre* to please — more at PLEASE] : the Roman Catholic vespers for the dead **2** \plə-'sē-\ [L, I shall please] **a (1)** : a medication prescribed more for the mental relief of the patient than for its actual effect on his disorder **(2)** : an inert or innocuous substance used esp. in controlled experiments testing the efficacy of another substance (as a drug) **b** : something tending to soothe

placebo effect *n* : improvement in the condition of a sick person that occurs in response to treatment but cannot be considered due to the specific treatment used

place·hold·er \'plās-ˌhōl-dər\ *n* : a symbol in a mathematical or logical expression that may be replaced by the name of any element of a set

[1]place·kick \'plā-ˌskik\ *n* : the kicking of a ball (as a football) placed or held in a stationary position on the ground

[2]placekick *vt* **1** : to kick (a ball) from a stationary position **2** : to score by means of a placekick — **place·kick·er** *n*

place·less \'plā-sləs\ *adj* : lacking a fixed location — **place·less·ly** *adv*

place·man \'plā-smən\ *n* : a political appointee to a public office esp. in 18th century Britain

place mat *n* : a small often rectangular table mat on which a place setting is laid

place·ment \'plā-smənt\ *n* **1** : an act or instance of placing: as **a** : an accurately hit ball (as in tennis) that an opponent cannot return **b** : the assignment of a person to a suitable place (as a job or a class in school) **2 a** : the position of a ball for a placekick **b** : PLACEKICK

placement test *n* : a test usu. given to a student entering an educational institution to determine his knowledge or proficiency in various subjects so that he may be assigned to appropriate courses or classes

place–name \'plā-ˌsnām\ *n* : the name of a geographical locality

pla·cen·ta \plə-'sent-ə\ *n, pl* **-centas** *or* **-cen·tae** \-'sent-(ˌ)ē\ [NL, fr. L, flat cake, fr. Gk *plakount-, plakous,* fr. *plak-, plax* flat surface — more at PLEASE] **1** : the vascular organ in mammals except monotremes and marsupials that unites the fetus to the maternal uterus and mediates its metabolic exchanges through a more or less intimate association of uterine mucosal with chorionic and usu. allantoic tissues; *also* : an analogous organ in another animal **2** : a sporangium-bearing surface; *esp* : the part of the carpel bearing ovules — **pla·cen·tal** \-'sent-ᵊl\ *adj or n*

pla·cen·ta·tion \ˌplas-ᵊn-'tā-shən, plə-ˌsen-\ *n* **1 a** : the development of the placenta and attachment of the fetus to the uterus during pregnancy **b** : the morphological type of a placenta **2** : the arrangement of placentas and ovules in a plant ovary

[1]plac·er \'plā-sər\ *n* : one that places: as **a** : one that deposits or arranges **b** : one of the winners in a competition

[2]plac·er \'plas-ər\ *n* [Sp, fr. Catal, submarine plain, fr. *plaza* place, fr. L *platea* broad street — more at PLACE] : an alluvial or glacial deposit containing particles of valuable mineral and esp. of gold

place setting *n* : a table service for one person

place value *n* : the value of the location of a digit in a numeral <in 425 the location of the digit 2 has a *place value* of ten while the digit itself indicates that there are two tens>

plac·id \'plas-əd\ *adj* [L *placidus,* fr. *placēre* to please — more at PLEASE] **1** : serenely free of interruption or disturbance : QUIET <~ summer skies> <a ~ disposition> **2** : COMPLACENT ***syn*** see

CALM *ant* choleric, ruffled — **pla·cid·i·ty** \plə-ˈsid-ət-ē, plə-\ *n* — **plac·id·ly** \ˈplas-əd-lē\ *adv* — **plac·id·ness** *n*

plack·et \ˈplak-ət\ *n* [origin unknown] **1 a :** a slit in a garment (as a skirt) often forming the closure **b** *archaic* **:** a pocket esp. in a woman's skirt **2** *archaic* **a :** PETTICOAT **b :** WOMAN

plac·oid \ˈplak-ˌȯid\ *adj* [Gk *plak-, plax* flat surface] **:** of, relating to, or being a scale of dermal origin with an enamel-tipped spine characteristic of the elasmobranchs

pla·fond \plä-fōⁿ\ *n* [F, fr. MF, fr. *plat* flat + *fond* bottom, fr. L *fundus* — more at PLATE, BOTTOM] **:** a usu. elaborate ceiling formed by the underside of a floor

pla·gal \ˈplā-gəl\ *adj* [ML *plagalis,* deriv. of Gk *plagios* oblique, sideways, fr. *plagos* side; akin to L *plaga* net, region, Gk *pelagos* sea — more at FLAKE] **1** *of a church mode* **:** having the keynote on the 4th scale step — compare AUTHENTIC 4a **2** *of a cadence* **:** progressing from the subdominant chord to the tonic — compare AUTHENTIC 4b

plage \ˈpläzh\ *n* [F, beach, luminous surface, fr. It *piaggia* beach, fr. LL *plagia,* fr. Gk *plagios* oblique] **:** a bright region on the sun that is caused by the light emitted by clouds of calcium or hydrogen and that is often associated with a sunspot

pla·gia·rism \ˈplā-jə-ˌriz-əm *also* -jē-ə-\ *n* **1 :** an act or instance of plagiarizing **2 :** something plagiarized — **pla·gia·rist** \-rəst\ *n* — **pla·gia·ris·tic** \ˌplā-jə-ˈris-tik *also* -jē-ə-\ *adj*

pla·gia·rize \ˈplā-jə-ˌrīz *also* -jē-ə-\ *vb* **-rized; -riz·ing** *vt* [*plagiary*] **:** to steal and pass off (the ideas or words of another) as one's own **:** use (a created production) without crediting the source ~ *vi* **:** to commit literary theft **:** present as new and original an idea or product derived from an existing source — **pla·gia·riz·er** *n*

pla·gia·ry \ˈplā-jē-ˌer-ē, -jə-rē\ *n, pl* **-ries** [L *plagiarius,* lit., plunderer, fr. *plagium* hunting net, fr. *plaga* net] **1** *archaic* **:** one that plagiarizes **2 :** PLAGIARISM

pla·gio·clase \ˈplā-j(ē-)ə-ˌklās, ˈplaj-(ē-)ə-, -ˌklāz\ *n* [Gk *plagios* + *klasis* breaking, fr. *klan* to break — more at HALT] **:** a triclinic feldspar; *esp* **:** one having calcium or sodium in its composition

pla·gio·tro·pic \ˌplā-j(ē-)ə-ˈtrō-pik, ˌplaj-(ē-)ə-, -ˈträp-\ *adj* [Gk *plagios* + ISV *-tropic*] **:** having the longer axis inclined away from the vertical <~ lateral branches> — **pla·gio·tro·pi·cal·ly** \-i-k(ə-)lē\ *adv* — **pla·gi·ot·ro·pism** \ˌplā-jē-ˈä-trə-ˌpiz-əm, ˌplaj-ē-\ *n*

¹plague \ˈplāg\ *n* [ME *plage,* fr. MF, fr. LL *plaga,* fr. L, blow; akin to L *plangere* to strike — more at PLAINT] **1 a :** a disastrous evil or affliction **:** CALAMITY **b :** a destructively numerous influx <a ~ of locusts> **2 a :** an epidemic disease causing a high rate of mortality **:** PESTILENCE **b :** a virulent contagious febrile disease that is caused by a bacterium (*Pasteurella pestis*) and that occurs in several forms **3 a :** a cause of irritation **:** NUISANCE **b :** a sudden unwelcome outbreak <a ~ of burglaries>

²plague *vt* **plagued; plagu·ing 1 :** to smite, infest, or afflict with or as if with disease, calamity, or natural evil **2 a :** to cause worry or distress to **:** HAMPER, BURDEN **b :** to disturb or annoy persistently *syn* see WORRY — **plagu·er** *n*

plague·some \ˈplāg-səm\ *adj* **1 :** TROUBLESOME **2 :** PESTILENTIAL

plagu·ey *or* **plaguy** \ˈplā-gē, ˈpleg-ē\ *adj, chiefly dial* **:** causing irritation or annoyance **:** TROUBLESOME — **plaguey** *adv* — **plagu·i·ly** \ˈplā-gə-lē, ˈpleg-ə-\ *adv*

plaice \ˈplās\ *n, pl* **plaice** [ME *plaice,* fr. OF *plaïs,* fr. LL *platensis*] **:** any of various flatfishes; *esp* **:** a large European flounder (*Pleuronectes platessa*)

plaid \ˈplad\ *n* [ScGael *plaide*] **1 :** a rectangular length of tartan worn over the left shoulder as part of the Scottish national costume **2 a :** a twilled woolen fabric with a tartan pattern **b :** a fabric with a pattern of tartan or an imitation of tartan **3 a :** TARTAN 1 **b :** a pattern of unevenly spaced repeated stripes crossing at right angles — **plaid** *adj* — **plaid·ed** \-əd\ *adj*

¹plain \ˈplān\ *vi* [ME *plainen,* fr. MF *plaindre,* fr. L *plangere* lament — more at PLAINT] *archaic* **:** COMPLAIN

²plain *n* [ME, fr. OF, fr. L *planum,* fr. neut. of *planus* flat, plain — more at FLOOR] **1 a :** an extensive area of level or rolling treeless country **b :** a broad unbroken expanse **2 :** something free from artifice, ornament, or extraneous matter

³plain *adj* **1** *archaic* **:** EVEN, LEVEL **2 :** lacking ornament **:** UNDECORATED **3 :** free of extraneous matter **:** PURE **4 :** free of impediments to view **:** UNOBSTRUCTED **5 a** (1) **:** evident to the mind or senses **:** OBVIOUS <it's perfectly ~ that they will resist> (2) **:** CLEAR <made his intentions ~> **b :** marked by outspoken candor **:** free from duplicity or subtlety **:** BLUNT **6 :** belonging to mankind in general **:** COMMON; *also* **:** lacking special distinction or affectation **:** ORDINARY **7 :** characterized by simplicity **:** not complicated <~ home-cooked meals> **8 :** lacking beauty or ugliness — **plain·ly** *adv* — **plain·ness** \ˈplān-nəs\ *n*

syn **1** see EVIDENT *ant* abstruse

2 PLAIN, HOMELY, SIMPLE, UNPRETENTIOUS *shared meaning element* **:** free from all ostentation or superficial embellishment. PLAIN stresses moderation and lack of anything likely to catch the attention <a *plain* house on a quiet street> Additionally, it may suggest quiet elegance <the furnishings were *plain* with very simple classic lines> or avoidance of waste and extravagance <she set a *plain* but ample meal before us> or, with reference to personal appearance, a lack of positive beauty that is by no means ugliness <a *plain* but very charming girl> HOMELY may suggest comfortable but unostentatious informality or easy familiarity <a book-learned language, wholly remote from anything personal, native, or *homely* —Willa Cather> <a comfortable *homely* scene> In application to personal appearance, especially in American use, *homely* is likely to imply something between *plain* and *ugly.* SIMPLE, very close to *plain* in its references to situations or things, may stress volition as the source of the quality described <what was then called the *simple* life . . . is recognizable as the austere luxury of a very cultivated poet —Agnes Repplier> and regularly connotes lack of complication or adornment <told the *simple* truth> <a *simple* gray dress> UNPRETENTIOUS stresses lack of vanity and affectation and may praise a person or a thing, especially when felt as a reflection of a personality <he drove a sturdy but *unpretentious* car> <a knowledgeable but quite *unpretentious* writer> *ant* lovely

3 see FRANK

4 see COMMON

⁴plain *adv* **:** in a plain manner **:** CLEARLY, SIMPLY <saw them clearly and told you ~ —*Amer. Documentation*>

⁵plain *adv* [partly fr. ME *plein* entire, complete, fr. MF, full, fr. L *plenus;* partly fr. ⁴*plain* — more at FULL] **:** ABSOLUTELY <it ~ galled me to pay fancy prices —F. R. Buckley>

plain·chant \ˈplān-ˌchant\ *n* [F *plain-chant,* lit., plain song] **:** PLAINSONG

plain·clothes·man \ˈplān-ˈklō(th)z-mən, -ˌman\ *n* **:** a police officer who does not wear a uniform while on duty **:** DETECTIVE

plain–laid \ˈplān-ˈlād\ *adj, of a rope* **:** consisting of three strands laid right-handed

Plain People *n* **:** members of any of various Protestant groups (as Mennonites) esp. in the U.S. who wear distinctively plain clothes and adhere to a simple and traditional style of life excluding many conveniences of modern technology (as motorcars)

Plains \ˈplānz\ *adj* **:** of or relating to No. American Indians of the Great Plains or to their culture

plain sailing *n* **:** easy progress over an unobstructed course

plains·man \ˈplānz-mən\ *n* [Great *Plains* + *man*] **:** an inhabitant of the plains

plain·song \ˈplān-ˌsȯŋ\ *n* **1 :** GREGORIAN CHANT **2 :** a liturgical chant of any of various Christian rites

plain·spo·ken \-ˈspō-kən\ *adj* **:** CANDID, FRANK — **plain·spo·ken·ness** \-kən-nəs\ *n*

plaint \ˈplānt\ *n* [ME, fr. MF, fr. L *planctus,* fr. *planctus,* pp. of *plangere* to strike, beat one's breast, lament; akin to OHG *fluokhōn* to curse, Gk *plēssein* to strike] **1 :** LAMENTATION, WAIL **2 :** PROTEST, COMPLAINT

plain·text \ˈplān-ˌtekst\ *n* **:** the intelligible form of an encrypted text or of its elements — compare CIPHERTEXT

plaint·ful \ˈplānt-fəl\ *adj* **:** MOURNFUL

plain·tiff \ˈplānt-əf\ *n* [ME *plaintif,* fr. MF, fr. *plaintif,* adj.] **1 :** one who commences a personal action or lawsuit to obtain a remedy for an injury to his rights **2 :** the complaining party in a litigation — compare DEFENDANT

plain·tive \ˈplānt-iv\ *adj* [ME *plaintif,* fr. MF, fr. *plaint*] **:** expressive of suffering or woe **:** MELANCHOLY — **plain·tive·ly** *adv* — **plain·tive·ness** *n*

plain weave *n* **:** a weave in which the threads interlace alternately

plais·ter \ˈplas-tər, ˈplās-\ *var of* PLASTER

¹plait \ˈplāt, ˈplat\ *n* [ME *pleit,* fr. MF, fr. (assumed) VL *plictus,* fr. *plictus,* pp. of L *plicare* to fold — more at PLY] **1 :** PLEAT **2 :** a braid of material (as hair or straw); *specif* **:** PIGTAIL

²plait *vt* **1 :** PLEAT 1 **2 a :** to interweave the strands or locks of **:** BRAID **b :** to make by plaiting — **plait·er** *n*

plait·ing *n* **:** the interlacing of strands **:** BRAIDING

¹plan \ˈplan\ *n* [F, plane, foundation, ground plan; partly fr. L *planum* level ground, fr. neut. of *planus* level; partly fr. F *planter* to plant, fix in place, fr. LL *plantare* — more at FLOOR, PLANT] **1 :** a drawing or diagram drawn on a plane: as **a :** a top or horizontal view of an object **b :** a large-scale map of a small area **2 a :** a method for achieving an end <working hard at a ~ to avoid work> **b :** an often customary method of doing something **:** PROCEDURE <the usual ~ is to both arrive and leave early> **c :** a detailed formulation of a program of action <the ~ called for increasing the bet whenever he won> **d :** GOAL, AIM <his ~ was to get a degree in medicine> **3 :** an orderly arrangement of parts of an overall design or objective — **plan·less** \-ləs\ *adj* — **plan·less·ly** *adv* — **plan·less·ness** *n*

syn PLAN, DESIGN, PLOT, SCHEME, PROJECT *shared meaning element* **:** a method devised for making or doing something or attaining an end

²plan *vb* **planned; plan·ning** *vt* **1 :** to arrange the parts of **:** DESIGN **2 :** to devise or project the realization or achievement of <~ a program> **3 :** to have in mind **:** INTEND ~ *vi* **:** to make plans — **plan·ner** *n*

¹plan- *or* **plano-** *comb form* [prob. fr. NL, fr. Gk, wandering, fr. *planos;* akin to Gk *planasthai* to wander — more at PLANET] **:** moving about **:** motile <*plano*blast>

²plan- *or* **plano-** *comb form* [L *planus*] **1 :** flat <*plano*sol> **2 :** flatly <*plano*spiral> **3 :** flat and <*plano*-concave>

pla·nar \ˈplā-nər, -ˌnär\ *adj* **1 :** of, relating to, or lying in a plane **2 :** two-dimensional in quality — **pla·nar·i·ty** \plā-ˈnar-ət-ē\ *n*

pla·nar·ia \plə-ˈnar-ē-ə, -ˈner-\ *n* [NL *Planaria,* genus name, fr. fem. of LL *planarius* lying on a plane, fr. *planum* plane] **:** PLANARIAN; *esp* **:** any of a genus (*Planaria*) of 2-eyed planarian worms

pla·nar·i·an \-ē-ən\ *n* [NL *Planaria,* type genus of the family] **:** any of a family (Planariidae) or order (Tricladida) of small soft-bodied ciliated mostly aquatic turbellarian worms

pla·na·tion \plā-ˈnā-shən\ *n* **:** the condition or process of becoming flattened; *esp* **:** mechanical erosion producing smoothed or flattened surfaces

planarian

plan·chet \ˈplan-chət\ *n* [dim. of *planch* (flat plate)] **1 :** a metal disk to be stamped as a coin **2 :** a small metal or plastic disk

plan·chette \plan-ˈshet\ *n* [F, fr. dim. of *planche* plank, fr. L *planca*] **:** a small triangular or heart-shaped board supported on casters at two points and a vertical pencil at a third and believed

ə abut ᵊ kitten ər further a back ā bake ä cot, cart
au̇ out ch chin e less ē easy g gift i trip ī life
j joke ŋ sing ō flow ȯ flaw ȯi coin th thin th this
ü loot u̇ foot y yet yü few yu̇ furious zh vision

to produce automatic writing when lightly touched by the fingers; *also* : a similar board without a pencil

Planck's constant \ˈplaŋ(k)s-, ˈpläŋ(k)s-\ *n* [Max K.E.L. *Planck*] : a proportionality constant *h* that relates the frequency of radiation to its quanta of energy and that has an approximate value of 6.625 10^{-27} erg second (gcm^2 per second)

¹plane \ˈplān\ *vb* **planed; plan·ing** [ME *planen*, fr. MF *planer*, fr. LL *planare*, fr. L *planus* level — more at FLOOR] *vt* **1 a :** to make smooth or even : LEVEL **b :** to make plane by use of a plane <*planed* the sides of the door> **2 :** to remove by planing — often used with *away* or *off* ~ *vi* **1 :** to work with a plane **2 :** to do the work of a plane — **plan·er** *n*

²plane *n* [ME, fr. MF, fr. L *platanus*, fr. Gk *platanos*; akin to Gk *platys* broad — more at PLACE] : any of a genus (*Platanus* of the family Platanaceae, the plane-tree family) of trees with large palmately lobed leaves and flowers in globose heads — called also *buttonwood, plane tree, sycamore*

³plane *n* [ME, fr. MF, fr. LL *plana*, fr. *planare*] : a tool for smoothing or shaping a wood surface

plane

⁴plane *n* [L *planum*, fr. neut. of *planus* level] **1 a :** a surface of such nature that a straight line joining any two of its points lies wholly in the surface **b :** a flat or level surface **2 :** a level of existence, consciousness, or development <on the intellectual ~> **3 a :** one of the main supporting surfaces of an airplane **b** [by shortening] : AIRPLANE

⁵plane *adj* [L *planus*] **1 :** having no elevations or depressions : FLAT **2 a :** of, relating to, or dealing with geometric planes **b :** lying in a plane <a ~ curve> ***syn*** see LEVEL

⁶plane *vi* **planed; plan·ing** [F *planer*, fr. *plan* plane; fr. the plane formed by the wings of a soaring bird] **1 a :** to fly while keeping the wings motionless **b :** to skim across the surface of the water **2 :** to travel by airplane

plane angle *n* **:** an angle formed by two intersecting lines each of which lies on a face of a dihedral angle and is perpendicular to the edge of the face

plane geometry *n* **:** a branch of elementary geometry that deals with plane figures

plane·load \ˈplān-ˈlōd\ *n* **:** a load that fills an airplane

pla·ner tree \ˈplā-nər-\ *n* [J. J. *Planer* †1789 G botanist] : a small-leaved No. American tree (*Planera aquatica*) of the elm family with an oval ribbed fruit

plan·et \ˈplan-ət\ *n* [ME *planete*, fr. OF, fr. LL *planeta*, modif. of Gk *planēt-, planēs*, lit., wanderer, fr. *planasthai* to wander; akin to ON *flana* to rush around] **1 a :** any of the seven celestial bodies sun, moon, Venus, Jupiter, Mars, Mercury, and Saturn that in ancient belief have motions of their own among the fixed stars **b** (1) : one of the bodies except a comet, meteor, or satellite that revolves around the sun in the solar system (2) : a similar body associated with another star **c :** EARTH — usu. used with *the* **2 :** a celestial body held to influence the fate of human beings **3 :** a person or thing of great importance : LUMINARY

PLANETS

SYMBOL	NAME	MEAN DISTANCE FROM THE SUN astronomical units	MEAN DISTANCE FROM THE SUN million miles	PERIOD OF REVOLUTION IN DAYS OR YEARS	EQUATORIAL DIAMETER IN MILES
☿	Mercury	0.387	36.0	88.0 d.	3,100
♀	Venus	0.723	67.2	224.7 d.	7,700
⊕	Earth	1.000	92.9	365.26 d.	7,926
♂	Mars	1.524	141.5	687.0 d.	4,200
♃	Jupiter	5.203	483.4	11.86 y.	88,700
♄	Saturn	9.539	886.0	29.46 y.	75,100
♅	Uranus	19.18	1782.0	84.01 y.	29,200
♆	Neptune	30.06	2792.0	164.8 y.	27,700
♇	Pluto	39.44	3664.0	247.7 y.	3,500

plane table *n* **:** an instrument that consists essentially of a drawing board on a tripod with a ruler pointed at the object observed and is used for plotting the lines of a survey directly from the observation

plan·e·tar·i·um \ˌplan-ə-ˈter-ē-əm\ *n, pl* **-iums** *or* **-ia** \-ē-ə\ **1 :** a model or representation of the solar system **2 a :** an optical device to project various celestial images and effects **b :** a building or room housing such a projector

plan·e·tary \ˈplan-ə-ˌter-ē\ *adj* **1 a :** of, relating to, or being a planet **b :** ERRATIC, WANDERING **c :** having a motion like that of a planet <~ electrons> **d :** IMMENSE <the scope of this project has reached ~ proportions> **2 a :** of, relating to, or belonging to the earth : TERRESTRIAL **b :** GLOBAL, WORLDWIDE **3 :** having or consisting of an epicyclic train of gear wheels

plan·e·tes·i·mal \ˌplan-ə-ˈtes-ə-məl, -ˈtez-\ *n* [*planet* + *-esimal* (as in *infinitesimal*)] **:** one of numerous small solid celestial bodies that may have existed at an early stage of the development of the solar system

planetesimal hypothesis *n* **:** a hypothesis in astronomy: the planets have evolved by aggregation from planetesimals

plan·e·toid \ˈplan-ə-ˌtȯid\ *n* **1 :** a body resembling a planet **2 :** ASTEROID — **plan·e·toi·dal** \ˌplan-ə-ˈtȯid-ᵊl\ *adj*

plan·e·tol·o·gy \ˌplan-ə-ˈtäl-ə-jē\ *n, pl* **-gies :** a study that deals with the condensed matter (as the planets, natural satellites, comets, and meteorites) of the solar system — **plan·e·to·log·i·cal** \ˌplan-ət-ᵊl-ˈäj-i-kəl\ *adj* — **plan·e·tol·o·gist** \ˌplan-ə-ˈtäl-ə-jəst\ *n*

plan·et–strick·en \ˈplan-ət-ˌstrik-ən\ *or* **plan·et–struck** \-ˌstrək\ *adj* **1 :** affected by the influence of a planet **2 :** PANIC-STRICKEN

planet wheel *n* **:** a gear wheel that revolves around the wheel with which it meshes in an epicyclic train

plan·form \ˈplan-ˌfȯrm\ *n* **:** the contour of an object (as an airplane) as viewed from above

plan·gen·cy \ˈplan-jən-sē\ *n* **:** the quality or state of being plangent

plan·gent \-jənt\ *adj* [L *plangent-, plangens*, prp. of *plangere* to strike, lament] **1 :** having a loud reverberating sound **2 :** having an expressive and esp. plaintive quality — **plan·gent·ly** *adv*

pla·nim·e·ter \plā-ˈnim-ət-ər, plə-\ *n* [F *planimètre*, fr. L *planum* plane + F *-mètre* -meter] **:** an instrument for measuring the area of a plane figure by tracing its boundary line

pla·ni·met·ric \ˌplā-nə-ˈme-trik\ *adj* **1 :** of, relating to, or made by means of a planimeter <~ measurements> **2** *of a map* **:** having no indications of contour

plan·ish \ˈplan-ish\ *vt* [MF *planiss-*, stem of *planir* to make smooth, fr. *plan* level, fr. L *planus*] **:** to toughen and finish (metal) by hammering lightly — **plan·ish·er** *n*

pla·ni·sphere \ˈplā-nə-ˌsfi(ə)r\ *n* [ML *planisphaerium*, fr. L *planum* plane + *sphaera* sphere] **:** a representation of the circles of the sphere on a plane; *esp* **:** a polar projection of the celestial sphere and the stars on a plane with adjustable circles or other appendages for showing celestial phenomena for any given time — **pla·ni·spher·ic** \ˌplā-nə-ˈsfi(ə)r-ik, -ˈsfer-\ *adj*

¹plank \ˈplaŋk\ *n* [ME, fr. ONF *planke*, fr. L *planca*] **1 a :** a heavy thick board; *specif* **:** one 2 to 4 inches thick and at least 8 inches wide **b :** an object made of a plank or planking **c :** PLANKING **2 a :** an article in the platform of a political party **b :** a principal item of a policy or program

²plank *vt* **1 :** to cover or floor with planks **2 :** to set down **3 :** to cook and serve on a board usu. with an elaborate garnish

plank·ing *n* **1 :** the act or process of covering or fitting with planks **2 :** a quantity of planks

plank·ter \ˈplaŋ(k)-tər\ *n* [Gk *planktēr* wanderer, fr. *plazesthai*] **:** a planktonic organism

plank·ton \ˈplaŋ(k)-tən, -ˌtän\ *n* [G, fr. Gk, neut. of *planktos* drifting, fr. *plazesthai* to wander, drift, pass. of *plazein* to drive astray; akin to L *plangere* to strike — more at PLAINT] **:** the passively floating or weakly swimming usu. minute animal and plant life of a body of water — **plank·ton·ic** \plaŋ(k)-ˈtän-ik\ *adj*

planned parenthood *n* **:** the practice of birth control measures (as contraception) designed to regulate the number and spacing of children in a family

plan·ning *n* **:** the act or process of making or carrying out plans; *specif* **:** the establishment of goals, policies, and procedures for a social or economic unit <city ~> <business ~>

plano- — see PLAN-

pla·no–con·cave \ˌplā-nō-(ˌ)kän-ˈkāv, -ˈkän-ˌ\ *adj* **:** flat on one side and concave on the other

pla·no–con·vex \-(ˌ)kän-ˈveks, -ˈkän-ˌ, -kən-ˈ\ *adj* **:** flat on one side and convex on the other

pla·nog·ra·phy \plā-ˈnäg-rə-fē, plə-\ *n* **:** a process (as lithography) for printing from a plane surface — **pla·no·graph** \ˈplā-nə-ˌgraf\ *vt* — **pla·no·graph·ic** \ˌplā-nə-ˈgraf-ik\ *adj*

pla·no·sol \ˈplā-nə-ˌsäl, -ˌsȯl\ *n* [²*plan-* + L *solum* ground, soil] **:** any of an intrazonal group of soils that have a strongly leached upper layer over a compacted clay or silt and occur on smooth flat uplands

plan position indicator *n* **:** PPI

¹plant \ˈplant\ *vb* [ME *planten*, fr. OE *plantian*, fr. LL *plantare* to plant, fix in place, fr. L, to plant, fr. *planta* plant] *vt* **1 a :** to put or set in the ground for growth <~ seeds> **b :** to set or sow with seeds or plants **c :** IMPLANT **2 a :** ESTABLISH, INSTITUTE **b :** COLONIZE, SETTLE **c :** to place (animals) in a new locality **d :** to stock with animals **3 a :** to place in or on the ground **b :** to place firmly or forcibly <~*ed* a hard blow on his chin> **4 a :** CONCEAL **b :** to covertly place for discovery, publication, or dissemination ~ *vi* **:** to plant something — **plant·able** \-ə-bəl\ *adj*

²plant *n* [ME *plante*, fr. OE, fr. L *planta*] **1 a :** a young tree, vine, shrub, or herb planted or suitable for planting **b :** any of a kingdom (Plantae) of living beings typically lacking locomotive movement or obvious nervous or sensory organs and possessing cellulose cell walls **2 a :** the land, buildings, machinery, apparatus, and fixtures employed in carrying on a trade or an industrial business **b :** a factory or workshop for the manufacture of a particular product **c :** the total facilities available for production or service **d :** the buildings and other physical equipment of an institution <the school ~> **3 :** an act of planting **4 :** something or someone planted <left muddy footprints as a ~ to confuse the police> — **plant·like** \-ˌlīk\ *adj*

Plan·tag·e·net \plan-ˈtaj-(ə-)nət\ *adj* [*Plantagenet*, nickname of the family adopted as surname] **:** of or relating to the English royal house that ruled from 1154 to 1399 — **Plantagenet** *n*

¹plan·tain \ˈplant-ᵊn\ *n* [ME, fr. OF, fr. L *plantagin-, plantago*, fr. *planta* sole of the foot; fr. its broad leaves — more at PLACE] **:** any of a genus (*Plantago* of the family Plantaginaceae, the plantain family) of short-stemmed elliptic-leaved herbs with spikes of minute greenish flowers

²plantain *n* [Sp *plántano* plane tree, banana tree, fr. ML *plantanus* plane tree, alter. of L *platanus* — more at PLANE] **1 :** a banana plant (*Musa paradisiaca*) **2 :** the angular greenish starchy fruit of the plantain that is a staple food in the tropics when cooked

plantain lily *n* **:** a plant (genus *Hosta*) of the lily family with plaited basal leaves and racemose white or violet flowers

plan·tar \ˈplant-ər, ˈplan-ˌtär\ *adj* [L *plantaris*, fr. *planta* sole — more at PLACE] **:** of or relating to the sole of the foot

plan·ta·tion \plan-ˈtā-shən\ *n* **1 :** a usu. large group of plants and esp. trees under cultivation **2 :** a settlement in a new country or region : COLONY <Plymouth *Plantation*> **3 a :** a place that is planted or under cultivation **b :** an agricultural estate usu. worked by resident labor under central direction

plant·er \ˈplant-ər\ *n* **1 :** one that cultivates plants: as **a :** FARMER **b :** one who owns or operates a plantation **2 :** one who settles or founds a place and esp. a new colony **3 :** a container in which ornamental plants are grown

planter's punch *n* **:** a punch of rum, lime or lemon juice, sugar, water, and sometimes bitters

plant food *n* **1 :** FOOD 1b **2 :** FERTILIZER

plant hormone *n* : an organic substance other than a nutrient that in minute amounts modifies a plant physiological process; *esp* : one produced by a plant and active elsewhere than at the site of production

plan·ti·grade \'plant-ə-,grād\ *adj* [F, fr. L *planta* sole + F *-grade*] : walking on the sole with the heel touching the ground <man is a ~ animal> — **plantigrade** *n*

plant·ing *n* : an area where plants are grown for commercial or decorative purposes

plant kingdom *n* : the one of the three basic groups of natural objects that includes all living and extinct plants — compare ANIMAL KINGDOM, MINERAL KINGDOM

plantlike flagellate *n* : any of various organisms that constitute a subclass (Phytomastigina), have many characteristics in common with typical algae, and are classified either as protozoans or as algae

plant louse *n* : APHID; *also* : any of various small insects (as a jumping plant louse) of similar habits

plan·u·la \'plan-yə-lə\ *n, pl* **-lae** \-,lē, -,lī\ [NL, fr. L *planus* level, flat — more at FLOOR] : the very young usu. flattened oval or oblong free-swimming ciliated larva of a coelenterate — **plan·u·lar** \-lər\ *adj* — **plan·u·loid** \-,lȯid\ *adj*

plaque \'plak\ *n* [F, fr. MF, metal sheet, fr. *plaquier* to plate, fr. MD *placken* to piece, patch; akin to MD *placke* piece, MHG *placke* patch] **1 a** : an ornamental brooch; *esp* : the badge of an honorary order **b** : a flat thin piece (as of metal) used for decoration **c** : a commemorative or identifying inscribed tablet **2 a** : a localized abnormal patch on a body part or surface **b** : a film of mucus harboring bacteria on a tooth **3** : a clear area in a bacterial culture produced by destruction of cells by a virus

¹plash \'plash\ *n* [prob. imit.] : SPLASH

²plash *vt* : to break the surface of (water) : SPLASH ~ *vi* : to cause a splashing or spattering effect

-pla·sia \'plā-zh(ē-)ə\ *or* **-pla·sy** \,plā-sē, ,plas-ē, p-lə-sē\ *n comb form* [NL *-plasia*, fr. Gk *plasis* molding, fr. *plassein*] : development : formation <hyper*plasia*> <homo*plasy*>

plasm \'plaz-əm\ *n* [LL *plasma* something molded] : PLASMA

plasm- *or* **plasmo-** *comb form* [F, fr. NL *plasma*] : plasma <*plasm*odium> <*plasmo*lysis>

-plasm \,plaz-əm\ *n comb form* [G *-plasma*, fr. NL *plasma*] : formative or formed material (as of a cell or tissue) <endo*plasm*>

plas·ma \'plaz-mə\ *n* [G, fr. LL, something molded, fr. Gk, fr. *plassein* to mold — more at PLASTER] **1** : a green faintly translucent quartz **2** [NL, fr. LL] **a** : the fluid part of blood, lymph, or milk as distinguished from suspended material **b** : the juice that can be expressed from muscle **3** : PROTOPLASM **4** : a collection of charged particles (as in the atmospheres of stars or in a metal) containing about equal numbers of positive ions and electrons and exhibiting some properties of a gas but differing from a gas in being a good conductor of electricity and in being affected by a magnetic field — **plas·mat·ic** \plaz-'mat-ik\ *adj*

plasma cell *n* : a mononuclear slightly amoeboid wandering cell that is usu. found in association with low-grade chronic inflammations or with various allergic processes

plas·ma·gel \'plaz-mə-,jel\ *n* : gelated protoplasm; *esp* : the outer firm zone of a pseudopodium

plas·ma·gene \-,jēn\ *n* [ISV] : an extranuclear determiner of hereditary characteristics with a capacity for replication similar to that of a nuclear gene — **plas·ma·gen·ic** \,plaz-mə-'jēn-ik, -'jen-\ *adj*

plasma jet *n* : a stream of very hot ionized plasma; *also* : a device for producing such a stream

plas·ma·lem·ma \,plaz-mə-'lem-ə\ *n* [NL, fr. *plasma* + Gk *lemma* husk — more at LEMMA] : the differentiated protoplasmic surface bounding a cell

plasma membrane *n* : a semipermeable limiting layer of cell protoplasm

plas·ma·pher·e·sis \,plaz-mə-'fer-ə-səs\ *n* [NL, fr. *plasma* + Gk *aphairesis* taking off — more at APHAERESIS] : a process in which red blood cells are separated from the plasma of a blood donor and returned to the donor's circulatory system

plas·ma·sol \'plaz-mə-,säl, -,sȯl, -,sōl\ *n* : solated protoplasm; *esp* : the inner fluid zone of a pseudopodium or amoeboid cell

plasma torch *n* : a device that heats a gas by electrical means to form a plasma for high-temperature operations (as melting metal)

plas·mid \'plaz-məd\ *n* [*plasma* + ²*-id*] : a cellular element that exists and replicates autonomously in the cytoplasm : PLASMAGENE

plas·min \-mən\ *n* : a proteolytic enzyme that dissolves the fibrin of blood clots

plas·min·o·gen \plaz-'min-ə-jən\ *n* : the precursor of plasmin that is found in blood plasma and serum

plas·mo·des·ma \,plaz-mə-'dez-mə\ *also* **plas·mo·desm** \'plaz-mə-,dez-əm\ *n, pl* **-des·ma·ta** \-'dez-mət-ə\ *or* **-des·mas** \-'dez-məz\ [NL *plasmodesma*, fr. *plasma* + Gk *desmat-, desma* bond, fr. *dein* to bind — more at DIADEM] : one of the cytoplasmic strands that pass through openings in some plant cell walls and provide living bridges between cells

plas·mo·di·um \plaz-'mōd-ē-əm\ *n, pl* **-dia** \-ē-ə\ [NL, fr. *plasm-* + *-odium* thing resembling, fr. Gk *-ōdēs* like] **1 a** : a motile multinucleate mass of protoplasm resulting from fusion of uninucleate amoeboid cells; *also* : an organism (as a stage of a slime mold) that consists of such a structure **b** : SYNCYTIUM 1 **2** : an individual malaria parasite

plas·mog·a·my \plaz-'mäg-ə-mē\ *n* [ISV] : fusion of the cytoplasm of two or more cells as distinguished from fusion of nuclei

plas·mol·y·sis \plaz-'mäl-ə-səs\ *n* [NL] : shrinking of the cytoplasm away from the wall of a living cell due to water loss by exosmosis — **plas·mo·lyt·ic** \,plaz-mə-'lit-ik\ *adj* — **plas·mo·lyt·i·cal·ly** \-i-k(ə-)lē\ *adv*

plas·mo·lyze \'plaz-mə-,līz\ *vb* **-lyzed; -lyz·ing** *vt* : to subject to plasmolysis ~ *vi* : to undergo plasmolysis

-plast \,plast\ *n comb form* [MF *-plaste* thing molded, fr. LL *-plastus*, fr. Gk *-plastos*, fr. *plastos* molded, fr. *plassein*] : organized particle or granule : cell <chromo*plast*>

¹plas·ter \'plas-tər\ *n* [ME, fr. OE, fr. L *emplastrum*, fr. Gk *emplastron*, fr. *emplassein* to plaster on, fr. *en-* + *plassein* to mold, plaster; akin to L *planus* level, flat — more at FLOOR] **1** : a medicated or protective dressing that consists of a film (as of cloth or plastic) spread with a usu. medicated substance <adhesive ~>; *broadly* : something applied to heal and soothe **2** : a pasty composition (as of lime, water, and sand) that hardens on drying and is used for coating walls, ceilings, and partitions — **plas·tery** \-t(ə-)rē\ *adj*

²plaster *vb* **plas·tered; plas·ter·ing** \-t(ə-)riŋ\ *vt* **1** : to overlay or cover with plaster : COAT **2** : to apply a plaster to **3 a** : to cover over or conceal as if with a coat of plaster **b** : to apply as a coating or incrustation **c** : to smooth down with a sticky or shiny substance <~*ed* his hair down> **4** : to fasten or apply tightly to another surface **5** : to treat with plaster of paris **6** : to affix to or place upon esp. conspicuously or in quantity **7** : to inflict heavy damage, injury, or casualties upon esp. by a concentrated or unremitting attack : strike heavily and effectively ~ *vi* : to apply plaster — **plas·ter·er** \-tər-ər\ *n*

plas·ter·board \'plas-tər-,bō(ə)rd, -,bȯ(ə)rd\ *n* : a board used in large sheets as a backing or as a substitute for plaster in walls and consisting of several piles of fiberboard, paper, or felt usu. bonded to a hardened gypsum plaster core

plaster cast *n* **1** : a sculptor's model in plaster of paris **2** : a rigid dressing of gauze impregnated with plaster of paris

plas·tered \'plas-tərd\ *adj* : DRUNK, INTOXICATED

plas·ter·ing *n* **1** : a coating of or as if of plaster **2** : a decisive defeat

plaster of par·is \-'par-əs\ *often cap 2d P* [*Paris*, France] : a white powdery slightly hydrated calcium sulfate $CaSO_4 \cdot \frac{1}{2}H_2O$ or $2CaSO_4 \cdot H_2O$ made by calcining gypsum and used chiefly for casts and molds in the form of a quick-setting paste with water

plas·ter·work \'plas-tər-,wərk\ *n* : plastering used to finish architectural constructions

¹plas·tic \'plas-tik\ *adj* [L *plasticus* of molding, fr. Gk *plastikos*, fr. *plassein* to mold, form] **1** : FORMATIVE, CREATIVE <~ forces in nature> **2 a** : capable of being molded or modeled <~ clay> **b** : capable of adapting to varying conditions : PLIABLE <ecologically ~ animals> **3** : SCULPTURAL **4** : made or consisting of a plastic **5** : capable of being deformed continuously and permanently in any direction without rupture **6** : of, relating to, or involving plastic surgery **7** : formed by or adapted to an artificial or conventional standard : SYNTHETIC <this is the ~ age, the era of the sham and the bogus — Logan Gourlay>

syn PLASTIC, PLIABLE, PLIANT, DUCTILE, MALLEABLE, ADAPTABLE *shared meaning element* : susceptible of being modified in form or nature

²plastic *n* : a plastic substance; *specif* : any of numerous organic synthetic or processed materials that are mostly thermoplastic or thermosetting polymers of high molecular weight and that can be molded, cast, extruded, drawn, or laminated into objects, films, or filaments — often used in pl. with sing. constr.

-plas·tic \'plas-tik\ *adj comb form* [Gk *-plastikos*, fr. *plassein*] **1** : developing : forming <thrombo*plastic*> **2** : of or relating to (something designated by a term ending in *-plasm, -plast, -plasty*, or *-plasy*) <homo*plastic*> <neo*plastic*>

plas·ti·cal·ly \'plas-ti-k(ə-)lē\ *adv* **1** : in a plastic manner **2** : with respect to plastic qualities

plastic art *n* **1** : art (as sculpture or bas-relief) characterized by modeling : three-dimensional art **2** : one of the visual arts (as painting, sculpture, or film) esp. as distinguished from those that are written (as poetry or music)

plastic foam *n* : EXPANDED PLASTIC

plas·tic·i·ty \pla-'stis-ət-ē\ *n* **1** : the quality or state of being plastic; *esp* : capacity for being molded or altered **2** : the ability to retain a shape attained by pressure deformation **3** : the capacity of organisms with the same genotype to vary in developmental pattern, in phenotype, or in behavior according to varying environmental conditions

plas·ti·cize \'plas-tə-,sīz\ *vt* **-cized; -ciz·ing** **1** : to make plastic **2** : to treat with a plastic <a *plasticized* mattress cover> — **plas·ti·ci·za·tion** \,plas-tə-sə-'zā-shən\ *n*

plas·ti·ciz·er \'plas-tə-,sī-zər\ *n* : one that plasticizes; *specif* : a chemical added esp. to rubbers and resins to impart flexibility, workability, or stretchability

plastic surgeon *n* : a specialist in plastic surgery

plastic surgery *n* : a branch of surgery concerned with the repair or restoration of lost, injured, or deformed parts of the body chiefly by transfer of tissue

plas·tid \'plas-təd\ *n* [G, fr. Gk *plastos* molded] : any of various cytoplasmic organelles of photosynthetic cells that serve in many cases as centers of special metabolic activities — **plas·tid·i·al** \pla-'stid-ē-əl\ *adj*

plas·ti·sol \'plas-tə-,säl, -,sȯl\ *n* [*plastic* + ⁴*sol*] : a substance consisting of a mixture of a resin and a plasticizer that can be molded, cast, or made into a continuous film by application of heat

plas·to·gene \'plas-tə-,jēn\ *n* [*plastid* + *-o-* + *-gene*] : a hereditary determinant in a plant cell plastid

plas·tral \'plas-trəl\ *adj* : of or relating to a plastron

plas·tron \'plas-trən\ *n* [MF, fr. OIt *piastrone*, aug. of *piastra* thin metal plate — more at PIASTER] **1 a** : a metal breastplate formerly worn under the hauberk **b** : a quilted pad worn in fencing practice to protect the chest, waist, and the side on which the weapon is held **2** : the ventral part of the shell of a tortoise or turtle consisting typically of nine symmetrically placed bones overlaid by horny plates **3 a** : a trimming like a bib for a woman's dress **b** : DICKEY

1a **4** : a thin film of air held by water-repellent hairs of some aquatic insects
-plas·ty \ˌplas-tē\ *n comb form* [F *-plastie,* fr. LGk *-plastia* molding, fr. Gk *-plastēs* molder, fr. *plassein*] : plastic surgery <osteo*plasty*>
-plasy — see -PLASIA
¹plat \ˈplat\ *vt* **plat·ted; plat·ting** [ME *platen,* alter. of *plaiten*] : PLAIT
²plat *n* : PLAIT
³plat *n* [prob. alter. of *plot*] **1** : a small piece of ground (as a lot or quadrat) : PLOT **2** : a plan, map, or chart of a piece of land with actual or proposed features (as lots); *also* : the land represented
⁴plat *vt* **plat·ted; plat·ting** : to make a plat of
⁵plat *abbr* **1** plateau **2** platoon
plat·an \ˈplat-ᵊn\ *n* [ME, fr. L *platanus*] : ²PLANE
plat du jour \ˌpläd-ə-ˈzhü(ə)r, ˌplad-\ *n, pl* **plats du jour** *same*\ [F, lit., plate of the day] : a dish that is featured by a restaurant on a particular day
¹plate \ˈplāt\ *n* [ME, fr. OF, fr. *plate,* fem. of *plat* flat, fr. (assumed) VL *plattus,* prob. fr. Gk *platys* broad, flat — more at PLACE] **1 a** : a smooth flat thin piece of material **b** (1) : forged, rolled, or cast metal in sheets usu. thicker than ¼ inch (2) : a very thin layer of metal deposited on a surface of base metal by plating **c** : one of the broad metal pieces used in armor; *also* : armor of such plates **d** (1) : a lamina or plaque (as of bone or horn) that forms part of an animal body; *esp* : SCUTE (2) : the thin under portion of the forequarter of beef; *esp* : the fatty back part — see BEEF illustration **e** : HOME PLATE **f** : any of the huge movable segments into which the earth's crust is divided **2** [ME; partly fr. OF *plate* plate, piece of silver; partly fr. OSp *plata* silver, fr. (assumed) VL *plattus* flat] **a** *obs* : a silver coin **b** : precious metal; *esp* : silver bullion **3** [ME, fr. MF *plat* dish, plate, fr. *plat* flat] **a** : domestic hollowware made of or plated with gold, silver, or base metals **b** : a shallow usu. circular vessel from which food is eaten or served **c** (1) : PLATEFUL (2) : a main course served on a plate (3) : food and service supplied to one person <a dinner at $10 a ~> **d** (1) : a prize given to the winner in a contest (2) : a horse race in which the contestants compete for a prize rather than stakes **e** : a dish or pouch passed in taking collections **f** : a flat glass dish used chiefly for culturing microorganisms **4 a** : a prepared surface from which printing is done **b** : a sheet of material (as glass) coated with a light-sensitive photographic emulsion **c** (1) : the usu. flat or grid-formed anode of an electron tube at which electrons collect (2) : a metallic grid with its interstices filled with active material that forms one of the structural units of a battery **d** : LICENSE PLATE **5** : a horizontal structural member (as a timber) that provides bearing and anchorage esp. for the trusses of a roof or the rafters **6** : the part of a denture that fits to the mouth; *broadly* : DENTURE **7** : a full-page illustration often on different paper from the text pages — **plate·like** \-ˌlīk\ *adj*
²plate *vt* **plat·ed; plat·ing** **1** : to cover or equip with plate: as **a** : to arm with armor plate **b** : to cover with an adherent layer mechanically, chemically, or electrically; *also* : to deposit (as a layer) on a surface **2** : to make a printing surface from or for **3** : to fix or secure with a plate
¹pla·teau \pla-ˈtō, ˈpla-ˌ\ *n, pl* **plateaus** *or* **pla·teaux** \-ˈtōz, -ˌtōz\ [F, fr. MF, platter, fr. *plat* flat] **1 a** : a usu. extensive land area having a relatively level surface raised sharply above adjacent land on at least one side : TABLELAND **b** : a similar undersea feature **2 a** : a region of little or no change in a graphical representation **b** : a relatively stable level, period, or condition
²plateau *vi* : to reach a level, period, or condition of stability
plate·ful \ˈplāt-ˌfu̇l\ *n* : as much or as many as a plate will hold
plate glass *n* : rolled, ground, and polished sheet glass
plate·let \ˈplāt-lət\ *n* : a minute flattened body (as of ice or a mineral); *esp* : BLOOD PLATELET
plate·mak·er \ˈplāt-ˌmā-kər\ *n* : a machine for making printing plates and esp. offset printing plates — **plate·mak·ing** \-kiŋ\ *n*
plat·en \ˈplat-ᵊn\ *n* [MF *plateine,* fr. *plate*] **1** : a flat plate (as of metal); *esp* : one that exerts or receives pressure **2** : the roller of a typewriter
plat·er \ˈplāt-ər\ *n* **1** : one that plates **2 a** : a horse that runs chiefly in plate races **b** : an inferior racehorse
plate rail *n* : a rail or narrow shelf along the upper part of a wall for holding plates or ornaments
plat·er·esque \ˌplat-ə-ˈresk\ *adj, often cap* [Sp *plateresco,* fr. *platero* silversmith, fr. *plata* silver] : of, relating to, or being a 16th century Spanish architectural style characterized by elaborate ornamentation suggestive of silver plate
plat·form \ˈplat-ˌfȯrm\ *n, often attrib* [MF *plate-forme* diagram, map, lit., flat form] **1** : PLAN, DESIGN **2** : a declaration of the principles on which a group of persons stand; *esp* : a declaration of principles and policies adopted by a political party or a candidate **3 a** (1) : a horizontal flat surface usu. higher than the adjoining area; *also* : a device incorporating or providing a platform (as for reaching high places) (2) : a raised flooring (as for speakers or performers) **b** : a place or opportunity for public discussion **4 a** : a layer (as of leather) between the inner sole and outer sole of a shoe **b** : a shoe having such a sole
platform rocker *n* : a chair that rocks on a stable platform
platform scale *n* : a weighing machine with a flat platform on which objects are weighed — called also *platform balance*
platform tennis *n* : a variation of paddle tennis that is played on a wooden platform enclosed by a wire fence
platin- *or* **platino-** *comb form* [NL *platinum*] : platinum <*platino*type> <*platin*iridium>
¹pla·ti·na \plə-ˈtē-nə\ *n* [Sp] : PLATINUM; *esp* : crude native platinum
²platina *adj* : of the color platinum
plat·ing \ˈplāt-iŋ\ *n* **1** : the act or process of plating **2 a** : a coating of metal plates **b** : a thin coating of metal
pla·tin·ic \plə-ˈtin-ik\ *adj* : of, relating to, or containing platinum esp. with a valence of four — compare PLATINOUS
plat·i·nize \ˈplat-ᵊn-ˌīz\ *vt* **-nized; -niz·ing** : to cover, treat, or combine with platinum or a compound of platinum
plat·i·no·cy·a·nide \ˌplat-ᵊn-ō-ˈsī-ə-ˌnīd\ *n* : a fluorescent complex salt formed by the union of platinous cyanide with another cyanide
plat·i·noid \ˈplat-ᵊn-ˌȯid\ *n* : an alloy chiefly of copper, nickel, and zinc used for forming electrical resistance coils and standards
plat·i·nous \ˈplat-nəs, -ᵊn-əs\ *adj* : of, relating to, or containing platinum esp. with a valence of two — compare PLATINIC
plat·i·num \ˈplat-nəm, -ᵊn-əm\ *n, often attrib* [NL, fr. Sp *platina,* fr. dim. of *plata* silver — more at PLATE] **1** : a heavy precious grayish white noncorroding ductile malleable metallic element that fuses with difficulty and is used esp. in chemical ware and apparatus, as a catalyst, and in dental and jewelry alloys — see ELEMENT table **2** : a moderate gray
platinum black *n* : a soft dull black powder of metallic platinum obtained by reduction and precipitation from solutions of its salts and used as a catalyst
platinum blonde *n* **1** : a pale silvery blonde color that in human hair is usu. produced by bleach and a bluish rinse **2** : a person whose hair is of the color platinum blonde
plat·i·tude \ˈplat-ə-ˌt(y)üd\ *n* [F, fr. *plat* flat, dull] **1** : the quality or state of being dull or insipid **2** : a banal, trite, or stale remark
plat·i·tu·di·nal \ˌplat-ə-ˈt(y)üd-nəl, -ᵊn-əl\ *adj* : PLATITUDINOUS
plat·i·tu·di·nar·i·an \-ˌt(y)üd-ᵊn-ˈer-ē-ən\ *n* : one given to the use of platitudes
plat·i·tu·di·nize \-ˈt(y)üd-ᵊn-ˌīz\ *vi* **-nized; -niz·ing** [*platitudinous*] : to utter platitudes
plat·i·tu·di·nous \-ˈt(y)üd-nəs, -ᵊn-əs\ *adj* [*platitude* + *-inous* (as in *multitudinous*)] : having the characteristics of a platitude : full of platitudes <~ remarks> — **plat·i·tu·di·nous·ly** *adv*
pla·ton·ic \plə-ˈtän-ik, plā-\ *adj* [L *platonicus,* fr. Gk *platōnikos* fr. *Platōn* Plato] **1** *cap* : of, relating to, or characteristic of Plato or Platonism **2 a** : relating to or based on platonic love; *also* : experiencing or professing platonic love **b** : NOMINAL, THEORETICAL — **pla·ton·i·cal·ly** \-i-k(ə-)lē\ *adv*
platonic love *n, often cap P* **1** : love conceived by Plato as ascending from passion for the individual to contemplation of the universal and ideal **2** : a close relationship between two persons in which sexual desire has been suppressed or sublimated
Pla·to·nism \ˈplāt-ᵊn-ˌiz-əm\ *n* **1 a** : the philosophy of Plato stressing esp. that actual things are copies of transcendent ideas and that these ideas are the objects of true knowledge apprehended by reminiscence **b** : NEOPLATONISM **2** : PLATONIC LOVE — **Pla·to·nist** \-ᵊn-əst\ *n* — **Pla·to·nis·tic** \ˌplāt-ᵊn-ˈis-tik\ *adj*
Pla·to·nize \ˈplāt-ᵊn-ˌīz\ *vb* **-nized; -niz·ing** *vi* : to adopt, imitate, or conform to Platonic opinions ~ *vt* : to explain in accordance with or adapt to Platonic doctrines; *esp* : IDEALIZE
¹pla·toon \plə-ˈtün, pla-\ *n* [F *peloton* small detachment, lit., ball, fr. *pelote* little ball — more at PELLET] **1** : a subdivision of a company-size military unit normally consisting of two or more squads or sections **2** : a group of persons sharing a common characteristic or activity <a ~ of waiters>: as **a** : a group of football players trained for either offense or defense and sent into or withdrawn from the game as a body **b** : two or more players (as in baseball) who alternate playing the same position
²platoon *vt* : to play (one player) alternately with another player in the same position (as on a baseball team) ~ *vi* **1** : to alternate with another player at the same position **2** : to use alternate players at the same position
platoon sergeant *n* : a noncommissioned officer in the army ranking above a staff sergeant and below a first sergeant
Platt·deutsch \ˈplat-ˌdȯich, ˈplät-\ *n* [G, fr. D *Platduitsch,* lit., Low German, fr. *plat* flat, low + *duitsch* German] : a colloquial language of northern Germany comprising several Low German dialects
plat·ter \ˈplat-ər\ *n* [ME *plater,* fr. AF, fr. MF *plat* plate] **1 a** : a large plate used esp. for serving meat **b** : PLATE 3c(2) **2** : a phonograph record — **plat·ter·ful** \-ˌfu̇l\ *n* — **on a platter** : without effort : very easily <can have the presidency *on a platter* —Jonathan Daniels>
¹platy \ˈplāt-ē\ *adj* : resembling a plate; *also* : consisting of plates or flaky layers — used chiefly of soil or mineral formations
²platy \ˈplat-ē\ *n, pl* **platy** *or* **plat·ys** *or* **plat·ies** [NL *Platypoecilus,* genus name] : any of various small stocky Mexican topminnows that are popular for tropical aquariums, are noted for variability and brilliant color, and are classified as a single species (*Platypoecilus maculatus*)
platy·hel·minth \ˌplat-i-ˈhel-ˌmin(t)th\ *n* [deriv. of Gk *platys* broad, flat + *helminth-, helmis* helminth] : any of a phylum (Platyhelminthes) of soft-bodied usu. much flattened worms (as the planarians, flukes, and tapeworms) — **platy·hel·min·thic** \-hel-ˈmin(t)-thik, -ˈmint-ik\ *adj*
platy·pus \ˈplat-i-pəs, -ˌpu̇s\ *n, pl* **platy·pus·es** *also* **platy·pi** \-ˌpī, -ˌpē\ [NL, fr. Gk *platypous* flat-footed, fr. *platys* broad, flat + *pous* foot — more at PLACE, FOOT] : a small aquatic oviparous mammal (*Ornithorhynchus anatinus*) of southern and eastern Australia and Tasmania that has a fleshy bill resembling that of a duck, dense fur, webbed feet, and a broad flattened tail

platypus

¹plat·yr·rhine \ˈplat-i-ˌrīn\ *adj* **1** [NL *Platyrrhina,* group name, fr. Gk *platyrrhin-, platyrrhis* broad-nosed] : of, relating to, or being any of a division (Platyrrhina) of monkeys all of which are New World monkeys and are characterized by a broad nasal septum, usu. 36 teeth, and often a prehensile tail **2** [Gk *platyrrhin-, platyrrhis,* fr. *platys* + *rhin-, rhis* nose] : having a short broad nose — **plat·yr·rhi·ny** \-ˌrī-nē\ *n*
²platyrrhine *n* : a platyrrhine individual

plau·dit \ˈplȯd-ət\ *n* [L *plaudite* applaud, pl. imper. of *plaudere* to applaud] **1 :** an act or round of applause **2 :** enthusiastic approval — usu. used in pl. <received the ~*s* of the critics>
plau·si·bil·i·ty \ˌplȯ-zə-ˈbil-ət-ē\ *n, pl* **-ties 1 :** the quality or state of being plausible **2 :** something plausible
plau·si·ble \ˈplȯ-zə-bəl\ *adj* [L *plausibilis* worthy of applause, fr. *plausus,* pp. of *plaudere*] **1 :** superficially fair, reasonable, or valuable but often specious <a ~ pretext> **2 :** superficially pleasing or persuasive <a swindler . . . , then a quack, then a smooth, ~ gentleman —R. W. Emerson> **3 :** appearing worthy of belief <his argument was both powerful and ~> — **plau·si·ble·ness** *n* — **plau·si·bly** \-blē\ *adv*
syn PLAUSIBLE, CREDIBLE, BELIEVABLE, COLORABLE, SPECIOUS *shared meaning element* **:** outwardly acceptable as true or genuine ***ant*** implausible
plau·sive \ˈplȯ-ziv, -siv\ *adj* [L *plausus,* pp.] **1 :** manifesting praise or approval **:** APPLAUDING **2** *obs* **:** PLEASING **3** *archaic* **:** SPECIOUS
¹play \ˈplā\ *n* [ME, fr. OE *plega;* akin to OE *plegan* to play, MD *pleyen*] **1 a :** SWORDPLAY **b** *archaic* **:** GAME, SPORT **c :** the conduct, course, or action of a game **d :** a particular act or maneuver in a game: as **(1) :** the action during an attempt to advance the ball in football **(2) :** the action in which a player is put out in baseball **e :** the action in which cards are played after bidding in a card game **f :** the moving of a piece in a board game (as chess) **2 a** *obs* **:** SEXUAL INTERCOURSE **b :** DALLIANCE **3 a :** recreational activity; *esp* **:** the spontaneous activity of children **b :** absence of serious or harmful intent **:** JEST <said it in ~> **c :** the act or an instance of playing on words or speech sounds **d :** GAMING, GAMBLING **4 a (1) :** an act, way, or manner of proceeding **:** MANEUVER <that was a ~ to get your fingerprints —Erle Stanley Gardner> **(2) :** DEAL, VENTURE **b (1) :** OPERATION, ACTIVITY <other motives surely come into ~ —M. R. Cohen> **(2) :** brisk, fitful, or light movement <the gem presented a dazzling ~ of colors> **(3) :** free or unimpeded motion (as of a part of a machine); *also* **:** the length or measure of such motion **(4) :** scope or opportunity for action **5 :** emphasis or publicity esp. in the news media <wished the country received a better ~ in the American press —Hugh MacLennan> **6 :** a move or series of moves calculated to arouse friendly feelings — usu. used with *make* <made a big ~ for the girl —Will Herman> **7 a :** the stage representation of an action or story **b :** a dramatic composition **:** DRAMA ***syn*** see FUN — **in play :** in condition or position to be legitimately played — **out of play :** not in play
²play *vi* **1 a :** to engage in sport or recreation **:** FROLIC **b :** to have sexual relations; *esp* **:** to have promiscuous or illicit sexual relations — usu. used in the phrase *play around* **c (1) :** to move aimlessly about **:** TRIFLE **(2) :** to deal or behave frivolously or mockingly **:** JEST **(3) :** to deal in a light, speculative, or sportive manner **(4) :** to make use of double meaning or of the similarity of sound of two words for stylistic or humorous effect **2 a :** to take advantage <~*ing* on fears> **b (1) :** FLUTTER, FRISK **(2) :** to move or operate in a lively, irregular, or intermittent manner **c :** to move or function freely within prescribed limits **d :** to discharge, eject, or fire repeatedly or so as to make a stream <hoses ~*ing* on a fire> **3 a (1) :** to perform music <~ on a violin> **(2) :** to sound in performance <the organ is ~*ing*> **(3) :** to emit sounds <his radio is ~*ing*> **(4) :** to reproduce recorded sounds <a record is ~*ing*> **b (1) :** to act in a dramatic production **(2) :** SHOW, RUN <what's ~*ing* at the theater> **c :** to be suitable for dramatic performance **d :** to act with special consideration so as to gain favor, approval, or sympathy <might ~ to popular prejudices to serve his political ends —V. L. Parrington> — often used in the phrase *play up to* **4 a :** to engage or take part in a game **b :** to perform in a position in a specified manner <the outfielders were ~*ing* deep> **c :** to play a card or move a piece during one's turn in a game **d :** GAMBLE **e (1) :** to behave or conduct oneself in a specified way <~ safe> **(2) :** to feign a specified state or quality <~ dead> **(3) :** to take part in or assent to some activity **:** COOPERATE <~ along with his scheme> **(4) :** to act so as to prove advantageous to another — usu. used in the phrase *play into the hands of* ~ *vt* **1 a (1) :** to engage in or occupy oneself with <~ baseball> **(2) :** to engage in as if in a game **(3) :** to deal with, handle, or manage **(4) :** EXPLOIT, MANIPULATE **b :** to pretend to engage in <children ~*ing* house> **c (1) :** to perform or execute for amusement or to deceive or mock <~ a trick> **(2) :** WREAK <~ havoc> **d :** to give an indicated degree of value, importance, or emphasis to — usu. used with *up* or *down* **2 a (1) :** to put on a performance of (a play) **(2) :** to act in the character or part of **(3) :** to act or perform in <~*ed* leading theaters> **b :** to perform or act the part of <~ the fool> **3 a (1) :** to contend against in a game **(2) :** to use as a contestant in a game <the coach did not ~ him> **(3) :** to perform the duties associated with (a certain position) <~*ed* quarterback> **(4) :** to guard or move into position to defend against (an opponent) in a specified manner **b (1) :** to wager in a game **:** STAKE **(2) :** to make wagers on <~ the races> **(3) :** to operate on the basis of <~ a hunch> **c :** to put into action in a game; *esp* **:** to remove (a playing card) from one's hand and place usu. face up on a table in one's turn either as part of a scoring combination or as one's contribution to a trick **d :** to catch or pick up (a batted ball) **:** FIELD <~*ed* the ball bare-handed> **e :** to direct the course of (as a ball) **:** HIT <~*ed* a wedge shot to the green>; *also* **:** to cause (a ball or puck) to rebound <~*ed* the ball off the backboard> **4 a :** to perform (music) on an instrument <~ a waltz> **b :** to perform music on <~ the violin> **c :** to perform music of (a certain composer) **d (1) :** to cause (as a radio or phonograph) to emit sounds **(2) :** to cause the recorded sounds of (as a record or a magnetic tape) to be reproduced **5 a :** WIELD, PLY **b :** to discharge, fire, or set off with continuous effect <~*ed* the hose on the burning building> **c :** to cause to move or operate lightly and irregularly or intermittently **d :** to keep (a hooked fish) in action — **play·abil·i·ty** \ˌplā-ə-ˈbil-ət-ē\ *n* — **play·able** \ˈplā-ə-bəl\ *adj* — **play ball :** COOPERATE — **play both ends against the middle :** to set opposing interests against each other to one's own ultimate profit — **play by ear :** to deal with something without previous planning or instructions — **play politics 1 :** to act from political considerations only **2 :** to seek to gain one's ends by scheming or intrigue — **play possum :** to pretend to be asleep or dead — **play second fiddle :** to take a subordinate position — **play the field :** to have dates with more than one member of the opposite sex — **play the game :** to act according to a code or set of standards — **play with oneself :** MASTURBATE
pla·ya \ˈplī-ə\ *n* [Sp, lit., beach] **:** the flat-floored bottom of an undrained desert basin that becomes at times a shallow lake
play–act \ˈplā-ˌakt\ *vb* [back-formation fr. *playacting*] *vi* **1 a :** to take part in theatrical performances esp. as a professional **b :** to make believe **2 :** to engage in theatrical or insincere behavior ~ *vt* **:** to act out
play–action pass *n* **:** a pass play in football in which the quarterback fakes a handoff before passing the ball
play·back \ˈplā-ˌbak\ *n* **1 :** the action of reproducing recorded sound or pictures often immediately after recording **2 :** a tape or disc sound or picture reproducing device
play back \(ˈ)plā-ˈbak\ *vt* **:** to perform a playback of (a usu. recently recorded disc or tape)
play·bill \ˈplā-ˌbil\ *n* **1 :** a bill advertising a play and usu. announcing the cast **2 :** a theater program
play·book \-ˌbu̇k\ *n* **1 :** one or more plays in book form **2 :** a notebook containing diagramed football plays
play·boy \-ˌbȯi\ *n* **:** a man who lives a life devoted chiefly to the pursuit of pleasure
play–by–play \ˌplā-bə-ˌplā, -ˌbī-\ *adj* **1 :** being a running commentary on a sports event **2 :** relating each event as it occurs
played out *adj* **1 :** worn out or used up **2 :** tired out **:** SPENT
play·er \ˈplā-ər\ *n* **:** one that plays: as **a :** a person who plays a game **b :** MUSICIAN **c :** ACTOR **d :** a mechanical device for automatically playing a musical instrument (as a piano)
player piano *n* **:** a piano containing a mechanical piano player
play·fel·low \ˈplā-ˌfel-(ˌ)ō, -ə(-w)\ *n* **:** PLAYMATE
play·field \-ˌfēld\ *n* **:** a playground designed for outdoor athletics
play·ful \ˈplā-fəl\ *adj* **1 :** full of play **:** FROLICSOME, SPORTIVE <a ~ kitten> **2 :** HUMOROUS, JOCULAR <the ~ tone of her voice —Ellen Glasgow> — **play·ful·ly** \-fə-lē\ *adv* — **play·ful·ness** *n*
play·girl \-ˌgər(-ə)l\ *n* **:** a female playboy
play·go·er \-ˌgō(-ə)r\ *n* **:** one who frequently attends plays
play·ground \-ˌgrau̇nd\ *n* **1 :** a piece of land used for and usu. equipped with facilities for recreation esp. by children **2 :** the area of a specific activity <that town was a gambling ~>
play·house \-ˌhau̇s\ *n* **1 :** THEATER **2 :** a small house for children to play in
playing card *n* **:** one of a set of 24 to 78 thin rectangular pieces of paperboard or plastic marked on one side to show its rank and suit and used in playing any of numerous games
playing field *n* **:** a field for various games; *esp* **:** the part of a field officially marked off for play
play·land \ˈplā-ˌland\ *n* **:** PLAYGROUND
play·let \-lət\ *n* **:** a short play
play·mak·er \-ˌmā-kər\ *n* **:** a player who leads the offense for a team (as in basketball or hockey)
play·mate \-ˌmāt\ *n* **:** a companion in play
play–off \ˈplā-ˌȯf\ *n* **1 :** a final contest or series of contests to determine the winner between contestants or teams that have tied **2 :** a series of contests played after the end of the regular season to determine a championship
play off \(ˈ)plā-ˈȯf\ *vt* **1 :** to complete the playing of (an interrupted contest) **2 :** to break (a tie) by a play-off **3 :** to set in opposition for one's own gain
play out *vt* **1 a :** to perform to the end <*play out* a role> **b :** to use up **:** FINISH **2 :** UNREEL, UNFOLD <*played out* a length of line —Gordon Webber> ~ *vi* **:** to become spent or exhausted
play·pen \ˈplā-ˌpen\ *n* **:** a portable usu. collapsible enclosure in which a baby or young child may play
play·room \-ˌrüm, -ˌru̇m\ *n* **:** RUMPUS ROOM
play·suit \-ˌsüt\ *n* **:** a sports and play outfit for women and children that consists usu. of a blouse and shorts
play therapy *n* **:** psychotherapy in which a child is encouraged to reveal his feelings and conflicts in play rather than by verbalization
play·thing \ˈplā-ˌthiŋ\ *n* **:** TOY
play·time \-ˌtīm\ *n* **:** a time for play or diversion
play·wear \ˈplā-ˌwa(ə)r, -ˌwe(ə)r\ *n* **:** informal clothing worn for leisure activities
play·wright \ˈplā-ˌrīt\ *n* [¹*play* + obs. *wright* (maker), fr. ME, fr. OE *wryhta* — more at WRIGHT] **:** a person who writes plays
pla·za \ˈplaz-ə, ˈpläz-\ *n* [Sp, fr. L *platea* broad street — more at PLACE] **1 :** a public square in a city or town **2 :** an open-air area used for the parking or servicing of motor vehicles **3 :** the section of a toll road at which the tollbooths are located <a toll ~> **4 :** an area adjacent to an expressway in which service facilities (as a restaurant, service station, and rest rooms) are located **5 :** SHOPPING CENTER
plea \ˈplē\ *n* [ME *plaid, plai,* fr. OF *plait, plaid,* fr. ML *placitum,* fr. L decision, decree, fr. neut. of *placitus,* pp. of *placēre* to please, be decided — more at PLEASE] **1 :** a legal suit or action **2 :** an allegation made by a party in support of his cause: as **a :** an allegation of fact — compare DEMURRER **b (1) :** a defendant's answer to a plaintiff's declaration in common-law practice **(2) :** an accused person's answer to a charge or indictment in criminal practice **c :** a plea of guilty to an indictment **3 :** something offered by way of excuse or justification <she left early with the ~

of a headache> **4 :** an earnest entreaty : APPEAL <their ~ for understanding must be answered> ***syn*** see APOLOGY

plea bargaining *n* **:** pleading guilty to a lesser charge in order to avoid standing trial for a more serious one

pleach \ˈplēch, ˈplāch\ *vt* [ME *plechen,* fr. ONF *plechier,* fr. L *plexus,* pp. of *plectere* to braid — more at PLY] **:** INTERLACE, PLAIT

plead \ˈplēd\ *vb* **plead·ed** \ˈplēd-əd\ *or* **pled** \ˈpled\; **plead·ing** [ME *plaiden* to institute a lawsuit, fr. OF *plaidier,* fr. *plaid* plea] *vi* **1 :** to argue a case or cause in a court of law **2 a :** to make an allegation in an action or other legal proceeding; *esp* **:** to answer the previous pleading of the other party by denying facts therein stated or by alleging new facts **b :** to conduct pleadings **3 :** to make a plea of a specified nature <~ not guilty> **4 a :** to argue for or against a claim **b :** to entreat or appeal earnestly : IMPLORE ~ *vt* **1 :** to maintain (as a case or cause) in a court of law or other tribunal **2 :** to allege in or by way of a legal plea **3 :** to offer as a plea usu. in defense, apology, or excuse — **plead·able** \ˈplēd-ə-bəl\ *adj* — **plead·er** *n* — **plead·ing·ly** \ˈplēd-iŋ-lē\ *adv*

plead·ing *n* **1 :** advocacy of a cause in a court of law **2 a :** one of the formal usu. written allegations and counter allegations made alternately by the parties in a legal action or proceeding **b :** the action or process performed by the parties in presenting such formal allegations until a single point at issue is produced **c :** the introduction of one of these allegations and esp. the first one **d :** the body of rules according to which these allegations are framed **3 :** the act or an instance of making a plea **4 :** a sincere entreaty

pleas·ance \ˈplez-ᵊn(t)s\ *n* **1 :** a feeling of pleasure : DELIGHT **2 :** a pleasant rest or recreation place usu. attached to a mansion

pleas·ant \ˈplez-ᵊnt\ *adj* [ME *plesaunt,* fr. MF *plaisant,* fr. prp. of *plaisir*] **1 :** having qualities that tend to give pleasure : AGREEABLE <a ~ day> **2 :** having or characterized by pleasing manners, behavior, or appearance — **pleas·ant·ly** *adv* — **pleas·ant·ness** *n*
syn PLEASANT, PLEASING, AGREEABLE, GRATEFUL, GRATIFYING, WELCOME *shared meaning element* **:** highly acceptable to the mind or senses ***ant*** unpleasant, distasteful

pleas·ant·ry \-ᵊn-trē\ *n, pl* **-ries 1 :** an agreeable playfulness in conversation : BANTER **2 :** a humorous act or remark : JEST

please \ˈplēz\ *vb* **pleased; pleas·ing** [ME *plesen,* fr. MF *plaisir,* fr. L *placēre;* akin to L *placare* to placate, OE *flōh* flat stone, Gk *plak-, plax* flat surface] *vi* **1 :** to afford or give pleasure or satisfaction **2 :** LIKE, WISH <do as you ~> **3** *archaic* **:** to have the kindness <will you ~ to enter the carriage —Charles Dickens> **4 :** to be willing to — usu. used in the imperative to express a polite request <~ come in> ~ *vt* **1 :** to give pleasure to : GRATIFY **2 :** to be the will or pleasure of <may it ~ your Majesty>

pleas·ing \ˈplē-ziŋ\ *adj* **:** giving pleasure : AGREEABLE <he found the sun's warmth ~> ***syn*** see PLEASANT ***ant*** displeasing, repellent — **pleas·ing·ly** \-ziŋ-lē\ *adv* — **pleas·ing·ness** *n*

plea·sur·able \ˈplezh-(ə-)rə-bəl, ˈplāzh-\ *adj* **:** PLEASANT, GRATIFYING — **plea·sur·abil·i·ty** \ˌplezh-(ə-)rə-ˈbil-ət-ē, ˌplāzh-\ *n* — **plea·sur·able·ness** \ˈplezh-(ə-)rə-bəl-nəs, ˈplāzh-\ *n* — **plea·sur·ably** \-blē\ *adv*

¹plea·sure \ˈplezh-ər, ˈplāzh-\ *n* [ME *plesure,* alter. of *plesir,* fr. MF *plaisir,* fr. *plaisir* to please] **1 :** DESIRE, INCLINATION <wait upon his ~ —Shak.> **2 :** a state of gratification **3 a :** sensual gratification **b :** frivolous amusement **4 :** a source of delight or joy

²pleasure *vb* **plea·sured; plea·sur·ing** \-(ə-)riŋ\ *vi* **1 :** to take pleasure : DELIGHT **2 :** to seek pleasure ~ *vt* **1 :** to give pleasure to : GRATIFY **2 :** to give sexual pleasure to

pleasure dome *n* **:** a place of pleasurable entertainment or recreation : RESORT

plea·sure·less \ˈplezh-ər-ləs, ˈplāzh-\ *adj* **:** giving no pleasure

pleasure principle *n* **:** a tendency for individual behavior to be directed toward immediate satisfaction of instinctual drives and immediate relief from pain or discomfort

¹pleat \ˈplēt\ *vt* [ME *pleten,* fr. *pleit, plete* plait] **1 :** FOLD; *esp* **:** to arrange in pleats <~ a skirt> **2 :** PLAIT 2 — **pleat·er** *n*

²pleat *n* [ME *plete*] **:** a fold in cloth made by doubling material over on itself; *also* **:** something resembling such a fold — **pleat·ed** *adj* — **pleat·less** \-ləs\ *adj*

pleb \ˈpleb\ *n* **:** PLEBEIAN

plebe \ˈplēb\ *n* [obs. *plebe* (common people), fr. F *plèbe,* fr. L *plebs*] **:** a freshman at a military or naval academy

¹ple·be·ian \pli-ˈbē-(y)ən\ *n* [L *plebeius* of the common people, fr. *plebs* common people; akin to Gk *plēthos* throng, *plēthein* to be full — more at FULL] **1 :** a member of the Roman plebs **2 :** one of the common people — **ple·be·ian·ism** \-ˌiz-əm\ *n*

²plebeian *adj* **1 :** of or relating to plebeians **2 :** crude or coarse in manner or style : COMMON — **ple·be·ian·ly** *adv*

pleb·i·scite \ˈpleb-ə-ˌsīt, -sət *also* -ˌsēt\ *n* [L *plebis scitum* law voted by the comitia, lit., decree of the common people] **:** a vote by which the people of an entire country or district express an opinion for or against a proposal esp. on a choice of government or ruler — **ple·bi·sci·ta·ry** \ple-ˈbis-ə-ˌter-ē, pli-; ˌpleb-ə-ˈsīt-ə-rē\ *adj*

plebs \ˈplebz, ˈpleps\ *n, pl* **ple·bes** \ˈplē-(ˌ)bēz, ˈplā-ˌbās\ [L] **1 :** the common people of ancient Rome **2 :** the general populace

ple·cop·ter·an \pli-ˈkäp-tə-rən\ *n* [NL *Plecoptera,* group name, fr. Gk *plekein* to braid + *pteron* wing — more at FEATHER] **:** STONE FLY — **plecopteran** *adj*

plec·to·gnath \ˈplek-ˌtäg-ˌnath, -tə(g)-\ *n* [deriv. of Gk *plektos* twisted (fr. *plekein* to braid) + *gnathos* jaw — more at PLY, GNATH-] **:** any of an order (Plectognathi) of bony fishes (as a filefish, a puffer, or a triggerfish) that usu. have the body covered with bony plates, spines, or ossicles — **plectognath** *adj*

plec·trum \ˈplek-trəm\ *n, pl* **plec·tra** \-trə\ *or* **plectrums** [L, fr. Gk *plēktron,* fr. *plēssein* to strike — more at PLAINT] **:** ⁵PICK 2c

¹pledge \ˈplej\ *n* [ME, security, fr. MF *plege,* fr. LL *plebium,* fr. (assumed) LL *plebere* to pledge] **1 a :** a bailment of a chattel as security for a debt or other obligation without involving transfer of title **b :** the chattel so delivered **c :** the contract incidental to such a bailment **2 a :** the state of being held as a security or guaranty **b :** something given as security for the performance of an act **3 :** a token, sign, or earnest of something else **4 :** a gage of battle **5 :** TOAST 3 **6 a :** a binding promise or agreement to do or forbear **b (1) :** a promise to join a fraternity or secret society **(2) :** a person who has so promised

²pledge *vt* **pledged; pledg·ing 1 :** to make a pledge of; *specif* **:** to deposit in pledge or pawn **2 :** to drink the health of : TOAST **3 :** to bind by a pledge : PLIGHT **4 :** to promise the performance of by a pledge : UNDERTAKE — **pledg·er** \ˈplej-ər\ *n* — **pled·gor** \ˈplej-ər, ple-ˈjȯ(ə)r\ *n*

pledg·ee \ple-ˈjē\ *n* **:** one to whom a pledge is given

pled·get \ˈplej-ət\ *n* [origin unknown] **:** a compress or pad used esp. to apply medication to or absorb discharges from a wound or ulcer

-ple·gia \ˈplē-j(ē-)ə\ *n comb form* [NL, fr. Gk *-plēgia,* fr. *plēssein* to strike — more at PLAINT] **:** paralysis <di*plegia*>

ple·iad \ˈplē-əd, -ˌad, *chiefly Brit* ˈplī-\ *n* [F *Pléiade,* group of 7 16th cent. F poets, fr. MF, group of 7 tragic poets of ancient Alexandria, fr. Gk *Pleiad-, Pleias,* fr. sing. of *Pleiades*] **:** a group of usu. seven illustrious or brilliant persons or things

Pleiad *n* **:** any of the Pleiades

Ple·ia·des \ˈplē-ə-ˌdēz, *chiefly Brit* ˈplī-\ *n pl* [L, fr. Gk] **1 :** the seven daughters of Atlas turned according to Greek mythology into a group of stars **2 :** a conspicuous loose cluster of stars in the constellation Taurus that includes six stars visible to the average eye

plein air \plā-ˈna(ə)r, ple-, -ˈne(ə)r\ *adj* [F, open air] **1 :** of or relating to painting in outdoor daylight **2 :** of or relating to a branch of impressionism that attempts to represent outdoor light and air — **plein-air·ism** \-ˌiz-əm\ *n* — **plein-air·ist** \-əst\ *n*

pleio- *or* **pleo-** *or* **plio-** *comb form* [Gk *pleiōn, pleōn* — more at PLUS] **:** more <*pleio*tropic> <*pleo*morphism> <*Plio*cene>

pleio·taxy \ˈplī-ə-ˌtak-sē\ *n* [ISV] **:** development of more than the normal number of parts (as bracts in a flower or inflorescence)

pleio·tro·pic \ˌplī-ə-ˈtrōp-ik, -ˈträp-\ *adj* **:** producing more than one genic effect; *specif* **:** having multiple phenotypic expressions <a ~ gene> — **pleio·tro·pi·cal·ly** \-i-k(ə-)lē\ *adv* — **plei·ot·ro·py** \plī-ˈä-trə-pē\ *n*

Pleis·to·cene \ˈplī-stə-ˌsēn\ *adj* [Gk *pleistos* most + ISV *-cene;* akin to Gk *pleiōn* more] **:** of, relating to, or being the earlier epoch of the Quaternary or the corresponding system of rocks — **Pleistocene** *n*

ple·na·ry \ˈplē-nə-rē, ˈplen-ə-\ *adj* [LL *plenarius,* fr. L *plenus* full — more at FULL] **1 :** complete in every respect : ABSOLUTE, UNQUALIFIED <~ power> **2 :** fully attended or constituted by all entitled to be present <a ~ session> ***syn*** see FULL ***ant*** limited

plenary indulgence *n* **:** a remission of the entire temporal punishment for sin

ple·nip·o·tent \pli-ˈnip-ət-ənt\ *adj* [LL *plenipotent-, plenipotens,* fr. L *plenus* + *potent-, potens* powerful — more at POTENT] **:** PLENIPOTENTIARY

¹pleni·po·ten·tia·ry \ˌplen-ə-pə-ˈtench-(ə-)rē, -ˈten-chē-ˌer-ē\ *adj* [ML *plenipotentiarius,* adj. & n., fr. (assumed) *plenipotentia,* investment with full power, fr. LL *plenipotent-, plenipotens*] **1 :** invested with full power **2 :** of or relating to a plenipotentiary

²plenipotentiary *n, pl* **-ries :** a person and esp. a diplomatic agent invested with full power to transact business

plen·ish \ˈplen-ish\ *vt* [ME (Sc) *plenyssen* to fill up, fr. MF *pleniss-,* stem of *plenir,* fr. *plen* full, fr. L *plenus*] *chiefly Brit* **:** EQUIP

plen·i·tude \ˈplen-ə-ˌt(y)üd\ *n* [ME *plenitude,* fr. MF or L; MF, fr. L *plenitudo,* fr. *plenus* full] **1 :** the quality or state of being full : COMPLETENESS **2 :** a great sufficiency : ABUNDANCE

plen·i·tu·di·nous \ˌplen-ə-ˈt(y)üd-nəs, -ᵊn-əs\ *adj* [L *plenitudin-, plenitudo* plenitude] **1 :** characterized by plenitude **2 :** PORTLY

plen·te·ous \ˈplent-ē-əs\ *adj* [ME *plentevous, plenteous,* fr. OF *plentiveus,* fr. *plentif* abundant, fr. *plenté* plenty] **1 :** FRUITFUL, PRODUCTIVE <a ~ harvest —J. G. Frazer> — usu. used with *in* or *of* <the seasons had been ~ in corn —George Eliot> **2 :** constituting or existing in plenty <~ grace with thee is found —Charles Wesley> — **plen·te·ous·ly** *adv* — **plen·te·ous·ness** *n*

plen·ti·ful \ˈplent-i-fəl\ *adj* **1 :** containing or yielding plenty <a ~ land> **2 :** characterized by, constituting, or existing in plenty — **plen·ti·ful·ly** \-f(ə-)lē\ *adv* — **plen·ti·ful·ness** *n*
syn PLENTIFUL, AMPLE, ABUNDANT, COPIOUS *shared meaning element* **:** more than sufficient without being excessive ***ant*** scanty, scant

plen·ti·tude \ˈplen(t)-ə-ˌt(y)üd\ *n* [by alter. (influenced by *plenty*)] **:** PLENITUDE

¹plen·ty \ˈplent-ē\ *n* [ME *plente,* fr. OF *plenté,* fr. LL *plenitat-, plenitas,* fr. L, fullness, fr. *plenus* full — more at FULL] **1 a :** a full or more than adequate amount or supply <had ~ of time to finish the job> **b :** a large number or amount <he's in ~ of trouble> **2 :** the quality or state of being copious : PLENTIFULNESS

²plenty *adj* **1 :** plentiful in amount, number, or supply <if reasons were as ~ as blackberries —Shak.> **2 :** AMPLE <~ work to be done —*Time*>

³plenty *adv* **:** to a considerable or extreme degree : ABUNDANTLY <the nights were ~ cold —F. B. Gipson>

ple·num \ˈplen-əm, ˈplēn-əm\ *n, pl* **-nums** *or* **-na** \-ə\ [NL, fr. L, neut. of *plenus*] **1 a :** a space or all space every part of which is full of matter **b (1) :** a condition in which the pressure of the air in an enclosed space is greater than that of the outside atmosphere **(2) :** an enclosed space in which such a condition exists **2 :** a general assembly of all members esp. of a legislative body **3 :** the quality or state of being full

ple·och·ro·ism \plē-ˈäk-rə-ˌwiz-əm\ *n* [ISV *pleochroic* (fr. *pleio-* + Gk *chrōs* skin, color) + *-ism* — more at GRIT] **:** the property of a crystal of showing different colors when viewed by light that vibrates parallel to different axes — **pleo·chro·ic** \ˌplē-ə-ˈkrō-ik\ *adj*

pleo·mor·phism \ˌplē-ə-ˈmȯr-ˌfiz-əm\ *n* [ISV] **1 :** the occurrence of more than one distinct form in the life cycle of a plant **2 :** the quality or state of having or assuming various forms : POLYMORPHISM — **pleo·mor·phic** \-fik\ *adj*

ple·o·nasm \ˈplē-ə-ˌnaz-əm\ *n* [LL *pleonasmus,* fr. Gk *pleonasmos,* fr. *pleonazein* to be excessive, fr. *pleiōn, pleōn* more — more at PLUS] **1 :** the use of more words than those necessary to denote mere sense (as in *the man he said*) : REDUNDANCY **2 :** an instance or example of pleonasm — **ple·o·nas·tic** \ˌplē-ə-ˈnas-tik\ *adj* — **ple·o·nas·ti·cal·ly** \-ti-k(ə-)lē\ *adv*

ple·oph·a·gous \plē-ˈäf-ə-gəs\ *adj* **1 :** eating a variety of foods **2** *of a parasite* **:** not restricted to a single kind of host

pleo·pod \ˈplē-ə-ˌpäd\ *n* [Gk *plein* to sail + E *-o-* + *-pod;* fr. its use in swimming — more at FLOW] **:** an abdominal limb of a crustacean

ple·ro·cer·coid \ˌplir-ō-ˈsər-ˌkȯid\ *n* [Gk *plērēs* full + *kerkos* tail — more at FULL] **:** the solid elongate infective larva of some tapeworms usu. occurring in the muscles of fishes

ple·sio·saur \ˈplē-sē-ə-ˌsȯ(ə)r, -zē-\ *n* [deriv. of Gk *plēsios* close (fr. *pelas* near) + *sauros* lizard — more at FELT] **:** any of a suborder (Plesiosauria) of Mesozoic marine reptiles with dorsoventrally flattened bodies and limbs modified into paddles

pleth·o·ra \ˈpleth-ə-rə\ *n* [ML, fr. Gk *plēthōra,* lit., fullness, fr. *plēthein* to be full — more at FULL] **1 :** a bodily condition characterized by an excess of blood and marked by turgescence and a florid complexion **2 :** SUPERFLUITY, EXCESS <a ~ of regulations> — **ple·tho·ric** \plə-ˈthȯr-ik, ple-, -ˈthär-; ˈpleth-ə-rik\ *adj*

ple·thys·mo·gram \ple-ˈthiz-mə-ˌgram, plə-\ *n* **:** a tracing made by a plethysmograph

ple·thys·mo·graph \-ˌgraf\ *n* [ISV, fr. Gk *plēthysmos* increase, fr. *plēthynein* to increase, fr. *plēthys* mass, quantity, fr. *plēthein* to be full] **:** an instrument for determining and registering variations in the size of an organ or limb and in the amount of blood present or passing through it — **ple·thys·mo·graph·ic** \-ˌthiz-mə-ˈgraf-ik\ *adj* — **ple·thys·mo·graph·i·cal·ly** \-i-k(ə-)lē\ *adv* — **pleth·ys·mog·ra·phy** \ˌpleth-iz-ˈmäg-rə-fē\ *n*

pleur- *or* **pleuro-** *comb form* [NL, fr. *pleura*] **1 a :** pleura <*pleuro*pneumonia> **b :** pleura and <*pleuro*peritoneum> **2** [Gk, fr. *pleura*] **:** side **:** lateral <*pleuro*dont>

pleu·ra \ˈplu̇r-ə\ *n, pl* **pleu·rae** \ˈplu̇(ə)r-ˌē, -ˌī\ *or* **pleuras** [Gk, rib, side] **:** the delicate serous membrane that lines each half of the thorax of mammals and is folded back over the surface of the lung of the same side — **pleu·ral** \ˈplu̇r-əl\ *adj*

pleu·ri·sy \ˈplu̇r-ə-sē\ *n* [ME *pluresie,* fr. MF *pleuresie,* fr. LL *pleurisis,* alter. of L *pleuritis,* fr. Gk, fr. *pleura* side] **:** inflammation of the pleura usu. with fever, painful and difficult respiration, cough, and exudation into the pleural cavity — **pleu·rit·ic** \plü-ˈrit-ik\ *adj*

¹pleur·odont \ˈplu̇r-ə-ˌdänt\ *n* **:** a lizard having pleurodont teeth

²pleurodont *adj* [Gk *pleura* side + ISV *-odont*] **1 :** consolidated with the inner surface of the alveolar ridge without sockets <~ teeth> **2 :** having pleurodont teeth

pleu·ro·per·i·to·ne·um \ˈplu̇r-ō-ˌper-ət-ᵊn-ˈē-əm\ *n* [NL] **:** the membrane lining the body cavity and covering the surface of the enclosed viscera of vertebrates that have no diaphragm

pleu·ro·pneu·mo·nia \-n(y)u̇-ˈmō-nyə\ *n* [NL] **1 :** combined inflammation of the pleura and lungs **2 :** an acute febrile and often fatal respiratory disorder of cattle and related animals caused by microorganisms (family Mycoplasmataceae) of uncertain affinities

pleuropneumonia–like organism *n* **:** MYCOPLASMA

pleus·ton \ˈplü-stən, -ˌstän\ *n* [(assumed) Gk *pleustos* (verbal of *plein* to sail, float) + ISV *-on* (as in *plankton*)] **:** macroscopic floating organisms forming mats on or near the surface of a body of fresh water — **pleus·ton·ic** \plü-ˈstän-ik\ *adj*

plexi·form \ˈplek-sə-ˌfȯrm\ *adj* [NL *plexus* + E *-iform*] **:** of, relating to, or having the form or characteristics of a plexus

Plexi·glas \-si-ˌglas\ *trademark* — used for acrylic plastic sheets and molding powders

plex·us \ˈplek-səs\ *n* [NL, fr. L, braid, network, fr. *plexus,* pp. of *plectere* to braid — more at PLY] **1 :** a network of anastomosing or interlacing blood vessels or nerves **2 :** an interwoven combination of parts or elements in a structure or system

plf *abbr* plaintiff

pli·able \ˈplī-ə-bəl\ *adj* [ME, fr. MF, fr. *plier* to bend, fold — more at PLY] **1 a :** supple enough to bend freely or repeatedly without breaking **b :** yielding readily to others **:** COMPLAISANT **2 :** adjustable to varying conditions **:** ADAPTABLE ***syn*** see PLASTIC ***ant*** obstinate — **pli·abil·i·ty** \ˌplī-ə-ˈbil-ət-ē\ *n* — **pli·able·ness** \ˈplī-ə-bəl-nəs\ *n* — **pli·ably** \-blē\ *adv*

pli·an·cy \ˈplī-ən-sē\ *n* **:** the quality or state of being pliant

pli·ant \ˈplī-ənt\ *adj* **1 :** PLIABLE 1a **2 :** easily influenced **:** YIELDING **3 :** suitable for varied uses ***syn*** see PLASTIC — **pli·ant·ly** *adv* — **pli·ant·ness** *n*

pli·ca \ˈplī-kə\ *n, pl* **pli·cae** \-ˌkē, -ˌsē\ [ML, fr. L *plicare* to fold — more at PLY] **:** a fold or folded part; *esp* **:** a groove or fold of skin — **pli·cal** \-kəl\ *adj*

pli·cate \ˈplī-ˌkāt\ *adj* [L *plicatus,* pp. of *plicare*] **1 :** folded lengthwise like a fan <a ~ leaf> **2 :** having the surface thrown up into or marked with parallel ridges <~ wing cases> — **pli·cate·ly** *adv* — **pli·cate·ness** *n*

pli·ca·tion \plī-ˈkā-shən\ *n* **1 :** the act or process of folding **:** the state of being folded **2 :** FOLD

plié \plē-ˈā\ *n* [F, fr. pp. of *plier* to bend] **:** a bending of the knees by a ballet dancer with the back held straight

pli·ers \ˈplī(-ə)rz\ *n pl but sing or pl in constr* **:** a small pincers with long jaws for holding small objects or for bending and cutting wire

¹plight \ˈplīt\ *vt* [ME *plighten,* fr. OE *plihtan* to endanger, fr. *pliht* danger; akin to OHG *pflegan* to take care of] **:** to put or give in pledge **:** ENGAGE <~ one's troth> — **plight·er** *n*

²plight *n* **:** a solemnly given pledge **:** ENGAGEMENT

³plight *n* [ME *plit,* fr. AF, fr. (assumed) VL *plictus* fold — more at PLAIT] **:** CONDITION, STATE; *esp* **:** bad state or condition

plim·soll \ˈplim(p)-səl, ˈplim-ˌsōl\ *n* [prob. fr. the supposed resemblance of the upper edge of the mudguard to the Plimsoll mark on a ship] *Brit* **:** a shoe with rubber sole, mudguard, and canvas top

Plimsoll mark *n* [Samuel *Plimsoll*] **:** a load line or a set of load-line markings on an oceangoing cargo ship — called also *Plimsoll line*

¹plink \ˈpliŋk\ *vb* [imit.] *vi* **1 :** to make a tinkling sound **2 :** to shoot at random targets ~ *vt* **1 :** to cause to make a tinkling sound **2 :** to shoot at esp. in a casual manner — **plink·er** *n*

²plink *n* **:** a tinkling metallic sound

plinth \ˈplin(t)th\ *n* [L *plinthus,* fr. Gk *plinthos*] **1 a :** the lowest member of a base **:** SUBBASE **b :** a block upon which the moldings of an architrave or trim are stopped at the bottom **2 :** a usu. square block serving as a base; *broadly* **:** any of various bases or lower parts — see BASE illustration **3 :** a course of stones forming a continuous foundation or base course

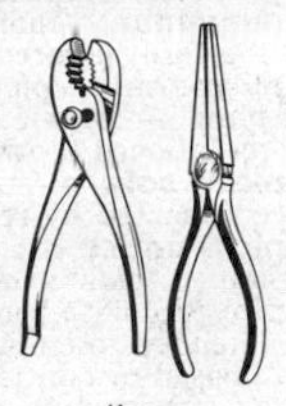

pliers

plio- — see PLEIO-

Plio·cene \ˈplī-ə-ˌsēn\ *adj* **:** of, relating to, or being the latest epoch of the Tertiary or the corresponding system of rocks — **Pliocene** *n*

Plio·film \ˈplī-ə-ˌfilm\ *trademark* — used for a glossy membrane made of rubber hydrochloride and used chiefly for water-resistant and packaging materials

pli·que–à–jour \ˌplē-(ˌ)kä-ˈzhu̇(ə)r\ *n* [F, lit., braid letting in daylight] **:** a style of enameling in which usu. transparent enamels are fused into the openings of a metal filigree to produce an effect suggestive of stained glass

plis·kie *or* **plis·ky** \ˈplis-kē\ *n, pl* **pliskies** [origin unknown] *chiefly Scot* **:** PRACTICAL JOKE, TRICK

plis·sé *or* **plis·se** \pli-ˈsā\ *n* [F *plissé,* fr. pp. of *plisser* to pleat, fr. MF, fr. *pli* fold, fr. *plier* to fold — more at PLY] **1 :** a textile finish of permanently puckered designs formed by treating with a caustic soda solution **2 :** a fabric usu. of cotton, rayon, or nylon with a plissé finish

plod \ˈpläd\ *vb* **plod·ded; plod·ding** [imit.] *vi* **1 a :** to walk heavily or slowly **:** TRUDGE **b :** to proceed slowly or tediously <the movie just ~*s* along> **2 :** to work laboriously and monotonously **:** DRUDGE <*plodding* through stacks of unanswered mail> ~ *vt* **:** to tread slowly or heavily along or over — **plod** *n* — **plod·der** *n* — **plod·ding·ly** \ˈpläd-iŋ-lē\ *adv*

-ploid \ˌplȯid\ *adj comb form* [ISV, fr. *diploid & haploid*] **:** having or being a chromosome number that bears (such) a relationship to or is (so many) times the basic chromosome number of a given group <poly*ploid*>

ploi·dy \ˈplȯid-ē\ *n* [fr. such words as *diploidy, hexaploidy*] **:** degree of repetition of the basic number of chromosomes

PL/1 \(ˌ)pē-ˌel-ˈwən\ *n* [*p*rogramming *l*anguage (version) *1*] **:** a general purpose language for programming a computer

¹plonk \ˈpläŋk, ˈplȯŋk\ *var of* PLUNK

²plonk *n* [short for earlier *plink-plonk,* perh. modif. of F *vin blanc* white wine] *chiefly Brit* **:** cheap or inferior wine

plop \ˈpläp\ *vb* **plopped; plop·ping** [imit.] *vi* **1 :** to fall, drop, or move suddenly with a sound like that of something dropping into water **2 :** to allow the body to drop heavily <*plopped* into a chair> ~ *vt* **:** to set, drop, or throw heavily — **plop** *n*

plo·sion \ˈplō-zhən\ *n* **:** EXPLOSION 2 — **plo·sive** \ˈplō-siv, -ziv\ *adj or n*

¹plot \ˈplät\ *n* [ME, fr. OE] **1 a :** a small area of planted ground <a vegetable ~> **b :** a small piece of land in a cemetery **c :** a measured piece of land **:** LOT **2 :** GROUND PLAN, PLAT **3 :** the plan or main story of a literary work **4 :** a secret plan for accomplishing a usu. evil or unlawful end **:** INTRIGUE **5 :** a graphic representation (as a chart) ***syn*** see PLAN — **plot·less** \-ləs\ *adj* — **plot·less·ness** *n*

²plot *vb* **plot·ted; plot·ting** *vt* **1 a :** to make a plot, map, or plan of **b :** to mark or note on or as if on a map or chart **2 :** to lay out in plots **3 a :** to locate (a point) by means of coordinates **b :** to locate (a curve) by plotted points **c :** to represent (an equation) by means of a curve so constructed **4 :** to plan or contrive esp. secretly **5 :** to invent or devise the plot of (a literary work) ~ *vi* **1 :** to form a plot **:** SCHEME **2 :** to be located by means of coordinates <the data ~ at a single point> — **plot·ter** *n*

Plo·ti·nism \plō-ˈtī-ˌniz-əm, ˈplōt-ᵊn-ˌiz-əm\ *n* **:** the Neoplatonic doctrines of the philosopher Plotinus — **Plo·ti·nist** \-ˈtī-nəst, -ᵊn-əst\ *n*

plot·tage \ˈplät-ij\ *n* **:** the area included in a plot of land

plot·ty \ˈplät-ē\ *adj* **plot·ti·er; -est :** marked by intricacy of plot or intrigue <as long as a modern novel and ever so much more ~ —*Harper's*>

plo·ver \ˈpləv-ər, ˈplō-vər\ *n, pl* **plover** *or* **plovers** [ME, fr. MF, fr. (assumed) VL *pluviarius,* fr. L *pluvia* rain — more at PLUVIAL] **1 :** any of numerous shore-inhabiting birds (family Charadriidae) that differ from the sandpipers in having a short hard-tipped bill and usu. a stouter more compact build **2 :** any of various birds (as a turnstone or sandpiper) related to the plovers

¹plow *or* **plough** \ˈplau̇\ *n* [ME, fr. OE *plōh* hide of land; akin to OHG *pfluog* plow] **1 :** an implement used to cut, lift, and turn over soil esp. in preparing a seedbed **2 :** any of various devices operating like a plow

²plow *or* **plough** *vt* **1 a :** to turn, break up, or work with a plow **b :** to make (as a furrow) with a plow **2 :** to cut into, open, or make furrows or ridges in with or as if with a plow — often used with *up* **3 :** to cleave the surface of or move through (water) <whales ~*ing* the ocean> ~ *vi* **1 a :** to use a plow **b :** to bear or admit of plowing **2 a :** to move in a way resembling that of a plow cutting into or going through the soil <the car ~*ed* into a group of spectators> **b :** to proceed steadily and laboriously **:** PLOD <had to ~ through a summer reading list> — **plow·able** \-ə-bəl\ *adj* — **plow·er** \ˈplau̇(-ə)r\ *n*

plow back *vt* **:** to retain (profits) for reinvestment in a business

plow·boy \ˈplau̇-ˌbȯi\ *n* **1 :** a boy who leads the team drawing a plow **2 :** a country youth

plow·head \-ˌhed\ *n* : the clevis of a plow

plow·man \-mən, -ˌman\ *n* **1** : a man who guides a plow **2** : a farm laborer

plow·share \ˈplau̇-ˌshe(ə)r, -ˌsha(ə)r\ *n* [ME *ploughshare*, fr. *plough* plow + *schare* plowshare — more at SHARE] : the part of a moldboard plow that cuts the furrow

plow sole *n* : a layer of earth at the bottom of the furrow compacted by repeated plowing at the same depth

plow under *vt* : to cause to disappear : BURY, OVERWHELM <let us not . . . *plow under* the family farmer —A. E. Stevenson †1965>

ploy \ˈplȯi\ *n* [prob. fr. *employ*] **1** : ESCAPADE, FROLIC **2** : a tactic intended to embarrass or frustrate an opponent; *also* : something devised or contrived : DEVICE <may have issued his threat merely as a bargaining ~ —*N.Y. Times*>

PLSS *abbr* portable life support system

[1]**pluck** \ˈplək\ *vb* [ME *plucken*, fr. OE *pluccian*; akin to MHG *pflücken* to pluck] *vt* **1** : to pull or pick off or out **2 a** : to remove something (as hairs) from by or as if by plucking <~ one's eyebrows> **b** : ROB, FLEECE **3** : to move or separate forcibly <~*ed* the child from the middle of the street> **4** : to pick, pull, or grasp at; *also* : to play (an instrument) in this manner **5** : to remove (a person) from one situation in life and transfer him to another ~ *vi* : to make a sharp pull or twitch — **pluck·er** *n*

[2]**pluck** *n* **1** : an act or instance of plucking or pulling **2** : the heart, liver, lungs, and windpipe of a slaughtered animal esp. as an item of food **3** : courageous readiness to fight or continue against odds : dogged resolution ***syn*** see FORTITUDE

plucky \ˈplək-ē\ *adj* **pluck·i·er; -est** : marked by courage : SPIRITED — **pluck·i·ly** \ˈplək-ə-lē\ *adv* — **pluck·i·ness** \ˈplək-ē-nəs\ *n*

[1]**plug** \ˈpləg\ *n* [D, fr. MD *plugge*; akin to MHG *pfloc* plug] **1 a** : a piece used to fill a hole : STOPPER **b** : an obtruding or obstructing mass of material resembling a stopper **2** : a flat compressed cake of tobacco **3** : SHOT **4** : a small core or segment removed from a larger object **5** : something inferior; *esp* : an inferior often aged or unsound horse; *also* : a quiet steady cold-blooded horse usu. of light or moderate weight **6 a** : FIREPLUG **b** : SPARK PLUG **7** : an artificial angling lure used primarily for casting and made with one or more sets of gang hooks **8** : any of various devices resembling or functioning like a plug: as **a** : a male fitting for making an electrical connection by insertion in a receptacle or body of electrical equipment to a circuit **b** : a device for connecting electric wires to a jack **9** : a piece of favorable publicity usu. incorporated in general matter

[2]**plug** *vb* **plugged; plug·ging** *vt* **1** : to stop, make tight, or secure by inserting a plug **2** : to hit with a bullet : SHOOT **3** : to advertise or publicize insistently ~ *vi* **1** : to become plugged — usu. used with *up* **2** : to work doggedly and persistently <*plugged* away at his homework> **3** : to fire shots — **plug·ger** *n*

plugged \ˈpləgd\ *adj* **1** : closed by or as if by a plug : OBSTRUCTED **2** *of a coin* : altered by the insertion of a plug of base metal

plug hat *n* : a man's stiff hat (as a bowler or top hat)

plug–in \ˈpləg-ˌin\ *adj* : designed to be connected to an electric circuit by plugging in <a ~ toy> — **plug–in** *n*

plug in \ˈpləg-ˈin, ˌpləg-\ *vi* : to establish an electric circuit by inserting a plug ~ *vt* : to attach or connect to a service outlet

plug–ug·ly \ˈpləg-ˌəg-lē\ *n* : THUG, TOUGH; *esp* : one hired to intimidate

plum \ˈpləm\ *n* [ME, fr. OE *plūme*; akin to OHG *pflūmo* plum tree; both fr. a prehistoric WGmc word borrowed fr. L *prunum* plum, fr. Gk *proumnon*] **1 a** : any of numerous trees and shrubs (genus *Prunus*) with globular to oval smooth-skinned fruits that are drupes with oblong seeds **b** : the edible fruit of a plum **2** : any of various trees with edible fruits resembling plums; *also* : its fruit **3 a** : a raisin when used in desserts (as puddings or cake) **b** : SUGARPLUM **4** : something excellent or superior; *esp* : something given as recompense for service **5** : a variable color averaging a dark reddish purple — **plum·like** \-ˌlīk\ *adj*

plum·age \ˈplü-mij\ *n* [ME, fr. MF, fr. OF, fr. *plume* feather — more at PLUME] : the entire clothing of feathers of a bird — **plum·aged** \-mijd\ *adj*

plu·mate \ˈplü-ˌmāt\ *adj* [NL *plumatus*, fr. L, covered with feathers, fr. *pluma* feather — more at FLEECE] : having a main shaft that bears small filaments <~ antennae of an insect>

[1]**plumb** \ˈpləm\ *n* [ME, fr. (assumed) OF *plomb*, fr. OF *plon* lead, fr. L *plumbum*] **1** : a lead weight attached to a line and used to indicate a vertical direction **2** : any of various weights (as a sinker for a fishing line or a lead for sounding) — **out of plumb** *or* **off plumb** : out of vertical or true

[2]**plumb** *adv* **1** : straight down or up : VERTICALLY **2** : in a direct manner : EXACTLY; *also* : without interval of time : IMMEDIATELY **3** *chiefly dial* : to a complete degree : ABSOLUTELY <'you're ~ crazy', she remarked, with easy candor —*Harper's Weekly*>

[3]**plumb** *vt* **1** : to weight with lead **2 a** : to measure the depth of with a plumb **b** : to examine minutely and critically <~*ing* the book's complexities> **3** : to adjust or test by a plumb line **4** : to seal with lead **5** [back-formation fr. *plumber*] : to supply with or install as plumbing ~ *vi* : to work as a plumber

[4]**plumb** *adj* **1** : exactly vertical or true **2** : DOWNRIGHT, COMPLETE ***syn*** see VERTICAL

plumb- *or* **plumbo-** *comb form* [L *plumb-*, fr. *plumbum*] : lead <*plumbism*>

plum·bag·i·nous \ˌpləm-ˈbaj-ə-nəs\ *adj* : resembling, consisting of, or containing graphite

plum·ba·go \ˌpləm-ˈbā-(ˌ)gō\ *n, pl* **-gos** [L *plumbagin-*, *plumbago* galena, leadwort, fr. *plumbum*] **1** : GRAPHITE **2** [NL, genus name, fr. L] : any of a genus (*Plumbago* of the family Plumbaginaceae, the plumbago family) of woody chiefly tropical plants with alternate leaves and spikes of showy flowers

plumb bob *n* : the metal bob of a plumb line

plum·be·ous \ˈpləm-bē-əs\ *adj* [L *plumbeus*, fr. *plumbum*] : consisting of or resembling lead; *esp* : of a leaden gray color

plumb·er \ˈpləm-ər\ *n* **1** *obs* : a dealer or worker in lead **2** : one who installs, repairs, and maintains piping, fittings, and fixtures involved in the distribution and use of water in a building

plumber's helper *n* : PLUNGER e — called also *plumber's friend*

plumber's snake *n* : a long flexible rod or cable usu. of steel that is used to free clogged pipes

plum·bic \ˈpləm-bik\ *adj* : of, relating to, or containing lead esp. with a valence of four

plum·bif·er·ous \ˌpləm-ˈbif-(ə-)rəs\ *adj* : containing lead

plumb·ing \ˈpləm-iŋ\ *n* **1** : the act of using a plumb **2** : a plumber's occupation or trade **3** : the apparatus (as pipes and fixtures) concerned in the distribution and use of water in a building

plum·bism \ˈpləm-ˌbiz-əm\ *n* : lead poisoning esp. when chronic

plumb line *n* **1** : a line (as of cord) that has at one end a weight (as a plumb bob) and is used esp. to determine verticality **2** : a line directed to the center of gravity of the earth : a vertical line

plum·bous \ˈpləm-bəs\ *adj* : of, relating to, or containing lead esp. with a valence of two

[1]**plume** \ˈplüm\ *n* [ME, fr. MF, fr. L *pluma* small soft feather — more at FLEECE] **1** : a feather of a bird: as **a** : a large conspicuous or showy feather **b** : CONTOUR FEATHER **c** : PLUMAGE **d** : a cluster of distinctive feathers **2 a** : material (as a feather, cluster of feathers, or a tuft of hair) worn as an ornament **b** : a token of honor or prowess : PRIZE **3** : something resembling a feather (as in shape, appearance, or lightness): as **a** : a plumose appendage of a plant **b** : an elongated and usu. open and mobile column or band (as of smoke, exhaust gases, or blowing snow) **c** : a plumate animal structure; *esp* : a full bushy tail

[2]**plume** *vt* **plumed; plum·ing** **1 a** : to provide or deck with feathers **b** : to array showily **2** : to indulge (oneself) in pride with an obvious or vain display of self-satisfaction **3 a** : to preen and arrange the feathers of (itself) — used of a bird **b** : to preen and arrange (feathers) ***syn*** see PRIDE

plumed \ˈplümd\ *adj* : provided with or adorned with or as if with a plume — often used in combination <a white-*plumed* egret>

plume·let \ˈplüm-lət\ *n* : a small tuft or plume

[1]**plum·met** \ˈpləm-ət\ *n* [ME *plomet*, fr. MF *plombet* ball of lead, fr. *plomb* lead, fr. (assumed) OF — more at PLUMB] : PLUMB; *also* : PLUMB LINE

[2]**plummet** *vi* **1** : to fall perpendicularly <the plane ~*ed* to earth> **2** : to drop sharply and abruptly <prices ~*ed*>

plum·my \ˈpləm-ē\ *adj* **plum·mi·er; -est** **1 a** : full of plums <a rich ~ cake> **b** : CHOICE, DESIRABLE <got a ~ role in the movie> **2 a** : having a plum color **b** : rich and mellow often to the point of affectation <a ~ singing voice>

plu·mose \ˈplü-ˌmōs\ *adj* **1** : having feathers or plumes : FEATHERED **2** : PLUMATE, FEATHERY — **plu·mose·ly** *adv*

[1]**plump** \ˈpləmp\ *vb* [ME *plumpen*, of imit. origin] *vi* **1** : to drop, sink, or come in contact suddenly or heavily <~*ed* down in the chair> **2** : to favor someone or something strongly — used with *for* ~ *vt* **1** : to drop, cast, or place suddenly or heavily **2** : to give support and favorable publicity to

[2]**plump** *adv* **1** : with a sudden or heavy drop **2 a** : straight down **b** : straight ahead **3** : without qualification : DIRECTLY

[3]**plump** *n* : a sudden plunge, fall, or blow; *also* : the sound made by a plump

[4]**plump** *n* [ME *plumpe*] *chiefly dial* : GROUP, FLOCK <a ~ of ducks rose at the same time —H. D. Thoreau>

[5]**plump** *adj* [ME, dull, blunt] **1** : having a full rounded usu. pleasing form <a ~ woman> **2** : AMPLE, ABUNDANT

[6]**plump** *vt* : to make plump ~ *vi* : to become plump

plump·en \ˈpləm-pən\ *vb* : [6]PLUMP

[1]**plump·er** \ˈpləm-pər\ *n* [[6]*plump*] : an object carried in the mouth to fill out the cheeks

[2]**plumper** *n* [[1]*plump*] *chiefly Brit* : a vote for only one candidate when two or more are to be elected to the same office

plump·ish \ˈpləm-pish\ *adj* : somewhat plump : moderately stout

[1]**plump·ly** \ˈpləm-plē\ *adv* : in a plump way <a ~ pretty girl>

[2]**plumply** *adv* [[2]*plump*] : in a wholehearted manner and without hesitation or circumlocution : FORTHRIGHTLY

[1]**plump·ness** \ˈpləmp-nəs\ *n* : the quality or state of being plump

[2]**plumpness** *n* : freedom from hesitation or circumlocution : FORTHRIGHTNESS

plum pudding *n* : a rich boiled or steamed pudding containing fruits and spices

plu·mu·late \ˈplü-myə-ˌlāt\ *adj* [L *plumula*, dim. of *pluma*] : finely plumose

plu·mule \ˈplü-(ˌ)myü(ə)l\ *n* [NL *plumula*, fr. L] **1** : the primary bud of a plant embryo usu. situated at the apex of the hypocotyl and consisting of leaves and an epicotyl **2** : a down feather — **plu·mu·lose** \ˈplü-myə-ˌlōs\ *adj*

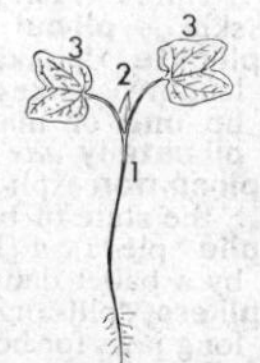

plumule of morning-glory seedling: *1* hypocotyl, *2* plumule, *3* cotyledons

plumy \ˈplü-mē\ *adj* **plum·i·er; -est** **1** : DOWNY **2** : having or resembling plumes

[1]**plun·der** \ˈplən-dər\ *vb* **plun·dered; plun·der·ing** \-d(ə-)riŋ\ [G *plündern*] *vt* **1** : PILLAGE, SACK **2** : to take esp. by force (as in war) : STEAL ~ *vi* : to commit robbery or looting — **plun·der·er** \-dər-ər\ *n*

[2]**plunder** *n* **1** : an act of plundering : PILLAGING **2** : something taken by force, theft, or fraud : LOOT **3** *chiefly dial* : personal or household effects ***syn*** see SPOIL

plun·der·able \ˈplən-d(ə-)rə-bəl\ *adj* **1** : capable of being plundered : subject to plunder **2** : worth plundering

plun·der·age \-d(ə-)rij\ *n* **1** : an act or instance of plundering; *esp* : embezzlement of goods on shipboard **2** : property obtained by plunderage

plun·der·ous \-d(ə-)rəs\ *adj* : given to plundering

[1]**plunge** \ˈplənj\ *vb* **plunged; plung·ing** [ME *plungen*, fr. MF *plonger*, fr. (assumed) VL *plumbicare*, fr. L *plumbum* lead — more at PLUMB] *vt* **1 a** : to cause to penetrate or enter quickly and forcibly into something **b** : to sink (a potted plant) in the ground

or a prepared bed **2 :** to cause to enter a state or course of action usu. suddenly, unexpectedly, or violently ~ *vi* **1 :** to thrust or cast oneself into or as if into water **2 a :** to become pitched or thrown headlong or violently forward and downward; *also* **:** to move oneself in such a manner **b :** to act with reckless haste **:** enter suddenly or unexpectedly **c :** to bet or gamble heavily and recklessly **3 :** to descend or dip suddenly <the road ~*s* along the slope>

syn PLUNGE, DIVE, PITCH *shared meaning element* **:** to throw oneself or throw or thrust something forward and downward into or as if into deep water

²plunge *n* **:** an act or instance of plunging **:** DIVE; *also* **:** SWIM

plung·er \ˈplən-jər\ *n* **:** one that plunges: as **a :** DIVER **b :** a reckless gambler or speculator **c :** the rod carrying the valves in the inner assembly of an automobile tire valve unit **d** (1) **:** a sliding reciprocating piece driven by or against fluid pressure; *esp* **:** PISTON (2) **:** a piece with a motion more or less like that of a ram or piston **e :** a rubber suction cup on a handle used to free plumbing traps and waste outlets of obstructions

plunging fire *n* **:** direct fire from a superior elevation resulting in the projectiles striking the target at a high angle

plunk \ˈpləŋk\ *vb* [imit.] *vt* **1 :** to pluck or hit so as to produce a quick, hollow, metallic, or harsh sound **2 :** to set down suddenly **:** PLUMP ~ *vi* **1 :** to make a plunking sound **2 :** to drop abruptly **:** DIVE **3 :** to come out in favor of someone or something — used with *for* — **plunk** *n* — **plunk·er** *n*

plunk down *vi* **:** to drop abruptly **:** settle into position ~ *vt* **1 a :** to put down usu. firmly or abruptly <*plunked* his money *down* on the counter> **b :** to settle (oneself) into position <*plunked* himself *down* on the bench> **2 :** to pay out

plu·per·fect \(ˈ)plü-ˈpər-fikt\ *adj* [modif. of LL *plusquamperfectus*, lit., more than perfect] **:** past perfect — **pluperfect** *n*

plu·ral \ˈplu̇r-əl\ *adj* [ME, fr. MF & L; MF *plurel*, fr. L *pluralis*, fr. *plur-*, *plus* more — more at PLUS] **1 :** of, relating to, or constituting a class of grammatical forms usu. used to denote more than one or in some languages more than two <*genetics* is ~ in form but takes a singular verb> **2 :** relating to or consisting of or containing more than one or more than one kind or class <a ~ society> — **plural** *n* — **plu·ral·ly** \-ə-lē\ *adv*

plu·ral·ism \ˈplu̇r-ə-ˌliz-əm\ *n* **1 :** the quality or state of being plural **2 :** the holding of two or more offices or positions (as benefices) at the same time **3 a :** a theory that there are more than one or more than two kinds of ultimate reality **b :** a theory that reality is composed of a plurality of entities **4 a :** a state of society in which members of diverse ethnic, racial, religious, or social groups maintain an autonomous participation in and development of their traditional culture or special interest within the confines of a common civilization **b :** a concept, doctrine, or policy advocating this state — **plu·ral·ist** \-ləst\ *adj or n* — **plu·ral·is·tic** \ˌplu̇r-ə-ˈlis-tik\ *adj* — **plu·ral·is·ti·cal·ly** \-ti-k(ə-)lē\ *adv*

plu·ral·i·ty \plu̇-ˈral-ət-ē\ *n, pl* **-ties 1 a :** the state of being plural **b :** the state of being numerous **c :** a large number or quantity **:** MULTITUDE **2:** PLURALISM 2; *also*: a benefice held by pluralism **3 a :** a number greater than another **b :** an excess of votes over those cast for an opposing candidate **c :** a number of votes cast for a candidate in a contest of more than two candidates that is greater than the number cast for any other candidate but not more than half the total votes cast

plu·ral·ize \ˈplu̇r-ə-ˌlīz\ *vt* **-ized; -iz·ing :** to make plural or express in the plural form — **plu·ral·iza·tion** \ˌplu̇r-ə-lə-ˈzā-shən\ *n*

pluri- *comb form* [L, fr. *plur-*, *plus*] **:** having or being more than one **:** MULTI- <*pluri*axial>

plu·ri·ax·i·al \ˌplu̇r-ē-ˈak-sē-əl\ *adj* **:** having more than one axis; *specif* **:** having flowers developed on secondary shoots

plu·rip·o·tent \plü-ˈrip-ət-ənt\ *adj* **:** not fixed as to developmental potentialities **:** having developmental plasticity

¹plus \ˈpləs\ *prep* [L, adv., more, fr. neut. of *plur-*, *plus*, adj., more; akin to Gk *pleiōn* more, L *plenus* full — more at FULL] **:** increased by **:** with the addition of <four ~ five> <the debt ~ interest>

²plus *n, pl* **plus·es** \ˈpləs-əz\ *also* **plus·ses 1 :** PLUS SIGN **2 :** an added quantity **3 :** a positive factor or quality **4 :** SURPLUS

³plus *adj* **1 :** algebraically positive **2 :** having, receiving, or being in addition to what is anticipated **3 a :** falling high in a specified range <a grade of C ~> **b :** greater than that specified **c :** possessing a specified quality to a high degree **4 :** electrically positive **5 :** relating to or being a particular one of the two mating types that are required for successful fertilization in sexual reproduction in some lower plants (as a fungus)

plus fours *n pl* **:** loose sports knickers made four inches longer than ordinary knickers

¹plush \ˈpləsh\ *n* [MF *peluche*] **:** a fabric with an even pile longer and less dense than velvet pile

²plush *adj* **1 :** relating to, resembling, or made of plush **2 :** notably luxurious — **plush·ly** *adv* — **plush·ness** *n*

plushy \ˈpləsh-ē\ *adj* **plush·i·er; -est 1 :** having the texture of or covered with plush **2 :** LUXURIOUS, SHOWY — **plush·i·ness** *n*

plus·sage \ˈpləs-ij\ *n* **:** amount over and above another

plus sign *n* **:** a sign + denoting addition or a positive quantity

Plu·to \ˈplüt-(ˌ)ō\ *n* [L *Pluton-*, *Pluto*, fr. Gk *Ploutōn*] **1 :** the Greek god of the underworld — compare DIS **2** [NL] **:** the planet farthest from the sun — see PLANET table

plu·toc·ra·cy \plü-ˈtäk-rə-sē\ *n, pl* **-cies** [Gk *ploutokratia*, fr. *ploutos* wealth] **1 :** government by the wealthy **2 :** a controlling class of rich men — **plu·to·crat** \ˈplüt-ə-ˌkrat\ *n* — **plu·to·crat·ic** \ˌplüt-ə-ˈkrat-ik\ *adj* — **plu·to·crat·i·cal·ly** \-i-k(ə-)lē\ *adv*

plu·ton \ˈplü-ˌtän\ *n* [prob. back-formation fr. *plutonic*] **:** a typically large body of intrusive igneous rock

plu·to·ni·an \plü-ˈtō-nē-ən\ *adj, often cap* **:** of, relating to, or characteristic of Pluto or the lower world **:** INFERNAL

plu·ton·ic \plü-ˈtän-ik\ *adj* [L *Pluton-*, *Pluto*] **1 :** formed by solidification of a molten magma deep within the earth and crystalline throughout <~ rock> **2** *often cap* **:** PLUTONIAN

plu·to·ni·um \plü-ˈtō-nē-əm\ *n* [NL, fr. *Pluton-*, *Pluto*, the planet Pluto] **:** a radioactive metallic element similar chemically to uranium that is formed as the isotope 239 by decay of neptunium and found in minute quantities in pitchblende, that undergoes slow disintegration with the emission of a helium nucleus to form uranium 235, and that is fissionable with slow neutrons to yield atomic energy — see ELEMENT table

¹plu·vi·al \ˈplü-vē-əl\ *adj* [L *pluvialis*, fr. *pluvia* rain, fr. fem. of *pluvius* rainy, fr. *pluere* to rain — more at FLOW] **1 a :** of or relating to rain **b :** characterized by abundant rain **2** *of a geologic change* **:** resulting from the action of rain

²pluvial *n* **:** a prolonged period of wet climate <the ~*s* of the early Pleistocene>

¹ply \ˈplī\ *vt* **plied; ply·ing** [ME *plien* to fold, fr. MF *plier*, fr. L *plicare*; akin to OHG *flehtan* to braid, L *plectere*, Gk *plekein*] **:** to twist together <~ two single yarns>

²ply *n, pl* **plies 1 a :** one of the strands in a yarn **b :** one of several layers (as of cloth) usu. sewn or laminated together **c :** one of the veneer sheets forming plywood **d :** a layer of a paper or paperboard **2 :** INCLINATION, BIAS

³ply *vb* **plied; ply·ing** [ME *plien*, short for *applien* to apply] *vt* **1 a :** to use or wield diligently <busily ~*ing* his pen> **b :** to practice or perform diligently <~*ing* his trade> **2 :** to keep furnishing or supplying something to <*plied* her with liquor> **3 :** to make a practice of rowing or sailing over or on <the boat *plies* the river> ~ *vi* **1 :** to apply oneself steadily **2 :** to go or travel regularly <a steamer ~*ing* between opposite shores of the lake>

Plym·outh Rock \ˌplim-əth-\ *n* [fr. *Plymouth Rock*, on which the Pilgrims are supposed to have landed in 1620] **:** any of an American breed of medium-sized single-combed dual-purpose domestic fowls

ply·wood \ˈplī-ˌwu̇d\ *n* **:** a structural material consisting of sheets of wood glued or cemented together with the grains of adjacent layers arranged at right angles or at a wide angle

pm *abbr* **1** phase modulation **2** premium

Pm *symbol* promethium

PM *abbr* **1** paymaster **2** permanent magnet **3** police magistrate **4** postmaster **5** post meridiem **6** postmortem **7** prime minister **8** provost marshal

PMH *abbr* production per man-hour

pmk *abbr* postmark

PMLA *abbr* Publications of the Modern Language Association of America

pmt *abbr* payment

PN *abbr* promissory note

-pnea *or* **-pnoea** \(p)-nē-ə\ *n comb form* [NL, fr. Gk *-pnoia*, fr. *pnoia*, fr. *pnein* to breathe] **:** breath **:** breathing <hyper*pnea*> <a*pnoea*>

pneum- *or* **pneumo-** *comb form* [NL, partly fr. Gk *pneum-*, (fr. *pneuma*), partly fr. Gk *pneumōn* lung] **1 :** air **:** gas <*pneumo*thorax> **2 :** lung <*pneum*ectomy> **:** pulmonary and <*pneumo*gastric> **3 :** respiration <*pneumo*graph> **4 :** pneumonia <*pneumo*coccus>

pneu·ma \ˈn(y)ü-mə\ *n* [Gk] **:** SOUL, SPIRIT

pneumat- *or* **pneumato-** *comb form* [Gk, fr. *pneumat-*, *pneuma*] **1 :** air **:** vapor **:** gas <*pneumat*ics> **2 :** respiration <*pneumato*meter>

pneu·mat·ic \n(y)u̇-ˈmat-ik\ *adj* [L *pneumaticus*, fr. Gk *pneumatikos*, fr. *pneumat-*, *pneuma* air, breath, spirit, fr. *pnein* to breathe — more at SNEEZE] **1 :** of, relating to, or using gas (as air or wind): **a :** moved or worked by air pressure **b** (1) **:** adapted for holding or inflated with compressed air (2) **:** having air-filled cavities **2 :** of or relating to the pneuma **:** SPIRITUAL — **pneu·mat·i·cal·ly** \-i-k(ə-)lē\ *adv*

pneu·ma·tic·i·ty \ˌn(y)ü-mə-ˈtis-ət-ē\ *n* **:** a condition marked by the presence of air cavities <~ of bird bones>

pneu·mat·ics \n(y)u̇-ˈmat-iks\ *n pl but sing in constr* **:** a branch of mechanics that deals with the mechanical properties of gases

pneu·ma·tol·o·gy \ˌn(y)ü-mə-ˈtäl-ə-jē\ *n* [NL *pneumatologia*, fr. Gk *pneumat-*, *pneuma* + NL *-logia* -logy] **:** the study of spiritual beings or phenomena

pneu·ma·tol·y·sis \-ˈtäl-ə-səs\ *n* [NL] **:** the process by which pneumatolytic minerals are formed

pneu·ma·to·lyt·ic \ˌn(y)ü-mət-ᵊl-ˈit-ik, (ˌ)n(y)ü-ˌmat-ᵊl-\ *adj* [ISV] **:** formed or forming by hot vapors or superheated liquids under pressure — used esp. of minerals and ores

pneu·ma·tom·e·ter \ˌn(y)ü-mə-ˈtäm-ət-ər\ *n* **1 :** an instrument for measuring the amount of force exerted by the lungs in respiration **2 :** SPIROMETER

pneu·mato·phore \n(y)u̇ˈmat-ə-ˌfō(ə)r, -ˌfȯ(ə)r\ *n* [ISV] **1 :** a muscular gas-containing sac that serves as a float on a siphonophore colony **2 :** a root often functioning as a respiratory organ in a marsh plant — **pneu·mato·phor·ic** \n(y)u̇-ˌmat-ə-ˈfȯr-ik, -ˈfär-\ *adj*

pneu·mec·to·my \n(y)u̇-ˈmek-tə-mē\ *n, pl* **-mies** [ISV] **:** the surgical removal of lung tissue

pneu·mo·ba·cil·lus \ˌn(y)ü-mō-bə-ˈsil-əs\ *n, pl* **-cil·li** \-ˌī *also* -ē\ [NL] **:** a bacterium (*Klebsiella pneumoniae*) associated with inflammations (as pneumonia) of the respiratory tract

pneu·mo·coc·cus \ˌn(y)ü-mə-ˈkäk-əs\ *n, pl* **-coc·ci** \-ˈkäk-(s)ī, -ˈkäk-(ˌ)(s)ē\ [NL] **:** a bacterium (*Diplococcus pneumoniae*) that causes an acute pneumonia involving one or more lobes of the lung — **pneu·mo·coc·cal** \-ˈkäk-əl\ *also* **pneu·mo·coc·cic** \-ˈkäk-(ˌ)sik\ *adj*

pneu·mo·co·ni·o·sis \ˈn(y)ü-mō-ˌkō-nē-ˈō-səs\ *n, pl* **-o·ses** \-ˌsēz\ [NL, fr. *pneum-* + Gk *konis* dust — more at INCINERATE] **:** a disease of the lungs caused by the habitual inhalation of irritant mineral or metallic particles — compare BLACK LUNG, SILICOSIS

pneu·mo·gas·tric \ˌn(y)ü-mə-ˈgas-trik\ *adj* **1 :** of or relating to the lungs and the stomach **2 :** VAGAL

pneu·mo·graph \ˈn(y)ü-mə-ˌgraf\ *n* [ISV] **:** an instrument for recording the thoracic movements or volume change during respiration

pneu·mo·nec·to·my \ˌn(y)ü-mə-ˈnek-tə-mē\ *n, pl* **-mies** [Gk *pneumōn* + ISV *-ectomy*] **:** excision of an entire lung or of one or more lobes of a lung

pneu·mo·nia \n(y)u̇-ˈmō-nyə\ *n* [NL, fr. Gk, fr. *pneumōn* lung, alter. of *pleumōn* — more at PULMONARY] **:** a disease of the lungs characterized by inflammation and consolidation followed by resolution and caused by infection or irritants

pneu·mon·ic \n(y)u̇-ˈmän-ik\ *adj* [NL *pneumonicus,* fr. Gk *pneumonikos,* fr. *pneumōn*] **1 :** of or relating to the lungs **:** PULMONIC **2 :** of, relating to, or affected with pneumonia

pneu·mo·no·ul·tra·mi·cro·scop·ic·sil·i·co·vol·ca·no·co·ni·o·sis \ˈn(y)ü-mə-(ˌ)nō-ˌəl-trə-ˌmī-krə-ˈskäp-ik-ˈsil-i-(ˌ)kō-(ˌ)väl-ˈkā-nō-ˌkō-nē-ˈō-səs\ *n*[NL, fr. Gk *pneumōn* + ISV *ultramicroscopic* + NL *silicon* + ISV *volcano* + Gk *konis* dust] **:** a pneumoconiosis caused by the inhalation of very fine silicate or quartz dust

pneu·mo·tho·rax \ˌn(y)ü-mə-ˈthō(ə)r-ˌaks, -ˈthȯ(ə)r-\ *n* [NL] **:** a state in which air or other gas is present in the pleural cavity and which occurs spontaneously as a result of disease or injury of lung tissue or puncture of the chest wall or is induced as a therapeutic measure to collapse the lung

pneu·mo·tro·pic \ˌn(y)ü-mə-ˈtrōp-ik, -ˈträp-\ *adj* **:** turning, directed toward, or having an affinity for lung tissues — used esp. of infective agents — **pneu·mot·ro·pism** \n(y)u̇-ˈmä-trə-ˌpiz-əm\ *n*

PNR *abbr* point of no return

pnxt *abbr* [L *pinxit*] he painted it

Po *symbol* polonium

PO *abbr* **1** petty officer **2** postal order **3** post office **4** purchase order

[1]**poach** \ˈpōch\ *vt* [ME *pochen,* fr. MF *pocher,* fr. OF *pochier,* lit., to put into a bag, fr. *poche* bag, pocket, of Gmc origin; akin to OE *pocca* bag — more at POKE] **:** to cook in simmering liquid

[2]**poach** *vb* [MF *pocher,* of Gmc origin; akin to ME *poken* to poke] *vt* **1 :** to trample or cut up (as sod) with or as if with hoofs **2 a :** to trespass on <what happens to a poet when he ~*es* upon a novelist's preserves —Virginia Woolf> **b :** to take (game or fish) by illegal methods ~ *vi* **1 a :** to sink into mud or mire while walking **b :** to become soft or muddy and full of holes when trampled on **2 :** to trespass for the purpose of stealing game; *also* **:** to take game or fish illegally

[1]**poach·er** \ˈpō-chər\ *n* [[2]*poach*] **1 :** one that trespasses or steals **2 :** one who kills or takes game or fish illegally

[2]**poacher** *n* [[1]*poach*] **1 :** a covered pan containing a plate with depressions or shallow cups in each of which an egg can be cooked over steam rising from boiling water in the bottom of the pan **2 :** a shallow baking dish in which food (as fish) can be poached

po' boy \ˈpō-ˌbȯi\ *var of* POOR BOY

POC *abbr* port of call

po·chard \ˈpō-chərd\ *n* [origin unknown] **:** any of numerous rather heavy-bodied diving ducks (esp. genus *Aythya*) with a large head and with feet and legs placed far back under the body

[1]**pock** \ˈpäk\ *n* [ME *pokke,* fr. OE *pocc;* akin to MLG & MD *pocke* pock, L *bucca* cheek, mouth] **:** a pustule in an eruptive disease (as smallpox); *also* **:** a spot suggesting such a pustule

[2]**pock** *vt* **:** to mark with or as if with pocks **:** PIT

[1]**pock·et** \ˈpäk-ət\ *n* [ME *poket,* fr. ONF *pokete,* dim. of *poke* bag, of Gmc origin; akin to OE *pocca* bag] **1 a :** a small bag carried by a person **:** PURSE **b :** a small bag that is sewed or inserted in a garment so that it is open at the top or side <coat ~> **2 :** supply of money **:** MEANS **3 :** RECEPTACLE, CONTAINER: as **a :** an opening at the corner or side of a billiard table **b :** a superficial pouch in some animals **4 :** a small isolated area or group <~*s* of unemployment>: **a (1) :** a cavity containing a deposit (as of gold or water) **(2) :** a small body of ore **b :** AIR HOLE **5 :** a place for a spar made by sewing a strip of canvas on a sail **6 a :** BLIND ALLEY **b :** the position of a contestant in a race hemmed in by others **c :** an area formed by blockers from which a football quarterback attempts to pass **7 :** the concave area at the base of the finger sections of a baseball glove or mitt in which the ball is normally caught — **pock·et·ful** \-ˌfu̇l\ *n* — **in one's pocket :** in one's control or possession — **in pocket 1 :** provided with funds **2 :** in the position of having made a profit — **out of pocket 1 :** low on money or funds **2 :** having suffered a loss

[2]**pocket** *vt* **1 a :** to put or enclose in or as if in one's pocket <~*ed* his change> **b :** to appropriate to one's own use **:** STEAL <~*ed* the money he had collected for charity> **c :** to refuse assent to (a bill) by a pocket veto **2 :** to put up with **:** ACCEPT **3 :** to set aside **:** SUPPRESS <~*ed* his pride> **4 a :** to hem in **b :** to drive (a ball) into a pocket of a pool table **5 :** to cover or supply with pockets

[3]**pocket** *adj* **1 a :** small enough to be carried in the pocket **b :** SMALL, MINIATURE <a ~ submarine> **2 a :** of or relating to money **b :** carried in or paid from one's own pocket

pocket battleship *n* **:** a small battleship built so as to come within treaty limitations of tonnage and armament

pocket billiards *n pl but usu sing in constr* **:** POOL 2b

pock·et·book \ˈpäk-ət-ˌbu̇k\ *n* **1** *usu* **pocket book :** a small esp. paperback book that can be carried in the pocket **2 a (1) :** a pocket-size container for money and personal papers **:** WALLET **(2) :** PURSE **b :** HANDBAG 2 **3 a :** financial resources **:** INCOME **b :** economic interests

pocket borough *n* **:** an English constituency controlled before parliamentary reform by a single person or family

pocket edition *n* **1 :** POCKETBOOK 1 **2 :** a miniature form of something

pocket gopher *n* **:** GOPHER 2a

pocket–handkerchief *n* **:** a handkerchief carried in the pocket

pock·et·knife \ˈpäk-ət-ˌnīf\ *n* **:** a knife that has one or more blades that fold into the handle and that can be carried in the pocket

pocket money *n* **:** money for small personal expenses

pocket mouse *n* **:** any of various nocturnal burrowing rodents (family Heteromyidae) that resemble mice, live in arid parts of western No. America, and have long hind legs and tail and fur-lined cheek pouches

pocket rat *n* **:** any of various rodents (as a pocket gopher) with cheek pouches

pock·et–size \ˈpäk-ət-ˌsīz\ *or* **pock·et–sized** \-ˌsīzd\ *adj* **1 :** of a size convenient for carrying in the pocket **2 :** SMALL <a ~ country>

pocket veto *n* **:** an indirect veto of a legislative bill by an executive through retention of the bill unsigned until after adjournment of the legislature — **pocket veto** *vt*

[1]**pock·mark** \ˈpäk-ˌmärk\ *n* **:** a mark, pit, or depressed scar caused by smallpox

[2]**pockmark** *vt* **:** to cover with or as if with pockmarks **:** PIT

pocky \ˈpäk-ē\ *adj* **1 a :** covered with pocks **b :** of, relating to, or infected with syphilis **2 :** relating to or being a pock or the pox

po·co \ˌpō-(ˌ)kō, ˌpȯ-\ *adv* [It, little, fr. L *paucus* — more at FEW] **:** to a slight degree **:** SOMEWHAT — used to qualify a direction in music <~ allegro>

po·co a po·co \ˌpō-kō-(ˌ)ä-ˈpō-(ˌ)kō, ˌpȯ-kō-(ˌ)ä-ˈpȯ-\ *adv* [It] **:** little by little **:** GRADUALLY — used as a direction in music

po·co·cu·ran·te \ˌpō-kō-k(y)u̇-ˈrant-ē\ *adj* [It *poco curante* caring little] **:** INDIFFERENT, NONCHALANT — **po·co·cu·ran·tism** \-ˈran-ˌtiz-əm\ *n*

po·co·sin \pə-ˈkōs-ᵊn\ *n* [Delaware *pâkwesen*] **:** an upland swamp of the coastal plain of the southeastern U.S.

[1]**pod** \ˈpäd\ *n* [origin unknown] **1 :** a bit socket in a brace **2 :** a straight groove or channel in the barrel of an auger

[2]**pod** *n* [prob. alter. of *cod* bag — more at CODPIECE] **1 :** a dry dehiscent seed vessel or fruit that is composed of one or more carpels; *esp* **:** LEGUME **2 a :** an anatomical pouch **b :** a grasshopper egg case **3 :** a tapered and roughly cylindrical body of ore or mineral **4 :** a streamlined compartment under the wings or fuselage of an aircraft used as a container (as for fuel); *broadly* **:** a protective container or housing <a submarine with its reactor in an external ~> **5 :** a detachable compartment (as for personnel, a power unit, or an instrument) on a spacecraft

[3]**pod** *vi* **pod·ded; pod·ding :** to produce pods

[4]**pod** *n* [origin unknown] **:** a number of animals (as seals) clustered together

POD *abbr* **1** pay on delivery **2** post office department

-pod \ˌpäd\ *n comb form* [Gk *-podos,* fr. *pod-, pous* foot — more at FOOT] **:** foot **:** part resembling a foot <pleo*pod*>

po·dag·ra \pə-ˈdag-rə\ *n* [ME, fr. L, fr. Gk, fr. *pod-, pous* + *agra* hunt, catch; akin to L *agere* to drive — more at AGENT] **:** GOUT — **po·dag·ral** \-rəl\ *adj*

pod corn *n* **:** an Indian corn that has each kernel enclosed in a chaffy shell similar to that of other cereals

po·de·sta \ˌpōd-ə-ˈstä\ *n* [It *podestà,* lit., power, fr. L *potestat-, postestas,* irreg. fr. *potis* able — more at POTENT] **:** a chief magistrate in a medieval Italian municipality

podgy \ˈpäj-ē\ *adj* **podg·i·er; -est** [*podge* (something pudgy)] **:** PUDGY

po·di·a·try \pə-ˈdī-ə-trē, pō-\ *n* [Gk *pod-, pous* + E *-iatry*] **:** the care and treatment of the human foot in health and disease — called also *chiropody* — **po·di·at·ric** \ˌpōd-ē-ˈa-trik\ *adj* — **po·di·a·trist** \pə-ˈdī-ə-trəst, pō-\ *n*

pod·ite \ˈpäd-ˌīt\ *n* [ISV *pod-* (fr. Gk *pod-, pous*) + *-ite*] **:** a limb segment of an anthropod — **po·dit·ic** \pä-ˈdit-ik\ *adj*

po·di·um \ˈpōd-ē-əm\ *n, pl* **podiums** *or* **po·dia** \-ē-ə\ [L — more at PEW] **1 :** a low wall serving as a foundation or terrace wall: as **a :** one around the arena of an ancient amphitheater serving as a base for the tiers of seats **b :** the masonry under the stylobate of a temple **2 a :** a dais esp. for an orchestral conductor **b :** LECTERN

-po·di·um \ˈpōd-ē-əm\ *n comb form, pl* **-po·dia** \-ē-ə\ [NL, fr. Gk *podion,* dim. of *pod-, pous* foot — more at FOOT] **:** foot **:** part resembling a foot <pseudo*podium*>

podo·phyl·lin \ˌpäd-ə-ˈfil-ən\ *n* [ISV, fr. NL *Podophyllum*] **:** a bitter irritant purgative resin obtained from the rhizome of the mayapple and used esp. as a cathartic

podo·phyl·lum \-ˈfil-əm\ *n, pl* **-phyl·li** \-ˈfil-ˌī\ *or* **-phyllums** [NL, fr. *Podophyllum,* genus of herbs including the mayapple] **:** the rhizome and rootlet of the mayapple that is used as a cathartic and as an agent intended to increase the flow of bile

Po·dunk \ˈpō-ˌdəŋk\ *n* [*Podunk,* village in Mass. or locality in Conn.] **:** a small, unimportant, and isolated town

pod·zol \ˈpäd-ˌzȯl\ *n* [Russ] **:** any of a group of zonal soils that develop in a moist climate esp. under coniferous or mixed forest and have an organic mat and a thin organic-mineral layer above a gray leached layer resting on a dark illuvial horizon enriched with amorphous clay — **pod·zol·ic** \päd-ˈzäl-ik, -ˈzȯl-\ *adj*

pod·zol·iza·tion \ˌpäd-ˌzȯ-lə-ˈzā-shən\ *n* **:** a process of soil formation esp. in humid regions involving principally leaching of the upper layers with accumulation of material in lower layers and development of characteristic horizons; *specif* **:** the development of a podzol — **pod·zol·ize** \ˈpäd-ˌzȯ-ˌlīz\ *vb*

POE *abbr* **1** port of embarkation **2** port of entry

po·em \ˈpō-əm, -ˌem\ *n* [MF *poeme,* fr. L *poema,* fr. Gk *poiēma,* fr. *poiein*] **1 :** a composition in verse **2 :** a piece of poetry communicating to the reader the sense of a complete experience **3 :** a creation, experience, or object suggesting a poem <the house we stayed in . . . was itself a ~ —H. J. Laski>

po·esy \ˈpō-ə-zē, -sē\ *n, pl* **po·esies** [ME *poesie,* fr. MF, fr. L *poesis,* fr. Gk *poiēsis,* lit., creation, fr. *poiein*] **1 a :** a poem or body of poems **b :** POETRY **2 :** poetic inspiration

po·et \ˈpō-ət\ *n* [ME, fr. OF *poete,* fr. L *poeta,* fr. Gk *poiētēs* maker, poet, fr. *poiein* to make, create; akin to Skt *cinoti* he heaps up] **1 :** one who writes poetry **:** a maker of verses **2 :** a creative artist of great imaginative and expressive gifts and special sensitivity to his medium — **po·et·ess** \-əs\ *n*

po·et·as·ter \ˈpō-ət-ˌas-tər\ *n* [NL, fr. L *poeta* + *-aster* -aster]

: an inferior poet

po·et·ic \pō-ˈet-ik\ *adj* **1 a :** of, relating to, or characteristic of poets or poetry **b :** given to writing poetry **2 :** written in verse

po·et·i·cal \-i-kəl\ *adj* **1 :** POETIC **2 :** being beyond or above the truth of history or nature : IDEALIZED <had ~ ideas about marriage> — **po·et·i·cal·ly** \-k(ə-)lē\ *adv*

po·et·i·cal·ness \-i-kəl-nəs\ *n* : poetic quality

po·et·i·cism \pō-ˈet-ə-ˌsiz-əm\ *n* : an archaic, trite, or strained expression in poetry

po·et·i·cize \-ˌsīz\ *vt* **-cized; -ciz·ing :** to give a poetic quality to

poetic justice *n* : an outcome in which vice is punished and virtue rewarded usu. in a manner peculiarly or ironically appropriate

poetic license *n* : LICENSE 4

po·et·ics \pō-ˈet-iks\ *n pl but sing or pl in constr* **1 a :** a treatise on poetry or aesthetics **b :** poetic theory or practice **2 :** poetic feelings or utterances

po·et·ize \ˈpō-ət-ˌīz\ *vb* **-ized; -iz·ing** *vi* : to compose poetry ~ *vt* : POETICIZE — **po·et·iz·er** *n*

poet laureate *n, pl* **poets laureate** *or* **poet laureates 1 :** a poet honored for achievement in his art **2 :** a poet appointed for life by an English sovereign as a member of the royal household and formerly expected to compose poems for court and national occasions **3 :** one regarded by a country or region as its most eminent or representative poet

po·et·ry \ˈpō-ə-trē, *esp South* -it-rē\ *n* **1 a :** metrical writing : VERSE **b :** the productions of a poet : POEMS **2 :** writing that formulates a concentrated imaginative awareness of experience in language chosen and arranged to create a specific emotional response through meaning, sound, and rhythm **3 a :** a quality that stirs the imagination **b :** a quality of spontaneity and grace

po·go·nia \pə-ˈgō-nē-ə\ *n* [NL, genus name, fr. Gk *pōgōn* beard] : any of a genus (*Pogonia*) of terrestrial orchids (as the snakemouth) of the north temperate zone that have terminal solitary flowers with a crested lip

pog·o·nip \ˈpäg-ə-ˌnip\ *n* [Paiute] : a dense winter fog containing frozen particles that is formed in deep mountain valleys of the western U.S.

po·go·noph·o·ran \ˌpō-gə-ˈnäf-ə-rən\ *n* [NL *Pogonophora*, group name, fr. Gk *pōgōnophora*, neut. pl. of *pōgōnophoros* wearing a beard] : any of a phylum or class (Pogonophora) of marine worms of uncertain systematic relationships that superficially resemble polychaetes but have a dorsal nervous system and obscure segmentation — **pogonophoran** *adj*

po·go stick \ˈpō-(ˌ)gō-\ *n* [fr. *Pogo*, a trademark] : a pole with a strong spring at the bottom and two footrests on which a person stands and propels himself along with a series of jumps

¹po·grom \pə-ˈgräm, ˈpō-grəm *also* ˈpäg-rəm\ *n* [Yiddish, fr. Russ, lit., devastation] : an organized massacre of helpless people; *specif* : such a massacre of Jews *syn* see MASSACRE

²progrom *vt* : to massacre or destroy in a pogrom

po·grom·ist \-əst\ *n* : one who organizes or takes part in a pogrom

po·gy \ˈpō-gē\ *n, pl* **pogies** [of Algonquian origin; akin to Abnaki *p8kangan* menhaden] : MENHADEN

poi \ˈpȯi\ *n, pl* **poi** *or* **pois** [Hawaiian & Samoan] : a Hawaiian food of taro root cooked, pounded, and kneaded to a paste and often allowed to ferment

-poi·e·sis \(ˌ)pȯi-ˈē-səs\ *n comb form, pl* **-poi·e·ses** \-ˈē-ˌsēz\ [NL, fr. Gk *poiēsis* creation — more at POESY] : production : formation <lympho*poiesis*>

-poi·et·ic \(ˌ)pȯi-ˈet-ik\ *adj comb form* [Gk *poiētikos* creative, fr. *poiētēs* maker — more at POET] : productive : formative <lympho*poietic*>

poi·gnan·cy \ˈpȯi-nyən-sē\ *n, pl* **-cies 1 :** the quality or state of being poignant **2 :** an instance of poignancy *syn* see PATHOS

poi·gnant \ˈpȯi-nyənt\ *adj* [ME *poinaunt*, fr. MF *poignant*, prp. of *poindre* to prick, sting, fr. L *pungere* — more at PUNGENT] **1 :** pungently pervasive <a ~ perfume> **2 a (1) :** painfully affecting the feelings : PIERCING **(2) :** deeply affecting : TOUCHING **b :** designed to make an impression : CUTTING <~ satire> **3 a :** pleasurably stimulating **b :** being to the point : APT *syn* **1** see PUNGENT *ant* dull (*as of sensation or reaction*) **2** see MOVING

poi·kilo·therm \pȯi-ˈkil-ə-ˌthərm\ *n* [Gk *poikilos* variegated + ISV *-therm*; akin to L *pingere* to paint — more at PAINT] : an organism (as a frog) with a variable body temperature that is usu. slightly higher than the temperature of its environment : a cold-blooded organism — **poi·ki·lo·ther·mic** \ˌpȯi-kə-lō-ˈthər-mik\ *adj* — **poi·ki·lo·ther·mism** \-ˈthər-ˌmiz-əm\ *n*

poi·lu \pwäl-ˈ(y)ü, ˈpwäl-ˌ; pwȧ-lᵫ\ *n* [F, fr. *poilu* hairy, fr. MF, fr. *poil* hair, fr. L *pilus* — more at PILE] : a French soldier; *esp* : a front-line soldier in World War I

poin·ci·ana \ˌpȯin(t)-sē-ˈan-ə, ˌp(w)än(t)-\ *n* [NL, genus name, fr. De *Poinci*, 17th cent. governor of part of the French West Indies] : any of a small genus (*Poinciana*) of ornamental tropical leguminous trees or shrubs with bright orange or red flowers; *also* : a showy closely related tree (*Delonix regia*) with immense racemes of scarlet and orange flowers, flat woody pods, and twice-pinnate leaves

poin·set·tia \pȯin-ˈset-ē-ə, -ˈset-ə\ *n* [NL, fr. Joel R. *Poinsett* †1851 Am diplomat] : any of various spurges (genus *Euphorbia*) with flower clusters subtended by showy involucral bracts; *esp* : a showy Mexican and So. American plant (*E. pulcherrima*) with tapering scarlet bracts that suggest petals and surround small yellow flowers

¹point \ˈpȯint\ *n* [ME, partly fr. OF, puncture, small spot, point in time or space, fr. L *punctum*, fr. neut. of *punctus*, pp. of *pungere* to prick; partly fr. OF *pointe* sharp end, fr. (assumed) VL *puncta*, fr. L, fem. of *punctus*, pp. — more at PUNGENT] **1 a (1) :** an individual detail : ITEM **(2) :** a distinguishing detail <tact is one of her strong ~*s*> **b :** the most important essential in a discussion or matter <missed the whole ~ of the joke> **c :** COGENCY **2** *obs* : physical condition **3 :** an end or object to be achieved : PURPOSE <did not see what ~ there was in continuing the discussion> **4 a (1) :** a geometric element of which it is postulated that at least two exist and that two suffice to determine a line **(2) :** a geometric element determined by an ordered set of coordinates **b (1) :** a narrowly localized place having a precisely indicated position <walked to a ~ 50 yards north of the building> **(2) :** a particular place : LOCALITY <have come from distant ~*s*> **c (1) :** an exact moment <at this ~ he was interrupted> **(2) :** a time interval immediately before something indicated : VERGE <at the ~ of death> **d (1) :** a particular step, stage, or degree in development <had reached the ~ where nothing seemed to matter anymore> **(2) :** a definite position in a scale **5 a :** the terminal usu. sharp or narrowly rounded part of something : TIP **b :** a weapon or tool having such a part and used for stabbing or piercing **c (1) :** the contact or discharge extremity of an electric device (as a spark plug or contact break) **(2)** *chiefly Brit* : an electric outlet **6 a :** a projecting usu. tapering piece of land or a sharp prominence **b (1) :** the tip of a projecting body part **(2) :** TINE 2 **(3)** *pl* : the extremities or markings of the extremities of an animal esp. when of a color differing from the rest of the body **c (1) :** a railroad switch **(2) :** the tip of the angle between two rails in a railroad frog **d :** the head of the bow of a stringed instrument **7 :** a short musical phrase; *esp* : a phrase in contrapuntal music **8 a :** a very small mark **b (1) :** PUNCTUATION MARK; *esp* : PERIOD **(2) :** DECIMAL POINT **9 :** a lace for tying parts of a garment together used esp. in the 16th and 17th centuries **10 :** one of usu. eleven divisions of a heraldic shield that determines the position of a charge **11 a :** one of the 32 equidistant spots of a compass card **b :** the difference of 11¼ degrees between two such successive points **12 :** a small detachment ahead of an advance guard or behind a rear guard **13 a :** NEEDLEPOINT 1 **b :** lace made with a bobbin **14 :** one of 12 spaces marked off on each side of a backgammon board **15 :** a unit of measurement: as **a (1) :** a unit of counting in the scoring of a game or contest **(2) :** a unit used in evaluating the strength of a bridge hand **b :** a unit of academic credit **c (1) :** a unit used in quoting prices (as of stocks, bonds, and commodities) **(2)** *pl* : a percentage of the face value of a loan often added as a placement fee or service charge **d :** a unit of about $^{1}/_{72}$ inch used to measure the belly-to-back dimension of printing type **16 :** the action of pointing: as **a :** the rigidly intent attitude of a hunting dog marking game for a gunner **b :** the action in dancing of extending one leg so that only the tips of the toes touch the floor **17 :** a position of a player in various games (as lacrosse); *also* : the player of such a position **18 :** a number thrown on the first roll of the dice in craps which the player attempts to repeat before throwing a seven — compare MISSOUT, PASS — **beside the point :** IRRELEVANT — **in point :** RELEVANT, PERTINENT — used predicatively or postpositively <mentioned a case *in point*> — **in point of :** with regard to : in the matter of <*in point of* law> — **to the point :** RELEVANT, PERTINENT <a suggestion that was *to the point*>

²point *vt* **1 a :** to furnish with a point : SHARPEN <~*ing* a pencil with a knife> **b :** to give added force, emphasis, or piquancy to <~ up a remark> **2 :** to scratch out the old mortar from the joints of (as a brick wall) and fill in with new material **3 a (1) :** to mark the pauses or grammatical divisions in : PUNCTUATE **(2) :** to separate (a decimal fraction) from an integer by a decimal point — usu. used with *off* **b :** to mark (as Hebrew words) **4 a (1) :** to indicate the position or direction of esp. by extending a finger <~ out a house> **(2) :** to direct somone's attention to <~ out a mistake> **b** *of a hunting dog* : to indicate the presence and place of (game) by a point **5 a :** to cause to be turned in a particular direction <~ a gun> <~*ed* the boat upstream> **b :** to extend (a leg) in executing a point in dancing ~ *vi* **1 a :** to indicate the fact or probability of something specified <everything ~*s* to a bright future> **b :** to indicate the position or direction of something esp. by extending a finger <~ at the map> **c :** to point game <a dog that ~*s* well> **2 a :** to lie extended, aimed, or turned in a particular direction <a directional arrow that ~*ed* to the north> **b :** to execute a point in dancing **3** *of a ship* : to sail close to the wind **4 :** to train for a particular contest

point–blank \ˈpȯint-ˈblaŋk\ *adj* **1 a :** marked by no appreciable drop below initial horizontal line of flight **b :** so close to a target that a missile fired will travel in a straight line to the mark **2 :** DIRECT, BLUNT <a ~ refusal> — **point–blank** *adv*

point count *n* : a method of evaluating the strength of a hand in bridge by counting points for each high card and often for long or short suits; *also* : the value of a hand so evaluated

point d'ap·pui \ˌpwaⁿ(n)-dap-ˈwē\ *n, pl* **points d'appui** *same*\ [F, lit., point of support] : a base esp. for a military operation

point–de·vice \ˌpȯint-di-ˈvīs\ *adj, archaic* [ME *at point devis* at a fixed point] : marked by punctilious attention to detail : METICULOUS — **point–device** *adv, archaic*

pointe \ˈpwaⁿ(n)t\ *n* [F, lit., point] : a ballet position in which the body is balanced on the extreme tip of the toe

¹point·ed \ˈpȯint-əd\ *adj* **1 a :** having a point **b :** having a pointed crown characteristic of Gothic architecture **2 a :** being to the point : PERTINENT **b :** aimed at a particular person or group **3 :** CONSPICUOUS, MARKED <~ indifference> — **point·ed·ly** *adv* — **point·ed·ness** *n*

²pointed *adj* [short for *appointed*] *obs* : SET, FIXED

point·er \ˈpȯint-ər\ *n* **1 :** one that furnishes with points **2 a :** one that points out; *specif* : a rod used to direct attention **b** *pl, cap* : the two stars in the Great Bear a line through which points to the North Star **3 :** a large strong slender smooth-haired gundog that hunts by scent and indicates the presence of game by pointing **4 :** a useful suggestion or hint : TIP

point estimate *n* : the single value assigned to a parameter in point estimation

---

ə abut	ə kitten	ər further	a back	ā bake	ä cot, cart	
aù out	ch chin	e less	ē easy	g gift	i trip	ī life
j joke	ŋ sing	ō flow	ȯ flaw	ȯi coin	th thin	t͟h this
ü loot	ù foot	y yet	yü few	yù furious	zh vision	

point estimation *n* : estimation in which a single value is assigned to a parameter

poin·til·lism \'pwa^{n}(n)-tē-,(y)iz-əm, 'pȯint-ᵊl-,iz-əm\ *n* [F *pointillisme,* fr. *pointiller* to stipple, fr. *point* spot — more at POINT] : the theory or practice in art of applying small strokes or dots of color to a surface so that from a distance they blend together — **poin·til·list** *also* **poin·til·liste** \,pwa^{n}(n)-tē-'(y)ēst, 'pȯint-ᵊl-əst\ *n or adj*

poin·til·lis·tic \,pwa^{n}(n)-tē-'(y)is-tik, ,pȯint-ᵊl-'is-\ *adj* : of, relating to, or characteristic of pointillism or pointillists

point lace *n* : NEEDLEPOINT 1

point·less \'pȯint-ləs\ *adj* **1** : devoid of meaning : SENSELESS <a ~ remark> **2** : devoid of effectiveness : FLAT <~ attempts to be funny> — **point·less·ly** *adv* — **point·less·ness** *n*

point of accumulation : LIMIT POINT

point of departure : a starting point esp. in a discussion

point of honor : a matter seriously affecting one's honor

point of inflection : INFLECTION POINT

point of no return **1** : the point in the flight of an aircraft (as over an ocean) beyond which the remaining fuel will be insufficient for a return to the starting point with the result that the craft must proceed **2** : a critical point (as in a course of action) at which turning back or reversal is not possible

point of view : a position from which something is considered or evaluated : STANDPOINT

point source *n* : a source of radiation (as light) that is concentrated at a point and considered as having no spatial extension

point system *n* : a system in which printing type and spacing materials are made in sizes that are exact multiples of the point

pointy \'pȯint-ē\ *adj* **point·i·er; -est** **1** : coming to a rather sharp point **2** : having parts that stick out sharply here and there

[1]**poise** \'pȯiz\ *vb* **poised; pois·ing** [ME *poisen* to weigh, ponder, fr. MF *pois-,* stem of *peser,* fr. L *pensare* — more at PENSIVE] *vt* **1 a** : BALANCE; *esp* : to hold or carry in equilibrium <walked along gracefully with a water jar *poised* on her head> **b** : to hold supported or suspended without motion in a steady position <*poised* her fork and gave her guest a knowing look —Louis Bromfield> **2** : to hold or carry (the head) in a particular way **3** : to put into readiness : BRACE ~ *vi* **1** : to become drawn up into readiness **2** : HOVER

[2]**poise** *n* [ME *poyse* weight, heaviness, fr. MF *pois,* fr. L *pensum,* fr. neut. of *pensus,* pp. of *pendere* to weigh — more at PENDANT] **1** : a stably balanced state : EQUILIBRIUM <a ~ between widely divergent impulses —F. R. Leavis> **2 a** : easy self-possessed assurance of manner : gracious tact in coping or handling; *also* : the pleasantly tranquil interaction between persons of poise <no angry outbursts marred the ~ of the meeting> **b** : a particular way of carrying oneself : BEARING, CARRIAGE ***syn*** see TACT

[3]**poise** \'pwäz\ *n* [F, fr. Jean Louis Marie *Poiseuille* †1869 F physician and anatomist] : a cgs unit of viscosity equal to the viscosity of a fluid that would require a shearing force of one dyne to move a square-centimeter area of either of two parallel layers of fluid one centimeter apart with a velocity of one centimeter per second relative to the other layer with the space between the layers being filled with the fluid

poised \'pȯizd\ *adj* : having poise: **a** : marked by balance or equilibrium **b** : marked by easy composure of manner or bearing

[1]**poi·son** \'pȯiz-ᵊn\ *n* [ME, fr. OF, drink, poisonous drink, poison, fr. L *potion-, potio* drink — more at POTION] **1 a** : a substance that through its chemical action usu. kills, injures, or impairs an organism **b** (1) : something destructive or harmful (2) : an object of aversion or abhorrence **2** : a substance that inhibits the activity of another substance or the course of a reaction or process <a catalyst ~>

[2]**poison** *vb* **poi·soned; poi·son·ing** \'pȯiz-niŋ, -ᵊn-iŋ\ *vt* **1 a** : to injure or kill with poison **b** : to treat, taint, or impregnate with poison **2** : to exert a baneful influence on : CORRUPT <~*ed* their minds> **3** : to inhibit the activity, course, or occurrence of <sulfur may ~ a fuel cell> ~ *vi* : to put poison into or on something — **poi·son·er** \'pȯiz-nər, -ᵊn-ər\ *n*

[3]**poison** *adj* **1** : POISONOUS <a ~ plant> : VENOMOUS <a ~ tongue> **2** : impregnated with poison : POISONED <a ~ arrow>

poison bean *n* : a leguminous shrub (*Daubentonia drummondii*) of the southern U.S. with poisonous seeds

poison gas *n* : a poisonous gas or a liquid or a solid giving off poisonous vapors designed (as in chemical warfare) to kill, injure, or disable by inhalation or contact

poison hemlock *n* **1** : a large branching biennial poisonous herb (*Conium maculatum*) of the carrot family with finely divided leaves and white flowers **2** : WATER HEMLOCK

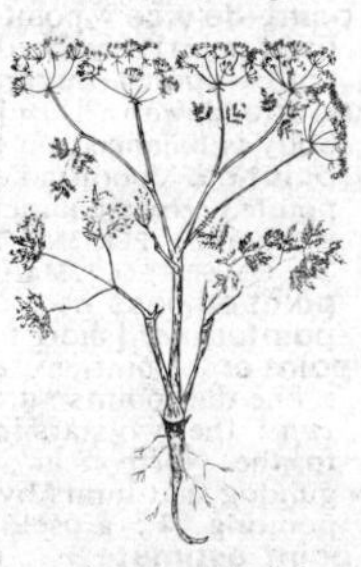

poison hemlock 1

poison ivy *n* : a climbing plant (*Rhus toxicodendron*) of the sumac family that is esp. common in the eastern and central U.S., that has ternate leaves, greenish flowers, and white berries, and that produces an acutely irritating oil causing a usu. intensely itching skin rash; *also* : any of several congeneric plants

poison oak *n* : any of several poison ivies: **a** : POISON SUMAC **b** : a bushy poison ivy (*Rhus diversiloba*) of the Pacific coast **c** : a bushy poison ivy (*Rhus quercifolia*) of the southeastern U.S.

poi·son·ous \'pȯiz-nəs, -ᵊn-əs\ *adj* : having the properties or effects of poison : VENOMOUS — **poi·son·ous·ly** *adv*

poison-pen *adj* : written with malice and spite and usu. anonymously <~ letter>

poison sumac *n* : a smooth shrubby American swamp poison ivy (*Rhus vernix*) with pinnate leaves, greenish flowers, and greenish white berries — called also *poison dogwood*

poi·son·wood \'pȯiz-ᵊn-,wu̇d\ *n* : a caustic or poisonous tree (*Metopium toxiferum*) of Florida and the West Indies that has compound leaves, greenish paniculate flowers, and orange-yellow fruits

poison ivy

Pois·son distribution \pwä-'sōⁿ-\ *n* [Siméon D. *Poisson* †1840 F mathematician] : a probability density function that is often used as a mathematical model of the number of outcomes (as traffic accidents, atomic disintegrations, or organisms) obtained in a suitable interval of time and space, that has the mean equal to the variance, that is used as an approximation to the binomial distribution, and that has the form

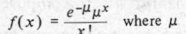

$$f(x) = \frac{e^{-\mu}\mu^x}{x!} \quad \text{where } \mu$$

is the mean and x takes on nonnegative integral values

[1]**poke** \'pōk\ *n* [ME, fr. ONF — more at POCKET] *chiefly South & Midland* : BAG, SACK

[2]**poke** *vb* **poked; pok·ing** [ME *poken;* akin to MD *poken* to poke] *vt* **1 a** (1) : PROD, JAB <*poked* him in the ribs and grinned broadly> (2) : to urge or stir by prodding or jabbing **b** (1) : PIERCE, STAB (2) : to produce by piercing, stabbing, or jabbing <~ a hole> **c** (1) : HIT, PUNCH <*poked* him in the nose> (2) : to deliver (a blow) with the fist **2 a** : to cause to project <*poked* her head out of the window> **b** : to interpose or interject in a meddlesome manner <asked him not to ~ his nose into other people's business> ~ *vi* **1 a** : to make a prodding, jabbing, or thrusting movement esp. repeatedly **b** : to strike out at something **2 a** : to look about or through something without system : RUMMAGE <*poking* around in the attic> **b** : MEDDLE **3** : to move or act slowly or aimlessly : DAWDLE <just *poked* around at home and didn't accomplish much> **4** : to become stuck out or forward : PROTRUDE — **poke fun at** : RIDICULE, MOCK

[3]**poke** *n* **1 a** : a quick thrust : JAB **b** : a blow with the fist : PUNCH **2** : a projecting brim on the front of a woman's bonnet

[4]**poke** *n* [modif. of *puccoon* (in some Algonquian language of Virginia), a plant used in dyeing] : POKEWEED

poke·ber·ry \'pōk-,ber-ē\ *n* : the berry of the pokeweed; *also* : POKEWEED

poke bonnet *n* : a woman's bonnet with a projecting brim at the front

poke check *n* : an act or instance of attempting to knock the puck away from an opponent in ice hockey by jabbing or thrusting at it with the stick

[1]**pok·er** \'pō-kər\ *n* : one that pokes; *esp* : a metal rod for stirring a fire

[2]**po·ker** \'pō-kər\ *n* [prob. modif. of F *poque,* a card game similar to poker] : one of several card games in which a player bets that the value of his hand is greater than that of the hands held by others, in which each subsequent player must either equal or raise the bet or drop out, and in which the player holding the highest hand at the end of the betting wins the pot

poker hands in descending value: *1* five of a kind, *2* royal flush, *3* straight flush, *4* four of a kind, *5* full house, *6* flush, *7* straight, *8* three of a kind, *9* two pairs, *10* one pair

poker face *n* [[2]*poker;* fr. the need of the poker player to conceal the true quality of his hand] : an inscrutable face that reveals no hint of a person's thoughts or feelings — **po·ker-faced** \,pō-kər-'fāst\ *adj*

poke·weed \'pō-,kwēd\ *n* : a coarse American perennial herb (*Phytolacca americana* of the family Phytolaccaceae, the pokeweed family) with racemose white flowers, dark purple juicy berries, a poisonous root, and young shoots sometimes used as potherbs

po·key \'pō-kē\ *n, pl* **pokeys** [origin unknown] *slang* : JAIL

poky *also* **pok·ey** \'pō-kē\ *adj* **pok·i·er; -est** [[2]*poke*] **1** : small and cramped **2** : SHABBY, DULL **3** : annoyingly slow — **pok·i·ly** \-kə-lē\ *adv* — **pok·i·ness** \-kē-nəs\ *n*

pol \'päl\ *n* : POLITICIAN

Pol *abbr* Poland; Polish

Po·la·bi·an \pō-'läb-ē-ən, -'lāb-\ *n* [*Polab,* of Slavic origin; akin to Pol *po* on, and to Pol *Laba,* Elbe river] **1** *or* **Polab** : a member of a Slavic people formerly dwelling in the basin of the Elbe and on the Baltic coast of Germany **2** : the extinct West Slavic language of the Polabians

Po·lack \'pō-,läk\ *n* [Pol *Polak*] **1** *obs* : POLE 1 **2** : a person of Polish birth or descent — usu. used disparagingly

Po·land Chi·na \,pō-lən(d)-'chī-nə\ *n* [*Poland,* Europe + *China,* Asia] : any of an American breed of large white-marked black swine of the lard type

[1]**po·lar** \ˈpō-lər\ *adj* [NL *polaris,* fr. L *polus* pole] **1 a :** of or relating to a geographical pole or the region around it **b :** coming from or having the characteristics of such a region **c (1) :** passing over a planet's north and south poles <a satellite in a ~ orbit> (2) : traveling in a polar orbit <a ~ satellite> **2 :** of or relating to one or more poles (as of a magnet) **3 :** serving as a guide **4 :** diametrically opposite **5 :** exhibiting polarity; *esp* **:** having a dipole or characterized by molecules having dipoles <a ~ solvent> **6 :** resembling a pole or axis around which all else revolves **:** PIVOTAL **7 :** of, relating to, or expressed in polar coordinates <~ equations>; *also* **:** of or relating to a polar coordinate system

[2]**polar** *n* **:** a straight line related to a point; *specif* **:** the straight line joining the points of contact of the tangents from a point exterior to a conic section

polar bear *n* **:** a large creamy-white bear (*Thalarctos maritimus* or *Ursus maritimus*) that inhabits arctic regions

polar bear

polar body *n* **:** a cell that separates from an oocyte during meiosis and that contains a nucleus produced in the first or second meiotic division but very little cytoplasm

polar circle *n* **:** one of the two parallels of latitude each at a distance from a pole of the earth equal to about 23 degrees 27 minutes

polar coordinate *n* **:** either of two numbers that locate a point in a plane by its distance from a fixed point on a line and the angle this line makes with a fixed line

polar front *n* **:** the boundary between the cold air of a polar region and the warmer air of lower latitudes

po·lar·im·e·ter \ˌpō-lə-ˈrim-ət-ər\ *n* [ISV, fr. *polarization*] **1 :** an instrument for determining the amount of polarization of light or the proportion of polarized light in a partially polarized ray **2 :** a polariscope for measuring the amount of rotation of the plane of polarization esp. by liquids — **po·lari·met·ric** \pō-ˌlar-ə-ˈme-trik\ *adj* — **po·lar·im·e·try** \ˌpō-lə-ˈrim-ə-trē\ *n*

Po·lar·is \pə-ˈlar-əs, -ˈlär-\ *n* [NL, fr. *polaris* polar] **:** NORTH STAR

po·lari·scope \pō-ˈlar-ə-ˌskōp\ *n* [ISV, fr. *polarization*] **1 :** an instrument for studying the properties of or examining substances in polarized light **2 :** POLARIMETER 2 — **po·lari·scop·ic** \-ˌlar-ə-ˈskäp-ik\ *adj*

po·lar·i·ty \pō-ˈlar-ət-ē, pə-\ *n, pl* **-ties 1 :** the quality or condition inherent in a body that exhibits opposite properties or powers in opposite parts or directions or that exhibits contrasted properties or powers in contrasted parts or directions **2 :** attraction toward a particular object or in a specific direction **3 :** the particular state either positive or negative with reference to the two poles or to electrification **4 a :** diametrical opposition **b :** an instance of such opposition

po·lar·iza·tion \ˌpō-lə-rə-ˈzā-shən\ *n* **1 :** the action of polarizing or state of being or becoming polarized: as **a (1) :** the action or process of affecting radiation and esp. light so that the vibrations of the wave assume a definite form **(2) :** the state of radiation affected by this process **b :** the deposition of gas on one or both electrodes of an electrolytic cell increasing the resistance and setting up a counter electromotive force **c :** MAGNETIZATION **2 a :** division into two opposites **b :** concentration about opposing extremes of groups or interests formerly ranged on a continuum

po·lar·ize \ˈpō-lə-ˌrīz\ *vb* **-ized; -iz·ing** [F *polariser,* fr. NL *polaris* polar] *vt* **1 :** to cause (as light waves) to vibrate in a definite pattern **2 :** to give physical polarity to **3 :** to break up into opposing factions or groupings ~ *vi* **:** to become polarized — **po·lar·iz·abil·i·ty** \ˌpō-lə-ˌrī-zə-ˈbil-ət-ē\ *n* — **po·lar·iz·able** \ˈpō-lə-ˌrī-zə-bəl\ *adj*

polar nucleus *n* **:** either of the two nuclei of a seed plant embryo sac that are destined to form endosperm

po·lar·og·ra·phy \ˌpō-lə-ˈräg-rə-fē\ *n* [ISV, fr. *polarization*] **:** a method of qualitative or quantitative analysis based on current-voltage curves obtained during electrolysis of a solution with a steadily increasing electromotive force — **po·laro·graph·ic** \pō-ˌlar-ə-ˈgraf-ik\ *adj* — **po·laro·graph·i·cal·ly** \-i-k(ə-)lē\ *adv*

Po·lar·oid \ˈpō-lə-ˌrȯid\ *trademark* — used esp. for a light-polarizing material used esp. in eyeglasses and lamps to prevent glare and in various optical devices

po·lar·on \ˈpō-lə-ˌrän\ *n* [ISV *polar* + [2]*-on*] **:** a conducting electron in an ionic crystal together with the induced polarization of the surrounding lattice

pol·der \ˈpōl-dər, ˈpäl-\ *n* [D] **:** a tract of low land reclaimed from a body of water (as the sea)

[1]**pole** \ˈpōl\ *n* [ME, fr. OE *pāl* stake, pole, fr. L *palus* stake; akin to L *pangere* to fix — more at PACT] **1 a :** a long slender usu. cylindrical object (as a length of wood) **b :** a shaft which extends from the front axle of a wagon between wheelhorses and by which the wagon is drawn **:** TONGUE **c :** a long staff of wood, metal, or fiberglass used in the pole vault **2 a :** a varying unit of length; *esp* **:** one measuring 16½ feet **b :** a unit of area equal to a square rod **3 :** a tree with a breast-high diameter of from 4 to 12 inches **4 :** the inside front row position on the starting line for a race

[2]**pole** *vb* **poled; pol·ing** *vt* **1 :** to act upon with a pole **2 :** to impel or push with a pole ~ *vi* **1 :** to propel a boat with a pole **2 :** to use ski poles to gain speed

[3]**pole** *n* [ME *pool,* fr. L *polus,* fr. Gk *polos* pivot, pole; akin to Gk *kyklos* wheel — more at WHEEL] **1 :** either extremity of an axis of a sphere and esp. of the earth's axis **2 a :** either of two related opposites **b :** a point of guidance or attraction **3 a :** one of the two terminals of an electric cell, battery, or dynamo **b :** one of two or more regions in a magnetized body at which the magnetic flux density is concentrated **4 :** either of two morphologically or physiologically differentiated areas at opposite ends of an axis in an organism or cell — see BLASTULA illustration **5 a :** the fixed point in a system of polar coordinates that serves as the origin **b :** the point of origin of two tangents to a conic that determine a polar

Pole \ˈpōl\ *n* [G, of Slavic origin; akin to Pol *Polak* Pole] **1 :** a native or inhabitant of Poland **2 :** a person of Polish descent

[1]**pole·ax** \ˈpō-ˌlaks\ *n* [ME *polax, pollax,* fr. *pol, polle* poll + *ax*] **1 :** a battle-ax with short handle and often a hook or spike opposite the blade; *also* **:** one with a long handle used as an ornamental weapon **2 :** an ax used in slaughtering cattle

[2]**poleax** *vt* **:** to attack, strike, or fell with or as if with a poleax

pole bean *n* **:** a cultivated bean that is usu. trained to grow upright on supports

pole·cat \ˈpōl-ˌkat\ *n, pl* **polecats** *or* **polecat** [ME *polcat,* prob. fr. MF *poul, pol* cock + ME *cat;* prob. fr. its preying on poultry — more at PULLET] **1 :** a European carnivorous mammal (*Mustela putorius*) of which the ferret is considered a domesticated variety **2 :** SKUNK

pole horse *n* **1 :** a horse harnessed beside the pole of a wagon **2 :** the horse having a starting position next to the inside rail in a harness race

pole·less \ˈpōl-ləs\ *adj* **:** having no pole

[1]**po·lem·ic** \pə-ˈlem-ik\ *n* [F *polémique,* fr. MF, fr. *polemique* controversial, fr. Gk *polemikos* warlike, hostile, fr. *polemos* war; akin to OE eal*felo* baleful, Gk *pallein* to brandish] **1 a :** an aggressive attack on or refutation of the opinions or principles of another **b :** the art or practice of disputation or controversy — usu. used in pl. but sing. or pl. in constr. **2 :** an aggressive controversialist **:** DISPUTANT — **po·lem·i·cist** \-ˈlem-ə-səst\ *n*

[2]**polemic** *or* **po·lem·i·cal** \-i-kəl\ *adj* **1 :** of, relating to, or being a polemic **:** CONTROVERSIAL **2 :** engaged in or addicted to polemics **:** DISPUTATIOUS — **po·lem·i·cal·ly** \-i-k(ə-)lē\ *adv*

po·lem·i·cize \-ˈlem-ə-ˌsīz\ *vi* **-cized; -ciz·ing :** POLEMIZE

po·le·mist \pə-ˈlem-əst, ˈpäl-ə-məst\ *n* [irreg. fr. *polemic*] **:** one skilled in or given to polemics

pol·e·mize \ˈpäl-ə-ˌmīz\ *vi* **-mized; -miz·ing :** to engage in controversy **:** dispute aggressively

pol·e·mo·ni·um \ˌpäl-ə-ˈmō-nē-əm\ *n* [NL, fr. Gk *polemōnion,* a plant] **:** JACOB'S LADDER

po·len·ta \pō-ˈlent-ə, pə-, -ˈlen-ˌtä\ *n* [It] **:** mush made of chestnut meal, cornmeal, semolina, or farina

pol·er \ˈpō-lər\ *n* **:** one that poles; *esp* **:** one that poles a boat

pole·star \ˈpōl-ˌstär\ *n* **1 :** NORTH STAR **2 a :** a directing principle **:** GUIDE **b :** a center of attraction

pole vault *n* **:** a vault with the aid of a pole; *specif* **:** a field event consisting of a vault for height over a crossbar — **pole–vault** *vi* — **pole–vault·er** *n*

pole·ward \ˈpōl-wərd\ *adv or adj* **:** toward or in the direction of a pole of the earth <as the sun moves ~> <~ variation in temperature>

[1]**po·lice** \pə-ˈlēs\ *n, pl* **police** *often attrib* [MF, government, fr. LL *politia,* fr. Gk *politeia,* fr. *politeuein* to be a citizen, engage in political activity, fr. *politēs* citizen, fr. *polis* city, state; akin to Skt *pur* city] **1 a :** the internal organization or regulation of a political unit through exercise of governmental powers esp. with respect to general comfort, health, morals, safety, or prosperity **b :** control and regulation of affairs affecting the general order and welfare of any unit or area **c :** the system of laws for effecting such control **2 a :** the department of government concerned primarily with maintenance of public order, safety, and health and enforcement of laws and possessing executive, judicial, and legislative powers **b :** the department of government charged with prevention, detection, and prosecution of public nuisances and crimes **3 a :** POLICE FORCE **b** *pl* **:** POLICEMEN **4 a :** a private organization resembling a police force <campus ~> **b** *pl* **:** the members of a private police organization **5 a :** the action or process of cleaning and putting in order **b :** military personnel detailed to perform this function

[2]**police** *vt* **po·liced; po·lic·ing 1** *archaic* **:** GOVERN **2 :** to control, regulate, or keep in order by use of police **3 :** to make clean and put in order **4 a :** to supervise the operation, execution, or administration of to prevent or detect and prosecute violations of rules and regulations **b :** to exercise such supervision over the policies and activities of **5 :** to perform the functions of a police force in or over

police action *n* **:** a localized military action undertaken without formal declaration of war by regular forces against persons held to be violators of international peace and order

police court *n* **:** a court of record that has jurisdiction over various minor offenses (as breach of the peace) and the power to bind over for trial in a superior court or for a grand jury persons accused of more serious offenses

police dog *n* **1 :** a dog trained to assist police esp. in tracking criminals **2 :** GERMAN SHEPHERD

police force *n* **:** a body of trained officers and men entrusted by a government with maintenance of public peace and order, enforcement of laws, and prevention and detection of crime

po·lice·man \pə-ˈlē-smən\ *n* **:** a member of a police force

police power *n* **:** the inherent power of a government to exercise reasonable control over persons and property within its jurisdiction in the interest of the general security, health, safety, morals, and welfare except where legally prohibited

police reporter *n* **:** a reporter regularly assigned to cover police news (as crimes and arrests)

police state *n* **:** a political unit characterized by repressive governmental control of political, economic, and social life usu. by an arbitrary exercise of power by police and esp. secret police in place of regular operation of administrative and judicial organs of the government according to publicly known legal procedures

police station *n* **:** the headquarters of the police for a particular locality

po·lice·wom·an \pə-ˈlē-ˌswu̇m-ən\ *n* **:** a woman who is a member of a police force

[1]**pol·i·cy** \ˈpäl-ə-sē\ *n, pl* **-cies** [ME *policie,* government, policy, fr. MF, government, regulation, fr. LL *politia* — more at POLICE] **1 a :** prudence or wisdom in the management of affairs **:** SAGACITY **b :** management or procedure based primarily on material interest **2 a :** a definite course or method of action selected from among alternatives and in light of given conditions to guide and determine present and future decisions **b :** a high-level overall plan embracing the general goals and acceptable procedures esp. of a governmental body

[2]**policy** *n, pl* **-cies** [alter. of earlier *police,* fr. MF, certificate, fr. OIt *polizza,* modif. of ML *apodixa* receipt, fr. MGk *apodeixis,* fr. Gk, proof, fr. *apodeiknynai* to demonstrate — more at APODICTIC] **1 :** a writing whereby a contract of insurance is made **2 a :** a daily lottery in which participants bet that certain numbers will be drawn from a lottery wheel **b :** NUMBER 6a

pol·i·cy·hold·er \ˈpäl-ə-sē-ˌhōl-dər\ *n* **:** the owner of an insurance policy

pol·i·cy·mak·ing \-ˌmā-kiŋ\ *n* **:** the high-level elaboration of policy and esp. of governmental policy — **pol·i·cy·mak·er** \-kər\ *n*

policy science *n* **:** a social science dealing with the making of high-level policy (as in a government or business)

po·lio \ˈpō-lē-ˌō\ *n* **:** POLIOMYELITIS

po·lio·my·elit·ic \ˌpō-lē-(ˌ)ō-ˌmī-ə-ˈlit-ik\ *adj* [ISV] **:** of, relating to, or affected with poliomyelitis

po·lio·my·eli·tis \-ˈlīt-əs\ *n* [NL, fr. Gk *polios* gray + *myelos* marrow — more at FALLOW, MYEL-] **:** an acute infectious virus disease characterized by fever, motor paralysis, and atrophy of skeletal muscles often with permanent disability and deformity and marked by inflammation of nerve cells in the anterior horns of the spinal cord — called also *infantile paralysis*

po·lio·vi·rus \ˈpō-lē-(ˌ)ō-ˌvī-rəs\ *n* [NL, fr. *polio*myelitis + *virus*] **:** an enterovirus that occurs in several antigenically distinct forms and is the causative agent of human poliomyelitis

po·lis \ˈpäl-əs\ *n, pl* **po·leis** \ˈpäl-ˌās\ [Gk — more at POLICE] **:** a Greek city-state; *broadly* **:** a state or society esp. when characterized by a sense of community

-p·o·lis \p-(ə-)ləs\ *n comb form* [LL, fr. Gk, fr. *polis*] **:** city <megalo*polis*>

[1]**pol·ish** \ˈpäl-ish\ *vb* [ME *polisshen,* fr. OF *poliss-,* stem of *polir,* fr. L *polire*] *vt* **1 :** to make smooth and glossy usu. by friction **:** BURNISH **2 :** to smooth, soften, or refine in manners or condition **3 :** to bring to a highly developed, finished, or refined state **:** PERFECT ~ *vi* **:** to become smooth or glossy by or as if by friction — **pol·ish·er** *n*

[2]**polish** *n* **1 a :** a smooth glossy surface **:** LUSTER **b :** freedom from rudeness or coarseness **:** CULTURE **c :** a state of high development or refinement **2 :** the action or process of polishing **3 :** a preparation that is used to produce a gloss and often a color for the protection and decoration of a surface <furniture ~> <nail ~>

[1]**Pol·ish** \ˈpō-lish\ *adj* [*Pole*] **:** of, relating to, or characteristic of Poland, the Poles, or Polish

[2]**Polish** *n* **:** the Slavic language of the Poles

polish off *vt* **:** to dispose of rapidly or completely

polit *abbr* political; politician

po·lit·bu·ro \ˈpäl-ət-ˌbyu̇(ə)r-(ˌ)ō, ˈpō-lət-, pə-ˈlit-\ *n* [Russ *politbyuro,* fr. *politicheskoye byuro* political bureau] **:** the principal policy-making and executive committee of a Communist party

po·lite \pə-ˈlīt\ *adj* **po·lit·er; -est** [L *politus,* fr. pp. of *polire*] **1 a :** of, relating to, or having the characteristics of advanced culture **b :** marked by refined cultural interests and pursuits esp. in arts and belles lettres **2 a :** showing or characterized by correct social usage **b :** marked by an appearance of consideration, tact, deference, or courtesy **c :** marked by a lack of roughness or crudities <uses terms seldom met with in ~ literature> ***syn*** see CIVIL ***ant*** impolite — **po·lite·ly** *adv* — **po·lite·ness** *n*

po·li·tesse \ˌpäl-i-ˈtes, ˌpó-li-\ *n* [F, fr. MF, cleanness, fr. OIt *pulitezza,* fr. *pulito,* pp. of *pulire* to polish, clean, fr. L *polire*] **:** formal politeness **:** DECOROUSNESS

pol·i·tic \ˈpäl-ə-ˌtik\ *adj* [ME *politik,* fr. MF *politique,* fr. L *politicus,* fr. Gk *politikos,* fr. *politēs* citizen — more at POLICE] **1 :** POLITICAL **2 :** characterized by shrewdness in managing, contriving, or dealing **3 :** sagacious in promoting a policy **4 :** shrewdly tactful ***syn*** see EXPEDIENT, SUAVE

po·lit·i·cal \pə-ˈlit-i-kəl\ *adj* [L *politicus*] **1 a :** of or relating to government, a government, or the conduct of government **b :** of, relating to, or concerned with the making as distinguished from the administration of governmental policy **2 a :** of, relating to, or involving politics and esp. party politics **b :** adept at, sensitive to, or engrossed in politics <highly ~ students> **3 :** organized in governmental terms <~ units> **4 :** involving or charged or concerned with acts against a government or a political system <~ criminals> — **po·lit·i·cal·ly** \-k(ə-)lē\ *adv*

political economy *n* **1 :** a 19th century social science comprising the modern science of economics **2 :** a modern social science dealing with the interrelationship of political and economic processes — **political economist** *n*

political science *n* **:** a social science concerned chiefly with the description and analysis of political and esp. governmental institutions and processes — **political scientist** *n*

pol·i·ti·cian \ˌpäl-ə-ˈtish-ən\ *n* **1 :** a person experienced in the art or science of government; *esp* **:** one actively engaged in conducting the business of a government **2 a :** a person engaged in party politics as a profession **b :** a person primarily interested in political offices from selfish or other narrow usu. short-run interests

po·lit·i·cize \pə-ˈlit-ə-ˌsīz\ *vb* **-cized; -ciz·ing** *vi* **:** to discuss or discourse on politics ~ *vt* **:** to give a political tone or character to — **po·lit·i·ci·za·tion** \-ˌlit-ə-sə-ˈzā-shən\ *n*

pol·i·tick \ˈpäl-ə-ˌtik\ *vi* [back-formation fr. *politicking,* n., fr. *politics* + *-ing*] **:** to engage in political discussion or activity — **pol·i·tick·er** *n*

po·lit·i·co \pə-ˈlit-i-ˌkō\ *n, pl* **-cos** *also* **-coes** [It *politico* or Sp *político,* derivs. of L *politicus* political] **:** POLITICIAN 2

politico- *comb form* [L *politicus*] **:** political and <*politico*-diplomatic>

pol·i·tics \ˈpäl-ə-ˌtiks\ *n pl but sing or pl in constr* [Gk *politika,* fr. neut. pl. of *politikos* political] **1 a :** the art or science of government **b :** the art or science concerned with guiding or influencing governmental policy **c :** the art or science concerned with winning and holding control over a government **2 :** political actions, practices, or policies **3 a :** political affairs or business; *specif* **:** competition between competing interest groups or individuals for power and leadership in a government or other group **b :** political life esp. as a principal activity or profession **c :** political activities characterized by artful and often dishonest practices **4 :** the political opinions or sympathies of a person **5 :** the total complex of relations between men in society

pol·i·ty \ˈpäl-ət-ē\ *n, pl* **-ties** [LL *politia* — more at POLICE] **1 :** political organization **2 :** a specific form of political organization **3 :** a politically organized unit **4 a :** the form or constitution of a politically organized unit **b :** the form of government of a religious denomination

pol·ka \ˈpōl-kə\ *n* [Czech, fr. Pol *Polka* Polish woman, fem. of *Polak* Pole] **1 :** a vivacious couple dance of Bohemian origin in duple time with a basic pattern of hop-step-close-step **2 :** a lively Bohemian dance tune in 2/4 time — **polka** *vi*

pol·ka dot \ˈpō-kə-ˌdät\ *n* **:** a dot in a pattern of regularly distributed dots in textile design — **polka–dot** *or* **pol·ka–dot·ted** \-ˌdät-əd\ *adj*

[1]**poll** \ˈpōl\ *n* [ME *pol, polle,* fr. MLG] **1 :** HEAD **2 a :** the prominent hairy top or back of the head **b :** NAPE **3 :** the broad or flat end of a striking tool (as a hammer) **4 a** (1) **:** the casting or recording of the votes of a body of persons (2) **:** a counting of votes cast **b :** the place where votes are cast or recorded — usu. used in pl. <at the ~*s*> **c :** the period of time during which votes may be cast at an election **d :** the total number of votes recorded <a heavy ~> **5 a :** a questioning or canvassing of persons selected at random or by quota to obtain information or opinions to be analyzed **b :** a record of the information so obtained

[2]**poll** *vt* **1 a :** to cut off or cut short the hair or wool of **:** CROP, SHEAR **b :** to cut off or cut short (as wool) **2 a :** to cut off or back the top of (as a tree); *specif* **:** POLLARD **b :** to cut off or cut short the horns of (cattle) **3 a :** to receive and record the votes of **b :** to request each member of to declare his vote individually <~ the assembly> **4 :** to receive (as votes) in an election **5 :** to question or canvass in a poll ~ *vi* **:** to cast one's vote at a poll — **poll·ee** \pō-ˈlē\ *n* — **poll·er** \ˈpō-lər\ *n*

[3]**poll** *n* [prob. fr. obs. E *poll,* adj., naturally hornless, short for E *polled*] **:** a polled animal

pol·lack *or* **pol·lock** \ˈpäl-ək\ *n, pl* **pollack** *or* **pollock** [Sc *podlok,* of unknown origin] **:** a commercially important north Atlantic food fish (*Pollachius virens*) related to and resembling the cods but darker

[1]**pol·lard** \ˈpäl-ərd\ *n* [[2]*poll*] **1 :** a hornless animal of a usu. horned kind **2 :** a tree cut back to the trunk to promote the growth of a dense head of foliage

[2]**pollard** *vt* **:** to make a pollard of (a tree)

polled \ˈpōld\ *adj* **:** having no horns

pol·len \ˈpäl-ən\ *n* [NL *pollin-, pollen,* fr. L, fine flour; akin to L *pulvis* dust, Gk *palē* fine meal] **1 :** a mass of microspores in a seed plant appearing usu. as a fine dust **2 :** a dusty bloom on the body of an insect — **pol·lin·ic** \pä-ˈlin-ik\ *adj*

pol·len·ate \ˈpäl-ə-ˌnāt\ *vt* **:** POLLINATE 1 — **pol·len·ation** \ˌpäl-ə-ˈnā-shən\ *n*

pollen basket *n* **:** a smooth area on each hind tibia of a bee that is edged by a fringe of stiff hairs and serves to collect and transport pollen — called also *corbicula*

bee with full pollen baskets

pollen grain *n* **:** one of the granular microspores that occur in pollen and give rise to the male gametophyte of a seed plant

pol·len·iz·er \ˈpäl-ə-ˌnī-zər\ *n* [*pollenize* (to pollinize)] **1 :** a plant that is a source of pollen **2 :** POLLINATOR a

pollen mother cell *n* **:** a cell that is derived from the hypodermis of the pollen sac and that gives rise by meiosis to four cells, each of which develops into a pollen grain

pollen sac *n* **:** one of the pouches of a seed plant anther in which pollen is formed

pollen tube *n* **:** a tube that is formed by a pollen grain, passes down the style, and conveys the sperm nuclei to the embryo sac of a flower

pol·lex \ˈpäl-ˌeks\ *n, pl* **pol·li·ces** \ˈpäl-ə-ˌsēz\ [NL *pollic-, pollex,* fr. L, thumb, big toe] **:** the first digit of the forelimb **:** THUMB — **pol·li·cal** \ˈpäl-i-kəl\ *adj*

pollin- *or* **pollini-** *comb form* [NL *pollin-, pollen*] **:** pollen <*pollinate*>

pol·li·nate \ˈpäl-ə-ˌnāt\ *vt* **-nat·ed; -nat·ing** **1 :** to place pollen on the stigma of **2 :** to mark or smudge with pollen

pol·li·na·tion \ˌpäl-ə-ˈnā-shən\ *n* **:** the transfer of pollen from a stamen to an ovule

pol·li·na·tor \ˈpäl-ə-ˌnāt-ər\ *n* **:** one that pollinates: as **a :** an agent that pollinates flowers **b :** POLLENIZER 1

pol·li·nif·er·ous \ˌpäl-ə-ˈnif-(ə-)rəs\ *adj* **1 :** bearing or producing pollen **2 :** adapted for the purpose of carrying pollen

pol·lin·i·um \pä-ˈlin-ē-əm\ *n, pl* **-ia** \-ē-ə\ [NL, fr. *pollin-*] **:** a coherent mass of pollen grains often with a stalk bearing an adhesive disk that clings to insects

pol·li·nize \ˈpäl-ə-ˌnīz\ *vt* **-nized; -niz·ing** [ISV] **:** POLLINATE 1

pol·li·niz·er \ˈ=ˌnī-zər\ *n* : POLLENIZER

pol·li·nose \ˈpäl-ə-ˌnōs\ *adj, of an insect* : covered with pollen

pol·li·no·sis *or* **pol·len·o·sis** \ˌpäl-ə-ˈnō-səs\ *n* [NL *pollinosis,* fr. *pollin-*] : an acute recurrent catarrhal disorder caused by allergic sensitivity to specific pollens

pol·li·wog *or* **pol·ly·wog** \ˈpäl-ē-ˌwäg, -ˌwȯg\ *n* [alter. of ME *polwygle,* prob. fr. *pol* poll + *wiglen* to wiggle] : TADPOLE

poll·ster \ˈpōl-stər\ *n* : one that conducts a poll or compiles data obtained by a poll

poll tax *n* : a tax of a fixed amount per person levied on adults and often payable as a requirement for voting

pol·lut·ant \pə-ˈlüt-ᵊnt\ *n* : something that pollutes

pol·lute \pə-ˈlüt\ *vt* **pol·lut·ed; pol·lut·ing** [ME *polluten,* fr. L *pollutus,* pp. of *polluere,* fr. *por-* (akin to L *per* through) + *-luere* (akin to L *lutum* mud, Gk *lyma* dirt, defilement) — more at FOR] **1** : to make ceremonially or morally impure : DEFILE **2** : to make physically impure or unclean : BEFOUL, DIRTY; *esp* : to contaminate (an environment) esp. with man-made waste ***syn*** see CONTAMINATE — **pol·lut·er** *n* — **pol·lut·ive** \-ˈlüt-iv\ *adj*

pol·lu·tion \pə-ˈlü-shən\ *n* **1** : emission of semen at other times than in coitus **2 a** : the action of polluting : the condition of being polluted **b** : POLLUTANT

Pol·lux \ˈpäl-əks\ *n* [L, modif. of Gk *Polydeukēs*] **1** : one of the Dioscuri **2** : a first-magnitude star in the constellation Gemini

Pol·ly·an·na \ˌpäl-ē-ˈan-ə\ *n* [*Pollyanna,* heroine of the novel *Pollyanna* (1913) by Eleanor Porter] : one characterized by irrepressible optimism and a tendency to find good in everything — **Pol·ly·an·na·ish** \-ˈan-ə-ish\ *or* **Pol·ly·an·nish** \-ˈan-ish\ *adj*

po·lo \ˈpō-(ˌ)lō\ *n* [Balti, ball] **1** : a game of oriental origin played by teams of players on horseback using mallets with long flexible handles to drive a wooden ball **2** : WATER POLO — **po·lo·ist** \ˈpō-(ˌ)lō-əst\ *n*

polo coat *n* : a tailored overcoat that is made of soft fabric and esp. tan camel's hair and often has stitched edges and a half-belt on the back

po·lo·naise \ˌpäl-ə-ˈnāz, ˌpō-lə-\ [F, fr. fem. of *polonais* Polish, fr. *Pologne* Poland, fr. ML *Polonia*] **1** : an elaborate overdress with a short-sleeved fitted waist and a draped cutaway overskirt **2 a** : a stately Polish processional dance popular in 19th century Europe **b** : music for this dance in moderate 3/4 time

po·lo·ni·um \pə-ˈlō-nē-əm\ *n* [NL, fr. ML *Polonia* Poland] : a radioactive metallic element that is similar chemically to tellurium and bismuth, occurs esp. in pitchblende and radium-lead residues, and emits a helium nucleus to form an isotope of lead — see ELEMENT table

Po·lo·ni·us \pə-ˈlō-nē-əs\ *n* : a garrulous courtier and father of Ophelia and Laertes in Shakespeare's *Hamlet*

polo shirt *n* : a close-fitting pullover knit shirt with short or long sleeves and turnover collar or banded neck

polonaise 1

pol·ter·geist \ˈpōl-tər-ˌgīst\ *n* [G, fr. *poltern* to knock + *geist* spirit, fr. OHG — more at GHOST] : a noisy usu. mischievous ghost held to be responsible for unexplained noises (as rappings)

¹pol·troon \päl-ˈtrün\ *n* [MF *poultron,* fr. OIt *poltrone,* fr. aug. of *poltro* colt, deriv. of L *pullus* young of an animal — more at FOAL] : a spiritless coward : CRAVEN

²poltroon *adj* : characterized by complete cowardice

pol·troon·ery \-ˈtrün-(ə-)rē\ *n* : mean pusillanimity : COWARDICE

pol·troon·ish \-ˈtrü-nish\ *adj* : resembling a poltroon : COWARDLY — **pol·troon·ish·ly** *adv*

¹poly \ˈpäl-ē\ *n, pl* **pol·ys** \-ēz\ [by shortening] : a polymorphonuclear leukocyte

²poly *abbr* polytechnic

poly- *comb form* [ME, fr. L, fr. Gk, fr. *polys;* akin to OE *full* full] **1 a** : many : several : much : MULTI- <*poly*chotomous> <*polygyny*> **b** : excessive : abnormal : HYPER- <*poly*phagia> **2 a** : containing an indefinite number more than one of a (specified) substance <*poly*sulfide> **b** : polymeric : polymer of a (specified) monomer <*poly*ethylene> <*poly*adenylic acid>

poly·acryl·amide \ˌpäl-ē-ə-ˈkril-ə-ˌmīd\ *n* : a polyamide of acrylic acid

polyacrylamide gel *n* : hydrated polyacrylamide that is used esp. for electrophoresis

poly·adel·phous \ˌpäl-ē-ə-ˈdel-fəs\ *adj* : united by the anthers into three or more groups <~ stamens>

poly·al·co·hol \ˌpäl-ē-ˈal-kə-ˌhȯl\ *n* : an alcohol (as ethylene glycol) that contains more than one hydroxy group

polyalphabetic substitution \ˌpäl-ē-ˌal-fə-ˈbet-ik-\ *n* : substitution in cryptography that uses several cipher alphabets so that each plaintext letter will have a continually changing cipher equivalent — compare MONOALPHABETIC SUBSTITUTION

poly·am·ide \ˌpäl-ē-ˈam-ˌīd\ *n* [ISV] : a compound characterized by more than one amide group; *esp* : a polymeric amide

poly·an·dric \-ˈan-drik\ *adj* : of or relating to polyandry

poly·an·drous \-drəs\ *adj* **1** [*poly-* + *-androus*] : having many usu. free hypogynous stamens **2** [*polyandry*] : relating to or practicing polyandry

poly·an·dry \ˈpäl-ē-ˌan-drē\ *n* [Gk *polyandros,* adj., having many husbands, fr. *poly-* + *andr-, anēr* man, husband — more at ANDR-] **1** : the state or practice of having more than one husband or male mate at one time — compare POLYGAMY, POLYGYNY **2** : the state of being polyandrous

poly·an·tha \ˌpäl-ē-ˈan(t)-thə\ *n* [NL, fr. Gk *polyanthos* blooming] : any of numerous dwarf hybrid bush roses characterized by many large clusters of small flowers

poly·an·thus \-ˈan(t)-thəs\ *n, pl* **-an·thus·es** *or* **-an·thi** \-ˈan-ˌthī, -ˌthē\ [NL, fr. Gk *polyanthos* blooming, fr. *poly-* + *anthos* flower — more at ANTHOLOGY] **1** : any of various hybrid primroses **2** : a narcissus (*Narcissus tazetta*) having small umbeled white or yellow flowers with a spreading perianth

poly·ba·site \ˌpäl-i-ˈbā-ˌsīt\ *n* [G *polybasit,* fr. *poly-* + *basi-*] : an iron-black metallic-looking ore $(Ag,Cu)_{16}Sb_2S_{11}$ of silver consisting of silver, copper, sulfur, and antimony

poly·car·bon·ate \ˌpäl-i-ˈkär-bə-ˌnāt, -nət\ *n* : any of various tough transparent thermoplastics characterized by high impact strength and high softening temperature

poly·car·pel·lary \-ˈkär-pə-ˌler-ē\ *adj* : consisting of several carpels

poly·car·pic \-ˈkär-pik\ *or* **poly·car·pous** \-pəs\ *adj* [prob. fr. NL *polycarpicus, polycarpus,* fr. *poly-* + *-carpicus* -carpic, *-carpus* -carpous] : having a gynoecium forming two or more distinct ovaries — **poly·car·py** \ˈpäl-i-ˌkär-pē\ *n*

poly·cen·trism \ˌpäl-i-ˈsen-ˌtriz-əm\ *n* : the doctrine of a plurality of centers of Communist thought and leadership

poly·chaete \ˈpäl-i-ˌkēt\ *adj* [deriv. of Gk *polychaitēs* having much hair, fr. *poly-* + *chaitē* long hair — more at CHAETA] : of or relating to a class (Polychaeta) of chiefly marine annelid worms usu. with paired segmental appendages, separate sexes, and a free-swimming trochophore larva — **polychaete** *n* — **poly·chae·tous** \ˌpäl-i-ˈkēt-əs\ *adj*

poly·cha·si·um \ˌpäl-i-ˈkā-z(h)ē-əm\ *n, pl* **-sia** \-z(h)ē-ə\ [NL, fr. *poly-* + *-chasium* (as in *dichasium*)] : a cymose inflorescence in which each main axis produces more than two branches

poly·chlo·ri·nat·ed biphenyl \-ˈklōr-ə-ˌnāt-əd-, -ˈklȯr-\ *n* : any of several compounds that are produced by replacing hydrogen atoms in biphenyl with chlorine, have various industrial applications, and are poisonous environmental pollutants which tend to accumulate in animal tissues — called also *PCB*

poly·chot·o·mous \-ˈkät-ə-məs\ *adj* [*poly-* + *-chotomous* (as in *dichotomous*)] : dividing or marked by division into many parts, branches, or classes — **poly·chot·o·my** \-mē\ *n*

poly·chro·mat·ic \-krō-ˈmat-ik\ *adj* [Gk *polychrōmatos,* fr. *poly-* + *chrōmat-, chrōma* color — more at CHROMATIC] **1** : showing a variety or a change of colors : MULTICOLORED **2** : being or relating to radiation that is composed of more than one wavelength

poly·chro·mato·phil·ia \-krō-ˌmat-ə-ˈfil-ē-ə\ *n* [NL] : the quality of being stainable with more than one type of stain and esp. with both acid and basic dyes

poly·chrome \ˈpäl-i-ˌkrōm\ *adj* [Gk *polychrōmos,* fr. *poly-* + *chrōma*] : relating to, made with, or decorated in several colors <~ pottery> — **poly·chro·my** \-ˌkrō-mē\ *n*

poly·cis·tron·ic \ˌpäl-i-sis-ˈträn-ik\ *adj* : containing the genetic information of a number of cistrons <~ messenger RNA>

poly·clin·ic \ˌpäl-i-ˈklin-ik\ *n* [ISV] : a clinic or hospital treating diseases of many sorts

poly·con·den·sa·tion \-ˌkän-ˌden-ˈsā-shən, -dən-\ *n* [ISV] : a chemical condensation leading to the formation of a compound of high molecular weight

poly·con·ic projection \ˌpäl-i-ˌkän-ik-\ *n* : a map projection of the earth's surface in which each narrow section is projected on the inside surface of a cone touching the sphere along this section and then the cone is unrolled

poly·cot \ˈpäl-i-ˌkät\ *or* **poly·cot·yl** \-ˌkät-ᵊl\ *n* : POLYCOTYLEDON

poly·cot·y·le·don \-ˌkät-ᵊl-ˈēd-ᵊn\ *n* [NL] : a plant having more than two cotyledons — **poly·cot·y·le·don·ous** \-ˈēd-nəs, -ᵊn-əs\ *adj*

poly·crys·tal·line \-ˈkris-tə-lən\ *adj* **1** : consisting of crystals variously oriented **2** : composed of more than one crystal — **poly·crys·tal** \ˈpäl-i-ˌkris-tᵊl\ *n*

poly·cy·clic \ˌpäl-i-ˈsī-klik, -ˈsik-lik\ *adj* [ISV] : having more than one cyclic component; *esp* : having two or more usu. fused rings in the molecule

poly·cy·the·mia \-(ˌ)sī-ˈthē-mē-ə\ *n* [NL, fr. *poly-* + *cyt-* + *-hemia*] : a condition marked by an abnormal increase in the number of circulating red blood cells; *specif* : POLYCYTHEMIA VERA — **poly·cy·the·mic** \-mik\ *adj*

polycythemia ve·ra \-ˈvir-ə\ *n* [NL, true polycythemia] : polycythemia of unknown cause that is characterized by increase in total blood volume and accompanied by nosebleed, distension of the circulatory vessels, and enlargement of the spleen — called also *erythremia*

poly·dac·tyl \ˌpäl-i-ˈdak-tᵊl\ *adj* [Gk *polydaktylos,* fr. *poly-* + *daktylos* digit] : having several to many and esp. abnormally many digits — **poly·dac·ty·ly** \-tə-lē\ *n*

poly·dac·ty·lous \-tə-ləs\ *adj* : POLYDACTYL

poly·dip·sia \ˌpäl-i-ˈdip-sē-ə\ *n* [NL, fr. *poly-* + Gk *dipsa* thirst] : excessive or abnormal thirst — **poly·dip·sic** \-sik\ *adj*

poly·dis·perse \-dis-ˈpərs\ *adj* [*poly-* + L *dispersus* dispersed, fr. pp. of *dispergere* to disperse] : of, relating to, or characterized by particles of varied sizes in the dispersed phase of a disperse system — **poly·dis·per·si·ty** \-ˈpər-sət-ē\ *n*

poly·elec·tro·lyte \ˌpäl-ē-ə-ˈlek-trə-ˌlīt\ *n* : a substance of high molecular weight (as a protein or a nucleotide) that is an electrolyte

poly·em·bry·o·ny \-ˈem-brē-ə-nē, -(ˌ)em-ˈbrī-\ *n* [ISV *poly-* + *embryon-* + *-y*] **1** : the condition of having several embryos **2** : the production of two or more embryos from one ovule or egg — **poly·em·bry·on·ic** \-ˌem-brē-ˈän-ik\ *adj*

poly·ene \ˈpäl-ē-ˌēn\ *n* [ISV] : an organic compound containing many double bonds; *esp* : one having the double bonds in a long aliphatic hydrocarbon chain — **poly·enic** \-ˈē-nik\ *adj*

poly·es·ter \ˈpäl-ē-ˌes-tər\ *n* [ISV] : a complex ester formed by polymerization or condensation and used esp. in making fibers or plastics — **poly·es·ter·i·fi·ca·tion** \-ē-ˌster-ə-fə-ˈkā-shən\ *n*

poly·es·trous \ˌpäl-ē-ˈes-trəs\ *adj* : having more than one period of estrus in a year

poly·eth·yl·ene \-ˈeth-ə-ˌlēn\ *n* **:** a polymer of ethylene; *esp* **:** any of various partially crystalline lightweight thermoplastics $(CH_2CH_2)_x$ that are resistant to chemicals and moisture, have good insulating properties, and are used esp. in packaging and insulation
po·lyg·a·la \pə-ˈlig-ə-lə\ *n* [NL, genus name, fr. L, milkwort, fr. Gk *polygalon,* fr. *poly-* + *gala* milk — more at GALAXY] **:** MILKWORT
poly·gam·ic \ˌpäl-i-ˈgam-ik\ *adj* **:** POLYGAMOUS — **poly·gam·i·cal** \-i-kəl\ *adj* — **poly·gam·i·cal·ly** \-i-k(ə-)lē\ *adv*
po·lyg·a·mous \pə-ˈlig-ə-məs\ *adj* [Gk *polygamos,* fr. *poly-* + *-gamos* -gamous] **1 a :** relating to or practicing polygamy **b :** having more than one mate at one time <baboons are ~> **2 :** bearing both hermaphrodite and unisexual flowers on the same plant — **po·lyg·a·mous·ly** *adv*
po·lyg·a·my \-mē\ *n* **1 :** marriage in which a spouse of either sex may have more than one mate at the same time — compare POLYANDRY, POLYGYNY **2 :** the state of being polygamous — **po·lyg·a·mist** \-məst\ *n* — **po·lyg·a·mize** \-ˌmīz\ *vi*
poly·gene \ˈpäl-i-ˌjēn\ *n* [ISV] **:** any of a group of nonallelic genes that collectively control the inheritance of a quantitative character or modify the expression of a qualitative character — **poly·gen·ic** \ˌpäl-i-ˈjē-nik\ *adj*
poly·gen·e·sis \ˌpäl-i-ˈjen-ə-səs\ *n* [NL] **:** polyphyletic origin — **poly·gen·e·sist** \-səst\ *n*
poly·ge·net·ic \-jə-ˈnet-ik\ *adj* **1 :** having many distinct sources **2 :** of or relating to polygenesis **:** POLYPHYLETIC — **poly·ge·net·i·cal·ly** \-i-k(ə-)lē\ *adv*
poly·glan·du·lar \-ˈglan-jə-lər\ *adj* [ISV] **:** of, relating to, or involving several glands <~ therapy>
[1]**poly·glot** \ˈpäl-i-ˌglät\ *n* [Gk *polyglōttos,* adj., polyglot, fr. *poly-* + *glōtta* language — more at GLOSS] **1 :** one who is polyglot **2** *cap* **:** a book containing versions of the same text in several languages; *esp* **:** the Scriptures in several languages **3 :** a mixture or confusion of languages or nomenclatures
[2]**polyglot** *adj* **1 a :** speaking or writing several languages **:** MULTILINGUAL **b :** composed of numerous linguistic groups <a ~ population> **2 :** containing matter in several languages <a ~ sign> **3 :** composed of elements from different languages
poly·glot·ism *or* **poly·glot·tism** \-ˌglät-ˌiz-əm\ *n* **:** the use of many languages **:** the ability to speak many languages
poly·gon \ˈpäl-i-ˌgän\ *n* [LL *polygonum,* fr. Gk *polygōnon,* fr. neut. of *polygōnos* polygonal, fr. *poly-* + *gōnia* angle — more at -GON] **1 :** a closed plane figure bounded by straight lines **2 :** a closed figure on a sphere bounded by arcs of great circles — **po·lyg·o·nal** \pə-ˈlig-ən-ᵊl\ *adj* — **po·lyg·o·nal·ly** \-ᵊl-ē\ *adv*

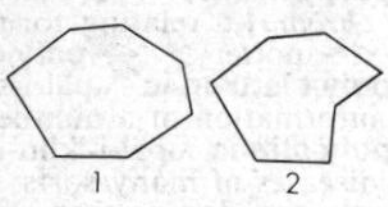

polygons 1: *1* convex, *2* concave

po·lyg·o·num \pə-ˈlig-ə-nəm\ *n* [NL, genus name, fr. Gk *polygonon* knotgrass, fr. *poly-* + *gony* knee — more at KNEE] **:** any of a genus (*Polygonum*) of herbs of the buckwheat family with prominent ocreae, thickened nodes, and flowers that are solitary and axillary or in spiked racemes — called also *knotweed*
poly·graph \ˈpäl-i-ˌgraf\ *n* **:** an instrument for recording variations of several different pulsations (as of physiological variables) simultaneously; *broadly* **:** LIE DETECTOR — **poly·graph·ic** \ˌpäl-i-ˈgraf-ik\ *adj*
poly·gy·noe·cial \ˌpäl-i-jin-ˈē-s(h)ē-əl, -i-(ˌ)gī-ˈnē-, -shəl\ *adj* [*poly-* + NL *gynoecium*] **:** made up of several to many united gynoecia
po·lyg·y·nous \pə-ˈlij-ə-nəs\ *adj* **1 :** relating to or practicing polygyny **2 :** having many pistils
po·lyg·y·ny \-nē\ *n* **:** the state or practice of having more than one wife or female mate at one time — compare POLYANDRY, POLYGAMY
polyhedral angle *n* **:** a portion of space partly enclosed by three or more planes whose intersections meet in a vertex
poly·he·dron \ˌpäl-i-ˈhē-drən\ *n, pl* **-drons** *or* **-dra** \-drə\ [NL] **:** a solid formed by plane faces — **poly·he·dral** \-drəl\ *adj*
poly·he·dro·sis \ˌpäl-i-hē-ˈdrō-səs\ *n, pl* **-droses** [NL, fr. *polyhedron*] **:** any of several virus diseases of insect larvae characterized by dissolution of tissues and accumulation of polyhedral granules in the resultant fluid
poly·his·tor \ˌpäl-i-ˈhis-tər\ *n* [Gk *polyistōr* very learned, fr. *poly-* + *istōr, histōr* learned — more at HISTORY] **:** POLYMATH — **poly·his·tor·ic** \-his-ˈtȯr-ik, -ˈtär-\ *adj*
poly·hy·droxy \-hī-ˈdräk-sē\ *adj* [*poly-* + *hydroxyl*] **:** containing more than one hydroxyl group in the molecule
Poly·hym·nia \ˌpäl-i-ˈhim-nē-ə\ *n* [L, fr. Gk *Polyymnia*] **:** the Greek Muse of sacred song
poly·mas·ti·gote \ˌpäl-i-ˈmas-tə-ˌgōt\ *adj* **:** having many flagella
poly·math \ˈpäl-i-ˌmath\ *n* [Gk *polymathēs* very learned, fr. *poly-* + *manthanein* to learn — more at MATHEMATICAL] **:** one of encyclopedic learning — **polymath** *or* **poly·math·ic** \ˌpäl-i-ˈmath-ik\ *adj* — **po·ly·ma·thy** \pə-ˈlim-ə-thē, ˈpäl-ə-ˌmath-ē\ *n*
poly·mer \ˈpäl-ə-mər\ *n* [ISV, back-formation fr. *polymeric*] **:** a chemical compound or mixture of compounds formed by polymerization and consisting essentially of repeating structural units
poly·mer·ase \-mə-ˌrās, -ˌrāz\ *n* [*polymer* + *-ase*] **:** any of several enzymes that catalyze the formation of DNA or RNA from precursor substances in the presence of preexisting DNA or RNA acting as a template
poly·mer·ic \ˌpäl-ə-ˈmer-ik\ *adj* [ISV, fr. Gk *polymerēs* having many parts, fr. *poly-* + *meros* part — more at MERIT] **1 :** of, relating to, or constituting a polymer **2 :** of, relating to, being, or involving nonallelic often identical genes that collectively control one or more hereditary traits — **poly·mer·i·cal·ly** \-i-k(ə-)lē\ *adv* — **po·ly·mer·ism** \pə-ˈlim-ə-ˌriz-əm, ˈpäl-ə-mə-\ *n*
po·ly·mer·iza·tion \pə-ˌlim-ə-rə-ˈzā-shən, ˌpäl-ə-mə-rə-\ *n* [ISV] **1 :** a chemical reaction in which two or more small molecules combine to form larger molecules that contain repeating structural units of the original molecules — compare ASSOCIATION 5 **2 :** reduplication of parts in an organism
po·ly·mer·ize \pə-ˈlim-ə-ˌrīz, ˈpäl-ə-mə-\ *vb* **-ized; -iz·ing** *vt* **:** to subject to polymerization ~ *vi* **:** to undergo polymerization
poly·morph \ˈpäl-i-ˌmȯrf\ *n* [ISV] **1 :** a polymorphic organism; *also* **:** one of the several forms of such an organism **2 :** any of the crystalline forms of a polymorphic substance
poly·mor·phic \ˌpäl-i-ˈmȯr-fik\ *or* **poly·mor·phous** \-fəs\ *adj* [Gk *polymorphos,* fr. *poly-* + *-morphos* -morphous] **:** having, assuming, or occurring in various forms, characters, or styles — **poly·mor·phi·cal·ly** \-fi-k(ə-)lē\ *or* **poly·mor·phous·ly** *adv* — **poly·mor·phism** \-ˌfiz-əm\ *n*
poly·mor·pho·nu·cle·ar \-ˌmȯr-fə-ˈn(y)ü-klē-ər\ *adj, of a leukocyte* **:** having the nucleus complexly lobed — **polymorphonuclear** *n*
poly·myx·in \ˌpäl-i-ˈmik-sən\ *n* [ISV, fr. NL *polymyxa* (specific epithet of *Bacillus polymyxa*), fr. *poly-* + Gk *myxa* mucus — more at MUCUS] **:** any of several toxic antibiotics obtained from a soil bacterium (*Bacillus polymyxa*) and active against gram-negative bacteria
Poly·ne·sian \ˌpäl-ə-ˈnē-zhən, -shən\ *n* **1 :** a member of any of the native peoples of Polynesia **2 :** a group of Austronesian languages spoken in Polynesia — **Polynesian** *adj*
poly·neu·ri·tis \ˌpäl-i-n(y)u̇-ˈrīt-əs\ *n* [NL] **:** neuritis of several peripheral nerves at the same time caused by alcoholism, poisons, infectious disease, or vitamin deficiency (as of thiamine)
Poly·ni·ces \ˌpäl-ə-ˈnī-sēz\ *n* [L, fr. Gk *Polyneikēs*] **:** a son of Oedipus in whose behalf the Seven against Thebes mounted their expedition
[1]**poly·no·mi·al** \ˌpäl-ə-ˈnō-mē-əl\ *n* [*poly-* + *-nomial* (as in *binomial*)] **:** a sum of two or more algebraic terms each of which consists of a constant multiplied by one or more variables raised to a nonnegative integral power <$a + bx + cx^2$ is a ~>
[2]**polynomial** *adj* **:** relating to, composed of, or expressed as one or more polynomials <~ functions> <~ equations>
poly·nu·cle·ar \ˌpäl-i-ˈn(y)ü-klē-ər\ *adj* [ISV] **:** chemically polycyclic esp. with respect to the benzene ring — used chiefly of aromatic hydrocarbons that are important as pollutants and possibly as carcinogens
poly·nu·cle·o·tide \-ˈn(y)ü-klē-ə-ˌtīd\ *n* [ISV] **:** a polymeric chain of mononucleotides
po·lyn·ya \ˌpäl-ən-ˈyä\ *n* [Russ *polyn'ya*] **:** an area of open water in sea ice
poly·oma virus \ˌpäl-ē-ˈō-mə-\ *n* [NL *polyoma,* fr. *poly-* + *-oma*] **:** a papovavirus of rodents that is associated with various kinds of tumors — called also *polyoma*
poly·on·y·mous \ˌpäl-ē-ˈän-ə-məs\ *adj* [Gk *polyōnymos,* fr. *poly-* + *onoma, onyma* name] **:** having or known by various names
pol·yp \ˈpäl-əp\ *n* [MF *polype* octopus, nasal tumor, fr. L *polypus,* fr. Gk *polypous,* fr. *poly-* + *pous* foot — more at FOOT] **1 :** a coelenterate that has typically a hollow cylindrical body closed and attached at one end and opening at the other by a central mouth surrounded by tentacles armed with nematocysts **2 :** a projecting mass of swollen and hypertrophied or tumorous membrane — **pol·yp·oid** \-ə-ˌpȯid\ *adj*
pol·yp·ary \ˈpäl-ə-ˌper-ē\ *n* **:** the common investing structure or tissue in which the polyps of compound coelenterates (as corals) are embedded
poly·pep·tide \ˌpäl-i-ˈpep-ˌtīd\ *n* [ISV] **:** a molecular chain of amino acids — **poly·pep·tid·ic** \-(ˌ)pep-ˈtid-ik\ *adj*
poly·pet·al·ous \-ˈpet-ᵊl-əs\ *adj* [NL *polypetalus,* fr. *poly-* + *petalum* petal] **:** having or consisting of separate petals
poly·pha·gia \-ˈfā-j(ē-)ə\ *n* [Gk *polyphagia,* fr. *polyphagos*] **:** excessive appetite or eating
po·lyph·a·gous \pə-ˈlif-ə-gəs\ *adj* [Gk *polyphagos* eating too much, fr. *poly-* + *-phagos* -phagous] **:** feeding on or utilizing many kinds of food — **po·lyph·a·gy** \-ə-jē\ *n*
poly·phase \ˈpäl-i-ˌfāz\ *adj* [ISV] **:** having or producing two or more phases <a ~ machine> <a ~ current>
poly·pha·sic \ˌpäl-i-ˈfā-zik\ *adj* **:** consisting of two or more phases
Poly·phe·mus \ˌpäl-ə-ˈfē-məs\ *n* [L, fr. Gk *Polyphēmos*] **:** a Cyclops whom Odysseus blinded in order to escape from his cave
poly·phe·nol \ˌpäl-i-ˈfē-ˌnōl, -fi-ˈ\ *n* [ISV] **:** a polyhydroxy phenol — **poly·phe·no·lic** \-fi-ˈnō-lik, -ˈnäl-ik\ *adj*
poly·phone \ˈpäl-i-ˌfōn\ *n* **:** a symbol or sequence of symbols having more than one phonemic value (as *a* in English)
poly·phon·ic \ˌpäl-i-ˈfän-ik\ *or* **po·lyph·o·nous** \pə-ˈlif-ə-nəs\ *adj* **1 :** of, relating to, or marked by polyphony **2 :** being a polyphone — **poly·phon·i·cal·ly** \ˌpäl-i-ˈfän-i-k(ə-)lē\ *or* **po·lyph·o·nous·ly** *adv*
polyphonic prose *n* **:** a freely rhythmical prose employing characteristic devices of verse (as alliteration and assonance)
po·lyph·o·ny \pə-ˈlif-ə-nē\ *n* [Gk *polyphōnia* variety of tones, fr. *polyphōnos* having many tones or voices, fr. *poly-* + *phōnē* voice — more at BAN] **:** a style of musical composition in which two or more independent but organically related voice parts sound against one another
poly·phy·let·ic \ˌpäl-i-(ˌ)fī-ˈlet-ik\ *adj* [ISV, fr. Gk *polyphylos* of many tribes, fr. *poly-* + *phylē* tribe — more at PHYL-] **:** of or relating to more than one stock; *specif* **:** derived from more than one ancestral line — **poly·phy·let·i·cal·ly** \-i-k(ə-)lē\ *adv* — **poly·phy·let·i·cism** \-ˈlet-ə-ˌsiz-əm\ *n*
pol·yp·ide \ˈpäl-ə-ˌpīd\ *n* [*polyp* + Gk *-idēs,* patronymic suffix] **:** one of the individual zooids of a bryozoan colony
poly·ploid \ˈpäl-i-ˌplȯid\ *adj* [ISV] **:** having or being a chromosome number that is a multiple greater than two of the monoploid number — **polyploid** *n* — **poly·ploi·dy** \-ˌplȯid-ē\ *n*
po·lyp·nea \pä-ˈlip-nē-ə, pə-\ *n* [NL] **:** rapid or panting respiration — **po·lyp·ne·ic** \-nē-ik\ *adj*
poly·po·dy \ˈpäl-ə-ˌpōd-ē\ *n, pl* **-dies** [ME *polypodie,* fr. L *polypodium,* fr. Gk *polypodion,* fr. *poly-* + *pod-, pous* foot — more at FOOT] **:** a widely distributed fern (*Polypodium vulgare*) that has creeping rootstocks and pinnatifid fronds with entire segments
pol·yp·ous \ˈpäl-ə-pəs\ *adj* **:** relating to, being, or resembling a polyp
poly·pro·pyl·ene \ˌpäl-i-ˈprō-pə-ˌlēn\ *n* **:** any of various thermoplastic plastics or fibers that are polymers of propylene
po·lyp·tych \ˈpäl-əp-ˌtik, pə-ˈlip-tik\ *n* [Gk *polyptychos* having many folds, fr. *poly-* + *ptychē* fold, fr. *ptyssein* to fold] **:** an

arrangement of four or more panels (as of a painting) usu. hinged and folding together
poly·rhythm \ˈpäl-i-ˌri*th*-əm\ *n* **:** the simultaneous combination of contrasting rhythms in a musical composition — **poly·rhyth·mic** \ˌpäl-i-ˈri*th*-mik\ *adj* — **poly·rhyth·mi·cal·ly** \-mi-k(ə-)lē\ *adv*
poly·ri·bo·nu·cle·o·tide \ˌpäl-i-ˌrī-bō-ˈn(y)ü-klē-ə-ˌtīd\ *n* **:** a polynucleotide in which the mononucleotides are ribonucleotides
poly·ri·bo·some \-ˈrī-bə-ˌsōm\ *n* **:** a cluster of ribosomes linked together by a molecule of messenger RNA and forming the site of protein synthesis — **poly·ri·bo·som·al** \-ˌrī-bə-ˈsō-məl\ *adj*
poly·sac·cha·ride \-ˈsak-ə-ˌrīd\ *n* [ISV] **:** a carbohydrate that can be decomposed by hydrolysis into two or more molecules of monosaccharides; *esp* **:** one of the more complex carbohydrates (as cellulose, starch, or glycogen)
poly·sa·pro·bic \-sə-ˈprō-bik\ *adj* [ISV] **:** living in a medium that is rich in decomposable organic matter and is nearly free from dissolved oxygen
po·ly·se·mous \ˌpäl-i-ˈsē-məs, pə-ˈlis-ə-məs\ *adj* [LL *polysemus*, fr. Gk *polysēmos*, fr. *poly-* + *sēma* sign] **:** marked by multiplicity of meaning — **po·ly·se·my** \-mē\ *n*
poly·sep·al·ous \ˌpäl-i-ˈsep-ə-ləs\ *adj* **:** having separate sepals
poly·some \ˈpäl-i-ˌsōm\ *n* **:** POLYRIBOSOME
poly·so·mic \ˌpäl-i-ˈsō-mik\ *adj* [ISV] **:** having one or a few chromosomes present in greater or smaller number than the rest — **polysomic** *n*
poly·sor·bate \-ˈsȯr-ˌbāt\ *n* **:** any of several emulsifiers used in the preparation of some pharmaceuticals or foods
po·lys·ti·chous \pə-ˈlis-ti-kəs\ *adj* [Gk *polystichos*, fr. *poly-* + *stichos* row — more at DISTICH] **:** arranged in several rows
poly·sty·rene \ˌpäl-i-ˈstī(ə)r-ˌēn\ *n* **:** a polymer of styrene; *esp* **:** a rigid transparent thermoplastic of good physical and electrical insulating properties used esp. in molded products, foams, and sheet materials
poly·sul·fide \-ˈsəl-ˌfīd\ *n* [ISV] **:** a sulfide containing two or more atoms of sulfur in the molecule
poly·syl·lab·ic \ˌpäl-i-sə-ˈlab-ik\ *adj* [ML *polysyllabus*, fr. Gk *polysyllabos*, fr. *poly-* + *syllabē* syllable] **1 :** having more than three syllables **2 :** characterized by polysyllabic words — **poly·syl·lab·i·cal·ly** \-i-k(ə-)lē\ *adv*
poly·syl·la·ble \ˈpäl-i-ˌsil-ə-bəl, ˌpäl-i-ˈ\ *n* [modif. of ML *polysyllaba*, fr. fem. of *polysyllabus*] **:** a polysyllabic word
poly·syn·ap·tic \ˌpäl-i-sə-ˈnap-tik\ *adj* **:** involving two or more synapses in the central nervous system <~ reflexes> — **poly·syn·ap·ti·cal·ly** \-ti-k(ə-)lē\ *adv*
poly·syn·de·ton \-ˈsin-də-ˌtän\ *n* [NL, fr. LGk, neut. of *polysyndetos* using many conjunctions, fr. Gk *poly-* + *syndetos* bound together, conjunctive — more at ASYNDETON] **:** repetition of conjunctions in close succession (as in *we have ships and men and money and stores*)
[1]**poly·tech·nic** \-ˈtek-nik\ *adj* [F *polytechnique*, fr. Gk *polytechnos* skilled in many arts, fr. *poly-* + *technē* art — more at TECHNICAL] **:** relating to or devoted to instruction in many technical arts or applied sciences
[2]**polytechnic** *n* **:** a polytechnic school
poly·tene \ˈpäl-i-ˌtēn\ *adj* [ISV] **:** relating to, being, or having chromosomes each of which consists of many strands with the corresponding chromomeres in contact — **poly·te·ny** \-ˌtē-nē\ *n*
poly·the·ism \ˈpäl-i-(ˌ)thē-ˌiz-əm\ *n* [F *polythéisme*, fr. L Gk *polytheos* polytheistic, fr. Gk, of many gods, fr. *poly-* + *theos* god] **:** belief in or worship of more than one god — **poly·the·ist** \-ˌthē-əst\ *adj or n* — **poly·the·is·tic** \ˌpäl-i-thē-ˈis-tik\ *also* **poly·the·is·ti·cal** \-ˈis-ti-kəl\ *adj*
poly·thene \ˈpäl-ə-ˌthēn\ *n* [by contr.] **:** POLYETHYLENE
po·lyt·o·cous \pə-ˈlit-ə-kəs\ *adj* [Gk *polytokos*, fr. *poly-* + *tiktein* to beget — more at THANE] **:** producing many eggs or young at one time
poly·to·nal·i·ty \ˌpäl-i-tō-ˈnal-ət-ē\ *n* **:** the simultaneous use of two or more musical keys — **poly·ton·al** \-ˈtōn-ᵊl\ *adj* — **poly·ton·al·ly** \-ᵊl-ē\ *adv*
poly·tro·phic \-ˈtrō-fik\ *adj* **:** deriving nourishment from more than one organic substance
poly·type \ˈpäl-i-ˌtīp\ *n* **:** a polymorphic crystal structure — **poly·typ·ism** \-ˌtī-ˌpiz-əm\ *n*
poly·typ·ic \ˌpäl-i-ˈtip-ik\ *adj* **1 :** represented by several or many types or subdivisions **2 :** of, relating to, or being a polytype
poly·un·sat·u·rat·ed \ˈpäl-ē-ˌən-ˈsach-ə-ˌrāt-əd\ *adj, of an oil or fatty acid* **:** rich in unsaturated chemical bonds
poly·ure·thane \ˌpäl-ē-ˈyu̇r-ə-ˌthān\ *n* [ISV] **:** any of various polymers that contain NHCOO linkages and are used esp. in flexible and rigid foams, elastomers, and resins
poly·uria \ˌpäl-ē-ˈyu̇r-ē-ə\ *n* [NL] **:** excessive secretion of urine
poly·va·lent \ˌpäl-i-ˈvā-lənt\ *adj* [ISV] **1 a :** having a valence greater usu. than two **b :** having variable valence **2 a :** effective against, sensitive toward, or counteracting more than one exciting agent (as a toxin or antigen) **b :** MULTIVALENT 2 — **poly·va·lence** \-lən(t)s\ *n*
poly·vi·nyl \-ˈvīn-ᵊl\ *adj* [ISV] **:** of, relating to, or being a polymerized vinyl compound, resin, or plastic — often used in combination
poly·wa·ter \ˈpäl-i-ˌwȯt-ər, -ˌwät-\ *n* [*poly*meric *water*] **:** water condensed into a glass capillary tube and held to be a stable form with special properties
poly·zo·an \ˌpäl-i-ˈzō-ən\ *n* **1** [NL *Polyzoa*, phylum name, fr. *poly-* + *-zoa*] **:** BRYOZOAN **2** [NL *Polyzoa*, subclass name, fr. *poly-* + *-zoa*] **:** CESTODE — **polyzoan** *adj*
poly·zo·ar·i·um \-zə-ˈwar-ē-əm, -ˈwer-\ *n, pl* **-ia** \-ē-ə\ [NL, fr. *Polyzoa*] **:** a bryozoan colony; *also* **:** the supporting skeleton of such a colony
poly·zo·ic \-ˈzō-ik\ *adj* **1 :** composed of many zooids **2 :** producing many sporozoites
pom·ace \ˈpəm-əs, ˈpäm-\ *n* [prob. fr. ML *pomacium* cider, fr. LL *pomum* apple, fr. L, fruit] **1 :** the dry or pulpy residue of material (as fruit, seeds, or fish) from which a liquid (as juice or oil) has been pressed or extracted **2 :** something crushed to a pulpy mass
po·ma·ceous \pō-ˈmā-shəs\ *adj* [NL *pomaceus*, fr. LL *pomum*] **1 :** of or relating to apples **2** [*pome*] **:** resembling a pome
po·made \pō-ˈmād, -ˈmäd\ *n* [MF *pommade* ointment formerly made from apples, fr. It *pomata*, fr. *pomo* apple, fr. LL *pomum*] **:** a perfumed ointment; *esp* **:** a fragrant unguent for the hair or scalp — **pomade** *vt*
po·man·der \ˈpō-ˌman-dər, pō-ˈ\ *n* [ME, modif. of MF *pome d'ambre*, lit., apple or ball of amber] **:** a mixture of aromatic substances enclosed in a perforated bag or box and formerly carried as a guard against infection
po·ma·tum \pō-ˈmāt-əm, -ˈmät-\ *n* [NL, fr. LL *pomum* apple] **:** OINTMENT; *esp* **:** a perfumed unguent for the hair or scalp
pome \ˈpōm\ *n* [ME, fr. MF *pome, pomme* apple, pome, ball, fr. LL *pomum* apple, fr. L, fruit] **:** a fleshy fruit consisting of an outer thickened fleshy layer and a central core with usu. five seeds enclosed in a capsule
pome·gran·ate \ˈpäm-(ə-)ˌgran-ət, ˈpəm-ˌgran-\ *n* [ME *poumgarnet*, fr. MF *pomme grenate*, lit., seedy apple] **1 :** a thick-skinned several-celled reddish berry that is about the size of an orange and has many seeds in a crimson pulp of tart flavor **2 :** a widely cultivated tropical Old World tree (*Punica granatum* of the family Punicaceae) bearing pomegranates

pomegranate 1

pom·e·lo \ˈpäm-ə-ˌlō\ *n, pl* **-los** [alter. of earlier *pompelmous*, fr. D *pompelmoes*] **1 :** SHADDOCK **2 :** GRAPEFRUIT
Pom·er·a·nian \ˌpäm-ə-ˈrā-nē-ən, -nyən\ *n* **1 :** a native or inhabitant of Pomerania **2 :** any of a breed of very small compact long-haired dogs — **Pomeranian** *adj*
po·mif·er·ous \pō-ˈmif-(ə-)rəs\ *adj* [L *pomifer* fruitbearing, fr. *pomum* + *-fer* -ferous] **:** bearing pomes
pom·mée \pä-ˈmā, ˌpə-\ *adj* [F, fr. MF *pomme* apple, ball] *of a heraldic cross* **:** having the end of each arm terminating in a ball or disk — see CROSS illustration
[1]**pom·mel** \ˈpəm-əl, ˈpäm-\ *n* [ME *pomel*, fr. MF, fr. (assumed) VL *pomellum* ball, knob, fr. dim. of LL *pomum* apple] **1 :** the knob on the hilt of a sword or saber **2 :** the protuberance at the front and top of a saddlebow **3 :** either of a pair of removable rounded or U-shaped handles used on the top of a side horse
[2]**pom·mel** \ˈpəm-əl\ *vt* **-meled** *or* **-melled; -mel·ing** *or* **-mel·ling** \-(ə-)liŋ\ [[1]*pommel*] **:** PUMMEL
po·mol·o·gy \pō-ˈmäl-ə-jē\ *n* [NL *pomologia*, fr. L *pomum* fruit + *-logia* -logy] **:** the science and practice of fruit growing — **po·mo·log·i·cal** \ˌpō-mə-ˈläj-i-kəl\ *adj* — **po·mo·log·i·cal·ly** \ˌpō-mə-ˈläj-i-k(ə-)lē\ *adv* — **po·mol·o·gist** \pō-ˈmäl-ə-jəst\ *n*
Po·mo·na \pə-ˈmō-nə\ *n* [L] **:** the Roman goddess of fruit trees
pomp \ˈpämp\ *n* [ME, fr. MF *pompe*, fr. L *pompa* procession, pomp, fr. Gk *pompē* act of sending, escort, procession, pomp] **1 :** a show of magnificence **:** SPLENDOR <every day begins . . . in a ~ of flaming colours —F. D. Ommanney> **2 :** a ceremonial or festal display (as a train of followers or a pageant) **3 a :** ostentatious display **:** VAINGLORY **b :** an ostentatious gesture or act
pom·pa·dour \ˈpäm-pə-ˌdō(ə)r, -ˌdȯ(ə)r\ *n* [Marquise de *Pompadour*] **1 a :** a woman's style of hairdressing in which the hair is brushed into a loose full roll around the face **b :** a man's style of hairdressing in which the hair is combed into a high mound in front to stand erect **2 :** hair dressed in a pompadour
pom·pa·no \ˈpäm-pə-ˌnō, ˈpəm-\ *n, pl* **-no** *or* **-nos** [Sp *pámpano* gilthead, lit., vine leaf, fr. L *pampinus*] **1 :** a marine percoid food fish (*Trachinotus carolinus*) of the southern Atlantic and Gulf coasts of No. America; *broadly* **:** any of several related fishes **2 :** a small bluish or greenish butterfish (*Peprilus simillimus*) of the Pacific coast
[1]**pom–pom** \ˈpäm-ˌpäm\ *n* [imit.] **:** an automatic gun of 20 to 40 millimeters mounted on ships in pairs, fours, or eights
[2]**pom–pom** *n* [alter. of *pompon*] **:** an ornamental ball or tuft used esp. on clothing, caps, or costumes
pom·pon \ˈpäm-ˌpän\ *n* [F, fr. MF *pompe* tuft of ribbons] **1 :** [2]POM-POM **2 :** a chrysanthemum or dahlia with small rounded flower heads
pom·pos·i·ty \päm-ˈpäs-ət-ē\ *n, pl* **-ties 1 :** pompous demeanor, speech, or behavior **2 :** a pompous gesture, habit, or act
pomp·ous \ˈpäm-pəs\ *adj* **1 :** relating to or suggestive of pomp **:** MAGNIFICENT **2 :** having or exhibiting self-importance **:** ARROGANT <a ~ politician> **3 :** excessively elevated or ornate <~ rhetoric> — **pomp·ous·ly** *adv* — **pomp·ous·ness** *n*
pon *abbr* pontoon
pon·cho \ˈpän-(ˌ)chō\ *n, pl* **ponchos** [AmerSp, fr. Araucanian *pontho* woolen fabric] **1 :** a cloak resembling a blanket with a slit in the middle for the head **2 :** a waterproof garment resembling a poncho worn chiefly as a raincoat
pond \ˈpänd\ *n* [ME *ponde* artificially confined body of water, alter. of *pounde* enclosure — more at POUND] **:** a body of water usu. smaller than a lake
pon·der \ˈpän-dər\ *vb* **pon·dered; pon·der·ing** \-d(ə-)riŋ\ [ME *ponderen*, fr. MF *ponderer*, fr. L *ponderare* to weigh, ponder, fr. *ponder-, pondus* weight — more at PENDANT] *vt* **1 :** to weigh in the mind **:** APPRAISE <~ *ed* their chances of success> **2 :** to deliberate about **3 :** to review mentally **:** think about <~ *ed* the events of the day> ~ *vi* **:** to think or consider esp. quietly, soberly, and deeply — **pon·der·er** \-dər-ər\ *n*

ə abut ᵊ kitten ər further a back ā bake ä cot, cart
au̇ out ch chin e less ē easy g gift i trip ī life
j joke ŋ sing ō flow ȯ flaw ȯi coin th thin *th* this
ü loot u̇ foot y yet yü few yu̇ furious zh vision

syn PONDER, MEDITATE, MUSE, RUMINATE *shared meaning element* : to consider or examine attentively or deliberately. PONDER implies a careful weighing of alternatives or prolonged, often inconclusive thinking <*ponder* over the best way to get out of a scrape> MEDITATE adds to *ponder* an implication of a definite directing or focusing of one's thought <*meditate* upon these things; give thyself wholly to them —1 Tim 4:15 (AV)> In transitive use it may imply such deep mental commitment (as to a plan) as to approach *intend* or *purpose* in meaning <he was *meditating* a book on Shakespearian questions —H. J. Oliver> MUSE, otherwise close to *meditate*, is likely to suggest a persistent but languid and inconclusive turning over in the mind <*musing* over old times> <he *mused* about the ultimate destiny of man> RUMINATE suggests going over something repeatedly in the mind often by way of casual reasoning or random speculation <sit at home and *ruminate* on the qualities of certain little books . . . which I can read and read again —L. P. Smith>

pon·der·a·ble \'pän-d(ə-)rə-bəl\ *adj* [LL *ponderabilis*, fr. *ponderare*] : capable of being weighed or appraised : APPRECIABLE **syn** see PERCEPTIBLE **ant** imponderable

pon·der·o·sa pine \ˌpän-də-ˌrō-sə-, -zə-\ *n* [NL *ponderosa*, specific epithet of *Pinus ponderosa*, species name, fr. L, fem. of *ponderosus* ponderous] : a tall timber tree (*Pinus ponderosa*) of western No. America with long needles in groups of two to five; *also* : its strong reddish straight-grained wood — called also *ponderosa*

pon·der·ous \'pän-d(ə-)rəs\ *adj* [ME, fr. MF *pondereux*, fr. L *ponderosus*, fr. *ponder-*, *pondus* weight] **1** : of very great weight **2** : unwieldy or clumsy because of weight and size **3** : oppressively or unpleasantly dull : PEDESTRIAN <~ prose> **syn** see HEAVY — **pon·der·ous·ly** *adv* — **pon·der·ous·ness** *n*

pond lily *n* : WATER LILY

pond scum *n* **1** : SPIROGYRA; *also* : any of various related algae **2** : a mass of tangled algal filaments in stagnant waters

pond·weed \'pän-ˌdwēd\ *n* : any of a genus (*Potamogeton* of the family Zannichelliaceae, the pondweed family) of aquatic plants with jointed usu. rooting stems, 2-ranked floating or submerged leaves, and spikes of greenish flowers

pone \'pōn\ *n* [of Algonquian origin; akin to Delaware *äpân* baked] *South & Midland* : CORN PONE

pon·gee \(ˈ)pän-'jē, 'pän-ˌ\ *n* [Chin (Pek) *pen*³ *chi*¹, fr. *pen*³ own + *chi*¹ loom] : a thin soft ecru or tan fabric of Chinese origin woven from raw silk; *also* : an imitation of this fabric in cotton or rayon

pon·gid \'pän-jəd, 'päŋ-gəd\ *n* [deriv. of Kongo *mpungu* ape] : an anthropoid ape — **pongid** *adj*

1**pon·iard** \'pän-yərd\ *n* [MF *poignard*, fr. *poing* fist, fr. L *pugnus* fist — more at PUNGENT] : a dagger with a usu. slender blade of triangular or square cross section

2**poniard** *vt* : to pierce or kill with a poniard

pons \'pänz\ *n, pl* **pon·tes** \'pän-ˌtēz\ [NL, short for *pons Varolii*] : a broad mass of chiefly transverse nerve fibers conspicuous on the ventral surface of the brain of man and lower mammals at the anterior end of the medulla oblongata — see BRAIN illustration

pons asi·no·rum \ˌpän-ˌzas-ə-'nōr-əm, -'nȯr-\ *n* [NL, lit., asses' bridge, name applied to the proposition that the base angles of an isosceles triangle are equal] : a critical test of ability imposed on the inexperienced or ignorant

pons Va·ro·lii \-və-'rō-lē-ˌī, -lē-ˌē\ *n* [NL, lit., bridge of Varoli, fr. Costanzo *Varoli* †1575 It surgeon and anatomist] : PONS

pon·ti·fex \'pänt-ə-ˌfeks\ *n, pl* **pon·tif·i·ces** \pän-'tif-ə-ˌsēz\ [L *pontific-*, *pontifex*, lit., bridge maker, fr. *pont-*, *pons* bridge + *facere* to make — more at FIND, DO] : a member of the council of priests in ancient Rome

pon·tiff \'pänt-əf\ *n* [F *pontif*, fr. L *pontific-*, *pontifex*] **1** : PONTIFEX **2** : BISHOP; *specif* : POPE

1**pon·tif·i·cal** \pän-'tif-i-kəl\ *adj* [L *pontificalis*, fr. *pontific-*, *pontifex*] **1 a** : of or relating to a pontiff or pontifex **b** : celebrated by a prelate of episcopal rank with distinctive ceremonies <~ mass> **2** : POMPOUS **3** : pretentiously dogmatic — **pon·tif·i·cal·ly** \-k(ə-)lē\ *adv*

2**pontifical** *n* **1** : episcopal attire; *specif* : the insignia of the episcopal order worn by a prelate when celebrating a pontifical mass — usu. used in pl. **2** : a book containing the forms for sacraments and rites performed by a bishop

1**pon·tif·i·cate** \pän-'tif-i-kət, -ə-ˌkāt\ *n* [L *pontificatus*, fr. *pontific-*, *pontifex*] : the state, office, or term of office of a pontiff

2**pon·tif·i·cate** \pän-'tif-ə-ˌkāt\ *vi* **-cat·ed**; **-cat·ing** [ML *pontificatus*, pp. of *pontificare*, fr. L *pontific-*, *pontifex*] **1 a** : to officiate as a pontiff **b** : to celebrate pontifical mass **2** : to deliver oracular utterances or dogmatic opinions — **pon·tif·i·ca·tion** \(ˌ)pän-ˌtif-ə-'kā-shən\ *n* — **pon·tif·i·ca·tor** \-ˌkāt-ər\ *n*

pon·tine \'pän-ˌtīn\ *adj* [ISV *pont-* (fr. NL *pont-*, *pons*) + *-ine*] : of or relating to the pons

Pont l'É·vêque \ˌpōⁿ-lā-'vek\ *n* [*Pont l'Évêque*, town in France] : a soft surface-ripened cheese firmer, yellower, and having less surface mold than Camembert

pon·ton \'pänt-ᵊn, pän-'tün\ *n* [F] : PONTOON

pon·ton·ier \ˌpänt-ᵊn-'i(ə)r\ *n* [F *pontonnier*, fr. *ponton*] : an individual engaged in constructing a pontoon bridge

pon·toon \pän-'tün\ *n* [F *ponton*, floating bridge, punt, fr. L *ponton-*, *ponto*, fr. *pont-*, *pons* bridge] **1** : a flat-bottomed boat (as a lighter); *esp* : a flat-bottomed boat or portable float used in building a floating temporary bridge **2** : a float esp. of an airplane

pontoon bridge *n* : a bridge whose deck is supported on pontoons

po·ny \'pō-nē\ *n, pl* **ponies** [prob. fr. obs. F *poulenet*, dim. of F *poulain* colt, fr. ML *pullanus*, fr. L *pullus* young of an animal, foal — more at FOAL] **1 a** : a small horse; *esp* : one of any of several breeds of very small stocky animals noted for their gentleness and endurance **b** : a bronco, mustang, or similar horse of the western U.S. **c** : RACEHORSE **2** : something smaller than standard **3** : a literal translation of a foreign language text; *esp* : one used surreptitiously by students in preparing or reciting lessons

pony car *n* [fr. its relatively small size and lively performance] : one of a group of 2-door American hardtops of different makes that are similar in sporty styling, high performance characteristics, and price range

pony express *n* : a rapid postal and express system that operated across the western U.S. in 1860–1861 by relays of horses and riders

po·ny·tail \'pō-nē-ˌtāl\ *n* : a style of arranging hair to resemble a pony's tail; *also* : hair arranged in this style

po·ny up \ˌpō-nē-'əp\ *vb* **po·nied up; po·ny·ing up** [origin unknown] *vt* : to pay (money) in settlement of an account <*ponied up* $12.50 for the fine —*Newsweek*> ~ *vi* : PAY

POO *abbr* post office order

pooch \'püch\ *n* [origin unknown] : DOG

pood \'püd, 'püt\ *n* [Russ *pud*, fr. ON *pund* pound — more at POUND] : a Russian unit of weight equal to about 36.11 pounds

poo·dle \'püd-ᵊl\ *n* [G *pudel*, short for *pudelhund*, fr. *pudeln* to splash (fr. *pudel* puddle, fr. LG) + *hund* dog (fr. OHG *hunt*) — more at PUDDLE, HOUND] : any of a breed of active intelligent heavy-coated solid-colored dogs

pooh \'pü, 'pu̇\ *interj* — used to express contempt or disapproval

pooh-bah \'pü-ˌbä, -ˌbȯ\ *n, often cap P&B* [*Pooh-Bah*, character in Gilbert and Sullivan's opera *The Mikado* (1885) bearing the title Lord-High-Everything-Else] **1** : a person holding many public or private offices **2** : a person in high position

pooh–pooh \'pü-(ˌ)pü, pü-'\ *also* **pooh** \'pü\ *vb* [*pooh*] *vi* : to express contempt or impatience ~ *vt* : to express contempt for

1**pool** \'pül\ *n* [ME, fr. OE *pōl*; akin to OHG *pfuol* pool] **1** : a small and rather deep body of usu. fresh water **2** : a small body of standing liquid : PUDDLE **3** : a continuous area of porous sedimentary rock which yields petroleum or gas

2**pool** *n* [F *poule*, lit., hen, fr. OF, fem. of *poul* cock — more at PULLET] **1 a** : an aggregate stake to which each player of a game has contributed **b** : all the money bet by a number of persons on a particular event **2 a** : a game played on an English billiard table in which each of the players stakes a sum and the winner takes all **b** : any of various games of billiards played on an oblong table having 6 pockets with usu. 15 object balls **3** : an aggregation of the interests or property of different persons made to further a joint undertaking by subjecting them to the same control and a common liability: as **a** : a common fund or combination of interests for the common adventure in buying or selling; *esp* : one for speculating in or manipulating the market price of securities or commodities (as grain) **b** : a combination between competing business houses for the control of traffic by removing competition **4** : a readily available supply: as **a** : the whole quantity of a particular material present in the body and available for function or the satisfying of metabolic demands **b** : a body product (as blood) collected from many donors and stored for later use

3**pool** *vt* : to contribute to a common stock (as of resources), sample, or effort

pool·room \'pül-ˌrüm, -ˌru̇m\ *n* **1** : a room in which bookmaking is carried on **2** : a room for the playing of pool

1**poop** \'püp\ *n* [MF *poupe*, fr. L *puppis*] **1** *obs* : STERN **2** : an enclosed superstructure at the stern of a ship above the main deck

2**poop** *vt* **1** : to break over the stern of **2** : to ship (a sea or wave) over the stern

3**poop** *vb* [origin unknown] *vt, slang* : to put out of breath; *also* : to tire out ~ *vi, slang* : to become exhausted <~ out>

4**poop** *n* [origin unknown] *slang* : INFORMATION

poop deck *n* : a partial deck above a ship's main afterdeck

poor \'pu̇(ə)r, 'pō(ə)r\ *adj* [ME *poure*, fr. OF *povre*, fr. L *pauper*; akin to L *pau*cus little and to L *parere* to produce, *parare* to acquire — more at FEW, PARE] **1 a** : lacking material possessions **b** : of, relating to, or characterized by poverty **2 a** : less than adequate : MEAGER **b** : small in worth **3** : exciting pity **4 a** : inferior in quality or value **b** : HUMBLE, UNPRETENTIOUS **c** : MEAN, PETTY **5** : LEAN, EMACIATED **6** : BARREN, UNPRODUCTIVE — used of land — **poor·ly** *adv* — **poor·ness** *n*

poor box *n* : a box (as in a church) for alms for the poor

poor boy \'pō(r)-ˌbȯi\ *n* : SUBMARINE 2

Poor Clare \-'kla(ə)r, -'kle(ə)r\ *n* : a member of an austere order of nuns founded by St. Clare under the direction of St. Francis in Assisi, Italy, in 1212

poor farm \'pu̇(ə)r-ˌfärm, 'pō(ə)r-\ *n* : a farm maintained at public expense for the support and employment of needy persons

poor·house \-ˌhau̇s\ *n* : a place maintained at public expense to house needy or dependent persons

poor·ish \'pu̇(ə)r-ish, 'pō(ə)r-\ *adj* : rather poor

poor law *n* : a law providing for or regulating the public relief or support of the poor

poor·ly \'pu̇(ə)r-lē, 'pō(ə)r-\ *adj* : somewhat ill : INDISPOSED

poor–mouth \-ˌmau̇th, -ˌmau̇th\ *vi* : to plead poverty as a defense or excuse ~ *vt* : to speak disparagingly of

poor mouth \-ˌmau̇th\ *n* : an exaggerated claim of poverty

poor–spir·it·ed \-'spir-ət-əd\ *adj* : lacking zest, confidence, or courage — **poor–spir·it·ed·ly** *adv* — **poor–spir·it·ed·ness** *n*

poor white *n* : a member of an inferior or underprivileged white social group — often taken to be offensive

1**pop** \'päp\ *vb* **popped; pop·ping** [ME *poppen*, of imit. origin] *vt* **1** : to strike or knock sharply : HIT **2** : to push, put, or thrust suddenly **3** : to cause to explode or burst open **4** : to fire at : SHOOT **5** : to take (drugs) orally or by injection <he *popped* pills> ~ *vi* **1 a** : to go, come, or enter suddenly **b** : to escape or break away from something (as a point of attachment) usu. suddenly or unexpectedly **2** : to make or burst with a sharp sound : EXPLODE **3** : to protrude from the sockets **4** : to shoot with a firearm **5** : to hit a pop fly — often used with *up* or *out* — **pop the question** : to propose marriage

2**pop** *n* **1** : a sharp explosive sound **2** : a shot from a gun **3** [fr. the sound made by pulling a cork from a bottle] : a flavored carbonated beverage **4** : POP FLY

3**pop** *adv* : like or with a pop : SUDDENLY

4**pop** *n* [short for *poppa*] : FATHER

5**pop** *adj* **1** : POPULAR <~ music>: as **a** : of or relating to pop music <~ singer> **b** : of, relating to, or constituting a mass culture esp. of the young widely disseminated through the mass media <~ society> **2 a :** of or relating to pop art <~ painter> **b :** having, using, or imitating themes or techniques characteristic of pop art <~ movie>

[6]**pop** *n* **1 :** pop music **2 :** POP ART **3 :** pop culture

[7]**pop** *abbr* population

pop art *n* **:** art in which commonplace objects (as road signs, hamburgers, comic strips, or soup cans) are used as subject matter and are often physically incorporated in the work — **pop artist** *n*

pop·corn \ˈpäp-ˌkȯ(ə)rn\ *n* **:** an Indian corn (*Zea mays everta*) whose kernels on exposure to heat burst open to form a white starchy mass; *also* **:** the popped kernels

pope \ˈpōp\ *n* [ME, fr. OE *pāpa,* fr. LL *papa,* fr. Gk *pappas, papas,* title of bishops, lit., papa] **1** *often cap* **:** a prelate who as bishop of Rome is the head of the Roman Catholic Church **2 :** one that resembles a pope (as in authority) **3 :** a priest of an Eastern church

pop·ery \ˈpō-p(ə-)rē\ *n* **:** ROMAN CATHOLICISM — usu. used disparagingly

pop eye \ˈpäp-ˌī\ *n* [back-formation fr. *pop-eyed*] **:** an eye staring and bulging (as from excitement) — **pop–eyed** \-ˈīd\ *adj*

pop fly *n* **:** a high fly ball in baseball

pop·gun \ˈpäp-ˌgən\ *n* **:** a toy gun that usu. shoots a cork and produces a popping sound

pop·in·jay \ˈpäp-ən-ˌjā\ *n* [ME *papejay* parrot, fr. MF *papegai, papejai,* fr. Ar *babghā'*] **:** a strutting supercilious person

pop·ish \ˈpō-pish\ *adj* [*pope*] **:** Roman Catholic — often used disparagingly

pop·ish·ly *adv* **:** in accordance with Roman Catholicism — often used disparagingly

pop·lar \ˈpäp-lər\ *n* [ME *poplere,* fr. MF *pouplier,* fr. *pouple* poplar, fr. L *populus*] **1 a :** any of a genus (*Populus*) of slender quick-growing trees (as an aspen or cottonwood) of the willow family **b :** the wood of a poplar **2 :** TULIP TREE 1

pop·lin \ˈpäp-lən\ *n* [F *papeline*] **:** a strong fabric in plain weave with crosswise ribs

pop·li·te·al \ˌpäp-lə-ˈtē-əl *also* päp-ˈlit-ē-\ *adj* [NL *popliteus,* fr. L *poplit-, poples* ham of the knee] **:** of or relating to the back part of the leg behind the knee joint

pop–off \ˈpäp-ˌȯf\ *n* **:** one who talks loosely or loudly

pop off \(ˈ)päp-ˈȯf\ *vi* **1 a :** to leave suddenly **b :** to die unexpectedly **2 :** to talk thoughtlessly and often loudly or angrily

pop·over \ˈpäp-ˌō-vər\ *n* **:** a hollow quick bread shaped like a muffin and made from a thin batter of eggs, milk, and flour

pop·pa \ˈpäp-ə\ *var of* PAPA

pop·per \ˈpäp-ər\ *n* **:** one that pops; *esp* **:** a utensil for popping corn

pop·pet \ˈpäp-ət\ *n* [ME *popet* doll, puppet — more at PUPPET] **1** *chiefly Brit* **:** DEAR **2 a** *Midland* **:** DOLL **b** *obs* **:** MARIONETTE **3 a :** an upright support or guide of a machine that is fastened at the bottom only **b :** a valve that rises perpendicularly to or from its seat **4 :** any of the small pieces of wood on a boat's gunwale supporting or forming the rowlocks

pop·pied \ˈpäp-ēd\ *adj* **1** *archaic* **:** growing or overgrown with poppies **2 :** DROWSY

[1]**pop·ple** \ˈpäp-əl\ *n* [ME *popul,* fr. OE, fr. L *populus*] *chiefly dial* **:** POPLAR 1

[2]**popple** *n* [*popple,* vb., fr. ME *poplen* to bubble, ripple, prob. of imit. origin] **:** a choppy sea

pop·py \ˈpäp-ē\ *n, pl* **pop·pies** [ME *popi,* fr. OE *popæg, popig,* modif. of L *papaver*] **1 a :** any of a genus (*Papaver* of the family Papaveraceae, the poppy family) of chiefly annual or perennial herbs with milky juice, showy regular flowers, and capsular fruits including one (*P. somniferum*) that is the source of opium and several that are cultivated as ornamentals **b :** an extract or decoction of poppy used medicinally **2 :** a strong reddish orange

poppy 1a

pop·py·cock \ˈpäp-ē-ˌkäk\ *n* [D dial. *pappekak,* lit., soft dung, fr. D *pap* pap + *kak* dung] **:** empty talk **:** NONSENSE

pop·py·head \-ˌhed\ *n* **:** a raised ornament often in the form of a finial generally used on the tops of the upright ends of seats in Gothic churches

Pop·si·cle \ˈpäp-ˌsik-əl\ *trademark* — used for flavored and colored water frozen in a rectangular shape on two flat handles

pop·u·lace \ˈpäp-yə-ləs\ *n* [MF, fr. It *popolaccio* rabble, pejorative of *popolo* the people, fr. L *populus*] **1 :** the common people **:** MASSES **2 :** POPULATION

pop·u·lar \ˈpäp-yə-lər\ *adj* [L *popularis,* fr. *populus* the people, a people] **1 :** of or relating to the general public **2 :** suitable to the majority: as **a :** easy to understand **:** PLAIN <a ~ history of the war> **b :** suited to the means of the majority **:** INEXPENSIVE <sold at ~ prices> **3 :** having general currency **4 :** commonly liked or approved <a very ~ girl> ***syn*** see COMMON ***ant*** unpopular, esoteric — **pop·u·lar·ly** *adv*

popular front *n, often cap P&F* **:** a working coalition esp. of leftist political parties against a common opponent; *specif* **:** one sponsored and dominated by Communists as a device for gaining power

pop·u·lar·i·ty \ˌpäp-yə-ˈlar-ət-ē\ *n* **:** the quality or state of being popular

pop·u·lar·ize \ˈpäp-yə-lə-ˌrīz\ *vb* **-ized; -iz·ing** *vi* **:** to cater to popular taste ~ *vt* **:** to make popular: as **a :** to cause to be liked or esteemed **b :** to present in generally understandable or interesting form — **pop·u·lar·i·za·tion** \ˌpäp-yə-lə-rə-ˈzā-shən\ *n* — **pop·u·lar·iz·er** \ˈpäp-yə-lə-ˌrī-zər\ *n*

popular sovereignty *n* **1 :** a doctrine in political theory that government is created by and subject to the will of the people **2 :** a pre-Civil War doctrine asserting the right of the people living in a newly organized territory to decide by vote of their territorial legislature whether or not slavery would be permitted there

pop·u·late \ˈpäp-yə-ˌlāt\ *vt* **-lat·ed; -lat·ing** [ML *populatus,* pp. of *populare* to people, fr. L *populus* people] **1 :** to have a place in **:** OCCUPY, INHABIT **2 a :** to furnish or provide with inhabitants **:** PEOPLE **b :** to provide with members

pop·u·la·tion \ˌpäp-yə-ˈlā-shən\ *n* [LL *population-, populatio,* fr. L *populus*] **1 a :** the whole number of people or inhabitants in a country or region **b :** the total of individuals occupying an area or making up a whole **c :** the total of particles in a particular energy level — used esp. of atoms in a laser **2 :** the act or process of populating **3 a :** a body of persons or individuals having a quality or characteristic in common **b (1) :** the organisms inhabiting a particular locality **(2) :** a group of interbreeding organisms that represents the level of organization at which speciation begins **4 :** a group of individual persons, objects, or items from which samples are taken for statistical measurement

population explosion *n* **:** a pyramiding of a living population; *esp* **:** the recent great increase in human numbers that is usu. related to both increased survival and increased reproduction

pop·u·list \ˈpäp-yə-ləst\ *n* [L *populus* the people] **1 :** a member of a political party claiming to represent the common people; *esp, often cap* **:** a member of a U.S. political party formed in 1891 primarily to represent agrarian interests and to advocate the free coinage of silver and government control of monopolies **2 :** a believer in the rights, wisdom, or virtues of the common people — **pop·u·lism** \-ˌliz-əm\ *n* — **populist** *also* **pop·u·lis·tic** \ˌpäp-yə-ˈlis-tik\ *adj, often cap*

pop·u·lous \ˈpäp-yə-ləs\ *adj* [L *populosus,* fr. *populus* people] **1 :** densely populated **2 a :** NUMEROUS **b :** filled to capacity **:** CROWDED — **pop·u·lous·ly** *adv* — **pop·u·lous·ness** *n*

pop–up \ˈpäp-ˌəp\ *n* **:** POP FLY

por *abbr* portrait

POR *abbr* pay on return

por·bea·gle \ˈpȯ(ə)r-ˌbē-gəl\ *n* [Corn *porgh-bugel*] **:** a small viviparous shark (*Lamna nasus*) of the north Atlantic and Pacific oceans with a pointed nose and crescent-shaped tail

por·ce·lain \ˈpōr-s(ə-)lən, ˈpȯr-\ *n* [ML *porcelaine* cowrie shell, porcelain, fr. It *porcellana,* fr. *porcello* vulva, lit., little pig, fr. L *porcellus,* dim. of *porcus* pig, vulva; fr. the shape of the shell — more at FARROW] **:** a hard, fine-grained, sonorous, nonporous, and usu. translucent and white ceramic ware that consists essentially of kaolin, quartz, and feldspar and is fired at high temperatures — **por·ce·lain·like** \-ˌlīk\ *adj* — **por·ce·la·ne·ous** *or* **por·cel·la·ne·ous** \ˌpōr-sə-ˈlā-nē-əs, ˌpȯr-\ *adj*

porcelain enamel *n* **:** VITREOUS ENAMEL

por·ce·lain·ize \ˈpōr-s(ə-)lə-ˌnīz, ˈpȯr-\ *vt* **-ized; -iz·ing :** to fire a vitreous coating on (as steel)

porch \ˈpō(ə)rch, ˈpȯ(ə)rch\ *n* [ME *porche,* fr. OF, fr. L *porticus* portico, fr. *porta* gate — more at FORD] **1 :** a covered entrance to a building usu. with a separate roof **:** VERANDA **2** *obs* **:** PORTICO

por·cine \ˈpȯr-ˌsīn\ *adj* [L *porcinus,* fr. *porcus* pig — more at FARROW] **:** of, relating to, or suggesting swine; *esp* **:** OBESE

por·cu·pine \ˈpȯr-kyə-ˌpīn\ *n, often attrib* [ME *porkepin,* fr. MF *porc espin,* fr. OIt *porcospino,* fr. L *porcus* pig + *spina* spine, prickle] **:** any of various relatively large rodents having stiff sharp erectile bristles mingled with the hair and constituting an Old World terrestrial family (Hystricidae) and a New World arboreal family (Erethizontidae)

porcupine

[1]**pore** \ˈpō(ə)r, ˈpȯ(ə)r\ *vi* **pored; por·ing** [ME *pouren*] **1 :** to gaze intently **2 :** to read studiously or attentively **3 :** to reflect or meditate steadily

[2]**pore** *n* [ME, fr. MF, fr. L *porus,* fr. Gk *poros* passage, pore — more at FARE] **1 :** a minute opening esp. in an animal or plant; *esp* **:** one by which matter passes through a membrane **2 :** a small interstice (as in soil) admitting absorption or passage of liquid — **pored** \ˈpō(ə)rd, ˈpȯ(ə)rd\ *adj*

pore fungus *n* **:** a fungus (family Boletaceae or Polyporaceae) having the spore-bearing surface within tubes or pores

por·gy \ˈpȯr-gē\ *n, pl* **porgies** *also* **porgy** [partly fr. earlier *pargo* (porgy); partly fr. earlier *scuppaug* (porgy)] **1 :** a blue-spotted crimson percoid food fish (*Pagrus pagrus*) of the coasts of Europe and America; *also* **:** any of various related fishes (family Sparidae) **2** [alter. of *pogy*] **:** any of various teleost fishes (as a menhaden) of families other than that of the porgy

po·rif·er·an \pə-ˈrif-ə-rən\ *n* [deriv. of L *porus* pore + *-fer* -ferous] **:** any of a phylum (Porifera) of primitive invertebrate animals comprising the sponges — **poriferan** *or* **po·rif·er·al** \-rəl\ *adj*

pork \ˈpō(ə)rk, ˈpȯ(ə)rk\ *n* [ME, fr. OF, pig, fr. L *porcus*] **1 :** the fresh or salted flesh of swine when dressed for food **2 :** government money, jobs, or favors used by politicians as patronage

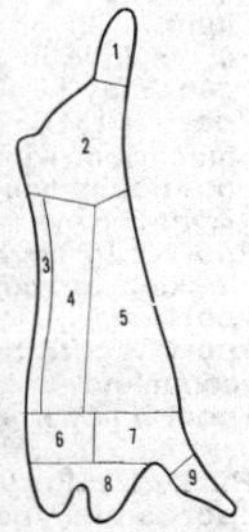

pork 1: *1* hind foot, *2* ham, *3* fatback, *4* loin, *5* side, *6* Boston butt, *7* picnic, *8* jowl, *9* forefoot

pork barrel *n* **:** a government project or appropriation yielding rich patronage benefits

pork·er \ˈpōr-kər, ˈpȯr-\ *n* **:** HOG; *esp* **:** a young pig fattened for table use as fresh pork

pork·pie hat \ˌpōrk-ˌpī-, ˌpȯrk-\ *n* [fr. its shape] **:** a felt, straw, or cloth hat with a low crown, flat top, and usu. a turned-up brim

ə abut ᵊ kitten ər further a back ā bake ä cot, cart
au̇ out ch chin e less ē easy g gift i trip ī life
j joke ŋ sing ō flow ȯ flaw ȯi coin th thin t͟h this
ü loot u̇ foot y yet yü few yu̇ furious zh vision

por·ky \ˈpȯr-kē\ *n, pl* **porkies** : PORCUPINE

por·nog·ra·pher \pȯr-ˈnäg-rə-fər\ *n* : one who produces pornography

por·nog·ra·phy \-fē\ *n* [Gk *pornographos,* adj., writing of harlots, fr. *pornē* harlot + *graphein* to write; akin to Gk *pernanai* to sell, *poros* journey — more at FARE, CARVE] **1** : the depiction of erotic behavior (as in pictures or writing) intended to cause sexual excitement **2** : material (as books or a photograph) that depicts erotic behavior and is intended to cause sexual excitement — **por·no·graph·ic** \ˌpȯr-nə-ˈgraf-ik\ *adj* — **por·no·graph·i·cal·ly** \-i-k(ə-)lē\ *adv*

po·rose \ˈpō(ə)r-ˌōs, ˈpȯ(ə)r-\ *adj* : divided into or forming a continuous series of pores <a ~ hymenium>

po·ros·i·ty \pə-ˈräs-ət-ē, pōr-ˈäs-, pȯ-ˈräs-\ *n, pl* **-ties** **1 a** : the quality or state of being porous **b** : the ratio of the volume of interstices of a material to the volume of its mass **2** : PORE

po·rous \ˈpōr-əs, ˈpȯr-\ *adj* **1 a** : possessing or full of pores **b** : containing vessels <hardwood is ~> **2** : permeable to liquids — **po·rous·ly** *adv* — **po·rous·ness** *n*

por·phyr·ia \pȯr-ˈfir-ē-ə\ *n* [NL, fr. ISV *porphyrin*] : a pathological state characterized by abnormalities of porphyrin metabolism, by excretion of excess porphyrins in the urine, and by extreme sensitivity to light

por·phy·rin \ˈpȯr-fə-rən\ *n* [ISV, fr. Gk *porphyra* purple] : any of various metal-free derivatives of pyrrole obtained esp. from chlorophyll or hemoglobin

por·phy·rit·ic \ˌpȯr-fə-ˈrit-ik\ *adj* [ML *porphyriticus,* fr. Gk *porphyritikos,* fr. *porphyritēs (lithos)* porphyry] **1** : of or relating to porphyry **2** : having distinct crystals (as of feldspar) in a relatively fine-grained base

por·phy·roid \ˈpȯr-fə-ˌrȯid\ *n* [*porphyry*] : a more or less schistose metamorphic rock with porphyritic texture

por·phy·rop·sin \ˌpȯr-fə-ˈräp-sən\ *n* [Gk *porphyra* purple + E *-opsin* (as in *rhodopsin*)] : a purple pigment in the retinal rods of freshwater fishes that resembles rhodopsin

por·phy·ry \ˈpȯr-f(ə-)rē\ *n, pl* **-ries** [ME *porfurie,* fr. ML *porphyrium,* alter. of L *porphyrites,* fr. Gk *porphyritēs (lithos),* lit., stone like Tyrian purple, fr. *porphyra* purple] **1** : a rock consisting of feldspar crystals embedded in a compact dark red or purple groundmass **2** : an igneous rock of porphyritic texture

por·poise \ˈpȯr-pəs\ *n* [ME *porpoys,* fr. MF *porpois,* fr. ML *porcopiscis,* fr. L *porcus* pig + *piscis* fish — more at FARROW, FISH] **1** : any of several small gregarious toothed whales (genus *Phocaena*); *esp* : a blunt-snouted usu. largely black whale (*P. phocaena*) of the north Atlantic and Pacific 5 to 8 feet long **2** : any of several dolphins

por·rect \pə-ˈrekt, pä-\ *adj* [L *porrectus,* pp. of *porrigere* to stretch out, fr. *por-* forward + *regere* to direct — more at PORTEND, RIGHT] : extended forward <~ antennae>

por·ridge \ˈpȯr-ij, ˈpär-\ *n* [alter. of *pottage*] : a soft food made by boiling meal of grains or legumes in milk or water until thick

por·rin·ger \-ən-jər\ *n* [alter. of ME *poteger, potinger,* fr. AF *potageer,* fr. MF *potager* of pottage, fr. *potage* pottage] : a low metal bowl with a single and often flat and pierced handle

[1]port \ˈpō(ə)rt, ˈpȯ(ə)rt\ *n* [ME, fr. OE & OF, fr. L *portus* — more at FORD] **1** : a place where ships may ride secure from storms : HAVEN **2 a** : a harbor town or city where ships may take on or discharge cargo **b** : AIRPORT **3** : PORT OF ENTRY

[2]port *n* [ME *porte,* fr. MF, gate, door, fr. L *porta* passage, gate; akin to L *portus* port] **1** *chiefly Scot* : GATE **2 a** : an opening for intake or exhaust of a fluid esp. in a valve seat or valve face **b** : the area of opening in a cylinder face of a passageway for the working fluid in an engine; *also* : such a passageway **c** : a means of access to a system **3 a** : an opening in a ship's side to admit light or air or to load cargo **b** *archaic* : the cover for a porthole **4** : a hole in an armored vehicle or fortification through which guns may be fired

[3]port *n* [ME, fr. MF, fr. *porter* to carry fr. L *portare*] **1** : the manner in which one bears himself **2** *archaic* : STATE 3 **3** : the position in which a military weapon is carried at the command *port arms*

[4]port *n* [prob. fr. [1]*port* or [2]*port*] : the left side of a ship or aircraft looking forward — called also *larboard;* compare STARBOARD — **port** *adj*

[5]port *vt* : to turn or put (a helm) to the left — used chiefly as a command

[6]port *n* [*Oporto,* Portugal] : a fortified sweet wine of rich taste and aroma

Port *abbr* Portugal; Portuguese

[1]por·ta·ble \ˈpōrt-ə-bəl, ˈpȯrt-\ *adj* [ME, fr. MF, fr. LL *portabilis,* fr. L *portare* to carry — more at FARE] **1** : capable of being carried or moved about <a ~ TV> <a ~ sawmill> **2** *obs* : BEARABLE — **por·ta·bil·i·ty** \ˌpōrt-ə-ˈbil-ət-ē, ˌpȯrt-\ *n* — **por·ta·bly** \ˈpōrt-ə-blē, ˈpȯrt-\ *adv*

[2]portable *n* : something that is portable

[1]por·tage \ˈpōrt-ij, ˈpȯrt-, *3 is also* pȯr-ˈtäzh\ *n* [ME, fr. MF, fr. *porter* to carry] **1** : the labor of carrying or transporting **2** *archaic* : the cost of carrying : PORTERAGE **3 a** : the carrying of boats or goods overland from one body of water to another **b** : the route followed in making such a transfer

[2]por·tage \ˈpōrt-ij, ˈpȯrt-; pȯr-ˈtäzh\ *vb* **por·taged; por·tag·ing** *vt* : to carry over a portage ~ *vi* : to move gear over a portage

[1]por·tal \ˈpōrt-ᵊl, ˈpȯrt-\ *n* [ME, fr. MF, fr. ML *portale* city gate, porch, fr. neut. of *portalis* of a gate, fr. L *porta* gate — more at PORT] **1** : DOOR, ENTRANCE; *esp* : a grand or imposing one **2** : the whole architectural composition surrounding and including the doorways and porches of a church **3** : the approach or entrance to a bridge or tunnel **4** : a communicating part or area of an organism; *specif* : the point at which something (as a pathogen) enters the body

[2]portal *adj* [NL *porta* transverse fissure of the liver, fr. L, gate] **1** : of or relating to the transverse fissure on the underside of the liver where most of the vessels enter **2** : of, relating to, or being a portal vein

portal system *n* [*portal vein*] : a system of veins that begins and ends in capillaries

portal–to–portal *adj* : of or relating to the time spent by a workman in traveling from the entrance to his employer's property to his actual working place (as in a mine) and in returning after work <~ pay>

portal vein *n* [[2]*portal*] : a vein that collects blood from one part of the body and distributes it in another through capillaries; *esp* : a vein carrying blood from the digestive organs and spleen to the liver

por·ta·men·to \ˌpōrt-ə-ˈmen-(ˌ)tō, ˌpȯrt-\ *n, pl* **-men·ti** \-(ˌ)tē\ [It, lit., act of carrying, fr. *portare* to carry, fr. L] : a continuous gliding movement from one tone to another by the voice, a trombone, or a bowed stringed instrument

port arms *n* [fr. the command *port arms!*] : a position in the manual of arms in which the rifle is held diagonally in front of the body with the muzzle pointing upward to the left; *also* : a command to assume this position

por·ta·tive \ˈpōrt-ət-iv, ˈpȯrt-\ *adj* [ME *portatif,* fr. MF, fr. L *portatus,* pp. of *portare*] : PORTABLE

port·cul·lis \pōrt-ˈkəl-əs, pȯrt-\ *n* [ME *port colice,* fr. MF *porte coleïce,* lit., sliding door] : a grating of iron hung over the gateway of a fortified place and lowered between grooves to prevent passage

portcullis

port de bras \ˌpȯrd-ə-ˈbrä\ *n* [F, lit., carriage of the arm] : the technique and practice of arm movement in ballet

Port du Sa·lut \ˌpōrd-ə-səl-ˈ(y)ü, ˌpȯrd-, -sal-\ *n* [F *port-du-salut, port-salut,* fr. *Port du Salut,* Trappist abbey in northwest France] : a semisoft pressed ripened cheese of mild flavor originated by Trappist monks in France — called also *Port Salut*

Porte \ˈpō(ə)rt, ˈpȯ(ə)rt\ *n* [F, short for *Sublime Porte,* lit., sublime gate; fr. the gate of the sultan's palace where justice was administered] : the government of the Ottoman Empire

porte co·chere \ˌpōrt-kō-ˈshe(ə)r, ˌpȯrt-\ *n* [F *porte cochère,* lit., coach door] **1** : a passageway through a building or screen wall designed to let vehicles pass from the street to an interior courtyard **2** : a roofed structure extending from the entrance of a building over an adjacent driveway and sheltering those getting in or out of vehicles

porte–mon·naie \ˈpōrt-ˌmən-ē\ *n* [F, fr. *porter* to carry + *monnaie* coined money, fr. MF *moneie* — more at PORT, MONEY] : a small pocketbook or purse

por·tend \pȯr-ˈtend, pōr-\ *vt* [ME *portenden,* fr. L *portendere,* fr. *por-* forward (akin to *per* through) + *tendere* to stretch — more at FOR, THIN] **1** : to give an omen or anticipatory sign of : BODE **2** : INDICATE, SIGNIFY

por·tent \ˈpȯ(ə)r-ˌtent, ˈpō(ə)r-\ *n* [L *portentum,* fr. neut. of *portentus,* pp. of *portendere*] **1** : something that foreshadows a coming event : OMEN **2** : prophetic indication or significance **3** : MARVEL, PRODIGY

por·ten·tous \pȯr-ˈtent-əs, pōr-\ *adj* **1** : of, relating to, or constituting a portent **2** : eliciting amazement or wonder : PRODIGIOUS **3** : self-consciously weighty : POMPOUS ***syn*** see OMINOUS — **por·ten·tous·ly** *adv* — **por·ten·tous·ness** *n*

[1]por·ter \ˈpōrt-ər, ˈpȯrt-\ *n* [ME, fr. OF *portier,* fr. LL *portarius,* fr. L *porta* gate — more at PORT] *chiefly Brit* : a person stationed at a door or gate to admit or assist those entering

[2]porter *n* [ME *portour,* fr. MF *porteour,* fr. LL *portator,* fr. L *portatus,* pp. of *portare* to carry — more at FARE] **1** : a person who carries burdens; *specif* : one employed to carry baggage for patrons at a hotel or transportation terminal **2** : a parlor-car or sleeping-car attendant who waits on passengers and makes up berths **3** [short for *porter's beer*] : a weak stout that is rich in saccharine matter and contains about four percent of alcohol **4** : a person who does routine cleaning of the premises, furniture, and equipment (as in a hospital or office)

por·ter·age \-ə-rij\ *n* : a porter's work; *also* : the charge for it

por·ter·house \ˈpōrt-ər-ˌhau̇s, ˈpȯrt-\ *n* **1** *archaic* : a house where malt liquor (as porter) is sold **2** : a large steak cut from the thick end of the short loin to contain a T-shaped bone and a large piece of tenderloin — see BEEF illustration

port·fo·lio \pōrt-ˈfō-lē-ˌō, pȯrt-\ *n, pl* **-lios** [It *portafoglio,* fr. *portare* to carry (fr. L) + *foglio* leaf, sheet, fr. L *folium* — more at BLADE] **1** : a hinged cover or flexible case for carrying loose papers, pictures, or pamphlets **2** [fr. the use of such a case to carry documents of state] : the office and functions of a minister of state or member of a cabinet **3** : the securities held by an investor : the commercial paper held by a financial house (as a bank)

port·hole \ˈpōrt-ˌhōl, ˈpȯrt-\ *n* [[2]*port*] **1** : an opening (as a window) with a cover or closure esp. in the side of a ship or aircraft **2** : a port through which to shoot **3** : [2]PORT 2

Por·tia \ˈpōr-shə, ˈpȯr-\ *n* : the heroine in Shakespeare's *The Merchant of Venice*

por·ti·co \ˈpōrt-i-ˌkō, ˈpȯrt-\ *n, pl* **-coes** *or* **-cos** [It, fr. L *porticus* — more at PORCH] : a colonnade or covered ambulatory esp. in classical architecture and often at the entrance of a building

por·tiere \pōr-ˈtye(ə)r, pȯr-, -ˈti(ə)r; ˈpōrt-ē-ər, ˈpȯrt-\ *n* [F *portière,* fr. OF, fem. of *portier* porter, doorkeeper] : a curtain hanging across a doorway

[1]por·tion \ˈpōr-shən, ˈpȯr-\ *n* [ME, fr. OF, fr. L *portion-, portio;* akin to L *part-, pars* part] **1** : an individual's part or share of something: as **a** : a share received by gift or inheritance **b** : DOWRY **c** : a helping of food **2** : an individual's lot, fate, or fortune : one's share of good and evil **3** : an often limited part set off or abstracted from a whole <give but that ~ which yourself proposed —Shak.> ***syn*** see PART, FATE

[2]**portion** *vt* **por·tioned; por·tion·ing** \-sh(ə-)niŋ\ **1 :** to divide into portions : DISTRIBUTE **2 :** to allot a dowry to : DOWER

por·tion·less \-shən-ləs\ *adj* **:** having no portion; *esp* **:** having no dowry or inheritance

port·land cement \ˌpōrt-lən(d)-, ˌpȯrt-\ *n* [Isle of *Portland,* England; fr. its resemblance to a limestone found there] **:** a hydraulic cement made by finely pulverizing the clinker produced by calcining to incipient fusion a mixture of argillaceous and calcareous materials

port·ly \ˈpōrt-lē, ˈpȯrt-\ *adj* **port·li·er; -est** [[1]*port*] **1 :** DIGNIFIED, STATELY **2 :** heavy or rotund of body **:** STOUT — **port·li·ness** *n*

[1]**port·man·teau** \pōrt-ˈman-(ˌ)tō, pȯrt-\ *n, pl* **-teaus** *or* **-teaux** \-(ˌ)tōz\ [MF *portemanteau,* fr. *porter* to carry + *manteau* mantle, fr. L *mantellum* — more at PORT] **:** a large traveling bag

[2]**portmanteau** *adj* **:** combining more than one use or quality

portmanteau word *n* **:** BLEND b

port of call **1 :** an intermediate port where ships customarily stop for supplies, repairs, or transshipment of cargo **2 :** a stop included on an itinerary

port of entry **1 :** a place where foreign goods may be cleared through a customhouse **2 :** a place where an alien may be permitted to enter a country

por·trait \ˈpōr-trət, ˈpȯr-, -ˌtrāt\ *n* [MF, fr. pp. of *portraire*] **1 :** PICTURE; *esp* **:** a pictorial representation (as a painting) of a person usu. showing his face **2 :** a sculptured figure **:** BUST, STATUE **3 :** a graphic portrayal in words

por·trait·ist \-əst\ *n* **:** a maker of portraits

por·trai·ture \ˈpōr-trə-ˌchu̇(ə)r, ˈpȯr-, -chər, -ˌt(y)u̇(ə)r\ *n* **1 :** the making of portraits **:** PORTRAYAL **2 :** PORTRAIT

por·tray \pōr-ˈtrā, pȯr-, pər-\ *vt* [ME *portraien,* fr. MF *portraire,* fr. L *protrahere* to draw forth, reveal, expose, fr. *pro-* forth + *trahere* to draw — more at PRO-, DRAW] **1 :** to make a picture of **:** DEPICT **2 a :** to describe in words **b :** to play the role of **:** ENACT — **por·tray·er** *n*

por·tray·al \-ˈtrā(-ə)l\ *n* **1 :** the act or process of portraying **:** REPRESENTATION **2 :** PORTRAIT

por·tress \ˈpōr-trəs, ˈpȯr-\ *n* **:** a female porter: as **a :** a doorkeeper in a convent or apartment house **b :** CHARWOMAN

Port Roy·al·ist \ˌpōrt-ˈrȯi-ə-ləst, pȯrt-\ *n* [F *port-royaliste,* fr. *Port-Royal,* a convent near Versailles, France] **:** a member or adherent of a 17th century French Jansenist lay community noted for its logicians and educators

Port Sa·lut \ˌpōr-səl-ˈ(y)ü, ˌpȯr-, -sal-\ *n* **:** PORT DU SALUT

Por·tu·guese \ˌpōr-chə-ˈgēz, ˌpȯr-, -ˈgēs\ *n, pl* **Portuguese** [Pg *português,* adj. & n., fr. *Portugal*] **1 a :** a native or inhabitant of Portugal **b :** one who is of Portuguese descent **2 :** the Romance language of Portugal and Brazil — **Portuguese** *adj*

Portuguese man-of-war *n* **:** any of several large siphonophores (genus *Physalia*) having a large bladderlike sac or cyst with a broad crest on the upper side by means of which the colony floats at the surface of the sea

por·tu·laca \ˌpōr-chə-ˈlak-ə, ˌpȯr-\ *n* [NL, genus name, fr. L, purslane, fr. *portula,* dim. of *porta* gate; fr. the lid of its capsule — more at PORT] **:** any of a genus (*Portulaca*) of mainly tropical succulent herbs of the purslane family; *esp* **:** a plant (*P. grandiflora*) cultivated for its showy flowers

pos *abbr* **1** position **2** positive

po·sa·da \pə-ˈsäd-ə\ *n* [Sp, fr. *posar* to lodge, fr. LL *pausare*] **:** an inn in Spanish-speaking countries

[1]**pose** \ˈpōz\ *vb* **posed; pos·ing** [ME *posen,* fr. MF *poser,* fr. (assumed) VL *pausare,* fr. LL, to stop, rest, pause, fr. L *pausa* pause] *vt* **1 a :** to put or set in place **b :** to place (as a model) in a studied attitude **2 a :** to put or set forth **:** OFFER <this attitude ~*s* a threat to our hopes for peace> **b :** to present for attention or consideration <let me ~ a question> ~ *vi* **1 :** to assume a posture or attitude usu. for artistic purposes **2 :** to affect an attitude or character **:** POSTURE ***syn*** see PROPOSE

[2]**pose** *n* **1 :** a sustained posture; *esp* **:** one assumed for artistic effect **2 :** an attitude assumed deliberately and usu. for a reason ***syn*** POSE, AIR, AFFECTATION, MANNERISM *shared meaning element* **:** an adopted way of speaking or acting

[3]**pose** *vt* **posed; pos·ing** [short for earlier *appose,* fr. ME *apposen,* alter. of *opposen* to oppose] **:** PUZZLE, BAFFLE

Po·sei·don \pə-ˈsīd-ᵊn\ *n* [L, fr. Gk *Poseidōn*] **:** the Greek god of the sea — compare NEPTUNE

[1]**pos·er** \ˈpō-zər\ *n* [[3]*pose*] **:** a puzzling or baffling question

[2]**poser** *n* [[1]*pose*] **:** a person who poses

po·seur \pō-ˈzər\ *n* [F, lit., poser, fr. *poser*] **:** an affected or insincere person

posh \ˈpäsh\ *adj* [origin unknown] **:** ELEGANT, FASHIONABLE

pos·it \ˈpäz-ət\ *vt* **pos·it·ed** \ˈpäz-ət-əd, ˈpäz-təd\; **pos·it·ing** \ˈpäz-ət-iŋ, ˈpäz-tiŋ\ [L *positus,* pp.] **1 :** to dispose or set firmly **:** FIX **2 :** to assume or affirm the existence of **:** POSTULATE

[1]**po·si·tion** \pə-ˈzish-ən\ *n* [MF, fr. L *position-, positio,* fr. *positus,* pp. of *ponere* to lay down, put, place, fr. (assumed) OL *posinere,* fr. *po-* away (akin to Gk *apo-*) + L *sinere* to lay, leave — more at SITE] **1 :** an act of placing or arranging: as **a :** the laying down of a proposition or thesis **b :** an arranging in order **2 :** a point of view adopted and held to <made his ~ on the issue clear> **3 :** a market commitment in securities or commodities; *also* **:** the inventory of a market trader **4 a :** the point or area occupied by a physical object <took her ~ at the head of the line> **b :** a certain arrangement of bodily parts <rose to a standing ~> **5 a :** relative place, situation, or standing <is now in a ~ to make important decisions on his own> **b :** social or official rank or status **c :** EMPLOYMENT, JOB **d :** a situation that confers advantage or preference
syn POSITION, STAND, ATTITUDE *shared meaning element* **:** a firmly held point of view or way of regarding something

[2]**position** *vt* **po·si·tioned; po·si·tion·ing** \-ˈzish-(ə-)niŋ\ **:** to put in proper position; *also* **:** LOCATE

po·si·tion·al \pə-ˈzish-nəl, -ən-ᵊl\ *adj* **1 :** of, relating to, or fixed by position <~ astronomy> **2 :** involving little movement <~ warfare> **3 :** dependent on position or environment or context <the front-articulated \k\ in \kē\ *key* and the back-articulated \k\ in \kül\ *cool* are ~ variants>

positional notation *n* **:** a system of expressing numbers in which the digits are arranged in succession, the position of each digit has a place value, and the number is equal to the sum of the products of each digit by its place value

position effect *n* **:** genic effect that is due to interaction of adjacent genes and that is modified when the spatial relationships of the genes change (as by chromosomal inversion)

position paper *n* **:** a detailed report that recommends a course of action on a particular issue

[1]**pos·i·tive** \ˈpäz-ət-iv, ˈpäz-tiv\ *adj* [ME, fr. OF *positif,* fr. L *positivus,* fr. *positus*] **1 a :** formally laid down or imposed **:** PRESCRIBED <~ laws> **b :** expressed clearly or peremptorily <her answer was a ~ *no*> **c :** fully assured **:** CONFIDENT **2 a :** of, relating to, or constituting the degree of comparison that is expressed in English by the unmodified and uninflected form of an adjective or adverb and denotes no increase or diminution **b (1) :** independent of changing circumstances **:** UNCONDITIONED **(2) :** relating to or constituting a motion or device that is definite, unyielding, constant, or certain in its action <a ~ system of levers> **c (1) :** INCONTESTABLE <~ proof> **(2) :** UNQUALIFIED <a ~ disgrace> **3 a :** not fictitious **:** REAL <a ~ influence for good in the community> **b :** active and effective in social or economic function rather than merely maintaining peace and order <a ~ government> **4 a :** having or expressing actual existence or quality as distinguished from deprivation or deficiency <~ change in temperature>: as **(1) :** logically affirmative <a ~ instance> **(2) :** not speculative **:** EMPIRICAL **b :** having rendition of light and shade similar in tone to the tones of the original subject <a ~ photographic image> **c (1) :** that is or is generated in a direction arbitrarily or customarily taken as that of increase or progression <~ rotation of the earth> <~ angles> **(2) :** directed or moving toward a source of stimulation <a ~ taxis> **d :** real and numerically greater than zero <+2 is a ~ integer> **5 a (1) :** being, relating to, or charged with electricity of which the proton is the elementary unit and which predominates in a glass body after being rubbed with silk **(2) :** losing electrons **b (1) :** having higher electric potential and constituting the part from which the current flows to the external circuit <the ~ terminal of a discharging storage battery> **(2) :** being an electron-collecting electrode of an electron tube **6 a :** marked by or indicating acceptance, approval, or affirmation **b :** affirming the presence of that sought or suspected to be present <a ~ test for blood> **7** *of a lens* **:** converging light rays and forming a real inverted image ***syn*** see SURE ***ant*** doubtful — **pos·i·tive·ly** \-lē, *for emphasis often* ˌpäz-ə-ˈtiv-\ *adv* — **pos·i·tive·ness** \ˈpäz-ət-iv-nəs, ˈpäz-tiv-\ *n*

[2]**positive** *n* **:** something positive: as **a (1) :** the positive degree of comparison in a language **(2) :** a positive form of an adjective or adverb **b :** something of which an affirmation can be made **:** REALITY **c :** a positive photograph or a print from a negative

positive law *n* **:** law established or recognized by governmental authority — compare NATURAL LAW

pos·i·tiv·ism \ˈpäz-ət-iv-ˌiz-əm, ˈpäz-tiv-\ *n* [F *positivisme,* fr. *positif* positive + *-isme* -ism] **1 a :** a theory that theology and metaphysics are earlier imperfect modes of knowledge and that positive knowledge is based on natural phenomena and their properties and relations as verified by the empirical sciences **b :** LOGICAL POSITIVISM **2 :** the quality or state of being positive — **pos·i·tiv·ist** \-əst\ *adj or n* — **pos·i·tiv·is·tic** \ˌpäz-ət-iv-ˈis-tik, ˌpäz-tiv-\ *adj*

pos·i·tiv·i·ty \ˌpäz-ə-ˈtiv-ət-ē\ *n, pl* **-ties** **1 :** the quality or state of being positive **2 :** something that is positive

pos·i·tron \ˈpäz-ə-ˌträn\ *n* [*posi*tive + *-tron* (as in *electron*)] **:** a positively charged particle having the same mass and magnitude of charge as the electron and constituting the antiparticle of the electron — called also *positive electron*

pos·i·tro·ni·um \ˌpäz-ə-ˈtrō-nē-əm\ *n* [*positron* + *-ium*] **:** a short-lived system suggestive of an atom and analogous to the hydrogen atom consisting of a positron and an electron bound together

poss *abbr* possessive

pos·se \ˈpäs-ē\ *n* [ML *posse comitatus,* lit., power or authority of the county] **1 :** a body of persons summoned by a sheriff to assist in preserving the public peace usu. in an emergency **2 :** a group of people temporarily organized to make a search (as for a lost child) **3 :** a large group often with a common interest

pos·sess \pə-ˈzes *also* -ˈses\ *vt* [ME *possessen,* fr. MF *possesser* to have possession of, take possession of, fr. L *possessus,* pp. of *possidēre,* fr. *potis* able, in power + *sedēre* to sit — more at POTENT, SIT] **1 a** *obs* **:** to instate in as owner **b :** to make the owner or holder — used with *of* or *with* **c :** to have possession of **2 a :** to have and hold as property **:** OWN **b :** to have as an attribute, knowledge, or skill **3 a :** to take into one's possession **b :** to enter into and control firmly **:** DOMINATE <whatever ~*ed* her to act like that?> **c :** to bring or cause to fall under the influence, possession, or control of some emotional or intellectual reaction <melancholy ~*es* her> ***syn*** see HAVE — **pos·ses·sor** *n*

pos·sessed *adj* **1** *obs* **:** held as a possession **2 a (1) :** influenced or controlled by something (as an evil spirit or a passion) **(2) :** MAD, CRAZED **b :** urgently desirous to do or have something **3 :** SELF-POSSESSED, CALM — **pos·sessed·ly** \-ˈzes-əd-lē, -ˈzes-tlē *also* -ˈses-\ *adv* — **pos·sessed·ness** \-ˈzes-əd-nəs, -ˈzest-nəs *also* -ˈses- & -ˈsest-\ *n*

pos·ses·sion \-ˈzesh-ən, *also* -ˈsesh-\ *n* **1 a :** the act of having or taking into control **b :** control or occupancy of property without regard to ownership **c :** OWNERSHIP **2 :** something owned, occupied, or controlled **:** PROPERTY **3 a :** domination by something (as an evil spirit, a passion, or an idea) **b :** a psychological state in which an individual's normal personality is replaced by another **c :** the fact or condition of being self-controlled — **pos·ses·sion·al** \-'zesh-nəl, -ən-ᵊl *also* -'sesh-\ *adj*

[1]**pos·ses·sive** \pə-'zes-iv *also* -'ses-\ *adj* **1 :** of, relating to, or constituting a word, a word group, or a grammatical case that denotes ownership or a relation analogous to ownership **2 :** manifesting possession or the desire to own or dominate — **pos·ses·sive·ly** *adv* — **pos·ses·sive·ness** *n*

[2]**possessive** *n* **1 a :** the possessive case **b :** a word in the possessive case **2 :** a possessive word or word group

possessive adjective *n* **:** a pronominal adjective expressing possession

possessive pronoun *n* **:** a pronoun that derives from a personal pronoun and denotes possession and analogous relationships

pos·ses·so·ry \pə-'zes-(ə-)rē *also* -'ses-\ *adj* **1 :** of, arising from, or having the nature of possession **2 :** having possession **3 :** characteristic of a possessor **:** POSSESSIVE

pos·set \'päs-ət\ *n* [ME *poshet, possot*] **:** a hot drink of sweetened and spiced milk curdled with ale or wine

pos·si·bil·i·ty \,päs-ə-'bil-ət-ē\ *n, pl* **-ties** **1 :** the condition or fact of being possible **2 :** something that is possible **3** *archaic* **:** one's utmost power, capacity, or ability **4 :** potential or prospective value — usu. used in pl. <the house had great *possibilities*>

pos·si·ble \'päs-ə-bəl\ *adj* [ME, fr. MF, fr. L *possibilis,* fr. *posse* to be able, fr. *potis, pote* able + *esse* to be — more at POTENT, IS] **1 a :** being within the limits of ability, capacity, or realization **b :** being what may be done or may occur according to nature, custom, or manners **2 :** being something that may or may not occur <it is ~ but not probable that he will win> **3 :** having an indicated potential <a ~ housing site> — **pos·si·bly** \-blē\ *adv*
syn **1** POSSIBLE, PRACTICABLE, FEASIBLE *shared meaning element* **:** capable of being realized *ant* impossible
2 see PROBABLE

pos·sum \'päs-əm\ *n* **:** OPOSSUM

[1]**post** \'pōst\ *n* [ME, fr. OE; akin to OHG *pfosto* post; both fr. a prehistoric WGmc word borrowed fr. L *postis;* akin to Gk *pro* before and to Gk *histasthai* to stand — more at FOR, STAND] **1 :** a piece (as of timber or metal) fixed firmly in an upright position esp. as a stay or support **:** PILLAR, COLUMN **2 :** a pole or stake set up to mark or indicate something; *esp* **:** a pole that marks the starting or finishing point of a horse race **3 :** a metallic fitting attached to an electrical device (as a storage battery) for convenience in making connections **4 :** GOALPOST

[2]**post** *vt* **1 :** to affix to a usual place (as a wall) for public notices **:** PLACARD **2 a :** to publish, announce, or advertise by or as if by use of a placard **b :** to denounce by public notice **c :** to enter on a public listing **d :** to forbid (property) to trespassers under penalty of legal prosecution by notices placed along the boundaries **e :** SCORE

[3]**post** *n* [MF *poste* relay station, courier, fr. OIt *posta* relay station, fr. fem. of *posto,* pp. of *porre* to place, fr. L *ponere* — more at POSITION] **1** *obs* **:** COURIER **2** *archaic* **a :** one of a series of stations for keeping horses for relays **b :** the distance between any two such consecutive stations **:** STAGE **3** *chiefly Brit* **a :** a nation's organization for handling mail; *also* **:** the mail handled **b :** a single dispatch of mail **c :** POST OFFICE **d :** POSTBOX

[4]**post** *vi* **1 :** to travel with post-horses **2 :** to ride or travel with haste **:** HURRY ~ *vt* **1** *archaic* **:** to dispatch in haste **2 :** MAIL <~ a letter> **3 a :** to transfer or carry from a book of original entry to a ledger **b :** to make transfer entries in **4 :** to make familiar with a subject **:** INFORM <kept her ~*ed* on the latest gossip>

[5]**post** *adv* **:** with post-horses **:** EXPRESS

[6]**post** *n* [MF *poste,* fr. OIt *posto,* fr. pp. of *porre* to place] **1 a :** the place at which a soldier is stationed; *esp* **:** a sentry's beat or station **b :** a station or task to which one is assigned **c :** the place at which a body of troops is stationed **:** CAMP **d :** a local subdivision of a veterans' organization **e :** one of two bugle calls sounded (as in the British Army) at tattoo **2 a :** an office or position to which a person is appointed **b :** a player position in basketball that is the focal point of the offense; *specif* **:** PIVOT 2b **3 a :** TRADING POST, SETTLEMENT **b :** a trading station on the floor of a stock exchange

[7]**post** *vt* **1 a :** to station in a given place <guards were ~*ed* at the doors> **b :** to carry ceremoniously to a position <~*ing* the colors> **2** *chiefly Brit* **:** to assign to a unit or location (as in the military or civil service) **3 :** to put up (as bond)

post- *prefix* [ME, fr. L, fr. *post;* akin to Skt *paśca* behind, after, Gk *apo* away from — more at OF] **1 a :** after **:** subsequent **:** later <*post*date> **b :** behind **:** posterior **:** following after <*post*lude> <*post*consonantal> **2 a :** subsequent to **:** later than <*post*operative> <*post*-Pleistocene> **b :** posterior to <*post*orbital>

post·age \'pō-stij\ *n* **1 :** the fee for postal service **2 :** adhesive stamps or printed indicia representing postal fees

postage–due stamp *n* **:** a special adhesive stamp that is applied by a post office to mail bearing insufficient postage to make up an amount equal to the deficient postage with often an additional fee and that is paid for by the addressee immediately prior to delivery

postage meter *n* **:** a machine that prints postal indicia on pieces of mail, records the amount of postage given in the indicia, and subtracts it from a total amount which has been paid at a post office and for which the machine has been set

postage stamp *n* **:** a government adhesive stamp or imprinted stamp for use on mail as evidence of prepayment of postage

post·al \'pōs-tᵊl\ *adj* **1 :** of or relating to the mails or the post office **2 :** conducted by mail <~ chess>

postal card *n* **1 :** a card officially stamped and issued by the government for use in the mail **2 :** POSTCARD

postal order *n, Brit* **:** MONEY ORDER

postal service *n* **:** POST OFFICE 1

postal union *n* **:** an association of governments setting up uniform regulations and practices for international mail

post·ax·i·al \(ˈ)pō-'stak-sē-əl\ *adj* **:** located behind an axis of the body; *esp* **:** of or relating to the posterior side of the axis of a vertebrate limb — **post·ax·i·al·ly** \-ə-lē\ *adv*

post·bag \'pōs(t)-,bag\ *n* **1** *Brit* **:** MAILBAG **2** *Brit* **:** a single batch of mail **:** LETTERS

post·bel·lum \(ˈ)pōs(t)-'bel-əm\ *adj* [L *post bellum* after the war] **:** of, relating to, or characteristic of the period following a war and esp. following the American Civil War

post·box \'pōs(t)-,bäks\ *n* **:** MAILBOX; *esp* **:** a public mailbox

post·boy \-,bȯi\ *n* **:** POSTILION

post·breed·ing \(ˈ)pōs(t)-'brēd-iŋ\ *adj* **:** following a period of physiological fitness for reproduction <~ regressive changes>

post·card \'pōs(t)-,kärd\ *n* **1 :** a card on which a message may be written for mailing without an envelope and to which the sender must affix a stamp **2 :** POSTAL CARD 1

post·ca·va \'pōs(t)-'kā-və\ *n* [NL] **:** the inferior vena cava of vertebrates higher than fishes — **post·ca·val** \-vəl\ *adj*

post chaise *n* **:** a carriage usu. having a closed body on four wheels and seating two to four persons

post·clas·si·cal \(ˈ)pōs(t)-'klas-i-kəl\ *or* **post·clas·sic** \-ik\ *adj* **:** of or relating to a period (as in art, literature, or civilization) following a classical one

post·co·lo·nial \,pōs(t)-kə-'lō-nyəl, -nē-əl\ *adj* **:** of or relating to the period following a colony's achieving independence

post–com·mu·nion \-kə-'myü-nyən\ *n, often cap P&C* [ML *post-communion-, postcommunio,* fr. L *post-* + LL *communio* communion] **:** a liturgically variable prayer following the communion at Mass

post·con·so·nan·tal \-,kän(t)-sə-'nant-ᵊl\ *adj* **:** immediately following a consonant

post·date \(ˈ)pōs(t)-'dāt\ *vt* **1 a :** to date with a date later than that of execution <~ a check> **b :** to assign (an event) to a date subsequent to that of actual occurrence **2 :** to follow in time

[1]**post·di·lu·vi·an** \,pōs(t)-də-'lü-vē-ən, -dī-\ *adj* [*post-* + L *diluvium* flood — more at DELUGE] **:** of or relating to the period after the flood described in the Bible

[2]**postdiluvian** *n* **:** one living after the flood described in the Bible

post·doc·tor·al \(ˈ)pōs(t)-'däk-t(ə-)rəl\ *also* **post·doc·tor·ate** \-t(ə-)rət\ *adj* **:** being beyond the doctoral level: **a :** of or relating to advanced academic or professional work beyond a doctor's degree <a ~ fellowship> **b :** engaged in such work <~ scholars>

post·em·bry·on·ic \,pō-,stem-brē-'än-ik\ *also* **post·em·bry·o·nal** \-'brī-ən-ᵊl\ *adj* **:** succeeding the embryonic stage

post·emer·gence \,pō-sti-'mər-jən(t)s\ *n* **:** a stage between the emergence of a seedling and the maturity of a crop plant — **postemergence** *adj*

[1]**post·er** \'pō-stər\ *n* [[4]*post*] **1** *archaic* **:** a swift traveler **2 :** POST-HORSE

[2]**poster** *n* [[2]*post*] **:** a bill or placard for posting often in a public place; *specif* **:** one that is decorative or pictorial

poster color *n* **:** an opaque watercolor paint with a gum or glue-size binder sold usu. in jars

poste res·tante \,pō-,stres-'tä(n)nt, -'täⁿt\ *n* [F, lit., waiting mail] *chiefly Brit* **:** GENERAL DELIVERY

pos·te·ri·ad \pō-'stir-ē-,ad, pä-\ *adv* [*posterior* + *-ad*] **:** toward the posterior part of the body

[1]**pos·te·ri·or** \pō-'stir-ē-ər, pä-\ *adj* [L, compar. of *posterus* coming after, fr. *post* after — more at POST-] **1 :** later in time **:** SUBSEQUENT **2 :** situated behind: as **a :** CAUDAL **b** *of the human body or its parts* **:** DORSAL **3** *of a plant part* **:** ADAXIAL, SUPERIOR — **pos·te·ri·or·ly** *adv*

[2]**pos·te·ri·or** \pä-'stir-ē-ər, pō-\ *n* **:** the hinder parts of the body; *specif* **:** BUTTOCKS

pos·te·ri·or·i·ty \(,)pō-,stir-ē-'ȯr-ət-ē, (,)pä-, -'är-\ *n* **:** the quality or state of being later or subsequent

pos·ter·i·ty \pä-'ster-ət-ē\ *n* [ME *posterite,* fr. MF *posterité,* fr. L *posteritat-, posteritas,* fr. *posterus* coming after] **1 :** the offspring of one progenitor to the furthest generation **:** DESCENDANTS **2 :** all future generations

pos·tern \'pōs-tərn, 'päs-\ *n* [ME *posterne,* fr. OF, alter. of *posterle,* fr. LL *posterula,* dim. of *postera* back door, fr. L, fem. of *posterus*] **1 :** a back door or gate **2 :** a private or side entrance or way — **postern** *adj*

post exchange *n* **:** a store at a military installation that sells merchandise and services to military personnel and authorized civilians

post·ex·il·ic \,pō-(,)steg-'zil-ik\ *adj* **:** of or relating to the period of Jewish history between the end of the exile in Babylon in 538 B.C. and A.D. 1

post·face \'pōs(t)-fəs, -,fās; pȯs-fås\ *n* [F, fr. *post-* + *-face* (as in *préface* preface)] **:** a brief article or note (as of explanation) placed at the end of a publication

post·form \(ˈ)pōs(t)-'fȯ(ə)rm\ *vt* **:** to shape (as a sheet of partially cured plastic material) subsequently

post–free \'pōs(t)-'frē\ *adj, chiefly Brit* **:** POSTPAID

post·gan·gli·on·ic \,pōs(t)-,gaŋ-glē-'än-ik\ *adj* **:** distal to a ganglion; *specif* **:** of, relating to, or being an axon arising from a cell body within an autonomic ganglion

post·gla·cial \(ˈ)pōs(t)-'glā-shəl\ *adj* [ISV] **:** occurring after a period of glaciation

[1]**post·grad·u·ate** \-'graj-(ə-)wət, -ə-,wāt\ *adj* **:** GRADUATE 2

[2]**postgraduate** *n* **:** a student continuing his education after graduation from high school or college

post·har·vest \'pōst-'här-vəst\ *adj* **:** relating to, taking place in, or used in the period after harvest <a ~ spray> <~ storage>

[1]**post·haste** \'pōst-'hāst\ *n* [[3]*post*] *archaic* **:** great haste

[2]**posthaste** *adv* **:** with all possible speed

[3]**posthaste** *adj, obs* **:** SPEEDY, IMMEDIATE <requires your . . . ~ appearance —Shak.>

post hoc \'pōst-'häk\ *n* [NL *post hoc, ergo propter hoc* after this, therefore because of this] **:** the fallacy of arguing from temporal sequence to a causal relation

post·hole \'pōst-,hōl\ *n* **:** a hole sunk in the ground to hold a fence post

post horn *n* : a simple straight or coiled brass or copper wind instrument with cupped mouthpiece used esp. by guards of mail coaches of the 18th and 19th centuries
post–horse \ˈpōst-ˌhȯ(ə)rs\ *n* [3*post*] : a horse for use esp. by couriers or mail carriers
post·hu·mous \ˈpäs-chə-məs *also* ˈpäs-t(h)ə-, pä-ˈst(y)ü-, pōst-ˈhyü\ *adj* [L *posthumus,* alter. of *postumus* late-born, posthumous, fr. superl. of *posterus* coming after — more at POSTERIOR] **1** : born after the death of the father **2** : published after the death of the author **3** : following or occurring after death <~ fame> — **post·hu·mous·ly** *adv* — **post·hu·mous·ness** *n*
post·hyp·not·ic \ˌpōst-(h)ip-ˈnät-ik\ *adj* [ISV] : of, relating to, or characteristic of the period following a hypnotic trance
pos·tiche \pȯ-stēsh\ *n* [F, fr. Sp. *postizo*] : WIG; *esp* : TOUPEE 2
pos·til·ion *or* **pos·til·lion** \pō-ˈstil-yən, pə-\ *n* [MF *postillon* mail carrier using post-horses, fr. It *postiglione,* fr. *posta* post] : one who rides as a guide on the near horse of one of the pairs attached to a coach or post chaise esp. without a coachman
Post·im·pres·sion·ism \ˌpō-stim-ˈpresh-ə-ˌniz-əm\ *n* [F *postimpressionisme,* fr. *post-* + *impressionisme* impressionism] : a theory or practice of art originating in France in the last quarter of the 19th century that in revolt against impressionism stresses variously volume, picture structure, or expressionism — **Post·im·pres·sion·ist** \-ˈpresh-(ə-)nəst\ *adj or n* — **Post·im·pres·sion·is·tic** \-ˌpresh-ə-ˈnis-tik\ *adj*
1**post·ing** *n* [4*post*] **1** : the act of transferring an entry or item from a book of original entry to the proper account in a ledger **2** : the record in a ledger account resulting from the transfer of an entry or item from a book of original entry
2**posting** *n* [7*post*] : appointment to a post or a command
post·ir·ra·di·a·tion \ˌpō-stir-ˌād-ē-ˈā-shən\ *adj* : occurring after irradiation
post–ju·ve·nal \(ˈ)pōs(t)-ˈjü-vən-ᵊl\ *adj* : following or terminating the juvenal stage of a bird's life history <a ~ molt>
post–Kant·ian \(ˈ)pōs(t)-ˈkant-ē-ən, -ˈkänt-\ *adj* : of or relating to the idealist philosophers (as Fichte, Schelling, and Hegel) following Kant and developing some of his ideas
post·lude \ˈpōst-ˌlüd\ *n* [*post-* + *-lude* (as in *prelude*)] **1** : a closing piece of music; *esp* : an organ voluntary at the end of a church service **2** : a closing phase (as of an epoch or a literary work)
post·man \ˈpōs(t)-mən, -ˌman\ *n* : MAILMAN
1**post·mark** \-ˌmärk\ *n* : an official postal marking on a piece of mail; *specif* : a cancellation mark showing the post office and date of mailing
2**postmark** *vt* : to put a postmark on
post·mas·ter \-ˌmas-tər\ *n* **1** : one who has charge of a post office **2** : one who has charge of a station for the accommodation of travelers or who supplies post-horses — **post·mas·ter·ship** \-ˌship\ *n*
postmaster general *n, pl* **postmasters general** : an official in charge of a national post office department or agency
post·meno·paus·al \ˌpōs(t)-ˌmen-ə-ˈpȯ-zəl\ *adj* **1** : having undergone menopause **2** : occurring after menopause
post me·ri·di·em \ˈpōs(t)-mə-ˈrid-ē-əm, -ē-ˌem\ *adj* [L] : being after noon
post·mil·le·nar·i·an·ism \ˈpōs(t)-ˌmil-ə-ˈner-ē-ə-ˌniz-əm\ *n* : POSTMILLENNIALISM — **postmillenarian** *adj or n*
post·mil·len·ni·al \ˌpōs(t)-mə-ˈlen-ē-əl\ *adj* **1** : coming after or relating to the period after the millennium **2** : holding or relating to postmillennialism
post·mil·len·ni·al·ism \-ē-ə-ˌliz-əm\ *n* : the view that Christ will return only at the end of the millennium — **post·mil·len·ni·al·ist** \-ē-ə-ləst\ *n*
post·mis·tress \ˈpōs(t)-ˌmis-trəs\ *n* : a female postmaster
post·mor·tem \(ˈ)pōs(t)-ˈmȯrt-əm\ *adj* [L *post mortem* after death] **1** : occurring after death **2** : following the event <a ~ appraisal of the game> — **postmortem** *n*
postmortem examination *n* : an examination of a body after death for determining the cause of death or the character and extent of changes produced by disease
1**post·na·sal** \(ˈ)pōs(t)-ˈnā-zəl\ *adj* : lying or occurring posterior to the nose
2**postnasal** *n* : a postnasal part
postnasal drip *n* : flow of mucous secretion from the posterior part of the nasal cavity onto the wall of the pharynx occurring usu. as a chronic accompaniment of an allergic state
post·na·tal \(ˈ)pōs(t)-ˈnāt-ᵊl\ *adj* [ISV] : subsequent to birth; *specif* : of or relating to an infant immediately after birth <~ care> — **post·na·tal·ly** \-ᵊl-ē\ *adv*
post·nup·tial \-ˈnəp-shəl, -chəl, *nonstand* -chə-wəl\ *adj* : made or occurring after marriage or mating — **post·nup·tial·ly** \-ē\ *adv*
1**post–obit** \pō-ˈstō-bət, *esp Brit* -ˈstäb-it\ *adj* [L *post obitum* after death] : occurring or taking effect after death
2**post–obit** *n* : POST-OBIT BOND
post–obit bond *n* : a bond made by a reversioner to secure a loan and payable out of his reversion
post office *n* **1** : a government department or agency handling the transmission of mail **2** : a local branch of a national post office handling the mail for a particular place or area **3** : a game in which a player acting as postmaster or postmistress may exact a kiss from one of the opposite sex as payment for the pretended delivery of a letter
post·op·er·a·tive \(ˈ)pō-ˈstäp-(ə-)rət-iv, -ˈstäp-ə-ˌrāt-\ *adj* [ISV] : following a surgical operation — **post·op·er·a·tive·ly** *adv*
post·or·bit·al \-ˈstȯr-bət-ᵊl\ *adj* : situated behind the eye socket
post·paid \ˈpōs(t)-ˈpād\ *adv* : with the postage paid by the sender and not chargeable to the receiver
post·par·tum \(ˈ)pōs(t)-ˈpärt-əm\ *adj* [NL *post partum* after birth] : following parturition <~ period> — **postpartum** *adv*
post·pi·tu·itary \ˌpōs(t)-pə-ˈt(y)ü-ə-ˌter-ē\ *adj* : arising in or derived from the posterior lobe of the pituitary body
post·pone \pōs(t)-ˈpōn\ *vt* **post·poned; post·pon·ing** [L *postponere* to place after, postpone, fr. *post-* + *ponere* to place — more at POSITION] **1** : to hold back to a later time : DEFER **2 a** : to place later (as in a sentence) than the normal position in English <~ an adjective> **b** : to place after in order of precedence, preference, or importance ***syn*** see DEFER — **post·pon·able** \-ˈpō-nə-bəl\ *adj* — **post·pone·ment** \-ˈpōn-mənt\ *n* — **post·pon·er** *n*
post·po·si·tion \ˌpōs(t)-pə-ˈzish-ən, ˈpōs(t)-pə-ˌ\ *n* [F, fr. *postposer* to place after, fr. L *postponere* (perf. indic. *postposui*)] : the placing of a grammatical element after a word to which it is primarily related in a sentence; *also* : such a word or particle esp. when functioning as a preposition — **post·po·si·tion·al** \ˌpōs(t)-pə-ˈzish-nəl, -ən-ᵊl\ *adj* — **post·po·si·tion·al·ly** \-ē\ *adv*
post·pos·i·tive \(ˈ)pōs(t)-ˈpäz-ət-iv, -ˈpäz-tiv\ *adj* : placed after or at the end of another word — **post·pos·i·tive·ly** *adv*
post·pran·di·al \pōs(t)-ˈpran-dē-əl\ *adj* : following a meal
post road *n* : a road used for the conveyance of mail
post·script \ˈpō(s)-ˌskript\ *n* [NL *postscriptum,* fr. L, neut. of *postscriptus,* pp. of *postscribere* to write after, fr. *post-* + *scribere* to write — more at SCRIBE] : a note or series of notes appended to a completed letter, article, or book
post·syn·ap·tic \ˌpōs(t)-sə-ˈnap-tik\ *adj* **1** : occurring after synapsis <a ~ chromosome> **2** : relating to, occurring in, or being part of a nerve cell by which a wave of excitation is conveyed away from a synapse — **post·syn·ap·ti·cal·ly** \-ti-k(ə-)lē\ *adv*
post·ten·sion \(ˈ)pōs(t)-ˈten-chən\ *vt* : to apply tension to (reinforcing steel) after concrete has set
post time *n* [1*post*] : the designated time for the start of a horse race
post·trau·mat·ic \ˌpōs(t)-trə-ˈmat-ik, -trȯ-, -trau̇-\ *adj* [ISV] : following or resulting from trauma
post·treat·ment \(ˈ)pōs(t)-ˈtrēt-mənt\ *adj* : relating to, typical of, or occurring in the stage following treatment <~ examinations> — **posttreatment** *adv*
pos·tu·lan·cy \ˈpäs-chə-lən-sē\ *n, pl* **-cies** **1** : the quality or state of being a postulant **2** : the period during which a person remains a postulant
pos·tu·lant \ˈpäs-chə-lənt\ *n* [F, petitioner, candidate, postulant, fr. MF, fr. prp. of *postuler* to demand, solicit, fr. L *postulare*] **1** : a person admitted to a religious house as a probationary candidate for membership **2** : a person on probation before being admitted as a candidate for holy orders in the Episcopal Church
1**pos·tu·late** \ˈpäs-chə-ˌlāt\ *vt* **-lat·ed; -lat·ing** [L *postulatus,* pp. of *postulare,* fr. (assumed) *postus,* pp. of L *poscere* to ask; akin to OHG *forsca* question, Skt *pṛcchati* he asks] **1** : DEMAND, CLAIM **2 a** : to assume or claim as true, existent, or necessary : depend upon or start from the postulate of **b** : to assume as a postulate or axiom (as in logic or mathematics) — **pos·tu·la·tion** \ˌpäs-chə-ˈlā-shən\ *n* — **pos·tu·la·tion·al** \-shnəl, -shən-ᵊl\ *adj*
2**pos·tu·late** \ˈpäs-chə-lət, -ˌlāt\ *n* [ML *postulatum,* fr. neut. of *postulatus,* pp. of *postulare* to assume, fr. L, to demand] **1** : a hypothesis advanced as an essential presupposition, condition, or premise of a train of reasoning **2** : AXIOM 2a
pos·tu·la·tor \-ˌlāt-ər\ *n* : an official who presents a plea for beatification or canonization in the Roman Catholic Church — compare DEVIL'S ADVOCATE
pos·tur·al \ˈpäs-chə-rəl\ *adj* : of, relating to, or involving posture
1**pos·ture** \ˈpäs-chər\ *n* [F, fr. It *postura,* fr. L *positura,* fr. *positus,* pp. of *ponere* to place — more at POSITION] **1 a** : the position or bearing of the body whether characteristic or assumed for a special purpose <erect ~> **b** : the pose of a model or artistic figure **2** : relative place or position : SITUATION **3** : state or condition at a given time esp. in relation to other persons or things <put the country in a ~ of defense> **4** : a conscious mental pose : ATTITUDE <his ~ of moral superiority>
2**posture** *vb* **pos·tured; pos·tur·ing** *vt* : to cause to assume a given posture : POSE ~ *vi* **1** : to assume a posture; *esp* : to strike a pose for effect **2** : to assume an artificial or pretended attitude : ATTITUDINIZE — **pos·tur·er** \-chər-ər\ *n*
post·vo·cal·ic \ˌpōst-vō-ˈkal-ik, -və-\ *adj* [ISV] : immediately following a vowel
post·war \ˈpōs-ˈtwȯ(ə)r\ *adj* : of or relating to the period after a war
po·sy \ˈpō-zē\ *n, pl* **posies** [alter. of *poesy*] **1** : a brief sentiment, motto, or legend **2** : BOUQUET, NOSEGAY
1**pot** \ˈpät\ *n* [ME, fr. OE *pott;* akin to MLG *pot* pot] **1 a** : a rounded metal or earthen container used chiefly for domestic purposes; *also* : any of various technical or industrial vessels or enclosures resembling or likened to a household pot <the ~ of a still> **b** : POTFUL <a ~ of coffee> **2** : an enclosed framework of wire, wood, or wicker for catching fish or lobsters **3 a** : a large amount (as of money) **b** (1) : the total of the bets at stake at one time (2) : one round in a poker game **c** : the total of a prize **d** : the common fund of a group **4** : POTSHOT **5** : POTBELLY **6** : RUIN, DETERIORATION <business went to ~> **7** *Brit* : a shot in snooker in which a ball is pocketed **8** : MARIJUANA
2**pot** *vb* **pot·ted; pot·ting** *vt* **1 a** : to place in a pot **b** : to preserve in a sealed pot, jar, or can <*potted* chicken> **2** : to shoot (as an animal) for food with a potshot **3** : to make or shape (earthenware) as a potter **4** : to embed (as electronic components) in a container with an insulating or protective material (as plastic) ~ *vi* : to take a potshot
3**pot** *abbr* **1** potential **2** potentiometer
1**po·ta·ble** \ˈpōt-ə-bəl\ *adj* [LL *potabilis,* fr. L *potare* to drink; akin to L *bibere* to drink, Gk *pinein*] : suitable for drinking — **po·ta·bil·i·ty** \ˌpōt-ə-ˈbil-ət-ē\ *n* — **po·ta·ble·ness** \ˈpōt-ə-bəl-nəs\ *n*
2**potable** *n* : a liquid that is suitable for drinking
po·tage \pȯ-ˈtäzh\ *n* [MF, fr. OF, pottage] : a thick soup

pot ale *n* **:** the residue of fermented wort left in a still after whiskey or alcohol has been distilled off and used for feeding swine

pot·ash \'pät-ˌash\ *n* [sing. of *pot ashes*] **1 a :** potassium carbonate esp. from wood ashes **b :** POTASSIUM HYDROXIDE **2 :** potassium or a potassium compound esp. as used in agriculture or industry

po·tas·sic \pə-'tas-ik\ *adj* **:** of, relating to, or containing potassium

po·tas·si·um \pə-'tas-ē-əm\ *n, often attrib* [NL, fr. *potassa* potash, fr. E *potash*] **:** a silver-white soft light low-melting univalent metallic element of the alkali metal group that occurs abundantly in nature esp. combined in minerals — see ELEMENT table

potassium–argon *adj* **:** being or relating to a method of dating archaeological or geological materials based on the radioactive decay of potassium to argon that has taken place in a specimen

potassium bromide *n* **:** a crystalline salt KBr with a saline taste that is used as a sedative and in photography

potassium carbonate *n* **:** a white salt K_2CO_3 that forms a strongly alkaline solution and is used in making glass and soap

potassium chlorate *n* **:** a crystalline salt $KClO_3$ that is used as an oxidizing agent in matches, fireworks, and explosives

potassium chloride *n* **:** a crystalline salt KCl occurring as a mineral and in natural waters and used as a fertilizer

potassium cyanide *n* **:** a very poisonous crystalline salt KCN used esp. in electroplating

potassium dichromate *n* **:** a soluble salt $K_2Cr_2O_7$ forming large orange-red crystals used esp. in dyeing, in photography, and as an oxidizing agent

potassium hydroxide *n* **:** a white deliquescent solid KOH that dissolves in water with much heat to form a strongly alkaline and caustic liquid and is used chiefly in making soap and as a reagent

potassium nitrate *n* **:** a crystalline salt KNO_3 that occurs as a product of nitrification in arable soils, is a strong oxidizer, and is used esp. in making gunpowder, in preserving meat, and in medicine

potassium permanganate *n* **:** a dark purple salt $KMnO_4$ used as an oxidizer and disinfectant

potassium phosphate *n* **:** any of various phosphates of potassium; *esp* **:** any of the three orthophosphates

potassium sulfate *n* **:** a while crystalline compound K_2SO_4 used as a fertilizer

po·ta·tion \pō-'tā-shən\ *n* [ME *potacioun,* fr. MF *potation,* fr. L *potation-, potatio* act of drinking, fr. *potatus,* pp. of *potare*] **1 :** a usu. alcoholic drink or brew **2 :** the act or an instance of drinking or inhaling; *also* **:** the portion taken in one such act

po·ta·to \pə-'tāt-(ˌ)ō, pət-'āt-, -ə(-w)\ *n, pl* **-toes** *often attrib* [Sp *batata,* fr. Taino] **1 :** SWEET POTATO **2 a :** an erect American herb (*Solanum tuberosum*) of the nightshade family widely cultivated as a vegetable crop **b :** the edible starchy tuber of a potato — called also *Irish potato, white potato*

potato 2a

potato beetle *n* **:** COLORADO POTATO BEETLE

potato blight *n* **:** any of several destructive fungus diseases of the potato

potato bug *n* **:** COLORADO POTATO BEETLE

potato chip *n* **:** a thin slice of white potato fried crisp and salted

potato leafhopper *n* **:** a small green white-spotted leafhopper (*Empoasca fabae*) of the eastern and southern U.S. that is a serious pest on many cultivated plants and esp. on the potato

potato psyllid *n* **:** a hemipterous insect (*Paratrioza cockerelli*) that feeds on tomato and potato plants and transmits a virus disease

potato tu·ber·worm \-'t(y)ü-bər-ˌwərm\ *n* **:** a grayish brown moth (*Phthorimaea operculella* of the family Gelechiidae) whose larva mines the leaves and bores in the stems esp. of potato and tobacco plants and commonly overwinters in potato tubers

pot–au–feu \ˌpät-ō-'fə(r), pȯ-tō-fœ̄\ *n, pl* **pot–au–feu** [F, lit., pot on the fire] **:** a French boiled dinner of meat and vegetables

pot·bel·lied \'pät-'bel-ēd\ *adj* **:** having a potbelly <a ~ man>

potbellied stove *n* **:** a stove with a rounded or bulging body — called also *potbelly stove*

pot·bel·ly \'pät-ˌbel-ē\ *n* **1 :** an enlarged, swollen, or protruding abdomen **2 :** POTBELLIED STOVE

pot·boil \-ˌbȯil\ *vi* **:** to produce potboilers

pot·boil·er \-ˌbȯi-lər\ *n* **:** a usu. inferior work (as of art or literature) produced chiefly for profit

pot·boy \-ˌbȯi\ *n* **:** a boy who serves drinks in a tavern

pot cheese *n* **:** COTTAGE CHEESE

po·teen *also* **po·theen** \pə-'tēn, -'chēn, -'tyēn, -'thēn\ *n* [IrGael *poitīn*] **:** illicitly distilled whiskey of Ireland

po·tence \'pōt-ᵊn(t)s\ *n* **:** POTENCY

po·ten·cy \'pōt-ᵊn-sē\ *n, pl* **-cies 1 a :** the quality or state of being potent **b :** FORCE, POWER **c :** the ability or capacity to achieve or bring about a particular result **2 :** POTENTIALITY 1

[1]**po·tent** \'pōt-ᵊnt\ *adj* [obs. E *potent* crutch] *of a heraldic cross* **:** having flat bars across the ends of the arms — see CROSS illustration

[2]**potent** *adj* [ME (Sc), fr. L *potent-, potens,* fr. prp. of (assumed) L *potēre* to be powerful, fr. L *potis, pote* able; akin to Goth brūth*faths* bridegroom, Gk *posis* husband, Skt *pati* master] **1 :** having or wielding force, authority, or influence **:** POWERFUL **2 :** achieving or bringing about a particular result **:** EFFECTIVE **3 a :** chemically or medicinally effective <a ~ vaccine> **b :** rich in a characteristic constituent <~ tea> **4 :** able to copulate — usu. used of the male — **po·tent·ly** *adv*

po·ten·tate \'pōt-ᵊn-ˌtāt\ *n* **:** one who wields controlling power

[1]**po·ten·tial** \pə-'ten-chəl\ *adj* [ME, fr. LL *potentialis,* fr. *potentia* potentiality, fr. L, power, fr. *potent-, potens*] **1 :** existing in possibility **:** capable of development into actuality <~ benefits> **2 :** expressing possibility; *specif* **:** of, relating to, or constituting a verb phrase expressing possibility, liberty, or power by the use of an auxiliary with the infinitive of the verb (as in "it may rain") ***syn*** see LATENT ***ant*** active, actual — **po·ten·tial·ly** \-'tench-(ə-)lē\ *adv*

[2]**potential** *n* **1 :** something that can develop or become actual <a ~ for violence> **2 a :** any of various functions from which the intensity or the velocity at any point in a field may be readily calculated **b :** the degree of electrification as referred to some standard

potential difference *n* **:** the voltage difference between two points that represents the work involved or the energy released in the transfer of a unit quantity of electricity from one point to the other

potential energy *n* **:** the energy that a piece of matter has because of its position or because of the arrangement of parts

po·ten·ti·al·i·ty \pə-ˌten-chē-'al-ət-ē\ *n, pl* **-ties 1 :** the ability to develop or come into existence **2 :** POTENTIAL 1

po·ten·ti·ate \pə-'ten-chē-ˌāt\ *vt* **-at·ed; -at·ing :** to make effective or more effective; *specif* **:** to augment (as a drug) synergistically — **po·ten·ti·a·tion** \-ˌten-chē-'ā-shən\ *n* — **po·ten·ti·a·tor** \-'ten-chē-ˌāt-ər\ *n*

po·ten·til·la \ˌpōt-ᵊn-'til-ə\ *n* [NL, genus name, fr. ML, garden heliotrope, fr. L *potent-, potens*] **:** any of a large genus (*Potentilla*) of herbs and shrubs (as a cinquefoil) of the rose family that have opposite pinnate or palmate leaves

po·ten·ti·om·e·ter \pə-ˌten-chē-'äm-ət-ər\ *n* [ISV *potential* + *-o-* + *-meter*] **1 :** an instrument for measuring electromotive forces **2 :** VOLTAGE DIVIDER — **po·ten·tio·met·ric** \-ch(ē-)ə-'me-trik\ *adj*

pot·ful \'pät-ˌfu̇l\ *n* **1 :** as much or as many as a pot will hold **2 :** a large amount <make a ~ of money —John Corry>

pot hat *n* **:** a hat with a stiff crown; *esp* **:** DERBY

pot·head \'pät-ˌhed\ *n* **:** one who smokes marijuana

[1]**poth·er** \'päth-ər\ *n* [origin unknown] **1 a :** confused or fidgety flurry or activity **:** COMMOTION **b :** agitated talk or controversy usu. over a trivial matter **2 :** a choking cloud of dust or smoke **3 :** mental turmoil ***syn*** see STIR

[2]**pother** *vb* **poth·ered; poth·er·ing** \-(ə-)riŋ\ *vt* **:** to put into a pother ~ *vi* **:** to be in a pother

pot·herb \'pät-ˌ(h)ərb\ *n* **:** an herb whose leaves or stems are cooked for use as greens; *also* **:** one (as mint) used to season food

pot holder *n* **:** a small cloth pad used for handling hot cooking utensils

pot·hole \'pät-ˌhōl\ *n* **1 a :** a circular hole formed in the rocky bed of a river by the grinding action of stones or gravel whirled round by the water **b :** a sizable, rounded, and often water-filled depression in land **2 :** a pot-shaped hole in a road surface — **pot·holed** \-ˌhōld\ *adj*

pot·hook \-ˌhu̇k\ *n* **1 :** an S-shaped hook for hanging pots and kettles over an open fire **2 :** a written character resembling a pothook

pot·house \-ˌhau̇s\ *n* **:** TAVERN 1

pot·hunt·er \-ˌhənt-ər\ *n* **1 :** one who hunts game for food **2 :** an amateur archeologist — **pot·hunt·ing** \-iŋ\ *n*

po·tion \'pō-shən\ *n* [ME *pocioun,* fr. MF *potion,* fr. L *potion-, potio* drink, potion, fr. *potus,* pp. of *potare* to drink — more at POTABLE] **:** a mixed drink (as of liquor) or dose (as of medicine)

[1]**pot·latch** \'pät-ˌlach\ *n* [Chinook Jargon, fr. Nootka *patshatl* giving] **1 :** a ceremonial feast of the Indians of the northwest coast marked by the host's lavish distribution of gifts requiring reciprocation **2** *Northwest* **:** a social event or celebration

[2]**potlatch** *vt* **1 :** to hold or give a potlatch for (as a tribe or group) **2 :** to give (as a gift) esp. with the expectation of a gift in return ~ *vi* **:** to hold or give a potlatch

pot liquor *n* **:** the liquid left in a pot after cooking

pot·luck \'pät-'lək\ *n* **1 :** the regular meal available to a guest for whom no special preparations have been made **2 :** the luck or chance of succeeding events or possibilities

pot marigold *n* **:** a calendula (*Calendula officinalis*) grown esp. for ornament

pot·pie \'pät-'pī\ *n* **:** pastry-covered meat and vegetables cooked in a deep dish

pot·pour·ri \ˌpō-pu̇-'rē\ *n* [F *pot pourri,* lit., rotten pot] **1 :** a mixture of flowers, herbs, and spices that is usu. kept in a jar and used for scent **2 :** a miscellaneous collection **:** MEDLEY <a ~ of the best songs and sketches —*Current Biog.*>

pot roast *n* **:** a piece of beef cooked by braising usu. on top of the stove — see BEEF illustration

pot·sherd \'pät-ˌshərd\ *n* [ME *pot-sherd,* fr. *pot* + *sherd* shard] **:** a pottery fragment

[1]**pot·shot** \-ˌshät\ *n* [fr. the notion that such a shot is unsportsmanlike and worthy only of one whose object is to fill his cooking pot] **1 :** a shot taken in a casual manner or at an easy target **2 :** a critical remark made in a random or sporadic manner

[2]**potshot** *vb* **potshot; pot·shot·ting** *vt* **:** to attack or shoot with a potshot ~ *vi* **:** to take a potshot

pot still *n* **:** a still used esp. in the distillation of Irish grain whiskey and Scotch malt whiskey in which the heat of the fire is applied directly to the pot containing the mash

pot·stone \'pät-ˌstōn\ *n* **:** a more or less impure steatite used esp. in prehistoric times to make cooking vessels

pot·tage \'pät-ij\ *n* [ME *potage,* fr. OF, fr. *pot* pot, of Gmc origin; akin to OE *pott* pot] **:** a thick soup of vegetables or vegetables and meat

pot·ted \'pät-əd\ *adj* **1 :** planted or grown in a pot **2** *chiefly Brit* **:** briefly and superficially summarized <a dull, pedestrian ~ history —*Times Lit. Supp.*> **3** *slang* **:** DRUNK, HIGH

[1]**pot·ter** \'pät-ər\ *n* **:** one that makes pottery

[2]**potter** *vi* [prob. freq. of E dial. *pote* to poke] **:** PUTTER <motorboats ~*ing* here and there —James Morris> — **pot·ter·er** \'pät-ər-ər\ *n* — **pot·ter·ing·ly** \'pät-ə-riŋ-lē\ *adv*

potter's clay *n* **:** a plastic clay suitable for making pottery — called also *potter's earth*

potter's field *n* [fr. the mention in Mt 27:7 of the purchase of a potter's field for use as a graveyard] **:** a public burial place for paupers, unknown persons, and criminals

potter's wheel *n* **:** a usu. horizontal disk revolving on a vertical spindle and carrying the clay being shaped by a potter

pot·tery \'pät-ə-rē\ *n, pl* **-ter·ies 1 :** a place where clayware is made and fired **2 a :** the art or craft of the potter **b :** the manufacture of clayware **3 :** CLAYWARE; *esp* **:** earthenware as distinguished on the one hand from porcelain and stoneware and on the other from brick and tile

potter's wheel

pot·tle \'pät-ᵊl\ *n* [ME *potel,* fr. OF, fr. *pot*] **1** *archaic* **:** a measure equal to a half gallon **2 :** a container holding a half gallon
pot·to \'pät-(,)ō\ *n, pl* **pottos** [of Niger-Congo origin; akin to Wolof *pata,* a tailless monkey] **:** any of several African primates (genera *Arctocebus* and *Perodicticus*); *esp* **:** a West African primate (*P. potto*) that has a vestigial index finger and tail
Pott's disease \'päts-\ *n* [Percivall *Pott* †1788 E surgeon] **:** tuberculosis of the spine with destruction of bone resulting in curvature of the spine
1pot·ty \'pät-ē\ *adj* **pot·ti·er; -est** [prob. fr. 1*pot*] **1** *Brit* **:** TRIVIAL, INSIGNIFICANT **2** *chiefly Brit* **:** slightly crazy **3 :** SNOBBISH
2potty *n, pl* **potties :** a small child's pot for urination or defecation
pot·ty–chair \-,che(ə)r, -,cha(ə)r\ *n* **:** a child's chair having an open seat under which a receptacle is placed for toilet training
1pouch \'pau̇ch\ *n* [ME *pouche,* fr. MF, of Gmc origin; akin to OE *pocca* bag] **1 :** a small drawstring bag carried on the person **2 a :** a bag of small or moderate size for storing or transporting goods; *specif* **:** a lockable bag for first class mail or diplomatic dispatches **b** *chiefly Scot* **:** POCKET **c :** PACKET **3 :** an anatomical structure resembling a pouch — **pouched** \'pau̇cht\ *adj*
2pouch *vt* **1 :** to put or form into or as if into a pouch **2 :** to transmit by pouch ~ *vi* **1 :** to form a pouch **2 :** to transmit mail or dispatches by pouch
pouchy \'pau̇-chē\ *adj* **pouch·i·er; -est :** having, tending to have, or resembling a pouch <~ insomniac eyes —Graham Greene>
pouf *also* **pouff** *or* **pouffe** \'püf\ *n* [F, something inflated, of imit. origin] **1 :** PUFF 3b(3) **2 :** a bouffant or fluffy part of a garment or accessory **3 :** OTTOMAN — **poufed** *or* **pouffed** \'püft\ *adj*
pou·larde *also* **pou·lard** \pü-'lärd\ *n* [F *poularde*] **:** a pullet sterilized to produce fattening
poult \'pōlt\ *n* [ME *polet, pulte* young fowl — more at PULLET] **:** a young fowl; *esp* **:** a young turkey
poul·ter·er \'pōl-tər-ər\ *n* [alter. of ME *pulter,* fr. MF *pouletier*] **:** one that deals in poultry
poul·ter's measure \'pōl-tərz-\ *n* [obs. *poulter* poulterer, fr. ME *pulter;* fr. the former practice of occasionally giving one or two extra when counting eggs by dozens] **:** a meter in which lines of 12 and 14 syllables alternate
1poul·tice \'pōl-təs\ *n* [ML *pultes* pap, fr. L, pl. of *pult-, puls* porridge] **:** a soft usu. heated and sometimes medicated mass spread on cloth and applied to sores or other lesions
2poultice *vt* **-ticed; -tic·ing :** to apply a poultice to
poul·try \'pōl-trē\ *n* [ME *pultrie,* fr. MF *pouleterie,* fr. OF, fr. *pouletier* poulterer, fr. *polet* — more at PULLET] **:** domesticated birds kept for eggs or meat
poul·try·man \-mən\ *n* **1 :** one who raises domestic fowls esp. on a commercial scale for the production of eggs and meat **2 :** one who deals in poultry or poultry products
1pounce \'pau̇n(t)s\ *n* [ME, talon] **:** the claw of a bird of prey
2pounce *vi* **pounced; pounc·ing 1 :** to swoop upon and seize something with or as if with talons **2 :** to make a sudden assault or approach
3pounce *n* **:** the act of pouncing
4pounce *vt* **pounced; pounc·ing :** to dust, rub, finish, or stencil with pounce
5pounce *n* [F *ponce* pumice, fr. LL *pomic-, pomex,* alter. of L *pumic-, pumex* — more at FOAM] **1 :** a fine powder formerly used to prevent ink from spreading **2 :** a fine powder for making stenciled patterns
poun·cet–box \'pau̇n(t)-sət-\ *n* [prob. fr. (assumed) MF *poncette* small pounce bag] *archaic* **:** a box for carrying pomander
1pound \'pau̇nd\ *n, pl* **pounds** *also* **pound** [ME, fr. OE *pund;* akin to ON *pund* pound; both fr. a prehistoric Gmc word borrowed fr. L *pondo* pound; akin to L *pondus* weight — more at PENDANT] **1 :** any of various units of mass and weight; *specif* **:** a unit now in general use among English-speaking peoples equal to 16 avoirdupois ounces or 7000 grains or 0.45359237 kilogram — called also *avoirdupois pound;* see WEIGHT table **2 a :** the basic monetary unit of the United Kingdom — called also *pound sterling* **b :** any of numerous basic monetary units of other countries — see MONEY table
2pound *vb* [alter. of ME *pounen,* fr. OE *pūnian*] *vt* **1 :** to reduce to powder or pulp by beating **2 a :** to strike heavily or repeatedly **b :** to produce by means of repeated vigorous strokes — usu. used with *out* <~ out a story on the typewriter> **c :** to inculcate by insistent repetition **:** DRIVE <day after day the facts were ~*ed* home to them —Ivy B. Priest> **3 :** to move along heavily or persistently <~*ed* the pavements looking for work> ~ *vi* **1 :** to strike heavy repeated blows **2 a :** to move with or make a heavy repetitive sound **b :** to work hard and continuously — used with *away*
3pound *n* **:** an act or sound of pounding
4pound *n* [ME, enclosure, fr. OE *pund-*] **1 a :** an enclosure for animals; *esp* **:** a public enclosure for stray or unlicensed animals <a dog ~> **b :** a depot for holding personal property until redeemed by the owner <a car ~> **2 :** a place or condition of confinement **3 a :** an enclosure within which fish are kept or caught; *esp* **:** the inner compartment of a fish trap or pound net **b :** an establishment selling live lobsters
5pound *vt, archaic* **:** IMPOUND
1pound·age \'pau̇n-dij\ *n* **1 a :** a tax levied in pounds sterling **b :** COMMISSION **2 a :** a charge per pound of weight **b :** weight in pounds
2poundage *n* **1 :** the act of impounding **:** the state of being impounded **2 :** a fee for the release of an impounded animal
pound·al \'pau̇n-dᵊl\ *n* [*pound* + *-al* (as in *quintal*)] **:** a unit of force equal to the force that would give a free mass of one pound an acceleration of one foot per second per second
pound cake *n* [fr. the original recipe prescribing a pound of each of the principal ingredients] **:** a rich butter cake made with a large proportion of eggs and shortening
1pound·er \'pau̇n-dər\ *n* **:** one that pounds
2pounder *n* **1 :** one having a usu. specified weight or value in pounds — usu. used in combination <caught a ten-*pounder* with his new fly rod> **2 :** a gun throwing a projectile of a specified weight — usu. used in combination <the ship was armed with six-*pounders*>
pound–fool·ish \'pau̇n(d)-'fü-lish\ *adj* [fr. the phrase *penny-wise and pound-foolish*] **:** imprudent in dealing with large sums or large matters
pound mile *n* **:** the transport of one pound of mail or express for one mile
pound net *n* **:** a fish trap consisting of a netting arranged into a directing wing and an enclosure with a narrow entrance
1pour \'pō(ə)r, 'pȯ(ə)r\ *vb* [ME *pouren*] *vt* **1 :** to cause to flow in a stream **2 :** to supply or produce freely or copiously ~ *vi* **1 :** to move with a continuous flow **2 :** to rain hard **3 :** to preside at a tea table — **pour·able** \'pōr-ə-bəl, 'pȯr-\ *adj* — **pour·er** \-ər\ *n* — **pour·ing·ly** \-iŋ-lē\ *adv*
syn POUR, STREAM, GUSH, SLUICE *shared meaning element* **:** to send forth or come forth abundantly
2pour *n* **1 :** the action of pouring **:** STREAM **2 a :** something that is poured <a ~ of concrete> **b :** a heavy fall of rain
pour·boire \pu̇(ə)rb-'wär\ *n* [F, fr. *pour boire* for drinking] **:** TIP, GRATUITY
pour·par·ler \,pu̇(ə)r-pär-'lā\ *n* [F] **:** a discussion preliminary to negotiations
pour·point \'pu̇(ə)r-,pȯint, -,pwant\ *n* [ME *purpoint,* fr. MF *pourpoint*] **:** a padded and quilted doublet
pour point \'pō(ə)r-,pȯint, 'pȯ(ə)r-\ *n* **:** the lowest temperature at which a substance flows under specified conditions
pousse–ca·fé \,pü-(,)ska-'fā\ *n* [F, lit., coffee chaser] **1 :** an after-dinner drink consisting of several liqueurs of different colors and specific gravities poured so as to remain in separate layers **2 :** a small drink of brandy or a liqueur taken with black coffee after dinner
pous·sette \pü-'set\ *vi* **pous·sett·ed; pous·sett·ing** [F, game in which contestants cross pins each attempting to get his pin on top, fr. *pousser* to push] **:** to swing in a semicircle with hands joined with one's partner in a country-dance
1pout \'pau̇t\ *n, pl* **pout** *or* **pouts** [prob. fr. (assumed) ME *poute,* a fish with a large head, fr. OE *-pūte;* akin to ME *pouten* to pout, Skt *budbuda* bubble] **:** any of several large-headed fishes (as a bullhead or eelpout)
2pout *vb* [ME *pouten*] *vi* **1 a :** to show displeasure by thrusting out the lips or wearing a sullen expression **b :** SULK **2 :** PROTRUDE ~ *vt* **:** to cause to protrude <~*ed* her lips>
3pout *n* **1 :** a protrusion of the lips expressive of displeasure **2** *pl* **:** a fit of pique
pout·er \'pau̇t-ər\ *n* **1 :** one that pouts **2 :** a domestic pigeon of a breed characterized by erect carriage and a distensible and dilatable crop
pouty \'pau̇t-ē\ *adj* **:** SULKY
pov·er·ty \'päv-ərt-ē\ *n, often attrib* [ME *poverte,* fr. OF *poverté,* fr. L *paupertat-, paupertas,* fr. *pauper* poor — more at POOR] **1 a :** the state of one who lacks a usual or socially acceptable amount of money or material possessions **b :** renunciation as a member of a religious order of the right as an individual to own property **2 :** SCARCITY, DEARTH **3 a :** debility due to malnutrition **b :** lack of fertility <~ of the soil>
syn POVERTY, INDIGENCE, PENURY, WANT, DESTITUTION *shared meaning element* **:** the state of one with insufficient resources ***ant*** riches
pov·er·ty–strick·en \-,strik-ən\ *adj* **:** very poor **:** DESTITUTE
1pow \'pō, 'pau̇\ *n* [by alter.] **:** HEAD, POLL
2pow \'pau̇\ *n* [imit.] **:** a sound of a blow or explosion
POW \,pē-(,)ō-'dəb-əl-(,)yü\ *abbr* prisoner of war
1pow·der \'pau̇d-ər\ *n, often attrib* [ME *poudre,* fr. OF, fr. L *pulver-, pulvis* dust — more at POLLEN] **1 :** matter in a finely divided state **:** particulate matter **2 a :** a preparation in the form of fine particles esp. for medicinal or cosmetic use **b :** fine dry light snow **3 :** any of various solid explosives used chiefly in gunnery and blasting
2powder *vb* **pow·dered; pow·der·ing** \'pau̇d-(ə-)riŋ\ *vt* **1 :** to sprinkle or cover with or as if with powder **2 :** to reduce or convert to powder **3 :** to hit (as a ball) very hard ~ *vi* **1 :** to become powder **2 :** to apply cosmetic powder — **pow·der·er** \-ər-ər\ *n*
powder blue *n* **:** a variable color averaging a pale blue
powder horn *n* **:** a flask for carrying gunpowder; *esp* **:** one made of the horn of an ox or cow
powder keg *n* **1 :** a small usu. metal cask for holding gunpowder or blasting powder **2 :** something liable to explode
powder metallurgy *n* **:** a branch of science or an art concerned with the production of powdered metals or of metallic objects by compressing a powdered metal or alloy with or without other

ə abut ᵊ kitten ər further a back ā bake ä cot, cart
au̇ out ch chin e less ē easy g gift i trip ī life
j joke ŋ sing ō flow ȯ flaw ȯi coin th thin t͟h this
ü loot u̇ foot y yet yü few yu̇ furious zh vision

materials and heating without thoroughly melting to solidify and strengthen

powder monkey *n* : one who carries or has charge of explosives (as in blasting operations)

powder-puff *adj* : of, relating to, or being a competitive activity or event for women <a ~ football game>

powder puff *n* : a small fluffy device (as a pad) for applying cosmetic powder

powder room *n* **1** : a rest room for women **2** : a lavatory in the main living area of a house

pow·dery \\'pau̇d-ə-rē\\ *adj* **1 a** : resembling or consisting of powder <~ snow> **b** : easily reduced to powder : CRUMBLING **2** : covered with or as if with powder

powdery mildew *n* **1** : a perfect fungus (family Erysiphaceae) or an imperfect fungus (genus *Oidium*) producing abundant powdery conidia on the host **2** : a plant disease caused by a powdery mildew

[1]**pow·er** \\'pau̇(-ə)r\\ *n, often attrib* [ME, fr. OF *poeir,* fr. *poeir* to be able, fr. (assumed) L *potēre* to be powerful — more at POTENT] **1 a** : possession of control, authority, or influence over others **b** : one having such power; *specif* : a sovereign state **c** : a controlling group : ESTABLISHMENT — often used in the phrase *the powers that be* **d** *archaic* : a force of armed men **e** *chiefly dial* : a large number or quantity **2 a (1)** : ability to act or produce an effect **(2)** : ability to get extra-base hits **(3)** : capacity for being acted upon or undergoing an effect **b** : legal or official authority, capacity, or right **3 a** : physical might **b** : mental or moral efficacy **c** : political control or influence **4** *pl* : an order of angels — see CELESTIAL HIERARCHY **5 a** : the number of times as indicated by an exponent that a number occurs as a factor in a product; *also* : the product itself **b** : CARDINAL NUMBER 2 **6 a** : a source or means of supplying energy; *esp* : ELECTRICITY **b** : MOTIVE POWER **c** : the time rate at which work is done or energy emitted or transferred **7** : MAGNIFICATION 2b **8** : SCOPE, COMPREHENSIVENESS **9** : the probability of rejecting the null hypothesis in a statistical test when a particular alternative hypothesis happens to be true

syn POWER, FACULTY, FUNCTION *shared meaning element* : ability of a living being to perform in a given way or capacity for a particular kind of performance

[2]**power** *vt* : to supply with power and esp. motive power

pow·er·boat \\'pau̇(-ə)r-ˌbōt\\ *n* : MOTORBOAT

pow·er–dive \\-ˌdīv\\ *vi* : to make a power dive ~ *vt* : to cause to power-dive

power dive *n* : a dive of an airplane accelerated by the power of the engine

pow·er·ful \\'pau̇(-ə)r-fəl\\ *adj* **1** : having great power, prestige, or influence **2** : leading to many or important deductions <a ~ set of postulates> — **pow·er·ful·ly** \\-f(ə-)lē\\ *adv*

power function *n* : a function of a parameter under statistical test whose value for a particular value of the parameter is the probability of rejecting the null hypothesis if that value of the parameter happens to be true

pow·er·house \\'pau̇(-ə)r-ˌhau̇s\\ *n* **1 a** : POWER PLANT 1 **b** : a source of influence or inspiration **2** : one having or wielding great power

pow·er·less \\-ləs\\ *adj* **1** : devoid of strength or resources **2** : lacking the authority or capacity to act : UNABLE — **pow·er·less·ly** *adv* — **pow·er·less·ness** *n*

power mower *n* : a motor-driven lawn mower

power of attorney : a legal instrument authorizing one to act as the attorney or agent of the grantor

power pack *n* : a unit for converting a power supply (as from a battery) to a voltage suitable for an electronic device

power plant *n* **1** : an electric utility generating station **2** : an engine and related parts supplying the motive power of a self-propelled object (as a rocket or automobile)

power play *n* **1** : an offensive maneuver (as in football or hockey) in which mass interference is provided at a particular point or in a particular zone **2** : a military, diplomatic, political, or administrative maneuver in which power is brought to bear

power politics *n pl but sing or pl in constr* : politics based primarily on the use of power as a coercive force rather than on ethical precepts; *esp* : international politics characterized by attempts to advance national interests through coercion on the basis of military and economic strength

power series *n* : an infinite series whose terms are successive integral powers of a variable multiplied by constants

power shovel *n* : a power-operated excavating machine consisting of a boom or crane that supports a dipper handle with a dipper at the end of it

power station *n* : POWER PLANT 1

power steering *n* : automotive steering with engine power used to amplify the torque applied at the steering wheel by the driver

power structure *n* **1** : a group of persons having control of an organization : ESTABLISHMENT **2** : the hierarchical interrelationships existing within a controlling group

power sweep *n* : SWEEP 3e

power take–off *n* : a supplementary mechanism (as on a tractor) enabling the engine power to be used to operate nonautomotive apparatus (as a pump or saw)

power train *n* : the intervening mechanism by which power is transmitted from an engine to a propeller or axle that it drives

[1]**pow·wow** \\'pau̇-ˌwau̇\\ *n* [of Algonquian origin; akin to Natick *pauwau* conjurer] **1** : an American Indian medicine man **2** : an American Indian ceremony (as for victory in war) **3 a** : a social get-together **b** : a meeting for discussion

[2]**powwow** *vi* : to hold a powwow

[1]**pox** \\'päks\\ *n, pl* **pox** *or* **pox·es** [alter. of *pocks,* pl. of *pock*] **1 a** : a virus disease (as chicken pox) characterized by pustules or eruptions **b** *archaic* : SMALLPOX **c** : SYPHILIS **2** : a disastrous evil : PLAGUE, CURSE <a ~ on him>

[2]**pox** *vt, archaic* : to infect with a pox and esp. with syphilis

pox·vi·rus \\'päks-ˌvī-rəs\\ *n* : any of a group of relatively large round, brick-shaped, or ovoid animal viruses (as the causative agent of smallpox) that have a fluffy appearance caused by a covering of tubules and threads

poz·zo·la·na \\ˌpät-sə-'län-ə\\ *or* **poz·zo·lan** \\'pät-sə-lən\\ *n* [It *pozzolana*] : finely divided siliceous or siliceous and aluminous material that reacts chemically with slaked lime at ordinary temperature and in the presence of moisture to form a strong slow-hardening cement — **poz·zo·la·nic** \\-'lan-ik, -'län-\\ *adj*

pp *abbr* **1** pages **2** [L *per procurationem*] by proxy **3** pianissimo

PP *abbr* **1** parcel post **2** past participle **3** postpaid **4** prepaid

ppa *abbr* per power of attorney

ppb *abbr* parts per billion

PPC *abbr* [F *pour prendre congé*] to take leave

ppd *abbr* **1** postpaid **2** prepaid

PPFA *abbr* Planned Parenthood Federation of America

[1]**PPI** \\ˌpē-(ˌ)pē-'ī\\ *n* [*p*lan *p*osition *i*ndicator] : a radarscope on which spots of light representing reflections of radar waves indicate the range and bearing of objects

[2]**PPI** *abbr* policy proof of interest

PPLO \\ˌpē-ˌpē-ˌel-'ō\\ *n, pl* **PPLO** [*p*leuro*p*neumonia-*l*ike *o*rganism] : MYCOPLASMA

ppm *abbr* parts per million

ppt *abbr* **1** parts per thousand **2** parts per trillion **3** precipitate

pptn *abbr* precipitation

PQ *abbr* **1** previous question **2** Province of Quebec

pr *abbr* **1** pair **2** price **3** printed

Pr *symbol* **1** praseodymium **2** propyl

PR *abbr* **1** payroll **2** proportional representation **3** public relations **4** Puerto Rico

prac·ti·ca·ble \\'prak-ti-kə-bəl\\ *adj* **1** : possible to practice or perform : FEASIBLE **2** : capable of being used : USABLE — **prac·ti·ca·bil·i·ty** \\ˌprak-ti-kə-'bil-ət-ē\\ *n* — **prac·ti·ca·ble·ness** \\'prak-ti-kə-bəl-nəs\\ *n* — **prac·ti·ca·bly** \\-blē\\ *adv*

syn **1** see POSSIBLE ***ant*** impracticable

2 PRACTICABLE, PRACTICAL *shared meaning element* : capable of being used or turned to account. In spite of the common element of meaning these terms are not interchangeable without loss of precision of expression. PRACTICABLE applies chiefly to something immaterial (as a plan, expedient, or design) which has not been tested in practice or to something material (as a machine or implement) that has not been proved in service or use; the term implies expectation rather than assurance of successful testing or proving <a serviceable concept on which to base a *practicable* policy —J. A. Hobson> PRACTICAL stresses opposition to all that is *theoretical, speculative, ideal, unrealistic,* or *imaginative* and implies a relation to the actual life of man, his daily needs, or problems that must be met. The term emphasizes actual established usefulness rather than discovered or theoretical usableness; thus, the modern low-slung high-speed automobile was *practicable* long before improved roads and fuels made it *practical;* a *practicable* expedient seems likely to meet the needs of a case, but a *practical* expedient has been proved effective in use.

[1]**prac·ti·cal** \\'prak-ti-kəl\\ *adj* [LL *practicus,* fr. Gk *praktikos,* fr. *prassein* to pass over, fare, do; akin to Gk *peran* to pass through — more at FARE] **1** : actively engaged in some course of action or occupation <a ~ farmer> **2 a** : of, relating to, or manifested in practice or action : not theoretical or ideal <a ~ question> <for all ~ purposes> **b** : being such in practice or effect : VIRTUAL <a ~ failure> **3** : capable of being put to use or account : USEFUL <he had a ~ knowledge of French> **4 a** : disposed to action as opposed to speculation or abstraction **b (1)** : qualified by practice or practical training <a good ~ mechanic> **(2)** : designed to supplement theoretical training by experience **5** : concerned with voluntary action and ethical decisions <~ reason> ***syn*** see PRACTICABLE — **prac·ti·cal·i·ty** \\ˌprak-ti-'kal-ət-ē\\ *n* — **prac·ti·cal·ness** \\'prak-ti-kəl-nəs\\ *n*

[2]**practical** *n* : an examination requiring demonstration of some practical skill <a zoology ~>

practical art *n* : an art (as woodworking) that serves ordinary or material needs — usu. used in pl.

practical joke *n* : a joke whose humor stems from the tricking or abuse of an individual placed somehow at a disadvantage — **practical joker** *n*

prac·ti·cal·ly \\'prak-ti-k(ə-)lē\\ *adv* **1** : in a practical manner <talked ~ about the problem> **2** : ALMOST, NEARLY <~ everyone went to the party>

practical nurse *n* : a nurse who cares for the sick professionally without having the training or experience required of a registered nurse; *esp* : LICENSED PRACTICAL NURSE

practical theology *n* : the study of the institutional activities of religion (as preaching, church administration, pastoral care, and liturgics)

[1]**prac·tice** *or* **prac·tise** \\'prak-təs\\ *vb* **prac·ticed** *or* **prac·tised; prac·tic·ing** *or* **prac·tis·ing** [ME *practisen,* fr. MF *practiser,* fr. *practique* practice, fr. LL *practice,* fr. Gk *praktikē,* fr. fem. of *praktikos*] *vt* **1 a** : to perform or work at repeatedly so as to become proficient <~ his act> **b** : to train by repeated exercises <~ pupils in penmanship> **2 a** : to carry out : APPLY <~ what he preaches> **b** : to do or perform often, customarily, or habitually <~ politeness> **c** : to be professionally engaged in <~ medicine> **3** *obs* : PLOT ~ *vi* **1** : to do repeated exercises for proficiency **2** : to pursue a profession actively **3** *archaic* : INTRIGUE **4** : to do something customarily **5** : to take advantage of someone <he *practised* on their credulity with huge success —*Times Lit. Supp.*> — **prac·tic·er** *n*

syn PRACTICE, EXERCISE, DRILL *shared meaning element* : to perform or make perform repeatedly

[2]**practice** *also* **practise** *n, often attrib* **1 a** : actual performance or application <ready to carry out in ~ what he advocated in principle> **b** : a repeated or customary action <he had an irritating ~ of watching his fellows> **c** : the usual way of doing something <it is wise to conform to local ~*s*> **d** : the form, manner, and order of conducting legal suits and prosecutions **2 a**

: systematic exercise for proficiency <~ makes perfect> **b** : the condition of being proficient through systematic exercise <get in ~> **3 a** : the continuous exercise of a profession **b** : a professional business; *esp* : one constituting an incorporeal property *syn* see HABIT

prac·ticed *or* **prac·tised** \'prak-təst\ *adj* **1** : EXPERIENCED, SKILLED **2** : learned by practice

prac·tice–teach \-təs-ˌtēch\ *vi* **-taught** \-ˌtȯt\; **-teach·ing** [back-formation fr. *practice teaching*] : to engage in practice teaching — **practice teacher** *n*

practice teaching *n* : teaching in which a student practices educational skills and methods under the supervision of an experienced teacher in preparation for professional teaching

prac·tic·ing *or* **prac·tis·ing** *adj* : actively engaged in a specified career or way of life <a ~ physician>

prac·ti·cum \'prak-ti-kəm\ *n* [G *praktikum,* fr. LL *practicum,* neut. of *practicus* practical] : a course of study designed esp. for the preparation of teachers and clinicians that involves the supervised practical application (as in a classroom or clinic) of previously studied theory

prac·ti·tio·ner \prak-'tish-(ə-)nər\ *n* [alter. of earlier *practician,* fr. ME (Sc) *pratician,* fr. MF *practicien,* fr. *pratique*] **1** : one who practices; *esp* : one who practices a profession **2** *Christian Science* : an authorized healer

prae·ci·pe *or* **pre·ci·pe** \'pres-ə-ˌpē, 'prēs-\ *n* [ME *precipe,* fr. ML, fr. L *praecipe,* imper. of *praecipere* to instruct — more at PRECEPT] **1** : any of various legal writs commanding a person to do something or to appear and show cause why he should not **2** : a written order requesting a clerk or prothonotary of a court to issue a writ and specifying the contents of the writ

prae·di·al *var of* PREDIAL

prae·mu·ni·re \ˌprē-myu̇-'nī(ə)r-ē\ *n* [ME *praemunire facias,* fr. ML, that you cause to warn; fr. prominent words in the writ] : an offense against the English Crown punishable chiefly by forfeiture and orig. committed by asserting papal legal supremacy in England

prae·no·men \prē-'nō-mən\ *n, pl* **-nomens** *or* **-no·mi·na** \-'näm-ə-nə, -'nō-mə-\ [L, fr. *prae-* pre- + *nomen* name — more at NAME] : the first of the usual three names of an ancient Roman

prae·sid·i·um *var of* PRESIDIUM

prae·tor \'prēt-ər\ *n* [ME *pretor,* fr. L *praetor*] : an ancient Roman magistrate ranking below a consul and having chiefly judicial functions — **prae·to·ri·al** \prē-'tōr-ē-əl, -'tȯr-\ *adj* — **prae·tor·ship** \'prēt-ər-ˌship\ *n*

prae·to·ri·an \prē-'tōr-ē-ən, -'tȯr-\ *adj* **1** : of or relating to a praetor **2** *often cap* : of, forming, or resembling the Roman imperial bodyguard — **praetorian** *n, often cap*

prag·mat·ic \prag-'mat-ik\ *also* **prag·mat·i·cal** \-i-kəl\ *adj* [L *pragmaticus* skilled in law or business, fr. Gk *pragmatikos,* fr. *pragmat-, pragma* deed, fr. *prassein* to do — more at PRACTICAL] **1** *archaic* **a** (1) : BUSY (2) : OFFICIOUS **b** : OPINIONATED **2** : relating to matters of fact or practical affairs often to the exclusion of intellectual or artistic matters : practical as opposed to idealistic <the problem-solving mentality, the product of science and ~ effort —T. F. O'Dea> <~ men of power have had no time or inclination to deal with . . . social morality —K. B. Clark> **3** : relating to or being in accordance with philosophical pragmatism — **pragmatic** *n* — **prag·mat·i·cal·ly** \-i-k(ə-)lē\ *adv*

prag·mat·i·cism \prag-'mat-ə-ˌsiz-əm\ *n* : the philosophic doctrine of C. S. Peirce — **prag·mat·i·cist** \-səst\ *n*

prag·mat·ics \prag-'mat-iks\ *n pl but sing or pl in constr* : a branch of semiotic that deals with the relation between signs or linguistic expressions and their users

pragmatic sanction *n* : a solemn decree of a sovereign on a matter of primary importance and with the force of fundamental law

prag·ma·tism \'prag-mə-ˌtiz-əm\ *n* **1** : a practical approach to problems and affairs <tried to strike a balance between principles and ~> **2** : an American movement in philosophy founded by C. S. Peirce and William James and marked by the doctrines that the meaning of conceptions is to be sought in their practical bearings, that the function of thought is to guide action, and that truth is preeminently to be tested by the practical consequences of belief — **prag·ma·tist** \-mət-əst\ *adj or n* — **prag·ma·tis·tic** \ˌprag-mə-'tis-tik\ *adj*

prai·rie \'pre(ə)r-ē\ *n, often attrib* [F, fr. (assumed) VL *prataria,* fr. L *pratum* meadow; akin to L *pravus* crooked, MIr *rāth* earthworks] : a tract of grassland: as **a** : a large area of level or rolling land in the Mississippi valley that in its natural uncultivated state usu. has deep fertile soil, a cover of tall coarse grasses, and few trees **b** : one of the dry treeless plateaus into which the prairies proper merge on the west

prairie breaker *n* : a plow with a long low moldboard designed to cut a wide shallow furrow and turn the slice completely over

prairie chicken *n* : a grouse (*Tympanuchus cupido pinnatus*) of the Mississippi valley; *also* : a closely related American grouse (*T. pallidicinctus*)

prairie dog *n* : a colonial American burrowing rodent (genus *Cynomys,* esp. *C. ludovicianus* of the prairies) related to the marmots

prairie schooner *n* : a covered wagon used by pioneers in cross-country travel — called also *prairie wagon*

prairie soil *n* : any of a zonal group of soils developed in a temperate relatively humid climate under tall grass

prairie wolf *n* : COYOTE

¹praise \'prāz\ *vb* **praised; prais·ing** [ME *praisen,* fr. MF *preisier* to prize, praise, fr. LL *pretiare* to prize, fr. L *pretium* price — more at PRICE] *vt* **1** : to express a favorable judgment of : COMMEND **2** : to glorify (a god or saint) esp. by the attribution of perfections ~ *vi* : to express praise — **prais·er** *n*

²praise *n* **1 a** : an expression of approval : COMMENDATION **b** : WORSHIP **2 a** : VALUE, MERIT **b** *archaic* : one that is praised

praise·wor·thy \'prāz-ˌwər-thē\ *adj* : LAUDABLE — **praise·wor·thi·ly** \-thə-lē\ *adv* — **praise·wor·thi·ness** \-thē-nəs\ *n*

Pra·krit \'präk-ˌrit, -rət\ *n* [Skt *prākṛta,* fr. *prākṛta* natural, vulgar] **1** : any or all of the ancient Indic languages or dialects other than Sanskrit — see INDO-EUROPEAN LANGUAGES table **2** : any of the modern Indic languages

pra·line \'prä-ˌlēn, 'prā-, 'prō-\ *n* [F, fr. Count Plessis-*Praslin* †1675 F soldier] : a confection of nut kernels: **a** : almonds roasted in boiling sugar until brown and crisp **b** : a patty of creamy brown sugar and pecan meats

prairie dog

prall·tril·ler \'präl-ˌtril-ər\ *n* [G] : a musical ornament made by a quick alternation of a principal tone with the tone above

¹pram \'präm, 'pram\ *n* [D *praam;* akin to MLG *prām* pram] : a small lightweight nearly flat-bottomed boat with a broad transom and usu. squared-off bow

²pram \'pram\ *n* [by shortening & alter. fr. *perambulator*] *chiefly Brit* : BABY CARRIAGE

prairie schooner

¹prance \'pran(t)s\ *vb* **pranced; pranc·ing** [ME *prauncen*] *vi* **1** : to spring from the hind legs or move by so doing **2** : to ride on a prancing horse **3** : to walk or move in a spirited manner : STRUT <*prancing* up and down, sublimely pleased with himself —Norman Douglas>; *also* : to dance about : CAPER <~ forward and back in rhythm to the music —Thomas Wolfe> ~ *vt* : to cause (a horse) to prance — **pranc·er** \'pran(t)-sər\ *n* — **pranc·ing·ly** \-siŋ-lē\ *adv*

²prance *n* : an act or instance of prancing; *specif* : a prancing movement

pran·di·al \'pran-dē-əl\ *adj* [L *prandium* late breakfast, luncheon] : of or relating to a meal

¹prang \'praŋ\ *vt* [imit.] : to have an accident with : cause to crash

²prang *n* : ACCIDENT, CRASH

¹prank \'praŋk\ *n* [obs. *prank* to play tricks] : TRICK: **a** *obs* : a malicious act **b** : a mildly mischievous act : PRACTICAL JOKE **c** : a ludicrous act

²prank *vb* [prob. fr. D *pronken* to strut; akin to MHG *gebrunkel* glitter of metal] *vt* : to dress or adorn gaily or showily ~ *vi* : to show oneself off

prank·ish \'praŋ-kish\ *adj* **1** : full of pranks <a ~ writer> **2** : having the nature of a prank <~ acts> — **prank·ish·ly** *adv* — **prank·ish·ness** *n*

prank·ster \'praŋ(k)-stər\ *n* : one who plays pranks

prase \'prāz, 'prās\ *n* [F, fr. L *prasius,* fr. Gk *prasios,* fr. *prasios,* adj., leek green, fr. *prason* leek; akin to L *porrum* leek] : a chalcedony that is translucent and leek green

pra·seo·dym·i·um \ˌprā-zē-ō-'dim-ē-əm, ˌprā-sē-\ *n* [NL, alter. of *praseodidymium,* irreg. fr. Gk *prasios,* adj. + NL *didymium*] : a yellowish white trivalent metallic element of the rare-earth group used chiefly in the form of its salts in coloring glass greenish yellow — see ELEMENT table

¹prate \'prāt\ *vi* **prat·ed; prat·ing** [ME *praten,* fr. MD; akin to MLG *pratten* to pout] : to talk long and idly : CHATTER — **prat·er** *n* — **prat·ing·ly** \'prāt-iŋ-lē\ *adv*

²prate *n* : empty or meaningless talk

prat·fall \'prat-ˌfȯl\ *n* [*prat* (buttocks) + *fall*] **1** : a fall on the buttocks **2** : a humiliating mishap or blunder

pra·tin·cole \'prat-ᵊn-ˌkōl, 'prāt-, -iŋ-\ *n* [deriv. of L *pratum* meadow + *incola* inhabitant, fr. *in-* + *colere* to cultivate — more at PRAIRIE, WHEEL] : any of a genus (*Glareola*) of Old World limicoline birds

pra·tique \pra-'tēk\ *n* [F, lit., practice — more at PRACTICE] : clearance given an incoming ship by the health authority of a port

¹prat·tle \'prat-ᵊl\ *vb* **prat·tled; prat·tling** \'prat-liŋ, -ᵊl-iŋ\ [LG *pratelen;* akin to MD *praten* to prate] *vi* **1** : PRATE **2** : to utter or make meaningless sounds suggestive of the chatter of children : BABBLE ~ *vt* : to say in an unaffected or childish manner — **prat·tler** \'prat-lər, -ᵊl-ər\ *n* — **prat·tling·ly** \-liŋ-lē, -ᵊl-iŋ-\ *adv*

²prattle *n* **1** : trifling or empty talk **2** : a sound that is meaningless, repetitive, and suggestive of the chatter of children

prau \'prau̇, 'prä-ˌü\ *n* [Malay *pĕrahu*] : any of several usu. undecked Indonesian boats propelled by sails, oars, or paddles

¹prawn \'prȯn, 'prän\ *n* [ME *prane*] : any of numerous widely distributed edible decapod crustaceans (as of the genera *Pandalus* and *Peneus*) that resemble shrimps with large compressed abdomens; *also* : SHRIMP

²prawn *vi* : to fish for or with prawns — **prawn·er** *n*

prax·e·ol·o·gy \ˌprak-sē-'äl-ə-jē\ *n* [alter. of earlier *praxiology,* fr. *praxis* + *-o-* + *-logy*] : the study of human action and conduct — **prax·e·o·log·i·cal** \-sē-ə-'läj-i-kəl\ *adj*

prax·is \'prak-səs\ *n, pl* **prax·es** \-ˌsēz\ [ML, fr. Gk, doing, action, fr. *prassein* to pass through, practice — more at PRACTICAL] **1** : exercise or practice of an art, science, or skill **2** : customary practice or conduct

pray \'prā\ *vb* [ME *prayen,* fr. OF *preier,* fr. L *precari,* fr. *prec-, prex* request, prayer; akin to OHG *frāgēn* to ask, Skt *pṛcchati* he asks] *vt* **1** : ENTREAT, IMPLORE — often used as a function word in introducing a question, request, or plea **2** : to get or bring by praying ~ *vi* **1** : to request in a humble manner **2** : to address God or a god with adoration, confession, supplication, or thanksgiving

[1]**prayer** \ˈpra(ə)r, ˈpre(ə)r\ *n, often attrib* [ME, fr. OF *preiere*, fr. ML *precaria*, fr. L, fem. of *precarius* obtained by entreaty, fr. *prec-, prex*] **1 a** (1) : an address (as a petition) to God or a god in word or thought <said a ~ for the success of the voyage> (2) : a set order of words used in praying <repeat a ~> **b** : an earnest request **2** : the act or practice of praying to God or a god <kneeling in ~> **3** : a religious service consisting chiefly of prayers — often used in pl. **4** : something prayed for **5** : a slight chance <tried hard but didn't have a ~>

[2]**pray·er** \ˈprā-ər, ˈpre(-ə)r\ *n* [ME *prayere*, fr. *prayen* to pray + *-er*] : one that prays : SUPPLIANT

prayer beads *n pl* : a string of beads by which prayers are counted; *specif* : ROSARY

prayer book *n* : a book containing prayers and often other forms and directions for worship

prayer·ful \ˈpra(ə)r-fəl, ˈpre(ə)r-\ *adj* **1** : DEVOUT **2** : EARNEST, SINCERE — **prayer·ful·ly** \-fə-lē\ *adv* — **prayer·ful·ness** *n*

prayer meeting *n* : a Protestant worship service usu. held on a week night — called also *prayer service*

prayer rug *n* : a small Oriental rug used by Muslims to kneel on when praying

prayer shawl *n* : TALLITH

prayer wheel *n* : a cylinder of wood or metal that revolves on an axis and contains written prayers and that is used in praying by Tibetan Buddhists

praying mantid *n* : MANTIS

praying mantis *n* : MANTIS

pre- *prefix* [ME, fr. OF & L; OF, fr. L *prae-*, fr. *prae* in front of, before — more at FOR] **1 a** (1) : earlier than : prior to : before <*Pre*cambrian> <*pre*historic> <*pre*-English> (2) : preparatory or prerequisite to <*pre*medical> <*pre*journalism> **b** : in advance : beforehand <*pre*cancel> <*pre*pay> **2 a** : in front of : anterior to <*pre*axial> <*pre*molar> **b** : front : anterior <*pre*abdomen>

preach \ˈprēch\ *vb* [ME *prechen*, fr. OF *prechier*, fr. LL *praedicare*, fr. L, to proclaim publicly, fr. *prae-* pre- + *dicare* to proclaim — more at DICTION] *vi* **1** : to deliver a sermon **2** : to urge acceptance or abandonment of an idea or course of action; *specif* : to exhort in an officious or tiresome manner ~ *vt* **1** : to set forth in a sermon <~ the gospel> **2** : to advocate earnestly <~*ed* revolution> **3** : to deliver (as a sermon) publicly **4** : to bring, put, or affect by preaching <~*ed* the . . . church out of debt —*Amer. Guide Series: Va.*> — **preach·er** *n* — **preach·ing·ly** \ˈprē-chiŋ-lē\ *adv*

preach·ify \ˈprē-chə-ˌfī\ *vi* **-ified; -ify·ing** : to preach ineptly or tediously

preach·ment \ˈprēch-mənt\ *n* **1** : the act or practice of preaching **2** : SERMON, EXHORTATION; *specif* : a tedious or unwelcome one

preachy \ˈprē-chē\ *adj* **preach·i·er; -est** : marked by obvious moral exhortation : DIDACTIC — **preach·i·ly** \-chə-lē\ *adv* — **preach·i·ness** \-chē-nəs\ *n*

pre·ad·ap·ta·tion \ˈprē-ˌad-ˌap-ˈtā-shən\ *n* **1** : the possession by an organism or group of characters that are not adapted to the ancestral environment but favor its survival in some other environment **2** : a preadaptive character

pre·adapt·ed \ˌprē-ə-ˈdap-təd\ *adj* : characterized by preadaptation

pre·adap·tive \-ˈdap-tiv\ *adj* : of, relating to, or characterized by preadaptation

pre·ad·o·les·cence \ˈprē-ˌad-ᵊl-ˈes-ᵊn(t)s\ *n* : the period of human development just preceding adolescence; *specif* : the period between the approximate ages of 9 and 12 — **pre·ad·o·les·cent** \-ᵊnt\ *adj or n*

pre·ag·ri·cul·tur·al \ˈprē-ˌag-rə-ˈkəlch-(ə-)rəl\ *adj* : existing or occurring before the practice of agriculture by men

pre·am·ble \ˈprē-ˌam-bəl, prē-ˈ\ *n* [ME, fr. MF *preambule*, fr. ML *preambulum*, fr. LL, neut. of *praeambulus* walking in front of, fr. L *prae-* + *ambulare* to walk] **1** : an introductory statement; *specif* : the introductory part of a constitution or statute that usu. states the reasons for and intent of the law **2** : an introductory fact or circumstance; *esp* : one indicating what is to follow

pre·am·pli·fi·er \(ˈ)prē-ˈam-plə-ˌfī(-ə)r\ *n* : an amplifier designed to amplify extremely weak signals from a device (as a microphone, phonograph pickup, tuner, or television camera) before the signals are fed to additional amplifier circuits

pre·ar·range \ˌprē-ə-ˈrānj\ *vt* : to arrange beforehand — **pre·ar·range·ment** \-ˈrānj-mənt\ *n*

pre·as·signed \ˌprē-ə-ˈsīnd\ *adj* : assigned beforehand

pre·atom·ic \-ə-ˈtäm-ik\ *adj* : of or relating to a time before the use of the atom bomb and atomic energy

pre·ax·i·al \(ˈ)prē-ˈak-sē-əl\ *adj* : situated in front of an axis of the body — **pre·ax·i·al·ly** \-ə-lē\ *adv*

preb·end \ˈpreb-ənd\ *n* [ME *prebende*, fr. MF, fr. ML *praebenda*, fr. LL, subsistence allowance granted by the state, fr. L, fem. of *praebendus*, gerundive of *praebēre* to offer, fr. *prae-* + *habēre* to hold — more at GIVE] **1** : a stipend furnished by a cathedral or collegiate church to a clergyman (as a canon) in its chapter **2** : PREBENDARY — **pre·ben·dal** \pri-ˈben-dᵊl, ˈpreb-ən-\ *adj*

preb·en·dary \ˈpreb-ən-ˌder-ē\ *n, pl* **-dar·ies** **1** : a clergyman receiving a prebend for officiating and serving in the church **2** : an honorary canon in a cathedral chapter

pre·bind \(ˈ)prē-ˈbīnd\ *vt* **-bound** \-ˈbau̇nd\; **-bind·ing** **1** : to bind (a book) in durable materials esp. for circulating library use **2** : to give (a book) a durable original binding

pre·bi·o·log·i·cal \ˈprē-ˌbī-ə-ˈläj-i-kəl\ *also* **pre·bi·o·log·ic** \-ik\ *adj* : of, relating to, or being chemical or environmental precursors of the origin of life <~ molecules>

pre·bi·ot·ic \ˌprē-bī-ˈät-ik\ *adj* : PREBIOLOGICAL

prec *abbr* preceding

pre·cal·cu·lus \(ˈ)prē-ˈkal-kyə-ləs\ *adj* : relating to or being mathematical prerequisites for the study of calculus

Pre·cam·bri·an \(ˈ)prē-ˈkam-brē-ən\ *adj* : of, relating to, or being the earliest era of geological history equivalent to the Archeozoic and Proterozoic eras or the corresponding system of rocks — **Precambrian** *n*

[1]**pre·can·cel** \(ˈ)prē-ˈkan(t)-səl\ *vt* : to cancel (a postage stamp) in advance of use — **pre·can·cel·la·tion** \ˌprē-ˌkan(t)-sə-ˈlā-shən\ *n*

[2]**precancel** *n* : a precanceled postage stamp

pre·can·cer·ous \(ˈ)prē-ˈkan(t)s-(ə-)rəs\ *adj* [ISV] : tending to become cancerous <a ~ lesion>

pre·cap·il·lary \(ˈ)prē-ˈkap-ə-ˌler-ē, *Brit usu* ˌprə-kə-ˈpil-ə-rē\ *adj* : being on the arterial side of and immediately adjacent to a capillary

pre·car·i·ous \pri-ˈkar-ē-əs, -ˈker-\ *adj* [L *precarius* obtained by entreaty, uncertain — more at PRAYER] **1** *archaic* : depending on the will or pleasure of another **2** : dependent on uncertain premises : DUBIOUS <~ generalizations> **3 a** : dependent on chance circumstances, unknown conditions, or uncertain developments **b** : characterized by a lack of security or stability that threatens with danger ***syn*** see DANGEROUS — **pre·car·i·ous·ly** *adv* — **pre·car·i·ous·ness** *n*

pre·cast \ˈprē-ˈkast\ *adj* : being concrete that is cast in the form of a structural element (as a panel or beam) before being placed in final position

prec·a·to·ry \ˈprek-ə-ˌtōr-ē, -ˌtȯr-\ *adj* [LL *precatorius*, fr. *precatus*, pp. of *precari* to pray — more at PRAY] : expressing a wish

pre·cau·tion \pri-ˈkȯ-shən\ *n* [F *précaution*, fr. LL *praecaution-, praecautio*, fr. L *praecautus*, pp. of *praecavēre* to guard against, fr. *prae-* + *cavēre* to be on one's guard — more at HEAR] **1** : care taken in advance : FORESIGHT <warned of the need for ~> **2** : a measure taken beforehand to prevent harm or secure good : SAFEGUARD — **pre·cau·tion·ary** \-shə-ˌner-ē\ *adj*

pre·cau·tious \-shəs\ *adj* : characterized by precaution

pre·ca·va \(ˈ)prē-ˈkā-və\ *n, pl* **-vae** \-(ˌ)vē\ [NL] : SUPERIOR VENA CAVA — **pre·ca·val** \-ˈkā-vəl\ *adj*

pre·cede \pri-ˈsēd\ *vb* **pre·ced·ed; pre·ced·ing** [ME *preceden*, fr. MF *preceder*, fr. L *praecedere*, fr. *prae-* pre- + *cedere* to go — more at CEDE] *vt* **1** : to surpass in rank, dignity, or importance **2** : to be, go, or come ahead or in front of **3** : to be earlier than **4** : to cause to be preceded : PREFACE ~ *vi* : to go or come before

pre·ce·dence \ˈpres-əd-ən(t)s, pri-ˈsēd-ᵊn(t)s\ *n* **1 a** *obs* : ANTECEDENT **b** : the fact of preceding in time **2 a** : the right to superior honor on a ceremonial or formal occasion **b** : the order of ceremonial or formal preference **c** : priority of importance : PREFERENCE ***syn*** see PRIORITY

pre·ce·den·cy \-ən-sē, -ᵊn-sē\ *n* : PRECEDENCE

[1]**pre·ce·dent** \pri-ˈsēd-ᵊnt, ˈpres-əd-ənt\ *adj* [ME, fr. MF, fr. L *praecedent-, praecedens*, prp. of *praecedere*] : prior in time, order, arrangement, or significance

[2]**prec·e·dent** \ˈpres-əd-ənt\ *n* **1** : an earlier occurrence of something similar **2 a** : something done or said that may serve as an example or rule to authorize or justify a subsequent act of the same or an analogous kind <a verdict that had no ~> **b** : the convention established by such a precedent or by long practice

pre·ced·ing \pri-ˈsēd-iŋ\ *adj* : that immediately precedes in time or place <the ~ day> <~ paragraphs>

syn PRECEDING, ANTECEDENT, FOREGOING, PREVIOUS, PRIOR, FORMER, ANTERIOR *shared meaning element* : being before ***ant*** following

pre·cen·sor \(ˈ)prē-ˈsen(t)-sər\ *vt* : to censor (a publication or film) before its release to the public

pre·cen·tor \pri-ˈsent-ər\ *n* [LL *praecentor*, fr. L *praecentus*, pp. of *praecinere* to sing before, fr. *prae-* + *canere* to sing — more at CHANT] : a leader of the singing of a choir or congregation — **pre·cen·to·ri·al** \ˌprē-ˌsen-ˈtōr-ē-əl, -ˈtȯr-\ *adj* — **pre·cen·tor·ship** \pri-ˈsent-ər-ˌship\ *n*

pre·cept \ˈprē-ˌsept\ *n* [ME, fr. L *praeceptum*, fr. neut. of *praeceptus*, pp. of *praecipere* to take beforehand, instruct, fr. *prae-* + *capere* to take — more at HEAVE] **1** : a command or principle intended as a general rule of action **2** : an order issued by legally constituted authority to a subordinate official

pre·cep·tive \pri-ˈsep-tiv\ *adj* : giving precepts : DIDACTIC — **pre·cep·tive·ly** *adv*

pre·cep·tor \pri-ˈsep-tər, ˈprē-ˌ\ *n* **1 a** : TEACHER, TUTOR **b** : the headmaster or principal of a school **2** : the head of a preceptory of Knights Templars — **pre·cep·tor·ship** \-tər-ˌship\ *n* — **pre·cep·tress** \-trəs\ *n*

[1]**pre·cep·to·ri·al** \pri-ˌsep-ˈtōr-ē-əl, ˌprē-, -ˈtȯr-\ *adj* : of, relating to, or making use of preceptors

[2]**preceptorial** *n* : a college course that emphasizes independent reading, discussion in small groups, and individual conferences with the teacher

pre·cep·to·ry \pri-ˈsep-t(ə-)rē, ˈprē-ˌ\ *n, pl* **-ries** **1** : a subordinate house or community of the Knights Templars; *broadly* : COMMANDERY 1 **2** : COMMANDERY 2

pre·cess \prē-ˈses, ˈprē-ˌ\ *vb* [back-formation fr. *precession*] *vi* : to progress with a movement of precession ~ *vt* : to cause to precess

pre·ces·sion \prē-ˈsesh-ən\ *n* [NL *praecession-, praecessio*, fr. ML, act of preceding, fr. L *praecessus*, pp. of *praecedere* to precede] : a comparatively slow gyration of the rotation axis of a spinning body about another line intersecting it so as to describe a cone caused by the application of a torque tending to change the direction of the rotation axis — **pre·ces·sion·al** \-ˈsesh-nəl, -ən-ᵊl\ *adj*

precession of the equinoxes : a slow westward motion of the equinoctial points along the ecliptic caused by the action of sun and moon upon the protuberant matter about the earth's equator

pre–Chel·le·an \(ˈ)prē-ˈshel-ē-ən\ *adj* : of or relating to a lower Paleolithic culture preceding the Abbevillian and characterized by crudely flaked stone hand axes

pre–Chris·tian \-ˈkris(h)-chən\ *adj* : of, relating to, or being a time before the beginning of the Christian era

pré·cieux \prā-syœ̄\ *or* **pré·cieuse** \-syœ̄z\ *adj* [F *précieux*, masc., & *précieuse*, fem., lit., precious, fr. OF *precios*] : PRECIOUS 3

pre·cinct \ˈprē-ˌsiŋ(k)t\ *n* [ME, fr. ML *praecinctum*, fr. L, neut. of *praecinctus*, pp. of *praecingere* to gird about, fr. *prae-* pre- + *cingere* to gird — more at CINCTURE] **1** : a part of a territory with definite bounds or functions often established for administrative purposes : DISTRICT: as **a** : a subdivision of a county, town, city, or ward for election purposes **b** : a division of a city for police control **2** : an enclosure bounded by the walls of a building — often used in pl. **3** *pl* : the region immediately surrounding a place : ENVIRONS **4** : BOUNDARY — often used in pl. <a ruined tower within the ~*s* of the squire's grounds —T. L. Peacock>

pre·ci·os·i·ty \ˌpres(h)-ē-ˈäs-ət-ē\ *n, pl* **-ties** **1** : fastidious refinement **2** : an instance of preciosity

1**pre·cious** \ˈpresh-əs\ *adj* [ME, fr. OF *precios,* fr. L *pretiosus,* fr. *pretium* price — more at PRICE] **1** : of great value or high price **2** : highly esteemed or cherished **3** : excessively refined : AFFECTED **4** : GREAT, THOROUGHGOING <~ scoundrel> ***syn*** see COSTLY — **pre·cious·ness** *n*

2**precious** *adv* : VERY, EXTREMELY <has ~ little to say>

pre·cious·ly *adv* **1** : in a precious manner **2** : PRECIOUS

prec·i·pice \ˈpres(-ə-)pəs\ *n* [MF, fr. L *praecipitium,* fr. *praecipit-, praeceps* headlong, fr. *prae-* + *caput* head — more at HEAD] **1** : a very steep or overhanging place **2** : the brink of disaster

pre·cip·i·ta·ble \pri-ˈsip-ət-ə-bəl\ *adj* : capable of being precipitated

pre·cip·i·tance \pri-ˈsip-ət-ən(t)s\ *n* : PRECIPITANCY

pre·cip·i·tan·cy \-ən-sē\ *n* : undue hastiness or suddenness

1**pre·cip·i·tant** \-ənt\ *adj* : PRECIPITATE — **pre·cip·i·tant·ly** *adv* — **pre·cip·i·tant·ness** *n*

2**precipitant** *n* : a precipitating agent; *esp* : one that causes the formation of a precipitate

1**pre·cip·i·tate** \pri-ˈsip-ə-ˌtāt\ *vb* **-tat·ed; -tat·ing** [L *praecipitatus,* pp. of *praecipitare,* fr. *praecipit-, praeceps*] *vt* **1 a** : to throw violently : HURL <the quandaries into which the release of nuclear energy has *precipitated* mankind —A. B. Arons> **b** : to throw down **2** : to bring about esp. abruptly <~ a scandal that would end with his expulsion —John Cheever> **3 a** : to cause to separate from solution or suspension **b** : to cause (vapor) to condense and fall or deposit ~ *vi* **1 a** : to fall headlong **b** : to fall or come suddenly into some condition **2** : to move or act precipitately **3 a** : to separate from solution or suspension **b** : to condense from a vapor and fall as rain or snow — **pre·cip·i·ta·tive** \-ˌtāt-iv\ *adj* — **pre·cip·i·ta·tor** \-ˌtāt-ər\ *n*

2**pre·cip·i·tate** \pri-ˈsip-ət-ət, -ə-ˌtāt\ *n* [NL *praecipitatum,* fr. L, neut. of *praecipitatus*] **1** : a substance separated from a solution or suspension by chemical or physical change usu. as an insoluble amorphous or crystalline solid **2** : a product, result, or outcome of some process or action

3**pre·cip·i·tate** \pri-ˈsip-ət-ət\ *adj* **1** : exhibiting violent or unwise speed **2 a** : falling, flowing, or rushing with steep descent **b** : PRECIPITOUS — **pre·cip·i·tate·ly** *adv* — **pre·cip·i·tate·ness** *n*
syn PRECIPITATE, HEADLONG, ABRUPT, IMPETUOUS, SUDDEN *shared meaning element* : showing undue haste or unexpectedness ***ant*** deliberate

pre·cip·i·ta·tion \pri-ˌsip-ə-ˈtā-shən\ *n* **1** : the quality or state of being precipitate : HASTE **2** : an act, process, or instance of precipitating; *esp* : the process of forming a precipitate **3** : something precipitated: as **a** : a deposit on the earth of hail, mist, rain, sleet, or snow; *also* : the quantity of water deposited **b** : PRECIPITATE 1

pre·cip·i·tin \pri-ˈsip-ət-ən\ *n* [ISV, fr. *precipitate*] : an antibody that forms an insoluble precipitate when it unites with its antigen

pre·cip·i·tin·o·gen \pri-ˌsip-ə-ˈtin-ə-jən\ *n* : an antigen that stimulates the production of a specific precipitin — **pre·cip·i·tin·o·gen·ic** \-ˌtin-ə-ˈjen-ik\ *adj*

pre·cip·i·tous \pri-ˈsip-ət-əs\ *adj* [F *précipiteux,* fr. MF, fr. L *precipitium* precipice] **1** : PRECIPITATE 1 **2 a** : very steep, perpendicular, or overhanging in rise or fall <a ~ slope> **b** : having precipitous sides <a ~ gorge> **c** : having a very steep ascent <a ~ street> ***syn*** see STEEP — **pre·cip·i·tous·ly** *adv* — **pre·cip·i·tous·ness** *n*

pré·cis \prā-ˈsē, ˈprā-(ˌ)sē\ *n, pl* **pré·cis** \-ˈsēz, -(ˌ)sēz\ [F, fr. *précis* precise] : a concise summary of essential points, statements, or facts

pre·cise \pri-ˈsīs\ *adj* [MF *precis,* fr. L *praecisus,* pp. of *praecidere* to cut off, fr. *prae-* + *caedere* to cut — more at CONCISE] **1** : exactly or sharply defined or stated **2** : minutely exact **3** : strictly conforming to a pattern, standard, or convention **4** : distinguished from every other : VERY <at just that ~ moment> ***syn*** see CORRECT ***ant*** imprecise, loose — **pre·cise·ly** *adv* — **pre·cise·ness** *n*

pre·ci·sian \pri-ˈsizh-ən\ *n* **1** : a person who stresses or practices scrupulous adherence to a strict standard esp. of religious observance or morality **2** : PURITAN 1 — **pre·ci·sian·ism** \-ə-ˌniz-əm\ *n*

1**pre·ci·sion** \pri-ˈsizh-ən\ *n* **1** : the quality or state of being precise : EXACTNESS **2 a** : the degree of refinement with which an operation is performed or a measurement stated **b** : the accuracy (as in binary or decimal places) with which a number can be represented usu. expressed in terms of computer words <double ~ arithmetic permits the representation of an expression by two computer words> **3** : RELEVANCE 2 — **pre·ci·sion·ist** \-ˈsizh-(ə-)nəst\ *n*

2**precision** *adj* **1** : adapted for extremely accurate measurement or operation **2** : held to low tolerance in manufacture **3** : marked by precision of execution

pre·clin·i·cal \(ˈ)prē-ˈklin-i-kəl\ *adj* : of or relating to the period preceding clinical manifestations

pre·clude \pri-ˈklüd\ *vt* **pre·clud·ed; pre·clud·ing** [L *praecludere,* fr. *prae-* + *claudere* to close — more at CLOSE] **1** *archaic* : CLOSE **2** : to make impossible by necessary consequence ***syn*** see PREVENT — **pre·clu·sion** \-ˈklü-zhən\ *n* — **pre·clu·sive** \-ˈklü-siv, -ziv\ *adj* — **pre·clu·sive·ly** *adv*

pre·co·cial \pri-ˈkō-shəl\ *adj* [NL *praecoces* precocial birds, fr. L, pl. of *praecoc-, precox*] : capable of a high degree of independent activity from birth <ducklings are ~> — compare ALTRICIAL

pre·co·cious \pri-ˈkō-shəs\ *adj* [L *praecoc-, praecox* early ripening, precocious, fr. *prae-* + *coquere* to cook — more at COOK] **1** : exceptionally early in development or occurrence **2** : exhibiting mature qualities at an unusually early age — **pre·co·cious·ly** *adv* — **pre·co·cious·ness** *n* — **pre·coc·i·ty** \pri-ˈkäs-ət-ē\ *n*

pre·cog·ni·tion \ˌprē-(ˌ)käg-ˈnish-ən\ *n* [LL *praecognition-, praecognitio,* fr. L *praecognitus,* pp. of *praecognoscere* to know beforehand, fr. *prae-* + *cognoscere* to know — more at COGNITION] : clairvoyance relating to an event or state not yet experienced — **pre·cog·ni·tive** \(ˈ)prē-ˈkäg-nət-iv\ *adj*

pre·col·lege \ˈprē-ˈkäl-ij\ *adj* : preceding and preparatory for college

pre·co·lo·nial \ˌprē-kə-ˈlō-nyəl, -nē-əl\ *adj* : of, relating to, or being the time before colonial status

pre–Co·lum·bi·an \ˌprē-kə-ˈləm-bē-ən\ *adj* : preceding or belonging to the time before the arrival of Columbus in America

pre·con·ceive \ˌprē-kən-ˈsēv\ *vt* : to form (as an opinion) prior to actual knowledge or experience <*preconceived* notions>

pre·con·cep·tion \-ˈsep-shən\ *n* **1** : a preconceived idea **2** : PREJUDICE

pre·con·cert \ˌprē-kən-ˈsərt\ *vt* : to settle by prior agreement

1**pre·con·di·tion** \-ˈdish-ən\ *n* : PREREQUISITE

2**precondition** *vt* : to put in a proper or desired condition or frame of mind esp. in preparation

pre·con·fer·ence \ˈprē-ˈkän-f(ə-)rən(t)s, -fərn(t)s\ *n* : a conference held prior to a conference or convention : a preliminary conference

pre·con·scious \(ˈ)prē-ˈkän-chəs\ *adj* : not present in consciousness but capable of being recalled without encountering any inner resistance or repression — **pre·con·scious·ly** *adv*

pre·con·so·nan·tal \ˌprē-ˌkän(t)-sə-ˈnant-ᵊl\ *adj* : immediately preceding a consonant

pre·con·ven·tion \ˌprē-kən-ˈven-chən\ *adj* : taking place prior to a convention <~ campaigning>

pre·cook \(ˈ)prē-ˈku̇k\ *vt* : to cook partially or entirely before final cooking or reheating

pre·cop·u·la·to·ry \-ˈkäp-yə-lə-ˌtōr-ē, -ˌtȯr-\ *adj* : preceding copulation <~ behavior>

pre·crit·i·cal \-ˈkrit-i-kəl\ *adj* : prior to the development of critical capacity

pre·cur·sor \pri-ˈkər-sər, ˈprē-ˌ\ *n* [L *praecursor,* fr. *praecursus,* pp. of *praecurrere* to run before, fr. *prae-* pre- + *currere* to run — more at CURRENT] **1 a** : one that precedes and indicates the approach of another **b** : PREDECESSOR **2** : a substance from which another substance is formed ***syn*** see FORERUNNER

pre·cur·so·ry \pri-ˈkərs-(ə-)rē\ *adj* : having the character of a precursor : PREMONITORY

pred *abbr* predicate

pre·da·ceous *or* **pre·da·cious** \pri-ˈdā-shəs\ *adj* [L *praedari* to prey upon (fr. *praeda* prey) + E *-aceous* or *-acious* (as in *rapacious*) — more at PREY] **1** : living by preying on other animals : PREDATORY **2** *usu predacious* : tending to devour or despoil : RAPACIOUS — **pre·da·ceous·ness** *n* — **pre·dac·i·ty** \-ˈdas-ət-ē\ *n*

pre·date \(ˈ)prē-ˈdāt\ *vt* : ANTEDATE

pre·da·tion \pri-ˈdā-shən\ *n* [L *praedation-, praedatio,* fr. *praedatus,* pp. of *praedari*] **1** : the act of preying or plundering : DEPREDATION **2** : a mode of life in which food is primarily obtained by the killing and consuming of animals

predation pressure *n* : the effects of predation on a natural community esp. with respect to the survival of species preyed upon

pred·a·tor \ˈpred-ət-ər, -ə-ˌtȯ(ə)r\ *n* **1** : one that preys, destroys, or devours **2** : an animal that lives by predation

pred·a·to·ri·al \ˌpred-ə-ˈtōr-ē-əl, -ˈtȯr-\ *adj* : PREDATORY

pred·a·to·ry \ˈpred-ə-ˌtōr-ē, -ˌtȯr-\ *adj* **1 a** : of, relating to, or practicing plunder, pillage, or rapine **b** : showing a disposition to injure or exploit others for one's own gain **2** : living by predation : PREDACEOUS; *also* : adapted to predation — **pred·a·to·ri·ly** \ˌpred-ə-ˈtōr-ə-lē, -ˈtȯr-\ *adv*

pre·dawn \ˈprē-ˈdȯn, -ˈdän\ *n* : the time just before dawn

pre·de·cease \ˌprēd-i-ˈsēs\ *vb* **-ceased; -ceas·ing** *vt* : to die before (another person) ~ *vi* : to die first — **predecease** *n*

pre·de·ces·sor \ˈpred-ə-ˌses-ər, ˈprēd-; ˌpred-ə-ˈ, ˌprēd-\ *n* [ME *predecessour,* fr. MF *predecesseur,* fr. LL *praedecessor,* fr. L *prae-* pre- + *decessor* retiring governor, fr. *decessus,* pp. of *decedere* to depart, retire from office — more at DECEASE] **1** : one that precedes; *esp* : a person who has previously occupied a position or office to which another has succeeded **2** *archaic* : ANCESTOR

pre·des·ig·nate \(ˈ)prē-ˈdez-ig-ˌnāt\ *vt* : to designate beforehand — **pre·des·ig·na·tion** \ˌprē-ˌdez-ig-ˈnā-shən\ *n*

pre·des·ti·nar·i·an \(ˌ)prē-ˌdes-tə-ˈner-ē-ən\ *n* [*predestin*ation + *-arian*] : one who believes in predestination — **predestinarian** *adj* — **pre·des·ti·nar·i·an·ism** \-ē-ə-ˌniz-əm\ *n*

1**pre·des·ti·nate** \prē-ˈdes-tə-nət, -ˌnāt\ *adj* [ME, fr. L *praedestinatus,* pp. of *praedestinare*] : destined, fated, or determined beforehand

2**pre·des·ti·nate** \-ˌnāt\ *vt* **-nat·ed; -nat·ing** [ME *predestinaten,* fr. L *praedestinatus,* pp.] **1** : to foreordain to an earthly or eternal lot or destiny by divine decree **2** *archaic* : PREDETERMINE

pre·des·ti·na·tion \(ˌ)prē-ˌdes-tə-ˈnā-shən\ *n* **1** : the act of predestinating : the state of being predestinated **2** : the doctrine that God in consequence of his foreknowledge of all events infallibly guides those who are destined for salvation

pre·des·ti·na·tor \prē-ˈdes-tə-ˌnāt-ər\ *n* **1** : one that predestinates **2** *archaic* : PREDESTINARIAN

pre·des·tine \(ˈ)prē-ˈdes-tən\ *vt* [ME *predestinen,* fr. MF or L; MF *predestiner,* fr. L *praedestinare,* fr. *prae-* + *destinare* to determine — more at DESTINE] : to destine, decree, determine, appoint, or settle beforehand; *esp* : PREDESTINATE 1

pre·de·ter·mi·na·tion \ˌprēd-i-ˌtər-mə-ˈnā-shən\ *n* **1 :** the act of predetermining **:** the state of being predetermined: as **a :** the ordaining of events beforehand **b :** a fixing or settling in advance **2 :** a purpose formed beforehand

pre·de·ter·mine \-ˈtər-mən\ *vt* [LL *praedeterminare,* fr. L *prae-* + *determinare* to determine] **1 a :** FOREORDAIN, PREDESTINE **b :** to determine beforehand **2 :** to impose a direction or tendency on beforehand

pre·de·ter·min·er \-ˈtərm-(ə-)nər\ *n* **:** a limiting noun modifier (as *both* or *all*) characterized by occurrence before the determiner in a noun phrase

pre·di·a·be·tes \ˌprē-ˌdī-ə-ˈbēt-ēz, -ˈbēt-əs\ *n* [*pre-* + *diabetes*] **:** an inapparent abnormal state that precedes the development of clinically evident diabetes — **pre·di·a·bet·ic** \-ˈbet-ik\ *adj or n*

pre·di·al \ˈprēd-ē-əl\ *adj* [ML *praedialis,* fr. L *praedium* landed property, fr. *praed-, praes* bondsman — more at PREST] **:** of or relating to land or its products

[1]pred·i·ca·ble \ˈpred-i-kə-bəl\ *n* [ML *praedicabile,* fr. neut. of *praedicabilis*]**:** something that may be predicated; *esp* **:** one of the five most general kinds of attribution in traditional logic that include genus, species, difference, property, and accident

[2]predicable *adj* [ML *praedicabilis,* fr. LL *praedicare* to predicate] **:** capable of being asserted

pre·dic·a·ment \pri-ˈdik-ə-mənt, *1 is usu* ˈpred-i-kə-\ *n* [ME, fr. LL *praedicamentum,* fr. *praedicare*] **1 :** the character, status, or classification assigned by a predication; *specif* **:** CATEGORY 1 **2 :** CONDITION, STATE; *esp* **:** a difficult, perplexing, or trying situation

[1]pred·i·cate \ˈpred-i-kət\ *n* [LL *praedicatum,* fr. neut. of *praedicatus*] **1 a :** something that is affirmed or denied of the subject in a proposition in logic <in "paper is white", whiteness is the ~> **b :** a term designating a property or relation **2 :** the part of a sentence or clause that expresses what is said of the subject and that usu. consists of a verb with or without objects, complements, or adverbial modifiers — **pred·i·ca·tive** \-kət-iv, ˈpred-ə-ˌkāt-\ *adj*

[2]pred·i·cate \ˈpred-ə-ˌkāt\ *vt* **-cat·ed; -cat·ing** [LL *praedicatus,* pp. of *praedicare* to assert, predicate logically, preach, fr. L, to proclaim publicly, assert — more at PREACH] **1 a :** AFFIRM, DECLARE **b** *archaic* **:** PREACH **2 a :** to assert to be a quality, attribute, or property — used with following *of* <~*s* intelligence of man> **b :** to make (a term) the predicate in a proposition **3 :** to cause to be based <his theory is *predicated* on recent findings> **4 :** IMPLY

predicate calculus *n* **:** the branch of symbolic logic that uses symbols for quantifiers and for subjects and predicates of propositions as well as for unanalyzed propositions and logical connectives — called also *functional calculus;* compare PROPOSITIONAL CALCULUS

predicate nominative *n* **:** a noun or pronoun in the nominative or common case completing the meaning of a linking verb

pred·i·ca·tion \ˌpred-ə-ˈkā-shən\ *n* **1** *archaic* **a :** an act of proclaiming or preaching **b :** SERMON **2 :** an act or instance of predicating: as **a :** the expression of action, state, or quality by a grammatical predicate **b :** the logical affirmation of something about another; *esp* **:** assignment of something to a class

pred·i·ca·to·ry \ˈpred-i-kə-ˌtōr-ē, -ˌtȯr-\ *adj* [LL *praedicatorius,* fr. *praedicatus,* pp. of *praedicare* to preach] **:** of or relating to preaching

pre·dict \pri-ˈdikt\ *vb* [L *praedictus,* pp. of *praedicere,* fr. *prae-* pre- + *dicere* to say — more at DICTION] *vt* **:** to declare in advance; *esp* **:** foretell on the basis of observation, experience, or scientific reason ~ *vi* **:** to make a prediction *syn* see FORETELL — **pre·dict·abil·i·ty** \-ˌdik-tə-ˈbil-ət-ē\ *n* — **pre·dict·able** \-ˈdik-tə-bəl\ *adj* — **pre·dict·ably** \-blē\ *adv* — **pre·dic·tor** \-ˈdik-tər\ *n*

pre·dic·tion \pri-ˈdik-shən\ *n* **1 :** an act of predicting **2 :** something that is predicted **:** FORECAST — **pre·dic·tive** \-ˈdik-tiv\ *adj* — **pre·dic·tive·ly** *adv*

pre·di·gest \ˌprēd-ī-ˈjest, ˌprēd-ə-\ *vt* **1 :** to subject to predigestion **2 :** to simplify for easy use <~*ed* classics for children>

pre·di·ges·tion \-ˈjes(h)-chən\ *n* **:** artificial partial digestion of food esp. for use in illness or impaired digestion

pre·di·lec·tion \ˌpred-ᵊl-ˈek-shən, ˌprēd-\ *n* [F *prédilection,* fr. ML *praedilectus,* pp. of *praediligere* to love more, prefer, fr. L *prae-* + *diligere* to love — more at DILIGENT] **:** a prepossession in favor of something **:** TASTE 6

syn PREDILECTION, PREPOSSESSION, PREJUDICE, BIAS *shared meaning element* **:** an attitude of mind that predisposes one to choosing, or judging, or taking a stand without full consideration or knowledge *ant* aversion

pre·dis·pose \ˌprēd-is-ˈpōz\ *vt* **1 :** to dispose in advance <a good teacher ~*s* children to learn> **2 :** to make susceptible <~ the miner to rheumatism —Lewis Mumford> ~ *vi* **:** to bring about susceptibility

pre·dis·po·si·tion \ˌprē-ˌdis-pə-ˈzish-ən\ *n* **:** a condition of being predisposed **:** INCLINATION <a hereditary ~ to disease>

pred·nis·o·lone \pred-ˈnis-ə-ˌlōn\ *n* [blend of *prednisone* and *-ol*] **:** a glucocorticoid $C_{21}H_{28}O_5$ that is a dehydrogenated analogue of cortisol and is used often in the form of an ester or methyl derivative esp. as an anti-inflammatory drug in the treatment of arthritis

pred·ni·sone \ˈpred-nə-ˌsōn *also* -ˌzōn\ *n* [prob. fr. *pre*gnane ($C_{21}H_{36}$) + *dien*e (compound containing two double bonds) + cort*isone*] **:** a glucocorticoid $C_{21}H_{26}O_5$ that is a dehydrogenated analogue of cortisone and is used as an anti-inflammatory agent esp. in the treatment of arthritis, as an antineoplastic agent, and as an immunosuppressant

pre·doc·tor·al \(ˈ)prē-ˈdäk-t(ə-)rəl\ *adj* **1 :** of or relating to the level before the doctoral in a program of academic study <a ~ fellowship> **2 :** being engaged in predoctoral academic work

pre·dom·i·nance \pri-ˈdäm(-ə)-nən(t)s\ *n* **:** the quality or state of being predominant

pre·dom·i·nan·cy \-nən-sē\ *n* **:** PREDOMINANCE

pre·dom·i·nant \-nənt\ *adj* [MF, fr. ML *praedominant-, praedominans,* prp. of *praedominari* to predominate, fr. L *prae-* + *dominari* to rule, govern — more at DOMINATE] **:** having superior strength, influence, or authority **:** PREVAILING *syn* see DOMINANT — **pre·dom·i·nant·ly** *adv*

[1]pre·dom·i·nate \-nət\ *adj* [alter. of *predominant*] **:** PREDOMINANT — **pre·dom·i·nate·ly** *adv*

[2]pre·dom·i·nate \pri-ˈdäm-ə-ˌnāt\ *vb* [ML *praedominatus,* pp. of *praedominari*] *vi* **1 :** to exert controlling power or influence **:** PREVAIL **2 :** to hold advantage in numbers or quantity **:** PREPONDERATE ~ *vi* **:** to exert control over **:** DOMINATE — **pre·dom·i·na·tion** \-ˌdäm-ə-ˈnā-shən\ *n*

pree \ˈprē\ *vt* **preed; pree·ing** [short for *preve* to prove, test, fr. ME *preven,* fr. OF *preuv-,* stem of *prover* to prove] *Scot* **:** to taste tentatively **:** SAMPLE

pre·emer·gence \ˌprē-ə-ˈmər-jən(t)s\ *adj* **:** used or occurring before emergence of seedlings aboveground <~ weed control>

pre·emer·gent \-jənt\ *adj* **:** PREEMERGENCE

pree·mie \ˈprē-mē\ *n* [*pre*mature + *-ie*]**:** a baby born prematurely

pre·em·i·nence \prē-ˈem-ə-nən(t)s\ *n* **:** the quality or state of being preeminent **:** SUPERIORITY

pre·em·i·nent \-nənt\ *adj* [LL *praeeminent-, praeeminens,* fr. L, prp. of *praeeminēre* to be outstanding, fr. *prae-* + *eminēre* to stand out — more at EMINENT] **:** having paramount rank, dignity, or importance **:** OUTSTANDING — **pre·em·i·nent·ly** *adv*

pre·em·ploy·ment \ˌprē-im-ˈplȯi-mənt\ *adj* **:** of, relating to, or occurring in the period prior to employment <~ interviews>

pre·empt \prē-ˈem(p)t\ *vb* [back-formation fr. *preemption*] *vt* **1 :** to acquire (as land) by preemption **2 :** to seize upon to the exclusion of others **:** take for oneself <the movement was then ~*ed* by a lunatic fringe> **3 :** to take the place of **:** REPLACE <the program did not appear, having been ~*ed* by a baseball game —Robert MacNeil> ~ *vi* **:** to make a preemptive bid in bridge *syn* see APPROPRIATE — **pre·emp·tor** \-ˈem(p)-tər\ *n*

pre·emp·tion \-ˈem(p)-shən\ *n* [ML *praeemptus,* pp. of *praeemere* to buy before, fr. L *prae-* pre- + *emere* to buy — more at REDEEM] **1 a :** the right of purchasing before others; *esp* **:** one given by the government to the actual settler upon a tract of public land **b :** the purchase of something under this right **2 :** a prior seizure or appropriation **:** a taking possession before others

pre·emp·tive \-ˈem(p)-tiv\ *adj* **1 a :** of or relating to preemption **b :** having power to preempt **2 :** of a bid in bridge that is higher than necessary and designed to shut out bids by the opponents **3 :** giving a stockholder first option to purchase new stock in an amount proportionate to his existing holdings <a ~ right> **4 :** marked by the seizing of the initiative **:** initiated by oneself <a ~ attack> — **pre·emp·tive·ly** *adv*

[1]preen \ˈprēn\ *n* [ME *prene,* fr. OE *prēon;* akin to MHG *pfrieme* awl] **1** *dial chiefly Brit* **:** PIN **2** *dial chiefly Brit* **:** BROOCH

[2]preen *vt, chiefly Scot* **:** [2]PIN

[3]preen *vb* [ME *preinen*] *vt* **1 :** to trim or dress with or as if with a bill **2 :** to dress or smooth (oneself) up **:** PRIMP **3 :** to pride or congratulate (oneself) for achievement ~ *vi* **1 :** to make oneself sleek **2 :** GLOAT, SWELL *syn* see PRIDE — **preen·er** *n*

pre–en·gi·neered \ˌprē-ˌen-jə-ˈni(ə)rd\ *adj* **:** constructed of or employing prefabricated modules <a ~ building>

pre·ex·il·ian \ˌprē-eg-ˈzil-ē-ən, -ˈzil-yən\ *or* **pre·ex·il·ic** \-ˈzil-ik\ *adj* **:** previous to the exile of the Jews to Babylon in about 600 B.C.

pre·ex·ist \ˌprē-ig-ˈzist\ *vi* **:** to exist earlier or before ~ *vt* **:** ANTEDATE

pre·ex·is·tence \-ˈzis-tən(t)s\ *n* **:** existence in a former state or previous to something else; *specif* **:** existence of the soul before its union with the body — **pre·ex·is·tent** \-tənt\ *adj*

pref *abbr* **1** preface **2** preference **3** preferred **4** prefix

pre·fab \(ˈ)prē-ˈfab, ˈprē-ˌ\ *n* **:** a prefabricated structure — **prefab** *adj*

pre·fab·ri·cate \(ˈ)prē-ˈfab-ri-ˌkāt\ *vt* **1 :** to fabricate the parts of at a factory so that construction consists mainly of assembling and uniting standardized parts **2 :** to give an artificial or synthetic quality to — **pre·fab·ri·ca·tion** \ˌprē-ˌfab-ri-ˈkā-shən\ *n*

[1]pref·ace \ˈpref-əs\ *n* [ME, fr. MF, fr. ML *prephatia,* alter. of L *praefation-, praefatio* foreword, fr. *praefatus,* pp. of *praefari* to say beforehand, fr. *prae-* pre- + *fari* to say — more at BAN] **1** *often cap* **:** a variable doxology beginning with the Sursum Corda and ending with the Sanctus in traditional eucharistic liturgies **2 :** the introductory remarks of a speaker or writer **:** FOREWORD **3 :** APPROACH, PRELIMINARY

[2]preface *vb* **pref·aced; pref·ac·ing** *vi* **:** to make introductory remarks ~ *vt* **1 :** to say or write as preface <a note *prefaced* to the manuscript> **2 :** PRECEDE, HERALD **3 :** to introduce by or begin with a preface **4 :** to stand in front of <a porch ~*s* the entrance> **5 :** to be a preliminary to — **pref·ac·er** *n*

pref·a·to·ri·al \ˌpref-ə-ˈtōr-ē-əl, -ˈtȯr-\ *adj* **:** PREFATORY — **pref·a·to·ri·al·ly** \-ē-ə-lē\ *adv*

pref·a·to·ry \ˈpref-ə-ˌtōr-ē, -ˌtȯr-\ *adj* [L *praefatus,* pp.] **1 :** of, relating to, or constituting a preface **2 :** located in front *syn* see PRELIMINARY — **pref·a·to·ri·ly** \ˌpref-ə-ˈtōr-ə-lē, -ˈtȯr-\ *adv*

pre·fect \ˈprē-ˌfekt\ *n* [ME, fr. MF, fr. L *praefectus,* fr. pp. of *praeficere* to place at the head of, fr. *prae-* + *facere* to make — more at DO] **1 :** any of various high officials or magistrates of differing functions and ranks in ancient Rome **2 :** a chief officer or chief magistrate **3 :** a student monitor in a private school

prefect apostolic *n* **:** a Roman Catholic clergyman and usu. a priest with quasi-episcopal jurisdiction over a district of a missionary territory

pre·fec·ture \ˈprē-ˌfek-chər\ *n* **1 :** the office or term of office of a prefect **2 :** the official residence of a prefect **3 :** the district governed by a prefect — **pre·fec·tur·al** \-chə-rəl, pri-ˈ\ *adj*

prefecture apostolic *n* **:** the district in which a prefect apostolic has ecclesiastical authority

pre·fer \pri-ˈfər\ *vt* **pre·ferred; pre·fer·ring** [ME *preferren,* fr. MF *preferer,* fr. L *praeferre* to put before, prefer, fr. *prae-* + *ferre* to carry — more at BEAR] **1** *archaic* **:** to promote or advance to a rank or position **2 :** to choose or esteem above another <~*s* sports to reading> **3 :** to give (a creditor) priority **4** *archaic* **:** to put or set forward or before someone **:** RECOMMEND **5 :** to bring or lay against someone <won't ~ charges> **6 :** to bring forward or lay before one for consideration — **pre·fer·rer** *n*

pref·er·a·ble \'pref-(ə-)rə-bəl, 'pref-ər-bəl\ *adj* **:** having greater value or desirability **:** being preferred — **pref·er·a·bil·i·ty** \ˌpref-(ə-)rə-'bil-ət-ē\ *n* — **pref·er·a·ble·ness** \'pref-(ə-)rə-bəl-nəs, 'pref-ər-bəl-\ *n* — **pref·er·a·bly** \-blē\ *adv*

pref·er·ence \'pref-ərn(t)s, 'pref-(ə-)rən(t)s\ *n* [F *préférence*, fr. ML *praeferentia*, fr. L *praeferent-*, *praeferens*, prp. of *praeferre*] **1 a :** the act of preferring **:** the state of being preferred **b :** the power or opportunity of choosing **2 :** one that is preferred **3 :** the act, fact, or principle of giving advantages to some over others **4 :** priority in the right to demand and receive satisfaction of an obligation ***syn*** see CHOICE

pref·er·en·tial \ˌpref-ə-'ren-chəl\ *adj* **1 :** showing preference <received ~ treatment> **2 :** employing or creating a preference in trade relations **3 :** designed to permit expression of preference among candidates <a ~ primary> **4 :** giving preference esp. in hiring to union members <a ~ shop> — **pref·er·en·tial·ly** \-'rench-(ə-)lē\ *adv*

pre·fer·ment \pri-'fər-mənt\ *n* **1 a :** advancement or promotion in dignity, office, or station **b :** a position or office of honor or profit **2 :** priority or seniority in right esp. to receive payment or to purchase property on equal terms with others **3 :** the act of bringing forward (as charges)

preferred stock *n* **:** stock guaranteed priority by a corporation's charter over common stock in the payment of dividends and usu. in the distribution of assets

pre·fig·u·ra·tion \(ˌ)prē-ˌfig-(y)ə-'rā-shən\ *n* **1 :** the act of prefiguring **:** the state of being prefigured **2 :** something that prefigures

pre·fig·u·ra·tive \(')prē-'fig-(y)ə-rət-iv\ *adj* **:** of, relating to, or showing by prefiguration **:** FORESHOWING — **pre·fig·u·ra·tive·ly** *adv* — **pre·fig·u·ra·tive·ness** *n*

pre·fig·ure \(')prē-'fig-yər, *esp Brit* -'fig-ər\ *vt* [ME *prefiguren*, fr. LL *praefigurare*, fr. L *prae-* pre- + *figurare* to shape, picture, fr. *figura* figure] **1 :** to show, suggest, or announce by an antecedent type, image, or likeness **2 :** to picture or imagine beforehand **:** FORESEE — **pre·fig·ure·ment** \-mənt\ *n*

[1]**pre·fix** *vt* [ME *prefixen*, fr. MF *prefixer*, fr. *pre-* + *fixer* to fix, fr. *fix* fixed, fr. L *fixus* — more at FIX] **1** \(')prē-'fiks\ **:** to fix or appoint beforehand **2** \'prē-ˌ, prē-'\ [[2]*prefix*] **:** to place in front **:** add as a prefix <~ a syllable to a word>

[2]**pre·fix** \'prē-ˌfiks\ *n* [NL *praefixum*, fr. L, neut. of *praefixus*, pp. of *praefigere* to fasten before, fr. *prae-* + *figere* to fasten — more at DIKE] **1 :** an affix attached to the beginning of a word, base, or phrase and serving to produce a derivative word or an inflectional form — compare SUFFIX **2 :** a title used before a person's name — **pre·fix·al** \'prē-ˌfik-səl, prē-'\ *adj* — **pre·fix·al·ly** \-sə-lē\ *adv*

pre·flight \'prē-'flīt\ *adj* **:** preparing for or preliminary to flight

pre·fo·cus \(')prē-'fō-kəs\ *vt* **:** to focus beforehand (as automotive headlights before installation)

pre·form \'prē-'fó(ə)rm\ *vt* [L *praeformare*, fr. *prae-* + *formare* to form, fr. *forma* form] **1 :** to form or shape beforehand **2 :** to bring to approximate shape and size — **pre·form** \-ˌfórm\ *n*

pre·for·ma·tion \ˌprē-fór-'mā-shən\ *n* **1 :** previous formation **2 :** the now discredited theory that every germ cell contains the organism of its kind fully formed and that development consists merely in increase in size

[1]**pre·fron·tal** \(')prē-'frənt-ᵊl\ *adj* **:** anterior to or involving the anterior part of a frontal structure <a ~ bone>

[2]**prefrontal** *n* **:** a prefrontal part (as a bone)

pre·gan·gli·on·ic \ˌprē-ˌgaŋ-glē-'än-ik\ *adj* **:** proximal to a ganglion; *specif* **:** of, relating to, or being a usu. medullated axon arising from a cell body in the central nervous system and terminating in an autonomic ganglion

preg·na·ble \'preg-nə-bəl\ *adj* [modif. of ME *prenable*, fr. MF — more at IMPREGNABLE] **:** vulnerable to capture <a ~ fort> — **preg·na·bil·i·ty** \ˌpreg-nə-'bil-ət-ē\ *n*

preg·nan·cy \'preg-nən-sē\ *n*, *pl* **-cies 1 :** the condition of being pregnant **:** GESTATION **2 :** the quality of being pregnant (as in meaning) **3 :** an instance of being pregnant

[1]**preg·nant** \'preg-nənt\ *adj* [ME *preignant*, fr. MF, fr. prp. of *preindre* to press, fr. L *premere* — more at PRESS] *archaic* **:** COGENT

[2]**pregnant** *adj* [ME, fr. L *praegnant-*, *praegnans*, alter. of *praegnas*, fr. *prae-* pre- + *-gnas* (akin to *gignere* to produce) — more at KIN] **1 :** abounding in fancy, wit, or resourcefulness **:** INVENTIVE <all this has been said . . . by great and ~ artists —*Times Lit. Supp.*> **2 :** rich in significance or implication **:** MEANINGFUL, PROFOUND <the ~ phrases of the Bible —Edmund Wilson> <a ~ pause> **3 :** containing unborn young within the body **:** GRAVID **4 :** having possibilities of development or consequence **:** involving important issues **:** MOMENTOUS <draw inspiration from the heroic achievements of that ~ age —Kemp Malone> **5** *obs* **:** INCLINED, DISPOSED <your own most ~ and vouchsafed ear —Shak.> **6 :** FULL, TEEMING <all nature seemed ~ with life —L. F. Herreshoff> <student movements . . . ~ with political possibilities —Daniel James> — **preg·nant·ly** *adv*

preg·nen·o·lone \preg-'nen-ᵊl-ˌōn\ *n* [ISV *pregnene* ($C_{21}H_{34}$) + *-ol* + *-one*] **:** an unsaturated hydroxy steroid ketone $C_{21}H_{32}O_2$ that is formed by the oxidation of steroids (as cholesterol) and yields progesterone on dehydrogenation

pre·heat \(')prē-'hēt\ *vt* **:** to heat beforehand; *esp* **:** to heat (an oven) to a designated temperature before using for cooking — **pre·heat·er** *n*

pre·hen·sile \prē-'hen(t)-səl, -'hen-ˌsīl\ *adj* [F *préhensile*, fr. L *prehensus*, pp. of *prehendere* to grasp, fr. *prae-* + *-hendere* (akin to ON *geta* to get) — more at GET] **1 :** adapted for seizing or grasping esp. by wrapping around <~ tail> **2 :** gifted with mental grasp or moral or aesthetic perception — **pre·hen·sil·i·ty** \(ˌ)prē-ˌhen-'sil-ət-ē\ *n*

pre·hen·sion \prē-'hen-chən\ *n* **1 :** the act of taking hold, seizing, or grasping **2 a :** mental understanding **:** COMPREHENSION **b :** apprehension by the senses

pre·his·to·ri·an \ˌprē-(h)is-'tōr-ē-ən, -'tór-\ *n* **:** an archaeologist who specializes in prehistoric man and his culture

pre·his·tor·ic \ˌprē-(h)is-'tór-ik, -'tär-\ *or* **pre·his·tor·i·cal** \-i-kəl\ *adj* **1 :** of, relating to, or existing in times antedating written history **2 :** of or relating to a language in a period of its development from which contemporary records of its sounds and forms have not been preserved — **pre·his·tor·i·cal·ly** \-i-k(ə-)lē\ *adv*

pre·his·to·ry \(')prē-'his-t(ə-)rē\ *n* **1 :** the study of prehistoric man **2 :** a history of the antecedents of an event or situation **3 :** the prehistoric period of man's evolution

pre·hom·i·nid \-'häm-ə-nəd\ *n* [deriv. of L *pre-* + *homin-*, *homo* man] **:** any of the extinct manlike primates that are often classified as a family (Prehominidae) — **prehominid** *adj*

pre·ig·ni·tion \ˌprē-ig-'nish-ən\ *n* **:** ignition in an internal-combustion engine while the inlet valve is open or before compression is completed

pre·in·duc·tion \ˌprē-in-'dək-shən\ *adj* **:** occurring prior to induction into military service <a ~ physical>

pre·in·dus·tri·al \-'dəs-trē-əl\ *adj* **:** of, relating to, or occurring in a period prior to the development of large-scale industry

pre·judge \(')prē-'jəj\ *vt* [MF *prejuger*, fr. L *praejudicare*, fr. *prae-* + *judicare* to judge — more at JUDGE] **:** to judge before hearing or before full and sufficient examination — **pre·judg·er** *n* — **pre·judg·ment** \-'jəj-mənt\ *n*

[1]**prej·u·dice** \'prej-əd-əs\ *n* [ME, fr. OF, fr. L *praejudicium* previous judgment, damage, fr. *prae-* + *judicium* judgment — more at JUDICIAL] **1 :** injury or damage resulting from some judgment or action of another in disregard of one's rights; *esp* **:** detriment to one's legal rights or claims **2 a (1) :** preconceived judgment or opinion **(2) :** an opinion or leaning adverse to anything without just grounds or before sufficient knowledge **b :** an instance of such judgment or opinion **c :** an irrational attitude of hostility directed against an individual, a group, a race, or their supposed characteristics ***syn*** see PREDILECTION

[2]**prejudice** *vt* **-diced; -dic·ing 1 :** to injure or damage by some judgment or action (as in a case of law) **2 :** to cause to have prejudice

prej·u·diced \-dəst\ *adj* **:** having a prejudice or bias for or esp. against

prej·u·di·cial \ˌprej-ə-'dish-əl\ *adj* **1 :** tending to injure or impair **:** DETRIMENTAL **2 :** leading to premature judgment or unwarranted opinion — **prej·u·di·cial·ly** \-'dish-(ə-)lē\ *adv* — **prej·u·di·cial·ness** \-əl-nəs\ *n*

prej·u·di·cious \-'dish-əs\ *adj* **:** PREJUDICIAL — **prej·u·di·cious·ly** *adv*

prel·a·cy \'prel-ə-sē\ *n*, *pl* **-cies 1 :** the office or dignity of a prelate **2 :** episcopal church government

pre·lap·sar·i·an \ˌprē-ˌlap-'ser-ē-ən\ *adj* [*pre-* + L *lapsus* slip, fall — more at LAPSE] **:** characteristic of or belonging to the time or state before the fall of man

prel·ate \'prel-ət *also* 'prē-ˌlāt\ *n* [ME *prelat*, fr. OF, fr. ML *praelatus*, lit., one receiving preferment, fr. L, (pp. of *praeferre* to prefer) fr. *prae-* + *latus*, pp. of *ferre* to carry — more at TOLERATE, BEAR] **:** an ecclesiastic (as a bishop or abbot) of superior rank

prelate nul·li·us \-nü-'lē-əs\ *n* [*nullius* fr. NL *nullius dioeceseos* of no diocese] **:** a Roman Catholic prelate who is usu. a titular bishop and who has ordinary jurisdiction over a district independent of any diocese

prel·a·ture \'prel-ə-ˌchü(ə)r, -chər, -ˌt(y)ù(ə)r\ *n* **1 :** PRELACY 1 **2 :** a body of prelates

pre·launch \'prē-'lónch, -'länch\ *adj* **:** preparing for or preliminary to launch (as of a spacecraft)

pre·lect \pri-'lekt\ *vi* [L *praelectus*, pp. of *praelegere*, fr. *prae-* + *legere* to read — more at LEGEND] **:** to discourse publicly **:** LECTURE — **pre·lec·tion** \-'lek-shən\ *n*

pre·li·ba·tion \ˌprē-lī-'bā-shən\ *n* [L *praelibation-*, *praelibatio*, fr. *praelibatus*, pp. of *praelibare* to taste beforehand, fr. *prae-* + *libare* to pour as an offering, taste — more at LIBATION] **:** FORETASTE

pre·lim \'prē-ˌlim, pri-'\ *n or adj* **:** PRELIMINARY

[1]**pre·lim·i·nary** \pri-'lim-ə-ˌner-ē\ *n*, *pl* **-nar·ies** [F *préliminaires*, pl., fr. ML *praeliminaris*, adj., preliminary, fr. L *prae-* pre- + *limin-*, *limen* threshold — more at LIMB] **:** something that precedes or is introductory or preparatory: as **a :** a preliminary scholastic examination **b** *pl*, *Brit* **:** FRONT MATTER **c :** a minor match preceding the main event (as of a boxing card)

[2]**preliminary** *adj* **:** coming before and usu. forming a necessary prelude to something else <held a ~ discussion to set up the agenda of the conference> — **pre·lim·i·nar·i·ly** \-ˌlim-ə-'ner-ə-lē\ *adv* ***syn*** PRELIMINARY, INTRODUCTORY, PREPARATORY, PREFATORY *shared meaning element* **:** serving to make ready the way for something that follows

pre·lit·er·ate \(')prē-'lit-ə-rət, -'li-trət\ *adj* **1 :** antedating the use of writing **2 :** not yet employing writing as a cultural medium — **preliterate** *n*

[1]**pre·lude** \'prel-ˌyüd, 'prā-ˌlüd, 'prel-ˌüd, 'prē-ˌlüd\ *n* [MF, fr. ML *praeludium*, fr. *praeludere* to play beforehand, fr. *prae-* + *ludere* to play — more at LUDICROUS] **1 :** an introductory performance, action, or event preceding and preparing for the principal or a more important matter **2 a :** a musical section or movement introducing the theme or chief subject (as of a fugue or suite) or serving as an introduction to an opera or oratorio **b :** an opening voluntary **c :** a separate concert piece usu. for piano or orchestra and based entirely on a short motive

2prelude *vb* **pre·lud·ed; pre·lud·ing** *vi* **:** to give or serve as a prelude; *esp* **:** to play a musical introduction ~ *vt* **1 :** to serve as prelude to **2 :** to play as a prelude — **pre·lud·er** *n*
pre·lu·sion \pri-ˈlü-zhən\ *n* [L *praelusion-, praelusio,* fr. *praelusus,* pp. of *praeludere*] **:** PRELUDE, INTRODUCTION
pre·lu·sive \-ˈlü-siv, -ziv\ *adj* **:** constituting or having the form of a prelude **:** INTRODUCTORY — **pre·lu·sive·ly** *adv*
pre·lu·so·ry \-ˈlüs-(ə-)rē, -ˈlüz-\ *adj* **:** PRELUSIVE
prem *abbr* premium
pre·ma·lig·nant \ˌprē-mə-ˈlig-nənt\ *adj* **:** PRECANCEROUS
pre·man \ˈprē-ˈman, -ˌman\ *n* **:** a hypothetical ancient primate constituting the immediate ancestor of man **:** PREHOMINID
pre·mar·i·tal \(ˈ)prē-ˈmar-ət-ᵊl\ *adj* **:** existing or occurring before marriage
pre·mar·ket·ing \(ˈ)prē-ˈmär-kət-iŋ\ *adj* **:** existing or occurring prior to marketing <~ clearance of a new drug>
pre·ma·ture \ˌprē-mə-ˈt(y)u̇(ə)r, -ˈchu̇(ə)r *also* ˌprem-ə-\ *adj* [L *praematurus* too early, fr. *prae-* + *maturus* ripe, mature] **:** happening, arriving, existing, or preformed before the proper or usual time; *esp* **:** born after a gestation period of less than 37 weeks <~ babies> — **premature** *n* — **pre·ma·ture·ly** *adv* — **pre·ma·ture·ness** *n* — **pre·ma·tu·ri·ty** \-ˈt(y)u̇r-ət-ē, -ˈchu̇r-\ *n*
pre·max·il·la \ˌprē-mak-ˈsil-ə\ *n* [NL]**:** either of a pair of bones of the upper jaw of vertebrates between and in front of the maxillae — **pre·max·il·lary** \(ˈ)prē-ˈmak-sə-ˌler-ē, *chiefly Brit* ˌprē-mak-ˈsil-ə-rē\ *adj or n*
1pre·med \ˈprē-ˈmed\ *adj* **:** PREMEDICAL
2premed *n* **:** a premedical student or course of study
pre·me·di·an \(ˈ)prē-ˈmēd-ē-ən\ *or* **pre·me·di·al** \-ē-əl\ *adj* **:** lying in front of the middle (as of the body)
pre·med·i·cal \(ˈ)prē-ˈmed-i-kəl\ *adj* **:** preceding and preparing for the professional study of medicine
pre·med·i·tate \pri-ˈmed-ə-ˌtāt, ˈprē-\ *vb* [L *praemeditatus,* pp. of *praemeditari,* fr. *prae-* + *meditari* to meditate] *vt* **:** to think about and revolve in the mind beforehand ~ *vi* **:** to think, consider, or deliberate beforehand — **pre·med·i·ta·tor** \-ˌtāt-ər\ *n*
pre·med·i·tat·ed *adj* **:** characterized by fully conscious willful intent and a measure of forethought and planning <~ murder> — **pre·med·i·tat·ed·ly** *adv*
pre·med·i·ta·tion \pri-ˌmed-ə-ˈtā-shən, ˌprē-\ *n* **:** an act or instance of premeditating; *specif* **:** consideration or planning of an act beforehand that shows intent to commit that act
pre·med·i·ta·tive \pri-ˈmed-ə-ˌtāt-iv, ˈprē-\ *adj* **:** given to or characterized by premeditation
pre·mei·ot·ic \ˌprē-mī-ˈät-ik\ *adj* **:** of, occurring in, or typical of a stage prior to meiosis <~ DNA synthesis> <~ tissue>
pre·men·stru·al \(ˈ)prē-ˈmen(t)-strə(-wə)l\ *adj* **:** of, relating to, or occurring in the period just preceding menstruation — **pre·men·stru·al·ly** \-ē\ *adv*
pre·mie *var of* PREEMIE
1pre·mier \pri-ˈm(y)i(ə)r; ˈprē-mē-ər, ˈprem-ē-\ *adj* [ME *primier,* fr. MF *premier* first, chief, fr. L *primarius* of the first rank — more at PRIMARY] **1 :** first in position, rank, or importance **:** PRINCIPAL **2 :** first in time **:** EARLIEST
2premier *n* [F, fr. *premier,* adj.] **:** PRIME MINISTER
pre·mier dan·seur \prə-myā-dä^{n}-sœr\ *n* [F] **:** the principal male dancer in a ballet company
1pre·miere \pri-ˈmye(ə)r, -ˈmi(ə)r; ˌprim-ē-ˈe(ə)r\ *n* [F *première,* fr. fem. of *premier* first] **1 :** a first performance or exhibition <the ~ of a play> **2 :** the leading lady of a group; *esp* **:** the chief actress of a theatrical cast
2premiere *or* **pre·mier** *like* 1PREMIERE\ *vb* **pre·miered; pre·mier·ing** *vt* **:** to give a first public performance of ~ *vi* **1 :** to have a first public performance **2 :** to appear for the first time as a star performer
3premiere *adj* [alter. of 1*premier*] **:** OUTSTANDING, CHIEF
pre·miere dan·seuse \prə-myer-dä^{n}-sœ̄z\ *n* [F *première danseuse*] **:** the principal female dancer in a ballet company
pre·mier·ship \pri-ˈm(y)i(ə)r-ˌship; ˈprē-mē-ər-, ˈprem-ē-\ *n* **:** the position or office of a premier
pre·mil·le·nar·i·an·ism \ˈprē-ˌmil-ə-ˈner-ē-ə-ˌniz-əm\ *n* **:** PREMILLENNIALISM — **pre·mil·le·nar·i·an** \-ē-ən\ *adj or n*
pre·mil·len·ni·al \ˌprē-mə-ˈlen-ē-əl\ *adj* [*pre-* + *millennium*] **1 :** coming before a millennium **2 :** holding or relating to premillennialism — **pre·mil·len·ni·al·ly** \-ē-ə-lē\ *adv*
pre·mil·len·ni·al·ism \-ē-ə-ˌliz-əm\ *n* **:** the view that Christ's return will precede and usher in a future millennium of Messianic rule mentioned in Revelation — **pre·mil·len·ni·al·ist** \-ē-ə-ləst\ *n*
1prem·ise \ˈprem-əs\ *n* [In sense 1, fr. ME *premisse,* fr. MF, fr. ML *praemissa,* fr. L, fem. of *praemissus,* pp. of *praemittere* to place ahead, fr. *prae-* pre- + *mittere* to send; in other senses, fr. ME *premisses,* fr. ML *praemissa,* fr. L, neut. pl. of *praemissus* — more at SMITE] **1 a :** a proposition antecedently supposed or proved as a basis of argument or inference; *specif* **:** either of the first two propositions of a syllogism from which the conclusion is drawn **b :** something assumed or taken for granted **:** PRESUPPOSITION **2** *pl* **:** matters previously stated; *specif* **:** the preliminary and explanatory part of a deed or of a bill in equity **3** *pl* [fr. its being identified in the premises of the deed] **a :** a tract of land with the buildings thereon **b :** a building or part of a building usu. with its appurtenances (as grounds)
2pre·mise \ˈprem-əs *also* pri-ˈmīz\ *vt* **pre·mised; pre·mis·ing 1 a :** to set forth beforehand as an introduction or a postulate **b :** to offer as a premise in an argument **2 :** to presuppose or imply as preexistent **:** POSTULATE
1pre·mi·um \ˈprē-mē-əm\ *n* [L *praemium* booty, profit, reward, fr. *prae-* + *emere* to take, buy — more at REDEEM] **1 a :** a reward or recompense for a particular act **b :** a sum over and above a regular price paid chiefly as an inducement or incentive <willing to pay a ~ for immediate delivery> **c :** a sum in advance of or in addition to the nominal value of something <bonds callable at a ~ of six percent> **d :** something given free or at a reduced price with the purchase of a product or service **2 :** the consideration paid for a contract of insurance **3 :** a high value or a value in excess of that normally or usu. expected <put a ~ on accuracy>
2premium *adj* **:** of exceptional quality or amount
1pre·mix \(ˈ)prē-ˈmiks\ *vt* **:** to mix far in advance of use
2pre·mix \ˈprē-ˌmiks\ *n* **:** a mixture of ingredients (as the dry materials for a cake batter) prepared beforehand and designed to be later mixed with other ingredients (as liquids)
pre·mo·lar \(ˈ)prē-ˈmō-lər\ *adj* **:** situated in front of or preceding the molar teeth; *esp* **:** being or relating to those teeth of a mammal in front of the true molars and behind the canines when the latter are present — **premolar** *n*
pre·mon·ish \-ˈmän-ish\ *vt, archaic* **:** FOREWARN ~ *vi, archaic* **:** to give warning in advance
pre·mo·ni·tion \ˌprē-mə-ˈnish-ən, ˌprem-ə-\ *n* [MF, fr. LL *praemonition-, praemonitio,* fr. L *praemonitus,* pp. of *praemonēre* to warn in advance, fr. *prae-* + *monēre* to warn — more at MIND] **1 :** previous notice or warning **:** FOREWARNING **2 :** anticipation of an event without conscious reason **:** PRESENTIMENT
pre·mon·i·to·ry \pri-ˈmän-ə-ˌtōr-ē, -ˌtȯr-\ *adj* **:** giving warning <a ~ symptom> — **pre·mon·i·to·ri·ly** \-ˌmän-ə-ˈtōr-ə-lē, -ˈtȯr-\ *adv*
Pre·mon·stra·ten·sian \ˌprē-ˌmän(t)-strə-ˈten-chən\ *n* [ML *praemonstratensis,* fr. *praemonstratensis* of Premontre, fr. *Praemonstratus* Prémontré] **:** a member of an order of canons regular founded by St. Norbert at Prémontré near Laon, France, in 1120
pre·morse \pri-ˈmȯ(ə)rs\ *adj* [L *praemorsus,* fr. pp. of *praemordēre* to bite off in front, fr. *prae-* + *mordēre* to bite — more at SMART] **:** terminated abruptly but irregularly as if bitten off <a ~ root>
pre·mune \(ˈ)prē-ˈmyün\ *adj* [back-formation fr. *premunition*] **:** exhibiting premunition
pre·mu·ni·tion \ˌprē-myu̇-ˈnish-ən\ *n* [L *praemunition-, praemunitio* advance fortification, fr. *praemunitus,* pp. of *praemunire* to fortify in advance, fr. *prae-* + *munire* to fortify — more at MUNITION] **1** *archaic* **:** an advance provision of protection **2 a :** resistance to a disease due to the existence of its causative agent in a state of physiological equilibrium in the host **b :** immunity to a particular infection due to previous presence of the causative agent
pre·name \ˈprē-ˌnām\ *n* **:** FORENAME
pre·na·tal \(ˈ)prē-ˈnāt-ᵊl\ *adj* **:** occurring, existing, or being in a stage before birth — **pre·na·tal·ly** \-ᵊl-ē\ *adv*
1pre·nom·i·nate \(ˈ)prē-ˈnäm-ə-nət\ *adj* [LL *praenominatus,* pp. of *praenominare* to name before, fr. L *prae-* + *nominare* to name — more at NOMINATE] *obs* **:** previously mentioned
2pre·nom·i·nate \-ˌnāt\ *vt, obs* **:** to mention previously — **pre·nom·i·na·tion** \(ˌ)prē-ˌnäm-ə-ˈnā-shən\ *n, obs*
pre·no·tion \(ˈ)prē-ˈnō-shən, ˈprē-ˌ\ *n* [L *praenotion-, praenotio* preconception, fr. *prae-* + *notio* idea, conception — more at NOTION] **1 :** PRESENTIMENT, PREMONITION **2 :** PRECONCEPTION
1pren·tice \ˈprent-əs\ *n* [ME *prentis,* short for *apprentis*] **:** APPRENTICE 1, LEARNER
2prentice *adj* **1 :** of, relating to, or characteristic of a prentice **2 :** not fully skilled; *also* **:** lacking in finish or polish
3prentice *vt* **pren·ticed; pren·tic·ing :** APPRENTICE
pre·oc·cu·pan·cy \(ˈ)prē-ˈäk-yə-pən-sē\ *n* **1 :** an act or the right of taking possession before another **2 :** the condition of being completely busied or preoccupied
pre·oc·cu·pa·tion \(ˌ)prē-ˌäk-yə-ˈpā-shən\ *n* [L *praeoccupation-, praeoccupatio* act of seizing beforehand, fr. *praeoccupatus,* pp. of *praeoccupare* to seize beforehand, fr. *prae-* + *occupare* to seize, occupy] **1 :** an act of preoccupying **:** the state of being preoccupied **2 a :** complete absorption of the mind or interests **b :** something that causes such absorption
pre·oc·cu·pied \(ˈ)prē-ˈäk-yə-ˌpīd\ *adj* **1 a :** lost in thought **:** ENGROSSED **b :** already occupied **2 :** previously applied to another group and unavailable for use in a new sense — used of a biological generic or specific name
pre·oc·cu·py \-ˌpī\ *vt* [*pre-* + *occupy*] **1 :** to engage or engross the interest or attention of beforehand or preferentially **2 :** to take possession of or fill beforehand or before another
pre·op·er·a·tive \(ˈ)prē-ˈäp-(ə-)rət-iv, -ˈäp-ə-ˌrāt-\ *adj* **:** occurring during the period preceding a surgical operation — **pre·op·er·a·tive·ly** *adv*
pre·or·bit·al \-ˈȯr-bət-ᵊl\ *adj* **:** occurring before going into orbit
pre·or·dain \ˌprē-ȯr-ˈdān\ *vt* **:** to decree or ordain in advance **:** FOREORDAIN — **pre·or·dain·ment** \-mənt\ *n* — **pre·or·di·na·tion** \(ˌ)prē-ˌȯrd-ᵊn-ˈā-shən\ *n*
pre·ovi·po·si·tion \ˌprē-ˌō-və-pə-ˈzish-ən\ *adj* **:** of, relating to, or being the period before oviposition of the first eggs by an adult female (as of an insect)
pre·ovu·la·to·ry \(ˈ)prē-ˈäv-yə-lə-ˌtōr-ē, -ˌtȯr-, -ˈōv-\ *adj* **:** occurring in or typical of the period immediately preceding ovulation
1prep \ˈprep\ *n* **1** *Brit* **:** preparation of lessons **:** HOMEWORK **2 :** PREPARATORY SCHOOL **3 :** a trial run in horse racing
2prep *vb* **prepped; prep·ping** *vi* **:** to attend preparatory school or engage in preparatory study or training ~ *vt* **:** to prepare for operation or examination
3prep *abbr* **1** preparatory **2** preposition
pre·pack·age \(ˈ)prē-ˈpak-ij\ *vt* **:** to package (as food or a manufactured article) before offering for sale to the consumer
prep·a·ra·tion \ˌprep-ə-ˈrā-shən\ *n* [ME *preparacion,* fr. MF *preparation,* fr. L *praeparation-, praeparatio,* fr. *praeparatus,* pp. of *praeparare*] **1 :** the action or process of making something ready for use or service or of getting ready for some occasion, test, or duty **2 :** a state of being prepared **:** READINESS **3 :** a preparatory act or measure **4 :** something that is prepared; *specif* **:** a medicinal substance made ready for use <a ~ for colds>
1pre·par·a·tive \pri-ˈpar-ət-iv\ *n* **:** something that prepares the way for or serves as a preliminary to something else **:** PREPARATION
2preparative *adj* **:** PREPARATORY — **pre·par·a·tive·ly** *adv*
pre·par·a·tor \pri-ˈpar-ət-ər\ *n* **:** one that prepares; *specif* **:** one that prepares scientific specimens
1pre·pa·ra·to·ry \pri-ˈpar-ə-ˌtōr-ē, -ˌtȯr- *also* ˈprep-(ə-)rə-\ *adj* **:** preparing or serving to prepare for something **:** INTRODUCTORY

syn see PRELIMINARY — **pre·pa·ra·to·ri·ly** \pri-ˌpar-ə-ˈtōr-ə-lē, -ˈtȯr- *also* ˌprep-(ə-)rə-\ *adv*

²preparatory *adv* **:** by way of preparation **:** in a preparatory manner — usu. used with *to* <took a deep breath ~ to drinking>

preparatory school *n* **1 :** a usu. private school preparing students primarily for college **2** *Brit* **:** a private elementary school preparing students primarily for public schools

pre·pare \pri-ˈpa(ə)r, -ˈpe(ə)r\ *vb* **pre·pared; pre·par·ing** [ME *preparen,* fr. MF *preparer,* fr. L *praeparare,* fr. *prae-* pre- + *parare* to procure, prepare — more at PARE] *vt* **1 :** to make ready beforehand for some purpose, use, or activity <~ food for dinner> <~ children for school> **2 :** to work out the details of **:** plan in advance <*preparing* his strategy for the coming campaign> **3 a :** to put together **:** COMPOUND <~ a prescription> **b :** to put into written form <~ a report> ~ *vi* **:** to get ready <*preparing* for a career in teaching> — **pre·par·er** *n*

syn PREPARE, FIT, QUALIFY, CONDITION, READY *shared meaning element* **:** to make someone or something ready (as for a use or an activity)

pre·pared \-ˈpa(ə)rd, -ˈpe(ə)rd\ *adj* **:** subjected to a special process or treatment — **pre·pared·ly** \-lē; -ˈpar-əd-lē, -ˈper-\ *adv*

pre·pared·ness \-ˈpar-əd-nəs, -ˈper- *also* -ˈpa(ə)rd-nəs *or* -ˈpe(ə)rd-nəs\ *n***:** the quality or state of being prepared; *specif* **:** a state of adequate preparation in case of war

pre·pay \(ˈ)prē-ˈpā\ *vt* **-paid** \-ˈpād\; **-pay·ing :** to pay or pay the charge on in advance — **pre·pay·ment** \-ˈpā-mənt\ *n*

prepd *abbr* prepared

pre·pense \pri-ˈpen(t)s\ *adj* [by shortening & alter. fr. earlier *purpensed,* fr. ME, pp. of *purpensen* to deliberate, premeditate, fr. MF *purpenser,* fr. OF, fr. *pur-* for + *penser* to think — more at PURCHASE, PENSIVE] **:** planned beforehand **:** PREMEDITATED — usu. used postpositively <malice ~> — **pre·pense·ly** *adv*

prepg *abbr* preparing

pre·plan \(ˈ)prē-ˈplan\ *vt* **:** to plan in advance <~ the week's menus> ~ *vi* **:** to make plans beforehand

pre·plant \ˈprē-ˈplant\ *also* **pre·plant·ing** \-iŋ\ *adj* **:** occurring or used before planting a crop <~ soil fertilization>

prepn *abbr* preparation

pre·pon·der·ance \pri-ˈpän-d(ə-)rən(t)s\ *n* **1 :** a superiority in weight or in power, importance, or strength **2 a :** a superiority or excess in number or quantity **b :** MAJORITY

pre·pon·der·an·cy \-d(ə-)rən-sē\ *n* **:** PREPONDERANCE

pre·pon·der·ant \pri-ˈpän-d(ə-)rənt\ *adj* **1 :** having superior weight, force, or influence **2 :** having greater prevalence ***syn*** see DOMINANT — **pre·pon·der·ant·ly** *adv*

¹pre·pon·der·ate \pri-ˈpän-də-ˌrāt\ *vb* **-at·ed; -at·ing** [L *praeponderatus,* pp. of *praeponderare,* fr. *prae-* + *ponder-, pondus* weight — more at PENDANT] *vt* **1** *archaic* **:** OUTWEIGH **2** *archaic* **:** to weigh down ~ *vi* **1 a :** to exceed in weight **b :** to descend or incline downward **2 :** to exceed in influence, power, or importance **:** PREDOMINATE **3 :** to exceed in numbers — **pre·pon·der·a·tion** \-ˌpän-də-ˈrā-shən, ˌprē-\ *n*

²pre·pon·der·ate \-ˈpän-də-rət\ *adj* **:** PREPONDERANT — **pre·pon·der·ate·ly** *adv*

prep·o·si·tion \ˌprep-ə-ˈzish-ən\ *n* [ME *preposicioun,* fr. L *praeposition-, praepositio,* fr. *praepositus,* pp. of *praeponere* to put in front, fr. *prae-* pre- + *ponere* to put — more at POSITION] **:** a linguistic form that combines with a noun, pronoun, or noun equivalent to form a phrase that typically has an adverbial, adjectival, or substantival relation to some other word — **prep·o·si·tion·al** \-ˈzish-nəl, -ən-ᵊl\ *adj* — **prep·o·si·tion·al·ly** \-ē\ *adv*

pre·pos·i·tive \pri-ˈpäz-ət-iv, -ˈpäz-tiv\ *adj* [LL *praepositivus,* fr. L *praepositus*] **:** put before **:** PREFIXED — **pre·pos·i·tive·ly** *adv*

pre·pos·sess \ˌprē-pə-ˈzes *also* -ˈses\ *vt* **1** *obs* **:** to take previous possession of **2 :** to cause to be preoccupied with an idea, belief, or attitude **3 a :** to influence beforehand for or against someone or something **b :** to induce to a favorable opinion beforehand

pre·pos·sess·ing *adj* **1** *archaic* **:** creating prejudice **2 :** tending to create a favorable impression **:** ATTRACTIVE — **pre·pos·sess·ing·ly** \-iŋ-lē\ *adv* — **pre·pos·sess·ing·ness** *n*

pre·pos·ses·sion \ˌprē-pə-ˈzesh-ən *also* -ˈsesh-\ *n* **1** *archaic* **:** prior possession **2 :** an attitude, belief, or impression formed beforehand **:** PREJUDICE **3 :** an exclusive concern with one idea or object **:** PREOCCUPATION ***syn*** see PREDILECTION

pre·pos·ter·ous \pri-ˈpäs-t(ə-)rəs\ *adj* [L *praeposterus,* lit., with the hindside in front, fr. *prae-* + *posterus* hinder, following — more at POSTERIOR] **:** contrary to nature, reason, or common sense **:** ABSURD — **pre·pos·ter·ous·ly** *adv* — **pre·pos·ter·ous·ness** *n*

pre·po·ten·cy \(ˈ)prē-ˈpōt-ᵊn-sē\ *n* **1 :** the quality or state of being prepotent **:** PREDOMINANCE **2 :** unusual ability of an individual or strain to transmit its characters to offspring because of homozygosity for numerous dominant genes

pre·po·tent \-ᵊnt\ *adj* [ME, fr. L *praepotent-, praepotens,* fr. *prae-* + *potens* powerful — more at POTENT] **1 a :** having exceptional power, authority, or influence **:** PREEMINENT **b :** exceeding others in power **2 :** exhibiting genetic prepotency — **pre·po·tent·ly** *adv*

prep·pie \ˈprep-ē\ *n* [¹*prep* + *-ie*] *slang* **:** one who attends or has attended preparatory school

pre·pran·di·al \(ˈ)prē-ˈpran-dē-əl\ *adj* **:** of, relating to, or suitable for the time just before dinner <a ~ drink>

¹pre·print \ˈprē-ˌprint, -ˈprint\ *n* **1 :** a printing of a speech or paper before its formal delivery; *esp* **:** an issue of a technical paper often in preliminary form before its publication in a journal **2 :** something (as an advertisement) printed before the rest of the publication in which it is to appear

²pre·print \(ˈ)prē-ˈprint\ *vt* **1 :** to print and issue as a preprint <~*ed* technical papers> **2 :** to print for use in a later printing

pre·pro·cess \(ˈ)prē-ˈpräs-ˌes, -ˈprōs-, -əs\ *vt* **:** to do preliminary processing of (as data) — **pre·pro·ces·sor** \-ˌes-ər, -ə-sər, -ə-ˌsȯ(ə)r\ *n*

pre·pro·fes·sion·al \ˌprē-prə-ˈfesh-nəl, -ən-ᵊl\ *adj* **:** of or relating to the period preceding specific study for or practice of a profession

pre·pro·gram \-ˈprō-ˌgram, -grəm\ *vt* **:** to program in advance of some intended use

prep school *n* **:** PREPARATORY SCHOOL

pre·pu·ber·al \(ˈ)prē-ˈpyü-b(ə-)rəl\ *adj* **:** of or relating to prepuberty — **pre·pu·ber·al·ly** \-ē\ *adv*

pre·pu·ber·tal \-bərt-ᵊl\ *adj* **:** PREPUBERAL — **pre·pu·ber·tal·ly** \-ᵊl-ē\ *adv*

pre·pu·ber·ty \-bərt-ē\ *n* **:** the period immediately preceding puberty

pre·pu·bes·cence \ˌprē-pyü-ˈbes-ᵊn(t)s\ *n* **:** PREPUBERTY

pre·pu·bes·cent \-ᵊnt\ *adj* **:** PREPUBERAL

pre·pub·li·ca·tion \ˌprē-ˌpəb-lə-ˈkā-shən\ *adj* **:** of or relating to a period before the official publication date of a book <~ price>

pre·puce \ˈprē-ˌpyüs\ *n* [ME, fr. MF, fr. L *praeputium,* fr. *prae-* + *-putium* (akin to Belorussian *potka* penis)] **:** FORESKIN; *also* **:** a similar fold investing the clitoris — **pre·pu·tial** \prē-ˈpyü-shəl\ *adj*

pre·punch \(ˈ)prē-ˈpənch\ *vt* **:** to punch in advance of some anticipated use

Pre–Ra·pha·el·ite \(ˈ)prē-ˈraf-ē-ə-ˌlīt, -ˈrā-fē-, -ˈräf-ē-\ *n* **1 a :** a member of a brotherhood of artists formed in England in 1848 to restore the artistic principles and practices regarded as characteristic of Italian art before Raphael **b :** an artist or writer influenced by this brotherhood **2 :** a modern artist dedicated to restoring early Renaissance ideals or methods **3 :** an Italian painter active before the time of Raphael's fame and influence — **Pre-Raphaelite** *adj* — **Pre–Ra·pha·el·it·ism** \-ˌlīt-ˌiz-əm\ *n*

pre·re·cord \ˌprē-ri-ˈkȯ(ə)rd\ *vt* **:** to record (as a radio or television program) in advance of presentation or use

pre–reg·is·tra·tion \ˌprē-ˌrej-ə-ˈstrā-shən\ *n* **:** a special registration (as for returning students) prior to an official registration period — **pre–reg·is·ter** \(ˈ)prē-ˈrej-ə-stər\ *vi*

pre·req·ui·site \(ˈ)prē-ˈrek-wə-zət\ *n* **:** something that is necessary to an end or to the carrying out of a function — **prerequisite** *adj*

pre·rog·a·tive \pri-ˈräg-ət-iv\ *n* [ME, fr. MF & L; MF, fr. L *praerogativa,* Roman century voting first in the comitia, privilege, fr. fem. of *praerogativus* voting first, fr. *praerogatus,* pp. of *praerogare* to ask for an opinion before another, fr. *prae-* + *rogare* to ask — more at RIGHT] **1 a :** an exclusive or special right, power, or privilege; as **(1) :** one belonging to an office or an official body **(2) :** one belonging to a person, group, or class of individuals **(3) :** one possessed by a nation as an attribute of sovereignty **b :** the discretionary power inhering in the British Crown **2 :** a distinctive excellence — **pre·rog·a·tived** \-ivd\ *adj*

pres *abbr* **1** present **2** president

pre·sa \ˈprā-sə, -(ˌ)sä, -zə\ *n, pl* **pre·se** \-(ˌ)sā, -(ˌ)zā\ [It, lit., act of taking, fr. *prendere* to take, fr. L *prehendere* to grasp — more at PREHENSILE] **:** a mark or cue (as :S:) indicating the point of entry of the successive voice parts of a canon

:S: + ⁜

three forms of prese

¹pres·age \ˈpres-ij, *archaic* pri-ˈsāj\ *n* [ME, fr. L *praesagium,* fr. *praesagire* to forebode, fr. *prae-* + *sagire* to perceive keenly — more at SEEK] **1 :** something that foreshadows or portends a future event **:** OMEN **2 :** an intuition or feeling of what is going to happen in the future **3** *archaic* **:** PROGNOSTICATION **4 :** warning or indication of the future — **pre·sage·ful** \pri-ˈsāj-fəl\ *adj*

²pre·sage \ˈpres-ij, pri-ˈsāj\ *vb* **pre·saged; pre·sag·ing** *vt* **1 :** to give an omen or warning of **:** FORESHADOW, PORTEND **2 :** FORETELL, PREDICT **3 :** to have a presentiment of ~ *vi* **:** to make or utter a prediction — **pre·sag·er** *n, obs*

pre·sanc·ti·fied \(ˈ)prē-ˈsaŋ(k)-ti-ˌfīd\ *adj* **:** consecrated at a previous service — used of eucharistic elements

Presb *abbr* Presbyterian

presby- *or* **presbyo-** *comb form* [NL, fr. Gk *presby-* elder, fr. *presbys* old man] **:** old age <*presby*opia> <*presbyo*phrenia>

pres·by·ope \ˈprez-bē-ˌōp; ˈpres-bē-, -pē-\ *n* [prob. fr. F, fr. Gk *presby-* + *ōps* eye — more at EYE] **:** a farsighted person

pres·by·opia \ˌprez-bē-ˈō-pē-ə, ˌpres-\ *n* [NL] **:** a visual condition of old age in which loss of elasticity of the lens of the eye causes defective accommodation and inability to focus sharply for near vision — **pres·by·opic** \-ˈō-pik, -ˈäp-ik\ *adj or n*

pres·by·ter \ˈprez-bət-ər, ˈpres-\ *n* [LL, elder, priest — more at PRIEST] **1 :** a member of the governing body of an early Christian church **2 :** a member of the order of priests in churches having episcopal hierarchies including bishops, priests, and deacons **3 :** ELDER 4b — **pres·byt·er·ate** \prez-ˈbit-ə-rət, pres-, -ˌrāt\ *n*

¹pres·by·te·ri·al \ˌprez-bə-ˈtir-ē-əl, ˌpres-\ *adj* **:** of or relating to presbyters or a presbytery — **pres·by·te·ri·al·ly** \-ē-ə-lē\ *adv*

²presbyterial *n, often cap* **:** an organization of Presbyterian women associated with a presbytery

¹Pres·by·te·ri·an \-ē-ən\ *adj* **1** *often not cap* **:** characterized by a graded system of representative ecclesiastical bodies (as presbyteries) exercising legislative and judicial powers **2 :** of, relating to, or constituting a Protestant Christian church that is presbyterian in government and traditionally Calvinistic in doctrine — **Pres·by·te·ri·an·ism** \-ē-ə-ˌniz-əm\ *n*

²Presbyterian *n* **:** a member of a Presbyterian church

pres·by·tery \ˈprez-bə-ˌter-ē, ˈpres-, -bə-trē\ *n, pl* **-ter·ies** [ME & LL; ME *presbytory* part of church reserved for clergy, fr. LL *presbyterium* group of presbyters, part of church reserved for clergy, fr. GK *presbyterion* group of presbyters, fr. *presbyteros* elder, priest — more at PRIEST] **1 :** the part of a church reserved for the officiating clergy **2 :** a ruling body in presbyterian churches consisting of the ministers and representative elders from congregations within a district **3 :** the jurisdiction of a presbytery **4 :** the house of a Roman Catholic parish priest

[1]**pre·school** \'prē-'skül\ *adj* : of, relating to, or constituting the period in a child's life from infancy to the age of five or six that ordinarily precedes attendance at elementary school

[2]**pre·school** \-,skül\ *n* : NURSERY SCHOOL, KINDERGARTEN

pre·school·er \-'skü-lər\ *n* **1** : a child not yet old enough for school **2** : a child attending a preschool

pre·science \'prēsh-(ē-)ən(t)s, 'presh-; 'prēs-ē-ən(t)s, 'pres-\ *n* [ME, fr. LL *praescientia,* fr. L *praescient-, praesciens,* prp. of *praescire* to know beforehand, fr. *prae-* + *scire* to know — more at SCIENCE] : foreknowledge of events: **a** : divine omniscience **b** : human anticipation of the course of events : FORESIGHT — **pre·scient** \-(ē-)ənt, -ē-ənt\ *adj* — **pre·scient·ly** *adv*

pre·sci·en·tif·ic \,prē-,sī-ən-'tif-ik\ *adj* [*pre-* + *scientific*] : of, relating to, or having the characteristics of a period before the rise of modern science or a state prior to the application of the scientific method

pre·scind \pri-'sind\ *vb* [L *praescindere* to cut off in front, fr. *prae-* + *scindere* to cut — more at SHED] *vt* : to detach for purposes of thought ~ *vi* : to withdraw one's attention

pre·score \(')prē-'skō(ə)r, -'skȯ(ə)r\ *vt* : to record (as sound) in advance for use when the corresponding scenes are photographed in making movies

pre·scribe \pri-'skrīb\ *vb* **pre·scribed; pre·scrib·ing** [L *praescribere* to write at the beginning, dictate, order, fr. *prae-* + *scribere* to write — more at SCRIBE] *vi* **1** [ME *prescriben,* fr. ML *praescribere,* fr. L, to write at the beginning] : to claim a title to something by right of prescription **2** : to lay down a rule : DICTATE **3** : to write or give medical prescriptions **4** : to become by prescription invalid or unenforceable ~ *vt* **1 a** : to lay down as a guide, direction, or rule of action : ORDAIN **b** : to specify with authority **2** : to designate or order the use of as a remedy — **pre·scrib·er** *n*

pre·script \'prē-,skript, pri-'\ *adj* [ME, fr. L *praescriptus,* pp.] : prescribed as a rule — **pre·script** \'prē-,skript\ *n*

pre·scrip·tion \pri-'skrip-shən\ *n* [partly fr. ME *prescripcion* establishment of a claim, fr. MF *prescription,* fr. LL *praescription-, praescriptio,* fr. L, act of writing at the beginning, order, limitation of subject matter, fr. *praescriptus,* pp. of *praescribere;* partly fr. L *praescription-, praescriptio* order] **1 a** : the establishment of a claim of title to something under common law usu. by use and enjoyment for a period fixed by statue **b** : the right or title acquired under common law by such possession **2** : the process of making claim to something by long use and enjoyment **3** : the action of laying down authoritative rules or directions **4 a** : a written direction for a therapeutic or corrective agent; *specif* : one for the preparation and use of a medicine **b** : a prescribed medicine **5 a** : ancient or long continued custom **b** : a claim founded upon ancient custom or long continued use **6** : something prescribed as a rule

prescription drug *n* : a drug that can be obtained only by means of a physician's prescription

pre·scrip·tive \pri-'skrip-tiv\ *adj* **1** : serving to prescribe **2** : acquired by, founded on, or determined by prescription or by long-standing custom — **pre·scrip·tive·ly** *adv*

pre·se·lect \,prē-sə-'lekt\ *vt* : to choose in advance usu. on the basis of a particular criterion — **pre·se·lec·tion** \-'lek-shən\ *n*

pre·sell \(')prē-'sel\ *vt* **-sold** \-'sōld\; **-sell·ing** : to precondition by advertising and devices of salesmanship for a subsequent purchase

pres·ence \'prez-ᵊn(t)s\ *n* **1** : the fact or condition of being present **2 a** : the part of space within one's immediate vicinity **b** : the neighborhood of one of superior esp. royal rank **3** *archaic* : COMPANY 2a **4** : one that is present: as **a** : the actual person or thing that is present **b** : something present of a visible or concrete nature **5 a** : the bearing, carriage, or air of a person; *esp* : stately or distinguished bearing **b** : a quality of poise and effectiveness that enables a performer to achieve a close relationship with his audience **6** : something (as a spirit) felt or believed to be present

presence chamber *n* : the room where a great personage receives those entitled to come into his presence

presence of mind : self-control so maintained in an emergency or in an embarrassing situation that one can say and do the right thing

[1]**pres·ent** \'prez-ᵊnt\ *n* [ME, fr. OF, fr. *presenter*] : something presented : GIFT

[2]**pre·sent** \pri-'zent\ *vb* [ME *presenten,* fr. OF *presenter,* fr. L *praesentare,* fr. *praesent-, praesens,* adj.] *vt* **1 a** : to bring or introduce into the presence of someone; *esp* : to introduce socially **b** : to bring (as a play) before the public **2** : to make a gift to **3** : to give or bestow formally **4 a** : to lay (as a charge) before a court as an object of inquiry **b** : to bring a formal public charge, indictment, or presentment against **5** : to nominate to a benefice **6** : to offer to view : SHOW **7** : to act the part of : PERFORM **8** : to aim, point, or direct (as a weapon) so as to face something or in a particular direction ~ *vi* **1** : to present a weapon **2** : to come forward or into view **syn** see GIVE — **pre·sent·er** *n*

[3]**pres·ent** \'prez-ᵊnt\ *adj* [ME, fr. OF, fr. L *praesent-, praesens,* fr. prp. of *praeesse* to be before one, fr. *prae-* pre- + *esse* to be — more at IS] **1** : now existing or in progress **2 a** : being in view or at hand **b** : existing in something mentioned or under consideration **3** : constituting the one actually involved, at hand, or being considered **4** : of, relating to, or constituting a verb tense that is expressive of present time or the time of speaking **5** *obs* : ATTENTIVE **6** *archaic* : INSTANT, IMMEDIATE — **pres·ent·ness** *n*

[4]**pres·ent** \'prez-ᵊnt\ *n* **1 a** *obs* : present occasion or affair **b** *pl* : the present words or statements; *specif* : the legal instrument or other writing in which these words are used **2 a** : the present tense of a language **b** : a verb form in the present tense **3** : the present time

pre·sent·able \pri-'zent-ə-bəl\ *adj* **1** : capable of being presented **2** : being in condition to be seen or inspected esp. by the critical — **pre·sent·abil·i·ty** \-,zent-ə-'bil-ət-ē\ *n* — **pre·sent·able·ness** \-'zent-ə-bəl-nəs\ *n* — **pre·sent·ably** \-blē\ *adv*

pre·sent arms \pri-,zent-\ *n* [fr. the command present arms!] **1** : a position in the manual of arms in which the rifle is held vertically in front of the body **2** : a command to assume the position of present arms or to give a hand salute

pre·sen·ta·tion \,prē-,zen-'tā-shən, ,prez-ᵊn-, ,prēz-ᵊn-\ *n* **1 a** : the act of presenting **b** : the act, power, or privilege esp. of a patron of applying to the bishop or ordinary for the institution of one nominated to a benefice **2** : something presented: as **a** : a symbol or image that represents something **b** : something offered or given : GIFT **c** : something set forth for the attention of the mind **d** : a descriptive or persuasive account (as by a salesman of his product) **3** : the position in which the fetus lies in the uterus in labor with respect to the mouth of the uterus **4** : an immediate object of perception, cognition, or memory **5** *often cap* : a church feast on November 21 celebrating the presentation of the Virgin Mary in the temple **6** : the method by which radio, navigation, or radar information is given to the operator (as the pilot of an airplane) — **pre·sen·ta·tion·al** \-shnəl, -shən-ᵊl\ *adj*

pre·sen·ta·tive \pri-'zent-ət-iv, 'prez-ᵊn-,tāt-\ *adj* : known, knowing, or capable of being known directly rather than through cogitation

pres·ent–day \'prez-ᵊnt-'dā\ *adj* : now existing or occurring

pre·sen·tee \,prez-ᵊn-'tē, pri-,zen-\ *n* : one who is presented or to whom something is presented

pre·sen·tient \pri-'sen-ch(ē-)ənt, 'prē-; pri-'zen-\ *adj* [L *praesentient-, praesentiens,* prp. of *praesentire*] : having a presentiment

pre·sen·ti·ment \pri-'zent-ə-mənt\ *n* [F *pressentiment,* fr. MF, fr. *pressentir* to have a presentiment, fr. L *praesentire* to feel beforehand, fr. *prae-* + *sentire* to feel — more at SENSE] : a feeling that something will or is about to happen : PREMONITION — **pre·sen·ti·men·tal** \-,zent-ə-'ment-ᵊl\ *adj*

pres·ent·ly \'prez-ᵊnt-lē\ *adv* **1** *archaic* : at once **2** : before long : without undue delay **3** : at the present time : NOW

syn PRESENTLY, SHORTLY, SOON, DIRECTLY *shared meaning element* : after a little while

pre·sent·ment \pri-'zent-mənt\ *n* **1** : the act of presenting to an authority a formal statement of a matter to be dealt with; *specif* : the notice taken or statement made by a grand jury of an offense from their own knowledge without a bill of indictment laid before them **2** : the act of offering at the proper time and place a document (as a bill of exchange) that calls for acceptance or payment by another **3 a** : the act of presenting to view or consciousness **b** : something set forth, presented, or exhibited **c** : the aspect in which something is presented

present participle *n* : a participle that typically expresses present action in relation to the time expressed by the finite verb in its clause and that in English is formed with the suffix *-ing* and is used in the formation of the progressive tenses

present perfect *adj* : of, relating to, or constituting a verb tense that is formed in English with *have* and that expresses action or state completed at the time of speaking — **present perfect** *n*

present tense *n* : the tense of a verb that expresses action or state in the present time and is used of what occurs or is true at the time of speaking and of what is habitual or characteristic or is always or necessarily true, that is sometimes used to refer to action in the past (as in the historical present), and that is sometimes used for future events

pres·er·va·tion·ist \,prez-ər-'vā-sh(ə-)nəst\ *n* : one that advocates preservation (as of a biological species or a historical landmark)

[1]**pre·ser·va·tive** \pri-'zər-vət-iv\ *adj* : having the power of preserving

[2]**preservative** *n* : something that preserves or has the power of preserving; *specif* : an additive used to protect against decay, discoloration, or spoilage

[1]**pre·serve** \pri-'zərv\ *vb* **pre·served; pre·serv·ing** [ME *preserven,* fr. MF *preserver,* fr. ML *praeservare,* fr. LL, to observe beforehand, fr. L *prae-* + *servare* to keep, guard, observe — more at CONSERVE] *vt* **1** : to keep safe from injury, harm, or destruction : PROTECT **2 a** : to keep alive, intact, or free from decay **b** : MAINTAIN **3 a** : to keep or save from decomposition **b** : to can, pickle, or similarly prepare for future use **4** : to keep up and reserve for personal or special use ~ *vi* **1** : to make preserves **2** : to raise and protect game for purposes of sport **3** : to stand preserving (as by canning) **syn** see SAVE — **pre·serv·able** \-'zər-və-bəl\ *adj* — **pres·er·va·tion** \,prez-ər-'vā-shən\ *n* — **pre·serv·er** \pri-'zər-vər\ *n*

[2]**preserve** *n* **1** : fruit canned or made into jams or jellies or cooked whole or in large pieces in a syrup so as to keep its shape — often used in pl. **2** : an area restricted for the protection and preservation of natural resources (as animals or trees); *esp* : one used primarily for regulated hunting or fishing **3** : something regarded as reserved for certain persons

pre·set \(')prē-'set\ *vt* **-set; -set·ting** : to set beforehand — **pre·set·ta·ble** \-'set-ə-bəl\ *adj*

pre·shrunk \'prē-'shrəŋk, *esp South* -'srəŋk\ *adj* : of, relating to, or being material (as a textile fabric) subjected to a shrinking process during manufacture usu. to reduce later shrinking

pre·side \pri-'zīd\ *vi* **pre·sid·ed; pre·sid·ing** [L *praesidēre* to guard, preside over, lit., to sit in front of, sit at the head of, fr. *prae-* + *sedēre* to sit — more at SIT] **1 a** : to occupy the place of authority : act as president, chairman, or moderator **b** : to occupy a position similar to that of a president or chairman **2** : to exercise guidance, direction, or control **3** : to occupy a position of featured instrumental performer — usu. used with *at* <*presided* at the organ> — **pre·sid·er** *n*

pres·i·den·cy \'prez-əd-ən-sē, 'prez-dən- *also* 'prez-ə-,den(t)-sē\ *n, pl* **-cies** **1 a** : the office of president **b** (1) : the office of president of the U.S. (2) : the American governmental institution comprising the office of president and various associated administrative and policy-making agencies **2** : the term during which a president holds office **3** : the action or function of one that presides : SUPERINTENDENCE **4** : a Mormon executive council of the church or a stake consisting of a president and two counselors

pres·i·dent \'prez-əd-ənt, 'prez-dənt *also* 'prez-ə-,dent\ *n* [ME, fr. MF, fr. L *praesident-, praesidens,* fr. prp. of *praesidēre*] **1** : an official chosen to preside over a meeting or assembly **2** : an appointed governor of a subordinate political unit **6 :** the chief officer of an organization (as a corporation or institution) usu. entrusted with the direction and administration of its policies **4 :** the presiding officer of a governmental body **5 a :** an elected official serving as both chief of state and chief political executive in a republic having a presidential government **b :** an elected official having the position of chief of state but usu. only minimal political powers in a republic having a parliamentary government — **pres·i·den·tial** \ˌprez-(ə-)ˈden-chəl\ *adj* — **pres·i·den·tial·ly** \-ˈdench-(ə-)lē\ *adv*

presidential government *n* **:** a system of government in which the president is constitutionally independent of the legislature

pres·i·dent·ship \ˈprez-əd-ənt-ˌship, ˈprez-dənt- *also* ˈprez-ə-ˌdent-\ *n* **:** PRESIDENCY

pre·sid·i·al \pri-ˈsid-ē-əl, prī-, -ˈzid-\ *adj* [LL *praesidialis,* fr. L *praesidium* garrison, fr. *praesid-, praeses* guard, governor, fr. *praesidēre*] **1 :** of, having, or constituting a garrison **2 :** of or relating to a president **:** PRESIDENTIAL **3** [F *présidial,* fr. MF, alter. of *presidal,* fr. LL *praesidalis* of a provincial governor, fr. L *praesid-, praeses*] **:** PROVINCIAL 1

pre·sid·i·ary \-ē-ˌer-ē\ *adj* **:** PRESIDIAL 1

pre·si·dio \pri-ˈsēd-ē-ˌō, -ˈsid-, -ˈzēd-, -ˈzid-\ *n, pl* **-di·os** [Sp, fr. L *praesidium*] **:** a garrisoned place; *esp* **:** a military post or fortified settlement in areas currently or orig. under Spanish control

pre·sid·i·um \pri-ˈsid-ē-əm, prī-, -ˈzid-\ *n, pl* **-ia** \-ē-ə\ *or* **-iums** [Russ *prezidium,* fr. L *praesidium* garrison] **:** a permanent executive committee selected esp. in Communist countries to act for a larger body

pre·sig·ni·fy \(ˌ)prē-ˈsig-nə-ˌfī\ *vt* [L *praesignificare,* fr. *prae-* + *significare* to signify] **:** to intimate or signify beforehand **:** PRESAGE

[1]**pre·soak** \(ˌ)prē-ˈsōk\ *vt* **:** to soak beforehand

[2]**pre·soak** \ˈprē-ˈsōk\ *n* **1 :** a preparation used in presoaking clothes **2 :** an instance of presoaking

pre–So·crat·ic \ˌprē-sə-ˈkrat-ik, -sō-\ *adj* **:** of or relating to Greek philosophers before Socrates — **pre–Socratic** *n*

[1]**press** \ˈpres\ *n* [ME *presse,* fr. OF, fr. *presser* to press] **1 a :** a crowd or crowded condition **:** THRONG **b :** a thronging or crowding forward or together **2 a :** an apparatus or machine by which a substance is cut or shaped, an impression of a body is taken, a material is compressed, pressure is applied to a body, liquid is expressed, or a cutting tool is fed into the work by pressure **b :** a building containing presses or a business using presses **3 :** CLOSET, CUPBOARD **4 a :** an action of pressing or pushing **:** PRESSURE **b :** an aggressive pressuring defense employed in basketball often over the entire court area **5 :** the properly smoothed and creased condition of a freshly pressed garment <out of ~> **6 a :** PRINTING PRESS **b :** the act or the process of printing **c :** a printing or publishing establishment **7 a :** the gathering and publishing or broadcasting of news **:** JOURNALISM **b :** newspapers, periodicals, and often radio and television news broadcasting **c :** news reporters, publishers, and broadcasters **d :** comment or notice in newspapers and periodicals <is getting a good ~> **8 :** any of various pressure devices (as one for keeping sporting gear from warping when not in use) **9 :** a lift in weight lifting in which the weight is raised to shoulder height and then smoothly extended overhead without assist from the legs — compare CLEAN AND JERK, SNATCH

[2]**press** *vb* [ME *pressen,* fr. MF *presser,* fr. L *pressare,* fr. *pressus* pp. of *premere* to press; akin to L *prelum* press and perh. to Russ *peret'* to press] *vt* **1 :** to act upon through steady pushing or thrusting force exerted in contact **:** SQUEEZE **2 a :** ASSAIL, HARASS **b :** AFFLICT, OPPRESS **3 a :** to squeeze out the juice or contents of **b :** to squeeze with apparatus or instruments to a desired density, smoothness, or shape **4 a :** to exert influence on **:** CONSTRAIN **b :** to try hard to persuade **:** BESEECH, ENTREAT **5 :** to move by means of pressure **6 a :** to lay stress or emphasis on **b :** to insist on or request urgently **7 :** to follow through (a course of action) **8 :** to clasp in affection or courtesy **9 :** to make (a phonograph record) from a matrix ~ *vi* **1 :** to crowd closely **:** MASS **2 :** to force or push one's way **3 :** to seek urgently **:** CONTEND **4 :** to require haste or speed in action **5 :** to exert pressure **6 :** to take or hold a press **7 :** to employ a press in basketball — **press·er** *n*

[3]**press** *vb* [alter. of obs. *prest* (to enlist by giving pay in advance)] *vt* **1 :** to force into service esp. in an army or navy **:** IMPRESS **2 a :** to take by authority esp. for public use **:** COMMANDEER **b :** to take and force into any usu. emergency service ~ *vi* **:** to impress men as soldiers or sailors

[4]**press** *n* **1 :** impressment into service esp. in a navy **2** *obs* **:** a warrant for impressing recruits

press agent *n* [[1]*press*] **:** an agent employed to establish and maintain good public relations through publicity — **press–agent** *vb* — **press–agent·ry** \-ˈā-jən-trē\ *n*

press·board \ˈpres-ˌbō(ə)rd, -ˌbȯ(ə)rd\ *n* **1 :** a strong highly glazed composition board resembling vulcanized fiber **2 :** IRONING BOARD; *esp* **:** a small one for sleeves

press box *n* **:** a space reserved for reporters (as at a stadium)

press conference *n* **:** an interview given by a public figure to newsmen by appointment

pressed \ˈprest\ *adj, of food* **:** shaped, molded, or having liquid or juices extracted under pressure <~ duck>

press–gang \ˈpres-ˌgaŋ\ *n* [[4]*press*] **:** a detachment of men under command of an officer empowered to force men into military or naval service — **press–gang** *vt*

press·ing *adj* **1 :** urgently important **:** CRITICAL **2 :** EARNEST, WARM — **press·ing·ly** \-iŋ-lē\ *adv*

press·man \ˈpres-mən, -ˌman\ *n* **1 :** an operator of a press; *esp* **:** the operator of a printing press **2** *Brit* **:** NEWSPAPERMAN

press·mark \-ˌmärk\ *n* [[1]*press* (closet)] *chiefly Brit* **:** a mark assigned to a book to indicate its location in a library

press of sail : the fullest amount of sail that a ship can crowd on — called also *press of canvas*

pres·sor \ˈpres-ˌȯ(ə)r, -ər\ *adj* [LL, one that presses, fr. L *pressus,* pp. of *premere* to press — more at PRESS] **:** raising or tending to raise blood pressure; *also* **:** involving vasoconstriction

press release *n* **:** HANDOUT 3

press·room \ˈpres-ˌrüm, -ˌrům\ *n* **1 :** a room in a printing plant containing the printing presses **2 :** a room (as at the White House) for the use of members of the press

press·run \-ˌrən, -ˈrən\ *n* **:** a continuous operation of a printing press producing a specified number of copies; *also* **:** the number of copies printed

[1]**pres·sure** \ˈpresh-ər\ *n* **1 a :** the burden of physical or mental distress **b :** the constraint of circumstance **:** the weight of social or economic imposition **2 :** the application of force to something by something else in direct contact with it **:** COMPRESSION **3** *archaic* **:** IMPRESSION, STAMP **4 a :** the action of a force against an opposing force **b :** the force or thrust exerted over a surface divided by its area **c :** ELECTROMOTIVE FORCE **5 :** the stress or urgency of matters demanding attention **:** EXIGENCY <people who work well under ~> **6 :** the force of selection that results from one or more agents and tends to reduce a population of organisms <population ~> <predation ~> **7 :** atmospheric pressure **8 :** a sensation aroused by moderate compression of a body part or surface

[2]**pressure** *vt* **pres·sured; pres·sur·ing** \-(ə-)riŋ\ **1 :** to apply pressure to **2 :** PRESSURIZE **3 :** to cook in a pressure cooker

pressure cabin *n* **:** a pressurized cabin

pressure cooker *n* **:** an airtight utensil for quick cooking or preserving of foods by means of superheated steam under pressure — **pressure–cook** *vb*

pressure gauge *n* **:** a gauge for indicating fluid pressure

pressure group *n* **:** an interest group organized to influence public and esp. governmental policy but not to elect candidates to office

pressure point *n* **:** a point where a blood vessel runs near a bone and can be compressed (as to check bleeding) by the application of pressure against the bone

pressure suit *n* **:** an inflatable suit for high-altitude or space flight to protect the body from low pressure

pres·sur·iza·tion \ˌpresh-(ə-)rə-ˈzā-shən\ *n* **:** the action or process of pressurizing **:** the state of being pressurized

pres·sur·ize \ˈpresh-ə-ˌrīz\ *vt* **-ized; -iz·ing 1 :** to maintain near-normal atmospheric pressure in during high-altitude or space flight (as by means of a supercharger) **2 :** to apply pressure to **3 :** to design to withstand pressure — **pres·sur·iz·er** *n*

press·work \ˈpres-ˌwərk\ *n* **:** the operation, management, or product of a printing press; *esp* **:** the branch of printing concerned with the actual transfer of ink from form or plates to paper

prest \ˈprest\ *adj* [ME, fr. OF, fr. L *praestus* — more at PRESTO] *obs* **:** READY

pre·ster·num \ˈprē-ˈstər-nəm\ *n* [NL] **:** the anterior segment of the sternum of a mammal **:** MANUBRIUM

pres·ti·dig·i·ta·tion \ˌpres-tə-ˌdij-ə-ˈtā-shən\ *n* [F, fr. *prestidigitateur* prestidigitator, fr. *preste* nimble, quick (fr. It *presto*) + L *digitus* finger — more at DIGIT] **:** SLEIGHT OF HAND, LEGERDEMAIN — **pres·ti·dig·i·ta·tor** \-ˈdij-ə-ˌtāt-ər\ *n*

pres·tige \pre-ˈstēzh, -ˈstēj\ *n, often attrib* [F, fr. MF, conjuror's trick, illusion, fr. LL *praestigium,* fr. L *praestigiae,* pl., conjuror's tricks, irreg. fr. *praestringere* to tie up, blindfold, fr. *prae-* + *stringere* to bind tight — more at STRAIN] **1 :** standing or estimation in the eyes of people **:** weight or credit in general opinion **2 :** commanding position in men's minds ***syn*** see INFLUENCE

pres·tige·ful \-fəl\ *adj* **:** PRESTIGIOUS 2

pres·ti·gious \pre-ˈstij-əs, *2 is oftener* -ˈstēj-\ *adj* [L *praestigiosus,* fr. *praestigiae*] **1** *archaic* **:** of, relating to, or marked by illusion, conjuring, or trickery **2 :** having prestige **:** HONORED — **pres·ti·gious·ly** *adv* — **pres·ti·gious·ness** *n*

pres·tis·si·mo \pres-ˈtis-ə-ˌmō\ *adv or adj* [It, fr. *presto* + *-issimo* suffix denoting a high degree] **:** faster than presto — used as a direction in music

[1]**pres·to** \ˈpres-(ˌ)tō\ *adv or adj* [It, quick, quickly, fr. L *praestus* ready, fr. *praesto,* adv., on hand; akin to L *prae* before — more at FOR] **1 :** at once **:** QUICKLY **2 :** at a rapid tempo — used as a direction in music

[2]**presto** *n, pl* **prestos :** a presto musical passage or movement

[1]**pre·stress** \(ˌ)prē-ˈstres\ *vt* **:** to introduce internal stresses into (as a structural beam) to counteract the stresses that will result from applied load (as in incorporating cables under tension in concrete)

[2]**pre·stress** \ˈprē-ˈstres\ *n* **1 :** the process of prestressing **2 :** the stresses introduced in prestress **3 :** the condition of being prestressed

pre·sum·able \pri-ˈzü-mə-bəl\ *adj* **:** capable of being presumed **:** acceptable as an assumption — **pre·sum·ably** \-blē\ *adv*

pre·sume \pri-ˈzüm\ *vb* **pre·sumed; pre·sum·ing** [ME *presumen,* fr. LL & MF; LL *praesumere* to dare, fr. L, to anticipate, assume, fr. *prae-* + *sumere* to take; MF *presumer* to assume, fr. L *praesumere* — more at CONSUME] *vt* **1 :** to undertake without leave or clear justification **:** DARE **2 :** to expect or assume esp. with confidence **3 :** to suppose to be true without proof <*presumed* innocent until proved guilty> **4 :** to take for granted **:** IMPLY ~ *vi* **1 :** to act or proceed presumptuously or on a presumption **2 :** to go beyond what is right or proper — **pre·sum·er** *n*

pre·sum·ing *adj* **:** PRESUMPTUOUS — **pre·sum·ing·ly** \-ˈzü-miŋ-lē\ *adv*

pre·sump·tion \pri-ˈzəm(p)-shən\ *n* [ME *presumpcioun,* fr. OF *presumption,* fr. LL & L; LL *praesumption-, praesumptio* presumptuous attitude, fr. L, assumption, fr. *praesumptus,* pp. of *praesumere*] **1 :** presumptuous attitude or conduct **:** AUDACITY **2 a :** an attitude or belief dictated by probability **:** ASSUMPTION **b :** the ground, reason, or evidence lending probability to a belief **3**

: a legal inference as to the existence or truth of a fact not certainly known that is drawn from the known or proved existence of some other fact

pre·sump·tive \-'zəm(p)-tiv\ *adj* **1 :** giving grounds for reasonable opinion or belief **2:** based on probability or presumption **3** : being an embryonic precursor with the potential for forming a particular structure or tissue in the normal course of development <~ neural tissue> — **pre·sump·tive·ly** *adv*

pre·sump·tu·ous \pri-'zəm(p)-ch(ə-w)əs, -shəs\ *adj* [ME, fr. MF *presumptueux,* fr. LL *praesumptuosus,* irreg. fr. *praesumptio*] : overstepping due bounds : taking liberties : OVERWEENING — **pre·sump·tu·ous·ly** *adv* — **pre·sump·tu·ous·ness** *n*

pre·sup·pose \ˌprē-sə-'pōz\ *vt* [ME *presupposen,* fr. MF *presupposer,* fr. ML *praesupponere* (perf. indic. *praesupposui*), fr. L *prae-* + ML *supponere* to suppose — more at SUPPOSE] **1 :** to suppose beforehand **2 :** to require as an antecedent in logic or fact — **pre·sup·po·si·tion** \(ˌ)prē-ˌsəp-ə-'zish-ən\ *n*

pre·syn·ap·tic \ˌprē-sə-'nap-tik\ *adj* : situated or occurring just before a nerve synapse — **pre·syn·ap·ti·cal·ly** \-ti-k(ə-)lē\ *adv*

pre·tax \'prē-'taks\ *adj* : existing before provision for taxes

pre·teen \-'tēn\ *n* : a preadolescent child — **preteen** *adj*

pre·tend \pri-'tend\ *vb* [ME *pretenden,* fr. L *praetendere* to allege as an excuse, lit., to stretch in front of like a curtain, fr. *prae-* pre- + *tendere* to stretch — more at THIN] *vt* **1 :** to give a false appearance of being, possessing, or performing : PROFESS <does not ~ that he is a psychiatrist> **2 a :** to make believe : FEIGN <he ~*ed* deafness> **b :** to claim, represent, or assert falsely <~*ing* an emotion he could not really feel> **3 :** VENTURE, UNDERTAKE ~ *vi* **1 :** to feign an action, part, or role in play **2** : to put in a claim ***syn*** see ASSUME

pre·tend·ed *adj* : professed or avowed but not genuine <~ affection> — **pre·tend·ed·ly** *adv*

pre·tend·er \pri-'ten-dər\ *n* : one that pretends: as **a :** one who lays claim to something; *specif* : a claimant to a throne who is held to have no just title **b :** one who makes a false or hypocritical show <a ~ to spirituality —Elaine L. Lawrence>

pre·tense *or* **pre·tence** \'prē-ˌten(t)s, pri-'\ *n* [ME, fr. MF *pretensse,* fr. (assumed) ML *praetensa,* fr. LL, fem. of *praetensus,* pp. of L *praetendere*] **1 :** a claim made or implied; *esp* : one not supported by fact **2 a :** mere ostentation : PRETENTIOUSNESS <confuse dignity with pomposity and ~ —Bennett Cerf> **b** : a pretentious act or assertion **3 :** an inadequate or insincere attempt to attain a certain condition or quality **4 :** professed rather than real intention or purpose : PRETEXT <was there under false ~*s*> **5 :** MAKE-BELIEVE, FICTION **6 :** false show : SIMULATION <saw through his ~ of indifference>

syn PRETENSE, PRETENSION, MAKE-BELIEVE *shared meaning element* : the offering of something false as real or true

[1]**pre·ten·sion** \pri-'ten-chən\ *n* **1 :** an allegation of doubtful value : PRETEXT **2 :** a claim or an effort to establish a claim **3** : a claim or right to attention or honor because of merit **4** : ASPIRATION, INTENTION **5 :** VANITY, PRETENTIOUSNESS ***syn*** see PRETENSE, AMBITION — **pre·ten·sion·less** \-ləs\ *adj*

[2]**pre·ten·sion** \(ˈ)prē-'ten-chən\ *vt* [*pre-* + [2]*tension*] : PRESTRESS

pre·ten·tious \pri-'ten-chəs\ *adj* [F *prétentieux,* fr. *prétention* pretension, fr. ML *praetention-, praetentio,* fr. L *praetentus,* pp. of *praetendere*] **1 :** making usu. unjustified or excessive claims (as of value or standing) <the ~ fraud who assumes a love of culture that is alien to him —Richard Watts> **2 :** making demands on one's skill, ability, or means : AMBITIOUS <the ~ daring of the Green Mountain Boys in crossing the lake —*Amer. Guide Series: Vt.*> ***syn*** see SHOWY — **pre·ten·tious·ly** *adv* — **pre·ten·tious·ness** *n*

pret·er·it *or* **pret·er·ite** \'pret-ə-rət\ *adj* [ME *preterit,* fr. MF, fr. L *praeteritus,* fr. pp. of *praeterire* to go by, pass, fr. *praeter* beyond, past, by (fr. compar. of *prae* before) + *ire* to go — more at FOR, ISSUE] **1** *archaic* : BYGONE, FORMER **2 :** of, relating to, or constituting a verb tense that indicates action in the past without reference to duration, continuance, or repetition — **preterit** *n*

pre·ter·mi·nal \(ˈ)prē-'tərm-nəl, -ən-ᵊl\ *adj* : occurring before death

pre·ter·mis·sion \ˌprēt-ər-'mish-ən\ *n* [L *praetermission-, praetermissio,* fr. *praetermissus,* pp. of *praetermittere*] : the act or an instance of pretermitting : OMISSION

pre·ter·mit \-'mit\ *vt* **-mit·ted; -mit·ting** [L *praetermittere,* fr. *praeter* by, past + *mittere* to let go, send — more at SMITE] **1** : to let pass without mention or notice : OMIT **2 :** to leave undone : NEGLECT **3 :** to break off : SUSPEND

pre·ter·nat·u·ral \ˌprēt-ər-'nach(-ə)-rəl\ *adj* [ML *praeternaturalis,* fr. L *praeter naturam* beyond nature] **1 :** existing outside of nature **2 :** exceeding what is natural or regular : EXTRAORDINARY <wits trained to ~ acuteness by the debates —G. L. Dickinson> **3 :** inexplicable by ordinary means; *esp* : PSYCHIC <~ phenomena> — **pre·ter·nat·u·ral·ly** \-rə-lē, -'nach-ər-lē\ *adv* — **pre·ter·nat·u·ral·ness** \-'nach(-ə)-rəl-nəs\ *n*

pre·test \(ˈ)prē-'\ *n* : a preliminary test serving for exploration rather than evaluation — **pretest** *vt*

pre·text \'prē-ˌtekst\ *n* [L *praetextus,* fr. *praetextus,* pp. of *praetexere* to assign as a pretext, lit., to weave in front, fr. *prae-* + *texere* to weave — more at TECHNICAL] : a purpose or motive alleged or an appearance assumed in order to cloak the real intention or state of affairs ***syn*** see APOLOGY

pre·tor, pre·to·ri·an *var of* PRAETOR, PRAETORIAN

pre·treat \(ˈ)prē-'trēt\ *vt* : to treat beforehand

[1]**pre·treat·ment** \-mənt\ *n* : the process of pretreating

[2]**pretreatment** *adj* : occurring in or typical of the period prior to treatment

pret·ti·fy \'prit-i-ˌfī, 'pu̇rt-, 'pru̇t-\ *vt* **-fied; -fy·ing :** to make pretty — **pret·ti·fi·ca·tion** \ˌprit-i-fə-'kā-shən, ˌpu̇rt-, ˌpru̇t-\ *n*

pret·ti·ness \'prit-ē-nəs, 'pu̇rt-, 'pru̇t-\ *n* **1 :** the quality or state of being pretty **2 :** something pretty

[1]**pret·ty** \'prit-ē, 'pu̇rt-, 'pru̇t-\ *adj* **pret·ti·er; -est** [ME *praty, prety,* fr. OE *prættig* tricky, fr. *prætt* trick; akin to ON *prettr* trick] **1 a** : ARTFUL, CLEVER **b :** PAT, APT **2 a :** pleasing by delicacy or grace **b :** having conventionally accepted elements of beauty **c** : appearing or sounding pleasant or nice but lacking strength, force, manliness, purpose, or intensity <~ words that make no sense —Elizabeth B. Browning> **3 a :** MISERABLE, TERRIBLE <a ~ mess you've gotten us into> **b** *chiefly Scot* : STOUT **4** : moderately large : CONSIDERABLE <a very ~ profit> ***syn*** see BEAUTIFUL ***ant*** plain — **pret·ti·ly** \-ᵊl-ē\ *adv* — **pret·ty·ish** \-ē-ish\ *adj*

[2]**pret·ty** \ˌpu̇rt-ē, pərt-ē (*unstressed* pərt-), ˌprit-ē, ˌpru̇t-ē; *before "near(ly)" often without* -ē\ *adv* **1 :** in some degree : MODERATELY <~ cold weather> **2** *archaic* : in a pretty manner : PRETTILY

[3]**pret·ty** \'prit-ē, 'pu̇rt-ē, 'pru̇t-ē\ *vt* **pret·tied; pret·ty·ing :** to make pretty — usu. used with *up* <curtains to ~ up the room>

[4]**pretty** *like*[3]\ *n, pl* **pretties** **1 :** a pretty person or thing **2** *pl* : dainty clothes; *esp* : LINGERIE

pre·tu·ber·cu·lous \ˌprē-t(y)u̇-'bər-kyə-ləs\ *or* **pre·tu·ber·cu·lar** \-lər\ *adj* **1 :** preceding the development of lesions definitely identifiable as tuberculous **2 :** likely to develop tuberculosis

pret·zel \'pret-səl\ *n* [G *brezel,* deriv. of L *brachiatus* having branches like arms, fr. *brachium* arm — more at BRACE] : a brittle glazed and salted cracker typically having the form of a loose knot

prev *abbr* previous; previously

pre·vail \pri-'vā(ə)l\ *vi* [ME *prevailen,* fr. L *praevalēre,* fr. *prae-* pre- + *valēre* to be strong — more at WIELD] **1 :** to gain ascendancy through strength or superiority : TRIUMPH **2 :** to be or become effective or effectual **3 :** to use persuasion successfully <~*ed* on him to sing> **4 :** to be frequent : PREDOMINATE <the west winds that ~ in the mountains> **5 :** to be or continue in use or fashion : PERSIST <a custom that still ~*s*> ***syn*** see INDUCE

pre·vail·ing \-'vā-liŋ\ *adj* **1 :** having superior force or influence **2 a :** most frequent <~ winds> **b :** generally current : COMMON — **pre·vail·ing·ly** \-liŋ-lē\ *adv*

syn PREVAILING, PREVALENT, RIFE, CURRENT *shared meaning element* : general (as in circulation, acceptance, or use) in a given place or at a given time

prev·a·lence \'prev(-ə)-lən(t)s\ *n* **1 :** the quality or state of being prevalent **2 :** the degree to which something is prevalent; *esp* : the percentage of a population that is affected with a particular disease at a given time

prev·a·lent \-lənt\ *adj* [L *praevalent-, praevalens* very powerful, fr. prp. of *praevalēre*] **1** *archaic* : POWERFUL **2** *archaic* : being in ascendancy : DOMINANT **3 :** generally or widely accepted, practiced, or favored : WIDESPREAD ***syn*** see PREVAILING — **prevalent** *n* — **prev·a·lent·ly** *adv*

pre·var·i·cate \pri-'var-ə-ˌkāt\ *vi* **-cat·ed; -cat·ing** [L *praevaricatus,* pp. of *praevaricari* to walk crookedly, fr. *prae-* + *varicus* having the feet spread apart, fr. *varus* bent, knock-kneed; prob. akin to OE *wōh* crooked, L *vacillare* to sway, *vagus* wandering] : to deviate from the truth : EQUIVOCATE ***syn*** see LIE — **pre·var·i·ca·tion** \-ˌvar-ə-'kā-shən\ *n* — **pre·var·i·ca·tor** \-'var-ə-ˌkāt-ər\ *n*

pré·ve·nance \prā-və-näⁿs, prev-näⁿs\ *n* [F, fr. *prévenant,* prp. of *prévenir* to anticipate, fr. L *praevenire*] : attentiveness to or anticipation of others' needs

pre·ve·nient \pri-'vē-nyənt\ *adj* [L *praevenient-, praeveniens,* prp. of *praevenire*] : ANTECEDENT, ANTICIPATORY — **pre·ve·nient·ly** *adv*

pre·vent \pri-'vent\ *vb* [ME *preventen* to anticipate, fr. L *praeventus,* pp. of *praevenire* to come before, anticipate, forestall, fr. *prae-* + *venire* to come — more at COME] *vt* **1** *archaic* **a :** to be in readiness for (as an occasion) **b :** to meet or satisfy in advance **c** : to act ahead of **d :** to arrive before **2** *archaic* : to go before with spiritual guidance <O let thy grace . . . ever ~, accompany, and follow me —Thomas Ken> **3 :** to deprive of power or hope of acting or succeeding **4 :** to keep from happening or existing <steps to ~ war> **5 :** to hold or keep back : HINDER, STOP — often used with *from* ~ *vi* : to interpose an obstacle — **pre·vent·abil·i·ty** \-ˌvent-ə-'bil-ət-ē\ *n* — **pre·vent·able** *also* **pre·vent·ible** \-'vent-ə-bəl\ *adj* — **pre·vent·er** *n*

syn PREVENT, PRECLUDE, OBVIATE, AVERT, WARD OFF *shared meaning element* : to stop from advancing or occurring ***ant*** permit

pre·ven·ta·tive \-'vent-ət-iv\ *adj or n* : PREVENTIVE

pre·ven·tion \pri-'ven-chən\ *n* : the act of preventing or hindering

[1]**pre·ven·tive** \-'vent-iv\ *n* : something that prevents; *esp* : something used to prevent disease

[2]**preventive** *adj* **1 :** devoted to or concerned with prevention : PRECAUTIONARY <~ steps against soil erosion> **2 :** undertaken to forestall anticipated hostile action <~ war> — **pre·ven·tive·ly** *adv* — **pre·ven·tive·ness** *n*

pre·ver·bal \(ˈ)prē-'vər-bəl\ *adj* **1 :** occurring before the verb **2** : having not yet acquired the faculty of speech <a ~ child>

[1]**pre·view** \'prē-ˌvyü\ *vt* **1 :** to see beforehand; *specif* : to view or to show in advance of public presentation **2 :** to give a preliminary survey of

[2]**preview** *n* **1 :** an advance showing or performance (as of a motion picture or play) **2** *also* **pre·vue** \-ˌvyü\ : a showing of snatches from a motion picture advertised for appearance in the near future **3 :** a statement giving advance information : FORETASTE **4 :** a preliminary survey

pre·vi·ous \'prē-vē-əs\ *adj* [L *praevius* leading the way, fr. *prae-* pre- + *via* way — more at VIA] **1 :** going before in time or order **2 :** acting too soon : PREMATURE ***syn*** see PRECEDING ***ant*** subsequent — **pre·vi·ous·ly** *adv* — **pre·vi·ous·ness** *n*

previous question *n* : a parliamentary motion that the pending question be put to an immediate vote without further debate or amendment and that if defeated has the effect of permitting resumption of debate

previous to *prep* : prior to : BEFORE

[1]**pre·vi·sion** \prē-'vizh-ən\ *n* [LL *praevision-, praevisio,* fr. L *praevisus,* pp. of *praevidēre* to foresee, fr. *prae-* + *vidēre* to see — more at WIT] **1 :** FORESIGHT, PRESCIENCE **2 :** FORECAST, PROGNOSTICATION — **pre·vi·sion·al** \-'vizh-nəl, -ən-ᵊl\ *adj* — **pre·vi·sion·ary** \-'vizh-ə-ˌner-ē\ *adj*

[2]**prevision** *vt* **pre·vi·sioned; pre·vi·sion·ing** \-'vizh-(ə-)niŋ\ : FORESEE

pre·vo·cal·ic \ˌprē-vō-'kal-ik, -və-\ *adj* [ISV] : immediately preceding a vowel

pre·vo·ca·tion·al \ˌprē-vō-ˈkā-shnəl, -shən-ᵊl\ *adj* **:** given or required before admission to a vocational school

pre·war \ˈprē-ˈwȯ(ə)r\ *adj* **:** occurring or existing before a war

prexy \ˈprek-sē\ *also* **prex** \ˈpreks\ *n, pl* **prex·ies** *also* **prex·es** [*prexy* fr. *prex,* by shortening & alter. fr. *president*] *slang* **:** PRESIDENT — used chiefly of a college president

¹prey \ˈprā\ *n, pl* **preys** [ME *preie,* fr. OF, fr. L *praeda;* akin to L *prehendere* to grasp, seize — more at PREHENSILE] **1** *archaic* **:** SPOIL, BOOTY **2 a :** an animal taken by a predator as food **b :** one that is helpless or unable to resist attack **:** VICTIM <was ~ to his own appetites> **3 :** the act or habit of preying

²prey *vi* [ME *preyen,* fr. OF *preier,* fr. L *praedari,* fr. *praeda*] **1 :** to make raids for the sake of booty **2 a :** to seize and devour prey **b :** to commit violence or robbery or fraud **3 :** to have an injurious, destructive, or wasting effect — **prey·er** *n*

prf *abbr* proof

PRF *abbr* **1** pulse recurrence frequency **2** pulse repetition frequency

Pri·am \ˈprī-əm, -ˌam\ *n* [L *Priamus,* fr. Gk *Priamos*] **:** the father of Hector and Paris and king of Troy during the Trojan War

pri·a·pic \prī-ˈā-pik, -ˈap-ik\ *adj* [L *priapus* lecher, fr. *Priapus*] **:** PHALLIC

Pri·a·pus \prī-ˈā-pəs\ *n* [L, fr. Gk *Priapos*] **:** the Roman god of male generative power

¹price \ˈprīs\ *n* [ME *pris,* fr. OF, fr. L *pretium* price, money; akin to Skt *prati-* against, in return — more at PROS-] **1** *archaic* **:** VALUE, WORTH **2 a :** the quantity of one thing that is exchanged or demanded in barter or sale for another **b :** the amount of money given or set as consideration for the sale of a specified thing **3 :** the terms for the sake of which something is done or undertaken: as **a :** an amount sufficient to bribe one <believed every man had his ~> **b :** a reward for the apprehension or death of a person <a man with a ~ on his head> **4 :** the cost at which something is obtained <the ~ of freedom is restraint —J. Irwin Miller>

²price *vt* **priced; pric·ing 1 :** to set a price on **2 :** to find out the price of **3 :** to drive by raising prices excessively <*priced* themselves out of the market> — **pric·er** *n*

price–cut·ter \ˈprī-ˌskət-ər\ *n* **:** one that reduces prices esp. to a level designed to cripple competition

-priced \ˈprīst\ *adj comb form* **:** having (such) a price set <low-*priced* merchandise>

price–earn·ings ratio \ˈprī-ˈsər-niŋz-\ *n* **:** a measure of the value of a common stock determined as the ratio of its market price to its earnings per share and usu. expressed as a simple numeral

price index *n* **:** an index number expressing the level of a group of commodity prices relative to the level of the prices of the same commodities during an arbitrarily chosen base period and used to indicate changes in the level of prices from one period to another

price·less \ˈprī-sləs\ *adj* **1 a :** having a value beyond any price **:** INVALUABLE **b :** costly because of rarity or quality **:** PRECIOUS **2 :** having worth in terms of other than market value **3 :** surprisingly amusing, odd, or absurd ***syn*** see COSTLY

price support *n* **:** artificial maintenance of prices (as of a raw material) at some predetermined level usu. through government action

price tag *n* **1 :** a tag on merchandise showing the price at which it is offered for sale **2 :** PRICE, COST

price war *n* **:** a period of commercial competition characterized by the repeated cutting of prices below those of competitors

pric·ey *also* **pricy** \ˈprī-sē\ *adj* **pric·i·er; -est** *chiefly Brit* **:** EXPENSIVE <a holiday abroad will be too ~ —Robin Dewhurst>

¹prick \ˈprik\ *n* [ME *prikke,* fr. OE *prica;* akin to MD *pric* prick] **1 :** a mark or shallow hole made by a pointed instrument **2 a :** a pointed instrument or weapon **b :** a sharp projecting organ or part **3 :** an instance of pricking or the sensation of being pricked: as **a :** a nagging or sharp feeling of remorse, regret, or sorrow **b :** a slight sharply localized discomfort <the ~ of a needle> **4 :** PENIS — usu. considered vulgar **5 :** a disagreeable or contemptible person

²prick *vt* **1 :** to pierce slightly with a sharp point **2 :** to affect with anguish, grief, or remorse <doubt began to ~ him —Philip Hale> **3 :** to ride, guide, or urge on with or as if with spurs **:** GOAD **4 :** to mark, distinguish, or note by means of a small mark **5 :** to trace or outline with punctures **6 :** to remove (a young seedling) from the seedbed to another suitable for further growth **7 :** to cause to be or stand erect <a dog ~*ing* his ears> ~ *vi* **1 a :** to prick something or cause a pricking sensation **b :** to feel discomfort as if from being pricked **2 a :** to urge a horse with the spur **b :** to ride fast **3 :** THRUST **4 :** to become directed upward **:** POINT — **prick up one's ears :** to listen intently

prick·er \ˈprik-ər\ *n* **1 :** one that pricks: as **a :** a rider of horses **b :** a military light horseman **2 :** BRIAR, PRICKLE, THORN

prick·et \ˈprik-ət\ *n* [ME *priket,* fr. *prikke*] **1 a :** a spike on which a candle is stuck **b :** a candlestick with such a point **2 :** a buck in his second year

¹prick·le \ˈprik-əl\ *n* [ME *prikle,* fr. OE *pricle;* akin to OE *prica* prick] **1 :** a fine sharp process or projection; *esp* **:** a sharp pointed emergence arising from the epidermis or bark of a plant **2 :** a prickling sensation

²prickle *vb* **prick·led; prick·ling** \-(ə-)liŋ\ *vt* **1 :** to prick slightly **2 :** to produce prickles in ~ *vi* **:** to cause or feel a prickling or stinging sensation **:** TINGLE

prick·ly \ˈprik-lē, -ə-lē\ *adj* **prick·li·er; -est 1 :** full of or covered with prickles; *esp* **:** distinguished from related kinds by the presence of prickles **2 :** marked by prickling **:** STINGING <a ~ sensation> **3 a :** TROUBLESOME, VEXATIOUS <~ issues> **b :** easily irritated <had a ~ disposition> — **prick·li·ness** *n*

prickly ash *n* **:** a prickly aromatic shrub or small tree (*Zanthoxylum americanum*) of the rue family with yellowish flowers

prickly heat *n* **:** a noncontagious cutaneous eruption of red pimples with intense itching and tingling caused by inflammation around the sweat ducts

prickly pear *n* **:** any of a large genus (*Opuntia*) of cacti with yellow flowers and flat or terete joints usu. studded with tubercles bearing spines or prickly hairs; *also* **:** its pulpy pear-shaped edible fruit

prickly pear

prickly poppy *n* **:** any of a genus (*Argemone*) of plants of the poppy family with prickly leaves and white or yellow flowers; *esp* **:** a yellow-flowered Mexican annual (*A. mexicana*)

pricky *adj* **prick·i·er; -est :** PRICKLY

¹pride \ˈprīd\ *n* [ME, fr. OE *prȳde,* fr. *prūd* proud — more at PROUD] **1 :** the quality or state of being proud: as **a :** inordinate self-esteem **:** CONCEIT **b :** a reasonable or justifiable self-respect **c :** delight or elation arising from some act, possession, or relationship <parental ~> **2 :** proud or disdainful behavior or treatment **:** DISDAIN **3 a :** ostentatious display **b :** highest pitch **:** PRIME **4 :** a source of pride **:** the best in a group or class <this pup is the ~ of the litter> **5 :** a company of lions

²pride *vt* **prid·ed; prid·ing :** to indulge in pride
syn PRIDE, PLUME, PIQUE, PREEN *shared meaning element* **:** to congratulate (oneself) because of something one is, has, or has done or achieved

pride·ful \ˈprīd-fəl\ *adj* **:** full of pride: as **a :** DISDAINFUL, HAUGHTY **b :** EXULTANT, ELATED — **pride·ful·ly** \-fə-lē\ *adv* — **pride·ful·ness** *n*

prie–dieu \(ˈ)prē-ˈdyə(r), prē-dyœ̄\ *n, pl* **prie–dieux** \-ˈdyə(r)(z), -dyœ̄(z)\ [F, lit., pray God] **1 :** a kneeling bench designed for use by a person at prayer and fitted with a raised shelf on which the elbows or a book may be rested **2 :** a low armless upholstered chair with a high straight back

pri·er \ˈprī(-ə)r\ *n* **:** one that pries; *esp* **:** an inquisitive person

priest \ˈprēst\ *n* [ME *preist,* fr. OE *prēost,* modif. of LL *presbyter,* fr. Gk *presbyteros* elder, priest, compar. of *presbys* old man] **:** one authorized to perform the sacred rites of a religion esp. as a mediatory agent between man and God; *specif* **:** an Anglican, Eastern Orthodox, or Roman Catholic clergyman ranking below a bishop and above a deacon — **priest·ess** \ˈprē-stəs\ *n*

priest·hood \ˈprēst-ˌhu̇d, ˈprē-ˌstu̇d\ *n* **1 :** the office, dignity, or character of a priest **2 :** the whole body of priests

priest·ly \ˈprēst-lē\ *adj* **1 :** of or relating to a priest or the priesthood **:** SACERDOTAL **2 :** characteristic of or befitting a priest — **priest·li·ness** *n*

priest–rid·den \ˈprē-ˌstrid-ᵊn\ *adj* **:** controlled or oppressed by a priest

¹prig \ˈprig\ *n* [*prig* (to steal)] **:** THIEF

²prig *n* [prob. fr. ¹*prig*] **1** *archaic* **:** FELLOW, PERSON **2** *archaic* **:** FOP **3 :** one who offends or irritates by observance of proprieties (as of speech or manners) in a pointed manner or to an obnoxious degree — **prig·gery** \-ə-rē\ *n* — **prig·gish** \ˈprig-ish\ *adj* — **prig·gish·ly** *adv* — **prig·gish·ness** *n*

prig·gism \ˈprig-ˌiz-əm\ *n* **:** stilted adherence to convention

¹prill \ˈpril\ *vt* [perh. fr. E dial. *prill* (a running stream)] **1 :** to convert (as a molten solid) into spherical pellets **2 :** to make (as granular material) free flowing

²prill *n* **:** prilled material **:** a prilled substance

¹prim \ˈprim\ *vt* **primmed; prim·ming** [origin unknown] **1 :** to give a prim or demure expression to <*primming* her thin lips after every mouthful —John Buchan> **2 :** to dress primly

²prim *adj* **prim·mer; prim·mest 1 a :** stiffly formal and proper **:** DECOROUS **b :** PRUDISH **2 :** NEAT, TRIM <~ hedges> — **prim·ly** *adv* — **prim·ness** *n*

³prim *abbr* **1** primary **2** primitive

pri·ma ballerina \ˌprē-mə-\ *n* [It, leading ballerina] **:** the principal female dancer in a ballet company

pri·ma·cy \ˈprī-mə-sē\ *n* **1 :** the state of being first (as in importance, order, or rank) **:** PREEMINENCE <the ~ of intellectual and esthetic over materialistic values —T. R. McConnell> **2 :** the office, rank, or preeminence of an ecclesiastical primate

pri·ma don·na \ˌprim-ə-ˈdän-ə, ˌprē-mə-\ *n, pl* **prima donnas** [It, lit., first lady] **1 :** a principal female singer in an opera or concert organization **2 :** an extremely sensitive, vain, or undisciplined person

¹pri·ma fa·cie \ˌprī-mə-ˈfā-shə, -s(h)ē *also* -s(h)ē-ˌē\ *adv* [L] **:** at first view **:** on the first appearance <the arguments . . . seem *prima facie* true —*Trans-Action*>

²prima facie *adj* **1 :** true, valid, or sufficient at first impression **:** APPARENT <the theory . . . gives a *prima facie* solution —R. J. Butler> **2 :** SELF-EVIDENT **3 :** legally sufficient to establish a fact or a case unless disproved <*prima facie* evidence>

pri·mal \ˈprī-məl\ *adj* [ML *primalis,* fr. L *primus* first — more at PRIME] **1 :** ORIGINAL, PRIMITIVE <village life continued in its ~ innocence —Van Wyck Brooks> **2 :** first in importance **:** FUNDAMENTAL <our ~ concern> — **pri·mal·i·ty** \prī-ˈmal-ət-ē\ *n*

pri·mar·i·ly \prī-ˈmer-ə-lē *also* prə-\ *adv* **1 :** for the most part **:** CHIEFLY <has now become ~ a residential town —S. P. B. Mais> **2 :** in the first place **:** ORIGINALLY

¹pri·ma·ry \ˈprī-ˌmer-ē, ˈprīm-(ə-)rē\ *adj* [LL *primarius* basic, primary, fr. L, principal, fr. *primus*] **1 a :** first in order of time or development **:** PRIMITIVE <the ~ stage of civilization> **b :** of or relating to formations of the Paleozoic and earlier periods **2 a :** of first rank, importance, or value **:** PRINCIPAL <the ~ purpose> **b :** BASIC, FUNDAMENTAL <security is a ~ need> **c :** of, relating to, or constituting the principal quills of a bird's wing **d :** of or relating to agriculture, forestry, and the extractive industries or their products **e :** expressive of present or future time <~ tense> **f :** of, relating to, or constituting the strongest of the three or four degrees of stress recognized by most linguists <the first syllable of *basketball* carries ~ stress> **3 a :** DIRECT, FIRSTHAND <~ sources of information> **b :** not derivable from other colors, odors, or tastes **c :** preparatory to something else in a continuing process <~ instruction> **d :** of or relating to a primary school <~ education> **e :** belonging to the first group or order in successive divisions, combinations, or ramifications <~ nerves> **f :** of, relating to, or constituting the inducing current or its circuit in an induction coil or transformer **g :** directly derived from ores <~ metals> **h :** of, relating to, or being the amino acid sequence in proteins <~ protein structure> **4 :** resulting from the substitution of one of two or more atoms or groups in a molecule; *esp* **:** being or characterized by a carbon atom united by a single valence to only one chain or ring member **5 :** of, relating to, involving, or derived from primary meristem <~ tissue> <~ growth> **6 :** of, relating to, or involved in the production of organic substances by green plants <~ productivity>

[2]**primary** *n, pl* **-ries** **1 :** something that stands first in rank, importance, or value **:** FUNDAMENTAL — usu. used in pl. **2 a** [short for *primary planet*] **:** a planet as distinguished from its satellites **b :** the brighter component of a double star **3 :** one of the usu. 9 or 10 strong quills on the distal joint of a bird's wing — see BIRD illustration **4 a :** any of a set of colors from which all other colors may be derived **b :** a primary-color sensation **5 a :** CAUCUS **b :** an election in which qualified voters nominate or express a preference for a particular candidate or group of candidates for political office, choose party officials, or select delegates for a party convention

primary atypical pneumonia *n* **:** a usu. mild pneumonia believed to be caused by a virus

primary cell *n* **:** a cell that converts chemical energy into electrical energy by irreversible chemical reactions

primary coil *n* **:** the coil through which the inducing current passes in an induction coil or transformer

primary consumer *n* **:** HERBIVORE

primary meristem *n* **:** meristem consisting of direct derivatives of embryonic cells that are always active in growth

primary root *n* **:** the root of a plant that develops first and originates from the radicle

primary school *n* **1 :** a school usu. including the first three grades of elementary school but sometimes also including kindergarten **2 :** ELEMENTARY SCHOOL

primary syphilis *n* **:** the first stage of syphilis that is marked by the development of a chancre and the spread of the causative spirochete in the tissues of the body

primary wall *n* **:** the first-formed wall of a plant cell that is produced around the protoplast and usu. has plasmodesmata

pri·mate \ˈprī-ˌmāt *or esp for 1* -mət\ *n* [ME *primat,* fr. OF, fr. ML *primat-, primas* archbishop, fr. L, leader, fr. *primus*] **1** *often cap* **:** a bishop who has precedence in a province, group of provinces, or a nation **2** *archaic* **:** one first in authority or rank **:** LEADER **3 :** any of an order (Primates) of mammals comprising man together with the apes, monkeys, and related forms (as lemurs and tarsiers) — **pri·mate·ship** \-ˌship\ *n* — **pri·ma·tial** \prī-ˈmā-shəl\ *adj*

pri·ma·tol·o·gy \ˌprī-mə-ˈtäl-ə-jē\ *n* **:** the study of primates esp. other than recent man — **pri·ma·to·log·i·cal** \-mət-ᵊl-ˈäj-i-kəl\ *adj* — **pri·ma·tol·o·gist** \-mə-ˈtäl-ə-jəst\ *n*

[1]**prime** \ˈprīm\ *n* [ME, fr. OE *prīm,* fr. L *prima hora* first hour] **1 a** *often cap* **:** the second of the canonical hours **b :** the first hour of the day **2 a :** the earliest stage **b :** SPRING **c :** YOUTH **3 :** the most active, thriving, or successful stage or period <in the ~ of his life> **4 :** the chief or best individual or part **:** PICK <~ of the flock, and choicest of the stall —Alexander Pope> **5 :** a positive integer that has no factor except itself and one **6 a :** the first note or tone of a musical scale **:** TONIC **b :** the interval between two notes on the same staff degree **7 :** the symbol ′

[2]**prime** *adj* [ME, fr. MF, fem. of *prin* first, fr. L *primus;* akin to L *prior*] **1 :** first in time **:** ORIGINAL **2 a :** having no factor except itself and one <3 is a ~ number> **b :** having no common factor except one <12 and 25 are relatively ~> **3 a :** first in rank, authority, or significance **:** PRINCIPAL **b :** having the highest quality or value <~ television time> **c :** of the highest grade regularly marketed — used of meat and esp. beef **4 :** not deriving from something else **:** PRIMARY — **prime·ly** *adv* — **prime·ness** *n*

[3]**prime** *vb* **primed; prim·ing** [prob. fr. [1]*prime*] *vt* **1 :** FILL, LOAD **2 :** to prepare for firing by supplying with priming or a primer **3 :** to apply the first color, coating, or preparation to <~ a wall> **4 :** to put into working order by filling or charging with something <~ a pump with water> **5 :** to instruct beforehand **:** COACH <*primed* the witness> **6 :** STIMULATE ~ *vi* **:** to become prime — **prime the pump :** to take steps to encourage the growth or functioning of something

prime cost *n* **:** the combined total of raw material and direct labor costs incurred in production

prime meridian *n* **:** the meridian of 0° longitude which runs through the original site of the Royal Observatory at Greenwich, England, and from which other longitudes are reckoned east and west

prime minister *n* **1 :** the chief minister of a ruler or state **2 :** the official head of a cabinet or ministry; *esp* **:** the chief executive of a parliamentary government — **prime ministership** *n* — **prime ministry** *n*

prime mover *n* [trans. of ML *primus motor*] **1 :** the self-moved being that is the source of all motion **2 a :** an initial source of motive power (as a windmill, water wheel, turbine, or internal-combustion engine) designed to receive and modify force and motion as supplied by some natural source and apply them to drive machinery **b :** a powerful tractor or truck usu. with all-wheel drive **3 :** the original or most effective force in an undertaking or work <education is . . . a *prime mover* of cultural and societal change —R. C. Buck>

[1]**prim·er** \ˈprim-ər, *esp Brit* ˈprī-mər\ *n* [ME, fr. ML *primarium,* fr. LL, neut. of *primarius* primary] **1 :** a small book for teaching children to read **2 :** a small introductory book on a subject

[2]**prim·er** \ˈprī-mər\ *n* **1 a :** a device for priming; *esp* **:** a cap, tube, or wafer containing percussion powder or compound used to ignite an explosive charge **b :** a molecule (as a DNA) whose presence is required for formation of more molecules of the same kind **2 :** material used in priming a surface — called also *prime coat*

prime rate *n* **:** an interest rate at which preferred customers can borrow from banks and which is the lowest commercial interest rate available at a particular time and place — called also *prime interest rate*

pri·me·ro \pri-ˈme(ə)r-(ˌ)ō, -ˈmi(ə)r-\ *n* [modif. of Sp *primera*] **:** a card game popular in the 16th and 17th centuries

pri·me·val \prī-ˈmē-vəl\ *adj* [L *primaevus,* fr. *primus* first + *aevum* age — more at AYE] **1 :** of or relating to the earliest ages <100 acres of ~ forest which has never felt an ax —Mary R. Zimmer> **2 :** existing in or persisting from the beginning (as of a solar system or universe) <a ~ gas cloud> — **pri·me·val·ly** \-və-lē\ *adv*

prim·ing *n* **1 :** the act of one that primes **2 :** the explosive used in priming a charge **3 :** [2]PRIMER 2

pri·mip·a·ra \prī-ˈmip-ə-rə\ *n, pl* **-ras** *or* **-rae** \-ˌrē, -ˌrī\ [L, fr. *primus* first + *-para*] **1 :** an individual bearing a first offspring **2 :** an individual that has borne only one offspring — **pri·mi·par·i·ty** \ˌprī-mə-ˈpar-ət-ē\ *n* — **pri·mip·a·rous** \prī-ˈmip-ə-rəs\ *adj*

[1]**prim·i·tive** \ˈprim-ət-iv\ *adj* [ME *primitif,* fr. L *primitivus,* fr. *primitus* originally, fr. *primus* first — more at PRIME] **1 a :** not derived **:** ORIGINAL, PRIMARY **b :** assumed as a basis; *esp* **:** AXIOMATIC <~ concepts> **2 a :** of or relating to the earliest age or period **:** PRIMEVAL <the ~ church> **b :** closely approximating an early ancestral type **:** little evolved **c :** belonging to or characteristic of an early stage of development **:** CRUDE, RUDIMENTARY <~ technology> **d :** of, relating to, or constituting the assumed parent speech of related languages <~ Germanic> **3 a :** ELEMENTAL, NATURAL <the noble savage endowed with ~ virtue —Oscar Handlin> **b :** of, relating to, or produced by a relatively simple people or culture <~ art> **c :** NAIVE **d (1) :** SELF-TAUGHT, UNTUTORED <~ craftsmen> **(2) :** produced by a self-taught artist <a ~ painting> — **prim·i·tive·ly** *adv* — **prim·i·tive·ness** *n* — **prim·i·tiv·i·ty** \ˌprim-ə-ˈtiv-ət-ē\ *n*

[2]**primitive** *n* **1 a :** something primitive; *specif* **:** a primitive idea, term, or proposition **b :** a root word **2 a (1) :** an artist of an early period of a culture or artistic movement **(2) :** a later imitator or follower of such an artist **b (1) :** a self-taught artist **(2) :** an artist whose work is marked by directness and naiveté **c :** a work of art produced by a primitive artist **3 a :** a member of a primitive people **b :** an unsophisticated person

primitive area *n* **:** a tract within a U.S. national forest set aside for preservation in natural condition with no alteration or development beyond measures for fire prevention being permitted

prim·i·tiv·ism \ˈprim-ət-iv-ˌiz-əm\ *n* **1 a :** belief in the superiority of a simple way of life close to nature **b :** belief in the superiority of nonindustrial society to that of the present **2 :** the style of art of primitive peoples or primitive artists — **prim·i·tiv·ist** \-iv-əst\ *n or adj* — **prim·i·tiv·is·tic** \ˌprim-ət-iv-ˈis-tik\ *adj*

[1]**pri·mo** \ˈprē-(ˌ)mō, ˈprī-\ *adv* [L, fr. *primus*] **:** in the first place

[2]**pri·mo** \ˈprē-(ˌ)mō\ *n, pl* **primos** [It, fr. *primo* first, fr. L *primus*] **:** the first or leading part (as in a duet or trio)

pri·mo·gen·i·tor \ˌprī-mō-ˈjen-ət-ər\ *n* [LL, fr. L *primus* + *genitor* begetter, fr. *genitus,* pp. of *gignere* to beget — more at KIN] **:** ANCESTOR, FOREFATHER

pri·mo·gen·i·ture \-ˈjen-ə-ˌchů(ə)r, -i-chər, -ə-ˌt(y)ů(ə)r\ *n* [LL *primogenitura,* fr. L *primus* + *genitura* birth, fr. *genitus,* pp.] **1 :** the state of being the firstborn of the children of the same parents **2 :** an exclusive right of inheritance belonging to the eldest son

pri·mor·di·al \prī-ˈmȯrd-ē-əl\ *adj* [ME, fr. LL *primordialis,* fr. L *primordium* origin, fr. neut. of *primordius* original, fr. *primus* first + *ordiri* to begin — more at PRIME, ORDER] **1 a :** first created or developed **:** PRIMEVAL **b :** earliest formed in the growth of an individual or organ **:** PRIMITIVE **2 :** FUNDAMENTAL, PRIMARY <~ human joys —Sir Winston Churchill> — **pri·mor·di·al·ly** \-ē-ə-lē\ *adv*

pri·mor·di·um \-ē-əm\ *n, pl* **-dia** \-ē-ə\ [NL, fr. L] **:** the rudiment or commencement of a part or organ

primp \ˈprimp\ *vb* [perh. alter. of [1]*prim*] *vt* **:** to dress, adorn, or arrange in a careful or finicky manner ~ *vi* **:** to dress or groom oneself carefully <~*s* for hours before a date>

prim·rose \ˈprim-ˌrōz\ *n* [ME *primerose,* fr. MF] **:** any of a genus (*Primula* of the family Primulaceae, the primrose family) of perennial herbs with large tufted basal leaves and showy variously colored flowers

primrose path *n* **1 :** a path of ease or pleasure and esp. sensual pleasure <himself the *primrose path* of dalliance treads —Shak.> **2 :** a path of least resistance

primrose yellow *n* **1 :** a light to moderate greenish yellow **2 :** a light to moderate yellow

prim·u·la \ˈprim-yə-lə\ *n* [ML, fr. *primula veris,* lit., firstling of spring] **:** PRIMROSE

pri·mum mo·bi·le \ˌprī-məm-ˈmō-bə-lē, ˌprē-\ *n, pl* **primum mobiles** [ME, fr. ML, lit., first moving thing] **:** the outermost concentric sphere conceived in medieval astronomy as carrying the spheres of the fixed stars and the planets in its daily revolution

pri·mus \ˈprī-məs\ *n, often cap* [ML, one who is first, magnate, fr. L, first — more at PRIME] **:** the presiding bishop of the Scottish Episcopal Church

pri·mus in·ter pa·res \ˈprī-mə-ˌsint-ər-ˈpar-ēz, ˈprē-\ *n* [L] **:** first among equals

prin *abbr* **1** principal **2** principle

prince \ˈprin(t)s\ *n* [ME, fr. OF, fr. L *princip-, princeps,* lit., one who takes the first part, fr. *primus* first + *capere* to take — more at HEAVE] **1 a :** MONARCH, KING **b :** the ruler of a principality or state **2 :** a male member of a royal family; *esp* **:** a son of the king **3 :** a nobleman of varying rank and status **4 :** a person of high rank or of high standing in his class or profession — **prince·ship** \ˈprin(t)s-ˌship\ *n*

Prince Al·bert \prin-ˈsal-bərt\ *n* [Prince *Albert* Edward (later Edward VII king of England) †1910] : a long double-breasted frock coat

prince charming *n* [*Prince Charming,* hero of the fairy tale *Cinderella* by Charles Perrault] : a suitor who fulfills the dreams of his beloved; *also* : a man of often specious charm toward women

prince consort *n, pl* **princes consort** : the husband of a reigning female sovereign

prince·dom \ˈprin(t)s-dəm, -təm\ *n* **1** : the jurisdiction, sovereignty, rank, or estate of a prince **2** : PRINCIPALITY 3 — usu. used in pl.

prince·kin \ˈprin(t)-skən\ *n* : a diminutive prince

prince·let \ˈprin(t)-slət\ *n* : PRINCELING

prince·li·ness \-slē-nəs\ *n* **1** : princely conduct or character **2** : LUXURY, MAGNIFICENCE

prince·ling \ˈprin(t)-sliŋ\ *n* : a petty or insignificant prince

prince·ly \ˈprin(t)-slē\ *adj* **prince·li·er; -est** **1** : of or relating to a prince : ROYAL **2** : befitting a prince : NOBLE, MAGNIFICENT <~ manners> <a ~ sum> — **princely** *adv*

Prince of Wales \-ˈwā(ə)lz\ : the male heir apparent to the British throne — used as a title only after it has been specif. conferred by the sovereign

prince's–feath·er \ˈprin(t)-səz-ˌfeth-ər\ *n* : a showy annual plant (*Amaranthus hybridus hypochondriacus*) of the amaranth family often cultivated for its dense usu. red spikes of bloom

[1]**prin·cess** \ˈprin(t)-səs, ˈprin-ˌses, (*usual Brit*) prin-ˈses\ *n* **1** *archaic* : a woman having sovereign power **2** : a female member of a royal family; *esp* : a daughter or granddaughter of a sovereign **3** : the consort of a prince **4** : one very outstanding in a specified respect <a ~ of a seamstress> <a winding ~ of a river>

[2]**princess** *like* [1]\ *or* **prin·cesse** \prin-ˈses\ *adj* [F *princesse* princess, fr. *prince*] : close-fitting and usu. with gores from neck to flaring hemline <a ~ gown>

princess royal *n, pl* **princesses royal** : the eldest daughter of a sovereign

[1]**prin·ci·pal** \ˈprin(t)-s(ə-)pəl, -sə-bəl\ *adj* [ME, fr. OF, fr. L *principalis,* fr. *princip-, princeps*] **1** : most important, consequential, or influential : CHIEF **2** : of, relating to, or constituting principal or a principal — **prin·ci·pal·ly** \-ē, ˈprin(t)-splē\ *adv*

[2]**principal** *n* **1** : a person who has controlling authority or is in a leading position: as **a** : a chief or head man or woman **b** : the chief executive officer of an educational institution (as a high school) **c** : one who employs another to act for him subject to his general control and instruction; *specif* : the person from whom an agent's authority derives **d** : the chief or an actual participant in a crime **e** : the person primarily or ultimately liable on a legal obligation **f** : a leading performer : STAR **2** : a matter or thing of primary importance: as **a** (1) : a capital sum placed at interest, due as a debt, or used as a fund (2) : the corpus of an estate, portion, devise, or bequest **b** : the construction that gives shape and strength to a roof and is usu. one of several trusses; *broadly* : the most important member of a piece of framing — **prin·ci·pal·ship** \ˈprin(t)-s(ə-)pəl-ˌship, -sə-bəl-\ *n*

principal diagonal *n* : the diagonal in a square matrix that runs from upper left to lower right

prin·ci·pal·i·ty \ˌprin(t)-sə-ˈpal-ət-ē\ *n, pl* **-ties** **1 a** : the state, office, or authority of a prince **b** : the position or responsibilities of a principal (as of a school) **2** : the territory or jurisdiction of a prince : the country that gives title to a prince **3** *pl* : an order of angels — see CELESTIAL HIERARCHY

principal parts *n pl* : a series of verb forms from which all the other forms of a verb can be derived including in English the infinitive, the past tense, and the present and past participles

prin·cip·i·al \prin-ˈsip-ē-əl\ *adj* [L *principium*] : INITIAL, PRIMARY

prin·cip·i·um \prin-ˈsip-ē-əm, priŋ-ˈkip-\ *n, pl* **-ia** \-ē-ə\ [L, beginning, basis] : a fundamental principle

prin·ci·ple \ˈprin(t)-s(ə-)pəl, -sə-bəl\ *n* [ME, modif. of MF *principe,* fr. L *principium* beginning, fr. *princip-, princeps* one taking the first part — more at PRINCE] **1 a** : a comprehensive and fundamental law, doctrine, or assumption **b** (1) : a rule or code of conduct (2) : habitual devotion to right principles <a man of ~> **c** : the laws or facts of nature underlying the working of an artificial device **2** : a primary source : ORIGIN **3** : an underlying faculty or endowment : an ingredient (as a chemical) that exhibits or imparts a characteristic quality <such ~*s* of human nature as greed and curiosity> **4** *cap, Christian Science* : a divine principle : GOD — **in principle** : with respect to fundamentals <prepared to accept the proposition *in principle*>

prin·ci·pled \-s(ə-)pəld, -sə-bəld\ *adj* : exhibiting, based on, or characterized by principle — often used in combination <high-*principled*>

prin·cox \ˈprin-ˌkäks, ˈpriŋ-\ *n* [origin unknown] *archaic* : a pert youth : COXCOMB

prink \ˈpriŋk\ *vb* [prob. alter. of [2]*prank*] : PRIMP — **prink·er** *n*

[1]**print** \ˈprint\ *n* [ME *preinte,* fr. OF, fr. *preint,* pp. of *preindre* to press, fr. L *premere* — more at PRESS] **1 a** : a mark made by pressure : IMPRESSION **b** : something impressed with a print or formed in a mold **2** : a device or instrument for impressing or forming a print **3 a** : printed state or form **b** : the printing industry **4** : printed matter **5** : printed letters : TYPE **6 a** (1) : a copy made by printing (2) : a reproduction of an original work of art (as a painting) made by a photomechanical process (3) : an original work of art (as a woodcut, etching, or lithograph) intended for graphic reproduction and produced by or under the supervision of the artist who designed it **b** : cloth with a pattern or figured design applied by printing; *also* : an article of such cloth **c** : a photographic copy; *esp* : one made from a negative — **in print** : procurable from the publisher — **out of print** : not procurable from the publisher

[2]**print** *vt* **1 a** : to impress something in or on **b** : to stamp (as a mark) in or on something **2 a** : to make a copy of by impressing paper against an inked printing surface **b** (1) : to impress (as wallpaper) with a design or pattern (2) : to impress (a pattern or design) on something **c** : to publish in print **3** : to write in letters shaped like those of ordinary roman text type **4** : to make (a positive picture) on sensitized photographic surface from a negative or a positive ~ *vi* **1 a** : to work as a printer **b** : to produce printed matter **2** : to produce something in printed form

print·able \ˈprint-ə-bəl\ *adj* **1** : capable of being printed or of being printed from **2** : considered fit to publish — **print·abil·i·ty** \ˌprin(t)-ə-ˈbil-ət-ē\ *n*

printed circuit *n* : a circuit for electronic apparatus made by depositing conductive material in continuous paths from terminal to terminal on an insulating surface

printed matter *n* : matter printed by any of various mechanical processes that is eligible for mailing at a special rate

print·er \ˈprint-ər\ *n* : one that prints: as **a** : a person engaged in printing **b** : a device used for printing; *esp* : a machine for printing from photographic negatives **c** : a device (as a chain printer) that produces printout

printer's devil *n* : an apprentice in a printing office

printer's mark *n* : IMPRINT b

print·ery \ˈprint-ə-rē\ *n, pl* **-er·ies** : PRINTING OFFICE

print·ing *n* **1** : reproduction in printed form **2** : the art, practice, or business of a printer **3** : IMPRESSION 4c **4** *pl* : paper to be printed on

printing ink *n* : ink made for use in printing

printing office *n* : an establishment where printing is done

printing press *n* : a machine that produces printed copies

print·less \ˈprint-ləs\ *adj* : making, bearing, or taking no imprint

print·mak·ing \-ˌmā-kiŋ\ *n* : the design and production of prints by an artist — **print·mak·er** \-kər\ *n*

print·out \ˈprint-ˌau̇t\ *n* : a printed record produced automatically (as by a computer)

print out \(ˈ)print-ˈau̇t\ *vt* : to make a printout of

[1]**pri·or** \ˈprī(-ə)r\ *n* [ME, fr. OE & MF, fr. ML, fr. LL, administrator, fr. L, former, superior] **1** : the superior ranking next to the abbot of a monastery **2** : the superior of a house or group of houses of any of various religious communities — **pri·or·ate** \ˈprī-ə-rət\ *n* — **pri·or·ship** \ˈprī(-ə)r-ˌship\ *n*

[2]**pri·or** \ˈprī(-ə)r\ *adj* [L, former, superior, compar. of OL *pri* before; akin to L *priscus* ancient, *prae* before — more at FOR] **1** : earlier in time or order **2** : taking precedence (as in importance) *syn* see PRECEDING — **pri·or·ly** *adv*

pri·or·ess \ˈprī-ə-rəs\ *n* : a nun corresponding in rank to a prior

pri·or·i·ty \prī-ˈȯr-ət-ē, -ˈär-\ *n, pl* **-ties** **1 a** (1) : the quality or state of being prior (2) : precedence in date or position of publication — used of taxa **b** (1) : superiority in rank, position, or privilege (2) : legal precedence in exercise of rights over the same subject matter **2** : a preferential rating; *esp* : one that allocates rights to goods and services usu. in limited supply **3** : something meriting prior attention

syn PRIORITY, PRECEDENCE *shared meaning element* : the act, the fact, or the right of preceding another

prior to *prep* : in advance of : BEFORE

pri·o·ry \ˈprī-(ə-)rē\ *n, pl* **-ries** : a religious house under a prior or prioress

prise \ˈprīz\ *chiefly Brit var of* PRIZE

pri·sere \ˈprī-ˌsi(ə)r\ *n* [[1]*primary* + *sere*] : the succession of vegetational stages that occurs in passing from bare earth or water to a climax community

prism \ˈpriz-əm\ *n* [LL *prismat-, prisma,* fr. Gk, lit., anything sawn, fr. *priein* to saw] **1** : a polyhedron with two polygonal faces lying in parallel planes and with the other faces parallelograms — see VOLUME table **2 a** : a transparent body that is bounded in part by two nonparallel plane faces and is used to deviate or disperse a beam of light **b** : a prism-shaped decorative glass luster **3** : a crystal form whose faces are parallel to one axis; *esp* : one whose faces are parallel to the vertical axis

prisms 1

pris·mat·ic \priz-ˈmat-ik\ *adj* **1** : relating to, resembling, or constituting a prism **2 a** : formed by a prism **b** : resembling the colors formed by refraction of light through a prism <~ effects> **3** : highly colored : BRILLIANT **4** : having such symmetry that a general form with faces cutting all axes at unspecified intercepts is a prism <~ crystals> — **pris·mat·i·cal·ly** \-i-k(ə-)lē\ *adv*

pris·ma·toid \ˈpriz-mə-ˌtȯid\ *n* [LL *prismat-, prisma* prism] : a polyhedron that has all of its vertexes in two parallel planes — **pris·ma·toi·dal** \ˌpriz-mə-ˈtȯid-ᵊl\ *adj*

pris·moid \ˈpriz-ˌmȯid\ *n* : a prismatoid with two parallel similar and not congruent bases and faces that are trapezoids — **pris·moi·dal** \priz-ˈmȯid-ᵊl\ *adj*

[1]**pris·on** \ˈpriz-ᵊn\ *n* [ME, fr. OF, fr. L *prehension-, prehensio* act of seizing, fr. *prehensus,* pp. of *prehendere* to seize — more at PREHENSILE] **1** : a state of confinement or captivity **2** : a place of confinement: as **a** : a building in which persons are confined for safe custody while on trial for an offense or for punishment after trial and conviction **b** : an institution for the imprisonment of persons convicted of serious crimes : PENITENTIARY

[2]**prison** *vt* : IMPRISON, CONFINE

prison camp *n* **1** : a camp for the confinement of reasonably trustworthy prisoners usu. employed on government projects **2** : a camp for prisoners of war

pris·on·er \ˈpriz-nər, -ᵊn-ər\ *n* : a person deprived of his liberty and kept under involuntary restraint, confinement, or custody; *esp* : one on trial or in prison
prisoner of war : a person captured in war; *esp* : a member of the armed forces of a nation who is taken by the enemy during combat
prisoner's base *n* : a game in which players on each of two teams seek to tag and imprison players of the other team who have ventured out of their home territory
prison fever *n* : typhus fever
pris·sy \ˈpris-ē\ *adj* **pris·si·er; -est** [prob. blend of *prim* and *sissy*] : being prim and precise : FINICKY — **pris·si·ly** \ˈpris-ə-lē\ *adv* — **pris·si·ness** \ˈpris-ē-nəs\ *n*
pris·tane \ˈpris-ˌtān\ *n* [L *pristis* shark, sawfish; fr. its occurrence in the liver oils of sharks] : an isoprenoid hydrocarbon $C_{19}H_{40}$ that usu. accompanies phytane
pris·tine \ˈpris-ˌtēn *also* pris-ˈtēn, *esp Brit* ˈpris-ˌtīn\ *adj* [L *pristinus*; akin to L *prior*] **1** : belonging to the earliest period or state <the hypothetical ~ lunar atmosphere> **2 a** : uncorrupted by civilization <~ innocence> **b** : free from soil or decay : being fresh and clean — **pris·tine·ly** *adv*
prith·ee \ˈprith-ē, ˈprith-\ *interj* [alter. of (*I*) *pray thee*] *archaic* — used to express a wish or request
priv *abbr* **1** private; privately **2** privative
pri·va·cy \ˈprī-və-sē, *Brit also* ˈpriv-ə-\ *n, pl* **-cies** **1** : the quality or state of being apart from company or observation : SECLUSION **2** *archaic* : a place of seclusion **3** : SECRECY
pri·vat·do·cent *or* **pri·vat·do·zent** \prī-ˈvät-dō(t)-ˌsent\ *n* [G *privatdozent*, fr. *privat* private + *dozent* teacher] : an unsalaried university lecturer or teacher in German-speaking countries remunerated directly by students' fees
[1]**pri·vate** \ˈprī-vət\ *adj* [ME *privat*, fr. L *privatus*, fr. pp. of *privare* to deprive, release, fr. *privus* private, set apart; akin to L *pro* for — more at FOR] **1 a** : intended for or restricted to the use of a particular person, group, or class <a ~ park> **b** : belonging to or concerning an individual person, company, or interest <a ~ house> **c** (1) : restricted to the individual or arising independently of others <~ opinion> (2) : carried on by the individual independently of the usual institutions <~ study>; *also* : being educated by independent study or a tutor or in a private school <~ students> **d** : not general in effect <a ~ statute> **e** : of, relating to, or receiving hospital service in which the patient has more privileges than a semiprivate or ward patient **2 a** (1) : not holding public office or employment <a ~ citizen> (2) : not related to one's official position : PERSONAL <~ correspondence> **b** : being a private <a ~ soldier> **3 a** : withdrawn from company or observation : SEQUESTERED <a ~ retreat> **b** : not known or intended to be known publicly : SECRET **c** : unsuitable for public use or display — **pri·vate·ly** *adv* — **pri·vate·ness** *n*
[2]**private** *n* **1** *archaic* : one not in public office **2** *obs* : PRIVACY **3 a** : a person of low rank in various organizations (as a police or fire department) **b** : an enlisted man of the lowest rank in the marine corps or of one of the two lowest ranks in the army — **in private** : not openly or in public
private detective *n* : a person concerned with the maintenance of lawful conduct or the investigation of crime either as a regular employee of a private interest (as a hotel) or as a contractor for fees
private enterprise *n* : FREE ENTERPRISE
pri·va·teer \ˌprī-və-ˈti(ə)r\ *n* **1** : an armed private ship commissioned to cruise against the commerce or warships of an enemy **2** : the commander or one of the crew of a privateer — **privateer** *vi*
private eye *n* : PRIVATE DETECTIVE
private first class *n* : an enlisted man ranking in the army above a private and below a corporal and in the marine corps above a private and below a lance corporal
private investigator *n* : PRIVATE DETECTIVE
private law *n* : a branch of law concerned with private persons, property, and relationships — compare PUBLIC LAW
private parts *n pl* : the external genital and excretory organs
private school *n* : a school that is established, conducted, and primarily supported by a nongovernmental agency
private treaty *n* : a sale of property on terms determined by conference of the seller and buyer — compare AUCTION
pri·va·tion \prī-ˈvā-shən\ *n* [ME *privacion*, fr. MF *privation*, fr. L *privation-, privatio*, fr. *privatus*, pp. of *privare*] **1** : an act or instance of depriving : DEPRIVATION **2** : the state of being deprived; *esp* : lack of what is needed for existence
pri·vat·ism \ˈprī-və-ˌtiz-əm\ *n* [*private*] : the attitude of being uncommitted to or avoiding involvement in anything beyond one's immediate interests
[1]**priv·a·tive** \ˈpriv-ət-iv\ *n* : a privative term, expression, or proposition; *also* : a privative prefix or suffix
[2]**privative** *adj* : constituting or predicating privation or absence of a quality <*a-, un-, non-* are ~ prefixes> <*blind* is a ~ term> — **priv·a·tive·ly** *adv*
priv·et \ˈpriv-ət\ *n* [origin unknown] : an ornamental shrub (*Ligustrum vulgare*) of the olive family with half-evergreen leaves and small white flowers widely used for hedges; *broadly* : any of various similar shrubs of the same genus
[1]**priv·i·lege** \ˈpriv(-ə)-lij\ *n* [ME, fr. OF, fr. L *privilegium* law for or against a private person, fr. *privus* private + *leg-, lex* law — more at LEGAL] : a right or immunity granted as a peculiar benefit, advantage, or favor : PREROGATIVE; *esp* : such a right or immunity attached specif. to a position or an office
[2]**privilege** *vt* **-leged; -leg·ing** : to grant a privilege to
priv·i·leged \-lijd\ *adj* **1** : having or enjoying one or more privileges <~ classes> **2** : not subject to the usual rules or penalties because of some special circumstance; *esp* : not subject to disclosure in a court of law <a ~ communication> **3** : having a plenary indulgence attached to a mass celebrated thereon <a ~ altar>
priv·i·ly \ˈpriv-ə-lē\ *adv* : in a privy manner : PRIVATELY, SECRETLY
priv·i·ty \ˈpriv-ət-ē\ *n, pl* **-ties** [ME *privite*, fr. OF, fr. ML *privitat-, privitas*, fr. L *privus* private — more at PRIVATE] **1** : private or joint knowledge of a private matter; *esp* : cognizance implying concurrence **2 a** : a relationship between persons who successively have a legal interest in the same right or property **b** : an interest in a transaction, contract, or legal action to which one is not a party arising out of a relationship to one of the parties
[1]**privy** \ˈpriv-ē\ *adj* [ME *prive*, fr. OF *privé*, fr. L *privatus* private] **1** : belonging or relating to a person in his individual rather than his official capacity **2 a** : PRIVATE, WITHDRAWN **b** : SECRET **3** : admitted as one sharing in a secret <~ to the conspiracy>
[2]**privy** *n, pl* **priv·ies** **1** : a person having a legal interest of privity **2 a** : a small building having a bench with holes through which the user may evacuate and usu. lacking means of automatic discharge **b** : TOILET 3b
privy council *n* **1** *archaic* : a secret or private council **2** *cap P&C* : a body of officials and dignitaries chosen by the British monarch as an advisory council to the Crown usu. functioning through its committees **3** : a usu. appointive advisory council to an executive — **privy councillor** *n*
privy purse *n, often cap both Ps* : an allowance for the private expenses of the British sovereign
prix fixe \ˈprē-ˈfēks, -ˈfiks\ *n* [F, fixed price] **1** : TABLE D'HÔTE **2** : the price charged for a table d'hôte meal
[1]**prize** \ˈprīz\ *n* [ME *pris* prize, price — more at PRICE] **1** : something offered or striven for in competition or in contests of chance; *also* : PREMIUM 1d **2** : something exceptionally desirable **3** *archaic* : a contest for a reward : COMPETITION
[2]**prize** *adj* **1 a** : awarded or worthy of a prize **b** : awarded as a prize **c** : entered for the sake of a prize <a ~ drawing> **2** : outstanding of a kind <raised ~ hogs>
[3]**prize** *vt* **prized; priz·ing** [ME *prisen*, fr. MF *prisier*, fr. LL *pretiare*, fr. L *pretium* price, value — more at PRICE] **1** : to estimate the value of : RATE **2** : to value highly : ESTEEM *syn* see APPRECIATE
[4]**prize** *n* [ME *prise*, fr. OF, act of taking, fr. *prendre* to take, fr. L *prehendere* — more at PREHENSILE] **1** : something taken by force, stratagem, or threat; *esp* : property lawfully captured at sea in time of war **2** : an act of capturing or taking; *esp* : the wartime capture of a ship and its cargo at sea *syn* see SPOIL
[5]**prize** \ˈprīz\ *vt* **prized; priz·ing** [*prize* (lever)] : to press, force, or move with a lever : PRY
prize·fight \ˈprīz-ˌfīt\ *n* : a professional boxing match — **prize·fight·er** \-ər\ *n*
prize·fight·ing \-iŋ\ *n* : [2]BOXING
prize money *n* **1** : a part of the proceeds of a captured ship formerly divided among the officers and men making the capture **2** : money offered in prizes
priz·er \ˈprī-zər\ *n, archaic* : one that contends for a prize
prize·win·ner \ˈprīz-ˌwin-ər\ *n* : a winner of a prize
prize·win·ning \-ˌwin-iŋ\ *adj* : having won or of a quality to win a prize <a ~ design>
PRN *abbr* [L *pro re nata*] for the emergency; as needed
[1]**pro** \ˈprō\ *n, pl* **pros** [ME, fr. L, prep., for — more at FOR] **1** : an argument or evidence in affirmation <an appraisal of the ~*s* and cons> **2** : the affirmative side or one holding it
[2]**pro** *adv* [*pro-*] : on the affirmative side : in affirmation <much has been written ~ and con>
[3]**pro** \(ˌ)prō\ *prep* [L] : in favor of : FOR
[4]**pro** \ˈprō\ *n or adj* : PROFESSIONAL
PRO *abbr* public relations officer
[1]**pro-** *prefix* [ME, fr. OF, fr. L, fr. Gk, before, forward, forth, for, fr. *pro* — more at FOR] **1 a** : earlier than : prior to : before <*pro*thalamion> **b** : rudimentary : PROT- <*pro*nucleus> **2 a** : located in front of or at the front of : anterior to <*pro*cephalic> <*pro*ventriculus> **b** : front : anterior <*pro*thorax> **3** : projecting <*pro*gnathous>
[2]**pro-** *prefix* [L *pro* in front of, before, for — more at FOR] **1** : taking the place of : substituting for <*pro*cathedral> <*pro*caine> **2** : favoring : supporting : championing <*pro*-American>
proa \ˈprō-ə\ *var of* PRAU
pro·ac·tive \(ˈ)prō-ˈak-tiv\ *adj* [L *pro-* forward] : involving modification by a factor which precedes that which is modified <~ inhibition of memory>
prob *abbr* **1** probable; probably **2** problem
prob·a·bi·lism \ˈpräb-ə-bə-ˌliz-əm\ *n* [F *probabilisme*, fr. L *probabilis* probable] **1** : a theory that certainty is impossible esp. in the sciences and that probability suffices to govern belief and action **2** : a theory that in disputed moral questions any solidly probable course may be followed even though an opposed course is or appears more probable — **prob·a·bi·list** \-ləst\ *adj or n*
prob·a·bi·lis·tic \ˌpräb-ə-bə-ˈlis-tik\ *adj* **1** : of or relating to probabilism **2** : of, relating to, or based on probability
prob·a·bil·i·ty \ˌpräb-ə-ˈbil-ət-ē\ *n, pl* **-ties** **1** : the quality or state of being probable **2** : something (as an occurrence or circumstance) that is probable **3 a** (1) : the ratio of the number of outcomes in an exhaustive set of equally likely outcomes that produce a given event to the total number of possible outcomes (2) : the chance that a given event will occur **b** : a branch of mathematics concerned with the study of probabilities **4** : a logical relation between statements such that evidence confirming one confirms the other to some degree
probability density *n* : PROBABILITY DENSITY FUNCTION; *also* : a particular value of a probability density function
probability density function *n* **1** : PROBABILITY FUNCTION **2** : a function of a continuous random variable whose integral over an interval gives the probability that its value will fall within the interval
probability distribution *n* : PROBABILITY FUNCTION; *also* : PROBABILITY DENSITY FUNCTION 2
probability function *n* : a function of a discrete random variable that gives the probability that a specified value will occur
prob·a·ble \ˈpräb-(ə-)bəl\ *adj* [ME, fr. MF, fr. L *probabilis*, fr. *probare* to test, approve, prove — more at PROVE] **1** : supported by evidence strong enough to establish presumption but not proof <a ~ hypothesis> **2** : establishing a probability <~ evidence>

3 **:** likely to be or become true or real <~ events> — **prob·a·bly** \ˈpräb-(ə-)blē, ˈpräb-lē\ *adv*
syn PROBABLE, POSSIBLE, LIKELY *shared meaning element* **:** being such as may become true or actual *ant* certain, improbable

probable cause *n* **:** a reasonable ground for supposing that a criminal charge is well-founded

pro·band \ˈprō-ˌband, prō-ˈ\ *n* [L *probandus*, gerundive of *probare*] **:** SUBJECT 3c(2)

pro·bang \ˈprō-ˌbaŋ\ *n* [origin unknown] **:** a slender flexible rod with a sponge on one end used esp. for removing obstructions from the esophagus

[1]pro·bate \ˈprō-ˌbāt, *esp Brit* -bit\ *n* [ME *probat*, fr. L *probatum*, neut. of *probatus*, pp. of *probare*] **1 a :** the action or process of proving before a competent judicial authority that a document offered for official recognition and registration as the last will and testament of a deceased person is genuine **b :** the judicial determination of the validity of a will **2 :** the officially authenticated copy of a probated will

[2]pro·bate \-ˌbāt\ *vt* **pro·bat·ed; pro·bat·ing 1 :** to establish (a will) by probate as genuine and valid **2 :** to put (a convicted offender) on probation

probate court *n* **:** a court that has jurisdiction chiefly over the probate of wills and administration of deceased persons' estates

pro·ba·tion \prō-ˈbā-shən\ *n* **1 :** critical examination and evaluation or subjection to such examination and evaluation **2 a :** subjection of an individual to a period of testing and trial to ascertain fitness (as for a job or school) **b :** the action of suspending the sentence of a convicted offender and giving him freedom during good behavior under the supervision of a probation officer **c :** the state or a period of being subject to probation — **pro·ba·tion·al** \-shnəl, -shən-ᵊl\ *adj* — **pro·ba·tion·al·ly** \-ē\ *adv* — **pro·ba·tion·ary** \-shə-ˌner-ē\ *adj*

pro·ba·tion·er \-sh(ə-)nər\ *n* **1 :** one (as a newly admitted student nurse) whose fitness is being tested during a trial period **2 :** a convicted offender on probation

probation officer *n* **:** an officer appointed to investigate, report on, and supervise the conduct of convicted offenders on probation

pro·ba·tive \ˈprō-bət-iv\ *adj* **1 :** serving to test or try **:** EXPLORATORY **2 :** serving to prove **:** SUBSTANTIATING

pro·ba·to·ry \ˈprō-bə-ˌtōr-ē, -ˌtȯr-\ *adj* **:** PROBATIVE

[1]probe \ˈprōb\ *n* [ML *proba* examination, fr. L *probare*] **1 :** a slender surgical instrument for examining a cavity **2 a :** a pointed metal tip for making electrical contact with a circuit element being checked **b :** a device used to penetrate or send back information esp. from outer space **c :** a pipe on the receiving airplane thrust into the drogue of the delivering airplane in air refueling **3 a :** the action of probing **b :** a penetrating or critical investigation **:** INQUIRY **c :** a tentative exploratory advance or survey

[2]probe *vb* **probed; prob·ing** *vt* **1 :** to examine with or as if with a probe **2 :** to investigate thoroughly ~ *vi* **:** to make an exploratory investigation *syn* see ENTER — **prob·er** *n*

pro·ben·e·cid \prō-ˈben-ə-səd\ *n* [irreg. fr. *propyl* + *benzoic acid*] **:** a drug $C_{13}H_{19}NO_4S$ that acts on renal tubular function and is used to inhibit the excretion of some drugs (as penicillin) and to increase the excretion of urates in gout

prob·it \ˈpräb-ət\ *n* [*probability unit*] **:** a unit of measurement of statistical probability based on deviations from the mean of a normal distribution

pro·bi·ty \ˈprō-bət-ē\ *n* [MF *probité*, fr. L *probitat-*, *probitas*, fr. *probus* honest — more at PROVE] **:** adherence to the highest principles and ideals **:** UPRIGHTNESS *syn* see HONESTY

[1]prob·lem \ˈpräb-ləm, ˈpräb-ᵊm, -ˌlem\ *n* [ME *probleme*, fr. MF, fr. L *problema*, fr. Gk *problēma*, lit., something thrown forward, fr. *proballein* to throw forward, fr. *pro-* forward + *ballein* to throw — more at PRO-, DEVIL] **1 a :** a question raised for inquiry, consideration, or solution **b :** a proposition in mathematics or physics stating something to be done **2 a :** an intricate unsettled question **b :** a source of perplexity, distress, or vexation *syn* see MYSTERY

[2]problem *adj* **1 :** dealing with a problem of human conduct or social relationship <a ~ play> **2 :** difficult to deal with <a ~ child>

prob·lem·at·ic \ˌpräb-lə-ˈmat-ik\ *or* **prob·lem·at·i·cal** \-i-kəl\ *adj* **1 a :** difficult to solve or decide **:** PUZZLING **b :** not definite or settled <their future remains ~> **c :** open to question or debate **:** QUESTIONABLE **2 :** expressing or supporting a possibility *syn* see DOUBTFUL — **prob·lem·at·i·cal·ly** \-i-k(ə-)lē\ *adv*

pro·bos·ci·de·an \prə-ˌbäs-ə-ˈdē-ən\ *or* **pro·bos·cid·i·an** \prə-ˌbäs-ˈid-ē-ən, (ˌ)prō-\ *n* [deriv. of L *proboscid-*, *proboscis*] **:** any of an order (Proboscidea) of large mammals comprising the elephants and extinct related forms — **proboscidean** *adj*

pro·bos·cis \prə-ˈbäs-əs\ *n, pl* **-boscises** *also* **-bos·ci·des** \-ˈbäs-ə-ˌdēz\ [L, fr. Gk *proboskis*, fr. *pro-* + *boskein* to feed; akin to Lith *gauja* herd] **1 a :** the trunk of an elephant; *also* **:** any long flexible snout **b :** the human nose esp. when prominent **2 :** any of various elongated or extensible tubular processes (as the sucking organ of a butterfly) of the oral region of an invertebrate

proc *abbr* proceedings

pro·caine \ˈprō-ˌkān\ *n* [ISV [2]*pro-* + *cocaine*] **:** a basic ester $C_{13}H_{20}N_2O_2$ of para-aminobenzoic acid; *also* **:** its crystalline hydrochloride used as a local anesthetic

pro·cam·bi·um \(ˈ)prō-ˈkam-bē-əm\ *n* [NL] **:** the part of a plant meristem that forms cambium and primary vascular tissues — **pro·cam·bi·al** \-bē-əl\ *adj*

pro·cary·ote \(ˈ)prō-ˈkar-ē-ˌōt\ *n* [*pro-* + Gk *karyōtos* provided with nuts — more at EUCARYOTE] **:** a cellular organism (as a bacterium or a blue-green alga) that does not have a distinct nucleus — compare EUCARYOTE — **pro·cary·ot·ic** \ˌprō-ˌkar-ē-ˈät-ik\ *adj*

pro·ca·the·dral \ˌprō-kə-ˈthē-drəl\ *n* **:** a parish church used as a cathedral

pro·ce·dur·al \prə-ˈsēj-(ə-)rəl\ *adj* **:** of or relating to procedure esp. of courts or other bodies administering substantive law — **pro·ce·dur·al·ly** \-ē\ *adv*

pro·ce·dure \prə-ˈsē-jər\ *n* [F *procédure*, fr. MF, fr. *proceder*] **1 a :** a particular way of accomplishing something or of acting **b :** a step in a procedure **2 :** a series of steps followed in a regular definite order <legal ~> **3 a :** a traditional or established way of doing things **b :** PROTOCOL 3

pro·ceed \prō-ˈsēd, prə-\ *vi* [ME *proceden*, fr. MF *proceder*, fr. L *procedere*, fr. *pro-* forward + *cedere* to go — more at PRO-, CEDE] **1 :** to come forth from a source **:** ISSUE **2 a :** to continue after a pause or interruption **b :** to go on in an orderly regulated way **3 a :** to begin and carry on an action, process, or movement **b :** to be in the process of being accomplished **4 :** to move along a course **:** ADVANCE *syn* see SPRING

pro·ceed·ing *n* **1 :** PROCEDURE **2** *pl* **:** EVENTS, HAPPENINGS **3** *pl* **:** legal action <divorce ~*s*> **4 :** AFFAIR, TRANSACTION **5** *pl* **:** an official record of things said or done

pro·ceeds \ˈprō-ˌsēdz\ *n pl* **1 :** the total amount brought in <the ~ of a sale> **2 :** the net amount received (as for a check or from an insurance settlement) after deduction of any discount or charges

pro·ce·phal·ic \ˌprō-sə-ˈfal-ik\ *adj* **:** relating to, forming, or situated on or near the front of the head

pro·cer·coid \(ˈ)prō-ˈsər-ˌkȯid\ *n* [*pro-* + Gk *kerkos* tail] **:** the solid first parasitic larva of some tapeworms that develops usu. in the body cavity of a copepod

[1]pro·cess \ˈpräs-ˌes, ˈprōs-, -əs\ *n, pl* **pro·cess·es** \-ˌes-əz, -ə-səz, -ə-ˌsēz\ [ME *proces*, fr. MF, fr. L *processus*, fr. *processus*, pp. of *procedere*] **1 a :** PROGRESS, ADVANCE **b :** something going on **:** PROCEEDING **2 a :** a natural phenomenon marked by gradual changes that lead toward a particular result <the ~ of growth> **b :** a series of actions or operations conducing to an end; *esp* **:** a continuous operation or treatment esp. in manufacture **3 a :** the whole course of proceedings in a legal action **b :** the summons, mandate, or writ used by a court to compel the appearance of the defendant in a legal action or compliance with its orders **4 :** a prominent or projecting part of an organism or organic structure <a bone ~> **5 :** [5]CONK

[2]process *vt* **1 a :** to proceed against by law **:** PROSECUTE **b (1) :** to take out a summons against **(2) :** to serve a summons on **2 a :** to subject to a special process or treatment (as in the course of manufacture) **b :** to work (hair) into a conk

[3]process *adj* **1 :** treated or made by a special process esp. when involving synthesis or artificial modification **2 :** made by or used in a mechanical or photomechanical duplicating process **3 :** of or involving illusory effects usu. introduced during processing of the film <a ~ motion-picture scene>

[4]pro·cess \prə-ˈses\ *vi* [back-formation fr. [1]*procession*] *chiefly Brit* **:** to move in a procession

pro·cess cheese \ˌpräs-ˌes-, ˌprōs-, -əs-\ *n* **:** a cheese made by blending several lots of cheese

pro·cess·ible *or* **pro·cess·able** \ˈpräs-ˌes-ə-bəl, ˈprōs-\ *adj* **:** suitable for processing **:** capable of being processed — **pro·cess·ibil·i·ty** *or* **pro·cess·abil·i·ty** \ˌpräs-ˌes-ə-ˈbil-ət-ē, ˌprōs-\ *n*

[1]pro·ces·sion \prə-ˈsesh-ən\ *n* **1 a :** continuous forward movement **:** PROGRESSION **b :** EMANATION <the Holy Ghost's ~ from the Father> **2 a :** a group of individuals moving along in an orderly often ceremonial way **b :** SUCCESSION, SEQUENCE

[2]procession *vi, archaic* **:** to go in procession

[1]pro·ces·sion·al \prə-ˈsesh-nəl, -ən-ᵊl\ *n* **1 :** a book containing material for a procession **2 :** a musical composition (as a hymn) designed for a procession **3 :** a ceremonial procession

[2]processional *adj* **:** of, relating to, or moving in a procession — **pro·ces·sion·al·ly** \-ē\ *adv*

pro·ces·sor \ˈpräs-ˌes-ər, ˈprōs-\ *n* **1 :** one that processes <food ~> **2 a (1) :** COMPUTER **(2) :** the part of a computer system that operates on data — called also *central processing unit* **b :** a computer program (as a compiler) that puts another program into a form acceptable to the computer

process printing *n* **:** a method of printing from halftone plates in usu. three or more colors so that nearly any hue may be reproduced

pro·cès–ver·bal \prō-ˌsā-vər-ˈbäl, -(ˌ)ver-\ *n, pl* **pro·cès–ver·baux** \-ˈbō\ [F, lit., verbal trial] **:** an official written record

pro·claim \prō-ˈklām, prə-\ *vt* [ME *proclamen*, fr. MF or L; MF *proclamer*, fr. L *proclamare*, fr. *pro-* before + *clamare* to cry out — more at PRO-, CLAIM] **1 a :** to declare publicly, typically insistently, proudly, or defiantly and in either speech or writing **:** ANNOUNCE **b :** to give outward indication of **:** SHOW **2 :** to declare or declare to be solemnly, officially, or formally <~ an amnesty> <~ the country a republic> **3 :** to praise or glorify openly or publicly **:** EXTOL *syn* see DECLARE — **pro·claim·er** *n*

proc·la·ma·tion \ˌpräk-lə-ˈmā-shən\ *n* [ME *proclamacion*, fr. MF *proclamation*, fr. L *proclamation-*, *proclamatio*, fr. *proclamatus*, pp. of *proclamare*] **1 :** the action of proclaiming **:** the state of being proclaimed **2 :** something proclaimed; *specif* **:** an official formal public announcement

pro·cli·max \(ˈ)prō-ˈklī-ˌmaks\ *n* **:** an ecological community that suggests a climax in stability and permanence but is not primarily the product of climate

pro·clit·ic \prō-ˈklit-ik\ *adj* [NL *procliticus*, fr. Gk *pro-* + LL *-cliticus* (as in *encliticus* enclitic)] **:** of, relating to, or constituting a word or particle without sentence stress that is accentually dependent upon a following stressed word and is pronounced with it as a phonetic unit — **proclitic** *n*

pro·cliv·i·ty \prō-ˈkliv-ət-ē\ *n, pl* **-ties** [L *proclivitas*, fr. *proclivis* sloping, prone, fr. *pro-* forward + *clivus* hill — more at PRO-, DECLIVITY] **:** an inclination or predisposition toward something; *esp* **:** a strong inherent inclination toward something objectionable *syn* see LEANING

Proc·ne \'präk-nē\ *n* [L, fr. Gk *Proknē*] **:** the wife of Tereus changed into a swallow while fleeing with her sister from Tereus

pro·con·sul \(ˌ)prō-'kän(t)-səl\ *n* [ME, fr. L, fr. *pro consule* for a consul] **1 :** a governor or military commander of an ancient Roman province **2 :** an administrator in a modern colony, dependency, or occupied area usu. with wide powers — **pro·con·su·lar** \-s(ə-)lər\ *adj* — **pro·con·su·late** \-s(ə-)lət\ *n* — **pro·con·sul·ship** \-səl-ˌship\ *n*

pro·cras·ti·nate \p(r)ə-'kras-tə-ˌnāt, prō-\ *vb* **-nat·ed; -nat·ing** [L *procrastinatus,* pp. of *procrastinare,* fr. *pro-* forward + *crastinus* of tomorrow, fr. *cras* tomorrow] *vt* **:** to put off intentionally and habitually ~ *vi* **:** to put off intentionally and reprehensibly the doing of something that should be done — **pro·cras·ti·na·tion** \-ˌkras-tə-'nā-shən\ *n* — **pro·cras·ti·na·tor** \-'kras-tə-ˌnāt-ər\ *n*

pro·cre·ant \'prō-krē-ənt\ *adj* **1 :** producing offspring **2** *archaic* **:** of or relating to procreation

pro·cre·ate \-ˌāt\ *vb* **-at·ed; -at·ing** [L *procreatus,* pp. of *procreare,* fr. *pro-* forth + *creare* to create — more at PRO-, CREATE] *vt* **:** to beget or bring forth (offspring) **:** PROPAGATE ~ *vi* **:** to beget or bring forth offspring **:** REPRODUCE — **pro·cre·ation** \ˌprō-krē-'ā-shən\ *n* — **pro·cre·ative** \'prō-krē-ˌāt-iv\ *adj* — **pro·cre·ator** \-ˌāt-ər\ *n*

pro·crus·te·an \p(r)ə-'krəs-tē-ən, prō-\ *adj, often cap* **1 :** of, relating to, or typical of Procrustes **2 :** marked by arbitrary often ruthless disregard of individual differences or special circumstances

procrustean bed *n, often cap P* **:** a scheme or pattern into which someone or something is arbitrarily forced

Pro·crus·tes \p(r)ə-'krəs-(ˌ)tēz, prō-\ *n* [L, fr. Gk *Prokroustēs*] **:** a giant of Eleusis who forced travelers to fit one of two unequally long beds by stretching their bodies or cutting off their legs

pro·cryp·tic \(ˌ)prō-'krip-tik\ *adj* [*pro-* (as in *protect*) + *cryptic*] **:** of, relating to, or being a concealing pattern or shade of coloring esp. in insects

proc·to·dae·um \ˌpräk-tə-'dē-əm\ *n, pl* **-daea** \-'dē-ə\ *or* **-dae·ums** [NL, fr. Gk *prōktos* anus + *hodos* way — more at CEDE] **:** the posterior ectodermal part of the alimentary canal formed in the embryo by invagination of the outer body wall

proc·tol·o·gy \präk-'täl-ə-jē\ *n* [Gk *prōktos* anus + E *-logy*] **:** a branch of medicine dealing with the structure and diseases of the anus, rectum, and sigmoid colon — **proc·to·log·ic** \ˌpräk-tə-'läj-ik\ *or* **proc·to·log·i·cal** \-i-kəl\ *adj* — **proc·tol·o·gist** \präk-'täl-ə-jəst\ *n*

proc·tor \'präk-tər\ *n* [ME *procutour* procurator, proctor, alter. of *procuratour*] **:** SUPERVISOR, MONITOR; *specif* **:** one appointed to supervise students (as at an examination) — **proctor** *vb* — **proc·to·ri·al** \präk-'tōr-ē-əl, -'tȯr-\ *adj* — **proc·tor·ship** \'präk-tər-ˌship\ *n*

pro·cum·bent \prō-'kəm-bənt\ *adj* [L *procumbent-, procumbens,* prp. of *procumbere* to fall or lean forward, fr. *pro-* forward + *-cumbere* to lie down — more at HIP] **1 :** being or having stems that trail along the ground without rooting **2 :** lying face down

proc·u·ra·tion \ˌpräk-yə-'rā-shən\ *n* [ME *procuracioun,* fr. MF *procuration,* fr. L *procuration-, procuratio,* fr. *procuratus,* pp. of *procurare*] **1 a :** the act of appointing another as one's agent or attorney **b :** the authority vested in one so appointed **2 :** the action of obtaining something (as supplies) **:** PROCUREMENT

proc·u·ra·tor \'präk-yə-ˌrāt-ər\ *n* **1 :** one that manages another's affairs **:** AGENT **2 :** an officer of the Roman empire entrusted with management of the financial affairs of a province and often having administrative powers as agent of the emperor — **proc·u·ra·to·ri·al** \ˌpräk-yə-rə-'tōr-ē-əl, -'tȯr-\ *adj*

pro·cure \prə-'kyu̇(ə)r, prō-\ *vb* **pro·cured; pro·cur·ing** [ME *procuren,* fr. LL *procurare,* fr. L, to take care of, fr. *pro-* for + *cura* care] *vt* **1 a :** to get possession of **:** obtain by particular care and effort **b :** to get and make available for promiscuous sexual intercourse **2 :** to bring about **:** ACHIEVE ~ *vi* **:** to procure women ***syn*** see GET — **pro·cur·able** \-'kyu̇r-ə-bəl\ *adj* — **pro·cur·ance** \-ən(t)s\ *n* — **pro·cure·ment** \-'kyu̇(ə)r-mənt\ *n*

pro·cur·er \-'kyu̇r-ər\ *n* **:** one that procures; *esp* **:** PANDER — **pro·cur·ess** \-əs\ *n*

Pro·cy·on \'prō-sē-ˌän, 'präs-ē-, -ən\ *n* [L, fr. Gk *Prokyōn,* lit., fore-dog; fr. its rising before the Dog Star] **:** a first-magnitude star in Canis Minor

[1]prod \'präd\ *vt* **prod·ded; prod·ding** [origin unknown] **1 a :** to thrust a pointed instrument into **:** PRICK **b :** to incite to action **:** STIR **2 :** to poke or stir as if with a prod — **prod·der** *n*

[2]prod *n* **1 :** a pointed instrument used to prod **2 :** an incitement to act

[3]prod *abbr* production

[1]prod·i·gal \'präd-i-gəl\ *adj* [L *prodigus,* fr. *prodigere* to drive away, squander, fr. *pro-, prod-* forth + *agere* to drive — more at PRO-, AGENT] **1 :** recklessly extravagant **2 :** characterized by wasteful expenditure **:** LAVISH **3 :** yielding abundantly **:** LUXURIANT ***syn*** see PROFUSE ***ant*** parsimonious, frugal — **prod·i·gal·i·ty** \ˌpräd-ə-'gal-ət-ē\ *n* — **prod·i·gal·ly** \'präd-i-g(ə-)lē\ *adv*

[2]prodigal *n* **:** one who spends or gives lavishly and foolishly ***syn*** see SPENDTHRIFT

pro·di·gious \prə-'dij-əs\ *adj* **1 a** *obs* **:** being an omen **:** PORTENTOUS **b** *archaic* **:** resembling or befitting a prodigy **:** STRANGE, UNUSUAL **2 :** exciting amazement or wonder **3 :** extraordinary in bulk, quantity, or degree **:** ENORMOUS ***syn*** see MONSTROUS — **pro·di·gious·ly** *adv* — **pro·di·gious·ness** *n*

prod·i·gy \'präd-ə-jē\ *n, pl* **-gies** [L *prodigium* omen, monster, fr. *pro-, prod-* + *-igium* (akin to *aio* I say) — more at ADAGE] **1 a :** a portentous event **:** OMEN **b :** something extraordinary or inexplicable **2 a :** an extraordinary, marvelous, or unusual accomplishment, deed, or event **b :** a highly talented child

pro·dro·mal \(ˌ)prō-'drō-məl\ *or* **pro·drom·ic** \-'dräm-ik\ *adj* **:** PRECURSORY; *esp* **:** marked by prodromes

pro·drome \'prō-ˌdrōm\ *n, pl* **pro·dro·ma·ta** \(ˌ)prō-'drō-mət-ə\ *or* **pro·dromes** \'prō-ˌdrōmz\ [F, lit., precursor, fr. Gk *prodromos,* fr. *pro-* before + *dromos* running — more at PRO-, DROMEDARY] **:** a premonitory symptom of disease

[1]pro·duce \prə-'d(y)üs, prō-\ *vb* **pro·duced; pro·duc·ing** [ME (Sc) *producen,* fr. L *producere,* fr. *pro-* forward + *ducere* to lead — more at TOW] *vt* **1 :** to offer to view or notice **:** EXHIBIT **2 :** to give birth or rise to **:** YIELD **3 :** to extend in length, area, or volume <~ a side of a triangle> **4 :** to present to the public on the stage or screen or over radio or television **5 :** to give being, form, or shape to **:** MAKE; *esp* **:** MANUFACTURE **6 :** to accrue or cause to accrue ~ *vi* **:** to bear, make, or yield something — **pro·duc·ible** \-'d(y)ü-sə-bəl\ *adj*

[2]pro·duce \'präd-(ˌ)üs, 'prōd- *also* -(ˌ)yüs\ *n* **1 a :** something produced **b :** the amount produced **:** YIELD **2 :** agricultural products and esp. fresh fruits and vegetables as distinguished from grain and other staple crops **3 :** the progeny usu. of a female animal

pro·duced \prə-'d(y)üst, prō-\ *adj* **:** disproportionately elongated <a ~ leaf>

pro·duc·er \prə-'d(y)ü-sər, prō-\ *n* **1 :** one that produces; *esp* **:** one that grows agricultural products or manufactures crude materials into articles of use **2 :** a furnace or apparatus that produces combustible gas to be used for fuel by circulating air or a mixture of air and steam through a layer of incandescent fuel **3 :** a person who supervises or finances the production of a stage or screen production or radio or television program **4 :** an organism (as a green plant) which produces its own organic compounds from simple precursors (as carbon dioxide and inorganic nitrogen) and many of which are food sources for other organisms — compare CONSUMER b

producer gas *n* **:** gas made in a producer and consisting chiefly of carbon monoxide, hydrogen, and nitrogen

producer goods *n pl* **:** goods (as tools and raw materials) that are used to produce other goods and satisfy human wants only indirectly

prod·uct \'präd-(ˌ)əkt\ *n* [in sense 1, fr. ME, fr. ML *productum,* fr. L, something produced, fr. neut. of *productus,* pp. of *producere;* in other senses, fr. L *productum*] **1 :** the number or expression resulting from the multiplication together of two or more numbers or expressions **2 :** something produced **3 :** the amount, quantity, or total produced **4 :** CONJUNCTION 5

pro·duc·tion \prə-'dək-shən, prō-\ *n* **1 a :** something produced **:** PRODUCT **b** (1) **:** a literary or artistic work (2) **:** a work presented on the stage or screen or over the air **c :** an exaggerated action **2 a :** the act or process of producing **b :** the creation of utility; *esp* **:** the making of goods available for human wants **3 :** total output esp. of a commodity or an industry — **pro·duc·tion·al** \-shnəl, -shən-ᵊl\ *adj*

production control *n* **:** systematic planning, coordinating, and directing of all manufacturing activities and influences to insure having goods made on time, of adequate quality, and at reasonable cost

production line *n* **:** LINE 6j

pro·duc·tive \prə-'dək-tiv, prō-\ *adj* **1 :** having the quality or power of producing esp. in abundance <~ fishing waters> **2 :** effective in bringing about **:** ORIGINATIVE <investigating committees have been ~ of much good —R. K. Carr> **3 a :** yielding or furnishing results, benefits, or profits **b :** yielding or devoted to the satisfaction of wants or the creation of utilities **4 :** continuing to be used in the formation of new words or constructions <*un-* is a ~ prefix> **5 :** raising mucus or sputum (as from the bronchi) <a ~ cough> — **pro·duc·tive·ly** *adv* — **pro·duc·tive·ness** *n*

pro·duc·tiv·i·ty \(ˌ)prō-ˌdək-'tiv-ət-ē, ˌpräd-(ˌ)ək-, prə-ˌdək-\ *n* **1 :** the quality or state of being productive **2 :** rate of production esp. of food by fixation of solar energy by producer organisms

pro·em \'prō-ˌem\ *n* [ME *proheme,* fr. MF, fr. L *prooemium,* fr. Gk *prooimion,* fr. *pro-* + *oimē* song] **1 :** preliminary comment **:** PREFACE **2 :** PRELUDE — **pro·emi·al** \prō-'ē-mē-əl, -'em-ē-\ *adj*

pro·en·zyme \(ˌ)prō-'en-ˌzīm\ *n* [ISV] **:** ZYMOGEN

pro·es·trus \(ˌ)prō-'es-trəs\ *n* [NL] **:** a period immediately preceding estrus characterized by preparatory physiological changes

[1]prof \'präf\ *n, slang* **:** PROFESSOR

[2]prof *abbr* professor; professional

pro·fa·na·tion \ˌpräf-ə-'nā-shən, ˌprō-fə-\ *n* **:** the act or an instance of profaning

syn PROFANATION, DESECRATION, SACRILEGE *shared meaning element* **:** a violation or misuse of something normally held sacred

pro·fa·na·to·ry \prō-'fan-ə-ˌtōr-ē, prə-, -'fā-nə-, -ˌtȯr-\ *adj* **:** tending to profane **:** DESECRATING

[1]pro·fane \prō-'fān, prə-\ *vt* **pro·faned; pro·fan·ing** **1 :** to treat (something sacred) with abuse, irreverence, or contempt **:** DESECRATE, VIOLATE **2 :** to debase by a wrong, unworthy, or vulgar use — **pro·fan·er** *n*

[2]profane *adj* [ME *prophane,* fr. MF, fr. L *profanus,* fr. *pro-* before + *fanum* temple — more at PRO-, FEAST] **1 :** not concerned with religion or religious purposes **:** SECULAR **2 :** not holy because unconsecrated, impure, or defiled **:** UNSANCTIFIED **3 :** serving to debase or defile what is holy **:** IRREVERENT **4 a :** not among the initiated **b :** not possessing esoteric or expert knowledge — **pro·fane·ly** *adv* — **pro·fane·ness** \-'fān-nəs\ *n*

pro·fan·i·ty \prō-'fan-ət-ē, prə-\ *n, pl* **-ties** **1 a :** the quality or state of being profane **b :** the use of profane language **2 a :** profane language **b :** an utterance of profane language

pro·fess \prə-'fes, prō-\ *vb* [in sense 1, fr. ME *professen,* fr. *profes,* adj., having professed one's vows, fr. OF, fr. LL *professus,* fr. L, pp. of *profiteri* to profess, confess, fr. *pro-* before + *fateri* to acknowledge; in other senses, fr. L *professus,* pp. — more at CONFESS] *vt* **1 :** to receive formally into a religious community following a novitiate by acceptance of the required vows **2 a :** to declare or admit openly or freely **:** AFFIRM **b :** to declare in words or appearances only **:** PRETEND **3 :** to confess one's faith in or allegiance to **4 :** to practice or claim to be versed in (a calling or profession) ~ *vi* **1 :** to make a profession or avowal **2** *obs* **:** to profess friendship

pro·fessed \-'fest\ *adj* **1 :** openly and freely declared or acknowledged **:** AFFIRMED **2 :** professing to be qualified; *also* **:** EXPERT

pro·fess·ed·ly \prə-'fes-əd-lē, -'fest-lē\ *adv* **1 :** by profession or declaration **:** AVOWEDLY **2 :** with pretense **:** ALLEGEDLY

pro·fes·sion \prə-'fesh-ən\ *n* **1 :** the act of taking the vows of a religious community **2 :** an act of openly declaring or publicly claiming a belief, faith, or opinion **:** PROTESTATION **3 :** an avowed religious faith **4 a :** a calling requiring specialized knowledge and often long and intensive academic preparation **b :** a principal calling, vocation, or employment **c :** the whole body of persons engaged in a calling

1pro·fes·sion·al \prə-'fesh-nəl, -ən-ᵊl\ *adj* **1 a :** of, relating to, or characteristic of a profession **b :** engaged in one of the learned professions **c :** characterized by or conforming to the technical or ethical standards of a profession **2 a :** participating for gain or livelihood in an activity or field of endeavor often engaged in by amateurs **b :** engaged in by persons receiving financial return <~ football> **3 :** following a line of conduct as though it were a profession <a ~ patriot> — **pro·fes·sion·al·ly** \-ē\ *adv*

2professional *n* **:** one that engages in a pursuit or activity professionally

pro·fes·sion·al·ism \-ˌiz-əm\ *n* **1 :** the conduct, aims, or qualities that characterize or mark a profession or a professional person **2 :** the following of a profession (as athletics) for gain or livelihood

pro·fes·sion·al·ize \-ˌīz\ *vt* **-ized; -iz·ing :** to give a professional character to — **pro·fes·sion·al·iza·tion** \-ˌfesh-nə-lə-'zā-shən, -ən-ᵊl-ə-\ *n*

pro·fes·sor \prə-'fes-ər\ *n* **1 :** one that professes, avows, or declares **2 a :** a faculty member of the highest academic rank at an institution of higher education **b :** a teacher at a university, college, or sometimes secondary school **c :** one that teaches or professes special knowledge of an art, sport, or occupation requiring skill — **pro·fes·so·ri·al** \ˌprō-fə-'sōr-ē-əl, ˌpräf-ə-, -'sȯr-\ *adj* — **pro·fes·so·ri·al·ly** \-ē-ə-lē\ *adv*

pro·fes·sor·ate \prə-'fes-ə-rət\ *n* **:** the office, term of office, or position of a professor

pro·fes·so·ri·at \ˌprō-fə-'sōr-ē-ət, ˌpräf-ə-, -'sȯr-, -ē-ˌat\ *or* **pro·fes·so·ri·ate** \-ət, -ˌät\ *n* [modif. of F *professorat,* fr. *professeur* professor, fr. L *professor,* fr. *professus*] **1 :** the body of college and university teachers at an institution or in society **2 :** PROFESSORSHIP

pro·fes·sor·ship \prə-'fes-ər-ˌship\ *n* **:** the office, duties, or position of an academic professor

1prof·fer \'präf-ər\ *vt* **prof·fered; prof·fer·ing** \-(ə-)riŋ\ [ME *profren,* fr. AF *profrer,* fr. OF *poroffrir,* fr. *por-* forth (fr. L *pro-*) + *offrir* to offer — more at PRO-] **:** to present for acceptance **:** TENDER, OFFER

2proffer *n* **:** OFFER, SUGGESTION

pro·fi·cien·cy \prə-'fish-ən-sē\ *n* **1 :** advancement in knowledge or skill **:** PROGRESS **2 :** the quality or state of being proficient

pro·fi·cient \prə-'fish-ənt\ *adj* [L *proficient-, proficiens,* prp. of *proficere* to go forward, accomplish, fr. *pro-* forward + *facere* to make — more at PRO-, DO] **:** well advanced in an art, occupation, or branch of knowledge — **proficient** *n* — **pro·fi·cient·ly** *adv*
syn PROFICIENT, ADEPT, SKILLED, SKILLFUL, EXPERT *shared meaning element* **:** having or manifesting the knowledge and experience needed for success in a trade or profession

1pro·file \'prō-ˌfīl\ *n* [It *profilo,* fr. *profilare* to draw in outline, fr. *pro-* forward (fr. L) + *filare* to spin, fr. LL — more at FILE] **1 :** a representation of something in outline; *esp* **:** a human head or face represented or seen in a side view **2 :** an outline seen or represented in sharp relief **:** CONTOUR **3 :** a side or sectional elevation: as **a :** a drawing showing a vertical section of the ground **b :** a vertical section of a soil exposing its various zones or inclusions **4 :** a set of data often in graphic form portraying the significant features of something <a corporation's earnings ~>; *esp* **:** a graph representing the extent to which an individual exhibits traits or abilities as determined by tests or ratings **5 :** a concise biographical sketch ***syn*** see OUTLINE

2profile *vt* **pro·filed; pro·fil·ing 1 :** to represent in profile or by a profile **:** produce (as by drawing, writing, or graphing) a profile of **2 :** to shape the outline of by passing a cutter around — **pro·fil·er** *n*

1prof·it \'präf-ət\ *n, often attrib* [ME, fr. MF, fr. L *profectus* advance, profit, fr. *profectus,* pp. of *proficere*] **1 :** a valuable return **:** GAIN **2 :** the excess of returns over expenditure in a transaction or series of transactions; *esp* **:** the excess of the selling price of goods over their cost **3 :** net income usu. for a given period of time **4 :** the ratio of profit for a given year to the amount of capital invested or to the value of sales **5 :** the compensation accruing to entrepreneurs for the assumption of risk in business enterprise as distinguished from wages or rent — **prof·it·less** \-ləs\ *adj*

2profit *vi* **1 :** to be of service or advantage **:** AVAIL **2 :** to derive benefit **:** GAIN ~ *vt* **:** to be of service to **:** BENEFIT

prof·it·able \'präf-ət-ə-bəl, 'präf-tə-bəl\ *adj* **:** affording profits **:** yielding advantageous returns or results ***syn*** see BENEFICIAL ***ant*** unprofitable — **prof·it·abil·i·ty** \ˌpräf-ət-ə-'bil-ət-ē\ *n* — **prof·it·able·ness** \'präf-ət-ə-bəl-nəs\ *n* — **prof·it·ably** \-blē\ *adv*

profit and loss *n* **:** a summary account used at the end of an accounting period to collect the balances of the nominal accounts so that the net profit or loss may be shown

prof·i·teer \ˌpräf-ə-'ti(ə)r\ *n* **:** one who makes what is considered an unreasonable profit esp. on the sale of essential goods during times of emergency — **profiteer** *vi*

profit sharing *n* **:** a system or process under which employees receive a part of the profits of an industrial or commercial enterprise

profit system *n* **:** FREE ENTERPRISE

prof·li·ga·cy \'präf-li-gə-sē\ *n* **:** the quality or state of being profligate

1prof·li·gate \'präf-li-gət, -lə-ˌgāt\ *adj* [L *profligatus,* fr. pp. of *profligare* to strike down, fr. *pro-* forward, down + *-fligare* (akin to *fligere* to strike); akin to Gk *thlibein* to squeeze] **1 :** completely given up to dissipation and licentiousness **2 :** wildly extravagant **:** PRODIGAL — **prof·li·gate·ly** *adv*

2profligate *n* **:** a person given to wildly extravagant and usu. grossly self-indulgent expenditure ***syn*** see SPENDTHRIFT

pro·flu·ent \'präf-ˌlü-ənt, 'prōf-; prō-'flü-\ *adj* [ME, fr. L *profluent-, profluens,* prp. of *profluere* to flow forth, fr. *pro-* forth + *fluere* to flow — more at PRO-, FLUENT] **:** flowing copiously or smoothly

pro for·ma \(ˈ)prō-'fȯr-mə\ *adj* [L] **1 :** made or carried out in a perfunctory manner or as a formality **2 :** provided in advance to prescribe form or describe items <*pro forma* invoice>

1pro·found \prə-'faund, prō-\ *adj* [ME, fr. MF *profond* deep, fr. L *profundus,* fr. *pro-* before + *fundus* bottom — more at PRO-, BOTTOM] **1 a :** having intellectual depth and insight **b :** difficult to fathom or understand **2 a :** extending far below the surface **b :** coming from, reaching to, or situated at a depth **:** DEEP-SEATED <a ~ sigh> **3 a :** characterized by intensity of feeling or quality **b :** all encompassing **:** COMPLETE <~ sleep> ***syn*** see DEEP ***ant*** shallow — **pro·found·ly** \-'faun-(d)lē\ *adv* — **pro·found·ness** \-'faun(d)-nəs\ *n*

2profound *n, archaic* **:** something that is very deep; *specif* **:** the depths of the sea

pro·fun·di·ty \prə-'fən-dət-ē\ *n, pl* **-ties** [ME *profundite,* fr. MF *profundité,* fr. L *profunditat-, profunditas* depth, fr. *profundus*] **1 a :** intellectual depth **b :** something profound or abstruse **2 :** the quality or state of being very profound or deep

pro·fuse \prə-'fyüs, prō-\ *adj* [ME, fr. L *profusus,* pp. of *profundere* to pour forth, fr. *pro-* forth + *fundere* to pour — more at FOUND] **1 :** pouring forth liberally **:** EXTRAVAGANT <~ in their thanks> **2 :** exhibiting great abundance **:** BOUNTIFUL <a ~ harvest> — **pro·fuse·ly** *adv* — **pro·fuse·ness** *n*
syn PROFUSE, LAVISH, PRODIGAL, LUXURIANT, LUSH, EXUBERANT *shared meaning element* **:** giving or given out in great abundance ***ant*** spare, scanty, scant

pro·fu·sion \-'fyü-zhən\ *n* **1 :** lavish expenditure **:** EXTRAVAGANCE **2 :** the quality or state of being profuse **3 :** lavish display

1prog \'präg\ *vi* **progged; prog·ging** [origin unknown] *chiefly dial* **:** to search about; *esp* **:** FORAGE

2prog *n, chiefly dial* **:** FOOD, VICTUALS

pro·ga·mete \ˌprō-gə-'mēt, (ˈ)prō-'gam-ˌēt\ *n* [ISV] **:** a cell giving rise to gametes: **a :** OOCYTE **b :** SPERMATOCYTE

pro·gen·i·tor \prō-'jen-ət-ər, prə-\ *n* [ME, fr. MF *progeniteur,* fr. L *progenitor,* fr. *progenitus,* pp. of *progignere* to beget, fr. *pro-* forth + *gignere* to beget — more at KIN] **1 a :** an ancestor in the direct line **:** FOREFATHER **b :** a biologically ancestral form **2 :** PRECURSOR, ORIGINATOR <~*s* of socialist ideas —*Times Lit. Supp.*>

prog·e·ny \'präj-(ə-)nē\ *n, pl* **-nies** [ME *progenie,* fr. OF, fr. L *progenies,* fr. *progignere*] **1 a :** DESCENDANTS, CHILDREN **b :** offspring of animals or plants **2 :** OUTCOME, PRODUCT **3 :** a body of followers, disciples, or successors

pro·ges·ta·tion·al \ˌprō-ˌjes-'tā-shnəl, -shən-ᵊl\ *adj* **:** preceding pregnancy or gestation; *esp* **:** of, relating to, inducing, or constituting the modifications of the female mammalian system associated with ovulation and corpus luteum formation <~ hormones>

pro·ges·ter·one \prō-'jes-tə-ˌrōn\ *n* [*progestin* + *sterol* + *-one*] **:** a steroid progestational hormone $C_{21}H_{30}O_2$

pro·ges·tin \-'jes-tən\ *n* [*pro-* + *gestation* + *-in*] **:** a progestational hormone; *esp* **:** PROGESTERONE

pro·ges·to·gen \-tə-jən\ *n* [*progestational* + *-ogen* (as in *estrogen*)] **:** any of several progestational steroids (as progesterone)

pro·glot·tid \(ˈ)prō-'glät-əd\ *n* [NL *proglottis*] **:** a segment of a tapeworm containing both male and female reproductive organs — **pro·glot·ti·de·an** \ˌprō-ˌglät-ə-'dē-ən, ˌprō-glä-'tid-ē-\ *adj*

pro·glot·tis \(ˈ)prō-'glät-əs\ *n, pl* **-glot·ti·des** \-'glät-ə-ˌdēz\ [NL *proglottid-, proglottis,* fr. Gk *proglōttis* tip of the tongue, fr. *pro-* + *glōtta* tongue — more at GLOSS] **:** PROGLOTTID

prog·na·thic \präg-'nath-ik, -'nā-thik\ *adj* **:** PROGNATHOUS

prog·na·thism \'präg-nə-ˌthiz-əm, präg-'nā-\ *n* **:** prognathous condition

prog·na·thous \-thəs\ *adj* **:** having the jaws projecting beyond the upper part of the face

prog·no·sis \präg-'nō-səs\ *n, pl* **-no·ses** \-ˌsēz\ [LL, fr. Gk *prognōsis,* lit., foreknowledge, fr. *progignōskein* to know before, fr. *pro-* + *gignōskein* to know — more at KNOW] **1 :** the prospect of recovery as anticipated from the usual course of disease or peculiarities of the case **2 :** FORECAST, PROGNOSTICATION

prog·nos·tic \präg-'näs-tik\ *n* [ME *pronostique,* fr. MF, fr. L *prognosticum,* fr. Gk *prognōstikon,* fr. neut. of *prognōstikos* foretelling, fr. *progignōskein*] **1 :** something that foretells **:** PORTENT **2 :** PROGNOSTICATION, PROPHECY — **prognostic** *adj*

prog·nos·ti·cate \präg-'näs-tə-ˌkāt\ *vt* **-cat·ed; -cat·ing 1 :** to foretell from signs or symptoms **:** PREDICT **2 :** FORESHOW, PRESAGE ***syn*** see FORETELL — **prog·nos·ti·ca·tive** \-ˌkāt-iv\ *adj* — **prog·nos·ti·ca·tor** \-ˌkāt-ər\ *n*

prog·nos·ti·ca·tion \(ˌ)präg-ˌnäs-tə-'kā-shən\ *n* **1 :** an indication in advance **:** FORETOKEN **2 a :** an act, the fact, or the power of prognosticating **:** FORECAST **b :** FOREBODING

pro·grade \'prō-ˌgrād\ *adj* [L *pro-* forward + *gradi* to go — more at PRO-, GRADE] **:** being or relating to orbital or rotational motion of a body that is in the same direction as that of another celestial body <~ orbit of a satellite>

1pro·gram *or* **pro·gramme** \'prō-ˌgram, -grəm\ *n* [F *programme* agenda, public notice, fr. Gk *programma,* fr. *prographein* to write before, fr. *pro-* before + *graphein* to write] **1** [LL *programma,* fr. Gk] **:** a public notice **2 a :** a brief usu. printed outline of the order to be followed, of the feature or features to be presented, and the persons participating (as in a public exercise, performance, or entertainment) **b :** the performance of a program; *esp* **:** a performance broadcast on radio or television **3 :** a plan or system

ə abut	ᵊ kitten	ər further	a back	ā bake	ä cot, cart
au̇ out	ch chin	e less	ē easy	g gift	i trip	ī life
j joke	ŋ sing	ō flow	ȯ flaw	ȯi coin	th thin	t͟h this
ü loot	u̇ foot	y yet	yü few	yu̇ furious	zh vision

under which action may be taken toward a goal **4 :** CURRICULUM **5 :** PROSPECTUS, SYLLABUS **6 a :** a plan for the programming of a mechanism (as a computer) **b :** a sequence of coded instructions that can be inserted into a mechanism (as a computer) or that is part of an organism **7 :** matter for programmed instruction

²program *also* **programme** *vt* **-grammed** *or* **-gramed; -gram·ming** *or* **-gram·ing 1 a :** to arrange or furnish a program of or for : BILL **b :** to enter in a program **2 :** to work out a sequence of operations to be performed by (a mechanism) : provide with a program **3 :** to insert a program for (a particular action) into or as if into a mechanism — **pro·gram·ma·bil·i·ty** \(,)prō-,gram-ə-'bil-ət-ē\ *n* — **pro·gram·ma·ble** \'prō-,gram-ə-bəl\ *adj*

program director *n* **:** one in charge of planning and scheduling program material for a radio or television station or network

pro·gram·mat·ic \,prō-grə-'mat-ik\ *adj* **1 :** relating to program music **2 :** of, resembling, or having a program — **pro·gram·mat·i·cal·ly** \-i-k(ə-)lē\ *adv*

pro·grammed *or* **pro·gramed** \'prō-,gramd, -grəmd\ *adj* **1 :** of or relating to learning by means of programmed instruction **2 :** produced in the form of programmed instruction

programmed instruction *n* **:** instruction through information given in small steps with each requiring a correct response by the learner before going on to the next step

pro·gram·mer *also* **pro·gram·er** \'prō-,gram-ər, -grə-mər\ *n* **:** one that programs: as **a :** one that prepares and tests programs for mechanisms **b :** a person or device that programs a mechanism **c :** one that prepares educational programs

pro·gram·ming *or* **pro·gram·ing** \-,gram-iŋ, -grə-miŋ\ *n* **:** the planning, scheduling, or performing of a program

program music *n* **:** music intended to suggest a sequence of images or incidents

¹prog·ress \'präg-rəs, -,res, *chiefly Brit* 'prō-,gres\ *n* [ME, fr. L *progressus* advance, fr. *progressus,* pp. of *progredi* to go forth, fr. *pro-* forward + *gradi* to go — more at PRO-, GRADE] **1 a** (1) **:** a royal journey marked by pomp and pageant (2) **:** a state procession **b :** a tour or circuit made by an official (as a judge) **c :** an expedition, journey, or march through a region **2 :** a forward or onward movement (as to an objective or to a goal) : ADVANCE **3 :** gradual betterment; *esp* **:** the progressive development of mankind — **in progress :** going on : OCCURRING

²pro·gress \prə-'gres\ *vi* **1 :** to move forward : PROCEED **2 :** to develop to a higher, better, or more advanced stage

pro·gres·sion \prə-'gresh-ən\ *n* **1 :** a sequence of numbers in which each term is related to its predecessor by a uniform law **2 a :** the action or process of progressing : ADVANCE **b :** a continuous and connected series : SEQUENCE **3 a :** succession of musical tones or chords **b :** the movement of musical parts in harmony **c :** SEQUENCE 2c — **pro·gres·sion·al** \-'gresh-nəl, -ən-ᵊl\ *adj*

pro·gres·sion·ist \-'gresh-(ə-)nəst\ *n* **:** one who believes in progress; *esp* **:** one who believes in the continuous progress of the human race or of society

pro·gres·sist \'präg-rəs-əst, -,res-; prə-'gres-\ *n* **1 :** PROGRESSIONIST **2 :** PROGRESSIVE 1

¹pro·gres·sive \prə-'gres-iv\ *adj* **1 a :** of, relating to, or characterized by progress **b :** making use of or interested in new ideas, findings, or opportunities **c :** of, relating to, or constituting an educational theory marked by emphasis on the individual child, informality of classroom procedure, and encouragement of self-expression **2 :** of, relating to, or characterized by progression **3 :** moving forward or onward : ADVANCING **4 :** increasing in extent or severity <a ~ disease> **5** *often cap* **:** of or relating to political Progressives **6 :** of, relating to, or constituting a verb form that expresses action or state in progress at the time of speaking or a time spoken of — **pro·gres·sive·ly** *adv* — **pro·gres·sive·ness** *n*

²progressive *n* **1 a :** one that is progressive **b :** one believing in moderate political change and esp. social improvement by governmental action **2** *cap* **:** a member of any of various U.S. political parties: as **a :** a member of a predominantly agrarian minor party that around 1912 split off from the Republicans; *specif* **:** BULL MOOSE **b :** a follower of Robert M. La Follette in the presidential campaign of 1924 **c :** a follower of Henry A. Wallace in the presidential campaign of 1948

Progressive Conservative *adj* **:** of or relating to a major political party in Canada traditionally advocating economic nationalism and close ties with the United Kingdom and the Commonwealth — **Progressive Conservative** *n*

progressive jazz *n* **:** jazz characterized by harmonic, contrapuntal, and rhythmic experimentation

pro·gres·siv·ism \prə-'gres-iv-iz-əm\ *n* **1 :** the principles or beliefs of progressives **2** *cap* **:** the political and economic doctrines advocated by the Progressives **3 :** the theories of progressive education — **pro·gres·siv·ist** \-iv-əst\ *n or adj* — **pro·gres·siv·is·tic** \-,gres-iv-'is-tik\ *adj*

pro·hib·it \prō-'hib-ət, prə-\ *vt* [ME *prohibiten,* fr. L *prohibitus,* pp. of *prohibēre* to hold away, fr. *pro-* forward + *habēre* to hold] **1 :** to forbid by authority : ENJOIN **2 a :** to prevent from doing something **b :** PRECLUDE ***syn*** see FORBID ***ant*** permit

pro·hi·bi·tion \,prō-ə-'bish-ən *also* ,prō-hə-\ *n* **1 :** the act of prohibiting by authority **2 :** an order to restrain or stop **3** *often cap* **:** the forbidding by law of the manufacture, transportation, and sale of alcoholic liquors except for medicinal and sacramental purposes

pro·hi·bi·tion·ist \-'bish-(ə-)nəst\ *n* **:** one who favors the prohibition of the sale or manufacture of alcoholic liquors; *specif, cap* **:** a member of a minor U.S. political party advocating prohibition

pro·hib·i·tive \prō-'hib-ət-iv, prə-\ *adj* **1 :** tending to prohibit or restrain **2 :** tending to preclude the use or acquisition of something — **pro·hib·i·tive·ly** *adv* — **pro·hib·i·tive·ness** *n*

pro·hib·i·to·ry \-'hib-ə-,tōr-ē, -,tȯr-\ *adj* **:** PROHIBITIVE

¹proj·ect \'präj-,ekt, -ikt\ *n* [ME *proiecte,* modif. of MF *pourjet,* fr. *pourjeter* to throw out, spy, plan, fr. *pour-* (fr. L *porro* forward) + *jeter* to throw; akin to Gk *pro* forward — more at FOR, JET] **1 :** a specific plan or design : SCHEME **2** *obs* **:** IDEA **3 :** a planned undertaking: as **a :** a definitely formulated piece of research **b :** a large usu. government-supported undertaking **c :** a task or problem engaged in usu. by a group of students to supplement and apply classroom studies **4 :** a group of houses or apartment buildings built and arranged according to a single plan ***syn*** see PLAN

²pro·ject \prə-'jekt\ *vb* [partly modif. of MF *pourjeter;* partly fr. L *projectus,* pp. of *proicere* to throw forward, fr. *pro-* + *jacere* to throw — more at JET] *vt* **1 a :** to devise in the mind : DESIGN **b :** to plan, figure, or estimate for the future <~ expenditures for the coming year> **2 :** to throw or cast forward <~ a missile> **3 :** to put or set forth : present for consideration **4 :** to cause to protrude **5 :** to cause (light or shadow) to fall into space or (an image) to fall on a surface <~ a beam of light> **6 :** to reproduce (as a point, line, or area) on a surface by motion in a prescribed direction **7 :** to communicate vividly esp. to an audience **8 :** to attribute (something in one's own mind) to a person, group, or object <a nation is an entity on which one can ~ many of the worst of one's instincts —*Times Lit. Supp.*> ~ *vi* **:** to jut out : PROTRUDE — **pro·ject·able** \-'jek-tə-bəl\ *adj*

¹pro·jec·tile \prə-'jek-tᵊl *also* -,tīl, *chiefly Brit* 'präj-ik-,tīl\ *n* **1 :** a body projected by external force and continuing in motion by its own inertia; *esp* **:** a missile for a weapon (as a firearm) **2 :** a self-propelling weapon (as a rocket)

²projectile *adj* **1 :** projecting or impelling forward <a ~ force> **2 :** capable of being thrust forward

pro·jec·tion \prə-'jek-shən\ *n* **1 a :** a systematic presentation of intersecting coordinate lines on a flat surface upon which features from the curved surface of the earth or the celestial sphere may be mapped **b :** the process or technique of reproducing a spatial object upon a plane or curved surface by projecting its points; *also* **:** the graphic reproduction so formed **2 :** a transforming change **3 :** the act of throwing or shooting forward : EJECTION **4 :** the forming of a plan : SCHEMING **5 a** (1) **:** a jutting out (2) **:** a part that juts out **b :** a view of a building or architectural element **6 a :** the act of perceiving a mental object as spatially and sensibly objective; *also* **:** something so perceived **b :** the attribution of one's own ideas, feelings, or attitudes to other people or to objects; *esp* **:** the externalization of blame, guilt, or responsibility as a defense against anxiety **7 :** the display of motion pictures by projecting an image from them upon a screen **8 :** an estimate of future possibilities based on a current trend — **pro·jec·tion·al** \-shnəl, -shən-ᵊl\ *adj*

syn PROJECTION, PROTRUSION, PROTUBERANCE, BULGE *shared meaning element* **:** an extension beyond the normal line or surface

projection booth *n* **:** a booth in a theater or hall for housing and operating a projector and esp. a motion-picture projector

pro·jec·tion·ist \prə-'jek-sh(ə-)nəst\ *n* **:** one that makes projections: as **a :** a map maker **b :** one that operates a motion-picture projector or television equipment

projection room *n* **1 :** PROJECTION BOOTH **2 :** a room equipped with a projector and screen for the private viewing of motion pictures

pro·jec·tive \prə-'jek-tiv\ *adj* **1 :** relating to, produced by, or involving geometric projection **2 :** jutting out : PROJECTING **3 :** of or relating to a test or device designed to analyze the psychodynamic constitution of an individual — **pro·jec·tive·ly** *adv*

projective geometry *n* **:** a branch of geometry that deals with the properties of configurations that are unaltered by projection

pro·jec·tor \prə-'jek-tər\ *n* **1 :** one that plans a project; *specif* **:** PROMOTER **2 :** one that projects: as **a :** a device for projecting a beam of light **b :** an optical instrument for projecting an image upon a surface **c :** a machine for projecting motion pictures on a screen **3 :** an imagined line from an object to a surface along which projection takes place

pro·jet \prō-'zhā, 'prō-,\ *n, pl* **projets** \-'zhā(z), -,zhā(z)\ [F, fr. MF *pourjet*] **1 :** PLAN; *esp* **:** a draft of a proposed measure or treaty **2 :** a projected or proposed design

prokaryote, prokaryotic *var of* PROCARYOTE, PROCARYOTIC

pro·lac·tin \prō-'lak-tən\ *n* [²*pro-* + *lact-* + *-in*] **:** a protein hormone of the anterior lobe of the pituitary that induces lactation in mammals

pro·la·min *or* **pro·la·mine** \'prō-lə-mən, -,mēn\ *n* [ISV *prol*ine + *am*monia + *-in, -ine*] **:** any of various simple proteins found esp. in seeds and insoluble in absolute alcohol or water

pro·lan \'prō-,lan\ *n* [G, fr. L *proles* progeny] **:** either of two gonadotrophic hormones: **a :** FOLLICLE-STIMULATING HORMONE **b :** LUTEINIZING HORMONE

¹pro·lapse \prō-'laps, 'prō-,\ *n* [NL *prolapsus,* fr. LL, fall, fr. L *prolapsus,* pp. of *prolabi* to fall or slide forward, fr. *pro-* forward + *labi* to slide — more at PRO-, SLEEP] **:** the falling down or slipping of a body part from its usual position or relations

²pro·lapse \prō-'laps\ *vi* **pro·lapsed; pro·laps·ing :** to undergo prolapse

pro·late \'prō-,lāt\ *adj* [L *prolatus* (pp. of *proferre* to bring forward, extend) fr. *pro-* forward + *latus,* pp. of *ferre* to carry] **:** EXTENDED; *esp* **:** elongated in the direction of a line joining the poles <a ~ spheroid>

prole \'prōl\ *n* **:** PROLETARIAN

pro·leg \'prō-,leg, -,lāg\ *n* **:** a fleshy leg that occurs on an abdominal segment of some insect larvae but does not occur in the adult

pro·le·gom·e·non \,prō-li-'gäm-ə-,nän, -nən\ *n, pl* **-e·na** \-nə\ [Gk, neut. pres. pass. part. of *prolegein* to say beforehand, fr. *pro-* before + *legein* to say] **:** prefatory remarks; *specif* **:** a formal essay or critical discussion serving to introduce and interpret an extended work — **pro·le·gom·e·nous** \-nəs\ *adj*

pro·lep·sis \prō-'lep-səs\ *n, pl* **-lep·ses** \-,sēz\ [Gk *prolēpsis,* fr. *prolambanein* to take beforehand, fr. *pro-* before + *lambanein* to take — more at LATCH] **:** ANTICIPATION; as **a :** the representation or assumption of a future act or development as if presently existing or accomplished **b :** the application of an adjective to a noun in anticipation of the result of the action of the verb (as in "while you slow oxen turn the *furrowed* plain") — **pro·lep·tic** \-'lep-tik\ *adj*

1pro·le·tar·i·an \ˌprō-lə-ˈter-ē-ən\ *n* [L *proletarius,* fr. *proles* progeny, fr. *pro-* forth + *-olescere* (fr. *alescere* to grow) — more at OLD] **:** a member of the proletariat

2proletarian *adj* **:** of, relating to, or representative of the proletariat

pro·le·tar·i·an·iza·tion \-ˌter-ē-ə-nə-ˈzā-shən\ *n* **:** reduction to a proletarian status or level

pro·le·tar·i·an·ize \-ˈter-ē-ə-ˌnīz\ *vt* **-ized; -iz·ing :** to cause to undergo proletarianization

pro·le·tar·i·at \ˌprō-lə-ˈter-ē-ət, -ˈtar-, -ē-ˌat\ *n, pl* **proletariat** [F *prolétariat,* fr. L *proletarius*] **1 :** the lowest social or economic class of a community **2 :** the laboring class; *esp* **:** the class of industrial workers who lack their own means of production and hence sell their labor to live

1pro·lif·er·ate \prə-ˈlif-ə-ˌrāt\ *vb* **-at·ed; -at·ing** [back-formation fr. *proliferation,* fr. F *prolifération,* fr. *proliférer* to proliferate, fr. *prolifère* proliferous, fr. L *proles* + *-fer* -ferous] *vi* **1 :** to grow by rapid production of new parts, cells, buds, or offspring **2 :** to increase in number as if by proliferation **:** MULTIPLY ~ *vt* **:** to cause to grow by proliferation — **pro·lif·er·a·tion** \-ˌlif-ə-ˈrā-shən\ *n* — **pro·lif·er·a·tive** \-ˈlif-ə-ˌrāt-iv\ *adj*

2pro·lif·er·ate \-ˈlif-ə-rət, -ˌrāt\ *adj* [back-formation fr. *proliferation*] **1 :** developing a leafy shoot from a normally terminal organ <~ flowers> **2 :** increased in number or quantity

pro·lif·er·ous \prə-ˈlif-(ə-)rəs\ *adj* **1 :** reproducing freely by vegetative means (as offsets, bulbils, gemmae) **2 :** undergoing proliferation; *specif* **:** producing a cluster of branchlets from a larger branch <a ~ coral> — **pro·lif·er·ous·ly** *adv*

pro·lif·ic \prə-ˈlif-ik\ *adj* [F *prolifique,* fr. L *proles* progeny] **1 :** producing young or fruit esp. freely **:** FRUITFUL **2** *archaic* **:** causing abundant growth, generation, or reproduction **3 :** marked by abundant inventiveness or productivity <a ~ writer> ***syn*** see FERTILE ***ant*** barren, unfruitful — **pro·lif·i·ca·cy** \-ˈlif-i-kə-sē\ *n* — **pro·lif·i·cal·ly** \-i-k(ə-)lē\ *adv* — **pro·lif·ic·ness** \-ik-nəs\ *n*

pro·li·fic·i·ty \ˌprō-lə-ˈfis-ət-ē\ *n* **:** prolific power or character

pro·line \ˈprō-ˌlēn\ *n* [G *prolin*] **:** an amino acid $C_5H_9NO_2$ that can be synthesized by animals from glutamate

pro·lix \prō-ˈliks, ˈprō-(ˌ)\ *adj* [ME, fr. MF & L; MF *prolixe,* fr. L *prolixus* extended, fr. *pro-* forward + *liquēre* to be fluid — more at LIQUID] **1 :** unduly prolonged or drawn out **2 :** given to verbosity and diffuseness in speaking or writing **:** LONG-WINDED ***syn*** see WORDY — **pro·lix·ly** *adv*

pro·lix·i·ty \prō-ˈlik-sət-ē\ *n* **:** the quality or state of being prolix

pro·loc·u·tor \prō-ˈläk-yət-ər\ *n* [L, fr. *pro-* for + *locutor* speaker, fr. *locutus,* pp. of *loqui* to speak] **1 :** one who speaks for another **:** SPOKESMAN **2 :** presiding officer **:** CHAIRMAN

pro·lo·gize \ˈprō-ˌlȯg-ˌīz, -ˌläg-; -lə-ˌjīz\ *or* **pro·logu·ize** \-ˌlȯg-ˌīz, -ˌläg-\ *vi* **-lo·gized** *or* **-logu·ized; -lo·giz·ing** *or* **-logu·iz·ing :** to write or speak a prologue

pro·logue *also* **pro·log** \ˈprō-ˌlȯg, -ˌläg\ *n* [ME *prolog,* fr. OF *prologue,* fr. L *prologus* preface to a play, fr. Gk *prologos* part of a Greek play preceding the entry of the chorus, fr. *pro-* before + *legein* to speak — more at PRO-, LEGEND] **1 :** the preface or introduction to a literary work **2 a :** a speech often in verse addressed to the audience by an actor at the beginning of a play **b :** the actor speaking such a prologue **3 :** an introductory or preceding event or development

pro·long \prə-ˈlȯŋ\ *vt* [ME *prolongen,* fr. MF *prolonguer,* fr. LL *prolongare,* fr. L *pro-* forward + *longus* long] **1 :** to lengthen in time **:** CONTINUE **2 :** to lengthen in extent, scope, or range ***syn*** see EXTEND ***ant*** curtail — **pro·long·er** \-ˈlȯŋ-ər\ *n*

pro·lon·gate \prə-ˈlȯŋ-ˌgāt, prō-\ *vt* **-gat·ed; -gat·ing :** PROLONG

pro·lon·ga·tion \(ˌ)prō-ˌlȯŋ-ˈgā-shən, prə-\ *n* **1 :** an extension or lengthening in time or duration **2 :** an expansion or continuation in extent, scope, or range

pro·lo·ther·a·py \ˌprō-lō-ˈther-ə-pē\ *n* [*proliferation* + *-o-* + *therapy*] **:** the rehabilitation of an incompetent structure (as a ligament or tendon) by the induced proliferation of new cells

pro·lu·sion \prō-ˈlü-zhən\ *n* [L *prolusion-, prolusio,* fr. *prolusus,* pp. of *proludere* to play beforehand, fr. *pro-* before + *ludere* to play — more at LUDICROUS] **1 :** a preliminary trial or exercise **:** PRELUDE **2 :** an introductory and often tentative discourse — **pro·lu·so·ry** \-ˈlüs-(ə-)rē, -ˈlüz-\ *adj*

1prom \ˈpräm\ *n* [short for *promenade*] **1 :** a formal dance given by a high school or college class **2** *Brit* **:** PROMENADE 2

2prom *abbr* promontory

1prom·e·nade \ˌpräm-ə-ˈnād, -ˈnäd\ *n* [F, fr. *promener* to take for a walk, fr. L *prominare* to drive forward, fr. *pro-* forward + *minare* to drive — more at AMENABLE] **1 :** a leisurely walk or ride esp. in a public place for pleasure or display **2 :** a place for strolling **3 a :** a ceremonious opening of a formal ball consisting of a grand march of all the guests **b :** a figure in a square dance in which couples move counterclockwise in a circle

2promenade *vb* **-nad·ed; -nad·ing** *vi* **1 :** to take or go on a promenade **2 :** to perform a promenade in a dance ~ *vt* **:** to walk about in or on — **prom·e·nad·er** *n*

promenade deck *n* **:** an upper deck or an area on a deck of a passenger ship where passengers stroll

Pro·me·the·an \prə-ˈmē-thē-ən\ *adj* **:** of, relating to, or resembling Prometheus, his experiences, or his art; *esp* **:** daringly original or creative

Pro·me·theus \-ˌth(y)üs, -thē-əs\ *n* [L, fr. Gk *Promētheus*] **:** a Titan who according to Greek myth stole fire from heaven, gave it to man, and was consequently put to extreme torture by Zeus

pro·me·thi·um \-thē-əm\ *n* [NL, fr. L *Prometheus*] **:** a metallic element of the rare-earth group obtained as a fission product of uranium or from neutron-irradiated neodymium — see ELEMENT table

prom·i·nence \ˈpräm(-ə)-nən(t)s\ *n* **1 :** the quality, state, or fact of being prominent or conspicuous **:** SALIENCE **2 :** something prominent **:** PROJECTION <a rocky ~> **3 :** a mass of gas resembling a cloud that arises from the chromosphere of the sun

prom·i·nent \-nənt\ *adj* [L *prominent-, prominens,* fr. prp. of *prominēre* to jut forward, fr. *pro-* forward + *-minēre* (akin to *mont-, mons* mountain) — more at MOUNT] **1 :** standing out or projecting beyond a surface or line **:** PROTUBERANT **2 a :** readily noticeable **:** CONSPICUOUS **b :** widely and popularly known **:** LEADING ***syn*** see NOTICEABLE — **prom·i·nent·ly** *adv*

pro·mis·cu·ity \ˌpräm-əs-ˈkyü-ət-ē, prə-ˌmis-\ *n, pl* **-ities 1 :** a miscellaneous mixture or mingling of persons or things **2 :** promiscuous sexual behavior

pro·mis·cu·ous \prə-ˈmis-kyə-wəs\ *adj* [L *promiscuus,* fr. *pro-* forth + *miscēre* to mix — more at PRO-, MIX] **1 :** composed of all sorts of persons or things **2 :** not restricted to one class, sort, or person **:** INDISCRIMINATE <a ~ and unprincipled attack on radicalism —A. M. Schlesinger *b*1917>; *specif* **:** not restricted to one sexual partner **3 :** CASUAL, IRREGULAR <~ eating habits> — **pro·mis·cu·ous·ly** *adv* — **pro·mis·cu·ous·ness** *n*

1prom·ise \ˈpräm-əs\ *n* [ME *promis,* fr. L *promissum,* fr. neut. of *promissus,* pp. of *promittere* to send forth, promise, fr. *pro-* forth + *mittere* to send — more at PRO-, SMITE] **1 a :** a declaration that one will do or refrain from doing something specified **b :** a legally binding declaration that gives the person to whom it is made a right to expect or to claim the performance or forbearance of a specified act **2 :** ground for expectation usu. of success, improvement, or excellence <show ~> **3 :** something that is promised

2promise *vb* **prom·ised; prom·is·ing** *vt* **1 :** to pledge oneself to do, bring about, or provide <~ aid> **2** *archaic* **:** WARRANT, ASSURE **3** *chiefly dial* **:** BETROTH **4 :** to suggest beforehand **:** FORETOKEN <dark clouds ~ rain> ~ *vi* **1 :** to make a promise **2 :** to give ground for expectation **:** be imminent

promised land *n* **:** a place or condition believed to promise final satisfaction or realization of hopes

prom·is·ee \ˌpräm-ə-ˈsē\ *n* **:** a person to whom a promise is made

prom·is·ing \ˈpräm-ə-siŋ\ *adj* **:** full of promise **:** likely to succeed or to yield good results — **prom·is·ing·ly** \-siŋ-lē\ *adv*

prom·i·sor \ˌpräm-ə-ˈsȯ(ə)r\ *also* **prom·is·er** \ˈpräm-ə-sər\ *n* **:** one who makes a promise

prom·is·so·ry \ˈpräm-ə-ˌsōr-ē, -ˌsȯr-\ *adj* [ML *promissorius,* fr. L *promissus,* pp.] **:** containing or conveying a promise or assurance

promissory note *n* **:** a written promise to pay at a fixed or determinable future time a sum of money to a specified individual or to bearer

prom·on·to·ry \ˈpräm-ən-ˌtōr-ē, -ˌtȯr-\ *n, pl* **-ries** [L *promunturium, promonturium;* prob. akin to *prominēre* to jut forth — more at PROMINENT] **1 a :** a high point of land or rock projecting into a body of water **:** HEADLAND **b :** a prominent mass of land (as a bluff) overlooking or projecting into a lowland **2 :** a bodily prominence

pro·mot·able \prə-ˈmōt-ə-bəl\ *adj* **1 :** capable of being advanced in rank, dignity, or position <~ managerial manpower> **2 :** capable of being promoted for consumer acceptance esp. through advertising — **pro·mot·abil·i·ty** \-ˌmōt-ə-ˈbil-ət-ē\ *n*

pro·mote \prə-ˈmōt\ *vt* **pro·mot·ed; pro·mot·ing** [L *promotus,* pp. of *promovēre,* lit., to move forward, fr. *pro-* forward + *movēre* to move] **1 a :** to advance in station, rank, or honor **:** RAISE **b :** to change (a pawn) into a piece in chess by moving to the eighth rank **c :** to advance (a student) from one grade to the next higher grade **2 a :** to contribute to the growth or prosperity of **:** FURTHER <~ international understanding> **b :** to help bring (as an enterprise) into being **:** LAUNCH **c :** to present (merchandise) for public acceptance through advertising and publicity **3** *slang* **:** to get possession of by doubtful means or by ingenuity ***syn*** see ADVANCE ***ant*** impede

pro·mot·er \-ˈmōt-ər\ *n* **1 :** one that promotes; *esp* **:** one who assumes the financial responsibilities of a sporting event (as a boxing match) including contracting with the principals, renting the site, and collecting gate receipts **2** *obs* **:** PROSECUTOR **3 :** a substance that in very small amounts is able to increase the activity of a catalyst

pro·mo·tion \prə-ˈmō-shən\ *n* **1 :** the act or fact of being raised in position or rank **:** PREFERMENT **2 :** the act of furthering the growth or development of something; *esp* **:** the furtherance of the acceptance and sale of merchandise through advertising and publicity — **pro·mo·tion·al** \-shnəl, -shən-ᵊl\ *adj*

pro·mo·tive \-ˈmōt-iv\ *adj* **1 :** tending to further or encourage **2 :** serving to promote **:** PROMOTIONAL — **pro·mo·tive·ness** *n*

1prompt \ˈpräm(p)t\ *vt* [ME *prompten,* fr. ML *promptare,* fr. L *promptus* prompt] **1 :** to move to action **:** INCITE <curiosity ~*ed* him to ask the question> **2 :** to assist (one acting or reciting) by suggesting or saying the next words of something forgotten or imperfectly learned **:** CUE **3 :** to serve as the inciting cause of **:** URGE <~*s* the question: has the danger of a severe recession passed? —S. H. Slichter> — **prompt·er** *n*

2prompt *adj* **:** of or relating to prompting actors

3prompt *adj* [ME, fr. MF or L; MF, fr. L *promptus* ready, prompt, fr. pp. of *promere* to bring forth, fr. *pro-* forth + *emere* to take — more at REDEEM] **1 :** being ready and quick to act as occasion demands **2 :** performed readily or immediately <~ assistance> ***syn*** see QUICK — **prompt·ly** \ˈpräm(p)-tlē, ˈpräm-plē\ *adv* — **prompt·ness** \ˈprämt-nəs, ˈprämp-nəs\ *n*

4prompt *n, pl* **prompts** \ˈpräm(t)s, ˈprämps\ **1** [1*prompt*] **:** the act or an instance of prompting **:** REMINDER **2** [3*prompt*] **:** a limit of time given for payment of an account for goods purchased; *also* **:** the contract by which this time is fixed

prompt·book \ˈprämt-ˌbu̇k, ˈprämp-ˌbu̇k\ *n* **:** a copy of a play with directions for performance used by a theater prompter

promp·ti·tude \'präm(p)-tə-,t(y)üd\ *n* [ME, fr. MF or LL; MF, fr. LL *promptitudo*, fr. L *promptus*] : the quality or habit of being prompt : PROMPTNESS
prompt side *n* **1 :** the side of the stage to the right of an actor facing the audience **2 :** the side of the stage adjacent to the prompter's corner
pro·mul·gate \'präm-əl-,gāt; prō-'məl-, prə-', 'prō-(,)\ *vt* **-gat·ed; -gat·ing** [L *promulgatus*, pp. of *promulgare*] **1 :** to make known by open declaration : PROCLAIM **2 a :** to make known or public the terms of (a proposed law) **b :** to put (a law) into action or force *syn* see DECLARE — **pro·mul·ga·tion** \,präm-əl-'gā-shən; ,prō-(,)məl-, (,)prō-, , prə-,\ *n* — **pro·mul·ga·tor** \'präm-əl-,gāt-ər; prō-'məl-, prə-', 'prō-(,)\ *n*
pron *abbr* **1** pronoun **2** pronounced **3** pronunciation
pro·nate \'prō-,nāt\ *vt* **pro·nat·ed; pro·nat·ing** [LL *pronatus*, pp. of *pronare* to bend forward, fr. L *pronus*] : to rotate (as the hand or forearm) so as to bring the palm facing downward or backward; *broadly* : to rotate (a joint or part) forward and toward the midline — **pro·na·tion** \prō-'nā-shən\ *n*
pro·na·tor \'prō-,nāt-ər\ *n* : a muscle that produces pronation
prone \'prōn\ *adj* [ME, fr. L *pronus* bent forward, tending; akin to L *pro* forward — more at FOR] **1 :** having a tendency or inclination : DISPOSED <man is ~ to error> <is ~ to overlook such things> **2 :** having the front or ventral surface downward — **prone** *adv* — **prone·ly** *adv* — **prone·ness** \'prōn-nəs\ *n*
syn PRONE, SUPINE, PROSTRATE, RECUMBENT *shared meaning element* : lying down
pro·neph·ros \(')prō-'nef-rəs, -,räs\ *n* [NL, fr. Gk *pro-* + *nephros* kidney — more at NEPHRITIS] : a member of the anterior pair of the three pairs of embryonic renal organs of higher vertebrates — **pro·neph·ric** \-rik\ *adj*
[1]**prong** \'prȯŋ, 'präŋ\ *n* [ME *pronge*] **1 :** FORK **2 :** a tine of a fork **3 :** a slender pointed or projecting part: as **a :** a fang of a tooth **b :** a point of an antler — **pronged** \'prȯŋd, 'präŋd\ *adj*
[2]**prong** *vt* : to stab, pierce, or break up with a pronged device
prong·horn \'prȯŋ-,hȯ(ə)rn, 'präŋ-\ *n, pl* **pronghorn** *also* **pronghorns :** a ruminant mammal (*Antilocapra americana*) of treeless parts of western No. America that resembles an antelope — called also *pronghorn antelope*
pro·nom·i·nal \prō-'näm-ən-ᵊl, -'näm-nəl\ *adj* [LL *pronominalis*, fr. L *pronomin-*, *pronomen*] **1 :** of, relating to, or constituting a pronoun **2 :** resembling a pronoun in identifying or specifying without describing <the ~ adjective *this* in *this* dog> — **pro·nom·i·nal·ly** \-ē\ *adv*
pro·noun \'prō-,naùn\ *n* [ME *pronom*, fr. L *pronomin-*, *pronomen*, fr. *pro-* for + *nomin-*, *nomen* name — more at PRO-, NAME] : a word belonging to one of the major form classes in any of a great many languages that is used as a substitute for a noun or noun equivalent, takes noun constructions, and refers to persons or things named or understood in the context

pronghorn

pro·nounce \prə-'naùn(t)s\ *vb* **pro·nounced; pro·nounc·ing** [ME *pronouncen*, fr. MF *prononcier*, fr. L *pronuntiare*, fr. *pro-* forth + *nuntiare* to report, fr. *nuntius* messenger — more at PRO-] *vt* **1 :** to declare officially or ceremoniously <the minister *pronounced* them man and wife> **2 :** to declare authoritatively or as an opinion <doctors *pronounced* him fit to resume duties> **3 a :** to employ the organs of speech to produce <~ these words>; *esp* : to say correctly <I can't ~ his name> **b :** to represent in printed characters the spoken counterpart of (an orthographic representation) <both dictionaries ~ *clique* the same> **4 :** RECITE <speak the speech, I pray you, as I *pronounced* it to you —Shak.> ~ *vi* **1 :** to pass judgment **2 :** to produce the components of spoken language — **pro·nounce·able** \-'naùn(t)-sə-bəl\ *adj* — **pro·nounc·er** *n*
pro·nounced \-'naùn(t)st\ *adj* : strongly marked : DECIDED — **pro·nounced·ly** \-'naùn(t)-səd-lē, -'naùn(t)s-tlē\ *adv*
pro·nounce·ment \prə-'naùn(t)-smənt\ *n* **1 :** a usu. formal declaration of opinion **2 :** an authoritative announcement
pro·nounc·ing *adj* : relating to or indicating pronunciation <a ~ dictionary>
pron·to \'prän-,tō\ *adv* [Sp, fr. L *promptus* prompt] : without delay
pro·nu·cle·us \(')prō-'n(y)ü-klē-əs\ *n* [NL] : either of the gamete nuclei which contribute to the formation of the zygote nucleus and which are in the stage after completion of maturation and entry of a sperm into the egg — **pro·nu·cle·ar** \-klē-ər\ *adj*
pro·nun·ci·a·men·to \prō-,nən(t)-sē-ə-'ment-(,)ō\ *n, pl* **-tos** *or* **-toes** [Sp *pronunciamiento*, fr. *pronunciar* to pronounce, fr. L *pronuntiare*] : PROCLAMATION, PRONOUNCEMENT
pro·nun·ci·a·tion \prə-,nən(t)-sē-'ā-shən\ *n* [ME *pronunciacion*, fr. MF *prononciation*, fr. L *pronuntiation-*, *pronuntiatio*, fr. *pronuntiatus*, pp. of *pronuntiare*] : the act or manner of pronouncing something — **pro·nun·ci·a·tion·al** \-shnəl, -shən-ᵊl\ *adj*
[1]**proof** \'prüf\ *n* [ME, alter. of *preove*, fr. OF *preuve*, fr. LL *proba*, fr. L *probare* to prove — more at PROVE] **1 a :** the cogency of evidence that compels acceptance by the mind of a truth or a fact **b :** the process or an instance of establishing the validity of a statement esp. by derivation from other statements in accordance with accepted or stipulated principles of reasoning **2** *obs* : EXPERIENCE **3 :** an act, effort, or operation designed to establish or discover a fact or truth : TEST **4** *archaic* : the quality or state of having been tested or tried; *esp* : unyielding hardness **5 :** evidence operating to determine the finding or judgment of a tribunal **6 a :** an impression (as from type) taken for correction

PROOFREADERS' MARKS

- or or — delete; take it out
- close up; print as one word
- delete and close up
- or or — caret; insert here (something
- # — insert a space
- eq# — space evenly where indicated
- stet — let marked text stand as set
- tr — transpose; change order the
- / — used to separate two or more marks and often as a concluding stroke at the end of an insertion
- set farther to the left
- set farther to the right
- set ae or fl as ligatures æ or ﬂ
- straighten alignment
- straighten or align
- x — imperfect or broken character
- indent or insert em quad space
- ¶ — begin a new paragraph
- (sp) — spell out (set 5 lbs. as five pounds)
- cap — set in capitals (CAPITALS)
- sm cap or s.c. — set in small capitals (SMALL CAPITALS)
- lc — set in Lowercase (lowercase)
- ital — set in italic (*italic*)
- rom — set in roman (roman)
- bf — set in boldface (**boldface**)
- = or -/ or or /H/ — hyphen
- 1/N or en or /N/ — en dash (1965–72)
- 1/M or em or /M/ — em — or long — dash
- superscript or superior (2 as in πr^2)
- subscript or inferior (2 as in H_2O)
- or — centered (· for a centered dot in $p \cdot q$)
- comma
- apostrophe
- period
- ; or ;/ — semicolon
- : or — colon
- or — quotation marks
- (/) — parentheses
- [/] — brackets
- OK/? — query to author: has this been set as intended?
- or [1] — push down a work-up
- [1] — turn over an inverted letter
- wf[1] — wrong font; a character of the wrong size or esp. style

[1] The last three symbols are unlikely to be needed in marking proofs of photocomposed matter.

or examination **b :** a proof impression of an engraving, etching, or lithograph **c :** a coin that is struck from a highly-polished die on a polished planchet, is not intended for circulation, and sometimes differs in metallic content from that of coins of identical design struck for circulation **d :** a test photographic print made from a negative **7 :** a test applied to articles or substances to determine whether they are of standard or satisfactory quality **8 a :** the minimum alcoholic strength of proof spirit **b :** strength with reference to the standard for proof spirit; *specif* **:** alcoholic strength indicated by a number that is twice the percent by volume of alcohol present <whiskey of 90 ~ is 45% alcohol>

[2]**proof** *adj* **1 :** designed for or successful in resisting or repelling — often used in combination <water*proof*> **2 :** used in proving or testing or a standard of comparison **3 :** of standard strength or quality or alcoholic content

[3]**proof** *vt* **1 a :** to make or take a proof or test of **b :** PROOFREAD **2 :** to bring (dough) to the proper lightness **3 :** to give a resistant quality to — **proof·er** *n*

proof·like \'prü-ˌflīk\ *adj* **:** resembling a proof coin esp. because of a mirrorlike surface

proof·read \'prü-ˌfrēd\ *vt* [back-formation fr. *proofreader*] **:** to read and mark corrections in (a proof) — **proof·read·er** *n*

proof·room \'prü-ˌfrüm, -ˌfru̇m\ *n* **:** a room in which proofreading is done

proof spirit *n* **:** alcoholic liquor or mixture of alcohol and water that contains one half of its volume of alcohol of a specific gravity 0.7939 at 60°F

[1]**prop** \'präp\ *n* [ME *proppe*, fr. MD, stopper; akin to MLG *proppe* stopper] **:** something that props or sustains **:** SUPPORT

[2]**prop** *vt* **propped; prop·ping 1 a :** to support by placing something under or against — often used with *up* **b :** to support by placing against something **2 :** SUSTAIN, STRENGTHEN

[3]**prop** *n* **:** PROPERTY 3

[4]**prop** *n* **:** PROPELLER

[5]**prop** *abbr* **1** property **2** proposition **3** proprietor

prop- *comb form* [ISV, fr. *propionic (acid)*] **:** related to propionic acid <*prop*ane> <*prop*yl>

[1]**pro·pae·deu·tic** \ˌprō-pi-'d(y)üt-ik\ *n* [Gk *propaideuein* to teach beforehand, fr. *pro-* before + *paideuein* to teach, fr. *paid-, pais* child — more at PRO-, FEW] **:** preparatory study or instruction

[2]**propaedeutic** *adj* **:** needed as preparation for learning or study

pro·pa·gan·da \ˌpräp-ə-'gan-də, ˌprō-pə-\ *n* [NL, fr. *Congregatio de propaganda fide* Congregation for propagating the faith, organization established by Pope Gregory XV] **1** *cap* **:** a congregation of the Roman curia having jurisdiction over missionary territories and related institutions **2 :** the spreading of ideas, information, or rumor for the purpose of helping or injuring an institution, a cause, or a person **3 :** ideas, facts, or allegations spread deliberately to further one's cause or to damage an opposing cause; *also* **:** a public action having such an effect

pro·pa·gan·dism \-'gan-ˌdiz-əm\ *n* **:** the action, practice, or art of propagating doctrines or of spreading or employing propaganda — **pro·pa·gan·dist** \-dəst\ *n or adj* — **pro·pa·gan·dis·tic** \-ˌgan-'dis-tik\ *adj* — **pro·pa·gan·dis·ti·cal·ly** \-ti-k(ə-)lē\ *adv*

pro·pa·gan·dize \-'gan-ˌdīz\ *vb* **-dized; -diz·ing** *vt* **:** to subject to propaganda ~ *vi* **:** to carry on propaganda

prop·a·gate \'präp-ə-ˌgāt\ *vb* **-gat·ed; -gat·ing** [L *propagatus*, pp. of *propagare* to set slips, propagate, fr. *propages* slip, offspring, fr. *pro-* before + *pangere* to fasten — more at PRO-, PACT] *vt* **1 :** to cause to continue or increase by sexual or asexual reproduction **2 :** to pass along to offspring **3 a :** to cause to spread out and affect a greater number or greater area **:** EXTEND **b :** PUBLICIZE **c :** TRANSMIT ~ *vi* **1 :** to multiply sexually or asexually **2 :** INCREASE, EXTEND **3 :** to travel through space or a material — used of wave energy (as light, sound, or radio waves) — **prop·a·ga·ble** \'präp-ə-gə-bəl\ *adj* — **prop·a·ga·tive** \-ˌgāt-iv\ *adj* — **prop·a·ga·tor** \-ˌgāt-ər\ *n*

prop·a·ga·tion \ˌpräp-ə-'gā-shən\ *n* **:** the act or action of propagating: as **a :** increase (as of a kind of organism) in numbers **b :** the spreading of something (as a belief) abroad or into new regions **:** DISSEMINATION **c :** enlargement or extension (as of a crack) in a solid body — **prop·a·ga·tion·al** \-shnəl, -shən-ᵊl\ *adj*

prop·a·gule \'präp-ə-ˌgyü(ə)l\ *n* [NL *propagulum*, fr. L *propages* slip] **:** a structure (as a cutting, a seed, or a spore) that propagates a plant

pro·pane \'prō-ˌpān\ *n* [ISV *prop-* + *-ane*] **:** a heavy flammable gaseous paraffin hydrocarbon C_3H_8 found in crude petroleum and natural gas and used esp. as fuel and in chemical synthesis

pro·par·oxy·tone \ˌprō-pə-'räk-si-ˌtōn, ˌprō-ˌpar-'äk-\ *adj* [Gk *proparoxytonos*, fr. *pro-* + *paroxytonos* paroxytone] **:** having or characterized by an acute accent or by stress on the antepenult — **proparoxytone** *n*

pro·pel \prə-'pel\ *vt* **pro·pelled; pro·pel·ling** [ME *propellen*, fr. L *propellere*, fr. *pro-* before + *pellere* to drive — more at FELT] **1 :** to drive forward or onward by means of a force that imparts motion **2 :** to urge on **:** MOTIVATE ***syn*** see PUSH

[1]**pro·pel·lant** *or* **pro·pel·lent** \-'pel-ənt\ *adj* **:** capable of propelling

[2]**propellant** *also* **propellent** *n* **:** something that propels: as **a :** an explosive for propelling projectiles **b :** fuel plus oxidizer used by a rocket engine **c :** a gas in a pressure bottle for expelling the contents when the pressure is released

pro·pel·ler *also* **pro·pel·lor** \prə-'pel-ər\ *n* **:** one that propels; *specif* **:** SCREW PROPELLER

pro·pend \prō-'pend\ *vi* [L *propendēre*, fr. *pro-* before + *pendēre* to hang — more at PENDANT] *obs* **:** INCLINE

pro·pense \prō-'pen(t)s\ *adj* [L *propensus*, pp. of *propendēre*] *archaic* **:** leaning or inclining toward **:** DISPOSED

pro·pen·si·ty \prə-'pen(t)-sət-ē\ *n, pl* **-ties :** an intense and often urgent natural inclination ***syn*** see LEANING

[1]**prop·er** \'präp-ər\ *adj* [ME *propre* proper, own, fr. OF, fr. L *proprius* own] **1 :** marked by suitability, rightness, or appropriateness **:** FIT **2 a :** appointed for the liturgy of a particular day **b :** belonging to one **:** OWN **c :** referring to one individual only **d :** represented heraldically in natural color **3 :** belonging characteristically to a species or individual **:** PECULIAR **4 :** very good **:** EXCELLENT **5** *chiefly Brit* **:** UTTER, ABSOLUTE **6** *chiefly dial* **:** BECOMING, HANDSOME **7 :** strictly limited to a specified thing, place, or idea <the city ~> **8 a :** strictly accurate **:** CORRECT **b** *archaic* **:** VIRTUOUS, RESPECTABLE **c :** strictly decorous **:** GENTEEL **9 :** being a mathematical subset (as a subgroup) that does not contain all the elements of the inclusive set from which it is derived ***syn*** see FIT ***ant*** improper — **prop·er·ness** *n*

[2]**proper** *n* **1 :** the parts of the mass that vary according to the liturgical calendar **2 :** the part of a missal or breviary containing the proper of the mass and the offices proper to the holy days of the liturgical year

[3]**proper** *adv, chiefly dial* **:** in a thorough manner **:** COMPLETELY

proper adjective *n* **:** an adjective that is formed from a proper noun and that is usu. capitalized in English

pro·per·din \prō-'pərd-ᵊn\ *n* [prob. fr. [1]*pro-* + L *perdere* to destroy + E *-in* — more at PERDITION] **:** a serum protein that participates in destruction of bacteria, neutralization of viruses, and lysis of red blood cells

proper fraction *n* **:** a fraction in which the numerator is less or of lower degree than the denominator

prop·er·ly \'präp-ər-lē\ *adv* **:** in a proper manner: as **a :** in a fit manner **:** SUITABLY **b :** strictly in accordance with fact **:** CORRECTLY **c** *chiefly Brit* **:** to the full extent **:** UTTERLY

proper noun *n* **:** a noun that designates a particular being or thing, does not take a limiting modifier, and is usu. capitalized in English — called also *proper name*

prop·er·tied \'präp-ərt-ēd\ *adj* **:** possessing property

prop·er·ty \'präp-ərt-ē\ *n, pl* **-ties** [ME *proprete*, fr. MF *propreté*, fr. L *proprietat-, proprietas*, fr. *proprius* own] **1 a :** a quality or trait belonging and esp. peculiar to an individual or thing **b :** an effect that an object has on another object or on the senses **c :** VIRTUE 3 **d :** an attribute common to all members of a class **2 a :** something owned or possessed; *specif* **:** a piece of real estate **b :** the exclusive right to possess, enjoy, and dispose of a thing **:** OWNERSHIP **c :** something to which a person has a legal title **3 :** an article or object used in a play or motion picture except painted scenery and costumes — **prop·er·ty·less** \-ē-ləs\ *adj*

property damage insurance *n* **:** insurance protecting against all or part of an individual's legal liability for damage done (as by his automobile) to the property of another

property man *n* **:** one who is in charge of stage properties

property right *n* **:** a legal right or interest in or against specific property

property tax *n* **:** a tax levied on real or personal property

pro·phage \'prō-ˌfāj, -ˌfäzh\ *n* **:** an intracellular form of a bacteriophage in which it is harmless to the host, is usu. integrated into the hereditary material of the host, and reproduces when the host does

pro·phase \-ˌfāz\ *n* [ISV] **1 :** the initial phase of mitosis in which chromosomes are condensed from the resting form and split into paired chromatids **2 :** the initial stage of meiosis in which the chromosomes become visible, homologous pairs of chromosomes undergo synapsis and become shortened and thickened, individual chromosomes become visibly double as paired chromatids, chiasmata occur, and the nuclear membrane disappears — compare DIAKINESIS, DIPLOTENE, LEPTOTENE, PACHYTENE, ZYGOTENE — **pro·pha·sic** \(ˈ)prō-'fā-zik\ *adj*

proph·e·cy *also* **proph·e·sy** \'präf-ə-sē\ *n, pl* **-cies** *also* **-sies** [ME *prophecie*, fr. OF, fr. LL *prophetia*, fr. Gk *prophēteia*, fr. *prophētēs* prophet] **1 :** the function or vocation of a prophet; *specif* **:** the inspired declaration of divine will and purpose **2 :** an inspired utterance of a prophet **3 :** a prediction of something to come

proph·e·sy \'präf-ə-ˌsī\ *vb* **-sied; -sy·ing** [ME *prophesien*, fr. MF *prophesier*, fr. OF, fr. *prophecie*] *vt* **1 :** to utter by or as if by divine inspiration **2 :** to predict with assurance or on the basis of mystic knowledge **3 :** FORESHOW, PREFIGURE ~ *vi* **1 :** to speak as if divinely inspired **2 :** to give instruction in religious matters **:** PREACH **3 :** to make a prediction ***syn*** see FORETELL — **proph·e·si·er** \-ˌsī(-ə)r\ *n*

proph·et \'präf-ət\ *n* [ME *prophete*, fr. OF, fr. L *propheta*, fr. Gk *prophētēs*, fr. *pro* for + *phanai* to speak — more at FOR, BAN] **1 :** one who utters divinely inspired revelations; *specif, often cap* **:** the writer of one of the prophetic books of the Old Testament **2 :** one gifted with more than ordinary spiritual and moral insight; *esp* **:** an inspired poet **3 :** one who foretells future events **:** PREDICTOR <a weather ~> **4 :** an effective or leading spokesman for a cause, doctrine, or group <he is first the student and then the ~ of power —Alfred Kazin> **5** *Christian Science* **a :** a spiritual seer **b :** disappearance of material sense before the conscious facts of spiritual Truth — **proph·et·ess** \-ət-əs\ *n*

pro·phet·ic \prə-'fet-ik\ *or* **pro·phet·i·cal** \-'fet-i-kəl\ *adj* **1 :** of, relating to, or characteristic of a prophet or prophecy **2 :** foretelling events **:** PREDICTIVE — **pro·phet·i·cal·ly** \-i-k(ə-)lē\ *adv*

Proph·ets \'präf-əts\ *n pl* **:** the second part of the Jewish scriptures — see BIBLE table

[1]**pro·phy·lac·tic** \ˌprō-fə-'lak-tik *also* ˌpräf-ə-\ *adj* [Gk *prophylaktikos*, fr. *prophylassein* to keep guard before, fr. *pro-* before + *phylassein* to guard, fr. *phylak-, phylax* guard] **1 :** guarding from or preventing disease **2 :** tending to prevent or ward off **:** PREVENTIVE <the purpose of this volume is ~ rather than remedial —Knight Dunlap> — **pro·phy·lac·ti·cal·ly** \-ti-k(ə-)lē\ *adv*

[2]**prophylactic** *n* **:** something that is prophylactic: as **a :** something (as a condom) for preventing venereal infection **b :** a contraceptive device

pro·phy·lax·is \-'lak-səs\ *n, pl* **-lax·es** \-'lak-,sēz\ [NL, fr. Gk *prophylaktikos*] : measures designed to preserve health (as of the body or of society) and prevent the spread of disease

¹pro·pine \prə-'pēn, -'pīn\ *vt* **pro·pined; pro·pin·ing** [ME *propinen,* fr. MF *propiner,* fr. L *propinare* to present, drink to someone's health, fr. Gk *propinein* lit., to drink first, fr. *pro-* ¹pro- + *pinein* to drink — more at POTABLE] *chiefly Scot* **1** : to present or give esp. as a token of friendship **2** : PLEDGE 2

²propine *n, Scot* : a gift in return for a favor

pro·pin·qui·ty \prə-'piŋ-kwət-ē\ *n* [ME *propinquite,* fr. L *propinquitat-, propinquitas* kinship, proximity, fr. *propinquus* near, akin, fr. *prope* near — more at APPROACH] **1** : nearness of blood : KINSHIP **2** : nearness in place or time : PROXIMITY

pro·pi·o·nate \'prō-pē-ə-,nāt\ *n* [ISV] : a salt or ester of propionic acid

pro·pi·on·ic acid \,prō-pē-,än-ik-\ *n* [ISV ¹*pro-* + Gk *piōn* fat; akin to L *opimus* fat — more at FAT] : a liquid sharp-odored fatty acid $C_3H_6O_2$ found in milk and distillates of wood, coal, and petroleum

pro·pi·ti·ate \prō-'pish-ē-,āt\ *vt* **-at·ed; -at·ing** [L *propitiatus,* pp. of *propitiare,* fr. *propitius* propitious] : to gain or regain the favor or goodwill of : APPEASE, CONCILIATE — **pro·pi·ti·able** \-ē-ə-bəl\ *adj* — **pro·pi·ti·ator** \-ē-,āt-ər\ *n*

pro·pi·ti·a·tion \prō-,pis(h)-ē-'ā-shən\ *n* **1** : the act of propitiating **2** : something that propitiates; *specif* : an atoning sacrifice

pro·pi·tia·to·ry \prō-'pish-(ē-)ə-,tōr-ē, -,tȯr-\ *adj* **1** : of or relating to propitiation **2** : intended to propitiate : EXPIATORY

pro·pi·tious \prə-'pish-əs\ *adj* [ME *propicious,* fr. L *propitius,* fr. *pro-* for + *petere* to seek — more at PRO-, FEATHER] **1** : favorably disposed : BENEVOLENT **2** : being of good omen : AUSPICIOUS <~ sign> **3** : tending to favor : ADVANTAGEOUS ***syn*** see FAVORABLE ***ant*** unpropitious, adverse — **pro·pi·tious·ly** *adv* — **pro·pi·tious·ness** *n*

prop·jet engine \,präp-,jet-\ *n* : TURBO-PROPELLER ENGINE

pro·plas·tid \(')prō-'plas-təd\ *n* [ISV] : a minute cytoplasmic body from which a plastid is formed

prop·man \'präp-,man\ *n* : PROPERTY MAN

prop·o·lis \'präp-ə-ləs\ *n* [L, fr. Gk, fr. *pro-* for + *polis* city — more at PRO-, POLICE] : a brownish resinous material of waxy consistency collected by bees from the buds of trees and used as a cement

pro·pone \prə-'pōn\ *vt* **pro·poned; pro·pon·ing** [ME (Sc) *proponen,* fr. L *proponere* — more at PROPOUND] **1** *Scot* : PROPOSE, PROPOUND **2** *Scot* : to put forward (a defense)

pro·po·nent \prə-'pō-nənt, 'prō-,\ *n* [L *proponent-, proponens,* prp. of *proponere*] : one who argues in favor of something : ADVOCATE

¹pro·por·tion \p(r)ə-'pōr-shən, -'pȯr-\ *n* [ME *proporcion,* fr. MF *proportion,* fr. L *proportion-, proportio,* fr. *pro* for + *portion-, portio* portion — more at FOR] **1** : the relation of one part to another or to the whole with respect to magnitude, quantity, or degree : RATIO **2** : harmonious relation of parts to each other or to the whole : BALANCE, SYMMETRY **3** : a relation of equality of two ratios in which the first of the four terms divided by the second equals the third divided by the fourth (as in $4/2=10/5$) **4 a** : proper or equal share <each did his ~ of the work> **b** : QUOTA, PERCENTAGE **5** : SIZE, DIMENSION

²proportion *vt* **pro·por·tioned; pro·por·tion·ing** \-sh(ə-)niŋ\ **1** : to adjust (a part or thing) in size relative to other parts or things **2** : to make the parts of harmonious or symmetrical **3** : APPORTION, ALLOT

pro·por·tion·able \-sh(ə-)nə-bəl\ *adj, archaic* : PROPORTIONAL, PROPORTIONATE — **pro·por·tion·ably** \-blē\ *adv, archaic*

¹pro·por·tion·al \p(r)ə-'pōr-shnəl, -'pȯr-, -shən-ᵊl\ *adj* **1 a** : being in proportion : PROPORTIONATE **b** : having the same or a constant ratio **2** : regulated or determined in size or degree with reference to proportions <a ~ system of immigration quotas> — **pro·por·tion·al·i·ty** \-,pōr-shə-'nal-ət-ē, -,pȯr-\ *n* — **pro·por·tion·al·ly** \-'pōr-shnə-lē, -'pȯr-, -shən-ᵊl-ē\ *adv*

²proportional *n* : a number or quantity in a proportion

proportional parts *n pl* : fractional parts of the difference between successive entries in a table for use in linear interpolation

proportional representation *n* : an electoral system designed to represent in a legislative body each political group or party in proportion to its actual voting strength in the electorate

proportional tax *n* : a tax in which the tax rate remains constant regardless of the amount of the tax base

¹pro·por·tion·ate \p(r)ə-'pōr-sh(ə-)nət, -'pȯr-\ *adj* : being in proportion — **pro·por·tion·ate·ly** *adv*

²pro·por·tion·ate \-shə-,nāt\ *vt* **-at·ed; -at·ing** : to make proportionate : PROPORTION

pro·pos·al \prə-'pō-zəl\ *n* **1** : an act of putting forward or stating something for consideration **2 a** : something proposed : SUGGESTION **b** : OFFER; *specif* : an offer of marriage

pro·pose \prə-'pōz\ *vb* **pro·posed; pro·pos·ing** [ME *proposen,* fr. MF *proposer,* fr. L *proponere* (perf. indic. *proposui*) — more at PROPOUND] *vi* **1** : to form or put forward a plan or intention <man ~*s,* but God disposes> **2** *obs* : to engage in talk or discussion **3** : to make an offer of marriage ~ *vt* **1 a** : to set before the mind (as for discussion, imitation, or action) <*proposed* a plan for settling the dispute> **b** : to set before someone and esp. oneself as an aim or intent <*proposed* to spend the summer in study> **2 a** : to set forth for acceptance or rejection <~ terms for peace> <~ a topic for debate> **b** : to recommend to fill a place or vacancy : NOMINATE <agreed to ~ him for membership> **c** : to offer as a toast <~ the health of the ladies> — **pro·pos·er** *n*

syn PROPOSE, PROPOUND, POSE *shared meaning element* : to set before the mind for consideration

¹prop·o·si·tion \,präp-ə-'zish-ən\ *n* **1 a** : something offered for consideration or acceptance : PROPOSAL; *specif* : a request for sexual intercourse **b** : the point to be discussed or maintained in argument usu. stated in sentence form near the outset **c** : a theorem or problem to be demonstrated or performed **2 a** : an expression in language or signs of something that can be believed, doubted, or denied or is either true or false **b** : the objective meaning of a proposition **3** : a project or situation requiring some action — **prop·o·si·tion·al** \-'zish-nəl, -ən-ᵊl\ *adj*

²proposition *vt* **prop·o·si·tioned; prop·o·si·tion·ing** \-'zish-(ə-)niŋ\ : to make a proposal to; *specif* : to suggest sexual intercourse to

propositional calculus *n* : the branch of symbolic logic that uses symbols for unanalyzed propositions and logical connectives only — called also *sentential calculus;* compare PREDICATE CALCULUS

propositional function *n* **1** : SENTENTIAL FUNCTION **2** : something that is designated or expressed by a sentential function

pro·pos·i·tus \prō-'päz-ət-əs\ *n, pl* **-i·ti** \-ə-,tī\ [NL, fr. L, pp. of *proponere*] : the person immediately concerned : SUBJECT

pro·pound \prə-'paund\ *vt* [alter. of earlier *propone,* fr. ME (Sc) *proponen,* fr. L *proponere* to display, propound, fr. *pro-* before + *ponere* to put, place — more at PRO-, POSITION] : to offer for discussion or consideration ***syn*** see PROPOSE — **pro·pound·er** *n*

pro·prae·tor *or* **pro·pre·tor** \(')prō-'prēt-ər\ *n* [L *propraetor,* fr. *pro-* (as in *proconsul*) + *praetor*] : a praetor of ancient Rome sent out to govern a province

pro·pran·o·lol \prō-'pran-ə-,lōl, -,lōl\ *n* [prob. alter. of earlier *propanolol,* fr. *propanol* (propyl alcohol) + *-ol*] : a beta-adrenergic blocking agent $C_{16}H_{21}NO_2$ used in the treatment of abnormal heart rhythms and angina pectoris

¹pro·pri·etary \p(r)ə-'prī-ə-,ter-ē\ *n, pl* **-etar·ies** **1 a** : PROPRIETOR, OWNER **b** : an owner or grantee of a proprietary colony **2** : a body of proprietors **3** : a drug that is protected by secrecy, patent, or copyright against free competition as to name, product, composition, or process of manufacture

²proprietary *adj* [LL *proprietarius,* fr. L *proprietas* property — more at PROPERTY] **1** : of, relating to, or characteristic of a proprietor <~ rights> **2** : made and marketed by one having the exclusive right to manufacture and sell <a ~ process> **3** : privately owned and managed <a ~ clinic>

proprietary colony *n* : a colony granted to a proprietor with full prerogatives of government

pro·pri·etor \p(r)ə-'prī-ət-ər\ *n* [alter. of ¹*proprietary*] **1** : PROPRIETARY 1b **2 a** : one who has the legal right or exclusive title to something : OWNER **b** : one having an interest (as control or present use) less than absolute and exclusive right — **pro·pri·etor·ship** \-,ship\ *n* — **pro·pri·etress** \-'prī-ə-trəs\ *n*

pro·pri·ety \p(r)ə-'prī-ət-ē\ *n, pl* **-eties** [ME *propriete,* fr. MF *proprieté* property, quality of a person or thing — more at PROPERTY] **1** *obs* : true nature **2** *obs* : a special characteristic : PECULIARITY **3** : the quality or state of being proper **4 a** : the standard of what is socially acceptable in conduct or speech : DECORUM **b** : fear of offending against conventional rules of behavior esp. as between the sexes **c** *pl* : the customs and manners of polite society

pro·prio·cep·tion \,prō-prē-ō-'sep-shən\ *n* [*proprioceptive* + *-ion*] : the reception of stimuli produced within the organism

pro·prio·cep·tive \-'sep-tiv\ *adj* [L *proprius* own + E *-ceptive* (as in *receptive*)] : of, relating to, or being stimuli arising within the organism

pro·prio·cep·tor \-tər\ *n* : a sensory receptor excited by proprioceptive stimuli

prop root *n* : a root that serves as a prop or support to the plant

pro·pto·sis \(')prō-'tō-səs, präp-'tō-\ *n* [NL, fr. LL, falling forward, fr. Gk *proptōsis,* fr. *propiptein* to fall forward, fr. *pro-* + *piptein* to fall — more at PRO-, FEATHER] : forward projection or displacement esp. of the eyeball

pro·pul·sion \prə-'pəl-shən\ *n* [L *propulsus,* pp. of *propellere* to propel] **1** : the action or process of propelling **2** : something that propels

pro·pul·sive \-'pəl-siv\ *adj* [L *propulsus*] : tending or having power to propel

pro·pyl \'prō-pəl\ *n* : either of two isomeric alkyl radicals C_3H_7 derived from propane or an isomer — **pro·pyl·ic** \prō-'pil-ik\ *adj*

pro·py·lae·um \,präp-ə-'lē-əm, ,prōp-\ *n, pl* **-laea** \-'lē-ə\ [L, fr. Gk *propylaion,* fr. *pro-* before + *pylē* gate — more at PRO-] : a vestibule or entrance of architectural importance before a building or enclosure — often used in pl.

pro·pyl·ene \'prō-pə-,lēn\ *n* : a flammable gaseous hydrocarbon C_3H_6 obtained by cracking petroleum hydrocarbons and used chiefly in organic synthesis

propylene glycol *n* : a sweet hygroscopic viscous liquid $C_3H_8O_2$ made esp. from propylene and used esp. as an antifreeze and solvent and in brake fluids

pro ra·ta \(')prō-'rāt-ə, -'rät-, -'rat-\ *adv* [L] : proportionately according to an exactly calculable factor (as share or liability) — **pro rata** *adj*

pro·rate \(')prō-'rāt\ *vb* **pro·rat·ed; pro·rat·ing** [*pro rata*] *vt* : to divide, distribute, or assess proportionately ~ *vi* : to make a pro rata distribution

pro·ra·tion \prō-'rā-shən\ *n* : an act or an instance of prorating; *specif* : the limitation of production of crude oil or gas to some fractional part of the total productive capacity of each producer

pro·ro·gate \'prōr-ō-,gāt, 'prȯr-\ *vt* **-gat·ed; -gat·ing** : PROROGUE — **pro·ro·ga·tion** \,prōr-ō-'gā-shən, ,prȯr-\ *n*

pro·rogue \p(r)ə-'rōg\ *vb* **pro·rogued; pro·rogu·ing** [ME *prorogen,* fr. MF *proroguer,* fr. L *prorogare,* fr. *pro-* before + *rogare* to ask — more at PRO-, RIGHT] *vt* **1** : DEFER, POSTPONE **2** : to terminate a session of (as a British parliament) by royal prerogative ~ *vi* : to suspend or end a legislative session ***syn*** see ADJOURN

¹pros *pl of* PRO

²pros *abbr* prosody

pros- *prefix* [LL, fr. Gk, fr. *proti, pros* face to face with, towards, in addition to, near; akin to Skt *prati-* near, towards, against, in return, Gk *pro* before — more at FOR] **1** : near : toward <*pros*enchyma> **2** : in front <*pros*encephalon>

pro·sa·ic \prō-'zā-ik\ *adj* [LL *prosaicus,* fr. L *prosa* prose] **1 a** : characteristic of prose as distinguished from poetry : FACTUAL **b** : DULL, UNIMAGINATIVE **2** : belonging to or suitable for the everyday world — **pro·sa·i·cal·ly** \-'zā-ə-k(ə-)lē\ *adv*

syn PROSAIC, PROSY, MATTER-OF-FACT *shared meaning element* : having a plain practical unimaginative quality or character

pro·sa·ism \'prō-(,)zā-,iz-əm\ *n* **1 :** a prosaic manner, style, or quality **2 :** a prosaic expression
pro·sa·ist *n* [L *prosa* prose] **1** \'prō-(,)zā-əst, -zā-,ist\ **:** a prose writer **2** \prō-'zā-əst\ **:** a prosaic person
pro·sa·teur \,prō-zə-'tər\ *n* [F, fr. It *prosatore,* fr. ML *prosator,* fr. L *prosa*] **:** a writer of prose
pro·sce·ni·um \prō-'sē-nē-əm\ *n* [L, fr. Gk *proskēnion* front of the building forming the background for a dramatic performance, stage, fr. *pro-* + *skēnē* building forming the background for a dramatic performance — more at SCENE] **1 a :** the stage of an ancient Greek or Roman theater **b :** the part of a modern stage in front of the curtain **c :** the wall that separates the stage from the auditorium and provides the arch that frames it **2 :** FOREGROUND
proscenium arch *n* **:** the arch that encloses the opening in the proscenium wall through which the spectator sees the stage
pro·sciut·to \prō-'shü-(,)tō\ *n, pl* **-tl** \-(,)tē\ *or* **-tos** [It, alter. of obs. *presciutto*] **:** dry-cured spiced Italian ham usu. sliced very thin
pro·scribe \prō-'skrīb\ *vt* **pro·scribed; pro·scrib·ing** [L *proscribere* to publish, proscribe, fr. *pro-* before + *scribere* to write — more at SCRIBE] **1 a :** to publish the name of (a person) as condemned to death with his property forfeited to the state **b :** OUTLAW **2 :** to condemn or forbid as harmful **:** PROHIBIT — **pro·scrib·er** *n*
pro·scrip·tion \prō-'skrip-shən\ *n* [ME *proscripcion,* fr. L *proscription-, proscriptio,* fr. *proscriptus,* pp. of *proscribere*] **1 :** the act of proscribing **:** the state of being proscribed **2 :** an imposed restraint or restriction **:** PROHIBITION — **pro·scrip·tive** \-'skrip-tiv\ *adj* — **pro·scrip·tive·ly** *adv*
¹prose \'prōz\ *n* [ME, fr. MF, fr. L *prosa,* fr. fem. of *prorsus, prosus,* straightforward, being in prose, contr. of *proversus,* pp. of *provertere* to turn forward, fr. *pro-* forward + *vertere* to turn — more at PRO-, WORTH] **1 a :** the ordinary language of men in speaking or writing **b :** a literary medium distinguished from poetry esp. by its greater irregularity and variety of rhythm and its closer correspondence to the patterns of everyday speech **2 :** a prosaic style, quality, character, or condition **:** ORDINARINESS, MATTER-OF-FACTNESS
²prose *vi* **prosed; pros·ing 1 :** to write prose **2 :** to write or speak in a dull prosaic manner
³prose *adj* **1 :** of, relating to, or written in prose **2 :** MATTER-OF-FACT, PROSAIC <dry, ~ people of superior intelligence —Mary McCarthy>
pro·sec·tor \prō-'sek-tər\ *n* [prob. fr. F *prosecteur,* fr. LL *prosector* anatomist, fr. L *prosectus,* pp. of *prosecare* to cut away, fr. *pro-* forth + *secare* to cut — more at PRO-, SAW] **:** one that makes dissections for anatomic demonstrations — **pro·sec·to·ri·al** \,prō-,sek-'tōr-ē-əl, -'tȯr-\ *adj*
pros·e·cute \'präs-i-,kyüt\ *vb* **-cut·ed; -cut·ing** [ME *prosecuten,* fr. L *prosecutus,* pp. of *prosequi* to pursue — more at PURSUE] *vt* **1 :** to follow to the end **:** pursue until finished <was . . . ordered to ~ the war with . . . vigor —Marjory S. Douglas> **2 :** to engage in **:** PERFORM **3 a :** to pursue for redress or punishment of a crime or violation of law in due legal form before a legal tribunal <*prosecuted* them for fraud> **b :** to institute legal proceedings with reference to <~ a claim> ~ *vi* **:** to institute and carry on a legal suit or prosecution — **pros·e·cut·able** \-,kyüt-ə-bəl\ *adj*
prosecuting attorney *n* **:** an attorney who conducts proceedings in a court on behalf of the government **:** DISTRICT ATTORNEY
pros·e·cu·tion \,präs-i-'kyü-shən\ *n* **1 :** the act or process of prosecuting; *specif* **:** the institution and continuance of a criminal suit involving the process of pursuing formal charges against an offender to final judgment **2 :** the party by whom criminal proceedings are instituted or conducted **3** *obs* **:** PURSUIT
pros·e·cu·tor \'präs-i-,kyüt-ər\ *n* **1 :** a person who institutes an official prosecution before a court **2 :** PROSECUTING ATTORNEY
¹pros·e·lyte \'präs-ə-,līt\ *n* [ME *proselite,* fr. LL *proselytus* proselyte, alien resident, fr. Gk *prosēlytos,* fr. *pros* near + *-ēlytos* (akin to *elthein* to go); akin to Gk *elaunein* to drive — more at PROS-, ELASTIC] **:** a new convert; *specif* **:** a convert to Judaism
²proselyte *vb* **-lyt·ed; -lyt·ing** *vt* **:** to convert from one religion, belief, or party to another ~ *vi* **1 :** to make proselytes **2 :** to recruit members esp. by the offer of special inducements
pros·e·ly·tism \'präs-ə-,līt-,iz-əm, 'präs-(ə-)lə-,tiz-\ *n* **1 :** the act of becoming or condition of being a proselyte **:** CONVERSION **2 :** the act or process of proselyting
pros·e·ly·tize \'präs-(ə-)lə-,tīz\ *vb* **-tized; -tiz·ing :** PROSELYTE — **pros·e·ly·ti·za·tion** \,präs-(ə-)lət-ə-'zā-shən, ,präs-ə-,līt-\ *n* — **pros·e·ly·tiz·er** \'präs-(ə-)lə-,tī-zər\ *n*
pro·sem·i·nar \(')prō-'sem-ə-,när\ *n* **:** a directed course of study conducted in the manner of a graduate seminar but often open to advanced undergraduate students
pros·en·ceph·a·lon \,präs-,en-'sef-ə-,län, -lən\ *n* [NL] **:** FOREBRAIN — **pros·en·ce·phal·ic** \-sə-'fal-ik\ *adj*
pros·en·chy·ma \prä-'seŋ-kə-mə\ *n, pl* **pros·en·chy·ma·ta** \,präs-ᵊn-'kim-ət-ə, -'kīm-\ *or* **prosenchymas** [NL] **:** a tissue of higher plants composed of elongated cells with little protoplasm and specialized for conduction and support — **pros·en·chy·ma·tous** \,präs-ᵊn-'kim-ət-əs, -'kīm-\ *adj*
prose poem *n* **:** a work in prose that has some of the qualities of a poem — **prose poet** *n*
pros·er \'prō-zər\ *n* **1 :** a writer of prose **2 :** one who talks or writes tediously
Pro·ser·pi·na \prō-'sər-pə-nə\ *or* **Pros·er·pine** \'präs-ər-,pīn\ *n* [L *Proserpina*] **:** PERSEPHONE
pro·sit \'prō-zət, -sət\ *or* **prost** \'prōst\ *interj* [G, fr. L *prosit* may it be beneficial, fr. *prodesse* to be useful — more at PROUD] — used to wish good health esp. before drinking
pro·so \'prō-(,)sō\ *n* [Russ] **:** MILLET 1a
proso·branch \'präs-ə-,braŋk\ *n, pl* **-branchs** [NL *Prosobranchia,* group name, fr. *proso-* in front (fr. Gk *prosō* forward) + *branchia*] **:** any of a subclass (Streptoneura, Prosobranchia, or Prosobranchiata) of gastropods that have the loop of visceral nerves twisted into a figure 8, the sexes usu. separate, and usu. an operculum
pro·sod·ic \prə-'säd-ik *also* -'zäd-\ *or* **pro·sod·i·cal** \-i-kəl\ *adj* **:** of or relating to prosody — **pro·sod·i·cal·ly** \-i-k(ə-)lē\ *adv*
pros·o·dy \'präs-əd-ē *also* 'präz-\ *n, pl* **-dies** [ME, fr. L *prosodia* accent of a syllable, fr. Gk *prosōidia* song sung to instrumental music, accent, fr. *pros* in addition to + *ōidē* song — more at PROS-, ODE] **1 :** the study of versification; *esp* **:** the systematic study of metrical structure **:** METRICS **2 :** a particular system, theory, or style of versification — **pros·o·dist** \-əd-əst\ *n*
pro·so·ma \(')prō-'sō-mə\ *n* [NL, fr. Gk *pro-* + *sōma* body; akin to L *tumēre* to swell — more at THUMB] **:** the anterior region of the body of an invertebrate when not readily analyzable into its primitive segmentation; *esp* **:** CEPHALOTHORAX — **pro·so·mal** \-məl\ *adj*
pros·o·pog·ra·phy \,präs-ə-'päg-rə-fē\ *n* [NL *prosopographia,* fr. Gk *prosōpon* person + *-graphia* -graphy] **:** a study that identifies and relates a group of persons or characters within a particular historical or literary context — **pros·o·po·graph·i·cal** \-pə-'graf-i-kəl\ *adj*
pro·so·po·poe·ia \prə-,sō-pə-'pē-(y)ə, ,präs-ə-pə-\ *n* [L, fr. Gk *prosōpopoiia,* fr. *prosōpon* mask, person (fr. *pros-* + *ōps* face) + *poiein* to make — more at EYE, POET] **1 :** a figure of speech in which an imaginary or absent person is represented as speaking or acting **2 :** PERSONIFICATION
¹pros·pect \'präs-,pekt\ *n* [ME, fr. L *prospectus* view, prospect, fr. *prospectus,* pp. of *prospicere* to look forward, exercise foresight, fr. *pro-* forward + *specere* to look — more at PRO-, SKY] **1 :** EXPOSURE 2b **2 a (1) :** an extensive view **(2) :** a mental consideration **:** SURVEY **b :** a place that commands an extensive view **:** LOOKOUT **c :** something extended to the view **:** SCENE **d** *archaic* **:** a sketch or picture of a scene **3** *obs* **:** ASPECT **4 a :** the act of looking forward **:** ANTICIPATION **b :** a mental picture of something to come **:** VISION **c :** something that is awaited or expected **:** POSSIBILITY **d** *pl* **(1) :** financial expectations **(2) :** CHANCES **5 a :** a place showing signs of containing a mineral deposit **b :** a partly developed mine **c :** the mineral yield of a tested sample of ore or gravel **6 a :** a potential buyer or customer **b :** a likely candidate
syn PROSPECT, OUTLOOK, ANTICIPATION, FORETASTE *shared meaning element* **:** an advance realization of something to come
²pros·pect \'präs-,pekt, *chiefly Brit* prəs-'\ *vi* **:** to explore an area esp. for mineral deposits ~ *vt* **:** to inspect (a region) for mineral deposits; *broadly* **:** EXPLORE — **pros·pec·tor** \-,pek-tər, -'pek-\ *n*
pro·spec·tive \prə-'spek-tiv *also* 'prä-, prō-', prä-'\ *adj* **1 :** likely to come about **:** EXPECTED <the ~ benefits of this law> **2 :** likely to be or become <a ~ mother> — **pro·spec·tive·ly** *adv*
pro·spec·tus \prə-'spek-təs, prä-\ *n* [L, prospect] **1 :** a preliminary printed statement that describes an enterprise (as a business or publication) and that is distributed to prospective buyers, investors, or participants **2 :** something (as a statement or situation) that forecasts the course or nature of something not yet existent or developed
pros·per \'präs-pər\ *vb* **pros·pered; pros·per·ing** \-p(ə-)riŋ\ [ME *prosperen,* fr. MF *prosperer,* fr. L *prosperare* to cause to succeed, fr. *prosperus* favorable] *vi* **1 :** to succeed in an enterprise or activity; *esp* **:** to achieve economic success **2 :** to become strong and flourishing ~ *vt* **:** to cause to succeed or thrive ***syn*** see SUCCEED
pros·per·i·ty \prä-'sper-ət-ē\ *n* **:** the condition of being successful or thriving; *esp* **:** economic well-being
Pros·pero \'präs-pə-,rō\ *n* **:** the rightful duke of Milan in Shakespeare's *The Tempest*
pros·per·ous \'präs-p(ə-)rəs\ *adj* [ME, fr. MF *prospereux,* fr. *prosperer* to prosper + *-eux* -ous] **1 :** AUSPICIOUS, FAVORABLE **2 a :** marked by success or economic well-being **b :** enjoying vigorous and healthy growth **:** FLOURISHING — **pros·per·ous·ly** *adv* — **pros·per·ous·ness** *n*
pros·ta·glan·din \,präs-tə-'glan-dən\ *n* [*prostate gland* + *-in;* fr. its occurrence in the sexual glands of animals] **:** any of various oxygenated unsaturated cyclic fatty acids of animals that may perform a variety of hormonelike actions (as in controlling blood pressure or smooth muscle contraction)
¹pros·tate \'präs-,tāt\ *n* **:** PROSTATE GLAND
²pros·tate \'präs-,tāt\ *also* **pros·tat·ic** \prä-'stat-ik\ *adj* [NL *prostata* prostate gland, fr. Gk *prostatēs,* fr. *proïstanai* to put in front, fr. *pro-* before + *histanai* to cause to stand — more at PRO-, STAND] **:** of, relating to, or being the prostate gland
pros·ta·tec·to·my \,präs-tə-'tek-tə-mē\ *n, pl* **-mies :** surgical removal of the prostate gland
prostate gland *n* **:** a firm partly muscular partly glandular body that is situated about the base of the mammalian male urethra and secretes an alkaline viscid fluid which is a major constituent of the ejaculatory fluid
prostatic utricle *n* **:** a small blind pouch that projects from the posterior wall of the urethra into the prostate
pros·ta·tism \'präs-tə-,tiz-əm\ *n* **:** disease of the prostate; *esp* **:** a disorder resulting from obstruction of the bladder neck by an enlarged prostate
pros·ta·ti·tis \,präs-tə-'tīt-əs\ *n* [NL] **:** inflammation of the prostate gland
pros·the·sis \präs-'thē-səs, 'präs-thə-\ *n, pl* **-the·ses** \-,sēz\ [NL, fr. Gk, addition, fr. *prostithenai* to add to, fr. *pros-* in addition to + *tithenai* to put — more at PROS-, DO] **:** an artificial device to replace a missing part of the body
pros·thet·ic \präs-'thet-ik\ *adj* **1 :** of or relating to a prosthesis or prosthetics **2 :** of, relating to, or constituting a nonprotein group of a conjugated protein — **pros·thet·i·cal·ly** \-i-k(ə-)lē\ *adv*

pros·thet·ics \-iks\ *n pl but sing or pl in constr* **:** the surgical and dental specialties concerned with the artificial replacement of missing parts

prosth·odon·tics \ˌpräs-thə-ˈdänt-iks\ *n pl but sing or pl in constr* [NL *prosthodontia,* fr. *prosthesis* + *-odontia*] **:** prosthetic dentistry — **prosth·odon·tist** \-ˈdänt-əst\ *n* **:** a specialist in prosthodontics

[1]**pros·ti·tute** \ˈpräs-tə-ˌt(y)üt\ *vt* **-tut·ed; -tut·ing** [L *prostitutus,* pp. of *prostituere,* fr. *pro-* before + *statuere* to station — more at PRO-, STATUTE] **1 :** to offer indiscriminately for sexual intercourse esp. for money **2 :** to devote to corrupt or unworthy purposes **:** DEBASE <~ one's talents> — **pros·ti·tu·tor** \-ˌt(y)üt-ər\ *n*

[2]**prostitute** *adj* **:** devoted to corrupt purposes **:** PROSTITUTED

[3]**prostitute** *n* **1 a :** a woman who engages in promiscuous sexual intercourse esp. for money **:** WHORE **b :** a male who engages in sexual practices for money **2 :** a person (as a writer or painter) who deliberately debases himself or his talents (as for money)

pros·ti·tu·tion \ˌpräs-tə-ˈt(y)ü-shən\ *n* **1 :** the act or practice of indulging in promiscuous sexual relations esp. for money **2 :** the state of being prostituted **:** DEBASEMENT

pro·sto·mi·um \prō-ˈstō-mē-əm\ *n, pl* **-mia** \-mē-ə\ [NL, fr. Gk *pro-* + *stoma* mouth — more at STOMACH] **:** the portion of the head of various worms and mollusks that is situated in front of the mouth and is usu. considered to be nonmetameric — **pro·sto·mi·al** \-mē-əl\ *adj*

[1]**pros·trate** \ˈpräs-ˌtrāt\ *adj* [ME *prostrat,* fr. L *prostratus,* pp. of *prosternere,* fr. *pro-* before + *sternere* to spread out, throw down — more at STREW] **1 a :** stretched out with face on the ground in adoration or submission **b :** extended in a horizontal position **:** FLAT **2 :** lacking in vitality or will **:** OVERCOME **3 :** trailing on the ground **:** PROCUMBENT <~ shrub> ***syn*** see PRONE

[2]**pros·trate** \ˈpräs-ˌtrāt, *esp Brit* präs-ˈ\ *vt* **pros·trat·ed; pros·trat·ing 1 :** to throw or put into a prostrate position **2 :** to put (oneself) in a humble and submissive posture or state <the whole town had to ~ itself in official apology —Claudia Cassidy> **3 :** to reduce to submission, helplessness, or exhaustion **:** OVERCOME <*prostrated* with grief>

pros·tra·tion \prä-ˈstrā-shən\ *n* **1 a :** the act of assuming a prostrate position **b :** the state of being in a prostrate position **:** ABASEMENT **2 a :** complete physical or mental exhaustion **:** COLLAPSE **b :** the process of being made powerless of the condition of powerlessness <the country suffered economic ~ after the war>

prosy \ˈprō-zē\ *adj* **pros·i·er; -est** [¹*prose*] **:** lacking in qualities that seize the attention or strike the imagination **:** COMMONPLACE; *esp* **:** tediously dull in speech or manner ***syn*** see PROSAIC — **pros·i·ly** \-zə-lē\ *adv* — **pros·i·ness** \-zē-nəs\ *n*

Prot *abbr* Protestant

prot- *or* **proto-** *comb form* [ME *protho-,* fr. MF, fr. LL *proto-,* fr. Gk *prōt-, prōto-,* fr. *prōtos;* akin to Gk *pro* before — more at FOR] **1 a :** first in time <*proto*lithic> <*proto*nymph> **b :** beginning **:** giving rise to <*proto*planet> **2 a :** first or lowest of a series and as such usu. having the smallest relative amount of a (specified) element or radical <*prot*oxide> **b :** parent substance of a (specified) substance <*prot*actinium> **3 :** first formed **:** primary <*proto*xylem> **4** *cap* **:** relating to or constituting the recorded or assumed language that is ancestral to a language or to a group of related languages or dialects <*Proto*-Indo-European>

prot·ac·tin·i·um \ˌprōt-ˌak-ˈtin-ē-əm\ *n* [NL] **:** a shiny metallic radioelement of relatively short life — see ELEMENT table

pro·tag·o·nist \prō-ˈtag-ə-nəst\ *n* [Gk *prōtagōnistēs,* fr. *prōt-* prot- + *agōnistēs* competitor at games, actor, fr. *agōnizesthai* to compete, fr. *agōn* contest, competition at games — more at AGONY] **1 :** one who takes the leading part in a drama, novel, or story **2 :** the leader of a cause **:** CHAMPION **3 :** a muscle that by its contraction actually causes a particular movement

prot·amine \ˈprōt-ə-ˌmēn\ *n* [ISV *prot-* + *amine*] **:** any of various strongly basic proteins of relatively low molecular weight that are associated with nucleic acids, can be obtained in quantity from sperm cells, and typically contain much arginine

prot·a·sis \ˈprät-ə-səs\ *n, pl* **-a·ses** \-ˌsēz\ [LL, fr. Gk, premise of a syllogism, conditional clause, fr. *proteinein* to stretch out before, put forward, fr. *pro-* + *teinein* to stretch — more at THIN] **1 :** the introductory part of a play or narrative poem **2 :** the subordinate clause of a conditional sentence — compare APODOSIS — **pro·tat·ic** \prä-ˈtat-ik, prō-\ *adj*

prote- *or* **proteo-** *comb form* [ISV, fr. F *protéine*] **:** protein <*proteo*lysis> <*prote*ose>

pro·tea \ˈprōt-ē-ə\ *n* [NL, genus name, fr. L *Proteus* Proteus] **:** any of a genus (*Protea* of the family Proteaceae, the protea family) of evergreen shrubs often grown for their showy bracts and dense flower heads

pro·te·an \ˈprōt-ē-ən, prō-ˈtē-\ *adj* **1 :** of or resembling Proteus **:** VARIABLE **2 :** readily assuming different shapes or roles **3 :** displaying great diversity

pro·te·ase \ˈprōt-ē-ˌās, -ˌāz\ *n* [ISV] **:** PROTEINASE, PEPTIDASE

pro·tect \prə-ˈtekt\ *vt* [L *protectus,* pp. of *protegere,* fr. *pro-* in front + *tegere* to cover — more at PRO-, THATCH] **1 a :** to cover or shield from injury or destruction **:** GUARD **b :** to save from contingent financial loss **2 :** to shield or foster by a protective tariff ***syn*** see DEFEND — **pro·tec·tive** \-ˈtek-tiv\ *adj* — **pro·tec·tive·ly** *adv* — **pro·tec·tive·ness** *n*

pro·tec·tant \prə-ˈtek-tənt\ *n* **:** a protecting agent

pro·tec·tion \prə-ˈtek-shən\ *n* **1 :** the act of protecting **:** the state of being protected **2 a :** one that protects **b :** supervision or support of one that is smaller and weaker **3 :** the freeing of the producers of a country from foreign competition in their home market by restrictions (as high duties) on foreign competitive goods **4 a :** immunity from prosecution purchased by criminals through bribery **b :** money extorted by racketeers posing as a protective association **5 :** COVERAGE 2a

pro·tec·tion·ist \-sh(ə-)nəst\ *n* **:** an advocate of government economic protection for domestic producers through restrictions on foreign competitors — **pro·tec·tion·ism** \-shə-ˌniz-əm\ *n* — **protectionist** *adj*

protective tariff *n* **:** a tariff intended primarily to protect domestic producers rather than to yield revenue — compare REVENUE TARIFF

pro·tec·tor \prə-ˈtek-tər\ *n* **1 a :** one that protects **:** GUARDIAN **b :** a device used to prevent injury **:** GUARD **2 a :** one having the care of a kingdom during the king's minority **:** REGENT **b :** the executive head of the Commonwealth of England, Scotland, and Ireland from 1653 to 1659 — called also *Lord Protector of the Commonwealth* — **pro·tec·tor·ship** \-ˌship\ *n* — **pro·tec·tress** \-ˈtek-trəs\ *n*

pro·tec·tor·al \-ˈtek-t(ə-)rəl\ *adj* **:** of or relating to a protector or protectorate

pro·tec·tor·ate \-ˈtek-t(ə-)rət\ *n* **1 a :** government by a protector **b :** the government of England (1653–59) under the Cromwells **c :** the rank, office, or period of rule of a protector **2 a :** the relationship of superior authority assumed by one power or state over a dependent one **b :** the dependent political unit in such a relationship

pro·tec·to·ry \-t(ə-)rē\ *n, pl* **-ries :** an institution for the protection and care usu. of homeless or delinquent children

pro·té·gé \ˈprōt-ə-ˌzhā, ˌprōt-ə-ˈ\ *n* [F, fr. pp. of *protéger* to protect, fr. L *protegere*] **:** a man under the care and protection of an influential person usu. for the furthering of his career

pro·té·gée \ˈprōt-ə-ˌzhā, ˌprōt-ə-ˈ\ *n* [F, fem. of *protégé*] **:** a female protégé

pro·teid \ˈprō-ˌtēd, ˈprōt-ē-əd\ *also* **pro·teide** \ˈprō-ˌtīd, ˈprōt-ē-ˌīd\ *n* [ISV, fr. *protein*] **:** PROTEIN 1

pro·tein \ˈprō-ˌtēn, ˈprōt-ē-ən\ *n, often attrib* [F *protéine,* fr. LGk *prōteios* primary, fr. Gk *prōtos* first — more at PROT-] **1 :** any of numerous naturally occurring extremely complex combinations of amino acids that contain the elements carbon, hydrogen, nitrogen, oxygen, usu. sulfur, and occas. other elements (as phosphorus or iron), are essential constituents of all living cells, and are synthesized from raw materials by plants but assimilated as separate amino acids by animals **2 :** the total nitrogenous material in plant or animal substances

pro·tein·aceous \ˌprōt-ᵊn-ˈā-shəs, ˌprō-ˌtēn-, ˌprōt-ē-ən-\ *adj* **:** of, relating to, resembling, or being protein

pro·tein·ase \ˈprōt-ᵊn-ˌās, ˈprō-ˌtēn-, ˈprōt-ē-ən-, -ˌāz\ *n* [ISV] **:** an enzyme that hydrolyzes proteins esp. to peptides

pro·tein·ate \-ˌāt\ *n* **:** a compound of a protein <silver ~>

pro·tein·uria \ˌprōt-ᵊn-ˈ(y)u̇r-ē-ə, ˌprō-ˌtēn-, ˌprōt-ē-ən-\ *n* [NL, fr. ISV *protein* + NL *-uria*] **:** the presence of protein in the urine — **pro·tein·uric** \-ˈ(y)u̇r-ik\ *adj*

pro tem \(ˈ)prō-ˈtem\ *adv* **:** pro tempore

pro tem·po·re \prō-ˈtem-pə-rē\ *adv* [L] **:** for the time being

pro·tend \prō-ˈtend\ *vb* [ME *protenden,* fr. L *protendere,* fr. *pro-* + *tendere* to stretch — more at THIN] *vt* **1** *archaic* **:** to stretch forth **2** *archaic* **:** EXTEND ~ *vi, archaic* **:** to stick out **:** PROTRUDE

pro·ten·sive \-ˈten(t)-siv\ *adj* [L *protensus,* pp. of *protendere*] **1** *archaic* **:** having continuance in time **2** *archaic* **:** having lengthwise extent or extensiveness — **pro·ten·sive·ly** *adv*

pro·teo·clas·tic \ˌprōt-ē-ō-ˈklas-tik\ *adj* [*prote-* + Gk *klan* to break — more at HALT] **:** PROTEOLYTIC

pro·te·ol·y·sis \ˌprōt-ē-ˈäl-ə-səs\ *n* [NL] **:** the hydrolysis of proteins or peptides with formation of simpler and soluble products

pro·teo·lyt·ic \ˌprōt-ē-ə-ˈlit-ik\ *adj* **:** of, relating to, or producing proteolysis

pro·te·ose \ˈprōt-ē-ˌōs, -ˌōz\ *n* [ISV] **:** any of various water-soluble protein derivatives formed by partial hydrolysis of proteins

pro·ter·an·thous \ˌprät-ə-ˈran(t)-thəs, ˌprōt-\ *adj* [Gk *proteros* + *anthos* flower — more at ANTHOLOGY] **:** having flowers appearing before the leaves — **pro·ter·an·thy** \ˈprät-ə-ˌran(t)-thē, ˈprōt-\ *n*

Pro·tero·zo·ic \ˌprät-ə-rə-ˈzō-ik, ˌprōt-\ *adj* [Gk *proteros* former, earlier (fr. *pro* before) + ISV *-zoic* — more at FOR] **:** of, relating to, or being an era of geological history that includes the interval between the Archeozoic and the Paleozoic, perhaps exceeds in length all of subsequent geological time, and is marked by rocks that contain a few fossils indicating the existence of annelid worms and algae; *also* **:** relating to the system of rocks formed in this era — see GEOLOGIC TIME table — **Proterozoic** *n*

[1]**pro·test** \ˈprō-ˌtest\ *n* **1 :** a solemn declaration of opinion and usu. of dissent: as **a :** a sworn declaration that payment of a note or bill has been refused and that all responsible signers or debtors are liable for resulting loss or damage **b :** a formal declaration of dissent by a member to an act or resolution of a legislature; *esp* **:** one made by a member of the House of Lords **c :** a declaration made esp. before or while paying that a tax is illegal and that payment is not voluntary **d :** a solemn declaration of disapproval **2 :** the act of protesting; *esp* **:** a usu. organized public demonstration of disapproval <staged a ~ against the war> **3 a :** a complaint, objection, or display of unwillingness usu. to an idea or a course of action <went to the dentist under ~> **b :** a gesture of extreme disapproval **4 :** an objection made to an official or a governing body of a sport

[2]**pro·test** \prə-ˈtest, ˈprō-ˌ, prō-ˈ\ *vb* [ME *protesten,* fr. MF *protester,* fr. L *protestari,* fr. *pro-* forth + *testari* to call to witness — more at PRO-, TESTAMENT] *vt* **1 :** to make solemn declaration or affirmation of **2 :** to execute or have executed a formal protest against (as a bill or note) **3 :** to make a protest against **4 :** to offer objection to in words or acts ~ *vi* **1 :** to make a protestation **2 :** to make or enter a protest ***syn* 1** see ASSERT **2** see OBJECT ***ant*** agree — **pro·test·er** *or* **pro·tes·tor** \-ˈtes-tər, -ˌtes-\ *n*

[1]**prot·es·tant** \ˈprät-əs-tənt, *2 is also* prə-ˈtes-\ *n* [MF, fr. L *protestant-, protestans,* prp. of *protestari*] **1** *cap* **a :** one of a group of German princes and cities presenting a defense of freedom of conscience against an edict of the Diet of Spires in 1529 intended to suppress the Lutheran movement **b :** a Christian denying the universal authority of the Pope and affirming the Reformation principles of justification by faith alone, the priesthood of all believers, and the primacy of the Bible as the only source of revealed truth **c :** a Christian not of a Catholic or Eastern church **2 :** one who makes or enters a protest — **Prot·es·tant·ism** \ˈprät-əs-tənt-ˌiz-əm\ *n*

²protestant *adj* **1** *cap* **:** of or relating to Protestants, their churches, or their religion **2 :** making or sounding a protest <the two ~ ladies up and marched out —*Time*>
pro·tes·ta·tion \ˌprät-əs-ˈtā-shən, ˌprō-ˌtes-, ˌprōt-əs-, ˌprät-ˌes-\ *n* **:** the act of protesting **:** a solemn declaration or avowal
pro·te·us \ˈprōt-ē-əs\ *n, pl* **-tei** \-ē-ˌī\ [NL, genus name, fr. L, Proteus] **:** any of a genus (*Proteus*) of aerobic gram-negative usu. motile bacteria that include saprophytes in decaying organic matter and forms associated with gastrointestinal disorders
Pro·teus \ˈprō-ˌt(y)üs, ˈprōt-ē-əs\ *n* [L, fr. Gk *Prōteus*] **:** a Greek sea god capable of assuming different forms
pro·tha·la·mi·on \ˌprō-thə-ˈlā-mē-ən, -ˌän\ *or* **pro·tha·la·mi·um** \-mē-əm\ *n, pl* **-mia** \-mē-ə\ [NL, fr. Gk *pro-* + *-thalamion* (as in *epithalamion*)] **:** a song in celebration of a marriage
pro·thal·li·um \prō-ˈthal-ē-əm\ *n, pl* **-thal·lia** \-ē-ə\ [NL, fr. *pro-* + *thallus*] **1 :** the gametophyte of a pteridophyte (as a fern) that is typically a small flat green thallus attached to the soil by rhizoids **2 :** a greatly reduced structure of a seed plant corresponding to the pteridophyte prothallium — **pro·thal·li·al** \-ē-əl\ *adj*
pro·thal·lus \(ˈ)prō-ˈthal-əs\ *n* [NL, fr. *pro-* + *thallus*] **:** PROTHALLIUM
proth·e·sis \ˈpräth-ə-səs\ *n, pl* **-e·ses** \-ˌsēz\ [LL, alter. of *prosthesis,* fr. Gk, lit., addition — more at PROSTHESIS] **:** the addition of a sound to the beginning of a word (as in Old French *estat* — whence English *estate* — from Latin *status*) — **pro·thet·ic** \prä-ˈthet-ik\ *adj*
prothe·tely \ˈpräth-ə-ˌtel-ē\ *n* [perh. fr. Gk *protithenai* to put before (fr. *pro-* + *tithenai* to put) + *telein* to complete, perfect, fr. *telos* end — more at DO, WHEEL] **:** relatively precocious differentiation of a structure usu. associated with a later stage of development — **prothe·tel·ic** \ˌpräth-ə-ˈtel-ik\ *adj*
pro·tho·no·ta·ry \prō-ˈthän-ə-ˌter-ē, ˌprō-thə-ˈnōt-ə-rē\ *or* **pro·to·no·ta·ry** \prō-ˈtän-ə-ˌter-ē, ˌprōt-ə-ˈnōt-ə-rē\ *n, pl* **-ries** [ME *prothonotarie,* fr. LL *protonotarius,* fr. *prot-* + L *notarius* notary] **:** a chief clerk of any of various courts of law — **pro·tho·no·tar·i·al** \prō-ˌthän-ə-ˈter-ē-əl, ˌpro-thə-nō-ˈter-ē-əl\ *adj*
pro·tho·rac·ic \ˌprō-thə-ˈras-ik\ *adj* **:** of or relating to the prothorax
prothoracic gland *n* **:** one of a pair of thoracic endocrine organs in some insects that control molting
pro·tho·rax \(ˈ)prō-ˈthō(ə)r-ˌaks, -ˈthȯ(ə)r-\ *n* [NL *prothorac-, prothorax,* fr. ¹*pro-* + *thorax*] **:** the anterior segment of the thorax of an insect — see INSECT illustration
pro·throm·bin \(ˈ)prō-ˈthräm-bən\ *n* [ISV] **:** a plasma protein produced in the liver in the presence of vitamin K and converted into thrombin in the clotting of blood
pro·tist \ˈprōt-əst, ˈprō-ˌtist\ *n* [deriv. of Gk *prōtistos* very first, primal, fr. superl. of *prōtos* first — more at PROT-] **:** any of a kingdom or other group (Protista) of unicellular or acellular organisms comprising bacteria, protozoans, various algae and fungi, and sometimes viruses — **pro·tis·tan** \prō-ˈtis-tən\ *adj or n*
pro·ti·um \ˈprōt-ē-əm, ˈprō-shē-\ *n* [NL, fr. Gk *prōtos* first] **:** the ordinary light hydrogen isotope of atomic mass 1
proto- — see PROT-
pro·to·col \ˈprōt-ə-ˌkȯl, -ˌkōl, -ˌkäl, -kəl\ *n* [MF *prothocole,* fr. ML *protocollum,* fr. LGk *prōtokollon* first sheet of a papyrus roll bearing data of manufacture, fr. Gk *prōt-* prot- + *kollan* to glue together, fr. *kolla* glue; akin to MD *helen* to glue] **1 :** an original draft, minute, or record of a document or transaction **2 a :** a preliminary memorandum often formulated and signed by diplomatic negotiators as a basis for a final convention or treaty **b :** the records or minutes of a diplomatic conference or congress that show officially the agreements arrived at by the negotiators **3 :** a code prescribing strict adherence to correct etiquette and precedence (as in diplomatic exchange and in the military services) **4 :** the plan of a scientific experiment or treatment
pro·to·derm \ˈprōt-ə-ˌdərm\ *n* [ISV] **:** DERMATOGEN — **pro·to·der·mal** \ˌprōt-ə-ˈdər-məl\ *adj*
pro·to·gal·axy \ˌprōt-ō-ˈgal-ək-sē\ *n* **:** a hypothetical cloud of gas believed to have condensed into stars and formed the galaxies
pro·to·his·to·ry \-ˈhis-t(ə-)rē\ *n* [ISV] **:** the study of man in the times that immediately antedate recorded history — **pro·to·his·to·ri·an** \-(h)is-ˈtōr-ē-ən, -ˈtȯr-\ *n* — **pro·to·his·tor·ic** \-ˈtȯr-ik, -ˈtär-\ *adj*
pro·to·hu·man \-ˈhyü-mən, -ˈyü-\ *adj* **:** of, relating to, or resembling an early primitive human or a manlike primate — **protohuman** *n*
pro·to·lan·guage \ˈprōt-ō-ˌlaŋ-gwij\ *n* **:** an assumed or recorded ancestral language
pro·to·lith·ic \ˌprōt-ə-ˈlith-ik\ *adj* **:** of or relating to the earliest period of the Stone Age **:** EOLITHIC
pro·to·mar·tyr \ˈprōt-ō-ˌmärt-ər\ *n* [ME *prothomartir,* fr. MF, fr. LL *protomartyr,* fr. LGk *prōtomartyr-, prōtomartys,* fr. Gk *prōt-* + *martyr-, martys* martyr] **:** the first martyr in a cause or region
pro·ton \ˈprō-ˌtän\ *n* [Gk *prōton,* neut. of *prōtos* first — more at PROT-] **:** an elementary particle that is identical with the nucleus of the hydrogen atom, that along with neutrons is a constituent of all other atomic nuclei, that carries a positive charge numerically equal to the charge of an electron, and that has a mass of 1.672×10^{-24} gram — **pro·ton·ic** \prō-ˈtän-ik\ *adj*
pro·ton·ate \ˈprōt-ə-ˌnāt\ *vb* **-at·ed; -at·ing** *vt* **:** to add a proton to ~ *vi* **:** to acquire an additional proton — **pro·ton·ation** \ˌprōt-ə-ˈnā-shən\ *n*
pro·to·ne·ma \ˌprōt-ə-ˈnē-mə\ *n, pl* **-ne·ma·ta** \-ˈnē-mət-ə, -ˈnem-ət-\ [NL *protonemat-, protonema,* fr. *prot-* + Gk *nēma* thread — more at NEMAT-] **:** the primary usu. filamentous thalloid stage of the gametophyte in mosses and in some liverworts comparable to the prothallium in ferns — **pro·to·ne·mal** \-ˈnē-məl\ *adj* — **pro·to·ne·ma·tal** \-ˈnē-mət-ᵊl, -ˈnem-ət-\ *adj*
protonotary apostolic *or* **prothonotary apostolic** *n, pl* **protonotaries apostolic** *or* **prothonotaries apostolic :** a priest of the chief college of the papal curia who keeps records of consistories and canonizations and signs papal bulls; *also* **:** an honorary member of this college
pro·ton–syn·chro·tron \ˈprō-ˌtän-ˈsiŋ-k(r)ə-ˌträn, -ˈsin-\ *n* **:** a synchrotron in which protons are accelerated by means of frequency modulation of the radio-frequency accelerating voltage so that they have energies of billions of electron volts
pro·to·nymph \ˈprōt-ə-ˌnim(p)f\ *n* **:** any of various acarids in their first developmental stage — **pro·to·nymph·al** \ˌprōt-ə-ˈnim(p)-fəl\ *adj*
pro·to·path·ic \ˌprōt-ə-ˈpath-ik\ *adj* [ISV, fr. MGk *prōtopathēs* affected first, fr. Gk *prōt-* prot- + *pathos* experience, suffering — more at PATHOS] **:** of, relating to, or being cutaneous sensory reception responsive only to rather gross stimuli
pro·to·phlo·em \-ˈflō-ˌem\ *n* **:** the first-formed phloem that develops from procambium, consists of narrow thin-walled cells capable of a limited amount of stretching, and is usu. associated with a region of rapid growth
pro·to·plan·et \ˈprōt-ō-ˌplan-ət\ *n* **:** a hypothetical whirling gaseous mass within a giant cloud of gas and dust that rotates around a sun and is believed to give rise to a planet
pro·to·plasm \ˈprōt-ə-ˌplaz-əm\ *n* [G *protoplasma,* fr. *prot-* + NL *plasma*] **1 :** the organized colloidal complex of organic and inorganic substances (as proteins and water) that constitutes the living nucleus, cytoplasm, plastids, and mitochondria of the cell and is regarded as the only form of matter in which the vital phenomena are manifested **2 :** CYTOPLASM — **pro·to·plas·mic** \ˌprōt-ə-ˈplaz-mik\ *adj*
pro·to·plast \ˈprōt-ə-ˌplast\ *n* [MF *protoplaste,* fr. LL *protoplastus* first man, fr. Gk *prōtoplastos* first formed, fr. *prōt-* prot- + *plastos* formed, fr. *plassein* to mold — more at PLASTER] **1 :** one that is formed first **:** PROTOTYPE **2 a :** the nucleus, cytoplasm, and plasma membrane of a cell constituting a living unit distinct from inert walls and inclusions **b :** ENERGID — **pro·to·plas·tic** \ˌprōt-ə-ˈplas-tik\ *adj*
pro·to·por·phy·rin \ˌprōt-ō-ˈpȯr-f(ə-)rən\ *n* [ISV] **:** a purple porphyrin acid $C_{34}H_{34}N_4O_4$ obtained from hemin or heme by removal of bound iron
pro·to·star \ˈprōt-ō-ˌstär\ *n* **:** a hypothetical cloud of dust and atoms in space believed to develop into a star
pro·to·stele \ˈprōt-ə-ˌstēl, ˌprōt-ə-ˈstē-lē\ *n* **:** a stele forming a solid rod with the phloem surrounding the xylem — **pro·to·ste·lic** \ˌprōt-ə-ˈstē-lik\ *adj*
pro·to·troph \ˈprōt-ə-ˌtrōf, -ˌträf\ *n* [back-formation fr. *prototrophic*] **:** a prototrophic individual
pro·to·tro·phic \ˌprōt-ə-ˈtrō-fik\ *adj* [ISV] **:** deriving nutriment from inorganic sources — **pro·to·tro·phy** \prō-ˈtä-trə-fē\ *n*
pro·to·typ·al \ˌprōt-ə-ˈtī-pəl\ *adj* **:** of, relating to, or constituting a prototype **:** ARCHETYPAL
pro·to·type \ˈprōt-ə-ˌtīp\ *n* [F, fr. Gk *prōtotypon,* fr. neut. of *prōtotypos* archetypal, fr. *prōt-* + *typos* type] **1 :** an original model on which something is patterned **:** ARCHETYPE **2 :** an individual that exhibits the essential features of a later type **3 :** a standard or typical example **4 :** a first full-scale and usu. functional form of a new type or design of a construction (as an airplane)
pro·to·typ·i·cal \ˌprōt-ə-ˈtip-i-kəl\ *also* **pro·to·typ·ic** \-ik\ *adj* **:** PROTOTYPAL — **pro·to·typ·i·cal·ly** \-i-k(ə-)lē\ *adv*
pro·to·xy·lem \ˌprōt-ə-ˈzī-ləm, -ˌlem\ *n* **:** the first-formed xylem developing from procambium and consisting of narrow cells with annular, spiral, or scalariform wall thickenings
pro·to·zo·al \ˌprōt-ə-ˈzō-əl\ *adj* **:** of or relating to protozoans
pro·to·zo·an \-ˈzō-ən\ *n* [NL *Protozoa,* phylum name, fr. *prot-* + *-zoa*] **:** any of a phylum or subkingdom (Protozoa) of minute protoplasmic acellular or unicellular animals which have varied morphology and physiology and often complex life cycles, which are represented in almost every kind of habitat, and some of which are serious parasites of man and domestic animals — **protozoan** *adj* — **pro·to·zo·ic** \-ˈzō-ik\ *adj*
pro·to·zo·ol·o·gy \-zō-ˈäl-ə-jē, -zə-ˈwäl-\ *n* [NL *Protozoa* + ISV *-logy*] **:** a branch of zoology dealing with protozoans — **pro·to·zoo·log·i·cal** \-ˌzō-ə-ˈläj-i-kəl\ *adj* — **pro·to·zo·ol·o·gist** \-zō-ˈäl-ə-jəst, -zə-ˈwäl-\ *n*
pro·to·zo·on \-ˈzō-ˌän\ *n, pl* **-zoa** \-ˈzō-ə\ [NL, fr. sing. of *Protozoa*] **:** PROTOZOAN
pro·tract \prō-ˈtrakt, p(r)ə-\ *vt* [L *protractus,* pp. of *protrahere,* lit., to draw forward, fr. *pro-* forward + *trahere* to draw — more at PRO-, DRAW] **1** *archaic* **:** DELAY, DEFER **2 :** to prolong in time or space **3 :** to lay down the lines and angles of with scale and protractor **:** PLOT **4 :** to extend forward or outward ***syn*** see EXTEND ***ant*** curtail — **pro·trac·tive** \-ˈtrak-tiv\ *adj*
protracted meeting *n* **:** a revival meeting extending over a period of time
pro·trac·tile \-ˈtrak-tᵊl, -ˌtīl\ *adj* [L *protractus*] **:** capable of being thrust out <~ jaws>
pro·trac·tion \-ˈtrak-shən\ *n* [LL *protraction-, protractio* act of drawing out, fr. *protractus*] **1 :** the act of protracting **:** the state of being protracted **2 :** the drawing to scale of an area of land
pro·trac·tor \-ˈtrak-tər\ *n* **1 a :** one that protracts, prolongs, or delays **b :** a muscle that extends a part **2 :** an instrument that is used for laying down and measuring angles in drawing and plotting
pro·trep·tic \prō-ˈtrep-tik\ *n* [LL *protrepticus* hortatory, encouraging, fr. Gk *protreptikos,* fr. *protrepein* to turn forward, urge on, fr. *pro-* + *trepein* to turn — more at TROPE] **:** an utterance (as a speech) designed to instruct and persuade — **protreptic** *adj*
pro·trude \prō-ˈtrüd\ *vb* **pro·trud·ed; pro·trud·ing** [L *protrudere,* fr. *pro-* + *trudere* to thrust — more at THREAT] *vt* **1** *archaic* **:** to thrust forward **2 :** to cause to project or stick out ~ *vi* **:** to jut out from the surrounding surface or context <a handker-

chief *protruding* from his breast pocket> — **pro·tru·si·ble** \-'trü-sə-bəl, -zə-\ *adj*

pro·tru·sion \prō-'trü-zhən\ *n* [L *protrusus,* pp. of *protrudere*] **1 :** the act of protruding **:** the state of being protruded **2 :** something (as a part or excrescence) that protrudes ***syn*** see PROJECTION

pro·tru·sive \-'trü-siv, -ziv\ *adj* **1** *archaic* **:** thrusting forward **2 :** PROMINENT, PROTUBERANT <a ~ jaw> **3 :** OBTRUSIVE, PUSHING <a coarse ~ manner> — **pro·tru·sive·ly** *adv* — **pro·tru·sive·ness** *n*

pro·tu·ber·ance \prō-'t(y)ü-b(ə-)rən(t)s\ *n* **1 :** the quality or state of being protuberant **2 :** something that is protuberant ***syn*** see PROJECTION

pro·tu·ber·ant \-b(ə-)rənt\ *adj* [LL *protuberant-, protuberans,* prp. of *protuberare* to bulge out, fr. L *pro-* forward + *tuber* hump, swelling] **1 :** thrusting out from a surrounding or adjacent surface often as a rounded mass **:** PROMINENT **2 :** forcing itself into consciousness **:** OBTRUSIVE — **pro·tu·ber·ant·ly** *adv*

proud \'prau̇d\ *adj* [ME, fr. OE *prūd,* prob. fr. OF *prod, prud, prou* capable, good, valiant, fr. LL *prode* advantage, advantageous, back-formation fr. L *prodesse* to be advantageous, fr. *pro-, prod-* for, in favor + *esse* to be — more at PRO-, IS] **1 :** feeling or showing pride: as **a :** having or displaying excessive self-esteem **b :** much pleased **:** EXULTANT **c :** having proper self-respect **2 a :** marked by stateliness **:** MAGNIFICENT **b :** giving reason for pride **:** GLORIOUS <the ~*est* moment in her life> **3 :** VIGOROUS, SPIRITED <a ~ steed> — **proud·ly** *adv*

syn PROUD, ARROGANT, HAUGHTY, LORDLY, INSOLENT, OVERBEARING, SUPERCILIOUS, DISDAINFUL *shared meaning element* **:** showing or feeling superiority toward others ***ant*** humble, ashamed

proud flesh *n* **:** an excessive growth of granulation tissue (as in an ulcer)

proud·ful \'prau̇d-fəl\ *adj, chiefly dial* **:** marked by or full of pride

proud·heart·ed \-'härt-əd\ *adj* **:** proud in spirit **:** HAUGHTY

prov *abbr* **1** province; provincial **2** provisional

Prov *abbr* Proverbs

prov·able \'prü-və-bəl\ *adj* **:** capable of being proved — **prov·able·ness** *n* — **prov·ably** \-blē\ *adv*

pro·vas·cu·lar \(ˈ)prō-'vas-kyə-lər\ *adj* **:** of, relating to, or being procambium

prove \'prüv\ *vb* **proved; proved** *or* **prov·en** \'prü-vən, *Brit also* 'prō-\; **prov·ing** \'prü-viŋ\ [ME *proven,* fr. OF *prover,* fr. L *probare* to test, approve, prove, fr. *probus* good, honest, fr. *pro-* for, in favor + *-bus* (akin to OE *bēon* to be)] *vt* **1** *archaic* **:** EXPERIENCE <we will all the pleasures ~ —Christopher Marlowe> **2 a :** to test the quality of **:** try out <the exception ~*s* the rule> **b :** to try or ascertain by an experiment or a standard; *esp* **:** to subject to a technical testing process **c :** to make a test of (as a mineral vein) — usu. used with *up* or *out* **3 a :** to establish the truth or validity of by evidence or demonstration <*proved* her innocence> <young people need to ~ themselves as competent adults> **b :** to check the correctness of (as an arithmetic operation) **4 a :** to ascertain the genuineness of **:** VERIFY; *specif* **:** to obtain probate of (a will) **b :** PROOF 1 ~ *vi* **:** to turn out esp. after trial or test <the new drug *proved* to be very effective> — **prov·er** \'prü-vər\ *n*

prov·e·nance \'präv(-ə)-nən(t)s, -ˌnän(t)s\ *n* [F, fr. *provenir* to come forth, originate, fr. L *provenire,* fr. *pro-* forth + *venire* to come — more at PRO-, COME] **:** ORIGIN, SOURCE

Pro·ven·çal \ˌpräv-ən-'säl, ˌprōv-, -ˌäⁿ-; prə-'ven(t)-səl\ *n* [MF, fr. *provençal* of Provence, fr. *Provence*] **1 :** a native or inhabitant of Provence **2 :** a Romance language spoken in southeastern France — **Provençal** *adj*

prov·en·der \'präv-ən-dər\ *n* [ME, fr. MF *provende, provendre,* fr. ML *provenda,* alter. of *praebenda* prebend] **1 :** dry food for domestic animals **:** FEED **2 :** FOOD, VICTUALS

pro·ve·nience \prə-'vē-nyən(t)s, -nē-ən(t)s\ *n* [alter. of *provenance*] **:** ORIGIN, SOURCE

prov·en·ly \'prü-vən-lē, *Brit also* 'prō-\ *adv* **:** demonstrably as stated **:** without doubt or uncertainty

pro·ven·tric·u·lus \ˌprō-ven-'trik-yə-ləs\ *n, pl* **-li** \-ˌlī, -ˌlē\ [NL] **1 :** the glandular or true stomach of a bird that is situated between the crop and gizzard **2 :** a muscular dilatation of the foregut in most mandibulate insects that is armed internally with chitinous teeth or plates for triturating food **3 :** the thin-walled sac in front of the gizzard of an earthworm

prove out *vi* **:** to turn out to be adequate or satisfactory

[1]**prov·erb** \'präv-ˌərb\ *n* [ME *proverbe,* fr. MF, fr. L *proverbium,* fr. *pro-* + *verbum* word — more at WORD] **1 :** a brief popular epigram or maxim **:** ADAGE **2 :** BYWORD 4

[2]**proverb** *vt* **1** *obs* **:** to provide with a proverb **2 :** to speak of proverbially <am I not sung and ~*ed* . . . in every street —John Milton>

pro–verb \'prō-ˌvərb, -'vərb\ *n* **:** a form of the verb *do* used to avoid repetition of a full verb <the word *do* in "act as I do" is a ~>

pro·ver·bi·al \prə-'vər-bē-əl\ *adj* **1 :** of, relating to, or resembling a proverb **2 :** that has become a proverb or byword **:** commonly spoken of — **pro·ver·bi·al·ly** \-ə-lē\ *adv*

Prov·erbs \'präv-ˌərbz\ *n pl but sing in constr* **:** a collection of moral sayings and counsels forming a book of canonical Jewish and Christian Scripture — see BIBLE table

pro·vide \prə-'vīd\ *vb* **pro·vid·ed; pro·vid·ing** [ME *providen,* fr. L *providēre,* lit., to see ahead, fr. *pro-* forward + *vidēre* to see — more at PRO-, WIT] *vi* **1 :** to take precautionary measures <~ for the common defense —*U.S. Constitution*> **2 :** to make a proviso or stipulation <the constitution . . . ~*s* for an elected two-chamber legislature —*Current Biog.*> **3 :** to supply what is needed for sustenance or support <~*s* for a large family> ~ *vt* **1** *archaic* **:** to procure in advance **:** PREPARE **2 a :** to fit out **:** EQUIP <~ the children with new shoes> **b :** to supply for use **:** AFFORD, YIELD <a string quartet *provided* the entertainment> <curtains ~ privacy> **3 :** STIPULATE

pro·vid·ed *conj* [pp. of *provide*] **:** on condition that **:** with the understanding **:** IF

prov·i·dence \'präv-əd-ən(t)s, -ə-ˌden(t)s\ *n* [ME, fr. MF, fr. L *providentia,* fr. *provident-, providens*] **1 a** *often cap* **:** divine guidance or care **b** *cap* **:** God conceived as the power sustaining and guiding human destiny **2 :** the quality or state of being provident

prov·i·dent \-əd-ənt, -ə-ˌdent\ *adj* [L *provident-, providens,* fr. prp. of *providēre*] **1 :** making provision for the future **:** PRUDENT **2 :** FRUGAL, SAVING — **prov·i·dent·ly** *adv*

prov·i·den·tial \ˌpräv-ə-'den-chəl\ *adj* **1** *archaic* **:** marked by foresight **:** PRUDENT **2 :** of, relating to, or determined by Providence **3 :** occurring by or as if by an intervention of Providence **:** OPPORTUNE <a ~ escape> ***syn*** see LUCKY — **prov·i·den·tial·ly** \-'dench-(ə-)lē\ *adv*

pro·vid·er \prə-'vīd-ər\ *n* **:** one that provides; *esp* **:** one that provides for his family

pro·vid·ing *conj* [prp. of *provide*] **:** on condition that **:** in case

prov·ince \'präv-ən(t)s\ *n* [F, fr. L *provincia*] **1 a :** a country or region brought under the control of the ancient Roman government **b :** an administrative district or division of a country **c** *pl* **:** all of a country except the metropolis **2 a :** a division of a country forming the jurisdiction of an archbishop or metropolitan **b :** a territorial unit of a religious order **3 a :** a biogeographic division of less rank than a region **b :** an area that exhibits essential continuity of geological history; *also* **:** one characterized by particular structural or petrological features **4 a :** proper or appropriate function or scope **:** SPHERE **b :** a department of knowledge or activity ***syn*** see FUNCTION

[1]**pro·vin·cial** \prə-'vin-chəl\ *n* **1 :** the superior of a province of a Roman Catholic religious order **2 :** one living in or coming from a province **3 a :** a person of local or restricted interests or outlook **b :** a person lacking urban polish or refinement

[2]**provincial** *adj* **1 :** of, relating to, or coming from a province **2 a :** limited in outlook **:** NARROW **b :** lacking the polish of urban society **:** UNSOPHISTICATED **3 :** of or relating to a decorative style (as in furniture) marked by simplicity, informality, and relative plainness — **pro·vin·cial·ly** \-'vinch-(ə-)lē\ *adv*

pro·vin·cial·ism \-chə-ˌliz-əm\ *n* **1 :** a dialectal or local word, phrase, or idiom **2 :** the quality or state of being provincial

pro·vin·cial·ist \-'vinch-(ə-)ləst\ *n* **:** a native or inhabitant of a province

pro·vin·ci·al·i·ty \prə-ˌvin-chē-'al-ət-ē\ *n, pl* **-ties** **1 :** PROVINCIALISM 2 **2 :** an act or instance of provincialism

pro·vin·cial·ize \-'vin-chə-ˌlīz\ *vt* **-ized; -iz·ing :** to make provincial — **pro·vin·cial·iza·tion** \-ˌvinch-(ə-)lə-'zā-shən\ *n*

proving ground *n* **1 :** a place designed for or used in scientific experimentation or testing **2 :** a place where something new is tried out

pro·vi·rus \(ˈ)prō-'vī-rəs\ *n* [NL] **:** a noninfectious intracellular form of a virus that behaves in the host cell like a plasmagene — **pro·vi·ral** \-rəl\ *adj*

[1]**pro·vi·sion** \prə-'vizh-ən\ *n* [ME, fr. MF, fr. LL & L; LL *provision-, provisio* act of providing, fr. L, foresight, fr. *provisus,* pp. of *providēre* to see ahead] **1 a :** the act or process of providing **b :** the quality or state of being prepared beforehand **c :** a measure taken beforehand **:** PREPARATION <lack of proper ~ for replacements —Alzada Comstock> **2 :** a stock of needed materials or supplies; *esp* **:** a stock of food **:** VICTUALS — usu. used in pl. **3 :** PROVISO, STIPULATION

[2]**provision** *vt* **pro·vi·sioned; pro·vi·sion·ing** \-'vizh-(ə-)niŋ\ **:** to supply with provisions

[1]**pro·vi·sion·al** \prə-'vizh-nəl, -ən-ᵊl\ *adj* **:** serving for the time being **:** TEMPORARY — **pro·vi·sion·al·ly** \-ē\ *adv*

[2]**provisional** *n* **:** a postage stamp for use until a regular issue appears

pro·vi·sion·ary \prə-'vizh-ə-ˌner-ē\ *adj* **:** PROVISIONAL

pro·vi·sion·er \-'vizh-(ə-)nər\ *n* **:** a furnisher of provisions

pro·vi·so \prə-'vī-(ˌ)zō\ *n, pl* **-sos** *or* **-soes** [ME, fr. ML *proviso quod* provided that] **1 :** an article or clause (as in a contract) that introduces a condition **2 :** a conditional stipulation **:** PROVISION

pro·vi·so·ry \-'vīz-(ə-)rē\ *adj* **1 :** containing or subject to a proviso **:** CONDITIONAL **2 :** PROVISIONAL

pro·vi·ta·min \(ˈ)prō-'vīt-ə-mən\ *n* **:** a precursor of a vitamin convertible into the vitamin in an organism

provocateur *n* **:** AGENT PROVOCATEUR

prov·o·ca·tion \ˌpräv-ə-'kā-shən\ *n* [ME *provocacioun,* fr. MF *provocation,* fr. L *provocation-, provocatio,* fr. *provocatus,* pp. of *provocare*] **1 :** the act of provoking **:** INCITEMENT **2 :** something that provokes, arouses, or stimulates

pro·voc·a·tive \prə-'väk-ət-iv\ *adj* **:** serving or tending to provoke, excite, or stimulate — **provocative** *n* — **pro·voc·a·tive·ly** *adv* — **pro·voc·a·tive·ness** *n*

pro·voke \prə-'vōk\ *vt* **pro·voked; pro·vok·ing** [ME *provoken,* fr. MF *provoquer,* fr. L *provocare,* fr. *pro-* forth + *vocare* to call — more at PRO-, VOICE] **1 a** *archaic* **:** AROUSE, STIR **b :** to incite to anger **:** INCENSE **2 a :** to call forth **:** EVOKE **b :** to stir up purposely **:** INDUCE **c :** to provide the needed stimulus for

syn **1** PROVOKE, EXCITE, STIMULATE, PIQUE, QUICKEN *shared meaning element* **:** to rouse one into doing or feeling or to produce by so rousing a person ***ant*** gratify

2 see IRRITATE

pro·vok·ing \-'vō-kiŋ\ *adj* **:** causing mild anger **:** ANNOYING — **pro·vok·ing·ly** \-kiŋ-lē\ *adv*

pro·vo·lo·ne \ˌprō-və-'lō-nē\ *n* [It, aug. of *provola,* a kind of cheese] **:** a hard smooth cheese of Italian origin that is made from curd that has been heated and kneaded, molded into various shapes, hung in strings to cure, and often smoked

pro·vost \'prō-ˌvōst, 'präv-əst, 'prō-vəst, *esp attrib* ˌprō-(ˌ)vō\ *n* [ME, fr. OE *profost* & OF *provost,* fr. ML *propositus,* alter. of *praepositus,* fr. L, one in charge, director, fr. pp. of *praeponere* to place at the head — more at PREPOSITION] **1 :** the chief dignitary of a collegiate or cathedral chapter **2 :** the chief magistrate of a Scottish burgh **3 :** the keeper of a prison **4 :** a high-ranking university administrative officer

provost court *n* **:** a military court usu. for the trial of minor offenses within an occupied hostile territory
provost guard *n* **:** a police detail of soldiers under the authority of the provost marshal
provost marshal *n* **:** an officer who supervises the military police of a command
[1]**prow** \ˈprau̇\ *adj* [ME, fr. MF *prou* — more at PROUD] *archaic* **:** VALIANT, GALLANT
[2]**prow** \ˈprau̇, *archaic* ˈprō\ *n* [MF *proue,* prob. fr. OIt dial. *prua,* fr. L *prora,* fr. Gk *prōira*] **1 :** the bow of a ship **:** STEM **2 :** a pointed projecting front part (as of an airplane)
prow·ess \ˈprau̇-əs *also* ˈprō-\ *n* [ME *prouesse,* fr. OF *proesse,* fr. *prou* valiant — more at PROUD] **1 :** distinguished bravery; *esp* **:** military valor and skill **2 :** extraordinary ability <his ~ on the football field> ***syn*** see HEROISM
[1]**prowl** \ˈprau̇(ə)l\ *vb* [ME *prollen*] *vi* **:** to move about or wander stealthily <submarines were ~*ing* along our coast —Owen Wister> ~ *vt* **:** to roam over in a predatory manner <they ~*ed* the premises —Cedric Adams> — **prowl·er** \ˈprau̇-lər\ *n*
[2]**prowl** *n* **:** an act or instance of prowling — **on the prowl :** in search of something; *specif* **:** in search of a sexual partner <his fourth wife had just left him, and he was *on the prowl* again —Mary McCarthy>
prowl car *n* **:** SQUAD CAR
prox *abbr* proximo
prox·e·mics \präk-ˈsē-miks\ *n pl but sing or pl in constr* [*prox*imity + *-emics* (as in *phonemics*)] **:** a branch of study dealing with the personal and cultural spatial needs of man and his interaction with his environing space — **prox·e·mic** \-mik\ *adj*
prox·i·mal \ˈpräk-sə-məl\ *adj* [L *proximus*] **1 :** situated close to **:** NEAREST, PROXIMATE **2 :** next to or nearest the point of attachment or origin, a central point, or the point of view; *esp* **:** located toward the center of the body — compare DISTAL — **prox·i·mal·ly** \-mə-lē\ *adv*
proximal convoluted tubule *n* **:** the convoluted portion of the vertebrate nephron that lies between Bowman's capsule and the loop of Henle, is made up of a single layer of cuboidal cells with striated borders, and is held to be concerned esp. with resorption of sugar, sodium and chloride ions, and water from the glomerular filtrate — called also *proximal tubule*
prox·i·mate \ˈpräk-sə-mət\ *adj* [L *proximatus,* pp. of *proximare* to approach, fr. *proximus* nearest, next, superl. of *prope* near — more at APPROACH] **1 a :** very near **:** CLOSE **b :** soon forthcoming **:** IMMINENT **2 :** next preceding or following <an interest in ~, rather than ultimate, goals —Reinhold Niebuhr> — **prox·i·mate·ly** *adv* — **prox·i·mate·ness** *n*
prox·im·i·ty \präk-ˈsim-ət-ē\ *n* [MF *proximité,* fr. L *proximitat-, proximitas,* fr. *proximus*] **:** the quality or state of being proximate
proximity fuze *n* **:** an electronic device that detonates a projectile within effective range of the target by means of the radio waves sent out from a tiny radio set in the nose of the projectile and reflected back to the set from the target
prox·i·mo \ˈpräk-sə-ˌmō\ *adj* [L *proximo mense* in the next month] **:** of or occurring in the next month after the present
proxy \ˈpräk-sē\ *n, pl* **prox·ies** [ME *procucie,* contr. of *procuracie,* fr. AF, fr. ML *procuratia,* alter. of L *procuratio* procuration] **1 :** the agency, function, or office of a deputy who acts as a substitute for another **2 a :** authority or power to act for another **b :** a document giving such authority; *specif* **:** a power of attorney authorizing a specified person to vote corporate stock **3 :** a person authorized to act for another **:** PROCURATOR — **proxy** *adj*
proxy marriage *n* **:** a marriage celebrated in the absence of one of the contracting parties who authorizes a proxy to represent him at the ceremony
prude \ˈprüd\ *n* [F, good woman, prudish woman, short for *prudefemme* good woman, fr. OF *prode femme*] **:** a person who is excessively or priggishly attentive to propriety or decorum; *esp* **:** a woman who shows or affects extreme modesty
pru·dence \ˈprüd-ᵊn(t)s\ *n* **1 :** the ability to govern and discipline oneself by the use of reason **2 :** sagacity or shrewdness in the management of affairs **3 :** skill and good judgment in the use of resources **4 :** caution or circumspection as to danger or risk
pru·dent \-ᵊnt\ *adj* [ME, fr. MF, fr. L *prudent-, prudens,* contr. of *provident-, providens* — more at PROVIDENT] **:** characterized by, arising from, or showing prudence: as **a :** marked by wisdom or judiciousness **b :** shrewd in the management of practical affairs **c :** marked by circumspection **:** DISCREET **d :** PROVIDENT, FRUGAL ***syn*** see WISE — **pru·dent·ly** *adv*
pru·den·tial \prü-ˈden-chəl\ *adj* **1 :** of, relating to, or proceeding from prudence **2 :** exercising prudence esp. in business matters — **pru·den·tial·ly** \-ˈdench-(ə-)lē\ *adv*
prud·ery \ˈprüd-(ə-)rē\ *n, pl* **-er·ies** **1 :** the characteristic quality or state of a prude **2 :** a prudish act or remark
prud·ish \ˈprüd-ish\ *adj* **:** marked by prudery **:** PRIGGISH — **prud·ish·ly** *adv* — **prud·ish·ness** *n*
pru·inose \ˈprü-ə-ˌnōs\ *adj* [L *pruinosus* covered with hoarfrost, fr. *pruina* hoarfrost] **:** covered with whitish dust or bloom <~ stems>
[1]**prune** \ˈprün\ *n* [ME, fr. MF, plum, fr. L *prunum* — more at PLUM] **:** a plum dried or capable of drying without fermentation
[2]**prune** *vb* **pruned; prun·ing** [ME *prouynen,* fr. MF *proignier,* prob. alter. of *provigner* to layer, fr. *provain* layer, fr. L *propagin-, propago,* fr. *pro-* forward + *pangere* to fix — more at PRO-, PACT] *vt* **1 :** to cut off or cut back parts of for better shape or more fruitful growth **2 a :** to reduce by eliminating superfluous matter <*pruned* the text> **b :** to remove as superfluous <~ away all ornamentation> **c :** to effect a reduction in <~ the budget> ~ *vi* **:** to cut away what is unwanted — **prun·er** *n*
pru·nel·la \prü-ˈnel-ə\ *also* **pru·nelle** \-ˈnel\ *n* [F *prunelle,* lit., sloe, fr. dim. of *prune* plum] **1 :** a twilled woolen dress fabric **2 :** a heavy woolen fabric used for the uppers of shoes
pruning hook *n* **:** a pole bearing a curved blade for pruning plants
pru·ri·ence \ˈpru̇r-ē-ən(t)s\ *n* **:** the quality or state of being prurient
pru·ri·en·cy \-ən-sē\ *n* **:** PRURIENCE
pru·ri·ent \-ənt\ *adj* [L *prurient-, pruriens,* prp. of *prurire* to itch, crave, be wanton; akin to L *pruna* glowing coal, Skt *plosati* he singes] **1 :** marked by restless craving **2 a :** having lascivious thoughts or desires **:** LEWD **b :** arousing such thoughts or desires — **pru·ri·ent·ly** *adv*
pru·rig·i·nous \prü-ˈrij-ə-nəs\ *adj* [L *pruriginosus* having the itch, fr. *prurigin-, prurigo*] **:** resembling, caused by, affected with, or being prurigo
pru·ri·go \prü-ˈrī-(ˌ)gō, -ˈrē-\ *n* [NL, fr. L, itch, fr. *prurire*] **:** a chronic inflammatory skin disease marked by itching papules
pru·rit·ic \-ˈrit-ik\ *adj* **:** of, relating to, or marked by itching
pru·ri·tus \-ˈrīt-əs, -ˈrēt-\ *n* [L, fr. *pruritus,* pp. of *prurire*] **:** ITCH 1
Prus·sian blue \ˌprəsh-ən-\ *n* [*Prussia,* Germany] **1 :** any of numerous blue iron pigments formerly regarded as ferric ferrocyanide **2 :** a dark blue crystalline hydrated ferric ferrocyanide $Fe_4[Fe(CN)_6]_3 \cdot xH_2O$ used as a test for ferric iron **3 :** a variable color averaging a moderate to strong greenish blue
Prus·sian·ism \ˈprəsh-ə-ˌniz-əm\ *n* **:** the practices or policies (as the advocacy of militarism) held to be typically Prussian
prus·sian·ize \-ˌnīz\ *vt* **-ized; -iz·ing** *often cap* **:** to make Prussian in character or principle (as in authoritarian control or rigid discipline) — **prus·sian·iza·tion** \ˌprəsh-ə-nə-ˈzā-shən\ *n*
prus·si·ate \ˈprəs-ē-ˌāt\ *n* [F, fr. (*acide*) *prussique*] **1 :** a salt of hydrocyanic acid **:** CYANIDE **2 a :** FERROCYANIDE **b :** FERRICYANIDE
pru·tah *or* **pru·ta** \prü-ˈtä\ *n, pl* **pru·toth** *or* **pru·tot** \-ˈtōt(h), -ˈtōs\ [NHeb *pĕrūṭāh,* fr. LHeb, a small coin] **1 :** a monetary unit of Israel equivalent to $^1/_{1000}$ pound **2 :** a coin representing one prutah
[1]**pry** \ˈprī\ *vi* **pried; pry·ing** [ME *prien*] **:** to look closely or inquisitively; *esp* **:** to make a nosy or presumptuous inquiry
[2]**pry** *vt* **pried; pry·ing** [alter. of [5]*prize*] **1 :** to raise, move, or pull apart with a pry or lever **:** PRIZE **2 :** to extract, detach, or open with difficulty <*pried* the secret out of his sister>
[3]**pry** *n* **1 :** a tool for prying **2 :** LEVERAGE
pry·er *var of* PRIER
pry·ing *adj* **:** impertinently or officiously inquisitive or interrogatory ***syn*** see CURIOUS — **pry·ing·ly** \-iŋ-lē\ *adv*
Ps *or* **Psa** *abbr* Psalms
PS *abbr* **1** [L *postscriptum*] postscript **2** power supply **3** public school
psalm \ˈsäm, ˈsälm\ *n, often cap* [ME, fr. OE *psealm,* fr. LL *psalmus,* fr. Gk *psalmos,* lit., twanging of a harp, fr. *psallein* to pluck, play a stringed instrument] **:** a sacred song or poem used in worship; *esp* **:** one of the biblical hymns collected in the Book of Psalms
psalm·book \-ˌbu̇k\ *n, archaic* **:** PSALTER
psalm·ist \ˈsäm-əst, ˈsäl-məst\ *n* **:** a writer or composer of esp. biblical psalms
psalm·o·dy \ˈsäm-əd-ē, ˈsäl-məd-\ *n* [ME *psalmodie,* fr. LL *psalmodia,* fr. LGk *psalmōidia,* lit., singing to the harp, fr. *psalmos* + *aidein* to sing — more at ODE] **1 :** the act, practice, or art of singing psalms in worship **2 :** a collection of psalms
Psalms \ˈsämz, ˈsälmz\ *n pl but sing in constr* **:** a collection of sacred poems forming a book of canonical Jewish and Christian Scripture — see BIBLE table
Psal·ter \ˈsȯl-tər\ *n* [ME, fr. OE *psalter* & OF *psaltier,* fr. LL *psalterium,* fr. LGk *psaltērion,* fr. Gk, psaltery] **:** the Book of Psalms; *also* **:** a collection of Psalms for liturgical or devotional use
psal·te·ri·um \sȯl-ˈtir-ē-əm\ *n, pl* **-ria** \-ē-ə\ [NL, fr. LL, psalter; fr. the resemblance of the folds to the pages of a book] **:** OMASUM
psal·tery *also* **psal·try** \ˈsȯl-t(ə-)rē\ *n, pl* **-ter·ies** *also* **-tries** [ME *psalterie,* fr. MF, fr. L *psalterium,* fr. Gk *psaltērion,* fr. *psallein* to play on a stringed instrument] **:** an ancient musical instrument resembling the zither
p's and q's \ˌpēz-ᵊn-ˈkyüz\ *n pl* [fr. the phrase *mind one's p's and q's,* alluding to the difficulty a child learning to write has in distinguishing between *p* and *q*] **1 :** something (as one's manners) that one should be mindful of <better watch his *p's and q's* when I get a six-gun of my own —Jean Stafford> **2 :** best behavior <being on her *p's and q's* for two solid days was too much —Guy McCrone>
PSAT *abbr* Preliminary Scholastic Aptitude Test
psec *abbr* picosecond
pse·phol·o·gy \sē-ˈfäl-ə-jē\ *n* [Gk *psēphos* pebble, ballot, vote; fr. the use of pebbles by the ancient Greeks in voting] **:** the scientific study of elections — **pse·pho·log·i·cal** \ˌsē-fə-ˈläj-i-kəl\ *adj* — **pse·phol·o·gist** \sē-ˈfäl-ə-jəst\ *n*
pseud *abbr* pseudonym; pseudonymous
pseud- *or* **pseudo-** *comb form* [ME, fr. LL, fr. Gk, fr. *pseudēs*] **:** false **:** spurious <*pseud*axis> <*pseudo*classic> <*pseudo*podium>
pseud·epi·graph \sü-ˈdep-ə-ˌgraf\ *n* **:** PSEUDEPIGRAPHON 2
pseud·epig·ra·phon \ˌsüd-i-ˈpig-rə-ˌfän\ *n, pl* **-pha** \-fə\ [NL, sing. of *pseudepigrapha,* fr. Gk, neut. pl. of *pseudepigraphos* falsely inscribed, fr. *pseud-* + *epigraphein* to inscribe — more at EPIGRAM] **1** *pl* **:** APOCRYPHA **2 :** any of various pseudonymous or anonymous Jewish religious writings of the period 200 B.C. to 200 A.D.; *esp* **:** one of such writings (as the Psalms of Solomon) not included in any canon of biblical Scripture — usu. used in pl.
pseud·epig·ra·phy \-fē\ *n* [Gk *pseudepigraphos*] **:** the ascription of false names of authors to works
pseu·do \ˈsüd-(ˌ)ō\ *adj* [ME, fr. *pseudo-*] **:** being apparently rather than actually as stated **:** SHAM, SPURIOUS <distinction between true and ~ humanism —K. F. Reinhardt>

ə abut ᵊ kitten ər further a back ā bake ä cot, cart
au̇ out ch chin e less ē easy g gift i trip ī life
j joke ŋ sing ō flow ȯ flaw ȯi coin th thin t͟h this
ü loot u̇ foot y yet yü few yu̇ furious zh vision

pseu·do·al·lele \ˌsüd-ō-ə-ˈlē(ə)l\ *n* **:** any of two or more closely linked genes that act usu. as if a single member of an allelic pair but occas. undergo crossing-over and recombination — **pseu·do·al·le·lic** \-ˈlē-lik, -ˈlel-ik\ *adj* — **pseu·do·al·lel·ism** \-ˈlē(ə)l-ˌiz-əm, -ˈlel-ˌiz-\ *n*

pseu·do·cho·lin·es·ter·ase \ˈsüd-ō-ˌkō-lə-ˈnes-tə-ˌrās, -ˌrāz\ *n* **:** CHOLINESTERASE 2

pseu·do·clas·sic \ˌsüd-ō-ˈklas-ik\ *adj* **:** pretending to be or erroneously regarded as classic — **pseudoclassic** *n*

pseu·do·clas·si·cism \-ˈklas-ə-ˌsiz-əm\ *n* **:** imitative representation of classicism in literature and art

pseu·do·coel \ˈsüd-ə-ˌsēl\ *n* **:** a body cavity that is not a product of gastrulation and is not lined with a well-defined mesodermal membrane

pseu·do·coe·lom·ate \ˌsüd-ō-ˈsē-lə-ˌmāt\ *adj* [*pseud-* + *coelomate*] **:** having a body cavity that is a pseudocoel — **pseudocoelomate** *n*

pseu·do·cy·e·sis \-sī-ˈē-səs\ *n* [NL, fr. *pseud-* + *cyesis* pregnancy, fr. Gk *kyēsis,* fr. *kyein* to be pregnant — more at CAVE] **:** a psychosomatic state that occurs without conception and is marked by some of the physical symptoms and changes in hormonal balance of pregnancy

pseu·do·mo·nad \ˌsüd-ə-ˈmō-ˌnad, -nəd\ *n* [NL *Pseudomonad-, Pseudomonas,* genus name] **:** any of a genus (*Pseudomonas*) of short rod-shaped bacteria many of which produce a greenish fluorescent water-soluble pigment and some of which are saprophytes or plant or animal pathogens

pseu·do·mo·nas \-nəs\ *n, pl* **-mo·na·des** \-ˈmō-nə-ˌdēz, -ˈmän-ə-\ [NL, genus name, fr. *pseud-* + *monad-, monas* monad] **:** PSEUDOMONAD

pseu·do·morph \ˈsüd-ə-ˌmȯrf\ *n* [prob. fr. F *pseudomorphe,* fr. *pseud-* + *-morphe* -morph] **1 :** a mineral having the characteristic outward form of another species **2 :** a deceptive or irregular form — **pseu·do·mor·phic** \ˌsüd-ə-ˈmȯr-fik\ *adj* — **pseu·do·mor·phism** \-ˌfiz-əm\ *n* — **pseu·do·mor·phous** \-fəs\ *adj*

pseu·do·my·ce·li·um \ˈsüd-ō-mī-ˈsē-lē-əm\ *n* [NL] **:** a cellular association which occurs among higher bacteria and yeasts and in which cells form chains resembling small mycelia — **pseu·do·my·ce·li·al** \-lē-əl\ *adj*

pseud·onym \ˈsüd-ᵊn-ˌim\ *n* [F *pseudonyme,* fr. Gk *pseudōnymos* bearing a false name] **:** a fictitious name; *esp* **:** PEN NAME

pseud·onym·i·ty \ˌsüd-ᵊn-ˈim-ət-ē\ *n* **:** the use of a pseudonym; *also* **:** the fact or state of being signed with a pseudonym

pseud·on·y·mous \sü-ˈdän-ə-məs\ *adj* [Gk *pseudōnymos,* fr. *pseud-* + *onoma, onyma* name] **:** bearing or using a fictitious name <a ~ report>; *also* **:** being a pseudonym — **pseud·on·y·mous·ly** *adv* — **pseud·on·y·mous·ness** *n*

pseu·do·pa·ren·chy·ma \ˌsüd-ō-pə-ˈreŋ-kə-mə\ *n* [NL] **:** compactly interwoven short-celled filaments in a thallophyte that resemble parenchyma of higher plants — **pseu·do·par·en·chy·ma·tous** \-ˌpar-ən-ˈkim-ət-əs, -ˈkī-mət-\ *adj*

pseu·do·pod \ˈsüd-ə-ˌpäd\ *n* [NL *pseudopodium*] **1 :** PSEUDOPODIUM **2 :** a supposed or apparent psychic projection (as from a medium's body) — **pseu·dop·o·dal** \sü-ˈdäp-əd-ᵊl\ *or* **pseu·do·po·di·al** \ˌsüd-ə-ˈpōd-ē-əl\ *adj*

pseu·do·po·di·um \ˌsüd-ə-ˈpōd-ē-əm\ *n* [NL] **1 :** a temporary protrusion or retractile process of the protoplasm of a cell that serves a locomotor or food-gathering function **2 :** a slender leafless branch of the gametophyte in various mosses that often bears gemmae

pseu·do·preg·nan·cy \ˌsüd-ō-ˈpreg-nən-sē\ *n* **1 :** PSEUDOCYESIS **2 :** an anestrous state resembling pregnancy that occurs in various mammals usu. after an infertile copulation — **pseu·do·preg·nant** \-nənt\ *adj*

pseu·do·ran·dom \-ˈran-dəm\ *adj* **:** being or involving numbers that are selected by a definite computational process (as one involving a computer) but that satisfy one or more standard tests for statistical randomness

pseu·do·salt \ˈsüd-ō-ˌsȯlt\ *n* **:** a compound analogous in formula to a salt but not ionized as such

pseu·do·sci·ence \ˌsüd-ō-ˈsī-ən(t)s\ *n* **:** a system of theories, assumptions, and methods erroneously regarded as scientific — **pseu·do·sci·en·tif·ic** \-ˌsī-ən-ˈtif-ik\ *adj* — **pseu·do·sci·en·tist** \-ˈsī-ənt-əst\ *n*

pseu·do·scor·pi·on \-ˈskȯr-pē-ən\ *n* [NL *Pseudoscorpiones,* group name, fr. *pseud-* + L *scorpion-, scorpio* scorpion] **:** any of an order (Pseudoscorpiones, Pseudoscorpionida, or Pseudoscorpionidea) of minute arachnids that have no caudal sting and feed on minute animals (as insects and mites)

pseu·do·so·phis·ti·ca·tion \ˈsüd-ō-sə-ˌfis-tə-ˈkā-shən\ *n* **:** false or feigned sophistication — **pseu·do·so·phis·ti·cat·ed** \-sə-ˈfis-ti-ˌkāt-əd\ *adj*

pseu·do·tu·ber·cu·lo·sis \-t(y)u̇-ˌbər-kyə-ˈlō-səs\ *n* [NL] **:** any of several diseases that are characterized by the formation of granulomas resembling tubercular nodules but are not caused by the tubercle bacillus

psf *abbr* pounds per square foot

PSG *abbr* platoon sergeant

pshaw \ˈshȯ\ *interj* — used to express irritation, disapproval, contempt, or disbelief

1psi \ˈsī, ˈpsī\ *n* [LGk, fr. Gk *psei*] **:** the 23d letter of the Greek alphabet — see ALPHABET table

2psi *abbr* pounds per square inch

psig *abbr* pounds per square inch gauge

psi·lo·cy·bin \ˌsī-lə-ˈsī-bən\ *n* [NL *Psilocybe,* genus name + *-in*] **:** a hallucinogenic organic compound $C_{12}H_{17}N_2O_4P$ obtained from a fungus (*Psilocybe mexicana*)

psi·lo·phyte \ˈsī-lə-ˌfīt\ *n* [NL *Psilophyton,* genus of plants, fr. Gk *psilos* bare, mere + *phyton* plant — more at PHYT-] **:** any of an order (Psilophytales) of Paleozoic simple dichotomously branched plants of Europe and eastern Canada that include the oldest known land plants with vascular structure — **psi·lo·phyt·ic** \ˌsī-lə-ˈfit-ik\ *adj*

psit·ta·ceous \sə-ˈtā-shəs, si-\ *adj* [L *psittacus* parrot] **1 :** PSITTACINE **2 :** resembling a parrot <~ chatter>

psit·ta·cine \ˈsit-ə-ˌsīn\ *adj* [L *psittacinus,* fr. *psittacus* parrot, fr. Gk *psittakos*] **:** of or relating to the parrots — **psittacine** *n*

psit·ta·co·sis \ˌsit-ə-ˈkō-səs\ *n* [NL, fr. L *psittacus*] **:** an infectious disease of birds caused by a rickettsia (*Miyagawanella psittaci*), marked by diarrhea and wasting, and transmissible to man in whom it usu. occurs as an atypical pneumonia accompanied by high fever — **psit·ta·co·tic** \-ˈkät-ik, -ˈkōt-\ *adj*

pso·cid \ˈsō-səd\ *n* [deriv. of NL *Psocus,* genus of lice] **:** any of an order (Corrodentia) of minute usu. winged primitive insects (as a book louse)

pso·ri·a·sis \sə-ˈrī-ə-səs\ *n* [NL, fr. Gk *psōriasis,* fr. *psōrian* to have the itch, fr. *psōra* itch; akin to Gk *psēn* to rub] **:** a chronic skin disease characterized by circumscribed red patches covered with white scales — **pso·ri·at·ic** \ˌsōr-ē-ˈat-ik, ˌsȯr-\ *adj or n*

PST *abbr* Pacific standard time

1psych *also* **psyche** \ˈsīk\ *vt* [by shortening] **1 :** PSYCHOANALYZE **2 a :** to anticipate correctly the intentions or actions of **:** OUTGUESS **b :** to analyze or figure out (as a problem or course of action) <I ~*ed* it all out by myself and decided —David Hulburd> **3 a :** to make psychologically uneasy **:** INTIMIDATE, SCARE <pressure doesn't ~ me —Jerry Quarry> — often used with *out* **b :** to make (oneself) psychologically ready for performance — usu. used with *up* <~*ed* himself up for the race>

2psych *abbr* psychology

psych- *or* **psycho-** *comb form* [Gk, fr. *psychē* breath, principle of life, life, soul; akin to Gk *psychein* to breathe, blow, cool, Skt *babhasti* he blows] **1 :** soul **:** spirit <*psycho*gnosis> **2 a :** mind **:** mental processes and activities <*psycho*dynamic> <*psycho*logy> **b :** psychological methods <*psycho*analysis> <*psycho*therapy> **c :** brain <*psycho*surgery> **d :** mental and <*psycho*somatic>

psych·as·the·nia \ˌsī-kəs-ˈthē-nē-ə\ *n* [NL] **:** an incapacity to resolve doubts or uncertainties or to resist phobias, obsessions, or compulsions that one knows are irrational — **psych·as·then·ic** \-ˈthen-ik\ *adj or n*

Psy·che \ˈsī-kē\ *n* [L, fr. Gk *psychē* soul] **1 :** a princess loved by Cupid **2** *not cap* [Gk *psychē*] **a :** SOUL, SELF **b :** MIND

psy·che·de·lia \ˌsī-kə-ˈdēl-yə\ *n* [NL, fr. E *psychedelic* + NL *-ia*] **:** the world of people or items associated with psychedelic drugs

1psy·che·del·ic \ˌsī-kə-ˈdel-ik\ *adj* [Gk *psychē* soul + *dēloun* to show] **1 a :** of, relating to, or being drugs (as LSD) capable of producing abnormal psychic effects (as hallucinations) and sometimes psychic states resembling mental illness **b :** produced by or associated with the use of psychedelic drugs <a ~ experience> <hippies escaping to their ~ lairs —T. E. Mullaney> **2 a :** imitating or reproducing effects (as distorted or bizarre images or sounds) resembling those produced by psychedelic drugs <a ~ light show> **b (1) :** brightly colored <ferryboats soon will take on a ~ look, with an overall coat of orange and touches of red and yellow —*N.Y. Times*> **(2)** *of colors* **:** FLUORESCENT — **psy·che·del·i·cal·ly** \-ˈdel-i-k(ə-)lē\ *adv*

2psychedelic *n* **1 :** a psychedelic drug (as LSD) **2 a :** a user or an advocate of psychedelic drugs **b :** a person with psychedelic social and cultural interests and orientation

Psy·che knot \ˌsī-kē-\ *n* [fr. the frequent representation of Psyche in works of art with this style] **:** a woman's hair style in which the hair is brushed back and twisted into a conical coil usu. just above the nape

psy·chi·a·try \sə-ˈkī-ə-trē, sī-\ *n* [prob. fr. (assumed) NL *psychiatria,* fr. *psych-* + *-iatria* -iatry] **:** a branch of medicine that deals with mental, emotional, or behavioral disorders — **psy·chi·at·ric** \ˌsī-kē-ˈa-trik\ *adj* — **psy·chi·at·ri·cal·ly** \-tri-k(ə-)lē\ *adv* — **psy·chi·a·trist** \sə-ˈkī-ə-trəst, sī-\ *n*

1psy·chic \ˈsī-kik\ *also* **psy·chi·cal** \-ki-kəl\ *adj* [Gk *psychikos* of the soul, fr. *psychē* soul] **1 :** of or relating to the psyche **:** PSYCHOGENIC **2 :** lying outside the sphere of physical science or knowledge **:** immaterial, moral, or spiritual in origin or force **3 :** sensitive to nonphysical or supernatural forces and influences **:** marked by extraordinary or mysterious sensitivity, perception, or understanding — **psy·chi·cal·ly** \-ki-k(ə-)lē\ *adv*

2psychic *n* **1 a :** a person apparently sensitive to nonphysical forces **b :** MEDIUM 2d **2 :** psychic phenomena

psychic energizer *n* **:** a drug with marked antidepressant properties that is used esp. to relieve depressive syndromes

psy·cho \ˈsī-(ˌ)kō\ *n, pl* **psychos** [short for *psychoneurotic*] **:** a victim of severe mental or emotional disorder; *esp* **:** a psychoneurotic person — **psycho** *adj*

psy·cho·acous·tic \ˌsī-kō-ə-ˈkü-stik\ *adj* **:** of or relating to psychoacoustics

psy·cho·acous·tics \-stiks\ *n pl but sing in constr* **:** a branch of science dealing with hearing, the sensations produced by sounds, and the problems of communication

psy·cho·ac·tive \ˌsī-kō-ˈak-tiv\ *adj* **:** affecting the mind or behavior <~ drugs>

psy·cho·anal·y·sis \ˌsī-kō-ə-ˈnal-ə-səs\ *n* [ISV] **:** a method of analyzing psychic phenomena and treating emotional disorders that emphasizes the importance of the patient's talking freely about himself while under treatment and esp. about early childhood experiences and about his dreams — **psy·cho·an·a·lyst** \-ˈan-ᵊl-əst\ *n*

psy·cho·an·a·lyt·ic \-ˌan-ᵊl-ˈit-ik\ *or* **psy·cho·an·a·lyt·i·cal** \-i-kəl\ *adj* **:** of, relating to, or employing psychoanalysis or its principles and techniques — **psy·cho·an·a·lyt·i·cal·ly** \-i-k(ə-)lē\ *adv*

psy·cho·an·a·lyze \-ˈan-ᵊl-ˌīz\ *vt* **:** to treat by means of psychoanalysis

psy·cho·bi·og·ra·phy \-bī-ˈäg-rə-fē, -bē-\ *n* **:** PSYCHOGRAPH 2 — **psy·cho·bio·graph·i·cal** \-ˌbī-ə-ˈgraf-i-kəl\ *adj*

psy·cho·bi·ol·o·gy \-bī-ˈäl-ə-jē\ *n* [ISV] **:** the study of mental life and behavior in relation to other biological processes — **psy·cho·bi·o·log·ic** \-ˌbī-ə-ˈläj-ik\ *or* **psy·cho·bi·o·log·i·cal** \-i-kəl\ *adj* — **psy·cho·bi·ol·o·gist** \-bī-ˈäl-ə-jəst\ *n*

psy·cho·chem·i·cal \-ˈkem-i-kəl\ *n* **:** a psychoactive chemical — **psychochemical** *adj*
psy·cho·dra·ma \ˌsī-kə-ˈdräm-ə, -ˈdram-\ *n* **:** an extemporized dramatization designed to afford catharsis and social relearning for one or more of the participants from whose life history the plot is abstracted — **psy·cho·dra·mat·ic** \-kō-drə-ˈmat-ik\ *adj*
psy·cho·dy·nam·ics \ˌsī-kō-dī-ˈnam-iks, -də-\ *n* **1 :** the psychology of mental or emotional forces or processes developing esp. in early childhood and their effects on behavior and mental states **2 :** explanation or interpretation (as of behavior or mental states) in terms of mental or emotional forces or processes **3 :** motivational forces acting esp. at the unconscious level — **psy·cho·dy·nam·ic** \-ik\ *adj* — **psy·cho·dy·nam·i·cal·ly** \-i-k(ə-)lē\ *adv*
psy·cho·gen·e·sis \ˌsī-kə-ˈjen-ə-səs\ *n* [NL] **1 :** the origin and development of mental functions, traits, or states **2 :** development from mental as distinguished from physical origins — **psy·cho·ge·net·ic** \-jə-ˈnet-ik\ *adj*
psy·cho·gen·ic \-ˈjen-ik\ *adj* **:** originating in the mind or in mental or emotional conflict — **psy·cho·gen·i·cal·ly** \-i-k(ə-)lē\ *adv*
psy·chog·no·sis \ˌsī-kəg-ˈnō-səs, -ˌkäg-\ *also* **psy·chog·no·sy** \sī-ˈkäg-nə-sē\ *n, pl* **-no·ses** \-ˈnō-ˌsēz\ *also* **-no·sies** \-nə-sēz\ [NL *psychognosis,* fr. *psych-* + *-gnosis*] **:** the study of the psyche in relation to character
psy·cho·graph \ˈsī-kə-ˌgraf\ *n* **1 :** PROFILE 4 **2 :** a biography written from a psychodynamic point of view; *also* **:** a character analysis
psy·cho·ki·ne·sis \ˌsī-kō-kə-ˈnē-səs, -kī-\ *n* [NL, fr. *psych-* + Gk *kinēsis* motion — more at KINESIOLOGY] **:** movement of physical objects by the mind without use of physical means — compare PRECOGNITION, TELEKINESIS — **psy·cho·ki·net·ic** \-ˈnet-ik\ *adj*
psychol *abbr* psychologist; psychology
psy·cho·lin·guist \ˌsī-kō-ˈliŋ-gwəst\ *n* **:** a student or specialist in psycholinguistics
psy·cho·lin·guis·tics \-liŋ-ˈgwis-tiks\ *n pl but sing in constr* **:** the study of linguistic behavior as conditioning and conditioned by psychological factors — **psy·cho·lin·guis·tic** \-tik\ *adj*
psy·cho·log·i·cal \ˌsī-kə-ˈläj-i-kəl\ *also* **psy·cho·log·ic** \-ik\ *adj* **1 a :** of or relating to psychology **b :** MENTAL **2 :** directed toward the will or toward the mind specif. in its conative function <~ warfare> — **psy·cho·log·i·cal·ly** \-i-k(ə-)lē\ *adv*
psychological hedonism *n* **:** the theory that conduct is fundamentally motivated by the pursuit of pleasure or the avoidance of pain
psychological moment *n* **:** the occasion when the mental atmosphere is most certain to be favorable to the full effect of an action or event
psy·chol·o·gism \sī-ˈkäl-ə-ˌjiz-əm\ *n* **:** a theory that applies psychological conceptions to the interpretation of historical events or logical thought
psy·chol·o·gize \-ˌjīz\ *vb* **-gized; -giz·ing** *vt* **:** to explain or interpret in psychological terms ~ *vi* **:** to speculate in psychological terms or upon psychological motivations
psy·chol·o·gy \-jē\ *n, pl* **-gies** [NL *psychologia,* fr. *psych-* + *-logia* -logy] **1 :** the science of mind and behavior **2 a :** the mental or behavioral characteristics of an individual or group **b :** the study of mind and behavior in relation to a particular field of knowledge or activity **3 :** a treatise on psychology — **psy·chol·o·gist** \-jəst\ *n*
psy·cho·met·ric \ˌsī-kə-ˈme-trik\ *adj* **:** of or relating to psychometrics or psychometry — **psy·cho·met·ri·cal·ly** \-tri-k(ə-)lē\ *adv*
psy·cho·met·rics \-ˈme-triks\ *n pl but sing in constr* **:** the psychological theory or technique of mental measurement
psy·chom·e·try \sī-ˈkäm-ə-trē\ *n* **1 :** divination of facts concerning an object or its owner through contact with or proximity to the object **2 :** PSYCHOMETRICS
psy·cho·mo·tor \ˌsī-kə-ˈmōt-ər\ *adj* [ISV] **:** of or relating to motor action directly proceeding from mental activity
psy·cho·neu·ro·sis \ˌsī-kō-n(y)u̇-ˈrō-səs\ *n* [NL] **:** NEUROSIS; *esp* **:** a neurosis based on emotional conflict in which an impulse that has been blocked seeks expression in a disguised response or symptom — **psy·cho·neu·rot·ic** \-ˈrät-ik\ *adj or n*
psy·cho·path \ˈsī-kə-ˌpath\ *n* [ISV] **:** a mentally ill or unstable person; *esp* **:** a person having a psychopathic personality
[1]**psy·cho·path·ic** \ˌsī-kə-ˈpath-ik\ *adj* **:** of, relating to, or characterized by psychopathy — **psy·cho·path·i·cal·ly** \-i-k(ə-)lē\ *adv*
[2]**psychopathic** *n* **:** PSYCHOPATH
psychopathic personality *n* **1 :** an emotionally and behaviorally disordered state characterized by clear perception of reality except for the individual's social and moral obligations and often by the pursuit of immediate personal gratification in criminal acts, drug addiction, or sexual perversion **2 :** an individual having a psychopathic personality
psy·cho·pa·thol·o·gy \ˌsī-kō-pə-ˈthäl-ə-jē, -pa-\ *n* [ISV *psych-* + *pathology*] **:** the study of psychologic and behavioral dysfunction occurring in mental disorder or in social disorganization; *also* **:** such dysfunction — **psy·cho·patho·log·ic** \ˌsī-kō-ˌpath-ə-ˈläj-ik\ *or* **psy·cho·patho·log·i·cal** \-i-kəl\ *adj* — **psy·cho·patho·log·i·cal·ly** \-i-k(ə-)lē\ *adv* — **psy·cho·pa·thol·o·gist** \-pə-ˈthäl-ə-jəst, -pa-\ *n*
psy·chop·a·thy \sī-ˈkäp-ə-thē\ *n* [ISV] **:** mental disorder; *esp* **:** extreme mental disorder marked usu. by egocentric and antisocial activity
psy·cho·phar·ma·ceu·ti·cal \ˈsī-kō-ˌfär-mə-ˈsüt-i-kəl\ *n* **:** a drug having an effect on the mental state of the user
psy·cho·phar·ma·col·o·gy \-mə-ˈkäl-ə-jē\ *n* **:** the study of the effect of drugs on the mind and behavior — **psy·cho·phar·ma·co·log·i·cal** \-mə-kə-ˈläj-i-kəl\ *or* **psy·cho·phar·ma·co·log·ic** \-ik\ *adj* — **psy·cho·phar·ma·col·o·gist** \-ˈkäl-ə-jəst\ *n*
psy·cho·phys·i·cal \ˌsī-kō-ˈfiz-i-kəl\ *adj* **:** of or relating to psychophysics; *also* **:** sharing mental and physical qualities — **psy·cho·phys·i·cal·ly** \-k(ə-)lē\ *adv*
psychophysical parallelism *n* **:** a theory that parallel physical and psychical events do not interact
psy·cho·phys·ics \ˌsī-kō-ˈfiz-iks\ *n pl but sing in constr* [ISV] **:** a branch of psychology that studies the effect of physical processes (as intensity of stimulation) upon the mental processes of an organism — **psy·cho·phys·i·cist** \-ˈfiz-(ə-)səst\ *n*
psy·cho·phys·i·o·log·i·cal \ˈsī-kō-ˌfiz-ē-ə-ˈläj-i-kəl\ *or* **psy·cho·phys·i·o·log·ic** \-ik\ *adj* **1 :** of or relating to physiological psychology **2 :** combining or involving mental and bodily processes — **psy·cho·phys·i·o·log·i·cal·ly** \-i-k(ə-)lē\ *adv*
psy·cho·phys·i·ol·o·gy \-ē-ˈäl-ə-jē\ *n* [ISV] **:** PHYSIOLOGICAL PSYCHOLOGY — **psy·cho·phys·i·ol·o·gist** \-jəst\ *n*
psy·cho·sex·u·al \ˌsī-kō-ˈseksh-(ə-)wəl, -ˈsek-shəl\ *adj* **1 :** of or relating to the mental, emotional, and behavioral aspects of sexual development **2 :** of or relating to mental or emotional attitudes concerning sexual activity **3 :** of or relating to the physiological psychology of sex — **psy·cho·sex·u·al·ly** \-ē\ *adv*
psy·cho·sex·u·al·i·ty \-ˌsek-shə-ˈwal-ət-ē\ *n* **:** the psychic factors of sex
psy·cho·sis \sī-ˈkō-səs\ *n, pl* **-cho·ses** \-ˌsēz\ [NL] **:** fundamental mental derangement (as paranoia) characterized by defective or lost contact with reality — **psy·chot·ic** \-ˈkät-ik\ *adj or n* — **psy·chot·i·cal·ly** \-i-k(ə-)lē\ *adv*
psy·cho·so·cial \ˌsī-kō-ˈsō-shəl\ *adj* **1 :** involving both psychological and social aspects <~ adjustment in marriage> **2 :** relating social conditions to mental health <~ medicine> — **psy·cho·so·cial·ly** \-ˈsōsh-(ə-)lē\ *adv*
[1]**psy·cho·so·mat·ic** \ˌsī-kə-sə-ˈmat-ik\ *adj* [ISV] **1 :** of, relating to, or resulting from the interaction and interdependence of psychological and somatic factors <~ medicine> <a ~ illness> **2 :** of or relating to psychosomatics or psychosomatic disorders — **psy·cho·so·mat·i·cal·ly** \-i-k(ə-)lē\ *adv*
[2]**psychosomatic** *n* **:** one who evidences bodily symptoms or bodily and mental symptoms as a result of mental conflict
psy·cho·so·mat·ics \ˌsī-kə-sə-ˈmat-iks\ *n pl but sing in constr* **:** a branch of medical science dealing with interrelationships between the mind or emotions and the body and esp. with the relation of psychic conflict to somatic symptomatology
psy·cho·sur·gery \ˌsī-kō-ˈsərj-(ə-)rē\ *n* **:** cerebral surgery employed in treating psychic symptoms — **psy·cho·sur·geon** \-ˈsər-jən\ *n* — **psy·cho·sur·gi·cal** \-ˈsər-ji-kəl\ *adj*
psy·cho·ther·a·peu·tic \-ˌther-ə-ˈpyüt-ik\ *adj* [ISV] **:** of or relating to psychotherapy — **psy·cho·ther·a·peu·ti·cal·ly** \-i-k(ə-)lē\ *adv*
psy·cho·ther·a·peu·tics \-iks\ *n pl but sing or pl in constr* **:** PSYCHOTHERAPY
psy·cho·ther·a·py \-ˈther-ə-pē\ *n* [ISV] **:** treatment of mental or emotional disorder or of related bodily ills by psychological means — **psy·cho·ther·a·pist** \-pəst\ *n*
psy·chot·o·gen \sī-ˈkät-ə-jən\ *n* [*psychotic* + *-o-* + *-gen*] **:** a chemical agent (as a drug) that induces a psychotic state — **psy·choto·gen·ic** \(ˌ)sī-ˌkät-ə-ˈjen-ik\ *adj*
[1]**psy·choto·mi·met·ic** \sī-ˌkät-ō-mə-ˈmet-ik, -mī-\ *adj* [*psychotic* + *-o-* + *mimetic*] **:** of, relating to, involving, or inducing psychotic alteration of behavior and personality <~ drugs> — **psy·choto·mi·met·i·cal·ly** \-i-k(ə-)lē\ *adv*
[2]**psychotomimetic** *n* **:** a psychotomimetic agent (as a drug)
psy·cho·tro·pic \ˌsī-kə-ˈtrō-pik\ *adj* **:** acting on the mind
psychro- *comb form* [Gk, fr. *psychros,* fr. *psychein* to cool — more at PSYCH-] **:** cold <*psychro*meter>
psy·chrom·e·ter \sī-ˈkräm-ət-ər\ *n* [ISV] **:** a hygrometer consisting essentially of two similar thermometers with the bulb of one being kept wet so that the cooling that results from evaporation makes it register a lower temperature than the dry one and with the difference between the readings constituting a measure of the dryness of the atmosphere — **psy·chro·met·ric** \ˌsī-krə-ˈme-trik\ *adj* — **psy·chrom·e·try** \sī-ˈkräm-ə-trē\ *n*
psy·chro·phil·ic \ˌsī-krō-ˈfil-ik\ *adj* **:** thriving at a relatively low temperature <~ bacteria>
psyl·la \ˈsil-ə\ *n* [NL, genus name, fr. Gk, flea; akin to L *pulex* flea, Skt *pluṣi*] **:** any of various plant lice (family Psyllidae) including economically important plant pests — compare PEAR PSYLLA
psyl·lid \ˈsil-əd\ *n* [deriv. of NL *Psylla*] **:** PSYLLA — **psyllid** *adj*
pt *abbr* **1** part **2** payment **3** pint **4** point **5** port
Pt *symbol* platinum
PT *abbr* **1** Pacific time **2** physical therapy **3** physical training
pta *abbr* peseta
PTA *abbr* Parent-Teacher Association
ptar·mi·gan \ˈtär-mi-gən\ *n, pl* **-gan** *or* **-gans** [modif. of ScGael *tàrmachan*] **:** any of various grouses (genus *Lagopus*) of northern regions with completely feathered feet

ptarmigan

P T boat \(ˈ)pē-ˈtē-\ *n* [*patrol torpedo*] **:** a high-speed 60 to 100 foot motorboat usu. equipped with torpedoes, machine guns, and depth charges — called also *PT*
PTC \ˌpē-ˌtē-ˈsē\ *n* **:** PHENYLTHIOCARBAMIDE
pte *abbr, Brit* private
pterid- *or* **pterido-** *comb form* [Gk *pterid-, pteris;* akin to Gk *pteron* wing, feather — more at FEATHER] **:** fern <*pterid*oid> <*pterido*logy>
pter·i·dine \ˈter-ə-ˌdēn\ *n* [ISV *pter-* (fr. Gk *pteron*) + *-id* + *-ine;* fr. its being a factor in the pigments of butterfly wings] **:** a yellow crystalline bicyclic base $C_6H_4N_4$ that is a structural constituent esp. of various animal pigments
pter·i·doid \ˈter-ə-ˌdoid\ *adj* **:** related to or resembling a fern

ə abut	ə kitten	ər further	a back	ā bake	ä cot, cart
au̇ out	ch chin	e less	ē easy	g gift	i trip
ī life	j joke	ŋ sing	ō flow	ȯ flaw	ȯi coin
th thin	t͟h this	ü loot	u̇ foot	y yet	yü few
yu̇ furious	zh vision				

pter·i·dol·o·gy \ˌter-ə-ˈdäl-ə-jē\ *n* : the study of ferns — **pter·i·do·log·i·cal** \ˌter-ə-də-ˈläj-i-kəl\ *adj* — **pter·i·dol·o·gist** \-ˈdäl-ə-jəst\ *n*

pte·ri·do·phyte \tə-ˈrid-ə-ˌfīt, ˈter-əd-ō-\ *n* [deriv. of Gk *pterid-*, *pteris* fern + *phyton* plant — more at PHYT-] : any of a division (Pteridophyta) of vascular plants (as a fern) that have roots, stems, and leaves but lack flowers or seeds — **pte·ri·do·phyt·ic** \tə-ˌrid-ə-ˈfit-ik, ˌter-əd-ō-\ *or* **pter·i·doph·y·tous** \ˌter-ə-ˈdäf-ət-əs\ *adj*

pte·ri·do·sperm \tə-ˈrid-ə-ˌspərm, ˈter-əd-ō-\ *n* [ISV] : SEED FERN

pter·in \ˈter-ən\ *n* [ISV *pter-* (fr. Gk *pteron* wing) + *-in*] : a compound that contains the bicyclic ring system characteristic of pteridine

ptero·dac·tyl \ˌter-ə-ˈdak-tᵊl\ *n* [NL *Pterodactylus*, genus of reptiles, fr. Gk *pteron* wing + *daktylos* finger — more at FEATHER] : any of an order (Pterosauria) of extinct flying reptiles existing from the Lower Jurassic nearly to the close of the Mesozoic and having a featherless wing membrane that extends from the side of the body along the arm to the end of the greatly enlarged fourth digit — **ptero·dac·ty·loid** \-tə-ˌlȯid\ *adj* — **ptero·dac·ty·lous** \-ləs\ *adj*

pte·ro·ic acid \tə-ˌrō-ik-\ *n* [*pter*in + *-oic*] : a crystalline amino acid $C_{14}H_{12}N_6O_3$ formed with glutamic acid by hydrolysis of folic acid or other pteroylglutamic acids

ptero·pod \ˈter-ə-ˌpäd\ *n* [NL *Pteropoda*, group name, fr. Gk *pteron* wing + NL *-poda*] : any of a group (Pteropoda) of small gastropod mollusks having the anterior lobes of the foot expanded into broad thin winglike organs with which they swim — **pteropod** *adj* — **pte·rop·o·dan** \tə-ˈräp-əd-ən\ *adj or n*

ptero·saur \ˈter-ə-ˌsȯ(ə)r\ *n* [deriv. of Gk *pteron* wing + *sauros* lizard] : PTERODACTYL

pter·o·yl·glu·tam·ic acid \ˈter-ə-ˌwil-glü-ˌtam-ik-\ *n* [ISV *pteroyl* (the radical $(C_{13}H_{11}N_6O)CO$) + *glutamic*] : an acid that is a conjugate of pteroic acid and glutamic acid; *esp* : FOLIC ACID

pter·y·goid \ˈter-ə-ˌgȯid\ *adj* [NL *pterygoides*, fr. Gk *ptergoeidēs*, lit., shaped like a wing, fr. *pteryg-*, *pteryx* wing; akin to Gk *pteron* wing — more at FEATHER] : of, relating to, or lying in the region of the inferior part of the sphenoid bone of the vertebrate skull — **pterygoid** *n*

pterygoid bone *n* : a horizontally placed bone or group of bones of the upper jaw or roof of the mouth in most lower vertebrates

pterygoid process *n* : a process extending downward from each side of the sphenoid bone in man and other mammals

pter·y·la \ˈter-ə-lə\ *n, pl* **-lae** \-ˌlē, -ˌlī\ [NL, fr. Gk *pteron* + *hylē* wood, forest] : one of the definite areas of the skin of a bird on which feathers grow

ptg *abbr* printing

pti·san \tiz-ˈan, ˈtiz-ᵊn\ *n* [ME *tisane*, fr. MF, fr. L *ptisana* — more at TISANE] : a decoction of barley with other ingredients; *broadly* : TEA, TISANE

PTO *abbr* please turn over

Ptol·e·ma·ic \ˌtäl-ə-ˈmā-ik\ *adj* [Gk *Ptolemaikos*, fr. *Ptolemaios* Ptolemy] **1** : of or relating to Ptolemy the geographer and astronomer who flourished at Alexandria about A.D. 130 **2** : of or relating to the Greco-Egyptian Ptolemies ruling Egypt from 323 B.C. to 30 B.C.

Ptolemaic system *n* [after Ptolemy the astronomer] : the system of planetary motions according to which the earth is at the center with the sun, moon, and planets revolving around it

Ptol·e·ma·ist \ˌtäl-ə-ˈmā-əst\ *n* : an adherent of the Ptolemaic system

pto·maine \ˈtō-ˌmān, tō-ˈ\ *n* [It *ptomaina*, fr. Gk *ptōma* fall, fallen body, corpse, fr. *piptein* to fall — more at FEATHER] : any of various organic bases which are formed by the action of putrefactive bacteria on nitrogenous matter and some of which are poisonous

ptomaine poisoning *n* : food poisoning caused by bacteria or bacterial products

pto·sis \ˈtō-səs\ *n, pl* **pto·ses** \-ˌsēz\ [NL, fr. Gk *ptōsis* act of falling, fr. *piptein*] : a sagging or prolapse of an organ or part; *esp* : a drooping of the upper eyelid

PTV *abbr* public television

pty *abbr* proprietary

pty·a·lin \ˈtī-ə-lən\ *n* [Gk *ptyalon* saliva, fr. *ptyein* to spit — more at SPEW] : an amylase found in the saliva of many animals

pty·a·lism \-ˌliz-əm\ *n* [NL *ptyalismus*, fr. Gk *ptyalismos*, fr. *ptyalizein* to salivate, fr. *ptyalon*] : an excessive flow of saliva

Pu *symbol* plutonium

PU *abbr* pickup

[1]**pub** \ˈpəb\ *n* **1** *chiefly Brit* : PUBLIC HOUSE 2 **2** : an establishment where alcoholic beverages are sold and consumed

[2]**pub** *abbr* **1** public **2** publication **3** published; publisher; publishing

pub crawler *n* : one who goes from bar to bar

pu·ber·tal \ˈpyü-bərt-ᵊl\ *or* **pu·ber·al** \ˈpyü-bə-rəl\ *adj* [*pubertal* fr. *puberty*; *puberal* fr. ML *puberalis*, fr. L *puber*] : of or relating to puberty

pu·ber·ty \ˈpyü-bərt-ē\ *n* [ME *puberte*, fr. L *pubertas*, fr. *puber* pubescent] **1** : the condition of being or the period of becoming first capable of reproducing sexually marked by maturing of the genital organs, development of secondary sex characteristics, and in the human and in higher primates by the first occurrence of menstruation in the female **2** : the age at which puberty occurs often construed legally as 14 in boys and 12 in girls

pu·ber·u·lent \pyü-ˈber-(y)ə-lənt\ *adj* [L *puber* pubescent + E *-ulent* (as in *pulverulent*)] : covered with fine pubescence

pu·bes \ˈpyü-(ˌ)bēz\ *n, pl* **pubes** [NL, fr. L, manhood, body hair, pubic region; akin to L *puber* pubescent] **1** : the hair that appears on the lower part of the hypogastric region at puberty **2** : the pubic region

pu·bes·cence \pyü-ˈbes-ᵊn(t)s\ *n* **1** : the quality or state of being pubescent **2** : a pubescent covering or surface

pu·bes·cent \-ᵊnt\ *adj* [L *pubescent-*, *pubescens*, prp. of *pubescere* to reach puberty, become covered as with hair, fr. *pubes*] **1** : arriving at or having reached puberty **2** : covered with fine soft short hairs — compare VILLOUS

pu·bic \ˈpyü-bik\ *adj* : of, relating to, or situated in or near the region of the pubes or the pubis

pu·bis \ˈpyü-bəs\ *n, pl* **pu·bes** \-(ˌ)bēz\ [NL *os pubis*, lit., bone of the pubic region] : the ventral and anterior of the three principal bones composing either half of the pelvis

publ *abbr* **1** publication **2** published; publisher

[1]**pub·lic** \ˈpəb-lik\ *adj* [ME *publique*, fr. MF, fr. L *publicus*, prob. alter. of *poplicus*, fr. *populus* the people] **1 a** : of, relating to, or affecting all the people or the whole area of a nation or state <~ law> **b** : of or relating to a government **c** : of, relating to, or being in the service of the community or nation <an eminent figure in ~ life> <~ affairs> **2 a** : of or relating to mankind in general : UNIVERSAL **b** : GENERAL, POPULAR **3** : of or relating to business or community interests as opposed to private affairs : SOCIAL **4** : devoted to the general or national welfare : HUMANITARIAN **5 a** : accessible to or shared by all members of the community **b** : capitalized in shares that can be freely traded on the open market <a ~ company> — compare CLOSE CORPORATION **6 a** : exposed to general view : OPEN **b** : WELL-KNOWN, PROMINENT **c** : PERCEPTIBLE, MATERIAL — **pub·lic·ness** *n*

[2]**public** *n* **1** : a place accessible or visible to the public — usu. used in the phrase *in public* **2** : the people as a whole : POPULACE **3** : a group of people having common interests or characteristics; *specif* : the group at which a particular activity or enterprise aims

public–address system *n* : an apparatus including a microphone and loudspeakers used for broadcasting to a large audience in an auditorium or out of doors

pub·li·can \ˈpəb-li-kən\ *n* [ME, fr. MF, fr. L *publicanus* tax farmer, fr. *publicum* public revenue, fr. neut. of *publicus*] **1 a** : a Jewish tax collector for the ancient Romans **b** : a collector of taxes or tribute **2** *chiefly Brit* : the licensee of a public house

public assistance *n* : government aid to needy, blind, aged, or disabled persons and to dependent children

pub·li·ca·tion \ˌpəb-lə-ˈkā-shən\ *n* [ME *publicacioun*, fr. MF *publication*, fr. LL *publication-*, *publicatio*, fr. L *publicatus*, pp. of *publicare*] **1** : the act or process of publishing **2** : a published work

public defender *n* : a lawyer usu. holding public office whose duty is to defend accused persons unable to pay for legal assistance

public domain *n* **1** : land owned directly by the government **2** : the realm embracing property rights that belong to the community at large, are unprotected by copyright or patent, and are subject to appropriation by anyone

public health *n* : the art and science dealing with the protection and improvement of community health by organized community effort and including preventive medicine and sanitary and social science

public house *n* **1** : INN, HOSTELRY **2** *chiefly Brit* : a licensed saloon or bar

pub·li·cist \ˈpəb-lə-səst\ *n* **1 a** : an expert in international law **b** : an expert or commentator on public affairs **2** : one that publicizes; *specif* : PRESS AGENT

pub·lic·i·ty \(ˌ)pə-ˈblis-ət-ē, -ˈblis-tē\ *n* **1** : the quality or state of being public **2 a** : an act or device designed to attract public interest; *specif* : information with news value issued as a means of gaining public attention or support **b** : the dissemination of information or promotional material **c** : paid advertising **d** : public attention or acclaim

pub·li·cize \ˈpəb-lə-ˌsīz\ *vt* **-cized; -ciz·ing** : to give publicity to

public land *n* : land owned by a government; *specif* : that part of the U.S. public domain subject to sale or disposal under the homestead laws

public law *n* **1** : a legislative enactment affecting the public at large **2** : a branch of law concerned with regulating the relations of individuals with the government and the organization and conduct of the government itself — compare PRIVATE LAW

pub·lic·ly \ˈpəb-li-klē\ *adv* **1** : in a manner observable by or in a place accessible to the public : OPENLY **2 a** : by the people generally **b** : by a government

public officer *n* : a person who holds a post to which he has been legally elected or appointed and who exercises governmental functions

public relations *n pl but usu sing in constr* : the business of inducing the public to have understanding for and goodwill toward a person, firm, or institution; *also* : the degree of understanding and goodwill achieved

public sale *n* : AUCTION 1

public school *n* **1** : an endowed secondary boarding school in Great Britain offering a classical curriculum and preparation for the universities or public service **2** : a free tax-supported school controlled by a local governmental authority

public servant *n* : a government official or employee

public service *n* **1** : the business of supplying a commodity (as electricity or gas) or service (as transportation) to any or all members of a community **2** : a service rendered in the public interest **3** : governmental employment; *esp* : CIVIL SERVICE

public–service corporation *n* : a quasi-public corporation

public speaking *n* **1** : the act or process of making speeches in public **2** : the art or science of effective oral communication with an audience <took a course in *public speaking*>

pub·lic–spir·it·ed \ˌpəb-lik-ˈspir-ət-əd\ *adj* : motivated by devotion to the general welfare — **pub·lic–spir·it·ed·ness** *n*

public television *n* : television that provides cultural, informational, and instructional programs for the public and that does not promote the sale of a product or service except for identifying the donors of program funds

public utility *n* : a business organization (as a public-service corporation) performing a public service and subject to special governmental regulation

public works *n pl* : works (as schools, highways, docks) constructed for public use or enjoyment esp. when financed and owned by the government

pub·lish \ˈpəb-lish\ *vb* [ME *publishen,* modif. of MF *publier,* fr. L *publicare,* fr. *publicus*] *vt* **1 a :** to make generally known **b :** to make public announcement of **2 a :** to place before the public : DISSEMINATE **b :** to produce or release for publication; *specif* **:** PRINT **c :** to issue the work of (an author) ~ *vi* **1 :** to put out an edition **2 :** to have one's work accepted for publication <a ~*ing* scholar> ***syn*** see DECLARE — **pub·lish·able** \-ə-bəl\ *adj*

pub·lish·er \-ər\ *n* **:** one that publishes; *esp* **:** a person or corporation whose business is publishing

pub·lish·ing \-iŋ\ *n* **:** the business or profession of the commercial production and issuance of literature, information, musical scores or sometimes recordings, or art <newspaper ~> <microfilm ~>

puc·coon \(ˌ)pə-ˈkün\ *n* [fr. *puccoon* (in some Algonquian language of Virginia)] **1 :** any of several American plants (as bloodroot) yielding a red or yellow pigment **2 :** a pigment from a puccoon

puce \ˈpyüs\ *n* [F, lit., flea, fr. L *pulic-, pulex* — more at PSYLLA] **:** a dark red

[1]**puck** \ˈpək\ *n* [ME *puke,* fr. OE *pūca;* akin to ON *pūki* devil] **1** *archaic* **:** an evil spirit **:** DEMON **2 :** a mischievous sprite **:** HOBGOBLIN; *specif, cap* **:** ROBIN GOODFELLOW

[2]**puck** *n* [E dial. *puck* to poke, hit, alter. of E [2]*poke*]**:** a vulcanized rubber disk used in ice hockey

pucka *var of* PUKKA

[1]**puck·er** \ˈpək-ər\ *vb* **puck·ered; puck·er·ing** \-(ə-)riŋ\ [prob. irreg. fr. [1]*poke*] *vi* **:** to become wrinkled or constricted ~ *vt* **:** to contract into folds or wrinkles

[2]**pucker** *n* **:** a fold or wrinkle in a normally even surface

puck·ery \ˈpək-(ə-)rē\ *adj* **:** that puckers or causes puckering

puck·ish \ˈpək-ish\ *adj* [[1]*puck*] **:** IMPISH, WHIMSICAL — **puck·ish·ly** *adv* — **puck·ish·ness** *n*

pud \ˈpu̇d\ *n, Brit* **:** PUDDING

PUD *abbr* pickup and delivery

pud·ding \ˈpu̇d-iŋ\ *n* [ME] **1 :** BLOOD SAUSAGE **2 a** (1) **:** a boiled or baked soft food usu. with a cereal base <corn ~> (2) **:** a dessert of a soft, spongy, or thick creamy consistency <chocolate ~> **b :** a dish often containing suet or having a suet crust and orig. boiled in a bag <steak and kidney ~>

pudding stone *n* **:** CONGLOMERATE

[1]**pud·dle** \ˈpəd-ᵊl\ *n* [ME *podel;* akin to LG *pudel* puddle, OE *pudd* ditch] **1 :** a very small pool of usu. dirty or muddy water **2 a :** an earthy mixture (as of clay, sand, and gravel) worked while wet into a compact mass that becomes impervious to water when dry **b :** a thin mixture of soil and water for puddling plants

[2]**puddle** *vb* **pud·dled; pud·dling** \ˈpəd-liŋ, -ᵊl-iŋ\ *vi* **:** to dabble or wade around in a puddle ~ *vt* **1 :** to make muddy or turbid **:** MUDDLE **2 a :** to work (a wet mixture of earth or concrete) into a dense impervious mass **b :** to subject (iron) to the process of puddling **3 a :** to strew with puddles **b :** to compact (soil) esp. by working when too wet **c :** to dip the roots of (a plant) in a thin mud before transplanting — **pud·dler** \-lər, -ᵊl-ər\ *n*

puddle duck *n* **:** DABBLER b

pud·dling \ˈpəd-liŋ, -ᵊl-iŋ\ *n* **:** the process of converting pig iron into wrought iron or rarely steel by subjecting it to heat and frequent stirring in a furnace in the presence of oxidizing substances

pu·den·cy \ˈpyüd-ᵊn-sē\ *n* [L *pudentia,* fr. *pudent-, pudens,* prp. of *pudēre* to be ashamed, make ashamed] **:** MODESTY

pu·den·dum \pyu̇-ˈden-dəm\ *n, pl* **-da** \-də\ [NL, sing. of L *pudenda,* fr. neut. pl. of *pudendus,* gerundive of *pudēre* to be ashamed] **:** the external genital organs of a human being and esp. of a woman — usu. used in pl. — **pu·den·dal** \-dᵊl\ *adj*

pudgy \ˈpəj-ē\ *adj* **pudg·i·er; -est** [origin unknown] **:** being short and plump **:** CHUBBY — **pudg·i·ness** *n*

pueb·lo \pü-ˈeb-(ˌ)lō, ˈpweb-, pyü-ˈeb-\ *n, pl* **-los** [Sp, village, lit., people, fr. L *populus*] **1 a :** the communal dwelling of an Indian village of Arizona, New Mexico, and adjacent areas consisting of contiguous flat-roofed stone or adobe houses in groups sometimes several stories high **b :** an Indian village of the southwestern U.S. **2** *cap* **a :** a group of Amerindian peoples of the southwestern U.S. **b :** a member of any of these peoples

pu·er·ile \ˈpyu̇(-ə)r-əl, -ˌīl\ *adj* [F or L; F *puéril,* fr. L *puerilis,* fr. *puer* boy, child; akin to Gk *pais* boy, child — more at FEW] **1 :** JUVENILE **2 :** CHILDISH, SILLY <~ remarks> — **pu·er·ile·ly** \-ə(l)-lē, -ˌīl-lē\ *adv* — **pu·er·il·i·ty** \ˌpyu̇(-ə)r-ˈil-ət-ē\ *n*

pu·er·il·ism \ˈpyu̇(-ə)r-ə-ˌliz-əm, ˈpyu̇(-ə)r-ˌī-\ *n* **:** childish behavior esp. as a symptom of mental disorder

pu·er·per·al \pyü-ˈər-p(ə-)rəl\ *adj* [L *puerpera* woman in childbirth, fr. *puer* child + *parere* to give birth to — more at PARE] **:** of or relating to parturition <~ infection>

puerperal fever *n* **:** an abnormal condition that results from infection of the placental site following delivery or abortion and is characterized in mild form by fever but in serious cases may spread through the uterine wall or pass into the bloodstream — called also *childbed fever, puerperal sepsis*

pu·er·pe·ri·um \ˌpyü-ər-ˈpir-ē-əm\ *n, pl* **-ria** \-ē-ə\ [L, fr. *puerpera*] **:** the condition of a woman immediately following childbirth

[1]**puff** \ˈpəf\ *vb* [ME *puffen,* fr. OE *pyffan,* of imit. origin] *vi* **1 a** (1) **:** to blow in short gusts (2) **:** to exhale forcibly **b :** to breathe hard **:** PANT **c :** to emit small whiffs or clouds (as of smoke) **2 :** to speak or act in a scornful, conceited, or exaggerated manner **3 a :** to become distended **:** SWELL — usu. used with *up* **b :** to open or appear in or as if in a puff **4 :** to form a chromosomal puff ~ *vt* **1 :** to emit, propel, blow, or expel by or as if by puffs **:** WAFT **2 a :** to distend with or as if with air or gas **:** INFLATE **b :** to make proud or conceited **:** ELATE **c** (1) **:** to praise extravagantly and usu. with exaggeration (2) **:** ADVERTISE

[2]**puff** *n* **1 a :** an act or instance of puffing **:** WHIFF **b :** a slight explosive sound accompanying a puff **c :** a perceptible cloud or aura emitted in a puff **d :** DRAW 1a **2 :** a light round hollow pastry made of puff paste **3 a :** a slight swelling **:** PROTUBERANCE **b :** a fluffy mass: as (1) **:** POUF 2 (2) **:** a small fluffy pad for applying cosmetic powder (3) **:** a soft loose roll of hair (4) **:** a quilted bed covering **4 :** a commendatory notice or review **5 :** an enlarged region of a chromosome that is associated with intensely active genes involved in RNA synthesis — **puff·i·ness** \ˈpəf-ē-nəs\ *n* — **puffy** \ˈpəf-ē\ *adj*

puff adder *n* **:** HOGNOSE SNAKE

puff·ball \ˈpəf-ˌbȯl\ *n* **:** any of various globose and often edible fungi (esp. family Lycoperdaceae) that discharge ripe spores in a smokelike cloud when pressed or struck — see FUNGUS illustration

puff·er \ˈpəf-ər\ *n* **1 :** one that puffs **2 :** GLOBEFISH; *broadly* **:** any of various similar fishes (order Plectognathi)

puff·ery \ˈpəf-(ə-)rē\ *n* **:** flattering publicity **:** exaggerated commendation esp. for promotional purposes

puf·fin \ˈpəf-ən\ *n* [ME *pophyn*]**:** any of several sea birds (genera *Fratercula* and *Lunda*) having a short neck and a deep grooved parti-colored laterally compressed bill

puffin

puff paste *n* **:** a rich dough containing a large quantity of butter that is used in making light flaky pastries

[1]**pug** \ˈpəg\ *n* [obs. *pug* (hobgoblin, monkey)] **1 :** a small sturdy compact dog of a breed of Asiatic origin with a close coat, tightly curled tail, and broad wrinkled face **2 a :** PUG NOSE **b :** a close knot or coil of hair **:** BUN

[2]**pug** *vt* **pugged; pug·ging** [perh. alter. of [2]*poke*] **1 :** to plug or pack with a substance (as clay or mortar) esp. for deadening sound **2 :** to work and mix (as clay) when wet esp. to make more homogeneous and easier to handle (as in throwing or molding wares)

[3]**pug** *n* [by shortening & alter. fr. *pugilist*] **:** [1]BOXER

[4]**pug** *n* [Hindi *pag* foot] **:** FOOTPRINT; *esp* **:** a print of a wild mammal

pug·ga·ree *or* **pug·a·ree** *or* **pug·gree** \ˈpəg-(ə-)rē\ *n* [Hindi *pagṛī* turban] **:** a light scarf wrapped around a sun helmet

pu·gi·lism \ˈpyü-jə-ˌliz-əm\ *n* [L *pugil* boxer; akin to L *pugnus* fist — more at PUNGENT] **:** [2]BOXING — **pu·gi·lis·tic** \ˌpyü-jə-ˈlis-tik\ *adj*

pu·gi·list \ˈpyü-jə-ləst\ *n* **:** FIGHTER; *esp* **:** a professional boxer

pug·mark \ˈpəg-ˌmärk\ *n* **:** [4]PUG

pug mill *n* [[2]*pug*]**:** a machine in which materials (as clay and water) are mixed, blended, or kneaded into a desired consistency

pug·na·cious \ˌpəg-ˈnā-shəs\ *adj* [L *pugnac-, pugnax,* fr. *pugnare* to fight — more at PUNGENT] **:** having a belligerent nature **:** TRUCULENT, COMBATIVE ***syn*** see BELLIGERENT ***ant*** pacific — **pug·na·cious·ly** *adv* — **pug·na·cious·ness** *n* — **pug·nac·i·ty** \-ˈnas-ət-ē\ *n*

pug nose *n* [[1]*pug*] **:** a nose having a slightly concave bridge and flattened nostrils — **pug–nosed** \ˈpəg-ˈnōzd\ *adj*

puis·ne \ˈpyü-nē\ *adj* [MF *puisné* younger — more at PUNY] *chiefly Brit* **:** inferior in rank <~ judge> — **puisne** *n*

puis·sance \ˈpwis-ᵊn(t)s, ˈpyü-ə-sən(t)s, pyü-ˈis-ᵊn(t)s\ *n* [ME, fr. MF, fr. OF, fr. *puissant* powerful, fr. *poeir* to be able, be powerful — more at POWER] **:** STRENGTH, POWER — **puis·sant** \-ᵊnt, -sənt\ *adj* — **puis·sant·ly** *adv*

puke \ˈpyük\ *vb* **puked; puk·ing** [perh. imit.] **:** VOMIT — **puke** *n*

puk·ka \ˈpək-ə\ *adj* [Hindi *pakkā* cooked, ripe, solid, fr. Skt *pakva;* akin to Gk *pessein* to cook — more at COOK] **:** GENUINE, AUTHENTIC; *also* **:** FIRST-CLASS

pul \ˈpül\ *n, pl* **puls** \ˈpülz\ *or* **pu·li** \ˈpü-lē\ [Per *pūl*] — see *afghani* at MONEY table

Pu·las·ki \pə-ˈlas-kē, pyü-\ *n* [Edward C. *Pulaski,* 20th cent. Am forest ranger] **:** a single-bit ax with an adz-shaped hoe extending from the back

pul·chri·tude \ˈpəl-krə-ˌt(y)üd\ *n* [ME, fr. L *pulchritudin-, pulchritudo,* fr. *pulchr-, pulcher* beautiful] **:** physical comeliness

pul·chri·tu·di·nous \ˌpəl-krə-ˈt(y)üd-nəs, -ᵊn-əs\ *adj* **:** having or marked by pulchritude

pule \ˈpyü(ə)l\ *vi* **puled; pul·ing** [prob. imit.] **:** WHINE, WHIMPER — **pul·er** *n*

pu·li \ˈpu̇l-ē, ˈpyül-\ *n, pl* **pu·lik** \-ik\ *or* **pulis** \-ēz\ [Hung] **:** an intelligent vigorous medium-sized farm dog of a Hungarian breed with a long usu. corded coat

pu·li·cide \ˈpyü-lə-ˌsīd\ *n* [blend of L *pulic-, pulex* flea and E *-cide*] **:** an agent used for destroying fleas

Pu·lit·zer prize \ˌpu̇l-ət-sər-, ˌpyü-lət-\ *n* **:** any of various annual prizes (as for outstanding literary or journalistic achievement) established by the will of Joseph Pulitzer

[1]**pull** \ˈpu̇l\ *vb* [ME *pullen,* fr. OE *pullian*] *vt* **1 a :** to draw out from the skin <~ feathers from a rooster's tail> **b :** to pluck from a plant or by the roots <~ flowers> <~ turnips> **c :** EXTRACT <~ a tooth> **2 a :** to exert force upon so as to cause or tend to cause motion toward the force **b :** to stretch (cooling candy) repeatedly <~ taffy> **c :** to strain abnormally <~ a tendon> **d :** to hold back (a racehorse) from winning **e :** to work (an oar) by drawing back strongly **3 :** to hit (a ball) toward the left from a right-handed swing or toward the right from a left-handed swing **4 :** to draw apart **:** REND, TEAR **5 :** to print (as a proof) by impression **6 :** REMOVE <~ a crankshaft> <~*ed* the pitcher in the third inning> **7 :** to bring (a weapon) into the open <~*ed* a knife> **8 :** COMMIT, PERPETRATE <~ a robbery> **9 :** to draw the support or attention of **:** ATTRACT <~ votes> ~ *vi* **1 a :** to use force in drawing, dragging, or tugging **b :** to move esp. through the exercise of mechanical energy <the car ~*ed* out of the driveway> **c** (1) **:** to take a drink (2) **:** to draw hard in smoking <~*ed* at his pipe> **d :** to strain against the bit **2**

: to draw a gun **3 :** to admit of being pulled **4 :** to feel or express strong sympathy : ROOT <~ *ing* for his team to win> **5** *of an offensive lineman in football* : to move back from the line of scrimmage and toward one flank to provide blocking for a ballcarrier — **pull·er** *n*

syn PULL, DRAW, DRAG, HAUL, TUG *shared meaning element* : to cause to move toward or after an applied force

— **pull a fast one :** to perpetrate a trick or fraud — **pull a punch** *or* **pull punches :** to refrain from using all the force at one's disposal — **pull oneself together :** to regain one's self-possession — **pull one's leg :** to deceive someone playfully : HOAX — **pull one's teeth :** to make one harmless — **pull one's weight :** to do one's full share of the work — **pull stakes** *or* **pull up stakes** : to move out : LEAVE — **pull strings** *or* **pull wires :** to exert secret influence or control — **pull the rug from under :** to remove support or assistance from — **pull the string :** to throw a slow pitch — **pull the wool over one's eyes :** to blind to the true situation : HOODWINK — **pull together :** to work in harmony : COOPERATE

[2]**pull** *n, often attrib* **1 a :** the act or an instance of pulling **b** (1) : a draft of liquid (2) : an inhalation of smoke **c :** the effort expended in moving <a long ~ uphill> **d :** force required to overcome resistance to pulling <trigger ~> **2 a :** ADVANTAGE **b :** special influence **3 :** PROOF 6a **4 :** a device for pulling something or for operating by pulling <drawer ~> **5 :** a force that attracts, compels, or influences : ATTRACTION

pull away *vi* **1 :** to draw oneself back or away : WITHDRAW **2** : to move off or ahead

pull·back \ˈpu̇l-ˌbak\ *n* : a pulling back; *esp* : an orderly withdrawal of troops from a position or area

pull down *vt* **1 a :** DEMOLISH, DESTROY **b :** to hunt down : OVERCOME **2 a :** to bring to a lower level : REDUCE **b** : to depress in health, strength, or spirits **3 :** to draw as wages or salary

pul·let \ˈpu̇l-ət\ *n* [ME *polet* young fowl, fr. MF *poulet,* fr. OF, dim. of *poul* cock, fr. LL *pullus,* fr. L, young of an animal, chicken, sprout — more at FOAL] : a young hen; *specif* : a hen of the common fowl less than a year old

pul·ley \ˈpu̇l-ē\ *n, pl* **pulleys** [ME *pouley,* fr. MF *poulie,* prob. deriv. of Gk *polos* axis, pole] **1 :** a sheave or small wheel with a grooved rim and with or without the block in which it runs used singly with a rope or chain to change the direction and point of application of a pulling force and in various combinations to increase the applied force esp. for lifting weights **2 :** a pulley or pulleys with ropes to form a tackle that constitutes one of the simple machines **3 :** a wheel used to transmit power by means of a band, belt, cord, rope, or chain passing over its rim

pull in *vt* **1 :** CHECK, RESTRAIN **2 :** ARREST ~ *vi* : to arrive at a destination or come to a stop

Pull·man \ˈpu̇l-mən\ *n* [George M. *Pullman*] **1 :** a railroad passenger car with specially comfortable furnishings for day or esp. for night travel **2 :** a large suitcase — called also *Pullman case*

pull off *vt* : to carry out despite difficulties : accomplish successfully against odds

pul·lo·rum disease \pə-ˈlōr-əm-, -ˈlȯr-\ *n* [NL *pullorum* (specific epithet of *Salmonella pullorum*), fr. L, of chickens (gen. pl. of *pullus*)] : a destructive typically diarrheal salmonellosis of the chicken and less often other birds caused by a bacterium (*Salmonella pullorum*) which is transmitted either through the egg or from chick to chick

pull·out \ˈpu̇l-ˌau̇t\ *n* **1 :** something that can be pulled out **2** : the action in which an airplane goes from a dive to horizontal flight **3 :** PULLBACK

pull out \pu̇l-ˈau̇t\ *vi* **1 :** LEAVE, DEPART **2 :** WITHDRAW **3 :** to emerge or escape from difficulty

[1]**pull·over** \ˌpu̇l-ˌō-vər\ *adj* : put on by being pulled over the head

[2]**pullover** \ˈpu̇l-ˌō-vər\ *n* : a pullover garment

pull over \pu̇-ˈlō-vər\ *vi* : to steer one's vehicle to the side of the road

pull round *vt* : to restore to good health ~ *vi* : to regain one's health

pull through *vt* : to help through a dangerous or difficult situation ~ *vi* : to survive a dangerous or difficult situation

pul·lu·late \ˈpəl-yə-ˌlāt\ *vi* **-lat·ed; -lat·ing** [L *pullulatus,* pp. of *pullulare,* fr. *pullulus,* dim. of *pullus* chicken, sprout] **1 a :** GERMINATE, SPROUT **b :** to breed or produce freely **2 :** SWARM, TEEM — **pul·lu·la·tion** \ˌpəl-yə-ˈlā-shən\ *n*

pull–up \ˈpu̇l-ˌəp\ *n* : CHIN-UP

pull up \pu̇l-ˈəp\ *vt* **1 :** CHECK, REBUKE **2 :** to bring to a stop : HALT ~ *vi* **1 a :** to check oneself **b :** to come to a halt : STOP **2 :** to draw even with others in a race

pul·mo·nary \ˈpu̇l-mə-ˌner-ē, ˈpəl-\ *adj* [L *pulmonarius,* fr. *pulmon-, pulmo* lung; akin to Gk *pleumōn* lung] **1 :** relating to, functioning like, or associated with the lungs **2 :** PULMONATE **3 :** carried on by the lungs

pulmonary artery *n* : an artery that conveys venous blood from the heart to the lungs — see HEART illustration

pulmonary vein *n* : a valveless vein that returns oxygenated blood from the lungs to the heart

[1]**pul·mo·nate** \ˈpu̇l-mə-ˌnāt, ˈpəl-\ *adj* [L *pulmon-, pulmo* lung] **1** : having lungs or organs resembling lungs **2 :** of or relating to a large order (Pulmonata) of gastropod mollusks having a lung or respiratory sac and comprising most land snails and slugs and many freshwater snails

[2]**pulmonate** *n* : a pulmonate gastropod

pul·mon·ic \pu̇l-ˈmän-ik, ˌpəl-\ *adj* [L *pulmon-, pulmo*] : PULMONARY

pul·mo·tor \ˈpu̇l-ˌmōt-ər, ˈpəl-\ *n* [fr. *Pulmotor,* a trademark] : a respiratory apparatus for pumping oxygen or air into and out of the lungs (as of an asphyxiated person)

[1]**pulp** \ˈpəlp\ *n* [MF *poulpe,* fr. L *pulpa* flesh, pulp] **1 a** (1) : the soft, succulent, usu. mesocarpic part of fruit (2) : stem pith when soft and spongy **b :** a soft mass of vegetable matter (as of apples) from which most of the water has been extracted by pressure **c :** the soft sensitive tissue that fills the central cavity of a tooth **d :** a material prepared by chemical or mechanical means from various materials (as rags but chiefly from wood) and used in making paper and cellulose products **2 :** pulverized ore mixed with water **3 a :** pulpy condition or character **b :** something in such a condition or having such a character **4 :** a magazine or book using rough-surfaced paper made of wood pulp and often dealing with sensational material — **pulp·i·ness** \ˈpəl-pē-nəs\ *n* — **pulpy** \ˈpəl-pē\ *adj*

[2]**pulp** *vt* **1 :** to reduce to pulp : cause to appear pulpy **2 :** to deprive of the pulp **3 :** to produce or reproduce (written matter) in pulp form ~ *vi* : to become pulp or pulpy — **pulp·er** *n*

pulp·al \ˈpəl-pəl\ *adj* : of or relating to pulp esp. of a tooth <a ~ abscess> — **pulp·al·ly** \ˈpəl-pə-lē\ *adv*

pul·pit \ˈpu̇l-ˌpit *also* ˈpəl-, -pət\ *n* [ME, fr. LL *pulpitum,* fr. L, staging, platform] **1 :** an elevated platform or high reading desk used in preaching or conducting a worship service **2 a :** the preaching profession **b :** a preaching position

pulp·wood \ˈpəlp-ˌwu̇d\ *n* : a wood (as of aspen, hemlock, pine, or spruce) used in making pulp for paper

pul·que \ˈpül-ˌkā; ˈpül-kē, ˈpu̇l-\ *n* [MexSp] : a fermented drink made in Mexico from the juice of various magueys

pul·sant \ˈpəl-sənt\ *adj* : pulsating with activity

pul·sar \ˈpəl-ˌsär\ *n* [*pulse* + *-ar* (as in *quasar*)] : a celestial source of pulsating radio waves characterized by a short interval (as .033 or 3.5 seconds) between pulses and uniformity of the repetition rate of the pulses

pul·sate \ˈpəl-ˌsāt *also* ˌpəl-ˈ\ *vi* **pul·sat·ed; pul·sat·ing** [L *pulsatus,* pp. of *pulsare,* fr. *pulsus,* pp. of *pellere*] **1 :** to exhibit a pulse : BEAT **2 :** to throb or move rhythmically : VIBRATE

pul·sa·tile \ˈpəl-sət-ᵊl, -sə-ˌtīl\ *adj* : marked by pulsation

pul·sa·tion \ˌpəl-ˈsā-shən\ *n* **1 :** rhythmical throbbing or vibrating (as of an artery); *also* : a single beat or throb **2 :** a periodically recurring alternate increase and decrease of a quantity (as pressure, volume, or voltage)

pul·sa·tor \ˈpəl-ˌsāt-ər, ˌpəl-ˈ\ *n* : something (as a pulsometer pump) that beats or throbs in working

pul·sa·to·ry \ˈpəl-sə-ˌtōr-ē, -ˌtȯr-\ *adj* : capable of or characterized by pulsation : THROBBING

[1]**pulse** \ˈpəls\ *n* [ME *puls,* fr. OF *pouls* porridge, fr. L *pult-, puls;* akin to L *pollen* fine flour — more at POLLEN] : the edible seeds of various leguminous crops (as peas, beans, or lentils); *also* : a plant yielding pulse

[2]**pulse** *n* [ME *puls,* fr. MF *pouls,* fr. L *pulsus,* lit., beating, fr. *pulsus,* pp. of *pellere* to drive, push, beat — more at FELT] **1 :** a regular throbbing caused in the arteries by the contractions of the heart; *also* : a single excursion of such throbbing **2 a :** underlying sentiment or opinion or an indication of it **b :** VITALITY **3 a** : rhythmical beating, vibrating, or sounding **b :** BEAT, THROB **4 a** : a transient variation of a quantity (as electrical current or voltage) whose value is normally constant **b** (1) : an electromagnetic wave or modulation thereof of brief duration (2) : a brief disturbance of pressure in a medium; *esp* : a sound wave or short train of sound waves

[3]**pulse** *vb* **pulsed; puls·ing** *vi* : to exhibit a pulse or pulsation : THROB ~ *vt* **1 :** to drive by or as if by a pulsation **2 :** to cause to pulsate **3 a :** to produce or modulate (as electromagnetic waves) in the form of pulses <*pulsed* waves> **b :** to cause (an apparatus) to produce pulses — **puls·er** *n*

pulse–jet engine \ˌpəls-ˌjet-\ *n* : a jet engine having in its forward end intermittent air-inlet valves designed to produce a pulsating thrust by the intermittent flow of hot gases

pul·sim·e·ter \ˌpəl-ˈsim-ət-ər\ *n* : an instrument for measuring the pulse and esp. its force and rate

pul·sion \ˈpəl-shən\ *n* [LL *pulsion-, pulsio,* fr. L *pulsus,* pp.] : PROPULSION

pul·som·e·ter \ˌpəl-ˈsäm-ət-ər\ *n* [ISV] : a pump with valves for raising water by steam and atmospheric pressure without intervention of a piston

pulv *abbr* [L *pulvis*] powder

pul·ver·a·ble \ˈpəlv-(ə-)rə-bəl\ *adj* : capable of being pulverized

pul·ver·ize \ˈpəl-və-ˌrīz\ *vb* **-ized; -iz·ing** [MF *pulveriser,* fr. LL *pulverizare,* fr. L *pulver-, pulvis* dust, powder — more at POLLEN] *vt* **1 :** to reduce (as by crushing, beating, or grinding) to very small particles : ATOMIZE **2 :** ANNIHILATE, DEMOLISH ~ *vi* : to become pulverized — **pul·ver·iz·able** \-ˌrī-zə-bəl\ *adj* — **pul·ver·i·za·tion** \ˌpəl-v(ə-)rə-ˈzā-shən\ *n* — **pul·ver·iz·er** \ˈpəl-və-ˌrī-zər\ *n*

pul·ver·u·lent \ˌpəl-ˈver-(y)ə-lənt\ *adj* [L *pulverulentus* dusty, fr. *pulver-, pulvis*] **1 :** consisting of or reducible to fine powder **2** : being or looking dusty : CRUMBLY

pul·vil·lus \ˌpəl-ˈvil-əs\ *n, pl* **-vil·li** \-ˈvil-ˌī, -(ˌ)ē\ [NL, fr. L, dim. of *pulvinus* cushion] : one of the lobed hairy adhesive organs that terminate the feet of true flies

pul·vi·nus \ˌpəl-ˈvī-nəs, -ˈvē-\ *n, pl* **-vi·ni** \-ˈvī-ˌnī, -ˈvē-(ˌ)nē\ [NL, fr. L, cushion] : a mass of large thin-walled cells surrounding a vascular strand at the base of a petiole or petiolule and functioning in turgor movements of leaves or leaflets

pu·ma \ˈp(y)ü-mə\ *n, pl* **pumas** *also* **puma** [Sp, fr. Quechua] : COUGAR; *also* : the fur or pelt of a cougar

[1]**pum·ice** \ˈpəm-əs\ *n* [ME *pomis,* fr. MF, fr. L *pumic-, pumex* — more at FOAM] : a volcanic glass full of cavities and very light in weight used esp. in powder form for smoothing and polishing — **pu·mi·ceous** \pyü-ˈmish-əs, ˌpə-\ *adj*

[2]**pumice** *vt* **pum·iced; pum·ic·ing :** to dress or finish with pumice

pum·ic·ite \ˈpəm-ə-ˌsīt\ *n* **1 :** PUMICE **2 :** an abrasive that is a gritty volcanic dust

pum·mel \ˈpəm-əl\ *vb* **-meled** *or* **-melled; -mel·ing** *or* **-mel·ling** \-(ə-)liŋ\ [alter. of *pommel*] : POUND, BEAT

[1]**pump** \ˈpəmp\ *n* [ME *pumpe, pompe,* fr. MLG *pumpe* or MD *pompe,* prob. fr. Sp *bomba,* of imit. origin] **1 :** a device that raises, transfers, or compresses fluids or that attenuates gases esp. by suction or pressure or both **2 :** HEART **3 :** an act or the process of pumping **4 :** electromagnetic radiation for pumping atoms or

molecules **5 :** a mechanism (as the sodium pump) for pumping atoms, ions, or molecules

2pump *vt* **1 a :** to raise (as water) with a pump **b :** to draw fluid from with a pump **2 :** to pour forth, deliver, or draw with or as if with a pump <~*ed* money into the economy> <~ new life into the classroom> **3 a :** to question persistently **b :** to elicit by persistent questioning **4 a :** to operate by manipulating a lever **b :** to manipulate as if operating a pump handle <~*ed* his hand warmly> **5 :** to fill with air by means of a pump or bellows **6 :** to transport (as ions) against a concentration gradient by the expenditure of energy **7 a :** to raise (atoms or molecules) to a higher energy level by exposure to usu. electromagnetic radiation at one of the resonant frequencies so that reemission may occur at another frequency resulting in amplification or sustained oscillation **b :** to expose (as a laser, semiconductor, or crystal) to radiation in the process of pumping ~ *vi* **1 :** to work a pump **:** raise or move a fluid with a pump **2 :** to move in a manner that resembles the action or operation of a pump handle **3 :** to spurt out intermittently

3pump *n* [origin unknown] **:** a low shoe that is not fastened on and that grips the foot chiefly at the toe and heel

pumped storage *n* **:** a hydroelectric system in which electricity is generated during periods of greatest consumption by the use of water that has been pumped into a reservoir at a higher altitude during periods of low consumption

pump·er \ˈpəm-pər\ *n* **:** one that pumps; *esp* **:** a fire truck equipped with a pump

pum·per·nick·el \ˈpəm-pər-ˌnik-əl\ *n* [G] **:** a dark coarse sourdough bread made of unbolted rye flour

pump·kin \ˈpəŋ-kən, ˈpəm(p)-kən\ *n, often attrib* [alter. of earlier *pumpion,* modif. of F *popon, pompon* melon, pumpkin, fr. L *pepon-, pepo,* fr. Gk *pepōn,* fr. *pepōn* ripened; akin to Gk *pessein* to cook, ripen — more at COOK] **1 a :** the usu. round deep yellow fruit of a vine (*Cucurbita pepo*) of the gourd family widely cultivated as food **b :** WINTER CROOKNECK **c** *Brit* **:** any of various large-fruited winter squashes (*C. maxima*) **2 :** a usu. hairy prickly vine that produces pumpkins

pump·kin·seed \-ˌsēd\ *n* **1 :** a small brilliantly colored No. American freshwater sunfish (*Lepomis gibbosus*) **2 :** BLUEGILL

pump priming *n* **:** government investment expenditures designed to induce a self-sustaining expansion of economic activity

1pun \ˈpən\ *n* [perh. fr. It *puntiglio* fine point, quibble — more at PUNCTILIO] **:** the humorous use of a word in such a way as to suggest different meanings or applications or of words having the same or nearly the same sound but different meanings

2pun *vi* **punned; pun·ning :** to make puns

pu·na \ˈpü-nə\ *n* [AmerSp, fr. Quechua] **1 :** a treeless windswept tableland or basin in the higher Andes **2 :** a cold mountain wind in Peru

1punch \ˈpənch\ *vb* [ME *punchen,* fr. MF *poinçonner* to prick, stamp, fr. *poinçon* puncheon] *vt* **1 a :** PROD, POKE **b :** DRIVE, HERD <~*ing* cattle> **2 a :** to strike with a forward thrust esp. of the fist **b :** to drive or push forcibly by or as if by a punch **c :** to hit (a ball) with less than a full swing **3 :** to emboss, cut, perforate, or make with or as if with a punch **4 :** to strike or press sharply the operating mechanism of ~ *vi* **:** to perform the action of punching something ***syn*** see STRIKE — **punch·er** *n*

2punch *n* **1 :** the action of punching **2 :** a quick blow with or as if with the fist **3 :** effective energy or forcefulness <an opening paragraph with a lot of ~> <a minority group with no political ~> — **punch·less** \ˈpənch-ləs\ *adj* — **to the punch :** to the first blow or to decisive action — usu. used with *beat*

3punch *n* [prob. short for *puncheon*] **1 a :** a tool usu. in the form of a short rod of steel that is variously shaped at one end for different operations (as forming, perforating, embossing, or cutting) **b :** a short tapering steel rod for driving the heads of nails below a surface **c :** a steel die faced with a letter in relief that is forced into a softer metal to form an intaglio matrix from which foundry type is cast **d :** a device for cutting holes or notches in paper or cardboard **2 :** a hole or notch from a perforating operation

4punch *n* [perh. fr. Hindi *pā̃c* five, fr. Skt *pañca;* akin to Gk *pente* five; fr. the number of ingredients] **:** a hot or cold beverage usu. composed of wine or alcoholic liquor, citrus juice, spices, tea, and water; *also* **:** a beverage composed of nonalcoholic liquids

Punch–and–Judy show \ˌpən-chən-ˈjüd-ē-\ *n* **:** a traditional puppet show in which the little hook-nosed humpback Punch fights comically with his wife Judy

punch·ball \ˈpənch-ˌbȯl\ *n* **:** baseball adapted to playing in small areas and marked by the use of a rubber ball hit with a closed fist instead of a bat

punch·board \-ˌbō(ə)rd, -ˌbȯ(ə)rd\ *n* **:** a small board that has many holes each filled with a rolled-up printed slip to be punched out on payment of a nominal sum in an effort to obtain a slip that entitles the player to a designated prize

punch bowl *n* **:** a large bowl from which a beverage (as punch) is served

punch card *n* **:** a card with holes punched in particular positions each with its own signification for use in data processing; *also* **:** a similar card with holes and notches cut along the edge — called also *Hollerith card, punched card*

punch–drunk \ˈpənch-ˌdrəŋk\ *adj* [[2]*punch*] **1 :** suffering cerebral injury from many minute brain hemorrhages as a result of repeated head blows received in boxing **2 :** behaving as if punch-drunk **:** DAZED, CONFUSED

1pun·cheon \ˈpən-chən\ *n* [ME *ponson,* fr. MF *poinçon* pointed tool, king post (perh. fr. its being marked by the builder with a pointed tool), fr. (assumed) VL *punction-, punctio* pointed tool, fr. *punctiare* to prick, fr. L *punctus,* pp. of *pungere* to prick — more at PUNGENT] **1 :** a pointed tool for piercing or for working on stone **2 a :** a short upright framing timber **b :** a split log or heavy slab with the face smoothed **3 :** a figured stamp die or punch used esp. by goldsmiths, cutlers, and engravers

2puncheon *n* [ME *poncion,* fr. MF *ponchon, poinçon,* of unknown origin] **1 :** a large cask of varying capacity **2 :** any of various units of liquid capacity (as a unit equal to 70 gallons)

punch in *vi* **:** to record the time of one's arrival or beginning work by punching a time clock

pun·chi·nel·lo \ˌpən-chə-ˈnel-(ˌ)ō\ *n* [modif. of It dial. *polecenella*] **1** *cap* **:** a fat short humpbacked clown or buffoon in Italian puppet shows **2** *pl* **-los :** a squat grotesque person

Punchinello

punching bag *n* **:** a stuffed or inflated bag that is usu. suspended for free movement and that is punched for exercise or for training in boxing

punch line *n* **:** the sentence, statement, or phrase (as in a joke) that makes the point

punch–out \ˈpən-ˌchau̇t\ *n* **:** a part of a surface marked off by perforations so that it may be forced out

punch out \ˌpən-ˈchau̇t\ *vi* **:** to record the time of one's stopping work or departure by punching a time clock

punch press *n* **:** a press equipped with cutting, shaping, or combination dies for working on material (as metal)

punch–up \ˈpən-ˌchəp\ *n, Brit* **:** FISTFIGHT

punchy \ˈpən-chē\ *adj* **punch·i·er; -est 1 :** having punch **:** FORCEFUL **2 :** PUNCH-DRUNK

punc·tate \ˈpəŋ(k)-ˌtāt\ *adj* [NL *punctatus,* fr. L *punctum* point — more at POINT] **1 :** marked with minute spots or depressions <a ~ leaf> **2 :** occurring in dots or points <~ skin lesions> — **punc·ta·tion** \ˌpəŋ(k)-ˈtā-shən\ *n*

punc·til·io \ˌpəŋ(k)-ˈtil-ē-ˌō\ *n, pl* **-i·os** [It & Sp; It *puntiglio* point of honor, scruple, fr. Sp *puntillo,* fr. dim. of *punto* point, fr. L *punctum*] **1 :** a minute detail of conduct in a ceremony or in observance of a code **2 :** careful observance of forms (as in social conduct)

punc·til·i·ous \-ē-əs\ *adj* **:** marked by or concerned about precise exact accordance with the details of codes or conventions ***syn*** see CAREFUL — **punc·til·i·ous·ly** *adv* — **punc·til·i·ous·ness** *n*

punc·tu·al \ˈpəŋ(k)-chə(-wə)l\ *adj* [ML *punctualis,* fr. L *punctus* pricking, point, fr. *punctus,* pp. of *pungere* to prick — more at PUNGENT] **1 :** relating to or having the nature of a point **2 :** being to the point **:** POINTED **3 :** PUNCTILIOUS **4 a :** being on time **:** PROMPT <a ~ businessman> **b :** characterized by regular occurrence <the ~ . . . small drop of water dripping somewhere in the rear —Thomas Wolfe> — **punc·tu·al·i·ty** \ˌpəŋ(k)-chə-ˈwal-ət-ē\ *n* — **punc·tu·al·ly** \ˈpəŋ(k)-chə(-wə)-lē\ *adv* — **punc·tu·al·ness** \-chə(-wə)l-nəs\ *n*

punc·tu·ate \ˈpəŋ(k)-chə-ˌwāt\ *vb* **-at·ed; -at·ing** [ML *punctuatus,* pp. of *punctuare* to point, provide with punctuation marks, fr. L *punctus* point] *vt* **1 :** to mark or divide (written matter) with punctuation marks **2 :** to break into or interrupt at intervals <the steady click of her needles *punctuated* the silence —Edith Wharton> ~ *vi* **:** to use punctuation marks — **punc·tu·a·tor** \-ˌwāt-ər\ *n*

punc·tu·a·tion \ˌpəŋ-(k)-chə-ˈwā-shən\ *n* **1 :** the act of punctuating **:** the state of being punctuated **2 :** the act or practice of inserting standardized marks or signs in written matter to clarify the meaning and separate structural units; *also* **:** a system of punctuation

PUNCTUATION MARKS

,	comma
;	semicolon
:	colon
.	period *or* full stop
—	dash *or* em dash
–	dash *or* en dash
~	swung dash
-	hyphen
⸗	double hyphen
?	question mark *or* interrogation point
¿ ?	question marks, Spanish
!	exclamation point
¡ !	exclamation points, Spanish
'	apostrophe
( )	parentheses *or* curves
[ ]	brackets *or* square brackets
〈 〉	brackets, angle
{ }	braces
" "	quotation marks
« » *or* » « *or* „ "	quotation marks, European
' '	quotation marks, single
. . . *or* . . . . *or* *** *or* ——	ellipsis
. . . *or*	suspension points

ə abut	ᵊ kitten	ər further	a back	ā bake	ä cot, cart
au̇ out	ch chin	e less	ē easy	g gift	i trip	ī life
j joke	ŋ sing	ō flow	ȯ flaw	ȯi coin	th thin	t͟h this
ü loot	u̇ foot	y yet	yü few	yu̇ furious	zh vision

punctuation mark *n* : any of various standardized marks or signs used in punctuation

1**punc·ture** \ˈpəŋ(k)-chər\ *n* [L *punctura,* fr. *punctus,* pp. of *pungere*] **1** : an act of puncturing **2** : a hole, slight wound, or other perforation made by puncturing **3** : a minute depression

2**puncture** *vb* **punc·tured; punc·tur·ing** \ˈpəŋ(k)-chə-riŋ, ˈpəŋ(k)-shriŋ\ *vt* **1** : to pierce with a pointed instrument or object **2** : to cause a puncture in **3** : to make useless or ineffective as if by a puncture : DESTROY <failures *punctured* his confidence> ~ *vi* : to become punctured

punc·tured *adj* : having the surface covered with minute indentations or dots : PUNCTATE

puncture vine *n* : a European annual prostrate weed (*Tribula terrestris* of the family Zygophyllaceae) that has been introduced into the western U.S. and has compound leaves and hard spiny pods noted for puncturing automobile tires and for lowering the quality of hay and forage crops — called also *caltrop, puncture-weed*

pun·dit \ˈpən-dət\ *n* [Hindi *paṇḍit,* fr. Skt *paṇḍita,* fr. *paṇḍita*] **1** : PANDIT **2** : a learned man : TEACHER **3** : one who gives opinions in an authoritative manner : AUTHORITY, CRITIC

pun·dit·ry \-də-trē\ *n* : the learning, methods, or pronouncements of pundits

pung \ˈpəŋ\ *n* [short for earlier *tow-pong,* of Algonquian origin; akin to Micmac *tobâgun* drag made with skin] *NewEng* : a sleigh with a box-shaped body

pun·gen·cy \ˈpən-jən-sē\ *n* : the quality or state of being pungent

pun·gent \-jənt\ *adj* [L *pungent-, pungens,* prp. of *pungere* to prick, sting; akin to L *pugnus* fist, *pugnare* to fight, Gk *pygmē* fist] **1** : having a stiff and sharp point <~ leaves> **2** : sharply painful; *also* : POIGNANT **3 a** : marked by a sharp incisive quality : CAUSTIC <a ~ denunciation> **b** : being to the point : highly expressive <~ prose> **4** : causing a sharp or irritating sensation; *esp* : ACRID — **pun·gent·ly** *adv*

syn PUNGENT, PIQUANT, POIGNANT, RACY *shared meaning element* : sharp and stimulating to the mind or senses ***ant*** bland

1**Pu·nic** \ˈpyü-nik\ *adj* [L *punicus,* fr. *Poenus* inhabitant of Carthage, modif. of Gk *Phoinix* Phoenician] **1** : of or relating to Carthage or the Carthaginians **2** : FAITHLESS, TREACHEROUS

2**Punic** *n* : the Phoenician dialect of ancient Carthage

pun·ish \ˈpən-ish\ *vb* [ME *punisshen,* fr. MF *puniss-,* stem of *punir,* fr. L *punire,* fr. *poena* penalty — more at PAIN] *vt* **1 a** : to impose a penalty on for a fault, offense, or violation **b** : to inflict a penalty for the commission of (an offense) in retribution or retaliation **2 a** : to deal with roughly or harshly **b** : to inflict injury on : HURT ~ *vi* : to inflict punishment — **pun·ish·abil·i·ty** \ˌpən-ish-ə-ˈbil-ət-ē\ *n* — **pun·ish·able** \ˈpən-ish-ə-bəl\ *adj* — **pun·ish·er** *n*

syn PUNISH, CHASTISE, CASTIGATE, CHASTEN, DISCIPLINE, CORRECT *shared meaning element* : to inflict a penalty on in requital for wrongdoing ***ant*** excuse, pardon

pun·ish·ment \ˈpən-ish-mənt\ *n* **1** : the act of punishing **2 a** : suffering, pain, or loss that serves as retribution **b** : a penalty inflicted on an offender through judicial procedure **3** : severe, rough, or disastrous treatment <the fighter had been subjected to heavy ~ in his losing bout —*N.Y. Times*>

pu·ni·tion \pyü-ˈnish-ən\ *n* [ME *punicion,* fr. MF *punition,* fr. L *punition-, punitio,* fr. *punitus*] : PUNISHMENT

pu·ni·tive \ˈpyü-nət-iv\ *adj* [F *punitif,* fr. ML *punitivus,* fr. L *punitus,* pp. of *punire*] : inflicting, involving, or aiming at punishment — **pu·ni·tive·ly** *adv* — **pu·ni·tive·ness** *n*

punitive damages *n pl* : damages awarded in excess of normal compensation to the plaintiff to punish a defendant for a serious wrong

Pun·jabi \ˌpən-ˈjäb-ē, -ˈjab-\ *n* [Hindi *pañjābī,* fr. *pañjābī* of Punjab, fr. Per, fr. *Pañjāb* Punjab] **1** : a native or inhabitant of the Punjab region of northwestern India **2** : PANJABI 1 — **Punjabi** *adj*

1**punk** \ˈpəŋk\ *n* [origin unknown] **1** *archaic* : PROSTITUTE **2** [prob. partly fr. 3*punk*] : NONSENSE, FOOLISHNESS **3 a** : a young inexperienced person : BEGINNER, NOVICE; *esp* : a young man **b** : a usu. petty gangster, hoodlum, or ruffian

2**punk** *adj* **1** : very poor : INFERIOR <played a ~ game> **2** : being in poor health <said that she was feeling ~>

3**punk** *n* [perh. alter. of *spunk*] **1** : wood so decayed as to be dry, crumbly, and useful for tinder **2** : a dry spongy substance prepared from fungi (genus *Fomes*) and used to ignite fuses esp. of fireworks

pun·kah \ˈpəŋ-kə\ *n* [Hindi *pākhā*] : a fan used esp. in India that consists of a canvas-covered frame suspended from the ceiling and that is operated by a cord

pun·kie *also* **pun·ky** \ˈpəŋ-kē\ *n, pl* **punkies** [D dial. *punki,* fr. Delaware *punk,* lit., fine ashes, powder] : BITING MIDGE

pun·kin *var of* PUMPKIN

punky \ˈpəŋ-kē\ *adj* **punk·i·er; -est** **1** : of, relating to, or resembling punk **2** : burning slowly : SMOLDERING — **punk·i·ness** *n*

pun·ny *adj* **pun·ni·er; -est** : constituting or involving a pun

pun·ster \ˈpən(t)-stər\ *n* : one who is given to punning

1**punt** \ˈpənt\ *n* [(assumed) ME, fr. OE, fr. L *ponton-, ponto* — more at PONTOON] : a long narrow flat-bottomed boat with square ends usu. propelled with a pole

2**punt** *vt* : to propel (as a punt) with a pole

3**punt** *vi* [F *ponter,* fr. *ponte* point in some games, play against the banker, fr. Sp *punto* point, fr. L *punctum* — more at POINT] **1** : to play at a gambling game against the banker **2** *Brit* : GAMBLE

4**punt** *vb* [origin unknown] *vt* : to kick (a football or soccer ball) with the top of the foot before the ball which is dropped from the hands hits the ground ~ *vi* : to punt a ball

5**punt** *n* : the act or an instance of punting a ball: as **a** : a kick used by a goalkeeper in soccer to clear the ball **b** : a kick used in football to give the opposing team possession of the ball away from the line of scrimmage esp. when a first down seems unlikely

punt·er \ˈpənt-ər\ *n* : one that punts: as **a** *chiefly Brit* : one that gambles; *esp* : one that bets against a bookmaker **b** : one that uses a punt in boating **c** : one that punts a ball

punt formation *n* : an offensive football formation in which a back making a punt stands approximately 10 yards behind the line and the other backs are in blocking position close to the line

pun·ty \ˈpənt-ē\ *n, pl* **punties** [F *pontil*] : a metal rod used for fashioning hot glass

pu·ny \ˈpyü-nē\ *adj* **pu·ni·er; -est** [MF *puisné* younger, lit., born afterward, fr. *puis* afterward + *né* born] : slight or inferior in power, size, or importance : WEAK — **pu·ni·ly** \ˈpyün-ᵊl-ē\ *adv* — **pu·ni·ness** \ˈpyü-nē-nəs\ *n*

1**pup** \ˈpəp\ *n* [short for *puppy*] : a young dog; *also* : one of the young of various animals (as a seal or rat)

2**pup** *vi* **pupped; pup·ping** : to give birth to pups

pu·pa \ˈpyü-pə\ *n, pl* **pu·pae** \-(ˌ)pē, -ˌpī\ *or* **pupas** [NL, fr. L *pupa* girl, doll] : an intermediate usu. quiescent stage of a metamorphic insect (as a bee, moth, or beetle) that occurs between the larva and the imago, is usu. enclosed in a cocoon or case, and undergoes internal changes by which larval structures are replaced by those typical of the imago — **pu·pal** \ˈpyü-pəl\ *adj*

pu·par·i·um \pyü-ˈpar-ē-əm, -ˈper-\ *n, pl* **pu·par·ia** \-ē-ə\ [NL, fr. *pupa*] : the outer shell formed from the larval skin that covers a coarctate pupa — **pu·par·i·al** \-ē-əl\ *adj*

pu·pate \ˈpyü-ˌpāt\ *vi* **pu·pat·ed; pu·pat·ing** : to become a pupa : pass through a pupal stage — **pu·pa·tion** \pyü-ˈpā-shən\ *n*

pup·fish \ˈpəp-ˌfish\ *n* : any of several cyprinodont fishes (esp. *Cyprinodon nevadensis* and *C. diabolis*) of warm streams and springs of the western U.S.

1**pu·pil** \ˈpyü-pəl\ *n* [ME *pupille* minor ward, fr. MF, fr. L *pupillus* male ward (fr. dim. of *pupus* boy) & *pupilla* female ward, fr. dim. of *pupa* girl, doll, puppet] **1** : a child or young person in school or in the charge of a tutor or instructor : STUDENT **2** : one who has been taught or influenced by a famous or distinguished person

2**pupil** *n* [MF *pupille,* fr. L *pupilla,* fr. dim. of *pupa* doll; fr. the tiny image of oneself seen reflected in another's eye] : the contractile usu. round aperture in the iris of the eye — **pu·pil·ar** \-pə-lər\ *adj* — **pu·pil·lary** \-ˌler-ē\ *adj*

pu·pil·age *or* **pu·pil·lage** \ˈpyü-pə-lij\ *n* : the state or period of being a pupil

pu·pip·a·rous \pyü-ˈpip-ə-rəs\ *adj* [NL *pupa* + E *-i-* + *-parous*] **1** : producing mature larvae that are ready to pupate at birth **2** : of or relating to a division (Pupipara) of two-winged flies with pupiparous larvae

pup·pet \ˈpəp-ət\ *n* [ME *popet,* fr. MF *poupette,* dim. of (assumed) *poupe* doll, fr. L *pupa*] **1 a** : a small-scale figure (as of a person or animal) usu. with a cloth body and hollow head that fits over and is moved by the hand **b** : MARIONETTE **2** : DOLL 1 **3** : one whose acts are controlled by an outside force or influence

pup·pe·teer \ˌpəp-ə-ˈti(ə)r\ *n* : one who manipulates puppets

pup·pet·ry \ˈpəp-ə-trē\ *n, pl* **-ries** **1** : the production or creation of puppets or puppet shows **2** : the art of manipulating puppets

pup·py \ˈpəp-ē\ *n, pl* **puppies** [ME *popi,* fr. MF *poupée* doll, toy, fr. (assumed) *poupe* doll] : a young domestic dog; *specif* : one less than a year old

puppy dog *n* : a domestic dog; *esp* : one having the lovable attributes of a puppy

pup·py·ish \ˈpəp-ē-ish\ *adj* : of, relating to, or characteristic of a puppy

puppy love *n* : transitory affection felt by a boy or girl for one of the opposite sex

pup tent *n* : a wedge-shaped shelter tent usu. without flooring or sidewalls

Pu·ra·na \pu̇-ˈrän-ə\ *n, often cap* [Skt *purāṇa,* fr. *purāṇa* ancient, fr. *purā* formerly; akin to OE *fore*] : one of a class of Hindu sacred writings chiefly from A.D. 300 to A.D. 750 comprising popular myths and legends and other traditional lore — **Pu·ra·nic** \-ik\ *adj*

pur·blind \ˈpər-ˌblīnd\ *adj* [ME *pur blind,* fr. *pur* purely, wholly, fr. *pur* pure] **1 a** *obs* : wholly blind **b** : partly blind **2** : lacking in vision, insight, or understanding : OBTUSE — **pur·blind·ly** \-ˌblīn-(d)lē\ *adv* — **pur·blind·ness** \-ˌblīn(d)-nəs\ *n*

1**pur·chase** \ˈpər-chəs\ *vb* **pur·chased; pur·chas·ing** [ME *purchacen,* fr. OF *purchacier* to seek to obtain, fr. *por-, pur-* for, forward (modif. of L *pro-*) + *chacier* to pursue, chase — more at PRO-] *vt* **1 a** *archaic* : GAIN, ACQUIRE **b** : to acquire (real estate) by means other than descent or inheritance **c** : to obtain by paying money or its equivalent : BUY **d** : to obtain by labor, danger, or sacrifice **2** : to apply a device for obtaining a mechanical advantage to (as something to be moved); *also* : to move by a purchase **3** : to constitute the means for buying <our dollars ~ less each year> ~ *vi* : to purchase something — **pur·chas·able** \-chə-sə-bəl\ *adj* — **pur·chas·er** *n*

2**purchase** *n* **1** : an act or instance of purchasing **2** : something obtained esp. for a price in money or its equivalent **3 a** (1) : a mechanical hold or advantage applied to the raising or moving of heavy bodies (2) : an apparatus or device by which advantage is gained **b** (1) : an advantage used in applying one's power (2) : a means of exerting power

pur·dah \ˈpərd-ə\ *n* [Hindi *parda,* lit., screen, veil] : seclusion of women from public observation among Muslims and some Hindus esp. in India

pure \ˈpyu̇(ə)r\ *adj* **pur·er; pur·est** [ME *pur,* fr. OF, fr. L *purus;* akin to Skt *punāti* he cleanses, MIr *ūr* fresh, green] **1 a** (1) : unmixed with any other matter <~ gold> (2) : free from dust, dirt, or taint <~ food> (3) : SPOTLESS, STAINLESS **b** : free from harshness or roughness and being in tune — used of a musical tone **c** *of a vowel* : characterized by no appreciable alteration of articulation during utterance **2 a** : SHEER, UNMITIGATED <~ folly> **b** (1) : ABSTRACT, THEORETICAL (2) : a priori <~ mechanics> **c** : not directed toward exposition of reality or solution of practical problems <~ literature> **d** : being nonobjective and to be appraised on formal and technical qualities only <~ form> **3 a** (1) : free from what vitiates, weakens, or pollutes (2) : containing nothing that does not properly belong **b** : free from moral fault or guilt **c** : marked by chastity : CONTINENT **d** (1) : of pure blood and unmixed ancestry (2) : homozygous in and breeding true for one or more characters **e :** ritually clean ***syn*** see CHASTE ***ant*** impure, immoral — **pure·ness** *n*

pure·blood \ˈpyu̇(ə)r-ˌbləd\ *or* **pure–blood·ed** \-ˈbləd-əd\ *adj* : of unmixed ancestry : PUREBRED — **pure·blood** \-ˌbləd\ *n*

pure·bred \-ˈbred\ *adj* : bred from members of a recognized breed, strain, or kind without admixture of other blood over many generations — **pure·bred** \-ˌbred\ *n*

pure democracy *n* : democracy in which the power is exercised directly by the people rather than through representatives

[1]pu·ree \pyu̇-ˈrā, -ˈrē\ *n* [F, fr. MF, fr. fem. of *puré,* pp. of *purer* to purify, strain, fr. L *purare* to purify, fr. *purus*] **1 :** a paste or thick liquid suspension usu. produced by rubbing cooked food through a sieve **2 :** a thick soup made of pureed vegetables

[2]puree *vt* **pu·reed; pu·ree·ing :** to reduce to a pulp by cooking and then rub through a sieve

pure imaginary *n* : the product of a real number other than zero and the imaginary unit

pure·ly \ˈpyu̇(ə)r-lē\ *adv* **1 :** without admixture of anything injurious or foreign **2 :** SIMPLY, MERELY <read ~ for relaxation> **3 :** in a chaste or innocent manner **4 :** WHOLLY, COMPLETELY <a selection based ~ on merit>

pur·fle \ˈpər-fəl\ *vt* **pur·fled; pur·fling** \-f(ə-)liŋ\ [ME *purfilen,* fr. MF *porfiler*] : to ornament the border or edges of — **purfle** *n*

pur·ga·tion \ˌpər-ˈgā-shən\ *n* : the act or result of purging

[1]pur·ga·tive \ˈpər-gət-iv\ *adj* [ME *purgatif,* fr. MF, fr. LL *purgativus,* fr. L *purgatus,* pp.] : purging or tending to purge

[2]purgative *n* : a purging medicine : CATHARTIC

pur·ga·to·ri·al \ˌpər-gə-ˈtōr-ē-əl, -ˈtȯr-\ *adj* **1 :** cleansing of sin : EXPIATORY **2 :** of or relating to purgatory

pur·ga·to·ry \ˈpər-gə-ˌtōr-ē, -ˌtȯr-\ *n, pl* **-ries** [ME, fr. AF or ML; AF *purgatorie,* fr. ML *purgatorium,* fr. LL, neut. of *purgatorius* purging, fr. L *purgatus,* pp. of *purgare*] **1 :** an intermediate state after death for expiatory purification; *specif* : a place or state of punishment wherein according to Roman Catholic doctrine the souls of those who die in God's grace may make satisfaction for past sins and so become fit for heaven **2 :** a place or state of temporary suffering or misery <the return trip was absolute ~>

[1]purge \ˈpərj\ *vb* **purged; purg·ing** [ME *purgen,* fr. OF *purgier,* fr. L *purigare, purgare* to purify, purge, fr. *purus* pure + *-igare* (akin to *agere* to drive, do) — more at ACT] *vt* **1 a :** to clear of guilt **b :** to free from moral or ceremonial defilement **2 a :** to cause evacuation from (as the bowels) **b (1) :** to make free of an unwanted substance (as an impurity or a foreign material) <~ a cabin of gas> **(2) :** to free (as a boiler) of sediment or relieve (as a steam pipe) of trapped air by bleeding **c (1) :** to rid (as a nation or party) by a purge **(2) :** to get rid of (as undesirable persons) : ELIMINATE ~ *vi* **1 :** to become purged **2 :** to have or produce frequent evacuations **3 :** to cause purgation — **purg·er** *n*

[2]purge *n* **1 a :** an act or instance of purging **b :** the removal of elements or members regarded as undesirable and esp. as treacherous or disloyal **2 :** something that purges; *esp* : PURGATIVE

pu·ri·fi·ca·tion \ˌpyu̇r-ə-fə-ˈkā-shən\ *n* : the act or an instance of purifying or of being purified

pu·ri·fi·ca·tor \ˈpyu̇r-ə-fə-ˌkāt-ər\ *n* **1 :** one that purifies **2 :** a linen cloth used to wipe the chalice after celebration of the Eucharist

pu·ri·fi·ca·to·ry \pyu̇-ˈrif-i-kə-ˌtōr-ē, ˈpyu̇r-(ə-)fə-kə-, -ˌtȯr-\ *adj* : serving, tending, or intended to purify

pu·ri·fy \ˈpyu̇r-ə-ˌfī\ *vb* **-fied; -fy·ing** [ME *purifien,* fr. MF *purifier,* fr. L *purificare,* fr. L *purus* + *-ificare* -ify] *vt* : to make pure: as **a :** to clear from material defilement or imperfection **b :** to free from guilt or moral or ceremonial blemish **c :** to free from undesirable elements ~ *vi* : to grow or become pure or clean — **pu·ri·fi·er** \-ˌfī(-ə)r\ *n*

Pu·rim \ˈpu̇r-(ˌ)im, pu̇r-ˈ\ *n* [Heb *pūrīm,* lit., lots; fr. the casting of lots by Haman (Esth 9:24–26)] : a Jewish holiday celebrated on the 14th of Adar in commemoration of the deliverance of the Jews from the massacre plotted by Haman

pu·rine \ˈpyu̇(ə)r-ˌēn\ *n* [G *purin,* fr. L *purus* pure + NL *uricus* uric, fr. E *uric*] **1 :** a crystalline base $C_5H_4N_4$ that is the parent of compounds of the uric-acid group **2 :** a derivative of purine; *esp* : a base (as adenine or guanine) that is a constituent of DNA or RNA

pur·ism \ˈpyu̇(ə)r-ˌiz-əm\ *n* **1 :** rigid adherence to or insistence on purity or nicety esp. in use of words **2 :** an example of purism; *esp* : a word, phrase, or sense used chiefly by purists

pur·ist \ˈpyu̇r-əst\ *n* : one who adheres strictly and often excessively to a tradition; *esp* : one preoccupied with the purity of a language and its protection from the use of foreign or altered forms — **pu·ris·tic** *adj*

[1]pu·ri·tan \ˈpyu̇r-ət-ᵊn\ *n* [prob. fr. LL *puritas* purity] **1** *cap* : a member of a 16th and 17th century Protestant group in England and New England opposing as unscriptural the ceremonial worship and the prelacy of the Church of England **2 :** one who practices or preaches a more rigorous or professedly purer moral code than that which prevails

[2]puritan *adj, often cap* : of or relating to puritans, the Puritans, or puritanism

pu·ri·tan·i·cal \ˌpyu̇r-ə-ˈtan-i-kəl\ *adj* **1 :** PURITAN **2 :** of, relating to, or characterized by a rigid morality : SEVERE, AUSTERE <~ censors of literature> — **pu·ri·tan·i·cal·ly** \-k(ə-)lē\ *adv*

pu·ri·tan·ism \ˈpyu̇r-ət-ᵊn-ˌiz-əm\ *n* **1** *cap* : the beliefs and practices characteristic of the Puritans **2 :** strictness and austerity esp. in matters of religion or conduct

pu·ri·ty \ˈpyu̇r-ət-ē\ *n* [ME *purete,* fr. OF *pureté,* fr. LL *puritat-, puritas,* fr. L *purus* pure] **1 :** the quality or state of being pure **2 :** SATURATION 4a

Pur·kin·je cell \(ˌ)pər-ˌkin-jē-\ *n* [Johannes E. *Purkinje*] : any of numerous nerve cells that occupy the middle layer of the cerebellar cortex and are characterized by a large globose body with massive dendrites directed outward and a single slender axon directed inward

Purkinje fiber *n* [J. E. *Purkinje*] : any of the modified cardiac muscle fibers that have few nuclei, granulated central cytoplasm, and sparse peripheral striations and make up a network of conducting tissue in the myocardium

[1]purl \ˈpər(-ə)l\ *n* [obs. *pirl* (to twist)] **1 :** gold or silver thread or wire for embroidering or edging **2 :** the intertwisting of thread that knots a stitch usu. along an edge **3 :** PURL STITCH

[2]purl *vt* **1 a :** to embroider with gold or silver thread **b :** to edge or border with gold or silver embroidery **2 :** to knit in purl stitch ~ *vi* : to do knitting in purl stitch

[3]purl *n* [perh. of Scand origin; akin to Norw *purla* to ripple] **1 :** a purling or swirling stream or rill **2 :** a gentle murmur or movement (as of purling water)

[4]purl *vi* **1 :** EDDY, SWIRL **2 :** to make a soft murmuring sound like that of a purling stream

pur·lieu \ˈpərl-(ˌ)(y)ü\ *n* [ME *purlewe* land severed from an English royal forest by perambulation, fr. AF *puralé* perambulation, fr. OF *puraler* to go through, fr. *pur-* for, through + *aler* to go — more at PURCHASE, ALLEY] **1 a :** a frequently visited place : HAUNT **b** *pl* : CONFINES, BOUNDS **2 a :** an outlying or adjacent district **b** *pl* : ENVIRONS, NEIGHBORHOOD

pur·lin \ˈpər-lən\ *n* [origin unknown] : a horizontal member in a roof supporting the rafters

pur·loin \(ˌ)pər-ˈlȯin, ˈpər-ˌ\ *vt* [ME *purloinen* to put away, render ineffectual, fr. AF *purloigner,* fr. OF *porloigner* to put off, delay, fr. *por-* forward + *loing* at a distance, fr. L *longe,* fr. *longus* long — more at PURCHASE] : to appropriate wrongfully and often by a breach of trust ***syn*** see STEAL — **pur·loin·er** *n*

purl stitch *n* [[1]*purl*] : a knitting stitch usu. made with the yarn at the front of the work by inserting the right needle into the front of a loop on the left needle from the right, catching the yarn with the right needle, and bringing it through to form a new loop — compare KNIT STITCH

pu·ro·my·cin \ˌpyu̇r-ə-ˈmīs-ᵊn\ *n* [*purine* + *-o-* + *-mycin*] : an antibiotic $C_{22}H_{29}N_7O_5$ that is obtained from an actinomycete (*Streptomyces alboniger*) and is used esp. as a potent inhibitor of protein synthesis in microorganisms and mammalian cells

[1]pur·ple \ˈpər-pəl\ *adj* **pur·pler** \-p(ə-)lər\; **pur·plest** \-p(ə-)ləst\ [ME *purpel,* alter. of *purper,* fr. OE *purpuran* of purple, gen. of *purpure* purple color, fr. L *purpura,* fr. Gk *porphyra*] **1 :** IMPERIAL, REGAL **2 :** of the color purple **3 a :** highly rhetorical : ORNATE **b :** marked by profanity

[2]purple *n* **1 a (1) :** TYRIAN PURPLE **(2) :** any of various colors that fall about midway between red and blue in hue **b (1) :** cloth dyed purple **(2) :** a garment of such color; *esp* : a purple robe worn as an emblem of rank or authority **c (1) :** a mollusk (as of the genus *Purpura*) yielding a purple dye and esp. the Tyrian purple of ancient times **(2) :** a pigment or dye that colors purple **2 a :** imperial or regal rank or power **b :** high rank or station

[3]purple *vb* **pur·pled; pur·pling** \-p(ə-)liŋ\ *vt* : to make purple ~ *vi* : to become purple

Purple Heart *n* : a U.S. military decoration awarded to any member of the armed forces wounded in action

purple loosestrife *n* : a marsh herb (*Lythrum salicaria*) of Europe and the eastern U.S. that has a long spike of purple flowers

purple passage *n* [trans. of L *pannus purpureus* purple patch; fr. the traditional splendor of purple cloth as contrasted with more shabby materials] **1 :** a passage conspicuous for brillance or effectiveness in a work that is dull, commonplace, or uninspired **2 :** a piece of obtrusively ornate writing — called also *purple patch*

purple scale *n* : a brownish or purplish armored scale (*Lepidosaphes beckii*) that is destructive to citrus fruit

pur·plish \ˈpər-p(ə-)lish\ *adj* : somewhat purple

pur·ply \ˈpər-p(ə-)lē\ *adj* : PURPLISH

[1]pur·port \ˈpər-ˌpō(ə)rt, -ˌpȯ(ə)rt\ *n* [ME, fr. AF, content, tenor, fr. *purporter* to contain, fr. OF *porporter* to convey, fr. *por-* forward + *porter* to carry — more at PURCHASE, PORT] : meaning conveyed, professed, or implied : IMPORT; *also* : SUBSTANCE, GIST

[2]pur·port \(ˌ)pər-ˈpō(ə)rt, -ˈpȯ(ə)rt\ *vt* **1 :** to have the often specious appearance of being, intending, or claiming (something implied or inferred) : PROFESS <a book that ~*s* to be an objective analysis> **2 :** INTEND, PURPOSE

pur·port·ed *adj* : REPUTED, RUMORED — **pur·port·ed·ly** *adv*

[1]pur·pose \ˈpər-pəs\ *n* [ME *purpos,* fr. OF, fr. *purposer* to purpose, fr. L *proponere* (perf. indic. *proposui*) to propose — more at PROPOSE] **1 a :** something set up as an object or end to be attained : INTENTION **b :** RESOLUTION, DETERMINATION **2 :** a subject under discussion or an action in course of execution ***syn*** see INTENTION — **on purpose :** by intent : INTENTIONALLY

[2]purpose *vt* **pur·posed; pur·pos·ing :** to propose as an aim to oneself

pur·pose·ful \ˈpər-pəs-fəl\ *adj* **1 :** full of determination <a ~ man> **2 :** having a purpose or aim : MEANINGFUL <~ activities> — **pur·pose·ful·ly** \-fə-lē\ *adv* — **pur·pose·ful·ness** *n*

pur·pose·less \-ləs\ *adj* : having no purpose : AIMLESS, MEANINGLESS — **pur·pose·less·ly** *adv* — **pur·pose·less·ness** *n*

pur·pose·ly \-lē\ *adv* : with a deliberate or express purpose

pur·po·sive \ˈpər-pə-siv, (ˌ)pər-ˈpō-\ *adj* **1 :** serving or effecting a useful function though not as a result of planning or design **2 :** having or tending to fulfill a conscious purpose or design : PURPOSEFUL — **pur·po·sive·ly** *adv* — **pur·po·sive·ness** *n*

pur·pu·ra \ˈpər-p(y)ə-rə\ *n* [NL, fr. L, purple color] : any of several hemorrhagic states characterized by patches of purplish discoloration resulting from extravasation of blood into the skin and mucous membranes — **pur·pu·ric** \ˌpər-ˈpyu̇(ə)r-ik\ *adj*

pur·pure \ˈpər-pyər\ *n* [ME, fr. OE, purple] : the heraldic color purple

1**purr** \ˈpər\ *n* [imit.] : a low vibratory murmur typical of an apparently contented or pleased cat

2**purr** *vi* **1** : to make a purr **2 a** : to speak in a manner that resembles a purr **b** : to speak in a malicious catty manner — **purr·ing·ly** \-iŋ-lē\ *adv*

1**purse** \ˈpərs\ *n* [ME *purs,* fr. OE, modif. of ML *bursa,* fr. LL, oxhide, fr. Gk *byrsa*] **1 a** (1) : a small bag for money (2) : a receptacle (as a pocketbook) for carrying money and often other small objects **b** : a receptacle (as a pouch) shaped like a purse **2 a** : RESOURCES, FUNDS **b** : a sum of money offered as a prize or present; *also* : the total amount of money offered in prizes for a given event — **purse·like** \-ˌlīk\ *adj*

2**purse** *vt* **pursed; purs·ing 1** : to put into a purse **2** : PUCKER, KNIT

purse crab *n* : a land crab (*Birgus latro*) that is widely distributed about islands of the tropical Indian and Pacific oceans where it burrows in the soil and feeds on coconuts and that is related to the hermit crabs but distinguished by its large size and broad symmetrical abdomen with edible oily flesh

purse–proud \ˈpər-ˌsprau̇d\ *adj* : proud because of one's wealth esp. in the absence of other distinctions

purs·er \ˈpər-sər\ *n* **1** : an official on a ship responsible for papers and accounts and on a passenger ship also for the comfort and welfare of passengers **2** : an official on an airliner responsible esp. for the comfort and welfare of passengers

purse seine *n* : a large seine designed to be set by two boats around a school of fish and so arranged that after the ends have been brought together the bottom can be closed — **purse seiner** *n*

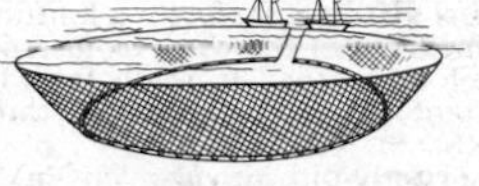
purse seine

purse strings *n pl* : financial resources

purs·lane \ˈpər-slən, -ˌslān\ *n* [ME, fr. MF *porcelaine,* fr. LL *porcillagin-, porcillago,* alter. of L *porcillaca,* alter. of *portulaca*] : any of a family (Portulacaceae, the purslane family) of usu. succulent herbs having perfect regular flowers with 2 sepals and 4 to 5 hypogynous petals; *esp* : a fleshy-leaved trailing plant (*Portulaca oleracea*) with tiny yellow flowers that is a common troublesome weed but is sometimes eaten as a potherb or in salads

pur·su·ance \pər-ˈsü-ən(t)s\ *n* : the act of pursuing; *esp* : a carrying out or into effect : PROSECUTION <in ~ of his duties>

pursuant to *prep* : in carrying out : in conformance to : according to

pur·sue \pər-ˈsü\ *vb* **pur·sued; pur·su·ing** [ME *pursuen,* fr. AF *pursuer,* fr. OF *poursuir,* fr. L *prosequi,* fr. *pro-* forward + *sequi* to follow — more at PRO-, SUE] *vt* **1** : to follow in order to overtake, capture, kill, or defeat **2** : to find or employ measures to obtain or accomplish : SEEK <~ a goal> **3** : to proceed along <~*s* a northern course> **4 a** : to engage in <~ a hobby> **b** : to follow up <~ an argument> **5** : to continue to afflict : HAUNT <was *pursued* by horrible memories> **6** : COURT, 1CHASE 1c <*pursued* by dozens of women> ~ *vi* : to go in pursuit ***syn*** see FOLLOW — **pur·su·er** *n*

pur·suit \pər-ˈsüt\ *n* [ME, fr. OF *poursuite,* fr. *poursuir*] **1** : the act of pursuing **2** : an activity that one engages in as a vocation, profession, or avocation : OCCUPATION

pursuit plane *n* : a fighter plane designed for pursuit of enemy airplanes

pur·sui·vant \ˈpər-s(w)i-vənt\ *n* [ME *pursevant* attendant of a herald, fr. MF *poursuivant,* lit., follower, fr. prp. of *poursuir, poursuivre* to pursue] **1** : an officer of arms ranking below a herald but having similar duties **2** : FOLLOWER, ATTENDANT

1**pur·sy** \ˈpəs-ē, ˈpər-sē\ *or* **pus·sy** \ˈpəs-ē\ *adj* **pur·si·er** *or* **pus·si·er; -est** [ME *pursy,* fr. AF *pursif,* alter. of MF *polsif,* fr. *poulser, polser* to beat, push, pant — more at PUSH] **1** : short-winded esp. because of corpulence **2** : FAT — **pur·si·ness** *n*

2**pursy** \ˈpər-sē\ *adj* **purs·i·er; -est** [*purse*] **1** : having a puckered appearance **2** : PURSE-PROUD

pur·te·nance \ˈpərt-nən(t)s, -ən-ən(t)s\ *n* [ME, lit., appendage, modif. of MF *partenance,* fr. *partenir* to pertain — more at PERTAIN] : ENTRAILS, PLUCK

pu·ru·lence \ˈpyu̇r-(y)ə-lən(t)s\ *n* : the quality or state of being purulent; *also* : PUS

pu·ru·lent \-lənt\ *adj* [L *purulentus,* fr. *pur-, pus* pus] **1** : containing, consisting of, or being pus <a ~ discharge> **2** : accompanied by suppuration

pur·vey \(ˌ)pər-ˈvā, ˈpər-ˌ\ *vt* **pur·veyed; pur·vey·ing** [ME *purveien,* fr. MF *porveeir,* fr. L *providēre* to provide] **1** : to supply (as provisions) usu. as a matter of business **2** : CIRCULATE, DISSEMINATE

pur·vey·ance \-ən(t)s\ *n* : the act or process of purveying or procuring

pur·vey·or \-ər\ *n* **1** : one that purveys **2** : VICTUALLER, CATERER

pur·view \ˈpər-ˌvyü\ *n* [ME *purveu,* fr. AF *purveu est* it is provided (opening phrase of a statute)] **1 a** : the body or enacting part of a statute **b** : the limit, purpose, or scope of a statute **2** : the range or limit of authority, competence, responsibility, concern, or intention **3** : range of vision, understanding, or cognizance

pus \ˈpəs\ *n* [L *pur-, pus* — more at FOUL] : thick opaque usu. yellowish white fluid matter formed by suppuration and composed of exudate containing leukocytes, tissue debris, and microorganisms

Pus \ˈpu̇s\ *n* [Hindi *pūs,* fr. Skt *puṣya*] : a month of the Hindu year — see MONTH table

Pu·sey·ism \ˈpyü-zē-ˌiz-əm, -sē-\ *n* [Edward Bouverie *Pusey*] : TRACTARIANISM — **Pu·sey·ite** \-ˌīt\ *n*

1**push** \ˈpu̇sh\ *vb* [ME *posshen,* fr. OF *poulser* to beat, push, fr. L *pulsare,* fr. *pulsus,* pp. of *pellere* to drive, strike — more at FELT] *vt* **1 a** : to press against with force in order to drive or impel **b** : to move or endeavor to move away or ahead by steady pressure without striking **2 a** : to thrust forward, downward, or outward **b** : to hit (a baseball) to the opposite side of a baseball field — compare PULL **3 a** : to press or urge forward to completion **b** : to urge or press the advancement, adoption, or practice of <~*ed* a bill in the legislature>; *specif* : to make aggressive efforts to sell <a drive to ~ canned goods> **c** : to engage in the illicit sale of (narcotics) **4** : to bear hard upon so as to involve in difficulty <grinding poverty ~*ed* them to the breaking point> **5** : to approach in age or number <the old man was ~*ing* seventy-five> ~ *vi* **1** : to press against something with steady force in or as if in order to impel **2** : to press forward energetically against opposition **3** : to exert oneself continuously, vigorously, or obtrusively to gain an end <unions ~*ing* for higher wages> ***syn*** PUSH, THRUST, SHOVE, PROPEL *shared meaning element* : to use force on so as to cause to move ahead or aside — **push one's luck** : to take an increasing risk

2**push** *n* **1** : a vigorous effort to attain an end : DRIVE: **a** : a military assault or offensive **b** : an advance that overcomes obstacles **c** : a campaign to promote a product **2** : a time for action : EMERGENCY **3 a** : an act of pushing : SHOVE **b** (1) : a physical force steadily applied in a direction away from the body exerting it <the ~ of the water against the wharf> (2) : a nonphysical pressure : INFLUENCE, URGE **c** : vigorous enterprise or energy **4 a** : an exertion of influence to promote another's interests **b** : stimulation to activity : IMPETUS

push around *vt* : to impose on contemptuously

push·ball \ˈpu̇sh-ˌbȯl\ *n* : a game in which each of two sides endeavors to push an inflated leather-covered ball six feet in diameter across its opponents' goal; *also* : the ball used

push–bike \-ˌbīk\ *n, Brit* : a pedal bicycle — called also *push bicycle*

push broom *n* : a long-handled wide brush that is designed to be pushed and is used for sweeping

push–button *adj* : using or dependent on complex and more or less self-operating mechanisms that are put in operation by a simple act comparable to pushing a button <~ warfare>

push button *n* : a small button or knob that when pushed operates something esp. by closing an electric circuit

push·cart \ˈpu̇sh-ˌkärt\ *n* : a cart or barrow pushed by hand

push·chair \-ˌche(ə)r, -ˌcha(ə)r\ *n, Brit* : STROLLER

push·down \-ˌdau̇n\ *n* : a store of data (as in a computer) from which the most recently stored item must be the first retrieved — called also *pushdown list, pushdown stack*

push·er \ˈpu̇sh-ər\ *n* : one that pushes; *esp* : one that pushes illegal drugs

push·ful \-fəl\ *adj* : PUSHING — **push·ful·ness** *n*

push·ing *adj* **1** : marked by ambition, energy, enterprise, and initiative **2** : marked by tactless forwardness or officious intrusiveness ***syn*** see AGGRESSIVE

push off *vi* : to set out <we *pushed off* for home>

push on *vi* : to continue on one's way : PROCEED

push·over \ˈpu̇sh-ˌō-vər\ *n* **1** : an opponent who is easy to defeat or a victim who is capable of no effective resistance <so kind, warmhearted and open that she's . . . a ~ for rivals —Virginia Bird> **2** : someone unable to resist an attraction or appeal : SUCKER **3** : something accomplished without difficulty : SNAP

push·pin \-ˌpin\ *n* : a pin that has a roughly cylindrical head and that is easily inserted into or withdrawn from a surface (as a map) with the fingers

push–pull \-ˈpu̇l\ *adj* : constituting or relating to an arrangement of two electron tubes such that an alternating input causes them to send current through a load alternately <a ~ circuit> — **push–pull** *n*

Push·tu \ˈpəsh-(ˌ)tü\ *var of* PASHTO

push–up \ˈpu̇sh-ˌəp\ *n* : a conditioning exercise performed in a prone position by raising and lowering the body with the straightening and bending of the arms while keeping the back straight and supporting the body on the hands and toes

pushy \ˈpu̇sh-ē\ *adj* **push·i·er; -est** : aggressive often to an objectionable degree : FORWARD — **push·i·ly** \ˈpu̇sh-ə-lē\ *adv* — **push·i·ness** \ˈpu̇sh-ē-nəs\ *n*

pu·sil·la·nim·i·ty \ˌpyü-sə-lə-ˈnim-ət-ē *also* ˌpyü-zə-\ *n* : the quality or state of being pusillanimous : COWARDLINESS

pu·sil·lan·i·mous \-ˈlan-ə-məs\ *adj* [LL *pusillanimis,* fr. L *pusillus* very small (dim. of *pusus* small child) + *animus* spirit; akin to L *puer* child — more at PUERILE, ANIMATE] : lacking courage and resolution : marked by contemptible timidity — **pu·sil·lan·i·mous·ly** *adv*

1**puss** \ˈpu̇s\ *n* [origin unknown] **1** : CAT **2** : GIRL

2**puss** *n* [IrGael *pus* mouth, fr. MIr *bus*] *slang* : FACE

puss·ley \ˈpəs-lē\ *n* [by alter.] : PURSLANE

1**pussy** \ˈpu̇s-ē\ *n, pl* **puss·ies 1** : PUSS **2** : a catkin of the pussy willow

2**pus·sy** \ˈpəs-ē\ *adj* **pus·si·er; -est** : full of or resembling pus

3**pus·sy** \ˈpəs-ē\ *var of* PURSY

4**pus·sy** \ˈpu̇s-ē\ *n, pl* **pussies** [earlier *puss* (perh. of LG or Scand origin) + *-y;* akin to ON *pūss* pocket, pouch, LG *pūse* vulva, OE *pusa* bag, Gk *byein* to stuff, plug] **1** : VULVA — usu. considered vulgar **2 a** : SEXUAL INTERCOURSE — usu. considered vulgar **b** : the female partner in sexual intercourse — usu. considered vulgar

pussy·cat \ˈpu̇s-ē-ˌkat\ *n* : CAT

pussy·foot \ˈpu̇s-ē-ˌfu̇t\ *vi* **1** : to tread or move warily or stealthily **2** : to refrain from committing oneself — **pussy·foot·er** *n*

pussy·toes \ˈpu̇s-ē-ˌtōz\ *or* **puss·y's–toes** \-ēz-\ *n pl but sing or pl in constr* : any of a genus (*Antennaria*) of woolly or hoary composite herbs that are natives mostly of temperate regions and have small whitish discoid flower heads and a pappus formed of club-shaped bristles

pussy willow \ˌpu̇s-ē-\ *n* : a willow (as the American *Salix discolor*) having large cylindrical silky aments

1**pus·tu·lant** \ˈpəs-chə-lənt, ˈpəs-t(y)ə-\ *adj* : producing pustules

2**pustulant** *n* : an agent (as a chemical) that induces pustule formation

pus·tu·lar \-lər\ *adj* **1 :** of, relating to, or resembling pustules **2 :** covered with pustular prominences : PUSTULATE

pus·tu·late \-lət, -ˌlāt\ *or* **pus·tu·lat·ed** \-ˌlāt-əd\ *adj* : covered with pustules

pus·tu·la·tion \ˌpəs-chə-ˈlā-shən, ˌpəs-t(y)ə-\ *n* **1 :** the act of producing pustules : the state of having pustules **2 :** PUSTULE

pus·tule \ˈpəs-(ˌ)chü(ə)l, -(ˌ)t(y)ü(ə)l\ *n* [ME, fr. L *pustula* — more at FOG] **1 :** a small circumscribed elevation of the skin containing pus and having an inflamed base **2 :** a small often distinctively colored elevation or spot resembling a blister or pimple

pussy willow

¹put \ˈpu̇t\ *vb* **put; put·ting** [ME *putten;* akin to OE *putung* instigation, MD *poten* to plant] *vt* **1 a :** to place in a specified position or relationship : LAY <~ the book on the table> **b :** to move in a specified direction **c (1) :** to send (as a weapon or missile) into or through something : THRUST **(2) :** to throw with an overhand pushing motion <~ the shot> **d :** to bring into a specified state or condition <a reapportionment . . . that was ~ into effect at the Semptember primaries —*Current Biog.*> **2 a :** to cause to endure or suffer something : SUBJECT <~ him to death> **b :** IMPOSE, INFLICT <~ a special tax on luxuries> **3 a :** to set before one for judgment or decision <~ the question> **b :** to call for a formal vote on <~ the motion> **4 a (1) :** to turn into language or literary form <~ his feelings into words> **(2) :** to translate into another language <~ the poem into English> **(3) :** ADAPT <lyrics ~ to music> **b :** EXPRESS, STATE <*putting* it mildly> **5 a :** to devote (oneself) to an activity or end <~ himself to winning back their confidence> **b :** APPLY <~ his mind to the problem> **c :** ASSIGN <~ them to work> **d :** to cause to perform an action : URGE <~ the horse over the fence> **e :** IMPEL, INCITE <~ them into a frenzy> **6 a :** REPOSE, REST <~*s* his faith in reason> **b :** INVEST <~ his money in the company> **7 a :** to give as an estimate <~ the time as about eleven> **b :** ATTACH, ATTRIBUTE <~*s* a high value on his friendship> **c :** IMPUTE <~ the blame on his partner> **8 :** BET, WAGER <~ two dollars on the favorite> ~ *vi* **1 :** to start in motion : GO; *esp* : to leave in a hurry **2** *of a ship* : to take a specified course <~ down the river> — **put forth 1 a :** ASSERT, PROPOSE **b :** to make public : ISSUE **2 :** to bring into action : EXERT **3 :** to produce or send out by growth <*put forth* leaves> **4 :** to start out — **put forward :** PROPOSE <*put forward* a theory> — **put in mind :** REMIND — **put one's finger on :** IDENTIFY <*put his finger on* the cause of the trouble> — **put one's foot down :** to take a firm stand — **put one's foot in one's mouth :** to make a tactless or embarrassing blunder — **put paid to** *Brit* : to finish off : wipe out — **put the arm on** *or* **put the bite on :** to ask for money — **put the finger on :** to inform on <*put the finger on* . . . heroin pushers —Barrie Zwicker> — **put to bed :** to make the final preparations for printing (as a newspaper) — **put together 1 :** to create as a unified whole : CONSTRUCT **2 :** ADD, COMBINE — **put to it :** to give difficulty to : press hard <had been *put to it* to keep up> — **put two and two together :** to draw the proper inference from given premises

²put *n* **1 :** a throw made with an overhand pushing motion; *specif* : the act or an instance of putting the shot **2 :** an option to sell a specified amount of a security (as a stock) or commodity (as wheat) at a fixed price at or within a specified time — compare ²CALL 3d

³put *adj* : being in place : FIXED, SET <stay ~ until I call>

put about *vi, of a ship* : to change direction : go on another tack ~ *vt* : to cause to change course or direction

put across *vt* **1 :** to achieve or carry through by deceit or trickery **2 :** to convey effectively or forcefully

put–and–take \ˌpu̇t-ᵊn-ˈtāk\ *n* : any of various games of chance played with a teetotum or with dice in which players contribute to a pool and take from it according to the instructions on the top or dice

pu·ta·tive \ˈpyüt-ət-iv\ *adj* [ME, fr. LL *putativus,* fr. L *putatus,* pp. of *putare* to think — more at PAVE] **1 :** commonly accepted or supposed **2 :** assumed to exist or to have existed — **pu·ta·tive·ly** *adv*

put away *vt* **1 a :** DISCARD, RENOUNCE <to *put* grief *away* is disloyal to the memory of the departed —H. A. Overstreet> **b :** DIVORCE **2 :** to eat or drink up : CONSUME **3 a :** to confine esp. in a mental institution **b :** BURY **c :** KILL

put by *vt* **1** *archaic* : REJECT **2 :** to lay aside : SAVE

put–down \ˈpu̇t-ˌdau̇n\ *n* : an act or instance of putting down; *esp* : a humiliating remark : SQUELCH

put down \ˌpu̇t-ˈdau̇n, ˈpu̇t-\ *vt* **1 :** to bring to an end : STOP <*put down* a riot> **2 a :** DEPOSE, DEGRADE **b :** DISPARAGE, BELITTLE <mentioned his poetry only to *put* it *down*> **c :** DISAPPROVE, CRITICIZE <was *put down* for the way she dressed> **d :** HUMILIATE, SQUELCH <*put* him *down* with a sharp retort> **3 :** to make ineffective : CHECK <*put down* the gossip> **4 a :** to put in writing <*put* it *down* truthfully> **b :** to enter in a list <*put* me *down* for a donation> **5 a :** to place in a category <I *put* him *down* as a hypochondriac —O. S. J. Gogarty> **b :** ATTRIBUTE <*put* it *down* to inexperience> **6 :** CONSUME <*putting down* helping after helping —Carson McCullers> **7 :** to pack or preserve for future use — **put down roots :** to establish a permanent residence

put in *vt* **1 :** to make a formal offer or declaration of <*put in* a plea of guilty> **2 :** to come in with : INTERPOSE <*put in* a word for his brother> **3 :** to spend (time) at some occupation or job <*put in* six hours at the office> **4 :** PLANT <*put in* a crop> ~ *vi* **1 :** to call at or enter a place; *esp* : to enter a harbor or port **2 :** to make an application, request, or offer — often used with *for* <had to retire and *put in* for a pension —Seymour Nagan>

put·log \ˈpu̇t-ˌlȯg, ˈpət-, -ˌläg\ *n* [prob. alter. of earlier *putlock,* perh. fr. ³*put* + *lock*] : one of the short timbers that support the flooring of a scaffold

put off *vt* **1 :** DISCONCERT, REPEL **2 a :** to hold back to a later time **b :** to induce to wait <*put* the bill collector *off*> **3 :** to take off : rid oneself of **4 :** to sell or pass fraudulently

¹put–on \ˌpu̇t-ˌȯn, -ˌän\ *adj* : PRETENDED, ASSUMED

²put–on \ˈpu̇t-ˌȯn, -ˌän\ *n* : an instance of putting someone on <conversational ~*s* are related to old-fashioned joshing —Jacob Brackman>; *also* : PARODY, SPOOF <a kind of *put-on* of every pretentious film ever made —C. A. Ridley>

put on \(ˈ)pu̇t-ˈȯn, -ˈän\ *vt* **1 a :** to dress oneself in : DON **b :** to make part of one's appearance or behavior **c :** FEIGN <*put* a saintly manner *on*> **2 :** to cause to act or operate : APPLY <*put on* more speed> **3 a :** ADD <*put on* weight> **b :** EXAGGERATE, OVERSTATE <he's *putting* it *on* when he makes such claims> **4 :** PERFORM, PRODUCE <*put on* a play> **5 a :** to mislead deliberately esp. for amusement <the interviewer . . . must be put down — or possibly, *put on* —Melvin Maddocks> **b :** KID <you're *putting* me *on*>

put·out \ˈpu̇t-ˌau̇t\ *n* : the retiring of a base runner or batter by a defensive player in baseball

put out \ˌpu̇t-ˈau̇t, ˈpu̇t-\ *vt* **1 :** EXERT, USE <*put out* considerable effort> **2 :** EXTINGUISH <*put* the fire *out*> **3 :** PUBLISH, ISSUE **4 :** to produce for sale **5 a :** DISCONCERT, EMBARRASS **b :** ANNOY, IRRITATE **c :** INCONVENIENCE <don't *put* yourself *out* for us> **6 :** to cause to be out (as in baseball or cricket) ~ *vi* **1 :** to set out from shore **2 :** to make an effort

put over *vt* **1 :** DELAY, POSTPONE **2 :** to put across

pu·tre·fac·tion \ˌpyü-trə-ˈfak-shən\ *n* [ME *putrefaccion,* fr. LL *putrefaction-, putrefactio,* fr. L *putrefactus,* pp. of *putrefacere*] **1 :** the decompostion of organic matter; *esp* : the typically anaerobic splitting of proteins by bacteria and fungi with the formation of foul-smelling incompletely oxidized products **2 :** the state of being putrefied : CORRUPTION — **pu·tre·fac·tive** \-ˈfak-tiv\ *adj*

pu·tre·fy \ˈpyü-trə-ˌfī\ *vb* **-fied; -fy·ing** [ME *putrefien,* fr. MF & L; MF *putrefier,* fr. L *putrefacere,* fr. *putrere* to be rotten + *facere* to make — more at DO] *vt* : to make putrid ~ *vi* : to undergo putrefaction **syn** see DECAY

pu·tres·cence \pyü-ˈtres-ᵊn(t)s\ *n* : the state of being putrescent

pu·tres·cent \-ᵊnt\ *adj* [L *putrescent-, putrescens,* prp. of *putrescere* to grow rotten, fr. *putrēre*] **1 :** undergoing putrefaction : becoming putrid **2 :** of or relating to putrefaction

pu·tres·ci·ble \-ˈtres-ə-bəl\ *adj* : liable to become putrid

pu·tres·cine \-ˈtres-ˌēn\ *n* [ISV, fr. L *putrescere*] : a crystalline slightly poisonous ptomaine $C_4N_{12}N_2$ that is formed by decarboxylation of ornithine, occurs widely but scantily in living things, and is found esp. in putrid flesh

pu·trid \ˈpyü-trəd\ *adj* [L *putridus,* fr. *putrēre* to be rotten, fr. *puter, putris* rotten; akin to L *putēre* to stink] **1 a :** being in a state of putrefaction : ROTTEN **b :** of, relating to, or characteristic of putrefaction : FOUL <a ~ odor> **2 a :** morally corrupt **b :** totally objectionable **syn** see MALODOROUS — **pu·trid·i·ty** \pyü-ˈtrid-ət-ē\ *n* — **pu·trid·ly** \ˈpyü-trəd-lē\ *adv* — **pu·trid·ness** *n*

putsch \ˈpu̇ch\ *n* [G] : a secretly plotted and suddenly executed attempt to overthrow a government

putsch·ist \ˈpu̇ch-əst\ *n* : one who takes part in a putsch

putt \ˈpət\ *n* [alter. of ¹*put*] : a golf stroke made on a putting green to cause the ball to roll into or near the hole — **putt** *vb*

put·tee \ˌpə-ˈtē, pu̇-; ˈpət-ē\ *n* [Hindi *paṭṭī* strip of cloth, fr. Skt *paṭṭikā*] **1 :** a cloth strip wrapped around the leg from ankle to knee **2 :** a usu. leather legging secured by a strap or catch or by laces

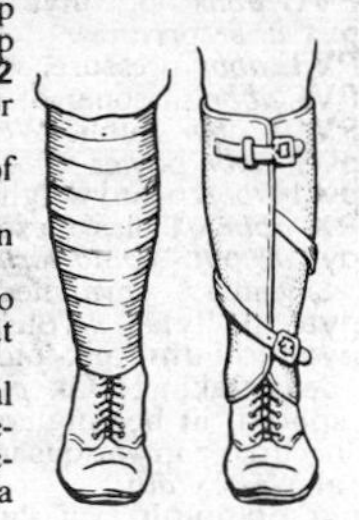

puttees

¹put·ter \ˈpu̇t-ər\ *n* : one that puts <a ~ of questions>

²putt·er \ˈpət-ər\ *n* **1 :** a golf club used in putting **2 :** one that putts

³put·ter \ˈpət-ər\ *vi* [alter. of *potter*] **1 :** to move or act aimlessly or idly **2 :** to work at random : TINKER — **put·ter·er** \-ər-ər\ *n*

put through *vt* **1 :** to carry to a successful conclusion <*put through* a number of reforms> **2 a :** to make a telephone connection for **b :** to obtain a connection for (a telephone call)

putt·ing green \ˈpət-iŋ-\ *n* : a smooth grassy area at the end of a golf fairway containing the hole into which the ball must be played

put to *vi, of a ship* : to put in to shore (as for shelter)

¹put·ty \ˈpət-ē\ *n, pl* **putties** [F *potée,* lit., potful, fr. OF, fr. *pot* — more at POTAGE] **1 :** a pasty substance consisting of hydrated lime and water **2 :** a polishing material containing chiefly an oxide of tin **3 a :** a cement usu. made of whiting and boiled linseed oil beaten or kneaded to the consistency of dough and used esp. in fastening glass in sashes and stopping crevices in woodwork **b :** any of various substances resembling such cement in appearance, consistency, or use: as **(1) :** an acid-resistant mixture of ferric oxide and boiled linseed oil **(2) :** a mixture of red and white lead and boiled linseed oil used as a lute in pipe fitting **4 :** a light brownish gray to light grayish brown textile color **5 :** one who is easily manipulated <is ~ in her hands>

²putty *vt* **put·tied; put·ty·ing** : to use putty on or apply putty to

put·ty·root \ˈpət-ē-ˌrüt, -ˌru̇t\ *n* : a No. American orchid (*Aplectrum hyemale*) having a slender naked rootstock and producing brown flowers

put–up \ˌpu̇t-ˌəp\ *adj* : arranged secretly beforehand

put up \ˌpu̇t-ˈəp, ˈpu̇t-\ *vt* **1 a :** to place in a container or receptacle <*put* his lunch *up* in a bag> **b :** to put away (a sword) in a scabbard : SHEATHE **c :** to prepare so as to preserve for later use : CAN **d :** to put in storage **2 :** to start (game) from cover **3 :** to nominate for election **4 :** to offer up (as a prayer) **5 :** SET 17 **6 :** to offer for public sale <*puts* his possessions *up* for auction> **7 :** to give food and shelter to : ACCOMMODATE **8 :** to arrange (as a plot or scheme) with others <*put up* a job to steal the jewels> **9 :** BUILD, ERECT **10 a :** to make a display of <*put up* a bluff> **b :** to carry on <*put up* a struggle against odds> **11 a :** CONTRIBUTE, PAY **b :** to offer as a prize or stake **12 :** to increase the amount of : RAISE ~ *vi* : LODGE — **put up to :** INCITE, INSTIGATE <they *put* him *up to* playing the prank> — **put up with :** to endure or tolerate without complaint or attempt at reprisal

put–up·on \ˈpu̇t-ə-ˌpȯn, -ˌpän\ *adj* **:** imposed upon : taken advantage of

[1]puz·zle \ˈpəz-əl\ *vb* **puz·zled; puz·zling** \-(ə-)liŋ\ [origin unknown] *vt* **1 :** to offer or represent to (a person or his mind) a problem difficult to solve or a situation difficult to resolve : challenge mentally <a schoolmaster *puzzled* by a hard sum —R. W. Emerson>; *also* : to exert (as oneself) over such a problem or situation <they *puzzled* their wits to find a solution> **2** *archaic* **:** COMPLICATE, ENTANGLE **3 :** to solve with difficulty or ingenuity <~ out an answer to a riddle> ~ *vi* **1 :** to be uncertain as to action or choice **2 :** to attempt a solution of a puzzle by guesswork or experiment — **puz·zler** \-(ə-)lər\ *n*

syn PUZZLE, PERPLEX, BEWILDER, DISTRACT, NONPLUS, CONFOUND, DUMBFOUND *shared meaning element* **:** to baffle and disturb mentally. PUZZLE implies presentation of a problem difficult to solve <a persistent fever which *puzzled* her doctor> PERPLEX adds a suggestion of worry and uncertainty especially about making a necessary decision <new and *perplexing* challenges face higher education today —M. S. Eisenhower> BEWILDER often implies perplexity but it stresses a confusion of mind that hampers clear and decisive thinking <the *bewildering* confusion of our times —Matthew Arnold> DISTRACT implies agitation or uncertainty induced by conflicting preoccupations or interests <that conflict of races and religions which had so long *distracted* the island —T. B. Macaulay> NONPLUS implies a bafflement that makes orderly planning or deciding impossible <doing the unexpected in a way likely to *nonplus* a conventionally-minded enemy —*Times Lit. Supp.*> CONFOUND implies temporary mental paralysis caused by astonishment or profound abasement <so spoke the son of God; and Satan stood a while as mute, *confounded* —John Milton> DUMBFOUND suggests intense but momentary confounding; often the idea of astonishment is so stressed that *dumbfound* becomes a near synonym of *astound* <I was *dumbfounded* to hear him say that I was on a quixotic enterprise —William Lawrence>

[2]puzzle *n* **1 :** the state of being puzzled : PERPLEXITY **2 a:** something that puzzles **b :** a question, problem, or contrivance designed for testing ingenuity ***syn*** see MYSTERY

puz·zle·head·ed \ˌpəz-əl-ˈhed-əd\ *adj* **:** having or based on confused attitudes or ideas — **puz·zle·head·ed·ness** *n*

puz·zle·ment \ˈpəz-əl-mənt\ *n* **1 :** the state of being puzzled **:** PERPLEXITY **2 :** PUZZLE

PV *abbr* polyvinyl

PVA *abbr* polyvinyl acetate

PVC *abbr* polyvinyl chloride

pvt *abbr* private

PVT *abbr* pressure, volume, temperature

PW *abbr* prisoner of war

PWA *abbr* Public Works Administration

pwr *abbr* power

pwt *abbr* pennyweight

PX *abbr* **1** please exchange **2** post exchange

py- *or* **pyo-** *comb form* [Gk, fr. *pyon* pus — more at FOUL] **:** pus <*py*emia> <*pyo*rrhea>

pya \pē-ˈ(y)ä\ *n* [Burmese] — see *kyat* at MONEY table

pyc·nid·i·um \pik-ˈnid-ē-əm\ *n, pl* **-ia** \-ē-ə\ [NL, fr. Gk *pyknos* dense; akin to Gk *pyka* thickly, Alb *puth* kiss] **:** a flask-shaped spore fruit bearing conidiophores and conidia on the interior and occurring in various imperfect fungi and ascomycetes — **pyc·nid·i·al** \-ē-əl\ *adj*

pyc·no·go·nid \pik-ˈnäg-ə-nəd, ˌpik-nə-ˈgän-əd\ *n* [deriv. of Gk *pyknos* + *gony* knee — more at KNEE] **:** SEA SPIDER

pyc·nom·e·ter \pik-ˈnäm-ət-ər\ *n* [Gk *pyknos* + ISV *-meter*] **:** a standard vessel often provided with a thermometer for measuring and comparing the densities of liquids or solids

pye–dog \ˈpī-ˌdȯg, -ˈdȯg\ *n* [prob. by shortening and alter. fr. *pariah dog*] **:** a half-wild dog common about Asian villages

pyel- *or* **pyelo-** *comb form* [NL, pelvis, fr. Gk *pyelos* trough; akin to Gk *plein* to sail — more at FLOW] **:** renal pelvis <*pyelo*graphy>

py·eli·tis \ˌpī-ə-ˈlīt-əs\ *n* [NL] **:** inflammation of the lining of the renal pelvis

py·elo·ne·phri·tis \ˌpī-(ə-)lō-ni-ˈfrīt-əs\ *n* [NL] **:** inflammation of both the lining of the pelvis and the parenchyma of the kidney — **py·elo·ne·phrit·ic** \-ˈfrit-ik\ *adj*

py·emia \pī-ˈē-mē-ə\ *n* [NL] **:** septicemia caused by pus-forming bacteria and accompanied by multiple abscesses — **py·emic** \-mik\ *adj*

py·gid·i·um \pī-ˈjid-ē-əm\ *n, pl* **-ia** \-ē-ə\ [NL, fr. Gk *pygidion*, dim. of *pygē* rump; akin to L *pustula* pustule] **:** a caudal structure or the terminal body region of various invertebrates — **py·gid·i·al** \-ē-əl\ *adj*

pyg·mae·an *or* **pyg·me·an** \pig-ˈmē-ən, ˈpig-mē-\ *adj* [L *pygmaeus*] **:** PYGMY

Pyg·ma·lion \pig-ˈmāl-yən, -ˈmā-lē-ən\ *n* [L, fr. Gk *Pygmaliōn*] **:** a king of Cyprus who made a female figure of ivory that was brought to life for him by Aphrodite

pyg·moid \ˈpig-ˌmȯid\ *adj* **:** resembling or having the characteristics of the Pygmies

pyg·my \ˈpig-mē\ *n, pl* **pygmies** [ME *pigmei*, fr. L *pygmaeus* of a pygmy, dwarfish, fr. Gk *pygmaios*, fr. *pygmē* fist, measure of length — more at PUNGENT] **1** *often cap* **:** one of a race of dwarfs described by ancient Greek authors **2** *cap* **:** one of a small people of equatorial Africa ranging under five feet in height **3 :** a short insignificant person **:** DWARF — **pygmy** *adj*

pyg·my·ish \-mē-ish\ *adj* **:** having the characteristics of a pygmy

pyg·my·ism \-ˌiz-əm\ *n* **:** a stunted or dwarfish condition

py·ja·mas \pə-ˈjä-məz\ *chiefly Brit var of* PAJAMAS

pyk·nic \ˈpik-nik\ *adj* [ISV, fr. Gk *pyknos* dense, stocky — more at PYCNIDIUM] **:** characterized by shortness of stature, broadness of girth, and powerful muscularity **:** ENDOMORPHIC 2b — **pyknic** *n*

py·lon \ˈpī-ˌlän, -lən\ *n* [Gk *pylōn*, fr. *pylē* gate] **1 a :** a usu. massive gateway **b :** an ancient Egyptian gateway building in a truncated pyramidal form **c :** a monumental mass flanking an entranceway or an approach to a bridge **2 :** a tower for supporting either end of a wire over a long span; *broadly* **:** any of various towerlike structures **3 :** a projection (as a post or tower) marking a prescribed course of flight for an airplane **4 :** a rigid structure on the outside of an aircraft for supporting something (as an engine, tank, or bomb) — see AIRPLANE illustration **5 :** a conical marker used on a road (as for directing traffic)

py·lo·ric \pī-ˈlōr-ik, pə-, -ˈlȯr-\ *adj* **:** of or relating to the pylorus; *also* **:** of, relating to, or situated in or near the posterior part of the stomach

py·lo·rus \-əs\ *n, pl* **py·lo·ri** \-ˈlō(ə)r-ˌī, -(ˌ)ē\ [LL, fr. Gk *pylōros*, lit., gatekeeper, fr. *pylē*] **:** the opening from the vertebrate stomach into the intestine

pyo·der·ma \ˌpī-ə-ˈdər-mə\ *n* [NL] **:** a bacterial skin inflammation marked by pus-filled lesions — **pyo·der·mic** \-mik\ *adj*

pyo·gen·ic \-ˈjen-ik\ *adj* [ISV] **:** producing pus <~ bacteria> **:** marked by pus production

py·or·rhea \ˌpī-ə-ˈrē-ə\ *n* [NL] **:** a discharge of pus; *specif* **:** purulent inflammation of the sockets of the teeth leading usu. to loosening of the teeth — **py·or·rhe·al** \-ˈrē-əl\ *adj*

pyr- *or* **pyro-** *comb form* [ME, fr. MF, fr. LL, fr. Gk, fr. *pyr* — more at FIRE] **1 :** fire **:** heat <*pyro*meter> <*pyr*heliometer> **2 a :** produced by or as if by the action of heat <*pyro*electricity> **b :** derived from a corresponding ortho acid by loss usu. of one molecule of water from two molecules of acid <*pyro*phosphoric acid> **3 :** fever <*pyro*toxin>

pyr·acan·tha \ˌpī-rə-ˈkan(t)-thə\ *n* [NL, genus name, fr. Gk *pyrakantha*, a tree, fr. *pyr-* + *akantha* thorn — more at ACANTH-] **:** any of a small genus (*Pyracantha*) of Eurasian thorny evergreen or half-evergreen shrubs of the rose family with alternate leaves, corymbs of white flowers, and small reddish pomes

py·ral·id \pī-ˈral-əd\ *n* [deriv. of L *pyralis*, fly fabled as living in fire, fr. Gk, fr. *pyr* fire] **:** any of a very large heterogeneous family (Pyralidae) of mostly small slender long-legged moths — **pyralid** *adj*

py·ral·i·did \pī-ˈral-əd-əd, -ə-ˌdid\ *n* [deriv. of L *pyralis*] **:** PYRALID — **pyralidid** *adj*

[1]pyr·a·mid \ˈpir-ə-ˌmid\ *n* [L *pyramid-*, *pyramis*, fr. Gk, of unknown origin] **1 a :** an ancient massive structure found esp. in Egypt having typically a square ground plan, outside walls in the form of four triangles that meet in a point at the top, and inner sepulchral chambers **b :** a structure or object of similar form **2 :** a polyhedron having for its base a polygon and for faces triangles with a common vertex — see VOLUME table **3 :** a crystalline form each face of which intersects the vertical axis and either two lateral axes or in the tetragonal system one lateral axis **4 :** an anatomical structure resembling a pyramid: as **a :** one of the conical masses that project from the renal medulla into the kidney pelvis **b :** either of two large bundles of motor fibers from the cerebral cortex that reach the medulla oblongata and are continuous with the pyramidal tracts of the spinal cord **5 :** an immaterial structure built on a broad supporting base and narrowing gradually to an apex <the socioeconomic ~> — **py·ra·mi·dal** \pə-ˈram-əd-ᵊl, ˌpir-ə-ˈmid-\ *adj* — **py·ra·mi·dal·ly** \-ē\ *adv* — **pyr·a·mid·i·cal** \ˌpir-ə-ˈmid-i-kəl\ *adj*

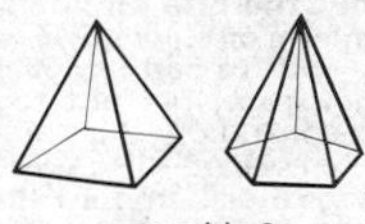

pyramids 2

[2]pyramid *vi* **1 :** to speculate (as on a security or commodity exchange) by using paper profits as margin for additional transactions **2 :** to increase rapidly and progressively step by step on a broad base ~ *vt* **1 :** to arrange or build up as if on the base of a pyramid **2 :** to use (as profits) in speculative pyramiding **3 :** to increase the impact of (as a tax assessed at the production level) on the ultimate consumer by treating as a cost subject to markup <they ~ every cost, with middlemen, tariffs, taxes, and overheads —D. D. Eisenhower>

pyramidal tract *n* **:** any of four columns of motor fibers that run in pairs on each side of the spinal cord and are continuations of the pyramids of the medulla oblongata

Py·ram·i·don \pə-ˈram-ə-ˌdän\ *trademark* — used for aminopyrine

Pyr·a·mus \ˈpir-ə-məs\ *n* [L, fr. Gk *Pyramos*] **:** a legendary youth of Babylon who dies for love of Thisbe

py·ran \ˈpī(ə)r-ˌan\ *n* [ISV] **:** either of two cyclic compounds C_5H_6O that contain five carbon atoms and one oxygen atom in the ring

py·ra·noid \ˈpī-rə-ˌnȯid\ *adj* **:** derived from or related to the pyrans

py·ra·nose \ˈpī-rə-ˌnōs, -ˌnōz\ *n* [ISV *pyran* + *-ose*] **:** a monosaccharide in the form of a cyclic hemiacetal containing a pyranoid ring

py·ran·o·side \pī-ˈran-ə-ˌsīd\ *n* **:** a glycoside containing the pyranoid ring

pyr·ar·gy·rite \pī-ˈrär-jə-ˌrīt\ *n* [G *pyrargyrit*, fr. Gk *pyr-* + *argyros* silver — more at ARGENT] **:** a mineral Ag_3SbS_3 consisting of silver antimony sulfide that occurs in rhombohedral crystals or massive and has a dark red or black color with a metallic adamantine luster

pyre \ˈpī(ə)r\ *n* [L *pyra*, fr. Gk, fr. *pyr* fire — more at FIRE] **:** a combustible heap for burning a dead body as a funeral rite; *broadly* **:** a pile of material to be burned <a ~ of dead leaves>

py·rene \ˈpī(ə)r-ˌēn, pī-ˈrēn\ *n* [NL *pyrena*, fr. Gk *pyrēn* stone of a fruit; akin to Gk *pyros* wheat — more at FURZE] **:** the stone of a drupelet; *broadly* **:** a small hard nutlet

qua·draph·o·ny \kwä-ˈdraf-ə-nē\ *n* [irreg. fr. *quadri-* + *-phony*] **:** the transmission, recording, or reproduction of sound by techniques that utilize four transmission channels — **quad·ra·phon·ic** \ˌkwäd-rə-ˈfän-ik\ *adj*

quad·rat \ˈkwäd-rət, -ˌrat\ *n* [alter. of [2]*quadrate*] **1 :** [2]QUAD **2 :** a usu. rectangular plot used for ecological or population studies

[1]**quad·rate** \ˈkwäd-ˌrāt, -rət\ *adj* [ME, fr. L *quadratus*, pp. of *quadrare* to make square, fit; akin to L *quattuor*] **1 :** being square or approximately square **2** *of a heraldic cross* **:** expanded into a square at the junction of the arms — see CROSS illustration **3 :** of, relating to, or constituting a bony or cartilaginous element of each side of the skull to which the lower jaw is articulated in most vertebrates below mammals

[2]**quadrate** *n* **1 :** an approximately square or cubical area, space, or body **2 :** a quadrate bone

[3]**quad·rate** \ˈkwäd-ˌrāt\ *vi* **quad·rat·ed; quad·rat·ing** *archaic* **:** AGREE, CORRESPOND

qua·drat·ic \kwä-ˈdrat-ik\ *adj* **:** involving terms of the second degree at most <~ function> — **quadratic** *n* — **qua·drat·i·cal·ly** \-i-k(ə-)lē\ *adv*

quadratic form *n* **:** a homogeneous polynomial of the second degree <$x^2 + 5xy + y^2$ is a *quadratic form*>

qua·drat·ics \kwä-ˈdrat-iks\ *n pl but sing or pl in constr* **:** a branch of algebra dealing with quadratic equations

quad·ra·ture \ˈkwäd-rə-ˌchu̇(ə)r, -chər, -ˌt(y)u̇(ə)r\ *n* **1 :** the process of finding a square equal in area to a given area **2 a :** a configuration in which two celestial bodies have a separation of 90 degrees **b :** either of two points on an orbit in a middle position between the syzygies

qua·dren·ni·al \kwä-ˈdren-ē-əl\ *adj* **1 :** consisting of or lasting for four years <a ~ term of office> **2 :** occurring or being done every four years <~ elections> — **quadrennial** *n* — **qua·dren·ni·al·ly** \-ē-ə-lē\ *adv*

qua·dren·ni·um \-ē-əm\ *n* [L *quadriennium*, fr. *quadri-* + *annus* year — more at ANNUAL] **:** a period of four years

quadri- *or* **quadr-** *or* **quadru-** *comb form* [ME, fr. L; akin to L *quattuor* four] **1 a :** four <*quadri*lingual> <*quadru*mana> **b :** square <*quadr*ic> **2 :** fourth <*quadri*centennial>

quad·ric \ˈkwäd-rik\ *adj* [ISV] **:** QUADRATIC <~ surface> — used where there are more than two variables — **quadric** *n*

quad·ri·cen·ten·ni·al \ˌkwäd-rə-sen-ˈten-ē-əl\ *n* **:** a 400th anniversary or its celebration

quad·ri·ceps \ˈkwäd-rə-ˌseps\ *n* [NL *quadricipit-, quadriceps*, fr. *quadri-* + *-cipit-, -ceps* (as in *bicipit-, biceps* biceps] **:** the great extensor muscle of the front of the thigh divided above into four parts

quad·ri·cip·i·tal \ˌkwäd-rə-ˈsip-ət-ᵊl\ *adj* **:** of, relating to, or being a quadriceps

quad·ri·fid \ˈkwäd-rə-fəd, -ˌfid\ *adj* [L *quadrifidus*, fr. *quadri-* + *-fidus* -fid] **:** divided or deeply cleft into four parts <a ~ petal>

qua·dri·ga \kwä-ˈdrē-gə\ *n, pl* **-gae** \-ˌgī\ [L, sing. of *quadrigae* team of four, contr. of *quadrijugae*, fem. pl. of *quadrijugus* yoked four abreast, fr. *quadri-* + *jungere* to yoke, join — more at JOIN] **:** a chariot drawn by four horses abreast

[1]**quad·ri·lat·er·al** \ˌkwäd-rə-ˈlat-ə-rəl, -ˈla-trəl\ *adj* [prob. fr. (assumed) NL *quadrilateralis*, fr. L *quadrilaterus*, fr. *quadri-* + *later-, latus* side] **:** having four sides

[2]**quadrilateral** *n* **1 :** a polygon of four sides **2 :** a combination or group that involves four parts or individuals

[1]**qua·drille** \kwä-ˈdril, k(w)ə-\ *n* [F, group of knights engaged in a carrousel, variant of ombre, fr. Sp *cuadrilla* troop] **1 :** a 4-handed variant of ombre popular esp. in the 18th century **2 :** a square dance for four couples made up of five or six figures chiefly in 6/8 and 2/4 time; *also* **:** music for this dance

[2]**quadrille** *adj* [F *quadrillé*] **:** marked with squares or rectangles

qua·dril·lion \kwä-ˈdril-yən\ *n* [F, fr. MF, fr. *quadri-* + *-illion* (as in *million*)] — see NUMBER table — **quadrillion** *adj* — **qua·dril·lionth** \-yən(t)th\ *adj or n*

quad·ri·par·tite \ˌkwäd-rə-ˈpär-ˌtīt\ *adj* [ME, fr. L *quadripartitus*, fr. *quadri-* + *partitus*, pp. of *partire* to divide, fr. *part-, pars* part] **1 :** consisting of or divided into four parts **2 :** shared or participated in by four parties or persons <a ~ agreement>

[1]**quad·ri·va·lent** \-ˈvā-lənt\ *adj* [ISV] **1 :** TETRAVALENT 1 **2 :** composed of four homologous chromosomes synapsed in meiotic prophase

[2]**quadrivalent** *n* **:** a quadrivalent chromosomal group

qua·driv·i·al \kwä-ˈdriv-ē-əl\ *adj* **1 :** of or relating to the quadrivium **2 :** having four ways or roads meeting in a point

qua·driv·i·um \-ē-əm\ *n* [LL, fr. L, crossroads, fr. *quadri-* + *via* way — more at VIA] **:** a group of studies consisting of arithmetic, music, geometry, and astronomy and forming the upper division of the seven liberal arts in medieval universities — compare TRIVIUM

qua·droon \kwä-ˈdrün\ *n* [modif. of Sp *cuarterón*, fr. *cuarto* fourth, fr. L *quartus*] **:** a person of one-quarter Negro ancestry

qua·dru·ma·na \kwä-ˈdrü-mə-nə\ *n pl* [NL, fr. *quadri-* + L *manus* hand — more at MANUAL] **:** primates excluding man considered as a group distinguished by hand-shaped feet — **qua·dru·ma·nal** \-mən-ᵊl\ *adj* — **quad·ru·mane** \ˈkwäd-ru̇-ˌmān\ *adj or n* — **qua·dru·ma·nous** \kwä-ˈdrü-mə-nəs\ *adj*

qua·drum·vir \kwä-ˈdrəm-vər\ *n* [back-formation fr. *quadrumvirate*] **:** a member of a quadrumvirate

qua·drum·vi·rate \-və-rət\ *n* [*quadri-* + *-umvirate* (as in *triumvirate*)] **:** a group or association of four men

quad·ru·ped \ˈkwäd-rə-ˌped\ *n* [L *quadruped-, quadrupes*, fr. *quadruped-, quadrupes*, adj., having four feet, fr. *quadri-* + *ped-, pes* foot — more at FOOT] **:** an animal having four feet — **quadruped** *adj* — **qua·dru·pe·dal** \kwä-ˈdrü-pəd-ᵊl, ˌkwäd-rə-ˈped-\ *adj*

[1]**qua·dru·ple** \kwä-ˈdrüp-əl, -ˈdrəp-; ˈkwäd-rəp-\ *vb* **qua·dru·pled; qua·dru·pling** \-(ə-)liŋ\ *vt* **:** to make four times as great or as many ~ *vi* **:** to become four times as great or as numerous

[2]**quadruple** *n* **:** a sum four times as great as another **:** a fourfold amount

[3]**quadruple** *adj* [MF or L; MF, fr. L *quadruplus*, fr. *quadri-* + *-plus* multiplied by — more at DOUBLE] **1 :** having four units or members **2 :** being four times as great or as many **3 :** marked by four beats per measure <~ meter> — **qua·dru·ply** \-ˈdrüp-lē, -ˈdrəp-, -rəp-\ *adv*

qua·dru·plet \kwä-ˈdrəp-lət, -ˈdrüp-; ˈkwäd-rəp-\ *n* **1 :** one of four offspring born at one birth **2 :** a combination of four of a kind **3 :** a group of four musical notes to be performed in the time ordinarily given to three of the same kind

[1]**qua·dru·pli·cate** \kwä-ˈdrü-pli-kət\ *adj* [L *quadruplicatus*, pp. of *quadruplicare* to quadruple, fr. *quadruplic-, quadruplex* fourfold, fr. *quadri-* + *-plic-, -plex* fold — more at SIMPLE] **1 :** consisting of or existing in four corresponding or identical parts or examples <~ invoices> **2 :** being the fourth of four things exactly alike <file the ~ copy>

[2]**qua·dru·pli·cate** \-plə-ˌkāt\ *vt* **-cat·ed; -cat·ing 1 :** to make quadruple or fourfold **2 :** to prepare in quadruplicate — **qua·dru·pli·ca·tion** \-ˌdrü-plə-ˈkā-shən\ *n*

[3]**qua·dru·pli·cate** \kwä-ˈdrü-pli-kət\ *n* **1 :** one of four things exactly alike; *specif* **:** one of four identical copies **2 :** four copies all alike — used with *in* <typed in ~>

quad·ru·plic·i·ty \ˌkwäd-ru̇-ˈplis-ət-ē\ *n* [L *quadruplic-, quadruplex* fourfold + E *-ity*] **:** the state of being quadruple

quad·ru·pole \ˈkwäd-rə-ˌpōl\ *n* [ISV *quadri-* + *pole*] **:** a system composed of two dipoles of equal but oppositely directed moment

quaere *n* [L, imper. of *quarere* to seek, question] *archaic* **:** QUERY

quaes·tor \ˈkwes-tər, ˈkwē-stər\ *n* [ME *questor*, fr. L *quaestor*, fr. *quaestus*, pp. of *quaerere*] **:** one of numerous ancient Roman officials concerned chiefly with financial administration

[1]**quaff** \ˈkwäf, ˈkwaf\ *vb* [origin unknown] *vi* **:** to drink deeply ~ *vt* **:** to drink (a beverage) deeply — **quaff·er** *n*

[2]**quaff** *n* **:** a deep drink

quag \ˈkwag, ˈkwäg\ *n* [origin unknown] **:** MARSH, BOG

quag·ga \ˈkwag-ə, ˈkwäg-\ *n* [obs. Afrik (now *kwagga*)] **:** an extinct wild ass (*Equus quagga*) of southern Africa related to the zebras

quag·gy \ˈkwag-ē, ˈkwäg-\ *adj* **1 :** MARSHY **2 :** FLABBY, YIELDING

quag·mire \ˈkwag-ˌmī(ə)r, ˈkwäg-\ *n* **1 :** soft miry land that shakes or yields under the foot **2 :** a difficult or precarious position **:** PREDICAMENT

qua·hog *also* **qua·haug** \ˈkō-ˌhȯg, ˈkwȯ-, ˈkwō-, -ˌhäg\ *n* [Narraganset *poquaûhock*] **:** a thick-shelled American clam (*Mercenaria mercenaria*)

quai \ˈkā\ *n* [F] **:** QUAY

quaich *or* **quaigh** \ˈkwāk\ *n* [ScGael *cuach*] *chiefly Scot* **:** a small shallow drinking vessel with ears for use as handles

[1]**quail** \ˈkwā(ə)l\ *n, pl* **quail** *or* **quails** [ME *quaille*, fr. MF, fr. ML *quaccula*, of imit. origin] **1 :** any of various Old World gallinaceous birds (genus *Coturnix*); *esp* **:** a migratory game bird (*C. coturnix* syn. *C. communis*) **2 :** any of various small American game birds (order Galliformes); *esp* **:** BOBWHITE

[2]**quail** *vb* [ME *quailen* to curdle, fr. MF *quailler*, fr. L *coagulare* — more at COAGULATE] *vi* **1 a** *chiefly dial* **:** WITHER, DECLINE **b :** to give way <his courage never ~*ed*> **2 :** to recoil in dread or terror **:** COWER <the strongest ~ before financial ruin —Samuel Butler †1902> ~ *vt, archaic* **:** to make fearful ***syn*** see RECOIL

quaint \ˈkwānt\ *adj* [ME *cointe*, fr. OF, fr. L *cognitus*, pp. of *cognoscere* to know — more at COGNITION] **1** *obs* **:** EXPERT, SKILLED **2 a :** marked by skillful design <~ with many a device in India ink —Herman Melville> **b :** marked by beauty or elegance <a body so fantastic, trim, and ~ —William Cowper> **3 a :** unusual or different in character or appearance **:** ODD <figures of fun, ~ people —Herman Wouk> **b :** pleasingly or strikingly old-fashioned or unfamiliar — **quaint·ly** *adv* — **quaint·ness** *n*

[1]**quake** \ˈkwāk\ *vi* **quaked; quak·ing** [ME *quaken*, fr. OE *cwacian*] **1 :** to shake or vibrate usu. from shock or instability **2 :** to tremble or shudder usu. from cold or fear

[2]**quake** *n* **:** an instance of shaking or trembling (as of the earth or moon); *esp* **:** EARTHQUAKE

quak·er \ˈkwā-kər\ *n* **1 :** one that quakes **2** *cap* **:** FRIEND 5 — **Quak·er·ish** \ˈkwā-k(ə-)rish\ *adj* — **Quak·er·ism** \-kə-ˌriz-əm\ *n* — **Quak·er·ly** \-kər-lē\ *adj*

Quaker gun *n* [fr. opposition to war as a basic Quaker tenet] **:** a dummy piece of artillery usu. made of wood

quak·er–la·dies \ˌkwā-kər-ˈlād-ēz\ *n pl* **:** BLUETS

quaking aspen *n* **:** an aspen (*Populus tremuloides*) of the U.S. and Canada that has small suborbicular leaves with flattened petioles and finely serrate margins

qual *abbr* qualitative

qua·le \ˈkwäl-ē, -ā\ *n, pl* **qua·lia** \ˈkwäl-ē-ə\ [L, neut. of *qualis* of what kind] **1 :** a property (as redness) considered apart from things having the property **:** UNIVERSAL **2 :** a property as it is experienced as distinct from any source it might have in a physical object

qual·i·fi·able \ˈkwäl-ə-ˌfī-ə-bəl\ *adj* **:** capable of qualifying or being qualified

qual·i·fi·ca·tion \ˌkwäl-ə-fə-ˈkā-shən\ *n* **1 :** a restriction in meaning or application **:** a limiting modification <this statement stands without ~> **2 a** *obs* **:** NATURE **b** *archaic* **:** CHARACTERISTIC **3 a :** a quality or skill that fits a person (as for an office) <the applicant with the best ~*s*> **b :** a condition that must be complied with (as for the attainment of a privilege) <a ~ for membership>

qual·i·fied \ˈkwäl-ə-ˌfīd\ *adj* **1 a :** fitted (as by training or experience) for a given purpose **:** COMPETENT **b :** having complied with the specific requirements or precedent conditions (as for an

quar·ry·man \ˈkwȯr-ē-mən, ˈkwär-\ *n* : QUARRIER

quart \ˈkwȯ(ə)rt\ *n* [ME, one fourth of a gallon, fr. MF *quarte,* fr. OF, fr. fem. of *quart,* adj., fourth, fr. L *quartus;* akin to L *quattuor* four — more at FOUR] **1** — see WEIGHT table **2 a** : a vessel or measure having a capacity of one quart **b** : any of various units for bottled wine; *esp* : a unit for champagne containing 26 fluid ounces

1quar·tan \ˈkwȯrt-ᵊn\ *adj* [ME *quarteyne,* fr. OF *(fievre) quartaine* quartan fever, fr. L *(febris) quartana,* fr. *quartanus* of the fourth, fr. *quartus*] : occurring every fourth day reckoning inclusively; *specif* : recurring at approximately 72-hour intervals

2quartan *n* : an intermittent fever that recurs at approximately 72-hour intervals; *esp* : a quartan malaria

1quar·ter \ˈkwȯ(r)t-ər\ *n* [ME, fr. OF *quartier,* fr. L *quartarius,* fr. *quartus* fourth] **1** : one of four equal parts into which something is divisible : a fourth part <in the top ~ of his class> **2** : any of various units of capacity or weight equal to or derived from one fourth of some larger unit **3** : any of various units of length or area equal to one fourth of some larger unit **4** : the fourth part of a measure of time: as **a** : one of a set of four 3-month divisions of a year <business was up during the third ~> **b** : a school term of about 12 weeks **c** : QUARTER HOUR <a ~ after three> **5 a** : a coin worth a quarter of a dollar **b** : the sum of 25 cents **6** : one limb of a quadruped with the adjacent parts; *esp* : one fourth part of the carcass of a slaughtered animal including a leg **7 a** : the region or direction lying under any of the four divisions of the horizon **b** : one of the four parts into which the horizon is divided or the cardinal point corresponding to it **c** : a compass point or direction other than the cardinal points **d** (1) : a person or group not definitely specified <financial help from many ~*s* —*Current Biog.*> (2) : a point, direction, or place not definitely identified <the view to the rear ~ —*Consumer Reports*> **8 a** : a division or district of a town or city <he describes the immigrant ~ —Alfred Kazin> **b** : the inhabitants of such a quarter **9 a** : an assigned station or post **b** *pl* : an assembly of a ship's company for ceremony, drill, or emergency **c** *pl* : living accommodations : LODGINGS <show you to your ~*s*> **10** : merciful consideration of an opponent; *specif* : the clemency of not killing a defeated enemy **11** : a fourth part of the moon's period **12** : the side of a horse's hoof between the toe and the heel — see HOOF illustration **13 a** : any of the four parts into which a heraldic field is divided **b** : a bearing or charge occupying the first fourth part of a heraldic field **14** : the state of two machine parts that are exactly at right angles to one another or are spaced about a circle so as to subtend a right angle at the center of the circle **15 a** : the stern area of a ship's side **b** : the part of the yardarm outside the slings **16** : one side of the upper of a shoe or boot from heel to vamp **17** : one of the four equal periods into which the playing time of some games is divided

2quarter *vt* **1 a** : to divide into four equal or nearly equal parts **b** : to separate into either more or fewer than four parts <~ an orange> **c** *archaic* : to divide (a human body) into four parts **2** : to provide with lodging or shelter **3** : to crisscross (an area) in many directions **4 a** : to arrange or bear (as different coats of arms) quarterly on one escutcheon **b** : to add (a coat of arms) to others on one escutcheon **c** : to divide (as by stripes) a shield into distinct sections **5** : to adjust or locate (as cranks) at right angles in a machine ~ *vi* **1** : LODGE, DWELL **2** : to crisscross a district **3** : to change from one quarter to another <the moon ~*s*> **4** : to strike on a ship's quarter <the wind was ~*ing*>

3quarter *adj* : consisting of or equal to a quarter

quar·ter·age \ˈkwȯ(r)t-ə-rij\ *n* : a quarterly payment, tax, wage, or allowance

1quar·ter·back \ˈkwȯ(r)t-ər-ˌbak\ *n* : an offensive back in football who usu. lines up behind the center, calls the signals, and directs the offensive play of his team

2quarterback *vt* **1** : to direct the offensive play of (as a football team) **2** : to give executive direction to : BOSS <~*ed* the original buying syndicate —*Time*> ~ *vi* : to play quarterback

quarterback sneak *n* : a usu. quick run with the ball by a quarterback into the middle of the offensive line

quar·ter–bound \ˌkwȯ(r)t-ər-ˈbau̇nd\ *adj, of a book* : bound in material of two qualities with the material of better quality on the spine only — **quarter binding** *n*

quarter crack *n* : a sand crack usu. in a horse's forefoot

quarter day *n* : the day which begins a quarter of the year and on which a quarterly payment often falls due

quar·ter·deck \ˈkwȯ(r)t-ər-ˌdek\ *n* **1** : the stern area of a ship's upper deck **2** : a part of a deck on a naval vessel set aside by the captain for ceremonial and official use

1, quarterdeck 1

1quar·ter·fi·nal \ˌkwȯ(r)t-ər-ˈfīn-ᵊl\ *adj* **1** : being next to the semifinal in an elimination tournament **2** : of or participating in a quarterfinal

2quarterfinal *n* **1** : a quarterfinal match **2** *pl* : a quarterfinal round — **quar·ter·fi·nal·ist** \-ᵊl-əst\ *n*

quarter horse *n* [fr. its high speed for distances up to a quarter of a mile] : an alert cobby muscular horse capable of high speed for short distances and of great endurance under the saddle

quarter hour *n* **1** : fifteen minutes **2** : any of the quarter points of an hour **3** : a unit of academic credit representing an hour of class (as lecture class) or three hours of laboratory work each week for an academic quarter

1quar·ter·ing \ˈkwȯ(r)t-ə-riŋ\ *n* **1 a** : the division of an escutcheon containing different coats of arms into four or more compartments **b** : a quarter of an escutcheon or the coat of arms on it **2** : a line of usu. noble or distinguished ancestry

2quartering *adj* **1** : coming from a point well abaft the beam of a ship but not directly astern <~ waves> **2** : lying at right angles

1quar·ter·ly \ˈkwȯ(r)t-ər-lē\ *adv* **1** : in heraldic quarters or quarterings **2** : at 3-month intervals

2quarterly *adj* **1** : computed for or payable at 3-month intervals <~ premium> **2** : recurring, issued, or spaced at 3-month intervals **3** : divided into heraldic quarters or compartments

3quarterly *n, pl* **-lies** : a periodical published four times a year

Quarterly Meeting *n* : an organizational unit of the Society of Friends usu. composed of several Monthly Meetings

quar·ter·mas·ter \ˈkwȯ(r)t-ər-ˌmas-tər\ *n* **1** : a petty officer who attends to a ship's helm, binnacle, and signals **2** : an army officer who provides clothing and subsistence for a body of troops

quar·tern \ˈkwȯ(r)t-ərn\ *n* [ME *quarteron,* fr. OF, quarter of a pound, quarter of a hundred, fr. *quartier* quarter] : a fourth part

quartern loaf *n* [fr. its being made from a quartern (¼ peck) of flour] *Brit* : a loaf of bread weighing about four pounds

quarter note *n* : a musical note with the time value of ¼ of a whole note — see NOTE illustration

quar·ter–phase \ˌkwȯ(r)t-ər-ˈfāz\ *adj* : DIPHASE

quarter rest *n* : a musical rest corresponding in time value to a quarter note

quar·ter·sawed \ˌkwȯ(r)t-ər-ˈsȯd\ *also* **quar·ter·sawn** \-ˈsȯn\ *adj* : sawed from quartered logs so that the annual rings are nearly at right angles to the wide face — used of boards and planks

quarter section *n* : a tract of land that is half a mile square and contains 160 acres in the U.S. government system of land surveying

quarter sessions *n pl* **1** : an English local court with limited original and appellate criminal and sometimes civil jurisdiction and often administrative functions held quarterly usu. by two justices of the peace in a county or by a recorder in a borough **2** : a local court with criminal jurisdiction and sometimes administrative functions in some states of the U.S.

quar·ter·staff \ˈkwȯ(r)t-ər-ˌstaf\ *n, pl* **-staves** \-ˌstavz, -ˌstāvz\ : a long stout staff formerly used as a weapon and wielded with one hand in the middle and the other between the middle and the end

quarter tone *n* **1** : a musical interval of one half a semitone **2** : a tone at an interval of one quarter

quar·tet *also* **quar·tette** \kwȯr-ˈtet\ *n* [It *quartetto,* fr. *quarto* fourth, fr. L *quartus* — more at QUART] **1** : a musical composition for four instruments or voices **2** : a group or set of four; *esp* : the performers of a quartet

quar·tic \ˈkwȯrt-ik\ *adj* [L *quartus* fourth] : of the fourth degree <~ equation> — **quartic** *n*

quar·tile \ˈkwȯr-ˌtīl, ˈkwȯrt-ᵊl\ *n* [ISV, fr. L *quartus*] : the value that marks the boundary between two consecutive intervals in a frequency distribution of four intervals with each containing one quarter of the total population

quar·to \ˈkwȯrt-(ˌ)ō\ *n, pl* **quartos** [L, abl. of *quartus* fourth] **1** : the size of a piece of paper cut four from a sheet; *also* : paper or a page of this size **2** : a book printed on quarto pages

quartz \ˈkwȯ(ə)rts\ *n* [G *quarz*] : a mineral SiO_2 consisting of a silicon dioxide that occurs in colorless and transparent or colored hexagonal crystals and also in crystalline masses — **quartz·ose** \ˈkwȯrt-ˌsōs\ *adj*

quartz battery *n* : STAMP MILL — called also *quartz mill*

quartz glass *n* : vitreous silica prepared from pure quartz and noted for its transparency to ultraviolet radiation

quartz·if·er·ous \kwȯrt-ˈsif-(ə-)rəs\ *adj* : bearing quartz

quartz–iodine lamp *n* : an incandescent lamp that has a quartz bulb and a tungsten filament with the bulb containing iodine which reacts with the vaporized tungsten to prevent excessive blackening of the bulb

quartz·ite \ˈkwȯrt-ˌsīt\ *n* [ISV] : a compact granular rock composed of quartz and derived from sandstone by metamorphism — **quartz·it·ic** \kwȯrt-ˈsit-ik\ *adj*

qua·sar \ˈkwā-ˌzär *also* -ˌsär\ *n* [*quasi*-stell*ar* radio source] : QUASI-STELLAR RADIO SOURCE

quash \ˈkwäsh, ˈkwȯsh\ *vt* [ME *quassen,* fr. MF *casser, quasser* to annul, fr. LL *cassare,* fr. L *cassus* void, without effect; akin to L *carēre* to be without — more at CASTE; in sense *2,* partly fr. ME *quashen* to smash, fr. MF *quasser, casser,* fr. L *quassare,* to shake violently, shatter, fr. *quassus,* pp. of *quatere* to shake; akin to OE *hūdenian* to shake] **1** : to nullify esp. by judicial action <~ an indictment> **2** : to suppress or extinguish summarily and completely : SUBDUE <~ a rebellion> ***syn*** see CRUSH

qua·si \ˈkwā-ˌzī, -ˌsī; ˈkwäz-ē, ˈkwäs-; ˈkwā-zē\ *adj* **1** : having some resemblance usu. by possession of certain attributes <a ~ corporation> **2** : having a legal status only by operation or construction of law and without reference to intent <a ~ contract>

quasi- *comb form* [L *quasi* as if, as it were, approximately, fr. *quam* as + *si* if — more at QUANTITY, SO] : in some sense or degree <*quasi*-historical> <*quasi*-officially>

qua·si–ju·di·cial \-jü-ˈdish-əl\ *adj* **1** : having a partly judicial character by possession of the right to hold hearings on and conduct investigations into disputed claims and alleged infractions of rules and regulations and to make decisions in the general manner of courts <~ bodies> **2** : essentially judicial in character but not within the judicial power or function esp. as constitutionally defined <~ review> — **qua·si–ju·di·cial·ly** \-ˈdish-(ə-)lē\ *adv*

qua·si–leg·is·la·tive \-ˈlej-ə-ˌslāt-iv\ *adj* **1** : having a partly legislative character by possession of the right to make rules and regulations having the force of law <a ~ agency> **2** : essentially legislative in character but not within the legislative power or function esp. as constitutionally defined <~ powers>

Qua·si·mo·do \ˌkwäs-i-ˈmōd-(ˌ)ō, ˌkwäz-\ *n* [ML *quasi modo geniti infantes* as newborn babes (words of the introit for Low Sunday)] : LOW SUNDAY

qua·si·par·ti·cle \-ˈpärt-i-kəl; *see* QUASI\ *n* **:** a composite entity (as a vibration in a solid) that is analogous in its behavior to a single particle

qua·si–pub·lic \-ˈpəb-lik\ *adj* **:** essentially public (as in services rendered) although under private ownership or control

quasi–stellar object *n* **:** QUASI-STELLAR RADIO SOURCE

qua·si–stel·lar radio source \-ˈstel-ər-\ *n* **:** any of various very distant celestial objects that resemble stars but emit unusually bright blue and ultraviolet light and radio waves

quas·sia \ˈkwäsh-ə\ *n* [NL, genus name, fr. *Quassi* 18th cent. Surinam Negro slave who discovered the medicinal value of quassia] **:** a drug from the heartwood of various tropical trees of the ailanthus family used esp. as a bitter tonic and remedy for roundworms in children and as an insecticide

qua·ter·cen·te·na·ry \ˌkwät-ər-sen-ˈten-ə-rē, -ˈsent-ᵊn-ˌer-ē, -sen-ˈtē-nə-rē\ *n* [L *quater* four times + E *centenary* — more at QUATERNION] **:** a year marking a 400th anniversary

1qua·ter·na·ry \ˈkwät-ə(r)-ˌner-ē, kwə-ˈtər-nə-rē\ *adj* [L *quaternarius,* fr. *quaterni* four each] **1 a :** of, relating to, or consisting of four units or members **b :** of, relating to, or being a number system with a base of four **2** *cap* **:** of, relating to, or being the geological period from the end of the Tertiary to the present time or the corresponding system of rocks **3 :** consisting of, containing, or being an atom united by four bonds to carbon atoms

2quaternary *n, pl* **-ries 1 :** a member of a group fourth in order or rank **2** *cap* **:** the Quaternary period or system of rocks

quaternary ammonium compound *n* **:** any of numerous strong bases and their salts derived from ammonium by replacement of the hydrogen atoms with organic radicals and important esp. as surface-active agents, disinfectants, and drugs

qua·ter·ni·on \kwə-ˈtər-nē-ən, kwä-\ *n* [ME *quaternyoun,* fr. LL *quaternion-, quaternio,* fr. L *quaterni* four each, fr. *quater* four times; akin to L *quattuor* four — more at FOUR] **1 :** a set of four parts, things, or persons **2 a :** a generalized complex number that is composed of a real number and a vector and that depends on one real and three imaginary units **b** *pl* **:** the calculus of quaternions

qua·ter·ni·ty \kwə-ˈtər-nət-ē, kwä-\ *n, pl* **-ties** [LL *quaternitas,* fr. L *quaterni* four each] **:** a union of a group or set of four

qua·train \ˈkwä-ˌtrān, kwä-ˈ\ *n* [F, fr. MF, fr. *quatre* four, fr. L *quattuor*] **:** a unit or group of four lines of verse

qua·tre·foil \ˈkat-ər-ˌfȯil, ˈka-trə-\ *n* [ME *quaterfoil* set of four leaves, fr. MF *quatre* + ME *-foil* (as in *trefoil*)] **1 :** a conventionalized representation of a flower with four petals or of a leaf with four leaflets **2 :** a 4-lobed foliation in architecture

quat·tro·cen·to \ˌkwä-trō-ˈchen-(ˌ)tō\ *n, often cap* [It, lit., four hundred, fr. *quattro* four (fr. L *quattuor*) + *cento* hundred — more at CINQUECENTO] **:** the 15th century esp. with reference to Italian literature and art

quat·tu·or·de·cil·lion \ˌkwät-ə-ˌwȯr-di-ˈsil-yən\ *n, often attrib* [L *quattuordecim* fourteen (fr. *quattuor* four + *decem* ten) + E *-illion* (as in *million*) — more at TEN] — see NUMBER table

1qua·ver \ˈkwā-vər\ *vb* **qua·vered; qua·ver·ing** \ˈkwāv-(ə-)riŋ\ [ME *quaveren,* freq. of *quaven* to tremble] *vi* **1 :** TREMBLE, SHAKE <~*ing* inwardly> **2 :** TRILL **3 :** to utter sound in tremulous tones ~ *vt* **:** to utter quaveringly — **qua·ver·ing·ly** \ˈkwāv-(ə-)riŋ-lē\ *adv* — **qua·very** \-(ə-)rē\ *adj*

2quaver *n* **1 :** EIGHTH NOTE **2 :** TRILL 1 **3 :** a tremulous sound

quay \ˈkē, ˈk(w)ā\ *n* [alter. of earlier *key,* fr. ME, fr. MF *cai,* of Celt origin; akin to Corn *kē* hedge, fence; akin to OE *hecg* hedge] **:** a stretch of paved bank or a solid artificial landing place beside navigable water for convenience in loading and unloading ships

quay·age \-ij\ *n* **1 :** a charge for use of a quay **2 :** room on or for quays **3 :** a system of quays

quay·side \-ˌsīd\ *n* **:** land bordering a quay

Que *abbr* Quebec

quean \ˈkwēn, ˈkwān\ *n* [ME *quene,* fr. OE *cwene;* akin to OE *cwēn* woman, queen] **1 :** a disreputable woman; *specif* **:** PROSTITUTE **2** *chiefly Scot* **:** WOMAN; *esp* **:** one that is young or unmarried

quea·sy *also* **quea·zy** \ˈkwē-zē\ *adj* **quea·si·er; -est** [ME *coysy, qwesye*] **1 :** full of doubt **:** HAZARDOUS **2 a :** causing nausea <~ motion> **b :** suffering from nausea **:** NAUSEATED **3 a :** causing uneasiness **b** (1) **:** DELICATE, SQUEAMISH (2) **:** ill at ease — **quea·si·ly** \-zə-lē\ *adv* — **quea·si·ness** \-zē-nəs\ *n*

Que·bec \kwi-ˈbek *also* ki-\ — a communications code word for the letter *q*

Que·be·cois *or* **Qué·be·cois** \ˌkā-bə-ˈkwä, -ˌbe-\ *n, pl* **Quebecois** *or* **Québecois** \-ˈkwä(z)\ [F *Québecois,* fr. *Québec* Quebec] **:** a native or inhabitant of Quebec; *specif* **:** a French-speaking native or inhabitant of Quebec

que·bra·cho \kā-ˈbräch-(ˌ)ō, ki-\ *n* [AmerSp, alter. of *quiebracha,* fr. Sp *quiebra* it breaks + *hacha* ax] **1 :** any of several trees of southern So. America with hard wood: as **a :** a tree (*Aspidosperma quebracho*) of the dogbane family which occurs in Argentina and Chile and whose dried bark is used as a respiratory sedative in dyspnea and in asthma **b :** a chiefly Argentine tree (*Schinopsis lorentzii*) of the sumac family with dense wood rich in tannins **2 a :** the wood of a quebracho **b :** a tannin-rich extract of the Argentine quebracho used in tanning leather

Que·chua \ˈkech-(ə-)wə, kə-ˈchü-ə\ *n, pl* **Quechua** *or* **Quechuas** [Sp, fr. Quechua *kkechúwa* plunderer, robber] **1 a :** a member of an Amerindian people of central Peru **b :** a group of peoples constituting the dominant element of the Inca Empire **2 a :** the language of the Quechua people widely spoken by other Indian peoples of Peru, Bolivia, Ecuador, Chile, and Argentina **b :** a language family comprising the Quechua language — **Que·chu·an** \-(ə-)wən, -ˈchü-ən\ *adj or n*

1queen \ˈkwēn\ *n* [ME *quene,* fr. OE *cwēn* woman, wife, queen; akin to Goth *qens* wife, Gk *gynē* woman, wife] **1 a :** the wife or widow of a king **b :** the wife or widow of a tribal chief **2 a :** a female monarch **b :** a female chieftain **3 a :** a woman eminent in rank, power, or attractions <a movie ~> **b :** a goddess or a thing personified as female and having supremacy in a specified realm **c :** an attractive girl or woman; *esp* **:** a beauty contest winner **4 :** the most privileged piece of each color in a set of chessmen having the power to move in any direction across any number of unoccupied squares **5 :** a playing card marked with a stylized figure of a queen **6 :** the fertile fully developed female of social bees, ants, and termites whose function is to lay eggs — see HONEYBEE illustration **7 :** a mature female cat kept esp. for breeding **8 :** HOMOSEXUAL

2queen *vi* **1 :** to act like a queen; *esp* **:** to put on airs — usu. used with *it* <~*s* it over her friends> **2 :** to become a queen in chess ~ *vt* **:** to promote (a pawn) to a queen in chess

Queen Anne \kwē-ˈnan\ *adj* [*Queen Anne* of England] **1 :** of, relating to, or having the characteristics of a style of furniture prevalent in England under Dutch influence esp. during the first half of the 18th century that is marked by extensive use of upholstery, marquetry, and Oriental fabrics **2 :** of, relating to, or having the characteristics of a style of English building of the early 18th century characterized by modified classic ornament and the use of red brickwork in which even relief ornament is carved

Queen Anne's lace *n* **:** WILD CARROT

queen consort *n, pl* **queens consort :** the wife of a reigning king

queen mother *n* **:** a queen dowager who is mother of the reigning sovereign

queen post *n* **:** one of two vertical tie posts in a truss (as of a roof)

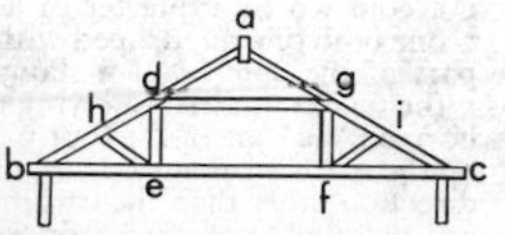

de, gf queen posts; *bc* beam; *dg* straining beam; *bd, cg* principal rafters; *ba, ca* rafters, *eh, fi* struts

queen regent *n, pl* **queens regent :** a queen ruling in behalf of another or in her own right

queen regnant *n, pl* **queens regnant :** a queen reigning in her own right

Queen's Bench *n* — used instead of *King's Bench* when the British monarch is a queen

Queen's Counsel *n* — used instead of *King's Counsel* when the British monarch is a queen

queen·ship \ˈkwēn-ˌship\ *n* **1 :** the rank, dignity, or state of being a queen **2 :** a regal quality like that of a queen

queen·side \-ˌsīd\ *n* **:** the side of a chessboard containing the file on which the queen sits at the beginning of the game

queen–size *adj* **1 :** having dimensions of approximately 60 inches by 80 inches — used of a bed; compare FULL-SIZE, KING-SIZE, TWIN-SIZE **2 :** of a size that fits a queen-size bed <a ~ sheet>

queen substance *n* **:** a pheromone that is secreted by queen bees, is consumed by worker bees, and inhibits the development of their ovaries

queen truss *n* **:** a truss framed with queen posts

1queer \ˈkwi(ə)r\ *adj* [origin unknown] **1 a :** differing in some odd way from what is usual or normal **b** (1) **:** ECCENTRIC, UNCONVENTIONAL (2) **:** mildly insane **:** TOUCHED **c :** absorbed or interested to an extreme or unreasonable degree **:** OBSESSED **d :** sexually deviate **:** HOMOSEXUAL **2 a :** WORTHLESS, COUNTERFEIT <~ money> **b :** QUESTIONABLE, SUSPICIOUS **3 :** not quite well — **queer·ish** \-ish\ *adj* — **queer·ly** *adv* — **queer·ness** *n*

2queer *vt* **1 :** to spoil the effect or success of <~ one's plans> **2 :** to put or get into an embarrassing or disadvantageous situation

3queer *n* **:** one that is queer; *esp* **:** HOMOSEXUAL

1quell \ˈkwel\ *vt* [ME *quellen* to kill, quell, fr. OE *cwellan* to kill; akin to OHG *quellen* to torture, kill, *quāla* torment, Gk *belonē* needle] **1 :** to thoroughly overwhelm and reduce to submission or passivity <~ a riot> **2 :** QUIET, PACIFY <~ fears> ***syn*** see CRUSH ***ant*** foment — **quell·er** *n*

2quell *n* [ME, fr. *quellen*] **1** *obs* **:** SLAUGHTER **2** *archaic* **:** the power of quelling

quench \ˈkwench\ *vb* [ME *quenchen,* fr. OE *-cwencan;* akin to OE *-cwincan* to vanish, OFris *quinka*] *vt* **1 a :** to put out (as a fire or light) **:** EXTINGUISH **b :** to put out the light or fire of <~ glowing coals with water> **c :** to cool (as heated metal) suddenly by immersion (as in oil or water); *broadly* **:** to cause to lose heat or warmth <you have ~*ed* the warmth of France toward you —Alfred Tennyson> **2 a :** to bring (something immaterial) to an end typically by satisfying, damping, cooling, or decreasing <a rational understanding of the laws of nature can ~ impossible desires —Lucius Garvin> <the praise that ~*es* all desire to read the book —T. S. Eliot> **b :** to terminate by or as if by destroying **:** ELIMINATE <the Commonwealth party ~*ed* a whole generation of play-acting —Margery Bailey> <~ a rebellion> **c :** to relieve or satisfy with liquid <~*ed* his thirst at a wayside spring> ~ *vi* **1 :** to become extinguished **:** COOL **2 :** to become calm **:** SUBSIDE ***syn*** see CRUSH — **quench·able** \ˈkwen-chə-bəl\ *adj* — **quench·er** *n* — **quench·less** \ˈkwench-ləs\ *adj*

quer·ce·tin \ˈkwər-sət-ən\ *n* [ISV, fr. L *quercetum* oak forest, fr. *quercus* oak — more at FIR] **:** a yellow crystalline pigment $C_{15}H_{10}O_7$ occurring usu. in the form of glycosides in various plants

quer·cit·ron \ˈkwər-ˌsi-trən, ˌkwər-ˈ\ *n* [blend of NL *Quercus* (genus name) and ISV *citron*] **1 :** a large timber oak (*Quercus velutina*) of the eastern and central U.S. **2 :** the bark of a quercitron that is rich in tannin and yellow coloring matter and is used in tanning and dyeing

que·rist \ˈkwi(ə)r-əst, ˈkwe(ə)r-\ *n* [L *quaerere* to ask] **:** one who inquires

quern \ˈkwərn\ *n* [ME, fr. OE *cweorn;* akin to OHG *quirn* mill, OSlav *žrŭny*] **:** a primitive hand mill for grinding grain

quer·u·lous \ˈkwer-(y)ə-ləs *also* ˈkwir-\ *adj* [L *querulus,* fr. *queri* to complain] **1 :** habitually complaining **2 :** FRETFUL, WHINING <a ~ voice> — **quer·u·lous·ly** *adv* — **quer·u·lous·ness** *n*

1que·ry \ˈkwi(ə)r-ē, ˈkwe(ə)r-\ *n, pl* **queries** [alter. of earlier *quere,* fr. L *quaere,* imper. of *quaerere* to ask] **1 :** QUESTION, INQUIRY **2 :** a question in the mind **:** DOUBT **3 :** QUESTION MARK

2query *vt* **que·ried; que·ry·ing 1 :** to put as a question **2 :** to ask questions about esp. in order to resolve a doubt **3 :** to ask questions of esp. with a desire for authoritative information **4 :** to mark with a query ***syn*** see ASK — **que·ri·er** *n*

1quest \ˈkwest\ *n* [ME, search, pursuit, investigation, inquest, fr. MF *queste* search, pursuit, fr. (assumed) VL *quaesta*, fr. L, fem. of *quaestus*] **1 a :** a jury of inquest **b :** INVESTIGATION **2 :** an act or instance of seeking: **a :** PURSUIT, SEARCH **b :** a chivalrous enterprise in medieval romance usu. involving an adventurous journey **3** *obs* **:** ones who search or make inquiry

2quest *vi* **1** *of a dog* **a :** to search a trail **b :** BAY **2 :** to go on a quest ~ *vt* **1 :** to search for **2 :** to ask for — **quest·er** *n*

1ques·tion \ˈkwes(h)-chən\ *n* [ME, fr. MF, fr. L *quaestion-, quaestio*, fr. *quaesitus quaestus*, pp. of *quaerere* to seek, ask] **1 a** (1) **:** an interrogative expression often used to test knowledge (2) **:** an interrogative sentence or clause **b :** a subject or aspect in dispute or open for discussion **:** ISSUE; *broadly* **:** PROBLEM, MATTER **c** (1) **:** a subject or point of debate or a proposition to be voted on in a meeting (2) **:** the bringing of such to a vote **d :** the specific point at issue **2 a :** an act or instance of asking **:** INQUIRY **b :** INTERROGATION; *also* **:** a judicial or official investigation **c :** torture as part of an examination **d** (1) **:** OBJECTION, DISPUTE <true beyond ~> (2) **:** room for doubt or objection <little ~ of his skill> (3) **:** CHANCE, POSSIBILITY <no ~ of escape>

2question *vt* **1 :** to ask a question of or about **2 :** to interrogate intensively **:** CROSS-EXAMINE **3 a :** DOUBT, DISPUTE **b :** to subject to analysis **:** EXAMINE ~ *vi* **:** to ask questions **:** INQUIRE ***syn*** see ASK — **ques·tion·er** *n*

ques·tion·able \ˈkwes(h)-chə-nə-bəl, *rapid* ˈkwesh-nə-\ *adj* **1** *obs* **:** inviting inquiry **2** *obs* **:** liable to judicial inquiry or action **3 :** affording reason for being doubted, questioned, or challenged **:** not certain or exact **:** PROBLEMATIC <milk of ~ purity> <a ~ decision> **4 :** attended by well-grounded suspicions of being immoral, crude, false, or unsound **:** DUBIOUS <~ motives> ***syn*** see DOUBTFUL ***ant*** authoritative, unquestionable — **ques·tion·able·ness** *n* — **ques·tion·ably** \-blē\ *adv*

ques·tion·ary \ˈkwes(h)-chə-ˌner-ē\ *n, pl* **-ar·ies :** QUESTIONNAIRE

ques·tion·less \ˈkwes(h)-chən-ləs\ *adj* **1 :** INDUBITABLE, UNQUESTIONABLE **2 :** UNQUESTIONING

question mark *n* **1 :** a mark ? used in writing and printing at the conclusion of a sentence to indicate a direct question **2 :** something unknown, unknowable, or uncertain

ques·tion·naire \ˌkwes(h)-chə-ˈna(ə)r, -ˈne(ə)r\ *n* [F, fr. *questionner* to question, fr. MF, fr. *question*, n.] **1 :** a set of questions for obtaining statistically useful or personal information from individuals **2 :** a written or printed questionnaire often with spaces for answers **3 :** a survey made by the use of a questionnaire

question time *n* **:** a period in a session of a British parliamentary body during which members may put to a minister questions on matters concerning his department

ques·tor \ˈkwes-tər\ *var of* QUAESTOR

quet·zal \ket-ˈsäl, -ˈsal\ *n, pl* **quetzals** *or* **quet·za·les** \-ˈsäl-(ˌ)ās, -ˈsal-\ [AmerSp, fr. Nahuatl *quetzaltototl*, fr. *quetzalli* brilliant tail feather + *tototl* bird] **1 :** a Central American trogon (*Pharomachrus mocino*) that has brilliant plumage and in the male long upper tail coverts **2** — see MONEY table

quetzal 1

Quet·zal·coatl \ket-ˈsäl-ˌkwät-ᵊl, -ˈsal-, -kə-ˌwät-\ *n* [Nahuatl] **:** a chief Toltec and Aztec god identified with the wind and air and represented by means of a feathered serpent

1queue \ˈkyü\ *n* [F, lit., tail, fr. L *cauda, coda*] **1 :** a braid of hair usu. worn hanging at the back of the head **2 :** a waiting line esp. of persons or vehicles

2queue *vb* **queued; queu·ing** *or* **queue·ing** *vt* **:** to arrange or form in a queue ~ *vi* **:** to line up or wait in a queue — **queu·er** *n*

1quib·ble \ˈkwib-əl\ *n* [prob. dim. of obs. *quib* (quibble)] **1 :** an evasion of or shift from the point **:** EQUIVOCATION **2 :** a minor objection or criticism

2quibble *vb* **quib·bled; quib·bling** \-(ə-)liŋ\ *vi* **1 :** EQUIVOCATE **2 a :** CAVIL, CARP **b :** BICKER ~ *vt* **:** to subject to quibbles — **quib·bler** \-(ə-)lər\ *n*

quiche \ˈkēsh\ *n* [F, fr. G dial. (Lorraine) *küche*, dim. of *kuchen* cake, fr. OHG *kuocho* — more at CAKE] **:** a pastry shell filled with a rich egg and cream custard and various other ingredients (as ham, seafood, or vegetables)

quiche Lor·raine \-lə-ˈrān, -lō-\ *n* [F, fr. *lorraine*, fem. of *lorrain* of Lorraine] **:** a quiche containing cheese and crisp bacon bits

1quick \ˈkwik\ *adj* [ME *quik*, fr. OE *cwic*; akin to ON *kvikr* living, L *vivus* living, *vivere* to live, Gk *bios, zōē* life] **1** *archaic* **:** not dead **:** LIVING, ALIVE **2 :** acting or capable of acting with speed: as **a** (1) **:** fast in understanding, thinking, or learning **:** mentally agile <a ~ mind> <~ thinking> (2) **:** reacting to stimuli with speed and keen sensitivity (3) **:** aroused immediately and intensely <~ tempers> **b** (1) **:** fast in development or occurrence <a ~ succession of events> (2) **:** done or taking place with rapidity <gave them a ~ look> **c :** marked by speed, readiness, or promptness of physical movement <walked with ~ steps> **d :** inclined to hastiness (as in action or response) <too ~ to criticize> **e :** capable of being easily and speedily prepared <a ~ and tasty dinner> **3** *archaic* **a :** not stagnant **:** RUNNING, FLOWING **b :** MOVING, SHIFTING <~ mud> **4** *archaic* **:** FIERY, GLOWING **5** *obs* **a :** PUNGENT **b :** CAUSTIC **6** *archaic* **:** PREGNANT **7 :** having a sharp angle <a ~ turn in the road> — **quick·ly** *adv* — **quick·ness** *n*

syn* 1** see FAST ***ant sluggish

2 QUICK, PROMPT, READY, APT *shared meaning element* **:** able to respond without delay or hesitation or indicative of such ability. QUICK stresses instancy of response and is likely to connote native rather than acquired power <very *quick* in perception> <a keen *quick* mind> PROMPT is more likely to connote training and discipline that fits one for instant response <*prompt* insight into the workings of complex apparatus —F. H. Garrison> READY suggests facility or fluency in response <reading maketh a full man, conference a *ready* man —Francis Bacon> APT stresses the possession of qualities (as intelligence, a particular talent, or a strong bent) that makes quick effective response possible <an *apt* student> <her answer was *apt* and to the point> ***ant*** sluggish

2quick *adv* **:** in a quick manner

3quick *n* **1 quick** *pl* **:** living beings **2** [prob. of Scand origin; akin to ON *kvika* sensitive flesh, fr. *kvikr* living] **a :** a painfully sensitive spot or area of flesh (as that underlying a fingernail or toenail) **b :** the inmost sensibilities <hurt to the ~ by the remark> **c :** the very center of something **:** HEART **3** *archaic* **:** LIFE 11

quick assets *n pl* **:** cash, accounts receivable, and other current assets excluding inventories

quick bread *n* **:** bread made with a leavening agent (as baking powder or baking soda) that permits immediate baking of the dough or batter mixture <biscuits and muffins are *quick bread*>

quick·en \ˈkwik-ən\ *vb* **quick·ened; quick·en·ing** \-(ə-)niŋ\ *vt* **1 a :** to make alive **:** REVIVE **b :** to cause to be enlivened **:** STIMULATE **2** *archaic* **a :** KINDLE **b :** to cause to burn more intensely **3 :** to make more rapid **:** HASTEN, ACCELERATE <~*ed* her steps> **4 a :** to make (a curve) sharper **b :** to make (a slope) steeper ~ *vi* **1 :** to quicken something **2 :** to come to life; *esp* **:** to enter into a phase of active growth and development <seeds ~*ing* in the soil> **3 :** to reach the stage of gestation at which fetal motion is felt **4 :** to shine more brightly <watched the dawn ~*ing* in the east> **5 :** to become more rapid <her pulse ~*ed* at the sight> — **quick·en·er** \-(ə-)nər\ *n*

syn* 1** QUICKEN, ANIMATE, ENLIVEN, VIVIFY *shared meaning element* **:** to make alive or lively ***ant deaden

2 see PROVOKE ***ant*** arrest

quick–freeze \ˈkwik-ˈfrēz\ *vt* **-froze** \-ˈfrōz\; **-fro·zen** \-ˈfrōz-ᵊn\; **-freez·ing :** to freeze (food) for preservation so rapidly that ice crystals formed are too small to rupture the cells and the natural juices and flavor are preserved

quick·ie \ˈkwik-ē\ *n* **:** something done or made in a hurry

quick kick *n* **:** a punt in football on first, second, or third down made from a running or passing formation and designed to take the opposing team by surprise

quick·lime \ˈkwik-ˌlīm\ *n* **:** the first solid product that is obtained by calcining limestone and that develops great heat and becomes crumbly when treated with water

quick–lunch \-ˈlənch\ *n* **:** a luncheonette specializing in short-order food

quick·sand \ˈkwik-ˌsand\ *n* **:** sand readily yielding to pressure; *esp* **:** a deep mass of loose sand mixed with water into which heavy objects readily sink

quick·set \-ˌset\ *n, chiefly Brit* **:** plant cuttings set in the ground to grow esp. in a hedgerow; *also* **:** a hedge or thicket esp. of hawthorn grown from quickset

quick·sil·ver \-ˌsil-vər\ *n* **:** MERCURY 2a — **quicksilver** *adj*

quick·step \-ˌstep\ *n* **:** a spirited march tune usu. accompanying a march in quick time

quick–tem·pered \-ˈtem-pərd\ *adj* **:** easily angered **:** IRASCIBLE

quick time *n* **:** a rate of marching in which 120 steps each 30 inches in length are taken in one minute

quick–wit·ted \ˈkwik-ˈwit-əd\ *adj* **:** quick in perception and understanding **:** mentally alert ***syn*** see INTELLIGENT — **quick–wit·ted·ly** *adv* — **quick–wit·ted·ness** *n*

1quid \ˈkwid\ *n, pl* **quid** *also* **quids** [origin unknown] *Brit* **:** a pound sterling **:** SOVEREIGN

2quid *n* [E dial., cud, fr. ME *quide*, fr. OE *cwidu* — more at CUD] **:** a cut or wad of something chewable

quid·di·ty \ˈkwid-ət-ē\ *n, pl* **-ties** [ML *quidditas* essence, lit., whatness, fr. L *quid* what, neut. of *quis* who — more at WHO] **1 a :** a trifling point **:** QUIBBLE **b :** CROTCHET, ECCENTRICITY **2 :** whatever makes something to be of the type that it is **:** ESSENCE

quid·nunc \ˈkwid-ˌnəŋk\ *n* [L *quid nunc* what now?] **:** one who seeks to know all the latest news or gossip **:** BUSYBODY

quid pro quo \ˌkwid-ˌprō-ˈkwō\ *n* [NL, something for something] **:** something given or received for something else

qui·es·cence \kwī-ˈes-ᵊn(t)s, kwē-\ *n* **:** the quality or state of being quiescent

qui·es·cent \-ᵊnt\ *adj* [L *quiescent-, quiescens*, prp. of *quiescere* to become quiet, rest, fr. *quies*] **1 :** being at rest **:** INACTIVE **2 :** causing no trouble or symptoms <~ gallstones> ***syn*** see LATENT — **qui·es·cent·ly** *adv*

1qui·et \ˈkwī-ət\ *n* [ME, fr. L *quiet-, quies* rest, quiet — more at WHILE] **:** the quality or state of being quiet **:** TRANQUILLITY — **on the quiet :** in a secretive manner

2quiet *adj* [ME, fr. MF, fr. L *quietus*, fr. pp. of *quiescere*] **1 a :** marked by little or no motion or activity **:** CALM <a ~ sea> **b :** GENTLE, EASYGOING <a ~ temperament> **c :** not disturbed **:** not interfered with <~ reading> **d :** enjoyed in peace and relaxation <a ~ cup of tea> **2 a :** free from noise or uproar **:** STILL **b :** UNOBTRUSIVE, CONSERVATIVE <~ clothes> **3 :** SECLUDED <a ~ nook> — **qui·et·ly** *adv* — **qui·et·ness** *n*

3quiet *adv* **:** in a quiet manner <a *quiet*-running engine>

4quiet *vt* **1 :** to cause to be quiet **:** CALM **2 :** to make secure by freeing from dispute or question <~ title to a property> ~ *vi* **:** to become quiet — usu. used with *down* — **qui·et·er** *n*

qui·et·en \ˈkwī-ət-ᵊn\ *vb* **qui·et·ened; qui·et·en·ing** \-ət-niŋ, -ᵊn-iŋ\ *chiefly Brit* **:** QUIET

qui·et·ism \ˈkwī-ət-ˌiz-əm\ *n* **1 a :** a system of religious mysticism teaching that perfection and spiritual peace are attained by annihilation of the will and passive absorption in contemplation of God and divine things **b :** a passive withdrawn attitude or policy toward the world or worldly affairs **2 :** a state of calmness or passivity — **qui·et·ist** \-ət-əst\ *adj or n*

qui·etude \ˈkwī-ə-ˌt(y)üd\ *n* [MF, fr. LL *quietudo,* fr. L *quietus*] **:** a quiet state **:** REPOSE

qui·etus \kwī-ˈēt-əs\ *n* [ME *quietus est,* fr. ML, he is quit, formula of discharge from obligation] **1 :** final settlement (as of a debt) **2 :** removal from activity; *esp* **:** DEATH **3 :** something that quiets or represses **4 :** a state of inactivity

quiff \ˈkwif\ *n* [origin unknown] *Brit* **:** a prominent forelock

[1]**quill** \ˈkwil\ *n* [ME *quil* hollow reed, bobbin; akin to MHG *kil* large feather] **1 a** (1) **:** a bobbin, spool, or spindle on which filling yarn is wound (2) **:** a hollow shaft often surrounding another shaft and used in various mechanical devices **b :** a roll of dried bark <cinnamon ~*s*> **2 a** (1) **:** the hollow horny barrel of a feather (2) **:** FEATHER; *esp* **:** one of the large stiff feathers of the wing or tail **b :** one of the hollow sharp spines of a porcupine or hedgehog **3 :** something made from or resembling the quill of a feather; *esp* **:** a pen for writing **4 :** a float for a fishing line

[2]**quill** *vt* **1 :** to pierce with quills **2 a :** to wind (thread or yarn) on a quill **b :** to make a series of small rounded ridges in (cloth)

quill·back \ˈkwil-ˌbak\ *n, pl* **quillback** *or* **quillbacks :** any of several suckers; *esp* **:** a small fish (*Carpiodes cyprinus*) of central and eastern No. America that has the first ray of the dorsal fin much elongated

[1]**quilt** \ˈkwilt\ *n* [ME *quilte* mattress, quilt, fr. OF *cuilte,* fr. L *culcita* mattress] **1 :** a bed coverlet of two layers of cloth filled with wool, cotton, or down and held in place by stitched designs **2 :** something that is quilted or resembles a quilt

[2]**quilt** *vt.* **1 a :** to fill, pad, or line like a quilt **b** (1) **:** to stitch, sew, or cover with lines or patterns like those used in quilts (2) **:** to stitch (designs) through layers of cloth **c :** to fasten between two pieces of material **2 :** to stitch or sew in layers with padding in between ~ *vi* **1 :** to make quilts **2 :** to do quilted work — **quilt·er** *n*

quilt·ing *n* **1 :** the process of quilting **2 :** material that is quilted or used for making quilts

quin- *or* **quino-** *comb form* [Sp *quina* — more at QUININE] **1 :** cinchona **:** cinchona bark <*quin*oline> **2 :** quinone <*quin*oid>

quin·a·crine \ˈkwin-ə-ˌkrēn\ *n* [*quin-* + *acridine*]**:** an antimalarial drug derived from acridine and used esp. as the dihydrochloride $C_{23}H_{30}ClN_3O.2HCl.2H_2O$

quince \ˈkwin(t)s\ *n* [ME *quynce* quinces, pl. of *coyn, quyn* quince, fr. MF *coin,* fr. L *cydonium,* fr. Gk *kydōnion*] **1 :** the fruit of a central Asiatic tree (*Cydonia oblonga*) of the rose family that resembles a hard-fleshed yellow apple and is used for marmalade, jelly, and preserves **2 :** the tree that bears quinces

quince 1

quin·cun·cial \kwin-ˈkən-chəl\ *or* **quin·cunx·ial** \-ˈkəŋ(k)-sē-əl\ *adj* **1 :** of, relating to, or arranged in a quincunx **2 :** having the members of a pentamerous bud or flower so imbricated that two are exterior, two are interior, and one has one edge exterior and one interior — **quin·cun·cial·ly** \-ˈkən-chə-lē\ *adv*

quin·cunx \ˈkwin-ˌkəŋ(k)s\ *n* [L *quincunc-, quincunx,* lit., five twelfths, fr. *quinque* five + *uncia* twelfth part — more at FIVE, OUNCE] **1 :** an arrangement of five things with one at each corner and one in the middle of a square or rectangle **2 :** a quincuncial arrangement of plant parts

quin·de·cil·lion \ˌkwin-di-ˈsil-yən\ *n, often attrib* [L *quindecim* fifteen (fr. *quinque* five + *decem* ten) + E *-illion* (as in *million*) — more at TEN] — see NUMBER table

quin·i·dine \ˈkwin-ə-ˌdēn\ *n* [ISV, fr. *quinine*] **:** an alkaloid $C_{20}H_{24}N_2O_2$ stereoisomeric with and resembling quinine that is used in treating cardiac rhythm irregularities

qui·nie·la \kēn-ˈyel-ə\ *or* **qui·nel·la** \kē-ˈnel-ə\ *n* [AmerSp *quiniela,* a game of chance resembling a lottery]**:** a system of betting (as on dog races) in which the bettor must pick the first and second place finishers but need not designate their order of finish in order to win — compare PERFECTA

qui·nine \ˈkwī-ˌnīn *also* ˈkwin-ˌīn *or* kwin-ˈīn *or* k(w)in-ˈēn\ *n* [Sp *quina* cinchona, short for *quinaquina,* fr. Quechua] **1 :** a bitter crystalline alkaloid $C_{20}H_{24}N_2O_2$ from cinchona bark used in medicine **2 :** a salt of quinine used as an antipyretic, antimalarial, antiperiodic, and bitter tonic

quinine water *n* **:** a carbonated beverage flavored with a small amount of quinine, lemon, and lime

qui·noa \ki-ˈnō-ə\ *n* [Sp, f. Quechua *quinua*] **:** a pigweed (*Chenopodium quinoa*) of the high Andes whose seeds are ground and widely used as food in Peru

quin·oid \ˈkwin-ˌȯid\ *n* **:** a quinonoid compound

qui·noi·dine \kwə-ˈnȯid-ᵊn\ *n* [ISV] **:** a bitter brownish resinous mixture of alkaloids obtained as a by-product in the extraction of cinchona bark for crystalline alkaloids and formerly used as a quinine substitute

quin·o·line \ˈkwin-ᵊl-ˌēn\ *n* [ISV *quin-* + *-ol* + *-ine*] **1 :** a pungent oily nitrogenous base C_9H_7N that is obtained usu. by distillation of coal tar or by synthesis from aniline and is the parent compound of many alkaloids, drugs, and dyes **2 :** a derivative of quinoline

qui·none \kwin-ˈōn, ˈkwin-ˌ\ *n* [ISV *quinine* + *-one*] **1 :** either of two isomeric cyclic crystalline compounds $C_6H_4O_2$ that are di-keto derivatives of dihydro-benzene **2 :** any of various usu. yellow, orange, or red quinonoid compounds including several that are biologically important as coenzymes, hydrogen acceptors, or vitamins

qui·no·noid \kwin-ˈō-ˌnȯid, ˈkwin-ə-\ *or* **quin·oid** \ˈkwin-ˌȯid\ *adj* **:** resembling quinone esp. in having a benzene nucleus containing two double bonds within the nucleus

Quin·qua·ge·si·ma \ˌkwiŋ-kə-ˈjes-ə-mə, -ˈjā-zə-\ *n* [ML, fr. L, fem. of *quinquagesimus* fiftieth, fr. *quinquaginta* fifty, fr. *quinque* + *-ginta* (akin to *viginti* twenty — more at VIGESIMAL)]**:** the Sunday before Lent

quinque- *or* **quinqu-** *comb form* [L, fr. *quinque* — more at FIVE] **:** five <*quinque*foliolate>

quin·quen·ni·al \kwin-ˈkwen-ē-əl, kwiŋ-\ *adj* **1 :** consisting of or lasting for five years **2 :** occurring or being done every five years — **quinquennial** *n* — **quin·quen·ni·al·ly** \-ē-ə-lē\ *adv*

quin·quen·ni·um \-ē-əm\ *n, pl* **-ni·ums** *or* **-nia** \-ē-ə\ [L, fr. *quinque-* + *annus* year — more at ANNUAL]**:** a period of five years

quin·que·va·lent *also* **quin·qui·va·lent** \ˌkwiŋ-kwi-ˈvā-lənt\ *adj* **:** PENTAVALENT

quin·sy \ˈkwin-zē\ *n* [ME *quinesie,* fr. MF *quinancie,* fr. LL *cynanche,* fr. Gk *kynanchē,* fr. *kyn-, kyōn* dog + *anchein* to strangle — more at HOUND, ANGER]**:** a severe inflammation of the throat or adjacent parts with swelling and fever

quint \ˈkwint\ *n* **:** QUINTUPLET

quin·tain \ˈkwint-ᵊn\ *n* [ME *quintaine,* fr. MF, fr. L *quintana* street in a Roman camp separating the fifth maniple from the sixth where military exercises were performed, fr. fem. of *quintanus* fifth in rank, fr. *quintus* fifth]**:** an object to be tilted at; *esp* **:** a post with a revolving crosspiece that has a target at one end and a sandbag at the other end

quin·tal \ˈkwint-ᵊl, ˈkant-\ *n* [ME, fr. MF, fr. ML *quintale,* fr. Ar *qinṭār,* fr. LGk *kentēnarion,* fr. LL *centenarium,* fr. L, neut. of *centenarius* consisting of a hundred — more at CENTENARY] **1 :** HUNDREDWEIGHT **2** — see METRIC SYSTEM table

quin·tes·sence \kwin-ˈtes-ᵊn(t)s\ *n* [ME, fr. MF *quinte essence,* fr. ML *quinta essentia,* lit., fifth essence] **1 :** the fifth and highest essence in ancient and medieval philosophy that permeates all nature and is the substance composing the heavenly bodies **2 :** the essence of a thing in its purest and most concentrated form **3 :** the most typical example or representative — **quint·es·sen·tial** \ˌkwint-ə-ˈsen-chəl\ *adj*

quin·tet *also* **quin·tette** \kwin-ˈtet\ *n* [*quintet* fr. It *quintetto,* fr. *quinto* fifth, fr. L *quintus; quintette* fr. F, fr. It *quintetto*] **1 :** a musical composition or movement for five instruments or voices **2 :** a group or set of five: as **a :** the performers of a quintet **b :** a basketball team

[1]**quin·tic** \ˈkwint-ik\ *adj* [L *quintus* fifth] **:** of the fifth degree

[2]**quintic** *n* **:** a polynomial or a polynomial equation of the fifth degree

quin·tile \ˈkwin-ˌtīl\ *n* [L *quintus* + E *-ile*]**:** any of the four values that divide the items of a frequency distribution into five classes

quin·til·lion \kwin-ˈtil-yən\ *n* [L *quintus* + E *-illion* (as in *million*)] — see NUMBER table — **quintillion** *adj* — **quin·til·lionth** \-yən(t)th\ *adj or n*

[1]**quin·tu·ple** \kwin-ˈt(y)üp-əl, -ˈtəp-; ˈkwint-əp-\ *adj* [MF, fr. LL *quintuplex,* fr. L *quintus* fifth + *-plex* -fold; akin to L *quinque* five — more at FIVE, SIMPLE] **1 :** having five units or members **2 :** being five times as great or as many **3 :** marked by five beats per measure <~ meter> — **quintuple** *n*

[2]**quintuple** *vb* **quin·tu·pled; quin·tu·pling** \-(ə-)liŋ\ *vt* **:** to make five times as great or as many ~ *vi* **:** to become five times as much or as numerous

quin·tu·plet \kwin-ˈtəp-lət, -ˈt(y)üp-; ˈkwint-əp-\ *n* **1 :** a combination of five of a kind **2 :** one of five offspring born at one birth

[1]**quin·tu·pli·cate** \kwin-ˈt(y)ü-pli-kət\ *adj* [L *quintuplicatus,* pp. of *quintuplicare* to quintuple, fr. *quintuplic-, quintuplex* quintuple] **1 :** consisting of or existing in five corresponding or identical parts or examples <~ invoices> **2 :** being the fifth of five things exactly alike <file the ~ copy>

[2]**quintuplicate** *n* **1 :** one of five things exactly alike; *specif* **:** one of five identical copies **2 :** five copies all alike — used with *in* <typed in ~>

[3]**quin·tu·pli·cate** \-plə-ˌkāt\ *vt* **-cat·ed; -cat·ing 1 :** to make quintuple or fivefold **2 :** to prepare in quintuplicate

[1]**quip** \ˈkwip\ *n* [earlier *quippy,* perh. fr. L *quippe* indeed, to be sure (often ironical), fr. *quid* what — more at QUIDDITY] **1 a :** a clever usu. taunting remark **:** GIBE **b :** a witty or funny observation or response usu. made on the spur of the moment **2 :** QUIBBLE, EQUIVOCATION **3 :** something strange, droll, curious, or eccentric **:** ODDITY ***syn*** see JEST — **quip·ster** \-stər\ *n*

[2]**quip** *vb* **quipped; quip·ping** *vi* **:** to make quips **:** GIBE ~ *vt* **:** to jest or gibe at

qui·pu \ˈkē-(ˌ)pü\ *n* [Sp *quipo,* fr. Quechua *quipu*]**:** a device made of a main cord with smaller varicolored cords attached and knotted and used by the ancient Peruvians (as for calculating)

[1]**quire** \ˈkwī(ə)r\ *n* [ME *quair* four sheets of paper folded once, collection of sheets, fr. MF *quaer,* fr. (assumed) VL *quadernum,* alter. of L *quaterni* four each, set of four — more at QUATERNION] **:** a collection of 24 or sometimes 25 sheets of paper of the same size and quality **:** one twentieth of a ream

[2]**quire** *var of* CHOIR

Qui·ri·nus \kwə-ˈrī-nəs, -ˈrē-\ *n* [L] **:** an early state god of the Romans later identified with Romulus

[1]**quirk** \ˈkwərk\ *n* [origin unknown] **1 a :** an abrupt twist or curve **b :** a peculiar trait **:** IDIOSYNCRASY **c :** ACCIDENT, VAGARY **2 :** a groove separating a bead or other molding from adjoining members — **quirk·i·ly** \ˈkwər-kə-lē\ *adv* — **quirk·i·ness** \-kē-nəs\ *n* — **quirky** \-kē\ *adj*

[2]**quirk** *vb* **:** CURL, TWIST

[1]**quirt** \ˈkwərt\ *n* [MexSp *cuarta*] **:** a riding whip with a short handle and a rawhide lash

[2]**quirt** *vt* **:** to strike or drive with a quirt

quis·ling \ˈkwiz-liŋ\ *n* [Vidkun *Quisling* †1945 Norw politician] **:** a traitor who collaborates with the invaders of his country esp. by serving in a puppet government — **quis·ling·ism** \-liŋ-ˌiz-əm\ *n*

1**quit** \ˈkwit\ *adj* [ME *quite, quit,* fr. OF *quite*] **:** released from obligation, charge, or penalty; *esp* **:** FREE

2**quit** *vb* **quit** *also* **quit·ted; quit·ting** [ME *quiten, quitten,* fr. MF *quiter, quitter,* fr. OF, fr. *quite* free of, released, lit., at rest, fr. L *quietus* quiet, at rest] *vt* **1 :** to set free **:** RELIEVE, RELEASE <~ oneself of fear> **2 :** to make full payment of **:** pay up <~ a debt> **3 :** CONDUCT, ACQUIT <the youths ~ themselves like men> **4 a :** to depart from or out of **b :** to leave the company of **c :** to relinquish, abandon, or give over (as a way of thinking, acting, or living) **:** FORSAKE **d :** to give up (an action, activity, or employment) **:** LEAVE <~ a job> ~ *vi* **1 :** to cease normal, expected, or necessary action **2 :** to give up employment **3 :** to give up **:** admit defeat ***syn*** see GO, STOP

3**quit** *n* **:** the act of quitting a job

quitch \ˈkwich\ *n* [(assumed) ME *quicche,* fr. OE *cwice;* akin to OHG *quecca* couch grass, OE *cwic* living — more at QUICK] **:** QUACK GRASS

quit·claim \ˈkwit-ˌklām\ *vt* **:** to release or relinquish a legal claim to; *esp* **:** to release a claim to or convey by a quitclaim deed — **quitclaim** *n*

quitclaim deed *n* **:** a legal instrument used to release one person's right, title, or interest to another without providing a guarantee or warranty of title

quite \ˈkwīt\ *adv* [ME, fr. *quite,* adj., quit] **1 :** WHOLLY, COMPLETELY <not ~ all> **2 :** to an extreme **:** POSITIVELY <~ sure> **3 :** to a considerable extent **:** RATHER <~ near>

quit·rent \ˈkwit-ˌrent\ *n* **:** a fixed rent payable to a feudal superior in commutation of services; *specif* **:** a fixed rent due from a socage tenant

quits \ˈkwits\ *adj* [ME, quit, prob. fr. ML *quittus,* alter. of L *quietus* at rest] **:** being on even terms by repayment or requital

quit·tance \ˈkwit-ᵊn(t)s\ *n* **1 a :** discharge from a debt or an obligation **b :** a document evidencing quittance **2 :** RECOMPENSE, REQUITAL

quit·ter \ˈkwit-ər\ *n* **:** one that quits; *esp* **:** one that gives up too easily **:** DEFEATIST

quit·tor \ˈkwit-ər\ *n* [ME *quiture* pus, prob. fr. OF, act of boiling, fr. L *coctura,* fr. *coctus,* pp. of *coquere* to cook — more at COOK] **:** a purulent inflammation of the feet esp. of horses and asses affecting chiefly the cartilage

1**quiv·er** \ˈkwiv-ər\ *n* [ME, fr. OF *quivre,* of Gmc origin; akin to OE *cocer* quiver, OHG *kohhari*] **1 :** a case for carrying or holding arrows **2 :** the arrows in a quiver

2**quiver** *vi* **quiv·ered; quiv·er·ing** \-(ə-)riŋ\ [ME *quiveren,* prob. fr. *quiver* agile, quick, fr. (assumed) OE *cwifer*] **:** to shake or move with a slight trembling motion

3**quiver** *n* **:** the act or action of quivering **:** TREMOR

qui vive \kē-ˈvēv\ *n* [F *qui-vive,* fr. *qui vive ?* long live who ?, challenge of a French sentry] **1 :** CHALLENGE **2 :** ALERT, LOOKOUT — used in the phrase *on the qui vive*

qui·xote \ˈkwik-sət, kē-ˈ(h)ōt-ē\ *n, often cap* [Don *Quixote*] **:** a quixotic person — **quix·o·tism** \ˈkwik-sə-ˌtiz-əm\ *n* — **quix·o·try** \-sə-trē\ *n*

quix·ot·ic \kwik-ˈsät-ik\ *adj* [Don *Quixote,* hero of the novel *Don Quixote de la Mancha* (1605, 1615) by Cervantes] **:** idealistic to an impractical degree; *esp* **:** marked by rash lofty romantic ideas or extravagantly chivalrous action — **quix·ot·i·cal** \-i-kəl\ *adj* — **quix·ot·i·cal·ly** \-i-k(ə-)lē\ *adv*

1**quiz** \ˈkwiz\ *n, pl* **quiz·zes** [origin unknown] **1 :** an eccentric person **2 :** PRACTICAL JOKE **3 :** the act or action of quizzing; *specif* **:** a short oral or written test

2**quiz** *vt* **quizzed; quiz·zing 1 :** to make fun of **:** MOCK **2 :** to look at inquisitively **3 :** to question closely — **quiz·zer** *n*

quiz·mas·ter \ˈkwiz-ˌmas-tər\ *n* **:** one who puts the questions to contestants in a quiz show

quiz show *n* **:** an entertainment program (as on radio or television) in which contestants answer questions — called also *quiz program*

quiz·zi·cal \ˈkwiz-i-kəl\ *adj* **1 :** slightly eccentric **:** ODD **2 :** marked or characterized by bantering or teasing **3 :** INQUISITIVE, QUESTIONING — **quiz·zi·cal·i·ty** \ˌkwiz-ə-ˈkal-ət-ē\ *n* — **quiz·zi·cal·ly** \ˈkwiz-i-k(ə-)lē\ *adv*

quod \ˈkwäd\ *n* [origin unknown] *slang Brit* **:** PRISON

quod·li·bet \ˈkwäd-lə-ˌbet\ *n* [ME, fr. ML *quodlibetum,* fr. L *quodlibet,* neut. of *quilibet* any whatever, fr. *qui* who, what + *libet* it pleases, fr. *libēre* to please — more at WHO, LOVE] **1 :** a philosophical or theological point proposed for disputation; *also* **:** a disputation on such a point **2 :** a whimsical combination of familiar melodies or texts

1**quoin** \ˈk(w)ȯin\ *n* [alter. of 1*coin*] **1 a :** a solid exterior angle (as of a building) usu. distinguished from the adjoining surfaces by material texture, color, size, or projection **b :** one of the blocks forming a quoin **2 :** the keystone or a voussoir of an arch **3 :** a wooden or expandable metal block used by printers to lock up a form within a chase

2**quoin** *vt* **1 :** to equip (a type form) with quoins **2 :** to provide with quoins <~*ed* walls>

1**quoit** \ˈkwāt, ˈk(w)ȯit\ *n* [ME *coite*] **1 :** a flattened ring of iron or circle of rope used in a throwing game **2** *pl but sing in constr* **:** a game in which the quoits are thrown at an upright pin in an attempt to ring the pin or come as near to it as possible

2**quoit** *vt* **:** to throw like a quoit

quon·dam \ˈkwän-dəm, -ˌdam\ *adj* [L, at one time, formerly, fr. *quom, cum* when; akin to L *qui* who — more at WHO] **:** FORMER, SOMETIME <a ~ friend>

Quon·set \ˌkwän(t)-sət, ˌkwän-zət\ *trademark* — used for a prefabricated shelter set on a foundation of bolted steel trusses and built of a semicircular arching roof of corrugated metal insulated with wood fiber

quo·rum \ˈkwōr-əm, ˈkwȯr-\ *n* [ME, quorum of justices of the peace, fr. L, of whom, gen. pl. of *qui* who; fr. the wording of the commission formerly issued to justices of the peace] **1 :** the number usu. a majority of officers or members of a body that when duly assembled is legally competent to transact business **2 :** a select group **3 :** a Mormon body comprising those in the same grade of priesthood

quot *abbr* quotation

quo·ta \ˈkwōt-ə\ *n* [ML, fr. L *quota pars* how great a part] **1 :** a proportional part or share; *esp* **:** the share or proportion assigned to each in a division or to each member of a body **2 :** the number or amount constituting a proportional share

quot·able \ˈkwōt-ə-bəl *also* ˈkōt-\ *adj* **:** fit for or worth quoting

quo·ta·tion \kwō-ˈtā-shən *also* kō-\ *n* **1 :** something that is quoted; *esp* **:** a passage referred to, repeated, or adduced **2 a :** the act or process of quoting **b** (1) **:** the naming or publishing of current bids and offers or prices of securities or commodities (2) **:** the bids, offers, or prices so named or published; *esp* **:** the highest bid and lowest offer for a particular security in a given market at a particular time

quotation mark *n* **:** one of a pair of punctuation marks " " or ' ' used chiefly to indicate the beginning and the end of a quotation in which the exact phraseology of another or of a text is directly cited

1**quote** \ˈkwōt *also* ˈkōt\ *vb* **quot·ed; quot·ing** [ML *quotare* to mark the number of, number references, fr. L *quotus* of what number or quantity, fr. *quot* how many, (as) many as; akin to L *qui* who — more at WHO] *vt* **1 a :** to speak or write (a passage) from another usu. with credit acknowledgment **b :** to repeat a passage from esp. in substantiation or illustration **2 :** to cite in illustration <~ cases> **3 a :** to name (the current price or bid-offer spread) of a commodity, stock, or bond **b :** to give exact information on **4 :** to set off by quotation marks ~ *vi* **:** to inform a hearer or reader that matter following is quoted

syn QUOTE, CITE, REPEAT *shared meaning element* **:** to say or write again something already said or written by another

2**quote** *n* **1 :** QUOTATION **2 :** QUOTATION MARK — often used orally to indicate the beginning of a direct quotation

quoth \(ˈ)kwōth\ *vb past* [ME, past of *quethen* to say, fr. OE *cwethan;* akin to OHG *quedan* to say] *archaic* **:** SAID — used chiefly in the first and third persons with a postpositive subject

quotha \ˈkwō-thə\ *interj* [alter. of *quoth he*] *archaic* — used esp. to express surprise or contempt

quo·tid·i·an \kwō-ˈtid-ē-ən\ *adj* [ME *cotidian,* fr. MF, fr. L *quotidianus, cotidianus,* fr. *quotidie* every day, fr. *quot* (as) many as + *dies* day — more at DEITY] **1 :** occurring every day <~ fever> **2 a :** belonging to each day **:** EVERYDAY <~ routine> **b :** COMMONPLACE, ORDINARY <~ drabness> ***syn*** see DAILY

quo·tient \ˈkwō-shənt\ *n* [ME *quocient,* modif. of L *quotiens* how many times, fr. *quot* how many] **1 :** the number resulting from the division of one number by another **2 :** the numerical ratio usu. multiplied by 100 between a test score and a measurement on which that score might be expected largely to depend **3 :** QUOTA, SHARE

quotient group *n* **:** a group whose elements are the cosets of a normal subgroup of a given group

quotient ring *n* **:** a ring whose elements are the cosets of an ideal in a given ring

quo war·ran·to \ˌkwō-wə-ˈränt(ˌ)ō-, -ˈrant-; (ˈ)kwō-ˈwȯr-ənt-ˌō, -ˈwär-\ *n* [ML, by what warrant; fr. the wording of the writ] **1 a :** an English writ formerly requiring a person to show by what authority he exercises a public office, franchise, or liberty **b :** a legal proceeding for a like purpose begun by an information **2 :** the legal action begun by a quo warranto

Qur·'an *or* **Qur·an** \kə-ˈran, -ˈrän; ku̇(ə)r-ˈan, -ˈän\ *var of* KORAN

qursh *n, pl* **qursh** \ˈku̇(ə)rsh\ [Ar. *qirsh*] — see *riyal* at MONEY table

qv *abbr* [L *quod vide*] which see

qy *abbr* query

1**r** \ˈär\ *n, pl* **r's** *or* **rs** \ˈärz\ *often cap, often attrib* **1 a :** the 18th letter of the English alphabet **b :** a graphic representation of this letter **c :** a speech counterpart of orthographic *r* **2 :** a graphic device for reproducing the letter *r* **3 :** one designated *r* esp. as the 18th in order or class **4 :** something shaped like the letter R

2**r** *abbr, often cap* **1** rabbi **2** radius **3** rain **4** range **5** Rankine **6** rare **7** real **8** Reaumur **9** red **10** Republican **11** resistance **12** right **13** river **14** roentgen **15** rook **16** rough **17** ruble **18** run **19** rupee

3**r** *symbol* correlation coefficient

1**R** \ˈär\ *adj* [restricted] *of a motion picture* **:** of such a nature that admission is restricted to persons over a specified age (as 17) unless accompanied by a parent or guardian — compare G, PG, X

2**R** *symbol* **1** radical — used esp. of a univalent hydrocarbon radical **2** recipe **3** registered trademark — often enclosed in a circle

1**Ra** \ˈrä, ˈrȯ\ *n* [Egypt *rʻ*] **:** the Egyptian sun-god and chief deity

2**Ra** *symbol* radium

RA *abbr* **1** regular army **2** right ascension **3** Royal Academician; Royal Academy

RAAF *abbr* Royal Australian Air Force

ra·ba·to \rə-ˈbät-(ˌ)ō\ *n, pl* **-tos** [modif. of MF *rabat,* lit., act of turning down] **:** a wide lace-edged collar of the early 17th century often stiffened to stand high at the back

1**rab·bet** \ˈrab-ət\ *n* [ME *rabet,* fr. MF *rabat* act of beating down, fr. OF *rabattre* to beat down, reduce — more at REBATE] **:** a channel, groove, or recess cut out of the edge or face of any body; *esp* **:** one intended to receive another member (as a panel)

2**rabbet** *vt* **1 :** to cut a rabbet in **2 :** to unite the edges of in a rabbet joint ~ *vi* **:** to become joined by a rabbet

rabbet joint *n* **:** a joint formed by fitting together rabbeted boards or timbers

rab·bi \ˈrab-ˌī\ *n* [LL, fr. Gk *rhabbi,* fr. Heb *rabbī* my master, fr. *rabh* master + *-ī* my] **1 :** MASTER, TEACHER — used by Jews as a term of address **2 :** a Jew qualified to expound and apply the halakah and other Jewish law **3 :** a Jew trained and ordained for professional religious leadership; *specif* **:** the official leader of a Jewish congregation

rab·bin \ˈrab-ən\ *n* [F] **:** RABBI

rab·bin·ate \ˈrab-ə-nət, -ˌnāt\ *n* **1 :** the office or tenure of a rabbi **2 :** the whole body of rabbis

rab·bin·ic \rə-ˈbin-ik, ra-\ *or* **rab·bin·i·cal** \-i-kəl\ *adj* **1 :** of or relating to rabbis or their writings **2 :** of or preparing for the rabbinate **3 :** comprising or belonging to any of several sets of Hebrew characters simpler than the square Hebrew letters — **rab·bin·i·cal·ly** \-i-k(ə-)lē\ *adv*

Rabbinic Hebrew *n* **:** the Hebrew used esp. by medieval rabbis

rab·bin·ism \ˈrab-ə-ˌniz-əm\ *n* **:** rabbinic teachings and traditions

1**rab·bit** \ˈrab-ət\ *n, pl* **rabbit** *or* **rabbits** *often attrib* [ME *rabet*] **1 a :** a small long-eared mammal (*Oryctolagus cuniculus*) that is related to the ordinary hares but differs from them in producing naked young and in its burrowing habits **b :** HARE **2 :** the pelt of a rabbit **3 :** WELSH RABBIT **4 a :** a figure of a rabbit sped mechanically along the edge of a dog track as an object of pursuit **b :** a runner on a track team who sets a fast pace for a teammate in the first part of a long-distance race — **rab·bity** \-ē\ *adj*

2**rabbit** *vi* **:** to hunt rabbits — **rab·bit·er** *n*

rabbit brush *n* **:** any of several low branching shrubs (genus *Chrysothamnus* and esp. *C. nauseosus*) of the alkali plains of western No. America that are characterized by linear entire leaves and clusters of golden yellow flowers

rabbit ears *n pl* **:** an indoor dipole television antenna consisting of two usu. extensible rods connected to a base to form a V shape

rab·bit-eye \ˈrab-ət-ˌī\ *n* **:** a blueberry (*Vaccinium ashei*) of the southeastern U.S.

rabbit fever *n* **:** TULAREMIA

rabbit punch *n* **:** a short chopping blow delivered to the back of the neck or the base of the skull

rab·bit·ry \ˈrab-ə-trē\ *n, pl* **-ries :** a place where domestic rabbits are kept; *also* **:** a rabbit-raising enterprise

1**rabble** \ˈrab-əl\ *n* [ME *rabel* pack of animals] **1 :** a disorganized or confused collection of things **2 a :** a disorganized or disorderly crowd of people **:** MOB **b :** the lowest class of people

2**rabble** *vt* **rab·bled; rab·bling** \-(ə-)liŋ\ **:** to insult or assault by or as a mob

3**rabble** *n* [F *râble* fire shovel, fr. ML *rotabulum,* alter. of L *rutabulum,* fr. *rutus,* pp. of *ruere* to dig up — more at RUG] **:** an iron bar with the end bent for use like a rake in puddling iron; *also* **:** a similar device used in a melting, refining, or roasting furnace

4**rabble** *vt* **rab·bled; rab·bling** \-(ə-)liŋ\ **:** to stir or skim with a rabble — **rab·bler** \ˈrab-(ə-)lər\ *n*

rab·ble·ment \ˈrab-əl-mənt\ *n* **1 :** RABBLE **2 :** DISTURBANCE

rab·ble–rous·er \ˈrab-əl-ˌrau̇-zər\ *n* **:** one that stirs up (as to hatred or violence) the masses of the people **:** DEMAGOGUE

Ra·be·lai·sian \ˌrab-ə-ˈlā-zhən, -zē-ən\ *adj* **1 :** of, relating to, or characteristic of Rabelais or his works **2 :** marked by gross robust humor, extravagance of caricature, or bold naturalism

Ra·bi \ˈrəb-ē\ *n* [Ar *rabīʻ*] **:** either of two months of the Muhammadan year: **a :** the 3d month **b :** the 4th month — see MONTH table

ra·bic \ˈrā-bik\ *adj* **:** of or relating to rabies

ra·bid \ˈrab-əd *also* ˈrā-bəd\ *adj* [L *rabidus* mad, fr. *rabere*] **1 a :** extremely violent **:** FURIOUS **b :** going to extreme lengths in expressing or pursuing a feeling, interest, or opinion **2 :** affected with rabies — **ra·bid·i·ty** \rə-ˈbid-ət-ē, ra-, rā-\ *n* — **ra·bid·ly** \ˈrab-əd-lē *also* ˈrā-bəd-\ *adv* — **ra·bid·ness** *n*

ra·bies \ˈrā-bēz\ *n, pl* **rabies** [NL, fr. L, madness, fr. *rabere* to rave — more at RAGE] **:** an acute virus disease of the nervous system of warm-blooded animals usu. transmitted through the bite of a rabid animal

rac·coon \ra-ˈkün *also* rə-\ *n, pl* **raccoon** *or* **raccoons** [*ärähkun* (in some Algonquian language of Virginia)] **1 a :** a small flesh-eating mammal (*Procyon lotor*) of No. America that is chiefly gray, has a bushy ringed tail, and lives chiefly in trees **b :** the pelt of this animal **2 :** any of several animals resembling or related to the raccoon

raccoon 1a

1**race** \ˈrās\ *n* [ME *ras,* fr. ON *rās;* akin to OE *rǣs* rush, L *rorarii* skirmishers, Gk *erōē* rush] **1** *chiefly Scot* **:** the act of running **2 a :** a strong or rapid current of water through a narrow channel **b :** a heavy or choppy sea **c :** a watercourse used industrially **d :** the current flowing in such a course **3 a :** a set course or duration of time **b :** the course of life **4 a :** a contest of speed **b** *pl* **:** a meeting in which several races (as for horses) are run **c :** a contest or rivalry involving progress toward a goal <pennant ~> **5 :** a track or channel in which something rolls or slides; *specif* **:** a groove (as for the balls) in a bearing **6 :** SLIPSTREAM

2**race** *vb* **raced; rac·ing** *vi* **1 :** to compete in a race **2 :** to go or move at top speed or out of control **3 :** to revolve too fast under a diminished load ~ *vt* **1 :** to engage in a race with **2 a :** to enter in a race **b :** to drive at high speed **c :** to transport or propel at maximum speed **3 :** to speed (as an engine) without a working load or with the transmission disengaged

3**race** *n* [MF, generation, fr. OIt *razza*] **1 :** a breeding stock of animals **2 a :** a family, tribe, people, or nation belonging to the same stock **b :** a class or kind of people unified by community of interests, habits, or characteristics <the English ~> **3 a :** an actually or potentially interbreeding group within a species; *also* **:** a taxonomic category (as a subspecies) representing such a group **b :** BREED **c :** a division of mankind possessing traits that are transmissible by descent and sufficient to characterize it as a distinct human type **4** *obs* **:** inherited temperament or disposition **5 :** distinctive flavor, taste, or strength

race·course \ˈrā-ˌskō(ə)rs, -ˌskȯ(ə)rs\ *n* **1 :** a course for racing **2 :** RACEWAY 1

race·horse \ˈrās-ˌhȯ(ə)rs\ *n* **:** a horse bred or kept for racing

ra·ce·mate \rā-ˈsē-ˌmāt, rə-; ˈras-ə-\ *n* **1 :** a salt or ester of racemic acid **2 :** a racemic compound or mixture

ra·ceme \rā-ˈsēm, rə-\ *n* [L *racemus* bunch of grapes] **:** a simple inflorescence (as in the lily-of-the-valley) in which the elongated axis bears flowers on short stems in succession toward the apex — see INFLORESCENCE illustration

ra·ce·mic \-ˈsē-mik\ *adj* **:** of, relating to, or constituting a compound or mixture that is composed of equal amounts of dextrorotatory and levorotatory forms of the same compound and is optically inactive

ra·ce·mi·za·tion \rā-ˌsē-mə-ˈzā-shən, rə-; ˌras-ə-mə-\ *n* **:** the action or process of changing from an optically active compound into a racemic compound or mixture — **ra·ce·mize** \rā-ˈsē-ˌmīz, rə-; ˈras-ə-\ *vb*

ra·ce·mose \ˈras-ə-ˌmōs; rā-ˈsē-, rə-\ *adj* [L *racemosus* full of clusters, fr. *racemus*] **:** having or growing in the form of a raceme

racemose gland *n* **:** a compound gland of freely branching ducts that end in acini

rac·er \ˈrā-sər\ *n* **1 :** one that races or is used for racing **2 :** any of various active American snakes (genus *Coluber* and *Mastigophis*); *esp* **:** BLACK RACER

race riot *n* **:** a riot caused by racial dissensions or hatreds

race runner *n* **:** a No. American lizard (*Cnemidophorus sexlineatus*) that moves swiftly

race·track \ˈrā-ˌstrak\ *n* **:** a usu. oval course on which races are run

race·track·er \ˈrā-ˌstrak-ər\ *n* **:** one who frequents a racetrack

race·way \ˈrā-ˌswā\ *n* **1 :** a canal for a current of water **2 :** a channel for loosely holding electrical wires in buildings **3 :** 1RACE 5 **4 :** a course for racing; *esp* **:** a track for harness racing

rach·et \ˈrach-ət\ *var of* RATCHET

rachi- *or* **rachio-** *comb form* [Gk *rhachi-,* fr. *rhachis;* akin to Gk *rhachos* thorn, Lith *ražas* stubble] **:** spine <*rachi*odont>

ra·chi·odont \ˈrā-kē-ō-ˌdänt, ˈrak-ē-\ *adj* **:** having gular teeth that are modified vertebral spines <a ~ snake>

ra·chis \ˈrā-kəs, ˈrak-əs\ *n, pl* **ra·chis·es** *also* **ra·chi·des** \ˈrak-ə-ˌdēz, ˈrā-kə-\ [NL *rachid-, rachis,* modif. of Gk *rhachis*] **1 :** SPINAL COLUMN **2 :** an axial structure: as **a** (1) **:** the elongated axis of an inflorescence (2) **:** an extension of the petiole of a compound leaf that bears the leaflets **b :** the distal part of the shaft of a feather that bears the web

ra·chit·ic \rə-ˈkit-ik\ *adj* **:** RICKETY

ra·chi·tis \rə-ˈkit-əs\ *n* [NL, fr. Gk *rhachitis* disease of the spine, fr. *rhachis*] **:** RICKETS

ra·cial \ˈrā-shəl\ *adj* **1 :** of, relating to, or based on a race **2 :** existing or occurring between races — **ra·cial·ly** \-shə-lē\ *adv*

ra·cial·ism \ˈrā-shə-ˌliz-əm\ *n* **1 :** racial prejudice or discrimination **2 :** RACISM 1 — **ra·cial·ist** \-ləst\ *n* — **ra·cial·is·tic** \ˌrā-shə-ˈlis-tik\ *adj*

rac·ing \ˈrā-siŋ\ *n* **:** the sport or profession of engaging in or holding races

racing form *n* **:** an information sheet giving pertinent data about horse races

rac·ism \ˈrā-ˌsiz-əm *also* -ˌshiz-\ *n* **1 :** a belief that race is the primary determinant of human traits and capacities and that racial differences produce an inherent superiority of a particular race **2 :** RACIALISM 1 — **rac·ist** \-səst *also* -shəst\ *n*

1**rack** \ˈrak\ *n* [ME *rak,* prob. of Scand origin; akin to Sw dial. *rak* wreck; akin to OE *wrecan* to drive — more at WREAK] **:** a wind-driven mass of high often broken clouds

[2]**rack** *vi* : to fly or scud in high wind
[3]**rack** *n* [ME, prob. fr. MD *rec* framework; akin to OE *reccan* to stretch, Gk *oregein* — more at RIGHT] **1** : a framework for holding fodder for livestock **2** : an instrument of torture on which a body is stretched **3 a** (1) : a cause of anguish or pain (2) : acute suffering **b** : the action of straining or wrenching **4** : a framework, stand, or grating on or in which articles are placed **5** : a frame placed in a stream to stop fish and floating or suspended matter **6 a** : a bar with teeth on one face for gearing with a pinion or worm gear **b** : a notched bar used as a ratchet to engage with a pawl, click, or detent **7** : a pair of antlers **8** : a triangular frame used to set up the balls in a pool game; *also* : the balls as set up — **on the rack** : under great mental or emotional stress

rack 6a with pinion

[4]**rack** *vt* **1** : to torture on the rack **2** : to cause to suffer torture, pain, or anguish **3 a** : to stretch or strain violently <~*ed* his brains> **b** : to raise (rents) oppressively **c** : to harass or oppress with high rents or extortions **4** : to work or treat (material) on a rack **5** : to work by a rack and pinion or worm so as to extend or contract <~ a camera> **6** : to seize (as parallel ropes of a tackle) together **7** : to place (as pool balls) in a rack ~ *vi* : to become forced out of shape or out of plumb *syn* see AFFLICT — **rack·er** *n*
[5]**rack** *vt* [ME *rakken,* fr. OProv *arraca*] : to draw off (as wine) from the lees
[6]**rack** *vi* [prob. alter. of [1]*rock*] *of a horse* : to go at a rack
[7]**rack** *n* : either of two gaits of a horse: **a** : PACE 4b **b** : a fast showy usu. artificial 4-beat gait
[8]**rack** *n* [perh. fr. [3]*rack*] **1** : the neck and spine of a forequarter of veal, pork, or esp. mutton **2** : the rib section of a foresaddle of lamb used for chops or as a roast — see LAMB **illustration**
[9]**rack** *n* [alter. of *wrack*] : DESTRUCTION <~ and ruin>
[1]**rack·et** *also* **rac·quet** \ˈrak-ət\ *n* [MF *raquette,* fr. Ar *rāhah* palm of the hand] **1 a** : a lightweight implement that consists of a netting (as of nylon) stretched in an oval open frame with a handle attached and that is used for striking the ball in any of various games (as tennis, racquets, or badminton) **b** : a paddle used in table tennis **2** *usu* **racquets** *pl but sing in constr* : a game for two or four players with ball and racket on a four-walled court
[2]**racket** *n* [prob. imit.] **1** : confused clattering noise : CLAMOR **2 a** : social whirl or excitement **b** : the strain of exciting or trying experiences **3 a** : a fraudulent scheme, enterprise, or activity **b** : a usu. illegitimate enterprise made workable by bribery or intimidation **c** : an easy and lucrative means of livelihood **d** *slang* : OCCUPATION, BUSINESS
[3]**racket** *vi* **1** : to engage in active social life **2** : to move with or make a racket
[1]**rack·e·teer** \ˌrak-ə-ˈti(ə)r\ *n* : one who extorts money or advantages by threats of violence, by blackmail, or by unlawful interference with business or employment
[2]**racketeer** *vi* : to carry on a racket ~ *vt* : to practice extortion on
rack·ety \ˈrak-ət-ē\ *adj* **1** : NOISY **2** : FLASHY, ROWDY **3** : RICKETY
rack·le \ˈrak-əl\ *adj* [ME *rakel*] *chiefly Scot* : IMPETUOUS, HEADSTRONG
rack railway *n* : a railway having between its rails a rack that meshes with a gear wheel or pinion of the locomotive for traction on steep grades
rack–rent *vt* : to subject to rack rent
rack rent *n* [[4]*rack*] **1** : an excessive or unreasonably high rent **2** *Brit* : the highest rent that can be earned on a property
rack–rent·er \ˈrak-ˈrent-ər\ *n* : one that pays or exacts rack rent
rack up *vt* : SCORE <*racked up* 30 points in the first half>
ra·clette \ra-ˈklet, rä-\ *n* [F, fr. *racler* to scrape] : a Swiss dish consisting of cheese melted over a fire and then scraped onto bread or boiled potatoes; *also* : the cheese used in this dish
ra·con \ˈrā-ˌkän\ *n* [*radar beacon*] : RADAR BEACON
ra·con·teur \ˌrak-ˌän-ˈtər, -ən-\ *n* [F, fr. MF, fr. *raconter* to tell, fr. OF, fr. *re-* + *aconter, acompter* to tell, count — more at ACCOUNT] : one who excels in telling anecdotes
ra·coon *var of* RACCOON
[1]**racy** \ˈrā-sē\ *adj* **rac·i·er; -est** [[3]*race*] **1** : having the distinctive quality of something in its original or most characteristic form **2 a** : full of zest or vigor **b** : having a strongly marked quality : PIQUANT <a ~ flavor> **c** : RISQUÉ, SUGGESTIVE *syn* see PUNGENT — **rac·i·ly** \ˈrā-sə-lē\ *adv* — **rac·i·ness** \-sē-nəs\ *n*
[2]**racy** *adj* **rac·i·er; -est** : having a body fitted for racing : long-bodied and lean
[1]**rad** \ˈrad\ *n* [*radiation*] : a unit of absorbed dose of ionizing radiation equal to an energy of 100 ergs per gram of irradiated material
[2]**rad** *abbr* **1** radical **2** radio **3** radius **4** radix
Rad *abbr* Radnorshire
ra·dar \ˈrā-ˌdär\ *n, often attrib* [*ra*dio *d*etecting *a*nd *r*anging] : a radio device or system for locating an object by means of ultrahigh-frequency radio waves reflected from the object and received, observed, and analyzed by the receiving part of the device in such a way that characteristics (as distance and direction) of the object may be determined
radar astronomy *n* : astronomy dealing with investigations of celestial bodies in the solar system by comparing the characteristics of a reflected radar wave with the characteristics of one transmitted from the earth
radar beacon *n* : a radar transmitter that upon receiving a radar signal emits a signal which reinforces the normal reflected signal or which introduces a code into the reflected signal esp. for identification purposes
ra·dar·scope \ˈrā-ˌdär-ˌskōp\ *n* [*radar* + oscillo*scope*] : the oscilloscope or screen serving as the visual indicator in a radar receiver
radar telescope *n* : a radar transmitter-receiver with an antenna for use in radar astronomy
[1]**rad·dle** \ˈrad-ᵊl\ *n* [prob. alter. of *ruddle*] : RED OCHER
[2]**raddle** *vt* **rad·dled; rad·dling** \ˈrad-liŋ, -ᵊl-iŋ\ : to mark or paint with raddle
[3]**raddle** *vt* **rad·dled; rad·dling** \ˈrad-liŋ, -ᵊl-iŋ\ [E dial. *raddle* (supple stick interwoven with others as in making a fence)] : to twist together : INTERWEAVE
rad·dled \ˈrad-ᵊld\ *adj* [origin unknown] **1** : being in a state of confusion : lacking composure **2** : broken down : WORN
radi- *or* **radio-** *comb form* [F, fr. L *radius* ray] **1 a** : radial : radially <*radio*symmetrical> **b** : radial and <*radio*bicipital> **2 a** : radiant energy : radiation <*radio*active> <*radi*opaque> **b** : radioactive <*radio*element> **c** : radium : X rays <*radio*therapy> **d** : radioactive isotopes esp. as produced artifically <*radio*carbon> **e** : radio <*radio*telegraphy>
[1]**ra·di·al** \ˈrād-ē-əl\ *adj* [ML *radialis,* fr. L *radius* ray] **1** : arranged or having parts arranged like rays <the ~ form of a starfish> **2 a** : relating to, placed like, or moving along a radius **b** : characterized by divergence from a center **3** : of, relating to, or adjacent to a bodily radius <the thumb is on the ~ aspect of the hand> **4** : developing uniformly around a central axis <~ cleavage of an egg> — **ra·di·al·ly** \-ē-ə-lē\ *adv*
[2]**radial** *n* **1 a** : a radial part **b** : RAY **2** : a body part (as an artery) lying near or following the course of the radius **3** : a pneumatic tire in which the ply cords that extend to the beads are laid at approximately 90 degrees to the center line of the tread — called also *radial-ply tire, radial tire*
ra·di·a·le \ˌrād-ē-ˈal-(ˌ)ē, -ˈāl-, -ˈäl-\ *n, pl* **-lia** \-ē-ə\ [NL, fr. ML, neut. of *radialis*] : a bone or cartilage of the carpus that articulates with the radius; *specif* : the navicular in man
radial engine *n* : a usu. internal-combustion engine with cylinders arranged radially like the spokes of a wheel
radial symmetry *n* : the condition of having similar parts regularly arranged around a central axis — **radially symmetrical** *adj*
ra·di·an \ˈrād-ē-ən\ *n* : a unit of plane angular measurement that is equal to the angle at the center of a circle subtended by an arc equal in length to the radius
ra·di·ance \ˈrād-ē-ən(t)s\ *n* **1** : the quality or state of being radiant **2** : a deep pink **3** : the flux density of radiant energy per unit solid angle and per unit projected area of radiating surface
ra·di·an·cy \-ən-sē\ *n* : RADIANCE
[1]**ra·di·ant** \ˈrād-ē-ənt\ *adj* **1 a** : radiating rays or reflecting beams of light **b** : vividly bright and shining : GLOWING **2** : marked by or expressive of love, confidence, or happiness **3 a** : emitted or transmitted by radiation **b** : emitting or relating to radiant heat **4** : of, relating to, or exhibiting biological radiation *syn* see BRIGHT — **ra·di·ant·ly** *adv*
[2]**radiant** *n* : something that radiates: as **a** : a point in the heavens at which the visible parallel paths of meteors appear to meet when traced backward **b** : a point or object from which light emanates **c** : the part of a gas or electric heater that becomes incandescent
radiant energy *n* : energy traveling as a wave motion; *specif* : the energy of electromagnetic waves
radiant flux *n* : the rate of emission or transmission of radiant energy
radiant heat *n* : heat transmitted by radiation as contrasted with that transmitted by conduction or convection <*radiant heat* from the sun>
radiant heating *n* : PANEL HEATING
[1]**ra·di·ate** \ˈrād-ē-ˌāt\ *vb* **-at·ed; -at·ing** [L *radiatus,* pp. of *radiare,* fr. *radius* ray] *vi* **1** : to send out rays : shine brightly **2 a** : to issue in rays **b** : to evolve by radiation **3** : to proceed in a direct line from or toward a center ~ *vt* **1** : to send out in rays **2** : IRRADIATE, ILLUMINATE **3** : to spread abroad or around as if from a center
[2]**ra·di·ate** \ˈrād-ē-ət, -ē-ˌāt\ *adj* : having rays or radial parts: as **a** : having ray flowers **b** : characterized by radial symmetry : radially symmetrical — **ra·di·ate·ly** *adv*
ra·di·a·tion \ˌrād-ē-ˈā-shən\ *n* **1 a** : the action or process of radiating **b** (1) : the process of emitting radiant energy in the form of waves or particles (2) : the combined processes of emission, transmission, and absorption of radiant energy **2 a** : something that is radiated **b** : energy radiated in the form of waves or particles **3** : radial arrangement **4** : biological evolution in a group of organisms that is characterized by spreading into different environments and by divergence of structure **5** : RADIATOR — **ra·di·a·tion·al** \-shnəl, -shən-ᵊl\ *adj* — **ra·di·a·tion·less** \-shən-ləs\ *adj* — **ra·di·a·tive** \ˈrād-ē-ˌāt-iv\ *adj*
radiation sickness *n* : sickness that results from exposure to radiation and is commonly marked by fatigue, nausea, vomiting, loss of teeth and hair, and in more severe cases by damage to blood-forming tissue with decrease in red and white blood cells and with bleeding
ra·di·a·tor \ˈrād-ē-ˌāt-ər\ *n* : one that radiates: as **a** : any of various devices (as a nest of pipes or tubes) for heating external objects or cooling internal substances **b** : a transmitting antenna
[1]**rad·i·cal** \ˈrad-i-kəl\ *adj* [ME, fr. LL *radicalis,* fr. L *radic-, radix* root — more at ROOT] **1** : of, relating to, or proceeding from a root: as **a** (1) : of or growing from the root of a plant <~ tubers> (2) : growing from the base of a stem, from a rootlike stem, or from a stem that does not rise above the ground <~ leaves> **b** : of, relating to, or constituting a linguistic root **c** : of or relating to a mathematical root **d** : designed to remove the root of a disease or all diseased tissue <~ surgery> **2** : of or relating to the origin : FUNDAMENTAL **3 a** : marked by a considerable departure from the usual or traditional : EXTREME **b** : tending or disposed to

make extreme changes in existing views, habits, conditions, or institutions **c :** of, relating to, or constituting a political group associated with views, practices, and policies of extreme change **d :** advocating extreme measures to retain or restore a political state of affairs <the ~ right> — **rad·i·cal·ness** *n*

2radical *n* **1 a :** a root part **b :** a basic principle : FOUNDATION **2 a :** ROOT 6 **b :** a sound or letter belonging to a radical **3 :** one who is radical **4 a :** a single replaceable atom of the reactive atomic form of an element **b :** a group of atoms that is replaceable by a single atom, that is capable of remaining unchanged during a series of reactions, or that may show a definite transitory existence in the course of a reaction **5 a :** RADICAL EXPRESSION **b :** RADICAL SIGN

radical expression *n* **:** a mathematical expression involving radical signs

rad·i·cal·ism \ˈrad-i-kə-ˌliz-əm\ *n* **1 :** the quality or state of being radical **2 :** the doctrines or principles of radicals

rad·i·cal·ize \-kə-ˌlīz\ *vt* **-ized; -iz·ing :** to make radical esp. in politics — **rad·i·cal·iza·tion** \ˌrad-i-kə-lə-ˈzā-shən\ *n*

rad·i·cal·ly \ˈrad-i-k(ə-)lē\ *adv* **1 :** in origin or essence **2 :** in a radical or extreme manner

radical sign *n* **:** the sign √ placed before an expression to denote that the square root is to be extracted or that some other root is to be extracted when a corresponding index is placed over the sign

rad·i·cand \ˌrad-ə-ˈkand\ *n* [L *radicandum,* neut. of *radicandus,* gerundive of *radicari*] **:** the quantity under a radical sign

rad·i·cate \ˈrad-ə-ˌkāt\ *vt* **-cat·ed; -cat·ing** [ME *radicaten,* fr. L *radicatus,* pp. of *radicari* to take root, fr. *radic-, radix* root] **:** to cause to take root

radices *pl of* RADIX

rad·i·cle \ˈrad-i-kəl\ *n* [L *radicula,* dim. of *radic-, radix*] **1 :** the lower part of the axis of a plant embryo or seedling: **a :** the embryonic root of a seedling **b :** HYPOCOTYL **c :** the hypocotyl and the root together **2 :** the rootlike beginning of an anatomical vessel or part **3 :** RADICAL — **ra·dic·u·lar** \ra-ˈdik-yə-lər\ *adj*

radii *pl of* RADIUS

1ra·dio \ˈrād-ē-ˌō\ *n, pl* **ra·di·os** [short for *radiotelegraphy*] **1 a :** the wireless transmission and reception of electric impulses or signals by means of electric waves **b :** the use of these waves for the wireless transmission of electric impulses into which sound is converted **2 :** a radio message **3 :** a radio receiving set **4 a :** a radio transmitting station **b :** a radio broadcasting organization **c :** the radio broadcasting industry **d :** communication by radio

2radio *adj* **1 :** of, relating to, or operated by radiant energy **2 :** of or relating to electric currents or phenomena of frequencies between about 15,000 and 10^{11} per second **3 a :** of, relating to, or used in radio or a radio set **b :** specializing in radio or associated with the radio industry **c** (1) **:** transmitted by radio (2) **:** making or participating in radio broadcasts **d :** controlled or directed by radio

3radio *vt* **1 :** to send or communicate by radio **2 :** to send a radio message to ~ *vi* **:** to send or communicate something by radio

ra·dio·ac·tive \ˌrād-ē-ō-ˈak-tiv\ *adj* [ISV] **:** of, caused by, or exhibiting radioactivity — **ra·dio·ac·tive·ly** *adv*

ra·dio·ac·tiv·i·ty \-ak-ˈtiv-ət-ē\ *n* [ISV] **:** the property possessed by some elements (as uranium) of spontaneously emitting alpha or beta rays and sometimes also gamma rays by the disintegration of the nuclei of atoms

radio astronomy *n* **:** astronomy dealing with electromagnetic radiations of radio frequency received from outside the earth's atmosphere

ra·dio·au·to·graph \ˌrād-ē-ō-ˈȯt-ə-ˌgraf\ *n* **:** AUTORADIOGRAPH — **ra·dio·au·to·graph·ic** \-ˌȯt-ə-ˈgraf-ik\ *adj* — **ra·dio·au·tog·ra·phy** \-ō-ȯ-ˈtäg-rə-fē\ *n*

radio beacon *n* **:** a radio transmitting station that transmits special radio signals for use (as on a landing field) in determining the direction or position of those receiving them

ra·dio·bi·ol·o·gy \ˌrād-ē-ō-bī-ˈäl-ə-jē\ *n* **:** a branch of biology dealing with the interaction of biological systems and radiant energy or radioactive materials — **ra·dio·bi·o·log·i·cal** \-ˌbī-ə-ˈläj-i-kəl\ *or* **ra·dio·bi·o·log·ic** \-ik\ *adj* — **ra·dio·bi·o·log·i·cal·ly** \-i-k(ə-)lē\ *adv* — **ra·dio·bi·ol·o·gist** \-bī-ˈäl-ə-jəst\ *n*

ra·dio·broad·cast \-ˈbrȯd-ˌkast\ *vt* **:** to broadcast (as music) by radio — **ra·dio·broad·cast·er** *n*

ra·dio·broad·cast·ing *n* **:** the act or process of radiobroadcasting something **:** an instance of such broadcasting

radio car *n* **:** an automobile equipped with radio communication

ra·dio·car·bon \ˌrād-ē-ō-ˈkär-bən\ *n* [ISV] **:** radioactive carbon; *esp* **:** CARBON 14

ra·dio·cast \ˈrād-ē-ō-ˌkast\ *vt* [*radio-* + broad*cast*] **:** RADIOBROADCAST — **ra·dio·cast·er** *n*

ra·dio·chem·is·try \ˌrād-ē-ō-ˈkem-ə-strē\ *n* **:** a branch of chemistry dealing with radioactive substances and phenomena including tracer studies — **ra·dio·chem·i·cal** \-ˈkem-i-kəl\ *adj* — **ra·dio·chem·i·cal·ly** \-k(ə-)lē\ *adv* — **ra·dio·chem·ist** \-ˈkem-əst\ *n*

radio compass *n* **:** a direction finder used in navigation

ra·dio·ecol·o·gy \ˌrād-ē-ō-i-ˈkäl-ə-jē\ *n* **:** the study of the interaction of ecological communities and radiations or radioactive substances — **ra·dio·eco·log·i·cal** \-ˌē-kə-ˈläj-i-kəl, -ˌek-ə-\ *adj* — **ra·dio·ecol·o·gist** \-i-ˈkäl-ə-jəst\ *n*

ra·dio·el·e·ment \-ˈel-ə-mənt\ *n* [ISV] **:** a radioactive element

radio frequency *n* **:** an electromagnetic wave frequency intermediate between audio frequencies and infrared frequencies used esp. in radio and television transmission

radio galaxy *n* **:** a galaxy containing a source from which radio energy is detected

ra·dio·gen·ic \ˌrād-ē-ō-ˈjen-ik\ *adj* **:** produced by radioactivity

ra·dio·gram \ˈrād-ē-ō-ˌgram\ *n* **1 :** RADIOGRAPH **2 :** a message transmitted by radiotelegraphy **3** *Brit* **:** a combined radio receiver and record player

1ra·dio·graph \-ˌgraf\ *n* **:** a picture produced on a sensitive surface by a form of radiation other than light; *specif* **:** an X ray or gamma ray photograph — **ra·dio·graph·ic** \ˌrād-ē-ō-ˈgraf-ik\ *adj* —

RADIO FREQUENCIES

CLASS	ABBREVIATION	RANGE
extremely low frequency	ELF	30 to 300 hertz
voice frequency	VF	300 to 3000 hertz
very low frequency	VLF	3 to 30 kilohertz
low frequency	LF	30 to 300 kilohertz
medium frequency	MF	300 to 3000 kilohertz
high frequency	HF	3 to 30 megahertz
very high frequency	VHF	30 to 300 megahertz
ultrahigh frequency	UHF	300 to 3000 megahertz
superhigh frequency	SHF	3 to 30 gigahertz
extremely high frequency	EHF	30 to 300 gigahertz

ra·dio·graph·i·cal·ly \-i-k(ə-)lē\ *adv*

2radiograph *vt* **:** to make a radiograph of

3radiograph *vt* [*radio-* + tele*graph*] **:** to send a radiogram to

ra·di·og·ra·phy \ˌrād-ē-ˈäg-rə-fē\ *n* [ISV] **:** the art, act, or process of making radiographs

ra·dio·im·mu·no·as·say \ˈrād-ē-ˌō-im-yə-nō-ˈas-ˌā, -im-ˌyü-, -a-ˈsā\ *n* **:** immunoassay of a substance (as insulin) that has been radioactively labeled

ra·dio·iso·tope \ˌrād-ē-ō-ˈī-sə-ˌtōp\ *n* [ISV] **:** a radioactive isotope — **ra·dio·iso·to·pic** \-ˌī-sə-ˈtäp-ik, -ˈtōp-ik\ *adj* — **ra·dio·iso·to·pi·cal·ly** \-i-k(ə-)lē\ *adv*

ra·dio·la·bel \-ˈlā-bəl\ *vt* **:** LABEL 2

ra·di·o·lar·i·an \ˌrād-ē-ō-ˈlar-ē-ən, -ˈler-\ *n* [deriv. of LL *radiolus* small sunbeam, fr. dim. of L *radius* ray — more at RAY] **:** any of a large order (Radiolaria) of marine protozoans having a siliceous skeleton of spicules and radiating threadlike pseudopodia

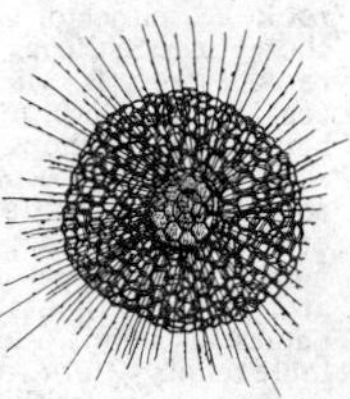
radiolarian

ra·dio·lo·ca·tion \-lō-ˈkā-shən\ *n* **:** the detection or the determination of the position and course of distant objects by radar

ra·dio·log·i·cal \ˌrād-ē-ə-ˈläj-i-kəl\ *or* **ra·dio·log·ic** \-ik\ *adj* **1 :** of or relating to radiology **2 :** of or relating to nuclear radiation — **ra·dio·log·i·cal·ly** \-k(ə-)lē\ *adv*

ra·di·ol·o·gist \ˌrād-ē-ˈäl-ə-jəst\ *n* **:** a specialist in the use of radiant energy

ra·di·ol·o·gy \-jē\ *n* **:** the science of radioactive substances and high-energy radiations; *also* **:** the use of radiant energy (as X rays and radium) in the diagnosis and treatment of disease

ra·dio·lu·cen·cy \ˌrād-ē-ō-ˈlüs-ᵊn-sē\ *n* **:** the quality or state of being permeable to radiation — **ra·dio·lu·cent** \-ᵊnt\ *adj*

ra·di·ol·y·sis \ˌrād-ē-ˈäl-ə-səs\ *n* [NL] **:** chemical decomposition by the action of radiation — **ra·dio·lyt·ic** \-ē-ə-ˈlit-ik\ *adj*

ra·dio·man \ˈrād-ē-ō-ˌman\ *n* **:** a radio operator or technician

ra·dio·me·te·or·o·graph \ˈrād-ē-ō-ˌmēt-ē-ˈȯr-ə-ˌgraf, -ˈär-\ *n* **:** RADIOSONDE

ra·di·om·e·ter \ˌrād-ē-ˈäm-ət-ər\ *n* **:** an instrument for measuring the intensity of radiant energy by the torsional twist of suspended vanes that are blackened on one side and exposed to a source of radiant energy; *also* **:** an instrument for measuring electromagnetic or acoustic radiation — **ra·di·om·e·try** \-ə-trē\ *n*

ra·dio·met·ric \ˌrād-ē-ō-ˈme-trik\ *adj* [ISV] **1 :** relating to, using, or measured by a radiometer **2 :** of or relating to the measurement of geologic time by means of the rate of disintegration of radioactive elements — **ra·dio·met·ri·cal·ly** \-tri-k(ə-)lē\ *adv*

ra·dio·mi·met·ic \-mə-ˈmet-ik, -mī-\ *adj* [ISV] **:** producing effects similar to those of radiation

ra·di·on·ics \ˌrād-ē-ˈän-iks\ *n pl but sing in constr* [*radio-* + electro*nics*] **:** ELECTRONICS

ra·dio·nu·clide \ˌrād-ē-ō-ˈn(y)ü-ˌklīd\ *n* **:** a radioactive nuclide

ra·di·opaque \ˌrād-ē-ō-ˈpāk\ *adj* **:** being opaque to various forms of radiation (as X rays)

ra·dio·phar·ma·ceu·ti·cal \ˈrād-ē-ō-ˌfär-mə-ˈsüt-i-kəl\ *n* **:** a radioactive drug used for diagnostic or therapeutic purposes

ra·dio·phone \ˈrād-ē-ə-ˌfōn\ *n* **1 :** an apparatus for the production of sound by radiant energy **2 :** RADIOTELEPHONE

ra·dio·pho·to \ˌrād-ē-ō-ˈfōt-(ˌ)ō\ *n* **1** *also* **ra·dio·pho·to·graph** \-ˈfōt-ə-ˌgraf\ **:** a picture transmitted by radio **2 :** the process of transmitting a picture by radio

ra·dio·pro·tec·tive \-prə-ˈtek-tiv\ *adj* **:** serving to protect or aiding in protecting against the injurious effect of radiations <~ drugs> — **ra·dio·pro·tec·tion** \-ˈtek-shən\ *n*

radio range *n* **:** a radio facility aiding in the navigation of airplanes

ra·dio·scop·ic \ˌrād-ē-ō-ˈskäp-ik\ *adj* **:** of or relating to radioscopy

ra·di·os·co·py \-ˈäs-kə-pē\ *n* [ISV] **:** direct observation of objects opaque to light by means of some other form of radiant energy

ra·dio·sen·si·tive \ˌrād-ē-ō-ˈsen(t)-sət-iv, -ˈsen(t)-stiv\ *adj* **:** sensitive to the effects of radiant energy <~ cancer cells> — **ra·dio·sen·si·tiv·i·ty** \-ˌsen(t)-sə-ˈtiv-ət-ē\ *n*

ra·dio·sonde \ˈrād-ē-ō-ˌsänd\ *n* [ISV] **:** a miniature radio transmitter that is carried (as by an unmanned balloon) aloft with instruments for broadcasting (as by means of precise tone signals) the humidity, temperature, and pressure

radio spectrum *n* **:** the region of the electromagnetic spectrum usu. including frequencies below 30,000 megacycles in which radio or radar transmission and detection techniques may be used

radio star *n* **:** a cosmic radio source of very small dimensions and relatively strong radiation

ra·dio·stron·tium \ˌrād-ē-ō-ˈsträn-ch(ē-)əm, -ˈstränt-ē-əm\ *n* [NL] **:** radioactive strontium; *esp* **:** STRONTIUM 90

ra·dio·sym·met·ri·cal \-sə-ˈme-tri-kəl\ *adj* **:** having the property of radial symmetry; *specif* **:** ACTINOMORPHIC

ra·dio·tele·graph \-'tel-ə-,graf\ *n* [ISV] : WIRELESS TELEGRAPHY — **ra·dio·tele·graph·ic** \-,tel-ə-'graf-ik\ *adj* — **ra·dio·te·leg·ra·phy** \-tə-'leg-rə-fē\ *n*
ra·dio·te·lem·e·try \-tə-'lem-ə-trē\ *n* : TELEMETRY — **ra·dio·tele·met·ric** \-,tel-ə-'me-trik\ *adj*
ra·dio·tele·phone \-'tel-ə-,fōn\ *n* [ISV] : an apparatus for carrying on wireless telephony by radio waves — **ra·dio·te·le·pho·ny** \-tə-'lef-ə-nē, -'tel-ə-,fō-nē\ *n*
radio telescope *n* : a radio receiver-antenna combination used for observation in radio astronomy
ra·dio·ther·a·py \,rād-ē-ō-'ther-ə-pē\ *n* [ISV] : the treatment of disease by means of X rays or radioactive substances — **ra·dio·ther·a·pist** \-pəst\ *n*
ra·dio·tho·ri·um \-'thōr-ē-əm, -'thȯr-\ *n* [NL] : a radioactive isotope of thorium with the mass number 228
ra·dio·trac·er \'rād-ē-ō-,trā-sər\ *n* : a radioactive tracer
ra·dio–ul·na \,rād-ē-ō-'əl-nə\ *n* [NL] : a bone in the forelimb of an amphibian (as a frog) that represents the fused radius and ulna of higher forms
radio wave *n* : an electromagnetic wave with radio frequency
rad·ish \'rad-ish, 'red-\ *n* [ME, alter. of OE *rædic*, fr. L *radic-, radix* root, radish — more at ROOT] : the pungent fleshy root of a plant (*Raphanus sativus*) of the mustard family usu. eaten raw; *also* : the plant that produces radishes
ra·di·um \'rād-ē-əm\ *n, often attrib* [NL, fr. L *radius* ray] : an intensely radioactive shining white metallic element that resembles barium chemically, occurs in combination in minute quantities in minerals (as pitchblende or carnotite), emits alpha particles and gamma rays to form radon, and is used chiefly in luminous materials and in the treatment of cancer — see ELEMENT table
radium therapy *n* : RADIOTHERAPY
ra·di·us \'rād-ē-əs\ *n, pl* **ra·dii** \-ē-,ī\ *also* **ra·di·us·es** [L, ray, radius] **1 a** : the bone on the thumb side of the human forearm; *also* : a corresponding part of vertebrates above fishes **b** : the third and usu. largest vein of an insect's wing **2** : a line segment extending from the center of a circle or sphere to the curve or surface **3 a** : the length of a radius <a truck with a short turning ~> **b** : the circular area defined by a stated radius **c** : a bounded or circumscribed area **4** : a radial part **5** : the distance from a center line or point to an axis of rotation **6** : an imaginary radial plane dividing the body of a radially symmetrical animal into similar parts
radius of curvature : the reciprocal of the curvature of a curve
radius vector *n* **1 a** : a line segment or its length from a fixed point to a variable point **b** : the linear polar coordinate of a variable point **2** : a straight line joining the center of an attracting body (as the sun) with that of a body (as a planet) in orbit around it
ra·dix \'rād-iks\ *n, pl* **ra·di·ces** \'rād-ə-,sēz, 'rad-\ *or* **ra·dix·es** \'rād-ik-səz\ [L, root] **1** : BASE 5d **2** : the primary source **3** : the root of a plant **4** : RADICLE; *esp* : a root of a cranial or spinal nerve
RADM *abbr* rear admiral
ra·dome \'rā-,dōm\ *n* [*ra*dar *dome*] : a plastic housing sheltering the antenna assembly of a radar set esp. on an airplane
ra·don \'rā-,dän\ *n* [ISV, fr. *radium*] : a heavy radioactive stable gaseous element formed by disintegration of radium — see ELEMENT table
rad·u·la \'raj-ə-lə\ *n, pl* **-lae** \-,lē, -,lī\ *also* **-las** [NL, fr. L, scraper, fr. *radere* to scrape — more at RAT] : a horny band or ribbon in mollusks other than bivalves that bears minute teeth on its dorsal surface and tears up food and draws it into the mouth — **rad·u·lar** \-lər\ *adj*
RAF *abbr* Royal Air Force
raff \'raf\ *n* [ME *raf* rubbish] : RIFFRAFF
raf·fia \'raf-ē-ə\ *n* [Malagasy *rafia*] : the fiber of the raffia palm used for tying plants and making baskets and hats
raffia palm *n* : a pinnate-leaved palm (*Raphia ruffia*) of Madagascar that is valued for the fiber from its leafstalks
raf·fi·nose \'raf-ə-,nōs, -,nōz\ *n* [F, fr. *raffiner* to refine, fr. *re-* + *affiner* to make fine, fr. *a-* ad- (fr. L *ad-*) + *fin* fine] : a crystalline slightly sweet sugar $C_{18}H_{32}O_{16}$ obtained commercially from cottonseed meal and present in many plant products
raff·ish \'raf-ish\ *adj* **1** : marked by or suggestive of flashy vulgarity or crudeness **2** : marked by a careless unconventionality : RAKISH — **raff·ish·ly** *adv* — **raff·ish·ness** *n*
[1]**raf·fle** \'raf-əl\ *n* [ME *rafle*, a dice game, fr. MF] : a lottery in which the prize is won by one of numerous persons buying chances
[2]**raffle** *vb* **raf·fled; raf·fling** \'raf-(ə-)liŋ\ *vi* : to engage in a raffle ~ *vt* : to dispose of by means of a raffle <~ off a turkey>
[3]**raffle** *n* [prob. fr. F *rafle* act of snatching, sweeping, fr. MF *rafle, raffe*, fr. MHG *raffen* to snatch; akin to OE *hreppan* to touch, *hearpe* harp — more at HARP] : RUBBISH; *specif* : a jumble or tangle of nautical equipment
raf·fle·sia \rə-'flē-zh(ē-)ə, ra-\ *n* [NL, fr. Sir Stamford *Raffles* †1826 E colonial administrator] : any of a genus (*Rafflesia* of the family Rafflesiaceae) of Malaysian dicotyledonous plants that are parasitic in other plants and have fleshy usu. foul-smelling apetalous flowers emerging from the host, imbricated scales in place of leaves, and no stems
[1]**raft** \'raft\ *n* [ME *rafte* rafter, raft, fr. ON *raptr* rafter] **1 a** : a collection of logs or timber fastened together for conveyance by water **b** : a flat structure for support or transportation on water **2** : a floating cohesive mass **3** : an aggregation of animals (as waterfowl) resting on the water
[2]**raft** *vt* **1** : to transport in the form of or by means of a raft **2** : to make into a raft ~ *vi* : to travel by raft
[3]**raft** *n* [alter. (influenced by [1]*raft*) of *raff* (jumble)] : a large collection
[1]**raf·ter** \'raf-tər\ *n* [ME, fr. OE *ræfter*; akin to ON *raptr* rafter] : any of the parallel beams that support a roof
[2]**raft·er** \'raf-tər\ *n* [[2]*raft*] : one who maneuvers logs into position and binds them into rafts
rafts·man \'raf(t)-smən\ *n* : a man engaged in rafting

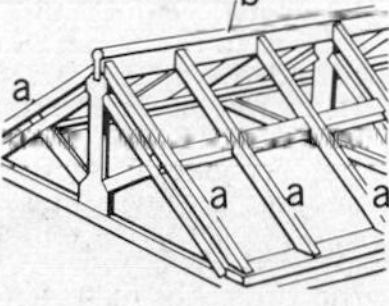

a rafters, *b* ridgepole

[1]**rag** \'rag\ *n* [ME *ragge*, fr. (assumed) OE *ragg*, fr. ON *rögg* tuft, shagginess — more at RUG] **1 a** : a waste piece of cloth **b** *pl* : clothes usu. in poor or ragged condition **2** : something resembling a rag **3** : NEWSPAPER **4** : the stringy axis and white fibrous membrane of a citrus fruit
[2]**rag** *n* [origin unknown] **1** : any of various hard rocks **2** : a large roofing slate that is rough on one side
[3]**rag** *vt* **ragged** \'ragd\; **rag·ging** [origin unknown] **1** : to rail at : SCOLD **2** : TORMENT, TEASE
[4]**rag** *n, chiefly Brit* : an outburst of boisterous fun; *also* : PRANK
[5]**rag** *n* [short for *ragtime*] : a composition in ragtime
ra·ga \'räg-ə\ *n* [Skt *rāga*, lit., color, tone] **1** : one of the ancient traditional melodic patterns or modes in Indian music **2** : an improvisation based on a traditional raga — compare TALA
rag·a·muf·fin \'rag-ə-,məf-ən\ *n* [*Ragamoffyn*, a demon in *Piers Plowman* (1393), attributed to William Langland] : a ragged often disreputable person; *esp* : a poorly clothed often dirty child
rag·bag \'rag-,bag\ *n* **1** : a bag for scraps **2** : a miscellaneous collection
rag doll *n* **1** : a stuffed usu. painted cloth doll **2** : a rolled strip of moist cloth for testing the germination of seed
[1]**rage** \'rāj\ *n* [ME, fr. MF, fr. LL *rabia*, fr. L *rabies* rage, madness, fr. *rabere* to be mad; akin to Skt *rabhas* violence] **1 a** : violent and uncontrolled anger **b** : a fit of violent wrath **c** *archaic* : INSANITY **2** : violent action (as of wind or sea) **3** : an intense feeling : PASSION **4** : a fad pursued with intense enthusiasm <was all the ~> ***syn*** see ANGER, FASHION
[2]**rage** *vi* **raged; rag·ing** **1** : to be in a rage **2** : to be in tumult **3** : to prevail uncontrollably
rag·ged \'rag-əd\ *adj* **1** : roughly unkempt **2** : having an irregular edge or outline **3 a** : torn or worn to tatters **b** : worn out from stress and strain <ran herself ~> **4** : wearing tattered clothes **5 a** : STRAGGLY **b** : executed in an irregular or uneven manner **c** *of a sound* : HARSH, DISSONANT — **rag·ged·ly** *adv* — **rag·ged·ness** *n*
ragged robin *n* : a perennial herb (*Lychnis floscuculi*) cultivated for its pink flowers with narrow-lobed petals
rag·gedy \'rag-əd-ē\ *adj* : RAGGED
rag·gle \'rag-əl\ *n* [*raggle* (to cut a raggle in)] : a groove cut in masonry
rag·gle–tag·gle \'rag-əl-,tag-əl\ *adj* [irreg. fr. *ragtag*] : MOTLEY
ra·gi \'rag-ē, 'räg-\ *n* [Hindi *rāgī*] : an East Indian cereal grass (*Eleusine coracana*) yielding a staple food crop in the Orient; *also* : the seeds of ragi used for food
rag·ing \'rā-jiŋ\ *adj* **1** : causing great pain or distress **2** : VIOLENT, WILD **3** : EXTRAORDINARY, TREMENDOUS
rag·lan \'rag-lən\ *n* [F.J.H. Somerset, Baron *Raglan* †1855 Brit field marshal] : a loose overcoat with raglan sleeves
raglan sleeve *n* : a sleeve that extends to the neckline with slanted seams from the underarm to the neck
rag·man \'rag-,man\ *n* : a man who collects or deals in rags
ra·gout \ra-'gü\ *n* [F *ragoût*, fr. *ragoûter* to revive the taste, fr. *re-* + *a-* ad- (fr. L *ad-*) + *goût* taste, fr. L *gustus*; akin to L *gustare* to taste — more at CHOOSE] **1** : well-seasoned meat and vegetables cooked in a thick sauce **2** : MIXTURE, MÉLANGE
rag·pick·er \'rag-,pik-ər\ *n* : one who collects rags and refuse for a livelihood
rag·tag \'rag-,tag\ *adj* [*ragtag and bobtail*] **1** : RAGGED, UNKEMPT **2** : RAMSHACKLE
ragtag and bobtail *n* [[1]*rag* + [1]*tag*] : RABBLE
rag·time \'rag-,tīm\ *n* [prob. fr. *ragged* + *time*] **1** : rhythm characterized by strong syncopation in the melody with a regularly accented accompaniment **2** : music having ragtime rhythm
rag·weed \-,wēd\ *n* **1** : any of various chiefly No. American weedy composite herbs (genus *Ambrosia*) that produce highly allergenic pollen **2** : FRANSERIA
rag·wort \-,wərt, -,wȯ(ə)rt\ *n* : any of several composite herbs (genus *Senecio*); *esp* : TANSY RAGWORT
rah \'rä, 'rȯ\ *interj* : HURRAH — used esp. to cheer on a team
rah–rah \'rä-(,)rä, 'rȯ-(,)rȯ\ *adj* [redupl. of *rah*] : marked by the enthusiastic expression of college spirit
[1]**raid** \'rād\ *n* [Sc dial., fr. OE *rād* ride, raid — more at ROAD] **1 a** : a hostile or predatory incursion **b** : a surprise attack by a small force **2 a** : a brief foray outside one's usual sphere **b** : a sudden invasion by officers of the law **c** : a daring operation against a competitor **3** : the act of mulcting public money **4** : an attempt by professional operators to depress stock prices by concerted selling
[2]**raid** *vt* : to make a raid on ~ *vi* : to conduct or take part in a raid
raid·er \'rād-ər\ *n* : one that raids: as **a** : a fast lightly armed ship operating against merchant shipping **b** : a soldier specially trained for close-range fighting
[1]**rail** \'rā(ə)l\ *n* [ME *raile*, fr. MF *reille* ruler, bar, fr. L *regula* ruler, fr. *regere* to keep straight, direct, rule — more at RIGHT] **1 a** : a bar extending from one post or support to another and serving as a guard or barrier **b** : a structural member or support **2 a** : RAILING 1 **b** : a light structure serving as a guard at the outer edge of a ship's deck **c** : a fence bounding a racetrack **3 a** : a bar of rolled steel forming a track for wheeled vehicles **b** : TRACK **c** : RAILROAD
[2]**rail** *vt* : to provide with a railing : FENCE

[3]**rail** *n, pl* **rail** *or* **rails** [ME *raile,* fr. MF *raale*] **:** any of numerous precocial wading birds (family Rallidae) that are structurally related to the cranes but are of small or medium size and have short rounded wings, a short tail, and usu. very long toes which enable them to run on the soft mud of swamps

[4]**rail** *vi* [ME *railen,* fr. MF *railler* to mock, fr. OProv *ralhar* to babble, joke, fr. (assumed) VL *ragulare* to bray, fr. LL *ragere* to neigh] **:** to revile or scold in harsh, insolent, or abusive language ***syn*** see SCOLD — **rail·er** *n*

rail·bird \ˈrā(ə)l-ˌbərd\ *n* **:** a racing enthusiast who sits on or near the track rail to watch a race or workout

rail fence *n* **:** a fence of posts and split rails

rail·head \ˈrā(ə)l-ˌhed\ *n* **1 :** a point on a railroad in a theater of operations at which military supplies are unloaded for distribution **2 :** the end of a railroad line

rail·ing \ˈrā-liŋ\ *n* **1 :** a barrier consisting of a rail and supports **2 :** RAILS; *also* **:** material for making rails

rail·lery \ˈrā-lə-rē\ *n, pl* **-ler·ies** [F *raillerie,* fr. MF, fr. *railler* to mock] **1 :** good-natured ridicule **:** BANTER **2 :** JEST

[1]**rail·road** \ˈrā(ə)l-ˌrōd\ *n* **:** a permanent road having a line of rails fixed to ties and laid on a roadbed and providing a track for cars or equipment drawn by locomotives or propelled by self-contained motors; *also* **:** such a road and its assets constituting a single property

[2]**railroad** *vt* **1 :** to transport by railroad **2 a :** to push through hastily or without due consideration **b :** to convict with undue haste and by means of false charges or insufficient evidence ~ *vi* **:** to work for a railroad company — **rail·road·er** *n*

railroad flat *n* **:** an apartment having a series of narrow rooms arranged in line

rail·road·ing *n* **:** construction or operation of a railroad

railroad worm *n* [fr. the rows of luminescent spots along its sides making it resemble a lighted train] **1 :** APPLE MAGGOT **2 :** the larva or wingless female of any of several So. American beetles (genus *Phrixothrix* of the family Cantharidae)

rail–split·ter \ˈrā(ə)l-ˌsplit-ər\ *n* **:** one that makes logs into fence rails

rail·way \-ˌwā\ *n* **1 :** RAILROAD; *esp* **:** a railroad operating with light equipment or within a small area **2 :** a line of track providing a runway for wheels

rai·ment \ˈrā-mənt\ *n* [ME *rayment,* short for *arrayment,* fr. *arrayen* to array] **:** CLOTHING, GARMENTS

[1]**rain** \ˈrān\ *n, often attrib* [ME *reyn,* fr. OE *regn, rēn;* akin to OHG *regan* rain] **1 a :** water falling in drops condensed from vapor in the atmosphere **b :** the descent of this water **c :** water that has fallen as rain **:** RAINWATER **2 a :** a fall of rain **:** RAINSTORM **b** *pl* **:** the rainy season **3 :** rainy weather **4 :** a heavy fall of particles or bodies

[2]**rain** *vi* **1 :** to fall as water in drops from the clouds **2 :** to send down rain **3 :** to fall like rain ~ *vt* **1 :** to pour down **2 :** to bestow abundantly

rain·bird \ˈrān-ˌbərd\ *n* **:** any of numerous birds (esp. of the family Cuculidae) whose cries are popularly believed to augur rain

rain·bow \-ˌbō\ *n* **1 :** an arc or circle that exhibits in concentric bands the colors of the spectrum and that is formed opposite the sun by the refraction and reflection of the sun's rays in raindrops, spray, or mist **2 a :** a multicolored array **b :** a wide assortment or range **3** [fr. the impossibility of reaching the rainbow, at whose foot a pot of gold is said to be buried] **:** an illusory goal or hope **4 :** RAINBOW TROUT

rainbow fish *n* **:** any of numerous brilliantly colored fishes (as a wrasse, parrot fish, or guppy)

rainbow perch *n* **:** a small brilliantly striped, red, orange, and blue surf fish (*Hypsurus caryi*) of the Pacific coast of No. America

rainbow runner *n* **:** a large brilliantly marked blue and yellow food and sport fish (*Elagatis bipinnulatus*) common in warm seas

rainbow trout *n* **:** a large stout-bodied and sometimes anadromous trout (*Salmo gairdneri*) of western No. America that typically is greenish above and white on the belly with a pink, red, or lavender stripe along each side of the body and with profuse black dots

rain check *n* **1 :** a ticket stub good for a later performance when the scheduled one is rained out **2 :** an assurance of a deferred extension of an offer; *esp* **:** an assurance that a customer can take advantage of a sale later if the item or service offered is not available (as by being sold out)

rain·coat \ˈrān-ˌkōt\ *n* **:** a coat of waterproof or water-resistant material

rain·drop \-ˌdräp\ *n* **:** a drop of rain

rain·fall \-ˌfȯl\ *n* **1 :** RAIN 2a **2 :** the amount of precipitation usu. measured by the depth in inches

rain forest *n* **:** a tropical woodland with an annual rainfall of at least 100 inches and marked by lofty broad-leaved evergreen trees forming a continuous canopy

rain gauge *n* **:** an instrument for measuring the quantity of precipitation

rain·mak·ing \ˈrān-ˌmā-kiŋ\ *n* **:** the action or process of producing or attempting to produce rain by artificial means — **rain·mak·er** \-kər\ *n*

rain out *vt* **:** to interrupt or prevent by rain

rain·proof \ˈrān-ˈprüf\ *adj* **:** impervious to rain

rain·spout \-ˌspau̇t\ *n* **:** a pipe, duct, or orifice draining a roof gutter

rain·squall \-ˌskwȯl\ *n* **:** a squall accompanied by rain

rain·storm \-ˌstȯ(ə)rm\ *n* **:** a storm of or with rain

rain tree *n* **:** MONKEYPOD

rain·wash \ˈrān-ˌwȯsh, -ˌwäsh\ *n* **:** the washing away of material by rain; *also* **:** the material so washed away

rain·wa·ter \-ˌwȯt-ər, -ˌwät-\ *n* **:** water fallen as rain that has not collected soluble matter from the soil and is therefore soft

rain·wear \-ˌwa(ə)r, -ˌwe(ə)r\ *n* **:** waterproof or water-resistant clothing

rainy \ˈrā-nē\ *adj* **rain·i·er; -est :** marked by, abounding with, or bringing rain

rainy day *n* **:** a period of want or need

[1]**raise** \ˈrāz\ *vb* **raised; rais·ing** [ME *raisen,* fr. ON *reisa* — more at REAR] *vt* **1 :** to cause or help to rise to a standing position **2 a :** AWAKEN, AROUSE **b :** to stir up **:** INCITE <~ a rebellion> **c :** to flush (game) from cover **d :** to recall from or as if from death **e :** to establish radio communication with **3 a :** to set upright by lifting or building **b :** to lift higher **c :** to place higher in rank or dignity **:** ELEVATE **d :** HEIGHTEN, INVIGORATE <~ the spirits> **e :** to end or suspend the operation or validity of <~ a siege> **4 :** to get together for a purpose **:** COLLECT <~ funds> **5 a :** to breed and bring (an animal) to maturity **b :** GROW, CULTIVATE <~ cotton> **c :** to bring up (a child) **:** REAR **6 a :** to give rise to **:** PROVOKE <~ a commotion> **b :** to give voice to <~ a cheer> **7 :** to bring up for consideration or debate <~ an issue> **8 a :** to increase the strength, intensity, or pitch of **b :** to increase the degree of **c :** to cause to rise in level or amount <~ the rent> **d (1) :** to increase the amount of (a poker bet) **(2) :** to bet more than (a previous bettor) **e (1) :** to make a higher bridge bid in (a partner's suit) **(2) :** to increase the bid of (one's partner) **9 :** to make light and porous <~ dough> **10 :** to cause to ascend **11 :** to multiply (a quantity) by itself a specified number of times **12 :** to bring in sight on the horizon by approaching <~ land> **13 a :** to bring up the nap of (cloth) **b :** to cause (as a blister) to form on the skin **14 :** to increase the nominal value of fraudulently <~ a check> **15 :** to articulate (a sound) with the tongue in a higher position ~ *vi* **1** *dial* **:** RISE **2 :** to increase a bet or bid ***syn*** see LIFT — **rais·er** *n* — **raise cain** *or* **raise hell 1 :** to act wildly **:** create a disturbance **2 :** to scold or upbraid someone esp. loudly — **raise eyebrows :** to cause surprise or astonishment

[2]**raise** *n* **1 :** an act of raising or lifting **2 :** a rising stretch of road **:** an upward grade **:** RISE **3 :** an increase in amount: as **a :** an increase of a bet or bid **b :** an increase in wages or salary **4 :** a vertical or inclined opening or passageway connecting one mine working area with another at a higher level

raised *adj* **1 a :** done in relief **b :** having a nap **2 :** leavened with yeast rather than with baking powder or baking soda

rai·sin \ˈrāz-ᵊn\ *n* [ME, fr. MF, grape, fr. L *racemus* cluster of grapes or berries] **:** a grape usu. of a special type dried in the sun or by artificial heat

rai·son d'être \ˌrā-ˌzō^{n}-ˈdetrᵊ\ *n* [F] **:** reason or justification for existence

raj \ˈräj\ *n* [Hindi *rāj,* fr. Skt *rājya;* akin to Skt *rājan* king] **:** REIGN

ra·ja *or* **ra·jah** \ˈräj-ə, ˈräj-(ˌ)ä, ˈräzh-\ *n* [Hindi *rājā,* fr. Skt *rājan* king — more at ROYAL] **1 :** an Indian or Malay prince or chief **2 :** the bearer of a title of nobility among the Hindus

Ra·jab \rə-ˈjab\ *n* [Ar] **:** the 7th month of the Muhammadan year — see MONTH table

Ra·jas·tha·ni \ˌräj-ə-ˈstän-ē, ˌräzh-\ *n* [Hindi *Rājasthānī,* fr. *Rājasthān* Rajputana] **:** the Indic language of Rajasthan

Raj·put *or* **Raj·poot** \ˈräj-ˌpu̇t, ˈräzh-\ *n* [Hindi *rājpūt,* fr. Skt *rājaputra* king's son, fr. *rājan* king + *putra* son — more at FEW] **:** a member of an Indo-Aryan caste of northern India

[1]**rake** \ˈrāk\ *n* [ME, fr. OE *racu;* akin to OHG *rehho* rake] **1 a :** an implement equipped with projecting prongs to gather material (as grass) or for loosening or smoothing the surface of the ground **b :** a machine for gathering hay **2 :** an implement like a rake

[2]**rake** *vt* **raked; rak·ing 1 :** to gather, loosen, or smooth with or as if with a rake **2 :** to gain rapidly or in abundance <~ in a fortune> **3 a :** to touch in passing over lightly **b :** SCRATCH **4 :** to censure severely **5 :** to search through **:** RANSACK **6 :** to sweep the length of esp. with gunfire **:** ENFILADE **7 :** to glance over rapidly — **rak·er** *n*

[3]**rake** *vi* **raked; rak·ing** [origin unknown] **:** to incline from the perpendicular

[4]**rake** *n* **1 :** inclination from the perpendicular; *esp* **:** the overhang of a ship's bow or stern **2 :** inclination from the horizontal **:** SLOPE **3 :** the angle between the top cutting surface of a tool and a plane perpendicular to the surface of the work **4 :** the angle between a wing-tip edge that is sensibly straight in planform and the plane of symmetry of an airplane

[5]**rake** *n* [short for *rakehell*] **:** a dissolute person **:** LIBERTINE

rake·hell \ˈrāk-ˌhel\ *n* **:** LIBERTINE 2 — **rakehell** *or* **rake·helly** \-ˌhel-ē\ *adj*

rake–off \ˈrā-ˌkȯf\ *n* [[2]*rake* + *off;* fr. the use of a rake by a croupier to collect the operator's profits in a gambling casino] **:** a percentage or cut taken (as by an operator)

rake up *vt* **:** to dig out **:** UNCOVER <*rake up* a scandal>

[1]**rak·ish** \ˈrā-kish\ *adj* **:** of, relating to, or characteristic of a rake **:** DISSOLUTE

[2]**rakish** *adj* [prob. fr. [3]*rake;* fr. the raking masts of pirate ships] **1 :** having a smart stylish appearance suggestive of speed <a ~ ship> **2 :** negligent of convention or formality **:** JAUNTY <~ clothes>

rak·ish·ly *adv* **:** in a rakish manner

rak·ish·ness *n* **:** the quality or state of being rakish

rale \ˈral, ˈräl\ *n* [F *râle*] **:** an abnormal sound that accompanies the normal respiratory sounds

ral·len·tan·do \ˌräl-ən-ˈtän-(ˌ)dō\ *adv or adj* [It, lit., slowing down, verbal of *rallentare* to slow down again, fr. *re-* + *allentare* to slow down] **:** with a gradual decrease in tempo — used as a direction in music

[1]**ral·ly** \ˈral-ē\ *vb* **ral·lied; ral·ly·ing** [F *rallier,* fr. OF *ralier,* fr. *re-* + *alier* to unite — more at ALLY] *vt* **1 a :** to muster for a common purpose **b :** to recall to order **2 a :** to arouse for action **b :** to rouse from depression or weakness ~ *vi* **1 :** to come together again to renew an effort **2 :** to join in a common cause **3 :** RECOVER, REBOUND **4 :** to engage in a rally

[2]**rally** *n, pl* **rallies 1 a :** a mustering of scattered forces to renew an effort **b :** a summoning up of strength or courage after weakness or dejection **c :** a recovery of price after a decline **d :** a renewed offensive **2 :** a mass meeting intended to arouse group enthusiasm **3 :** a series of strokes interchanged between players (as in tennis) before a point is won **4** *also* **ral·lye** [F *rallye,* fr. E [1]*rally*] **:** a competitive automobile run over public roads and under ordinary traffic rules with the object of maintaining a

specified average speed between checkpoints over a route unknown to the participants until the start of the run

3rally *vt* **ral·lied; ral·ly·ing** [F *railler* to mock, rally — more at RAIL] : to attack with raillery : BANTER *syn* see RIDICULE

ral·ly·ing \'ral-ē-iŋ\ *n* : the sport of driving in automobile rallies

ral·ly·ist \'ral-ē-əst\ *n* : one who participates in an automobile rally

ral·ly·mas·ter \-ˌmas-tər\ *n* : one who organizes and conducts an automobile rally

1ram \'ram\ *n* [ME, fr. OE *ramm;* akin to OHG *ram*] **1 a :** a male sheep **b** *cap* : ARIES **2 a :** BATTERING RAM **b :** a warship with a heavy beak at the prow for piercing an enemy ship **3** : any of various guided pieces for exerting pressure or for driving or forcing something by impact: as **a :** the plunger of a hydrostatic press or force pump **b :** the weight that strikes the blow in a pile driver

2ram *vb* **rammed; ram·ming** [ME *rammen*] *vi* **1 :** to strike with violence : CRASH **2 :** to move with extreme rapidity ~ *vt* **1** : to force in by driving **2 a :** to make compact (as by pounding) **b :** CRAM, CROWD **3 :** to force passage or acceptance of <~ home an idea> **4 :** to strike against violently — **ram·mer** *n*

RAM *abbr* Royal Academy of Music

Ra·ma \'räm-ə\ *n* [Skt *Rāma*] : a deity or deified hero of later Hinduism worshiped as an avatar of Vishnu

Ram·a·dan \'ram-ə-ˌdän, -ˌdan\ *n* [Ar *Ramaḍān*] : the 9th month of the Muhammadan year observed as sacred with fasting practiced daily from dawn to sunset — see MONTH table

ra·mate \'rā-ˌmāt\ *adj* [L *ramus* branch] : having branches

1ram·ble \'ram-bəl\ *vb* **ram·bled; ram·bling** \-b(ə-)liŋ\ [perh. fr. ME *romblen,* freq. of *romen* to roam] *vi* **1 a :** to move aimlessly from place to place **b :** to explore idly **2 :** to talk or write in a desultory or long-winded wandering fashion **3 :** to grow or extend irregularly ~ *vt* : to wander over : ROAM — **ram·bling·ly** \-b(ə-)liŋ-lē\ *adv*

2ramble *n* : a leisurely excursion for pleasure; *esp* : an aimless walk

ram·bler \'ram-blər\ *n* **1 :** one that rambles **2 :** any of various climbing roses with rather small often double flowers in large clusters

ram·bouil·let \ˌram-bə-'lā, -bü-'yā\ *n, often cap* [*Rambouillet,* France] : a large sturdy sheep developed in France

ram·bunc·tious \ram-'bəŋ(k)-shəs\ *adj* [prob. irreg. fr. *robust*] : marked by uncontrollable exuberance : UNRULY — **ram·bunc·tious·ly** *adv* — **ram·bunc·tious·ness** *n*

ram·bu·tan \ram-'büt-^{ə}n\ *n* [Malay] : a bright red spiny Malayan fruit closely related to the litchi; *also* : a tree (*Nephelium lappaceum*) of the soapberry family that bears this fruit

ram·e·kin *or* **ram·e·quin** \'ram-(i-)kən\ *n* [F *ramequin,* fr. LG *ramken,* dim. of *ram* cream] **1 :** a preparation of cheese with bread crumbs, puff paste, or eggs baked in a mold or shell **2** : an individual baking dish

ra·men·tum \rə-'ment-əm\ *n, pl* **-ta** \-ə\ [NL, fr. L, a shaving, fr. *radere* to scratch, scrape — more at RAT] : a thin brownish scale on a leaf or young shoot of a fern

ra·met \'rā-ˌmet\ *n* [L *ramus* branch] : an independent member of a clone

ra·mie \'rā-mē, 'ram-ē\ *n* [Malay *rami*] : an Asian perennial plant (*Boehmeria nivea*) of the nettle family; *also* : the strong lustrous bast fiber of this plant

ram·i·fi·ca·tion \ˌram-ə-fə-'kā-shən\ *n* **1 a :** the act or process of branching **b :** arrangement of branches (as on a plant) **2 a** : BRANCH, OFFSHOOT **b :** a branched structure **3 :** OUTGROWTH, CONSEQUENCE <the ~*s* of a problem>

ra·mi·form \'ram-ə-ˌfȯrm, 'rā-mə-\ *adj* [L *ramus* + E *-iform*] : resembling or constituting branches : BRANCHED

ram·i·fy \'ram-ə-ˌfī\ *vb* **-fied; -fy·ing** [MF *ramifier,* fr. ML *ramificare,* fr. L *ramus* branch; akin to L *radix* root — more at ROOT] *vt* **1 :** to cause to branch **2 :** to separate into divisions ~ *vi* **1 :** to split up into branches or constituent parts **2 :** to send forth branches or extensions

Ra·mism \'rā-ˌmiz-əm\ *n* : the doctrines of the French philosopher Ramus (†1572) based on opposition to Aristotelianism and advocacy of a new logic blended with rhetoric — **Ra·mist** \-məst\ *n or adj*

ram·jet engine \ˌram-ˌjet-\ *n* : a jet engine having in its forward end a continuous inlet of air that depends on the speed of flight for the compressing effect produced on the air rather than on a mechanical compressor

ra·mose \'rā-ˌmōs\ *adj* [L *ramosus,* fr. *ramus* branch] : consisting of or having branches <a ~ sponge> — **ra·mose·ly** *adv*

ra·mous \'rā-məs\ *adj* [L *ramosus*] **1 :** RAMOSE **2 :** resembling branches

1ramp \'ramp\ *vi* [ME *rampen,* fr. OF *ramper* to crawl, rear, of Gmc origin; akin to OHG *rimpfan* to wrinkle — more at RUMPLE] **1 a :** to stand or advance menacingly with forelegs or with arms raised **b :** to move or act furiously : STORM **2 :** to creep up — used esp. of plants

2ramp *n* : the act or an instance of ramping

3ramp *n* [F *rampe,* fr. *ramper*] **1 :** a short bend, slope, or curve usu. in the vertical plane where a handrail or coping changes its direction **2 :** a sloping way: as **a :** a sloping floor, walk, or roadway leading from one level to another **b :** a stairway for entering or leaving the main door of an airplane **c :** a slope for launching boats **3 :** APRON 2j

1ram·page \'ram-ˌpāj, (')ram-'\ *vi* **ram·paged; ram·pag·ing** [Sc] : to rush wildly about

2ram·page \'ram-ˌpāj\ *n* : a course of violent, riotous, or reckless action or behavior — **ram·pa·geous** \ram-'pā-jəs\ *adj* — **ram·pa·geous·ly** *adv* — **ram·pa·geous·ness** *n*

ram·pan·cy \'ram-pən-sē\ *n* : the quality or state of being rampant

ram·pant \'ram-pənt *also* -ˌpant\ *adj* [ME, fr. MF, prp. of *ramper*] **1 a :** rearing upon the hind legs with forelegs extended **b** : standing on one hind foot with one foreleg raised above the other and the head in profile — used of a heraldic animal **2 a :** marked by a menacing wildness, extravagance, or absence of restraint **b** : WIDESPREAD **3 :** having one impost or abutment higher than the other <a ~ arch> — **ram·pant·ly** *adv*

ram·part \'ram-ˌpärt, -pərt\ *n* [MF] **1 :** a broad embankment raised as a fortification and usu. surmounted by a parapet **2** : a protective barrier : BULWARK **3 :** a wall-like ridge (as of rock fragments, earth, or debris)

ram·pike \-ˌpīk\ *n* [origin unknown] : an erect broken or dead tree

ram·pi·on \'ram-pē-ən\ *n* [prob. modif. of MF *raiponce,* fr. OIt *raponzo*] : a European bellflower (*Campanula rapunculus*) with a tuberous root used with the leaves in salad

1ram·rod \'ram-ˌräd\ *n* **1 :** a rod for ramming home the charge in a muzzle-loading firearm **2 :** a cleaning rod for small arms

2ramrod *adj* : marked by rigidity, severity, or stiffness

ram·shack·le \'ram-ˌshak-əl\ *adj* [alter. of earlier *ransackled,* fr. pp. of obs. *ransackle,* freq. of *ransack*] **1 :** appearing ready to collapse : RICKETY **2 :** carelessly or loosely constructed

rams·horn \'ramz-ˌhȯ(ə)rn\ *n* : a snail (genus *Planorbis*) often used as an aquarium scavenger

ram·til \'ram-ˌtil, 'räm\ *n* [Hindi *rāmtil,* fr. Skt *Rāma* Rama + *tila* sesame] : a tropical composite herb (*Guizotia abyssinica*) cultivated in India for its oil seeds

ra·mus \'rā-məs\ *n, pl* **ra·mi** \-ˌmī\ [NL, fr. L, branch — more at RAMIFY] : a projecting part, elongated process, or branch: as **a** : the posterior more or less vertical part on each side of the lower jaw that articulates with the skull **b :** a branch of a nerve

ran *past of* RUN

1ranch \'ranch\ *n* [MexSp *rancho* small ranch, fr. Sp, camp, hut & Sp dial., small farm, fr. OSp *ranchear (se)* to take up quarters, fr. MF *(se) ranger* to take up a position, fr. *ranger* to set in a row — more at RANGE] **1 :** a large farm for raising horses, beef cattle, or sheep **2 :** a farm or area devoted to a particular specialty **3** : RANCH HOUSE

2ranch *vi* : to live or work on a ranch ~ *vt* **1 :** to work as a rancher on **2 :** to raise on a ranch

ranch·er \'ran-chər\ *n* : one who owns or works on a ranch

ran·che·ro \ran-'che(ə)r-(ˌ)ō, rän-\ *n, pl* **-ros** [MexSp, fr. *rancho*] : RANCHER

ranch house *n* : a one-story house typically with a low-pitched roof and an open plan

ranch·land \'ranch-ˌland\ *n* : land suitable for ranching

ranch·man \'ranch-mən\ *n* : RANCHER

ran·cho \'ran-(ˌ)chō, 'rän-\ *n, pl* **ranchos** [MexSp, small ranch] : RANCH 1

ran·cid \'ran(t)-səd\ *adj* [L *rancidus,* fr. *rancēre* to be rancid] **1** : having a rank smell or taste **2 :** OFFENSIVE *syn* see MALODOROUS — **ran·cid·i·ty** \ran-'sid-ət-ē\ *n* — **ran·cid·ness** \'ran(t)-səd-nəs\ *n*

ran·cor \'raŋ-kər, -ˌkȯ(ə)r\ *n* [ME *rancour,* fr. MF *ranceur,* fr. LL *rancor* rancidity, rancor, fr. L *rancēre*] : bitter deep-seated ill will *syn* see ENMITY

ran·cor·ous \'raŋ-k(ə-)rəs\ *adj* : marked by rancor — **ran·cor·ous·ly** *adv*

ran·cour *Brit var of* RANCOR

rand \'rand, 'ränd, 'ränt\ *n, pl* **rand** [the *Rand,* So. Africa] — see MONEY table

R & B *abbr* rhythm and blues

R and D *abbr* research and development

1ran·dom \'ran-dəm\ *n* [ME, impetuosity, fr. MF *randon,* fr. OF, fr. *randir* to run, of Gmc origin; akin to OHG *rinnan* to run — more at RUN] : a haphazard course — **at random :** without definite aim, direction, rule, or method

2random *adj* **1 :** lacking a definite plan, purpose, or pattern **2 a** : relating to, having, or being elements or events with definite probability of occurrence <~ processes> **b :** being or relating to a set or to an element of a set each of whose elements has equal probability of occurrence <a ~ sample>; *also* : characterized by procedures designed to obtain such sets or elements <~ sampling> — **ran·dom·ly** *adv* — **ran·dom·ness** *n*

syn RANDOM, HAPHAZARD, CASUAL, DESULTORY *shared meaning element* : determined by accident rather than design

3random *adv* : in a random manner

random–access *adj* : permitting access to stored data in any order the user desires <a ~ computer memory>

ran·dom·iza·tion \ˌran-də-mə-'zā-shən\ *n* : arrangement (as of samples or experimental treatments) so as to simulate a chance distribution, reduce interference by irrelevant variables, and yield unbiased statistical data

ran·dom·ize \'ran-də-ˌmīz\ *vt* **-ized; -iz·ing :** to use randomization on — **ran·dom·iz·er** *n*

randomized block *n* : an experimental design (as in horticulture) in which different treatments are distributed in random order in a block or plot — called also *randomized block design*

random variable *n* : a variable that is itself a function of the result of a statistical experiment in which each outcome has a definite probability of occurrence <the number of spots showing if two dice are thrown is a ~> — called also *variate*

random walk *n* : a process (as Brownian movement or genetic drift) consisting of a sequence of steps (as movements or changes in gene frequency) each of whose characteristics (as magnitude and direction) are determined by chance

R and R *abbr* rest and recreation; rest and recuperation

1randy \'ran-dē\ *adj* [prob. fr. obs. *rand* (to rant)] **1** *chiefly Scot* : having a coarse manner **2 :** LUSTFUL, LECHEROUS

2randy *n, pl* **rand·ies** *chiefly Scot* : a scolding or dissolute woman

rang *past of* RING

1range \ˈrānj\ *n, often attrib* [ME, row of persons, fr. OF *renge,* fr. *rengier* to range] **1 a** (1) **:** a series of things in a line **:** ROW (2) **:** a series of mountains (3) **:** one of the north-south rows of a township in a U.S. public-land survey that are numbered east and west from the principal meridian of the survey **b :** an aggregate of individuals in one order **c :** a direction line **2 :** a cooking stove that has an oven and a flat top with burners or heating elements **3 a :** a place that may be ranged over **b :** an open region over which livestock may roam and feed **c :** the region throughout which a kind of organism or ecological community naturally lives or occurs **4 :** the act of ranging about **5 a** (1) **:** the horizontal distance to which a projectile can be propelled (2) **:** the horizontal distance between a weapon and target **b :** the maximum distance a vehicle can travel without refueling **c :** a place where shooting or golf driving is practiced **6 a :** the space or extent included, covered, or used **:** SCOPE **b :** the extent of pitch covered by a melody or lying within the capacity of a voice or instrument **7 a :** a sequence, series, or scale between limits <a wide ~ of patterns> **b :** the limits of a series **:** the distance or extent between possible extremes **c :** the difference between the least and greatest values of an attribute or of the variable of a frequency distribution **8 a :** the set of values a function may take on **b :** the class of admissible values of a variable **9 :** LINE 11

2range *vb* **ranged; rang·ing** [ME *rangen,* fr. MF *ranger,* fr. OF *rengier,* fr. *renc, reng* line, place, row — more at RANK] *vt* **1 a :** to set in a row or in the proper order **b :** to place among others in a position or situation **c :** to assign to a category **:** CLASSIFY **2 a :** to rove over or through **b :** to sail or pass along **3 :** to arrange (an anchor cable) on deck **4 :** to graze (livestock) on a range **5 :** to determine or give the elevation necessary for (a gun) to propel a projectile to a given distance ~ *vi* **1 a :** to roam at large or freely **b :** to move over an area so as to explore it **2 :** to take a position **3 a :** to correspond in direction or line **:** ALIGN **b :** to extend in a particular direction **4 :** to have range **5 :** to change or differ within limits **6** *of an organism* **:** to live or occur in or be native to a region ***syn*** see LINE

range finder *n* **1 :** an instrument used in gunnery to determine the distance of a target **2 :** TACHYMETER 1 **3 :** a device for measuring the distance between a camera and an object

range·land \ˈrānj-ˌland\ *n* **:** land used or suitable for range

range paralysis *n* **:** an avian leukosis involving flaccid paralysis esp. of the legs and wings of maturing chickens

rang·er \ˈrān-jər\ *n* **1 a :** the keeper of a British royal park or forest **b :** FOREST RANGER **2 :** one that ranges **3 a :** one of a body of organized armed men who range over a region esp. to enforce the law **b :** a soldier specially trained in close-range fighting and in raiding tactics

rangy \ˈrān-jē\ *adj* **rang·i·er; -est 1 :** able to range for considerable distances **2 a :** long-limbed and long-bodied <~ cattle> **b :** being tall and slender **3 :** having room for ranging **4 :** having great scope — **rang·i·ness** *n*

ra·ni *or* **ra·nee** \rä-ˈnē, ˈrän-ˌē\ *n* [Hindi rānī, fr. Skt *rājñī,* fem. of *rājan* king — more at ROYAL] **:** a Hindu queen **:** a rajah's wife

ra·nid \ˈran-əd, ˈrā-nəd\ *n* [deriv. of L *rana* frog] **:** any of a large family (Ranidae) of frogs distinguished by slightly dilated transverse sacral processes

1rank \ˈraŋk\ *adj* [ME, fr. OE *ranc* overbearing, strong; akin to OE *riht* right — more at RIGHT] **1 :** luxuriantly or excessively vigorous in growth **2 :** offensively gross or coarse **:** FOUL **3** *obs* **:** grown too large **4 a :** shockingly conspicuous <must lecture him on his ~ disloyalty —David Walden> **b :** COMPLETE — used as an intensive <~ beginners> **5** *archaic* **:** LUSTFUL, RUTTISH **6 :** offensive in odor or flavor; *esp* **:** RANCID **7 :** PUTRID, FESTERING **8 :** high in amount **:** EXCESSIVE ***syn*** see MALODOROUS, FLAGRANT — **rank·ly** *adv* — **rank·ness** *n*

2rank *n* [MF *renc, reng,* of Gmc origin; akin to OHG *hring* ring — more at RING] **1 a :** ROW, SERIES **b :** a row of people **c** (1) **:** a line of soldiers ranged side by side in close order (2) *pl* **:** ARMED FORCES (3) *pl* **:** the body of enlisted men **d :** any of the rows of squares that extend across a chessboard perpendicular to the files **e** *Brit* **:** STAND 6 **2 :** an orderly arrangement **:** FORMATION **3 :** a social class **4 a :** relative standing or position **b :** a degree or position of dignity, eminence, or excellence **:** DISTINCTION <soon took ~ as a leading attorney —J. D. Hicks> **c :** high social position <the privileges of ~> **d :** a grade of official standing **5 :** the order according to some statistical characteristic (as score on a test) **6 :** any of a series of classes of coal based on increasing alteration of the parent vegetable matter, increasing carbon content, and increasing fuel value **7 :** the number of linearly independent rows in a matrix

3rank *vt* **1 :** to arrange in lines or in a regular formation **2 :** to determine the relative position of **:** RATE **3 :** to take precedence of ~ *vi* **1 :** to form or move in ranks **2 :** to take or have a position in relation to others

rank and file *n* **1 :** the enlisted men of an armed force **2 :** the individuals who constitute the body of an organization, society, or nation as distinguished from the leaders — **rank and fil·er** \-ˈfī-lər\ *n*

rank correlation *n* **:** a measure of correlation depending on rank

rank·er \ˈraŋ-kər\ *n* **:** one who serves or has served in the ranks; *esp* **:** a commissioned officer promoted from the ranks

Ran·kine \ˈraŋ-kən\ *adj* [William J. M. *Rankine* †1872 Sc engineer & physicist] **:** being, according to, or relating to an absolute temperature scale on which the unit of measurement equals a Fahrenheit degree and on which the freezing point of water is 491.69° and the boiling point 671.69°

rank·ing *adj* **:** having a high position: as **a :** FOREMOST <~ poet> **b :** being next to the chairman in seniority <~ committee member>

ran·kle \ˈraŋ-kəl\ *vb* **ran·kled; ran·kling** \-k(ə-)liŋ\ [ME *ranclen* to fester, fr. MF *rancler,* fr. OF *draoncler, raoncler,* fr. *draoncle, raoncle* festering sore, fr. (assumed) VL *dracunculus,* fr. L, dim. of *draco* serpent — more at DRAGON] *vi* **1 :** to cause anger, irritation, or deep bitterness **2 :** to feel anger and irritation ~ *vt* **:** to cause irritation or bitterness in

ran·sack \ˈran-ˌsak, (ˈ)ran-ˈ\ *vt* [ME *ransaken,* fr. ON *rannsaka,* fr. *rann* house + *-saka* (akin to OE *sēcan* to seek)] **1 a :** to search thoroughly **b :** to examine closely and carefully **2 :** to search through to commit robbery **:** PLUNDER — **ran·sack·er** *n*

1ran·som \ˈran(t)-səm\ *n* [ME *ransoun,* fr. OF *rançon,* fr. L *redemption-, redemptio* — more at REDEMPTION] **1 :** a consideration paid or demanded for the redemption of a captured person **2 :** the act of ransoming

2ransom *vt* **1 :** to deliver esp. from sin or its penalty **2 :** to free from captivity or punishment by paying a price ***syn*** see RESCUE — **ran·som·er** *n*

1rant \ˈrant\ *vb* [obs. D *ranten, randen*] *vi* **1 :** to talk in a noisy, excited, or declamatory manner **2 :** to scold vehemently ~ *vt* **:** to utter in a bombastic declamatory fashion — **rant·er** *n* — **rant·ing·ly** \-iŋ-lē\ *adv*

2rant *n* **1 a :** a bombastic extravagant speech **b :** bombastic extravagant language **2** *dial Brit* **:** a rousing good time ***syn*** see BOMBAST

ran·u·la \ˈran-yə-lə\ *n* [NL, fr. L, swelling on the tongue of cattle, fr. dim. of *rana* frog] **:** a cyst formed under the tongue by obstruction of a gland duct

ra·nun·cu·lus \rə-ˈnəŋ-kyə-ləs\ *n, pl* **-lus·es** *or* **-li** \-ˌlī, -ˌlē\ [NL, genus name, fr. L, tadpole, crowfoot, dim. of *rana* frog] **:** any of a large widely distributed genus (*Ranunculus*) of dicotyledonous herbs (as a buttercup) that have simple or variously lobed leaves and usu. yellow flowers with five deciduous sepals and five nectar-producing petals

1rap \ˈrap\ *n* [ME *rappe*] **1 :** a sharp blow or knock **2 :** a sharp rebuke or criticism **3** *slang* **a :** the responsibility for or adverse consequences of an action **b :** a criminal charge **c :** a prison sentence

2rap *vb* **rapped; rap·ping** *vt* **1 :** to strike with a sharp blow **2 :** to utter suddenly and forcibly **3 :** to cause to be or come by raps <~ the meeting to order> **4 :** to criticize sharply **5** *slang* **:** to arrest, hold, or sentence on a criminal charge ~ *vi* **1 :** to strike a quick sharp blow **2 :** to make a short sharp sound

3rap *vt* **rapped** *also* **rapt; rap·ping** [back-formation fr. *rapt*] **1 :** to snatch away or upward **2 :** ENRAPTURE

4rap *n* [perh. fr. [1]*rap*] **:** a minimum amount or degree (as of care or consideration) **:** the least bit <doesn't care a ~>

5rap *n* [perh. by shortening & alter. fr. *repartee*] **:** TALK, CONVERSATION

6rap *vi* **rapped; rap·ping :** to talk freely and frankly <a center where they could meet and ~ congenially . . . with people . . . with similar interests and problems —Robert Liebert>

7rap *abbr* rapid

ra·pa·cious \rə-ˈpā-shəs\ *adj* [L *rapac-, rapax,* fr. *rapere* to seize] **1 :** excessively grasping or covetous <in an age of unscrupulous plunder he was among the most ~ — *Times Lit. Supp.*> **2 :** living on prey **3 :** RAVENOUS, VORACIOUS — **ra·pa·cious·ly** *adv* — **ra·pa·cious·ness** *n*

ra·pac·i·ty \rə-ˈpas-ət-ē\ *n* **:** the quality of being rapacious

1rape \ˈrāp\ *n* [ME, fr. L *rapa, rapum* turnip, rape; akin to OHG *rāba* turnip, rape] **:** a European herb (*Brassica napus*) of the mustard family grown as a forage crop for sheep and hogs and for its seeds which yield rape oil and are a bird food

2rape *vt* **raped; rap·ing** [ME *rapen,* fr. L *rapere*] **1 a** *archaic* **:** to seize and take away by force **b :** DESPOIL **2 :** to commit rape on — **rap·er** *n* — **rap·ist** \ˈrā-pəst\ *n*

3rape *n* **1 :** an act or instance of robbing or despoiling or carrying away a person by force **2 a :** sexual intercourse with a woman by a man without her consent and chiefly by force or deception — compare STATUTORY RAPE **b :** unlawful sexual intercourse by force or threat other than by a man with a woman **3 :** an outrageous violation

4rape *n* [F *râpe* grape stalk] **:** grape pomace

rape oil *n* **:** a nondrying or semidrying oil obtained from rapeseed and turnip seed and used chiefly as a lubricant, illuminant, and food — called also *rapeseed oil*

rape·seed \ˈrāp-ˌsēd\ *n* **:** the seed of the rape plant

Ra·pha·el \ˈraf-ē-əl, ˈrā-fē-\ *n* [LL, fr. Gk *Rhaphaēl,* fr. Heb *Rĕphā'ēl*] **:** one of the four archangels named in Hebrew tradition

ra·phe \ˈrā-(ˌ)fē\ *n* [NL, fr. Gk *rhaphē* seam, fr. *rhaptein* to sew — more at RHAPSODY] **1 :** the seamlike union of the two lateral halves of a part or organ (as the tongue) having externally a ridge or furrow **2 a :** the part of the stalk of an anatropous ovary that is united in growth to the outside covering and forms a ridge along the body of the ovule **b :** the median line of a diatom's valve

ra·phia \ˈrā-fē-ə, ˈraf-ē-\ *n* [NL, genus of palms, fr. Malagasy *rafia* raffia] **:** RAFFIA

raph·ide \ˈraf-ˌīd\ *n, pl* **raph·ides** \ˈraf-ˌīdz, ˈraf-ə-ˌdēz\ [F & NL; F *raphide,* fr. NL *raphides,* pl., modif. of Gk *rhaphides,* pl. of *rhaphid-, rhaphis* needle, fr. *rhaptein*] **:** one of the needle-shaped crystals, usu. of calcium oxalate that develop as metabolic byproducts in plant cells

1rap·id \ˈrap-əd\ *adj* [L *rapidus* seizing, sweeping, rapid, fr. *rapere* to seize, sweep away; akin to OE *refsan* to blame] **:** marked by a fast rate of motion, activity, succession, or occurrence ***syn*** see FAST ***ant*** deliberate, leisurely — **rap·id·ly** *adv* — **rap·id·ness** *n*

2rapid *n* **:** a part of a river where the current is fast and the surface is usu. broken by obstructions — usu. used in pl. but sing. or pl. in constr.

rapid eye movement *n* **:** a rapid conjugate movement of the eyes that is associated with paradoxical sleep

rap·id–fire \ˌrap-əd-ˈfī(ə)r\ *adj* **1 :** firing or adapted for firing shots in rapid succession **2 :** marked by rapidity, liveliness, or sharpness

ra·pid·i·ty \rə-ˈpid-ət-ē, ra-\ *n* **:** the quality or state of being rapid

rapid transit *n* **:** fast passenger transportation (as by subway) in urban areas

ra·pi·er \ˈrā-pē-ər\ *n* [MF (*espee*) *rapiere*] **:** a straight 2-edged sword with a narrow pointed blade

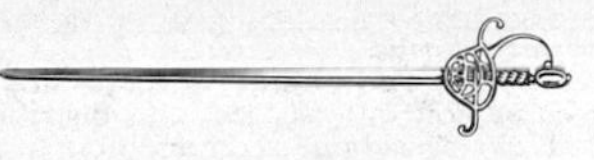

rapier

rap·ine \ˈrap-ən, -ˌīn\ *n* [ME *rapyne,* fr. L *rapina,* fr. *rapere* to seize, rob] **:** PILLAGE, PLUNDER

rap·pa·ree \ˌrap-ə-ˈrē\ *n* [IrGael *rāpaire*] **1 :** an Irish irregular soldier or bandit **2 :** VAGABOND, PLUNDERER

rap·pee \ra-ˈpē\ *n* [F *(tabac) râpé,* lit., grated tobacco] **:** a pungent snuff made from dark rank tobacco leaves

rap·pel \rə-ˈpel, ra-\ *n* [F, lit., recall, fr. OF *rapel,* fr. *rapeler* to recall, fr. *re-* + *apeler* to appeal, call — more at APPEAL] **:** descent (as of a cliff) by means of a rope passed under one thigh, across the body, and over the opposite shoulder — **rappel** *vi*

rap·pen \ˈräp-ən\ *n, pl* **rappen** [G, lit., raven; akin to OHG *hraban* raven — more at RAVEN] **:** the centime of Switzerland

rap·per \ˈrap-ər\ *n* **:** one that raps or is used for rapping; *specif* **:** a door knocker

rap·pi·ni \ra-ˈpē-nē\ *n pl* [It *rapini,* pl. of *rapino,* dim. of *rapo* turnip, fr. L *rapum* — more at RAPE] **:** immature turnip plants for use as greens

rap·port \ra-ˈpō(ə)r, rə-, -ˈpȯ(ə)r\ *n* [F, fr. *rapporter* to bring back, refer, fr. OF *raporter* to bring back, fr. *re-* + *aporter* to bring, fr. L *apportare,* fr. *ad-* + *portare* to carry — more at FARE] **:** RELATION; *esp* **:** relation marked by harmony, conformity, accord, or affinity

rap·por·teur \ˌra-ˌpōr-ˈtər, -ˌpȯr-\ *n* [F, fr. *rapporter* to bring back, report] **:** one that gives reports (as at a meeting of a learned society)

rap·proche·ment \ˌrap-ˌrōsh-ˈmäⁿ, -ˌrȯsh-; ra-ˈprōsh-ˌ\ *n* [F, fr. *rapprocher* to bring together, fr. MF, fr. *re-* + *approcher* to approach, fr. OF *aprochier*] **:** establishment or state of cordial relations

rap·scal·lion \rap-ˈskal-yən\ *n* [alter. of earlier *rascallion,* fr. 1*rascal*] **:** RASCAL, NE'ER-DO-WELL

rapt \ˈrapt\ *adj* [ME, fr. L *raptus,* pp. of *rapere* to seize — more at RAPID] **1 :** lifted up and carried away **2 :** transported with emotion **:** ENRAPTURED **3 :** wholly absorbed **:** ENGROSSED — **rapt·ly** \ˈrap-(t)lē\ *adv* — **rapt·ness** \ˈrap(t)-nəs\ *n*

rap·tor \ˈrap-tər, -ˌtȯ(ə)r\ *n* [deriv. of L *raptor* plunderer, fr. *raptus*] **:** a bird of prey

rap·to·ri·al \rap-ˈtōr-ē-əl, -ˈtȯr-\ *adj* **1 :** PREDACEOUS 1 **2 :** adapted to seize prey **3 :** of, relating to, or being a bird of prey

1**rap·ture** \ˈrap-chər\ *n* [L *raptus*] **1 a :** a state or experience of being carried away by overwhelming emotion **b :** a mystical experience in which the spirit is exalted to a knowledge of divine things **2 :** an expression or manifestation of ecstasy or passion *syn* see ECSTASY — **rap·tur·ous** \ˈrap-chə-rəs, ˈrap-shrəs\ *adj* — **rap·tur·ous·ly** *adv* — **rap·tur·ous·ness** *n*

2**rapture** *vt* **rap·tured; rap·tur·ing :** ENRAPTURE

rapture of the deep : NITROGEN NARCOSIS

ra·ra avis \ˌrar-ə-ˈā-vəs, ˌrer-; ˌrär-ə-ˈä-wəs\ *n, pl* **ra·ra avis·es** \-ˈā-və-səz\ *or* **ra·rae aves** \ˌrär-ˌī-ˈä-ˌwās\ [L, rare bird] **:** a rare person or thing **:** RARITY

1**rare** \ˈra(ə)r, ˈre(ə)r\ *adj* **rar·er; rar·est** [alter. of earlier *rere,* fr. ME, fr. OE *hrēre* boiled lightly; akin to OE *hrēran* to stir, OHG *hruoren*] **:** cooked so that the inside is still red <~ roast beef>

2**rare** *adj* **rar·er; rar·est** [ME, fr. L *rarus*] **1 :** marked by wide separation of component particles **:** THIN <~ air> **2 a :** marked by unusual quality, merit, or appeal **:** DISTINCTIVE **b :** superlative or extreme of its kind **3 :** seldom occurring or found **:** UNCOMMON *syn* see CHOICE, INFREQUENT — **rare·ness** *n*

rare·bit \ˈra(ə)r-bət, ˈre-(ə)r-\ *n* [(*Welsh*) *rarebit*] **:** WELSH RABBIT

rare earth *n* **1 :** any of a group of similar oxides of metals or a mixture of such oxides occurring together in widely distributed but relatively scarce minerals **2 :** RARE EARTH ELEMENT

rare earth element *n* **:** any of a series of metallic elements of which the oxides are classed as rare earths and which include the elements with atomic numbers 58 through 71, usu. lanthanum, and sometimes yttrium and scandium — called also *rare earth metal;* compare ELEMENT table

rar·ee–show \ˈrar-ē-ˌshō, ˈrer-\ *n* [alter. of *rare show*] **1 :** PEEP SHOW **2 :** SHOW, SPECTACLE; *specif* **:** a cheap street show

rar·efac·tion \ˌrar-ə-ˈfak-shən, ˌrer-\ *n* [F or ML; F *raréfaction,* fr. ML *rarefaction-, rarefactio,* fr. L *rarefactus,* pp. of *rarefacere* to rarefy] **1 :** the action or process of rarefying **2 :** the quality or state of being rarefied **3 :** a state or region of minimum pressure in a medium transversed by compression waves (as sound waves) — **rar·efac·tion·al** \-shnəl, -shən-ᵊl\ *adj* — **rar·e·fac·tive** \-ˈfak-tiv\ *adj*

rar·efied *also* **rar·i·fied** \ˈrar-ə-ˌfīd, ˈrer-\ *adj* **1 :** of, relating to, or interesting to a select group **:** ESOTERIC **2 :** very high

rar·efy *also* **rar·i·fy** \-ə-ˌfī\ *vb* **-efied; -efy·ing** [ME *rarefien, rarifien,* fr. MF *rarefier,* modif. of L *rarefacere,* fr. *rarus* rare + *facere* to make — more at DO] *vt* **1 :** to make rare, thin, porous, or less dense **:** to expand without the addition of matter **2 :** to make more spiritual, refined, or abstruse ~ *vi* **:** to become less dense

rare·ly \ˈra(ə)r-lē, ˈre(ə)r-\ *adv* **1 :** not often **:** SELDOM **2 :** with rare skill **:** EXCELLENTLY **3 :** in an extreme or exceptional manner

1**rare·ripe** \ˈra(ə)r-ˌrīp, ˈre(ə)r-\ *adj* [E dial. *rare* (early) + E *ripe*] **:** ripe before others or earlier than usual

2**rareripe** *n* **1 :** an early ripening fruit or vegetable **2** *dial* **:** GREEN ONION

rar·ing \ˈra(ə)r-ən, ˈre(ə)r-, -iŋ\ *adj* [fr. prp. of E dial. *rare* to rear, alter. of E *rear*] **:** full of enthusiasm or eagerness

rar·i·ty \ˈrar-ət-ē, ˈrer-\ *n, pl* **-ties 1 :** the quality, state, or fact of being rare **2 :** one that is rare

ras·bo·ra \raz-ˈbōr-ə, -ˈbȯr-\ *n* [NL, genus name, fr. native name in the East Indies] **:** any of a genus (*Rasbora*) of tiny brilliantly colored cyprinid freshwater fishes often kept in tropical aquariums

1**ras·cal** \ˈras-kəl\ *n* [ME *rascaile* rabble, one of the rabble] **1 :** a mean, unprincipled, or dishonest person **2 :** a mischievous person or animal

2**rascal** *adj* **:** of, forming, or befitting the rabble **:** LOW

ras·cal·i·ty \ra-ˈskal-ət-ē\ *n, pl* **-ties 1 :** RABBLE **2 a :** the character or actions of a rascal **:** KNAVERY **b :** a rascally act

ras·cal·ly \ˈras-kə-lē\ *adj* **:** of or characteristic of a rascal — **ras·cally** *adv*

rase \ˈrāz\ *vt* **rased; ras·ing** [ME *rasen,* fr. MF *raser,* fr. (assumed) VL *rasare,* fr. L *rasus,* pp. of *radere* to scrape, shave] **1 :** ERASE **2 :** RAZE 1

1**rash** \ˈrash\ *adj* [ME (northern dial.) *rasch* quick; akin to OHG *rasc* fast] **1 :** marked by or proceeding from undue haste or lack of deliberation or caution **2** *obs* **:** quickly effective *syn* see ADVENTUROUS *ant* calculating — **rash·ly** *adv* — **rash·ness** *n*

2**rash** *adv, archaic* **:** in a rash manner

3**rash** *n* [obs. F *rache* scurf, fr. (assumed) VL *rasica,* fr. *rasicare* to scratch, fr. L *rasus,* pp. of *radere*] **1 :** an eruption on the body **2 :** a large number of instances in a short period

rash·er \ˈrash-ər\ *n* [perh. fr. obs. *rash* to cut, fr. ME *rashen*] **:** a thin slice of bacon or ham broiled or fried; *also* **:** a portion consisting of several such slices

ra·so·ri·al \rə-ˈzōr-ē-əl, -ˈsōr-, -ˈzȯr-, -ˈsȯr-\ *adj* [deriv. of LL *rasor* scraper, fr. L *rasus*] **1 :** habitually scratching the ground in search of food <~ birds> **2 :** GALLINACEOUS

1**rasp** \ˈrasp\ *vb* [ME *raspen,* fr. (assumed) MF *rasper,* of Gmc origin; akin to OHG *raspōn* to scrape together] *vt* **1 :** to rub with something rough; *specif* **:** to abrade with a rasp **2 :** to grate upon **:** IRRITATE **3 :** to utter in an irritated tone ~ *vi* **1 :** SCRAPE **2 :** to produce a grating sound — **rasp·er** *n* — **rasp·ing·ly** \ˈras-piŋ-lē\ *adv*

2**rasp** *n* **1 :** a coarse file with cutting points instead of lines **2 :** something used for rasping **3 a :** an act of rasping **b :** a rasping sound, sensation, or effect

rasp·ber·ry \ˈraz-ˌber-ē, -b(ə-)rē\ *n* [E dial. *rasp* (raspberry) + E *berry*] **1 a :** any of various usu. black or red edible berries that are aggregate fruits consisting of numerous small drupes on a fleshy receptacle and that are usu. rounder and smaller than the closely related blackberries **b :** a plant (genus *Rubus*) that bears raspberries **2 :** a sound of contempt made by protruding the tongue between the lips and expelling air forcibly to produce a vibration

raspy \ˈras-pē\ *adj* **1 :** HARSH, GRATING **2 :** IRRITABLE

ras·ter \ˈras-tər\ *n* [G, fr. L *raster, rastrum* rake, fr. *radere* to scrape] **:** the area on which the image is reproduced in a kinescope

ra·sure \ˈrā-shər, -zhər\ *n* [MF, fr. L *rasura,* fr. *rasus,* pp. of *radere*] **:** ERASURE, OBLITERATION

1**rat** \ˈrat\ *n* [ME, fr. OE *ræt;* akin to OHG *ratta* rat, L *rodere* to gnaw, *radere* to scrape, shave] **1 a :** any of numerous rodents (*Rattus* and related genera) differing from the related mice by considerably larger size and by structural details (as of the teeth) **b :** any of various similar rodents **2 :** a contemptible person: as **a :** one who betrays or deserts his party, friends, or associates **b :** SCAB 3b **c :** INFORMER 2 **3 :** a pad over which a woman's hair is arranged — **rat·like** \-ˌlīk\ *adj*

2**rat** *vb* **rat·ted; rat·ting** *vi* **1 :** to betray, desert, or inform on one's associates — usu. used with *on* **2 :** to catch or hunt rats **3 :** to work as a scab ~ *vt* **:** to give (hair) the effect of greater quantity by use of a rat — **rat on :** to go back on (as an agreement or statement) **:** welsh on <*ratted on* her debts —Ellery Sedgwick>

rat·able *or* **rate·able** \ˈrāt-ə-bəl\ *adj* **:** capable of being rated, estimated, or apportioned — **rat·ably** \-blē\ *adv*

rat·a·fia \ˌrat-ə-ˈfē-ə\ *n* [F] **1 :** a liqueur flavored with fruit kernels and bitter almonds **2 :** a sweet biscuit made of almond paste

rat·a·plan \ˈrat-ə-ˌplan\ *n* [F, of imit. origin] **:** the iterative sound of beating <a rolling ~ of drums —*Time*>

rat–a–tat \ˈrat-ə-ˌtat\ *or* **rat–a–tat–tat** \ˌrat-ə-ˌta(t)-ˈtat\ *n* [imit.] **:** a sharp repeated knocking, tapping, or cracking sound

rat–bite fever *n* **:** either of two febrile bacterial diseases of man usu. transmitted by the bite of a rat

ratch \ˈrach\ *n* [G *ratsche,* fr. *ratschen* to rattle, fr. MHG *ratzen;* akin to MHG *razzeln* to rattle] **1 :** RATCHET 2 **2 :** a notched bar with which a pawl or detent works to prevent reversal of motion

rat cheese *n* **:** CHEDDAR

ratch·et \ˈrach-ət\ *n* [alter. of earlier *rochet,* fr. F, alter. of MF *rocquet* lance head, of Gmc origin; akin to OHG *rocko* distaff — more at ROCK] **1 :** a mechanism that consists of a bar or wheel having inclined teeth into which a pawl drops so that motion can be imparted to the wheel or bar, governed, or prevented and that is used in a hand tool (as a brace or screwdriver) to allow effective motion in one direction only **2 :** a pawl or detent for holding or propelling a ratchet wheel

ratchet wheel *n* **:** a toothed wheel held in position or turned by an engaging pawl

1**rate** \ˈrāt\ *vb* **rat·ed; rat·ing** [ME *raten*] *vt* **1 :** to rebuke angrily or violently **2** *obs* **:** to drive away by scolding ~ *vi* **:** to voice angry reprimands

2**rate** *n* [ME, fr. MF, fr. ML *rata,* fr. L (*pro*) *rata* (*parte*) according to a fixed proportion] **1 a :** reckoned value **:** VALUATION **b** *obs* **:** ESTIMATION **2** *obs* **:** a fixed quantity **3 a :** a fixed ratio between two things **b :** a charge, payment, or price fixed according to a ratio, scale, or standard: as **(1) :** a charge per unit of a public-service commodity **(2) :** a charge per unit of freight or passenger service **(3) :** a unit charge or ratio used by a government for assessing property taxes **(4)** *Brit* **:** a local tax **4 a :** a quantity, amount, or degree of something measured per unit of

ə abut ᵊ kitten ər further a back ā bake ä cot, cart
au̇ out ch chin e less ē easy g gift i trip ī life
j joke ŋ sing ō flow ȯ flaw ȯi coin th thin t͟h this
ü loot u̇ foot y yet yü few yu̇ furious zh vision

something else **b :** an amount of payment or charge based on another amount; *specif* **:** the amount of premium per unit of insurance **5 :** relative condition or quality **:** CLASS — **at any rate :** in any case **:** ANYWAY

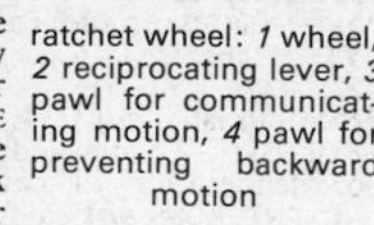

ratchet wheel: *1* wheel, *2* reciprocating lever, *3* pawl for communicating motion, *4* pawl for preventing backward motion

[3]**rate** *vb* **rat·ed; rat·ing** *vt* **1** *obs* **:** ALLOT **2 :** CONSIDER, REGARD <was *rated* an excellent pianist> **3 a :** to set an estimate on **:** VALUE, ESTEEM <black is *rated* very high this season> **b :** to determine or assign the relative rank or class of **:** GRADE <~ a seaman> **c :** to estimate the normal capacity or power of **4 :** to fix the amount of premium to be charged per unit of insurance on **5 :** to have a right to **:** DESERVE <she *rated* special privileges> ~ *vi* **:** to enjoy a status of special privilege <really ~*s* with her boss> *syn* see ESTIMATE

rated load *n* **:** the load a machine is designed to carry

ra·tel \ˈrāt-ᵊl, ˈrät-\ *n* [Afrik, lit., rattle, fr. MD — more at RATTLE] **:** an African or Asiatic nocturnal carnivorous mammal (genus *Mellivora*) resembling the badger

rate·me·ter \ˈrāt-ˌmēt-ər\ *n* **:** an instrument that indicates the counting rate of an electronic counter

rate of change : a value that results from dividing the change of a function of a variable by the change in the variable <velocity is the *rate of change* of distance with respect to time>

rate of exchange : the amount of one currency that will buy a given amount of another

rate of interest : the percentage usu. on an annual basis that is paid for the use of money belonging to another

rate·pay·er \ˈrāt-ˌpā-ər\ *n, Brit* **:** TAXPAYER

rat·er \ˈrāt-ər\ *n* **1 :** one that rates; *specif* **:** a person who estimates or determines a rating **2 :** one having a specified rating or class — usu. used in combination <first-*rater*>

rat fink *n* **:** FINK 3

rat·fish \ˈrat-ˌfish\ *n* **:** CHIMAERA; *esp* **:** a silvery iridescent white-spotted chimaera (*Hydrolagus colliei*) of cold deep waters of the Pacific coast of No. America

rathe \ˈrāth, ˈrath\ *adj* [ME, quick, fr. OE *hræth*, alter. of *hræd;* akin to OHG *hrad* quick] *archaic* **:** EARLY <bring the ~ primrose that forsaken dies —John Milton>

rath·er \ˈrath-ər, ˈrəth-, ˈräth-; *interjectionally* ˈra-ˈthər, ˈrə-, ˈrä-\ *adv* [ME, fr. OE *hrathor*, compar. of *hrathe* quickly; akin to OHG *rado* quickly, OE *hræd* quick] **1 :** with better reason or more propriety <pity ~ than despise —Shak.> **2 :** more readily or willingly **:** PREFERABLY <I'd ~ not go> — often used interjectionally to express affirmation **3 :** more properly or truly <my father, or ~ my stepfather> **4 :** to the contrary **:** INSTEAD <was no better but ~ grew worse —Mk 5:26 (RSV)> **5 :** in some degree **:** SOMEWHAT <it's ~ warm>

raths·kel·ler \ˈrät-ˌskel-ər, ˈrat(h)-\ *n* [obs. G (now *ratskeller*), city-hall basement restaurant, fr. *rat* council + *keller* cellar] **:** a restaurant which is patterned after the cellar of a German city hall and in which beer is sold

rat·icide \ˈrat-ə-ˌsīd\ *n* **:** a substance for killing rats

rat·i·fy \ˈrat-ə-ˌfī\ *vt* **-fied; -fy·ing** [ME *ratifien*, fr. MF *ratifier*, fr. ML *ratificare*, fr. L *ratus* determined, fr. pp. of *reri* to calculate — more at REASON] **:** to approve and sanction formally **:** CONFIRM <~ a treaty> — **rat·i·fi·ca·tion** \ˌrat-ə-fə-ˈkā-shən\ *n*

ra·ti·né \ˌrat-ə-ˈnā\ *or* **ra·tine** \ˌrat-ə-ˈnā, ra-ˈtēn\ *n* [F *ratiné*] **1 :** a nubby ply yarn of various fibers made by twisting under tension a thick and a thin yarn **2 :** a rough bulky fabric usu. woven loosely in plain weave from ratiné yarns

rat·ing \ˈrāt-iŋ\ *n* **1 :** a classification according to grade; *specif* **:** a military or naval specialist classification **2** *chiefly Brit* **:** a naval enlisted man **3 a :** relative estimate or evaluation **:** STANDING <the school has a good academic ~> **b :** an estimate of an individual's or business's credit and responsibility **4 :** a stated operating limit of a machine expressible in power units (as kilowatts of a direct-current generator) or in characteristics (as voltage)

ra·tio \ˈrā-(ˌ)shō, -shē-ˌō\ *n, pl* **ra·tios** [L, computation, reason — more at REASON] **1 a :** the indicated quotient of two mathematical expressions **b :** the relationship in quantity, amount, or size between two or more things **:** PROPORTION **2 :** the expression of the relative values of gold and silver as determined by a country's currency laws

ra·ti·o·ci·nate \ˌrat-ē-ˈōs-ᵊn-ˌāt, ˌrash-ē-, -ˈäs-\ *vi* **-nat·ed; -nat·ing** [L *ratiocinatus*, pp. of *ratiocinari* to reckon, fr. *ratio*] **:** REASON — **ra·ti·o·ci·na·tor** \-ˌāt-ər\ *n*

ra·ti·o·ci·na·tion \-ˌōs-ᵊn-ˈā-shən, -ˌäs-\ *n* **1 :** the process of exact thinking **:** REASONING **2 :** a reasoned train of thought — **ra·ti·o·ci·na·tive** \-ˈōs-ᵊn-ˌāt-iv, -ˈäs-\ *adj*

[1]**ra·tion** \ˈrash-ən, ˈrā-shən\ *n* [F, fr. L *ration-, ratio* computation, reason] **1 a :** a food allowance for one day **b** *pl* **:** FOOD, PROVISIONS **2 :** a share esp. as determined by supply

syn RATION, ALLOWANCE, DOLE, PITTANCE *shared meaning element* **:** the amount of food, supplies, or money allotted to an individual. RATION implies apportionment and, often, equal sharing; basically, it applies to the daily supply of food provided for one individual (as a prisoner or a milk cow) but it is freely extended to scarce things made available either equally or equitably in accord with need <gasoline *rations* in wartime vary with the special needs of individuals> ALLOWANCE, though often interchangeable with *ration,* is of wider application, for it stresses granting, rather than sharing what is available in restricted supply <provided each man with a weekly *allowance* of tobacco> <a regular *allowance* teaches children to handle money> DOLE tends to imply a grudging allowance to needy or grasping recipients <cold charity's unwelcome *dole* —P. B. Shelley> In modern and especially British use, *dole* applies specifically to a public payment to the needy or unemployed. PITTANCE stresses meagerness or miserliness and may apply indifferently to a ration, an allowance, an alms, a dole, or a wage <and gained, by spinning hemp, a *pittance* for herself —William Wordsworth>

[2]**ration** *vt* **ra·tioned; ra·tion·ing** \ˈrash-(ə-)niŋ, ˈrāsh-\ **1 :** to supply with or put on rations **2 a :** to distribute as rations — often used with *out* <~*ed* out sugar and flour> **b :** to distribute equitably **c :** to use sparingly

[1]**ra·tio·nal** \ˈrash-nəl, -ən-ᵊl\ *adj* [ME *racional*, fr. L *rationalis*, fr. *ration-, ratio*] **1 a :** having reason or understanding **b :** relating to, based on, or agreeable to reason **:** REASONABLE <a ~ explanation> <~ behavior> **2 :** involving only multiplication, division, addition, and subtraction and only a finite number of times **3 :** relating to, consisting of, or being one or more rational numbers — **ra·tio·nal·ly** \-ē\ *adv* — **ra·tio·nal·ness** *n*

[2]**rational** *n* **:** something rational; *specif* **:** RATIONAL NUMBER

ra·tio·nale \ˌrash-ə-ˈnal\ *n* [L, neut. of *rationalis*] **1 :** an explanation of controlling principles of opinion, belief, practice, or phenomena **2 :** an underlying reason **:** BASIS

rational function *n* **1 :** POLYNOMIAL **2 :** a function that is the quotient of two polynomials

ra·tio·nal·ism \ˈrash-nə-ˌliz-əm, -ən-ᵊl-ˌiz-\ *n* **1 :** reliance on reason as the basis for establishment of religious truth **2 a :** a theory that reason is in itself a source of knowledge superior to and independent of sense perceptions **b :** a view that reason and experience rather than the nonrational are the fundamental criteria in the solution of problems **3 :** FUNCTIONALISM — **ra·tio·nal·ist** \-nə-ləst, -ən-ᵊl-əst\ *n* — **rationalist** *or* **ra·tio·nal·is·tic** \ˌrash-nə-ˈlis-tik, -ən-ᵊl-ˈis-\ *adj* — **ra·tio·nal·is·ti·cal·ly** \-ti-k(ə-)lē\ *adv*

ra·tio·nal·i·ty \ˌrash-ə-ˈnal-ət-ē\ *n, pl* **-ties 1 :** the quality or state of being rational **2 :** the quality or state of being agreeable to reason **:** REASONABLENESS **3 :** a rational opinion, belief, or practice — usu. used in pl.

ra·tio·nal·ize \ˈrash-nə-ˌlīz, -ən-ᵊl-ˌīz\ *vb* **-ized; -iz·ing** *vt* **1 :** to free (a mathematical expression) from irrational parts <~ a denominator> **2 :** to bring into accord with reason or cause something to seem reasonable: as **a :** to substitute a natural for a supernatural explanation of <~ a myth> **b :** to attribute (one's actions) to rational and creditable motives without analysis of true and esp. unconscious motives <*rationalized* his dislike of his brother> ~ *vi* **:** to provide plausible but untrue reasons for conduct — **ra·tio·nal·iza·tion** \ˌrash-nə-lə-ˈzā-shən, -ən-ᵊl-ə-\ *n* — **ra·tio·nal·iz·er** \ˈrash-nə-ˌlī-zər, -ən-ᵊl-ˌī-\ *n*

rational number *n* **:** an integer or the quotient of two integers

[1]**rat·ite** \ˈra-ˌtīt\ *adj* [deriv. of L *ratitus* marked with the figure of a raft, fr. *ratis* raft] **:** having a flat breastbone

[2]**ratite** *n* **:** a bird with a flat breastbone; *esp* **:** any of a superorder (Ratitae) of birds (as an ostrich, an emu, a moa, and a kiwi) that have small or rudimentary wings and no keel to the breastbone

rat·line \ˈrat-lən\ *n* [origin unknown] **:** one of the small transverse ropes attached to the shrouds of a ship so as to form the steps of a rope ladder

ratlines

rat mite *n* **:** a widely distributed mite (*Bdellonyssus bacoti*) that usu. feeds on rodents but may cause dermatitis in and transmit typhus to man

[1]**ra·toon** \ra-ˈtün\ *n* [Sp *retoño*, fr. *retoñar* to sprout, fr. *re-* (fr. L) + *otoñar* to grow in autumn, fr. *otoño* autumn, fr. L *autumnus*] **1 :** a shoot of a perennial plant (as sugarcane) **2 :** a crop (as of bananas) produced on ratoons

[2]**ratoon** *vi* **:** to sprout or spring up from the root ~ *vt* **:** to grow or produce (a crop) from or on ratoons

ra·to unit \ˈrāt-(ˌ)ō-\ *n* [*r*ocket-*a*ssisted *t*ake*o*ff] **:** JATO UNIT

rat race *n* **:** strenuous, wearisome, and usu. competitive activity or rush

rat snake *n* **:** any of numerous large harmless rat-eating colubrid snakes — called also *chicken snake*

rat·tail \ˈrat-ˌtāl\ *n* **1 :** a horse's tail with little or no hair **2 :** GRENADIER 2

rattail cactus *n* **:** a commonly cultivated tropical American cactus (*Aporocactus flagelliformis*) with creeping stems and showy crimson flowers

rat–tail file *n* **:** a round slender tapered file

rat·tan \ra-ˈtan, rə-\ *n* [Malay *rotan*] **1 a :** a climbing palm (esp. of the genera *Calamus* and *Daemonorops*) with very long tough stems **b :** a part of the stem of a rattan used esp. for walking sticks and wickerwork **2 :** a rattan cane or switch

rat·teen \ra-ˈtēn\ *n* [F *ratine*] *archaic* **:** a coarse woolen fabric

rat·ter \ˈrat-ər\ *n* **:** one that catches rats; *specif* **:** a rat-catching dog or cat

[1]**rat·tle** \ˈrat-ᵊl\ *vb* **rat·tled; rat·tling** \ˈrat-liŋ, -ᵊl-iŋ\ [ME *ratelen;* akin to MD *ratel* rattle, OE *hratian* to rush — more at CARDINAL] *vi* **1 :** to make a rapid succession of short sharp noises <the windows *rattled* in the wind> **2 :** to chatter incessantly and aimlessly **3 a :** to move with a clatter or rattle **b :** to have room to move about aimlessly ~ *vt* **1 :** to say, perform, or affect in a brisk lively fashion <*rattled* off four magnificent backhands —Kim Chapin> **2 :** to cause to make a rattling sound **3 :** ROUSE; *specif* **:** to beat (a cover) for game **4 :** to upset to the point of loss of poise and composure *syn* see EMBARRASS

[2]**rattle** *n* **1 a :** a rapid succession of sharp clattering sounds **b :** NOISE, RACKET **2 a :** a device that produces a rattle; *specif* **:** a case containing pellets used as a baby's toy **b :** the sound-producing organ on a rattlesnake's tail **3 :** a throat noise caused by air passing through mucus and heard esp. at the approach of death

[3]**rattle** *vt* **rat·tled; rat·tling** \ˈrat-liŋ, -ᵊl-iŋ\ [irreg. fr. *ratline*] **:** to furnish with ratlines

rat·tle·brain \ˈrat-ᵊl-ˌbrān\ *n* **:** a flighty or thoughtless person — **rat·tle·brained** \ˌrat-ᵊl-ˈbrānd\ *adj*

rat·tler \ˈrat-lər, -ᵊl-ər\ *n* **1 :** one that rattles **2 :** RATTLESNAKE

rat·tle·snake \ˈrat-ᵊl-ˌsnāk\ *n* **:** any of various thick-bodied American venomous snakes (family Crotalidae, genera *Sistrurus* and *Crotalus*) with horny interlocking joints at the end of the tail that make a sharp rattling sound when shaken

rattlesnake

rattlesnake plantain *n* **:** an orchid (genus *Goodyera*) with checked or mottled leaves

rattlesnake root *n* **:** any of various plants formerly believed to be distasteful to rattlesnakes or effective against their venom: as **a :** any of a genus (*Prenanthes* and esp. *P. altissima*) of composite plants that have lobed or pinnatifid leaves and small heads of drooping ligulate flowers **b :** SENECA SNAKEROOT

rattlesnake weed *n* **1 :** a hawkweed (*Hieracium venosum*) with purple-veined leaves **2 :** a weedy herb (*Daucus pusillus*) of the western U.S. related to the carrot

rat·tle·trap \ˈrat-ᵊl-ˌtrap\ *n* **:** something rattly or rickety; *esp* **:** an old car — **rattletrap** *adj*

[1]**rat·tling** \ˈrat-liŋ\ *adj* **1 :** LIVELY, BRISK <moved at a ~ pace> **2 :** extraordinarily good **:** SPLENDID <played a ~ game —*Sunday Independent (Dublin)*> — **rat·tling·ly** \-liŋ-lē\ *adv*

[2]**rattling** *adv* **:** to an extreme degree **:** VERY <a ~ good argument —E. A. Betts>

rat·tly \ˈrat-lē, -ᵊl-ē\ *adj* **:** likely to rattle **:** making a rattle

rat·ton \ˈrat-ᵊn, ˈrät-\ *n* [ME *ratoun*, fr. MF *raton*, dim. of *rat*, prob. of Gmc origin; akin to OE *ræt* rat] *chiefly dial* **:** RAT

rat·trap \ˈra(t)-ˌtrap\ *n* **1 :** a trap for rats **2 :** a dirty dilapidated structure **3 :** a hopeless situation

rat trap cheese *n* **:** CHEDDAR

rat·ty \ˈrat-ē\ *adj* **rat·ti·er; -est** **1 a :** infested with rats **b :** of, relating to, or suggestive of a rat **2 :** SHABBY, UNKEMPT <a ~ brown overcoat —John Lardner> **3 a :** DESPICABLE, TREACHEROUS <she was forever taking up with ~ people —Frances G. Patton> **b :** IRRITABLE <feeling ~ as hell —Richard Bissell>

rau·cous \ˈrȯ-kəs\ *adj* [L *raucus* hoarse; akin to OE *rēon* to lament — more at RUMOR] **1 :** disagreeably harsh or strident **:** HOARSE <~ voices> **2 :** boisterously disorderly <a . . . ~ frontier town —Truman Capote> — **rau·cous·ly** *adv* — **rau·cous·ness** *n*

raun·chy \ˈrȯn-chē, ˈrän-\ *adj* **raun·chi·er; -est** [origin unknown] **1 :** SLOVENLY, DIRTY <a ~ panhandler> **2 :** OBSCENE, SMUTTY <~ jokes> — **raun·chi·ly** \ˈrȯn-chə-lē\ *adv* — **raun·chi·ness** \-chē-nəs\ *n*

rau·wol·fia \rau̇-ˈwu̇l-fē-ə, rȯ-\ *n* [NL, genus name, fr. Leonhard *Rauwolf* †1596 G botanist] **1 :** any of a large pantropic genus (*Rauwolfia*) of the dogbane family of somewhat poisonous trees and shrubs yielding emetic and purgative substances **2 :** a medicinal extract from the root of an Indian rauwolfia (*Rauwolfia serpentina*) used in the treatment of hypertension and mental disorders

[1]**rav·age** \ˈrav-ij\ *n* [F, fr. MF, fr. *ravir* to ravish — more at RAVISH] **1 :** an act or practice of ravaging **2 :** damage resulting from ravaging **:** violently destructive effect <the ~*s* of time>

[2]**ravage** *vb* **rav·aged; rav·ag·ing** *vt* **:** to wreak havoc on **:** visit destructively and often violently ~ *vi* **:** to commit destructive actions — **rav·age·ment** \-ij-mənt\ *n* — **rav·ag·er** *n*
syn RAVAGE, DEVASTATE, WASTE, SACK, PILLAGE *shared meaning element* **:** to lay waste by plundering or destroying

[1]**rave** \ˈrāv\ *vb* **raved; rav·ing** [ME *raven*] *vi* **1 a :** to talk irrationally in or as if in delirium **b :** to declaim wildly **c :** to talk with extreme enthusiasm <*raved* about her beauty> **2 :** to move or advance violently **:** STORM <the iced gusts still ~ and beat —John Keats> ~ *vt* **:** to utter in madness or frenzy — **rav·er** *n*

[2]**rave** *n* **1 :** an act or instance of raving **2 :** an extravagantly favorable criticism <the play received the critics' ~*s*>

[1]**rav·el** \ˈrav-əl\ *vb* **-eled** *or* **-elled; -el·ing** *or* **-el·ling** \-(ə-)liŋ\ [D *rafelen*, fr. *rafel* loose thread; akin to OE *ræfter* rafter] *vt* **1 a :** to separate or undo the texture of **:** UNRAVEL **b :** to undo the intricacies of **:** DISENTANGLE **2 :** ENTANGLE, CONFUSE ~ *vi* **1** *obs* **:** to become entangled or confused **2 :** to become unwoven, untwisted, or unwound **:** FRAY **3 :** to break up **:** CRUMBLE — **rav·el·er** \-(ə-)lər\ *n* — **rav·el·ment** \-əl-mənt\ *n*

[2]**ravel** *n* **:** an act or result of raveling: as **a :** something tangled **b :** something raveled out; *specif* **:** a loose thread

rav·el·ing *or* **rav·el·ling** \ˈrav(-ə)-liŋ, -lən\ *n* **:** RAVEL b

[1]**ra·ven** \ˈrā-vən\ *n* [ME, fr. OE *hræfn;* akin to OHG *hraban* raven, L *corvus*, Gk *korax*, L *crepare* to rattle, crack] **:** a glossy black corvine bird (*Corvus corax*) of northern Europe, Asia, and America — compare CROW

raven

[2]**raven** *adj* **:** of the color or glossy sheen of the raven <~ hair>

[3]**rav·en** \ˈrav-ən\ *vb* **rav·ened; rav·en·ing** \-(ə-)niŋ\ [MF *raviner* to rush, take by force, fr. *ravine* rapine] *vt* **1 :** to devour greedily **2 :** DESPOIL <men . . . ~ the earth, destroying its resources —*New Yorker*> ~ *vi* **1 :** to feed greedily **2 :** to prowl for food **:** PREY **3 :** PLUNDER — **rav·en·er** \-(ə-)nər\ *n*

rav·en·ous \ˈrav-(ə-)nəs\ *adj* **1 :** RAPACIOUS, VORACIOUS <~ wolves> **2 :** very eager for food, satisfaction, or gratification <a ~ appetite> — **rav·en·ous·ly** *adv* — **rav·en·ous·ness** *n*

rav·in \ˈrav-ən\ *n* [ME, fr. MF *ravine*] **1 :** PLUNDER, PILLAGE **2 a :** an act or habit of preying **b :** something seized as prey <red in tooth and claw with ~ —Alfred Tennyson>

ra·vine \rə-ˈvēn\ *n* [F, fr. MF, rapine, rush, fr. L *rapina* rapine] **:** a small narrow steep-sided valley that is larger than a gully and smaller than a canyon and that is usu. worn by running water

rav·ined \ˈrav-ənd\ *adj, obs* **:** RAVENOUS

[1]**rav·ing** \ˈrā-viŋ\ *n* **:** irrational, incoherent, wild, or extravagant utterance or declamation — usu. used in pl.

[2]**raving** *adj* **1 :** talking wildly or irrationally <a ~ lunatic> **2 :** RAVISHING <a ~ beauty>

rav·i·o·li \ˌrav-ē-ˈō-lē, ˌräv-\ *n* [It, fr. It dial., pl. of *raviolo*, lit., little turnip, dim. of *rava* turnip, fr. L *rapa* — more at RAPE] **:** little cases of dough containing a savory filling (as of meat or cheese); *also* **:** a dish consisting of ravioli in a tomato sauce

rav·ish \ˈrav-ish\ *vt* [ME *ravisshen*, fr. MF *raviss-*, stem of *ravir*, fr. (assumed) VL *rapire*, alter. of L *rapere* to seize, rob — more at RAPID] **1 a :** to seize and take away by violence **b :** to overcome with emotion (as joy or delight) <~*ed* by the beauty of the scene> **c :** RAPE, VIOLATE **2 :** PLUNDER, ROB ***syn*** see TRANSPORT — **rav·ish·er** *n* — **rav·ish·ment** \-ish-mənt\ *n*

rav·ish·ing \ˈrav-ish-iŋ\ *adj* **:** unusually attractive, pleasing, or striking — **rav·ish·ing·ly** \-iŋ-lē\ *adv*

[1]**raw** \ˈrȯ\ *adj* **raw·er** \ˈrȯ(-ə)r\; **raw·est** \ˈrȯ-əst\ [ME, fr. OE *hrēaw;* akin to OHG *hrō* raw, L *crudus* raw, *cruor* blood, Gk *kreas* flesh] **1 :** not cooked **2 a (1) :** being in or nearly in the natural state **:** not processed or purified <~ fibers> <~ sewage> **(2) :** not diluted or blended <~ spirits> **b :** unprepared or imperfectly prepared for use **c :** not being in polished, finished, or processed form <~ data> <a ~ draft of a thesis> **3 a (1) :** having the surface abraded or chafed **(2) :** very irritated <a ~ sore throat> **b :** lacking covering **:** NAKED **4 a :** lacking experience or understanding **:** GREEN <a ~ recruit> **b (1) :** marked by absence of refinements **(2) :** VULGAR, COARSE <a ~ joke> **5 :** disagreeably damp or cold ***syn*** see RUDE — **raw·ly** *adv* — **raw·ness** *n*

[2]**raw** *n* **:** a raw place or state — **in the raw** **1 :** in the natural or crude state <life *in the raw*> **2 :** NAKED <slept *in the raw*>

raw·boned \ˈrȯ-ˈbōnd\ *adj* **1 :** having little flesh **:** GAUNT **2 :** having a coarse heavy frame that seems inadequately covered with flesh ***syn*** see LEAN

raw deal *n* **:** an instance of unfair treatment

[1]**raw·hide** \ˈrȯ-ˌhīd\ *n* **1 :** untanned cattle skin **2 :** a whip of untanned hide

[2]**rawhide** *vt* **raw·hid·ed; raw·hid·ing** **:** to whip or drive with or as if with a rawhide

ra·win·sonde \ˈrā-wən-ˌsänd\ *n* [*ra*dar + *win*d + radio*sonde*] **:** a radiosonde tracked by a radio direction-finding device to determine the velocity of winds aloft

raw material *n* **:** material whether crude or processed that can be converted by manufacture, processing, or combination into a new and useful product <wheat, the finished product of the farmer, is *raw material* for the flour mill —C. A. Koepke>; *broadly* **:** something with a potential for improvement, development, or elaboration <perplexities are often the *raw material* of discoveries —Agnes M. Clerke>

raw score *n* **:** an individual's actual achievement (as on a test) usu. expressed numerically and unadjusted for relative position in the group tested

rax \ˈraks\ *vb* [ME (northern dial.) *raxen*, fr. OE *raxan;* akin to OE *reccan* to stretch — more at RACK] *chiefly Scot* **:** STRETCH

[1]**ray** \ˈrā\ *n* [ME *raye*, fr. MF *raie*, fr. L *raia*] **:** any of numerous elasmobranch fishes (order Hypotremata) having the body flattened dorsoventrally, the eyes on the upper surface, and a much-reduced caudal region

[2]**ray** *n* [ME, fr. MF *rai*, fr. L *radius* rod, ray] **1 a :** one of the lines of light that appear to radiate from a bright object **b :** a beam of light or other radiant energy of small cross section **c (1) :** a stream of material particles traveling in the same line (as in radioactive phenomena) **(2) :** a single particle of such a stream **2 a :** light cast by rays **:** RADIANCE **b :** a moral or intellectual light **3 :** a thin line suggesting a ray: as **a :** any of a group of lines diverging from a common center **b :** HALF LINE **4 a :** one of the bony rods that extend and support the membrane in the fin of a fish **b :** one of the radiating divisions of the body of a radiate animal **c :** a longitudinal vein of an insect's wing **5 a :** a branch or flower stalk of an umbel **b (1) :** MEDULLARY RAY **(2) :** VASCULAR RAY **c :** RAY FLOWER 1 **6 :** PARTICLE, TRACE <~ of hope>

[3]**ray** *vi* **1 a :** to shine in or as if in rays **b :** to issue as rays **2 :** to extend like the radii of a circle **:** RADIATE ~ *vt* **1 :** to emit in rays **2 :** to furnish or mark with rays

rayed \ˈrād\ *adj* **:** having ray flowers

ray floret *n* **:** RAY FLOWER 1

ray flower *n* **1 :** one of the marginal flowers of the head in a composite plant (as the aster) that also has disk flowers **2 :** the entire head in a plant (as chicory) that lacks disk flowers

ray·less \ˈrā-ləs\ *adj* **1 :** having, admitting, or emitting no rays; *esp* **:** DARK **2 :** lacking ray flowers — **ray·less·ness** *n*

rayless goldenrod *n* **:** any of several composite plants (*Haplopappus* or related genera) some of which produce trembles in cattle

ray·on \ˈrā-ˌän\ *n* [irreg. fr. [2]*ray*] **1 :** any of a group of smooth textile fibers made in filament and staple form from cellulosic material by extrusion through minute holes **2 :** a rayon yarn, thread, or fabric

raze \ˈrāz\ *vt* **razed; raz·ing** [alter. of *rase*] **1 :** to destroy to the ground : DEMOLISH **2 a :** to scrape, cut, or shave off **b** *archaic* : ERASE — **raz·er** *n*

[1]**ra·zee** \rā-ˈzē\ *n* [F (*vaisseau*) *rasé*, lit., cut-off ship] : a wooden ship with the upper deck cut away

[2]**razee** *vt* **ra·zeed; ra·zee·ing :** to convert to a razee

ra·zor \ˈrā-zər\ *n* [ME *rasour*, fr. OF *raseor*, fr. *raser* to raze, shave — more at RASE] : a keen-edged cutting instrument for shaving or cutting hair

ra·zor·back \ˈrā-zər-ˌbak\ *n* : a thin-bodied long-legged half-wild mongrel hog chiefly of the southeastern U.S.

ra·zor–backed \ˌrā-zər-ˈbakt\ *or* **ra·zor·back** \ˈrā-zər-ˌbak\ *adj* : having a sharp narrow back <a ~ horse>

ra·zor·bill \ˈrā-zər-ˌbil\ *n* : a No. Atlantic auk (*Alca torda*) with the plumage black above and white below and a compressed sharp-edged bill — called also *razor-billed auk*

razor clam *n* : any of numerous marine bivalve mollusks (family Solenidae) having a long narrow curved thin shell

[1]**razz** \ˈraz\ *n* [short for *razzberry* (sound of contempt), alter. of *raspberry*] : RASPBERRY 2

[2]**razz** *vt* : HECKLE, DERIDE <the fans ~*ed* the visiting players>

raz·zle–daz·zle \ˌraz-əl-ˈdaz-əl\ *n* [irreg. redupl. of *dazzle*] **1 :** a state of confusion or hilarity **2 :** a complex maneuver (as in sports) designed to confuse an opponent **3 :** a confusing or colorful often gaudy action or display

razz·ma·tazz \ˌraz-mə-ˈtaz\ *n* [prob. alter. of *razzle-dazzle*] **1** : RAZZLE-DAZZLE 3 **2 :** DOUBLE-TALK 2 <the ~ of TV commercials> **3 :** VIM, ZING <that ballplayer has a lot of ~>

Rb *symbol* rubidium

RBA *abbr* Royal Society of British Artists

RBC *abbr* red blood cells; red blood count

RBE *abbr* relative biological effectiveness

RBI \ˌär-(ˌ)bē-ˈī, ˈrib-ē\ *n, pl* **RBIs** *or* **RBI** [*r*un *b*atted *i*n] : a run scored in baseball by an action by a batter (as a base hit)

RBS *abbr* Royal Society of British Sculptors

RC *abbr* **1** Red Cross **2** resistance-capacitance **3** Roman Catholic

RCAF *abbr* Royal Canadian Air Force

RCMP *abbr* Royal Canadian Mounted Police

RCN *abbr* Royal Canadian Navy

r color *n* : an acoustic effect of a simultaneously articulated \r\ imparted to a vowel by retroflexion or constriction of the tongue — **r–col·ored** \ˈär-ˌkəl-ərd\ *adj*

RCP *abbr* Royal College of Physicians

RCS *abbr* Royal College of Surgeons

rct *abbr* recruit

rd *abbr* **1** road **2** rod **3** round

RD *abbr* **1** refer to drawer **2** rural delivery

RDF *abbr* radio direction finder; radio direction finding

[1]**re** \ˈrā\ *n* [ML, fr. the syllable sung to this note in a medieval hymn to St. John the Baptist] : the 2d tone of the diatonic scale in solmization

[2]**re** \(ˈ)rā, (ˈ)rē\ *prep* [L, abl. of *res* thing — more at REAL] : with regard to : in re

Re *symbol* rhenium

re- *prefix* [ME, fr. OF, fr. L *re-*, *red-* back, again, against] **1 :** again : anew <*re*tell> **2 :** back : backward <*re*call>

reaccommodate
reaccredit
reaccreditation
reaccumulation
reachieve
reachievement
reacquaint
reacquire
reacquisition
reactuate
readapt
readdict
readdiction
readdress
readjust
readjustable
readjustment
readmission
readmit
readmittance
readopt
readoption
reaffirm
reaffirmation
reaffix
reallocate
reallocation
reanalysis
reanalyze
reanesthetize
reanimate
reanimation
reannex
reannexation
reappear
reappearance
reapplication
reapply
reappoint
reappointment
reappraisal
reappraise
rearousal
rearouse
rearrange
rearrangement
rearranger
rearrest
reascend
reascent
reassail
reassemble
reassembly
reassert
reassertion
reassess
reassessment
reassign
reassignment
reassort
reassortment
reassume
reassumption
reattach
reattachment
reattack
reattain
reattainment
reattempt
reattribute
reattribution
reauthorize
reawake
reawaken
rebait
rebalance
rebaptism
rebaptize
rebid
rebiddable
rebind
reboard
reboil
reburial
rebury
rebutton
recalibrate
recane
recarbonize
recatalog
recatalogue
recentralization
recertification
recertify
rechannel
recheck
rechristen
rechromatograph
recirculate
recirculation
reclassification
reclassify
reclean
recoal
recock
recodification
recodify
recolonization
recolonize
recolor
recombine
recommence
recommencement
recommission
recompilation
recompile
recomplete
recompletion
recompound
recompress
recompression
recomputation
recompute
reconceive
reconcentrate
reconcentration
reconception
reconceptualization
reconceptualize
recondensation
recondense
reconduct
reconfine
reconnect
reconnection
reconquer
reconquest
reconsecrate
reconsecration
reconsign
reconsignment
reconsult
reconsultation
recontact
recontaminate
recontamination
recontour
recontract
reconvene
reconvict
reconviction
reconvince
recook
recopy
recouple
recross
recut
redate
rededicate
rededication
redelegate
redeliver
redelivery
redemand
redemandable
redemocratize
redeposit
redesignate
redifferentiation
redigest
redigestion
redip
rediscover
rediscovery
redispose
redisposition
redissolve
redistill
redistillation
redivide
redivision
redomesticate
redraft
redraw
redrawer
reeligibility
reeligible
reembodiment
reembody
reemerge
reemergence
reemergent
reemission
reemit
reemphasis
reemphasize
reenchant
reenergize
reengineer
reenlist
reenlistment
reequip
reerect
reerection
reescalate
reescalation
reestablish
reestablishment
reevaluate
reevaluation
reevaporation
reevoke
reexamination
reexamine
reexchange
reexperience
reexploration
reexplore
reexport
reexportation
reexporter
reface
refall
refasten
refeed
refight
refigure
refilm
refilter
refind
refix
refloat
reflood
reflourish
reflower
refly
refold
reformat
reformulate
reformulation
refortification
refortify
refound
reframe
refreeze
refront
refurnish
regather
regild
regive
reglaze
reglow
reglue
regrade
regrind
regroove
regrowth
rehammer
rehandle
reheat
rehire
rehospitalization
rehospitalize
reidentification
reidentify
reignite
reimage
reimmerse
reimmersion
reimplantation
reimpose
reimposition
reinclude
reinclusion
reincorporate
reindex
reinfestation
reinfiltrate
reinfiltration
reinitiate
reinjure
reinnervate
reinnervation
reinsert
reinsertion
reinspect
reinspection
reinstall
reinstitute
reinstitution
reinter
reintroduce
reintroduction
reinvasion
reinvestigate
reinvestigation
rejudge
rejustify
rekey
rekeyboard
relabel
relearn
relend
relet
reletter
relicense
relight
reload
reloader
relubricate
relubrication
remachine
remarriage
remarry
remeet
remelt
remigrate
remigration
remineralization
remix
remobilize
remold
remotivate
rename
renationalization
renationalize
renature
reoccupation
reoccupy
reoccur
reoccurrence
reordination
reorient
reorientate
reorientation
reoxidation
reoxidize
repack
repaint
repattern
repave
repeople
reperk
rephotograph
rephrase
replan
replaster
replate
repolarize
repolymerize
repopularization
repopularize
reprecipitate
repressurize
reprice
repropose
repurchase
repurify
reread
rerecord
reregister
reregistration
reroll
reroller
reroute
resample
resaw
resay
reschedule
rescore
rescreen
reseal
reseat
resecrete
resediment
resee
resegregate
resegregation
resell
reseller
resensitize
resentence
resettle
resettlement
resew
reshoot
reshoulder
reshow
resilver
resize
resmelt
resmooth
resolidify
resow
respring
restaff
restimulate
restimulation
restock
restraighten
restrengthen
restring
restuff
restyle
resublime
resubmission
resubmit
resummon
resurge
resurrender
resurvey
resuspend
resuspension
resynthesis
resynthesize
retabulate
retailor
retaste
reteach
rethink
rethread
retie
retime
retint
retitle
retrack
retransform
retransformation
retransmission
retransmit
retraverse
retune
retype
reupholster
reutilize
revaccinate
revaccination
revaporize
reverification
reverify
revote
rewarm
rewash
rewater
reweave
rewed
reweigh
reweigher
reweld
rewire

're \(ə)r\ *vb* : ARE <you'*re* right>

REA *abbr* **1** Railway Express Agency **2** Rural Electrification Administration

re·ab·sorb \ˌrē-əb-ˈsȯ(ə)rb, -ˈzȯ(ə)rb\ *vt* **:** to take up (something previously secreted) <sugars ~*ed* in the kidney>; *also* **:** RESORB 2

[1]reach \ˈrēch\ *vb* [ME *rechen,* fr. OE *rǣcan;* akin to OHG *reichen* to reach, Lith *raižytis* to stretch oneself repeatedly] *vt* **1 a :** to stretch out **:** EXTEND **b :** THRUST **2 a :** to touch or grasp by extending a part of the body (as a hand) or an object <couldn't ~ the apple> **b :** to pick up and draw toward one **:** TAKE **c** (1) **:** to extend to <the shadow ~*ed* the wall> (2) **:** to get up to or as far as **:** come to <your letter ~*ed* me yesterday> <his voice ~*ed* the last rows> <they hoped to ~ an agreement> **d** (1) **:** ENCOMPASS (2) **:** to make an impression on (3) **:** to communicate with **3 :** to hand over **:** PASS ~ *vi* **1 a :** to make a stretch with or as if with one's hand **b :** to strain after something **2 a :** PROJECT, EXTEND <his land ~*es* to the river> **b :** to arrive at or come to something <as far as the eye could ~> **3 :** to sail on a reach — **reach·able** \ˈrē-chə-bəl\ *adj* — **reach·er** *n*
syn REACH, GAIN, COMPASS, ACHIEVE, ATTAIN *shared meaning element* **:** to arrive at a point or end by work or effort

[2]reach *n* **1 a** (1) **:** the action or an act of reaching (2) **:** an individual part of a progression or journey **b :** the distance or extent of reaching or of ability to reach **c :** COMPREHENSION, RANGE **2 :** a continuous stretch or expanse; *esp* **:** a straight portion of a stream or river **3 :** a bearing shaft or coupling pole; *esp* **:** the rod joining the hind axle to the forward bolster of a wagon **4 :** the tack sailed by a ship with the wind coming just forward of the beam or with the wind directly abeam or abaft the beam **5** *pl* **:** positions of importance <the higher ~*es* of academic life>

reach–me–down \ˈrēch-mē-ˌdau̇n\ *adj or n, chiefly Brit* **:** HAND-ME-DOWN

re·act \rē-ˈakt\ *vb* [NL *reactus,* pp. of *reagere,* fr. L *re-* + *agere* to act — more at AGENT] *vi* **1 :** to exert a reciprocal or counteracting force or influence — often used with *on* or *upon* **2 :** to respond to a stimulus **3 :** to act in opposition to a force or influence — usu. used with *against* **4 :** to move or tend in a reverse direction **5 :** to undergo chemical reaction ~ *vt* **:** to cause to react

re·ac·tance \rē-ˈak-tən(t)s\ *n* **:** the part of the impedance of an alternating-current circuit that is due to capacitance or inductance or both and that is expressed in ohms

re·ac·tant \-tənt\ *n* **:** a substance that enters into and is altered in the course of a chemical reaction

re·ac·tion \rē-ˈak-shən\ *n* **1 a :** the act or process or an instance of reacting **b :** tendency toward a former and usu. outmoded political or social order or policy **2 :** bodily response to or activity aroused by a stimulus: **a :** an action induced by vital resistance to another action; *esp* **:** the response of tissues to a foreign substance (as an antigen or infective agent) **b :** depression or exhaustion due to excessive exertion or stimulation **c :** heightened activity and overaction succeeding depression or shock **d :** a mental or emotional disorder forming an individual's response to his life situation **3 :** the force that a body subjected to the action of a force from another body exerts in the opposite direction **4 a** (1) **:** chemical transformation or change **:** the interaction of chemical entities (2) **:** the state resulting from such a reaction **b :** a process involving change in atomic nuclei — **re·ac·tion·al** \-shnəl, -shən-ᵊl\ *adj* — **re·ac·tion·al·ly** \-ē\ *adv*

[1]re·ac·tion·ary \rē-ˈak-shə-ˌner-ē\ *adj* **:** relating to, marked by, or favoring reaction and esp. political reaction — **re·ac·tion·ary·ism** \-ˌiz-əm\ *n*

[2]reactionary *n, pl* **-ar·ies :** a reactionary person

reaction engine *n* **:** an engine (as a jet engine) that develops thrust by expelling a jet of fluid or a stream of particles

re·ac·ti·vate \(ˈ)rē-ˈak-tə-ˌvāt\ *vt* **:** to activate again ~ *vi* **:** to become active again — **re·ac·ti·va·tion** \(ˌ)rē-ˌak-tə-ˈvā-shən\ *n*

re·ac·tive \rē-ˈak-tiv\ *adj* **1 :** of, relating to, or marked by reaction or reactance **2 a :** readily responsive to a stimulus **b :** occurring as a result of stress or emotional upset <~ depression> — **re·ac·tive·ly** *adv* — **re·ac·tive·ness** *n* — **re·ac·tiv·i·ty** \(ˌ)rē-ˌak-ˈtiv-ət-ē\ *n*

re·ac·tor \rē-ˈak-tər\ *n* **1 :** one that reacts **2 :** a device (as a coil, winding, or conductor of small resistance) used to introduce reactance into an alternating-current circuit **3 a :** a vat for an industrial chemical reaction **b :** an apparatus in which a chain reaction of fissionable material is initiated and controlled

[1]read \ˈrēd\ *vb* **read** \ˈred\; **read·ing** \ˈrēd-iŋ\ [ME *reden* to advise, interpret, read, fr. OE *rǣdan;* akin to OHG *rātan* to advise, Gk *arariskein* to fit — more at ARM] *vt* **1 a** (1) **:** to receive or take in the sense of (as letters or symbols) by scanning (2) **:** to study the movements of (as lips) with mental formulation of the communication expressed (3) **:** to utter aloud the printed or written words of <~ them a story> (4) **:** to understand the meaning of (written or printed matter) <students who can really ~ the classics> **b :** to learn from what one has seen or found in writing or printing **c :** to deliver aloud by or as if by reading; *specif* **:** to utter interpretively **d** (1) **:** to become acquainted with or look over the contents of (as a book) **:** PERUSE (2) **:** to make a study of <~ law> (3) **:** to read the works of **e** (1) **:** COPYREAD (2) **:** PROOFREAD **f** (1) **:** to receive and understand (a voice message) by radio (2) **:** UNDERSTAND, COMPREHEND **2 a :** to interpret the meaning or significance of <~ palms> **b :** FORETELL, PREDICT <able to ~ his fortune> **3 a :** to learn the nature of by observing outward expression or signs <~*s* him like a book> **b :** to note the action of in order to anticipate what will happen <a good canoeist ~*s* the rapids>; *also* **:** to anticipate correctly <an experienced linebacker able to ~ plays> **4 a :** to attribute a meaning to (as something read) **:** INTERPRET <how do you ~ this passage> **b :** to attribute (a meaning) to something read or considered <~ a nonexistent meaning into her words> **5 :** to use as a substitute for or in preference to another word or phrase in a particular passage, text, or version <~ *hurry* for *harry*> **6 :** INDICATE <the thermometer ~*s* zero> **7 :** to interpret (a musical work) in performance **8 a :** to sense the meaning of (information) in recorded and coded form (as in storage) **:** acquire (information) from storage — used of a computer or data processor **b :** to read the coded information on (as tape or a punch card) **c :** to cause to be read and transferred to storage <~ the contents of a punch card into a core> ~ *vi* **1 a :** to perform the act of reading words **:** read something **b** (1) **:** to learn something by reading (2) **:** to pursue a course of study **2 a :** to yield a particular meaning or impression when read **b :** to have qualities that affect comprehension or enjoyment **3 :** to consist of specific words, phrases, or other similar elements <a passage that ~*s* differently in older versions> — **read between the lines :** to understand more than is directly stated — **read the riot act 1 :** to order a mob to disperse **2 a :** to order or warn to cease something **b :** to protest vehemently **c :** to reprimand severely

[2]read \ˈrēd\ *n* **1** *chiefly Brit* **:** a period of reading <it was a night . . . for a ~ and a long sleep —William Sansom> **2 :** something (as a book) for reading <a moving novel, intelligent . . . on the whole, a pretty good ~ —Eliot Fremont-Smith> **3 :** the action or an instance of reading

[3]read \ˈred\ *adj* **:** instructed by or informed through reading

read·able \ˈrēd-ə-bəl\ *adj* **:** able to be read easily: as **a :** LEGIBLE **b :** interesting to read — **read·abil·i·ty** \ˌrēd-ə-ˈbil-ət-ē\ *n* — **read·able·ness** \ˈrēd-ə-bəl-nəs\ *n* — **read·ably** \-blē\ *adv*

read·er \ˈrēd-ər\ *n* **1 a :** one that reads **b :** one appointed to read to others: as (1) **:** LECTOR (2) **:** one chosen to read aloud selected material in a Christian Science church or society **c** (1) **:** PROOFREADER (2) **:** one who evaluates manuscripts (3) **:** one who reads periodical literature to discover items of special interest or value **d :** an employee who reads and records the indications of meters **e :** a teacher's assistant who reads and marks student papers **2** *Brit* **:** one who reads lectures or expounds subjects to students **3 a :** a device for projecting a readable image of a transparency **b :** a unit that scans material recorded (as on punch cards) for storage or computation **4 a :** a book for instruction and practice esp. in reading **b :** ANTHOLOGY

read·er·ship \-ˌship\ *n* **1 a :** the quality or state of being a reader **b :** the office or position of a reader **2 :** the mass or a particular group of readers

readi·ly \ˈred-ᵊl-ē\ *adv* **:** in a ready manner: as **a :** without hesitating **:** WILLINGLY <he ~ accepted advice> **b :** without much difficulty **:** EASILY <for reasons that anyone could ~ understand>

read·ing \ˈrēd-iŋ\ *n* **1 :** the act of reading **2 a :** material read or for reading **b :** extent of material read **3 a :** a particular version **b :** data indicated by an instrument **4 a :** a particular interpretation of something (as a law) **b :** a particular performance of something (as a musical work) **5 :** an indication of a certain state of affairs <a study to get some ~ of shoppers' preferences>

reading chair *n* **:** a chair with a narrow back, high short arms, a small slanted shelf attached to the top of the back, and a seat designed for straddling and for permitting one to sit facing the shelf

reading desk *n* **:** a desk to support a book in a convenient position for a standing reader

read·out \ˈrēd-ˌau̇t\ *n* **1 :** the process of reading **2 a :** the process of removing information from an automatic device (as an electronic computer) and displaying it in an understandable form **b :** the information removed from such a device and displayed or recorded (as by magnetic tape or printing device) **c :** a device used for readout **3 :** the radio transmission of data or pictures from a space vehicle either immediately upon acquisition or later by means of playback of a tape recording

read out \(ˈ)rēd-ˈau̇t\ *vt* **1 a :** to read aloud **b :** to produce a readout of **2 :** to expel from an organization

[1]ready \ˈred-ē\ *adj* **readi·er; -est** [ME *redy;* akin to OHG *reiti* ready, Goth ga*raiths* arrayed, Gk *arariskein* to fit — more at ARM] **1 a :** prepared mentally or physically for some experience or action **b :** prepared for immediate use <dinner is ~> **2 a** (1) **:** willingly disposed **:** INCLINED <~ to agree to his proposal> (2) **:** likely to do something indicated <~ to cry with vexation> **b :** spontaneously prompt **3 :** notably dexterous, adroit, or skilled **4 :** immediately available <had little ~ cash> ***syn*** see QUICK — **readi·ness** *n*

[2]ready *vt* **read·ied; ready·ing :** to make ready ***syn*** see PREPARE

[3]ready *n* **:** the state of being ready; *esp* **:** preparation of a gun for immediate aiming and firing <kept their guns at the ~>

ready box *n* **:** a box placed near a gun (as on a ship) to hold ammunition kept ready for immediate use

[1]ready–made \ˌred-ē-ˈmād\ *adj* **1 :** made beforehand esp. for general sale <~ suits> **2 :** lacking originality or individuality **3 :** readily available <her illness provided a ~ excuse>

[2]ready–made *n* **1 :** something that is ready-made **2** *usu* **ready-made :** an artifact (as a comb or a pair of ice tongs) selected and displayed as a work of art

ready room *n* **:** a room in which pilots are briefed and await orders

ready–to–wear \ˌred-ēt-ə-ˈwa(ə)r, -ˈwe(ə)r\ *adj* **:** READY-MADE; *also* **:** dealing in ready-made clothes <~ stores>

ready–wit·ted \ˌred-ē-ˈwit-əd\ *adj* **:** QUICK-WITTED

re·af·for·est \ˌrē-ə-ˈfȯr-əst, -ˈfär-\ *vt, chiefly Brit* **:** REFOREST — **re·af·for·es·ta·tion** \-ˌfȯr-ə-ˈstā-shən, -ˌfär-\ *n, chiefly Brit*

re·agent \rē-ˈā-jənt\ *n* [NL *reagent-, reagens,* prp. of *reagere* to react — more at REACT] **:** a substance used (as in detecting or measuring a component, in preparing a product, or in developing photographs) because of its chemical or biological activity

re·ag·gre·gate \(ˈ)rē-ˈag-ri-ˌgāt\ *vt* **:** to reform into an aggregate or a whole <~ the subunits of a macromolecule> — **re·ag·gre·gate** \-gət\ *n* — **re·ag·gre·ga·tion** \(ˌ)rē-ˌag-ri-ˈgā-shən\ *n*

re·agin \rē-ˈā-jən\ *n* [ISV, fr. *reagent*] **1 :** a substance in the blood of persons with syphilis responsible for positive serological reactions for syphilis **2 :** an antibody in the blood of individuals with some forms of allergy possessing the power of passively sensitizing the skin of normal individuals — **re·agin·ic** \ˌrē-ə-ˈjin-ik\ *adj* — **re·agin·i·cal·ly** \-i-k(ə-)lē\ *adv*

[1]**re·al** \ˈrē(-ə)l, ˈri(-ə)l\ *adj* [ME, real, relating to things (in law), fr. MF, fr. ML & LL; ML *realis* relating to things (in law), fr. LL, real, fr. L *res* thing, fact; akin to Skt *rai* property] **1 :** of or relating to fixed, permanent, or immovable things (as lands or tenements) **2 a :** not artificial, fraudulent, illusory, or apparent : GENUINE; *also* : being precisely what the name implies <~ economic growth equals apparent growth less the current inflationary increment> **b** (1) : occurring in fact <a story of ~ life> (2) : of or relating to practical or everyday concerns or activities <left school to live in the ~ world> **c :** having objective independent existence <unable to believe that what he saw was ~> **d :** FUNDAMENTAL, ESSENTIAL **e** (1) : belonging to the set of real numbers <the ~ roots of an equation> (2) : concerned with or containing real numbers <~ analysis> (3) : REAL-VALUED <~ variable> **f :** measured by purchasing power <~ income> **g :** COMPLETE, UTTER <considered him a ~ idiot> **3 :** exact as regards repetition of musical intervals in transposition — **re·al·ness** *n*

syn REAL, ACTUAL, TRUE *shared meaning element* : corresponding to known facts ***ant*** unreal, apparent, imaginary

[2]**real** *n* **:** a real thing; *esp* : a mathematical real quantity — **for real 1 :** in earnest : SERIOUSLY <they were fighting *for real*> **2 :** GENUINE <couldn't believe the threats were *for real*>

[3]**real** *adv* **:** VERY <there was only one word for him. He was ~ cool —H. M. McLuhan>

[4]**re·al** \rā-ˈäl\ *n, pl* **reals** *or* **re·ales** \-ˈäl-(ˌ)ās\ [Sp, fr. *real* royal, fr. L *regalis* — more at ROYAL] **1 :** a former monetary unit of Spain and its possessions **2 :** a coin representing one real

[5]**re·al** \rā-ˈäl\ *n, pl* **reals** *or* **reis** \ˈrās(h), ˈrāz(h)\ [Pg, fr. *real* royal, fr. L *regalis*] **1 :** a former monetary unit of Portugal or Brazil **2 :** a coin representing one real

real estate *n* **:** property in buildings and land

real focus *n* **:** a point at which rays (as of light) converge or from which they diverge

re·al·gar \rē-ˈal-ˌgär, -gər\ *n* [ME, fr. ML, fr. Catal, fr. Ar *rahj al-ghār* powder of the mine] **:** an orange-red mineral consisting of arsenic sulfide and having a resinous luster

re·alia \rē-ˈal-ē-ə, -ˈā-lē-\ *n pl* [LL, neut. pl. of *realis* real] **:** objects or activities used to relate classroom teaching to the real life esp. of peoples studied

re·align \ˌrē-ə-ˈlīn\ *vt* **:** to align again; *esp* : to reorganize or make new groupings of — **re·align·ment** \-mənt\ *n*

real image *n* **:** an optical image formed of real foci

re·al·ism \ˈrē-ə-ˌliz-əm, ˈri-ə-\ *n* **1 :** concern for fact or reality and rejection of the impractical and visionary **2 a :** a doctrine that universals exist outside the mind; *specif* : the conception that an abstract term names an independent and unitary reality **b :** the conception that objects of sense perception or cognition exist independently of the mind **3 :** fidelity in art and literature to nature or to real life and to accurate representation without idealization — **re·al·ist** \-ləst\ *adj or n* — **re·al·is·tic** \ˌrē-ə-ˈlis-tik, ˌri-ə-\ *adj* — **re·al·is·ti·cally** \-ti-k(ə-)lē\ *adv*

re·al·i·ty \rē-ˈal-ət-ē\ *n, pl* **-ties 1 :** the quality or state of being real **2 a** (1) : a real event, entity, or state of affairs <his dream became a ~> (2) : the totality of real things and events <trying to escape from ~> **b :** something that is neither derivative nor dependent but exists necessarily — **in reality :** in actual fact

re·al·iza·tion \ˌrē-ə-lə-ˈzā-shən, ˌri-ə-\ *n* **1 :** the action of realizing : the state of being realized **2 :** something realized

re·al·ize \ˈrē-ə-ˌlīz, ˈri-ə-\ *vt* **-ized; -iz·ing** [F *réaliser,* fr. MF *realiser,* fr. *real* real] **1 a :** to bring into concrete existence : ACCOMPLISH <finally *realized* his goal> **b :** to cause to seem real : make appear real <a book in which the characters are carefully *realized*> **2 a :** to convert into actual money <*realized* assets> **b :** to bring or get by sale, investment, or effort : GAIN **3 :** to conceive vividly as real : be fully aware of <he did not ~ the risk he was taking> ***syn*** see THINK — **re·al·iz·able** \-ˌlī-zə-bəl\ *adj* — **re·al·iz·er** *n*

re·al·ly \ˈrē-(ə-)lē, ˈri(-ə)l-ē\ *adv* **1 a :** in reality : ACTUALLY <~ didn't know the answer> **b :** TRULY, UNQUESTIONABLY <~ beautiful diamonds> **2 :** INDEED 1 <~, you're being ridiculous>

realm \ˈrelm\ *n* [ME *realme,* fr. OF, modif. of L *regimen* rule — more at REGIMEN] **1 :** KINGDOM **2 :** SPHERE, DOMAIN <within the ~ of possibility> **3 :** a primary marine or terrestrial biogeographic division of the earth's surface

real number *n* **:** one of the numbers that have no imaginary parts and comprise the rationals and the irrationals

re·al·po·li·tik \rā-ˈäl-ˌpō-li-ˌtēk\ *n* [G, fr. *real* practical + *politik* politics] **:** politics based on practical and material factors rather than on theoretical or ethical objectives

real presence *n, often cap R&P* **:** the doctrine that Christ is actually present in the Eucharist

real time *n* **1 :** the actual time in which a physical process takes place — used in reference to a process controlled by a computer **2 :** the actual time in which an event takes place with the reporting on or recording of the event practically simultaneous with its occurrence — **real–time** *adj*

Re·al·tor \ˈrē(-ə)l-tər, -ˌtȯ(ə)r *also* rē-ˈal-\ *service mark* — used for a real estate agent who is a member of the National Association of Real Estate Boards

re·al·ty \ˈrē(-ə)l-tē\ *n* [*real* + *-ty* (as in *property*)] **:** REAL ESTATE

re·al–val·ued \ˌrē-əl-ˈval-(ˌ)yüd, -yəd\ *adj* **:** taking on only real numbers for values <a ~ function>

[1]**ream** \ˈrēm\ *n* [ME *reme,* fr. MF *raime,* fr. Ar *rizmah,* lit., bundle] **1 :** a quantity of paper being 20 quires or variously 480, 500, or 516 sheets **2 :** a great amount — usu. used in pl.

[2]**ream** *vt* [perh. fr. (assumed) ME dial. *remen* to open up, fr. OE dial. *rēman;* akin to OE *rȳman* to open up, *rūm* roomy — more at ROOM] **1 a :** to widen the opening of (a hole) : COUNTERSINK **b** (1) : to enlarge or dress out (a hole) with a reamer (2) : to enlarge the bore of (as a gun) in this way **c :** to remove by reaming **2 a :** to press out with a reamer **b :** to press out the juice of (as an orange) with a reamer **3 :** CHEAT, VICTIMIZE

ream·er \ˈrē-mər\ *n* **:** one that reams: as **a :** a rotating finishing tool with cutting edges used to enlarge or shape a hole **b :** a fruit juice extractor with a ridged and pointed center rising from a shallow dish

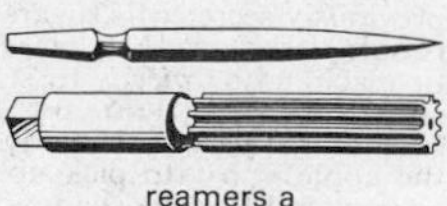
reamers a

reap \ˈrēp\ *vb* [ME *repen,* fr. OE *reopan;* akin to OE *rāw* row — more at ROW] *vt* **1 a** (1) : to cut with a sickle, scythe, or reaping machine (2) : to clear of a crop by reaping **b :** to gather by reaping : HARVEST **2 :** OBTAIN, WIN ~ *vi* **:** to reap something

reap·er \ˈrē-pər\ *n* **:** one that reaps; *esp* : any of various machines for reaping grain

reap·hook \ˈrēp-ˌhu̇k\ *n* **:** a hand implement with a hook-shaped blade used in reaping

re·ap·por·tion \ˌrē-ə-ˈpōr-shən, -ˈpȯr-\ *vt* **:** to apportion (as a house of representatives) anew ~ *vi* **:** to make a new apportionment — **re·ap·por·tion·ment** \-shən-mənt\ *n*

[1]**rear** \ˈri(ə)r, *vt4 & vi2 are also* ˈra(ə)r *or* ˈre(ə)r\ *vb* [ME *reren,* fr. OE *rǣran;* akin to ON *reisa* to raise, OE *rīsan* to rise] *vt* **1 :** to erect by building : CONSTRUCT **2 :** to raise upright **3 a** (1) : to breed and raise (an animal) for use or market (2) : to bring up (a person) **b :** to cause (as plants) to grow **4 :** to cause (a horse) to rise up on the hind legs ~ *vi* **1 :** to rise high **2** *of a horse* **:** to rise up on the hind legs ***syn*** see LIFT — **rear·er** *n*

[2]**rear** \ˈri(ə)r\ *n* [prob. fr. *rear-* (in such terms as *rear guard*)] **1 :** the back part of something: as **a :** the unit (as of an army) or area farthest from the enemy **b :** the part of something located opposite its front <the ~ of a house> **c :** BUTTOCKS **2 :** the space or position at the back <moved to the ~>

[3]**rear** \ˈri(ə)r\ *adj* **:** being at the back

[4]**rear** \ˈri(ə)r\ *adv* **:** toward or from the rear — usu. used in combination <a *rear*-driven car>

rear admiral *n* **:** a commissioned officer in the navy or coast guard who ranks above a captain and whose insignia is two stars

rear echelon *n* **:** an element of a military headquarters or unit located at a considerable distance from the front and concerned esp. with administrative and supply duties

rear·guard \ˈri(ə)r-ˌgärd\ *adj* **:** of or relating to resistance esp. to sweeping social forces <fought a ~ action against automation>

rear guard \-ˈgärd, -ˌgärd\ *n* [ME *reregarde,* fr. MF, fr. OF, fr. *rere* backward, behind (fr. L *retro*) + *garde* guard — more at RETRO-] **:** a military detachment detailed to bring up and protect the rear of a main body or force

rear·horse \ˈri(ə)r-ˌhȯ(ə)rs, ˈra(ə)r-, ˈre(ə)r-\ *n* [fr. the way it rears up when disturbed] **:** MANTIS

re·arm \(ˈ)rē-ˈärm\ *vt* **:** to arm (as a nation or a military force) again with new or better weapons ~ *vi* **:** to become armed again — **re·ar·ma·ment** \-ˈär-mə-mənt\ *n*

rear·most \ˈri(ə)r-ˌmōst\ *adj* **:** farthest in the rear : LAST

rear·view mirror \ˌri(ə)r-ˌvyü-\ *n* **:** a mirror (as in an automobile) that gives a view of the area behind a vehicle

[1]**rear·ward** \ˈri(ə)r-ˌwȯrd\ *n* [ME *rerewarde,* fr. AF; akin to OF *reregarde* rear guard] **:** REAR; *esp* : the rear division (as of an army)

[2]**rear·ward** \-wərd\ *adj* [[2]*rear* + *-ward*] **1 :** located at, near, or toward the rear **2 :** directed toward the rear — **rear·ward·ly** *adv*

[3]**rear·ward** \-wərd\ *also* **rear·wards** \-wərdz\ *adv* **:** at, near, or toward the rear : BACKWARD

[1]**rea·son** \ˈrēz-ᵊn\ *n* [ME *resoun,* fr. OF *raison,* fr. L *ration-, ratio* reason, computation; akin to Goth *garathjan* to count, L *reri* to calculate, think, Gk *arariskein* to fit — more at ARM] **1 a :** a statement offered in explanation or justification <gave ~*s* that were quite satisfactory> **b :** a rational ground or motive <a good ~ to act soon> **c :** a sufficient ground of explanation or of logical defense; *esp* : something (as a principle or law) that supports a conclusion or explains a fact <outlined the ~*s* behind his client's action> **d :** the thing that makes some fact intelligible : CAUSE <wanted to know the ~ for earthquakes> **2 a** (1) : the power of comprehending, inferring, or thinking esp. in orderly rational ways : INTELLIGENCE (2) : proper exercise of the mind (3) : SANITY **b :** the sum of the intellectual powers **3** *archaic* **:** treatment that affords satisfaction

***syn* 1** see CAUSE

2 REASON, UNDERSTANDING, INTUITION *shared meaning element* : the power of the intellect by which man attains to truth or knowledge

— **in reason :** RIGHTLY, JUSTIFIABLY — **within reason :** within reasonable limits — **with reason :** with good cause

[2]**reason** *vb* **rea·soned; rea·son·ing** \ˈrēz-niŋ, -ᵊn-iŋ\ *vi* **1 :** to use the faculty of reason so as to arrive at conclusions : THINK **2 a** *obs* **:** to take part in conversation, discussion, or argument **b :** to talk with another so as to influence his actions or opinions <can't ~ with her> ~ *vt* **1** *archaic* **:** to justify or support with reasons **2 :** to persuade or influence by the use of reason **3 :** to discover, formulate, or conclude by the use of reason <a carefully ~*ed* analysis> ***syn*** see THINK — **rea·son·er** \-nər, -ᵊn-ər\ *n*

rea·son·able \ˈrēz-nə-bəl, -ᵊn-ə-bəl\ *adj* **1 a :** agreeable to reason <a ~ theory> **b :** not extreme or excessive <~ requests> **c :** MODERATE, FAIR <a ~ boss> <a ~ price> **d :** INEXPENSIVE **2 a :** having the faculty of reason **b :** possessing sound judgment — **rea·son·abil·i·ty** \ˌrēz-nə-ˈbil-ət-ē, -ᵊn-ə-\ *n* — **rea·son·able·ness** \ˈrēz-nə-bəl-nəs, -ᵊn-ə-\ *n* — **rea·son·ably** \-blē\ *adv*

rea·son·ing *n* **1 :** the use of reasons; *esp* : the drawing of inferences or conclusions through the use of reason **2 :** an instance of the use of reason : ARGUMENT

rea·son·less \ˈrēz-ᵊn-ləs\ *adj* **1 :** not having the faculty of reason <a ~ brute> **2 :** not reasoned : SENSELESS <~ hostility> **3 :** not based on or supported by reasons <a ~ accusation> — **rea·son·less·ly** *adv*

re·as·sur·ance \ˌrē-ə-ˈshu̇r-ən(t)s\ *n* **1 :** the action of reassuring **:** the state of being reassured **2 :** REINSURANCE

re·as·sure \ˌrē-ə-ˈshu̇(ə)r\ *vt* **1 :** to assure anew <*reassured* him that the work was on schedule> **2 :** to restore to confidence **3 :** REINSURE — **re·as·sur·ing·ly** \-ˈshu̇r-iŋ-lē\ *adv*

re·ata \rē-ˈat-ə, -ˈät-\ *n* [AmerSp] **:** LARIAT

Re·au·mur \ˌrā-ō-ˈmyu̇(ə)r; rā-ˈō-mər, -ˌmyu̇(ə)r\ *adj* [René Antoine Ferchault de *Réaumur*] **:** relating or conforming to a thermometric scale on which the boiling point of water is at 80° above the zero of the scale and the freezing point is at zero

¹reave \ˈrēv\ *vb* **reaved** *or* **reft** \ˈreft\; **reav·ing** [ME *reven,* fr. OE *rēafian;* akin to OHG *roubōn* to rob, L *rumpere* to break, *ruere* to rush, dig up — more at RUG] *vi* **:** PLUNDER, ROB ~ *vt* **1** *archaic* **a :** to deprive of **:** ROB **b :** SEIZE **2** *archaic* **:** to carry or tear away — **reav·er** *n*

²reave *vt* **reaved** *or* **reft** \ˈreft\; **reav·ing** [ME *reven,* prob. modif. of ON *rifa* to rive] *archaic* **:** BURST

reb \ˈreb\ *n* [short for *rebel*] **:** JOHNNY REB

Reb \(ˈ)reb\ *n* [Yiddish, fr. Heb *rabbī* my master, rabbi] **:** RABBI, MISTER — used as a title

re·bar·ba·tive \ri-ˈbär-bət-iv\ *adj* [F *rébarbatif,* fr. MF, fr. *rebarber* to be repellent, fr. *re-* + *barbe* beard, fr. L *barba* — more at BEARD] **:** REPELLENT, IRRITATING — **re·bar·ba·tive·ly** *adv*

¹re·bate \ˈrē-ˌbāt, ri-ˈ\ *vb* **re·bat·ed; re·bat·ing** [ME *rebaten,* fr. MF *rabattre* to beat down again, fr. OF, fr. *re-* + *abattre* to beat down, fr. *a-* (fr. L *ad-*) + *battre* to beat, fr. L *battuere* — more at BATTLE] *vt* **1 :** to reduce the force or activity of **:** DIMINISH **2 :** to reduce the sharpness of **:** BLUNT **3 a :** to make a rebate of **b :** to give a rebate to ~ *vi* **:** to give rebates — **re·bat·er** *n*

²re·bate \ˈrē-ˌbāt\ *n* **:** a return of a part of a payment **:** ABATEMENT

³re·bate \ˈrab-ət, ˈrē-ˌbāt\ *var of* RABBET

re·ba·to \ri-ˈbät-(ˌ)ō\ *var of* RABATO

reb·be \ˈreb-ə\ *n* [Yiddish, fr. Heb *rabbī* rabbi] **:** a Jewish spiritual leader or teacher **:** RABBI

re·bec *or* **re·beck** \ˈrē-ˌbek\ *n* [MF *rebec,* alter. of OF *rebebe,* fr. OProv *rebeb,* fr. Ar *rebāb*] **:** an ancient bowed usu. 3-stringed musical instrument with a pear-shaped body and slender neck

Re·bek·ah \ri-ˈbek-ə\ *n* [Heb *Ribhqāh*] **:** the wife of Isaac

¹reb·el \ˈreb-əl\ *adj* [ME, fr. OF *rebelle,* fr. L *rebellis,* fr. *re-* + *bellum* war, fr. OL *duellum* — more at DUEL] **1 a :** opposing or taking arms against a government or ruler **b :** of or relating to rebels <the ~ camp> **2 :** DISOBEDIENT, REBELLIOUS

²rebel *n* **:** one who rebels or participates in a rebellion

³rebel \ri-ˈbel\ *vi* **re·belled; re·bel·ling** **1 a :** to oppose or disobey one in authority or control **b :** to renounce and resist by force the authority of one's government **2 a :** to act in or show opposition or disobedience <*rebelled* against the conventions of polite society> **b :** to feel or exhibit anger or revulsion <*rebelled* at the injustice of life>

re·bel·lion \ri-ˈbel-yən\ *n* **1 :** opposition to one in authority or dominance **2 a :** open, armed, and usu. unsuccessful defiance of or resistance to an established government **b :** an instance of such defiance or resistance

syn REBELLION, REVOLUTION, UPRISING, REVOLT, INSURRECTION, MUTINY *shared meaning element* **:** an armed outbreak against a government or powers in authority

re·bel·lious \-yəs\ *adj* **1 a :** given to or engaged in rebellion <~ troops> **b :** of, relating to, or characteristic of a rebel or rebellion <a ~ speech> **2 :** resisting treatment or management **:** REFRACTORY — **re·bel·lious·ly** *adv* — **re·bel·lious·ness** *n*

rebel yell *n* **:** a prolonged high-pitched yell traditionally given by Confederate soldiers in the U.S. Civil War

re·birth \(ˈ)rē-ˈbərth, ˈrē-ˌ\ *n* **1 a :** a new or second birth **:** METEMPSYCHOSIS **b :** spiritual regeneration **2 :** RENAISSANCE, REVIVAL <a ~ of nationalism>

reb·o·ant \ˈreb-ə-wənt\ *adj* [L *reboant-, reboans,* prp. of *reboare* to resound, fr. *re-* + *boare* to cry aloud, roar, fr. Gk *boan,* of imit. origin] **:** marked by reverberation

re·born \(ˈ)rē-ˈbȯ(ə)rn\ *adj* **:** born again **:** REGENERATED, REVIVED

¹re·bound \ˈrē-ˈbau̇nd, ri-ˈ\ *vb* [ME *rebounden,* fr. MF *rebondir,* fr. OF, fr. *re-* + *bondir* to bound — more at BOUND] *vi* **1 a :** to spring back on or as if on collision or impact with another body **b :** to recover from setback or frustration **2 :** REECHO **3 :** to gain possession of a rebound in basketball ~ *vt* **:** to cause to rebound

²re·bound \ˈrē-ˌbau̇nd, ri-ˈ\ *n* **1 a :** the action of rebounding **:** RECOIL **b :** an upward leap or movement **:** RECOVERY <a sharp ~ in prices> **2 a :** a basketball or hockey puck that rebounds **b :** the act or an instance of gaining possession of a basketball rebound <leads the league in ~*s*> **3 :** a reaction to setback, frustration, or crisis <on the ~ from an unhappy love affair>

re·bound·er \ˈrē-ˈbau̇n-dər, ˈrē-ˌ, ri-ˈ\ *n* **:** a basketball player skilled at rebounding

re·bo·zo \ri-ˈbō-(ˌ)zō, -(ˌ)sō\ *n, pl* **-zos** [Sp, shawl, fr. *rebozar* to muffle, fr. *re-* (fr. L) + *bozo* mouth, fr. (assumed) VL *bucceum,* fr. L *bucca* cheek] **:** a long scarf worn chiefly by Mexican women

re·branch \(ˈ)rē-ˈbranch\ *vi* **:** to form secondary branches

re·broad·cast \(ˈ)rē-ˈbrȯd-ˌkast\ *vt* **-cast; -cast·ing** **1 :** to broadcast again (a radio or television program being simultaneously received from another source) **2 :** to repeat (a broadcast) at a later time — **rebroadcast** *n*

re·buff \ri-ˈbəf\ *vt* [MF *rebuffer,* fr. OIt *ribuffare* to reprimand] **:** to refuse or check sharply **:** SNUB — **rebuff** *n*

re·build \(ˈ)rē-ˈbild\ *vb* **-built** \-ˈbilt\; **-build·ing** *vt* **1 a :** to make extensive repairs to **:** RECONSTRUCT <~ a war-torn city> **b :** to restore to a previous state <~ inventories> **2 :** to make extensive changes in **:** REMODEL <~ society> ~ *vi* **:** to build again <planned to ~ after the fire> *syn* see MEND

¹re·buke \ri-ˈbyük\ *vt* **re·buked; re·buk·ing** [ME *rebuken,* fr. ONF *rebuker*] **1 a :** to criticize sharply **:** REPRIMAND **b :** to serve as a rebuke to **2 :** to turn back or keep down **:** CHECK *syn* see REPROVE — **re·buk·er** *n*

²rebuke *n* **:** an expression of strong disapproval **:** REPRIMAND

re·bus \ˈrē-bəs\ *n* [L, by things, abl. pl. of *res* thing — more at REAL] **:** a representation of words or syllables by pictures of objects or by symbols whose names resemble the intended words or syllables in sound; *also* **:** a riddle made up of such pictures or symbols

rebus

re·but \ri-ˈbət\ *vb* **re·but·ted; re·but·ting** [ME *rebuten,* fr. OF *reboter,* fr. *re-* + *boter* to butt — more at BUTT] *vt* **1 :** to drive or beat back **:** REPEL **2 a :** to contradict or oppose by formal legal argument, plea, or countervailing proof **b :** to expose the falsity of **:** REFUTE ~ *vi* **:** to make or furnish an answer or counter proof *syn* see DISPROVE — **re·but·ta·ble** \-ˈbət-ə-bəl\ *adj*

re·but·tal \ri-ˈbət-ᵊl\ *n* **:** the act of rebutting esp. in a legal suit; *also* **:** argument or proof that rebuts

¹re·but·ter \-ˈbət-ər\ *n* [AF *rebuter,* fr. OF *reboter* to rebut] **:** the answer of a defendant in matter of fact to a plaintiff's surrejoinder

²rebutter *n* **:** something that rebuts **:** REFUTATION

rec *abbr* **1** receipt **2** record; recording **3** recreation

re·cal·ci·trance \ri-ˈkal-sə-trən(t)s\ *n* **:** the state of being recalcitrant

re·cal·ci·tran·cy \-trən-sē\ *n* **:** RECALCITRANCE

re·cal·ci·trant \-trənt\ *adj* [LL *recalcitrant-, recalcitrans,* prp. of *recalcitrare* to be stubbornly disobedient, fr. L, to kick back, fr. *re-* + *calcitrare* to kick, fr. *calc-, calx* heel — more at CALK] **1 :** obstinately defiant of authority or restraint **2 a :** difficult to handle or operate **b :** not responsive to treatment **c :** RESISTANT <this subject is ~ both to observation and to experiment —G. G. Simpson> *syn* see UNRULY *ant* amenable — **recalcitrant** *n*

re·cal·cu·late \(ˈ)rē-ˈkal-kyə-ˌlāt\ *vt* **:** to calculate again esp. in order to discover the source of an error or formulate new conclusions — **re·cal·cu·la·tion** \(ˌ)rē-ˌkal-kyə-ˈlā-shən\ *n*

re·ca·les·cence \ˌrē-kə-ˈles-ᵊn(t)s\ *n* [L *recalescere* to grow warm again, fr. *re-* + *calescere* to grow warm, incho. of *calēre* to be warm — more at LEE] **:** an increase in temperature that occurs while cooling metal through a range of temperatures in which change in structure occurs

¹re·call \ri-ˈkȯl\ *vt* **1 a :** to call back <was ~*ed* to active duty> **b :** to bring back to mind <~*s* his early years> **c :** to remind one of **:** RESEMBLE <a playwright who ~*s* the Elizabethan dramatists> **2 :** CANCEL, REVOKE **3 :** RESTORE, REVIVE *syn* see REMEMBER — **re·call·abil·i·ty** \-ˌkȯ-lə-ˈbil-ət-ē\ *n* — **re·call·able** \-ˈkȯ-lə-bəl\ *adj* — **re·call·er** *n*

²re·call \ri-ˈkȯl, ˈrē-ˌ\ *n* **1 :** a call to return <a ~ of workers after a layoff> **2 :** the right or procedure by which an official may be removed by vote of the people **3 :** remembrance of what has been learned or experienced **4 :** the act of revoking **5 :** the return to a dealer of a product (as an automobile) specified as defective by the manufacturer so that the dealer may make repairs **6 :** the ability (as of an information retrieval system) to retrieve stored material

re·can·a·li·za·tion \(ˌ)rē-ˌkan-ᵊl-ə-ˈzā-shən\ *n* **:** the process of reuniting an interrupted channel of a bodily tube (as a vas deferens)

re·cant \ri-ˈkant\ *vb* [L *recantare,* fr. *re-* + *cantare* to sing — more at CHANT] *vt* **1 :** to withdraw or repudiate (a statement or belief) formally and publicly **:** RENOUNCE **2 :** REVOKE ~ *vi* **:** to make an open confession of error *syn* see ABJURE — **re·can·ta·tion** \ˌrē-ˌkan-ˈtā-shən\ *n*

¹re·cap \(ˈ)rē-ˈkap\ *vt* **re·capped; re·cap·ping** **:** to cement, mold, and vulcanize a strip of camelback on the buffed and roughened surface of the tread of (a worn pneumatic tire) — **re·cap·pa·ble** \-ˈkap-ə-bəl\ *adj*

²re·cap \ˈrē-ˌkap\ *n* **:** a recapped tire

³re·cap \ˈrē-ˌkap, ri-ˈ\ *vt* **re·capped; re·cap·ping** [by shortening] **:** RECAPITULATE

⁴re·cap \ˈrē-ˌkap\ *n* **:** RECAPITULATION

re·cap·i·tal·iza·tion \(ˌ)rē-ˌkap-ət-ᵊl-ə-ˈzā-shən, -ˌkap-tᵊl-\ *n* **:** a revision of the capital structure of a corporation

re·cap·i·tal·ize \(ˈ)rē-ˈkap-ət-ᵊl-ˌīz, -ˈkap-tᵊl-\ *vt* **:** to change the capital structure of

re·ca·pit·u·late \ˌrē-kə-ˈpich-ə-ˌlāt\ *vt* **-lat·ed; -lat·ing** [LL *recapitulatus,* pp. of *recapitulare* to restate by heads, sum up, fr. L *re-* + *capitulum* division of a book] **:** to repeat the principal points or stages of **:** SUMMARIZE

re·ca·pit·u·la·tion \-ˌpich-ə-ˈlā-shən\ *n* **1 :** a concise summary **2 :** the hypothetical occurrence in an individual organism's development of successive stages resembling the series of ancestral types from which it has descended so that the ontogeny of the individual is a recapitulation of the phylogeny of its group **3 :** the third section of a sonata form

¹re·cap·ture \(ˈ)rē-ˈkap-chər\ *n* **1 a :** the act of retaking **b :** an instance of being retaken **2 :** the retaking of a prize or goods under international law **3 :** a government seizure under law of earnings or profits beyond a fixed amount

²recapture *vt* **1 a :** to capture again **b :** to experience again <by no effort of the imagination could she ~ the ecstasy —Ellen Glasgow> **2 :** to take (as a portion of earnings or profits above a fixed amount) by law or through negotiations under law

re·cast \(ˈ)rē-ˈkast\ *vt* **-cast; -cast·ing** **:** to cast again <~ a gun> <~ a play>; *also* **:** REMODEL, REFASHION <~*s* his political image to fit the times> — **re·cast** \ˈrē-ˌkast, (ˈ)rē-ˈ\ *n*

recd *abbr* received

¹re·cede \ri-ˈsēd\ *vi* **re·ced·ed; re·ced·ing** [L *recedere* to go back, fr. *re-* + *cedere* to go — more at CEDE] **1 a :** to move back or away **:** WITHDRAW **b :** to slant backward **2 :** to grow less or smaller **:** DIMINISH *syn* RECEDE, RETREAT, RETROGRADE, RETRACT, BACK *shared meaning element* : to move backward *ant* proceed, advance

[2]**re·cede** \(ˈ)rē-ˈsēd\ *vt* [*re-* + *cede*] : to cede back to a former possessor

[1]**re·ceipt** \ri-ˈsēt\ *n* [ME *receite*, fr. ONF, fr. ML *recepta*, prob. fr. L, neut. pl. of *receptus*, pp. of *recipere* to receive] **1** : RECIPE **2 a** *obs* : RECEPTACLE **b** *archaic* : a revenue office **3** : the act or process of receiving **4** : something received — usu. used in pl. **5** : a writing acknowledging the receiving of goods or money

[2]**receipt** *vt* **1** : to give a receipt for or acknowledge the receipt of **2** : to mark as paid

re·ceiv·able \ri-ˈsē-və-bəl\ *adj* **1** : capable of being received **2** : subject to call for payment <notes ~>

re·ceiv·ables \-bəlz\ *n pl* : amounts of money receivable

re·ceive \ri-ˈsēv\ *vb* **re·ceived; re·ceiv·ing** [ME *receiven*, fr. ONF *receivre*, fr. L *recipere*, fr. *re-* + *capere* to take — more at HEAVE] *vt* **1** : to come into possession of : ACQUIRE <~ a gift> **2 a** : to act as a receptacle or container for <the cistern ~*s* water from the roof> **b** : to assimilate through the mind or senses <~ new ideas> **3 a** : to permit to enter : ADMIT **b** : WELCOME, GREET **4** : to accept as authoritative or true : BELIEVE **5 a** : to support the weight or pressure of : BEAR **b** : to take (a mark or impression) from the weight of something <some clay ~*s* clear impressions> **c** : ACQUIRE, EXPERIENCE <*received* his early schooling at home> **d** : to suffer the hurt or injury of <*received* a broken nose> ~ *vi* **1** : to be a recipient **2** : to be at home to visitors <~*s* on Tuesdays> **3** : to convert incoming radio waves into perceptible signals **4** : to catch or gain possession of a kicked ball in football

syn RECEIVE, ACCEPT, ADMIT, TAKE *shared meaning element* : to permit to come into one's possession, presence, group, mind, or substance

Received Pronunciation *n* : the pronunciation of Received Standard

Received Standard *n* : the form of English spoken at the English public schools, at the universities of Oxford and Cambridge, and by many educated Englishmen elsewhere

re·ceiv·er \ri-ˈsē-vər\ *n* : one that receives: as **a** : TREASURER **b** (1) : a person appointed to hold in trust and administer property under litigation (2) : a person appointed to wind up the affairs of a business involving a public interest or to manage a corporation during reorganization **c** : one that receives stolen goods : FENCE **d** : a vessel to receive and contain gases **e** : the portion of a telegraphic or telephonic apparatus that converts the electric currents or waves into visible or audible signals **f** (1) : CATCHER (2) : a member of the offensive team in football eligible to catch a forward pass

receiver general *n, pl* **receivers general** : a public officer in charge of the treasury (as of Massachusetts)

re·ceiv·er·ship \ri-ˈsē-vər-ˌship\ *n* **1** : the office or function of a receiver **2** : the state of being in the hands of a receiver

receiving blanket *n* : a small lightweight blanket used to wrap an infant (as after bathing)

receiving end *n* : the position of being a recipient or esp. a victim — usu. used in the phrase *on the receiving end*

receiving line *n* : a group of people who stand in a line and individually welcome arriving guests (as at a wedding reception)

re·cen·cy \ˈrēs-ᵊn-sē\ *n* : the quality or state of being recent <the eagerness of the people for ~ in their news —F. L. Mott>

re·cen·sion \ri-ˈsen-chən\ *n* [L *recension-*, *recensio* enumeration, fr. *recensēre* to review, fr. *re-* + *censēre* to assess, tax] **1** : a critical revision of a text **2** : a text established by critical revision

re·cent \ˈrēs-ᵊnt\ *adj* [MF or L; MF, fr. L *recent-*, *recens;* akin to Gk *kainos* new] **1 a** : of or relating to a time not long past **b** : having lately come into existence : NEW, FRESH **2** *cap* : of, relating to, or being the present or post-Pleistocene geologic epoch *syn* see MODERN — **re·cent·ness** *n*

re·cent·ly *adv* : during a recent period of time : LATELY

re·cep·ta·cle \ri-ˈsep-ti-kəl\ *n* [L *receptaculum*, fr. *receptare* to receive, fr. *receptus*, pp. of *recipere* to receive] **1** : one that receives and contains something : CONTAINER **2** [NL *receptaculum*, fr. L] **a** : an intercellular cavity containing products of secretion **b** : the end of the flower stalk upon which the floral organs are borne **c** : a modified branch bearing sporangia in a cryptogamous plant **3** : a mounted female electrical fitting that contains the live parts of the circuit

re·cep·tac·u·lum \ˌrē-ˌsep-ˈtak-yə-ləm\ *n, pl* **-la** \-lə\ [NL, fr. L] : RECEPTACLE 2

re·cep·tion \ri-ˈsep-shən\ *n* [ME *recepcion*, fr. MF or L; MF *reception*, fr. L *reception-*, *receptio*, fr. *receptus*, pp. of *recipere*] **1** : the act or action or an instance of receiving: as **a** : RECEIPT <the ~ of American capital> **b** : ADMISSION <his ~ into the church> **c** : RESPONSE, REACTION <the play met with a mixed ~> **d** : the receiving of a radio or television broadcast **2** : a social gathering often for the purpose of extending a formal welcome

re·cep·tion·ist \-sh(ə-)nəst\ *n* : one employed to greet callers

re·cep·tive \ri-ˈsep-tiv\ *adj* **1** : able or inclined to receive; *esp* : open and responsive to ideas, impressions, or suggestions **2 a** *of a sensory end organ* : fit to receive and transmit stimuli **b** : SENSORY — **re·cep·tive·ly** *adv* — **re·cep·tive·ness** *n* — **re·cep·tiv·i·ty** \ˌrē-ˌsep-ˈtiv-ət-ē, ri-\ *n*

re·cep·tor \ri-ˈsep-tər\ *n* : RECEIVER: as **a** : a cell or group of cells that receives stimuli : SENSE ORGAN **b** : a chemical group having a specific affinity for a particular antibody or a virus **c** : a cellular entity (as a beta-receptor or alpha-receptor) that is a postulated intermediary between a chemical agent (as a neurohumor) acting on nervous tissue and the physiological or pharmacological response

[1]**re·cess** \ˈrē-ˌses, ri-ˈ\ *n* [L *recessus*, fr. *recessus*, pp. of *recedere* to recede] **1** : the action of receding : RECESSION **2** : a hidden, secret, or secluded place **3 a** : INDENTATION, CLEFT <a deep ~ in the hill> **b** : ALCOVE <a pleasant ~ lined with books> **4** : a suspension of business or procedure often for rest or relaxation <children playing at ~> *syn* see PAUSE

[2]**recess** *vt* **1** : to put into a recess <~*ed* lighting> **2** : to make a recess in **3** : to interrupt for a recess ~ *vi* : to take a recess

[1]**re·ces·sion** \ri-ˈsesh-ən\ *n* **1** : the act or action of receding : WITHDRAWAL **2** : a departing procession (as of clergy and choir at the end of a church service) **3** : a period of reduced economic activity — **re·ces·sion·ary** \-ə-ˌner-ē\ *adj*

[2]**re·ces·sion** \(ˈ)rē-ˈsesh-ən\ *n* [*re-* + *cession*] : the act of ceding back to a former possessor

[1]**re·ces·sion·al** \ri-ˈsesh-nəl, -ən-ᵊl\ *adj* : of or relating to a withdrawal

[2]**recessional** *n* **1** : a hymn or musical piece at the conclusion of a service or program **2** : [1]RECESSION 2

[1]**re·ces·sive** \ri-ˈses-iv\ *adj* **1 a** : tending to go back : RECEDING **b** : RETIRING, WITHDRAWN **2 a** : producing little or no phenotypic effect when occurring in heterozygous condition with a contrasting allele <~ genes> **b** : expressed only when the determining gene is in the homozygous condition <~ traits> — **re·ces·sive·ly** *adv* — **re·ces·sive·ness** *n*

[2]**recessive** *n* **1** : a recessive character or gene **2** : an organism possessing one or more recessive characters

re·charge \(ˈ)rē-ˈchärj\ *vi* : to make a new attack ~ *vt* : to charge again; *esp* : to restore anew the active materials in (a storage battery) — **re·charge** \(ˈ)rē-ˈchärj, ˈrē-ˌ\ *n* — **re·charge·able** \(ˈ)rē-ˈchär-jə-bəl\ *adj* — **re·charg·er** \-jər\ *n*

ré·chauf·fé \ˌrā-shō-ˈfā, -ˈshō-ˌ\ *n* [F] **1** : a warmed-over dish of food **2** : REHASH

re·cheat \ri-ˈchēt\ *n* [ME *rechate*, fr. *rechaten* to blow the recheat, fr. MF *rachater* to assemble, rally, fr. *re-* + *achater* to acquire, fr. (assumed) VL *accaptare*, fr. L *ac-* + *captare* to seek to obtain, intens. of *capere* to take, receive — more at HEAVE] : a hunting call sounded on a horn to assemble the hounds

re·cher·ché \rə-ˌsher-ˈshā, -ˈshe(ə)r-ˌ\ *adj* [F] **1 a** : EXQUISITE, CHOICE **b** : EXOTIC, RARE **2** : excessively refined : AFFECTED **3** : OVERBLOWN, PRETENTIOUS

re·cid·i·vism \ri-ˈsid-ə-ˌviz-əm\ *n* : a tendency to relapse into a previous condition or mode of behavior; *esp* : relapse into criminal behavior

re·cid·i·vist \-vəst\ *n* [F *récidiviste*, fr. *récidiver* to relapse, fr. ML *recidivare*, fr. L *recidivus* recurring, fr. *recidere* to fall back, fr. *re-* + *cadere* to fall — more at CHANCE] : one who relapses; *specif* : an habitual criminal — **recidivist** *adj* — **re·cid·i·vis·tic** \-ˌsid-ə-ˈvis-tik\ *adj*

recip *abbr* reciprocal; reciprocity

rec·i·pe \ˈres-ə-(ˌ)pē\ *n* [L, take, imper. of *recipere* to take, receive — more at RECEIVE] **1** : PRESCRIPTION 4 **2** : a set of instructions for making something (as a food dish) from various ingredients **3** : a procedure for doing or attaining something <a ~ for success>

re·cip·i·ent \ri-ˈsip-ē-ənt\ *n* [L *recipient-*, *recipiens*, prp. of *recipere*] : one that receives : RECEIVER — **recipient** *adj*

[1]**re·cip·ro·cal** \ri-ˈsip-rə-kəl\ *adj* [L *reciprocus* returning the same way, alternating, irreg. fr. *re-* + *pro-*] **1 a** : inversely related : OPPOSITE **b** : of, constituting, or resulting from paired crosses in which the kind that supplies the male parent of the first cross supplies the female parent of the second cross and vice versa **2** : shared, felt, or shown by both sides **3** : serving to reciprocate : consisting of or functioning as a return in kind <the ~ devastation of nuclear war> **4 a** : mutually corresponding <agreed to extend ~ privileges to each other's citizens> **b** : marked by or based on reciprocity <~ trade agreements> — **re·cip·ro·cal·ly** \-k(ə-)lē\ *adv*

syn RECIPROCAL, MUTUAL, COMMON *shared meaning element* : shared, experienced, or shown by each of those involved

[2]**reciprocal** *n* **1** : something in a reciprocal relationship to another **2** : one of a pair of numbers (as $\frac{2}{3}$, $\frac{3}{2}$) whose product is one; *broadly* : MULTIPLICATIVE INVERSE

reciprocal pronoun *n* : a pronoun (as *each other*) used to denote mutual action or cross relationship between the members comprised in a plural subject

re·cip·ro·cate \ri-ˈsip-rə-ˌkāt\ *vb* **-cat·ed; -cat·ing** *vt* **1** : to give and take mutually **2** : to return in kind or degree <~ a compliment gracefully> ~ *vi* **1** : to make a return for something <we hope to ~ for your kindness> **2** : to move forward and backward alternately <a *reciprocating* valve> — **re·cip·ro·ca·tor** \-ˌkāt-ər\ *n*

syn RECIPROCATE, RETALIATE, REQUITE, RETURN *shared meaning element* : to give back, usually in kind or quantity. RECIPROCATE is likely to imply mutuality and a reasonably equivalent exchange or a paying back of what one has received <the love of Lavinia for the hero, most correctly *reciprocated* by him —H. O. Taylor> <few men *reciprocate* evil with good> RETALIATE usually applies to a paying back of injury in exact measure and kind by way of revenge <the students charged the policy with brutality and *retaliated* with some brutality of their own —S. T. Wise> REQUITE can imply a simple reciprocation or a paying back in terms of what one considers the merits of the case without regard to mutual satisfaction <hospitality should be *requited* in kind —Agnes M. Miall> <his servility was *requited* with cold comtempt —T. B. Macaulay> RETURN stresses a paying back of whatever has been given, sometimes in kind, sometimes by way of contrast <*return* blow for blow> <he *returns* my envy with pity —Richard Steele>

reciprocating engine *n* : an engine in which the to-and-fro motion of a piston is transformed into circular motion of the crankshaft

re·cip·ro·ca·tion \ri-ˌsip-rə-ˈkā-shən\ *n* **1 a** : a mutual exchange **b** : a return in kind or of like value **2** : an alternating motion — **re·cip·ro·ca·tive** \-ˈsip-rə-ˌkāt-iv, -kət-\ *adj*

rec·i·proc·i·ty \ˌres-ə-ˈpräs-ət-ē, -ˈpräs-tē\ *n, pl* **-ties** **1** : the quality or state of being reciprocal : mutual dependence, action, or influence **2** : a mutual exchange of privileges; *specif* : a recognition by one of two countries or institutions of the validity of licenses or privileges granted by the other

re·ci·sion \ri-ˈsizh-ən\ *n* [MF, alter. of *rescision*, fr. LL *rescission-*, *rescissio* rescission] : CANCELLATION

re·cit·al \ri-ˈsīt-ᵊl\ *n* **1 a** : the act or process or an instance of reciting **b** : a detailed account : ENUMERATION <the ~ of his troubles> **c** : DISCOURSE, NARRATION <a colorful ~ of a night on

the town> **2 a :** a concert given by an individual musician or dancer or by a dance troupe **b :** a public exhibition of skill given by music or dance pupils — **re·cit·al·ist** \-ᵊl-əst\ *n*

rec·i·ta·tion \ˌres-ə-ˈtā-shən\ *n* **1 :** the act of enumerating <a ~ of relevant details> **2 :** the act or an instance of reading or repeating aloud esp. publicly **3 a :** a student's oral reply to questions **b :** a class period

rec·i·ta·tive \ˌres-(ə-)tə-ˈtēv\ *n* [It *recitativo,* fr. *recitare* to recite, fr. L] **1 :** a rhythmically free declamatory vocal style for delivering a narrative text; *also* **:** a passage to be delivered in this style **2 :** RECITATION — **recitative** *adj*

rec·i·ta·ti·vo \ˌres-(ə-)tə-ˈtē-(ˌ)vō\ *n, pl* **-vi** \-(ˌ)vē\ *or* **-vos** [It] **:** RECITATIVE 1

re·cite \ri-ˈsīt\ *vb* **re·cit·ed; re·cit·ing** [ME *reciten* to state formally, fr. MF or L; MF *reciter* to recite, fr. L *recitare,* fr. *re-* + *citare* to summon — more at CITE] *vt* **1 :** to repeat from memory or read aloud publicly **2 a :** to relate in full <~*s* dull anecdotes> **b :** ENUMERATE, DETAIL <*recited* a catalog of offenses> **3 :** to repeat or answer questions about (a lesson) ~ *vi* **1 :** to repeat or read aloud something memorized or prepared **2 :** to reply to a teacher's question on a lesson — **re·cit·er** *n*

reck \ˈrek\ *vb* [ME *recken* to take heed, fr. OE *reccan;* akin to OHG *ruohhen* to take heed] *vi* **1 :** WORRY, CARE **2** *archaic* **:** to be of account or interest **:** MATTER ~ *vt* **1** *archaic* **:** to care for **:** REGARD **2** *archaic* **:** to matter to **:** CONCERN

reck·less \ˈrek-ləs\ *adj* **1 :** marked by lack of proper caution **:** careless of consequences **2 :** NEGLIGENT <~ mining practices devastated the countryside> ***syn*** see ADVENTUROUS ***ant*** calculating — **reck·less·ly** *adv* — **reck·less·ness** *n*

reck·on \ˈrek-ən\ *vb* **reck·oned; reck·on·ing** \-(ə-)niŋ\ [ME *rekenen,* fr. OE *-recenian* (as in *gerecenian* to narrate); akin to OE *reccan*] *vt* **1 a :** COUNT <~ the days till Christmas> **b :** ESTIMATE, COMPUTE <~ the height of a building> **c :** to determine by reference to a fixed basis <the existence of the U.S. is ~*ed* from the Declaration of Independence> **2 :** to regard or think of as **:** CONSIDER **3** *chiefly dial* **:** SUPPOSE, THINK <I ~ I've outlived my time —Ellen Glasgow> ~ *vi* **1 :** to settle accounts **2 :** to make a calculation **3 a :** JUDGE **b** *chiefly dial* **:** SUPPOSE, THINK **4 :** to accept something as certain **:** place reliance <I ~ on your promise to help> ***syn*** see RELY — **reckon with :** to take into consideration — **reckon without :** to fail to consider **:** IGNORE

reck·on·ing *n* **1 :** the act or an instance of reckoning: as **a :** ACCOUNT, BILL **b :** COMPUTATION **c :** calculation of a ship's position **2 :** a settling of accounts <day of ~> **3 :** a summing up

re·claim \ri-ˈklām\ *vt* [ME *reclamen,* fr. OF *reclamer* to call back, fr. L *reclamare* to cry out against, fr. *re-* + *clamare* to cry out — more at CLAIM] **1 a :** to recall from wrong or improper conduct **:** REFORM **b :** TAME, SUBDUE **2 a :** to rescue from an undesirable state **b :** to make available for human use by changing natural conditions <~ swampland> **3 :** to obtain from a waste product or by-product **:** RECOVER ***syn*** see RESCUE — **re·claim·able** \-ˈklā-mə-bəl\ *adj*

re–claim \(ˈ)rē-ˈklām\ *vt* **:** to demand or obtain the return of

rec·la·ma·tion \ˌrek-lə-ˈmā-shən\ *n* [MF, fr. L *reclamation-, reclamatio,* fr. *reclamatus,* pp. of *reclamare*] **:** the act or process of reclaiming: as **a :** REFORMATION, REHABILITATION **b :** restoration to use **:** RECOVERY

ré·clame \rā-ˈkläm\ *n* [F, advertising, fr. *réclamer* to appeal, fr. OF *reclamer*] **1 :** public acclaim **:** VOGUE **2 :** a gift for dramatization or publicity **:** SHOWMANSHIP

rec·li·nate \ˈrek-lə-ˌnāt\ *adj* **:** bent downward so that the apex is below the base <~ leaves>

re·cline \ri-ˈklīn\ *vb* **re·clined; re·clin·ing** [ME *reclinen,* fr. MF or L; MF *recliner,* fr. L *reclinare,* fr. *re-* + *clinare* to bend — more at LEAN] *vt* **:** to cause or permit to incline backwards ~ *vi* **1 :** to lean or incline backwards **2 :** REPOSE, LIE

re·clos·able \(ˈ)rē-ˈklō-zə-bəl\ *adj* **:** capable of being closed again tightly after opening <~ packages of bacon>

[1]**re·cluse** \ˈrek-ˌlüs, ri-ˈklüs, ˈrek-ˌlüz\ *adj* [ME, fr. OF *reclus,* lit., shut up, fr. LL *reclusus,* pp. of *recludere* to shut up, fr. L *re-* + *claudere* to close — more at CLOSE] **:** marked by withdrawal from society **:** SOLITARY — **re·clu·sive** \ri-ˈklü-siv, -ziv\ *adj*

[2]**recluse** *n* **:** a person who leads a secluded or solitary life

re·clu·sion \ri-ˈklü-zhən\ *n* **:** the state of being recluse

rec·og·ni·tion \ˌrek-ig-ˈnish-ən, -əg-\ *n* [L *recognition-, recognitio,* fr. *recognitus,* pp. of *recognoscere*] **1 :** the action of recognizing **:** the state of being recognized: as **a :** ACKNOWLEDGMENT; *esp* **:** formal acknowledgment of the political existence of a government or nation **b :** knowledge or feeling that an object present has been met before **2 :** special notice or attention **3 :** the sensing and encoding of printed or written data by a machine <optical character ~> <magnetic ink character ~>

syn RECOGNITION, IDENTIFICATION, ASSIMILATION, APPERCEPTION *shared meaning element* **:** a form of cognition that relates a perception of something new to knowledge already possessed

re·cog·ni·zance \ri-ˈkäg-nə-zən(t)s, -ˈkän-ə-\ *n* [alter. of ME *reconissaunce,* fr. MF *reconoissance* recognition, fr. *reconoistre* to recognize] **1 a :** an obligation of record entered into before a court or magistrate requiring the performance of an act (as appearance in court) usu. under penalty of a money forfeiture **b :** the sum liable to forfeiture upon such an obligation **2** *archaic* **:** TOKEN, PLEDGE

rec·og·nize \ˈrek-ig-ˌnīz, -əg-\ *vt* **-nized; -niz·ing** [modif. of MF *reconoiss-,* stem of *reconoistre,* fr. L *recognoscere,* fr. *re-* + *cognoscere* to know — more at COGNITION] **1 a :** to perceive to be something previously known <*recognized* the word> **b :** to perceive clearly **:** REALIZE **2 :** to acknowledge or take notice of in some definite way: as **a :** to acknowledge with a show of appreciation <~ an act of bravery with the award of a medal> **b :** to acknowledge acquaintance with <~ an old crony with a nod> **c :** to admit the fact of <~*s* his obligation> **3 :** to acknowledge formally: as **a :** to admit as being lord or sovereign **b :** to admit as being of a particular status **c :** to admit as being one entitled to be heard **d :** to acknowledge the de facto existence or the independence of — **rec·og·niz·abil·i·ty** \ˌrek-ig-ˌnī-zə-ˈbil-ət-ē, -əg-\ *n* — **rec·og·niz·able** \ˈrek-əg-ˌnī-zə-bəl, -ig-\ *adj* — **rec·og·niz·ably** \-blē\ *adv* — **rec·og·niz·er** *n*

[1]**re·coil** \ri-ˈkȯi(ə)l\ *vi* [ME *reculen,* fr. OF *reculer,* fr. *re-* + *cul* backside — more at CULET] **1 a :** to fall back under pressure **b :** to shrink back physically or emotionally **2 :** to spring back to or as if to a starting point **:** REBOUND **3** *obs* **:** DEGENERATE

syn RECOIL, SHRINK, FLINCH, WINCE, BLENCH, QUAIL *shared meaning element* **:** to draw back through fear or distaste ***ant*** confront, defy

[2]**re·coil** \ˈrē-ˌkȯil, ri-ˈkȯi(ə)l\ *n* **1 :** the act or action of recoiling; *esp* **:** the kickback of a gun upon firing **2 :** REACTION <the ~ from the rigors of Calvinism —Edmund Wilson>

re·coil·less \-ˌkȯil-ləs, -ˈkȯi(ə)l-\ *adj* **:** having a minimum of recoil

re·coil–op·er·at·ed \ˌrē-ˌkȯil-ˈäp-(ə-)ˌrāt-əd\ *adj, of a firearm* **:** utilizing the movement of parts in recoil to operate the action

re·coin \(ˈ)rē-ˈkȯin\ *vt* **:** to coin again or anew — **re·coin·age** \-ˈkȯi-nij\ *n*

rec·ol·lect \ˌrek-ə-ˈlekt\ *vb* [ML *recollectus,* pp. of *recolligere,* fr. L, to gather again] *vt* **1 :** to bring back to the level of conscious awareness **:** REMEMBER <trying to ~ a forgotten address> **2 :** to remind (oneself) of something temporarily forgotten ~ *vi* **:** to call something to mind ***syn*** see REMEMBER

re–col·lect \ˌrē-kə-ˈlekt\ *vt* [partly fr. L *recollectus,* pp. of *recolligere,* fr. *re-* + *colligere* to collect; partly fr. *re-* + *collect*] **:** to collect again; *esp* **:** RALLY, RECOVER <~*ing* all my force, and drawing my sword —Henry Brooke>

rec·ol·lect·ed \ˌrek-ə-ˈlek-təd\ *adj* **:** COMPOSED, CALM

rec·ol·lec·tion \ˌrek-ə-ˈlek-shən\ *n* **1 a :** tranquillity of mind **b :** religious contemplation **2 a :** the action or power of recalling to mind **b :** something recalled to the mind ***syn*** see MEMORY

re·com·bi·nant \(ˈ)rē-ˈkäm-bə-nənt\ *adj* **:** exhibiting genetic recombination <~ progeny> — **recombinant** *n*

re·com·bi·na·tion \ˌrē-ˌkäm-bə-ˈnā-shən\ *n* **:** the formation by the processes of crossing-over and independent assortment of new combinations of genes in progeny that did not occur in the parents — **re·com·bi·na·tion·al** \-shnəl, -shən-ᵊl\ *adj*

rec·om·mend \ˌrek-ə-ˈmend\ *vt* [ME *recommenden* to praise, fr. ML *recommendare,* fr. L *re-* + *commendare* to commend] **1 a :** to present as worthy of acceptance or trial <~*ed* the medicine> **b :** to endorse as fit, worthy, or competent <~*s* her for the position> **2 :** ENTRUST, COMMIT <~*ed* his soul to God> **3 :** to make acceptable <has other points to ~ it> **4 :** ADVISE <~ that the matter be dropped> — **rec·om·mend·able** \-ˈmen-də-bəl\ *adj* — **rec·om·men·da·to·ry** \-də-ˌtōr-ē, -ˌtȯr-\ *adj* — **rec·om·mend·er** *n*

rec·om·men·da·tion \ˌrek-ə-mən-ˈdā-shən, -ˌmen-\ *n* **1 a :** the act of recommending **b :** something (as a course of action) recommended **2 :** something that recommends or expresses commendation

re·com·mit \ˌrē-kə-ˈmit\ *vt* **1 :** to refer (as a bill) back to a committee **2 :** to entrust or consign again — **re·com·mit·ment** \-mənt\ *n* — **re·com·mit·tal** \-ˈmit-ᵊl\ *n*

[1]**rec·om·pense** \ˈrek-əm-ˌpen(t)s\ *vt* **-pensed; -pens·ing** [ME *recompensen,* fr. MF *recompenser,* fr. LL *recompensare,* fr. L *re-* + *compensare* to compensate] **1 a :** to give something to by way of compensation (as for a service rendered or damage incurred) **b :** to pay for **2 :** to return in kind **:** REQUITE ***syn*** see PAY

[2]**recompense** *n* **:** an equivalent or a return for something done, suffered, or given **:** COMPENSATION <offered in ~ for injuries>

re·com·pose \ˌrē-kəm-ˈpōz\ *vt* **1 :** to compose again **:** REARRANGE **2 :** to restore to composure — **re·com·po·si·tion** \(ˌ)rē-ˌkäm-pə-ˈzish-ən\ *n*

rec·on·cil·able \ˌrek-ən-ˈsī-lə-bəl, ˈrek-ən-ˌ\ *adj* **:** capable of being reconciled — **rec·on·cil·abil·i·ty** \ˌrek-ən-ˌsī-lə-ˈbil-ət-ē\ *n* — **rec·on·cil·able·ness** \ˌrek-ən-ˈsī-lə-bəl-nəs, ˈrek-ən-ˌ\ *n*

rec·on·cile \ˈrek-ən-ˌsīl\ *vb* **-ciled; -cil·ing** [ME *reconcilen,* fr. MF or L; MF *reconcilier,* fr. L *reconciliare,* fr. *re-* + *conciliare* to conciliate] *vt* **1 a :** to restore to friendship or harmony <*reconciled* the factions> **b :** SETTLE, RESOLVE <~ differences> **2 :** to make consistent or congruous <~ an ideal with reality> **3 :** to cause to submit to or accept <was *reconciled* to hardship> ~ *vi* **:** to become reconciled ***syn*** see ADAPT — **rec·on·cile·ment** \-ˌsīl-mənt\ *n* — **rec·on·cil·er** *n*

rec·on·cil·i·a·tion \ˌrek-ən-ˌsil-ē-ˈā-shən\ *n* [ME, fr. L *reconciliation-, reconciliatio,* fr. *reconciliatus,* pp. of *reconciliare*] **:** the action of reconciling **:** the state of being reconciled — **rec·on·cil·ia·to·ry** \-ˈsil-yə-ˌtōr-ē, -ˈsil-ē-ə-, -ˌtȯr-\ *adj*

re·con·dite \ˈrek-ən-ˌdīt, ri-ˈkän-\ *adj* [L *reconditus,* pp. of *recondere* to conceal, fr. *re-* + *condere* to store up, fr. *com-* + *-dere* to put — more at DO] **1 :** hidden from sight **:** CONCEALED <produced some ~ flasks of wine —T. L. Peacock> **2 :** incomprehensible to one of ordinary understanding or knowledge **:** DEEP <a ~ subject> **3 :** of, relating to, or dealing with something little known or obscure <~ fact about the origin of the holiday —Floyd Dell> — **re·con·dite·ly** *adv* — **re·con·dite·ness** *n*

re·con·di·tion \ˌrē-kən-ˈdish-ən\ *vt* **1 :** to restore to good condition (as by replacing parts) **2 :** to condition (as a person or his attitudes) anew; *also* **:** to reinstate (a response) in an organism

re·con·firm \ˌrē-kən-ˈfərm\ *vt* **:** to confirm again; *also* **:** to establish more strongly — **re·con·fir·ma·tion** \(ˌ)rē-ˌkän-fər-ˈmā-shən\ *n*

re·con·nais·sance \ri-ˈkän-ə-zən(t)s *also* -sən(t)s\ *n* [F, lit., recognition, fr. MF *reconoissance*] **:** a preliminary survey to gain

information; *esp* : an exploratory military survey of enemy territory
re·con·noi·ter \ˌrē-kə-ˈnȯit-ər *also* ˌrek-ə-\ *vb* **re·con·noi·tered; re·con·noi·ter·ing** \-ˈnȯit-ə-riŋ, -ˈnȯi-triŋ\ [obs. F *reconnoître,* lit., to recognize, fr. MF *reconoistre* — more at RECOGNIZE] *vt* : to make a reconnaissance of ~ *vi* : to engage in reconnaissance
re·con·sid·er \ˌrē-kən-ˈsid-ər\ *vt* : to consider again with a view to changing or reversing; *specif* : to take up again in a meeting ~ *vi* : to consider something again — **re·con·sid·er·a·tion** \-ˌsid-ə-ˈrā-shən\ *n*
re·con·sti·tute \(ˈ)rē-ˈkän(t)-stə-ˌt(y)üt\ *vt* : to constitute again or anew; *esp* : to restore to a former condition by adding water <~ powdered milk> — **re·con·sti·tu·tion** \(ˌ)rē-ˌkän(t)-stə-ˈt(y)ü-shən\ *n*
re·con·struct \ˌrē-kən-ˈstrəkt\ *vt* : to construct again : REESTABLISH, REASSEMBLE — **re·con·struct·ible** \-ˈstrək-tə-bəl\ *adj* — **re·con·struc·tive** \-tiv\ *adj* — **re·con·struc·tor** \-tər\ *n*
re·con·struc·tion \ˌrē-kən-ˈstrək-shən\ *n* **1 a** : the action of reconstructing : the state of being reconstructed **b** *often cap* : the reorganization and reestablishment of the seceded states in the Union after the American Civil War **2** : something reconstructed
re·con·struc·tion·ism \-shə-ˌniz-əm\ *n, often cap* **1** : advocacy of post-Civil War reconstruction **2** : a movement in 20th century American Judaism that advocates a creative adjustment to contemporary conditions through the cultivation of traditions and folkways shared by all Jews — **re·con·struc·tion·ist** \-sh(ə-)nəst\ *n, often cap*
re·con·ver·sion \ˌrē-kən-ˈvər-zhən, -shən\ *n* : conversion back to a previous state
re·con·vert \ˌrē-kən-ˈvərt\ *vt* : to cause to undergo reconversion ~ *vi* : to undergo reconversion
re·con·vey \ˌrē-kən-ˈvā\ *vt* : to convey back to a previous position or owner — **re·con·vey·ance** \-ˈvā-ən(t)s\ *n*
1re·cord \ri-ˈkȯ(ə)rd\ *vb* [ME *recorden,* lit., to recall, fr. OF *recorder,* fr. L *recordari,* fr. *re-* + *cord-, cor* heart — more at HEART] *vt* **1 a** (1) : to set down in writing : furnish written evidence of (2) : to deposit an authentic official copy of <~ a deed> **b** : to state as if for a record <spoke in favor of the bill but also said he wanted to ~ certain reservations> **c** (1) : to register permanently by mechanical means <earthquake shocks ~*ed* by a seismograph> (2) : INDICATE, READ <the thermometer ~*ed* 90°> **2** : to give evidence of <the intensity of the explosion is ~*ed* on the charred tree trunks> **3** : to cause (as sound) to be registered on something (as a phonograph disc) in reproducible form ~ *vi* : to record something — **re·cord·able** \-ˈkȯrd-ə-bəl\ *adj*
2rec·ord \ˈrek-ərd *also* -ˌȯ(ə)rd\ *n* **1** : the state or fact of being recorded **2** : something that records: as **a** : something that recalls or relates past events **b** : an official document that records the acts of a public body or officer **c** : an authentic official copy of a document deposited with a legally designated officer **d** : the official copy of the papers used in a law case **3 a** : a body of known or recorded facts regarding something or someone **b** : an attested top performance **4** : something on which sound or visual images have been recorded; *specif* : a disc with a spiral groove carrying recorded sound for phonograph reproduction — **off the record** : not for publication <spoke *off the record*> <remarks that were *off the record*> — **of record** **1** : appearing on the record of a court proceeding **2 a** : documented or otherwise attested <a partner *of record* in several firms> **b** : furnished with documents <a book *of record*> — **on record** **1** : in the position of having publicly declared oneself <went *on record* as opposed to higher taxes> **2** : in the status of being known, published, or documented <his friends left *on record* a marvelous description of him>
3record *like*2\ *adj* : surpassing others of the kind
re·cor·da·tion \ˌrek-ˌȯr-ˈdā-shən; ˌrē-ˌkȯr-, ri-\ *n* : the action or process of recording
record changer *n* : a phonograph with a device that automatically positions and plays successively each of a stack of records; *also* : the automatic device on a record changer
re·cord·er \ri-ˈkȯrd-ər\ *n* **1** : one that records **2 a** : the chief judicial magistrate of some British cities and boroughs **b** : a municipal judge with criminal jurisdiction of first instance and sometimes limited civil jurisdiction **3** : one of a group of wind instruments ranging from treble to bass that are characterized by a conical tube, a whistle mouthpiece, and eight finger holes

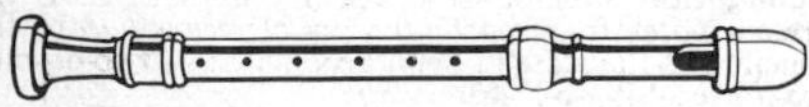

recorder 3

re·cord·ing \ri-ˈkȯrd-iŋ\ *n* : RECORD 4
re·cord·ist \ri-ˈkȯrd-əst\ *n* : one who records sound (as on magnetic tape)
record player *n* : an electronic instrument for playing phonograph records through a loudspeaker
1re·count \ri-ˈkau̇nt\ *vt* [ME *recounten,* fr. MF *reconter,* fr. *re-* + *conter* to count, relate — more at COUNT] : to relate in detail : NARRATE — **re·count·er** *n*
2re·count \(ˈ)rē-ˈkau̇nt\ *vt* [*re-* + *count*] : to count again
3re·count \ˈrē-ˌkau̇nt, (ˈ)rē-ˈ\ *n* : a second or fresh count
re·coup \ri-ˈküp\ *vb* [F *recouper* to cut back, fr. OF, fr. *re-* + *couper* to cut — more at COPE] *vt* **1** : to withhold rightfully part of (a sum legally claimed) instead of filing a counterclaim **2 a** : to get an equivalent for (as losses) : make up for **b** : REIMBURSE, COMPENSATE <~ a person for losses> **3** : REGAIN <an attempt to ~ his fortune> ~ *vi* : to make up for something lost — **re·coup·able** \-ˈkü-pə-bəl\ *adj* — **re·coup·ment** \-ˈküp-mənt\ *n*
re·course \ˈrē-ˌkō(ə)rs, -ˌkȯ(ə)rs, ri-ˈ\ *n* [ME *recours,* fr. MF, fr. LL *recursus,* fr. L, act of running back, fr. *recursus,* pp. of *recurrere* to run back — more at RECUR] **1 a** : a turning to someone or something for help or protection **b** : a source of help or strength : RESORT **2** : the right to demand payment from the maker or endorser of a negotiable instrument (as a check)
re·cov·er \ri-ˈkəv-ər\ *vb* **re·cov·ered; re·cov·er·ing** \-(ə-)riŋ\ [ME *recoveren,* fr. MF *recoverer,* fr. L *recuperare;* akin to L *recipere* to receive — more at RECEIVE] *vt* **1** : to get back : REGAIN **2 a** : to bring back to normal position or condition <stumbled, then ~*ed* himself> **b** *archaic* : RESCUE **3 a** : to make up for <~ increased costs through higher prices> **b** : to gain by legal process **4** *archaic* : REACH **5** : to find or identify again <~ a comet> **6 a** : to obtain from an ore, a waste product, or a by-product **b** : to save from loss and restore to usefulness : RECLAIM ~ *vi* **1** : to regain a normal position or condition (as of health) <~*ing* from a cold> **2** : to obtain a final legal judgment in one's favor — **re·cov·er·abil·i·ty** \-ˌkəv-(ə-)rə-ˈbil-ət-ē\ *adj* — **re·cov·er·able** \-ˈkəv-(ə-)rə-bəl\ *adj* — **re·cov·er·er** \-ˈkəv-ər-ər\ *n*
re–cov·er \(ˈ)rē-ˈkəv-ər\ *vt* : to cover again or anew
re·cov·ery \ri-ˈkəv-(ə-)rē\ *n, pl* **-er·ies** : the act, process, or an instance of recovering; *esp* : an economic upturn (as after a depression)
recovery room *n* : a hospital room equipped for meeting postoperative emergencies
1rec·re·ant \ˈrek-rē-ənt\ *adj* [ME, fr. MF, fr. prp. of *recroire* to renounce one's cause in a trial by battle, fr. *re-* + *croire* to believe, fr. L *credere* — more at CREED] **1** : crying for mercy : COWARDLY **2** : unfaithful to duty or allegiance
2recreant *n* **1** : COWARD **2** : APOSTATE, DESERTER
1rec·re·ate \ˈrek-rē-ˌāt\ *vb* **-at·ed; -at·ing** [L *recreatus,* pp.] *vt* : to give new life or freshness to : REFRESH ~ *vi* : to take recreation — **rec·re·ative** \-ˌāt-iv\ *adj*
2re·cre·ate \ˌrē-krē-ˈāt\ *vt* : to create again; *esp* : to form anew in the imagination — **re·cre·at·able** \-ˈāt-ə-bəl\ *adj* — **re·cre·ation** \-ˈā-shən\ *n* — **re·cre·ative** \-ˈāt-iv\ *adj*
rec·re·ation \ˌrek-rē-ˈā-shən\ *n* [ME *recreacion,* fr. MF *recreation,* fr. L *recreation-, recreatio* restoration to health, fr. *recreatus,* pp. of *recreare* to create anew, restore, refresh, fr. *re-* + *creare* to create] : refreshment of strength and spirits after work; *also* : a means of refreshment or diversion — **rec·re·ation·al** \-shnəl, -shən-ᵊl\ *adj*
rec·re·ation·ist \-sh(ə-)nəst\ *n* : one who seeks recreation esp. in the outdoors
recreation room *n* **1** : a room (as a rumpus room) used for recreation and relaxation **2** : a public room (as in a hospital) for recreation and social activities — called also *rec room*
re·crim·i·nate \ri-ˈkrim-ə-ˌnāt\ *vi* **-nat·ed; -nat·ing** [ML *recriminatus,* pp. of *recriminare,* fr. L *re-* + *criminari* to accuse — more at CRIMINATE] **1** : to make a retaliatory charge against an accuser **2** : to retort bitterly — **re·crim·i·na·tion** \-ˌkrim-ə-ˈnā-shən\ *n* — **re·crim·i·na·tive** \-ˈkrim-ə-ˌnāt-iv\ *adj* — **re·crim·i·na·to·ry** \-ˈkrim-(ə-)nə-ˌtōr-ē, -ˌtȯr-\ *adj*
re·cru·desce \ˌrē-krü-ˈdes\ *vi* **-desced; -desc·ing** [L *recrudescere* to become raw again, fr. *re-* + *crudescere* to become raw, fr. *crudus* raw — more at RAW] : to break out or become active again ***syn*** see RETURN
re·cru·des·cence \-ˈdes-ᵊn(t)s\ *n* : a new outbreak after a period of abatement or inactivity : RENEWAL
re·cru·des·cent \-ᵊnt\ *adj* : breaking out again : RENEWING
1re·cruit \ri-ˈkrüt\ *n* [F *recrute, recrue* fresh growth, new levy of soldiers, fr. MF, fr. *recroistre* to grow up again, fr. L *recrescere,* fr. *re-* + *crescere* to grow — more at CRESCENT] **1** : a fresh or additional supply **2** : a newcomer to a field or activity; *specif* : a newly enlisted or drafted member of the armed forces **3** : a former enlisted man of the lowest rank in the army
2recruit *vt* **1 a** (1) : to fill up the number of (as an army) with new members : REINFORCE (2) : to enlist as a member of an armed service **b** : to increase or maintain the number of <American ~*ed* her population from Europe> **c** : to secure the services of : ENGAGE, HIRE **d** : to enroll or seek to enroll <a college that ~*s* students from the ghettos> **2** : REPLENISH **3** : to restore or increase the health, vigor, or intensity of ~ *vi* : to enlist new members — **re·cruit·er** *n* — **re·cruit·ment** \-ˈkrüt-mənt\ *n*
re·crys·tal·lize \(ˈ)rē-ˈkris-tə-ˌlīz\ *vb* : to crystallize again or repeatedly — **re·crys·tal·li·za·tion** \(ˌ)rē-ˌkris-tə-lə-ˈzā-shən\ *n*
rec sec *abbr* recording secretary
rect *abbr* **1** rectangle; rectangular **2** receipt **3** rectified
rect- *or* **recto-** *comb form* [NL *rectum*] : rectum <*rectal*>
rec·tal \ˈrek-tᵊl\ *adj* : relating to, affecting, or being near the rectum — **rec·tal·ly** \-ē\ *adv*
rect·an·gle \ˈrek-ˌtaŋ-gəl\ *n* [ML *rectangulus* having a right angle, fr. L *rectus* right + *angulus* angle — more at RIGHT, ANGLE] : a parallelogram all of whose angles are right angles
rect·an·gu·lar \rek-ˈtaŋ-gyə-lər\ *adj* **1** : shaped like a rectangle <a ~ area> **2 a** : crossing, lying, or meeting at a right angle <~ axes> **b** : having edges, surfaces, or faces that meet at right angles : having faces or surfaces shaped like rectangles <~ parallelepipeds> <~ blocks> — **rect·an·gu·lar·i·ty** \(ˌ)rek-ˌtaŋ-gyə-ˈlar-ət-ē\ *n* — **rect·an·gu·lar·ly** \rek-ˈtaŋ-gyə-lər-lē\ *adv*

rectangles

rectangular coordinate *n* : a Cartesian coordinate of a Cartesian coordinate system whose straight-line axes or coordinate planes are perpendicular
rec·ti·fi·able \ˈrek-tə-ˌfī-ə-bəl\ *adj* [*rectify* (to determine the length of an arc)] : having finite length <a ~ curve> — **rec·ti·fi·abil·i·ty** \ˌrek-tə-ˌfī-ə-ˈbil-ət-ē\ *n*
rec·ti·fi·er \ˈrek-tə-ˌfī(-ə)r\ *n* : one that rectifies; *specif* : a device for converting alternating current into direct current
rec·ti·fy \ˈrek-tə-ˌfī\ *vt* **-fied; -fy·ing** [ME *rectifien,* fr. MF *rectifier,* fr. ML *rectificare,* fr. L *rectus* right] **1** : to set right : REMEDY **2** : to purify (as alcohol) esp. by repeated or fractional distillation **3** : to correct by removing errors : ADJUST <~ the calendar> **4** : to make (an alternating current) unidirectional ***syn*** see CORRECT — **rec·ti·fi·ca·tion** \ˌrek-tə-fə-ˈkā-shən\ *n*

rec·ti·lin·ear \ˌrek-tə-ˈlin-ē-ər\ *adj* [LL *rectilineus,* fr. L *rectus* + *linea* line] **1 :** moving in or forming a straight line <~ motion> **2 :** characterized by straight lines **3 :** PERPENDICULAR 3 **4 :** corrected for distortion so that straight lines are imaged accurately <~ lens> — **rec·ti·lin·ear·ly** *adv*

rec·ti·tude \ˈrek-tə-ˌt(y)üd\ *n* [ME, fr. MF, fr. LL *rectitudo,* fr. L *rectus* straight, right] **1 :** the quality or state of being straight **2 :** moral integrity : RIGHTEOUSNESS **3 :** the quality or state of being correct in judgment or procedure

rec·ti·tu·di·nous \ˌrek-tə-ˈt(y)üd-nəs, -ᵊn-əs\ *adj* [LL *rectitudin-, rectitudo* rectitude] **1 :** characterized by rectitude **2 :** piously self-righteous

rec·to \ˈrek-(ˌ)tō\ *n, pl* **rectos** [NL *recto (folio)* the page being straight] **1 :** the side of a leaf (as of a manuscript) that is to be read first **2 :** a right-hand page — compare VERSO

rec·tor \ˈrek-tər\ *n* [L, fr. *rectus,* pp. of *regere* to direct — more at RIGHT] **1 :** one that directs : LEADER **2 a :** a clergyman (as of the Protestant Episcopal Church) in charge of a parish **b :** an incumbent of a Church of England benefice in full possession of its rights **c :** a Roman Catholic priest directing a church with no pastor or one whose pastor has other duties **3 :** the head of a university or school — **rec·tor·ate** \-t(ə-)rət\ *n* — **rec·to·ri·al** \rek-ˈtōr-ē-əl, -ˈtȯr-\ *adj* — **rec·tor·ship** \ˈrek-tər-ˌship\ *n*

rec·to·ry \ˈrek-t(ə-)rē\ *n, pl* **-ries** **1 :** a benefice held by a rector **2 :** a rector's residence

rec·trix \ˈrek-triks\ *n, pl* **rec·tri·ces** \ˈrek-trə-ˌsēz, rek-ˈtrī-(ˌ)sēz\ [NL, fr. L, fem. of *rector* one that directs] **:** any of the quill feathers of a bird's tail that are important in controlling flight direction

rec·tum \ˈrek-təm\ *n, pl* **rectums** *or* **rec·ta** \-tə\ [NL, fr. *rectum intestinum,* lit., straight intestine] **:** the terminal part of the intestine from the sigmoid flexure to the anus

rec·tus \ˈrek-təs\ *n, pl* **rec·ti** \-ˌtī, -ˌtē\ [NL, fr. *rectus musculus* straight muscle] **:** any of several straight muscles (as of the abdomen)

re·cum·ben·cy \ri-ˈkəm-bən-sē\ *n, pl* **-cies** **:** the state of leaning, resting, or reclining : REPOSE; *also* **:** a recumbent position

re·cum·bent \-bənt\ *adj* [L *recumbent-, recumbens,* prp. of *recumbere* to lie down, fr. *re-* + *-cumbere* to lie down (akin to L *cubare* to lie, recline) — more at HIP] **1 a :** suggestive of repose : LEANING, RESTING **b :** lying down **c :** representing a person lying down <a ~ statue> **2** *of an anatomical structure* **:** tending to rest upon the surface from which it extends ***syn*** see PRONE — **re·cum·bent·ly** *adv*

re·cu·per·ate \ri-ˈk(y)ü-pə-ˌrāt\ *vb* **-at·ed; -at·ing** [L *recuperatus,* pp. of *recuperare* — more at RECOVER] *vt* **:** to get back : REGAIN ~ *vi* **:** to regain a former state or condition; *esp* **:** to recover health or strength — **re·cu·per·a·tion** \-ˌk(y)ü-pə-ˈrā-shən\ *n*

re·cu·per·a·tive \-ˈk(y)ü-pə-ˌrāt-iv\ *adj* **1 :** of or relating to recuperation <~ powers> **2 :** aiding in recuperation : RESTORATIVE

re·cur \ri-ˈkər\ *vi* **re·curred; re·cur·ring** [ME *recurren* to return, fr. L *recurrere,* lit., to run back, fr. *re-* + *currere* to run — more at CURRENT] **1 :** to have recourse : RESORT **2 :** to go back in thought or discourse **3 a :** to come up again for consideration **b :** to come again to mind **4 :** to occur again after an interval ***syn*** see RETURN — **re·cur·rence** \-ˈkər-ən(t)s, -ˈkə-rən(t)s\ *n*

re·cur·rent \-ˈkər-ənt, -ˈkə-rənt\ *adj* [L *recurrent-, recurrens,* prp. of *recurrere*] **1 :** running or turning back in a direction opposite to a former course — used of various nerves and branches of vessels in the arms and legs **2 :** returning or happening time after time <~ complaints> ***syn*** see INTERMITTENT — **re·cur·rent·ly** *adv*

recurring decimal *n* **:** REPEATING DECIMAL

re·cur·sion \ri-ˈkər-zhən\ *n* [LL *recursion-, recursio,* fr. *recursus,* pp. of *recurrere* to run back — more at RECUR] **1 :** RETURN **2 :** the determination of a succession of elements (as numbers or functions) by operation on one or more preceding elements according to a rule or formula involving a finite number of steps

re·cur·sive \ri-ˈkər-siv\ *adj* **1 :** of, relating to, or involving mathematical recursion **2 :** of, relating to, or constituting a procedure that can repeat itself indefinitely or until a specified condition is met <a ~ rule in a grammar> — **re·cur·sive·ly** *adv* — **re·cur·sive·ness** *n*

re·curved \(ˈ)rē-ˈkərvd\ *adj* **:** curved backward or inward

re·cu·san·cy \ˈrek-yə-zən-sē, ri-ˈkyüz-ᵊn-\ *n* [*recusant,* n., fr. L *recusant-, recusans,* prp. of *recusare* to refuse, fr. *re-* + *causari* to give a reason, fr. *causa* cause, reason] **:** refusal to accept or obey established authority; *specif* **:** the refusal of Roman Catholics to attend services of the Church of England constituting a statutory offense from about 1570 till 1791 — **re·cu·sant** \-zənt, -ᵊnt\ *n or adj*

re·cy·cle \(ˈ)rē-ˈsī-kəl\ *vt* **:** to pass again through a series of changes or treatments: as **a :** to process (as liquid body waste, glass, or cans) in order to regain material for human use **b :** RECOVER 6 ~ *vi* **1 :** to return to an earlier point in a countdown **2 :** to return to an original condition so that operation can begin again — used of an electronic device — **re·cy·cla·ble** \-k(ə-)lə-bəl\ *adj*

¹red \ˈred\ *adj* **red·der; red·dest** [ME, fr. OE *rēad;* akin to OHG *rōt* red, L *ruber & rufus,* Gk *erythros*] **1 a :** of the color red **b :** having red as a distinguishing color **2 a** (1) **:** flushed esp. with anger or embarrassment (2) **:** RUDDY, FLORID (3) **:** of a coppery hue **b :** BLOODSHOT <eyes ~ from crying> **c :** in the color range between a moderate orange and russet or bay **d :** tinged with red : REDDISH **3 :** heated to redness : GLOWING **4 a :** inciting or endorsing radical social or political change esp. by force **b :** COMMUNIST **c :** of or relating to a communist country and esp. to the U.S.S.R. **5 :** failing to show a profit <a ~ financial statement> — compare BLACK

²red *n* **1 :** a color whose hue resembles that of blood or of the ruby or is that of the long-wave extreme of the visible spectrum **2 :** one that is of a red or reddish color; *esp* **:** an animal with a reddish coat **3 a :** a pigment or dye that colors red **b :** a shade or tint of red **4 a :** one who advocates the violent overthrow of an existing social or political order **b** *cap* **:** COMMUNIST **5** [fr. the bookkeeping practice of entering debit items in red ink] **:** the condition of showing a loss <in the ~>

³red *abbr* reduce; reduction

re·dact \ri-ˈdakt\ *vt* [back-formation fr. *redaction*] **1 :** to put in writing : FRAME **2 :** to select or adapt for publication : EDIT

re·dac·tion \-ˈdak-shən\ *n* [F *rédaction,* fr. LL *redaction-, redactio* act of reducing, compressing, fr. L *redactus,* pp. of *redigere* to bring back, reduce, fr. *re-, red-* re- + *agere* to lead — more at AGENT] **1 :** an act or instance of redacting **2 :** a work that has been redacted : EDITION, VERSION — **re·dac·tion·al** \-shnəl, -shən-ᵊl\ *adj*

re·dac·tor \-ˈdak-tər\ *n* **:** one who redacts; *esp* **:** EDITOR

red admiral *n* **:** a nymphalid butterfly (*Vanessa atalanta*) that is common in both Europe and America, has broad orange-red bands on the fore wings, and feeds on nettles in the larval stage

red alert *n* **:** the final stage of alert in which enemy attack appears imminent

red alga *n* **:** an alga (division Rhodophyta) that has predominantly red pigmentation

red ant *n* **:** any of various reddish ants (as the pharaoh ant)

red·ar·gue \ri-ˈdär-(ˌ)gyü\ *vt* **-gued; -gu·ing** [ME *redarguen,* fr. L *redarguere,* fr. *red-* + *arguere* assert, make clear — more at ARGENT] *archaic* **:** CONFUTE, DISPROVE

red–bait \ˈred-ˌbāt\ *vb, often cap R, vt* **:** to subject (as a person or group) to red-baiting ~ *vi* **:** to engage in red-baiting

red–bait·ing *n, often cap R* **:** the act of attacking or persecuting as a Communist or as communistic

red bay *n* **:** a small tree (*Persea borbonia*) of the southern U.S. that has dark red heartwood

red·bel·ly dace \ˌred-ˌbel-ē-\ *n* **:** either of two small brightly marked No. American cyprinid fishes (*Chrosomus eos* and *C. erythrogaster*) — called also *red-bellied dace*

red birch *n* **1 :** the heartwood lumber of the yellow birch (*Betula lutea*) and of the sweet birch (*Betula lenta*) **2 :** a valuable New Zealand timber tree (*Nothofagus fusca*); *also* **:** its hard wood

red·bird \ˈred-ˌbərd\ *n* **:** any of several birds (as a cardinal, several tanagers, or the bullfinch) with predominantly red plumage

red blood cell *n* **:** one of the hemoglobin-containing cells that carry oxygen to the tissues and are responsible for the red color of vertebrate blood — called also *erythrocyte, red blood corpuscle, red cell, red corpuscle*

red–blood·ed \ˈred-ˈbləd-əd\ *adj* **:** VIGOROUS, LUSTY

red·bone \ˈred-ˌbōn\ *n* **:** a moderate-sized speedy dark red or red and tan American hound that is used esp. for hunting raccoons

red·breast \ˈred-ˌbrest\ *n* **1 :** a bird (as a robin) with a reddish breast **2 :** a reddish-bellied sunfish (*Lepomis auritus*) of the eastern U.S. — called also *red-breasted bream*

red·brick \-ˌbrik\ *adj* [fr. the common use of red brick in constructing the buildings of recently founded universities] **:** of, relating to, or being the British universities founded in modern times

red·bud \-ˌbəd\ *n* **:** an American leguminous tree (genus *Cercis*) with usu. pale rosy pink flowers

red bug *n, South & Midland* **:** CHIGGER 2

red·cap \ˈred-ˌkap\ *n* **:** a baggage porter (as at a railroad station)

red–carpet *adj* [fr. the traditional laying down of a red carpet for important guests to walk on] **:** marked by ceremonial courtesy <~ treatment>

red carpet *n* **:** a greeting or reception marked by ceremonial courtesy — usu. used in the phrase *roll out the red carpet*

red cedar *n* **1 :** an American juniper (*Juniperus virginiana*) that is common east of the Rocky mountains and has dark green closely imbricated needle-shaped leaves **2 :** the fragrant close-grained red wood of the red cedar

red cent *n* **:** a trivial amount : PENNY 4, WHIT

red clover *n* **:** a Eurasian clover (*Trifolium pratense*) with globose heads of reddish purple flowers widely cultivated as a hay, forage, and cover crop

red·coat \ˈred-ˌkōt\ *n* **:** a British soldier esp. in America during the Revolutionary War

red coral *n* **:** a gorgonian (*Corallium nobile*) of the Mediterranean and adjacent parts of the Atlantic having a hard stony skeleton of a delicate red or pink color used for ornaments and jewelry

red deer 1

Red Cross *n* **:** a red Greek cross on a white background used as the emblem of the International Red Cross

¹redd \ˈred\ *vb* **redd·ed** *or* **redd; redd·ing** [ME *redden* to clear, prob. alter. of *ridden* — more at RID] *vt, chiefly dial* **:** to set in order ~ *vi, chiefly dial* **:** to make things tidy

²redd *n* [origin unknown] **:** the spawning ground or nest of various fishes

red deer *n* **1 :** the common deer of temperate Europe and Asia (*Cervus elaphus*) which is related to but smaller than the elk **2 :** the whitetail in its summer coat

red·den \ˈred-ᵊn\ *vb* **red·dened; red·den·ing** \ˈred-niŋ, -ᵊn-iŋ\ *vt* **:** to make red or reddish ~ *vi* **:** to become red; *esp* **:** BLUSH

red·dish \ˈred-ish\ *adj* **:** tinged with red — **red·dish·ness** *n*

red dog *n* **:** BLITZ 2b — **red dog** *vb*

---

[1]**rede** \'rēd\ *vt* [ME *reden* — more at READ] **1** *dial* : to give counsel to : ADVISE **2** *dial* : INTERPRET, EXPLAIN
[2]**rede** *n* **1** *chiefly dial* : COUNSEL, ADVICE **2** *archaic* : ACCOUNT, STORY
red·ear \'red-ˌi(ə)r\ *n* : a common sunfish (*Lepomis microlophus*) of the southern and eastern U.S. resembling the bluegill but having the back part of the gill cover bright orange-red — called also *shellcracker*
re·dec·o·rate \(ˈ)rē-'dek-ə-ˌrāt\ *vt* : to freshen or change in appearance : REFURBISH ~ *vi* : to freshen or change a decorative scheme — **re·dec·o·ra·tion** \(ˌ)rē-ˌdek-ə-'rā-shən\ *n* — **re·dec·o·ra·tor** \(ˈ)rē-'dek-ə-ˌrāt-ər\ *n*
re·deem \ri-'dēm\ *vt* [ME *redemen*, modif. of MF *redimer*, fr. L *redimere*, fr. *re-*, *red-* re- + *emere* to take, buy; akin to Lith *imti* to take] **1 a** : to buy back : REPURCHASE **b** : to get or win back **2** : to free from what distresses or harms: as **a** : to free from captivity by payment of ransom **b** : to extricate from or help to overcome something detrimental <new interests that ~*ed* his life from futility> **c** : to release from blame or debt : CLEAR **d** : to free from the consequences of sin **3** : to change for the better : REFORM **4** : REPAIR, RESTORE **5 a** : to free from a lien by payment of an amount secured thereby **b** (1) : to remove the obligation of by payment <the U.S. Treasury ~*s* savings bonds on demand> (2) : to convert into something of value <~ trading stamps> **c** : to make good : FULFILL **6 a** : to atone for : EXPIATE **b** (1) : to offset the bad effect of (2) : to make worthwhile : RETRIEVE ***syn*** see RESCUE — **re·deem·able** \-'dē-mə-bəl\ *adj*
re·deem·er \-'dē-mər\ *n* : a person who redeems; *esp, cap* : JESUS
re·de·fine \ˌrēd-i-'fīn\ *vt* **1** : to define (a concept) again <had to ~ their terms in order to deal with the problem> **2** : to reexamine or reevaluate esp. with a view to change — **re·def·i·ni·tion** \(ˌ)rē-ˌdef-ə-'nish-ən\ *n*
re·demp·tion \ri-'dem(p)-shən\ *n* [ME *redempcioun*, fr. MF *redemption*, fr. L *redemption-*, *redemptio*, fr. *redemptus*, pp. of *redimere* to redeem] : the act, process, or an instance of redeeming — **re·demp·tion·al** \-shnəl, -shən-ᵊl\ *adj*
re·demp·tion·er \-sh(ə-)nər\ *n* : an immigrant to America in the 18th and 19th centuries who obtained passage by becoming an indentured servant
re·demp·tive \-'dem(p)-tiv\ *adj* : of, relating to, or bringing about redemption
Re·demp·tor·ist \ri-'dem(p)-t(ə-)rəst\ *n* [F *rédemptoriste*, fr. LL *redemptor* redeemer, fr. L, contractor, fr. *redemptus*] : a member of the Congregation of the Most Holy Redeemer founded by St. Alphonsus Liguori in Scala, Italy, in 1732 and devoted to preaching
re·demp·to·ry \ri-'dem(p)-t(ə-)rē\ *adj* : serving to redeem
re·de·ploy \ˌrēd-i-'plȯi\ *vt* : to transfer from one area or activity to another ~ *vi* : to relocate men or equipment — **re·de·ploy·ment** \-mənt\ *n*
re·de·scribe \ˌrēd-i-'skrīb\ *vt* : to describe anew or again; *esp* : to give a new and more complete description to (a biological taxon)
re·de·scrip·tion \-'skrip-shən\ *n* : a new and more complete description of a biological taxon
re·de·sign \ˌrēd-i-'zīn\ *vt* : to revise in appearance, function, or content — **redesign** *n*
re·de·ter·mine \ˌrēd-i-'tər-mən\ *vt* : to determine again : CONFIRM — **re·de·ter·mi·na·tion** \-ˌtər-mə-'nā-shən\ *n*
re·de·vel·op \ˌrēd-i-'vel-əp\ *vt* : to develop again; *esp* : REDESIGN, REBUILD — **re·de·vel·op·er** *n*
re·de·vel·op·ment \-əp-mənt\ *n* : the act or process of redeveloping; *esp* : renovation of a blighted area
red–eye \'red-ˌī\ *n* : cheap whiskey
red·eye gravy \ˌred-ˌī-\ *n* : gravy made from the juices of ham
red feed *n* : small red marine planktonic copepods that are a leading food of some commercial fishes
red fescue *n* : a perennial pasture and turf grass (*Festuca rubra*) of Europe and America with creeping rootstocks, erect culms, and reddish spikelets
red·fish \'red-ˌfish\ *n* : any of various reddish fishes: as **a** (1) : a marine scorpaenid food fish (*Sebastes marinus*) of the northern coasts of Europe and America that is usu. bright rose-red when mature (2) : a fish (*Sebastes mentella*) related to the redfish **b** : CHANNEL BASS
red fox *n* : a fox (*Vulpes vulpes*) with bright orange-red to dusky reddish brown fur
red giant *n* : a star that has low surface temperature and a diameter that is large relative to the sun
red–green blindness *n* : dichromatism in which the spectrum is seen in tones of yellow and blue — called also *red-green color blindness*
Red Guard *n* : a member of a teenage activist organization in China serving the Maoist party
red gum *n* **1** : any of several Australian trees of the genus *Eucalyptus* (esp. *E. camaldulensis, E. amygdalina*, and *E. calophylla*) **2** : eucalyptus gum
red–hand·ed \'red-'han-dəd\ *adv or adj* : in the act of committing a crime or misdeed <caught ~>
red·head \'red-ˌhed\ *n* **1** : a person having red hair **2** : an American duck (*Aythya americana*) related to the canvasback but having in the male a brighter reddish head and shorter bill
red·head·ed *adj* : having red hair or a red head
red heat *n* : the state of being red-hot; *also* : the temperature at which a substance is red-hot
red herring *n* **1** : a herring cured by salting and slow smoking to a dark brown color **2** [fr. the practice of drawing a red herring across a trail to confuse hunting dogs] : something that distracts attention from the real issue
red·horse \'red-ˌhȯrs\ *n* : any of numerous large suckers (genera *Moxostoma* and *Placopharynx*) of No. American rivers and lakes that have in the male red fins esp. in the breeding season

[1]**red–hot** \'red-'hät\ *adj* **1** : glowing with heat : extremely hot **2** : exhibiting or marked by intense emotion, enthusiasm, or violence <a ~ political campaign> **3** : FRESH, NEW <~ news>
[2]**red–hot** \-ˌhät\ *n* **1** : one who shows intense emotion or partisanship **2** : HOT DOG **3** : a small red candy strongly flavored with cinnamon
re·dia \'rēd-ē-ə\ *n, pl* **re·di·ae** \-ē-ˌē\ *also* **re·di·as** [NL, fr. Francesco *Redi* †1698? It naturalist] : a larva produced within the sporocyst of many trematodes that produces another generation of rediae or develops into a cercaria — **re·di·al** \-ē-əl\ *adj*
Red Indian *n* : AMERICAN INDIAN
red·in·gote \'red-iŋ-ˌgōt\ *n* [F, modif. of E *riding coat*] : a fitted outer garment: as **a** : a double-breasted coat with wide flat cuffs and collar worn by men in the 18th century **b** : a woman's lightweight coat open at the front **c** : a dress with a front gore of contrasting material
red ink *n* [fr. the use of red ink in financial statements to indicate a loss] **1** : a business loss : DEFICIT **2** : the condition of showing a business loss
red·in·te·grate \ri-'dint-ə-ˌgrāt, re-\ *vt* [ME *redintegraten*, fr. L *redintegratus*, pp. of *redintegrare*, fr. *re-*, *red-* re- + *integrare* to make complete — more at INTEGRATE] *archaic* : to restore to a former and esp. sound state
red·in·te·gra·tion \ri-ˌdint-ə-'grā-shən, re-\ *n* **1** *archaic* : restoration to a former state **2 a** : revival of the whole of a previous mental state when a phase of it recurs **b** : arousal of any response by a part of the complex of stimuli that originally aroused that response — **red·in·te·gra·tive** \-'dint-ə-ˌgrāt-iv\ *adj*
re·di·rect \ˌrēd-ə-'rekt, ˌrē-(ˌ)dī-\ *vt* : to change the course or direction of — **re·di·rec·tion** \-'rek-shən\ *n*
[1]**re·dis·count** \(ˈ)rē-'dis-ˌkau̇nt, ˌrē-dis-'\ *vt* : to discount again (as commercial paper) — **re·dis·count·able** \-ə-bəl\ *adj*
[2]**re·dis·count** \(ˈ)rē-'dis-ˌkau̇nt\ *n* **1** : the act or process of rediscounting **2** : negotiable paper that is rediscounted
re·dis·trib·ute \ˌrēd-ə-'strib-yət\ *vt* **1** : to alter the distribution of : REALLOCATE **2** : to spread to other areas — **re·dis·tri·bu·tion** \(ˌ)rē-ˌdis-trə-'byü-shən\ *n* — **re·dis·trib·u·tive** \ˌrēd-ə-'strib-yət-iv\ *adj* — **re·dis·trib·u·to·ry** \-yə-ˌtōr-ē, -ˌtȯr-\ *adj*
re·dis·trict \(ˈ)rē-'dis-(ˌ)trikt\ *vt* : to divide anew into districts; *specif* : to revise the legislative districts of ~ *vi* : to revise legislative districts
red·i·vi·vus \ˌred-ə-'vī-vəs, -'vē-\ *adj* [LL, fr. L, renovated] : brought back to life : REBORN
red jasmine *n* **1** : a widely cultivated frangipani (*Plumeria rubra*) with large terminal cymes of pink, red, or purple fragrant flowers **2** : CYPRESS VINE
red lead *n* : an orange-red to brick-red lead oxide Pb_3O_4 used in storage-battery plates, in glass and ceramics, and as a paint pigment — called also *minium*
red leaf *n* : any of several plant diseases characterized by reddening of the foliage
red·leg \'red-ˌleg, -ˌlāg\ *n* : any of several birds (as a redshank) with red legs
red–legged grasshopper \ˌred-ˌleg(-ə)d-, -ˌlāg(-ə)d-\ *n* : a widely distributed and sometimes highly destructive small No. American grasshopper (*Melanoplus femur-rubrum*) with red hind legs — called also *red-legged locust*
red–let·ter \ˌred-ˌlet-ər\ *adj* [fr. the practice of marking holy days in red letters in church calendars] : of special significance
red light *n* **1** : a warning signal; *esp* : a red traffic signal **2** : a cautionary sign : DETERRENT
red–light district *n* : a district in which houses of prostitution are numerous
red·ly \'red-lē\ *adv* : in a red manner : with red color
red man *n* **1** : AMERICAN INDIAN **2** *cap R&M* [Improved Order of *Red Men*] : a member of a major benevolent and fraternal order
red maple *n* : a common tree (*Acer rubrum*) of the eastern and central U.S. that grows chiefly on moist soils, has reddish twigs and somewhat pubescent leaves, and yields a lighter and softer wood than the sugar maple
red marrow *n* : reddish bone marrow that is the seat of blood-cell production
red mass *n, often cap R & M* : a votive mass of the Holy Ghost celebrated in red vestments esp. at the opening of courts and congresses
red mite *n* : any of several mites having a red color: as **a** : EUROPEAN RED MITE **b** : CITRUS RED MITE
red mulberry *n* : a No. American forest tree (*Morus rubra*) with soft weak but durable wood; *also* : its edible purple fruit
red mullet *n* : MULLET 2
red–neck \'red-ˌnek\ *n* : a white member of the Southern rural laboring class
red·ness \-nəs\ *n* : the quality or state of being red or red-hot
re·do \(ˈ)rē-'dü\ *vt* **1** : to do over or again **2** : REDECORATE — **re·do** \'rē-ˌdü, -'dü\ *n*
red oak *n* **1** : any of numerous American oaks (as *Quercus rubra* and *Quercus falcata*) that have four stamens in each floret, acorns with the inner surface of the shell lined with woolly hairs, the acorn cap covered with thin scales, and leaf veins that usu. run beyond the margin of the leaf to form bristles **2** : the wood of red oak
red ocher *n* : a red earthy hematite used as a pigment
red·o·lence \'red-ᵊl-ən(t)s\ *n* **1** : the quality or state of being redolent **2** : SCENT, AROMA
red·o·lent \-ᵊl-ənt\ *adj* [ME, fr. MF, fr. L *redolent-*, *redolens*, prp. of *redolēre* to emit a scent, fr. *re-*, *red-* + *olēre* to smell — more at ODOR] **1** : exuding fragrance : AROMATIC **2 a** : full of a specified fragrance : SCENTED <air ~ of seaweed> **b** : EVOCATIVE, SUGGESTIVE <a city ~ of antiquity> — **red·o·lent·ly** *adv*
red osier *n* : a common No. American shrub (*Cornus stolonifera*) with reddish purple twigs, white flowers, and globose blue or whitish fruit
re·dou·ble \(ˈ)rē-'dəb-əl\ *vt* **1** : to make twice as great in size or amount : INTENSIFY **2 a** *obs* : to echo back **b** *archaic* : REPEAT

~ *vi* **1 :** to become redoubled **2** *archaic* **:** RESOUND **3 :** to double an opponent's double in bridge — **redouble** *n*

re·doubt \ri-ˈdau̇t\ *n* [F *redoute,* fr. It *ridotto,* fr. ML *reductus* secret place, fr. L, withdrawn, fr. pp. of *reducere* to lead back — more at REDUCE] **1 a :** a small usu. temporary enclosed defensive work **b :** a defended position **:** protective barrier **2 :** a secure place **:** STRONGHOLD

re·doubt·able \ri-ˈdau̇t-ə-bəl\ *adj* [ME *redoutable,* fr. MF, fr. *redouter* to dread, fr. *re-* + *douter* to doubt] **1 :** causing fear or alarm **:** FORMIDABLE **2 :** inspiring or worthy of awe or reverence **:** ILLUSTRIOUS — **re·doubt·ably** \-blē\ *adv*

re·dound \ri-ˈdau̇nd\ *vi* [ME *redounden,* fr. MF *redonder,* fr. L *redundare,* fr. *re-, red-* re- + *unda* wave — more at WATER] **1** *archaic* **:** to become swollen **:** OVERFLOW **2 :** to lead to a usu. unplanned end as if by an inevitable flow of consequences **3 :** to become transferred or added **:** ACCRUE **4 :** REBOUND, REFLECT ***syn*** see CONDUCE

red·out \ˈred-ˌau̇t\ *n* **:** a condition in which centripetal acceleration drives blood to the head and causes reddening of the visual field and headache

re·dox \ˈrē-ˌdäks\ *n* [*red*uction + *ox*idation] **:** OXIDATION-REDUCTION

red oxide of zinc *n* **:** ZINCITE

red–pen·cil \ˈred-ˈpen(t)-səl\ *vt* **1 :** CENSOR **2 :** CORRECT, REVISE

red pepper *n* **:** CAYENNE PEPPER

red pine *n* **1 :** a No. American pine (*Pinosa resinosa*) that has reddish bark **2 :** the hard but not durable wood of the red pine that consists chiefly of sapwood

red·poll \ˈred-ˌpōl\ *n* **:** any of several small finches (genus *Carduelis* or *Acanthis*) which resemble siskins and in which the males usu. have a red or rosy crown

red poll *n, often cap R&P* [alter. of *red polled*] **:** any of a British breed of large hornless dual-purpose cattle that are red with a little white on the switch and belly

¹re·dress \ri-ˈdres\ *vt* [ME *redressen,* fr. MF *redresser,* fr. OF *redrecier,* fr. *re-* + *drecier* to make straight — more at DRESS] **1 a (1) :** to set right **:** REMEDY **(2) :** to make up for **:** COMPENSATE **b :** to remove the cause of (a grievance or complaint) **c :** to exact reparation for **:** AVENGE **2** *archaic* **a :** to requite (a person) for a wrong or loss **b :** HEAL ***syn*** see CORRECT — **re·dress·er** *n*

²re·dress \ri-ˈdres, ˈrē-ˌ\ *n* **1 a :** relief from distress **b :** means or possibility of seeking a remedy <without ~> **2 :** compensation for wrong or loss **:** REPARATION **3 a :** an act or instance of redressing **b :** CORRECTION, RETRIBUTION

red ribbon *n* **:** a red ribbon usu. with appropriate words or markings awarded the second-place winner in a competition

red·root \ˈred-ˌrüt, -ˌru̇t\ *n* **1 :** a perennial herb (*Lachnanthes tinctoria*) of the bloodwort family of the eastern U.S. whose red root is the source of a dye **2 :** BLOODROOT **3 :** a pigweed (*Amaranthus retroflexus*) that bears greenish flowers in dense spikes with bracts almost twice as long as the sepals

red rust *n* **1 :** the uredinial stage of a rust **2 :** the diseased condition produced by red rust

red salmon *n* **:** SOCKEYE

red seaweed *n* **:** RED ALGA; *specif* **:** any of a genus (*Polysiphonia*) having a filamentous much-branched thallus

red·shank \ˈred-ˌshaŋk\ *n* **:** a common Old World limicoline bird (*Tringa totanus*) with pale red legs and feet

red shift *n* **:** a displacement of the spectrum of a celestial body toward longer wavelengths that is a consequence of the Doppler effect or the gravitational field of the source

red·shirt \ˈred-ˌshərt\ *n* [fr. the red jersey commonly worn by such a player in practice scrimmages against the regulars] **:** a college athlete who is kept out of varsity competition for a year in order to extend the period of his eligibility — **redshirt** *vt*

red–shoul·dered hawk \ˌred-ˌshōl-dərd-\ *n* **:** a common hawk (*Buteo lineatus*) of eastern No. America that has a banded tail and a light spot on the underside of the wings toward the tips

red sin·dhi \-ˈsin-dē\ *n* [¹*red* + *sindhi* (one belonging to Sind, Pakistan)] **:** any of an Indian breed of rather small red humped dairy cattle extensively used for crossbreeding with European stock in tropical areas

red siskin *n* **:** a finch (*Carduelis cucullata*) of northern So. America that is scarlet with black head, wings, and tail and that is often kept as a cage bird

red·skin \ˈred-ˌskin\ *n* **:** AMERICAN INDIAN

red snapper *n* **:** any of various reddish fishes (as of the genera *Lutjanus* and *Sebastodes*) including several food fishes

red snow *n* **:** snow colored by various airborne dusts or by a growth of algae (as of the genus *Chlamydomonas*) that contain red pigment and live in the upper layer of snow; *also* **:** an alga causing red snow

red soil *n* **:** any of a group of zonal soils that develop in a warm temperate moist climate under deciduous or mixed forests and that have thin organic and organic-mineral layers overlying a yellowish brown leached layer resting on an illuvial red horizon — called also *red podzolic soil*

red spider *n* **:** any of several small web-spinning mites (family Tetranychidae) that attack forage and crop plants

red spruce *n* **:** a coniferous tree (*Picea rubens*) of eastern No. America that has deeply furrowed brown or purplish bark and is an important source of lumber and pulpwood

red squill *n* **:** a European squill (*Urginea maritima*) having a reddish brown bulb that is used chiefly in rat poison

red squirrel *n* **:** a common and widely distributed No. American squirrel (*Tamiasciurus hudsonicus* or *Sciurus hudsonicus*) that has the upper parts chiefly red and is smaller than the gray squirrel

red star *n* **:** a star having a very low surface temperature and a red color

red·start \ˈred-ˌstärt\ *n* [*red* + obs. *start* (handle, tail)] **1 :** a small European singing bird (*Phoenicurus phoenicurus*) related to the redbreast **2 :** a fly-catching warbler (*Setophaga ruticilla*) chiefly of eastern No. America

red–tailed hawk \ˌred-ˌtāld-\ *n* **:** a widely distributed New World buteonine hawk (*Buteo jamaicensis*); *esp* **:** a common rodent-eating hawk (*Buteo jamaicensis borealis*) of eastern No. America that is mottled dusky above and white streaked dusky and tinged with buff below and has a rather short typically reddish tail

red tape *n* [fr. the red tape formerly used to bind legal documents in England] **:** official routine or procedure marked by excessive complexity which results in delay or inaction

red tide *n* **:** seawater discolored by the presence of large numbers of dinoflagellates (esp. of the genera *Gonyaulax* and *Gymnodinium*) in a density fatal to many forms of marine life

red·top \ˈred-ˌtäp\ *n* **:** any of various grasses (genus *Agrostis*) with usu. reddish panicles; *esp* **:** an important forage and lawn grass (*A. alba*) of eastern No. America

re·duce \ri-ˈd(y)üs\ *vb* **re·duced; re·duc·ing** [ME *reducen* to lead back, fr. L *reducere,* fr. *re-* + *ducere* to lead — more at TOW] *vt* **1 a :** to draw together or cause to converge **:** CONSOLIDATE <~ all the questions to one> **b :** to diminish in size, amount, extent, or number <~ taxes> <~ the likelihood of war> **c :** to narrow down **:** RESTRICT <the Indians were *reduced* to small reservations> **d :** to make shorter **:** ABRIDGE **2** *archaic* **:** to restore to righteousness **:** SAVE **3 :** to bring to a specified state or condition <were *reducing* to order the chaos following the war> **4 a :** to force to capitulate **b :** FORCE, COMPEL **5 a :** to bring to a systematic form or character <~ natural events to laws> **b :** to put down in written or printed form <~ an agreement to writing> **6 :** to correct (as a fracture) by bringing displaced or broken parts back into their normal positions **7 a :** to lower in grade or rank **:** DEMOTE **b :** to lower in condition or status **:** DOWNGRADE **8 a :** to diminish in strength or density **b :** to diminish in value **9 a (1) :** to change the denominations or form of without changing the value **(2) :** to construct a geometrical figure similar to but smaller than (a given figure) **b :** to transpose from one form into another **:** CONVERT **c :** to change (an expression) to an equivalent but more fundamental expression <~ a fraction> **10 :** to break down (as by crushing or grinding) **:** PULVERIZE **11 a :** to bring to the metallic state by removal of nonmetallic elements <~ an ore by heat> **b :** DEOXIDIZE **c :** to combine with or subject to the action of hydrogen **d (1) :** to change (an element or ion) from a higher to a lower oxidation state **(2) :** to add one or more electrons to (an atom or ion or molecule) **12 :** to change (a stressed vowel) to an unstressed vowel ~ *vi* **1 a (1) :** to become diminished or lessened; *esp* **:** to lose weight by dieting **(2) :** to become reduced <ferrous iron ~*s* to ferric iron> **b :** to become concentrated or consolidated **c :** to undergo meiosis **2 :** to become converted or equated ***syn*** see DECREASE — **re·duc·er** *n* — **re·duc·ibil·i·ty** \-ˌd(y)ü-sə-ˈbil-ət-ē\ *n* — **re·duc·ible** \-ˈd(y)ü-sə-bəl\ *adj* — **re·duc·ibly** \-blē\ *adv*

reducing agent *n* **:** a substance that reduces a chemical compound usu. by donating electrons

re·duc·tant \ri-ˈdək-tənt\ *n* **:** REDUCING AGENT

re·duc·tase \-ˌtās, -ˌtāz\ *n* **:** an enzyme that catalyzes reduction

re·duc·tio ad ab·sur·dum \ri-ˈdək-tē-ˌō-ˌad-əb-ˈsərd-əm, -s(h)ē-ˌō-, -ˈzərd-\ *n* [LL, lit., reduction to the absurd] **:** disproof of a proposition by showing an absurdity to which it leads when carried to its logical conclusion

re·duc·tion \ri-ˈdək-shən\ *n* [ME *reduccion* restoration, fr. MF *reduction,* fr. LL & L; LL *reduction-, reductio* reduction (in a syllogism), fr. L, restoration, fr. *reductus,* pp. of *reducere*] **1 :** the act or process of reducing **:** the state of being reduced **2 a :** something made by reducing **b :** the amount by which something is reduced **3 :** MEIOSIS; *specif* **:** production of the gametic chromosome number in the first meiotic division — **re·duc·tion·al** \-shnəl, -shən-ᵊl\ *adj*

reduction division *n* **:** the usu. first division of meiosis in which chromosome reduction occurs; *also* **:** MEIOSIS

reduction gear *n* **:** a combination of gears used to reduce the input speed (as of a marine turbine) to a lower output speed (as of a ship's propeller)

re·duc·tion·ism \ri-ˈdək-shə-ˌniz-əm\ *n* **1 :** a procedure or theory that reduces complex data or phenomena to simple terms; *esp* **:** OVERSIMPLIFICATION **2 :** the attempt to explain all biological processes by the same explanations (as by physical laws) that chemists and physicists use to interpret inanimate matter; *also* **:** the theory that complete reductionism is possible — **re·duc·tion·ist** \-sh(ə-)nəst\ *n or adj* — **re·duc·tion·is·tic** \-ˌdək-shə-ˈnis-tik\ *adj*

re·duc·tive \ri-ˈdək-tiv\ *adj* **1 :** of, relating to, causing, or involving reduction **2 :** of or relating to reductionism **:** REDUCTIONISTIC

re·dun·dan·cy \ri-ˈdən-dən-sē\ *n, pl* **-cies** **1 a :** the quality or state of being redundant **:** SUPERFLUITY **b** *chiefly Brit* **:** dismissal from a job **2 :** PROFUSION, ABUNDANCE **3 a :** superfluous repetition **:** PROLIXITY **b :** an act or instance of needless repetition **4 :** the part of a message that can be eliminated without loss of essential information

re·dun·dant \-dənt\ *adj* [L *redundant-, redundans,* prp. of *redundare* to overflow — more at REDOUND] **1 a :** exceeding what is necessary or normal **:** SUPERFLUOUS **b :** characterized by or containing an excess; *specif* **:** using more words than necessary **c :** characterized by similarity or repetition <a group of particularly ~ brick buildings> **d** *chiefly Brit* **:** unnecessary or unfit for a job **2 :** PROFUSE, LAVISH **3 :** serving as a duplicate for preventing failure of an entire system (as a spacecraft) upon failure of a single component ***syn*** see WORDY ***ant*** concise — **re·dun·dant·ly** *adv*

---

re·du·pli·cate \ri-ˈd(y)ü-pli-ˌkāt, ˈrē-\ *vt* [LL *reduplicatus*, pp. of *reduplicare*, fr. L *re-* + *duplicare* to double — more at DUPLICATE] **1** : to make or perform again : COPY, REPEAT **2** : to form (a word) by reduplication — **re·du·pli·cate** \-kət\ *adj*
re·du·pli·ca·tion \ri-ˌd(y)ü-pli-ˈkā-shən, ˌrē-\ *n* **1** : an act or instance of doubling or reiterating **2 a** : an often grammatically functional repetition of a radical element or a part of it occurring usu. at the beginning of a word and often accompanied by change of the radical vowel **b (1)** : a word or form produced by reduplication **(2)** : the repeated element in such a word or form **3** : ANADIPLOSIS — **re·du·pli·ca·tive** \ri-ˈd(y)ü-pli-ˌkāt-iv, ˈrē-\ *adj* — **re·du·pli·ca·tive·ly** *adv*
re·du·vi·id \ri-ˈd(y)ü-vē-əd\ *n* [deriv. of L *reduvia* hangnail] : any of a large and widely distributed family (Reduviidae) of blood-sucking hemipterous insects comprising the assassin bugs — **reduviid** *adj*
red water *n* : a disease of cattle marked by hematuria
red wheat *n* : a wheat that has red grains
red wine *n* : a wine with a predominantly red color derived during fermentation from the natural pigment in the skins of dark-colored grapes
red·wing \ˈred-ˌwiŋ\ *n* **1** : a European thrush (*Turdus musicus*) having the underwing coverts red **2** : REDWING BLACKBIRD
redwing blackbird *n* : a No. American blackbird (*Agelaius phoeniceus*) of which the adult male is black with a patch of bright scarlet at the bend of the wings bordered behind with yellow or buff — called also *red-winged blackbird*
red·wood \ˈred-ˌwu̇d\ *n* **1** : a wood yielding a red dye **2** : a tree that yields a red dyewood or produces red or reddish wood **3 a** : a commercially important coniferous timber tree (*Sequoia sempervirens*) of California that often reaches a height of 300 feet **b** : the brownish red light wood of the California redwood
red worm *n* : BLOODWORM; *esp* : a small reddish aquatic oligochaete worm (genus *Tubifex*)
red zinc ore *n* : ZINCITE
re·echo \(ˈ)rē-ˈek-(ˌ)ō\ *vi* : to repeat or return an echo : echo again or repeatedly : REVERBERATE ~ *vt* : to echo back : REPEAT
[1]**reed** \ˈrēd\ *n* [ME *rede*, fr. OE *hrēod*; akin to OHG *hriot* reed, Lith *krutėti* to stir] **1 a** : any of various tall grasses with slender often prominently jointed stems that grow esp. in wet areas **b** : a stem of a reed **c** : a person or thing too weak to rely on : one easily swayed or overcome **2** : a growth or mass of reeds; *specif* : reeds for thatching **3** : ARROW **4** : a wind instrument made from the hollow joint of a plant **5** : an ancient Hebrew unit of length equal to 6 cubits **6 a** : a thin elastic tongue (as of cane, wood, metal, or plastic) fastened at one end over an air opening in a wind instrument (as a clarinet, organ pipe, or accordion) and set in vibration by an air current **b** : a woodwind instrument that produces sound by the vibrating of a reed against the mouthpiece <the ~*s* of an orchestra> **7** : a device on a loom resembling a comb and used to space warp yarns evenly **8** : REEDING 1a

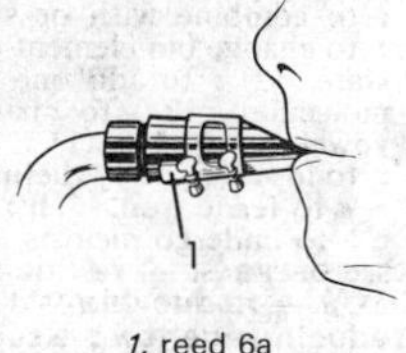

1, reed 6a

[2]**reed** *vt* : to make corrugations on (the edge of a coin)
reed·buck \ˈrēd-ˌbək\ *n, pl* **reedbuck** *also* **reedbucks** : any of a genus (*Redunca*) of fawn-colored African antelopes in which the females are hornless
re·ed·i·fy \(ˈ)rē-ˈed-ə-ˌfī\ *vt* **-fied; -fy·ing** [ME *reedifien*, fr. MF *reedifier*, fr. LL *reaedificare*, fr. L *re-* + *aedificare* to build] : REBUILD
reed·ing \ˈrēd-iŋ\ *n* **1 a** : a small convex molding — see MOLDING illustration **b** : decoration by series of reedings **2** : corrugations on the edge of a coin
reed organ *n* : a keyboard wind instrument in which the wind acts on a set of free reeds
reed pipe *n* : a pipe-organ pipe producing its tone by vibration of a beating reed in a current of air
re·ed·u·cate \(ˈ)rē-ˈej-ə-ˌkāt\ *vt* : to train again; *esp* : to rehabilitate through education — **re·ed·u·ca·tion** \(ˌ)rē-ˌej-ə-ˈkā-shən\ *n* — **re·ed·u·ca·tive** \(ˈ)rē-ˈej-ə-ˌkāt-iv\ *adj*
reedy \ˈrēd-ē\ *adj* **reed·i·er; -est** **1** : abounding in or covered with reeds **2** : made of or resembling reeds; *esp* : SLENDER, FRAIL **3** : having the tone quality of a reed instrument
[1]**reef** \ˈrēf\ *n* [ME *riff*, fr. ON *rif*] **1** : a part of a sail taken in or let out in regulating size **2** : reduction in sail area by reefing
[2]**reef** *vt* **1** : to reduce the area of (a sail) by rolling or folding a portion **2** : to lower or bring inboard (a spar) wholly or partially ~ *vi* : to reduce a sail by taking in a reef
[3]**reef** *n* [D *rif*, prob. of Scand origin; akin to ON *rif* reef of a sail] **1 a** : a chain of rocks or ridge of sand at or near the surface of water **b** : a hazardous obstruction **2** : VEIN, LODE — **reefy** \ˈrē-fē\ *adj*
[1]**reef·er** \ˈrē-fər\ *n* **1** : one that reefs **2** : a close-fitting usu. double-breasted jacket of thick cloth
[2]**reefer** *n* [[2]*reef*] : a marijuana cigarette
[3]**ree·fer** \ˈrē-fər\ *n* [by shortening & alter.] **1** : REFRIGERATOR **2** : a refrigerator car, truck, trailer, or ship
reef knot *n* : a square knot used in reefing a sail — see KNOT illustration
[1]**reek** \ˈrēk\ *n* [ME *rek*, fr. OE *rēc*; akin to OHG *rouh* smoke] **1** *chiefly dial* : SMOKE **2** : VAPOR, FOG **3** : a strong or disagreeable fume or odor
[2]**reek** *vi* **1** : to emit smoke or vapor **2 a** : to give off or become permeated with a strong or offensive odor **b** : to give a strong impression of some constituent quality or feature <a neighborhood that ~*s* of poverty> **3** : EMANATE ~ *vt* **1** : to subject to the action of smoke or vapor **2** : to give off : EXUDE <a man who ~*s* charm> — **reek·er** *n* — **reeky** \ˈrē-kē\ *adj*
[1]**reel** \ˈrē(ə)l\ *n* [ME, fr. OE *hrēol*; akin to ON *hræll* weaver's reed, Gk *krekein* to weave] **1** : a revolvable device on which something flexible is wound: as **a** : a small windlass at the butt of a fishing rod for the line **b** *chiefly Brit* : a spool or bobbin for sewing thread **c** : a flanged spool for photographic film **2** : a quantity of something wound on a reel **3** : a frame for drying clothes usu. having radial arms on a vertical pole
[2]**reel** *vt* **1** : to wind on or as if on a reel **2** : to draw by reeling a line <~ a fish in> ~ *vi* : to turn a reel — **reel·able** \ˈrē-lə-bəl\ *adj* — **reel·er** *n*
[3]**reel** *vb* [ME *relen*, prob. fr. *reel*, n.] *vi* **1 a** : to turn or move round and round : WHIRL **b** : to be giddy : be in a whirl <his mind was ~*ing*> **2** : to behave in a violent disorderly manner **3** : to waver or fall back (as from a blow) : RECOIL **4** : to walk or move unsteadily : SWAY ~ *vt* : to cause to reel
[4]**reel** *n* : a reeling motion
[5]**reel** *n* [prob. fr. [4]*reel*] : a lively Scottish-Highland dance; *also* : the music for this dance
re·elect \ˌrē-ə-ˈlekt\ *vt* : to elect for another term in office — **re·elec·tion** \-ˈlek-shən\ *n*
reel off *vt* **1** : to tell or recite readily and usu. at length <*reel off* a few jokes to break the ice> **2** : to chalk up usu. as a series
reel–to–reel *adj* : of, relating to, or utilizing magnetic tape that requires threading on a take-up reel <a ~ tape recorder>
re·em·broi·der \ˌrē-əm-ˈbrȯid-ər\ *vt* : to outline a design (as on lace) with embroidery stitching
re·em·ploy \ˌrē-əm-ˈplȯi\ *vt* : to employ again; *esp* : to hire back — **re·em·ploy·ment** \-mənt\ *n*
re·en·act \ˌrē-ə-ˈnakt\ *vt* **1** : to enact (as a law) again **2** : to act or perform again **3** : to repeat the actions of (an earlier event or incident) — **re·en·act·ment** \-ˈnak(t)-mənt\ *n*
re·en·force \ˌrē-ən-ˈfō(ə)rs, -ˈfȯ(ə)rs\ *var of* REINFORCE
re·en·ter \(ˈ)rē-ˈent-ər\ *vt* **1** : to enter (something) again **2** : to return to and enter ~ *vi* : to enter again
re·en·trance \(ˈ)rē-ˈen-trən(t)s\ *n* : REENTRY
[1]**re·en·trant** \-trənt\ *adj* : directed inward
[2]**reentrant** *n* **1** : one that reenters **2** : one that is reentrant
re·en·try \(ˈ)rē-ˈen-trē\ *n* **1** : a retaking possession; *esp* : entry by a lessor on leased premises on the tenant's failure to perform the conditions of the lease **2** : a second or new entry **3** : a playing card that will enable a player to regain the lead **4** : the action of reentering the earth's atmosphere after travel in space
reest \ˈrēst\ *vi* [prob. short for Sc *arreest* to arrest, fr. ME (Sc) *arreisten*, fr. MF *arester* — more at ARREST] *chiefly Scot* : BALK
[1]**reeve** \ˈrēv\ *n* [ME *reve*, fr. OE *gerēfa*, fr. *ge-* (associative prefix) + *-rēfa* (akin to OE *-rōf* number, OHG *ruova*) — more at CO-] **1** : a local administrative agent of an Anglo-Saxon king **2** : a medieval English manor officer responsible chiefly for overseeing the discharge of feudal obligations **3 a** : the council president in some Canadian municipalities **b** : a local official charged with enforcement of specific regulations <deer ~>
[2]**reeve** *vb* **rove** \ˈrōv\ *or* **reeved; reev·ing** [origin unknown] *vt* **1** : to pass (as a rope) through a hole or opening **2** : to fasten by passing through a hole or around something **3** : to pass a rope through ~ *vi, of a rope* : to pass through a block or similar device
[3]**reeve** *n* [prob. alter. of *ruff*] : the female of the ruff
[1]**ref** \ˈref\ *n* : a referee in a game or sport
[2]**ref** *abbr* **1** reference **2** referred **3** refining **4** reformed **5** refunding
re·fash·ion \(ˈ)rē-ˈfash-ən\ *vt* : to make over : ALTER
re·fect \ri-ˈfekt\ *vt* [L *refectus*, pp.] *archaic* : to refresh with food or drink
re·fec·tion \ri-ˈfek-shən\ *n* [ME *refeccioun*, fr. MF *refection*, fr. L *refection-, refectio*, fr. *refectus*, pp. of *reficere* to restore, fr. *re-* + *facere* to make — more at DO] **1** : refreshment of mind, spirit, or body; *esp* : NOURISHMENT **2 a** : the taking of refreshment **b** : food and drink together : REPAST
re·fec·to·ry \ri-ˈfek-t(ə-)rē\ *n, pl* **-ries** [LL *refectorium*, fr. L *refectus*] : a dining hall esp. in a monastery
refectory table *n* : a long table with heavy legs
re·fel \ri-ˈfel\ *vt* **re·felled; re·fel·ling** [L *refellere* to prove false, refute, fr. *re-* + *fallere* to deceive] *obs* : REJECT, REPULSE
re·fer \ri-ˈfər\ *vb* **re·ferred; re·fer·ring** [ME *referren*, fr. L *referre* to bring back, report, refer, fr. *re-* + *ferre* to carry — more at BEAR] *vt* **1 a (1)** : to think of, regard, or classify within a general category or group **(2)** : to explain in terms of a general cause **b** : to allot to a particular place, stage, or period **c** : to regard as coming from or located in a specific area **2 a** : to send or direct for treatment, aid, information, or decision <~ a patient to a specialist> <~ a bill back to a committee> **b** : to direct for testimony or guaranty as to character or ability ~ *vi* **1 a** : to have relation or connection : RELATE **b** : to direct attention usu. by clear and specific mention <no one *referred* to yesterday's quarrel> **2** : to have recourse : glance briefly <*referred* frequently to his notes while speaking> — **re·fer·able** \ˈref-(ə-)rə-bəl, ri-ˈfər-ə-\ *adj* — **re·fer·rer** \ri-ˈfər-ər\ *n*
syn **1** see ASCRIBE
2 REFER, ALLUDE, ADVERT *shared meaning element* : to call or direct attention to something
[1]**ref·er·ee** \ˌref-ə-ˈrē\ *n* **1** : one to whom a thing is referred: as **a** : a person to whom a legal matter is referred for investigation and report or for settlement **b** : a person who reviews an esp. technical paper before publication **c** : REFERENCE 4a **2** : a sports official usu. having final authority in administering a game
[2]**referee** *vb* **-eed; -ee·ing** *vt* **1** : to conduct (as a match or game) as referee **2 a** : to arbitrate (as a legal matter) as a judge or third party **b** : to review (as a technical paper) before publication ~ *vi* : to act as a referee
[1]**ref·er·ence** \ˈref-ərn(t)s, ˈref-(ə-)rən(t)s\ *n* **1** : the act of referring or consulting **2** : a bearing on a matter : RELATION <in ~ to your recent letter> **3** : something that refers: as **a** : ALLUSION, MENTION **b** : something (as a sign or indication) that refers a reader or consulter to another source of information (as a book or passage) **c** : consultation of sources of information **4** : one referred to or consulted: as **a** : a person to whom inquiries as to character or ability can be made **b** : a statement of the qualifica-

tions of a person seeking employment or appointment given by someone familiar with him **c** (1) **:** a source of information (as a book or passage) to which a reader or consulter is referred (2) **:** a work (as a dictionary or encyclopedia) containing useful facts or information **d :** DENOTATION, MEANING

²**reference** *vt* **-enced; -enc·ing 1 a :** to supply with references **b :** to cite in or as a reference **2 :** to put in a form (as a table) adapted to easy reference

³**reference** *adj* **:** used or usable for reference; *esp* **:** constituting a standard for measuring or constructing

reference mark *n* **:** a conventional mark (as *, †, or ‡) placed in written or printed text to direct the reader's attention esp. to a footnote

ref·er·en·dum \ˌref-ə-ˈren-dəm\ *n, pl* **-da** \-də\ *or* **-dums** [NL, fr. L, neut. of *referendus,* gerundive of *referre* to refer] **1 a :** the principle or practice of submitting to popular vote a measure passed upon or proposed by a legislative body or by popular initiative **b :** a vote on a measure so submitted **2 :** a diplomatic agent's note asking his government for instructions

ref·er·ent \ˈref-(ə-)rənt\ *n* [L *referent-, referens,* prp. of *referre*] **:** one that refers or is referred to; *esp* **:** the thing that a symbol (as a word or sign) stands for — **referent** *adj*

ref·er·en·tial \ˌref-ə-ˈren-chəl\ *adj* **:** containing or constituting a reference — **ref·er·en·tial·ly** \-ˈrench-(ə-)lē\ *adv*

re·fer·ral \ri-ˈfər-əl\ *n* **1 :** the act, action, or an instance of referring **2 :** one that is referred

¹**re·fill** \(ˈ)rē-ˈfil\ *vt* **:** to fill again **:** REPLENISH ~ *vi* **:** to become filled again — **re·fill·able** \-ə-bəl\ *adj*

²**re·fill** \ˈrē-ˌfil\ *n* **1 :** a product or a container and a product used to refill the exhausted supply of a device **2 :** something provided again; *esp* **:** a second filling of a medical prescription

re·fi·nance \ˌrē-fə-ˈnan(t)s, (ˈ)rē-ˈfī-ˌ, ˌrē-(ˌ)fī-ˈ\ *vt* **:** to renew or reorganize the financing of ~ *vi* **:** to finance something anew

re·fine \ri-ˈfīn\ *vb* **re·fined; re·fin·ing** *vt* **1 :** to reduce to a pure state <~ sugar> **2 :** to free from moral imperfection **:** ELEVATE **3 :** to improve or perfect by pruning or polishing <~ a poetic style> **4 :** to reduce in vigor or intensity **5 :** to free from what is coarse, vulgar, or uncouth ~ *vi* **1 :** to become pure or perfected **2 :** to make improvement by introducing subtleties or distinctions — **re·fin·er** *n*

re·fined \ri-ˈfīnd\ *adj* **1 :** free from impurities **2 :** FASTIDIOUS, CULTIVATED **3 :** PRECISE, EXACT <a ~ test for radioactivity>

re·fine·ment \ri-ˈfīn-mənt\ *n* **1 :** the action or process of refining **2 :** the quality or state of being refined **:** CULTIVATION **3 a :** a refined feature or method **b :** a highly refined distinction **:** SUBTLETY **c :** a contrivance or device intended to improve or perfect

re·fin·ery \ri-ˈfīn-(ə-)rē\ *n, pl* **-er·ies :** a building and equipment for refining or purifying metals, oil, or sugar

re·fin·ish \(ˈ)rē-ˈfin-ish\ *vt* **:** to give (as furniture) a new surface ~ *vi* **:** to refinish furniture — **re·fin·ish·er** *n*

¹**re·fit** \(ˈ)rē-ˈfit\ *vt* **:** to fit out or supply again ~ *vi* **:** to obtain repairs or fresh supplies or equipment

²**re·fit** \ˈrē-ˌfit, (ˈ)rē-ˈ\ *n* **:** the action of refitting; *esp* **:** a refitting and renovating of a ship

refl *abbr* reflex; reflexive

re·fla·tion \(ˈ)rē-ˈflā-shən\ *n* [*re-* + *-flation* (as in *deflation*)] **:** restoration of deflated prices to a desirable level — **re·fla·tion·ary** \-shə-ˌner-ē\ *adj*

re·flect \ri-ˈflekt\ *vb* [ME *reflecten,* fr. L *reflectere* to bend back, fr. *re-* + *flectere* to bend] *vt* **1** *archaic* **:** to turn into or away from a course **:** DEFLECT **2 :** to turn, throw, or bend off or backward at an angle <a mirror ~*s* light> **3 :** to bend or fold back **4 :** to give back or exhibit as an image, likeness, or outline **:** MIRROR <the clouds were ~*ed* in the water> **5 :** to bring or cast as a result <his attitude ~*s* little credit on his judgment> **6 :** to make manifest or apparent **:** SHOW <the pulse ~*s* the condition of the heart> **7 :** REALIZE, CONSIDER ~ *vi* **1 :** to throw back light or sound **2 a :** to think quietly and calmly **b :** to express a thought or opinion resulting from reflection **3 a :** to tend to bring reproach or discredit <an investigation that ~*s* on all the members of the department> **b :** to bring about a specified appearance or characterization <an act which ~*s* well on him> **c :** to have a bearing or influence ***syn*** see THINK

re·flec·tance \ri-ˈflek-tən(t)s\ *n* **:** the fraction of the total radiant flux incident upon a surface that is reflected and that varies according to the wavelength distribution of the incident radiation

reflecting telescope *n* **:** REFLECTOR 2

re·flec·tion \ri-ˈflek-shən\ *n* [ME, alter. of *reflexion,* fr. LL *reflexion-, reflexio* act of bending back, fr. L *reflexus,* pp. of *reflectere*] **1 :** an instance of reflecting; *esp* **:** the return of light or sound waves from a surface **2 :** the production of an image by or as if by a mirror **3 a :** the action of bending or folding back **b :** a reflected part **:** FOLD **4 :** something produced by reflecting: as **a :** an image given back by a reflecting surface **b :** an effect produced by an influence <a high crime rate is a ~ of an unstable society> **5 :** an often obscure or indirect criticism **:** REPROACH <the book was suppressed as a ~ on the regime> **6 :** a thought, idea, or opinion formed or a remark made as a result of meditation **7 :** consideration of some subject matter, idea, or purpose **8** *obs* **:** turning back **:** RETURN **9 a :** a transformation of a figure in which each point is replaced by a point symmetric with respect to a line **b :** a transformation that involves reflection in more than one axis of a rectangular coordinate system ***syn*** see ANIMADVERSION — **re·flec·tion·al** \-shnəl, -shən-ᵊl\ *adj*

re·flec·tive \ri-ˈflek-tiv\ *adj* **1 :** capable of reflecting light, images, or sound waves **2 :** marked by reflection **:** THOUGHTFUL, DELIBERATIVE **3 :** of, relating to, or caused by reflection <~ glare of the snow> **4 :** REFLEXIVE <~ verb> — **re·flec·tive·ly** *adv* — **re·flec·tive·ness** *n* — **re·flec·tiv·i·ty** \ˌrē-ˌflek-ˈtiv-ət-ē, ri-\ *n*

re·flec·tom·e·ter \ˌrē-ˌflek-ˈtäm-ət-ər, ri-\ *n* **:** a device for measuring the reflectance of radiant energy (as light) — **re·flec·tom·e·try** \-ə-trē\ *n*

re·flec·tor \ri-ˈflek-tər\ *n* **1 :** one that reflects; *esp* **:** a polished surface for reflecting light or other radiation **2 :** a telescope in which the principal focusing element is a mirror

re·flec·tor·ize \-tə-ˌrīz\ *vt* **-ized; -iz·ing 1 :** to make reflecting **2 :** to provide with reflectors

¹**re·flex** \ˈrē-ˌfleks\ *n* [L *reflexus,* pp. of *reflectere* to reflect] **1 a :** reflected heat, light, or color **b :** a mirrored image **c :** a copy exact in essential or peculiar features **2 a :** an automatic and often inborn response to a stimulus that involves a nerve impulse passing inward from a receptor to a nerve center and thence outward to an effector (as a muscle or gland) without reaching the level of consciousness — called also *reflex act;* compare HABIT **b :** the process that culminates in a reflex and comprises reception, transmission, and reaction **c** *pl* **:** the power of acting or responding with adequate speed **d :** a way of thinking or behaving

²**reflex** *adj* [L *reflexus*] **1 :** bent, turned, or directed back **:** REFLECTED <a stem with ~ leaves> **2 :** directed back upon the mind or its operations **:** INTROSPECTIVE **3 :** produced or carried out in reaction, resistance, or return **4** *of an angle* **:** being between 180° and 360° **5 :** of, relating to, or produced by reflex action without intervention of consciousness — **re·flex·ly** *adv*

reflex arc *n* **:** the complete nervous path involved in a reflex

reflex camera *n* **:** a single- or double-lens camera in which the image formed by the focusing lens is reflected onto a usu. ground-glass screen for viewing

re·flexed \ˈrē-ˌflekst, ri-ˈ\ *adj* [L *reflexus* + E *-ed*] **:** bent or curved backward or downward <~ petals> <~ leaves>

re·flex·ion *chiefly Brit var of* REFLECTION

¹**re·flex·ive** \ri-ˈflek-siv\ *adj* [ML *reflexivus,* fr. L *reflexus*] **1 a :** directed or turned back on itself **b :** marked by or capable of reflection **:** REFLECTIVE **2 :** relating to, characterized by, or being a relation that exists between an entity and itself <the relation *is equal to* is ~ but the relation *is the father of* is not> **3 :** of, relating to, or constituting an action (as in "he perjured himself") directed back upon the agent or the grammatical subject **4 :** characterized by habitual and unthinking behavior — **re·flex·ive·ly** *adv* — **re·flex·ive·ness** *n* — **re·flex·iv·i·ty** \ˌrē-ˌflek-ˈsiv-ət-ē, ri-\ *n*

²**reflexive** *n* **:** REFLEXIVE PRONOUN

reflexive pronoun *n* **:** a pronoun referring to the subject of the sentence, clause, or verbal phrase in which it stands; *specif* **:** a personal pronoun compounded with *-self*

re·flex·ol·o·gy \ˌrē-ˌflek-ˈsäl-ə-jē\ *n* [ISV] **:** the study and interpretation of behavior in terms of simple and complex reflexes

re·flo·res·cence \ˌrē-flə-ˈres-ᵊn(t)s, -flō-\ *n* [L *reflorescere* to blossom again, fr. *re-* + *florescere* to bloom — more at FLORESCENCE] **:** a renewed blossoming

re·flo·res·cent \-ᵊnt\ *adj* **:** flowering again

re·flow \(ˈ)rē-ˈflō\ *vi* **1 :** to flow back **:** EBB **2 :** to flow in again — **re·flow** \ˈrē-ˌflō\ *n*

ref·lu·ence \ˈref-ˌlü-ən(t)s, re-ˈflü-\ *n* **:** REFLUX 1

re·flu·ent \-ənt\ *adj* [L *refluent-, refluens,* prp. of *refluere* to flow back, fr. *re-* + *fluere* to flow — more at FLUID] **:** flowing back

¹**re·flux** \ˈrē-ˌfləks\ *n* [ME, fr. ML *refluxus,* fr. L *re-* + *fluxus* flow — more at FLUX] **1 :** a flowing back **:** EBB **2 :** a process of refluxing or condition of being refluxed

²**re·flux** \ri-ˈfləks, ˈrē-ˌ\ *vt* **:** to cause to flow back or return; *esp* **:** to heat so that the vapors formed condense and return to be heated again

re·fo·cus \(ˈ)rē-ˈfō-kəs\ *vt* **1 :** to focus again **2 :** to change the emphasis or direction of <had ~*ed* his life> ~ *vi* **1 :** to focus something again **2 :** to change emphasis or direction

re·for·est \(ˈ)rē-ˈfȯr-əst, -ˈfär-\ *vt* **:** to renew forest cover on by seeding or planting — **re·for·es·ta·tion** \(ˌ)rē-ˌfȯr-ə-ˈstā-shən, -ˌfär-\ *n*

re·forge \(ˈ)rē-ˈfō(ə)rj, -ˈfȯ(ə)rj\ *vt* [ME *reforgen,* fr. MF *reforgier,* fr. *re-* + *forgier* to forge] **:** to forge again **:** make over

¹**re·form** \ri-ˈfō(ə)rm\ *vb* [ME *reformen,* fr. MF *reformer,* fr. L *reformare,* fr. *re-* + *formare* to form] *vt* **1 a :** to amend or improve by change of form or removal of faults or abuses **b :** to put or change into an improved form or condition **2 :** to put an end to (an evil) by enforcing or introducing a better method or course of action **3 :** to induce or cause to abandon evil ways <~ a drunkard> **4 a :** to subject (hydrocarbons) to cracking **b :** to produce (as gasoline or gas) by cracking ~ *vi* **:** to become changed for the better ***syn*** see CORRECT — **re·form·abil·i·ty** \-ˌfȯr-mə-ˈbil-ət-ē\ *n* — **re·form·able** \-ˈfȯr-mə-bəl\ *adj*

²**reform** *n* **1 :** amendment of what is defective, vicious, corrupt, or depraved **2 :** a removal or correction of an abuse, a wrong, or errors **3** *cap* **:** REFORM JUDAISM

³**reform** *adj* **:** relating to or favoring reform

re-form \(ˈ)rē-ˈfō(ə)rm\ *vt* **:** to form again ~ *vi* **:** to take form again <the ice ~*ed* on the lake>

re·for·mate \ri-ˈfȯr-ˌmāt, -mət\ *n* **:** a product of hydrocarbon reforming

ref·or·ma·tion \ˌref-ər-ˈmā-shən\ *n* **1 :** the act of reforming **:** the state of being reformed **2** *cap* **:** a 16th century religious movement marked ultimately by rejection or modification of some Roman Catholic doctrine and practice and establishment of the Protestant churches — **ref·or·ma·tion·al** \-shnəl, -shən-ᵊl\ *adj*

re·for·ma·tive \ri-ˈfȯr-mət-iv\ *adj* **:** intended or tending to reform

¹**re·for·ma·to·ry** \ri-ˈfȯr-mə-ˌtōr-ē, -ˌtȯr-\ *adj* **:** REFORMATIVE

²**reformatory** *n, pl* **-ries :** a penal institution to which young or first offenders or women are committed for training and reformation

---

ə abut ᵊ kitten ər further a back ā bake ä cot, cart
aù out ch chin e less ē easy g gift i trip ī life
j joke ŋ sing ō flow ȯ flaw ȯi coin th thin t͟h this
ü loot u̇ foot y yet yü few yu̇ furious zh vision

re·formed *adj* **1 :** changed for the better **2** *cap* **:** PROTESTANT; *specif* **:** of or relating to the chiefly Calvinist Protestant churches formed in various continental European countries

reformed spelling *n* **:** any of several methods of spelling English words that use letters with more phonetic consistency than conventional spelling and that usu. discard some silent letters (as in *pedagog* for *pedagogue*)

re·form·er \ri-ˈfȯr-mər\ *n* **1 :** one that works for or urges reform **2** *cap* **:** a leader of the Protestant Reformation

re·form·ism \ri-ˈfȯr-ˌmiz-əm\ *n* **:** a doctrine, policy, or movement of reform — **re·form·ist** \-məst\ *n*

Reform Judaism *n* **:** Judaism marked by a liberal approach in nonobservance of much legal tradition regarded as irrelevant to the present and in shortening and simplification of traditional ritual

reform school *n* **:** a reformatory for boys or girls

refr *abbr* refraction

re·fract \ri-ˈfrakt\ *vt* [L *refractus,* pp. of *refringere* to break open, break up, refract, fr. *re-* + *frangere* to break — more at BREAK] **1 :** to subject to refraction **2 :** to determine the refracting power of

re·frac·tile \-ˈfrak-tᵊl, -ˌtīl\ *adj* **:** capable of refracting **:** REFRACTIVE

refracting telescope *n* **:** REFRACTOR

re·frac·tion \ri-ˈfrak-shən\ *n* **1 :** deflection from a straight path undergone by a light ray or energy wave in passing obliquely from one medium (as air) into another (as glass) in which its velocity is different **2 :** the change in the apparent position of a celestial body due to bending of the light rays emanating from it as they pass through the atmosphere; *also* **:** the correction to be applied to the apparent position of a body because of this bending

re·frac·tive \ri-ˈfrak-tiv\ *adj* **1 :** having power to refract **2 :** relating or due to refraction — **re·frac·tive·ly** *adv* — **re·frac·tive·ness** *n* — **re·frac·tiv·i·ty** \ˌrē-ˌfrak-ˈtiv-ət-ē, ri-\ *n*

refractive index *n* **:** INDEX OF REFRACTION

re·frac·tom·e·ter \ˌrē-ˌfrak-ˈtäm-ət-ər, ri-\ *n* [ISV] **:** an instrument for measuring indices of refraction — **re·frac·to·met·ric** \ri-ˌfrak-tə-ˈme-trik\ *adj* — **re·frac·tom·e·try** \ˌrē-ˌfrak-ˈtäm-ə-trē, ri-\ *n*

re·frac·tor \ri-ˈfrak-tər\ *n* **:** a telescope whose principal focusing element is usu. an achromatic lens

[1]re·frac·to·ry \ri-ˈfrak-t(ə-)rē\ *adj* [alter. of *refractory,* fr. L *refractarius,* irreg. fr. *refragari* to oppose, fr. *re-* + *-fragari* (as in *suffragari* to support with one's vote) — more at SUFFRAGE] **1 :** resisting control or authority **:** STUBBORN, UNMANAGEABLE **2 a :** resistant to treatment or cure <a ~ lesion> **b :** unresponsive to stimulus **c :** IMMUNE, INSUSCEPTIBLE <after recovery they were ~ to infection> **3 :** difficult to fuse, corrode, or draw out; *esp* **:** capable of enduring high temperature ***syn*** see UNRULY ***ant*** malleable, amenable — **re·frac·to·ri·ly** \-t(ə-)rə-lē; ˌrē-ˌfrak-ˈtōr-ə-lē, ri-, -ˈtȯr-\ *adv* — **re·frac·to·ri·ness** \ri-ˈfrak-t(ə-)rē-nəs\ *n*

[2]refractory *n, pl* **-ries :** a refractory person or thing; *esp* **:** a heat-resisting ceramic material

refractory period *n* **:** the brief period immediately following the response esp. of a muscle or nerve before it recovers the capacity to make a second response — called also *refractory phase*

[1]re·frain \ri-ˈfrān\ *vb* [ME *refreynen,* fr. MF *refraindre* fr. L *refringere* to break up, destroy, check — more at REFRACT] *vt, archaic* **:** CURB, RESTRAIN ~ *vi* **:** to keep oneself from doing, feeling, or indulging in something and esp. from following a passing impulse — **re·frain·ment** \-mənt\ *n*

syn REFRAIN, ABSTAIN, FORBEAR *shared meaning element* **:** to keep oneself from doing or indulging in something

[2]refrain *n* [ME *refreyn,* fr. MF *refrain,* fr. *refraindre* to resound, fr. L *refringere* to break up, refract] **:** a regularly recurring phrase or verse esp. at the end of each stanza or division of a poem or song **:** CHORUS; *also* **:** the musical setting of a refrain

re·fran·gi·ble \ri-ˈfran-jə-bəl\ *adj* [irreg. fr. L *refringere* to refract] **:** capable of being refracted — **re·fran·gi·bil·i·ty** \-ˌfran-jə-ˈbil-ət-ē\ *n* — **re·fran·gi·ble·ness** \-ˈfran-jə-bəl-nəs\ *n*

re·fresh \ri-ˈfresh\ *vb* [ME *refresshen,* fr. MF *refreschir,* fr. OF, fr. *re-* + *freis* fresh — more at FRESH] *vt* **1 :** to restore strength and animation to **:** REVIVE **2 :** to freshen up **:** RENOVATE **3 a :** to restore or maintain by renewing supply **:** REPLENISH **b :** AROUSE, STIMULATE <let me ~ your memory> **4 :** to restore water to ~ *vi* **1 :** to become refreshed **2 :** to take refreshment **3 :** to lay in fresh provisions ***syn*** see RENEW

re·fresh·en \ri-ˈfresh-ən, (ˈ)rē-\ *vt* [*re-* + *freshen*] **:** REFRESH

re·fresh·er \ri-ˈfresh-ər\ *n* **1 :** something (as a drink) that refreshes **2 :** REMINDER **3 :** review or instruction designed esp. to keep one abreast of professional developments

re·fresh·ing \-iŋ\ *adj* **:** serving to refresh; *esp* **:** agreeably stimulating because of freshness or newness — **re·fresh·ing·ly** \-iŋ-lē\ *adv*

re·fresh·ment \ri-ˈfresh-mənt\ *n* **1 :** the act of refreshing **:** the state of being refreshed **2 a :** something (as food or drink) that refreshes **b** *pl* (1) **:** a light meal (2) **:** assorted light foods

refrig *abbr* refrigerating; refrigeration

[1]re·frig·er·ant \ri-ˈfrij-(ə-)rənt\ *adj* **:** allaying heat or fever

[2]refrigerant *n* **:** a refrigerant agent or agency: as **a :** a medication for reducing body heat **b :** a substance used in refrigeration

re·frig·er·ate \ri-ˈfrij-ə-ˌrāt\ *vt* **-at·ed; -at·ing** [L *refrigeratus,* pp. of *refrigerare,* fr. *re-* + *frigerare* to cool, fr. *frigor-, frigus* cold — more at FRIGID] **:** to make or keep cold or cool; *specif* **:** to freeze or chill (as food) for preservation — **re·frig·er·a·tion** \-ˌfrij-ə-ˈrā-shən\ *n*

re·frig·er·a·tor \ri-ˈfrij-ə-ˌrāt-ər\ *n* **:** something that refrigerates or keeps cool: **a :** a cabinet or room for keeping food or other items cool **b :** an apparatus for rapidly cooling heated liquids or vapors in a distilling process

re·frin·gent \ri-ˈfrin-jənt\ *adj* [L *refringent-, refringens,* prp. of *refringere* to refract] **:** REFRACTIVE, REFRACTING

reft *past of* REAVE

re·fu·el \(ˈ)rē-ˈfyü-əl\ *vt* **:** to provide with additional fuel ~ *vi* **:** to take on additional fuel

[1]ref·uge \ˈref-(ˌ)yüj\ *n* [ME, fr. MF, fr. L *refugium,* fr. *refugere* to escape, fr. *re-* + *fugere* to flee — more at FUGITIVE] **1 :** shelter or protection from danger or distress **2 :** a place that provides shelter or protection **3 :** a means of resort for help in difficulty

[2]refuge *vb* **ref·uged; ref·ug·ing** *vt* **:** to give refuge to ~ *vi* **:** to seek or take refuge

ref·u·gee \ˌref-yu̇-ˈjē\ *n* [F *réfugié,* pp. of (*se*) *réfugier* to take refuge, fr. L *refugium*] **:** one that flees for safety; *esp* **:** one who flees to a foreign country or power to escape danger or persecution — **ref·u·gee·ism** \-ˌiz-əm\ *n*

re·fu·gi·um \ri-ˈfyü-jē-əm\ *n, pl* **-gia** \-jē-ə\ [NL, fr. L, refuge] **:** an area of relatively unaltered climate that is inhabited by plants and animals during a period of continental climatic change (as a glaciation) and remains as a center of relict forms from which a new dispersion and speciation may take place after climatic readjustment

re·ful·gence \ri-ˈfu̇l-jən(t)s, -ˈfəl-\ *n* [L *refulgentia,* fr. *refulgent-, refulgens,* prp. of *refulgēre* to shine brightly, fr. *re-* + *fulgēre* to shine — more at FULGENT] **:** a radiant or resplendent quality or state **:** BRILLIANCE — **re·ful·gent** \-jənt\ *adj*

[1]re·fund \ri-ˈfənd, ˈrē-ˌ\ *vt* [ME *refunden,* fr. MF & L; MF *refonder,* fr. L *refundere,* lit., to pour back, fr. *re-* + *fundere* to pour — more at FOUND] **1 :** to give or put back **2 :** to return (money) in restitution, repayment, or balancing of accounts — **re·fund·abil·i·ty** \ri-ˌfən-də-ˈbil-ət-ē, (ˌ)rē-\ *n* — **re·fund·able** \-ə-bəl\ *adj*

[2]re·fund \ˈrē-ˌfənd\ *n* **1 :** the act of refunding **2 :** a sum refunded

[3]re·fund \(ˈ)rē-ˈfənd\ *vt* [*re-* + *fund*] **:** to fund (a debt) again

re·fur·bish \ri-ˈfər-bish\ *vt* **:** to brighten or freshen up **:** RENOVATE — **re·fur·bish·er** *n* — **re·fur·bish·ment** \-bish-mənt\ *n*

re·fus·al \ri-ˈfyü-zəl\ *n* **1 :** the act of refusing or denying **2 :** the opportunity or right of refusing or taking before others

[1]re·fuse \ri-ˈfyüz\ *vb* **re·fused; re·fus·ing** [ME *refusen,* fr. MF *refuser,* fr. (assumed) VL *refusare,* fr. L *refusus,* pp. of *refundere* to pour back] *vt* **1 :** to express oneself as unwilling to accept <~ a gift> <~ a promotion> **2 a :** to show or express unwillingness to do or comply with <the motor *refused* to start> **b :** DENY <they were *refused* admittance to the game> **3** *obs* **:** to give up **:** RENOUNCE **4** *of a horse* **:** to decline to jump or leap over ~ *vi* **:** to withhold acceptance, compliance, or permission ***syn*** see DECLINE — **re·fus·er** *n*

[2]ref·use \ˈref-ˌyüs, -ˌyüz\ *n* [ME, fr. MF *refus* rejection, fr. OF, fr. *refuser*] **1 :** the worthless or useless part of something **:** LEAVINGS **2 :** TRASH, GARBAGE

[3]ref·use \ˈref-ˌyüs, -ˌyüz\ *adj* **:** thrown aside or left as worthless

ref·u·ta·tion \ˌref-yu̇-ˈtā-shən\ *n* **:** the act or process of refuting

re·fute \ri-ˈfyüt\ *vt* **re·fut·ed; re·fut·ing** [L *refutare,* fr. *re-* + *-futare* to beat — more at BEAT] **1 :** to prove wrong by argument or evidence **:** show to be false or erroneous **2 :** to deny the truth or accuracy of <*refuted* the election returns which showed him the loser> ***syn*** see DISPROVE — **re·fut·able** \-ˈfyüt-ə-bəl\ *adj* — **re·fut·ably** \-blē\ *adv* — **re·fut·er** *n*

reg *abbr* **1** region **2** register; registered **3** regular **4** regulation

re·gain \ri-ˈgān\ *vt* **:** to gain or reach again **:** RECOVER

re·gal \ˈrē-gəl\ *adj* [ME, fr. MF or L; MF, fr. L *regalis* — more at ROYAL] **1 :** of, relating to, or suitable for a king **2 :** of notable excellence or magnificence **:** SPLENDID — **re·gal·i·ty** \ri-ˈgal-ət-ē\ *n* — **re·gal·ly** \ˈrē-gə-lē\ *adv*

[1]re·gale \ri-ˈgā(ə)l\ *vb* **re·galed; re·gal·ing** [F *régaler,* fr. MF, fr. *regale,* n.] *vt* **1 :** to entertain sumptuously **:** feast with delicacies **2 :** to give pleasure or amusement to <*regaled* us with stories of his exploits> ~ *vi* **:** to feast oneself **:** FEED

[2]regale *n* [F *régal,* fr. MF *regale,* fr. *re-* + *galer* to have a good time — more at GALLANT] **1 :** a sumptuous feast **2 :** a choice piece esp. of food

re·ga·lia \ri-ˈgāl-yə\ *n pl* [ML, fr. L, neut. pl. of *regalis*] **1 :** royal rights or prerogatives **2 a :** the emblems, symbols, or paraphernalia indicative of royalty **b :** decorations or insignia indicative of an office or membership **3 :** special dress; *esp* **:** FINERY

[1]re·gard \ri-ˈgärd\ *n* [ME, fr. MF, fr. OF, fr. *regarder*] **1** *archaic* **:** APPEARANCE **2 :** LOOK, GAZE **3 a :** ATTENTION, CONSIDERATION <due ~ should be given to all facets of the question> **b :** a protective interest **:** CARE <ought to have more ~ for his health> **4 a :** the worth or estimation in which something is held <a man of small ~> **b** (1) **:** a feeling of respect and affection **:** ESTEEM <his hard work won him the ~ of his colleagues> (2) *pl* **:** friendly greetings implying such feeling <give him my ~*s*> **5 :** a basis of action or opinion **:** MOTIVE **6 :** an aspect to be taken into consideration **:** RESPECT <is a small school, and is fortunate in this ~> **7** *obs* **:** INTENTION — **in regard to :** with respect to **:** CONCERNING — **with regard to :** in regard to

[2]regard *vb* [ME *regarden,* fr. MF *regarder* to look back at, regard, fr. OF, fr. *re-* + *garder* to guard, look at] *vt* **1 :** to pay attention to **:** take into consideration or account **2 a :** to show respect or consideration for **b :** to hold in high esteem **3 :** to look at **4** *archaic* **:** to relate to **5 :** to consider and appraise usu. from a particular point of view <he is highly ~*ed* as a mechanic> ~ *vi* **1 :** to look attentively **:** GAZE **2 :** to pay attention **:** HEED

syn REGARD, RESPECT, ESTEEM, ADMIRE *shared meaning element* **:** to recognize the worth of a person or thing — **as regards :** with respect to **:** CONCERNING

re·gar·dant \ri-ˈgärd-ᵊnt\ *adj* [ME, fr. MF, prp. of *regarder*] **:** looking backward over the shoulder — used of a heraldic animal

re·gard·ful \ri-ˈgärd-fəl\ *adj* **1 :** HEEDFUL, OBSERVANT **2 :** full or expressive of regard or respect **:** RESPECTFUL — **re·gard·ful·ly** \-fə-lē\ *adv* — **re·gard·ful·ness** *n*

re·gard·ing *prep* **:** with respect to **:** CONCERNING

[1]re·gard·less \ri-ˈgärd-ləs\ *adj* **:** HEEDLESS, CARELESS — **re·gard·less·ly** *adv* — **re·gard·less·ness** *n*

[2]regardless *adv* **:** despite everything <went ahead with their plans ~>

regardless of *prep* **:** in spite of <*regardless of* our mistakes>

re·gat·ta \ri-ˈgät-ə, -ˈgat-\ *n* [It] **:** a rowing, speedboat, or sailing race or a series of such races

regd *abbr* registered
re·ge·la·tion \ˌrē-jə-'lā-shən\ *n* **:** the freezing again of water derived from ice melting under pressure when the pressure is relieved
1**re·gen·cy** \'rē-jən-sē\ *n, pl* **-cies** **1 :** the office, jurisdiction, or government of a regent or body of regents **2 :** a body of regents **3 :** the period of rule of a regent or body of regents
2**regency** *adj, often cap* [fr. the regency of George, Prince of Wales (afterwards George IV) during the period 1811–20] **:** of, relating to, or resembling the styles (as of furniture or dress) of the regency of George, Prince of Wales
re·gen·er·a·cy \ri-'jen-(ə-)rə-sē\ *n* **:** the state of being regenerated
1**re·gen·er·ate** \ri-'jen-(ə-)rət\ *adj* [ME *regenerat,* fr. L *regeneratus,* pp. of *regenerare* to regenerate, fr. *re-* + *generare* to beget — more at GENERATE] **1 :** formed or created again **2 :** spiritually reborn or converted **3 :** restored to a better, higher, or more worthy state — **re·gen·er·ate·ly** *adv* — **re·gen·er·ate·ness** *n*
2**regenerate** *n* **:** one that is regenerated: as **a :** an individual who is spiritually reborn **b** (1) **:** an organism that has undergone regeneration (2) **:** a regenerated body part
3**re·gen·er·ate** \ri-'jen-ə-ˌrāt\ *vi* **1 :** to become formed again **2 :** to become regenerate **:** REFORM **3 :** to undergo regeneration ~ *vt* **1 a :** to subject to spiritual regeneration **b :** to change radically and for the better **2 a :** to generate or produce anew; *esp* **:** to replace (a body part) by a new growth of tissue **b :** to produce again chemically sometimes in a physically changed form **3 :** to restore to original strength or properties **4 :** to increase the amplification of (an electron current) by causing part of the power in the output circuit to act upon the input circuit — **re·gen·er·a·ble** \-'jen-(ə-)rə-bəl\ *adj*
regenerated cellulose *n* **:** cellulose obtained in a changed form by chemical treatment (as of a cellulose solution or derivative)
re·gen·er·a·tion \ri-ˌjen-ə-'rā-shən, ˌrē-\ *n* **1 :** an act or the process of regenerating **:** the state of being regenerated **2 :** spiritual renewal or revival **3 :** renewal or restoration of a body or bodily part after injury or as a normal process **4 :** utilization by special devices of heat or other products that would ordinarily be lost
re·gen·er·a·tive \ri-'jen-ə-ˌrāt-iv, -'jen-(ə-)rət-\ *adj* **1 :** of, relating to, or marked by regeneration **2 :** tending to regenerate — **re·gen·er·a·tive·ly** *adv*
re·gen·er·a·tor \ri-'jen-ə-ˌrāt-ər\ *n* **1 :** one that regenerates **2 :** a device used esp. with hot-air engines or gas furnaces in which incoming air or gas is heated by contact with masses (as of brick) previously heated by outgoing hot air or gas
re·gent \'rē-jənt\ *n* [ME, fr. MF or ML; MF, fr. ML *regent-, regens,* fr. L, prp. of *regere* to rule — more at RIGHT] **1 :** one who rules or reigns **:** GOVERNOR **2 :** one who governs a kingdom in the minority, absence, or disability of the sovereign **3 :** a member of a governing board (as of a state university) — **regent** *adj* — **re·gent·al** \-jənt-ᵊl\ *adj*
reg·i·cide \'rej-ə-ˌsīd\ *n* **1** [prob. fr. (assumed) NL *regicida,* fr. L *reg-, rex* king + *-cida* -cide — more at ROYAL] **:** one who kills a king **2** [prob. fr. (assumed) NL *regicidium,* fr L *reg-, rex* + *-cidium* -cide] **:** the killing of a king — **reg·i·cid·al** \ˌrej-ə-'sīd-ᵊl\ *adj*
re·gime *also* **ré·gime** \rā-'zhēm, ri- *also* ri-'jēm\ *n* [F *régime,* fr. L *regimin-, regimen*] **1 a :** REGIMEN 1 **b :** a regular pattern of occurrence or action (as of seasonal rainfall) **c :** the characteristic behavior or orderly procedure of a natural phenomenon or process **2 a :** mode of rule or management **b :** a form of government <a socialist ~> **c :** a government in power <predicted that the new ~ would fall> **d :** a period of rule <during the Stalin ~>
reg·i·men \'rej-ə-mən *also* 'rezh-ə-\ *n* [ME, fr. L *regimin-, regimen* rule, fr. *regere*] **1 a :** a systematic plan (as of diet, therapy, or medication) esp. when designed to improve and maintain the health of a patient **b :** a regular course of strenuous training <the daily ~ of a top ballet dancer> **2 :** GOVERNMENT, RULE **3 :** REGIME 1c
1**reg·i·ment** \'rej-(ə-)mənt\ *n* [ME, fr. MF, fr. LL *regimentum,* fr. L *regere*] **1 :** governmental rule **2 :** a military unit consisting usu. of a number of battalions
2**reg·i·ment** \'rej-ə-ˌment\ *vt* **1 :** to form into or assign to a regiment **2 a :** to organize rigidly esp. for the sake of regulation or control <~ an entire country> **b :** to subject to order or uniformity — **reg·i·men·ta·tion** \ˌrej-ə-mən-'tā-shən, -ˌmen-\ *n*
reg·i·men·tal \ˌrej-ə-'ment-ᵊl\ *adj* **1 :** of or relating to a regiment **2 :** AUTHORITATIVE, DICTATORIAL — **reg·i·men·tal·ly** \-ᵊl-ē\ *adv*
reg·i·men·tals \-ᵊlz\ *n pl* **1 :** a regimental uniform **2 :** military dress
re·gion \'rē-jən\ *n* [ME, fr. MF, fr. L *region-, regio,* fr. *regere* to rule] **1 :** an administrative area, division, or district **2 a :** an indefinite area of the world or universe <few unknown ~*s* left on earth> **b :** a broad homogeneous geographical area <the Appalachian ~> **c** (1) **:** a major world area that supports a characteristic fauna (2) **:** an area characterized by the prevalence of one or more vegetational climax types **3 a :** one of the major subdivisions into which the body or one of its parts is divisible **b :** an indefinite area surrounding a specified body part <a pain in the ~ of the heart> **4 :** a sphere of activity of interest **:** FIELD **5 :** one of the zones into which the atmosphere is divided according to height or the sea according to depth **6 :** an open connected set together with none, some, or all of the points on its boundary <a simple closed curve divides the plane into two ~*s*>
1**re·gion·al** \'rēj-nəl, -ən-ᵊl\ *adj* **1 :** of, relating to, or characteristic of a region **2 :** affecting a particular region **:** LOCALIZED
2**regional** *n* **:** something (as a branch of an organization or an edition of a magazine) that serves a region
re·gion·al·ism \'rēj-nəl-ˌiz-əm, -ən-ᵊl-\ *n* **1 a :** consciousness of and loyalty to a distinct region with a homogeneous population **b :** development of a political or social system based on one or more such areas **2 :** emphasis on regional locale and characteristics in art or literature **3 :** a characteristic feature (as of speech) of a geographic area — **re·gion·al·ist** \-əst\ *n or adj* — **re·gion·al·is·tic** \ˌrēj-nəl-'is-tik, -ən-ᵊl-\ *adj*
re·gion·al·ize \'rēj-nəl-ˌīz, -ən-ᵊl-\ *vt* **-ized; -iz·ing :** to divide into regions or administrative districts **:** arrange regionally — **re·gion·al·iza·tion** \ˌrēj-nəl-ə-'zā-shən, -ən-ᵊl-ə-\ *n*
regional library *n* **:** a public library system serving several adjacent counties usu. in the same state
re·gion·al·ly \'rēj-nə-lē, -ən-ᵊl-ē\ *adv* **:** on a regional basis
re·gis·seur \ˌrā-zhi-'sər\ *n* [F *régisseur*] **:** a director responsible for staging a theatrical work (as a ballet)
1**reg·is·ter** \'rej-ə-stər\ *n* [ME *registre,* fr. MF, fr. ML *registrum,* alter. of LL *regesta,* pl., register, fr. L, neut. pl. of *regestus,* pp. of *regerere* to bring back, fr. *re-* + *gerere* to bear — more at CAST] **1 :** a written record containing regular entries of items or details **2 a :** a book or system of public records **b :** a roster of qualified or available individuals <a civil service ~> **3 :** an entry in a register **4 a :** a set of organ pipes of like quality **:** STOP **b** (1) **:** the range of a human voice or a musical instrument (2) **:** a portion of such a range similarly produced or of the same quality **5 a :** a device regulating admission of air to fuel **b :** a grille often with shutters for admitting heated air or for ventilation **6 :** REGISTRATION, REGISTRY **7 a :** an automatic device registering a number or a quantity **b :** a number or quantity so registered **8 :** a condition of correct alignment or proper relative position **9 :** a device (as in a computer) for storing small amounts of data; *esp* **:** one in which data can be both stored and operated on
2**register** *vb* **reg·is·tered; reg·is·ter·ing** \-st(ə-)riŋ\ *vt* **1 a :** to make or secure official entry of in a register **b :** to enroll formally esp. as a voter or student **c :** to record automatically **:** INDICATE **d :** to make a record of **:** NOTE **2 :** to make or adjust so as to correspond exactly **3 :** to secure special protection for (a piece of mail) by prepayment of a fee **4 :** to convey an impression of **:** EXPRESS <~*ed* surprise at the telegram> **5 :** ACHIEVE, WIN <~*ed* an impressive victory> ~ *vi* **1 a :** to enroll one's name in a register <~*ed* at the hotel> **b :** to enroll one's name officially as a prerequisite for voting **c :** to enroll formally as a student **2 a :** to correspond exactly **b :** to be in correct alignment or register **3 :** to make or convey an impression <the name didn't ~>
3**register** *n* [prob. alter. of ME *registrer*] **:** REGISTRAR
reg·is·tered *adj* **1 a :** having the owner's name entered in a register <~ security> **b :** recorded as the owner of a security **2 :** recorded on the basis of pedigree or breed characteristics in the studbook of a breed association **3 :** qualified formally or officially
registered mail *n* **:** mail recorded in the post office of mailing and at each successive point of transmission and guaranteed special care in delivery
registered nurse *n* **:** a graduate trained nurse who has been licensed by a state authority after passing qualifying examinations for registration
register ton *n* **:** TON 2a
reg·is·tra·ble \'rej-ə-st(ə-)rə-bəl\ *adj* **:** capable of being registered
reg·is·trant \'rej-ə-strənt\ *n* **:** one that registers or is registered
reg·is·trar \'rej-ə-ˌsträr\ *n* [alter. of ME *registrer,* fr. MF *registreur,* fr. *registrer* to register, fr. ML *registrare,* fr. *registrum*] **:** an official recorder or keeper of records: as **a :** an officer of an educational institution responsible for registering students, keeping academic records, and corresponding with applicants and evaluating their credentials **b :** an admitting officer at a hospital
reg·is·tra·tion \ˌrej-ə-'strā-shən\ *n* **1 :** the act of registering **2 :** an entry in a register **3 :** the number of individuals registered **:** ENROLLMENT **4 a :** the art or act of selecting and adjusting pipe organ stops **b :** the combination of stops selected for performing a particular organ work **5 :** a document certifying an act of registering
reg·is·try \'rej-ə-strē\ *n, pl* **-tries** **1 :** REGISTRATION, ENROLLMENT **2 :** the nationality of a ship according to its entry in a register **:** FLAG **3 :** a place of registration **4 a :** an official record book **b :** an entry in a registry
re·gius professor \ˌrē-j(ē-)əs-\ *n* [NL, royal professor] **:** a holder of a professorship founded by royal subsidy at a British university
reg·let \'reg-lət\ *n* [F *réglet,* fr. MF *reglet* straightedge, fr. *regle,* fr. L *regula* — more at RULE] **1 :** a flat narrow architectural molding **2 :** a strip of wood used like a lead between lines of type
reg·nal \'reg-nᵊl\ *adj* [ML *regnalis,* fr. L *regnum* reign — more at REIGN] **:** of or relating to a king or his reign; *specif* **:** calculated from a monarch's accession to the throne <in his eighth ~ year>
reg·nant \'reg-nənt\ *adj* [L *regnant-, regnans,* prp. of *regnare* to reign, fr. *regnum*] **1 :** exercising rule **:** REIGNING **2 a :** having the chief power **b :** of common or widespread occurrence
reg·num \'reg-nəm\ *n, pl* **reg·na** \-nə\ [L] **:** KINGDOM
rego·lith \'reg-ə-ˌlith\ *n* [Gk *rhēgos* blanket + E *-lith;* akin to Skt *rāga* color] **:** MANTLEROCK
re·gorge \(ˈ)rē-'gȯ(ə)rj\ *vt* **re·gorged; re·gorg·ing** [F *regorger,* fr. MF, fr. *re-* + *gorger* to gorge] **:** DISGORGE
rego·sol \'reg-ə-ˌsäl, -ˌsȯl\ *n* [*rego-* (as in *regolith*) + L *solum* soil — more at SOLE] **:** an azonal soil consisting chiefly of imperfectly consolidated material and having no clear-cut and specific morphology
re·grant \(ˈ)rē-'grant\ *vt* **:** to grant back or again — **re·grant** \(ˈ)rē-'grant, 'rē-ˌ\ *n*
re·greet \(ˈ)rē-'grēt\ *vt, archaic* **:** to greet in return
regreets *n pl, obs* **:** GREETINGS
1**re·gress** \'rē-ˌgres\ *n* [ME, fr. L *regressus,* fr. *regressus,* pp. of *regredi* to go back, fr. *re-* + *gradi* to go — more at GRADE] **1 a :** an act or the privilege of going or coming back **b :** REENTRY 1 **2 :** movement backward to a previous and esp. worse or more primitive state or condition **3 :** the act of reasoning backward

ə abut ᵊ kitten ər further a back ā bake ä cot, cart
au̇ out ch chin e less ē easy g gift i trip ī life
j joke ŋ sing ō flow ȯ flaw ȯi coin th thin th this
ü loot u̇ foot y yet yü few yu̇ furious zh vision

[2]**re·gress** \ri-'gres\ *vi* **1 a :** to make or undergo regress **:** RETROGRADE **b :** to be subject to or exhibit regression **2 :** to tend to approach or revert to a mean ~ *vt* **:** to induce a state of psychological regression in — **re·gres·sor** \-'gres-ər\ *n*

re·gres·sion \ri-'gresh-ən\ *n* **1 :** the act or an instance of regressing **2 :** a trend or shift toward a lower or less perfect state: as **a :** progressive decline of a manifestation of disease **b** (1) **:** gradual loss of differentiation and function by a body part esp. as a physiological change accompanying aging (2) **:** gradual loss of memories and acquired skills **c :** reversion to an earlier mental or behavioral level **d :** a functional relationship between two or more correlated variables that is often empirically determined from data and is used esp. to predict values of one variable when given values of the others <the ~ of *y* on *x* is linear>; *specif* **:** a function that yields the mean value of a random variable under the condition that one or more independent variables have specified values **3 :** retrograde motion esp. of an astronomical orbital characteristic

re·gres·sive \ri-'gres-iv\ *adj* **1 :** tending to regress or produce regression **2 :** being, characterized by, or developing in the course of an evolutionary process involving increasing simplification of bodily structure **3 :** decreasing in rate as the base increases <a ~ tax> — **re·gres·sive·ly** *adv* — **re·gres·sive·ness** *n*

[1]**re·gret** \ri-'gret\ *vb* **re·gret·ted; re·gret·ting** [ME *regretten,* fr. MF *regreter,* fr. OF, fr. *re-* + *-greter* (of Scand origin; akin to ON *grāta* to weep) — more at GREET] *vt* **1 a :** to mourn the loss or death of **b :** to miss very much **2 :** to be very sorry for <~*s* his mistakes> ~ *vi* **:** to experience regret — **re·gret·ter** *n*

[2]**regret** *n* **1 :** grief or pain tinged with emotion (as disappointment, longing, or remorse) **2 a :** an expression of distressing emotion (as sorrow or disappointment) **b** *pl* **:** a note politely declining an invitation ***syn*** see SORROW — **re·gret·ful** \-'gret-fəl\ *adj* — **re·gret·ful·ly** \-fə-lē\ *adv* — **re·gret·ful·ness** *n*

re·gret·less \ri-'gret-ləs\ *adj* **:** feeling no regret

re·gret·ta·ble \ri-'gret-ə-bəl\ *adj* **:** deserving regret

re·gret·ta·bly \-blē\ *adv* **1 :** in a regrettable manner **:** to a regrettable extent <a ~ steep decline in wages> **2 :** it is regrettable that — used as a sentence modifier <~, we had failed to consider alternatives>

re·group \(')rē-'grüp\ *vt* **:** to form into a new grouping <in order to subtract 129 from 531 ~ 531 into 5 hundreds, 2 tens, and 11 ones> <~ military forces> ~ *vi* **1 :** to reorganize (as after a setback) for renewed activity **2 :** to alter the tactical formation of a military force

re·grow \(')rē-'grō\ *vb* **-grew** \-'grü\; **-grown** \-'grōn\; **-grow·ing** *vt* **:** to grow (as a missing part) anew ~ *vi* **:** to continue growth after interruption or injury

regt *abbr* regiment

[1]**reg·u·lar** \'reg-yə-lər\ *adj* [ME *reguler,* fr. MF, fr. LL *regularis* regular, fr. L, of a bar, fr. *regula* rule — more at RULE] **1 :** belonging to a religious order **2 a :** formed, built, arranged, or ordered according to some established rule, law, principle, or type **b** (1) **:** both equilateral and equiangular <a ~ polygon> (2) **:** having faces that are congruent regular polygons and all the polyhedral angles congruent <a ~ polyhedron> **c** *of a flower* **:** having the arrangement of floral parts exhibiting radial symmetry with members of the same whorl similar in form **d :** having or constituting an isometric system <~ crystals> **3 a :** ORDERLY, METHODICAL <~ habits> **b :** recurring or functioning at fixed or uniform intervals <a ~ income> **4 a :** constituted, conducted, or done in conformity with established or prescribed usages, rules, or discipline **b :** NORMAL, CORRECT: as (1) **:** COMPLETE, ABSOLUTE <a ~ fool> <the office seemed like a ~ madhouse> (2) **:** thinking or behaving in an acceptable manner <wanted to prove he was a ~ guy> **c** (1) **:** conforming to the normal or usual manner of inflection (2) **:** WEAK 7 **5 a :** of, relating to, or constituting the regular army of a state **b :** constituting or made up of individuals properly recognized as legitimate combatants in war — **reg·u·lar·ly** *adv*

syn REGULAR, NORMAL, TYPICAL, NATURAL *shared meaning element* **:** being of the sort or kind that is expected as usual, ordinary, or average ***ant*** irregular

[2]**regular** *n* **1 :** one who is regular: as **a :** one of the regular clergy **b :** a soldier in a regular army **c :** one who can be trusted or depended on <a party ~> **d :** a player on an athletic team who usu. starts every game **e :** one who is usu. present or participating **2 :** a clothing size designed to fit a person of average height

regular army *n* **:** a permanently organized body constituting the standing army of a state

reg·u·lar·i·ty \,reg-yə-'lar-ət-ē\ *n, pl* **-ties 1 :** the quality or state of being regular **2 :** something that is regular

reg·u·lar·ize \'reg-yə-lə-,rīz\ *vt* **-ized; -iz·ing :** to make regular by conformance to law, rules, or custom — **reg·u·lar·iza·tion** \,reg-yə-lə-rə-'zā-shən\ *n* — **reg·u·lar·iz·er** \'reg-yə-lə-,rī-zər\ *n*

regular solid *n* **:** any of the five regular polyhedrons

regular year *n* **:** a common year of 354 days or a leap year of 384 days in the Jewish calendar

reg·u·late \'reg-yə-,lāt\ *vt* **-lat·ed; -lat·ing** [LL *regulatus,* pp. of *regulare,* fr. L *regula*] **1 a :** to govern or direct according to rule **b** (1) **:** to bring under the control of law or constituted authority (2) **:** to make regulations for or concerning <~ the industries of a country> **2 :** to bring order, method, or uniformity to <~ one's habits> **3 :** to fix or adjust the time, amount, degree, or rate of <~ the pressure of a tire> — **reg·u·la·tive** \-,lāt-iv\ *adj* — **reg·u·la·to·ry** \-lə-,tōr-ē, -,tȯr-\ *adj*

[1]**reg·u·la·tion** \,reg-yə-'lā-shən\ *n* **1 :** the act of regulating **:** the state of being regulated **2 a :** an authoritative rule dealing with details or procedure <safety ~*s* in a factory> **b :** a rule or order having the force of law issued by an executive authority of a government **3 a :** the process of redistributing material (as in an embryo) to restore a damaged or lost part independent of new tissue growth **b :** the mechanism by which an early embryo maintains normal development

[2]**regulation** *adj* **:** conforming to regulations **:** OFFICIAL

reg·u·la·tor \'reg-yə-,lāt-ər\ *n* **1 :** one that regulates **2 :** REGULATOR GENE

regulator gene *n* **:** a gene controlling the production of a genetic repressor

reg·u·lus \'reg-yə-ləs\ *n* [NL, fr. L, petty king, fr. *reg-, rex* king — more at ROYAL] **1** *cap* **:** a first-magnitude star in the constellation Leo **2** [ML, metallic antimony, fr. L] **:** the more or less impure mass of metal formed beneath the slag in smelting and reducing ores

re·gur·gi·tate \(')rē-'gər-jə-,tāt\ *vb* **-tat·ed; -tat·ing** [ML *regurgitatus,* pp. of *regurgitare,* fr. L *re-* + LL *gurgitare* to engulf, fr. L *gurgit-, gurges* whirlpool — more at VORACIOUS] *vi* **:** to become thrown or poured back ~ *vt* **:** to throw or pour back or out (as from a cavity) — **re·gur·gi·ta·tive** \-,tāt-iv\ *adj*

re·gur·gi·ta·tion \(,)rē-,gər-jə-'tā-shən\ *n* **:** an act of regurgitating: as **a :** the casting up of incompletely digested food (as by some birds in feeding their young) **b :** the backward flow of blood through a defective heart valve

re·ha·bil·i·tant \,rē-(h)ə-'bil-ə-tənt\ *n* **:** a disabled person undergoing rehabilitation

re·ha·bil·i·tate \,rē-(h)ə-'bil-ə-,tāt\ *vt* **-tat·ed; -tat·ing** [ML *rehabilitatus,* pp. of *rehabilitare,* fr. L *re-* + LL *habilitare* to habilitate] **1 a :** to restore to a former capacity **:** REINSTATE **b :** to restore to good repute **:** reestablish the good name of **2 a :** to restore to a former state (as of efficiency, good management, or solvency) <~ slum areas> **b :** to restore to a condition of health or useful and constructive activity — **re·ha·bil·i·ta·tive** \-,tāt-iv\ *adj* — **re·ha·bil·i·ta·tor** \-,tāt-ər\ *n*

re·ha·bil·i·ta·tion \-,bil-ə-'tā-shən\ *n* **:** the action or process of rehabilitating or of being rehabilitated **:** the state of being rehabilitated — **re·ha·bil·i·ta·tion·ist** \-sh(ə-)nəst\ *n*

[1]**re·hash** \(')rē-'hash\ *vt* **1 :** to talk over or discuss again **2 :** to present or use again in another form without substantial change or improvement

[2]**re·hash** \'rē-,hash\ *n* **1 :** a product of rehashing **:** something presented in a new form without change of substance <a book that was a ~ of stale ideas> **2 :** the action or process of rehashing

re·hear \(')rē-'hi(ə)r\ *vt* **-heard** \-'hərd\; **-hear·ing** \-'hi(ə)r-iŋ\ **:** to hear judicially again or anew

re·hear·ing *n* **:** a second or new hearing by the same tribunal

re·hears·al \ri-'hər-səl\ *n* **1 :** something recounted or told again **:** RECITAL **2 a :** a private performance or practice session preparatory to a public appearance **b :** a practice exercise **:** TRIAL

re·hearse \ri-'hərs\ *vb* **re·hearsed; re·hears·ing** [ME *rehersen,* fr. MF *rehercier,* lit., to harrow again, fr. *re-* + *hercier* to harrow, fr. *herce* harrow — more at HEARSE] *vt* **1 a :** to say again **:** REPEAT **b :** to recite aloud in a formal manner **2 :** to present an account of **:** NARRATE, RELATE <~ a familiar story> **3 :** to recount in order **:** ENUMERATE <had *rehearsed* their grievances in a letter to the governor> **4 a :** to give a rehearsal of **b :** to train or make proficient by rehearsal **5 :** to perform or practice as if in a rehearsal ~ *vi* **:** to engage in a rehearsal — **re·hears·er** *n*

re·house \(')rē-'hau̇z\ *vt* **:** to house again or anew; *esp* **:** to establish in a new or different housing unit of a better quality

re·hu·man·ize \(')rē-'(h)yü-mə-,nīz\ *vt* **1 :** to make compatible with human rights and dignity **2 :** to restore to a rich full life — **re·hu·man·iza·tion** \(,)rē-,(h)yü-mə-nə-'zā-shən\ *n*

re·hy·drate \(')rē-'hī-,drāt\ *vt* **:** to restore fluid lost in dehydration to — **re·hy·drat·able** \-,drāt-ə-bəl\ *adj* — **re·hy·dra·tion** \,rē-,hī-'drā-shən\ *n*

reichs·mark \'rīk-,smärk\ *n, pl* **reichsmarks** *also* **reichsmark** [G, fr. *reichs* (gen. of *reich* empire, kingdom, fr. OHG *rihhi*) + *mark* — more at RICH] **:** the German mark from 1925 to 1948

re·ifi·ca·tion \,rā-ə-fə-'kā-shən, ,rē-\ *n* **:** the process or result of reifying

re·ify \'rā-ə-,fī, rē-\ *vt* **re·ified; re·ify·ing** [L *res* thing — more at REAL] **:** to regard (something abstract) as a material thing

[1]**reign** \'rān\ *n* [ME *regne,* fr. OF, fr. L *regnum,* fr. *reg-, rex* king — more at ROYAL] **1 a :** royal authority **:** SOVEREIGNTY <under the ~ of the Stuart kings> **b :** the dominion, sway, or influence of one resembling a monarch <the ~ of the Puritan ministers> **2 :** the time during which one (as a sovereign) reigns

[2]**reign** *vi* **1 a :** to possess or exercise sovereign power **:** RULE **b :** to hold office as chief of state although possessing little governing power <in England the sovereign ~*s* but does not rule> **2 :** to exercise authority in the manner of a monarch **3 :** to be predominant or prevalent <chaos ~*ed* in the classroom>

reign of terror [*Reign of Terror,* a period of the French Revolution that was conspicuous for mass executions of political suspects] **:** a state or a period of time marked by violence often committed by those in power that produces widespread terror

re·im·burse \,rē-əm-'bərs\ *vt* **-bursed; -bursing** [*re-* + obs. E *imburse* (to put in the pocket, pay)] **1 :** to pay back to someone **:** REPAY <~ travel expenses> **2 :** to make restoration or payment of an equivalent to <~ an agent for his traveling expenses> ***syn*** see PAY — **re·im·burs·able** \-'bər-sə-bəl\ *adj* — **re·im·burse·ment** \-'bər-smənt\ *n*

re·im·pres·sion \,rē-əm-'presh-ən\ *n* **:** REPRINT a

[1]**rein** \'rān\ *n* [ME *reine,* fr. MF *rene,* fr. (assumed) VL *retina,* fr. L *retinēre* to restrain — more at RETAIN] **1 :** a line fastened to a bit by which a rider or driver controls an animal — usu. used in pl. **2 a :** a restraining influence **:** CHECK <regulations impose ~*s* on personal freedom> **b :** controlling or guiding power <the ~*s* of government> **3 :** opportunity for unhampered activity or use

[2]**rein** *vt* **1 :** to check or stop by or as if by a pull at the reins <~*ed* in his horse> <couldn't ~ his impatience> **2 :** to control or direct with or as if with reins ~ *vi* **1** *archaic* **:** to submit to the use of reins **2 :** to stop or slow up one's horse or oneself by or as if by pulling the reins

re·in·car·nate \,rē-ən-'kär-,nāt, (')rē-'in-,\ *vt* **:** to incarnate again

re·in·car·na·tion \(,)rē-,in-,kär-'nā-shən\ *n* **1 a :** the action of reincarnating **:** the state of being reincarnated **b :** rebirth in new bodies or forms of life; *esp* **:** a rebirth of a soul in a new human body **2** : a fresh embodiment — **re·in·car·na·tion·ist** \-sh(ə-)nəst\ *n*

rein·deer \'rān-ˌdi(ə)r\ *n* [ME *reindere,* fr. ON *hreinn* reindeer + ME *deer*] : any of several deer (genus *Rangifer*) inhabiting northern Europe, Asia, and America and having antlers in both sexes

reindeer moss *n* : a gray, erect, tufted, and much-branched lichen (*Cladonia rangiferina*) that forms extensive patches in arctic and north-temperate regions, constitutes a large part of the food of reindeer, and is sometimes eaten by man — called also *reindeer lichen*

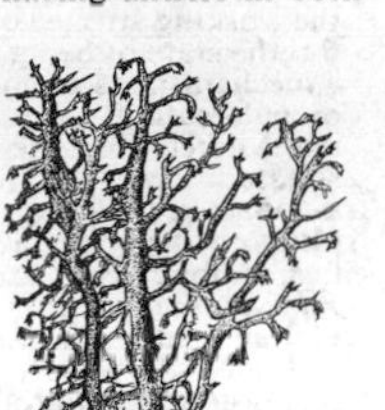
reindeer moss

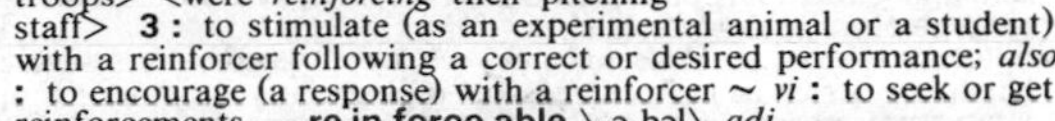

re·in·fec·tion \ˌrē-ən-'fek-shən\ *n* : infection following recovery from or superimposed on infection of the same type

re·in·force \ˌrē-ən-'fō(ə)rs, -'fȯ(ə)rs\ *vb* [*re-* + *inforce,* alter. of *enforce*] *vt* **1** : to strengthen by additional assistance, material, or support : make stronger or more pronounced <~ the elbows of a jacket> <claimed that the media ~ destructive impulses> **2** : to strengthen or increase by fresh additions <~ the regular troops> <were *reinforcing* their pitching staff> **3** : to stimulate (as an experimental animal or a student) with a reinforcer following a correct or desired performance; *also* : to encourage (a response) with a reinforcer ~ *vi* : to seek or get reinforcements — **re·in·force·able** \-ə-bəl\ *adj*

reinforced concrete *n* : concrete in which metal (as steel) is embedded so that the two materials act together in resisting forces

re·in·force·ment \ˌrē-ən-'fōr-smənt, -'fȯr-\ *n* **1** : the action of reinforcing : the state of being reinforced **2** : something that reinforces

re·in·forc·er \-'fōr-sər, -'fȯr-\ *n* : a stimulus (as a reward or the removal of discomfort) that is effective esp. in operant conditioning because it regularly follows a desired response

rein·less \'rān-ləs\ *adj* : having no reins; *also* : UNRESTRAINED, UNCHECKED

reins \'rānz\ *n pl* [ME, fr. MF & L; MF, fr. L *renes*] **1 a** : KIDNEYS **b** : the region of the kidneys : LOINS **2** : the seat of the feelings or passions

reins·man \'rānz-mən\ *n* : a skilled driver or rider of horses

re·in·state \ˌrē-ən-'stāt\ *vt* **-stat·ed; -stat·ing 1** : to place again (as in possession or in a former position) **2** : to restore to a previous effective state — **re·in·state·ment** \-'stāt-mənt\ *n*

re·in·sur·ance \ˌrē-ən-'shu̇r-ən(t)s, *esp South* (ˈ)rē-'in-ˌ\ *n* : insurance by another insurer of all or a part of a risk previously assumed by an insurance company

re·in·sure \ˌrē-ən-'shu̇(ə)r\ *vt* **1** : to insure again by transferring to another insurance company all or a part of a liability assumed **2** : to insure again by assuming all or a part of the liability of an insurance company already covering a risk ~ *vi* : to provide increased insurance — **re·in·sur·er** *n*

re·in·te·grate \(ˈ)rē-'int-ə-ˌgrāt\ *vt* [ML *reintegratus,* pp. of *reintegrare* to renew, reinstate, fr. L *re-* + *integrare* to integrate] : to integrate again into an entity : restore to unity — **re·in·te·gra·tion** \(ˌ)rē-ˌint-ə-'grā-shən\ *n* — **re·in·te·gra·tive** \(ˈ)rē-'int-ə-ˌgrāt-iv\ *adj*

re·in·ter·pret \ˌrē-ən-'tər-prət, *rapid* -pət\ *vt* : to interpret again; *specif* : to give a new or different interpretation to — **re·in·ter·pre·ta·tion** \-ˌtər-prə-'tā-shən, *rapid* -pə-\ *n*

re·in·vent \ˌrē-ən-'vent\ *vt* **1** : to make as if for the first time something already invented <realized they were ~*ing* a machine that had been designed a century before> **2** : to remake or redo completely <radicals who want to ~ America> **3** : to bring into use again : REESTABLISH — **re·in·ven·tion** \-'ven-chən\ *n*

re·in·vest \ˌrē-ən-'vest\ *vt* **1** : to invest again or anew **2 a** : to invest (as income from investments) in additional securities **b** : to invest (as earnings) in a business rather than distribute as dividends or profits

re·in·vest·ment \-'ves(t)-mənt\ *n* **1** : the action of reinvesting : the state of being reinvested **2** : a second or repeated investment

re·in·vig·o·rate \ˌrē-ən-'vig-ə-ˌrāt\ *vt* : to give renewed or fresh vigor to <a long walk ~*s* the mind> — **re·in·vig·o·ra·tion** \-ˌvig-ə-'rā-shən\ *n* — **re·in·vig·o·ra·tor** \-'vig-ə-ˌrāt-ər\ *n*

reis *pl of* REAL

re·is·sue \(ˈ)rē-'ish-(ˌ)ü, -'ish-ə(-w), *chiefly Brit* -'is-(ˌ)yü\ *vi* : to come forth again ~ *vt* : to issue again; *esp* : to cause to become available again — **reissue** *n*

re·it·er·ate \rē-'it-ə-ˌrāt\ *vt* **-at·ed; -at·ing** [L *reiteratus,* pp. of *reiterare* to repeat, fr. *re-* + *iterare* to iterate] : to say or do over again or repeatedly sometimes with wearying effect ***syn*** see REPEAT — **re·it·er·a·tion** \(ˌ)rē-ˌit-ə-'rā-shən\ *n* — **re·it·er·a·tive** \rē-'it-ə-ˌrāt-iv, -rət-iv; -'i-trət-iv\ *adj* — **re·it·er·a·tive·ly** *adv* — **re·it·er·a·tive·ness** *n* — **re·it·er·a·tor** \-'it-ə-ˌrāt-ər\ *n*

Rei·ter's syndrome \'rīt-ərz-\ *n* [Hans *Reiter b*1881 G physician] : a disease of uncertain cause that is characterized by arthritis, conjunctivitis, and urethritis — called also *Reiter's disease*

reive \'rēv\ *vb* **reived; reiv·ing** [ME (Sc) *reifen,* fr. OE *rēafian* to rob — more at REAVE] *Scot* : RAID — **reiv·er** *n, Scot*

¹re·ject \ri-'jekt\ *vt* [ME *rejecten,* fr. L *rejectus,* pp. of *reicere,* fr. *re-* + *jacere* to throw — more at JET] **1 a** : to refuse to accept, consider, submit to, take for some purpose, or use <thought about her suggestion and then ~*ed* it> <~ a manuscript> <~*ed* the weevily grain as unfit for use> **b** : to refuse to hear, receive, or admit : REBUFF, REPELL <parents who ~ their children> **c** : to refuse as lover or spouse **2** *obs* : to cast off **3** : to throw back : REPULSE **4** : to spew out ***syn*** see DECLINE ***ant*** accept : choose, select — **re·ject·er** *or* **re·jec·tor** \-'jek-tər\ *n* — **re·ject·ing·ly** \-tiŋ-lē\ *adv* — **re·jec·tive** \-'jek-tiv\ *adj*

²re·ject \'rē-ˌjekt\ *n* : a rejected person or thing

re·ject·ee \ri-ˌjek-'tē, ˌrē-\ *n* : one that is rejected; *specif* : a person rejected as unfit for military service

re·jec·tion \ri-'jek-shən\ *n* **1 a** : the action of rejecting : the state of being rejected **b** : the immunological process of sloughing off foreign tissue or an organ (as a transplant) by the recipient organism **2** : something rejected

rejection slip *n* : a printed slip enclosed with a rejected manuscript returned by an editor to an author

re·jig·ger \(ˈ)rē-'jig-ər\ *vt* [*re-* + *¹jigger*] : ALTER, REARRANGE

re·joice \ri-'jȯis\ *vb* **re·joiced; re·joic·ing** [ME *rejoicen,* fr. MF *rejoiss-,* stem of *rejoir,* fr. *re-* + *joir* to rejoice, fr. L *guadēre* — more at JOY] *vt* : to give joy to : GLADDEN ~ *vi* : to feel joy or great delight — **re·joic·er** *n* — **re·joic·ing·ly** \-'jȯi-siŋ-lē\ *adv* — **rejoice in** : HAVE, POSSESS

re·joic·ing *n* **1** : the action of one that rejoices **2** : an instance, occasion, or expression of joy : FESTIVITY

re·join \ri-'jȯin, *vt 1 is* (ˈ)rē-\ *vb* [ME *rejoinen* to answer to a legal charge, fr. MF *rejoin-,* stem of *rejoindre,* fr. *re-* + *joindre* to join — more at JOIN] *vi* : to answer the replication of the plaintiff ~ *vt* **1** : to join again **2** : to say often sharply or critically in response esp. as a reply to a reply ***syn*** see ANSWER

re·join·der \ri-'jȯin-dər\ *n* [ME *rejoiner,* fr. MF *rejoindre* to rejoin] **1** : the defendant's answer to the plaintiff's replication **2** : REPLY; *specif* : an answer to a reply

re·ju·ve·nate \ri-'jü-və-ˌnāt\ *vb* **-nat·ed; -nat·ing** [*re-* + L *juvenis* young — more at YOUNG] *vt* **1 a** : to make young or youthful again : REINVIGORATE **b** : to restore to an original or new state <~ old cars> **2 a** : to stimulate (as by uplift) to renewed erosive activity — used of streams **b** : to develop youthful features of topography in ~ *vi* : to cause or undergo rejuvenation ***syn*** see RENEW — **re·ju·ve·na·tion** \ri-ˌjü-və-'nā-shən, ˌrē-\ *n* — **re·ju·ve·na·tor** \ri-'jü-və-ˌnāt-ər\ *n*

re·ju·ve·nes·cence \ri-ˌjü-və-'nes-ən(t)s, ˌrē-\ *n* [ML *rejuvenescere* to become young again, fr. L *re-* + *juvenescere* to become young, fr. *juvenis*] : a renewal of youthfulness : REJUVENATION — **re·ju·ve·nes·cent** \-ᵊnt\ *adj*

re·kin·dle \(ˈ)rē-'kin-dᵊl\ *vt* : to kindle again ~ *vi* : to ignite anew <in case the fire ~*s*> — **re·kin·dler** \-(d)lər, -dᵊl-ər\ *n*

re·knit \(ˈ)rē-'nit\ *vt* : to knit up or together again ~ *vi* : to engage in reknitting something

rel *abbr* **1** relating; relative **2** released **3** religion; religious

¹re·lapse \ri-'laps, 'rē-ˌ\ *n* [L *relapsus,* pp. of *relabi* to slide back, fr. *re-* + *labi* to slide — more at SLEEP] **1** : the act or an instance of backsliding, worsening, or subsiding **2** : a recurrence of symptoms of a disease after a period of improvement

²re·lapse \ri-'laps\ *vi* **re·lapsed; re·laps·ing 1** : to slip or fall back into a former worse state **2** : SINK, SUBSIDE <~ into deep thought> ***syn*** see LAPSE — **re·laps·er** *n*

relapsing fever *n* : a variable acute epidemic disease that is marked by recurring high fever lasting 5 to 7 days and that is caused by a spirochete (genus *Borrelia*) transmitted by the bites of lice and ticks

re·late \ri-'lāt\ *vb* **re·lat·ed; re·lat·ing** [L *relatus* (pp. of *referre* to carry back), fr. *re-* + *latus,* pp. of *ferre* to carry — more at TOLERATE, BEAR] *vt* **1** : to give an account of : TELL **2** : to show or establish logical or causal connection between ~ *vi* **1** : to apply or take effect retroactively **2** : to have relationship or connection : REFER **3** : to have or establish a relationship : INTERACT <the way a child ~*s* to a psychiatrist> **4** : to respond esp. favorably <can't ~ to that kind of music> ***syn*** see JOIN — **re·lat·able** \-'lāt-ə-bəl\ *adj* — **re·lat·er** *n*

re·lat·ed *adj* **1** : connected by reason of an established or discoverable relation **2** : connected by common ancestry or sometimes by marriage **3** : having close harmonic connection — used of tones, chords, or tonalities — **re·lat·ed·ly** *adv* — **re·lat·ed·ness** *n*

syn RELATED, COGNATE, KINDRED, ALLIED, AFFILIATED *shared meaning element* : connected by or as if by close family ties

re·la·tion \ri-'lā-shən\ *n* **1** : the act of telling or recounting : ACCOUNT **2** : an aspect or quality (as resemblance) that connects two or more things or parts as being or belonging or working together or as being of the same kind <the ~ of time and space>; *specif* : a property (as one expressed by *is equal to, is less than,* or *is the brother of*) that holds between an ordered pair of objects **3** : the referring by a legal fiction of an act to a prior date as the time of its taking effect **4 a** (1) : a person connected by consanguinity or affinity : RELATIVE (2) : a person legally entitled to a share of the property of an intestate **b** : relationship by consanguinity or affinity : KINSHIP **5** : REFERENCE, RESPECT <in ~ to> **6** : the attitude or stance which two or more persons or groups assume toward one another <race ~*s*> **7 a** : the state of being mutually or reciprocally interested (as in social or commercial matters) **b** *pl* (1) : DEALINGS, AFFAIRS <foreign ~*s*> (2) : INTERCOURSE (3) : SEXUAL INTERCOURSE

re·la·tion·al \-shnəl, -shən-ᵊl\ *adj* **1** : of or relating to kinship **2** : characterized or constituted by relations **3** : having the function chiefly of indicating a relation of syntax <*has* is notional in *he has luck,* ~ in *he has gone*> — **re·la·tion·al·ly** \-ē\ *adv*

re·la·tion·ship \-shən-ˌship\ *n* **1** : the state or character of being related or interrelated : CONNECTION <show the ~ between two things> **2** : KINSHIP; *also* : a specific instance or type of kinship **3** : a state of affairs existing between those having relations or dealings <had a good ~ with his family>

¹rel·a·tive \'rel-ət-iv\ *n* **1** : a word referring grammatically to an antecedent **2** : a thing having a relation to or connection with or necessary dependence on another thing **3 a** : a person connected with another by blood or affinity **b** : an animal or plant related to another by common descent **4** : a relative term

ə abut ᵊ kitten ər further a back ā bake ä cot, cart
au̇ out ch chin e less ē easy g gift i trip ī life
j joke ŋ sing ō flow ȯ flaw ȯi coin th thin t͟h this
ü loot u̇ foot y yet yü few yu̇ furious zh vision

[2]**relative** *adj* **1 :** introducing a subordinate clause qualifying an expressed or implied antecedent <~ pronoun>; *also* **:** introduced by such a connective <~ clause> **2 :** RELEVANT, PERTINENT <matters ~ to world peace> **3 :** not absolute or independent **:** COMPARATIVE <the ~ isolation of life in the country> **4 :** having the same key signature — used of major and minor keys and scales **5 :** expressed as the ratio of the specified quantity (as an error in measuring) to the total magnitude (as the value of a measured quantity) or to the mean of all the quantities involved — **rel·a·tive·ly** *adv* — **rel·a·tive·ness** *n*

relative humidity *n* **:** the ratio of the amount of water vapor actually present in the air to the greatest amount possible at the same temperature

relative to *prep* **:** with regard to **:** in connection with

relative wind *n* **:** the motion of the air relative to a body in it

rel·a·tiv·ism \ˈrel-ət-iv-ˌiz-əm\ *n* **1 a :** a theory that knowledge is relative to the limited nature of the mind and the conditions of knowing **b :** a view that ethical truths depend on the individuals and groups holding them **2 :** RELATIVITY 3 — **rel·a·tiv·ist** \-əst\ *n*

rel·a·tiv·is·tic \ˌrel-ət-iv-ˈis-tik\ *adj* **1 :** of, relating to, or characterized by relativity or relativism **2 :** moving at a velocity such that there is a significant change in properties (as mass) in accordance with the theory of relativity <a ~ electron> — **rel·a·tiv·is·ti·cal·ly** \-ˈis-ti-k(ə-)lē\ *adv*

rel·a·tiv·i·ty \ˌrel-ə-ˈtiv-ət-ē\ *n, pl* **-ties 1 a :** the quality or state of being relative **b :** something that is relative **2 :** the state of being dependent for existence on or determined in nature, value, or quality by relation to something else **3 a :** a theory which is based on the two postulates (1) that the speed of light in a vacuum is constant and independent of the source or observer and (2) that the mathematical forms of the laws of physics are invariant in all inertial systems and which leads to the assertion of the equivalence of mass and energy and of change in mass, dimension, and time with increased velocity — called also *special theory of relativity* **b :** an extension of the theory to include gravitation and related acceleration phenomena — called also *general theory of relativity* **4 :** RELATIVISM 1b

rel·a·tiv·ize \ˈrel-ət-iv-ˌīz\ *vt* **-ized; -iz·ing :** to treat or describe as relative

re·la·tor \ri-ˈlāt-ər\ *n* **:** one who relates **:** NARRATOR

re·lax \ri-ˈlaks\ *vb* [ME *relaxen* to make less compact, fr. L *relaxare*, fr. *re-* + *laxare* to loosen, fr. *laxus* loose — more at SLACK] *vt* **1 :** to make less tense or rigid **:** SLACKEN <~*ed* his muscles> **2 :** to make less severe or stringent **:** MODIFY <~ immigration laws> **3 :** to make soft or enervated **4 :** to relieve from nervous tension ~ *vi* **1 :** to become lax, weak, or loose **:** REST **2 :** to become less intense or severe <hoped the committee would ~ in its opposition> **3** *of a muscle or muscle fiber* **:** to become inactive and lengthen **4 :** to cast off social restraint, nervous tension, or anxiety <couldn't ~ in crowds> **5 :** to seek rest or recreation <~ at the seashore> **6 :** to relieve constipation **7 :** to attain an equilibrium state following the abrupt removal of some influence (as light, high temperature, or stress) — **re·lax·er** *n*

[1]**re·lax·ant** \ri-ˈlak-sənt\ *adj* **:** of, relating to, or producing relaxation

[2]**relaxant** *n* **:** a substance (as a drug) that relaxes; *specif* **:** one that relieves muscular tension

re·lax·ation \ˌrē-ˌlak-ˈsā-shən, ri-ˌlak- *esp Brit* ˌrel-ək-\ *n* **1 :** the act or fact of relaxing or of being relaxed **2 :** a relaxing or recreative state, activity, or pastime **:** DIVERSION **3 :** the lengthening that characterizes inactive muscle fibers or muscles

re·laxed \ri-ˈlakst\ *adj* **1 :** freed from or lacking in precision or stringency **2 :** set or being at rest or at ease **3 :** easy of manner **:** INFORMAL ***syn*** see LOOSE ***ant*** strict — **re·laxed·ly** \-ˈlak-səd-lē, -ˈlaks-tlē\ *adv* — **re·laxed·ness** \-ˈlak-səd-nəs, -ˈlaks(t)-nəs\ *n*

re·lax·in \ri-ˈlak-sən\ *n* **:** a sex hormone of the corpus luteum that facilitates birth by causing relaxation of the pelvic ligaments

[1]**re·lay** \ˈrē-ˌlā\ *n* **1 a :** a supply (as of horses) arranged beforehand for successive relief **b :** a number of men who relieve others in some work <worked in ~*s* around the clock> **2 a :** a race between teams in which each team member successively covers a specified portion of the course **b :** one of the divisions of a relay **3 :** an electromagnetic device for remote or automatic control that is actuated by variation in conditions of an electric circuit and that operates in turn other devices (as switches) in the same or a different circuit **4 :** SERVOMOTOR **5 :** the act of passing along (as a message or ball) by stages; *also* **:** one of such stages

[2]**re·lay** \ˈrē-ˌlā, ri-ˈlā\ *vt* **re·layed; re·lay·ing** [ME *relayen*, fr. MF *relaier*, fr. OF, fr. *re-* + *laier* to leave — more at DELAY] **1 a :** to place or dispose in relays **b :** to provide with relays **2 :** to pass along by relays <news was ~*ed* to distant points> **3 :** to control or operate by a relay

[3]**re·lay** \(ˈ)rē-ˈlā\ *vt* **-laid** \-ˈlād\; **-lay·ing :** to lay again <~ track>

re·leas·able \ri-ˈlē-sə-bəl\ *adj* **1 :** capable of being released **2 :** designed to release (as in a fall) <~ ski bindings> — **re·leas·abil·i·ty** \-ˌlē-sə-ˈbil-ət-ē\ *n* — **re·leas·ably** \-ˈlē-sə-blē\ *adv*

[1]**re·lease** \ri-ˈlēs\ *vt* **re·leased; re·leas·ing** [ME *relesen*, fr. OF *relessier*, fr. L *relaxare* to relax] **1 :** to set free from restraint, confinement, or servitude **2 :** to relieve from something that confines, burdens, or oppresses <was *released* from her promise> **3 :** to give up in favor of another **:** RELINQUISH <~ a claim to property> **4 :** to give permission for publication, performance, exhibition, or sale of on but not before a specified date; *also* **:** PUBLISH, PRESENT <the commission *released* its findings> ***syn*** see FREE ***ant*** detain (*as a prisoner*), check (*as thoughts, feelings*)

[2]**release** *n* **1 :** relief or deliverance from sorrow, suffering, or trouble **2 a :** discharge from obligation or responsibility **b** (1) **:** relinquishment of a right or claim (2) **:** an act by which a legal right is discharged; *specif* **:** a conveyance of a right in lands or tenements to another having an estate in possession **3 a :** the act or an instance of liberating or freeing <an early ~ from jail> **b :** the act or manner of concluding a musical tone or phrase **c :** the act or manner of ending a sound **:** the movement of one or more vocal organs in quitting the position for a speech sound **4 :** an instrument effecting a legal release **5 a :** the permitting of a working fluid (as steam) to escape from the cylinder at the end of the working stroke **b :** the point in a cycle at which this act occurs **6 :** the state of being freed **7 :** a device adapted to hold or release a mechanism as required **8 a :** the act of permitting performance or publication; *also* **:** PERFORMANCE, PUBLICATION <a record that immediately became a best seller on its ~> **b :** the matter released; *esp* **:** a statement prepared for the press

re–lease \(ˈ)rē-ˈlēs\ *vt* **:** to lease again

released time *n* **:** a scheduled time when children are dismissed from public school to receive religious instruction — called also *release time*

release print *n* **:** a motion-picture film released for public showing

re·leas·er \ri-ˈlē-sər\ *n* **:** one that releases; *specif* **:** a stimulus that serves as the initiator of complex reflex behavior

rel·e·gate \ˈrel-ə-ˌgāt\ *vt* **-gat·ed; -gat·ing** [L *relegatus*, pp. of *relegare*, fr. *re-* + *legare* to send with a commission — more at LEGATE] **1 :** to send into exile **:** BANISH **2 :** ASSIGN: as **a :** to assign to a place of insignificance or of oblivion **:** put out of sight or mind **b :** to assign to an appropriate place or situation on the basis of classification or appraisal **c :** to submit to someone or something for appropriate action **:** DELEGATE ***syn*** see COMMIT — **rel·e·ga·tion** \ˌrel-ə-ˈgā-shən\ *n*

re·lent \ri-ˈlent\ *vb* [ME *relenten*] *vi* **1 :** to become less severe, harsh, or strict usu. from reasons of humanity **2 :** to let up **:** SLACKEN ~ *vt, obs* **:** SOFTEN, MOLLIFY ***syn*** see YIELD

re·lent·less \-ləs\ *adj* **:** PERSISTENT, UNRELENTING — **re·lent·less·ly** *adv* — **re·lent·less·ness** *n*

rel·e·vance \ˈrel-ə-vən(t)s\ *n* **1 :** relation to the matter at hand **:** practical and esp. social applicability **:** PERTINENCE <giving ~ to college courses>; *also* **:** social importance <a community's struggle for ~> **2 :** the ability (as of an information retrieval system) to retrieve material that satisfies the needs of the user

rel·e·van·cy \-vən-sē\ *n* **:** RELEVANCE

rel·e·vant \ˈrel-ə-vənt\ *adj* [ML *relevant-, relevans*, fr. L, prp. of *relevare* to raise up — more at RELIEVE] **1 a :** having significant and demonstrable bearing upon the matter at hand **b :** affording evidence tending to prove or disprove the matter at issue or under discussion <~ testimony> **2 :** PROPORTIONAL, RELATIVE — **rel·e·vant·ly** *adv*

syn RELEVANT, GERMANE, MATERIAL, PERTINENT, APPOSITE, APPLICABLE, APROPOS *shared meaning element* **:** relating to or bearing upon the matter in hand ***ant*** extraneous

re·li·abil·i·ty \ri-ˌlī-ə-ˈbil-ət-ē\ *n* **1 :** the quality or state of being reliable **2 :** the extent to which an experiment, test, or measuring procedure yields the same results on repeated trials

re·li·able \ri-ˈlī-ə-bəl\ *adj* **1 :** suitable or fit to be relied on **:** DEPENDABLE **2 :** giving the same result on successive trials — **re·li·able·ness** *n* — **re·li·ably** \-blē\ *adv*

re·li·ance \ri-ˈlī-ən(t)s\ *n* **1 :** the act of relying **:** the condition or attitude of one who relies **:** DEPENDENCE <~ on military power to achieve political ends> **2 :** something or someone relied on

re·li·ant \-ənt\ *adj* **:** having reliance on something or someone **:** DEPENDENT — **re·li·ant·ly** *adv*

rel·ic \ˈrel-ik\ *n* [ME *relik*, fr. OF *relique*, fr. ML *reliquia*, fr. LL *reliquiae*, pl., remains of a martyr, fr. L, remains, fr. *relinquere* to leave behind — more at RELINQUISH] **1 a :** an object esteemed and venerated because of association with a saint or martyr **b :** SOUVENIR, MEMENTO **2** *pl* **:** REMAINS, CORPSE **3 :** something left behind after decay, disintegration, or disappearance <~*s* of ancient cities> **4 :** a trace of some past or outmoded practice, custom, or belief

[1]**rel·ict** \ˈrel-ikt\ *n* [in sense 1, fr. LL *relicta*, fr. L, fem. of *relictus*, pp. of *relinquere;* in senses 2 & 3, fr. *relict* (residual), adj., fr. L *relictus*] **1 :** WIDOW **2 :** a persistent remnant of an otherwise extinct flora or fauna or kind of organism **3 a :** a relief feature or rock remaining after other parts have disappeared **b :** something left unchanged

[2]**relict** *adj* **:** of, relating to, or being a relict

re·lic·tion \ri-ˈlik-shən\ *n* [L *reliction-, relictio* act of leaving behind, fr. *relictus*] **1 :** the gradual recession of water leaving land permanently uncovered **2 :** land uncovered by reliction

[1]**re·lief** \ri-ˈlēf\ *n* [ME, fr. MF, fr. OF, fr. *relever*] **1 :** a payment made by a feudal tenant to his lord upon succeeding to an inherited estate **2 a :** removal or lightening of something oppressive, painful, or distressing <sought ~ from asthma by moving out of the city> **b :** aid in the form of money or necessities for the poor, aged, or handicapped **c :** military assistance to an endangered post or force **d :** means of breaking or avoiding monotony or boredom **:** DIVERSION **3 :** release from a post or from the performance of duty <~ of a sentry> **4 :** one that relieves another from duty by taking his place <explaining the duties to their ~*s*> **5 :** legal remedy or redress **6** [F] **a :** a mode of sculpture in which forms and figures are distinguished from a surrounding plane surface **b :** sculpture or a sculptural form executed in this mode **c :** projecting detail, ornament, or figures **7 :** sharpness of outline due to contrast <a roof in bold ~ against the sky> **8 :** the elevations or inequalities of a land surface

relief 6b

[2]**relief** *adj* **1 :** providing relief **2 :** characterized by surface inequalities **3 :** of or used in letterpress

relief map *n* **:** a map representing topographic relief

relief pitcher *n* **:** a baseball pitcher who takes over for another during a game; *esp* **:** one who is regularly held in readiness for relief

relief printing *n* : LETTERPRESS 1a
re·lieve \ri-ˈlēv\ *vb* **re·lieved; re·liev·ing** [ME *releven,* fr. MF *relever* to raise, relieve, fr. L *relevare,* fr. *re-* + *levare* to raise — more at LEVER] *vt* **1 a :** to free from a burden : give aid or help to **b :** to set free from an obligation, condition, or restriction **c :** to ease of a burden, wrong, or oppression by judicial or legislative interposition **2 a :** to bring about the removal or alleviation of : MITIGATE **b :** ROB, DEPRIVE <was *relieved* of his watch> **3 a :** to release from a post, station, or duty **b :** to take the place of **4 :** to remove or lessen the monotony of **5 a :** to set off by contrast **b :** to raise in relief **6 :** to relieve the bladder or bowels of (oneself) ~ *vi* **1 :** to bring or give relief **2 :** to stand out in relief **3 :** to serve as a relief pitcher — **re·liev·able** \-ˈlē-və-bəl\ *adj* — **re·liev·er** *n*
syn RELIEVE, ALLEVIATE, LIGHTEN, ASSUAGE, MITIGATE, ALLAY *shared meaning element* : to make less grievous or more tolerable ***ant*** intensify
re·lieved \ri-ˈlēvd\ *adj* : experiencing or showing relief esp. from anxiety or pent-up emotions — **re·liev·ed·ly** \-ˈlē-vəd-lē\ *adv*
re·lie·vo \ri-ˈlē-(ˌ)vō, rēl-ˈyā-\ *n, pl* **-vos** [It *rilievo,* fr. *rilevare* to raise, fr. L *relevare*] : RELIEF 6
relig *abbr* religion
re·li·gio- \ri-ˈlij-(ē-)ō\ *comb form* : religion <*religio*centric> : religion and <*religio*philosophical>
re·li·gion \ri-ˈlij-ən\ *n* [ME *religioun,* fr. L *religion-, religio* reverence, religion] **1 a (1) :** the service and worship of God or the supernatural **(2) :** commitment or devotion to religious faith or observance **b :** the state of a religious <a nun in her twentieth year of ~> **2 :** a personal set or institutionalized system of religious attitudes, beliefs, and practices **3** *archaic* **:** scrupulous conformity : CONSCIENTIOUSNESS **4 :** a cause, principle, or system of beliefs held to with ardor and faith
re·li·gion·ist \-ˈlij-(ə-)nəst\ *n* : a person adhering to a religion
re·li·gi·ose \ri-ˈlij-ē-ˌōs\ *adj* : RELIGIOUS; *esp* : excessively, obtrusively, or sentimentally religious — **re·li·gi·os·i·ty** \-ˌlij-ē-ˈäs-ət-ē\ *n*
[1]**re·li·gious** \ri-ˈlij-əs\ *adj* [ME, fr. OF *religieus,* fr. L *religiosus,* fr. *religio*] **1 :** relating to or manifesting faithful devotion to an acknowledged ultimate reality or deity <a ~ man> <~ attitudes> **2 :** of, relating to, or devoted to religious beliefs or observances **3 a :** scrupulously and conscientiously faithful **b :** FERVENT, ZEALOUS ***syn*** see DEVOUT ***ant*** irreligious — **re·li·gious·ly** *adv* — **re·li·gious·ness** *n*
[2]**religious** *n, pl* **religious** [ME, fr. OF *religieus,* fr. *religieus,* adj.] : a member of a religious order under monastic vows
re·line \(ˈ)rē-ˈlīn\ *vt* : to put new lines on or a new lining in
re·lin·quish \ri-ˈliŋ-kwish, -ˈlin-\ *vt* [ME *relinquisshen,* fr. MF *relinquiss-,* stem of *relinquir,* fr. L *relinquere* to leave behind, fr. *re-* + *linquere* to leave — more at LOAN] **1 :** to withdraw or retreat from : leave behind <immigrants sadly ~*ing* their native land> **2 a :** to desist from <he ~*ed* law to resume teaching> **b :** to give up : RENOUNCE <~*ed* their claims to the estate> **3 a :** to stop holding physically : RELEASE <slowly ~*ed* his grip on the bar> **b :** to give over possession or control of : YIELD <few leaders willingly ~ power> — **re·lin·quish·ment** \-mənt\ *n*
syn RELINQUISH, YIELD, RESIGN, SURRENDER, ABANDON, WAIVE *shared meaning element* : to give up completely. RELINQUISH is likely to stress regretful emotion as involved in giving something up <he had let something go . . . : something very precious, that he could not consciously have *relinquished* —Willa Cather> YIELD implies concession or compliance or submission to force <*yield* not thy neck to fortune's yoke —Shak.> <unwilling to *yield* or share their privileges> RESIGN emphasizes voluntary and usually formal relinquishment or sacrifice without a struggle <*resign* a position> and may connote acceptance of the inevitable <*resigned* to the loss of his hair> SURRENDER usually implies the existence of external compulsion or demands and commonly presupposes some degree of antecedent resistance <he *surrendered* to his daughter's pleas for a car of her own> ABANDON stresses finality and completeness in giving up <*abandoning* standards that seem outmoded> <*abandoned* the dance and went for a swim> WAIVE implies essentially voluntary conceding or forgoing <*waive* a right> ***ant*** keep
rel·i·quary \ˈrel-ə-ˌkwer-ē\ *n, pl* **-quar·ies** [F *reliquaire,* fr. ML *reliquiarium,* fr. *reliquia* relic — more at RELIC] : a container or shrine in which sacred relics are kept
re·lique \ri-ˈlēk, ˈrel-ik\ *archaic var of* RELIC
re·liq·ui·ae \ri-ˈlik-wē-ˌī, -wē-ˌē\ *n pl* [L — more at RELIC] : remains of the dead : RELICS
[1]**rel·ish** \ˈrel-ish\ *n* [alter. of ME *reles* taste, fr. OF, something left behind, release, fr. *relessier* to release] **1 :** characteristic flavor; *esp* : pleasing or zestful flavor **2 :** a quantity just sufficient to flavor or characterize : TRACE **3 a :** enjoyment of or delight in something that satisfies one's tastes, inclinations, or desires <eat with ~> **b :** a strong liking : INCLINATION <a boy with little ~ for sports> **4 a :** something adding a zestful flavor; *esp* : a highly seasoned sauce (as of pickles or mustard) eaten with other food to add flavor **b :** APPETIZER, HORS D'OEUVRE ***syn*** see TASTE
[2]**relish** *vt* **1 :** to add relish to **2 :** to be pleased or gratified by : ENJOY **3 :** to eat or drink with pleasure **4 :** to appreciate with taste and discernment ~ *vi* : to have a characteristic or pleasing taste — **rel·ish·able** \-ə-bəl\ *adj*
re·live \(ˈ)rē-ˈliv\ *vt* : to live over again; *esp* : to experience again in the imagination ~ *vi* : to live again
re·lo·cate \(ˈ)rē-ˈlō-ˌkāt, ˌrē-lō-ˈ\ *vt* : to locate again : establish or lay out in a new place ~ *vi* : to move to a new location — **re·lo·ca·tion** \ˌrē-lō-ˈkā-shən\ *n*
re·lo·cat·ee \ˌrē-lə-ˌkāt-ˈē, ˌrē-ˌlō-kə-ˈtē\ *n* : one who moves to a new location : one that is relocated
re·lu·cent \ri-ˈlüs-ᵊnt\ *adj* [L *relucent-, relucens,* pp. of *relucēre* to shine back, fr. *re-* + *lucēre* to shine — more at LIGHT] : reflecting light : SHINING
re·luct \ri-ˈləkt\ *vi* [L *reluctari*] : to feel or show repugnance or opposition : REVOLT
re·luc·tance \ri-ˈlək-tən(t)s\ *n* **1 :** the quality or state of being reluctant **2 :** the opposition offered by a magnetic substance to magnetic flux; *specif* : the ratio of the magnetic potential difference to the corresponding flux
re·luc·tan·cy \-tən-sē\ *n* : RELUCTANCE
re·luc·tant \ri-ˈlək-tənt\ *adj* [L *reluctant-, reluctans,* prp. of *reluctari* to struggle against, fr. *re-* + *luctari* to struggle — more at LOCK] **1 :** struggling against : OPPOSING **2 :** holding back : AVERSE, UNWILLING <~ to condemn him> ***syn*** see DISINCLINED — **re·luc·tant·ly** *adv*
re·luc·tate \ri-ˈlək-ˌtāt\ *vi* **-tat·ed; -tat·ing :** to show reluctance — **re·luc·ta·tion** \ri-ˌlək-ˈtā-shən, ˌrē-\ *n*
re·luc·tiv·i·ty \ri-ˌlək-ˈtiv-ət-ē, ˌrē-\ *n* [*reluct*ance + *-ivity* (as in *conductivity*)] : the reciprocal of magnetic permeability
re·lume \(ˈ)rē-ˈlüm\ *vt* **re·lumed; re·lum·ing** [irreg. fr. LL *reluminare*] : to light or light up again : REKINDLE
re·lu·mine \-ˈlü-mən\ *vt* **-mined; -min·ing** [LL *reluminare,* fr. L *re-* + *luminare* to light up — more at ILLUMINATE] : RELUME
re·ly \ri-ˈlī\ *vi* **re·lied; re·ly·ing** [ME *relien* to rally, fr. MF *relier* to connect, rally, fr. L *religare* to tie back, fr. *re-* + *ligare* to tie — more at LIGATURE] **1 :** to have confidence based on experience <her husband was a man she could ~ on> **2 :** to be dependent <they ~ on a spring for their water> — **re·li·er** \-ˈlī(-ə)r\ *n*
syn RELY, TRUST, DEPEND, COUNT, RECKON *shared meaning element* : to place full confidence
rem *n* [*r*oentgen *e*quivalent *m*an] : the dosage of an ionizing radiation that will cause the same biological effect as one roentgen of X-ray or gamma-ray dosage
REM \ˈrem\ *n* : RAPID EYE MOVEMENT
[1]**re·main** \ri-ˈmān\ *vi* [ME *remainen,* fr. MF *remaindre,* fr. L *remanēre,* fr. *re-* + *manēre* to remain — more at MANSION] **1 a :** to be a part not destroyed, taken, or used up <only a few ruins ~> **b :** to be something yet to be shown, done, or treated <it ~*s* to be seen> **2 :** to stay in the same place or with the same person or group; *specif* : to stay behind **3 :** to continue unchanged <the fact ~*s* that nothing can be done> ***syn*** see STAY
[2]**remain** *n* **1** *obs* : STAY **2 :** a remaining part or trace — usu. used in pl. <threw away the ~*s* of the meal> **3** *pl* **:** writings left unpublished at a writer's death **4** *pl* **:** a dead body
[1]**re·main·der** \ri-ˈmān-dər\ *n* [ME, fr. AF, fr. MF *remaindre*] **1 :** an interest or estate in property that follows and is dependent upon the termination of a prior intervening possessory estate created at the same time by the same instrument **2 a :** a remaining group, part, or trace **b (1) :** the number left after a subtraction **(2) :** the final undivided part after division that is less or of lower degree than the divisor **3 :** a book sold at a reduced price by the publisher after sales have slowed
[2]**remainder** *adj* : LEFTOVER, REMAINING
[3]**remainder** *vt* **re·main·dered; re·main·der·ing** \-d(ə-)riŋ\ **:** to dispose of as remainders
[1]**re·make** \(ˈ)rē-ˈmāk\ *vt* **-made** \-ˈmād\; **-mak·ing :** to make anew or in a different form
[2]**re·make** \ˈrē-ˌmāk\ *n* : one that is remade; *esp* : a new version of a motion picture
re·man \(ˈ)rē-ˈman\ *vt* **1 :** to man again or anew **2 :** to imbue with courage again
re·mand \ri-ˈmand\ *vt* [ME *remaunden,* fr. MF *remander,* fr. LL *remandare* to send back word, fr. L *re-* + *mandare* to order — more at MANDATE] : to order back: as **a :** to send back (a case) to another court or agency for further action **b :** to return to custody pending trial or for further detention — **remand** *n*
re·ma·nence \ˈrem-ə-nən(t)s, ri-ˈmā-\ *n* : the magnetic induction remaining in a magnetized substance when the magnetizing force has become zero
re·ma·nent \-nənt\ *adj* [ME, fr. L *remanent-, remanens,* prp. of *remanēre* to remain] **1 :** RESIDUAL, REMAINING **2 :** of, relating to, or characterized by remanence
re·man·u·fac·ture \(ˌ)rē-ˌman-(y)ə-ˈfak-chər\ *vt* : to manufacture (as produce or used material) into a new product <~ tomatoes in making sauces> <~ carburetors> — **remanufacture** *n* — **re·man·u·fac·tur·er** \-chər-ər\ *n*
re·map \(ˈ)rē-ˈmap\ *vt* : to map again or anew; *also* : to lay out in a new pattern <~ a congressional district> <~ an expressway>
[1]**re·mark** \ri-ˈmärk\ *vb* [F *remarquer,* fr. MF, fr. *re-* + *marquer* to mark — more at MARQUE] *vt* **1 :** to take notice of : OBSERVE **2 :** to express as an observation or comment : SAY ~ *vi* : to notice something and comment thereon — used with *on* or *upon*
syn REMARK, COMMENT, COMMENTATE, ANIMADVERT *shared meaning element* : to make observations and pass on one's judgment
[2]**remark** *n* **1 :** the act of remarking : NOTICE **2 :** mention of that which deserves attention or notice **3 :** an expression of opinion or judgment
re·mark·able \ri-ˈmär-kə-bəl\ *adj* : worthy of being or likely to be noticed esp. as being uncommon or extraordinary ***syn*** see NOTICEABLE — **re·mark·able·ness** *n* — **re·mark·ably** \-blē\ *adv*
re·marque \ri-ˈmärk\ *n* [F *remarque* remark, note, fr. MF, fr. *remarquer*] **1 :** a drawn, etched, or incised scribble or sketch done on the margin of a plate or stone and removed before the regular printing **2 :** a proof taken before remarques have been removed
re·match \(ˈ)rē-ˈmach, ˈrē-ˌ\ *n* : a second match between the same contestants or teams
re·me·di·a·ble \ri-ˈmēd-ē-ə-bəl\ *adj* : capable of being remedied — **re·me·di·a·ble·ness** *n* — **re·me·di·a·bly** \-blē\ *adv*
re·me·di·al \ri-ˈmēd-ē-əl\ *adj* **1 :** intended as a remedy **2 :** concerned with the correction of faulty study habits and the rais-

ing of a pupil's general competence <~ reading courses> — **re·me·di·al·ly** \-ə-lē\ *adv*

remediate *adj, obs* : REMEDIAL

re·me·di·a·tion \ri-ˌmēd-ē-ˈā-shən\ *n* : the act or process of remedying <~ of reading problems>

rem·e·di·less \ˈrem-əd-ē-ləs\ *adj* **1** : having no remedy : IRREMEDIABLE **2** : having no legal remedy — **rem·e·di·less·ly** *adv*

[1]rem·e·dy \ˈrem-əd-ē\ *n, pl* **-dies** [ME *remedie,* fr. AF, fr. L *remedium,* fr. *re-* + *mederi* to heal — more at MEDICAL] **1** : a medicine, application, or treatment that relieves or cures a disease **2** : something that corrects or counteracts an evil **3** : the legal means to recover a right or to prevent or obtain redress for a wrong

[2]remedy *vt* **-died; -dy·ing** : to provide or serve as a remedy for : RELIEVE ***syn*** see CURE, CORRECT

re·mem·ber \ri-ˈmem-bər\ *vb* **re·mem·bered; re·mem·ber·ing** \-b(ə-)riŋ\ [ME *remembren,* fr. MF *remembrer,* fr. LL *rememorari,* fr. L *re-* + LL *memorari* to be mindful of, fr. L *memor* mindful — more at MEMORY] *vt* **1** : to bring to mind or think of again <~*s* the old days> **2** *archaic* **a** : BETHINK **b** : REMIND **3 a** : to keep in mind for attention or consideration <~*s* friends at Christmas> **b** : REWARD <was ~*ed* in the will> **4** : to retain in the memory <~ the facts until the test is over> **5** : to convey greetings from **6** : RECORD, COMMEMORATE ~ *vi* **1** : to exercise or have the power of memory **2** : to have a recollection or remembrance — **re·mem·ber·abil·i·ty** \-ˌmem-b(ə-)rə-ˈbil-ət-ē\ *n* — **re·mem·ber·able** \-ˈmem-b(ə-)rə-bəl\ *adj* — **re·mem·ber·er** \-bər-ər\ *n*

syn REMEMBER, RECOLLECT, RECALL, REMIND, REMINISCE *shared meaning element* : to bring an image or idea from the past into the mind ***ant*** forget

re·mem·brance \ri-ˈmem-brən(t)s *also* -bə-rən(t)s\ *n* **1** : the state of bearing in mind <occupation troops kept them in ~ of their defeat> **2 a** : the ability to remember : MEMORY **b** : the period over which one's memory extends **3** : an act of recalling to mind <~ of the offense angered him all over again> **4** : a memory of a person, thing, or event <had only a dim ~ of that night> **5 a** : something that serves to keep in or bring to mind : REMINDER **b** : COMMEMORATION, MEMORIAL **c** : a greeting or gift recalling or expressing friendship or affection ***syn*** see MEMORY

re·mem·branc·er \ri-ˈmem-brən-sər\ *n* : one that reminds; *esp, cap* : one of several English officials having originally the duty of bringing a matter to the attention of the proper authority

Remembrance Sunday *n* : a Sunday that is usu. closest to November 11 and that in Great Britain is set aside in commemoration of the end of hostilities in 1918 and 1945 — compare VETERANS DAY

re·mex \ˈrē-ˌmeks\ *n, pl* **rem·i·ges** \ˈrem-ə-ˌjēz\ [NL *remig-, remex,* fr. L, oarsman, fr. *remus* oar + *agere* to drive — more at ROW, AGENT] : a primary or secondary quill feather of the wing of a bird — **re·mi·gial** \ri-ˈmij-(ē-)əl\ *adj*

re·mil·i·ta·rize \(ˈ)rē-ˈmil-ə-tə-ˌrīz\ *vt* : to equip again with military forces and installations — **re·mil·i·ta·ri·za·tion** \(ˌ)rē-ˌmil-ət-ə-rə-ˈzā-shən\ *n*

re·mind \ri-ˈmīnd\ *vt* : to put in mind of something : cause to remember <the view ~*ed* him of his old home> ***syn*** see REMEMBER — **re·mind·er** *n*

re·mind·ful \-ˈmīn(d)-fəl\ *adj* **1** : MINDFUL **2** : tending to remind : SUGGESTIVE, EVOCATIVE

rem·i·nisce \ˌrem-ə-ˈnis\ *vi* **-nisced; -nisc·ing** [back-formation fr. *reminiscence*] : to indulge in reminiscence ***syn*** see REMEMBER

rem·i·nis·cence \-ˈnis-ᵊn(t)s\ *n* **1** : apprehension of a Platonic idea as if it had been known in a previous existence **2 a** : recall to mind of a long-forgotten experience or fact **b** : the process or practice of thinking or telling about past experiences **3 a** : a remembered experience **b** : an account of a memorable experience — often used in pl. <published the ~*s* of the old settler> **4** : something so like another as to be regarded as an unconscious repetition, imitation, or survival ***syn*** see MEMORY

rem·i·nis·cent \-ᵊnt\ *adj* [L *reminiscent-, reminiscens,* prp. of *reminisci* to remember, fr. *re-* + *-minisci* (akin to L *ment-, mens* mind) — more at MIND] **1** : of the character of or relating to reminiscence **2** : marked by or given to reminiscence **3** : tending to remind one (as of something seen or known before) : SUGGESTIVE <a technology ~ of the Stone Age> — **rem·i·nis·cent·ly** *adv*

rem·i·nis·cen·tial \ˌrem-ə-(ˌ)nis-ˈen-chəl\ *adj* : REMINISCENT

re·mint \(ˈ)rē-ˈmint\ *vt* : to melt down (old or worn coin) and make into new coin

re·mise \ri-ˈmīz\ *vt* **re·mised; re·mis·ing** [ME *remisen,* fr. MF *remis,* pp. of *remettre* to put back, fr. L *remittere* to send back] : to give, grant, or release a claim to : DEED

re·miss \ri-ˈmis\ *adj* [ME, fr. L *remissus,* fr. pp. of *remittere* to send back, relax] **1** : negligent in the performance of work or duty : CARELESS <he would be ~ if he failed to report the accident> **2** : showing neglect or inattention : LAX <service was ~ in most of the hotels> ***syn*** see NEGLIGENT — **re·miss·ly** *adv* — **re·miss·ness** *n*

re·mis·si·ble \ri-ˈmis-ə-bəl\ *adj* : capable of being forgiven <~ sins> — **re·mis·si·bly** \-blē\ *adv*

re·mis·sion \ri-ˈmish-ən\ *n* **1** : the act or process of remitting **2** : a state or period during which something (as symptoms) is remitted

[1]re·mit \ri-ˈmit\ *vb* **re·mit·ted; re·mit·ting** [ME *remitten,* fr. L *remittere* to send back, fr. *re-* + *mittere* to send — more at SMITE] *vt* **1 a** : to release from the guilt or penalty of <~ sins> **b** : to refrain from exacting <~ a tax> **c** : to cancel or refrain from inflicting <~ the penalty of loss of pay> **d** : to give relief from (suffering) **2 a** : to lay aside (a mood or disposition) partly or wholly **b** : to desist from (an activity) **c** : to let (as attention or diligence) slacken : RELAX **3** : to submit or refer for consideration, judgment, decision, or action; *specif* : REMAND **4** : to restore or consign to a former status or condition **5** : POSTPONE, DEFER **6** : to send (money) to a person or place esp. in payment of a demand, account, or draft ~ *vi* **1 a** : to abate in force or intensity : MODERATE **b** *of a disease or abnormality* : to abate symptoms for a period **2** : to send money (as in payment) — **re·mit·ment** \-ˈmit-mənt\ *n* — **re·mit·ta·ble** \-ˈmit-ə-bəl\ *adj* — **re·mit·ter** *n*

[2]re·mit \ri-ˈmit, ˈrē-ˌ\ *n* **1** : an act of remitting **2** : something remitted to another person or authority

re·mit·tal \ri-ˈmit-ᵊl\ *n* : REMISSION

re·mit·tance \ri-ˈmit-ᵊn(t)s\ *n* **1 a** : a sum of money remitted **b** : an instrument by which money is remitted **2** : transmittal of money (as to a distant place)

remittance man *n* : a person living abroad on remittances from home

re·mit·tent \ri-ˈmit-ᵊnt\ *adj* [L *remittent-, remittens,* prp. of *remittere*] *of a disease* : marked by alternating periods of abatement and increase of symptoms — **re·mit·tent·ly** *adv*

[1]rem·nant \ˈrem-nənt\ *n* [ME, contr. of *remenant,* fr. MF, fr. prp. of *remenoir* to remain, fr. L *remanēre* — more at REMAIN] **1 a** : a usu. small part, member, or trace remaining **b** : a small surviving group — often used in pl. **2** : an unsold or unused end of piece goods

[2]remnant *adj* : still remaining

re·mod·el \(ˈ)rē-ˈmäd-ᵊl\ *vt* : to alter the structure of : RECONSTRUCT <~ an old house>

re·mon·e·tize \(ˈ)rē-ˈmän-ə-ˌtīz, -ˈmən-\ *vt* : to restore to use as legal tender <~ silver> — **re·mon·e·ti·za·tion** \(ˌ)rē-ˌmän-ət-ə-ˈzā-shən, -ˌmən-\ *n*

re·mon·strance \ri-ˈmän(t)-strən(t)s\ *n* **1** *archaic* : REPRESENTATION, DEMONSTRATION; *specif* : a document formally stating points of opposition or grievance **2** : an act or instance of remonstrating

re·mon·strant \-strənt\ *adj* : vigorously objecting or opposing — **remonstrant** *n* — **re·mon·strant·ly** *adv*

re·mon·strate \ri-ˈmän-ˌstrāt *also* ˈrem-ən-\ *vb* **-strat·ed; -strat·ing** [ML *remonstratus,* pp. of *remonstrare* to demonstrate, fr. L *re-* + *monstrare* to show — more at MUSTER] *vt* : to say or plead in protest, reproof, or opposition ~ *vi* : to present and urge reasons in opposition : EXPOSTULATE ***syn*** see OBJECT — **re·mon·stra·tion** \ri-ˌmän-ˈstrā-shən, ˌrem-ən-\ *n* — **re·mon·stra·tive** \ri-ˈmän(t)-strət-iv\ *adj* — **re·mon·stra·tive·ly** *adv* — **re·mon·stra·tor** \ri-ˈmän-ˌstrāt-ər *also* ˈrem-ən-\ *n*

rem·o·ra \ˈrem-ə-rə *also* ri-ˈmōr-ə *or* -ˈmȯr-\ *n* [L, lit., delay, fr. *remorari* to delay, fr. *re-* + *morari* to delay — more at MORATORIUM] **1** : any of several specialized fishes (of *Echeneis* and related genera) that have the anterior dorsal fin converted into a suctorial disk on the head by means of which they cling to other fishes and to ships **2** : HINDRANCE, DRAG — **rem·o·rid** \ˈrem-ə-rəd\ *adj*

remora 1

re·morse \ri-ˈmȯ(ə)rs\ *n* [ME, fr. MF *remors,* fr. ML *remorsus,* fr. LL, act of biting again, fr. L *remorsus,* pp. of *remordēre* to bite again, fr. *re-* + *mordēre* to bite — more at SMART] **1** : a gnawing distress arising from a sense of guilt for past wrongs : SELF-REPROACH **2** *obs* : COMPASSION ***syn*** see PENITENCE

re·morse·ful \-ˈmȯrs-fəl\ *adj* : motivated or marked by remorse — **re·morse·ful·ly** \-fə-lē\ *adv* — **re·morse·ful·ness** *n*

re·morse·less \-ˈmȯr-sləs\ *adj* **1** : having no remorse : MERCILESS <~ cruelty> **2** : PERSISTENT, INDEFATIGABLE — **re·morse·less·ly** *adv* — **re·morse·less·ness** *n*

re·mote \ri-ˈmōt\ *adj* **re·mot·er; -est** [L *remotus,* fr. pp. of *removēre* to remove] **1** : separated by great intervals **2** : far removed in space, time, or relation : DIVERGENT <the ~ past> <comments ~ from the truth> **3** : OUT-OF-THE-WAY, SECLUDED **4** : acting on or controlling indirectly or from a distance <~ computer operation> **5** : not arising from a primary or proximate action **6** : small in degree : SLIGHT <a ~ possibility> **7** : distant in manner : ALOOF ***syn*** see DISTANT — **re·mote·ly** *adv* — **re·mote·ness** *n*

re·mo·tion \ri-ˈmō-shən\ *n* **1** : the quality or state of being remote **2** : the act of removing : REMOVAL **3** *obs* : DEPARTURE

[1]re·mount \(ˈ)rē-ˈmau̇nt\ *vb* [ME *remounten,* partly fr. *re-* + *mounten* to mount, partly fr. MF *remonter,* fr. *re-* + *monter* to mount] *vt* **1** : to mount (something) again <~ a picture> **2** : to furnish remounts to ~ *vi* **1** : to mount again **2** : REVERT

[2]re·mount \ˈrē-ˌmau̇nt, (ˈ)rē-ˈ\ *n* : a fresh horse to replace one no longer available

re·mov·able \ri-ˈmü-və-bəl\ *adj* : capable of being removed — **re·mov·abil·i·ty** \-ˌmü-və-ˈbil-ət-ē\ *n* — **re·mov·able·ness** \-ˈmü-və-bəl-nəs\ *n* — **re·mov·ably** \-blē\ *adv*

re·mov·al \ri-ˈmü-vəl\ *n* : the act or process of removing : the fact of being removed

[1]re·move \ri-ˈmüv\ *vb* **re·moved; re·mov·ing** [ME *removen,* fr. OF *removoir,* fr. L *removēre,* fr. *re-* + *movēre* to move] *vt* **1 a** : to change the location, position, station, or residence of <~ soldiers to the front> **b** : to transfer (a legal proceeding) from one court to another **2** : to move by lifting, pushing aside, or taking away or off <~*s* his hat in church> **3** : to dismiss from office **4** : to get rid of : ELIMINATE <~ a tumor surgically> ~ *vi* **1** : to change location, station, or residence <*removing* from the city to the suburbs> **2** : to go away **3** : to be capable of being removed — **re·mov·er** *n*

[2]remove *n* **1** : REMOVAL; *specif* : MOVE 2c **2 a** : a distance or interval separating one person or thing from another **b** : a degree or stage of separation

re·moved *adj* **1 a** : distant in degree of relationship **b** : of a younger or older generation <a second cousin's child is a second cousin once ~> **2** : separate or remote in space, time, or character ***syn*** see DISTANT

REM sleep *n* : PARADOXICAL SLEEP

re·mu·da \ri-ˈm(y)üd-ə\ *n* [AmerSp, relay of horses, fr. Sp, exchange] : the herd of horses from which those to be used for the day are chosen

re·mu·ner·ate \ri-ˈmyü-nə-ˌrāt\ *vt* **-at·ed; -at·ing** [L *remuneratus,* pp. of *remunerare* to recompense, fr. *re-* + *munerare* to give, fr. *muner-, munus* gift — more at MEAN] **1** : to pay an equivalent for

<his services were generously *remunerated*> **2 :** to pay an equivalent to for a service, loss, or expense : RECOMPENSE ***syn*** see PAY — **re·mu·ner·a·tor** \-ˌrāt-ər\ *n* — **re·mu·ner·a·to·ry** \-rə-ˌtōr-ē, -ˌtȯr-\ *adj*

re·mu·ner·a·tion \ri-ˌmyü-nə-ˈrā-shən\ *n* **1 :** an act or fact of remunerating **2 :** something that remunerates : RECOMPENSE, PAY

re·mu·ner·a·tive \ri-ˈmyü-nə-rət-iv, -ˌrāt-\ *adj* **1 :** serving to remunerate **2 :** providing remuneration : PROFITABLE — **re·mu·ner·a·tive·ly** *adv* — **re·mu·ner·a·tive·ness** *n*

Re·mus \ˈrē-məs\ *n* [L] : a son of Mars slain by his twin brother Romulus

re·nais·sance \ˌren-ə-ˈsän(t)s, -ˈzän(t)s, -ˈsäⁿs, -ˈzäⁿs, *chiefly Brit* ri-ˈnās-ᵊn(t)s\ *n, often attrib* [F, fr. MF, rebirth, fr. *renaistre* to be born again, fr. L *renasci*, fr. *re-* + *nasci* to be born — more at NATION] **1** *cap* **a :** the transitional movement in Europe between medieval and modern times beginning in the 14th century in Italy, lasting into the 17th century, and marked by a humanistic revival of classical influence expressed in a flowering of the arts and literature and by the beginnings of modern science **b :** the period of the Renaissance **c :** the neoclassic style of architecture prevailing during the Renaissance **2** *often cap* **:** a movement or period of vigorous artistic and intellectual activity **3 :** REBIRTH, REVIVAL

Renaissance man *n* : a person who has wide interests and is expert in several areas

re·nal \ˈrēn-ᵊl\ *adj* [F or LL; F *rénal*, fr. LL *renalis*, fr. L *renes* kidneys] : relating to, involving, or located in the region of the kidneys : NEPHRITIC

re·na·scence \ri-ˈnas-ᵊn(t)s, -ˈnās-\ *n, often cap* : RENAISSANCE

re·na·scent \-ᵊnt\ *adj* [L *renascent-, renascens*, prp. of *renasci*] : rising again into being or vigor

re·na·ture \(ˈ)rē-ˈnā-chər\ *vt* **re·na·tured; re·na·tur·ing** \-ˈnāch-(ə-)riŋ\ [*re-* + *-nature* (as in *denature*)] : to restore (as a denatured protein) to an original or normal condition — **re·na·tur·ation** \(ˌ)rē-ˌnā-chə-ˈrā-shən\ *n*

ren·con·tre \räⁿ-kōⁿtrᵊ, ren-ˈkänt-ər\ *or* **ren·coun·ter** \ren-ˈkau̇nt-ər\ *n* [*rencounter* fr. MF *rencontre*, fr. *rencontrer*; *rencontre* fr. F] **1 :** a hostile meeting or a contest between forces or individuals : COMBAT **2 :** a casual meeting

ren·coun·ter \ren-ˈkau̇nt-ər\ *vt* [MF *rencontrer* to meet by chance or in hostility, fr. *re-* + *encontrer* to encounter] : to meet casually

rend \ˈrend\ *vb* **rent** \ˈrent\; **rend·ing** [ME *renden*, fr. OE *rendan*; akin to OFris *renda* to tear, Skt *randhra* hole] *vt* **1 :** to remove from place by violence : WREST **2 :** to split or tear apart or in pieces by violence **3 :** to tear (the hair or clothing) as a sign of anger, grief, or despair **4 a :** to lacerate mentally or emotionally **b :** to pierce with sound **c :** to divide (as a nation) into contesting factions ~ *vi* **1 :** to perform an act of tearing or splitting **2 :** to become torn or split ***syn*** see TEAR

[1]ren·der \ˈren-dər\ *vb* **ren·dered; ren·der·ing** \-d(ə-)riŋ\ [ME *rendren*, fr. MF *rendre* to give back, yield, fr. (assumed) VL *rendere*, alter. of L *reddere*, partly fr. *re-* + *dare* to give & partly fr. *re-* + *-dere* to put — more at DATE, DO] *vt* **1 a :** to melt down : extract by melting <~ lard> **b :** to treat so as to convert into industrial fats and oils or fertilizer **2 a :** to transmit to another : DELIVER **b :** to give up : YIELD **c :** to furnish for consideration, approval, or information: as **(1) :** to hand down (a legal judgment) **(2) :** to agree upon and report (a verdict) **3 a :** to give in return or retribution **b (1) :** to give back : RESTORE **(2) :** REFLECT, ECHO **c :** to give in acknowledgment of dependence or obligation : PAY **d :** to do (a service) for another **4 a (1) :** to cause to be or become : MAKE <enough rainfall . . . to ~ irrigation unnecessary —P. E. James> <~ a person helpless> **(2) :** IMPART **b (1) :** to reproduce or represent by artistic or verbal means : DEPICT **(2) :** to give a performance of **(3) :** to produce a copy or version of <the documents are ~*ed* in the original French> **(4) :** to execute the motions of <~ a salute> **c :** TRANSLATE **5 :** to direct the execution of : ADMINISTER <~ justice> **6 :** to apply a coat of plaster or cement directly to ~ *vi* : to give recompense — **ren·der·able** \-d(ə-)rə-bəl\ *adj* — **ren·der·er** \-dər-ər\ *n*

[2]render *n* : a return esp. in goods or services due from a feudal tenant to his lord

[1]ren·dez·vous \ˈrän-di-ˌvü, -dā-\ *n, pl* **ren·dez·vous** \-ˌvüz\ [MF, fr. *rendez vous* present yourselves] **1 a :** a place appointed for assembling or meeting **b :** a place of popular resort : HAUNT **2 :** a meeting at an appointed place and time **3 :** the process of bringing two spacecraft together

[2]rendezvous *vb* **ren·dez·voused** \-ˌvüd\; **ren·dez·vous·ing** \-ˌvü-iŋ\; **ren·dez·vouses** \-ˌvüz\ *vi* : to come together at a rendezvous ~ *vt* **1 :** to bring together at a rendezvous **2 :** to meet at a rendezvous

ren·di·tion \ren-ˈdish-ən\ *n* [obs. F, fr. MF, alter. of *reddition*, fr. LL *reddition-, redditio*, fr. L *redditus*, pp. of *reddere*] : the act or result of rendering: as **a :** SURRENDER **b :** TRANSLATION **c :** PERFORMANCE, INTERPRETATION

ren·dzi·na \ren-ˈjē-nə\ *n* [Pol *rędzina* rich limy soil] : a dark grayish brown intrazonal soil developed in grassy regions of high to moderate humidity from soft calcareous marl or chalk

[1]ren·e·gade \ˈren-i-ˌgād\ *n* [Sp *renegado*, fr. ML *renegatus*, fr. pp. of *renegare* to deny, fr. L *re-* + *negare* to deny — more at NEGATE] **1 :** a deserter from one faith, cause, or allegiance to another **2 :** an individual who rejects lawful or conventional behavior

[2]renegade *vi* **-gad·ed; -gad·ing :** to become a renegade

[3]renegade *adj* **1 :** having deserted a faith, cause, or religion for a hostile one **2 :** having rejected tradition : UNCONVENTIONAL

ren·e·ga·do \ˌren-i-ˈgäd-(ˌ)ō, -ˈgād-\ *n, pl* **-does** [Sp] : RENEGADE

re·nege \ri-ˈnig, -ˈneg, -ˈnēg, -ˈnāg\ *vb* **re·neged; re·neg·ing** [ML *renegare*] *vt* : DENY, RENOUNCE ~ *vi* **1** *obs* **:** to make a denial **2 :** REVOKE **3 :** to go back on a promise or commitment — **re·neg·er** *n*

re·ne·go·tia·ble \ˌrē-ni-ˈgō-sh(ē-)ə-bəl\ *adj* : subject to renegotiation

re·ne·go·ti·ate \ˌrē-ni-ˈgō-shē-ˌāt\ *vt* : to negotiate again; *esp* : to readjust by negotiation to eliminate or recover excessive profits — **re·ne·go·ti·a·tion** \ˌrē-ni-ˌgō-s(h)ē-ˈā-shən\ *n*

re·new \ri-ˈn(y)ü\ *vt* **1 :** to make like new : restore to freshness, vigor, or perfection <as we ~ our strength in sleep> **2 :** to make new spiritually : REGENERATE **3 a :** to restore to existence : REVIVE **b :** to make extensive changes in : REBUILD **4 :** to do again : REPEAT **5 :** to begin again : RESUME **6 :** REPLACE, REPLENISH <~ water in a tank> **7 a :** to grant or obtain an extension of or on **b :** to grant or obtain an extension on the loan of <~ a library book> ~ *vi* **1 :** to become new or as new **2 :** to begin again : RESUME **3 :** to make a renewal (as of a lease) — **re·new·abil·i·ty** \-ˌn(y)ü-ə-ˈbil-ət-ē\ *n* — **re·new·ably** \-ˈn(y)ü-ə-blē\ *adv* — **re·new·er** *n*

syn RENEW, RESTORE, REFRESH, RENOVATE, REJUVENATE *shared meaning element* : to make like new

re·new·able \-ˈn(y)ü-ə-bəl\ *adj* : capable of being renewed; *esp* : capable of being replaced by natural ecological cycles or sound management practices

re·new·al \ri-ˈn(y)ü-əl\ *n* **1 :** the act or process of renewing : REPETITION **2 :** the quality or state of being renewed **3 :** something (as a subscription to a magazine) renewed **4 :** something used for renewing; *specif* **:** an expenditure that betters existing fixed assets **5 :** the rebuilding of a large area (as of a city) by a public authority

Renf *abbr* Renfrewshire

reni- *or* **reno-** *comb form* [L *renes* kidneys] : kidney <*reni*form>

re·ni·form \ˈrē-nə-ˌfȯrm, ˈren-ə-\ *adj* [NL *reniformis*, fr. *reni-* + *-formis* -form] : suggesting a kidney in outline

re·nig \ri-ˈnig\ *vi* **re·nigged; re·nig·ging :** RENEGE

re·nin \ˈrē-nən, ˈren-ən\ *n* [ISV, fr. L *renes*] : a proteolytic enzyme of the kidney that plays a major role in the release of angiotensin

re·ni·ten·cy \ˈren-ə-tən-sē, ri-ˈnīt-ᵊn-\ *n* : RESISTANCE, OPPOSITION

re·ni·tent \ˈren-ə-tənt, ri-ˈnīt-ᵊnt\ *adj* [F or L; F *rénitent*, fr. L *renitent-, renitens*, prp. of *reniti* to struggle against, fr. *re-* + *niti* to strive — more at NISUS] **1 :** resisting physical pressure **2 :** resisting constraint or compulsion : RECALCITRANT

ren·net \ˈren-ət\ *n* [ME, fr. (assumed) ME *rennen* to cause to coagulate, fr. OE *gerennan*, fr. *ge-* together + (assumed) OE *rennan* to cause to run; akin to OHG *rennen* to cause to run, OE *rinnan* to run — more at CO-, RUN] **1 a :** the contents of the stomach of an unweaned animal and esp. a calf **b :** the lining membrane of a stomach (as the fourth of a ruminant) used for curdling milk; *also* **:** a preparation of the stomach of animals used for this purpose **2 a :** RENNIN **b :** a substitute for rennin

ren·nin \ˈren-ən\ *n* : an enzyme that coagulates milk and is used in making cheese and junkets; *esp* : one from the mucous membrane of the stomach of a calf

re·no·gram \ˈrē-nə-ˌgram\ *n* : a photographic depiction of the course of renal excretion of a radioactively labeled substance — **re·no·graph·ic** \ˌrē-nə-ˈgraf-ik\ *adj* — **re·nog·ra·phy** \rē-ˈnäg-rə-fē\ *n*

re·nom·i·nate \(ˈ)rē-ˈnäm-ə-ˌnāt\ *vt* : to nominate again esp. for a succeeding term — **re·nom·i·na·tion** \(ˌ)rē-ˌnäm-ə-ˈnā-shən\ *n*

[1]re·nounce \ri-ˈnau̇n(t)s\ *vb* **re·nounced; re·nounc·ing** [ME *renouncen*, fr. MF *renoncer*, fr. L *renuntiare*, fr. *re-* + *nuntiare* to report, fr. *nuntius* messenger] *vt* **1 :** to give up, refuse, or resign usu. by formal declaration <~ his errors> **2 :** to refuse to follow, obey, or recognize any further : REPUDIATE <~ the authority of the church> **3 :** to fail to follow with a card from (the suit led) ~ *vi* : to make a renounce or renunciation ***syn* 1** see ABDICATE ***ant*** arrogate **2** see ABJURE ***ant*** confess, claim — **re·nounce·ment** \-ˈnau̇n(t)-smənt\ *n* — **re·nounc·er** *n*

[2]re·nounce \ri-ˈnau̇n(t)s, ˈrē-ˌ\ *n* : failure to follow suit in a card game

ren·o·vate \ˈren-ə-ˌvāt\ *vt* **-vat·ed; -vat·ing** [L *renovatus*, pp. of *renovare*, fr. *re-* + *novare* to make new, fr. *novus* new — more at NEW] **1 :** to restore to life, vigor, or activity : REVIVE <the church was *renovated* by a new ecumenical spirit> **2 :** to restore to a former better state (as by cleaning, repairing, or rebuilding) ***syn*** see RENEW — **ren·o·va·tion** \ˌren-ə-ˈvā-shən\ *n* — **ren·o·va·tor** \ˈren-ə-ˌvāt-ər\ *n*

[1]re·nown \ri-ˈnau̇n\ *n* [ME, fr. MF *renon*, fr. OF, fr. *renomer* to celebrate, fr. *re-* + *nomer* to name, fr. L *nominare*, fr. *nomin-, nomen* name — more at NAME] **1 :** a state of being widely acclaimed and highly honored : FAME **2** *obs* **:** REPORT, RUMOR

[2]renown *vt* : to give renown to

re·nowned *adj* : having renown : CELEBRATED ***syn*** see FAMOUS

[1]rent \ˈrent\ *n* [ME *rente*, fr. OF, income from a property, fr. (assumed) VL *rendita*, fr. fem. of *renditus*, pp. of *rendere* to yield — more at RENDER] **1 :** property (as a house) rented or for rent **2 a :** a usu. fixed periodical return made by a tenant or occupant of property to the owner for the possession and use thereof; *esp* : an agreed sum paid at fixed intervals by a tenant to his landlord for the use of land or its appendages **b :** the amount paid by a hirer of personal property to the owner for the use thereof **3 a :** the portion of the income of an economy (as of a nation) attributable to land as a factor of production in addition to capital and labor **b :** ECONOMIC RENT — **for rent :** available for use or service in return for payment

[2]rent *vt* **1 :** to take and hold under an agreement to pay rent **2 :** to grant the possession and enjoyment of for rent ~ *vi* **1 :** to be for rent **2 a :** to obtain the possession and use of a place or article for rent **b :** to allow the possession and use of property for rent ***syn*** see HIRE — **rent·abil·i·ty** \ˌrent-ə-ˈbil-ət-ē\ *n* — **rent·able** \ˈrent-ə-bəl\ *adj*

[3]rent *past of* REND

[4]rent *n* [E dial. *rent* (to rend)] **1 :** an opening made by or as if by rending **2 :** a split in a party or organized group : SCHISM **3 :** an act or instance of rending
rent–a–car \ˈrent-ə-ˌkär\ *n* [fr. the imper. phrase *rent a car*] : a rented car
[1]rent·al \ˈrent-ᵊl\ *n* **1 :** an amount paid or collected as rent **2 :** something that is rented **3 :** an act of renting **4 :** a business that rents something
[2]rental *adj* **1 a :** of or relating to rent **b :** available for rent **2 :** dealing in rental property <a ~ agency>
rental library *n* : a commercially operated library (as in a store) that lends books at a fixed charge per book per day — called also *lending library*
rent control *n* : government regulation of the amount charged as rent for housing and often also of eviction
rente \ˈrä^n(n)t\ *n* [F] **1 :** annual income under French law resembling an annuity **2 a :** interest payable by the French and other European governments on the consolidated debt **b :** a government security yielding rente
rent·er \ˈrent-ər\ *n* : one that rents; *specif* : the lessee or tenant of property
ren·tier \rä^n-tyā\ *n* [F, fr. OF, fr. *rente*] **1 :** one who owns rentes **2 :** a person who receives a fixed income (as from land or stocks)
rent strike *n* : a refusal by a group of tenants to pay rent (as in protest against high rates)
re·num·ber \(ˈ)rē-ˈnəm-bər\ *vt* : to number again or differently
re·nun·ci·a·tion \ri-ˌnən(t)-sē-ˈā-shən\ *n* [ME, fr. L *renuntiation-, renuntiatio*, fr. *renuntiatus*, pp. of *renuntiare*] : the act or practice of renouncing : REPUDIATION; *specif* : ascetic self-denial — **re·nun·ci·a·tive** \ri-ˈnən(t)-sē-ˌāt-iv\ *adj* — **re·nun·ci·a·to·ry** \-sē-ə-ˌtōr-ē, -ˌtȯr-\ *adj*
re·of·fer \(ˈ)rē-ˈȯf-ər, -ˈäf-\ *vt* : to offer (a security issue) for public sale
re·open \(ˈ)rē-ˈō-pən, -ˈōp-ᵊm\ *vt* **1 :** to open again **2 a :** to take up again : RESUME <~ discussion> **b :** to resume discussion or consideration of <~ a contract> **3 :** to begin again ~ *vi* : to open again <school ~*s* in September>
[1]re·or·der \(ˈ)rē-ˈȯrd-ər\ *vt* **1 :** to arrange in a different way **2 :** to give a reorder for ~ *vi* : to place a reorder
[2]reorder *n* : an order like a previous order placed with the same supplier
re·or·ga·ni·za·tion \(ˌ)rē-ˌȯrg-(ə-)nə-ˈzā-shən\ *n* : the act or process of reorganizing : the state of being reorganized; *esp* : the financial reconstruction of a business concern — **re·or·ga·ni·za·tion·al** \-shnəl, -shən-ᵊl\ *adj*
re·or·ga·nize \(ˈ)rē-ˈȯr-gə-ˌnīz\ *vt* : to organize again or anew ~ *vi* : to reorganize something — **re·or·ga·niz·er** *n*
reo·vi·rus \ˌrē-ō-ˈvī-rəs\ *n* [*r*espiratory *e*nteric *o*rphan (i.e. unidentified) *virus*] : any of a group of rather large, widely distributed, and possibly tumorigenic viruses with double-stranded RNA
[1]rep \ˈrep\ *n, slang* : REPUTATION; *esp* : status in a group (as a gang)
[2]rep *or* **repp** \ˈrep\ *n* [F *reps*, modif. of E *ribs*, pl. of *rib*] : a plain-weave fabric with prominent rounded crosswise ribs
[3]rep *n* : REPRESENTATIVE
[4]rep *n* [*r*oentgen *e*quivalent *p*hysical] : the dosage of an ionizing radiation that will develop the same amount of energy upon absorption in human tissue as one roentgen of X-ray or gamma-ray dosage
[5]rep *n* : REPERTORY 2b
[6]rep *abbr* **1** repair **2** report; reporter **3** republic
Rep *abbr* Republican
re·pack·age \(ˈ)rē-ˈpak-ij\ *vt* : to package again or anew; *specif* : to put into a more efficient or attractive form <~ a candidate's public image> — **re·pack·ag·er** *n*
[1]re·pair \ri-ˈpa(ə)r, -ˈpe(ə)r\ *vi* [ME *repairen*, fr. MF *repairier* to go back to one's country, fr. LL *repatriare*, fr. L *re-* + *patria* native country — more at EXPATRIATE] **1 a :** to betake oneself : GO <~*ed* to his home> **b :** RALLY **2** *obs* : RETURN
[2]repair *n* **1 :** the act of repairing : RESORT **2 :** a popular gathering place
[3]repair *vb* [ME *repairen*, fr. MF *reparer*, fr. L *reparare*, fr. *re-* + *parare* to prepare — more at PARE] *vt* **1 a :** to restore by replacing a part or putting together what is torn or broken : FIX <~ a shoe> **b :** to restore to a sound or healthy state : RENEW <~ his strength> **2 :** to make good : compensate for : REMEDY <will ~ his earlier failure> ~ *vi* : to make repairs **syn** see MEND — **re·pair·abil·i·ty** \-ˌpar-ə-ˈbil-ət-ē, -ˌper-\ *n* — **re·pair·able** \-ˈpar-ə-bəl, -ˈper-\ *adj* — **re·pair·er** \-ˈpar-ər, -ˈper-\ *n*
[4]repair *n* **1 a :** the act or process of repairing **b :** an instance or result of repairing **c :** the replacement of destroyed cells or tissues by new formations **2 a :** relative condition with respect to soundness or need of repairing **b :** the state of being in good or sound condition
re·pair·man \ri-ˈpa(ə)r-ˌman, -ˈpe(ə)r-\ *n* : one who repairs; *specif* : one whose occupation is to make repairs in a mechanism
re·pand \ri-ˈpand\ *adj* [L *repandus* bent backward, fr. *re-* + *pandus* bent; akin to ON *fattr* bent backward] : having a slightly undulating margin <a ~ leaf>
rep·a·ra·ble \ˈrep-(ə-)rə-bəl\ *adj* : capable of being repaired
rep·a·ra·tion \ˌrep-ə-ˈrā-shən\ *n* [ME, fr. MF, fr. LL *reparation-, reparatio*, fr. L *reparatus*, pp. of *reparare*] **1 a :** a repairing or keeping in repair **b** *pl* : REPAIRS **2 a :** the act of making amends, offering expiation, or giving satisfaction for a wrong or injury **b :** something done or given as amends or satisfaction **3 :** the payment of damages : INDEMNIFICATION; *specif* : compensation in money or materials payable by a defeated nation for damages to or expenditures sustained by another nation as a result of hostilities with the defeated nation — usu. used in pl.
re·par·a·tive \ri-ˈpar-ət-iv\ *adj* **1 :** of, relating to, or effecting repair **2 :** serving to make amends
rep·ar·tee \ˌrep-ər-ˈtē, -ˌär-, -ˈtā\ *n* [F *repartie*, fr. *repartir* to retort, fr. MF, fr. *re-* + *partir* to divide — more at PART] **1 a :** a quick and witty reply **b :** a succession or interchange of clever retorts : amusing and usu. light sparring with words **2 :** adroitness and cleverness in reply : skill in repartee **syn** see WIT
[1]re·par·ti·tion \ˌrep-ˌär-ˈtish-ən, ˌrē-ˌpär-\ *n* [prob. fr. Sp *repartición*, fr. *repartir* to distribute, fr. *re-* + *partir* to divide, fr. L *partire* — more at PART] : DISTRIBUTION
[2]re·par·ti·tion \ˌrē-ˌpär-ˈtish-ən\ *n* [*re-* + *partition*] : a second or additional dividing or distribution
re·pass \(ˈ)rē-ˈpas\ *vb* [ME *repassen*, fr. MF *repasser*, fr. OF, fr. *re-* + *passer* to pass] *vi* : to pass again esp. in the opposite direction : RETURN ~ *vt* **1 :** to pass through, over, or by again <~ the house> **2 :** to cause to pass again **3 :** to adopt again <~*ed* the resolution> — **re·pas·sage** \-ˈpas-ij\ *n*
[1]re·past \ri-ˈpast, ˈrē-ˌ\ *n* [ME, fr. MF, fr. OF, fr. *repaistre* to feed, fr. *re-* + *paistre* to feed, fr. L *pascere* — more at FOOD] **1 :** something taken as food : MEAL **2 :** the act or time of taking food
[2]re·past \ri-ˈpast\ *vt, obs* : FEED ~ *vi* : to take food : FEAST
re·pa·tri·ate \(ˈ)rē-ˈpā-trē-ˌāt, -ˈpa-\ *vt* **-at·ed; -at·ing** [LL *repatriatus*, pp. of *repatriare* to go back to one's country — more at REPAIR] : to restore or return to the country of origin, allegiance, or citizenship <~ prisoners of war> — **re·pa·tri·ate** \-trē-ət, -trē-ˌāt\ *n* — **re·pa·tri·a·tion** \(ˌ)rē-ˌpā-trē-ˈā-shən, -ˌpa-\ *n*
re·pay \(ˈ)rē-ˈpā\ *vb* **-paid** \-ˈpād\; **-pay·ing** *vt* **1 a :** to pay back : REFUND <~ a loan> **b :** to give or inflict in return or requital <~ evil for evil> **2 :** to make a return payment to : COMPENSATE, REQUITE **3 :** to make requital for : RECOMPENSE <a company which ~*s* hard work> ~ *vi* : to make return payment or requital **syn** see PAY — **re·pay·able** \-ˈpā-ə-bəl\ *adj* — **re·pay·ment** \-ˈpā-mənt\ *n*
re·peal \ri-ˈpē(ə)l\ *vt* [ME *repelen*, fr. MF *repeler*, fr. OF, fr. *re-* + *apeler* to appeal, call] **1 :** to rescind or annul by authoritative act; *esp* : to revoke or abrogate by legislative enactment **2 :** ABANDON, RENOUNCE **3** *obs* : to summon to return : RECALL — **repeal** *n* — **re·peal·able** \-ˈpē-lə-bəl\ *adj*
re·peal·er \ri-ˈpē-lər\ *n* : one that repeals; *specif* : a legislative act that abrogates an earlier act
[1]re·peat \ri-ˈpēt\ *vb* [ME *repeten*, fr. MF *repeter*, fr. L *repetere*, fr. *re-* + *petere* to go to, seek — more at FEATHER] *vt* **1 a :** to say or state again **b :** to say over from memory : RECITE **c :** to say after another **2 a :** to make, do, or perform again <~ an experiment> **b :** to make appear again : REPRODUCE <a program ~*ed* on tape> **c :** to go through or experience again <had to ~ third grade> **3 :** to express or present (oneself) again in the same words, terms, or form ~ *vi* : to say, do, or accomplish something again; *esp* : to vote illegally by casting more than one ballot in an election — **re·peat·abil·i·ty** \-ˌpēt-ə-ˈbil-ət-ē\ *n* — **re·peat·able** \-ˈpēt-ə-bəl\ *adj*
syn 1 REPEAT, ITERATE, REITERATE *shared meaning element* : to say or do again
2 see QUOTE
[2]re·peat \ri-ˈpēt, ˈrē-ˌ\ *n* **1 :** the act of repeating **2 a :** something repeated : REPETITION **b :** a musical passage to be repeated in performance; *also* : a sign placed before and after such a passage **c :** a usu. transcribed repetition of a radio or television program

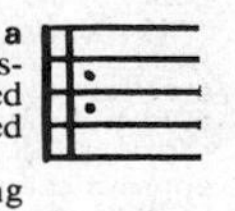

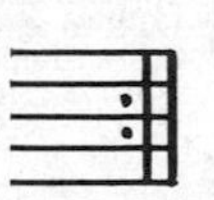

repeats 2b

re·peat·ed \ri-ˈpēt-əd\ *adj* **1 :** renewed or recurring again and again <~ changes of plan> **2 :** said, done, or presented again
re·peat·ed·ly *adv* : again and again
re·peat·er \ri-ˈpēt-ər\ *n* : one that repeats: as **a :** one who relates or recites **b :** a watch or clock with a striking mechanism that upon pressure of a spring will indicate the time in hours or quarters and sometimes minutes **c :** a firearm having a magazine that holds a number of cartridges loaded into the firing chamber automatically by the action of the piece **d :** an habitual violator of the laws **e :** one who votes illegally by casting more than one ballot in an election **f :** a student enrolled in a class or course for a second or subsequent time
re·peat·ing *adj, of a firearm* : designed to fire several bullets rapidly in succession
repeating decimal *n* : a decimal in which after a certain point a particular digit or sequence of digits repeats itself indefinitely — compare TERMINATING DECIMAL
re·pe·chage \ˌrep-ə-ˈshäzh, rə-ˌpesh-ˈäzh\ *n* [F *repêchage* second chance, reexamination for a candidate who has failed, fr. *repêcher* to fish out, rescue, fr. *re-* + *pêcher* to fish, fr. L *piscari* — more at PISCATORY] : a trial heat (as in rowing) in which first-round losers are given another chance to qualify for the semifinals
re·pel \ri-ˈpel\ *vb* **re·pelled; re·pel·ling** [ME *repellen*, fr. L *repellere*, fr. *re-* + *pellere* to drive — more at FELT] *vt* **1 a :** to drive back : REPULSE **b :** to fight against : RESIST **2 :** to turn away : REJECT <*repelled* the insinuation> **3 a :** to drive away : DISCOURAGE <foul words and frowns must not ~ a lover — Shak.> **b :** to be incapable of adhering to, mixing with, taking up, or holding **c :** to force away or apart or tend to do so by mutual action at a distance **4 :** to cause aversion in : DISGUST ~ *vi* : to cause aversion — **re·pel·ler** *n*
re·pel·len·cy \ri-ˈpel-ən-sē\ *n* : the quality or capacity of repelling
[1]re·pel·lent *also* **re·pel·lant** \ri-ˈpel-ənt\ *adj* [L *repellent-, repellens*, prp. of *repellere*] **1 :** serving or tending to drive away or ward off — often used in combination <a mosquito-*repellent* spray> **2 :** arousing aversion or disgust : REPULSIVE **syn** see REPUGNANT **ant** attractive, pleasing — **re·pel·lent·ly** *adv*
[2]repellent *also* **repellant** *n* : something that repels; *esp* : a substance used to prevent insect attacks
[1]re·pent \ri-ˈpent\ *vb* [ME *repenten*, fr. OF *repentir*, fr. *re-* + *pentir* to be sorry, fr. L *paenitēre* — more at PENITENCE] *vi* **1 :** to turn from sin and dedicate oneself to the amendment of one's life **2 a :** to feel regret or contrition **b :** to change one's mind ~ *vt* **1 :** to cause to feel regret or contrition **2 :** to feel sorrow, regret, or contrition for — **re·pent·er** *n*
[2]re·pent \ˈrē-pənt\ *adj* [L *repent-, repens*, prp. of *repere* to creep — more at REPTILE] : CREEPING, PROSTRATE

re·pen·tance \ri-ˈpent-ᵊn(t)s\ *n* **:** the action or process of repenting esp. for misdeeds or moral shortcomings ***syn*** see PENITENCE

re·pen·tant \-ᵊnt\ *adj* **1 :** experiencing repentance **:** PENITENT **2 :** expressive of repentance — **re·pen·tant·ly** *adv*

re·per·cus·sion \ˌrē-pər-ˈkəsh-ən, ˌrep-ər-\ *n* [L *repercussion-, repercussio,* fr. *repercussus,* pp. of *repercutere* to drive back, fr. *re-* + *percutere* to beat — more at PERCUSSION] **1 :** REFLECTION, REVERBERATION **2 a :** an action or effect given or exerted in return **:** a reciprocal action or effect **b :** a widespread, indirect, or unforeseen effect of an act, action, or event — usu. used in pl. — **re·per·cus·sive** \-ˈkəs-iv\ *adj*

rep·er·toire \ˈrep-ə(r)-ˌtwär\ *n* [F *répertoire,* fr. LL *repertorium*] **1 a :** a list or supply of dramas, operas, pieces, or parts that a company or person is prepared to perform **b :** a supply of skills, devices, or expedients <part of the ~ of a quarterback>; *broadly* **:** AMOUNT, SUPPLY <an endless ~ of summer clothes> **2 a :** the complete list or supply of dramas, operas, or musical works available for performance <our modern orchestral ~> **b :** the complete list or supply of skills, devices, or ingredients used in a particular field, occupation, or practice <the ~ of literary criticism> **c :** a list or supply of capabilities <the instruction ~ of a computer>

rep·er·to·ry \ˈrep-ə(r)-ˌtōr-ē, -ˌtȯr-\ *n, pl* **-ries** [LL *repertorium* list, fr. L *repertus,* pp. of *reperire* to find, fr. *re-* + *parere* to produce — more at PARE] **1 :** a place where something may be found **:** REPOSITORY **2 a :** REPERTOIRE **b :** a theater in which several different plays are presented in a season by a resident company

rep·e·tend \ˈrep-ə-ˌtend\ *n* [L *repetendus* to be repeated, gerundive of *repetere* to repeat] **:** a repeated sound, word, or phrase; *specif* **:** REFRAIN

rep·e·ti·tion \ˌrep-ə-ˈtish-ən\ *n* [L *repetition-, repetitio,* fr. *repetitus,* pp. of *repetere* to repeat] **1 :** the act or an instance of repeating or being repeated **2 :** MENTION, RECITAL — **rep·e·ti·tion·al** \-ˈtish-nəl, -ən-ᵊl\ *adj*

rep·e·ti·tious \-ˈtish-əs\ *adj* **:** characterized or marked by repetition; *esp* **:** tediously repeating — **rep·e·ti·tious·ly** *adv* — **rep·e·ti·tious·ness** *n*

re·pet·i·tive \ri-ˈpet-ət-iv\ *adj* **:** REPETITIOUS — **re·pet·i·tive·ly** *adv* — **re·pet·i·tive·ness** *n*

re·pine \ri-ˈpīn\ *vi* **re·pined; re·pin·ing 1 :** to feel or express dejection or discontent **2 :** to long for something — **re·pin·er** *n*

repl *abbr* replace; replacement

re·place \ri-ˈplās\ *vt* **1 :** to restore to a former place or position <~ cards in a file> **2 :** to take the place of esp. as a substitute or successor **3 :** to put something new in the place of <~ a worn carpet> — **re·place·able** \-ˈplā-sə-bəl\ *adj* — **re·plac·er** *n*

syn REPLACE, DISPLACE, SUPPLANT, SUPERSEDE *shared meaning element* **:** to put out of a usual or proper place or into the place of another

re·place·ment \ri-ˈplā-smənt\ *n* **1 :** the action or process of replacing **:** the state of being replaced **:** SUBSTITUTION **2 :** something that replaces; *esp* **:** an individual assigned to a military unit to replace a loss or complete a quota

re·plant \(ˈ)rē-ˈplant\ *vt* **1 :** to plant again or anew **2 :** to provide with new plants

1**re·play** \(ˈ)rē-ˈplā\ *vt* **:** to play again or over

2**re·play** \ˈrē-ˌplā\ *n* **1 a :** an act or instance of replaying **b :** the playing of a tape (as a videotape) **2 :** REPETITION, REENACTMENT <don't want a ~ of our old mistakes>

re·plead·er \(ˈ)rē-ˈplēd-ər\ *n* [*replead* (to plead again) + *-er* (as in *misnomer*)] **1 :** a second legal pleading **2 :** the right of pleading again granted usu. when the issue raised is immaterial or insufficient

re·plen·ish \ri-ˈplen-ish\ *vb* [ME *replenisshen,* fr. MF *repleniss-,* stem of *replenir* to fill, fr. OF, fr. *re-* + *plein* full, fr. L *plenus* — more at FULL] *vt* **1 a :** to fill with persons or animals **:** STOCK **b** *archaic* **:** to supply fully **:** PERFECT **c :** to fill with inspiration or power **:** NOURISH **2 a :** to fill or build up again <~*ed* his glass> **b :** to make good **:** REPLACE ~ *vi* **:** to become full **:** fill up again — **re·plen·ish·er** *n* — **re·plen·ish·ment** \-ish-mənt\ *n*

re·plete \ri-ˈplēt\ *adj* [ME, fr. MF & L; MF *replet,* fr. L *repletus,* pp. of *replēre* to fill up, fr. *re-* + *plēre* to fill — more at FULL] **1 :** fully or abundantly provided or filled **2 a :** abundantly fed **b :** FAT, STOUT **3 :** COMPLETE ***syn*** see FULL — **re·plete·ness** *n*

re·ple·tion \ri-ˈplē-shən\ *n* **1 :** the act of eating to excess **:** the state of being fed to excess **:** SURFEIT **2 :** the condition of being filled up or overcrowded **3 :** fulfillment of a need or desire **:** SATISFACTION

1**re·plev·in** \ri-ˈplev-ən\ *n* [ME, fr. AF *replevine,* fr. *replevir* to give security, fr. OF, fr. *re-* + *plevir* to pledge, fr. (assumed) LL *plebere*] **1 :** the recovery by a person of goods or chattels claimed to be wrongfully taken or detained upon the person's giving security to try the matter in court and return the goods if defeated in the action **2 :** the writ or the common-law action whereby goods and chattels are replevied

2**replevin** *vt* **:** REPLEVY

1**re·plevy** \ri-ˈplev-ē\ *n, pl* **re·plev·ies** [ME, fr. AF *replevir,* v.] **:** REPLEVIN

2**replevy** *vt* **re·plev·ied; re·plevy·ing :** to take or get back by a writ for replevin — **re·plevi·able** \-ē-ə-bəl\ *adj*

rep·li·ca \ˈrep-li-kə\ *n* [It, repetition, fr. *replicare* to repeat, fr. LL, fr. L, to fold back — more at REPLY] **1 :** a close reproduction or facsimile esp. by the maker of the original **2 :** COPY, DUPLICATE

1**rep·li·cate** \ˈrep-lə-ˌkāt\ *vb* **-cat·ed; -cat·ing** [LL *replicatus,* pp. of *replicare*] *vt* **1 :** DUPLICATE, REPEAT <~ a statistical experiment> **2** [L *replicatus*] **:** to fold or bend back <*replicated* leaf> ~ *vi* **:** to undergo replication **:** produce a replica of itself <*replicating* virus particles> — **rep·li·ca·tive** \-ˌkāt-iv\ *adj*

2**rep·li·cate** \-li-kət\ *n* **:** one of several identical experiments, procedures, or samples

3**replicate** \-li-kət\ *adj* **:** MANIFOLD, REPEATED

rep·li·ca·tion \ˌrep-lə-ˈkā-shən\ *n* **1 a :** an answer **:** REPLY **b (1) :** an answer to a reply **:** REJOINDER **(2) :** a plaintiff's reply to a defendant's plea, answer, or counterclaim **2 :** ECHO, REVERBERATION **3 a :** COPY, REPRODUCTION **b :** the action or process of reproducing **4 :** performance of an experiment or procedure more than once; *esp* **:** systematic or random repetition of agricultural test rows or plats to reduce error

1**re·ply** \ri-ˈplī\ *vb* **re·plied; re·ply·ing** [ME *replien,* fr. MF *replier* to fold again, fr. L *replicare* to fold back, fr. *re-* + *plicare* to fold — more at PLY] *vi* **1 a :** to respond in words or writing **b :** ECHO, RESOUND **c :** to make a legal replication **2 :** to do something in response; *specif* **:** to return gunfire or an attack ~ *vt* **:** to give as an answer ***syn*** see ANSWER — **re·pli·er** \-ˈplī(-ə)r\ *n*

2**reply** *n, pl* **replies 1 :** something said, written, or done in answer or response **2 :** REPLICATION 1b(2)

1**re·port** \ri-ˈpō(ə)rt, -ˈpȯ(ə)rt\ *n* [ME, fr. MF, fr. OF, fr. *reporter* to report, fr. L *reportare,* fr. *re-* + *portare* to carry — more at FARE] **1 a :** common talk or an account spread by common talk **:** RUMOR **b :** quality of reputation <a man of good ~> **2 a :** a usu. detailed account or statement <a news ~> **b :** an account or statement of a judicial opinion or decision **c :** a usu. formal record of the proceedings of a meeting or session **3 :** an explosive noise — **on report :** subject to disciplinary action

syn REPORT, RUMOR, GOSSIP, HEARSAY *shared meaning element* **:** common talk or an instance of it that spreads rapidly

2**report** *vt* **1 a :** to give an account of **:** RELATE **b :** to describe as being in a specified state <~*ed* him much improved> **2 a :** to serve as carrier of (a message) **b :** to relate the words or sense of (something said) **c :** to make a written record or summary of **d (1) :** to watch for and write about the newsworthy aspects or developments of **:** COVER **(2) :** to prepare or present an account of for broadcast **3 a (1) :** to give a formal or official account or statement of <the treasurer ~*ed* a balance of ten dollars> **(2) :** to return or present (a matter referred for consideration) with conclusions or recommendations **b :** to announce or relate as the result of investigation <~*ed* no sign of disease> **c :** to announce the presence, arrival, or sighting of **d :** to make known to the proper authorities <~ a fire> **e :** to make a charge of misconduct against ~ *vi* **1 a :** to give an account **:** TELL **b :** to present oneself **c :** to account for oneself <~*ed* sick on Friday> **2 :** to make, issue, or submit a report **3 :** to act in the capacity of a reporter — **re·port·able** \-ˈpōrt-ə-bəl, -ˈpȯrt-\ *adj*

re·port·age \ri-ˈpōrt-ij, -ˈpȯrt-, *esp for 2* ˌrep-ər-ˈtäzh, ˌrep-ˌȯr-\ *n* [F, fr. *reporter* to report] **1 a :** the act or process of reporting news **b :** something (as news) that is reported **2 :** writing intended to give an account of observed or documented events

report card *n* **:** a report on a student that is periodically submitted by a school to the student's parents or guardian

re·port·ed·ly \ri-ˈpōrt-əd-lē, -ˈpȯrt-\ *adv* **:** according to report

re·port·er \ri-ˈpōrt-ər, -ˈpȯrt-\ *n* **:** one that reports: as **a :** one who makes authorized statements of law decisions or legislative proceedings **b :** one who makes a shorthand record of a speech or proceeding **c (1) :** one employed by a newspaper or magazine to gather and write news **(2) :** one who broadcasts news — **re·por·to·ri·al** \ˌrep-ə(r)-ˈtōr-ē-əl, ˌrēp-, -ˈtȯr-\ *adj* — **re·por·to·ri·al·ly** \-ē-ə-lē\ *adv*

report out *vt* **:** to return after consideration and often with revisions to a legislative body for action <after much debate the committee *reported* the bill *out*>

report stage *n* **:** the stage in the British legislative process preceding the third reading and concerned esp. with amendments and details

re·pos·al \ri-ˈpō-zəl\ *n, obs* **:** the act of reposing

1**re·pose** \ri-ˈpōz\ *vt* **re·posed; re·pos·ing** [ME *reposen* to replace, fr. L *reponere* (perf. indic. *reposui*)] **1** *archaic* **:** to put away or set down **:** DEPOSIT **2 a :** to place (as confidence or trust) in someone or something **b :** to place for control, management, or use

2**repose** *vb* **re·posed; re·pos·ing** [ME *reposen,* fr. MF *reposer,* fr. OF, fr. LL *repausare,* fr. L *re-* + LL *pausare* to stop — more at PAUSE] *vt* **:** to lay at rest ~ *vi* **1 a :** to lie at rest **b :** to lie dead <*reposing* in state> **c :** to remain still or concealed **2 :** to take a rest **3** *archaic* **:** RELY **4 :** to rest for support **:** LIE

3**repose** *n* **1 a :** a state of resting after exertion or strain; *esp* **:** rest in sleep **b :** eternal or heavenly rest <pray for the ~ of a soul> **2 a :** a place of rest **b :** PEACE, TRANQUILLITY <the ~ of the bayous> **c :** a harmony in the arrangement of parts and colors that is restful to the eye **3 a :** lack of activity **:** QUIESCENCE **b :** cessation or absence of activity, movement, or animation <the appearance of his face in ~> **4 :** composure of manner **:** POISE

re·pose·ful \ri-ˈpōz-fəl\ *adj* **:** of a kind to induce ease and relaxation — **re·pose·ful·ly** \-fə-lē\ *adv* — **re·pose·ful·ness** *n*

re·pos·it *vt* **re·pos·it·ed** \-ˈpäz-ət-əd, -ˈpäz-təd\; **re·pos·it·ing** \-ˈpäz-ət-iŋ, -ˈpäz-tiŋ\ [L *repositus,* pp. of *reponere* to replace, fr. *re-* + *ponere* to place — more at POSITION] **1** \ri-ˈpäz-ət\ **:** DEPOSIT, STORE **2** \(ˈ)rē-\ **:** to put back in place **:** REPLACE

1**re·po·si·tion** \ˌrē-pə-ˈzish-ən, ˌrep-ə-\ *n* **:** the act of repositing **:** the state of being reposited

2**re·po·si·tion** \ˌrē-pə-ˈzish-ən\ *vt* **:** to change the position of

1**re·pos·i·to·ry** \ri-ˈpäz-ə-ˌtōr-ē, -ˌtȯr-\ *n, pl* **-ries 1 :** a place, room, or container where something is deposited or stored **:** DEPOSITORY **2 :** a side altar in a Roman Catholic church where the consecrated Host is reserved from Maundy Thursday until Good Friday **3 :** one that contains or stores something nonmaterial <considered the book a ~ of knowledge> **4 :** a place or region richly supplied with a natural resource **5 :** a person to whom something is confided or entrusted

2**repository** *adj, of a drug* **:** designed to act over a prolonged period

re·pos·sess \ˌrē-pə-ˈzes *also* -ˈses\ *vt* **1 a :** to regain possession of **b :** to resume possession of in default of the payment of installments due **2 :** to restore to possession — **re·pos·ses·sion** \-ˈzesh-ən *also* -ˈsesh-\ *n*

1re·pous·sé \rə-ˌpü-ˈsā, -ˈpü-ˌ\ *adj* [F] **1 :** shaped or ornamented with patterns in relief made by hammering or pressing on the reverse side — used esp. of metal **2 :** formed in relief

2repoussé *n* **1 :** repoussé work **2 :** repoussé decoration

re·pow·er \(ˈ)rē-ˈpau̇(-ə)r\ *vt* **:** to provide again or anew with power; *esp* **:** to provide (as a boat) with a new engine ~ *vi* **:** to repower something (as a boat)

repp *var of* REP

rep·re·hend \ˌrep-ri-ˈhend\ *vt* [ME *reprehenden,* fr. L *reprehendere,* lit., to hold back, fr. *re-* + *prehendere* to grasp — more at PREHENSILE] **:** to voice disapproval of **:** CENSURE ***syn*** see CRITICIZE

rep·re·hen·si·ble \ˌrep-ri-ˈhen(t)-sə-bəl\ *adj* **:** worthy of or deserving reprehension **:** CULPABLE — **rep·re·hen·si·bil·i·ty** \-ˌhen(t)-sə-ˈbil-ət-ē\ *n* — **rep·re·hen·si·ble·ness** \-ˈhen(t)-sə-bəl-nəs\ *n* — **rep·re·hen·si·bly** \-blē\ *adv*

rep·re·hen·sion \-ˈhen-chən\ *n* [ME *reprehensioun,* fr. MF or L; MF *reprehension,* fr. L *reprehension-, reprehensio,* fr. *reprehensus,* pp. of *reprehendere*] **:** the act of reprehending **:** CENSURE

rep·re·hen·sive \-ˈhen(t)-siv\ *adj* **:** serving to reprehend **:** conveying reprehension or reproof

rep·re·sent \ˌrep-ri-ˈzent\ *vb* [ME *representen,* fr. MF *representer,* fr. L *repraesentare,* fr. *re-* + *praesentare* to present] *vt* **1 :** to bring clearly before the mind **:** PRESENT <a book which ~*s* the character of early America> **2 :** to serve as a sign or symbol of <the flag ~*s* our country> **3 :** to portray or exhibit in art **:** DEPICT **4 :** to serve as the counterpart or image of **:** TYPIFY <a movie hero who ~*s* the ideals of the culture> **5 a :** to produce on the stage **b :** to act the part or role of **6 a** (1) **:** to take the place of in some respect (2) **:** to act in the place of or for usu. by legal right **b :** to serve esp. in a legislative body by delegated authority usu. resulting from election **7 :** to describe as having a specified character or quality <~*s* himself as a friend of the workingman> **8 a :** to give one's impression and judgment of **:** state in a manner intended to affect action or judgment **:** ADVOCATE **b :** to point out in protest or remonstrance **9 :** to serve as a specimen, example, or instance of **10 a :** to form an image or representation of in the mind **b** (1) **:** to apprehend (an object) by means of an idea (2) **:** to recall in memory **11 :** to correspond to in essence **:** CONSTITUTE ~ *vi* **:** to make representations against something **:** PROTEST — **rep·re·sent·able** \-ə-bəl\ *adj* — **rep·re·sent·er** *n*

re–pre·sent \ˌrē-pri-ˈzent\ *vt* **:** to present again or anew — **re–pre·sen·ta·tion** \ˈrē-ˌprē-ˌzen-ˈtā-shən, -ˌprez-ᵊn-, -ˌprēz-ᵊn-\ *n*

rep·re·sen·ta·tion \ˌrep-ri-ˌzen-ˈtā-shən, -zən-\ *n* **1 :** one that represents: as **a :** an artistic likeness or image **b** (1) **:** a statement or account made to influence opinion or action (2) **:** an incidental or collateral statement of fact on the faith of which a contract is entered into **c :** a dramatic production or performance **d** (1) **:** a usu. formal statement made against something or to effect a change (2) **:** a usu. formal protest **2 :** the act or action of representing **:** the state of being represented: as **a :** REPRESENTATIONALISM 2 **b** (1) **:** the action or fact of one person standing for another so as to have the rights and obligations of the person represented (2) **:** the substitution of an individual or class in place of a person (as a child for a deceased parent) **c :** the action of representing or the fact of being represented esp. in a legislative body **3 :** the body of persons representing a constituency — **rep·re·sen·ta·tion·al** \-shnəl, -shən-ᵊl\ *adj*

rep·re·sen·ta·tion·al·ism \-shnəl-ˌiz-əm, -shən-ᵊl-\ *n* **1 :** the doctrine that the immediate object of knowledge is an idea in the mind distinct from the external object which is the occasion of perception **2 :** the theory or practice of realistic representation in art — **rep·re·sen·ta·tion·al·ist** \-əst\ *n*

1rep·re·sen·ta·tive \ˌrep-ri-ˈzent-ət-iv\ *adj* **1 :** serving to represent <a painting ~ of battle> **2 a :** standing or acting for another esp. through delegated authority **b :** of, based on, or constituting a government in which the many are represented by persons chosen from among them usu. by election **3 :** serving as a typical or characteristic example <a ~ housewife> **4 :** of or relating to representation or representationalism — **rep·re·sen·ta·tive·ly** *adv* — **rep·re·sen·ta·tive·ness** *n* — **rep·re·sen·ta·tiv·i·ty** \-ˌzent-ə-ˈtiv-ət-ē\ *n*

2representative *n* **1 :** a typical example of a group, class, or quality **:** SPECIMEN **2 :** one that represents another or others: as **a** (1) **:** one that represents a constituency as a member of a legislative body (2) **:** a member of the house of representatives of the U.S. Congress or a state legislature **b :** one that represents another as agent, deputy, substitute, or delegate usu. being invested with the authority of the principal **c :** one that represents a business organization **d :** one that represents another as successor or heir

re·press \ri-ˈpres\ *vb* [ME *repressen,* fr. L *repressus,* pp. of *reprimere* to check, fr. *re-* + *premere* to press — more at PRESS] *vt* **1 a :** to check by or as if by pressure **:** CURB <injustice was ~*ed*> **b :** to put down by force **:** SUBDUE <~ a disturbance> **2 a :** to hold in by self-control <~*ed* a laugh> **b :** to prevent the natural or normal expression, activity, or development of <~*ed* his anger> **3 :** to exclude from consciousness **4 :** to inactivate (a gene) by blocking ~ *vi* **:** to take repressive action ***syn*** see SUPPRESS — **re·press·ibil·i·ty** \-ˌpres-ə-ˈbil-ət-ē\ *n* — **re·press·ible** \-ˈpres-ə-bəl\ *adj* — **re·pres·sive** \-ˈpres-iv\ *adj* — **re·pres·sive·ly** *adv* — **re·pres·sive·ness** *n*

re–press \(ˈ)rē-ˈpres\ *vt* **:** to press again <~ a record>

re·pressed \ri-ˈprest\ *adj* **1 :** subjected to or marked by repression **2 :** characterized by restraint

re·pres·sion \ri-ˈpresh-ən\ *n* **1 a :** the action or process of repressing **:** the state of being repressed <~ of unpopular opinions> **b :** an instance of repressing <racial ~*s*> **2 a :** a process by which unacceptable desires or impulses are excluded from consciousness and left to operate in the unconscious **b :** an item so excluded — **re·pres·sion·ist** \-(ə-)nəst\ *adj*

re·pres·sor \ri-ˈpres-ər\ *n* [NL] **:** one that represses; *esp* **:** a product of the action of a regulator gene that interacts with a genetic operator and inhibits its function

re·priev·al \ri-ˈprē-vəl\ *n, archaic* **:** REPRIEVE

1re·prieve \ri-ˈprēv\ *vt* **re·prieved; re·priev·ing** [perh. fr. MF *repris,* pp. of *reprendre* to take back] **1 :** to delay the punishment of (as a condemned prisoner) **2 :** to give relief or deliverance to for a time

2reprieve *n* **1 a :** the act of reprieving **:** the state of being reprieved **b :** a formal temporary suspension of the execution of a sentence esp. of death **2 :** an order or warrant for a reprieve **3 :** a temporary respite (as from pain or trouble)

1rep·ri·mand \ˈrep-rə-ˌmand\ *n* [F *réprimande,* fr. L *reprimenda,* fem. of *reprimendus,* gerundive of *reprimere* to check] **:** a severe or formal reproof

2reprimand *vt* **:** to reprove sharply or censure formally usu. from a position of authority ***syn*** see REPROVE

1re·print \(ˈ)rē-ˈprint\ *vt* **:** to print again **:** make a reprint of

2re·print \ˈrē-ˌprint, (ˈ)rē-ˈ\ *n* **:** a reproduction of printed matter: as **a :** a subsequent printing of a book already published that preserves the identical text of the previous printing **b :** OFFPRINT **c :** matter (as an article) that has appeared in print before

re·print·er \(ˈ)rē-ˈprint-ər\ *n* **:** one that publishes a reprint

re·pri·sal \ri-ˈprī-zəl\ *n* [ME *reprisail,* fr. MF *reprisaille,* fr. OIt *ripresaglia,* fr. *ripreso,* pp. of *riprendere* to take back, fr. *ri-* re- (fr. L *re-*) + *prendere* to take, fr. L *prehendere* — more at PREHENSILE] **1 a :** the act or practice in international law of resorting to force short of war in retaliation for damage or loss suffered **b :** an instance of such action **2** *obs* **:** PRIZE **3 :** the regaining of something (as by recapture) **4 :** something (as a sum of money) given or paid in restitution — usu. used in pl. **5 :** a retaliatory act

1re·prise \ri-ˈprēz, *1 is also* -ˈprīz\ *n* [ME, fr. MF, lit., action of taking back, fr. OF, fr. *reprendre* to take back, fr. *re-* + *prendre* to take, fr. L *prehendere*] **1 :** a deduction or charge made yearly out of a manor or estate — usu. used in pl. **2 :** a recurrence, renewal, or resumption of an action **3 a :** a musical repetition: (1) **:** the repetition of the exposition preceding the development (2) **:** RECAPITULATION **b :** a repeated performance **:** REPETITION

2re·prise \ri-ˈprīz, *3 is* -ˈprēz\ *vt* **re·prised; re·pris·ing** [MF *reprise* action of taking back] **1** *archaic* **:** to take back; *esp* **:** to recover by force **2** *archaic* **:** COMPENSATE **3 :** to repeat the performance of <~ a song>

re·pris·ti·nate \(ˈ)rē-ˈpris-tə-ˌnāt\ *vt* **-nat·ed; -nat·ing** [*re-* + *pristine* + *-ate*] **:** to restore to an original state or condition — **re·pris·ti·na·tion** \(ˌ)rē-ˌpris-tə-ˈnā-shən\ *n*

re·pro \ˈrē-(ˌ)prō\ *n, pl* **repros** [short for *reproduction*] **:** a clear sharp proof made esp. from a letterpress printing surface to serve as photographic copy for a printing plate

1re·proach \ri-ˈprōch\ *n* [ME *reproche,* fr. MF, fr. OF, fr. *reprochier* to reproach, fr. (assumed) VL *repropiare,* fr. L *re-* + *prope* near — more at APPROACH] **1 a :** a cause or occasion of blame, discredit, or disgrace <the poverty of millions is a constant ~> **b :** DISCREDIT, DISGRACE <their methods brought ~ on them> **2 :** the act or action of reproaching or disapproving <was beyond ~> **3 :** an expression of rebuke or disapproval **4** *obs* **:** one subjected to censure or scorn — **re·proach·ful** \-fəl\ *adj* — **re·proach·ful·ly** \-fə-lē\ *adv* — **re·proach·ful·ness** *n*

2reproach *vt* **1 :** to make (something) a matter of reproach **2 :** to express disappointment in or displeasure with (a person) for conduct that is blameworthy or in need of amendment **3 :** to bring into discredit ***syn*** see REPROVE — **re·proach·able** \-ˈprō-chə-bəl\ *adj* — **re·proach·er** *n* — **re·proach·ing·ly** \-ˈprō-chiŋ-lē\ *adv*

rep·ro·bance \ˈrep-rə-bən(t)s\ *n, archaic* **:** REPROBATION

1rep·ro·bate \ˈrep-rə-ˌbāt\ *vt* **-bat·ed; -bat·ing** [ME *reprobaten,* fr. LL *reprobatus,* pp. of *reprobare* — more at REPROVE] **1 :** to condemn strongly as unworthy, unacceptable, or evil <*reprobating* the laxity of the age> **2 :** to foreordain to damnation **3 :** to refuse to accept **:** REJECT ***syn*** see CRITICIZE — **rep·ro·ba·tion** \ˌrep-rə-ˈbā-shən\ *n* — **rep·ro·ba·tive** \ˈrep-rə-ˌbāt-iv\ *adj* — **rep·ro·ba·to·ry** \-bə-ˌtōr-ē, -ˌtȯr-\ *adj*

2reprobate *adj* **1** *archaic* **:** rejected as worthless or not standing a test **:** CONDEMNED **2 a :** foreordained to damnation **b :** morally abandoned **:** DEPRAVED **3 :** expressing or involving reprobation **4 :** of, relating to, or characteristic of a reprobate **:** CORRUPT

3reprobate *n* **:** a reprobate person

re·pro·cess \(ˈ)rē-ˈpräs-ˌes, -ˈprōs-, -əs\ *vt* **:** to subject to a special process or treatment in preparation for reuse

re·pro·duce \ˌrē-prə-ˈd(y)üs\ *vt* **:** to produce again: as **a :** to produce (new individuals of the same kind) by a sexual or asexual process **b :** to cause to exist again or anew <~ water from steam> **c :** to imitate closely <sound-effects men can ~ the sound of thunder> **d :** to present again **e :** to make a representation (as an image or copy) of <~ a face on canvas> **f :** to revive mentally **:** RECALL **g :** to translate (a recording) into sound ~ *vi* **1 :** to undergo reproduction **2 :** to produce offspring — **re·pro·duc·er** *n* — **re·pro·duc·ibil·i·ty** \-ˌd(y)ü-sə-ˈbil-ət-ē\ *n* — **re·pro·duc·ible** \-ˈd(y)ü-sə-bəl\ *adj*

re·pro·duc·tion \ˌrē-prə-ˈdək-shən\ *n* **1 :** the act or process of reproducing; *specif* **:** the process by which plants and animals give rise to offspring and which fundamentally consists of the segregation of a portion of the parental body by a sexual or an asexual process and its subsequent growth and differentiation into a new individual **2 :** something reproduced **:** COPY **3 :** young seedling trees in a forest

1re·pro·duc·tive \ˌrē-prə-ˈdək-tiv\ *adj* **:** of, relating to, or capable of reproduction — **re·pro·duc·tive·ly** *adv*

2reproductive *n* **:** an actual or potential parent; *specif* **:** a sexually functional social insect

re·pro·gram \(ˈ)rē-ˈprō-ˌgram, -grəm\ *vt* **:** to rewrite a program for (as a computer) ~ *vi* **:** to rewrite a computer program

re·prog·ra·phy \ri-ˈpräg-rə-fē\ *n* [*reproduction* + *-graphy*] **:** facsimile reproduction (as by photocopying) of graphic matter

re·proof \ri-ˈprüf\ *n* [ME *reprof,* fr. MF *reprove,* fr. OF, fr. *reprover*] : criticism for a fault : REBUKE

re·pro·por·tion \ˌrē-p(r)ə-ˈpōr-shən, -ˈpȯr-\ *vt* : to change the proportions of

re·prove \ri-ˈprüv\ *vb* **re·proved; re·prov·ing** [ME *reproven,* fr. MF *reprover,* fr. LL *reprobare* to disapprove, condemn, fr. L *re-* + *probare* to test, approve — more at PROVE] *vt* **1** : to call attention to the remissness of usu. with a kindly intent to correct or assist <~ a child's bad manners> **2** : to express disapproval of : CENSURE <~ a child for his bad manners> **3** *obs* : DISPROVE, REFUTE **4** *obs* : CONVINCE, CONVICT ~ *vi* : to express rebuke or reproof — **re·prov·er** *n* — **re·prov·ing·ly** \-ˈprü-viŋ-lē\ *adv*

syn REPROVE, REBUKE, REPRIMAND, ADMONISH, REPROACH, CHIDE *shared meaning element* : to criticize adversely

rept *abbr* report

1rep·tile \ˈrep-tᵊl, -ˌtīl\ *n* [ME *reptil,* fr. MF or LL; MF *reptile* (fem.), fr. LL *reptile* (neut.), fr. neut. of *reptilis* reptant, fr. L *reptus,* pp. of *repere* to creep; akin to OHG *reba* tendril] **1** : an animal that crawls or moves on its belly (as a snake) or on small short legs (as a lizard) **2 a** : any of a class (Reptilia) of air-breathing vertebrates that include the alligators and crocodiles, lizards, snakes, turtles, and extinct related forms and are characterized by a completely ossified skeleton with a single occipital condyle, a distinct quadrate bone usu. immovably articulated with the skull, ribs attached to the sternum, and a body usu. covered with scales or bony plates **b** : AMPHIBIAN **3** : a groveling or despised person

2reptile *adj* : characteristic of a reptile : REPTILIAN

1rep·til·ian \rep-ˈtil-ē-ən, -ˈtil-yən\ *adj* **1** : resembling or having the characteristics of the reptiles **2** : of or relating to the reptiles

2reptilian *n* : REPTILE 2a

re·pub·lic \ri-ˈpəb-lik\ *n* [F *république,* fr. MF *republique,* fr. L *respublica,* fr. *res* thing, wealth + *publica,* fem. of *publicus* public — more at REAL, PUBLIC] **1 a** (1) : a government having a chief of state who is not a monarch and who in modern times is usu. a president (2) : a political unit (as a nation) having such a form of government **b** (1) : a government in which supreme power resides in a body of citizens entitled to vote and is exercised by elected officers and representatives responsible to them and governing according to law (2) : a political unit (as a nation) having such a form of government **c** : a usu. specified republican government of a political unit <the French Fourth *Republic*> **2** : a body of persons freely engaged in a specified activity <the ~ of letters> **3** : a constituent political and territorial unit of the U.S.S.R. or Yugoslavia

1re·pub·li·can \ri-ˈpəb-li-kən\ *adj* **1 a** : of, relating to, or having the characteristics of a republic **b** : favoring, supporting, or advocating a republic **c** : belonging or appropriate to one living in or supporting a republic <~ simplicity> **2** *cap* **a** : DEMOCRATIC-REPUBLICAN **b** : of, relating to, or constituting the one of the two major political parties evolving in the U.S. in the mid-19th century that is usu. primarily associated with business, financial, and some agricultural interests and is held to favor a restricted governmental role in social and economic life

2republican *n* **1** : one that favors or supports a republican form of government **2** *cap* **a** : a member of a political party advocating republicanism **b** : a member of the Democratic-Republican party or of the Republican party of the U.S.

re·pub·li·can·ism \ri-ˈpəb-li-kə-ˌniz-əm\ *n* **1** : adherence to or sympathy for a republican form of government **2** : the principles or theory of republican government **3** *cap* **a** : the principles, policy, or practices of the Republican party of the U.S. **b** : the Republican party or its members

re·pub·li·can·ize \-kə-ˌnīz\ *vt* **-ized; -iz·ing** : to make republican in character, form, or principle

re·pub·li·ca·tion \(ˌ)rē-ˌpəb-lə-ˈkā-shən\ *n* **1** : the act or action of republishing : the state of being republished **2** : something that has been republished

re·pub·lish \(ˈ)rē-ˈpəb-lish\ *vt* **1** : to publish again or anew **2** : to execute (a will) anew — **re·pub·lish·er** *n*

re·pu·di·ate \ri-ˈpyüd-ē-ˌāt\ *vt* **-at·ed; -at·ing** [L *repudiatus,* pp. of *repudiare,* fr. *repudium* divorce] **1** : to divorce or separate formally from (a woman) **2** : to refuse to have anything to do with : DISOWN **3 a** : to refuse to accept; *esp* : to reject as unauthorized or as having no binding force **b** : to reject as untrue or unjust <~ a charge> **4** : to refuse to acknowledge or pay ***syn*** see DECLINE ***ant*** adopt — **re·pu·di·a·tor** \-ˌāt-ər\ *n*

re·pu·di·a·tion \ri-ˌpyüd-ē-ˈā-shən\ *n* : the act of repudiating : the state of being repudiated; *esp* : the refusal of public authorities to acknowledge or pay a debt — **re·pu·di·a·tion·ist** \-sh(ə-)nəst\ *n*

re·pugn \ri-ˈpyün\ *vb* [ME *repugnen,* fr. MF & L; MF *repugner,* fr. L *repugnare*] *vi, archaic* : to offer opposition, objection, or resistance ~ *vt* : to contend against : OPPOSE

re·pug·nance \ri-ˈpəg-nən(t)s\ *n* **1 a** : the quality or fact of being contradictory or inconsistent **b** : an instance of such contradiction or inconsistency **2** : strong dislike, distaste, or antagonism

re·pug·nan·cy \-nən-sē\ *n, pl* **-cies** : REPUGNANCE

re·pug·nant \-nənt\ *adj* [ME, opposed, contradictory, incompatible, fr. MF, fr. L *repugnant-, repugnans,* prp. of *repugnare* to fight against, fr. *re-* + *pugnare* to fight — more at PUNGENT] **1** : INCOMPATIBLE, INCONSISTENT **2** *archaic* : HOSTILE **3** : exciting distaste or aversion — **re·pug·nant·ly** *adv*

syn REPUGNANT, REPELLENT, ABHORRENT, DISTASTEFUL, OBNOXIOUS, INVIDIOUS *shared meaning element* : so alien or unlikable as to arouse antagonism and aversion ***ant*** congenial

1re·pulse \ri-ˈpəls\ *vt* **re·pulsed; re·puls·ing** [L *repulsus,* pp. of *repellere* to repel] **1** : to drive or beat back : REPEL **2** : to repel by discourtesy, coldness, or denial **3** : to cause repulsion in

2repulse *n* **1** : REBUFF, REJECTION **2** : the action of repelling an attacker : the fact of being repelled

re·pul·sion \ri-ˈpəl-shən\ *n* **1** : the action of repulsing : the state of being repulsed **2** : the action of repelling : the force with which bodies, particles, or like forces repel one another **3** : a feeling of aversion : REPUGNANCE

re·pul·sive \-siv\ *adj* **1** : tending to repel or reject : COLD, FORBIDDING **2** : serving or able to repulse **3** : arousing aversion or disgust — **re·pul·sive·ly** *adv* — **re·pul·sive·ness** *n*

rep·u·ta·ble \ˈrep-yət-ə-bəl\ *adj* **1** : enjoying good repute : held in esteem **2** : employed widely or sanctioned by good writers — **rep·u·ta·bil·i·ty** \ˌrep-yət-ə-ˈbil-ət-ē\ *n* — **rep·u·ta·bly** \ˈrep-yət-ə-blē\ *adv*

rep·u·ta·tion \ˌrep-yə-ˈtā-shən\ *n* **1 a** : overall quality or character as seen or judged by people in general **b** : recognition by other people of some characteristic or ability <has the ~ of being clever> **2** : a place in public esteem or regard : good name

1re·pute \ri-ˈpyüt\ *vt* **re·put·ed; re·put·ing** [ME *reputen,* fr. MF *reputer,* fr. L *reputare* to reckon up, think over, fr. *re-* + *putare* to reckon — more at PAVE] : BELIEVE, CONSIDER

2repute *n* **1** : the character or status commonly ascribed to one : REPUTATION **2** : the state of being favorably known, spoken of, or esteemed

re·put·ed *adj* **1** : having a good repute : REPUTABLE **2** : being such according to reputation or popular belief

re·put·ed·ly *adv* : according to reputation or general belief

req *abbr* **1** require; required **2** requisition

reqd *abbr* required

1re·quest \ri-ˈkwest\ *n* [ME *requeste,* fr. MF, fr. (assumed) VL *requaesta,* fr. fem. of *requaestus,* pp. of *requaerere* to require] **1** : the act or an instance of asking for something **2** : something asked for **3** : the condition or fact of being requested <available on ~> **4** : the state of being sought after : DEMAND

2request *vt* **1** : to make a request to or of <~*ed* her to write a paper> **2** : to ask as a favor or privilege <he ~*s* to be excused> **3** *obs* : to ask (a person) to come or go to a thing or place **4** : to ask for <~*ed* a brief delay> ***syn*** see ASK — **re·quest·er** *or* **re·quest·or** \-ˈkwes-tər\ *n*

re·qui·em \ˈrek-wē-əm *also* ˈrāk- *or* ˈrēk-\ *n* [ME, fr. L (first word of the introit of the requiem mass), accus. of *requies* rest, fr. *re-* + *quies* quiet, rest — more at WHILE] **1** : a mass for the dead **2 a** : a solemn chant (as a dirge) for the repose of the dead **b** : something that resembles such a solemn chant **3** *cap* **a** : a musical setting of the mass for the dead **b** : a musical composition in honor of the dead

re·qui·es·cat \ˌrek-wē-ˈes-ˌkät; -ˌat; ˌrā-kwē-ˈes-ˌkät\ *n* [L, may he (or she) rest, fr. *requiescere* to rest, fr. *re-* + *quiescere* to be quiet, fr. *quies*] : a prayer for the repose of a dead person

re·quin \rə-ˈkan\ *n* [F] : any of several voracious sharks (family Carcharhinidae)

re·quire \ri-ˈkwī(ə)r\ *vb* **re·quired; re·quir·ing** [ME *requeren,* fr. MF *requerre,* fr. (assumed) VL *requaerere* to seek for, need, require, alter. of L *requirere,* fr. *re-* + *quaerere* to seek, ask] *vt* **1 a** : to claim or ask for by right and authority <this night your soul is *required* of you —Lk 12:20 (RSV)> **b** *archaic* : REQUEST **2 a** : to call for as suitable or appropriate <the occasion ~*s* formal dress> **b** : to demand as necessary or essential : have a compelling need for <all living beings ~ food> **3** : to impose a compulsion or command on : COMPEL **4** *chiefly Brit* : to feel or be obliged — used with a following infinitive <one does not ~ to be a specialist —Elizabeth Bowen> ~ *vi, archaic* : ASK ***syn*** see DEMAND, LACK

re·quire·ment \-ˈkwī(ə)r-mənt\ *n* : something required: **a** : something wanted or needed : NECESSITY <production was not sufficient to satisfy ~*s* for cars> **b** : an essential requisite : CONDITION <failed to meet the school's ~*s*>

req·ui·site \ˈrek-wə-zət\ *adj* [ME, fr. L *requisitus,* pp. of *requirere*] : ESSENTIAL, NECESSARY — **requisite** *n* — **req·ui·site·ness** *n*

req·ui·si·tion \ˌrek-wə-ˈzish-ən\ *n* [MF or ML; MF, fr. ML *requisition-, requisitio,* fr. L, act of searching, fr. *requisitus*] **1 a** : the act of formally requiring or calling upon someone to perform an action **b** : a formal demand made by one nation upon another for the surrender or extradition of a fugitive from justice **2 a** : the act of requiring something to be furnished **b** : a demand or application made usu. with authority: as (1) : a demand made by military authorities upon civilians for supplies or other needs (2) : a written request for something authorized but not made available automatically **3** : the state of being in demand or use — **requisition** *vt*

re·quit·al \ri-ˈkwīt-ᵊl\ *n* **1** : the act or action of requiting : the state of being requited **2** : something given in return, compensation, or retaliation

re·quite \ri-ˈkwīt\ *vt* **re·quit·ed; re·quit·ing** [*re-* + obs. *quite* (to quit, pay), fr. ME *quiten* — more at QUIT] **1 a** : to make return for : REPAY **b** : to make retaliation for : AVENGE **2** : to make suitable return to for a benefit or service or for an injury ***syn*** see RECIPROCATE — **re·quit·er** *n*

re·ra·di·ate \(ˈ)rē-ˈrād-ē-ˌāt\ *vt* : to radiate again or anew; *esp* : to emit (energy) in the form of radiation after absorbing incident radiation — **re·ra·di·a·tion** \(ˌ)rē-ˌrād-ē-ˈā-shən\ *n*

rere·dos \ˈrer-ə-ˌdäs *also* ˈrir-ə-ˌdäs *or* ˈri(ə)r-ˌdäs\ *n* [ME, fr. AF *areredos,* fr. MF *arrere* behind + *dos* back, fr. L *dorsum* — more at ARREAR] **1** : a usu. ornamental wood or stone screen or partition wall behind an altar **2** : the back of a fireplace or open hearth

1re·re·lease \ˌrē-ri-ˈlēs\ *vt* : to release (as a movie or record) again

2rerelease *n* : something that is rereleased

rere·mouse \ˈri(ə)r-ˌmau̇s\ *n* [ME *reremous,* fr. OE *hrēremūs,* prob. fr. *hrēran* to stir + *mūs* mouse] *chiefly dial* : BAT

rereward *n* [ME *rerewarde,* fr. AF, fr. OF *rere* behind + ONF *warde* guard; akin to OF *garde* guard — more at REAR GUARD] *obs* : REAR GUARD

---

[1]**re·run** \(ˈ)rē-ˈrən\ *vt* **-ran** \-ˈran\; **-run; -run·ning :** to run again or anew
[2]**re·run** \ˈrē-ˌrən, (ˈ)rē-ˈ\ *n* **:** the act or action or an instance of rerunning **:** REPETITION; *esp* **:** a presentation of a motion-picture film or television program after its first run
[1]**res** \ˈrās, ˈrēz\ *n, pl* **res** [L — more at REAL] **:** a particular thing **:** MATTER — used esp. in legal phrases
[2]**res** *abbr* **1** research **2** reserve **3** residence **4** resolution
RES *abbr* reticuloendothelial system
res ad·ju·di·ca·ta \ˈrē-zə-ˌjüd-i-ˈkät-ə\ *n* [LL] **:** RES JUDICATA
re·sail \(ˈ)rē-ˈsā(ə)l\ *vi* **:** to sail back or again
re·sal·able \(ˈ)rē-ˈsā-lə-bəl\ *adj* **:** fit for resale
re·sale \ˈrē-ˌsāl, (ˈ)rē-ˈsā(ə)l\ *n* **1 :** the act of selling again usu. to a new party **2 a :** a secondhand sale **b :** an additional sale to the same buyer
re·scale \(ˈ)rē-ˈskā(ə)l\ *vt* **:** to plan, establish, or formulate on a new and usu. smaller scale
re·scind \ri-ˈsind\ *vt* [L *rescindere* to annul, fr. *re-* + *scindere* to cut — more at SHED] **1 :** to take away **:** REMOVE **2 a :** to take back **:** ANNUL, CANCEL <refused to ~ his harsh order> **b :** to abrogate (a contract) by restoring to the opposite party what one has received from him **3 :** to make void (as an act) by action of the enacting authority or a superior authority **:** REPEAL — **re·scind·er** *n* — **re·scind·ment** \-ˈsin(d)-mənt\ *n*
re·scis·sion \ri-ˈsizh-ən\ *n* [LL *rescission-, rescissio,* fr. L *rescissus,* pp. of *rescindere*] **:** an act of rescinding
re·scis·so·ry \-ˈsiz-ə-rē, -ˈsis-\ *adj* **:** relating to or tending to or having the effect of rescission
re·script \ˈrē-ˌskript\ *n* [L, *rescriptum,* fr. neut. of *rescriptus,* pp. of *rescribere* to write in reply, fr. *re-* + *scribere* to write — more at SCRIBE] **1 :** a written answer of a Roman emperor or of a pope to a legal inquiry or petition **2 :** an official or authoritative order, decree, edict, or announcement **3 :** an act or instance of rewriting
res·cue \ˈres-(ˌ)kyü\ *vt* **res·cued; res·cu·ing** [ME *rescuen,* fr. MF *rescourre,* fr. OF, fr. *re-* + *escourre* to shake out, fr. L *excutere,* fr. *ex-* + *quatere* to shake — more at QUASH] **:** to free from confinement, danger, or evil **:** SAVE, DELIVER: as **a :** to take (as a prisoner) forcibly from legal custody **b :** to recover (as a prize) by force **c :** to deliver (as a place under seige) by armed force — **rescue** *n* — **res·cu·er** *n*
syn RESCUE, DELIVER, REDEEM, RANSOM, RECLAIM, SAVE *shared meaning element* **:** to set free (as from confinement or risk)
rescue mission *n* **:** a city religious mission seeking to convert and rehabilitate the down-and-out
[1]**re·search** \ri-ˈsərch, ˈrē-ˌ\ *n* [MF *recerche,* fr. *recerchier* to investigate thoroughly, fr. OF, fr. *re-* + *cerchier* to search — more at SEARCH] **1 :** careful or diligent search **2 :** studious inquiry or examination; *esp* **:** investigation or experimentation aimed at the discovery and interpretation of facts, revision of accepted theories or laws in the light of new facts, or practical application of such new or revised theories or laws
[2]**research** *vt* **1 :** to search or investigate exhaustively <~ a problem> **2 :** to do research for <~ a book> ~ *vi* **:** to engage in research — **re·search·able** \-ə-bəl\ *adj* — **re·search·er** *n*
re·search·ist \-ˈsər-chəst, -ˌsər-\ *n* **:** one engaged in research
re·seau \rā-ˈzō, ri-\ *n, pl* **re·seaux** \-ˈzōz\ [F *réseau,* fr. OF *resel,* dim. of *rais* net, fr. L *retis, rete* — more at RETINA] **1 :** a system of lines forming small squares of standard size photographed by a separate exposure on the same plate with star images to facilitate measurements **2 :** a net ground or foundation in lace **3 :** a screen with minute elements of three colors in a regular geometric pattern used for taking color photographs
re·sect \ri-ˈsekt\ *vt* [L *resectus,* pp. of *resecare* to cut off, fr. *re-* + *secare* to cut — more at SAW] **:** to perform resection on — **re·sect·abil·i·ty** \-ˌsek-tə-ˈbil-ət-ē\ *n* — **re·sect·able** \-ˈsek-tə-bəl\ *adj*
re·sec·tion \ri-ˈsek-shən\ *n* **:** the surgical removal of part of an organ or structure
[1]**re·se·da** \ri-ˈsed-ə\ *n* [NL, genus name, fr. L, a plant used to reduce tumors] **:** any of a genus (*Reseda*) of Old World herbs of the mignonette family having racemose flowers with cleft petals and numerous stamens
[2]**reseda** \ˈrā-zə-ˌdä\ *n* [F *réséda,* fr. *réséda* reseda plant] **:** a variable color averaging a grayish green
re·seed \(ˈ)rē-ˈsēd\ *vt* **1 :** to sow seed on again or anew **2 :** to maintain (itself) by self-sown seed ~ *vi* **:** to maintain itself by self-sown seed
re·sem·blance \ri-ˈzem-blən(t)s\ *n* **1 a :** the quality or state of resembling; *esp* **:** correspondence in appearance or superficial qualities **b :** a point of likeness **2 :** REPRESENTATION, IMAGE **3** *archaic* **:** characteristic appearance **4** *obs* **:** PROBABILITY ***syn*** see LIKENESS ***ant*** difference, distinction
re·sem·blant \-blənt\ *adj* **:** marked by or showing resemblance
re·sem·ble \ri-ˈzem-bəl\ *vt* **re·sem·bled; re·sem·bling** \-b(ə-)liŋ\ [ME *resemblen,* fr. MF *resembler,* fr. OF, fr. *re-* + *sembler* to be like, seem, fr. L *similare* to copy, fr. *similis* like — more at SAME] **1 :** to be like or similar to **2** *archaic* **:** to represent as like
re·send \(ˈ)rē-ˈsend\ *vt* **-sent** \-ˈsent\; **-send·ing :** to send again or back
re·sent \ri-ˈzent\ *vt* [F *ressentir* to be emotionally sensible of, fr. OF, fr. *re-* + *sentir* to feel, fr. L *sentire* — more at SENSE] **:** to feel or express annoyance or ill will at
re·sent·ful \-fəl\ *adj* **1 :** full of resentment **:** inclined to resent **2 :** caused or marked by resentment — **re·sent·ful·ly** \-fə-lē\ *adv* — **re·sent·ful·ness** *n*
re·sent·ment \ri-ˈzent-mənt\ *n* **:** a feeling of indignant displeasure or persistent ill will at something regarded as a wrong, insult, or injury ***syn*** see OFFENSE
re·ser·pine \ri-ˈsər-ˌpēn, -pən\ *n* [G *reserpin,* prob. irreg. fr. NL *Rauwolfia serpentina,* a species of rauwolfia] **:** a drug $C_{33}H_{40}N_2O_9$ extracted esp. from the root of rauwolfias and used in the treatment of hypertension, mental disorders, and tension states
res·er·va·tion \ˌrez-ər-ˈvā-shən\ *n* **1 :** an act of reserving something: as **a (1) :** the act or fact of a grantor's reserving some newly created thing out of the thing granted **(2) :** the right or interest so reserved **b :** the setting of limiting conditions or withholding from complete exposition <answered without ~> **c :** an arrangement to have something (as a hotel room or a theater seat) held for one's use; *also* **:** a promise, guarantee, or record of such engagement **2 :** something reserved: as **a :** a tract of public land set aside (as for the use of Indians) **b :** an area in which hunting is not permitted; *esp* **:** one set aside as a secure breeding place **3 a :** a limiting condition <agreed, but with ~*s*> **b :** a specific objection <had ~*s* about the finding>
[1]**re·serve** \ri-ˈzərv\ *vt* **re·served; re·serv·ing** [ME *reserven,* fr. MF *reserver,* fr. L *reservare,* lit., to keep back, fr. *re-* + *servare* to keep — more at CONSERVE] **1 a :** to hold in reserve **:** keep back <~ grain for seed> **b (1) :** to retain power of absolution of to oneself — used of a religious superior **(2) :** to set aside (part of the consecrated elements) at the Eucharist for future use **c :** to retain or hold over to a future time or place **:** DEFER <~ one's judgment on a plan> **d :** to make legal reservation of **2 :** to set or have set aside or apart <~ a hotel room> ***syn*** see KEEP
[2]**reserve** *n, often attrib* **1 :** something stored or kept available for future use or need **:** STOCK **2 :** something reserved or set aside for a particular purpose, use, or reason: as **a (1) :** a military force withheld from action for later decisive use — usu. used in pl. **(2) :** forces not in the field but available **(3) :** the military forces of a country not part of the regular services; *also* **:** RESERVIST **b :** a tract (as of public land) set apart **:** RESERVATION **3 :** an act of reserving **:** QUALIFICATION **4 a :** restraint, closeness, or caution in one's words and actions **b :** forebearance from making a full explanation, complete disclosure, or free expression of one's mind **5** *archaic* **:** SECRET **6 a :** money or its equivalent kept in hand or set apart usu. to meet liabilities **b :** the liquid resources of a nation for meeting international payments **7 :** the capacity of blood or bacteriological media to react with acid or alkali within predetermined usu. physiological limits of hydrogen-ion concentration **8 :** SUBSTITUTE — **in reserve :** held back for future or special use
reserve bank *n* **:** a central bank holding reserves of other banks
reserve clause *n* **:** the clause in a professional athlete's contract that reserves for the club the exclusive right to the athlete's services until he is sold, traded, or released
re·served \ri-ˈzərvd\ *adj* **1 :** restrained in words and actions **2 :** kept or set apart or aside for future or special use ***syn*** see SILENT ***ant*** expansive, blatant — **re·serv·ed·ly** \-ˈzər-vəd-lē\ *adv* — **re·serv·ed·ness** \-ˈzər-vəd-nəs\ *n*
reserved power *n* **:** a political power reserved by a constitution to the exclusive jurisdiction of a specified political authority
reserve price *n* **:** a price announced at an auction as the lowest that will be considered
re·serv·ist \ri-ˈzər-vəst\ *n* **:** a member of a military reserve
res·er·voir \ˈrez-ə(r)v-ˌwär, -ə(r)v-ˌ(w)ȯr *also* -ər-ˌvȯi\ *n* [F *réservoir,* fr. MF, fr. *reserver*] **1 :** a place where something is kept in store: as **a :** an artificial lake where water is collected and kept in quantity for use **b :** a part of an apparatus in which a liquid is held **c :** SUPPLY, STORE <a large ~ of educated people> **2 :** an extra supply **:** RESERVE **3 :** an organism in which a parasite that is pathogenic for some other species lives and multiples without damaging its host; *also* **:** a noneconomic organism within which a pathogen of economic or medical importance flourishes
re·set \(ˈ)rē-ˈset\ *vt* **-set; -set·ting 1 :** to set again or anew <~ type> <~ a diamond> **2 :** to change the reading of <~ an odometer> — **re·set·table** \-ˈset-ə-bəl\ *adj*
res ges·tae \ˈrās-ˈges-ˌtī, ˈrēz-ˈjes-(ˌ)tē\ *n pl* [L] **:** things done; *esp* **:** the facts that form the environment of a litigated issue and are admissible in evidence
resh \ˈrāsh\ *n* [Heb *rēsh*] **:** the 20th letter of the Hebrew alphabet — see ALPHABET table
re·shape \(ˈ)rē-ˈshāp\ *vt* **:** to give a new form or orientation to **:** REORGANIZE — **re·shap·er** *n*
re·ship \(ˈ)rē-ˈship\ *vt* **:** to ship again; *specif* **:** to put on board a second time ~ *vi* **:** to embark on a ship again or anew; *specif* **:** to sign again for service on a ship — **re·ship·ment** \-mənt\ *n* — **re·ship·per** *n*
re·shuf·fle \(ˈ)rē-ˈshəf-əl\ *vt* **1 :** to shuffle (as cards) again **2 :** to reorganize usu. by the redistribution of existing elements <the cabinet was *reshuffled* by the prime minister> — **reshuffle** *n*
re·sid \ri-ˈzid\ *n* **:** RESIDUAL OIL
re·side \ri-ˈzīd\ *vi* **re·sid·ed; re·sid·ing** [ME *residen,* fr. MF or L; MF *resider,* fr. L *residēre* to sit back, remain, abide, fr. *re-* + *sedēre* to sit — more at SIT] **1 a :** to be in residence as the incumbent of a benefice or office **b :** to dwell permanently or continuously **:** occupy a place as one's legal domicile **2 a :** to be present as an element or quality **b :** to be vested as a right — **re·sid·er** *n*
syn RESIDE, LIVE, DWELL, SOJOURN *shared meaning element* **:** to have as one's habitation or domicile
res·i·dence \ˈrez-əd-ən(t)s, ˈrez-dən(t)s, ˈrez-ə-ˌden(t)s\ *n* **1 a :** the act or fact of dwelling in a place for some time **b :** the act or fact of living or regularly staying at or in some place for the discharge of a duty or the enjoyment of a benefit **2 a (1) :** the place where one actually lives as distinguished from his domicile or a place of temporary sojourn **(2) :** DOMICILE 2a **b :** the place where a corporation is actually or officially established **c :** the status of a legal resident **3 a :** a building used as a home **:** DWELLING **b :** housing or a unit of housing provided for students **4 a :** the period or duration of abode in a place <after a ~ of 30 years> **b :** a period of active and esp. full-time study, research, or teaching at a college or university **5 :** the persistence of a substance that is suspended or dissolved in a medium <the ~ time of a pollutant> — **in residence :** engaged to live and work at a particular place often for a specified time <poet *in residence* at a university>
res·i·den·cy \ˈrez-əd-ən-sē, ˈrez-dən-, ˈrez-ə-ˌden(t)-\ *n, pl* **-cies 1 :** a usu. official place of residence **2 :** a territory in a protected state in which the powers of the protecting state are executed by a resident agent **3 :** a period of advanced training in a medical specialty

[1]**res·i·dent** \'rez-əd-ənt, 'rez-dənt, 'rez-ə-ˌdent\ *adj* [ME, fr. L *resident-, residens,* prp. of *residēre*] **1 a :** living in a place for some length of time : RESIDING **b :** serving in a regular or full-time capacity <the ~ engineer for a highway department>; *also* : being in residence **2 :** PRESENT, INHERENT **3 :** not migratory

[2]**resident** *n* **1 :** one who resides in a place **2 :** a diplomatic agent residing at a foreign court or seat of government; *esp* : one exercising authority in a protected state as representative of the protecting power **3 :** a physician serving a residency

resident commissioner *n* **1 :** a nonvoting representative of a dependency in the U.S. House of Representatives **2 :** a resident administrator in a British colony or possession

res·i·den·tial \ˌrez(-ə)-'den-chəl\ *adj* **1 a :** used as a residence or by residents **b :** providing living accommodations for students <a ~ college> **2 :** restricted to or occupied by residences <a ~ neighborhood> **3 :** of or relating to residence or residences — **res·i·den·tial·ly** \-'dench-(ə-)lē\ *adv*

[1]**re·sid·u·al** \ri-'zij-(ə-)wəl, -'zij-əl\ *adj* [L *residuum* residue] **1 :** of, relating to, or constituting a residue **2 :** leaving a residue that remains effective for some time — **re·sid·u·al·ly** \-ē\ *adv*

[2]**residual** *n* **1 :** REMAINDER, RESIDUUM: as **a :** the difference between results obtained by observation and by computation from a formula or between the mean of several observations and any one of them **b :** a residual product or substance **c :** an internal aftereffect of experience or activity that influences later behavior; *esp* : a disability remaining from a disease or operation **2 :** a payment (as to an actor or writer) for each rerun after an initial showing (as of a taped TV show)

residual oil *n* **:** fuel oil that remains after the removal of valuable distillates (as gasoline) from petroleum and that is used esp. by industry — called also *resid*

residual power *n* **:** power held to remain at the disposal of a governmental authority after an enumeration or delegation of specified powers to other authorities

re·sid·u·ary \ri-'zij-ə-ˌwer-ē\ *adj* **:** of, relating to, or constituting a residue

res·i·due \'rez-ə-ˌd(y)ü\ *n* [ME, fr. MF *residu,* fr. L *residuum,* fr. neut. of *residuus* left over, fr. *residēre* to remain] **:** something that remains after a part is taken, separated, or designated : REMNANT, REMAINDER: as **a :** the part of a testator's estate remaining after the satisfaction of all debts, charges, allowances, and previous devises and bequests **b :** the remainder after subtracting a multiple of a modulus from an integer or a power of the integer : the second of two terms in a congruence <2 and 7 are ~*s* of 12 modulo 5> <9 is a quadratic ~ of 7 modulo 5 since 7^2–8x5=9> **c :** a constituent structural unit (as a group or monomer) of a usu. complex molecule <amino acid ~*s* left after hydrolysis of protein>

residue class *n* **:** the set of elements (as integers) that leave the same remainder when divided by the same modulus

re·sid·u·um \ri-'zij-ə-wəm\ *n, pl* **re·sid·ua** \-ə-wə\ [L] **:** something residual: as **a :** RESIDUE a **b :** a residual product (as from the distillation of petroleum)

re·sign \ri-'zīn\ *vb* [ME *resignen,* fr. MF *resigner,* fr. L *resignare,* lit., to unseal, cancel, fr. *re-* + *signare* to sign, seal — more at SIGN] *vt* **1 :** to give up deliberately; *esp* : to renounce (as a right or position) by a formal act **2 :** RELEGATE, CONSIGN: *esp* : to give (oneself) over without resistance <~*ed* herself to her fate> ~ *vi* **1 :** to give up one's office or position : QUIT **2 :** to accept something as inevitable : SUBMIT *syn* see RELINQUISH, ABDICATE — **re·sign·ed·ly** \-'zī-nəd-lē\ *adv* — **re·sign·ed·ness** \-'zī-nəd-nəs\ *n* — **re·sign·er** \-'zī-nər\ *n*

res·ig·na·tion \ˌrez-ig-'nā-shən\ *n* **1 a :** an act or instance of resigning something : SURRENDER **b :** a formal notification of resigning **2 :** the quality or state of being resigned : SUBMISSIVENESS

re·sile \ri-'zī(ə)l\ *vi* **re·siled; re·sil·ing** [LL & L; LL *resilire* to withdraw, fr. L, to recoil] **:** RECOIL, RETRACT: *esp* : to return to a prior position

re·sil·ience \ri-'zil-yən(t)s\ *n* **1 :** the capability of a strained body to recover its size and shape after deformation caused esp. by compressive stress **2 :** an ability to recover from or adjust easily to misfortune or change

re·sil·ien·cy \-yən-sē\ *n* **:** RESILIENCE

re·sil·ient \-yənt\ *adj* [L *resilient-, resiliens,* prp. of *resilire* to jump back, recoil, fr. *re-* + *salire* to leap — more at SALLY] **:** characterized or marked by resilience: as **a :** capable of withstanding shock without permanent deformation or rupture **b :** tending to recover from or adjust easily to misfortune or change — **re·sil·ient·ly** *adv*

[1]**res·in** \'rez-ᵊn\ *n* [ME, fr. MF *resine,* fr. L *resina,* fr. Gk *rhētinē* pine resin] **1 a :** any of various solid or semisolid amorphous fusible flammable natural organic substances that are usu. transparent or translucent and yellowish to brown, are formed esp. in plant secretions, are soluble in organic solvents (as ether) but not in water, are electrical nonconductors, and are used chiefly in varnishes, printing inks, plastics, and sizes and in medicine **b :** ROSIN **2 a :** any of a large class of synthetic products that have some of the physical properties of natural resins but are different chemically and are used chiefly as plastics **b :** any of various products made from a natural resin or a natural polymer

[2]**resin** *vt* **res·ined; res·in·ing** \'rez-ᵊn-iŋ, 'rez-niŋ\ **:** to treat with resin

res·in·ate \'rez-ᵊn-ˌāt\ *vt* **-at·ed; -at·ing :** to impregnate or flavor with resin

resin canal *n* **:** a tubular intercellular space in gymnosperms and some angiosperms that is lined with epithelial cells which secrete resin — called also *resin duct*

re·sin·i·fy \re-'zin-ə-ˌfī\ *vt* **-fied; fy·ing :** to convert into or treat with resin

re·sin·oid \'rez-ᵊn-ˌȯid\ *n* **1 a :** a somewhat resinous substance **b :** a thermosetting synthetic resin **2 :** GUM RESIN

res·in·ous \'rez-nəs, -ᵊn-əs\ *adj* **:** of, relating to, resembling, containing, or derived from resin

[1]**re·sist** \ri-'zist\ *vb* [ME *resisten,* fr. MF or L; MF *resister,* fr. L *resistere,* fr. *re-* + *sistere* to take a stand; akin to L *stare* to stand — more at STAND] *vt* **1 :** to withstand the force or effect of **2 :** to exert oneself so as to counteract or defeat ~ *vi* **:** to exert force in opposition ***syn*** see OPPOSE

[2]**resist** *n* **:** something (as a protective coating) that resists or prevents a particular action

re·sis·tance \ri-'zis-tən(t)s\ *n* **1 a :** an act or instance of resisting : OPPOSITION **b :** a means of resisting **2 :** the ability to resist; *esp* : the inherent capacity of a living being to resist untoward circumstances (as disease, malnutrition, or toxic agents) **3 :** an opposing or retarding force **4 a :** the opposition offered by a body or substance to the passage through it of a steady electric current **b :** a source of resistance **5** *often cap* **:** an underground organization of a conquered country engaging in sabotage and secret operations against occupation forces and collaborators

[1]**re·sis·tant** \-tənt\ *adj* **:** giving or capable of resistance — often used in combination <wrinkle-*resistant* clothes>

[2]**resistant** *n* **:** one that resists : RESISTER

re·sist·er \ri-'zis-tər\ *n* **:** one that resists; *esp* : one who actively opposes the policies of a government

re·sist·ibil·i·ty \ri-ˌzis-tə-'bil-ət-ē\ *n* **1 :** the quality or state of being resistible **2 :** ability to resist

re·sist·ible *or* **re·sist·able** \ri-'zis-tə-bəl\ *adj* **:** capable of being resisted

re·sis·tive \ri-'zis-tiv\ *adj* **:** marked by resistance — often used in combination <fire-*resistive* material> — **re·sis·tive·ly** *adv* — **re·sis·tive·ness** *n*

re·sis·tiv·i·ty \ri-ˌzis-'tiv-ət-ē, ˌrē-\ *n, pl* **-ties 1 :** capacity for resisting : RESISTANCE **2 :** the longitudinal electrical resistance of a uniform rod of unit length and unit cross-sectional area : the reciprocal of conductivity

re·sist·less \ri-'zist-ləs\ *adj* **1 :** IRRESISTIBLE **2 :** offering no resistance — **re·sist·less·ly** *adv* — **re·sist·less·ness** *n*

re·sis·tor \ri-'zis-tər\ *n* **:** a device that has electrical resistance and that is used in an electric circuit for protection, operation, or current control

re·sit·ting \(')rē-'sit-iŋ\ *n* **:** a sitting (as of a legislature) for a second time : another sitting

res ju·di·ca·ta \'rēz-ˌjüd-i-'kät-ə\ *n* [L, judged matter] **:** a matter finally decided on its merits by a court having competent jurisdiction and not subject to litigation again between the same parties

reso·jet engine \ˌrez-ō-ˌjet-\ *n* [*reso*nance + *jet* + *engine*] **:** a jet engine that consists of a continuously open air inlet, a diffuser, a combustion chamber, and an exhaust nozzle, has fuel admitted continuously, and has resonance established within the engine so that there is a pulsating thrust produced by the intermittent flow of hot gases

re·sole \(')rē-'sōl\ *vt* **:** to furnish (a shoe) with a new sole ~ *vi* **:** to resole a shoe

re·sol·u·ble \ri-'zäl-yə-bəl\ *adj* [LL *resolubilis,* fr. L *resolvere* to resolve] **:** capable of being resolved

[1]**res·o·lute** \'rez-ə-ˌlüt, -lət\ *adj* [L *resolutus,* pp. of *resolvere*] **1 :** marked by firm determination : RESOLVED **2 :** BOLD, STEADY ***syn*** see FAITHFUL — **res·o·lute·ly** \-ˌlüt-lē, -lət-; ˌrez-ə-'lüt-\ *adv* — **res·o·lute·ness** \-ˌlüt-nəs, -lət-, -'lüt-\ *n*

[2]**resolute** *n* **:** one who is resolute

res·o·lu·tion \ˌrez-ə-'lü-shən\ *n* **1 :** the act or process of reducing to simpler form: as **a :** the act of analyzing a complex notion into simpler ones **b :** the act of answering : SOLVING **c :** the act of determining **d :** the passing of a voice part from a dissonant to a consonant tone or the progression of a chord from dissonance to consonance **e :** the separating of a chemical compound or mixture into its constitutents **f (1) :** the division of a prosodic element into its component parts **(2) :** the substitution in Greek or Latin prosody of two short syllables for a long syllable **g :** the analysis of a vector into two or more vectors of which it is the sum **h :** the process or capability of making distinguishable the individual parts of an object, closely adjacent optical images, or sources of light **2 :** the subsidence of inflammation esp. in a lung **3 a :** something that is resolved **b :** firmness of resolve **4 :** a formal expression of opinion, will, or intent voted by an official body or assembled group **5 :** the point in a literary work at which the chief dramatic complication is worked out ***syn*** see COURAGE

[1]**re·solve** \ri-'zälv, -'zȯlv\ *vb* **re·solved; re·solv·ing** [L *resolvere* to unloose, dissolve, fr. *re-* + *solvere* to loosen, release — more at SOLVE] *vt* **1** *obs* **:** DISSOLVE, MELT **2 a :** to break up : SEPARATE <the prism *resolved* the light into a play of color>; *also* : to change by disintegration **b :** to reduce by analysis <~ the problem into simple elements> **c :** to distinguish between or make independently visible adjacent parts of **d :** to separate (a racemic compound or mixture) into the two components **3 :** to cause resolution of (as inflammation) **4 a :** to deal with successfully : clear up <~ doubts> <~ a dispute> **b :** to find an answer to **c :** to make clear or understandable **d :** to find a mathematical solution of **e :** to split up (as a vector) into two or more components esp. in assigned directions **5 :** to reach a firm decision about <~ to get more sleep> <~ disputed points in a text> **6 a :** to declare or decide by a formal resolution and vote **b :** to change by resolution or formal vote <the house *resolved* itself into a committee> **7 :** to make (as voice parts) progress from dissonance to consonance **8 :** to work out the resolution of (as a play) ~ *vi* **1 :** to become separated into component parts; *also* : to become reduced by dissolving or analysis **2 :** to form a resolution : DETERMINE **3 :** CONSULT, DELIBERATE **4 :** to progress

from dissonance to consonance ***syn*** **1** see ANALYZE ***ant*** blend **2** see DECIDE — **re·solv·able** \-ˈzäl-və-bəl, -ˈzȯl-\ *adj* — **re·solv·er** *n*

2**resolve** *n* **1 :** something that is resolved **2 :** fixity of purpose **:** RESOLUTENESS **3 :** a legal or official determination; *esp* **:** a formal resolution

1**re·sol·vent** \ri-ˈzäl-vənt, -ˈzȯl-\ *adj* [L *resolvent, resolvens,* prp. of *resolvere*] **:** having power to resolve <a ~ drug>

2**resolvent** *n* **1 :** an agent capable of dispersing or absorbing inflammatory products **2 :** SOLVENT **3 :** a means of solving something

resolving power *n* **1 :** the ability of an optical system to form distinguishable images of objects separated by small angular distances **2 :** the ability of a photographic film or plate to reproduce the fine detail of an optical image

res·o·nance \ˈrez-ᵊn-ən(t)s, ˈrez-nən(t)s\ *n* **1 a :** the quality or state of being resonant **b (1) :** a vibration of large amplitude in a mechanical or electrical system caused by a relatively small periodic stimulus of the same or nearly the same period as the natural vibration period of the system **(2) :** the state of adjustment that produces resonance in a mechanical or electrical system **2 a :** the intensification and enriching of a musical tone by supplementary vibration **b :** a quality imparted to voiced sounds by the resonance-chamber action of mouth and pharynx configurations and in some cases also of the nostrils **c :** a quality of richness or variety **3 :** the sound elicited on percussion of the chest **4 :** a phenomenon that is shown by a molecule, ion, or radical to which two or more structures differing only in the distribution of electrons can be assigned and which gives rise to a stable structure intermediate among the assigned structures **5 a :** the enhancement of an atomic, nuclear, or particle reaction or a scattering event by excitation of internal motion in the system **b :** MAGNETIC RESONANCE **6 :** an extremely short-lived elementary particle

res·o·nant \ˈrez-ᵊn-ənt, ˈrez-nənt\ *adj* **1 :** continuing to sound **:** ECHOING **2 a :** capable of inducing resonance **b :** relating to or exhibiting resonance **3 a :** intensified and enriched by resonance **b :** marked by grandiloquence — **resonant** *n* — **res·o·nant·ly** *adv*

res·o·nate \ˈrez-ᵊn-ˌāt\ *vb* **-nat·ed; -nat·ing** [L *resonatus,* pp. of *resonare* to resound — more at RESOUND] *vi* **1 :** to produce or exhibit resonance **2 :** to respond as if by resonance <a child learning to talk ~*s* to his family>; *also* **:** to have a repetitive pattern that resembles resonance ~ *vt* **:** to subject to resonating

res·o·na·tor \-ˌāt-ər\ *n* **:** something that resounds or resonates: as **a :** a hollow metallic container for producing microwaves or a piezoelectric crystal put into oscillation by the oscillations of an outside source **b :** a device for increasing the resonance of a musical instrument

re·sorb \(ˈ)rē-ˈsȯ(ə)rb, -ˈzȯ(ə)rb\ *vb* [L *resorbēre,* fr. *re-* + *sorbēre* to suck up — more at ABSORB] *vt* **1 :** to swallow or suck in again **2 :** to break down and assimilate (something previously differentiated) ~ *vi* **:** to undergo resorption

res·or·cin \rə-ˈzȯrs-ᵊn\ *n* [ISV *res-* (fr. L *resina* resin) + *orcin* (a phenol $C_7H_8O_2$)] **:** RESORCINOL

res·or·cin·ol \-ˌȯl, -ˌōl\ *n* **:** a crystalline phenol $C_6H_6O_2$ obtained from various resins or artificially and used esp. in making dyes, pharmaceuticals, and resins

re·sorp·tion \(ˈ)rē-ˈsȯrp-shən, -ˈzȯrp-\ *n* [L *resorptus,* pp. of *resorbēre*] **:** the action or process of resorbing something — **re·sorp·tive** \-tiv\ *adj*

1**re·sort** \ri-ˈzȯ(ə)rt\ *n* [ME, fr. MF, resource, recourse, fr. *resortir* to rebound, resort, fr. OF, fr. *re-* + *sortir* to escape, sally] **1 a :** one who is looked to for help **:** REFUGE, RESOURCE **b :** RECOURSE **2 a :** frequent, habitual, or general visiting <a place of popular ~> **b :** persons who frequent a place **:** THRONG **c (1) :** a frequently visited place **:** HAUNT **(2) :** a place providing recreation and entertainment esp. to vacationers ***syn*** see RESOURCE

2**resort** *vi* **1 :** to go esp. frequently or habitually **:** REPAIR **2 :** to have recourse <~ to force>

re·sort·er \ri-ˈzȯrt-ər\ *n* **:** a frequenter of resorts

re·sound \ri-ˈzaund *also* -ˈsaund\ *vb* [ME *resounen,* fr. MF *resoner,* fr. L *resonare,* fr. *re-* + *sonare* to sound; akin to L *sonus* sound — more at SOUND] *vi* **1 :** to become filled with sound **:** REVERBERATE **2 a :** to sound loudly **b :** to produce a sonorous or echoing sound **3 :** to become renowned ~ *vt* **1 :** to extol loudly or widely **:** CELEBRATE **2 :** ECHO, REVERBERATE **3 :** to sound or utter in full resonant tones

re·sound·ing *adj* **1 :** producing or characterized by resonant sound **:** RESONATING **2 a :** impressively sonorous **b :** EMPHATIC, UNEQUIVOCAL <a ~ success> — **re·sound·ing·ly** \-ˈzau̇n-diŋ-lē *also* -ˈsau̇n-\ *adv*

re·source \ˈrē-ˌsō(ə)rs, -ˌsȯ(ə)rs, -ˌzō(ə)rs, -ˌzȯ(ə)rs, ri-ˈ\ *n* [F *ressource,* fr. OF *ressourse* relief, resource, fr. *resourdre* to relieve, lit., to rise again, fr. L *resurgere* — more at RESURRECTION] **1 a :** a source of supply or support **:** an available means — usu. used in pl. **b :** a natural source of wealth or revenue — usu. used in pl. **c :** computable wealth — usu. used in pl. **d :** a source of information or expertise **2 :** something to which one has recourse in difficulty **:** EXPEDIENT **3 :** a possibility of relief or recovery **4 :** a means of spending one's leisure time **5 :** an ability to meet and handle a situation **:** RESOURCEFULNESS

syn RESOURCE, RESORT, EXPEDIENT, SHIFT, MAKESHIFT, STOPGAP *shared meaning element* **:** something one turns to in the absence of a usual means or source of supply

re·source·ful \ri-ˈsōrs-fəl, -ˈsȯrs-, -ˈzōrs-, -ˈzȯrs-\ *adj* **:** able to meet situations **:** capable of devising ways and means — **re·source·ful·ly** \-fə-lē\ *adv* — **re·source·ful·ness** *n*

resp *abbr* respective; respectively

1**re·spect** \ri-ˈspekt\ *n* [ME, fr. L *respectus,* lit., act of looking back, fr. *respectus,* pp. of *respicere* to look back, regard, fr. *re-* + *specere* to look — more at SPY] **1 :** a relation to or concern with something usu. specified **:** REFERENCE <with ~ to your last letter> **2 :** an act of giving particular attention **:** CONSIDERATION **3 a :** high or special regard **:** ESTEEM **b :** the quality or state of being esteemed **c** *pl* **:** expressions of respect or deference <paid his ~*s*> **4 :** PARTICULAR, DETAIL <a good plan in some ~*s*>

2**respect** *vt* **1 a :** to consider worthy of high regard **:** ESTEEM **b :** to refrain from interfering with **2 :** to have reference to **:** CONCERN ***syn*** see REGARD ***ant*** abuse, misuse — **re·spect·er** *n*

re·spect·abil·i·ty \ri-ˌspek-tə-ˈbil-ət-ē\ *n, pl* **-ties :** the quality or state of being respectable

1**re·spect·able** \ri-ˈspek-tə-bəl\ *adj* **1 :** worthy of respect **:** ESTIMABLE **2 :** decent or correct in character or behavior **:** PROPER **3 a :** fair in size or quantity <~ amount> **b :** moderately good **:** TOLERABLE **4 :** fit to be seen **:** PRESENTABLE <~ clothes> — **re·spect·able·ness** *n* — **re·spect·ably** \-blē\ *adv*

2**respectable** *n* **:** a respectable person

re·spect·ful \ri-ˈspekt-fəl\ *adj* **:** marked by or showing respect or deference — **re·spect·ful·ly** \-fə-lē\ *adv* — **re·spect·ful·ness** *n*

re·spect·ing *prep* **1 :** in view of **:** CONSIDERING **2 :** with regard to **:** CONCERNING

re·spec·tive \ri-ˈspek-tiv\ *adj* **1** *obs* **:** PARTIAL, DISCRIMINATIVE **2 :** PARTICULAR, SEPARATE <their ~ homes> — **re·spec·tive·ness** *n*

re·spec·tive·ly *adv* **1 :** in particular **:** SEPARATELY <could not recognize the solutions as salty or sour, ~> **2 :** in the order given <Mary and Anne were ~ 12 and 16 years old>

re·spell \(ˈ)rē-ˈspel\ *vt* **:** to spell again or in another way; *esp* **:** to spell out according to a phonetic system

res·pi·ra·ble \ˈres-p(ə-)rə-bəl, ri-ˈspī-rə-\ *adj* **:** fit for breathing; *also* **:** capable of being taken in by breathing <~ particles of ash>

res·pi·ra·tion \ˌres-pə-ˈrā-shən\ *n* **1 a :** the placing of air or dissolved gases in intimate contact with the circulating medium of a multicellular organism (as by breathing) **b :** a single complete act of breathing **2 :** the physical and chemical processes by which an organism supplies its cells and tissues with the oxygen needed for metabolism and relieves them of the carbon dioxide formed in energy-producing reactions **3 :** any of various energy-yielding oxidative reactions in living matter — **res·pi·ra·tion·al** \-shnəl, -shən-ᵊl\ *adj* — **re·spi·ra·to·ry** \ˈres-p(ə-)rə-ˌtōr-ē, ri-ˈspī-rə-, -ˌtȯr-\ *adj*

res·pi·ra·tor \ˈres-pə-ˌrāt-ər\ *n* **1 :** a device worn over the mouth or nose for protecting the respiratory tract **2 :** a device for maintaining artificial respiration

respiratory pigment *n* **:** any of various permanently or intermittently colored conjugated proteins that function in the transfer of oxygen in cellular respiration

respiratory quotient *n* **:** a ratio indicating the relation of the volume of carbon dioxide given off in respiration to that of the oxygen consumed

respiratory system *n* **:** a system of organs subserving the function of respiration and in air-breathing vertebrates consisting typically of the lungs and their nervous and circulatory supply and the channels by which these are continuous with the outer air

re·spire \ri-ˈspī(ə)r\ *vb* **re·spired; re·spir·ing** [ME *respiren,* fr. L *respirare,* fr. *re-* + *spirare* to blow, breathe — more at SPIRIT] *vi* **1 :** BREATHE; *specif* **:** to inhale and exhale air successively **2** *of a cell or tissue* **:** to take up oxygen and produce carbon dioxide through oxidation ~ *vt* **:** BREATHE

res·pi·rom·e·ter \ˌres-pə-ˈräm-ət-ər\ *n* **:** an instrument for studying the character and extent of respiration — **res·pi·ro·met·ric** \-rō-ˈme-trik\ *adj* — **res·pi·rom·e·try** \-ˈräm-ə-trē\ *n*

1**re·spite** \ˈres-pət *also* ri-ˈspīt, *Brit usu* ˈres-ˌpīt\ *n* [ME *respit,* fr. OF, fr. ML *respectus,* fr. L, act of looking back — more at RESPECT] **1 :** a period of temporary delay; *esp* **:** REPRIEVE 1b **2 :** an interval of rest or relief ***syn*** see PAUSE

2**respite** *vt* **re·spit·ed; re·spit·ing 1 :** to grant a respite to **2 :** to put off **:** DELAY

re·splen·dence \ri-ˈsplen-dən(t)s\ *n* **:** the quality or state of being resplendent **:** SPLENDOR

re·splen·den·cy \-dən-sē\ *n* **:** RESPLENDENCE

re·splen·dent \-dənt\ *adj* [L *resplendent-, resplendens,* prp. of *resplendēre* to shine back, fr. *re-* + *splendēre* to shine — more at SPLENDID] **:** shining brilliantly **:** characterized by a glowing splendor <how great and ~ a thing love could be —J. W. Krutch> ***syn*** see SPLENDID — **re·splen·dent·ly** *adv*

1**re·spond** \ri-ˈspänd\ *vb* [MF *respondre,* fr. L *respondēre* to promise in return, answer, fr. *re-* + *spondēre* to promise — more at SPOUSE] *vi* **1 :** to say something in return **:** make an answer **2 a :** to react in response **b :** to show favorable reaction <~ to surgery> **3 :** to be answerable <~ in damages> ~ *vt* **:** REPLY ***syn*** see ANSWER

2**respond** *n* **:** an engaged pillar supporting an arch or closing a colonnade or arcade

1**re·spon·dent** \ri-ˈspän-dənt\ *n* [L *respondent-, respondens,* prp. of *respondēre*] **1 :** one who responds: as **a :** one who maintains a thesis in reply **b (1) :** one who answers in various legal proceedings (as in equity cases) **(2) :** the prevailing party in the lower court **c :** a person who responds to a poll **2 :** a reflex that occurs in response to a specific external stimulus <the knee jerk is a typical ~> — compare OPERANT

2**respondent** *adj* **:** making response **:** RESPONSIVE; *esp* **:** being a respondent at law

re·spond·er \ri-ˈspän-dər\ *n* **:** one that responds; *esp* **:** the part of a transponder that transmits a radio signal

re·sponse \ri-ˈspän(t)s\ *n* [ME & L; ME *respounse,* fr. MF *respons,* fr. L *responsum* reply, fr. neut. of *responsus,* pp. of *respondēre*] **1 :** an act of responding **2 :** something constituting a reply or a reaction: as **a :** a verse, phrase, or word sung or said by the people or choir after or in reply to the officiant in a liturgical service **b :** the activity or inhibition of previous activity of an organism or any of its parts resulting from stimulation **c :** the output of a transducer or detecting device resulting from a given input

re·spon·si·bil·i·ty \ri-ˌspän(t)-sə-ˈbil-ət-ē\ *n, pl* **-ties 1 :** the quality or state of being responsible: as **a :** moral, legal, or mental accountability **b :** RELIABILITY, TRUSTWORTHINESS **2 :** something for which one is responsible **:** BURDEN

re·spon·si·ble \ri-ˈspän(t)-sə-bəl\ *adj* **1 a :** liable to be called on to answer **b (1) :** liable to be called to account as the primary cause, motive, or agent <a committee ~ for the job> (2) : being the cause or explanation <mechanical defects were ~ for the accident> **c** : liable to legal review or in case of fault to penalties **2 a** : able to answer for one's conduct and obligations : TRUSTWORTHY **b** : able to choose for oneself between right and wrong **3** : marked by or involving responsibility or accountability <~ financial policies> <a ~ job> **4** : politically answerable; *esp* : required to submit to the electorate if defeated by the legislature — used esp. of the British cabinet — **re·spon·si·ble·ness** *n* — **re·spon·si·bly** \-blē\ *adv*

re·spon·sions \ri-ˈspän-chənz\ *n pl* : an examination required for matriculation as an undergraduate at Oxford

re·spon·sive \ri-ˈspän(t)-siv\ *adj* **1** : giving response : constituting a response : ANSWERING <a ~ glance> <~ aggression> **2** : quick to respond or react appropriately or sympathetically : SENSITIVE **3** : using responses <~ worship> — **re·spon·sive·ly** *adv* — **re·spon·sive·ness** *n*

re·spon·so·ry \-ˈspän(t)s-(ə-)rē\ *n, pl* **-ries** : a set of versicles and responses sung or said after or during a lection

re·spon·sum \ri-ˈspän(t)-səm\ *n, pl* **-sa** \-sə\ [NL, fr. L, reply, formal opinion of a jurisconsult] : a written decision from a rabbinic authority in response to a submitted question or problem

res pu·bli·ca \(ˈ)rā-ˈspü-bli-ˌkä\ *n* [L — more at REPUBLIC] **1** : COMMONWEALTH, STATE, REPUBLIC **2** : COMMONWEAL

res·sen·ti·ment \rəs-ˌäⁿ-tē-ˈmäⁿ\ *n* [F, resentment, fr. *ressentir* to resent] : resentment expressed indirectly esp. by belittling the values held by the hated individual

[1]rest \ˈrest\ *n* [ME, fr. OE; akin to OHG *rasta* rest, *ruowa* calm, Gk *erōē* respite] **1** : REPOSE, SLEEP; *specif* : a bodily state characterized by minimal functional and metabolic activities — compare PARADOXICAL SLEEP **2 a** : freedom from activity or labor **b** : a state of motionlessness or inactivity **c** : the repose of death **3** : a place for resting or lodging **4** : peace of mind or spirit **5 a** (1) : a rhythmic silence in music (2) : a character representing such a silence **b** : a brief pause in reading **6** : something used for support — **at rest 1** : resting or reposing esp. in sleep or death **2** : QUIESCENT, MOTIONLESS **3** : free of anxieties

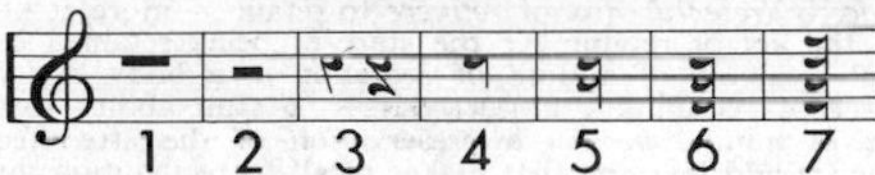

rests 5a(2): *1* whole, *2* half, *3* quarter, *4* eighth, *5* sixteenth, *6* thirty-second, *7* sixty-fourth

[2]rest *vi* **1 a** : to get rest by lying down; *esp* : SLEEP **b** : to lie dead **2** : to cease from action or motion : refrain from labor or exertion **3** : to be free from anxiety or disturbance **4** : to sit or lie fixed or supported <a column ~*s* on its pedestal> **5 a** : to remain confident : TRUST <cannot ~ on that assumption> **b** : to be based or founded <the verdict ~*ed* on several sound precedents> **6** : to remain for action or accomplishment <the answer ~*s* with him> **7** *of farmland* : to remain idle or uncropped **8** : to bring to an end voluntarily the introduction of evidence in a law case ~ *vt* **1** : to give rest to **2** : to set at rest **3** : to place on or against a support **4 a** : to cause to be firmly fixed <~*ed* all hope in his son> **b** : to stop voluntarily from presenting evidence pertinent to (a case at law) — **rest·er** *n*

[3]rest *n* [ME *reste,* lit., stoppage, short for *areste,* fr. MF, fr. OF, fr. *arester* to arrest] : a projection or attachment on the side of the breastplate of medieval armor for supporting the butt of a lance

[4]rest *n* [ME, fr. MF *reste,* fr. *rester* to remain, fr. L *restare,* lit., to stand back, fr. *re-* + *stare* to stand — more at STAND] : something that remains over : REMAINDER <ate the ~ of the candy> — **for the rest** : with regard to remaining issues or needs

re·stage \(ˈ)rē-ˈstāj\ *vt* : to present again or anew on the stage

[1]re·start \(ˈ)rē-ˈstärt\ *vt* **1** : to start anew **2** : to resume (as an activity) after interruption ~ *vi* : to resume operation — **re·start·able** \-ə-bəl\ *adj*

[2]re·start \ˈrē-ˌstärt, (ˈ)rē-ˈ\ *n* : the act or an instance of restarting

re·state \(ˈ)rē-ˈstāt\ *vt* : to state again or in another way

re·state·ment \-mənt\ *n* **1** : the act of restating **2** : something that is restated

res·tau·rant \ˈres-t(ə-)rənt, -tə-ˌränt, -ˌtränt, -tərnt\ *n* [F, fr. prp. of *restaurer* to restore, fr. L *restaurare*] : a public eating place

res·tau·ra·teur \ˌres-tə-rə-ˈtər\ *also* **res·tau·ran·teur** \-ˌrän-\ *n* [F *restaurateur,* fr. LL *restaurator* restorer, fr. L *restauratus,* pp. of *restaurare*] : the operator or proprietor of a restaurant

rest·ful \ˈrest-fəl\ *adj* **1** : marked by, affording, or suggesting rest and repose <a ~ color scheme> **2** : being at rest : QUIET ***syn*** see COMFORTABLE — **rest·ful·ly** \-fə-lē\ *adv* — **rest·ful·ness** *n*

rest home *n* : an establishment that provides housing and general care for the aged or the convalescent

rest house *n* : a building used for shelter by travelers

rest·ing *adj* **1** : being or characterized by dormancy : QUIESCENT <a ~ spore> <bulbs in the ~ state> **2** : not undergoing or marked by division : VEGETATIVE <a ~ nucleus>

res·ti·tute \ˈres-tə-ˌt(y)üt\ *vb* **-tut·ed; -tut·ing** [L *restitutus,* pp.] *vt* **1** : to restore to a former state or position **2** : to give back; *esp* : REFUND ~ *vi* : to undergo restitution

res·ti·tu·tion \ˌres-tə-ˈt(y)ü-shən\ *n* [ME, fr. OF, fr. L *restitution-, restitutio,* fr. *restitutus,* pp. of *restituere* to restore, fr. *re-* + *statuere* to set up — more at STATUTE] **1** : an act of restoring or a condition of being restored: as **a** : a restoration of something to its rightful owner **b** : a making good of or giving an equivalent for some injury **2** : a legal action serving to cause restoration of a previous state

res·tive \ˈres-tiv\ *adj* [ME, fr. MF *restif,* fr. *rester* to stop behind, remain] **1** : stubbornly resisting control : BALKY **2** : marked by restlessness : FIDGETY ***syn*** see CONTRARY — **res·tive·ly** *adv* — **res·tive·ness** *n*

rest·less \ˈrest-ləs\ *adj* **1** : lacking or giving no rest : UNEASY <a ~ night> **2** : continuously moving : UNQUIET <the ~ sea> **3** : characterized by or manifesting unrest esp. of mind <~ pacing>; *also* : CHANGEFUL, DISCONTENTED — **rest·less·ly** *adv* — **rest·less·ness** *n*

rest mass *n* : the mass of a body exclusive of additional mass acquired by the body when in motion according to the theory of relativity

re·stor·able \ri-ˈstōr-ə-bəl, -ˈstȯr-\ *adj* : fit for restoring or reclaiming

re·stor·al \-əl\ *n* : RESTORATION

res·to·ra·tion \ˌres-tə-ˈrā-shən\ *n* **1** : an act of restoring or the condition of being restored: as **a** : a bringing back to a former position or condition : REINSTATEMENT <the ~ of peace> **b** : RESTITUTION **c** : a restoring to an unimpaired or improved condition <the ~ of a painting> **d** : the replacing of missing teeth or crowns **2** : something that is restored; *specif* : a representation or reconstruction of the original form (as of a fossil or a building) **3** *cap* **a** : the reestablishing of the monarchy in England in 1660 under Charles II **b** : the period in English history usu. held to coincide with the reign of Charles II but sometimes to extend through the reign of James II

[1]re·stor·ative \ri-ˈstōr-ət-iv, -ˈstȯr-\ *adj* : of or relating to restoration; *esp* : having power to restore — **re·stor·ative·ly** *adv* — **re·stor·ative·ness** *n*

[2]restorative *n* : something that serves to restore to consciousness, vigor, or health

re·store \ri-ˈstō(ə)r, -ˈstȯ(ə)r\ *vt* **re·stored; re·stor·ing** [ME *restoren,* fr. OF *restorer,* fr. L *restaurare* to renew, rebuild, alter. of *instaurare* to renew — more at STORE] **1** : to give back : RETURN **2** : to put or bring back into existence or use **3** : to bring back to or put back into a former or original state : RENEW **4** : to put again in possession of something ***syn*** see RENEW — **re·stor·er** *n*

re·strain \ri-ˈstrān\ *vt* [ME *restraynen,* fr. MF *restraindre,* fr. L *restringere* to restrain, restrict, fr. *re-* + *stringere* to bind tight — more at STRAIN] **1 a** : to prevent from doing, exhibiting, or expressing something <~*ed* the boy from jumping> **b** : to limit, restrict, or keep under control <he found it hard to ~ his anger> **2** : to moderate or limit the force, effect, development, or full exercise of <~ trade> **3** : to deprive of liberty; *esp* : to place under arrest or restraint — **re·strain·able** \-ˈstrā-nə-bəl\ *adj* — **re·strain·er** *n*

syn RESTRAIN, CHECK, CURB, BRIDLE *shared meaning element* : to hold back from or control in doing something ***ant*** impel, incite, activate, abandon (*oneself*)

re·strained \ri-ˈstrānd\ *adj* : marked by restraint : being without excess or extravagance — **re·strain·ed·ly** \-ˈstrā-nəd-lē\ *adv*

restraining order *n* : a preliminary legal order sometimes issued to keep a situation unchanged pending decision upon an application for an injunction

re·straint \ri-ˈstrānt\ *n* [ME, fr. MF *restrainte,* fr. *restraindre*] **1 a** : an act of restraining : the state of being restrained **b** (1) : a means of restraining : a restraining force of influence (2) : a device that restricts movement <a ~ for children riding in cars> **2** : a control over the expression of one's emotions or thoughts

re·strict \ri-ˈstrikt\ *vt* [L *restrictus,* pp. of *restringere*] **1** : to confine within bounds : RESTRAIN **2** : to place under restrictions as to use or distribution ***syn*** see LIMIT

re·strict·ed *adj* : subject or subjected to restriction: as **a** : not general : LIMITED <the decision had a ~ effect> **b** : available to the use of particular groups or specif. excluding others <a ~ neighborhood> **c** : not intended for general circulation or release <a ~ document> — **re·strict·ed·ly** *adv*

re·stric·tion \ri-ˈstrik-shən\ *n* **1** : something that restricts: as **a** : a regulation that restricts or restrains <~*s* for hunters> **b** : a limitation on the use or enjoyment of property or a facility **2** : an act of restricting : the condition of being restricted

re·stric·tion·ism \-shə-ˌniz-əm\ *n* : a policy or philosophy advocating restriction (as of trade) — **re·stric·tion·ist** \-sh(ə-)nəst\ *adj or n*

re·stric·tive \ri-ˈstrik-tiv\ *adj* **1 a** : of or relating to restriction **b** : serving or tending to restrict <~ regulations> **2** : limiting the reference of a modified word or phrase <~ clause> **3** : prohibiting further negotiation — **restrictive** *n* — **re·stric·tive·ly** *adv* — **re·stric·tive·ness** *n*

re·strike \(ˈ)rē-ˈstrīk, ˈrē-ˌ\ *n* : a coin or medal struck from an orginal die at some time after the original issue

rest room *n* : a room or suite of rooms providing personal facilities (as toilets)

re·struc·ture \(ˈ)rē-ˈstrək-chər\ *vt* : to change the makeup, organization, or pattern of ~ *vi* : to restructure something

re·study \(ˈ)rē-ˈstəd-ē\ *vt* : to study again or anew : make a new appraisal or evaluation of — **restudy** *n*

[1]re·sult \ri-ˈzəlt\ *vi* [ME *resulten,* fr. ML *resultare,* fr. L, to rebound, fr. *re-* + *saltare* to leap — more at SALTATION] **1** : to proceed or arise as a consequence, effect, or conclusion : have an issue or result <injuries ~*ing* from skiing> **2** : REVERT 2

[2]result *n* **1** : something that results as a consequence, issue, or conclusion; *also* : beneficial or tangible effect : FRUIT **2** : something obtained by calculation or investigation <showed us the ~ of the calculations> ***syn*** see EFFECT — **re·sult·ful** \-fəl\ *adj* — **re·sult·ful·ness** *n* — **re·sult·less** \-ləs\ *adj*

[1]re·sul·tant \ri-ˈzəlt-ᵊnt\ *adj* : derived from or resulting from something else — **re·sul·tant·ly** *adv*

[2]resultant *n* : something that results : OUTCOME; *specif* : the single vector that is the sum of a given set of vectors

re·sume \ri-ˈzüm\ *vb* **re·sumed; re·sum·ing** [ME *resumen,* fr. MF or L; MF *resumer,* fr. L *resumere,* fr. *re-* + *sumere* to take up, take — more at CONSUME] *vt* **1 :** to assume or take again : REOCCUPY <*resumed* his seat by the fire —Thomas Hardy> **2 :** to return to or begin again after interruption <*resumed* her work> **3 :** to take back to oneself **4 :** to pick up again **5 :** REITERATE, SUMMARIZE ~ *vi* **:** to begin again something interrupted

ré·su·mé *or* **re·su·me** *or* **re·su·mé** \ˈrez-ə-ˌmā, ˌrez-ə-ˈ*also* ˈrāz- *or* ˌrāz-\ *n* [F *résumé,* fr. pp. of *résumer* to resume, summarize] **:** SUMMARY; *specif* **:** a short account of one's career and qualifications prepared typically by an applicant for a position

re·sump·tion \ri-ˈzəm(p)-shən\ *n* [ME, fr. MF or LL; MF *resomption,* fr. LL *resumption-, resumptio,* fr. L *resumptus,* pp. of *resumere*] **1 :** an act or instance of resuming : RECOMMENCEMENT **2 :** a return to payment in specie

re·su·pi·nate \ri-ˈsü-pə-ˌnāt\ *adj* [L *resupinatus,* pp. of *resupinare* to bend back to a supine position, fr. *re-* + *supinus* supine] **:** inverted in position; *also* **:** appearing by a twist of the axis to be upside down

re·su·pi·na·tion \ri-ˌsü-pə-ˈnā-shən\ *n* **:** a twisting to an inverted or apparently inverted position

res·u·pine \ˌres-ə-ˈpīn\ *adj* [L *resupinus,* back-formation fr. *resupinare*] **:** SUPINE 1

re·sup·ply \ˌrē-sə-ˈplī\ *vt* **:** to supply again : provide anew with supplies — **resupply** *n*

re·sur·face \(ˈ)rē-ˈsər-fəs\ *vt* **:** to provide with a new or fresh surface ~ *vi* **:** to come again to the surface (as of the water); *broadly* **:** to appear or show up again

re·surge \ri-ˈsərj\ *vi* **re·surged; re·surg·ing** [L *resurgere*] **:** to undergo a resurgence

re·sur·gence \ri-ˈsər-jən(t)s\ *n* **:** a rising again into life, activity, or prominence : RENASCENCE

re·sur·gent \-jənt\ *adj* [L *resurgent-, resurgens,* prp. of *resurgere*] **:** undergoing or tending to produce resurgence

res·ur·rect \ˌrez-ə-ˈrekt\ *vt* [back-formation fr. *resurrection*] **1 :** to raise from the dead **2 :** to bring to view, attention, or use again

res·ur·rec·tion \ˌrez-ə-ˈrek-shən\ *n* [ME, fr. LL *resurrection-, resurrectio* act of rising from the dead, fr. *resurrectus,* pp. of *resurgere* to rise from the dead, fr. L, to rise again, fr. *re-* + *surgere* to rise — more at SURGE] **1 a** *cap* **:** the rising of Christ from the dead **b** *often cap* **:** the rising again to life of all the human dead before the final judgment **c :** the state of one risen from the dead **2 :** RESURGENCE, REVIVAL **3** *Christian Science* **:** a spiritualization of thought : material belief that yields to spiritual understanding — **res·ur·rec·tion·al** \-shnəl, -shən-ᵊl\ *adj*

res·ur·rec·tion·ist \-sh(ə-)nəst\ *n* **1 :** BODY SNATCHER **2 :** one who resurrects

re·sus·ci·tate \ri-ˈsəs-ə-ˌtāt\ *vb* **-tat·ed; -tat·ing** [L *resuscitatus,* pp. of *resuscitare,* lit., to stir up again, fr. *re-* + *suscitare* to stir up, fr. *sub-, sus-* up + *citare* to put in motion, stir — more at SUB-, CITE] *vt* **:** to revive from apparent death or from unconsciousness; *also* **:** REVITALIZE ~ *vi* **:** to come to : REVIVE — **re·sus·ci·ta·tion** \ri-ˌsəs-ə-ˈtā-shən, ˌrē-\ *n* — **re·sus·ci·ta·tive** \ri-ˈsəs-ə-ˌtāt-iv\ *adj*

re·sus·ci·ta·tor \ri-ˈsəs-ə-ˌtāt-ər\ *n* **:** one that resuscitates; *specif* **:** an apparatus used to restore the respiration of a partially asphyxiated person

[1]**ret** \ˈret\ *vb* **ret·ted; ret·ting** [ME *reten,* fr. MD] *vt* **:** to soak (as flax) to loosen the fiber from the woody tissue ~ *vi* **:** to become retted

[2]**ret** *abbr* **1** retain **2** retired **3** return

re·ta·ble \ˈrē-ˌtā-bəl, ˈret-ə-bəl\ *n* [F, fr. Sp *retablo,* deriv. of L *retro-* + *tabula* board, tablet] **:** a raised shelf above an altar for the altar cross, the altar lights, and flowers

[1]**re·tail** \ˈrē-ˌtāl, *esp for 2 also* ri-ˈtā(ə)l\ *vb* [ME *retailen,* fr. MF *retaillier* to cut back, divide into pieces, fr. OF, fr. *re-* + *taillier* to cut — more at TAILOR] *vt* **1 :** to sell in small quantities directly to the ultimate consumer **2 :** TELL, RETELL ~ *vi* **:** to sell at retail — **re·tail·er** *n*

[2]**re·tail** \ˈrē-ˌtāl\ *n* **:** the sale of commodities or goods in small quantities to ultimate consumers — **at retail 1 :** at a retailer's price **2 :** [4]RETAIL

[3]**re·tail** \ˈrē-ˌtāl\ *adj* **:** of, relating to, or engaged in the sale of commodities at retail <~ trade>

[4]**re·tail** \ˈrē-ˌtāl\ *adv* **:** in small quantities : from a retailer

re·tail·ing \ˈrē-ˌtā-liŋ\ *n* **:** the activities involved in the selling of goods to ultimate consumers for personal or household consumption

re·tain \ri-ˈtān\ *vt* [ME *reteinen, retainen,* fr. MF *retenir,* fr. L *retinēre* to hold back, keep, restrain, fr. *re-* + *tenēre* to hold — more at THIN] **1 a :** to keep in possession or use **b :** to keep in one's pay or service; *specif* **:** to employ by paying a retainer **c :** to keep in mind or memory : REMEMBER **2 :** to hold secure or intact <lead ~*s* heat> ***syn*** see KEEP

retained object *n* **:** an object in a passive construction <*me* in *a book was given me* and *book* in *I was given a book* are *retained objects*>

[1]**re·tain·er** \ri-ˈtā-nər\ *n* [ME *reteiner* act of withholding, fr. *reteinen* + AF *-er* (as in *weyver* waiver)] **1 :** the act of a client by which he engages the services of a lawyer, counselor, or adviser **2 :** a fee paid to a lawyer or professional adviser for advice or services or for a claim on his services in case of need

[2]**retainer** *n* [*retain*] **1 :** one that retains **2 a :** a person attached or owing service to a household; *esp* **:** SERVANT **b :** EMPLOYEE **3 :** any of various devices used for holding something

[1]**re·take** \(ˈ)rē-ˈtāk\ *vt* **-took** \-ˈtu̇k\; **-tak·en** \-ˈtā-kən\; **-tak·ing 1 :** to take or receive again **2 :** RECAPTURE **3 :** to photograph again

[2]**re·take** \ˈrē-ˌtāk\ *n* **:** a second photographing or photograph

re·tal·i·ate \ri-ˈtal-ē-ˌāt\ *vb* **-at·ed; -at·ing** [LL *retaliatus,* pp. of *retaliare,* fr. *re-* + *talio* legal retaliation] *vt* **:** to repay (as an injury) in kind ~ *vi* **:** to return like for like; *esp* **:** to get revenge ***syn*** see RECIPROCATE — **re·tal·i·a·tion** \ri-ˌtal-ē-ˈā-shən, ˌrē-\ *n* — **re·tal·i·a·tive** \ri-ˈtal-ē-ˌāt-iv\ *adj* — **re·tal·ia·to·ry** \-ˈtal-yə-ˌtōr-ē, -ˈtal-ē-ə-, -ˌtȯr-\ *adj*

[1]**re·tard** \ri-ˈtärd\ *vb* [L *retardare,* fr. *re-* + *tardus* slow] *vt* **1 :** to slow up esp. by preventing or hindering advance or accomplishment : IMPEDE **2 :** to delay academic progress by failure to promote ~ *vi* **:** to undergo retardation ***syn*** see DELAY ***ant*** accelerate, advance, further — **re·tard·er** *n*

[2]**retard** *n* **:** a holding back or slowing down : RETARDATION

re·tar·dant \ri-ˈtärd-ᵊnt\ *adj* **:** serving or tending to retard <flame-retardant fabrics> — **retardant** *n*

re·tar·date \-ˈtärd-ˌāt, -ət\ *n* **:** a mentally retarded person

re·tar·da·tion \ˌrē-ˌtär-ˈdā-shən, ri-\ *n* **1 :** an act or instance of retarding **2 :** the extent to which something is retarded **3 :** a musical suspension; *specif* **:** one that resolves upward **4 a :** an abnormal slowness of thought or action; *also* **:** less than normal intellectual competence usu. characterized by an IQ of less than 70 **b :** slowness in development or progress

re·tard·ed \ri-ˈtärd-əd\ *adj* **:** slow or limited in intellectual or emotional development or academic progress

retch \ˈrech, *esp Brit* ˈrēch\ *vb* [(assumed) ME *rechen* to spit, retch, fr. OE *hrǣcan* to spit, hawk; akin to L *crepare* to rattle — more at RAVEN] *vi* **:** to make an effort to vomit ~ *vt* **:** VOMIT — **retch** *n*

retd *abbr* **1** retained **2** retired **3** returned

re·te \ˈrēt-ē, ˈrāt-\ *n, pl* **re·tia** \ˈrēt-ē-ə, ˈrāt-\ [NL, fr. L, net — more at RETINA] **1 :** a network esp. of blood vessels or nerves : PLEXUS **2 :** an anatomical part resembling or including a network

re·tell \(ˈ)rē-ˈtel\ *vt* **-told** \-ˈtōld\; **-tell·ing 1 :** to count again **2 :** to tell again or in another form

re·tell·ing *n* **:** a new version of a story <a ~ of a Greek legend>

re·tem \rə-ˈtem, ˈret-əm\ *n* [Ar *ratam*] **:** a desert shrub (*Retama raetam*) of western Asia that is the juniper of the Old Testament and has tiny white flowers

re·tene \ˈrē-ˌtēn, ˈret-ˌēn\ *n* [Gk *rhētinē* resin] **:** a crystalline hydrocarbon $C_{18}H_{18}$ isolated esp. from pine tar and fossil resins or prepared artificially

re·ten·tion \ri-ˈten-chən\ *n* [ME *retencioun,* fr. L *retention-, retentio,* fr. *retentus,* pp. of *retinēre* to retain — more at RETAIN] **1 a :** the act of retaining : the state of being retained **b :** abnormal retaining of a fluid or secretion in a body cavity **2 a :** power of retaining : RETENTIVENESS **b :** an ability to retain things in mind; *specif* **:** a preservation of the aftereffects of experience and learning that makes recall or recognition possible **3 :** something retained

re·ten·tive \-ˈtent-iv\ *adj* **:** having the power, property, or capacity of retaining <soils ~ of moisture>; *esp* **:** retaining knowledge easily — **re·ten·tive·ly** *adv* — **re·ten·tive·ness** *n*

re·ten·tiv·i·ty \ˌrē-ˌten-ˈtiv-ət-ē, ri-\ *n* **:** the power of retaining; *specif* **:** the capacity for retaining magnetism after the action of the magnetizing force has ceased

[1]**re·test** \(ˈ)rē-ˈtest\ *vt* **:** to test again

[2]**re·test** \ˈrē-ˌtest, (ˈ)rē-ˈ\ *n* **:** a repeated test

re·think \(ˈ)rē-ˈthiŋk\ *vb* **-thought** \-ˈthȯt\; **-think·ing** *vt* **:** to think about again : RECONSIDER ~ *vi* **:** to engage in reconsideration — **re·think** \ˈrē-ˌthiŋk, -ˈthiŋk\ *n* — **re·think·er** *n*

re·ti·a·ri·us \ˌrēt-ē-ˈar-ē-əs\ *n, pl* **-a·rii** \-ē-ˌē\ [L, fr. *rete* net] **:** a Roman gladiator armed with a net and a trident

ret·i·cence \ˈret-ə-sən(t)s\ *n* **1 :** the quality or state of being reticent : RESERVE, RESTRAINT **2 :** an instance of being reticent

ret·i·cen·cy \-sən-sē\ *n, pl* **-cies :** RETICENCE

ret·i·cent \-sənt\ *adj* [L *reticent-, reticens,* prp. of *reticēre* to keep silent, fr. *re-* + *tacēre* to be silent — more at TACIT] **1 :** inclined to be silent or uncommunicative in speech : RESERVED **2 :** restrained in expression, presentation, or appearance <the room has an aspect of ~ dignity —A. N. Whitehead> ***syn*** see SILENT ***ant*** frank — **ret·i·cent·ly** *adv*

ret·i·cle \ˈret-i-kəl\ *n* [L *reticulum* network] **:** a system of lines, dots, cross hairs, or wires in the focus of the eyepiece of an optical instrument

re·tic·u·lar \ri-ˈtik-yə-lər\ *adj* **1 :** RETICULATE; *esp* **:** of, relating to, or forming a reticulum **2 :** INTRICATE

[1]**re·tic·u·late** \-lət, -ˌlāt\ *adj* [L *reticulatus,* fr. *reticulum*] **1 :** resembling a net; *esp* **:** having veins, fibers, or lines crossing <a ~ leaf> **2 :** of, relating to, or constituting evolutionary change dependent on genetic recombination involving diverse interbreeding populations — **re·tic·u·late·ly** *adv*

[2]**re·tic·u·late** \-ˌlāt\ *vb* **-lat·ed; -lat·ing** [back-formation fr. *reticulated,* adj. (reticulate)] *vt* **1 :** to divide, mark, or construct so as to form a network **2 :** to distribute (as electricity, water, or goods) by a network ~ *vi* **:** to become reticulated

re·tic·u·la·tion \ri-ˌtik-yə-ˈlā-shən\ *n* **:** a reticulated formation : NETWORK; *also* **:** something reticulated

ret·i·cule \ˈret-i-ˌkyü(ə)l\ *n* [F *réticule,* fr. L *reticulum* network, network bag, fr. dim. of *rete* net] **1 :** RETICLE **2 :** a woman's drawstring bag used esp. as a carryall

re·tic·u·lo·cyte \ri-ˈtik-yə-lō-ˌsīt\ *n* [NL *reticulum* + ISV *-cyte*] **:** a young red blood cell that contains a fine basophilic reticulum and appears esp. during active regeneration of lost blood — **re·tic·u·lo·cyt·ic** \-ˌtik-yə-lō-ˈsit-ik\ *adj*

re·tic·u·lo·en·do·the·li·al \ri-ˈtik-yə-lō-ˌen-də-ˈthē-lē-əl\ *adj* [NL *reticulum* + *endothelium*] **:** of, relating to, or being the reticuloendothelial system

reticuloendothelial system *n* **:** a diffuse system of cells arising from mesenchyme and comprising all the phagocytic cells of the body except the circulating leukocytes

re·tic·u·lose \ri-ˈtik-yə-ˌlōs\ *adj* **:** RETICULATE

re·tic·u·lum \ri-ˈtik-yə-ləm\ *n* [NL, fr. L, network] **1 :** the second stomach of a ruminant in which folds of the mucous membrane form hexagonal cells **2 :** a reticular formation : NETWORK; *esp* **:** interstitial tissue composed of reticulum cells

reticulum cell *n* **:** one of the branched anastomosing reticuloendothelial cells that form an intricate interstitial network ramifying through other tissues and organs

re·ti·form \ˈrēt-ə-ˌfȯrm, ˈret-\ *adj* [NL *retiformis,* fr. L *rete* + *-iformis* -iform] **:** composed of crossing lines and interstices **:** RETICULAR

retin- *or* **retino-** *comb form* [*retina*] **:** retina <*retinitis*> <*retinoscopy*>

ret·i·na \ˈret-ᵊn-ə, ˈret-nə\ *n, pl* **retinas** *or* **ret·i·nae** \-ᵊn-ˌē, -ˌī\ [ME *rethina,* fr. ML *retina,* prob. fr. L *rete* net; akin to Gk *erēmos* lonely, solitary, Lith *retis* sieve] **:** the sensory membrane that lines the eye, receives the image formed by the lens, is the immediate instrument of vision, and is connected with the brain by the optic nerve — see EYE illustration — **ret·i·nal** \ˈret-ᵊn-əl, ˈret-nəl\ *adj*

ret·i·nac·u·lum \ˌret-ᵊn-ˈak-yə-ləm\ *n, pl* **-la** \-lə\ [NL, fr. L, halter, cable, fr. *retinēre* to hold back — more at RETAIN] **:** a connecting or retaining band or body — **ret·i·nac·u·lar** \-lər\ *n*

ret·i·nal \ˈret-ᵊn-ˌal, -ˌȯl\ *n* [*retin-* + 3*-al*] **:** a yellowish to orange aldehyde $C_{20}H_{28}O$ derived from vitamin A that in combination with proteins forms the visual pigments of the retinal rods and cones

ret·i·nene \ˈret-ᵊn-ˌēn\ *n* **:** RETINAL

ret·i·nis·po·ra \ˌret-ᵊn-ˈis-pə-rə\ *or* **ret·i·nos·po·ra** \-ˈäs-\ *n* [NL, fr. Gk *rhētinē* resin + NL *spora* spore] **1 :** any of various Japanese ornamental dwarf shrubs (genus *Chamaecyparis*) that resemble cypresses **2 :** any of several shrubs (genus *Thuja*) that retain the needlelike juvenile foliage permanently

ret·i·ni·tis \ˌret-ᵊn-ˈīt-əs\ *n* [NL] **:** inflammation of the retina

ret·i·nol \ˈret-ᵊn-ˌȯl, -ˌōl\ *n* [*retin-* + 1*-ol;* fr. its being the source of retinal] **:** the chief and typical vitamin A

ret·i·nop·a·thy \ˌret-ᵊn-ˈäp-ə-thē\ *n* **:** any of various noninflammatory disorders of the retina including some that are major causes of blindness

ret·i·nos·co·py \ˌret-ᵊn-ˈäs-kə-pē\ *n* **:** observation of the retina of the eye esp. to determine the state of refraction

ret·i·nue \ˈret-ᵊn-ˌ(y)ü\ *n* [ME *retenue,* fr. MF, fr. fem. of *retenu,* pp. of *retenir* to retain] **:** a group of retainers or attendants

re·tin·u·la \re-ˈtin-yə-lə\ *n, pl* **-lae** \-ˌlē, -ˌlī\ *also* **-las** [NL, dim. of ML *retina*] **:** the neural receptor of a single facet of an arthropod compound eye — **re·tin·u·lar** \-lər\ *adj*

re·tir·ant \ri-ˈtī-rənt\ *n* **:** RETIREE

re·tire \ri-ˈtī(ə)r\ *vb* **re·tired; re·tir·ing** [MF *retirer,* fr. *re-* + *tirer* to draw — more at TIRADE] *vi* **1 :** to withdraw from action or danger **:** RETREAT **2 :** to withdraw esp. for privacy **3 :** to fall back **:** RECEDE **4 :** to withdraw from one's position or occupation **:** conclude one's working or professional career **5 :** to go to bed ~ *vt* **1 :** WITHDRAW: as **a :** to march (a military force) away from the enemy **b :** to withdraw from circulation or from the market **:** RECALL **c :** to withdraw from usual use or service **2 :** to cause to retire from one's position or occupation **3 a :** to put out (a batter or batsman) in baseball or cricket **b :** to cause (a side) to end a turn at bat in baseball **4 :** to win permanent possession of (as a trophy) *syn* see GO

re·tired \ri-ˈtī(ə)rd\ *adj* **1 :** SECLUDED <~ village> **2 :** withdrawn from one's position or occupation **:** having concluded one's working or professional career **3 :** received by or due to one in retirement — **re·tired·ly** \-ˈtī-rəd-lē, -ˈtī(ə)rd-\ *adv* — **re·tired·ness** \-ˈtī(ə)rd-nəs\ *n*

re·tir·ee \ri-ˌtī-ˈrē\ *n* **:** a person who has retired from his vocation or profession

1**re·tire·ment** \ri-ˈtī(ə)r-mənt\ *n* **1 a :** an act of retiring **:** the state of being retired **b :** withdrawal from one's position or occupation or from active working life **c :** the age at which one normally retires <reached ~ but was asked to work another year> **2 :** a place of seclusion or privacy

2**retirement** *adj* **:** of, relating to, or designed for retired persons

re·tir·ing \ri-ˈtī(ə)r-iŋ\ *adj* **:** RESERVED, SHY — **re·tir·ing·ly** \-iŋ-lē\ *adv* — **re·tir·ing·ness** *n*

re·tool \(ˈ)rē-ˈtül\ *vt* **1 :** to reequip with tools **2 :** REORGANIZE

1**re·tort** \ri-ˈtȯ(ə)rt\ *vb* [L *retortus,* pp. of *retorquēre,* lit., to twist back, hurl back, fr. *re-* + *torquēre* to twist — more at TORTURE] *vt* **1 :** to pay or hurl back **:** RETURN <~ an insult> **2 a :** to make a reply to **b :** to say in reply **3 :** to answer (as an argument) by a counter argument ~ *vi* **1 :** to answer back usu. sharply **2 :** to return an argument or charge **3 :** RETALIATE *syn* see ANSWER

2**retort** *n* **:** a quick, witty, or cutting reply; *esp* **:** one that turns the first speaker's words against him

3**re·tort** \ri-ˈtȯ(ə)rt, ˈrē-ˌ\ *n* [MF *retorte,* fr. ML *retorta,* fr. L, fem. of *retortus,* pp.; fr. its shape] **:** a vessel in which substances are distilled or decomposed by heat

4**re·tort** \ri-ˈtȯ(ə)rt, ˈrē-ˌ\ *vt* **:** to treat (as oil shale) by heating in a retort

retorts

re·tor·tion \ri-ˈtȯr-shən\ *n* **:** an act of retorting

1**re·touch** \(ˈ)rē-ˈtəch\ *vb* [F *retoucher,* fr. MF, fr. *re-* + *toucher* to touch] *vt* **1 :** to touch up **:** rework in order to improve **2 :** to alter (as a photographic negative) to produce a more desirable appearance **3 :** to color (new growth of hair) to match previously dyed, tinted, or bleached hair ~ *vi* **:** to make or give retouches — **re·touch·er** *n*

2**re·touch** \ˈrē-ˌtəch, (ˈ)rē-ˈ\ *n* **:** the act, process, or an instance of retouching; *esp* **:** the retouching of a new growth of hair

re·trace \(ˈ)rē-ˈtrās\ *vt* [F *retracer,* fr. MF *retracier,* fr. *re-* + *tracier* to trace] **:** to trace again or back

re·tract \ri-ˈtrakt\ *vb* [ME *retracten,* fr. L *retractus,* pp. of *retrahere* — more at RETREAT] *vt* **1 :** to draw back or in <cats ~ their claws> **2 a :** to take back **:** WITHDRAW <~ a confession> **b :** DISAVOW ~ *vi* **1 :** to draw back **2 :** to recant or disavow something *syn* **1** see RECEDE *ant* protract **2** see ABJURE — **re·tract·able** \-ˈtrak-tə-bəl\ *adj*

re·trac·tile \ri-ˈtrak-tᵊl, -ˌtīl\ *adj* **:** capable of being drawn back or in <~ claws> — **re·trac·til·i·ty** \ˌrē-ˌtrak-ˈtil-ət-ē, ri-\ *n*

re·trac·tion \ri-ˈtrak-shən\ *n* **1 :** an act of recanting; *specif* **:** a statement made by one retracting **2 :** an act of retracting **:** the state of being retracted **3 :** the ability to retract

re·trac·tor \ri-ˈtrak-tər\ *n* **:** one that retracts: as **a :** a surgical instrument for holding open the edges of a wound **b :** a muscle that draws in an organ or part

re·train \(ˈ)rē-ˈtrān\ *vt* **:** to train again or anew ~ *vi* **:** to become trained again — **re·train·able** \-ˈtrā-nə-bəl\ *adj*

re·train·ee \(ˌ)rē-ˌtrā-ˈnē\ *n* **:** a person who is being retrained

re·tral \ˈrē-trəl, ˈre-\ *adj* [L *retro* back — more at RETRO-] **1 :** situated at or toward the back **:** POSTERIOR **2 :** BACKWARD, RETROGRADE — **re·tral·ly** \-trə-lē\ *adv*

re·trans·late \ˌrē-tran(t)s-ˈlāt, -tranz-\ *vt* **:** to translate (a translation) into another language; *also* **:** to give a new form to ~ *vi* **:** to retranslate something — **re·trans·la·tion** \-ˈlā-shən\ *n*

1**re·tread** \(ˈ)rē-ˈtred\ *vt* **re·tread·ed; re·tread·ing 1 :** to cement, mold, and vulcanize a new tread of camelback upon the bare cord fabric of (a worn tire) **2 :** to make over as if new <~ an old plot>

2**re·tread** \ˈrē-ˌtred\ *n* **1 :** a new tread on a tire **2 :** a retreaded tire **3 :** one (as a retired person) who is retrained for work

re–tread \(ˈ)rē-ˈtred\ *vt* **-trod** \-ˈträd\; **-trod·den** \-ˈträd-ᵊn\ *or* **trod; -tread·ing :** to tread again

1**re·treat** \ri-ˈtrēt\ *n* [ME *retret,* fr. MF *retrait,* fr. pp. of *retraire* to withdraw, fr. L *retrahere,* lit., to draw back, fr. *re-* + *trahere* to draw — more at DRAW] **1 a (1) :** an act or process of withdrawing esp. from what is difficult, dangerous, or disagreeable **(2) :** the process of receding from a position or state attained <the ~ of a glacier> <the slow ~ of an epidemic> **b (1) :** the usu. forced withdrawal of troops from an enemy or from an advanced position **(2) :** a signal for retreating **c (1) :** a signal given by bugle at the beginning of a military flag-lowering ceremony **(2) :** a military flag-lowering ceremony **2 :** a place of privacy or safety **:** REFUGE **3 :** a period of group withdrawal for prayer, meditation, study, and instruction under a director

2**retreat** *vi* **1 :** to make a retreat **:** WITHDRAW **2 :** to slope backward ~ *vt* **:** to draw or lead back **:** REMOVE; *specif* **:** to move (a piece) back in chess *syn* see RECEDE — **re·treat·er** *n*

re·treat·ant \-ˈtrēt-ᵊnt\ *n* **:** one who is on a religious retreat

re·trench \ri-ˈtrench\ *vb* [obs. F *retrencher* (now *retrancher*), fr. MF *retrenchier,* fr. *re-* + *trenchier* to cut] *vt* **1 a :** to cut down **:** REDUCE **b :** to cut out **:** EXCISE **2 :** to pare away **:** REMOVE ~ *vi* **:** to make retrenchments; *specif* **:** ECONOMIZE *syn* see SHORTEN

re·trench·ment \-mənt\ *n* **:** REDUCTION, CURTAILMENT; *specif* **:** a cutting of expenses

re·tri·al \(ˈ)rē-ˈtrī(-ə)l\ *n* **:** a second trial, experiment, or test

ret·ri·bu·tion \ˌre-trə-ˈbyü-shən\ *n* [ME *retribucioun,* fr. MF *retribution,* fr. LL *retribution-, retributio,* fr. L *retributus,* pp. of *retribuere* to pay back, fr. *re-* + *tribuere* to pay — more at TRIBUTE] **1 :** RECOMPENSE, REWARD **2 :** the dispensing or receiving of reward or punishment esp. in the hereafter **3 :** something given or exacted in recompense; *esp* **:** PUNISHMENT

re·trib·u·tive \ri-ˈtrib-yət-iv\ *adj* **:** of, relating to, or marked by retribution — **re·trib·u·tive·ly** *adv*

re·trib·u·to·ry \-yə-ˌtōr-ē, -ˌtȯr-\ *adj* **:** RETRIBUTIVE

re·triev·al \ri-ˈtrē-vəl\ *n* **1 :** an act or process of retrieving **2 :** possibility of being retrieved or of recovering <beyond ~>

1**re·trieve** \ri-ˈtrēv\ *vb* **re·trieved; re·triev·ing** [ME *retreven,* modif. of MF *retrouver* to find again, fr. *re-* + *trouver* to find, prob. fr. (assumed) VL *tropare* to compose — more at TROUBADOUR] *vt* **1 :** to discover and bring in (killed or wounded game) **2 :** to call to mind again **3 :** to get back again **:** REGAIN **4 a :** RESCUE, SALVAGE **b :** to return (as a ball or shuttlecock that is difficult to reach) successfully **5 :** RESTORE, REVIVE <his writing ~*s* the past> **6 :** to remedy the evil consequences of **:** CORRECT **7 :** to get and bring back; *esp* **:** to recover (as information) from storage ~ *vi* **:** to bring in game <a dog that ~*s* well>; *also* **:** to bring back an object thrown by a person — **re·triev·abil·i·ty** \-ˌtrē-və-ˈbil-ət-ē\ *n* — **re·triev·able** \-ˈtrē-və-bəl\ *adj*

2**retrieve** *n* **1 :** RETRIEVAL **2 :** the successful return of a ball that is difficult to reach or control (as in tennis)

re·triev·er \ri-ˈtrē-vər\ *n* **:** one that retrieves; *specif* **:** a vigorous active medium-sized dog with heavy water-resistant coat developed by crossbreeding and used esp. for retrieving game

retro- *prefix* [ME, fr. L, fr. *retro,* fr. *re-* + *-tro* (as in *intro* within) — more at INTRO-] **1 :** backward **:** back <*retro*-rocket> **2 :** situated behind <*retro*choir>

ret·ro·ac·tion \ˌre-trō-ˈak-shən\ *n* **1** [*retroactive* + *-ion*] **:** retroactive operation (as of a law or tax) **2** [*retro-* + *action*] **:** a reciprocal action **:** REACTION

ret·ro·ac·tive \-ˈak-tiv\ *adj* [F *retroactif,* fr. L *retroactus,* pp. of *retroagere* to drive back, reverse, fr. *retro-* + *agere* to drive — more at AGENT] **:** extending in scope or effect to a prior time or to conditions that existed or originated in the past; *esp* **:** made effective as of a date prior to enactment, promulgation, or imposition <~ tax> — **ret·ro·ac·tive·ly** *adv* — **ret·ro·ac·tiv·i·ty** \-ˌak-ˈtiv-ət-ē\ *n*

ret·ro·cede \ˌre-trō-ˈsēd\ *vb* **-ced·ed; -ced·ing** [L *retrocedere,* fr. *retro-* + *cedere* to go, cede — more at CEDE] *vi* **:** to go back **:** RECEDE ~ *vt* [F *rétrocéder,* fr. ML *retrocedere,* fr. L *retro-* + *cedere* to cede] **:** to cede back (as a territory) — **ret·ro·ces·sion** \-ˈsesh-ən\ *n*

ret·ro·fire \ˈre-trō-ˌfī(ə)r\ *vi, of a retro-rocket* **:** to become ignited ~ *vt* **:** to cause to retrofire — **retrofire** *n*

ret·ro·fit \ˌre-trō-ˈfit\ *vt* **:** to furnish (as an aircraft) with new parts or equipment not available at the time of manufacture

ret·ro·flex \ˈre-trə-ˌfleks\ *or* **ret·ro·flexed** \-ˌflekst\ *adj* [ISV, fr.

ə abut   ᵊ kitten   ər further   a back   ā bake   ä cot, cart
aù out   ch chin   e less   ē easy   g gift   i trip   ī life
j joke   ŋ sing   ō flow   ȯ flaw   ȯi coin   th thin   t͟h this
ü loot   ù foot   y yet   yü few   yù furious   zh vision

NL *retroflexus,* fr. L *retro-* + *flexus,* pp. of *flectere* to bend] **1** : turned or bent abruptly backward **2** : articulated with the tongue tip turned up or curled back just under the hard palate <~ vowel>

ret·ro·flex·ion *or* **ret·ro·flec·tion** \ˌre-trə-ˈflek-shən\ *n* **1 :** the act or process of bending back **2 :** the state of being bent back; *esp* **:** the bending back of an organ (as a uterus) upon itself **3 :** retroflex articulation

ret·ro·gra·da·tion \ˌre-trō-grā-ˈdā-shən, -grə-\ *n* **:** the action or process of retrograding

[1]**ret·ro·grade** \ˈre-trə-ˌgrād\ *adj* [ME, fr. L *retrogradus,* fr. *retro-* + *gradi* to go] **1 a** (1) *of a celestial body* **:** having a direction contrary to that of the general motion of similar bodies (2) **:** being or relating to the rotation of a satellite in a direction opposite to that of the body orbited **b :** moving, directed, or treading backward <a ~ step> **c :** contrary to the normal order **:** INVERSE **2 :** tending toward or resulting in a worse state **3** *archaic* **:** CONTRADICTORY, OPPOSED **4 :** characterized by retrogression **5 :** affecting a period immediately prior to a precipitating cause <~ amnesia> — **ret·ro·grade·ly** *adv*

[2]**retrograde** *adv* **:** BACKWARD, REVERSELY

[3]**retrograde** *vb* [L *retrogradi,* fr. *retro-* + *gradi* to go — more at GRADE] *vt, archaic* **:** to turn back **:** REVERSE ~ *vi* **1 a :** to go back **:** RETREAT <a glacier ~*s*> **b :** to go back over (as a narrative or an argument) **:** RECAPITULATE **2 :** to decline to a worse condition *syn* see RECEDE

ret·ro·gress \ˌre-trə-ˈgres\ *vi* [L *retrogressus,* pp. of *retrogradi*] **:** to move backward **:** REVERT

ret·ro·gres·sion \-ˈgresh-ən\ *n* **1 :** REGRESSION 3 **2 :** a reversal in development or condition; *esp* **:** a passing from a higher to a lower or from a more to a less specialized state or type in the course of development (as of an organism)

ret·ro·gres·sive \-ˈgres-iv\ *adj* **:** characterized by retrogression: as **a :** going or directed backward **b :** declining from a better to a worse state **c :** passing from a higher to a lower organization — **ret·ro·gres·sive·ly** *adv*

ret·ro·len·tal \ˌre-trō-ˈlent-^{ə}l\ *adj* [*retro-* + L *lent-, lens* lens] **:** situated or occurring behind a lens (as of the eye)

ret·ro·lin·gual \-ˈliŋ-g(yə-)wəl\ *adj* **:** situated behind or near the base of the tongue <~ salivary glands>

ret·ro·pack \ˈre-trō-ˌpak\ *n* **:** a system of auxiliary rockets on a spacecraft that produces thrust in the direction opposite to the motion of the spacecraft and that is used to reduce speed

ret·ro·per·i·to·ne·al \-ˌper-ət-^{ə}n-ˈē-əl\ *adj* **:** situated behind the peritoneum — **ret·ro·per·i·to·ne·al·ly** \-ə-lē\ *adv*

ret·ro·re·flec·tion \ˌre-trō-ri-ˈflek-shən\ *n* **:** the action or use of a retroreflector — **ret·ro·re·flec·tive** \-ˈflek-tiv\ *adj*

ret·ro·re·flec·tor \-ˈflek-tər\ *n* **:** a device that reflects radiation (as light) so that the paths of the rays are parallel to those of the incident rays

ret·ro–rock·et \ˈre-trō-ˌräk-ət\ *n* **:** an auxiliary rocket on an airplane, missile, or spacecraft that produces thrust in a direction opposite to or at an oblique angle to the motion of the object for deceleration

re·trorse \ˈrē-ˌtrȯ(ə)rs\ *adj* [L *retrorsus,* contr. of *retroversus* — more at RETROVERSION] **:** bent backward or downward — **re·trorse·ly** *adv*

ret·ro·ser·rate \ˌre-trō-ˈse(ə)r-ˌāt, -sə-ˈrāt\ *adj* **:** having retrorse teeth or barbs <a ~ leaf>

[1]**ret·ro·spect** \ˈre-trə-ˌspekt\ *n* [*retro-* + *-spect* (as in *prospect*)] **1** *archaic* **:** reference to or regard of a precedent or authority **2 :** a review of or meditation on past events — **in retrospect :** in considering the past or a past event

[2]**retrospect** *adj* **:** RETROSPECTIVE

[3]**retrospect** *vb* [L *retrospectus,* pp. of *retrospicere* to look back at, fr. *retro-* + *specere* to look — more at SPY] *vi* **1 :** to engage in retrospection **2 :** to refer back **:** REFLECT ~ *vt* **:** to go back over in thought

ret·ro·spec·tion \ˌre-trə-ˈspek-shən\ *n* **:** the act or process or an instance of surveying the past

[1]**ret·ro·spec·tive** \-ˈspek-tiv\ *adj* **1 a** (1) **:** of, relating to, or given to retrospection (2) **:** based on memory <a ~ report> **b :** being a retrospective <a ~ exhibition> **2 :** affecting things past **:** RETROACTIVE — **ret·ro·spec·tive·ly** *adv*

[2]**retrospective** *n* **:** a generally comprehensive exhibition showing the work of an artist over a span of years

re·trous·sé \rə-ˌtrü-ˈsā, rə-ˈtrü-ˌ, ˌre-trü-ˈ\ *adj* [F, fr. pp. of *retrousser* to tuck up, fr. MF, fr. *re-* + *trousser* to truss, tuck up] **:** turned up <~ nose>

ret·ro·ver·sion \ˌre-trō-ˈvər-zhən *also* -shən\ *n* [L *retroversus* turned backward, fr. *retro-* + *versus,* pp. of *vertere* to turn — more at WORTH] **1 :** the act or process of turning back or regressing **2 :** the bending backward of the uterus and cervix

re–try \(ˈ)rē-ˈtrī\ *vt* **:** to try again

ret·si·na \ret-ˈsē-nə\ *n* [NGk, perh. fr. It *resina* resin, fr. L] **:** a resin-flavored Greek wine

[1]**re·turn** \ri-ˈtərn\ *vb* [ME *retournen,* fr. MF *retourner,* fr. *re-* + *tourner* to turn — more at TURN] *vi* **1 a :** to go back or come back again <~ home> **b :** to go back in thought or practice **:** REVERT <soon ~*ed* to her old habit> **2 :** to pass back to an earlier possessor <the estate ~*ed* to a distant branch of the family> **3 :** REPLY, RETORT ~ *vt* **1 a :** to give (as an official account) to a superior **b :** to elect (a candidate) as attested by official report or returns **c :** to bring back (as a writ or verdict) to an office or tribunal **2 a :** to bring, send, or put back to a former or proper place <~ the gun to its holster> **b :** to restore to a former or to a normal state **3 a :** to send back **:** VISIT — usu. used with *on* or *upon* **b** *obs* **:** RETORT **4 :** to bring in (as profit) **:** YIELD **5 a :** to give or perform in return **:** REPAY <~ a compliment> **b :** to give back to the owner **c :** REFLECT <~ an echo> **6 :** to cause (as a wall) to continue in a different direction (as at a right angle) **7 :** to lead (a specified suit or specified card of a suit) in response to a partner's earlier lead **8 a :** to play (a ball or shuttlecock) served by an opponent **b :** to run with (a football) after a kick by the opposing team — **re·turn·er** *n*
syn **1** RETURN, REVERT, RECUR, RECRUDESCE *shared meaning element* **:** to go or come back
2 see RECIPROCATE

[2]**return** *n* **1 a :** the act of coming back to or from a place or condition **b :** a regular or frequent returning **:** RECURRENCE **2 a** (1) **:** the delivery of a legal order (as a writ) to the proper officer or court (2) **:** the endorsed certificate of an official stating his action in the execution of such an order (3) **:** the sending back of a commission with the certificate of the commissioners **b :** an account or formal report **c** (1) **:** a report of the results of balloting — usu. used in pl. <election ~*s*> (2) **:** an official declaration of the election of a candidate (3) *chiefly Brit* **:** ELECTION **d** (1) **:** a formal statement on a required legal form showing taxable income, allowable deductions and exemptions, and the computation of the tax due (2) **:** a list of taxable property **3 a :** the continuation usu. at a right angle of the face or of a member of a building or of a molding or group of moldings **b :** a turn, bend, or winding back (as in a rod, stream, or trench) **c :** a means for conveying something (as water) back to its starting point **4 a :** a quantity of goods, consignment, or cargo coming back in exchange for goods sent out as a mercantile venture **b :** the value of or profit from such venture **c** (1) **:** the profit from labor, investment, or business **:** YIELD (2) *pl* **:** RESULTS **d :** the rate of profit in a process of production per unit of cost **5 a :** the act of returning something to a former place, condition, or ownership **:** RESTITUTION **b :** something returned; *esp, pl* **:** unsold publications returned to the publisher for cash or credit **6 a :** something given in repayment or reciprocation **b :** ANSWER, RETORT **7 :** an answering play: as **a :** a lead in a suit previously led by one's partner in a card game **b :** the action of returning a ball (as in football or tennis) — **in return :** in compensation or repayment

[3]**return** *adj* **1 a :** having or formed by a change of direction <a ~ facade> **b :** doubled on itself <a ~ flue> **2 :** played, delivered, or given in return **:** taking place for the second time <a ~ meeting for the two champions> **3 :** used or taken on returning <the ~ road> **4 :** returning or permitting return <a ~ valve> **5 :** of, relating to, or causing a return to a place or condition

re·turn·able \ri-ˈtər-nə-bəl\ *adj* **1 :** legally required to be returned, delivered, or argued at a specified time or place <a writ ~ on the date indicated> **2 a :** capable of returning or of being returned (as for reuse) **b :** permitted to be returned

re·turn·ee \ri-ˌtər-ˈnē\ *n* **:** one who returns; *esp* **:** one returning to the U.S. after military service overseas

re·tuse \ri-ˈt(y)üs\ *adj* [L *retusus* blunted, fr. pp. of *retundere* to pound back, blunt, fr. *re-* + *tundere* to beat, pound — more at STINT] **:** having the apex rounded or obtuse with a slight notch <a ~ leaf>

[1]**Reu·ben** \ˈrü-bən\ *n* [Heb *Rĕʼūbhēn*] **:** a son of Jacob and the traditional eponymous ancestor of one of the tribes of Israel

[2]**Reuben** *n* [*Reuben* L. Goldberg †1970 Am cartoonist] **:** a statuette awarded annually by a professional organization for notable achievement in cartoon artistry

re·uni·fy \(ˈ)rē-ˈyü-nə-ˌfī\ *vt* **:** to restore unity to — **re·uni·fi·ca·tion** \(ˌ)rē-ˌyü-nə-fə-ˈkā-shən\ *n*

re·union \(ˈ)rē-ˈyü-nyən\ *n* **1 :** an act of reuniting **:** the state of being reunited **2 :** a reuniting of persons after separation

re·union·ist \-nyə-nəst\ *n* **:** an advocate of reunion (as of sects or parties) — **re·union·is·tic** \(ˌ)rē-ˌyü-nyə-ˈnis-tik\ *adj*

re·unite \ˌrē-yü-ˈnīt\ *vb* [ML *reunitus,* pp. of *reunire,* fr. L *re-* + LL *unire* to unite — more at UNITE] *vt* **:** to bring together again ~ *vi* **:** to come together again **:** REJOIN

re–up \(ˈ)rē-ˈəp\ *vi* [*re-* + sign *up*] **:** to enlist again

re·us·able \(ˈ)rē-ˈyü-zə-bəl\ *adj* **:** capable of being used again or repeatedly

[1]**re·use** \(ˈ)rē-ˈyüz\ *vt* **:** to use again esp. after reclaiming or reprocessing <the need to ~ scarce resources>

[2]**reuse** \-ˈyüs\ *n* **:** further or repeated use

[1]**rev** \ˈrev\ *n* [short for *revolution*] **:** a revolution of a motor

[2]**rev** *vb* **revved; rev·ving** *vt* **1 a :** to step up the number of revolutions per minute of — often used with *up* <~ up the engine> **b :** INCREASE — used with *up* <~ up production> **2 :** to drive or operate esp. at high speed — often used with *up* **3 :** to make more active or effective — used with *up* ~ *vi* **1 :** to operate at an increased speed of revolution — usu. used with *up* **2 :** to increase in amount or activity — used with *up*

[3]**rev** *abbr* **1** revenue **2** reverse **3** review; reviewed **4** revised; revision

Rev *abbr* **1** Revelation **2** reverend

REV *abbr* reentry vehicle

re·val·i·date \(ˈ)rē-ˈval-ə-ˌdāt\ *vt* **:** to make valid again — **re·val·i·da·tion** \(ˌ)rē-ˌval-ə-ˈdā-shən\ *n*

re·val·u·ate \(ˈ)rē-ˈval-yə-ˌwāt\ *vt* [back-formation fr. *revaluation*] **:** REVALUE; *specif* **:** to increase the value of (currency) — **re·val·u·a·tion** \(ˌ)rē-ˌval-yə-ˈwā-shən\ *n*

re·val·ue \(ˈ)rē-ˈval-(ˌ)yü, -yə(-w)\ *vt* **1 :** to value (as currency) anew **2 :** to make a new valuation of **:** REAPPRAISE

re·vamp \(ˈ)rē-ˈvamp\ *vt* **1 :** RENOVATE, RECONSTRUCT **2 :** to make over **:** REVISE

re·vanche \rə-ˈvä^{n}sh\ *n* [F, fr. MF, alter. of *revenche* — more at REVENGE] **:** REVENGE; *esp* **:** a usu. political policy designed to recover lost territory or status

[1]**re·vanch·ist** \-ˈvä^{n}-shəst\ *n* **:** one who advocates a policy of revanche

[2]**revanchist** *adj* **:** of or relating to a policy of revanche

[1]**re·veal** \ri-ˈvē(ə)l\ *vt* [ME *revelen,* fr. MF *reveler,* fr. L *revelare* to uncover, reveal, fr. *re-* + *velare* to cover, veil, fr. *velum* veil] **1 :** to make known through divine inspiration **2 :** to make (something secret or hidden) publicly or generally known <~ a secret> **3 :** to open up to view **:** DISPLAY <the uncurtained window ~*ed* a cluttered room> — **re·veal·able** \-ˈvē-lə-bəl\ *adj* — **re·veal·er** *n*

syn REVEAL, DISCOVER, DISCLOSE, DIVULGE, TELL, BETRAY *shared meaning element* : to make known what has been or should be concealed *ant* conceal

2**reveal** *n* [alter. of earlier *revale,* fr. ME *revalen* to lower, fr. MF *revaler,* fr. *re-* + *val* valley — more at VALE] : the side of an opening (as for a window) between a frame and the outer surface of a wall; *also* : JAMB

re·veal·ing *adj* : full of import : SIGNIFICANT

re·veal·ment \ri-ˈvē(ə)l-mənt\ *n* : an act of revealing

re·veg·e·tate \(ˈ)rē-ˈvej-ə-ˌtāt\ *vt* : to provide (barren or denuded land) with a new vegetative cover — **re·veg·e·ta·tion** \(ˌ)rē-ˌvej-ə-ˈtā-shən\ *n*

re·ve·hent \ˈrev-ə-hənt, ri-ˈvē-ənt\ *adj* [L *revehent-, revehens,* prp. of *revehere* to carry back, fr. *re-* + *vehere* to carry — more at WAY] : carrying back <~ veins>

rev·eil·le \ˈrev-ə-lē, *Brit* ri-ˈval-i *or* -ˈvel-\ *n* [modif. of F *réveillez,* imper. pl. of *réveiller* to awaken, fr. *re-* + *eveiller* to awaken, fr. (assumed) VL *exvigilare,* fr. L *ex-* + *vigilare* to keep watch, stay awake — more at VIGILANT] **1 :** a bugle call at about sunrise signaling the first military formation of the day; *also* : the formation so signaled **2 :** a signal to get up mornings

1**rev·el** \ˈrev-əl\ *vi* **-eled** *or* **-elled; -el·ing** *or* **-el·ling** \-(ə-)liŋ\ [ME *revelen,* fr. MF *reveler,* lit., to rebel, fr. L *rebellare*] **1 :** to take part in a revel : CAROUSE **2 :** to take intense satisfaction

2**revel** *n* : a usu. wild party or celebration

rev·e·la·tion \ˌrev-ə-ˈlā-shən\ *n* [ME, fr. MF, fr. LL *revelation-, revelatio,* fr. L *revelatus,* pp. of *revelare* to reveal] **1 a :** an act of revealing or communicating divine truth **b :** something that is revealed by God to man **2** *cap* : an apocalyptic writing addressed to early Christians of Asia Minor and included as a book in the New Testament — see BIBLE table **3 a :** an act of revealing to view or making known **b :** something that is revealed; *esp* : an enlightening or astonishing disclosure

Rev·e·la·tions \-shənz\ *n pl but sing in constr* [alter. (influenced by such titles as *Galatians*) of *Revelation*] : REVELATION 2

rev·e·la·tor \ˈrev-ə-ˌlāt-ər\ *n* : one that reveals; *esp* : one that reveals the will of God

re·ve·la·to·ry \ˈrev-ə-lə-ˌtōr-ē, -ˌtȯr-, ri-ˈvel-ə-\ *adj* : of or relating to revelation : serving to reveal something

rev·el·er *or* **rev·el·ler** \ˈrev-(ə-)lər\ *n* : one who engages in revelry

rev·el·ry \ˈrev-əl-rē\ *n* : noisy partying or merrymaking

rev·e·nant \ˈrev-ə-ˌnäⁿ, -nənt\ *n* [F, fr. prp. of *revenir* to return] : one that returns after death or a long absence — **revenant** *adj*

1**re·venge** \ri-ˈvenj\ *vt* **re·venged; re·veng·ing** [ME *revengen,* fr. MF *revengier,* fr. OF, fr. *re-* + *vengier* to avenge — more at VENGEANCE] **1 :** to inflict injury in return for <~ an insult> **2 :** to avenge (as oneself) usu. by retaliating in kind or degree *syn* see AVENGE — **re·veng·er** *n*

2**revenge** *n* [MF *revenge, revenche,* fr. *revengier, revenchier* to revenge] **1 :** an act or instance of retaliating in order to get even **2 :** a desire for revenge **3 :** an opportunity for getting satisfaction

re·venge·ful \ri-ˈvenj-fəl\ *adj* : full of or prone to revenge : determined to get even *syn* see VINDICTIVE — **re·venge·ful·ly** \-fə-lē\ *adv* — **re·venge·ful·ness** *n*

rev·e·nue \ˈrev-ə-ˌn(y)ü\ *n, often attrib* [ME, fr. MF, fr. *revenir* to return, fr. L *revenire,* fr. *re-* + *venire* to come — more at COME] **1 :** the gross income returned by an investment **2 :** the yield of sources of income (as taxes) that a political unit (as a nation or state) collects and receives into the treasury for public use **3 :** the total income produced by a given source <a property expected to yield a large annual ~> **4 :** a government department concerned with the collection of the national revenue

revenue bond *n* : a bond issued by a public agency authorized to build, acquire, or improve a revenue-producing property (as a toll road or a water system) and payable solely out of revenue derived from such property

rev·e·nu·er \ˈrev-ə-ˌn(y)ü-ər\ *n* : a revenue officer or boat

revenue stamp *n* : a stamp (as on a cigar box) for use as evidence of payment of a tax

revenue tariff *n* : a tariff intended wholly or primarily to produce public revenue — compare PROTECTIVE TARIFF

re·verb \ri-ˈvərb, ˈrē-ˌ\ *n* [short for *reverberation*] : an electronically produced echo effect in recorded music; *also* : a device for producing reverb

re·ver·ber·ant \ri-ˈvər-b(ə-)rənt\ *adj* **1 :** tending to reverberate **2 :** marked by reverberation : RESONANT — **re·ver·ber·ant·ly** *adv*

1**re·ver·ber·ate** \-bə-ˌrāt\ *vb* **-at·ed; -at·ing** [L *reverberatus,* pp. of *reverberare,* fr. *re-* + *verberare* to lash, fr. *verber* rod — more at VERVAIN] *vt* **1 :** to force back: as **a :** REPEL **b :** ECHO <~ sound> **c :** REFLECT <~ light or heat> **2 :** to subject to the action of a reverberatory furnace ~ *vi* **1 a :** to become driven back **b :** to become reflected **2 :** to continue in or as if in a series of echoes : RESOUND

2**re·ver·ber·ate** \-b(ə-)rət\ *adj* : REVERBERANT, REVERBERATED

re·ver·ber·a·tion \ri-ˌvər-bə-ˈrā-shən\ *n* **1 :** an act of reverberating : the state of being reverberated **2 a :** something that is reverberated **b :** an effect or impact that resembles an echo

re·ver·ber·a·tive \ri-ˈvər-bə-ˌrāt-iv, -b(ə-)rət-\ *adj* **1 :** constituting reverberation **2 :** tending to reverberate : REFLECTIVE

1**re·ver·ber·a·to·ry** \ri-ˈvər-b(ə-)rə-ˌtōr-ē, -bə-ˌtōr-, -ˌtȯr-\ *adj* : acting by reverberation; *esp* : forced back or diverted onto material under treatment

2**reverberatory** *n, pl* **-ries :** a furnace or kiln in which heat is radiated from the roof onto the material treated

1**re·vere** \ri-ˈvi(ə)r\ *vt* **re·vered; re·ver·ing** [L *revereri,* fr. *re-* + *vereri* to fear, respect — more at WARY] : to show devoted deferential honor to

syn REVERE, REVERENCE, VENERATE, WORSHIP, ADORE *shared meaning element* : to honor and admire profoundly and respectfully. REVERE stresses deference and tenderness of feeling <that makes her loved at home, *revered* abroad —Robert Burns> REVERENCE presupposes an intrinsic merit and inviolability in the one honored and a corresponding depth of feeling in the one honoring <sincerity and simplicity! if I could only say how I *reverence* them —A. C. Benson> VENERATE implies a holding as holy or sacrosanct because of character, association, or age <those who *venerate* . . . Dante and Shakespeare and Milton —Havelock Ellis> <a *venerated* tradition> WORSHIP implies homage usually expressed in words or ceremony and, in other than divine application, may impute exalted character or outstanding merit to the one worshiped or weakness (as of judgment or sense) to the worshiper <admire the poetry and *worship* the memory of the poet —William DuBois> <foolish mothers *worshiping* and indulging spoiled children> ADORE, otherwise close to *worship,* may stress the notion of an individual and personal approach or attachment <his staff *adored* him, his men worshiped him —W. A. White> *ant* flout

2**revere** *n* [by alter.] : REVERS

1**rev·er·ence** \ˈrev-(ə-)rən(t)s, ˈrev-ərn(t)s\ *n* **1 :** honor or respect felt or shown : DEFERENCE; *esp* : profound adoring awed respect **2 :** a gesture of respect (as a bow) **3 :** the state of being revered **4 :** one held in reverence — used as a title for a clergyman

syn **1** see HONOR

2 REVERENCE, AWE, FEAR *shared meaning element* : the emotion inspired by what arouses one's deep respect or veneration

2**reverence** *vt* **-enced; -enc·ing :** to regard or treat with reverence *syn* see REVERE — **rev·er·enc·er** *n*

1**rev·er·end** \ˈrev-(ə-)rənd, ˈrev-ərnd\ *adj* [ME, fr. MF, fr. L *reverendus,* gerundive of *revereri*] **1 :** worthy of reverence : REVERED **2 a :** of or relating to the clergy **b :** being a member of the clergy — used as a title usu. preceded by *the* and followed by a title or a full name <the *Reverend* Mr. Doe> <the *Reverend* John Doe>

2**reverend** *n* : a member of the clergy — used with *the*

rev·er·ent \ˈrev-(ə-)rənt, ˈrev-ərnt\ *adj* [ME, fr. L *reverent-, reverens,* prp. of *revereri*] : expressing or characterized by reverence : WORSHIPFUL — **rev·er·ent·ly** *adv*

rev·er·en·tial \ˌrev-ə-ˈren-chəl\ *adj* **1 :** expressing or having a quality of reverence <~ awe> **2 :** inspiring reverence — **rev·er·en·tial·ly** \-ˈrench-(ə-)lē\ *adv*

rev·er·ie *or* **rev·ery** \ˈrev-(ə-)rē\ *n, pl* **rev·er·ies** [F *rêverie,* fr. MF, delirium, fr. *resver, rever* to wander, be delirious] **1 :** DAYDREAM **2 :** the condition of being lost in thought

re·vers \ri-ˈvi(ə)r, -ˈve(ə)r\ *n, pl* **re·vers** \-ˈvi(ə)rz, -ˈve(ə)rz [F, lit., reverse, fr. MF, fr. *revers,* adj.] : a lapel esp. on a woman's garment

re·ver·sal \ri-ˈvər-səl\ *n* **1 :** an act or the process of reversing: as **a :** a change or overthrowing of a legal proceeding or judgment **b :** a causing to move or face in an opposite direction or to appear in an inverted position **2 :** a conversion of a photographic positive into a negative or vice versa **3 :** a change for the worse

1**re·verse** \ri-ˈvərs\ *adj* [ME *revers,* fr. MF, fr. L *reversus,* pp. of *revertere* to turn back — more at REVERT] **1 a :** opposite or contrary to a previous or normal condition <~ order> **b :** having the back presented to the observer or opponent **2 :** coming from the rear of a military force **3 :** acting, operating, or arranged in a manner contrary to the usual **4 :** effecting reverse movement <~ gear> **5 :** so made that the part normally black is white and vice versa <~ photoengraving> — **re·verse·ly** *adv*

2**reverse** *vb* **re·versed; re·vers·ing** *vt* **1 a :** to turn completely about in position or direction **b :** to turn upside down : INVERT **2 :** ANNUL: as **a :** to overthrow, set aside, or make void (a legal decision) by a contrary decision **b :** to cause to take an opposite point of view **c :** to change to the contrary <~ a policy> **3 :** to cause to go in the opposite direction; *esp* : to cause (as an engine) to perform its action in the opposite direction ~ *vi* **1 :** to turn or move in the opposite direction **2 :** to put a mechanism (as an engine) in reverse — **re·vers·er** *n* — **reverse one's field :** to turn and head in the opposite direction

3**reverse** *n* **1 :** something directly contrary to something else : OPPOSITE **2 :** an act or instance or reversing; *specif* : a change for the worse **3 :** the back part of something; *esp* : the back cover of a book **4 a (1) :** a gear that reverses something; *also* : the whole mechanism brought into play when such a gear is used **(2) :** movement in reverse **b :** an offensive play in football in which a back moving in one direction gives the ball to a player moving in the opposite direction — **in reverse :** in an opposite manner or direction

1**re·vers·ible** \ri-ˈvər-sə-bəl\ *adj* : capable of being reversed or of reversing: as **a :** capable of going through a series of actions (as changes) either backward or forward <a ~ chemical reaction> **b (1) :** having two finished usable sides <~ fabric> **(2) :** wearable with either side out <~ coat> — **re·vers·ibil·i·ty** \-ˌvər-sə-ˈbil-ət-ē\ *n* — **re·vers·ibly** \-ˈvər-sə-blē\ *adv*

2**reversible** *n* : a reversible cloth or article of clothing

reversing thermometer *n* : a thermometer for registering temperature in deep water by means of the breaking of a column of mercury when the thermometer inverts at a specified depth

re·ver·sion \ri-ˈvər-zhən, -shən\ *n* [ME, fr. MF, fr. L *reversion-, reversio* act of returning, fr. *reversus,* pp.] **1 a :** the part of a simple estate remaining in the control of its owner after he has granted therefrom a lesser particular estate **b :** a future interest in property left in the control of a grantor or his successor **2 :** the right of succession or future possession or enjoyment **3 a :** an act or the process of returning (as to a former condition) **b :** a return toward an ancestral type or condition : reappearance of an ancestral character **4 :** an act or instance of turning the opposite way : the state of being so turned **5 :** a product of reversion; *specif* : an organism with an atavistic character : THROWBACK

re·ver·sion·al \-ˈvərzh-nəl, -ˈvərsh-, -ən-ᵊl\ *adj* : REVERSIONARY

re·ver·sion·ary \-ˈvər-zhə-ˌner-ē, -shə-\ *adj* : of, relating to, constituting, or involving esp. a legal reversion

re·ver·sion·er \-ˈvərzh-nər, -ˈvərsh-, -ə-nər\ *n* : one that has or is entitled to a reversion

re·vert \ri-ˈvərt\ *vi* [ME *reverten,* fr. MF *revertir,* fr. L *revertere,* v.t., to turn back & *reverti,* v.i., to return, come back, fr. *re-* + *vertere, verti* to turn — more at WORTH] **1 :** to come or go back esp. to a lower or worse condition <many ~*ed* to savagery> **2 :** to return to the proprietor or his heirs at the end of a reversion **3 :** to return to an ancestral type ***syn*** see RETURN — **re·vert·er** *n* — **re·vert·ible** \-ˈvərt-ə-bəl\ *adj*

re·vert·ed \ri-ˈvərt-əd\ *adj* **1 :** turned or curled back or the wrong way <~ leaf> **2 :** affected with reversion <a ~ bacteria culture>

re·vest \(ˈ)rē-ˈvest\ *vt* : REINSTATE, REINVEST

re·vet \ri-ˈvet\ *vt* **re·vet·ted; re·vet·ting** [F *revêtir,* lit., to clothe again, dress up, fr. L *revestire,* fr. *re-* + *vestire* to clothe — more at VEST] : to face (as an embankment) with a revetment

re·vet·ment \-ˈvet-mənt\ *n* **1 :** a facing (as of stone or concrete) to sustain an embankment **2 :** EMBANKMENT; *esp* : a barricade to provide shelter (as against bomb splinters or strafing)

re·vict·ual \(ˈ)rē-ˈvit-ᵊl\ *vt* : to supply with a fresh stock of provisions ~ *vi* : to obtain fresh stocks of provisions

[1]re·view \ri-ˈvyü\ *n* [MF *revue,* fr. *revoir* to look over, fr. *re-* + *voir* to see — more at VIEW] **1 :** REVISION 1 **2 a :** a formal military inspection **b :** a military ceremony honoring a person or an event **3 :** a general survey (as of the events of a period) **4 :** an act of inspecting or examining **5 :** judicial reexamination (as of the proceedings of a lower tribunal by a higher) **6 a :** a critical evaluation (as of a book or play) **b :** a magazine devoted chiefly to reviews and essays **7 a :** a retrospective view or survey (as of one's life) **b** (1) : renewed study of material previously studied (2) : an exercise facilitating such study **8 :** REVUE

[2]re·view \ri-ˈvyü, *1 is also* ˈrē-\ *vb* [in senses 1 & 2, fr. *re-* + *view;* in other senses, fr. [1]*review*] *vt* **1 :** to view or see again **2 :** to examine or study again; *esp* : to reexamine judicially **3 :** to look back on : take a retrospective view of **4 a :** to go over or examine critically or deliberately <~*ed* the results of the study> **b :** to give a critical evaluation of <~ a novel> **5 :** to hold a review of <~ troops> ~ *vi* **1 :** to study material again : make a review <~ for a test> **2 :** to write reviews

re·view·er \ri-ˈvyü-ər\ *n* : one that reviews; *esp* : a writer of critical reviews

re·vile \ri-ˈvī(ə)l\ *vb* **re·viled; re·vil·ing** [ME *revilen,* fr. MF *reviler* to despise, fr. *re-* + *vil* vile] *vt* : to subject to verbal abuse : VITUPERATE ~ *vi* : to use abusive language : RAIL ***syn*** see SCOLD — **re·vile·ment** \-ˈvī(ə)l-mənt\ *n* — **re·vil·er** *n*

re·vis·al \ri-ˈvī-zəl\ *n* : an act of revising : REVISION

[1]re·vise \ri-ˈvīz\ *vt* **re·vised; re·vis·ing** [F *reviser,* fr. L *revisere* to look at again, fr. *revisus,* pp. of *revidēre* to see again, fr. *re-* + *vidēre* to see — more at WIT] **1 :** to look over again in order to correct or improve <~ a manuscript> **2 a :** to make a new, amended, improved, or up-to-date version of <~ a dictionary> **b :** to provide with a new taxonomic arrangement <*revising* the alpine ferns> ***syn*** see CORRECT — **re·vis·able** \-ˈvī-zə-bəl\ *adj* — **re·vis·er** *or* **re·vi·sor** \-ˈvī-zər\ *n*

[2]re·vise \ˈrē-ˌvīz, ri-ˈ\ *n* **1 :** an act of revising : REVISION **2 :** a printing proof taken from matter that incorporates changes marked in a previous proof

Revised Standard Version *n* : a revision of the American Standard Version of the Bible published in 1946 and 1952

Revised Version *n* : a British revision of the Authorized Version of the Bible published in 1881 and 1885

re·vi·sion \ri-ˈvizh-ən\ *n* **1 :** an act of revising (as a manuscript) **2 :** a revised version — **re·vi·sion·ary** \-ə-ˌner-ē\ *adj*

re·vi·sion·ism \ri-ˈvizh-ə-ˌniz-əm\ *n* **1 :** advocacy of revision (as of a doctrine or policy or in historical analysis) **2 :** a movement in revolutionary Marxian socialism favoring an evolutionary rather than a revolutionary spirit

[1]re·vi·sion·ist \-ˈvizh-(ə-)nəst\ *n* **1 :** an advocate of revision (as of an accepted attitude) **2 :** an advocate of revisionism

[2]revisionist *adj* : advocating revision or revisionism

[1]re·vis·it \(ˈ)rē-ˈviz-ət\ *vt* : to visit again : return to

[2]revisit *n* : a second or subsequent visit

re·vi·so·ry \ri-ˈvīz-(ə-)rē\ *adj* : having the power or purpose to revise <a ~ committee> <a ~ function>

re·vi·tal·iza·tion \(ˌ)rē-ˌvīt-ᵊl-ə-ˈzā-shən\ *n* **1 :** an act or instance of revitalizing **2 :** something revitalized

re·vi·tal·ize \(ˈ)rē-ˈvīt-ᵊl-ˌīz\ *vt* **-ized; -iz·ing :** to give new life or vigor to

re·viv·al \ri-ˈvī-vəl\ *n* **1 :** an act or instance of reviving : the state of being revived: as **a :** renewed attention to or interest in something **b :** a new presentation or publication **c** (1) : a period of renewed religious interest (2) : an often highly emotional evangelistic meeting or series of meetings **d :** REVITALIZATION 1 **2 :** restoration of force, validity, or effect (as to a contract)

re·viv·al·ism \-ˈvī-və-ˌliz-əm\ *n* **1 :** the spirit or methods characteristic of religious revivals **2 :** a tendency or desire to revive or restore

re·viv·al·ist \-ˈvīv-(ə-)ləst\ *n* **1 :** one who conducts religious revivals; *specif* : a clergyman who travels about to conduct revivals **2 :** one who revives or restores something disused

re·viv·al·is·tic \-ˌvī-və-ˈlis-tik\ *or* **re·viv·al·ist** \-ˈvīv-(ə-)ləst\ *adj* : of or relating to revivalists or religious revivals

re·vive \ri-ˈvīv\ *vb* **re·vived; re·viv·ing** [ME *reviven,* fr. MF *revivre,* fr. L *revivere* to live again, fr. *re-* + *vivere* to live — more at QUICK] *vi* : to return to consciousness or life : to become active or flourishing again ~ *vt* **1 :** to restore to consciousness or life : REANIMATE **2 :** to restore from a depressed, inactive, or unused state : bring back **3 :** to renew in the mind or memory : RECALL — **re·viv·able** \-ˈvī-və-bəl\ *adj* — **re·viv·er** *n*

re·viv·i·fy \rē-ˈviv-ə-ˌfī\ *vt* [F *révivifier,* fr. LL *revivificare,* fr. L *re-* + LL *vivificare* to vivify] : to give new life to : REVIVE — **re·viv·i·fi·ca·tion** \-ˌviv-ə-fə-ˈkā-shən\ *n*

re·vi·vis·cence \ˌrē-ˌvī-ˈvis-ᵊn(t)s, ri-\ *n* [L *reviviscere* to come to life again, fr. *re-* + *viviscere* to come to life, fr. *vivus* alive, living — more at QUICK] : an act of reviving : the state of being revived — **re·vi·vis·cent** \-ᵊnt\ *adj*

re·vo·ca·ble \ˈrev-ə-kə-bəl *also* ri-ˈvō-\ *also* **re·vok·able** \ri-ˈvō-kə-bəl\ *adj* [ME, fr. MF, fr. L *revocabilis,* fr. *revocare*] : capable of being revoked

re·vo·ca·tion \ˌrev-ə-ˈkā-shən; ri-ˌvō-, ˌrē-\ *n* [ME, fr. MF, fr. L *revocation-, revocatio,* fr. *revocatus,* pp. of *revocare*] : an act or instance of revoking

[1]re·voke \ri-ˈvōk\ *vb* **re·voked; re·vok·ing** [ME *revoken,* fr. MF *revoquer,* fr. L *revocare,* fr. *re-* + *vocare* to call — more at VOICE] *vt* **1 :** to bring or call back **2 :** to annul by recalling or taking back : RESCIND <~ a will> ~ *vi* : to fail to follow suit when able in a card game in violation of the rules — **re·vok·er** *n*

[2]revoke *n* : an act or instance of revoking in a card game

[1]re·volt \ri-ˈvōlt *also* -ˈvȯlt\ *vb* [MF *revolter,* fr. OIt *rivoltare* to overthrow, fr. (assumed) VL *revolvitare,* freq. of L *revolvere* to revolve, roll back] *vi* **1 :** to renounce allegiance or subjection (as to a government) : REBEL **2 a :** to experience disgust or shock **b :** to turn away with disgust ~ *vt* : to cause to turn away or shrink with disgust or abhorrence : NAUSEATE — **re·volt·er** *n*

[2]revolt *n* **1 :** a renouncing of allegiance (as to a government or party); *esp* : a determined armed uprising **2 :** a movement or expression of vigorous dissent ***syn*** see REBELLION

re·volt·ing *adj* : extremely offensive : NAUSEATING

rev·o·lute \ˈrev-ə-ˌlüt\ *adj* [L *revolutus,* pp.] : rolled backward or downward <a leaf with ~ margins>

rev·o·lu·tion \ˌrev-ə-ˈlü-shən\ *n* [ME *revolucioun,* fr. MF *revolution,* fr. LL *revolution-, revolutio,* fr. L *revolutus,* pp. of *revolvere*] **1 a** (1) : the action by a celestial body of going round in an orbit or elliptic course; *also* : apparent movement of such a body round the earth (2) : the time taken by a celestial body to make a complete round in its orbit (3) : the rotation of a celestial body on its axis **b :** completion of a course (as of years); *also* : the period made by the regular succession of a measure of time or by a succession of similar events **c** (1) : a progressive motion of a body round a center or axis so that any line of the body remains parallel to and returns to its initial position (2) : motion of any figure about a center or axis <~ of a right triangle about one of its legs generates a cone> (3) : ROTATION 1b **2 a :** a sudden, radical, or complete change **b :** a fundamental change in political organization; *esp* : the overthrow or renunciation of one government or ruler and the substitution of another by the governed **c :** activity or movement designed to effect fundamental changes in the socioeconomic situation (as of a racial or cultural segment of the population) ***syn*** see REBELLION

[1]rev·o·lu·tion·ary \-shə-ˌner-ē\ *adj* **1 a :** of, relating to, or constituting a revolution <~ war> **b :** tending to or promoting revolution <a ~ speech>; *also* : RADICAL, EXTREMIST <a ~ outlook> **2** *cap* : of or relating to the American Revolution or to the period in which it occurred — **rev·o·lu·tion·ari·ly** \-ˌlü-shə-ˈner-ə-lē\ *adv* — **rev·o·lu·tion·ari·ness** \-ˈlü-shə-ˌner-ē-nəs\ *n*

[2]revolutionary *n, pl* **-ar·ies :** REVOLUTIONIST

Revolutionary calendar *n* : the calendar of the first French republic adopted in 1793, dated from September 22, 1792, and divided into 12 months of 30 days with 5 extra days in a regular year

rev·o·lu·tion·ist \ˌrev-ə-ˈlü-sh(ə-)nəst\ *n* **1 :** one engaged in a revolution **2 :** an adherent or advocate of revolutionary doctrines — **revolutionist** *adj*

rev·o·lu·tion·ize \-shə-ˌnīz\ *vb* **-ized; -iz·ing** *vt* **1 :** to overthrow the established government of **2 :** to imbue with revolutionary doctrines **3 :** to change fundamentally or completely ~ *vi* : to undergo revolution — **rev·o·lu·tion·iz·er** *n*

re·volve \ri-ˈvälv, -ˈvȯlv\ *vb* **re·volved; re·volv·ing** [ME *revolven,* fr. L *revolvere* to roll back, cause to return, fr. *re-* + *volvere* to roll — more at VOLUBLE] *vt* **1 :** to turn over at length in the mind : PONDER <~ a scheme> **2 a :** to cause to go round in an orbit **b :** to cause to turn round on or as if on an axis : ROTATE ~ *vi* **1 :** RECUR **2 a :** to ponder something **b :** to remain under consideration <ideas *revolved* in his mind> **3 a :** to move in a curved path round a center or axis **b :** to turn or roll round on an axis **4 :** to center on : have as a main point <the dispute *revolved* around wages> — **re·volv·able** \-ˈväl-və-bəl, -ˈvȯl-\ *adj*

re·volv·er \ri-ˈväl-vər, -ˈvȯl-\ *n* **1 :** one that revolves **2 :** a handgun with a cylinder of several chambers brought successively into line with the barrel and discharged with the same hammer

re·volv·ing *adj* : tending to revolve or recur; *esp* : recurrently available

revolving charge account *n* : a charge account under which payment is made in monthly installments and includes a carrying charge

revolving credit *n* : a credit which may be used repeatedly up to the limit specified after partial or total repayments have been made

revolving fund *n* : a fund set up for specified purposes with the proviso that repayments to the fund may be used again for these purposes

re·vue \ri-ˈvyü\ *n* [F, fr. MF, review — more at REVIEW] : a theatrical production consisting typically of brief loosely connected often satirical skits, songs, and dances — called also *review*

re·vulsed \ri-ˈvəlst\ *adj* [L *revulsus,* pp. + E *-ed*] : affected with or having undergone revulsion

re·vul·sion \ri-ˈvəl-shən\ *n* [L *revulsion-, revulsio* act of tearing away, fr. *revulsus,* pp. of *revellere* to pluck away, fr. *re-* + *vellere* to pluck — more at VULNERABLE] **1 :** a strong pulling or drawing away : WITHDRAWAL **2 a :** a sudden or strong reaction or change <he puzzled people with the ~*s* of his moods> **b :** a sense of utter distaste or repugnance — **re·vul·sive** \-ˈvəl-siv\ *adj*

re·wake \(ˈ)rē-ˈwāk\ *vb* **-waked** *or* **-woke** \-ˈwōk\; **-waked** *or* **-wo·ken** \-ˈwō-kən\ *or* **-woke; -wak·ing** *vt* : to waken again or anew ~ *vi* : to become awake again

re·wak·en \(ˈ)rē-ˈwā-kən\ *vb* : REWAKE

[1]**re·ward** \ri-ˈwȯ(ə)rd\ *vt* [ME *rewarden,* fr. ONF *rewarder* to regard, reward, fr. *re-* + *warder* to watch, guard, of Gmc origin; akin to OHG *wartēn* to watch — more at WARD] **1 :** to give a reward to or for **2 :** RECOMPENSE — **re·ward·able** \-ˈwȯrd-ə-bəl\ *adj* — **re·ward·er** *n*

[2]**reward** *n* **:** something that is given in return for good or evil done or received and esp. that is offered or given for some service or attainment

re·ward·ing *adj* **1 :** yielding or likely to yield a reward **:** VALUABLE, SATISFYING <a ~ experience> **2 :** offered by way of reward **:** serving as a reward <a ~ smile of thanks>

[1]**re·wind** \(ˈ)rē-ˈwīnd\ *vt* **-wound** \-ˈwau̇nd\; **-wind·ing :** to wind again; *esp* **:** to reverse the winding of (as film)

[2]**re·wind** \ˈrē-ˌwīnd, (ˈ)rē-ˈ\ *n* **1 :** something that rewinds or is rewound **2 :** an act of rewinding

re·word \(ˈ)rē-ˈwərd\ *vt* **1 :** to repeat in the same words **2 :** to alter the wording of; *also* **:** to restate in other words

re·work \(ˈ)rē-ˈwərk\ *vt* **:** to work again or anew: as **a :** REVISE **b :** to reprocess (as used material) for further use

[1]**re·write** \(ˈ)rē-ˈrīt\ *vb* **-wrote** \-ˈrōt\; **-writ·ten** \-ˈrit-ᵊn\; **-writ·ing** \-ˈrīt-iŋ\ *vt* **1 :** to write in reply **2 :** to make a revision of (as a story) **:** cause to be revised: as **a :** to put (contributed material) into form for publication **b :** to alter (previously published material) for use in another publication ~ *vi* **:** to revise something previously written — **re·writ·er** *n*

[2]**re·write** \ˈrē-ˌrīt\ *n* **1 :** a piece of writing (as a news story) constructed by rewriting **2 :** an act or instance of rewriting

re·write man \ˈrē-ˌrīt-ˌman\ *n* **:** a newspaperman who specializes in rewriting

re·write rule \ˈrē-ˌrīt-\ *n* **:** a rule in a grammar which specifies the constituents of a single symbol

rey·nard \ˈrān-ərd, ˈren-, -ˌär(d)\ *n, often cap* [ME *Renard,* name of the fox who is hero of the F beast epic *Roman de Renart,* fr. MF *Renart, Renard*] **:** FOX

re·zone \(ˈ)rē-ˈzōn\ *vt* **:** to alter the zoning of

rf *abbr* refunding

RF *abbr* radio frequency

R factor \ˈär-\ *n* [*r*esistance] **:** a factor that is present in some bacteria, is a basis of resistance to antibiotics, and can be transferred from cell to cell by conjugation

RFD *abbr* rural free delivery

RGS *abbr* Royal Geographical Society

rh *abbr* relative humidity

[1]**Rh** \ˈär-ˈāch\ *adj* **:** of, relating to, or being an Rh factor <~ antigens> <~ sensitization in pregnancy>

[2]**Rh** *symbol* rhodium

RH *abbr* right hand

rhab·do·coele \ˈrab-də-ˌsēl\ *n* [deriv. of Gk *rhabdos* rod + *koilos* hollow — more at CAVE] **:** a turbellarian worm (order Rhabdocoela) with an unbranched intestine

rhab·dom \ˈrab-ˌdäm, -dəm\ *or* **rhab·dome** \-ˌdōm\ *n* [LGk *rhabdōma* bundle of rods, fr. Gk *rhabdos* rod] **:** one of the minute rodlike structures in the retinulae in the compound eyes of arthropods

rhab·do·man·cy \ˈrab-də-ˌman(t)-sē\ *n* [LGk *rhabdomanteia,* fr. Gk *rhabdos* rod + *-manteia* -mancy — more at VERVAIN] **:** divination by rods or wands

rhab·do·mere \-ˌmi(ə)r\ *n* [blend of *rhabdom* and *-mere*] **:** a division of a rhabdom

rhad·a·man·thine \ˌrad-ə-ˈman(t)-thən, -ˈman-ˌthīn\ *adj, often cap* [*Rhadamanthus,* mythical judge in the lower world] **:** rigorously strict or just

Rhae·to–Ro·man·ic \ˌrēt-ō-rō-ˈman-ik\ *n* [L *Rhaetus* of Rhaetia, ancient Roman province + E *Romanic*] **:** a Romance language of eastern Switzerland, northeastern Italy, and adjacent parts of Austria

rham·na·ceous \ram-ˈnā-shəs\ *adj* [deriv. of Gk *rhamnos*] **:** of, relating to, or being the buckthorn family (Rhamnaceae)

rham·nose \ˈram-ˌnōs, -ˌnōz\ *n* [ISV, fr. NL *Rhamnus,* genus of the buckthorn; fr. its being produced from a plant of this genus] **:** a crystalline sugar $C_6H_{12}O_5$ that occurs combined in many plants and is obtained in the common dextrorotatory L form

rham·nus \ˈram-nəs\ *n* [NL, genus name, fr. Gk *rhamnos* buckthorn; akin to Gk *rhabdos* rod] **:** any of a genus (*Rhamnus*) of trees and shrubs of the buckthorn family having pinnately veined leaves, small perfect or polygamous flowers with the ovary free from the disk, and a fruit that is a drupe

rhaphe *var of* RAPHE

rhap·sod·ic \rap-ˈsäd-ik\ *adj* **1 :** resembling or characteristic of a rhapsody **2 :** extravagantly emotional **:** RAPTUROUS — **rhap·sod·i·cal** \-i-kəl\ *adj* — **rhap·sod·i·cal·ly** \-i-k(ə-)lē\ *adv*

rhap·so·dist \ˈrap-səd-əst\ *n* **1 :** a professional reciter of epic poems **2 :** one who writes or speaks rhapsodically

rhap·so·dize \-sə-ˌdīz\ *vi* **-dized; -diz·ing :** to speak or write in a rhapsodic manner <~ about a new book>

rhap·so·dy \ˈrap-səd-ē\ *n, pl* **-dies** [L *rhapsodia,* fr. Gk *rhapsōidia* recitation of selections from epic poetry, rhapsody, fr. *rhaptein* to sew, stitch together + *aidein* to sing; akin to OHG *worf* scythe handle, Gk *rhepein* to bend, incline — more at ODE] **1 :** a portion of an epic poem adapted for recitation **2** *archaic* **:** a miscellaneous collection **3 a (1) :** a highly emotional utterance **(2) :** a highly emotional literary work **(3) :** effusively rapturous or extravagant discourse **b :** RAPTURE, ECSTASY **4 :** a musical composition of irregular form having an improvisatory character *syn* see BOMBAST

rhat·a·ny \ˈrat-ᵊn-ē\ *n* [Sp *ratania* & Pg *ratânhia,* fr. Quechua *ratánya*] **1 :** the dried root of either of two American shrubs (*Krameria triandra* and *K. argentea*) used as an astringent **2 :** a plant yielding rhatany

rhea \ˈrē-ə\ *n* [NL, genus of birds, prob. fr. L *Rhea,* mother of Zeus, fr. Gk] **:** any of several large tall flightless So. American birds (order Rheiformes) that resemble but are smaller than the African ostrich, have three toes, a fully feathered head and neck, an undeveloped tail, and pale gray to brownish feathers that droop over the rump and back

rhe·bok \ˈrē-ˌbäk\ *n* [Afrik *reebok,* fr. MD, male roe deer, fr. *ree* roe + *boc* buck] **:** a large gray southern African antelope (*Pelea capreolus*)

rhe·ni·um \ˈrē-nē-əm\ *n* [NL, fr. L *Rhenus* Rhine river] **:** a rare heavy metallic element that resembles manganese, is obtained either as a powder or as a silver-white hard metal, and is used in catalysts and thermocouples — see ELEMENT table

rheo- *comb form* [Gk *rhein* to flow — more at STREAM] **:** flow **:** current <*rheo*stat>

rhe·ol·o·gy \rē-ˈäl-ə-jē\ *n* [ISV] **:** a science dealing with the deformation and flow of matter — **rhe·o·log·i·cal** \ˌrē-ə-ˈläj-i-kəl\ *adj* — **rhe·o·log·i·cal·ly** \-k(ə-)lē\ *adv* — **rhe·ol·o·gist** \rē-ˈäl-ə-jəst\ *n*

rhe·om·e·ter \rē-ˈäm-ət-ər\ *n* [ISV] **:** an instrument for measuring the flow of viscous substances

rheo·phile \ˈrē-ə-ˌfīl\ *or* **rheo·phil·ic** \ˌrē-ə-ˈfil-ik\ *also* **rheo·phil** \ˈrē-ə-ˌfil\ *adj* [ISV] **:** preferring or living in flowing water <~ fauna>

rheo·stat \ˈrē-ə-ˌstat\ *n* **:** a resistor for regulating a current by means of variable resistances — **rheo·stat·ic** \ˌrē-ə-ˈstat-ik\ *adj*

rhe·sus monkey \ˌrē-səs-\ *n* [NL *Rhesus,* genus of monkeys, fr. L, a mythical king of Thrace, fr. Gk *Rhēsos*] **:** a pale brown Indian monkey (*Macaca mulatta*) often kept in zoos and used in medical research

rhet *abbr* rhetoric

rhe·tor \ˈrē-ˌtȯ(ə)r, ˈre-; ˈrēt-ər, ˈret-\ *n* [ME *rethor,* fr. L *rhetor,* fr. Gk *rhētōr*] **:** RHETORICIAN 1

rhet·o·ric \ˈret-ə-rik\ *n* [ME *rethorik,* fr. MF *rethorique,* fr. L *rhetorica,* fr. Gk *rhētorikē,* lit., art of oratory, fr. fem. of *rhētorikos* of an orator, fr. *rhētōr* orator, rhetorician, fr. *eirein* to say, speak — more at WORD] **1 :** the art of speaking or writing effectively; *specif* **:** the study of principles and rules of composition formulated by critics of ancient times **2 a :** skill in the effective use of speech **b :** a type or mode of language or speech; *also* **:** insincere or grandiloquent language **3 :** verbal communication **:** DISCOURSE

rhe·tor·i·cal \ri-ˈtȯr-i-kəl, -ˈtär-\ *also* **rhe·tor·ic** \ri-ˈtȯr-ik, -ˈtär-\ *adj* **1 a :** of, relating to, or concerned with rhetoric **b :** employed for rhetorical effect **2 a :** given to rhetoric **:** GRANDILOQUENT **b :** VERBAL — **rhe·tor·i·cal·ly** \-i-k(ə-)lē\ *adv* — **rhe·tor·i·cal·ness** \-i-kəl-nəs\ *n*

rhetorical question *n* **:** a question asked merely for effect with no answer expected

rhet·o·ri·cian \ˌret-ə-ˈrish-ən\ *n* **1 a :** a master or teacher of rhetoric **b :** ORATOR **2 :** an eloquent or grandiloquent writer or speaker

rheum \ˈrüm\ *n* [ME *reume,* fr. MF, fr. L *rheuma,* fr. Gk, lit., flow, flux, fr. *rhein* to flow — more at STREAM] **1 :** a watery discharge from the mucous membranes esp. of the eyes or nose **2** *archaic* **:** TEARS — **rheumy** \ˈrü-mē\ *adj*

[1]**rheu·mat·ic** \ru̇-ˈmat-ik\ *adj* [ME *rewmatik* subject to rheum, fr. L *rheumaticus,* fr. Gk *rheumatikos,* fr. *rheumat-, rheuma*] **:** of, relating to, characteristic of, or affected with rheumatism — **rheu·mat·i·cal·ly** \-i-k(ə-)lē\ *adv*

[2]**rheumatic** *n* **:** one affected with rheumatism

rheumatic disease *n* **:** any of several diseases (as rheumatic fever or fibrositis) characterized by inflammation and pain in muscles or joints

rheumatic fever *n* **:** an acute disease that occurs chiefly in children and young adults and is characterized by fever, by inflammation and pain in and around the joints, and by inflammatory involvement of the pericardium and heart valves

rheu·ma·tism \ˈrü-mə-ˌtiz-əm, ˈru̇m-ə-\ *n* [L *rheumatismus* flux, rheum, fr. Gk *rheumatismos,* fr. *rheumatizesthai* to suffer from a flux, fr. *rheumat-, rheuma* flux] **1 :** any of various conditions characterized by inflammation or pain in muscles, joints, or fibrous tissue <muscular ~> **2 :** RHEUMATOID ARTHRITIS

rheu·ma·tiz \-ˌtiz\ *n, chiefly dial* **:** RHEUMATISM

rheu·ma·toid \-ˌtȯid\ *adj* [ISV, fr. *rheumatism*] **:** characteristic of or affected with rheumatoid arthritis

rheumatoid arthritis *n* **:** a constitutional disease of unknown cause and progressive course that is characterized by inflammation and swelling of joint structures

rheu·ma·tol·o·gy \ˌrü-mə-ˈtäl-ə-jē, ˌru̇m-ə-\ *n* **:** a branch of medicine dealing with rheumatic diseases — **rheu·ma·tol·o·gist** \-jəst\ *n*

Rh factor \ˈär-ˈāch-\ *n* [*rh*esus monkey (in which it was first detected)] **:** any of one or more substances present in the red blood cells of most persons and of higher animals, inherited according to Mendelian principles, and capable of inducing intense antigenic reactions

rhin- *or* **rhino-** *comb form* [NL, fr. Gk, fr. *rhin-, rhis*] **:** nose **:** nose and <*rhin*itis> <*rhino*laryngology>

rhi·nal \ˈrīn-ᵊl\ *adj* **:** of or relating to the nose **:** NASAL

-rhine — see -RRHINE

rhin·en·ceph·a·lon \ˌrī-(ˌ)nen-ˈsef-ə-ˌlän, -lən\ *n* [NL] **:** the chiefly olfactory part of the forebrain — **rhin·en·ce·phal·ic** \ˌrī-ˌnen-sə-ˈfal-ik\ *adj*

rhine·stone \ˈrīn-ˌstōn\ *n* [*Rhine* river] **:** a colorless imitation stone of high luster made of glass, paste, or gem quartz

Rhine wine \ˈrīn-\ *n* **1 :** a typically light-bodied dry white wine produced in the Rhine valley **2 :** a wine similar to Rhine wine produced elsewhere

rhi·ni·tis \rī-ˈnīt-əs\ *n* [NL] **:** inflammation of the mucous membrane of the nose

[1]**rhi·no** \ˈrī-(ˌ)nō\ *n* [origin unknown] **:** MONEY, CASH

[2]**rhino** *n, pl* **rhino** *or* **rhinos :** RHINOCEROS

rhi·noc·er·os \rī-ˈnäs-(ə-)rəs, rə-\ *n, pl* **-noc·er·os·es** *or* **-noc·eros** *or* **-noc·eri** \-ˈnäs-ə-ˌrī\ [ME *rinoceros,* fr. L *rhinocerot-, rhinoceros,* fr. Gk *rhinokerōt-, rhinokerōs,* fr. *rhin-* + *keras* horn — more at HORN] : any of various large powerful herbivorous thick-skinned perissodactyl mammals (family Rhinocerotidae) that have one or two heavy upright horns on the snout — **rhi·noc·er·ot·ic** \(ˌ)rī-ˌnäs-ə-ˈrät-ik, rə-\ *adj*

rhinoceros beetle *n* : any of various large chiefly tropical beetles (of *Dynastes* and closely related genera) having projecting horns on thorax and head

rhi·no·lar·yn·gol·o·gy \ˈrī-nō-ˌlar-ən-ˈgäl-ə-jē\ *n* : a branch of medical science dealing with the nose and larynx

rhi·no·phar·yn·gi·tis \-ˌfar-ən-ˈjīt-əs\ *n* [NL] : inflammation of the mucous membrane of the nose and pharynx

rhi·nos·co·py \rī-ˈnäs-kə-pē\ *n* [ISV] : examination of the nasal passages

rhi·no·spo·rid·i·um \ˌrī-nō-spə-ˈrid-ē-əm\ *n* [NL, genus name, fr. *rhin-* + *sporidium* small spore] : any of a genus (*Rhinosporidium*) of microparasites of uncertain relationship associated with some nasal polyps in man and in horses

rhi·no·vi·rus \-ˈvī-rəs\ *n* [NL] : any of a group of picornaviruses that are related to the enteroviruses and are associated with disorders of the upper respiratory tract

rhiz- *or* **rhizo-** *comb form* [NL, fr. Gk, fr. *rhiza* — more at ROOT] : root <*rhiz*anthous> <*rhizo*carpous>

-rhi·za *or* **-r·rhi·za** \ˈrī-zə\ *n comb form, pl* **-zae** \-(ˌ)zē\ *or* **-zas** [NL, fr. Gk *rhiza*] : root : part resembling or connected with a root <coleo*rhiza*> <myco*rrhiza*>

rhiz·an·thous \rī-ˈzan(t)-thəs\ *adj* [ISV *rhiz-* + Gk *anthos* flower — more at ANTHOLOGY] : producing flowers apparently directly from the root

rhi·zo·bi·um \rī-ˈzō-bē-əm\ *n, pl* **-bia** \-bē-ə\ [NL, genus name, fr. *rhiz-* + Gk *bios* life — more at QUICK] : any of a genus (*Rhizobium*) of small heterotrophic soil bacteria capable of forming symbiotic nodules on the roots of leguminous plants and of there becoming bacteroids that fix atmospheric nitrogen

rhi·zo·car·pous \ˌrī-zə-ˈkär-pəs\ *or* **rhi·zo·car·pic** \-pik\ *adj* [ISV] : having perennial underground parts but annual stems and foliage <~ herbs>

rhi·zo·ceph·a·lan \ˌrī-zō-ˈsef-ə-lən\ *or* **rhi·zo·ceph·a·lid** \-ləd\ *n* [deriv. of Gk *rhiza* root + *kephalē* head — more at ROOT, CEPHALIC] : a crustacean of an order (Rhizocephala) comprising degenerate forms that live as parasites on crabs and hermit crabs

rhi·zoc·to·nia \ˌrī-ˌzäk-ˈtō-nē-ə\ *n* [NL, genus name, fr. *rhiz-* + Gk *-ktonos* killing, fr. *kteinein* to kill; akin to Skt *kṣaṇoti* he wounds] : a fungus of a form genus (*Rhizoctonia*) that includes major plant pathogens

rhizoctonia disease *n* : a plant disease caused by a rhizoctonia; *esp* : one of potatoes characterized esp. by black scurfy spots on the tubers

rhi·zo·gen·e·sis \-ˈjen-ə-səs\ *n* [NL] : root development

rhi·zo·gen·ic \ˌrī-zə-ˈjen-ik\ *or* **rhi·zo·ge·net·ic** \-jə-ˈnet-ik\ *adj* : producing roots <~ tissue>

rhi·zoid \ˈrī-ˌzȯid\ *n* : a rootlike structure — **rhi·zoi·dal** \rī-ˈzȯid-ᵊl\ *adj*

rhi·zo·ma·tous \rī-ˈzō-mət-əs\ *adj* [ISV, fr. NL *rhizomat-, rhizoma*] : having or resembling a rhizome

rhi·zome \ˈrī-ˌzōm\ *n* [NL *rhizomat-, rhizoma,* fr. Gk *rhizōmat-, rhizōma* mass of roots, fr. *rhizoun* to cause to take root, fr. *rhiza* root — more at ROOT] : a somewhat elongate usu. horizontal subterranean plant stem that is often thickened by deposits of reserve food material, produces shoots above and roots below, and is distinguished from a true root in possessing buds, nodes, and usu. scalelike leaves — **rhi·zo·mic** \rī-ˈzō-mik, -ˈzäm-ik\ *adj*

rhi·zo·mor·phous \ˌrī-zə-ˈmȯr-fəs\ *adj* [ISV] : shaped like a root

rhi·zo·plane \ˈrī-zə-ˌplān\ *n* : the external surface of roots together with closely adhering soil particles and debris

rhi·zo·pod \ˈrī-zə-ˌpäd\ *n* [deriv. of Gk *rhiza* + *pod-, pous* foot — more at FOOT] : any of a subclass (Rhizopoda) of usu. creeping protozoans (as an amoeba or a foraminifer) having lobate or rootlike pseudopods — **rhi·zop·o·dal** \rī-ˈzäp-əd-ᵊl\ *adj* — **rhi·zop·o·dous** \-əd-əs\ *adj*

rhi·zo·pus \ˈrī-zə-pəs, -ˌpu̇s\ *n* [NL, genus name, fr. *rhiz-* + Gk *pous* foot] : any of a genus (*Rhizopus*) of mold fungi including economic pests causing decay — see FUNGUS illustration

rhi·zo·sphere \-ˌsfi(ə)r\ *n* [ISV] : soil that surrounds and is influenced by the roots of a plant

rhi·zot·o·my \rī-ˈzät-ə-mē\ *n, pl* **-mies** [ISV] : the operation of cutting the anterior or posterior spinal nerve roots for therapeutic purposes

Rh–neg·a·tive \ˌär-ˌāch-ˈneg-ət-iv\ *adj* : lacking Rh factor in the blood

rho \ˈrō\ *n* [Gk *rhō,* of Sem origin; akin to Heb *rēsh* resh] **1** : the 17th letter of the Greek alphabet — see ALPHABET table **2** : a very short-lived unstable meson with mass 1490 times the mass of an electron — called also *rho particle*

rhod- *or* **rhodo-** *comb form* [NL, fr. L, fr. Gk, fr. *rhodon* rose] : rose : red <*rhod*ium> <*rhodo*lite>

rho·da·mine \ˈrōd-ə-ˌmēn\ *n, often cap* [ISV] : any of a group of yellowish red to blue fluorescent dyes; *esp* : a brilliant bluish red dye made by fusing an amino derivative of phenol with phthalic anhydride and used esp. in coloring paper and as a biological stain — called also *rhodamine B*

Rhode Is·land bent \rō-ˌdī-lən(d)-\ *n* [*Rhode Island,* U.S.] : a lawn grass (*Agrostis tenuis*) of eastern No. America

Rhode Island Red *n* : any of an American breed of general-purpose domestic fowls having a long heavy body, smooth yellow or reddish legs, and rich brownish red plumage

Rhode Island White *n* : any of an American breed of domestic fowls resembling Rhode Island Reds but having pure white plumage

Rhodes grass \ˈrōdz-\ *n* [Cecil J. *Rhodes*] : an African perennial grass (*Chloris gayana*) widely cultivated as a forage grass esp. in dry regions

Rho·de·sian man \rō-ˌdē-zh(ē-)ən-\ *n* [Northern *Rhodesia,* Africa] : an extinct African man (*Homo rhodesiensis* or *Africanthropus rhodesiensis*) having long bones of modern type, a skull with prominent brow ridges and large face but human palate and dentition, and a simple but relatively large brain

Rhodesian Ridge·back \-ˈrij-ˌbak\ *n* : any of an African breed of powerful long-bodied hunting dogs having a dense harsh short tan coat with a characteristic crest of reversed hair along the spine

Rhodes scholar \ˈrōd(z)-\ *n* : a holder of one of numerous scholarships founded under the will of Cecil J. Rhodes that can be used at Oxford University for two or three years and are open to candidates from the British Commonwealth and the U.S.

rho·di·um \ˈrōd-ē-əm\ *n* [NL, fr. Gk *rhodon* rose] : a white hard ductile metallic element that is chiefly trivalent and resistant to attack by acids, occurs in platinum ores, and is used in alloys with platinum — see ELEMENT table

rho·do·chro·site \ˌrōd-ə-ˈkrō-ˌsīt, rə-ˈdäk-rə-\ *n* [G *rhodocrosit,* fr. Gk *rhodochrōs* rose-colored, fr. *rhod-* + *chrōs* color; akin to Gk *chrōma* color — more at CHROMATIC] : a rose red mineral $MnCO_3$ consisting essentially of manganese carbonate

rho·do·den·dron \ˌrōd-ə-ˈden-drən\ *n* [NL, genus name, fr. L, rosebay, fr. Gk, fr. *rhod-* + *dendron* tree — more at DENDR-] : any of a genus (*Rhododendron*) of the heath family of widely cultivated shrubs and trees with alternate leaves and showy flowers; *esp* : one with leathery evergreen leaves as distinguished from a deciduous azalea

rho·do·lite \ˈrōd-ᵊl-ˌīt\ *n* : a pink or purple garnet used as a gem

rhodomontade *var of* RODOMONTADE

rho·do·nite \ˈrōd-ᵊn-ˌīt\ *n* [G *rhodonit,* fr. Gk *rhodon* rose] : a pale red triclinic mineral $MnSiO_3$ that consists essentially of manganese silicate and is used as an ornamental stone

rho·do·plast \ˈrōd-ə-ˌplast\ *n* [ISV] : one of the reddish chromatophores occurring in the red algae

rho·dop·sin \rō-ˈdäp-sən\ *n* [ISV *rhod-* + Gk *opsis* sight, vision + ISV *-in* — more at OPTIC] : a red photosensitive pigment in the retinal rods of marine fishes and most higher vertebrates that is important in vision in dim light — called also *visual purple*

rho·do·ra \rō-ˈdōr-ə, -ˈdȯr-\ *n* [NL, genus name, fr. L, a plant] : any of a genus (*Rhodora*) of the heath family of shrubs that are found in Canada and New England and have delicate pink flowers produced before or with the leaves in the spring

rhomb \ˈräm(b)\ *n, pl* **rhombs** \ˈrämz\ [MF *rhombe,* fr. L *rhombus*] **1** : RHOMBUS **2** : RHOMBOHEDRON

rhomb- *or* **rhombo-** *comb form* [MF, fr. L, fr. Gk, fr. *rhombos*] : rhomb <*rhomb*encephalon> <*rhombo*hedron>

rhomb·en·ceph·a·lon \ˌräm-(ˌ)ben-ˈsef-ə-ˌlän, -lən\ *n* [NL] : the parts of the vertebrate brain that develop from the embryonic hindbrain; *also* : HINDBRAIN 1a

rhom·bic \ˈräm-bik\ *adj* **1** : having the form of a rhombus **2** : ORTHORHOMBIC

rhom·bo·he·dron \ˌräm-bō-ˈhē-drən\ *n, pl* **-drons** *or* **-dra** \-drə\ [NL] : a parallelepiped whose faces are rhombuses — **rhom·bo·he·dral** \-drəl\ *adj*

¹rhom·boid \ˈräm-ˌbȯid\ *n* [MF *rhomboïde,* fr. L *rhomboides,* fr. Gk *rhomboeidēs* resembling a rhombus, fr. *rhombos*] : a parallelogram in which the angles are oblique and adjacent sides are unequal

²rhom·boid \ˈräm-ˌbȯid\ *or* **rhom·boi·dal** \räm-ˈbȯid-ᵊl\ *adj* : shaped somewhat like a rhombus or rhomboid

rhomboid

rhom·boi·de·us \räm-ˈbȯid-ē-əs\ *n, pl* **-dei** \-ē-ˌī\ [NL, fr. L *rhomboides* rhomboid] : either of two muscles that lie beneath the trapezius muscle and connect the spinous processes of various vertebrae with the medial border of the scapula

rhom·bus \ˈräm-bəs\ *n, pl* **rhom·bus·es** *or* **rhom·bi** \-ˌbī, -ˌbē\ [L, fr. Gk *rhombos*] : an equilateral parallelogram usu. having oblique angles

rhon·chus \ˈräŋ-kəs\ *n, pl* **rhon·chi** \ˈräŋ-ˌkī\ [LGk, fr. *rhenchein* to snore, wheeze; akin to OIr *srennim* I snore] : a whistling or snoring sound heard on auscultation of the chest when the air channels are partly obstructed

Rh–pos·i·tive \ˌär-ˌāch-ˈpäz-ət-iv, -ˈpäz-tiv\ *adj* : containing Rh factor in the red blood cells

rhu·barb \ˈrü-ˌbärb\ *n* [ME *rubarbe,* fr. MF *reubarbe,* fr. ML *reubarbarum,* alter. of *rha barbarum,* lit., barbarian rhubarb] **1** : any of several plants (genus *Rheum*) of the buckwheat family having large leaves with thick succulent petioles often used as food **2** : the dried rhizome and roots of any of several rhubarbs grown in China and Tibet and used as a purgative and stomachic **3** : a heated dispute or controversy

rhumb \ˈrəm(b)\ *n, pl* **rhumbs** \ˈrəmz\ [Sp *rumbo* rhumb, rhumb line] : any of the points of the mariner's compass

rhumba *var of* RUMBA

rhumb line *n* [Sp *rumbo*] : a line on the surface of the earth that makes equal oblique angles with all meridians and that is a spiral coiling round the poles but never reaching them

rhus \ˈrüs\ *n, pl* **rhus·es** *or* **rhus** [NL, genus name, fr. L, sumac, fr. Gk *rhous*] : any of a genus (*Rhus*) of shrubs and trees (as sumac or poison ivy) that are native to temperate and warm regions, have simple or pinnate leaves, and sometimes produce substances causing dermatitis

¹rhyme \ˈrīm\ *n* [alter. of ME *rime,* fr. OF] **1 a** : correspondence in terminal sounds of units of composition or utterance (as two or more words or lines of verse) **b** : one of two or more words thus corresponding in sound **c** : correspondence of other than terminal word sounds: as (1) : ALLITERATION (2) : INTERNAL RHYME **2 a** (1) : rhyming verse (2) : POETRY **b** : a composition in verse that rhymes **3** : RHYTHM, MEASURE

²rhyme *vb* **rhymed; rhym·ing** *vi* **1** : to make rhymes; *also* : to compose rhyming verse **2 a** *of a word or verse* : to end in syllables that rhyme **b** : to be a rhyme <*date* ~*s* with *fate*> **3** : to be in accord : HARMONIZE ~ *vt* **1** : to relate or praise in rhyming verse **2 a** : to put into rhyme **b** : to compose (verse) in rhyme **c**

: to cause to rhyme : use as rhyme
rhym·er \'rī-mər\ *n* : one that makes rhymes; *specif* : RHYMESTER
rhyme royal \-'rȯi(-ə)l\ *n* : a stanza of seven lines in iambic pentameter with a rhyme scheme of *ababbcc*
rhyme scheme *n* : the arrangement of rhymes in a stanza or a poem
rhyme·ster \'rīm(p)-stər\ *n* : an inferior poet
[1]**rhyn·cho·ce·pha·lian** \ˌriŋ-kō-sə-'fāl-yən\ *adj* [deriv. of Gk *rhynchos* beak, snout + *kephalē* head] : of or relating to an order (Rhynchocephalia) of reptiles resembling lizards
[2]**rhynchocephalian** *n* : a rhynchocephalian reptile : TUATARA
rhyn·choph·o·ran \riŋ-'käf-ə-rən\ *or* **rhyn·cho·phore** \'riŋ-kə-ˌfō(ə)r, -ˌfȯ(ə)r\ *n* [deriv. of Gk *rhynchos* + *pherein* to bear] : any of a group (Rhynchophora) of beetles with the head usu. prolonged as a snout : SNOUT BEETLE, WEEVIL
rhy·o·lite \'rī-ə-ˌlīt\ *n* [G *rhyolith*, fr. Gk *rhyax* stream, stream of lava (fr. *rhein*) + G *-lith* -lite] : a very acid volcanic rock that is the lava form of granite — **rhy·o·lit·ic** \ˌrī-ə-'lit-ik\ *adj*
rhythm *n* [MF & L; MF *rhythme*, fr. L *rhythmus*, fr. Gk *rhythmos*, fr. *rhein* to flow — more at STREAM] **1 a** : an ordered recurrent alternation of strong and weak elements in the flow of sound and silence in speech **b** : a particular example or form of rhythm <iambic ~> **2 a** : the aspect of music comprising all the elements (as accent, meter, and tempo) that relate to forward movement **b** : a characteristic rhythmic pattern <rumba ~>; *also* : [1]METER 2 **c** : the group of instruments in a band supplying the rhythm — called also *rhythm section* **3 a** : movement or fluctuation marked by the regular recurrence or natural flow of related elements **b** : the repetition in a literary work of phrase, incident, character type, or symbol **4** : a regularly recurrent quantitative change in a variable biological process **5** : the effect created by the elements in a play, movie, or novel that relate to the temporal development of the action **6** : RHYTHM METHOD
rhythm and blues *n* : popular music with elements of blues and Negro folk music
rhythm band *n* : a band usu. composed of school children who play simple percussion instruments (as rhythm sticks, sleigh bells, or tambourines) to learn fundamentals of coordination and music
rhyth·mic \'rith-mik\ *or* **rhyth·mi·cal** \-mi-kəl\ *adj* **1** : of, relating to, or involving rhythm **2** : marked by or moving in pronounced rhythm — **rhyth·mi·cal·ly** \-mi-k(ə-)lē\ *adv*
rhyth·mic·i·ty \rith-'mis-ət-ē\ *n* : the state of being rhythmic or of responding rhythmically
rhyth·mics \'rith-miks\ *n pl but sing or pl in constr* : the science or theory of rhythms
rhyth·mist \'rith-(ə-)məst\ *n* : one who studies or has a feeling for rhythm
rhyth·mize \'rith-(ə-)ˌmīz\ *vt* **-mized; -miz·ing** : to order or compose rhythmically — **rhyth·mi·za·tion** \ˌrith-(ə-)mə-'zā-shən\ *n*
rhythm method *n* : a method of birth control involving continence during the period in which ovulation is most likely to occur
rhythm stick *n* : one of a pair of plain or notched wood sticks that are struck or rubbed together to produce various percussive sounds and are used esp. by young children in rhythm bands
rhyt·i·dome \'rit-ə-ˌdōm, 'rīt-\ *n* [prob. fr. (assumed) NL *rhytidoma*, fr. Gk *rhytidōma* wrinkle, fr. *rhytidoun* to wrinkle, fr. *rhytid-*, *rhytis* wrinkle] : the bark external to the last formed periderm
RI *abbr* **1** refractive index **2** Rhode Island
[1]**ri·al** \rē-'ȯl, -'äl\ *n* [Per, fr. Ar *riyāl* riyal] — see MONEY table
[2]**rial** *var of* RIYAL
ri·al·to \rē-'al-(ˌ)tō\ *n, pl* **-tos** [*Rialto*, island and district in Venice] **1** : EXCHANGE, MARKETPLACE **2** : a theater district
ri·ant \'rī-ənt, 'rē-; rē-'äⁿ\ *adj* [MF, prp. of *rire* to laugh, fr. L *ridēre* — more at RIDICULOUS] : GAY, MIRTHFUL — **ri·ant·ly** \'rī-ənt-lē, 'rē-\ *adv*
ri·a·ta \rē-'at-ə, -'ät-\ *n* [modif. of AmerSp *reata*] : LARIAT
[1]**rib** \'rib\ *n* [ME, fr. OE; akin to OHG *rippi* rib, Gk *erephein* to roof over] **1 a** : one of the paired curved bony or partly cartilaginous rods that stiffen the walls of the body of most vertebrates and protect the viscera **b** : a cut of meat including a rib — see BEEF illustration **c** [fr. the account of Eve's creation from Adam's rib, Gen 2:21–22] : WIFE **2** : something resembling a rib in shape or function: as **a** (1) : a traverse member of the frame of a ship that runs from keel to deck (2) : a light fore-and-aft member in an airplane's wing **b** : one of the stiff strips supporting an umbrella's fabric **c** : one of the arches in Romanesque and Gothic vaulting meeting and crossing one another and dividing the whole vaulted space into triangles **3** : an elongated ridge: as **a** (1) : a vein of an insect's wing (2) : one of the primary veins of a leaf **b** : one of the ridges in a knitted or woven fabric
[2]**rib** *vt* **ribbed; rib·bing** **1** : to furnish or enclose with ribs **2** : to form vertical ridges in knitting — **rib·ber** *n*
[3]**rib** *vt* **ribbed; rib·bing** [prob. fr. [1]*rib*; fr. the tickling of the ribs to cause laughter] : to poke fun at : KID — **rib·ber** *n*
[4]**rib** *n* **1** : JOKE **2** : PARODY
RIBA *abbr* Royal Institute of British Architects
[1]**rib·ald** \'rib-əld *also* 'rib-ˌȯld, 'rī-ˌbȯld\ *n* [ME, fr. OF *ribaut*, *ribauld* wanton, rascal, fr. *riber* to be wanton, of Gmc origin; akin to OHG *rīban* to be wanton, lit., to twist; akin to Gk *rhiptein* to throw] : a ribald person
[2]**ribald** *adj* **1** : CRUDE, OFFENSIVE <~ language> **2** : characterized by or using coarse indecent humor **syn** see COARSE
rib·ald·ry \'rib-əl-drē *also* 'rib-\ *n, pl* **-ries** **1** : a ribald quality or element **2** : ribald language or humor
rib·and \'rib-ənd\ *n* [ME, alter. of *riban*] : a ribbon used esp. as a decoration
rib·band \'rib-ˌ(b)and, 'rib-ən(d)\ *n* [[1]*rib* + *band*] : a long narrow strip or bar used in shipbuilding; *esp* : one bent and bolted longitudinally to the frames to hold them in position during construction
rib·bing \'rib-iŋ\ *n* : an arrangement of ribs
[1]**rib·bon** \'rib-ən\ *n* [ME *riban*, fr. MF *riban*, *ruban*] **1 a** : a flat or tubular narrow closely woven fabric (as of silk or rayon) used for trimmings or knitting **b** : a narrow fabric used for tying packages **c** : a piece of usu. multicolored ribbon worn as a military decoration or in place of a medal **d** : a strip of colored satin given for winning a place in a competition **2** : a long narrow strip resembling a ribbon: as **a** : a board framed into the studs to support the ceiling or floor joists **b** : a strip of inked fabric (as in a typewriter) **3** *pl* : reins for controlling an animal **4** : TATTER, SHRED — usu. used in pl. **5** : RIBBAND — **rib·bon·like** \-ˌlīk\ *adj*
[2]**ribbon** *vt* **1 a** : to adorn with ribbons **b** : to divide into ribbons **c** : to cover with or as if with ribbons **2** : to rip to shreds
ribbon candy *n* : a thin brittle usu. colored sugar candy folded back and forth upon itself
ribbon development *n* : a system of buildings built side by side along a road
rib·bon·fish \'rib-ən-ˌfish\ *n* : any of various elongate greatly compressed marine fishes (as a dealfish or oarfish)
ribbon worm *n* : NEMERTEAN
rib·by \'rib-ē\ *adj* : showing or marked by ribs
rib cage *n* : the bony enclosing wall of the chest consisting chiefly of the ribs and their connectives
ri·bes \'rī-(ˌ)bēz\ *n, pl* **ribes** [NL, genus name, fr. ML, currant, fr. Ar *rībās* rhubarb] : any of a genus (*Ribes*) of shrubs (as a currant or a gooseberry) of the saxifrage family that have small racemose variously colored flowers and pulpy two-seeded to many-seeded berries
rib eye *n* : the large piece of meat that lies along the outer side of the rib (as of a steer)
rib·grass \'rib-ˌgras\ *n* : [1]PLANTAIN; *specif* : an Old World plantain (*Plantago lanceolata*) with long narrow ribbed leaves
rib·let \'rib-lət\ *n* : one of the rib ends in the strip of breast of lamb or veal — see LAMB illustration
ri·bo·fla·vin \ˌrī-bə-'flā-vən, 'rī-bə-ˌ\ *n* [ISV *ribose* + L *flavus* yellow — more at BLUE] : a yellow crystalline compound $C_{17}H_{20}N_4O_6$ that is a growth-promoting member of the vitamin B complex and occurs both free (as in milk) and combined (as in liver) — called also *vitamin B_2*, *vitamin G*
ri·bo·nu·cle·ase \ˌrī-bō-'n(y)ü-klē-ˌās, -ˌāz\ *n* [*ribonucleic* (acid) + *-ase*] : an enzyme that catalyzes the hydrolysis of RNA
ri·bo·nu·cle·ic acid \ˌrī-bō-n(y)ü-ˌklē-ik-, -ˌklā-\ *n* [*ribose* + *nucleic acid*] : RNA
ri·bo·nu·cleo·pro·tein \-ˌn(y)ü-klē-ō-'prō-ˌtēn, -'prōt-ē-ən\ *n* [*ribonucleic* + *-o-* + *protein*] : a nucleoprotein that contains RNA
ri·bo·nu·cle·o·side \-'n(y)ü-klē-ə-ˌsīd\ *n* [*ribose* + *nucleoside*] : a nucleoside that contains ribose
ri·bo·nu·cle·o·tide \-ˌtīd\ *n* [*ribose* + *nucleotide*] : a nucleotide that contains ribose and occurs esp. as a constituent of RNA
ri·bose \'rī-ˌbōs, -ˌbōz\ *n* [ISV, fr. *ribonic acid* (an acid $C_5H_{10}O_6$ obtained by oxidation of ribose)] : a pentose $C_5H_{10}O_5$ found esp. in the D-form and obtained esp. from RNA
ribosomal RNA *n* : the part of RNA that is a fundamental structural element of the ribosomes
ri·bo·some \'rī-bə-ˌsōm\ *n* [*ribonucleic* (acid) + *-some*] : one of the RNA-rich cytoplasmic granules that are sites of protein synthesis — **ri·bo·som·al** \ˌrī-bə-'sō-məl\ *adj*
rib roast *n* : a cut of meat containing the large piece that lies along the outer side of the rib — see BEEF illustration
rib·wort \'rib-ˌwərt, -ˌwȯ(ə)rt\ *n* : RIBGRASS
rice \'rīs\ *n, pl* **rice** [ME *rys*, fr. OF *ris*, fr. OIt *riso*, fr. Gk *oryza*, *oryzon*] **1** : an annual cereal grass (*Oryza sativa*) widely cultivated in warm climates for its seed that is used for food and for its by-products **2** : the seed of rice
rice·bird \'rīs-ˌbərd\ *n* : any of several small birds common in rice fields; *esp* : BOBOLINK
rice paper *n* [fr. its resemblance to paper made from rice straw] : a thin papery material made from rice-paper tree pith
rice-paper tree *n* : a small Asiatic tree or shrub (*Tetrapanax papyriferum*) of the ginseng family
rice polishings *n pl* : the inner bran layer of rice rubbed off in milling
ric·er \'rī-sər\ *n* : a kitchen utensil in which soft foods are pressed through a perforated container to produce strings about the diameter of a rice grain

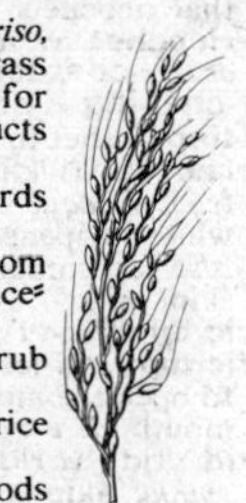
rice 1

ri·cer·car \ˌrē-cher-'kär\ *n* [It, fr. *ricercare* to seek again, fr. *ri-* re- (fr. L *re-*) + *cercare* to seek, fr. LL *circare* to go about; fr. the disguising of the subjects by various alterations] : any of various contrapuntal instrumental forms esp. of the 16th and 17th centuries employing fugal expositions on one or more subjects
rich \'rich\ *adj* [ME *riche*, fr. OE *rīce*; akin to OHG *rīhhi* rich, OE *rīce* kingdom, OHG *rīhhi*; all fr. prehistoric Gmc words borrowed fr. Celt words akin to OIr *rī* (gen. *rīg*) king — more at ROYAL] **1** : having abundant possessions and esp. material wealth **2 a** : having high value or quality **b** : well supplied **3** : magnificently impressive : SUMPTUOUS **4 a** : vivid and deep in color <a ~ red> **b** : full and mellow in tone and quality <a ~ voice> **c** : PUNGENT <~ odors> **5** : highly productive or remunerative <a ~ mine> **6 a** : having abundant plant nutrients <~ soil> **b** : highly seasoned, fatty, oily, or sweet <~ foods> **c** : high in the combustible component <a ~ fuel mixture> **7 a** : AMUSING; *also* : LAUGHABLE **b** : MEANINGFUL, SIGNIFICANT <~ allusions> **c** : LUSH <~ meadows> **8** : pure or nearly pure <~ lime> — **rich·ness** *n*

ə abut	ᵊ kitten	ər further	a back	ā bake	ä cot, cart
aů out	ch chin	e less	ē easy	g gift	i trip ī life
j joke	ŋ sing	ō flow	ȯ flaw	ȯi coin	th thin th this
ü loot	ů foot	y yet	yü few	yů furious	zh vision

syn RICH, WEALTHY, AFFLUENT, WELL-OFF, WELL-TO-DO, OPULENT *shared meaning element* : having goods, property, and money in abundance *ant* poor
Rich·ard Roe \ˌrich-ər-ˈdrō\ *n* : a party to legal proceedings whose true name is unknown — compare JOHN DOE
rich·en \ˈrich-ən\ *vt* **rich·ened; rich·en·ing** \-(ə-)niŋ\ : to make rich or richer
rich·es \ˈrich-əz\ *n pl* [ME, sing. or pl., fr. *richesse*, lit., richness, fr. OF, fr. *riche* rich, of Gmc origin; akin to OE *rice* rich] : things that make one rich : WEALTH
rich·ly \ˈrich-lē\ *adv* **1** : in a rich manner **2** : in full measure : AMPLY <praise ~ deserved>
Rich·ter scale \ˈrik-tər-\ *n* [after Charles R. *Richter* b1900 Am seismologist] : a logarithmic scale for expressing the magnitude of a seismic disturbance (as an earthquake) in terms of the energy dissipated in it with 1.5 indicating the smallest earthquake that can be felt, 4.5 an earthquake causing slight damage, and 8.5 a very devastating earthquake
ri·cin \ˈrīs-ᵊn, ˈris-\ *n* [L *ricinus* castor-oil plant] : a poisonous protein in the castor bean
ri·cin·ole·ic acid \ˌrīs-ᵊn-ō-ˌlē-ik-, ˌris-, -ˌlā-\ *n* [L *ricin*us + E *oleic*] : an oily unsaturated hydroxy fatty acid $C_{18}H_{34}O_3$ that occurs in castor oil as a glyceride and yields esters important as plasticizers
ric·i·nus \ˈris-ᵊn-əs\ *n* [NL, genus name, fr. L, castor-oil plant] : any of a genus (*Ricinus*) of plants (as the castor-oil plant) of the spurge family with large palmate leaves
1rick \ˈrik\ *n* [ME *reek*, fr. OE *hrēac*; akin to ON *hraukr* rick] **1** : a stack (as of hay) in the open air **2** : a pile of material (as cordwood) split from short logs
2rick *vt* : to pile (as hay) in ricks
3rick *vt* [perh. fr. ME *wrikken* to move unsteadily] *chiefly Brit* : WRENCH, SPRAIN
rick·ets \ˈrik-əts\ *n pl but sing in constr* [origin unknown] : a childhood disease that is characterized esp. by soft and deformed bones and that is caused by failure to assimilate and use calcium and phosphorus normally due to inadequate sunlight or vitamin D
rick·ett·sia \rik-ˈet-sē-ə\ *n, pl* **-si·as** *or* **-si·ae** \-sē-ˌē, -ˌī\ [NL, genus of microorganisms, fr. Howard T. *Ricketts* †1910 Am pathologist] : any of a family (Rickettsiaceae) of pleomorphic rod-shaped nonfilterable microorganisms that cause various diseases (as typhus) — **rick·ett·si·al** \-sē-əl\ *adj*
rick·ety \ˈrik-ət-ē\ *adj* **1** : affected with rickets **2 a** : feeble in the joints <a ~ old man> **b** : SHAKY, UNSOUND <~ stairs>
rick·ey \ˈrik-ē\ *n, pl* **rickeys** [prob. fr. the name *Rickey*] : a drink containing liquor, lime juice, sugar, and soda water; *also* : a similar drink without liquor
rick·rack *or* **ric·rac** \ˈrik-ˌrak\ *n* [redupl. of 4*rack*] : a flat braid woven to form zigzags and used esp. as trimming on clothing
rick·sha *or* **rick·shaw** \ˈrik-ˌshȯ\ *n* [alter. of *jinrikisha*] : a small covered 2-wheeled vehicle usu. for one passenger that is pulled by one man and that was used orig. in Japan

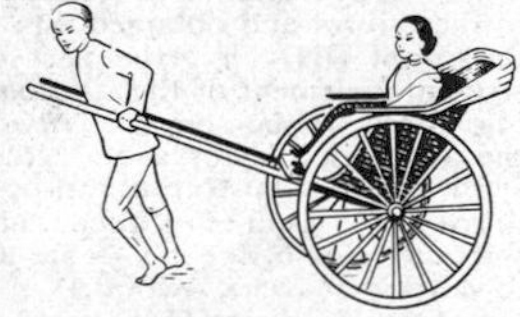
ricksha

1ric·o·chet \ˈrik-ə-ˌshā, *Brit also* -ˌshet\ *n* [F] : a glancing rebound (as of a projectile off a flat surface); *also* : an object that ricochets
2ricochet *vi* **-cheted** \-ˌshād\ *or* **-chet·ted** \-ˌshet-əd\; **-chet·ing** \-ˌshā-iŋ\ *or* **-chet·ting** \-ˌshet-iŋ\ : to skip with or as if with glancing rebounds
ri·cot·ta \ri-ˈkät-ə\ *n* [It, fr. fem. of pp. of *ricuocere* to cook again, fr. L *recoquere*, fr. *re-* + *coquere* to cook — more at COOK] : a white unripened whey cheese of Italy that resembles cottage cheese; *also* : a similar cheese made in the United States from whole or skim milk
ric·tal \ˈrik-tᵊl\ *adj* : of or relating to the rictus
ric·tus \ˈrik-təs\ *n* [NL, fr. L, open mouth, fr. *rictus*, pp. of *ringi* to open the mouth; akin to OSlav *ręgnǫti*] **1** : the gape of a bird's mouth **2 a** : the mouth orifice **b** : a gaping grin or grimace
rid \ˈrid\ *vt* **rid** *also* **rid·ded; rid·ding** [ME *ridden* to clear, fr. ON *rythja*; akin to L *ruere* to dig up — more at RUG] **1** *archaic* : SAVE, RESCUE **2** : to make free : RELIEVE, DISENCUMBER <~ himself of his troubles> <be ~ of worries> <get ~ of that junk>
rid·able *or* **ride·able** \ˈrīd-ə-bəl\ *adj* : fit for riding
rid·dance \ˈrid-ᵊn(t)s\ *n* **1** : an act of ridding **2** : DELIVERANCE, RELIEF — often used in the phrase *good riddance*
rid·den \ˈrid-ᵊn\ *adj* **1** : extremely concerned with or bothered by — usu. used in combination <conscience-*ridden*> **2** : excessively full of or supplied with — usu. used in combination <slum-*ridden*>
1rid·dle \ˈrid-ᵊl\ *n* [ME *redels*, *ridel*, fr. OE *rǣdelse* opinion, conjecture, riddle; akin to OE *rǣdan* to interpret — more at READ] **1** : a mystifying, misleading, or puzzling question posed as a problem to be solved or guessed : CONUNDRUM, ENIGMA **2** : something or someone difficult to understand *syn* see MYSTERY
2riddle *vb* **rid·dled; rid·dling** \ˈrid-liŋ, -ᵊl-iŋ\ *vt* **1** : to find the solution of : EXPLAIN **2** : to set a riddle for : PUZZLE ~ *vi* : to speak in or propound riddles — **rid·dler** \-lər, -ᵊl-ər\ *n*
3riddle *n* [ME *riddil*, fr. OE *hriddel*; akin to L *cribrum* sieve, *cernere* to sift — more at CERTAIN] : a coarse sieve
4riddle *vt* **rid·dled; rid·dling** \ˈrid-liŋ, -ᵊl-iŋ\ **1** : to separate (as grain from the chaff) with a riddle : pass through a riddle : SCREEN **2 a** : to fill (something or someone) as full of holes as a sieve : puncture often and thoroughly <*riddled* the ship with a broadside> **b** : to corrupt throughout : PERMEATE
rid·dling \ˈrid-liŋ,-ᵊl-iŋ\ *adj* : containing or presenting riddles
1ride \ˈrīd\ *vb* **rode** \ˈrōd\ *or chiefly dial* **rid** \ˈrid\; **rid·den** \ˈrid-ᵊn\ *or chiefly dial* **rid** *or* **rode; rid·ing** \ˈrīd-iŋ\ [ME *riden*, fr. OE *rīdan*; akin to OHG *rītan* to ride] *vi* **1 a** : to sit and travel on the back of an animal that one directs **b** : to travel in or on a conveyance **2** : to become sustained <*rode* on a wave of popularity> **3 a** : to lie moored or anchored <a ship ~*s* at anchor> **b** : SAIL **c** : to move like a floating object <the moon *rode* in the sky> **4** : to become supported on a point or surface **5** : to travel over a surface <the car ~*s* well> **6** : to continue without interference <let it ~> **7** : to be contingent : DEPEND <plans ~ on his nomination> **8** : to climb up on the body <shorts that ~ up> **9** : to become bet <his money is *riding* on the favorite> ~ *vt* **1 a** : to mount and travel on while controlling <~ a bike> **b** : to move with <~ the waves> **2 a** : to traverse by conveyance <*rode* 500 miles> **b** : to ride a horse in <~ a race> **3** : SURVIVE, OUTLAST — usu. used with *out* <*rode* out the gale> **4** : to traverse on horseback to inspect or maintain <~ fence> **5** : to mount in copulation **6 a** : OBSESS, OPPRESS <*ridden* by anxiety> **b** : to harass persistently : NAG **c** : TEASE, RIB **7** : CARRY, CONVEY **8** : to project over : OVERLAP **9** : to give with (a punch) to soften the impact **10** : to keep in partial engagement by resting a foot continuously on the pedal <~ the clutch> — **ride circuit** : to hold court in the various towns of a judicial circuit — **ride for a fall** : to court disaster — **ride herd on** : to keep a check on — **ride high** : to experience success — **ride roughshod over** : to treat with disdain or abuse
2ride *n* **1** : an act of riding; *esp* : a trip on horseback or by vehicle **2** : a way (as a road or path) suitable for riding **3** : any of various mechanical devices (as at an amusement park) for riding on **4 a** : a trip on which gangsters take a victim to murder him **b** : DECEPTION <take the taxpayers for a ~> **5** : a means of transportation **6** : the qualities of travel comfort in a vehicle **7** : a job as a driver in an automobile race
rid·er \ˈrīd-ər\ *n* **1** : one that rides **2 a** : an addition to a document often attached on a separate piece of paper **b** : a clause appended to a legislative bill to secure a usu. distinct object **3** : something used to overlie another or to move along on another piece — **rid·er·less** \-ləs\ *adj*
1ridge \ˈrij\ *n* [ME *rigge*, fr. OE *hrycg*; akin to OHG *hrukki* ridge, back, L *cruc-*, *crux* cross, *curvus* curved — more at CROWN] **1** : an elevated body part (as along the backbone) **2 a** : a range of hills or mountains **b** : an elongate elevation on an ocean bottom **3** : an elongate crest or a linear series of crests **4** : a raised strip (as of plowed ground) **5** : the line of intersection at the top between the opposite slopes or sides of a roof — **ridged** \ˈrijd\ *adj*
2ridge *vb* **ridged; ridg·ing** *vt* : to form into a ridge ~ *vi* : to extend in ridges
ridge·ling *or* **ridg·ling** \ˈrij-liŋ\ *n* [perh. fr. 1*ridge*, fr. the supposition that the undescended testis remains near the animal's back] **1** : a male animal having one or both testes retained in the inguinal canal **2** : an imperfectly castrated male animal
ridge·pole \ˈrij-ˌpōl\ *n* **1** : the highest horizontal timber in a roof and the receiver of the upper ends of the rafters — see RAFTER illustration **2** : the horizontal pole at the top of a tent
ridgy \ˈrij-ē\ *adj* : having or rising in ridges
1rid·i·cule \ˈrid-ə-ˌkyü(ə)l\ *n* [F or L; F, fr. L *ridiculum* jest] : the act of exposing to laughter : DERISION, MOCKERY
2ridicule *vt* **-culed; -cul·ing** : to make fun of — **rid·i·cul·er** *n*
syn RIDICULE, DERIDE, MOCK, TAUNT, TWIT, RALLY *shared meaning element* : to make an object of laughter
ri·dic·u·lous \rə-ˈdik-yə-ləs\ *adj* [L *ridiculosus* (fr. *ridiculum* jest, fr. neut. of *ridiculus*) or *ridiculus*, lit., laughable, fr. *ridēre* to laugh; akin to Skt *vrīḍate* he is ashamed] : arousing or deserving ridicule : ABSURD, PREPOSTEROUS *syn* see LAUGHABLE — **ri·dic·u·lous·ly** *adv* — **ri·dic·u·lous·ness** *n*
1ri·ding \ˈrīd-iŋ\ *n* [ME, alter. of (assumed) OE *thriding*, fr. ON *thrithjungr* third part, fr. *thrithi* third; akin to OE *thridda* third — more at THIRD] **1** : one of the three administrative jurisdictions into which Yorkshire, England, is divided **2** : an administrative jurisdiction or electoral district in a British dominion (as Canada)
2rid·ing \ˈrīd-iŋ\ *n* : the action or state of one that rides
3rid·ing *adj* **1** : used for or when riding <a ~ horse> **2** : operated by a rider <a ~ plow>
rid·ley \ˈrid-lē\ *n* [prob. fr. the name *Ridley*] : a marine turtle (*Caretta kempii* or *Lepidochelys kempii*) found off the Atlantic coast of the U.S.
ri·dot·to \ri-ˈdät-(ˌ)ō\ *n, pl* **-tos** [It, retreat, place of entertainment, redoubt] : a public entertainment consisting of music and dancing often in masquerade popular in 18th century England
ri·el \rē-ˈel\ *n* [origin unknown] — see MONEY table
Rie·mann·ian geometry \rē-ˌmän-ē-ən-\ *n* [G. F. B. *Riemann*] : a non-Euclidean geometry in which straight lines are geodesics and in which the parallel postulate is replaced by the postulate that every pair of straight lines intersects
Rie·mann integral \ˌrē-ˌmän-, -mən-\ *n* [G. F. B. *Riemann*] : DEFINITE INTEGRAL
Ries·ling \ˈrēz-liŋ, ˈrē-sliŋ\ *n* [G] : a dry white table wine resembling Rhine wine
ri·fam·pi·cin \rī-ˈfam-pə-sən\ *n* [*rif*amycin (an antibiotic produced from a bacterium, from which it is derived) + *ampicill*in (which it resembles in efficacy)] : a semisynthetic antibiotic that acts against some viruses and bacteria esp. by inhibiting RNA synthesis
rife \ˈrīf\ *adj* [ME *ryfe*, fr. OE *rȳfe*; akin to ON *rifr* abundant] **1** : prevalent esp. to an increasing degree <fear was ~ in the people> **2** : ABUNDANT, COMMON **3** : copiously supplied : ABOUNDING — usu. used with *with* <~ with rumors> *syn* see PREVAILING — **rife** *adv* — **rife·ly** *adv*
1riff \ˈrif\ *vb* [short for *riffle*] : RIFFLE, SKIM <~ pages>
2riff *n* [prob. by shortening & alter. fr. *refrain*] : an ostinato phrase in jazz typically supporting a solo improvisation; *also* : a piece based on such a phrase
3riff *vi* : to perform a jazz riff
Riff \ˈrif\ *n, pl* **Riffs** *or* **Riffi** \ˈrif-ē\ *or* **Riff** : a Berber of the Rif in northern Morocco
Riff·ian \ˈrif-ē-ən\ *n* : RIFF
1rif·fle \ˈrif-əl\ *n* [perh. alter. of *ruffle*] **1 a** : a shallow extending across a stream bed and causing broken water **b** : a stretch of water flowing over a riffle **2** : a small wave or succession of small waves : RIPPLE **3** [2*riffle*] **a** : the act or process of shuffling (as cards) **b** : the sound made while doing this

2riffle *vb* **rif·fled; rif·fling** \'rif-(ə-)liŋ\ *vi* **1 :** to form, flow over, or move in riffles **2 :** to flip cursorily : THUMB <~ through files> ~ *vt* **1 :** to ruffle slightly : RIPPLE **2 a :** to leaf through hastily; *specif* **:** to leaf (as a stack of paper) by sliding a thumb along the edge of the leaves **b :** to shuffle (playing cards) by separating the deck into two parts and riffling with the thumbs so the cards intermix **3 :** to manipulate (small objects) idly between the fingers

3riffle *n* [prob. fr. [1]*riffle*] **1 a :** any of various contrivances (as blocks or rails) laid on the bottom of a sluice or launder to make a series of grooves or interstices to catch and retain a mineral (as gold) **b :** a groove or interstice so formed **2 :** a cleat or bar fastened to an inclined surface in a gold-washing apparatus to catch and hold mineral grains

4riffle *vt* **rif·fled; rif·fling** \'rif-(ə-)liŋ\ **:** to run through a riffle or over a series of riffles <~ ground ore>

rif·fler \'rif-lər\ *n* [F *rifloir,* fr. *rifler* to file, rifle] **:** a small filing or scraping tool

riff·raff \'rif-ˌraf\ *n* [ME *riffe raffe,* fr. *rif and raf* every single one, fr. MF *rif et raf* completely, fr. *rifler* to plunder + *raffe* act of sweeping] **1 a :** disreputable persons **b :** RABBLE **c :** one of the riffraff **2 :** REFUSE, RUBBISH — **riffraff** *adj*

1ri·fle \'rī-fəl\ *vb* **ri·fled; ri·fling** \-f(ə-)liŋ\ [ME *riflen,* fr. MF *rifler* to scratch, file, plunder, of Gmc origin; akin to obs. D *rijffelen* to scrape] *vt* **1 :** to ransack esp. with the intent to steal **2 :** to steal and carry away ~ *vi* **:** to engage in ransacking and stealing — **ri·fler** \-f(ə-)lər\ *n*

2rifle *vt* **ri·fled; ri·fling** \-f(ə-)liŋ\ [F *rifler* to scratch, file] **:** to cut spiral grooves into the bore of <*rifled* arms> <*rifled* pipe>

3rifle *n* **1 a :** a shoulder weapon with a rifled bore **b :** a rifled artillery piece **2** *pl* **:** a body of soldiers armed with rifles — **ri·fle·man** \-fəl-mən\ *n*

4rifle *vt* **ri·fled; ri·fling** \-f(ə-)liŋ\ [[3]*rifle*] **:** to propel (as a ball) with great force or speed

ri·fle·bird \'rī-fəl-ˌbərd\ *n* **:** any of several birds of paradise

ri·fle·ry \'rī-fəl-rē\ *n* **:** the practice of shooting at targets with a rifle

ri·fle·scope \'rī-fəl-ˌskōp\ *n* **:** a telescopic sight for a rifle

ri·fling \'rī-f(ə-)liŋ\ *n* **1 :** the act or process of making spiral grooves **2 :** a system of spiral grooves in the surface of the bore of a gun causing a projectile when fired to rotate about its longer axis

1rift \'rift\ *n* [ME, of Scand origin; akin to Dan & Norw *rift* fissure, ON *rīfa* to rive — more at RIVE] **1 a :** FISSURE, CREVASSE **b :** a normal geological fault **2 :** a clear space or interval **3 :** BREACH, ESTRANGEMENT

2rift *vt* **1 :** CLEAVE, DIVIDE **2 :** PENETRATE ~ *vi* **:** to burst open

3rift *n* [prob. alter. of E dial. *riff* (reef)] **:** a shallow or rocky place in a stream

rift valley *n* **:** an elongated valley formed by the depression of a block of the earth's crust between two faults or groups of faults of approximately parallel strike

1rig \'rig\ *vt* **rigged; rig·ging** [ME *riggen*] **1 :** to fit out (as a ship) with rigging **2 :** CLOTHE, DRESS — usu. used with *out* **3 :** to furnish with special gear : EQUIP **4 a :** to put in condition or position for use : ADJUST, ARRANGE <a car *rigged* for manual control> **b :** CONSTRUCT <~ up a temporary shelter>

2rig *n* **1 :** the distinctive shape, number, and arrangement of sails and masts of a ship **2 :** EQUIPAGE; *esp* **:** a carriage with its horse **3 :** DRESS, CLOTHING **4 :** tackle, equipment, or machinery fitted for a specified purpose <an oil-drilling ~>

3rig *vt* **rigged; rig·ging** [*rig* (swindle)] **1 :** to manipulate or control usu. by deceptive or dishonest means <~ an election> **2 :** to fix in advance for a desired result <~ a quiz program>

rig·a·doon \ˌrig-ə-'dün\ *or* **ri·gau·don** \rē-gō-dōⁿ\ *n* [F *rigaudon*] **:** a lively dance of the 17th and 18th centuries; *also* **:** the music for a rigadoon

rig·a·ma·role *var of* RIGMAROLE

rig·a·to·ni \ˌrig-ə-'tō-nē\ *n* [It, pl., fr. *rigato* furrowed, fluted, fr. pp. of *rigare* to furrow, flute, fr. *riga* line, of Gmc origin; akin to OHG *rīga* line — more at ROW] **:** macaroni made in short curved fluted pieces

Ri·gel \'rī-jəl, -gəl; 'rij-əl\ *n* [Ar *Rijl,* lit., foot] **:** a first-magnitude star in the left foot of the constellation Orion

rig·ger \'rig-ər\ *n* **1 :** one that rigs **2 :** a long slender pointed sable paintbrush **3 :** a ship of a specified rig <square-*rigger*>

rig·ging \'rig-iŋ, -ən\ *n* **1 a :** lines and chains used aboard a ship esp. in working sail and supporting masts and spars **b :** a similar network (as in theater scenery) used for support and manipulation **2 :** CLOTHING

1right \'rīt\ *adj* [ME, fr. OE *riht;* akin to OHG *reht* right, L *rectus* straight, right, *regere* to lead straight, direct, rule, *rogare* to ask, Gk *oregein* to stretch out] **1 :** RIGHTEOUS, UPRIGHT **2 :** being in accordance with what is just, good, or proper <~ conduct> **3 a :** agreeable to a standard **b :** conforming to facts or truth : CORRECT <the ~ answer> **4 :** SUITABLE, APPROPRIATE <the ~ man for the job> **5 :** STRAIGHT <a ~ line> **6 :** GENUINE, REAL **7 a :** of, relating to, situated on, or being the side of the body which is away from the heart and on which the hand is stronger in most people **b :** located nearer to the right hand than to the left <the ~ pocket>; *esp* **:** located on the right hand when facing in the same direction as an observer <the ~ wing of an army> <stage ~> **8 :** having its axis perpendicular to the base <~ cone> **9 :** of, relating to, or constituting the principal or more prominent side of an object <made sure his socks were ~ side out> **10 :** acting or judging in accordance with truth or fact <time proved him ~> **11 a :** being in good physical or mental health or order <not in his ~ mind> **b :** being in a correct or proper state <put things ~> **12 :** most favorable or desired : PREFERABLE; *also* **:** socially acceptable <knew all the ~ people> **13** *often cap* **:** of, adhering to, or constituted by the Right esp. in politics ***syn*** see CORRECT ***ant*** wrong — **right·ness** *n*

2right *n* [ME, fr. OE *riht,* fr. *riht,* adj.] **1 :** qualities (as adherence to duty or obedience to lawful authority) that together constitute the ideal of moral propriety or merit moral approval **2 :** something to which one has a just claim: as **a :** the power or privilege to which one is justly entitled **b (1) :** the interest that one has in a piece of property — often used in pl. <mineral ~*s*> **(2)** *pl* **:** the property interest possessed under law or custom and agreement in an intangible thing esp. of a literary and artistic nature <film ~*s* of the novel> **3 :** something that one may properly claim as due **4 :** the cause of truth or justice **5 a :** the right hand; *also* **:** a blow struck with this hand <gave him a hard ~ on the jaw> **b :** the location or direction of the right side <woods on his ~> **c :** the part on the right side **6 a :** the true account or correct interpretation **b :** the quality or state of being factually correct **7** *often cap* **a :** the part of a legislative chamber located to the right of the presiding officer **b :** the members of a continental European legislative body occupying the right as a result of holding more conservative political views than other members **8 a (1)** *cap* **:** individuals sometimes professing opposition to change in the established order and favoring traditional attitudes and practices and sometimes advocating the forced establishment of an authoritarian political order **(2) :** a group or party in another organization that favors conservative, traditional, or sometimes authoritarian attitudes and policies **b** *often cap* **:** a conservative position **9 a :** a privilege given stockholders to subscribe pro rata to a new issue of securities generally below market price **b :** the negotiable certificate evidencing such privilege — usu. used in pl. — **by rights :** with reason or justice : PROPERLY — **in one's own right :** by virtue of one's own qualifications or properties — **to rights :** into proper order

3right *adv* **1 :** according to right <live ~> **2 :** in the exact location or position : PRECISELY <~ at his fingertips> <~ in the middle of the floor> **3 :** in a suitable, proper, or desired manner <knew he wasn't doing it ~> **4 :** in a direct line or course : DIRECTLY, STRAIGHT <go ~ home> **5 :** according to fact or truth : TRULY <guessed ~> **6 a :** all the way <windows ~ to the floor> **b :** in a complete manner <felt ~ at home> **7 :** without delay : IMMEDIATELY <~ after lunch> **8 :** to a great degree : VERY <a ~ pleasant day> **9 :** on or to the right <looked left and ~> — **right now :** at the present : just now

4right *vt* **1 a :** to do justice to : redress the injuries of <so just is God to ~ the innocent —Shak.> **b :** JUSTIFY, VINDICATE <felt the need to ~ himself in court> **2 :** AVENGE <vows to ~ the injustice done to his family> **3 a :** to adjust or restore to the proper state or condition <helps to ~ the imbalance of his previous work> **b :** to bring or restore to an upright position <~ a capsized boat> ~ *vi* **:** to become upright — **right·er** *n*

right angle *n* **:** the angle bounded by two lines perpendicular to each other : an angle of 90° or $^1/_2\pi$ radians — **right–an·gled** \'rīt-'aŋ-gəld\ *or* **right–an·gle** \-gəl\ *adj*

right ascension *n* **:** the arc of the celestial equator between the vernal equinox and the point where the hour circle through the given body intersects the equator reckoned eastward commonly in terms of the corresponding interval of sidereal time in hours, minutes, and seconds

right away *adv* **:** without delay or hesitation : IMMEDIATELY

right circular cone *n* **:** CONE 2a

right circular cylinder *n* **:** a cylinder with circular bases such that any line lying wholly in the surface and joining the bases is perpendicular to them

righ·teous \'rī-chəs\ *adj* [alter. of earlier *rightuous,* alter. of ME *rightwise, rightwos,* fr. OE *rihtwīs,* fr. *riht,* n., right + *wīs* wise] **1 :** acting in accord with divine or moral law : free from guilt or sin **2 a :** morally right or justifiable <a ~ decision> **b :** arising from an outraged sense of justice or morality <~ indignation> ***syn*** see MORAL ***ant*** iniquitous — **righ·teous·ly** *adv* — **righ·teous·ness** *n*

right field *n* **1 :** the part of the baseball outfield to the right looking out from the plate **2 :** the position of the player defending right field — **right fielder** *n*

right·ful \'rīt-fəl\ *adj* **1 :** JUST, EQUITABLE **2 a :** having a just or legally established claim : LEGITIMATE <the ~ owner> **b :** held by right or just claim : LEGAL <~ authority> **3 :** FITTING, PROPER <thought her ~ place was in the home> — **right·ful·ly** \-fə-lē\ *adv* — **right·ful·ness** *n*

right–hand \'rīt-ˌhand\ *adj* **1 :** situated on the right **2 :** RIGHT-HANDED **3 :** chiefly relied on <~ man>

right hand *n* **1 a :** the hand on a person's right side **b :** a reliable or indispensable person **2 a :** the right side **b :** a place of honor

right–hand·ed \-'han-dəd\ *adj* **1 :** using the right hand habitually or more easily than the left; *also* **:** swinging from right to left <a ~ batter> **2 :** relating to, designed for, or done with the right hand **3 a :** having the same direction or course as the movement of the hands of a watch viewed from in front : CLOCKWISE — used of a twist, rotary motion, or spiral curve as viewed from a given direction with respect to the axis of rotation **b** *of a rope* **:** formed of strands twisted clockwise so that if held vertically the strands spiral upward to the right **4** *of a door* **:** opening to the right away from one — **right–handed** *adv* — **right–hand·ed·ly** *adv* — **right–hand·ed·ness** *n*

right–hand·er \-'han-dər\ *n* **1 :** a blow struck with the right hand **2 :** a right-handed person

right·ism \'rīt-ˌiz-əm\ *n, often cap* **1 :** the principles and views of the Right **2 :** advocacy of or adherence to the doctrines of the Right — **right·ist** \'rīt-əst\ *n or adj, often cap*

right·ly \'rīt-lē\ *adv* **1 :** in accordance with right conduct : FAIRLY, JUSTLY **2 :** in the right or proper manner : PROPERLY, FITLY **3 :** according to truth or fact : CORRECTLY, EXACTLY

right–mind·ed \-'mīn-dəd\ *adj* **:** having a right or honest mind : purposing well <a ~ citizen> — **right–mind·ed·ness** *n*

right off *adv* **:** right away **:** at once — **right off the bat :** right off

right of search : the right to stop a merchant vessel on the high seas and make a reasonable search to determine its liability to capture by violation of international or revenue law

right–of–way \ˌrīt-ə(v)-ˈwā\ *n, pl* **rights–of–way** *also* **right–of–ways 1 :** a legal right of passage over another person's ground **2 a :** the area over which a right-of-way exists **b :** the strip of land over which is built a public road **c :** the land occupied by a railroad esp. for its main line **d :** the land used by a public utility (as for a transmission line) **3 a :** a precedence in passing accorded to one vehicle over another by custom, decision, or statute **b :** the right of traffic to take precedence **c :** the right to take precedence over others <gave the bill the ~ in the Senate>

right on *interj* — used to express agreement or to give encouragement

Right Reverend — used as a title for high ecclesiastical officials

right shoulder arms *n* **:** a position in the manual of arms in which the butt of the rifle is held in the right hand with the barrel resting on the right shoulder; *also* **:** a command to assume this position

right–to–work law *n* **:** any of various state laws banning the closed shop and the union shop

right triangle *n* **:** a triangle having a right angle

right·ward \ˈrīt-wərd\ *adj* **:** being toward or on the right

right whale *n* **:** a large whalebone whale (family Balaenidae) having no dorsal fin, very long baleen, a large head, an unwrinkled throat, and small eyes near the angles of the mouth

right wing *n, often attrib* **1 :** the rightist division of a group or party **2 :** RIGHT 8 — **right–wing·er** \-ˈwiŋ-ər\ *n*

rig·id \ˈrij-əd\ *adj* [MF or L; MF *rigide,* fr. L *rigidus,* fr. *rigēre* to be stiff] **1 a :** deficient in or devoid of flexibility <~ price controls> <a ~ bar of metal> **b :** appearing stiff and unyielding <his face ~ with pain> **2 a :** inflexibly set in opinion **b :** strictly observed <adheres to a ~ schedule> **3 :** firmly inflexible rather than lax or indulgent <a ~ disciplinarian> **4 :** precise and accurate in procedure **5 a :** having the gas containers enclosed within compartments of a fixed fabric-covered framework <a ~ airship> **b :** having the outer shape maintained by a fixed framework — **rig·id·ly** *adv* — **rig·id·ness** *n*
syn* 1** see STIFF ***ant elastic
2 RIGID, RIGOROUS, STRICT, STRINGENT *shared meaning element* **:** extremely severe or stern ***ant*** lax

ri·gid·i·fy \rə-ˈjid-ə-ˌfī\ *vb* **-fied; -fy·ing** *vt* **:** to make rigid ~ *vi* **:** to become rigid — **ri·gid·i·fi·ca·tion** \-ˌjid-ə-fə-ˈkā-shən\ *n*

ri·gid·i·ty \rə-ˈjid-ət-ē\ *n, pl* **-ties 1 :** the quality or state of being rigid **2 :** one that is rigid (as in form or conduct)

rig·ma·role \ˈrig-(ə-)mə-ˌrōl\ *n* [alter. of obs. *ragman roll* (long list, catalog)] **1 :** confused or meaningless talk **2 :** a complex and ritualistic procedure

rig·or \ˈrig-ər\ *n* [ME *rigour,* fr. MF *rigueur,* fr. L *rigor,* lit., stiffness, fr. *rigēre* to be stiff] **1 a (1) :** harsh inflexibility in opinion, temper, or judgment **:** SEVERITY **(2) :** the quality of being unyielding or inflexible **:** STRICTNESS **(3) :** severity of life **:** AUSTERITY **b :** an act or instance of strictness, severity, or cruelty **2 :** a tremor caused by a chill **3 :** a condition that makes life difficult, challenging, or uncomfortable; *esp* **:** extremity of cold **4 :** strict precision **:** EXACTNESS <logical ~> **5 a** *obs* **:** RIGIDITY, STIFFNESS **b :** rigidness or torpor of organs or tissue that prevents response to stimuli ***syn*** see DIFFICULTY

rig·or·ism \ˈrig-ə-ˌriz-əm\ *n* **:** rigidity in principle or practice — **rig·or·ist** \-ə-rəst\ *n or adj* — **rig·or·is·tic** \ˌrig-ə-ˈris-tik\ *adj*

rig·or mor·tis \ˌrig-ər-ˈmȯrt-əs *also chiefly Brit* ˌrī-ˌgȯ(ə)r-\ *n* [NL, stiffness of death] **:** temporary rigidity of muscles occurring after death

rig·or·ous \ˈrig-(ə-)rəs\ *adj* **1 :** manifesting, exercising, or favoring rigor **:** very strict **2 a :** marked by extremes of temperature or climate **b :** HARSH, SEVERE **3 :** scrupulously accurate **:** PRECISE ***syn*** see RIGID — **rig·or·ous·ly** *adv* — **rig·or·ous·ness** *n*

rig·our *chiefly Brit var of* RIGOR

Riks·mål *or* **Riks·maal** \ˈrik-ˌsmȯl, ˈrēk-\ *n* [Norw, fr. *rik* kingdom + *mål* speech, fr. ON *māl;* akin to OE *rīce* kingdom — more at RICH, MAIL] **:** BOKMÅL

rile \ˈrī(ə)l\ *vt* **riled; ril·ing** [by alter.] **1 :** ROIL 1 **2 :** to make agitated and angry **:** UPSET ***syn*** see IRRITATE

ril·ey \ˈrī-lē\ *adj* **1 :** TURBID **2 :** ANGRY

[1]rill \ˈril\ *n* [D *ril* or LG *rille;* akin to OE *rīth* rivulet] **:** a very small brook

[2]rill *vi* **:** to flow like a rill

[3]rill \ˈril\ *or* **rille** \ˈril, ˈril-ə\ *n* [G *rille,* lit., channel made by a small stream, fr. LG, rill] **:** any of several long narrow valleys on the moon's surface

rill·et \ˈril-ət\ *n* **:** a little rill

[1]rim \ˈrim\ *n* [ME, fr. OE *rima;* akin to ON *rimi* strip of land, Gk *ērema* gently, Lith *remti* to support] **1 a :** the outer often curved or circular edge or border of something **b :** BRINK **2 a :** the outer part of a wheel joined to the hub usu. by spokes **b :** a removable outer metal band on an automobile wheel to which the tire is attached **3 :** FRAME 3d(1) ***syn*** see BORDER — **rim·less** \-ləs\ *adj*

[2]rim *vb* **rimmed; rim·ming** *vt* **1 :** to serve as a rim for **:** BORDER <cliffs *rimming* the camp> **2 :** to run around the rim of <putts that ~ the cup> ~ *vi* **:** to form or show a rim

[1]rime \ˈrīm\ *n* [ME *rim,* fr. OE *hrīm;* akin to ON *hrīm* frost, Latvian *kreims* cream] **1 :** FROST 1c **2 :** an accumulation of granular ice tufts on the windward sides of exposed objects that is formed from supercooled fog or cloud and built out directly against the wind **3 :** CRUST, INCRUSTATION <a ~ of snow>

[2]rime *vt* **rimed; rim·ing :** to cover with or as if with rime

[3]rime, rimer, rimester *var of* RHYME, RHYMER, RHYMESTER

rim·land \ˈrim-ˌland\ *n* **:** a region on the periphery of the heartland

rimmed \ˈrimd\ *adj* **:** having a rim — usu. used in combination <dark-*rimmed* glasses> <red-*rimmed* eyes>

ri·mose \ˈrī-ˌmōs\ *or* **ri·mous** \-məs\ *adj* [L *rimosus,* fr. *rima* slit, crack — more at ROW] **:** having numerous clefts, cracks, or fissures <~ tree bark>

rim·rock \ˈrim-ˌräk\ *n* **1 :** a top stratum or overlying strata of resistant rock of a plateau that outcrops to form a vertical face **2 :** the edge or face of a rimrock outcrop

rimy \ˈrī-mē\ *adj* **rim·i·er; -est :** covered with rime **:** FROSTY

rind \ˈrīnd, ˈrīn\ *n* [ME, fr. OE; akin to OHG *rinda* bark, OE *rendan* to rend] **:** the bark of a tree; *also* **:** a usu. hard or tough outer layer **:** PEEL, CRUST <grated lemon ~> — **rind·ed** \-əd\ *adj*

rin·der·pest \ˈrin-dər-ˌpest\ *n* [G, fr. *rinder,* pl., cattle + *pest* pestilence] **:** an acute infectious febrile disease esp. of cattle caused by a filterable virus and marked by diphtheritic inflammation of mucous membranes

[1]ring \ˈriŋ\ *n* [ME, fr. OE *hring;* akin to OHG *hring* ring, L *curvus* curved — more at CROWN] **1 :** a circular band for holding, connecting, hanging, pulling, packing, or sealing <a key ~> <a towel ~> **2 :** a circlet usu. of precious metal worn on the finger **3 a :** a circular line, figure, or object <smoke ~> **b :** an encircling arrangement <a ~ of suburbs> **c :** a circular or spiral course — often used in pl. in the phrase *run rings around* **4 a (1) :** an often circular space esp. for exhibitions or competitions; *esp* **:** such a space at a circus **(2) :** a structure containing such a ring **b :** a square enclosure in which boxers or wrestlers contest **5 :** one of three concentric bands usu. believed to be composed of meteoric fragments revolving around the planet Saturn **6 :** ANNUAL RING **7 :** an exclusive combination of persons for a selfish and often corrupt purpose (as to control the market) <a drug ~> **8 :** the field of a political contest **:** RACE **9 :** food in the shape of a circle **10 :** an arrangement of atoms represented in formulas or models in a cyclic manner as a closed chain — called also *cycle* **11 :** a set of elements subject to two operations which is a commutative group under the first operation, in which the second operation is associative, in which each pair of elements uniquely determines another element of the set when subjected to the second operation, and in which the second operation is distributive relative to the first **12** *pl* **a :** a pair of usu. rubber-covered metal rings suspended from a ceiling or crossbar to a height of approximately eight feet above the floor and used for hanging, swinging, and balancing feats in gymnastics **b :** an event in gymnastics competition in which the rings are used **13 :** [2]BOXING <ended his ~ career> — **ring·like** \ˈriŋ-ˌlīk\ *adj*

[2]ring *vb* **ringed; ring·ing** \ˈriŋ-iŋ\ *vt* **1 :** to place or form a ring around **:** ENCIRCLE <police ~*ed* the building> **2 :** to provide with a ring **3 :** GIRDLE 3 **4 :** to throw a ringer over (the peg) in a game (as horseshoes or quoits) ~ *vi* **1 a :** to move in a ring **b :** to rise in the air spirally **2 :** to form or take the shape of a ring

[3]ring *vb* **rang** \ˈraŋ\; **rung** \ˈrəŋ\; **ring·ing** \ˈriŋ-iŋ\ [ME *ringen,* fr. OE *hringan;* akin to MD *ringen* to ring, Lith *krankti* to croak] *vi* **1 :** to sound resonantly or sonorously <the doorbell *rang*> <cheers *rang* out> **2 a :** to be filled with a reverberating sound **:** RESOUND <the halls *rang* with laughter> **b :** to have the sensation of being filled with a humming sound <his ears *rang*> **3 :** to cause something to ring <~ for the waitress> **4 a :** to be filled with talk or report <the whole land *rang* with his fame> **b :** to have great renown **c :** to sound repetitiously <their praise *rang* in his ears> **5 :** to have a sound or character expressive of some quality <a story that ~*s* true> **6** *chiefly Brit* **:** to make a telephone call — usu. used with *up* ~ *vt* **1 :** to cause to sound esp. by striking **2 :** to make (a sound) by or as if by ringing a bell **3 :** to announce by or as if by ringing **4 :** to repeat often, loudly, or earnestly **5 a :** to summon esp. by bell **b** *chiefly Brit* **:** TELEPHONE — usu. used with *up* — **ring a bell :** to arouse a response <that name *rings a bell*> — **ring down the curtain :** to conclude a performance or an action — **ring the changes** *or* **ring changes :** to run through the range of possible variations — **ring up the curtain :** to begin a performance or an action

[4]ring *n* **1 :** a set of bells **2 :** a clear resonant sound made by or resembling that made by vibrating metal **3 :** resonant tone **:** SONORITY **4 :** a loud sound continued, repeated, or reverberated **5 :** a sound or character expressive of some particular quality <the sermon had a familiar ~> **6 a :** the act or an instance of ringing **b :** a telephone call <give me a ~ in the morning>

ring–a–lie·vo \ˌriŋ-ə-ˈlē-(ˌ)vō\ *or* **ring–a–le·vio** \-vē-ˌō\ *n* [alter. of earlier *ring relievo,* fr. [1]*ring* + *relieve*] **:** a game in which players on one team are given time to hide and are then sought out by members of the other team who try to capture them, keep them in a place of confinement, and keep them from being released by their teammates

ring–around–a–rosy \ˌriŋ-ə-ˌraun-də-ˈrō-zē\ *or* **ring–around–the–rosy** \-ˌraun(d)-thə-\ *n* **:** a children's singing game in which players dance around in a circle and at a given signal squat — called also *ring-a-rosy*

ring·bark \ˈriŋ-ˌbärk\ *vt* **:** GIRDLE 3

ring binder *n* **:** a loose-leaf binder in which split metal rings attached to a metal back hold the perforated sheets of paper

ring·bolt \ˈriŋ-ˌbōlt\ *n* **:** an eyebolt with a ring through its eye

ring·bone \-ˌbōn\ *n* **:** an exostosis on the pastern bones of the horse usu. producing lameness — **ring·boned** \-ˌbōnd\ *adj*

ring dance *n* **:** ROUND DANCE 1

ring·dove \ˈriŋ-ˌdəv\ *n* **1 :** a common European pigeon (*Columba palumbus*) with a whitish patch on each side of the neck and wings edged with white **2 :** a small dove (*Streptopelia risoria*) of southeastern Europe and Asia

ringed \ˈriŋd\ *adj* **1 :** encircled or marked with or as if with rings **2 :** composed or formed of rings

rin·gent \ˈrin-jənt\ *adj* [L *ringent-, ringens,* prp. of *ringi* to open the mouth — more at RICTUS] **:** having lips separated like an open mouth <a ~ corolla>

[1]ring·er \ˈriŋ-ər\ *n* **1 :** one that sounds esp. by ringing **2 a (1) :** one that enters a competition under false representations **(2) :** IMPOSTER, FAKE **b :** one that strongly resembles another — often used with *dead* <he's a dead ~ for the senator>

2**ringer** *n* : one that encircles or puts a ring around (as a quoit or horseshoe that lodges so as to surround the peg)
Ring·er's solution \'riŋ-ərz-\ *or* **Ring·er solution** \'riŋ-ər-\ *n* [Sidney *Ringer* †1910 E physician] : a balanced aqueous solution that contains chloride, sodium, potassium, calcium, bicarbonate, and phosphate ions and that is used in physiological experiments to provide a medium essentially isotonic to many animal tissues
ring finger *n* : the third finger of the left hand counting the index finger as the first
ring·ing \'riŋ-iŋ\ *adj* **1** : clear and full in tone : RESOUNDING <a ~ baritone> **2** : vigorously unequivocal : DECISIVE <a ~ condemnation of immorality> — **ring·ing·ly** \-iŋ-lē\ *adv*
ring·lead·er \'riŋ-ˌlēd-ər\ *n* : a leader of a group of individuals engaged esp. in improper or unlawful activities
ring·let \'riŋ-lət\ *n* **1** *archaic* : a small ring or circle **2** : CURL; *esp* : a long curl of hair
ring·mas·ter \'riŋ-ˌmas-tər\ *n* : one in charge of performances in a ring (as of a circus)
ring·neck \-ˌnek\ *n* : a ring-necked bird or animal
ring–necked \'riŋ-'nekt\ *or* **ring–neck** \ˌriŋ-ˌnek\ *adj* : having a ring of color about the neck
ring–necked duck *n* : an American scaup duck (*Aythya collaris*) the male of which has a narrow chestnut ring encircling the neck, a black back, and light gray sides with a conspicuous white mark in front of the wings
ring–necked pheasant *n* : any of various pheasants with white neck rings that have been widely introduced in temperate regions as game birds and that are varieties of or hybrids between varieties of the common Old World pheasant (*Phasianus colchicus*)
Ring of the Ni·be·lung \-'nē-bə-ˌlüŋ\ : a ring made by the dwarf Alberich whose story is the theme of a tetralogy of music dramas by Richard Wagner
ring–po·rous \'riŋ-ˌpōr-əs, -ˌpȯr-\ *adj* : having vessels more numerous and usu. larger in cross section in the springwood with a resulting more or less distinct line between the springwood and the wood of the previous season — compare DIFFUSE-POROUS
1**ring·side** \'riŋ-ˌsīd\ *n* **1** : the area just outside a ring esp. in which a contest occurs **2** : a place from which one may have a close view
2**ringside** *adj* : being at the ringside <a ~ seat>
ring spot *n* **1** : a lesion of plant tissue consisting of yellowish, purplish, or necrotic, often concentric rings **2** : a plant disease of which ring spots are the characteristic lesion
ring·straked \'riŋ-ˌstrākt\ *adj, archaic* : marked with circular stripes
ring·tail \-ˌtāl\ *n* **1** : CACOMISTLE **2** : RACCOON **3** : CAPUCHIN 3
ring–tailed \-'tā(ə)ld\ *adj* **1** : having a tail marked with rings of differing colors **2** : having a tail carried in the form of a circle <a ~ dog>
ring·taw \-ˌtȯ\ *n* : a game of marbles in which marbles are placed in a circle on the ground and shot at from the edge of the circle with the object being to knock them out of the circle
ring·toss \-ˌtȯs, -ˌtäs\ *n* : a game in which the object is to toss a ring so that it will fall over an upright stick
ring up *vt* [fr. the bell that rings when a sum is recorded by a cash register] **1** : to total and record esp. by means of a cash register **2** : RECORD <*rang up* many social triumphs>
ring·worm \'riŋ-ˌwərm\ *n* : any of several contagious diseases of the skin, hair, or nails of man and domestic animals caused by fungi and characterized by ring-shaped discolored patches on the skin that are covered with vesicles and scales
rink \'riŋk\ *n* [ME (Sc) *rinc* area in which a contest takes place, fr. MF *renc* place, row — more at RANK] **1 a** : a smooth extent of ice marked off for curling or ice hockey **b** : a surface of ice for ice-skating; *also* : a building containing such a rink **c** : an enclosure for roller-skating **2** : an alley for lawn bowling **3** : a team in bowls or curling
rink·tum dit·ty \ˌriŋ(k)-təm-'dit-ē\ *n* [origin unknown] : a mixture of seasoned tomato sauce, cheese, and egg served on toast
1**rinse** \'rin(t)s, *esp dial* 'rench\ *vt* **rinsed; rins·ing** [ME *rincen*, fr. MF *rincer*, fr. (assumed) VL *recentiare*, fr. L *recent-, recens* fresh, recent] **1** : to cleanse by flushing with liquid (as water) — often used with *out* <~ out the mouth> **2 a** : to cleanse (as from soap used in washing) by clear water **b** : to treat (hair) with a rinse **3** : to remove (dirt or impurities) by washing lightly or in water only — **rins·er** *n*
2**rinse** *n* **1** : the act or process of rinsing **2 a** : liquid used for rinsing **b** : a solution that temporarily tints hair
rins·ing *n* **1** : water that has been used for rinsing — usu. used in pl. **2** : DREGS, RESIDUE — usu. used in pl.
1**ri·ot** \'rī-ət\ *n, often attrib* [ME, fr. OF, dispute] **1** *archaic* **a** : profligate behavior : DEBAUCHERY **b** : unrestrained revelry **c** : noise, uproar, or disturbance made by revelers **2 a** : public violence, tumult, or disorder **b** : a violent public disorder; *specif* : a tumultuous disturbance of the public peace by three or more persons assembled together and acting with a common intent **3** : a random or disorderly profusion <the woods were a ~ of color> **4** : one that is wildly amusing <the new comedy is a ~>
2**riot** *vi* **1** : to indulge in revelry or wantonness **2** : to create or engage in a riot ~ *vt* : to waste or spend recklessly <~*ed* away his whole inheritance> — **ri·ot·er** *n*
riot act *n* [the *Riot Act*, English law of 1715 providing for the dispersal of riots upon command of legal authority] : a vigorous reprimand or warning — used in the phrase *read the riot act*
riot gun *n* : a small arm used to disperse rioters rather than to inflict serious injury or death; *esp* : a short-barreled shotgun
ri·ot·ous \'rī-ət-əs\ *adj* **1** : ABUNDANT, EXUBERANT <the garden was ~ with flowers> **2 a** : of the nature of a riot : TURBULENT **b** : participating in riot — **ri·ot·ous·ly** *adv* — **ri·ot·ous·ness** *n*
1**rip** \'rip\ *vb* **ripped; rip·ping** [prob. fr. Flem *rippen* to strip off roughly] *vt* **1 a** : to tear or split apart or open **b** : to saw or split (wood) with the grain **2** : to slash or slit with or as if with a sharp blade **3** : to hit sharply <*ripped* a double to left field> **4** : to utter violently : spit out <*ripped* out an oath> ~ *vi* **1** : to become ripped : REND **2** : to rush headlong <*ripped* past second base> *syn* see TEAR — **rip into** : to tear into : ATTACK
2**rip** *n* : a rent made by ripping : TEAR
3**rip** *n* [perh. fr. 2*rip*] **1** : a body of water made rough by the meeting of opposing tides, currents, or winds **2** : a current of water roughened by passing over an irregular bottom
4**rip** *n* [perh. by shortening & alter. fr. *reprobate*] **1** : a worn-out worthless horse **2** : a dissolute person : LIBERTINE
RIP *abbr* **1** [L *requiescat in pace*] may he rest in peace **2** [L *requiescant in pace*] may they rest in peace
ri·par·i·an \rə-'per-ē-ən, rī-\ *adj* [L *riparius* — more at RIVER] : relating to or living or located on the bank of a natural watercourse (as a river) or sometimes of a lake or a tidewater
riparian right *n* : a right (as access to or use of the shore, bed, and water) of one owning riparian land
rip cord *n* **1** : a cord by which the gasbag of a balloon may be ripped open for a limited distance to release the gas quickly and so cause immediate descent **2** : a cord or wire pulled in making a descent to release the pilot parachute which lifts the main parachute out of its container
rip current *n* : a strong usu. narrow surface current flowing outward from a shore that results from the return flow of waves and wind-driven water
ripe \'rīp\ *adj* **rip·er; rip·est** [ME, fr. OE *rīpe*; akin to OE *rīpan* to reap — more at REAP] **1** : fully grown and developed : MATURE **2** : having mature knowledge, understanding, or judgment **3** : of advanced years : LATE <lived to a ~ old age> **4 a** : fully arrived : SUITABLE <the time seemed ~ for the experiment> **b** : fully prepared : READY <the colonies were ~ for revolution> **5** : brought by aging to full flavor or the best state : MELLOW <~ cheese> **6** : ruddy, plump, or full like ripened fruit *syn* see MATURE *ant* unripe, green — **ripe·ly** *adv* — **ripe·ness** *n*
rip·en \'rī-pən, 'rip-ᵊm\ *vb* **rip·ened; rip·en·ing** \'rīp-(ə-)niŋ\ *vi* : to grow or become ripe ~ *vt* **1** : to make ripe **2 a** : to bring to completeness or perfection **b** : to age or cure (cheese) to develop characteristic flavor, odor, body, texture, and color **c** : to improve flavor and tenderness of (beef or game) through a period of refrigeration — **rip·en·er** \'rīp-(ə-)nər\ *n*
ri·pie·no \ri-'pyā-(ˌ)nō, -'pyen-(ˌ)ō\ *n, pl* **-ni** \-(ˌ)nē, -(ˌ)ē\ *or* **-nos** [It, lit., filled up] : TUTTI
rip–off \'rip-ˌȯf\ *n* : an act or instance of stealing : THEFT; *also* : a financial exploitation
rip off \(')rip-'ȯf\ *vb* : ROB; *also* : STEAL
ri·poste \ri-'pōst\ *n* [F, modif. of It *risposta*, lit., answer, fr. *rispondere* to respond, fr. L *respondēre*] **1** : a fencer's quick return thrust following a parry **2** : a retaliatory verbal sally : RETORT **3** : a retaliatory maneuver or measure — **riposte** *vi*
rip·per \'rip-ər\ *n* **1** : one that rips: as **a** : RIPSAW **b** : a machine used to break up solid material (as rock or ore) **2** : an excellent example or instance of its kind
rip·ping \'rip-iŋ\ *adj* [prob. fr. prp. of 1*rip*] : EXCELLENT, DELIGHTFUL <wrote me some ~ letters> <had a ~ time>
1**rip·ple** \'rip-əl\ *vb* **rip·pled; rip·pling** \-(ə-)liŋ\ [perh. freq. of 1*rip*] *vi* **1 a** : to become lightly ruffled or covered with small waves **b** : to flow in small waves **c** : to fall in soft undulating folds <her dress *rippled* to the floor> **2** : to flow with a light rise and fall of sound or inflection <laughter *rippled* over the audience> **3** : to move with an undulating motion or so as to cause ripples <the canoe *rippled* through the water> **4** : to run irregularly through a group or a population <the news gradually *rippled* outwards> ~ *vt* **1** : to stir up small waves on **2** : to impart a wavy motion or appearance to <*rippling* his arm muscles> **3** : to utter or play with a slight rise and fall of sound — **rip·pler** \-(ə-)lər\ *n*
2**ripple** *n* **1 a** : a shallow stretch of rough water in a stream **b** (1) : the ruffling of the surface of water (2) : a small wave **2 a** : RIPPLE MARK **b** : a sound like that of rippling water <a ~ of laughter>
ripple mark *n* **1** : one of a series of small ridges produced esp. on sand by the action of wind, a current of water, or waves **2** : a striation across the grain of wood esp. on the tangential surface — **rip·ple–marked** \'rip-əl-ˌmärkt\ *adj*
1**rip·rap** \'rip-ˌrap\ *n* [obs. *riprap* (sound of rapping)] **1** : a foundation or sustaining wall of stones thrown together without order (as in deep water or on an embankment slope to prevent erosion) **2** : stone used for riprap
2**riprap** *vt* **1** : to form a riprap in or upon **2** : to strengthen or support with a riprap
rip–roar·ing \'rip-'rōr-iŋ, -'rȯr-\ *adj* : noisily excited or exciting
rip·saw \'rip-ˌsȯ\ *n* : a coarse-toothed saw having teeth slightly set that is used to cut wood in the direction of the grain — compare CROSSCUT SAW
rip·snort·er \'rip-'snȯrt-ər\ *n* : something extraordinary : HUMDINGER <the finale was a ~> — **rip·snort·ing** \-iŋ\ *adj*
rip·tide \'rip-ˌtīd\ *n* : RIP CURRENT
Rip·u·ar·i·an \ˌrip-yə-'wer-ē-ən\ *adj* [ML *Ripuarius*] : of, relating to, or constituting a group of Franks settling in the 4th century on the Rhine near Cologne
Rip van Win·kle \ˌrip-(ˌ)van-'wiŋ-kəl, -vən-\ *n* : a ne'er-do-well in a story in Washington Irving's *Sketch Book* who sleeps for 20 years
1**rise** \'rīz\ *vi* **rose** \'rōz\; **ris·en** \'riz-ᵊn\; **ris·ing** \'rī-ziŋ\ [ME *risen*, fr. OE *rīsan*; akin to OHG *rīsan* to rise, L *oriri* to rise, *rivus* stream, Gk *ornynai* to rouse] **1 a** : to assume an upright position esp. from lying, kneeling, or sitting **b** : to get up from sleep or from one's bed **2** : to return from death **3** : to take up arms <~ in rebellion> **4** : to respond warmly : APPLAUD — usu. used with *to* <the audience *rose* to his verve and wit> **5** : to end a session

: ADJOURN **6** : to appear above the horizon <the sun ~*s* at six> **7 a** : to move upward : ASCEND **b** : to increase in height, size, or volume <the river *rose* after the heavy rains> **8** : to extend above other objects <mountain peaks *rose* between the valleys> **9 a** : to become heartened or elated <his spirits *rose*> **b** : to increase in fervor or intensity <his anger *rose* as he thought about the insult> **10 a** : to attain a higher level or rank <officers who *rose* from the ranks> **b** : to increase in quantity or number **11 a** : to take place : HAPPEN **b** : to come into being : ORIGINATE **12** : to follow as a consequence : RESULT **13** : to exert oneself to meet a challenge <~ to the occasion> ***syn*** see SPRING

[2]**rise** \'rīz *also* 'rīs\ *n* **1** : an act of rising or a state of being risen: as **a** : a movement upward : ASCENT **b** : emergence (as of the sun) above the horizon **c** : the upward movement of a fish to seize food or bait **2** : BEGINNING, ORIGIN <the river had its ~ in the mountain> **3** : the distance or elevation of one point above another **4 a** : an increase esp. in amount, number, or volume **b** : an increase in price, value, rate, or sum <a ~ in the cost of living> **5 a** : an upward slope <a ~ in the road> **b** : a spot higher than surrounding ground : HILLTOP **6** : an angry reaction <got a ~ out of him>

ris·er \'rī-zər\ *n* **1** : one that rises (as from sleep) **2** : the upright member between two stair treads **3** : a movable stage platform on which performers are placed for greater visibility **4** : one of the straps that connects a parachutist's harness with the shroud lines

ris·i·bil·i·ty \ˌriz-ə-'bil-ət-ē\ *n, pl* **-ties 1** : the ability or inclination to laugh — often used in pl. <our *risibilities* support us as we skim over the surface of a deep issue —J. A. Pike> **2** : LAUGHTER

ris·i·ble \'riz-ə-bəl\ *adj* [LL *risibilis*, fr. L *risus*, pp. of *ridēre* to laugh — more at RIDICULOUS] **1 a** : capable of laughing **b** : disposed to laugh **2** : arousing or provoking laughter : FUNNY **3** : associated with, relating to, or used in laughter <~ muscles>

ris·i·bles \-bəlz\ *n pl* : sense of the ridiculous : sense of humor

[1]**ris·ing** \'rī-ziŋ\ *n* : INSURRECTION, UPRISING

[2]**rising** *adv* : approaching a stated age : NEARLY <a red cow ~ four years old —*Lancaster (Pa.) Jour.*>

rising diphthong *n* : a diphthong in which the second element is more prominent that the first (as \wi\ in \'kwit\ *quit*)

rising rhythm *n* : rhythm with stress occurring regularly on the last syllable of each foot — compare FALLING RHYTHM

[1]**risk** \'risk\ *n* [F *risque*, fr. It *risco*] **1** : possibility of loss or injury : PERIL **2** : a dangerous element or factor **3 a** : the chance of loss or the perils to the subject matter of an insurance contract; *also* : the degree of probability of such loss **b** : a person or thing that is a specified hazard to an insurer <a poor ~ for insurance> **c** : an insurance hazard from a specified cause or source <war ~>

[2]**risk** *vt* **1** : to expose to hazard or danger <~*ed* his life> **2** : to incur the risk or danger of <~*ed* breaking his neck> — **risk·er** *n*

risk capital *n* : VENTURE CAPITAL

risky \'ris-kē\ *adj* **risk·i·er**; **-est** : attended with risk or danger : HAZARDOUS ***syn*** see DANGEROUS — **risk·i·ness** *n*

ri·sor·gi·men·to \(ˌ)rē-ˌzȯr-ji-'men-(ˌ)tō, -ˌsȯr-\ *n, pl* **-tos** [It, lit., rising again] : a time of renewal or renaissance : REVIVAL; *specif* : the 19th century movement for Italian political unity

ri·sot·to \ri-'sȯt-(ˌ)ō, -'zȯt-\ *n, pl* **-tos** [It] : rice cooked in meat stock and seasoned (as with Parmesan cheese or saffron)

ris·qué \ri-'skā\ *adj* [F, fr. pp. of *risquer* to risk, fr. *risque*] : verging on impropriety or indecency : OFF-COLOR

rit *abbr* ritardando

ri·tard \ri-'tärd, 'rē-ˌ\ *n* : RITARDANDO

[1]**ri·tar·dan·do** \ri-ˌtär-'dän-(ˌ)dō, ˌrē-\ *adv or adj* [It, fr. L *retardandum*, gerund of *retardare* to retard] : with a gradual slackening in tempo — used as a direction in music

[2]**ritardando** *n, pl* **-dos** : a ritardando passage

rite \'rīt\ *n* [ME, fr. L *ritus*; akin to OE *rīm* number, Gk *arithmos* number — more at ARITHMETIC] **1 a** : a prescribed form or manner governing the words or actions for a ceremony **b** : the liturgy of a church or group of churches **2** : a ceremonial act or action <initiation ~*s*> **3** : a division of the Christian church using a distinctive liturgy

rite de pas·sage \ˌrēt-də-pa-'säzh, -pä-\ *n, pl* **rites de passage** \ˌrēt(s)-də-\ [F] : RITE OF PASSAGE

rite of passage [trans. of F *rite de passage*] : a ritual associated with a crisis or a change of status (as marriage, illness, or death) for an individual

ri·tor·nel·lo \ˌrit-ər-'nel-(ˌ)ō, ˌri-ˌtȯr-\ *n, pl* **-nel·li** \-'nel-(ˌ)ē\ *or* **-nellos** [It] **1 a** : a short recurrent instrumental passage in a vocal composition **b** : an instrumental interlude in early opera **2** : a tutti passage in a concerto or rondo refrain

[1]**rit·u·al** \'rich-(ə-)wəl, 'rich-əl\ *adj* **1** : of or relating to rites or a ritual : CEREMONIAL <a ~ dance> **2** : according to religious law or social custom <~ purity> — **rit·u·al·ly** \-ē\ *adv*

[2]**ritual** *n* **1** : the established form for a ceremony; *specif* : the order of words prescribed for a religious ceremony **2 a** : ritual observance; *specif* : a system of rites **b** : a ceremonial act or action **c** : any formal and customarily repeated act or series of acts

rit·u·al·ism \-ˌiz-əm\ *n* **1** : the use of ritual **2** : excessive devotion to ritual — **rit·u·al·ist** \-əst\ *n* — **rit·u·al·is·tic** \ˌrich-(ə-)wəl-'is-tik, ˌrich-əl-\ *adj* — **rit·u·al·is·ti·cal·ly** \-ti-k(ə-)lē\ *adv*

rit·u·al·ize \'rich-(ə-)wə-ˌlīz, 'rich-əl-\ *vb* **-ized**; **-iz·ing** *vi* : to practice ritualism ~ *vt* **1** : to make a ritual of **2** : to impose a ritual on — **rit·u·al·iza·tion** \ˌrich-(ə-)wəl-ə-'zā-shən, ˌrich-əl-\ *n*

ritzy \'rit-sē\ *adj* **ritz·i·er**; **-est** [*Ritz* hotels, noted for their opulence] **1** : ostentatiously smart : FASHIONABLE, POSH **2** : SNOBBISH — **ritz·i·ness** *n*

riv *abbr* river

[1]**ri·val** \'rī-vəl\ *n* [MF or L; MF, fr. L *rivalis* one using the same stream as another, rival in love, fr. *rivalis* of a stream, fr. *rivus* stream — more at RISE] **1 a** : one of two or more striving to reach or obtain something that only one can possess **b** : one who tries to excel **2** *obs* : ASSOCIATE, COMPANION **3** : one that equals another in desired qualities : PEER

[2]**rival** *adj* : having the same pretensions or claims : COMPETING

[3]**rival** *vb* **ri·valed** *or* **ri·valled**; **ri·val·ing** *or* **ri·val·ling** \'rīv-(ə-)liŋ\ *vi* : to act as a rival : COMPETE ~ *vt* **1** : to be in competition with **2** : to strive to equal or excel : EMULATE **3** : to possess qualities or aptitudes that approach or equal (those of another)
***syn* 1** RIVAL, COMPETE, VIE, EMULATE *shared meaning element* : to strive to equal or surpass
2 see MATCH

ri·val·rous \'rī-vəl-rəs\ *adj* : given to rivalry : COMPETITIVE

ri·val·ry \'rī-vəl-rē\ *n, pl* **-ries** : the act of rivaling : the state of being a rival : COMPETITION

rive \'rīv\ *vb* **rived** \'rīvd\; **riv·en** \'riv-ən\ *also* **rived**; **riv·ing** \'rī-viŋ\ [ME *riven*, fr. ON *rīfa*; akin to L *ripa* shore, Gk *ereipein* to tear down, OE *rāw* row] *vt* **1 a** : to wrench open or tear apart or to pieces : REND **b** : to split with force or violence <lightning *rived* the tree> **2 a** : to divide into pieces : SHATTER **b** : FRACTURE ~ *vi* : to become split : CRACK ***syn*** see TEAR

riv·er \'riv-ər\ *n* [ME *rivere*, fr. OF, fr. (assumed) VL *riparia*, fr. L, fem. of *riparius* riparian, fr. *ripa*] **1 a** : a natural stream of water of considerable volume **b** : WATERCOURSE **2 a** : something resembling a river <a ~ of lava> **b** *pl* : large or overwhelming quantities <drank ~*s* of coffee> — **up the river** : to or in prison <takes the rap and goes *up the river* —Nigel Balchin>

riv·er·bank \'riv-ər-ˌbaŋk\ *n* : the bank of a river

riv·er·bed \-ˌbed\ *n* : the channel occupied by a river

riv·er·boat \-ˌbōt\ *n* : a boat for use on a river

river duck *n* : DABBLER b

riv·er–god \'riv-ər-ˌgäd\ *n* : a deity believed to preside over a river as its tutelary divinity

river horse *n* : HIPPOPOTAMUS

riv·er·ine \'riv-ə-ˌrīn, -ˌrēn\ *adj* **1** : relating to, formed by, or resembling a river **2** : living or situated on the banks of a river

riv·er·side \'riv-ər-ˌsīd\ *n* : the side or bank of a river

riv·er·ward \-wərd\ *or* **riv·er·wards** \-wərdz\ *adv* [[1]*river* + *-ward, -wards*] : toward a river

riv·er·weed \-ˌwēd\ *n* : any of a widely-distributed genus (*Podostemon* of the family Podostemaceae) of rock-inhabiting submerged aquatic herbs that have sessile involucrate flowers and poorly developed leaves

[1]**riv·et** \'riv-ət\ *n* [ME *rivette*, fr. MF *river* to be attached] : a headed pin or bolt of metal used for uniting two or more pieces by passing the shank through a hole in each piece and then beating or pressing down the plain end so as to make a second head

[2]**rivet** *vt* **1** : to fasten with or as if with rivets **2** : to upset the end or point of (as a metallic pin, rod, or bolt) by beating or pressing so as to form a head **3** : to fasten firmly <they ~ these feelings . . . tightly together —Michael Novak> **4** : to attract and hold (as the attention) completely — **riv·et·er** *n*

ri·vi·era \ˌriv-ē-'er-ə, ri-'vyer-\ *n, often cap* [fr. the *Riviera*, region in southeastern France and northwestern Italy] : a coastal region frequented as a resort area and usu. marked by a mild climate

ri·vi·ère \ˌriv-ē-'e(ə)r, ri-'vye(ə)r\ *n* [F, lit., river, fr. OF *rivere*] : a necklace of precious stones (as diamonds)

riv·u·let \'riv-(y)ə-lət\ *n* [It *rivoletto*, dim. of *rivolo*, fr. L *rivulus*, dim. of *rivus* stream — more at RISE] : a small stream : BROOK

[1]**ri·yal** \rē-'(y)ȯl, -'(y)äl\ *n* [Ar *riyāl*, fr. Sp *real* real] **1** — see *dinar* at MONEY table **2** — see MONEY table

[2]**riyal** *var of* RIAL

RJ *abbr* road junction

rm *abbr* **1** ream **2** room

rms *abbr* root-mean-square

RMS *abbr* **1** Royal Mail Service **2** royal mail steamer; royal mail steamship

Rn *symbol* radon

RN *abbr* **1** registered nurse **2** Royal Navy

RNA \ˌär-ˌen-'ā\ *n* [*ribo*nucleic *a*cid] : any of various nucleic acids that contain ribose and uracil as structural components and are associated with the control of cellular chemical activities — compare MESSENGER RNA, RIBOSOMAL RNA, TRANSFER RNA

RNase *or* **RNA·ase** \ˌär-ˌen-'ā-ˌās, -'ā-ˌāz\ *n* [*RNA* + *-ase*] : RIBONUCLEASE

rnd *abbr* round

RNR *abbr* Royal Naval Reserve

RNVR *abbr* Royal Naval Volunteer Reserve

RNZAF *abbr* Royal New Zealand Air Force

[1]**roach** \'rōch\ *n, pl* **roach** *also* **roach·es** [ME *roche*, fr. MF] **1** : a silver-white European freshwater cyprinid fish (*Rutilus rutilus*) with a greenish back; *also* : any of various related fishes (as some shiners) **2** : any of several American freshwater sunfishes (family Centrarchidae)

[2]**roach** *vt* [origin unknown] **1** : to cause to arch; *specif* : to brush (the hair) in a roach — often used with *up* **2** : to cut (as a horse's mane) so that the remainder stands upright

[3]**roach** *n* **1** : a curved cut in the edge of a sail to prevent chafing or to secure a better fit **2** : a roll of hair brushed straight back from the forehead or side of the head

[4]**roach** *n* **1** : COCKROACH **2** : the butt of a marijuana cigarette

roach back *n* : an arched back (as of a dog)

roach clip *n* : a metal clip that resembles tweezers and is used by marijuana smokers to hold a roach — called also *roach holder*

road \'rōd\ *n* [ME *rode*, fr. OE *rād* ride, journey; akin to OE *rīdan* to ride] **1** : a place less enclosed than a harbor where ships may ride at anchor — often used in pl.; called also *roadstead* **2 a** : an open way for vehicles, persons, and animals; *esp* : one lying outside of an urban district : HIGHWAY **b** : ROADBED 2b **3** : ROUTE, PATH **4** : RAILWAY — **road·less** \'rōd-ləs\ *adj* — **on the road 1** : away from home usu. in regular travel or on business **2** : in transit through a circuit of scheduled performances or games in several locations <the team is *on the road*>

road·abil·i·ty \ˌrōd-ə-'bil-ət-ē\ *n* : the qualities (as steadiness and balance) desirable in an automobile on the road

road agent *n* : a highwayman who formerly operated esp. on stage routes in unsettled districts

road·bed \'rōd-,bed\ *n* **1 a :** the bed on which the ties, rails, and ballast of a railroad rest **b :** the ballast or the upper surface of the ballast on which the ties rest **2 a :** the earth foundation of a road prepared for surfacing **b :** the part of the surface of a road traveled by vehicles

road·block \-,bläk\ *n* **1 a :** a barricade often with traps or mines for holding up an enemy at a point on a road covered by fire **b :** a road barricade set up esp. by law enforcement officers **2 :** an obstruction in a road **3 :** something (as a fact, condition, or countermeasure) that blocks progress or prevents accomplishment of an objective — **roadblock** *vt*

road hog *n* **:** a driver of an automotive vehicle who obstructs others esp. by occupying part of another's traffic lane

road·house \'rōd-,haùs\ *n* **:** an inn usu. outside city limits providing liquor and usu. meals, dancing, and often gambling

road metal *n* **:** broken stone or cinders used in making and repairing roads or ballasting railroads

road racing *n* **:** racing (as in automobiles) over public roads or over a closed course designed to simulate public roads (as with left- and right-hand turns, sharp corners, and hills)

road roller *n* **:** one that rolls roadways; *specif* **:** a machine equipped with heavy wide smooth rollers for compacting roads and pavements

road·run·ner \'rō-,drən-ər\ *n* **:** a largely terrestrial bird (*Geococcyx californianus*) of the cuckoo family that is a speedy runner and ranges from California to Mexico and eastward to Texas; *also* **:** a closely related Mexican bird (*G. velox*)

roadrunner

road show *n* **1 :** a theatrical performance given by a troupe on tour **2 :** a special engagement of a new motion picture usu. at increased prices

¹road·side \'rōd-,sīd\ *n* **:** the strip of land along a road **:** the side of a road

²roadside *adj* **:** situated at the side of a road <a ~ diner>

road·stead \'rōd-,sted\ *n* **:** ROAD 1

road·ster \'rōd-stər\ *n* **1 a :** a horse for riding or driving on roads **b :** a utility saddle horse of the hackney type **2 a :** a light carriage **:** BUGGY **b :** an automobile with an open body that seats two and that has a luggage compartment or rumble seat in the rear

road test *n* **1 :** a test of a vehicle under practical operating conditions on the road **2 :** a test on the road of a person's driving ability as a requirement for a driver's license — **road test** *vt*

road·way \'rōd-,wā\ *n* **1 a :** the strip of land over which a road passes **b :** ROAD; *specif* **:** ROADBED 2b **2 :** a railroad right-of-way with tracks, structures, and appurtenances **3 :** the part of a bridge used by vehicles

road·work \-,wərk\ *n* **:** conditioning for an athletic contest (as a boxing match) consisting mainly of long runs

road·wor·thy \-,wər-thē\ *adj* **:** fit for use on the road — **road·wor·thi·ness** *n*

roam \'rōm\ *vb* [ME *romen*] *vi* **1 :** to go from place to place without purpose or direction **:** WANDER **2 :** to travel purposefully unhindered through a wide area <cattle ~*ing* in search of water> ~ *vt* **:** to range or wander over — **roam** *n* — **roam·er** *n*

¹roan \'rōn *also* 'rō-ən\ *adj* [MF, fr. OSp *roano*] **:** having the base color (as black, red, gray, or brown) muted and lightened by admixture of white hairs <a ~ horse> <a ~ calf>

²roan *n* **1 :** an animal (as a horse) with a roan coat — usu. used of a red roan when unqualified **2 :** the color of a roan horse — used esp. when the base color is red **3 :** a sheepskin tanned with sumac and colored and finished to imitate morocco

¹roar \'rō(ə)r, 'rò(ə)r\ *vb* [ME *roren*, fr. OE *rārian;* akin to OHG *rērēn* to bleat, Skt *rāyati* he barks] *vi* **1 a :** to utter or emit a full loud prolonged sound **b :** to sing or shout with full force **2 a :** to make or emit a loud confused sound (as background reverberation or rumbling) **b :** to laugh loudly **3 :** to be boisterous or disorderly **4 :** to make a loud noise in breathing (as horses afflicted with roaring) ~ *vt* **1 :** to utter or proclaim with a roar <~*ed* his commands> **2 :** to cause to roar

²roar *n* **1 :** the deep cry of a wild animal **2 :** a loud deep cry (as of pain or anger) **3 :** a loud continuous confused sound <the ~ of conversation in the bar> **4 :** a boisterous outcry

roar·er \'rōr-ər, 'ròr-\ *n* **1 :** one that roars **2 :** a horse subject to roaring

¹roar·ing \'rōr-iŋ, 'ròr-\ *n* **:** noisy respiration in a horse caused by nerve paralysis and muscular atrophy and constituting an unsoundness in the horse

²roaring *adj* **1 :** making or characterized by a sound resembling a roar **:** LOUD <~ applause> **2 :** marked by prosperity esp. of a temporary nature **:** THRIVING, BOOMING <did a ~ business>

³roaring *adv* **:** EXTREMELY <was ~ hungry —Herman Wouk>

roaring boy *n* **:** a noisy street bully of Elizabethan and Jacobean England who intimidated passersby

¹roast \'rōst\ *vb* [ME *rosten*, fr. OF *rostir*, of Gmc origin; akin to OHG *rōsten* to roast] *vt* **1 a :** to cook by exposing to dry heat (as in an oven or before a fire) or by surrounding with hot embers, sand, or stones <~ a potato in ashes> **b :** to dry and parch by exposure to heat <~ coffee> <~ chestnuts> **2 :** to heat (inorganic material) with access of air and without fusing to effect change (as expulsion of volatile matter, oxidation, or removal of sulfur from sulfide ores) **3 :** to heat to excess <the sun no longer ~*ed* the valley —Oliver La Farge> **4 :** to criticize severely <films have been ~*ed* by most critics —H. J. Seldes> ~ *vi* **1 :** to cook food by heat **2 :** to undergo being roasted

²roast *n* **1 :** a piece of meat suitable for roasting **2 :** a gathering at which food is roasted before an open fire or in hot ashes or sand **3 :** an act or process of roasting; *specif* **:** severe banter or criticism

³roast *adj* **:** that has been roasted <~ beef>

roast·er \'rō-stər\ *n* **1 :** one that roasts **2 :** a device for roasting **3 :** something adapted to roasting: as **a :** a suckling pig **b :** a young domestic fowl

roasting ear *n* **1 :** an ear of young corn roasted or suitable for roasting usu. in the husk **2** *chiefly South & Midland* **:** an ear of corn suitable for boiling or steaming

rob \'räb\ *vb* **robbed; rob·bing** [ME *robben*, fr. OF *rober*, of Gmc origin; akin to OHG *roubōn* to rob — more at REAVE] *vt* **1 a** (1) **:** to take something away from by force **:** steal from (2) **:** to take personal property from by violence or threat **b** (1) **:** to remove valuables without right from (a place) (2) **:** to take the contents of (a receptacle) **c :** to take away as loot **:** STEAL <~ jewelry> **2 a :** to deprive of something due, expected, or desired <air power had . . . *robbed* sea power of its sovereign values —S. L. A. Marshall> **b :** to withhold unjustly or injuriously ~ *vi* **:** to commit robbery — **rob·ber** *n*

ro·ba·lo \rō-'bäl-(,)ō\ *n, pl* **-los** *or* **-lo** [Sp] **:** SNOOK 1

ro·band \'rō-,band, -bənd\ *n* [prob. fr. MD *rabant*] **:** a piece of spun yarn or marline used to fasten the head of a sail to a spar

robber baron *n* **1 :** a medieval lord who subsisted by robbing, holding for ransom, or taxing travelers through his domain **2 :** an American capitalist of the latter part of the 19th century who became wealthy through exploitation (as of natural resources, governmental influence, or low wage scales)

robber fly *n* **:** any of numerous predaceous flies (family Asilidae) some of which closely resemble the bumblebees

rob·bery \'räb-(ə-)rē\ *n, pl* **-ber·ies :** the act or practice of robbing; *specif* **:** larceny from the person or presence of another by violence or threat

¹robe \'rōb\ *n* [ME, fr. OF, robe, booty, of Gmc origin; akin to OHG *roubōn* to rob] **1 a :** a long flowing outer garment; *esp* **:** one used for ceremonial occasions or as a symbol of office or profession **b :** a loose garment (as a bathrobe) for informal wear esp. at home **2 :** COVERING, MANTLE <peaks on the axis of the range in their ~*s* of snow and light —John Muir †1914> **3 :** a covering of pelts or fabric for the lower body used while driving or at outdoor events

²robe *vb* **robed; rob·ing** *vt* **:** to clothe or cover with or as if with a robe ~ *vi* **1 :** to put on a robe **2 :** DRESS

robe de cham·bre \,rōb-də-'shäⁿbrᵊ, -'shäm-brə\ *n, pl* **robes de chambre** \,rōb(z)-\ [F] **:** DRESSING GOWN

rob·in \'räb-ən\ *n* [short for *robin redbreast*] **1 a :** a small European thrush (*Erithacus rubecola*) resembling a warbler and having a brownish olive back and yellowish red throat and breast **b :** any of various Old World songbirds that are related to or resemble the European robin **2 :** a large No. American thrush (*Turdus migratorius*) with olivaceous gray upperparts, blackish head and tail, black and whitish streaked throat, and chiefly dull reddish breast and underparts

Rob·in Good·fel·low \,räb-ən-'gùd-,fel-(,)ō, -ə(-w)\ *n* **:** a mischievous sprite in English folklore

Robin Hood \-'hùd\ *n* **:** a legendary outlaw famed for his archery and for robbing the rich and giving to the poor

robin red·breast \-'red-,brest\ *n* [ME, fr. *Robin*, nickname for *Robert*] **:** ROBIN

Rob·in·son Cru·soe \,räb-ə(n)-sən-'krü-(,)sō\ *n* **:** a shipwrecked sailor in Defoe's *Robinson Crusoe* who lives for many years on a desert island

ro·ble \'rō-(,)blā\ *n* [AmerSp, fr. Sp, oak, fr. L *robur*] **:** any of several oaks of California and Mexico

ro·bot \'rō-,bät, -bət\ *n* [Czech, fr. *robota* work; akin to OHG *arabeit* trouble, L *orbus* orphaned] **1 a :** a machine that looks like a human being and performs various complex acts (as walking or talking) of a human being; *also* **:** a similar but fictional machine whose lack of capacity for human emotions is often emphasized **b :** an efficient, insensitive, often brutalized person **2 :** an automatic apparatus or device that performs functions ordinarily ascribed to human beings or operates with what appears to be almost human intelligence **3 :** a mechanism guided by automatic controls — **ro·bot·ism** \-,iz-əm\ *n*

robot bomb *n* **:** a small pilotless jet-propelled airplane that is heavily loaded with explosives and that descends as an aerial bomb

ro·bot·ics \rō-'bät-iks\ *n pl but sing in constr* **:** a field of interest concerned with the construction, maintenance, and behavior of robots <~ is a major science-fiction theme>

ro·bot·iza·tion \,rō-,bät-ə-'zā-shən, -bət-\ *n* **1 :** AUTOMATION **2 :** the process of turning a human being into a robot

ro·bot·ize \'rō-,bät-,īz, -bət-\ *vt* **-ized; -iz·ing 1 :** to make automatic **2 :** to turn (a human being) into a robot

Rob Roy \'räb-'ròi\ *n* [prob. fr. *Rob Roy*, nickname of Robert McGregor †1734 Scot freebooter] **:** a manhattan made with Scotch whisky

ro·bust \rō-'bəst, 'rō-(,)bəst\ *adj* [L *robustus* oaken, strong, fr. *robor-*, *robur* oak, strength] **1 a :** having or exhibiting strength or vigorous health **:** VIGOROUS **b :** firm in purpose or outlook <a ~ faith> **c :** strongly formed or constructed **:** STURDY <a ~ plastic> **2 :** ROUGH, RUDE <stories . . . laden with ~, down-home imagery —*Playboy*> **3 :** requiring strength or vigor <~ work> **4 :** FULL-BODIED <~ coffee> ***syn*** see HEALTHY ***ant*** frail, feeble — **ro·bust·ly** *adv* — **ro·bust·ness** \-'bəs(t)-nəs, -(,)bəs(t)-\ *n*

ro·bus·ta coffee \rō-,bəs-tə-\ *n* [NL *robusta*, specific epithet of *Coffea robusta*, syn. of *Coffea canephora*] **1 :** a coffee (*Coffea* *canephora*) that is indigenous to Central Africa but has been introduced elsewhere (as in Java) **2 a :** the seed of robusta coffee **b :** coffee brewed from the seed of robusta coffee

ro·bus·tious \rō-ˈbəs-chəs\ *adj* **1 :** ROBUST **2 :** vigorous in a rough or unrefined way : BOISTEROUS — **ro·bus·tious·ly** *adv* — **ro·bus·tious·ness** *n*

roc \ˈräk\ *n* [Ar *rukhkh*] **:** a legendary bird of great size and strength believed to inhabit the Indian ocean area

roc·am·bole \ˈräk-əm-ˌbōl\ *n* [F, fr. G *rockenbolle,* fr. *rocken, roggen* rye + *bolle* bulb] **:** a European leek (*Allium scorodoprasum*) used for flavoring

Ro·chelle salt \rō-ˌshel-\ *n* **:** a crystalline salt $KNaC_4H_4O_6.4H_2O$ that is a mild purgative

roche mou·ton·née \ˈrōsh-ˌmüt-ᵊn-ˈā, ˈrōsh-\ *n, pl* **roches mou·ton·nées** *same or* -ˈāz\ [F, lit., fleecy rock] **:** an elongate rounded ice-sculptured hillock of bedrock

roch·et \ˈräch-ət\ *n* [ME, fr. MF, fr. OF, fr. (assumed) OF *roc* coat, of Gmc origin; akin to OHG *roc* coat] **:** a white linen vestment resembling a surplice with close-fitting sleeves worn esp. by bishops and privileged prelates

¹rock \ˈräk\ *vb* [ME *rokken,* fr. OE *roccian;* akin to OHG *rucken* to cause to move] *vt* **1 a :** to move back and forth in or as if in a cradle **b :** to wash (placer gravel) in a cradle **2 a :** to cause to sway back and forth **b** (1) **:** DAZE, STUN (2) **:** DISTURB, UPSET ~ *vi* **1 :** to become moved backward and forward under impact **2 :** to move oneself or itself rhythmically back and forth ***syn*** see SHAKE — **rock the boat :** to do something that disturbs the equilibrium of a situation <don't *rock the boat* and you'll get your promotions and salary increases —K. M. Cottam>

²rock *n* **1 :** a rocking movement **2 :** popular music usu. played on electronically amplified instruments and characterized by a persistent heavily accented beat, much repetition of simple phrases, and often country, folk, and blues elements

³rock *n* [ME *roc,* fr. MD *rocke;* akin to OHG *rocko* distaff, *roc* coat] **1 :** DISTAFF **2 :** the wool or flax on a distaff

⁴rock *n* [ME *rokke,* fr. ONF *roque,* fr. (assumed) VL *rocca*] **1 :** a large mass of stone forming a cliff, promontory, or peak **2 :** a concreted mass of stony material; *also* **:** broken pieces of such masses **3 :** consolidated or unconsolidated solid mineral matter; *also* **:** a particular mass of it **4 a :** something like a rock in firmness: (1) **:** FOUNDATION, SUPPORT (2) **:** REFUGE <a ~ of independent thought . . . in an ocean of parochialism —Thomas Molnar> **b :** something that threatens or causes disaster — often used in pl. **5 a :** a flavored stick candy with color running through **b :** ROCK CANDY 1 **6** *slang* **a :** GEM **b :** DIAMOND — **rock** *adj* — **rock·like** \ˈräk-ˌlīk\ *adj* — **on the rocks 1 :** in or into a state of destruction or wreckage <their marriage went *on the rocks*> **2 :** on ice cubes <bourbon *on the rocks*>

rock·a·bil·ly \ˈräk-ə-ˌbil-ē\ *n* [²*rock* + *-billy* (as in *hillbilly*)] **:** pop music marked by features of rock and country music

rock and roll *var of* ROCK 'N' ROLL

rock and rye *n* **:** a drink made with rye whiskey and rock candy and flavored with orange, lemon, and occas. pineapple and cherry

rock·a·way \ˈräk-ə-ˌwā\ *n* [perh. fr. *Rockaway,* New Jersey] **:** a light low four-wheeled carriage with a fixed top and open sides

rock bass *n* **1 :** a sunfish (*Ambloplites rupestris*) found esp. in the upper Mississippi valley and Great Lakes region **2 a :** a striped bass (*Morone saxatilis*) **b :** any of several sea basses (genus *Paralabrax*) of the California and adjoining Mexican coast

rock–bottom *adj* **:** being the very lowest <~ off-season rates>

rock bottom *n* **:** the lowest or most fundamental part or level

rock·bound \ˈräk-ˌbaund\ *adj* **:** fringed, surrounded, or covered with rocks : ROCKY

rock brake *n* **:** any of several ferns that grow chiefly on or among rocks

rock candy *n* **1 :** boiled sugar crystallized in large masses on string and used esp. in rock and rye **2 :** ⁴ROCK 5a

Rock Cornish *n* **:** a crossbred domestic fowl produced by interbreeding Cornish and white Plymouth Rock fowls and used esp. for small roasters

rock crystal *n* **:** transparent quartz

rock·er \ˈräk-ər\ *n* **1 a :** either of two curving pieces of wood or metal on which an object (as a cradle) rocks **b :** any of various objects (as an infant's toy having a seat placed between side pieces) that rock on rockers **c :** any of various objects in the form of a rocker or with parts resembling a rocker (as a skate with a curved blade) **d :** one of the curved stripes at the lower part of a chevron worn by a noncommissioned officer above the rank of sergeant **2 :** any of various devices that work with a rocking motion — **off one's rocker :** in a state of extreme confusion or insanity <went *off her rocker,* and had to be put away —Mervyn Wall>

rocker arm *n* **:** a center-pivoted lever to push an automotive engine valve down

¹rock·et \ˈräk-ət, rä-ˈket\ *n* [MF *roquette,* fr. OIt *rochetta,* dim. of *ruca* garden rocket, fr. L *eruca*] **1 :** a yellowish flowered European herb (*Eruca sativa*) of the mustard family that is sometimes grown for salad **2 a :** DAME'S VIOLET **b :** any of several plants resembling dame's violet

²rock·et \ˈräk-ət\ *n, often attrib* [It *rocchetta,* lit., small distaff, fr. dim. of *rocca* distaff, of Gmc origin; akin to OHG *rocko* distaff] **1 a :** a firework consisting of a case partly filled with a combustible composition fastened to a guiding stick and projected through the air by the reaction resulting from the rearward discharge of the gases liberated by combustion **b :** such a device used as an incendiary weapon or as a propelling unit (as for a lifesaving line or a whaling harpoon) **2 :** a jet engine that operates on the same principle as the firework rocket, consists essentially of a combustion chamber and an exhaust nozzle, carries either liquid or solid propellants which provide the fuel and oxygen needed for combustion and thus make the engine independent of the oxygen of the air, and is used esp. for the propulsion of a missile (as a bomb or shell) or a vehicle (as an airplane) **3 :** a rocket-propelled bomb, missile, or projectile

³rock·et \ˈräk-ət\ *vt* **:** to convey by means of a rocket ~ *vi* **1 :** to rise up swiftly, spectacularly, and with force **2 :** to travel rapidly in or as if in a rocket

rocket bomb *n* **1 :** an aerial bomb designed for release at low altitude and equipped with a rocket apparatus for giving it added momentum **2 :** a rocket-propelled bomb launched from the ground

rock·e·teer \ˌräk-ə-ˈti(ə)r\ *n* **1 :** one who fires, pilots, or rides in a rocket **2 :** a scientist who specializes in rocketry

rocket plane *n* **:** an airplane propelled by rockets or armed with rocket launchers

rocket propulsion *n* **:** propulsion by means of a rocket engine

rock·et·ry \ˈräk-ə-trē\ *n* **:** the study of, experimentation with, or use of rockets

rocket ship *n* **:** a rocket-propelled craft capable of navigation beyond the earth's atmosphere

rocket sled *n* **:** a rocket-propelled vehicle that runs usu. on a single rail and that is used esp. in aeronautical experimentation

rock·fall \ˈräk-ˌfȯl\ *n* **:** a mass of falling or fallen rocks

rock·fish \-ˌfish\ *n* **:** any of various important market fishes that live among rocks or on rocky bottoms: as **a :** any of several scorpaenid fishes **b :** a striped bass (*Morone saxatilis*) **c :** any of several groupers **d :** GREENLING 1

rock garden *n* **:** a garden laid out among rocks or decorated with rocks and adapted for the growth of particular kinds of plants (as alpines)

rock hind *n* **:** any of various spotted groupers commonly found about rocky coasts or reefs

rock hound *n* **1 a :** a specialist in geology **b :** one who searches for oil **2 :** an amateur rock and mineral collector

rock·i·ness \ˈräk-ē-nəs\ *n* **:** the quality or state of being rocky

rocking chair *n* **:** a chair mounted on rockers

rocking horse *n* **:** a toy horse mounted on rockers — called also *hobbyhorse*

rock·ling \ˈräk-liŋ\ *n* **:** any of several small rather elongate marine cods (family Gadidae)

rock lobster *n* **1 :** SPINY LOBSTER **2 :** the flesh of the Cape crawfish esp. when canned or frozen for use as food

rock maple *n* **:** a sugar maple (*Acer saccharum*)

rock 'n' roll \ˌräk-ən-ˈrōl\ *n* **:** ²ROCK 2

rock oil *n* **:** PETROLEUM

rock·oon \rä-ˈkün\ *n* [²*rock*et + ball*oon*] **:** a small research rocket carried to a high altitude by a balloon and then fired

rock pigeon *n* **:** a bluish gray wild pigeon (*Columba livia*) of Europe and Asia

rock rabbit *n* **1 :** HYRAX **2 :** PIKA

rock–ribbed \ˈräk-ˈribd\ *adj* **1 :** ROCKY **2 :** firm and inflexible in doctrine or integrity <a ~ conservative community —John Hale>

rock·rose \ˈräk-ˈrōz\ *n* **:** any of various shrubs or woody herbs (family Cistaceae, the rockrose family) with simple entire leaves and a capsular fruit

rock salt *n* **:** common salt occurring in solid form as a mineral; *also* **:** salt artificially prepared in large crystals or masses

rock·shaft \ˈräk-ˌshaft\ *n* **:** a shaft that oscillates on its journals instead of revolving

rock·skip·per \-ˌskip-ər\ *n* **:** any of several blennies

rock tripe *n* **:** any of various dark leathery umbilicate foliose lichens (as of the genus *Umbilicaria*) that are widely distributed on rocks in boreal and alpine areas and that are sometimes used as emergency food

rock wallaby *n* **:** any of various medium-sized kangaroos (genus *Petrogale*)

rock·weed \ˈräk-ˌwēd\ *n* **:** a coarse brown seaweed (family Fucaceae) growing attached to rocks

rock wool *n* **:** mineral wool made by blowing a jet of steam through molten rock (as limestone or siliceous rock) or through slag and used chiefly for heat and sound insulation

¹rocky \ˈräk-ē\ *adj* **rock·i·er; -est** [⁴*rock*] **1 :** abounding in or consisting of rocks **2 :** difficult to impress or affect : INSENSITIVE **3 :** firmly held : STEADFAST

²rocky *adj* **rock·i·er; -est** [¹*rock*] **1 :** UNSTABLE, WOBBLY **2 :** physically upset (as from drinking excessively) **3 :** marked by obstacles : DIFFICULT <a financially ~ year —Michael Murray>

Rocky Mountain sheep *n* [*Rocky mountains,* No. America] **:** BIGHORN

Rocky Mountain spotted fever *n* **:** an acute rickettsial disease characterized by chills, fever, prostration, pains in muscles and joints, and a red to purple eruption and transmitted by the bite of a wood tick (*Dermacentor andersoni*)

¹ro·co·co \rə-ˈkō-(ˌ)kō, ˌrō-kə-ˈkō\ *adj* [F, irreg. fr. *rocaille* rock-work, fr. *roc* rock, alter. of MF *roche,* fr. (assumed) VL *rocca*] **1 a :** of or relating to an artistic style esp. of the 18th century characterized by fanciful curved spatial forms and ornament of pierced shellwork **b :** of or relating to an 18th century musical style marked by light gay ornamentation and departure from thoroughbass and polyphony **2 :** excessively ornate or intricate

²rococo *n* **:** rococo work or style

rod \ˈräd\ *n* [ME, fr. OE *rodd;* akin to ON *rudda* club] **1 a** (1) **:** a straight slender stick growing on or cut from a tree or bush (2) **:** OSIER (3) **:** a stick or bundle of twigs used to punish; *also* **:** PUNISHMENT (4) **:** a shepherd's cudgel (5) **:** a pole with a line and usu. a reel attached for fishing **b** (1) **:** a slender bar (as of wood or metal) (2) **:** a bar or staff for measuring (3) **:** SCEPTER; *also* **:** a wand or staff carried as a badge of office (as of marshal) **2 a :** a unit of length — see WEIGHT table **b :** a square rod **3 :** any of the long rod-shaped photosensitive receptors in the retina responsive to faint light **4 :** a bacterium shaped like a rod **5** *slang* **:** PISTOL — **rod·less** \-ləs\ *adj* — **rod·like** \-ˌlīk\ *adj*

rode *past of* RIDE

ro·dent \ˈrōd-ᵊnt\ *n* [deriv. of L *rodent-, rodens,* prp. of *rodere* to gnaw — more at RAT] **:** any of an order (Rodentia) of relatively small gnawing mammals (as a mouse, a squirrel, or a beaver) that have in the upper jaw a single pair of incisors with a chisel-shaped edge; *also* **:** a small mammal (as a rabbit or a shrew) — **rodent** *adj*

ro·den·ti·cide \rō-ˈdent-ə-ˌsīd\ *n* **:** an agent that kills, repels, or controls rodents

rodent ulcer *n* [L *rodent-, rodens* gnawing] **:** a chronic persisting ulcer of the exposed skin and esp. of the face that is destructive locally, spreads slowly, and is usu. a carcinoma derived from basal cells — called also *rodent cancer*

ro·deo \ˈrōd-ē-ˌō, rə-ˈdā-(ˌ)ō\ *n, pl* **ro·de·os** [Sp, fr. *rodear* to surround, fr. *rueda* wheel, fr. L *rota* — more at ROLL] **1 :** ROUNDUP **2 a :** a public performance featuring bronco riding, calf roping, steer wrestling, and Brahma bull riding **b :** a contest resembling a rodeo

rod·man \ˈräd-mən, -ˌman\ *n* **:** a surveyor's assistant who holds the leveling rod

ro·do·mon·tade \ˌräd-ə-mən-ˈtād, ˌrōd-, -ˈtäd\ *n* [MF, fr. It *Rodomonte,* character in *Orlando Innamorato* by Matteo M. Boiardo] **1 :** a bragging speech **2 :** vain boasting or bluster **:** RANT — **rodomontade** *adj*

¹roe \ˈrō\ *n, pl* **roe** *or* **roes** [ME *ro,* fr. OE *rā;* akin to OHG *rēh* roe, OIr *ríabach* dappled] **:** DOE

²roe *n* [ME *roof;* akin to OHG *rogo* roe, Lith *kurkulai* frog's eggs] **1 a :** the eggs of a fish esp. when still enclosed in the ovarian membrane **b :** the eggs or ovaries of an invertebrate (as the coral of a lobster) **2 :** a dark mottled or flecked figure appearing esp. in quartersawed lumber

roe·buck \ˈrō-ˌbək\ *n, pl* **roebuck** *or* **roebucks :** ROE DEER; *esp* **:** the male roe deer

roe deer *n* **:** a small European and Asiatic deer (*Capreolus capreolus*) that has erect cylindrical antlers forked at the summit, is reddish brown in summer and grayish in winter, has a white rump patch, and is noted for its nimbleness and grace

¹roent·gen \ˈrent-gən, ˈrənt-, -jən; ˈren-chən, ˈrən-\ *adj* [ISV, fr. Wilhelm *Röntgen*] **:** of or relating to X rays <~ examinations>

²roentgen *n* **:** the international unit of X-radiation or gamma radiation equal to the amount of radiation that produces in one cubic centimeter of dry air at 0°C and standard atmospheric pressure ionization of either sign equal to one electrostatic unit of charge

roent·gen·ize \-ˌīz\ *vt* **-ized; -iz·ing 1 :** to make (air or other gas) conducting by the passage of X rays **2 :** to subject to the action of X rays

roent·gen·o·gram \-ə-ˌgram\ *n* [ISV] **:** a photograph made with X rays

roent·gen·o·graph \-ˌgraf\ *n* **:** ROENTGENOGRAM

roent·gen·og·ra·phy \ˌrent-gən-ˈäg-rə-fē, ˌrənt-, -jən-; ˌren-chən-, ˌrən-\ *n* [ISV] **:** photography by means of X rays — **roent·gen·o·graph·ic** \-ə-ˈgraf-ik\ *adj* — **roent·gen·o·graph·i·cal·ly** \-i-k(ə-)lē\ *adv*

roent·gen·ol·o·gy \-ˈäl-ə-jē\ *n* [ISV] **:** a branch of radiology that deals with the use of X rays for diagnosis or treatment of disease — **roent·gen·o·log·ic** \-ə-ˈläj-ik\ *or* **roent·gen·o·log·i·cal** \-i-kəl\ *adj* — **roent·gen·o·log·i·cal·ly** \-i-k(ə-)lē\ *adv* — **roent·gen·ol·o·gist** \-ˈäl-ə-jəst\ *n*

roent·gen·o·scope \ˈrent-gən-ə-ˌskōp, ˈrənt-, -jən-; ˈren-chən-, ˈrən-\ *n* **:** FLUOROSCOPE — **roent·gen·o·scop·ic** \ˌrent-gən-ə-ˈskäp-ik, ˌrənt-, -jən-; ˌren-chən-, ˌrən-\ *adj* — **roent·gen·os·co·py** \-ˈäs-kə-pē\ *n*

roent·gen·o·ther·a·py \ˌrent-gən-ə-ˈther-ə-pē, ˌrənt-, -jən-; ˌren-chən-, ˌrən-\ *n* [ISV] **:** X-RAY THERAPY

roentgen ray *n, often cap 1st R* **:** X RAY

ROG *abbr* receipt of goods

ro·ga·tion \rō-ˈgā-shən\ *n* [ME *rogacion,* fr. LL *rogation-, rogatio,* fr. L, questioning, fr. *rogatus,* pp. of *rogare* to ask — more at RIGHT] **1** *obs* **:** LITANY, SUPPLICATION **2 :** the religious observance of the Rogation Days — often used in pl.

Rogation Day *n* **:** one of the days of prayer esp. for the harvest observed on the three days before Ascension Day and by Roman Catholics also on April 25

rog·er \ˈräj-ər\ *interj* [fr. *Roger,* former communications code word for the letter *r*] — used esp. in radio and signaling to indicate that a message has been received and understood

¹rogue \ˈrōg\ *n* [origin unknown] **1 :** VAGRANT, TRAMP **2 :** a dishonest or worthless person **:** SCOUNDREL **3 :** a mischievous person **:** SCAMP **4 :** a horse inclined to shirk or misbehave **5 :** an individual exhibiting a chance and usu. inferior biological variation — **rogu·ish** \ˈrō-gish\ *adj* — **rogu·ish·ly** *adv* — **rogu·ish·ness** *n*

²rogue *vi* **rogued; rogu·ing** *or* **rogue·ing :** to weed out inferior, diseased, or nontypical individuals from a crop plant or a field

³rogue *adj, of an animal* **:** being vicious and destructive

rogue elephant *n* **:** a vicious elephant that separates from the herd and roams alone

rogu·ery \ˈrō-g(ə-)rē\ *n, pl* **-er·ies 1 :** an act characteristic of a rogue **2 :** mischievous play

rogues' gallery *n* **:** a collection of pictures of persons arrested as criminals

roil \ˈrȯi(ə)l, *vt 2 is also* ˈrī(ə)l\ *vb* [origin unknown] *vt* **1 a :** to make turbid by stirring up the sediment or dregs of **b :** to stir up **:** DISTURB, DISORDER **2 :** RILE 2 ~ *vi* **:** to move turbulently

roily \ˈrȯi-lē\ *adj* **1 :** full of sediment or dregs **:** MUDDY **2 :** TURBULENT <the ~ waters rushed out in a wasting flood —V. L. Parrington> ***syn*** see TURBID

rois·ter \ˈrȯi-stər\ *vi* **rois·tered; rois·ter·ing** \-st(ə-)riŋ\ [earlier *roister* (roisterer)] **:** to engage in noisy revelry **:** CAROUSE — **rois·ter·er** \-stər-ər\ *n* — **rois·ter·ous** \-st(ə-)rəs\ *adj*

rol·a·mite \ˈrō-lə-ˌmīt\ *n* [*roll* + *-amite,* of unknown origin] **:** a nearly frictionless elementary mechanism consisting of two or more rollers inserted in the loops of a flexible band with the band acting to turn the rollers whose movement can be directed to perform various functions

Ro·land \ˈrō-lənd\ *n* [F] **:** a stalwart defender of the Christians against the Saracens in the Charlemagne legends who was killed at Roncesvalles

role *also* **rôle** \ˈrōl\ *n* [F *rôle,* lit., roll, fr. OF *rolle*] **1 a (1) :** a character assigned or assumed **(2) :** a socially expected behavior pattern usu. determined by an individual's status in a particular society **b :** a part played by an actor or singer **2 :** FUNCTION **3 :** an identifier attached to an index term to show functional relationships between terms

¹roll \ˈrōl\ *n* [ME *rolle,* fr. OF, fr. L *rotula,* dim. of *rota* wheel; akin to OHG *rad* wheel, Skt *ratha* wagon] **1 a (1) :** a written document that may be rolled up **:** SCROLL; *specif* **:** a document containing an official or formal record <the ~*s* of parliament> **(2) :** a manuscript book **b :** a list of names or related items **:** CATALOG **c :** an official list: as **(1) :** MUSTER ROLL **(2) :** a list of members of a school or class or of members of a legislative body **2 :** something that is rolled up into a cylinder or ball: as **a :** a quantity (as of fabric or paper) rolled up to form a single package **b :** a hairdo in which some or all of the hair is rolled or curled up or under <a pageboy ~> **c :** any of various food preparations rolled up for cooking or serving; *specif* **:** a small piece of baked yeast dough **d :** a cylindrical twist of tobacco **e :** a flexible case (as of leather) in which articles may be rolled and fastened by straps or clasps **f (1) :** paper money folded or rolled into a wad **(2)** *slang* **:** BANKROLL **3 :** something that performs a rolling action or movement **:** ROLLER: as **a :** a wheel for making decorative lines on book covers; *also* **:** a design impressed by such a tool **b :** a typewriter platen

²roll *vt* **1 a :** to impel forward by causing to turn over and over on a surface **b :** to cause to revolve by turning over and over on or as if on an axis **c :** to cause to move in a circular manner **d :** to form into a mass by turning over and over **e :** to impel forward with an easy continuous motion **2 a :** to put a wrapping around **:** ENFOLD, ENVELOP **b :** to wrap round on itself **:** shape into a ball or roll **3 a :** to press, spread, or level with a roller **:** make smooth, even, or compact **b :** to spread out **:** EXTEND <~ out the red carpet> **4 a :** to move on rollers or wheels **b :** to cause to begin operating or moving <~ the cameras> **5 a :** to sound with a full reverberating tone <~*ed* out the words> **b :** to make a continuous beating sound upon **:** sound a roll upon <~*ed* their drums> **c :** to utter with a trill <~*ed* his *r*'s> **d :** to play (a chord) in arpeggio style **6 :** to rob (a drunk, sleeping, or unconscious person) usu. by going through the pockets ~ *vi* **1 a :** to move along a surface by rotation without sliding **b (1) :** to turn over and over <the children ~*ed* in the grass> **(2) :** to luxuriate in an abundant supply **:** WALLOW <fairly ~*ing* in money> **2 a :** to move onward or around as if by completing a revolution **:** ELAPSE, PASS <the months ~ on> **b :** to shift the gaze continually <eyes ~*ing* in terror> **c :** to revolve on an axis **3 :** to move about **:** ROAM, WANDER **4 a :** to flow with a rising and falling motion <the waves ~*ed* in> **b :** to flow in a continuous stream **:** POUR <money was ~*ing* in> **c :** to have an undulating contour <~*ing* prairie> **d :** to lie extended **:** STRETCH **5 a :** to travel in a vehicle **b :** to become carried on a stream **c :** to move on wheels **6 a :** to make a deep reverberating sound <the thunder ~*s*> **b :** TRILL **7 a :** to swing from side to side <the ship heaved and ~*ed*> **b :** to walk with a swinging gait **:** SWAY **c :** to move so as to cushion the impact of a blow — used with *with* <~*ed* with the punch> **8 a :** to take the form of a cylinder or ball **b :** to respond to rolling in a specified way or to be in a specified condition after being rolled **9 a :** to get under way **:** begin to move or operate **b :** to move forward **:** develop and maintain impetus **10 a :** BOWL **b :** to execute a somersault **11** *of a football quarterback* **:** to run toward one flank usu. parallel to the line of scrimmage esp. before throwing a pass — often used with *out* — **roll the bones :** to shoot craps

³roll *n* **1 a :** a sound produced by rapid strokes on a drum **b :** a sonorous and often rhythmical flow of speech **c :** a heavy reverberatory sound <the ~ of cannon> **d :** a chord in arpeggio style **e :** a trill of some birds (as a canary) **2 :** a rolling movement or an action or process involving such movement <a ~ of the dice>: as **a :** a swaying movement of the body **b :** a side-to-side movement (as of a ship or train) **c :** a flight maneuver in which a complete revolution about the longitudinal axis of an airplane is made with the horizontal direction of flight being approximately maintained; *also* **:** the motion of a spacecraft about its longitudinal axis **d :** SOMERSAULT **e :** the movement of a curling stone after impact with another stone

roll·back \ˈrōl-ˌbak\ *n* **:** the act or an instance of rolling back

roll back \ˈrōl-ˈbak\ *vt* **1 :** to reduce (as a commodity price) to or toward a previous level on a national scale by government control devices **2 :** to cause to retreat or withdraw **:** push back

roll bar *n* **:** an overhead metal bar on an automobile that is designed to protect the occupant in case of a turnover

roll call *n* **:** the act or an instance of calling off a list of names (as for checking attendance); *also* **:** a time for a roll call

¹roll·er \ˈrō-lər\ *n* **1 a :** a revolving cylinder over or on which something is moved or which is used to press, shape, or smooth something **b :** a cylinder or rod on which something (as a shade) is rolled up **2 a :** a long heavy wave on a coast **b :** a tumbler pigeon **3 :** one that rolls or performs a rolling operation

²rol·ler \ˈrō-lər\ *n* [G, fr. *rollen* to roll, reverberate, fr. MF *roller,* fr. (assumed) VL *rotulare,* fr. L *rotula*] **1 :** any of numerous mostly brightly colored nonpasserine Old World birds (family Coraciidae) related to the motmots and todies **2 :** a canary having a song in which the notes are soft and run together

roller bearing *n* **:** a bearing in which the journal rotates in peripheral contact with a number of rollers usu. contained in a cage

roll·er coast·er \ˈrō-lər-ˌkō-stər, ˈrō-lē-ˌkō-\ *n* **:** an elevated railway (as in an amusement park) constructed with curves and inclines on which cars roll

roller derby *n* : a contest between two roller-skating teams on a banked oval track in which each team attempts to maneuver a skater into position to score points by circling the track and passing members of the opposing team within a given time period
roller skate *n* : a shoe with a set of wheels attached for skating over a flat surface (as a floor or sidewalk); *also* : a metal frame with wheels attached that can be fitted to the sole of a shoe — **roller-skate** *vi* — **roller skater** *n*
roller towel *n* : an endless towel hung from a roller
Rolle's theorem \'rȯlz-, 'rōlz-\ *n* [Michel *Rolle* †1719 F mathematician] : a theorem in mathematics: if a curve is continuous, crosses the x-axis at two points, and has a tangent at every point between the two intercepts, its tangent is parallel to the x-axis at some point between the intercepts
roll film *n* : a strip of film for still camera use wound on a spool
rol·lick \'räl-ik\ *vi* [origin unknown] : to move or behave in a carefree joyous manner : FROLIC — **rollick** *n*
rolling hitch *n* : a hitch for fastening a line to a spar or to the standing part of another line that will not slip when the pull is parallel to the spar or line
rolling mill *n* : an establishment where metal is rolled into plates and bars
rolling pin *n* : a long cylinder for rolling out dough
rolling stock *n* : the wheeled vehicles owned and used by a railroad or motor carrier
roll-off \'rō-ˌlȯf\ *n* : a play-off match in bowling
roll·out \'rō-ˌlau̇t\ *n* **1** : the public introduction of a new aircraft **2** : a football play in which the quarterback rolls to his left or right
roll out \(')rō-'lau̇t\ *vi* : to get out of bed
roll·over \'rō-ˌlō-vər\ *n* **1** : the act or process of rolling over **2** : a motor vehicle accident in which the vehicle overturns
roll-over arm *n* : a fully upholstered chair or sofa arm curving outward from the seat
roll·top desk \ˌrōl-ˌtäp-\ *n* : a writing desk with a sliding cover often of parallel slats fastened to a flexible backing
roll up *vt* : to increase by successive accumulations : ACCUMULATE <*rolled up* a large majority> ~ *vi* **1** : to become larger by successive accumulations **2** : to arrive in a vehicle
[1]**ro·ly-po·ly** \ˌrō-lē-'pō-lē\ *n, pl* **-lies** [redupl. of *roly,* fr. [2]*roll*] **1** : a sweet dough spread with a filling, rolled, and baked or steamed **2** : a roly-poly person or thing
[2]**roly-poly** *adj* : being short and pudgy : ROTUND
Rom *abbr* **1** Roman **2** Romance **3** Romania; Romanian
ROM *abbr* read-only memory
Ro·ma·ic \rō-'mā-ik\ *n* [NGk *Rhōmaiikos,* fr. Gk *Rhōmaïkos* Roman, fr. *Rhōmē* Rome] : the modern Greek vernacular — **Romaic** *adj*
ro·maine \rō-'mān\ *n* [F, fr. fem. of *romain* Roman, fr. L *Romanus*] : COS LETTUCE
ro·man \rō-'mäⁿ\ *n* [MF, fr. OF *romans* romance] : a metrical romance
[1]**Ro·man** \'rō-mən\ *n* [partly fr. ME, fr. OE, fr. L *Romanus,* adj. & n., fr. *Roma* Rome; partly fr. ME *Romain,* fr. OF, fr. L *Romanus*] **1** : a native or resident of Rome **2** : ROMAN CATHOLIC — often taken to be offensive **3** *not cap* : roman letters or type
[2]**Roman** *adj* **1** : of or relating to Rome or the people of Rome; *specif* : characteristic of the ancient Romans <~ fortitude> **2** : LATIN **3** *not cap* : UPRIGHT — used of numbers and letters whose capital forms are modeled on ancient Roman inscriptions **4** : of or relating to the see of Rome or the Roman Catholic Church **5** : having a semicircular intrados <~ arch> **6** : having a prominent slightly aquiline bridge <~ nose>
ro·man à clef \rō-ˌmäⁿ-(ⁿ)n-(ˌ)ä-'klā\ *n, pl* **romans à clef** \-ˌmäⁿ-(ˌ)zä-\ [F, lit., novel with a key] : a novel in which real persons or actual events figure under disguise
Roman calendar *n* : a calendar of ancient Rome preceding the Julian calendar and having 12 months with the days of the month reckoned backward from fixed points — compare CALENDS
Roman candle *n* : a cylindrical firework that discharges at intervals balls or stars of fire
[1]**Roman Catholic** *n* : a member of the Roman Catholic Church
[2]**Roman Catholic** *adj* : of or relating to the body of Christians being in communion with the pope and having a hierarchy of priests and bishops under the pope, a liturgy centered in the Mass, and a body of dogma formulated by the church as the infallible interpreter of revealed truth; *specif* : of or relating to the Western rite of this church marked by a Latin liturgy — **Roman Catholicism** *n*
[1]**ro·mance** \rō-'man(t)s, rə-; 'rō-ˌ\ *n* [ME *romauns,* fr. OF *romans* French, something written in French, fr. L *romanice* in the Roman manner, fr. *romanicus* Roman, fr. *Romanus*] **1 a** (1) : a medieval tale in verse or prose based on legend, chivalric love and adventure, or the supernatural (2) : a prose narrative treating imaginary characters involved in events remote in time or place and usu. heroic, adventurous, or mysterious (3) : a love story **b** : a class of such literature **2** : something that lacks basis in fact **3** : an emotional attraction or aura belonging to an esp. heroic era, adventure, or calling **4** : LOVE AFFAIR **5** *cap* : the Romance languages
[2]**romance** *vb* **ro·manced; ro·manc·ing** *vi* **1** : to exaggerate or invent detail or incident **2** : to entertain romantic thoughts or ideas ~ *vt* : to carry on a love affair with
[3]**romance** *n* : a short instrumental piece in ballad style
Ro·mance \rō-'man(t)s, rə-; 'rō-ˌ\ *adj* : of, relating to, or constituting the languages developed from Latin — see INDO-EUROPEAN LANGUAGES table
ro·manc·er \-ər\ *n* **1** : a writer of romance **2** : one that romances
Roman collar *n* : CLERICAL COLLAR
Ro·man·esque \ˌrō-mə-'nesk\ *adj* : of or relating to a style of architecture developed in Italy and western Europe between the Roman and the Gothic styles and characterized in its development after 1000 by the use of the round arch and vault, substitution of piers for columns, decorative use of arcades, and profuse ornament — **Romanesque** *n*
ro·man-fleuve \rō-ˌmäⁿ-'flœv, -'flə(r)v\ *n, pl* **ro·mans-fleuves** \-ˌmäⁿ-'flœv, 'flə(r)v(z)\ [F, lit., river novel] : a distinctively French novel in the form of a long usu. easygoing chronicle of a social group (as a family or a community)
Roman holiday *n* **1** : a time of debauchery or of sadistic enjoyment **2** : a violent, destructive, or tumultuous disturbance : RIOT
Ro·ma·nian \ru̇-'mā-nē-ən, rō-, -nyən\ *var of* RUMANIAN
Ro·man·ic \rō-'man-ik\ *adj* : ROMANCE — **Romanic** *n*
Ro·man·ism \'rō-mə-ˌniz-əm\ *n* : ROMAN CATHOLICISM — often taken to be offensive
Ro·man·ist \-nəst\ *n* **1** : ROMAN CATHOLIC — often taken to be offensive **2** : a specialist in the language, culture, or law of ancient Rome — **Romanist** *or* **Ro·man·is·tic** \ˌrō-mə-'nis-tik\ *adj*
ro·man·ize \'rō-mə-ˌnīz\ *vt* **-ized; -iz·ing** **1** *often cap* : to make Roman : LATINIZE **2** : to write or print (as a language) in the roman alphabet <~ Chinese> — **ro·man·iza·tion** \ˌrō-mə-nə-'zā-shən\ *n, often cap*
roman law *n, often cap R* : the legal system of the ancient Romans that includes written and unwritten law, is based on the traditional law and the legislation of the city of Rome, and in form comprises legislation of the assemblies, resolves of the senate, enactments of the emperors, edicts of the praetors, writings of the jurisconsults, and the codes of the later emperors
Roman numeral *n* : a numeral in a system of notation that is based on the ancient Roman system — see NUMBER table
Ro·ma·no \rə-'män-(ˌ)ō, rō-\ *n* [It, Roman, fr. L *Romanus*] : a hard Italian cheese that is sharper than Parmesan
Ro·mans \'rō-mənz\ *n pl but sing in constr* : a letter on doctrine written by St. Paul to the Christians of Rome and included as a book in the New Testament — see BIBLE table
Ro·mansh *or* **Ro·mansch** \rō-'mänch, -'manch\ *n* [Romansh *romonsch*] : the Rhaeto-Romanic dialects spoken in the Grisons, Switzerland, and in adjacent parts of Italy
[1]**ro·man·tic** \rō-'mant-ik, rə-\ *adj* [F *romantique,* fr. obs. *romant* romance, fr. OF *romans*] **1** : consisting of or resembling a romance **2** : having no basis in fact : IMAGINARY **3** : impractical in conception or plan : VISIONARY **4 a** : marked by the imaginative or emotional appeal of the heroic, adventurous, remote, mysterious, or idealized **b** *often cap* : of, relating to, or having the characteristics of romanticism **c** : of or relating to music of the 19th century characterized by an emphasis on subjective emotional qualities and freedom of form; *also* : of or relating to a composer of this music **5 a** : having an inclination for romance **b** : ARDENT, FERVENT; *esp* : marked by or constituting passionate love **6** : of, relating to, or constituting the part of the hero esp. in a light comedy — **ro·man·ti·cal·ly** \-i-k(ə-)lē\ *adv*
[2]**romantic** *n* **1** : a romantic person, trait, or component **2** *cap* : a romantic writer, artist, or composer
ro·man·ti·cism \rō-'mant-ə-ˌsiz-əm, rə-\ *n* **1** : the quality or state of being romantic **2** *often cap* **a** (1) : a literary, artistic, and philosophical movement originating in the 18th century, characterized chiefly by a reaction against neoclassicism and an emphasis on the imagination and emotions, and marked esp. in English literature by sensibility and the use of autobiographical material, an exaltation of the primitive and the common man, an appreciation of external nature, an interest in the remote, a predilection for melancholy, and the use in poetry of older verse forms (2) : an aspect of romanticism **b** : adherence to or practice of romantic doctrine or assumptions — **ro·man·ti·cist** \-səst\ *n, often cap*
ro·man·ti·cize \-'mant-ə-ˌsīz\ *vb* **-cized; -ciz·ing** *vt* : to make romantic ~ *vi* **1** : to hold romantic ideas **2** : to present details, incidents, or people in a romantic way — **ro·man·ti·ci·za·tion** \-ˌmant-ə-sə-'zā-shən\ *n*
Ro·ma·ny \'räm-ə-nē, 'rō-mə-\ *n, pl* **Romanies** [Romany *romani,* adj., gypsy, fr. *rom* gypsy man, fr. Skt *ḍomba* man of a low caste of musicians] **1** : GYPSY 1 **2** : the Indic language of the Gypsies — **Romany** *adj*
ro·maunt \rō-'mȯnt, -'mänt\ *n* [ME, fr. MF *romant*] *archaic* : ROMANCE 1a(1)
rom·el·dale \'räm-əl-ˌdāl\ *n, often cap* [blend of *Romney, Rambouillet,* and *Corriedale*] : any of an American breed of utility sheep yielding a heavy fleece of fine wool and producing a quickly maturing high-grade market lamb
[1]**Ro·meo** \'rō-mē-ˌō, *in Shak also* 'rōm-(ˌ)yō\ *n, pl* **Ro·me·os** **1** : the hero of Shakespeare's *Romeo and Juliet* who dies for love of Juliet **2** : a male lover
[2]**Romeo** — a communications code word for the letter *r*
Rom·ish \'rō-mish\ *adj* : Roman Catholic — usu. used disparagingly — **Rom·ish·ly** *adv* — **Rom·ish·ness** *n*
Rom·ney Marsh \ˌräm-nē-, ˌrəm-\ *n* [*Romney Marsh,* pasture tract in England] : any of a British breed of hardy long-wooled mutton-type sheep esp. adapted to damp or marshy regions — called also *Romney*
[1]**romp** \'rämp, 'rȯmp\ *n* [partly alter. of [2]*ramp;* partly alter. of *ramp* (bold woman)] **1** : one that romps; *esp* : a romping girl or woman **2** : boisterous play : FROLIC **3** : an easy winning pace
[2]**romp** *vi* [alter. of [1]*ramp*] **1** : to play in a boisterous manner **2** : to proceed in a gay or animated manner **3** : to win easily
romp·er \'räm-pər, 'rȯm-\ *n* **1** : one that romps **2** : a one-piece garment esp. for children with the lower part shaped like bloomers — usu. used in pl.
Rom·u·lus \'räm-yə-ləs\ *n* [L] : a son of Mars and legendary founder of Rome
ron·deau \'rän-(ˌ)dō, rän-'dō\ *n, pl* **ron·deaux** \-(ˌ)dōz, -'dōz\ [MF *rondel, rondeau*] **1 a** : a fixed form of verse running on two rhymes and consisting usu. of 15 lines of 8 or 10 syllables divided into three stanzas in which the opening words of the first line of the first stanza serve as the refrain of the second and third stanzas — called also *rondel* **b** : a poem in this form **2** : a monophonic trouvère song with a 2-part refrain

rondeau re·dou·blé \-rə-ˌdü-ˈblā\ *n, pl* **rondeaux redoublés** *same*\ [F, lit., double rondeau] **1 :** a fixed form of verse running on two alternating rhymes that usu. consists of five quatrains in which the lines of the first quatrain are used consecutively to end each of the remaining four quatrains which are in turn sometimes followed by an envoi of four lines that terminates with the opening words of the poem **2 :** a poem in the rondeau redoublé form

ron·del \ˈrän-dᵊl, rän-ˈdel\ *or* **ron·delle** \rän-ˈdel\ *n* [ME, fr. OF, lit., small circle — more at ROUNDEL] **1** *usu rondelle* **:** a circular object **2 a** *usu rondel* **:** a fixed form of verse running on two rhymes and consisting usu. of 14 lines of 8 or 10 syllables divided into three stanzas in which the first two lines of the first stanza serve as the refrain of the second and third stanzas **b :** a poem in this form **c :** RONDEAU 1

ron·de·let \ˌrän-də-ˈlet, -ˈlā\ *n* **:** a modified rondeau running on two rhymes and consisting usu. of seven lines in which the first line of four syllables is repeated as the third line and as the final line or refrain and the remaining lines are made up of eight syllables each

ron·do \ˈrän-(ˌ)dō, rän-ˈdō\ *n, pl* **rondos** [It *rondò,* fr. MF *rondeau*] **1 :** an instrumental composition typically with a refrain recurring four times in the tonic and with three couplets in contrasting keys **2 :** the musical form of a rondo used esp. for a movement in a concerto or sonata

ron·dure \ˈrän-jər, -(ˌ)d(y)ù(ə)r\ *n* [F *rondeur* roundness, fr. MF, fr. *rond* round, fr. OF *roont* — more at ROUND] **1 :** ROUND 1a **2 :** gracefully rounded curvature

ron·nel \ˈrän-ᵊl\ *n* [fr. *Ronnel,* a trademark]**:** an organophosphate $C_8H_8Cl_3O_3PS$ that is used esp. as a systemic insecticide to protect cattle from pests

röntgen *var of* ROENTGEN

ron·yon \ˈrən-yən, ˈrän-\ *n* [perh. modif. of F *rogne* scab] *obs* **:** a mangy or scabby creature

rood \ˈrüd\ *n* [ME, fr. OE *rōd* rod, rood; akin to OHG *ruota* rod, OSlav *ratište* shaft of a lance] **1 :** a cross or crucifix symbolizing the cross on which Jesus Christ died; *specif* **:** a large crucifix on a beam or screen at the entrance of the chancel of a medieval church **2 a :** any of various units of land area; *esp* **:** a British unit equal to ¼ acre **b :** any of various units of length; *esp* **:** a British unit equal to seven or eight yards or sometimes a rod

[1]**roof** \ˈrüf, ˈrùf\ *n, pl* **roofs** \ˈrüfs, ˈrùfs *also* ˈrüvz, ˈrùvz\ [ME, fr. OE *hrōf;* akin to ON *hrōf* roof of a boathouse, OSlav *stropŭ* roof] **1 a :** the cover of a building **b :** DWELLING, HOME **c :** ROOFING **2 a (1) :** the highest point **:** SUMMIT **(2) :** CEILING 5 **b :** something resembling a roof in form or function **3 a :** the vaulted upper boundary of the mouth **b :** a covering structure of any of various parts of the body <~ of the skull> — **roofed** \ˈrüft, ˈrùft\ *adj* — **roof·less** \ˈrüf-ləs, ˈrùf-\ *adj* — **roof·like** \-ˌlīk\ *adj*

[2]**roof** *vt* **1 a :** to cover with or as if with a roof **b :** to provide (a roof) with a protective exterior **2 :** to constitute a roof over — **roof·er** *n*

roof garden *n* **:** a restaurant at the top of a building usu. with facilities for music and dancing

roof·ing *n* **:** material for a roof

roof·line \ˈrüf-ˌlīn, ˈrùf-\ *n* **:** the profile of a roof (as of a house)

[1]**roof·top** \-ˌtäp\ *n* **:** ROOF; *esp* **:** the outer surface of a usu. flat roof <sunning themselves on the ~>

[2]**rooftop** *adj* **:** situated on a rooftop

roof·tree \ˈrüf-ˌtrē, ˈrùf-\ *n* **:** RIDGEPOLE

[1]**rook** \ˈrùk\ *n* [ME, fr. OE *hrōc;* akin to OE *hræfn* raven — more at RAVEN]**:** a common Old World gregarious bird (*Corvus frugilegus*) about the size and color of the related American crow

[2]**rook** *vt* **:** to defraud by cheating or swindling

[3]**rook** *n* [ME *rok,* fr. MF *roc,* fr. Ar *rukhkh,* fr. Per]**:** either of two pieces of the same color in a set of chessmen having the power to move along the ranks or files across any number of unoccupied squares — called also *castle*

rook·ery \ˈrùk-ə-rē\ *n, pl* **-er·ies 1 a :** the nests or breeding place of a colony of rooks; *also* **:** a colony of rooks **b :** a breeding ground or haunt of gregarious birds or mammals; *also* **:** a colony of such birds or mammals **2 :** a crowded dilapidated tenement or group of dwellings **3 :** a place teeming with like individuals

rook·ie \ˈrùk-ē\ *n* [perh. alter. of *recruit*] **1 :** RECRUIT; *also* **:** NOVICE **2 :** one who is in his first year of participation in a major professional sport

rooky \ˈrùk-ē\ *adj* **:** full of or containing rooks

[1]**room** \ˈrüm, ˈrùm\ *n* [ME, fr. OE *rūm;* akin to OHG *rūm* room, L *rur-, rus* open land] **1 :** an extent of space occupied by or sufficient or available for something <houseplants that take up very little ~> <in the country where there is ~ to run and play> <make ~ for me to squeeze by> **2 a** *obs* **:** a place or station assigned or in a hierarchy **:** POST **b :** a place or station formerly occupied by another **3 a :** a partitioned part of the inside of a building; *esp* **:** such a part used as a lodging **b :** the people in a room **4 :** a suitable or fit occasion **:** OPPORTUNITY <left no ~ for doubt>

[2]**room** *vi* **:** to occupy a room ~ *vt* **:** to accommodate with lodgings

room and board *n* **:** lodging and food usu. specifically earned or furnished

room·er \ˈrü-mər, ˈrùm-ər\ *n* **:** LODGER

room·ette \rü-ˈmet, rùm-ˈet\ *n* **1 :** a small private single room on a railroad sleeping car **2 :** a small room (as in a dormitory)

room·ful \ˈrüm-ˌfùl, ˈrùm-\ *n* **:** as much or as many as a room will hold; *also* **:** the persons or objects in a room

rooming house *n* **:** LODGING HOUSE

room·mate \ˈrüm-ˌmāt, ˈrùm-\ *n* **:** one of two or more persons occupying the same room

roomy \ˈrü-mē, ˈrùm-ē\ *adj* **room·i·er; -est 1 :** having ample room **:** SPACIOUS **2** *of a female mammal* **:** having a large or well-proportioned body suited for breeding — **room·i·ness** *n*

roor·back \ˈrù(ə)r-ˌbak\ *n* [fr. an attack on James K. Polk in 1844 purporting to quote from an invented book by a Baron von *Roorback*]**:** a defamatory falsehood published for political effect

roose \ˈrüz\ *vt* [ME *rusen,* fr. ON *hrōsa*] *chiefly dial* **:** PRAISE

[1]**roost** \ˈrüst\ *n* [ME, fr. OE *hrōst;* akin to MD *roest* roost, OSlav *krada* pile of wood] **1 a :** a support on which birds rest **b :** a place where birds customarily roost **2 :** a group of birds (as fowl) roosting together

[2]**roost** *vi* **1 :** to settle down for rest or sleep **:** PERCH **2 :** to settle oneself as if on a roost ~ *vt* **:** to supply a roost for or put to roost

roost·er \ˈrüs-tər *also* ˈrùs-\ *n* **1 a :** an adult male domestic fowl **:** COCK **b :** an adult male of various birds other than the domestic fowl **2 :** a cocky or vain person

[1]**root** \ˈrüt, ˈrùt\ *n, often attrib* [ME, fr. OE *rōt,* fr. ON; akin to OE *wyrt* root, L *radix,* Gk *rhiza*] **1 a :** the usu. underground part of a seed plant body that originates usu. from the hypocotyl, functions as an organ of absorption, aeration, and food storage or as a means of anchorage and support, and differs from a stem esp. in lacking nodes, buds, and leaves **b :** any subterranean plant part (as a true root or a bulb, tuber, rootstock, or other modified stem) esp. when fleshy and edible **2 a :** the part of a tooth within the socket — see TOOTH illustration **b :** the enlarged basal part of a hair within the skin **c :** the proximal end of a nerve **d :** the part of an organ or physical structure by which it is attached to the body <the ~ of the tongue> **3 a :** something that is an origin or source (as of a condition or quality) <the love of money is the ~ of all evil —1 Tim 6:10 (AV)> **b :** one or more progenitors of a group of descendants **c :** an underlying support **:** BASIS **d :** the essential core **:** HEART **e :** close relationship with an environment **:** TIE — usu. used in pl. **4 a :** a quantity taken an indicated number of times as an equal factor <2 is a fourth ~ of 16> **b :** a number that reduces an equation to an identity when it is substituted for one variable **5 a :** the lower part **:** BASE **b :** the part by which an object is attached to something else **6 :** the simple element inferred as the basis from which a word is derived by phonetic change or by extension (as composition or the addition of an affix or inflectional ending) **7 :** the tone from whose overtones a chord is composed **:** the lowest tone of a chord in normal position ***syn*** see ORIGIN — **root·ed** \-əd\ *adj* — **root·like** \-ˌlīk\ *adj*

[2]**root** *vt* **1 a :** to furnish with or enable to develop roots **b :** to fix or implant by or as if by roots **2 :** to remove altogether often by force <~ out dissenters> ~ *vi* **1 :** to grow roots or take root **2 :** to have an origin or base

[3]**root** *vb* [ME *wroten,* fr. OE *wrōtan;* akin to OHG *ruozzan* to root] *vi* **1 :** to turn up or dig in the earth with the snout **:** GRUB **2 :** to poke or dig about ~ *vt* **:** to turn over, dig up, or discover and bring to light — usu. used with *out*

[4]**root** \ˈrüt *also* ˈrùt\ *vi* [perh. alter. of [2]*rout*] **1 :** to noisily applaud or encourage a contestant or team **:** CHEER **2 :** to wish the success of or lend support to someone or something — **root·er** *n*

root·age \ˈrüt-ij, ˈrùt-\ *n* **1 :** a developed system of roots **2 :** ROOT 3a

root beer *n* **:** a sweetened effervescent beverage flavored with extracts of roots and herbs

root cap *n* **:** a protective cap of parenchyma cells that covers the terminal meristem in most root tips

root cellar *n* **:** a pit used for the storage esp. of root crops

root crop *n* **:** a crop (as turnips or sweet potatoes) grown for its enlarged roots

root·ed·ness \ˈrüt-əd-nəs, ˈrùt-\ *n* **:** the quality or state of having roots

root graft *n* **1 :** a plant graft in which the stock is a root or piece of a root **2 :** a natural anastomosis between roots of compatible plants

root hair *n* **:** a filamentous extension of an epidermal cell near the tip of a rootlet that functions in absorption of water and minerals

root hairs on bean rootlet

root·hold \ˈrüt-ˌhōld, ˈrùt-\ *n* **1 :** the anchorage of a plant to soil through the growing and spreading of roots **2 :** a place where plants may obtain a roothold

root knot *n* **:** a plant disease caused by nematodes that produce characteristic enlargements on the roots and stunt the growth of the plant

root–knot nematode *n* **:** any of several small plant-parasitic nematodes (genus *Meloidogyne*) that cause root knot

root·less \ˈrüt-ləs, ˈrùt-\ *adj* **:** having no roots <~ nomads> — **root·less·ness** *n*

root·let \-lət\ *n* **:** a small root

root–mean–square *n* **:** the square root of the arithmetic mean of the squares of a set of numbers

root pressure *n* **:** the chiefly osmotic pressure by which water rises into the stems of plants from the roots

root rot *n* **:** a plant disease characterized by a decay of the roots

root·stalk \ˈrüt-ˌstȯk, ˈrùt-\ *n* **:** RHIZOME

root·stock \-ˌstäk\ *n* **1 :** a rhizomatous underground part of a plant **2 :** a stock for grafting consisting of a root or a piece of root; *broadly* **:** STOCK

rooty \ˈrüt-ē, ˈrùt-\ *adj* **:** full or consisting of roots <~ soil>

ROP *abbr* **1** record of production **2** run-of-paper

[1]**rope** \ˈrōp\ *n* [ME, fr. OE *rāp;* akin to OHG *reif* hoop] **1 a :** a large stout cord of strands of fibers or wire twisted or braided together **b :** a long slender strip of material used as rope <rawhide ~> **c :** a hangman's noose **2 :** a row or string consisting of things united by or as if by braiding, twining, or threading **3** *pl* **:** special techniques or procedures <show him the ~*s*>

[2]**rope** *vb* **roped; rop·ing** *vt* **1 a :** to bind, fasten, or tie with a rope or cord **b :** to partition, separate, or divide by a rope <~ off the street> **c :** LASSO **2 :** to draw as if with a rope **:** LURE ~ *vi* **:** to take the form of or twist in the manner of rope — **rop·er** *n*

rope·danc·er \'rōp-ˌdan(t)-sər\ *n* **:** one that dances, walks, or performs acrobatic feats on a rope high in the air — **rope·danc·ing** \-siŋ\ *n*

rop·ery \'rō-p(ə-)rē\ *n* [prob. fr. the thought that the perpetrator deserved the gallows] *archaic* **:** roguish tricks or banter

rope·walk \'rōp-ˌwȯk\ *n* **:** a long covered walk, building, or room where ropes are manufactured

rope·walk·er \-ˌwȯ-kər\ *n* **:** an acrobat that walks on a rope high in the air

rope·way \-ˌwā\ *n* **1 :** a fixed cable or a pair of fixed cables between supporting towers serving as a track for suspended passenger or freight carriers **2 :** an endless aerial cable moved by a stationary engine and used to transport freight (as logs and ore)

ropy \'rō-pē\ *adj* **rop·i·er; -est 1 a :** capable of being drawn into a thread **:** VISCOUS **b :** having a gelatinous or slimy quality from bacterial or fungal contamination <~ milk> <~ flour> **2 a :** resembling rope **b :** MUSCULAR, SINEWY — **rop·i·ness** *n*

roque \'rōk\ *n* [alter. of *croquet*] **:** croquet played on a hard-surfaced court with a raised border

Roque·fort \'rōk-fərt\ *trademark* — used for a cheese made of ewes' milk and ripened in caves

ro·que·laure \ˌrō-kə-'lō(ə)r, ˌräk-ə-, -'lȯ(ə)r\ *n* [F, fr. the Duc de *Roquelaure* †1738 F marshal] **:** a knee-length cloak worn esp. in the 18th and 19th centuries

ror·qual \'rȯ(ə)r-kwəl, -ˌkwȯl\ *n* [F, fr. Norw *røhval,* fr. ON *reytharhvalr,* fr. *reythr* rorqual + *hvalr* whale] **:** a large whalebone whale (genus *Balaenoptera*) having the skin of the throat marked with deep longitudinal furrows

Ror·schach \'rȯ(ə)r-ˌshäk\ *adj* **:** of, relating to, used in connection with, or resulting from the Rorschach test

Rorschach test *n* [Hermann *Rorschach* †1922 Swiss psychiatrist] **:** a personality and intelligence test in which a subject interprets inkblot designs in terms that reveal intellectual and emotional factors — called also *Rorschach inkblot test*

Ros *or* **Rosc** *abbr* Roscommon

ro·sa·ceous \rō-'zā-shəs\ *adj* [deriv. of L *rosa*] **1 :** of or relating to the rose family **2 :** of, relating to, or resembling a rose esp. in having a 5-petaled regular corolla

ros·an·i·line \rō-'zan-ᵊl-ən\ *n* [L *rosa* rose + ISV *aniline*] **1 :** a white crystalline base $C_{20}H_{21}N_3O$ that is the parent of many dyes **2 :** FUCHSINE

ro·sar·i·an \rō-'zar-ē-ən, -'zer-\ *n* **:** a cultivator of roses

ro·sa·ry \'rōz-(ə-)rē\ *n, pl* **-ries** [ML *rosarium,* fr. L, rose garden, fr. neut. of *rosarius* of roses, fr. *rosa* rose] **1 :** a string of beads used in counting prayers esp. of the Roman Catholic rosary **2** *often cap* **:** a Roman Catholic devotion consisting of meditation on usu. five sacred mysteries during recitation of five decades of Hail Marys of which each begins with an Our Father and ends with a Gloria

rosary pea *n* **1 :** an East Indian leguminous twining herb (*Abrus precatorius*) that bears jequirity beans and has a root used as a substitute for licorice — called also *Indian licorice, jequirity bean* **2 :** JEQUIRITY BEAN 1

ros·coe \'räs-(ˌ)kō\ *n* [prob. fr. the name *Roscoe*] *slang* **:** PISTOL

[1]**rose** *past of* RISE

[2]**rose** \'rōz\ *n* [ME, fr. OE, fr. L *rosa*] **1 a :** any of a genus (*Rosa* of the family Rosaceae, the rose family) of usu. prickly shrubs with pinnate leaves and showy flowers having five petals in the wild state but being often double or semidouble under cultivation **b :** the flower of a rose **2 :** something resembling a rose in form: as **a** (1) **:** COMPASS CARD (2) **:** a circular card with radiating lines used in other instruments **b :** a rosette esp. on a shoe **c** (1) **:** a form in which gems (as diamonds) are cut that usu. has a flat circular base and facets in two ranges rising to a point (2) **:** a gem with a rose cut **3 :** a variable color averaging a moderate purplish red **4 :** a plane curve which consists of three or more loops meeting at the origin and whose equation in polar coordinates is of the form $\rho = a \sin n\theta$ or $\rho = a \cos n\theta$ where *n* is an integer greater than 1 — **rose·like** \-ˌlīk\ *adj* — **under the rose :** in secret or private **:** sub rosa

[3]**rose** *adj* **1 a :** of or relating to a rose **b :** containing or used for roses **c :** flavored, scented, or colored with or like roses **2 :** of the color rose

ro·sé \rō-'zā\ *n* [F] **:** a light pink table wine made from red grapes by removing the skins after fermentation has begun

ro·se·ate \'rō-zē-ət, -zē-ˌāt\ *adj* [L *roseus* rosy, fr. *rosa*] **1 :** resembling a rose esp. in color **2 :** overly optimistic **:** viewed favorably — **ro·se·ate·ly** *adv*

roseate spoonbill *n* **:** a spoonbill (*Ajaia ajaja*) that is found from the southern U.S. to Patagonia and has chiefly pink plumage

rose·bay \'rōz-ˌbā\ *n* **1 :** OLEANDER **2 :** RHODODENDRON; *esp* **:** GREAT LAUREL **3 :** FIREWEED b

rose–breast·ed grosbeak \ˌrōz-ˌbres-təd-\ *n* **:** a grosbeak (*Pheucticus ludovicianus*) of eastern No. America that in the male is chiefly black and white with a rose-red breast and in the female is grayish brown with a streaked breast

rose·bush \'rōz-ˌbu̇sh\ *n* **:** a shrubby rose

rose chafer *n* **:** a common No. American beetle (*Macrodactylus subspinosus*) that feeds on plant roots as a larva and on leaves and flowers (as of rose or grapevines) as an adult — called also *rose bug*

rose–col·ored \'rōz-ˌkəl-ərd\ *adj* **1 :** having a rose color **2 :** seeing or seen in a promising light **:** OPTIMISTIC

rose–colored glasses *n pl* **:** favorably disposed opinions **:** optimistic eyes <views the world through *rose-colored glasses*>

rose comb *n* **:** a flat broad comb of a domestic fowl having the upper surface studded with small tubercles and terminating posteriorly in a fleshy spike

rose daphne *n* **:** a low evergreen shrub (*Daphne cneorum*) with trailing pubescent branches and fragrant rose-pink flowers

rose fever *n* **:** hay fever occurring in the spring or early summer — called also *rose cold*

rose·fish \'rōz-ˌfish\ *n* **:** REDFISH a(1)

rose geranium *n* **:** any of several pelargoniums grown for their fragrant 3- to 5-lobed leaves and small pink flowers

ro·se·ma·ling \'rō-zə-ˌmäl-iŋ, -sə-\ *n* [Norw, fr. *rose* rose + *maling* painting] **:** painted or sometimes carved decoration (as on furniture, walls, or wooden dinnerware) in Scandinavian peasant style that consists esp. of floral designs and inscriptions

rose mallow *n* **1 :** any of several plants (genus *Hibiscus*) with large rose-colored flowers; *esp* **:** a showy plant (*H. moscheutos*) of the salt marshes of the eastern U.S. **2 :** HOLLYHOCK

rose·mary \'rōz-ˌmer-ē\ *n, pl* **-mar·ies** [ME *rosmarine,* fr. L *rosmarinus,* fr. *ror-, ros* dew + *marinus* of the sea; akin to ON *rās* race — more at RACE, MARINE] **1 :** a fragrant shrubby mint (*Rosmarinus officinalis*) of southern Europe and Asia Minor used in cookery and in perfumery **2 :** COSTMARY

rose of Jer·i·cho \-'jer-i-ˌkō\ [ME, fr. *Jericho,* ancient city in Palestine] **:** an Asiatic plant (*Anastatica hierochuntica*) that rolls up when dry and expands when moistened

rose of Shar·on \-'shar-ən, -'sher-\ [Plain of *Sharon,* Palestine] **1 :** a Eurasian St.-John's-wort (*Hypericum calycinum*) often cultivated for its large yellow flowers **2 :** a commonly cultivated Asiatic small shrubby tree (*Hibiscus syriacus*) having showy bell-shaped rose, purple, or white flowers

rose oil *n* **:** a fragrant essential oil obtained from roses and used chiefly in perfumery and in flavoring

ro·se·o·la \ˌrō-zē-'ō-lə, rō-'zē-ə-lə\ *n* [NL, fr. L *roseus* rosy, fr. *rosa* rose] **:** a rose-colored eruption in spots or a disease marked by such an eruption: as **a :** GERMAN MEASLES **b :** a mild disease of infants and children characterized by fever lasting three days followed by an eruption of rose-colored spots — **ro·se·o·lar** \-lər\ *adj*

roseola in·fan·tum \-in-'fant-əm\ *n* **:** ROSEOLA b

rose pink *n* **:** a variable color averaging a moderate pink

ros·ery \'rōz-(ə-)rē\ *n, pl* **-er·ies :** a place where roses are grown

rose slug *n* **:** the slimy green larva of either of two sawflies (*Claudius isomerus* and *Endelomyia aethiops*) that feed on the parenchyma of and skeletonize the leaves of roses

ro·set \'rō-zət\ *n* [alter. of ME *rosin*] *chiefly Scot* **:** RESIN

Ro·set·ta stone \rō-ˌzet-ə-\ *n* [*Rosetta,* Egypt] **:** a black basalt stone found in 1799 that bears an inscription in hieroglyphics, demotic characters, and Greek and is celebrated for having given the first clue to the decipherment of Egyptian hieroglyphics

ro·sette \rō-'zet\ *n* [F, lit., small rose, fr. OF, fr. *rose,* fr. L *rosa*] **1 :** an ornament usu. made of material gathered or pleated so as to resemble a rose and worn as a badge of office, as evidence of having won a decoration (as the Medal of Honor), or as trimming **2 :** a disk of foliage or a floral design usu. in relief used as a decorative motif **3 :** a structure or color marking on an animal suggestive of a rosette; *esp* **:** one of the groups of spots on a leopard **4 :** a cluster of leaves in crowded circles or spirals arising basally from a crown (as in the dandelion) or apically from an axis with greatly shortened internodes (as in many tropical palms)

rose·wa·ter \'rōz-ˌwȯt-ər, -ˌwät-\ *adj* **1 :** having the odor of rose water **2 :** affectedly nice or delicate

rose water *n* **:** a watery solution of the odoriferous constituents of the rose used as a perfume

rose window *n* **:** a circular window filled with tracery

rose window

rose·wood \'rōz-ˌwu̇d\ *n* **1 :** any of various tropical trees (as of the genus *Dalbergia*) yielding valuable cabinet woods of a dark red or purplish color streaked and variegated with black **2 :** the wood of a rosewood

Rosh Ha·sha·nah \ˌrōsh-(h)ə-'shō-nə, ˌräsh-, -'shän-ə\ *n* [LHeb *rōsh hashshānāh,* lit., beginning of the year] **:** the Jewish New Year observed on the first and by Orthodox and Conservative Jews also on the second of Tishri

Ro·si·cru·cian \ˌrō-zə-'krü-shən, ˌräz-ə-\ *n* [Christian *Rosenkreutz* (NL *Rosae Crucis*) reputed 15th cent. founder of the movement] **1 :** an adherent of a 17th and 18th century movement devoted to esoteric wisdom with emphasis on psychic and spiritual enlightenment **2 :** a member of one of several organizations held to be descended from the Rosicrucians — **Rosicrucian** *adj* — **Ro·si·cru·cian·ism** \-shə-ˌniz-əm\ *n*

ros·i·ly \'rō-zə-lē\ *adv* **1 :** with a rosy color or tinge **2 :** PLEASANTLY, CHEERFULLY

[1]**ros·in** \'räz-ᵊn, 'rȯz-, *dial* 'rō-zəm\ *n* [ME, modif. of MF *resine* resin] **:** a translucent amber-colored to almost black brittle friable resin that is obtained by chemical means from the oleoresin or dead wood of pine trees or from tall oil and used esp. in making varnish, paper size, soap, and soldering flux and in rosining violin bows

[2]**rosin** *vt* **ros·ined; ros·in·ing** \'räz-niŋ, 'rȯz-, -ᵊn-iŋ\ **:** to rub or treat (as the bow of a violin) with rosin

ros·in·ous \'räz-ᵊn-əs, 'räz-nəs, 'rȯz-\ *adj* **:** containing or resembling rosin

ros·in·weed \'räz-ᵊn-ˌwēd, 'rȯz-\ *n* **:** any of various American plants having resinous foliage or a resinous odor; *esp* **:** a coarse yellow-flowered composite herb (*Silphium laciniatum*)

Ross *abbr* Ross and Cromarty

ros·tel·lar \rä-'stel-ər\ *adj* **:** of, relating to, or having the form of a rostellum

ros·tel·late \'räs-tə-ˌlāt, rä-'stel-ət\ *adj* **:** having a rostellum

ros·tel·lum \rä-'stel-əm\ *n* [NL, fr. L, dim. of *rostrum* beak] **:** a small process resembling a beak **:** a diminutive rostrum; as **a :** the apex of the gynoecium of an orchid flower **b :** the sucking beak of an insect (as a louse or aphid) **c :** an anterior prolongation of the head of a tapeworm bearing hooks

ros·ter \'räs-tər *also* 'rȯs- *or* 'rōs-\ *n* [D *rooster,* lit., gridiron; fr. the parallel lines] **1 a :** a roll or list of personnel; *esp* **:** one that gives the order in which a duty is to be performed **b :** the persons listed on a roster **2 :** an itemized list

ros·trate \'räs-ˌtrāt, -trət *also* 'rȯs-\ *adj* **:** having a rostrum

ros·trum \'räs-trəm *also* 'rȯs-\ *n, pl* **rostrums** *or* **ros·tra** \-trə\ [L, beak, ship's beak, fr. *rodere* to gnaw — more at RAT] **1** [L *Rostra,* pl., a platform for speakers in the Roman Forum decorated with the beaks of captured ships, fr. pl. of *rostrum*] **a :** an ancient Roman platform for public orators **b :** a stage for public speaking **c :** a raised platform on a stage **2 :** the curved end of a ship's prow; *esp* **:** the beak of a war galley **3 :** a bodily part or process (as a snout or beak of an insect or a median projection of the carapace of a crustacean) suggesting a bird's bill — **ros·tral** \-trəl\ *adj*

ro·su·late \'räz(h)-ə-ˌlāt, 'rōz(h)-\ *adj* [LL *rosula*, dim. of L *rosa* rose] **:** arranged in the form of a rosette or in rosettes

rosy \'rō-zē\ *adj* **ros·i·er; -est** **1 a :** of the color rose **b :** having a rosy complexion **:** BLOOMING **c :** marked by blushes **2 :** characterized by or tending to promote optimism — **ros·i·ness** *n*

¹rot \'rät\ *vb* **rot·ted; rot·ting** [ME *roten*, fr. OE *rotian*; akin to OHG *rōzzēn* to rot, L *rudus* rubble — more at RUDE] *vi* **1 a :** to undergo decomposition from the action of bacteria or fungi **b :** to become unsound or weak (as from use or chemical action) **2 a :** to go to ruin **:** DETERIORATE **b :** to become morally corrupt **:** DEGENERATE ~ *vt* **:** to cause to decompose or deteriorate with rot **syn** see DECAY

²rot *n* **1 a :** the process of rotting **:** the state of being rotten **:** DECAY **b :** something rotten or rotting **2 a** *archaic* **:** a wasting putrescent disease **b :** any of several parasitic diseases esp. of sheep marked by necrosis and wasting **c :** plant disease marked by breakdown of tissues and caused esp. by fungi or bacteria **3 :** NONSENSE — often used interjectionally

³rot *abbr* rotating; rotation

ro·ta \'rōt-ə\ *n* [L, wheel — more at ROLL] **1** *chiefly Brit* **a :** a fixed order of rotation (as of persons or duties) **b :** a roll or list of persons **:** ROSTER **2** *cap* [ML, fr. L] **:** a tribunal of the papal curia exercising jurisdiction esp. in matrimonial cases appealed from diocesan courts

ro·ta·me·ter \'rōt-ə-ˌmēt-ər, rō-'tam-ət-\ *n* [L *rota* + E *-meter*] **:** a gauge that consists of a graduated glass tube containing a free float for measuring the flow of a fluid

Ro·tar·i·an \rō-'ter-ē-ən\ *n* [*Rotary* (*club*)] **:** a member of a major national and international service club

¹ro·ta·ry \'rōt-ə-rē\ *adj* [ML *rotarius*, fr. L *rota* wheel] **1 a :** turning on an axis like a wheel **b :** taking place about an axis <~ motion> **2 :** having an important part that turns on an axis <~ cutter> **3 :** characterized by rotation **4 :** of, relating to, or being a press in which paper is printed by rotation in contact with a curved printing surface attached to a cylinder

²rotary *n, pl* **-ries** **1 :** a rotary machine **2 :** a road junction formed around a central circle about which traffic moves in one direction only — called also *circle, traffic circle*

rotary cultivator *n* **:** an implement having blades or claws that revolve rapidly and till or stir the soil

rotary engine *n* **1 :** any of various engines (as a turbine) in which power is applied to vanes or similar parts constrained to move in a circular path **2 :** a radial engine in which the cylinders revolve about a stationary crankshaft

rotary plow *n* **1 :** a plow having a rotating propeller-shaped element for throwing snow aside **2 :** ROTARY CULTIVATOR

rotary-wing aircraft *n* **:** ROTORCRAFT

¹ro·tate \'rō-ˌtat\ *adj* [L *rota*] **:** having the parts flat and spreading or radiating like the spokes of a wheel <~ blue flowers>

²ro·tate \'rō-ˌtāt, *esp Brit* rō-'\ *vb* **ro·tat·ed; ro·tat·ing** [L *rotatus*, pp. of *rotare*, fr. *rota* wheel — more at ROLL] *vi* **1 :** to turn about an axis or a center **:** REVOLVE; *specif* **:** to move in such a way that all particles follow circles with a common angular velocity about a common axis **2 a :** to perform an act, function, or operation in turn **b :** to pass or alternate in a series ~ *vt* **1 :** to cause to turn about an axis or a center **:** REVOLVE **2 :** to cause to grow in rotation <~ crops> **3 :** to cause to pass or act in a series **:** ALTERNATE **4 :** to exchange (individuals or units) with other personnel — **ro·tat·able** \'rō-ˌtāt-ə-bəl *also* rō-'\ *adj*

ro·ta·tion \rō-'tā-shən\ *n* **1 a (1) :** the action or process of rotating on or as if on an axis or center **(2) :** the act or an instance of rotating something **b :** one complete turn **:** the angular displacement required to return a rotating body or figure to its original orientation **2 a :** return or succession in a series <~ of the seasons> **b :** the growing of different crops in succession in one field usu. in a regular sequence **3 :** the turning of a body part about its long axis as if on a pivot **4 :** a game of pool in which all 15 object balls are shot in numerical order — **ro·ta·tion·al** \-shnəl, -shən-ᵊl\ *adj*

ro·ta·tive \'rō-ˌtāt-iv *also* rō-'\ *adj* **1 :** turning like a wheel **:** ROTARY **2 :** relating to, occurring in, or characterized by rotation — **ro·ta·tive·ly** *adv*

ro·ta·tor \'rō-ˌtāt-ər *also* rō-'\ *n* **:** one that rotates or causes rotation: as **a :** a muscle that partially rotates a part on its axis **b :** a device for rotating a directional antenna **c :** a rotating planet or galaxy

ro·ta·to·ry \'rōt-ə-ˌtōr-ē, -ˌtòr-, *Brit* -t(ə-)ri *also* rō-'tā-tə-ri\ *adj* **1 :** of, relating to, or producing rotation **2 :** occurring in rotation

ROTC *abbr* Reserve Officers' Training Corps

¹rote \'rōt\ *n* [ME, fr. OF, of Gmc origin; akin to OHG *hruozza* crowd] **:** ³CROWD 1

²rote *n* [ME] **1 :** the use of memory usu. with little intelligence <learn by ~> **2 :** routine or repetition carried out mechanically or unthinkingly <a joyless sense of order, ~, and commercial hustle —L. L. King>

³rote *n* [perh. of Scand origin; akin to ON *rauta* to roar — more at ROUT] **:** the noise of surf on the shore

ro·te·none \'rōt-ᵊn-ˌōn\ *n* [ISV, fr. Jap *roten* derris plant] **:** a crystalline insecticide $C_{23}H_{22}O_6$ that is of low toxicity for warm-blooded animals and is used esp. in home gardens

rot·gut \'rät-ˌgət\ *n* **:** bad liquor

ro·ti·fer \'rōt-ə-fər\ *n* [deriv. of L *rota* + *-fer*] **:** any of a class (Rotifera) of minute usu. microscopic but many-celled aquatic invertebrate animals having the anterior end modified into a retractile disk bearing circles of strong cilia that often give the appearance of rapidly revolving wheels

ro·tis·ser·ie \rō-'tis-(ə-)rē\ *n* [F *rôtisserie*, fr. MF *rostisserie*, fr. *rostir* to roast — more at ROAST] **1 :** a restaurant specializing in broiled and barbecued meats **2 :** an appliance fitted with a spit on which food is rotated before or over a source of heat

rotifer

rotl \'rät-ᵊl\ *n* [Ar *raṭl*] **:** any of various units of weight of Mediterranean and Near Eastern countries ranging from slightly less than one pound to more than six pounds

ro·to \'rōt-(ˌ)ō\ *n, pl* **rotos** **:** ROTOGRAVURE

ro·to·gra·vure \ˌrōt-ə-grə-'vyu̇(ə)r\ *n* [L *rota* + E *-o-* + *gravure*] **1 a :** a photogravure process in which the impression is produced by a rotary press **b :** a print made by rotogravure **2 :** a section of a newspaper devoted to rotogravure pictures

ro·tor \'rōt-ər\ *n* [contr. of *rotator*] **1 :** a part that revolves in a stationary part; *esp* **:** the rotating member of an electrical machine **2 :** a revolving vertical cylinder of a rotor ship **3 :** a complete system of more or less horizontal blades that supplies all or a major part of the force supporting an aircraft in flight

ro·tor·craft \-ˌkraft\ *n* **:** an aircraft (as a helicopter) supported in flight partially or wholly by rotating airfoils

rotor ship *n* **:** a ship propelled by the pressure and suction of the wind acting on one or more revolving vertical cylinders

ro·to·till \'rōt-ə-ˌtil\ *vt* [back-formation fr. *Rototiller*] **:** to stir with a rotary cultivator

Ro·to·till·er \-ˌtil-ər\ *trademark* — used for a rotary cultivator

rot·ten \'rät-ᵊn\ *adj* [ME *roten*, fr. ON *rotinn*; akin to OE *rotian* to rot] **1 :** having rotted **:** PUTRID **2 :** morally corrupt **3 :** extremely unpleasant or inferior <it was a ~ show —M. J. Arlen> **4 :** marked by weakness or unsoundness <feeling ~> — **rot·ten·ly** *adv* — **rot·ten·ness** \-ᵊn-(n)əs\ *n*

rotten borough *n* **:** an election district that has many fewer inhabitants than other election districts with the same voting power

rot·ten·stone \'rät-ᵊn-ˌstōn\ *n* **:** a decomposed siliceous limestone used for polishing

rot·ter \'rät-ər\ *n* **:** a thoroughly objectionable person

rott·wei·ler \'rät-ˌwī-lər, 'ròt-ˌvī-\ *n, often cap* [G, fr. *Rottweil*, Germany] **:** any of a German breed of tall vigorous black shorthaired cattle dogs

ro·tund \rō-'tənd, 'rō-ˌ\ *adj* [L *rotundus* — more at ROUND] **1 :** marked by roundness **:** ROUNDED **2 :** marked by fullness of sound or cadence **:** OROTUND, SONOROUS <a master of ~ phrase> **3 :** notably plump **:** CHUBBY — **ro·tun·di·ty** \rō-'tən-dət-ē\ *n* — **ro·tund·ly** \-'tən-dlē, 'rō-ˌ\ *adv* — **ro·tund·ness** \rō-'tən(d)-nəs, 'rō-ˌ\ *n*

ro·tun·da \rō-'tən-də\ *n* [It *rotonda*, fr. L *rotunda*, fem. of *rotundus*] **1 :** a round building; *esp* **:** one covered by a dome **2 a :** a large round room **b :** a large central area (as in a hotel)

ro·tu·ri·er \rō-'t(y)u̇r-ē-ˌā\ *n* [MF] **:** a person not of noble birth

rou·ble *var of* RUBLE

roué \ru̇-'ā\ *n* [F, lit., broken on the wheel, fr. pp. of *rouer* to break on the wheel, fr. ML *rotare*, fr. L, to rotate; fr. the feeling that such a person deserves this punishment] **:** a man devoted to a life of sensual pleasure **:** RAKE

rou·en \rü-'äⁿ, -'än\ *n* [*Rouen*, France] *often cap* **:** any of a breed of domestic ducks resembling wild mallards in coloring

¹rouge \'rüzh, *esp South* 'rüj\ *n* [F, fr. MF, fr. *rouge* red, fr. L *rubeus* reddish — more at RUBY] **1 :** any of various cosmetics for coloring the cheeks or lips red **2 :** a red powder consisting essentially of ferric oxide used in polishing glass, metal, or gems and as a pigment

²rouge *vb* **rouged; roug·ing** *vt* **1 :** to apply rouge to **2 :** to cause to redden ~ *vi* **:** to use rouge

¹rough \'rəf\ *adj* **rough·er; rough·est** [ME, fr. OE *rūh*; akin to L *ruga* wrinkle, Gk *oryssein* to dig, ON *rögg* tuft — more at RUG] **1 a :** marked by inequalities, ridges, or projections on the surface **:** COARSE **b :** covered with or made up of coarse and often shaggy hair **c (1) :** having a broken, uneven, or bumpy surface <~ terrain> **(2) :** difficult to travel through or penetrate **:** WILD <into the ~ woods —P. B. Shelley> **2 a :** TURBULENT, TEMPESTUOUS <~ seas> **b (1) :** characterized by harshness, violence, or force **(2) :** presenting a challenge **:** DIFFICULT <~ to deal with —R. M. McAlmon> **3 :** coarse or rugged in character or appearance: as **a :** harsh to the ear **b :** crude in style or expression **c :** INDELICATE **d :** marked by a lack of refinement or grace **:** UNCOUTH **4 a :** CRUDE, UNFINISHED <~ carpentry> **b :** executed or ventured hastily, tentatively, or imperfectly <a ~ draft> <~ estimate> — **rough·ness** *n*

syn 1 ROUGH, HARSH, UNEVEN, RUGGED, SCABROUS *shared meaning element* **:** not smooth or even **ant** smooth
2 see RUDE **ant** gentle

²rough *n* **1 :** uneven ground covered with high grass, brush, and stones; *specif* **:** such ground bordering a golf fairway **2 :** the rugged or disagreeable side or aspect <hiking-camping admirers of nature in the ~ —Eleanor Stirling> **3 a :** something in a crude, unfinished, or preliminary state **b :** broad outline **:** general terms <the question . . . has been discussed in ~ —*Manchester Guardian Weekly*> **c :** a hasty preliminary drawing or layout **4 :** ROWDY

³rough *vt* **1 :** ROUGHEN **2 a :** to subject to violence **:** MANHANDLE, BEAT — usu. used with *up* **b :** to subject to unnecessary and intentional violence in a sport **3 :** to calk or otherwise roughen (a horse's shoes) to prevent slipping **4 a :** to shape, make, or dress in a rough or preliminary way **b :** to indicate the chief lines of <~

out the structure of a building> — **rough·er** *n* — **rough it :** to live under harsh or primitive conditions

rough·age \'rəf-ij\ *n* **:** coarse bulky food (as bran) that is relatively high in fiber and low in digestible nutrients and that by its bulk stimulates peristalsis

rough–and–ready \,rəf-ən-'red-ē\ *adj* **:** crude in nature, method, or manner but effective in action or use

1rough–and–tum·ble \-'təm-bəl\ *n* **:** rough disorderly unrestrained fighting or struggling

2rough–and–tumble *adj* **1 :** marked by rough-and-tumble <grew up in a ~ atmosphere —E. J. Kahn> **2 :** put together haphazardly **:** MAKESHIFT <a ~ fence>

rough bluegrass *n* **:** a European forage grass (*Poa trivialis*) naturalized in eastern No. America

rough breathing *n* **1 :** a mark ʽ used in Greek over some initial vowels or over ρ to show that they are aspirated (as in ὡς pronounced \'hōs\ or ῥήτωρ pronounced \'hrā-,tōr\) **2 :** the sound indicated by a mark ʽ over a Greek vowel or ρ

1rough·cast \'rəf-,kast\ *n* **1 :** a rough model **2 :** a plaster of lime mixed with shells or pebbles used for covering buildings **3 :** a rough surface finish (as of a plaster wall)

2roughcast \-,kast, *for 2 also* -'kast\ *vt* **-cast; -cast·ing 1 :** to plaster (as a wall) with roughcast **2 :** to shape or form roughly

1rough–dry \'rəf-'drī\ *vt* **:** to dry (laundry) without smoothing or ironing

2rough–dry \,rəf-,drī\ *adj* **:** being dry after laundering but not ironed or smoothed over <~ clothes>

rough·en \'rəf-ən\ *vb* **rough·ened; rough·en·ing** \-(ə-)niŋ\ *vt* **:** to make rough or rougher <her hands were ~*ed* by work —Ellen Glasgow> ~ *vi* **:** to become rough

rough fish *n* **:** a fish that is neither a sport fish nor an important food for sport fishes

rough–hew \'rəf-'hyü\ *vt* **-hewed; -hewn** \-'hyün\; **-hew·ing 1 :** to hew (as timber) coarsely without smoothing or finishing **2 :** to form crudely

rough–hewn \-'hyün\ *adj* **1 :** being in a rough, unsmoothed, or unfinished state **:** crudely formed <~ beams> **2 :** lacking polish <he was rather attractive, in a ~ kind of way —Jan Speas>

1rough·house \'rəf-,haùs\ *n* **:** violence or rough boisterous play

2rough·house \-,haùs, -,haùz\ *vb* **rough·housed; rough·hous·ing** *vt* **:** to treat in a boisterously rough manner ~ *vi* **:** to engage in roughhouse

rough·ish \'rəf-ish\ *adj* **:** somewhat rough

rough·leg \'rəf-,leg, -,lāg\ *n* **:** ROUGH-LEGGED HAWK

rough–legged hawk \,rəf-,leg(-ə)d-, -,lāg(-ə)d-\ *n* **:** any of several large heavily built hawks (genus *Buteo*) that have the tarsus feathered to the base of the toes and feed chiefly on rodents

rough lemon *n* **1 :** a hybrid lemon that forms a large spreading thorny tree, bears rough-skinned nearly globular acid fruit, and is important chiefly as a rootstock for other citrus trees **2 :** the fruit of a rough lemon

rough·ly \'rəf-lē\ *adv* **1 :** in a rough manner: as **a :** with harshness or violence <treated the prisoner ~> **b :** in crude fashion **:** IMPERFECTLY <~ dressed lumber> **2 :** without completeness or exactness **:** APPROXIMATELY <~ 20 percent>

rough·neck \'rəf-,nek\ *n* **1 a :** a rough or uncouth person **b :** ROWDY, TOUGH **2 :** a worker of an oil-well-drilling crew other than the driller

rough·rid·er \'rəf-'rīd-ər\ *n* **1 :** one who is accustomed to riding unbroken or little-trained horses **2** *cap* **:** a member of the 1st U.S. Volunteer Cavalry regiment in the Spanish-American War commanded by Theodore Roosevelt

rough·shod \-'shäd\ *adj* **1 :** shod with calked shoes **2 :** marked by main force without justice or consideration <a tyrant's ~ rule>

rou·lade \rü-'läd\ *n* [F, lit., act of rolling] **1 :** a florid vocal embellishment sung to one syllable **2 :** a slice of usu. stuffed meat that is rolled, browned, and steamed or braised

rou·leau \rü-'lō\ *n, pl* **rou·leaux** \-'lōz\ [F] **:** a little roll; *esp* **:** a roll of coins put up in paper

1rou·lette \rü-'let\ *n* [F, lit., small wheel, fr. OF *roelete,* dim. of *roele* small wheel, fr. LL *rotella,* dim. of L *rota* wheel — more at ROLL] **1 :** a gambling game in which players bet on which compartment of a revolving wheel a small ball will come to rest in **2 a :** any of various toothed wheels or disks (as for producing rows of dots on engraved plates or for making short consecutive incisions in paper to facilitate subsequent division) **b :** tiny slits between rows of stamps in a sheet that are made by a roulette and serve as an aid in separation — compare PERFORATION

2roulette *vt* **rou·lett·ed; rou·lett·ing :** to make roulettes in

Rou·ma·nian \rù-'mā-nē-ən, -nyən\ *var of* RUMANIAN

1round \'raùnd\ *vt* [ME *rounen,* fr. OE *rūnian;* akin to OE *rūn* mystery — more at RUNE] **1 :** WHISPER **2 :** to speak to in a whisper

2round *adj* [ME, fr. OF *roont,* fr. L *rotundus;* akin to L *rota* wheel — more at ROLL] **1 a** (1) **:** having every part of the surface or circumference equidistant from the center (2) **:** CYLINDRICAL <a ~ peg> **b :** approximately round <a ~ face> **2 :** well filled out **:** PLUMP, SHAPELY **3 a :** COMPLETE, FULL <a ~ dozen> <a ~ ton> **b :** approximately correct; *esp* **:** exact only to a specific decimal **c :** substantial in amount **:** AMPLE <a good ~ price —T. B. Costain> **4 :** direct in utterance **:** OUTSPOKEN <a ~ oath> **5 :** moving in or forming a circle **6 a :** brought to completion or perfection **:** FINISHED **b :** presented with lifelike fullness or vividness **7 :** delivered with a swing of the arm <a ~ blow> **8 a :** having full or unimpeded resonance or tone **:** SONOROUS **b :** pronounced with rounded lips **:** LABIALIZED **9 :** of or relating to handwriting predominantly curved rather than angular — **round·ly** \'raùn-(d)lē\ *adv* — **round·ness** \'raùn(d)-nəs\ *n*

3round *adv* **1 :** in a circular or curved path or progression **2 :** AROUND **3 :** with revolving or rotating motion <the wheel turns ~> **4 :** to a particular person or place <send ~ for the doctor>

4round \(')raùnd\ *prep* **1 :** AROUND **2 :** all during **:** THROUGHOUT <~ the year>

5round \'raùnd\ *n* **1 a :** something (as a circle, globe, or ring) that is round **b** (1) **:** a knot of people (2) **:** a circle of things **2 :** ROUND DANCE 1 **3 :** a musical canon sung in unison in which each part is continuously repeated **4 a :** a rung of a ladder or a chair **b :** a rounded molding **5 a :** a circling or circuitous path or course **b :** motion in a circle or a curving path **6 a :** a route or circuit habitually covered (as by a watchman or policeman) **b :** a series of professional calls on hospital patients made by a doctor or nurse — usu. used in pl. **c :** a series of similar or customary calls or stops <making the ~*s* of his friends —*Current Biog.*> **7 :** a drink of liquor apiece served at one time to each person in a group <I'll buy the next ~> **8 :** a sequence of recurring routine or repetitive actions or events <went about his ~ of chores> **9 :** a period of time that recurs in a fixed pattern <the daily ~> **10 a :** one shot fired by a weapon or by each man in a military unit **b :** a unit of ammunition consisting of the parts necessary to fire one shot **11 a :** a unit of action in a contest or game which comprises a stated period, covers a prescribed distance, includes a specified number of plays, or gives each player one turn **b :** a division of a tournament in which each contestant plays an opponent **12 :** a prolonged burst (as of applause) **13 :** a cut of beef esp. between the rump and the lower leg — see BEEF illustration **14 :** a rounded or curved part — **in the round 1 :** in full sculptured form unattached to a background **2 :** with an inclusive or comprehensive view or representation **3 :** with a center stage surrounded by an audience <theater *in the round*>

6round \'raùnd\ *vt* **1 a :** to make round **b** (1) **:** to make (the lips) round and protruded (as in the pronunciation of \ü\) (2) **:** to pronounce with lip rounding **:** LABIALIZE **2 a :** to go around **b :** to pass part of the way around **3 :** ENCIRCLE, ENCOMPASS **4 :** to bring to completion or perfection — often used with *off* or *out* **5 :** to express as a round number — often used with *off* <11.3572 ~*ed* off to three decimals becomes 11.357> ~ *vi* **1 a :** to become round, plump, or shapely **b :** to reach fullness or completion **2 :** to follow a winding course **:** BEND <~*ing* into the home stretch> — **round on :** to turn against **:** ASSAIL

1round·about \'raùn-də-,baùt\ *n* **1 :** a circuitous route **:** DETOUR **2** *Brit* **:** MERRY-GO-ROUND **3 :** a short close-fitting jacket worn by men and boys esp. in the 19th century **4** *Brit* **:** ROTARY 2

2roundabout *adj* **:** CIRCUITOUS, INDIRECT <had to take a ~ course> — **round·about·ness** *n*

round angle *n* **:** an angle of 360° or 2 π radians

round clam *n* **:** QUAHOG

round dance *n* **1 :** a folk dance in which participants form a ring and move in a prescribed direction **2 :** a ballroom dance in which couples progress around the room

round·ed \'raùn-dəd\ *adj* **1 :** made round **:** flowing rather than jagged or angular **2 :** fully developed — **round·ed·ness** *n*

roun·del \'raùn-dᵊl\ *n* [ME, fr. OF *rondel,* fr. *roont* round — more at ROUND] **1 :** a round figure or object; *esp* **:** a circular panel, window, or niche **2 a :** RONDEL 2a **b :** an English modified rondeau

roun·de·lay \'raùn-də-,lā\ *n* [modif. of MF *rondelet,* dim. of *rondel*] **1 :** a simple song with a refrain **2 :** a poem with a refrain recurring frequently or at fixed intervals as in a rondel

round·er \'raùn-dər\ *n* **1 :** a dissolute person **:** WASTREL **2** *pl but sing in constr* **:** a game of English origin that is played with ball and bat and that somewhat resembles baseball **3 a :** one that rounds by hand or by machine **b :** a tool for making an edge or a surface round **4 :** a boxing match lasting a specified number of rounds — usu. used in combination <a 10-*rounder*>

round·head \'raùnd-,hed\ *n* **1** *cap* [fr. the Puritans' cropping their hair short in contrast to the Cavaliers] **a :** PURITAN 1 **b :** a member of the parliamentary party in England at the time of Charles I and Oliver Cromwell **2 :** a brachycephalic person

round·head·ed \-'hed-əd\ *adj* **:** having a round head; *specif* **:** BRACHYCEPHALIC — **round·head·ed·ness** *n*

round·house \'raùnd-,haùs\ *n* **1** *archaic* **:** LOCKUP **2 :** a circular building for housing and repairing locomotives **3 :** a cabin or apartment on the stern of a quarterdeck **4 :** a blow in boxing delivered with a wide swing

round·ish \'raùn-dish\ *adj* **:** somewhat round

round·let \'raùn-(d)lət\ *n* [ME *roundelet,* fr. MF *rondelet* — more at ROUNDELAY] **:** a small circle or round object **:** DISK

round lot *n* **:** the standard unit of trading in a security market usu. amounting to 100 shares of stock

round robin *n* [fr. the name *Robin*] **1 a :** a written petition, memorial, or protest to which the signatures are affixed in a circle so as not to indicate who signed first **b :** a statement signed by several persons **c :** a letter sent in turn to the members of a group each of whom signs and forwards it sometimes after adding comment **2 :** ROUND TABLE 2 **3 :** a tournament in which every contestant meets every other contestant in turn **4 :** SERIES, ROUND

round–shoul·dered \'raùn(d)-'shōl-dərd\ *adj* **:** having the shoulders stooping or rounded

rounds·man \'raùn(d)z-mən\ *n* **1 :** one that makes rounds **2 :** a supervisory police officer of the grade of sergeant or just below

round steak *n* **:** a steak cut from the round of beef — see BEEF illustration

round table *n* **1 a** *cap R & T* **:** a large circular table for King Arthur and his knights **b :** the knights of King Arthur **2 :** a conference for discussion or deliberation by several participants; *also* **:** the participants in such a conference

round–the–clock *adj* **:** AROUND-THE-CLOCK

round trip *n* **:** a trip to a place and back usu. over the same route

round·up \'raùn-,dəp\ *n* **1 a** (1) **:** the act or process of collecting cattle by riding around them and driving them in (2) **:** the men and horses so engaged **b :** a gathering in of scattered persons or things <a ~ of all suspects> **2 :** a summary of information (as from news bulletins)

round up \'raùn-'dəp\ *vt* **1 :** to collect (cattle) by means of a roundup **2 :** to gather in or bring together from various quarters

round window *n* **:** the cochlear fenestra of the ear

round·wood \ˈrau̇n-ˌdwu̇d\ *n* **:** timber used (as for poles) without being squared by sawing or hewing
round·worm \ˈrau̇n-ˌdwərm\ *n* **:** NEMATODE; *also* **:** a related round-bodied unsegmented worm (as an acanthocephalan) as distinguished from a flatworm
roup \ˈrüp, ˈrau̇p\ *n* [origin unknown] **:** a virus disease of poultry marked by cheesy lesions of the mouth, throat, and eyes
[1]**rouse** \ˈrau̇z\ *vb* **roused; rous·ing** [ME *rousen*] *vi* **1 :** to become aroused **:** AWAKEN **2 :** to become stirred ~ *vt* **1** *archaic* **:** to cause to break from cover **2 a :** to stir up **:** EXCITE <was *roused* to fury> **b :** to arouse from sleep or repose **:** AWAKEN — **rouse·ment** \ˈrau̇z-mənt\ *n* — **rous·er** *n*
[2]**rouse** *n* **:** an act or instance of rousing; *esp* **:** an excited stir
[3]**rouse** *n* [alter. (resulting fr. incorrect division of *to drink carouse*) of *carouse*] **1** *obs* **:** DRINK, TOAST **2** *archaic* **:** CAROUSAL
rouse·about \ˈrau̇-zə-ˌbau̇t\ *n, Austral* **:** an unskilled worker
rous·ing \ˈrau̇-ziŋ\ *adj* **1 a :** giving rise to excitement **:** STIRRING **b :** BRISK, LIVELY **2 :** EXCEPTIONAL, SUPERLATIVE
Rous sarcoma \ˈrau̇s-\ *n* [F. Peyton *Rous* †1970 Am physician] **:** a readily transplantable malignant spindle-cell sarcoma of chickens that is caused by a specific carcinogenic virus
Rous·seau·ism \ru̇-ˈsō-ˌiz-əm\ *n* **1 :** the philosophical, educational, and political doctrines of Jean Jacques Rousseau **2 :** the return to or glorification of a simpler and more primitive way of life — **Rous·seau·ist** \-əst\ *n* — **Rous·seau·is·tic** \ˌrü-ˌsō-ˈis-tik, ru̇-\ *adj*
roust \ˈrau̇st\ *vt* [alter. of [1]*rouse*] **:** to drive (as from bed) roughly or unceremoniously
roust·about \ˈrau̇-stə-ˌbau̇t\ *n* **1 a :** DECKHAND **b :** LONGSHOREMAN **2 :** an unskilled or semiskilled laborer esp. in an oil field or refinery **3 :** a circus worker who erects and dismantles tents, cares for the grounds, and handles animals and equipment
roust·er \ˈrau̇-stər\ *n* **:** ROUSTABOUT 1
[1]**rout** \ˈrau̇t\ *n* [ME *route*, fr. MF, troop, defeat, fr. (assumed) VL *rupta*, fr. L, fem. of *ruptus*, pp. of *rumpere* to break — more at REAVE] **1 :** a crowd of people **:** THRONG; *specif* **:** RABBLE 2b **2 a :** DISTURBANCE **b** *archaic* **:** FUSS **3 :** a fashionable gathering
[2]**rout** \ˈrōt, ˈrüt\ *vi* [ME *rowten*, fr. ON *rauta*; akin to OE *rēotan* to weep, L *rudere* to roar] *dial chiefly Brit* **:** to low loudly **:** BELLOW — used of cattle
[3]**rout** \ˈrau̇t\ *vb* [alter. of [3]*root*] *vi* **1 :** to poke around with the snout **:** ROOT <pigs ~*ing* in the earth> **2 :** to search haphazardly ~ *vt* **1 a** *archaic* **:** to dig up with the snout **b :** to gouge out or make a furrow in (as wood or metal); *specif* **:** to cut away (as blank parts) from a printing surface (as an engraving or electrotype) with a router **2 a :** to expel by force — usu. used with *out* **b :** to cause to emerge esp. from bed **3 :** to come up with **:** UNCOVER
[4]**rout** \ˈrau̇t\ *n* [MF *route* troop, defeat] **1 :** a state of wild confusion or disorderly retreat **2 a :** a disastrous defeat **:** DEBACLE **b :** a precipitate flight
[5]**rout** \ˈrau̇t\ *vt* **1 a :** to disorganize completely **:** DEMORALIZE **b :** to put to precipitate flight **c :** to defeat decisively or disastrously <the discomfiture of seeing their party ~*ed* at the polls —A. N. Holcombe> **2 :** to drive out **:** DISPEL
[1]**route** \ˈrüt, ˈrau̇t\ *n* [ME, fr. OF, fr. (assumed) VL *rupta* (*via*), lit., broken way, fr. L *rupta*, fem. of *ruptus*, pp.] **1 a :** a traveled way **:** HIGHWAY <the main ~ north> **b :** a means of access **:** CHANNEL <the ~ to social mobility —T. F. O'Dea> **2 :** a line of travel **:** COURSE **3 a :** an established or selected course of travel or action **b :** an assigned territory to be systematically covered <a newspaper ~>
[2]**route** *vt* **rout·ed; rout·ing** **1 a :** to send by a selected route **:** DIRECT <was *routed* along the scenic shore road> **b :** to divert in a specified direction **2 :** to prearrange and direct the order and execution of (a series of operations)
route·man \ˈrüt-mən, ˈrau̇t-ˌman\ *n* **:** one who is responsible for making sales or deliveries on an assigned route
route march *n* **:** ROUTE STEP
[1]**rout·er** \ˈrau̇t-ər\ *n* **:** one that routs: as **a :** a routing plane **b :** a machine with a revolving vertical spindle and cutter for milling out the surface of wood or metal
[2]**rout·er** \ˈrüt-ər, ˈrau̇t-\ *n* **:** one that routes
[3]**rout·er** \ˈrüt-ər, ˈrau̇t-\ *n* [*route* (race of a mile or more)] **:** a horse trained for distance races
route step *n* **:** a style of marching in which troops maintain prescribed intervals but are not required to keep in step or to maintain silence — called also *route march*
route·way \ˈrüt-ˌwā, ˈrau̇t-\ *n* **:** ROUTE 3a
routh \ˈrau̇th, ˈrüth\ *n* [origin unknown] *chiefly Scot* **:** PLENTY
[1]**rou·tine** \rü-ˈtēn\ *n* [F, fr. MF, fr. *route* traveled way] **1 a :** a regular course of procedure <if resort to legal action becomes a campus ~ —J. A. Perkins> **b :** habitual or mechanical performance of an established procedure <settled into the ~ of factory work> **2 :** a reiterated speech or formula <the old "After you" ~ —Ray Russell> **3 :** a fixed piece of entertainment often repeated <a dance ~>; *specif* **:** a theatrical number **4 :** a sequence of computer instructions for performing a particular task
[2]**rou·tine** \rü-ˈtēn, ˌrü-ˌ\ *adj* **1 :** of a commonplace or repetitious character **:** ORDINARY **2 :** of, relating to, or being in accordance with established procedure <~ business> — **rou·tine·ly** *adv*
rou·tin·ize \rü-ˈtē-ˌnīz, ˈrüt-ᵊn-ˌīz\ *vt* **-ized; -iz·ing :** to discipline in or reduce to a routine — **rou·tin·iza·tion** \(ˌ)rü-ˌtē-nə-ˈzā-shən, ˌrüt-ᵊn-ə-\ *n*
roux \ˈrü\ *n, pl* **roux** \ˈrüz\ [F, fr. *beurre roux* browned butter] **:** a cooked mixture of flour and fat used as a thickening agent in a soup or a sauce
[1]**rove** \ˈrōv\ *vb* **roved; rov·ing** [ME *roven* to shoot at rovers] *vi* **:** to move aimlessly **:** ROAM ~ *vt* **:** to wander through or over
[2]**rove** *n* **:** an act or instance of wandering
[3]**rove** *past of* REEVE
[4]**rove** *vt* **roved; rov·ing** [origin unknown] **:** to join (textile fibers) with a slight twist and draw out into roving
[5]**rove** *n* **:** ROVING

rove beetle *n* [perh. fr. [1]*rove*] **:** any of numerous often predatory active beetles (family Staphylinidae) having a long body and very short wing covers beneath which the wings are folded transversely
[1]**ro·ver** \ˈrō-vər\ *n* [ME, fr. MD, fr. *roven* to rob; akin to OE *rēafian* to reave — more at REAVE] **:** PIRATE
[2]**rov·er** \ˈrō-vər\ *n* [ME, fr. *roven* to shoot at random, wander] **1 :** a random or long-distance mark in archery — usu. used in pl. **2 :** WANDERER, ROAMER **3 :** a player who is not assigned to a specific position on a team and who plays wherever he is needed
[1]**rov·ing** \ˈrō-viŋ\ *adj* [[1]*rove*] **1 a :** capable of being shifted from place to place **:** MOBILE **b :** not restricted as to location or area of concern **2 :** inclined to ramble or stray <a ~ fancy>
[2]**roving** *n* [[4]*rove*] **:** a slightly twisted roll or strand of usu. textile fibers
[1]**row** \ˈrō\ *vb* [ME *rowen*, fr. OE *rōwan*; akin to MHG *rüejen* to row, L *remus* oar] *vi* **1 :** to propel a boat by means of oars **2 :** to move by or as if by the propulsion of oars ~ *vt* **1 a :** to propel with or as if with oars **b :** to be equipped with (a specified number of oars) **c (1) :** to participate in (a rowing match) **(2) :** to compete against in rowing **(3) :** to pull (an oar) in a crew **2 :** to transport in an oar-propelled boat — **row·er** \ˈrō(-ə)r\ *n*
[2]**row** *n* **:** an act or instance of rowing
[3]**row** *n* [ME *rawe*; akin to OE *rǣw* row, OHG *rīga* line, L *rima* slit] **1 :** a number of objects arranged in a usu. straight line <a ~ of bottles>; *also* **:** the line along which such objects are arranged <planted the corn in parallel ~*s*> **2 a :** WAY, STREET **b :** an urban area (as along one street) dominated by a specific kind of enterprise or occupancy <doctors living elsewhere come back to doctors' ~ along 116th Street —Jonathan Randal> **3 :** TWELVE-TONE ROW — **in a row :** one after another **:** SUCCESSIVELY
[4]**row** *vt* **:** to form into rows
[5]**row** \ˈrau̇\ *n* [origin unknown] **:** a noisy disturbance or quarrel
[6]**row** \ˈrau̇\ *vi* **:** to engage in a row **:** have a quarrel
row·an \ˈrau̇-ən, ˈrō-ən\ *n* [of Scand origin; akin to ON *reynir* rowan; akin to OE *rēad* red — more at RED] **1 a :** a Eurasian tree (*Sorbus aucuparia*) of the rose family with flat corymbs of white flowers followed by small red pomes **b :** an American mountain ash (*Sorbus americana*) **2 :** the fruit of a rowan
row·an·ber·ry \-ˌber-ē\ *n* **:** ROWAN 2
row·boat \ˈrō-ˌbōt\ *n* **:** a small boat designed to be rowed
[1]**row·dy** \ˈrau̇d-ē\ *adj* **row·di·er; -est** [perh. irreg. fr. [5]*row*] **:** coarse or boisterous in behavior **:** ROUGH — **row·di·ly** \ˈrau̇d-ᵊl-ē\ *adv* — **row·di·ness** \ˈrau̇d-ē-nəs\ *n* — **row·dy·ish** \-ē-ish\ *adj*
[2]**rowdy** *n, pl* **rowdies :** a rowdy person **:** TOUGH
row·dy·ism \ˈrau̇d-ē-ˌiz-əm\ *n* **:** rowdy character or behavior
[1]**row·el** \ˈrau̇(-ə)l\ *n* [ME *rowelle*, fr. MF *rouelle* small wheel, fr. OF *roele* — more at ROULETTE] **:** a revolving disk at the end of a spur with sharp marginal points
[2]**rowel** *vt* **-eled** *or* **-elled; -el·ing** *or* **-el·ling** **1 :** to goad with or as if with a rowel **2 :** VEX, TROUBLE
row·en \ˈrau̇-ən\ *n* [ME *rowein*, fr. (assumed) ONF *rewain*; akin to OF *regaïn* aftermath, fr. *re-* + *gaaignier* to till — more at GAIN] **1 :** a stubble field left unplowed for late grazing **2 :** AFTERMATH 1 — often used in pl.
row house \ˈrō-\ *n* **:** one of a series of houses connected by common sidewalls and forming a continuous group
row·ing \ˈrō-iŋ\ *n* **:** the sport of racing in shells
row·lock \ˈräl-ək, ˈrəl-; ˈrō-ˌläk\ *n* [prob. by alter.] *chiefly Brit* **:** OARLOCK
Rox *abbr* Roxburghshire
[1]**roy·al** \ˈrȯi(-ə)l\ *adj* [ME *roial*, fr. MF, fr. L *regalis*, fr. *reg-, rex* king; akin to OIr *rī* (gen. *rig*) king, Skt *rājan*, L *regere* to rule — more at RIGHT] **1 a :** of kingly ancestry <the ~ family> **b :** of, relating to, or subject to the crown <the ~ estates> **c :** being in the crown's service <*Royal* Air Force> **2 a :** suitable for royalty **:** MAGNIFICENT <the ~ gift of such poets —Kathleen Raine> **b :** requiring no exertion **:** EASY <there is no ~ road to logic —Justus Buchler> **3 a :** of superior size, magnitude, or quality <a patronage of ~ dimensions —J. H. Plumb> **b :** established or chartered by the crown **4 :** of, relating to, or being a part (as a mast, sail, or yard) next above the topgallant — **roy·al·ly** \ˈrȯi-ə-lē\ *adv*
[2]**royal** *n* **1 :** a stag of 8 years or more having antlers with at least 12 points **2 :** a small sail on the royal mast immediately above the topgallant sail **3 :** a person of royal blood **4 :** a size of paper usu. 20 x 25 or 19 x 24 inches
royal antler *n* **:** the third tine above the base of a stag's antler — see ANTLER illustration
royal blue *n* **:** a variable color averaging a vivid purplish blue
royal flush *n* **:** a straight flush having an ace as the highest card — see POKER illustration
roy·al·ism \ˈrȯi-ə-ˌliz-əm\ *n* **:** MONARCHISM
roy·al·ist \-ə-ləst\ *n* **1** *often cap* **:** an adherent of a king or of monarchical government: as **a :** CAVALIER 3 **b :** TORY 4 **2 :** a reactionary business tycoon — **royalist** *adj*
royal jelly *n* **:** a highly nutritious secretion of the pharyngeal glands of the honeybee that is fed to the very young larvae in a colony and to all queen larvae
royal palm *n* **:** any of several palms (genus *Roystonea*); *esp* **:** a tall graceful pinnate-leaved palm (*R. regia*) of southern Florida and Cuba that is widely planted for ornament
royal poinciana *n* **:** a showy tropical tree (*Delonix regia* syn. *Poinciana regia*) widely planted for its immense racemes of scarlet and orange flowers — called also *flamboyant, peacock flower*
royal purple *n* **:** a dark reddish purple

roy·al·ty \'rȯi(-ə)l-tē\ *n, pl* **-ties** [ME *roialte,* fr. MF *roialté,* fr. OF, fr. *roial*] **1 a :** royal status or power **:** SOVEREIGNTY **b :** a right or perquisite of a sovereign (as a percentage paid to the crown of gold or silver taken from mines) **2 :** regal character or bearing **:** NOBILITY **3 a :** persons of royal lineage **b :** a person of royal rank <how to address *royalties* —George Santayana> **c :** a privileged class **4 :** a right of jurisdiction granted to an individual or corporation by a sovereign **5 a :** a share of the product or profit reserved by the grantor esp. of an oil or mining lease **b :** a payment made to an author or composer for each copy of his work sold or to an inventor for each article sold under a patent
royster *var of* ROISTER
roz·zer \'räz-ər\ *n* [origin unknown] *slang Brit* **:** POLICEMAN
RP *abbr* **1** Received Pronunciation **2** relief pitcher **3** reply paid **4** reprint; reprinting
RPG \ˌär-(ˌ)pē-'jē\ *n* [*r*eport *p*rogram *g*enerator] **:** a computer language that generates programs from the user's specifications esp. to produce business reports
RPM *abbr* revolutions per minute
RPO *abbr* railway post office
RPS *abbr* revolutions per second
rpt *abbr* **1** repeat **2** report
RQ *abbr* respiratory quotient
RR *abbr* **1** railroad **2** rural route
RRB *abbr* Railroad Retirement Board
-r·rha·gia \'rā-j(ē-)ə, 'rā-zhə; 'räj-ə, 'räzh-\ *n comb form* [NL, fr. Gk, fr. *rhēgnynai* to break, burst; akin to OSlav *rězati* to cut] **:** abnormal or excessive discharge or flow <metro*rrhagia*>
-r·rhea *also* **-r·rhoea** \'rē-ə\ *n comb form* [ME *-ria,* fr. LL *-rrhoea,* fr. Gk *-rrhoia,* fr. *rhoia,* fr. *rhein* to flow — more at STREAM] **:** flow **:** discharge <logo*rrhea*> <leuko*rrhea*>
-r·rhine *or* **-rhine** \ˌrīn\ *adj comb form* [ISV, fr. Gk *-rrhin-, -rrhis,* fr. *rhin-, rhis* nose] **:** having (such) a nose <platy*rrhine*>
-r·rhi·za — see -RHIZA
RS *abbr* **1** recording secretary **2** revised statutes **3** right side **4** Royal Society
RSA *abbr* Royal Scottish Academy
RSE *abbr* Royal Society of Edinburgh
RSFSR *abbr* [Russ *Rossiĭskaya Sovetskaya Federativnaya Sotsialisticheskaya Respublika*] Russian Soviet Federated Socialist Republic
RSV *abbr* Revised Standard Version
RSVP *abbr* [F *répondez s'il vous plaît*] please reply
RSWC *abbr* right side up with care
rt *abbr* right
RT *abbr* **1** radiotelephone **2** room temperature
rte *abbr* route
Ru *symbol* ruthenium
[1]**rub** \'rəb\ *vb* **rubbed; rub·bing** [ME *rubben;* akin to Icel *rubba* to scrape] *vi* **1 a :** to move along the surface of a body with pressure **:** GRATE **b (1) :** to fret or chafe with friction **(2) :** to cause discontent, irritation, or anger **2 :** to continue in a situation usu. with slight difficulty <in spite of financial difficulties, he is *rubbing* along> **3 :** to admit of being rubbed (as for erasure or obliteration) ~ *vt* **1 a :** to subject to the action of something moving esp. back and forth with pressure and friction **b (1) :** to cause (a body) to move with pressure and friction along a surface **(2) :** to treat in any of various ways by rubbing **c :** to bring into reciprocal back-and-forth or rotary contact **2 :** ANNOY, IRRITATE <his attitude tended to ~ her> — **rub elbows** *or* **rub shoulders :** to associate closely **:** MINGLE — **rub the wrong way :** to arouse the antagonism or displeasure of **:** IRRITATE
[2]**rub** *n* **1 a :** an unevenness of surface (as of the ground in lawn bowling) **b :** OBSTRUCTION, DIFFICULTY <the ~ is that so few of the scholars have any sense of this truth themselves —Benjamin Farrington> **c :** something grating to the feelings (as a gibe or harsh criticism) **d :** something that mars serenity **2 :** the application of friction with pressure <an alcohol ~>
rub–a–dub \'rəb-ə-ˌdəb\ *n* [imit.] **:** the sound of drumbeats
Ru·bai·yat stanza \'rü-bē-ˌät-, -ˌat-; -ˌbī-(y)ät-, -ˌ(y)at-\ *n* [*The Rubáiyát of Omar Khayyám,* quatrains translated by Edward Fitzgerald (1859)] **:** an iambic pentameter quatrain with a rhyme scheme *aaba* — called also *Omar stanza*
Ru·barth's disease \'rü-ˌbärt(h)s-\ *n* [C. Sven *Rubarth b*1905 Sw veterinarian] **:** an often fatal febrile virus hepatitis of dogs
ru·basse \rü-'bas, 'rü-ˌ\ *n* [F *rubace,* irreg. fr. *rubis* ruby — more at RUBY] **:** a quartz stained a ruby red
ru·ba·to \rü-'bät-(ˌ)ō\ *n, pl* **-tos** [It, lit., robbed] **:** a fluctuation of speed within a musical phrase typically against a rhythmically steady accompaniment
[1]**rub·ber** \'rəb-ər\ *n, often attrib* **1 a :** one that rubs **b :** an instrument or object (as a rubber eraser) used in rubbing, polishing, scraping, or cleaning **c :** something that prevents rubbing or chafing **2** [fr. its use in erasers] **a :** an elastic substance that is obtained by coagulating the milky juice of any of various tropical plants (as of the genera *Hevea* and *Ficus*), is essentially a polymer of isoprene, and is prepared as sheets and then dried — called also *caoutchouc, india rubber* **b :** any of various synthetic rubberlike substances **c :** natural or synthetic rubber modified by chemical treatment to increase its useful properties (as toughness and resistance to wear) and used esp. in tires, electrical insulation, and waterproof materials **3 :** something made of or resembling rubber: as **a :** a rubber overshoe **b (1) :** a rubber tire **(2) :** the set of tires on a vehicle **c :** a rectangular slab of white rubber in the middle of a baseball infield on which a pitcher stands while pitching **d :** CONDOM — **rubber** *adj*
[2]**rubber** *n* [origin unknown] **1 :** a contest consisting of an odd number of games won by the side that takes a majority (as two out of three) **2 :** an odd game played to determine the winner of a tie
rubber band *n* **:** an endless band of rubber used in various ways (as for holding together a sheaf of papers)
rubber–base paint *n* **:** a paint having a rubber derivative or a synthetic resin as its binder or vehicle
rubber bridge *n* **:** a form of contract bridge in which settlement is made at the end of each rubber
rubber cement *n* **:** an adhesive consisting typically of a dispersion of vulcanized rubber in an organic solvent
rubber check *n* [fr. its coming back like a bouncing rubber ball] **:** a check returned by the bank as not good
rub·ber·ize \'rəb-ə-ˌrīz\ *vt* **-ized; -iz·ing :** to coat or impregnate with rubber or a rubber solution
rub·ber·like \'rəb-ər-ˌlīk\ *adj* **:** resembling rubber esp. in physical properties (as elasticity and toughness)
[1]**rub·ber·neck** \-ˌnek\ *also* **rub·ber·neck·er** \-ər\ *n* **1 :** an inquisitive person **2 :** TOURIST; *esp* **:** one on a guided tour
[2]**rubberneck** *vi* **1 :** to look about, stare, or listen with exaggerated curiosity **2 :** to go on a tour **:** SIGHTSEE
rubber plant *n* **:** a plant that yields rubber; *esp* **:** a tall tropical Asian tree (*Ficus elastica*) frequently dwarfed as an ornamental
rubber–stamp *vt* **1 :** to mark with a rubber stamp **2 :** to approve, endorse, or dispose of as a matter of routine or at the command of another
rubber stamp *n* **1 :** a stamp of rubber for making imprints **2 a :** a person who echoes or imitates others **b :** a body or person that approves or endorses a program or policy with little or no dissent or discussion **3 a :** a stereotyped copy or expression <the usual *rubber stamps* of criticism —H. L. Mencken> **b :** a routine endorsement or approval
rubber tree *n* **:** a tree that yields rubber; *esp* **:** a So. American tree (*Hevea brasiliensis*) of the spurge family that is cultivated in plantations and is a chief source of rubber
rub·bery \'rəb-(ə-)rē\ *adj* **:** resembling rubber (as in elasticity, consistency, or texture) <~ legs>
rub·bing \'rəb-iŋ\ *n* **:** an image of a raised, incised, or textured surface obtained by placing paper over it and rubbing the paper with a colored substance
rub·bish \'rəb-ish, *nonstand* -ij\ *n* [ME *robys*] **1 :** useless waste or rejected matter **:** TRASH **2 :** something that is worthless or nonsensical <few real masterpieces are forgotten and not much ~ survives —William Bridges-Adams> — **rub·bishy** \-ē\ *adj*
[1]**rub·ble** \'rəb-əl\ *n* [ME *robyl*] **1 a :** broken fragments (as of rock) resulting from the decay or destruction of a building <fortifications knocked into ~ —C. S. Forester> **b :** a miscellaneous confused mass or group of usu. broken or worthless things <the human ~ . . . washed up by the roily wake of the war —John Woodburn> **2 :** waterworn or rough broken stones or bricks used in coarse masonry or in filling courses of walls; *also* **:** RUBBLEWORK **3 :** rough stone as it comes from the quarry
[2]**rubble** *vt* **rub·bled; rub·bling** \-(ə-)liŋ\ **:** to reduce to rubble
rub·ble·work \'rəb-əl-ˌwərk\ *n* **:** masonry of unsquared or rudely squared stones that are irregular in size and shape
rub·down \'rəb-ˌdau̇n\ *n* **:** a brisk rubbing of the body
rube \'rüb\ *n* [*Rube,* nickname for *Reuben*] **:** an awkward unsophisticated person **:** RUSTIC
[1]**ru·be·fa·cient** \ˌrü-bə-'fā-shənt\ *adj* [L *rubefacient-, rubefaciens,* prp. of *rubefacere* to make red, fr. *rubeus* reddish + *facere* to make — more at RUBY, DO] **:** causing redness (as of the skin)
[2]**rubefacient** *n* **:** a substance for external application that produces redness of the skin
Rube Gold·berg \'rüb-'gōl(d)-ˌbərg\ *adj* [Reuben (*Rube*) L. *Goldberg* †1970 Am cartoonist] **:** accomplishing by complex means what seemingly could be done simply <a kind of *Rube Goldberg* contraption . . . with five hundred moving parts —L. T. Grant>
ru·bel·la \rü-'bel-ə\ *n* [NL, fr. L, fem. of *rubellus* reddish, fr. *ruber* red — more at RED] **:** GERMAN MEASLES
ru·bel·lite \rü-'bel-ˌīt, 'rü-bə-ˌlīt\ *n* [L *rubellus*] **:** a red tourmaline used as a gem
ru·be·o·la \ˌrü-bē-'ō-lə, rü-'bē-ə-lə\ *n* [NL, fr. neut. pl. of (assumed) NL *rubeolus* reddish, fr. L *rubeus* — more at RUBY] **:** MEASLES — **ru·be·o·lar** \-lər\ *adj*
Ru·bi·con \'rü-bi-ˌkän\ *n* [L *Rubicon-, Rubico,* river of northern Italy forming part of the boundary between Cisalpine Gaul and Italy whose crossing by Julius Caesar in 49 B.C. was regarded by the Senate as an act of war] **:** a bounding or limiting line; *esp* **:** one that when crossed commits a person irrevocably
ru·bi·cund \'rü-bi-(ˌ)kənd\ *adj* [L *rubicundus,* fr. *rubēre* to be red; akin to L *rubeus*] **:** RUDDY — **ru·bi·cun·di·ty** \ˌrü-bi-'kən-dət-ē\ *n*
ru·bid·i·um \rü-'bid-ē-əm\ *n* [NL, fr. L *rubidus* red, fr. *rubēre*] **:** a soft silvery metallic element that decomposes water with violence and bursts into flame spontaneously in air — see ELEMENT table
ru·big·i·nous \rü-'bij-ə-nəs\ *adj* [L *robiginosus, rubiginosus* rusty, fr. *robigin-, robigo* rust; akin to L *rubēre*] **:** of a rusty red color
rub in *vt* **:** to harp on (as something unpleasant) **:** EMPHASIZE
ru·bi·ous \'rü-bē-əs\ *adj* **:** RED, RUBY
ru·ble \'rü-bəl\ *n* [Russ *rubl'*] — see MONEY table
rub out *vt* **1 :** to obliterate or extinguish by rubbing **2 :** to destroy completely; *specif* **:** KILL, MURDER <somebody *rubbed* him *out* . . . with a twenty-two —Raymond Chandler>
ru·bric \'rü-brik, -ˌbrik\ *n* [ME *rubrike* red ocher, heading in red letters of part of a book, fr. MF *rubrique,* fr. L *rubrica,* fr. *rubr-, ruber* red] **1 :** a heading of a part of a book or manuscript done or underlined in a color (as red) different from the rest **2 a (1) :** NAME, TITLE; *specif* **:** the title of a statute **(2) :** something under which a thing is classed **:** CATEGORY <the sensations falling under the general ~, "pressure" —F. A. Geldard> **b :** an authoritative rule; *esp* **:** a rule for conduct of a liturgical service **c :** an explanatory or introductory commentary **:** GLOSS; *specif* **:** an editorial interpolation **3 :** an established rule or custom — **rubric** *or* **ru·bri·cal** \-bri-kəl\ *adj* — **ru·bri·cal·ly** \-bri-k(ə-)lē\ *adv*
ru·bri·cate \'rü-bri-ˌkāt\ *vt* **-cat·ed; -cat·ing 1 :** to write or print as a rubric **2 :** to provide with a rubric — **ru·bri·ca·tion** \ˌrü-bri-'kā-shən\ *n* — **ru·bri·ca·tor** \'rü-bri-ˌkāt-ər\ *n*
rub up *vt* **1 :** to revive or refresh knowledge of **:** RECALL **2 :** to improve the keenness of (a mental faculty)
ru·bus \'rü-bəs\ *n, pl* **rubus** [NL, genus name, fr. L, blackberry] **:** any of a genus (*Rubus*) of plants (as a blackberry or a raspberry) of the rose family having 3- to 7-foliolate or simple lobed leaves,

white or pink flowers, and a mass of carpels ripening into an aggregate fruit composed of many drupelets

1**ru·by** \'rü-bē\ *n, pl* **rubies** [ME, fr. MF *rubis, rubi,* irreg. fr. L *rubeus* reddish; akin to L *ruber* red — more at RED] **1 a :** a precious stone that is a red corundum **b :** something made of ruby; *esp* **:** a watch bearing or other part of ruby or a substitute material **2 a :** the dark red color of the ruby **b :** something resembling a ruby in color **3 :** a Brazilian hummingbird (genus *Clytolaema*) whose male has a ruby throat or breast

2**ruby** *adj* **:** of the color ruby

ruby glass *n* **:** glass of a deep red color containing selenium, an oxide of copper, or a chloride of gold

ruby spinel *n* **:** a usu. red spinel used as a gem

ru·by–throat \'rü-bē-ˌthrōt\ *n* **:** RUBY-THROATED HUMMINGBIRD

ru·by–throat·ed hummingbird \ˌrü-bē-ˌthrōt-əd-\ *n* **:** a hummingbird (*Archilochus colubris*) of eastern No. America having a bright bronzy green back, whitish underparts, and in the adult male a red throat with metallic reflections

ruche \'rüsh\ *or* **ruch·ing** \'rü-shiŋ\ *n* [F *ruche*] **:** a pleated, fluted, or gathered strip of fabric used for trimming

1**ruck** \'rək\ *n* [ME *ruke* pile of combustible material, of Scand origin; akin to ON *hraukr* rick — more at RICK] **1 a :** an indistinguishable gathering **:** JUMBLE **b :** the usual run of persons or things **:** GENERALITY <his verse compares well with the general ~ of poets of his day —Bonamy Dobrée> **2 :** the persons or things following the vanguard

2**ruck** *vb* [*ruck,* n. (wrinkle)] **:** PUCKER, WRINKLE

ruck·sack \'rək-ˌsak, 'ru̇k-\ *n* [G] **:** KNAPSACK

ruck·us \'rək-əs, 'rük-, 'ru̇k-\ *n* [prob. blend of *ruction* and *rumpus*] **:** ROW, DISTURBANCE <raise a ~>

ruc·tion \'rək-shən\ *n* [perh. by shortening & alter. fr. *insurrection*] **1 :** a noisy fight **2 :** DISTURBANCE, UPROAR

rud·beck·ia \ˌrəd-'bek-ē-ə, rüd-\ *n* [NL, genus name, fr. Olof *Rudbeck* †1702 Sw scientist] **:** any of a genus (*Rudbeckia*) of No. American perennial composite herbs having showy flower heads with mostly yellow ray flowers and a conical chaffy receptacle

rudd \'rəd, 'ru̇d\ *n* [prob. fr. *rud* redness, red ocher, fr. ME *rude,* fr. OE *rudu* — more at RUDDY] **:** a freshwater European cyprinid fish (*Scardinius erythrophthalmus*) resembling the roach

rud·der \'rəd-ər\ *n* [ME *rother,* fr. OE *rōther* paddle; akin to OE *rōwan* to row] **1 :** a flat piece or structure of wood or metal attached upright to a ship's stern so that it can be turned causing the ship's head to turn in the same direction **2 :** a movable auxiliary airfoil usu. attached at the rear end that serves to control direction of flight of an airplane in the horizontal plane — see AIRPLANE illustration — **rud·der·less** \-ləs\ *adj*

rud·der·post \-ˌpōst\ *n* **1 :** RUDDERSTOCK **2 :** an additional sternpost in a ship with a single screw propeller to which the rudder is attached

rud·der·stock \-ˌstäk\ *n* **:** the shaft of a rudder

1**rud·dle** \'rəd-ᵊl\ *n* [dim. of *rud* red ocher] **:** RED OCHER

2**ruddle** *vt* **rud·dled; rud·dling** \'rəd-liŋ, -ᵊl-iŋ\ **:** to color with or as if with red ocher **:** REDDEN

rud·dle·man \'rəd-ᵊl-mən\ *n* **:** a dealer in red ocher

rud·dock \'rəd-ək, 'ru̇d-\ *n* [ME *ruddok,* fr. OE *rudduc;* akin to OE *rudu*] **:** ROBIN 1a

rud·dy \'rəd-ē\ *adj* **rud·di·er; -est** [ME *rudi,* fr. OE *rudig,* fr. *rudu* redness; akin to OE *rēad* red — more at RED] **1 :** having a healthy reddish color **2 :** RED, REDDISH **3** *Brit* — used as an intensive <a ~ lie> — **rud·di·ly** \'rəd-ᵊl-ē\ *adv* — **rud·di·ness** \'rəd-ē-nəs\ *n*

rude \'rüd\ *adj* **rud·er; rud·est** [ME, fr. MF, fr. L *rudis;* akin to L *rudus* rubble, *ruere* to fall — more at RUG] **1 a :** being in a rough or unfinished state **:** CRUDE **b :** NATURAL, RAW <~ cotton> **c :** PRIMITIVE, UNDEVELOPED <peasants use ~ wooden plows —Jack Raymond> **d :** SIMPLE, ELEMENTAL <landscape done in ~ whites, blacks, deep browns —Richard Harris> **2 :** lacking refinement or delicacy: **a :** IGNORANT, UNLEARNED **b :** INELEGANT, UNCOUTH **c :** offensive in manner or action **:** DISCOURTEOUS **d :** UNCIVILIZED, SAVAGE **e :** COARSE, VULGAR **3 :** marked by or suggestive of lack of training or skill **:** INEXPERIENCED <~ workmanship> **4 :** ROBUST, STURDY **5 :** FORCEFUL, ABRUPT <a ~ awakening> — **rude·ly** *adv*

syn RUDE, ROUGH, CRUDE, RAW, CALLOW, GREEN *shared meaning element* **:** lacking in social refinement

rude·ness *n* **1 :** the quality or state of being rude **2 :** a rude action

1**ru·der·al** \'rüd-ə-rəl\ *adj* [NL *ruderalis,* fr. L *ruder-, rudus* rubble] **:** growing where the natural vegetational cover has been disturbed by man <~ weeds of old fields and roadsides>

2**ruderal** *n* **:** a weedy and commonly introduced plant growing where the vegetational cover has been interrupted

rudes·by \'rüdz-bē\ *n, pl* **rudesbies** [*rude* + *-sby* (as in the name *Crosby*)] *archaic* **:** a rude person

ru·di·ment \'rüd-ə-mənt\ *n* [L *rudimentum* beginning, fr. *rudis* raw, rude] **1 :** a basic principle or element or a fundamental skill — usu. used in pl. <students . . . teaching themselves the ~*s* of rational government —G. B. Galanti> **2 a :** something unformed or undeveloped **:** BEGINNING — usu. used in pl. <the ~*s* of a plan> **b** (1) **:** a body part or organ so deficient in size or structure as to entirely prevent its performing its normal function (2) **:** an organ just beginning to develop **:** ANLAGE — **ru·di·men·tal** \ˌrüd-ə-'ment-ᵊl\ *adj*

ru·di·men·ta·ry \ˌrüd-ə-'ment-ə-rē, -'men-trē\ *adj* **1 :** consisting in first principles **:** FUNDAMENTAL <these ~ truths —M. R. Cohen> **2 :** of a primitive kind **:** ELEMENTARY <the equipment of these past empire-builders was ~ —A. J. Toynbee> **3 :** very imperfectly developed or represented only by a vestige <the ~ tail of a hyrax> — **ru·di·men·tari·ly** \-ˌmen-'ter-ə-lē, -'men-trə-lē\ *adv* — **ru·di·men·tari·ness** \-'ment-ə-rē-nəs, -'men-trē-\ *n*

1**rue** \'rü\ *vb* **rued; ru·ing** [ME *ruen,* fr. OE *hrēowan;* akin to OHG *hriuwan* to regret] *vt* **:** to feel penitence, remorse, or regret for ~ *vi* **:** to feel sorrow, remorse, or regret

2**rue** *n* **:** REGRET, SORROW

3**rue** *n* [ME, fr. MF, fr. L *ruta,* fr. Gk *rhytē*] **:** a strong-scented perennial woody herb (*Ruta graveolens* of the family Rutaceae, the rue family) that has bitter leaves used in medicine

rue anemone *n* **:** a delicate vernal herb (*Anemonella thalictroides*) of the buttercup family with white flowers resembling those of the wood anemone

rue·ful \'rü-fəl\ *adj* **1 :** exciting pity or sympathy **:** PITIABLE <~ squalid poverty . . . by every wayside —John Morley> **2 :** MOURNFUL, REGRETFUL <troubled her with a ~ disquiet —W. M. Thackeray> — **rue·ful·ly** \-fə-lē\ *adv* — **rue·ful·ness** *n*

ru·fes·cent \rü-'fes-ᵊnt\ *adj* [L *rufescent-, rufescens,* prp. of *rufescere* to become reddish, fr. *rufus* red — more at RED] **:** REDDISH

1**ruff** \'rəf\ *n* [ME *ruf*] **1** *also* **ruffe** \'rəf\ **:** a small freshwater European perch (*Acerina cernua*) **2 :** PUMPKINSEED 1

2**ruff** *n* [prob. back-formation fr. *ruffle*] **1 :** a wheel-shaped stiff collar worn by men and women of the late 16th and early 17th centuries **2 :** a fringe or frill of long hairs or feathers growing around or on the neck **3 :** a common Eurasian sandpiper (*Philomachus pugnax*) whose male during the breeding season has a large ruff of erectile feathers on the neck — **ruffed** \'rəft\ *adj*

1, ruff 1

3**ruff** *n* [MF *roffle*] **:** the act of trumping

4**ruff** *vt* **:** to play a trump on (a card previously led or played) ~ *vi* **:** to take a trick with a trump

ruffed grouse *n* **:** a No. American grouse (*Bonasa umbellus*) valued as a game bird in the eastern U.S. and Canada

ruffed grouse

ruf·fi·an \'rəf-ē-ən\ *n* [MF *rufian*] **:** a brutal person **:** BULLY — **ruffian** *adj* — **ruf·fi·an·ism** \-ē-ə-ˌniz-əm\ *n* — **ruf·fi·an·ly** *adj*

1**ruf·fle** \'rəf-əl\ *vb* **ruf·fled; ruf·fling** \-(ə-)liŋ\ [ME *ruffelen;* akin to LG *ruffelen* to crumple] *vt* **1 a :** ROUGHEN, ABRADE **b :** TROUBLE, VEX <*ruffled* his composure> **2 :** to erect (as feathers) in or like a ruff **3 a :** to flip through (as pages) **b :** SHUFFLE **4 :** to make into a ruffle ~ *vi* **:** to become ruffled <their dispositions ~ perceptively —*Life*>

2**ruffle** *n* **1 :** a state or cause of irritation **2 :** COMMOTION, BRAWL **3 :** an unevenness or disturbance of surface **:** RIPPLE **4 a :** a strip of fabric gathered or pleated on one edge **b :** 2RUFF 2 — **ruf·fly** \'rəf-(ə-)lē\ *adj*

3**ruffle** *n* [*ruff* (a drumbeat)] **:** a low vibrating drumbeat less loud than a roll

ru·fous \'rü-fəs\ *adj* [L *rufus* red — more at RED] **:** REDDISH

rug \'rəg\ *n* [(assumed) ME, rag, tuft, of Scand origin; akin to ON *rögg* tuft; akin to L *ruere* to rush, fall, dig up, Skt *ravate* he breaks up] **1 :** a piece of thick heavy fabric that usu. has a nap or pile and is used as a floor covering **2 :** a floor mat of an animal pelt <a bearskin ~> **3 :** LAP ROBE

ru·ga \'rü-gə\ *n, pl* **ru·gae** \-ˌgī, -ˌgē, -ˌjē\ [NL, fr. L, wrinkle — more at ROUGH] **:** an anatomical fold or wrinkle esp. of the viscera — usu. used in pl. — **ru·gal** \'rü-gəl\ *adj* — **ru·gate** \-ˌgāt\ *adj*

rug·by \'rəg-bē\ *n, often cap* [*Rugby* School, Rugby, England] **:** a football game in which play is continuous without time-outs or substitutions, interference and forward passing are not permitted, and kicking, dribbling, lateral passing, and tackling are featured

rug·ged \'rəg-əd\ *adj* [ME, fr. (assumed) ME *rug*] **1** *obs* **:** SHAGGY, HAIRY **2 :** having a rough uneven surface **:** JAGGED <~ mountains> **3 :** TURBULENT, STORMY **4 a :** seamed with wrinkles and furrows **:** WEATHERED **b :** showing signs of strength **:** STURDY <there was a certain ~ air of fidelity about him —Charles Dickens> **5 a :** AUSTERE, STERN **b :** COARSE, RUDE **6 a :** strongly built or constituted <those that survive are stalwart, ~ men —L. D. Stamp> **b :** presenting a severe test of ability, stamina, or resolution ***syn*** see ROUGH — **rug·ged·ly** *adv* — **rug·ged·ness** *n*

rug·ged·ize \'rəg-əd-ˌīz\ *vt* **-ized; -iz·ing :** to strengthen (as a machine) for better resistance to wear, stress, and abuse <a *ruggedized* camera> — **rug·ged·iza·tion** \ˌrəg-əd-ə-'zā-shən\ *n*

rug·ger \'rəg-ər\ *n* [by alter.] *Brit* **:** RUGBY

ru·go·sa rose \rü-ˌgō-sə-, -zə-\ *n* [NL *rugosa,* specific epithet of *Rosa rugosa* rugose rose] **:** any of various garden roses descended from a rose introduced from China and Japan

ru·gose \'rü-ˌgōs\ *adj* [L *rugosus,* fr. *ruga*] **1 :** full of wrinkles <~ cheeks> **2 :** having the veinlets sunken and the spaces between elevated <~ leaves of the sage> — **ru·gose·ly** *adv* — **ru·gos·i·ty** \rü-'gäs-ət-ē\ *n*

ru·gu·lose \'rü-gyə-ˌlōs\ *adj* [prob. fr. (assumed) NL *rugulosus,* fr. NL *rugula,* dim. of L *ruga*] **:** having small rugae **:** finely wrinkled

Ruhm·korff coil \ˌrüm-ˌkȯrf-, ˌrəm-\ *n* [Heinrich *Ruhmkorff* †1877 G physicist] **:** INDUCTION COIL

1ru·in \'rü-ən, -ˌin\ *n* [ME *ruine,* fr. MF, fr. L *ruina;* akin to L *ruere* to fall — more at RUG] **1 a** *archaic* **:** a falling down **:** COLLAPSE <from age to age . . . the crash of ~ fitfully resounds —William Wordsworth> **b :** physical, moral, economic, or social collapse **2 a :** the state of being ruined <the city lay in ~s> **b :** the remains of something destroyed — usu. used in pl. <the ~s of the ancient world —William Hazlitt †1830> **3 :** a cause of destruction **4 a :** the action of destroying, laying waste, or wrecking **b :** DAMAGE, INJURY **5 :** a ruined building, person, or object — **ru·in·ate** \-ə-ˌnət, -ˌnāt\ *adj* — **ru·in·ate** \-ˌnāt\ *vt*

syn RUIN, HAVOC, DEVASTATION, DESTRUCTION *shared meaning element* **:** the bringing about of or the results of disaster

2ruin *vt* **1 :** to reduce to ruins **:** DEVASTATE **2 a :** to damage irreparably **b :** BANKRUPT, IMPOVERISH <~*ed* by speculation> **3 :** to subject to frustration, failure, or disaster <~*ed* his chances of promotion> ~ *vi* **:** to become ruined — **ru·in·er** *n*

syn RUIN, WRECK, DILAPIDATE *shared meaning element* **:** to subject to forces that are destructive of soundness, worth, or usefulness

ru·in·ation \ˌrü-ə-'nā-shən\ *n* **:** RUIN, DESTRUCTION

ru·in·ous \'rü-ə-nəs\ *adj* **1 :** DILAPIDATED, RUINED **2 :** causing or tending to cause ruin — **ru·in·ous·ly** *adv* — **ru·in·ous·ness** *n*

1rule \'rül\ *n* [ME *reule,* fr. OF, fr. L *regula* straightedge, rule, fr. *regere* to lead straight — more at RIGHT] **1 a :** a prescribed guide for conduct or action **b :** the laws or regulations prescribed by the founder of a religious order for observance by its members **c :** an accepted procedure, custom, or habit **d (1) :** a usu. written order or direction made by a court regulating court practice or the action of parties **(2) :** a legal precept or doctrine **e :** a regulation or bylaw governing procedure or controlling conduct **2 a (1) :** a usu. valid generalization <such statements . . . should be the ~, rather than the exception —J. K. Javits> **(2) :** a generally prevailing quality, state, or mode <fair weather was the ~ yesterday —*N.Y. Times*> **b :** a standard of judgment **:** CRITERION **c :** a regulating principle **3 a :** the exercise of authority or control **:** DOMINION **b :** a period during which a specified ruler or government exercises control **4 a :** a strip of material marked off in units used for measuring or ruling off lengths **b :** a metal strip with a type-high face that prints a linear design; *also* **:** the design so printed — **as a rule :** for the most part **:** GENERALLY

2rule *vb* **ruled; rul·ing** *vt* **1 a :** to exert control, direction, or influence on <the superstitions that ~ primitive minds> **b :** to exercise control over esp. by curbing or restraining <~ a fractious horse> <*ruled* his appetites firmly> **2 a :** to exercise authority or power over often harshly or arbitrarily <the speaker *ruled* the legislature with an iron hand> **b :** to be preeminent in **:** DOMINATE **3 :** to determine and declare authoritatively; *esp* **:** to command or determine judicially **4 a (1) :** to mark with lines drawn along or as if along the straight edge of a ruler **(2) :** to mark (a line) on a paper with a ruler **b :** to arrange in a line ~ *vi* **1 a :** to exercise supreme authority **b :** to be first in importance or prominence **:** PREDOMINATE <the physical did not ~ in her nature —Sherwood Anderson> **2 :** to exist in a specified state or condition **3 :** to lay down a legal rule ***syn*** see GOVERN, DECIDE

ruled surface *n* **:** a surface generated by a moving straight line with the result that through every point on the surface a line can be drawn lying wholly in the surface

rule·less \'rül-ləs\ *adj* **:** not restrained or regulated by law

rule of the road : a customary practice (as driving always on a particular side of the road or yielding the right of way) developed in the interest of safety and often subsequently reinforced by law; *esp* **:** any of the rules making up a code governing ships in matters relating to mutual safety

rule of thumb 1 : a method of procedure based upon experience and common sense **2 :** a general principle regarded as roughly correct but not intended to be scientifically accurate

rule out *vt* **1 :** EXCLUDE, ELIMINATE **2 :** to make impossible **:** PREVENT <heavy rain *ruled out* the picnic>

rul·er \'rü-lər\ *n* **1 :** one that rules; *specif* **:** SOVEREIGN **2 :** a worker or a machine that rules paper **3 :** a smooth-edged strip (as of wood or metal) that is usu. marked off in units (as inches) and is used for guiding a pen or pencil in drawing lines or for measuring — **rul·er·ship** \-ˌship\ *n*

1rul·ing \'rü-liŋ\ *n* **:** an official or authoritative decision, decree, statement, or interpretation (as by a judge on a point of law)

2ruling *adj* **1 a :** exerting power or authority <the ~ party> **b :** CHIEF, PREDOMINATING <a ~ passion> **2 :** generally prevailing

1rum \'rəm\ *adj* **rum·mer; rum·mest** [earlier *rome,* perh. fr. Romany *rom* gypsy man] **1** *chiefly Brit* **:** QUEER, ODD <writing is a ~ trade . . . and what is all right one day is all wrong the next —Angela Thirkell> **2** *chiefly Brit* **:** DIFFICULT, DANGEROUS

2rum *n* [prob. short for obs. *rumbullion* (rum)] **1 :** an alcoholic liquor distilled from a fermented cane product (as molasses) **2 :** alcoholic liquor <the demon ~>

Rum *abbr* Rumania; Rumanian

Ru·ma·nian \rù-'mā-nē-ən, -nyən\ *n* **1 :** a native or inhabitant of Rumania **2 :** the Romance language of the Rumanians — **Rumanian** *adj*

rum·ba \'rəm-bə, 'rùm-, 'rüm-\ *n* [AmerSp] **:** a ballroom dance of Cuban Negro origin in 2/4 or 4/4 time with a basic pattern of step-close-step and marked by a delayed transfer of weight and pronounced hip movements; *also* **:** the music for this dance

1rum·ble \'rəm-bəl\ *vb* **rum·bled; rum·bling** \-b(ə-)liŋ\ [ME *rumblen;* akin to MHG *rummeln* to rumble] *vi* **1 :** to make a low heavy rolling sound <thunder *rumbling* in the distance> **2 :** to travel with a low reverberating sound <wagons *rumbled* into town> **3 :** to speak in a low rolling tone **4 :** to engage in a rumble ~ *vt* **1 :** to utter or emit in a low rolling voice **2 :** to polish or otherwise treat (metal parts) in a tumbling barrel — **rum·bler** \-b(ə-)lər\ *n*

2rumble *n* **1 a :** a low heavy continuous reverberating often muffled sound (as of thunder) **b :** low frequency noise in phonographic playback caused by the transmission of mechanical vibrations by the turntable to the pickup **2 :** a seat for servants behind the body of a carriage **3 :** TUMBLING BARREL **4 a :** widespread expression of dissatisfaction or unrest **b :** a street fight esp. among gangs

rumble seat *n* **:** a folding seat in the back of an automobile (as a coupe or roadster) not covered by the top

rum·bling \'rəm-bliŋ\ *n* **1 :** RUMBLE **2 :** general but unofficial talk or opinion often of dissatisfaction — usu. used in pl. <occasional ~s about . . . government spending —Paul Potter>

rum·bly \'rəm-b(ə-)lē\ *adj* **:** tending to rumble or rattle

rum·bus·tious \ˌrəm-'bəs-chəs\ *adj* [alter. of *robustious*] *chiefly Brit* **:** RAMBUNCTIOUS

ru·men \'rü-mən\ *n, pl* **ru·mi·na** \-mə-nə\ *or* **rumens** [NL *rumin-, rumen,* fr. L, gullet] **:** the large first compartment of the stomach of a ruminant in which cellulose is broken down by the action of symbionts — **ru·mi·nal** \-mən-ᵊl\ *adj*

1ru·mi·nant \'rü-mə-nənt\ *n* **:** a ruminant mammal

2ruminant *adj* **1 a (1) :** chewing the cud **(2) :** characterized by chewing again what has been swallowed **b :** of or relating to a suborder (Ruminantia) of even-toed hoofed mammals (as sheep, giraffes, deer, and camels) that chew the cud and have a complex 3- or 4-chambered stomach **2 :** given to or engaged in contemplation **:** MEDITATIVE <stood there with her hands clasped in this attitude of ~ relish —Thomas Wolfe> — **ru·mi·nant·ly** *adv*

ru·mi·nate \'rü-mə-ˌnāt\ *vb* **-nat·ed; -nat·ing** [L *ruminatus,* pp. of *ruminari* to chew the cud, muse upon, fr. *rumin-, rumen* gullet; akin to Skt *romantha* ruminant] *vt* **1 :** to go over in the mind repeatedly and often casually or slowly **2 :** to chew repeatedly for an extended period ~ *vi* **1 :** to chew again what has been chewed slightly and swallowed **:** chew the cud **2 :** to engage in contemplation **:** REFLECT ***syn*** see PONDER — **ru·mi·na·tion** \ˌrü-mə-'nā-shən\ *n* — **ru·mi·na·tive** \'rü-mə-ˌnāt-iv\ *adj* — **ru·mi·na·tive·ly** *adv* — **ru·mi·na·tor** \-ˌnāt-ər\ *n*

1rum·mage \'rəm-ij\ *n* [obs. E *rummage* act of packing cargo, modif. of MF *arrimage*] **1 :** a thorough search esp. among a confusion of objects **2 a :** a confused miscellaneous collection **b :** items for sale at a rummage sale

2rummage *vb* **rum·maged; rum·mag·ing** *vt* **1 :** to make a thorough search through **:** RANSACK <*rummaged* the attic> **2 :** to discover by searching **3 :** to examine minutely and completely ~ *vi* **1 :** to make a thorough search or investigation **2 :** to engage in an undirected or haphazard search — **rum·mag·er** *n*

rummage sale *n* **:** a usu. informal sale of miscellaneous goods; *esp* **:** a sale of donated articles conducted by a nonprofit organization (as a church or charity) to help support its programs

rum·mer \'rəm-ər\ *n* [G or D; G *römer,* fr. D *roemer*] **:** a large-bowled footed drinking glass often elaborately etched or engraved

1rum·my \'rəm-ē\ *adj* **rum·mi·er; -est :** QUEER, ODD <were still feeling a little ~ from our trip up the escalator —*New Yorker*>

2rummy *n, pl* **rummies :** DRUNKARD

3rummy *n* [perh. fr. 1*rummy*] **:** any of several card games for two or more players in which each player tries to assemble groups of three or more cards of the same rank or suit and to be the first to meld all his cards

1ru·mor \'rü-mər\ *n* [ME *rumour,* fr. MF, fr. L *rumor;* akin to OE *rēon* to lament, Gk *ōryesthai* to howl] **1 :** talk or opinion widely disseminated with no discernible source **:** HEARSAY **2 :** a statement or report current without known authority for its truth **3 :** a soft low indistinct sound **:** MURMUR ***syn*** see REPORT

2rumor *vt* **ru·mored; ru·mor·ing** \'rüm-(ə-)riŋ\ **:** to tell or spread by rumor

ru·mor·mon·ger \-ˌməŋ-gər, -ˌmäŋ-\ *n* **:** one who spreads rumors

ru·mour \'rü-mər\ *chiefly Brit var of* RUMOR

rump \'rəmp\ *n* [ME, of Scand origin; akin to Icel *rumpr* rump; akin to MHG *rumph* torso] **1 a :** the upper rounded part of the hindquarters of a quadruped mammal **b :** BUTTOCKS **c :** the sacral or dorsal part of the posterior end of a bird **2 :** a cut of beef between the loin and round — see BEEF illustration **3 :** a small fragment remaining after the separation of the larger part of a group or an area; *esp* **:** a group (as a parliament) carrying on in the name of the original body after the departure or expulsion of a large number of its members

1rum·ple \'rəm-pəl\ *n* **:** FOLD, WRINKLE

2rumple *vb* **rum·pled; rum·pling** \-p(ə-)liŋ\ [D *rompelen;* akin to OHG *rimpfan* to wrinkle, L *curvus* curved] *vt* **1 :** WRINKLE, CRUMPLE **2 :** to make unkempt **:** TOUSLE <~ his hair> ~ *vi* **:** to become rumpled

rum·ply \'rəm-p(ə-)lē\ *adj* **rum·pli·er; -est :** having rumples

rum·pus \'rəm-pəs\ *n* [origin unknown] **:** a usu. noisy commotion

rumpus room *n* **:** a room usu. in the basement of a home that is used for games, parties, and recreation

rum·run·ner \'rəm-ˌrən-ər\ *n* **:** a person or ship engaged in bringing prohibited liquor ashore or across a border — **rum–run·ning** \-ˌrən-iŋ\ *adj*

1run \'rən\ *vb* **ran** \'ran\; **run; run·ning** [ME *ronnen,* alter. of *rinnen,* v.i. (fr. OE *iernan, rinnan* & ON *rinna*) & of *rennen,* v.t., fr. ON *renna;* akin to OHG *rinnan,* v.i., to run, OE *rīsan* to rise] *vi* **1 a :** to go faster than a walk; *specif* **:** to go steadily by springing steps so that both feet leave the ground for an instant in each step **b** *of a horse* **:** to move at a fast gallop **c :** FLEE, RETREAT, ESCAPE <dropped his gun and *ran*> **d :** to utilize a running play on offense — used of a football team **2 a :** to go without restraint **:** move freely about at will <let his chickens ~ loose> **b :** to keep company **:** CONSORT <a ram *running* with ewes> <*ran* with a wild crowd when he was young> **c :** to sail before the wind in distinction from reaching or sailing close-hauled **d :** ROAM, ROVE <*running* about with no overcoat> **3 a :** to go rapidly or hurriedly **:** HASTEN <~ and fetch the doctor> **b :** to go in urgency or distress **:** RESORT <~*s* to his mother at every little difficulty> **c :** to make a quick, easy, or casual trip or visit <*ran* over to borrow some sugar> **4 a :** to contend in a race **b :** to enter into an election contest **5 a :** to move on or as if on wheels **:** GLIDE <file drawers *running* on ball bearings> **b :** to roll forward rapidly or freely **c :** to pass or slide freely <a rope ~*s*

through the pulley> d : to ravel lengthwise <stockings guaranteed not to ~> 6 : to sing or play a musical passage quickly <~ up the scale> 7 a : to go back and forth : PLY <the train ~s between New York and Washington> b *of fish* : to migrate or move in schools; *esp* : to ascend a river to spawn 8 a : TURN, ROTATE <a swiftly *running* grindstone> b : FUNCTION, OPERATE <the engine ~s on gasoline> 9 a : to continue in force or operation <the contract has two more years to ~> b : to accompany as a valid obligation or right <a right-of-way that ~s with the land> c : to continue to accrue or become payable <interest on the loan ~s from July 1st> 10 : to pass from one state to another <~ into debt> 11 a : to flow rapidly or under pressure b : MELT, FUSE c : SPREAD, DISSOLVE <colors guaranteed not to ~> d : to discharge pus or serum <a *running* sore> 12 a : to develop rapidly in some specific direction; *esp* : to throw out an elongated shoot of growth b : to tend to produce or develop a specified quality or feature <they ~ to big noses in that family> 13 a : to lie in or take a certain direction <the boundary line ~s east> b : to lie or extend in relation to something c : to go back : REACH d (1) : to be in a certain form or expression <the letter ~s as follows> (2) : to be in a certain order of succession 14 a : to occur persistently <musical talent ~s in his family> b : to remain of a specified size, character, or quality <profits were *running* high> c : to exist or occur in a continuous range of variation <shades ~ from white to dark gray> d : to play on a stage a number of successive days or nights <the musical *ran* for six months> 15 a : to spread or pass quickly from point to point <chills *ran* up his spine> b : to be current : CIRCULATE <speculation *ran* rife on who would win> ~ *vt* 1 a : to cause (an animal) to go rapidly : ride or drive fast b : to bring to a specified condition by or as if by running <*ran* himself to death> c : to go in pursuit of : HUNT, CHASE <dogs that ~ deer> d : to follow the trail of backward : TRACE <*ran* the rumor to its source> e : to enter, register, or enroll as a contestant in a race f : to put forward as a candidate for office 2 a : to drive (livestock) esp. to a grazing place b : to provide pasturage for (livestock) c : to keep or maintain (livestock) on or as if on pasturage 3 a : to pass over or traverse with speed b : to accomplish or perform by or as if by running <*ran* a great race> <*running* errands for a bank> c : to slip through or past <~ a blockade> 4 a : to cause to penetrate or enter : THRUST <*ran* a splinter into his toe> b : STITCH c : to cause to pass : LEAD <~ a wire in from the antenna> d : to cause to collide <*ran* his head into a post> e : SMUGGLE <~ guns> 5 : to cause to pass lightly or quickly over, along, or into something <*ran* his eye down the list> 6 a : to cause or allow (as a vehicle or a vessel) to go in a specified manner or direction <*ran* his car off the road> b : OPERATE <~ a lathe> c : to carry on : MANAGE, CONDUCT <~ a factory> 7 a : to be full of or drenched with <streets *ran* blood> b : CONTAIN, ASSAY 8 : to cause to move or flow in a specified way or into a specified position <~ cards into a file> 9 a : to melt and cast in a mold <~ bullets> b : TREAT, PROCESS, REFINE <~ oil in a still> <~ a problem through a computer> 10 : to make oneself liable to : INCUR <*ran* the risk of discovery> 11 : to mark out : DRAW <~ a contour line on a map> 12 : to permit (as charges) to accumulate before settling <~ an account at the grocery> 13 a : to run off <a book to be ~ on lightweight paper> b : to carry in a printed medium : PRINT 14 a : to make (a series of counts) without a miss <~ 19 in an inning in billiards> b : to lead winning cards of (a suit) successively 15 : to make (a golf ball) roll forward after alighting — **run across** : to meet with or discover by chance — **run after** 1 : PURSUE, CHASE; *esp* : to seek the company of 2 : to take up with : FOLLOW <*run after* new theories> — **run against** 1 : to meet suddenly or unexpectedly 2 : to work or take effect unfavorably to : DISFAVOR, OPPOSE — **run a temperature** : to have a fever — **run false** : to save distance by running directly for the game instead of following the scent or track — **run foul of** 1 : to collide with <*ran foul of* a hidden reef> 2 : to come into conflict with <*run foul of* the law> — **run into** 1 a : to change or transform into : BECOME b : to merge with c : to mount up to <his yearly income often *runs into* six figures> 2 a : to collide with b : ENCOUNTER, MEET <*ran into* an old classmate the other day> — **run rings around** : to show marked superiority over : defeat decisively or overwhelmingly — **run riot** 1 : to act wildly or without restraint 2 : to occur in profusion — **run short** : to become insufficient — **run short of** : to use up — **run to** : to mount up to <the book *runs to* 500 pages> — **run upon** : to run across : meet with

[2]run *n* 1 a : an act or the action of running : continued rapid movement b : a quickened gallop c (1) : the act of migrating or ascending a river to spawn (2) : an assemblage of fish that migrate or ascend a river to spawn d : a running race <a mile ~> e : a score made in baseball by a runner reaching home plate safely f : strength or ability to run <two laps took most of the ~ out of him> g : a gain of a usu. specified distance made on a running play in football <a 25-yard ~> 2 a *chiefly Midland* : CREEK 2 b : something that flows in the course of a certain operation or during a certain time <the first ~ of sap in sugar maples> 3 a : the stern of the underwater body of a ship from where it begins to curve or slope upward and inward b : the direction in which a vein of ore lies c : a direction of secondary or minor cleavage : GRAIN <the ~ of a mass of granite> d (1) : the horizontal distance covered by a flight of steps (2) : the horizontal distance from the wall plate to the center line of a building e : general tendency or direction 4 : a continuous series esp. of things of identical or similar sort: as a : a rapid passage up or down a scale in vocal or instrumental music b : a number of rapid small dance steps executed in even tempo c : the act of making successively a number of successful shots or strokes; *also* : the score thus made <a ~ of 20 in billiards> d : an unbroken course of performances or showings e : a set of consecutive measurements, readings, or observations f : persistent and heavy demands from depositors, creditors, or customers <a ~ on a bank> g : SEQUENCE 2b 5 : the quantity of work turned out in a continuous operation <a newspaper press ~> 6 : the usual or normal kind, character, type, or group <the average ~ of students> 7 a : the distance covered in a period of continuous traveling or sailing b : a course or route esp. if mapped out and traveled with regularity : TRIP c : a news reporter's regular territory : BEAT d : the distance a golf ball travels after touching the ground e : freedom of movement in or access to a place or area <has the ~ of the house> 8 a : the period during which a machine or plant is in continuous operation b : the use of machinery for a single set of processing procedures <a computer ~> 9 a : a way, track, or path frequented by animals b : an enclosure for livestock where they may feed or exercise c *Austral* (1) : a large area of land used for grazing <a sheep ~> (2) : RANCH, STATION <*run*-holder> d : an inclined passageway 10 a : an inclined course (as for skiing or bobsledding) b : a support (as a track, pipe, or trough) on which something runs 11 a : a ravel in a knitted fabric (as in hosiery) caused by the breaking of stitches b : a paint defect caused by excessive flow — **in the long run** : in the course of sufficiently prolonged time, trial, or experience — **in the short run** : in the immediate future — **on the run** 1 : in haste : without pausing 2 : in retreat : running away

[3]run *adj* 1 a : being in a melted state <~ butter> b : made from molten material : cast in a mold <~ metal> 2 *of fish* : having made a migration or spawning run <a fresh ~ salmon> 3 : exhausted or winded from running

run·about \ˈrən-ə-ˌbau̇t\ *n* 1 : one who wanders about : STRAY 2 : a light open wagon, roadster, or motorboat

run·a·gate \ˈrən-ə-ˌgāt\ *n* [alter. of *renegate*, fr. ML *renegatus* — more at RENEGADE] 1 : FUGITIVE, RUNAWAY 2 : VAGABOND

run along *vi* : to go away : be on one's way : DEPART

run·around \ˈrən-ə-ˌrau̇nd\ *n* 1 : matter typeset in shortened measure to run around something (as a cut) 2 : deceptive or delaying action esp. in response to a request

[1]run·away \ˈrən-ə-ˌwā\ *n* 1 : FUGITIVE 2 : the act of running away out of control; *also* : something (as a horse) that is running out of control 3 : a one-sided or overwhelming victory

[2]runaway *adj* 1 a : running away : FUGITIVE b : leaving to gain special advantages (as lower wages) or avoid disadvantages (as governmental or union restrictions) <~ shipping firms> 2 : accomplished by elopement or during flight 3 : won by or having a long lead 4 : subject to uncontrolled changes <~ inflation>

run away \ˌrən-ə-ˈwā\ *vi* 1 a : FLEE, DESERT b : to leave home; *esp* : ELOPE 2 : to run out of control : STAMPEDE, BOLT 3 : to gain a substantial lead : win by a large margin — **run away with** 1 : to take away in haste or secretly; *esp* : STEAL 2 : to outshine the others in (a theatrical performance) 3 : to carry or drive beyond prudent or reasonable limits <his imagination *ran away with* him>

run·back \ˈrən-ˌbak\ *n* : a run made in football after catching an opponent's kick or intercepting a pass

run·ci·ble spoon \ˌrən(t)-sə-bəl-\ *n* [coined with an obscure meaning by Edward Lear] : a sharp-edged fork with three broad curved prongs

run·ci·nate \ˈrən(t)-sə-ˌnāt\ *adj* [L *runcinatus*, pp. of *runcinare* to plane off, fr. *runcina* plane] : pinnately cut with the lobes pointing downward <~ leaves of the dandelion>

run·dle \ˈrən-d^{ə}l\ *n* [ME *roundel* circle — more at ROUNDEL] 1 : a step of a ladder : RUNG 2 : the drum of a windlass or capstan

rund·let *or* **run·let** \ˈrən-(d)lət\ *n* [ME *roundelet* — more at ROUNDLET] 1 : a small barrel : KEG 2 : an old unit of liquid capacity equal to 18 U.S. gallons

run·down \ˈrən-ˌdau̇n\ *n* 1 : a maneuver in baseball in which a base runner who is caught off base is chased by two or more opposing players who throw the ball from one to another in an attempt to tag him out 2 : an item-by-item report : SUMMARY

run–down \ˈrən-ˈdau̇n\ *adj* 1 : being in poor repair : DILAPIDATED 2 : worn out : EXHAUSTED 3 : completely unwound

run down \ˈrən-ˈdau̇n, ˌrən-\ *vt* 1 a : to collide with and knock down b : to run against and cause to sink 2 a : to chase to exhaustion or until captured b : to find by search : trace the source of c : to tag out (a base runner) between bases on a rundown 3 : DISPARAGE ~ *vi* 1 : to cease to operate because of the exhaustion of motive power <that clock *ran down* hours ago> 2 : to decline in physical condition

rune \ˈrün\ *n* [ON & OE *rūn* mystery, runic character, writing;

f u th o r k g
w h n i j ch p eo s t
b e m l ng oe d a ae y ea

the runic alphabet

akin to OHG *rūna* secret discussion] **1** : one of the characters of an alphabet prob. derived from Latin and Greek and used by the Germanic peoples from about the 3d to the 13th centuries **2** : MYSTERY, MAGIC **3** [Finn *runo,* of Gmc origin; akin to ON *rūn*] **a** : a Finnish or Old Norse poem **b** : POEM, SONG — **ru·nic** \'rü-nik\ *adj*

[1]**rung** *past part of* RING

[2]**rung** \'rəŋ\ *n* [ME, fr. OE *hrung;* akin to OE *hring* ring — more at RING] **1** *Scot* : a heavy staff or cudgel **2** : a spoke of a wheel **3 a** : a rounded part placed as a crosspiece between the legs of a chair **b** : one of the crosspieces of a ladder **4** : a stage in an ascent <rise a few ~*s* on the social scale —H. W. Van Loon>

run–in \'rən-ˌin\ *n* **1** : something inserted as a substantial addition in copy or typeset matter **2** : ALTERCATION, QUARREL

run in \'rən-'in, ˌrən-\ *vt* **1 a** : to make (typeset matter) continuous without a paragraph or other break **b** : to insert as additional matter **2** : to arrest for a minor offense **3** : to break in ~ *vi* : to pay a casual visit

run·less \'rən-ləs\ *adj* : scoring no runs

run·let \'rən-lət\ *n* : RUNNEL

run·nel \'rən-ᵊl\ *n* [alter. of ME *rinel,* fr. OE *rynel;* akin to OE *rinnan* to run — more at RUN] : RIVULET, STREAMLET

run·ner \'rən-ər\ *n* **1 a** : one that runs : RACER **b** : BASE RUNNER **c** : BALLCARRIER **2 a** : MESSENGER **b** : one that smuggles or distributes illicit or contraband goods (as drugs, liquor, or guns) **3** : any of various large active carangid fishes **4 a** : either of the longitudinal pieces on which a sled or sleigh slides **b** : the part of a skate that slides on the ice : BLADE **c** : the support of a drawer or a sliding door **5 a** : a growth produced by a plant in running; *esp* : STOLON 1a **b** : a plant that forms or spreads by means of runners **c** : a twining vine (as a scarlet runner) **6 a** : a long narrow carpet for a hall or staircase **b** : a narrow decorative cloth cover for a table or dresser top

runner bean *n, chiefly Brit* : SCARLET RUNNER

run·ner–up \'rən-ə-ˌrəp, ˌrən-ə-'\ *n, pl* **runners–up** *also* **runner–ups** : the competitor that finishes next to the winner in a contest involving several competitors

[1]**run·ning** \'rən-iŋ\ *n* **1 a** : the action of running **b** : RACE **2** : physical condition for running **3** : MANAGEMENT, CARE — **in the running 1** : competing in a contest **2** : having a chance to win a contest — **out of the running 1** : not competing in a contest **2** : having no chance of winning a contest

[2]**running** *adj* **1** : FLUID, RUNNY **2 a** : INCESSANT, CONTINUOUS <a ~ battle> **b** : made during the course of a process or activity <a ~ commentary on the game> **3** : measured in a straight line <cost of lumber per ~ foot> **4** : CURSIVE, FLOWING **5 a** : initiated or performed while running or with a running start <~ catch> **b** : of, relating to, used in, or being a football play in which the ball is advanced by running rather than by passing <their ~ game was off> <a ~ back> **c** : designed for use for foot races <a ~ track> **6** : fitted or trained for running rather than walking, trotting, or jumping <a ~ horse>

[3]**running** *adv* : in succession : CONSECUTIVELY <for three days ~>

running board *n* : a footboard esp. at the side of an automobile

running gear *n* **1** : the parts of an automobile chassis not used in developing, transmitting, and controlling power **2** : the working and carrying parts of a machine (as a locomotive)

running hand *n* : handwriting in which the letters are usu. slanted and the words formed without lifting the pen

running head *n* : a headline repeated on consecutive pages (as of a book) — called also *running headline*

running knot *n* : a knot that slips along the rope or line round which it is tied; *esp* : an overhand slipknot

running light *n* : one of the lights carried by a vehicle (as a ship) under way at night that indicate size, position, and direction

running mate *n* **1** : a horse entered in a race to set the pace for a horse of the same owner or stable **2** : a candidate running for a subordinate place on a ticket; *esp* : the candidate for vice-president **3** : COMPANION

running start *n* : FLYING START

running stitch *n* : a small even stitch run in and out in cloth

running title *n* : the title or short title of a volume printed at the top of left-hand text pages or sometimes of all text pages

run·ny \'rən-ē\ *adj* : having a tendency to run <a ~ nose>

run·off \'rən-ˌȯf\ *n* **1** : the portion of the precipitation on the land that ultimately reaches streams; *esp* : the water from rain or melted snow that flows over the surface **2** : a final race, contest, or election to decide an earlier one that has not resulted in a decision in favor of any one competitor

run off \'rən-'ȯf, ˌrən-\ *vt* **1 a** : to recite or compose rapidly or glibly **b** : to produce copies (as with a printing press) **c** : to cause to be run or played to a finish **d** : to decide (as a race) by a runoff **e** : to carry out (a test) **2** : to draw off : drain off **3 a** : to drive off (as trespassers) **b** : to steal (as cattle) by driving away ~ *vi* : to run away — **run off with** : to carry off : STEAL

run–of–paper \ˌrən-əv-'pā-pər\ *adj* : to be placed anywhere in a newspaper at the option of the editor <~ advertisement>

run–of–the–mill \ˌrən-ə(v)-t͟hə-'mil\ *adj* : not outstanding in quality or rarity : AVERAGE

run–of–the–mine \-'mīn\ *or* **run–of–mine** \-əv-'mīn\ *adj* **1** : not graded <~ coal> **2** : RUN-OF-THE-MILL

[1]**run–on** \'rən-'ȯn, -'än\ *adj* : continuing without rhetorical pause from one line of verse into another

[2]**run–on** \-ˌȯn, -ˌän\ *n* : something (as a dictionary entry) that is run on

run on \'rən-'ȯn, ˌrən-, -'än\ *vi* **1** : to keep going : CONTINUE **2** : to talk or narrate at length ~ *vt* **1** : to continue (matter in type) without a break or a new paragraph : run in **2** : to place or add (as an entry in a dictionary) at the end of a paragraphed item

run–on sentence *n* : a sentence containing a comma fault

run out *vi* **1 a** : to come to an end : EXPIRE <time *ran out*> **b** : to become exhausted or used up : FAIL <the gasoline *ran out*> **2** : to jut out ~ *vt* **1** : to finish out (as a course, series, or contest) : COMPLETE **2 a** : to fill out (a line) with quads, leaders, or ornaments **b** : to set (as the first line of a paragraph) with a hanging indention **3** : to exhaust (oneself) in running **4** : to cause to leave by force or coercion : EXPEL — **run out of** : to use up the available supply of — **run out on** : DESERT

run·over \'rən-ˌō-vər\ *n* : matter for publication that exceeds the space allotted

run–over \'rən-'ō-vər\ *adj* : extending beyond the allotted space

run over \ˌrən-'ō-vər\ *vi* **1** : OVERFLOW **2** : to exceed a limit ~ *vt* **1** : to go over, examine, repeat, or rehearse quickly **2** : to collide with, knock down, and often drive over <*ran over* a dog>

runt \'rənt\ *n* [origin unknown] **1** *chiefly Scot* : a hardened stalk or stem of a plant **2** : an animal unusually small of its kind; *esp* : the smallest of a litter of pigs **3** : a person of small stature — **runt·i·ness** \'rənt-ē-nəs\ *n* — **runty** \'rənt-ē\ *adj*

run–through \'rən-ˌthrü\ *n* : a cursory reading, summary, or rehearsal

run through \ˌrən-'thrü\ *vt* **1** : PIERCE **2** : to spend or consume wastefully and rapidly **3** : to read or rehearse without pausing **4 a** : to carry out : DO **b** : to subject to a process

run up *vi* : to grow rapidly : shoot up ~ *vt* **1** : to increase by bidding : bid up **2** : to stitch together quickly **3** : to erect hastily **4** : to run (an aircraft engine) at high speed for testing, checking, or warming

run·way \'rən-ˌwā\ *n* **1** : the channel of a stream **2 a** : a beaten path made by animals **b** : a passageway for animals **3** : an artificially surfaced strip of ground on a landing field for the landing and takeoff of airplanes **4** : a narrow platform from a stage into an auditorium **5** : RUN 10b

ru·pee \rü-'pē, 'rü-ˌpē\ *n* [Hindi *rūpaiyā,* fr. Skt *rūpya* coined silver] — see MONEY table

ru·pi·ah \rü-'pē-ə\ *n, pl* **rupiah** *or* **rupiahs** [Hindi *rūpaiyā*] — see MONEY table

ru·pic·o·lous \rü-'pik-ə-ləs\ *or* **ru·pic·o·line** \-ˌlīn\ *adj* [L *rupes* rock + *-cola* inhabitant; akin to L *rumpere* — more at WHEEL] : living among, inhabiting, or growing on rocks

[1]**rup·ture** \'rəp-chər\ *n* [ME *ruptur,* fr. MF or L; MF *rupture,* fr. L *ruptura* fracture, fr. *ruptus,* pp. of *rumpere* to break — more at REAVE] **1** : breach of peace or concord; *specif* : open hostility or war between nations **2 a** : the tearing apart of a tissue <~ of the heart muscle> <~ of an intervertebral disk> **b** : HERNIA **3** : a breaking apart or the state of being broken apart

[2]**rupture** *vb* **rup·tured; rup·tur·ing** \-chə-riŋ, -shriŋ\ *vt* **1 a** : to part by violence : BREAK, BURST **b** : to create or induce a breach of **2** : to produce a rupture in ~ *vi* : to have or undergo a rupture

ru·ral \'ru̇r-əl\ *adj* [ME, fr. MF, fr. L *ruralis,* fr. *rur-, rus* open land — more at ROOM] : of or relating to the country, country people or life, or agriculture — **ru·ral·i·ty** \ru̇-'ral-ət-ē\ *n* — **ru·ral·ly** \-ə-lē\ *adv*

syn RURAL, RUSTIC, PASTORAL, BUCOLIC *shared meaning element* : relating to or characteristic of the country. RURAL, the comprehensive turn, implies a contrast to *urban* <they were well-off by *rural* standards> <a peaceful *rural* scene> RUSTIC, often interchangeable with *rural,* is more likely to be chosen to describe less pleasing aspects of country life <rude carts, bespattered with *rustic* mire —Charles Dickens> or to stress a contrast with the refinements of city or town <if education had not meddled with her *rustic* nature —Jean Stafford> PASTORAL implies an idealized rusticity and separation from urban bustle <*pastoral* dales, thin-set with modest farms —William Wordsworth> BUCOLIC, a curiously dichotomous word, may come close to *pastoral* in stressing rural peace and charm <there is here a *bucolic* atmosphere of peculiar beauty and inspiration —Sacheverell Sitwell> or approach *rustic* in emphasizing the crudity and lack of refinement of rural life or people <unable long to stand the *bucolic* tedium>

rural dean *n* : DEAN 1b

rural free delivery *n* : free delivery of mail to a rural area — called also *rural delivery*

ru·ral·ist \'ru̇r-ə-ləst\ *n* : one who lives in a rural area

rural route *n* : a mail-delivery route in a rural free delivery area

rur·ban \'rər-bən, 'ru̇(ə)r-\ *adj* [blend of *rural* and *urban*] : of, relating to, or constituting an area which is chiefly residential but where some farming is carried on

Ru·ri·tan \'ru̇r-ə-tən\ *n* [*Ruritan National* (club)] : a member of a major national service club

ruse \'rüs, 'rüz\ *n* [F, fr. MF, fr. *ruser* to dodge, deceive] : a wily subterfuge ***syn*** see TRICK

[1]**rush** \'rəsh\ *n* [ME, fr. OE *risc;* akin to MHG *rusch* rush, L *restis* rope] : any of various monocotyledonous often tufted marsh plants (as of the genera *Juncus* and *Scirpus* of the family Juncaceae, the rush family) with cylindrical often hollow stems which are used in bottoming chairs and plaiting mats — **rushy** \-ē\ *adj*

[2]**rush** *vb* [ME *russhen,* fr. MF *ruser* to put to flight, repel, deceive, fr. L *recusare* to refuse — more at RECUSANCY] *vi* **1** : to move forward, progress, or act with haste or eagerness or without preparation **2** : to advance a football by running plays <~*ed* for a total of 150 yards> ~ *vt* **1** : to push or impel on or forward with speed, impetuosity, or violence **2** : to perform in a short time or at high speed **3** : to urge to an unnatural or extreme speed **4** : to run toward or against in attack : CHARGE **5 a** : to carry (a ball) forward in a running play **b** : to move in quickly on (a kicker or passer) to hinder, prevent, or block a kick or pass — used esp. of defensive linemen **6 a** : to lavish attention on : COURT **b** : to try to secure a pledge of membership (as in a fraternity) from

[3]**rush** *n* **1 a** : a violent forward motion **b** : ONSET, ATTACK **c** : a surging of emotion **2 a** : a burst of activity, productivity, or speed **b** : a sudden insistent demand **3** : a thronging of people usu. to a new place in search of wealth <gold ~> **4** : the act of carrying a football during a game : running play **5** : a round of attention usu. involving extensive social activity **6** : a print of a motion-picture scene processed directly after the shooting for review by the director or producer **7** : the first rapid excitation produced by a narcotic drug

[4]rush *adj* : requiring or marked by special speed or urgency <~ orders> <the ~ season>
rush candle *n* : RUSHLIGHT
rush·ee \ˌrəsh-ˈē\ *n* : a college or university student who is being rushed by a fraternity or sorority
rush·er \ˈrəsh-ər\ *n* : one that rushes; *esp* : BALLCARRIER
rush hour *n* : a period of the day when the demands esp. of traffic or business are at a peak
rush·ing *n* : the act of advancing a football by running plays : the use of running plays; *also* : yardage gained by running plays
rush·light \ˈrəsh-ˌlīt\ *n* : a candle that consists of the pith of a rush dipped in grease
rusk \ˈrəsk\ *n* [modif. of Sp & Pg *rosca* coil, twisted roll] **1** : hard crisp bread orig. used as ship's stores **2** : a sweet or plain bread baked, sliced, and baked again until dry and crisp
[1]Russ \ˈrəs, ˈrüs, ˈrůs\ *n, pl* **Russ** *or* **Russ·es** [Russ *Rus'*] : RUSSIAN — **Russ** *adj*
[2]Russ *abbr* Russia; Russian
[1]rus·set \ˈrəs-ət\ *n* [ME, fr. OF *rousset,* fr. *rousset,* adj., russet, fr. *rous* russet, fr. L *russus* red; akin to L *ruber* red — more at RED] **1** : coarse homespun usu. reddish brown cloth **2** : a variable color averaging a strong brown **3** : any of various winter apples having russet rough skins
[2]russet *adj* : of the color russet
rus·set·ing *also* **rus·set·ting** \ˈrəs-ət-iŋ\ *n* : a brownish roughened area on the skin of fruit (as apples) caused by injury
Rus·sia leather \ˌrəsh-ə-\ *n* [*Russia,* Europe] : leather made by tanning various skins with willow, birch, or oak and then rubbing the flesh side with a phenolic oil distilled from a European birch — called also *Russia calf*
Rus·sian \ˈrəsh-ən\ *n* **1 a** : a native or inhabitant of Russia; *esp* : a member of the dominant Slavic-speaking Great Russian ethnic group of Russia **b** : one that is of Russian descent **2 a** : a Slavic language of the Russian people that is the official language of the U.S.S.R. **b** : the three Slavic languages of the Russian people including Belorussian and Ukrainian — **Russian** *adj*
Russian blue *n, often cap B* : a slender long-bodied large-eared domestic cat with short silky bluish gray fur
Russian dressing *n* : a dressing (as of mayonnaise or oil and vinegar) with added chili sauce, chopped pickles, or pimientos
rus·sian·ize \ˈrəsh-ə-ˌnīz\ *vt* **-ized; -iz·ing** *often cap* : to make Russian — **rus·sian·iza·tion** \ˌrəsh-ə-nə-ˈzā-shən\ *n*
Russian olive *n* : a chiefly silvery Eurasian large shrub or small tree (*Elaeagnus angustifolia*) cultivated in arid windy regions esp. as a shelterbelt plant
Russian roulette *n* : an act of bravado consisting of spinning the cylinder of a revolver loaded with one cartridge, pointing the muzzle at one's own head, and pulling the trigger
Russian thistle *n* : a prickly European herb (*Salsola kali tenuifolia*) that is a serious pest in No. America — called also *Russian tumbleweed*
Russian wolfhound *n* : BORZOI
rus·si·fy \ˈrəs-ə-ˌfī\ *vt* **-fied; -fy·ing** *often cap* : RUSSIANIZE — **rus·si·fi·ca·tion** \ˌrəs-ə-fə-ˈkā-shən\ *n*
Rus·so- *comb form* [*Russia & Russian*] **1** \ˌrəs-ə, ˈrəs-, -ō\ : Russia : Russians <*Russo*phobia> **2** \ˈrəs(h)-(ˌ)ō, ˌrəs(h)-\ : Russian and <*Russo*-Japanese>
[1]rust \ˈrəst\ *n* [ME, fr. OE *rūst;* akin to OE *rēad* red — more at RED] **1 a** : the reddish brittle coating formed on iron esp. when chemically attacked by moist air and composed essentially of hydrated ferric oxide **b** : a comparable coating produced on a metal other than iron by corrosion **c** : something resembling rust : ACCRETION **2** : corrosive or injurious influence or effect **3** : any of numerous destructive diseases of plants produced by fungi (order Uredinales) and characterized by reddish brown pustular lesions; *also* : a fungus causing this **4** : a strong brown

rust 3: natural size on wheat; magnified to show spores

[2]rust *vi* **1** : to form rust : become oxidized <iron ~*s*> **2** : to degenerate esp. from inaction, lack of use, or passage of time <most men would . . . have allowed their faculties to ~ —T. B. Macaulay> **3** : to become reddish brown as if with rust <the leaves slowly ~*ed*> **4** : to be affected with a rust fungus ~ *vt* **1** : to cause (a metal) to form rust <keep up your bright swords, for the dew will ~ them —Shak.> **2** : to impair or corrode by or as if by time, inactivity, or deleterious use **3** : to cause to become reddish brown : turn the color of rust
[1]rus·tic \ˈrəs-tik\ *also* **rus·ti·cal** \-ti-kəl\ *adj* [ME *rustik,* fr. MF *rustique,* fr. L *rusticus,* fr. *rus* open land — more at ROOM] **1** : of, relating to, or suitable for the country : RURAL **2 a** : made of the rough limbs of trees <~ furniture> **b** : finished by rusticating <a ~ joint in masonry> **3 a** : characteristic of or resembling country people **b** : lacking in social graces or polish **4** : appropriate to the country (as in plainness or sturdiness) <heavy ~ boots> ***syn*** see RURAL — **rus·ti·cal·ly** \-ti-k(ə-)lē\ *adv* — **rus·tic·i·ty** \ˌrəs-ˈtis-ət-ē\ *n*
[2]rustic *n* **1** : an inhabitant of a rural area **2 a** : an awkward coarse person **b** : an unsophisticated rural person
rus·ti·cate \ˈrəs-ti-ˌkāt\ *vb* **-cat·ed; -cat·ing** *vi* : to go into or reside in the country : follow a rustic life ~ *vt* **1** : to suspend from school or college **2** : to bevel or rebate (as the edges of stone blocks) to make the joints conspicuous <a *rusticated* stone wall> **3 a** : to compel to reside in the country **b** : to cause to become rustic : implant rustic mannerisms in — **rus·ti·ca·tion** \ˌrəs-ti-ˈkā-shən\ *n* — **rus·ti·ca·tor** \ˈrəs-ti-ˌkāt-ər\ *n*
[1]rus·tle \ˈrəs-əl\ *vb* **rus·tled; rus·tling** \ˈrəs-(ə-)liŋ\ [ME *rustelen*] *vi* **1** : to make or cause a rustle **2 a** : to act or move with energy or speed **b** : to forage food **3** : to steal cattle ~ *vt* **1** : to cause to rustle **2** : to procure by rustling; *esp* : FORAGE **3** : to take (as cattle) feloniously : STEAL — **rus·tler** \-(ə-)lər\ *n*
[2]rustle *n* : a quick succession or confusion of small sounds
rust mite *n* : any of various small gall mites that burrow in the surface of leaves or fruits usu. producing brown or reddish patches
rust·proof \ˈrəst-ˈprüf\ *adj* : incapable of rusting
[1]rusty \ˈrəs-tē\ *adj* **rust·i·er; -est** **1** : affected by or as if by rust; *esp* : stiff with or as if with rust **2** : inept and slow through lack of practice or old age **3 a** : of the color rust **b** : dulled in color or appearance by age and use <a ~ old suit of clothes> **4** : OUTMODED **5** : HOARSE, GRATING — **rust·i·ly** \-tə-lē\ *adv* — **rust·i·ness** \-tē-nəs\ *n*
[2]rus·ty \ˈrəs-tē\ *adj* **rus·ti·er; -est** [alter. of *restive*] *chiefly dial* : ill-tempered : SURLY
[1]rut \ˈrət\ *n* [ME *rutte,* fr. MF *rut* roar, fr. LL *rugitus,* fr. L *rugitus,* pp. of *rugire* to roar; akin to OE *rēoc* wild, MIr *rucht* roar] **1** : an annually recurrent state of sexual excitement in the male deer; *broadly* : sexual excitement in a mammal esp. when periodic : ESTRUS, HEAT **2** : the period during which rut normally occurs — often used with *the*
[2]rut *vi* **rut·ted; rut·ting** : to be in or enter into a state of rut
[3]rut *n* [perh. modif. of MF *route* way, route] **1 a** : a track worn by a wheel or by habitual passage **b** : a groove in which something runs **c** : CHANNEL, FURROW **2** : a usual or fixed practice; *esp* : a monotonous routine <fall easily into a conversational ~>
[4]rut *vt* **rut·ted; rut·ting** : to make a rut in : FURROW
ru·ta·ba·ga \ˌrüt-ə-ˈbā-gə, ˌrůt-, -ˈbeg-ə\ *n* [Sw dial. *rotabagge,* fr. *rot* root + *bagge* bag] : a turnip (*Brassica napobrassica*) commonly with a very large yellowish root
ruth \ˈrüth\ *n* [ME *ruthe,* fr. *ruen* to rue] **1** : compassion for the misery of another **2** : sorrow for one's own faults : REMORSE ***syn*** see SYMPATHY
Ruth \ˈrüth\ *n* [Heb *Rūth*] **1** : a Moabite woman who accompanied Naomi to Bethlehem and became the ancestress of David **2** : a short narrative book of canonical Jewish and Christian Scriptures — see BIBLE table
ru·the·nic \rü-ˈthen-ik, -ˈthē-nik\ *adj* : of, relating to, or derived from ruthenium esp. with a relatively high valence
ru·the·ni·ous \rü-ˈthē-nē-əs\ *adj* : of, relating to, or derived from ruthenium esp. with a relatively low valence
ru·the·ni·um \-nē-əm\ *n* [NL, fr. ML *Ruthenia* Russia] : a hard brittle grayish polyvalent rare metallic element occurring in platinum ores and used in hardening platinum alloys — see ELEMENT table
Ruth·er·ford atom \ˌrət͟h-ə(r)-fərd-\ *n* [Baron Ernest *Rutherford*] : the atom held to consist of a small dense positively charged nucleus surrounded by planetary electrons
ruth·ful \ˈrüth-fəl\ *adj* **1** : full of ruth : TENDER **2** : full of sorrow : WOEFUL **3** : causing sorrow — **ruth·ful·ly** \-fə-lē\ *adv* — **ruth·ful·ness** *n*
ruth·less \ˈrüth-ləs *also* ˈrůth-\ *adj* : having no ruth : MERCILESS, CRUEL — **ruth·less·ly** *adv* — **ruth·less·ness** *n*
ru·ti·lant \ˈrüt-ᵊl-ənt\ *adj* [ME *rutilaunt,* fr. L *rutilant-, rutilans,* pp. of *rutilare* to be reddish, fr. *rutilus* reddish; akin to L *ruber* red — more at RED] : having a reddish glow
ru·tile \ˈrü-ˌtēl\ *n* [G *rutil,* fr. L *rutilus* reddish] : a mineral TiO_2 that consists of titanium dioxide usu. with a little iron, is typically of a reddish brown color but sometimes deep red or black, and has a brilliant metallic or adamantine luster
Rutland *abbr* Rutlandshire
rut·tish \ˈrət-ish\ *adj* : inclined to rut : LUSTFUL — **rut·tish·ly** *adv* — **rut·tish·ness** *n*
rut·ty \ˈrət-ē\ *adj* **rut·ti·er; -est** : full of ruts
RW *abbr* **1** radiological warfare **2** right worshipful **3** right worthy
rwy *or* **ry** *abbr* railway
Rx \ˈär-ˈeks\ *n* [alter. of ℞ symbol used at the beginning of a prescription, abbr. for L *recipe* — more at RECIPE] : a medical prescription
-ry \rē\ *n suffix* [ME *-rie,* fr. OF, short for *-erie* -ery] : -ERY <wizard*ry*> <citizen*ry*> <ancient*ry*>
rya \ˈrē-ə\ *n* [*Rya,* village in southwest Sweden] : a Scandinavian handwoven rug with a deep resilient comparatively flat pile; *also* : the weave typical of this rug
[1]rye \ˈrī\ *n* [ME, fr. OE *ryge;* akin to OHG *rocko* rye, Lith *rugys*] **1** : a hardy annual grass (*Secale cereale*) that is widely grown for grain and as a cover crop **2** : the seeds of rye **3** : RYE BREAD **4** : RYE WHISKEY
[2]rye *n* [Romany *rai,* fr. Skt *rājan* king — more at ROYAL] : a male gypsy
rye bread *n* : bread made wholly or in part of rye flour; *esp* : a light bread often with caraway seeds
rye·grass \ˈrī-ˌgras\ *n* : any of several grasses (genus *Lolium*); *esp* : either of two grasses (*L. perenne* and *L. multiflorum*) that are used esp. for pasture and as cover crops in the southern U.S. and in New Zealand
rye whiskey *n* : a whiskey distilled from rye or from rye and malt

[1]**s** \'es\ *n, pl* **s's** *or* **ss** \'es-əz\, *often cap, often attrib* **1 a :** the 19th letter of the English alphabet **b :** a graphic representation of this letter **c :** a speech counterpart of orthographic *s* **2 :** a graphic device for reproducing the letter *s* **3 :** one designated *s* esp. as the 19th in order or class **4** [abbr. for *satisfactory*] **a :** a grade rating a student's work as satisfactory **b :** one graded or rated with an S **5 :** something shaped like the letter S

[2]**s** *abbr, often cap* **1** sabbath **2** saint **3** schilling **4** second; secondary **5** section **6** semi **7** senate **8** series **9** shilling **10** [L *signa*] label **11** signor **12** sine **13** singular **14** small **15** smooth **16** snow **17** society **18** son **19** sou **20** south; southern **21** stere **22** subject **23** symmetrical

[1]**-s** \s *after a voiceless consonant sound,* z *after a voiced consonant sound or a vowel sound*\ *n pl suffix* [ME *-es, -s,* fr. OE *-as,* nom. & acc. pl. ending of some masc. nouns; akin to OS *-os*] **1** — used to form the plural of most nouns that do not end in *s, z, sh, ch,* or postconsonantal *y* <head*s*> <book*s*> <boy*s*> <belief*s*>, to form the plural of proper nouns that end in postconsonantal *y* <Mary*s*>, and with or without a preceding apostrophe to form the plural of abbreviations, numbers, letters, and symbols used as nouns <MC*s*> <Ph.D.'*s*> <4*s*> <the 1940'*s*> <$*s*> <B'*s*>; compare [1]-ES 1 **2** [ME *-es, -s,* pl. ending of nouns, fr. *-es,* gen. sing. ending of nouns (functioning adverbially), fr. OE *-es*] — used to form adverbs denoting usual or repeated action or state <always at home Sunday*s*> <morning*s* he stops by the newsstand>

[2]**-s** *vb suffix* [ME (Northern & North Midland dial.) *-es,* fr. OE (Northumbrian dial.) *-es, -as,* prob. fr. OE *-es, -as,* 2d sing. pres. indic. ending — more at -EST] — used to form the third person singular present of most verbs that do not end in *s, z, sh, ch,* or postconsonantal *y* <fall*s*> <take*s*> <play*s*>; compare [2]-ES

[1]**'s** *like* -'s\ *vb* [contr. of *is, has, does*] **1 :** IS <she*'s* here> **2 :** HAS <he*'s* seen them> **3 :** DOES <what*'s* he want?>

[2]**'s** \s\ *pron* [by contr.] **:** US — used with *let* <let*'s*>

-'s \s *after voiceless consonant sounds other than* s, sh, ch; z *after vowel sounds and voiced consonant sounds other than* z, zh, j; əz *after* s, sh, ch, z, zh, j\ *n suffix or pron suffix* [ME *-es, -s,* gen. sing. ending, fr. OE *-es;* akin to OHG *-es,* gen. sing. ending, Gk *-oio, -ou,* Skt *-asya*] — used to form the possessive of singular nouns <boy*'s*>, of plural nouns not ending in *s* <children*'s*>, of some pronouns <anyone*'s*>, and of word groups functioning as nouns <the man in the corner*'s* hat> or pronouns <someone else*'s*>

S *symbol* **1** entropy **2** standard deviation of a sample **3** sulfur **4** svedberg

SA *abbr* **1** Salvation Army **2** seaman apprentice **3** sex appeal **4** [L *sine anno* without year] without date **5** South Africa **6** South America **7** South Australia **8** subject to approval

Saa·nen \'sän-ən, 'zän-\ *n* [*Saanen,* locality in southwest Switzerland] **:** any of a Swiss breed of usu. white and hornless short-haired dairy goats

sab·a·dil·la \,sab-ə-'dil-ə, -'dē-(y)ə\ *n* [Sp *cebadilla*] **:** a Mexican plant (*Schoenocaulon officinalis*) of the lily family; *also* **:** its seeds that are used as a source of veratrine and in insecticides

sab·bat \'sab-ət, sa-'bä\ *n, often cap* [F, lit., sabbath, fr. L *sabbatum*] **:** a midnight assembly of diabolists (as witches and sorcerers) held esp. in medieval and Renaissance times to renew allegiance to the devil through mystic rites and orgies

[1]**Sab·ba·tar·i·an** \,sab-ə-'ter-ē-ən\ *n* [L *sabbatarius,* fr. *sabbatum* sabbath] **1 :** one who observes the Sabbath on Saturday in conformity with the letter of the fourth commandment **2 :** an adherent of Sabbatarianism

[2]**Sabbatarian** *adj* **1 :** of or relating to the Sabbath **2 :** of or relating to Sabbatarians or Sabbatarianism

Sab·ba·tar·i·an·ism \-,iz-əm\ *n* **:** strict and often rigorous observance of the Sabbath

Sab·bath \'sab-əth\ *n* [ME *sabat,* fr. OF & OE, fr. L *sabbatum,* fr. Gk *sabbaton,* fr. Heb *shabbāth,* lit., rest] **1** *often cap* **a :** the seventh day of the week observed from Friday evening to Saturday evening as a day of rest and worship by Jews and some Christians **b :** Sunday observed among Christians as a day of rest and worship **2 :** a time of rest

[1]**sab·bat·i·cal** \sə-'bat-i-kəl\ *or* **sab·bat·ic** \-ik\ *adj* [LL *sabbaticus,* fr. Gk *sabbatikos,* fr. *sabbaton*] **1 :** of or relating to the sabbath <~ laws> **2 :** of or relating to a sabbatical year

[2]**sabbatical** *n* **1 :** SABBATICAL YEAR 2 **2 :** LEAVE 1b

sabbatical year *n* **1** *often cap S* **:** a year of rest for the land observed every seventh year in ancient Judea **2 :** a leave often with pay granted usu. every seventh year (as to a college professor) for rest, travel, or research — called also *sabbatical leave*

Sa·bel·li·an \sə-'bel-ē-ən\ *n* [L *Sabellus* Sabine] **1 :** a member of one of a group of early Italian peoples including Sabines and Samnites **2 :** one or all of several little known languages or dialects of ancient Italy presumably closely related to Oscan and Umbrian — see INDO-EUROPEAN LANGUAGES table — **Sabellian** *adj*

[1]**sa·ber** *or* **sa·bre** \'sā-bər\ *n* [F *sabre,* modif. of G dial. *sabel,* fr. MHG, of Slav origin; akin to Russ *sablya* saber] **1 :** a cavalry sword with a curved blade, thick back, and guard **2 a :** a light fencing or dueling sword having an arched guard that covers the back of the hand and a tapering flexible blade with a full cutting edge along one side and an 8-inch cutting edge on the back at the tip — compare ÉPÉE, FOIL **b :** the sport of fencing with the saber

saber 1

[2]**saber** *or* **sabre** *vt* **sa·bered** *or* **sa·bred; sa·ber·ing** *or* **sa·bring** \-b(ə-)riŋ\ **:** to strike, cut, or kill with a saber

saber rattling *n* **:** ostentatious display of military power

saber saw *n* **:** a light portable electric saw with a pointed reciprocating blade

sa·ber·tooth \'sā-bər-,tüth\ *n* **:** SABER-TOOTHED TIGER

sa·ber–toothed \,sā-bər-'tütht\ *adj* **:** having long sharp canine teeth

saber–toothed tiger \-,tüth(t)-\ *n* **:** any of numerous extinct cats (as genus *Smilodon*) widely distributed from the Oligocene through the Pleistocene and characterized by extreme development of the upper canines into curved swordlike piercing or slashing weapons

sa·bin \'sā-bən\ *n* [Wallace C. W. *Sabine* †1919 Am physicist] **:** a unit of acoustic absorption equivalent to the absorption by one square foot of a perfect absorber

Sa·bine \'sā-,bīn, *esp Brit* 'sab-,īn\ *n* [ME, *Sabin,* fr. L *Sabinus*] **1 :** a member of an ancient people of the Apennines northeast of Latium **2 :** the Italic language of the Sabine people — **Sabine** *adj*

[1]**sa·ble** \'sā-bəl\ *n, pl* **sables** [ME, sable or its fur, the heraldic color black, black, fr. MF, sable or its fur, the heraldic color black, fr. MLG *sabel* sable or its fur, fr. MHG *zobel,* of Slav origin; akin to Russ *sobol'* sable or its fur] **1 a :** the color black **b :** black clothing worn in mourning — usu. used in pl. **2 a** *or pl* **sable** (1) **:** a carnivorous mammal (*Martes zibellina*) of northern Europe and parts of northern Asia related to the martens and supplying a valuable fur (2) **:** any of various animals related to the sable **b :** the fur or pelt of a sable **3 a :** the usu. dark brown color of the fur of the sable **b :** a grayish yellowish brown

[2]**sable** *adj* **1 :** of the color black **2 :** DARK

sa·ble·fish \'sā-bəl-,fish\ *n* **:** a large spiny-finned gray to blackish fish (*Anoplopoma fimbria*) of the Pacific coast that is a leading market fish and has a liver rich in vitamins

sa·bot \sa-'bō, 'sab-(,)ō, *for 1b also* 'sab-ət\ *n* [F] **1 a :** a wooden shoe worn in various European countries **b** (1) **:** a strap across the instep in a shoe esp. of the sandal type (2) **:** a shoe having a sabot strap **2 :** a thrust-transmitting carrier that positions a missile in a gun barrel or launching tube and that prevents the escape of gas ahead of the missile

[1]**sab·o·tage** \'sab-ə-,täzh\ *n* [F, fr. *saboter* to clatter with sabots, botch, sabotage, fr. *sabot*] **1 :** destruction of an employer's property (as tools or materials) or the hindering of manufacturing by discontented workmen **2 :** destructive or obstructive action carried on by a civilian or enemy agent designed to hinder a nation's war effort **3 a :** an act or process tending to hamper or hurt **b :** deliberate subversion

[2]**sabotage** *vt* **-taged; -tag·ing :** to practice sabotage on

sab·o·teur \,sab-ə-'tər, -'t(y)ů(ə)r\ *n* [F, fr. *saboter*] **:** one that commits sabotage

sa·bra \'säb-rə\ *n, often cap* [NHeb *sabrāh*] **:** a native-born Israeli

sac \'sak\ *n* [F, lit., bag, fr. L *saccus* — more at SACK] **:** a pouch within an animal or plant often containing a fluid <a synovial ~> — **sac·like** \-,līk\ *adj*

SAC \'sak\ *abbr* Strategic Air Command

sa·ca·huis·te \,sak-ə-'wis-tə, ,säk-, -tē\ *n* [AmerSp *zacahuiscle,* of AmerInd origin; akin to Nahuatl *zacatl* coarse grass] **:** a bear grass (*Nolina texana*) with long linear leaves that is used for forage

sac·a·ton \'sak-ə-,tōn\ *n* [AmerSp *zacatón,* fr. *zacate* coarse grass, fr. Nahuatl *zacatl*] **:** a coarse perennial grass (*Sporobolus wrightii*) of the southwestern U.S. that is used for hay in alkaline regions

sac·cade \sa-'käd\ *n* [F, twitch, jerk, fr. MF, fr. *saquer* to pull, draw] **:** a small rapid jerky movement of the eye esp. as it jumps from fixation on one point to another (as in reading) — **sac·cad·ic** \-'käd-ik\ *adj*

sac·cate \'sak-,āt\ *adj* [NL *saccatus,* fr. L *saccus*] **:** having the form of a sac or pouch <~ pollen grains>

sacchar- *or* **sacchari-** *or* **sacchar0-** *comb form* [L *saccharum,* fr. Gk *sakcharon,* fr. Pali *sakkharā,* fr. Skt *śarkarā* gravel, sugar] **:** sugar <*sacchar*ic> <*sacchari*fy> <*saccharo*meter>

sac·cha·rase \'sak-ə-,rās, -,rāz\ *n* [ISV] **:** INVERTASE

sac·cha·rate \-,rāt\ *n* **:** a compound of a sugar usu. with a bivalent metal; *esp* **:** a metallic derivative of sucrose

sac·cha·ride \'sak-ə-,rīd\ *n* **:** a simple sugar, combination of sugars, or polymerized sugar **:** CARBOHYDRATE

sac·char·i·fy \sə-'kar-ə-,fī, sa-\ *vt* **-fied; -fy·ing :** to break (as a complex carbohydrate) into simple sugars — **sac·char·i·fi·ca·tion** \-,kar-ə-fə-'kā-shən\ *n*

sac·cha·rim·e·ter \,sak-ə-'rim-ət-ər\ *n* [ISV] **:** a device for measuring the amount of sugar in a solution; *esp* **:** a polarimeter so used — **sac·cha·rim·e·try** \-'rim-ə-trē\ *n*

sac·cha·rin \'sak-(ə-)rən\ *n* [ISV] **:** a crystalline compound $C_7H_5NO_3S$ that is unrelated to the carbohydrates, is several hundred times sweeter than cane sugar, and is used as a calorie-free sweetener

sac·cha·rine \'sak-(ə-)rən, -ə-,rēn, -ə-,rīn\ *adj* [L *saccharum*] **1 a :** of, relating to, or resembling that of sugar <~ taste> **b :** yielding or containing sugar <~ vegetables> **2 :** overly or sickishly sweet <~ flavor> **3 :** ingratiatingly or affectedly agreeable or friendly — **sac·cha·rin·i·ty** \,sak-ə-'rin-ət-ē\ *n*

sac·cha·roi·dal \,sak-ə-'rȯid-ᵊl\ *adj* **:** having or being a fine granular texture like that of loaf sugar <~ marble>

sac·cha·rom·e·ter \-'räm-ət-ər\ *n* **:** SACCHARIMETER; *esp* **:** a hydrometer with a special scale

sac·cha·ro·my·ces \-rō-'mī-(,)sēz\ *n* [NL, genus name, fr. *sacchar-* + *-myces* fungus, fr. Gk *mykēs* — more at MYC-] **:** any of a genus (*Saccharomyces* family Saccharomycetaceae) of usu. unicellular yeasts (as a brewer's yeast) that are distinguished by their sparse or absent mycelium and by their facility in reproducing asexually by budding

sac·cha·rose \'sak-ə-,rōs, -,rōz\ *n* **:** SUCROSE; *broadly* **:** DISACCHARIDE

sac·cu·lar \'sak-yə-lər\ *adj* **:** resembling a sac <a ~ aneurysm>

sac·cu·late \-,lāt, -lət\ *or* **sac·cu·lat·ed** \,lāt-əd\ *adj* **:** having or formed of a series of saccular expansions — **sac·cu·la·tion** \,sak-yə-'lā-shən\ *n*

sac·cule \'sak-(,)yü(ə)l\ *n* [NL *sacculus,* fr. L, dim. of *saccus* bag — more at SACK] **:** a little sac; *specif* **:** the smaller chamber of the membranous labyrinth of the ear

sac·cu·lus \'sak-yə-ləs\ *n, pl* **-li** \-,lī, -,lē\ [NL] : SACCULE

sac·er·do·tal \,sas-ər-'dōt-ᵊl, ,sak-\ *adj* [ME, fr. MF, fr. L *sacerdotalis,* fr. *sacerdot-, sacerdos* priest, fr. *sacer* sacred + *-dot-, -dos* (akin to *facere* to make) — more at SACRED, DO] **1** : of or relating to priests or a priesthood : PRIESTLY **2** : of, relating to, or suggesting sacerdotalism — **sac·er·do·tal·ly** \-ᵊl-ē\ *adv*

sac·er·do·tal·ism \-ᵊl-,iz-əm\ *n* : religious belief emphasizing the powers of priests as essential mediators between God and man — **sac·er·do·tal·ist** \-ᵊl-əst\ *n*

sac fungus *n* : ASCOMYCETE

sa·chem \'sā-chəm, 'sach-əm\ *n* [Narraganset & Pequot *sachima*] **1** : a No. American Indian chief; *esp* : the chief of a confederation of the Algonquian tribes of the north Atlantic coast **2** : a Tammany leader — **sa·chem·ic** \sā-'chem-ik, sa-\ *adj*

sa·chet \sa-'shā\ *n* [F, fr. OF, dim. of *sac* bag — more at SAC] **1** : a small bag or packet **2** : a small bag containing a perfumed powder used to scent clothes and linens — **sa·cheted** \-'shād\ *adj*

[1]**sack** \'sak\ *n* [ME *sak* bag, sackcloth, fr. OE *sacc;* akin to OHG *sac* bag; both fr. a prehistoric Gmc word borrowed fr. L *saccus* bag & LL *saccus* sackcloth, both fr. Gk *sakkos* bag, sackcloth, of Sem origin; akin to Heb *śaq* bag, sackcloth] **1** : a usu. rectangular-shaped bag (as of paper, burlap, or canvas) **2** : the amount contained in a sack; *esp* : a fixed amount of a commodity used as a unit of measure **3 a** : a woman's loose-fitting dress **b** : a short usu. loose-fitting coat for women and children **c** : SACQUE 2 **4** : DISMISSAL — usu. used with *get* or *give* **5 a** : HAMMOCK, BUNK **b** : BED **6** : a base in baseball — **sack·ful** \-,fu̇l\ *n*

[2]**sack** *vt* **1** : to put or place in a sack **2** : to dismiss esp. summarily — **sack·er** *n*

[3]**sack** *n* [modif. of MF *sec* dry, fr. L *siccus;* akin to OHG *sīhan* to filter, Gk *hikmas* moisture] : a white wine imported to England from the south of Europe during the 16th and 17th centuries

[4]**sack** *n* [MF *sac,* fr. OIt *sacco,* lit., bag, fr. L *saccus*] : the plundering of a captured town

[5]**sack** *vt* **1** : to plunder (as a town) after capture **2** : to strip of valuables : LOOT ***syn*** see RAVAGE — **sack·er** *n*

sack·but \'sak-(,)bət\ *n* [MF *saqueboute,* lit., hooked lance, fr. OF, fr. *saquer* to pull + *bouter* to push — more at BUTT] : the medieval trombone

sack·cloth \'sak-,(k)lȯth\ *n* [[1]*sack*] **1** : a coarse cloth of goat or camel's hair or of flax, hemp, or cotton **2** : a garment of sackcloth worn as a sign of mourning or penitence

sack coat *n* : a man's jacket with a straight unfitted back

sack·ing \'sak-iŋ\ *n* : material for sacks; *esp* : a coarse fabric (as burlap or gunny)

sack out \'sak-'au̇t\ *vi* [[1]*sack*] : to go to bed : lie down

sack race *n* : a jumping race in which each contestant has his legs enclosed in a sack

sacque \'sak\ *n* [alter. of [1]*sack*] **1** : SACK 3a, 3b **2** : an infant's usu. short jacket that fastens at the neck

sacr- *or* **sacro-** *comb form* [NL, fr. *sacrum,* fr. L, neut. of *sacr-, sacer* sacred] **1** : sacrum <*sacral*> **2** : sacral and <*sacroiliac*>

[1]**sa·cral** \'sak-rəl, 'sā-krəl\ *adj* : of, relating to, or lying near the sacrum

[2]**sa·cral** \'sā-krəl, 'sak-rəl\ *adj* [L *sacr-, sacer* — more at SACRED] : HOLY, SACRED

sac·ra·ment \'sak-rə-mənt\ *n* [ME *sacrement, sacrament,* fr. OF & LL; OF, fr. LL *sacramentum,* fr. L, oath of allegiance, obligation, fr. *sacrare* to consecrate] **1** : a formal religious act that is sacred as a sign or symbol of a spiritual reality; *esp* : one believed to have been instituted or recognized by Jesus Christ **2** *cap* : the eucharistic elements; *specif* : BLESSED SACRAMENT

[1]**sac·ra·men·tal** \,sak-rə-'ment-ᵊl\ *adj* **1** : of, relating to, or having the character of a sacrament **2** : suggesting a sacrament (as in sacredness) — **sac·ra·men·tal·ly** \-ᵊl-ē\ *adv*

[2]**sacramental** *n* : an action or object (as the rosary) of ecclesiastical origin that serves as an indirect means of grace by producing devotion

sac·ra·men·tal·ism \-ᵊl-,iz-əm\ *n* : belief in or use of sacramental rites, acts, or objects; *specif* : belief that the sacraments are inherently efficacious and necessary for salvation

sac·ra·men·tal·ist \-ᵊl-əst\ *n* **1** : SACRAMENTARIAN **2** : an adherent of sacramentalism

Sac·ra·men·tar·i·an \,sak-rə-,men-'ter-ē-ən, -mən-\ *n* **1** : one who interprets sacraments as merely visible symbols **2** : SACRAMENTALIST — **Sacramentarian** *adj* — **Sac·ra·men·tar·i·an·ism** \-ē-ə-,niz-əm\ *n*

sa·crar·i·um \sə-'krer-ē-əm, sa-, sā-\ *n, pl* **-ia** \-ē-ə\ [ML, fr. L, pagan Roman shrine, fr. *sacr-, sacer* sacred] **1 a** : SANCTUARY 1b **b** : SACRISTY **c** : PISCINA **2** : an ancient Roman shrine or sanctuary in a temple or a home holding sacred objects

sa·cred \'sā-krəd\ *adj* [ME, fr. pp. of *sacren* to consecrate, fr. OF *sacrer,* fr. L *sacrare,* fr. *sacr-, sacer* holy, cursed; akin to L *sancire* to make sacred, Hitt *saklais* rite] **1 a** : dedicated or set apart for the service or worship of deity <a tree ~ to the gods> **b** : devoted exclusively to one service or use (as of a person or purpose) <a fund ~ to charity> **2 a** : worthy of religious veneration : HOLY **b** : entitled to reverence and respect **3** : of or relating to religion : not secular or profane <~ music> **4** *archaic* : ACCURSED — **sa·cred·ly** *adv* — **sa·cred·ness** *n*

syn SACRED, SACROSANCT, INVIOLATE, INVIOLABLE *shared meaning element* : protected (as by law, custom, or human respect) against abuse

sacred baboon *n* [fr. its veneration by the ancient Egyptians] : HAMADRYAD 2b

sacred cow *n* [fr. the veneration of the cow by the Hindus] : a person or thing immune from criticism

sacred mushroom *n* **1** : any of various New World hallucinogenic fungi (as genus *Psilocybe*) used esp. in some Indian ceremonies **2** : MESCAL BUTTON

[1]**sac·ri·fice** \'sak-rə-,fīs, -fəs *also* -,fīz\ *n* [ME, fr. OF, fr. L *sacrificium,* fr. *sacr-, sacer* + *facere* to make — more at DO] **1** : an act of offering to deity something precious; *esp* : the killing of a victim on an altar **2** : something offered in sacrifice **3 a** : destruction or surrender of something for the sake of something else **b** : something given up or lost <the ~*s* made by parents> **4** : LOSS <goods sold at a ~> **5** : SACRIFICE HIT

[2]**sac·ri·fice** \-,fīs, -,fīz *also* -fəs\ *vb* **-ficed; -fic·ing** *vt* **1** : to offer as a sacrifice **2** : to suffer loss of, give up, renounce, injure, or destroy for an ideal, belief, or end **3** : to sell at a loss ~ *vi* **1** : to offer up or perform rites of a sacrifice **2** : to make a sacrifice hit in baseball — **sac·ri·fic·er** *n*

sacrifice fly *n* : an outfield fly in baseball caught by a fielder after which a runner scores

sacrifice hit *n* : a bunt in baseball that allows a runner to advance one base while the batter is put out

sac·ri·fi·cial \,sak-rə-'fish-əl\ *adj* : of, relating to, of the nature of, or involving sacrifice — **sac·ri·fi·cial·ly** \-ə-lē\ *adv*

sac·ri·lege \'sak-rə-lij\ *n* [ME, fr. OF, fr. L *sacrilegium,* fr. *sacrilegus* one who steals sacred things, fr. *sacr-, sacer* + *legere* to gather, steal — more at LEGEND] **1** : a technical and not necessarily intrinsically outrageous violation (as improper reception of a sacrament) of what is sacred because consecrated to God **2** : gross irreverence toward a hallowed person, place, or thing ***syn*** see PROFANATION — **sac·ri·le·gious** \,sak-rə-'lij-əs, -'lē-jəs\ *adj* — **sac·ri·le·gious·ly** *adv* — **sac·ri·le·gious·ness** *n*

sac·ris·tan \'sak-rə-stən\ *n* : a person in charge of the sacristy and ceremonial equipment; *also* : SEXTON

sac·ris·ty \'sak-rə-stē\ *n, pl* **-ties** [ML *sacristia,* fr. *sacrista* sacristan, fr. L *sacr-, sacer*] : a room in a church where sacred vessels and vestments are kept and where the clergy vests

[1]**sa·cro·il·i·ac** \,sak-rō-'il-ē-,ak, ,sā-krō-\ *adj* [ISV] : of, relating to, or being the region of juncture of the sacrum and ilium

[2]**sacroiliac** *n* : the sacroiliac region; *also* : its firm fibrous cartilage

sac·ro·sanct \'sak-rō-,saŋ(k)t\ *adj* [L *sacrosanctus,* prob. fr. *sacro sanctus* hallowed by a sacred rite] : most sacred or holy; *also* : having an imputed rather than a genuine sacred character <~ institutions that have outlived their usefulness to society> ***syn*** see SACRED — **sac·ro·sanc·ti·ty** \,sak-rō-'saŋ(k)-tət-ē\ *n*

sa·crum \'sak-rəm, 'sā-krəm\ *n, pl* **sa·cra** \'sak-rə, 'sā-krə\ [NL, fr. LL *os sacrum* last bone of the spine, lit., holy bone] : the part of the vertebral column that is directly connected with or forms a part of the pelvis and in man consists of five united vertebrae

sad \'sad\ *adj* **sad·der; sad·dest** [ME, fr. OE *sæd* sated; akin to OHG *sat* sated, L *satis* enough] **1 a** : affected with or expressive of grief or unhappiness : DOWNCAST **b** (1) : causing or associated with grief or unhappiness : DEPRESSING <~ news> (2) : DEPLORABLE, REGRETTABLE <a ~ relaxation of morals —C. W. Cunnington> **c** : of little worth **2** : of a dull somber color — **sad·ly** *adv* — **sad·ness** *n*

sad·den \'sad-ᵊn\ *vb* **sad·dened; sad·den·ing** \'sad-niŋ, -ᵊn-iŋ\ *vt* : to make sad ~ *vi* : to become sad

saddle 1a (1)

[1]**sad·dle** \'sad-ᵊl\ *n, often attrib* [ME *sadel,* fr. OE *sadol;* akin to OHG *satul* saddle] **1 a** (1) : a girthed usu. padded and leather-covered seat for the rider of an animal (as a horse) (2) : a part of a driving harness comparable to a saddle that is used to keep the breeching in place **b** : a seat to be straddled by the rider of a vehicle (as a bicycle) **2** : an often shaped mounted support for an object **3 a** : a ridge connecting two higher elevations **b** : COL 2 **4 a** : both sides of the unsplit back of a carcass including both loins **b** : a colored marking on the back of an animal **c** : the rear part of a male fowl's back extending to the tail — see COCK illustration **5** : the central part of the backbone of the binding of a book **6** : a piece of leather across the instep of a shoe — **sad·dle·less** \-ᵊl-(l)əs\ *adj* — **in the saddle** : in control

[2]**saddle** *vb* **sad·dled; sad·dling** \'sad-liŋ, -ᵊl-iŋ\ *vt* **1** : to put a saddle on **2 a** : to place under a burden or encumbrance **b** : to place (an onerous responsibility) on a person or group ~ *vi* : to mount a saddled horse

sad·dle·bag \'sad-ᵊl-,bag\ *n* : one of a pair of covered pouches laid across the back of a horse behind the saddle or hanging over the rear wheel of a bicycle or motorcycle

saddle blanket *n* : a folded blanket or pad under a saddle to prevent galling the horse

sad·dle·bow \'sad-ᵊl-,bō\ *n* : the arch in or the pieces forming the front of a saddle

sad·dle·cloth \-,klȯth\ *n* : a cloth placed under or over a saddle

sad·dled prominent \,sad-ᵊld-\ *n* [fr. the hump or prominence on the back of the larva] : a moth (*Heterocampa guttivitta*) whose larva is a serious defoliator of hardwood trees in the eastern and midwestern U.S.

saddle horn *n* : a hornlike prolongation of the pommel of a stock saddle

saddle horse *n* : a horse suited for or trained for riding

saddle leather *n* : leather made of the hide of cattle that is vegetable tanned and used for saddlery; *also* : smooth polished leather simulating this

sad·dler \'sad-lər\ *n* : one that makes, repairs, or sells saddles and other furnishings for horses

saddle roof *n* : a roof having two gables and one ridge

sad·dlery \'sad-lə-rē, 'sad-ᵊl-rē\ *n, pl* **-dler·ies** : the trade, articles of trade, or shop of a saddler

saddle seat *n* : a slightly concave chair seat (as of a Windsor chair) with sometimes a thickened ridge at the center front

S T

saddle shoe *n* **:** an oxford-style shoe having a saddle of contrasting color or leather — called also *saddle oxford*
saddle soap *n* **:** a mild soap made with added unsaponified oil and used for cleansing and conditioning leather
saddle sore *n* **1 :** a gall or open sore developing on the back of a horse at points of pressure from an ill-fitting or ill-adjusted saddle **2 :** an irritation or sore on parts of the rider chafed by the saddle
sad·dle·tree \'sad-ᵊl-ˌtrē\ *n* **:** the frame of a saddle
Sad·du·ce·an \ˌsaj-ə-'sē-ən, ˌsad-yə-\ *adj* **:** of or relating to the Sadducees
Sad·du·cee \'saj-ə-ˌsē, 'sad-yə-\ *n* [ME *saducee,* fr. OE *sadduce,* fr. LL *sadducaeus,* fr. Gk *saddoukaios,* fr. LHeb *ṣaddūqi*] **:** a member of a Jewish party of the intertestamental period consisting of a traditional ruling class of priests and rejecting doctrines not in the Law (as resurrection, retribution in a future life, and the existence of angels) — **Sad·du·cee·ism** \-ˌiz-əm\ *n*
sa·dhe \'(t)säd-ə, -ē\ *n* [Heb *ṣādhē*] **:** the 18th letter of the Hebrew alphabet — see ALPHABET table
sa·dhu *or* **sad·dhu** \'säd-(ˌ)ü\ *n* [Skt *sādhu*] **:** a usu. Hindu mendicant ascetic
sad·iron \'sad-ˌī(-ə)rn\ *n* [*sad* (compact, heavy) + *iron*] **:** a flatiron pointed at both ends and having a removable handle
sa·dism \'sā-ˌdiz-əm, 'sad-ˌiz-\ *n* [ISV, fr. Marquis de *Sade*] **1 :** a sexual perversion in which gratification is obtained by the infliction of physical or mental pain on others (as upon a love object) — compare MASOCHISM **2 a :** delight in cruelty **b :** excessive cruelty — **sa·dist** \'sād-əst, 'sad-\ *adj or n* — **sa·dis·tic** \sə-'dis-tik *also* sā- *or* sa-\ *adj* — **sa·dis·ti·cal·ly** \-ti-k(ə-)lē\ *adv*
sa·do·mas·och·ism \ˌsād-(ˌ)ō-'mas-ə-ˌkiz-əm, ˌsad-, -'maz-\ *n* [ISV *sad*ism + *-o-* + *masochism*] **:** the derivation of pleasure from the infliction of physical or mental pain either on others or on oneself — **sa·do·mas·och·ist** \-kəst\ *n* — **sa·do·mas·och·is·tic** \-ˌmas-ə-'kis-tik, -ˌmaz-\ *adj*
sad sack *n* **:** an inept person; *esp* **:** an inept serviceman
Sa·far \sə-'fär\ *n* [Ar *ṣafar*] **:** the 2d month of the Muhammadan year — see MONTH table
sa·fa·ri \sə-'fär-ē, -'far-\ *n* [Ar *safarīy* of a trip] **1 :** the caravan and equipment of a hunting expedition esp. in eastern Africa **2 :** a hunting expedition in eastern Africa **3 :** JOURNEY, EXPEDITION <an arctic ~> — **safari** *vi*
[1]**safe** \'sāf\ *adj* **saf·er; saf·est** [ME *sauf,* fr. OF, fr. L *salvus* safe, healthy; akin to L *salus* health, safety, *salubris* healthful, *solidus* solid, Gk *holos* whole, safe] **1 :** freed from harm or risk **:** UNHURT **2 a :** secure from threat of danger, harm, or loss **b :** successful in reaching base in baseball without being put out **3 :** affording safety from danger **4** *obs, of mental or moral faculties* **:** HEALTHY, SOUND **5 a :** not threatening danger **:** HARMLESS **b :** unlikely to produce controversy **6 a :** not liable to take risks **:** CAUTIOUS **b :** TRUSTWORTHY, RELIABLE — **safe** *or* **safe·ly** *adv* — **safe·ness** *n*
syn SAFE, SECURE *shared meaning element* **:** free from danger or risk ***ant*** dangerous, unsafe
[2]**safe** *n* **:** a place or receptacle to keep articles (as valuables) safe
safe-con·duct \(')sāf-'kän-(ˌ)dəkt\ *n* [ME *sauf conduit,* fr. OF, safe conduct] **1 :** protection given a person passing through a military zone or occupied area **2 :** a document authorizing safe-conduct
safe·crack·er \'sāf-ˌkrak-ər\ *n* **:** one that breaks open safes to steal — **safe·crack·ing** \-iŋ\ *n*
safe-deposit box *n* **:** a box (as in the vault of a bank) for safe storage of valuables — called also *safety-deposit box*
[1]**safe·guard** \'sāf-ˌgärd\ *n* [ME *saufgarde,* fr. MF *saufegarde,* fr. OF, fr *sauve* safe + *garde* guard] **1 a :** CONVOY, ESCORT **b :** PASS, SAFE-CONDUCT **2 a :** a precautionary measure or stipulation **b :** a technical contrivance to prevent accident
[2]**safeguard** *vt* **1 :** to provide a safeguard for **2 :** to make safe **:** PROTECT ***syn*** see DEFEND
safe·keep·ing \'sāf-'kē-piŋ\ *n* **1 :** the act or process of preserving in safety **2 :** the state of being preserved in safety
safe·light \'sā-ˌflīt\ *n* **:** a darkroom lamp with a filter to screen out rays that are harmful to sensitive film or paper
[1]**safe·ty** \'sāf-tē\ *n, pl* **safeties** [ME *saufte,* fr. MF *sauveté,* fr. OF, fr. *sauve,* fem. of *sauf* safe] **1 :** the condition of being safe from undergoing or causing hurt, injury, or loss **2 :** a device (as on a gun, a mine, or a machine) designed to prevent inadvertent or hazardous operation **3 a (1) :** a situation in football in which a member of the offensive team is tackled behind its own goal line that counts two points for the defensive team — compare TOUCHBACK **(2) :** a member of a defensive backfield in football who occupies the deepest position in order to receive a kick, defend against a forward pass, or stop a ballcarrier — called also *safetyman* **b :** a billiard shot made with no attempt to score or so as to leave the balls in an unfavorable position for the opponent **c :** BASE HIT
[2]**safety** *vt* **safe·tied; safe·ty·ing :** to protect against failure, breakage, or accident <~ a rifle>
safety belt *n* **:** a belt fastening a person to an object to prevent falling or injury
safety glass *n* **:** transparent material that is prepared by laminating a sheet of transparent plastic between sheets of clear glass and is used esp. for windows (as of automobiles) likely to be subjected to shock or impact
safety island *n* **:** an area within a roadway from which vehicular traffic is excluded (as by pavement markings or curbing)
safety lamp *n* **:** a miner's lamp constructed to avoid explosion in an atmosphere containing flammable gas usu. by enclosing the flame in fine wire gauze
safe·ty·man \'sāf-tē-ˌman\ *n* **:** SAFETY 3a(2)
safety match *n* **:** a match capable of being struck and ignited only on a specially prepared friction surface
safety pin *n* **:** a pin in the form of a clasp with a guard covering its point when fastened
safety razor *n* **:** a razor provided with a guard for the blade to prevent deep cuts in the skin
safety valve *n* **1 :** an automatic escape or relief valve (as for a steam boiler) **2 :** an outlet for pent-up energy or emotion <a *safety valve* for many of the frustrations of life —N. L. Gerrard>
safety zone *n* **:** a safety island for pedestrians or for streetcar or bus passengers
saf·flow·er \'saf-ˌlau̇(-ə)r\ *n* [MF *saffleur,* fr. OIt *saffiore,* fr. Ar *aṣfar* a yellow plant] **:** a widely grown Old World composite herb (*Carthamus tinctorius*) with large orange or red flower heads and seeds rich in oil; *also* **:** a red dyestuff prepared from the flower heads
safflower oil *n* **:** an edible drying oil obtained from the seeds of the safflower
saf·fron \'saf-rən\ *n* [ME, fr. OF *safran,* fr. ML *safranum,* fr. Ar *za'farān*] **1 :** a purple-flowered crocus (*Crocus sativus*) **2 :** the deep orange aromatic pungent dried stigmas of saffron used to color and flavor foods and formerly as a dyestuff and in medicine **3 :** a moderate orange to orange yellow
saf·ra·nine \'saf-rə-ˌnēn, -nən\ *or* **saf·ra·nin** \-nən\ *n* [ISV, fr. F or G *safran* saffron] **1 :** any of various usu. red synthetic dyes that are amino derivatives of bases **2 :** any of various mixtures of safranine salts used in dyeing and as microscopic stains
saf·role \'saf-ˌrōl\ *n* [ISV, fr. F or G *safran*] **:** a poisonous oily cyclic ether $C_{10}H_{10}O_2$ that is the principal component of sassafras oil and is used chiefly for perfuming and flavoring
[1]**sag** \'sag\ *vb* **sagged; sag·ging** [ME *saggen,* prob. of Scand origin; akin to Sw *sacka* to sag] *vi* **1 :** to droop, sink, or settle from or as if from pressure or loss of tautness **2 a :** to lose firmness, resiliency, or vigor <spirits *sagging* from overwork> **b :** to fall from a thriving state **3 :** DRIFT **4 :** to fail to stimulate or retain interest ~ *vt* **:** to cause to sag **:** leave slack in
[2]**sag** *n* **1 :** a tendency to drift (as of a ship to leeward) **2 a :** a sagging part <the ~ in a rope> **b :** a drop or depression below the surrounding area **c :** an instance or amount of sagging <~ is inevitable in a heavy unsupported span> **3 :** a temporary economic decline (as in the price of a commodity)
sa·ga \'säg-ə *also* 'sag-\ *n* [ON — more at SAW] **1 :** a prose narrative recorded in Iceland in the 12th and 13th centuries of historic or legendary figures and events of the heroic age of Norway and Iceland **2 :** a modern heroic narrative resembling the Icelandic saga **3 :** a long detailed account <the ~ of the winning of the West> <the great ~ of changing race relations —H. S. Ashmore>
syn see MYTH
sa·ga·cious \sə-'gā-shəs, sig-'ā-\ *adj* [L *sagac-, sagax* sagacious; akin to L *sagire* to perceive keenly — more at SEEK] **1** *obs* **:** keen in sense perception **2 a :** of keen and farsighted penetration and judgment **:** DISCERNING <~ judge of character> **b :** caused by or indicating acute discernment <~ purchase of stock> ***syn*** see SHREWD — **sa·ga·cious·ly** *adv* — **sa·ga·cious·ness** *n*
sa·gac·i·ty \sə-'gas-ət-ē, sig-'as-\ *n* **:** the quality of being sagacious
sag·a·more \'sag-ə-ˌmō(ə)r, -ˌmȯ(ə)r\ *n* [Abnaki *sāgimau,* lit., he prevails over] **1 :** a subordinate chief of the Algonquian Indians of the north Atlantic coast **2 :** SACHEM 1
saga novel *n* **:** ROMAN-FLEUVE
[1]**sage** \'sāj\ *adj* [ME, fr. OF, fr. (assumed) VL *sapius,* fr. L *sapere* to taste, have good taste, be wise; akin to OE *sefa* mind, Oscan *sipus* knowing] **1 a :** wise through reflection and experience **b** *archaic* **:** GRAVE, SOLEMN **2 :** proceeding from or characterized by wisdom, prudence, and good judgment <~ counsel> ***syn*** see WISE — **sage·ly** *adv* — **sage·ness** *n*
[2]**sage** *n* **1 :** one (as a profound philosopher) distinguished for wisdom **2 :** a mature or venerable man of sound judgment
[3]**sage** *n* [ME, fr. MF *sauge,* fr. L *salvia,* fr. *salvus* healthy; fr. its use as a medicinal herb — more at SAFE] **1 :** a mint (*Salvia officinalis*) with grayish green aromatic leaves used esp. in flavoring meats; *broadly* **:** SALVIA **2 :** SAGEBRUSH
sage·brush \'sāj-ˌbrəsh\ *n* **:** any of several No. American hoary composite undershrubs (genus *Artemisia*); *esp* **:** a common plant (*A. tridentata*) having a bitter juice and an odor resembling sage and often covering vast tracts of alkaline plains in the western U.S.
sage cheese *n* **:** a cheese similar to mild cheddar flecked with green and flavored with sage
sag·ger *or* **sag·gar** \'sag-ər\ *n* [prob. alter. of *safeguard*] **:** a box made of fireclay in which delicate ceramic pieces are fired
sag·it·tal \'saj-ət-ᵊl\ *adj* [L *sagitta* arrow] **1 :** of or relating to the suture between the parietal bones of the skull **2 :** of, relating to, situated in, or being the median plane of the body or any plane parallel thereto — **sag·it·tal·ly** \-ᵊl-ē\ *adv*
Sag·it·tar·i·us \ˌsaj-ə-'ter-ē-əs\ *n* [L (gen. *Sagittarii*), lit., archer, fr. *sagitta*] **1 :** a southern constellation pictured as a centaur shooting an arrow **2 a :** the 9th sign of the zodiac in astrology — see ZODIAC table **b :** one born under this sign
sag·it·tate \'saj-ə-ˌtāt\ *adj* [L *sagitta*] **:** shaped like an arrowhead; *specif* **:** elongated, triangular, and having the two basal lobes prolonged downward <~ leaf>
sa·go \'sā-(ˌ)gō\ *n, pl* **sagos** [Malay *sagu* sago palm] **:** a dry granulated or powdered starch prepared from the pith of a sago palm and used in foods and as textile stiffening
sago palm *n* **:** a plant that yields sago; *esp* **:** any of various lofty pinnate-leaved Indian and Malaysian palms (genus *Metroxylon*)
sa·gua·ro \sə-'wär-ə, -'(g)wär-(ˌ)ō\ *n, pl* **-ros** [MexSp] **:** an arborescent cactus (*Carnegiea gigantea*) of desert regions of the southwestern U.S. and Mexico that has a tall columnar simple or sparsely branched trunk of up to 60 feet and bears white flowers and edible fruit
sa·hib \'sä-(h)ib\ *n* [Hindi *sāhib,* fr. Ar] **:** SIR, MASTER — used esp. among Hindus and Muslims in colonial India when addressing or speaking of a European of some social or official status
sa·hi·wal \'sä-hē-ˌwäl\ *n, often cap* [*Sahiwal,* town in Pakistan] **:** any of an Indian breed of humped short-horned solid-colored dairy cattle
said \'sed\ *adj* [pp. of *say*] **:** AFOREMENTIONED
[1]**sail** \'sā(ə)l, *as last element in compounds often* səl\ *n* [ME, fr. OE *segl;* akin to OHG *segal* sail, L *secare* to cut — more at SAW] **1 a (1) :** an extent of fabric (as canvas) by means of which wind is

used to propel a ship through water (2) : the sails of a ship **b** *pl usu* **sail** : a ship equipped with sails **2** : an extent of fabric used in propelling a wind-driven vehicle (as an iceboat) **3** : something that resembles a sail **4** : a passage by a sailing ship : CRUISE — **sailed** \ˈsā(ə)ld\ *adj* — **under sail** : in motion with sails set

saguaro

²sail *vi* **1 a** : to travel on water in a ship **b** : YACHT **2 a** : to travel on water by the action of wind upon sails or by other means **b** : to move without visible effort or in a stately manner (as through water) <swans ~*ing* on the lake> <~*ed* gracefully into the room —L. C. Douglas> **3** : to begin a water voyage <~ with the tide> ~ *vt* **1 a** : to travel upon (water) by means of motive power (as sail) **b** : to glide through **2** : to direct or manage the motion of (as a ship) — **sail·able** \ˈsā-lə-bəl\ *adj* — **sail into** : to attack vigorously or sharply <*sailed into* his dinner> <*sailed into* me for being late>

sail·board \ˈsā(ə)l-ˌbō(ə)rd, -ˌbȯ(ə)rd\ *n* : a small flat sailboat that is designed for one or two passengers

sail·boat \ˈsā(ə)l-ˌbōt\ *n* : a boat usu. propelled by sail — **sail·boat·er** \-ər\ *n* — **sail·boat·ing** \-iŋ\ *n*

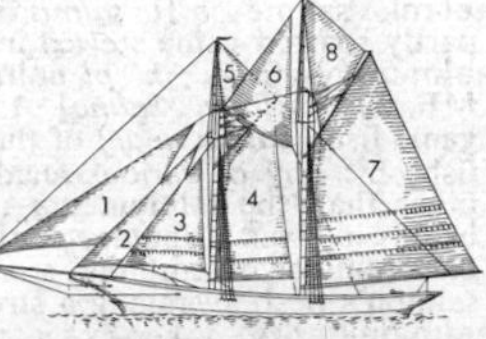

schooner's sails: *1* flying jib, *2* jib, *3* forestaysail, *4* foresail, *5* fore gaff-topsail, *6* main-topmast staysail, *7* mainsail, *8* main gaff-topsail

sail·cloth \-ˌklȯth\ *n* : a heavy canvas used for sails, tents, or upholstery; *also* : a lightweight canvas used for clothing

sail·er \ˈsā-lər\ *n* : a ship or boat esp. having specified sailing qualities

sail·fish \ˈsā(ə)l-ˌfish\ *n* : any of a genus (*Istiophorus*) of large pelagic fishes related to the swordfish but having teeth, scales, and a very large dorsal fin

sail·ing \ˈsā-liŋ\ *n* **1 a** : the technical skill of managing a ship : NAVIGATION **b** : the method of determining the course to be followed to reach a given point **2 a** : the sport of handling or riding in a sailboat **b** : a departure from a port

sail·or \ˈsā-lər\ *n* [alter. of *sailer*] **1 a** : one that sails; *esp* : MARINER **b** (1) : a member of a ship's crew (2) : SEAMAN 2b **2** : a traveler by water **3** : a stiff straw hat with a low flat crown and straight circular brim

sailor collar *n* : a broad collar having a square flap across the back and tapering to a V in the front

sail·or's–choice \ˌsā-lərz-ˈchȯis\ *n* : any of several small grunts of the Western Atlantic: as **a** : PINFISH **b** : PIGFISH 1

sail·plane \ˈsā(ə)l-ˌplān\ *n* : a glider of such design that it is able to rise in an upward air current — **sailplane** *vi* — **sail·plan·er** *n*

sain \ˈsān\ *vt* [ME *sainen*, fr. OE *segnian*, fr. LL *signare*, fr. L, to mark — more at SIGN] **1** *dial Brit* : to make the sign of the cross on (oneself) **2** *dial Brit* : BLESS

sain·foin \ˈsān-ˌfȯin, ˈsan-\ *n* [F, fr. MF, fr. *sain* healthy (fr. L *sanus*) + *foin* hay, fr. L *fenum*] : a Eurasian pink-flowered perennial leguminous forage herb (*Onobrychis viciaefolia*); *also* : any of several New World legumes

¹saint \ˈsānt, *before a name* (ˌ)sānt *or* sənt\ *n* [ME, fr. MF, fr. LL *sanctus*, fr. L, sacred, fr. pp. of *sancire* to make sacred — more at SACRED] **1** : one officially recognized esp. through canonization as preeminent for holiness **2 a** : one of the spirits of the departed in heaven **b** : ANGEL 1a **3 a** : one of God's chosen and usu. Christian people **b** *cap* : a member of any of various Christian bodies; *specif* : LATTER-DAY SAINT **4** : one eminent for piety or virtue **5** : an illustrious predecessor — **saint·like** \ˈsānt-ˌlīk\ *adj*

²saint \ˈsānt\ *vt* : to recognize or designate as a saint; *specif* : CANONIZE

Saint Ag·nes' Eve \-ˌag-nəs-(əz-)ˈēv\ *n* [*St. Agnes*] : the night of January 20 when a woman is traditionally held to have a revelation of her future husband

Saint An·drew's cross \-ˌan-ˌdrüz-\ *n* [*St. Andrew* †*ab* A.D. 60, one of the twelve apostles] : a figure of a cross that has the form of two intersecting oblique bars — see CROSS illustration

Saint An·tho·ny's cross \-ˌan(t)-thə-nēz-, *chiefly Brit* -ˌan-tə-\ *n* [*St. Anthony*] : TAU CROSS

Saint Anthony's fire *n* : any of several inflammations or gangrenous conditions (as erysipelas or ergotism) of the skin

saint au·gus·tine grass \-ˌȯ-gə-ˌstēn-\ *n, often cap S&A* [prob. fr. *St. Augustine*, Fla.] **1** : a perennial much-branched creeping grass (*Stenotaphrum secundatum*) of the southern U.S. that is valuable as a sand binder and as sod grass **2** : a grass (*Manisuris rugosa*) similar to Saint Augustine grass

Saint Ber·nard \-bər-ˈnärd\ *n* [the hospice of Grand *St. Bernard*, where such dogs were first bred] : any of a Swiss alpine breed of tall powerful working dogs used esp. formerly in aiding lost travelers

saint·dom \ˈsānt-dəm\ *n* : the quality or state of being a saint

saint·ed \ˈsānt-əd\ *adj* **1** : befitting or relating to a saint **2** : SAINTLY, PIOUS **3** : entered into heaven : DEAD

Saint El·mo's fire \-ˌel-(ˌ)mōz-\ *n* [*St. Elmo* (*Erasmus*) †303 It bishop & patron saint of sailors] : a flaming phenomenon sometimes seen in stormy weather at prominent points on an airplane or ship and on land that is of the nature of a brush discharge of electricity — called also *Saint Elmo's light*

saint·hood \ˈsānt-ˌhu̇d\ *n* **1** : the quality or state of being a saint **2** : saints as a group

Saint–John's–wort \-ˈjänz-ˌwərt, -ˌwȯ(ə)rt\ *n* [*St. John* the Baptist] : any of a genus (*Hypericum* of the family Guttiferae, the Saint-John's-wort family) of herbs and shrubs with showy pentamerous yellow flowers

Saint Lawrence skiff *n* [*Saint Lawrence* (river)] : SKIFF 3

Saint Lou·is encephalitis \-ˌlü-əs-\ *n* [*St. Louis*, Mo.] : a No. American viral encephalitis that is transmitted by several culex mosquitoes

saint·ly \ˈsānt-lē\ *adj* : relating to, resembling, or befitting a saint : HOLY — **saint·li·ness** *n*

Saint Mar·tin's summer \-ˌmärt-ᵊn(z)-ˈsəm-ər\ *n* [*Saint Martin's* Day, November 11] : Indian summer when occurring in November

Saint Pat·rick's Day \-ˈpa-triks-\ *n* : March 17 observed by the Roman Catholic Church in honor of St. Patrick and celebrated in Ireland in commemoration of his death

saint's day *n* : a day in a church calendar on which a saint is commemorated

saint·ship \ˈsānt-ˌship\ *n* : SAINTHOOD 1

Saint Val·en·tine's Day \-ˈval-ən-ˌtīnz-\ *n* [*St. Valentine* †*ab*270 It priest] : February 14 observed in honor of St. Valentine and as a time for sending valentines

Saint Vi·tus's dance \-ˌvīt-əs(-əz)-\ *n* [*St. Vitus*, 3d cent. Christian child martyr] : CHOREA

saith \(ˈ)seth, ˈsā-əth\ *archaic pres 3d sing of* SAY

saithe \ˈsāth, ˈsāth\ *n, pl* **saithe** [of Scand origin; akin to ON *seithr* coalfish] : POLLACK

Sai·va \ˈs(h)ī-və\ *n* [Skt *Śaiva*, fr. *Śiva* Siva] : a member of a major Hindu sect devoted to the cult of Siva — **Sai·vism** \-ˌviz-əm\ *n*

¹sake \ˈsāk\ *n* [ME, dispute, guilt, purpose, fr. OE *sacu* guilt, action at law; akin to OHG *sahha* action at law, cause, OE *sēcan* to seek — more at SEEK] **1** : END, PURPOSE <for the ~ of argument> **2 a** : the good, advantage, or enhancement of some entity (as an ideal) <free to pursue learning for its own ~ —M. S. Eisenhower> **b** : personal or social welfare, safety, or benefit

²sa·ke *or* **sa·ki** \ˈsäk-ē\ *n* [Jap *sake*] : a Japanese alcoholic beverage of fermented rice usu. served hot

sa·ker \ˈsā-kər\ *n* [ME *sagre*, fr. MF *sacre*, fr. Ar *ṣaqr*] : an Old World falcon (*Falco cherrug*) used in falconry

Sakti \ˈs(h)äk-tē\, **Saktism** *var of* SHAKTI, SHAKTISM

sal \ˈsal\ *n* [L — more at SALT] : SALT

¹sa·laam \sə-ˈläm\ *n* [Ar *salām*, lit., peace] **1** : a salutation or ceremonial greeting in the East **2** : an obeisance performed by bowing very low and placing the right palm on the forehead

²salaam *vt* : to greet or pay homage to with a salaam <the attendant opened the door, ~*ed* him in —J. A. Phillips> ~ *vi* : to perform a salaam

sal·able *or* **sale·able** \ˈsā-lə-bəl\ *adj* : capable of being or fit to be sold : MARKETABLE — **sal·abil·i·ty** \ˌsā-lə-ˈbil-ət-ē\ *n*

sa·la·cious \sə-ˈlā-shəs\ *adj* [L *salac-*, *salax* fond of leaping, lustful, fr. *salire* to leap — more at SALLY] **1** : arousing or appealing to sexual desire or imagination : LASCIVIOUS **2** : LECHEROUS, LUSTFUL — **sa·la·cious·ly** *adv* — **sa·la·cious·ness** *n*

sal·ad \ˈsal-əd\ *n* [ME *salade*, fr. MF, fr. OProv *salada*, fr. *salar* to salt, fr. *sal* salt, fr. L — more at SALT] **1 a** : green vegetables (as lettuce, endive, or romaine) and often tomatoes, cucumbers, or radishes served wtih dressing **b** : a cold dish of meat, fish, or shellfish served with fruits, vegetables, or hard-boiled eggs and a dressing usu. on lettuce **2** : a green vegetable or herb grown for salad; *esp* : LETTUCE

salad days *n pl* : time of youthful inexperience or indiscretion <my *salad days* when I was green in judgment —Shak.>

salad dressing *n* : a dressing either uncooked (as French dressing) or cooked (as a boiled dressing) that is used for salad

salad oil *n* : an edible vegetable oil (as olive oil) suitable for using in salad dressings

sal·a·man·der \ˈsal-ə-ˌman-dər *also* ˌsal-ə-ˈ\ *n* [ME *salamandre*, fr. MF, fr. L *salamandra*, fr. Gk] **1** : a mythical animal having the power to endure fire without harm **2** : an elemental being in the theory of Paracelsus inhabiting fire **3** : any of numerous amphibians (order Caudata) superficially resembling lizards but scaleless and covered with a soft moist skin and breathing by gills in the larval stage **4** : an article (as a cooking utensil for browning pastry or a portable stove or incinerator) used in connection with fire — **sal·a·man·drine** \ˌsal-ə-ˈman-drən\ *adj*

sa·la·mi \sə-ˈläm-ē\ *n* [It, pl. of *salame* salami, fr. *salare* to salt, fr. *sale* salt, fr. L *sal* — more at SALT] : highly seasoned sausage of pork and beef either dried or fresh

sal am·mo·ni·ac \ˌsal-ə-ˈmō-nē-ˌak\ *n* [ME *sal armoniak*, fr. L *sal ammoniacus*, lit., salt of Ammon] : AMMONIUM CHLORIDE

sa·lar·i·at \sə-ˈlar-ē-ət, -ˈler-\ *n* [F, fr. *salaire* salary (fr. L *salarium*) + *-ariat* (as in *prolétariat* proletariat)] : the class or body of salaried persons usu. as distinguished from wage earners <the proletariat, the ~, the peasantry —Harvey Wheeler>

sal·a·ry \ˈsal(-ə)-rē\ *n, pl* **-ries** [ME *salarie*, fr. L *salarium* salt money, pension, salary, fr. neut. of *salarius* of salt, fr. *sal* salt — more at SALT] : fixed compensation paid regularly for services *syn* see WAGE — **sal·a·ried** \-rēd\ *adj*

sale \ˈsā(ə)l\ *n* [ME, fr. OE *sala*, fr. ON — more at SELL] **1** : the act of selling; *specif* : the transfer of ownership of and title to property from one person to another for a price **2** : availability for purchase — usu. used in the phrases *for sale* and *on sale* **3 a** : opportunity of selling or being sold : DEMAND **b** : distribution by selling **4** : public disposal to the highest bidder : AUCTION **5** : a selling of goods at bargain prices **6** *pl* **a** : operations and activities involved in promoting and selling goods or services <vice-president in charge of ~*s*> **b** : gross receipts

sa·lep \ˈsal-əp, sə-ˈlep\ *n* [F or Sp, fr. Ar dial. *sahlab*, alter. of Ar (*khusy ath-*) *thaʽlab*, lit., testicles of the fox] : the starchy or mucilaginous dried tubers of various Old World orchids (esp. genus *Orchis*) used for food or in medicine

sal·era·tus \ˌsal-ə-ˈrāt-əs\ *n* [NL *sal aeratus* aerated salt] **:** a leavening agent consisting of potassium or sodium bicarbonate
sale·room \ˈsā(ə)l-ˌrüm, -ˌru̇m\ *chiefly Brit var of* SALESROOM
sales \ˈsā(ə)lz\ *adj* **:** of, relating to, or used in selling
sales check *n* **:** a strip or piece of paper used by retail stores as a memorandum, record, or receipt of a purchase or sale
sales·clerk \ˈsā(ə)lz-ˌklərk\ *n* **:** a salesman or saleswoman in a store
sales·girl \-ˌgər(-ə)l\ *n* **:** SALESWOMAN
Sa·le·sian \sə-ˈlē-zhən, sā-\ *n* **:** a member of the Society of St. Francis de Sales founded by St. John Bosco in Turin, Italy in the 19th century and devoted chiefly to education
sales·la·dy \ˈsā(ə)lz-ˌlād-ē\ *n* **:** SALESWOMAN
sales·man \ˈsā(ə)lz-mən\ *n* **:** one who sells either in a given territory or in a store — **sales·man·ship** \-ˌship\ *n*
sales·peo·ple \-ˌpē-pəl\ *n pl* **:** persons employed to sell goods or services
sales register *n* **:** CASH REGISTER
sales·room \ˈsā(ə)lz-ˌrüm, -ˌru̇m\ *n* **:** a place where goods are displayed for sale; *esp* **:** an auction room
sales slip *n* **:** SALES CHECK
sales tax *n* **:** a tax levied on the sale of goods and services that is usu. calculated as a percentage of the purchase price and collected by the seller
sales·wom·an \ˈsā(ə)lz-ˌwu̇m-ən\ *n* **:** a woman employed to sell merchandise esp. in a store
sali- *comb form* [L, fr. *sal* — more at SALT] **:** salt <*sali*ferous>
sal·ic \ˈsal-ik\ *adj* [by alter.] **:** SIALIC
Sa·lic \ˈsā-lik, ˈsal-ik\ *adj* [MF or ML; MF *salique,* fr. ML *Salicus,* fr. LL *Salii* Salic Franks] **:** of, relating to, or being a Frankish people that settled on the IJssel river early in the 4th century
sal·i·cin \ˈsal-ə-sən\ *n* [F *salicine,* fr. L *salic-, salix* willow — more at SALLOW] **:** a bitter white crystalline glucoside $C_{13}H_{18}O_7$ found in the bark and leaves of several willows and poplars and used in medicine like salicylic acid
Salic law *n* **1 :** the legal code of the Salic Franks **2 :** a rule held to derive from the Salic code excluding females from the line of succession to a throne
sa·lic·y·late \sə-ˈlis-ə-ˌlāt\ *n* **:** a salt or ester of salicylic acid
sal·i·cyl·ic acid \ˌsal-ə-ˌsil-ik-\ *n* [ISV, fr. *salicyl* (the radical HOC_6H_4CO)] **:** a crystalline phenolic acid $C_7H_6O_3$ used esp. in the form of salts as an analgesic and antipyretic and in the treatment of rheumatism
sa·lience \ˈsā-lyən(t)s, -lē-ən(t)s\ *n* **1 :** the quality or state of being salient **2 :** a striking point or feature **:** HIGHLIGHT
sa·lien·cy \-lyən-sē, -lē-ən-\ *n, pl* **-cies :** SALIENCE
[1]**sa·lient** \ˈsā-lyənt, -lē-ənt\ *adj* [L *sallent-, saliens,* prp. of *salire* to leap — more at SALLY] **1 :** moving by leaps or springs **:** JUMPING; *specif* **:** of, relating to, or being a salientian <a ~ amphibian> **2 :** jetting upward <a ~ fountain> **3 a :** projecting beyond a line, surface, or level **b :** standing out conspicuously **:** PROMINENT, STRIKING <~ traits> ***syn*** see NOTICEABLE — **sa·lient·ly** *adv*
[2]**salient** *n* **:** something (as a promontory) that projects outward or upward from its surroundings; *esp* **:** an outwardly projecting part of a fortification, trench system, or line of defense
sa·li·en·tian \ˌsā-lē-ˈen-chən\ *n* [deriv. of L *salient-, saliens*] **:** any of an order (Salientia) of amphibians comprising the frogs, toads, and tree toads all of which lack a tail in the adult stage and have long strong hind limbs suited to leaping and swimming — **salientian** *adj*
sa·lim·e·ter \sā-ˈlim-ət-ər, -sə-\ *n* **:** a hydrometer for indicating the percentage of a salt in a solution
sa·li·na \sə-ˈlī-nə, -ˈlē-\ *n* [Sp, fr. L *salinae* saltworks, fr. fem. pl. of *salinus*] **1 :** a salt-encrusted playa or flat **2 :** a salt marsh, pond, or lake
[1]**sa·line** \ˈsā-ˌlēn, -ˌlīn\ *adj* [ME, fr. L *salinus,* fr. *sal* salt — more at SALT] **1 :** consisting of or containing salt <a ~ solution> **2 :** of, relating to, or resembling salt **:** SALTY <a ~ taste> **3 :** consisting of or relating to the salts of the alkali metals or of magnesium <a ~ cathartic> — **sa·lin·i·ty** \sā-ˈlin-ət-ē, sə-\ *n*
[2]**saline** *n* **1 :** a metallic salt; *esp* **:** a salt of potassium, sodium, or magnesium with a cathartic action **2 :** a saline solution; *esp* **:** one isotonic with body fluids
sa·li·nize \ˈsal-ə-ˌnīz *also* ˈsā-lə-\ *vt* **-nized; -niz·ing :** to treat or impregnate with salt — **sa·li·ni·za·tion** \ˌsal-ə-nə-ˈzā-shən *also* ˌsā-lə-\ *n*
sa·li·nom·e·ter \ˌsal-ə-ˈnäm-ət-ər, ˌsā-lə-\ *n* [ISV *saline* + *-o-* + *-meter*] **:** an instrument (as a hydrometer) for measuring the amount of salt in a solution
Sa·lique \ˈsā-lik, ˈsal-ik; sa-ˈlēk, sā-\ *var of* SALIC
Salis·bury steak \ˌsȯlz-ˌber-ē-, ˌsalz-, -b(ə-)rē-\ *n* [J. H. *Salisbury,* 19th cent. E physician] **:** ground beef mixed with egg, milk, bread crumbs, and seasonings and formed into a large patty and cooked
Sa·lish \ˈsā-lish\ *n* **1 :** a language stock of the Mosan phylum **2 :** the peoples speaking Salish dialects — **Sa·lish·an** \-ən\ *adj*
sa·li·va \sə-ˈlī-və\ *n* [L — more at SALLOW] **:** a slightly alkaline secretion of water, mucin, protein, salts, and often a starch-splitting enzyme that is secreted into the mouth by salivary glands, lubricates ingested food, and often begins the breakdown of starches
sal·i·vary \ˈsal-ə-ˌver-ē\ *adj* **:** of or relating to saliva or the glands that secrete it; *esp* **:** producing or carrying saliva
salivary chromosome *n* **:** one of the very large polytene chromosomal strands that are made up of many chromatids and are typical of the salivary gland cells of various insects
sal·i·vate \ˈsal-ə-ˌvāt\ *vb* **-vat·ed; -vat·ing** *vt* **:** to produce an abnormal flow of saliva in (as by the use of mercury) ~ *vi* **:** to have a flow of saliva esp. in excess — **sal·i·va·tion** \ˌsal-ə-ˈvā-shən\ *n*
Salk vaccine \ˈsȯ(l)k-\ *n* [Jonas *Salk b*1914 Am physician] **:** a vaccine consisting of poliomyelitis virus inactivated with formaldehyde
sal·let \ˈsal-ət\ *n* [ME, fr. MF *sallade*] **:** a light 15th century helmet with or without a visor and with a projection over the neck
[1]**sal·low** \ˈsal-(ˌ)ō, -ə(-w)\ *n* [ME, fr. OE *sealh;* akin to OHG *salha* sallow, L *salix* willow] **:** any of various Old World broad-leaved willows (as *Salix caprea*) including important sources of charcoal and tanbark
[2]**sallow** *adj* [ME *salowe,* fr. OE *salu;* akin to OHG *salo* murky, L *saliva* spittle] **:** of a grayish greenish yellow color — **sal·low·ish** \ˈsal-ə-wish\ *adj* — **sal·low·ness** \ˈsal-ō-nəs, ˈsal-ə-\ *n*
[1]**sal·ly** \ˈsal-ē\ *n, pl* **sallies** [MF *saillie,* fr. OF, fr. *saillir* to rush forward, fr. L *salire* to leap; akin to Gk *hallesthai* to leap] **1 :** an action of rushing or bursting forth; *esp* **:** a sortie of troops from a defensive position to attack the enemy **2 a :** a brief outbreak **:** OUTBURST **b :** a witty or imaginative saying **:** QUIP **3 :** a venture or excursion usu. off the beaten track **:** JAUNT
[2]**sally** *vi* **sal·lied; sal·ly·ing 1 :** to leap out or burst forth suddenly **2 :** to set out **:** DEPART — usu. used with *forth*
Sal·ly Lunn \ˌsal-ē-ˈlən\ *n* [*Sally Lunn,* 18th cent. E baker] **:** a slightly sweetened yeast-leavened bread
sally port *n* **:** a gate or passage in a fortified place for use by troops making a sortie
sal·ma·gun·di \ˌsal-mə-ˈgən-dē\ *n* [F *salmigondis*] **1 :** a salad plate of chopped meats, anchovies, eggs, and vegetables arranged in rows for contrast and dressed with a salad dressing **2 :** a heterogeneous mixture **:** POTPOURRI
sal·mi \ˈsal-mē\ *n* [F *salmis,* short for *salmigondis*] **:** a ragout of partly roasted game stewed in a rich sauce
salm·on \ˈsam-ən\ *n, pl* **salmon** *also* **salmons** [ME *samon,* fr. MF, fr. L *salmon-, salmo*] **1 a :** a large soft-finned anadromous game fish (*Salmo salar*) of the northern Atlantic noted as a food fish **b :** any of various anadromous fishes (family Salmonidae) other than the salmon; *esp* **:** a fish (genus *Oncorhynchus*) that breeds in rivers tributary to the northern Pacific **c :** a fish (as a barramunda) resembling a salmon **2 :** the variable color of salmon's flesh averaging a strong yellowish pink
salm·on·ber·ry \-ˌber-ē\ *n* **:** a showy red-flowered raspberry (*Rubus spectabilis*) of the Pacific coast; *also* **:** its edible salmon-colored fruit
sal·mo·nel·la \ˌsal-mə-ˈnel-ə\ *n, pl* **-nel·lae** \-ˈnel-(ˌ)ē, -ˌī\ *or* **-nellas** *or* **-nella** [NL, genus name, fr. Daniel E. *Salmon* †1914 Am veterinarian] **:** any of a genus (*Salmonella*) of aerobic rod-shaped usu. motile bacteria that are pathogenic for man and other warm-blooded animals and cause food poisoning, gastrointestinal inflammation, or diseases of the genital tract
sal·mo·nel·lo·sis \ˌsal-mə-ˌnel-ˈō-səs\ *n, pl* **-lo·ses** \-ˌsēz\ [NL] **:** infection with or disease caused by salmonellae
sal·mo·nid \ˈsa(l)m-ə-(ˌ)nid\ *n* [NL *Salmonidae* group name, fr. *Salmon-, Salmo,* genus name, fr. L *salmo* salmon] **:** any of a family (Salmonidae) of elongate soft-finned fishes (as a salmon or trout) that have the last vertebrae upturned — **salmonid** *adj*
salm·on·oid \ˈsam-ə-ˌnȯid\ *n* **:** SALMONID; *also* **:** a related fish — **salmonoid** *adj*
salmon pink *n* **:** a strong yellowish pink that is lighter and slightly redder than average salmon
Sa·lo·me \sə-ˈlō-mē\ *n* [LL, fr. Gk *Salōmē*] **:** a niece of Herod Antipas given the head of John the Baptist as a reward for her dancing
sa·lom·e·ter \sā-ˈläm-ət-ər, sə-\ *n* [L *sal* salt + E *-o-* + *-meter*] **:** SALIMETER
sa·lon \sə-ˈlän, ˈsal-ˌän, sa-ˈlōⁿ\ *n* [F] **1 :** an elegant apartment or living room (as in a fashionable home) **2 :** a fashionable assemblage of notables (as literary figures, artists, or statesmen) held by custom at the home of a prominent person **3 a :** a hall for exhibition of art **b** *cap* **:** an annual exhibition of works of art **4 :** a stylish business establishment or shop <a beauty ~>
sa·loon \sə-ˈlün\ *n* [F *salon,* fr. It *salone,* aug. of *sala* hall, of Gmc origin; akin to OHG *sal* hall; akin to Lith *sala* village] **1 :** SALON 1 **2 :** SALON 2 **3 a :** an often elaborately decorated public apartment or hall (as a large cabin for social use of a ship's passengers) **b :** SALON 4 **c :** a room or establishment in which alcoholic beverages are sold and consumed **4** *Brit* **a :** PARLOR CAR **b :** SEDAN 2a
sa·loop \sə-ˈlüp\ *n* [modif. of F or Sp *salep*] **1 :** SALEP **2 :** a hot drink made from an infusion of salep or sassafras
sal·pa \ˈsal-pə\ *n* [NL, genus name, fr. L, a kind of stockfish, fr. Gk *salpē*] **:** a transparent barrel-shaped or fusiform free-swimming oceanic tunicate (family Salpidae and esp. genus *Salpa*) that is abundant in warm seas
sal·pi·glos·sis \ˌsal-pə-ˈgläs-əs\ *n* [NL, genus name, irreg. fr. Gk *salpinx* trumpet + *glōssa* tongue — more at GLOSS] **:** any of a small genus (*Salpiglossis*) of Chilean herbs of the nightshade family with large funnel-shaped varicolored flowers often strikingly marked
salping- *or* **salpingo-** *comb form* [NL, fr. *salping-, salpinx*] **:** salpinx <*salping*itis>
sal·pin·gian \sal-ˈpin-j(ē-)ən\ *adj* **:** of or relating to a salpinx
sal·pin·gi·tis \ˌsal-pən-ˈjīt-əs\ *n* [NL] **:** inflammation of a fallopian or eustachian tube
sal·pinx \ˈsal-(ˌ)piŋ(k)s\ *n, pl* **sal·pin·ges** \sal-ˈpin-(ˌ)jēz\ [NL *salping-, salpinx,* fr. Gk, trumpet] **1 :** EUSTACHIAN TUBE **2 :** FALLOPIAN TUBE
sal·si·fy \ˈsal-sə-fē, -ˌfī\ *n* [F *salsifis,* modif. of It *sassefrica,* fr. LL *saxifrica,* any of various herbs, fr. L *saxum* rock + *fricare* to rub — more at SAXIFRAGE, FRICTION] **:** a European biennial composite herb (*Tragopogon porrifolius*) with a long fusiform edible root — called also *oyster plant, vegetable oyster*
sal soda \ˈsal-ˈsōd-ə\ *n* **:** a transparent crystalline hydrated sodium carbonate $Na_2CO_3 10H_2O$ — called also *washing soda*
[1]**salt** \ˈsȯlt\ *n* [ME, fr. OE *sealt;* akin to OHG *salz* salt, L *sal,* Gk *hals* salt, sea] **1 a :** a crystalline compound NaCl that is the chloride of sodium, abundant in nature, and used esp. for seasoning or preserving food or in industry — called also *common salt* **b :** a substance (as sal soda) resembling common salt in some property **c** *pl* (1) **:** a mineral or saline mixture (as Epsom salts) used as an aperient or cathartic (2) **:** SMELLING SALTS **d :** any of numerous compounds that result from replacement of part or all of the acid hydrogen of an acid by a metal or a radical acting like a metal **:** an ionic or electrovalent crystalline compound **2 a :** an ingredient that gives savor, piquancy, or zest **:** FLAVOR <a peo-

ple . . . full of life, vigor, and the ~ of personality —Clifton Fadiman> **b :** sharpness of wit : PUNGENCY <songs that have the ~ of wit —John Simon> **c :** COMMON SENSE **d :** RESERVE, SKEPTICISM — often used in the phrase *with a grain of salt* **e :** a scattered elite — usu. used in the phrase *salt of the earth* **3 :** SAILOR <a tale worthy of an old ~> **4 :** KEEP 3 — usu. used in the phrases *earn one's salt* and *worth one's salt* — **salt·like** \-ˌlīk\ *adj*

²salt *vt* **1 a :** to treat, provide, or season with common salt **b :** to preserve (food) with salt or in brine **c :** to supply (as an animal) with salt **2 :** to give flavor or piquancy to (as a story) **3 :** to enrich (as a mine) artificially by secretly placing valuable mineral in some of the working places **4 :** to sprinkle with or as if with a salt <~*ing* clouds with silver iodide>

³salt *adj* **1 a :** SALINE, SALTY **b :** being or inducing one of the four basic taste sensations — compare BITTER, SOUR, SWEET **2 :** cured or seasoned with salt : SALTED **3 :** overflowed with salt water <a ~ pond> **4 :** SHARP, PUNGENT — **salt·ness** *n*

⁴salt *adj* [by shortening & alter. fr. *assaut,* fr. ME *a sawt,* fr. MF *a saut,* lit., on the jump] *obs* : LUSTFUL, LASCIVIOUS

sal·ta·rel·lo \ˌsal-tə-ˈrel-(ˌ)ō, ˌsäl-\ *n, pl* **-los** [It] **:** an Italian dance with a lively hop step beginning each measure

sal·ta·tion \sal-ˈtā-shən, sȯl-\ *n* [L *saltation-, saltatio,* fr. *saltatus,* pp. of *saltare* to leap, dance, fr. *saltus,* pp. of *salire* to leap — more at SALLY] **1 a :** the action or process of leaping or jumping **b :** DANCE **2 a :** the direct transformation of one organismic form into another when it occurs according to some evolutionary theories by major evolutionary steps; *broadly* **:** discontinuous variation **b :** MUTATION — used esp. of bacteria and fungi

sal·ta·to·ri·al \ˌsal-tə-ˈtōr-ē-əl, ˌsȯl-, -ˈtȯr-\ *adj* **:** relating to, marked by, or adapted for leaping <~ legs of a grasshopper>

sal·ta·to·ry \ˈsal-tə-ˌtōr-ē, ˈsȯl-, -ˌtȯr-\ *adj* **1 :** of or relating to dancing <the ~ art> **2 :** proceeding by leaps rather than by gradual transitions : DISCONTINUOUS

salt away *vt* **:** to lay away (as money) safely : SAVE

salt·box \ˈsȯlt-ˌbäks\ *n* **:** a frame dwelling with two stories in front and one behind and a roof with a long rear slope

saltbox

salt·bush \-ˌbu̇sh\ *n* **:** any of various shrubby plants of the goosefoot family that thrive in dry alkaline soil; *esp* **:** one of the oraches that are important browse plants in dry regions

salt·cel·lar \ˈsȯlt-ˌsel-ər\ *n* [ME *salt saler,* fr. *salt* + *saler* salt cellar, fr. MF, fr. L *salarius* of salt — more at SALARY] **:** a small vessel for holding salt at the table

salt dome *n* **:** a domical anticline in sedimentary rock that has a mass of rock salt as its core

salt·ed \ˈsȯl-təd\ *adj, of an animal* **:** immune to a contagious disease because of prior infection and recovery

salt·er \ˈsȯl-tər\ *n* **1 :** one that manufactures or deals in salt **2 :** one that salts something (as meat, fish, or hides)

sal·tern \ˈsȯl-tərn\ *n* [OE *sealtern,* fr. *sealt* salt + *ærn* house; akin to ON *rann* house] **:** a place where salt is made (as by boiling)

salt flat *n* **:** a salt-encrusted flat area resulting from evaporation of a former body of water

salt gland *n* **:** a gland (as of a marine bird) capable of excreting a concentrated salt solution

salt grass *n* **:** a grass native to an alkaline habitat (as a salt meadow)

sal·tine \sȯl-ˈtēn\ *n* **:** a thin crisp cracker sprinkled with salt

sal·tire \ˈsȯl-ˌtī(ə)r, ˈsal-\ *n* [ME *sautire,* fr. MF *saultoir* X-shaped animal barricade that can be jumped over by people, saltire, fr. *saulter* to jump, fr. L *saltare* — more at SALTATION] **:** a heraldic charge consisting of a cross formed by a bend and a bend sinister crossing in the center

salt lake *n* **:** a landlocked body of water that has become salty through evaporation

salt·less \ˈsȯlt-ləs\ *adj* **1 :** having no salt **2 :** INSIPID

salt lick *n* **:** LICK 3

salt marsh *n* **:** flat land subject to overflow by salt water

salt–marsh caterpillar *n* **:** an American moth (*Estigmene acrea* of the family Arctiidae) whose larva is destructive to various crop plants

salt out *vt* **:** to precipitate, coagulate, or separate (as a dissolved substance or lyophilic sol) esp. from a solution by the addition of salt ~ *vi* **:** to become salted out

salt·pe·ter \ˈsȯlt-ˈpēt-ər\ *n* [alter. of earlier *saltpeter,* fr. ME, fr. MF *saltpetre,* fr. ML *sal petrae,* lit., salt of the rock] **1 :** POTASSIUM NITRATE **2 :** SODIUM NITRATE

salt pork *n* **:** fat pork cured in salt or brine

salt·shak·er \ˈsȯlt-ˌshā-kər\ *n* **:** a container with a perforated top for sprinkling salt

salt·wa·ter \ˌsȯlt-ˌwȯt-ər, -ˌwät-\ *adj* **:** relating to, living in, or consisting of salt water

salt·works \ˈsȯlt-ˌwərks\ *n pl but sing or pl in constr* **:** a plant where salt is prepared commercially

salt·wort \-ˌwərt, -ˌwȯ(ə)rt\ *n* **1 :** any of a genus (*Salsola*) of plants of the goosefoot family used in making soda ash **2 :** GLASSWORT **3 :** a low-growing strong-smelling coastal shrub (*Batis maritima*) of warm parts of the New World

salty \ˈsȯl-tē\ *adj* **salt·i·er; -est** **1 :** of, seasoned with, or containing salt **2 :** smacking of the sea or nautical life **3 a :** PIQUANT **b :** EARTHY 3b — **salt·i·ly** \-tə-lē\ *adv* — **salt·i·ness** \-tē-nəs\ *n*

sa·lu·bri·ous \sə-ˈlü-brē-əs\ *adj* [L *salubris* — more at SAFE] **:** favorable to or promoting health or well-being — **sa·lu·bri·ous·ly** *adv* — **sa·lu·bri·ous·ness** *n* — **sa·lu·bri·ty** \-brət-ē\ *n*

sa·lu·ki \sə-ˈlü-kē\ *n* [Ar *salūqīy* of Saluq, fr. *Salūq* Saluq, ancient city in Arabia] **:** any of an old northern African and Asiatic breed of tall slender swift-footed keen-eyed hunting dogs having long narrow skulls, long silky ears, and a smooth silky coat ranging from white or cream to black or black and tan

sal·u·tary \ˈsal-yə-ˌter-ē\ *adj* [MF *salutaire,* fr. L *salutaris,* fr. *salut-, salus* health] **1 :** promoting health : CURATIVE **2 :** producing a beneficial effect : REMEDIAL <~ advice> — **sal·u·tari·ly** \ˌsal-yə-ˈter-ə-lē\ *adv* — **sal·u·tari·ness** \ˈsal-yə-ˌter-ē-nəs\ *n*

sal·u·ta·tion \ˌsal-yə-ˈtā-shən\ *n* **1 a :** an expression of greeting, goodwill, or courtesy by word, gesture, or ceremony **b** *pl* **:** REGARDS **2 :** the word or phrase of greeting (as *Gentlemen* or *Dear Sir*) that conventionally comes immediately before the body of a letter — **sal·u·ta·tion·al** \-shnəl, -shən-ᵊl\ *adj*

sa·lu·ta·to·ri·an \sə-ˌlüt-ə-ˈtōr-ē-ən, -ˈtȯr-\ *n* **:** the student usu. having the second highest rank in a graduating class who delivers the salutatory address at the commencement exercises

¹sa·lu·ta·to·ry \sə-ˈlüt-ə-ˌtōr-ē, -ˌtȯr-\ *adj* **:** of or relating to a salutation : expressing or containing a welcome or greeting

²salutatory *n, pl* **-ries** **:** an address or statement of welcome or greeting

¹sa·lute \sə-ˈlüt\ *vb* **sa·lut·ed; sa·lut·ing** [ME *saluten,* fr. L *salutare,* fr. *salut-, salus* health, safety, greeting — more at SAFE] *vt* **1 a :** to address with expressions of kind wishes, courtesy, or honor **b :** to give a sign of respect, courtesy, or goodwill to : GREET **2 :** to become apparent to (one of the senses) **3 a :** to honor (as a person, nation, or event) by a conventional military or naval ceremony **b :** to show respect and recognition to (a military superior) by assuming a prescribed position **c :** to express commendation of : PRAISE ~ *vi* **:** to make a salute — **sa·lut·er** *n*

²salute *n* **1 :** GREETING, SALUTATION **2 a :** a sign, token, or ceremony expressing goodwill, compliment, or respect <the festival was a ~ to the arts> **b :** the position (as of the hand) or the entire attitude of a person saluting a superior **3 :** FIRECRACKER

sal·u·tif·er·ous \ˌsal-yə-ˈtif-(ə-)rəs\ *adj* [L *salutifer,* fr. *salut-, salus* + *-i-* + *-fer* -ferous] **:** SALUTARY

salv·able \ˈsal-və-bəl\ *adj* [LL *salvare* to save — more at SAVE] **:** capable of being saved or salvaged

Sal·va·dor·an \ˌsal-və-ˈdōr-ən, -ˈdȯr-\ *n* **:** a native or inhabitant of El Salvador — **Salvadoran** *adj*

¹sal·vage \ˈsal-vij\ *n* [F; fr. MF, fr. *salver* to save — more at SAVE] **1 a :** compensation paid for saving a ship or its cargo from the perils of the sea or for the lives and property rescued in a wreck **b :** the act of saving or rescuing a ship or its cargo **c :** the act of saving or rescuing property in danger (as from fire) **2 a :** property saved from destruction in a calamity (as a wreck or fire) **b :** something extracted (as from rubbish) as valuable or useful

²salvage *vt* **sal·vaged; sal·vag·ing** **:** to rescue or save (as from wreckage or ruin) — **sal·vage·abil·i·ty** \ˌsal-vij-ə-ˈbil-ət-ē\ *n* — **sal·vage·able** \-ə-bəl\ *adj* — **sal·vag·er** *n*

Sal·var·san \ˈsal-vər-ˌsan\ *trademark* — used for arsphenamine

sal·va·tion \sal-ˈvā-shən\ *n* [ME, fr. OF, fr. LL *salvation-, salvatio,* fr. *salvatus,* pp. of *salvare* to save — more at SAVE] **1 a :** deliverance from the power and effects of sin **b :** the agent or means that effects salvation **c** *Christian Science* **:** the realization of the supremacy of infinite Mind over all bringing with it the destruction of the illusion of sin, sickness, and death **2 :** liberation from ignorance or illusion <science is authoritative truth and the promise of ~ —L. H. Harshbarger> **3 a :** preservation from destruction or failure **b :** deliverance from danger or difficulty — **sal·va·tion·al** \-shnəl, -shən-ᵊl\ *adj*

Salvation Army *n* **:** an international religious and charitable group organized on military lines and founded in 1865 by William Booth for evangelizing and social betterment (as of the poor)

sal·va·tion·ism \sal-ˈvā-shə-ˌniz-əm\ *n* **:** religious teaching emphasizing the saving of the soul

Sal·va·tion·ist \-sh(ə-)nəst\ *n* **1 :** a soldier or officer of the Salvation Army **2** *often not cap* **:** EVANGELIST — **salvationist** *adj, often cap*

¹salve \ˈsav, ˈsȧv\ *n* [ME, fr. OE *sealf;* akin to OHG *salba* salve, Gk *olpē* oil flask] **1 :** an unctuous adhesive substance for application to wounds or sores **2 :** a remedial or soothing influence or agency <a ~ to their hurt feelings>

²salve *vt* **salved; salv·ing** **1 :** to remedy (as disease) with or as if with a salve **2 :** QUIET, ASSUAGE <give him a raise in salary to ~ his feelings —Upton Sinclair>

³salve \ˈsalv\ *vt* **salved; salv·ing** [back-formation fr. *salvage*] **:** SALVAGE <returned to the wreck to supervise the *salving* of the cargo —*Times Lit. Supp.*> — **sal·vor** \ˈsal-vər, -ˌvȯ(ə)r\ *n*

sal·ver \ˈsal-vər\ *n* [modif. of F *salve,* fr. Sp *salva* sampling of food to detect poison, tray, fr. *salvar* to save, sample food to detect poison, fr. LL *salvare* to save — more at SAVE] **:** a tray esp. for serving food or beverages

sal·ver·form \ˈsal-vər-ˌfȯrm\ *adj* **:** tubular with a spreading limb — used of a gamopetalous corolla

sal·ver–shaped \ˈsal-vər-ˌshāpt\ *adj* **:** SALVERFORM

sal·via \ˈsal-vē-ə\ *n* [NL, genus name, fr. L, sage — more at SAGE] **:** any of a large and widely distributed genus (*Salvia*) of herbs or shrubs of the mint family having a 2-lipped open calyx and two anthers; *esp* **:** one (*S. splendens*) with scarlet flowers

sal·vif·ic \sal-ˈvif-ik\ *adj* [LL *salvificus,* fr. L *salvus* safe + *-ficus* -fic] **:** having the intent or power to save or redeem <the ~ life and death of Christ —E. A. Walsh>

¹sal·vo \ˈsal-(ˌ)vō\ *n, pl* **salvos** *or* **salvoes** [It *salva,* fr. F *salve,* fr. L, hail!, imper. of *salvēre* to be healthy, fr. *salvus* healthy — more at SAFE] **1 a :** a simultaneous discharge of two or more guns in military action or as a salute **b :** the release all at one time of a rack of bombs or rockets (as from an airplane) **c :** a series of shots by an artillery battery with each gun firing one round in turn after a prescribed interval **d :** the bombs or projectiles released in a salvo **2 :** SALUTE, TRIBUTE <received ~*s* of praise from . . .

the . . . critics —Janet Flanner> **3 :** a sudden burst (as of cheers) <laughed heartily, in great ~*s* —S. E. White>
[2]**salvo** *vt* **:** to release a salvo of ~ *vi* **:** to fire a salvo
[3]**salvo** *n, pl* **salvos** [ML *salvo jure* with the right reserved] **1 :** a mental reservation **:** PROVISO **2 :** a means of safeguarding one's name or honor or allaying one's conscience **:** SALVE
sal vo·la·ti·le \ˌsal-və-ˈlat-ᵊl-ē\ *n* [NL, lit., volatile salt] **:** an aromatic solution of ammonium carbonate in alcohol or ammonia water or both
Sam *or* **Saml** *abbr* Samuel
SAM \ˈsam, ˌes-(ˌ)ā-ˈem\ *abbr* surface-to-air missile
sa·ma·ra \ˈsam-ə-rə; sə-ˈmar-ə, -ˈmär-\ *n* [NL, fr. L, seed of the elm] **:** a dry indehiscent usu. one-seeded winged fruit (as of an ash or elm tree) — called also *key*

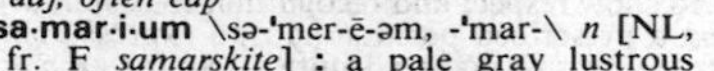

samaras: *1* ash, *2* elm, *3* maple

Sa·mar·i·tan \sə-ˈmar-ət-ᵊn, -ˈmer-\ *n* [ME, fr. LL *samaritanus,* n. & adj., fr. Gk *samaritēs* inhabitant of Samaria, fr. *Samaria*] **1 :** a native or inhabitant of Samaria **2** *often not cap* [fr. the parable of the good Samaritan, Lk 10:30–37] **:** one ready and generous in helping those in distress — **samaritan** *adj, often cap*
sa·mar·i·um \sə-ˈmer-ē-əm, -ˈmar-\ *n* [NL, fr. F *samarskite*] **:** a pale gray lustrous metallic element used esp. in alloys that form permanent magnets — see ELEMENT table
sa·mar·skite \sə-ˈmär-ˌskīt, ˈsam-ər-\ *n* [F, fr. Col. von *Samarski,* 19th cent. Russ mine official] **:** a velvety or brownish black orthorhombic mineral that is a complex oxide of rare earths, uranium, iron, lead, thorium, columbium, tantalum, titanium, and tin
sam·ba \ˈsam-bə, ˈsäm-\ *n* [Pg] **:** a Brazilian dance of African origin with a basic pattern of step-close-step-close and characterized by a dip and spring upward at each beat of the music; *also* **:** the music for this dance — **samba** *vi*
sam·bar *or* **sam·bur** \ˈsäm-bər, ˈsam-\ *n* [Hindi *sā̃bar,* fr. Skt *śambara*] **:** a large Asiatic deer (*Cervus unicolor*) having strong three-pointed antlers and long coarse hair on the throat
Sam Browne belt \ˌsam-ˌbrau̇n-\ *n* [Sir *Sam*uel James *Browne* †1901 Brit army officer] **:** a leather belt for a dress uniform supported by a light strap passing over the right shoulder
[1]**same** \ˈsām\ *adj* [ME, fr. ON *samr;* akin to OHG *sama* same, L *simulis* like, *simul* together, at the same time, *sem-* one, Gk *homos* same, *hama* together, *hen-, heis* one] **1 a :** resembling in every relevant respect **b :** conforming in every respect — used with *as* **2 a :** being one without addition, change, or discontinuance **:** IDENTICAL **b :** being the one under discussion or already referred to **3 :** corresponding so closely as to be indistinguishable <the ~ day last year> **4 :** of equal value or importance
syn SAME, SELFSAME, VERY, IDENTICAL, EQUIVALENT, EQUAL *shared meaning element* **:** not different from another or others or not differing from each other. SAME may imply, and SELFSAME invariably implies, that the things under consideration are in reality one and not two or more different but like things <they take their children to the *same* doctor> <this is the *selfsame* book I borrowed from you> But *same* may also apply to things distinct in fact but not in kind <all received the *same* ration> VERY, like *selfsame,* implies identity <there's the *very* man I mentioned> or, like *same,* likeness in kind <that is the *very* thing that I was saying —P. B. Shelley> IDENTICAL can imply selfsameness <went back to the *identical* spot where we had stopped> or absolute agreement in all pertinent details <their dresses were *identical*> EQUIVALENT describes what amounts (as in worth or import) to the same thing as another <barter involves the exchange of one thing for another of *equivalent* value> EQUAL implies complete correspondence (as in number, size, or value) and, therefore, equivalence but not selfsameness <receive *equal* pay for *equal* work> ***ant*** different
[2]**same** *pron* **1 :** something identical with or similar to another **2 :** something previously defined or described
[3]**same** *adv* **:** in the same manner
sa·mekh \ˈsäm-ˌek\ *n* [Heb *sāmekh*] **:** the 15th letter of the Hebrew alphabet — see ALPHABET table
same·ness \ˈsām-nəs\ *n* **1 :** the quality or state of being the same **:** IDENTITY, SIMILARITY **2 :** MONOTONY, UNIFORMITY
sam·i·sen \ˈsam-ə-ˌsen\ *n* [Jap] **:** a 3-stringed Japanese musical instrument resembling a banjo
sa·mite \ˈsam-ˌīt, ˈsā-ˌmīt\ *n* [ME *samit,* fr. MF, fr. ML *examitum, samitum,* fr. MGk *hexamiton,* fr. Gk, neut. of *hexamitos* of six threads, fr. *hexa-* + *mitos* thread of the warp] **:** a rich medieval silk fabric interwoven with gold or silver
sam·let \ˈsam-lət\ *n* [irreg. fr. *salmon* + *-let*] **:** PARR
Sam·nite \ˈsam-ˌnīt\ *n* [*Samnium,* Italy] **:** a member of an ancient people of central Italy
Sa·mo·an \sə-ˈmō-ən\ *n* **1 :** a native or inhabitant of Samoa **2 :** the Polynesian language of the Samoans — **Samoan** *adj*
sam·o·var \ˈsam-ə-ˌvär\ *n* [Russ, fr. *samo-* self + *varit'* to boil] **1 :** an urn with a spigot at its base used esp. in Russia to boil water for tea **2 :** an urn similar to a Russian samovar with a device for heating the contents
Sam·o·yed *also* **Sam·o·yede** \ˈsam-ə-ˌyed, ˈsam-ˌȯi-ˌed\ *n* [Russ *samoed*] **1 :** a member of a people of the Nenets district of the Arkhangelsk region of the U.S.S.R. **2 :** any of a group of Uralic languages spoken by the Samoyed people **3 :** any of a Siberian breed of medium-sized deep-chested white or cream-colored arctic dogs — **Samoyed** *adj* — **Sam·o·yed·ic** \ˌsam-ə-ˈyed-ik, -ˌȯi-ˈed-\ *adj*
samp \ˈsamp\ *n* [Narraganset *nasaump* corn mush] **:** coarse hominy or a boiled cereal made from it
sam·pan \ˈsam-ˌpan\ *n* [Chin (Pek) *san*¹ *pan*³, fr. *san*¹ three + *pan*³ board, plank] **:** a flat-bottomed Chinese skiff usu. propelled by two short oars
sam·phire \ˈsam-ˌfī(ə)r\ *n* [alter. of earlier *sampiere,* fr. MF (*herbe de*) *Saint Pierre,* lit., St. Peter's herb] **1 :** a fleshy European seacoast plant (*Crithmum maritimum*) of the carrot family that is sometimes pickled **2 :** a common glasswort (*Salicornia europaea*) that is sometimes pickled

samovar 1

[1]**sam·ple** \ˈsam-pəl\ *n* [ME, fr. MF *essample,* fr. L *exemplum* — more at EXAMPLE] **1 :** a representative part or a single item from a larger whole or group presented for inspection or shown as evidence of quality **:** SPECIMEN **2 :** a finite part of a statistical population whose properties are studied to gain information about the whole ***syn*** see INSTANCE
[2]**sample** *vt* **sam·pled; sam·pling** \-p(ə-)liŋ\ **:** to take a sample of or from; *esp* **:** to judge the quality of by a sample **:** TEST <*sampled* his output for defects>
[3]**sample** *adj* **:** serving as an illustration or example <~ questions>
[1]**sam·pler** \ˈsam-plər\ *n* **:** a decorative piece of needlework typically having letters or verses embroidered on it in various stitches as an example of skill
[2]**sam·pler** \-p(ə-)lər\ *n* **1 :** one that collects, prepares, or examines samples **2 :** something containing representative specimens or selections <a ~ of nineteen poets —K. E. Judd>

sampan

sample room *n* **:** a room in which samples are displayed; *esp* **:** a hotel room in which salesmen display merchandise for the inspection of buyers for retail stores
sample space *n* **:** a set in which all of the possible outcomes of a statistical experiment are represented as points
sam·pling \ˈsam-pliŋ *for 2 & 3* -p(ə-)liŋ\ *n* **1 :** a small part selected as a sample for inspection or analysis <ask a ~ of people why they didn't buy one client's product —Vance Packard> **2 :** the act, process, or technique of selecting a suitable sample; *specif* **:** the act, process, or technique of selecting a representative part of a population for the purpose of determining parameters or characteristics of the whole population **3 :** the introduction or promotion of a product by distributing trial packages of it
sam·sa·ra \səm-ˈsär-ə\ *n* [Skt *saṁsāra,* lit., passing through] **:** the indefinitely repeated cycles of birth, misery, and death caused by karma
sam·shu \ˈsam-(ˌ)shü, -ˈshü\ *n* [perh. fr. Chin (Pek) *shao*¹ *chiu*³, lit., spirits that will burn] **:** an alcoholic liquor distilled in China usu. from rice or large millet
Sam·son \ˈsam(p)-sən\ *n* [LL, fr. Gk *Sampsōn,* fr. Heb *Shimshōn*] **:** a Hebrew hero who wreaked havoc among the Philistines by means of his great strength
Sam·so·ni·an \sam(p)-ˈsō-nē-ən\ *adj* [*Samson*] **:** of heroic strength or proportions **:** MIGHTY
Sam·u·el \ˈsam-yə(-wə)l\ *n* [LL, fr. Gk *Samouel,* fr. Heb *Shĕmū'ēl*] **1 :** the early Hebrew judge who successively anointed Saul and David king **2 :** either of two narrative and historical books of canonical Jewish and Christian Scriptures — see BIBLE table
sam·u·rai \ˈsam-(y)ə-ˌrī\ *n, pl* **samurai** [Jap] **1 :** a military retainer of a Japanese daimyo practicing the chivalric code of Bushido **2 :** the warrior aristocracy of Japan
san·a·tar·i·um \ˌsan-ə-ˈter-ē-əm\ *n, pl* **-iums** *or* **-ia** \-ē-ə\ [by alter.] **:** SANATORIUM
san·a·tive \ˈsan-ət-iv\ *adj* [ME *sanatif,* fr. MF, fr. LL *sanativus,* fr. L *sanatus,* pp. of *sanare* to cure, fr. *sanus* healthy] **:** having the power to cure or heal **:** CURATIVE, RESTORATIVE
san·a·to·ri·um \ˌsan-ə-ˈtōr-ē-əm, -ˈtȯr-\ *n, pl* **-riums** *or* **-ria** \-ē-ə\ [NL, fr. LL, neut. of *sanatorius* curative, fr. *sanatus*] **1 :** an establishment that provides therapy combined with a regimen (as of diet and exercise) for treatment or rehabilitation **2 a :** an institution for rest and recuperation (as of convalescents) **b :** an establishment for the treatment of the chronically ill
san·be·ni·to \ˌsan-bə-ˈnēt-(ˌ)ō, ˌsam-\ *n, pl* **-tos** [Sp *sambenito,* fr. *San Benito* St. Benedict of Nursia] **1 :** a sackcloth coat worn by penitents on being reconciled to the church **2 :** a Spanish Inquisition garment resembling a scapular and being either yellow with red crosses for the penitent or black with painted devils and flames for the impenitent condemned to an auto-da-fé
San·cho Pan·za \ˌsan-chō-ˈpan-zə\ *n* [Sp] **:** the squire of Don Quixote in Cervantes' *Don Quixote*
sanc·ti·fi·ca·tion \ˌsaŋ(k)-tə-fə-ˈkā-shən\ *n* **1 :** an act of sanctifying **2 a :** the state of being sanctified **b :** the state of growing in divine grace as a result of Christian commitment after baptism or conversion
sanc·ti·fi·er \ˈsaŋ(k)-tə-ˌfī(-ə)r\ *n* **:** one that sanctifies; *specif, cap* **:** HOLY SPIRIT
sanc·ti·fy \-ˌfī\ *vt* **-fied; -fy·ing** [ME *sanctifien,* fr. MF *sanctifier,* fr. LL *sanctificare,* fr. L *sanctus* sacred — more at SAINT] **1 :** to set apart to a sacred purpose or to religious use **:** CONSECRATE **2 :** to free from sin **:** PURIFY **3 :** to give moral or social sanction to <we ~ education and overflow our colleges —Hal Borland> **4 :** to make productive of holiness or piety <observe the day of the sabbath, to ~ it —Deut 5:12 (DV)>
sanc·ti·mo·nious \ˌsaŋ(k)-tə-ˈmō-nē-əs, -nyəs\ *adj* **1 :** affecting piousness **:** hypocritically devout **2** *obs* **:** possessing sanctity **:** HOLY ***syn*** see DEVOUT, HYPOCRITICAL — **sanc·ti·mo·nious·ly** *adv* — **sanc·ti·mo·nious·ness** *n*
sanc·ti·mo·ny \ˈsaŋ(k)-tə-ˌmō-nē\ *n, pl* **-nies** [MF *sanctimonie,* fr. L *sanctimonia,* fr. *sanctus*] **1** *obs* **:** HOLINESS **2 :** assumed or hypocritical holiness
[1]**sanc·tion** \ˈsaŋ(k)-shən\ *n* [MF or L; MF, fr. L *sanction-, sanctio,* fr. *sanctus,* pp. of *sancire* to make holy — more at SACRED] **1 :** a formal decree; *esp* **:** an ecclesiastical decree **2 a** *obs* **:** a solemn agreement **:** OATH **b :** something that makes an oath binding **3 :** the detriment, loss of reward, or coercive intervention

annexed to a violation of a law as a means of enforcing the law **4 a :** a consideration, principle, or influence (as of conscience) that impels to moral action or determines moral judgment **b :** a mechanism of social control for enforcing a society's standards **c :** explicit or official permission or ratification : APPROBATION **5 :** an economic or military coercive measure adopted usu. by several nations in concert for forcing a nation violating international law to desist or yield to adjudication

²**sanction** *vt* **sanc·tioned; sanc·tion·ing** \-sh(ə-)niŋ\ **1 :** to make valid or binding usu. by a formal procedure (as ratification) **2 :** to give effective or authoritative approval or consent to ***syn*** see APPROVE ***ant*** interdict

sanc·ti·ty \ˈsaŋ(k)-tət-ē\ *n, pl* **-ties** [ME *sauntite,* fr. MF *saincteté,* fr. L *sanctitat-, sanctitas,* fr. *sanctus* sacred] **1 :** holiness of life and character : GODLINESS **2 a :** the quality or state of being holy or sacred : INVIOLABILITY **b** *pl* **:** sacred objects, obligations, or rights

sanc·tu·ary \ˈsaŋ(k)-chə-ˌwer-ē\ *n, pl* **-ar·ies** [ME *sanctuarie,* fr. MF *saintuarie,* fr. LL *sanctuarium,* fr. L *sanctus*] **1 :** a consecrated place: as **a :** the ancient Hebrew temple at Jerusalem or its holy of holies **b (1) :** the most sacred part of a religious building (as the part of a Christian church in which the altar is placed) **(2) :** the room in which general worship services are held **(3) :** a place (as a church or a temple) for worship **2 a (1) :** a place of refuge and protection **(2) :** a refuge for wildlife where predators are controlled and hunting is illegal **b :** the immunity from law attached to a sanctuary

sanc·tum \ˈsaŋ(k)-təm\ *n, pl* **sanctums** *also* **sanc·ta** \-tə\ [LL, fr. L, neut. of *sanctus* sacred] **1 :** a sacred place **2 :** a place (as a study or office) where one is free from intrusion <an editor's ~>

sanc·tum sanc·to·rum \ˌsaŋ(k)-təm-ˌsaŋ(k)-ˈtōr-əm, -ˈtȯr-\ *n* [LL] **1 :** HOLY OF HOLIES **2 :** SANCTUM 2

Sanc·tus \ˈsaŋ(k)-təs; ˈsäŋ(k)-təs, -ˌtüs\ *n* [ME, fr. LL *Sanctus, sanctus, sanctus* Holy, holy, holy, opening of a hymn sung by the angels in Isa 6:3] **:** an ancient Christian hymn of adoration sung or said immediately before the prayer of consecration in traditional eucharistic liturgies

Sanctus bell *n* **:** a bell rung by the server at several points (as at the Sanctus) during the mass

¹**sand** \ˈsand\ *n* [ME, fr. OE; akin to OHG *sant* sand, L *sabulum,* Gk *psammos & ammos* sand, *psēn* to rub] **1 a :** a loose granular material that results from the disintegration of rocks, consists of particles smaller than gravel but coarser than silt, and is used in mortar, glass, abrasives, and foundry molds **b :** soil containing 85 percent or more of sand and a maximum of 10 percent of clay; *broadly* **:** sandy soil **2 a :** a tract of sand : BEACH **b :** a sandbank or sandbar **3 :** the sand in an hourglass; *also* **:** the moments of a lifetime — usu. used in pl. <the ~*s* of this government run out very rapidly —H. J. Laski> **4 :** an oil-producing formation of sandstone or unconsolidated sand **5 :** firm resolution **6 :** a variable color averaging a yellowish gray ***syn*** see FORTITUDE

²**sand** *vt* **1 :** to sprinkle or dust with or as if with sand **2 :** to cover or fill with sand **3 :** to smooth or dress by grinding or rubbing with an abrasive (as sandpaper)

san·dal \ˈsan-dᵊl\ *n* [ME *sandalie,* fr. L *sandalium,* fr. Gk *sandalion,* dim. of *sandalon* sandal] **1 :** a shoe consisting of a sole strapped to the foot **2 :** a low-cut shoe that fastens by an ankle strap **3 :** a strap to hold on a slipper or low shoe **4 :** a rubber overshoe cut very low

san·dal·wood \-ˌwu̇d\ *n* [*sandal* (sandalwood) (fr. ME, fr. MF, fr. ML *sandalum,* fr. LGk *santalon,* deriv. of Skt *candana,* of Dravidian origin; akin to Tamil *cāntu* sandalwood tree) + *wood*] **1 :** the compact close-grained fragrant yellowish heartwood of an Indo-Malayan parasitic tree (*Santalum album* of the family Santalaceae, the sandalwood family) much used in ornamental carving and cabinetwork; *also* **:** the tree that yields this wood **2 :** any of various trees other than sandalwood some of which yield dyewoods; *also* **:** the fragrant wood of such a tree

sandalwood oil *n* **:** an essential oil obtained from sandalwood: as **a :** a pale yellow somewhat viscous aromatic liquid obtained from a sandalwood (*Santalum album*) and used chiefly in perfumes and soaps **b :** an oil obtained from a sandalwood (*Eucarya spicata*) of Western Australia

san·da·rac \ˈsan-də-ˌrak\ *n* [L *sandaraca* red coloring, fr. Gk *sandarakē* realgar, red pigment from realgar] **:** a brittle faintly aromatic translucent resin obtained esp. from the African sandarac tree and used chiefly in making varnish and as incense

sandarac tree *n* **:** a large northern African tree (*Callitris articulata*) of the pine family with a hard durable fragrant wood much used in building; *also* **:** any of several related Australian trees

¹**sand·bag** \ˈsan(d)-ˌbag\ *n* **:** a bag filled with sand and used in fortifications, as ballast, or as a weapon

²**sandbag** *vt* **1 :** to bank, stop up, or weight with sandbags **2 a :** to hit or stun with a sandbag **b :** to coerce by crude means <are raiding the Treasury and *sandbagging* the government —C. W. Ferguson> — **sand·bag·ger** *n*

sand·bank \ˈsan(d)-ˌbaŋk\ *n* **:** a large deposit of sand (as in a hillside or forming a bar or shoal)

sand·bar \-ˌbär\ *n* **:** a ridge of sand built up by currents esp. in a river or in coastal waters

¹**sand·blast** \-ˌblast\ *n* **:** a stream of sand projected by air or steam (as for engraving, cutting, or cleaning glass or stone)

²**sandblast** *vt* **:** to use a sandblast on — **sand·blast·er** *n*

sand–blind \ˈsan(d)-ˌblīnd\ *adj* [ME, prob. fr. (assumed) ME *samblind,* fr. OE *sam-* half + *blind;* akin to OHG *sāmi-* half — more at SEMI-] **:** having poor eyesight : PURBLIND

sand bluestem *n* **:** a tall rhizomatous American grass (*Andropogon hallii*) used for forage and as a soil binder

sand·box \ˈsan(d)-ˌbäks\ *n* **:** a box or receptacle containing loose sand: as **a :** a shaker for sprinkling sand upon wet ink **b :** a box that contains sand for children to play in

sand·bur \ˈsan(d)-ˌbər\ *n* **:** any of several weeds with burry fruit that occur esp. in waste places: as **a :** a No. American nightshade (*Solanum rostratum*) with prickly foliage and racemose yellow flowers **b :** an annual bristly herb (*Franseria acanthicarpa*) of western No. America that is related to the cocklebur

sand–cast \-ˌkast\ *vt* **-cast; -cast·ing :** to make (a casting) by pouring metal in a sand mold

sand casting *n* **:** a casting made in a mold of sand

sand crack *n* **:** a fissure in the wall of a horse's hoof often causing lameness

sand dollar *n* **:** any of numerous flat circular sea urchins (order Exocycloida) that live chiefly in shallow water on sandy bottoms

sand dollar

sand·er \ˈsan-dər\ *n* **:** one that sands: as **a :** a device for spreading sand on newly surfaced or icy roads; *also* **:** the device together with the truck that bears it **b :** a machine or device that smooths, polishes, or scours by means of abrasive material usu. in the form of a disk or belt — called also *sanding machine*

sand·er·ling \ˈsan-dər-liŋ\ *n* [perh. irreg. fr. *sand* + *-ling*] **:** a small sandpiper (*Crocethia alba*) with largely gray-and-white plumage

sand flea *n* **1 :** a flea (as a chigoe) found in sandy places **2 :** BEACH FLEA

sand fly *n* **:** any of various small biting two-winged flies (families Psychodidae, Simuliidae, and Ceratopogonidae)

sand·fly fever \ˌsan(d)-ˌflī-\ *n* **:** a virus disease of brief duration that is characterized by fever, headache, pain in the eyes, malaise, and leukopenia and is transmitted by the bite of a sand fly (*Phlebotomus papatasii*) — called also *phlebotomus fever*

sand·glass \ˈsan(d)-ˌglas\ *n* **:** an instrument (as an hourglass) for measuring time by the running of sand

sand grouse *n* **:** any of numerous birds (family Pteroclidae) of arid parts of southern Europe, Asia, and Africa that are closely related to the pigeons but have precocial downy young

san·dhi \ˈsan-dē, ˈsän-\ *n* [Skt *saṁdhi,* lit., placing together] **:** modification of the sound of a morpheme (as a word or affix) conditioned by context in which it is uttered <pronunciation of *-ed* as \d\ in *glazed* and as \t\ in *paced,* and occurrence of *a* in *a cow* and of *an* in *an old cow,* are examples of ~>

sand·hill crane \ˌsand-ˌhil-\ *n* **:** a crane (*Grus canadensis*) of eastern and central No. America that is chiefly bluish gray tinged with a sandy yellow

sand·hog \ˈsand-ˌhȯg, -ˌhäg\ *n* **:** a laborer who works in a caisson in driving underwater tunnels

sand jack *n* **:** a device for lowering a heavy weight (as a bridge section) into place by allowing sand on which it is supported to run out

sand lance *n* **:** any of several small elongate marine teleost fishes (genus *Ammodytes*) that associate in large schools and remain buried in sandy beaches at ebb tide — called also *sand eel, sand launce*

sand lily *n* **:** a western No. American spring herb (*Leucocrinum montanum*) of the lily family with narrow linear leaves and fragrant salver-shaped flowers

sand·ling \ˈsan-(d)liŋ\ *n* **:** a small flounder

sand·lot \ˈsan-ˌ(d)lät\ *n* **:** a vacant lot esp. when used for the unorganized sports of boys — **sand·lot·ter** \-ˌ(d)lät-ər\ *n*

sand·man \ˈsan(d)-ˌman\ *n* **:** the genie of folklore who makes children sleepy supposedly by sprinkling sand in their eyes

sand myrtle *n* **:** a variable low-branching evergreen upland shrub (*Leiophyllum buxifolium*) of the heath family found in the southeastern U.S.

sand painting *n* **:** a Navaho and Pueblo Indian ceremonial design made of various materials (as colored sands) upon a flat surface of sand or buckskin

¹**sand·pa·per** \ˈsan(d)-ˌpā-pər\ *n* **:** paper covered on one side with abrasive material (as sand) glued fast and used for smoothing and polishing — **sand·pa·pery** \-p(ə-)rē\ *adj*

²**sandpaper** *vt* **:** to rub with or as if with sandpaper

sand·pile \ˈsan(d)-ˌpīl\ *n* **:** a pile of sand; *esp* **:** sand for children to play in

sand·pip·er \-ˌpī-pər\ *n* **:** any of numerous small shorebirds (suborder Charadrii) distinguished from the related plovers chiefly by the longer and soft-tipped bill

sand rat *n* **:** any of various rodents (as of Africa) native to sandy or desert areas

sand smelt *n* **:** SILVERSIDES

sand·soap \ˈsan(d)-ˌsōp\ *n* **:** a gritty soap for all-purpose cleaning

sand·stone \-ˌstōn\ *n* **:** a sedimentary rock consisting of usu. quartz sand united by some cement (as silica or calcium carbonate)

sand·storm \-ˌstȯ(ə)rm\ *n* **:** a windstorm (as in a desert) driving clouds of sand before it

sand table *n* **1 :** a table holding sand for children to mold **2 :** a table bearing a relief model of a terrain built to scale for study or demonstration esp. of military tactics

sand trap *n* **:** an artificial hazard on a golf course consisting of a depression containing sand

sand verbena *n* **:** any of several western American herbs (genus *Abronia*) of the four-o'clock family having flowers like the verbena; *esp* **:** either of two plants (*A. latifolia* and *A. umbellata*) of the Pacific coast

¹**sand·wich** \ˈsan-(ˌ)(d)wich\ *n* [John Montagu, 4th Earl of *Sandwich* †1792 E diplomat] **1 :** a slice of bread covered with a filling (as of meat, cheese, fish, or various mixtures) which is usu. covered with another slice of bread; *also* **:** a partially split long or

round roll stuffed with a filling **2 :** something resembling a sandwich

[2]**sandwich** *vt* **1 :** to make into or as if into a sandwich; *esp* **:** to insert or enclose between usu. two things of another quality or character **2 :** to make a place for — often used with *in* or *between*

sandwich board *n* **:** two usu. hinged boards designed for hanging from the shoulders with one board before and one behind and used esp. for advertising or picketing

sandwich coin *n* **:** a clad coin

sandwich man *n* **:** one who advertises or pickets a place of business by wearing a sandwich board

sand·worm \ˈsan-ˌ(d)wərm\ *n* **:** any of various sand-dwelling polychaete worms: as **a :** any of several large burrowing worms (esp. genus *Nereis*) often used as bait **b :** LUGWORM

sand·wort \ˈsan-ˌ(d)wərt, -ˌ(d)wȯ(ə)rt\ *n* **:** any of a genus (*Arenaria*) of low tufted herbs of the pink family growing usu. in dry sandy regions

sandy \ˈsan-dē\ *adj* **sand·i·er; -est 1 :** consisting of, containing, or sprinkled with sand **2 :** of the color sand — **sand·i·ness** *n*

sane \ˈsān\ *adj* **san·er; san·est** [L *sanus* healthy, sane] **1 :** free from hurt or disease **:** HEALTHY **2 :** mentally sound; *esp* **:** able to anticipate and appraise the effect of one's actions **3 :** proceeding from a sound mind **:** RATIONAL ***syn*** see WISE ***ant*** insane — **sane·ly** *adv* — **sane·ness** \ˈsān-nəs\ *n*

San·for·ized \ˈsan-fə-ˌrīzd\ *trademark* — used for fabrics that are shrunk by a mechanical process before being manufactured into articles (as clothing)

sang *past of* SING

san·ga·ree \ˌsaŋ-gə-ˈrē\ *n* [Sp *sangría*] **:** a sweetened iced drink of wine or sometimes of ale, beer, or liquor garnished with nutmeg

sang·froid \ˈsäⁿ-ˈf(r)wä, ˌsäⁿ-frə-ˈwä\ *n* [F *sang-froid,* lit., cold blood] **:** self-possession or imperturbability esp. under strain ***syn*** see EQUANIMITY

San·greal \san-ˈgrā(ə)l, ˈsaŋ-\ *n* [ME *Sangrayll,* fr. MF *Saint Graal* Holy Grail] **:** GRAIL

san·gria \saŋ-ˈgrē-ə, san-\ *n* [Sp] **:** a punch made of red wine, fruit juice, and soda water

san·gui·nar·ia \ˌsaŋ-gwə-ˈner-ē-ə, -ˈnar-\ *n* [NL, fr. L, an herb that stanches blood, fr. fem. of *sanguinarius* sanguinary] **1 :** BLOODROOT **2 :** the rhizome and roots of a bloodroot used as an expectorant and emetic

san·gui·nary \ˈsaŋ-gwə-ˌner-ē\ *adj* [L *sanguinarius,* fr. *sanguin-, sanguis* blood] **1 :** BLOODTHIRSTY, MURDEROUS <~ hatred> **2 :** attended by bloodshed **:** BLOODY <this bitter and ~ war —T. H. D. Mahoney> **3 :** consisting of blood <a ~ stream> — **san·gui·nari·ly** \ˌsaŋ-gwə-ˈner-ə-lē\ *adv*

[1]**san·guine** \ˈsaŋ-gwən\ *adj* [ME *sanguin,* fr. MF, fr. L *sanguineus,* fr. *sanguin-, sanguis*] **1 :** BLOODRED **2 a :** consisting of or relating to blood **b :** SANGUINARY 1 **c** *of the complexion* **:** RUDDY **3 :** having blood as the predominating bodily humor; *also* **:** having the bodily conformation and temperament held characteristic of such predominance and marked by sturdiness, high color, and cheerfulness **4 :** CONFIDENT, OPTIMISTIC — **san·guine·ly** *adv* — **san·guine·ness** \-gwən-nəs\ *n* — **san·guin·i·ty** \saŋ-ˈgwin-ət-ē, san-\ *n*

[2]**sanguine** *n* **:** a moderate to strong red

san·guin·e·ous \san-ˈgwin-ē-əs, saŋ-\ *adj* [L *sanguineus*] **1 :** BLOODRED **2 :** of, relating to, or involving bloodshed **:** BLOODTHIRSTY **3 :** of, relating to, or containing blood

san·guin·o·lent \-ˈgwin-ᵊl-ənt\ *adj* [L *sanguinolentus,* fr. *sanguin-, sanguis*] **:** of, containing, or tinged with blood <~ sputum>

san·gui·no·pu·ru·lent \ˌsaŋ-gwə-nō-ˈpyůr-(y)ə-lənt\ *adj* [L *sanguin-, sanguis* blood + E *-o-* + *purulent*] **:** containing blood and pus <~ discharge>

San·he·drin \san-ˈhed-rən, sän-; san-ˈhēd-, ˈsan-əd-\ *n* [LHeb *sanhedhrīn gĕdhōlāh* great council] **:** the supreme council and tribunal of the Jews during post-exilic times headed by a High Priest and having religious, civil, and criminal jurisdiction

san·i·cle \ˈsan-i-kəl\ *n* [ME, fr. MF, fr. ML *sanicula*] **:** any of several plants sometimes held to have healing powers; *esp* **:** a plant (genus *Sanicula*) of the carrot family with a root used in folk medicine as an anodyne or astringent

sa·ni·ous \ˈsā-nē-əs\ *adj* [L *saniosus,* fr. *sanies* corrupted blood] **:** thin and seropurulent with a slightly bloody tinge

sanit *abbr* sanitary; sanitation

san·i·tar·i·an \ˌsan-ə-ˈter-ē-ən\ *n* **:** a specialist in sanitary science and public health <milk ~>

san·i·tari·ly \-ˈter-ə-lē\ *adv* **:** in a sanitary manner **:** with regard to sanitation

san·i·tar·i·um \ˌsan-ə-ˈter-ē-əm\ *n, pl* **-i·ums** *or* **-ia** \-ē-ə\ [NL, fr. L *sanitat-, sanitas* health] **:** SANATORIUM

san·i·tary \ˈsan-ə-ˌter-ē\ *adj* [F *sanitaire,* fr. L *sanitas*] **1 :** of or relating to health <~ measures> **2 :** of, relating to, or used in the disposal esp. of domestic waterborne waste <~ sewage> **3 :** characterized by or readily kept in cleanliness <~ packages>

sanitary landfill *n* **:** LANDFILL

sanitary napkin *n* **:** a disposable absorbent pad (as of cellulose) in a gauze covering used postpartum or during menstruation to absorb the uterine flow

sanitary ware *n* **:** ceramic plumbing fixtures (as sinks, lavatories, or toilet bowls)

san·i·tate \ˈsan-ə-ˌtāt\ *vt* **-tat·ed; -tat·ing** [back-formation fr. *sanitation*] **:** to make sanitary esp. by providing with sanitary appliances or facilities

san·i·ta·tion \ˌsan-ə-ˈtā-shən\ *n* **1 :** the act or process of making sanitary **2 :** the promotion of hygiene and prevention of disease by maintenance of sanitary conditions

san·i·tize \ˈsan-ə-ˌtīz\ *vt* **-tized; -tiz·ing** [L *sanitas*] **1 :** to make sanitary (as by cleaning or sterilizing) **2 :** to make more acceptable by removing unpleasant or undesired features <~ a document> — **san·i·ti·za·tion** \ˌsan-ət-ə-ˈzā-shən\ *n*

san·i·to·ri·um \ˌsan-ə-ˈtōr-ē-əm, -ˈtȯr-\ *n, pl* **-ri·ums** *or* **-ria** \-ē-ə\ [by alter. (influenced by *sanitarium*)] **:** SANATORIUM

san·i·ty \ˈsan-ət-ē\ *n* [ME *sanite,* fr. L *sanitat-, sanitas* health, sanity, fr. *sanus* healthy, sane] **:** the quality or state of being sane; *esp* **:** soundness or health of mind

San Ja·cin·to Day \ˌsan-jə-ˈsint-ə-\ *n* **:** April 21 observed as a legal holiday in Texas in commemoration of the battle of San Jacinto in 1836

San Jo·se scale \ˌsan-ə-ˌzā-, -(h)ō-\ *n* [*San Jose,* Calif.] **:** a scale insect (*Aspidiotus perniciosus*) that is naturalized in the U.S. prob. from Asia and is a most damaging pest to fruit trees

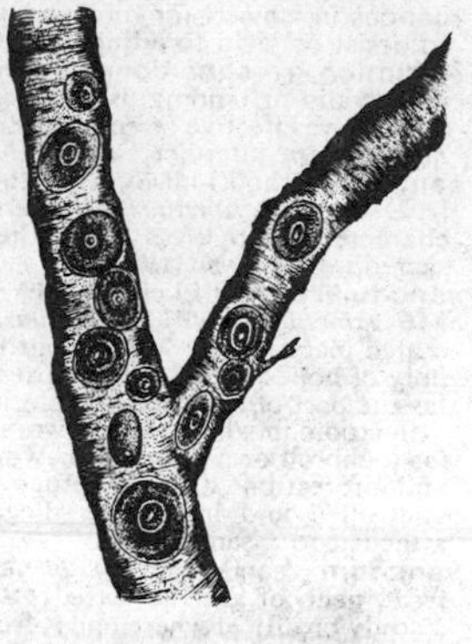

San Jose scale on tree branch

sank *past of* SINK

San·khya \ˈsäŋ-kyə\ *n* [Skt *sāṁkhya,* lit., based on calculation] **:** an orthodox Hindu philosophy teaching salvation through knowledge of the distinction between matter and souls

sann hemp \ˈsən-, ˈsän-\ *n* [Hindi *san*] **:** SUNN

san·nup \ˈsan-əp\ *n* [Abnaki *senanbe*] **:** a married male American Indian

sann·ya·si \(ˌ)sən-ˈyäs-ē\ *or* **sann·ya·sin** \-ˈyäs-ᵊn\ *n* [Hindi *sannyāsī,* fr. Skt *sannyāsin*] **:** a Hindu mendicant ascetic

[1]**sans** \(ˌ)sanz\ *prep* [ME *saun, sans,* fr. MF *san, sans,* modif. of L *sine* without — more at SUNDER] **:** WITHOUT <my love to thee is sound, ~ crack or flaw —Shak.>

[2]**sans** \ˈsanz\ *n, pl* **sans :** SANS SERIF

sans·cu·lotte \ˌsan-skyů-ˈlät\ *n* [F *sans-culotte,* lit., without breeches] **1 :** an extreme radical republican in France at the time of the Revolution **2 :** a person of the lower class: as **a :** one lacking culture and refinement **b :** a radical or violent extremist in politics — **sans·cu·lott·ic** \-ˈlät-ik\ *adj* — **sans·cu·lott·ish** \-ish\ *adj* — **sans·cu·lott·ism** \-ˌiz-əm, ˈsan-skyů-ˌlät-\ *n*

san·sei \(ˈ)sän-ˈsā, ˈsän-ˌ\ *n, pl* **sansei** *also* **sanseis** *often cap* [Jap *san* third + *sei* generation] **:** a son or daughter of nisei parents who is born and educated in America and esp. in the U.S.

san·se·vie·ria \ˌsan(t)-sə-ˈvir-ē-ə\ *n* [NL, genus name, fr. Raimondo di Sangro, prince of *San Severo* †1774 It scholar] **:** any of a genus (*Sansevieria*) of tropical herbs of the lily family with showy mottled sword-shaped leaves usu. yielding a strong fiber

San·skrit \ˈsan-ˌskrit, ˈsan(t)-skrət\ *n* [Skt *saṁskṛta,* lit., perfected, fr. *sam* together + *karoti* he makes] **1 :** an ancient Indic language that is the classical language of India and of Hinduism as described by the Indian grammarians **2 :** classical Sanskrit together with the older Vedic and various later modifications of classical Sanskrit — see INDO-EUROPEAN LANGUAGES table — **Sanskrit** *adj* — **San·skrit·ist** \-əst\ *n*

San·skrit·ic \san-ˈskrit-ik\ *n* **1 :** INDIC **2 :** a group of Indic languages developed directly from Sanskrit — see INDO-EUROPEAN LANGUAGES table — **Sanskritic** *adj*

sans ser·if *or* **san·ser·if** \san-ˈser-əf, ˈsanz-\ *n* [prob. fr. *sans* + modif. of D *schreef* stroke — more at SERIF] **:** a letter or typeface with no serifs

sans serif

San·ta Claus \ˈsant-ē-ˌklȯz, ˈsant-ə-\ *n* [modif. of D *Sinterklaas,* alter. of *Sint Nikolaas* Saint Nicholas *fl*4th cent., bishop of Myra, Asia Minor and patron saint of children] **:** a plump white-bearded and red-suited old man of modern myth who delivers presents to good children at Christmas time

San·ta Ger·tru·dis \ˌsant-ə-(ˌ)gər-ˈtrüd-əs\ *n* [*Santa Gertrudis,* section of the King Ranch, Kingsville, Texas] **:** any of a breed of cherry-red beef cattle developed from a Brahman-Shorthorn cross and valued for their hardiness in hot climes and thrifty growth on grass

san·tir \san-ˈti(ə)r\ *or* **san·tour** \-ˈtů(ə)r\ *n* [Ar *santīr, santūr,* fr. Gk *psaltērion* psaltery] **:** a Persian dulcimer

san·to·li·na \ˌsant-ᵊl-ˈē-nə\ *n* [NL, genus name, alter. of L *santonica*] **:** any of a genus (*Santolina*) of Mediterranean composite undershrubs that have dissected leaves and clustered flower heads lacking ray flowers

san·ton·i·ca \san-ˈtän-i-kə\ *n* [NL, fr. L (*herba*) *santonica* an herb, prob. wormwood, fem. of *santonicus* of the Santoni, fr. *Santoni,* a people of Aquitania] **1 :** a European wormwood (*Artemisia pauciflora*) **2 :** the unexpanded dried flower heads of santonica or a related plant used as an anthelmintic

san·to·nin \ˈsant-ᵊn-ən, san-ˈtän-ən\ *n* [ISV, fr. NL *santonica*] **:** a poisonous slightly bitter crystalline compound $C_{15}H_{18}O_3$ found esp. in santonica and used as an anthelmintic

San·tos \ˈsant-əs\ *n* [*Santos,* Brazil] **:** a Brazilian coffee of moderate body and somewhat acid flavor produced chiefly in the state of São Paulo

[1]**sap** \ˈsap\ *n* [ME, fr. OE *sæp;* akin to OHG *saf* sap] **1 a :** the fluid part of a plant; *specif* **:** a watery solution that circulates through a plant's vascular system **b** (1) **:** a body fluid (as blood) essential to life, health, or vigor (2) **:** bodily health and vigor **2 :** a foolish gullible person **3 :** BLACKJACK, BLUDGEON

[2]**sap** *vt* **sapped; sap·ping 1 :** to drain or deprive of sap **2 :** to knock out with a sap

[3]**sap** *n* [MF & OIt; MF *sappe* hoe, fr. OIt *zappa*] **:** the extension of a trench from within the trench itself to a point beneath an enemy's fortifications

[4]**sap** *vb* **sapped; sap·ping** *vi* **:** to proceed by digging a sap ~ *vt* **1 :** to subvert by digging or eroding the substratum or foundation **:** UNDERMINE <*sapped* by floods, their houses fell —John Dryden> **2 :** to weaken or exhaust the energy or vitality of **3**

: to operate against or pierce by a sap *syn* see WEAKEN

sap green *n* : a strong yellow green

sap·head \'sap-ˌhed\ *n* : a weak-minded stupid person : SAP — **sap·head·ed** \-'hed-əd\ *adj*

sa·phe·nous \sə-'fē-nəs, 'saf-ə-nəs\ *adj* [*saphena* (saphenous vein), fr. ME, fr. ML, fr. Ar *ṣāfin*] : of, relating to, or being either of the two chief superficial veins of the leg

sap house *n* : a maple sugarhouse

sap·id \'sap-əd\ *adj* [L *sapidus* tasty, fr. *sapere* to taste — more at SAGE] **1 a** : affecting the organs of taste : possessing flavor **b** : having a strong agreeable flavor **2** : agreeable to the mind — **sa·pid·i·ty** \sa-'pid-ət-ē\ *n*

sa·pi·ence \'sā-pē-ən(t)s, 'sap-ē-\ *n* : WISDOM, SAGENESS

sa·pi·ens \'sap-ē-ənz, 'sā-pē-, -ˌenz\ *adj* [NL (specific epithet of *Homo sapiens*), fr. L, pp. of *sapere*] : of, relating to, or being recent man (*Homo sapiens*) as distinguished from various fossil men

sa·pi·ent \'sā-pē-ənt, 'sap-ē-\ *adj* [ME, fr. MF, fr. L *sapient-, sapiens*, fr. prp. of *sapere* to taste, be wise] : possessing or expressing great sagacity or discernment *syn* see WISE — **sa·pi·ent·ly** *adv*

sap·less \'sap-ləs\ *adj* **1** : destitute of sap : DRY **2** : lacking vitality or vigor : FEEBLE — **sap·less·ness** *n*

sap·ling \'sap-liŋ, -lən\ *n* **1** : a young tree; *specif* : one not over four inches in diameter at breast height **2** : YOUTH 2a

sap·o·dil·la \ˌsap-ə-'dil-ə, -'dē-(y)ə\ *n* [Sp *zapotillo*, dim. of *zapote* sapodilla — more at SAPOTA] : a tropical evergreen tree (*Achras zapota* of the family Sapotaceae, the sapodilla family) with hard reddish wood, a latex that yields chicle, and a rough-skinned brownish edible fruit; *also* : its fruit

sa·po·ge·nin \ˌsap-ə-'jen-ən, sə-'päj-ə-nən\ *n* [ISV *sapo*nin + *-genin* (compound formed from another compound)] : an aglycon of a sapogenin that is typically obtained by hydrolysis, has either a complex terpenoid or a steroidal structure, and in the latter case forms a practicable starting point in the synthesis of steroid hormones

sap·o·na·ceous \ˌsap-ə-'nā-shəs\ *adj* [NL *saponaceus*, fr. L *sapon-, sapo* soap, of Gmc origin; akin to OE *sāpe* soap] : resembling or having the qualities of soap — **sap·o·na·ceous·ness** *n*

sa·pon·i·fy \sə-'pän-ə-ˌfī\ *vb* **-fied; -fy·ing** [F *saponifier*, fr. L *sapon-, sapo*] *vt* : to convert (as fat) into soap; *specif* : to hydrolyze (a fat) with alkali to form a soap and glycerol ~ *vi* : to undergo saponifying — **sa·pon·i·fi·able** \-ˌfī-ə-bəl\ *adj* — **sa·pon·i·fi·ca·tion** \-ˌpän-ə-fə-'kā-shən\ *n* — **sa·pon·i·fi·er** \-ˌfī(-ə)r\ *n*

sa·po·nin \'sap-ə-nən, sə-'pō-\ *n* [F *saponine*, fr. L *sapon-, sapo*] : any of various mostly toxic surfactant glucosides that occur in plants (as soapwort or soapbark) and are characterized by the property of producing a soapy lather; *esp* : a hygroscopic amorphous saponin mixture used esp. as a foaming and emulsifying agent and detergent

sap·o·nite \'sap-ə-ˌnīt\ *n* [Sw *saponit*, fr. L *sapon-, sapo* soap] : a hydrous magnesium aluminum silicate occurring in soft soapy amorphous masses and filling veins and cavities (as in serpentine)

sa·por \'sā-pər, -ˌpȯ(ə)r\ *n* [ME, fr. L — more at SAVOR] : a property (as bitterness) that affects the sense of taste : SAVOR, FLAVOR — **sa·po·rous** \'sā-pə-rəs, 'sap-ə-\ *adj*

sa·po·ta \sə-'pōt-ə\ *n* [modif. of Sp *zapote*, fr. Nahuatl *tzapotl*] : SAPODILLA

sap·pan·wood \sə-'pan-ˌwu̇d; 'sap-ˌan-, -ən-\ *n* [Malay *sapang* heartwood of sappanwood + E *wood*] : a red brazilwood that is obtained from an East Indian leguminous tree (*Caesalpinia sappan*); *also* : this tree

sap·per \'sap-ər\ *n* **1** : a military specialist in field fortification work (as sapping) **2** : a military specialist who lays, detects, and disarms mines

¹sap·phic \'saf-ik\ *adj* **1** *cap* : of or relating to the Greek lyric poet Sappho **2** : of, relating to, or consisting of a 4-line strophe made up of chiefly trochaic and dactylic feet **3** : LESBIAN 2

²sapphic *n* **1** : a sapphic strophe **2** : a verse having the metrical pattern of one of the first three lines of a sapphic strophe

sap·phire \'saf-ˌī(ə)r\ *n* [ME *safir*, fr. OF, fr. L *sapphirus*, fr. Gk *sappheiros*, fr. Heb *sappīr*, fr. Skt *śanipriya*, lit., dear to the planet Saturn, fr. *Śani* Saturn + *priya* dear] **1 a** : a gem variety of corundum in transparent or translucent crystals of a color other than red; *esp* : one of a transparent rich blue **b** : a gem of such corundum **2** : a variable color averaging a deep purplish blue — **sapphire** *adj*

sap·phi·rine \'saf-ə-ˌrīn, 'saf-ˌī(ə)r-ˌēn, sa-'fī-rən\ *adj* **1** : made of sapphire **2** : resembling sapphire esp. in color

sap·phism \'saf-ˌiz-əm\ *n* [*Sappho* + *-ism*; fr. the belief that Sappho was homosexual] : LESBIANISM

sap·pi·ness \'sap-ē-nəs\ *n* **1** : the state of being full of or smelling of sap **2** : the quality or state of being sappy : FOOLISHNESS

sap·py \'sap-ē\ *adj* **sap·pi·er; -est** **1** : abounding with sap **2** : resembling or consisting largely of sapwood **3 a** : foolishly or immaturely sentimental **b** : lacking in good sense : SILLY

sapr- *or* **sapro-** *comb form* [Gk, fr. *sapros*] **1** : rotten : putrid <*sapremia*> **2** : dead or decaying organic matter <*sapro*phyte>

sa·pre·mia \sa-'prē-mē-ə\ *n* [NL] : a toxic state in which toxic products of putrefactive bacteria are present in the blood — **sa·pre·mic** \-mik\ *adj*

sap·robe \'sap-ˌrōb\ *n* [ISV *sapr-* + Gk *bios* life — more at QUICK] : a saprobic organism

sa·pro·bic \sa-'prō-bik\ *adj* : SAPROPHYTIC; *also* : living in or being an environment rich in organic matter and relatively free from oxygen — **sa·pro·bi·cal·ly** \-bi-k(ə-)lē\ *adv*

sap·ro·gen·ic \ˌsap-rə-'jen-ik\ *adj* : of, causing, or resulting from putrefaction — **sap·ro·ge·nic·i·ty** \-rō-jə-'nis-ət-ē\ *n*

sap·ro·lite \'sap-rə-ˌlīt\ *n* : disintegrated rock that lies in its original place

sap·ro·pe·lic \ˌsap-rə-'pel-ik, -'pē-lik\ *adj* [ISV *sapr-* + Gk *pēlos* clay, mud] : living in mud or ooze rich in decaying organic matter

sa·proph·a·gous \sa-'präf-ə-gəs\ *adj* [NL *saprophagus*, fr. *sapr-* + *-phagus* -phagous] : feeding on decaying matter

sap·ro·phyte \'sap-rə-ˌfīt\ *n* [ISV] : a saprophytic organism; *esp* : a plant living on dead or decaying organic matter

sap·ro·phyt·ic \ˌsap-rə-'fit-ik\ *adj* : obtaining food by absorbing dissolved organic material; *esp* : obtaining nourishment osmotically from the products of organic breakdown and decay — **sap·ro·phyt·i·cal·ly** \-i-k(ə-)lē\ *adv*

sap·ro·zo·ic \ˌsap-rə-'zō-ik\ *adj* : SAPROPHYTIC — used of animals (as protozoans)

sap·sa·go \sap-'sā-(ˌ)gō, 'sap-sə-ˌgō\ *n* [modif. of G *schabziger*] : a very hard green skim-milk cheese flavored with the powdered leaves of an aromatic legume (*Trigonella coerulea*) and shaped in truncated cones

sap·suck·er \'sap-ˌsək-ər\ *n* : any of various small American woodpeckers (esp. genus *Sphyrapicus*) that drill holes in trees in order to obtain sap and insects for food

sap·wood \-ˌwu̇d\ *n* : the younger softer living or physiologically active outer portion of wood that lies between the cambium and the heartwood and is more permeable, less durable, and usu. lighter in color than the heartwood

sar·a·band *or* **sar·a·bande** \'sar-ə-ˌband\ *n* [F *sarabande*, fr. Sp *zarabanda*] **1** : a stately court dance of the 17th and 18th centuries resembling the minuet **2** : the music for the saraband in slow triple time with accent on the second beat

Sar·a·cen \'sar-ə-sən\ *n* [ME, fr. LL *Saracenus*, fr. LGk *Sarakēnos*] : a member of a nomadic people of the deserts between Syria and Arabia; *broadly* : ARAB — **Saracen** *adj* — **Sar·a·cen·ic** \ˌsar-ə-'sen-ik\ *adj*

Sa·rah \'ser-ə, 'sar-ə, 'sā-rə\ *n* [Heb *Śārāh*] **1** : the wife of Abraham and mother of Isaac **2** : a kinswoman of Tobias married to him

Sa·ran \sə-'ran\ *trademark* — used for a tough flexible thermoplastic

sarape \sə-'räp-ē\ *var of* SERAPE

Sar·a·to·ga trunk \ˌsar-ə-ˌtō-gə-\ *n* [*Saratoga* Springs, N.Y.] : a large traveling trunk usu. with a rounded top

sarc- *or* **sarco-** *comb form* [Gk *sark-, sarko-*, fr. *sark-, sarx*] **1** : flesh <*sarc*ous> **2** : striated muscle <*sarco*lemma>

sar·casm \'sär-ˌkaz-əm\ *n* [F *sarcasme*, fr. LL *sarcasmos*, fr. Gk *sarkasmos*, fr. *sarkazein* to tear flesh, bite the lips in rage, sneer, fr. *sark-, sarx* flesh; akin to Av *thwarəs* to cut] **1** : a sharp and often satirical or ironic utterance designed to cut or give pain <tired of his contemptuous ~*s*> **2 a** : a mode of satirical wit depending for its effect on bitter, caustic, and often ironic language that is usu. directed against an individual <~ is another mode of humor that requires a master hand —E. P. J. Corbett> **b** : the use or language of sarcasm <this is no time to indulge in ~> *syn* see WIT

sar·cas·tic \sär-'kas-tik\ *adj* [fr. *sarcasm*, after such pairs as E *enthusiasm: enthusiastic*] **1** : having the character of sarcasm <~ criticism> **2** : given to the use of sarcasm : CAUSTIC <a ~ critic> — **sar·cas·ti·cal·ly** \-ti-k(ə-)lē\ *adv*

syn SARCASTIC, SATIRIC, IRONIC, SARDONIC *shared meaning element* : marked by bitterness and a power or will to cut or sting

sarce·net *or* **sarse·net** \'sär-snət\ *n* [ME *sarcenet*, fr. AF *sarzinett*] : a soft thin silk in plain or twill weaves used for dresses, veilings, or trimmings — **sarcenet** *adj*

sar·co·carp \'sär-kə-ˌkärp\ *n* [F *sarcocarpe*, fr. *sarc-* + *-carpe* -carp] **1** : a usu. thickened and fleshy mesocarp **2** : a fleshy fruit

sar·coid \'sär-ˌkȯid\ *n* **1** : any of various diseases characterized esp. by the formation of nodules in the skin **2** : a nodule characteristic of sarcoid or of sarcoidosis

sar·coid·osis \ˌsär-ˌkȯid-'ō-səs\ *n, pl* **-o·ses** \-ˌsēz\ [NL] : a chronic disease of unknown cause that is characterized by the formation of nodules resembling true tubercles esp. in the lymph nodes, lungs, bones, and skin

sar·co·lem·ma \ˌsär-kə-'lem-ə\ *n* [NL, fr. *sarc-* + Gk *lemma* husk — more at LEMMA] : the thin transparent homogeneous sheath enclosing a striated muscle fiber — **sar·co·lem·mal** \-əl\ *adj*

sar·co·ma \sär-'kō-mə\ *n, pl* **-mas** *or* **-ma·ta** \-mət-ə\ [NL, fr. Gk *sarkōmat-, sarkōma* fleshy growth, fr. *sarkoun* to grow flesh, fr. *sark-, sarx*] : a malignant neoplasm arising in tissue of mesodermal origin (as connective tissue, bone, cartilage, or striated muscle) — **sar·co·ma·tous** \sär-'kō-mət-əs\ *adj*

sar·co·ma·to·sis \(ˌ)sär-ˌkō-mə-'tō-səs\ *n, pl* **-to·ses** \-ˌsēz\ [NL] : a disease characterized by the presence and spread of sarcomas

sar·co·mere \'sär-kə-ˌmi(ə)r\ *n* : one of the repeating structural units of striated muscle fibrils — **sar·co·mer·ic** \ˌsär-kə-'mi(ə)r-ik, -'mer-\ *adj*

sar·coph·a·gous \sär-'käf-ə-gəs\ *or* **sar·co·phag·ic** \ˌsär-kə-'faj-ik\ *adj* [L *sarcophagus* flesh-eating, fr. Gk *sarkophagos*] : CARNIVOROUS — **sar·coph·a·gy** \sär-'käf-ə-jē\ *n*

sar·coph·a·gus \sär-'käf-ə-gəs\ *n, pl* **-gi** \-ˌgī, -ˌjī, -ˌgē\ *also* **-gus·es** [L *sarcophagus* (*lapis*) limestone used for coffins, fr. Gk (*lithos*) *sarkophagos*, lit., flesh-eating stone, fr. *sark-* sarc- + *phagein* to eat — more at BAKSHEESH] : a stone coffin

sar·co·plasm \'sär-kə-ˌplaz-əm\ *n* [NL *sarcoplasma*] : the cytoplasm of a striated muscle fiber — **sar·co·plas·mic** \ˌsär-kə-'plaz-mik\ *adj*

sar·co·plas·ma \ˌsär-kə-'plaz-mə\ *n, pl* **-ma·ta** \-mət-ə\ [NL] : SARCOPLASM — **sar·co·plas·mat·ic** \-ˌplaz-'mat-ik\ *adj*

sarcoplasmic reticulum *n* : the endoplasmic reticulum of a striated muscle fiber

sar·cop·tic mange \(ˌ)sär-ˌkäp-tik-\ *n* [NL *Sarcoptes*, genus of mites, fr. *sarc-* + Gk *koptein* to cut — more at CAPON] : mange caused by mites (genus *Sarcoptes*) burrowing in the skin esp. of the head and face

sar·co·some \'sär-kə-ˌsōm\ *n* [NL *sarcosoma,* fr. *sarc-* + *-soma* -some]: a mitochondrion of a striated muscle fiber — **sar·co·som·al** \ˌsär-kə-'sō-məl\ *adj*

sard \'särd\ *n* [F *sarde,* fr. L *sarda*] **:** a deep orange-red variety of chalcedony classed by some as a variety of carnelian

sardar *var of* SIRDAR

sar·dine \sär-'dēn\ *n, pl* **sardines** *also* **sardine** [ME *sardeine,* fr. MF *sardine,* fr. L *sardina*] **1 :** any of several small or immature clupeid fishes; *esp* **:** the young of the European pilchard (*Sardinia pilchardus*) when of a size suitable for preserving for food **2 :** any of various small fishes (as an anchovy) resembling the true sardines or similarly preserved for food

Sar·din·ian \sär-'din-ē-ən, -'din-yən\ *n* **1 :** a native or inhabitant of Sardinia **2 :** the Romance language of central and southern Sardinia — **Sardinian** *adj*

sar·don·ic \sär-'dän-ik\ *adj* [F *sardonique,* fr. Gk *sardonios*] **:** disdainfully or skeptically humorous **:** derisively mocking <a ~ comment> <his ~ expression> ***syn*** see SARCASTIC — **sar·don·i·cal·ly** \-i-k(ə-)lē\ *adv*

sar·don·i·cism \sär-'dän-ə-ˌsiz-əm\ *n* **:** sardonic quality or humor

sard·onyx \sär-'dän-iks *also* 'särd-ᵊn-\ *n* [ME *sardonix,* fr. L *sardonyx,* fr. Gk] **:** an onyx having parallel layers of sard

sar·gas·so \sär-'gas-(ˌ)ō\ *n, pl* **-sos** [Pg *sargaço*] **1 :** GULFWEED, SARGASSUM **2 :** a mass of floating vegetation and esp. sargassums

sar·gas·sum \sär-'gas-əm\ *n* [NL, genus name, fr. ISV *sargasso*] **:** any of a genus (*Sargassum*) of brown algae that have a branching thallus with lateral outgrowths differentiated as leafy segments, air bladders, or spore-bearing structures **:** GULFWEED

sarge \'särj\ *n* [by shortening & alter.] **:** SERGEANT

sa·ri *or* **sa·ree** \'sär-ē\ *n* [Hindi *sārī,* fr. Skt *śāṭī*] **:** a garment of Hindu women that consists of yards of lightweight cloth draped so that one end forms a skirt and the other a head or shoulder covering

sari

sa·rin \'sär-ən, zä-'rēn\ *n* [G] **:** an extremely toxic chemical warfare agent $C_4H_{10}FO_2P$ that is a powerful cholinesterase inhibitor

sark \'särk\ *n* [ME (Sc) *serk,* fr. OE *serc;* akin to ON *serkr* shirt] *dial chiefly Brit* **:** SHIRT

sa·rod *also* **sa·rode** \sə-'rōd\ *n* [Hindi *sarod,* fr. Per] **:** a lute of northern India — **sa·rod·ist** \-'rōd-əst\ *n*

sa·rong \sə-'rȯŋ, -'räŋ\ *n* [Malay *kain sarong* cloth sheath] **1 :** a loose skirt made of a long strip of cloth wrapped around the body and worn by men and women of the Malay archipelago and the Pacific islands **2 :** cloth for sarongs

Sar·pe·don \sär-'pēd-ᵊn\ *n* [L, fr. Gk *Sarpēdōn*] **:** a son of Zeus and Europa and king of Lycia killed in the Trojan War

sar·ra·ce·nia \ˌsar-ə-'sē-nē-ə, -'sen-ē-\ *n* [NL, genus name, fr. Michel *Sarrazin* †1734 F physician & naturalist] **:** any of a genus (*Sarracenia* of the family Sarraceniaceae) that includes the insectivorous bog herbs of eastern No. America with pitcher-shaped or tubular leaves having an arched or hooded flap at the apex

sar·sa·pa·ril·la \ˌsas-(ə-)pə-'ril-ə, ˌsärs-, -'rel-\ *n* [Sp *zarzaparilla*] **1 a :** any of various tropical American greenbriers **b :** the dried roots of a sarsaparilla used esp. as a flavoring **2 :** any of various plants (as wild sarsaparilla) that resemble or are used as a substitute for sarsaparilla **3 :** a sweetened carbonated beverage flavored with birch oil and sassafras

sar·to·ri·al \sär-'tōr-ē-əl, sə(r)-, -'tȯr-\ *adj* [L *sartor*] **:** of or relating to a tailor or tailored clothes — **sar·to·ri·al·ly** \-ē-ə-lē\ *adv*

sar·to·ri·us \sär-'tōr-ē-əs, -'tȯr-\ *n, pl* **-rii** \-ē-ˌī, -ē-ˌē\ [NL, fr. L *sartor* tailor, fr. *sartus,* pp. of *sarcire* to mend — more at EXORCISE] **:** a muscle that crosses the front of the thigh obliquely, assists in rotating the leg to the position assumed in sitting like a tailor, and in man is the longest muscle

Sar·um \'sar-əm, 'ser-\ *adj* [*Sarum,* old borough near Salisbury, England] **:** of or relating to the Roman rite as modified in Salisbury and used in England, Wales, and Ireland before the Reformation

[1]**sash** \'sash\ *n* [Ar *shāsh* muslin] **:** a band worn about the waist or over one shoulder and used as a dress accessory or the emblem of an honorary or military order — **sashed** \'sasht\ *adj*

[2]**sash** *n, pl* **sash** *also* **sash·es** [prob. modif. of F *châssis* chassis (taken as pl.)] **:** the framework in which panes of glass are set in a window or door; *also* **:** such a framework together with its panes forming a usu. movable part of a window

[1]**sa·shay** \sa-'shā, sī-\ *vi* [alter. of *chassé*] **1 :** to make a chassé **2 a :** WALK, GLIDE, GO **b :** to strut or move about in an ostentatious or conspicuous manner **c :** to proceed or move in a diagonal or sideways manner

[2]**sashay** *n* [by alter.] **1 :** CHASSE **2 :** TRIP, EXCURSION **3 :** a square-dance figure in which partners sidestep in a circle around each other with the man moving behind the woman

sa·shi·mi \'säsh-ə-mē\ *n* [Jap] **:** a Japanese dish consisting of thinly sliced raw fish

Sask *abbr* Saskatchewan

sas·ka·toon \ˌsas-kə-'tün\ *n* [*Saskatoon,* Saskatchewan, Canada] **:** SERVICEBERRY 2; *esp* **:** a shrubby western serviceberry (*Amelanchier alnifolia*) with sweet usu. purple fruit

[1]**sass** \'sas\ *n* [back-formation fr. *sassy*] **:** impudent speech

[2]**sass** *vt* **:** to talk impudently or disrespectfully to

sas·sa·fras \'sas-(ə-)ˌfras\ *n* [Sp *sasafrás*] **1 :** a tall eastern No. American tree (*Sassafras albidum*) of the laurel family with mucilaginous twigs and leaves **2 :** the dried root bark of the sassafras used esp. as a diaphoretic or flavoring agent

[1]**Sas·sa·ni·an** *or* **Sa·sa·ni·an** \sə-'sā-nē-ən, sa-'sā-\ *adj* **:** of, relating to, or having the characteristics of the Sassanid dynasty of ancient Persia or its art or architecture

[2]**Sassanian** *or* **Sasanian** *n* **:** SASSANID

Sas·sa·nid \sə-'sän-əd, -'san-; 'sas-ᵊn-\ *n* [NL *Sassanidae* Sassanids, fr. *Sassan,* founder of the dynasty] **:** a member of a dynasty of Persian kings of the 3d to 7th centuries — **Sassanid** *adj*

sass·wood \'sas-ˌwu̇d\ *n* [earlier *sassywood,* fr. *sassy* sasswood + *wood*] **:** a western African leguminous tree (*Erythrophloeum guineënse*) with a poisonous bark and a hard strong insect-resistant wood

sassy \'sas-ē\ *adj* **sass·i·er; -est** [by alter.] **1 :** IMPUDENT, SAUCY **2 :** VIGOROUS, LIVELY **3 :** distinctively smart and stylish <a ~ black-and-white bow tie —Jean Stafford>

sas·sy bark \'sas-ē-\ *n* [*sassy* sasswood, prob. of African origin; akin to Ewe *se^3 se^3 wu^3,* an African timber tree] **:** sasswood bark formerly used (as by tribal Africans) as poison in ordeals

[1]**sat** *past of* SIT

[2]**sat** *abbr* saturate; saturated; saturation

Sat *abbr* Saturday

SAT *abbr* Scholastic Aptitude Test

Sa·tan \'sāt-ᵊn\ *n* [ME, fr. OE, fr. LL, fr. Gk, fr. Heb *śāṭān*] **:** the adversary of God and lord of evil in Judaism and Christianity

sa·tang \sə-'täŋ\ *n, pl* **satang** *or* **satangs** [Thai *satāṅ*] — see *baht* at MONEY table

sa·tan·ic \sə-'tan-ik, sā-\ *adj* **1 :** of, relating to, or characteristic of Satan or satanism <~ pride> <~ rites> **2 :** characterized by extreme cruelty or viciousness — **sa·tan·i·cal·ly** \-i-k(ə-)lē\ *adv*

sa·tan·ism \'sāt-ᵊn-ˌiz-əm\ *n, often cap* **1 :** innate wickedness **:** DIABOLISM **2 :** obsession with or affinity for evil; *specif* **:** the worship of Satan marked by the travesty of Christian rites — **sa·tan·ist** \-ᵊn-əst\ *n, often cap*

satch·el \'sach-əl\ *n* [ME *sachel,* fr. MF, fr. L *sacellus,* dim. of *saccus* bag — more at SACK] **:** a small bag often with a shoulder strap <schoolboys with their ~*s*> — **satch·el·ful** \-ˌfu̇l\ *n*

satd *abbr* saturated

[1]**sate** \'sāt, 'sat\ *archaic past of* SIT

[2]**sate** \'sāt\ *vt* **sat·ed; sat·ing** [prob. by shortening & alter. fr. *satiate*] **1 :** to cloy with overabundance **:** GLUT **2 :** to appease (as a thirst) by indulging to the full ***syn*** see SATIATE

sa·teen \sa-'tēn, sə-\ *n* [alter. of *satin*] **:** a smooth durable lustrous fabric usu. made of cotton in satin weave

sat·el·lite \'sat-ᵊl-ˌīt\ *n* [MF, fr. L *satellit-, satelles* attendant] **1 :** a hired agent or obsequious follower **:** MINION, SYCOPHANT **2 a :** a celestial body orbiting another of larger size **b :** a man-made object or vehicle intended to orbit the earth, the moon, or another celestial body **3 :** someone or something attendant, subordinate, or dependent; *esp* **:** a country politically and economically dominated or controlled by another more powerful country **4 :** a usu. independent urban community situated near but not immediately adjacent to a large city ***syn*** see FOLLOWER — **satellite** *adj*

sa·tem \'sät-əm\ *adj* [Av *satəm* hundred; fr. the fact that its initial sound (derived fr. an alveolar fricative) is the representative of an IE palatal stop — more at HUNDRED] **:** of, relating to, or constituting that part of the Indo-European language family in which the palatal stops became in prehistoric times palatal or alveolar fricatives — compare CENTUM

sa·ti \(ˌ)sə-'tē, 'sə-ˌtē\ *var of* SUTTEE

sa·tia·ble \'sā-shə-bəl\ *adj* **:** capable of being appeased or satisfied

[1]**sa·tiate** \'sā-sh(ē-)ət\ *adj* **:** filled to satiety **:** SATIATED

[2]**sa·ti·ate** \'sā-shē-ˌāt\ *vt* **-at·ed; -at·ing** [L *satiatus,* pp. of *satiare,* fr. *satis* enough — more at SAD] **:** to satisfy (as a need or desire) fully or to excess — **sa·ti·a·tion** \ˌsā-s(h)ē-'ā-shən\ *n*

syn SATIATE, SATE, SURFEIT, CLOY, PALL, GLUT, GORGE *shared meaning element* **:** to fill to repletion

sa·ti·ety \sə-'tī-ət-ē *also* 'sā-sh(ē-)ət-\ *n* [MF *satieté,* fr. L *satietat-, satietas,* fr. *satis*] **1 :** the quality or state of being fed or gratified to or beyond capacity **:** SURFEIT, FULLNESS **2 :** the revulsion or disgust caused by overindulgence or excess

[1]**sat·in** \'sat-ᵊn\ *n* [ME, fr. MF] **:** a fabric (as of silk) in satin weave with lustrous face and dull back

[2]**satin** *adj* **1 :** made of or covered with satin <~ shoes> **2 :** suggestive of satin esp. in smooth lustrous appearance or sleekness to touch <panels with an oiled ~ finish>

sat·in·et \ˌsat-ᵊn-'et\ *n* **1 :** a thin silk satin or imitation satin **2 :** a variation of satin weave used in making satinet

satin stitch *n* **:** an embroidery stitch nearly alike on both sides and worked so closely as to resemble satin

satin weave *n* **:** a weave in which warp threads interlace with filling threads to produce a smooth-faced fabric

sat·in·wood \'sat-ᵊn-ˌwu̇d\ *n* **1 a :** an East Indian tree (*Chloroxylon swietenia*) of the mahogany family that yields a lustrous yellowish brown wood **b :** a tree (as a yellowwood) with wood resembling true satinwood **2 :** the wood of a satinwood

sat·iny \'sat-nē, 'sat-ᵊn-ē\ *adj* **:** having or resembling the soft lustrous smoothness of satin

sat·ire \'sa-ˌtī(ə)r\ *n* [MF, fr. L *satura, satira,* fr. (*lanx*) *satura* full plate, medley, fr. fem. of *satur* sated; akin to L *satis* enough — more at SAD] **1 :** a literary work holding up human vices and follies to ridicule or scorn **2 :** trenchant wit, irony, or sarcasm used to expose and discredit vice or folly ***syn*** see WIT

sa·tir·ic \sə-'tir-ik\ *or* **sa·tir·i·cal** \-i-kəl\ *adj* **1 :** of, relating to, or constituting satire <~ writers> <the ~ undertone of his essay> **2 :** manifesting or given to satire <watched by his ~ companion> ***syn*** see SARCASTIC — **sa·tir·i·cal·ly** \-i-k(ə-)lē\ *adv*

sat·i·rist \'sat-ə-rəst\ *n* **:** one that satirizes; *esp* **:** a writer of satire

sat·i·rize \-ˌrīz\ *vb* **-rized; -riz·ing** *vi* **:** to utter or write satire ~ *vt* **:** to censure or ridicule by means of satire

sat·is·fac·tion \ˌsat-əs-'fak-shən\ *n* [ME, fr. MF, fr. LL *satisfaction-, satisfactio,* fr. L, reparation, amends, fr. *satisfactus,* pp. of *satisfacere* to satisfy] **1 a :** the payment through penance of the temporal punishment incurred by a sin **b :** reparation for sin that meets the demands of divine justice **2 a :** fulfillment of a need or want **b :** the quality or state of being satisfied **:** CONTENTMENT **c :** a source or means of enjoyment **:** GRATIFICATION **3 a :** compensation for a loss or injury **:** ATONEMENT, RESTITUTION **b :** the discharge of a legal obligation or claim **c :** VINDICATION **4 :** convinced assurance or certainty <proved to the ~ of the court>

sat·is·fac·to·ri·ly \-'fak-t(ə-)rə-lē\ *adv* : in a satisfactory manner
sat·is·fac·to·ry \ˌsat-əs-'fak-t(ə-)rē\ *adj* : giving satisfaction : ADEQUATE — **sat·is·fac·to·ri·ness** *n*
sat·is·fi·able \'sat-əs-ˌfī-ə-bəl\ *adj* : capable of being satisfied
sat·is·fy \'sat-əs-ˌfī\ *vb* **-fied; -fy·ing** [ME *satisfien,* fr. MF *satisfier,* modif. of L *satisfacere,* fr. *satis* enough + *facere* to do, make — more at SAD, DO] *vt* **1 a :** to carry out the terms of (as a contract) : DISCHARGE **b :** to meet a financial obligation to **2 :** to make reparation to (an injured party) : INDEMNIFY **3 a :** to make happy : PLEASE **b :** to gratify to the full : APPEASE **4 a** : CONVINCE **b :** to put an end to (doubt or uncertainty) : DISPEL **5 a :** to conform to (as specifications) : be adequate to (an end in view) **b :** to make true by fulfilling a condition <values that ~ an equation> <~ a hypothesis> **6 :** to respond to by chemical union <~ valences> ~ *vi* : to be adequate : SUFFICE; *also* : PLEASE — **sat·is·fy·ing·ly** \-iŋ-lē\ *adv*
syn **1** SATISFY, FULFILL, MEET, ANSWER *shared meaning element* : to measure up to a set of criteria or requirements
2 see PAY
sa·to·ri \sə-'tōr-ē, sä-, -'tȯr-\ *n* [Jap] : a state of intuitive illumination sought in Zen Buddhism
sa·trap \'sā-ˌtrap *also* 'sa-ˌtrap *or* 'sa-trəp\ *n* [ME, fr. L *satrapes,* fr. Gk *satrapēs,* fr. OPer *xshathrapāvan,* lit., protector of the dominion] **1 :** the governor of a province in ancient Persia **2 a :** RULER **b :** a subordinate official : HENCHMAN
sa·tra·py \'sā-trə-pē, 'sa-, -ˌtrap-ē\ *n, pl* **-pies** : the territory or jurisdiction of a satrap
sat·u·ra·ble \'sach-(ə-)rə-bəl\ *adj* : capable of being saturated
sat·u·rant \'sach-(ə-)rənt\ *n* : something that saturates
[1]**sat·u·rate** \'sach-ə-ˌrāt\ *vt* **-rat·ed; -rat·ing** [L *saturatus,* pp. of *saturare,* fr. *satur* sated — more at SATIRE] **1 :** to satisfy fully : SATIATE **2 :** to treat, furnish, or charge with something to the point where no more can be absorbed, dissolved, or retained <water *saturated* with salt> **3 a :** to fill completely with something that permeates or pervades <moonglow . . . ~*s* an empty sky —Henry Miller> **b :** to load to capacity **4 :** to cause to combine till there is no further tendency to combine *syn* see SOAK — **sat·u·ra·tor** \-ˌrāt-ər\ *n*
[2]**sat·u·rate** \'sach-(ə-)rət\ *adj* : SATURATED
sat·u·rat·ed \'sach-ə-ˌrāt-əd\ *adj* **1 :** full of moisture : made thoroughly wet **2 a :** being the most concentrated solution that can persist in the presence of an excess of the dissolved substance **b :** being a compound that does not tend to unite directly with another compound — used esp. of organic compounds containing no double or triple bonds
sat·u·ra·tion \ˌsach-ə-'rā-shən\ *n* **1 a :** the act of saturating : the state of being saturated **b :** SATIETY, SURFEIT **2 :** conversion of an unsaturated to a saturated chemical compound (as by hydrogenation) **3 :** a state of maximum impregnation: as **a** : complete infiltration : PERMEATION **b :** the presence in air of the most water possible under existent pressure and temperature **c** : magnetization to the point beyond which a further increase in the intensity of the magnetizing force will produce no further magnetization **4 a :** chromatic purity : freedom from dilution with white **b** (1) : degree of difference from the gray having the same lightness — used of an object color (2) : degree of difference from the achromatic light-source color of the same brightness — used of a light-source color **5 :** the supplying of a market with all the goods it will absorb **6 :** an overwhelming concentration of military forces or firepower
Sat·ur·day \'sat-ərd-ē\ *n* [ME *saterday,* fr. OE *sæterndæg;* akin to OFris *sāterdei;* both fr. a prehistoric WGmc compound whose first component was borrowed fr. L *Saturnus* Saturn and whose second component is represented by OE *dæg* day] : the seventh day of the week — **Sat·ur·days** \-ēz\ *adv*
Sat·urn \'sat-ərn\ *n* [L *Saturnus*] **1 :** a Roman god of agriculture and father by Ops of Jupiter **2 :** the planet 6th in order from the sun — see PLANET table
sat·ur·na·lia \ˌsat-ər-'nāl-yə, -'nā-lē-ə\ *n pl but sing or pl in constr* [L, fr. neut. pl. of *saturnalis* of Saturn, fr. *Saturnus*] **1** *cap* : the festival of Saturn in ancient Rome beginning on Dec. 17 **2** *sing, pl* **saturnalias** *also* **saturnalia a :** an unrestrained often licentious celebration : ORGY **b :** EXCESS, EXTRAVAGANCE — **sat·ur·na·lian** \-'nāl-yən, -'nā-lē-ən\ *adj* — **sat·ur·na·lian·ly** *adv*
Sa·tur·ni·an \sa-'tər-nē-ən, sə-\ *adj* **1 :** of, relating to, or influenced by the planet Saturn **2** *archaic* : of or relating to the god Saturn or the golden age of his reign
sa·tur·ni·id \-nē-əd\ *n* [deriv. of NL *Saturnia,* genus of moths, fr. L, daughter of the god Saturn] : any of a large family (Saturniidae) of stout strong-winged moths (as a luna moth or a cecropia moth) with hairy bodies — **saturniid** *adj*
sat·ur·nine \'sat-ər-ˌnīn\ *adj* **1 :** born under or influenced astrologically by the planet Saturn **2 a :** cold and steady in mood : slow to act or change **b :** of a gloomy or surly disposition **c** : having a sardonic aspect <a ~ smile> **3 :** of, relating to, or produced by the absorption of lead into the system <~ poisoning> — **sat·ur·nine·ly** *adv*
sat·urn·ism \'sat-ər-ˌniz-əm\ *n* [*saturn* (lead)] : LEAD POISONING
sa·tya·gra·ha \(ˌ)sə-'tyä-grə-hə\ *n* [Skt *satyāgraha,* lit., insistence on truth] : pressure for social and political reform through friendly passive resistance practiced by M. K. Gandhi and his followers in India
sa·tyr \'sāt-ər, 'sat-\ *n* [ME, fr. L *satyrus,* fr. Gk *satyros*] **1** *often cap* : a sylvan deity of Greek mythology having certain characteristics of a horse or goat and fond of Dionysian revelry **2 :** a lecherous man : one having satyriasis **3 :** any of many usu. brown and gray butterflies (family Satyridae) often with ocelli on the wings — **sa·tyr·ic** \sā-'tir-ik, sə-, sa-\ *adj*
sa·ty·ri·a·sis \ˌsāt-ə-'rī-ə-səs, ˌsat-\ *n* [LL, fr. Gk, fr. *satyros*] : excessive or abnormal sexual craving in the male
sa·ty·rid \sə-'tī-rəd\ *n* [NL *Satyridae,* group name, deriv. of Gk *satyros*] : any of a family (Satyridae) of usu. brownish butterflies that feed on grasses as larvae and have one or more main wing veins swollen basally — **satyrid** *adj*

satyr play *n* : a comic play of ancient Greece burlesquing a mythological subject and having a chorus representing satyrs

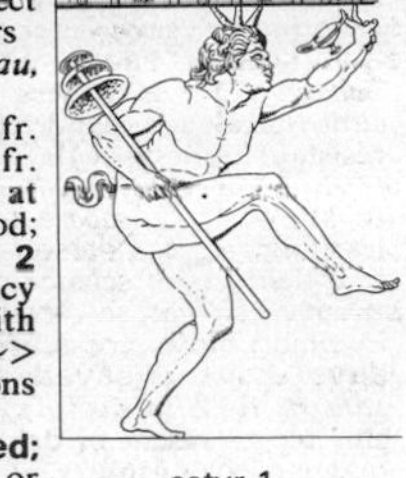
satyr 1

sau \sə-'ü\ *n, pl* **sau** [Vietnamese *xu, sau,* fr. F *sou* sou] : XU
[1]**sauce** \'sȯs, *usu* 'sas *for 4*\ *n* [ME, fr. MF, fr. L *salsa,* fem. of *salsus* salted, fr. pp. of *sallere* to salt, fr. *sal* salt — more at SALT] **1 :** a condiment or relish for food; *esp* : a fluid dressing or topping **2** : something that adds zest or piquancy **3 :** stewed or canned fruit eaten with other food or as a dessert <cranberry ~> **4 :** pert or impudent language or actions **5** *slang* : LIQUOR
[2]**sauce** \'sȯs, *usu* 'sas *for 3*\ *vt* **sauced; sauc·ing 1 :** to dress with relish or seasoning **2 a** *archaic* : to modify the harsh or unpleasant characteristics of **b :** to give zest or piquancy to **3 :** to be rude or impudent to
sauce·box \'sas-ˌbäks *also* 'sȯs-\ *n* : a saucy impudent person
sauce·pan \'sȯ-ˌspan, *esp Brit* -spən\ *n* : a small deep cooking pan with a handle
sau·cer \'sȯ-sər\ *n* [ME, plate containing sauce, fr. MF *saussier,* fr. *sausse, sauce*] **1 :** a small shallow dish in which a cup is set at table **2 :** something resembling a saucer esp. in shape; *esp* : FLYING SAUCER — **sau·cer·like** \-ˌlīk\ *adj*
saucy \'sas-ē *also* 'sȯs-ē\ *adj* **sauc·i·er; -est 1 a :** impertinently bold and impudent **b :** amusingly forward and flippant : IRREPRESSIBLE **2 :** SMART, TRIM <a ~ ship> — **sauc·i·ly** \-ə-lē\ *adv* — **sauc·i·ness** \-ē-nəs\ *n*
syn SAUCY, PERT, ARCH *shared meaning element* : flippant and bold in manner or attitude
sau·er·bra·ten \'saů(-ə)r-ˌbrät-ᵊn\ *n* [G, fr. *sauer* sour + *braten* roast meat] : oven-roasted or pot-roasted beef marinated before cooking in vinegar with peppercorns, garlic, onions, and bay leaves
sau·er·kraut \'saů(-ə)r-ˌkraůt\ *n* [G, fr. *sauer* sour + *kraut* cabbage] : cabbage cut fine and fermented in a brine made of its own juice with salt
sau·ger \'sȯ-gər\ *n* [origin unknown] **1 :** a pike perch (*Stizostedion canadense*) similar to but smaller than the walleye **2** : WALLEYE
saugh *or* **sauch** \'säk, 'sȯk\ *n* [ME (Sc) *sauch,* fr. OE *salh,* alter. of *sealh*] *chiefly Scot* : SALLOW
Saul \'sȯl\ *n* [LL *Saulus,* fr. Gk *Saulos,* fr. Heb *Shā'ūl*] **1 :** the first king of Israel **2 :** the apostle Paul — called also *Saul of Tarsus*
sault \'sü\ *n* [obs. F, lit., leap, fr. L *saltus,* fr. *saltus,* pp. of *salire* to leap — more at SALLY] : a falls or rapids in a river
sau·na \'saů-nə\ *n* [Finn] **1 :** a Finnish steam bath in which the steam is provided by water thrown on hot stones; *also* : a bathhouse or room used for such a bath **2 :** a dry heat bath; *also* : a room or cabinet used for such a bath
saun·ter \'sȯnt-ər, 'sänt-\ *vi* [prob. fr. ME *santren* to muse] : to walk about in an idle or leisurely manner : STROLL — **saunter** *n* — **saun·ter·er** \-ər-ər\ *n*
sau·rel \sȯ-'rel\ *n* [F, fr. LL *saurus* horse mackerel, fr. Gk *sauros*] : either of two carangid fishes (genus *Trachurus*): **a :** a horse mackerel (*T. trachurus*) **b :** a jack mackerel (*T. symmetricus*)
sau·ri·an \'sȯr-ē-ən\ *n* [deriv. of Gk *sauros* horse mackerel, lizard; akin to Gk *psauein* to touch, graze] : any of a group (Sauria) of reptiles including the lizards and in older classifications the crocodiles and various extinct forms (as the dinosaurs and ichthyosaurs) that resemble lizards — **saurian** *adj*
sau·ro·pod \'sȯr-ə-ˌpäd\ *n* [NL *Sauropoda,* suborder of dinosaurs, fr. Gk *sauros* lizard + NL *-poda*] : any of a suborder (Sauropoda) of dinosaurs comprising herbivorous forms with long neck and tail, small head, and more or less plantigrade 5-toed limbs — **sauropod** *adj* — **sau·rop·o·dous** \sȯ-'räp-əd-əs\ *adj*
sau·ry \'sȯr-ē\ *n, pl* **sauries** [NL *saurus* lizard, fr. Gk *sauros*] : a slender long-beaked fish (*Scombresox saurus*) related to the needlefishes and found in temperate parts of the Atlantic
sau·sage \'sȯ-sij\ *n* [ME *sausige,* fr. ONF *saussiche,* fr. LL *salsicia,* fr. L *salsus* salted — more at SAUCE] : a highly seasoned minced meat (as pork) usu. stuffed in casings of prepared animal intestine
S Aust *abbr* South Australia
[1]**sau·té** \sȯ-'tā, sō-\ *n* [F, pp. of *sauter* to jump, fr. L *saltare* — more at SALTATION] : a sautéed dish — **sauté** *adj*
[2]**sauté** *vt* **sau·téed** *or* **sau·téd; sau·té·ing :** to fry in a small amount of fat
sau·terne \sō-'tərn, sȯ-, -'te(ə)rn\ *n, often cap* [F *sauternes,* fr. *Sauternes,* commune in France] : a usu. semisweet golden-colored table wine
[1]**sav·age** \'sav-ij\ *adj* [ME *sauvage,* fr. MF, fr. ML *salvaticus,* alter. of L *silvaticus* of the woods, wild, fr. *silva* wood, forest] **1 a** : not domesticated or under human control : UNTAMED <~ beasts> **b :** lacking the restraints normal to civilized man : FIERCE, FEROCIOUS **2 :** WILD, UNCULTIVATED <seldom have I seen such ~ scenery —Douglas Carruthers> **3 :** BOORISH, RUDE <the ~ bad manners of most motorists —M. P. O'Connor> **4 :** lacking complex or advanced culture : UNCIVILIZED *syn* see BARBARIAN, FIERCE — **sav·age·ly** *adv* — **sav·age·ness** *n*
[2]**savage** *n* **1 :** a person belonging to a primitive society **2 :** a brutal person **3 :** a rude or unmannerly person
[3]**savage** *vt* **sav·aged; sav·ag·ing :** to attack or treat brutally

ə abut	ᵊ kitten	ər further	a back	ā bake	ä cot, cart
aů out	ch chin	e less	ē easy	g gift	i trip	ī life
j joke	ŋ sing	ō flow	ȯ flaw	ȯi coin	th thin	t͟h this
ü loot	ů foot	y yet	yü few	yů furious	zh vision

sav·age·ry \'sav-ij-(ə-)rē\ *n, pl* **-ries** **1 a :** the quality of being savage **b :** an act of cruelty or violence **2 :** an uncivilized state

sav·ag·ism \'sav-ij-ˌiz-əm\ *n* **:** SAVAGERY

sa·van·na *or* **sa·van·nah** \sə-'van-ə\ *n* [Sp *zavana,* fr. Taino *zabana*] **1 :** a treeless plain esp. in Florida **2 :** a tropical or subtropical grassland containing scattered trees and drought-resistant undergrowth

sa·vant \sa-'vänt, sə-, -'väⁿ; sə-'vant, 'sav-ənt\ *n* [F, fr. prp. of *savoir* to know, fr. L *sapere* to be wise — more at SAGE] **:** a man of learning; *esp* **:** a person with detailed knowledge in some specialized field (as of science or literature)

sa·vate \sə-'vät, sa-, -'vat\ *n* [F, lit., old shoe] **:** a form of boxing in which blows are delivered with either the hands or the feet

1save \'sāv\ *vb* **saved; sav·ing** [ME *saven,* fr. OF *salver,* fr. LL *salvare,* fr. L *salvus* safe — more at SAFE] *vt* **1 a :** to deliver from sin **b :** to rescue or deliver from danger or harm **c :** to preserve or guard from injury, destruction, or loss **2 :** to put aside as a store or reserve **:** ACCUMULATE **3 a :** to make unnecessary **:** AVOID <it ~*s* an hour's waiting> **b (1) :** to keep from being lost to an opponent **(2) :** to prevent an opponent from scoring or winning **4 :** MAINTAIN, PRESERVE <~ appearances> ~ *vi* **1 :** to rescue or deliver someone **2 a :** to put aside money **b :** to avoid unnecessary waste or expense **:** ECONOMIZE **3 :** to make a save — **sav·able** *or* **save·able** \'sā-və-bəl\ *adj* — **sav·er** *n*
syn **1** see RESCUE
2 SAVE, PRESERVE, CONSERVE ***shared meaning element*** **:** to keep secure from injury, decay, or loss ***ant*** spend, consume

2save *n* **1 :** a play that prevents an opponent from scoring or winning **2 :** a baseball game in which a relief pitcher successfully protects a team's lead

3save \(ˌ)sāv\ *prep* [ME *sauf,* fr. OF, fr. *sauf,* adj., safe — more at SAFE] **:** other than **:** BUT, EXCEPT <no hope ~ one>

4save \(ˌ)sāv\ *conj* **1 :** were it not **:** ONLY — used with *that* **2 :** BUT, EXCEPT — used before a word often taken to be the subject of a clause <no one knows about it ~ she>

save–all \'sā-ˌvȯl\ *n* **:** something that prevents waste, loss, or damage: as **a :** a device to hold a candle end in a candlestick and permit it to burn to the very end **b (1) :** a small sail sometimes set under the foot of another sail or between two sails **(2) :** a net hung between ship and pier to catch articles lost over the side **c :** a receptacle for catching waste products for further utilization

sav·e·loy \'sav-ə-ˌlȯi\ *n* [modif. of F *cervelas*] *Brit* **:** a ready-cooked highly seasoned dry sausage

sav·in \'sav-ən\ *n* [ME, fr. MF *savine,* fr. L *sabina*] **1 :** a Eurasian juniper (*Juniperus sabina*) with dark foliage and small yellowish green berries **2 :** RED CEDAR 1; *also* **:** a related shrubby juniper (*Juniperus horizontalis*)

1sav·ing \'sā-viŋ\ *n* [gerund of *save*] **1 :** preservation from danger or destruction **:** DELIVERANCE **2 :** the act or an instance of economizing **3 a** *pl* **:** money put by **b :** the excess of income over consumption expenditures — often used in pl.

2sav·ing \ˌsā-viŋ, 'sā-\ *prep* [prp. of *save*] **1 :** EXCEPT, SAVE **2 :** without disrespect to

3sav·ing \ˌsā-viŋ, 'sā-\ *conj* **:** EXCEPT, SAVE

saving grace *n* **:** a redeeming quality or factor

savings account *n* **:** an account (as in a bank) on which interest is usu. paid and from which withdrawals can be made usu. only by presentation of a passbook or by written authorization on a prescribed form

savings and loan association *n* **:** a cooperative association that solicits savings in the form of share capital and invests its funds in mortgages

savings bank *n* **:** a bank organized to receive savings accounts only

savings bond *n* **:** a nontransferable registered U.S. bond issued in denominations of $25 to $1000

sav·ior *or* **sav·iour** \'sāv-yər *also* -ˌyȯ(ə)r\ *n* [ME *saveour,* fr. MF, fr. LL *salvator,* fr. *salvatus,* pp. of *salvare* to save] **1 :** one that saves from danger or destruction **2 :** one who brings salvation; *specif, cap* **:** the savior acknowledged by Christians

sa·voir faire \ˌsav-ˌwär-'fa(ə)r, -'fe(ə)r\ *n* [F *savoir-faire,* lit., knowing how to do] **:** capacity for appropriate action; *esp* **:** a polished sureness in social behavior ***syn*** see TACT

1sa·vor *also* **sa·vour** \'sā-vər\ *n* [ME, fr. OF, fr. L *sapor;* akin to L *sapere* to taste — more at SAGE] **1 :** the taste or smell of something **2 :** a particular flavor or smell **3 :** a distinctive quality — **sa·vor·less** \-ləs\ *adj* — **sa·vor·ous** \'sāv-(ə-)rəs\ *adj*

2savor *also* **savour** *vb* **sa·vored; sa·vor·ing** \'sāv-(ə-)riŋ\ *vi* **:** to have a specified smell or quality **:** SMACK ~ *vt* **1 :** to give flavor to **:** SEASON **2 a :** to have experience of **:** TASTE **b :** to taste or smell with pleasure **:** RELISH **c :** to delight in **:** ENJOY — **sa·vor·er** \'sā-vər-ər\ *n*

1sa·vory *also* **savoury** \'sāv(-ə)-rē\ *adj* **:** having savor: as **a :** piquantly pleasant to the mind <a ~ collection of essays> **b :** morally attractive **:** EDIFYING <his reputation was anything but ~> **c :** pleasing to the sense of taste esp. by reason of effective seasoning ***syn*** see PALATABLE ***ant*** bland, acrid — **sa·vor·i·ly** \-rə-lē\ *adv* — **sa·vor·i·ness** \-rē-nəs\ *n*

2savory *also* **savoury** *n, pl* **sa·vor·ies** *Brit* **:** a dish of stimulating flavor served usu. at the end of dinner but sometimes as an appetizer

3sa·vo·ry \'sāv(-ə)-rē\ *n, pl* **-ries** [ME *saverey*] **:** an aromatic mint (genus *Satureia*); *esp* **:** SUMMER SAVORY

Sa·voy·ard \sə-'vȯi-ˌärd, ˌsav-ˌȯi-'ärd, ˌsav-ˌwä-'yär(d)\ *n* [*Savoy* theater, London, built for the presentation of Gilbert and Sullivan operas] **:** a devotee, performer, or producer of the comic operas of W. S. Gilbert and A. S. Sullivan

sa·voy cabbage \sə-ˌvȯi-, ˌsav-ˌȯi-\ *n* [trans. of F *chou de Savoie* cabbage of Savoy] **:** a cabbage with compact heads of wrinkled and curled leaves

1sav·vy \'sav-ē\ *vb* **sav·vied; sav·vy·ing** [modif. of Sp *sabe* he knows, fr. *saber* to know, fr. L *sapere* to be wise — more at SAGE] **:** COMPREHEND, UNDERSTAND

2savvy *n* **:** practical know-how <political ~> — **savvy** *adj*

1saw *past of* SEE

2saw \'sȯ\ *n* [ME *sawe,* fr. OE *sagu;* akin to OHG *sega* saw, L *secare* to cut, *secula* sickle] **1 :** a hand or power tool used to cut hard material (as wood, metal, or bone) and equipped usu. with a toothed blade or disk **2 :** a tool or machine that incorporates a saw <a power ~> — **saw·like** \-ˌlīk\ *adj*

3saw *vb* **sawed** \'sȯd\; **sawed** *or* **sawn** \'sȯn\; **saw·ing** \'sȯ(-)iŋ\ *vt* **1 :** to cut with a saw **2 :** to produce or form by cutting with a saw **3 :** to slash as though with a saw ~ *vi* **1 a :** to use a saw **b :** to cut with or as if with a saw **2 :** to undergo cutting with a saw **3 :** to make motions as though using a saw <~*ed* at the reins> — **saw·er** \'sȯ(-ə)r\ *n*

4saw *n* [ME *sawe,* fr. OE *sagu* discourse; akin to OHG & ON *saga* tale, OE *secgan* to say — more at SAY] **:** MAXIM, PROVERB

Sa·wan \'sä-wən\ *n* [Hindi *sāwan,* fr. Skt *śrāvaṇa*] **:** a month of the Hindu year — see MONTH table

saw·bones \'sȯ-ˌbōnz\ *n, pl* **sawbones** *or* **saw·bones·es** *slang* **:** PHYSICIAN, SURGEON

saw·buck \'sȯ-ˌbək\ *n* **1 :** SAWHORSE **2** [prob. fr. the resemblance of the Roman numeral X to the ends of a sawhorse] *slang* **:** a 10-dollar bill

saw·dust \'sȯd-(ˌ)əst\ *n* **:** fine particles (as of wood) made by a saw in cutting

saw–edged \'sȯ-'ejd\ *adj* **:** having a toothed or badly nicked edge

sawed–off \'sȯd-ˌȯf\ *adj* **1 :** having an end sawed off <a ~ shotgun> **2 :** of less than average height

saw·fish \'sȯ-ˌfish\ *n* **:** any of a family (Pristidae) of several large elongate viviparous rays having a long flattened snout with a row of stout serrate structures along each edge and living in warm shallow seas and in or near the mouths of rivers principally in tropical America and Africa

saw·fly \-ˌflī\ *n* **:** any of numerous hymenopterous insects (superfamily Tenthredinoidea) whose female usu. has a pair of serrated blades in her ovipositor and whose larva resembles a plant-feeding caterpillar

saw grass *n* **:** a sedge (as of the genus *Cladium*) having the edges of the leaves set with minute sharp teeth

saw·horse \'sȯ-ˌhȯ(ə)rs\ *n* **:** a rack on which wood is laid for sawing by hand; *esp* **:** one with X-shaped ends

saw·log \-ˌlȯg, -ˌläg\ *n* **:** a log of suitable size for sawing into lumber

saw·mill \-ˌmil\ *n* **:** a mill or machine for sawing logs

saw·ney \'sȯ-nē\ *n* [prob. alter. of *zany*] *chiefly Brit* **:** FOOL, SIMPLETON — **sawney** *adj*

saw palmetto *n* **:** any of several shrubby palms with spiny-toothed leafstalks esp. of the southern U.S. and West Indies; *esp* **:** a common stemless palm (*Serenoa repens*) of the southern U.S.

saw set *n* **:** an instrument used to set the teeth of saws

saw·tim·ber \'sȯ-ˌtim-bər\ *n* **:** timber suitable for sawing into lumber

saw·tooth \-ˌtüth\ *adj* **:** having serrations **:** arranged or having parts arranged like the teeth of a saw <a ~ roof>

saw–toothed \-'tütht\ *adj* **1 :** having teeth like those of a saw <a ~ shark> **2 :** SAWTOOTH

saw–whet \'sȯ-ˌ(h)wet\ *n* [fr. the resemblance of its cry to the sound made in filing a saw] **:** a very small harsh-voiced No. American owl (*Cryptoglaux acadica*) that is largely dark brown above and white beneath

saw·yer \'sȯ-yər, 'sȯi-ər\ *n* **1 :** one that saws **2 :** any of several large longicorn beetles whose larvae bore large holes in timber or dead wood **3 :** a tree fast in the bed of a stream with its branches projecting to the surface

sax \'saks\ *n* **:** SAXOPHONE

sax·horn \'saks-ˌhȯ(ə)rn\ *n* [Antoine *Sax* †1894 + E *horn*] **:** one of a group of valved brass instruments ranging from soprano to bass and characterized by a conical tube, oval shape, and cup-shaped mouthpiece

sax·ic·o·lous \sak-'sik-ə-ləs\ *or* **sax·ic·o·line** \-ˌlīn\ *adj* [L *saxum* rock + *-cola* inhabitant; akin to L *colere* to inhabit — more at WHEEL] **:** inhabiting or growing among rocks <~ lichens>

sax·i·frage \'sak-sə-frij, -ˌfrāj\ *n* [ME, fr. MF, fr. LL *saxifraga,* fr. L, fem. of *saxifragus* breaking rocks, fr. *saxum* rock + *frangere* to break; akin to OE *sæx* knife, *sagu* saw — more at SAW, BREAK] **:** any of a genus (*Saxifraga* of the family Saxifragaceae, the saxifrage family) of mostly perennial herbs with showy pentamerous flowers and often with basal tufted leaves

saxi·tox·in \ˌsak-sə-'täk-sən\ *n* [NL *Saxidomus giganteus,* species of butter clam from which it is isolated + E *toxin*] **:** a potent nonprotein poison $C_{10}H_{17}N_7O_4.2HCl$ that originates in a causative agent (*Gonyaulax catenella*) of red tide and sometimes occurs in normally edible mollusks

Sax·on \'sak-sən\ *n* [ME, fr. LL *Saxones* Saxons, of Gmc origin; akin to OE *Seaxan* Saxons] **1 a (1) :** a member of a Germanic people that entered and conquered England with the Angles and Jutes in the 5th century A.D. and merged with them to form the Anglo-Saxon people **(2) :** an Englishman or lowlander as distinguished from a Welshman, Irishman, or Highlander **b :** a native or inhabitant of Saxony **2 a :** the Germanic language or dialect of any of the Saxon peoples **b :** the Germanic element in the English language esp. as distinguished from the French and Latin — **Saxon** *adj*

sax·o·ny \'sak-s(ə-)nē\ *n, pl* **-nies** *often cap* [*Saxony,* Germany] **1 a :** a fine soft woolen fabric **b :** a fine closely twisted knitting yarn **2 :** a Wilton jacquard carpet

sax·o·phone \'sak-sə-ˌfōn\ *n* [F, fr. Antoine J. (known as Adolphe) *Sax* †1894 Belgian maker of musical instruments + F *-phone*] **:** one of a group of single-reed woodwind instruments ranging from soprano to bass and characterized by a conical metal tube and finger keys — **sax·o·phon·ic** \ˌsak-sə-'fōn-ik, -'fän-\ *adj* — **sax·o·phon·ist** \'sak-sə-ˌfō-nəst, *esp Brit* sak-'säf-ə-\ *n*

sax·tu·ba \'sak-'st(y)ü-bə\ *n* [Antoine *Sax* + E *tuba*] **:** a bass saxhorn

1say \'sā, *South also* 'se\ *vb* **said** \'sed, *esp when subject follows* səd\; **say·ing** \'sā-iŋ\; **says** \'sez, *esp when subject follows* səz\ [ME *sayen,* fr. OE *secgan;* akin to OHG *sagēn* to say, Gk en*nepein*

to speak, tell] *vt* **1 a :** to express in words : STATE **b :** to state as opinion or belief : DECLARE **2 a :** UTTER, PRONOUNCE **b :** RECITE, REPEAT <*said* his prayers> **3 a :** INDICATE, SHOW <the clock ~*s* five minutes after twelve> **b :** to give expression to : COMMUNICATE <a glance that *said* all that was necessary> ~ *vi* **:** to express oneself : SPEAK — **say·er** \ˈsā-ər, ˈse(-ə)r\ *n* — **say uncle :** to admit defeat — **that is to say :** in other words : in effect

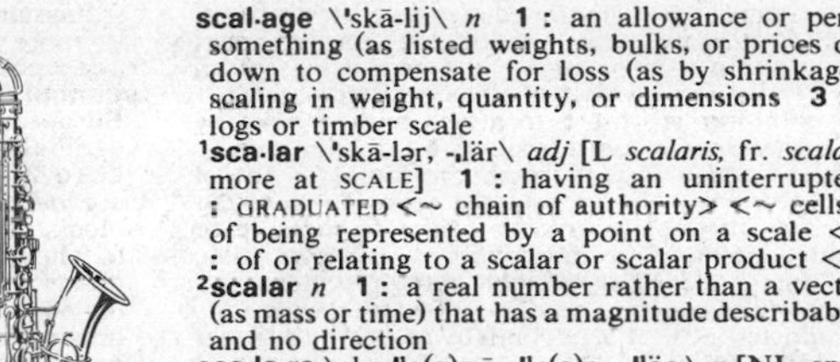
alto saxophone

[2]**say** *n, pl* **says** \ˈsāz, *South also* ˈsez\ **1** *archaic* **:** something that is said : STATEMENT **2 :** an expression of opinion <had his ~> **3 :** a right or power to influence action or decision; *esp* **:** the authority to make final decisions

[3]**say** *adv* [fr. imper. of [1]*say*] **1 :** ABOUT, APPROXIMATELY <the property is worth, ~, four million dollars> **2 :** for example : AS <if we compress any gas, ~ oxygen>

say·able \ˈsā-ə-bəl, ˈse-\ *adj* **1 :** capable of being said **2 :** capable of being spoken effectively or easily <readings in ~ Chinese —*Linguistic Reporter*>

say·ing \ˈsā-iŋ, ˈse-\ *n* **:** something said; *esp* **:** ADAGE

say–so \ˈsā-(ˌ)sō, ˈse-\ *n* **1 a :** one's unsupported assertion : one's bare word or assurance **b :** an authoritative pronouncement <left the hospital on the ~ of his doctor> **2 :** a right of final decision

say·yid \ˈsī-(y)əd, ˈsēd-ē\ *n* [Ar] **1 :** an Islamic chief or leader **2 :** LORD, SIR — used as a courtesy title for a Muslim of rank or lineage

Saz·e·rac \ˈsaz-ə-ˌrak\ *n* [origin unknown] **:** a cocktail of bourbon, absinthe flavoring, bitters, and sugar with lemon peel

sb *abbr* substantive

Sb *symbol* [L *stibium*] antimony

SB *abbr* **1** [NL *Scientiae Baccalaureus*] bachelor of science **2** simultaneous broadcast **3** southbound

SBA *abbr* Small Business Administration

SBN *abbr* Standard Book Number

sc *abbr* **1** scale **2** scene **3** science **4** screw **5** [L *sculpsit*] he carved it; he engraved it

[1]**Sc** *abbr* **1** Scots **2** stratocumulus

[2]**Sc** *symbol* scandium

SC *abbr* **1** Sisters of Charity **2** South Carolina **3** supercalendered **4** supreme court

[1]**scab** \ˈskab\ *n* [ME, of Scand origin; akin to OSw *skabbr* scab; akin to OE *sceabb* scab, L *scabies* mange, *scabere* to scratch — more at SHAVE] **1 :** scabies of domestic animals **2 :** a crust of hardened blood and serum over a wound **3 a :** a contemptible person **b (1) :** one who refuses to join a labor union **(2) :** a union member who refuses to strike or returns to work before a strike has ended **(3) :** a worker who accepts employment or replaces a union worker during a strike **(4) :** one who works for less than union wages or on nonunion terms **4 :** any of various bacterial or fungous diseases of plants characterized by crustaceous spots; *also* **:** one of the spots

[2]**scab** *vi* **scabbed; scab·bing 1 :** to become covered with a scab **2 :** to act as a scab

[1]**scab·bard** \ˈskab-ərd\ *n* [ME *scaubert,* fr. AF *escaubers*] **:** a sheath for a sword, dagger, or bayonet

[2]**scabbard** *vt* **:** to put in a scabbard

scab·ble \ˈskab-əl\ *vt* **scab·bled; scab·bling** \-(ə-)liŋ\ [ME *scaplen,* fr. MF *escapler* to dress timber] **:** to dress (as stone) roughly

scab·by \ˈskab-ē\ *adj* **scab·bi·er; -est 1 a :** covered with or full of scabs <~ skin> **b :** diseased with scab <a ~ animal> <~ potatoes> **2 :** MEAN, CONTEMPTIBLE <a ~ trick>

sca·bies \ˈskā-bēz\ *n, pl* **scabies** [L] **:** itch or mange esp. with exudative crusts — **sca·bi·et·ic** \ˌskā-bē-ˈet-ik\ *adj*

sca·bi·o·sa \ˌskā-bē-ˈō-sə, ˌskab-ē-, -zə\ *n* [NL, genus name, fr. ML, scabious, n.] **:** any of a genus (*Scabiosa*) of herbs of the teasel family with terminal flower heads subtended by a leafy involucre

[1]**sca·bi·ous** \ˈskā-bē-əs, ˈskab-ē-\ *n* [ME *scabiose,* fr. ML *scabiosa,* fr. L, fem. of *scabiosus,* adj.] **1 :** SCABIOSA **2 :** any of several fleabanes (genus *Erigeron*)

[2]**scabious** *adj* [L *scabiosus,* fr. *scabies*] **1 :** SCABBY **2 :** of, relating to, or resembling scabies <~ eruptions>

sca·brous \ˈskab-rəs *also* ˈskāb-\ *adj* [L *scabr-, scaber* rough, scurfy; akin to L *scabies* mange — more at SCAB] **1 :** DIFFICULT, KNOTTY <a ~ problem> **2 :** rough to the touch: as **a :** having small raised dots, scales, or points <a ~ leaf> **b :** covered with raised, roughened, or unwholesome patches <~ paint> <yellowed ~ skin> **3 :** dealing with suggestive, indecent, or scandalous themes : SALACIOUS; *also* **:** SQUALID **syn** see ROUGH **ant** glabrous, smooth — **sca·brous·ly** *adv* — **sca·brous·ness** *n*

[1]**scad** \ˈskad\ *n, pl* **scad** *also* **scads** [origin unknown] **:** any of several carangid fishes (esp. of the genus *Decapterus*)

[2]**scad** *n* [prob. alter. of E dial. *scald* a multitude, fr. [3]*scald*] **1 :** a large number or quantity <hooked a ~ of little fish —*Field & Stream*> **2** *pl* **:** a great abundance <~*s* of money>

scaf·fold \ˈskaf-əld *also* -ˌōld\ *n* [ME, fr. ONF *escafaut,* modif. of (assumed) VL *catafalicum,* fr. Gk *kata-* cata- + L *fala* tower] **1 a :** a temporary or movable platform for workmen (as bricklayers, painters, or miners) to stand or sit on when working at a height above the floor or ground **b :** a platform on which a criminal is executed (as by hanging or beheading) **c :** a platform at a height above ground or floor level **2 :** a supporting framework

scaf·fold·ing \-iŋ\ *n* **:** a system of scaffolds; *also* **:** material for scaffolds

scag \ˈskag\ *n* [origin unknown] *slang* **:** HEROIN

sca·glio·la \skal-ˈyō-lə, -ˈyȯ-\ *n* [It, lit., little chip] **:** an imitation of ornamental marble consisting of finely ground gypsum mixed with glue

scal·able \ˈskā-lə-bəl\ *adj* **:** capable of being scaled

sca·lade \skə-ˈlād, -ˈläd\ *or* **sca·la·do** \-ˈlād-(ˌ)ō, -ˈläd-\ *n, pl* **-lades** *or* **-la·dos** [obs. It *scalada,* fr. *scalare* to scale, fr. *scala* ladder, staircase, fr. LL — more at SCALE] *archaic* **:** ESCALADE

scal·age \ˈskā-lij\ *n* **1 :** an allowance or percentage by which something (as listed weights, bulks, or prices of goods) is scaled down to compensate for loss (as by shrinkage) **2 :** the act of scaling in weight, quantity, or dimensions **3 :** the amount that logs or timber scale

[1]**sca·lar** \ˈskā-lər, -ˌlär\ *adj* [L *scalaris,* fr. *scalae* stairs, ladder — more at SCALE] **1 :** having an uninterrupted series of steps : GRADUATED <~ chain of authority> <~ cells> **2 a :** capable of being represented by a point on a scale <~ quantity> **b :** of or relating to a scalar or scalar product <~ multiplication>

[2]**scalar** *n* **1 :** a real number rather than a vector **2 :** a quantity (as mass or time) that has a magnitude describable by a real number and no direction

sca·la·re \skə-ˈla(ə)r-ē, -ˈle(ə)r-, -ˈlär-\ *n* [NL, specific epithet, fr. L, neut. of *scalaris;* fr. the barred pattern on its body] **:** a black and silver laterally compressed So. American cichlid fish (*Pterophyllum scalare*) popular in aquariums

sca·lari·form \skə-ˈlar-ə-ˌfȯrm\ *n* [NL *scalariformis,* fr. L *scalaris* + *-iformis* -iform] **:** resembling a ladder esp. in having transverse bars or markings like the rounds of a ladder <~ cells in plants> — **sca·lari·form·ly** *adv*

scalar product *n* **:** a real number that is the product of the lengths of two vectors and the cosine of the angle between them — called also *dot product, inner product*

scal·ation \skā-ˈlā-shən\ *n* [[3]*scale*] **:** LEPIDOSIS

scal·a·wag \ˈskal-i-ˌwag\ *n* [origin unknown] **1 :** SCAMP, REPROBATE **2 :** an animal of little value esp. because of poor feeding, smallness, or age **3 :** a white Southerner acting as a Republican in the time of reconstruction after the Civil War

[1]**scald** \ˈskȯld\ *vb* [ME *scalden,* fr. ONF *escalder,* fr. LL *excaldare* to wash in warm water, fr. L *ex-* + *calida, calda* warm water, fr. fem. of *calidus* warm — more at CALDRON] *vt* **1 :** to burn with or as if with hot liquid or steam **2 a :** to subject to the action of boiling water or steam **b :** to bring to a temperature just below the boiling point <~ milk> **3 :** SCORCH ~ *vi* **1 :** to scald something **2 :** to become scalded

[2]**scald** *n* **1 :** an injury to the body caused by scalding **2 :** an act or process of scalding **3 a :** a plant disease marked esp. by discoloration suggesting injury by heat **b :** a burning and browning of plant tissues resulting from high temperatures or high temperature and intense light

[3]**scald** *adj* [*scall* + *-ed*] **1** *archaic* **:** SCABBY, SCURFY **2** *archaic* **:** SHABBY, CONTEMPTIBLE <~ rogues>

[4]**scald** \ˈskȯld, ˈskäld\ *var of* SKALD

[5]**scald** \ˈskȯld\ *adj* [alter. of *scalded*] **:** subjected to scalding <like coffee . . . with ~ cream —Charles Kingsley>

scald·ing \ˈskȯl-diŋ\ *adj* **1 :** causing the sensation of scalding or burning **2 :** BOILING **3 :** ARDENT, SCORCHING <the ~ sun> **4 :** BITING, SCATHING <a series of ~ editorials>

[1]**scale** \ˈskā(ə)l\ *n* [ME, bowl, scale of a balance, fr. ON *skāl;* akin to ON *skel* shell — more at SHELL] **1 a :** either pan or tray of a balance **b :** a beam that is supported freely in the center and has two pans of equal weight suspended from its ends — usu. used in pl. **2 :** an instrument or machine for weighing

[2]**scale** *vb* **scaled; scal·ing** *vt* **:** to weigh in scales ~ *vi* **:** to have a specified weight on scales

[3]**scale** *n* [ME, fr. MF *escale,* of Gmc origin; akin to OE *scealu* shell, husk — more at SHELL] **1 a :** a small, flattened, rigid, and definitely circumscribed plate forming part of the external body covering esp. of a fish **b :** a small thin plate suggesting a fish scale <~*s* of mica> <the ~*s* on a moth's wing> **c :** the scaly covering of a scaled animal **2 :** a small thin dry lamina shed (as in many skin diseases) from the skin **3 :** a thin coating, layer, or incrustation: **a (1) :** a black scaly coating of oxide (as magnetic oxide) forming on the surface of iron when heated for processing **(2) :** a similar coating forming on other metals **b :** a hard incrustation usu. rich in sulfate of calcium that is deposited on the inside of a vessel (as a boiler) in which water is heated **4 a :** a modified leaf protecting a seed plant bud before expansion **b :** a thin, membranous, chaffy, or woody bract **5 a :** one of the small overlapping usu. metal pieces forming the outer surface of scale armor **b :** SCALE ARMOR **6 a :** SCALE INSECT **b :** infestation with or disease caused by scale insects — **scaled** \ˈskā(ə)ld\ *adj* — **scale·less** \ˈskā(ə)l-ləs\ *adj*

[4]**scale** *vb* **scaled; scal·ing** *vt* **1 :** to remove the scale or scales from (as by scraping) <~ a fish> **2 :** to take off in thin layers or scales **3 :** to form scale on <hard water ~*s* a boiler> **4 :** to throw (as a thin flat stone) so that the edge cuts the air or so that it skips on water : SKIM ~ *vi* **1 :** to separate and come off in scales : FLAKE **2 :** to shed scales <*scaling* skin> **3 :** to become encrusted with scale

[5]**scale** *n* [ME, fr. LL *scala* ladder, staircase, fr. L *scalae,* pl., stairs, rungs, ladder; akin to L *scandere* to climb — more at SCAN] **1 a** *obs* **:** LADDER **b** *archaic* **:** a means of ascent **2 :** a graduated series of musical tones ascending or descending in order of pitch according to a specified scheme of their intervals **3 :** something graduated esp. when used as a measure or rule: as **a :** a series of spaces marked by lines and used to measure distances or to register something (as the height of the mercury in a thermometer) **b :** a divided line on a map or chart indicating the length used to represent a larger unit of measure (as an inch to a mile) **c :** an instrument consisting of a strip (as of wood, plastic, or metal) with one or more sets of spaces graduated and numbered on its surface for measuring or laying off distances or dimensions **4 :** a graduated series or scheme of rank or order <a ~ of taxation> **5 :** a proportion between two sets of dimensions (as between those of a

drawing and its original) **6 :** a graded series of tests or of performances used in rating individual intelligence or achievement — **scale** *adj* — **to scale :** according to the proportions of an established scale of measurement <floor plans drawn *to scale*>

6**scale** *vb* **scaled; scal·ing** *vt* **1 a :** to attack with or take by means of scaling ladders <~ a castle wall> **b :** to climb up or reach by means of a ladder **c :** to reach the highest point of **:** SURMOUNT **2 a :** to arrange in a graduated series <~ a test> **b** (1) **:** to measure by or as if by a scale (2) **:** to measure or estimate the sound content of (as logs) **c :** to pattern, make, regulate, set, or estimate according to some rate or standard <a production schedule *scaled* to actual need> — often used with *down* or *up* <~ down imports> ~ *vi* **1 :** to climb by or as if by a ladder **2 :** to rise in a graduated series **3 :** MEASURE ***syn*** see ASCEND

7**scale** *n* [6*scale*] **1** *obs* **:** ESCALADE **2 :** an estimate of the amount of sound lumber in logs or standing timber

scale armor *n* **:** armor of small metallic scales on leather or cloth

scale–down \'skā(ə)l-ˌdau̇n\ *n* **:** a reduction according to a fixed ratio <a ~ of debts>

scale insect *n* **:** any of numerous small but very prolific homopterous insects (esp. family Coccidae) which have winged males, degenerated scale-covered females attached to the host plant, and young that suck the juices of plants and some of which are economic pests — compare LAC

scale leaf *n* **:** a modified usu. small and scaly leaf (as a bud scale or bract or the leaf of cypress)

scale·like \'skā(ə)l-ˌlīk\ *adj* **:** resembling a scale <~ design>; *specif* **:** reduced to a minute appressed element resembling a scale

sca·lene \'skā-ˌlēn, skā-'\ *adj* [LL *scalenus,* fr. Gk *skalēnos,* lit., uneven; akin to Gk *skolios* crooked — more at CYLINDER] *of a triangle* **:** having the three sides of unequal length

scale·pan \'skā(ə)l-ˌpan\ *n* **:** a pan of a scale for weighing

scal·er \'skā-lər\ *n* **1 :** one that scales **2 :** an electronic device that operates a recorder or produces an output pulse after a specified number of input impulses

scale–up \'skā-ˌləp\ *n* **:** an increase according to a fixed ratio

scall \'skȯl\ *n* [ME, fr. ON *skalli* bald head] **:** a scurf or scabby disorder (as of the scalp)

scal·lion \'skal-yən\ *n* [ME *scaloun,* fr. AF *scalun,* fr. (assumed) VL *escalonia,* fr. L *ascalonia* (*caepa*) onion of Ascalon, fr. fem. of *ascalonius* of Ascalon, fr. *Ascalon-, Ascalo* Ascalon, seaport in southern Palestine] **1 :** SHALLOT **2 :** LEEK **3 :** an onion forming a thick basal portion without a bulb; *also* **:** GREEN ONION

1**scal·lop** \'skäl-əp, 'skal-\ *n* [ME *scalop,* fr. MF *escalope* shell, of Gmc origin; akin to MD *schelpe* shell] **1 a :** any of many marine bivalve mollusks (family Pectinidae) that have a radially ribbed shell with the edge undulated and that swim by opening and closing the valves **b :** the adductor muscle of a scallop as an article of food **2 :** a scallop-shell valve or a similarly shaped dish used for baking **3 :** one of a continuous series of circle segments or angular projections forming a border **4 :** CYMLING **5** [F *escalope,* perh. fr. E 1*scallop;* fr. its being served curled like a scallop-shell valve] **:** a thin slice of boneless meat (as veal)

2**scallop** *vt* **1** [fr. earlier *escallop* scallop shell, alter. (influenced by MF *escalope* shell) of 1*scallop*] **:** to bake in a sauce usu. covered with seasoned bread or cracker crumbs <~*ed* potatoes> **2** [1*scallop*] **a :** to shape, cut, or finish in scallops **b :** to form scallops in ~ *vi* **:** to gather or dredge scallops — **scal·lop·er** *n*

scal·lo·pi·ni \ˌskäl-ə-'pē-nē, ˌskal-\ *n* [modif. of It *scaloppine*] **:** thin slices of meat (as veal) sautéed or coated with flour and fried

scal·ly·wag *var of* SCALAWAG

sca·lo·gram \'skā-lə-ˌgram\ *n* [5*scale* + *-o-* + *-gram*] **:** an arrangement of items (as of a psychological or sociological test) in ascending order of difficulty <analysis by ~>

1**scalp** \'skalp\ *n* [ME, of Scand origin; akin to ON *skālpr* sheath; akin to MD *schelpe* shell] **1 a :** the part of the integument of the human head usu. covered with hair in both sexes **b :** the part of a lower animal (as a wolf or fox) corresponding to the human scalp **2 a :** a part of the human scalp with attached hair cut or torn from an enemy as a token of victory esp. by Indian warriors of No. America **b :** a trophy of victory **3** *chiefly Scot* **:** a projecting mass of bare ground or rock

2**scalp** *vt* **1 a :** to deprive of the scalp **b :** to remove an upper part from **2 a :** to screen or sift (as ore or meal) in order to remove foreign materials or to separate out coarser grades **b :** to remove a desired constituent from and discard the rest **3 a :** to buy and sell so as to make small quick profits <~ stocks> <~ grain> **b :** to obtain and resell at greatly increased prices <~ theater tickets> ~ *vi* **1 :** to take scalps **2 :** to profit by slight market fluctuations — **scalp·er** *n*

scal·pel \'skal-pəl *also* skal-'pel\ *n* [L *scalpellus, scalpellum,* dim. of *scalper, scalprum* chisel, knife, fr. *scalpere* to carve — more at SHELF] **:** a small straight thin-bladed knife used esp. in surgery

scalp lock *n* **:** a long tuft of hair on the crown of the otherwise shaved head of a warrior of some Amerindian tribes

scaly \'skā-lē\ *adj* **scal·i·er; -est 1 a :** covered with, composed of, or rich in scale or scales **b :** FLAKY **2 :** of or relating to scaly animals **3 :** DESPICABLE, POOR **4 :** infested with scale insects <~ fruit> — **scal·i·ness** *n*

scaly anteater *n* **:** PANGOLIN

scam·mo·ny \'skam-ə-nē\ *n, pl* **-nies** [ME *scamonie,* fr. L *scammonia,* fr. Gk *skammōnia*] **1 :** a twining convolvulus (*Convolvulus scammonia*) of Asia Minor with a large thick root **2 a :** the dried root of scammony **b :** a cathartic resin obtained from scammony

1**scamp** \'skamp\ *n* [obs. *scamp* (to roam about idly)] **1** RASCAL, ROGUE **2 :** an impish or playful young person — **scamp·ish** \'skam-pish\ *adj*

2**scamp** *vt* [perh. of Scand origin; akin to ON *skammr* short — more at SCANT] **:** to perform in a hasty, neglectful, or imperfect manner <brief, but never hurried or ~*ed* —Crane Brinton>

1**scam·per** \'skam-pər\ *vi* **scam·pered; scam·per·ing** \-p(ə-)riŋ\ [prob. fr. obs. D *schampen* to flee, fr. MF *escamper,* fr. It *scampare,* fr. (assumed) VL *excampare* to decamp, fr. L *ex-* + *campus* field — more at CAMP] **:** to run nimbly and playfully about

2**scamper** *n* **:** a playful scurry

scam·pi \'skam-pē, 'skäm-\ *n, pl* **scampi** [It, pl. of *scampo,* a European lobster] **:** SHRIMP; *esp* **:** large shrimp prepared with a garlic-flavored sauce

1**scan** \'skan\ *vb* **scanned; scan·ning** [ME *scannen,* fr. LL *scandere,* fr. L, to climb; akin to Gk *skandalon* trap, stumbling block, offense, Skt *skandati* he leaps] *vt* **1 :** to read or mark so as to show metrical structure **2 :** to examine by point-by-point observation or checking: **a :** to investigate thoroughly by checking point by point and often repeatedly <a fire lookout *scanning* the hills with binoculars> **b :** to glance from point to point of often hastily, casually, or in search of a particular item <~ the want ads looking for a job> **3 a :** to examine successive small portions of (as an object) with a sensing device (as a photometer or a beam of radiation) **b :** to make a detailed examination of (as the human body) for the presence or localization of radioactive material **c :** to bring under a moving electron beam for conversion of light and dark picture or image values into corresponding electrical values to be transmitted by facsimile or television; *also* **:** to bring under a moving electron beam in the reconstruction of the image or picture **d :** to direct a succession of radar beams over in searching for a target **e :** to check (as a magnetic tape or a punch card) for recorded data by means of a mechanical or electronic device ~ *vi* **1 :** to scan verse **2 :** to conform to a metrical pattern ***syn*** see SCRUTINIZE — **scan·na·ble** \'skan-ə-bəl\ *adj*

2**scan** *n* **1 :** the act or process of scanning **2 :** a radar display **3 :** a radar or television trace **4 :** a depiction (as a photograph) of the distribution of a radioactive material in something (as a bodily organ)

Scand *abbr* Scandinavia; Scandinavian

1**scan·dal** \'skan-dᵊl\ *n* [LL *scandalum* stumbling block, offense, fr. Gk *skandalon*] **1 a :** discredit brought upon religion by unseemly conduct in a religious person **b :** conduct that causes or encourages a lapse of faith or of religious obedience in another **2 :** loss of or damage to reputation caused by actual or apparent violation of morality or propriety **:** DISGRACE **3 a :** a circumstance or action that offends propriety or established moral conceptions or disgraces those associated with it **b :** a person whose conduct offends propriety or morality **4 :** malicious or defamatory gossip **5 :** indignation, chagrin, or bewilderment brought about by a flagrant violation of morality, propriety, or religious opinion ***syn*** see OFFENSE

2**scandal** *vt* **1** *obs* **:** DISGRACE **2** *chiefly dial* **:** DEFAME, SLANDER

scan·dal·ize \'skan-də-ˌlīz\ *vt* **-ized; -iz·ing 1 :** to speak falsely or maliciously of **2** *archaic* **:** to bring into reproach **3 :** to offend the moral sense of **:** SHOCK — **scan·dal·iza·tion** \ˌskan-də-lə-'zā-shən\ *n* — **scan·dal·iz·er** \'skan-də-ˌlī-zər\ *n*

scan·dal·mon·ger \'skan-dᵊl-ˌməŋ-gər, -ˌmäŋ-\ *n* **:** a person who circulates scandal

scan·dal·ous \'skan-d(ə-)ləs\ *adj* **1 :** LIBELOUS, DEFAMATORY **2 :** offensive to propriety or morality **:** SHOCKING — **scan·dal·ous·ly** *adv* — **scan·dal·ous·ness** *n*

scandal sheet *n* **:** a newspaper or periodical dealing to a large extent in scandal and gossip

scan·dent \'skan-dənt\ *adj* [L *scandent-, scandens,* prp. of *scandere* to climb — more at SCAN] **:** characterized by a climbing mode of growth <~ stems>

Scan·di·an \'skan-dē-ən\ *adj* [L *Scandia*] **1 :** SCANDINAVIAN **2 :** of or relating to the languages of Scandinavia — **Scandian** *n*

Scan·di·na·vian \ˌskan-də-'nā-vē-ən, -vyən\ *n* **1 a :** a native or inhabitant of Scandinavia **b :** a person of Scandinavian descent **2 :** the No. Germanic languages — **Scandinavian** *adj*

scan·di·um \'skan-dē-əm\ *n* [NL, fr. L *Scandia,* ancient name of southern Scandinavian peninsula] **:** a white trivalent metallic element found in association with rare-earth elements — see ELEMENT table

scan·ner \'skan-ər\ *n* **:** one that scans: as **a :** a device that automatically checks a process or condition and may initiate a desired corrective action **b :** a device for sensing recorded data

scanning electron microscope *n* **:** an electron microscope in which a beam of focused electrons moves across the object with the secondary electrons produced by the object and the electrons scattered by the object being collected to form a three-dimensional image on a cathode-ray tube — called also *scanning microscope*

scan·sion \'skan-chən\ *n* [LL *scansion-, scansio,* fr. L, act of climbing, fr. (assumed) L *scansus,* pp. of L *scandere*] **:** the analysis of verse to show its meter

1**scant** \'skant\ *adj* [ME, fr. ON *skamt,* neut. of *skammr* short; akin to Gk *koptein* to cut — more at CAPON] **1** *dial* **a :** excessively frugal **b :** not prodigal **:** CHARY **2 a :** barely or scarcely sufficient; *specif* **:** not quite coming up to a stated measure **b :** lacking in amplitude or quantity **3 :** having a small or insufficient supply <he's fat, and ~ of breath —Shak.> ***syn*** see MEAGER ***ant*** plentiful, profuse — **scant·ly** *adv* — **scant·ness** *n*

2**scant** *adv, dial* **:** SCARCELY, HARDLY

3**scant** *vt* **1 :** to provide with a meager or inadequate portion or allowance **:** STINT **2 :** to make small, narrow, or meager **:** SKIMP **3 :** to provide an incomplete supply of **:** WITHHOLD **4 :** to give scant attention to **:** SLIGHT

scant·ies \'skant-ēz\ *n pl* [blend of 1*scant* and *panties*] **:** abbreviated panties for women

scant·ling \'skant-liŋ, -lən\ *n* [alter. of ME *scantilon,* lit., mason's or carpenter's gauge, fr. ONF *escantillon*] **1 a :** the dimensions of timber and stone used in building **b :** the dimensions of a frame or strake used in shipbuilding **2 :** a small quantity, amount, or proportion **:** MODICUM **3 :** a small piece of lumber (as an upright piece in house framing)

scanty \'skant-ē\ *adj* **scant·i·er; -est** [E dial. *scant* scanty supply, fr. ME, fr. ON *skant,* fr. neut. of *skammr* short] **1 :** barely sufficient **2 :** somewhat less than is needed or normal **:** INSUFFICIENT ***syn*** see MEAGER ***ant*** ample, plentiful, profuse — **scant·i·ly** \'skant-ᵊl-ē\ *adv* — **scant·i·ness** \'skant-ē-nəs\ *n*

¹scape \'skāp\ *vb* **scaped; scap·ing** [ME *scapen,* short for *escapen*] : ESCAPE

²scape *n* [L *scapus* shaft, stalk — more at SHAFT] **1 :** a peduncle arising at or beneath the surface of the ground in an acaulescent plant (as the tulip); *broadly* : a flower stalk **2 a :** the shaft of a column **b :** the small concave curve at the top or bottom of the shaft of a column where it joins the capital or the base **3 :** the shaft of an animal part (as an antenna or feather)

-scape \ˌskāp\ *n comb form* [*landscape*] : view or picture of a (specified) type of scene <city*scape*>

¹scape·goat \'skāp-ˌgōt\ *n* [¹*scape;* intended as trans. of Heb *'azāzēl* (prob. name of a demon), as if *'ēz 'ōzēl* goat that departs, Lev 16:8 (AV)] **1 :** a goat upon whose head are symbolically placed the sins of the people after which he is sent into the wilderness in the biblical ceremony for Yom Kippur **2 :** a person or thing bearing the blame for others

²scapegoat *vt* : to make a scapegoat of

scape·goat·ing \'skāp-ˌgōt-iŋ\ *n* : the action or process of casting blame for shortcomings or failure on an innocent or at most only partly responsible individual or group

scape·goat·ism \-ˌgōt-ˌiz-əm\ *n* : SCAPEGOATING

scape·grace \'skāp-ˌgrās\ *n* [¹*scape*] : an incorrigible rascal

¹scaph·oid \'skaf-ˌȯid\ *adj* [NL *scaphoides,* fr. Gk *skaphoeidēs,* fr. *skaphos* boat] : shaped like a boat : NAVICULAR

²scaphoid *n* : the navicular of the carpus or tarsus

scap·o·lite \'skap-ə-ˌlīt\ *n* [F, fr. L *scapus* shaft + F *-o-* + *-lite;* fr. the prismatic shape of its crystals] : any of a group of minerals that are essentially complex silicates of aluminum, calcium, and sodium and that include some used as semiprecious stones

sca·pose \'skā-ˌpōs\ *adj* : bearing, resembling, or consisting of a scape

scap·u·la \'skap-yə-lə\ *n, pl* **-lae** \-ˌlē, -ˌlī\ *or* **-las** [NL, fr. L, shoulder blade, shoulder] : either of a pair of large triangular bones lying one in each dorsal lateral part of the thorax, forming the principal bone of the corresponding half of the shoulder girdle, and articulating with the corresponding clavicle or coracoid — called also *shoulder blade*

¹scap·u·lar \-lər\ *n* [ME *scapulare,* fr. LL, fr. L *scapula* shoulder] **1 a :** a long wide band of cloth with an opening for the head worn front and back over the shoulders as part of a monastic habit **b :** a pair of small cloth squares joined by shoulder tapes and worn under the clothing on the breast and back as a sacramental and often also as a badge of a third order or confraternity **2 a :** SCAPULA **b :** one of the feathers covering the base of a bird's wing — see BIRD illustration

²scapular *adj* [NL *scapularis,* fr. *scapula*] : of or relating to the shoulder, the scapula, or scapulars

scapular medal *n* : a medal worn in place of a sacramental scapular

¹scar \'skär\ *n* [ME *skere,* fr. ON *sker* skerry; akin to ON *skera* to cut — more at SHEAR] **1 :** an isolated or protruding rock **2 :** a steep rocky eminence : a bare place on the side of a mountain

²scar *n* [ME *escare, scar,* fr. MF *escare* scab, fr. LL *eschara,* fr. Gk, hearth, scab] **1 :** a mark left (as in the skin) by the healing of injured tissue **2 a :** a mark left on a stem or branch by a fallen leaf or harvested fruit **b :** CICATRIX 2 **3 :** a mark or indentation resulting from damage or wear <the ~*s* of bullets on the . . . church door —Kay Boyle> **4 :** a lasting moral or emotional injury <one of his men had been killed . . . in a manner that left a ~ upon his mind —H. G. Wells> — **scar·less** \-ləs\ *adj*

³scar *vb* **scarred; scar·ring** *vt* **1 :** to mark with a scar **2 :** to do lasting injury to ~ *vi* **1 :** to form a scar **2 :** to become scarred

scar·ab \'skar-əb\ *n* [MF *scarabee,* fr. L *scarabaeus*] **1 :** SCARABAEUS 1; *broadly* : a scarabaeid beetle **2 :** SCARABAEUS 2

scar·a·bae·id \ˌskar-ə-'bē-əd\ *n* [deriv. of L *scarabaeus*] : any of a family (Scarabaeidae) of stout-bodied beetles with lamellate antennae including the dung beetles — **scarabaeid** *adj*

scar·a·bae·us \ˌskar-ə-'bē-əs\ *n* [L] **1** *pl* **-bae·us·es** *or* **-baei** \-'bē-ˌī\ : a large black or nearly black dung beetle (*Scarabaeus sacer*) **2 :** a stone or faience beetle used in ancient Egypt as a talisman, ornament, and a symbol of the resurrection

scarabaeus 1

scar·a·mouch *or* **scar·a·mouche** \'skar-ə-ˌmüsh, -ˌmüch, -ˌmau̇ch\ *n* [F *Scaramouche,* fr. It *Scaramuccia*] **1** *cap* : a stock character in the Italian commedia dell'arte that burlesques the Spanish don and is characterized by boastfulness and cowardliness **2 a :** a cowardly buffoon **b :** RASCAL, SCAMP

¹scarce \'ske(ə)rs, 'ska(ə)rs\ *adj* **scarc·er; scarc·est** [ME *scars,* fr. ONF *escars,* fr. (assumed) VL *excarpsus,* lit., plucked out, pp. of L *excerpere* to pluck out — more at EXCERPT] : deficient in quantity or number compared with the demand : not plentiful or abundant ***syn*** see INFREQUENT ***ant*** abundant — **scarce·ness** *n*

²scarce *adv* : SCARCELY, HARDLY

scarce·ly *adv* **1 a :** by a narrow margin : only just <had ~ rung the bell when the door flew open —Agnes S. Turnbull> **b :** almost not <~ ever wore this mantle —Arnold Bennett> **2 a :** certainly not <could ~ interfere between another man and his own beast —Owen Wister> **b :** probably not <there could ~ have been found a leader better equipped —V. L. Parrington>

scar·ci·ty \'sker-sət-ē, 'sker-stē, 'skar-\ *n, pl* **-ties :** the quality or state of being scarce; *esp* : want of provisions for the support of life

¹scare \'ske(ə)r, 'ska(ə)r\ *vb* **scared; scar·ing** [ME *skerren,* fr. ON *skirra,* fr. *skjarr* shy, timid] *vt* : to frighten suddenly : ALARM ~ *vi* : to become scared — **scar·er** *n*

²scare *n* **1 :** a sudden fright **2 :** a widespread state of alarm : PANIC — **scare** *adj*

scare·crow \'ske(ə)r-ˌkrō, 'ska(ə)r-\ *n* **1 a :** an object usu. suggesting a human figure that is set up to frighten birds (as crows) away from crops **b :** something frightening but harmless **2 :** a skinny or ragged person

scared *adj* : thrown into or living in a state of fear, fright, or panic

scaredy-cat \'ske(ə)rd-ē-ˌkat, 'ska(ə)rd-\ *n* [*scared,* pp. of *scare* + *-y* + *cat*] : an unduly fearful person

scare·head \'ske(ə)r-ˌhed, 'ska(ə)r-\ *n* : a big, sensational, or alarming newspaper headline

scare·mon·ger \-ˌməŋ-gər, -ˌmäŋ-\ *n* : one inclined to raise or excite alarms esp. needlessly

scare up *vt* : to bring to light or get together with considerable labor or difficulty : scrape up <managed to *scare up* the money>

¹scarf \'skärf\ *n, pl* **scarves** \'skärvz\ *or* **scarfs** [ONF *escarpe* sash, sling] **1 :** a broad band of cloth worn about the shoulders, around the neck, or over the head **2 a :** a military or official sash usu. indicative of rank **b** *archaic* : TIPPET 3 **3 :** RUNNER 6b

²scarf *vt* **1 :** to wrap, cover, or adorn with or as if with a scarf **2 :** to wrap or throw on (a scarf or mantle) loosely

³scarf *n, pl* **scarfs** [ME *skarf,* prob. of Scand origin; akin to ON *skarfr* scarf; akin to Gk *skorpios* scorpion] **1 :** either of the chamfered or cutaway ends that fit together to form a scarf joint **2 :** a joint made by chamfering, halving, or notching two pieces to correspond and lapping and bolting them — called also *scarf joint*

⁴scarf *or* **scarph** \'skärf\ *vt* **1 :** to unite by a scarf joint **2 :** to form a scarf on

scarfs 2

scarf·pin \'skärf-ˌpin\ *n* : TIEPIN

scarf·skin \'skärf-ˌskin\ *n* [¹*scarf*] : EPIDERMIS; *esp* : that forming the cuticle of a nail

scar·i·fi·ca·tion \ˌskar-ə-fə-'kā-shən, ˌsker-\ *n* **1 :** the act or process of scarifying **2 :** a mark or marks made by scarifying

¹scar·i·fy \'skar-ə-ˌfī, 'sker-\ *vt* **-fied; -fy·ing** [MF *scarifier,* fr. LL *scarificare,* alter. of L *scarifare,* fr. Gk *skariphasthai* to scratch an outline, sketch — more at SCRIBE] **1 :** to make scratches or small cuts in (as the skin) <~ an area for vaccination> **2 :** to lacerate the feelings of <denounces, *scarifies,* blasts the pedantic schoolmasters —Gilbert Highet> **3 :** to break up and loosen the surface of (as a field or road) **4 :** to cut or soften the wall of (a hard seed) to hasten germination — **scar·i·fi·er** \-ˌfī(-ə)r\ *n*

²scar·ify \'sker-ə-ˌfī, 'skar-\ *vt* **-fied; -fy·ing :** SCARE, FRIGHTEN

scar·i·ous \'sker-ē-əs, 'skar-\ *adj* [NL *scariosus*] : dry and membranous in texture <a ~ bract>

scar·la·ti·na \ˌskär-lə-'tē-nə\ *n* [NL, fr. ML *scarlata* scarlet] : SCARLET FEVER — **scar·la·ti·nal** \-'tēn-ᵊl\ *adj*

¹scar·let \'skär-lət\ *n* [ME *scarlat, scarlet,* fr. OF or ML; OF *escarlate,* fr. ML *scarlata,* fr. Per *saqalāt,* a kind of rich cloth] **1 :** scarlet cloth or clothes **2 :** any of various bright reds

²scarlet *adj* **1 :** of the color scarlet **2 a :** grossly and glaringly offensive <sinning in flagrant and ~ fashion —G. W. Johnson> **b** [fr. the use of the word in Isa 1:18 & Rev 17:1–6 (AV)] : WHORISH <~ women who became the hostesses of the gambling dens and nightclubs —Mabel Elliot>

scarlet fever *n* : an acute contagious febrile disease caused by a hemolytic streptococcus and characterized by inflammation of the nose, throat, and mouth, generalized toxemia, and a red rash

scarlet letter *n* [fr. the novel *The Scarlet Letter* (1850) by Nathaniel Hawthorne] : a scarlet A worn as a punitive mark of adultery

scarlet pimpernel *n* **1 :** a common pimpernel (*Anagallis arvensis*) having scarlet, white, or purplish flowers that close in cloudy weather **2** [*The Scarlet Pimpernel,* assumed name of the hero of *The Scarlet Pimpernel* (1905), novel by Baroness Orczy] : a person who rescues others from mortal danger by smuggling them across a border

scarlet runner *n* : a tropical American high-climbing bean (*Phaseolus coccineus*) that has large bright red flowers and red-and-black seeds and is grown widely as an ornamental and in Great Britain as a preferred food bean

scarlet sage *n* : a garden salvia (*Salvia splendens*) of Brazil with long racemes of intense scarlet flowers

scarlet tanager *n* : a common American tanager (*Piranga olivacea*) of which the male is scarlet with black wings and the female and young are chiefly olive

¹scarp \'skärp\ *n* [It *scarpa*] **1 :** the inner side of a ditch below the parapet of a fortification **2 a :** a line of cliffs produced by faulting or erosion **b :** a low steep slope along a beach caused by wave erosion

²scarp *vt* : to cut down vertically or to a steep slope

scar·per \'skär-pər\ *vi* [perh. fr. It *scappare,* fr. (assumed) VL *excappare* — more at ESCAPE] *Brit* : to run away

scar·ry \'skär-ē\ *adj* [²*scar*] : bearing marks of wounds : SCARRED

¹scart \'skärt\ *vb* [ME *skarten,* alter. of *scratten*] *chiefly Scot* : SCRATCH, SCRAPE

²scart *n, chiefly Scot* : SCRATCH, MARK; *esp* : one made in writing

scar tissue *n* : the connective tissue forming a scar and composed chiefly of fibroblasts in recent scars and largely of dense collagenous fibers in old scars

scary *also* **scar·ey** \'ske(ə)r-ē, 'ska(ə)r-\ *adj* **scar·i·er; -est 1 :** causing fright : ALARMING <told us a ~ story> **2 :** easily scared : TIMID **3 :** feeling alarm or fright : FRIGHTENED

¹scat \'skat\ *vi* **scat·ted; scat·ting** [*scat,* interj. used to drive away a cat] **1 :** to go away quickly **2 :** to move fast : SCOOT

²scat *n* [Gk *skat-, skōr* excrement — more at SCAT-] : an animal fecal dropping

---

[3]**scat** *n* [perh. imit.] : jazz singing with nonsense syllables
[4]**scat** *vi* **scat·ted; scat·ting :** to improvise nonsense syllables to an instrumental accompaniment : sing scat
SCAT *abbr* **1** School and College Ability Test **2** supersonic commercial air transport
scat- *or* **scato-** *comb form* [Gk *skato-*, fr. *skat-*, *skōr* excrement; akin to OE *scearn* dung, L mus*cerda* mouse dropping] : ordure <*scato*logy>
scat·back \'skat-ˌbak\ *n* [[1]*scat* + *back*] : an offensive back in football who is an esp. fast and elusive ballcarrier
[1]**scathe** \'skāth, 'skāth\ *n* [ME *skathe*, fr. ON *skathi;* akin to OE *sceatha* injury, Gk *askēthēs* unharmed] : HARM, INJURY — **scathe·less** \-ləs\ *adj*
[2]**scathe** \'skāth\ *vt* **scathed; scath·ing 1 :** to do harm to; *specif* : SCORCH, SEAR **2 :** to assail with withering denunciation
scath·ing \'skā-thiŋ\ *adj* **:** bitterly severe <a ~ condemnation> — **scath·ing·ly** \-thiŋ-lē\ *adv*
sca·tol·o·gy \ska-'täl-ə-jē, skə-\ *n* **1 :** the biologically oriented study of excrement (as for taxonomic purposes or for the determination of diet) **2 :** interest in or treatment of obscene matters esp. in literature — **scat·o·log·i·cal** \ˌskat-ᵊl-'äj-i-kəl\ *adj*
scatt \'skat\ *n* [ON *skattr;* akin to OE *sceat* property, money, a small coin] *archaic* : TAX, TRIBUTE
[1]**scat·ter** \'skat-ər\ *vb* [ME *scateren*] *vt* **1** *archaic* **:** to fling away heedlessly : SQUANDER **2 a :** to cause to separate widely **b :** to cause to vanish **3 :** to distribute irregularly **4 :** to sow by casting in all directions : STREW **5 a :** to reflect irregularly and diffusely **b :** to diffuse or disperse (a beam of radiation) **6 :** to divide into ineffectual small portions ~ *vi* **1 :** to separate and go in various directions : DISPERSE **2 :** to occur or fall irregularly or at random — **scat·ter·er** \-ər-ər\ *n* — **scat·ter·ing·ly** \'skat-ə-riŋ-lē\ *adv*
syn SCATTER, DISPERSE, DISSIPATE, DISPEL *shared meaning element* : to cause to separate or break up
[2]**scatter** *n* **1 :** the act of scattering **2 :** a small supply or number irregularly distributed or strewn about **3 :** the state or extent of being scattered; *esp* : DISPERSION
scat·ter·ation \ˌskat-ə-'rā-shən\ *n* **1 :** the act or process of scattering : the state of being scattered **2 :** the movement of people and industry away from the city; *also* : the resulting regional urbanization **3 :** a policy of distributing funds and energies in too many ineffectively small units
scat·ter·brain \'skat-ər-ˌbrān\ *n* **:** a giddy heedless person
scat·ter·brained \-ˌbrānd\ *adj* **:** having the characteristics of a scatterbrain
scatter diagram *n* **:** a two-dimensional graph in rectangular coordinates consisting of points whose coordinates represent values of two variables under study
scat·ter·good \'skat-ər-ˌgu̇d\ *n* **:** a wasteful person : SPENDTHRIFT
scat·ter·gram \-ˌgram\ *n* **:** SCATTER DIAGRAM
scat·ter·graph \-ˌgraf\ *n* **:** SCATTER DIAGRAM
scat·ter–gun \-ˌgən\ *n* **:** SHOTGUN
[1]**scat·ter·ing** *n* **1 :** an act or process in which something scatters or is scattered **2 :** something scattered; *esp* : a small number or quantity interspersed here and there <a ~ of visitors>
[2]**scattering** *adj* **1 :** going in various directions **2 :** found or placed far apart and in no order **3 :** divided among many or several <~ votes> — **scat·ter·ing·ly** \-ə-riŋ-lē\ *adv*
scatter pin *n* **:** a small ornamental pin worn usu. in groups of two or more on a woman's dress
scatter rug *n* **:** a rug of such a size that several can be used (as to fill vacant places) in a room
scat·ter·shot \'skat-ər-ˌshät\ *adj* **:** broadly inclusive : SHOTGUN
scat·ty \'skat-ē\ *adj* **scat·ti·er; -est** [prob. fr. *scatter*brain + *-y*] *Brit* : CRAZY
scaup \'sko̊p\ *n, pl* **scaup** *or* **scaups** [perh. alter. of *scalp* (bed of shellfish); fr. its fondness for shellfish] **:** any of several diving ducks (genus *Aythya* and esp. *A. affinis* and *A. marila*)
scav·enge \'skav-ənj, -inj\ *vb* **scav·enged; scav·eng·ing** [back-formation fr. *scavenger*] *vt* **1 a** (1) **:** to remove (as dirt or refuse) from an area (2) **:** to clean away dirt or refuse from : CLEANSE <~ a street> **b :** to feed on (carrion or refuse) **2 a :** to remove (burned gases) from the cylinder of an internal-combustion engine after a working stroke **b :** to remove (as an undesirable constituent) from a substance or region by chemical or physical means **c** : to clean and purify (molten metal) by taking up foreign elements in chemical union **3 :** to salvage from discarded or refuse material; *also* **:** to salvage usable material from ~ *vi* **:** to work or act as a scavenger
scav·en·ger \'skav-ən-jər\ *n* [alter. of earlier *scavager*, fr. ME *skawager* collector of a toll on goods sold by nonresident merchants, fr. *skawage* toll on goods sold by nonresident merchants, fr. ONF *escauwage* inspection] **1** *chiefly Brit* : a person employed to remove dirt and refuse from streets **2 :** one that scavenges: as **a :** a garbage collector **b :** a junk collector **c** : a chemically active substance acting to make innocuous or remove an undesirable substance **3 :** an organism that feeds habitually on refuse or carrion
scavenger hunt *n* **:** a party contest in which usu. couples are sent out with a time limit in which to acquire without buying one or more articles that are esp. difficult to obtain
SCCA *abbr* Sports Car Club of America
sce·na \'shā-(ˌ)nä\ *n* [It, lit., scene, fr. L] **:** an elaborate solo vocal composition that consists of a recitative usu. followed by one or more aria sections
sce·nar·io \sə-'nar-ē-ˌō, -'ner-\ *n, pl* **-i·os** [It, fr. L *scaenarium*, fr. *scaena* stage] **1 a :** an outline or synopsis of a play; *esp* : a plot outline used by actors of the commedia dell'arte **b :** the libretto of an opera **2 a :** SCREENPLAY **b :** SHOOTING SCRIPT **3 :** an account or synopsis of a projected course of action or events <his ~ for a settlement envisages . . . reunification —Selig Harrison>
sce·nar·ist \-'nar-əst, -'ner-\ *n* **:** a writer of scenarios
[1]**scend** \'send\ *vi* [alter. of *send*] **:** to rise or heave upward under the influence of a natural force (as on a wave)
[2]**scend** *n* **1 :** the upward movement of a pitching ship **2 :** the lift of a wave : SEND
scene \'sēn\ *n* [MF, stage, fr. L *scena, scaena* stage, scene, fr. Gk *skēnē* temporary shelter, tent, building forming the background for a dramatic performance, stage; akin to Gk *skia* shadow — more at SHINE] **1 :** one of the subdivisions of a play: as **a :** a division of an act presenting continuous action in one place **b :** a single situation or unit of dialogue in a play <the love ~> **c :** a motion-picture or television episode or sequence **2 a :** a stage setting **b :** a real or imaginary prospect suggesting a stage setting <a sylvan ~> **3 :** the place of an occurrence or action : LOCALE <~ of the crime> **4 :** an exhibition of anger or indecorous behavior <make a ~> **5 a :** sphere of activity <the drug ~> **b :** SITUATION <your ~ . . . was unimportant, nobody wanted to hear about it —Michael Herr> — **behind the scenes 1 :** out of public view : in secret **2 :** in a position to see the hidden workings <taken *behind the scenes* and told just how in fact the actual government . . . has operated —William Clark>
scene dock *n* **:** a space near the stage in a theater where scenery is stored
scen·ery \'sēn-(ə-)rē\ *n, pl* **-er·ies 1 :** the painted scenes or hangings and accessories used on a theater stage **2 :** a picturesque view or landscape
scene·shift·er \-ˌshif-tər\ *n* **:** a worker who moves the scenes in a theater
scene–steal·er \'sēn-ˌstē-lər\ *n* **:** an actor who diverts attention to himself when he is not intended to be the center of attention
sce·nic \'sēn-ik *also* 'sen-\ *also* **sce·ni·cal** \-i-kəl\ *adj* **1 :** of or relating to the stage, a stage setting, or stage representation **2** : of or relating to natural scenery <a ~ view> **3 :** representing graphically an action, event, or episode <a ~ bas-relief> — **sce·ni·cal·ly** \-i-k(ə-)lē\ *adv*
scenic railway *n* **:** a miniature railway (as in an amusement park) with artificial scenery along the way
sce·nog·ra·phy \sē-'näg-rə-fē\ *n* [Gk *skēnographia* painting of scenery, fr. *skēnē* + *-graphia* -graphy] **:** the art of perspective representation esp. as applied to the painting of stage scenery (as by the ancient Greeks) — **sce·no·graph·ic** \ˌsē-nə-'graf-ik\ *adj* — **sce·no·graph·i·cal·ly** \-i-k(ə-)lē\ *adv*
[1]**scent** \'sent\ *vb* [ME *senten*, fr. MF *sentir* to feel, smell, fr. L *sentire* to perceive, feel — more at SENSE] *vt* **1 a :** to perceive by the olfactory organs : SMELL **b :** to get or have an inkling of <~ trouble> **2 :** to imbue or fill with odor <~*ed* the air with perfume> ~ *vi* **1 :** to yield an odor of some specified kind <this ~*s* of sulfur>; *also* **:** to bear indication or suggestions <the very air ~*s* of treachery> **2 :** to use the nose in seeking or tracking prey
[2]**scent** *n* **1 :** effluvia from a substance that affect the sense of smell: as **a :** an odor left by an animal on a surface passed over **b :** a characteristic or particular odor; *esp* : one that is agreeable **2 a :** power of smelling : sense of smell <a keen ~> **b :** power of detection : NOSE <a ~ for heresy> **3 :** a course of pursuit or discovery <throw one off the ~> **4 :** INKLING, INTIMATION <a ~ of trouble> **5 :** PERFUME 2 **6 :** bits of paper dropped in the game of hare and hounds **7 :** a mixture prepared for use as a lure in hunting or fishing ***syn*** see FRAGRANCE, SMELL — **scent·less** \'sent-ləs\ *adj*
scent·ed *adj* **:** having scent: as **a :** having the sense of smell **b** : having a perfumed smell **c :** having or exhaling an odor
[1]**scep·ter** \'sep-tər\ *n* [ME *sceptre*, fr. OF *ceptre*, fr. L *sceptrum*, fr. Gk *skēptron* staff, scepter — more at SHAFT] **1 :** a staff or baton borne by a sovereign as an emblem of authority **2 :** royal or imperial authority : SOVEREIGNTY
[2]**scepter** *vt* **scep·tered; scep·ter·ing** \-t(ə-)riŋ\ **:** to endow with the scepter in token of royal authority
scep·tered \'sep-tərd\ *adj* **1 :** invested with a scepter or sovereign authority **2 :** of or relating to a sovereign or to royalty
scep·tic \'skep-tik\ *var of* SKEPTIC
scep·tre \'sep-tər\ *Brit var of* SCEPTER
sch *abbr* school
scha·den·freu·de \'shäd-ᵊn-ˌfrȯid-ə\ *n* [G, fr. *schaden* damage + *freude* joy] **:** enjoyment obtained from others' troubles
[1]**sched·ule** \'skej-(ˌ)ü(ə)l, 'skej-əl, *Canad also* 'shej-, *Brit usu* 'shed-(ˌ)yü(ə)l\ *n* [ME *cedule*, fr. MF, slip of paper, note, fr. LL *schedula* slip of paper, dim. of L *scheda*, *scida* sheet of papyrus, fr. (assumed) Gk *schidē;* akin to Gk *schizein* to split — more at SHED] **1 a** *obs* **:** a written document **b :** a statement of supplementary details appended to a legal or legislative document **2 :** a written or printed list, catalog, or inventory; *also* **:** TIMETABLE **3 :** PROGRAM, PROPOSAL **4:** a body of items to be dealt with : AGENDA
[2]**schedule** *vt* **sched·uled sched·ul·ing 1 a :** to place in a schedule **b :** to make a schedule of **2 :** to appoint, assign, or designate for a fixed time — **sched·ul·er** *n*
schee·lite \'shā-ˌlīt\ *n* [G *scheelit*, fr. Karl W. *Scheele* †1786 Sw chemist] **:** a mineral $CaWO_4$ consisting of the tungstate of calcium that is a source of tungsten and its compounds
Sche·her·a·zade \shə-ˌher-ə-'zäd(-ə), -'zäd(-ē)\ *n* [G *Scheherezade*, fr. Per *Shīrazād*] **:** the fictional wife of an oriental king and the narrator of the tales in the *Arabian Nights' Entertainment*
sche·ma \'skē-mə\ *n, pl* **sche·ma·ta** \-mət-ə\ [Gk *schēmat-*, *schēma*] **:** a diagrammatic presentation; *specif* : FIGURE 6
[1]**sche·mat·ic** \ski-'mat-ik\ *adj* [NL *schematicus*, fr. Gk *schēmat-*, *schēma*] **:** of or relating to a scheme or schema : DIAGRAMMATIC — **sche·mat·i·cal·ly** \-i-k(ə-)lē\ *adv*
[2]**schematic** *n* **:** a schematic drawing or diagram
sche·ma·tism \'skē-mə-ˌtiz-əm\ *n* **:** the disposition of constituents in a pattern or according to a scheme : DESIGN; *also* **:** a particular systematic disposition of parts
sche·ma·tize \'skē-mə-ˌtīz\ *vt* **-tized; -tiz·ing** [Gk *schēmatizein*, fr. *schēmat-*, *schēma*] **1 :** to form or to form into a scheme or systematic arrangement **2 :** to express or depict schematically — **sche·ma·ti·za·tion** \ˌskē-mət-ə-'zā-shən\ *n*
[1]**scheme** \'skēm\ *n* [L *schemat-*, *schema* arrangement, figure, fr. Gk *schēmat-*, *schēma*, fr. *echein* to have, hold, be in (such) a

condition; akin to OE *sige* victory, Skt *sahate* he prevails] **1 a** *archaic* (1) **:** a mathematical or astronomical diagram (2) **:** a representation of the astrological aspects of the planets at a particular time **b :** a graphic sketch or outline **2 :** a concise statement or table **:** EPITOME **3 :** a plan or program of action; *esp* **:** a crafty or secret one **4 :** a systematic or organized framework **:** DESIGN ***syn*** see PLAN

²scheme *vb* **schemed; schem·ing** *vt* **:** to form a scheme for ~ *vi* **:** to form plans; *also* **:** PLOT, INTRIGUE — **schem·er** *n*

schem·ing *adj* **:** given to forming schemes; *esp* **:** shrewdly devious and intriguing

¹scher·zan·do \skert-ˈsän-(ˌ)dō\ *adv or adj* [It, fr. verbal of *scherzare* to joke, of Gmc origin; akin to MHG *scherzen* to leap for joy, joke; akin to Gk *skairein* to gambol — more at CARDINAL] **:** in sportive manner **:** PLAYFULLY — used as a direction in music indicating style and tempo <allegretto ~>

²scherzando *n, pl* **-dos :** a passage or movement in scherzando style

scher·zo \ˈske(ə)rt-(ˌ)sō\ *n, pl* **scherzos** *or* **scher·zi** \-(ˌ)sē\ [It, lit., joke, fr. *scherzare*] **:** a sprightly humorous instrumental musical composition or movement commonly in quick triple time

Schick test \ˈshik-\ *n* [Béla *Schick*] **:** a serological test by cutaneous injection of a diluted diphtheria toxin that causes an area of reddening and induration in a subject susceptible to diphtheria

Schiff reagent \ˌshif-\ *n* [Hugo *Schiff* †1915 G chemist] **:** a solution of fuchsine decolorized by treatment with sulfur dioxide that gives a useful test for aldehydes because they restore the reddish violet color of the dye — called also *Schiff's reagent;* compare FEULGEN REACTION

schil·ler \ˈshil-ər\ *n* [G] **:** a bronzy iridescent luster (as of a mineral)

schil·ling \ˈshil-iŋ\ *n* [G, fr. OHG *skilling,* a gold coin — more at SHILLING] — see MONEY table

schip·per·ke \ˈskip-ər-kē, -ərk(-ə)\ *n* [Flem, dim. of *schipper* skipper; fr. its use as a watchdog on boats — more at SKIPPER] **:** any of a Belgian breed of small stocky black dogs with foxy head and erect triangular ears

schism \ˈsiz-əm, ˈskiz-; ˈskiz- *is rare among churchmen*\ *n* [ME *scisme,* fr. MF *cisme,* fr. LL *schismat-, schisma,* fr. Gk, cleft, division, fr. *schizein* to split] **1 :** DIVISION, SEPARATION; *also* **:** DISCORD, DISHARMONY **2 a :** formal division in or separation from a church or religious body **b :** the offense of promoting schism

¹schis·mat·ic \siz-ˈmat-ik, skiz-\ *n* **:** one who creates or takes part in schism

²schismatic *also* **schis·mat·i·cal** \-i-kəl\ *adj* **:** of, relating to, or guilty of schism — **schis·mat·i·cal·ly** \-i-k(ə-)lē\ *adv*

schis·ma·tist \ˈsiz-mət-əst, ˈskiz-\ *n* [prob. fr. *schismatize*] **:** SCHISMATIC

schis·ma·tize \-mə-ˌtīz\ *vb* **-tized; -tiz·ing** *vi* **:** to take part in schism; *esp* **:** to make a breach of union (as in the church) ~ *vt* **:** to induce into schism

schist \ˈshist\ *n* [F *schiste,* fr. L *schistos* (*lapis*), lit., fissile stone, fr. Gk *schistos* that may be split, fr. *schizein*] **:** a metamorphic crystalline rock having a closely foliated structure and admitting of division along approximately parallel planes

schis·tose \ˈshis-ˌtōs\ *also* **schis·tous** \-təs\ *adj* **:** of or relating to schist **:** having the character or structure of a schist — **schis·tos·i·ty** \shis-ˈtäs-ət-ē\ *n*

schis·to·some \ˈshis-tə-ˌsōm\ *n* [NL *Schistosoma,* genus name, fr. Gk *schistos* + *sōma* body — more at SOMAT-] **:** any of a genus (*Schistosoma*) of elongated trematode worms with the sexes separate that parasitize the blood vessels of birds and mammals and in man cause destructive schistosomiases; *broadly* **:** a worm of the family (Schistosomatidae) that includes this genus — **schis·to·som·al** \ˌshis-tə-ˈsō-məl\ *adj* — **schistosome** *adj*

schis·to·so·mi·a·sis \ˌshis-tə-sō-ˈmī-ə-səs\ *n, pl* **-a·ses** \-ˌsēz\ [NL, fr. *Schistosoma*] **:** infestation with or disease caused by schistosomes; *specif* **:** a severe endemic disease of man in much of Asia, Africa, and So. America marked esp. by blood loss and tissue damage

schiz- *or* **schizo-** *comb form* [NL, fr. Gk *schizo-,* fr. *schizein* to split] **1 :** split **:** cleft <*schizo*carp> **2 :** characterized by or involving cleavage <*schizo*genesis> **3 :** schizophrenia <*schizo*thymia>

schizo \ˈskit-(ˌ)sō\ *n, pl* **schiz·os :** a schizophrenic individual

schizo·carp \ˈskiz-ə-ˌkärp, ˈskit-sə-\ *n* [ISV] **:** a dry compound fruit that splits at maturity into several indehiscent one-seeded carpels

schi·zog·o·ny \skiz-ˈäg-ə-nē, skit-ˈsäg-\ *n* [NL *schizogonia,* fr. *schiz-* + L *-gonia* -gony] **:** asexual reproduction by multiple segmentation characteristic of sporozoans (as the malaria parasite) — **schi·zog·o·nous** \-nəs\ *or* **schizo·gon·ic** \ˌskiz-ə-ˈgän-ik, ˌskit-sə-\ *adj*

schiz·oid \ˈskit-ˌsȯid\ *adj* [ISV] **:** characterized by, resulting from, tending toward, or suggestive of schizophrenia — **schizoid** *n*

schizo·my·cete \ˌskiz-ə-ˈmī-ˌsēt, ˌskit-sə-, -ˌmī-ˈ\ *n* [deriv. of Gk *schizo-* schiz- + *mykēt-, mykēs* fungus — more at MYC-] **:** BACTERIUM — **schizo·my·ce·tous** \-ˌmī-ˈsēt-əs\ *adj*

schiz·ont \ˈskiz-ˌänt, ˈskit-ˌsänt\ *n* [ISV] **:** a multinucleate sporozoan that reproduces by schizogony

schizo·phrene \ˈskit-sə-ˌfrēn\ *n* [ISV, prob. back-formation fr. NL *schizophrenia*] **:** one affected with schizophrenia **:** SCHIZOPHRENIC

schizo·phre·nia \ˌskit-sə-ˈfrē-nē-ə\ *n* [NL] **:** a psychotic disorder characterized by loss of contact with the environment and by disintegration of personality expressed as disorder of feeling, thought, and conduct — **schizo·phren·ic** \-ˈfren-ik\ *adj or n* — **schizo·phren·i·cal·ly** \-ˈfren-i-k(ə-)lē\ *adv*

schizo·phyte \ˈskiz-ə-ˌfīt, ˈskit-sə-\ *n* [deriv. of Gk *schizo-* + *phyton* plant — more at PLANT] **:** any of a division (*Schizophyta*) of plants comprising the blue-green algae and bacteria and characterized by unicellular or loosely colonial and often filamentous organization, by lack of an obvious nucleus, and by chiefly asexual reproduction — **schizo·phyt·ic** \ˌskiz-ə-ˈfit-ik, ˌskit-sə-\ *adj*

schizo·thy·mic \ˌskit-sə-ˈthī-mik\ *adj* [NL *schizothymia* state of being schizothymic, fr. *schiz-* + *-thymia*] **:** tending toward an introverted temperament that while remaining within the bounds of normality somewhat resembles schizophrenia

schle·miel \shlə-ˈmē(ə)l\ *n* [Yiddish *shlumiel*] **:** an unlucky bungler **:** CHUMP

schlepp \ˈshlep\ *vb* [Yiddish *shleppen,* fr. MHG *sleppen,* fr. MLG *slēpen*] *slang* **:** DRAG, HAUL

schlie·ren \ˈshlir-ən\ *n pl* [G] **1 :** small masses or streaks in an igneous rock that differ in composition from the main body **2 :** regions of varying refraction in a transparent medium often caused by pressure or temperature differences and detectable esp. by photographing the passage of a beam of light — **schlie·ric** \ˈshli(ə)r-ik\ *adj*

schlock \ˈshläk\ *adj* [Yiddish *shlak,* fr. *shlak* curse, cheap merchandise, lit., blow, fr. MHG *slag, slac,* fr. OHG *slag,* fr. *slahan* to strike — more at SLAY] **:** of low quality or value — **schlock** *n*

schmaltz *or* **schmalz** \ˈshmȯlts, ˈshmälts\ *n* [Yiddish *shmalts,* lit., rendered fat, fr. MHG *smalz;* akin to OHG *smelzan* to melt — more at SMELT] **:** sentimental or florid music or art — **schmaltzy** \-ē\ *adj*

Schmidt system \ˈs(h)mit-\ *n* [B. *Schmidt* †1935 G optical scientist] **:** an optical system (as for a telescope or camera) that utilizes an objective composed of a concave spherical mirror having in front of it a transparent plate to offset spherical aberration

schmo *or* **schmoe** \ˈshmō\ *n, pl* **schmoes** [prob. modif. of Yiddish *shmok* penis, fool, fr. G *schmuck* adornment] *slang* **:** JERK 4

schmuck \ˈshmək\ *n* [Yiddish *shmok* penis, fool, fr. G *schmuck* adornment] *slang* **:** JERK 4

schnapps \ˈshnaps\ *n, pl* **schnapps** [G *schnaps,* lit., dram of liquor, fr. LG, fr. *snappen* to snap] **:** any of various distilled liquors; *esp* **:** strong Holland gin

schnau·zer \ˈshnaut-sər, ˈs(h)nau̇-zər\ *n* [G, fr. *schnauze* snout — more at SNOUT] **:** a dog of any of three breeds that originated in Germany and are characterized by a long head, small ears, heavy eyebrows, mustache and beard, and a wiry coat: **a :** STANDARD SCHNAUZER **b :** GIANT SCHNAUZER **c :** MINIATURE SCHNAUZER

schnit·zel \ˈs(h)nit-səl\ *n* [G, lit., shaving, chip, fr. MHG, dim. of *sniz* slice; akin to OHG *snīdan* to cut, OE *snithan,* Czech *snět* bough] **:** a seasoned and garnished veal cutlet

schnook \ˈshnu̇k\ *n* [origin unknown] *slang* **:** a stupid or unimportant person **:** DOLT

schnor·kel \ˈs(h)nȯr-kəl\ *var of* SNORKEL

schnor·rer \ˈshnȯr-ər, ˈshnōr-\ *n* [Yiddish *shnorer*] **:** BEGGAR; *esp* **:** one who wheedles others into supplying his wants

schnoz·zle \ˈs(h)näz-əl\ *n* [prob. modif. of Yiddish *shnoitsl,* dim. of *shnoits* snout, fr. G *schnauze* snout, muzzle — more at SNOUT] *slang* **:** NOSE

scho·la can·to·rum \ˌskō-lə-kan-ˈtōr-əm, -ˈtȯr-\ *n, pl* **scho·lae cantorum** \-ˌlē-, -ˌlā-, -ˌlī-\ [ML, school of singers] **1 :** a singing school esp. for church choristers; *specif* **:** the choir or choir school of a monastery or of a cathedral **2 :** an enclosure designed for a choir and located in the center of the nave in early church buildings

schol·ar \ˈskäl-ər\ *n* [ME *scoler,* fr. OE *scolere* & OF *escoler,* fr. ML *scholaris,* fr. LL, of a school, fr. L *schola* school] **1 :** one who attends a school or studies under a teacher **:** PUPIL **2 a :** one who has done advanced study in a special field **b :** a learned person **3 :** a holder of a scholarship

schol·ar·ly \-ər-lē\ *adj* **:** characteristic of or suitable to learned persons **:** LEARNED, ACADEMIC

schol·ar·ship \-ər-ˌship\ *n* **1 :** a grant-in-aid to a student (as by a college or foundation) **2 :** the character, qualities, or attainments of a scholar **:** LEARNING **3 :** a fund of knowledge and learning <drawing on the ~ of the ancients> ***syn*** see KNOWLEDGE

¹scho·las·tic \skə-ˈlas-tik\ *adj* [ML & L; ML *scholasticus* of the schoolmen, fr. L, of a school, fr. Gk *scholastikos,* fr. *scholazein* to keep a school, fr. *scholē* school] **1 a** *often cap* **:** of or relating to Scholasticism <~ theology> <~ philosophy> **b :** suggestive or characteristic of a scholastic esp. in subtlety or aridity **:** PEDANTIC <turned out dull ~ reports> **2 :** of or relating to schools or scholars; *esp* **:** of or relating to high school or secondary school ***syn*** see PEDANTIC — **scho·las·ti·cal·ly** \-ti-k(ə-)lē\ *adv*

²scholastic *n* **1 a** *cap* **:** a Scholastic philosopher **b :** PEDANT, FORMALIST **2** [NL *scholasticus,* fr. L *scholasticus,* adj.] **:** a student in a scholasticate **3 :** one who adopts academic or traditional methods in art

scho·las·ti·cate \skə-ˈlas-tə-ˌkāt, -ti-kət\ *n* [NL *scholasticatus,* fr. *scholasticus* student in a scholasticate] **:** a college-level school of general study for those preparing for membership in a Roman Catholic religious order

scho·las·ti·cism \skə-ˈlas-tə-ˌsiz-əm\ *n* **1** *cap* **a :** a philosophical movement dominant in western Christian civilization from the 9th until the 17th century and combining religious dogma with the mystical and intuitional tradition of patristic philosophy esp. of St. Augustine and later with Aristotelianism **b :** NEO-SCHOLASTICISM **2 a :** close adherence to the traditional teachings or methods of a school or sect **b :** pedantic adherence to scholarly methods

scho·li·ast \ˈskō-lē-ˌast, -lē-əst\ *n* [MGk *scholiastēs,* fr. *scholiazein* to write scholia on, fr. Gk *scholion*] **:** a maker of scholia **:** COMMENTATOR, ANNOTATOR — **scho·li·as·tic** \ˌskō-lē-ˈas-tik\ *adj*

scho·li·um \ˈskō-lē-əm\ *n, pl* **-lia** \-lē-ə\ *or* **-li·ums** [NL, fr. Gk *scholion* comment, scholium, fr. dim. of *scholē* lecture] **1 :** a marginal annotation or comment (as on the text of a classic by an early grammarian) **2 :** a remark or observation subjoined but not essential to a demonstration or a train of reasoning

[1]**school** \'skül\ *n* [ME *scole,* fr OE *scōl,* fr. L *schola,* fr. Gk *scholē* leisure, discussion, lecture, school; akin to Gk *echein* to hold — more at SCHEME] **1 :** an organization that provides instruction: as **a :** an institution for the teaching of children **b :** COLLEGE, UNIVERSITY **c** (1) **:** a group of scholars and teachers pursuing knowledge together that with similar groups constituted a medieval university (2) **:** one of the four faculties of a medieval university (3) **:** an institution for specialized higher education often associated with a university <the ~ of engineering> **d :** an establishment offering specialized instruction <a ~ of beauty culture> <driving ~*s*> **2 a** (1) **:** the process of teaching or learning esp. at a school (2) **:** attendance at a school (3) **:** a session of a school **b :** a school building **c :** the students attending a school; *also* **:** its teachers and students **3 :** a source of knowledge <experience was his ~> **4 a :** persons who hold a common doctrine or follow the same teacher (as in philosophy, theology, or medicine) <the Aristotelian ~> **b :** a group of artists under a common influence **c :** persons of similar opinions or behavior <other ~*s* of thought> **5 :** the regulations governing military drill of individuals or units; *also* **:** the exercises carried out <the ~ of the soldier>

[2]**school** *vt* **1 :** to educate in an institution of learning **2 a :** to teach or drill in a specific knowledge or skill <well ~*ed* in languages> **b :** to discipline or habituate to something <~ oneself in patience> ***syn*** see TEACH

[3]**school** *n* [ME *scole,* fr MD *schole;* akin to OE *scolu* multitude, *scylian* to separate — more at SKILL] **:** a large number of fish or aquatic animals of one kind swimming together

[4]**school** *vi* **:** to swim or feed in a school <bluefish are ~*ing*>

school age *n* **:** the period of life during which a child is considered mentally and physically fit to attend school and is commonly required to do so by law

school·bag \'skül-,bag\ *n* **:** a usu. cloth bag for carrying schoolbooks and school supplies

school board *n* **:** a board in charge of local public schools

school·book \-,bu̇k\ *n* **:** a textbook for use in schoolwork

school·boy \-,bȯi\ *n* **:** a boy attending school

school bus *n* **:** a vehicle that is either publicly owned or privately owned and operated for compensation and that is used for transporting children to or from school or on activities connected with school

school·child \'skül-,chīld\ *n* **:** a child attending school

school district *n* **:** an area within a state often comprising several towns that has its own board and power of taxation and that serves as the unit for administration of a public-school system

school edition *n* **:** an edition of a book issued esp. for use in schools and usu. simplified, condensed, or emended esp. with glossarial or explanatory matter

-school·er \'skü-lər\ *comb form* **:** one who attends (such) a school <grade-*schooler*>

school·fel·low \'skül-,fel-(,)ō, -ə(-w)\ *n* **:** SCHOOLMATE

school·girl \-,gər(-ə)l\ *n* **:** a girl attending school

school·house \-,hau̇s\ *n* **:** a building used as a school and esp. as an elementary school

school·ing *n* **1 a :** instruction in school **b :** discipline derived from experience **2** *archaic* **:** chastisement for correction **:** REPROOF **3 :** the cost of instruction and maintenance at school **4 :** the training of a horse to service; *esp* **:** the teaching and exercising of horse and rider in the formal techniques of equitation

school–leav·er \'skül-,lē-vər\ *n, Brit* **:** a pupil who has recently left school often without completing his course of studies

school·man \'skül-mən, -,man\ *n* **1 a :** one skilled in academic disputation **b** *cap* **:** SCHOLASTIC 1a **2 :** a schoolteacher or school administrator

school·marm \-,mä(r)m\ *or* **school·ma'am** \-,mäm, -,mam\ *n* [*school* + *marm,* alter. of ma'am] **1 :** a female schoolteacher esp. in a rural or small-town school **2 :** a person who exhibits characteristics (as pedantry and priggishness) attributed to schoolteachers

school·mas·ter \-,mas-tər\ *n* **1 :** a male schoolteacher **2 :** one that disciplines or directs **3 :** a reddish brown edible snapper (*Lutjanus apodus*) of the tropical Atlantic and the Gulf of Mexico

school·mate \-,māt\ *n* **:** a companion at school

school·mis·tress \-,mis-trəs\ *n* **:** a female schoolteacher

school·room \-,rüm, -,ru̇m\ *n* **:** CLASSROOM

school·teach·er \-,tē-chər\ *n* **:** a person who teaches in a school

school·time \-,tīm\ *n* **1 :** the time for beginning a session of school or during which school is held **2 :** the period of life spent in school or in study

school·work \-,wərk\ *n* **:** lessons done in classes at school or assigned to be done at home

schoo·ner \'skü-nər\ *n* [origin unknown] **1 :** a fore-and-aft rigged ship having two masts with a smaller sail on the foremast and with the mainmast stepped nearly amidships; *broadly* **:** any of various larger fore-and-aft rigged ships with three to seven masts **2 :** a large tall drinking glass (as for beer or ale) **3 :** PRAIRIE SCHOONER

schooner rig *n* **:** FORE-AND-AFT RIG — **schoo·ner–rigged** \,skü-nə(r)-'rigd\ *adj*

schorl \'shȯr(ə)l\ *n* [G *schörl*] **:** TOURMALINE; *esp* **:** tourmaline of the black variety — **schorl·aceous** \shȯr-'lā-shəs\ *adj*

schot·tische \'shät-ish, shä-'tēsh\ *n* [G, fr. *schottisch* Scottish, fr. *Schotte* Scotchman; akin to OE *Scottas* Scotchmen] **1 :** a round dance in duple measure resembling a slow polka **2 :** music for the schottische

schtick *var of* SHTICK

[1]**schuss** \'shu̇s, 'shüs\ *n* [G, lit., shot, fr. OHG *scuz* — more at SHOT] **1 :** a straight high-speed run on skis **2 :** a straightaway downhill skiing course

[2]**schuss** *vt* **:** to make a schuss over <~ a slope> ~ *vi* **:** to ski directly down a slope

schuss·boom·er \-,bü-mər\ *n* [*schuss* + [3]*boom* + *-er*] **:** one who skis usu. straight downhill at high speed

schwa \'shwä\ *n* [G, fr. Heb *shĕwā*] **1 :** an unstressed mid-central vowel that is the usual sound of the first and last vowels of the English word *America* **2 :** the symbol ə used for the schwa sound and less widely for a similarly articulated stressed vowel (as in *cut*)

Schwann cell \'shwän-\ *n* [Theodor *Schwann* †1882 G naturalist] **:** a cell of the neurilemma of a nerve fiber

schwar·me·rei \,shfer-mə-'rī\ *n* [G *schwärmerei,* fr. *schwärmen* to be enthusiastic, lit., to swarm] **:** excessive or unwholesome sentiment

sci *abbr* science; scientific

sci·ae·nid \sī-'ē-nəd\ *n* [deriv. of Gk *skiaina,* a fish] **:** any of a family (Sciaenidae) of carnivorous mostly marine percoid fishes comprising the croakers and including numerous food fishes — **sciaenid** *adj* — **sci·ae·noid** \-,nȯid\ *adj or n*

sci·at·ic \sī-'at-ik\ *adj* [MF *sciatique,* fr. LL *sciaticus,* alter. of L *ischiadicus* of sciatica, fr. Gk *ischiadikos,* fr. *ischiad-, ischias* sciatica, fr. *ischion* ischium] **1 :** of, relating to, or situated near the hip **2 :** of, relating to, or caused by sciatica <~ pains>

sci·at·i·ca \sī-'at-i-kə\ *n* [ME, fr. ML, fr. LL, fem. of *sciaticus*] **:** pain along the course of a sciatic nerve esp. in the back of the thigh; *broadly* **:** pain in the lower back, buttocks, hips, or adjacent parts

sciatic nerve *n* **:** either of the pair of largest nerves in the body that arise one on each side from the nerve plexus supplying the posterior limb and pelvic region and that pass out of the pelvis and down the back of the thigh

sci·ence \'sī-ən(t)s\ *n* [ME, fr. MF, fr. L *scientia,* fr. *scient-, sciens* having knowledge, fr. prp. of *scire* to know; akin to L *scindere* to cut — more at SHED] **1 a :** possession of knowledge as distinguished from ignorance or misunderstanding **b :** knowledge attained through study or practice **2 a :** a department of systematized knowledge as an object of study <the ~ of theology> **b :** something (as a sport or technique) that may be studied or learned like systematized knowledge **c :** one of the natural sciences **3 a :** knowledge covering general truths or the operation of general laws esp. as obtained and tested through scientific method **b :** such knowledge concerned with the physical world and its phenomena **:** NATURAL SCIENCE **4 :** a system or method based or purporting to be based on scientific principles **5** *cap* **:** CHRISTIAN SCIENCE

science fiction *n* **:** fiction dealing principally with the impact of actual or imagined science upon society or individuals; *broadly* **:** literary fantasy including a scientific factor as an essential orienting component

sci·en·tial \sī-'en-chəl\ *adj* **1 :** relating to or producing knowledge or science **2 :** having efficient knowledge **:** CAPABLE

sci·en·tif·ic \,sī-ən-'tif-ik\ *adj* [ML *scientificus* producing knowledge, fr. L *scient-, sciens* + *-i-* + *-ficus* -fic] **:** of, relating to, or exhibiting the methods or principles of science — **sci·en·tif·i·cal·ly** \-i-k(ə-)lē\ *adv*

scientific method *n* **:** principles and procedures for the systematic pursuit of knowledge involving the recognition and formulation of a problem, the collection of data through observation and experiment, and the formulation and testing of hypotheses

scientific notation *n* **:** a widely used system in which numbers are expressed as products consisting of a number between 1 and 10 multiplied by an appropriate power of 10

sci·en·tism \'sī-ən-,tiz-əm\ *n* **1 :** methods and attitudes typical of or attributed to the natural scientist **2 :** an exaggerated trust in the efficacy of the methods of natural science to explain social or psychological phenomena, to solve pressing human problems, or to provide a comprehensive unified picture of the meaning of the cosmos

sci·en·tist \'sī-ənt-əst\ *n* [L *scientia*] **1 :** one learned in science and esp. natural science **:** a scientific investigator **2** *cap* **:** CHRISTIAN SCIENTIST

sci·en·tol·o·gy \,sī-ən-'täl-ə-jē\ *n* [L *scientia* science + E *-o-* + *-logy*] **:** a religious movement begun in 1952 by L. Ron Hubbard which teaches immortality and reincarnation and claims a sure psychotherapeutic method for freeing the individual from personal problems, increasing human abilities (as intelligence), and speeding recovery from sickness, injury, and mental disorder — **sci·en·tol·o·gist** \-jəst\ *n*

sci–fi \'sī-'fī\ *adj* [*science fiction*] **:** of, relating to, or being science fiction <a ~ story>

scil *abbr* scilicet

sci·li·cet \'skē-li-,ket, 'sī-lə-,set\ *adv* [ME, fr. L, surely, to wit, fr. *scire* to know + *licet* it is permitted, fr. *licēre* to be permitted — more at LICENSE] **:** to wit **:** NAMELY

scil·la \'s(k)il-ə\ *n* [NL, genus name, fr. L, squill — more at SQUILL] **:** any of a genus (*Scilla*) of Old World bulbous herbs of the lily family with narrow basal leaves and pink, blue, or white racemose flowers

scim·i·tar \'sim-ət-ər, -ə-,tär\ *n* [It *scimitarra*] **:** a saber made of a curved blade with the edge on the convex side and used chiefly by Arabs and Turks

scin·tig·ra·phy \sin-'tig-rə-fē\ *n* [*scintillation* + *-graphy;* fr. the scintillation counter used to record radiation on the picture] **:** a diagnostic technique in which a two dimensional picture of a bodily radiation source is obtained by the use of radioisotopes — **scin·ti·graph·ic** \,sint-ə-'graf-ik\ *adj*

scin·til·la \sin-'til-ə\ *n* [L] **:** SPARK, TRACE

scin·til·lant \'sint-ᵊl-ənt\ *adj* **:** that scintillates **:** SPARKLING — **scin·til·lant·ly** *adv*

scimitar

scin·til·late \'sint-ᵊl-,āt\ *vb* **-lat·ed; -lat·ing** [L *scintillatus,* pp. of *scintillare* to sparkle, fr. *scintilla* spark] *vi* **1 :** to emit sparks **:** SPARK **2 :** to emit quick flashes as if throwing off sparks; *also* **:** SPARKLE, TWINKLE ~ *vt* **:** to throw off as a spark or as sparkling flashes <~ witticisms> — **scin·til·la·tor** \-,āt-ər\ *n*

scin·til·la·tion \,sint-ᵊl-'ā-shən\ *n* **1 :** an act or instance of scintillating; *esp* **:** rapid changes in the brightness of a celestial body **2 a :** a spark or flash emitted in scintillating **b :** a flash of light produced in a phosphor by an ionizing event **3 :** a brilliant outburst (as of wit) **4 :** a flash of the eye

scintillation counter *n* : a device for detecting and registering individual scintillations (as in radioactive emission)
scin·til·lom·e·ter \ˌsint-ᵊl-ˈäm-ət-ər\ *n* [L *scintilla* + ISV *-o-* + *-meter*] : SCINTILLATION COUNTER
sci·o·lism \ˈsī-ə-ˌliz-əm\ *n* [LL *sciolus* smatterer, fr. dim. of L *scius* knowing, fr. *scire* to know — more at SCIENCE] : a superficial show of learning — **sci·o·list** \-ləst\ *n* — **sci·o·lis·tic** \ˌsī-ə-ˈlis-tik\ *adj*
scio·man·cy \ˈsī-ə-ˌman(t)-sē, ˈskē-ə-\ *n* [LL *sciomantia*, fr. L Gk *skiomanteia*, fr. Gk *skia* shadow, shade + *-manteia* -mancy — more at SHINE] : divination by consulting the ghosts of the dead — **scio·man·tic** \ˌsī-ə-ˈmant-ik, ˌskē-ə-\ *adj*
sci·on \ˈsī-ən\ *n* [ME, fr. MF *cion*, of Gmc origin; akin to OHG *chīnan* to sprout, split open, OE *cīnan* to gape] **1 :** a detached living portion of a plant joined to a stock in grafting and usu. supplying solely aerial parts to a graft **2 :** DESCENDANT, CHILD
sci·re fa·cias \ˌsī-rē-ˈfā-sh(ē-)əs\ *n* [ME, fr. ML, you should cause to know] **1 :** a judicial writ founded upon some matter of record and requiring the party proceeded against to show cause why the record should not be enforced, annulled, or vacated **2 :** a legal proceeding instituted by a scire facias
sci·roc·co \shi-ˈräk-(ˌ)ō, sə-\ *var of* SIROCCO
scir·rhous \ˈs(k)ir-əs\ *adj* **1 :** of, relating to, or being a scirrhus **2 :** hard or indurated with or as if with fibrous tissue
scir·rhus \ˈs(k)ir-əs\ *n, pl* **scir·rhi** \ˈs(k)i(ə)r-ˌī, ˈski(ə)r-ˌē\ [NL, fr. Gk *skiros*, *skirrhos*, fr. *skiros* hard] : a hard slow-growing malignant tumor having a preponderance of fibrous tissue
scis·sile \ˈsis-əl, -ˌīl\ *adj* [F, fr. L *scissilis*, fr. *scissus*, pp. of *scindere* to split — more at SHED] : capable of being cut smoothly or split easily <a ~ peptide bond>
scis·sion \ˈsizh-ən\ *n* [F, fr. LL *scission-*, *scissio*, fr. L *scissus*, pp.] **1 :** a division or split in a group or union : SCHISM **2 :** an action or process of cutting, dividing, or splitting : the state of being cut, divided, or split
[1]**scis·sor** \ˈsiz-ər\ *n* [ME *sisoure*, fr. MF *cisoire*, fr. LL *cisorium* cutting instrument, irreg. fr. L *caesus*, pp. of *caedere* to cut — more at CONCISE] : SCISSORS
[2]**scissor** *vt* **scis·sored; scis·sor·ing** \-(ə-)riŋ\ : to cut, cut up, or cut off with scissors or shears
scis·sors \ˈsiz-ərz\ *n pl but sing or pl in constr* **1 :** a cutting instrument having two blades whose cutting edges slide past each other **2 a :** a gymnastic feat in which the leg movements suggest the opening and closing of scissors **b :** SCISSORS HOLD
scissors hold *n* : a wrestling hold in which the legs are locked around the head or body of an opponent
scissors kick *n* : a swimming kick used in trudgen strokes and sidestrokes in which the legs move like scissors
scis·sor·tail \ˈsiz-ər-ˌtāl\ *n* : a flycatcher (*Muscivora forficata*) of the southern U.S. and Mexico with a deeply forked tail
[1]**sclaff** \ˈsklaf\ *n* [prob. imit.] : a golf stroke in which the club head strikes the ground behind the ball before touching the ball
[2]**sclaff** *vi* : to make a sclaff in golf ~ *vt* **1 :** to cause (a golf club) to make a sclaff **2 :** to strike (the ground) in making a sclaff — **sclaff·er** *n*
scler- *or* **sclero-** *comb form* [NL, fr. Gk *sklēr-*, *sklēro-*, fr. *sklēros* — more at SKELETON] **1 a :** hard <*scler*ite> <*sclero*derma> **b :** hardness <*sclero*meter> **2 :** sclera <*scler*itis>
sclera \ˈskler-ə\ *n* [NL, fr. Gk *sklēros* hard] : the dense fibrous opaque white outer coat enclosing the eyeball except the part covered by the cornea — see EYE illustration — **scler·al** \-əl\ *adj*
scler·e·id \ˈskler-ē-əd\ *n* [*scler*enchyma + *-id*] : a sclerenchymatous cell of a higher plant that is nearly isodiametric
scle·ren·chy·ma \sklə-ˈreŋ-kə-mə\ *n* [NL] : a protective or supporting tissue in higher plants composed of cells with walls thickened and lignified and often mineralized — **scler·en·chy·ma·tous** \ˌskler-ən-ˈkim-ət-əs, -ˈkī-mət-\ *adj*
scler·ite \ˈskle(ə)r-ˌīt\ *n* [ISV] : a hard chitinous or calcareous plate, piece, or spicule (as of the arthropod integument)
sclero·der·ma \ˌskler-ə-ˈdər-mə\ *n* [NL] : a disease of the skin characterized by thickening and hardening of the subcutaneous tissues
sclero·der·ma·tous \-mət-əs\ *adj* : having a hard external covering (as of bony plates or horny scales)
scle·rom·e·ter \sklə-ˈräm-ət-ər\ *n* [ISV] : an instrument for determining the relative hardnesses of materials
sclero·pro·tein \ˌskler-ō-ˈprō-ˌtēn, -ˈprōt-ē-ən\ *n* [ISV] : any of various fibrous proteins esp. from connective and skeletal tissues
scle·rose \sklə-ˈrōz, -ˈrōs\ *vb* [back-formation fr. *sclerosis*] *vt* : to cause sclerosis in : INDURATE ~ *vi* : to undergo sclerosis
scle·ro·sis \sklə-ˈrō-səs\ *n* [ME *sclirosis*, fr. ML, fr. Gk *sklērōsis* hardening, fr. *sklēroun* to harden, fr. *sklēros*] **1 :** pathological hardening of tissue esp. from overgrowth of fibrous tissue or increase in interstitial tissue; *also* : a disease characterized by sclerosis **2 :** hardening of plant cell walls usu. by lignification
[1]**scle·rot·ic** \sklə-ˈrät-ik\ *adj* **1 :** being or relating to the sclera **2 :** of, relating to, or affected with sclerosis
[2]**sclerotic** *n* [ML *sclerotica*, fr. (assumed) Gk *sklērōtos*, verbal of Gk *sklēroun* to harden] : SCLERA
scler·o·tin \ˈskler-ə-tən, sklə-ˈrōt-ᵊn\ *n* [(assumed) Gk *sklērōtos* + ISV *-in*] : an insoluble tanned protein permeating and stiffening the chitin of the cuticle of arthropods
scle·ro·tium \sklə-ˈrō-sh(ē-)əm\ *n, pl* **-tia** \-sh(ē-)ə\ [NL, fr. (assumed) Gk *sklērōtos*, verbal of Gk *sklēroun* to harden] : a compact mass of hardened mycelium stored with reserve food material that in some higher fungi becomes detached and remains dormant until a favorable opportunity for growth occurs — **scle·ro·tial** \-ˈrō-shəl\ *adj*
scler·o·ti·za·tion \ˌskler-ət-ə-ˈzā-shən\ *n* : the quality or state of being sclerotized
scler·o·tized \ˈskler-ə-ˌtīzd\ *adj* [(assumed) Gk *sklērōtos* + E *-ize* + *-ed*] : hardened by substances other than chitin — used chiefly of the cuticle of an insect
[1]**scoff** \ˈskäf, ˈskȯf\ *n* [ME *scof*, prob. of Scand origin; akin to obs. Dan *skof* jest; akin to OFris *skof* mockery] **1 :** an expression of scorn, derision, or contempt : GIBE **2 :** an object of scorn, mockery, or derision
[2]**scoff** *vi* : to show contempt by derisive acts or language : MOCK ~ *vt* : to treat or address with derision : mock at — **scoff·er** *n*
syn SCOFF, JEER, GIBE, FLEER, SNEER, FLOUT *shared meaning element* : to show contempt in derision or mockery
scoff·law \-ˌlȯ\ *n* : a contemptuous law violator
[1]**scold** \ˈskōld\ *n* [ME *scald*, *scold*, prob. of Scand origin; akin to ON *skāld* poet, skald, Icel *skālda* to make scurrilous verse] **1 :** one addicted to abusive ribald speech **2 :** one who scolds habitually or persistently **3 :** scolding remarks
[2]**scold** *vi* **1** *obs* : to quarrel noisily : BRAWL **2 :** to find fault noisily and wordily ~ *vt* : to censure usu. severely or angrily : rebuke or reprove sharply — **scold·er** *n*
syn SCOLD, UPBRAID, BERATE, RAIL, REVILE, VITUPERATE *shared meaning element* : to reproach angrily and abusively
scold·ing *n* **1 :** the action of one who scolds **2 :** a harsh or severe reproof
sco·le·cite \ˈskäl-ə-ˌsīt, ˈskō-lə-\ *n* [G *skolezit*, fr. Gk *skōlēk-*, *skōlēx* worm; fr. the motion of some forms when heated] : a zeolite mineral $CaAl_2Si_3O_{10}.3H_2O$ that is a hydrous calcium aluminum silicate and occurs in radiating groups of crystals, in fibrous masses, and in nodules
sco·lex \ˈskō-ˌleks\ *n, pl* **sco·li·ces** \-lə-ˌsēz\ [NL *scolic-*, *scolex*, fr. Gk *skōlēk-*, *skōlēx* worm; akin to Gk *skelos* leg — more at CYLINDER] : the head of a tapeworm either in the larva or adult stage
sco·li·o·sis \ˌskō-lē-ˈō-səs\ *n, pl* **-o·ses** \-ˌsēz\ [NL, fr. Gk *skoliōsis* crookedness of a bodily part, fr. *skolios* crooked — more at CYLINDER] : a lateral curvature of the spine — **sco·li·ot·ic** \-ˈät-ik\ *adj*
scol·lop \ˈskäl-əp\ *var of* SCALLOP
scol·o·pen·dra \ˌskäl-ə-ˈpen-drə\ *n* [NL, genus of centipedes, fr. L, a kind of millipede, fr. Gk *skolopendra*] : CENTIPEDE
scom·broid \ˈskäm-ˌbrȯid\ *n* [deriv. of Gk *skombros* mackerel] : any of a suborder (Scombroidea) of marine spiny-finned fishes (as mackerels, tunas, albacores, bonitos, and swordfishes) of great economic importance as food fishes — **scombroid** *adj*
[1]**sconce** \ˈskän(t)s\ *n* [ME, fr. MF *esconse* screened lantern, fr. OF, fr. fem. of *escons*, pp. of *escondre* to hide, fr. L *abscondere* — more at ABSCOND] : a bracket candlestick or group of candlesticks; *also* : an electric light fixture patterned on a candle sconce
[2]**sconce** *n* [D *schans*, fr. G *schanze*] : a detached defensive work
scone \ˈskōn, ˈskän\ *n* [perh. fr. D *schoonbrood* fine white bread, fr. *schoon* pure, clean + *brood* bread] : a quick bread of oatmeal or barley flour rolled round, cut into quarters, and baked on a griddle
[1]**scoop** \ˈsküp\ *n* [ME *scope*, fr. MD *schope*; akin to OHG *skepfen* to shape — more at SHAPE] **1 a :** a large ladle **b :** a deep shovel or similar implement for digging, dipping, or shoveling **c :** a hemispherical utensil for dipping soft food **d :** a small spoon-shaped utensil or instrument for cutting or gouging **2 :** the action of scooping **3 a :** a hollow place : CAVITY **b :** a part forming or surrounding an opening for channeling a fluid (as air) into a desired path **4 a :** information esp. of immediate interest **b :** BEAT 7b — **scoop·ful** \-ˌfu̇l\ *n*
[2]**scoop** *vt* **1 :** to take out or up with or as if with a scoop : DIP **2 :** to empty by lading **3 :** to make hollow : dig out **4 :** BEAT 5a(2) — **scoop·er** *n*
scoot \ˈsküt\ *vi* [prob. of Scand origin; akin to ON *skjōta* to shoot — more at SHOOT] : to go suddenly and swiftly — **scoot** *n*
scoot·er \ˈsküt-ər\ *n* **1 :** a child's foot-operated vehicle consisting of a narrow board mounted between two wheels tandem with an upright steering handle attached to the front wheel **2 :** MOTOR SCOOTER
scop \ˈskäp, ˈskōp, ˈshōp\ *n* [OE; akin to OHG *schof* poet] : an Old English bard or poet
[1]**scope** \ˈskōp\ *n* [It *scopo* purpose, goal, fr. Gk *skopos*, fr. *skeptesthai* to watch, look at — more at SPY] **1 :** space or opportunity for unhampered motion, activity, or thought **2 :** INTENTION, OBJECT **3 :** extent of treatment, activity, or influence **4 :** range of operation
[2]**scope** *n* [*-scope*] **1 :** any of various instruments for viewing: as **a :** MICROSCOPE **b :** TELESCOPE **c :** OSCILLOSCOPE **d :** RADARSCOPE **2 :** HOROSCOPE
-scope \ˌskōp\ *n comb form* [NL *-scopium*, fr. Gk *-skopion*, fr. *skeptesthai*] : means (as an instrument) for viewing or observing <micro*scope*>
sco·pol·amine \skō-ˈpäl-ə-ˌmēn, -mən\ *n* [G *scopolamin*, fr. NL *Scopolia*, genus of plants + G *amin* amine] : a poisonous alkaloid $C_{17}H_{21}NO_4$ found in the roots of various plants (esp. genus *Scopolia*) of the nightshade family and used esp. as a truth serum or usu. with morphine as a sedative in surgery and obstetrics
scop·u·la \ˈskäp-yə-lə\ *n* [NL, fr. LL, dim. of L *scopa* broom — more at SCULLION] : a bushy tuft of hairs — **scop·u·late** \-ˌlāt\ *adj*
-s·co·py \s-kə-pē\ *n comb form* [Gk *-skopia*, fr. *skeptesthai*] : viewing : observation <radio*scopy*>
scor·bu·tic \skȯr-ˈbyüt-ik\ *adj* [NL *scorbuticus*, fr. *scorbutus* scurvy, prob. of Gmc origin; akin to OE *scurf*] : of, relating to, or resembling scurvy; *also* : diseased with scurvy — **scor·bu·ti·cal·ly** \-i-k(ə-)lē\ *adv*
[1]**scorch** \ˈskȯ(ə)rch\ *vb* [ME *scorcnen*, *scorchen*, prob. of Scand origin; akin to ON *skorpna* to shrivel up — more at SHRIMP] *vt* **1 :** to burn a surface so as to change its color and texture **2 a :** to parch with or as if with intense heat **b :** to afflict painfully with or as if with censure or sarcasm **3 :** to devastate completely

esp. before abandoning — used in the phrase *scorched earth* esp. of property of possible use to an enemy ~ *vi* **1 :** to become scorched **2 :** to travel at great and usu. excessive speed — **scorch·ing·ly** \'skȯr-chiŋ-lē\ *adv*

[2]**scorch** *n* **1 :** a result of scorching **2 :** a browning of plant tissues usu. from disease or heat

[3]**scorch** *vt* [alter. of [2]*score*] *dial Brit* **:** CUT, SLASH

scorched *adj* **:** parched or discolored by scorching

scorch·er \'skȯr-chər\ *n* **:** one that scorches; *esp* **:** a very hot day

[1]**score** \'skō(ə)r, 'skȯ(ə)r\ *n, pl* **scores** [ME *scor,* fr. ON *skor* notch, tally, twenty; akin to OE *scieran* to cut — more at SHEAR] **1** *or pl* **score a :** TWENTY **b :** a group of 20 things — often used in combination with a cardinal number <five*score*> **c** *pl* **:** a group of an indefinite large number **2 a :** a line (as a scratch or incision) made with or as if with a sharp instrument **b** (1) **:** a mark used as a starting point or goal (2) **:** a mark used for keeping account **3 a :** an account or reckoning kept by making marks on a tally **b :** ACCOUNT **c :** amount due **:** INDEBTEDNESS **4 :** an obligation or injury kept in mind for requital **:** GRUDGE **5 a :** REASON, GROUND **b :** SUBJECT, TOPIC **6 a :** the copy of a musical composition in written or printed notation **b :** a musical composition; *specif* **:** the music for a movie or theatrical production **c :** a complete description of a dance composition in choreographic notation **7 a :** a number that expresses accomplishment (as in a game or test) or excellence (as in quality) either absolutely in points gained or by comparison to a standard **b :** an act (as a goal, run, or touchdown) in any of various games or contests that gains points **c :** success esp. in obtaining marijuana or narcotics **8 :** the stark inescapable facts of a situation <knows the ~>

[2]**score** *vb* **scored; scor·ing** *vt* **1 a :** to keep a record or account of by or as if by notches on a tally **:** RECORD **b :** to enter in a record **c :** to mark with significant lines or notches (as in keeping account) **2 :** to mark with lines, grooves, scratches, or notches **3 :** BERATE, SCOLD **4 a** (1) **:** to make (a score) in a game or contest <*scored* a touchdown> <*scored* three points> (2) **:** to enable (a base runner) to make a score (3) **:** to have as a value in a game or contest **:** COUNT <a touchdown ~*s* six points> **b :** ACHIEVE, WIN **5 :** to determine the merit of **:** GRADE **6 a :** to write or arrange (music) for a specific performance medium **b :** to make an orchestration of **c :** to compose a score for (a movie) ~ *vi* **1 :** to keep score in a game or contest **2 :** to make a score in a game or contest **3 a :** to gain or have the advantage **b** (1) **:** to be successful (2) **:** to obtain marijuana or narcotics **c :** [3]RATE — **scor·er** *n*

score·board \'skō(ə)r-ˌbō(ə)rd, 'skȯ(ə)r-ˌbȯ(ə)rd\ *n* **:** a large board for displaying the score of a game or match and sometimes other information

score·card \-ˌkärd\ *n* **:** a card for recording the score of a game

score·keep·er \-ˌkē-pər\ *n* **:** an official who records the score during the progress of a game or contest

score·less \-ləs\ *adj* **:** having no score; *specif* **:** involving no points

sco·ria \'skōr-ē-ə, 'skȯr-\ *n, pl* **-ri·ae** \-ē-ˌē, -ē-ˌī\ [ME, fr. L, fr. Gk *skōria,* fr. *skōr* excrement — more at SCAT-] **1 :** the refuse from melting of metals or reduction of ores **:** SLAG **2 :** rough vesicular cindery lava — **sco·ri·a·ceous** \ˌskōr-ē-'ā-shəs, ˌskȯr-\ *adj*

[1]**scorn** \'skȯ(ə)rn\ *n* [ME, fr. OF *escarn,* of Gmc origin; akin to OHG *scern* jest; akin to Gk *skairein* to gambol — more at CARDINAL] **1 :** an emotion involving both anger and disgust **:** vigorous contempt **:** DISDAIN **2 :** an expression of extreme contempt **3 :** an object of extreme disdain, contempt, or derision

[2]**scorn** *vt* **1 :** to reject with vigorous or angry contempt **:** CONTEMN <~*ed* all warnings of disaster> **2 :** to refuse because of scorn **:** DISDAIN <~*ed* to reply to the charge> ~ *vi* **:** to show disdain or derision **:** SCOFF ***syn*** see DESPISE — **scorn·er** *n*

scorn·ful \'skȯrn-fəl\ *adj* **:** full of scorn **:** CONTEMPTUOUS — **scorn·ful·ly** \-fə-lē\ *adv* — **scorn·ful·ness** *n*

scor·pae·nid \skȯr-'pē-nəd\ *n* [deriv. of Gk *skorpaina,* a kind of fish] **:** any of a family (Scorpaenidae) of marine spiny-finned fishes comprising the scorpion fishes — **scorpaenid** *adj*

Scor·pio \'skȯr-pē-ˌō\ *n* [L (gen. *Scorpionis*), fr. Gk *Skorpios,* lit., scorpion] **1 :** SCORPIUS **2 a :** the 8th sign of the zodiac in astrology — see ZODIAC table **b :** one born under this sign

scor·pi·oid \-pē-ˌȯid\ *adj* [Gk *skorpioeidēs* resembling a scorpion, fr. *skorpios*] **:** curved at the end like a scorpion's tail **:** CIRCINATE <a ~ inflorescence>

scor·pi·on \'skȯr-pē-ən\ *n* [ME, fr. OF, fr. L *scorpion-, scorpio,* fr. Gk *skorpios;* akin to OE *scieran* to cut — more at SHEAR] **1 a :** any of an order (Scorpionida) of arachnids that have an elongated body and a narrow segmented tail bearing a venomous sting at the tip **b** *cap* **:** SCORPIO **2 :** a scourge prob. studded with metal **3 :** something that incites to action like the sting of an insect

scorpion

scorpion fish *n* **:** a scorpaenid fish; *esp* **:** one with a venomous spine on the dorsal fin

scorpion fly *n* **:** any of a family (Panorpidae) of mecopterous insects that have cylindrical bodies and the male genitalia enlarged into a swollen bulb; *broadly* **:** a mecopterous insect

Scor·pi·us \'skȯr-pē-əs\ *n* [L (gen. *Scorpii*), fr. Gk *Skorpios,* lit., scorpion] **:** a southern constellation partly in the Milky Way and next to Libra

scot \'skät\ *n* [ME, fr. ON *skot* shot, contribution — more at SHOT] **:** money assessed or paid

[1]**Scot** \'skät\ *n* [ME *Scottes* Scotchmen, fr. OE *Scottas* Irishmen, Scotchmen, fr. LL *Scotus* Irishman] **1 :** one of a Gaelic people of northern Ireland settling in Scotland about A.D. 500 **2 a :** a native or inhabitant of Scotland **b :** a person of Scotch descent

[2]**Scot** *abbr* Scotland; Scottish

scot and lot *n* **1 :** a parish assessment formerly laid on subjects in Great Britain according to their ability to pay **2 :** obligations of all kinds taken as a whole

[1]**scotch** \'skäch\ *vt* [ME *scocchen* to gash] **1 :** to injure so as to make temporarily harmless **2 a :** to stamp out **:** CRUSH **b :** to end decisively by demonstrating the falsity of

[2]**scotch** *n* **:** a slight cut **:** SCORE

[3]**scotch** *n* [origin unknown] **:** a chock to prevent rolling or slipping

[4]**scotch** *vt* **1 :** to block with a chock **2 :** HINDER, THWART

[1]**Scotch** \'skäch\ *adj* [contr. of *Scottish*] **1 :** of, relating to, or characteristic of Scotland, the Scotch, or Scots **2 :** inclined to frugality

syn SCOTCH, SCOTTISH, SCOTS *shared meaning element* **:** constituting, belonging to, or deriving from Scotland or its people. SCOTCH is more widely used outside Scotland and is likely to occur in casual context or in the spoken language <we referred to ourselves as *Scotch* and not Scots. When, years later, I learned that the usage was different it seemed to me rather an affectation —J. K. Galbraith> SCOTTISH has a more literary, less casual flavor and use <the *Scottish* Universities> <when Mary assumed the *Scottish* crown> SCOTS, otherwise interchangeable with *Scottish,* may be preferred in reference to law and in historical reference to money <a pound *Scots*> In Scotland itself *Scottish* and *Scots* are often preferred to *Scotch* <a delegation of *Scottish* editors —*Scotsman*> <the *Scots* community in New York —*Scotsman*> but *Scotch* is also used <I'm pure *Scotch* . . . the correct term is *Scottish,* but that sounds so pompous —Margaret, Duchess of Argyll>

[2]**Scotch** *n* **1 :** SCOTS **2** *pl in constr* **:** the people of Scotland **3** *often cap* **:** SCOTCH WHISKY

[3]**Scotch** *trademark* —used for any of numerous adhesive tapes

Scotch broom *n* **:** a deciduous broom (*Cytisus scoparius*) of western Europe that is widely cultivated for its bright yellow or partly red flowers and that has become a pest in some areas (as California)

Scotch broth *n* **:** a soup made from beef or mutton and vegetables and thickened with barley

Scotch–Irish *adj* **1 :** of, relating to, or characteristic of the population of northern Ireland that is descended from Scotch settlers **2 :** of, relating to, or characteristic of the people of Scotch descent emigrating from northern Ireland to the U.S. before 1846 or their descendants

Scotch·man \'skäch-mən\ *n* **:** a man of Scotch descent **:** a male Scot

Scotch pine *n* **:** a pine (*Pinus sylvestris*) of northern Europe and Asia with spreading or pendulous branches, short rigid twisted needles, and hard yellow wood that provides valuable timber

Scotch terrier *n* **:** SCOTTISH TERRIER

Scotch verdict *n* **1 :** a verdict of not proven that is allowed by Scottish criminal law in some cases instead of a verdict of not guilty **2 :** an inconclusive decision or pronouncement

Scotch whisky *n* **:** whiskey distilled in Scotland esp. from malted barley

Scotch·wom·an \'skäch-ˌwu̇m-ən\ *n* **:** a woman who is Scotch

Scotch woodcock *n* **:** buttered toast spread with anchovy paste and scrambled egg

sco·ter \'skōt-ər\ *n, pl* **scoters** *or* **scoter** [origin unknown] **:** any of several sea ducks (genera *Oidemia* and *Melanitta*) of northern coasts of Europe and No. America and some larger inland waters

scot–free \'skät-'frē\ *adj* [*scot* + *free*] **:** completely free from obligation, harm, or penalty

sco·tia \'skō-sh(ē-)ə, 'skōt-ē-ə\ *n* [L, fr. Gk *skotia,* fr. fem. of *skotios* dark, shadowy, fr. *skotos* darkness — more at SHADE] **:** a concave molding used esp. in classical architecture in the bases of columns — see BASE illustration, MOLDING illustration

Scot·ic \'skät-ik\ *adj* **:** of or relating to the ancient Scots

Sco·tism \'skōt-ˌiz-əm\ *n* **:** the doctrines of Duns Scotus (as voluntarism, logical realism, and the plurality of substantial forms) — **Sco·tist** \'skōt-əst\ *n*

Scot·land Yard \ˌskät-lən(d)-'yärd\ *n* [*Scotland Yard,* street in London formerly the headquarters of the metropolitan police] **:** the detective department of the metropolitan police force of London

sco·to·ma \skə-'tō-mə\ *n, pl* **-mas** *or* **-ma·ta** \-mət-ə\ [NL *scotomat-, scotoma,* fr. ML, dimness of vision, fr. Gk *skotōmat-, skotōma,* fr. *skotoun* to darken, fr. *skotos*] **:** a blind or dark spot in the visual field — **sco·to·ma·tous** \-mət-əs\ *adj*

sco·to·pic \skə-'tō-pik, -'täp-ik\ *adj* [NL *scotopia* scotopic vision, fr. Gk *skotos* darkness + NL *-opia*] **:** relating to or being vision in dim light with dark-adapted eyes that is mediated by the retinal rods

[1]**Scots** \'skäts\ *adj* [ME *Scottis,* alter. of *Scottish*] **:** SCOTCH 1 — used esp. of the people and language and in legal context ***syn*** see SCOTCH

[2]**Scots** *n* **:** the English language of Scotland

Scots·man \'skät-smən\ *n* **:** SCOTCHMAN

Scots pine *n* **:** SCOTCH PINE

Scot·ti·cism \'skät-ə-ˌsiz-əm\ *n* [LL *scotticus* of the ancient Scots, fr. *Scotus* Scot] **:** a characteristic feature of Scottish English esp. as contrasted with standard English

scot·tie \'skät-ē\ *n* **1** *cap* **:** SCOTCHMAN **2 :** SCOTTISH TERRIER

[1]**Scot·tish** \'skät-ish\ *adj* [ME, fr. *Scottes* Scotchmen] **:** SCOTCH 1 — often preferred by natives of Scotland ***syn*** see SCOTCH

[2]**Scottish** *n* **:** SCOTS

Scottish deerhound *n* **:** any of a breed of large tall dogs that have the general form of a greyhound but are larger and taller with a rough usu. blue-gray coat

Scottish Gaelic *n* **:** the Gaelic language of Scotland

Scottish rite *n* **1 :** a ceremonial observed by one of the Masonic systems **2 :** a system or organization that observes the Scottish rite and confers 33 degrees

Scottish terrier *n* **:** any of an old Scottish breed of terrier that has short legs, a large head with small erect ears and a powerful muzzle, a broad deep chest, and a very hard coat of wiry hair

scoun·drel \'skau̇n-drəl\ *n* [origin unknown] **:** a mean worthless fellow **:** VILLAIN — **scoundrel** *adj* — **scoun·drel·ly** \-drə-lē\ *adj*

[1]**scour** \'skau̇(ə)r\ *vb* [ME *scuren,* prob. of Scand origin; akin to Sw *skura* to rush] *vi* **:** to move about quickly esp. in search ~ *vt* **1**

: to move through or range over usu. rapidly **2 :** to examine minutely and rapidly

[2]**scour** *vb* [ME *scouren*] *vt* **1 a :** to rub hard for the purpose of cleansing **b :** to remove by rubbing hard and washing **2** *archaic* **:** to make (a region) free (as from undesired occupants) **3 :** to clean by purging : PURGE **4 :** to clear (as a pipe or ditch) by removing dirt and debris **5 :** to free from foreign matter or impurities by or as if by washing <~ wool> **6 :** to clear, dig, or remove by or as if by a powerful current of water ~ *vi* **1 :** to perform a process of scouring **2 :** to suffer from diarrhea or dysentery : PURGE **3 :** to become clean and bright by rubbing

[3]**scour** *n* **1 :** a place scoured by running water **2 :** scouring action (as of a glacier) **3 :** DIARRHEA, DYSENTERY — usu. used in pl. but sing. or pl. in constr. **4 :** SCOURING 1; *also* **:** damage done by scouring action

scour·er \ˈskau̇r-ər\ *n* **:** one that scours

[1]**scourge** \ˈskərj *also* ˈskō(ə)rj, ˈskȯ(ə)rj, ˈsku̇(ə)rj\ *n* [ME, fr. AF *escorge*, fr. (assumed) OF *escorgier* to whip, fr. OF *es-* ex- + L *corrigia* whip] **1 :** WHIP; *esp* **:** one used to inflict pain or punishment **2 a :** an instrument of punishment or criticism **b :** a cause of widespread or great affliction

[2]**scourge** *vt* **scourged; scourg·ing 1 :** to whip severely : FLOG **2 a :** to punish severely **b :** to subject to affliction : DEVASTATE **c :** to force as if by blows of a whip **d :** to subject to severe criticism or satire — **scourg·er** *n*

scour·ing \ˈskau̇(ə)r-iŋ\ *n* **1 :** material removed by scouring or cleaning **2 :** the lowest rank of society — usu. used in pl.

scouring rush *n* **:** HORSETAIL; *esp* **:** one (*Equisetum hyemale*) with strongly siliceous stems formerly used for scouring

scouse \ˈskau̇s\ *n* **:** LOBSCOUSE

[1]**scout** \ˈskau̇t\ *vb* [ME *scouten*, fr. MF *escouter* to listen, fr. L *auscultare* — more at AUSCULTATION] *vi* **1 :** to explore an area to obtain information (as about an enemy) **2 a :** to make a search **b :** to act as an athletic or entertainment scout ~ *vt* **1 :** to observe in order to obtain information or evaluate **2 :** to explore in order to obtain information **3 :** to find by making a search

[2]**scout** *n* **1 a :** the act of scouting **b :** a scouting expedition : RECONNAISSANCE **2 a :** one sent to obtain information; *esp* **:** a soldier, ship, or plane sent out in war to reconnoiter **b :** WATCHMAN, LOOKOUT **c :** a person who searches for talented newcomers **3 a :** BOY SCOUT **b :** GIRL SCOUT **4 :** FELLOW, GUY

[3]**scout** *vb* [of Scand origin; akin to ON *skūti* taunt; akin to OE *scēotan* to shoot — more at SHOOT] *vt* **1 :** to make fun of : MOCK **2 :** to reject scornfully as absurd or unworthy of consideration <~ a new theory> ~ *vi* **:** SCOFF ***syn*** see DESPISE

scout car *n* **:** a fast armored military reconnaissance vehicle with four-wheel drive and open top

scout·craft \ˈskau̇t-ˌkraft\ *n* **:** the craft, skill, or practice of a scout

scout·er \ˈskau̇t-ər\ *n* **1 :** one that scouts **2 :** a member of the Boy Scouts of America over 18 years of age

scouth \ˈsküth, ˈskau̇th\ *n* [origin unknown] *Scot* **:** PLENTY

scout·ing \ˈskau̇t-iŋ\ *n* **1 :** the action of one that scouts **2 :** the activities of the various boy scout and girl scout movements

scout·mas·ter \ˈskau̇t-ˌmas-tər\ *n* **:** the leader of a band of scouts; *specif* **:** the adult leader of a troop of boy scouts

scow \ˈskau̇\ *n* [D *schouw*; akin to OHG *scalta* punt pole]**:** a large flat-bottomed boat with broad square ends used chiefly for transporting bulk material (as ore, sand, or refuse)

[1]**scowl** \ˈskau̇(ə)l\ *vb* [ME *skoulen*, prob. of Scand origin; akin to Dan *skule* to scowl] *vi* **1 :** to draw down the forehead and make a face in expression of displeasure **2 :** to exhibit a threatening aspect ~ *vt* **:** to express with a scowl ***syn*** see FROWN — **scowl·er** *n*

[2]**scowl** *n* **:** a facial expression of displeasure : FROWN

SCPO *abbr* senior chief petty officer

[1]**scrab·ble** \ˈskrab-əl\ *vb* **scrab·bled; scrab·bling** \-(ə-)liŋ\ [D *schrabbelen* to scratch] *vi* **1 :** SCRAWL, SCRIBBLE **2 :** to scratch or claw about clumsily or frantically **3 a :** SCRAMBLE, CLAMBER **b :** to struggle by or as if by scraping or scratching ~ *vt* **1 :** SCRAMBLE **2 :** SCRIBBLE — **scrab·bler** \-(ə-)lər\ *n*

[2]**scrabble** *n* **1 :** SCRIBBLE **2 :** a repeated scratching or clawing **3 :** SCRAMBLE

scrab·bly \ˈskrab-(ə-)lē\ *adj* **1 :** SCRATCHY, RASPY **2 :** SPARSE, SCRUBBY

[1]**scrag** \ˈskrag\ *n* [perh. alter. of [2]*crag*] **1 :** a rawboned or scrawny person or animal **2 :** the lean end of a neck of mutton or veal; *broadly* **:** NECK

[2]**scrag** *vt* **scragged; scrag·ging 1 a :** to execute by hanging or garroting **b :** to wring the neck of **2 :** CHOKE

scrag·gly \ˈskrag-(ə-)lē\ *adj* **:** IRREGULAR; *also* **:** RAGGED, UNKEMPT

scrag·gy \ˈskrag-ē\ *adj* **scrag·gi·er; -est 1 :** ROUGH, JAGGED **2 :** being lean and long : SCRAWNY

scram \ˈskram\ *vi* **scrammed; scram·ming** [short for *scramble*] **:** to go away at once <~, you're not wanted>

[1]**scram·ble** \ˈskram-bəl\ *vb* **scram·bled; scram·bling** \-b(ə-)liŋ\ [perh. alter. of [1]*scrabble*] *vi* **1 a :** to move or climb hastily on all fours **b :** to move with urgency or panic **2 a :** to struggle eagerly or unceremoniously for possession of something <~ for front seats> **b :** to get or gather something with difficulty or in irregular ways <~ for a living> **3 a :** to spread or grow irregularly : SPRAWL, STRAGGLE **b** *of a plant* **:** to climb over a support **4 :** to take off quickly in response to an alert **5** *of a football quarterback* **:** to run with the ball after the pass protection breaks down ~ *vt* **1 :** to collect by scrambling **2 a :** to toss or mix together : JUMBLE **b :** to prepare (eggs) by stirring during frying **3 :** to cause or order (a fighter-interceptor group) to scramble **4 :** to disarrange the elements of telephone, teletype, facsimile, or television transmissions in order to make unintelligible to interception — **scram·bler** \-b(ə-)lər\ *n*

[2]**scramble** *n* **1 :** a scrambling movement or struggle **2 :** a disordered mess : JUMBLE **3 :** a rapid emergency takeoff of fighter-interceptor planes

scran·nel \ˈskran-ᵊl\ *adj* [origin unknown] **:** HARSH, UNMELODIOUS

[1]**scrap** \ˈskrap\ *n* [ME, fr. ON *skrap* scraps; akin to ON *skrapa* to scrape] **1** *pl* **:** fragments of discarded or leftover food **2 a :** a small detached piece : BIT <a ~ of paper> **b :** a fragment of something written or printed **c :** the least piece <not a ~ of evidence> **3** *pl* **:** CRACKLINGS **4 a :** fragments of stock removed in manufacturing **b :** manufactured articles or parts rejected or discarded and useful only as material for reprocessing; *esp* **:** waste and discarded metal

[2]**scrap** *vt* **scrapped; scrap·ping 1 :** to convert into scrap **2 :** to abandon or get rid of as no longer of enough worth or effectiveness to retain <~ outworn methods> ***syn*** see DISCARD

[3]**scrap** *n* [origin unknown] **:** FIGHT

[4]**scrap** *vi* **scrapped; scrap·ping :** QUARREL, FIGHT

scrap·book \ˈskrap-ˌbu̇k\ *n* **:** a blank book in which miscellaneous items (as newspaper clippings or pictures) may be pasted or inserted

[1]**scrape** \ˈskrāp\ *vb* **scraped; scrap·ing** [ME *scrapen*, fr. ON *skrapa*; akin to OE *scrapian* to scrape, L *scrobis* ditch, Gk *keirein* to cut — more at SHEAR] *vt* **1 a :** to remove (excrescent matter) from a surface by usu. repeated strokes of an edged instrument **b :** to make (a surface) smooth or clean with strokes of an edged instrument or an abrasive **2 a :** to grate harshly over or against **b :** to damage or injure the surface of by contact with a rough surface **c :** to draw roughly or noisily over a surface **3 :** to collect by or as if by scraping — often used with *up* or *together* <~ up the price of a bottle> ~ *vi* **1 :** to move in sliding contact with a rough surface **2 :** to accumulate money by small economies **3 :** to draw back the foot along the ground in making a bow **4 :** to make one's way with difficulty or succeed by a narrow margin — **scrap·er** *n* — **scrape a leg :** to make a low bow

[2]**scrape** *n* **1 a :** the act or process of scraping **b :** a sound made by scraping **2 :** a bow made with a drawing back of the foot along the ground **3 a :** a disagreeable predicament **b :** QUARREL, FIGHT

scrap heap *n* **1 :** a pile of discarded metal **2 :** the place to which useless things are relegated : DISCARD

scra·pie \ˈskrā-pē\ *n* [[1]*scrape*] **:** a usu. fatal virus disease of sheep that is characterized by twitching, excitability, intense itching, excessive thirst, emaciation, weakness, and finally paralysis

scrap·per \ˈskrap-ər\ *n* **:** FIGHTER, QUARRELER

scrap·pi·ness \ˈskrap-ē-nəs\ *n* **:** the quality or state of being scrappy

scrap·ple \ˈskrap-əl\ *n* [dim. of [1]*scrap*] **:** a seasoned mixture of ground meat (as pork) and cornmeal set in a mold and served sliced and fried

[1]**scrap·py** \ˈskrap-ē\ *adj* **scrap·pi·er; -est :** consisting of scraps

[2]**scrappy** *adj* **scrap·pi·er; -est 1 :** QUARRELSOME **2 :** aggressive and determined in spirit

[1]**scratch** \ˈskrach\ *vb* [blend of E dial. *scrat* (to scratch) and obs. E *cratch* (to scratch)] *vt* **1 :** to scrape or dig with the claws or nails **2 :** to rub and tear or mark the surface of with something sharp or jagged **3 :** to scrape or rub lightly (as to relieve itching) **4 :** to scrape together **5 :** to write or draw on a surface **6 a :** to cancel or erase by or as if by drawing a line through **b :** to withdraw (an entry) from competition **7 :** SCRIBBLE, SCRAWL **8 :** to scrape along a rough surface <~ a match> ~ *vi* **1 :** to use the claws or nails in digging, tearing, or wounding **2 :** to scrape or rub oneself lightly (as to relieve itching) **3 :** to gather money or get a living by hard work and saving **4 :** to make a thin grating sound **5 :** to withdraw from a contest or engagement **6 :** to make a scratch in billiards or pool — **scratch·er** *n*

[2]**scratch** *n* **1 :** a mark or injury produced by scratching; *also* **:** a slight wound **2 :** SCRAWL, SCRIBBLE **3 :** the sound made by scratching **4 a :** the starting line in a race **b :** a point at which everything remains to be done <build a school system from ~> **5 a :** a test of courage **b :** satisfactory condition or performance <not up to ~> **6 :** a contestant whose name is withdrawn **7 :** poultry feed (as mixed grains) scattered on the litter or ground esp. to induce birds to exercise — called also *scratch feed* **8 a :** a shot in billiards or pool that involves a penalty; *specif* **:** a shot in pool in which the cue ball falls into the pocket **b :** a shot that scores by chance : FLUKE **9** *slang* **:** MONEY, FUNDS

[3]**scratch** *adj* **1 :** made as or used for a tentative effort **2 :** made or done by chance and not as intended <a ~ shot> **3 :** arranged or put together with little selection : HAPHAZARD <a ~ team> **4 :** without handicap or allowance <a ~ golfer>

scratch hit *n* **:** a batted ball not solidly hit yet credited to the batter as a base hit

scratch line *n* **1 :** a starting line for a race **2 :** a line that marks the extreme limit of the takeoff for a long jump **3 :** a line from which the javelin is thrown and which must not be overstepped by the thrower

scratch pad *n* **:** a pad of scratch paper

scratch paper *n* **:** paper that may be used for casual writing

scratch sheet *n* **:** a racing publication listing horses scratched from races and giving the handicapper's grading of the horses in order of winning chances

scratch test *n* **:** a test for allergic susceptibility made by rubbing an extract of an allergy-producing substance into small breaks or scratches in the skin

scratchy \ˈskrach-ē\ *adj* **scratch·i·er; -est 1 :** likely to scratch : PRICKLY <~ undergrowth> **2 :** making a scratching noise **3 :** marked or made with scratches <~ drawing> <~ handwriting> **4 :** uneven in quality : RAGGED **5 :** causing tingling or itching : IRRITATING <~ wool> — **scratch·i·ness** *n*

scrawl \'skrȯl\ *vb* [origin unknown] *vt* : to write or draw awkwardly, hastily, or carelessly ~ *vi* : to write awkwardly or carelessly — **scrawl** *n* — **scrawl·er** *n* — **scrawly** \'skrȯ-lē\ *adj*
scraw·ny \'skrȯ-nē\ *adj* **scraw·ni·er; -est** [origin unknown] : exceptionally thin and slight or meager in body <~ scrub cattle> ***syn*** see LEAN ***ant*** brawny, fleshy — **scraw·ni·ness** *n*
screak \'skrēk\ *vi* [of Scand origin; akin to ON *skrækja* to screak; akin to ME *scremen* to scream] : to make a harsh shrill noise : SCREECH — **screak** *n* — **screaky** \-ē\ *adj*
[1]**scream** \'skrēm\ *vb* [ME *scremen;* akin to OHG *scrian* to scream] *vi* **1 a** (1) : to voice a sudden sharp loud cry (2) : to produce harsh high tones **b** : to move with or make a noise resembling a scream **2 a** : to speak or write with intense hysterical expressions **b** : to protest violently **3** : to produce a vivid startling effect ~ *vt* : to utter with or as if with a scream
[2]**scream** *n* **1** : a loud sharp penetrating cry or noise **2** : one that provokes mirth
scream·er \'skrē-mər\ *n* **1** : one that screams **2** : any of several So. American birds (family Anhimidae) with large stout bills, spurred wings, and more or less webbed feet **3** : a sensationally startling headline
scream·ing·ly \'skrē-miŋ-lē\ *adv* : to an extreme degree
scree \'skrē\ *n* [of Scand origin; akin to ON *skritha* landslide, fr. *skrītha* to creep; akin to OHG *scrītan* to go, Lith *skrytis* felly, n.] : an accumulation of stones or rocky debris lying on a slope or at the base of a hill or cliff : TALUS
[1]**screech** \'skrēch\ *vb* [alter. of earlier *scritch,* fr. ME *scrichen;* akin to ON *skrækja* to screak] *vi* **1** : to utter a high shrill piercing cry : make an outcry usu. in terror or pain **2** : to make a sound resembling a screech ~ *vt* : to utter with or as if with a screech — **screech·er** *n*
[2]**screech** *n* **1** : a high shrill piercing cry usu. expressing pain or terror **2** : a sound resembling a screech
screech owl *n* : any of numerous New World owls (genus *Otus*); *esp* : a small No. American owl (*O. asio*) with a pair of tufts of lengthened feathers on the head resembling ears
screed \'skrēd\ *n* [ME *screde* fragment, fr. OE *scrēade* — more at SHRED] **1 a** : a lengthy discourse **b** : an informal piece of writing **2** : a strip (as of plaster of the thickness planned for the coat) laid on as a guide **3** : a leveling device drawn over freshly poured concrete
[1]**screen** \'skrēn\ *n* [ME *screne,* fr. MF *escren,* fr. MD *scherm;* akin to OHG *skirm* screen, L *corium* skin — more at CUIRASS] **1 a** : a device used as a protection from heat or drafts or as an ornament **b:** a nonbearing partition often ornamental carried up to a height necessary for separation and protection **2 a** : something that shelters, protects, or conceals; *esp* : a body of troops, ships, or planes whose function is to protect a command, an area, or a larger force **b** : a shield for secret usu. evil practices **c** : a maneuver in various sports whereby an opponent is legally cut off from the play; *specif* : a maneuver in basketball in which an offensive player positions himself in such a way as to momentarily impede the movement of a defensive player attempting to guard his man **d** : SCREEN PASS **3 a** : a perforated plate or cylinder or a meshed wire or cloth fabric usu. mounted and used to separate coarser from finer parts **b** : a system for examining and separating into different groups **c** : a piece of apparatus designed to prevent agencies in one part from affecting other parts <an optical ~> <an electric ~> <a magnetic ~> **d** : a frame holding a usu. metallic netting used esp. in a window or door to exclude pests (as insects) **4 a** : a flat surface upon which a picture or series of pictures is projected or reflected **b** : something that receives or retains a mental image or impression **c** : the surface upon which the image appears in a television or radar receiver **5** : a glass plate ruled with crossing opaque lines through which an image is photographed in making a halftone **6** : the motion-picture industry
[2]**screen** *vt* **1** : to guard from injury or danger **2 a** : to give shelter or protection to with or as if with a screen **b** : to separate with or as if with a screen; *also* : to shield (an opponent) from a play or from view of a play **3 a** : to pass (as coal, gravel, or ashes) through a screen to separate the fine part from the coarse; *also* : to remove by a screen **b** (1) : to examine usu. methodically in order to make a separation into different groups (2) : to select or eliminate by a screening process **4** : to provide with a screen to keep out pests (as insects) **5 a** : to project (as a motion-picture film) on a screen **b** : to present in a motion picture ~ *vi* **1** : to appear on a motion-picture screen **2** : to provide a screen in a game or sport ***syn*** see HIDE — **screen·able** \'skrē-nə-bəl\ *adj* — **screen·er** *n*
screen·ing \'skrē-niŋ\ *n* **1** *pl but sing or pl in constr* : material (as waste or fine coal) separated out by passage through or retention on a screen **2** : metal or plastic mesh (as for window screens) **3** : a showing of a motion picture
screen·land \'skrēn-ˌland\ *n* : FILMDOM
screen memory *n* : a recollection of early childhood that may be falsely recalled or magnified in importance and that masks another memory of deep emotional significance
screen pass *n* : a forward pass in football to a receiver at or behind the line of scrimmage who is protected by a screen of blockers
screen·play \'skrēn-ˌplā\ *n* : the written form of a story prepared for motion-picture production including description of characters, details of scenes and settings, dialogue, and stage directions
screen test *n* : a short film sequence testing the ability of a prospective motion-picture actor — **screen–test** *vt*
screen·writ·er \'skrēn-ˌrīt-ər\ *n* : a writer of screenplays
[1]**screw** \'skrü\ *n* [ME, fr. MF *escroe* female screw, nut, fr. ML *scrofa,* fr. L, sow] **1 a** : a simple machine of the inclined plane type in which the applied force acts along a spiral path about a cylinder while the resisting force acts along the axis of the cylinder **b** : a usu. pointed and headed cylindrical fastener that is helically or spirally threaded and designed for insertion into material by rotating (as with a screwdriver) **2 a** : a screwlike form : SPIRAL **b** : a turn of a screw; *also* : a twist like the turn of a screw **c** : a screwlike device (as a corkscrew) **3** : a worn-out horse **4** *chiefly Brit* : a small packet (as of tobacco) **5** : one who bargains shrewdly; *also* : SKINFLINT **6** : a prison guard : TURNKEY **7** : SCREW PROPELLER **8** : THUMBSCREW 2 **9** : an act of sexual intercourse — usu. considered vulgar — **screw·like** \-ˌlīk\ *adj*
[2]**screw** *vt* **1 a** (1) : to attach, fasten, or close by means of a screw (2) : to unite or separate by means of a screw or a twisting motion <~ the two pieces together> (3) : to press tightly in a device (as a vise) operated by a screw (4) : to operate, tighten, or adjust by means of a screw (5) : to torture by means of a thumbscrew **b** : to cause to rotate spirally about an axis **2 a** (1) : to twist into strained configurations : CONTORT <~*ed* up his face> (2) : SQUINT (3) : CRUMPLE **b** : to furnish with a spiral groove or ridge : THREAD **3** : to increase the intensity, quantity, or capability of **4 a** : to practice extortion upon : OPPRESS **b** : to extract by pressure or threat **5** : to copulate with — usu. considered vulgar ~ *vi* **1** : to rotate like or as a screw **2** : to turn or move with a twisting or writhing motion **3** : COPULATE — usu. considered vulgar — **screw·er** *n*
[1]**screw·ball** \'skrü-ˌbȯl\ *n* **1** : a baseball pitch that spins and breaks in the opposite direction to a curve **2** : a whimsical, eccentric, or crazy person : ZANY
[2]**screwball** *adj* : crazily eccentric or whimsical : ZANY
screw bean *n* **1** : a leguminous shrub or small tree (*Prosopis pubescens*) of the southwestern U.S. — called also *screwbean mesquite* **2** : a spirally twisted sweet pod that is the fruit of the screwbean
screw·driv·er \'skrü-ˌdrī-vər\ *n* **1** : a tool for turning screws **2** : vodka and orange juice served with ice
screw eye *n* : a wood screw with a head in the form of a loop
screw jack *n* : JACKSCREW
screw pine *n* : any of a genus (*Pandanus* of the family Pandanaceae, the screw-pine family) of tropical monocotyledonous plants with slender palmlike stems, often huge prop roots, and terminal crowns of swordlike leaves
screw propeller *n* : a device that consists of a central hub with radiating blades placed and twisted so that each forms part of a helical surface and that is used to propel a vehicle (as a ship or airplane)
screw thread *n* **1** : the projecting helical rib of a screw **2** : one complete turn of a screw thread
screw up *vt* **1** : to tighten, fasten, or lock by or as if by a screw **2** : BUNGLE, BOTCH ~ *vi* : to botch an activity or undertaking
screw·worm \'skrü-ˌwərm\ *n* : a two-winged fly (*Cochliomyia hominivorax*) of the warmer parts of America whose larva develops in sores or wounds or in the nostrils of mammals including man with serious or sometimes fatal results; *broadly* : any of several flies whose larvae parasitize the flesh of mammals
screwy \'skrü-ē\ *adj* **screw·i·er; -est** **1** : crazily absurd, eccentric, or unusual **2** : CRAZY, INSANE — **screw·i·ness** *n*
scrib·al \'skrī-bəl\ *adj* : of, relating to, or due to a scribe
scrib·ble \'skrib-əl\ *vb* **scrib·bled; scrib·bling** \-(ə-)liŋ\ [ME *scriblen,* fr. ML *scribillare,* fr. L *scribere* to write] *vt* **1** : to write hastily or carelessly without regard to legibility or thought **2** : to cover with careless or worthless writings or drawings ~ *vi* : to write or draw hastily and carelessly — **scribble** *n*
scrib·bler \'skrib-(ə-)lər\ *n* **1** : one that scribbles **2** : a minor or worthless author
[1]**scribe** \'skrīb\ *n* [ME, fr. L *scriba* official writer, fr. *scribere* to write; akin to Gk *skariphasthai* to scratch an outline, *keirein* to cut — more at SHEAR] **1** : one of a learned class in ancient Israel through New Testament times studying the Scriptures and serving as copyists, editors, teachers, and jurists **2 a** : an official or public secretary or clerk **b** : a copier of manuscripts **3** : AUTHOR; *specif* : JOURNALIST
[2]**scribe** *vi* **scribed; scrib·ing** : to work as a scribe : WRITE
[3]**scribe** *vt* **scribed; scrib·ing** [prob. short for *describe*] **1** : to mark a line on by cutting or scratching with a pointed instrument **2** : to make by cutting or scratching
[4]**scribe** *n* : SCRIBER
scrib·er \'skrī-bər\ *n* : a sharp-pointed tool for making marks and esp. for marking off material (as wood or metal) to be cut
scrieve \'skrēv\ *vi* [of Scand origin; akin to ON *skrefa* to stride] *Scot* : to move along swiftly and smoothly
scrim \'skrim\ *n* [origin unknown] **1** : a durable plain-woven usu. cotton fabric for use in clothing, curtains, building, and industry **2** : a transparent or translucent theater drop or section of a drop
[1]**scrim·mage** \'skrim-ij\ *n* [alter. of [1]*skirmish*] **1 a** : a minor battle : SKIRMISH **b** : a confused fight : SCUFFLE **2 a** : SCRUMMAGE **b** : the interplay between two football teams that begins with the snap of the ball and continues until the ball is dead **c** (1) : a play that begins at a line of scrimmage as opposed to a runback in football <raced 93 yards from ~ —*N.Y. Times*> (2) : LINE OF SCRIMMAGE **d** : practice play (as in football or basketball) between a team's squads
[2]**scrimmage** *vi* **scrim·maged; scrim·mag·ing** : to take part in a scrimmage — **scrim·mag·er** *n*
scrimp \'skrimp\ *vb* [perh. of Scand origin; akin to Sw *skrympa* to shrink, ON *skorpna* to shrivel up — more at SHRIMP] *vt* **1** : to be niggardly in providing for **2** : to make too small, short, or scanty ~ *vi* : to be frugal or niggardly — **scrimpy** \'skrim-pē\ *adj*
[1]**scrim·shaw** \'skrim-ˌshȯ\ *n* [origin unknown] **1** : any of various carved or engraved articles made esp. by American whalers usu. from whalebone or whale ivory **2** : scrimshawed work **3** : the art, practice, or technique of producing scrimshaw
[2]**scrimshaw** *vt* : to carve or engrave into scrimshaw ~ *vi* : to produce scrimshaw
[1]**scrip** \'skrip\ *n* [ME *scrippe,* fr. ML *scrippum* pilgrim's knapsack] *archaic* : a small bag or wallet
[2]**scrip** *n* [short for *script*] **1** : a short writing (as a certificate, schedule, or list) **2** : a small piece **3 a** : any of various documents used as evidence that the holder or bearer is entitled to receive something (as a fractional share of stock or an allotment of

land) **b :** paper currency or a token issued for temporary use in an emergency

[1]script \ˈskript\ *n* [L *scriptum* thing written, fr. neut. of *scriptus,* pp. of *scribere* to write — more at SCRIBE] **1 a :** something written **:** TEXT **b :** an original or principal instrument or document **c** (1) **:** MANUSCRIPT 1 (2) **:** the written text of a stage play, screenplay, or broadcast; *specif* **:** the one used in production or performance **2 a :** printed lettering resembling handwritten lettering **b :** written characters **:** HANDWRITING **c :** ALPHABET **3 :** a plan of action

[2]script *vt* **:** to prepare a script for or from

[3]script *abbr* scripture

scrip·to·ri·um \skrip-ˈtōr-ē-əm, -ˈtȯr-\ *n, pl* **-ria** \-ē-ə\ [ML, fr. L *scriptus*] **:** a copying room in a medieval monastery set apart for the scribes

scrip·tur·al \ˈskrip-chə-rəl, ˈskrip-shrəl\ *adj* **:** of, relating to, contained in, or according to a sacred writing; *specif* **:** BIBLICAL — **scrip·tur·al·ly** \-ē\ *adv*

scrip·ture \ˈskrip-chər\ *n* [ME, fr. LL *scriptura,* fr. L, act or product of writing, fr. *scriptus*] **1 a** (1) *cap* **:** the books of the Old and New Testaments or of either of them **:** BIBLE — often used in pl. (2) *often cap* **:** a passage from the Bible **b :** the sacred writings of a religion **c :** a body of writings considered as authoritative **2 :** something written <the primitive man's awe for any ~ —George Santayana>

script·writ·er \ˈskrip-ˌtrīt-ər\ *n* **:** one that writes screenplays or radio or television programs

scriv·en·er \ˈskriv-(ə-)nər\ *n* [ME *scriveiner,* alter. of *scrivein,* fr. MF *escrivein,* fr. (assumed) VL *scriban-, scriba,* alter. of L *scriba* scribe] **1 :** a professional or public copyist or writer **:** SCRIBE **2 :** NOTARY PUBLIC

scrod \ˈskräd\ *n* [perh. fr. obs. D *schrood* shred; akin to OE *scrēade* shred — more at SHRED] **:** a young fish (as a cod or haddock); *esp* **:** one split and boned for cooking

scrof·u·la \ˈskrȯf-yə-lə, ˈskräf-\ *n* [ML, fr. LL *scrofulae,* pl., swellings of the lymph glands of the neck, fr. pl. of *scrofula,* dim. of L *scrofa* breeding sow] **:** tuberculosis of lymph glands esp. in the neck

scrof·u·lous \-ləs\ *adj* **1 :** of, relating to, or affected with scrofula **2 a :** having a diseased appearance **b :** morally contaminated

scroll \ˈskrōl\ *n* [ME *scrowle,* alter. of *scrowe,* fr. MF *escroue* scrap, scroll, of Gmc origin; akin to OE *scrēade* shred] **1 a :** a roll (as of papyrus, leather, or parchment) for writing a document **b** *archaic* **:** a written message **c :** ROSTER, LIST **d :** a riband with rolled ends often inscribed with a motto **2 a :** something resembling a scroll in shape; *esp* **:** a spiral or convoluted form in ornamental design derived from the curves of a loosely or partly rolled parchment scroll **b :** the curved head of a bowed stringed musical instrument — see VIOLIN illustration

scroll saw *n* **1 :** a thin handsaw for cutting curves or irregular designs **2 :** FRETSAW **3 :** JIGSAW 1

scroll·work \ˈskrōl-ˌwərk\ *n* **:** ornamentation characterized by scrolls; *esp* **:** fancy designs in wood often made with a scroll saw

scrooge \ˈskrüj\ *n, often cap* [Ebenezer *Scrooge,* character in *A Christmas Carol,* story by Charles Dickens] **:** a miserly person

scro·tum \ˈskrōt-əm\ *n, pl* **scro·ta** \-ə\ *or* **scrotums** [L; akin to L *scrupus* sharp stone — more at SHRED] **:** the external pouch that in most mammals contains the testes — **scro·tal** \ˈskrōt-ᵊl\ *adj*

scrouge \ˈskrau̇j, ˈskrüj\ *vb* **scrouged; scroug·ing** [alter. of E dial. *scruze* (to squeeze)] *chiefly dial* **:** CROWD, PRESS

scrounge \ˈskrau̇nj\ *vb* **scrounged; scroung·ing** [alter. of E dial. *scrunge* (to wander about idly)] *vt* **1 :** to collect by or as if by foraging **2 :** CADGE, WHEEDLE ~ *vi* **1 :** FORAGE, HUNT **2 :** WHEEDLE — **scroung·er** *n*

[1]scrub \ˈskrəb\ *n, often attrib* [ME, alter. of *schrobbe* shrub — more at SHRUB] **1 a :** a stunted tree or shrub **b :** vegetation consisting chiefly of scrubs **c :** a tract covered with scrub **2 :** a domestic animal of mixed or unknown parentage and usu. inferior conformation **:** MONGREL **3 :** a person of insignificant size or standing **4 :** a player not belonging to the first string

[2]scrub *vb* **scrubbed; scrub·bing** [of LG or Scand origin; akin to MLG & MD *schrubben* to scrub, Sw *skrubba*] *vt* **1 a** (1) **:** to clean with hard rubbing **:** SCOUR (2) **:** to remove by scrubbing **b :** to subject to friction **:** RUB **2 :** WASH 6c(2) **3 :** CANCEL, ELIMINATE ~ *vi* **:** to use hard rubbing in cleaning

[3]scrub *n* **1 :** an act or instance of scrubbing; *esp* **:** CANCELLATION **2 :** one that scrubs

scrub·bed \ˈskrəb-əd\ *adj* [[1]*scrub*] *archaic* **:** SCRUBBY 1

scrub·ber \ˈskrəb-ər\ *n* **:** one that scrubs; *esp* **:** an apparatus for removing impurities esp. from gases

scrub brush *n* **:** a brush with hard bristles for heavy cleaning — called also *scrubbing brush*

scrub·by \ˈskrəb-ē\ *adj* **scrub·bi·er; -est** [[1]*scrub*] **1 :** inferior in size or quality **:** STUNTED <~ cattle> **2 :** covered with or consisting of scrub **3 :** lacking distinction **:** PALTRY

scrub·land \ˈskrəb-ˌland\ *n* **:** land covered with scrub

scrub pine *n* **:** a pine of dwarf, straggly, or scrubby growth usu. by reason of environmental conditions; *specif* **:** a pine tree unsuitable for lumber by reason of inferior or defective growth

scrub typhus *n* **:** TSUTSUGAMUSHI DISEASE

scrub·wom·an \ˈskrəb-ˌwu̇m-ən\ *n* **:** a woman who hires herself out for cleaning **:** CHARWOMAN

scruff \ˈskrəf\ *n* [alter. of earlier *scuff,* of unknown origin] **:** the back of the neck **:** NAPE

scruffy \ˈskrəf-ē\ *adj* **scruff·i·er; -est** [E dial. *scruff* (something worthless)] **:** SHABBY, CONTEMPTIBLE — **scruff·i·ness** *n*

scrum \ˈskrəm\ *or* **scrum·mage** \ˈskrəm-ij\ *n* [*scrum* short for *scrummage,* alter. of *scrimmage*] **:** a Rugby play in which the forwards of each side crouch in a tight formation with locked arms and with the two front rows of each team meeting head to head so that the ball can be put in play between them — **scrummage** *vi*

scrump·tious \ˈskrəm(p)-shəs\ *adj* [prob. alter. of *sumptuous*] **:** DELIGHTFUL, EXCELLENT — **scrump·tious·ly** *adv*

[1]scrunch \ˈskrənch, ˈskru̇nch\ *vb* [alter. of [1]*crunch*] *vt* **1 :** CRUNCH, CRUSH **2 a :** CONTRACT, HUNCH **b :** CRUMPLE, RUMPLE ~ *vi* **1 :** to move with or make a crunching sound **2 :** CROUCH, SQUEEZE

[2]scrunch *n* **:** a crunching sound

[1]scru·ple \ˈskrü-pəl\ *n* [ME *scriple,* fr. L *scrupulus* a unit of weight, fr. *scrupulus* small sharp stone] **1** — see WEIGHT table **2 :** a minute part or quantity **:** IOTA

[2]scruple *n* [MF *scrupule,* fr. L *scrupulus* small sharp stone, cause of mental discomfort, scruple, dim. of *scrupus* sharp stone — more at SHRED] **1 :** an ethical consideration or principle that inhibits action **2 :** the quality or state of being scrupulous ***syn*** see QUALM

[3]scruple *vi* **scru·pled; scru·pling** \-p(ə-)liŋ\ **1 :** to have scruples **2 :** to be reluctant on grounds of conscience **:** HESITATE

scru·pu·los·i·ty \ˌskrü-pyə-ˈläs-ət-ē\ *n* **1 :** the quality or state of being scrupulous **2 :** SCRUPLE 1

scru·pu·lous \ˈskrü-pyə-ləs\ *adj* [ME, fr. L *scrupulosus,* fr. *scrupulus*] **1 :** having moral integrity **:** inclined to scruple **:** high-principled **2 :** punctiliously exact **:** PAINSTAKING <working with ~ care> ***syn*** **1** see CAREFUL ***ant*** remiss **2** see UPRIGHT ***ant*** unscrupulous — **scru·pu·lous·ly** *adv* — **scru·pu·lous·ness** *n*

scru·ta·ble \ˈskrüt-ə-bəl\ *adj* [LL *scrutabilis* searchable, fr. L *scrutari* to search, investigate, examine — more at SCRUTINY] **:** capable of being deciphered **:** COMPREHENSIBLE

scru·ta·tor \ˈskrü-ˌtāt-ər, skrü-ˈ\ *n* [L, fr. *scrutatus,* pp. of *scrutari* to search] **:** OBSERVER, EXAMINER

scru·ti·neer \ˌskrüt-ᵊn-ˈi(ə)r\ *n* **1 :** one that examines **2** *Brit* **:** one who takes or counts votes

scru·ti·nize \ˈskrüt-ᵊn-ˌīz\ *vb* **-nized; -niz·ing** *vt* **:** to examine closely and minutely ~ *vi* **:** to make a scrutiny — **scru·ti·niz·er** *n*

syn SCRUTINIZE, SCAN, INSPECT, EXAMINE *shared meaning element* **:** to look at or over carefully and usu. critically

scru·ti·ny \ˈskrüt-ᵊn-ē, ˈskrüt-nē\ *n, pl* **-nies** [L *scrutinium,* fr. *scrutari* to search, examine, fr. *scruta* trash] **1 :** a searching study, inquiry, or inspection **:** EXAMINATION **2 :** a searching look **3 :** close watch **:** SURVEILLANCE

sct *abbr* scout

sctd *abbr* scattered

scu·ba \ˈsk(y)ü-bə\ *n* [*s*elf-*c*ontained *u*nderwater *b*reathing *a*pparatus] **:** an apparatus used for breathing while swimming under water

scuba diver *n* **:** one who swims under water with the aid of scuba gear — **scuba dive** *vi*

[1]scud \ˈskəd\ *vi* **scud·ded; scud·ding** [prob. of Scand origin; akin to Norw *skudda* to push; akin to L *quatere* to shake — more at QUASH] **1 :** to move or run swiftly esp. as if driven forward **2 :** to run before a gale

[2]scud *n* **1 :** the action of scudding **:** RUSH **2 a :** loose vapory clouds driven swiftly by the wind **b** (1) **:** a slight sudden shower (2) **:** mist, rain, snow, or spray driven by the wind **c :** a gust of wind

scu·do \ˈsküd-(ˌ)ō\ *n, pl* **scu·di** \-(ˌ)ē\ [It, lit., shield] **1 :** a gold coin first issued in the 15th century or a silver coin first issued in the 16th century, used in Italy to the 19th century, and approximately equivalent to a dollar **2 :** a unit of value equivalent to a scudo

[1]scuff \ˈskəf\ *vb* [prob. of Scand origin; akin to Sw *skuffa* to push] *vi* **1 a :** to walk without lifting the feet **:** SHUFFLE **b :** to poke or shuffle a foot in exploration or embarrassment **2 :** to become scratched, chipped, or roughened by wear ~ *vt* **1 :** [3]CUFF **2 a :** to scrape (the feet) along a surface while walking or back and forth while standing **b :** to poke at with the toe **3 :** to scratch, gouge, or wear away the surface of

[2]scuff *n* **1 a :** a noise of or as if of scuffing **b :** the act or an instance of scuffing **c :** a mark or injury caused by scuffing **2 :** a flat-soled slipper without quarter or heel strap

scuf·fle \ˈskəf-əl\ *vi* **scuf·fled; scuf·fling** \-(ə-)liŋ\ [prob. of Scand origin; akin to Sw *skuffa* to push] **1 :** to struggle at close quarters with disorder and confusion **2 a :** to move with a quick shuffling gait **:** SCURRY **b :** SHUFFLE — **scuffle** *n*

scuffle hoe *n* **:** a garden hoe that has both edges sharpened and can be pushed forward or drawn back

[1]scull \ˈskəl\ *n* [ME *sculle*] **1 a :** an oar used at the stern of a boat to propel it forward with a thwartwise motion **b :** one of a pair of oars usu. less than 10 feet in length and operated by one person **2 :** a racing shell propelled by one or two persons using sculls

[2]scull *vt* **:** to propel (a boat) by sculls or by a large oar worked thwartwise ~ *vi* **:** to scull a boat — **scull·er** *n*

sculpin 1

scul·lery \ˈskəl-(ə-)rē\ *n, pl* **-ler·ies** [ME, department of household in charge of dishes, fr. MF *escuelerie,* fr. *escuelle* bowl, fr. L *scutella* drinking bowl — more at SCUTTLE] **:** a room for cleaning and storing dishes and culinary utensils, washing vegetables, and similar coarse work

scul·lion \ˈskəl-yən\ *n* [ME *sculion,* fr. MF *escouillon* dishcloth, alter. of *escouvillon,* fr. *escouve* broom, fr. L *scopa,* lit., twig; akin to L *scapus* stalk — more at SHAFT] **:** a kitchen helper

scul·pin \ˈskəl-pən\ *n, pl* **sculpins** *also* **sculpin** [origin unknown] **1 :** any of a family (Cottidae) of numerous spiny large-headed broad-mouthed usu. scaleless fishes **2 :** a scorpion fish (*Scorpaena guttata*) of the southern California coast caught for food and sport

sculpt \ˈskəlpt\ *vb* [F *sculpter,* alter. of obs. *sculper,* fr. L *sculpere*] **:** CARVE, SCULPTURE

ə abut	ᵊ kitten	ər further	a back	ā bake	ä cot, cart
au̇ out	ch chin	e less	ē easy	g gift	i trip	ī life
j joke	ŋ sing	ō flow	ȯ flaw	ȯi coin	th thin	t͟h this
ü loot	u̇ foot	y yet	yü few	yu̇ furious	zh vision

sculp·tor \'skəlp-tər\ *n* [L, fr. *sculptus,* pp. of *sculpere*] **:** one that sculptures **:** an artist who produces works of sculpture

sculp·tress \-trəs\ *n* **:** a female sculptor

sculp·tur·al \'skəlp-chə-rəl, 'skəlp-shrəl\ *adj* **1 :** of or relating to sculpture **2 :** resembling sculpture **:** SCULPTURESQUE — **sculp·tur·al·ly** \-ē\ *adv*

[1]**sculp·ture** \'skəlp-chər\ *n* [ME, fr. L *sculptura,* fr. *sculptus,* pp. of *sculpere* to carve, alter. of *scalpere* — more at SHELF] **1 a :** the action or art of processing (as by carving, modeling, or welding) plastic or hard materials into works of art **b** (1) **:** work produced by sculpture (2) **:** a three-dimensional work of art (as a statue) **2 :** impressed or raised markings or a pattern of such esp. on a plant or animal part

[2]**sculpture** *vb* **sculp·tured; sculp·tur·ing** \'skəlp-chə-riŋ, 'skəlp-shriŋ\ *vt* **1 a :** to form an image or representation of from solid material (as wood or stone) **b :** to form into a three-dimensional work of art **2 :** to change (the form of the earth's surface) by natural processes (as erosion and deposition) **3 :** to shape by or as if by carving or molding ~ *vi* **:** to work as a sculptor

sculp·tur·esque \ˌskəlp-chə-'resk\ *adj* **:** done in the manner of or resembling sculpture — **sculp·tur·esque·ly** *adv*

[1]**scum** \'skəm\ *n* [ME, fr. MD *schum;* akin to OHG *scūm* foam] **1 a :** extraneous matter or impurities risen to or formed on the surface of a liquid often as a foul filmy covering **b :** the scoria of metals in a molten state **:** DROSS **2 a :** REFUSE **b :** the lowest class **:** RABBLE — **scum·my** \'skəm-ē\ *adj*

[2]**scum** *vi* **scummed; scum·ming :** to become covered with or as if with scum

[1]**scum·ble** \'skəm-bəl\ *vt* **scum·bled; scum·bling** \-b(ə-)liŋ\ [freq. of [2]*scum*] **1 a :** to make (as color or a painting) less brilliant by covering with a thin coat of opaque or semiopaque color **b :** to apply (a color) in this manner **2 :** to soften the lines or colors of (a drawing) by rubbing lightly

[2]**scumble** *n* **1 :** the act or effect of scumbling **2 :** a material used for scumbling

[1]**scun·ner** \'skən-ər\ *vi* [ME (Sc dial.) *skunniren*] *chiefly Scot* **:** to be in a state of disgusted irritation

[2]**scunner** *n* **:** an unreasonable or extreme dislike or prejudice

scup \'skəp\ *n, pl* **scup** *also* **scups** [Narraganset *mishcùp*] **:** a porgy (*Stenostomus chrysops*) that is distributed along the Atlantic coast of the U.S. from So. Carolina to Maine and that is used as a panfish

scup·per \'skəp-ər\ *n* [ME *skopper*] **1 :** an opening cut through the waterway and bulwarks of a ship so that water falling on deck may flow overboard **2 :** an opening in the wall of a building through which water can drain from a floor or flat roof

scup·per·nong \-ˌnȯŋ, -ˌnäŋ\ *n* [*Scuppernong,* river and lake in No. Carolina] **1 :** MUSCADINE; *esp* **:** a cultivated muscadine with yellowish green plum-flavored fruits **2 :** a white aromatic table wine made from scuppernongs

scurf \'skərf\ *n* [ME, of Scand origin; akin to Icel *skurfa* scurf; akin to OHG *scorf* scurf, L *carpere* to pluck — more at HARVEST] **1 :** thin dry scales detached from the epidermis esp. in an abnormal skin condition **2 a :** something like flakes or scales adhering to a surface **b :** the foul remains of something adherent **3 a :** a scaly deposit or covering on some plant parts; *also* **:** a localized or general darkening and roughening of a plant surface usu. more pronounced than russeting **b :** a plant disease characterized by scurf — **scurfy** \'skər-fē\ *adj*

scur·rile *or* **scur·ril** \'skər-əl, 'skə-rəl\ *adj* [MF *scurrile,* fr. L *scurrilis,* fr. *scurra* buffoon] **:** SCURRILOUS

scur·ril·i·ty \skə-'ril-ət-ē\ *n, pl* **-ties 1 :** the quality or state of being scurrilous **2 a :** scurrilous or abusive language **b :** an offensively rude or abusive remark *syn* see ABUSE

scur·ri·lous \'skər-ə-ləs, 'skə-rə-\ *adj* **1 a :** using or given to coarse language **b :** being vulgar and evil <~ imposters who used a religious exterior to rob poor people —Edwin Benson> **2 :** containing obscenities or coarse abuse <a . . . campaign filled with ~ charges and countercharges —A. D. Graeff> — **scur·ri·lous·ly** *adv* — **scur·ri·lous·ness** *n*

scur·ry \'skər-ē, 'skə-rē\ *vi* **scur·ried; scur·ry·ing** [short for *hurry-scurry,* redupl. of *hurry*] **1 :** to move in or as if in a brisk rapidly alternating step **:** SCAMPER **2 :** to circulate in an agitated, confused, or fluttering manner — **scurry** *n*

[1]**scur·vy** \'skər-vē\ *adj* [*scurf*] **:** disgustingly mean or contemptible **:** DESPICABLE <a ~ trick> *syn* see CONTEMPTIBLE — **scur·vi·ly** \-və-lē\ *adv* — **scur·vi·ness** \-vē-nəs\ *n*

[2]**scurvy** *n* **:** a disease marked by spongy gums, loosening of the teeth, and a bleeding into the skin and mucous membranes and caused by a lack of ascorbic acid

scurvy grass *n* **:** a cress (as *Cochlearia officinalis*) formerly believed useful in preventing or treating scurvy

scut \'skət\ *n* [origin unknown] **:** a short erect tail (as of a hare)

scu·tage \'sk(y)üt-ij\ *n* [ME, fr. ML *scutagium,* fr. L *scutum* shield — more at ESQUIRE] **:** a tax levied upon a tenant of a knight's estate in place of military service

[1]**scutch** \'skəch\ *vt* [(assumed) F *escoucher* to beat, fr. (assumed) VL *excuticare* to beat out, fr. L *executere,* fr. *ex-* + *quatere* to shake, strike — more at QUASH] **:** to separate the woody fiber from (flax or hemp) by beating

[2]**scutch** *n* **1 :** SCUTCHER **2 :** a bricklayer's hammer for cutting, trimming, and dressing bricks

scutch·eon \'skəch-ən\ *n* [ME *scochon,* fr. MF *escuchon*] **:** ESCUTCHEON

scutch·er \'skəch-ər\ *n* **:** an implement or machine for scutching flax or cotton

scute \'sk(y)üt\ *n* [NL *scutum,* fr. L, shield — more at ESQUIRE] **:** an external bony or horny plate or large scale

scu·tel·late \sk(y)ü-'tel-ət, 'sk(y)üt-ᵊl-ˌāt\ *adj* **1 :** of or resembling a scutellum **2** *or* **scu·tel·lat·ed** \'sk(y)üt-ᵊl-ˌāt-əd\ **:** having or covered with scutella

scu·tel·la·tion \ˌsk(y)üt-ᵊl-'ā-shən\ *n* **:** LEPIDOSIS

scu·tel·lum \sk(y)ü-'tel-əm\ *n, pl* **-la** \-ə\ [NL, dim. of L *scutum* shield] **1 :** any of several small shield-shaped plant structures **2 :** a hard plate or scale (as on the thorax of an insect or the tarsus of a bird) — **scu·tel·lar** \-ər\ *adj*

scut·ter \'skət-ər\ *vi* [alter. of [4]*scuttle*] **:** SCURRY, SCAMPER

[1]**scut·tle** \'skət-ᵊl\ *n* [ME *scutel,* fr. L *scutella* drinking bowl, tray, dim. of *scutra* platter] **1 :** a shallow open basket for carrying something (as grain or garden produce) **2 :** a metal pail that usu. has a bail and a sloped lip and is used esp. for carrying coal

[2]**scuttle** *n* [ME *skottell*] **1 :** a small opening in a wall or roof furnished with a lid: as **a :** a small opening or hatchway in the deck of a ship large enough to admit a man and with a lid for covering it **b :** a small hole in the side or bottom of a ship furnished with a lid or glazed **2 :** a lid that closes a scuttle

[3]**scuttle** *vt* **scut·tled; scut·tling** \'skət-liŋ, -ᵊl-iŋ\ **1 :** to cut a hole through the bottom, deck, or side of (a ship); *specif* **:** to sink or attempt to sink by making holes through the bottom **2 :** DESTROY, WRECK

[4]**scuttle** *vi* **scut·tled; scut·tling** \'skət-liŋ, -ᵊl-iŋ\ [prob. blend of *scud* and *shuttle*] **:** SCURRY

[5]**scuttle** *n* **1 :** a quick shuffling pace **2 :** a short swift run

scut·tle·butt \'skət-ᵊl-ˌbət\ *n* [[2]*scuttle*] **1 a :** a cask on shipboard to contain fresh water for a day's use **b :** a drinking fountain on a ship or at a naval or marine installation **2 :** RUMOR, GOSSIP

scu·tum \'sk(y)üt-əm\ *n, pl* **scu·ta** \-ə\ [NL, fr. L, shield — more at ESQUIRE] **:** a bony, horny, or chitinous plate **:** SCUTE

Scyl·la \'sil-ə\ *n* [L, fr. Gk *Skyllē*] **:** a nymph changed into a monster who terrorized Odysseus and other mariners in the Straits of Messina — **between Scylla and Cha·ryb·dis** \-kə-'rib-dəs\ **:** between two equally hazardous alternatives

scy·phis·to·ma \sī-'fis-tə-mə\ *n, pl* **-mae** \-(ˌ)mē\ *also* **-mas** [NL, fr. L *scyphus* cup + Gk *stoma* mouth] **:** a sexually produced scyphozoan larva that ultimately repeatedly constricts transversely to form free-swimming medusae

scy·pho·zo·an \ˌsī-fə-'zō-ən\ *n* [NL *Scyphozoa,* class name, fr. L *scyphus* + NL *-zoa*] **:** any of a class (Scyphozoa) of coelenterates that comprise jellyfishes lacking a true polyp and usu. a velum — **scyphozoan** *adj*

[1]**scythe** \'sīth\ *n* [ME *sithe,* fr. OE *sīthe;* akin to OE *sagu* saw — more at SAW] **:** an implement used for mowing (as grass) and composed of a long curving blade fastened at an angle to a long handle

[2]**scythe** *vt* **scythed; scyth·ing :** to cut with or as if with a scythe

Scyth·i·an \'sith-ē-ən, 'sith-\ *n* [L *Scytha,* fr. Gk *Skythēs*] **1 :** a member of an ancient nomadic people inhabiting Scythia **2 :** the Iranian language of the Scythians — **Scythian** *adj*

sd *abbr* **1** said **2** sewed

SD *abbr* **1** sea-damaged **2** sight draft **3** sine die **4** South Dakota **5** special delivery **6** stage direction **7** standard deviation

SDA *abbr* **1** specific dynamic action **2** Students for Democratic Action

S Dak *abbr* South Dakota

SDI *abbr* selective dissemination of information

SDS *abbr* Students for a Democratic Society

Se *symbol* selenium

SE *abbr* **1** southeast **2** stock exchange **3** straight edge

sea \'sē\ *n* [ME *see,* fr. OE *sǣ;* akin to OS & OHG *sē* sea] **1 a :** a great body of salty water that covers much of the earth; *broadly* **:** the waters of the earth as distinguished from the land and air **b :** a body of salt water of second rank more or less landlocked <the Mediterranean ~> **c :** OCEAN **d :** an inland body of water esp. if large or if salt or brackish <the Caspian ~> **e :** a small freshwater lake <the *Sea* of Galilee> **2 a :** surface motion on a large body of water or its direction; *also* **:** rough water **:** a heavy swell or wave **b :** the disturbance of the ocean or other body of water due to the wind **3 :** something vast or overwhelming likened to the sea **4 :** the seafaring life **5 :** [3]MARE — **sea** *adj* — **at sea 1 :** on the sea; *specif* **:** on a sea voyage **2 :** LOST, BEWILDERED — **to sea :** to or upon the open waters of the sea

sea anchor *n* **:** a drag typically of canvas thrown overboard to retard the drifting of a ship or seaplane and to keep its head to the wind

sea anemone *n* **:** any of numerous usu. solitary polyps (order Actiniaria) whose form, bright and varied colors, and cluster of tentacles superficially resemble a flower

sea anemone

sea·bag \'sē-ˌbag\ *n* **:** a cylindrical canvas bag used esp. by a sailor for clothes and other gear

sea bass *n* **1 :** any of numerous marine fishes (family Serranidae) that are usu. smaller and more active than the groupers; *esp* **:** a food and sport fish (*Centropristes striatus*) of the Atlantic coast of the U.S. **2 :** any of numerous croakers or drums including noted sport and food fishes

sea·beach \'sē-ˌbēch\ *n* **:** a beach lying along the sea

sea·bed \-ˌbed\ *n* **:** the floor of a sea or ocean

Sea·bee \'sē-(ˌ)bē\ *n* [alter. of *cee* + *bee;* fr. the initials of *construction battalion*] **:** a member of one of the U.S. Navy construction battalions for building naval shore facilities in combat zones

sea·bird \'sē-ˌbərd\ *n* **:** a bird (as a gull or albatross) frequenting the open ocean

sea biscuit *n* **:** hard biscuit or bread for use on shipboard

sea·board \'sē-ˌbō(ə)rd, -ˌbȯ(ə)rd\ *n* **:** SEACOAST; *also* **:** the country bordering a seacoast — **seaboard** *adj*

sea·boot \-ˌbüt\ *n* **:** a very high waterproof boot used esp. by sailors and fishermen

sea·borne \-ˌbō(ə)rn, -ˌbȯ(ə)rn\ *adj* **1 :** borne over or upon the sea <a ~ invasion> **2 :** engaged in or carried on by oversea shipping <~ trade>

sea bread *n* **:** HARDTACK

sea bream *n* : any of numerous marine percoid fishes (as of the families Sparidae or Bramidae)
sea breeze *n* : a cooling breeze blowing generally in the daytime inland from the sea
sea captain *n* : the master esp. of a merchant vessel
sea change *n* 1 *archaic* : a change brought about by the sea 2 : TRANSFORMATION
sea chest *n* : a sailor's storage chest for personal property
sea·coast \ˈsē-ˌkōst\ *n* : the shore or border of the land adjacent to the sea
sea cow *n* : MANATEE, DUGONG
sea·craft \ˈsē-ˌkraft\ *n* 1 : seagoing ships 2 : skill in navigation
sea crawfish *n* : SPINY LOBSTER
sea crayfish *n* : SPINY LOBSTER
sea cucumber *n* : HOLOTHURIAN; *esp* : one whose contracted body suggests a cucumber in form
sea devil *n* 1 : DEVILFISH 1 2 : any of a family (Certiidae) of deep-sea fishes that often have luminous organs and are related to the anglers but are black in color

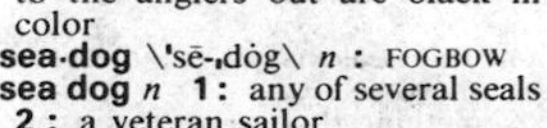

sea cucumber

sea·dog \ˈsē-ˌdȯg\ *n* : FOGBOW
sea dog *n* 1 : any of several seals 2 : a veteran sailor
sea·drome \-ˌdrōm\ *n* : a usu. floating airdrome on water serving esp. as an intermediate or emergency landing place
sea duck *n* : a diving duck (as a scoter, merganser, or eider) that frequents the sea
sea duty *n* : duty in the U.S. Navy performed outside the continental U.S. or specified dependencies thereof
sea eagle *n* 1 : any of various fish-eating eagles 2 : OSPREY
sea–ear \ˈsē-ˌi(ə)r\ *n* : ABALONE
sea fan *n* : a gorgonian with a fan-shaped skeleton; *esp* : one (*Gorgonia flabellum*) of Florida and the West Indies
sea·far·er \ˈsē-ˌfar-ər, -ˌfer-\ *n* [*sea* + [1]*fare* + *-er*] : MARINER
sea·far·ing \-ˌfar-iŋ, -ˌfer-\ *n* : a mariner's calling — **seafaring** *adj*
sea feather *n* : a gorgonian with a plumose skeleton; *esp* : SEA PEN
sea fight *n* : an engagement between ships at sea
sea fire *n* : marine bioluminescence
sea·floor \ˈsē-ˌflō(ə)r, -ˌflȯ(ə)r\ *n* : SEABED
sea·food \-ˌfüd\ *n* : edible marine fish and shellfish
sea·fowl \-ˌfau̇l\ *n* : SEABIRD
sea·front \-ˌfrənt\ *n* : the waterfront of a seaside place
sea gate *n* : a way (as a gate, beach, or channel) that gives access to the sea
sea·girt \ˈsē-ˌgərt\ *adj* : surrounded by the sea
sea·go·ing \-ˌgō-iŋ, -ˌgȯ(-)iŋ\ *adj* : OCEANGOING
sea grape *n* : a variable plant (*Coccoloba uvifera*) of sandy shores of Florida and tropical America that has rounded leaves with cordate bases and bears clusters of bluish edible berries
sea green *n* 1 : a moderate green or bluish green 2 : a moderate yellow green
sea gull *n* : a gull frequenting the sea; *broadly* : GULL
sea hare *n* : any of various large naked mollusks (genus *Aplysia*) with arched backs and anterior tentacles that project like ears
sea holly *n* : a European coastal herb (*Eryngium maritimum*) of the carrot family with spiny leaves and pale blue flowers
sea horse *n* 1 : WALRUS 2 : a fabulous creature half horse and half fish 3 : any of numerous small fishes (family Syngnathidae) related to the pipefishes but stockier with the head and forepart of the body sharply flexed like the head and neck of a horse
sea is·land cotton \ˌsē-ˌī-lən(d)-\ *n, often cap S&I* [*Sea islands*, chain of islands in the Atlantic] : a cotton (*Gossypium barbadense*) with esp. long silky fiber — called also *sea island*
sea kale *n* : a European fleshy plant (*Crambe maritima*) of the mustard family used as a potherb
sea king *n* : a Norse pirate chief
[1]seal \ˈsē(ə)l\ *n, pl* **seals** *also* **seal** [ME *sele*, fr. OE *seolh*; akin to OHG *selah* seal] 1 : any of numerous marine aquatic carnivorous mammals (families Phocidae and Otariidae) that occur chiefly in cold regions and have limbs modified into webbed flippers adapted primarily to swimming; *esp* : FUR SEAL 2 a : the pelt of a fur seal b : leather made from the skin of a seal 3 : a dark grayish yellowish brown
[2]seal *vi* : to hunt seal
[3]seal *n* [ME *seel*, fr. OF, fr. L *sigillum* seal, fr. dim. of *signum* sign, seal] 1 a : something that confirms, ratifies, or makes secure : GUARANTEE, ASSURANCE b (1) : a device with a cut or raised emblem, symbol, or word used to certify a signature or authenticate a document (2) : a medallion or ring face bearing such a device incised so that it can be impressed on wax or moist clay; *also* : a piece of wax or a wafer bearing such an impression c : an impression, device, or mark given the effect of a common-law seal by statute law or by American local custom recognized by judicial decision d : a usu. ornamental adhesive stamp that may be used to close a letter or package; *esp* : one given in a fund-raising campaign 2 a : something that secures (as a wax seal on a document) b : a closure that must be broken to be opened and that thus reveals tampering c (1) : a tight and perfect closure (as against the passage of gas or water) (2) : a device to prevent the passage or return of gas or air into a pipe or container 3 : a seal that is a symbol or mark of office — **under seal** : with an authenticating seal affixed
[4]seal *vt* 1 a : to confirm or make secure by or as if by a seal b : to solemnize for eternity (as a marriage) by a Mormon rite 2 a : to set or affix an authenticating seal to; *also* : AUTHENTICATE, RATIFY b : to mark with a stamp or seal usu. as an evidence of standard exactness, legal size, weight, or capacity, or merchantable quality 3 a : to fasten with or as if with a seal to prevent tampering b : to close or make secure against access, leakage, or passage by a fastening or coating c : to fix in position or close breaks in with a filling (as of plaster) 4 : to determine irrevocably or indisputably <that answer ~*ed* our fate>
sea ladder *n* 1 : a rope ladder or set of steps to be lowered over a ship's side for use in coming aboard (as at sea) 2 : SEA STEPS
sea lamprey *n* : a large anadromous lamprey (*Petromyzon marinus*) that is sometimes used as food and is a pest destructive of native fish fauna in the Great Lakes
sea–lane \ˈsē-ˌlān\ *n* : an established sea route
seal·ant \ˈsē-lənt\ *n* : a sealing agent <radiator ~>
sea lavender *n* : any of a genus (*Limonium*) of mostly coastal plants of the plumbago family
sea lawyer *n* : an argumentative captious sailor
sealed–beam \ˈsē(ə)l(d)-ˈbēm\ *adj* : of, relating to, or being an electric light with prefocussed reflector and lens sealed in the lamp vacuum
sea legs *n pl* : bodily adjustment to the motion of a ship indicated esp. by ability to walk steadily and by freedom from seasickness
[1]seal·er \ˈsē-lər\ *n* 1 : an official who attests or certifies conformity to a standard of correctness 2 : a coat (as of size) applied to prevent subsequent coats of paint or varnish from sinking in
[2]sealer *n* : a mariner or a ship engaged in hunting seals
seal·ery \ˈsē-lə-rē\ *n, pl* **-er·ies** : a seal fishery
sea lettuce *n* : any of several seaweeds (esp. genus *Ulva*, of the family Ulvaceae) with green fronds sometimes eaten as salad
sea level *n* : the level of the surface of the sea esp. as its mean position midway between mean high and low water
sea lily *n* : CRINOID; *esp* : a stalked crinoid
sealing wax *n* : a resinous composition that is plastic when warm and is used for sealing (as letters, dry cells, or cans)
sea lion *n* : any of several large Pacific eared seals (genus *Zalophus* and *Otaria*) that are related to the fur seals but lack their valuable coat
seal off *vt* : to close tightly
seal point *n* [[1]*seal* (the color)] : a Siamese cat with cream or fawn-colored body and dark grayish yellowish brown points
seal ring *n* : a finger ring engraved with a seal : SIGNET RING
seal·skin \ˈsē(ə)l-ˌskin\ *n* 1 : the fur or pelt of a fur seal 2 : a garment (as a jacket, coat, or cape) of sealskin — **sealskin** *adj*
Sea·ly·ham terrier \ˌsē-lē-ˌham-, *esp Brit* -lē-əm-\ *n* [*Sealyham*, Pembrokeshire, Wales] : a short-legged long-headed strong-jawed heavy-boned chiefly white terrier of a breed developed in Wales
[1]seam \ˈsēm\ *n* [ME *seem*, fr. OE *sēam*; akin to OE *sīwian* to sew — more at SEW] 1 a : the joining of two pieces (as of cloth or leather) by sewing usu. near the edge b : the stitching used in such a joining 2 : the space between adjacent planks or strakes of a ship 3 a : a line, groove, or ridge formed by the abutment of edges b : a thin layer or stratum (as of rock) between distinctive layers; *also* : a bed of valuable mineral and esp. coal irrespective of thickness c : a line left by a cut or wound; *also* : WRINKLE — **seam·like** \-ˌlīk\ *adj*
[2]seam *vt* 1 a : to join by sewing b : to join as if by sewing (as by welding, riveting, or heat-sealing) 2 : to mark with lines suggesting seams ~ *vi* : to become fissured or ridgy — **seam·er** *n*
sea–maid \ˈsē-ˌmād\ *or* **sea–maid·en** \-ˌmād-ᵊn\ *n* : MERMAID; *also* : a goddess or nymph of the sea
sea·man \ˈsē-mən\ *n* 1 : SAILOR, MARINER 2 a : one of the three ranks below petty officer in the navy or coast guard b : an enlisted man in the navy or coast guard ranking above a seaman apprentice and below a petty officer
seaman apprentice *n* : an enlisted man in the navy or coast guard ranking above a seaman recruit and below a seaman
sea·man·like \ˈsē-mən-ˌlīk\ *adj* : characteristic of or befitting a competent seaman
sea·man·ly \-lē\ *adj* : SEAMANLIKE
seaman recruit *n* : an enlisted man of the lowest rank in the navy or coast guard
sea·man·ship \ˈsē-mən-ˌship\ *n* : the art or skill of handling, working, and navigating a ship
sea·mark \-ˌmärk\ *n* 1 : a line on a coast marking the tidal limit 2 : an elevated object serving as a beacon to mariners
sea mew *n* : SEA GULL; *esp* : a European gull (*Larus canus*)
sea mile *n* : NAUTICAL MILE
seam·less \ˈsēm-ləs\ *adj* : having no seam — **seam·less·ly** *adv* — **seam·less·ness** *n*
sea·mount \ˈsē-ˌmau̇nt\ *n* : a submarine mountain rising above the deep-sea floor
sea mouse *n* : a large broad marine polychaete worm (esp. genus *Aphrodite*) covered with hairlike setae
seam·ster \ˈsēm(p)-stər *also* ˈsem(p)-\ *n* [ME *semester, semster*, fr. OE *sēamestre* seamstress, tailor, fr. *sēam* seam] : a person employed at sewing; *esp* : TAILOR
seam·stress \-strəs\ *n* : a woman whose occupation is sewing
seamy \ˈsē-mē\ *adj* **seam·i·er; -est** 1 *archaic* : having the rough side of the seam showing 2 a : UNPLEASANT b : DEGRADED, SORDID — **seam·i·ness** *n*
sé·ance \ˈsā-ˌän(t)s, -ˌäⁿs, sā-ˈ\ *n* [F, fr. *seoir* to sit, fr. L *sedēre* — more at SIT] 1 : SESSION, SITTING 2 : a spiritualist meeting to receive spirit communications
sea nettle *n* : a stinging jellyfish
sea oats *n pl but sing or pl in constr* : a tall grass (*Uniola panicolata*) that has panicles resembling those of the oat, grows on the coast of the southern U.S., and is useful as a sand binder
sea onion *n* : SQUILL 1a
sea otter *n* : a rare large marine otter (*Enhydra lutris*) of the northern Pacific coasts that attains a maximum length of nearly six

feet and feeds largely on shellfish

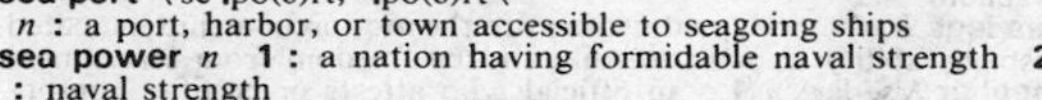
sea otter

sea–otter's–cabbage *n* : a gigantic kelp (*Nereocystis lütkeana*) of the northern Pacific

sea pen *n* : any of numerous anthozoans (as of the genus *Pennatula*) whose colonies have a feathery form

sea·piece \'sē-ˌpēs\ *n* : SEASCAPE 2

sea·plane \-ˌplān\ *n* : an airplane designed to take off from and land on the water

sea·port \'sē-ˌpō(ə)rt, -ˌpȯ(ə)rt\ *n* : a port, harbor, or town accessible to seagoing ships

sea power *n* **1** : a nation having formidable naval strength **2** : naval strength

sea purse *n* : the horny egg case of skates and of some sharks

sea puss \-ˌpu̇s\ *n* [by folk etymology fr. a word of Algonquian origin; akin to Delaware *sepus* small brook] : a swirling or along-shore undertow

sea·quake \'sē-ˌkwāk\ *n* [*sea* + *-quake* (as in *earthquake*)] : a submarine earthquake

[1]**sear** *var of* SERE

[2]**sear** \'si(ə)r\ *vb* [ME *seren,* fr. OE *sēarian* to become sere, fr. *sēar* sere] *vi* : to cause withering or drying ~ *vt* **1** : to make withered and dry : PARCH **2** : to burn, scorch, or injure with or as if with sudden application of intense heat — **sear·ing·ly** \-iŋ-lē\ *adv*

[3]**sear** *n* : a mark or scar left by searing

[4]**sear** *n* [prob. fr. MF *serre* grasp, fr. *serrer* to press, grasp, fr. LL *serare* to bolt, latch, fr. L *sera* bar for fastening a door] : the catch that holds the hammer of a gunlock at cock or half cock

sea raven *n* : a large sculpin (*Hemitripterus americanus*) of the northern Atlantic coast of America

[1]**search** \'sərch\ *vb* [ME *cerchen,* fr. MF *cerchier* to go about, survey, search, fr. LL *circare* to go about, fr. L *circum* round about] *vt* **1** : to look into or over carefully or thoroughly in an effort to find or discover something: as **a** : to examine in seeking something <~*ed* the north field> **b** : to look through or explore by inspecting possible places of concealment or investigating suspicious circumstances **c** : to read thoroughly : CHECK; *esp* : to examine a public record or register for information about <~ land titles> **d** : to examine for articles concealed on the person **e** : to look at as if to discover or penetrate intention or nature **2** : to uncover, find, or come to know by inquiry or scrutiny ~ *vi* **1** : to look or inquire carefully <~*ed* for the papers> **2** : to make painstaking investigation or examination — **search·able** \'sər-chə-bəl\ *adj* — **search·er** *n* — **search·ing·ly** \-chiŋ-lē\ *adv*

[2]**search** *n* **1 a** : an act of searching **b** : an act of boarding and inspecting a ship on the high seas in exercise of right of search **2** *obs* : a party that searches **3** : power or range of penetrating; *also* : a penetrating effect

search·less \'sərch-ləs\ *adj* : INSCRUTABLE, IMPENETRABLE

search·light \-ˌlīt\ *n* **1** : an apparatus for projecting a beam of light; *also* : a beam of light projected by it **2** : FLASHLIGHT 3

search warrant *n* : a warrant authorizing a search (as of a house) for stolen goods or unlawful possessions (as gambling implements)

sea robin *n* : any of various marine fishes (family Triglidae) with a spiny armored head and three pairs of modified fin rays used as feelers and in crawling — called also *gurnard*

sea room *n* : room for maneuver at sea

sea rover *n* : one that roves the sea; *specif* : PIRATE

sea–run \ˌsē-ˌrən\ *adj* : ANADROMOUS <a ~ salmon>

sea·scape \'sē-ˌskāp\ *n* **1** : a view of the sea **2** : a picture representing a scene at sea

sea scorpion *n* : SCULPIN

sea scout *n* : a boy enrolled in the boy-scout program that provides training for older boys in seamanship and water activities

sea serpent *n* : a large marine animal resembling a serpent often reported to have been seen but never proved to exist

sea·shell \'sē-ˌshel\ *n* : the shell of a marine animal and esp. a mollusk

sea·shore \-ˌshō(ə)r, -ˌshȯ(ə)r\ *n* **1 a** : land adjacent to the sea : SEACOAST **b** : NATIONAL SEASHORE **2** : all the ground between the ordinary high-water and low-water marks : FORESHORE

sea·sick \-ˌsik\ *adj* : affected with or suggestive of seasickness

sea·sick·ness \-nəs\ *n* : motion sickness experienced on the water

sea·side \'sē-ˌsīd\ *n* : the district or land bordering the sea : country adjacent to the sea : SEASHORE

sea slater *n* : SLATER 2b

sea slug *n* **1** : HOLOTHURIAN **2** : a naked marine gastropod; *specif* : NUDIBRANCH

sea snake *n* **1** : any of numerous venomous aquatic viviparous snakes (family Hydrophidae) of warm seas **2** : SEA SERPENT

[1]**sea·son** \'sēz-ᵊn\ *n* [ME, fr. OF *saison,* fr. L *sation-, satio* action of sowing, fr. *satus,* pp. of *serere* to sow — more at SOW] **1 a** : a time characterized by a particular circumstance or feature <at the age of eighteen, in a ~ of religious awakening —F. A. Christie> **b** : a suitable or natural time or occasion <when my ~ comes to sit on David's throne —John Milton> **c** : an indefinite period of time : WHILE <sent home again to her father for a ~ —Francis Hackett> **2 a** : a period of the year characterized by or associated with a particular activity or phenomenon <hay fever ~>: as (1) : a period associated with some phase or activity of agriculture (as growth or harvesting) (2) : a period in which an animal engages in some activity (as migrating or mating) (3) : the period normally characterized by a particular kind of weather <a long rainy ~> (4) : a period marked by special activity in some field <the theatrical ~> <the hunting ~> (5) : a period in which a place is most frequented **b** : one of the four quarters into which the year is commonly divided **c** : the time of a major holiday **3** : YEAR <a boy of seven ~*s*> **4** [ME *sesoun,* fr. *sesounen* to season] *obs* : SEASONING **5** : the total schedule of games played or to be played by a sports team during a playing season <try to get through the ~ undefeated> **6** : OFF-SEASON <closed for the ~> — **in season 1** : at the right time **2** : at the stage of greatest fitness (as for eating) <peaches are *in season*> **3** : legally available to be hunted or caught — **out of season** : not in season

[2]**season** *vb* **sea·soned; sea·son·ing** \'sēz-niŋ, -ᵊn-iŋ\ [ME *sesounen,* fr. MF *assaisoner* to ripen, season, fr. OF, fr. *a-* (fr. L *ad-*) + *saison* season] *vt* **1 a** : to give (food) more flavor or zest by adding seasoning or savory ingredients; *also* : to add seasoning to **b** : to make more agreeable <advice ~*ed* with wit> **c** *archaic* : to qualify by admixture : TEMPER **2 a** : to treat (as lumber) so as to prepare for use **b** : to make fit by experience <a ~*ed* veteran> ~ *vi* : to become seasoned

sea·son·able \'sēz-nə-bəl, -ᵊn-ə-bəl\ *adj* **1** : occurring in good or proper time : OPPORTUNE <a ~ time for discussion> **2** : suitable to the season or circumstances : TIMELY <a ~ frost> — **sea·son·able·ness** *n* — **sea·son·ably** \-blē\ *adv*

syn SEASONABLE, TIMELY, OPPORTUNE, PAT *shared meaning element* : appropriate to the time or situation ***ant*** unseasonable

sea·son·al \'sēz-nəl, -ᵊn-əl\ *adj* **1** : of, relating to, or occurring at a particular season <~ storms> **2** : affected or caused by seasonal need or availability <~ unemployment> <~ industries> — **sea·son·al·ly** \-ē\ *adv*

sea·son·er \'sēz-nər, -ᵊn-ər\ *n* : one that seasons: as **a** : a user of seasonings <a heavy ~> **b** : SEASONING

sea·son·ing \'sēz-niŋ, -ᵊn-iŋ\ *n* : something that serves to season; *esp* : an ingredient (as a condiment, spice, or herb) added to food primarily for the savor that it imparts

season ticket *n* : a ticket (as to all of a club's home games or for specified daily transportation) valid during a specified time

sea spider *n* : any of various small long-legged marine arthropods (class Pycnogonida) that superficially resemble spiders

sea squirt *n* : a sessile tunicate : ASCIDIAN

sea star *n* : STARFISH

sea steps *n pl* : projecting metal plates or bars attached to the side of a ship by which it may be boarded

sea stores *n pl* : supplies (as of foodstuffs) laid in before starting on a sea voyage

sea·strand \'sē-ˌstrand\ *n* : SEASHORE

[1]**seat** \'sēt\ *n* [ME *sete,* fr. ON *sæti;* akin to OE *sittan* to sit] **1 a** : a special chair of one in eminence; *also* : the status represented by it **b** : a chair, stool, or bench intended to be sat in or on **c** : the particular part of something on which one rests in sitting <the ~ of a chair> <trouser ~>; *also* : the part of the body that bears the weight in sitting : BUTTOCKS **2 a** : a seating accommodation <a ~ for the game> <a 200-*seat* restaurant> **b** : a right of sitting <lost his ~ in Congress> **c** : membership on an exchange **3 a** : a place occupied by something **b** : a place from which authority is exercised <the county ~> **c** : a bodily part in which some function or condition is centered <the brain as the ~ of the mind> **4** : posture in or way of sitting on horseback **5 a** : a part at or forming the base of something **b** : a part (as a socket) or surface on or in which another part or surface rests

[2]**seat** *vt* **1 a** : to install in a seat of dignity or office **b** (1) : to cause to sit or assist in finding a seat (2) : to provide seats for <a theater ~*ing* 1000 persons> **c** : to put in a sitting position **2** : to repair the seat of or provide a new seat for **3** : to fit to or with a seat <~ a valve> ~ *vi* **1** *archaic* : to take one's seat or place **2** : to fit correctly on a seat — **seat·er** *n*

seat belt *n* : an arrangement of straps designed to hold a person steady in a seat (as during the takeoff of an airplane or while driving an automobile)

-seat·er \'sēt-ər\ *n comb form* : one that has a specified number of seats <the car was a four-*seater*>

seat·ing \'sēt-iŋ\ *n* **1** : the act of providing with seats **2 a** : material for covering or upholstering seats **b** : a seat on or in which something rests <a valve ~>

seat·mate \'sēt-ˌmāt\ *n* : one with whom one shares a seat

SEATO \'sē-ˌtō\ *abbr* Southeast Asia Treaty Organization

sea·train \'sē-ˌtrān\ *n* : a seagoing ship equipped for carrying a train of railroad cars

sea trout *n* **1** : any of various trouts or chars that as adults inhabit the sea but ascend rivers to spawn **2** : any of various marine fishes felt to resemble trouts: as **a** (1) : WEAKFISH 1 (2) : SPOTTED SEA TROUT **b** : a greenling (*Hexagrammos decagrammus*)

sea urchin *n* : any of a class (Echinoidea) of echinoderms usu. enclosed in thin brittle shells that are flattened and globular and covered with movable spines

sea urchin

sea·wall \'sē-ˌwȯl\ *n* : a wall or embankment to protect the shore from erosion or to act as a breakwater

[1]**sea·ward** \'sē-wərd\ *also* **sea·wards** \-wərdz\ *adv* : toward the sea

[2]**seaward** *n* : the direction or side away from land and toward the open sea

[3]**seaward** *adj* **1** directed or situated toward the sea **2** : coming from the sea <a ~ wind>

sea·ware \'sē-ˌwa(ə)r, -ˌwe(ə)r\ *n* : sea wrack for use as manure

sea wasp *n* : any of various scyphozoan jellyfishes (order or suborder Cubomedusae) that sting virulently and sometimes fatally

sea·wa·ter \'sē-ˌwȯt-ər, -ˌwät-\ *n* : water in or from the sea

sea·way \-ˌwā\ *n* **1** : a moderate or rough sea **2** : a ship's headway **3** : the sea as a route for travel; *also* : an ocean traffic lane **4** : a deep inland waterway that admits ocean shipping

sea·weed \-ˌwēd\ *n* **1** : a mass or growth of marine plants **2** : a plant growing in the sea; *esp* : a marine alga (as a kelp)

sea whip *n* : a gorgonian with an elongated flexible unbranched or little-branched axis

sea·wor·thy \'sē-ˌwər-t͟hē\ *adj* : fit or safe for a sea voyage <a ~ ship> — **sea·wor·thi·ness** \-t͟hē-nəs\ *n*

sea wrack *n* : SEAWEED; *esp* : that cast ashore in masses

se·ba·ceous \si-ˈbā-shəs\ *adj* [L *sebaceus* made of tallow, fr. *sebum* tallow — more at SOAP] **1 :** of, relating to, or being fatty material : FATTY <a ~ exudate> **2 :** secreting sebum <~ glands>

se·ba·cic acid \si-ˌbas-ik-, ˌsē-, -ˌbā-sik-\ *n* [ISV, fr. L *sebaceus*] : a crystalline dicarboxylic acid $C_{10}H_{18}O_4$ used esp. in the manufacture of synthetic resins

seb·or·rhea \ˌseb-ə-ˈrē-ə\ *n* [NL, fr. L *sebum* + NL *-rrhea*] : abnormally increased secretion and discharge of sebum — **seb·or·rhe·ic** \-ˈrē-ik\ *adj*

se·bum \ˈsē-bəm\ *n* [L, tallow, grease] : fatty lubricant matter secreted by sebaceous glands of the skin

[1]**sec** \ˈsek\ *adj* [F, lit., dry — more at SACK] *of champagne* : containing three to five percent sugar by volume : DRY

[2]**sec** *abbr* **1** second; secondary **2** secretary **3** section **4** [L *secundum*] according to

[3]**sec** *symbol* secant

SEC *abbr* Securities and Exchange Commission

se·cant \ˈsē-ˌkant, -kənt\ *n* [NL *secant-, secans,* fr. L, prp. of *secare* to cut — more at SAW] **1 :** a straight line cutting a curve at two or more points **2 a :** a straight line drawn from the center of a circle through one end of a circular arc to a tangent drawn from the other end of the arc **b :** the trigonometric function that for an acute angle is the ratio of the hypotenuse of a right triangle of which the angle is considered part and the side adjacent to the angle

sec·a·teur \ˌsek-ə-ˈtər\ *n* [F *sécateur,* fr. L *secare* to cut] *chiefly Brit* : pruning shears — usu. used in pl.

[1]**sec·co** \ˈsek-(ˌ)ō\ *n* [It, fr. *secco* dry, fr. L *siccus* — more at SACK] : the art of painting on dry plaster

[2]**secco** *adj or adv* [It, lit., dry] **1 :** short and very staccato — used as a direction in music **2** *of a recitative* : accompanied only by the instruments playing the continuo

se·cede \si-ˈsēd\ *vi* **se·ced·ed; se·ced·ing** [L *secedere,* fr. *sed-, se-* apart (*fr. sed, se* without) + *cedere* to go — more at IDIOT, CEDE] : to withdraw from an organization or communion (as a church or political party) — **se·ced·er** *n*

se·cern \si-ˈsərn\ *vt* [L *secernere* to separate — more at SECRET] : to discriminate in thought : DISTINGUISH

se·ces·sion \si-ˈsesh-ən\ *n* [L *secession-, secessio,* fr. *secessus,* pp. of *secedere*] **1 :** withdrawal into privacy or solitude : RETIREMENT **2 :** formal withdrawal from an organization (as a religious communion or political party or federation)

se·ces·sion·ism \-ˈsesh-ə-ˌniz-əm\ *n* : the doctrine or policy of secession

se·ces·sion·ist \-ˈsesh-(ə-)nəst\ *n* : one who joins in a secession or maintains that secession is a right

se·clude \si-ˈklüd\ *vt* **se·clud·ed; se·clud·ing** [ME *secluden* to keep away, fr. L *secludere* to separate, seclude, fr. *se-* apart + *claudere* to close — more at SECEDE, CLOSE] **1 :** to remove or separate from intercourse or outside influence : ISOLATE **2** *obs* : to exclude from a privilege, rank, or dignity : DEBAR **3** *obs* : to shut off : SCREEN

se·clud·ed *adj* **1 :** screened or hidden from view : SEQUESTERED <a ~ valley> **2 :** living in seclusion : SOLITARY <~ monks> — **se·clud·ed·ly** *adv* — **se·clud·ed·ness** *n*

se·clu·sion \si-ˈklü-zhən\ *n* [ML *seclusion-, seclusio,* fr. L *seclusus,* pp. of *secludere*] **1 :** the act of secluding : the condition of being secluded **2 :** a secluded or isolated place ***syn*** see SOLITUDE — **se·clu·sive** \-ˈklü-siv, -ziv\ *adj* — **se·clu·sive·ly** *adv* — **se·clu·sive·ness** *n*

seco·bar·bi·tal \ˌsek-ō-ˈbär-bə-ˌtȯl\ *n* [*seco*nal + *barbital*] : a barbiturate $C_{12}H_{18}N_2O_3$ that is used chiefly in the form of its bitter hygroscopic powdery sodium salt as a hypnotic and sedative

[1]**sec·ond** \ˈsek-ənd *also* -ənt, *esp before a consonant* -ən, -ᵊŋ\ *adj* [ME, fr. OF, fr. L *secundus* second, following, favorable, fr. *sequi* to follow — more at SUE] **1 a :** next to the first in place or time <was ~ in line> **b (1) :** next to the first in value, excellence, or degree <his ~ choice of schools> **(2) :** INFERIOR, SUBORDINATE <was ~ to none> **c :** ranking next below the top of a grade or degree in authority or precedence <~ mate> **d :** ALTERNATE, OTHER <elects a mayor every ~ year> **e :** resembling or suggesting a prototype : ANOTHER <a ~ Thoreau> **f :** ingrained by discipline, training, or effort : ACQUIRED <~ nature> **g :** being the forward gear or speed next higher than first in a motor vehicle **2 :** relating to or having a part typically subordinate to and lower in pitch than the first part in concerted or ensemble music — **second** *or* **sec·ond·ly** *adv*

[2]**second** *n* **1 a** — see NUMBER table **b :** one that is next after the first in rank, position, authority, or precedence <the ~ in line> **2 :** one that assists or supports another; *esp* : the assistant of a duelist or boxer **3 a :** the musical interval embracing two diatonic degrees **b :** a tone at this interval; *specif* : SUPERTONIC **c :** the harmonic combination of two tones a second apart **4 a** *pl* : merchandise that is usu. slightly flawed and does not meet the manufacturer's standard for firsts or irregulars **b :** an article of such merchandise **5 :** the act or declaration by which a parliamentary motion is seconded **6 :** a place next below the first in a competition, examination, or contest **7 :** SECOND BASE **8 :** the second forward gear or speed of a motor vehicle **9** *pl* : a second helping of food

[3]**second** *n* [ME *secunde,* fr. ML *secunda,* fr. L, fem. of *secundus* second; fr. its being the second sexagesimal division of a unit, as a minute is the first] **1 :** the 60th part of a minute of time or of a minute of angular measure **2 :** an instant of time : MOMENT

[4]**second** *vt* [L *secundare,* fr. *secundus* second, favorable] **1 a :** to give support or encouragement to : ASSIST **b :** to support (a fighting man) in combat : to bring up reinforcements for **2 a :** to support or assist in contention or debate **b :** to endorse (a motion or a nomination) so that debate or voting may begin **3** *chiefly Brit* : to release (as a military officer) from a regularly assigned position for temporary duty with another unit or organization — **sec·ond·er** *n*

[1]**sec·ond·ary** \ˈsek-ən-ˌder-ē\ *adj* **1 a :** of second rank, importance, or value **b :** of, relating to, or constituting the second strongest of the three or four degrees of stress recognized by most linguists <the fourth syllable of *basketball team* carries ~ stress> **c** *of a tense* : expressive of past time **2 a :** immediately derived from something original, primary, or basic **b :** of or relating to the induced current or its circuit in an induction coil or transformer <a ~ coil> <~ voltage> **c :** characterized by or resulting from the substitution of two atoms or groups in a molecule <a ~ salt>; *esp* : being or characterized by a carbon atom united by two valences to chain or ring members **d (1) :** not first in order of occurrence or development **(2) :** produced by activity of formative tissue and esp. cambium other than that at a growing point <~ growth> <~ phloem> **3 a :** of or relating to the second order or stage in a series **b :** of, relating to, or being the second segment of the wing of a bird or the quills of this segment **c :** of or relating to a secondary school <~ education> — **sec·ond·ari·ly** \ˌsek-ən-ˈder-ə-lē\ *adv* — **sec·ond·ari·ness** \ˈsek-ən-ˌder-ē-nəs\ *n*

[2]**secondary** *n, pl* **-ar·ies** **1 :** one occupying a subordinate or auxiliary position rather than that of a principal **2 :** a defensive football backfield **3 :** a secondary electrical circuit or coil **4 :** any of the quill feathers of the forearm of a bird — see BIRD illustration

secondary cell *n* : STORAGE CELL

secondary color *n* : a color formed by mixing primary colors in equal or equivalent quantities

secondary emission *n* : the emission of electrons from a surface that is bombarded by particles (as electrons or ions) from a primary source

secondary radiation *n* : rays (as X rays or beta rays) emitted by molecules or atoms as the result of the incidence of a primary radiation

secondary road *n* **1 :** a road not of primary importance **2 :** a feeder road

secondary root *n* : one of the branches of a primary root

secondary school *n* : a school intermediate between elementary school and college and usu. offering general, technical, vocational, or college-preparatory courses

secondary sex characteristic *n* : a physical or mental characteristic (as the breasts of a female mammal or the nuptial plumage of a male bird) that appears in members of one sex at puberty or in seasonal breeders at the breeding season and is not directly concerned with reproduction — called also *secondary sexual characteristic*

secondary syphilis *n* : the second stage of syphilis that appears from 2 to 6 months after primary infection, that is marked by lesions esp. in the skin but also in organs and tissues, and that lasts from 3 to 12 weeks

second base *n* **1 :** the base that must be touched second by a base runner in baseball **2 :** the player position for defending the area of the baseball infield on the first-base side of second base — **second baseman** *n*

sec·ond–best \ˌsek-ən-ˈbest, -ᵊŋ-\ *adj* : next to the best

[1]**second best** *n* : one that is below or after the best

[2]**second best** *adv* : in second place

second blessing *n* : sanctification as a second gift of the Holy Spirit that follows an initial experience of conversion

second childhood *n* : DOTAGE

second–class *adj* **1 :** of or relating to a second class **2 :** INFERIOR, MEDIOCRE; *also* : socially, politically, or economically deprived <~ citizens>

second class *n* **1 :** the second and usu. next to highest group in a classification **2 :** CABIN CLASS **3 :** a class of U.S. or Canadian mail comprising newspapers and periodicals sent to regular subscribers

Second Coming *n* : the coming of Christ as judge on the last day

second consonant shift *n* : CONSONANT SHIFT b

second–degree burn *n* : a burn marked by pain, blistering, and superficial destruction of dermis with edema and hyperemia of the tissues beneath the burn

Second Empire \ˌsek-ən-ˈdem-ˌpī(ə)r\ *adj* : of, relating to, or characteristic of a style (as of furniture) developed in France under Napoleon III and marked by heavy ornate modification of Empire styles

second estate *n, often cap S&E* : the second of the traditional political classes; *specif* : NOBILITY

second growth *n* : forest trees that come up naturally after removal of the first growth by cutting or by fire

sec·ond–guess \ˌsek-ᵊŋ-ˈges, -ən-\ *vt* **1 :** to think out alternative strategies or explanations for after the event **2 a :** OUTGUESS **b :** PREDICT — **sec·ond–guess·er** *n*

[1]**sec·ond·hand** \ˌsek-ən-ˈ\ *adj* **1 a :** received from or through an intermediary : BORROWED **b :** DERIVATIVE <~ ideas> **2 a :** acquired after being used by another : not new <~ books> **b :** dealing in secondhand merchandise <a ~ bookstore>

[2]**secondhand** \ˌsek-ən-ˈ\ *adv* : at second hand : INDIRECTLY

[1]**second hand** \ˌsek-ən-ˈhand\ *n* : an intermediate person or means : INTERMEDIARY — usu. used in the phrase *at second hand*

[2]**second hand** \ˈsek-ən-ˌ\ *n* : the hand marking seconds on a timepiece

second lieutenant *n* : a commissioned officer of the lowest rank in the army, air force, or marine corps

second mortgage *n* : a mortgage the lien of which is subordinate to that of a first mortgage

se·con·do \si-ˈkōn-(ˌ)dō, -ˈkän-\ *n, pl* **-di** \-(ˌ)dē\ [It, fr. *secondo,* adj., second, fr. L *secundus*] : the second part in a concerted piece; *esp* : the lower part (as in a piano duet)

second person *n* **1 a :** a set of linguistic forms (as verb forms, pronouns, and inflectional affixes) referring to the person or thing

addressed in the utterance in which they occur **b :** a linguistic form belonging to such a set **2 :** reference of a linguistic form to the person or thing addressed in the utterance in which it occurs
sec·ond–rate \ˌsek-ən-ˈ(d)rāt\ *adj* **:** of second or inferior quality or value **:** MEDIOCRE — **sec·ond–rate·ness** *n* — **sec·ond–rat·er** \-ˈ(d)rāt-ər\ *n*
Second Reader *n* **:** a member of a Christian Science church or society chosen for a term of office to assist the First Reader in conducting services by reading aloud selections from the Bible
second reading *n* **1 :** the stage in the British legislative process following the first reading and usu. providing for debate on the principal features of a bill before its submission to a committee for consideration of details **2 :** the stage in the U.S. legislative process that occurs when a bill has been reported back from committee and that provides an opportunity for full debate and amendment before a vote is taken on the question of a third reading
second sight *n* **:** the capacity to see remote or future objects or events **:** CLAIRVOYANCE, PRECOGNITION
second–story man *n* **:** a burglar who enters a house by an upstairs window
sec·ond–string \ˌsek-ən-ˌstriŋ, ˌsek-ᵊŋ-\ *adj* [fr. the reserve bowstring carried by an archer in case the first breaks] **:** being a substitute as distinguished from a regular (as on a ball team)
second thought *n* **:** reconsideration or a revised opinion of a previous often hurried decision <began to have *second thoughts*>
second wind *n* **:** renewed energy or endurance
se·cre·cy \ˈsē-krə-sē\ *n, pl* **-cies** [alter. of earlier *secretie,* fr. ME *secretee,* fr. *secre* secret, fr. MF *secré,* fr. L *secretus*] **1 :** the habit or practice of keeping secrets or maintaining privacy or concealment **2 :** the condition of being hidden or concealed
1se·cret \ˈsē-krət\ *adj* [ME, fr. MF, fr. L *secretus,* fr. pp. of *secernere* to separate, distinguish, fr. *se-* apart + *cernere* to sift — more at SECEDE, CERTAIN] **1 a :** kept from knowledge or view **:** HIDDEN **b :** marked by the habit of discretion **:** CLOSEMOUTHED **c :** working with hidden aims or methods **:** UNDERCOVER <a ~ agent> **d :** not acknowledged **:** UNAVOWED <a ~ bride> **e :** conducted in secret <a ~ trial> **2 :** remote from human frequentation or notice **:** SECLUDED **3 :** revealed only to the initiated **:** ESOTERIC **4 :** constructed so as to elude observation or detection <a ~ panel> **5 :** containing information whose unauthorized disclosure could endanger national security — compare CONFIDENTIAL, TOP SECRET — **se·cret·ly** *adv*
syn SECRET, COVERT, STEALTHY, FURTIVE, CLANDESTINE, SURREPTITIOUS, UNDERHAND, UNDERHANDED ***shared meaning element* :** existing or done in such a way as to elude attention or observation
2secret *n* **1 a :** something kept hidden or unexplained **:** MYSTERY **b :** something kept from the knowledge of others or shared only confidentially with a few **c :** a method, formula, or process used in an art or a manufacturing operation and divulged only to those of one's own company or craft **d** *pl* **:** the practices or knowledge making up the shared discipline or culture of an esoteric society **2 :** a prayer traditionally said inaudibly by the celebrant just before the preface of the mass **3 :** something taken to be a specific or key to a desired end <the ~ of longevity> — **in secret :** in a private place or manner **:** in secrecy
se·cre·ta·gogue \si-ˈkrēt-ə-ˌgäg\ *n* [*secretion* + *-agogue*] **:** a substance stimulating secretion (as by the stomach or pancreas)
sec·re·tar·i·at \ˌsek-rə-ˈter-ē-ət\ *n* [F *secrétariat,* fr. ML *secretariatus,* fr. *secretarius*] **1 :** the office of secretary **2 :** a secretarial corps; *specif* **:** the clerical staff of an organization **3 :** the administrative department of a governmental organization
sec·re·tary \ˈsek-rə-ˌter-ē\ *n, pl* **-tar·ies** [ME *secretarie,* fr. ML *secretarius,* confidential employee, secretary, fr. L *secretum* secret, fr. neut. of *secretus,* pp.] **1 :** one employed to handle correspondence and manage routine and detail work for a superior **2 a :** an officer of a business concern who may keep records of directors' and stockholders' meetings and of stock ownership and transfer and help supervise the company's legal interests **b :** an officer of an organization or society responsible for its records and correspondence **3 :** an officer of state who superintends a government administrative department **4 a :** WRITING DESK, ESCRITOIRE **b :** a writing desk with a top section for books — **sec·re·tari·al** \ˌsek-rə-ˈter-ē-əl\ *adj* — **sec·re·tary·ship** \ˈ-sek-rə-ˌter-ē-ˌship\ *n*

secretary 4b

secretary bird *n* [prob. fr. the resemblance of its crest to a bunch of quill pens stuck behind the ear] **:** a large long-legged African bird of prey (*Sagittarius serpentarius*) that feeds largely upon reptiles
secretary–general *n, pl* **secretaries–general :** a principal administrative officer
secret ballot *n* **:** AUSTRALIAN BALLOT
1se·crete \si-ˈkrēt\ *vt* **se·cret·ed; se·cret·ing** [back-formation fr. *secretion*] **:** to form and give off (a secretion)
2se·crete \si-ˈkrēt, ˈsē-krət\ *vt* **se·cret·ed; se·cret·ing** [alter. of obs. *secret,* fr. *1secret*] **1 :** to deposit or conceal in a hiding place **2 :** to appropriate secretly **:** ABSTRACT ***syn*** see HIDE
se·cre·tin \si-ˈkrēt-ᵊn\ *n* [*secretion* + *-in*] **:** an intestinal hormone capable of stimulating the pancreas and liver to secrete
se·cre·tion \si-ˈkrē-shən\ *n* [F *sécrétion,* fr. L *secretion-, secretio* separation, fr. *secretus,* pp. of *secernere* to separate — more at SECRET] **1 a :** the process of segregating, elaborating, and releasing some material either functionally specialized (as saliva) or isolated for excretion (as urine) **b :** a product of secretion formed by an animal or plant; *esp* **:** one performing a specific useful function in the organism **2** [*2secrete*] **:** the act of hiding something **:** CONCEALMENT — **se·cre·tion·ary** \-shə-ˌner-ē\ *adj*
se·cre·tive \ˈsē-krət-iv, si-ˈkrēt-\ *adj* [back-formation fr. *secretiveness,* part trans. of F *secrétivité*] **:** disposed to secrecy **:** not open or outgoing in speech, activity, or purposes ***syn*** see SILENT ***ant*** frank — **se·cre·tive·ly** *adv* — **se·cre·tive·ness** *n*
se·cre·tor \si-ˈkrēt-ər\ *n* **:** an individual of blood group A, B, or AB who secretes the antigens characteristic of these blood groups in bodily fluids (as saliva)
se·cre·to·ry \si-ˈkrēt-ə-rē\ *adj* **:** of, relating to, or promoting secretion; *also* **:** produced by secretion
secret partner *n* **:** a partner whose membership in a partnership is kept secret from the public
secret police *n* **:** a police organization operating for the most part in secrecy and esp. for the political purposes of its government often with terroristic methods
secret service *n* **1 :** a governmental service of a secret nature **2** *cap both Ss* **:** a division of the U.S. Treasury Department charged chiefly with the suppression of counterfeiting and the protection of the president
secret society *n* **:** any of various oath-bound societies often devoted to brotherhood, moral discipline, and mutual assistance
1sect \ˈsekt\ *n* [ME *secte,* fr. MF & LL & L; MF, group, sect, fr. LL *secta* organized ecclesiastical body, fr. L, way of life, class of persons, fr. *sequi* to follow] **1 a :** a dissenting or schismatic religious body; *esp* **:** one regarded as extreme or heretical **b :** a religious denomination **2** *archaic* **:** SEX <so is all her ~ —Shak.> **3 a :** a group adhering to a distinctive doctrine or to a leader **b :** PARTY **c :** FACTION
2sect *abbr* section; sectional
1-sect \ˌsekt\ *adj comb form* [L *sectus,* pp. of *secare* to cut — more at SAW] **:** cut **:** divided <pinnati*sect*>
2-sect \ˌsekt, ˈsekt\ *vb comb form* [L *sectus*] **:** cut **:** divide <bi*sect*>
1sec·tar·i·an \sek-ˈter-ē-ən\ *adj* **1 :** of, relating to, or characteristic of a sect or sectarian **2 :** limited in character or scope **:** PAROCHIAL — **sec·tar·i·an·ism** \-ē-ə-ˌniz-əm\ *n*
2sectarian *n* **1 :** an adherent of a sect **2 :** a narrow or bigoted person
sec·tar·i·an·ize \sek-ˈter-ē-ə-ˌnīz\ *vb* **-ized; -iz·ing** *vi* **:** to act as sectarians ~ *vt* **:** to make sectarian
sec·ta·ry \ˈsek-tə-rē\ *n, pl* **-ries :** a member of a sect
sec·tile \ˈsek-tᵊl, -ˌtīl\ *adj* [L *sectilis,* fr. *sectus*] **:** capable of being severed by a knife with a smooth cut — **sec·til·i·ty** \sek-ˈtil-ət-ē\ *n*
1sec·tion \ˈsek-shən\ *n* [L *section-, sectio,* fr. *sectus*] **1 a :** the action or an instance of cutting or separating by cutting **b :** a part set off by or as if by cutting **2 :** a distinct part or portion of a writing: as **a :** a subdivision of a chapter **b :** a division of a law **c :** a distinct component part of a newspaper **3 a :** the profile of something as it would appear if cut through by an intersecting plane **b :** the plane figure resulting from the cutting of a solid by a plane **4 :** a natural subdivision of a taxonomic group **5:** a character § commonly used in printing as a mark for the beginning of a section and as the fourth in series of the reference marks **6 :** a piece of land one square mile in area forming one of the 36 subdivisions of a township **7 :** a distinct part of a territorial or political area, community, or group of people **8 a :** a part that is, may be, or is viewed as separated <chop the stalks into ~*s*> <the northern ~ of the route> **b :** one segment of a fruit **:** CARPEL **9 :** a basic military unit usu. having a special function **10 :** a very thin slice (as of tissue) suitable for microscopic examination **11 a :** one of the classes formed by dividing the students taking a course **b :** one of the discussion groups into which a conference or organization is divided **12 a :** a division of a railroad sleeping car with an upper and a lower berth **b :** a part of a permanent railroad way under the care of a particular set of men **c :** one of two or more vehicles or trains which run on the same schedule **13 :** one of several component parts that may be assembled or reassembled <a bookcase in ~*s*> **14 :** a division of an orchestra composed of one class of instruments **15 :** SIGNATURE 3b ***syn*** see PART
2section *vb* **sec·tioned; sec·tion·ing** \-sh(ə-)niŋ\ *vt* **1 :** to cut or separate into sections **2 :** to represent in sections ~ *vi* **:** to become cut or separated into parts
1sec·tion·al \ˈsek-shnəl, -shən-ᵊl\ *adj* **1 a :** of or relating to a section **b :** local or regional rather than general in character <~ interests> **2 :** consisting of or divided into sections <~ furniture> — **sec·tion·al·ly** \-ē\ *adv*
2sectional *n* **:** a piece of furniture made up of modular units capable of use separately or in various combinations
sec·tion·al·ism \ˈsek-shnə-ˌliz-əm, -shən-ᵊl-ˌiz-\ *n* **:** an exaggerated devotion to the interests of a region
Section Eight *n* [*Section VIII,* Army Regulation 615-360, in effect from December 1922 to July 1944] **1 :** a discharge from the U.S. Army for military inaptitude or undesirable habits or traits of character **2 :** a soldier discharged for military inaptitude or undesirable habits or traits of character
section gang *n* **:** a crew of track workers employed to maintain a railroad section
section hand *n* **:** a laborer belonging to a section gang
1sec·tor \ˈsek-tər, -ˌtȯ(ə)r\ *n* [LL, fr. L, cutter, fr. *sectus,* pp. of *secare* to cut — more at SAW] **1 a :** a geometrical figure bounded by two radii and the included arc of a circle **b (1) :** a subdivision of a defensive military position **(2) :** a portion of a military front or area of operation **2 :** a mathematical instrument consisting of two rulers connected at one end by a joint and marked with several scales **3 :** a distinctive part (as of an economy)
2sec·tor \-tər\ *vt* **sec·tored; sec·tor·ing** \-t(ə-)riŋ\ **:** to divide into or furnish with sectors
sec·to·ri·al \sek-ˈtōr-ē-əl, -ˈtȯr-\ *adj* **1 :** of, relating to, or having the shape of a sector of a circle **2** *of a chimera* **:** having a sector of variant growth interposed in an otherwise normal body of tissue
1sec·u·lar \ˈsek-yə-lər\ *adj* [ME, fr. OF *seculer,* fr. LL *saecularis,* fr. L, coming once in an age, fr. *saeculum* breed, generation; akin to L *serere* to sow — more at SOW] **1 a :** of or relating to the worldly or temporal <~ concerns> **b :** not overtly or specif. religious <~ music> **c :** not ecclesiastical or clerical <~ courts> <~ landowners> **2 :** not bound by monastic vows or rules; *specif* **:** of, relating to, or forming clergy not belonging to a religious order

or congregation <a ~ priest> **3 a :** occurring once in an age or a century **b :** existing or continuing through ages or centuries **c :** of or relating to a long term of indefinite duration — **sec·u·lar·i·ty** \ˌsek-yə-ˈlar-ət-ē\ *n* — **sec·u·lar·ly** \ˈsek-yə-lər-lē\ *adv*

²secular *n, pl* **seculars** *or* **secular** **1 :** a secular ecclesiastic (as a parish priest) **2 :** LAYMAN

sec·u·lar·ism \ˈsek-yə-lə-ˌriz-əm\ *n* **:** indifference to or rejection or exclusion of religion and religious considerations — **sec·u·lar·ist** \-rəst\ *n* — **secularist** *or* **sec·u·lar·is·tic** \ˌsek-yə-lə-ˈris-tik\ *adj*

sec·u·lar·ize \ˈsek-yə-lə-ˌrīz\ *vt* **-ized; -iz·ing** **1 :** to make secular **2 :** to transfer from ecclesiastical to civil or lay use, possession, or control **3 :** to convert to or imbue with secularism — **sec·u·lar·iza·tion** \ˌsek-yə-lə-rə-ˈzā-shən\ *n* — **sec·u·lar·iz·er** *n*

se·cund \si-ˈkənd, ˈsē-ˌ\ *adj* [L *secundus* following — more at SECOND] **:** having some part or element arranged on one side only **:** UNILATERAL <~ racemes>

¹se·cure \si-ˈkyu̇(ə)r\ *adj* **se·cur·er; -est** [L *securus* safe, secure, fr. *se* without + *cura* care — more at IDIOT, CURE] **1 a** *archaic* **:** unwisely free from fear or distrust **:** OVERCONFIDENT **b :** easy in mind **:** CONFIDENT **c :** assured in opinion or expectation **:** having no doubt **2 a :** free from danger **b :** free from risk of loss **c :** affording safety **:** INVIOLABLE <a ~ hideaway> **d :** TRUSTWORTHY, DEPENDABLE <~ foundation> **3 :** ASSURED, CERTAIN <~ victory> ***syn*** see SAFE ***ant*** precarious, dangerous — **se·cure·ly** *adv* — **se·cure·ness** *n*

²secure *vb* **se·cured; se·cur·ing** *vt* **1 a :** to relieve from exposure to danger **:** act to make safe against adverse contingencies <he locked the door to ~ them from interruption> <~ a supply line from enemy raids> **b :** to put beyond hazard of losing or of not receiving **:** GUARANTEE <~ the blessings of liberty —*U.S. Constitution*> **c :** to give pledge of payment to (a creditor) or of (an obligation) <~ a note by a pledge of collateral> **2 a :** to take (a person) into custody **:** hold fast **:** PINION **b :** to make fast **:** SEAL <~ a door> **3 a :** to get secure usu. lasting possession or control of <~ employment> **b :** to bring about **:** EFFECT **4 :** to release (naval personnel) from work or duty ~ *vi* **1** *of naval personnel* **:** to stop work **:** go off duty **2** *of a ship* **:** to tie up **:** BERTH ***syn*** see ENSURE, GET — **se·cur·er** *n*

se·cure·ment \si-ˈkyu̇(ə)r-mənt\ *n* **1** *obs* **:** PROTECTION **2 :** the act or process of securing

se·cu·ri·ty \si-ˈkyu̇r-ət-ē\ *n, pl* **-ties** **1 :** the quality or state of being secure: as **a :** freedom from danger **:** SAFETY **b :** freedom from fear or anxiety **c :** freedom from want or deprivation <job ~> **2 a :** something given, deposited, or pledged to make certain the fulfillment of an obligation **b :** SURETY **3 :** an evidence of debt or of ownership (as a stock certificate or bond) **4 a :** something that secures **:** PROTECTION **b (1) :** measures taken to guard against espionage or sabotage, crime, attack, or escape **(2) :** an organization or department whose task is security

security blanket *n* **1 :** a blanket carried by a child as a protection against anxiety **2 :** a usu. familiar object whose presence dispels anxiety

Security Council *n* **:** a permanent council of the United Nations having primary responsibility for the maintenance of peace and security

security interest *n* **:** the rights that a creditor has in the personal property of a debtor that secures an obligation **:** LIEN

security police *n* **1 :** police engaged in counterespionage **2 :** AIR POLICE

secy *abbr* secretary

sed *abbr* sediment; sedimentation

se·dan \si-ˈdan\ *n* [origin unknown] **1 :** a portable often covered chair that is designed to carry one person and that is borne on poles by two men **2 a :** an enclosed automobile seating four to seven persons including the driver and having a single compartment, two or four doors, and a permanent top **b :** a motorboat having one passenger compartment

sedan 1

¹se·date \si-ˈdāt\ *adj* [L *sedatus*, fr. pp. of *sedare* to calm; akin to *sedēre* to sit — more at SIT] **:** keeping a quiet steady attitude or pace **:** UNRUFFLED ***syn*** see SERIOUS ***ant*** flighty — **se·date·ly** *adv* — **se·date·ness** *n*

²sedate *vt* **se·dat·ed; se·dat·ing** [back-formation fr. *sedative*] **:** to dose with sedatives

se·da·tion \si-ˈdā-shən\ *n* **1 :** the inducing of a relaxed easy state esp. by the use of sedatives **2 :** a state resulting from or like that resulting from sedation

¹sed·a·tive \ˈsed-ət-iv\ *adj* **:** tending to calm, moderate, or tranquilize nervousness or excitement

²sedative *n* **:** a sedative agent or drug

sed·en·tary \ˈsed-ᵊn-ˌter-ē\ *adj* [MF *sedentaire*, fr. L *sedentarius*, fr. *sedent-*, *sedens*, prp. of *sedēre* to sit] **1 :** not migratory **:** SETTLED <~ birds> **2 :** doing or requiring much sitting **3 :** permanently attached <~ barnacles>

se·der \ˈsād-ər\ *n, often cap* [Heb *sēdher* order] **:** a Jewish home or community service including a ceremonial dinner held on the first evening of the Passover and repeated on the second by Orthodox Jews except in Israel in commemoration of the exodus from Egypt

se·de·runt \sə-ˈdir-ənt, -ˈder-\ *n* [L, there sat (fr. *sedēre* to sit), word used to introduce list of those attending a session — more at SIT] **:** a prolonged sitting (as for discussion)

sedge \ˈsej\ *n* [ME *segge*, fr. OE *secg*; akin to MHG *segge* sedge, OE *sagu* saw — more at SAW] **:** any of a family (Cyperaceae, the sedge family) of usu. tufted marsh plants differing from the related grasses in having achenes and solid stems; *esp* **:** any of a cosmopolitan genus (*Carex*) — **sedgy** \ˈsej-ē\ *adj*

se·di·lia \sə-ˈdēl-yə, -ˈdil-, *esp Brit* -ˈdil-\ *n pl* [L, pl. of *sedile* seat, fr. *sedēre*] **:** seats on the south side of the chancel for the celebrant, deacon, and subdeacon

¹sed·i·ment \ˈsed-ə-mənt\ *n* [MF, fr. L *sedimentum* settling, fr. *sedēre* to sit, sink down] **1 :** the matter that settles to the bottom of a liquid **2 :** material deposited by water, wind, or glaciers

²sed·i·ment \-ˌment\ *vt* **:** to deposit as sediment ~ *vi* **1 :** to settle to the bottom in a liquid **2 :** to deposit sediment

sed·i·men·ta·ry \ˌsed-ə-ˈment-ə-rē, -ˈmen-trē\ *adj* **1 :** of, relating to, or containing sediment <~ deposits> **2 :** formed by or from deposits of sediment

sedimentary rock *n* **:** rock formed of mechanical, chemical, or organic sediment: as **a :** rock (as sandstone or shale) formed of fragments transported from their source and deposited elsewhere by water **b :** rock (as rock salt or gypsum) formed by precipitation or solution **c :** rock (as limestone) formed from inorganic remains (as shells and skeletons) of organisms

sed·i·men·ta·tion \ˌsed-ə-mən-ˈtā-shən, -ˌmen-\ *n* **:** the action or process of forming or depositing sediment **:** SETTLING

sed·i·men·tol·o·gy \ˌsed-ə-mən-ˈtäl-ə-jē, -ˌmen-\ *n* **:** a branch of science that deals with sedimentary rocks and their inclusions — **sed·i·men·to·log·ic** \-ˌment-ᵊl-ˈäj-ik\ *or* **sed·i·men·to·log·i·cal** \-i-kəl\ *adj* — **sed·i·men·to·log·i·cal·ly** \-i-k(ə-)lē\ *adv* — **sed·i·men·tol·o·gist** \-mən-ˈtäl-ə-jəst, -ˌmen-\ *n*

se·di·tion \si-ˈdish-ən\ *n* [ME, fr. MF, fr. L *sedition-*, *seditio*, lit., separation, fr. *se-* apart + *ition-*, *itio* act of going, fr. *itus*, pp. of *ire* to go — more at SECEDE, ISSUE] **:** incitement of resistance to or insurrection against lawful authority

se·di·tious \si-ˈdish-əs\ *adj* **1 :** disposed to arouse or take part in or guilty of sedition **2 :** of, relating to, or tending to incite to sedition — **se·di·tious·ly** *adv* — **se·di·tious·ness** *n*

se·duce \si-ˈd(y)üs\ *vt* **se·duced; se·duc·ing** [LL *seducere*, fr. L, to lead away, fr. *se-* apart + *ducere* to lead — more at TOW] **1 :** to persuade to disobedience or disloyalty **2 :** to lead astray usu. by persuasion or false promises **3 :** to carry out the physical seduction of **4 :** ATTRACT ***syn*** see LURE — **se·duc·er** *n*

se·duce·ment \-ˈd(y)ü-smənt\ *n* **1 :** SEDUCTION **2 :** something that serves to seduce

se·duc·tion \si-ˈdək-shən\ *n* [MF, fr. LL *seduction-*, *seductio*, fr. L, act of leading aside, fr. *seductus*, pp. of *seducere*] **1 :** the act of seducing to wrong; *specif* **:** the enticement of a female to unlawful sexual intercourse without use of force **2 :** something that seduces **:** TEMPTATION **3 :** something that attracts or charms

se·duc·tive \-ˈdək-tiv\ *adj* **:** tending to seduce **:** having alluring or tempting qualities <a ~ woman> <a ~ spring morning> — **se·duc·tive·ly** *adv* — **se·duc·tive·ness** *n*

se·duc·tress \-ˈdək-trəs\ *n* [obs. *seductor* male seducer, fr. LL, fr. *seductus*, pp. of *seducere* to seduce] **:** a female seducer

se·du·li·ty \si-ˈd(y)ü-lət-ē\ *n* **:** sedulous activity **:** DILIGENCE

sed·u·lous \ˈsej-ə-ləs\ *adj* [L *sedulus*, fr. *sedulo* sincerely, diligently, fr. *se* without + *dolus* guile — more at IDIOT, TALE] **1 :** involving or accomplished with careful perseverance <~ craftmanship> **2 :** diligent in application or pursuit <a ~ student> ***syn*** see BUSY — **sed·u·lous·ly** *adv* — **sed·u·lous·ness** *n*

se·dum \ˈsēd-əm\ *n* [NL, genus name, fr. L, houseleek] **:** any of a genus (*Sedum*) of fleshy widely distributed herbs of the orpine family **:** STONECROP

¹see \ˈsē\ *vb* **saw** \ˈsȯ\; **seen** \ˈsēn\; **see·ing** \ˈsē-iŋ\ [ME *seen*, fr. OE *sēon*; akin to OHG *sehan* to see, OE *secgan* to say — more at SAY] *vt* **1 :** to perceive by the eye **2 a :** to have experience of **:** UNDERGO <~ army service> **b :** to come to know **:** DISCOVER **3 a :** to form a mental picture of **:** VISUALIZE <can still ~ her as she was years ago> **b :** to perceive the meaning or importance of **:** UNDERSTAND **c :** to be aware of **:** RECOGNIZE <~*s* only his faults> **d :** to imagine as a possibility **:** SUPPOSE <couldn't ~ him as a crook> **4 a :** EXAMINE, WATCH <want to ~ how he handles the problem> **b (1) :** READ **(2) :** to read of **c :** to attend as a spectator <~ a play> **5 a :** to take care of **:** provide for <had enough money to ~ us through> **b :** to make sure <~ that order is kept> **6 a :** to regard as **:** JUDGE **b :** to prefer to have <I'll ~ him hanged first> <I'll ~ you dead before I accept your terms> **c :** to find acceptable or attractive <can't understand what he ~*s* in her> **7 a :** to call on **:** VISIT **b (1) :** to keep company with esp. in courtship or dating <had been ~*ing* each other for a year> **(2) :** to grant an interview to **:** RECEIVE <the president will ~ you> **8 :** ACCOMPANY, ESCORT <~ the girls home> **9 :** to meet (a bet) in poker or to equal the bet of (a player) **:** CALL ~ *vi* **1 a :** to give or pay attention **b :** to look about **2 a :** to have the power of sight **b :** to apprehend objects by sight **3 :** to grasp something mentally **4 :** to make investigation or inquiry
syn SEE, LOOK, WATCH *shared meaning element* **:** to perceive something by use of the eyes
— **see after :** to attend to **:** care for — **see eye to eye :** to have a common viewpoint **:** AGREE — **see things :** HALLUCINATE — **see through :** to grasp the true nature of <*saw through* his deceptions> — **see to :** to attend to **:** care for

²see *n* [ME *se*, fr. OF, fr. L *sedes* seat; akin to L *sedēre* to sit — more at SIT] **1 a** *archaic* **:** CATHEDRA **b :** a cathedral town **c :** a seat of a bishop's office, power, or authority **2 :** the authority or jurisdiction of a bishop

see·able \ˈsē-ə-bəl\ *adj* **:** capable of being seen

¹seed \ˈsēd\ *n, pl* **seed** *or* **seeds** [ME, fr. OE *sǣd*; akin to OHG *sāt* seed, OE *sāwan* to sow — more at SOW] **1 a (1) :** the grains or ripened ovules of plants used for sowing **(2) :** the fertilized ripened ovule of a flowering plant containing an embryo and capable normally of germination to produce a new plant; *broadly* **:** a propagative plant structure (as a spore or small dry fruit) **b :** a propagative animal structure: **(1) :** MILT, SEMEN **(2) :** a small egg (as of an insect) **(3) :** a developmental form of a lower animal

ə abut	ᵊ kitten	ər further	a back	ā bake	ä cot, cart
au̇ out	ch chin	e less	ē easy	g gift	i trip	ī life
j joke	ŋ sing	ō flow	ȯ flaw	ȯi coin	th thin	th this
ü loot	u̇ foot	y yet	yü few	yu̇ furious	zh vision

suitable for transplanting; *specif* : SPAT **c** : the condition or stage of bearing seed <in ~> **2** : PROGENY **3** : a source of development or growth : GERM <sowed the ~*s* of discord> **4** : something (as a tiny particle or a bubble in glass) that resembles a seed in shape or size — **seed** *adj* — **seed·ed** \-əd\ *adj* — **seed·less** \-ləs\ *adj* — **seed·like** \-ˌlīk\ *adj* — **go to seed** *or* **run to seed 1** : to develop seed **2** : DECAY

²**seed** *vi* **1** : to sow seed : PLANT **2** : to bear or shed seed ~ *vt* **1 a** : to plant seeds in : SOW <~ land to grass> **b** : to furnish with something that causes or stimulates growth or development **c** : INOCULATE **d** : to supply with nuclei (as of crystallization or condensation); *esp* : to treat (a cloud) with solid particles to convert water droplets into ice crystals in an attempt to produce precipitation **2** : PLANT 1a **3** : to extract the seeds from (as raisins) **4 a** : to schedule (tournament players or teams) so that superior ones will not meet in early rounds **b** : to rank (a contestant) relative to others in a tournament on the basis of previous record <the top-*seeded* tennis star>

seed·bed \'sēd-ˌbed\ *n* **1** : soil or a bed of soil prepared for planting seed **2** : a place or source of growth or development

seed·cake \-ˌkāk\ *n* **1** : a cake or cookie containing aromatic seeds (as sesame or caraway) **2** : OIL CAKE

seed coat *n* : an outer protective covering of a seed

seed·eat·er \'sēd-ˌēt-ər\ *n* : a bird (as a finch) whose diet consists basically of seeds — called also *hard-bill*

seed·er \'sēd-ər\ *n* **1** : an implement for planting or sowing seeds **2** : a device for seeding fruit **3** : one that seeds clouds

seed fern *n* : any of an order (Cycadofilicales) of extinct plants with foliage like that of ferns and with naked seeds

seed leaf *n* : COTYLEDON 2

seed·ling \'sēd-liŋ\ *n* **1** : a plant grown from seed **2** : a young plant: as **a** : a tree smaller than a sapling **b** : a nursery plant not yet transplanted — **seedling** *adj*

seed money *n* : money used for setting up a new enterprise

seed oyster *n* : a young oyster esp. of a size for transplantation

seed pearl *n* **1** : a very small and often irregular pearl **2** : minute pearls imbedded in some binding material

seed plant *n* : a plant that bears seeds; *specif* : SPERMATOPHYTE

seed·pod \'sēd-ˌpäd\ *n* : ²POD 1

seeds·man \'sēdz-mən\ *n* **1** : one who sows seeds **2** : a dealer in seeds

seed stock *n* : a supply (as of seed) for planting; *broadly* : a source of new individuals <leaving a *seed stock* of trout in the streams>

seed tick *n* : the 6-legged larva of a tick

seed·time \'sēd-ˌtīm\ *n* **1** : the season of sowing **2** : a period of original development

seed vessel *n* : PERICARP

seedy \'sēd-ē\ *adj* **seed·i·er; -est 1 a** : containing or full of seeds <a ~ fruit> **b** : containing many small similar inclusions <glass ~ with air bubbles> **2** : inferior in condition or quality: as **a** : SHABBY, RUN-DOWN <~ clothes> **b** : somewhat disreputable : SQUALID <a ~ district> <~ entertainment> **c** : slightly unwell : DEBILITATED <felt ~ and went home early> — **seed·i·ly** \'sēd-ᵊl-ē\ *adv* — **seed·i·ness** \'sēd-ē-nəs\ *n*

see·ing \'sē-iŋ\ *conj* : inasmuch as

Seeing Eye *trademark* — used for a guide dog trained to lead the blind

seek \'sēk\ *vb* **sought** \'sȯt\; **seek·ing** [ME *seken,* fr. OE *sēcan;* akin to OHG *suohhen* to seek, L *sagire* to perceive keenly, Gk *hēgeisthai* to lead] *vt* **1** : to resort to : go to **2 a** : to go in search of : look for **b** : to try to discover **3** : to ask for : REQUEST <~*s* advice> **4** : to try to acquire or gain : aim at <~ fame> **5** : to make an attempt : TRY — used with an infinitive <governments . . . ~ to keep the bulk of their people contented —D. M. Potter> ~ *vi* **1** : to make a search or inquiry **2 a** : to be sought **b** : to be lacking <in critical judgment . . . they were sadly to ~ —*Times Lit. Supp.*> — **seek·er** *n*

seel \'sē(ə)l\ *vt* [alter. of ME *silen,* fr. MF *siller,* fr. ML *ciliare,* fr. L *cilium* eyelid] **1** : to close the eyes of (as a hawk) by drawing threads through the eyelids **2** *archaic* : to close up (one's eyes)

see·ly \'sē-lē\ *adj* [ME *sely* — more at SILLY] *archaic* : pitiable esp. because of weak physical or mental condition : FRAIL

seem \'sēm\ *vi* [ME *semen,* of Scand origin; akin to ON *sōma* to beseem, *samr* same — more at SAME] **1** : to give the impression of being **2** : to appear to the observation or understanding
syn SEEM, LOOK, APPEAR *shared meaning element* : to give the impression of being as stated without necessarily being so in fact

¹**seem·ing** *n* : external appearance as distinguished from true character : LOOK

²**seeming** *adj* : having an often deceptive or delusive appearance on superficial examination <their wealth gave them a ~ security> *syn* see APPARENT — **seem·ing·ly** \'sē-miŋ-lē\ *adv*

seem·ly \'sēm-lē\ *adj* **seem·li·er; -est** [ME *semely,* fr. ON *sœmiligr,* fr. *sœmr* becoming; akin to ON *sōma* to beseem] **1 a** : good-looking : HANDSOME **b** : agreeably fashioned : ATTRACTIVE **2** : conventionally proper : DECOROUS **3** : suited to the occasion, purpose, or person : FIT — **seem·li·ness** *n* — **seemly** *adv*

¹**seep** \'sēp\ *vi* [alter. of earlier *sipe,* fr. ME *sipen,* fr. OE *sipian;* akin to MLG *sipen* to seep] : to flow or pass slowly through fine pores or small openings : OOZE <water ~*ed* in through a crack>

²**seep** *n* **1 a** : a spot where a fluid (as water, oil, or gas) contained in the ground oozes slowly to the surface and often forms a pool **b** : a small spring **2** : SEEPAGE — **seepy** \'sē-pē\ *adj*

seep·age \'sē-pij\ *n* **1** : the process of seeping : OOZING **2** : a quantity of fluid that has seeped (as through porous material)

¹**seer** \'si(ə)r, *esp for 1 also* 'sē-ər\ *n* **1** : one that sees **2 a** : one that predicts events or developments **b** : a person credited with extraordinary moral and spiritual insight **3** : one that practices divination esp. by concentrating on a glass or crystal globe

²**seer** \'si(ə)r\ *n, pl* **seers** *or* **seer** [Hindi *ser*] **1** : any of various Indian units of weight; *esp* : a unit equal to 2.057 pounds **2** : an Afghan unit of weight equal to 15.6 pounds

seer·ess \'si(ə)r-əs\ *n* : a female seer : PROPHETESS

seer·suck·er \'si(ə)r-ˌsək-ər\ *n* [Hindi *śīrśaker,* fr. Per *shīr-o-shakar,* lit., milk and sugar] : a light fabric of linen, cotton, or rayon usu. striped and slightly puckered

¹**see·saw** \'sē-ˌsȯ\ *n* [prob. fr. redupl. of ³*saw*] **1** : an alternating up-and-down or backward-and-forward motion or movement; *also* : a contest or struggle in which now one side now the other has the lead **2** : a game in which two children or groups of children ride on opposite ends of a plank balanced in the middle so that one end goes up as the other goes down **b** : the plank or apparatus so used — **seesaw** *adj*

²**seesaw** *vi* **1 a** : to move backward and forward or up and down **b** : to play at seesaw **2** : ALTERNATE ~ *vt* : to cause to move in seesaw fashion

¹**seethe** \'sēth\ *vb* **seethed; seeth·ing** [ME *sethen,* fr. OE *sēothan;* akin to OHG *siodan* to seethe, Lith *siausti* to rage] *vt* **1** *archaic* : BOIL, STEW **2** : to soak or saturate in a liquid ~ *vi* **1** *archaic* : BOIL **2 a** : to be in a state of rapid agitated movement **b** : to churn or foam as if boiling **3** : to suffer violent internal excitement

²**seethe** *n* : a state of seething : EBULLITION

seeth·ing *adj* **1** : intensely hot : BOILING <a ~ inferno> **2** : constantly moving or active : AGITATED

see–through \'sē-ˌthrü\ *adj* : TRANSPARENT

seg·e·tal \'sej-ət-ᵊl\ *adj* [LL *segetalis,* fr. L *seget-, seges* field of grain, crop] : growing in fields of grain

¹**seg·ment** \'seg-mənt\ *n* [L *segmentum,* fr. *secare* to cut — more at SAW] **1 a** : a separate piece of something : BIT, FRAGMENT <chop the stalks into short ~*s*> **b** : one of the constituent parts into which a body, entity, or quantity is divided or marked off by or as if by natural boundaries <all ~*s* of the population agree> **2** : a portion cut off from a geometrical figure by one or more points, lines, or planes: as **a** : the part of a circular area bounded by a chord and an arc of that circle or so much of the area as is cut off by the chord **b** : the part of a sphere cut off by a plane or included between two parallel planes **c** : the finite part of a line between two points in the line *syn* see PART — **seg·men·tary** \-mən-ˌter-ē\ *adj*

²**seg·ment** \'seg-ˌment\ *vt* : to separate into segments : give off as segments

seg·men·tal \seg-'ment-ᵊl\ *adj* **1** : of, relating to, or having the form of a segment and esp. the sector of a circle <~ fanlight> <~ pediment> **2** : of, relating to, or composed of somites or metameres : METAMERIC **3 a** : divided into segments <~ knowledge> **b** : PARTIAL, INCOMPLETE **c** : resulting from segmentation — **seg·men·tal·ly** \-ᵊl-ē\ *adv*

seg·men·ta·tion \ˌseg-mən-'tā-shən, -ˌmen-\ *n* : the process of dividing into segments; *esp* : the formation of many cells from a single cell (as in a developing egg)

segmentation cavity *n* : BLASTOCOEL

seg·ment·ed \'seg-ˌment-əd, seg-'\ *adj* : divided into or composed of segments or sections <~ worms>

se·gno \'sān-(ˌ)yō\ *n, pl* **segnos** [It, sign, fr. L *signum*] : a notational sign; *specif* : the sign that marks the beginning or end of a musical repeat

segno

sego lily \ˌsē-(ˌ)gō-\ *n* [*sego* (the bulb of the sego lily), fr. Paiute] : a western No. American perennial herb (*Calochortus nuttallii*) of the lily family with bell-shaped flowers white within and largely green without

seg·re·gant \'seg-ri-gənt\ *n* : SEGREGATE

¹**seg·re·gate** \'seg-ri-ˌgāt\ *vb* **-gat·ed; -gat·ing** [L *segregatus,* pp. of *segregare,* fr. *se-* apart + *greg-, grex* herd — more at SECEDE, GREGARIOUS] *vt* **1** : to separate or set apart from others or from the general mass : ISOLATE **2** : to cause or force the separation of (as from the rest of society) ~ *vi* **1** : SEPARATE, WITHDRAW **2** : to practice or enforce a policy of segregation **3** : to undergo genetic segregation — **seg·re·ga·tive** \-ˌgāt-iv\ *adj*

²**seg·re·gate** \'seg-ri-gət, -ˌgāt\ *n* : one that is in some respect segregated; *esp* : one that differs genetically from the parental line because of genetic segregation

seg·re·gat·ed *adj* **1 a** : set apart or separated from others of the same kind or group <a ~ account in a bank> **b** : divided in facilities or administered separately for members of different groups or races <~ education> **c** : restricted to members of one group or one race by a policy of segregation <~ schools> **2** : practicing or maintaining segregation esp. of races <~ states>

seg·re·ga·tion \ˌseg-ri-'gā-shən\ *n* **1** : the act or process of segregating : the state of being segregated **2 a** : the separation or isolation of a race, class, or ethnic group by enforced or voluntary residence in a restricted area, by barriers to social intercourse, by separate educational facilities, or by other discriminatory means **b** : the separation for special treatment or observation of individuals or items from a larger group <~ of gifted children into accelerated classes> <~ of incorrigibles at a prison> **3** : the separation of allelic genes that occurs typically during meiosis

seg·re·ga·tion·ist \-sh(ə-)nəst\ *n* : a person who believes in or practices segregation esp. of races — **segregationist** *adj*

¹**se·gue** \'säg-(ˌ)wā, 'seg-\ *v imper* [It, there follows, fr. *seguire* to follow, fr. L *sequi* — more at SUE] **1** : proceed to what follows without pause — used as a direction in music **2** : perform the music that follows like that which has preceded — used as a direction in music

²**segue** *vi* **se·gued; se·gue·ing** : to proceed without pause from one musical number or theme to another

³**segue** *n* : a transition from one musical number to another

se·gui·di·lla \ˌseg-ə-'dē-(y)ə, -'dēl-yə\ *n* [Sp] **1** : a Spanish stanza of four or seven short partly assonant verses **2 a** : a Spanish dance with many regional variations **b** : the music for such a dance

sei \'sā, 'sī\ *n* [short for *sei whale,* part trans. of Norw *seihval,* fr. *sei* coalfish + *hval* whale; fr. its habit of following the coalfish in search of food] : a common and widely distributed small white-spotted rorqual (*Balaenopterus borealis*) — called also *sei whale*

sei·cen·to \sā-ˈchen-(ˌ)tō\ *n* [It, lit., six-hundred, fr. *sei* six (fr. L *sex*) + *cento* hundred — more at SIX, CINQUECENTO] : the 17th century; *specif* : the 17th century period in Italian literature and art

seiche \ˈsāsh, ˈsēch\ *n* [F] : an oscillation of the surface of a lake or landlocked sea that varies in period from a few minutes to several hours

sei·del \ˈsīd-ᵊl, ˈzīd-\ *n* [G, fr. L *situla* bucket] : a large glass for beer

Seid·litz powders \ˈsed-ləts-\ *n pl* [*Sedlitz*, Bohemia, Czechoslovakia; fr. the similarity of their effect to that of the water of the village] : effervescing salts consisting of one powder of sodium bicarbonate and Rochelle salt and another of tartaric acid that are mixed in water and drunk as a mild cathartic

sei·gneur \sān-ˈyər\ *n, often cap* [MF, fr. ML *senior*, fr. L, adj., elder — more at SENIOR] : LORD, SEIGNIOR

sei·gneur·ial \-ˈyu̇r-ē-əl, -ˈyər-\ *adj* : of, relating to, or befitting a seigneur

sei·gneury \ˈsān-yə-rē\ *n, pl* **-gneur·ies** **1 a** : the territory under the government of a feudal lord **b** : a landed estate held in Canada by feudal tenure until 1854 **2** : the manor house of a Canadian seigneur

sei·gnior \sān-ˈyō(ə)r, ˈsān-ˌ\ *n* [ME *seignour*, fr. MF *seigneur*] : a man of rank or authority; *esp* : the feudal lord of a manor

sei·gnior·age *or* **sei·gnor·age** \ˈsān-yə-rij\ *n* [ME *seigneurage*, fr. MF, right of the lord (esp. to coin money), fr. *seigneur*] : a government revenue from the manufacture of coins calculated as the difference between the face value and the metal value of the coins

sei·gniory *or* **sei·gnory** \ˈsān-yə-rē\ *n, pl* **-gnior·ies** *or* **-gnor·ies** **1** : LORDSHIP, DOMINION; *specif* : the power or authority of a feudal lord **2** : the territory over which a lord holds jurisdiction

sei·gno·ri·al \sān-ˈyōr-ē-əl, -ˈyȯr-\ *adj* : of, relating to, or befitting a seignior : MANORIAL

[1]**seine** \ˈsān\ *n* [ME, fr. OE *segne*; akin to OHG *segīna* seine; both fr. a prehistoric WGmc word borrowed fr. L *sagena* seine, fr. Gk *sagēnē*] : a large net with sinkers on one edge and floats on the other that hangs vertically in the water and is used to enclose fish when its ends are pulled together or are drawn ashore

[2]**seine** *vb* **seined; sein·ing** *vi* : to fish with or catch fish with a seine ~ *vt* : to fish for or in with a seine — **sein·er** *n*

sei·sin *or* **sei·zin** \ˈsēz-ᵊn\ *n* [ME *seisine*, fr. OF *saisine*, fr. *saisir* to seize — more at SEIZE] **1** : the possession of land or chattels **2** : the possession of a freehold estate in land by one having title thereto

seism \ˈsī-zəm\ *n* [Gk *seismos*] : EARTHQUAKE

seism- *or* **seismo-** *comb form* [Gk, fr. *seismos*] : earthquake : vibration <*seismo*meter>

seis·mic \ˈsīz-mik, ˈsīs-\ *adj* [Gk *seismos* shock, earthquake, fr. *seiein* to shake; akin to Skt *tveṣati* he is violently moved] **1** : of, subject to, or caused by an earthquake; *also* : of or relating to an earth vibration caused by something else (as an explosion or the impact of a meteorite) **2** : of or relating to a vibration on a celestial body (as the moon) comparable to a seismic event on earth — **seis·mic·i·ty** \sīz-ˈmis-ət-ē, sīs-\ *n*

seis·mo·gram \ˈsīz-mə-ˌgram, ˈsīs-\ *n* [ISV] : the record of an earth tremor by a seismograph

seis·mo·graph \-ˌgraf\ *n* [ISV] : an apparatus to measure and record vibrations within the earth and of the ground — **seis·mog·ra·pher** \sīz-ˈmäg-rə-fər, sīs-\ *n* — **seis·mo·graph·ic** \ˌsīz-mə-ˈgraf-ik, ˌsīs-\ *adj* — **seis·mog·ra·phy** \sīz-ˈmäg-rə-fē, sīs-\ *n*

seis·mol·o·gy \sīz-ˈmäl-ə-jē, sīs-\ *n* [ISV] : a science that deals with earthquakes and with artificially produced vibrations of the earth — **seis·mo·log·i·cal** \ˌsīz-mə-ˈläj-i-kəl, ˌsīs-\ *adj* — **seis·mol·o·gist** \sīz-ˈmäl-ə-jəst, sīs-\ *n*

seis·mom·e·ter \sīz-ˈmäm-ət-ər, sīs-\ *n* : a seismograph measuring the actual movements of the ground (as on the earth or the moon) — **seis·mo·met·ric** \ˌsīz-mə-ˈme-trik, ˌsīs-\ *adj*

seis·mom·e·try \sīz-ˈmäm-ə-trē, sīs-\ *n* [ISV] : the scientific study of earthquakes

seize \ˈsēz\ *vb* **seized; seiz·ing** [ME *saisen*, fr. OF *saisir* to put in possession of, fr. ML *sacire*, of Gmc origin; akin to OHG *sezzen* to set — more at SET] *vt* **1 a** *usu* **seise** \ˈsēz\ : to vest ownership of a freehold estate in **b** *often* **seise** : to put in possession of something <the biographer will be *seized* of all pertinent papers> **2 a** : to take possession of : CONFISCATE **b** : to take possession of by legal process **3 a** : to possess or take by force : CAPTURE **b** : to take prisoner : ARREST **4 a** : to take hold of : CLUTCH **b** : to possess oneself of : GRASP **c** : to understand fully and distinctly : APPREHEND **5 a** : to attack or overwhelm physically : AFFLICT <suddenly *seized* with an acute illness —H. G. Armstrong> **b** : to possess (one's mind) completely or overwhelmingly <*seized* the popular imagination —Basil Davenport> **6** : to bind or fasten together with a lashing of small stuff (as yarn, marline, or fine wire) ~ *vi* **1** : to take or lay hold suddenly or forcibly **2 a** : to cohere to a relatively moving part through excessive pressure, temperature, or friction — used esp. of machine parts (as bearings, brakes, or pistons) **b** : to fail to operate due to the seizing of a part — used of an engine ***syn*** see TAKE — **seiz·er** *n*

seiz·ing *n* **1** : the operation of fastening together or lashing with tarred small stuff **2 a** : the cord or lashing used in seizing **b** : the fastening so made — see KNOT illustration

sei·zure \ˈsē-zhər\ *n* **1 a** : the act, action, or process of seizing : the state of being seized **b** : the taking possession of person or property by legal process **2** : a sudden attack (as of disease)

se·jant \ˈsē-jənt\ *adj* [modif. of MF *seant*, prp. of *seoir* to sit, fr. L *sedēre* — more at SIT] : SITTING — used of a heraldic animal

[1]**sel** \ˈsel\ *chiefly Scot var of* SELF

[2]**sel** *abbr* select; selected; selection

se·la·chi·an \sə-ˈlā-kē-ən\ *n* [deriv. of Gk *selachos* cartilaginous phosphorescent fish; akin to Gk *selas* brightness — more at SELENIUM] : any of a variously defined group (Selachii) of elasmobranch fishes that includes all the elasmobranchs or all elasmobranchs except the chimaeras, the existing sharks and rays or in its most restricted use the existing sharks as distinguished from the rays — **selachian** *adj*

se·lag·i·nel·la \sə-ˌlaj-ə-ˈnel-ə\ *n* [NL, genus name, fr. L *selagin-*, *selago*, a plant resembling the savin] : any of a genus (*Selaginella*) of mossy lower tracheophytes that have branching stems and scalelike leaves and produce one-celled sporangia containing both megaspores and microspores

selaginella

se·lah \ˈsē-lə, -ˌlä\ *interj* [Heb *selāh*] — a term of uncertain meaning found in the Hebrew text of the Psalms and Habakkuk carried over untranslated into some English versions

sel·couth \ˈsel-ˌküth\ *adj* [ME, fr. OE *seldcūth*, fr. *seldan* seldom + *cūth* known — more at UNCOUTH] *archaic* : UNUSUAL, STRANGE

[1]**sel·dom** \ˈsel-dəm\ *adv* [ME, fr. OE *seldan*; akin to OHG *seltan* seldom, L *sed*, *se* without — more at IDIOT] : in few instances : RARELY, INFREQUENTLY

[2]**seldom** *adj* : RARE, INFREQUENT

[1]**se·lect** \sə-ˈlekt\ *adj* [L *selectus*, pp. of *seligere* to select, fr. *se-* apart (fr. *sed*, *se* without) + *legere* to gather, select — more at LEGEND] **1** : chosen from a number or group by fitness or preference **2 a** : of special value or excellence : SUPERIOR, CHOICE **b** : exclusively or fastidiously chosen often with regard to social, economic, or cultural characteristics **3** : judicious or restrictive in choice : DISCRIMINATING <pleased with the ~ appreciation of his books —Osbert Sitwell> — **se·lect·ness** \sə-ˈlek(t)-nəs\ *n*

[2]**select** *n* : one that is select — often used in pl.

[3]**select** *vt* : to take by preference from a number or group : pick out : CHOOSE ~ *vi* : to make a choice

se·lect·ed *adj* : SELECT; *specif* : of a higher grade or quality than the ordinary

se·lect·ee \sə-ˌlek-ˈtē\ *n* : one inducted into military service under selective service

se·lec·tion \sə-ˈlek-shən\ *n* **1** : the act or process of selecting : the state of being selected **2** : one that is selected : CHOICE; *also* : a collection of selected things **3** : a natural or artificial process that results or tends to result in the survival and propagation of some individuals or organisms but not of others with the result that the inherited traits of the survivors are perpetuated

se·lec·tive \sə-ˈlek-tiv\ *adj* **1** : of, relating to, or characterized by selection : selecting or tending to select **2** : of, relating to, or constituting the ability of a radio circuit or apparatus to respond to a specific frequency without interference — **se·lec·tive·ly** *adv* — **se·lec·tive·ness** *n* — **se·lec·tiv·i·ty** \sə-ˌlek-ˈtiv-ət-ē, ˌsē-\ *n*

selective service *n* : a system under which men are called up for military service : DRAFT

se·lect·man \si-ˈlek(t)-ˌman, -ˌlek(t)-ˈman, -ˈlek(t)-mən; ˈsē-ˌlek(t)-ˌman\ *n* : one of a board of officials elected in towns of all New England states except Rhode Island to serve as the chief administrative authority of the town

se·lec·tor \sə-ˈlek-tər\ *n* : one that selects

[1]**selen-** *or* **seleno-** *comb form* [L *selen-*, fr. Gk *selēn-*, fr. *selēnē* — more at SELENIUM] : moon <*selen*ium> <*seleno*graphy>

[2]**selen-** *or* **seleni-** *or* **seleno-** *comb form* [Sw, fr. NL *selenium*] : selenium <*seleni*ferous> <*selen*ious>

sel·e·nate \ˈsel-ə-ˌnāt\ *n* [Sw *selenat*, fr. *selen* selenic] : a salt ester of selenic acid

se·le·nic \sə-ˈlēn-ik, -ˈlen-\ *adj* [Sw *selen*, fr. NL *selenium*] : of, relating to, or containing selenium esp. with a relatively high valence

selenic acid *n* : a strong acid H_2SeO_4 whose aqueous solution attacks gold and platinum

sel·e·nide \ˈsel-ə-ˌnīd\ *n* : a binary compound of selenium usu. with a more electropositive element or radical

sel·e·nif·er·ous \ˌsel-ə-ˈnif-(ə-)rəs\ *adj* [ISV] : containing or yielding selenium <~ vegetation> <~ soils>

se·le·ni·ous \sə-ˈlē-nē-əs\ *adj* [ISV] : of, relating to, or containing selenium esp. with a relatively low valence

sel·e·nite \ˈsel-ə-ˌnīt\ *n* [L *selenites*, fr. Gk *selēnitēs* (*lithos*), lit., stone of the moon, fr. *selēnē*; fr. the belief that it waxed and waned with the moon] : a variety of gypsum occurring in transparent crystals or crystalline masses

se·le·ni·um \sə-ˈlē-nē-əm\ *n* [NL, fr. Gk *selēnē* moon; akin to Gk *selas* brightness, L *sol* sun — more at SOLAR] : a nonmetallic element that resembles sulfur and tellurium chemically, is obtained chiefly as a by-product in copper refining, and occurs in allotropic forms of which a gray stable form varies in electrical conductivity with the intensity of its illumination and is used in electronic devices — see ELEMENT table

selenium cell *n* : an insulated strip of selenium mounted with electrodes and used as a photoconductive element

se·le·no·cen·tric \sə-ˌlē-nə-ˈsen-trik\ *adj* [ISV] : of or relating to the center of the moon; *also* : referred to or involving the moon as a center

sel·e·nog·ra·phy \ˌsel-ə-ˈnäg-rə-fē\ *n* **1** : the science of the physical features of the moon **2** : the physical geography of the moon — **sel·e·nog·ra·pher** \-fər\ *n* — **se·le·no·graph·ic** \ˌsel-ə-nō-ˈgraf-ik, sə-ˌlē-nə-\ *adj* — **sel·e·nog·ra·phist** \ˌsel-ə-ˈnäg-rə-fəst\ *n*

sel·e·nol·o·gy \ˌsel-ə-ˈnäl-ə-jē\ *n* : a branch of astronomy that deals with the moon — **se·le·no·log·i·cal** \ˌsel-ə-nō-ˈläj-i-kəl, sə-ˌlēn-ᵊl-ˈäj-\ *adj* — **selenologist** *n*

sel·e·no·sis \ˌsel-ə-ˈnō-səs\ *n* [NL] : poisoning of livestock by selenium due to ingestion of plants grown in seleniferous soils

[1]**self** \ˈself, *South also* ˈsef\ *pron* [ME (intensive pron.), fr. OE; akin to OHG *selb,* intensive pron., L *sui* (reflexive pron.) of oneself — more at SUICIDE] : MYSELF, HIMSELF, HERSELF <check payable to ~>

[2]**self** *adj* **1** *obs* : belonging to oneself : OWN **2** *obs* : IDENTICAL, SAME **3 a** : having a single character or quality throughout; *specif* : having one color only <a ~ flower> **b** : of the same kind (as in color, material, or pattern) as something with which it is used <a ~ belt> <~ trimming>

[3]**self** *n, pl* **selves** \ˈselvz, *South also* ˈsevz\ **1 a** : the entire person of an individual **b** : the realization or embodiment of an abstraction **2 a (1)** : an individual's typical character or behavior <his true ~ was revealed> **(2)** : an individual's temporary behavior or character <his better ~> **b** : a person in his best condition <looked like his old ~> **3** : the union of elements (as body, emotions, thoughts, and sensations) that constitute the individuality and identity of a person **4** : personal interest or advantage

[4]**self** *vt* **1** : INBREED **2** : to pollinate with pollen from the same flower or plant ~ *vi* : to undergo self-pollination

self- *comb form* [ME, fr. OE, fr. *self*] **1 a** : oneself or itself <*self*-supporting> **b** : of oneself or itself <*self*-abasement> **c** : by oneself or itself <*self*-propelled> <*self*-acting> **2 a** : to, with, for, or toward oneself or itself <*self*-consistent> <*self*-addressed> <*self*-love> **b** : of or in oneself or itself inherently <*self*-evident> **c** : from or by means of oneself or itself <*self*-fertile>

self-aban·doned \ˌsel-fə-ˈban-dənd\ *adj* : abandoned by oneself; *esp* : given up to one's impulses

self-aban·don·ment \-dən-mənt\ *n* **1** : a surrender of one's selfish interests or desires **2** : a lack of self-restraint

self-abase·ment \ˌsel-fə-ˈbā-smənt\ *n* : humiliation of oneself based on feelings of inferiority, guilt, or shame

self-ab·ne·gat·ing \ˈsel-ˈfab-ni-ˌgāt-iŋ\ *adj* : SELF-DENYING

self-ab·ne·ga·tion \ˌsel-ˌfab-ni-ˈgā-shən\ *n* : SELF-DENIAL

self-ab·sorbed \ˌsel-fəb-ˈsȯ(ə)rbd, -ˈzȯ(ə)rbd\ *adj* : absorbed in one's own thoughts, activities, or interests

self-ab·sorp·tion \-ˈsȯrp-shən, -ˈzȯrp-\ *n* : preoccupation with oneself

self-abuse \ˌsel-fə-ˈbyüs\ *n* **1** : reproach of oneself **2** : MASTURBATION

self-ac·cu·sa·tion \ˌsel-ˌfak-yə-ˈzā-shən\ *n* : the act or an instance of accusing oneself

self-ac·cu·sa·to·ry \ˌsel-fə-ˈkyü-zə-ˌtōr-ē, -ˌtȯr-\ *adj* : SELF-ACCUSING

self-ac·cus·ing \-ˈkyü-ziŋ\ *adj* : acting or serving to accuse oneself

self-ac·quired \ˌsel-fə-ˈkwī(ə)rd\ *adj* : acquired by oneself

self-act·ing \ˈsel-ˈfak-tiŋ\ *adj* : acting or capable of acting of or by itself : AUTOMATIC

self-ac·tiv·i·ty \ˌsel-ˌfak-ˈtiv-ət-ē\ *n* : independent and esp. self-determined activity

self-ac·tu·al·ize \ˈsel-ˈfak-ch(ə-w)ə-ˌlīz, -ˈfaksh-wə-\ *vi* : to realize fully one's potential — **self-ac·tu·al·iza·tion** \ˌsel-ˌfak-ch(ə-w)ə-lə-ˈzā-shən, -ˌfaksh-wə-\ *n* — **self-ac·tu·al·iz·er** \ˈsel-ˈfak-ch(ə-w)ə-ˌlī-zər, -ˈfaksh-wə-\ *n*

self-ad·dressed \ˌsel-fə-ˈdrest, ˈsel-ˈfad-ˌrest\ *adj* : addressed for return to the sender <a ~ envelope>

self-ad·just·ing \ˌsel-fə-ˈjəs-tiŋ\ *adj* : adjusting by itself

self-ad·just·ment \-ˈjəs(t)-mənt\ *n* : adjustment to oneself or one's environment

self-ad·min·is·tered \ˌsel-fəd-ˈmin-ə-stərd\ *adj* : administered, managed, or dispensed by oneself

self-ad·mi·ra·tion \ˌsel-ˌfad-mə-ˈrā-shən\ *n* : SELF-CONCEIT

self-ad·vance·ment \ˌsel-fəd-ˈvan(t)-smənt\ *n* : the act of advancing oneself

self-af·fect·ed \ˌsel-fə-ˈfek-təd\ *adj* : CONCEITED, SELF-LOVING

self-ag·gran·dize·ment \ˌsel-fə-ˈgran-dəz-mənt, -ˌdīz-; ˌsel-ˌfag-rən-ˈdīz-\ *n* : the act or process of making oneself greater

self-ag·gran·diz·ing \ˌsel-fə-ˈgran-ˌdī-ziŋ, ˈsel-ˈfag-rən-\ *adj* : acting or seeking to make oneself greater

self-anal·y·sis \ˌsel-fə-ˈnal-ə-səs\ *n* : a systematic attempt by an individual to understand his own personality without the aid of another person

self-an·a·lyt·i·cal \ˌsel-ˌfan-ᵊl-ˈit-i-kəl\ *also* **self-an·a·lyt·ic** *adj* : using self-analysis

self-an·ni·hi·la·tion \ˌsel-fə-ˌnī-ə-ˈlā-shən\ *n* : annihilation of the self (as in mystical contemplation of God)

self-ap·plaud·ing \ˌsel-fə-ˈplȯd-iŋ\ *adj* : marked by self-applause

self-ap·plause \-ˈplȯz\ *n* : an expression or feeling of approval of oneself

self-ap·point·ed \ˌsel-fə-ˈpȯint-əd\ *adj* : appointed by oneself usu. without warrant or qualifications <a ~ guardian of public morals>

self-ap·pro·ba·tion \ˌsel-ˌfap-rə-ˈbā-shən\ *n* : satisfaction with one's actions and achievements

self-as·sert·ing \ˌsel-fə-ˈsərt-iŋ\ *adj* **1** : asserting oneself or one's own rights, claims, or opinions **2 a** : SELF-ASSURED, CONFIDENT **b** : ARROGANT — **self-as·sert·ing·ly** \-iŋ-lē\ *adv*

self-as·ser·tion \ˌsel-fə-ˈsər-shən\ *n* **1** : the act of asserting oneself or one's own rights, claims, or opinions **2** : the act of asserting one's superiority over others

self-as·sert·ive \-ˈsərt-iv\ *adj* : given to or characterized by self-assertion *syn* see AGGRESSIVE — **self-as·sert·ive·ly** *adv* — **self-as·sert·ive·ness** *n*

self-as·sump·tion \ˌsel-fə-ˈsəm(p)-shən\ *n* : SELF-CONCEIT

self-as·sur·ance \ˌsel-fə-ˈshu̇r-ən(t)s\ *n* : SELF-CONFIDENCE

self-as·sured \-ˈshu̇(ə)rd\ *adj* : sure of oneself : SELF-CONFIDENT — **self-as·sured·ly** \-ˈshu̇r-əd-lē, -ˈshu̇(ə)rd-\ *adv* — **self-as·sured·ness** \-ˈshu̇r-əd-nəs, -ˈshu̇(ə)rd-\ *n*

self-aware \ˌsel-fə-ˈwa(ə)r, -ˈwe(ə)r\ *adj* : characterized by self-awareness

self-aware·ness *n* : an awareness of one's own personality or individuality

self-be·tray·al \ˌself-bi-ˈtrā(-ə)l\ *n* : SELF-REVELATION

self-bind·er \ˈself-ˈbīn-dər\ *n* : a harvesting machine that cuts grain and binds it into bundles

self-born \-ˈbȯ(ə)rn\ *adj* **1** : arising within the self <~ sorrows> **2** : springing from a prior self <phoenix rising ~ from the fire>

self-care \-ˈke(ə)r, -ˈka(ə)r\ *n* : care for oneself

self-cas·ti·ga·tion \ˌself-ˌkas-tə-ˈgā-shən\ *n* : SELF-PUNISHMENT

self-cen·tered \ˈself-ˈsent-ərd\ *adj* **1** : independent of outside force or influence : SELF-SUFFICIENT **2** : concerned solely with one's own desires, needs, or interests : SELFISH — **self-cen·tered·ly** *adv* — **self-cen·tered·ness** *n*

self-charg·ing \-ˈchär-jiŋ\ *adj* : that charges itself

self-clos·ing \-ˈklō-ziŋ\ *adj* : closing or shutting automatically after being opened

self-cock·ing \-ˈkäk-iŋ\ *adj* : cocked by the operation of some part of the action <~ on closing the bolt>

self-col·lect·ed \ˌself-kə-ˈlek-təd\ *adj* : SELF-POSSESSED

self-col·ored \ˈself-ˈkəl-ərd\ *adj* : of a single color <a ~ flower>

self-com·mand \ˌself-kə-ˈmand\ *n* : control of one's own behavior and emotions : SELF-CONTROL

self-com·pat·i·ble \-kəm-ˈpat-ə-bəl\ *adj* : capable of effective self-pollination that results in the production of seeds and fruits — **self-com·pat·i·bil·i·ty** \-ˌpat-ə-ˈbil-ət-ē\ *n*

self-com·pla·cen·cy \-ˈplās-ᵊn-sē\ *n* : SELF-SATISFACTION

self-com·pla·cent \-ᵊnt\ *adj* : SELF-SATISFIED — **self-com·pla·cent·ly** *adv*

self-com·posed \ˌself-kəm-ˈpōzd\ *adj* : having control over one's emotions : CALM — **self-com·pos·ed·ly** \-ˈpō-zəd-lē\ *adv* — **self-com·posed·ness** \-ˈpō-zəd-nəs, -ˈpōz(d)-nəs\ *n*

self-con·ceit \ˌself-kən-ˈsēt\ *n* : an exaggerated opinion of one's own qualities or abilities : VANITY — **self-con·ceit·ed** \-əd\ *adj*

self-con·cept \ˈself-ˈkän-ˌsept\ *n* : the mental image one has of oneself

self-con·cep·tion \ˌself-kən-ˈsep-shən\ *n* : SELF-CONCEPT

self-con·cern \-ˈsərn\ *n* : a selfish or morbid concern for oneself — **self-con·cerned** \-ˈsərnd\ *adj*

self-con·dem·na·tion \ˌself-ˌkän-ˌdem-ˈnā-shən, -dəm-\ *n* : condemnation of one's own character or actions

self-con·demned \-kən-ˈdemd\ *adj* : condemned by oneself

self-con·fessed \-ˈfest\ *adj* : openly acknowledged : AVOWED

self-con·fes·sion \-ˈfesh-ən\ *n* : open acknowledgment : AVOWAL

self-con·fi·dence \ˈself-ˈkän-fəd-ən(t)s, -fə-ˌden(t)s\ *n* : confidence in oneself and in one's powers and abilities — **self-con·fi·dent** \-fəd-ənt, -fə-ˌdent\ *adj* — **self-con·fi·dent·ly** *adv*

self-con·grat·u·la·tion \ˌself-kən-ˌgrach-ə-ˈlā-shən\ *n* : congratulation of oneself; *esp* : a complacent acknowledgment of one's own superiority or good fortune

self-con·grat·u·la·to·ry \-ˈgrach-(ə-)lə-ˌtōr-ē, -ˌtȯr-\ *adj* : indulging in self-congratulation

self-con·scious \ˈself-ˈkän-chəs\ *adj* **1 a** : conscious of one's own acts or states as belonging to or originating in oneself : aware of oneself as an individual **b** : intensely aware of oneself : CONSCIOUS <a rising and ~ social class>; *also* : produced or done with such awareness <~ art> **2** : uncomfortably conscious of oneself as an object of the observation of others : ill at ease — **self-con·scious·ly** *adv* — **self-con·scious·ness** *n*

self-con·se·cra·tion \ˌself-ˌkän(t)-sə-ˈkrā-shən\ *n* : the act or an instance of consecrating oneself

self-con·se·quence \ˈself-ˈkän(t)-sə-ˌkwen(t)s, -si-kwən(t)s\ *n* : SELF-IMPORTANCE

self-con·sis·ten·cy \ˌself-kən-ˈsis-tən-sē\ *n* : the quality or state of being self-consistent

self-con·sis·tent \-tənt\ *adj* : having each part logically consistent with the rest

self-con·sti·tut·ed \ˈself-ˈkän(t)-stə-ˌt(y)üt-əd\ *adj* : constituted by oneself or itself

self-con·tained \ˌself-kən-ˈtānd\ *adj* **1 a** : complete in itself : INDEPENDENT <a ~ machine> <a ~ program of study> **b** : BUILT-IN <a lectern with a ~ light fixture> **2 a** : showing self-command **b** : formal and reserved in manner — **self-con·tained·ly** \-ˈtā-nəd-lē, -ˈtān-dlē\ *adv* — **self-con·tained·ness** \-ˈtā-nəd-nəs, -ˈtān(d)-nəs\ *n* — **self-con·tain·ment** \-ˈtān-mənt\ *n*

self-con·tam·i·na·tion \ˌself-kən-ˌtam-ə-ˈnā-shən\ *n* **1** : contamination by oneself **2** : contamination from within

self-con·tem·pla·tion \ˌself-ˌkänt-əm-ˈplā-shən, -ˌkän-ˌtem-\ *n* : the act or an instance of contemplating oneself

self-con·tempt \ˌself-kən-ˈtem(p)t\ *n* : contempt for oneself

self-con·tent \-ˈtent\ *n* : SELF-SATISFACTION

self-con·tent·ed \-əd\ *adj* : SELF-SATISFIED — **self-con·tent·ed·ly** *adv* — **self-con·tent·ed·ness** *n*

self-con·tent·ment \-ˈtent-mənt\ *n* : SELF-SATISFACTION

self-con·tra·dic·tion \ˌself-ˌkän-trə-ˈdik-shən\ *n* **1** : contradiction of oneself **2** : a self-contradictory statement or proposition

self-con·tra·dic·to·ry \-ˈdik-t(ə-)rē\ *adj* : consisting of two contradictory members or parts

self-con·trol \ˌself-kən-ˈtrōl\ *n* : restraint exercised over one's own impulses, emotions, or desires — **self-con·trolled** \-ˈtrōld\ *adj*

self-cor·rect·ing \ˌself-kə-ˈrek-tiŋ\ *adj* : correcting or compensating for one's own errors or weaknesses

self-cor·rec·tive \-ˈrek-tiv\ *adj* : SELF-CORRECTING

self-cre·at·ed \ˌself-krē-ˈāt-əd, ˈself-ˈkrē-ˌ\ *adj* : created or appointed by oneself

self-crit·i·cal \ˈself-ˈkrit-i-kəl\ *adj* : critical of oneself or itself

self-crit·i·cism \-ˈkrit-ə-ˌsiz-əm\ *n* : the act of or capacity for criticizing one's own faults or shortcomings

self-cul·ti·va·tion \ˌself-ˌkəl-tə-ˈvā-shən\ *n* : the act of cultivating oneself

self-cul·ture \ˈself-ˈkəl-chər\ *n* : the development of one's mind or capacities through one's own efforts

self-de·ceit \ˌself-di-ˈsēt\ *n* : SELF-DECEPTION

self–de·ceived \-ˈsēvd\ *adj* : deceived or misled by one's own misconceptions

self–de·ceiv·er \-ˈsē-vər\ *n* : one who practices self-deception

self–de·ceiv·ing \-ˈsē-viŋ\ *adj* **1** : given to self-deception <a ~ hypocrite> **2** : serving to deceive oneself <~ excuses>

self–de·cep·tion \-ˈsep-shən\ *n* : the act of deceiving oneself : the state of being deceived by oneself

self–de·cep·tive \-ˈsep-tiv\ *adj* : SELF-DECEIVING

self–ded·i·ca·tion \ˌself-ˌded-i-ˈkā-shən\ *n* : dedication of oneself to a cause or ideal

self–de·feat·ing \ˌself-di-ˈfēt-iŋ\ *adj* : acting to defeat its own purpose

self–de·fense \-ˈfen(t)s\ *n* **1** : the act of defending oneself, one's property, or a close relative **2** : a plea of justification for the use of force or for homicide

self–de·fen·sive \-ˈfen(t)-siv\ *adj* : of, relating to, or given to self-defense <a ~ person> <a ~ attitude>

self–de·lud·ed \-ˈlüd-əd\ *adj* : SELF-DECEIVED

self–de·lu·sion \-ˈlü-zhən\ *n* : SELF-DECEPTION

self–de·ni·al \ˌself-di-ˈnī(-ə)l\ *n* : a restraint or limitation of one's own desires or interests

self–de·ny·ing \-ˈnī-iŋ\ *adj* : showing self-denial — **self–de·ny·ing·ly** \-iŋ-lē\ *adv*

self–de·pen·dence \-ˈpen-dən(t)s\ *n* : SELF-RELIANCE

self–de·pen·dent \-dənt\ *adj* : showing or marked by self-dependence

self–dep·re·cat·ing \ˈself-ˈdep-ri-ˌkāt-iŋ\ *adj* : given to self-depreciation — **self–dep·re·cat·ing·ly** \-iŋ-lē\ *adv*

self–dep·re·ca·to·ry \-kə-ˌtōr-ē, -ˌtȯr-\ *adj* : SELF-DEPRECATING

self–de·pre·ci·a·tion \ˌself-di-ˌprē-shē-ˈā-shən\ *n* : disparagement or undervaluation of oneself

self–de·spair \-di-ˈspa(ə)r, -ˈspe(ə)r\ *n* : despair of oneself : HOPELESSNESS

self–de·stroy·er \-di-ˈstrȯi(-ə)r\ *n* : one who destroys himself

self–de·stroy·ing \-ˈstrȯi-iŋ\ *adj* : SELF-DESTRUCTIVE

self–de·struct \ˌself-di-ˈstrəkt\ *vi* : to destroy itself

self–de·struc·tion \-ˈstrək-shən\ *n* : destruction of oneself; *esp* : SUICIDE

self–de·struc·tive \-ˈstrək-tiv\ *adj* : acting or tending to harm or destroy oneself; *also* : SUICIDAL — **self–de·struc·tive·ness** *n*

self–de·ter·mi·na·tion \ˌself-di-ˌtər-mə-ˈnā-shən\ *n* **1** : free choice of one's own acts or states without external compulsion **2** : determination by the people of a territorial unit of their own future political status

self–de·ter·mined \-ˈtər-mənd\ *adj* : determined by oneself

self–de·ter·min·ing \-ˈtərm-(ə-)niŋ\ *adj* : capable of determining one's own acts

self–de·ter·min·ism \-ˈtər-mə-ˌniz-əm\ *n* : a doctrine that the actions of a self are determined by itself

self–de·vel·op·ment \ˌself-di-ˈvel-əp-mənt\ *n* : development of the capabilities or possibilities of oneself

self–de·vot·ed \-ˈvōt-əd\ *adj* : characterized by self-devotion — **self–de·vot·ed·ly** *adv* — **self–de·vot·ed·ness** *n*

self–de·vot·ing \-ˈvōt-iŋ\ *adj* : SELF-DEVOTED

self–de·vo·tion \-ˈvō-shən\ *n* : devotion of oneself esp. in service or sacrifice <his ~ to science cost him his life>

self–de·vour·ing \-ˈvau̇(ə)r-iŋ\ *adj* : devouring itself

self–di·ges·tion \ˌself-(ˌ)dī-ˈjes(h)-chən, -də-\ *n* : decomposition of plant or animal tissue by internal process : AUTOLYSIS

self–di·rect·ed \ˌself-də-ˈrek-təd, -(ˌ)dī-\ *adj* : directed by oneself; *specif* : not guided or impelled by an outside force or agency

self–di·rect·ing \-ˈrek-tiŋ\ *adj* : directing oneself

self–di·rec·tion \-ˈrek-shən\ *n* : guidance of oneself

self–dis·ci·pline \ˈself-ˈdis-ə-plən\ *n* : correction or regulation of oneself for the sake of improvement

self–dis·ci·plined \-plənd\ *adj* : capable of or subject to self-discipline

self–dis·cov·ery \ˌself-dis-ˈkəv-(ə-)rē\ *n* : the act or process of achieving self-knowledge

self–dis·trib·ut·ing \-ˈtrib-yət-iŋ\ *adj* : distributing itself automatically

self–dis·trust \-ˈtrəst\ *n* : a lack of confidence in oneself : DIFFIDENCE — **self–dis·trust·ful** \-fəl\ *adj*

self·dom \ˈself-dəm, -təm\ *n* : the essence of one's self : INDIVIDUALITY

self–doubt \ˈself-ˈdau̇t\ *n* : a lack of faith in oneself — **self–doubt·ing** \-iŋ\ *adj*

self–dra·ma·ti·za·tion \ˌself-ˌdram-ət-ə-ˈzā-shən, -ˌdräm-\ *n* : the act or an instance of dramatizing oneself

self–dra·ma·tiz·ing \ˈself-ˈdram-ə-ˌtī-ziŋ, -ˈdräm-\ *adj* : seeing and presenting oneself as an important or dramatic figure

self–drive \ˈself-ˈdrīv\ *adj, chiefly Brit* : being a rental car

self–ed·u·cat·ed \ˈsel-ˈfej-ə-ˌkāt-əd\ *adj* : educated by one's own efforts without formal instruction — **self–ed·u·ca·tion** \ˌsel-ˌfej-ə-ˈkā-shən\ *n*

self–ef·face·ment \ˌsel-fə-ˈfā-smənt\ *n* : the placing or keeping of oneself in the background

self–ef·fac·ing \-ˈfā-siŋ\ *adj* : RESERVED, SHY — **self–ef·fac·ing·ly** \-siŋ-lē\ *adv*

self–elect·ed \ˌsel-fə-ˈlek-təd\ *adj* : SELF-APPOINTED

self–em·ployed \ˌsel-fim-ˈplȯid\ *adj* : earning income directly from one's own business, trade, or profession rather than as a specified salary or wages from an employer

self–em·ploy·ment \-ˈplȯi-mənt\ *n* : the state of being self-employed

self–en·er·giz·ing \ˈsel-ˈfen-ər-ˌjī-ziŋ\ *adj* : containing means for augmentation of power within itself <a ~ brake>

self–en·forc·ing \ˌsel-fin-ˈfōr-siŋ, -ˈfȯr-\ *adj* : containing in itself the authority or means that provide for its enforcement

self–en·rich·ment \ˌsel-fin-ˈrich-mənt\ *n* : the act or process of increasing one's intellectual or spiritual resources

self–es·teem \ˌsel-fə-ˈstēm\ *n* **1** : a confidence and satisfaction in oneself : SELF-RESPECT **2** : SELF-CONCEIT

self–ev·i·dence \ˈsel-ˈfev-əd-ənts, -ə-ˌden(t)s\ *n* : the quality or state of being self-evident

self–ev·i·dent \-əd-ənt, -ə-ˌdent\ *adj* : evident without proof or reasoning — **self–ev·i·dent·ly** *adv*

self–ex·al·ta·tion \ˌsel-ˌfeg-ˌzȯl-ˈtā-shən, -ˌfek-ˌsȯl-\ *n* : exaltation of oneself : VAINGLORY

self–ex·alt·ing \ˌsel-fig-ˈzȯl-tiŋ\ *adj* : VAINGLORIOUS — **self–ex·alt·ing·ly** \-tiŋ-lē\ *adv*

self–ex·am·i·na·tion \ˌsel-fig-ˌzam-ə-ˈnā-shən\ *n* : a reflective examination (as of one's beliefs or motives) : INTROSPECTION

self–ex·cit·ed \ˌsel-fik-ˈsīt-əd\ *adj* : excited by a current produced by the dynamo itself <~ generator>

self–ex·e·cut·ing \ˈsel-ˈfek-sə-ˌkyüt-iŋ\ *adj* : taking effect immediately without implementing legislation <a ~ treaty>

self–ex·ile \ˈsel-ˈfeg-ˌzīl, -ˈfek-ˌsīl\ *n* : one who is self-exiled

self–ex·iled \-ˌzīld, -ˌsīld\ *adj* : exiled by one's own wish or decision

self–ex·is·tence \ˌsel-fig-ˈzis-tən(t)s\ *n* : the quality or state of being self-existent

self–ex·is·tent \-tənt\ *adj* : existing of or by itself

self–ex·plain·ing \ˌsel-fik-ˈsplā-niŋ\ *adj* : SELF-EXPLANATORY

self–ex·plan·a·to·ry \ˌsel-fik-ˈsplan-ə-ˌtōr-ē, -ˌtȯr-\ *adj* : explaining itself : capable of being understood without explanation

self–ex·pres·sion \ˌsel-fik-ˈspresh-ən\ *n* : the expression of one's own personality : assertion of one's individual traits — **self–ex·pres·sive** \-ˈspres-iv\ *adj*

self–feed \ˈself-ˈfēd\ *vt* **-fed** \-ˈfed\; **-feed·ing** : to provide rations to (animals) in bulk so as to permit selecting food in kind and quantity as wanted — compare HAND-FEED

self–feed·er \-ər\ *n* : a device for feeding livestock that is equipped with a feed hopper that automatically supplies a trough below

self–feel·ing \ˈself-ˈfē-liŋ\ *n* : self-centered emotion

self–fer·tile \ˈself-ˈfərt-ᵊl\ *adj* : fertile by means of its own pollen or sperm — **self–fer·til·i·ty** \ˌself-(ˌ)fər-ˈtil-ət-ē\ *n*

self–fer·til·iza·tion \ˌself-ˌfərt-ᵊl-ə-ˈzā-shən\ *n* : fertilization effected by union of ova with pollen or sperm from the same individual

self–fer·til·ized \ˈself-ˈfərt-ᵊl-ˌīzd\ *adj* : fertilized by one's own pollen or sperm

self–fer·til·iz·ing \-ˌī-ziŋ\ *adj* : SELF-FERTILIZED

self–flag·el·la·tion \ˌself-ˌflaj-ə-ˈlā-shən\ *n* : extreme criticism of oneself

self–flat·ter·ing \ˈself-ˈflat-ə-riŋ\ *adj* : given to self-flattery

self–flat·tery \-ə-rē\ *n* : the glossing over of one's own weaknesses or mistakes and the exaggeration of one's own good qualities and achievements

self–for·get·ful \ˌself-fər-ˈget-fəl\ *adj* : having or showing no thought of self or selfish interests — **self–for·get·ful·ly** \-fə-lē\ *adv* — **self–for·get·ful·ness** *n*

self–for·get·ting \-ˈget-iŋ\ *adj* : SELF-FORGETFUL — **self–for·get·ting·ly** \-iŋ-lē\ *adv*

self–formed \ˈself-ˈfȯ(ə)rmd\ *adj* : formed or developed by one's own efforts

self–fruit·ful \-ˈfrüt-fəl\ *adj* : capable of setting a crop of self-pollinated fruit — **self–fruit·ful·ness** *n*

self–ful·fill·ing \ˌself-fu̇l-ˈfil-iŋ\ *adj* **1** : marked by or achieving self-fulfillment **2** : attaining fulfillment by virtue of having been predicted or assumed beforehand <a ~ prophecy>

self–ful·fill·ment \-ˈfil-mənt\ *n* : fulfillment of oneself

self–gen·er·at·ed \ˈself-ˈjen-ə-ˌrāt-əd\ *adj* : generated from within oneself <~ humor>

self–giv·en \ˈself-ˈgiv-ən\ *adj* **1** : derived from itself <a ~ entity> **2** : given by oneself <~ authority>

self–giv·ing \-ˈgiv-iŋ\ *adj* : giving completely of oneself : SELF-SACRIFICING, UNSELFISH

self–glo·ri·fi·ca·tion \ˌself-ˌglōr-ə-fə-ˈkā-shən, -ˌglȯr-\ *n* : a feeling or expression of one's own superiority

self–glo·ri·fy·ing \ˈself-ˈglōr-ə-ˌfī-iŋ, -ˈglȯr-\ *adj* : given to or marked by boasting : BOASTFUL

self–glo·ry \-ˈglōr-ē, -ˈglȯr-ē\ *n* : personal vanity : PRIDE

self–gov·er·nance \-ˈgəv-ər-nən(t)s\ *n* : SELF-GOVERNMENT 2

self–gov·erned \-ˈgəv-ərnd\ *adj* **1** : not influenced or controlled by others **2** : exercising self-control

self–gov·ern·ing \-ˈgəv-ər-niŋ\ *adj* : having control or rule over oneself; *specif* : having self-government : AUTONOMOUS

self–gov·ern·ment \-ˈgəv-ər(n)-mənt, -ˈgəv-ᵊm-ənt\ *n* **1** : SELF-COMMAND, SELF-CONTROL **2** : government under the control and direction of the inhabitants of a political unit rather than by an outside authority; *broadly* : control of one's own affairs

self–grat·i·fi·ca·tion \ˌself-ˌgrat-ə-fə-ˈkā-shən\ *n* : the act of pleasing oneself or of satisfying one's desires

self–grat·u·la·tion \-ˌgrach-ə-ˈlā-shən\ *n* : SELF-CONGRATULATION

self–grat·u·la·to·ry \ˈself-ˈgrach-(ə-)lə-ˌtōr-ē, -ˌtȯr-\ *adj* : SELF-CONGRATULATORY

self–hard·en·ing \-ˈhärd-niŋ, -ᵊn-iŋ\ *adj* : hardening by itself or without quenching after heating <~ steel>

self–hate \-ˈhāt\ *n* : hatred redirected toward oneself

self–hat·ing \-ˈhāt-iŋ\ *adj* : given to self-hate

self–ha·tred \-ˈhā-trəd\ *n* : SELF-HATE

self–heal \ˈself-ˌhēl\ *n* : any of several plants sometimes believed to possess healing properties; *esp* : a blue-flowered Eurasian mint (*Prunella vulgaris*) naturalized throughout No. America

self–help \ˈself-ˈhelp\ *n* : the act or an instance of providing for or helping oneself without dependence on others

self·hood \-ˌhu̇d\ *n* **1** : INDIVIDUALITY **2** : the quality or state of being selfish

self-hum·bling \-'həm-b(ə-)liŋ, -'əm-\ *adj* : acting or serving to humble oneself
self-hu·mil·i·a·tion \ˌself-hyü-ˌmil-ē-'ā-shən, ˌself-yü-\ *n* : the act or an instance of humbling oneself
self-hyp·no·sis \ˌself-(h)ip-'nō-səs\ *n* : hypnosis of oneself
self-iden·ti·cal \ˌsel-ˌfī-'dent-i-kəl, -fə-\ *adj* : having self-identity
self-iden·ti·fi·ca·tion \-ˌdent-ə-fə-'kā-shən\ *n* : identification with someone or something outside oneself
self-iden·ti·ty \-'den(t)-ət-ē\ *n* **1** : sameness of a thing with itself **2** : INDIVIDUALITY <self-understanding is the necessary condition of a sense of ~—J. C. Murray>
self-ig·nite \ˌsel-fig-'nīt\ *vi* : to become ignited without flame or spark (as under high compression)
self-ig·ni·tion \-'nish-ən\ *n* : ignition without flame or spark
self-im·age \'sel-'fim-ij\ *n* : one's conception of oneself or of one's role
self-im·mo·la·tion \ˌsel-ˌfim-ə-'lā-shən\ *n* : a deliberate and willing sacrifice of oneself
self-im·por·tance \ˌsel-fim-'pȯrt-ᵊn(t)s, -ən(t)s\ *n* **1** : an exaggerated estimate of one's own importance : SELF-CONCEIT **2** : arrogant or pompous behavior — **self-im·por·tant** \-ᵊnt, -ənt\ *adj* — **self-im·por·tant·ly** *adv*
self-imposed \-'pōzd\ *adj* : imposed on one by oneself : voluntarily assumed
self-im·prove·ment \-'prüv-mənt\ *n* : improvement of oneself by one's own action
self-in·clu·sive \ˌsel-fin-'klü-siv, -ziv\ *adj* **1** : enclosing itself **2** : complete in itself
self-in·com·pat·i·ble \ˌsel-ˌfin-kəm-'pat-ə-bəl\ *adj* : incapable of effective self-pollination — **self-in·com·pat·i·bil·i·ty** \-ˌpat-ə-'bil-ət-ē\ *n*
self-in·crim·i·nat·ing \ˌsel-fin-'krim-ə-ˌnāt-iŋ\ *adj* : serving or tending to incriminate oneself
self-in·crim·i·na·tion \-ˌkrim-ə-'nā-shən\ *n* : incrimination of oneself; *specif* : the giving of evidence or answering of questions the tendency of which would be to subject one to criminal prosecution
self-in·duced \ˌsel-fin-'d(y)üst\ *adj* : induced by oneself; *specif* : produced by self-induction <a ~ voltage>
self-in·duc·tance \-'dək-tən(t)s\ *n* : inductance that induces an electromotive force in the same circuit as the one in which the current varies
self-in·duc·tion \-'dək-shən\ *n* : induction of an electromotive force in a circuit by a varying current in the same circuit
self-in·dul·gence \-'dəl-jən(t)s\ *n* : excessive or unrestrained gratification of one's own appetites, desires, or whims — **self-in·dul·gent** \-jənt\ *adj* — **self-in·dul·gent·ly** *adv*
self-in·flict·ed \ˌsel-fin-'flik-təd\ *adj* : inflicted by oneself; *esp* : inflicted by one's own hand <a ~ wound>
self-ini·ti·at·ed \ˌsel-fin-'ish-ē-ˌāt-əd\ *adj* : initiated by oneself
self-in·struct·ed \ˌsel-fin-'strək-təd\ *adj* : SELF-TAUGHT
self-in·struc·tion·al \-'strək-shnəl, -shən-ᵊl\ *adj* : of, relating to, or designed for independent study
self-in·sur·ance \ˌsel-fin-'shu̇r-ən(t)s, 'sel-'fin-ˌ\ *n* : insurance of oneself or of one's own interests by the setting aside of money at regular intervals to provide a fund to cover possible losses
self-in·sured \ˌsel-fin-'shu̇(ə)rd\ *adj* : insured by oneself
self-in·sur·er \-'shu̇r-ər\ *n* : one who practices self-insurance
self-in·ter·est \'sel-'fin-trəst; -'fint-ə-rəst, -ə-ˌrest, -ərst; -'fin-ˌtrest\ *n* **1** : one's own interest or advantage <~ requires that we be generous in foreign aid> **2** : a concern for one's own advantage and well-being <acted out of ~ and fear> — **self-in·ter·est·ed** \-əd\ *adj* — **self-in·ter·est·ed·ness** *n*
self-in·volved \ˌsel-fin-'välvd, -'vȯlvd\ *adj* : SELF-ABSORBED
self·ish \'sel-fish\ *adj* **1** : concerned excessively or exclusively with oneself : seeking or concentrating on one's own advantage, pleasure, or well-being without regard for others **2** : arising from concern with one's own welfare or advantage in disregard of others <a ~ act> — **self·ish·ly** *adv* — **self·ish·ness** *n*
self-jus·ti·fi·ca·tion \ˌself-ˌjəs-tə-fə-'kā-shən\ *n* : the act or an instance of making excuses for oneself
self-jus·ti·fy·ing \'self-'jəs-tə-ˌfī-iŋ\ *adj* **1** : seeking to justify oneself **2** : automatically justifying itself <a ~ typewriter>
self-know·ing \'self-'nō-iŋ\ *adj* : having self-knowledge
self-knowl·edge \'self-'näl-ij\ *n* : knowledge or understanding of one's own capabilities, character, feelings, or motivations
self·less \'sel-fləs\ *adj* : having no concern for self : UNSELFISH — **self·less·ly** *adv* — **self·less·ness** *n*
self-lim·i·ta·tion \ˌsel-ˌflim-ə-'tā-shən\ *n* : the quality or state of being self-limiting
self-lim·it·ed \'sel-'flim-ət-əd\ *adj* : limited by one's or its own nature; *specif* : running a definite and limited course <a ~ disease>
self-lim·it·ing \-ət-iŋ\ *adj* : limiting oneself or itself
self-liq·ui·dat·ing \'sel-'flik-wə-ˌdāt-iŋ\ *adj* **1** : of or relating to a commercial transaction in which goods are converted into cash in a short time **2** : generating funds from its own operations to repay the investment made to create it <a ~ housing project>
self-load·er \'sel-'flōd-ər\ *n* : a semiautomatic firearm
self-load·ing \'sel-'flōd-iŋ\ *adj, of a firearm* : SEMIAUTOMATIC
self-lock·ing \'sel-'fläk-iŋ\ *adj* : locking by its own action
self-love \'sel-'fləv\ *n* : love of self: **a** : CONCEIT **b** : regard for one's own happiness or advantage — **self-lov·ing** \-'fləv-iŋ\ *adj*
self-lu·bri·cat·ing \'sel-'flü-brə-ˌkāt-iŋ\ *adj* : lubricating itself
self-lu·mi·nous \'sel-'flü-mə-nəs\ *adj* : having in itself the property of emitting light
self-made \'self-'mād\ *adj* **1** : made such by one's own actions **2** : raised from poverty or obscurity by one's own efforts <a ~ man>
self-mail·er \-'mā-lər\ *n* : a folder that can be sent by mail without enclosure in an envelope by use of a gummed sticker or a precanceled stamp to hold the leaves together
self-mail·ing \-liŋ\ *adj* : capable of being mailed without being enclosed in an envelope
self-mas·tery \'self-'mas-t(ə-)rē\ *n* : SELF-COMMAND, SELF-CONTROL
self-moved \-'müvd\ *adj* : moved by inherent power
self-mur·der \-'mərd-ər\ *n* : SELF-DESTRUCTION, SUICIDE
self-naught·ing \'self-'nȯt-iŋ, -'nät-\ *n* : SELF-EFFACEMENT
self·ness \'self-nəs\ *n* **1** : EGOISM, SELFISHNESS **2** : PERSONALITY, SELFHOOD
self-ob·ser·va·tion \ˌsel-ˌfäb-sər-'vā-shən, -zər-\ *n* **1** : observation of one's own appearance **2** : INTROSPECTION
self-op·er·at·ing \'sel-'fäp-(ə-)ˌrāt-iŋ\ *adj* : SELF-ACTING
self-op·er·a·tive \-'fäp-(ə-)rət-iv, -'fäp-ə-ˌrāt-\ *adj* : SELF-ACTING
self-opin·ion \ˌsel-fə-'pin-yən\ *n* : high or exaggerated opinion of oneself : SELF-CONCEIT
self-opin·ion·at·ed \-yə-ˌnāt-əd\ *adj* **1** : CONCEITED **2** : stubbornly holding to one's own opinion : OPINIONATED — **self-opin·ion·at·ed·ness** *n*
self-opin·ioned \ˌsel-fə-'pin-yənd\ *adj* : SELF-OPINIONATED
self-or·ga·ni·za·tion \ˌsel-ˌfȯrg-(ə-)nə-'zā-shən\ *n* : organization of oneself or itself; *specif* : the act or process of forming or joining a labor union
self-orig·i·nat·ed \ˌsel-fə-'rij-ə-ˌnāt-əd\ *adj* : originated by oneself
self-orig·i·nat·ing \-ˌnāt-iŋ\ *adj* : originating by or from oneself
self-par·o·dy \'self-'par-əd-ē\ *n* : parody of oneself
self-par·tial·i·ty \ˌself-ˌpär-shē-'al-ət-ē, -ˌpär-'shal-\ *n* **1** : an excessive estimate of oneself as compared with others **2** : a prejudice in favor of one's own claims or interests
self-per·cep·tion \ˌself-pər-'sep-shən\ *n* : perception of oneself; *esp* : SELF-IMAGE
self-per·pet·u·at·ing \-'pech-ə-ˌwāt-iŋ\ *adj* : capable of continuing or renewing oneself or itself indefinitely <~ board of trustees>
self-per·pet·u·a·tion \-ˌpech-ə-'wā-shən\ *n* : perpetuation of oneself or itself
self-pity \'self-'pit-ē\ *n* : pity for oneself; *esp* : a self-indulgent dwelling on one's own sorrows or misfortunes — **self-pity·ing** \-ē-iŋ\ *adj* — **self-pity·ing·ly** \-iŋ-lē\ *adv*
self-pleased \-'plēzd\ *adj* : SELF-SATISFIED
self-pleas·ing \-'plē-ziŋ\ *adj* : pleasing to oneself
self-poise \-'pȯiz\ *n* : the quality or state of being self-poised
self-poised \-'pȯizd\ *adj* **1** : balanced without support **2** : having poise through self-command
self-pol·li·nate \'self-'päl-ə-ˌnāt\ *vi* : to undergo self-pollination ~ *vt* : SELF 2
self-pol·li·na·tion \ˌself-ˌpäl-ə-'nā-shən\ *n* : the transfer of pollen from the anther of a flower to the stigma of the same flower or sometimes to that of a genetically identical flower (as of the same plant or clone)
self-por·trait \'self-'pōr-trət, -'pȯr-, -ˌtrāt\ *n* : a portrait of oneself done by oneself
self-pos·sessed \ˌself-pə-'zest, *also* -'sest\ *adj* : having or showing self-possession : composed in mind or manner : CALM — **self-pos·sessed·ly** \-'zes-əd-lē, -'ses-; -'zest-lē, -'sest-\ *adv*
self-pos·ses·sion \ˌself-pə-'zesh-ən, *also* -'sesh-\ *n* : control of one's emotions or reactions esp. when under stress : PRESENCE OF MIND, COMPOSURE ***syn*** see CONFIDENCE
self-praise \'self-'prāz\ *n* : praise of oneself
self-pres·er·va·tion \ˌself-ˌprez-ər-'vā-shən\ *n* **1** : preservation of oneself from destruction or harm **2** : a natural or instinctive tendency to act so as to preserve one's own existence
self-pre·serv·ing \ˌself-pri-'zər-viŋ\ *adj* : acting or tending to preserve oneself
self-pride \'self-'prīd\ *n* : pride in oneself or in that which relates to oneself
self-pro·claimed \ˌself-prō-'klāmd, -prə-\ *adj* : SELF-STYLED
self-pro·duced \ˌself-prə-'d(y)üst, -prō-\ *adj* : produced by oneself
self-pro·pelled \ˌself-prə-'peld\ *adj* **1** : containing within itself the means for its own propulsion <a ~ vehicle> **2** : mounted on or fired from a moving vehicle <a ~ gun>
self-pro·pel·ling \-'pel-iŋ\ *adj* : SELF-PROPELLED 1
self-pro·pul·sion \-'pəl-shən\ *n* : propulsion by one's own power
self-pro·tec·tion \-'tek-shən\ *n* : protection of oneself : SELF-DEFENSE
self-pro·tec·tive \-'tek-tiv\ *adj* : serving or tending to protect oneself — **self-pro·tec·tive·ness** *n*
self-pun·ish·ment \'self-'pən-ish-mənt\ *n* : punishment of oneself
self-pu·ri·fi·ca·tion \ˌself-ˌpyu̇r-ə-fə-'kā-shən\ *n* **1** : purification by natural process <~ of water> **2** : purification of oneself
self-ques·tion \'self-'kwes(h)-chən\ *n* : a question put to a person by himself
self-ques·tion·ing \-chə-niŋ\ *n* : examination of one's own actions and motives
self-raised \'sel-'frāzd\ *adj* : raised by one's own power or effort
self-rat·ing \'sel-'frāt-iŋ\ *n* : determination of one's own rating with reference to a standard scale
self-re·al·iza·tion \ˌsel-ˌfrē-ə-lə-'zā-shən, -ˌfri-ə-\ *n* : fulfillment by oneself of the possibilities of one's character or personality
self-re·al·iza·tion·ism \-shə-ˌniz-əm\ *n* : the ethical theory that the highest good for man consists in realizing or fulfilling himself usu. on the assumption that he has certain inborn abilities constituting his real or ideal self
self-re·al·iza·tion·ist \-sh(ə-)nəst\ *n* : an advocate of self-realizationism
self-re·cord·ing \ˌsel-fri-'kȯrd-iŋ\ *adj* : making an automatic record <~ instruments>
self-re·crim·i·na·tion \-ˌkrim-ə-'nā-shən\ *n* : the act of accusing or blaming oneself
self-re·flec·tion \-'flek-shən\ *n* : SELF-EXAMINATION
self-re·flec·tive \-'flek-tiv\ *adj* : marked by or engaging in self-reflection
self-ref·or·ma·tion \ˌsel-ˌfref-ər-'mā-shən\ *n* : the act or an instance of reforming oneself
self-re·gard \ˌsel-fri-'gärd\ *n* **1** : regard for or consideration of oneself or one's own interests **2** : SELF-RESPECT

self-re·gard·ing \-iŋ\ *adj* : concerned with oneself or one's own interests

self-reg·is·ter·ing \'sel-'frej-ə-st(ə-)riŋ\ *adj* : registering automatically <a ~ barometer>

self-reg·u·lat·ing \'sel-'freg-yə-ˌlāt-iŋ\ *adj* : regulating oneself or itself; *esp* : AUTOMATIC <a ~ mechanism>

self-reg·u·la·tion \ˌsel-ˌfreg-yə-'lā-shən\ *n* : regulation of or by oneself or itself

self-reg·u·la·tive \'sel-'freg-yə-ˌlāt-iv\ *adj* : serving or tending to regulate oneself or itself

self-reg·u·la·to·ry \-lə-ˌtōr-ē, -ˌtȯr-\ *adj* : SELF-REGULATIVE

self-re·li·ance \ˌsel-fri-'lī-ənts\ *n* : reliance upon one's own efforts and abilities

self-re·li·ant \-ənt\ *adj* : having confidence in and exercising one's own powers or judgment

self-re·nounc·ing \ˌsel-fri-'naun(t)-siŋ\ *adj* : marked by self-renunciation

self-re·nun·ci·a·tion \-ˌnən(t)-sē-'ā-shən\ *n* : renunciation of one's own desires or ambitions

self-rep·li·cat·ing \'sel-'frep-lə-ˌkāt-iŋ\ *adj* : reproducing itself autonomously <DNA is a ~ molecule>

self-re·pres·sion \ˌsel-fri-'presh-ən\ *n* : the keeping to oneself of one's thoughts, wishes, or feelings

self-re·proach \ˌsel-fri-'prōch\ *n* : the act of blaming or accusing oneself — **self-re·proach·ful** \-fəl\ *adj*

self-re·proach·ing \-'prō-chiŋ\ *adj* : of, relating to, or characterized by self-reproach — **self-re·proach·ing·ly** \-chiŋ-lē\ *adv* — **self-re·proach·ing·ness** *n*

self-re·proof \ˌsel-fri-'prüf\ *n* : the act of reproving oneself

self-re·prov·ing \-'prü-viŋ\ *adj* : feeling or expressing self-reproof — **self-re·prov·ing·ly** \-viŋ-lē\ *adv*

self-re·spect \ˌsel-fri-'spekt\ *n* **1** : a proper respect for oneself as a human being **2** : regard for one's own standing or position

self-re·spect·ing \-'spek-tiŋ\ *adj* : having or characterized by self-respect

self-re·strain·ing \-'strā-niŋ\ *adj* : marked by self-restraint

self-re·straint \-'strānt\ *n* : restraint imposed on oneself

self-re·veal·ing \ˌsel-fri-'vē-liŋ\ *adj* : marked by self-revelation

self-rev·e·la·tion \ˌsel-ˌfrev-ə-'lā-shən\ *n* : revelation of one's own thoughts, feelings, and attitudes esp. without deliberate intent

self-re·ward·ing \ˌsel-fri-'wȯrd-iŋ\ *adj* : containing or producing its own reward <a ~ virtue>

self-righ·teous \'sel-'frī-chəs\ *adj* : convinced of one's own righteousness esp. in contrast with the actions and beliefs of others : narrow-mindedly moralistic — **self-righ·teous·ly** *adv* — **self-righ·teous·ness** *n*

self-right·ing \'sel-'frīt-iŋ\ *adj* : capable of righting itself when capsized <a ~ boat>

self-ris·ing flour \ˌsel-ˌfrī-ziŋ-\ *n* : a commercially prepared mixture of flour, salt, and a leavening agent

self-rule \'sel-'frül\ *n* : SELF-GOVERNMENT

self-rul·ing \-'frü-liŋ\ *adj* : SELF-GOVERNING

self-sac·ri·fice \'self-'sak-rə-ˌfīs, -fəs *also* -ˌfīz\ *n* : sacrifice of oneself or one's interest for others or for a cause or ideal

self-sac·ri·fic·er \-ˌfīs-ər, -ˌfīz- *also* -fəs-\ *n* : one that practices self-sacrifice

self-sa·cri·fic·ing \-ˌfīs-iŋ, -ˌfīz- *also* -fəs-\ *adj* : sacrificing oneself for others — **self-sac·ri·fic·ing·ly** \-iŋ-lē\ *adv*

self·same \'self-ˌsām\ *adj* : being the one mentioned or in question : IDENTICAL <he left the ~ day> ***syn*** see SAME ***ant*** diverse — **self·same·ness** \-ˌsām-nəs, -'sām-\ *n*

self-sat·is·fac·tion \ˌself-ˌsat-əs-'fak-shən\ *n* : a usu. smug satisfaction with oneself or one's position or achievements

self-sat·is·fied \'self-'sat-əs-ˌfīd\ *adj* : feeling or showing self-satisfaction

self-sat·is·fy·ing \-ˌfī-iŋ\ *adj* : giving satisfaction to oneself

self-scru·ti·ny \'self-'skrüt-ᵊn-ē, -'skrüt-nē\ *n* : SELF-EXAMINATION

self-seal·ing \'self-'sē-liŋ\ *adj* **1** : capable of sealing itself (as after puncture) <a ~ tire> **2** : capable of being sealed by pressure without the addition of moisture <~ envelopes>

self-search·ing \-'sər-chiŋ\ *adj* : SELF-QUESTIONING

self-seek·er \-'sē-kər\ *n* : one who is self-seeking

¹self-seek·ing \-kiŋ\ *n* : the act or practice of selfishly advancing one's own ends

²self-seeking *adj* : seeking only to further one's own interests

self-se·lec·tion \ˌself-sə-'lek-shən\ *n* : selection of or by oneself; *esp* : selection of goods by retail customers from display racks or counters in a store

self-ser·vice \'self-'sər-vəs\ *n* : the serving of oneself (as in a cafeteria or supermarket) with things to be paid for at a cashier's desk usu. upon leaving — **self-service** *adj*

self-serv·ing \-'sər-viŋ\ *adj* : serving one's own interests often in disregard of the truth or the interests of others

self-slaugh·ter \-'slȯt-ər\ *n* : SUICIDE

self-slaugh·tered \-ərd\ *adj* : killed by oneself

self-slay·er \'self-ˌslā-ər\ *n* : one who kills himself

self-sow \-'sō\ *vi* **-sowed** \-'sōd\; **-sown** \-'sōn\ *or* **-sowed; -sow·ing** : to sow itself by dropping seeds or by natural action (as of wind or water)

self-start·er \-'stärt-ər\ *n* **1** : a more or less automatic attachment for starting an engine; *esp* : an electric motor used to start an internal-combustion engine **2** : a person who has initiative

self-start·ing \-'stärt-iŋ\ *adj* : capable of starting by oneself or itself

self-ster·ile \-'ster-əl\ *adj* : sterile to its own pollen or sperm — **self-ste·ril·i·ty** \ˌself-stə-'ril-ət-ē\ *n*

self-stim·u·la·tion \ˌself-ˌstim-yə-'lā-shən\ *n* : stimulation of oneself as a result of one's own activity or behavior <electrical ~ of the brain in rats>

self-study \'self-'stəd-ē\ *n* : study of oneself; *also* : a record of observations from such study

self-styled \-'stī(ə)ld\ *adj* : called by oneself <~ experts>

self-sub·sis·tence \ˌself-səb-'sis-tən(t)s\ *n* : the quality or state of being self-subsistent

self-sub·sis·tent \-tənt\ *adj* : subsisting independently of anything external to itself

self-sub·sist·ing \-'sis-tiŋ\ *adj* : SELF-SUBSISTENT

self-suf·fi·cien·cy \ˌself-sə-'fish-ən-sē\ *n* : the quality or state of being self-sufficient

self-suf·fi·cient \-'fish-ənt\ *adj* **1** : able to maintain oneself or itself without outside aid : capable of providing for one's own needs **2** : having an extreme confidence in one's own ability or worth : HAUGHTY, OVERBEARING

self-suf·fic·ing \-'fī-siŋ *also* -ziŋ\ *adj* : SELF-SUFFICIENT — **self-suf·fic·ing·ly** \-siŋ-lē, -ziŋ-\ *adv* — **self-suf·fic·ing·ness** *n*

self-sug·ges·tion \ˌself-sə(g)-'jes(h)-chən\ *n* : AUTOSUGGESTION

self-sup·port \ˌself-sə-'pō(ə)rt, -'pȯ(ə)rt\ *n* : independent support of oneself or itself — **self-sup·port·ed** \-əd\ *adj*

self-sup·port·ing \-iŋ\ *adj* : characterized by self-support: as **a** : meeting one's needs by one's own efforts or output **b** : supporting itself or its own weight <a ~ wall>

self-sur·ren·der \-sə-'ren-dər\ *n* : surrender of the self : a yielding up (as to some influence) of oneself or one's will

self-sus·tained \-sə-'stānd\ *adj* : sustained by oneself or itself

self-sus·tain·ing \-'stā-niŋ\ *adj* **1** : maintaining or able to maintain oneself or itself by independent effort **2** : maintaining or able to maintain itself once commenced <a ~ nuclear reaction>

self-taught \'self-'tȯt\ *adj* **1** : having knowledge or skills acquired by one's own efforts without formal instruction <a ~ musician> **2** : learned by oneself <~ knowledge>

self-tor·ment \'self-'tȯr-ˌment\ *n* : the act of tormenting oneself — **self-tor·ment·ing** \ˌself-tȯr-'ment-iŋ, 'self-'tȯr-ˌ\ *adj* — **self-tor·men·tor** \ˌself-tȯr-'ment-ər, 'self-'tȯr-ˌ\ *n*

self-tran·scen·dence \ˌself-ˌtran(t)s-'en-dən(t)s\ *n* : the capacity to transcend oneself

self-treat·ment \'self-'trēt-mənt\ *n* : medication of oneself or treatment of one's own disease without medical supervision or prescription

self-trust \-'trəst\ *n* : SELF-CONFIDENCE

self-un·der·stand·ing \ˌsel-ˌfən-dər-'stan-diŋ\ *n* : SELF-KNOWLEDGE

self-un·fruit·ful \ˌsel-ˌfən-'früt-fəl\ *adj* : setting few or no fruits in the absence of cross-pollination — **self-un·fruit·ful·ness** *n*

self-will \'self-'wil\ *n* : stubborn or willful adherence to one's own desires or ideas : OBSTINACY

self-willed \-'wild\ *adj* : governed by one's own will : not yielding to the wishes of others : OBSTINATE — **self-willed·ly** \-'wil-(d)lē\ *adv* — **self-willed·ness** \-'wil(d)-nəs\ *n*

self-wind·ing \-'wīn-diŋ\ *adj* : not needing to be wound by hand <a ~ watch>

self-wor·ship \-'wər-shəp\ *n* : worship of oneself — **self-wor·ship·er** *n*

Sel·juk \'sel-ˌjük, sel-'\ *or* **Sel·ju·ki·an** \sel-'jü-kē-ən\ *adj* [Turk *Selçuk*, eponymous ancestor of the dynasties] **1** : of or relating to any of several Turkish dynasties ruling over a great part of western Asia in the 11th, 12th, and 13th centuries **2** : of, relating to, or characteristic of a Turkish people ruled over by a Seljuk dynasty — **Seljuk** *or* **Seljukian** *n*

Selk *abbr* Selkirkshire

¹sell \'sel\ *vb* **sold** \'sōld\; **sell·ing** [ME *sellen*, fr. OE *sellan*; akin to OHG *sellen* to sell, ON *sala* sale, Gk *helein* to take] *vt* **1** : to deliver or give up in violation of duty, trust, or loyalty : BETRAY — often used with *out* **2 a** (1) : to give up (property) to another for money or other valuable consideration (2) : to offer for sale **b** : to give up in return for something else esp. foolishly or dishonorably <*sold* his birthright for a mess of pottage> **c** : to exact a price for <*sold* their lives dearly> **3 a** : to deliver into slavery for money **b** : to give into the power of another <*sold* his soul to the devil> **c** : to deliver the personal services of for money **4** : to dispose of or manage for profit instead of in accordance with conscience, justice, or duty <*sold* his vote> **5 a** : to develop a belief in the truth, value, or desirability of : gain acceptance for <a campaign manager trying to ~ his candidate> **b** : to persuade or influence to a course of action or to the acceptance of something <~ children on reading> **6** : to impose on : CHEAT <realized that he had been *sold*> **7 a** : to cause or promote the sale of <advertising ~*s* newspapers> **b** : to make or attempt to make sales to **c** : to influence or induce to make a purchase **8** : to achieve a sale of <*sold* a million copies> ~ *vi* **1** : to dispose of something by sale **2** : to achieve a sale; *also* : to achieve satisfactory sales <hoped that the new line would ~> **3** : to have a specified price — **sell·able** \'sel-ə-bəl\ *adj* — **sell a bill of goods** : to take unfair or unjust advantage of — **sell down the river** : to betray the faith of — **sell short 1** : to make a short sale **2** : to fail to value properly : UNDERESTIMATE

²sell *n* **1** : a deliberate deception : HOAX **2** : the act or an instance of selling

³sell *or* **selle** \'sel\ *n* [ME *selle*, fr. MF, fr. L *sella* — more at SETTLE] *archaic* : SADDLE

⁴sell *chiefly Scot var of* SELF

sell·er \'sel-ər\ *n* **1** : one that offers for sale **2** : a product offered for sale and selling well, to a specified extent, or in a specified manner <a million-copy ~> <a poor ~>

seller's market *n* : a market in which goods are scarce, buyers have a limited range of choice, and prices are high — compare BUYER'S MARKET

selling climax *n* : a sharp decline in stock prices for a short time on very heavy trading volume followed by a rally

sell·ing-plat·er \'sel-iŋ-ˌplāt-ər\ *n* : a horse that runs in selling races

selling point *n* : an aspect or detail of something that is emphasized (as in selling or promoting)
selling race *n* : a claiming race in which the winning horse is put up for auction
sell–off \'sel-ˌȯf\ *n* : a usu. sudden sharp decline in security prices accompanied by increased volume of trading
sell off \(ˈ)sel-ˈȯf\ *vt* : to dispose of completely by selling ~ *vi* : to suffer a drop in prices
sell·out \'sel-ˌau̇t\ *n* **1 :** the act or an instance of selling out **2 :** a show, exhibition, or contest for which all seats are sold **3 :** one who sells out
sell out \(ˈ)sel-ˈau̇t\ *vt* **1 :** to dispose of entirely by sale **2 a :** to sell the goods of (a debtor) in order to satisfy creditors **b :** to sell security or commodity holdings of usu. to satisfy an uncovered margin ~ *vi* **1 :** to dispose of one's goods by sale; *esp* : to sell one's business **2 :** to betray one's cause or associates
sel·syn \'sel-ˌsin\ *n* [*self-syn*chronizing] : a system comprising a generator and a motor so connected by wire that angular rotation or position in the generator is reproduced simultaneously in the motor — called also *synchro*
selt·zer \'selt-sər\ *n* [modif. of G *Selterser (wasser)* water of Selters, fr. Nieder *Selters,* Germany] : an artificially prepared mineral water containing carbon dioxide
sel·vage *or* **sel·vedge** \'sel-vij\ *n* [ME *selvage,* prob. fr. MFlem *selvegge, selvage,* fr. *selv* self + *egge* edge; akin to OE *self* and to OE *ecg* edge — more at EDGE] **1 a :** the edge on either side of a woven or flat-knitted fabric so finished as to prevent raveling; *specif* : a narrow border often of different or heavier threads than the fabric and sometimes in a different weave **b :** an edge (as of fabric or paper) meant to be cut off and discarded **2 :** an outer or peripheral part: as **a :** BORDER, EDGE **b :** the edge plate of a lock through which the bolt is projected — **sel·vaged** *or* **sel·vedged** \-vijd\ *adj*
selves *pl of* SELF
sem *abbr* **1** seminar **2** seminary
Sem *abbr* Semitic
SEM *abbr* scanning electron microscope
se·man·tic \si-'mant-ik\ *also* **se·man·ti·cal** \-i-kəl\ *adj* [Gk *sēmantikos* significant, fr. *sēmainein* to signify, mean, fr. *sēma* sign, token; akin to Skt *dhyāti* he thinks] **1 :** of or relating to meaning in language **2 :** of or relating to semantics — **se·man·ti·cal·ly** \-i-k(ə-)lē\ *adv*
se·man·ti·cist \-'mant-ə-səst\ *n* : a specialist in semantics
se·man·tics \si-'mant-iks\ *n pl but sing or pl in constr* **1 :** the study of meanings: **a :** the historical and psychological study and the classification of changes in the signification of words or forms viewed as factors in linguistic development **b (1) :** SEMIOTIC **(2) :** a branch of semiotic dealing with the relations between signs and what they refer to and including theories of denotation, extension, naming, and truth **2 :** GENERAL SEMANTICS **3 a :** the meaning or relationship of meanings of a sign or set of signs; *esp* : connotative meaning **b :** the exploitation of connotation and ambiguity (as in propaganda)
¹sema·phore \'sem-ə-ˌfō(ə)r, -ˌfȯ(ə)r\ *n* [Gk *sēma* sign, signal + ISV *-phore*] **1 :** an apparatus for visual signaling (as by the position of one or more movable arms) **2 :** a system of visual signaling by two flags held one in each hand

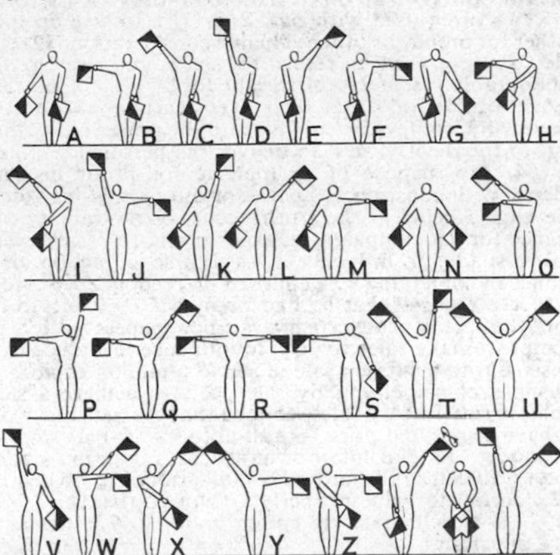

semaphore 2: alphabet; 3 positions following Z: error, end of word, numerals follow; numerals 1,2, 3,4,5,6,7,8,9,0 same as A through J

²semaphore *vb* **-phored; -phor·ing** *vt* : to convey (information) by or as if by semaphore ~ *vi* : to send signals by or as if by semaphore
se·ma·si·ol·o·gy \si-ˌmā-sē-'äl-ə-jē, -ˌmā-zē-\ *n* [ISV, fr. Gk *sēmasia* meaning, fr. *sēmainein* to mean] : SEMANTICS 1 — **se·ma·si·o·log·i·cal** \-sē-ə-'läj-i-kəl, -zē-\ *adj* — **se·ma·si·ol·o·gist** \-sē-'äl-ə-jəst, -zē-\ *n*
se·mat·ic \si-'mat-ik\ *adj* [Gk *sēmat-, sēma* sign] : warning of danger — used of conspicuous colors of a poisonous or noxious animal <the ~ coloration of the skunk>
¹sem·bla·ble \'sem-blə-bəl\ *adj* [ME, fr. MF, fr. OF, fr. *sembler* to be like, seem] **1 :** SIMILAR **2 :** SUITABLE **3 :** APPARENT, SEEMING — **sem·bla·bly** \-blə-blē\ *adv*
²semblable *n* **1** *archaic* : something similar : LIKE **2 :** one that is like oneself : one's fellow
sem·blance \'sem-blən(t)s\ *n* [ME, fr. MF, fr. OF *sembler* to be like, seem — more at RESEMBLE] **1 a :** outward and often specious appearance or show : FORM <wrapped in a ~ of composure —Harry Hervey> **b :** MODICUM <has been struggling to get some ~ of justice for his people —Bayard Rustin> **2 :** COUNTENANCE, ASPECT **3 a :** phantasmal form : APPARITION **b :** IMAGE, LIKENESS **4 :** actual or apparent resemblance
se·mé \sə-'mā, 'sem-(ˌ)ā\ *adj* [MF, pp. of *semer* to sow, fr. L *seminare,* fr. *semen*] : having an ornamental pattern consisting of usu. regularly disposed separate objects or groups of small figures (as flowers or stars) : SOWN, DOTTED — **semé** *n*
se·mei·ol·o·gy *var of* SEMIOLOGY
Sem·e·le \'sem-ə-ˌlē\ *n* [L, fr. Gk *Semelē*] : a daughter of Cadmus consumed by flames when visited by Zeus in his divine splendor
se·men \'sē-mən\ *n* [NL, fr. L, seed; akin to OHG *sāmo* seed, L *serere* to sow — more at SOW] : a viscid whitish fluid of the male reproductive tract consisting of spermatozoa suspended in secretions of accessory glands
se·mes·ter \sə-'mes-tər\ *n* [G, fr. L *semestris* half-yearly, fr. *sex* six + *mensis* month — more at SIX, MOON] **1 :** a period of six months **2 :** either of the two usu. 18-week periods of instruction into which an academic year is often divided — **se·mes·tral** \-trəl\ *or* **se·mes·tri·al** \-trē-əl\ *adj*
semester hour *n* : a unit of academic credit representing an hour of class (as lecture class) or three hours of laboratory work each week for an academic semester
semi \'sem-ē, -ˌī\ *n* : SEMITRAILER
semi- \ˌsem-i, 'sem-, -ˌī\ *prefix* [ME, fr. L; akin to OHG *sāmi-* half, Gk *hēmi-*] **1 a :** precisely half of: **(1) :** forming a bisection of <*semi*ellipse> <*semi*oval> **(2) :** being a usu. vertically bisected form of (a specified architectural feature) <*semi*arch> <*semi*dome> **b :** half in quantity or value : half of or occurring halfway through a specified period of time <*semi*annual> <*semi*centenary> — compare BI- **2 :** to some extent : partly : incompletely <*semi*civilized> <*semi*-independent> <*semi*dry> — compare DEMI-, HEMI- **3 a :** partial : incomplete <*semi*consciousness> <*semi*darkness> **b :** having some of the characteristics of <*semi*porcelain> **c :** quasi <*semi*governmental> <*semi*monastic>
semi·ab·stract \ˌsem-ē-ab-'strakt, ˌsem-ˌī-, -'ab-ˌ\ *adj* : having subject matter that is easily recognizable although the form is stylized <~ art> — **semi·ab·strac·tion** \-ab-'strak-shən\ *n*
semi·an·nu·al \-'an-yə(-wə)l\ *adj* : occurring every six months or twice a year — **semi·an·nu·al·ly** \-ē\ *adv*
semi·aquat·ic \-ə-'kwät-ik, -'kwat-\ *adj* : growing equally well in or adjacent to water; *also* : frequenting but not living wholly in water
semi·ar·bo·re·al \-är-'bōr-ē-əl, -'bȯr-\ *adj* : often inhabiting and frequenting trees but not completely arboreal
semi·ar·id \-'ar-əd\ *adj* : characterized by light rainfall; *specif* : having from about 10 to about 20 inches of annual precipitation — **semi·arid·i·ty** \-ə-'rid-ət-ē, -a-'rid-\ *n*
semi·au·to·mat·ic \-ˌȯt-ə-'mat-ik\ *adj* : not fully automatic: as **a :** operated partly automatically and partly by hand **b** *of a firearm* : employing gas pressure or force of recoil and mechanical spring action to eject the empty cartridge case after the first shot and load the next cartridge from the magazine but requiring release and another pressure of the trigger for each successive shot — **semiautomatic** *n* — **semi·au·to·mat·i·cal·ly** \-i-k(ə-)lē\ *adv*
semi·au·ton·o·mous \-ȯ-'tän-ə-məs\ *adj* : largely self-governing within a larger political or organizational entity
semi·base·ment \ˌsem-i-'bā-smənt, ˌsem-ˌī-\ *n* : a basement that is below ground level for only part of its depth
semi·breve \'sem-i-ˌbrēv, 'sem-ˌī-, -ˌbrev\ *n* : WHOLE NOTE
semi·cen·te·na·ry \ˌsem-i-sen-'ten-ə-rē, ˌsem-ˌī-, -'sent-ᵊn-ˌer-ē, -sen-'tē-nə-rē\ *n* : SEMICENTENNIAL — **semicentenary** *adj*
semi·cen·ten·ni·al \-sen-'ten-ē-əl\ *n* : a 50th anniversary or its celebration — **semicentennial** *adj*
semi·cir·cle \'sem-i-ˌsər-kəl\ *n* [L *semicirculus,* fr. *semi-* + *circulus* circle] **1 :** a half of a circle **2 :** an object or arrangement of objects in the form of a half circle — **semi·cir·cu·lar** \ˌsem-i-'sər-kyə-lər\ *adj*
semicircular canal *n* : any of the loop-shaped tubular parts of the labyrinth of the ear that together constitute a sensory organ associated with the maintenance of bodily equilibrium — see EAR illustration
semi·civ·i·lized \ˌsem-i-'siv-ə-ˌlīzd, ˌsem-ˌī-\ *adj* : partly civilized
semi·clas·sic \-'klas-ik\ *n* : a semiclassical work (as of music)
semi·clas·si·cal \-i-kəl\ *adj* : having some of the characteristics of the classical: as **a :** of, relating to, or being a musical composition that acts as a bridge between classical and popular music **b :** of, relating to, or being a classical composition that has developed popular appeal
semi·co·lon \'sem-i-ˌkō-lən\ *n* : a punctuation mark ; used chiefly in a coordinating function between major sentence elements (as independent clauses of a compound sentence)
semi·co·lo·nial \ˌsem-i-kə-'lō-nyəl, ˌsem-ˌī-, -nē-əl\ *adj* **1 :** nominally independent but actually under foreign domination **2 :** dependent on foreign nations as suppliers of manufactured goods and as purchasers of raw materials — **semi·co·lo·nial·ism** \-ˌiz-əm\ *n*
semi·col·o·ny \-'käl-ə-nē\ *n* : a semicolonial state
semi·com·mer·cial \-kə-'mər-shəl\ *adj* : of, relating to, adapted to, or characterized by limited marketing of an experimental product
semi·con·duct·ing \ˌsem-i-kən-'dək-tiŋ, ˌsem-ˌī-\ *adj* : of, relating to, or having the characteristics of a semiconductor
semi·con·duc·tor \-'dək-tər\ *n* : any of a class of solids (as germanium or silicon) whose electrical conductivity is between that of a conductor and that of an insulator in being nearly metallic at high temperatures and nearly absent at low temperatures
semi·con·scious \-'kän-chəs\ *adj* : incompletely conscious : imperfectly aware or responsive — **semi·con·scious·ly** *adv* — **semi·con·scious·ness** *n*

semi·con·ser·va·tive \-kən-ˈsər-vət-iv\ *adj* **:** relating to or being replication (as of DNA) in which the original separates into parts each of which is incorporated into a new whole and serves as a template for the formation of the missing parts — **semi·con·ser·va·tive·ly** *adv*
semi·crys·tal·line \-ˈkris-tə-lən\ *adj* **:** incompletely or imperfectly crystalline
semi·cy·lin·dri·cal \-sə-ˈlin-dri-kəl\ *adj* **:** having the shape of a longitudinal half of a cylinder
semi·dark·ness \-ˈdärk-nəs\ *n* **:** partial darkness
semi·de·ify \-ˈdē-ə-ˌfī, -ˈdā-\ *vt* **:** to regard as somewhat godlike
semi·des·ert \-ˈdez-ərt\ *n* **:** an area that has some of the characteristics of a desert and is often located between a desert and grassland or woodland
semi·de·tached \-di-ˈtacht\ *adj* **:** forming one of a pair of residences joined into one building by a common sidewall
semi·di·am·e·ter \ˌsem-i-dī-ˈam-ət-ər\ *n* **:** RADIUS; *specif* **:** the apparent radius of a generally spherical celestial body
semi·di·ur·nal \-dī-ˈərn-ᵊl\ *adj* **1 :** relating to or accomplished in half a day **2 :** occurring twice a day **3 :** occurring approximately every half day <the ~ tides>
semi·di·vine \ˌsem-i-də-ˈvīn, ˌsem-ˌī-\ *adj* **:** more than mortal but not fully divine
semi·doc·u·men·ta·ry \-ˌdäk-yə-ˈment-ə-rē, -ˈmen-trē\ *n* **:** a motion picture that uses many details taken from actual events or situations in presenting a fictional story — **semidocumentary** *adj*
semi·dome \ˈsem-i-ˌdōm, ˈsem-ˌī-\ *n* **:** a roof or ceiling covering a semicircular or nearly semicircular room or recess — **semi·domed** \-ˌdōmd\ *adj*
semi·do·mes·ti·cat·ed \ˌsem-i-də-ˈmes-ti-ˌkāt-əd, ˌsem-ˌī-\ *or* **semi·do·mes·tic** \-ˈmes-tik\ *adj* **:** of, relating to, or living in semidomestication
semi·do·mes·ti·ca·tion \-ˌmes-ti-ˈkā-shən\ *n* **:** a captive state (as in a zoo) of a wild animal in which its living conditions and often its breeding are controlled by man
semi·dom·i·nant \-ˈdäm-(ə-)nənt\ *adj* **:** producing an intermediate phenotype in the heterozygous condition <a ~ mutant gene>
semi·dou·ble \-ˈdəb-əl\ *adj* **:** having more than the normal number of petals or ray florets though retaining some pollen-bearing stamens or some perfect disk florets <a ~ daisy>
semi·dry \ˌsem-i-ˈdrī\ *adj* **:** moderately dry
semi·dry·ing \-ˈdrī-iŋ\ *adj* **:** that dries imperfectly or slowly — used of some oils (as cottonseed oil)
semi·el·lipse \ˌsem-ē-ə-ˈlips, ˌsem-ˌī-\ *n* **:** the part of an ellipse from one end of usu. the transverse diameter to the other — **semi·el·lip·tic** \-ˈlip-tik\ *or* **semi·el·lip·ti·cal** \-ti-kəl\ *adj*
semi·erect \-ə-ˈrekt\ *adj* **1 :** incompletely upright in bodily posture <~ primates> **2 :** erect for half the length <~ stems>
semi·ev·er·green \-ˈev-ər-ˌgrēn\ *adj* **:** HALF-EVERGREEN
[1]semi·fi·nal \ˌsem-i-ˈfīn-ᵊl\ *adj* **1 :** being next to the last in an elimination tournament **2 :** of or participating in a semifinal
[2]semi·fi·nal \ˈsem-i-ˌ\ *n* **1 :** a semifinal match **2 :** a semifinal round — **semi·fi·nal·ist** \ˌsem-i-ˈfīn-ᵊl-əst\ *n*
semi·fin·ished \ˌsem-i-ˈfin-isht, ˌsem-ˌī-\ *adj* **:** partially finished or processed; *esp, of steel* **:** rolled from raw ingots into shapes (as bars, billets, or plates) suitable for further processing
semi·fit·ted \-ˈfit-əd\ *adj* **:** conforming somewhat to the lines of the body
semi·flex·i·ble \-ˈflek-sə-bəl\ *adj* **1 :** somewhat flexible **2** *of a book cover* **:** consisting of a heavy flexible board under the covering material
semi·flu·id \-ˈflü-əd\ *adj* **:** having the qualities of both a fluid and a solid **:** VISCOUS <fluid and ~ lubricants> — **semifluid** *n*
semi·for·mal \-ˈfȯr-məl\ *adj* **:** being or suitable for an occasion of moderate formality <a ~ dinner> <~ gowns>
semi·fos·sil \-ˈfäs-əl\ *adj* **:** incompletely fossilized
semi·gloss \ˈsem-i-ˌgläs, ˈsem-ˌī-, -ˌglȯs\ *adj* **:** having a low luster; *specif* **:** producing a finish midway between gloss and flat
semi·gov·ern·men·tal \ˌsem-i-ˌgəv-ər(n)-ˈment-ᵊl, ˌsem-ˌī-, -ˌgəv-ᵊm-ˈent-\ *adj* **:** having some governmental functions and powers
semi·group \ˈsem-i-ˌgrüp, ˈsem-ˌī-\ *n* **:** a mathematical set that is closed under an associative binary operation
semi–in·de·pen·dent \ˈsem-ē-ˌin-də-ˈpen-dənt, ˈsem-ˌī-\ *adj* **:** partially independent; *specif* **:** SEMIAUTONOMOUS
semi–in·di·rect \-ˌin-də-ˈrekt, -dī-\ *adj, of lighting* **:** using a translucent reflector that transmits some primary light while reflecting most of it
semi·leg·end·ary \ˌsem-i-ˈlej-ən-ˌder-ē, ˌsem-ˌī-\ *adj* **:** having historical foundation but elaborated in legend
semi·le·thal \-ˈlē-thəl\ *n* **:** a mutation that in the homozygous condition produces more than 50 percent mortality but not complete mortality — **semilethal** *adj*
semi·liq·uid \-ˈlik-wəd\ *adj* **:** having the qualities of both a liquid and a solid **:** SEMIFLUID <~ manure> — **semiliquid** *n*
semi·lit·er·ate \-ˈlit-ə-rət, -ˈli-trət\ *adj* **1 a :** able to read and write on an elementary level **b :** able to read but unable to write **2 :** having limited knowledge or understanding **:** not well-versed <differentiate . . . between efforts of professional engineers and of ~ technicians —L. A. Orleans>
semi·log \-ˈlȯg, -ˈläg\ *adj* **:** SEMILOGARITHMIC
semi·log·a·rith·mic \-ˌlȯg-ə-ˈrith-mik, -ˌläg-\ *adj* **:** having one scale logarithmic and the other arithmetic — used of graph paper or of a graph on such paper
semi·lu·nar \-ˈlü-nər\ *adj* [NL *semilunaris,* fr. L *semi-* + *lunaris* lunar] **:** shaped like a crescent
semilunar valve *n* **:** any of the crescentic cusps that occur as a set of three between the heart and the aorta and another of three between the heart and the pulmonary artery, are forced apart by pressure in the ventricles during systole and pushed together by pressure in the arteries during diastole, and prevent regurgitation of blood into the ventricles; *also* **:** either set of three cusps
semi·lus·trous \ˌsem-i-ˈləs-trəs, ˌsem-ˌī-\ *adj* **:** slightly lustrous
semi·man·u·fac·tures \-ˌman-(y)ə-ˈfak-chərz\ *n pl* **:** products (as steel or newsprint) that are made from raw materials and that require further processing to become finished goods
semi·mat *or* **semi·matt** *or* **semi·matte** \-ˈmat\ *adj* [*semi-* + [4]*mat*] **:** having a slight luster
semi·met·al \-ˈmet-ᵊl\ *n* **:** an element (as arsenic) possessing metallic properties in an inferior degree and not malleable — **semi·me·tal·lic** \-mə-ˈtal-ik\ *adj*
semi·mi·cro \-ˈmī-(ˌ)krō\ *adj* **:** of, relating to, or dealing with quantities intermediate between those treated as micro and macro <~ analysis for chlorine> <a ~ balance>
semi·moist \-ˈmȯist\ *adj* **:** slightly moist
semi·mo·nas·tic \-mə-ˈnas-tik\ *adj* **:** having some features characteristic of a monastic order
[1]semi·month·ly \-ˈmən(t)th-lē\ *adj* **:** occurring twice a month
[2]semimonthly *n* **:** a semimonthly publication
[3]semimonthly *adv* **:** twice a month
semi·mys·ti·cal \ˌsem-i-ˈmis-ti-kəl, ˌsem-ˌī-\ *adj* **:** having some of the qualities of mysticism
sem·i·nal \ˈsem-ən-ᵊl\ *adj* [ME, fr. MF, fr. L *seminalis,* fr. *semin-, semen* seed — more at SEMEN] **1 :** of, relating to, or consisting of seed or semen **2 :** containing or contributing the seeds of later development **:** CREATIVE, ORIGINAL <a ~ book> <one of the most ~ of the great poets> — **sem·i·nal·ly** \-ᵊl-ē\ *adv*
seminal duct *n* **:** a tube or passage serving esp. or exclusively as an efferent duct of the testis and in man being made up of the tubules of the epididymis, the vas deferens, and the ejaculatory duct
seminal fluid *n* **1 :** SEMEN **2 :** the part of the semen that is produced by various accessory glands **:** semen excepting the spermatozoa
seminal vesicle *n* **:** a pouch on either side of the male reproductive tract that is variously formed in different mammals, is connected with the seminal duct, and serves for temporary storage of semen
sem·i·nar \ˈsem-ə-ˌnär\ *n* [G, fr. L *seminarium* seminary] **1 :** a group of advanced students studying under a professor with each doing original research and all exchanging results through reports and discussions **2 a (1) :** a course of study pursued by a seminar **(2) :** an advanced or graduate course often featuring informality and discussion **b :** a scheduled meeting of a seminar or a room for such meetings **3 :** a meeting for giving and discussing information
sem·i·nar·i·an \ˌsem-ə-ˈner-ē-ən\ *n* **:** a student in a seminary esp. of the Roman Catholic Church
sem·i·na·rist \ˈsem-ə-nə-rəst\ *n* **:** SEMINARIAN
sem·i·nary \ˈsem-ə-ˌner-ē\ *n, pl* **-nar·ies** [ME, seedbed, nursery, seminary, fr. L *seminarium,* fr. *semin-, semen* seed] **1 :** an environment in which something originates and from which it is propagated <a ~ of vice and crime> **2 a :** an institution of secondary or higher education; *esp* **:** an academy for girls **b :** an institution for the training of candidates for the priesthood, ministry, or rabbinate
sem·i·nif·er·ous \ˌsem-ə-ˈnif-(ə-)rəs\ *adj* [L *semin-, semen* seed + E *-iferous*] **:** producing or bearing seed or semen
seminiferous tubule *n* **:** any of the coiled threadlike tubules that make up the bulk of the testis and are lined with a germinal epithelium from which the spermatozoa are produced
Sem·i·nole \ˈsem-ə-ˌnōl\ *n, pl* **Seminoles** *or* **Seminole** [Creek *simaló-ni, simanó-li,* lit., wild, fr. AmerSp *cimarrón*] **:** a member of an Amerindian people of Florida
semi·no·mad \ˌsem-i-ˈnō-ˌmad, ˌsem-ˌī-\ *n* **:** a member of a people living usu. in portable or temporary dwellings and practicing seasonal migration but having a base camp at which some crops are cultivated — **semi·no·mad·ic** \-nō-ˈmad-ik\ *adj*
semi·nude \-ˈn(y)üd\ *adj* **:** partially nude — **semi·nu·di·ty** \-ˈn(y)üd-ət-ē\ *n*
semi·of·fi·cial \ˌsem-ē-ə-ˈfish-əl, ˌsem-ˌī-\ *adj* **:** having some official authority or standing — **semi·of·fi·cial·ly** \-ˈfish-(ə-)lē\ *adv*
se·mi·ol·o·gy \ˌsē-ˌmī-ˈäl-ə-jē\ *n* [Gk *sēmeion* sign] **:** the study of signs; *esp* **:** SEMIOTIC — **se·mi·o·log·i·cal** \(ˌ)sē-ˌmī-ə-ˈläj-i-kəl\ *adj*
semi·opaque \ˌsem-ē-ō-ˈpāk, ˌsem-ˌī-\ *adj* **:** nearly opaque
se·mi·o·sis \ˌsē-ˌmī-ˈō-səs\ *n* [NL, fr. Gk *sēmeiōsis* observation of signs, fr. *sēmeioun*] **:** a process in which something functions as a sign to an organism
se·mi·ot·ic \ˌsē-ˌmī-ˈät-ik\ *or* **se·mi·ot·ics** \-iks\ *n, pl* **semiotics** [Gk *sēmeiōtikos* observant of signs, fr. *sēmeiousthai* to interpret signs, fr. *sēmeion* sign; akin to Gk *sēma* sign — more at SEMANTIC] **:** a general philosophical theory of signs and symbols that deals esp. with their function in both artificially constructed and natural languages and comprises syntactics, semantics, and pragmatics — **semiotic** *also* **semi·ot·i·cal** \-i-kəl\ *adj* — **se·mi·o·ti·cian** \(ˌ)sē-ˌmī-ə-ˈtish-ən\ *n*
semi·pal·mat·ed \ˌsem-i-ˈpal-ˌmāt-əd, ˌsem-ˌī-, -ˈpä(l)m-ˌāt-\ *adj* **:** having the anterior toes joined only part way down with a web <the ~ feet of the plover>
semi·par·a·sit·ic \-ˌpar-ə-ˈsit-ik\ *adj* **:** of, relating to, or being a hemiparasite
semi·per·ma·nent \-ˈpərm-(ə-)nənt\ *adj* **:** lasting or intended to last for a long time but not permanent
semi·per·me·able \-ˈpər-mē-ə-bəl\ *adj* **:** partially but not freely or wholly permeable; *specif* **:** permeable to some usu. small molecules but not to other usu. larger particles <a ~ membrane> — **semi·per·me·abil·i·ty** \-ˌpər-mē-ə-ˈbil-ət-ē\ *n*
semi·po·lit·i·cal \-pə-ˈlit-i-kəl\ *adj* **:** of, relating to, or involving some political features or activity
semi·por·ce·lain \-ˈpȯr-s(ə-)lən, -ˈpȯr-\ *n* **:** any of several ceramic wares resembling or imitative of porcelain; *esp* **:** a relatively

---

ə abut ᵊ kitten ər further a back ā bake ä cot, cart
au̇ out ch chin e less ē easy g gift i trip ī life
j joke ŋ sing ō flow ȯ flaw ȯi coin th thin th this
ü loot u̇ foot y yet yü few yu̇ furious zh vision

high-fired and hard-glazed white earthenware widely used for tableware

semi·post·al \ˌsem-i-'pōs-tᵊl, ˌsem-ˌī-\ *n* : a postage stamp sold at a premium over its postal value esp. for a humanitarian purpose

semi·pre·cious \-'presh-əs\ *adj, of a gemstone* : of less commercial value than a precious stone

semi·pri·vate \-'prī-vət\ *adj* : of, receiving, or associated with hospital service giving a patient more privileges than a ward patient but fewer than a private patient

semi·pro \'sem-i-ˌprō, 'sem-ˌī-\ *adj or n* : SEMIPROFESSIONAL

1**semi·pro·fes·sion·al** \ˌsem-i-prə-'fesh-nəl, -ən-ᵊl, ˌsem-ˌī-\ *adj* **1** : engaging in an activity for pay or gain but not as a full-time occupation **2** : engaged in by semiprofessional players <~ baseball> — **semi·pro·fes·sion·al·ly** \-ē\ *adv*

2**semiprofessional** *n* : one who engages in an activity (as a sport) semiprofessionally

semi·pub·lic \ˌsem-i-'pəb-lik, ˌsem-ˌī-\ *adj* **1** : having some features of a public institution; *specif* : maintained as a public service by a private nonprofit organization **2** : open to some persons outside the regular constituency

semi·quan·ti·ta·tive \-'kwän(t)-ə-ˌtāt-iv\ *adj* : constituting or involving less than quantitative precision — **semi·quan·ti·ta·tive·ly** *adv*

semi·qua·ver \'sem-i-ˌkwā-vər, 'sem-ˌī-\ *n* : SIXTEENTH NOTE

semi·re·li·gious \-ri-'lij-əs\ *adj* : somewhat religious in character

semi·re·tired \-ri-'tī(ə)rd\ *adj* : working only part-time esp. because of age or ill health

semi·re·tire·ment \-'tī(ə)r-mənt\ *n* : the state or condition of being semiretired

semi·rig·id \ˌsem-i-'rij-əd, ˌsem-ˌī-\ *adj* **1** : rigid to some degree or in some parts **2** *of an airship* : having a flexible cylindrical gas container with an attached stiffening keel that carries the load

semi·sa·cred \-'sā-krəd\ *adj* : SEMIRELIGIOUS

semi·se·cret \-'sē-krət\ *adj* : not publicly announced but widely known nevertheless

semi·sed·en·tary \-'sed-ᵊn-ˌter-ē\ *adj* : sedentary during part of the year and nomadic otherwise <~ tribes>

semi·shrub \'sem-i-ˌshrəb, 'sem-ˌī-, *esp South* -ˌsrəb\ *n* : SUBSHRUB, UNDERSHRUB — **semi·shrub·by** \-ē\ *adj*

semi·skilled \ˌsem-i-'skild, ˌsem-ˌī-\ *adj* : having or requiring less training than skilled labor and more than unskilled labor

semi·soft \-'sȯft\ *adj* : moderately soft; *specif* : firm but easily cut <~ cheese>

semi·sol·id \-'säl-əd\ *adj* : having the qualities of both a solid and a liquid : highly viscous — **semisolid** *n*

semi·sweet \-'swēt\ *adj* : slightly sweetened <~ chocolate>

semi·syn·thet·ic \-sin-'thet-ik\ *adj* **1** : produced by chemical alteration of a natural starting material <~ penicillins> **2** : containing both chemically identified and complex natural ingredients <a ~ diet>

Sem·ite \'sem-ˌīt, *esp Brit* 'sē-ˌmīt\ *n* [F *sémite*, fr. *Sem* Shem, fr. LL, fr. Gk *Sēm*, fr. Heb *Shēm*] : a member of any of a group of peoples of southwestern Asia chiefly represented now by the Jews and Arabs but in ancient times also by the Babylonians, Assyrians, Aramaeans, Canaanites, and Phoenicians

semi·ter·res·tri·al \ˌsem-i-tə-'res-trē-əl, ˌsem-ˌī-, -'res(h)-chəl\ *adj* **1** : growing on boggy ground **2** : frequenting but not living wholly on land

1**Se·mit·ic** \sə-'mit-ik\ *adj* **1** : of, relating to, or characteristic of the Semites; *specif* : JEWISH **2** : of, relating to, or constituting a subfamily of the Afro-Asiatic language family that includes Hebrew, Aramaic, Arabic, and Ethiopic

2**Semitic** *n* : any or all of the Semitic languages

Se·mit·i·cist \sə-'mit-ə-səst\ *n* : SEMITIST

Se·mit·ics \-'mit-iks\ *n pl but sing in constr* : the study of the language, literature, and history of Semitic peoples; *specif* : Semitic philology

Sem·i·tism \'sem-ə-ˌtiz-əm\ *n* **1 a** : Semitic character or qualities **b** : a characteristic feature of a Semitic language occurring in another language **2** : policy favorable to Jews : predisposition in favor of Jews

Sem·i·tist \-ət-əst\ *n* **1** : a scholar of the Semitic languages, cultures, or histories **2** *often not cap* : a person favoring or disposed to favor the Jews

semi·ton·al \ˌsem-i-'tōn-ᵊl, ˌsem-ˌī-\ *adj* : CHROMATIC 3a, SEMITONIC — **semi·ton·al·ly** \-ᵊl-ē\ *adv*

semi·tone \'sem-i-ˌtōn, 'sem-ˌī-\ *n* : the tone at a half step; *also* : HALF STEP — **semi·ton·ic** \ˌsem-i-'tän-ik, ˌsem-ˌī-\ *adj* — **semi·ton·i·cal·ly** \-i-k(ə-)lē\ *adv*

semi·trail·er \'sem-i-ˌtrā-lər, 'sem-ˌī-\ *n* **1** : a freight trailer that when attached is supported at its forward end by the fifth wheel device of the truck tractor **2** : a trucking rig made up of a tractor and a semitrailer

semi·trans·lu·cent \ˌsem-i-ˌtran(t)s-'lüs-ᵊnt, -ˌtranz-\ *adj* : somewhat translucent

semi·trans·par·ent \-ˌtran(t)s-'par-ənt, -'per-\ *adj* : imperfectly transparent

semi·trop·i·cal \-'träp-i-kəl\ *also* **semi·trop·ic** \-ik\ *adj* : SUBTROPICAL

semi·trop·ics \-iks\ *n pl* : SUBTROPICS

semi·vow·el \'sem-i-ˌvau̇(-ə)l\ *n* **1** : one of the glides (as English \y\, \w\, or \r\) **2** : a letter representing a semivowel

1**semi·week·ly** \ˌsem-i-'wē-klē, ˌsem-ˌī-\ *adj* : occurring twice a week — **semiweekly** *adv*

2**semiweekly** *n* : a semiweekly publication

semi·works \'sem-i-ˌwərks, 'sem-ˌī-\ *n pl, often attrib* : a manufacturing plant operating on a limited commercial scale to provide final tests of a new product or process

semi·year·ly \ˌsem-i-'yi(ə)r-lē, ˌsem-ˌī-\ *adj* : occurring twice a year

sem·o·li·na \ˌsem-ə-'lē-nə\ *n* [It *semolino*, dim. of *semola* bran, fr. L *simila* finest wheat flour] : the purified middlings of hard wheat (as durum) used for pasta (as macaroni or spaghetti)

sem·per·vi·vum \ˌsem-pər-'vī-vəm\ *n* [NL, fr. L, neuter of *sempervivus* ever-living, fr. *semper* ever + *vivus* living — more at QUICK] : any of a large genus (*Sempervivum*) of Old World fleshy herbs of the orpine family often grown as ornamentals

sem·pi·ter·nal \ˌsem-pi-'tərn-ᵊl\ *adj* [ME, fr. LL *sempiternalis*, fr. L *sempiternus*, fr. *semper* ever, always, fr. *sem-* one, same (akin to ON *samr* same) + *per* through — more at SAME, FOR] : of never-ending duration : ETERNAL — **sem·pi·ter·nal·ly** \-ᵊl-ē\ *adv*

sem·pi·ter·ni·ty \-'tər-nət-ē\ *n* : ETERNITY

sem·ple \'sem-pəl\ *adj* [alter. of *simple*] *Scot* : of humble birth

sem·pli·ce \'sem-pli-ˌchā\ *adj or adv* [It, fr. L *simplic-, simplex* — more at SIMPLE] : SIMPLE — used as a direction in music

sem·pre \'sem-(ˌ)prā\ *adv* [It, fr. L *semper*] : ALWAYS — used in music directions <~ legato>

semp·stress \'sem(p)-strəs\ *var of* SEAMSTRESS

1**sen** \'sen\ *n, pl* **sen** [Jap] — see *yen* at MONEY table

2**sen** *n, pl* **sen** [Indonesian *sén*, prob. fr. E *cent*] — see *rupiah* at MONEY table

3**sen** *n, pl* **sen** [prob. from Indonesian *sén*] — see *dollar, riel* at MONEY table

4**sen** *abbr* **1** senate; senator **2** senior

se·nar·i·us \si-'nar-ē-əs, -'ner-\ *n, pl* **se·nar·ii** \-ē-ˌī, -ē-ˌē\ [L, fr. *senarius* consisting of six each, fr. *seni* six each, fr. *sex* six — more at SIX] : a verse consisting of six feet esp. in Latin prosody

se·na·ry \'sen-ə-rē, 'sēn-\ *adj* [L *senarius* consisting of six] : of, based upon, or characterized by six : compounded of six things or six parts <~ scale> <~ division>

sen·ate \'sen-ət\ *n* [ME *senat*, fr. OF, fr. L *senatus*, lit., council of elders, fr. *sen-, senex* old, old man — more at SENIOR] **1** : an assembly or council usu. possessing high deliberative and legislative functions: as **a** : the supreme council of the ancient Roman republic and empire **b** : the second chamber in the bicameral legislature of a major political unit (as a nation, state, or province) **2** : the hall or chamber in which a senate meets **3** : a governing body of some universities charged with maintaining academic standards and regulations and usu. composed of the principal or representative members of the faculty

sen·a·tor \'sen-ət-ər, *as a title also* 'sen-tər\ *n* [ME *senatour*, fr. OF *senateur*, fr. L *senator*, fr. *senatus*] : a member of a senate

sen·a·to·ri·al \ˌsen-ə-'tōr-ē-əl, -'tȯr-\ *adj* : of, relating to, or befitting a senator or a senate <~ office> <~ rank>

senatorial courtesy *n* : a custom of the U.S. Senate of refusing to confirm a presidential appointment of an official in or from a state when the appointment is opposed by the senators or senior senator of the president's party from that state

senatorial district *n* : a territorial division from which a senator is elected — compare CONGRESSIONAL DISTRICT

sen·a·to·ri·an \ˌsen-ə-'tōr-ē-ən, -'tȯr-\ *adj* : SENATORIAL; *specif* : of or relating to the ancient Roman senate

sen·a·tor·ship \'sen-ət-ər-ˌship\ *n* : the office or position of senator

se·na·tus con·sul·tum \sə-ˌnät-ə-skən-'səl-təm, -'su̇l-\ *n, pl* **senatus con·sul·ta** \-tə\ [L, decree of the senate] : a decree of the ancient Roman senate

1**send** \'send\ *vb* **sent** \'sent\; **send·ing** [ME *senden*, fr. OE *sendan*; akin to OHG *sendan* to send, OE *sith* road, journey, OIr *sēt*] *vt* **1** : to cause to go: as **a** : to propel or throw in a particular direction **b** : DELIVER <*sent* a blow to his chin> **c** : DRIVE <*sent* the ball between the goalposts> **2** : to cause to happen <whatever fate may ~> **3** : to dispatch by a means of communication **4 a** : to direct, order, or request to go **b** : to permit or enable to attend a term or session <~ a child to college> **c** : to direct by advice or reference **d** : to cause or order to depart : DISMISS **5 a** : to force to go : drive away **b** : to cause to assume a specified state <*sent* him into a rage> **6** : to cause to issue: as **a** : to pour out : DISCHARGE <clouds ~*ing* forth rain> **b** : UTTER <~ forth a cry> **c** : EMIT <*sent* out waves of perfume> **d** : to grow out (parts) in the course of development <a plant ~*ing* forth shoots> **7** : to cause to be carried to a destination; *esp* : to consign to death or a place of punishment **8** : to convey or cause to be conveyed or transmitted by an agent **9** : to strike or thrust so as to impel violently <*sent* him sprawling> **10** : DELIGHT, THRILL ~ *vi* **1 a** : to dispatch someone to convey a message or do an errand — often used with *out* <~ out for coffee> **b** : to dispatch a request or order — often used with *away* **2** : SCEND **3** : TRANSMIT — **send·er** *n* — **send for** : to request by message to come : SUMMON — **send packing** : to send off or dismiss roughly or in disgrace

2**send** *n* **1** : the lift of a wave **2** : SCEND 1

send down *vt, Brit* : to suspend or expel from a university

send in *vt* **1** : to cause to be delivered <*send in* a letter of complaint> **2** : to give (one's name or card) to a servant when making a call **3** : to send (a player) into an athletic contest

send–off \'sen-ˌdȯf\ *n* : a demonstration of goodwill and enthusiasm for the beginning of a new venture (as a trip)

send out *vt* **1** : ISSUE <had *sent* the invitations *out*> **2** : to dispatch (as an order) from a store or similar establishment

send round *vt* **1** : CIRCULATE <a notice is being *sent round*> **2** : to dispatch (as a messenger) for some object or purpose

send up *vt* : to sentence to imprisonment : send to jail

se·ne \'sā-(ˌ)nā\ *n* [Samoan, fr. E *cent*] — see *tala* at MONEY table

Sen·e·ca \'sen-i-kə\ *n, pl* **Seneca** *or* **Senecas** [D *Sennecaas*, pl., the Seneca, Oneida, Onondaga, and Cayuga people collectively, fr. Mahican *A'sinnika* Oneida] **1 a** : an Amerindian people of western New York **b** : a member of this people **2** : the language of the Seneca people

seneca snakeroot *n* : a No. American milkwort (*Polygala senega*) with tufted leafy stems terminated by small white flowers — called also *rattlesnake root, senega root;* compare SENEGA

se·ne·cio \si-'nē-sh(ē-ˌ)ō\ *n, pl* **-cios** [NL, genus name, fr. L, old man, groundsel (fr. its hoary pappus), fr. *sen-, senic-, senex* old man] : any of a genus (*Senecio*) of widely distributed composite plants that have alternate or basal leaves and flower heads with both tubular and radiate or only tubular flowers and with the ray flowers mostly yellow and pistillate

se·nec·ti·tude \si-ˈnek-tə-ˌt(y)üd\ *n* [ML *senectitudo,* alter. of L *senectus* old age, fr. *sen-, senic-, senex* old, old man — more at SENIOR] : the final stage of the normal life span
sen·e·ga \ˈsen-i-gə\ *or* **sen·e·ca** \-kə\ *n* **1 :** the dried root of seneca snakeroot that contains an irritating saponin **2 :** the dried root of a plant (*Polygala alba*) related to seneca snakeroot
senega root *n* [alter. of *Seneca root;* fr. its use by the Seneca as a remedy for snakebite] **1 :** SENECA SNAKEROOT **2 :** SENEGA 1
se·nes·cence \si-ˈnes-ᵊn(t)s\ *n* [*senescent,* fr. L *senescent-, senescens,* prp. of *senescere* to grow old, fr. *sen-, senex* old] **1 :** the state of being old : the process of becoming old **2 :** the plant growth phase from full maturity to death that is characterized by an accumulation of metabolic products, increase in respiratory rate, and a loss in dry weight esp. in leaves and fruit — **se·nes·cent** \-ᵊnt\ *adj*
sen·e·schal \ˈsen-ə-shəl\ *n* [ME, fr. MF, of Gmc origin; akin to Goth *sineigs* old, and to OHG *scalc* servant — more at SENIOR] : an agent or bailiff in charge of a lord's estate in feudal times
sen·gi \ˈseŋ-gē\ *n, pl* **sengi** [native name in Zaire] — see *zaire* at MONEY table
se·nhor \si-ˈnyō(ə)r, -ˈnyȯ(ə)r\ *n, pl* **senhors** *or* **se·nho·res** \-ˈnyōr-ēs(h), -ˈnyȯr-, -ēz(h)\ [Pg, fr. ML *senior* superior, lord, fr. L, adj., elder] : a Portuguese or Brazilian gentleman — used as a title equivalent to *Mister*
se·nho·ra \-ˈnyōr-ə, -ˈnyȯr-\ *n* [Pg, fem. of *senhor*] : a married Portuguese or Brazilian woman — used as a title equivalent to *Mrs.*
se·nho·ri·ta \ˌsē-nyə-ˈrēt-ə\ *n* [Pg, fr. dim. of *senhora*] : an unmarried Portuguese or Brazilian girl or woman — used as a title equivalent to *Miss*
se·nile \ˈsēn-ˌīl *also* ˈsen-\ *adj* [L *senilis,* fr. *sen-, senex* old, old man] **1 :** of, relating to, exhibiting, or characteristic of old age <~ weakness>; *esp* **:** exhibiting a loss of mental faculties associated with old age **2 :** approaching the end of a geological cycle of erosion — **se·nile·ly** \-ˌīl-lē\ *adv*
se·nil·i·ty \si-ˈnil-ət-ē *also* se-\ *n* **:** the quality or state of being senile; *specif* **:** the physical and mental infirmity of old age
¹**se·nior** \ˈsē-nyər\ *n* [ME, fr. L, fr. *senior,* adj.] **1 :** a person older than another <five years his ~> **2 a :** a person with higher standing or rank **b :** a senior fellow of a college at an English university **c :** a student in the year preceding graduation from a school of secondary or higher level
²**senior** *adj* [ME, fr. L, older, elder, compar. of *sen-, senex* old; akin to Goth *sineigs* old, Gk *henos*] **1 a :** of prior birth, establishment, or enrollment — often used to distinguish a father with the same given name as his son **b :** having reached the age of retirement <~ citizens> **2 :** SUPERIOR <the ~ officers> **3 :** of or relating to seniors <the ~ class> **4 :** having a claim on corporate assets and income prior to other securities
senior chief petty officer *n* **:** an enlisted man in the navy or coast guard ranking above a chief petty officer and below a master chief petty officer
senior high school *n* **:** a school usu. including grades 10–12
se·nior·i·ty \sēn-ˈyȯr-ət-ē, -ˈyär-\ *n* **1 :** the quality or state of being senior **:** PRIORITY **2 :** a privileged status attained by length of continuous service (as in a company)
senior master sergeant *n* **:** a noncommissioned officer in the air force ranking above a master sergeant and below a chief master sergeant
sen·i·ti \ˈsen-ə-tē\ *n, pl* **seniti** [Tongan, modif. of E *cent*] — see *pa'anga* at MONEY table
sen·na \ˈsen-ə\ *n* [NL, fr. Ar *sanā*] **1 :** any of a genus (*Cassia*) of leguminous herbs, shrubs, and trees native to warm regions; *esp* **:** one used medicinally **2 :** the dried leaflets of various sennas (esp. *Cassia acutifolia* and *C. angustifolia*) used as a purgative
sen·net \ˈsen-ət\ *n* [prob. alter. of obs. *signet* (signal)] **:** a signal call on a trumpet or cornet for entrance or exit on the stage
sen·night *also* **se'n·night** \ˈsen-ˌīt\ *n* [ME, fr. OE *seofon nihta* seven nights] *archaic* **:** the space of seven nights and days **:** WEEK
sen·nit \ˈsen-ət\ *n* [perh. fr. F *coussinet,* dim. of *coussin* cushion; fr. its use to protect cables from fraying] **1 :** a braided cord or fabric (as of plaited rope yarns) **2 :** a straw or grass braid for hats
se·nor *or* **se·ñor** \sān-ˈyō(ə)r\ *n, pl* **senors** *or* **se·ño·res** \-ˈyō(ə)r-(ˌ)ās, -ˈyȯ(ə)r-\ [Sp *señor,* fr. ML *senior* superior, lord, fr. L, adj., elder] **:** a Spanish or Spanish-speaking man — used as a title equivalent to *Mister*
se·no·ra *or* **se·ño·ra** \sān-ˈyōr-ə, -ˈyȯr-\ *n* [Sp *señora,* fem. of *señor*] **:** a married Spanish or Spanish-speaking woman — used as a title equivalent to *Mrs.*
se·no·ri·ta *or* **se·ño·ri·ta** \ˌsān-yə-ˈrēt-ə\ *n* [Sp *señorita,* fr. dim. of *señora*]**:** an unmarried Spanish or Spanish-speaking girl or woman — used as a title equivalent to *Miss*
sen·sate \ˈsen-ˌsāt\ *adj* [ML, fr. LL, endowed with sense, fr. L *sensus* sense] **1 :** relating to, apprehending, or apprehended through the senses **2 :** preoccupied with things that can be experienced through a sense modality — **sen·sate·ly** *adv*
sen·sa·tion \sen-ˈsā-shən, sən-\ *n* [ML *sensation-, sensatio,* fr. LL *sensatus* endowed with sense] **1 a :** a mental process (as seeing, hearing, or smelling) due to immediate bodily stimulation often as distinguished from awareness of the process — compare PERCEPTION **b :** awareness (as of heat or pain) due to stimulation of a sense organ **c :** a state of consciousness of a kind usu. due to physical objects or internal bodily changes <a binding ~ in his chest> **d :** an indefinite bodily feeling <a ~ of buoyancy> **2 :** something (as a physical object, sense-datum, pain, or afterimage) that causes or is the object of sensation **3 a :** a state of excited interest or feeling <their elopement caused a ~> **b :** a cause of such excitement <the fire was the ~ of the season>; *esp* **:** one (as a person) in some respect exceptional or outstanding
syn SENSATION, SENSE, FEELING, SENSIBILITY *shared meaning element* **:** the power to respond or the capacity for or act of responding to stimuli. SENSATION may center attention on the fact of perception through or as if through the sense organs whether with or without a higher intellectual component <the stage of *sensation* precedes that of rational comprehension> <the visual impression is a *sensation* and is derived from past experience —Adelbert Ames Jr.> SENSE may differ little from *sensation* <as the fire burned lower a *sense* of chill crept over them> or it may be applied specifically to any of the basic sensory powers <the *sense* of smell> but in its typical application to the power or act of responding it is likely to stress intellectual awareness and full consciousness <the *sense* of frustration felt among students —J. M. Feron> <her life was shadowed by a deep *sense* of loss> FEELING may apply to sensations (as touch, heat, cold, or pressure) that are perceived through the skin <a *feeling* of warmth> or to a complex response to stimulation involving sensation, emotion, and a degree of thought <the plea left her with the *feeling* that she ought to help> or to the power to respond <a person of strong *feeling* and responsive spirit> SENSIBILITY often replaces *feeling* in this last use, especially when a keenly impressionable nature is to be implied <the extreme *sensibility* to physical suffering which characterizes modern civilization —W. R. Inge> or excessive or affected responsiveness suggested <the . . . sentimentalist . . . who spends his life in a weltering sea of *sensibility* —William James>
sen·sa·tion·al \-shnəl, -shən-ᵊl\ *adj* **1 :** of or relating to sensation or the senses **2 :** arousing or tending to arouse (as by lurid details) a quick, intense, and usu. superficial interest, curiosity, or emotional reaction **3 :** exceedingly or unexpectedly excellent or great — **sen·sa·tion·al·ly** \-ē\ *adv*
sen·sa·tion·al·ism \-ˌiz-əm\ *n* **1 :** the use or effect of sensational subject matter or treatment **2 :** empiricism that limits experience as a source of knowledge to sensation or sense perceptions — **sen·sa·tion·al·ist** \-əst\ *n* — **sen·sa·tion·al·is·tic** \-ˌsā-shnəl-ˈis-tik, -shən-ᵊl-\ *adj*
¹**sense** \ˈsen(t)s\ *n* [MF or L; MF *sens* sensation, feeling, mechanism of perception, meaning, fr. L *sensus,* fr. *sensus,* pp. of *sentire* to perceive, feel; akin to OHG *sin* mind, sense, OE *sith* journey — more at SEND] **1 :** a meaning conveyed or intended **:** IMPORT, SIGNIFICATION; *esp* **:** one of a set of meanings a word or phrase may bear esp. as segregated in a dictionary entry **2 a :** the faculty of perceiving by means of sense organs **b :** a specialized animal function or mechanism (as sight, hearing, smell, taste, or touch) basically involving a stimulus and a sense organ **c :** the sensory mechanisms constituting a unit distinct from other functions (as movement or thought) **3 :** conscious awareness or rationality — usu. used in pl. <when he came to his *~s* he was shocked to hear what he had done> **4 a :** a particular sensation or kind or quality of sensation <a good ~ of balance> **b :** a definite but often vague awareness or impression <felt a ~ of insecurity> <a ~ of danger> **c :** a motivating awareness <a ~ of shame> **d :** a discerning awareness and appreciation <her ~ of humor> **5 :** CONSENSUS <the ~ of the meeting> **6 a :** capacity for effective application of the powers of the mind as a basis for action or response **:** INTELLIGENCE **b :** sound mental capacity and understanding typically marked by shrewdness and practicality; *also* **:** agreement with or satisfaction of such power <this decision makes ~> **7 :** one of two opposite directions of motion (as of a point, line, or surface)
syn **1** see SENSATION
2 SENSE, COMMON SENSE, GUMPTION, JUDGMENT, WISDOM *shared meaning element* **:** ability to reach intelligent conclusions
3 see MEANING
²**sense** *vt* **sensed; sens·ing 1 a :** to perceive by the senses **b :** to be or become conscious of <~ danger> **2 :** GRASP, COMPREHEND **3 :** to detect (as a symbol or radiation) automatically
sense–datum *n, pl* **sense–data :** an immediate unanalyzable private object of sensation
sense·ful \ˈsen(t)s-fəl\ *adj* **:** REASONABLE, JUDICIOUS
sense·less \ˈsen(t)-sləs\ *adj* **:** destitute of, deficient in, or contrary to sense; as **a :** UNCONSCIOUS <knocked ~> **b :** FOOLISH, STUPID <it was some ~ practical joke —A. Conan Doyle> **c :** MEANINGLESS, PURPOSELESS <a ~ murder> — **sense·less·ly** *adv* — **sense·less·ness** *n*
sense organ *n* **:** a bodily structure that receives a stimulus (as heat or sound waves) and is affected in such a manner as to initiate a wave of excitation in associated sensory nerve fibers which convey specific impulses to the central nervous system where they are interpreted as corresponding sensations **:** RECEPTOR
sen·si·bil·ia \ˌsen(t)-sə-ˈbil-ē-ə, -ˈbil-yə\ *n pl* [LL, fr. neut. pl. of L *sensibilis* sensible] **:** what may be sensed
sen·si·bil·i·ty \ˌsen(t)-sə-ˈbil-ət-ē\ *n, pl* **-ties 1 :** ability to receive sensations **:** SENSITIVENESS <tactile ~> **2 :** peculiar susceptibility to a pleasurable or painful impression (as from praise or a slight) — often used in pl. **3 :** awareness of and responsiveness toward something (as emotion in another) **4 :** refined or excessive sensitiveness in emotion and taste with especial responsiveness to the pathetic ***syn*** see SENSATION
¹**sen·si·ble** \ˈsen(t)-sə-bəl\ *adj* [ME, fr. MF, fr. L *sensibilis,* fr. *sensus,* pp.] **1 :** of a kind to be felt or perceived: as **a :** perceptible to the senses or to reason or understanding <felt a ~ chill> <his distress was ~ from his manner> **b :** perceptibly large **:** CONSIDERABLE <a ~ error> **c** (1) **:** perceptible as real or material **:** SUBSTANTIAL <the ~ world in which we live> (2) **:** of a kind to arouse emotional response <his whipping was a ~ expression of his father's anger> **2 a :** capable of receiving sensory impressions <~ to pain> **b :** receptive to external influences **:** SENSITIVE <disturbed in the most ~ reaches of his spirit> **3 a :** perceiving through the senses or mind **:** COGNIZANT <~ of the increasing heat>; *also* **:** convinced by perceived evidence **:** SATISFIED <~ of my error> **b :** emotionally aware and responsive <we are ~ of your problems> **c :** CONSCIOUS **4 :** having,

containing, or indicative of good sense or reason : RATIONAL, REASONABLE <~ men> <made a ~ answer> ***syn*** 1 see MATERIAL ***ant*** intelligible 2 see PERCEPTIBLE ***ant*** insensible 3 see AWARE ***ant*** insensible (*of or to*) 4 see WISE ***ant*** absurd, foolish, fatuous — **sen·si·ble·ness** *n* — **sen·si·bly** \-blē\ *adv*

²**sensible** *n* : something that can be sensed

sen·sil·lum \sen-'sil-əm\ *n, pl* **-sil·la** \-'sil-ə\ [NL, dim. of ML *sensus* sense organ, fr. L, sense] : a simple epithelial sense organ usu. in the form of a spine, plate, rod, cone, or peg that is composed of one or a few cells with a nerve connection

¹**sen·si·tive** \'sen(t)-sət-iv, 'sen(t)-stiv\ *adj* [ME, fr. MF *sensitif*, fr. ML *sensitivus*, irreg. fr. L *sensus*] 1 : SENSORY 2 2 a : receptive to sense impressions b : capable of being stimulated or excited by external agents (as light, gravity, or contact) <a photographic emulsion ~ to red light> <~ protoplasm> 3 : highly responsive or susceptible: as a (1) : easily hurt or damaged; *esp* : easily hurt emotionally (2) : delicately aware of the attitudes and feelings of others or of the nuances of a work of art b : excessively or abnormally susceptible : HYPERSENSITIVE <~ to egg protein> c : readily fluctuating in price or demand <~ commodities> d : capable of indicating minute differences : DELICATE <~ scales> e : readily affected or changed by various agents (as light or mechanical shock) f : high in radio sensitivity 4 : concerned with highly classified government information or involving discretionary authority over important policy matters — **sen·si·tive·ly** *adv* — **sen·si·tive·ness** *n*

²**sensitive** *n* 1 : a person having occult or psychical abilities 2 : a sensitive person

sensitive plant *n* : any of several mimosas (esp. *Mimosa pudica*) with leaves that fold or droop when touched; *broadly* : a plant responding to touch with movement

sen·si·tiv·i·ty \,sen(t)-sə-'tiv-ət-ē\ *n, pl* **-ties** : the quality or state of being sensitive: as a : the capacity of an organism or sense organ to respond to stimulation : IRRITABILITY b : the quality or state of being hypersensitive c : the degree to which a radio receiving set responds to incoming waves d : the capacity of being easily hurt e : awareness of the needs and emotions of others

sen·si·ti·za·tion \,sen(t)-sət-ə-'zā-shən, ,sen(t)-stə-'zā-\ *n* 1 : the quality or state of being sensitized (as to an antigen) 2 : the action or process of sensitizing

sen·si·tize \'sen(t)-sə-,tīz\ *vb* **-tized; -tiz·ing** [*sensitive* + *-ize*] *vt* : to make sensitive or hypersensitive ~ *vi* : to become sensitive — **sen·si·tiz·er** *n*

sen·si·tom·e·ter \,sen(t)-sə-'täm-ət-ər\ *n* [ISV *sensitive* + *-o-* + *-meter*] : an instrument for measuring sensitivity of photographic material — **sen·si·to·met·ric** \,sen(t)-sət-ə-'me-trik\ *adj* — **sen·si·tom·e·try** \-sə-'täm-ə-trē\ *n*

sen·sor \'sen-,sȯ(ə)r, 'sen(t)-sər\ *n* [L *sensus*, pp. of *sentire* to perceive — more at SENSE] : a device that responds to a physical stimulus (as heat, light, sound, pressure, magnetism, or a particular motion) and transmits a resulting impulse (as for measurement or operating a control); *also* : SENSE ORGAN

sen·so·ri·al \sen-'sōr-ē-əl, -'sȯr-\ *adj* : SENSORY — **sen·so·ri·al·ly** \-ə-lē\ *adv*

sen·so·ri·mo·tor \,sen(t)s-(ə-)rē-'mōt-ər\ *adj* : of, relating to, or functioning in both sensory and motor aspects of bodily activity

sen·so·ri·neu·ral \-'n(y)u̇r-əl\ *adj* [*sensory* + *neural*] : of, relating to, or involving the aspects of sense perception mediated by nerves <~ hearing loss>

sen·so·ri·um \sen-'sōr-ē-əm, -'sȯr-\ *n, pl* **-ri·ums** *or* **-ria** \-ē-ə\ [LL, sense organ, fr. L *sensus* sense] : the parts of the brain or the mind concerned with the reception and interpretation of sensory stimuli; *broadly* : the entire sensory apparatus

sen·so·ry \'sen(t)s-(ə-)rē\ *adj* 1 : of or relating to sensation or to the senses 2 : conveying nerve impulses from the sense organs to the nerve centers : AFFERENT

sen·su·al \'sench-(ə-)wəl, 'sen-shəl\ *adj* [ME, fr. LL *sensualis*, fr. L *sensus* sense + *-alis* -al] 1 : SENSORY 2 : relating to or consisting in the gratification of the senses or the indulgence of appetite : FLESHLY 3 a : devoted to or preoccupied with the senses or appetites b : VOLUPTUOUS c : deficient in moral, spiritual, or intellectual interests : WORLDLY; *esp* : IRRELIGIOUS ***syn*** see CARNAL — **sen·su·al·i·ty** \,sen-chə-'wal-ət-ē\ *n* — **sen·su·al·ly** \'sench-(ə-)wə-lē, 'sen-shə-lē\ *adv*

sen·su·al·ism \'sench-(ə-)wə-,liz-əm, 'sen-shə-,liz-\ *n* : persistent or excessive pursuit of sensual pleasures and interests — **sen·su·al·ist** \-ləst\ *n* — **sen·su·al·is·tic** \,sench-(ə-)wə-'lis-tik, ,sen-shə-'lis-\ *adj*

sen·su·al·ize \'sench-(ə-)wə-,līz, 'sen-shə-,līz\ *vt* **-ized; -iz·ing** : to make sensual — **sen·su·al·iza·tion** \,sench-(ə-)wə-lə-'zā-shən, ,sen-shə-lə-\ *n*

sen·sum \'sen(t)-səm\ *n, pl* **sen·sa** \-sə\ [ML, fr. L, neut. of *sensus*, pp. of *sentire* to feel — more at SENSE] : SENSE-DATUM

sen·su·ous \'sench-(ə-)wəs\ *adj* [L *sensus* sense + E *-ous*] 1 a : of or relating to the senses or sensible objects b : producing or characterized by gratification of the senses : having strong sensory appeal <~ pleasure> 2 : characterized by sense impressions or imagery aimed at the senses <~ verse> 3 : highly susceptible to influence through the senses — **sen·su·os·i·ty** \,sen-chə-'wäs-ət-ē\ *n* — **sen·su·ous·ly** \'sench-ə-wə-slē\ *adv* — **sen·su·ous·ness** *n*

sent *past of* SEND

¹**sen·tence** \'sent-ᵊn(t)s, -ᵊnz\ *n* [ME, fr. OF, fr. L *sententia*, lit., feeling, opinion, fr. (assumed) *sentent-, sentens*, irreg. prp. of *sentire* to feel — more at SENSE] 1 *obs* : OPINION; *esp* : a conclusion given on request or reached after deliberation 2 a : JUDGMENT 2a; *specif* : one formally pronounced by a court or judge in a criminal proceeding and specifying the punishment to be inflicted upon the convict b : the punishment so imposed <serve out a ~> 3 *archaic* : MAXIM, SAW 4 : a grammatically self-contained speech unit consisting of a word or a syntactically related group of words that expresses an assertion, a question, a command, a wish, or an exclamation, that in writing usu. begins with a capital letter and concludes with appropriate end punctuation, and that in speaking is phonetically distinguished by various patterns of **stress, pitch,** and pauses 5 : PERIOD 1b 6 : a meaningful logical formula : PROPOSITION 2a — **sen·ten·tial** \sen-'ten-chəl\ *adj* — **sen·ten·tial·ly** \-chə-lē\ *adv*

²**sentence** *vt* **sen·tenced; sen·tenc·ing** 1 : to impose a sentence on 2 : to cause to suffer something <*sentenced* these most primitive cultures to extinction —E. W. Count>

sentence fragment *n* : a word, phrase, or clause that usu. has in speech the intonation of a sentence but lacks the grammatically self-contained structure usu. found in the sentences of formal and esp. written composition

sentence stress *n* : the manner in which stresses are distributed on the syllables of words assembled into sentences — called also *sentence accent*

sen·ten·tia \sen-'ten-ch(ē-)ə\ *n, pl* **-ti·ae** \-chē-,ē\ [L, lit., feeling, opinion — more at SENTENCE] : APHORISM — usu. used in pl.

sentential calculus *n* : PROPOSITIONAL CALCULUS

sentential function *n* : an expression that contains one or more variables and becomes a declarative sentence when constants are substituted for the variables

sen·ten·tious \sen-'ten-chəs\ *adj* [ME, fr. L *sententiosus*, fr. *sententia* sentence, maxim] 1 : terse, aphoristic, or moralistic in expression : PITHY, EPIGRAMMATIC 2 a : given to or abounding in aphoristic expression b : given to or abounding in excessive moralizing — **sen·ten·tious·ly** *adv* — **sen·ten·tious·ness** *n*

sen·ti \'sent-ē\ *n, pl* **senti** [Swahili, modif. of E *cent*] — see *shilingi* at MONEY table

sen·tience \'sen-ch(ē-)ən(t)s, 'sent-ē-ən(t)s\ *n* 1 : a sentient quality or state 2 : feeling or sensation as distinguished from perception and thought

sen·tient \'sen-ch(ē-)ənt, 'sent-ē-ənt\ *adj* [L *sentient-, sentiens*, prp. of *sentire* to perceive, feel] 1 : responsive to or conscious of sense impressions 2 : AWARE 3 : finely sensitive in perception or feeling — **sen·tient·ly** *adv*

sen·ti·ment \'sent-ə-mənt\ *n* [F or ML; F, fr. ML *sentimentum*, fr. L *sentire*] 1 a : an attitude, thought, or judgment prompted by feeling : PREDILECTION b : a specific view or notion : OPINION 2 a : EMOTION b : refined feeling : delicate sensibility esp. as expressed in a work of art c : emotional idealism d : a romantic or nostalgic feeling verging on sentimentality 3 a : an idea colored by emotion b : the emotional significance of a passage or expression as distinguished from its verbal context ***syn*** see FEELING, OPINION

sen·ti·men·tal \,sent-ə-'ment-ᵊl\ *adj* 1 a : marked or governed by feeling, sensibility, or emotional idealism b : resulting from feeling rather than reason or thought 2 : having an excess of sentiment or sensibility — **sen·ti·men·tal·ly** \-ᵊl-ē\ *adv*

sen·ti·men·tal·ism \,sent-ə-'ment-ᵊl-,iz-əm\ *n* 1 : the disposition to favor or indulge in sentimentality 2 : an excessively sentimental conception or statement — **sen·ti·men·tal·ist** \-ᵊl-əst\ *n*

sen·ti·men·tal·i·ty \,sent-ə-,men-'tal-ət-ē, -mən-\ *n, pl* **-ties** 1 : the quality or state of being sentimental esp. to excess or in affectation 2 : a sentimental idea or its expression

sen·ti·men·tal·ize \-'ment-ᵊl-,īz\ *vb* **-ized; -iz·ing** *vi* : to indulge in sentiment ~ *vt* : to look upon or imbue with sentiment — **sen·ti·men·tal·iza·tion** \-,ment-ᵊl-ə-'zā-shən\ *n*

sen·ti·mo \sen-'tē-(,)mō\ *n, pl* **-mos** [Pilipino, fr. Sp *céntimo*] — see *peso* at MONEY table

¹**sen·ti·nel** \'sent-nəl, -ᵊn-əl\ *n* [MF *sentinelle*, fr. OIt *sentinella*, fr. *sentina* vigilance, fr. *sentire* to perceive, fr. L] : SENTRY

²**sentinel** *vt* **-neled** *or* **-nelled; -nel·ing** *or* **-nel·ling** 1 : to watch over as a sentinel 2 : to furnish with a sentinel 3 : to post as sentinel

sen·try \'sen-trē\ *n, pl* **sentries** [perh. fr. obs. *sentry* (sanctuary, watch tower)] : GUARD, WATCH; *esp* : a soldier standing guard at a point of passage (as a gate)

sentry box *n* : a shelter for a sentry on his post

sep *abbr* separate; separated

Sep *abbr* September

se·pal \'sēp-əl, 'sep-\ *n* [NL *sepalum*, fr. *sepa-* (fr. Gk *skepē* covering) + *-lum* (as in *petalum* petal); akin to Lith *kepurė* head covering] : one of the modified leaves comprising a calyx — see FLOWER illustration

se·pal·oid \-ə-,lȯid\ *adj* : resembling or functioning as a sepal

-sep·al·ous \'sep-ə-ləs\ *adj comb form* [*sepal*] : having (such or so many) sepals <gamo*sepalous*>

sep·a·ra·ble \'sep-(ə-)rə-bəl\ *adj* 1 : capable of being separated or dissociated 2 *obs* : causing separation — **sep·a·ra·bil·i·ty** \,sep-(ə-)rə-'bil-ət-ē\ *n* — **sep·a·ra·ble·ness** *n* — **sep·a·ra·bly** \-blē\ *adv*

¹**sep·a·rate** \'sep-(ə-),rāt\ *vb* **-rat·ed; -rat·ing** [ME *separaten*, fr. L *separatus*, pp. of *separare*, fr. *se-* apart + *parare* to prepare, procure — more at SECEDE, PARE] *vt* 1 a : to set or keep apart : DISCONNECT, SEVER b : to make a distinction between : DISCRIMINATE, DISTINGUISH <~ religion from magic> c : SORT <~ mail> d : to disperse in space or time : SCATTER <widely *separated* homesteads> 2 *archaic* : to set aside for a special purpose : CHOOSE, DEDICATE 3 : to part by a legal separation: a : to sever conjugal ties with b : to sever contractual relations with : DISCHARGE <*separated* from the army> 4 : to block off : SEGREGATE 5 a : to isolate from a mixture : EXTRACT <~ cream from milk> b : to divide into constituent parts ~ *vi* 1 : to become divided or detached 2 a : to sever an association : WITHDRAW b : to cease to live together as man and wife 3 : to go in different directions 4 : to become isolated from a mixture

syn SEPARATE, PART, DIVIDE, SEVER, SUNDER, DIVORCE *shared meaning element* : to become or cause to become disunited or disjoined ***ant*** combine

²**sep·a·rate** \'sep-(ə-)rət\ *adj* 1 a *archaic* : SOLITARY, SECLUDED b : IMMATERIAL, DISEMBODIED c : set or kept apart : DETACHED 2 a : not shared with another : INDIVIDUAL <~ rooms> b *often cap* : estranged from a parent body <*separate* churches> 3 a : existing by itself : AUTONOMOUS b : dissimilar in nature or identity ***syn*** see DISTINCT, SINGLE — **sep·a·rate·ly** \-(ə-)rət-lē, 'sep-ərt-lē\ *adv* — **sep·a·rate·ness** \-(ə-)rət-nəs\ *n*

[3]**sep·a·rate** \'sep-(ə-)rət\ *n* **1 :** OFFPRINT **2 :** an article of dress designed to be worn interchangeably with others to form various costume combinations — usu. used in pl.
sep·a·ra·tion \,sep-ə-'rā-shən\ *n* **1 :** the act or process of separating **:** the state of being separated **2 a :** a point, line, or means of division **b :** an intervening space **:** GAP **3 a :** cessation of cohabitation between husband and wife by mutual agreement or judicial decree **b :** termination of a contractual relationship (as employment or military service)
sep·a·ra·tion·ist \-sh(ə-)nəst\ *n* **:** SEPARATIST
sep·a·rat·ism \'sep-(ə-)rət-,iz-əm\ *n* **:** a belief in, movement for, or state of separation (as schism, secession, or segregation)
sep·a·rat·ist \'sep-(ə-)rət-əst, 'sep-ə-,rāt-\ *n, often cap* **:** one that favors separatism: as **a** *cap* **:** one of a group of 16th and 17th century English Protestants preferring to separate from rather than to reform the Church of England **b :** an advocate of independence or autonomy for a part of a political unit (as a nation) **c :** an advocate of racial or cultural separation — **separatist** *adj, often cap* — **sep·a·ra·tis·tic** \,sep-(ə-)rə-'tis-tik\ *adj*
sep·a·ra·tive \'sep-ə-,rāt-iv, 'sep-(ə-)rət-\ *adj* **:** tending toward, causing, or expressing separation
sep·a·ra·tor \'sep-(ə-),rāt-ər\ *n* **:** one that separates; *specif* **:** a device for separating liquids of different specific gravities (as cream from milk) or liquids from solids
sepd *abbr* separated
sepg *abbr* separating
Se·phar·di \sə-'färd-ē\ *n, pl* **Se·phar·dim** \-'färd-əm\ [LHeb *sĕphāradhi*, fr. *sĕphāradh* Spain, fr. Heb, region where Jews were once exiled (Obad 1: 20)] **:** a member of the occidental branch of European Jews or one of their descendants that settled in Spain and Portugal — **Se·phar·dic** \-'färd-ik\ *adj*
[1]**se·pia** \'sē-pē-ə\ *n* [NL, genus comprising cuttlefish, fr. L, cuttlefish, fr. Gk *sēpia*; akin to Gk *sēpein* to make putrid, *sapros* rotten] **1 a :** the inky secretion of a cuttlefish **b :** a brown melanin-containing pigment from the ink of cuttlefishes **2 :** a print or photograph of a brown color resembling sepia **3 :** a brownish gray to dark olive brown
[2]**sepia** *adj* **1 :** of the color sepia **2 :** made of or done in sepia
se·pi·o·lite \'sē-pē-ə-,līt\ *n* [G *sepiolith*, fr. Gk *sēpion* cuttlebone (fr. *sēpia*) + G *-lith* -lite] **:** MEERSCHAUM 1
sepn *abbr* separation
se·poy \'sē-,pȯi\ *n* [Pg *sipai*, fr. Hindi *sipāhī*, fr. Per, cavalryman] **:** a native of India employed as a soldier by a European power
sep·pu·ku \se-'pü-(,)kü, 'sep-ə-,kü\ *n* [Jap] **:** HARA-KIRI
sep·sis \'sep-səs\ *n, pl* **sep·ses** \'sep-,sēz\ [NL, fr. Gk *sēpsis* decay, fr. *sēpein* to make putrid] **:** a toxic condition resulting from the spread of bacteria or their products from a focus of infection; *esp* **:** SEPTICEMIA
sept \'sept\ *n* [prob. alter. of *sect*] **:** a branch of a family; *esp* **:** CLAN
Sept *abbr* September
sep·tal \'sep-tᵊl\ *adj* **:** of or relating to a septum
sep·tate \'sep-,tāt\ *adj* **:** divided by or having a septum
Sep·tem·ber \sep-'tem-bər, səp-\ *n* [ME *Septembre*, fr. OF, fr. L *September* (seventh month), fr. *septem* seven — more at SEVEN] **:** the 9th month of the Gregorian calendar
sep·te·nar·i·us \,sep-tə-'nar-ē-əs, -'ner-\ *n, pl* **-nar·ii** \-ē-,ī, -ē-,ē\ [L, fr. *septenarius* of seven, fr. *septeni* seven each, fr. *septem* seven] **:** a verse consisting of seven feet esp. in Latin prosody
sep·ten·de·cil·lion \(,)sep-,ten-di-'sil-yən\ *n, often attrib* [L *septendecim* seventeen (fr. *septem* seven + *decem* ten) + E *-illion* (as in *million*) — more at TEN] — see NUMBER table
sep·ten·ni·al \sep-'ten-ē-əl\ *adj* [LL *septennium* period of seven years, fr. L *septem* + *-ennium* (as in *biennium*)] **1 :** consisting of or lasting for seven years **2 :** occurring or being done every seven years — **sep·ten·ni·al·ly** \-ə-lē\ *adv*
sep·ten·tri·on \sep-'ten-trē-,än, -trē-ən\ *n* [ME, fr. MF, fr. L *septentrio*, sing. of *septentriones* the seven stars of Ursa Major or Ursa Minor, lit., the seven plow oxen, fr. *septem* seven + *trio* plow ox] *obs* **:** the northern regions **:** NORTH
sep·ten·tri·o·nal \-trē-ən-ᵊl\ *adj* **:** NORTHERN
sep·tet \sep-'tet\ *n* [G *septet*, fr. L *septem*] **1 :** a musical composition for seven instruments or voices **2 :** a group or set of seven; *esp* **:** the performers of a septet
sep·tic \'sep-tik\ *adj* [L *septicus*, fr. Gk *sēptikos*, fr. *sēpein* to make putrid — more at SEPIA] **1 :** PUTREFACTIVE **2 :** relating to, involving, or characteristic of sepsis
sep·ti·ce·mia \,sep-tə-'sē-mē-ə\ *n* [NL, fr. L *septicus* + NL *-emia*] **:** invasion of the bloodstream by virulent microorganisms from a local seat of infection accompanied esp. by chills, fever, and prostration — called also *blood poisoning*; compare SEPSIS — **sep·ti·ce·mic** \-'sē-mik\ *adj*
sep·ti·ci·dal \,sep-tə-'sīd-ᵊl\ *adj* [NL *septum* + L *-cidere* to cut, fr. *caedere* — more at CONCISE] **:** dehiscent longitudinally at or along a septum <a ~ fruit>
septic sore throat *n* **:** an inflammatory sore throat caused by hemolytic streptococci and marked by fever, prostration, and toxemia
septic tank *n* **:** a tank in which the solid matter of continuously flowing sewage is disintegrated by bacteria
sep·tif·ra·gal \sep-'tif-ri-gəl\ *adj* [NL *septum* + L *frangere* to break — more at BREAK] **:** dehiscing by breaking away from the dissepiments <a ~ pod>
sep·til·lion \sep-'til-yən\ *n, often attrib* [F, fr. L *septem* + F *-illion* (as in *million*) — more at SEVEN] — see NUMBER table
sep·tu·a·ge·nar·i·an \(,)sep-,t(y)ü-ə-jə-'ner-ē-ən, ,sep-tə-,waj-ə-\ *n* [LL *septuagenarius* 70 years old, fr. L, of or containing 70, fr. *septuageni* 70 each, fr. *septuaginta*] **:** a person who is in his seventies — **septuagenarian** *adj*
Sep·tu·a·ges·i·ma \,sep-tə-wə-'jes-ə-mə, -'jā-zə-\ *n* [ME, fr. LL, fr. L, fem. of *septuagesimus* 70th, fr. *septuginta* seventy; fr. its being the 70th day before Easter] **:** the third Sunday before Lent
Sep·tu·a·gint \sep-'t(y)ü-ə-jənt, 'sep-tə-wə-,jint\ *n* [LL *Septuaginta*, fr. L, seventy, irreg. fr. *septem* seven + *-ginta* (akin to L *viginti* twenty); fr. the approximate number of its translators — more at SEVEN, VIGESIMAL] **:** a pre-Christian Greek version of the Jewish Scriptures redacted by Jewish scholars and adopted by Greek-speaking Christians — **Sep·tu·a·gin·tal** \(,)sep-,t(y)ü-ə-'jint-ᵊl, ,sep-tə-wə-\ *adj*
sep·tum \'sep-təm\ *n, pl* **sep·ta** \-tə\ [NL, fr. L *saeptum* enclosure, fence, wall, fr. *saepire* to fence in, fr. *saepes* fence, hedge; akin to Gk *haimasia* stone wall] **:** a dividing wall or membrane esp. between bodily spaces or masses of soft tissue — compare DISSEPIMENT
[1]**sep·ul·cher** *or* **sep·ul·chre** \'sep-əl-kər\ *n* [ME *sepulcre*, fr. OF, fr. L *sepulcrum, sepulchrum*, fr. *sepelire* to bury; akin to Gk *hepein* to care for, Skt *sapati* he serves] **1 :** a place of burial **:** TOMB **2 :** a receptacle for religious relics esp. in an altar
[2]**sepulcher** *or* **sepulchre** *vt* **-chered** *or* **-chred; -chering** *or* **-chring** \-k(ə-)riŋ\ **1** *archaic* **:** to place in a sepulcher **:** BURY **2** *archaic* **:** to serve as a sepulcher for
se·pul·chral \sə-'pəl-krəl *also* -'pu̇l-\ *adj* **1 :** MORTUARY **2 :** suited to or suggestive of a sepulcher **:** FUNEREAL — **se·pul·chral·ly** \-krə-lē\ *adv*
sep·ul·ture \'sep-əl-,chu̇(ə)r\ *n* [ME, fr. OF, fr. L *sepultura*, fr. *sepultus*, pp. of *sepelire*] **1 :** BURIAL **2 :** SEPULCHER
seq *abbr* [L *sequens, sequentes, sequentia*] the following
seqq *abbr* [L *sequentes, sequentia*] the following
se·qua·cious \si-'kwā-shəs\ *adj* [L *sequac-, sequax* inclined to follow, fr. *sequi*] **1** *archaic* **:** SUBSERVIENT, TRACTABLE **2 :** intellectually servile — **se·qua·cious·ly** *adv* — **se·quac·i·ty** \-'kwas-ət-ē\ *n*
se·quel \'sē-kwəl *also* -,kwel\ *n* [ME, fr. MF *sequelle*, fr. L *sequela*, fr. *sequi* to follow — more at SUE] **1 :** CONSEQUENCE, RESULT **2 a :** subsequent development **b :** the next installment (as of a speech or narrative); *esp* **:** a literary work continuing the course of a narrative begun in a preceding one
se·quela \si-'kwel-ə\ *n, pl* **se·quel·ae** \-'kwel-(,)ē\ [NL, fr. L, sequel] **1 :** an aftereffect of disease or injury **2 :** a secondary result
[1]**se·quence** \'sē-kwən(t)s, -,kwen(t)s\ *n* [ME, fr. ML *sequentia*, fr. LL, sequel, lit., act of following, fr. L *sequent-, sequens*, prp. of *sequi*] **1 :** a hymn in irregular meter between the gradual and Gospel in masses for special occasions (as Easter) **2 :** a continuous or connected series: as **a :** an extended series of poems united by a single theme <a sonnet ~> **b :** three or more playing cards usu. of the same suit in consecutive order of rank **c :** a succession of repetitions of a melodic phrase or harmonic pattern each in a new position **d :** a set of elements ordered as are the natural numbers **e (1) :** a succession of related shots or scenes developing a single subject or phase of a film story **(2) :** EPISODE **3 a :** order of succession **b :** an arrangement of the tenses of successive verbs in a sentence designed to express a coherent relationship esp. between main and subordinate parts **4 a :** CONSEQUENCE, RESULT **b :** a subsequent development **5 :** continuity of progression
[2]**sequence** *vt* **se·quenced; se·quenc·ing :** to arrange in a sequence
se·quenc·er \'sē-kwən-sər, -,kwen(t)-sər\ *n* **:** any of various devices for arranging (as informational items or the events in the launching of a rocket) into or separating (as amino acids from protein) in a sequence
se·quen·cy \'sē-kwən-sē\ *n* [LL *sequentia*] **:** SEQUENCE 3a, 5
se·quent \'sē-kwənt\ *adj* [L *sequent-, sequens*, prp.] **1 :** CONSECUTIVE, SUCCEEDING **2 :** CONSEQUENT, RESULTANT
se·quen·tial \si-'kwen-chəl\ *adj* **1 :** of, relating to, or arranged in a sequence **:** SERIAL <~ file systems> **2 :** following in sequence **3 :** relating to or based on a method of testing a statistical hypothesis that involves examination of a sequence of samples for each of which the decision is made to accept or reject the hypothesis or to continue sampling — **se·quen·tial·ly** \-'kwench-(ə-)lē\ *adv*
[1]**se·ques·ter** \si-'kwes-tər\ *vt* **se·ques·tered; se·ques·ter·ing** \-t(ə-)riŋ\ [ME *sequestren*, fr. MF *sequestrer*, fr. LL *sequestrare* to surrender for safekeeping, set apart, fr. L *sequester* agent, depositary, bailee; akin to L *sequi* to follow] **1 a :** to set apart **:** SEGREGATE **b :** SECLUDE, WITHDRAW **2 a :** to seize esp. by a writ of sequestration **b :** to place (property) in custody esp. in sequestration **3 :** to hold (as a metallic ion) in solution usu. by inclusion in an appropriate coordination complex
[2]**sequester** *n, obs* **:** SEPARATION, ISOLATION
se·ques·trate \'sēk-wəs-,trāt, 'sek-; si-'kwes-\ *vt* **-trat·ed; -trat·ing** [LL *sequestratus*, pp. of *sequestrare*] **:** SEQUESTER
se·ques·tra·tion \,sēk-wəs-'trā-shən, ,sek-; (,)sē-,kwes-\ *n* **1 :** the act of sequestering **:** the state of being sequestered **2 a :** a legal writ authorizing a sheriff or commissioner to take into custody the property of a defendant who is in contempt until he complies with the orders of a court **b :** a deposit whereby a neutral depositary agrees to hold property in litigation and to restore it to the party to whom it is adjudged to belong **3 :** the formation of a sequestrum
se·ques·trum \si-'kwes-trəm\ *n, pl* **-trums** *also* **-tra** \-trə\ [NL, fr. L, legal sequestration; akin to L *sequester* bailee] **:** a fragment of dead bone detached from adjoining sound bone
se·quin \'sē-kwən\ *n* [F, fr. It *zecchino*, fr. *zecca* mint, fr. Ar *sikkah* die, coin] **1 :** an old gold coin of Italy and Turkey **2 :** SPANGLE
se·quined *or* **se·quinned** \-kwənd\ *adj* **:** ornamented with or as if with sequins
se·qui·tur \'sek-wət-ər, -wə-,tu̇(ə)r\ *n* [L, it follows, 3d pers. sing. pres. indic. of *sequi* to follow — more at SUE] **:** the conclusion of an inference **:** CONSEQUENCE

ə abut	ᵊ kitten	ər further	a back	ā bake	ä cot, cart
au̇ out	ch chin	e less	ē easy	g gift	i trip	ī life
j joke	ŋ sing	ō flow	ȯ flaw	ȯi coin	th thin	th this
ü loot	u̇ foot	y yet	yü few	yu̇ furious	zh vision

se·quoia \si-ˈkwȯi-(y)ə\ *n* [NL, genus name, fr. *Sequoya* (George Guess) †1843 Am Indian scholar] : either of two huge coniferous California trees of the pine family that reach a height of over 300 feet: **a** : BIG TREE **b** : REDWOOD 3a
ser *abbr* **1** serial **2** series **3** service
sera *pl of* SERUM
se·rac \sə-ˈrak, sā-\ *n* [F *sérac,* lit., a kind of white cheese, fr. ML *seracium* whey, fr. L *serum* whey — more at SERUM] : a pinnacle, sharp ridge, or block of ice among the crevasses of a glacier
se·ra·glio \sə-ˈral-(ˌ)yō, -ˈräl-\ *n, pl* **-glios** [It *serraglio* enclosure, seraglio, partly fr. ML *serraculum* bar of a door, bolt, fr. LL *serare* to bolt; partly fr. Turk *saray* palace — more at SEAR] **1** : HAREM 1a **2** : a palace of a sultan
se·rai \sə-ˈrī\ *n* [Turk & Per; Turk *saray* mansion, palace, fr. Per *sarāī* mansion, inn] **1** : CARAVANSARY **2** : SERAGLIO 2
ser·al \ˈsir-əl\ *adj* : of, relating to, or constituting an ecological sere
se·ra·pe \sə-ˈräp-ē, -ˈrap-\ *n* [MexSp *sarape*] : a colorful woolen shawl worn over the shoulders esp. by Mexican men
ser·aph \ˈser-əf\ *also* **ser·a·phim** \-ə-ˌfim\ *n, pl* **seraphim** *or* **seraphs** [LL *seraphim,* pl., seraphs, fr. Heb *śĕrāphīm*] **1** : one of the 6-winged angels standing in the presence of God **2** *pl* : an order of angels — see CELESTIAL HIERARCHY — **se·raph·ic** \sə-ˈraf-ik\ *adj* — **se·raph·i·cal·ly** \-i-k(ə-)lē\ *adv*
Se·ra·pis \sə-ˈrā-pəs\ *n* [L, fr. Gk *Sarapis*] : an Egyptian god combining attributes of Osiris and Apis and having a widespread cult throughout Greece and Rome
1**Serb** \ˈsərb\ *n* [Serb *Srb*] **1** : a native or inhabitant of Serbia **2** : SERBIAN 2 — **Serb** *adj*
2**Serb** *abbr* Serbian
Ser·bi·an \ˈsər-bē-ən\ *n* **1** : SERB 1 **2 a** : the Serbo-Croatian language as spoken in Serbia **b** : a literary form of Serbo-Croatian using the Cyrillic alphabet — **Serbian** *adj*
Ser·bo–Cro·atian \ˌsər-(ˌ)bō-krō-ˈā-shən\ *n* **1** : the Slavic language of the Serbs and Croats consisting of Serbian written in the Cyrillic alphabet and Croatian written in the Roman alphabet **2** : one whose native language is Serbo-Croatian — **Serbo–Croatian** *adj*
1**sere** \ˈsi(ə)r\ *adj* [ME, fr. OE *sēar* dry; akin to OHG *sōrēn* to wither, Gk *hauos* dry] **1** : WITHERED **2** *archaic* : THREADBARE
2**sere** *n* [L *series* series] : a series of ecological communities that succeed one another in the biotic development of an area or formation
1**ser·e·nade** \ˌser-ə-ˈnād\ *n* [F *sérénade,* fr. It *serenata,* fr. *sereno* clear, calm (of weather), fr. L *serenus*] **1 a** : a complimentary vocal or instrumental performance; *esp* : one given outdoors at night for a woman **b** : a work so performed **2** : an instrumental composition in several movements, written for a small ensemble, and midway between the suite and the symphony in style
2**serenade** *vb* **-nad·ed; -nad·ing** *vt* : to perform a serenade in honor of ~ *vi* : to play a serenade — **ser·e·nad·er** *n*
ser·e·na·ta \ˌser-ə-ˈnät-ə\ *n* [It, serenade] : an 18th century secular cantata of a dramatic character usu. composed in honor of an individual or event
ser·en·dip·i·tous \ˌser-ən-ˈdip-ət-əs\ *adj* : obtained or characterized by serendipity <~ discoveries> — **ser·en·dip·i·tous·ly** *adv*
ser·en·dip·i·ty \-ˈdip-ət-ē\ *n* [fr. its possession by the heroes of the Per fairy tale *The Three Princes of Serendip*] : the faculty of finding valuable or agreeable things not sought for
1**se·rene** \sə-ˈrēn\ *adj* [L *serenus;* akin to OHG *serawēn* to become dry, Gk *xēros* dry] **1 a** : clear and free of storms or unpleasant change <~ skies> **b** : shining bright and steady <the moon, ~ in glory —Alexander Pope> **2** : marked by or suggestive of utter calm and unruffled repose or quietude <a ~ smile> **3** : AUGUST — used as part of a title <His *Serene* Highness> ***syn*** see CALM — **se·rene·ly** *adv* — **se·rene·ness** \-ˈrēn-nəs\ *n*
2**serene** *n* **1** : a serene condition or expanse (as of sky, sea, or light) **2** : SERENITY, TRANQUILLITY
se·ren·i·ty \sə-ˈren-ət-ē\ *n* : the quality or state of being serene
serf \ˈsərf\ *n* [F, fr. L *servus* slave, servant, serf — more at SERVE] : a member of a servile feudal class bound to the soil and subject to the will of his lord — **serf·age** \ˈsər-fij\ *n* — **serf·dom** \ˈsərf-dəm, -təm\ *n*
serg *or* **sergt** *abbr* sergeant
serge \ˈsərj\ *n* [ME *sarge,* fr. MF, fr. (assumed) VL *sarica,* fr. L *serica,* fem. of *sericus* silken — more at SERICEOUS] : a durable twilled fabric having a smooth clear face and a pronounced diagonal rib on the front and the back
ser·gean·cy \ˈsär-jən-sē\ *n* : the function, office, or rank of a sergeant
ser·geant \ˈsär-jənt\ *n* [ME, servant, attendant, sergeant, fr. OF *sergent, serjant,* fr. L *servient-, serviens,* prp. of *servire* to serve] **1** : SERGEANT AT ARMS **2** *obs* : an officer who enforces the judgments of a court or the commands of one in authority **3** : an officer in a police force ranking in the U.S. just below captain or sometimes lieutenant and in England just below inspector **4** : a noncommissioned officer ranking in the army and marine corps above a corporal and below a staff sergeant and in the air force above an airman first class and below a staff sergeant; *broadly* : NONCOMMISSIONED OFFICER
sergeant at arms : an officer of an organization (as a legislative body or court of law) who preserves order and executes commands
sergeant first class *n* : a noncommissioned officer in the army ranking above a staff sergeant and below a master sergeant
sergeant fish *n* **1** : COBIA **2** : SNOOK 1
sergeant major *n, pl* **sergeants major** *or* **sergeant majors** **1** : a noncommissioned officer in the army, air force, or marine corps serving as chief administrative assistant in a headquarters **2** : a noncommissioned officer in the marine corps ranking above a first sergeant **3** : a bluish green to yellow percoid fish (*Abudefduf saxatilis*) with black vertical stripes on the sides that is widely distributed in the western tropical Atlantic ocean
sergeant major of the army : the ranking noncommissioned officer of the army serving as adviser to the chief of staff
sergeant major of the marine corps : the ranking noncommissioned officer of the marine corps serving as adviser to the commandant
ser·geanty \ˈsär-jənt-ē\ *n, pl* **-geant·ies** [ME *sergeantie,* fr. MF *sergentie,* fr. *sergent* sergeant] : any of numerous feudal services of a personal nature by which an estate is held of the king or other lord distinct from military tenure and from socage tenure
serg·ing \ˈsər-jiŋ\ *n* [*serge*] : the process of overcasting the raw edges of a fabric (as a carpet) to prevent raveling
1**se·ri·al** \ˈsir-ē-əl\ *adj* **1** : of, relating to, consisting of, or arranged in a series, rank, or row <~ order> **2** : appearing in successive parts or numbers <a ~ story> **3** : belonging to a series maturing periodically rather than on a single date <~ bonds> **4** : of, relating to, or being music based on a series of tones in an arbitrary but fixed pattern without regard for traditional tonality <~ technique> — **se·ri·al·ly** \-ə-lē\ *adv*
2**serial** *n* **1 a** : a work appearing (as in a magazine or on television) in parts at intervals **b** : one part of a serial work : INSTALLMENT **2** : a publication (as a newspaper or journal) issued as one of a consecutively numbered and indefinitely continued series — **se·ri·al·ist** \-ə-ləst\ *n*
se·ri·al·ism \ˈsir-ē-ə-ˌliz-əm\ *n* : serial music; *also* : the theory or practice of composing serial music
se·ri·al·iza·tion \ˌsir-ē-ə-lə-ˈzā-shən\ *n* : the act or process of serializing
se·ri·al·ize \ˈsir-ē-ə-ˌlīz\ *vt* **-ized; -iz·ing** : to arrange or publish in serial form
serial number *n* : a number indicating place in a series and used as a means of identification
1**se·ri·ate** \ˈsir-ē-ˌāt, -ē-ət\ *adj* [(assumed) NL *seriatus,* fr. L *series*] : arranged in a series or succession — **se·ri·ate·ly** *adv*
2**se·ri·ate** \ˈsir-ē-ˌāt\ *vt* **-at·ed; -at·ing** : to arrange in a series
1**se·ri·a·tim** \ˌsir-ē-ˈāt-əm, -ˈat-\ *adv* [ML, fr. L *series*] : in a series
2**seriatim** *adj* : following seriatim
se·ri·ceous \sə-ˈrish-əs\ *adj* [LL *sericeus* silken, fr. L *sericum* silk garment, silk, fr. neut. of *sericus* silken, fr. Gk *sērikos,* fr. *Sēres,* an eastern Asiatic people producing silk in ancient times] : finely pubescent <~ leaf>
ser·i·cin \ˈser-ə-sən\ *n* [ISV, fr. L *sericum* silk] : a gelatinous protein that cements the two fibroin filaments in a silk fiber
seri·cul·ture \ˈser-ə-ˌkəl-chər\ *n* [L *seri*cum silk + E *culture*] : the production of raw silk by raising silkworms — **seri·cul·tur·al** \-ˈkəlch(-ə)-rəl\ *adj* — **seri·cul·tur·ist** \-rəst\ *n*
se·ries \ˈsi(ə)r-(ˌ)ēz\ *n, pl* **series** *often attrib* [L, fr. *serere* to join, link together; akin to Gk *eirein* to string together, *hormos* chain, necklace] **1** : a number of things or events of the same class coming one after another in spatial or temporal succession <a concert ~> <the hall opened into a ~ of small rooms> **2** : the indicated sum of a usu. infinite sequence of numbers **3 a** : the coins or currency of a particular country and period **b** : a group of postage stamps in different denominations **4** : a succession of volumes or issues published with related subjects or authors, similar format and price, or continuous numbering **5** : a division of rock formations that is smaller than a system and comprises rocks deposited during an epoch **6** : a group of chemical compounds related in composition and structure **7** : an arrangement of the parts of or elements in an electric circuit whereby the whole current passes through each part or element without branching **8** : a set of vowels connected by ablaut (as *i, a, u* in *ring, rang, rung*) **9 a** : a number of games (as of baseball) played usu. on consecutive days between two teams <in town for a 3-game ~> **b** : WORLD SERIES **10** : a group of successive coordinate sentence elements joined together <an a, b, and c ~> **11** : SOIL SERIES **12** : three consecutive games in bowling — **in series** : in a serial arrangement
series winding *n* : a winding in which the armature coil and the field-magnet coil are in series with the external circuit — **se·ries–wound** \ˌsir-ēz-ˈwau̇nd\ *adj*
ser·if \ˈser-əf\ *n* [prob. fr. D *schreef* stroke, line, fr. MD, fr. *schriven* to write, fr. L *scribere* — more at SCRIBE] : any of the short lines stemming from and at an angle to the upper and lower ends of the strokes of a letter

1 serifs

seri·graph \ˈser-ə-ˌgraf\ *n* [L *seri*cum silk + Gk *graphein* to write, draw — more at CARVE] : an original color print made by pressing pigments through a silk screen with a stencil design — **se·rig·ra·pher** \sə-ˈrig-rə-fər\ *n* — **se·rig·ra·phy** \-fē\ *n*
se·rin \sə-ˈraⁿ\ *n* [F] : a small European finch (*Serinus canarius*) related to the canary
ser·ine \ˈse(ə)r-ˌēn\ *n* [ISV *ser*icin + *-ine*] : a crystalline amino acid $C_3H_7NO_3$ that occurs as a structural part of many proteins or cephalins
se·rio·com·ic \ˌsir-ē-ō-ˈkäm-ik\ *adj* [*seri*ous + *-o-* + *comic*] : having a mixture of the serious and the comic <a ~ novel> — **se·rio·com·i·cal·ly** \-i-k(ə-)lē\ *adv*
se·ri·ous \ˈsir-ē-əs\ *adj* [ME *seryows,* fr. MF or LL; MF *serieux,* fr. LL *seriosus,* alter. of L *serius*] **1** : thoughtful or subdued in appearance or manner : SOBER **2 a** : requiring much thought or work <~ study> **b** : of or relating to a matter of importance <a ~ play> **3 a** : not joking or trifling : being in earnest **b** *archaic* : PIOUS **c** : deeply interested : DEVOTED <~ fishermen> **4 a** : not easily answered or solved <~ objections> **b** : having important or dangerous possible consequences <a ~ injury>
syn SERIOUS, GRAVE, SOLEMN, SEDATE, STAID, SOBER, EARNEST *shared meaning element* : not light or frivolous ***ant*** light, flippant
se·ri·ous·ly *adv* **1** : in a sincere manner : EARNESTLY **2** : to a serious extent : SEVERELY
se·ri·ous–mind·ed \ˌsir-ē-ə-ˈsmīn-dəd\ *adj* : having a serious disposition or trend of thought — **se·ri·ous–mind·ed·ly** *adv* — **se·ri·ous–mind·ed·ness** *n*

se·ri·ous·ness *n* **:** the quality or state of being serious
ser·jeant, ser·jeanty *var of* SERGEANT, SERGEANTY
ser·jeant–at–law \ˌsär-jənt-ət-ˈlȯ\ *n, pl* **ser·jeants–at–law :** a member of a former class of barristers of the highest rank
ser·mon \ˈsər-mən\ *n* [ME, fr. OF, fr. ML *sermon-, sermo,* fr. L, speech, conversation, fr. *serere* to link together — more at SERIES] **1 :** a religious discourse delivered in public usu. by a clergyman as a part of a worship service **2 :** a speech on conduct or duty — **ser·mon·ic** \ˌsər-ˈmän-ik\ *adj*
ser·mon·ize \ˈsər-mə-ˌnīz\ *vb* **-ized; -iz·ing** *vi* **1 :** to compose or deliver a sermon **2 :** to speak didactically or dogmatically ~ *vt* **:** to preach at length — **ser·mon·iz·er** *n*
Sermon on the Mount : an ethical discourse delivered by Jesus and recorded in Matthew 5–7 and paralleled briefly in Luke 6:20–49
sero- *comb form* [L *serum*] **:** serum <*sero*logy>
se·ro·di·ag·no·sis \ˈsir-ō-ˌdī-ig-ˈnō-səs\ *n* [NL] **:** diagnosis by the use of serum (as in the Wassermann test) — **se·ro·di·ag·nos·tic** \-ˈnäs-tik\ *adj*
se·rol·o·gy \sə-ˈräl-ə-jē, sir-ˈäl-\ *n* [ISV] **:** a science dealing with serums and esp. their reactions and properties — **se·ro·log·i·cal** \ˌsir-ə-ˈläj-i-kəl\ *or* **se·ro·log·ic** \-ik\ *adj* — **se·ro·log·i·cal·ly** \-i-k(ə-)lē\ *adv* — **se·rol·o·gist** \sə-ˈräl-ə-jəst, sir-ˈäl-\ *n*
se·ro·pu·ru·lent \ˌsir-ō-ˈpyu̇r-(y)ə-lənt, ˌser-\ *adj* **:** consisting of a mixture of serum and pus <a ~ exudate>
se·ro·sa \sə-ˈrō-zə\ *n* [NL, fr. fem. of *serosus* serous, fr. L *serum*] **:** a usu. enclosing serous membrane — **se·ro·sal** \-zəl\ *adj*
se·ro·ti·nal \sə-ˈrät-nəl, -ᵊn-əl; ˌser-ə-ˈtīn-ᵊl\ *adj* [L *serotinus* coming late] **:** of or relating to the latter and usu. drier part of summer
se·rot·i·nous \sə-ˈrät-nəs, -ᵊn-əs; ˌser-ə-ˈtī-nəs\ *adj* [L *serotinus* coming late, fr. *sero* late — more at SOIREE] **:** late esp. in developing or flowering
se·ro·to·nin \ˌsir-ə-ˈtō-nən, ˌser-\ *n* [*sero-* + *tonic* + *-in*] **:** a phenolic amine $C_{10}H_{12}N_2O$ that is a powerful vasoconstrictor and is found esp. in the blood serum and gastric mucosa of mammals
se·ro·type \ˈsir-ə-ˌtīp, ˈser-\ *n* [*sero-* + *type*] **:** a group of intimately related organisms distinguished by a common set of antigens; *also* **:** the set of antigens characteristic of such a group
se·rous \ˈsir-əs\ *adj* [MF *sereux,* fr. *serum,* fr. L] **:** of, relating to, or resembling serum; *esp* **:** of thin watery constitution <a ~ exudate>
serous membrane *n* **:** a thin membrane (as the peritoneum) with cells that secrete a serous fluid; *esp* **:** SEROSA
se·row \sə-ˈrō\ *n* [Lepcha *să-ro* long-haired Tibetan goat] **:** any of several goat antelopes (genus *Capricornis*) of eastern Asia which are usu. rather dark and heavily built and some of which have distinct manes
ser·pent \ˈsər-pənt\ *n* [ME, fr. MF, fr. L *serpent-, serpens,* fr. prp. of *serpere* to creep; akin to Gk *herpein* to creep, Skt *sarpati* he creeps] **1 a** *archaic* **:** a noxious creature that creeps, hisses, or stings **b :** SNAKE **2 :** DEVIL 1 **3 :** a treacherous person
¹ser·pen·tine \ˈsər-pən-ˌtēn, -ˌtīn\ *adj* [ME, fr. MF *serpentin,* fr. LL *serpentinus,* fr. L *serpent-, serpens*] **1 :** of or resembling a serpent (as in form or movement) **2 :** subtly wily or tempting **3 a :** winding or turning one way and another **b :** having a compound curve whose central curve is convex — **ser·pen·tine·ly** *adv*
²serpentine *n* **:** something that winds sinuously
³ser·pen·tine \-ˌtēn\ *n* [ME, fr. ML *serpentina, serpentinum,* fr. LL fem. & neut. of *serpentinus* resembling a serpent] **:** a mineral or rock consisting essentially of a hydrous magnesium silicate $Mg_3Si_2O_7 \cdot 2H_2O$ usu. having a dull green color and often a mottled appearance
ser·pig·i·nous \(ˌ)sər-ˈpij-ə-nəs\ *adj* [ML *serpigin-, serpigo* creeping skin disease, fr. L *serpere* to creep] **:** CREEPING, SPREADING; *esp* **:** healing over in one portion while continuing to advance in another <~ ulcer> — **ser·pig·i·nous·ly** *adv*
ser·ra·nid \sə-ˈran-əd, ˈser-ə-nəd\ *n* [deriv. of L *serra* saw] **:** any of a large family (Serranidae) of carnivorous marine percoid fishes which have an oblong compressed body covered with ctenoid scales and many of which are important food and sport fishes (as the sea basses) esp. of warm seas — **serranid** *adj* — **ser·ra·noid** \ˈser-ə-ˌnȯid\ *adj or n*
¹ser·rate \sə-ˈrāt, ˈse(ə)r-ˌāt\ *vt* **ser·rat·ed; ser·rat·ing** [LL *serratus,* pp. of *serrare* to saw, fr. L *serra*] **:** to mark with serrations
²ser·rate \ˈse(ə)r-ˌāt, sə-ˈrāt\ *adj* [L *serratus,* fr. *serra* saw] **:** notched or toothed on the edge; *specif* **:** having marginal teeth pointing forward or toward the apex <a ~ leaf>
ser·ra·tion \sə-ˈrā-shən, se-\ *n* **1 :** the condition of being serrate **2 :** a formation resembling the toothed edge of a saw **3 :** one of the teeth in a serrate margin
ser·ried \ˈser-ēd\ *adj* **1 :** crowded or pressed together **:** COMPACT <the crowd collected in a ~ mass —W. S. Maugham> **2** [by alter.] **:** marked by ridges **:** SERRATE <the ~ contours of the . . . mountains —*Amer. Guide Series: Oregon*> — **ser·ried·ly** *adv* — **ser·ried·ness** *n*
ser·ry \ˈser-ē\ *vb* **ser·ried; ser·ry·ing** [MF *serré,* pp. of *serrer* to press, crowd — more at SEAR] *vi, archaic* **:** to press together esp. in ranks ~ *vt* **:** to crowd together
Ser·to·man \(ˌ)sər-ˈtō-mən\ *n* [*Sertoma* (club)] **:** a member of a major international service club
ser·tu·lar·i·an \ˌsər-chə-ˈler-ē-ən, ˌsərt-ᵊl-ˈer-\ *n* [NL *Sertularia,* genus name, fr. L *sertula,* dim. of *serta* melilot, fr. fem. of *sertus,* pp. of *serere* to link together, entwine — more at SERIES] **:** any of a genus (*Sertularia*) of delicate branching hydroids — **sertularian** *adj*
se·rum \ˈsir-əm\ *n, pl* **serums** *or* **se·ra** \-ə\ [L, whey, serum; akin to Gk *oros* whey, serum, *hormē* onset, assault, Skt *sarati* it flows] **1 :** the watery portion of an animal fluid remaining after coagulation: **a :** BLOOD SERUM; *esp* **:** immune blood serum that contains specific immune bodies (as antitoxins or agglutinins) <antitoxin ~> **b :** WHEY **c :** a normal or pathological serous fluid (as in a blister) **2 :** the watery part of a plant fluid
serum albumin *n* **:** a crystallizable albumin or mixture of albumins that normally constitutes more than half of the protein in blood serum and serves to maintain the osmotic pressure of the blood
serum globulin *n* **:** a globulin or mixture of globulins occurring in blood serum and containing most of the antibodies of the blood
serum sickness *n* **:** an allergic reaction to the injection of foreign serum manifested by urticaria, swelling, eruption, arthritis, and fever
serv *abbr* service
ser·val \ˈsər-vəl, (ˌ)sər-ˈval\ *n* [F, fr. Pg *lobo cerval* lynx, fr. ML *lupus cervalis,* lit., cervine wolf] **:** a long-legged African wildcat (*Felis capensis*) having large untufted ears and a tawny black-spotted coat
ser·vant \ˈsər-vənt\ *n* [ME, fr. OF, fr. prp. of *servir*] **:** one that serves others; *specif* **:** one that performs duties about the person or home of a master or personal employer
¹serve \ˈsərv\ *vb* **served; serv·ing** [ME *serven,* fr. OF *servir,* fr. L *servire* to be a slave, serve, fr. *servus* slave, servant, perh. of Etruscan origin] *vi* **1 a :** to be a servant **b :** to do military or naval service **2 :** to assist a celebrant as server at mass **3 a :** to be of use <in a day when few people could write, seals *served* as signatures —Elizabeth W. King> **b :** to be favorable, opportune, or convenient **c :** to stand by **:** ASSIST **d :** to hold an office **:** discharge a duty or function <~ on a jury> **4 :** to prove adequate or satisfactory **:** SUFFICE <a safe-conduct that *served* not only for him but for the entire party> **5 :** to help persons to food: as **a :** to wait at table **b :** to set out portions of food or drink **6 :** to wait on customers **7 :** to put the ball or shuttlecock in play in any of various games (as tennis, volleyball, or badminton) ~ *vt* **1 a :** to be a servant to **:** ATTEND **b :** to give the service and respect due to (a superior) **c :** to comply with the commands or demands of **:** GRATIFY **d :** to give military or naval service to **e :** to perform the duties of (an office or post) **2 :** to act as server at (mass) **3** *archaic* **:** to pay a lover's or suitor's court to (a lady) <that gentle lady, whom I love and ~ —Edmund Spenser> **4 a :** to work through or perform (a term of service) <*served* his time as a mate> **b :** to put in (a term of imprisonment) **5 a :** to wait on at table **b :** to bring (food) to a diner **6 a :** to furnish or supply with something needed or desired **b :** to wait on (a customer) in a store **c :** to furnish professional service to **7 a :** to answer the needs of **:** AVAIL **b :** to be enough for **:** SUFFICE **c :** to contribute or conduce to **:** PROMOTE **8 :** to treat or act toward in a specified way **:** REQUITE <he *served* me ill> **9 a :** to bring to notice, deliver, or execute as required by law **b :** to make legal service upon (a person named in a process) **10** *of an animal* **:** to copulate with **11 :** to wind yarn or wire tightly around (a rope or stay) for protection **12 :** to provide services that benefit or help **13 :** to put (the ball or shuttlecock) in play (as in tennis or badminton) — **serve one right :** to be deserved
²serve *n* **:** the act of putting the ball or shuttlecock in play in any of various games (as volleyball, badminton, or tennis); *also* **:** a turn to serve
serv·er \ˈsər-vər\ *n* **1 :** one that serves food or drink **2 :** the player who serves (as in tennis) **3 :** something used in serving food or drink **4 :** one that serves legal processes upon another **5 :** the celebrant's assistant at low mass
¹ser·vice \ˈsər-vəs\ *n* [ME, fr. OF, fr. L *servitium* condition of a slave, body of slaves, fr. *servus* slave] **1 a :** the occupation or function of serving <in active ~> **b :** employment as a servant <entered his ~> **2 a :** the work performed by one that serves <gives good ~> **b :** HELP, USE, BENEFIT <be of ~ to them> **c :** contribution to the welfare of others **d :** disposal for use <put the capability of the entire system at his ~ —C. R. Bowen> **3 a :** a form followed in worship or in a religious ceremony <the burial ~> **b** *often pl* **:** a meeting for worship <held evening ~*s*> **4 :** the act of serving: as **a :** a helpful act <did him a ~> **b :** useful labor that does not produce a tangible commodity — usu. used in pl. <charge for professional ~*s*> **c :** SERVE **5 :** a set of articles for a particular use <a silver ~ for 12> **6 a :** an administrative division (as of a government or business) <the consular ~> **b :** one of a nation's military forces (as the army or navy) **7 a :** a facility supplying some public demand <telephone ~> <bus ~> **b :** a facility providing maintenance and repair <television ~> **8 :** the materials (as spun yarn, small lines, or canvas) used for serving a rope **9 :** the act of bringing a legal writ, process, or summons to notice as prescribed by law **10 :** the act of copulating with a female animal **11 :** a branch of a hospital medical staff devoted to a particular specialty <obstetrical ~>
²service *adj* **1 :** of or relating to the armed services **2 :** used in serving or supplying <delivery men use the ~ entrance> **3 :** intended for hard or everyday use **4 a :** providing services <the ~ trades—from filling stations to universities —John Fischer> **b :** offering repair, maintenance, or incidental services
³service *vt* **ser·viced; ser·vic·ing :** to perform services for: as **a :** to repair or provide maintenance for **b :** to meet interest and sinking fund payments on (as government debt) **c :** to perform any of the business functions auxiliary to production or distribution of **d** *of an animal* **:** SERVE 10 — **ser·vic·er** *n*
⁴ser·vice \ˈsər-vəs\ *n* [ME *serves,* pl. of *serve* serviceberry, service tree, fr. OE *syrfe,* fr. (assumed) VL *sorbea,* fr. L *sorbus* service tree] **:** an Old World tree (*Sorbus domestica*) resembling the related mountain ashes but having larger flowers and larger edible fruit; *also* **:** a related Old World tree (*S. torminalis*) with bitter fruits
ser·vice·able \ˈsər-və-sə-bəl\ *adj* **1 :** HELPFUL, USEFUL **2 :** wearing well in use — **ser·vice·abil·i·ty** \ˌsər-və-sə-ˈbil-ət-ē\ *n* — **ser·vice·able·ness** \ˈsər-və-sə-bəl-nəs\ *n* — **ser·vice·ably** \-blē\ *adv*

ser·vice·ber·ry \'sər-vəs-ˌber-ē, *2 is also* 'sär-\ *n* **1 :** the fruit of a service tree **2 :** any of various No. American trees and shrubs (genus *Amelanchier*) of the rose family sometimes cultivated for their showy white flowers or edible purple or red fruits — called also *Juneberry, shadbush*

service book *n* **:** a book setting forth forms of worship used in religious services

service box *n* **:** the area in which a player stands while serving in various court games (as squash racquets or handball)

service break *n* **:** a point won on an opponent's serve (as in tennis)

service cap *n* **:** a flat-topped visor cap worn as part of a military uniform — compare GARRISON CAP

service ceiling *n* **:** the altitude at which under standard air conditions a particular airplane can no longer rise at a rate greater than a small designated rate (as 100 feet per minute)

service charge *n* **:** a fee charged for a particular service often in addition to a standard or basic fee

service club *n* **1 :** a club of business or professional men or women organized for their common benefit and active in community service **2 :** a recreation center for enlisted men provided by one of the armed services

service court *n* **:** a part of the court into which the ball or shuttlecock must be served

service line *n* **:** a line marked on a court in various games (as handball or tennis) parallel to the front wall or to the net to mark a boundary which must not be overstepped in serving

ser·vice·man \'sər-və-ˌsman, -smən\ *n* **1 :** a male member of the armed forces **2 :** a man employed to repair or maintain equipment **3 :** a service station attendant

service mark *n* **:** a mark or device used to identify a service (as transportation or insurance) offered to customers

service medal *n* **:** a medal awarded to an individual for military service in a specified war or campaign

service module *n* **:** a space vehicle module that contains propellant tanks, fuel cells, and the main rocket engine

service road *n* **:** FRONTAGE ROAD

service sideline *n* **:** either of the lines on a doubles tennis court inside and parallel to the sidelines and marking the edges of the service courts

service station *n* **1 :** a retail station for servicing motor vehicles esp. with gasoline and oil **2 :** a place at which some service is offered

service stripe *n* **:** a stripe worn on an enlisted man's left sleeve to indicate three years of service in the army or four years in the navy

ser·vice tree \'sər-vəs-\ *n* [[4]*service*] **:** [4]SERVICE

ser·vi·ette \ˌsər-vē-'et\ *n* [F, fr. MF, fr. *servir* to serve] *chiefly Brit* **:** a table napkin

ser·vile \'sər-vəl, -ˌvīl\ *adj* [ME, fr. L *servilis,* fr. *servus* slave — more at SERVE] **1 :** of or befitting a slave or a menial position **2 :** meanly or cravenly submissive **:** ABJECT ***syn*** see SUBSERVIENT ***ant*** authoritative — **ser·vile·ly** \-və(l)-lē, -ˌvīl-lē\ *adv* — **ser·vile·ness** \-vəl-nəs, -ˌvīl-\ *n* — **ser·vil·i·ty** \(ˌ)sər-'vil-ət-ē\ *n*

serv·ing \'sər-viŋ\ *n* **:** a helping of food or drink

Ser·vite \'sər-ˌvīt\ *n* [ML *Servitae,* pl. Servites, fr. L *servus*] **:** a member of the mendicant Order of Servants of Mary founded in Florence, Italy, in 1233 — **Servite** *adj*

ser·vi·tor \'sər-vət-ər, -və-ˌtȯ(ə)r\ *n* [ME *servitour,* fr. MF, fr. LL *servitor,* fr. L *servitus,* pp. of *servire* to serve] **:** a male servant

ser·vi·tude \'sər-və-ˌt(y)üd\ *n* [ME, fr. MF, fr. L *servitudo* slavery, fr. *servus* slave] **1 :** a condition in which one lacks liberty esp. to determine one's course of action or way of life **2 :** a right by which something (as a piece of land) owned by one person is subject to a specified use or enjoyment by another

syn SERVITUDE, SLAVERY, BONDAGE *shared meaning element* **:** the state of being subject to a master

ser·vo \'sər-(ˌ)vō\ *n, pl* **servos 1 :** SERVOMOTOR **2 :** SERVOMECHANISM

ser·vo·mech·a·nism \'sər-vō-ˌmek-ə-ˌniz-əm\ *n* [*servo-* (as in *servomotor*) + *mechanism*] **:** an automatic device for controlling large amounts of power by means of very small amounts of power and automatically correcting performance of a mechanism

ser·vo·mo·tor \'sər-vō-ˌmōt-ər\ *n* [F *servo-moteur,* fr. L *servus* slave, servant + F *-o-* + *moteur* motor, fr. L *motor* one that moves — more at MOTOR] **:** a power-driven mechanism that supplements a primary control operated by a comparatively feeble force (as in a servomechanism)

-ses *pl of* -SIS

ses·a·me \'ses-ə-mē *also* 'sez-\ *n* [alter. of earlier *sesam, sesama,* fr. L *sesamum, sesama,* fr. Gk *sēsamon, sēsamē,* of Sem origin; akin to Assyr *šamaššamu* sesame, Ar *simsim*] **1 :** an East Indian annual erect herb (*Sesamum indicum* of the family Pedaliaceae); *also* **:** its small somewhat flat seeds used as a source of oil and a flavoring agent **2 :** OPEN SESAME

sesame oil *n* **:** a pale yellow bland semidrying fatty oil obtained from sesame seeds and used chiefly as an edible oil, as a vehicle for various pharmaceuticals, and in cosmetics and soaps

ses·a·moid \'ses-ə-ˌmȯid\ *adj* [Gk *sēsamoeidēs,* lit., resembling sesame seed, fr. *sēsamon*] **:** of, relating to, or being a nodular mass of bone or cartilage in a tendon esp. at a joint or bony prominence — **sesamoid** *n*

sesqui- *comb form* [L, one and a half, half again, lit., and a half, fr. *semis* half (fr. *semi-*) + *-que* (enclitic) and; akin to Gk *te* and, Skt *ca,* Goth *-h, -uh*] **1 :** one and a half times <*sesqui*centennial> **2 a :** containing three atoms or equivalents of a specified element or radical esp. combined with two of another <*sesqui*oxide> **b :** intermediate **:** combination <*sesqui*carbonate>

ses·qui·car·bon·ate \ˌses-kwi-'kär-bə-ˌnāt, -nət\ *n* **:** a salt that is neither a simple normal carbonate nor a simple bicarbonate but often a combination of the two

ses·qui·cen·te·na·ry \-kwi-sen-'ten-ə-rē, -'sent-ᵊn-ˌer-ē, -sen-'tē-nə-rē\ *n* **:** SESQUICENTENNIAL

ses·qui·cen·ten·ni·al \-sen-'ten-ē-əl\ *n* **:** a 150th anniversary or its celebration — **sesquicentennial** *adj*

ses·qui·pe·da·lian \ˌses-kwə-pə-'dāl-yən\ *adj* [L *sesquipedalis,* lit., a foot and a half long, fr. *sesqui-* + *ped-, pes* foot — more at FOOT] **1 :** having many syllables **:** LONG <~ terms> **2 :** given to or characterized by the use of long words <a ~ orator>

ses·sile \'ses-īl, -əl\ *adj* [L *sessilis* of or fit for sitting, low, dwarf (of plants), fr. *sessus,* pp.] **1 :** attached directly by the base **:** not raised upon a stalk or peduncle <a ~ leaf> <~ bubbles> **2 :** permanently attached or established **:** not free to move about <~ polyps> <~ wealth> — **ses·sil·i·ty** \se-'sil-ət-ē\ *n*

ses·sion \'sesh-ən\ *n* [ME, fr. MF, fr. L *session-, sessio,* lit., act of sitting, fr. *sessus,* pp. of *sedēre* to sit — more at SIT] **1 :** a meeting or series of meetings of a body (as a court or legislature) for the transaction of business <morning ~> **2** *pl* **a (1) :** a sitting of English justices of peace in execution of the powers conferred by their commissions **(2) :** an English court holding such sessions **b :** any of various courts similar to the English sessions **3 :** the period between the first meeting of a legislative or judicial body and the prorogation or final adjournment **4 :** the ruling body of a Presbyterian congregation consisting of the elders in active service **5 :** the period during the year or day in which a school conducts classes **6 :** a meeting or period devoted to a particular activity <a recording ~> — **ses·sion·al** \'sesh-nəl, -ən-ᵊl\ *adj*

ses·terce \'ses-ˌtərs\ *n* [L *sestertius,* fr. *sestertius* two and a half times as great (fr. its being equal originally to two and a half asses), fr. *semis* half (fr. *semi-*) + *tertius* third — more at THIRD] **:** an ancient Roman coin equal to ¼ denarius

ses·ter·tium \se-'stər-sh(ē-)əm\ *n, pl* **-tia** \-sh(ē-)ə\ [L, fr. gen. pl. of *sestertius* (in the phrase *milia sestertium* thousands of sesterces)] **:** a unit of value in ancient Rome equal to 1000 sesterces

ses·ti·na \se-'stē-nə\ *n* [It, fr. *sesto* sixth] **:** a lyrical fixed form consisting of six six-line usu. unrhymed stanzas in which the end words of the first stanza recur as end words of the following five stanzas in a successively rotating order and as the middle and end words of the three verses of the concluding tercet

ses·tet \se-'stet\ *n* [It *sestetto,* fr. *sesto* sixth, fr. L *sextus* — more at SEXT] **:** a stanza or a poem of six lines; *specif* **:** the last six lines of an Italian sonnet

[1]**set** \'set\ *vb* **set; set·ting** [ME *setten,* fr. OE *settan;* akin to OHG *sezzen* to set, OE *sittan* to sit] *vt* **1 :** to cause to sit **:** place in or on a seat **2 a :** to put (a fowl) on eggs to hatch them **b :** to put (eggs) for hatching under a fowl or into an incubator **3 :** to place (oneself) in position to start running in a race **4 a :** to place with care or deliberate purpose and with relative stability <~ a ladder against the wall> <~ a stone on the grave> **b :** TRANSPLANT 1 <~ seedlings> **c (1) :** to make (as a trap) ready to catch prey **(2) :** to fix (a hook) firmly into the jaw of a fish **d :** to put aside (as dough containing yeast) for fermenting **5 :** to direct with fixed attention <~ your mind to it> **6 :** to cause to assume a specified condition, relation, or occupation <slaves were ~ free> **7 a :** to appoint or assign to an office or duty **b :** POST, STATION **8 :** to cause to assume a specified posture or position <~ the door ajar> **9 a :** to fix as a distinguishing imprint, sign, or appearance <the years have ~ their mark on him> **b :** AFFIX **c :** APPLY <~ a match to kindling> **10 :** to fix or decide on as a time, limit, or regulation **:** PRESCRIBE <~ a wedding day> <~ the rules for the game> **11 a :** to establish as the highest level or best performance <~ a record for the half mile> **b :** to furnish as a pattern or model <~ an example of generosity> **c :** to allot as a task <*setting* lessons for the children to work upon at home — *Manchester Examiner*> **12 a :** to adjust a device and esp. a measuring device to a desired position <~ the alarm for 7:00> <~ a thermostat at 70>; *also* **:** to adjust (as a clock) in conformity with a standard **b :** to restore to normal position or connection when dislocated or fractured <~ a broken bone> **c :** to spread to the wind <~ the sails> **13 a :** to put in order for use <~ a place for a guest> **b :** to make scenically ready for a performance <~ the stage> **c (1) :** to arrange (type) for printing <~ type by hand> **(2) :** to put into type or its equivalent (as on film) <~ the first word in italic> **14 a :** to put a fine edge on by grinding or honing <~ a razor> **b :** to bend slightly the tooth points of (a saw) alternately in opposite directions **c :** to sink (the head of a nail) below the surface **15 :** to fix in a desired position (as by heating or stretching) **16 :** to wave, curl, or arrange (hair) **17 a :** to adorn with something affixed or infixed **:** STUD, DOT <clear sky ~ with stars> **b :** to fix (as a precious stone) in a border of metal **:** place in a setting **18 a :** to hold something in regard or esteem at the rate of <~*s* a great deal by daily exercise> **b :** to place in a relative rank or category <~ duty before pleasure> **c :** to fix at a certain amount <~ bail at $500> **d :** VALUE, RATE <his promises were ~ at naught> **e :** to place as an estimate of worth <~ a high value on life> **19 :** to place in relation for comparison or balance <theory ~ against practice> **20 a :** to direct to action **b :** to incite to attack or antagonism <war ~*s* brother against brother> **21 a :** to place by transporting <was ~ ashore on the island> **b :** to put in motion **c :** to put and fix in a direction <~ our faces toward home once more> **d** *of a dog* **:** to point out the position of (game) by holding a fixed attitude **22 :** to defeat (an opponent or his contract) in bridge **23 a :** to fix firmly **:** make immobile **:** give rigid form or condition to <~ his jaw in determination> **b :** to make unyielding or obstinate **24 :** to cause to become firm or solid <~ milk for cheese> **25 :** to cause (as fruit) to develop ~ *vi* **1** *chiefly dial* **:** SIT **2 :** to be becoming **:** be suitable **:** FIT <his behavior does not ~ well with his years> **3 :** to cover and warm eggs to hatch them **4 a :** to become lodged or fixed <the pudding ~ heavily on his stomach> **b :** to place oneself in position in preparation for an action (as running) **5** *of a plant part* **:** to undergo development usu. as a result of pollination **6 a :** to pass below the horizon **:** go down <the sun ~*s*> **b :** to sink out of sight **:** pass away **7 :** to apply oneself to some activity <~ to work> **8 :** to have a specified direction in motion **:** FLOW, TEND <the wind was *setting* from Pine Hill to the farm —Esther Forbes> **9** *of a dog* **:** to indicate the position of game by crouching or pointing **10 :** to dance face to face with another in a square dance <~ to your

partner and turn> **11 a :** to become solid or thickened by chemical or physical alteration <the cement ~*s* rapidly> **b** *of a dye or color* **:** to become permanent **c** *of a bone* **:** to become whole by knitting **d** *of metal* **:** to acquire a permanent twist or bend from strain
syn SET, SETTLE, FIX, ESTABLISH *shared meaning element* **:** to put securely in position
— set about : to begin to do **— set apart 1 :** to reserve to a particular use **2 :** to make noticeable or outstanding **— set aside 1 :** to put to one side **:** DISCARD **2 :** to set apart for a purpose **:** RESERVE, SAVE **3 :** DISMISS **4 :** ANNUL, OVERRULE **— set at :** to mount an attack on **:** ASSAIL <would go although . . . devils should *set at* me —Charlotte Yonge> **— set eyes on :** to catch sight of **— set foot in :** ENTER **— set foot on :** to step **— set forth 1 :** PUBLISH **2 :** to give an account or statement of **3 :** to start out on a journey **— set forward 1 :** FURTHER **2 :** to start out on a journey **— set in motion :** to give impulse to <*sets* the story *in motion* vividly —Howard Thompson> **— set one's hand to :** to become engaged in **— set one's heart on :** RESOLVE <she *set her heart* on succeeding> **— set one's house in order :** to organize one's affairs **— set one's sights on :** to determine to pursue **— set one straight :** to inform fully **— set sail :** to begin a voyage <*set sail* for Europe> **— set store :** to consider valuable, trustworthy, or worthwhile — used with *by* or *on* **— set the stage :** to provide the basis for **— set to music :** to provide music or instrumental accompaniment for (a text) **— set upon :** to attack usu. with violence <the dogs *set upon* the trespassers>

[2]set *adj* [ME *sett,* fr. pp. of *setten* to set] **1 :** INTENT, DETERMINED <~ upon going> **2 :** fixed by authority or appointment **:** PRESCRIBED, SPECIFIED <~ hours of study> **3 :** INTENTIONAL PREMEDITATED <did it of ~ purpose> **4 :** reluctant to change <~ in his ways> **5 a :** IMMOVABLE, RIGID <~ frown> **b :** BUILT-IN **6 :** SETTLED, PERSISTENT <~ defiance> **7 :** being in readiness **:** PREPARED <~ for an early morning start>

[3]set *n* **1 a :** the act or action of setting **b :** the condition of being set **2 a :** mental inclination, tendency, or habit **:** BENT <a ~ toward mathematics> **b :** a state of psychological preparedness usu. of limited duration for action in response to an anticipated stimulus or situation <the influence of mental ~ on the effect experienced with marijuana> **3 :** a number of things of the same kind that belong or are used together **4 :** direction of flow <the ~ of the wind> **5 :** form or carriage of the body or of its parts **6 :** the manner of fitting or of being placed or suspended <in order to give the skirt a pretty ~ —Mary J. Howell> **7 :** amount of deflection from a straight line **8 :** permanent change of form (as of metal) due to repeated or excessive stress **9 :** the act of arranging hair by curling or waving **10 a :** a young plant or rooted cutting ready for transplanting **b :** a small bulb, corm, or tuber or a piece of tuber used for propagation <onion ~*s*> **11 :** the width of the body of a piece of type **12 :** an artificial setting for a scene of a theatrical or film production **13 :** a division of a tennis match won by the side that wins at least six games beating the opponent by two games or by winning a tie breaker **14 :** a collection of books or periodicals forming a unit **15 :** a clutch of eggs **16 :** the basic formation in a country-dance or square dance **17 :** a session of music (as jazz or dance music) usu. followed by an intermission; *also* **:** the music played at one session **18 :** a group of persons associated by common interests **19 :** a collection of mathematical elements (as numbers or points) — called also *class* **20 :** an apparatus of electronic components assembled so as to function as a unit <a radio ~> **21 :** a usu. offensive formation in football
syn SET, CIRCLE, COTERIE, CLIQUE *shared meaning element* **:** a more or less closed and exclusive group of persons

se·ta \ˈsēt-ə\ *n, pl* **se·tae** \ˈsē-ˌtē\ [NL, fr. L *saeta, seta* bristle — more at SINEW] **:** a slender usu. rigid or bristly and springy organ or part of an animal or plant **— se·tal** \ˈsēt-ᵊl\ *adj*

se·ta·ceous \si-ˈtā-shəs\ *adj* [L *saeta, seta*] **1 :** set with or consisting of bristles **2 :** resembling a bristle in form or texture **— se·ta·ceous·ly** *adv*

set–aside \ˈset-ə-ˌsīd\ *n* **:** something (as a portion of receipts or production) that is set aside for a specified purpose

set·back \ˈset-ˌbak\ *n* **1 :** a checking of progress **2 :** DEFEAT, REVERSE **3 :** [4]PITCH 7 **4 :** a placing of the face of a building on a line some distance to the rear of the building line or of the wall below

[1]set back \(ˈ)set-ˈbak\ *vt* [[1]*set* + [2]*back*] **1 :** to slow the progress of **:** HINDER, DELAY **2 :** COST <a new suit *set* him *back* $65>

[2]set back \ˈset-ˌbak\ *n* [*set,* pp. of [1]*set* + [1]*back*] **:** an offensive football back who usu. lines up behind the quarterback — compare FLANKER, SLOTBACK

set by *vt* **:** to set apart for future use

set down *vt* **1 :** to cause to sit down **:** SEAT **2 :** to place at rest on a surface or on the ground **3 :** to suspend (a jockey) from racing **4 :** to cause or allow to get off a vehicle **:** DELIVER **5 :** to land (an airplane) on the ground or water **6 a :** ORDAIN, ESTABLISH **b :** to put in writing **7 a :** REGARD, CONSIDER <*set* him *down* as a liar> **b :** ATTRIBUTE

se te·nant \sə-ˈten-ənt, ˌset-ə-ˈnä^{n}\ *adj* [F, lit., holding one another] *of postage stamps* **:** joined together as in the original sheet but differing in design, overprint, color, or perforation

Seth \ˈseth\ *n* [Heb *Shēth*] **:** a son of Adam

[1]set–in \ˌset-ˌin\ *adj* **1 :** placed, located, or built as a part of some other construction <a ~ bookcase> <a ~ washbasin> **2 :** cut separately and stitched in <~ sleeves>

[2]set–in \ˈset-ˌin\ *n* **:** INSERT

set in *vt* **1 :** INSERT; *esp* **:** to stitch (a small part) within a large article <*set in* a sleeve of a dress> **2 :** to direct (a ship) towards shore ~ *vi* **1 :** to become established **2 :** to blow or flow toward shore <the wind was beginning to *set in*>

set·line \ˈset-ˌlīn\ *n* **:** a long heavy fishing line to which several hooks are attached in series

set·off \ˈset-ˌȯf\ *n* **1 :** something that is set off against another thing**: a :** DECORATION, ORNAMENT **b :** COMPENSATION, COUNTERBALANCE **2 :** the discharge of a debt by setting against it a distinct claim in favor of the debtor; *also* **:** the claim itself **3 :** OFFSET 7a

set off \(ˈ)set-ˈȯf\ *vt* **1 a :** to put in relief **:** show up by contrast **b :** ADORN, EMBELLISH **c :** to set apart **:** make distinct or outstanding **2 a :** OFFSET, COMPENSATE <more variety in the Lancashire weather to *set off* its most disagreeable phases —*Geog. Jour.*> **b :** to make a setoff of <the respective totals shall be *set off* against one another —O. R. Hobson> **3 a :** to set in motion **b :** to cause to explode **4 :** to measure off on a surface ~ *vi* **1 :** to start out on a course or a journey <*set off* for home> **2 :** OFFSET

set on *vt* **1 :** ATTACK **2 a** *obs* **:** PROMOTE **b :** to urge (as a dog) to attack or pursue **c :** to incite to action **:** INSTIGATE **d :** to set to work ~ *vi* **:** to go on **:** ADVANCE

se·tose \ˈsē-ˌtōs\ *adj* [L *saetosus,* fr. *saeta*] **:** SETACEOUS, BRISTLY

set·out \ˈset-ˌau̇t\ *n* **1 a** (1) **:** ARRAY, DISPLAY (2) **:** ARRANGEMENT, LAYOUT **b :** BUFFET, SPREAD **c :** TURNOUT 5 **2 :** PARTY, ENTERTAINMENT **3 :** BEGINNING, OUTSET

set out \(ˈ)set-ˈau̇t\ *vt* **1 :** to state, describe, or recite at length <distributed copies of a pamphlet *setting out* his ideas in full —S. F. Mason> **2 a :** to arrange and present graphically or systematically **b :** to mark out (as a design) **:** lay out the plan of **3 :** to begin with a definite purpose **:** INTEND, UNDERTAKE ~ *vi* **:** to start out on a course, a journey, or a career

set piece *n* **1 :** a realistic piece of stage scenery standing by itself **2 :** a composition (as in literature) executed in a fixed or ideal form often with studied artistry and brilliant effect **3 :** a precisely planned and conducted military operation

set point *n* **:** a situation (as in tennis) in which one player will win the game and set by winning the next point; *also* **:** the point won

set·screw \ˈset-ˌskrü\ *n* **1 :** a screw screwed through one part tightly upon or into another part to prevent relative movement **2 :** a screw for regulating a valve opening or a spring tension

set·tee \se-ˈtē\ *n* [alter. of *settle*] **1 :** a long seat with a back **2 :** a medium-sized sofa with arms and a back

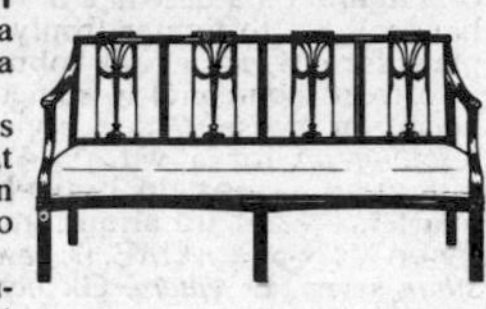
settee 2

set·ter \ˈset-ər\ *n* **1 :** one that sets **2 :** a large bird dog of a type that was formerly trained to crouch on finding game but is now expected to point

set theory *n* **:** a branch of mathematics or of symbolic logic that deals with the nature and relations of sets **— set theoretic** *adj*

set·ting \ˈset-iŋ\ *n* **1 :** the manner, position, or direction in which something is set **2 :** the frame or bed in which a gem is set; *also* **:** style of mounting **3 a :** BACKGROUND, ENVIRONMENT **b :** the time and place of the action of a literary, dramatic, or cinematic work **c :** the scenery used in a theatrical or film production **4 :** the music composed for a text (as a poem) **5 :** the articles of tableware for setting a place at table <two ~*s* of sterling silver> **6 :** a batch of eggs for incubation

[1]set·tle \ˈset-ᵊl\ *n* [ME, place for sitting, seat, chair, fr. OE *setl;* akin to OHG *sezzal* seat, L *sella* seat, chair, saddle, OE *sittan* to sit] **:** a wooden bench with arms, a high solid back, and an enclosed foundation which can be used as a chest

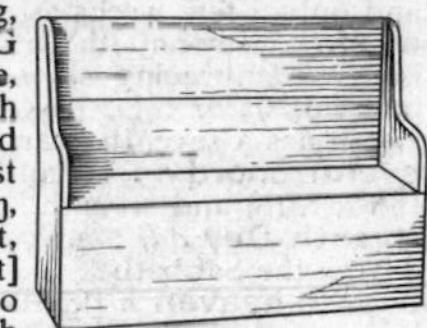
settle

[2]set·tle *vb* **set·tled; set·tling** \ˈset-liŋ, -ᵊl-iŋ\ [ME *settlen* to seat, bring to rest, come to rest, fr. OE *setlan,* fr. *setl* seat] *vt* **1 :** to place so as to stay **2 a :** to establish in residence **b :** to furnish with inhabitants **:** COLONIZE **3 a :** to cause to pack down **b :** to clarify by causing dregs or impurities to sink **4 :** to make quiet or orderly **5 a :** to fix or resolve conclusively <~ the question> **b :** to establish or secure permanently <~ the order of royal succession> **6 :** to arrange in a desired position **7 :** to make or arrange for final disposition of <*settled* his affairs> **8** *of an animal* **:** IMPREGNATE ~ *vi* **1 :** to come to rest **2 a :** to sink gradually or to the bottom **b :** to become clear by the deposit of sediment or scum **c :** to become compact by sinking **3 a :** to become fixed, resolved, or established <a cold *settled* in his chest> **b :** to establish a residence or colony <*settled* in Europe for a few years> **4 a :** to become quiet or orderly **b :** to take up an ordered or stable life — often used with *down* <marry and ~ down> **5 :** to adjust differences or accounts **6** *of an animal* **:** CONCEIVE ***syn* 1** see SET ***ant*** unsettle **2** see DECIDE **— settle for :** to be content with **— settle the stomach :** to remove or relieve the distress or nausea of indigestion in the stomach

set·tle·ment \ˈset-ᵊl-mənt\ *n* **1 :** the act or process of settling **2 :** an act of bestowing or giving possession under legal sanction **b :** the sum, estate, or income secured to one by such a settlement **3 a :** a place or region newly settled **b :** a small village **4 :** an institution providing various community services esp. to large city populations **5 :** an agreement composing differences

settlement house *n* **:** SETTLEMENT 4

set·tler \ˈset-lər, -ᵊl-ər\ *n* **:** one that settles (as a new region)

set·tling \ˈset-liŋ, -ᵊl-iŋ\ *n* **:** SEDIMENT, DREGS — usu. used in pl.

set·tlor \ˈset-ˌlȯ(ə)r, -ᵊl-ˌȯ(ə)r\ *n* **:** one that makes a settlement or creates a trust of property

set–to \'set-ˌtü\ *n, pl* **set–tos** : a usu. brief and vigorous contest

set to \(ˈ)set-'tü\ *vi* **1** : to begin actively and earnestly **2** : to begin fighting

set·up \'set-ˌəp\ *n* **1 a** : carriage of the body; *esp* : erect and soldierly bearing **b** : CONSTITUTION, MAKEUP **2 a** : the assembly and arrangement of the tools and apparatus required for the performance of an operation **b** : the preparation and adjustment of machines for an assigned task **3 a** : a table setting **b** : glass, ice, and mixer served to patrons who supply their own liquor **4 a** : a camera position from which a scene is filmed; *also* : the footage taken from one camera position **b** : the final arrangement of the scenery and properties for a scene of a theatrical or cinematic production **5 a** : a position of the balls in billiards or pool from which it is easy to score **b** : a task or contest purposely made easy **c** : something easy to get or accomplish **6 a** : the manner in which the elements or components of a machine, apparatus, or mechanical, electrical, or hydraulic system are arranged, designed, or assembled **b** : the patterns within which political, social, or administrative forces operate : customary or established practice **7** : PROJECT, PLAN

set up \(ˈ)set-'əp\ *vt* **1 a** : to raise to and place in a high position **b** : to place in view : POST **c** : to put forward (as a plan) for acceptance **2 a** : to place upright : ERECT <*set up* a statue> **b** : to assemble the parts of and erect in position <*set up* a printing press> **c** : to put (a machine) in readiness or adjustment for a tooling operation **3** : CAUSE, CREATE <*set up* a clamor> **4** : to place in power or in office <*set up* the general as dictator> **5 a** : to raise from depression : ELATE, GRATIFY **b** : to make proud or vain **6 a** : to put forward or extol as a model **b** : to claim oneself to be <*sets* himself *up* as an authority> **7** : FOUND, INAUGURATE <*set up* a home for orphans> **8 a** : to provide with means of making a living <*set* him *up* in business> **b** : to bring or restore to normal health **c** : to cause (one) to take on a soldierly or athletic appearance esp. through drill **9** : to erect (a perpendicular or a figure) on a base in a drawing **10 a** : to make taut (a stay or hawser) **b** : to tighten firmly **11** : to make carefully worked out plans for <*set up* a bank robbery> **12 a** : to pay for (drinks) **b** : to treat (someone) to something ~ *vi* **1** : to come into active operation or use **2** : to begin business **3** : to make pretensions <*setting up* for a wit> **4** : to become firm or consolidated : HARDEN — **set up housekeeping** : to establish one's living quarters — **set up shop** : to establish one's business

sev·en \'sev-ən\ *n* [ME, fr. *seven*, adj., fr. OE *seofon;* akin to OHG *sibun* seven, L *septem*, Gk *hepta*] **1** — see NUMBER table **2** : the seventh in a set or series <the ~ of diamonds> **3** : something having seven units or members — **seven** *adj or pron*

sev·en·fold \'sev-ən-ˌfōld\ *adj* **1** : having seven units or members **2** : being seven times as great or as many — **sevenfold** *adv*

seven seas *n pl* : all the waters or oceans of the world

sev·en·teen \ˌsev-ən-'tēn\ *n* [*seventeen*, adj., fr. ME *seventene*, fr. OE *seofontēne;* akin to OE *tien* ten] — see NUMBER table — **seventeen** *adj or pron* — **sev·en·teenth** \-'tēn(t)th\ *adj or n*

seventeen–year locust *n* : a cicada (*Cicada septendecim*) of the U.S. that has in the North a life of seventeen years and in the South of thirteen years of which most is spent underground as a nymph and only a few weeks as a winged adult

sev·enth \'sev-ən(t)th\ *n* **1** — see NUMBER table **2 a** : a musical interval embracing seven diatonic degrees **b** : a tone at this interval; *specif* : LEADING TONE **c** : the harmonic combination of two tones a seventh apart — **seventh** *adj or adv*

seventh chord *n* : a chord comprising a fundamental tone with its third, fifth, and seventh

Seventh–Day *adj* : advocating or practicing observance of Saturday as the Sabbath

seventh heaven *n* [fr. the seventh being the highest of the seven heavens of Muslim and cabalist doctrine] : a state of extreme joy

sev·en·ty \'sev-ən-tē, -dē\ *n, pl* **-ties** [*seventy*, adj., fr. ME, fr. OE *seofontig*, short for *hundseofontig*, fr. *hundseofontig*, n., group of 70, fr. *hund* hundred + *seofon* seven + *-tig* group of ten — more at HUNDRED, EIGHTY] **1** — see NUMBER table **2** *pl* : the numbers 70 to 79; *specif* : the years 70 to 79 in a lifetime or century **3** *cap* : a Mormon elder ordained for missionary work under the apostles — **sev·en·ti·eth** \-tē-əth, -dē-\ *adj or n* — **seventy** *adj or pron*

sev·en·ty–eight \ˌsev-ən-tē-'āt, -ən-dē-\ *n* **1** — see NUMBER table **2** : a phonograph record designed to be played at 78 revolutions per minute — usu. written 78 — **seventy–eight** *adj or pron*

sev·en–up \ˌsev-ə-'nəp\ *n* : an American variety of all fours in which a total of seven points constitutes game

sev·er \'sev-ər\ *vb* **sev·ered; sev·er·ing** \-(ə-)riŋ\ [ME *severen*, fr. MF *severer*, fr. L *separare* — more at SEPARATE] *vt* : to put or keep apart : DIVIDE; *esp* : to remove (as a part) by or as if by cutting ~ *vi* : to become separated *syn* see SEPARATE

sev·er·able \'sev-(ə-)rə-bəl\ *adj* : capable of being severed; *esp* : capable of being divided into legally independent rights or obligations — **sev·er·abil·i·ty** \ˌsev-(ə-)rə-'bil-ət-ē\ *n*

[1]**sev·er·al** \'sev-(ə-)rəl\ *adj* [ME, fr. AF, fr. ML *separalis*, fr. L *separ* separate, back-formation fr. *separare* to separate] **1 a** : separate or distinct from one another <federal union of the ~ states> **b (1)** : individually owned or controlled : EXCLUSIVE <a ~ fishery> — compare COMMON **(2)** : of or relating separately to each individual involved <a ~ judgment> **c** : being separate and distinctive : RESPECTIVE <specialists in their ~ fields> **2 a** : more than one <~ pleas> **b** : more than two but fewer than many <moved ~ inches> **c** *chiefly dial* : being a great many *syn* see DISTINCT — **sev·er·al·ly** \-ē\ *adv*

[2]**several** *pron, pl in constr* : an indefinite number more than two and fewer than many <~ of the guests>

sev·er·al·fold \ˌsev-(ə-)rəl-'fōld\ *adj* **1** : having several parts or aspects **2** : being several times as large, as great, or as many as some understood size, degree, or amount <a ~ increase> — **severalfold** *adv*

sev·er·al·ty \'sev-(ə-)rəl-tē\ *n* [MF *severalte*, fr. AF *severalté*, fr. *several*] **1** : the quality or state of being several : DISTINCTNESS, SEPARATENESS **2 a** : a sole, separate, and exclusive possession, dominion, or ownership : one's own right without a joint interest in any other person <tenants in ~> **b** : the quality or state of being individual or particular **3 a** : land owned in severalty **b** : the quality or state of being held in severalty

sev·er·ance \'sev-(ə-)rən(t)s\ *n* : the act or process of severing : the state of being severed

severance pay *n* : an allowance usu. based on length of service that is payable to an employee on termination of employment

se·vere \sə-'vi(ə)r\ *adj* **se·ver·er; -est** [MF or L; MF, fr. L *severus*] **1 a** : strict in judgment, discipline, or government **b** : of a strict or stern bearing or manner : AUSTERE **2** : rigorous in restraint, punishment, or requirement : STRINGENT, RESTRICTIVE **3** : strongly critical or condemnatory : CENSORIOUS <a ~ critic> **4 a** : maintaining a scrupulously exacting standard of behavior or self-discipline **b** : establishing exacting standards of accuracy and integrity in intellectual processes <a ~ logician> **5** : sober or restrained in decoration or manner : PLAIN **6 a** : inflicting physical discomfort or hardship : HARSH <~ winters> **b** : inflicting pain or distress : GRIEVOUS <a ~ wound> **7** : requiring great effort : ARDUOUS <a ~ test> **8** : of a great degree : MARKED, SERIOUS <~ depression> — **se·vere·ly** *adv* — **se·vere·ness** *n*

syn SEVERE, STERN, AUSTERE, ASCETIC *shared meaning element* : given to or marked by strict discipline and firm restraint ***ant*** tolerant, tender

se·ver·i·ty \sə-'ver-ət-ē\ *n* : the quality or state of being severe

Sevres \'sev-rə, 'sev(rᵊ)\ *n* [*Sèvres*, France] : an often elaborately decorated French porcelain

sew \'sō\ *vb* **sewed; sewn** \'sōn\ *or* **sewed; sew·ing** [ME *sewen*, fr. OE *sīwian;* akin to OHG *siuwen* to sew, L *suere*] *vt* **1** : to unite or fasten by stitches **2** : to close or enclose by sewing <~ the money in a bag> ~ *vi* : to practice or engage in sewing

sew·age \'sü-ij\ *n* [[3]*sewer*] : refuse liquids or waste matter carried off by sewers

[1]**sew·er** \'sü-ər, 'sü(-ə)r\ *n* [ME, fr. AF *asseour*, lit., seater, fr. OF *asseoir* to seat — more at ASSIZE] : a medieval household officer often of high rank in charge of serving the dishes at table and sometimes of seating and tasting

[2]**sew·er** \'sō(-ə)r\ *n* : one that sews

[3]**sew·er** \'sü-ər, 'sü(-ə)r\ *n* [ME, fr. MF *esseweur, seweur*, fr. *essewer* to drain, fr. (assumed) VL *exaquare*, fr. L *ex-* + *aqua* water — more at ISLAND] : an artificial usu. subterranean conduit to carry off sewage and sometimes surface water (as from rainfall)

sew·er·age \'sü-ə-rij, 'sü(-ə)r-ij\ *n* **1** : SEWAGE **2** : the removal and disposal of sewage and surface water by sewers **3** : a system of sewers

sew·ing \'sō-iŋ\ *n* **1** : the act, method, or occupation of one that sews **2** : material that has been or is to be sewed

sew up *vt* **1** : to mend completely by sewing **2** : to get exclusive use or control of **3** : to make certain of : ASSURE

[1]**sex** \'seks\ *n* [ME, fr. L *sexus*] **1** : either of two divisions of organisms distinguished respectively as male or female **2** : the sum of the structural, functional, and behavioral characteristics of living beings that subserve reproduction by two interacting parents and that distinguish males and females **3 a** : sexually motivated phenomena or behavior **b** : SEXUAL INTERCOURSE **4** : GENITALIA

[2]**sex** *vt* **1** : to identify the sex of <~ chicks> **2 a** : to increase the sexual appeal of **b** : to arouse the sexual desires of

sex- *or* **sexi-** *comb form* [L *sex* — more at SIX] : six <*sexi*valent> <*sex*partite>

sex·a·ge·nar·i·an \ˌsek-sə-jə-'ner-ē-ən, (ˌ)sek-ˌsaj-ə-\ *n* [L *sexagenarius* of or containing 60, 60 years old, fr. *sexageni* 60 each, fr. *sexaginta* sixty, irreg. fr. *sex* six + *-ginta* (akin to L *viginti* twenty) — more at SIX, VIGESIMAL] : a person who is in his sixties — **sexagenarian** *adj*

Sex·a·ges·i·ma \ˌsek-sə-'jes-ə-mə, -'jā-zə-\ *n* [LL, fr. L, fem. of *sexagesimus* sixtieth; fr. its being approximately 60 days before Easter] : the second Sunday before Lent

[1]**sex·a·ges·i·mal** \-'jes-ə-məl\ *adj* [L *sexagesimus* sixtieth, fr. *sexaginta* sixty] : of, relating to, or based on the number 60

[2]**sexagesimal** *n* : a sexagesimal fraction

sex appeal *n* **1** : personal appeal or physical attractiveness for members of the opposite sex **2** : potential for popularity : general attractiveness

sex cell *n* : GAMETE; *also* : its cellular precursor

sex chromosome *n* : a chromosome that is inherited differently in the two sexes, that is or is held to be concerned directly with the inheritance of sex, and that is the seat of factors governing the inheritance of various sex-linked and sex-limited characters

sex·de·cil·lion \ˌseks-di-'sil-yən\ *n, often attrib* [L *sedecim*, *sexdecim* sixteen (fr. *sex* six + *decem* ten) + E *-illion* (as in *million*) — more at TEN] — see NUMBER table

sexed \'sekst\ *adj* **1** : having sex or sexual instincts **2** : having sex appeal

sex gland *n* : GONAD

sex hormone *n* : a hormone (as from the gonads or adrenal cortex) that affects the growth or function of the reproductive organs or the development of secondary sex characteristics

sex·ism \'sek-ˌsiz-əm\ *n* [[1]*sex* + *-ism* (as in *racism*)] : prejudice or discrimination against women — **sex·ist** \sek-səst\ *adj or n*

sex kitten *n* : a woman who has sex appeal

sex·less \'sek-sləs\ *adj* **1** : lacking sex : NEUTER **2** : lacking sexiness — **sex·less·ly** *adv* — **sex·less·ness** *n*

sex–lim·it·ed \'sek-'slim-ət-əd\ *adj* : expressed in the phenotype of only one sex

sex–link·age \'sek-ˌsliŋ-kij\ *n* : the quality or state of being sex-linked

sex–linked \'sek-ˌsliŋ(k)t\ *adj* **1** : located in a sex chromosome <a ~ gene> **2** : mediated by a sex-linked gene <a ~ character>

sex·ol·o·gy \sek-'säl-ə-jē\ *n* : the study of sex or of the interaction of the sexes esp. among human beings

sex·pot \'sek-ˌspät\ *n* : a conspicuously sexy woman

sext \'sekst\ *n, often cap* [ME *sexte*, fr. LL *sexta*, fr. L, sixth hour of the day, fr. fem. of *sextus* sixth, fr. *sex* six] : the fourth of the canonical hours

Sex·tans \ˈsek-ˌstanz\ *n* [NL (gen. *Sextantis*), lit., sextant] **:** a constellation on the equator south of Leo
sex·tant \ˈsek-stənt\ *n* [NL *sextant-, sextans* sixth part of a circle, fr. L, sixth part, fr. *sextus* sixth] **:** an instrument for measuring angular distances used esp. in navigation to observe altitudes of celestial bodies (as in ascertaining latitude and longitude)
sex·tet \sek-ˈstet\ *n* [alter. of *sestet*] **1 :** a musical composition for six instruments or voices **2 :** a group or set of six: as **a :** the performers of a sextet **b :** a hockey team
sex·til·lion \sek-ˈstil-yən\ *n, often attrib* [F, irreg. fr. *sex-* (fr. L *sex*) + *-illion* (as in *million*)] — see NUMBER table
sex·to \ˈsek-(ˌ)stō\ *n, pl* **sextos** [L *sexto,* abl. of *sextus* sixth] **:** SIXMO

sextant

sex·to·dec·i·mo \ˌsek-stə-ˈdes-ə-ˌmō\ *n, pl* **-mos** [L, abl. of *sextus decimus* sixteenth, fr. *sextus* sixth + *decimus* tenth — more at DIME] **:** SIXTEENMO
sex·ton \ˈsek-stən\ *n* [ME *secresteyn, sexteyn,* fr. MF *secrestain,* fr. ML *sacristanus* — more at SACRISTAN] **:** a church officer or employee who takes care of the church property and at some churches rings the bell for services and digs graves
1sex·tu·ple \sek-ˈst(y)üp-əl, -ˈstəp-; ˈsek-stəp-\ *adj* [prob. fr. ML *sextuplus,* fr. L *sextus* sixth + *-plus* multiplied by — more at DOUBLE] **1 :** having six units or members **2 :** being six times as great or as many **3 :** marked by six beats per measure of music <~ time> — **sextuple** *n*
2sextuple *vb* **sex·tu·pled; sex·tu·pling** \-(ə-)liŋ\ *vt* **:** to make six times as much or as many ~ *vi* **:** to become six times as much or as numerous
sex·tu·plet \sek-ˈstəp-lət, -ˈst(y)üp-; ˈsek-st(y)əp-\ *n* **1 :** a combination of six of a kind **2 :** one of six offspring born at one birth **3 :** a group of six equal musical notes performed in the time ordinarily given to four of the same value
1sex·tu·pli·cate \sek-ˈst(y)ü-pli-kət\ *adj* [blend of *sextuple* and *-plicate* (as in *duplicate*)] **1 :** repeated six times **2 :** SIXTH <file the ~ copy> — **sextuplicate** *n*
2sex·tu·pli·cate \-plə-ˌkāt\ *vt* **-cat·ed; -cat·ing 1 :** SEXTUPLE **2 :** to provide in sextuplicate
sex·u·al \ˈseksh-(ə-)wəl, ˈsek-shəl\ *adj* [LL *sexualis,* fr. L *sexus* sex] **1 :** of, relating to, or associated with sex or the sexes <~ differentiation> <~ conflict> **2 :** having or involving sex <~ reproduction> — **sex·u·al·ly** \ˈseksh-(ə-)wə-lē, ˈseksh-(ə-)lē\ *adv*
sexual generation *n* **:** the generation of an organism with alternation of generations that reproduces sexually
sexual intercourse *n* **:** sexual connection esp. between humans **:** COITUS, COPULATION
sex·u·al·i·ty \ˌsek-shə-ˈwal-ət-ē\ *n* **:** the quality or state of being sexual: **a :** the condition of having sex **b :** sexual activity **c :** expression of sexual receptivity or interest esp. when excessive
sex·u·al·ize \ˈseksh-(ə-)wə-ˌlīz, ˈsek-shə-ˌlīz\ *vt* **-ized; -iz·ing :** to make sexual **:** endow with a sexual character or cast
sexual relations *n pl* **:** COITUS
sexy \ˈsek-sē\ *adj* **sex·i·er; -est :** sexually suggestive or stimulating **:** EROTIC — **sex·i·ly** \-sə-lē\ *adv* — **sex·i·ness** \-sē-nəs\ *n*
Sey·fert galaxy \ˌsē-fərt-, ˌsī-\ *n* [Carl K. *Seyfert* †1960 Am astronomer] **:** any of a class of spiral galaxies that have small compact bright nuclei characterized by variability in light intensity, emission of radio waves, and spectra which indicate hot gases in rapid motion
sf *or* **sfz** *abbr* sforzando
SF *abbr, often not cap* **1** sacrifice fly **2** science fiction **3** sinking fund
SFC *abbr* sergeant first class
sfer·ics \ˈsfi(ə)r-iks, ˈsfer-\ *n pl* [by shortening & alteration] **1 :** ATMOSPHERICS **2** *sing in constr* **:** an electronic detector of storms
1sforzando \sfort-ˈsän-(ˌ)dō, -ˈsan-\ *adj or adv* [It, verbal of *sforzare* to force] **:** played with prominent stress or accent — used as a direction in music
2sforzando *n, pl* **-dos** *or* **-di** \-(ˌ)dē\ **:** an accented tone or chord
sfu·ma·to \sfü-ˈmä-(ˌ)tō\ *n* [It, fr. pp. of *sfumare* to evaporate, fr *s-* (fr. L *ex-*) + *fumare* to smoke, fr. L] **:** the definition of form without abrupt outline by the delicate blending of one tone into another
SG *abbr* **1** senior grade **2** sergeant **3** solicitor general **4** *often not cap* specific gravity **5** surgeon general
sgd *abbr* signed
sgraf·fi·to \zgra-ˈfē-(ˌ)tō, skra-\ *n, pl* **-ti** \-(ˌ)tē\ [It, fr. pp. of *sgraffire* to scratch, produce sgraffito] **1 :** decoration by cutting away parts of a surface layer (as of plaster or clay) to expose a different colored ground — compare GRAFFITO **2 :** something (as traditional Pennsylvania Dutch pottery) decorated with sgraffito
Sgt *abbr* sergeant
Sgt Maj *abbr* sergeant major
1sh \sh *often prolonged*\ *interj* — used often in prolonged or reduplicated form to urge or command silence
2sh *abbr* share
Sha'·ban \shə-ˈbän\ *n* [Ar *sha'bān*] **:** the 8th month of the Muhammadan year — see MONTH table
Shab·bat \shə-ˈbät, ˈshäb-əs\ *n, pl* **Shab·ba·tim** \shə-ˈbät-əm, -ˈbō-səm\ [Heb *shabbāth*] **:** the Jewish Sabbath
shab·by \ˈshab-ē\ *adj* **shab·bi·er; -est** [obs. E *shab* (a low fellow)] **1 a :** threadbare and faded from wear <a ~ sofa> **b :** ill kept **:** DILAPIDATED <a ~ neighborhood> **2 :** clothed with worn or seedy garments <a ~ hobo> **3 a :** MEAN, DESPICABLE <must feel ~ . . . because of his compromises —Nat Hentoff> **b :** UNGENEROUS, UNFAIR <laments the ~ way in which this country often treated a poet —Paul Engle> **c :** inferior in quality **:** SLOVENLY <his reasoning is weak, even ~ —J. T. Farrell> — **shab·bi·ly** \ˈshab-ə-lē\ *adv* — **shab·bi·ness** \ˈshab-ē-nəs\ *n*

Sha·bu·oth \shə-ˈvü-ˌōt(h), -ˌōs, -əs\ *n* [Heb *shābhūʽōth,* lit., weeks] **:** a Jewish holiday observed on the 6th and 7th of Sivan in commemoration of the revelation of the Ten Commandments at Mt. Sinai
shack \ˈshak\ *n* [prob. back-formation fr. E dial. *shackly* (rickety)] **1 :** HUT, SHANTY **2 :** a room or similar enclosed structure for a particular person or use <a cook's ~> <a radio ~>
1shack·le \ˈshak-əl\ *n* [ME *schakel,* fr. OE *sceacul;* akin to ON *skökull* pole of a cart] **1 :** something (as a manacle or fetter) that confines the legs or arms **2 :** something that checks or prevents free action as if by fetters — usu. used in pl. **3 :** any of various devices for making something (as a clevis) fast **4 :** a length of cable or anchor chain usu. 15 feet
2shackle *vt* **shack·led; shack·ling** \-(ə-)liŋ\ **1 a :** to bind with shackles **:** FETTER **b :** to make fast with a shackle **2 :** to deprive of freedom esp. of action by means of restrictions or handicaps **:** IMPEDE *syn* see HAMPER — **shack·ler** \-(ə-)lər\ *n*
shack·le·bone \ˈshak-əl-ˌbōn, ˈshāk-\ *n, Scot* **:** WRIST
shack up \(ˈ)shak-ˈəp\ *vi* **:** to become established in a dwelling or shelter esp. when involving cohabitation **:** spend the night
shad \ˈshad\ *n, pl* **shad** [(assumed) ME, fr. OE *sceadd;* akin to L *scatēre* to bubble] **:** any of several clupeid fishes (genus *Alosa*) that differ from the typical herrings in having a relatively deep body and in being anadromous and that are extremely important food fishes of Europe and No. America
shad·ber·ry \-ˌber-ē\ *n* **1 :** the fruit of the serviceberry **2 :** SERVICEBERRY 2
shad·blow \ˈshad-ˌblō\ *n* **:** SERVICEBERRY 2
shad·bush \-ˌbu̇sh\ *n* **:** SERVICEBERRY 2
shad·dock \ˈshad-ək\ *n* [Captain *Shaddock,* 17th cent. E ship commander] **:** a very large thick-rinded usu. pear-shaped citrus fruit differing from the closely related grapefruit esp. in its loose rind and often coarse dry pulp; *also* **:** the tree (*Citrus grandis*) that bears it
1shade \ˈshād\ *n* [ME, fr. OE *sceadu;* akin to OHG *scato* shadow, Gk *skotos* darkness] **1 a :** comparative darkness or obscurity owing to interception of the rays of light **b :** relative obscurity or retirement **2 a :** shelter (as by foliage) from the heat and glare of sunlight **b :** a place sheltered from the sun **3 :** an evanescent or unreal appearance **4** *pl* **a :** the shadows that gather as darkness comes on **b :** NETHERWORLD, HADES **5 :** a disembodied spirit **:** GHOST **6 :** something that intercepts or shelters from light, sun, or heat: as **a :** a device partially covering a lamp so as to reduce glare **b :** a flexible screen usu. mounted on a roller for regulating the light or the view through a window **c** *pl* **:** SUNGLASSES **7 a :** the reproduction of the effect of shade in painting or drawing **b :** a subdued or somber feature **8 a :** a color produced by a pigment or dye mixture having some black in it **b :** a color slightly different from the one under consideration **9 a :** a minute difference or variation **b :** a minute degree or quantity **10 :** a facial expression of sadness or displeasure — **shade·less** \-ləs\ *adj*
2shade *vb* **shad·ed; shad·ing** *vt* **1 a :** to shelter or screen by intercepting radiated light or heat **b :** to cover with a shade **2 :** to hide partly by or as if by a shadow **3 :** to darken with or as if with a shadow **4 :** to cast into the shade (as by some exhibition of superiority) **:** OBSCURE **5 a :** to represent the effect of shade or shadow on **b :** to add shading to **c :** to color so that the shades pass gradually from one to another **6 :** to change by gradual transition or qualification **7 :** to reduce slightly (as a price) ~ *vi* **1 :** to pass by slight changes or imperceptible degrees into something else **2 :** to undergo or exhibit minute difference or variation — **shad·er** *n*
shade–grown \ˈshād-ˌgrōn\ *adj* **:** grown in the shade; *specif* **:** grown under cloth <~ tobacco>
shade tree *n* **:** a tree grown primarily to produce shade
shad·ing \ˈshād-iŋ\ *n* **:** the filling up within outlines to suggest three-dimensionality, shadow, or more or less darkness in a picture or drawing
sha·doof *also* **sha·duf** \shə-ˈdüf, sha-\ *n* [Ar. *shādūf*] **:** a counterbalanced sweep used since ancient times esp. in Egypt for raising water (as for irrigation)
1shad·ow \ˈshad-(ˌ)ō, -ə(-w)\ *n* [ME *shadwe,* fr. OE *sceaduw-, sceadu* shade, shadow] **1 :** partial darkness or obscurity within a part of space from which rays from a source of light are cut off by an interposed opaque body **2 :** a reflected image **3 :** shelter from danger or observation **4 a :** an imperfect and faint representation **b :** an imitation of something **:** COPY **5 :** the dark figure cast upon a surface by a body intercepting the rays from a source of light **6 :** PHANTOM **7** *pl* **:** DARKNESS **8 :** a shaded or darker portion of a picture **9 :** an attenuated form or a vestigial remnant **10 a :** an inseparable companion or follower **b :** one (as a spy or detective) that shadows **11 :** a small degree or portion **:** TRACE **12 :** a source of gloom or unhappiness **13 a :** an area within the shadow cast by an object **:** an area near an object **:** VICINITY **b :** pervasive and dominant influence — **shad·ow·less** \ˈshad-ō-ləs, -ə-ləs\ *adj* — **shad·ow·like** \-ˌlīk\ *adj*
2shadow *vt* **1** *archaic* **:** SHELTER, PROTECT **2 :** to cast a shadow upon **:** CLOUD **3** *obs* **:** to shelter from the sun **4** *obs* **:** CONCEAL **5 :** to represent or indicate obscurely or faintly — often used with *forth* or *out* **6 :** to follow esp. secretly **:** TRAIL **7** *archaic* **:** SHADE 5 ~ *vi* **1 :** to pass gradually or by degrees **2 :** to become overcast with or as if with shadows — **shad·ow·er** \-ə-wər\ *n*
3shadow *adj* **1 :** not functioning in an official capacity <a ~ government in exile> **2 a :** having an indistinct pattern <~ plaid> **b :** having darker sections of design <~ lace>

shad·ow·box \ˈshad-ō-ˌbäks, -ə-ˌbäks\ *vi* **:** to box with an imaginary opponent esp. as a form of training
shadow box *n* **:** a shallow enclosing case usu. with a glass front in which something is set for protection and display
shadow cabinet *n* **:** a group of leaders of a parliamentary opposition who constitute the probable membership of the cabinet when their party is returned to power
shadow dance *n* **:** a dance shown by throwing the shadows of dancers on a screen
shad·ow·graph \ˈshad-ō-ˌgraf, -ə-ˌgraf\ *n* **1 :** SHADOW PLAY **2 :** a photographic image resembling a shadow
shadow play *n* **:** a drama exhibited by throwing shadows of puppets or actors on a screen — called also *shadow show*
shad·owy \ˈshad-ə-wē\ *adj* **1 a :** of the nature of or resembling a shadow **:** UNSUBSTANTIAL **b :** faintly perceptible **:** INDISTINCT **2 :** being in or obscured by shadow <deep ~ interiors> **3 :** SHADY 1 — **shad·ow·i·ly** \-wə-lē\ *adv* — **shad·ow·i·ness** \-wē-nəs\ *n*
shady \ˈshād-ē\ *adj* **shad·i·er; -est 1 :** producing or affording shade **2 :** sheltered from the sun's rays **3 a :** of questionable merit **:** UNCERTAIN, UNRELIABLE **b :** DISREPUTABLE — **shad·i·ly** \ˈshād-ᵊl-ē\ *adv* — **shad·i·ness** \ˈshād-ē-nəs\ *n*
[1]**shaft** \ˈshaft\ *n, pl* **shafts** \ˈshaf(t)s, *for 1b usu* ˈshavz\ [ME, fr. OE *sceaft;* akin to OHG *scaft* shaft, L *scapus* shaft, stalk, Gk *skēptron* staff, L *capo* capon — more at CAPON] **1 a (1) :** the long handle of a spear or similar weapon **(2) :** SPEAR, LANCE **b :** POLE; *specif* **:** either of two long pieces of wood between which a horse is hitched to a vehicle **c (1) :** an arrow esp. for a longbow **(2) :** the body or stem of an arrow extending from the nock to the head **2 :** a sharply delineated beam of light shining through an opening **3 :** something suggestive of the shaft of a spear or arrow esp. in long slender cylindrical form: as **a :** the trunk of a tree **b :** the cylindrical pillar between the capital and the base **c :** the handle or helve of a tool or instrument (as a hammer or golf club) **d :** a commonly cylindrical bar used to support rotating pieces or to transmit power or motion by rotation **e :** the stem or midrib of a feather **f :** the upright member of a cross esp. below the arms **g :** a small architectural column (as at each side of a doorway) **h :** a column, obelisk, or other spire-shaped or columnar monument **i :** a vertical or inclined opening of uniform and limited cross section made for finding or mining ore, raising water, or ventilating underground workings (as in a cave) **j :** a vertical opening or passage through the floors of a building **4 a :** a projectile thrown like a spear or shot like an arrow **b :** a scornful, satirical, or pithily critical remark **c :** harsh or unfair treatment
[2]**shaft** *vt* **1 :** to fit with a shaft **2** *slang* **:** to treat unfairly or harshly
shaft horsepower *n* **:** horsepower transmitted by an engine shaft
shaft·ing \ˈshaf-tiŋ\ *n* **:** shafts or material for shafts
[1]**shag** \ˈshag\ *n* [(assumed) ME *shagge,* fr. OE *sceacga;* akin to ON *skegg* beard, OSlav *skokŭ* leap] **1 a :** a shaggy tangled mass or covering (as of hair) **b :** long coarse or matted fiber or nap **2 :** a strong coarse tobacco cut into fine shreds **3 :** CORMORANT
[2]**shag** *adj* **:** SHAGGY
[3]**shag** *vb* **shagged; shag·ging** *vi* **:** to fall or hang in shaggy masses ~ *vt* **:** to make rough or shaggy
[4]**shag** *vt* **shagged; shag·ging** [origin unknown] **1 a :** to chase after; *esp* **:** to chase after and return (a ball) hit usu. out of play **b :** to catch (a fly) in baseball practice **2 :** to chase away
[5]**shag** *vi* **shagged; shag·ging** [perh. alter. of *shack* (to lumber along)] **1 :** to move or lope along **2 :** to dance the shag
[6]**shag** *n* **:** a dance step executed by hopping livelily on each foot in turn
shag·bark \ˈshag-ˌbärk\ *n* **:** SHAGBARK HICKORY
shagbark hickory *n* **:** a hickory (*Carya ovata*) with sweet edible nuts and a gray shaggy outer bark that peels off in long strips; *also* **:** its wood
shag·gy \ˈshag-ē\ *adj* **shag·gi·er; -est 1 a :** covered with or consisting of long, coarse, or matted hair **b :** covered with or consisting of thick, tangled, or unkempt vegetation **c :** having a rough nap, texture, or surface **d :** having hairlike processes **2 a :** UNKEMPT **b :** confused or unclear in conception or thinking — **shag·gi·ly** \ˈshag-ə-lē\ *adv* — **shag·gi·ness** \ˈshag-ē-nəs\ *n*
shag·gy–dog story \ˌshag-ē-ˈdȯg-\ *n* **:** a long-drawn-out circumstantial story concerning an inconsequential happening that impresses the teller as humorous but the hearer as boring and pointless; *also* **:** a similar humorous story whose humor lies in the pointlessness or irrelevance of the punch line
shag·gy·mane \ˈshag-ē-ˌmān\ *n* **:** a common edible mushroom (*Coprinus comatus*) having an elongated shaggy white pileus and black spores — called also *shaggy cap*
sha·green \sha-ˈgrēn, shə-\ *n* [by folk etymology fr. F *chagrin,* fr. Turk *sağrı*] **1 :** an untanned leather covered with small round granulations and usu. dyed green **2 :** the rough skin of various sharks and rays when covered with small close-set tubercles — **shagreen** *adj*
shah \ˈshä, ˈshȯ\ *n, often cap* [Per *shāh* king — more at CHECK] **:** the sovereign of Iran — **shah·dom** \ˈshäd-əm, ˈshȯd-\ *n*
Sha·hap·ti·an \shə-ˈhap-tē-ən\ *n, pl* **Shahaptian** *or* **Shahaptians 1 :** a member of an Indian people of a large territory along the Columbia river and its tributaries **2 :** the language of the Shahaptian people including Nez Percé and Yakima
shai·tan \shā-ˈtän, shī-\ *n* [Ar *shaytān*] **:** an evil spirit; *specif* **:** an evil jinn
Shak *abbr* Shakespeare
shak·able *or* **shake·able** \ˈshā-kə-bəl\ *adj* **:** capable of being shaken
[1]**shake** \ˈshāk\ *vb* **shook** \ˈshu̇k\; **shak·en** \ˈshā-kən\; **shak·ing** [ME *shaken,* fr. OE *sceacan;* akin to ON *skaka* to shake, Skt *khajati* he agitates] *vi* **1 :** to move irregularly to and fro **2 :** to vibrate esp. as the result of a blow or shock **3 :** to tremble as a result of physical or emotional disturbance **4 :** to experience a state of instability **:** TOTTER **5 :** to briskly move something to and fro or up and down esp. in order to mix **6 :** to clasp hands **7 :** TRILL ~ *vt* **1 :** to brandish, wave, or flourish often in a threatening manner **2 :** to cause to move in a usu. quick jerky manner **3 :** to cause to quake, quiver, or tremble **4 a :** to free oneself from <~ a habit> <~ off a cold> **b :** to get away from **:** get rid of <can you ~ your friend? I want to talk to you alone —Elmer Davis> **5 :** to cause to waver **:** WEAKEN <~ one's faith> **6 :** to bring to a specified condition by repeated quick jerky movements <*shook* himself loose from the man's grasp> **7 :** to dislodge or eject by quick jerky movements of the support or container <*shook* the dust from the cloth> **8 :** to clasp (hands) in greeting or farewell or as a sign of goodwill or agreement **9 :** to stir the feelings of **:** UPSET <*shook* her up> **10 :** TRILL
syn SHAKE, AGITATE, ROCK, CONVULSE *shared meaning element* **:** to cause to move up and down or to and fro with some degree of violence
— **shake a leg 1 :** DANCE **2 :** to hurry up
[2]**shake** *n* **1 :** an act of shaking: as **a :** an act of shaking hands **b :** an act of shaking oneself **2 a :** a blow or shock that upsets the equilibrium or disturbs the balance of something **b :** EARTHQUAKE **3** *pl* **a :** a condition of trembling (as from chill); *specif* **:** DELIRIUM TREMENS **b :** MALARIA 2a **4 :** something produced by shaking: as **a :** a fissure separating annual rings of growth in timber **b :** a fissure in strata **c :** MILK SHAKE **5 :** a wavering, quivering, or alternating motion caused by a blow or shock **6 :** TRILL **7 :** a very brief period of time **8** *pl* **:** one of importance or ability — usu. used in the phrase *no great shakes* **9 :** a shingle split from a piece of log usu. three or four feet long **10 :** [3]DEAL 3 <a fair ~>
shake·down \ˈshāk-ˌdau̇n\ *n* **1 :** an improvised bed (as one made up on the floor) **2 :** a boisterous dance **3 :** an act or instance of shaking someone down; *esp* **:** EXTORTION **4 :** a thorough search **5 :** a process or period of adjustment **6 :** a testing under operating conditions of something new (as a ship) for possible faults and defects and for familiarizing the operators with it
shake down \(ˈ)shāk-ˈdau̇n\ *vi* **1 a :** to take up temporary quarters **b :** to occupy an improvised or makeshift bed **2 a :** to become accustomed esp. to new surroundings or duties **b :** to settle down ~ *vt* **1 :** to obtain money from in a dishonest or illegal manner **2 :** to make a thorough search of **3 :** to bring about a reduction of **4 :** to give a shakedown test to
shake·out \ˈshā-ˌkau̇t\ *n* **1 a :** a minor economic recession **b :** a sharp break in a particular industry that usu. follows overproduction or excessive competition and tends to force out weaker producers **2 :** a sharp lowering of prices; *esp* **:** a sharp usu. brief decline in a commodity or security market that drives weak or frightened speculators from the market
shak·er \ˈshā-kər\ *n* **1 :** one that shakes: as **a :** a utensil or machine used in shaking <pepper ~> <cocktail ~> **b :** one who incites or promotes action **2** *cap* [fr. a dance with shaking movements performed as part of worship] **:** a member of a millenarian sect originating in England in 1747 and practicing celibacy and an ascetic communal life — **Shaker** *adj* — **Shak·er·ism** \-kə-ˌriz-əm\ *n*
[1]**Shake·spear·ean** *or* **Shake·spear·ian** *also* **Shak·sper·ean** *or* **Shak·sper·ian** \shāk-ˈspir-ē-ən\ *adj* **:** of, relating to, or having the characteristics of Shakespeare or his writings
[2]**Shakespearean** *or* **Shakespearian** *also* **Shaksperean** *or* **Shaksperian** *n* **:** an authority on or devotee of Shakespeare
Shake·spear·eana *or* **Shake·spear·iana** \(ˌ)shāk-ˌspir-ē-ˈan-ə, -ˈän-ə, -ˈā-nə\ *n pl* **:** collected items by, about, or relating to Shakespeare
Shakespearean sonnet *n* **:** ENGLISH SONNET
shake–up \ˈshā-ˌkəp\ *n* **:** an act or instance of shaking up; *specif* **:** an extensive and often drastic reorganization
shake up \(ˈ)shā-ˈkəp\ *vt* **1** *obs* **:** CHIDE, SCOLD **2 :** to jar by or as if by a physical shock <the collision *shook up* both drivers> **3 :** to effect an extensive and often drastic reorganization of
shaking palsy *n* **:** PARALYSIS AGITANS
sha·ko \ˈshak-(ˌ)ō, ˈshāk-, ˈshäk-\ *n, pl* **shakos** *or* **shakoes** [F, fr. Hung *csákó*] **:** a stiff military hat with a high crown and plume

shako

Shak·ta \ˈs(h)äk-tə\ *n or adj* [Skt *śākta,* fr. *Śakti*] **:** an adherent of Shaktism
Shak·ti \-tē\ *n* [Skt *Śakti*] **:** the dynamic energy of a Hindu god personified as his female consort; *broadly* **:** cosmic energy as conceived in Hindu thought
Shak·tism \-ˌtiz-əm\ *n* **:** a Hindu sect worshiping Shakti under various names (as Kali or Durga) in a cult of devotion to the female principle often with magical or orgiastic rites
shaky \ˈshā-kē\ *adj* **shak·i·er; -est 1 :** characterized by shakes <~ timber> **2 a :** lacking stability **:** PRECARIOUS **b :** lacking in firmness (as of beliefs or principles) **c :** lacking in authority or reliability **:** QUESTIONABLE **3 a :** somewhat unsound in health **b :** characterized by shaking **4 :** likely to give way or break down — **shak·i·ly** \-kə-lē\ *adv* — **shak·i·ness** \-kē-nəs\ *n*
shale \ˈshā(ə)l\ *n* [ME, shell, scale, fr. OE *scealu* — more at SHELL] **:** a fissile rock that is formed by the consolidation of clay, mud, or silt, has a finely stratified or laminated structure, and is composed of minerals essentially unaltered since deposition
shale oil *n* **:** a crude dark oil obtained from oil shale by heating
shall \shəl, (ˈ)shal\ *vb, past* **should** \shəd, (ˈ)shu̇d\; *pres sing & pl* **shall** [ME *shal* (1st & 3d sing. pres. indic.), fr. OE *sceal;* akin to OHG *scal* (1st & 3d sing. pres. indic.) ought to, must, Lith *skola* debt] *verbal auxiliary* **1** *archaic* **a :** will have to **:** MUST **b :** will be able to **:** CAN **2 a** — used to express a command or exhortation <you ~ go> **b** — used in laws, regulations, or directives to express what is mandatory <it ~ be unlawful to carry firearms> **3 a** — used to express what is inevitable or seems likely to happen in the future <we ~ have to be ready> <we ~ see> **b** — used to express simple futurity <when ~ we expect you> **4** — used to express determination <they ~ not pass> ~ *vi* **:** will go <he to England ~ along with you —Shak.>

shal·loon \shə-'lün, sha-\ *n* [*Châlons*-sur-Marne, France] : a lightweight twilled fabric of wool or worsted used chiefly for the linings of coats and uniforms
shal·lop \'shal-əp\ *n* [MF *chaloupe*] **1** : a usu. two-masted ship with lugsails **2** : a small open boat propelled by oars or sails and used chiefly in shallow waters
shal·lot \shə-'lät *also* 'shal-ət\ *n* [modif. of F *échalote,* deriv. of (assumed) VL *escalonia* — more at SCALLION] **1** : a bulbous perennial herb (*Allium ascalonicum*) that resembles an onion and produces small clustered bulbs used in seasoning **2** : GREEN ONION
[1]**shal·low** \'shal-(,)ō, -ə(-w)\ *adj* [ME *schalowe*] **1** : having little depth <~ water> **2** : having little extension inwards or backwards <office buildings have taken the form of ~ slabs —Lewis Mumford> **3 a** : penetrating only the easily or quickly perceived <~ generalizations> **b** : lacking in depth of knowledge, thought, or feeling <a ~ demagogue> **4** : displacing comparatively little air : WEAK <~ breathing> ***syn*** see SUPERFICIAL ***ant*** deep — **shal·low·ly** \-ō-lē, -ə-lē\ *adv* — **shal·low·ness** *n*
[2]**shallow** *vt* : to make shallow ~ *vi* : to become shallow
[3]**shallow** *n* : a shallow place or area in a body of water — usu. used in pl. but sing. or pl. in constr.
sha·lom \shä-'lōm, shə-\ *interj* [Heb *shālōm* peace] — used as a Jewish greeting and farewell
sha·lom alei·chem \,shȯ-lə-mə-'lā-kəm, ,shō-, -kəm\ *interj* [Heb *shālōm 'alēkhem* peace unto you] — used as a traditional Jewish greeting
shalt \shəlt, (')shalt\ *archaic pres 2d sing of* SHALL
[1]**sham** \'sham\ *n* [perh. fr. E dial. *sham* shame, alter. of E *shame*] **1** : a trick that deludes : HOAX **2** : cheap falseness : HYPOCRISY **3** : a decorative piece of cloth made to simulate an article of personal or household linen and used in place of or over it **4** : an imitation or counterfeit purporting to be genuine **5** : a person who shams ***syn*** see IMPOSTURE
[2]**sham** *vb* **shammed; sham·ming** *vt* : to go through the external motions necessary to counterfeit ~ *vi* : to act intentionally so as to give a false impression : FEIGN ***syn*** see ASSUME
[3]**sham** *adj* **1** : not genuine : FALSE <~ pearls> **2** : having such poor quality as to seem false : ADULTERATED
sha·man \'shäm-ən, 'shā-mən *also* shə-'män\ *n* [Russ or Tungus; Russ, fr. Tungus *šaman*] : a priest who uses magic for the purpose of curing the sick, divining the hidden, and controlling events
sha·man·ism \-,iz-əm\ *n* : a religion of the Ural-Altaic peoples of northern Asia and Europe characterized by belief in an unseen world of gods, demons, and ancestral spirits responsive only to the shamans; *also* : any similar religion — **sha·man·ist** \-əst\ *n* — **sha·man·is·tic** \,shäm-ən-'is-tik, ,shā-mən-\ *adj*
sham·ble \'sham-bəl\ *vi* **sham·bled; sham·bling** \-b(ə-)liŋ\ [*shamble* (bowed, malformed)] : to walk awkwardly with dragging feet : SHUFFLE — **shamble** *n*
sham·bles \'sham-bəlz\ *n pl but sing or pl in constr* [*shamble* (meat market) & obs. E *shamble* (table for exhibition of meat for sale)] **1** *archaic* : a meat market **2** : SLAUGHTERHOUSE **3 a** : a place of mass slaughter or bloodshed **b** : a scene or a state of great destruction : WRECKAGE **c** : a state of great disorder or confusion
sham·bling *adj* : characterized by slow awkward movement
[1]**shame** \'shām\ *n* [ME, fr. OE *scamu;* akin to OHG *scama* shame] **1 a** : a painful emotion caused by consciousness of guilt, shortcoming, or impropriety **b** : the susceptibility to such emotion **2** : a condition of humiliating disgrace or disrepute : IGNOMINY **3 a** : something that brings strong regret, censure, or reproach **b** : a cause of feeling shame ***syn*** see DISGRACE ***ant*** glory, pride
[2]**shame** *vt* **shamed; sham·ing** **1** : to bring shame to : DISGRACE **2** : to put to shame by outdoing **3** : to cause to feel shame **4** : to force by causing to feel guilty <*shamed* into confessing>
shame·faced \'shām-'fāst\ *adj* [alter. of *shamefast*] **1** : showing modesty : BASHFUL **2** : showing shame : ASHAMED — **shame·faced·ly** \-'fā-səd-lē, -'fāst-lē\ *adv* — **shame·faced·ness** \-'fā-səd-nəs, -'fās(t)-nəs\ *n*
shame·fast \'shām-,fast\ *adj* [ME, fr. OE *scamfæst,* fr. *scamu* + *fæst* fixed, fast] *archaic* : SHAMEFACED
shame·ful \'shām-fəl\ *adj* **1 a** : bringing shame : DISGRACEFUL **b** : arousing the feeling of shame : INDECENT **2** *archaic* : full of the feeling of shame : ASHAMED — **shame·ful·ly** \-fə-lē\ *adv* — **shame·ful·ness** *n*
shame·less \'shām-ləs\ *adj* **1** : having no shame : insensible to disgrace **2** : showing lack of shame : DISGRACEFUL — **shame·less·ly** *adv* — **shame·less·ness** *n*
sham·mer \'sham-ər\ *n* : one that shams
sham·mes \'shäm-əs\ *n, pl* **sham·mo·sim** \shä-'mȯ-səm\ [Yiddish *shames,* fr. MHeb *shāmmāsh*] **1** : the sexton of a synagogue **2** : the candle or taper used to light the other candles in a Hanukkah menorah
sham·my \'sham-ē\ *var of* CHAMOIS
[1]**sham·poo** \sham-'pü\ *vt* [Hindi *cāpo,* imper. of *cāpnā* to press, shampoo] **1** *archaic* : MASSAGE **2 a** : to wash (as the hair) with soap and water or with a special preparation **b** : to wash the hair of — **sham·poo·er** *n*
[2]**shampoo** *n, pl* **shampoos** **1** : an act or instance of shampooing **2** : a preparation used in shampooing
sham·rock \'sham-,räk\ *n* [IrGael *seamrōg*] : a trifoliolate leguminous plant used as a floral emblem by the Irish: as **a** : a yellow-flowered clover (*Trifolium dubium*) often regarded as the true shamrock **b** : WOOD SORREL 1 **c** : WHITE DUTCH CLOVER **d** : a yellow-flowered medic (*Medicago lupulina*) with black pods
sha·mus \'shäm-əs, 'shā-məs\ *n* [prob. fr. Yiddish *shames* shammes; prob. fr. a jocular comparison of the duties of a sexton and those of a store detective] **1** *slang* : POLICEMAN **2** *slang* : a private detective
Shan \'shän, 'shan\ *n, pl* **Shan** *or* **Shans** **1 a** : a group of Mongoloid peoples of southeastern Asia **b** : a member of any of these peoples **2** : the Thai languages of the Shan
shan·dry·dan \'shan-drē-,dan\ *n* [origin unknown] **1** : a chaise with a hood **2** : a rickety vehicle
shan·dy \'shan-dē\ *n, pl* **shandies** **1** : SHANDYGAFF **2** : a drink consisting of beer and lemonade
shan·dy·gaff \'shan-dē-,gaf\ *n* [origin unknown] : a drink consisting of beer and ginger beer or ginger ale
shang·hai \shaŋ-'hī\ *vt* **shang·haied; shang·hai·ing** [*Shanghai,* China; fr. the formerly widespread use of this method to secure sailors for voyages to the Orient] **1 a** : to put aboard a ship by force often with the help of liquor or a drug **b** : to put by force or threat of force into or as if into a place of detention **2** : to put by trickery into an undesirable position — **shang·hai·er** \-'hī(-ə)r\ *n*
Shan·gri–la \,shaŋ-gri-'lä\ *n* [*Shangri-La,* imaginary land depicted in the novel *Lost Horizon* (1933) by James Hilton] **1** : a remote beautiful imaginary place where life approaches perfection : UTOPIA **2** : a remote usu. idyllic hideaway
[1]**shank** \'shaŋk\ *n* [ME *shanke,* fr. OE *scanca;* akin to ON *skakkr* crooked, Gk *skazein* to limp] **1 a** : the part of the leg between the knee and the ankle in man or the corresponding part in various other vertebrates **b** : LEG **c** : a cut of beef, veal, mutton, or lamb from the upper or the lower part of the leg : SHIN — see BEEF illustration **2** : a straight narrow usu. essential part of an object: as **a** : the straight part of a nail or pin **b** : a straight part of a plant : STEM, STALK **c** : the part of an anchor between the ring and the crown **d** : the part of a fishhook between the eye and the bend **e** : the part of a key between the handle and the bit **f** : the stem of a tobacco pipe or the part between the stem and the bowl **g** : TANG 1 **h** (1) : the narrow part of the sole of a shoe beneath the instep (2) : SHANKPIECE **3** : a part of an object by which it can be attached: as **a** (1) : a projection on the back of a solid button (2) : a short stem of thread that holds a sewn button away from the cloth **b** : the projecting part of a knob handle that contains the spindle socket **c** : the end (as of a drill) that is gripped in a chuck **4** : BODY 7 **5 a** : the latter part of a period of time **b** : the early or main part of a period of time — **shanked** \'shaŋ(k)t\ *adj*
[2]**shank** *vt* : to hit (a golf ball) with the extreme heel of the club so that the ball goes sharply to the right
shank·piece \'shaŋk-,pēs\ *n* : a support for the arch of the foot inserted in the shank of a shoe
shan't \(')shant, (')shȧnt\ : shall not
shantey *or* **shanty** *var of* CHANTEY
shan·tung \(')shan-'təŋ\ *n* [*Shantung,* China] : a fabric in plain weave having a slightly irregular surface due to uneven slubbed filling yarns
shan·ty \'shant-ē\ *n, pl* **shanties** [CanF *chantier,* fr. F, gantry, fr. L *cantherius* trellis] : a small crudely built dwelling or shelter usu. of wood
shan·ty·man \-ē-mən, -,man\ *n* : one who lives in a shanty
shan·ty·town \-,taün\ *n* : a town or section of a town consisting mostly of shanties
shap·able *or* **shape·able** \'shā-pə-bəl\ *adj* **1** : capable of being shaped **2** : SHAPELY
[1]**shape** \'shāp\ *vb* **shaped; shap·ing** [ME *shapen,* alter. of OE *scieppan;* akin to OHG *skepfen* to shape] *vt* **1** : FORM, CREATE; *esp* : to give a particular form or shape to **2** *obs* : ORDAIN, DECREE **3** : to adapt in shape so as to fit neatly and closely <a dress *shaped* to her figure> **4 a** : DEVISE, PLAN **b** : to embody in definite form <*shaping* a folktale into an epic> **5 a** : to make fit for (as a particular use or purpose) : ADAPT **b** : to determine or direct the course of (as life) **c** : to modify (behavior) by rewarding changes that tend toward a desired response ~ *vi* **1** : HAPPEN, BEFALL <if things ~ right> **2** : to take on or approach a mature form (as in proficiency) — often used with *up* ***syn*** see MAKE — **shap·er** *n*
[2]**shape** *n* **1 a** : the visible makeup characteristic of a particular item or kind of item **b** (1) : spatial form (2) : a standard or universally recognized spatial form **2** : the appearance of the body as distinguished from that of the face : FIGURE **3 a** : PHANTOM, APPARITION **b** : assumed appearance : GUISE **4** : form of embodiment **5** : a mode of existence or form of being having identifying features **6** : something having a particular form **7** : the condition in which someone or something exists at a particular time <in excellent ~ for his age> ***syn*** see FORM — **shaped** \shāpt\ *adj* — **in shape** : in an original, normal, or fit condition <exercises to keep *in shape*>
shape·less \'shā-pləs\ *adj* **1** : having no definite shape **2 a** : deprived of usual or normal shape : MISSHAPEN <a ~ old hat> **b** : not shapely — **shape·less·ly** *adv* — **shape·less·ness** *n*
shape·ly \'shā-plē\ *adj* **shape·li·er; -est** : having a regular or pleasing shape — **shape·li·ness** *n*
shap·en \'shā-pən\ *adj* [archaic pp. of *shape*] : fashioned in or provided with a definite shape — usu. used in combination <an ill-*shapen* body>
shape note *n* : one of a system of seven notes showing the musical scale degree by the shape of the note head
shape–up \'shā-,pəp\ *n* : a system of hiring workers and esp. longshoremen by the day or shift by having applicants gather usu. in a semicircle for selection by a union-appointed hiring boss; *also* : an instance of such hiring practice
shard \'shärd\ *also* **sherd** \'shərd\ *n* [ME, fr. OE *sceard;* akin to OE *scieran* to cut — more at SHEAR] **1 a** : a piece or fragment of a brittle substance; *broadly* : a small piece **b** : SHELL, SCALE; *esp* : ELYTRON **2** *usu sherd* : fragments of pottery vessels found on sites and in refuse deposits where pottery-making peoples have lived **3** : highly angular curved glass fragments of tuffaceous sediments
[1]**share** \'she(ə)r, 'sha(ə)r\ *n* [ME, fr. OE *scearu* cutting, tonsure; akin to OE *scieran* to cut — more at SHEAR] **1 a** : a portion

ə abut	ᵊ kitten	ər further	a back	ā bake	ä cot, cart
aù out	ch chin	e less	ē easy	g gift	i trip	ī life
j joke	ŋ sing	ō flow	ȯ flaw	ȯi coin	th thin	th this
ü loot	ù foot	y yet	yü few	yù furious	zh vision

belonging to, due to, or contributed by an individual **b :** one's full or fair portion **2 a :** the part allotted or belonging to one of a number owning together property or interest **b :** any of the equal portions into which property or invested capital is divided; *specif* **:** any of the equal interests or rights into which the entire capital stock of a corporation is divided and ownership of which is regularly evidenced by one or more certificates **c** *pl, chiefly Brit* **:** STOCK 7c(1)

[2]**share** *vb* **shared; shar·ing** *vt* **1 :** to divide and distribute in shares **:** APPORTION — usu. used with *out* or *with* **2 :** to partake of, use, experience, or enjoy with others **3 :** to grant or give a share in ~ *vi* **1 :** to have a share — used with *in* **2 :** to apportion and take shares of something — **shar·er** *n*

syn SHARE, PARTICIPATE, PARTAKE *shared meaning element* **:** to have, get, or use in common with another or others

[3]**share** *n* [ME *schare,* fr. OE *scear;* akin to OHG *scaro* plowshare, OE *scieran* to cut] **:** PLOWSHARE

share·able *or* **shar·able** \ˈsher-ə-bəl, ˈshar-\ *adj* **:** capable of being shared — **share·abil·i·ty** \ˌsher-ə-ˈbil-ət-ē, ˌshar-\ *n*

share·crop \ˈshe(ə)r-ˌkräp, ˈsha(ə)r-\ *vb* [back-formation fr. *sharecropper*] *vi* **:** to farm as a sharecropper ~ *vt* **:** to farm (land) or produce (a crop) as a sharecropper

share·crop·per \-ˌkräp-ər\ *n* **:** a tenant farmer esp. in the southern U.S. who is provided with credit for seed, tools, living quarters, and food, works the land, and receives an agreed share of the value of the crop minus charges

share·hold·er \-ˌhōl-dər\ *n* **:** one that holds or owns a share in property; *esp* **:** STOCKHOLDER

sha·rif \shə-ˈrēf\ *n* [Ar *sharīf,* lit., illustrious] **:** a descendant of the prophet Muhammad through his daughter Fatima; *broadly* **:** one of noble ancestry or political preeminence in predominantly Islamic countries — **sha·rif·ian** \-ˈrē-fē-ən\ *adj*

[1]**shark** \ˈshärk\ *n* [origin unknown] **:** any of numerous mostly marine elasmobranch fishes of medium to large size that have a fusiform body, lateral branchial clefts, and a tough usu. dull gray skin roughened by minute tubercles, are typically active predators sometimes dangerous to man, and are of economic importance esp. for their large livers which are a source of oil and for their hides from which leather is made

[2]**shark** *n* [prob. modif. of G *schurke* scoundrel] **1 :** a rapacious crafty person who preys upon others through usury, extortion, or trickery **2 :** one who excels greatly esp. in a particular field

[3]**shark** *vt* **1** *archaic* **:** to gather hastily **2** *archaic* **:** to obtain by some irregular means ~ *vi* **1** *archaic* **:** to practice fraud or trickery **2** *archaic* **:** SNEAK

shark·skin \ˈshärk-ˌskin\ *n* **1 :** the hide of a shark or leather made from it **2 a :** a smooth durable woolen or worsted suiting in twill or basket weave with small woven designs **b :** a smooth crisp fabric with a dull finish made usu. of rayon in basket weave

shark sucker *n* **:** REMORA 1

[1]**sharp** \ˈshärp\ *adj* [ME, fr. OE *scearp;* akin to OE *scieran* to cut — more at SHEAR] **1 :** adapted to cutting or piercing: as **a :** having a thin keen edge or fine point **b :** briskly or bitingly cold **:** NIPPING <a ~ wind> **c :** composed of hard angular particles **:** GRITTY <~ sand> **2 a :** keen in intellect **:** QUICK-WITTED **b :** keen in perception **:** ACUTE <~ sight> **c :** keen in attention **:** VIGILANT <keep a ~ lookout> **d :** keen in attention to one's own interest sometimes to the point of being unethical <a ~ trader> **3 :** keen in spirit or action: as **a :** full of activity or energy **:** BRISK <~ blows> **b :** capable of acting or reacting strongly; *esp* **:** CAUSTIC **4 :** SEVERE, HARSH: as **a :** inclined to or marked by irritability or anger <a ~ temper> **b :** causing intense mental or physical distress <a ~ pain> **c :** cutting in language or import <a ~ rebuke> **5 :** affecting the senses or sense organs intensely: as **a** (1) **:** having a strong odor or flavor <~ cheese> (2) **:** ACRID **b :** having a strong piercing sound **c :** having the effect of or involving a sudden brilliant display of light <a ~ flash> **6 a :** terminating in a point or edge <~ features> **b :** involving an abrupt change in direction <a ~ turn> **c :** clear in outline or detail **:** DISTINCT <a ~ image> **d :** set forth with clarity and distinctness <~ contrast> **7 a** *of a tone* **:** raised a half step in pitch **b :** higher than the proper pitch **c :** MAJOR, AUGMENTED — used of an interval in music **8 :** STYLISH, DRESSY — **sharp·ly** *adv* — **sharp·ness** *n*

syn SHARP, KEEN, ACUTE *shared meaning element* **:** possessing or indicative of alert competence and clear understanding *ant* dull, blunt

[2]**sharp** *vt* **:** to raise (as a musical tone) in pitch; *esp* **:** to raise in pitch by a half step ~ *vi* **:** to sing or play above the proper pitch

[3]**sharp** *adv* **1 :** in a sharp manner **:** SHARPLY **2 :** EXACTLY, PRECISELY <4 o'clock ~>

[4]**sharp** *n* **:** one that is sharp: as **a :** a sharp edge or point **b** (1) **:** a musical note or tone one half step higher than a note or tone named (2) **:** a character on a line or space of the musical staff indicating a pitch a half step higher than the degree would indicate without it **c :** a long sewing needle with sharp point **d :** a real or self-styled expert; *also* **:** SHARPER

sharp b(2)

sharp·en \ˈshär-pən\ *vb* **sharp·ened; sharp·en·ing** \ˈshärp-(ə-)niŋ\ *vt* **:** to make sharp or sharper ~ *vi* **:** to grow or become sharp or sharper — **sharp·en·er** \ˈshärp-(ə-)nər\ *n*

sharp·er \ˈshär-pər\ *n* **:** CHEAT, SWINDLER; *esp* **:** a cheating gambler

sharp–eyed \ˈshär-ˈpīd\ *adj* **:** having keen sight; *also* **:** keen in observing or penetrating

sharp–fanged \ˈshärp-ˈfaŋd\ *adj* **1 :** having sharp teeth **2 :** SARCASTIC

sharp–freeze \-ˈfrēz\ *vt* **:** QUICK-FREEZE

sharp·ie *or* **sharpy** \ˈshär-pē\ *n, pl* **sharp·ies** [[1]*sharp*] **1 :** a long narrow shallow-draft boat with flat or slightly V-shaped bottom and one or two masts that bear a triangular sail **2 a :** SHARPER **b :** an exceptionally keen or alert person

sharp–nosed \ˈshärp-ˈnōzd\ *adj* **1 :** having a pointed nose or snout **2 :** keen in smelling

sharp practice *n* **:** the act of dealing in which advantage is taken or sought unscrupulously

sharp–set \ˈshärp-ˈset\ *adj* **1 :** set at a sharp angle or so as to present a sharp edge **2 :** eager in appetite or desire — **sharp–set·ness** *n*

sharp–shinned hawk \ˌshärp-ˌshind-\ *n* **:** a common widely distributed No. American bird-eating hawk (*Accipiter striatus*) with a long square-tipped tail and short rounded wings

sharp·shoot·er \ˈshärp-ˌshüt-ər\ *n* **:** a good marksman

sharp·shoot·ing \-ˌshüt-iŋ\ *n* **1 :** shooting with great precision **2 :** accurate and usu. unexpected attack (as in words)

sharp–sight·ed \-ˈsīt-əd\ *adj* **1 :** having acute sight **2 :** mentally keen or alert — **sharp–sight·ed·ly** *adv* — **sharp–sight·ed·ness** *n*

sharp–tongued \-ˈtəŋd\ *adj* **:** having a sharp tongue **:** harsh or bitter in speech <a ~ shrew>

sharp–wit·ted \-ˈwit-əd\ *adj* **:** having or showing an acute mind

shash·lik *also* **shash·lick** *or* **shas·lik** \shäsh-ˈlik, ˈshäsh-lik\ *n* [Russ *shashlyk,* of Turkic origin; akin to Kazan Tatar *šyšlyk* kabob] **:** KABOB

[1]**shat·ter** \ˈshat-ər\ *vb* [ME *schateren*] *vt* **1 :** to cause to drop or be dispersed **2 a :** to break at once into pieces **b :** to damage badly **:** RUIN **3 :** to cause the disruption or annihilation of **:** DEMOLISH ~ *vi* **1 :** to break apart **:** DISINTEGRATE **2 :** to drop off parts (as leaves, petals, or fruit) <the wheat ~*ed* in the fields> — **shat·ter·ing·ly** \-ə-riŋ-lē\ *adv*

[2]**shatter** *n* **1 :** FRAGMENT, SHRED <the broken vase lay in ~*s*> **2 :** an act of shattering **:** the state of being shattered **3 :** a result of shattering **:** SHOWER

shatter cone *n* **:** a conical fragment of rock that has striations radiating from the apex and that is formed by high pressure (as from volcanism or meteorite impact)

shat·ter·proof \ˌshat-ər-ˈprüf\ *adj* **:** proof against shattering

[1]**shave** \ˈshāv\ *vb* **shaved; shaved** *or* **shav·en** \ˈshā-vən\; **shav·ing** [ME *shaven,* fr. OE *scafan;* akin to L *scabere* to shave, *capo* capon] *vt* **1 a :** to remove a thin layer from **b :** to cut off in thin layers or shreds **:** SLICE **c :** to cut off closely **2 a :** to sever the hair from (the head or another part of the body) close to the roots **b :** to cut off (hair or beard) close to the skin **3 a :** to discount (a note) at an exorbitant rate **b :** DEDUCT, REDUCE **4 :** to come close to or touch lightly in passing ~ *vi* **1 :** to cut off hair or beard close to the skin **2 :** to proceed with difficulty **:** SCRAPE

[2]**shave** *n* **1 :** SHAVER 3 **2 :** a thin slice **:** SHAVING **3 :** an act or process of shaving **4 :** an act of passing very near to so as almost to graze

shave·ling \ˈshāv-liŋ\ *n* **1 :** a tonsured clergyman **:** PRIEST — usu. used disparagingly **2 :** STRIPLING

shav·er \ˈshā-vər\ *n* **1 :** a person who shaves **2** *archaic* **:** SWINDLER **3 :** a tool or machine for shaving; *specif* **:** an electric-powered razor **4 :** BOY, YOUNGSTER

shaves *pl of* SHAFT

shave·tail \ˈshāv-ˌtāl\ *n* [fr. the practice of shaving the tails of newly broken mules to distinguish them from untrained ones] **1 :** a pack mule esp. when newly broken in **2 :** SECOND LIEUTENANT — usu. used disparagingly

Sha·vi·an \ˈshā-vē-ən\ *n* [NL *Shavius,* latinized form of George Bernard *Shaw*] **:** an admirer or devotee of G. B. Shaw, his writings, or his social and political theories — **Shavian** *adj*

shav·ie \ˈshā-vē\ *n* [*shave* (swindle) + *-ie*] *Scot* **:** PRANK

shav·ing \ˈshā-viŋ\ *n* **1 :** the act of one that shaves **2 :** something shaved off <wood ~*s*>

[1]**shaw** \ˈshȯ\ *n* [ME, fr. OE *sceaga;* akin to ON *skegg* beard — more at SHAG] *dial* **:** COPPICE, THICKET

[2]**shaw** *n* [prob. alter. of *show*] *chiefly Brit* **:** the tops and stalks of a cultivated crop (as potatoes or turnips)

[1]**shawl** \ˈshȯl\ *n* [Per *shāl*] **:** a square or oblong usu. fabric garment or wrapper used esp. as a covering for the head or shoulders

[2]**shawl** *vt* **:** to wrap in or as if in a shawl

shawl collar *n* **:** an attached collar rolled back in a continuous tapering line that follows the surplice neckline of a garment

shawm \ˈshȯm\ *n* [ME *schalme,* fr. MF *chalemie,* modif. of LL *calamellus,* dim. of L *calamus* reed, fr. Gk *kalamos* — more at HAULM] **:** an early double-reed woodwind instrument

Shaw·nee \shȯ-ˈnē, shä-\ *n, pl* **Shawnee** *or* **Shawnees** [back-formation fr. obs. E *Shawnese,* fr. Shawnee *Shaawanwaaki*] **1 :** a member of an Amerindian people orig. of the central Ohio valley **2 :** the language of the Shawnee people

Shaw·wal \shə-ˈwäl\ *n* [Ar *shawwāl*] **:** the 10th month of the Muhammadan year — see MONTH table

shay \ˈshā\ *n* [back-formation fr. *chaise,* taken as pl.] *chiefly dial* **:** CHAISE 1

[1]**she** \(ˈ)shē\ *pron* [ME, prob. alter. of *hye* alter. of OE *hēo* she — more at HE] **1 :** that female one who is neither speaker nor hearer <~ is my wife> — compare HE, HER, HERS, IT, THEY **2** — used to refer to one regarded as feminine (as by personification) <~ was a fine ship>

[2]**she** \ˈshē\ *n* **:** a female person or animal — often used in combination <*she*-cat> <*she*-cousin>

shea butter \ˈshē-, ˈshā-\ *n* **:** a pale solid fat from the seeds of the shea tree used in food, soap, and candles

sheaf \ˈshēf\ *n, pl* **sheaves** \ˈshēvz\ [ME *sheef,* fr. OE *scēaf;* akin to OHG *scoub* sheaf, Russ *chub* forelock] **1 :** a quantity of the stalks and ears of a cereal grass or sometimes other plant material bound together **2 :** something resembling a sheaf of grain <a ~ of papers> — **sheaf·like** \ˈshē-ˌflīk\ *adj*

shea nut *n* **:** the seed of the shea tree

[1]**shear** \ˈshi(ə)r\ *vb* **sheared; sheared** *or* **shorn** \ˈshō(ə)rn, ˈshȯ(ə)rn\; **shear·ing** [ME *sheren,* fr. OE *scieran;* akin to ON *skera* to cut, L *curtus* shortened, Gk *keirein* to cut, shear] *vt* **1 a :** to cut off the hair from <with crown *shorn*> **b :** to cut or clip (as

hair or wool) from someone or something; *also* : to cut something from <~ a lawn> **c** *chiefly Scot* : to reap with a sickle **d** : to cut with shears or a similar instrument **2** : to cut with something sharp **3** : to deprive of something as if by cutting **4 a** : to subject to a shear force **b** : to cause (as a rock mass) to move along the plane of contact ~ *vi* **1** : to cut through something with or as if with a sharp instrument **2** *chiefly Scot* : to reap crops with a sickle **3** : to become divided under the action of a shear <the bolt may ~ off> — **shear·er** *n*

[2]**shear** *n* **1 a** (1) : a cutting implement similar or identical to a pair of scissors but typically larger — usu. used in pl. (2) : one blade of a pair of shears **b** : any of various cutting tools or machines operating by the action of opposed cutting edges of metal — usu. used in pl. **c** (1) : something resembling a shear or a pair of shears (2) : a hoisting apparatus consisting of two or sometimes more upright spars fastened together at their upper ends and having tackle for masting or dismasting ships or lifting heavy loads (as guns) — usu. used in pl. but sing. or pl. in constr. **2** *chiefly Brit* : the action or process or an instance of shearing — used in combination to indicate the approximate age of sheep in terms of shearings undergone **3 a** : internal force tangential to the section on which it acts — called also *shearing force* **b** : an action or stress resulting from applied forces that causes or tends to cause two contiguous parts of a body to slide relatively to each other in a direction parallel to their plane of contact

sheared *adj* : formed or finished by shearing; *esp* : cut to uniform length <a ~ raccoon coat>

shearing force *n* : SHEAR 3a

shear pin *n* : an easily replaceable pin inserted at a critical point in a machine and designed to break when subjected to excess stress

shear·wa·ter \ˈshi(ə)r-ˌwȯt-ər, -ˌwät-\ *n* : any of numerous oceanic birds (esp. genus *Puffinus*) that are related to the petrels and albatrosses and usu. skim close to the waves in flight

sheat·fish \ˈshēt-ˌfish\ *n* [alter. of *sheathfish*, fr. *sheath* + *fish*] : a large catfish (*Silurus glanis*) of central and eastern Europe

sheath \ˈshēth\ *n, pl* **sheaths** \ˈshēt͟hz, ˈshēths\ [ME *shethe*, fr. OE *scēath*; akin to OHG *sceida* sheath, L *scindere* to cut — more at SHED] **1** : a case for a blade (as of a knife) **2** : an investing cover or case of a plant or animal body or body part: as **a** : the tubular fold of skin into which the penis of many mammals is retracted **b** (1) : the lower part of a leaf (as of a grass) when surrounding the stem (2) : an ensheathing spathe **3** : any of various covering or supporting structures that are applied like or resemble the sheath of a blade: as **a** : SHEATHING 2 **b** : a woman's close-fitting dress usu. worn without a belt

sheath·bill \ˈshēth-ˌbil\ *n* : any of several white shore birds (family Chionididae) of colder parts of the southern hemisphere that have a horny sheath over the base of the upper mandible and suggest the pigeons in general appearance

sheathe \ˈshēt͟h\ *also* **sheath** \ˈshēth\ *vt* **sheathed; sheath·ing** [ME *shethen*, fr. *shethe* sheath] **1** : to put into or furnish with a sheath **2** : to plunge or bury (as a sword) in flesh **3** : to withdraw (a claw) into a sheath **4** : to case or cover with something (as sheets of metal) that protects — **sheath·er** *n*

sheath·ing \ˈshē-t͟hiŋ, -thiŋ\ *n* **1** : the action of one that sheathes something **2** : material used to sheathe something; *esp* : the first covering of boards or of waterproof material on the outside wall of a frame house or on a timber roof

sheath knife *n* : a knife having a fixed blade and designed to be carried in a sheath

shea tree \ˈshē-, ˈshā-\ *n* [Bambara *si*] : a tropical African tree (*Butyrospermum parkii*) of the sapodilla family with fatty nuts that yield shea butter

[1]**sheave** \ˈshiv, ˈshēv\ *n* [ME *sheve*; akin to OE *scēath* sheath] : a grooved wheel or pulley (as of a pulley block)

[2]**sheave** \ˈshēv\ *vt* **sheaved; sheav·ing** [*sheaf*] : to gather and bind into a sheaf

she·bang \shi-ˈbaŋ\ *n* [perh. alter. of *shebeen*] : CONTRIVANCE, AFFAIR, CONCERN <he's head of the whole ~>

She·bat \shə-ˈbät, -ˈvät\ *n* [Heb *shĕbhāṭ*] : the 5th month of the civil year or the 11th month of the ecclesiastical year in the Jewish calendar — see MONTH table

she·been \shə-ˈbēn\ *n* [IrGael *sībín* bad ale] *chiefly Irish* : an unlicensed or illegally operated drinking establishment

She·chi·nah \shə-ˈke̲-nə, -ˈkē-nə, -ˈkī-nə\ *n* [Heb *shĕkhīnāh*] : the presence of God in the world as conceived in Jewish theology

[1]**shed** \ˈshed\ *vb* **shed; shed·ding** [ME *sheden* to divide, separate, fr. OE *scēadan*; akin to OHG *skeidan* to separate, L *scindere* to cut, split, Gk *schizein* to split] *vt* **1** *chiefly dial* : to set apart : SEGREGATE **2** : to cause to be dispersed without penetrating <duck's plumage ~*s* water> **3 a** : to cause (blood) to flow by cutting or wounding **b** : to pour forth in drops <~ tears> **c** : to give off in a stream <fish *shedding* their eggs in spawning> **d** : to give off or out <his book ~*s* some light on this subject> **4 a** (1) : to cast off (as a body covering) : MOLT (2) : to let fall (as leaves) (3) : to eject (as seed or spores) from a natural receptacle **b** : to rid oneself of temporarily or permanently as superfluous or unwanted ~ *vi* **1** : to pour out : SPILL **2** : to become dispersed : SCATTER **3** : to cast off some natural covering <the cat is *shedding*> ***syn*** see DISCARD — **shed blood** : to cause death by violence

[2]**shed** *n* **1** *obs* : DISTINCTION, DIFFERENCE **2** : something (as the skin of a snake) that is discarded in shedding **3** : a divide of land

[3]**shed** *n* [alter. of earlier *shadde*, prob. fr. ME *shade*] **1 a** : a slight structure built for shelter or storage; *esp* : a single-storied building with one or more sides unenclosed **b** : a building held to resemble a shed **2** *archaic* : HUT

[4]**shed** *vt* **shed·ded; shed·ding** : to put or house in a shed

she'd \(ˌ)shēd\ : she had : she would

shed·der \ˈshed-ər\ *n* : one that sheds something: as **a** : a crab or lobster about to molt **b** : a newly molted crab

shed dormer *n* : a dormer with a roof sloping in the same direction as the roof from which the dormer projects

[1]**sheen** \ˈshēn\ *adj* [ME *shene*, fr. OE *sciene*; akin to OE *scēawian* to look — more at SHOW] **1** *archaic* : BEAUTIFUL **2** *archaic* : SHINING, RESPLENDENT

[2]**sheen** *vi* : to be bright : show a sheen

[3]**sheen** *n* **1 a** : a bright or shining condition : BRIGHTNESS **b** : a subdued glitter approaching but short of optical reflection **c** : a lustrous surface imparted to textiles through finishing processes or use of shiny yarns **2** : a textile exhibiting notable sheen — **sheeny** \ˈshē-nē\ *adj*

sheep \ˈshēp\ *n, pl* **sheep** *often attrib* [ME, fr. OE *scēap*; akin to OHG *scāf* sheep] **1** : any of numerous ruminant mammals (genus *Ovis*) related to the goats but stockier and lacking a beard in the male; *specif* : one (*O. aries*) long domesticated esp. for its flesh and wool **2 a** : a timid defenseless creature **b** : a stupid docile person; *esp* : one easily influenced or led **3** : leather prepared from the skins of sheep : SHEEPSKIN

sheep·ber·ry \-ˌber-ē\ *n* : an often shrubby No. American viburnum (*Viburnum lentago*) with white flowers in flat cymes; *also* : its black edible berry

sheep·cote \-ˌkōt, -ˌkät\ *n, chiefly Brit* : SHEEPFOLD

sheep–dip \-ˌdip\ *n* : a liquid preparation of toxic chemicals into which sheep are plunged esp. to destroy parasitic arthropods

sheep dog *n* : a dog used to tend, drive, or guard sheep

sheep fescue *n* : a hardy fine-foliaged European perennial grass (*Festuca ovina*) widely used as a lawn grass

sheep·fold \ˈshēp-ˌfōld\ *n* : a pen or shelter for sheep

sheep·herd·er \ˈshēp-ˌhərd-ər\ *n* : a worker in charge of sheep esp. on open range

sheep·herd·ing \-ˌhərd-iŋ\ *n* : the activities of a worker engaged in tending sheep

sheep·ish \ˈshē-pish\ *adj* **1** : resembling a sheep in meekness, stupidity, or timidity **2** : embarrassed by consciousness of a fault <a ~ look> — **sheep·ish·ly** *adv* — **sheep·ish·ness** *n*

sheep ked \ˈshēp-ˌked\ *n* [*sheep* + *ked* (sheep ked), of unknown origin] : a wingless bloodsucking dipterous fly (*Melophagus ovinus*) that feeds chiefly on sheep and is a vector of sheep trypanosomiasis — called also *sheep tick*

sheep laurel *n* : a No. American dwarf shrub (*Kalmia angustifolia*) that is poisonous to young stock and resembles mountain laurel but has narrower leaves and smaller bright red flowers — called also *lambkill*

sheep's eye *n* : a shy, longing, and usu. amorous glance — usu. used in pl.

sheep·shank \ˈshēp-ˌshaŋk\ *n* **1** : a knot for shortening a line — see KNOT illustration **2** *Scot* : something of no worth or importance

sheeps·head \ˈshēps-ˌhed\ *n* **1** : a marine percoid food fish (*Archosargus probatocephalus* of the family Sparidae) of the Atlantic and Gulf coasts of the U.S. with broad incisor teeth **2** : a large croaker (*Aplodinotus grunniens*) of the Great Lakes and Mississippi valley **3** : a common largely red or rose California wrasse (*Pimelometopon pulchrum*)

sheep·shear·er \ˈshēp-ˌshir-ər\ *n* : one that shears sheep

sheep·shear·ing \ˈshēp-ˌshi(ə)r-iŋ\ *n* **1** : the act of shearing sheep **2** : the time or season for shearing sheep; *also* : a festival held at this time

sheep·skin \-ˌskin\ *n* **1 a** : the skin of a sheep; *also* : leather prepared from it **b** : PARCHMENT **c** : a garment made of or lined with sheepskin **2** : DIPLOMA

sheep sorrel *n* : a small acid dock (*Rumex acetosella*)

sheep walk *n, chiefly Brit* : a pasture or range for sheep

[1]**sheer** \ˈshi(ə)r\ *adj* [ME *schere* freed from guilt, prob. alter. of *skere*, fr. ON *skærr* pure; akin to OE *scīnan* to shine] **1** *obs* : BRIGHT, SHINING **2** : of very thin or transparent texture : DIAPHANOUS **3 a** : UNQUALIFIED, UTTER <~ folly> <~ ignorance> **b** : being free from an adulterant : PURE, UNMIXED **c** : viewed or acting in dissociation from all else <won through by ~ determination> **4** : marked by great and unrelieved steepness ***syn*** see STEEP — **sheer·ly** *adv* — **sheer·ness** *n*

[2]**sheer** *adv* **1** : in a complete manner : ALTOGETHER **2** : straight up or down without a break : PERPENDICULARLY

[3]**sheer** *vb* [perh. alter. of [1]*shear*] *vi* : to deviate from a course : SWERVE ~ *vt* : to cause to sheer

[4]**sheer** *n* **1** : a turn, deviation, or change in a course (as of a ship) **2** : the position of a ship riding to a single anchor and heading toward it

[5]**sheer** *n* [perh. alter. of [2]*shear*] : the fore-and-aft curvature from bow to stern of a ship's deck as shown in side elevation

sheer·legs \ˈshi(ə)r-ˌlegz, -ˌlāgz\ *n pl but sing or pl in constr* : SHEAR 1c(2)

[1]**sheet** \ˈshēt\ *n* [ME *shete*, fr. OE *scȳte*; akin to OE *scēotan* to shoot — more at SHOOT] **1 a** : a broad piece of cloth; *esp* : an oblong of usu. linen or cotton cloth used as an article of bedding **b** : SAIL 1a(1) **2 a** (1) : a usu. rectangular piece of paper; *esp* : one manufactured for printing (2) : a rectangular piece of heavy paper with a plant specimen mounted on it <an herbarium of 100,000 ~*s*> **b** : a printed signature for a book esp. before it has been folded, cut, or bound — usu. used in pl. **c** : a newspaper, periodical, or occasional publication <a gossip ~> **d** : the unseparated postage stamps printed by one impression of a plate on a single piece of paper; *also* : a pane of stamps **3** : a broad stretch or surface of something <a ~ of ice> **4** : a suspended or moving expanse (as of fire or rain) **5 a** : a portion of something that is thin in comparison to its length and breadth **b** : a flat baking utensil of tinned metal <a cookie ~> **6** : a surface or part of a surface in which it is possible to pass from any one point of it to

any other without leaving the surface <a hyperboloid of two ~*s*> — **sheet·like** \-ˌlīk\ *adj*
[2]**sheet** *vt* **1 :** to cover with a sheet : SHROUD **2 :** to furnish with sheets **3 :** to form into sheets ~ *vi* : to fall, spread, or flow in a sheet <the rain ~*ed* against the windows> — **sheet·er** *n* — **sheet home 1 :** to extend (a sail) and set as flat as possible by hauling upon the sheets **2 :** to fix the responsibility for : bring home to one
[3]**sheet** *adj* **1 :** rolled or spread out in a sheet **2 :** of, relating to, or concerned with the making of sheet metal
[4]**sheet** *n* [ME *shete,* fr. OE *scēata* lower corner of a sail; akin to OE *scӯte* sheet] **1 :** a rope or chain that regulates the angle at which a sail is set in relation to the wind **2** *pl* **:** the spaces at either end of an open boat not occupied by thwarts : foresheets and stern sheets together — **three sheets in the wind** *or* **three sheets to the wind :** DRUNK
sheet anchor *n* **1 :** a large strong anchor formerly carried in the waist of a ship and used as a spare in an emergency **2 :** something that constitutes a main support or dependence esp. in danger
sheet bend *n* **:** a bend or hitch used for temporarily fastening a rope to the bight of another rope or to an eye — see KNOT illustration
sheet·fed \ˈshēt-ˌfed\ *adj* **:** of, relating to, or printed by a press that prints on paper in sheet form
sheet glass *n* **:** glass made in large sheets directly from the furnace or by making a cylinder and then flattening it
sheet·ing \ˈshēt-iŋ\ *n* **1 :** material in the form of sheets or suitable for forming into sheets **2 :** a lining (as wood or steel) used to support an embankment or the walls of an excavation
sheet lightning *n* **:** lightning in diffused or sheet form due to reflection and diffusion by the clouds and sky
sheet metal *n* **:** metal in the form of a sheet
sheet music *n* **:** music printed on large unbound sheets of paper
Sheet·rock \ˈshēt-ˌräk\ *trademark* — used for plasterboard
sheikh *or* **sheik** \ˈshēk, *also* ˈshāk *for 1*\ *n* [Ar *shaykh*] **1 :** an Arab chief **2** *usu sheik* **:** a man held to be irresistibly attractive to romantic young women
sheikh·dom *or* **sheik·dom** \-dəm, -təm\ *n* **:** a region under the rule of a sheikh
shek·el \ˈshek-əl\ *n* [Heb *sheqel*] **1 a :** any of various ancient units of weight; *esp* **:** a Hebrew unit equal to about 252 grains troy **b :** a unit of value based on a shekel weight of gold or silver **2 :** a coin weighing one shekel **3** *pl* **:** MONEY
Shekinah *var of* SHECHINAH
shel·drake \ˈshel-ˌdrāk\ *n* [ME, fr. *sheld-* (akin to MD *schillede* parti-colored) + *drake*] **1 :** any of various Old World ducks (genus *Tadorna*); *esp* **:** a common mostly black-and-white European duck (*T. tadorna*) slightly larger than the mallard **2 :** MERGANSER
shel·duck \-ˌdək\ *n* [*shel-* (as in *sheldrake*) + *duck*] **:** SHELDRAKE
shelf \ˈshelf\ *n, pl* **shelves** \ˈshelvz\ [ME, prob. fr. OE *scylfe;* akin to L *scalpere, sculpere* to carve, OE *sciell* shell] **1 a :** a thin flat usu. long and narrow piece of material (as wood) fastened horizontally (as on a wall) at a distance from the floor to hold objects **b :** one of several similar pieces in a closet, bookcase, or similar structure **c :** the contents of a shelf **2 :** something resembling a shelf in form or position: as **a :** a sandbank or ledge of rocks usu. partially submerged **b :** a stratum with a shelflike surface **c :** a flat projecting layer of rock **d :** the submerged border of a continent or island : CONTINENTAL SHELF — **shelf·ful** \ˈshelf-ˌfu̇l\ *n* — **shelf·like** \ˈshel-ˌflīk\ *adj* — **off the shelf :** available from stock : not made to order <*off the shelf* equipment> — **on the shelf :** in a state of inactivity or uselessness
shelf ice *n* **:** an extensive ice sheet originating on land but continuing out to sea beyond the depths at which it rests on the sea bottom
shelf life *n* **:** the period of time during which a material may be stored and remain suitable for use
[1]**shell** \ˈshel\ *n* [ME, fr. OE *sciell;* akin to OE *scealu* shell, ON *skel,* L *silex* pebble, flint, Gk *skallein* to hoe] **1 a :** a hard rigid usu. largely calcareous covering of an animal **b :** the hard or tough outer covering of an egg esp. of a bird — see EGG illustration **2 :** the covering or outside part of a fruit or seed esp. when hard or fibrous **3 :** shell material (as of mollusks or turtles) or their substance **4 :** something that resembles a shell: as **a :** a framework or exterior structure; *esp* **:** a building with an unfinished interior **b :** an external case or outside covering <the ~ of a ship> **c :** a casing without substance <mere effigies and ~*s* of men —Thomas Carlyle> **d :** an edible case for holding a filling <a pastry ~> **e :** a reinforced concrete arched or domed roof that is used primarily over large unpartitioned areas **f :** a small beer glass **5 :** a thin hard layer of rock **6 :** a shell-bearing mollusk **7 :** an impersonal attitude or manner that conceals the presence or absence of feeling **8 :** a narrow light racing boat propelled by one or more oarsmen **9 :** any of the spaces occupied by the orbits of a group of electrons of approximately equal energy surrounding the nucleus of an atom **10 a :** a projectile for cannon containing an explosive bursting charge **b :** a metal or paper case which holds the charge of powder and shot or bullet used with breech-loading small arms **11 :** a plain usu. sleeveless blouse or sweater — **shell** *adj* — **shelly** \ˈshel-ē\ *adj*
[2]**shell** *vt* **1 a :** to take out of a natural enclosing cover (as a shell, husk, pod, or capsule) <~ peanuts> **b :** to separate the kernels of (as an ear of Indian corn, wheat, or oats) from the cob, ear, or husk **2 :** to throw shells at, upon, or into : BOMBARD **3 :** to score heavily against (as an opposing pitcher in baseball) ~ *vi* **1 :** to fall or scale off in thin pieces **2 :** to cast the shell or exterior covering : fall out of the pod or husk <nuts which ~ in falling> **3 :** to gather shells (as from a beach) : collect shells
she'll \(ˌ)shē(ə)l, shil\ **:** she will : she shall
[1]**shel·lac** \shə-ˈlak\ *n* [[1]*shell* + *lac*] **1 :** purified lac usu. prepared in thin orange or yellow flakes by heating and filtering and often bleached white **2 :** a preparation of lac dissolved usu. in alcohol and used chiefly as a wood filler and finish **3 a :** a composition containing shellac used for making phonograph records **b :** an old 78 rpm phonograph record
[2]**shellac** *vt* **shel·lacked; shel·lack·ing 1 :** to coat or otherwise treat with shellac or a shellac varnish **2 :** to defeat decisively
shel·lack·ing *n* **:** a decisive defeat : DRUBBING
shell·back \ˈshel-ˌbak\ *n* **:** an old or veteran sailor
shell bean *n* **1 :** a bean grown primarily for its edible seeds — compare SNAP BEAN **2 :** the edible seed of a bean
shell·crack·er \ˈshel-ˌkrak-ər\ *n* **:** REDEAR
shelled \ˈsheld\ *adj* **1 :** having a shell esp. of a specified kind — often used in combination <pink-*shelled*> <thick-*shelled*> **2 a :** having the shell removed <~ oysters><~ nuts> **b :** removed from the cob <~ corn>
shell·er \ˈshel-ər\ *n* **1 :** one that shells <a peanut ~> **2 :** one that collects seashells
shell·fire \ˈshel-ˌfī(ə)r\ *n* **:** firing or shooting of shells
shell·fish \-ˌfish\ *n* **:** an aquatic invertebrate animal with a shell; *esp* **:** an edible mollusk or crustacean
shell game *n* **:** thimblerig played esp. with three walnut shells
shell jacket *n* **1 :** a short tight military jacket worn buttoned up the front **2 :** MESS JACKET
shell out *vb* **:** PAY
shell pink *n* **:** a variable color averaging a light yellowish pink
shell·proof \ˈshel-ˈprüf\ *adj* **:** capable of resisting shells or bombs
shell shock *n* **:** any of numerous often hysterical psychoneurotic conditions appearing in soldiers under fire in modern warfare — **shell–shock** *vt*
shell·work \ˈshel-ˌwərk\ *n* **:** work adorned with shells or composed of a pattern of shells
[1]**shel·ter** \ˈshel-tər\ *n* [origin unknown] **1 :** something that covers or affords protection <a bomb ~> **2 :** the state of being covered and protected <took ~> — **shel·ter·less** \-ləs\ *adj*
[2]**shelter** *vb* **shel·tered; shel·ter·ing** \-t(ə-)riŋ\ *vt* **1 :** to constitute or provide a shelter for : PROTECT <has led a ~*ed* life> **2 :** to place under shelter or protection <~*ed* himself in a mountain cave> ~ *vi* **:** to take shelter — **shel·ter·er** \-tər-ər\ *n*
shel·ter·belt \ˈshel-tər-ˌbelt\ *n* **:** a barrier of trees and shrubs that protects (as crops) from wind and storm and lessens erosion
shelter half *n* **:** one of the halves of a two-man shelter tent
shelter tent *n* **:** a small tent usu. consisting of two interchangeable pieces of waterproof cotton duck fixed for buttoning or tying
shel·ty *or* **shel·tie** \ˈshel-tē\ *n, pl* **shelties** [prob. of Scand origin; akin to ON *Hjalti* Shetlander] **1 :** SHETLAND PONY **2 :** SHETLAND SHEEPDOG
shelve \ˈshelv\ *vb* **shelved; shelv·ing** [*shelf*] *vt* **1 :** to furnish with shelves **2 :** to place on a shelf **3 a :** to remove from active service **b :** to put off or aside <~ a project> ~ *vi* **:** to slope in a formation like a shelf — **shelv·er** *n*
[1]**shelv·ing** \ˈshel-viŋ\ *n* **1 :** the state or degree of sloping **2 :** a sloping surface or place
[2]**shelving** *n* **1 :** material for shelves **2 :** SHELVES
Shem \ˈshem\ *n* [Heb *Shēm*] **:** the eldest son of Noah and ancestor of the Semitic peoples
She·ma \shə-ˈmä\ *n* [Heb *shĕma'* hear, first word of Deut 6:4] **:** the Jewish confession of faith comprising Deut 6:4–9 and 11:13–21 and Num 15:37–41
She·mi·ni Atze·reth \shə-ˌmē-nē-ät-ˈser-ət(h), -əs\ *n* [Heb *shĕmīnī 'aṣereth,* fr. Heb *shĕmīnī* eighth + *'aṣereth* assembly] **:** a Jewish festival following the seventh day of Sukkoth and marked by a special prayer for seasonal rain
Shem·ite \ˈshem-ˌīt\ *n* [*Shem*] **:** SEMITE — **She·mit·ic** \shə-ˈmit-ik\ *or* **Shem·it·ish** \ˈshem-ˌīt-ish\ *adj*
she·nan·i·gan \shə-ˈnan-i-gən\ *n* [origin unknown] **1 :** a devious trick used esp. for an underhand purpose **2 a :** tricky or questionable practices or conduct **b :** high-spirited or mischievous activity — usu. used in pl.
shend \ˈshend\ *vt* **shent** \ˈshent\; **shend·ing** [ME *shenden,* fr. OE *scendan;* akin to OE *scamu* shame — more at SHAME] **1** *archaic* **:** to put to shame or confusion **2** *archaic* **:** REPROVE, REVILE **3** *chiefly dial* **a :** INJURE, MAR **b :** RUIN, DESTROY
she–oak \ˈshē-ˌōk\ *n* **:** any of several casuarinas
She·ol \shē-ˈōl, ˈshē-ˌ\ *n* [Heb *Shĕ'ōl*] **:** the abode of the dead in early Hebrew thought
[1]**shep·herd** \ˈshep-ərd\ *n* [ME *sheepherde,* fr. OE *scēaphyrde,* fr. *scēap* sheep + *hierde* herdsman; akin to OE *heord* herd] **1 :** a man who tends sheep esp. in a flock that is grazing **2 :** PASTOR 1
[2]**shepherd** *vt* **1 :** to tend as a shepherd **2 :** to guide or guard in the manner of a shepherd <~*ed* the children onto the train>
shepherd dog *n* **:** SHEEP DOG
shep·herd·ess \ˈshep-ərd-əs\ *n* **1 :** a woman or girl who tends sheep **2 :** a rural lass
shepherd's check *n* **:** a pattern of small even black-and-white checks; *also* **:** a fabric woven in this pattern — called also *shepherd's plaid*

shepherd's check

shepherd's pie *n* **:** a meat pie with a mashed potato crust
shepherd's purse *n* **:** a white-flowered weedy annual herb (*Capsella bursa-pastoris*) of the mustard family with flat heart-shaped pods
Sher·a·ton \ˈsher-ət-ᵊn\ *adj* [Thomas *Sheraton*] **:** of, relating to, or being a style of furniture that originated in England around 1800 and is characterized by straight lines and graceful proportions
sher·bet \ˈshər-bət\ *or* **sher·bert** \-bərt\ *n* [Turk & Per; Turk *şerbet,* fr. Per *sharbat,* fr. Ar *sharbah* drink] **1 :** a cold drink of sweetened and diluted fruit juice **2 :** an ice with milk, egg white, or gelatin added
sherd *var of* SHARD
she·rif \shə-ˈrēf\ *var of* SHARIF

sher·iff \'sher-əf\ *n* [ME *shirreve,* fr. OE *scīrgerēfa,* fr. *scīr* shire + *gerēfa* reeve — more at REEVE] **:** an important official of a shire or county charged primarily with judicial duties (as executing the processes and orders of courts and judges) — **sher·iff·dom** \-əf-dəm, -əf-təm\ *n*

sher·lock \'shər-ˌläk, 'she(ə)r-\ *n, often cap* [*Sherlock* Holmes, detective in stories by Sir Arthur Conan Doyle] **:** DETECTIVE

Sher·pa \'she(ə)r-pə, 'shər-\ *n* **:** a member of a Tibetan people living on the high southern slopes of the Himalayas and skilled in mountain climbing

sher·ris \'sher-is\ *archaic var of* SHERRY

sher·ry \'sher-ē\ *n, pl* **sherries** [alter. of earlier *sherris* (taken as pl.), fr. *Xeres* (now *Jerez*), Spain] **:** a fortified wine of Spanish origin with a distinctive nutty flavor; *also* **:** a similar wine produced elsewhere

she's \(ˌ)shēz\ **:** she is **:** she has

Shet·land \'shet-lənd\ *n* **1 a :** SHETLAND PONY **b :** SHETLAND SHEEPDOG **2** *often not cap* **a :** a lightweight loosely twisted yarn of Shetland wool used for knitting and weaving **b :** a fabric or a garment made from Shetland wool

Shet·land pony \ˌshet-lən(d)-\ *n* **:** any of a breed of small stocky shaggy hardy ponies that originated in the Shetland islands

Shetland sheepdog *n* **:** any of a breed of small dogs developed in the Shetland islands that resemble miniature collies and have a short dense undercoat and a profuse outer coat of long hair

Shetland wool *n* **:** fine wool from sheep raised in the Shetland islands; *also* **:** yarn spun from this

sheugh \'shük\ *n* [ME *sough,* fr. *swoughen* to sough — more at SOUGH] *chiefly Scot* **:** DITCH, TRENCH

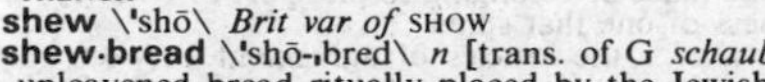
Shetland pony

shew \'shō\ *Brit var of* SHOW

shew·bread \'shō-ˌbred\ *n* [trans. of G *schaubrot*] **:** consecrated unleavened bread ritually placed by the Jewish priests of ancient Israel on a table in the sanctuary of the Tabernacle on the Sabbath

SHF *abbr* superhigh frequency

Shia \'shē-(ˌ)ä\ *n, pl* **Shi·as** [Ar *shī'ah* sect] **:** the Muslims of the branch of Islam comprising sects believing in Ali and the Imams as the only rightful successors of Muhammad and in the concealment and messianic return of the last recognized Imam — compare SUNNI — **Shi·ite** \'shē-ˌīt\ *n*

shib·bo·leth \'shib-ə-ləth *also* -ˌleth\ *n* [Heb *shibbōleth* stream; fr. the use of this word as a test to distinguish Gileadites from Ephraimites, who pronounced it *sibbōleth*] **1 a :** CATCHWORD, SLOGAN **b :** a use of language regarded as distinctive of a particular group **c :** a commonplace idea or saying **2 :** a custom or usage regarded as a criterion for distinguishing members of one group

shiel \'shē(ə)l\ *n* [ME (northern dial.) *schele*] *chiefly Scot* **:** SHIELING

¹shield \'shē(ə)ld\ *n* [ME *sheld,* fr. OE *scield;* akin to OE *sciell* shell] **1 :** a broad piece of defensive armor carried on the arm **2 :** one that protects or defends **:** DEFENSE **3 :** an adjunct of dress worn inside a part of the clothing (as the underarm) liable to be soiled by perspiration **4 :** a fixture designed to protect persons from injury from moving parts of machinery or parts carrying electricity **5 :** ESCUTCHEON; *esp* **:** one that is wide at the top and rounds to a point at the bottom **6 :** an armored screen protecting an otherwise exposed gun **7 :** an iron or steel framework moved forward in excavating to support the ground ahead of the lining **8 :** a protective structure (as a carapace, scale, or plate) of some animals **9 :** the Precambrian nuclear mass of a continent that is surrounded and sometimes covered by sedimentary rocks **10 :** something resembling a shield: as **a :** APOTHECIUM **b :** a policeman's badge **c :** a decorative or identifying emblem

²shield *vt* **1 a :** to protect with or as if with a shield **:** provide with a protective cover or shelter **b :** to cut off from observation **:** HIDE **2** *obs* **:** FORBID ***syn*** see DEFEND — **shield·er** *n*

shield law *n* **:** a law that protects journalists from forced disclosure of confidential news sources

shiel·ing \'shē-lən\ *n* **1** *dial Brit* **:** a mountain hut used as a shelter by shepherds **2** *dial Brit* **:** a summer pasture in the mountains

shier *comparative of* SHY

shiest *superlative of* SHY

¹shift \'shift\ *vb* [ME *shiften,* fr. OE *sciftan* to divide, arrange; akin to OE *scēadan* to divide — more at SHED] *vt* **1 :** to exchange for or replace by another **:** CHANGE **2 a :** to change the place, position, or direction of **:** MOVE **b :** to make a change in (place) **3 :** to change phonetically ~ *vi* **1 a :** to change place or position <~*ing* uneasily in his chair> **b :** to change direction <the wind~*ed*> **c :** to change the gear rotating the transmission shaft of an automobile **d :** to depress the shift key (as on a typewriter) **2 a :** to assume responsibility <had to ~ for herself> **b :** to resort to expedients **3 a :** to go through a change **b :** to change one's clothes **c :** to become changed phonetically — **shift·able** \'shif-tə-bəl\ *adj* — **shift·er** *n* — **shift gears :** to make a change

²shift *n* **1 a :** a means or device for effecting an end **b (1) :** a deceitful or underhand scheme **:** DODGE **(2) :** an expedient tried in difficult circumstances **:** EXTREMITY **2 a** *chiefly dial* **:** a change of clothes **b (1)** *chiefly dial* **:** SHIRT **(2) :** a woman's slip or chemise **(3) :** a woman's usu. loose-fitting or semi-fitted dress **3 a :** a change in direction <a ~ in the wind> **b :** a change in emphasis, judgment, or attitude **4 a :** a group of people who work or occupy themselves in turn with other groups **b (1) :** a change of one group of people (as workers) for another in regular alternation **(2) :** a scheduled period of work or duty **5 :** a change in place or position: as **a :** a change in the position of the hand on a fingerboard (as of a violin) **b (1) :** FAULT 5 **(2) :** the relative displacement of rock masses on opposite sides of a fault or fault zone **c (1) :** a simultaneous change of position in football by two or more players from one side of the line to the other **(2) :** a change of positions (as from one side of the infield to the other) made by one or more players in baseball to provide better defense against a particular hitter **d :** a change in frequency resulting in a change in position of a spectral line or band — compare DOPPLER EFFECT **e :** a movement of bits in a computer register to the right or left a specified number of places **6 :** a removal from one person or thing to another **:** TRANSFER **7 :** CONSONANT SHIFT **8 :** a bid in bridge in a suit other than the suit one's partner has bid — compare JUMP **9 :** GEARSHIFT ***syn*** see RESOURCE

shift key *n* **:** a key on a keyboard (as of a typewriter) that when pressed permits the characters on the upper part of the typefaces to print

shift·less \'shif(t)-ləs\ *adj* [*shift* (resourcefulness)] **1 :** lacking in resourcefulness **:** INEFFICIENT **2 :** lacking in ambition or incentive **:** LAZY — **shift·less·ly** *adv* — **shift·less·ness** *n*

shifty \'shif-tē\ *adj* **shift·i·er; -est 1 :** full of or ready with expedients **:** RESOURCEFUL **2 a :** given to deception, evasion, or fraud **:** TRICKY **b :** capable of evasive movement **:** ELUSIVE <a ~ boxer> **3 :** indicative of a tricky nature <~ eyes> — **shift·i·ly** \-tə-lē\ *adv* — **shift·i·ness** \-tē-nəs\ *n*

shi·gel·la \shi-'gel-ə\ *n, pl* **-gel·lae** \-'gel-(ˌ)ē, -(ˌ)ī\ *also* **-gellas** [NL, genus name, fr. Kiyoshi *Shiga* †1957 Jap bacteriologist] **:** any of a genus (*Shigella*) of nonmotile aerobic bacteria that form acid but no gas on many carbohydrates and that cause dysenteries in animals and esp. man

Shih Tzu \'shēd-'zü\ *n* [Chin (Pek) *shi*¹ *tzŭ*³ *kou*³ Pekingese dog, fr. *shi*¹ lion + *tzŭ*³ son + *kou*³ dog] **:** a small alert active dog of an old Chinese breed that has a square short unwrinkled muzzle, short muscular legs, massive amounts of long dense hair, and a face that is sometimes compared to a chrysanthemum esp. because of hair that grows upward on the muzzle

Shi·ism \'shē-ˌiz-əm\ *n* **:** Islam as taught by the Shia

¹shi·kar \shi-'kär\ *n* [Hindi *shikār,* fr. Per] *India* **:** HUNTING

²shikar *vb* **shi·karred; shi·kar·ring** *India* **:** HUNT

shi·ka·ri \shi-'kär-ē, -'kar-\ *n* [Hindi *shikārī,* fr. Per, fr. *shikār*] *India* **:** a big game hunter; *esp* **:** a professional hunter or guide

shik·sa *or* **shik·se** \'shik-sə\ *n* [Yiddish *shikse,* fem. of *sheykets, sheygets* non-Jewish boy, fr. Heb *sheqeṣ* blemish, abomination] **1 :** a non-Jewish girl — often used disparagingly **2 :** a Jewish girl who does not observe Jewish precepts — used esp. by Orthodox Jews

shi·lingi \shil-'iŋ-ē\ *n, pl* **shilingi** [Swahili, fr. E *shilling*] — see MONEY table

shill \'shil\ *n* [prob. short for *shillaber,* of unknown origin] **:** one who acts as a decoy (as for a pitchman or gambler) — **shill** *vi*

shil·le·lagh *also* **shil·la·lah** \shə-'lā-lē\ *n* [*Shillelagh,* town in Ireland famed for its oak trees] **:** CUDGEL

shil·ling \'shil-iŋ\ *n* [ME, fr. OE *scilling;* akin to OHG *skilling,* a gold coin; both fr. a prehistoric Gmc compound represented by OE *sceld* shield and by OE *-ling*] **1 a :** a former monetary unit of the United Kingdom equal to 12 pence or $^1/_{20}$ pound **b :** a monetary unit equal to $^1/_{20}$ pound of any of various other countries in or formerly in the British Commonwealth — see *pound* at MONEY table **2 :** a coin representing one shilling **3 :** any of several early American coins **4 —** see MONEY table **5 :** SHILINGI

Shil·luk \shil-'ük\ *n, pl* **Shilluk** *or* **Shilluks 1 :** a member of a Nilotic Negro people of the Sudan dwelling mainly on the west bank of the White Nile **2 :** the language of the Shilluk people

¹shilly–shally \'shil-ē-ˌshal-ē\ *adv* [irreg. redupl. of *shall I*] **:** in an irresolute, undecided, or hesitating manner

²shilly–shally *adj* **:** IRRESOLUTE, VACILLATING

³shilly–shally *n* **:** INDECISION, IRRESOLUTION

⁴shilly–shally *vi* **shilly–shall·ied; shilly–shally·ing 1 :** to show hesitation or lack of decisiveness or resolution **2 :** DAWDLE

shil·pit \'shil-pət\ *adj* [origin unknown] **1** *Scot* **:** pinched and starved in appearance **2** *Scot* **:** WEAK, INSIPID — used of drink

¹shim \'shim\ *n* [origin unknown] **:** a thin often tapered piece of material (as wood, metal, or stone) used to fill in space between things (as for support, leveling, or adjustment of fit)

²shim *vt* **shimmed; shim·ming :** to fill out or level up by the use of a shim

¹shim·mer \'shim-ər\ *vb* **shim·mered; shim·mer·ing** \-(ə-)riŋ\ [ME *schimeren,* fr. OE *scimerian;* akin to OE *scīnan* to shine — more at SHINE] *vi* **1 :** to shine with a soft tremulous or fitful light **:** GLIMMER **2 :** to reflect a wavering sometimes distorted visual image ~ *vt* **:** to cause to shimmer ***syn*** see FLASH

²shimmer *n* **1 :** a light that shimmers **:** subdued sparkle or sheen **:** GLIMMER **2 :** a wavering sometimes distorted visual image usu. resulting from heat induced changes in atmospheric refraction — **shim·mery** \'shim-(ə-)rē\ *adj*

¹shim·my \'shim-ē\ *n, pl* **shimmies 1** [by alter.] **:** CHEMISE **2** [short for *shimmy-shake*] **:** a jazz dance characterized by a shaking of the body from the shoulders down **3 :** an abnormal vibration esp. in the front wheels of a motor vehicle

²shimmy *vi* **shim·mied; shim·my·ing 1 :** to shake, quiver, or tremble in or as if in dancing a shimmy **2 :** to vibrate abnormally — used esp. of automobiles

¹shin \'shin\ *n* [ME *shine,* fr. OE *scinu;* akin to OHG *scina* shin, OE *scēadan* to divide — more at SHED] **:** the front part of the vertebrate leg below the knee

ə abut	ᵊ kitten	ər further	a back	ā bake	ä cot, cart
au̇ out	ch chin	e less	ē easy	g gift	i trip ī life
j joke	ŋ sing	ō flow	ȯ flaw	ȯi coin	th thin th this
ü loot	u̇ foot	y yet	yü few	yu̇ furious	zh vision

[2]**shin** *vb* **shinned; shin·ning** *vi* **1 :** to climb by moving oneself up or down by alternate use of the arms or hands and the legs **2 :** to move forward rapidly on foot ~ *vt* **1 :** to kick or strike on the shins **2 :** to climb by shinning

[3]**shin** \'shēn, 'shin\ *n* [Heb *shīn*] **:** the 22d letter of the Hebrew alphabet — see ALPHABET table

Shin \'shin, 'shēn\ *n* [Jap, lit., belief, faith] **:** a major Japanese Buddhist sect that emphasizes salvation by faith in exclusive worship of Amida Buddha

Shi·na \'shē-nə\ *n* **:** the Dard language of Gilgit in northern Kashmir

shin·bone \'shin-'bōn, -ˌbōn\ *n* **:** TIBIA 1

shin·dig \'shin-ˌdig\ *n* [prob. alter. of *shindy*] **1 a :** a social gathering with dancing **b :** a usu. large or lavish party **2 :** SHINDY 2

shin·dy \'shin-dē\ *n, pl* **shindys** *or* **shindies** [prob. alter. of *shinny*] **1 :** SHINDIG 1 **2 :** FRACAS, UPROAR

[1]**shine** \'shīn\ *vb* **shone** \'shōn, *esp Canad & Brit* 'shän\ *or* **shined; shin·ing** [ME *shinen,* fr. OE *scīnan;* akin to OHG *skīnan* to shine, Gk *skia* shadow] *vi* **1 :** to emit rays of light **2 :** to be bright by reflection of light **3 :** to be eminent, conspicuous, or distinguished <she always ~*s* in math class> **4 :** to have a bright glowing appearance <his face *shone* with enthusiasm> **5 :** to be conspicuously evident or clear ~ *vt* **1 a :** to cause to emit light **b :** to throw or flash the light of **2** *past & past part* **shined :** to make bright by polishing <*shined* his shoes>

[2]**shine** *n* **1 :** brightness caused by the emission of light **2 :** brightness caused by the reflection of light **:** LUSTER **3:** BRILLIANCE, SPLENDOR **4 :** fair weather **:** SUNSHINE <rain or ~> **5 :** TRICK, CAPER — usu. used in pl. **6 :** LIKING, FANCY <took a ~ to him> **7 a :** a polish or gloss given to shoes **b :** a single polishing of a pair of shoes

shin·er \'shī-nər\ *n* **1 :** one that shines **2 :** a silvery fish; *esp* **:** any of numerous small freshwater American cyprinid fishes (esp. genus *Notropis*) **3 :** BLACK EYE 1

[1]**shin·gle** \'shiŋ-gəl\ *n* [ME *schingel*] **1 :** a small thin piece of building material often with one end thicker than the other for laying in overlapping rows as a covering for the roof or sides of a building **2 :** a small signboard **3 :** a woman's haircut with the hair trimmed short from the back of the head to the nape

[2]**shingle** *vt* **shin·gled; shin·gling** \-g(ə-)liŋ\ **1 :** to cover with or as if with shingles **2 :** to bob and shape (the hair) in a shingle **3 :** to lay out or arrange so as to overlap

[3]**shingle** *n* [prob. of Scand origin; akin to Norw *singel* coarse gravel] **1 :** coarse rounded detritus or alluvial material esp. on the seashore that differs from ordinary gravel only in the larger size of the stones **2 :** a place strewn with shingle — **shin·gly** \-g(ə-)lē\ *adj*

[4]**shingle** *vt* **shin·gled; shin·gling** \-g(ə-)liŋ\ [F dial. *chingler,* lit., to whip, fr. MF dial., fr. *chingle* strap, fr. L *cingula,* fr. *cingere* to gird — more at CINCTURE] **:** to subject (as iron) to the process of expelling cinder and impurities by hammering and squeezing

shin·gler \-g(ə-)lər\ *n* **:** one that shingles

shin·gles \'shiŋ-gəlz\ *n pl but sing in constr* [ME *schingles,* by folk etymology fr. ML *cingulus,* fr. L *cingulum* girdle — more at CINGULUM] **:** HERPES ZOSTER

Shin·gon \'shin-ˌgän, 'shēn-\ *n* [Jap, lit., true word] **:** an esoteric Japanese Buddhist sect claiming the achievement of Buddhahood in this life through its prescribed rituals

shin·ing \'shī-niŋ\ *adj* **1 :** emitting or reflecting light **2 :** bright and often splendid in appearance **:** RESPLENDENT **3 :** possessing a distinguished quality **:** ILLUSTRIOUS **4 :** full of sunshine

shin·leaf \'shin-ˌlēf\ *n, pl* **shinleafs :** any of several pyrolas (esp. *Pyrola elliptica*) with lustrous evergreen basal leaves and racemose white or pinkish flowers

shin·nery \'shin-ə-rē\ *n, pl* **-ner·ies** [modif. of LaF *chênière,* fr. F *chêne* oak] **:** a dense growth of small trees or an area of such growth; *esp* **:** one of scrub oak in the West and Southwest

[1]**shin·ny** *also* **shin·ney** \'shin-ē\ *n* [perh. fr. [1]*shin*] **:** a variation of hockey played by schoolboys with a curved stick and a ball or block of wood; *also* **:** the stick used

[2]**shinny** *vi* **shin·nied; shin·ny·ing** [alter. of [2]*shin*] **:** SHIN 1

shin·plas·ter \'shin-ˌplas-tər\ *n* **1 :** a piece of privately-issued paper currency; *esp* **:** one poorly secured and depreciated in value **2 :** a piece of fractional currency

shin·splints \'shin-ˌsplin(t)s\ *n pl but sing in constr* **:** injury to and inflammation of the tibial and toe extensor muscles or their fasciae that is caused by repeated minimal traumas (as by running on a wood or cement floor)

Shin·to \'shin-(ˌ)tō\ *n* [Jap *shintō*] **:** the indigenous religion of Japan consisting chiefly in the cultic devotion to deities of natural forces and veneration of the Emperor as a descendant of the sun-goddess — **Shinto** *adj* — **Shin·to·ism** \-(ˌ)tō-ˌiz-əm\ *n* — **Shin·to·ist** \-ˌtō-əst\ *n or adj* — **Shin·to·is·tic** \ˌshin-tō-'is-tik\ *adj*

shiny \'shī-nē\ *adj* **shin·i·er; -est 1 a :** bright with the rays of the sun **:** SUNSHINY **b :** filled with light **2 :** bright in appearance **:** POLISHED <~ new shoes> **3 :** rubbed or worn smooth **4 :** lustrous with natural secretions <a ~ nose> — **shin·i·ness** *n*

[1]**ship** \'ship\ *n, often attrib* [ME, fr. OE *scip;* akin to OHG *skif* ship, OE *scēadan* to divide — more at SHED] **1 a :** a large seagoing vessel **b :** a sailing vessel having a bowsprit and usu. three masts each composed of a lower mast, a topmast, and a topgallant mast **2 :** BOAT; *esp* **:** one propelled by power or sail **3 :** a ship's crew **4 :** FORTUNE <when his ~ comes in he'll be able to live in better style> **5 :** AIRSHIP, AIRPLANE, SPACECRAFT

[2]**ship** *vb* **shipped; ship·ping** *vt* **1 a :** to place or receive on board a ship for transportation by water **b :** to cause to be transported <*shipped* him off to prep school> **2** *obs* **:** to provide with a ship **3 :** to put in place for use <~ the tiller> **4 :** to take into a ship or boat <~ the gangplank> **5 :** to engage for service on a ship **6 :** to take (as water) over the side — used of a boat or a ship ~ *vi* **1 :** to embark on a ship **2 :** to go or travel by ship **3 :** to engage to serve on shipboard — **ship·pa·ble** \'ship-ə-bəl\ *adj*

-ship \ˌship\ *n suffix* [ME, fr. OE *-scipe;* akin to OHG *-scaft* -ship, OE *scieppan* to shape — more at SHAPE] **1 :** state **:** condition **:** quality <friend*ship*> **2 :** office **:** dignity **:** profession <clerk*ship*> **3 :** art **:** skill <horseman*ship*> **4 :** something showing, exhibiting, or embodying a quality or state <town*ship*> **5 :** one entitled to a (specified) rank, title, or appellation <his Lord*ship*>

ship biscuit *n* **:** HARDTACK — called also *ship bread*

[1]**ship·board** \'ship-ˌbō(ə)rd, -ˌbȯ(ə)rd\ *n* **1 :** the side of a ship **2 :** SHIP <met on ~>

[2]**shipboard** *adj* **:** existing or taking place on board a ship

ship·borne \'ship-ˌbō(ə)rn, -ˌbȯ(ə)rn\ *adj* **:** transported or designed to be transported by ship <~ aircraft>

ship·build·er \'ship-ˌbil-dər\ *n* **:** one who designs or constructs ships — **ship·build·ing** \-diŋ\ *n*

ship fever *n* **:** TYPHUS

ship·fit·ter \'ship-ˌfit-ər\ *n* **1 :** one that fits together the structural members of ships and puts them into position for riveting or welding **2 :** a naval enlisted man who works in sheet metal and performs the work of a plumber aboard ship

ship·lap \-ˌlap\ *n* **:** wooden sheathing in which the boards are rabbeted so that the edges of each board lap over the edges of adjacent boards to make a flush joint

ship·load \-'lōd, -ˌlōd\ *n* **1 :** as much or as many as will fill or load a ship **2 :** an indefinitely large amount or number

ship·man \-mən\ *n* **1 :** SEAMAN, SAILOR **2 :** SHIPMASTER

ship·mas·ter \-ˌmas-tər\ *n* **:** the master or commander of a ship other than a warship

ship·mate \-ˌmāt\ *n* **:** a fellow sailor

ship·ment \-mənt\ *n* **1 :** the act or process of shipping **2 :** the goods shipped

ship money *n* **:** an impost levied at various times in England to provide ships for the national defense

ship of the line : a ship of war large enough to have a place in the line of battle

ship·own·er \'ship-ˌō-nər\ *n* **:** the owner of a ship or of a share in a ship

ship·per \'ship-ər\ *n* **:** one that sends goods by any form of conveyance

ship·ping \'ship-iŋ\ *n* **1 a :** passage on a ship **b :** SHIPS **c :** the body of ships in one place or belonging to one port or country **2 :** the act or business of one that ships

shipping articles *n pl* **:** the articles of agreement between the captain of a ship and the seamen in respect to wages, length of time for which they are shipped, and related matters

shipping clerk *n* **:** one who is employed in a shipping room to assemble, pack, and send out or receive goods

ship–rigged \'ship-'rigd\ *adj* **:** SQUARE-RIGGED

ship·shape \'ship-'shāp\ *adj* [short for earlier *shipshapen,* fr. *ship* + *shapen,* archaic pp. of *shape*] **:** TRIM, TIDY

ship·side \-ˌsīd\ *n* **:** the area adjacent to shipping that is used for storage and loading of freight and passengers **:** DOCK

ship's papers *n pl* **:** the papers with which a ship is legally required to be provided for due inspection to show the character of the ship and cargo

ship's service *n* **:** a ship or navy post exchange — called also *navy exchange*

ship's stores *n pl* **:** the supplies and equipment required for the operation and upkeep of a ship

shipt *abbr* shipment

ship·way \'ship-ˌwā\ *n* **1 :** the ways on which a ship is built **2 :** a ship canal

ship·worm \-ˌwərm\ *n* **:** any of various elongated marine clams (esp. family Teredinidae) that resemble worms, burrow in submerged wood, and damage wharf piles and wooden ships

[1]**ship·wreck** \-ˌrek\ *n* [alter. of earlier *shipwrack,* fr. ME *schipwrak,* fr. OE *scipwræc,* fr. *scip* ship + *wræc* something driven by the sea — more at WRACK] **1 :** a wrecked ship or its parts **2 :** the destruction or loss of a ship **3 :** an irretrievable loss or failure

[2]**shipwreck** *vt* **1 a :** to cause to experience shipwreck **b :** RUIN **2 :** to destroy (a ship) by grounding or foundering

ship·wright \'ship-ˌrīt\ *n* **:** a carpenter skilled in ship construction and repair

ship·yard \-ˌyärd\ *n* **:** a yard, place, or enclosure where ships are built or repaired

shire \'shī(ə)r, *in place-name compounds* ˌshi(ə)r, shər\ *n* [ME, fr. OE *scīr* office, shire; akin to OHG *scīra* care] **1 :** an administrative subdivision; *esp* **:** a county in England **2 :** any of a British breed of large heavy draft horses with heavily feathered legs

shire town *n* **1 :** a town that is the seat of the government of a county **:** COUNTY SEAT **2 :** a town where a court of superior jurisdiction (as a circuit court or a court with a jury) sits

shirk \'shərk\ *vb* [origin unknown] *vi* **1 :** to go stealthily **:** SNEAK **2 :** to evade the performance of an obligation ~ *vt* **:** AVOID, EVADE <~ one's duty> — **shirk·er** *n*

Shir·ley poppy \ˌshər-lē-\ *n* [*Shirley* vicarage, Croydon, Eng.] **:** a variable annual garden poppy with bright solitary single or double flowers

shirr \'shər\ *vt* [origin unknown] **1 :** to draw (as cloth) together in a shirring **2 :** to bake (eggs removed from the shell) until set

shirr·ing \'shər-iŋ\ *n* **:** a decorative gathering (as of cloth) made by drawing up the material along two or more parallel lines of stitching

shirt \'shərt\ *n* [ME *shirte,* fr. OE *scyrte;* akin to ON *skyrta* shirt, OE *scort* short] **1 :** a garment for the upper part of the body: as **a :** a cloth garment usu. having a collar, sleeves, a front opening, and a tail long enough to be tucked inside trousers or a skirt **b :** UNDERSHIRT **2 :** all or a large part of one's possessions <lost his ~ on that business deal>

shirt·front \-ˌfrənt\ *n* **:** the front of a shirt; *also* **:** the part of a man's shirt not covered by coat or vest

shirt·ing \-iŋ\ *n* **:** fabric suitable for shirts

shirt·mak·er \'shərt-ˌmā-kər\ *n* **:** one that makes shirts

shirt–sleeve \-ˌslēv\ *also* **shirt–sleeves** \-ˌslēvz\ *or* **shirt–sleeved** \-ˌslēvd\ *adj* **1 a :** being without a coat <a ~ audience> **b :** calling for the removal of coats for the sake of comfort or

efficiency <~ weather> **2 :** marked by informality and directness <~ diplomacy>
1shirt·tail \'shərt-ˌtāl\ *n* **1 :** the part of a shirt that reaches below the waist esp. in the back **2 a :** a short addition at the end of a newspaper article **b :** something small or inadequate
2shirttail *adj* **1 :** very young : IMMATURE <~ boys fishing in the creek> **2 :** distantly and indefinitely related <a ~ cousin on her father's side> **3 :** small, trivial, or short typically to the point of inadequacy <has a gullied ~ ranch in the hills>
shirt·waist \'shərt-ˌwāst\ *n* **:** a woman's tailored garment (as a blouse or dress) with details copied from men's shirts

shirtwaist dress

shirty \'shərt-ē\ *adj* **:** ANGRY, IRRITATED
shish ke·bab \'shish-kə-ˌbäb\ *n* [Arm *shish kabab*] **:** kabob cooked on skewers
1shit \'shit\ *vb* **shit; shit·ting** [alter. (influenced by 2*shit* and the past and pp. forms) of earlier *shite,* fr. ME *shiten,* fr. OE *-scītan;* akin to MLG & MD *schiten* to defecate, OHG *scīzan,* ON *skīta* to defecate, OE *scēadan* to divide, separate — more at SHED] *vi* **:** DEFECATE — usu. considered vulgar ~ *vt* **:** to defecate in — usu. considered vulgar
2shit *n* [fr. (assumed) ME, fr. OE *scite* (attested only in place names); akin to MD *schit, schitte* excrement, OE *scītan* to defecate] **1 :** EXCREMENT — usu. considered vulgar **2 :** an act of defecation — usu. considered vulgar **3 :** NONSENSE, FOOLISHNESS — usu. considered vulgar
shit·tah \'shit-ə\ *n, pl* **shittahs** *or* **shit·tim** \'shit-əm\ [Heb *shiṭṭāh*] **:** a tree of uncertain identity but prob. an acacia (as *Acacia seyal*) from the wood of which the ark and fittings of the Hebrew tabernacle were made
shit·tim·wood \'shit-əm-ˌwu̇d\ *also* **shittim** *n* [Heb *shiṭṭīm* (pl. of *shiṭṭāh*) + E *wood*] **1 :** the wood of the shittah tree **2 :** any of several buckthorns; *also* **:** their hard heavy dense wood used for turning and for inlay
shiv \'shiv\ *n* [prob. fr. Romany *chiv* blade] *slang* **:** KNIFE
Shi·va \'shiv-ə, 'shē-və\ *var of* SIVA
shiv·a·ree \ˌshiv-ə-'rē, 'shiv-ə-ˌ\ *n* [F *charivari*] **:** a noisy mock serenade to a newly married couple — **shivaree** *vt*
1shiv·er \'shiv-ər\ *n* [ME; akin to OE *scēadan* to divide — more at SHED] **:** one of the small pieces into which a brittle thing is broken by sudden violence
2shiver *vb* **shiv·ered; shiv·er·ing** \-(ə-)riŋ\ **:** to break into many small pieces **:** SHATTER
3shiver *vb* **shiv·ered; shiv·er·ing** \-(ə-)riŋ\ [ME *shiveren,* alter. of *chiveren*] *vi* **1 :** to undergo trembling **:** QUIVER **2 :** to tremble in the wind as it strikes first one and then the other side (of a sail) ~ *vt* **:** to cause (a sail) to shiver by steering close to the wind
4shiver *n* **:** an instance of shivering **:** TREMBLE
1shiv·ery \'shiv-(ə-)rē\ *adj* **:** inclined to break into flakes **:** BRITTLE
2shivery *adj* **1 :** characterized by shivers **2 :** causing shivers
shlemiehl *var of* SCHLEMIEL
shlock *var of* SCHLOCK
1shoal \'shōl\ *adj* [alter. of ME *shold,* fr. OE *sceald* — more at SKELETON] **:** SHALLOW
2shoal *n* **1 :** SHALLOW **2 :** a sandbank or sandbar that makes the water shoal; *specif* **:** an elevation which is not rocky and on which there is a depth of water of six fathoms or less
3shoal *vi* **:** to become shallow ~ *vt* **1 :** to come to a shallow or less deep part of **2 :** to cause to become shallow or less deep
4shoal *n* [(assumed) ME *shole,* fr. OE *scolu* multitude — more at SCHOOL] **:** a large group (as of fish) **:** CROWD
5shoal *vi* **:** THRONG, SCHOOL
shoat \'shōt\ *n* [ME *shote;* akin to Flem *schote* shoat] **:** a young hog usu. less than one year old
1shock \'shäk\ *n* [ME; akin to MHG *schoc* heap, OE *hēah* high — more at HIGH] **:** a pile of sheaves of grain or stalks of Indian corn set up in a field with the butt ends down
2shock *vt* **:** to collect into shocks
3shock *n, often attrib* [MF *choc,* fr. *choquer* to strike against, fr. OF *choquier,* prob. of Gmc origin; akin to MD *schocken* to jolt] **1 :** the impact or encounter of individuals or groups in combat **2 a :** a violent shake or jar **:** CONCUSSION **b :** an effect of such violence **3 a (1) :** a disturbance in the equilibrium or permanence of something **(2) :** a sudden or violent disturbance in the mental or emotional faculties **b :** something that causes such disturbance **4 :** a state of profound depression of the vital processes associated with reduced blood volume and pressure and caused usu. by severe esp. crushing injuries, hemorrhage, or burns **5 :** sudden stimulation of the nerves and convulsive contraction of the muscles caused by the discharge of electricity through the animal body **6 a :** APOPLEXY **b :** CORONARY THROMBOSIS
4shock *vt* **1 a :** to strike with suprise, terror, horror, or disgust **b :** to cause to undergo a physical or nervous shock **c :** to subject to the action of an electrical discharge **2 :** to drive by or as if by a shock ~ *vi* **:** to meet with a shock **:** COLLIDE
5shock *n* [perh. fr. 1*shock*] **:** a thick bushy mass (as of hair)
6shock *adj* **:** BUSHY, SHAGGY
7shock *n* **:** SHOCK ABSORBER
shock absorber *n* **:** any of several devices for absorbing the energy of sudden impulses or shocks in machinery or structures
shock·er \'shäk-ər\ *n* **:** one that shocks; *esp* **:** something horrifying or offensive (as a sensational work of fiction or drama)
shock front *n* **:** the advancing edge of a shock wave
shock·ing *adj* **:** extremely startling and offensive — **shock·ing·ly** \-iŋ-lē\ *adv*
shocking pink *n* **:** a striking, vivid, bright, or intense pink
shock·proof \'shäk-'prüf\ *adj* **1 :** incapable of being shocked **2 a :** resistant to shock **b :** unlikely to cause shock **:** protectively insulated <a ~ switch>
shock therapy *n* **:** the treatment of mental disorder by the artificial induction of coma or convulsions through use of drugs or electricity — called also *shock treatment*
shock troops *n pl* **:** troops esp. suited and chosen for offensive work because of their high morale, training, and discipline
shock tube *n* **:** a usu. enclosed tube in which experimental shock waves are produced as a result of the rupturing of a diaphragm separating two chambers containing a gas or gases at differential pressure
shock wave *n* **1 :** BLAST 5c **2 :** a compressional wave formed whenever the speed of a body or fluid relative to a medium exceeds that at which the medium can transmit sound **3 :** a violent pulsating disturbance or reaction <*shock waves* of rebellion>
shod \'shäd\ *adj* [ME, fr. pp. of *shoen* to shoe, fr. OE *scōgan,* fr. *scōh* shoe — more at SHOE] **1 a :** wearing footgear (as shoes) **b :** equipped with tires **2 :** furnished or equipped with a shoe
1shod·dy \'shäd-ē\ *n* [origin unknown] **1 a :** a wool of better quality and longer staple than mungo reclaimed from materials that are not felted **b :** a fabric often of inferior quality manufactured wholly or partly from reclaimed wool **2 a :** inferior, imitation, or pretentious articles or matter **b :** pretentious vulgarity
2shoddy *adj* **shod·di·er; -est** **1 :** made wholly or partly of shoddy **2 a :** cheaply imitative **:** vulgarly pretentious **b :** hastily or poorly done **:** INFERIOR **c :** SHABBY — **shod·di·ly** \'shäd-ᵊl-ē\ *adv* — **shod·di·ness** \'shäd-ē-nəs\ *n*
1shoe \'shü\ *n* [ME *shoo,* fr. OE *scōh;* akin to OHG *scuoh* shoe, OE *hȳd* hide] **1 a :** an outer covering for the human foot usu. made of leather with a thick or stiff sole and an attached heel **b :** a metal plate or rim for the hoof of an animal **2 :** something resembling a shoe: as **a :** a metal band on the runner of a sled **b :** the casing of a pneumatic tire; *broadly* **:** TIRE **3** *pl* **:** STATUS, POSITION; *also* **:** PLIGHT **4 :** a device that retards, stops, or controls the motion of an object; *esp* **:** the part of a brake that presses on the brake drum **5 a :** any of various devices that are inserted in or run along a track or groove to guide a movement, provide a contact or friction grip, or protect against wear, damage, or slipping **b :** a device (as a clip or track) on a camera that permits attachment of accessory items — called also *accessory shoe*
2shoe *vt* **shod** \'shäd\ *also* **shoed** \'shüd\; **shoe·ing** \'shü-iŋ\ **1 :** to furnish with a shoe **2 :** to cover for protection, strength, or ornament
shoe·bill \'shü-ˌbil\ *n* **:** a large broad-billed wading bird (*Balaeniceps rex*) of the valley of the White Nile that is related to the storks and herons
shoe·black \-ˌblak\ *n* **:** BOOTBLACK
1shoe·horn \-ˌhȯ(ə)rn\ *n* **:** a curved piece (as of horn, wood, or metal) used in putting on a shoe
2shoehorn *vt* **:** to force into a small, narrow, or insufficient space
shoe·lace \'shü-ˌlās\ *n* **:** a lace or string for fastening a shoe
shoe·mak·er \-ˌmā-kər\ *n* **:** one whose occupation is making or repairing shoes
shoe·pac *or* **shoe·pack** \'shü-ˌpak\ *n* [by folk etymology fr. Del *shipak*] **:** a waterproof laced boot worn esp. over heavy socks in cold weather
1shoe·string \'shü-ˌstriŋ\ *n* **1 :** SHOELACE **2** [fr. shoestrings being a typical item sold by itinerant vendors] **:** a small sum of money **:** capital inadequate or barely adequate to the needs of a transaction <start a business on a ~>
2shoestring *adj* **1 :** narrow and long like a shoestring <a ~ tie> **2 :** operating on, accomplished by, or consisting of a small amount of capital <a ~ budget>
shoestring catch *n* **:** a catch (as in baseball) made very close to the ground
shoe tree *n* **:** a foot-shaped device for inserting in a shoe to preserve its shape
sho·far \'shō-ˌfär, -fər\ *n, pl* **sho·froth** \shō-'frōt(h), -'frōs\ [Heb *shōphār*] **:** a ram's-horn trumpet blown by the ancient Hebrews in battle and high religious observances and used in synagogues before and during Rosh Hashanah and at the conclusion of Yom Kippur
1shog \'shäg\ *vi* **shogged; shog·ging** [ME *shoggen*] *chiefly dial* **:** to move along
2shog *n, chiefly dial* **:** SHAKE, JOLT
sho·gun \'shō-gən\ *n* [Jap *shōgun* general] **:** one of a line of military governors ruling Japan until the revolution of 1867–68 — **sho·gun·ate** \'shō-gə-nət, -ˌnāt\ *n*
sho·ji \'shō-(ˌ)jē\ *n, pl* **shoji** *also* **shojis** [Jap *shōji*] **:** a paper screen serving as a wall, partition, or sliding door
sho·lom \shä-'lōm, shə-\ *var of* SHALOM
shone *past of* SHINE
1shoo \'shü\ *interj* [ME *schowe*] — used in frightening away an animal (as a hen)
2shoo *vt* **:** to scare, drive, or send away by or as if by crying *shoo*
shoo·fly \'shü-ˌflī\ *n* [1*shoo* + *fly*] **1 :** a child's rocker having the seat built on or usu. between supports representing an animal figure **2 :** any of several plants held to repel flies
shoofly pie *n* **:** a rich pie of Pennsylvania-Dutch origin made of molasses or brown sugar sprinkled with a crumbly mixture of flour, sugar, and butter
shoo–in \'shü-ˌin\ *n* **:** one that is a certain and easy winner
1shook *past or chiefly dial past part of* SHAKE
2shook \'shu̇k\ *n* [origin unknown] **1 a :** a set of staves and headings for one hogshead, cask, or barrel **b :** a bundle of parts (as of boxes) ready to be put together **2 :** 1SHOCK
shook–up \(ˈ)shu̇k-'əp\ *adj* [*shook,* substandard pp. of *shake*] **:** nervously upset **:** AGITATED
shoon \'shün, 'shōn\ *chiefly dial pl of* SHOE

[1]shoot \'shüt\ *vb* **shot** \'shät\; **shoot·ing** [ME *sheten, shuten,* fr. OE *scēotan;* akin to ON *skjōta* to shoot, Lith *skudrus* quick] *vt* **1 a** (1) **:** to eject or impel or cause to be ejected or impelled by a sudden release of tension (as of a bowstring or slingshot or by a flick of a finger) <~ an arrow> <~ a spitball> <~ a marble> (2) **:** to drive forth or cause to be driven forth by an explosion (as of a powder charge in a firearm or of ignited fuel in a rocket) (3) **:** to drive forth or cause to be driven forth by a sudden release of gas or air <~ darts from a blowgun> <a steam catapult ~*s* planes from a carrier> (4) **:** to drive forth or away (as a ball or puck) by striking or pushing with the arm or hand or with an implement (5) **:** to throw or cast off or out often with force <~ dice> <the horse *shot* his rider out of the saddle> **b** (1) **:** to utter (as words or sounds) rapidly or suddenly or with force <~ out a stream of invective> (2) **:** to emit (as light, flame, or fumes) suddenly and rapidly (3) **:** to send forth with suddenness or intensity <*shot* a look of anger at him> **c :** to discharge, dump, or empty esp. by overturning, upending, or directing into a slide **2 :** to affect by shooting: as **a :** to strike with a missile esp. from a bow or gun; *esp* **:** to wound or kill with a missile discharged from a bow or firearm **b :** to remove or destroy by use of firearms <*shot* out the light>; *also* **:** WRECK, EXPLODE **3 a :** to push or slide (as the bolt of a door or lock) into or out of a fastening **b :** to pass (a shuttle) through the warp threads in weaving **c :** to push or thrust forward **:** stick out <toads ~*ing* out their tongues> **d :** to put forth in growing **e :** to place, send, or bring into position abruptly **4 a :** to engage in (a sport or game or a portion of a game that involves shooting) **:** PLAY <~ pool> <~ a round of golf> <~ craps> **b :** to score by shooting <~ a basket> <*shot* a 73 on the first 18 holes> **c** (1) **:** to place or offer (a bet) on the result of casting dice <~ $5> (2) **:** to use up by or as if by betting **:** EXHAUST <*shot* his whole wad on a shady deal> **5 a :** to practice the killing of (as game) with firearms esp. as a sport <~ woodcock> **b :** to hunt over <~ a tract of woodland> **6 a :** to cause to move suddenly or swiftly forward <*shot* the car onto the highway> **b :** to send or carry quickly **:** DISPATCH <~ the letter on to me as soon as you receive it> **7 :** to variegate as if by sprinkling color in streaks, flecks, or patches **8 :** to pass swiftly by, past, or along <~*ing* rapids> **9 :** to plane (as the edge of a board) straight or true **10 a :** to set off **:** DETONATE, IGNITE <~ a charge of dynamite> **b :** to effect by blasting **11 :** to determine the altitude of **12 :** to take a picture or series of pictures or television images of **:** PHOTOGRAPH, FILM **13 a :** to give an injection to **b :** to take (a drug) by hypodermic needle ~ *vi* **1 a :** to go or pass rapidly and precipitately <sparks ~*ing* up> <his feet *shot* out from under him> **b :** to move ahead by force of momentum **c :** to stream out suddenly **:** SPURT **d :** to dart in or as if in rays from a source of light **e :** to dart with a piercing sensation <pain *shot* up his arm> **2 a :** to cause an engine or weapon to discharge a missile **b :** to use a firearm or bow esp. for sport (as in hunting) **3 :** to propel a missile <guns that ~ many miles> **4 :** PROTRUDE, PROJECT **5 a :** to grow or sprout by or as if by putting forth shoots **b :** DEVELOP, MATURE **6 a :** to propel an object (as a ball) in a particular way **b :** to drive the ball or puck toward a goal **7 :** to cast dice **8 :** to slide into or out of a fastening <a bolt that ~*s* in either direction> **9 a :** to record visually (as on movie film or videotape) a scene of a motion picture or television production **b :** to operate a camera or set cameras in operation **:** FILM — **shoot at** *or* **shoot for :** to aim at **:** strive for — **shoot one's bolt :** to exhaust one's capabilities and resources — **shoot the breeze :** to converse idly **:** GOSSIP — **shoot the works 1 :** to venture all one's capital on one play **2 :** to put forth all one's efforts

[2]shoot *n* **1 :** a sending out of new growth or the growth sent out: as **a :** a stem or branch with its leaves and appendages esp. when not yet mature **b :** OFFSHOOT **c :** a similar formation of crystal **2 a :** an act of shooting (as with a bow or a firearm): (1) **:** SHOT (2) **:** the firing of a missile esp. by artillery **b** (1) **:** a hunting trip or party (2) **:** the right to shoot game in a particular area or land over which it is held **c** (1) **:** a shooting match <skeet ~> (2) **:** a round of shots in a shooting match **d** (1) **:** the action of shooting with a camera (2) **:** a launching of a rocket device or a guided missile esp. experimentally **3 a :** a motion or movement of rapid thrusting: as (1) **:** a sudden or rapid advance (2) [perh. by folk etymology fr. F *chute* — more at CHUTE] **:** a rush of water down a steep or rapid (3) **:** a momentary darting sensation **:** TWINGE (4) **:** THRUST 2b (5) **:** a falling of a detached mass of earth or ice (6) **:** the pace between strokes in rowing **b :** a bar of rays **:** BEAM <a ~ of sunlight> **4** [prob. by folk etymology fr. F *chute* — more at CHUTE] **a :** a place where a stream runs or descends swiftly **b :** any of various inclined channels or troughs through which something (as water, logs, or grain) is moved **5 :** an elongated usu. vertical body of ore in a vein

[3]shoot *interj* [euphemism for *shit*] — used to express annoyance or surprise

shoot–'em–up \'shüt-ə-ˌməp\ *n* **:** a movie or television show with much shooting and bloodshed

shoot·er \'shüt-ər\ *n* **1 :** one that shoots: as **a :** a person who fires a missile-discharging device (as a rifle or bow) **b :** the person who is rolling the dice in craps **2 :** something that is used in shooting: as **a :** a marble shot from the hand **b :** a repeating pistol — usu. used in combination <six-*shooter*>

shooting gallery *n* **:** a usu. covered range equipped with targets for practice with firearms

shooting iron *n* **:** FIREARM

shooting script *n* **1 :** the final completely detailed version of a motion-picture script in which scenes are grouped in the order most convenient for shooting **2 :** the final version of a television script used in the production of a program

shooting star *n* **1 :** a visual meteor appearing as a temporary streak of light in the night sky **2 :** a No. American perennial herb (*Dodecatheon meadia*) of the primrose family that has entire oblong leaves and showy flowers with reflexed petals

shooting stick *n* **:** a spiked stick with a top that opens into a seat

shoot–out \'shüt-ˌau̇t\ *n* **:** a battle fought with handguns or rifles

shoot–the–chutes \ˌshüt-t͟hə-'shüts\ *n pl but sing in constr* **:** an amusement ride consisting of a steep incline down which boats with flat bottoms slide usu. to continue across a body of water at the bottom

shoot up \(ˈ)shüt-'əp\ *vt* **:** to inject (a narcotic drug) into a vein ~ *vi* **:** to inject a narcotic into a vein — **shoot–up** \'shüt-ˌəp\ *n*

[1]shop \'shäp\ *n, often attrib* [ME *shoppe,* fr. OE *sceoppa* booth; akin to OHG *scopf* shed] **1 :** a handicraft establishment **:** ATELIER **2 a :** a building or room stocked with merchandise for sale **:** STORE **b** *or* **shoppe** \'shäp\ **:** a small retail establishment or a department in a large one offering a specified line of goods or services <a millinery ~> <a sandwich ~> **3 :** FACTORY, MILL **4 a :** a school laboratory equipped for instruction in manual arts **b :** the art or science of working with tools and machinery **5 a :** a business establishment; *esp* **:** OFFICE **b :** SHOPTALK

[2]shop *vb* **shopped; shop·ping** *vi* **1 a :** to examine goods or services with intent to buy **b :** to probe a market in search of the best buy **2 :** to make a search **:** HUNT ~ *vt* **:** to examine the stock or offerings of <~ the stores for Christmas gift ideas>

shop·keep·er \'shäp-ˌkē-pər\ *n* **:** STOREKEEPER 2

shop·lift \-ˌlift\ *vb* [back-formation fr. *shoplifter*] *vt* **:** to steal (goods on display) from a store ~ *vi* **:** to steal displayed goods from a store

shop·lift·er \-ˌlif-tər\ *n* **:** one who shoplifts

shop·per \'shäp-ər\ *n* **1 :** one that shops **2 :** one whose occupation is shopping as an agent for customers or for an employer **3 :** a usu. free paper carrying advertising and sometimes local news

shopping center *n* **:** a group of retail stores and service establishments usu. with ample parking facilities and usu. designed to serve a community or neighborhood — called also SHOPPING PLAZA

shopping mall *n* **1 :** an area restricted to pedestrians in a city and lined by shops **2 :** a shopping center with stores facing an enclosed area for pedestrians

shop steward *n* **:** a union member elected as the union representative of a shop or department in dealings with the management

shop·talk \'shäp-ˌtȯk\ *n* **:** the jargon or subject matter peculiar to an occupation or a special area of interest

shop·worn \-ˌwō(ə)rn, -ˌwȯ(ə)rn\ *adj* **1 :** faded, soiled, or otherwise impaired by remaining too long in a store **2 :** stale from excessive use or familiarity <~ clichés>

sho·ran \'shō(ə)r-ˌan, 'shȯ(ə)r-\ *n* [*sho*rt-*ra*nge *n*avigation] **:** a system of short-range navigation in which two radar signals transmitted by an airplane are intercepted and rebroadcast to the airplane by two ground stations of known position so as to determine the position of the airplane

[1]shore \'shō(ə)r, 'shȯ(ə)r\ *n, often attrib* [ME, fr. (assumed) OE *scor;* akin to OE *scieran* to cut — more at SHEAR] **1 :** the land bordering a usu. large body of water; *specif* **:** COAST **2 :** land as distinguished from the sea <shipboard and ~ duty>

[2]shore *vt* **shored; shor·ing** [ME *shoren;* akin to ON *skortha* to prop] **1 :** to support by a shore **:** PROP **2 :** to give support to **:** BRACE — usu. used with *up*

[3]shore *n* **:** a prop for preventing sinking or sagging

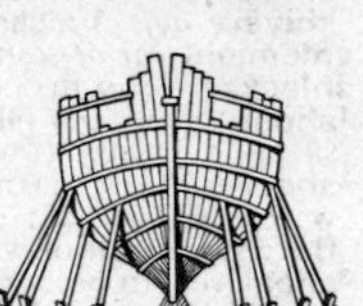
shores supporting a ship

shore·bird \'shō(ə)r-ˌbərd, 'shȯ(ə)r-\ *n* **:** any of a suborder (Charadrii) of birds (as a plover or snipe) that frequent the seashore

shore dinner *n* **:** a dinner consisting chiefly of seafoods

shore·front \-ˌfrənt\ *n* **:** land along a shore; *specif* **:** BEACHFRONT

shore leave *n* **:** a leave of absence to go on shore granted to a sailor or naval officer

shore·line \-ˌlīn\ *n* **:** the line where a body of water and the shore meet; *also* **:** the strip of land along this line

shore patrol *n* **1 :** a branch of a navy that exercises guard and police functions — compare MILITARY POLICE **2 :** petty officers detailed to perform police duty while a ship is in port

shore·side \-ˌsīd\ *adj* **:** situated at or near a shore

shore·ward \-wərd\ *or* **shore·wards** \-wərdz\ *adv* **:** toward the shore

shor·ing \'shōr-iŋ, 'shȯr-\ *n* **1 :** the act of supporting with or as if with a prop **2 :** a system or group of shores

shorn *past part of* SHEAR

[1]short \'shȯ(ə)rt\ *adj* [ME, fr. OE *scort*] **1 a :** having little length **b :** not tall or high **:** LOW **2 a :** not extended in time **:** BRIEF <a ~ vacation> **b :** not retentive <a ~ memory> **c :** EXPEDITIOUS, QUICK <made ~ work of the problem> **d :** seeming to pass quickly <made great progress in just a few ~ years> **3 a** *of a speech sound* **:** having a relatively short duration **b :** being the member of a pair of similarly spelled vowel or vowel-containing sounds that is descended from a vowel that was short in duration but is no longer so and that does not necessarily have duration as its chief distinguishing feature <~ *i* in *sin*> **c** *of a syllable in prosody* (1) **:** of relatively brief duration (2) **:** UNSTRESSED **4 :** limited in distance <a ~ trip> **5 a :** not coming up to a measure or requirement **:** INSUFFICIENT <in ~ supply> **b :** not reaching far enough <the throw to first was ~> **c :** enduring privation **d :** insufficiently supplied <~ of cash> <~ on brains> **6 a :** ABRUPT, CURT **b :** quickly provoked **7 :** [3]CHOPPY 1 **8 :** payable at an early date **9 a :** containing or cooked with shortening **:** FLAKY <~ pastry> **b** *of metal* **:** brittle under certain conditions **10 a :** not lengthy or drawn out **b :** made briefer **:** ABBREVIATED **11 a :** not having goods or property that one has sold in anticipation of a fall in prices **b :** consisting of or relating to a sale of securities or commodities that the seller does not possess or has not contracted for at the time of the sale <~ sale> **12 :** near the end of a tour of duty — **short·ish** \'shȯrt-ish\ *adj* — **in short order :** with dispatch **:** QUICKLY

[2]**short** *adv* **1 :** in a curt manner **2 :** for or during a brief time <*short*-lasting> **3 :** at a disadvantage : UNAWARES <caught ~> **4 :** so as to interrupt <took him up ~> **5 :** in an abrupt manner : SUDDENLY <the car stopped ~> **6 :** at some point or degree before a goal or limit aimed at or under consideration <the shells fell ~> <quit a month ~ of graduation> **7 :** clean across <the axle was snapped ~> **8 :** by or as if by a short sale

[3]**short** *n* **1 :** the sum and substance : UPSHOT **2 a :** a short syllable **b :** a short sound or signal **3** *pl* **a :** a by-product of wheat milling that includes the germ, fine bran, and some flour **b :** refuse, clippings, or trimmings discarded in various manufacturing processes **4 a** *pl* **:** knee-length or less than knee-length trousers **b** *pl* **:** short drawers **c :** a size in clothing for short men **5 a :** one who operates on the short side of the market **b** *pl* **:** short-term bonds **6** *pl* **:** DEFICIENCIES **7 :** SHORT CIRCUIT **8 :** SHORTSTOP 1 **9 :** SHORT SUBJECT — **in short :** by way of summary : BRIEFLY

[4]**short** *vt* **1 :** SHORTCHANGE, CHEAT **2 :** SHORT-CIRCUIT

short account *n* **1 :** the account of a short seller **2 :** the total of open short sales in a given subject of trade or in the market as a whole

short·age \'shȯrt-ij\ *n* **:** LACK, DEFICIT

short ballot *n* **:** a ballot limiting the number of elective offices to the most important legislative and executive posts and leaving minor positions to be filled by appointment

short·bread \'shȯrt-ˌbred\ *n* **:** a thick cookie made of flour, sugar, and a large amount of shortening

short·cake \-ˌkāk\ *n* **1 :** a crisp and often unsweetened biscuit or cookie **2 a :** a dessert made typically of very short baking-powder-biscuit dough spread with sweetened fruit **b :** a dish consisting of a rich biscuit split and covered with a meat mixture

short·change \-'chānj\ *vt* **1 :** to give less than the correct amount of change to **2 :** to deprive of something due : CHEAT — **short·chang·er** *n*

short–cir·cuit *vt* **1 :** to apply a short circuit to or establish a short circuit in **2 :** BYPASS **3 :** FRUSTRATE, IMPEDE

short circuit *n* **:** a connection of comparatively low resistance accidentally or intentionally made between points on a circuit between which the resistance is normally much greater

short·com·ing \'shȯrt-ˌkəm-iŋ, (ˈ)shȯrt-'\ *n* **:** DEFICIENCY, DEFECT

short covering *n* **:** buying in property (as securities) to close out a short sale

short·cut \'shȯrt-ˌkət, -'kət\ *n* **1 :** a route more direct than the one ordinarily taken **2 :** a method of doing something more directly and quickly than by ordinary procedure

short–day \'shȯrt-ˌdā\ *adj* **:** responding to or relating to a short photoperiod — used of a plant; compare DAY-NEUTRAL, LONG-DAY

short division *n* **:** mathematical division in which the successive steps are performed without writing out the remainders

short·en \'shȯrt-ᵊn\ *vb* **short·ened; short·en·ing** \'shȯrt-niŋ, -ᵊn-iŋ\ *vt* **1 a :** to reduce the length or duration of **b :** to cause to seem short **2 a :** to reduce in power or efficiency <is my hand ~*ed*, that it cannot redeem —Isa 50:2 (RSV)> **b** *obs* **:** to deprive of effect **3 :** to add fat to (pastry dough) in order to make tender and flaky ~ *vi* **:** to become short or shorter — **short·en·er** \-nər, -ᵊn-ər\ *n*

syn SHORTEN, CURTAIL, ABBREVIATE, ABRIDGE, RETRENCH *shared meaning element* **:** to reduce in extent. SHORTEN implies reduction in length or duration, real or apparent <*shorten* a rope> <their pleasant chat *shortened* the time of waiting> CURTAIL adds an implication of cutting that in some way deprives of completeness or adequacy <*curtail* expenditures> <laws that *curtail* our freedom> ABBREVIATE implies a shortening usually by cutting off or omitting some normally present part; thus, one *abbreviates* a word or phrase by cutting out or cutting off letters so that what remains stands for the whole <a . . . man of great . . . energy, though of *abbreviated* intelligence —W. L. Shirer> ABRIDGE may imply reduction in compass or scope <the danger of *abridging* the liberties of the people —Abraham Lincoln> or a shortening that retains all essential elements <*abridge* a course of study for an accelerated program> RETRENCH stresses reduction in scope of something (as expenses) felt to be excessive <a long speech . . . I could be glad you would *retrench* it —Thomas Gray> *ant* lengthen, elongate, extend

short·en·ing \'shȯrt-niŋ, -ᵊn-iŋ\ *n* **1 :** the action or process of making or becoming short; *specif* **:** the dropping of the latter part of a word so as to produce a new and shorter word of the same meaning **2 :** an edible fat used to shorten baked goods

short·fall \'shȯrt-ˌfȯl\ *n* **:** a failure to come up to a goal or need; *also* **:** the amount of such failure : DEFICIENCY

short·hand \-ˌhand\ *n* **1 :** a method of writing rapidly by substituting characters, abbreviations, or symbols for letters, words, or phrases : STENOGRAPHY **2 :** a system or instance of rapid or abbreviated communication — **shorthand** *adj*

short·hand·ed \-'han-dəd\ *adj* **:** short of the regular or necessary number of people

short·horn \-ˌhȯ(ə)rn\ *n, often cap* **:** any of a breed of red, roan, or white beef cattle originating in the north of England and including good milk-producing strains — called also *Durham*

short–horned grasshopper \ˌshȯrt-ˌhȯrn(d)-\ *n* **:** any of a family (Acrididae) of grasshoppers with short antennae

short hundredweight *n* **:** HUNDREDWEIGHT 1a

short·leaf pine \ˌshȯrt-ˌlēf-\ *n* **:** a pine (*Pinus echinata*) of the southern U.S. that has short flexible leaves and cinnamon-colored bark; *also* **:** its yellow wood

short line *n* **:** a transportation system (as a railroad) operating over a relatively short distance

short–lived \'shȯrt-'līvd, -ˌlivd\ *adj* **:** not living or lasting long *syn* see TRANSIENT *ant* agelong

short loin *n* **:** a portion of the hindquarter of beef immediately behind the ribs that is usu. cut into steaks

short·ly \'shȯrt-lē\ *adv* **1 a :** in a few words : BRIEFLY **b :** in an abrupt manner **2 a :** in a short time <we will be there ~> **b :** at a short interval <~ after sunset> *syn* see PRESENTLY

short·ness \-nəs\ *n* **:** the quality or state of being short

short–nosed cattle louse \ˌshȯrt-ˌnōz(d)-\ *n* **:** a large bluish broad-bodied and short-headed sucking louse (*Haematopinus eurysternus*) that attacks domestic cattle

short order *n* **:** an order for food that can be quickly cooked

short–range \'shȯrt-'rānj\ *adj* **1 :** involving or taking into account a short period of time <~ plans> **2 :** relating to or fit for short distances

short ribs *n pl* **:** a cut of beef consisting of rib ends between the rib roast and the plate — see BEEF illustration

short run *n* **:** a relatively brief period of time — often used in the phrase *in the short run*

short shrift *n* **1 :** a brief respite for confession before execution **2 :** summary treatment

short sight *n* **:** MYOPIA

short·sight·ed \'shȯrt-'sīt-əd\ *adj* **1 :** NEARSIGHTED **2 :** lacking foresight — **short·sight·ed·ly** *adv* — **short·sight·ed·ness** *n*

short–spo·ken \-'spō-kən\ *adj* **:** CURT

short·stop \-ˌstäp\ *n* **1 :** the player position in baseball for defending the infield area on the third-base side of second base **2 :** the player stationed in the shortstop position

short–stop \-ˌstäp\ *n* **:** STOP BATH

short story *n* **:** a brief invented prose narrative usu. dealing with a few characters and aiming at unity of effect and often concentrating on the creation of mood rather than plot

short subject *n* **:** a brief often documentary or educational film

short–tem·pered \'shȯrt-'tem-pərd\ *adj* **:** having a quick temper

short–term \-'tərm\ *adj* **1 :** occurring over or involving a relatively short period of time **2 a :** of, relating to, or constituting a financial operation or obligation based on a brief term and esp. one of less than a year **b :** generated by assets held for less than six months

short ton *n* — see WEIGHT table

short·wave \'shȯrt-'wāv\ *n, often attrib* **1 :** a radio wave of 60-meter wavelength or less **2 :** a radio transmitter using shortwaves **3 :** electromagnetic radiation having a wavelength equal to or less than that of visible light

short–wind·ed \-'win-dəd\ *adj* **1 :** affected with or characterized by shortness of breath **2 a :** BRIEF **b :** broken up into short units

shorty *or* **short·ie** \'shȯrt-ē\ *n, pl* **short·ies** *often attrib* **:** one that is short

Sho·sho·ne *or* **Sho·sho·ni** \shə-'shō-nē\ *n, pl* **Shoshones** *or* **Shoshoni** *also* **Shoshone** *or* **Shoshonis** **1 :** a group of Amerindian peoples orig. ranging through California, Colorado, Idaho, Nevada, Utah, and Wyoming **2 :** a member of any of the Shoshone peoples

Sho·sho·ne·an \-nē-ən\ *n* **:** a language family of the Uto-Aztecan phylum comprising the languages of most of the Uto-Aztecan peoples in the U.S.

[1]**shot** \'shät\ *n* [ME, fr. OE *scot;* akin to ON *skot* shot, OHG *scuz,* OE *scēotan* to shoot — more at SHOOT] **1 a :** an action of shooting **b :** a directed propelling of a missile; *specif* **:** a directed discharge of a firearm **c :** a stroke or throw in a game (as tennis, pool, or basketball); *also* **:** HOME RUN **d :** BLAST **e :** a medical or narcotics injection **2 a** *pl* **shot :** something propelled by shooting; *esp* **:** small lead or steel pellets esp. forming a charge for a shotgun **b :** a metal sphere of iron or brass that is put for distance in a field event **3 a :** the distance that a missile is or can be thrown **b :** RANGE, REACH **4 :** a charge to be paid : SCOT **5 :** one that shoots; *esp* **:** MARKSMAN **6 a :** ATTEMPT, TRY **b :** GUESS, CONJECTURE **c :** CHANCE **7 :** an effective remark **8 a :** a single photographic exposure; *esp* **:** SNAPSHOT **b :** a single sequence of a motion picture or a television program shot by one camera without interruption **9 :** a charge of explosives **10 a :** a single drink of liquor **b :** a small amount applied at one time : DOSE — **like a shot :** very rapidly — **shot in the arm :** STIMULUS, BOOST — **shot in the dark 1 :** a wild guess **2 :** an attempt that has little chance of success

[2]**shot** *adj* **1 a** *of a fabric* **:** having contrasting and changeable color effects : IRIDESCENT **b :** suffused or streaked with a color <hair ~ with gray> **c :** infused or permeated with a quality or element <~ through with wit> **2 :** having the form of pellets resembling shot **3 :** reduced to a state of ruin, prostration, or uselessness <his nerves are ~>

[1]**shot·gun** \'shät-'gən\ *n* **1 :** an often double-barreled smoothbore shoulder weapon for firing shot at short ranges **2 :** an offensive football formation in which the quarterback plays a few yards behind the line of scrimmage and the other backs are scattered as flankers or slotbacks

[2]**shotgun** *adj* **1 :** of, relating to, or using a shotgun **2 :** involving coercion **3 :** covering a wide field with hit-or-miss effectiveness

shotgun marriage *n* **:** a marriage forced or required because of pregnancy — called also *shotgun wedding*

shot hole *n* **1 :** a drilled hole in which a charge of dynamite is exploded **2 :** the dropping out of small rounded fragments of leaves that produces a shot-riddled appearance and is caused esp. by parasitic action

shot put *n* **:** a field event consisting in putting the shot for distance — **shot–put·ter** \'shät-ˌpu̇t-ər\ *n*

shot·ten \'shät-ᵊn\ *adj* [ME *shotyn,* fr. pp. of *shuten* to shoot] **:** having ejected the spawn and so of inferior food value <~ herring>

should \shəd, (ˈ)shu̇d\ [ME *sholde,* fr. OE *sceolde* owed, was obliged to; akin to OHG *scolta* owed, was obliged to] *past of* SHALL **1** — used in auxiliary function to express condition <if he ~ leave his father, his father would die —Gen 44:22 (RSV)> **2** — used in auxiliary function to express obligation, propriety, or expediency <'tis commanded I ~ do so —Shak.> <this is as it ~ be —H. L. Savage> <you ~ brush your teeth after each meal> **3** — used in auxiliary function to express futurity from a point of view in the past <realized that she ~ have to do most of her farm work before sunrise —Ellen Glasgow> **4** — used in auxiliary function to express what is probable or expected <with an early start, they ~ be here by noon> **5** — used in auxiliary function to express a request in a polite manner or to soften direct statement <I ~ suggest that a guide . . . is the first essential —L. D. Reddick>

[1]**shoul·der** \'shōl-dər\ *n* [ME *sholder*, fr. OE *sculdor;* akin to OHG *scultra* shoulder, OE *sciell* shell — more at SHELL] **1 a :** the laterally projecting part of the human body formed of the bones and joints by which the arm is connected with the trunk and the muscles covering them **b :** the region of the body of a lower vertebrate that corresponds to the shoulder but is less projecting **2 a:** the two shoulders and the upper part of the back — usu. used in pl. **b** *pl* **:** capacity for bearing a task or blame <placed the guilt squarely on his ~*s*> **3 :** a cut of meat including the upper joint of the foreleg and adjacent parts — see LAMB illustration **4 :** the part of a garment at the wearer's shoulder **5 :** an area adjacent to or along the edge of a higher, more prominent, or more important part: as **a** (1) **:** the part of a hill or mountain near the top (2) **:** a lateral protrusion or extension of a hill or mountain **b :** the flat top of the body of a piece of printing type from which the bevel rises to join the face — see TYPE illustration **c :** either edge of a roadway; *specif* **:** the part of a roadway outside of the traveled way **6 :** a rounded or sloping part (as of a stringed instrument or a bottle) where the neck joins the body — **shoul·dered** \-dərd\ *adj*

[2]**shoulder** *vb* **shoul·dered; shoul·der·ing** \-d(ə-)riŋ\ *vt* **1 :** to push or thrust with the shoulder **:** JOSTLE <~*ed* his way through the crowd> **2 a :** to place or bear on the shoulder <~*ed* his knapsack> **b :** to assume the burden or responsibility of <~ the blame> ~ *vi* **:** to push with the shoulders aggressively

shoulder bag *n* **:** a woman's handbag looped over the shoulder by a strap

shoulder belt *n* **:** an anchored belt worn across the upper torso and over the shoulders to hold a person steady in a seat esp. in case of an automobile collision — called also *shoulder harness*

shoulder blade *n* **:** SCAPULA

shoulder board *n* **:** one of a pair of broad pieces of stiffened cloth worn on the shoulders of a military uniform and carrying insignia

shoulder girdle *n* **:** PECTORAL GIRDLE

shoulder knot *n* **1 :** an ornamental knot of ribbon or lace worn on the shoulder in the 17th and 18th centuries **2 :** a detachable ornament of braided wire cord worn on the shoulders of a uniform of ceremony by a commissioned officer

shoulder mark *n* **:** SHOULDER BOARD

shoulder patch *n* **:** a cloth patch bearing an identifying mark and worn on one sleeve of a uniform below the shoulder

shoulder strap *n* **:** a strap that passes across the shoulder and holds up an article or garment

should·est \'shu̇d-əst\ *archaic past 2d sing of* SHALL

shouldn't \'shu̇d-ᵊnt\ **:** should not

shouldst \shədst, (')shu̇dst, shətst, (')shu̇tst\ *archaic past 2d sing of* SHALL

[1]**shout** \'shau̇t\ *vb* [ME *shouten*] *vi* **:** to utter a sudden loud cry ~ *vt* **:** to utter in a loud voice — **shout·er** *n*

[2]**shout** *n* **:** a loud cry or call

shouting distance *n* **:** a short distance **:** easy reach — usu. used with *within* <lived within *shouting distance* of his cousins>

shout song *n* **:** a rhythmic religious song used esp. by Negroes and characterized by responsive singing or shouting between leader and congregation

[1]**shove** \'shəv\ *vb* **shoved; shov·ing** [ME *shoven*, fr. OE *scūfan* to thrust away; akin to OHG *scioban* to push, OSlav *skubati* to tear] *vt* **1 :** to push along **2 :** to push or put in a rough, careless, or hasty manner **:** THRUST **3 :** to force by other than physical means **:** COMPEL <~ a bill through the legislature> ~ *vi* **1 :** to move by forcing a way <bargain hunters *shoving* up to the counter> **2 a :** to move something by exerting force **b :** LEAVE <put on his hat and *shoved off* for home> ***syn*** see PUSH — **shov·er** *n*

[2]**shove** *n* **:** an act or instance of shoving **:** a forcible push

[1]**shov·el** \'shəv-əl\ *n* [ME, fr. OE *scofl;* akin to OHG *scūfla* shovel, OE *scūfan* to thrust away] **1 a :** a hand implement consisting of a broad scoop or a more or less hollowed out blade with a handle used to lift and throw material **b :** something that resembles a shovel **2 :** SHOVELFUL

[2]**shovel** *vb* **-eled** *or* **-elled; -el·ing** *or* **-el·ling** \-(ə-)liŋ\ *vt* **1 :** to take up and throw with a shovel **2 :** to dig or clean out with a shovel **3 :** to throw or convey roughly or in the mass as if with a shovel <~*ed* his food into his mouth> ~ *vi* **:** to use a shovel

shov·el·er *or* **shov·el·ler** \'shəv-(ə-)lər\ *n* **1 :** one that shovels **2 :** any of several river ducks (genus *Anas*) having a large and very broad bill

shov·el·ful \'shəv-əl-ˌfu̇l\ *n, pl* **shovelfuls** \-ˌfu̇lz\ *also* **shov·els·ful** \-əlz-ˌfu̇l\ **:** as much as a shovel will hold

shovel hat *n* **:** a shallow-crowned hat with a wide brim curved up at the sides that is worn by some clergymen

shov·el·head \'shəv-əl-ˌhed\ *n* **:** any of several fishes with heads resembling a shovel; *esp* **:** a shark (*Sphyrna tiburo*) that is smaller than the related hammerhead and has a narrower head

shov·el·man \-ˌman, -mən\ *n* **:** one who works with a shovel or a power shovel

shov·el·nose \-ˌnōz\ *n* **:** a shovel-nosed animal and esp. a fish

shov·el–nosed \ˌshəv-əl-'nōzd\ *adj* **:** having a broad flat head, nose, or beak

[1]**show** \'shō\ *vb* **showed** \'shōd\; **shown** \'shōn\ *or* **showed; show·ing** [ME *shewen, showen*, fr. OE *scēawian* to look, look at, see; akin to OHG *scouwōn* to look, look at, L *cavēre* to be on one's guard] *vt* **1 :** to cause or permit to be seen **:** EXHIBIT <~*ed* every mark of extreme agitation> **2 :** to set out for sale **:** OFFER <stores were ~*ing* new spring suits> **3 :** to present as a public spectacle **:** PERFORM **4 :** to display for the notice of others **5 :** to reveal by one's condition, nature, or behavior **6 :** to give indication of by record **7 a :** to point out to someone <~*ed* him the house> **b :** CONDUCT, USHER <~*ed* me to an aisle seat> **8 :** ACCORD, BESTOW **9 a :** to set forth **:** DECLARE **b :** ALLEGE, PLEAD — used esp. in law <~ cause> **10 a :** to demonstrate or establish by argument or reasoning <~ a plan to be faulty> **b :** INFORM, INSTRUCT <~*ed* me how to solve the problem> **11 :** to present (an animal) for judging in a show ~ *vi* **1 a :** to be or come in view <anger ~*ed* in his face> **b :** to put in an appearance <failed to ~> **2 a :** to appear in a particular way <his nature ~*ed* strong in adversity> **b :** SEEM, APPEAR **3 a :** to give a theatrical performance **b :** to be staged or presented **4 :** to finish third or at least third in a horse race

syn SHOW, MANIFEST, EVIDENCE, EVINCE, DEMONSTRATE *shared meaning element* **:** to reveal outwardly or make apparent

— **show one's hand 1 :** to display one's cards faceup **2 :** to declare one's intentions or reveal one's resources — **show the door :** to tell someone to get out

[2]**show** *n* **1 :** a demonstrative display <a ~ of strength> **2 a** *archaic* **:** outward appearance **b :** a false semblance **:** PRETENSE <he made a ~ of friendship> **c :** a more or less true appearance of something **:** SIGN **d :** an impressive display **e :** OSTENTATION **3 :** CHANCE <gave him a ~ in spite of his background> **4 :** something exhibited esp. for wonder or ridicule **:** SPECTACLE **5 a :** a large display or exhibition arranged to arouse interest or stimulate sales <the national auto ~> **b :** a competitive exhibition of animals (as dogs) to demonstrate quality in breeding **6 a :** a theatrical presentation **b :** a radio or television program **c :** ENTERTAINMENT 3a **7 :** ENTERPRISE, AFFAIR <he ran the whole ~> **8 :** an indication of metal in a mine or of gas or oil in a well **9 :** third place at the finish of a horse race

show bill *n* **:** an advertising poster

show biz \-ˌbiz\ *n* [by shortening & alter.] **:** SHOW BUSINESS

show·boat \'shō-ˌbōt\ *n* **:** a river steamship containing a theater and carrying a troupe of actors to give plays at river communities

showbread *var of* SHEWBREAD

show business *n* **:** the arts, occupations, and businesses (as theater, motion pictures, and television) that comprise the entertainment industry

[1]**show·case** \'shō-ˌkās\ *n* **1 :** a glazed case, box, or cabinet for displaying and protecting wares in a store or articles in a museum **2 a :** a setting or framework for exhibiting something esp. at its best **b :** a medium or vehicle for exhibiting a tentative offering or tryout of something

[2]**showcase** *vt* **show·cased; show·cas·ing :** EXHIBIT

show·down \'shō-ˌdau̇n\ *n* **1 :** the placing of poker hands faceup on the table to determine the winner of a pot **2 :** the final settlement of a contested issue or the test of strength by which it is settled

[1]**show·er** \'shau̇(-ə)r\ *n* [ME *shour*, fr. OE *scūr;* akin to OHG *scūr* shower, L *caurus* northwest wind] **1 a :** a fall of rain of short duration **b :** a similar fall of sleet, hail, or snow **2 :** something resembling a rain shower **3 :** a party given by friends who bring gifts often of a particular kind **4 :** a bath in which water is showered on the body; *also* **:** the apparatus that provides a shower — **show·ery** \-ē\ *adj* — **to the showers :** out of the ball game

[2]**shower** *vi* **1 :** to rain or fall in or as if in a shower <letters ~*ed* on him in praise and protest> **2 :** to bathe in a shower bath ~ *vt* **1 a :** to wet (as with water) in a spray, fine stream, or drops **b :** to cause to fall in a shower <factory chimneys ~*ed* the district with soot> **2 :** to give in abundance <~*ed* him with honors>

[3]**show·er** \'shō(-ə)r\ *n* **:** one that shows **:** EXHIBITOR

shower bath *n* **:** SHOWER 4

show·ing \'shō-iŋ\ *n* **1 :** an act of putting something on view **:** DISPLAY **2 :** PERFORMANCE, RECORD <made a good ~ in competition> **3 a :** a statement or presentation of a case **b :** APPEARANCE, EVIDENCE

show·man \'shō-mən\ *n* **1 :** the producer of a play or other theatrical show **2 :** a person having a sense or knack for dramatically effective presentation — **show·man·ship** \-ˌship\ *n*

show–me \'shō-mē\ *adj* **:** insistent on proof or evidence

show–off \'shō-ˌȯf\ *n* **1 :** the act of showing off **2 :** one that shows off **:** EXHIBITIONIST

show off \(')shō-'ȯf\ *vt* **:** to display proudly <wanted to *show* his new car *off*> ~ *vi* **:** to seek to attract attention by conspicuous behavior <boys *showing off* for the girls>

show·piece \'shō-ˌpēs\ *n* **:** a prime or outstanding example used for exhibition

show·place \-ˌplās\ *n* **:** a place (as an estate or building) that is regarded as an example of beauty or excellence

show·room \-ˌrüm, -ˌru̇m\ *n* **:** a room where merchandise is exposed for sale or where samples are displayed

show·stop·per \-ˌstäp-ər\ *n* **:** an act, song, or performer that wins applause so prolonged as to interrupt a performance

show up *vt* **:** to reveal the true nature of **:** EXPOSE <*showed up* her ignorance> ~ *vi* **1 :** ARRIVE <*showed up* late for his own wedding> **2 :** to be plainly evident

show window *n* **1 :** an outside display window in which a store exhibits merchandise **2 :** a sample or setting used to exhibit or illustrate something at its best

showy \'shō-ē\ *adj* **show·i·er; -est 1 :** making an attractive show **:** STRIKING **2 :** given to or marked by a flashy often meretricious display **:** GAUDY — **show·i·ly** \'shō-ə-lē\ *adv* — **show·i·ness** \'shō-ē-nəs\ *n*

syn SHOWY, PRETENTIOUS, OSTENTATIOUS *shared meaning element* **:** given to or marked by excessive outward display

SHP *abbr* shaft horsepower

shpt *abbr* shipment

shrank *past of* SHRINK

shrap·nel \'shrap-nᵊl, *esp South* 'srap-\ *n, pl* **shrapnel** [Henry *Shrapnel* †1842 E artillery officer] **1 :** a projectile that consists of a case provided with a powder charge and a large number of usu. lead balls and that is exploded in flight **2 :** bomb, mine, or shell fragments

1**shred** \ˈshred, *esp South* ˈsred\ *n* [ME *shrede,* fr. OE *scrēade;* akin to OHG *scrōt* piece cut off, L *scrupus* sharp stone, OE *scieran* to cut — more at SHEAR] **:** a long narrow strip cut or torn off; *also* **:** PARTICLE, SCRAP

2**shred** *vb* **shred·ded; shred·ding** *vt* **1** *archaic* **:** to cut off **2 :** to cut or tear into shreds ~ *vi* **:** to come apart in or break up into shreds — **shred·der** *n*

shredded wheat *n* **:** a breakfast cereal made from cooked partially dried wheat that is shredded and molded into biscuits which are then oven-baked and toasted

1**shrew** \ˈshrü, *esp South* ˈsrü\ *n* [ME *shrewe* evil or scolding person, fr. OE *scrēawa* shrewmouse] **1 :** any of numerous small chiefly nocturnal mammals (family Soricidae) related to the moles and distinguished by a long pointed snout, very small eyes, and velvety fur **2 :** an ill-tempered scolding woman

shrew 1

2**shrew** *vt, obs* **:** CURSE

shrewd \ˈshrüd, *esp South* ˈsrüd\ *adj* [ME *shrewe* + *-ed*] **1** *archaic* **:** MISCHIEVOUS **2** *obs* **:** SHREWISH, ABUSIVE **3** *obs* **:** OMINOUS, DANGEROUS **4 a :** SEVERE, HARD <a ~ knock> **b :** SHARP, PIERCING <a ~ wind> **5 a :** marked by clever discerning awareness and hardheaded acumen <~ common sense> **b :** given to wily and artful ways or dealing <a ~ operator> — **shrewd·ly** *adv* — **shrewd·ness** *n*

syn SHREWD, SAGACIOUS, PERSPICACIOUS, ASTUTE *shared meaning element* **:** acute in perception and sound in judgment

shrew·ish \ˈshrü-ish, *esp South* ˈsrü-\ *adj* **:** ill-tempered **:** INTRACTABLE — **shrew·ish·ly** *adv* — **shrew·ish·ness** *n*

shrew·mouse \-ˌmau̇s\ *n* **:** SHREW 1

shri \ˈs(h)rē\ *var of* SRI

1**shriek** \ˈshrēk, *esp South* ˈsrēk\ *vb* [prob. irreg. fr. ME *shriken* to shriek; akin to ME *scremen* to scream] *vi* **1 :** to utter a sharp shrill sound **2 a :** to cry out in a high-pitched voice **:** SCREECH **b :** to suggest such a cry (as by vividness of expression) ~ *vt* **1 :** to utter with a shriek or sharply and shrilly <~ an alarm> **2 :** to express in a manner suggestive of a shriek

2**shriek** *n* **1 :** a shrill usu. wild or involuntary cry **2 :** a sound resembling a shriek <the ~ of chalk on the blackboard>

shrie·val \ˈshrē-vəl, *esp South* ˈsrē-\ *adj* [obs. *shrieve* sheriff, fr. ME *shirreve* — more at SHERIFF] **:** of or relating to a sheriff

shrie·val·ty \-vəl-tē\ *n, chiefly Brit* **1 :** the office of a sheriff **2 :** the term of office of a sheriff **3 :** the jurisdiction of a sheriff

shrieve \ˈshrēv, *esp South* ˈsrēv\ *archaic var of* SHRIVE

shrift \ˈshrift, *esp South* ˈsrift\ *n* [ME, fr. OE *scrift,* fr. *scrīfan* to shrive — more at SHRIVE] **1** *archaic* **a :** the act of shriving **:** CONFESSION **b :** a remission of sins pronounced by a priest in the sacrament of penance **2** *obs* **:** CONFESSIONAL

shrike \ˈshrīk, *esp South* ˈsrīk\ *n* [perh. fr. (assumed) ME *shrik,* fr. OE *scric* thrush; akin to ME *shriken* to shriek] **:** any of numerous usu. largely gray or brownish oscine birds (family Laniidae) that have a strong notched bill hooked at the tip, feed chiefly on insects, and often impale their prey on thorns

1**shrill** \ˈshril, *esp South* ˈsril\ *vb* [ME *shrillen*] *vi* **:** to utter or emit an acute piercing sound <alarm clocks ~ at five a.m. —Lucy Cook> ~ *vt* **:** SCREAM

2**shrill** *adj* **1 a :** having or emitting a sharp high-pitched tone or sound **:** PIERCING **b :** accompanied by sharp high-pitched sounds or cries <~ gaiety> **2 :** having a sharp or vivid effect on the senses <~ light> **3 :** STRIDENT, INTEMPERATE <~ anger> — **shrill** *adv* — **shrillness** *n* — **shril·ly** \ˈs(h)ril-lē\ *adv*

3**shrill** *n* **:** a shrill sound <the ~ of the ship's whistle>

1**shrimp** \ˈshrimp, *esp South* ˈsrimp\ *n, pl* **shrimps** *also* **shrimp** [ME *shrimpe;* akin to ON *skorpna* to shrivel up, L *curvus* curved — more at CROWN] **1 :** any of numerous mostly small and marine decapod crustaceans (suborder Natantia) having a slender elongated body, compressed abdomen, long legs, and a long, spiny rostrum; *also* **:** a small crustacean (as an amphipod or a branchiopod) resembling the true shrimps **2 :** a very small or puny person or thing — usu. used disparagingly — **shrimpy** \ˈs(h)rim-pē\ *adj*

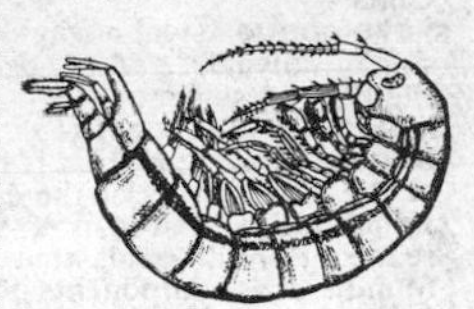

shrimp 1

2**shrimp** *vi* **:** to fish for or catch shrimps

shrimp pink *n* **:** a variable color averaging a deep pink

1**shrine** \ˈshrīn, *esp South* ˈsrīn\ *n* [ME, fr. OE *scrīn,* fr. L *scrinium* case, chest] **1 a :** a case, box, or receptacle; *esp* **:** one in which sacred relics (as the bones of a saint) are deposited **b :** a place in which devotion is paid to a saint or deity **:** SANCTUARY **c :** a niche containing a religious image **2 :** a receptacle (as a tomb) for the dead **3 :** a place or object hallowed by its associations

2**shrine** *vt* **:** ENSHRINE

Shrin·er \ˈshrī-nər, *esp South* ˈsrī-\ *n* [Ancient Arabic Order of Nobles of the Mystic *Shrine*] **:** a member of a secret fraternal society that is non-Masonic but admits only Knights Templars and 32d-degree Masons to membership

1**shrink** \ˈshriŋk, *esp South* ˈsriŋk\ *vb* **shrank** \ˈs(h)raŋk\ *also* **shrunk** \ˈs(h)rəŋk\; **shrunk** *or* **shrunk·en** \ˈs(h)rəŋ-kən\ [ME *shrinken,* fr. OE *scrincan;* akin to MD *schrinken* to draw back, L *curvus* curved — more at CROWN] *vi* **1 :** to contract or curl up the body or part of it **:** HUDDLE, COWER **2 a :** to contract to a less extent or compass **b :** to become smaller or more compacted **c :** to lose substance or weight **d :** to lessen in value **:** DWINDLE **3 :** to recoil instinctively (as from something painful or horrible) ~ *vt* **:** to cause to contract or shrink; *specif* **:** to compact (cloth) by causing to contract when subjected to washing, boiling, steaming, or other processes *syn* see CONTRACT, RECOIL *ant* swell, stretch — **shrink·able** \ˈs(h)riŋ-kə-bəl\ *adj* — **shrink·er** *n*

2**shrink** *n* **1 :** the act of shrinking **2 :** SHRINKAGE **3** [short for *headshrinker*] **a :** one who practices the principles or techniques of psychoanalysis **b :** a physician who specializes in psychiatry

shrink·age \ˈshriŋ-kij, *esp South* ˈsriŋ-\ *n* **1 :** the act or process of shrinking **2 :** the loss in weight of livestock during shipment and in the process of preparing the meat for consumption **3 :** the amount lost by shrinkage

shrinking violet *n* **:** a bashful or retiring person

shrink–wrap \ˈshriŋk-ˌrap, *esp South* ˈsriŋk-\ *vt* **:** to wrap (as a book or meat) in tough clear plastic film that is then shrunk (as by heating) to form a tightly fitting package

shrive \ˈshrīv, *esp South* ˈsrīv\ *vb* **shrived** *or* **shrove** \ˈs(h)rōv\; **shriv·en** \ˈs(h)riv-ən\ *or* **shrived** [ME *shriven,* fr. OE *scrīfan* to shrive, prescribe; akin to OHG *scrīban* to write; both fr. a prehistoric WGmc word borrowed fr. L *scribere* to write — more at SCRIBE] *vt* **1 :** to administer the sacrament of penance to **2 :** to free from guilt ~ *vi, archaic* **:** to confess one's sins esp. to a priest

shriv·el \ˈshriv-əl, *esp South* ˈsriv-\ *vb* **shriv·eled** *or* **shriv·elled; shriv·el·ing** *or* **shriv·el·ling** \-(ə-)liŋ\ [origin unknown] *vi* **1 :** to draw into wrinkles esp. with a loss of moisture **2 :** to become reduced to inanition, helplessness, or inefficiency ~ *vt* **:** to cause to shrivel

1**shroff** \ˈshräf, ˈshrȯf, *esp South* ˈsräf, ˈsrȯf\ *n* [Hindi *ṣarrāf,* fr. Ar] **:** a banker or money changer in the Far East; *esp* **:** one who tests and evaluates coin

2**shroff** *vt* **:** to sort (coins) into good and bad pieces

Shrop·shire \ˈshräp-ˌshi(ə)r, -shər, *esp US* -ˌshī(ə)r, *esp South* ˈsräp-\ *n* [*Shropshire,* England] **:** any of an English breed of dark-faced hornless sheep that are raised primarily for mutton and secondarily for their fine dense wool

1**shroud** \ˈshrau̇d, *esp South* ˈsrau̇d\ *n* [ME, fr. OE *scrūd;* akin to OE *scrēade* shred — more at SHRED] **1 :** burial garment **:** WINDING-SHEET, CEREMENT **2** *obs* **:** SHELTER, PROTECTION **3 :** something that covers, screens, or guards: as **a :** one of two flanges that give peripheral support to turbine or fan bedding **b :** a usu. fiberglass guard that protects a spacecraft from the heat of launching **4 a :** one of the ropes leading usu. in pairs from a ship's mastheads to give lateral support to the masts **b :** one of the cords that suspend the harness of a parachute from the canopy

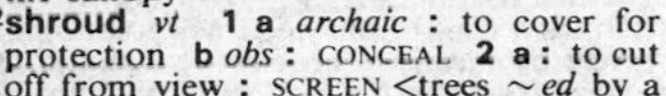

1, shrouds 4a

2**shroud** *vt* **1 a** *archaic* **:** to cover for protection **b** *obs* **:** CONCEAL **2 a :** to cut off from view **:** SCREEN <trees ~*ed* by a heavy fog> **b :** to veil under another appearance <information ~*ed* in cipher> **3 :** to dress for burial ~ *vi, archaic* **:** to seek shelter **:** take refuge

shroud–laid \-ˌlād\ *adj, of a rope* **:** composed of four strands and laid right-handed with a core

Shrove·tide \ˈshrōv-ˌtīd, *esp South* ˈsrōv-\ *n* [ME *schroftide,* fr. *schrof-* (fr. *shriven* to shrive) + *tide*] **:** the period usu. of three days immediately preceding Ash Wednesday

Shrove Tuesday *n* [ME *schroftewesday,* fr. *schrof-* (as in *schroftide*) + *tewesday* Tuesday] **:** the Tuesday before Ash Wednesday

1**shrub** \ˈshrəb, *esp South* ˈsrəb\ *n* [ME *schrobbe,* fr. OE *scrybb* brushwood; akin to Norw *skrubbebær* a cornel of a dwarf species] **:** a low usu. several-stemmed woody plant

2**shrub** *n* [Ar *sharāb* beverage] **1 :** a beverage that consists of an alcoholic liquor, fruit juice, fruit rind, and sugar **2 :** a beverage made by adding acidulated fruit juice to iced water

shrub·bery \ˈshrəb-(ə-)rē, *esp South* ˈsrəb-\ *n, pl* **-ber·ies :** a planting or growth of shrubs

shrub·by \ˈshrəb-ē, *esp South* ˈsrəb-\ *adj* **shrub·bi·er; -est 1 :** consisting of or covered with shrubs **2 :** resembling a shrub

1**shrug** \ˈshrəg, *esp South* ˈsrəg\ *vb* **shrugged; shrug·ging** [ME *schruggen*] *vi* **:** to raise or draw in the shoulders esp. to express aloofness, indifference, or aversion ~ *vt* **:** to lift or contract (the shoulders) esp. to express aloofness, indifference, or dislike

2**shrug** *n* **1 :** an act of shrugging **2 :** a woman's small waist-length or shorter jacket

shrug off *vt* **1 :** to brush aside **:** MINIMIZE <*shrugs off* the problem> **2 :** to shake off <*shrugging off* sleep> **3 :** to remove (a garment) by wriggling out

sht *abbr* sheet

shtetl *also* **shte·tel** \ˈshtet-ᵊl, ˈshtāt-\ *n, pl* **shtet·lach** \ˈshtet-ˌläk, ˈshtāt-\ [Yiddish, fr. MHG *stetel,* dim. of *stat* place, town, city, fr. OHG, place — more at STEAD] **:** a small Jewish town or village formerly found in Eastern Europe

shtg *abbr* shortage

shtick \ˈshtik\ *n* [Yiddish *shtik,* lit., piece, fr. MHG *stücke,* fr. OHG *stucki*] **:** an entertainment routine **:** BIT

1**shuck** \ˈshək\ *n* [origin unknown] **1 :** SHELL, HUSK: as **a :** the outer covering of a nut or of Indian corn **b :** the shell of an oyster or clam **2 :** something of little value — usu. used in pl. often interjectionally <not worth ~*s*> <~*s,* it was nothing>

2**shuck** *vt* **1 :** to strip of shucks **2 a :** to peel off (as clothing) — often used with *off* **b :** to lay aside — usu. used with *off* <bad habits are being ~*ed* off —A. W. Smith> — **shuck·er** *n*

ə abut	ᵊ kitten	ər further	a back	ā bake	ä cot, cart
au̇ out	ch chin	e less	ē easy	g gift	i trip	ī life
j joke	ŋ sing	ō flow	ȯ flaw	ȯi coin	th thin	t͟h this
ü loot	u̇ foot	y yet	yü few	yu̇ furious	zh vision

[1]shud·der \'shəd-ər\ *vi* **shud·dered; shud·der·ing** \-(ə-)riŋ\ [ME *shoddren;* akin to OHG *skutten* to shake, Lith *kuteti* to shake up] **1 :** to tremble convulsively : SHIVER **2 :** QUIVER
[2]shudder *n* **:** an act of shuddering — **shud·dery** \-(ə-)rē\ *adj*
[1]shuf·fle \'shəf-əl\ *vb* **shuf·fled; shuf·fling** \-(ə-)liŋ\ [perh. irreg. fr. [1]*shove*] *vt* **1 :** to mix in a mass confusedly : JUMBLE **2 :** to put or thrust aside or under cover <*shuffled* the whole matter out of his mind> **3 a :** to rearrange (as playing cards, dominoes, or tiles) to produce a random order **b :** to move about, back and forth, or from one place to another : SHIFT <~ funds among various accounts> **4 a :** to move (as the feet) by sliding along or back and forth without lifting **b :** to perform (as a dance) with a dragging, sliding step ~ *vi* **1 :** to work into or out of trickily : WORM <*shuffled* out of the difficulty somehow> **2 :** to act or speak in a shifty or evasive manner **3 a :** to move or walk in a sliding dragging manner without lifting the feet **b :** to dance in a lazy nonchalant manner with sliding and tapping motions of the feet **c :** to execute in a perfunctory or clumsy manner **4 :** to mix playing cards or counters by shuffling — **shuf·fler** \-(ə-)lər\ *n*
[2]shuffle *n* **1 :** an evasion of the issue : EQUIVOCATION **2 a :** an act of shuffling (as of cards) **b :** a right or turn to shuffle <was reminded that it was his ~> **c :** JUMBLE <lost in the ~ of papers> **3 a :** a dragging sliding movement; *specif* **:** a sliding or scraping step in dancing **b :** a dance characterized by such a step
shuf·fle·board \'shəf-əl-ˌbō(ə)rd, -ˌbȯ(ə)rd\ *n* [alter. of obs. E *shove-board*] **1 :** a game in which players use long-handled cues to shove wooden disks into scoring areas of a diagram marked on a smooth surface **2 :** a diagram on which shuffleboard is played

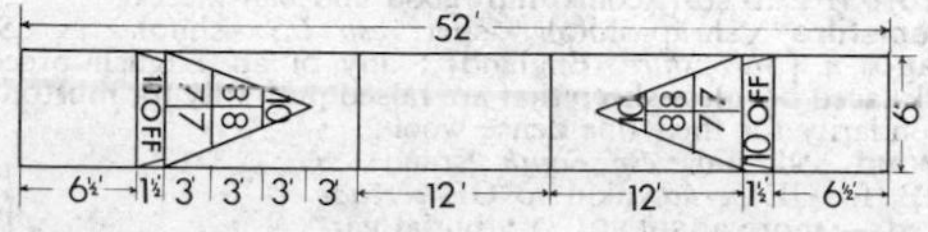

shuffleboard 2

shul \'shül\ *n* [Yiddish, fr. MHG *schuol,* lit., school] **:** SYNAGOGUE
shun \'shən\ *vt* **shunned; shun·ning** [ME *shunnen,* fr. OE *scunian*] **:** to avoid deliberately and esp. habitually ***syn*** see ESCAPE — **shun·ner** *n*
shun·pike \'shən-ˌpīk\ *n* **:** a side road used to avoid the toll on or the speed and traffic of a superhighway
shun·pik·ing \'shən-ˌpī-kiŋ\ *n* **:** the practice of avoiding superhighways esp. for the pleasure of driving on back roads — **shun·pik·er** \-kər\ *n*
[1]shunt \'shənt\ *vb* [ME *shunten* to flinch] *vt* **1 :** to turn off to one side : SHIFT; *esp* **:** to switch (as a train) from one track to another **2 :** to provide with or divert by means of an electrical shunt **3 :** to divert (blood) from one part to another by a surgical shunt ~ *vi* **1 :** to move to the side **2 :** to travel back and forth <~*ed* between the two towns> — **shunt·er** *n*
[2]shunt *n* **:** a means or mechanism for turning or thrusting aside: as **a** *chiefly Brit* **:** a railroad switch **b :** a conductor joining two points in an electrical circuit so as to form a parallel or alternative path through which a portion of the current may pass (as for regulating the amount passing in the main circuit) **c :** a surgical passage created between two blood vessels to divert blood from one part to another
[3]shunt *n* [origin unknown] **:** an accident (as a collision between two cars) in auto racing
shunt winding *n* **:** a winding so arranged as to divide the armature current and lead a portion of it around the field-magnet coils — **shunt–wound** \'shənt-'waünd\ *adj*
shush \'shəsh\ *n* [imit.] **:** a sibilant sound uttered to demand silence — **shush** *vt*
[1]shut \'shət\ *vb* **shut; shut·ting** [ME *shutten,* fr. OE *scyttan;* akin to OE *scēotan* to shoot — more at SHOOT] *vt* **1 a :** to move into position to close an opening <~ the lid> **b :** to prevent entrance to or passage to or from **2 :** to confine by or as if by enclosure <~ him in the closet> **3 :** to fasten with a lock or bolt **4 :** to close by bringing enclosing or covering parts together <~ the eyes> **5 :** to cause to cease or suspend operation — often used with *down* ~ *vi* **1 :** to close itself or become closed <flowers that ~ at night> **2 :** to cease or suspend an operation — often used with *down*
[2]shut *n* **1 :** the act of shutting **2 :** the line of union at a welded joint
shut·down \'shət-ˌdaün\ *n* **:** the cessation or suspension of an activity (as work in a mine or factory)
shut down \'shət-'daün, ˌshət-\ *vi* **:** to settle so as to obscure vision : close in <the night *shut down* early>
shute *var of* CHUTE
shut–eye \'shət-ˌī\ *n* **:** SLEEP
[1]shut–in \ˌshət-ˌin\ *adj* **1 :** confined to one's home or an institution by illness or incapacity **2 a :** SECRETIVE, BROODING <a bitter, ~ face —Claudia Cassidy> **b :** tending to avoid social contact : WITHDRAWN <the ~ personality type —S. K. Weinberg>
[2]shut–in \'shət-ˌin\ *n* **1 :** an invalid confined to his home, room, or bed **2 :** a narrow gorge-shaped part of an otherwise wide valley
shut in \ˌshət-'in\ *vt* **:** CONFINE, ENCLOSE
shut·off \'shət-ˌȯf\ *n* **1 :** something (as a valve) that shuts off **2 :** STOPPAGE, INTERRUPTION
shut off \ˌshət-'ȯf\ *vt* **1 a :** to cut off (as flow or passage) : STOP <*shuts off* the oxygen supply> **b :** to stop the operation of (as a machine) <*shut* the motor *off*> **2 :** to close off : SEPARATE — usu. used with *from* <*shut off* from the rest of the world> ~ *vi* **:** to cease operating : STOP <*shuts off* automatically>
shut·out \'shət-ˌaüt\ *n* **1 :** a game or contest in which one side fails to score **2 :** a preemptive bid in bridge
shut out \ˌshət-'aüt\ *vt* **1 :** EXCLUDE **2 :** to prevent (an opponent) from scoring in a game or contest **3 :** to forestall the bidding of (bridge opponents) by making a high or preemptive bid

[1]shut·ter \'shət-ər\ *n* **1 :** one that shuts **2 :** a usu. movable cover or screen for a window or door **3 :** a mechanical device that limits the passage of light; *esp* **:** a camera attachment that exposes the film or plate by opening and closing an aperture **4 :** the movable louvers in a pipe organ by which the swell box is opened — **shut·ter·less** \-ləs\ *adj*
[2]shutter *vt* **1 :** to close with or by shutters **2 :** to furnish with shutters
shut·ter·bug \'shət-ər-ˌbəg\ *n* **:** a photography enthusiast
[1]shut·tle \'shət-ᵊl\ *n* [ME *shittle,* prob. fr. OE *scytel* bar, bolt; akin to ON *skutill* bolt, OE *scēotan* to shoot — more at SHOOT] **1 a :** a device used in weaving for passing the thread of the woof between the threads of the warp **b :** a spindle-shaped device holding the thread in tatting, knotting, or netting **c :** a sliding thread holder for the lower thread of a sewing machine that carries the lower thread through a loop of the upper thread to make a stitch **2 :** SHUTTLECOCK **3 a :** a going back and forth regularly over a specified and often short route by a vehicle (as an airplane) **b :** an established route used in a shuttle; *also* **:** a vehicle used in a shuttle
[2]shuttle *vb* **shut·tled; shut·tling** \'shət-liŋ, -ᵊl-iŋ\ *vt* **1 :** to cause to move or travel back and forth frequently **2 :** to transport in, by, or as if by a shuttle ~ *vi* **1 :** to move or travel back and forth frequently **2 :** to move by or as if by a shuttle
[1]shut·tle·cock \'shət-ᵊl-ˌkäk\ *n* **:** a lightweight conical-shaped object with a rounded often rubber-covered nose that is used in badminton and that consists of a feathered cork or of molded plastic

shuttlecock

[2]shuttlecock *vt* **:** to send or toss to and fro : BANDY
shut up *vt* **:** to cause (a person) to stop talking ~ *vi* **:** to cease writing or speaking
[1]shy \'shī\ *adj* **shi·er** *or* **shy·er** \'shī(-ə)r\; **shi·est** *or* **shy·est** \'shī-əst\ [ME *schey,* fr. OE *scēoh;* akin to OHG *sciuhen* to frighten off, OSlav *šćuti* to chase] **1 :** easily frightened : TIMID **2 :** disposed to avoid a person or thing : DISTRUSTFUL **3 :** hesitant in committing oneself : CIRCUMSPECT **4 :** sensitively diffident or retiring : RESERVED <a ~ seclusive person>; *also* **:** expressive of such a state or nature <spoke in a ~ voice> **5 :** SECLUDED, HIDDEN **6 :** having less than the full or specified amount or number : SHORT <looks about 10 years ~ of his 62 —E. P. Snow> **7 :** DISREPUTABLE <gambling hells and ~ saloons —*Blackwood's*> — **shy·ly** *adv* — **shy·ness** *n*
syn SHY, BASHFUL, DIFFIDENT, MODEST, COY *shared meaning element* **:** disinclined to obtrude oneself ***ant*** obtrusive
[2]shy *vi* **shied; shy·ing** **1 :** to develop or show a dislike or distaste : RECOIL **2 :** to start suddenly aside through fright or alarm
[3]shy *n, pl* **shies :** a sudden start aside (as from fright)
[4]shy *vb* **shied; shy·ing** [perh. fr. [1]*shy*] *vt* **:** to throw (an object) with a jerk : FLING ~ *vi* **:** to make a sudden throw
[5]shy *n, pl* **shies** **1 :** the act of shying : TOSS, THROW **2 :** a verbal fling <took a few *shies* at the integrity of his opponent> **3 :** COCKSHY
[1]shy·lock \'shī-ˌläk\ *n* **1** *cap* **:** the Jewish usurer and antagonist of Antonio in Shakespeare's *The Merchant of Venice* **2 :** an extortionate creditor : LOAN SHARK
[2]shylock *vi* **:** to lend money at high rates of interest <exposé of systematic thievery . . . ~*ing,* and murder —*Current Biog.*>
shy·ster \'shī-stər\ *n* [prob. fr. *Scheuster fl*1840 Am attorney frequently rebuked in a New York court for pettifoggery] **:** one who is professionally unscrupulous esp. in the practice of law or politics : PETTIFOGGER
si \'sē\ *n* [It] **:** the 7th tone of the diatonic scale in solmization : TI
Si *symbol* silicon
SI *abbr* [F *Système International d'Unités*] International System of Units
si·al·a·gogue \sī-'al-ə-ˌgäg\ *n* [NL *sialogogus* promoting the expulsion of saliva, fr. *sial-* + *-ogogus* -ogogue] **:** an agent that promotes the flow of saliva
Si·al·ic \sī-'al-ik\ *adj* [ISV *Si* + *Al*] **:** of, relating to, or being relatively light rock that is rich in silica and alumina and is typical of the outer layers of the earth
si·al·ic acid \(ˌ)sī-ˌal-ik-\ *n* [*sial-* + *-ic*] **:** any of a group of reducing amido acids that are essentially carbohydrates and are found esp. as components of blood glycoproteins and mucoproteins
si·a·mang \'sē-ə-ˌmaŋ, sē-'am-əŋ\ *n* [Malay] **:** a black gibbon (*Symphalangus syndactylus*) of Sumatra that is the largest of the gibbons
[1]Si·a·mese \ˌsī-ə-'mēz, -'mēs\ *adj* [*Siam* (Thailand); in senses 2 & 3, fr. *Siamese twin*] **1 :** of, relating to, or characteristic of Thailand, the Thais, or their language **2 :** exhibiting great resemblance : very like **3** *not cap* **:** connecting two or more pipes or hose so as to permit discharge in a single stream
[2]Siamese *n, pl* **Siamese** **1 :** THAI 1 **2 :** THAI 2 **3 :** SIAMESE CAT
Siamese cat *n* **:** a slender blue-eyed short-haired domestic cat of a breed of oriental origin with pale fawn or gray body and darker ears, paws, tail, and face
Siamese fighting fish *n* **:** a brightly colored highly aggressive betta (*Betta splendens*) that is a popular aquarium fish
Siamese twin *n* [fr. Chang †1874 and Eng †1874 congenitally united twins born in Siam] **:** one of a pair of congenitally united twins in man or lower animals
[1]sib \'sib\ *adj* [ME, fr. OE *sibb,* fr. *sibb* kinship; akin to OHG *sippa* kinship, family, L *suus* one's own — more at SUICIDE] **:** related by blood : AKIN
[2]sib *n* **1 a :** KINDRED, RELATIVES **b :** a blood relation : KINSMAN **2 :** a brother or sister considered irrespective of sex; *broadly* **:** any plant or animal of a group sharing a degree of genetic relationship corresponding to that of human sibs **3 :** a group of persons unilaterally descended from a real or supposed ancestor
Si·be·ri·an husky \sī-ˌbir-ē-ən-\ *n*: a medium-sized compact dog of a breed that was developed in northeastern Siberia for use as a sled dog and that resembles the larger Alaskan malamute

1sib·i·lant \ˈsib-ə-lənt\ *adj* [L *sibilant-, sibilans,* prp. of *sibilare* to hiss, whistle, of imit. origin] **:** having, containing, or producing the sound of or a sound resembling that of the *s* or the *sh* in *sash* <a ~ affricate> <a ~ snake> — **sib·i·lant·ly** *adv*

2sibilant *n* **:** a sibilant speech sound (as English \s\, \z\, \sh\, \zh\, \ch(=tsh)\, or \j(=dzh)\)

sib·i·late \ˈsib-ə-ˌlāt\ *vb* **-lat·ed; -lat·ing** [L *sibilatus,* pp. of *sibilare*] *vi* **1 :** HISS **2 :** to utter an initial sibilant **:** prefix an \s\-sound ~ *vt* **1 :** HISS **2 :** to pronounce with an initial sibilant **:** prefix an \s\-sound to — **sib·i·la·tion** \ˌsib-ə-ˈlā-shən\ *n*

sib·ling \ˈsib-liŋ\ *n* **:** SIB 2; *also* **:** one of two or more individuals having one common parent

sibling species *n* **:** one of two or more species that are nearly indistinguishable morphologically

sib·yl \ˈsib-əl\ *n, often cap* [ME *sibile, sybylle,* fr. MF & L; MF *sibile,* fr. L *sibylla,* fr. Gk] **1 :** any of several prophetesses usu. accepted as 10 in number and credited to widely separate parts of the ancient world (as Babylonia, Egypt, Greece, and Italy) **2 a :** a female prophet **b :** FORTUNE-TELLER — **si·byl·ic** *or* **si·byl·lic** \sə-ˈbil-ik\ *adj* — **sib·yl·line** \ˈsib-ə-ˌlīn, -ˌlēn\ *adj*

1sic \(ˈ)sik\ *chiefly Scot var of* SUCH

2sic *or* **sick** \ˈsik\ *vt* **sicced** *or* **sicked** \ˈsikt\; **sic·cing** *or* **sick·ing** [alter. of *seek*] **1 :** CHASE, ATTACK — usu. used as an imperative esp. to a dog <~ ʼem> **2 :** to incite or urge to an attack, pursuit, or harassment **:** SET

3sic \ˈsik, ˈsēk\ *adv* [L, so thus — more at SO] **:** intentionally so written — used after a printed word or passage to indicate that it is intended exactly as printed or to indicate that it exactly reproduces an original <said he seed [~] it all>

sic·ca·tive \ˈsik-ət-iv\ *n* [LL *siccativus* making dry, fr. L *siccatus,* pp. of *siccare* to dry, fr. *siccus* dry — more at SACK] **:** DRIER 2

sick \ˈsik\ *adj* [ME *sek, sik,* fr. OE *sēoc;* akin to OHG *sioh* sick, MIr *socht* depression] **1 a (1) :** affected with disease or ill health **:** AILING **(2) :** of, relating to, or intended for use in sickness <~ pay> <a ~ ward> **b :** QUEASY, NAUSEATED <~ to one's stomach> <was ~ in the car> **c :** undergoing menstruation **2 :** spiritually or morally unsound or corrupt **3 a :** sickened by strong emotion (as shame or fear) <~ with fear> <worried ~> **b :** having a strong distaste from surfeit **:** SATIATED <~ of flattery> **c :** filled with disgust or chagrin <gossip that makes one ~> **d :** depressed and longing for something <~ for one's home> **4 a :** mentally or emotionally unsound or disordered **:** MORBID <~ thoughts> **b :** MACABRE, SADISTIC <~ jokes> **5 :** lacking vigor **:** SICKLY: as **a :** badly outclassed <looked ~ in the contest> **b :** declining or inactive after a period of speculative activity <grain futures were ~> **c :** incapable of yielding a profitable crop esp. because of buildup of disease organisms <clover-*sick* soils>

sick and tired *adj* **:** thoroughly fatigued or bored

sick bay *n* **:** a compartment in a ship used as a dispensary and hospital; *broadly* **:** a place for the care of the sick or injured

sick·bed \ˈsik-ˌbed\ *n* **:** the bed upon which one lies sick

sick call *n* **1 :** a usu. daily formation at which individuals report as sick to the medical officer **2 :** the period during which sick call is held

sick·en \ˈsik-ən\ *vb* **sick·ened; sick·en·ing** \-(ə-)niŋ\ *vt* **1 :** to make sick **2 :** to cause revulsion in as a result of weariness or satiety ~ *vi* **1 :** to become sick **2 :** to become weary or satiated

sick·en·er \ˈsik(-ə)-nər\ *n* **:** something that sickens, disgusts, or overwhelms

sick·en·ing \-niŋ\ *adj* **:** causing sickness **:** NAUSEATING <a ~ odor> — **sick·en·ing·ly** \-niŋ-lē\ *adv*

sick·er \ˈsik-ər\ *adj* [ME *siker,* fr. OE *sicor;* akin to OHG *sichor* secure; both fr. a prehistoric WGmc word borrowed fr. L *securus* secure] *chiefly Scot* **:** SECURE, SAFE; *also* **:** DEPENDABLE — **sicker** *adv*

sick·er·ly \-lē\ *adv, chiefly Scot* **:** in a secure manner **:** SAFELY

sick headache *n* **:** MIGRAINE

sick·ish \ˈsik-ish\ *adj* **1** *archaic* **:** somewhat ill **:** SICKLY **2 :** somewhat nauseated **:** QUEASY **3 :** somewhat sickening <a ~ odor> — **sick·ish·ly** *adv* — **sick·ish·ness** *n*

1sick·le \ˈsik-əl\ *n* [ME *sikel,* fr. OE *sicol;* akin to OHG *sichila* sickle; both fr. a prehistoric WGmc word borrowed fr. L *secula* sickle — more at SAW] **1 a :** an agricultural implement consisting of a curved metal blade with a short handle fitted on a tang **b :** the cutting mechanism (as of a reaper, combine, or mower) consisting of a bar with a series of cutting elements **2** *cap* **:** a group of six stars in the constellation Leo

2sickle *adj* **:** having the form of a sickle blade **:** having a curve similar to that of a sickle blade <the ~ moon>

3sickle *vb* **sick·led; sick·ling** \ˈsik-(ə-)liŋ\ *vt* **1 :** to mow or reap with a sickle **2 :** to form (a red blood cell) into a crescent ~ *vi* **:** to form into a crescent <the ability of red blood cells to ~>

sick leave *n* **1 :** an absence from work permitted because of illness **2 :** the number of days per year for which an employer agrees to pay employees who are sick

sick·le·bill \ˈsik-əl-ˌbil\ *n* **:** any of various birds (as a curlew or thrasher) with a strongly curved bill

sickle cell *n* **:** an abnormal red blood cell of crescent shape

sickle–cell anemia *n* **:** a chronic inherited anemia in which a large proportion or the majority of the red blood cells tend to sickle, which occurs primarily in individuals of Negro ancestry, and which is held to result from homozygosity for a semidominant gene

sickle–cell trait *n* **:** an inherited blood condition in which some red blood cells tend to sickle but usu. not enough to produce anemia, which occurs primarily in individuals of Negro ancestry, and which is held to result from heterozygosity for a semidominant gene — called also *sicklemia*

sickle feather *n* **:** one of the long curved tail feathers of a cock — see COCK illustration

sickl·emia \ˌsik-ə-ˈlē-mē-ə\ *n* [NL, fr. E *sickle* (cell) + NL *-emia*] **:** SICKLE-CELL TRAIT

1sick·ly \ˈsik-lē\ *adj* **1 :** somewhat unwell; *also* **:** habitually ailing **2 :** produced by or associated with sickness <a ~ complexion> <a ~ appetite> **3 :** producing or tending to produce disease **:** UNWHOLESOME <a ~ climate> **4 :** appearing as if sick: **a :** LANGUID, PALE <a ~ flame> **b :** WRETCHED, UNEASY <a ~ smile> **c :** lacking in vigor **:** WEAK <a ~ plant> <~ beer> **5 a :** tending to produce nausea <a ~ odor> **b :** MAWKISH — **sick·li·ness** *n* — **sick·ly** *or* **sick·li·ly** \ˈsik-lə-lē\ *adv*

2sickly *vt* **sick·lied; sick·ly·ing :** to make sick or sickly

sick·ness \ˈsik-nəs\ *n* **1 a :** ill health **:** ILLNESS **b :** a disordered, weakened, or unsound condition (as of society or a particular institution) **2 :** a specific disease **3 :** NAUSEA, QUEASINESS

sick pay *n* **:** salary or wages paid to an employee while on sick leave

sick·room \ˈsik-ˌrüm-ˌru̇m\ *n* **:** a room in which a person is confined by sickness

sic pas·sim \ˈsik-ˈpas-əm, ˈsēk-ˈpäs-im\ *adv* [L] **:** so throughout — used of a word or idea to be found throughout a book or a writer's work

sid·dur \ˈsid-ər, -ˌu̇(ə)r\ *n, pl* **sid·du·rim** \sə-ˈdu̇r-əm\ [MHeb *siddūr,* lit., order, arrangement] **:** a Jewish prayer book containing both Hebrew and Aramaic prayers used in the Ashkenazic daily liturgy

1side \ˈsīd\ *n* [ME, fr. OE *sīde;* akin to OHG *sīta* side, OE *sīd* ample, wide, *sāwan* to sow — more at SOW] **1 a :** the right or left part of the wall or trunk of the body <a pain in the ~> **b (1) :** one of the halves of the animal body on either side of the mesial plane **(2) :** a cut of meat including that about the ribs of one half of the body — used chiefly of smoked pork products **c :** one longitudinal half of a hide **2 :** a place, space, or direction with respect to a center or to a line of division (as of an aisle, river, or street) **3 :** a surface forming a border or face of an object **4 :** an outer portion of something considered as facing in a particular direction <the upper ~ of a sphere> **5 :** a slope or declivity of a hill or ridge **6 a :** a bounding line of a geometrical figure <each ~ of a square> **b :** one of the surfaces that delimit a solid; *esp* **:** one of the longer surfaces **c :** either surface of a thin object <one ~ of a record> <right ~ of the cloth> **7 :** the space beside one <he never left her ~> **8 :** the attitude or activity of one person or group with respect to another **:** PART **9 :** a body of partisans or contestants <victory for neither ~> **10 :** a line of descent traced through one's parent <grandfather on his mother's ~> **11 :** an aspect or part of something viewed as contrasted with some other aspect or part <the better ~ of his nature> **12 :** a position viewed as opposite to or contrasted with another <two ~*s* to every question> **13** *Brit* **:** sideways spin imparted to a billiard ball **14 :** a sheet containing the lines and cues for a single theatrical role *syn* see PHASE — **on the side 1 :** in addition to the main portion **2 :** in addition to a principal occupation

2side *adj* **1 a :** of or relating to the side **b :** situated on the side <~ window> **2 a :** directed toward or from the side <~ thrust> <~ wind> **b :** INCIDENTAL, INDIRECT <~ issue> <~ remark> **c :** made on the side <~ payment> **d :** additional to the main portion <~ order of french fries>

3side *vb* **sid·ed; sid·ing** *vt* **1 :** to agree with **:** SUPPORT **2 :** to be side by side with **3 :** to set or put aside **:** clear away <~ dishes> **4 :** to furnish with sides or siding <~ a house> ~ *vi* **:** to take sides **:** join or form sides <*sided* with the rebels>

4side *n* [obs. E *side* (proud, boastful)] **:** swaggering or arrogant manner **:** PRETENTIOUSNESS

side·arm \ˈsīd-ˌärm\ *adj* **:** of, relating to, or constituting a baseball pitching style in which the arm is not raised above the shoulder and the ball is thrown with a sideways sweep of the arm between shoulder and hip <~ delivery> — **sidearm** \ˈsī-\ *adv*

side arm *n* **:** a weapon (as a sword, revolver, or bayonet) worn at the side or in the belt

side·band \-ˌband\ *n* **:** the band of frequencies (as of radio waves) on either side of the carrier frequency produced by modulation

side bearing *n* **:** the space provided at each side of a typeset letter to prevent its touching adjoining letters

side·board \ˈsīd-ˌbō(ə)rd, -ˌbȯ(ə)rd\ *n* **:** a piece of dining-room furniture having compartments and shelves for holding articles of table service

side·burns \-ˌbərnz\ *n pl* [anagram of *burnsides*] **1 :** SIDE-WHISKERS; *esp* **:** short side-whiskers worn with a smooth chin **2 :** continuations of the hairline in front of the ears — **side·burned** \-ˌbərnd\ *adj*

side by side *adv* **1 :** beside one another <walked *side by side* down the aisle> **2 :** in the same place, time, or circumstance <lived peacefully *side by side* for many years> — **side–by–side** *adj*

side·car \ˈsīd-ˌkär\ *n* **1 :** a car attached to a motorcycle for a passenger seated abreast of the cyclist **2 :** a cocktail consisting of a liqueur with lemon juice and brandy

sid·ed \ˈsīd-əd\ *adj* **:** having sides often of a specified number or kind <one-*sided*> <glass-*sided*> — **sid·ed·ness** *n*

side dish *n* **:** one of the foods subordinate to the main course

side·dress \ˈsīd-ˌdres\ *n* **1 :** plant nutrients used to side-dress a crop **2 :** the act or process of side-dressing a crop

side–dress *vt* **:** to place plant nutrients on or in the soil near the roots of (a growing crop) often by means of a cultivator having a fertilizer-distributing attachment

side–dressing *n* **:** SIDEDRESS

side drum *n* **:** SNARE DRUM

side effect *n* **:** a secondary and usu. adverse effect (as of a drug) <toxic *side effects*> — called also *side reaction*

side–glance \ˈsīd-ˌglan(t)s\ *n* **1 :** a glance directed to the side **2 :** a passing allusion **:** an indirect or slight reference

1side·hill \-ˌhil\ *n* **:** HILLSIDE

2**sidehill** \ˌsīd-\ *adj* **:** used or located on or designed for a sidehill
side horse **1 :** a leather-covered rectangular or cylindrical form that has two pommels on the top, that is supported in a horizontal position by an adjustable frame, and that is used for swinging and balancing feats in gymnastics **2 :** an event in gymnastics competition in which the side horse is used
side issue *n* **:** an issue apart from the main point
side·kick \ˈsīd-ˌkik\ *n* **:** a person closely associated with another as subordinate or partner
side·light \-ˌlīt\ *n* **1 a :** light coming or produced from the side **b :** incidental light or information **2 :** the red light on the port bow or the green light on the starboard bow carried by ships under way at night
1**side·line** \-ˌlīn\ *n* **1 :** a line at right angles to a goal line or end line and marking a side of a court or field of play for athletic games **2 a :** a line of goods sold in addition to one's principal line **b :** a business or activity pursued in addition to one's regular occupation **3 a :** the space immediately outside the lines along either side of an athletic field or court **b :** the standpoint of persons not immediately participating (as in an athletic contest) — usu. used in pl. <his injury put him on the ~*s* for the rest of the season>
2**sideline** *vt* **:** to put out of action **:** put on the sidelines
side·lin·er \ˈsīd-ˌlī-nər\ *n* **:** one that remains on the sidelines during an activity **:** one that does not participate
1**side·ling** *or* **si·dling** \ˈsīd-liŋ\ *adv* [ME *sidling,* fr. 1*side* + *-ling*] **:** in a sidelong direction **:** SIDEWAYS
2**sideling** *or* **sidling** *adj* **1 :** directed toward one side **:** OBLIQUE **2 :** having an inclination **:** SLOPING <~ ground>
1**side·long** \ˈsīd-ˌlȯŋ\ *adv* [alter. of 1*sidelong*] **1 :** SIDEWAYS, OBLIQUELY **2 :** on the side
2**sidelong** \ˌsīd-\ *adj* **1 :** lying or inclining to one side **:** SLANTING **2 a :** directed to one side <~ looks> **b :** indirect rather than straightforward
side·man \ˈsīd-ˌman\ *n* **:** a member of a band or orchestra and esp. of a jazz or swing orchestra
side·piece \-ˌpēs\ *n* **:** a piece forming or contained in the side of something <the ~ of a carriage>
sider- *or* **sidero-** *comb form* [MF, fr. L, fr. Gk *sidēr-, sidēro-,* fr. *sidēros*] **:** iron <*sidero*lite> <*sider*osis>
-sid·er \ˈsīd-ər\ *comb form* **:** one placed or living in a usu. specified side (as a section of the city) <an east-*sider*>
si·de·re·al \sī-ˈdir-ē-əl, sə-\ *adj* [L *sidereus,* fr. *sider-, sidus* star, constellation; akin to Lith *svidus* shining] **:** of, relating to, or expressed in relation to stars or constellations **:** ASTRAL
sidereal day *n* **:** the interval between two successive transits of the March equinox over the upper meridian of a place **:** 23 hours, 56 minutes, 4.09 seconds of mean time
sidereal hour *n* **:** the 24th part of a sidereal day
sidereal minute *n* **:** the 60th part of a sidereal hour
sidereal month *n* **:** the mean time of the moon's revolution in its orbit from a star back to the same star **:** 27 days, 7 hours, 43 minutes, 11.5 seconds of mean time
sidereal second *n* **:** the 60th part of a sidereal minute
sidereal time *n* **1 :** time based on the sidereal day **2 :** the hour angle of the March equinox at a place
sidereal year *n* **:** the time in which the earth completes one revolution in its orbit around the sun measured with respect to the fixed stars **:** 365 days, 6 hours, 9 minutes, and 9.54 seconds of solar time
1**sid·er·ite** \ˈsid-ə-ˌrīt\ *n* [G *siderit,* fr. Gk *sidēros* iron] **:** a native ferrous carbonate $FeCO_3$ that is a valuable iron ore
2**siderite** *n* **:** a nickel-iron meteorite
sid·er·it·ic \ˌsid-ə-ˈrit-ik\ *adj* **:** of, relating to, or containing siderite
si·de·ro·lite \sī-ˈdir-ə-ˌlīt, ˈsid-ə-rə-\ *n* **:** a stony iron meteorite
side·sad·dle \ˈsīd-ˌsad-ᵊl\ *n* **:** a saddle for women in which the rider sits with both legs on the same side of the horse — **sidesaddle** *adv*

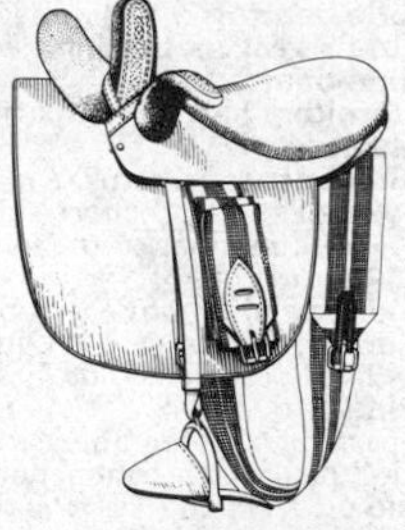
sidesaddle

side·show \-ˌshō\ *n* **1 :** a minor show offered in addition to a main exhibition (as of a circus) **2 :** an incidental diversion
side·slip \-ˌslip\ *vi* **1 :** to skid sideways — used esp. of an automobile **2 :** to slide sideways through the air in a downward direction in an airplane along an inclined lateral axis **3 :** to slide sideways in a downward direction in skiing
side·spin \-ˌspin\ *n* [1*side* + *spin*] **:** a rotary motion that causes a ball to revolve horizontally
side·split·ting \-ˌsplit-iŋ\ *adj* **:** extremely funny
side·step \ˈsīd-ˌstep\ *vi* **1 :** to take a side step **2 :** to avoid an issue or decision <men who know how to dodge, trim, and ~ —C. M. Fassett> ~ *vt* **1 :** to move out of the way of **:** AVOID <~ a blow> **2 :** BYPASS, EVADE <adept at *sidestepping* awkward questions> — **side·step·per** *n*
side step *n* **1 :** a step aside (as in boxing to avoid a blow) **2 :** a step taken sideways (as when climbing on skis)
side–strad·dle hop \ˌsīd-ˌstrad-ᵊl-\ *n* **:** JUMPING JACK 2
side·stroke \ˈsīd-ˌstrōk\ *n* **:** a swimming stroke which is executed on the side and in which the arms are swept backward and downward and the legs do a scissors kick
1**side·swipe** \-ˌswīp\ *vt* **:** to strike with a glancing blow along the side <*sideswiped* a parked car>
2**sideswipe** *n* **1 a :** the action of sideswiping **b :** an instance of sideswiping **:** a glancing blow **2 :** an incidental deprecatory remark, allusion, or reference
side table *n* **:** a table designed to be placed against a wall
1**side·track** \ˈsīd-ˌtrak\ *n* **1 :** SIDING 2 **2 :** a position or condition of secondary importance to which one may be diverted
2**sidetrack** *vt* **1 :** to transfer to a railroad siding **2 a :** to turn aside from a purpose **:** DEFLECT **b :** to prevent action upon by diversionary tactics <~ an issue>
side·walk \ˈsīd-ˌwȯk\ *n* **:** a usu. paved walk for pedestrians at the side of a street
sidewalk artist *n* **:** an artist who makes drawings usu. with chalk directly on the sidewalk to obtain money from passersby
sidewalk superintendent *n* **:** a spectator at a building or demolition job
side·wall \ˈsīd-ˌwȯl\ *n* **1 :** a wall forming the side of something **2 :** the side of an automotive tire between the tread shoulder and the rim bead
side·ward \ˈsīd-wərd\ *or* **side·wards** \-wərdz\ *adv* **:** toward a side
side·way \ˈsīd-ˌwā\ *adv or adj* **:** SIDEWAYS
side·ways \-ˌwāz\ *adv or adj* **1 :** from one side **2 :** with one side forward <turn ~> **3 :** obliquely or downward to one side; *also* **:** ASKANCE <look ~ at someone>
side–wheel \ˌsīd-ˌhwēl, ˈsīd-ˌwēl\ *adj* **:** of or constituting a steamer having a paddle wheel on each side
side–wheel·er \-ər\ *n* **:** a side-wheel steamer
side–whiskers \ˈsīd-ˌhwis-kərz, ˈsīd-ˌwis-\ *n pl* **:** whiskers on the side of the face usu. worn long — **side–whis·kered** \-kərd\ *adj*
side·wind·er \ˈsīd-ˌwīn-dər\ *n* **1 :** a heavy swinging blow from the side **2 :** a small pale-colored desert rattlesnake (*Crotalus cerastes*) of the southwestern U.S. that moves by thrusting its body diagonally forward in a series of flat S-shaped loops
side·wise \ˈsīd-ˌwīz\ *adv* **:** SIDEWAYS
sid·ing \ˈsīd-iŋ\ *n* **1** *archaic* **:** the taking of sides **:** PARTISANSHIP **2 :** a short railroad track connected with the main track — called also *sidetrack* **3 :** material (as boards or metal pieces) forming the exposed surface of outside walls of frame buildings
si·dle \ˈsīd-ᵊl\ *vb* **si·dled; si·dling** \ˈsīd-liŋ, -ᵊl-iŋ\ [prob. back-formation fr. 2*sideling*] *vi* **:** to go or move with one side foremost esp. in a furtive advance ~ *vt* **:** to cause to move or turn sideways <the pilot *sidled* the boat up to the dock> — **sidle** *n*
1**siege** \ˈsēj\ *n* [ME *sege,* fr. OF, seat, blockade, fr. (assumed) VL *sedicum,* fr. *sedicare,* to settle, fr. L *sedēre* to sit — more at SIT] **1** *obs* **:** a seat of distinction **:** THRONE **2 a :** a military blockade of a city or fortified place to compel it to surrender **b :** a persistent attack (as of illness) — **lay siege to 1 :** to besiege militarily <*laid siege to* the town> **2 :** to pursue diligently or persistently
2**siege** *vt* **sieged; sieg·ing :** BESIEGE
Siege Perilous *n* **:** a seat at King Arthur's Round Table reserved for the knight destined to achieve the quest of the Holy Grail and fatal to any other occupying it
Sieg·fried \ˈsig-ˌfrēd, ˈsēg-\ *n* [G] **:** a hero of the *Nibelungenlied* who slays a dragon guarding a gold hoard and wakes Brunhild from her enchanted sleep
Siegfried line *n* [*Siegfried,* Germanic hero] **:** a line of German defensive fortifications facing the Maginot Line
si·en·na \sē-ˈen-ə\ *n* [It *terra di Siena,* lit., Siena earth, fr. *Siena,* Italy] **:** an earthy substance containing oxides of iron and usu. of manganese that is brownish yellow when raw and orange red or reddish brown when burnt and is used as a pigment
si·ero·zem \sē-ˌer-ə-ˈzhȯm\ *n* [Russ *serozem,* fr. *seryĭ* gray + *zemlya* earth] **:** any of a zonal group of soils brownish gray at the surface and lighter below, based in a carbonate or hardpan layer, and characteristic of temperate to cool arid regions
si·er·ra \sē-ˈer-ə\ *n* [Sp, lit., saw, fr. L *serra*] **1 a :** a range of mountains esp. with a serrated or irregular outline **b :** the country about a sierra **2 :** any of various large fishes (genus *Scomberomorus*) that resemble mackerel
Sierra — a communication code word for the letter *s*
si·er·ran \sē-ˈer-ən\ *adj* **1 :** of or relating to a sierra <~ foothills> **2** *cap* **:** of or relating to the Sierra Nevada mountains of the western U.S.
Sierran *n* **:** a native or inhabitant of the region around the Sierra Nevada mountains
si·es·ta \sē-ˈes-tə\ *n* [Sp, fr. L *sexta* (*hora*) noon, lit., sixth hour — more at SEXT] **:** an afternoon nap or rest
sie·va bean \ˈsē-və-, ˈsiv-ē-\ *n* [origin unknown] **:** any of several small-seeded beans closely related to and sometimes classed as lima beans; *also* **:** the seed of a sieva bean
1**sieve** \ˈsiv\ *n* [ME *sive,* fr. OE *sife;* akin to OHG *sib* sieve, Serb *sípiti* to drizzle] **:** a device with meshes or perforations through which finer particles of a mixture (as of ashes, flour, or sand) of various sizes are passed to separate them from coarser ones, through which the liquid is drained from liquid-containing material, or through which soft materials are forced for reduction to fine particles
2**sieve** *vb* **sieved; siev·ing :** SIFT
sieve plate *n* **:** a perforated wall or part of a wall at the end of one of the individual cells making up a sieve tube
sieve tube *n* **:** a tube consisting of an end-to-end series of thin-walled living cells characteristic of the phloem and held to function chiefly in translocation of organic solutes
sift \ˈsift\ *vb* [ME *siften,* fr. OE *siftan;* akin to OE *sife* sieve] *vt* **1 a :** to put through a sieve <~ flour> **b :** to separate or separate out by or as if by putting through a sieve **2 a :** to screen out the valuable or good **:** SELECT **b :** to study or investigate thoroughly **:** PROBE **3 :** to scatter by or as if by sifting <~ sugar on a cake> ~ *vi* **1 :** to use a sieve **2 :** SCREEN, SELECT — **sift·er** *n*
sift·ing *n* **1 :** the act or process of sifting **2** *pl* **:** sifted material
sig *abbr* **1** signal **2** signature **3** signor
Sig *abbr* [L *signa*] label
SIG *abbr* special interest group
1**sigh** \ˈsī\ *vb* [ME *sihen,* alter. of *sichen,* fr. OE *sīcan;* akin to MD *versiken* to sigh] *vi* **1 :** to take a deep audible breath (as in weariness or grief) **2 :** to make a sound like sighing <wind ~*ing* in the branches> **3 :** GRIEVE, YEARN <~*ing* for the days of his youth> ~ *vt* **1 :** to express by sighs **2** *archaic* **:** to utter sighs over **:** MOURN — **sigh·er** \ˈsī(-ə)r\ *n*

[2]**sigh** *n* **1 :** an act of sighing esp. when involuntary and expressing an emotion or feeling (as weariness or relief) **2 :** the sound of gently moving or escaping air <~*s* of the summer breeze>

[1]**sight** \ˈsīt\ *n* [ME, fr. OE *gesiht* faculty or act of sight, thing seen; akin to OHG *gisiht* sight, OE *sēon* to see] **1 :** something that is seen : SPECTACLE **2 a :** a thing regarded as worth seeing — usu. used in pl. <a tour of the ~*s* of the city> **b :** something ludicrous or disorderly in appearance <you must get some sleep, you look a ~> **3** *chiefly dial* **:** a great number or quantity **4 a :** the process, power, or function of seeing; *specif* **:** the animal sense of which the end organ is the eye and by which the position, shape, and color of objects are perceived **b :** mental or spiritual perception **c :** mental view; *specif* **:** JUDGMENT **5 a :** the act of looking at or beholding **b :** INSPECTION, PERUSAL <this letter is for your ~ only> **c :** VIEW, GLIMPSE **d :** an observation to determine direction or position (as by a navigator) **6 a :** a perception of an object by the eye **b :** the range of vision **7 :** presentation of a note or draft to the maker or draftee : DEMAND **8 a :** a device for guiding the eye (as in aiming a firearm or bomb) **b :** a device with a small aperture through which objects are to be seen and by which their direction is ascertained — **out of sight 1 :** beyond comparison **2 :** beyond all expectation or reason — **sight for sore eyes :** one whose appearance or arrival is an occasion for joy or relief

[2]**sight** *adj* **1 :** based on recognition or comprehension without previous study <a ~ translation> **2 :** payable on presentation

[3]**sight** *vt* **1 :** to get or catch sight of <several whales were ~*ed*> **2 :** to look at through or as if through a sight; *esp* **:** to test for straightness **3 :** to aim by means of sights **4 a :** to equip with sights **b :** to adjust the sights of ~ *vi* **1 :** to take aim **2 :** to look carefully in a particular direction

sight draft *n* **:** a draft payable on presentation

sight·ed \ˈsīt-əd\ *adj* **:** having sight <clear-*sighted*>

sight gag *n* **:** a comic bit or episode whose effect is produced by pantomime or camera shot rather than by words

sight·less \ˈsīt-ləs\ *adj* **1 :** lacking sight : BLIND **2 :** INVISIBLE — **sight·less·ness** *n*

sight·ly \-lē\ *adj* **1 :** pleasing to the sight : ATTRACTIVE **2 :** affording a fine view — **sight·li·ness** *n* — **sightly** *adv*

sight–read \-ˌrēd\ *vb* **-read** \-ˌred\; **-read·ing** \-ˌrēd-iŋ\ [back-formation fr. *sight reader*] *vt* **:** to read (as a foreign language) or perform (music) without previous preparation or study ~ *vi* **:** to read at sight; *esp* **:** to perform music at sight — **sight reader** *n*

sight rhyme *n* **:** EYE RHYME

sight·see \ˈsīt-ˌsē\ *vi* [back-formation fr. [2]*sightseeing*] **:** to go about seeing sights of interest — **sight·se·er** \-ˌsē-ər, -ˌsi(ə)r\ *n*

[1]**sight–see·ing** \ˈsīt-ˌsē-iŋ\ *adj* **:** devoted to or used for seeing sights

[2]**sight–seeing** *n* **:** the act or pastime of seeing sights

sight unseen *adv* **:** without inspection or appraisal

sig·il \ˈsij-əl, ˈsig-ˌil\ *n* [L *sigillum* — more at SEAL] **1 :** SEAL, SIGNET **2 :** a sign, word, or device of supposed occult power in astrology or magic

sigill *abbr* [L *sigillum*] seal

sig·ma \ˈsig-mə\ *n* [Gk] **1 :** the 18th letter of the Greek alphabet — see ALPHABET table **2 :** an unstable elementary particle of the baryon family existing in positive, negative, and neutral charge states with masses respectively 2328, 2343, and 2333 times the mass of an electron — called also *sigma particle*

sig·moid \ˈsig-ˌmȯid\ *also* **sig·moi·dal** \sig-ˈmȯid-ᵊl\ *adj* [Gk *sigmoeidēs*, fr. *sigma*; fr. a common form of sigma shaped like the Roman letter C] **1 a :** curved like the letter C **b :** curved in two directions like the letter S **2 :** of, relating to, or being the sigmoid flexure of the intestine — **sig·moi·dal·ly** \sig-ˈmȯid-ᵊl-ē\ *adv*

sigmoid flexure *n* **:** the contracted and crooked part of the colon immediately above the rectum — called also *sigmoid colon*

[1]**sign** \ˈsīn\ *n* [ME *signe*, fr. OF, fr. L *signum* mark, token, sign, image, seal; prob. akin to L *secare* to cut — more at SAW] **1 a :** a motion or gesture by which a thought is expressed or a command or wish made known **b :** SIGNAL 2a **c :** a fundamental linguistic unit that designates an object or relation or has a purely syntactic function **d :** one of a set of gestures used to represent language **2 :** a mark having a conventional meaning and used in place of words or to represent a complex notion **3 :** one of the 12 divisions of the zodiac **4 a** (1) **:** a character (as a flat or sharp) used in musical notation (2) **:** SEGNO **b :** a character (as ÷) indicating a mathematical operation; *also* **:** one of two characters + and − that form part of the symbol of a number and characterize it as positive or negative **5 a :** a lettered board or other display used to identify or advertise a place of business **b :** a posted command, warning, or direction **c :** SIGNBOARD **6 a :** something material or external that stands for or signifies something spiritual **b :** something that serves to indicate the presence or existence of something : TOKEN <removed their hats as a ~ of respect> **c :** PRESAGE, PORTENT <~*s* of an early spring> **d :** an objective evidence of plant or animal disease **7 :** a remarkable event supposed to indicate the will of a deity : PRODIGY

[2]**sign** *vb* [ME *signen*, fr. MF *signer*, fr. L *signare* to mark, sign, seal, fr. *signum*] *vt* **1 a :** to place a sign upon **b :** CROSS 2 **c :** to represent or indicate by a sign **2 a :** to affix a signature to : ratify or attest by hand or seal <~ a bill into law> <the prisoner ~*ed* a confession> **b :** to assign or convey formally <~*ed* over his property to his brother> **c :** to write down (one's name) **3 :** to communicate by making a sign **4 :** to engage or hire by securing the signature of on a contract of employment ~ *vi* **1 :** to write one's name in token of assent, responsibility, or obligation **2 :** to make a sign or signal — **sign·er** *n*

[1]**sig·nal** \ˈsig-nᵊl\ *n* [ME, fr. MF, fr. ML *signale*, fr. LL, neut. of *signalis* of a sign, fr. L *signum*] **1** *archaic* **:** TOKEN, INDICATION **2 a :** an act, event, or watchword that has been agreed upon as the occasion of concerted action <waited for the ~ to begin the attack> **b :** something that incites to action **3 a :** a sound or gesture made to give warning or command <a ~ that warns of an air raid> **b :** an object placed to convey notice or warning **4 :** an object (as a flag on a pole) centered over a point so as to be observed from other positions in surveying **5 a :** an object used to transmit or convey information beyond the range of human voice **b :** the sound or image conveyed in telegraphy, telephony, radio, radar, or television **c :** a detectable physical quantity or impulse (as a voltage, current, or magnetic field strength) by which messages or information can be transmitted

[2]**signal** *vb* **sig·naled** *or* **sig·nalled; sig·nal·ing** *or* **sig·nal·ling** \-nə-liŋ\ *vt* **1 :** to notify by a signal <~*ed* the fleet to turn back> **2 a :** to communicate by signals **b :** to constitute a characteristic feature of (a meaningful linguistic form) ~ *vi* **:** to make or send a signal — **sig·nal·er** *or* **sig·nal·ler** *n*

[3]**signal** *adj* [modif. of F *signalé*, pp. of *signaler* to distinguish, fr. OIt *segnalare* to signal, distinguish, fr. *segnale* signal, fr. ML *signale*] **1 :** distinguished from the ordinary <~ achievement> **2 :** used in signaling <~ beacon> ***syn*** see NOTICEABLE

sig·nal·ize \ˈsig-nə-ˌlīz\ *vt* **-ized; -iz·ing** [[3]*signal*] **1 :** to make conspicuous : DISTINGUISH **2 :** to point out carefully or distinctly **3 :** to make signals to : SIGNAL; *also* **:** INDICATE **4 :** to place traffic signals at or on — **sig·nal·i·za·tion** \ˌsig-nə-lə-ˈzā-shən\ *n*

sig·nal·ly \ˈsig-nə-lē\ *adv* **:** in a signal manner : NOTABLY

sig·nal·man \ˈsig-nᵊl-mən, -ˌman\ *n* **:** one who signals or works with signals

sig·nal·ment \-mənt\ *n* [F *signalement*, fr. *signaler*] **:** description by peculiar, appropriate, or characteristic marks; *specif* **:** the systematic description of a person for purposes of identification

sig·na·to·ry \ˈsig-nə-ˌtōr-ē, -ˌtȯr-\ *n, pl* **-ries** [L *signatorius* of sealing, fr. *signatus*, pp.] **:** a signer with another or others <*signatories* to a petition>; *esp* **:** a government bound with others by a signed convention — **signatory** *adj*

sig·na·ture \ˈsig-nə-ˌchu̇(ə)r, -chər, -ˌt(y)u̇(ə)r\ *n* [MF or ML; MF, fr. ML *signatura*, fr. L *signatus*, pp. of *signare* to sign, seal] **1 a :** the name of a person written with his own hand **b :** the act of signing one's name **2 :** a feature in the appearance or qualities of a natural object formerly held to indicate its utility in medicine **3 a :** a letter or figure placed usu. at the bottom of the first page on each sheet of printed pages (as of a book) as a direction to the binder in arranging and gathering the sheets **b :** the sheet itself which when folded becomes one unit of the book **4 a :** KEY SIGNATURE **b :** TIME SIGNATURE **5 :** the part of a medical prescription which contains the directions to the patient **6 :** a tune, musical number, or sound effect or in television a characteristic title or picture used to identify a program, entertainer, or orchestra

sign·board \ˈsīn-ˌbō(ə)rd, -ˌbȯ(ə)rd\ *n* **:** a board bearing a notice or sign

[1]**sig·net** \ˈsig-nət\ *n* [ME, fr. MF, dim. of *signe* sign, seal] **1 :** a seal used officially to give personal authority to a document in lieu of signature **2 :** the impression made by or as if by a signet **3 :** a small intaglio seal (as in a finger ring)

[2]**signet** *vt* **:** to stamp or authenticate with a signet

signet ring *n* **:** a finger ring engraved with a signet, seal, or monogram : SEAL RING

sig·ni·fi·able \ˈsig-nə-ˌfī-ə-bəl\ *adj* **:** capable of being represented by a sign or symbol

sig·nif·i·cance \sig-ˈnif-i-kən(t)s\ *n* **1 a :** something that is conveyed as a meaning often obscurely or indirectly **b :** the quality of conveying or implying **2 a :** the quality of being important : MOMENT **b :** the quality of being statistically significant ***syn* 1** see MEANING **2** see IMPORTANCE ***ant*** insignificance

significance level *n* **:** LEVEL OF SIGNIFICANCE

sig·nif·i·can·cy \sig-ˈnif-i-kən-sē\ *n* **:** SIGNIFICANCE

sig·nif·i·cant \-kənt\ *adj* [L *significant-*, *significans*, prp. of *significare* to signify] **1 :** having meaning; *esp* **:** SUGGESTIVE, EXPRESSIVE <the painter's task to pick out the ~ details — Herbert Read> **2 :** suggesting or containing a disguised or special meaning <perhaps her glance was ~> **3 a :** having or likely to have influence or effect : IMPORTANT, WEIGHTY **b :** probably caused by something other than mere chance <statistically ~ correlation between vitamin deficiency and disease> — **sig·nif·i·cant·ly** *adv*

significant figures *n pl* **:** the figures of a number that begin with the first figure to the left that is not zero and end with the last figure to the right that is not zero or is a zero that is considered to be exact — called also *significant digits*

sig·ni·fi·ca·tion \ˌsig-nə-fə-ˈkā-shən\ *n* **1 a :** the act or process of signifying by signs or other symbolic means **b :** a formal notification **2 :** IMPORT; *esp* **:** the meaning that a term, symbol, or character regularly conveys or is intended to convey **3** *chiefly dial* **:** IMPORTANCE, CONSEQUENCE ***syn*** see MEANING

sig·nif·i·ca·tive \sig-ˈnif-ə-ˌkāt-iv\ *adj* **1 :** INDICATIVE <symptoms ~ of malaria> **2 :** SIGNIFICANT, SUGGESTIVE — **sig·nif·i·ca·tive·ly** *adv* — **sig·nif·i·ca·tive·ness** *n*

sig·nif·ics \sig-ˈnif-iks\ *n pl but sing or pl in constr* [*signify*] **:** SEMIOTIC, SEMANTICS

sig·ni·fi·er \ˈsig-nə-ˌfī(-ə)r\ *n* **:** one that signifies : SIGN

sig·ni·fy \ˈsig-nə-ˌfī\ *vb* **-fied; -fy·ing** [ME *signifien*, fr. OF *signifier*, fr. L *significare* to indicate, signify, fr. *signum* sign] *vt* **1 a :** MEAN, DENOTE **b :** IMPLY **2 :** to show esp. by a conventional token (as word, signal, or gesture) ~ *vi* **:** to have significance : MATTER

sign in *vi* **:** to make a record of arrival by signing a register or punching a time clock ~ *vt* **:** to record arrival of (a person) or receipt of (an article) by signing

si·gnior \sēn-ˈyō(ə)r, -ˈyȯ(ə)r\ *n* [It *signor*] **:** SIGNOR

sign language *n* **1 :** a system of hand gestures used for communication (as by the deaf) **2 :** an unsystematic method of communicating chiefly by manual gestures used by people speaking different languages

sign manual *n, pl* **signs manual** [[1]*sign* + *manual,* adj.] : SIGNATURE, *specif* : the king's signature on a royal grant or charter placed at the top of the document
sign of aggregation : any of various conventional devices (as braces, brackets, parentheses, or vinculums) used in mathematics to indicate that two or more terms are to be treated as one quantity
sign off \(ˈ)sī-ˈnȯf\ *vi* : to announce the end of a message, program, or broadcast and discontinue transmitting — **sign–off** \ˈsī-ˌnȯf\ *n*
sign of the cross : a gesture of the hand forming a cross esp. on forehead, shoulders, and breast to profess Christian faith or invoke divine protection or blessing
sign on \(ˈ)sī-ˈnȯn, -ˈnän\ *vi* **1** : to engage oneself for duty by signature or agreement : ENLIST <*signed on* as a member of the crew> **2** : to announce the start of broadcasting for the day ~ *vt* : to secure the signature of — **sign–on** \ˈsī-ˌnȯn, -ˌnän\ *n*
si·gnor \sēn-ˈyȯ(ə)r, -ˈyō(ə)r\ *n, pl* **signors** *or* **si·gno·ri** \sēn-ˈyōr-(ˌ)ē, -ˈyȯr-\ [It *signore, signor,* fr. ML *senior* superior, lord — more at SENOR] : a usu. Italian man of rank or gentility — used as a title equivalent to *Mister*
si·gno·ra \sēn-ˈyōr-ə, -ˈyȯr-\ *n, pl* **signoras** *or* **si·gno·re** \-ˈyōr-(ˌ)ā, -ˈyȯr-\ [It, fem. of *signore, signor*] : an Italian married woman usu. of rank or gentility — used as a title equivalent to *Mrs.*
si·gno·re \sēn-ˈyōr-(ˌ)ā, -ˈyȯr-\ *n, pl* **si·gno·ri** \-ˈyōr-(ˌ)ē, -ˈyȯr-\ [It] : SIGNOR
si·gno·ri·na \ˌsē-nyə-ˈrē-nə\ *n, pl* **-nas** *or* **-ne** \-(ˌ)nā\ [It, fr. dim. of *signora*] : an unmarried Italian woman — used as a title equivalent to *Miss*
si·gno·ri·no \-(ˌ)nō\ *n, pl* **-ni** \-(ˌ)nē\ [It, fr. dim. of *signore*] : a young Italian esp. of rank — used as a title equivalent to *Master*
si·gnory *or* **si·gniory** \ˈsē-nyə-rē\ *n, pl* **si·gnor·ies** *or* **si·gnior·ies** [ME *signorie,* fr. MF *seigneurie*] : SEIGNIORY
sign out *vi* : to indicate departure by signing a register <*signed out* of the hospital> ~ *vt* : to record or approve the release or departure of <*sign* books *out* of a library>
[1]**sign·post** \ˈsīn-ˌpōst\ *n* : a post bearing a sign; *specif* : a post (as at the fork of a road) with signs on it to direct travelers
[2]**signpost** *vt* : to provide with signposts or guides
sign up *vi* : to join an organization or accept an obligation by signing a contract <*sign up* for a set of reference volumes> ~ *vt* : to induce to sign a contract <*sign* a customer *up*>
Sig·urd \ˈsig-ˌu̇(ə)rd, ˈsig-ərd\ *n* [ON *Sigurthr*] : a hero in Norse mythology who slays the dragon Fafnir
sike \ˈsīk\ *n* [ME, fr. OE *sīc;* akin to ON *sīk* sike, OE *sicerian* to trickle] **1** *dial chiefly Brit* : a small stream; *esp* : one that dries up in summer **2** *dial chiefly Brit* : DITCH
[1]**Sikh** \ˈsēk\ *n* [Hindi, lit., disciple] : an adherent of a monotheistic religion of India founded about 1500 by a Hindu under Islamic influence and marked by rejection of idolatry and caste — **Sikh·ism** \-ˌiz-əm\ *n*
[2]**Sikh** *adj* : of or relating to Sikhs or Sikhism
si·lage \ˈsī-lij\ *n* [short for *ensilage*] : fodder converted into succulent feed for livestock through processes of anaerobic acid fermentation (as in a silo)
si·lane \ˈsil-ˌān, ˈsī-ˌlān\ *n* [ISV *sil*icon + meth*ane*] : any of various silicon hydrides that have the general formula Si_nH_{2n+2} and are analogous to hydrocarbons of the methane series
sild \ˈsil(d)\ *n, pl* **sild** *or* **silds** [Norw] : a young herring other than a brisling that is canned as a sardine in Norway
[1]**si·lence** \ˈsī-lən(t)s\ *n* [ME, fr. OF, fr. L *silentium,* fr. *silent-, silens*] **1** : forbearance from speech or noise : MUTENESS — often used interjectionally **2** : absence of sound or noise : STILLNESS **3** : absence of mention: **a** : OBLIVION, OBSCURITY **b** : SECRECY
[2]**silence** *vt* **si·lenced; si·lenc·ing** **1** : to compel or reduce to silence : STILL **2** : to restrain from expression : SUPPRESS **3** : to cause to cease hostile firing by return fire or bombing
si·lenc·er \ˈsī-lən-sər\ *n* : one that silences: as **a** *chiefly Brit* : the muffler of an internal-combustion engine **b** : a silencing device for small arms
si·lent \ˈsī-lənt\ *adj* [L *silent-, silens,* fr. prp. of *silēre* to be silent; akin to Goth ana*silan* to subside, L *sinere* to let go, lay — more at SITE] **1 a** : making no utterance : MUTE, SPEECHLESS **b** : indisposed to speak : not loquacious **2** : free from sound or noise : STILL **3** : performed or borne without utterance : UNSPOKEN <~ prayer> <~ grief> **4 a** : making no mention <history is ~ about this man> **b** : not widely or generally known or appreciated <the ~ pressures on a man in public office> **c** : taking no active part in the conduct of a business **5** : UNPRONOUNCED <~ *b* in *doubt*> **6** : not exhibiting the usual signs or symptoms of presence <a ~ infection> **7** : lacking spoken dialogue <a ~ motion picture> — **si·lent·ly** *adv* — **si·lent·ness** *n*
syn SILENT, TACITURN, RETICENT, RESERVED, SECRETIVE *shared meaning element* : showing restraint in speaking. SILENT implies a habit of saying no more than is needed <a stern, *silent* man, long a widower —Willa Cather> TACITURN implies a temperamental disinclination to speech and usually connotes unsociability <the farmer was *taciturn* and drove them speechlessly to the house —Pearl Buck> RETICENT implies a reluctance to speak out or at length, especially about one's own affairs <had been . . . *reticent* regarding the details of his own financial affairs —J. P. Marquand> RESERVED implies reticence and suggests the restraining influence of caution or formality in checking easy informal conversational exchange <a certain vulgar gusto . . . divided him from the *reserved,* watchful rest of the family —D. H. Lawrence> SECRETIVE, too, implies reticence but usually carries a disparaging suggestion of deviousness and lack of frankness or of an often ostentatious will to conceal <the king was a *secretive* child, and showed little of his mind —Edith Sitwell> ***ant*** talkative
silent butler *n* : a receptacle with hinged lid for collecting table crumbs and the contents of ashtrays
silent partner *n* **1** : a partner who is known to the public but has no voice in the conduct of a firm's business **2** : SECRET PARTNER
si·lents \ˈsī-lən(t)s\ *n pl* : motion pictures without spoken dialogue
silent service *n* **1** : NAVY — used with *the* **2** : the submarine service — used with *the*
silent treatment *n* : an act of completely ignoring a person or thing by resort to silence esp. as a means of expressing contempt or disapproval
si·le·nus \sī-ˈlē-nəs\ *n, pl* **-ni** \-ˌnī\ [L, fr. Gk *silēnos,* fr. *Silēnos* foster father of Dionysus] : a minor woodland deity and companion of Dionysus in ancient Greek mythology with a horse's ears and tail
si·le·sia \sī-ˈlē-zh(ē-)ə, sə-, -sh(ē-)ə\ *n* [*Silesia,* former Prussian province] **1** *archaic* : a linen cloth of Silesian origin **2** : a soft sturdy lightweight cotton twill
si·lex \ˈsī-ˌleks\ *n* [L *silic-, silex* flint, quartz — more at SHELL] : silica or a siliceous material (as powdered tripoli) esp. for use as a filler in paints or wood or as a dental material
Silex *trademark* — used for a vacuum coffee maker
[1]**sil·hou·ette** \ˌsil-ə-ˈwet\ *n* [F, fr. Étienne de *Silhouette* †1767 F controller general of finances; fr. his petty economies] **1** : a likeness cut from dark material and mounted on a light ground or one sketched in outline and solidly colored in **2** : the outline of a body viewed as circumscribing a mass <the ~ of an airplane>
[2]**silhouette** *vt* **-ett·ed; -ett·ing** : to represent by a silhouette; *also* : to project upon a background like a silhouette

silhouette 1

silic- *or* **silico-** *comb form* [*silicon*] : silicon <*silic*one>
sil·i·ca \ˈsil-i-kə\ *n* [NL, fr. L *silic-, silex* flint, quartz] : silicon dioxide SiO_2 occurring in crystalline, amorphous, and impure forms (as in quartz, opal, and sand respectively)
silica gel *n* : colloidal silica resembling coarse white sand in appearance but possessing many fine pores and therefore extremely adsorbent
sil·i·cate \ˈsil-ə-ˌkāt, ˈsil-i-kət\ *n* [*silicic (acid)*] : a salt or ester derived from a silicic acid; *esp* : any of numerous insoluble often complex metal salts that contain silicon and oxygen in the anion, constitute the largest class of minerals, and are used in building materials (as cement, bricks, and glass)
si·li·ceous *or* **si·li·cious** \sə-ˈlish-əs\ *adj* [L *siliceus* of flint, fr. *silic-, silex* flint, quartz] : of, relating to, or containing silica or a silicate <~ limestone>
silici- *comb form* [NL *silica*] : silica <*silici*ferous>
si·lic·ic \sə-ˈlis-ik\ *adj* [NL *silica* & NL *silicium* silicon (fr. *silica*)] : of, relating to, or derived from silica or silicon
silicic acid *n* : any of various weakly acid substances obtained as gelatinous masses by treating silicates with acids
sil·i·cic·o·lous \ˌsil-ə-ˈsik-ə-ləs\ *adj* : growing or thriving in siliceous soil <~ plants>
sil·i·cide \ˈsil-ə-ˌsīd\ *n* [ISV *silic-* + *-ide*] : a binary compound of silicon usu. with a more electropositive element or radical
si·lic·i·fi·ca·tion \sə-ˌlis-ə-fə-ˈkā-shən\ *n* : the action or process of silicifying : the state of being silicified
silicified wood *n* : chalcedony in the form of petrified wood
si·lic·i·fy \sə-ˈlis-ə-ˌfī\ *vb* **-fied; -fy·ing** *vt* : to convert into or impregnate with silica ~ *vi* : to become silicified
sil·i·cle \ˈsil-i-kəl\ *n* [L *silicula,* dim. of *siliqua*] : a broad short silique
sil·i·con \ˈsil-i-kən, ˈsil-ə-ˌkän\ *n* [NL *silica* + E *-on* (as in *carbon*)] : a tetravalent nonmetallic element that occurs combined as the most abundant element next to oxygen in the earth's crust and is used esp. in alloys — see ELEMENT table
silicon carbide *n* : a very hard dark crystalline compound SiC of silicon and carbon that is used as an abrasive and as a refractory and in electric resistors
sil·i·cone \ˈsil-ə-ˌkōn\ *n* [*silic-* + *-one*] : any of various polymeric organic silicon compounds obtained as oils, greases, or plastics and used esp. for water-resistant and heat-resistant lubricants, varnishes, binders, and electric insulators
silicone rubber *n* : rubber made from silicone elastomers and noted for its retention of flexibility, resilience, and tensile strength over a wide temperature range
sil·i·co·sis \ˌsil-ə-ˈkō-səs\ *n* [NL] : a condition of massive fibrosis of the lungs marked by shortness of breath and caused by prolonged inhalation of silica dusts — **sil·i·cot·ic** \-ˈkät-ik\ *adj or n*
sil·i·co·ther·mic \-kō-ˈthər-mik\ *adj* : of, relating to, or being a method of producing heat and chemical reduction (as of a metallic oxide) by oxidizing silicon or an alloy of silicon with oxygen taken from the oxide that it is desired to reduce
si·lique \sə-ˈlēk\ *n* [F, fr. NL *siliqua,* fr. L, pod, husk; akin to L *silic-, silex* flint — more at SHELL] : a narrow elongated two-valved usu. many-seeded capsule that is characteristic of the mustard family, opens by sutures at either margin, and has two parietal placentas
[1]**silk** \ˈsilk\ *n, often attrib* [ME, fr. OE *seolc;* prob. of Baltic or Slav origin; akin to OPruss *silkas* silk, OSlav *shelkŭ*] **1** : a fine continuous protein fiber produced by various insect larvae usu. for cocoons; *esp* : a lustrous tough elastic fiber produced by silkworms and used for textiles **2** : thread, yarn, or fabric made from silk filaments **3 a** : a garment of silk **b (1)** : a distinctive silk gown worn by a King's or Queen's Counsel **(2)** : a King's or Queen's Counsel **c** *pl* : the colored cap and blouse of a jockey or harness horse driver made in the registered racing color of his stable **4 a** : a filament resembling silk (as that produced by a spider) **b** : silky material <milkweed ~>; *esp* : the styles of an ear of Indian corn **5** : PARACHUTE
[2]**silk** *vi, of corn* : to develop the silk
silk·aline *or* **silk·oline** \ˌsil-kə-ˈlēn\ *n* [[1]*silk* + *-oline* (as in *crinoline*)] : a soft light cotton fabric with a smooth lustrous finish like that of silk
silk cotton *n* : the silky or cottony covering of seeds of various silk-cotton trees; *esp* : KAPOK

silk–cotton tree *n* : any of various tropical trees (family Bombacaceae, the silk-cotton family) with palmate leaves and large fruits with the seeds enveloped by silk cotton; *esp* : CEIBA 1

silk·en \'sil-kən\ *adj* **1** : made or consisting of silk **2** : resembling silk: as **a** : SOFT, LUSTROUS **b** (1) : agreeably smooth : HARMONIOUS (2) : INGRATIATING <sheathed her dagger-sharp comments in ~ tones —Harriet Pike> **3 a** : dressed in silk <~ ankles> **b** : LUXURIOUS

silk gland *n* : a gland that produces a viscid fluid, is extruded in filaments and hardens into silk on exposure to air: as **a** : either of a pair of greatly enlarged and modified salivary glands of an insect larva that produce a compound filament from which a larval or pupal cover (as a cocoon) is spun **b** : any of two or more abdominal glands of a spider that open through spinnerets and produce a filament used chiefly in the spinning of webs

silk grass *n* : any of several strong lustrous commercial fibers from bromeliads

silk hat *n* : a hat with a tall cylindrical crown and a silk-plush finish worn by men as a dress hat

silk oak *n* : any of various Australian timber trees (family Protaceae and esp. genus *Grevillea*) with mottled wood used in cabinetmaking and veneering — called also *silky oak*

silk screen *n* : a stencil process in which coloring matter is forced onto the material to be printed through the meshes of a silk or organdy screen so prepared as to have pervious printing areas and impervious nonprinting areas —called also *silk-screen process* — **silk–screen** *vt*

silk–stock·ing \'silk-'stäk-iŋ\ *adj* **1** : fashionably dressed <a ~ audience> **2** : ARISTOCRATIC, WEALTHY <a ~ district> **3** : of or relating to the American Federalist party

silk stocking *n* **1** : a fashionably dressed person **2** : an aristocratic or wealthy person **3** : FEDERALIST 2

silk·weed \'sil-ˌkwēd\ *n* : MILKWEED

silk·worm \'sil-ˌkwərm\ *n* : a moth whose larva spins a large amount of strong silk in constructing its cocoon; *esp* : an Asiatic moth (*Bombyx mori*) whose rough wrinkled hairless yellowish caterpillar produces the silk of commerce

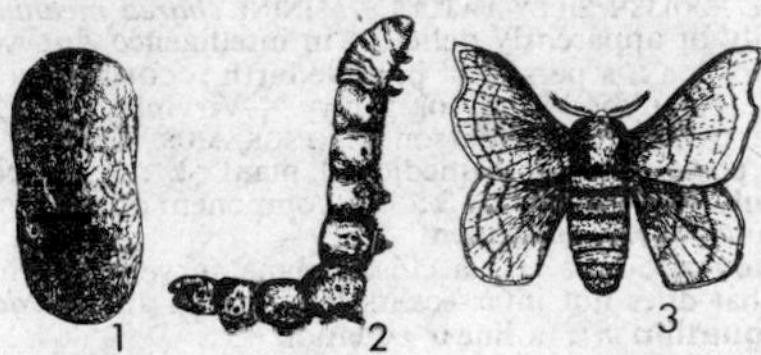

silkworm: *1* cocoon, *2* larva, *3* adult female

silky \'sil-kē\ *adj* **silk·i·er; -est** **1 a** : resembling or consisting of silk **b** : INGRATIATING <~ insinuations> **2** : having or covered with fine soft hairs, plumes, or scales — **silk·i·ly** \-kə-lē\ *adv* — **silk·i·ness** \-kē-nəs\ *n*

silky terrier *n* : a low-set toy terrier that weighs 8 to 10 pounds, has a flat silky glossy coat colored blue with tan on the head, chest, and legs, and is derived from crosses of the Australian terrier with the Yorkshire terrier — called also *silky*

sill \'sil\ *n* [ME *sille*, fr. OE *syll;* akin to OHG *swelli* beam, threshold, Gk *selis* crossbeam] **1** : a horizontal piece (as a timber) that forms the lowest member or one of the lowest members of a framework or supporting structure: as **a** : the horizontal member at the base of a window **b** : the threshold of a door **2** : a tabular body of igneous rock injected while molten between sedimentary or volcanic beds or along foliation planes of metamorphic rocks **3** : a submerged ridge at relatively shallow depth separating the basins of two bodies of water

sillabub *var of* SYLLABUB

sil·li·man·ite \'sil-ə-mə-ˌnīt\ *n* [Benjamin *Silliman* †1864 Am geologist] : a brown, grayish, or pale green mineral Al_2SiO_5 that consists of an aluminum silicate in orthorhombic crystals often occurring in fibrous or columnar forms

sil·ly \'sil-ē\ *adj* **sil·li·er; -est** [ME *sely, silly* happy, innocent, pitiable, feeble, fr. (assumed) OE *sǣlig*, fr. OE *sǣl* happiness; akin to OHG *sālig* happy, L *solari* to console, Gk *hilaros* cheerful] **1** *archaic* : HELPLESS, WEAK **2 a** : RUSTIC, PLAIN **b** *obs* : lowly in station : HUMBLE **3 a** : weak in intellect : FOOLISH **b** : exhibiting or indicative of a lack of common sense or sound judgment <a very ~ mistake> **c** : TRIFLING, FRIVOLOUS **4** : being stunned or dazed <scared ~> <knocked me ~> ***syn*** see SIMPLE — **sil·li·ly** \'sil-ə-lē\ *adv* — **sil·li·ness** \'sil-ē-nəs\ *n* — **silly** *n or adv*

silly season *n* : a period (as late summer) when newspapers must resort to minor or fantastic matters for lack of major news stories

si·lo \'sī-(ˌ)lō\ *n, pl* **silos** [Sp] **1** : a trench, pit, or esp. a tall cylinder (as of wood or concrete) usu. sealed to exclude air and used for making and storing silage **2 a** : a deep bin for storing material (as cement or coal) **b** : an underground structure for housing a guided missile

si·lox·ane \sə-'läk-ˌsān, sī-\ *n* [*sil*icon + *ox*ygen + meth*ane*] : any of various compounds containing alternate silicon and oxygen atoms in either a linear or cyclic arrangement usu. with one or two organic groups attached to each silicon atom

¹silt \'silt\ *n* [ME *cylte*, prob. of Scand origin; akin to Dan *sylt* salt marsh; akin to OHG *sulza* salt marsh, OE *sealt* salt] **1** : loose sedimentary material with rock particles usu. $\frac{1}{20}$ millimeter or less in diameter; *also* : soil containing 80 percent or more of such silt and less than 12 percent of clay **2** : a deposit of sediment (as by a river) — **silty** \'sil-tē\ *adj*

²silt *vi* : to become choked or obstructed with silt — often used with *up* <the channel ~*ed* up> ~ *vt* : to choke, fill, cover, or obstruct with silt or mud <the beaver had ~*ed* the creek —Hugh Fosburgh> — **silt·ation** \sil-'tā-shən\ *n*

silt·stone \'silt-ˌstōn\ *n* : a rock composed chiefly of indurated silt

Si·lu·res \'sil-yə-ˌrēz\ *n* [L] : a people of ancient Britain described by Tacitus as occupying chiefly southern Wales

Si·lu·ri·an \sī-'lu̇r-ē-ən, sə-\ *adj* [L *Silures*] **1** : of or relating to the Silures or their place of habitation **2** : of, relating to, or being a period of the Paleozoic era between the Ordovician and Devonian or the corresponding system of rocks marked by the beginning of coral-reef building and the appearance of some great crustaceans — **Silurian** *n*

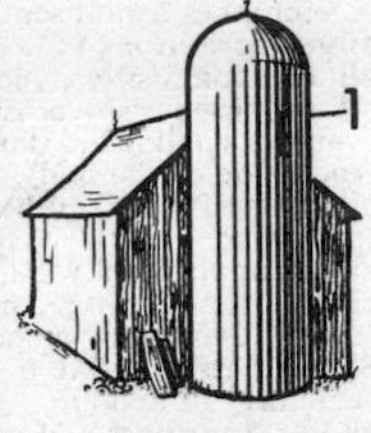

1, silo 1

sil·u·roid \'sil-yə-ˌrȯid\ *n* [deriv. of Gk *silouros*, a large river fish] : any of a suborder (Siluroidea) of fishes comprising the catfishes — **siluroid** *adj*

sil·va \'sil-və\ *n* [NL, fr. L, wood, forest] : the forest trees of a region or country

silvan *var of* SYLVAN

¹sil·ver \'sil-vər\ *n* [ME, fr. OE *seolfor;* akin to OHG *silbar* silver] **1** : a white metallic element that is sonorous, ductile, very malleable, capable of a high degree of polish, and chiefly univalent in compounds, and that has the highest thermal and electric conductivity of any substance — see ELEMENT table **2** : silver as a commodity <the value of ~ has risen> **3** : coin made of silver **4** : articles (as hollowware or table flatware) made of or plated with silver; *also* : similar articles and esp. flatware of other metals (as stainless steel) **5** : a nearly neutral slightly brownish medium gray

²silver *adj* **1** : made of silver **2** : resembling silver: as **a** : having a white lustrous sheen **b** : giving a soft resonant sound : dulcet in tone **c** : eloquently persuasive **3** : consisting of or yielding silver **4** : of, relating to, or characteristic of silver **5** : advocating the use of silver as a standard of currency

³silver *vt* **sil·vered; sil·ver·ing** \'silv-(ə-)riŋ\ **1 a** : to cover with silver (as by electroplating) **b** : to coat with a substance (as a metal) resembling silver **2 a** : to give a silvery luster to **b** : to make white like silver — **sil·ver·er** \'sil-vər-ər\ *n*

silver age *n* : an historical period of achievement secondary to that of a golden age

silver bell *n* : a medium-sized tree (*Halesia carolina*) of the storax family of the southeastern U.S. cultivated for its bell-shaped white flowers

sil·ver·ber·ry \'sil-vər-ˌber-ē\ *n* : a silvery No. American shrub (*Elaeagnus argentea*) related to the buffalo berry

silver bromide *n* : a compound AgBr that is extremely sensitive to light and is much used in the preparation of sensitive emulsion coatings for photographic materials

silver certificate *n* : a certificate formerly issued against the deposit of silver coin as legal tender in the U.S. and its possessions

silver chloride *n* : a compound AgCl sensitive to light and used esp. for photographic materials

silver cord *n* [*The Silver Cord* (1926), play by Sidney Howard] : the emotional tie between mother and child

silver fir *n* : any of various firs (genus *Abies*) with leaves that are white or silvery white beneath; *esp* : a valuable European timber tree (*A. alba*)

sil·ver·fish \'sil-vər-ˌfish\ *n* **1** : any of various silvery fishes (as a tarpon or silversides) **2** : any of various small wingless insects (order Thysanura); *esp* : one (*Lepisma saccharina*) found in houses and sometimes injurious to sized papers or starched clothes

silver fox *n* : a genetically determined color phase of the common red fox in which the pelt is black tipped with white

silver glance *n* : ARGENTITE

silver hake *n* : a common hake (*Merluccius bilinearis*) of the northern New England coast that is an important food fish

silver iodide *n* : a compound AgI that darkens on exposure to light and is used in photography, rainmaking, and medicine

silver–lace vine *n* : a twining Asiatic perennial (*Polygonum aubertii*) of the buckwheat family widely grown for its racemes of fragrant greenish flowers

silver lining *n* **1** : a white edge on a cloud **2** : a consoling or hopeful prospect

sil·ver·ly \'sil-vər-lē\ *adv* : with silvery appearance or sound

silver maple *n* **1** : a common No. American maple (*Acer saccharinum*) with deeply cut leaves that are light green above and silvery white below **2** : the hard close-grained but brittle light brown wood of the silver maple

sil·vern \'sil-vərn\ *adj* **1** : made of silver **2** : resembling or characteristic of silver : SILVERY

silver nitrate *n* : an irritant compound $AgNO_3$ that in contact with organic matter turns black and is used as a chemical reagent, in photography, and in medicine esp. as an antiseptic — called also *lunar caustic*

silver paper *n* : a metallic paper with a coating or lamination resembling silver — called also *tinfoil*

silver perch *n* : any of various somewhat silvery fishes that resemble perch: as **a** : a drum (*Bairdiella chrysura*) that occurs along the more southern Atlantic coast of the U.S. — called also *mademoiselle, yellowtail* **b** : WHITE PERCH 1

silver plate *n* **1** : a plating of silver **2** : domestic flatware and hollowware of silver or of a silver-plated base metal

silver protein *n* : any of several colloidal light-sensitive preparations of silver and protein used in aqueous solution on mucous membranes as antiseptics

silver screen *n* **1 :** a motion-picture screen **2 :** MOTION PICTURES

sil·ver·side \'sil-vər-ˌsīd\ *n* : SILVERSIDES

sil·ver·sides \'sil-vər-ˌsīdz\ *n pl but sing or pl in constr* : any of various small fishes (family Atherinidae) with a silvery stripe along each side of the body

sil·ver·smith \-ˌsmith\ *n* : an artisan who makes articles of silverware

silver spoon *n* : WEALTH; *esp* : inherited wealth

silver standard *n* : a monetary standard under which the currency unit is defined by a stated quantity of silver

Silver Star Medal *n* : a U.S. military decoration awarded for gallantry in action

sil·ver–tongued \ˌsil-vər-'təŋd\ *adj* : ELOQUENT

sil·ver·ware \'sil-vər-ˌwa(ə)r, -ˌwe(ə)r\ *n* : SILVER PLATE, FLATWARE

sil·ver·weed \-ˌwēd\ *n* : any of various somewhat silvery plants; *esp* : a cinquefoil (as the European *Potentilla anserina*) with leaves silvery or white-tomentose beneath

sil·very \'silv-(ə-)rē\ *adj* **1 :** having a soft clear musical tone : RESONANT <a ~ voice> **2 :** having the luster of silver **3 :** containing or consisting of silver — **sil·ver·i·ness** *n*

sil·vi·cal \'sil-vi-kəl\ *adj* : of or relating to silvics

sil·vic·o·lous \sil-'vik-ə-ləs\ *adj* [L *silvicola* inhabitant of a wood, fr. *silva* wood + *colere* to inhabit — more at WHEEL] : living in woodlands

sil·vics \'sil-viks\ *n pl but sing in constr* [NL *silva*] : the study of the life history, characteristics, and ecology of forest trees esp. in stands

sil·vi·cul·ture \'sil-və-ˌkəl-chər\ *n* [F, fr. L *silva, sylva* forest + *cultura* culture] : a branch of forestry dealing with the development and care of forests — **sil·vi·cul·tur·al** \ˌsil-və-'kəlch(-ə)-rəl\ *adj* — **sil·vi·cul·tur·al·ly** \-rə-lē\ *adv* — **sil·vi·cul·tur·ist** \ˌsil-və-'kəlch-(ə-)rəst\ *n*

si·ma·zine \'sī-mə-ˌzēn\ *n* [*sim-* (prob. alter. of *sym-* symmetrical, prefix used in names of organic compounds) + tri*azine*] : a selective herbicide used to control weeds among crop plants

Sim·chas To·rah \ˌsim-kə-'stōr-ə, -'stòr-\ *n* [Heb *śimḥath tōrāh* rejoicing of the Torah] : a Jewish holiday observed on the 23d of Tishri in celebration of the completion of the annual reading of the Torah

Sim·e·on \'sim-ē-ən\ *n* [LL, fr. Gk *Symeōn*, fr. Heb *Shim'ōn*] **1 :** a son of Jacob and the traditional eponymous ancestor of one of the tribes of Israel **2 :** a devout man of Jerusalem held to have uttered the Nunc Dimittis on seeing the infant Jesus in the temple

[1]**sim·i·an** \'sim-ē-ən\ *adj* [L *simia* ape, fr. *simus* snub-nosed, fr. Gk *simos*] : of, relating to, or resembling monkeys or apes

[2]**simian** *n* : MONKEY, APE

sim·i·lar \'sim-(ə-)lər\ *adj* [F *similaire*, fr. L *similis* like, similar — more at SAME] **1 :** having characteristics in common : strictly comparable **2 :** alike in substance or essentials : CORRESPONDING <no two animal habitats are exactly ~ —W. H. Dowdeswell> **3 :** not differing in shape but only in size or position <~ triangles> <~ polygons> — **sim·i·lar·ly** *adv*

syn SIMILAR, ALIKE, AKIN, ANALOGOUS, PARALLEL, IDENTICAL, UNIFORM *shared meaning element* : closely resembling each other ***ant*** dissimilar

sim·i·lar·i·ty \ˌsim-ə-'lar-ət-ē\ *n, pl* **-ties** **1 :** the quality or state of being similar : RESEMBLANCE **2 :** a comparable aspect : CORRESPONDENCE ***syn*** see LIKENESS ***ant*** dissimilarity

sim·i·le \'sim-ə-(ˌ)lē\ *n* [L, comparison, fr. neut. of *similis*] : a figure of speech comparing two unlike things that is often introduced by *like* or *as* (as in *cheeks like roses*) — compare METAPHOR

si·mil·i·tude \sə-'mil-ə-ˌt(y)üd\ *n* [ME, fr. MF, resemblance, likeness, fr. L *similitudo*, fr. *similis*] **1 a :** COUNTERPART, DOUBLE **b :** a visible likeness : IMAGE **2 :** an imaginative comparison : SIMILE **3 a :** correspondence in kind or quality **b :** a point of comparison ***syn*** see LIKENESS ***ant*** dissimilarity, dissimilitude

sim·mer \'sim-ər\ *vb* **sim·mered; sim·mer·ing** \-(ə-)riŋ\ [alter. of E dial. *simper*, fr. ME *simperen*, of imit. origin] *vi* **1 :** to stew gently below or just at the boiling point **2 a :** to be in a state of incipient development : FERMENT <ideas ~*ing* in the back of his mind> **b :** to be in inward turmoil : SEETHE ~ *vt* : to cook slowly in a liquid just below the boiling point

simmer down *vi* **1 :** to become reduced by or as if by simmering **2 :** to become calm or peaceful

sim·nel \'sim-nᵊl\ *n* [ME *simenel*, fr. OF, fr. L *simila* fine wheat flour] **1 :** a bun or bread of fine wheat flour **2** *Brit* : a rich fruitcake sometimes coated with almond paste and baked for mid-Lent, Easter, and Christmas

si·mo·le·on \sə-'mō-lē-ən\ *n* [origin unknown] *slang* : DOLLAR

Si·mon \'sī-mən\ *n* [Gk *Simōn*, fr. Heb *Shim'ōn*] **1 :** PETER — called also *Simon Peter* **2 :** one of the twelve disciples of Jesus — called also *Simon the Zealot* **3 :** a kinsman of Jesus **4 :** a Cyrenian constrained to help Jesus bear his cross to his place of crucifixion — called also *Simon the Cyrenian* **5 :** a Samaritan sorcerer converted by the evangelist Philip

si·mo·ni·ac \si-'mō-nē-ˌak, sə-\ *n* [ME, fr. MF or ML; MF *simoniaque*, fr. ML *simoniacus*, fr. LL *simonia* simony] : one who practices simony — **simoniac** *or* **si·mo·ni·a·cal** \ˌsī-mə-'nī-ə-kəl, ˌsim-ə-\ *adj* — **si·mo·ni·a·cal·ly** \-k(ə-)lē\ *adv*

si·mo·nize \'sī-mə-ˌnīz\ *vt* **-nized; -niz·ing** [fr. *Simoniz*, a trademark] : to polish with or as if with wax

Si·mon Le·gree \ˌsī-mən-lə-'grē\ *n* : a slave owner who has Tom flogged to death in Harriet B. Stowe's novel *Uncle Tom's Cabin*

Simon Ma·gus \-'mā-gəs\ *n* : SIMON 5

si·mon–pure \ˌsī-mən-'pyù(ə)r\ *adj* [fr. *the real Simon Pure*, alluding to a character impersonated by another in the play *A Bold Stroke for a Wife* (1718) by Susanna Centlivre] : of untainted purity or integrity; *also* : pretentiously or hypocritically pure

si·mo·ny \'sī-mə-nē, 'sim-ə-\ *n* [LL *simonia*, fr. *Simon* Magus 1st cent. A.D. Samaritan sorcerer (Acts 8:9–24)] : the buying or selling of a church office or ecclesiastical preferment

si·moom \sə-'müm, sī-\ *or* **si·moon** \-'mün\ *n* [Ar *samūm*] : a hot dry violent dust-laden wind from Asian and African deserts

simp \'simp\ *n* : SIMPLETON

sim·pa·ti·co \sim-'pät-i-ˌkō, -'pat-\ *adj* [It *simpatico* & Sp *simpático*, deriv. of *sympathia* sympathy] : CONGENIAL, LIKABLE

[1]**sim·per** \'sim-pər\ *vb* **sim·pered; sim·per·ing** \-p(ə-)riŋ\ [perh. of Scand origin; akin to Dan dial. *simper* affected, coy] *vi* : to smile in a silly manner ~ *vt* : to say with a simper <~*ed* her apologies> — **sim·per·er** \-pər-ər\ *n*

[2]**simper** *n* : a silly smile : SMIRK

[1]**sim·ple** \'sim-pəl\ *adj* **sim·pler** \-p(ə-)lər\; **sim·plest** \-p(ə-)ləst\ [ME, fr. OF, plain, uncomplicated, artless, fr. L *simplus, simplex*, lit., single; L *simplus* fr. *sem-, sim-* one + *-plus* multiplied by; L *simplic-, simplex* fr. *sem-, sim-* + *-plic-, -plex* -fold; akin to Gk di*plak-*, di*plax* double — more at SAME, DOUBLE] **1 :** free from guile : INNOCENT **2 a :** free from vanity : MODEST **b :** free from ostentation or display **3 :** of humble origin or modest position <a ~ farmer> **4 a :** lacking in knowledge or expertise <a ~ amateur of the arts> **b :** STUPID; *esp* : mentally retarded **c :** not socially or culturally sophisticated : NAIVE; *also* : CREDULOUS **5 a :** SHEER, UNMIXED <~ honesty> **b :** free of secondary complications <a ~ fracture> **c :** having only one main clause and no subordinate clauses <a ~ sentence> **d :** constituting a basic element : FUNDAMENTAL **e :** not made up of many like units <a ~ eye> **6 :** free from elaboration or figuration <~ harmony> **7 a** (1) : not subdivided into branches <a ~ stem> (2) : consisting of a single carpel (3) : developing from a single ovary <a ~ fruit> **b :** controlled by a single gene <~ inherited characters> **8 :** not limited or restricted : UNCONDITIONAL <a ~ obligation> **9 :** readily understood or performed <a ~ statement> <the adjustment was ~ to make> **10** *of a statistical hypothesis* : specifying exact values for one or more statistical parameters — compare COMPOSITE 3 — **sim·ple·ness** \-pəl-nəs\ *n*

syn **1** see PLAIN

2 SIMPLE, FOOLISH, SILLY, FATUOUS, ASININE *shared meaning element* : actually or apparently deficient in intelligence ***ant*** wise

[2]**simple** *n* **1 a :** a person of humble birth : COMMONER <thought very little of anybody, ~*s* or gentry —Virginia Woolf> **b** (1) : a rude or credulous person : IGNORAMUS (2) : a mentally retarded person **2 a :** a medicinal plant **b :** a vegetable drug having only one ingredient **3 :** one component of a complex; *specif* : an unanalyzable constituent

simple closed curve *n* : a closed plane curve (as a circle or an ellipse) that does not intersect itself — called also *Jordan curve*

simple equation *n* : a linear equation

simple fraction *n* : a fraction having whole numbers for the numerator and denominator — compare COMPLEX FRACTION

simple interest *n* : interest paid or computed on the original principal only of a loan or on the amount of an account often on the assumption that each day is 1/360 of a year

simple machine *n* : any of various elementary mechanisms formerly considered as the elements of which all machines are composed and including the lever, the wheel and axle, the pulley, the inclined plane, the wedge, and the screw

sim·ple·mind·ed \ˌsim-pəl-'mīn-dəd\ *adj* : devoid of subtlety : UNSOPHISTICATED; *also* : FOOLISH — **sim·ple·mind·ed·ly** *adv* — **sim·ple·mind·ed·ness** *n*

simple motion *n* : a motion in a straight line, circle or circular arc, or helix

simple sugar *n* : MONOSACCHARIDE

sim·ple·ton \'sim-pəl-tən\ *n* [[1]*simple* + *-ton* (as in surnames such as *Washington*)] : a person lacking in common sense ***syn*** see FOOL

simple vow *n* : a public vow taken by a religious in the Roman Catholic Church under which retention of property by the individual is permitted and marriage though illicit is valid under canon law

[1]**sim·plex** \'sim-ˌpleks\ *adj* [L *simplic-, simplex* — more at SIMPLE] **1 :** SIMPLE, SINGLE **2 :** allowing telecommunication in only one direction at a time <~ system>

[2]**simplex** *n, pl* **sim·plex·es** **1** *or pl* **sim·pli·ces** \-plə-ˌsēz\ *or* **sim·pli·cia** \sim-'plish-(ē-)ə\ : a simple word **2 :** a spatial configuration of *n* dimensions determined by *n* + 1 points in a space of dimension equal to or greater than *n* <a triangle together with its interior determined by its three vertices is a two-dimensional ~ in the plane or any space of higher dimension>

sim·pli·cial \sim-'plish-əl\ *adj* : of or relating to simplexes — **sim·pli·cial·ly** \-ə-lē\ *adv*

sim·plic·i·ty \sim-'plis-ət-ē, -'plis-tē\ *n* [ME *simplicite*, fr. MF *simplicité*, fr. L *simplicitat-, simplicitas*, fr. *simplic-, simplex*] **1 :** the state of being simple or uncompounded **2 a :** lack of subtlety or penetration : INNOCENCE, NAIVETÉ **b :** FOLLY, SILLINESS **3 :** freedom from pretense or guile : CANDOR **4 a :** directness of expression : CLARITY **b :** restraint in ornamentation : AUSTERITY

sim·pli·fy \'sim-plə-ˌfī\ *vt* **-fied; -fy·ing** [F *simplifier*, fr. ML *simplificare*, fr. L *simplus* simple] : to make simple or simpler: as **a :** to reduce to basic essentials **b :** to diminish in scope or complexity : STREAMLINE **c :** to make more intelligible : CLARIFY — **sim·pli·fi·ca·tion** \ˌsim-plə-fə-'kā-shən\ *n* — **sim·pli·fi·er** \'sim-plə-ˌfī(-ə)r\ *n*

sim·plism \'sim-ˌpliz-əm\ *n* : the act or an instance of oversimplifying; *esp* : the reduction of a problem to a false simplicity by ignoring complicating factors — **sim·plis·tic** \sim-'plis-tik\ *adj* — **sim·plis·ti·cal·ly** \-ti-k(ə-)lē\ *adv*

sim·ply \'sim-plē, *for 1 also* -pə-lē\ *adv* **1 a :** without ambiguity : CLEARLY **b :** without embellishment : PLAINLY **c :** DIRECTLY, CANDIDLY **2 a :** SOLELY, MERELY <eats ~ to keep alive> **b :** REALLY, LITERALLY <the concert was ~ marvelous>

simply connected *adj* : being or characterized by a surface which is divided into two separate parts by every closed curve it contains

simply ordered *adj* : having any two elements equal or connected by a relationship that is not symmetric and any three elements transitively related

sim·u·la·cre \'sim-yə-ˌlāk-ər, -ˌlak-\ *n* [ME, fr. MF, fr. L *simulacrum*] *archaic* : SIMULACRUM

sim·u·la·crum \ˌsim-yə-'lak-rəm, -'lāk-\ *n, pl* **-cra** \-rə\ *also* **-crums** [L, fr. *simulare*] **1** : IMAGE, REPRESENTATION <a reasonable ~ of reality —Martin Mayer> **2** : an insubstantial form or semblance of something : TRACE

¹sim·u·lar \'sim-yə-lər, -ˌlär\ *n* [irreg. fr. L *simulare* to simulate] *archaic* : one that simulates : DISSEMBLER

²simular *adj, archaic* : COUNTERFEIT, PRETENDED

sim·u·late \'sim-yə-ˌlāt\ *vt* **-lat·ed; -lat·ing** [L *simulatus*, pp. of *simulare* to copy, represent, feign, fr. *similis* like — more at SAME] **1** : to assume the outward qualities or appearance of usu. with the intent to deceive **2** : to make a simulation of (as a physical system) ***syn*** see ASSUME — **sim·u·la·tive** \-ˌlāt-iv\ *adj*

sim·u·lat·ed *adj* : made to look genuine : FAKE <~ pearls>

simulated rank *n* : a civilian status equivalent to a military rank

sim·u·la·tion \ˌsim-yə-'lā-shən\ *n* **1** : the act or process of simulating : FEIGNING **2** : a sham object : COUNTERFEIT **3 a** : the imitative representation of the functioning of one system or process by means of the functioning of another <a computer ~ of an industrial process> **b** : examination of a problem often not subject to direct experimentation by means of a simulating device

sim·u·la·tor \'sim-yə-ˌlāt-ər\ *n* : one that simulates; *esp* : a device that enables the operator to reproduce or represent under test conditions phenomena likely to occur in actual performance

si·mul·cast \'sī-məl-ˌkast *also* 'sim-əl-\ *vi* [*simul*taneous broad*cast*] : to broadcast simultaneously by AM and FM radio or by radio and television — **simulcast** *n*

si·mul·ta·neous \ˌsī-məl-'tā-nē-əs, -nyəs *also* ˌsim-əl-\ *adj* [(assumed) ML *simultaneus*, fr. L *simul* at the same time — more at SAME] **1** : existing or occurring at the same time : exactly coincident **2** : satisfied by the same values of the variables <~ equations> ***syn*** see CONTEMPORARY — **si·mul·ta·ne·ity** \-tə-'nē-ət-ē, -'nā-\ *n* — **si·mul·ta·neous·ly** \-'tā-nē-ə-slē, -nyə-\ *adv* — **si·mul·ta·neous·ness** *n*

¹sin \'sin\ *n* [ME *sinne*, fr. OE *synn*; akin to OHG *sunta* sin] **1 a** : an offense against religious or moral law **b** : an action that is or is felt to be highly reprehensible <it's a ~ to waste food> **2 a** : transgression of the law of God **b** : a vitiated state of human nature in which the self is estranged from God ***syn*** see OFFENSE

²sin *vi* **sinned; sin·ning** **1** : to commit a sin **2** : to commit an offense or fault

³sin \'sēn, 'sin\ *n* [Heb *śīn*] : the 21st letter of the Hebrew alphabet — see ALPHABET table

⁴sin *symbol* sine

Sin·an·thro·pus \si-'nan(t)-thrə-pəs, sə-; ˌsīn-ˌan-'thrō-, ˌsin-\ *n* [NL, fr. LL *Sinae*, pl., Chinese + Gk *anthrōpos* man — more at SINOLOGUE] : PEKING MAN

sin·a·pism \'sin-ə-ˌpiz-əm\ *n* [LL *sinapismus*, deriv. of Gk *sinapi* mustard] : MUSTARD PLASTER

¹since \(ˈ)sin(t)s\ *adv* [ME *sins*, contr. of *sithens*, fr. *sithen*, fr. OE *siththan*, fr. *sith tham* since that, fr. *sith* since + *tham*, dat. of *thæt* that; akin to OHG *sīd* since, L *serus* late, OE *sāwan* to sow] **1** : from a definite past time until now <has stayed there ever ~> **2** : before the present time : AGO <long ~ dead> **3** : after a time in the past : SUBSEQUENTLY <has ~ become rich>

²since *prep* : in the period after a specified time in the past : from a specified time in the past

³since *conj* **1** : at a time in the past after or later than <has held two jobs ~ he graduated> : from the time in the past when <ever ~ he was a child> **2** *obs* : WHEN **3** : in view of the fact that : BECAUSE <~ it was raining he wore a hat>

sin·cere \sin-'si(ə)r, sən-\ *adj* [MF, fr. L *sincerus*] **1 a** : free of dissimulation : HONEST <~ interest> **b** : free from adulteration : PURE <a ~ doctrine> <~ wine> **2** : marked by genuineness : TRUE — **sin·cere·ly** *adv* — **sin·cere·ness** *n*

syn SINCERE, WHOLEHEARTED, HEARTFELT, HEARTY, UNFEIGNED *shared meaning element* : genuine in feeling ***ant*** insincere

sin·cer·i·ty \-'ser-ət-ē, -'sir-\ *n* : the quality or state of being sincere : honesty of mind : freedom from hypocrisy

sin·cip·i·tal \sin-'sip-ət-ᵊl\ *adj* : of or relating to the sinciput

sin·ci·put \'sin(t)-sə-(ˌ)pət\ *n, pl* **sinciputs** *or* **sin·cip·i·ta** \sin-'sip-ət-ə\ [L *sincipit-, sinciput*, fr. *semi-* + *caput* head — more at HEAD] **1** : FOREHEAD **2** : the upper half of the skull

Sind·bad \'sin-ˌbad\ *n* : a citizen of Baghdad whose adventures at sea are told in the *Arabian Nights' Entertainments*

Sind·hi \'sin-dē\ *n, pl* **Sindhi** *or* **Sindhis** [Ar *Sindi*] **1** : a member of a mostly Muslim people of Sind **2** : the Indic language of Sind

sine \'sīn\ *n* [ML *sinus*, fr. L, curve] : the trigonometric function that for an acute angle is the ratio between the side opposite the angle when it is considered part of a right triangle and the hypotenuse

si·ne·cure \'sī-ni-ˌkyů(ə)r, 'sin-i-\ *n* [ML *sine cura* without cure of souls] **1** *archaic* : an ecclesiastical benefice without cure of souls **2** : an office or position that requires little or no work and that usu. provides an income

sine curve *n* : the graph in rectangular coordinates of the equation $y = a \sin bx$ where a and b are constants

si·ne die \ˌsī-ni-'dī-(ˌ)ē, ˌsin-ā-'dē-ˌā\ *adv* [L, without day] : without any future date being designated (as for resumption) : INDEFINITELY <the meeting adjourned *sine die*>

si·ne qua non \ˌsin-i-ˌkwä-'nän, -'nōn *also* ˌsēn-; *also* ˌsī-ni-ˌkwā-'nän\ *n* [LL, without which not] : an absolutely indispensable or essential thing

¹sin·ew \'sin-(ˌ)yü, -yə(-w) *also* 'sin-(ˌ)ü\ *n* [ME *sinewe*, fr. OE *seono*; akin to OHG *senawa* sinew, L *saeta* bristle] **1** : TENDON; *esp* : one dressed for use as a cord or thread **2** *obs* : NERVE **3 a** : solid resilient strength : POWER <intellectual and moral ~ —G. K. Chalmers> **b** : the chief supporting force : MAINSTAY — usu. used in pl. <providing the ~*s* of better living —Sam Pollock>

²sinew *vt* : to strengthen as if with sinews

sine wave *n* : a wave form that represents periodic oscillations in which the amplitude of displacement at each point is proportional to the sine of the phase angle of the displacement and that is visualized as a sine curve

sin·ewy \'sin-yə-wē *also* 'sin-ə-\ *adj* **1** : full of sinews : TOUGH, STRINGY <~ meat> **2** : STRONG <~ arms>

sin·fo·nia \ˌsin-fə-'nē-ə\ *n, pl* **-nie** \-'nē-ˌā\ [It, fr. L *symphonia* symphony] **1** : an orchestral musical composition serving as an introduction to choral works (as opera) esp. in the 18th century : OVERTURE **2** : SYMPHONY 2a, 2c

sinfonia con·cer·tante \-ˌkän(t)-sər-'tänt(-ē), -ˌkän-cher-'tän-ˌtā\ *n* [It, lit., symphony in concerto style] : a concerto for more than one solo instrument

sin·fo·niet·ta \ˌsin-fən-'yet-ə, -fōn-\ *n* [It, dim. of *sinfonia*] **1** : a symphony of less than standard length or for fewer instruments **2** : a small symphony orchestra; *esp* : an orchestra of strings only

sin·ful \'sin-fəl\ *adj* : tainted with, marked by, or full of sin : WICKED — **sin·ful·ly** \-fə-lē\ *adv* — **sin·ful·ness** *n*

¹sing \'siŋ\ *vb* **sang** \'saŋ\ *or* **sung** \'səŋ\; **sung; sing·ing** \'siŋ-iŋ\ [ME *singen*, fr. OE *singan*; akin to OHG *singan* to sing, Gk *omphē* voice] *vi* **1 a** : to produce musical tones by means of the voice **b** : to utter words in musical tones and with musical inflections and modulations **c** : to deliver songs as a trained or professional singer **2** : to make a shrill whining or whistling sound **3 a** : to relate or celebrate something in verse **b** : to compose poetry **4** : to produce musical or harmonious sounds **5** : BUZZ, RING **6** : to make a cry : CALL **7** : to give information or evidence ~ *vt* **1** : to utter with musical inflections; *esp* : to interpret in musical tones produced by the voice **2** : to relate or celebrate in verse **3** : CHANT, INTONE **4** : to bring or accompany to a place or state by singing <~*s* the child to sleep> — **sing·able** \'siŋ-ə-bəl\ *adj*

²sing *n* : a session of group singing

³sing *abbr* singular

sing–along \'siŋ-ə-ˌlȯŋ\ *n* : SONGFEST

¹singe \'sinj\ *vt* **singed; singe·ing** \'sin-jiŋ\ [ME *sengen*, fr. OE *sengan*; akin to OHG bi*sengan* to singe, OSlav i*sočiti* to dry] : to burn superficially or lightly : SCORCH; *esp* : to remove the hair, down, or fuzz from usu. by passing rapidly over a flame

²singe *n* : a slight burn : SCORCH

¹sing·er \'siŋ-ər\ *n* : one that sings

²sing·er \'sin-jər\ *n* : one that singes

singing game *n* : a children's game in which the players accompany their actions with the singing of a narrative song

¹sin·gle \'siŋ-gəl\ *adj* [ME, fr. MF, fr. L *singulus* one only; akin to L *sem-* one — more at SAME] **1 a** : not married **b** : of or relating to celibacy **2** : unaccompanied by others : LONE, SOLE <the ~ survivor of the disaster> **3 a** (1) : consisting of or having only one part, feature, or portion <~ consonants> (2) : consisting of one as opposed to or in contrast with many : UNIFORM <a ~ standard for men and women> (3) : consisting of only one in number <holds to a ~ ideal> **b** : having but one whorl of petals or ray flowers <a ~ rose> **4 a** : consisting of a separate unique whole : INDIVIDUAL <every ~ citizen> **b** : of, relating to, or involving only one person **5 a** : FRANK, HONEST <a ~ devotion> **b** : exclusively attentive <an eye ~ to the truth> **6** : UNBROKEN, UNDIVIDED **7** : having no equal or like : SINGULAR **8** : designed for the use of one person or family only <a ~ room>

syn SINGLE, SOLE, UNIQUE, SEPARATE, SOLITARY, PARTICULAR *shared meaning element* : one as distinguished from two or more or all others

²single *n* **1 a** : a separate individual person or thing **b** : a young unmarried adult **c** : a phonograph record (as a 45) having one short tune on each side **2** : a base hit that allows the batter to reach first base **3** *pl* **a** : a tennis match or similar game with one player on each side **b** : a golf match between two players

³single *vb* **sin·gled; sin·gling** \-g(ə-)liŋ\ *vt* **1** : to select or distinguish (a person or thing) from a number or group — usu. used with *out* **2 a** : to advance or score (a base runner) by a single **b** : to bring about the scoring of (a run) by a single ~ *vi* : to make a single in baseball

single–blind \ˌsiŋ-gəl-'blīnd\ *adj* : of, relating to, or being an experimental procedure in which the experimenters but not the subjects know the makeup of the test and control groups during the actual course of the experiments — compare DOUBLE-BLIND

sin·gle–breast·ed \-'bres-təd\ *adj* : having a center closing with one row of buttons and no lap <a ~ coat>

single combat *n* : combat between two persons

single cross *n* : a first-generation hybrid between two selected and usu. inbred lines — compare DOUBLE CROSS

single entry *n* : a method of bookkeeping that recognizes only one side of a business transaction and usu. consists only of a record of cash and personal accounts with debtors and creditors

single file *n* : a line (as of persons) moving one behind another — **single file** *adv*

¹sin·gle–foot \'siŋ-gəl-ˌfůt\ *n, pl* **single–foots** : ⁷RACK b

²single–foot *vi, of a horse* : to go at a rack — **sin·gle–foot·er** *n*

¹sin·gle–hand·ed \ˌsiŋ-gəl-'han-dəd\ *adj* **1** : managed or done by one person or with one on a side **2** : working alone or unassisted by others — **sin·gle–hand·ed·ly** *adv* — **sin·gle–hand·ed·ness** *n*

²single–handed *adv* : in a single-handed manner

sin·gle–heart·ed \ˌsiŋ-gəl-'härt-əd\ *adj* : characterized by sincerity and unity of purpose or dedication — **sin·gle–heart·ed·ly** *adv* — **sin·gle–heart·ed·ness** *n*

single knot *n* : OVERHAND KNOT

ə abut ᵊ kitten ər further a back ā bake ä cot, cart
aů out ch chin e less ē easy g gift i trip ī life
j joke ŋ sing ō flow ȯ flaw ȯi coin th thin t͟h this
ü loot ů foot y yet yü few yů furious zh vision

sin·gle–mind·ed \ˌsiŋ-gəl-ˈmīn-dəd\ *adj* **1 :** GUILELESS, SINCERE **2 :** having one unifying and overriding purpose — **sin·gle–mind·ed·ly** *adv* — **sin·gle–mind·ed·ness** *n*

sin·gle·ness \ˈsiŋ-gəl-nəs\ *n* **:** the quality or state of being single

sin·gle–phase \ˌsiŋ-gəl-ˈfāz\ *adj* **:** of or relating to a circuit energized by a single alternating electromotive force

sin·gle–space \-ˈspās\ *vt* **:** to type or print with no blank lines between lines of text

sin·gle·stick \ˈsiŋ-gəl-ˌstik\ *n* **:** fighting or fencing with a wooden stick or sword held in one hand; *also* **:** the weapon used

sin·glet \ˈsiŋ-glət\ *n* **1** [fr. its having only one thickness of cloth] *chiefly Brit* **:** an athletic jersey **:** UNDERSHIRT **2 :** an elementary particle that is not part of a multiplet

single tax *n* **:** a tax to be levied on a single item (as real estate) as the sole source of public revenue

sin·gle·ton \ˈsiŋ-gəl-tən\ *n* [F, fr. E *single*] **1 :** a card that is the only one of its suit orig. held in a hand **2 :** an individual member or thing distinct from others grouped with it; *specif* **:** an offspring born singly

sin·gle–track \ˌsiŋ-gəl-ˌtrak\ *adj* **1 :** having only one track **2 :** lacking intellectual range, receptiveness, or flexibility **:** ONE-TRACK

sin·gle·tree \ˈsiŋ-gəl-(ˌ)trē\ *n* **:** WHIFFLETREE

sin·gle–val·ued \ˌsiŋ-gəl-ˈval-(ˌ)yüd, -yəd\ *adj* **:** having one and only one value of the range associated with each value of the domain <a ~ function> — compare MULTIPLE-VALUED

single wing *n* **:** an offensive football formation in which one back plays as a flanker and two backs line up four or five yards behind the line in position to receive a direct snap from center

sin·gly \ˈsiŋ-g(ə-)lē\ *adv* **1 :** without the company of others **:** INDIVIDUALLY **2 :** SINGLE-HANDED

1**sing·song** \ˈsiŋ-ˌsȯŋ\ *n* **1 :** verse with marked and regular rhythm and rhyme **:** a jingling song **2 :** a voice delivery characterized by a narrow range or monotonous pattern of pitch — **sing·songy** \-ˌsȯŋ-ē\ *adj*

2**singsong** *adj* **:** having a monotonous cadence or rhythm

sing·spiel \ˈsiŋ-ˌspēl, ˈziŋ-ˌshpēl\ *n* [G, fr. *singen* to sing + *spiel* play] **:** a usu. comic dramatic musical work popular in Germany esp. in the latter part of the 18th century characterized by spoken dialogue interspersed with popular or folk songs

1**sin·gu·lar** \ˈsiŋ-gyə-lər\ *adj* [ME *singuler*, fr. MF, fr. L *singularis*, fr. *singulus* only one — more at SINGLE] **1 a :** of or relating to a separate person or thing **:** INDIVIDUAL **b :** of, relating to, or being a word form denoting one person, thing, or instance **c :** of or relating to a single instance or to something considered by itself **2 :** distinguished by superiority **:** EXCEPTIONAL <a man of ~ attainments> **3 :** set apart or memorable as being out of the ordinary **:** UNUSUAL <on the way home we had a ~ adventure> **4 :** departing from general usage or expectation **:** PECULIAR, ODD <the air had a ~ chill> **5 a** *of a matrix* **:** having a determinant equal to zero **b** *of a linear transformation* **:** having the property that the matrix of coefficients of the new variables has a determinant equal to zero ***syn*** see STRANGE — **sin·gu·lar·ly** *adv*

2**singular** *n* **1 :** the singular number, the inflectional form denoting it, or a word in that form **2 :** a singular term

sin·gu·lar·i·ty \ˌsiŋ-gyə-ˈlar-ət-ē\ *n, pl* **-ties 1 :** something that is singular: as **a :** a separate unit **b :** unusual or distinctive manner or behavior **:** PECULIARITY **2 :** the quality or state of being singular **3 :** a point at which the derivative of a given function of a complex variable does not exist but every neighborhood of which contains points for which the derivative exists

sin·gu·lar·ize \ˈsiŋ-gyə-lə-ˌrīz\ *vt* **-ized; -iz·ing :** to make singular

singular point *n* **:** SINGULARITY 3

Sin·ha·lese *or* **Sin·gha·lese** \ˌsiŋ-gə-ˈlēz, ˌsin-(h)ə-, -ˈlēs\ *n, pl* **Sinhalese** *or* **Singhalese** [Skt *Siṁhala* Ceylon] **1 :** a member of a people that inhabit Ceylon and form a major part of its population **2 :** the Indic language of the Sinhalese people — **Sinhalese** *or* **Singhalese** *adj*

si·ni·cize \ˈsī-nə-ˌsīz, ˈsin-ə-\ *vt* **-cized; -ciz·ing** *often cap* [ML *sinicus* Chinese, fr. LL *Sinae*, pl., Chinese — more at SINOLOGUE] **:** to modify by Chinese influence

sin·is·ter \ˈsin-əs-tər, *archaic* sə-ˈnis-\ *adj* [ME *sinistre*, fr. L *sinistr-*, *sinister* on the left side, unlucky, inauspicious] **1** *archaic* **:** UNFAVORABLE, UNLUCKY **2** *archaic* **:** FRAUDULENT **3 :** singularly evil or productive of evil **4 a :** of, relating to, or situated to the left or on the left side of something; *esp* **:** being or relating to the side of a heraldic shield at the left of the person bearing it **b :** of ill omen by reason of being on the left **5 :** presaging ill fortune or trouble **6 :** accompanied by or leading to disaster or unfavorable developments — **sin·is·ter·ly** *adv* — **sin·is·ter·ness** *n*
syn SINISTER, BALEFUL, MALIGN *shared meaning element* **:** seriously threatening disaster

si·nis·tral \ˈsin-əs-trəl, sə-ˈnis-\ *adj* **:** of, relating to, or inclined to the left: as **a :** LEFT-HANDED **b :** having whorls turning from the right toward the left as viewed with the apex toward the observer <~ coiling of a gastropod shell> — **si·nis·tral·ly** \-trə-lē\ *adv*

sin·is·trorse \ˈsin-ə-ˌstrȯ(ə)rs\ *adj* [NL *sinistrorsus*, fr. L, toward the left side, fr. *sinistr-*, *sinister* + *versus*, pp. of *vertere* to turn — more at WORTH] **1** *of a plant* **:** twining spirally upward around an axis from right to left — compare DEXTRORSE **2 :** SINISTRAL b

si·nis·trous \ˈsin-əs-trəs, sə-ˈnis-\ *adj, archaic* **:** SINISTER

Si·nit·ic \sī-ˈnit-ik, sə-\ *adj* [LL *Sinae*, pl., Chinese + E *-itic* (as in *Semitic*) — more at SINOLOGUE] **:** of or relating to the Chinese, their language, or their culture

1**sink** \ˈsiŋk\ *vb* **sank** \ˈsaŋk\ *or* **sunk** \ˈsəŋk\; **sunk; sink·ing** [ME *sinken*, fr. OE *sincan*; akin to OHG *sinkan* to sink, Arm *ankanim* I fall] *vi* **1 a :** to go to the bottom **:** SUBMERGE **b :** to become partly buried (as in mud) **c :** to become engulfed **2 a** (1) **:** to fall or drop to a lower place or level (2) **:** to flow at a lower depth or level (3) **:** to burn with lower intensity (4) **:** to fall to a lower pitch or volume <his voice *sank* to a whisper> **b :** to subside gradually **:** SETTLE **c :** to disappear from view **d :** to slope gradually **:** DIP **3 a :** to soak or become absorbed **:** PENETRATE **b :** to become impressively known or felt <the lesson had *sunk* in> **4 :** to become deeply absorbed <*sank* into reverie> **5 a :** to go downward in quality, state, or condition **b :** to grow less in amount or worth **6 a :** to fall or drop slowly for lack of strength **b :** to become depressed **c :** to fail in health or strength ~ *vt* **1 a :** to cause to sink <~ a battleship> **b :** to force down esp. below the earth's surface **c :** to cause (something) to penetrate **2 :** to engage deeply the attention of **:** IMMERSE **3 a :** to dig or bore (a well or shaft) in the earth **:** EXCAVATE **b :** to form by cutting or excising <~ words in stone> **4 :** to cast down or bring to a low condition or state **:** OVERWHELM, DEFEAT **5 :** to lower in standing or reputation **:** ABASE **6 a :** to lessen in value or amount **b :** to lower or soften (the voice) in speaking **7 :** RESTRAIN, SUPPRESS <~*s* her pride and approaches the despised neighbor —Richard Harrison> **8 :** to pay off (as a debt) **:** LIQUIDATE **9 :** INVEST — **sink·able** \ˈsiŋ-kə-bəl\ *adj*

2**sink** *n* **1 a :** a pool or pit for the deposit of waste or sewage **:** CESSPOOL **b :** a ditch or tunnel for carrying off sewage **:** SEWER **c :** a stationary basin connected with a drain and usu. a water supply for washing and drainage **2 :** a place where vice, corruption, or evil collect **3 :** SUMP **4 a :** a depression in the land surface; *esp* **:** one having a saline lake with no outlet **b :** SINKHOLE **5 :** a body or process that acts as a storage device or disposal mechanism: as **a :** HEAT SINK; *broadly* **:** a device that collects or dissipates energy (as radiation) **b :** a reactant with or absorber of a substance <soil is a ~ for carbon dioxide>

sink·age \ˈsiŋ-kij\ *n* **1 :** the process or degree of sinking **2 :** DEPRESSION, INDENTATION **3 :** the distance from the top line of a full page to the first line of sunk matter

sink·er \ˈsiŋ-kər\ *n* **1 :** one that sinks; *specif* **:** a weight for sinking a fishing line, seine, or sounding line **2 :** DOUGHNUT **3 :** a fastball that sinks as it reaches the plate — called also *sinkerball*

sink·hole \ˈsiŋk-ˌhōl\ *n* **1 :** a hollow place or depression in which drainage collects **2 :** a hollow in a limestone region that communicates with a cavern or passage

sinking fund *n* **:** a fund set up and accumulated by usu. regular deposits for paying off the principal of a debt when it falls due

sin·less \ˈsin-ləs\ *adj* **:** free from sin **:** IMPECCABLE — **sin·less·ly** *adv* — **sin·less·ness** *n*

sin·ner \ˈsin-ər\ *n* **1 :** one that sins **2 :** REPROBATE, SCAMP

Si·no- *comb form* [F, fr. LL *Sinae* — more at SINOLOGUE] **1 :** Chinese <*Sino*phile> **2** \ˌsī-(ˌ)nō, ˈsī-\ **:** Chinese and <*Sino*-Tibetan>

si·no·atri·al \ˌsī-nō-ˈā-trē-əl\ *also* **si·nu·atri·al** \ˌsī-n(y)ə-ˈwā-, ˌsin-yə-ˈwā-\ *adj* [NL *sinus* + *atrium*] **:** of, involving, or being the sinoatrial node <~ block>

sinoatrial node *n* **:** a small mass of tissue that is embedded in the musculature of the right auricle of higher vertebrates and that originates the impulses stimulating the heartbeat

si·no·logue \ˈsin-ᵊl-ˌȯg, ˈsin-, -ˌäg\ *n* [F, fr. LL *Sinae*, pl., Chinese (fr. Gk *Sinai*, fr. Ar *Sīn* China) + F *-logue*] **:** a specialist in sinology

si·nol·o·gy \sī-ˈnäl-ə-jē, sə-\ *n* [prob. fr. F *sinologie*, fr. *sino-* + *-logie* -logy] **:** the study of the Chinese and esp. their language, literature, history, and culture — **si·no·log·i·cal** \ˌsīn-ᵊl-ˈäj-i-kəl, ˌsin-\ *adj* — **si·nol·o·gist** \sī-ˈnäl-ə-jəst, sə-\ *n*

si·no·pia \sə-ˈnō-pē-ə\ *n, pl* **-pi·as** *or* **-pie** \-pē-ˌā\ [It, fr. L *sinopis*, fr. Gk *sinōpis*, *fr. Sinōpē* Sinop, ancient seaport in Asia Minor] **1 :** a red to reddish brown earth pigment used by the ancients that depends for its color on its content of red ferric oxide **2 :** a preliminary drawing for a fresco done in sinopia

Si·no–Ti·bet·an \ˌsī-nō-tə-ˈbet-ᵊn, ˈsī-\ *n* **:** a language group comprising Tibeto-Burman and Chinese

sin·syne \ˈsin-ˌsīn\ *adv* [ME (Sc) *sensyne*, fr. *sen* since (contr. of ME *sithen*) + *syne* since — more at SINCE, SYNE] *chiefly Scot* **:** since that time

1**sin·ter** \ˈsint-ər\ *n* [G, fr. OHG *sintar* slag — more at CINDER] **:** a deposit formed by the evaporation of spring or lake water

2**sinter** *vt* **:** to cause to become a coherent mass by heating without melting ~ *vi* **:** to undergo sintering — **sin·ter·abil·i·ty** \ˌsint-ə-rə-ˈbil-ət-ē\ *n*

sin·u·ate \ˈsin-yə-wət, -ˌwāt\ *adj* [L *sinuatus*, pp. of *sinuare* to bend, fr. *sinus* curve] **:** having the margin wavy with strong indentations <~ leaves> — **sin·u·ate·ly** *adv*

sin·u·os·i·ty \ˌsin-yə-ˈwäs-ət-ē\ *n, pl* **-ties 1 :** the quality or state of being sinuous **2 :** something that is sinuous

sin·u·ous \ˈsin-yə-wəs\ *adj* [L *sinuosus*, fr. *sinus*] **1 a :** of a serpentine or wavy form **:** WINDING **b :** marked by strong lithe movements **2 :** INTRICATE, COMPLEX — **sin·u·ous·ly** *adv* — **sin·u·ous·ness** *n*

si·nus \ˈsī-nəs\ *n* [NL, fr. L, curve, fold, hollow] **:** CAVITY, HOLLOW: as **a :** a narrow elongated tract extending from a focus of suppuration and serving for the discharge of pus **b** (1) **:** a cavity in the substance of a bone of the skull that usu. communicates with the nostrils and contains air (2) **:** a channel for venous blood (3) **:** a dilatation in a bodily canal or vessel **c :** a cleft or indentation between adjoining lobes

si·nus·itis \ˌsī-n(y)ə-ˈsīt-əs\ *n* **:** inflammation of a sinus of the skull

si·nu·soid \ˈsī-n(y)ə-ˌsȯid\ *n* [ML *sinus* sine] **1 :** SINE CURVE **2** [NL *sinus*] **:** a minute endothelium-lined space or passage for blood in the tissues of an organ (as the liver) — **si·nu·soi·dal** \ˌsī-n(y)ə-ˈsȯid-ᵊl\ *adj* — **si·nu·soi·dal·ly** \-ᵊl-ē\ *adv*

sinusoidal projection *n* **:** an equal-area map projection capable of showing the entire surface of the earth with all parallels as straight lines evenly spaced, the central meridian as one half the length of the equator, and all other meridians as curved lines

si·nus ve·no·sus \ˌsī-nəs-vi-ˈnō-səs\ *n* [NL, venous sinus] **:** an enlarged pouch that adjoins the heart, is formed by the union of the large systemic veins, and is the passage through which venous blood enters the heart in lower vertebrates and in embryos of higher forms

Si·on \ˈsī-ən\ *var of* ZION

Siou·an \ˈsü-ən\ *n* **1 :** a language stock of central and eastern No. America **2 :** a member of any of the peoples speaking Siouan languages

Sioux \ˈsü\ *n, pl* **Sioux** \ˈsü(z)\ [F, short for *Nadowessioux,* fr. Ojibwa *Nadoweisiw*] **1 :** DAKOTA **2 :** SIOUAN

¹sip \ˈsip\ *vb* **sipped; sip·ping** [ME *sippen;* akin to LG *sippen* to sip] *vi* **:** to take a sip of something esp. repeatedly ~ *vt* **1 :** to drink in small quantities **2 :** to take sips from — **sip·per** *n*

²sip *n* **1 :** the act of sipping **2 :** a small draft taken with the lips

¹si·phon \ˈsī-fən\ *n* [F *siphon,* fr. L *siphon-, sipho* tube, pipe, siphon, fr. Gk *siphōn*] **1 a :** a tube bent to form two legs of unequal length by which a liquid can be transferred to a lower level over an intermediate elevation by the pressure of the atmosphere in forcing the liquid up the shorter branch of the tube immersed in it while the excess of weight of the liquid in the longer branch when once filled causes a continuous flow **b** *usu* **syphon :** a bottle for holding aerated water that is driven out through a bent tube in its neck by the pressure of the gas when a valve in the tube is opened **2 :** any of various tubular organs in animals and esp. mollusks or arthropods that are used for drawing in or ejecting fluids — see CLAM illustration

siphon 1a

²siphon *vb* **si·phoned; si·phon·ing** \ˈsīf-(ə-)niŋ\ *vt* **:** to convey, draw off, or empty by or as if by a siphon ~ *vi* **:** to pass by or as if by a siphon

si·pho·no·phore \sī-ˈfän-ə-ˌfō(ə)r, ˈsī-fə-nə-, -ˌfȯ(ə)r\ *n* [deriv. of Gk *siphōn* + *pherein* to carry — more at BEAR] **:** any of an order (Siphonophora) of compound free-swimming or floating pelagic hydrozoans that are mostly delicate, transparent, and colored and have specialized zooids

si·pho·no·stele \sī-ˈfän-ə-ˌstēl, ˌsī-fə-nə-ˈstē-lē\ *n* [Gk *siphōn* tube, siphon] **:** a stele consisting of vascular tissue surrounding a central core of pith parenchyma — **si·pho·no·ste·lic** \ˌsī-fə-nə-ˈstē-lik, (ˌ)sī-ˌfän-ə-\ *adj* — **si·pho·no·ste·ly** \ˈsī-fə-nə-ˌstē-lē, sī-ˈfän-ə-\ *n*

sip·pet \ˈsip-ət\ *n, chiefly Brit* [alter. of *sop*] **:** a small bit of toast or fried bread esp. for garnishing

sir \(ˈ)sər\ *n* [ME, fr. *sire*] **1 a :** a man of rank or position **b :** a man entitled to be addressed as *sir* — used as a title before the given name of a knight or baronet and formerly sometimes before the given name of a priest **2 a** — used as a usu. respectful form of address **b** *cap* — used as a conventional form of address in the salutation of a letter

sir·dar \ˈsər-ˌdär, sər-ˈ\ *n* [Hindi *sardār,* fr. Per] **1 a :** a person of high rank (as an hereditary noble) esp. in India **b :** the commander of the Anglo-Egyptian army **2 :** one holding a responsible position in India: as **a :** FOREMAN **b :** TENANT FARMER

¹sire \ˈsī(ə)r\ *n* [ME, fr. OF, fr. L *senior* older — more at SENIOR] **1 a :** FATHER **b** *archaic* **:** male ancestor **:** FOREFATHER **c :** ORIGINATOR, AUTHOR **2 a** *archaic* **:** a man of rank or authority; *esp* **:** LORD — used formerly as a form of address and as a title **b** *obs* **:** an elderly man **:** SENIOR **3 :** the male parent of an animal and esp. of a domestic animal

²sire *vt* **sired; siring** **1 :** BEGET — used esp. of male domestic animals **2 :** to bring into being **:** ORIGINATE

¹si·ren \ˈsī-rən, *for 3 also* sī-ˈrēn\ *n* [ME, fr. MF & L; MF *sereine,* fr. LL *sirena,* fr. L *siren,* fr. Gk *seirēn*] **1** *often cap* **:** one of a group of female and partly human creatures in Greek mythology that lured mariners to destruction by their singing **2 a :** a woman who sings with bewitching sweetness **b :** a temptingly beautiful woman; *esp* **:** one who is insidiously seductive **:** TEMPTRESS **3 a :** an apparatus producing musical tones esp. in acoustical studies by the rapid interruption of a current of air, steam, or fluid by a perforated rotating disk **b :** a device often electrically operated for producing a penetrating warning sound <ambulance ~> <air-raid ~> **4** [NL, genus name, fr. L] **:** any of a genus (*Siren*) of eel-shaped amphibians with small forelimbs but neither hind legs nor pelvis and with permanent external gills as well as lungs

²si·ren \ˈsī-rən\ *adj* **:** resembling that of a siren **:** ENTICING

si·re·ni·an \sī-ˈrē-nē-ən\ *n* [NL *Sirenia* order name, fr. L *siren*] **:** any of an order (Sirenia) of aquatic herbivorous mammals including the manatee and dugong

siren song *n* **:** an alluring utterance or appeal; *esp* **:** one that is seductive or deceptive

Sir·i·us \ˈsir-ē-əs\ *n* [ME, fr. L, fr. Gk *Seirios,* lit., glowing] **:** a star of the constellation Canis Major constituting the brightest star in the heavens — called also *Dog Star*

sir·loin \ˈsər-ˌlȯin\ *n* [alter. of earlier *surloin,* modif. of MF *surlonge,* fr. *sur* over (fr. L *super*) + *loigne, longe* loin — more at OVER] **:** a cut of meat and esp. of beef from the part of the hindquarter just in front of the round — see BEEF illustration

si·roc·co \sə-ˈräk-(ˌ)ō\ *n, pl* **-cos** [It *scirocco, sirocco,* fr. Ar *sharq* east] **1 a :** a hot dust-laden wind from the Libyan deserts that blows on the northern Mediterranean coast chiefly in Italy, Malta, and Sicily **b :** a warm moist oppressive southeast wind in the same regions **2 :** a hot or warm wind of cyclonic origin from an arid or heated region

sir·rah *also* **sir·ra** \ˈsir-ə\ *n* [alter. of *sir*] *obs* — used as a form of address implying inferiority in the person addressed

sir·ree *also* **sir·ee** \(ˌ)sər-ˈē\ *n* [by alter.] **:** SIR — used as an emphatic form usu. after *yes* or *no*

sir–reverence *n* [prob. alter. of *save-reverence,* trans. of ML *salva reverentia* saving (your) reverence] **1** *obs* — used as an expression of apology before a statement that might be taken as offensive **2** *obs* **:** human feces; *also* **:** a lump of human feces

Sir Rog·er de Cov·er·ley \sə(r)-ˌräj-ərd-i-ˈkəv-ər-lē\ *n* [alter. (influenced by *Sir Roger de Coverley,* fictitious country gentleman appearing in many of the *Spectator* papers by Joseph Addison and Sir Richard Steele, fr. *roger of coverley*) of *roger of coverley,* prob. fr. *Roger,* the name + *of* + *Coverley,* a fictitious place name] **:** an English country-dance that resembles the Virginia reel

sirup, sirupy *var of* SYRUP, SYRUPY

sir·vente \si(ə)r-ˈvänt\ *or* **sir·ven·tes** \-ˈvent-əs\ *n, pl* **sir·ventes** \-ˈvänt, -ˈvän(t)s, -ˈvent-əs\ [F, fr. Prov *sirventes,* lit., servant's song, fr. *sirvent* servant, fr. L *servient-, serviens,* prp. of *servire* to serve] **:** a usu. moral or religious song of the Provençal troubadours satirizing social vices

sis \ˈsis\ *n* **:** SISTER — used in direct address

-sis \səs\ *n suffix, pl* **-ses** \ˌsēz\ [L, fr. Gk, fem. suffix of action] **:** process **:** action <peristal*sis*>

si·sal \ˈsī-səl, -zəl\ *n* [MexSp, fr. *Sisal,* Yucatán, Mexico] **1 a :** a strong durable white fiber used esp. for hard fiber cordage and twine — called also *sisal hemp* **b :** a widely cultivated West Indian agave (*Agave sisalana*) whose leaves yield sisal **2 :** any of several fibers similar to true sisal

sis·kin \ˈsis-kən\ *n* [G dial. *sisschen,* dim. of MHG *zîse* siskin, of Slav origin; akin to Czech *čížek* siskin] **:** a small sharp-billed chiefly greenish and yellowish finch (*Spinus spinus*) of temperate Europe and Asia related to the goldfinch — compare PINE SISKIN, RED SISKIN

sis·si·fied \ˈsis-i-ˌfīd\ *adj* **:** of, relating to, or having the characteristics of a sissy

sis·sy \ˈsis-ē\ *n, pl* **sissies** [*sis*] **:** an effeminate man or boy; *also* **:** a timid or cowardly person — **sissy** *adj*

sis·ter \ˈsis-tər\ *n* [ME *suster, sister,* partly fr. OE *sweostor* and partly of Scand origin; akin to ON *systir* sister; akin to L *soror* sister] **1 a** (1) **:** a female human being having the same parents as another person (2) **:** HALF SISTER (3) **:** SISTER-IN-LAW **b :** a female of a lower animal having a parent in common with another **2** *often cap* **a :** a member of a women's religious order (as of nuns or deaconesses); *specif* **:** one of a Roman Catholic congregation under simple vows **b :** a female member of a Christian church **3 a :** a woman related to another person by a common tie or interest **b :** one having similar characteristics to another <~ ships> **4** *chiefly Brit* **:** NURSE **5 a :** GIRL, WOMAN **b :** PERSON — usu. used in the phrase *weak sister*

sis·ter·hood \-ˌhu̇d\ *n* **1 a :** the state of being a sister **b :** sisterly relationship **2 :** a community or society of sisters; *specif* **:** a society of women religious

sis·ter–in–law \ˈsis-t(ə-)rən-ˌlȯ, -tərn-ˌlȯ\ *n, pl* **sis·ters–in–law** \-tər-zən-\ **1 :** the sister of one's spouse **2 a :** the wife of one's brother **b :** the wife of one's spouse's brother

sis·ter·ly \ˈsis-tər-lē\ *adj* **:** of, relating to, or having the characteristics of a sister — **sisterly** *adv*

Sis·tine \ˈsis-ˌtēn, sis-ˈ\ *adj* [It *sistino,* fr. NL *sixtinus,* fr. *Sixtus,* name of some popes] **1 :** of or relating to any of the popes named Sixtus **2** [fr. Pope *Sixtus* IV †1484] **:** of or relating to the Sistine chapel in the Vatican

sis·trum \ˈsis-trəm\ *n, pl* **sistrums** *or* **sis·tra** \-trə\ [ME, fr. L, fr. Gk *seistron,* fr. *seiein* to shake — more at SEISMIC] **:** an ancient percussion instrument used esp. in Egypt and consisting of a thin metal frame with numerous metal rods or loops that jingle when shaken

Sis·y·phe·an \ˌsis-ə-ˈfē-ən\ *or* **Si·syph·i·an** \sis-ˈif-ē-ən\ *adj* **:** of, relating to, or suggestive of the labors of Sisyphus

Sis·y·phus \ˈsis-ə-fəs\ *n* [L, fr. Gk *Sisyphos*] **:** a legendary king of Corinth condemned to roll a heavy rock up a hill in Hades only to have it roll down again as it nears the top

¹sit \ˈsit\ *vb* **sat** \ˈsat\; **sit·ting** [ME *sitten,* fr. OE *sittan;* akin to OHG *sizzen* to sit, L *sedēre,* Gk *hezesthai* to sit, *hedra* seat] *vi* **1 a :** to rest on the buttocks or haunches <~ in a chair> **b :** PERCH, ROOST **2 :** to occupy a place as a member of an official body <~ in Congress> **3 :** to hold a session **:** be in session for official business **4 :** to cover eggs for hatching **:** BROOD **5 a :** to take a position for having one's portrait painted or for being photographed **b :** to serve as a model **6** *archaic* **:** to have one's dwelling place **:** DWELL **7 a :** to lie or hang relative to a wearer <the collar ~*s* awkwardly> **b :** to affect one with or as if with weight <the food *sat* heavily on his stomach> **8 :** LIE, REST <a kettle *sitting* on the stove> **9 a :** to have a location <the house ~*s* well back from the road> **b** *of wind* **:** to blow from a certain direction **10 :** to remain inactive or quiescent <the car ~*s* in the garage> **11 :** to take an examination **12 :** BABY-SIT ~ *vt* **1 :** to cause to be seated **:** place on or in a seat **2 :** to sit on (eggs) **3 :** to keep one's seat on <~ a horse> **4 :** to provide seats or seating room for <the car will ~ six people> — **sit on 1 :** to hold deliberations concerning **2 :** REPRESS, SQUELCH **3 :** to delay action or decision concerning — **sit on one's hands 1 :** to withhold applause **2 :** to fail to take action — **sit pretty :** to be in a highly favorable situation — **sit tight 1 :** to maintain one's position without change **2 :** to remain quiet in or as if in hiding — **sit under :** to attend religious service under the instruction or ministrations of; *also* **:** to attend the classes or lectures of

²sit *n* **1 :** an act or period of sitting **2 :** the manner in which a garment fits

si·tar \si-ˈtär\ *n* [Hindi *sitār*] **:** an Indian lute with a long neck and a varying number of strings — **si·tar·ist** \-əst\ *n*

sit–down \ˈsit-ˌdau̇n, ˈsid-ˌau̇n\ *n* **1 :** a cessation of work by employees while maintaining continuous occupation of their place of employment as a protest and means toward forcing compliance with demands **2 :** a mass obstruction of an activity by sitting down to demonstrate a grievance or to get the activity modified or halted

¹site \ˈsīt\ *n* [ME, place, position, fr. MF or L; MF, fr. L *situs,* fr. *situs,* pp. of *sinere* to leave, place, lay; akin to L *serere* to sow — more at SOW] **1 a :** the spatial location of an actual or planned structure or set of structures (as a building, town, or monuments) **b :** a space of ground occupied or to be occupied by a building **2 :** the place, scene, or point of something

²site *vt* **sit·ed; sit·ing :** to place on a site or in position **:** LOCATE

sith \(ˈ)sith\ *or* **sith·ence** \ˈsith-ən(t)s\ *or* **sith·ens** \ˈsith-ənz\ *archaic var of* SINCE
sit–in \ˈsit-ˌin\ *n* **1 :** SIT-DOWN 1 **2 a :** an act of occupying seats in a racially segregated establishment in organized protest against discrimination **b :** an act of sitting in the seats or on the floor of an establishment as a means of organized protest
sit in \sit-ˈin\ *vi* **1 :** to take part in or be present at a session of music or discussion as a visitor **2 :** to participate in a sit-in
Sit·ka spruce \ˌsit-kə-\ *n* [*Sitka*, Alaska] **:** a tall spruce (*Picea sitchensis*) of the northern Pacific coast that has thin reddish brown bark and flat needles
si·tos·ter·ol \si-ˈtäs-tə-ˌrōl, sə-, -ˌrōl\ *n* [Gk *sitos* grain + E *sterol*] **:** any of several sterols that are widespread esp. in plant products (as wheat germ or soy bean oil) and are used as starting materials for the synthesis of steroid hormones
sit out *vt* **:** to refrain from participating in <*sit out* the next dance>
sit·ter \ˈsit-ər\ *n* **:** one that sits; *specif* **:** BABY-SITTER
1**sit·ting** \ˈsit-iŋ\ *n* **1 a :** the act of one that sits **b :** a single occasion of continuous sitting (as for a portrait or meal) **2 a :** a brooding over eggs for hatching **b :** SETTING 6 **3 :** SESSION <a ~ of the legislature>
2**sitting** *adj* **1 :** that is setting <a ~ hen> **2 :** occupying a judicial or legislative seat **:** being in office **3 :** easily hit or played <a ~ target> **4 a :** used in or for sitting <a ~ position> **b :** performed while sitting <a ~ shot>
sitting duck *n* **:** an easy or defenseless target for attack or criticism or unscrupulous dealings
sitting room *n* **:** LIVING ROOM 1
1**sit·u·ate** \ˈsich-(ə-)wət, -ə-ˌwāt\ *adj* [ML *situatus*, pp. of *situare* to place, fr. L *situs*] **:** having a site **:** LOCATED
2**sit·u·ate** \ˈsich-ə-ˌwāt\ *vt* **-at·ed; -at·ing :** to place in a site, situation, or category **:** LOCATE
sit·u·at·ed *adj* **1 :** having a site, situation, or location **:** LOCATED **2 :** provided with money or possessions <comfortably ~>
sit·u·a·tion \ˌsich-ə-ˈwā-shən\ *n* **1 a :** the way in which something is placed in relation to its surroundings **b :** SITE **c** *archaic* **:** LOCALITY **2** *archaic* **:** state of health **3 a :** position or place of employment **:** POST, JOB **b :** position in life **:** STATUS **4 a :** position with respect to conditions and circumstances <the military ~ remains obscure> **b :** the sum total of internal and external stimuli that act upon an organism within a given time interval **5 a :** relative position or combination of circumstances at a certain moment **b :** a critical, trying, or unusual state of affairs **:** PROBLEM **c :** a particular or striking complex of affairs at a stage in the action of a narrative or drama ***syn*** see STATE
sit·u·a·tion·al \-shnəl, -shən-ᵊl\ *adj* **1 :** of, relating to, or appropriate to a situation **2 :** of or relating to situation ethics — **sit·u·a·tion·al·ly** \-ē\ *adv*
situation comedy *n* **:** a radio or television comedy series that involves a continuing cast of characters in a succession of unconnected episodes
situation ethics *n* **:** a system of ethics which is based on love and by which acts are judged within their contexts instead of by categorical principles
sit–up \ˈsit-ˌəp\ *n* **:** a conditioning exercise performed from a supine position by raising the trunk to a sitting position usu. while keeping the legs straight and returning to the original position
sit up \sit-ˈəp\ *vi* **1 a :** to rise from a lying to a sitting position **b :** to sit with the back erect **2 :** to show interest, alertness, or surprise <*sit up* and take notice> **3 :** to stay up after the usual time for going to bed <*sat up* late to watch the movie>
si·tus \ˈsīt-əs\ *n* [L — more at SITE] **:** the place where something exists or originates; *specif* **:** the place where something (as a right) is held to be located in law
sitz bath \ˈsits-\ *n* [part trans. of G *sitzbad*, fr. *sitz* act of sitting + *bad* bath] **:** a tub in which one bathes in a sitting posture; *also* **:** a bath so taken esp. therapeutically
sitz·krieg \ˈsit-ˌskrēg, ˈzit-\ *n* [G, fr. *sitz* + *krieg* war] **:** static or nonaggressive warfare
sitz·mark \ˈsit-ˌsmärk, ˈzit-\ *n* [part trans. of G *sitzmarke*, fr. *sitz* + *marke* mark] **:** a depression left in the snow by a skier falling backward
Si·va \ˈs(h)iv-ə, ˈs(h)ē-və\ *n* [Skt *Śiva*] **:** the god of destruction and regeneration in the Hindu sacred triad — compare BRAHMA, VISHNU
Si·van \ˈsiv-ən\ *n* [Heb *Sīwān*] **:** the 9th month of the civil year or the 3d month of the ecclesiastical year in the Jewish calendar — see MONTH table
Si·wash \ˈsi-ˌwósh, -ˌwäsh\ *n* [*Siwash*, fictional college in stories by George Fitch †1915 Am author] **:** a small usu. inland college that is notably provincial in outlook <cheer for dear old *Siwash*>
six \ˈsiks\ *n* [ME, fr. *six*, adj., fr. OE *siex*; akin to OHG *sehs* six, L *sex*, Gk *hex*] **1** — see NUMBER table **2 :** the sixth in a set or series <the ~ of spades> **3 :** something having six units or members: as **a :** an ice-hockey team **b :** a 6-cylinder engine or automobile — **six** *adj or pron* — **at sixes and sevens :** being in disorder
six·fold \ˈsiks-ˌfōld, -ˈfōld\ *adj* **1 :** having six units or members **2 :** being six times as great or as many — **six·fold** \-ˈfōld\ *adv*
six–gun \ˈsiks-ˌgən\ *n* **:** a 6-chambered revolver
six·mo \ˈsik-(ˌ)smō\ *n, pl* **sixmos :** the size of a piece of paper cut six from a sheet; *also* **:** a book, a page, or paper of this size
six–o–six *or* **606** \ˌsik-ˌsō-ˈsiks\ *n* [fr. its having been the 606th compound tested and introduced by Paul Ehrlich] **:** ARSPHENAMINE
six–pack \ˈsik-ˌspak\ *n* **1 :** a container for six bottles or cans purchased together **2 :** the contents of a six-pack
six·pence \ˈsik-spən(t)s, *US also* -ˌspen(t)s\ *n* **1 :** the sum of six British pennies **2** *pl* **sixpence** *or* **six·penc·es :** a coin worth sixpence
six·pen·ny \ˈsik-spə-nē, *US also* -ˌspen-ē\ *adj* **:** costing or worth sixpence
sixpenny bit *n* **:** SIXPENCE 2
six·pen·ny nail \ˌsik-ˌspen-ē-\ *n* **:** a nail about two inches long
six–shoot·er \ˈsik(s)-ˈshüt-ər\ *n* **:** SIX-GUN
six·teen \(ˈ)sik-ˈstēn\ *n* [ME *sixtene*, fr. OE *sixtȳne*, adj.; akin to OE *tien* ten] — see NUMBER table — **sixteen** *adj or pron* — **six·teenth** \-ˈstēn(t)th\ *adj or n*
six·teen·mo \sik-ˈstēn-(ˌ)mō\ *n, pl* **-mos :** the size of a piece of paper cut 16 from a sheet; *also* **:** a book, a page, or paper of this size
sixteenth note *n* **:** a musical note with the time value of 1/16 of a whole note — see NOTE illustration
sixteenth rest *n* **:** a musical rest corresponding in time value to a sixteenth note
sixth \ˈsiks(t)th\ *n* **1** — see NUMBER table **2 a :** a musical interval embracing six diatonic degrees **b :** a tone at this interval; *specif* **:** SUBMEDIANT **c :** the harmonic combination of two tones a sixth apart — **sixth** *adj or adv* — **sixth·ly** \ˈsikst(h)-lē\ *adv*
sixth chord *n* **:** a musical chord consisting of a tone with its third and its sixth above and usu. being the first inversion of a triad
sixth sense *n* **:** a power of perception like but not one of the five senses **:** a keen intuitive power
Six·tine \ˈsik-ˌstīn, -ˌstēn\ *var of* SISTINE
six·ty \ˈsik-stē\ *n, pl* **sixties** [ME, fr. *sixty*, adj., fr. OE *siextig*, n., group of sixty, fr. *siex* six + *-tig* group of ten — more at EIGHTY] **1** —see NUMBER table **2** *pl* **:** the numbers 60-69; *specif* **:** the years 60 to 69 in a lifetime or century — **six·ti·eth** \ˈsik-stē-əth\ *adj or n* — **sixty** *adj or pron*
sixty–fourth note \ˌsik-stē-ˈfōrth-, -ˈfȯrth-\ *n* **:** a musical note with the time value of 1/64 of a whole note — see NOTE illustration
sixty–fourth rest *n* **:** a musical rest corresponding in time value to a sixty-fourth note
six·ty–nine \ˌsik-stē-ˈnīn\ *n* **1** — see NUMBER table **2 :** mutual cunnilingus and fellatio **:** mutual fellatio **:** mutual cunnilingus
siz·able *or* **size·able** \ˈsī-zə-bəl\ *adj* **:** fairly large **:** CONSIDERABLE — **siz·able·ness** *n* — **siz·ably** \-blē\ *adv*
siz·ar *also* **siz·er** \ˈsī-zər\ *n* [*sizar* alter. of *sizer*, fr. 1*size*] **:** a student (as in the university of Cambridge) who receives an allowance toward his college expenses and who orig. acted as a servant to other students in return for this allowance
1**size** \ˈsīz\ *n* [ME *sise* assize, fr. MF, fr. OF, short for *assise* — more at ASSIZE] **1** *dial Brit* **:** ASSIZE 5a — usu. used in pl. **2** *obs* **:** a fixed portion of food or drink **3 a :** physical magnitude, extent, or bulk **:** relative or proportionate dimensions **b :** relative aggregate amount or number **c :** considerable proportions **:** BIGNESS **4:** one of a series of graduated measures esp. of manufactured articles (as of clothing) conventionally identified by numbers or letters <a ~ 7 hat> **5 :** character, quality, or status of a person or thing esp. with reference to importance, relative merit, or correspondence to needs <try this idea on for ~> **6 :** actual state of affairs <that's about the ~ of it>
2**size** *vb* **sized; siz·ing** *vt* **1 :** to make a particular size **:** bring to proper or suitable size **2 :** to arrange, grade, or classify according to size or bulk **3 :** to form a judgment of — usu. used with *up* ~ *vi* **:** to equal in size or other particular characteristic **:** COMPARE — usu. used with *up* and often with *to* or *with*
3**size** *n* [ME *sise*] **:** any of various glutinous materials (as preparations of glue, flour, varnish, or resins) used for filling the pores in surfaces (as of paper, textiles, leather, or plaster) or for applying color or metal leaf (as to book edges or covers)
4**size** *vt* **sized; siz·ing :** to cover, stiffen, or glaze with or as if with size
5**size** \ˈsīz, ˌsīz\ *adj* **:** SIZED — usu. used in combination <bite-*size*>
sized \ˈsīzd, ˌsīzd\ *adj* **1 :** having a specified size or bulk — usu. used in combination <a small-*sized* house> **2 :** arranged or adjusted according to size
siz·ing \ˈsī-ziŋ\ *n* **:** 3SIZE
1**siz·zle** \ˈsiz-əl\ *vb* **siz·zled; siz·zling** \-(ə-)liŋ\ [perh. freq. of *siss* (to hiss)] *vt* **:** to burn up or sear with or as if with a hissing sound ~ *vi* **1 :** to make a hissing sound in or as if in burning or frying **2 :** to seethe with deep anger or resentment
2**sizzle** *n* **:** a hissing sound (as of something frying over a fire)
siz·zler \ˈsiz-(ə-)lər\ *n* **:** one that sizzles; *esp* **:** SCORCHER
SJ *abbr* Society of Jesus
SJD *abbr* [NL *scientiae juridicae doctor*] doctor of juridical science
skag \ˈskag\ *n* [origin unknown] *slang* **:** HEROIN
skald \ˈskȯld, ˈskäld\ *n* [ON *skāld* — more at SCOLD] **:** an ancient Scandinavian poet or historiographer; *broadly* **:** BARD — **skald·ic** \-ik\ *adj*
skat \ˈskät, ˈskat\ *n* [G, modif. of It *scarto* discard, fr. *scartare* to discard, fr. *s-* (fr. L *ex-*) + *carta* card] **1 :** a three-handed card game played with 32 cards in which players bid for the privilege of attempting any of several contracts **2 :** a widow of two cards in skat that may be used by the winner of the bid
1**skate** \ˈskāt\ *n, pl* **skates** *also* **skate** [ME *scate*, fr. ON *skata*] **:** any of numerous rays (as of the genus *Raja*) with the pectoral fins greatly developed giving the animal a rhomboidal shape

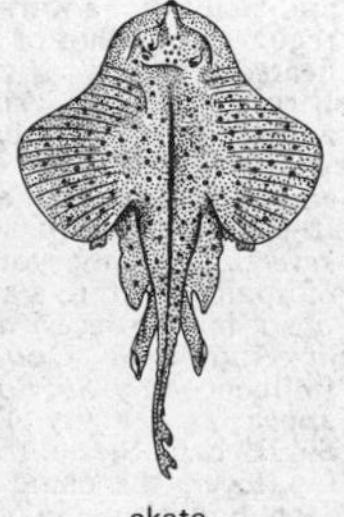
skate

2**skate** *n* [modif. of D *schaats* stilt, skate, fr. (assumed) ONF *escache* stilt; akin to OF *eschace* stilt] **1 a :** a metal frame that can be fitted to the sole of a shoe and to which is attached a runner or a set of wheels for gliding over ice or a surface other than ice **b :** ROLLER SKATE **c :** ICE SKATE **2 :** a period of skating
3**skate** *vb* **skat·ed; skat·ing** *vi* **1 :** to glide along on skates propelled by the alternate action of the legs **2 :** to slip or glide as if on skates **3 :** to proceed in a superficial manner ~ *vt* **:** to go along or through by skating
4**skate** *n* [prob. alter. of E dial. *skite* (an offensive person)] **1 :** a thin awkward-looking or decrepit horse **:** NAG **2 :** FELLOW

skate·board \'skāt-ˌbō(ə)rd, -ˌbȯ(ə)rd\ *n* : a narrow board about two feet long mounted on roller-skate wheels — **skate·board·er** \-ˌbōrd-ər, -ˌbȯrd-\ *n* — **skate·board·ing** \-iŋ\ *n*

skat·er \'skāt-ər\ *n* **1** : one that skates **2** : WATER STRIDER

skat·ing \'skāt-iŋ\ *n* : the act, art, or sport of gliding on skates

ska·tole \'skat-ˌōl, 'skāt-\ *also* **ska·tol** \-ˌȯl, -ˌōl\ *n* [ISV, fr. Gk *skat-, skōr* excrement — more at SCAT-] : a foul-smelling compound C_9H_9N found in the intestines and feces, in civet, and in several plants or made synthetically and used in perfumes as a fixative

skean *or* **skene** \'skē(-ə)n\ *n* [IrGael *scian* & ScGael *sgian*] : DAGGER, DIRK

ske·dad·dle \ski-'dad-ᵊl\ *vi* **ske·dad·dled; ske·dad·dling** \-'dad-liŋ, -ᵊl-iŋ\ [origin unknown] : to run away; *specif* : to flee in a panic — **ske·dad·dler** \-'dad-lər, -ᵊl-ər\ *n*

skeet \'skēt\ *n* [modif. of ON *skjōta* to shoot — more at SHOOT] : trapshooting in which clay targets are thrown in such a way as to simulate the angles of flight of birds

¹**skee·ter** \'skēt-ər\ *n* [by shortening & alter.] **1** : MOSQUITO **2** : an iceboat about 16 feet in length equipped with a single sail

²**skeet·er** \'skēt-ər\ *n* : a skeet shooter

skeg \'skeg\ *also* **skag** \'skag\ *n* [D *scheg;* akin to OSlav *skokŭ* leap — more at SHAG] **1** : the stern of the keel of a ship near the sternpost; *esp* : the part connecting the keel with the bottom of the rudderpost in a single-screw ship **2** : a fin situated on the rear bottom of a surfboard that is used for steering and stability

skeigh \'skēk\ *adj* [perh. of Scand origin; akin to Sw *skygg* shy; akin to OE *scēoh* shy — more at SHY] *chiefly Scot* : proudly spirited : SKITTISH

¹**skein** \'skān\ *n* [ME *skeyne,* fr. MF *escaigne*] **1** *or* **skean** *or* **skeane** \'skān\ : a loosely coiled length of yarn or thread wound on a reel **2** : something suggesting the twists or coils of a skein : TANGLE **3** : a flock of wildfowl (as geese or ducks) in flight

²**skein** *vt* : to wind into skeins <~ yarn>

skel·e·tal \'skel-ət-ᵊl\ *adj* : of, relating to, forming, attached to, or resembling a skeleton — **skel·e·tal·ly** \-ᵊl-ē\ *adv*

¹**skel·e·ton** \'skel-ət-ᵊn\ *n* [NL, fr. Gk, neut. of *skeletos* dried up; akin to Gk *skellein* to dry up, *sklēros* hard, OE *sceald* shallow] **1** : a usu. rigid supportive or protective structure or framework of an organism; *esp* : the bony or more or less cartilaginous framework supporting the soft tissues and protecting the internal organs of a vertebrate (as a fish or man) **2** : something reduced to its minimum form or essential parts **3** : an emaciated person or animal **4 a** : something forming a structural framework **b** : the straight or branched chain or ring of atoms that forms the basic structure of an organic molecule **5** : something shameful and kept secret (as in a family) — often used in the phrase *skeleton in the closet*

²**skeleton** *adj* : of, consisting of, or resembling a skeleton

skel·e·ton·ize \-ˌīz\ *vt* **-ized; -iz·ing** : to produce in or reduce to skeleton form <~ a leaf> <~ a news story> <~ a regiment>

skel·e·ton·iz·er \-ˌī-zər\ *n* : any of various lepidopterous larvae that eat the parenchyma of leaves reducing them to a skeleton of veins

skeleton key *n* : a key with a large part of the bit filed away to enable it to open low quality locks as a master key

skel·lum \'skel-əm\ *n* [D *schelm,* fr. LG; akin to OHG *skelmo* person deserving death] *chiefly Scot* : SCOUNDREL, RASCAL

¹**skelp** \'skelp\ *vb* **skelped** \'skelpt\ *also* **skel·pit** \'skel-pət\; **skelp·ing** [ME *skelpen*] *vt, dial Brit* : STRIKE, SLAP, BEAT ~ *vi* : to step lively : HUSTLE

²**skelp** *n, dial Brit* : a smart blow : SLAP

skel·ter \'skel-tər\ *vi* **skel·tered; skel·ter·ing** \-t(ə-)riŋ\ [fr. *-skelter* (in *helter-skelter*)] : SCURRY

Skel·ton·ics \skel-'tän-iks\ *n pl* [John *Skelton*] : short verses of an irregular meter with two or three stresses sometimes in falling and sometimes in rising rhythm and usu. with rhymed couplets

skep \'skep\ *n* [ME *skeppe* basket, basketful, fr. OE *sceppe,* fr. ON *skeppa* bushel; akin to OE *scieppan* to form, create — more at SHAPE] : BEEHIVE; *esp* : a domed hive made of twisted straw

skep·sis \'skep-səs\ *n* [NL, fr. Gk *skepsis* examination, doubt, skeptical philosophy, fr. *skeptesthai*] : philosophic doubt as to the objective reality of phenomena; *broadly* : a skeptical outlook or attitude

skep·tic \'skep-tik\ *n* [L or Gk; L *scepticus,* fr. Gk *skeptikos,* fr. *skeptikos* thoughtful, fr. *skeptesthai* to look, consider — more at SPY] **1** : an adherent or advocate of skepticism **2** : a person disposed to skepticism esp. regarding religion or religious principles

skep·ti·cal \-ti-kəl\ *adj* : relating to, characteristic of, or marked by skepticism <a ~ listener> — **skep·ti·cal·ly** \-k(ə-)lē\ *adv*

skep·ti·cism \'skep-tə-ˌsiz-əm\ *n* **1 a** : the doctrine that true knowledge or knowledge in a particular area is uncertain **b** : the method of suspended judgment, systematic doubt, or criticism characteristic of skeptics **2** : an attitude of doubt or a disposition to incredulity either in general or toward a particular object **3** : doubt concerning basic religious principles (as immortality, providence, and revelation) *syn* see UNCERTAINTY

sker·ry \'sker-ē\ *n, pl* **skerries** [of Scand origin; akin to ON *sker* skerry and to ON *ey* island; akin to L *aqua* water — more at SCAR, ISLAND] : a rocky isle : REEF

¹**sketch** \'skech\ *n* [D *schets,* fr. It *schizzo,* fr. *schizzare* to splash] **1 a** : a rough drawing representing the chief features of an object or scene and often made as a preliminary study **b** : a tentative draft (as for a literary work) **2** : a brief description (as of a person) or outline **3 a** : a short literary composition somewhat resembling the short story and the essay but intentionally slight in treatment, discursive in style, and familiar in tone **b** : a short instrumental composition usu. for piano **c** : a slight theatrical piece having a single scene; *esp* : a comic variety act

²**sketch** *vt* : to make a sketch, rough draft, or outline of ~ *vi* : to draw or paint a sketch — **sketch·er** *n*

sketch·book \'skech-ˌbu̇k\ *n* : a book of or for sketches

sketchy \'skech-ē\ *adj* **sketch·i·er; -est** **1** : of the nature of a sketch : roughly outlined **2** : wanting in completeness, clearness, or substance : SLIGHT, SUPERFICIAL — **sketch·i·ly** \'skech-ə-lē\ *adv* — **sketch·i·ness** \'skech-ē-nəs\ *n*

¹**skew** \'skyü\ *vb* [ME *skewen* to escape, skew, fr. ONF *escuer* to shun, of Gmc origin; akin to OHG *sciuhen* to frighten off — more at SHY] *vi* **1** : to take an oblique course **2** : to look askance ~ *vt* **1** : to make, set, or cut on the skew **2** : to distort from a true value or symmetrical form <~*ed* statistical data>

²**skew** *adj* **1** : set, placed, or running obliquely : SLANTING **2** : more developed on one side or in one direction than another : not symmetrical

³**skew** *n* : a deviation from a straight line : SLANT

skew arch *n* : an arch whose jambs are not at right angles with the face

skew·back \'skyü-ˌbak\ *n* : a course of masonry, a stone, or an iron plate having an inclined face against which the voussoirs of a segmental arch abut

skew·bald \-ˌbȯld\ *adj* [*skewed* (skewbald) + *bald*] *of an animal* : marked with spots and patches of white and some other color

skew curve *n* : a curve in three-dimensional space that does not lie in a single plane

skew distribution *n* : an unsymmetrical frequency distribution having the mode at a different value from the mean

¹**skew·er** \'skyü-ər, 'skyu̇(-ə)r\ *n* [prob. alter. of *skiver*] **1** : a pin of wood or metal for fastening meat to keep it in form while roasting or to hold small pieces of meat and vegetables for broiling **2** : any of various things shaped or used like a meat skewer

²**skewer** *vt* : to fasten or pierce with or as if with a skewer

skew field *n* : a mathematical field in which multiplication is not commutative

skew lines *n pl* : straight lines that do not intersect and are not in the same plane

skew·ness \'skyü-nəs\ *n* : lack of straightness or symmetry : DISTORTION; *esp* : lack of symmetry in a frequency distribution

¹**ski** \'skē, *Brit also* 'shē\ *n, pl* **skis** [Norw, fr. ON *skīth* stick of wood, ski; akin to OHG *skīt* stick of wood, OE *scēadan* to divide — more at SHED] **1 a** : one of a pair of narrow strips of wood, metal, or plastic curving upward in front that are used esp. for gliding over snow **b** : WATER SKI **2** : a piece of material that resembles a ski and is used as a runner on a vehicle

²**ski** *vb* **skied** \'skēd, 'shēd\; **ski·ing** *vi* : to glide on skis in travel or as a sport ~ *vt* : to travel or pass over on skis — **ski·able** \'skē-ə-bəl\ *adj* — **ski·er** *n*

skia- *comb form* [NL, fr. Gk *skia* — more at SCENE] : shadow <*skia*graph>

skia·gram \'skī-ə-ˌgram\ *n* [ISV] **1** : a figure formed by shading in the outline of a shadow **2** : RADIOGRAPH

skia·graph \-ˌgraf\ *n* : RADIOGRAPH

ski·ag·ra·phy \skī-'ag-rə-fē\ *n* [ISV] : the making of skiagrams

skia·scope \'skī-ə-ˌskōp\ *n* : a device for determining the refractive state of the eye from the movements of retinal lights and shadows — **ski·as·co·py** \skī-'as-kə-pē\ *n*

ski·bob \'skē-ˌbäb\ *n* [¹*ski* + ⁸*bob*] : a vehicle that has two short skis one behind the other, a steering handle attached to the forward ski, and a low upholstered seat over the rear ski and that is used for gliding downhill over snow by a rider wearing miniature skis for balance — **ski·bob·ber** \-ˌbäb-ər\ *n* — **ski·bob·bing** \-ˌbäb-iŋ\ *n*

ski boot *n* : a rigid padded shoe usu. of leather or plastic that extends just above the ankle, is securely fastened to the foot (as with laces, buckles, or hinges), and is locked into position in a ski binding

¹**skid** \'skid\ *n* [perh. of Scand origin; akin to ON *skīth* stick of wood] **1** : one of a group of objects (as planks or logs) used to support or elevate a structure or object **2** : a wooden fender hung over a ship's side to protect it in handling cargo **3** : a usu. iron shoe or clog attached to a chain and placed under a wheel to prevent its turning when descending a steep hill : DRAG **4** : a timber, bar, rail, pole, or log used in pairs or sets to form a slideway (as for an incline from a truck to the sidewalk) **5** : the act of skidding : SLIP, SIDESLIP **6** : a runner used as a member of the landing gear of an airplane or helicopter **7** *pl* : a route to defeat or downfall <on the ~*s*> **8** : a low platform mounted (as on wheels) on which material is set for handling and moving

²**skid** *vb* **skid·ded; skid·ding** *vt* **1** : to apply a brake or skid to : slow or halt by a skid **2** : to haul along, slide, hoist, or store on skids ~ *vi* **1** : to slide without rotating (as a wheel held from turning while a vehicle moves onward) **2 a** : to fail to grip the roadway; *specif* : to slip sideways on the road **b** *of an airplane* : to slide sidewise away from the center of curvature when turning **c** : SLIDE, SLIP **3** : to fall rapidly, steeply, or far

skid·der \'skid-ər\ *n* : one that skids or uses a skid

skid·doo *or* **ski·doo** \skid-'ü\ *vi* [prob. alter. of *skedaddle*] : to go away : DEPART

skid·dy \'skid-ē\ *adj* **skid·di·er; -est** : likely to skid or cause skidding <a wet ~ road>

skid fin *n* : a fore-and-aft vertical surface usu. placed above the upper wing of a biplane to provide lateral stability

skid road *n* **1** : a road along which logs are skidded **2 a** *West* : the part of a town frequented by loggers **b** : SKID ROW

skid row \-'rō\ *n* [alter. of *skid road*] : a district of cheap saloons and flophouses frequented by vagrants and alcoholics

ski·ey *var of* SKYEY

skiff \'skif\ *n* [MF or OIt; MF *esquif,* fr. OIt *schifo,* of Gmc origin; akin to OE *scip* ship] **1** : a small light sailing ship **2** : a light rowboat **3** : a boat with centerboard and spritsail light enough to be rowed — called also *St. Lawrence skiff* **4** : a small fast motorboat

---

ə abut	ᵊ kitten	ər further	a back	ā bake	ä cot, cart	
au̇ out	ch chin	e less	ē easy	g gift	i trip	ī life
j joke	ŋ sing	ō flow	ȯ flaw	ȯi coin	th thin	t͟h this
ü loot	u̇ foot	y yet	yü few	yu̇ furious	zh vision	

skif·fle \'skif-əl\ *n* [perh. imit.] **:** jazz or folk music played by a group consisting of or including nonstandard instruments or noisemakers (as jugs, washboards, or Jew's harps)

ski·ing *n* **:** the art or sport of sliding and jumping on skis

ski·jor·ing \'skē-ˌjōr-iŋ, -ˌjór-, (ˈ)skē-'\ *n* [modif. of Norw *skikjøring,* fr. *ski* + *kjøring* driving] **:** a winter sport in which a person wearing skis is drawn over snow or ice by a horse or vehicle

ski jump *n* **:** a jump made by a person wearing skis; *also* **:** a course or track esp. prepared for such jumping — **ski jump** *vi*

ski lift *n* **:** a motor-driven conveyor consisting usu. of a series of bars or seats suspended from an overhead moving cable and used for transporting skiers or sightseers up a long slope or mountainside

1**skill** \'skil\ *n* [ME *skil,* fr. ON, distinction, knowledge; akin to OE *scylian* to separate, *sciell* shell — more at SHELL] **1** *obs* **:** CAUSE, REASON **2 a :** the ability to use one's knowledge effectively and readily in execution or performance **b :** dexterity or coordination esp. in the execution of learned physical tasks **3 :** a learned power of doing something competently **:** a developed aptitude or ability <language ~*s*> ***syn*** see ART

2**skill** *vi, archaic* **:** to make a difference **:** MATTER, AVAIL

skilled \'skild\ *adj* **1 :** having acquired mastery of or skill in something (as a technique or a trade) **2 :** of, relating to, or requiring workers or labor with skill and training in a particular occupation, craft, or trade ***syn*** see PROFICIENT ***ant*** unskilled

skil·let \'skil-ət\ *n* [ME *skelet*] **1** *chiefly Brit* **:** a small kettle or pot usu. having three or four often long feet and used for cooking on the hearth **2 :** FRYING PAN

skill·ful *or* **skil·ful** \'skil-fəl\ *adj* **1 :** possessed of or displaying skill **:** EXPERT **2 :** accomplished with skill ***syn*** see PROFICIENT ***ant*** unskillful — **skill·ful·ly** \-fə-lē\ *adv* — **skill·ful·ness** *n*

skil·ling \'skil-iŋ, 'shil-\ *n* [Sw, Norw, & Dan, fr. ON *skillingr,* a gold coin; akin to OE *scilling* shilling] **1 :** any of various old Scandinavian units of value **2 :** any of the small coins representing one skilling

skill–less *or* **skil·less** \'skil-ləs\ *adj* **:** having no skill — **skill–less·ness** *n*

1**skim** \'skim\ *vb* **skimmed; skim·ming** [ME *skimmen*] *vt* **1 a :** to clear (a liquid) of scum or floating substance <~ boiling syrup> **b :** to remove (as film or scum) from the surface of a liquid **c :** to remove cream from by skimming **d :** to remove the best or most easily obtainable contents from **2 :** to read, study, or examine superficially and rapidly; *specif* **:** to glance through (as a book) for the chief ideas or the plot **3 :** to throw in a gliding path; *specif* **:** to throw so as to ricochet along the surface of water **4 :** to cover with or as if with a film, scum, or coat **5 :** to pass swiftly or lightly over ~ *vi* **1 a :** to pass lightly or hastily **:** glide or skip along, above, or near a surface **b :** to give a cursory glance or consideration **2 :** to become coated with a thin layer of film or scum **3 :** to put on a finishing coat of plaster

2**skim** *n* **1 :** a thin layer, coating, or film **2 :** the act of skimming **3 :** something skimmed; *specif* **:** SKIM MILK

3**skim** *adj* **1 :** having the cream removed by skimming **2 :** made of skim milk <~ cheese>

ski mask *n* **:** a knit fabric mask that covers the head, has openings for the eyes, mouth, and sometimes the nose, and is worn esp. by skiers for protection from the cold

skim·ble–skam·ble \ˌskim-bəl-'skam-bəl\ *adj* [redupl. of E dial. *scamble* to stumble along] **:** DISCURSIVE, SENSELESS

skim·mer \'skim-ər\ *n* **1 :** one that skims; *specif* **:** a flat perforated scoop or spoon used for skimming **2 a :** any of several long-winged marine birds (genus *Rhynchops*) related to the terns **b :** WATER STRIDER **3 :** a usu. straw flat-crowned hat with a wide straight brim **4 :** a fitted sleeveless usu. flaring sheathlike dress

skim milk *n* **:** milk from which the cream has been taken — called also *skimmed milk*

skim·ming *n* **1 :** that which is skimmed from a liquid **2 :** the practice of fraudulently reporting gambling income (as of a casino) so as to avoid full tax payments

ski·mo·bile \'skē-mō-ˌbēl\ *n* **:** SNOWMOBILE

1**skimp** \'skimp\ *adj* [perh. alter. of *scrimp*] **:** SCANTY, MEAGER

2**skimp** *vt* **:** to give insufficient or barely sufficient attention or effort to or funds for ~ *vi* **:** to save by or as if by skimping

skimpy \'skim-pē\ *adj* **skimp·i·er; -est :** deficient in supply or execution esp. through skimping **:** SCANTY ***syn*** see MEAGER — **skimp·i·ly** \-pə-lē\ *adv* — **skimp·i·ness** \-pē-nəs\ *n*

1**skin** \'skin\ *n, often attrib* [ME, fr. ON *skinn;* akin to OE *scinn* skin, MHG *schint* fruit peel, W *ysgythru* to cut] **1 a (1) :** the integument of an animal (as a fur-bearing mammal or a bird) separated from the body usu. with its hair or feathers **(2) :** a usu. unmounted specimen of a vertebrate (as in a museum) **b :** the hide or pelt of a game or domestic animal **c (1) :** the pelt of an animal prepared for use as a trimming or in a garment <it took 40 ~*s* to make the coat> — compare 3HIDE **(2) :** a sheet of parchment or vellum made from a hide **(3) :** BOTTLE 1b **2 a :** the external limiting layer of an animal body esp. when forming a tough but flexible cover relatively impermeable from without while intact **b :** any of various outer or surface layers (as a rind, husk, or pellicle) <a sausage ~> **3 :** the life or physical well-being of a person <made sure to save his ~> **4 :** a sheathing or casing forming the outside surface of a structure (as a ship or airplane) — **skin·less** \-ləs\ *adj* — **by the skin of one's teeth :** by a very narrow margin — **under one's skin :** so deeply penetrative as to irritate, stimulate, provoke thought, or otherwise excite — **under the skin :** beneath apparent or surface differences **:** at heart

2**skin** *vb* **skinned; skin·ning** *vt* **1 a :** to cover with or as if with skin **b :** to heal over with skin **2 a :** to strip, scrape, or rub off an outer covering (as the skin or rind) of **b :** to strip or peel off **c :** to cut, chip, or damage the surface of <fell and *skinned* his knee> **3 a :** to strip of money or property **:** FLEECE **b :** DEFEAT **c :** CENSURE, CASTIGATE **4 :** to urge on and direct the course of (as a draft animal) ~ *vi* **1 :** to become covered with or as if with skin **2 a :** SHIN **b :** to pass or get by with scant room to spare

skin–deep \'skin-'dēp\ *adj* **1 :** as deep as the skin **2 :** not thorough or lasting in impression **:** SUPERFICIAL

skin–dive \'skin-ˌdīv\ *vi* **:** to engage in skin diving — **skin diver** *n*

skin diving *n* **:** the sport of swimming under water with a face mask and flippers and esp. without a portable breathing device

skin effect *n* **:** an effect characteristic of current distribution in a conductor at high frequencies that results from a greater current density near the surface of the conductor than in its interior

skin flick *n* **:** a motion picture characterized by nudity and explicit sexual situations

skin·flint \'skin-ˌflint\ *n* **:** a person who would save, gain, or extort money by any means **:** MISER, NIGGARD

skin·ful \-ˌfu̇l\ *n* **1 :** the contents of a skin bottle **2 :** a large or satisfying quantity esp. of liquor

skin game *n* **:** a swindling game or trick

skin graft *n* **:** a piece of skin that is taken from a donor area to replace skin in a defective or denuded area (as one that has been burned)

skin grafting *n* **:** the action or process of making a skin graft

skin·head \'skin-ˌhed\ *n* **1 :** one whose hair is cut very short **2 :** a young short-haired working-class British hoodlum

1**skink** \'skiŋk\ *vt* [ME *skinken,* fr. MD *schenken;* akin to OE *scencan* to pour out drink, *scanca* shank] *chiefly dial* **:** to draw, pour out, or serve (drink)

2**skink** *n* [L *scincus,* fr. Gk *skinkos*] **:** any of a family (Scincidae) of mostly small pleurodont lizards that have small scales

skink·er \'skiŋ-kər\ *n* **:** one that serves liquor **:** TAPSTER

skinned \'skind\ *adj* **:** having skin esp. of a specified kind — usu. used in combination <dark-*skinned*>

skin·ner \'skin-ər\ *n* **1 a :** one that deals in skins, pelts, or hides **b :** one that removes, cures, or dresses skins **2 :** SHARPER **3 :** a driver of draft animals **:** TEAMSTER

Skin·ner box \ˌskin-ər-'bäks\ *n* [B. F. *Skinner b*1904 Am psychologist] **:** a laboratory apparatus in which an animal is caged for experiments in operant conditioning and which typically contains a lever that must be pressed by the animal to gain reward or avoid punishment

skin·ny \'skin-ē\ *adj* **skin·ni·er; -est 1 :** resembling skin **:** MEMBRANOUS **2 a :** lacking sufficient flesh **:** very thin **:** EMACIATED **b :** lacking usual or desirable bulk, quantity, qualities, or significance ***syn*** see LEAN ***ant*** fleshy — **skin·ni·ness** *n*

skin·ny–dip·ping \'skin-ē-ˌdip-iŋ\ *n* **:** swimming in the nude — **skin·ny–dip·per** \-ˌdip-ər\ *n*

skin–pop·ping \'skin-ˌpäp-iŋ\ *n* **:** injection of a drug subcutaneously rather than into a vein

skint \'skint\ *adj* [alter. of *skinned,* pp. of 2*skin*] *Brit* **:** PENNILESS

skin test *n* **:** a test (as a scratch test) performed on the skin and used in detecting allergic hypersensitivity

skin·tight \'skin-'tīt\ *adj* **:** closely fitted to the figure

ski·ör·ing \'skē-ˌər-iŋ, (ˈ)skē-'\ *var of* SKIJORING

1**skip** \'skip\ *vb* **skipped; skip·ping** [ME *skippen,* perh. of Scand origin; akin to Sw dial. *skopa* to hop] *vi* **1 a :** to move or proceed with leaps and bounds **:** CAPER **b :** to bound off one point after another **:** RICOCHET **2 :** to leave hurriedly or secretly <*skipped* out without paying his bill> **3 a :** to pass over or omit an interval, item, or step **b :** to omit a grade in school in advancing to the next **c :** MISFIRE 1 ~ *vt* **1 a :** to pass over without notice or mention **:** OMIT **b :** to pass by or leave out (a step in a progression or series) **2 a :** to cause to skip (a grade in school) **b :** to cause to bound or skim over a surface <~ a stone across a pond> **3 :** to leap over lightly and nimbly **4 a :** to depart from quickly and secretly <*skipped* town> **b :** to fail to attend <~ the staff meeting> — **skip bail :** to jump bail — **skip rope :** to jump rope

2**skip** *n* **1 a :** a light bounding step **b :** a gait composed of alternating hops and steps **2 :** an act of omission or the thing omitted

3**skip** *n* [short for 2*skipper*] **1 :** the captain of a side in a game (as curling or lawn bowling) who advises his men as to the play and controls the action **2 :** SKIPPER

4**skip** *vt* **skipped; skip·ping :** to act as skipper of

skip bomb *vt* **:** to attack by releasing delayed-action bombs from a low-flying airplane so that they skip along a land or water surface and strike a target

skip·jack \'skip-ˌjak\ *n, pl* **skipjacks** *or* **skipjack :** any of various fishes (as a bonito, tenpounder, or bluefish) that jump above or play at the surface of the water

ski pole *n* **:** one of a pair of lightweight usu. metal poles that have a handgrip and a wrist strap at one end and an encircling disk set a little above the point at the other end and that are used in skiing

1**skip·per** \'skip-ər\ *n* **1 :** any of various erratically active insects (as a click beetle or a water strider) **2 :** one that skips **3 :** the Atlantic saury (*Scombresox saurus*) or a related fish that jumps freely above the water **4 :** any of numerous small stout-bodied lepidopterous insects (superfamily Hesperioidea) that differ from the typical butterflies in wing venation and the form of the antennae

2**skipper** *n* [ME, fr. MD *schipper,* fr. *schip* ship; akin to OE *scip* ship — more at SHIP] **1 :** the master of a ship; *esp* **:** the master of a fishing, small trading, or pleasure boat **2 :** the captain or first pilot of an airplane

3**skip·per** *vt* **skip·pered; skip·per·ing** \'skip-(ə-)riŋ\ **1 :** to act as skipper of (as a boat) **2 :** to act as coach of (as a team)

1**skirl** \'skər(-ə)l, 'skir(ə)l\ *vb* [ME (Sc) *skrillen, skirlen,* of Scand origin; akin to OSw *skrælla* to rattle; akin to OE *scrallettan* to sound loudly] *vi, of a bagpipe* **:** to emit the high shrill tone of the chanter; *also* **:** to give forth music ~ *vt* **:** to play (music) on the bagpipe

2**skirl** *n* **:** a high shrill sound produced by the chanter of a bagpipe

1**skir·mish** \'skər-mish\ *n* [ME *skyrmissh,* alter. of *skarmish,* fr. MF *escarmouche,* fr. OIt *scaramuccia,* of Gmc origin; akin to OHG *skirmen* to defend] **1 :** a minor fight in war usu. incidental to larger movements **2 a :** a brisk preliminary verbal conflict **b :** a minor dispute or contest between opposing parties

2**skirmish** *vi* **1 :** to engage in a skirmish **2 :** to search about (as for supplies) **:** scout around — **skir·mish·er** *n*

1skirr \'skər, 'ski(ə)r\ *vb* [perh. alter. of 1*scour*] *vi* **1 :** to leave hastily **:** FLEE <birds ~*ed* off from the bushes —D. H. Lawrence> **2 :** to run, fly, sail, or otherwise move rapidly ~ *vt* **1 :** to search about in <~ the country round —Shak.> **2 a :** to pass rapidly over **:** SKIM **b** *dial* **:** to cause to skim

2skirr *n* [prob. imit.] **:** WHIR, ROAR

1skirt \'skərt\ *n* [ME, fr. ON *skyrta* shirt, kirtle — more at SHIRT] **1 a** (1) **:** a free-hanging part of an outer garment or undergarment extending from the waist down (2) **:** a separate free-hanging outer garment or undergarment for women and girls covering the body from the waist down **b :** either of two usu. leather flaps on a saddle covering the bars on which the stirrups are hung **c :** a cloth facing that hangs loosely and usu. in folds or pleats from the bottom edge or across the front of a piece of furniture **d :** the lower branches of a tree when near the ground **2 a :** the rim, periphery, or environs of an area **b** *pl* **:** outlying parts (as of a town or city) **3 :** a part or attachment serving as a rim, border, or edging **4 :** GIRL, WOMAN

2skirt *vt* **1 :** to form or run along the border or edge of **:** BORDER **2 a :** to provide a skirt for <a full-*skirted* coat> **b :** to furnish a border or shield for **3 a :** to go or pass around or about; *specif* **:** to go around or keep away from in order to avoid danger or discovery **b :** to avoid because of difficulty or fear of controversy <~*ed* the important issues> **c :** to evade or miss by a narrow margin <having ~*ed* disaster —Edith Wharton> ~ *vi* **:** to be, lie, or move along an edge, border, or margin — **skirt·er** *n*

skirt·ing \'skərt-iŋ\ *n* **1 :** something that skirts: as **a :** BORDER, EDGING **b** *Brit* **:** BASEBOARD **2 :** fabric suitable for skirts

ski run *n* **:** a slope or trail suitable for skiing

skit \'skit\ *n* [origin unknown] **1 :** a jeering or satirical remark **:** TAUNT **2 a :** a satirical or humorous story or sketch **b** (1) **:** a brief burlesque or comic sketch included in a dramatic performance (as a revue) (2) **:** a short serious dramatic piece; *esp* **:** one done by amateurs

ski touring *n* **:** cross-country skiing for pleasure

ski tow *n* **1 :** a motor-driven conveyor that is used for pulling skiers up a slope and that consists usu. of an endless moving rope which a skier grasps **2 :** SKI LIFT

skit·ter \'skit-ər\ *vb* [prob. freq. of E dial. *skite* to move quickly] *vi* **1 :** to glide or skip lightly or quickly along a surface **2 :** to twitch the hook of a fishing line through or along the surface of water ~ *vt* **:** to cause to skitter

skit·tery \'skit-ə-rē\ *adj* **:** SKITTISH

skit·tish \'skit-ish\ *adj* [ME] **1 a :** lively or frisky in action **:** CAPRICIOUS **b :** VARIABLE, FLUCTUATING **2 :** easily frightened **:** RESTIVE <a ~ horse> **3 a :** COY, BASHFUL **b :** marked by extreme caution **:** WARY — **skit·tish·ly** *adv* — **skit·tish·ness** *n*

skit·tle \'skit-ᵊl\ *n* [perh. of Scand origin; akin to ON *skutill* bolt — more at SHUTTLE] **1** *pl but sing in constr* **:** English ninepins played with a wooden disk or wooden ball **2 :** one of the pins used in skittles

skive \'skīv\ *vt* **skived; skiv·ing** [of Scand origin; akin to ON *skīfa* to slice; akin to OE *scēadan* to divide — more at SHED] **:** to cut off (as leather or rubber) in thin layers or pieces **:** PARE

skiv·er \'skī-vər\ *n* **1 :** a thin soft leather made of the grain side of a split sheepskin, usu. tanned in sumac and dyed **2 :** one that skives something (as leather)

skiv·vy \'skiv-ē\ *n, pl* **skivvies** [origin unknown] *Brit* **:** a female domestic servant

ski·wear \'skē-ˌwa(ə)r, -ˌwe(ə)r\ *n* **:** clothing suitable for wear while skiing

sklent \'sklent\ *vb* [ME *sclenten* to strike obliquely, alter. of *slenten* — more at SLANT] *vi* **1** *chiefly Scot* **:** to look askance **2** *chiefly Scot* **:** to cast aspersions ~ *vt, Scot* **:** to direct sideways **:** SLANT

skoal \'skōl\ *n* [Dan *skaal*, lit., cup; akin to ON *skāl* bowl — more at SCALE] **:** TOAST, HEALTH — often used interjectionally

Skt *abbr* Sanskrit

skua \'skyü-ə\ *n* [NL, fr. Faeroese *skūgvur*; akin to ON *skūfr* tassel, skua, OE *scēaf* sheaf — more at SHEAF] **:** JAEGER 2; *esp* **:** GREAT SKUA

skul·dug·gery *or* **skull·dug·gery** \ˌskəl-'dəg-(ə-)rē, 'skəl-ˌ\ *n, pl* **-ger·ies** [origin unknown] **:** a devious device or trick; *also* **:** underhanded or unscrupulous behavior

1skulk \'skəlk\ *vi* [ME *skulken*, of Scand origin; akin to Dan *skulke* to shirk, play truant] **1 :** to move in a stealthy or furtive manner **2 a :** to hide or conceal something (as oneself) often out of cowardice or fear or with sinister intent **b** *chiefly Brit* **:** MALINGER *syn* see LURK — **skulk·er** *n*

2skulk *n* **1 :** one that skulks **2 :** a group of foxes

skull \'skəl\ *n* [ME *skulle*, of Scand origin; akin to Sw *skulle* skull] **1 :** the skeleton of the head of a vertebrate forming a bony or cartilaginous case that encloses and protects the brain and chief sense organs and supports the jaws **2 :** the seat of understanding or intelligence **:** MIND — **skulled** \'skəld\ *adj*

skull and cross·bones \-'krós-ˌbōnz\ *n, pl* **skulls and cross·bones :** a representation of a human skull over crossbones usu. used as a warning of danger to life

skull·cap \'skəl-ˌkap\ *n* **1 :** a close-fitting cap; *esp* **:** a light cap without brim for indoor wear **2 :** any of various mints (genus *Scutellaria*) having a calyx that when inverted resembles a helmet

skull practice *n* **1 :** a strategy class for an athletic team **2 :** a meeting for consultation, discussion, or the interchange of ideas or information — called also *skull session*

1skunk \'skəŋk\ *n, pl* **skunks** *also* **skunk** [of Algonquian origin; akin to Abnaki *segākw* skunk] **1 a :** any of various common omnivorous black-and-white New World mammals (esp. genus *Mephitis*) related to the weasels and having a pair of perineal glands from which a secretion of pungent and offensive odor is ejected **b :** any of various offensive-smelling Old World animals **c :** the fur of a skunk **2 :** an obnoxious person

2skunk *vt* **1 a :** DEFEAT **b :** to shut out in a game **2 :** to fail to pay; *also* **:** CHEAT

skunk cabbage *n* **:** an eastern No. American perennial herb (*Symplocarpus foetidus*) of the arum family that sends up in early spring a cowl-shaped brownish purple spathe having an unpleasant odor; *also* **:** a related plant (*Lysichiton camstschatcense*) of the Pacific coast region

skunk cabbage (*Lysichiton camstschatcense*)

1sky \'skī\ *n, pl* **skies** [ME, cloud, sky, fr. ON *ský* cloud; akin to OE *scēo* cloud, L *cutis* skin — more at HIDE] **1 :** the upper atmosphere that constitutes an apparent great vault or arch over the earth **2 :** HEAVEN 2 **3 a :** weather in the upper atmosphere **b :** CLIMATE <temperate English *skies* —G. G. Coulton>

2sky *vt* **skied** *or* **skyed; sky·ing 1** *chiefly Brit* **:** to throw or toss up **:** FLIP **2 :** to hang (as a painting) above the line of vision

sky blue *n* **:** a variable color averaging a pale to light blue

sky·borne \'skī-ˌbō(ə)rn, -ˌbȯ(ə)rn\ *adj* **:** AIRBORNE <~ troops>

sky·cap \-ˌkap\ *n* [1*sky* + *-cap* (as in *redcap*)] **:** one employed to carry hand luggage at an airport — compare REDCAP

sky·div·ing \-ˌdī-viŋ\ *n* **:** the sport of jumping from an airplane at a moderate altitude (as 6000 feet) and executing various body maneuvers before pulling the rip cord of a parachute — **sky diver** *n*

Skye terrier \'skī-\ *n* [*Skye*, Scotland] **:** any of a Scottish breed of terriers with a long head, a long low body, and short straight legs

sky·ey \'skī-ē\ *adj* **:** of or resembling the sky **:** ETHEREAL

sky-high \'skī-'hī\ *adv or adj* **1 a :** high into the air **b :** to a high level or degree **2 :** in an enthusiastic manner **3 :** to bits **:** APART <blown ~> **4 :** in an exorbitant manner <prices rose ~>

sky·hook \-ˌhu̇k\ *n* **:** a hook conceived as being suspended from the sky

sky·jack·er \-ˌjak-ər\ *n* [*sky* + *-jacker* (as in *hijacker*)] **:** one who commandeers a flying airplane (as by coercing the pilot at gunpoint) — **sky·jack·ing** \-ˌjak-iŋ\ *n*

1sky·lark \'skī-ˌlärk\ *n* **1 :** a common largely brown Old World lark (*Alauda arvensis*) noted for its song esp. as uttered in vertical flight **2 :** any of various birds resembling the skylark

2skylark *vi* **1 :** to run up and down the rigging of a ship in sport **2 :** FROLIC, SPORT — **sky·lark·er** *n*

sky·light \'skī-ˌlīt\ *n* **1 :** the diffused and reflected light of the sky **2 :** an opening in a house roof or ship's deck that is covered with translucent or transparent material and that is designed to admit light

sky·line \-ˌlīn\ *n* **1 :** the apparent juncture of earth and sky **:** HORIZON **2 :** an outline (as of buildings or a mountain range) against the background of the sky

sky·lounge \-ˌlau̇nj\ *n* **:** a vehicle that picks up passengers and is then carried by helicopter between a downtown terminal and an airport

sky marshal *n* **:** an armed federal plainclothesman assigned to prevent skyjackings

sky·phos \'skī-ˌfäs, 'skē-ˌfós\ *n, pl* **sky·phoi** \'skī-ˌfȯi, 'skē-ˌfē\ **:** a deep drinking vessel with two horizontal handles used esp. in ancient Greece

sky pilot *n* **:** CLERGYMAN; *specif* **:** CHAPLAIN

1sky·rock·et \'skī-ˌräk-ət\ *n* **:** 2ROCKET 1a

2skyrocket *vi* **:** to shoot up abruptly <prices are ~*ing*> ~ *vt* **1 :** to cause to rise or increase abruptly and rapidly **2 :** CATAPULT

sky·sail \'skī-ˌsāl, -səl\ *n* **:** the sail above the royal

sky·scrap·er \-ˌskrā-pər\ *n* **:** a very tall building

sky·ward \-wərd\ *adv* **1 :** toward the sky **2 :** UPWARD

sky wave *n* **:** a radio wave that is propagated by means of the ionosphere

sky·way \'skī-ˌwā\ *n* **1 :** a route used by airplanes **:** AIR LANE **2 :** an elevated highway

sky·write \-ˌrīt\ *vb* **-wrote** \-ˌrōt\; **-writ·ten** \-ˌrit-ᵊn\; **-writ·ing** \-ˌrīt-iŋ\ [back-formation from *skywriting*] *vi* **:** to do skywriting ~ *vt* **:** to letter by skywriting — **sky·writ·er** *n*

sky·writ·ing \-ˌrīt-iŋ\ *n* **:** writing formed in the sky by means of a visible substance (as smoke) emitted from an airplane

sl *abbr* **1** slightly **2** slow

SL *abbr* **1** salvage loss **2** sea level **3** south latitude

1slab \'slab\ *n* [ME *slabbe*] **:** a thick plate or slice (as of stone, wood, or bread): as **a :** the outside piece cut from a log in squaring it **b :** concrete pavement (as of a road); *specif* **:** a strip of concrete pavement laid as a single unjointed piece

2slab *vt* **slabbed; slab·bing 1 a :** to divide or form into slabs **b :** to remove an outer slab from (as a log) **2 :** to cover or support (as a roadbed or roof) with slabs **3 :** to put on thickly

3slab *adj* [prob. of Scand origin; akin to obs. Dan *slab* slippery] *dial chiefly Eng* **:** THICK, VISCOUS

1slab·ber \'slab-ər\ *vb* **slab·bered; slab·ber·ing** \-(ə-)riŋ\ [prob. fr. D *slabberen*, freq. of *slabben* to slaver — more at SLAVER] **:** SLOBBER, DROOL

2slabber *n* **:** SLOBBER, SLAVER

slab-sid·ed \'slab-'sīd-əd\ *adj* **:** having flat sides; *also* **:** being tall or long and lank

1slack \'slak\ *adj* [ME *slak*, fr. OE *sleac*; akin to OHG *slah* slack, L *laxus* slack, loose, *languēre* to languish, Gk *lēgein* to stop] **1 :** not using due diligence, care, or dispatch **:** NEGLIGENT **2 a**

ə abut · ᵊ kitten · ər further · a back · ā bake · ä cot, cart
au̇ out · ch chin · e less · ē easy · g gift · i trip · ī life
j joke · ŋ sing · ō flow · ȯ flaw · ȯi coin · th thin · t͟h this
ü loot · u̇ foot · y yet · yü few · yu̇ furious · zh vision

: characterized by slowness, sluggishness, or lack of energy <a ~ pace> **b** : moderate in some quality; *esp* : moderately warm <a ~ oven> **c** : blowing or flowing at low speed <the tide was ~> **3 a** : not tight or taut <a ~ rope> **b** : lacking in usual or normal firmness and steadiness : WEAK <~ muscles> <~ supervision> **4** : wanting in activity : DULL <a ~ market> **5** : lacking in completeness, finish, or perfection <a very ~ piece of work> **6** : not watertight <~ cooperage> ***syn*** see NEGLIGENT, LOOSE — **slack·ly** *adv* — **slack·ness** *n*

^{2}slack *vt* **1 a** : to be slack or negligent in performing or doing **b** : LESSEN, MODERATE **2** : to release tension on : LOOSEN **3 a** : to cause to abate **b** : SLAKE 3 ~ *vi* **1** : to be or become slack **2** : to shirk or evade work or duty

^{3}slack *n* **1** : cessation in movement or flow **2** : a part of something that hangs loose without strain <take up the ~ of a rope> **3** *pl* : trousers esp. for casual wear **4** : a dull season or period

^{4}slack *n* [ME *slak,* fr. ON *slakki*] *dial Eng* : a pass between hills

^{5}slack *n* [ME *sleck*] : the finest screenings of coal produced at a mine unusable as fuel unless cleaned

slack–baked \ˈslak-ˈbākt\ *adj* **1** : UNDERDONE **2** : physically or mentally inferior : HALF-BAKED

slack·en \ˈslak-ən\ *vb* **slack·ened; slack·en·ing** \-(ə-)niŋ\ *vt* **1** : to make less active : slow up <~ speed at a crossing> **2** : to make slack (as by lessening tension or firmness) <~ sail> ~ *vi* **1** : to become slack or slow or negligent : slow down **2** : to become less active : SLACK ***syn*** see DELAY ***ant*** quicken

slack·er \ˈslak-ər\ *n* : a person who shirks work or obligation; *esp* : one who evades military service in time of war

slack water *n* : the period at the turn of the tide when there is little or no horizontal motion of tidal water — called also *slack tide*

slag \ˈslag\ *n* [MLG *slagge*] **1** : the dross or scoria of a metal : CINDER **2** : the scoriaceous lava from a volcano

slain *past part of* SLAY

slake \ˈslāk, *vi 2 & vt 3 are also* ˈslak\ *vb* **slaked; slak·ing** [ME *slaken,* fr. OE *slacian,* fr. *sleac* slack] *vi* **1** *archaic* : to die down : ABATE **2** : to become slaked : CRUMBLE <lime may ~ spontaneously in moist air> ~ *vt* **1** *archaic* : to lessen the force of : MODERATE **2** : SATISFY, QUENCH <~ your thirst> **3 a** : to cause (as lime) to heat and crumble by treatment with water : HYDRATE **b** : to alter (as lime) by exposure to air with conversion at least in part to a carbonate

sla·lom \ˈsläl-əm\ *n* [Norw, lit., sloping track] **1** : skiing in a zigzag or wavy course between upright obstacles (as flags); *also* : a race against time over such a course **2** : a race against time (as for automobiles or motorcycles) over a zigzag course usu. marked with traffic cones

^{1}slam \ˈslam\ *n* [origin unknown] **1** : GRAND SLAM **2** : LITTLE SLAM

^{2}slam *n* [prob. of Scand origin; akin to Icel *slæma* to slam] **1** : a heavy blow or impact **2 a** : a noisy violent closing **b** : a banging noise; *esp* : one made by the slam of a door **3** : a cutting or violent criticism

^{3}slam *vb* **slammed; slam·ming** *vt* **1** : to strike or beat hard : KNOCK **2** : to shut forcibly and noisily : BANG **3 a** : to set or slap down violently or noisily <*slammed* his fist on the table> **b** : to propel, thrust, or produce by striking hard <~ on the brakes> **4** : to criticize harshly ~ *vi* **1** : to make a banging noise **2** : to work or act noisily **3** : to utter verbal abuse

slam–bang \ˈslam-ˈbaŋ\ *adj* **1** : unduly loud or violent <a ~ clatter> **2** : notably vigorous <made a ~ effort to win>

SLAN *abbr* [L *sine loco, anno, (vel) nomine*] without place, year, or name

^{1}slan·der \ˈslan-dər\ *n* [ME *sclaundre, slaundre,* fr. OF *esclandre,* fr. LL *scandalum* stumbling block, offense — more at SCANDAL] **1** : the utterance of false charges or misrepresentations which defame and damage another's reputation **2** : a false and defamatory oral statement about a person — compare LIBEL — **slan·der·ous** \-d(ə-)rəs\ *adj* — **slan·der·ous·ly** *adv* — **slan·der·ous·ness** *n*

^{2}slander *vt* **slan·dered; slan·der·ing** \-d(ə-)riŋ\ : to utter slander against : DEFAME ***syn*** see MALIGN — **slan·der·er** \-dər-ər\ *n*

^{1}slang \ˈslaŋ\ *n* [origin unknown] **1** : language peculiar to a particular group: as **a** : ARGOT **b** : JARGON 2 **2** : an informal nonstandard vocabulary composed typically of coinages, arbitrarily changed words, and extravagant, forced, or facetious figures of speech ***syn*** see DIALECT — **slang** *adj* — **slang·i·ly** \ˈslaŋ-ə-lē\ *adv* — **slang·i·ness** \ˈslaŋ-ē-nəs\ *n* — **slangy** \ˈslaŋ-ē\ *adj*

^{2}slang *vt* : to abuse with harsh or coarse language ~ *vi* : to use slang or vulgar abuse

^{1}slant \ˈslant\ *vb* [ME *slenten* to fall obliquely, of Scand origin; akin to Sw *slinta* to slide; akin to OE *slīdan* to slide] *vi* **1** : to turn or incline from a right line or a level : SLOPE **2** : to take a diagonal course, direction, or path ~ *vt* **1** : to give an oblique or sloping direction to **2** : to interpret or present in line with a special interest : ANGLE <stories ~*ed* toward youth>; *specif* : to maliciously or dishonestly distort or falsify — **slant·ing·ly** \-iŋ-lē\ *adv*

syn SLANT, SLOPE, INCLINE, LEAN *shared meaning element* : to diverge from the vertical or horizontal

^{2}slant *n* **1** : a slanting direction, line, or plane : SLOPE **2 a** : something that slants **b** : DIAGONAL 3 **c** : a football running play in which the ballcarrier runs obliquely toward the line of scrimmage **3 a** : a peculiar or personal point of view, attitude, or opinion **b** : a slanting view : GLANCE — **slant** *adj* — **slant·ways** \-ˌwāz\ *adv* — **slant·wise** \-ˌwīz\ *adv or adj*

slant height *n* **1** : the length of an element of a right circular cone **2** : the altitude of a side of a regular pyramid

^{1}slap \ˈslap\ *n* [ME *slop,* fr. MD; akin to MD *slippen* to slip] *dial Brit* : OPENING, BREACH

^{2}slap *n* [LG *slapp,* of imit. origin] **1 a** : a blow with the open hand **b** : a quick sharp blow **2** : a noise like that of a slap; *esp* : a noise resulting from play or slackness between parts of a machine **3** : REBUFF, INSULT

^{3}slap *vt* **slapped; slap·ping** **1** : to strike sharply with or as if with the open hand **2** : to put, place, or throw with careless haste or force **3** : to assail verbally : INSULT ***syn*** see STRIKE

^{4}slap *adv* [prob. fr. LG *slapp,* fr. *slapp,* n.] : DIRECTLY, SMACK

slap·dash \ˈslap-ˈdash, -ˌdash\ *adj* : HAPHAZARD, SLIPSHOD

slap down *vt* **1** : to prohibit or restrain usu. abruptly and with censure from acting in a specified way : SQUELCH **2** : to put an abrupt stop to : SUPPRESS

slap·hap·py \ˈslap-ˌhap-ē\ *adj* **1** : PUNCH-DRUNK **2** : buoyantly or recklessly carefree or foolish : HAPPY-GO-LUCKY

slap·jack \-ˌjak\ *n* [^{3}*slap* + *-jack* (as in *flapjack*)] **1** : PANCAKE **2** : a card game in which each player tries to be the first to slap his hand on any jack that appears face up

slap shot *n* : a shot in ice hockey made with a swinging stroke

slap·stick \ˈslap-ˌstik\ *n* **1** : a device made of two flat pieces of wood fastened at one end so as to make a loud noise when used by an actor to strike a person **2** : comedy stressing farce and horseplay — **slapstick** *adj*

^{1}slash \ˈslash\ *vb* [ME *slaschen*] *vt* **1** : to cut with rough sweeping strokes **2** : CANE, LASH **3** : to cut slits in (as a garment) so as to reveal a color beneath **4** : to criticize cuttingly **5** : to reduce sharply : CUT ~ *vi* : to cut, lash at, or hit recklessly or savagely with or as if with an edged blade — **slash·er** *n*

^{2}slash *n* **1** : the act of slashing; *also* : a long cut or stroke made by or as if by slashing **2** : an ornamental slit in a garment **3** : an open tract in a forest strewn with debris (as from logging); *also* : the debris in such a tract

^{3}slash *n* [prob. alter. of *plash* (marshy pool)] : a low swampy area often overgrown with brush

slash–and–burn *adj* : characterized or developed by girdling, felling, and burning trees to make land arable usu. for a temporary purpose

^{1}slash·ing \ˈslash-iŋ\ *n* **1** : the act or process of slashing **2** : an insert or underlayer of contrasting color revealed by a slash (as in a garment) **3** : SLASH 3

^{2}slashing *adj* **1** : incisively satiric or critical **2** : DRIVING, PELTING **3** : VIVID, BRILLIANT — **slash·ing·ly** \-iŋ-lē\ *adv*

slash pine *n* [^{3}*slash*] : a southern pine (*Pinus elliottii*) that is an important source of turpentine and lumber

slash pocket *n* : a pocket suspended on the wrong side of a garment from a finished slit on the right side that serves as its opening

^{1}slat \ˈslat\ *n* [ME, slate, fr. MF *esclat* splinter, fr. OF, fr. *esclater* to burst, splinter] **1** : a thin narrow flat strip esp. of wood or metal: as **a** : LATH **b** : LOUVER **c** : STAVE **d** : one of the thin flat members in the back of a ladder-back chair **2** *pl, slang* : RIBS — **slat** *adj*

^{2}slat *vt* **slat·ted; slat·ting** : to make or equip with slats

^{3}slat *vt* **slat·ted; slat·ting** [prob. of Scand origin; akin to ON *sletta* to slap, throw] **1** : to hurl or throw smartly **2** : STRIKE, PUMMEL

^{1}slate \ˈslāt\ *n* [ME, fr. MF *esclat* splinter] **1** : a piece of construction material (as laminated rock) prepared as a shingle for roofing and siding **2** : a dense fine-grained metamorphic rock produced by the compression of various sediments (as clay or shale) so as to develop a characteristic cleavage **3** : a tablet of material (as slate) used for writing on **4** : a list of candidates for nomination or election **5 a** : a dark purplish gray **b** : any of various grays similar in color to common roofing slates — **slate** *adj* — **slate·like** \-ˌlīk\ *adj*

^{2}slate *vt* **slat·ed; slat·ing** **1** : to cover with slate or a slatelike substance <~ a roof> **2** : to register, schedule, or designate for action or appointment

^{3}slate *vt* **slat·ed; slat·ing** [prob. alter. of ^{3}*slat*] **1** : to thrash or pummel severely **2** *chiefly Brit* : to criticize or censure severely

slate black *n* : a nearly neutral slightly purplish black

slate blue *n* : a variable color averaging a grayish blue

slat·er \ˈslāt-ər\ *n* **1** : one that slates **2** [^{1}*slate;* fr. its color] **a** : WOOD LOUSE 1 **b** : any of various marine isopods — called also *sea slater*

^{1}slath·er \ˈslat͟h-ər\ *n* [origin unknown] : a great quantity — often used in pl.

^{2}slather *vt* **slath·ered; slath·er·ing** \-(ə-)riŋ\ **1 a** : to spread thickly or lavishly **b** : to spread something thickly or lavishly on **2** : to use or spend in a wasteful or lavish manner : SQUANDER

slat·ing \ˈslāt-iŋ\ *n* **1** : the work of a slater **2** : material used for slating : SLATES

^{1}slat·tern \ˈslat-ərn\ *n* [prob. fr. G *schlottern* to hang loosely, slouch; akin to D *slodderen* to hang loosely, *slodder* slut] : an untidy slovenly woman; *also* : SLUT, PROSTITUTE

^{2}slattern *adj* : SLATTERNLY

slat·tern·ly \ˈslat-ərn-lē\ *adj* **1** : untidy and dirty through habitual neglect; *also* : CARELESS, DISORDERLY **2** : of, relating to, or characteristic of a slut or prostitute — **slat·tern·li·ness** *n*

slaty \ˈslāt-ē\ *adj* : of, containing, or characteristic of slate; *also* : gray like slate

^{1}slaugh·ter \ˈslȯt-ər\ *n* [ME, of Scand origin; akin to ON *slātra* to slaughter; akin to OE *sleaht* slaughter, *slēan* to slay — more at SLAY] **1** : the act of killing; *specif* : the butchering of livestock for market **2** : killing of great numbers of human beings (as in battle or a massacre) : CARNAGE ***syn*** see MASSACRE

^{2}slaughter *vt* **1** : to kill (animals) for food : BUTCHER **2 a** : to kill in a bloody or violent manner : SLAY **b** : to kill in large numbers : MASSACRE — **slaugh·ter·er** \-ər-ər\ *n*

slaugh·ter·house \ˈslȯt-ər-ˌhau̇s\ *n* : an establishment where animals are butchered

slaugh·ter·ous \ˈslȯt-ə-rəs\ *adj* : of or relating to slaughter : MURDEROUS — **slaugh·ter·ous·ly** *adv*

^{1}Slav \ˈsläv, ˈslav\ *n* [ME *Sclav,* fr. ML *Sclavus,* fr. LGk *Sklabos,* fr. *Sklabēnoi* Slavs, of Slav origin; akin to OSlav *Slověne,* a Slavic people in the area of Salonika] : a person who speaks a Slavic language as his native tongue

^{2}Slav *abbr* Slavic

^{1}slave \ˈslāv\ *n* [ME *sclave,* fr. OF or ML; OF *esclave,* fr. ML *sclavus,* fr. *Sclavus* Slav; fr. the reduction to slavery of many Slavic peoples of central Europe] **1 :** a person held in servitude as the chattel of another : BONDMAN **2 :** a person who has lost control of himself and is dominated by something or someone <a ~ to drink> **3 :** a mechanical device (as the typewriter unit of a computer) that is directly responsive to another **4 :** DRUDGE, TOILER — **slave** *adj*

2slave *vb* **slaved; slav·ing** *vt* **1** *archaic* **:** ENSLAVE **2 :** to make directly responsive to another mechanism ~ *vi* **1 :** to work like a slave : DRUDGE **2 :** to traffic in slaves

slave ant *n* **:** an ant enslaved by a slave-making ant

slave driver *n* **1 :** a supervisor of slaves at work **2 :** a harsh taskmaster

slave·hold·er \'slāv-ˌhōl-dər\ *n* **:** an owner of slaves — **slave·hold·ing** \-diŋ\ *adj or n*

slave–mak·ing ant \'slāv-ˌmā-kiŋ-\ *n* **:** an ant that attacks the colonies of ants of other species and carries off the larvae and pupae to be reared in its own nest as slaves

1sla·ver \'slav-ər, 'slāv-, 'släv-\ *vb* **sla·vered; sla·ver·ing** \-(ə-)riŋ\ [ME *slaveren,* of Scand origin; akin to ON *slafra* to slaver; akin to MD *slabben* to slaver, L *labi* to slip — more at SLEEP] *vi* **:** DROOL, SLOBBER ~ *vt, archaic* **:** to smear with or as if with saliva

2slaver *n* **:** saliva dribbling from the mouth

3slav·er \'slā-vər\ *n* **1 a :** a person engaged in the slave trade **b :** a ship used in the slave trade **2 :** WHITE SLAVER

slav·ery \'slāv-(ə-)rē\ *n* **1 :** DRUDGERY, TOIL **2 :** submission to a dominating influence **3 a :** the state of a person who is a chattel of another **b :** the practice of slaveholding ***syn*** see SERVITUDE

slave state *n* **1 :** a state of the U.S. in which Negro slavery was legal until the Civil War **2 :** a nation subjected to totalitarian rule

slave trade *n* **:** traffic in slaves; *esp* **:** the buying and selling of Negroes for profit prior to the American Civil War

slav·ey \'slā-vē\ *n, pl* **slaveys :** DRUDGE; *esp* **:** a household servant who does general housework

1Slav·ic \'slav-ik, 'släv-\ *adj* **:** of, relating to, or characteristic of the Slavs or their languages

2Slavic *n* **:** a branch of the Indo-European language family containing Belorussian, Bulgarian, Czech, Polish, Serbo-Croatian, Slovene, Russian, and Ukrainian — see INDO-EUROPEAN LANGUAGES table

Slav·i·cist \'slav-ə-səst, 'släv-\ *n* **:** a specialist in the Slavic languages or literatures

slav·ish \'slā-vish\ *adj* **1 a :** of or characteristic of a slave; *esp* **:** basely or abjectly servile **b** *archaic* **:** DESPICABLE, LOW **2** *archaic* **:** OPPRESSIVE, TYRANNICAL **3 :** copying obsequiously or without originality : IMITATIVE ***syn*** see SUBSERVIENT — **slav·ish·ly** *adv* — **slav·ish·ness** *n*

Slav·ist \'släv-əst, 'slav-\ *n* **:** SLAVICIST

slav·oc·ra·cy \slā-'väk-rə-sē\ *n* **:** a powerful faction of slaveholders and advocates of slavery in the South before the Civil War

1Sla·vo·ni·an \slə-'vō-nē-ən\ *n* [*Slavonia,* region of southeast Europe, fr. ML *Sclavonia, Slavonia* land of the Slavs, fr. *Sclavus* Slav] **:** SLOVENE 1b

2Slavonian *adj* **1 :** SLOVENE **2** *archaic* **:** SLAVIC

1Sla·von·ic \slə-'vän-ik\ *adj* [NL *slavonicus,* fr. ML *Sclavonia, Slavonia* land of the Slavs] **:** SLAVIC

2Slavonic *n* **1 :** SLAVIC **2 :** OLD CHURCH SLAVONIC

Slav·o·phile \'slav-ə-ˌfil, 'släv-\ *or* **Slav·o·phil** \-ˌfil\ *n* **:** an admirer of the Slavs : an advocate of Slavophilism

Slav·oph·i·lism \sla-'väf-ə-ˌliz-əm, 'slav-ə-ˌfi-ˌliz-\ *n* **:** advocacy of Slavic and specif. Russian culture over that of the West esp. as practiced among some members of the Russian intelligentsia in the middle 19th century

slaw \'slȯ\ *n* **:** COLESLAW

slay \'slā\ *vb* **slew** \'slü\; **slain** \'slān\; **slay·ing** [ME *slen,* fr. OE *slēan* to strike, slay; akin to OHG *slahan* to strike, MIr *slacain* I beat] *vt* **1 :** to kill violently, wantonly, or in great numbers **2** *slang* **:** to affect overpoweringly : OVERWHELM ~ *vi* **:** KILL, MURDER ***syn*** see KILL — **slay·er** *n*

sld *abbr* **1** sailed **2** sealed **3** sold

1sleave \'slēv\ *vt* [(assumed) ME *sleven,* fr. OE *-slǣfan* to cut — more at SLIVER] *obs* **:** to separate (silk thread) into filaments

2sleave *n* **:** SKEIN <sleep that knits up the raveled ~ of care —Shak.>

sleave silk *n, obs* **:** floss silk that is easily separated into filaments for embroidery

slea·zy \'slē-zē *also* 'slā-\ *adj* **slea·zi·er; -est** [origin unknown] **1 a :** lacking firmness of texture : FLIMSY **b :** carelessly made of inferior materials : SHODDY **2 :** marked by cheapness of character or quality ***syn*** see LIMP — **slea·zi·ly** \-zə-lē\ *adv* — **slea·zi·ness** \-zē-nəs\ *n*

1sled \'sled\ *n* [ME *sledde,* fr. MD; akin to OE *slīdan* to slide] **1 :** a vehicle on runners for transportation esp. on snow or ice; *esp* **:** a small one for coasting down snow-covered hills **2 :** a sled used esp. by children for coasting down snow-covered hills

2sled *vb* **sled·ded; sled·ding** *vt* **:** SLEDGE ~ *vi* **:** to ride on a sled or sleigh — **sled·der** *n*

sled·ding *n* **1 a :** the use of a sled **b :** the conditions under which one may use a sled **2 :** GOING 4

sled dog *n* **:** a dog trained to draw a sledge esp. in the Arctic regions — called also *sledge dog*

1sledge \'slej\ *n* [ME *slegge,* fr. OE *slecg;* akin to ON *sleggja* sledgehammer, OE *slēan* to strike — more at SLAY] **:** SLEDGEHAMMER

2sledge *vb* **sledged; sledg·ing :** SLEDGEHAMMER

3sledge *n* [D dial. *sleedse;* akin to MD *sledde* sled] **1** *Brit* **:** SLEIGH **2 :** a vehicle with low runners that is used for transporting loads esp. over snow or ice

4sledge *vb* **sledged; sledg·ing** *vi* **1** *Brit* **:** to ride in a sleigh **2 :** to travel with a sledge ~ *vt* **:** to transport on a sledge

1sledge·ham·mer \'slej-ˌham-ər\ *n* [*1sledge*] **:** a large heavy hammer that is wielded with both hands — **sledgehammer** *adj*

2sledgehammer *vt* **:** to strike with or as if with a sledgehammer ~ *vi* **:** to strike blows with or as if with a sledgehammer

1sleek \'slēk\ *vb* [ME *sleken,* alter. of *sliken*] *vt* **1 :** SLICK **2 :** to cover up : gloss over ~ *vi* **:** SLICK

2sleek *adj* [alter. of *2slick*] **1 a :** smooth and glossy as if polished <~ dark hair> **b :** having a smooth well-groomed look <~ cattle grazing> **c :** healthy-looking **2 :** SLICK 3 **3 a :** having a prosperous air : THRIVING **b :** ELEGANT, STYLISH — **sleek·ly** *adv* — **sleek·ness** *n*

sleek·en \'slē-kən\ *vt* **sleek·ened; sleek·en·ing** \'slēk-(ə-)niŋ\ **:** to make sleek

sleek·it \'slē-kət\ *adj* [Sc, fr. pp. of *1sleek*] **1** *chiefly Scot* **:** SLEEK, SMOOTH **2** *chiefly Scot* **:** CRAFTY, DECEITFUL

1sleep \'slēp\ *n* [ME *slepe,* fr. OE *slǣp;* akin to OHG *slāf* sleep, L *labi* to slip, slide and perh. to Gk *lobos* pod, lobe] **1 :** the natural periodic suspension of consciousness during which the powers of the body are restored **2 :** a state resembling sleep: as **a :** a state of torpid inactivity **b :** DEATH <put a pet cat to ~>; *also* **:** TRANCE, COMA **c :** the closing of leaves or petals esp. at night **d :** a state marked by a diminution of feeling followed by tingling <his foot went to ~> **e :** the state of an animal during hibernation <the groundhog's winter ~> **3 a :** a period spent sleeping **b :** NIGHT **c :** a day's journey — **sleep·like** \'slē-ˌplīk\ *adj*

2sleep *vb* **slept** \'slept\; **sleep·ing** *vi* **1 :** to rest in a state of sleep **2 :** to be in a state (as of quiescence or death) resembling sleep **3 :** to have sexual relations ~ *vt* **1 :** to be slumbering in <*slept* the sleep of the dead> **2 :** to get rid of or spend in or by sleep <~ away the hours> <~ off a drunk> **3 :** to provide sleeping accommodations for <the boat ~*s* six>

sleep·er \'slē-pər\ *n* **1 :** one that sleeps **2 :** a piece of timber, stone, or steel on or near the ground to support a superstructure, keep railroad rails in place, or receive floor joists : STRINGPIECE **3 :** SLEEPING CAR **4 :** someone or something unpromising or unnoticed that suddenly attains prominence or value **5 :** a calf earmarked but not branded **6** *pl* **:** children's pajamas usu. with feet

sleep–in \ˌslē-ˌpin\ *adj* **:** that lives at the place of employment <a ~ maid>

sleep in \'slē-'pin\ *vi* **1 :** to sleep where one is employed **2 a :** OVERSLEEP **b :** to sleep late intentionally

sleeping bag *n* **:** a bag that is warmly lined or padded for sleeping outdoors or in a camp or tent

Sleeping Beauty *n* **:** a princess of a fairy tale who is wakened from an enchanted sleep by the kiss of a prince

sleeping car *n* **:** a railroad passenger car having berths for sleeping

sleeping partner *n* **:** a silent partner whose connection with the business is not publicly known

sleeping pill *n* **:** a drug and esp. a barbiturate that is taken as a tablet or capsule to induce sleep — called also *sleeping tablet*

sleeping porch *n* **:** a porch or room having open sides or many windows arranged to permit sleeping in the open air

sleeping sickness *n* **1 :** a serious disease that is prevalent in much of tropical Africa, is marked by fever, protracted lethargy, tremors, and loss of weight, is caused by either of two trypanosomes (*Trypanosoma gambiense* and *T. rhodesiense*), and is transmitted by tsetse flies **2 :** any of various viral encephalitides or encephalomyelitides of which lethargy or somnolence is a prominent feature

sleep·less \'slē-pləs\ *adj* **1 :** not able to sleep : INSOMNIAC **2 :** affording no sleep **3 :** unceasingly active — **sleep·less·ly** *adv* — **sleep·less·ness** *n*

sleep out *vi* **1 :** to sleep outdoors **2 :** to go home at night from one's place of employment **3 :** to sleep away from home

sleep·walk·er \'slēp-ˌwȯ-kər\ *n* **:** one that walks in his sleep : SOMNAMBULIST — **sleep·walk** \-ˌwȯk\ *vi*

sleepy \'slē-pē\ *adj* **sleep·i·er; -est 1 a :** ready to fall asleep **b :** of, relating to, or characteristic of sleep **2 :** sluggish as if from sleep : LETHARGIC; *also* **:** INACTIVE **3 :** sleep-inducing — **sleep·i·ly** \-pə-lē\ *adv* — **sleep·i·ness** \-pē-nəs\ *n*

syn SLEEPY, DROWSY, SOMNOLENT, SLUMBEROUS *shared meaning element* **:** affected by or inducing a desire to sleep

sleepy·head \'slē-pē-ˌhed\ *n* **:** a sleepy person

1sleet \'slēt\ *n* [ME *slete;* akin to MHG *slōz* hailstone, ME *sloor* mud — more at SLUR] **1 :** frozen or partly frozen rain **2 :** GLAZE 1 — **sleety** \-ē\ *adj*

2sleet *vi* **:** to shower sleet

sleeve \'slēv\ *n* [ME *sleve,* fr. OE *slīefe;* akin to OE *slēfan* to slip (clothes) on, *slūpan* to slip, OHG *sliofan,* L *lubricus* slippery] **1 a :** a part of a garment covering an arm **b :** SLEEVELET **2 :** a tubular machine part (as a hollow axle or a bushing) designed to fit over another part **3 :** JACKET 3c(4) — **sleeved** \'slēvd\ *adj* — **sleeve·less** \'slēv-ləs\ *adj* — **up one's sleeve :** held secretly in reserve

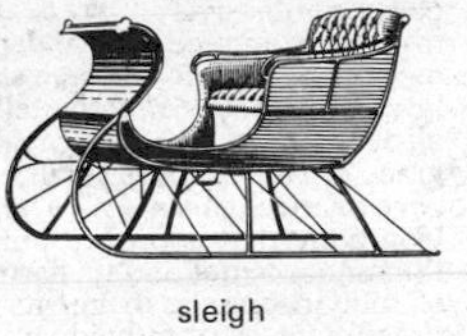

sleigh

sleeve·let \'slēv-lət\ *n* **:** a covering for the forearm to protect clothing from wear or dirt

1sleigh \'slā\ *n* [D *slee,* alter. of *slede;* akin to MD *sledde* sled] **:** a vehicle on runners used for transporting persons or goods on snow or ice

2sleigh *vi* **:** to drive or travel in a sleigh

sleigh bed *n* **:** a bed common esp. in the first half of the 19th century having a solid headboard and footboard that roll outward at the top

sleigh bell *n* **:** any of various bells commonly attached to a sleigh or to the harness of a horse drawing a sleigh: as **a :** CASCABEL 2 **b :** a hemispherical bell with an attached clapper

sleight \'slīt\ *n* [ME, fr. ON *slœgth,* fr. *slœgr* sly — more at SLY] **1 :** deceitful craftiness; *also* **:** STRATAGEM **2 :** DEXTERITY, SKILL

sleight of hand **1 a :** skill and dexterity in juggling or conjuring tricks **b :** adroitness in deception **2 :** a conjuring or juggling trick requiring sleight of hand

slen·der \'slen-dər\ *adj* [ME *sclendre, slendre*] **1 a :** spare in frame or flesh; *esp* **:** gracefully slight **b :** small or narrow in circumference or width in proportion to length or height **2 :** limited or inadequate in amount **:** MEAGER ***syn*** see THIN — **slen·der·ly** *adv* — **slen·der·ness** *n*

slen·der·ize \-də-ˌrīz\ *vt* **-ized; -iz·ing :** to make slender

[1]**sleuth** \'slüth\ *n* [short for *sleuthhound*] **:** DETECTIVE

[2]**sleuth** *vi* **:** to act as a detective

sleuth·hound \'slüth-ˌhau̇nd\ *n* [ME, fr. *sleuth* track of an animal or person (fr. ON *slōth*) + *hound*] **1 :** a hound that tracks by scent; *specif* **:** BLOODHOUND **2 :** DETECTIVE

[1]**slew** \'slü\ *past of* SLAY

[2]**slew** *var of* SLOUGH

[3]**slew** *var of* SLUE

[4]**slew** *n* [IrGael *sluagh*] **:** a large number

[1]**slice** \'slīs\ *n* [ME, fr. MF *esclice* splinter, fr. OF, fr. *esclicier* to splinter, of Gmc origin; akin to OHG *slīzan* to tear apart — more at SLIT] **1 a :** a thin flat piece cut from something **b :** a wedge-shaped piece (as of pie or cake) **2 :** a spatula for spreading paint or ink **3 :** a serving knife with wedge-shaped blade <a fish ~> **4 :** a flight of a ball that deviates from a straight course in the direction of the dominant hand of the player propelling it; *also* **:** a ball following such a course — compare HOOK **5 :** PORTION, SHARE <a ~ of the profits>

[2]**slice** *vb* **sliced; slic·ing** *vt* **1 :** to cut with or as if with a knife **2 :** to stir or spread with a slice **3 :** to hit (a ball) so that a slice results ~ *vi* **:** to slice something — **slic·er** *n*

slice bar *n* **:** a steel bar with a broad flat blade for chipping or scraping (as in breaking up clinkers)

slice–of–life *adj* [fr. the n. phrase *slice of life,* trans. of F *tranche de vie*] **:** of, relating to, or marked by the accurate transcription (as into drama) of a segment of actual life experience

[1]**slick** \'slik\ *vb* [ME *sliken;* akin to OHG *slīhhan* to glide, Gk *leios* smooth] *vt* **:** to make sleek or smooth ~ *vi* **:** SPRUCE — usu. used with *up*

[2]**slick** *adj* **1 a :** having a smooth surface **:** SLIPPERY **b :** having surface plausibility **:** GLIB **c :** based on stereotype **:** TRITE **2** *archaic* **:** SLEEK 1 **3 a :** characterized by subtlety or nimble wit **:** CLEVER; *esp* **:** WILY **b :** DEFT, SKILLFUL **4 :** extremely good **:** FIRST-RATE — **slick** *adv* — **slick·ly** *adv* — **slick·ness** *n*

[3]**slick** *n* **1 a :** something that is smooth or slippery; *esp* **:** a smooth patch of water covered with a film of oil **b :** a film of oil **2 :** an implement for producing a slick surface: as **a :** a flat paddle usu. of steel for smoothing a sample of flour **b :** a foundry tool for smoothing the surface of a sand mold or unbaked core **3 :** a popular magazine printed on coated stock **4 :** an automobile tire made without a tread for maximum traction (as in drag racing)

slick–ear \'slik-ˌi(ə)r\ *n* **:** a range animal lacking an earmark

slick·en·side \'slik-ən-ˌsīd\ *n* [E dial. *slicken* smooth (alter. of E [2]*slick*) + E *side*] **:** a smooth often striated surface produced on rock by movement along a fault or a subsidiary fracture — usu. used in pl.

slick·er \'slik-ər\ *n* **1** [[2]*slick*] **:** OILSKIN; *broadly* **:** RAINCOAT **2** [*slick* (to defraud cleverly)] **a :** a clever crook **:** SWINDLER **b :** a city dweller esp. of natty appearance or sophisticated mannerisms

[1]**slide** \'slīd\ *vb* **slid** \'slid\; **slid·ing** \'slīd-iŋ\ [ME *sliden,* fr. OE *slīdan;* akin to MHG *slīten* to slide, Gk *leios* smooth — more at LIME] *vi* **1 a :** to move smoothly along a surface **:** SLIP **b :** to coast over snow or ice **c :** to approach a base in baseball by gliding along the ground usu. feet first with the weight of the body supported esp. on one hip **2 a :** to slip or fall by loss of footing **b :** to change position or become dislocated **:** SHIFT **3 a :** to slither along the ground **:** CRAWL **b :** to stream along **:** FLOW **4 :** to take a natural course **:** DRIFT <let his affairs ~> **5 a :** to pass unobtrusively **:** STEAL **b :** to pass by gradations <the economy *slid* from recession to depression> ~ *vt* **1 a :** to cause to glide or slip **b :** to traverse in a sliding manner **2 :** to put unobtrusively or stealthily <*slid* the bill into his hand>

[2]**slide** *n* **1 a :** an act or instance of sliding **b** (1) **:** a musical grace of two or more small notes (2) **:** PORTAMENTO **2 :** a sliding part or mechanism: as **a** (1) **:** a U-shaped section of tube in the trombone that is pushed out and in to produce the tones between the fundamental and its harmonics (2) **:** a short U-shaped section of tube in brass instruments that is used to adjust the pitch of the instrument or of individual valves **b** (1) **:** a moving piece (as the ram of a punch press) that is guided by a part along which it slides (2) **:** a guiding surface (as a feeding mechanism) along which something slides **c :** SLIDING SEAT **3 a :** the descent of a mass of earth, rock, or snow down a hill or mountainside **b :** a dislocation in which one rock mass in a mining lode has slid on another **:** FAULT **4 a** (1) **:** a slippery surface for coasting (2) **:** a chute with a slippery bed down which children slide in play **b :** a channel or track on which something is slid **c :** a sloping trough down which objects are carried by gravity <a log ~> **5 a :** a flat piece of glass on which an object is mounted for microscopic examination **b :** a photographic transparency on a small plate or film arranged for projection

slide fastener *n* **:** ZIPPER

slid·er \'slīd-ər\ *n* **1 :** one that slides **2 :** a fastball that breaks slightly in the same direction as a curve

slide rule *n* **:** an instrument consisting in its simple form of a ruler and a medial slide that are graduated with similar logarithmic scales, labeled with the corresponding antilogarithms, and used for rapid calculation

slide valve *n* **:** a valve that opens and closes a passageway by sliding over a port; *specif* **:** such a valve often used in steam engines for admitting steam to the piston and releasing it

slide·way \'slīd-ˌwā\ *n* **:** a way along which something slides

sliding scale *n* **1 :** a wage scale geared to the selling price of the product or to the cost-of-living index but usu. guaranteeing a minimum below which the wage will not fall **2 a :** a system for raising or lowering tariffs in accord with price changes **b :** a flexible scale (as of fees or subsidies) adjusted to the needs or income of individuals <the *sliding scale* of medical fees>

sliding seat *n* **:** a rower's seat (as in a racing shell) that slides fore and aft — called also *slide*

slier *comparative of* SLY

sliest *superlative of* SLY

[1]**slight** \'slīt\ *adj* [ME, smooth, slight, prob. fr. MD *slicht;* akin to OHG *slīhhan* to glide — more at SLICK] **1 a :** having a slim or delicate build **:** not stout or massive in body **b :** lacking in strength or substance **:** FLIMSY, FRAIL **c :** deficient in weight, solidity, or importance **:** TRIVIAL **2 :** small of its kind or in amount **:** SCANTY, MEAGER ***syn*** see THIN — **slight·ly** *adv* — **slight·ness** *n*

[2]**slight** *vt* **1 :** to treat as slight or unimportant **:** make light of **2 :** to treat with disdain or indifference **3 :** to perform or attend to carelessly and inadequately **4 :** [1]SLUR 3 ***syn*** see NEGLECT

[3]**slight** *n* **1 :** an act or an instance of slighting **2 :** an instance of being slighted **:** a humiliating discourtesy

slight·ing *adj* **:** characterized by disregard or disrespect **:** DISPARAGING <a ~ remark> — **slight·ing·ly** \-iŋ-lē\ *adv*

sli·ly *var of* SLYLY

[1]**slim** \'slim\ *adj* **slim·mer; slim·mest** [D, bad, inferior, fr. MD *slimp* crooked, bad; akin to MHG *slimp* awry] **1 :** of small diameter or thickness in proportion to the height or length **:** SLENDER **2 a :** MEAN, WORTHLESS **b :** ADROIT, CRAFTY **3 a :** inferior in quality or amount **:** SLIGHT **b :** SCANTY, SMALL <a ~ chance> ***syn*** see THIN ***ant*** chubby (*of persons*) — **slim·ly** *adv* — **slim·ness** *n*

[2]**slim** *vb* **slimmed; slim·ming** *vt* **:** to make slender ~ *vi* **:** to become slender

[1]**slime** \'slīm\ *n* [ME, fr. OE *slīm;* akin to OHG *slīmen* to smooth, L *lima* file — more at LIME] **1 :** soft moist earth or clay; *esp* **:** viscous mud **2 :** a viscous or glutinous substance: as **a :** a mucous or mucoid secretion of various animals (as slugs and catfishes) **b :** a product of wet crushing consisting of ore ground so fine as to pass a 200-mesh screen

[2]**slime** *vb* **slimed; slim·ing** *vt* **1 :** to smear or cover with slime **2 :** to remove slime from (as fish for canning) **3 :** to crush or grind (ore) to a slime ~ *vi* **:** to become slimy

slime mold *n* **:** any of a group (Myxomycetes or Mycetozoa) of organisms usu. held to be lower fungi but sometimes considered protozoan that exist vegetatively as mobile plasmodia and reproduce by spores

slim–jim \'slim-'jim, -ˌjim\ *n* [[1]*slim* + *Jim,* nickname for *James*] **:** one that is notably slender — **slim–jim** *adj*

slim·ming *adj* **:** giving an effect of slenderness

slim·sy *or* **slimp·sy** \'slim-zē, 'slim(p)-sē\ *adj* [blend of *slim* and *flimsy*] **:** FLIMSY, FRAIL

slimy \'slī-mē\ *adj* **slim·i·er; -est** **1 :** of, relating to, or resembling slime **:** VISCOUS; *also* **:** covered with or yielding slime **2 :** VILE, OFFENSIVE — **slim·i·ly** \-mə-lē\ *adv* — **slim·i·ness** \-mē-nəs\ *n*

[1]**sling** \'sliŋ\ *vt* **slung** \'sləŋ\; **sling·ing** \'sliŋ-iŋ\ [ME *slingen,* prob. fr. ON *slyngva* to hurl; akin to OE & OHG *slingan* to worm, twist, Lith *slinkti*] **1 :** to cast with a sudden and usu. sweeping or swirling motion <*slung* the sweater over her shoulder> **2 :** to throw with a sling ***syn*** see THROW — **sling·er** \'sliŋ-ər\ *n*

[2]**sling** *n* **:** a slinging or hurling of or as if of a missile

[3]**sling** *n* **1 a :** an instrument for throwing stones that usu. consists of a short strap with strings fastened to its ends and is whirled round to discharge its missile by centrifugal force **b :** SLINGSHOT 1 **2 a :** a usu. looped line (as of strap, chain, or rope) used to hoist, lower, or carry something; *esp* **:** a hanging bandage suspended from the neck to support an arm or hand **b :** a chain or rope attached to a lower yard at the middle and passing around a mast near the masthead to support a yard **c :** a chain hooked at the bow and stern of a boat for lowering or hoisting **d :** a device (as a rope net) for enclosing material to be hoisted by a tackle or crane

[4]**sling** *vt* **slung** \'sləŋ\; **sling·ing** \'sliŋ-iŋ\ **:** to place in a sling for hoisting or lowering

[5]**sling** *n* [origin unknown] **:** an alcoholic drink usu. made of whiskey, brandy, or esp. gin with plain or carbonated water, sugar, and sometimes bitters and often garnished with lemon or lime peel if cold or dusted with nutmeg if hot <gin ~> <rum ~>

slinger ring *n* **:** a tubular ring fitted round the propeller hub of an airplane through which a spray of antifreeze solution is spread by centrifugal force over the propeller blades to prevent icing

sling·shot \'sliŋ-ˌshät\ *n* **1 :** a forked stick with an elastic band attached for shooting small stones **2 a :** a maneuver in auto racing in which a drafting car accelerates past the car in front by taking advantage of reserve power **b :** a dragster in which the driver sits behind the rear wheels

[1]**slink** \'sliŋk\ *vb* **slunk** \'sləŋk\ *also* **slinked** \'sliŋ(k)t\; **slink·ing** [ME *slinken,* fr. OE *slincan* to creep; akin to OE *slingan* to worm, twist] *vi* **1 :** to go or move stealthily or furtively (as in fear or shame) **:** STEAL **2 :** to move in a sinuous provocative manner ~ *vt* **:** to give premature birth to — used esp. of a domestic animal <a cow that ~*s* her calf> ***syn*** see LURK

[2]**slink** *n* **:** the young of an animal (as a calf) brought forth prematurely; *also* **:** the flesh or skin of such an animal

[3]**slink** *adj* **:** born prematurely or abortively <a ~ calf>

slinky \'sliŋ-kē\ *adj* **slink·i·er; -est** **1 :** characterized by slinking **:** stealthily quiet <~ movements> **2 :** sleek and sinuous in movement or outline; *esp* **:** following the lines of the figure in a gracefully flowing manner <a ~ evening gown> — **slink·i·ly** \-kə-lē\ *adv* — **slink·i·ness** \-kē-nəs\ *n*

[1]**slip** \'slip\ *vb* **slipped; slip·ping** [ME *slippen,* fr. MD or MLG; akin to Gk *olibros* slippery, *leios* smooth — more at LIME] *vi* **1 a** : to move with a smooth sliding motion **b** : to move quietly and cautiously : STEAL **c** : ELAPSE, PASS **2 a** (1) : to escape from memory or consciousness (2) : to become uttered through inadvertence **b** : to pass quickly or easily away : become lost <let an opportunity ~> **3** : to fall into error or fault : LAPSE **4 a** : to slide out of place or away from a support or one's grasp **b** : to slide on or down a slippery surface <~ on the stairs> **c** : to flow smoothly **5** : to get speedily into or out of clothing <*slipped* into his coat> **6** : to fall off from a standard or accustomed level by degrees : DECLINE **7** : SIDESLIP ~ *vt* **1** : to cause to move easily and smoothly : SLIDE **2 a** : to get away from : ELUDE, EVADE <*slipped* his pursuers> **b** : to free oneself from <the dog *slipped* his collar> **c** : to escape from (one's memory or notice) **3** : CAST, SHED <the snake *slipped* its skin> **4** : to put on (a garment) hurriedly **5 a** : to let loose from a restraining leash or grasp **b** : to cause to slip open : RELEASE, UNDO <~ a lock> **c** : to let go of **d** : to disengage from (an anchor) instead of hauling **6 a** : to insert, place, or pass quietly or secretly **b** : to give or pay on the sly **7** : SLINK, ABORT **8** : DISLOCATE <*slipped* his shoulder> **9** : to transfer (a stitch) from one needle to another without working a stitch **10** : to avoid (a punch) by moving the body or head quickly to one side — **slip something over** : to foist something on another : get the better of another by trickery

[2]**slip** *n* **1 a** : a sloping ramp extending out into the water to serve as a place for landing or repairing ships **b** : a ship's or boat's berth between two piers **2** : the act or an instance of departing secretly or hurriedly <gave his pursuer the ~> **3 a** : a mistake in judgment, policy, or procedure **b** : an unintentional and trivial mistake or fault : LAPSE **4** : a leash so made that it can be quickly slipped **5 a** : the act or an instance of slipping down or out of a place <a ~ on the ice>; *also* : a sudden mishap <many a ~ between the cup and the lip> **b** : a movement dislocating parts (as of a rock or soil mass); *also* : the result of such movement **c** : a fall from some level or standard : DECLINE <a ~ in stock prices> **6 a** : an undergarment made in dress length with shoulder straps **b** : a case into which something is slipped; *specif* : PILLOWCASE **7 a** : the motion of the center of resistance of the float of a paddle wheel or the blade of an oar through the water horizontally **b** : retrograde movement of a belt on a pulley **c** : the amount of leakage past the piston of a pump or the impellers of a blower **8** : a disposition or tendency to slip easily **9** : the action of sideslipping : an instance of sideslipping *syn* see ERROR

[3]**slip** *adj* **1 a** : operating by slipping <~ bar> **b** : capable of being detached <~ compartment> **2** : having a slipknot <~ cord> **3** : capable of being released quickly <~ bolt>

[4]**slip** *n* [ME *slippe,* prob. fr. MD or MLG, split, slit, flap] **1 a** : a small shoot or twig cut for planting or grafting : SCION **b** : DESCENDANT, OFFSPRING **2 a** : a long narrow strip of material **b** : a small piece of paper **3** : a young and slender person <a ~ of a girl> **4** : a long seat or narrow pew

[5]**slip** *vt* **slipped; slip·ping** : to take cuttings from (a plant) : divide into slips <~ a geranium>

[6]**slip** *n* [ME *slyp* slime, fr. OE *slypa* slime paste; akin to OE *slūpan* to slip — more at SLEEVE] : a mixture of finely divided clay and water used by potters (as for casting or decorating wares or in cementing separately formed parts)

slip·case \'slip-ˌkās\ *n* : a protective container with one open end for books

slip·cov·er \'slip-ˌkəv-ər\ *n* **1** : a cover that may be slipped off and on; *specif* : a removable protective covering for an article of furniture **2** : a protective cover readily slipped on or off a book

slip·form \'slip-ˌfȯrm\ *vt* : to construct with the use of a slip form

slip form *n* : a form that is moved slowly as concrete is placed during construction (as of a building or pavement)

slip·knot \'slip-ˌnät\ *n* : a knot that slips along the rope or line around which it is made; *esp* : one made by tying an overhand knot around the standing part of a rope — see KNOT illustration

slip noose *n* : a noose with a slipknot

slip–on \'slip-ˌȯn, -ˌän\ *n* : an article of clothing that is easily slipped on or off: as **a** : a glove or shoe without fastenings **b** : a garment (as a girdle) that one steps into and pulls up **c** : PULLOVER

slip·over \-ˌō-vər\ *n* : a garment or cover that slips on and off easily; *specif* : a pullover sweater

slip·page \'slip-ij\ *n* **1** : an act, instance, or process of slipping **2** : a loss in transmission of power; *also* : the difference between theoretical and actual output (as of power)

slipped disk *n* : a protrusion of one of the cartilage disks between vertebrae with pressure on spinal nerves resulting in low back pain or sciatic pain

[1]**slip·per** \'slip-ər\ *adj* [ME] *chiefly dial* : SLIPPERY

[2]**slipper** *n* [ME, fr. *slippen* to slip] : a light low-cut shoe that is easily slipped on the foot and is worn esp. while resting at home

slip·pery \'slip-(ə-)rē\ *adj* **slip·peri·er; -est** [alter. of ME *slipper,* fr. OE *slipor;* akin to MLG *slipper* slippery, *slippen* to slip] **1 a** : causing or tending to cause something to slide or fall <~ roads> **b** : tending to slip from the grasp **2** : not firmly fixed : UNSTABLE **3** : not to be trusted : TRICKY — **slip·peri·ness** *n*

slip·py \'slip-ē\ *adj* **slip·pi·er; -est** : SLIPPERY

slip ring *n* [[2]*slip*] : one of two or more continuous conducting rings from which the brushes take or to which they deliver current in a dynamo or motor

slip–sheet \'slip-ˌshēt\ *vt* : to insert slip sheets between (newly printed sheets)

slip sheet *n* [[1]*slip*] : a sheet of paper placed between newly printed sheets to prevent offsetting

slip·shod \'slip-'shäd\ *adj* [[1]*slip*] **1 a** : wearing loose shoes or slippers **b** : down at the heel : SHABBY **2** : CARELESS, SLOVENLY

slip·slop \-ˌsläp\ *n* [redupl. of [2]*slop*] **1** *archaic* : watery food : SLOPS **2** *archaic* : shallow talk or writing : TWADDLE — **slip–slop** *adj*

slip·sole \-ˌsōl\ *n* **1** : a thin insole **2** : a half sole inserted between the insole or welt and the outsole of a shoe to give additional height — called also *slip tap*

slip·stick \-ˌstik\ *n* : SLIDE RULE

slip stitch *n* **1** : a concealed stitch for sewing folded edges (as hems) made by alternately running the needle inside the fold and picking up a thread or two from the body of the article **2** : an unworked stitch; *esp* : a knitting stitch that is shifted from one needle to another without knitting it

[1]**slip·stream** \'slip-ˌstrēm\ *n* **1** : a stream of fluid (as air or water) driven aft by a propeller **2** : an area of reduced air pressure and forward suction immediately behind a rapidly moving racing car

[2]**slipstream** *vi* : to drive in the slipstream of a racing car

slip·up \'slip-ˌəp\ *n* **1** : MISTAKE **2** : MISCHANCE

slip up \slip-'əp\ *vi* : to make a mistake : BLUNDER

[1]**slit** \'slit\ *vt* **slit; slit·ting** [ME *slitten;* akin to MHG *slitzen* to slit, OHG *slīzan* to tear apart, OE *sciell* shell — more at SHELL] **1 a** : to make a slit in **b** : to cut off or away : SEVER **c** : to form into a slit **2** : to cut into long narrow strips — **slit·ter** *n*

[2]**slit** *n* : a long narrow cut or opening — **slit** *adj* — **slit·less** \'slit-ləs\ *adj*

slith·er \'slith-ər\ *vb* [ME *slideren,* fr. OE *slidrian,* freq. of *slīdan* to slide] *vi* **1** : to slide on or as if on a loose gravelly surface **2** : to slip or slide like a snake ~ *vt* : to cause to slide

slith·ery \'slith-ə-rē\ *adj* : having a slippery surface, texture, or quality

slit trench *n* : a narrow trench esp. for shelter in battle from bomb and shell fragments

[1]**sliv·er** \'sliv-ər, *2 is usu* 'slīv-\ *n* [ME *slivere,* fr. *sliven* to slice off, fr. OE *-slīfan;* akin to OE *-slǣfan* to cut] **1** : a long slender piece cut or torn off : SPLINTER **2** : an untwisted strand or rope of textile fiber produced by a carding or combing machine and ready for drawing, roving, or spinning

[2]**sliv·er** \'sliv-ər\ *vb* **sliv·ered; sliv·er·ing** \-(ə-)riŋ\ *vt* : to cut into slivers : SPLINTER ~ *vi* : to become split into slivers

sliv·o·vitz \'sliv-ə-ˌvits, 'slēv-, -ˌwits\ *n* [Serbo-Croatian *šljivovica,* fr. *šljiva, sliva* plum; akin to Russ *sliva* plum — more at LIVID] : a dry usu. colorless plum brandy made esp. in Hungary and the Balkan countries

Slo *abbr* Sligo

slob \'släb\ *n* [Ir *slab* mud] **1** : a heavy sludge of sea ice **2** : a slovenly or boorish person — **slob·bish** \'släb-ish\ *adj*

[1]**slob·ber** \'släb-ər\ *vb* **slob·bered; slob·ber·ing** \-(ə-)riŋ\ [ME *sloberen;* akin to LG *slubberen* to sip, Lith *lūpa* lip] *vi* **1** : to let saliva dribble from the mouth : DROOL **2** : to indulge the feelings effusively and without restraint ~ *vt* : to smear with or as if with dribbling saliva or food — **slob·ber·er** \-ər-ər\ *n*

[2]**slobber** *n* **1** : saliva drooled from the mouth **2** : driveling, sloppy, or incoherent utterance — **slob·bery** \'släb-(ə-)rē\ *adj*

sloe \'slō\ *n* [ME *slo,* fr. OE *slāh* — more at LIVID] : the small dark globose astringent fruit of the blackthorn; *also* : BLACKTHORN 1

sloe–eyed \'slō-'īd\ *adj* **1** : having soft dark bluish or purplish black eyes **2** : having slanted eyes

sloe gin *n* : a sweet reddish liqueur consisting of grain spirits flavored chiefly with sloes

[1]**slog** \'släg\ *vb* **slogged; slog·ging** [origin unknown] *vt* **1** : to hit hard : BEAT **2** : to plod (one's way) perseveringly esp. against difficulty ~ *vi* **1** : to plod heavily : TRAMP <*slogged* through the snow> **2** : to work hard and steadily : PLUG — **slog·ger** *n*

[2]**slog** *n* **1** : hard persistent work **2** : a hard dogged march or tramp

slo·gan \'slō-gən\ *n* [alter. of earlier *slogorn,* fr. ScGael *sluagh-ghairm* army cry] **1 a** : a war cry or rallying cry esp. of a Scottish clan **b** : a word or phrase used to express a characteristic position or stand or a goal to be achieved **2** : a brief attention-getting phrase used in advertising or promotion

slo·gan·eer \ˌslō-gə-'ni(ə)r\ *n* : a maker or user of slogans — **sloganeer** *vi*

slo·gan·ize \'slō-gə-ˌnīz\ *vt* **-ized; -iz·ing** : to express as a slogan

sloop \'slüp\ *n* [D *sloep*] : a fore-and-aft rigged boat with one mast and a single headsail jib

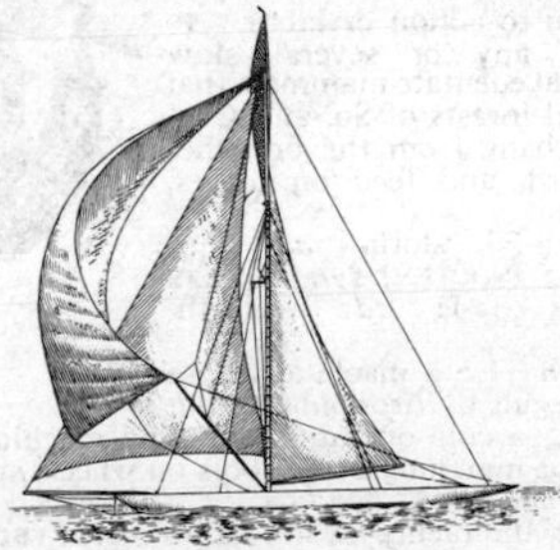

sloop

sloop of war **1** : a warship rigged as a ship, brig, or schooner mounting from 10 to 32 guns **2** : a warship larger than a gunboat with guns on one deck only

[1]**slop** \'släp\ *n* [ME *sloppe,* prob. fr. MD *slop;* akin to OE *oferslop* slop] **1 :** a loose smock or overall **2** *pl* **:** short full breeches worn by men in the 16th century **3** *pl* **:** articles (as clothing) sold to sailors

[2]**slop** *n* [ME *sloppe*] **1 :** soft mud : SLUSH **2 :** thin tasteless drink or liquid food — usu. used in pl. **3 :** liquid spilled or splashed **4 a :** food waste (as garbage) or a thin gruel fed to animals **b :** excreted body waste — usu. used in pl. **5 :** sentimental effusiveness in speech or writing : GUSH

[3]**slop** *vb* **slopped; slop·ping** *vt* **1 a :** to spill from a container **b :** to splash or spill liquid on **c :** to cause (a liquid) to splash **2 :** to dish out messily **3 :** to eat or drink greedily or noisily **4 :** to feed slop to <~ the hogs> ~ *vi* **1 :** to tramp in mud or slush **2 :** to become spilled or splashed **3 :** to be effusive : GUSH **4 :** to pass beyond or exceed a boundary or limit

slop basin *n, Brit* **:** a bowl for receiving the leavings of tea or coffee cups at table — called also *slop bowl*

slop chest *n* [[1]*slop*] **:** a store of clothing and personal requisites (as tobacco) carried on merchant ships for issue to the crew usu. as a charge against their wages

[1]**slope** \'slōp\ *adj* [ME *slope,* adv., obliquely] **:** that slants : SLOPING — often used in combination <*slope*-sided>

[2]**slope** *vb* **sloped; slop·ing** *vi* **1 :** to take an oblique course **2 :** to lie or fall in a slant : INCLINE **3 :** GO, TRAVEL <~*s* off into the night —Wolcott Gibbs> ~ *vt* **:** to cause to incline or slant ***syn*** see SLANT — **slop·er** *n*

[3]**slope** *n* **1 :** ground that forms a natural or artificial incline **2 :** upward or downward slant or inclination or degree of slant **3 :** the part of a continent draining to a particular ocean **4 a :** the tangent of the angle made by a straight line with the x-axis **b :** the slope of the line tangent to a plane curve at a point

slo–pitch \'slō-'pich, -ˌpich\ *n* [alter. of *slow pitch*] **:** a form of softball which is played with 10 men on each side and in which each pitch must travel in an arc 3 to 10 feet high and base stealing is not permitted

slop jar *n* **:** a large pail used as a chamber pot or to receive waste water from a washbowl or the contents of chamber pots

slop pail *n* **:** a pail for toilet or household slops

slop·py \'släp-ē\ *adj* **slop·pi·er; -est 1 a :** wet so as to spatter easily : SLUSHY <a ~ racetrack> **b :** wet or smeared with or as if with something slopped over **2 :** SLOVENLY, CARELESS <she's a ~ dresser> <did ~ work> **3 :** disagreeably effusive <~ sentimentalism> — **slop·pi·ly** \'släp-ə-lē\ *adv* — **slop·pi·ness** *n*

slop·work \'släp-ˌwərk\ *n* **1 :** the manufacture of cheap ready-made clothing **2 :** hasty slovenly work — **slop·work·er** \-ˌwər-kər\ *n*

[1]**slosh** \'släsh, 'slȯsh\ *n* [prob. blend of *slop* and *slush*] **1 :** SLUSH **2 :** the slap or splash of liquid

[2]**slosh** *vi* **1 :** to flounder or splash through water, mud, or slush **2 :** to move with a splashing motion <the water ~*ed* around him —Bill Alcine> ~ *vt* **1 :** to splash about in liquid **2 :** to splash (a liquid) about or on something **3 :** to splash with liquid

[1]**slot** \'slät\ *n* [ME, the hollow running down the middle of the breast, fr. MF *esclot*] **1 a :** a narrow opening or groove : SLIT, NOTCH <a mail ~ in a door> **b :** a narrow passage or enclosure **c :** a passage through the wing of an airplane or of a missile that is located usu. near the leading edge and formed between a main and an auxiliary airfoil for improving flow conditions over the wing so as to increase lift and delay stalling of the wing **2 :** a place or position in an organization or sequence : NICHE **3 :** a gap between an end and a tackle in an offensive football line

[2]**slot** *vt* **slot·ted; slot·ting 1 :** to cut a slot in **2 :** to place in or assign to a slot

[3]**slot** *n, pl* **slot** [MF *esclot* track] **:** the track of an animal (as a deer)

slot·back \'slät-ˌbak\ *n* **:** an offensive football halfback who lines up just behind the slot between an offensive end and tackle

slot car *n* **:** an electric toy racing automobile that has an arm underneath to fit into a groove of a track having parallel metal strips to supply electricity and that is remotely controlled by the operator's hand-held rheostat

sloth \'slȯth, 'slōth\ *n, pl* **sloths** *with* ths *or* th̲z\ [ME *slouthe,* fr. *slow*] **1 :** disinclination to action or labor : INDOLENCE **2 :** any of several slow-moving arboreal edentate mammals that inhabit tropical forests of So. and Central America, hang from the branches back downward, and feed on leaves, shoots, and fruits

sloth·ful \'slȯth-fəl, 'slōth-\ *adj* **:** inclined to sloth : INDOLENT ***syn*** see LAZY — **sloth·ful·ly** \-fə-lē\ *adv* — **sloth·ful·ness** *n*

sloth 2

slot machine *n* **1 :** a machine whose operation is begun by dropping a coin into a slot **2 :** a coin-operated gambling machine that pays off according to the matching of symbols on wheels spun by a handle — called also *one-armed bandit*

slot racing *n* **:** the racing of slot cars — **slot racer** *n*

[1]**slouch** \'slau̇ch\ *n* [origin unknown] **1 a :** an awkward fellow : LOUT **b :** a lazy or incompetent person **2 :** a gait or posture characterized by ungainly stooping of head and shoulders or excessive relaxation of body muscles

[2]**slouch** *vi* **1 :** to walk with or assume a slouch **2 :** DROOP ~ *vt* **:** to cause to droop <~*ed* his shoulders> — **slouch·er** *n*

slouch hat *n* **:** a soft usu. felt hat with a wide flexible brim

slouchy \'slau̇-chē\ *adj* **slouch·i·er; -est :** lacking erectness esp. in gait or posture — **slouch·i·ly** \-chə-lē\ *adv* — **slouch·i·ness** \-chē-nəs\ *n*

[1]**slough** \'slü, 'slau̇; *in the US* (*exc New Eng*) 'slü *is usual for sense 1 with those to whom the sense is familiar; for sense 2,* 'slau̇ *is more frequent than* 'slü\ *n* [ME *slogh,* fr. OE *slōh;* akin to MHG *slouche* ditch] **1 a :** a place of deep mud or mire **b** (1) **:** SWAMP (2) **:** an inlet from a river; *also* **:** BACKWATER (3) **:** a creek in a marsh or tide flat **2 :** a state of moral degradation or spiritual dejection

[2]**slough** *vt* **:** to engulf in a slough ~ *vi* **:** to plod through or as if through mud : SLOG

[3]**slough** \'sləf\ *or* **sluff** *n* [ME *slughe;* akin to MHG *slūch* snakeskin, Lith *šliaužti* to crawl] **1 :** the cast-off skin of a snake **2 :** a mass of dead tissue separating from an ulcer **3 :** something that may be shed or cast off

[4]**slough** \'sləf\ *or* **sluff** *vi* **1 a :** to become shed or cast off **b :** to cast off one's skin **c :** to separate in the form of dead tissue from living tissue **2 :** to crumble slowly and fall away ~ *vt* **1 :** to cast off **2 a :** to get rid of or discard as irksome, objectionable, or disadvantageous — usu. used with *off* **b :** to dispose of (a losing card in bridge) by discarding ***syn*** see DISCARD

slough of de·spond \ˌslau̇-əv-di-'spänd, ˌslü-\ [fr. the *Slough of Despond,* deep bog into which Christian falls on the way from the City of Destruction and from which Help saves him in the allegory *Pilgrim's Progress* (1678) by John Bunyan] **:** a state of extreme depression

slough over \ˌsləf-\ *vt* **:** to treat as slight or unimportant

sloughy \'slü-ē, 'slau̇- — *see* [1]SLOUGH\ *adj* **:** full of sloughs : MIRY

Slo·vak \'slō-ˌväk, -ˌvak\ *n* [Slovak *Slovák*] **1 :** a member of a Slavic people of eastern Czechoslovakia **2 :** the Slavic language of the Slovak people — **Slovak** *adj* — **Slo·va·ki·an** \slō-'väk-ē-ən, -'vak-\ *adj or n*

[1]**slov·en** \'sləv-ən\ *n* [ME *sloveyn* rascal, perh. fr. Flem *sloovin* woman of low character] **:** one habitually negligent of neatness or cleanliness esp. in personal appearance

[2]**sloven** *adj* **:** SLOVENLY

Slo·vene \'slō-ˌvēn\ *n* [G, fr. Slovene *Sloven*] **1 a :** a member of a southern Slavic group of people usu. classed with the Serbs and Croats and living in Yugoslavia **b :** a native or inhabitant of Slovenia **2 :** the language of the Slovenes — **Slovene** *adj* — **Slo·ve·nian** \slō-'vē-nē-ən, -nyən\ *adj or n*

slov·en·ly \'sləv-ən-lē\ *adj* **1 a :** untidy esp. in personal appearance **b :** lazily slipshod <~ in thought> **2 :** characteristic of a sloven <~ workmanship> — **slo·ven·li·ness** *n* — **slovenly** *adv*

[1]**slow** \'slō\ *adj* [ME, fr. OE *slāw;* akin to OHG *slēo* dull, Skt *srēvayati* he causes to fail] **1 a :** mentally dull : STUPID <a ~ student> **b :** naturally inert or sluggish **2 a :** lacking in readiness, promptness, or willingness **b :** not hasty or precipitate <was ~ to anger> **3 a :** moving, flowing, or proceeding without speed or at less than usual speed <traffic was ~> **b :** exhibiting or marked by retarded speed <he moved with ~ deliberation> **c :** not acute **d :** LOW, GENTLE <~ fire> **4 :** requiring a long time : GRADUAL <a ~ convalescence> **5 :** having qualities that hinder or stop rapid progress or action **6 a :** registering behind or below what is correct <his clock is ~> **b :** less than the time indicated by another method of reckoning **c :** that is behind the time at a specified time or place **7 a :** lacking in life, animation, or gaiety : BORING **b :** marked by reduced sales or patronage <business was ~> — **slow·ish** \'slō-ish\ *adj* — **slow·ness** *n*

[2]**slow** *adv* **:** SLOWLY

[3]**slow** *vt* **:** to make slow or slower : slacken the speed of <~ a car> — often used with *down* or *up* ~ *vi* **:** to go or become slower <production of new cars ~*ed* sharply> ***syn*** see DELAY ***ant*** speed

slow·down \'slō-ˌdau̇n\ *n* **:** a slowing down <a business ~>

slow–foot·ed \-'fu̇t-əd\ *adj* **:** moving at a very slow pace : PLODDING <a ~ novel> <a ~ ship> — **slow–footed·ness** *n*

slow·ly \-lē\ *adv* **:** in a slow manner : not quickly, fast, early, rashly, or readily

slow match *n* **:** a match or fuse made so as to burn slowly and evenly and used for firing (as of blasting charges)

slow motion *n* **:** the action in a projected motion picture apparently taking place at a speed much slower than that of the photographed action

slow–pitch \'slō-'pich, -ˌpich\ *n* **:** SLO-PITCH

slow·poke \'slō-ˌpōk\ *n* **:** a very slow person

slow–wit·ted \-'wit-əd\ *adj* **:** mentally slow : DULL

slow·worm \-ˌwərm\ *n* [ME *sloworm,* fr. OE *slāwyrm,* fr. *slā-* (akin to Sw *slå* earthworm) + *wyrm* worm] **:** BLINDWORM

[1]**slub** \'sləb\ *vt* **slubbed; slub·bing** [back-formation fr. *slubbing*] **:** to draw out and twist (as slivers of wool) slightly

[2]**slub** *n* **:** SLUBBING

slub·ber \'sləb-ər\ *vt* **slub·bered; slub·ber·ing** \-(ə-)riŋ\ [prob. fr. obs. D *slubberen*] **1** *dial chiefly Eng* **:** STAIN, SULLY **2 :** to perform in a slipshod fashion

slub·bing \'sləb-iŋ\ *n* [origin unknown] **:** slightly twisted roving

sludge \'sləj\ *n* [prob. alter. of *slush*] **1 :** MUD, MIRE; *esp* **:** a muddy deposit (as on a riverbed) : OOZE **2 :** a muddy or slushy mass, deposit, or sediment: as **a :** precipitated solid matter produced by water and sewage treatment processes **b :** muddy sediment in a steam boiler **c :** a precipitate or settling (as a mixture of impurities and acid) from a mineral oil **3 :** new sea ice forming in thin detached crystals

sludgy \'sləj-ē\ *adj* **sludg·i·er; -est :** containing or full of sludge

[1]**slue** \'slü\ *var of* SLOUGH

[2]**slue** *also* **slew** \'slü\ *vb* **slued; slu·ing** [origin unknown] *vt* **1** *usu slew* **:** to turn (as a telescope or a ship's spar) about a fixed point that is usu. the axis **2 :** to cause to skid : VEER <~ a car around a turn> ~ *vi* **1 :** to turn, twist, or swing about : PIVOT <*slued* around in the saddle —A. B. Guthrie> **2 :** SKID

[3]**slue** *n* **1 :** position or inclination after sluing **2 :** SKID 5

[4]**slue** *var of* SLEW

[1]**slug** \'sləg\ *n* [ME *slugge,* of Scand origin; akin to Norw dial. *slugga* to walk sluggishly; akin to ME *sloor* mud — more at SLUR] **1 :** SLUGGARD **2 :** any of numerous chiefly terrestrial pulmonate gastropods (family Limacidae) that are found in most parts of the world where there is a reasonable supply of moisture and are closely related to the land snails but are long and wormlike and have only a rudimentary shell often buried in the mantle or entirely absent **3 :** a smooth soft larva of a sawfly or moth that creeps like a mollusk

[2]**slug** *n* [prob. fr. [1]*slug*] **1 :** a lump, disk, or cylinder of material (as plastic or metal): as **a** (1) **:** a musket ball (2) **:** BULLET **b :** a piece of metal roughly shaped for subsequent processing **c :** a $50 gold piece **d :** a disk for insertion in a slot machine; *esp* **:** one used illegally instead of a coin **2 a :** a strip of metal thicker than a printer's lead **b :** a line of type cast as one piece **c :** a usu. temporary type line serving to instruct or identify **3 a :** a single drink of liquor **:** SHOT **b :** a detached mass of fluid (as water vapor or oil) that causes impact (as in a circulating system) **4 :** the gravitational unit of mass in the fps system to which a pound force can impart an acceleration of one foot per second per second
[3]**slug** *vt* **slugged; slug·ging :** to add a printer's slug to
[4]**slug** *n* [perh. fr. *slug* (to load with slugs)] **:** a heavy blow esp. with the fist
[5]**slug** *vt* **slugged; slug·ging :** to strike heavily with or as if with the fist or a bat
slug·abed \'sləg-ə-ˌbed\ *n* **:** one who stays in bed after his usual or proper time of getting up; *broadly* **:** SLUGGARD
slug·fest \'sləg-ˌfest\ *n* **:** a fight marked by the exchange of heavy blows
[1]**slug·gard** \'sləg-ərd\ *n* [ME *sluggart*] **:** an habitually lazy person
[2]**sluggard** *adj* **:** SLUGGARDLY — **slug·gard·ness** *n*
slug·gard·ly \'sləg-ərd-lē\ *adj* **:** lazily inactive
slug·ger \'sləg-ər\ *n* **:** one that strikes hard or with heavy blows: as **a :** a prizefighter who punches hard but has usu. little defensive skill **b :** a hard-hitting batter in baseball
slugging average *n* **:** the ratio (as a rate per thousand) of the total number of bases reached on base hits to official times at bat for a baseball player
slug·gish \'sləg-ish\ *adj* **1 :** averse to activity or exertion **:** INDOLENT; *also* **:** TORPID **2 :** slow to respond (as to stimulation or treatment) **3 a :** markedly slow in movement, flow, or growth **b :** economically inactive or slow ***syn*** see LETHARGIC ***ant*** brisk, quick (*of mind*) — **slug·gish·ly** *adv* — **slug·gish·ness** *n*
[1]**sluice** \'slüs\ *n* [alter. of ME *scluse,* fr. MF *escluse,* fr. LL *exclusa,* fr. L, fem. of *exclusus,* pp. of *excludere* to exclude] **1 a :** an artificial passage for water (as in a millstream) fitted with a valve or gate for stopping or regulating flow **b :** a body of water pent up behind a floodgate **2 :** a dock gate **:** FLOODGATE **3 a :** a stream flowing through a floodgate **b :** a channel to drain or carry off surplus water **4 :** a long inclined trough usu. on the ground (as for floating logs); *esp* **:** such a contrivance paved usu. with riffles to hold quicksilver for catching gold
[2]**sluice** *vb* **sluiced; sluic·ing** *vt* **1 :** to draw off by or through a sluice **2 a :** to wash with or in water running through or from a sluice **b :** to drench with a sudden flow **:** FLUSH **3 :** to transport (as logs) in a sluice ~ *vi* **:** to pour as if from a sluice ***syn*** see POUR
sluice·way \'slü-ˌswā\ *n* **:** an artificial channel into which water is let by a sluice
sluicy \'slü-sē\ *adj* **:** falling copiously or in streams **:** STREAMING
[1]**slum** \'sləm\ *n, often attrib* [origin unknown] **:** a densely populated usu. urban area marked by crowding, dirty run-down housing, poverty, and social disorganization
[2]**slum** *vi* **slummed; slum·ming :** to visit slums or places considered slums esp. out of curiosity — **slum·mer** *n*
[1]**slum·ber** \'sləm-bər\ *vi* **slum·bered; slum·ber·ing** \-b(ə-)riŋ\ [ME *slumberen,* freq. of *slumen* to doze, prob. fr. *slume* slumber, fr. OE *slūma;* akin to Lith *slugti* to diminish — more at SLUR] **1 a :** to sleep lightly **:** DOZE **b :** SLEEP **2 a :** to be in a torpid, slothful, or negligent state **b :** to lie dormant or latent — **slum·ber·er** \-bər-ər\ *n*
[2]**slumber** *n* **1 a :** SLEEP **b :** a light sleep **2 :** LETHARGY, TORPOR
slum·ber·ous *or* **slum·brous** \'sləm-b(ə-)rəs\ *adj* **1 :** heavy with sleep **:** SLEEPY **2 :** inducing slumber **:** SOPORIFIC **3 :** marked by or suggestive of a state of sleep or lethargy <a ~ peace pervaded every province —Pearl Buck> ***syn*** see SLEEPY
slumber party *n* **:** an overnight gathering of teenage girls usu. at one of their homes at which they dress in nightclothes but pass the night more in talking than sleeping
slum·bery \'sləm-b(ə-)rē\ *adj, archaic* **:** SLUMBEROUS
slum·gul·lion \'sləm-ˌgəl-yən, ˌsləm-'\ *n* [perh. fr. *slum* (slime) + E dial. *gullion* (mud, cesspool)] **:** a meat stew
slum·lord \'sləm-ˌlȯ(ə)rd\ *n* [[1]*slum* + land*lord*] **:** a landlord who receives unusually large profits from substandard properties
slum·my \'sləm-ē\ *adj* **slum·mi·er; -est :** of, relating to, or suggestive of a slum <~ streets>
[1]**slump** \'sləmp\ *vi* [prob. of Scand origin; akin to Norw *slumpa* to fall; akin to L *labi* to slide — more at SLEEP] **1 a :** to fall or sink suddenly **b :** to drop or slide down suddenly **:** COLLAPSE <~*ed* to the floor> **2 :** to assume a drooping posture or carriage **:** SLOUCH **3 :** to go into a slump <sales ~*ed*>
[2]**slump** *n* **1 a :** a marked or sustained decline esp. in economic activity or prices **b :** a period of poor or losing play by a team or individual <one spring I was in a batting ~ —Ted Williams> **2 :** a downward slide of land that usu. exhibits a backward rotating motion
slung *past of* SLING
slung·shot \'sləŋ-ˌshät\ *n* **:** a striking weapon consisting of a small mass of metal or stone fixed on a flexible handle or strap
slunk *past of* SLINK
[1]**slur** \'slər\ *vb* **slurred; slur·ring** [prob. fr. LG *slurrn* to shuffle; akin to ME *sloor* mud] *vt* **1 a :** to slide or slip over without due mention, consideration, or emphasis <*slurred* over certain facts> **b :** to perform hurriedly **:** SKIMP <let him not ~ his lesson —R. W. Emerson> **2 :** to perform (successive tones of different pitch) in a smooth or connected manner **3 a :** to reduce, make a substitution for, or omit (sounds that would normally occur in an utterance) **b :** to utter with such reduction, substitution, or omission of sounds <his speech was *slurred* to an indistinct murmur> ~ *vi* **1** *dial chiefly Eng* **:** SLIP, SLIDE **2 :** DRAG, SHUFFLE
[2]**slur** *n* **1 a :** a curved line connecting notes to be sung to the same syllable or performed without a break **b :** the combination of two or more slurred tones **2 :** a slurring manner of speech

slur 1a

[3]**slur** *vb* **slurred; slur·ring** [obs. E dial. *slur* thin mud, fr. ME *sloor;* akin to MHG *slier* mud, Lith *slugti* to diminish] *vt* **1 :** to cast aspersions on **:** DISPARAGE **2 :** to make indistinct **:** OBSCURE ~ *vi* **:** to slip so as to cause a slur — used of a sheet being printed
[4]**slur** *n* **1 a :** an insulting or disparaging remark or innuendo **:** ASPERSION **b :** a shaming or degrading effect **:** STAIN, STIGMA **2 :** a blurred spot in printed matter **:** SMUDGE
slurp \'slərp\ *vb* [D *slurpen;* akin to MLG *slorpen* to slurp] *vi* **:** to make a sucking noise while eating or drinking ~ *vt* **:** to eat or drink noisily or with a sucking sound — **slurp** *n*
[1]**slur·ry** \'slər-ē, 'slə-rē\ *n, pl* **slur·ries** [ME *slory*] **:** a watery mixture of insoluble matter (as mud, lime, or plaster of paris)
[2]**slurry** *vt* **slur·ried; slur·ry·ing :** to convert into a slurry
[1]**slush** \'sləsh\ *n* [perh. of Scand origin; akin to Norw *slusk* slush] **1 a :** partly melted or watery snow **b :** loose ice crystals formed during the early stages of freezing of salt water **2 a :** soft mud **:** MIRE **b :** grout made of portland cement, sand, and water **3 :** refuse grease and fat from cooking esp. on shipboard **4 :** a soft mixture of grease or oil and other materials for protecting the surface of metal parts against corrosion; *esp* **:** a mixture of white lead and lime for painting the bright parts of machines to preserve them from oxidation **5 :** paper pulp in water suspension **6 :** trashy and usu. cheaply sentimental material
[2]**slush** *vt* **1 :** to wet, splash, or paint with slush **2 :** to fill in (as joints) with slush or grout ~ *vi* **1 :** to make one's way through slush **2 :** to make a splashing sound
slush fund *n* **1 :** a fund raised from the sale of refuse to obtain small luxuries or pleasures for a warship's crew **2 :** a fund for bribing public officials or carrying on corruptive propaganda
slushy \'sləsh-ē\ *adj* **slush·i·er; -est :** being, involving, or resembling slush: as **a :** full of or covered with slush <~ streets> **b :** made up of or having the consistency of slush <~ snow> <a ~ mixture> **c :** having a cheaply sentimental quality **:** TRASHY <a ~ novel> — **slush·i·ness** *n*
slut \'slət\ *n* [ME *slutte*] **1 :** a slovenly woman **:** SLATTERN **2 a :** a lewd woman; *esp* **:** PROSTITUTE **b :** a saucy girl **:** MINX **3 :** a female dog **:** BITCH — **slut·tish** \'slət-ish\ *adj* — **slut·tish·ly** *adv* — **slut·tish·ness** *n*
SLV *abbr* satellite launch vehicle
sly \'slī\ *adj* **sli·er** *also* **sly·er** \'slī(-ə)r\; **sli·est** *also* **sly·est** \'slī-əst\ [ME *sli,* fr. ON *slœgr;* akin to OE *slēan* to strike — more at SLAY] **1** *chiefly dial* **a :** wise in practical affairs **b :** displaying cleverness **:** INGENIOUS **2 a :** clever in concealing one's aims or ends **:** FURTIVE <the ~ fox> **b :** lacking in straightforwardness and candor **:** DISSEMBLING <a ~ scheme> **3 :** lightly mischievous **:** ROGUISH <a ~ jest> — **sly·ly** *adv* — **sly·ness** *n*
syn SLY, CUNNING, CRAFTY, TRICKY, FOXY, ARTFUL *shared meaning element* **:** attaining or seeking to attain one's ends by devious means. SLY implies furtiveness, lack of candor, and skill in concealing one's aims and methods <with knowing leer and words of *sly* import —Washington Irving> CUNNING suggests the effective use of sometimes limited intelligence in overreaching or circumventing <all gods are cruel . . . but women-gods are mean and *cunning* as well —Gordon Bottomley> CRAFTY implies clever cunning and subtlety of method <as a *crafty* envoy does his country's business by dint of flirting and conviviality —C. E. Montague> TRICKY is more likely to suggest shiftiness and unreliability than skill in deception and maneuvering <he avoided the mean and *tricky;* he was always an honorable foe —W. C. Ford> FOXY implies a shrewd and wary craftiness usually involving devious dealing <this *foxy* publicity man turned fumbling poet —Sherwood Anderson> ARTFUL can imply insinuating alluring indirectness in dealing and often connotes sophistication or coquetry or cleverness <they stayed sober. The *artful* Henry had told them all the wine . . . was poisoned —D. B. Chidsey> <an *artful* approach to a problem>
— **on the sly :** in a manner intended to avoid notice
sly·boots \'slī-ˌbüts\ *n pl but sing in constr* **:** a sly tricky person; *esp* **:** one who is cunning or mischievous in an engaging way
slype \'slīp\ *n* [prob. fr. Flem *slijpe* place for slipping in and out] **:** a narrow passage; *specif* **:** one between the transept and chapter house or deanery in an English cathedral
sm *abbr* small
Sm *symbol* samarium
SM *abbr* **1** [NL *scientiae magister*] master of science **2** sergeant major **3** short meter **4** Society of Mary **5** soldier's medal **6** stage manager **7** station master
SMA *abbr* sergeant major of the army
[1]**smack** \'smak\ *n* [ME, fr. OE *smæc;* akin to OHG *smac* taste, Lith *smaguriauti* to nibble] **1 :** characteristic taste or flavor; *also* **:** a perceptible taste or tincture **2 :** a small quantity
[2]**smack** *vi* **1 :** to have a taste or flavor **2 :** to have a trace, vestige, or suggestion <a proposal that ~*s* of treason>
[3]**smack** *vb* [akin to MD *smacken* to strike] *vt* **1 :** to close and open (lips) noisily and in rapid succession esp. in eating **2 a :** to kiss with or as if with a smack **b :** to strike so as to produce a smack ~ *vi* **:** to make or give a smack
[4]**smack** *n* **1 :** a quick sharp noise made by rapidly compressing and opening the lips **2 :** a loud kiss **3 :** a sharp slap or blow
[5]**smack** *adv* **:** squarely and sharply **:** DIRECTLY
[6]**smack** *n* [D *smak* or LG *smack*] **:** a sailing ship (as a sloop or cutter) used chiefly in coasting and fishing
[7]**smack** *n* [origin unknown] *slang* **:** HEROIN

smack–dab \ˈsmak-ˈdab\ *adv* : EXACTLY, SQUARELY

smack·er \ˈsmak-ər\ *n* **1** : one that smacks **2** *slang* : DOLLAR

smack·ing \ˈsmak-iŋ\ *adj* : BRISK, LIVELY <a ~ breeze>

SMaj *abbr* sergeant major

1**small** \ˈsmȯl\ *adj* [ME *smal,* fr. OE *smæl;* akin to OHG *smal* small, L *malus* bad] **1 a** : having comparatively little size or slight dimensions **b** : LOWERCASE **2 a** : minor in influence, power, or rank **b** : operating on a limited scale **3** : lacking in strength <a ~ voice> **4 a** : little in an objectively measurable aspect (as quantity, amount, or value) **b** : made up of few or little units **5 a** : of little consequence : TRIVIAL, INSIGNIFICANT **b** : HUMBLE, MODEST <a ~ beginning> **6** : limited in degree **7 a** : MEAN, PETTY **b** : reduced to a humiliating position — **small·ish** \ˈsmȯ-lish\ *adj* — **small·ness** \ˈsmȯl-nəs\ *n*

syn SMALL, DIMINUTIVE, MINUTE, PETITE, TINY, MINIATURE, WEE *shared meaning element* : noticeably below average in magnitude *ant* large

2**small** *adv* **1** : in or into small pieces **2** : without force or loudness <speak as ~ as you will —Shak.> **3** : in a small manner

3**small** *n* **1** : a part smaller and esp. narrower than the remainder <the ~ of the back> **2 a** *pl* : small-sized products **b** *pl, Brit* : SMALLCLOTHES; *esp* : UNDERWEAR

small ale *n* : a weak ale brewed with little malt and little or no hops as a mild and cheap drink

small arm *n* : a firearm fired while held in the hands

small beer *n* **1** : weak or inferior beer **2** : something of small importance : TRIVIA

small calorie *n* : CALORIE 1a

small capital *n* : a letter having the form of but smaller than a capital letter (as in THESE WORDS)

small change *n* **1** : coins of low denomination **2** : something trifling or petty

small–claims court *n* : a special court intended to simplify and expedite the handling of small claims on debts — called also *small-debts court*

small·clothes \ˈsmȯl-ˌklō(th)z\ *n pl* **1** : close-fitting knee breeches worn in the 18th century **2** : small articles of clothing (as underclothing or handkerchiefs)

smaller *comparative of* SMALL *syn* see LESS *ant* larger

smaller European elm bark beetle *n* : ELM BARK BEETLE b

small–fry \ˈsmȯl-ˌfrī\ *adj* **1** : MINOR, UNIMPORTANT <a ~ politician> **2** : of, relating to, or intended for children : CHILDISH

small game *n* : game birds and mammals not classed as big game

small hours *n pl* : the early morning hours

small intestine *n* : the part of the intestine that lies between the stomach and colon, consists of duodenum, jejunum, and ileum, secretes digestive enzymes, and is the chief site of the absorption of digested nutrients

small–mind·ed \ˈsmȯl-ˈmīn-dəd\ *adj* **1** : having narrow interests, sympathies, or outlook <a ~ man> **2** : typical of a small-minded person : marked by pettiness, narrowness, or meanness <~ conduct> — **small–mind·ed·ly** *adv* — **small–mind·ed·ness** *n*

small·mouth bass \ˌsmȯl-ˌmau̇th-\ *n* : a black bass (*Micropterus dolomieu*) of clear rivers and lakes that is bronzy green above and lighter below and has the angle of the jaw falling below the eye — called also *smallmouth, smallmouth black bass*

small octave *n* : the musical octave that begins on the first C below middle C — see PITCH illustration

small potato *n* : one that is of trivial importance or worth — usu. used in pl. but sing. or pl. in constr.

small·pox \ˈsmȯl-ˌpäks\ *n* : an acute contagious febrile virus disease characterized by skin eruption with pustules, sloughing, and scar formation

small–scale \-ˈskā(ə)l\ *adj* **1** : small in scope; *esp* : small in output or operation **2** *of a map* : having a scale (as one inch to 25 miles) that permits plotting of comparatively little detail

small screen *n* : TELEVISION

small stores *n pl* : articles of clothing sold by a naval supply officer to naval personnel

small stuff *n* : small rope (as spun yarn or marline) usu. identified by the number of threads or yarns which it contains

small·sword \ˈsmȯl-ˌsō(ə)rd, -ˌsȯ(ə)rd\ *n* : a light tapering sword for thrusting used chiefly in dueling and fencing

small talk *n* : light or casual conversation : CHITCHAT

small–time \ˈsmȯl-ˈtīm\ *adj* : insignificant in performance and standing : PETTY <~ hoodlums> — **small–tim·er** \-ˈtī-mər\ *n*

smalt \ˈsmȯlt\ *n* [MF, fr. OIt *smalto,* of Gmc origin; akin to OHG *smelzan* to melt — more at SMELT] : a deep blue pigment used esp. as a ceramic color and prepared by fusing together silica, potash, and oxide of cobalt and grinding to powder the resultant glass

smalt·ite \ˈsmȯl-ˌtīt\ *n* [alter. of *smaltine,* fr. F, fr. *smalt*] : a bluish white or gray isometric mineral of metallic luster that is essentially an arsenide of cobalt and nickel

smal·to \ˈsmäl-(ˌ)tō, ˈsmȯl-\ *n, pl* **smal·ti** \-(ˌ)tē\ [It, smalt, smalto] : colored glass or enamel or a piece of either used in mosaic work

sma·ragd \smə-ˈragd, ˈsmar-ˌagd\ *n* [ME *smaragde,* fr. L *smaragdus*] : EMERALD — **sma·rag·dine** \smə-ˈrag-dən, ˈsmar-əg-ˌdīn\ *adj*

sma·rag·dite \smə-ˈrag-ˌdīt, ˈsmar-əg-ˌdīt\ *n* [F, fr. L *smaragdus* emerald — more at EMERALD] : a green foliated amphibole

smarmy \ˈsmär-mē\ *adj* [*smarm* (to gush, slobber)] : revealing or marked by a smug, ingratiating, or false earnestness : UNCTUOUS <a tone of ~ self-satisfaction — *New Yorker*>

1**smart** \ˈsmärt\ *vi* [ME *smerten,* fr. OE *smeortan;* akin to OHG *smerzan* to pain, L *mordēre* to bite, Gk *marainein* to waste away] **1** : to cause or be the cause or seat of a sharp poignant pain; *also* : to feel or have such a pain **2** : to feel or endure distress, remorse, or embarrassment <~*ing* from wounded vanity —W. L. Shirer> **3 a** : to endure sharp distress **b** : to pay a heavy or stinging penalty <would have to ~ for this foolishness>

2**smart** *adj* **1** : making one smart : causing a sharp stinging **2** : marked by often sharp forceful activity or vigorous strength <a ~ pull of the starter cord> **3** : BRISK, SPIRITED **4 a** : mentally alert : BRIGHT **b** : KNOWLEDGEABLE **c** : SHREWD <a ~ investment> **5 a** : WITTY, CLEVER **b** : PERT, SAUCY <was fired for being ~ with his boss> **6 a** : NEAT, TRIM **b** : stylish or elegant in dress or appearance <she's a ~ dresser> **c** (1) : SOPHISTICATED (2) : characteristic of or patronized by fashionable society — **smart·ly** *adv* — **smart·ness** *n*

3**smart** *adv* : in a smart manner : SMARTLY

4**smart** *n* **1** : a smarting pain; *esp* : a stinging local pain **2** : poignant grief or remorse <was not the sort to get over ~*s* —Sir Winston Churchill> **3** : an affectedly witty or fashionable person

smart al·eck \ˈsmärt-ˌal-ik, -ˌel-\ *n* [*Aleck,* nickname for *Alexander*] : an obnoxiously conceited and self-assertive person with pretensions to smartness or cleverness — **smart–al·ecky** \-ˌal-ə-kē, -ˌel-\ *or* **smart–aleck** \-ik\ *adj*

smart·en \ˈsmärt-ᵊn\ *vb* **smart·ened; smart·en·ing** \ˈsmärt-niŋ, -ᵊn-iŋ\ *vt* : to make smart or smarter; *esp* : SPRUCE — usu. used with *up* ~ *vi* : to smarten oneself — used with *up*

1**smart money** \ˈsmärt-ˌmən-ē\ *n* [4*smart*] : PUNITIVE DAMAGES

2**smart money** \-ˈmən-ē, -ˌmən-\ *n* [2*smart*] : money ventured by one having inside information or much experience

smart set *n* : ultrafashionable society

smart·weed \ˈsmärt-ˌwēd\ *n* **1** : any of various polygonums with strong acid juice **2** : a plant (as a nettle) that causes a burning sensation on contact with the skin

smarty *or* **smart·ie** \ˈsmärt-ē\ *n, pl* **smart·ies** : SMART ALECK

smarty–pants \-ˌpan(t)s\ *n pl but sing in constr* : SMART ALECK

1**smash** \ˈsmash\ *vb* [perh. blend of *smack* and *mash*] *vt* **1** : to break in pieces by violence : SHATTER **2 a** : to drive or throw violently esp. with a shattering or battering effect; *also* : to effect in this way **b** (1) : to hit (as a tennis ball) with a hard overhand stroke (2) : to drive (a ball) with a forceful stroke **3** : to destroy utterly : WRECK ~ *vi* **1** : to move or become propelled with violence or crashing effect <~*ed* into a tree> **2** : to become wrecked **3** : to go to pieces suddenly under collision or pressure **4** : to execute a smash (as in tennis) — **smash·er** *n*

2**smash** *n* **1 a** : a smashing blow or attack **b** : a hard overhand stroke (as in tennis or badminton) **2** : the condition of being smashed **3 a** : the action or sound of smashing; *esp* : a wreck due to collision : CRASH **b** : utter collapse : RUIN; *esp* : BANKRUPTCY **4** : a fruit beverage made with crushed or squeezed fruit **5** : a striking success : HIT

3**smash** *adv* : with a resounding crash

4**smash** *adj* : being a smash : OUTSTANDING <a ~ hit>

smashed \ˈsmasht\ *adj, slang* : DRUNK, INTOXICATED

smash·ing \ˈsmash-iŋ\ *adj* **1** : that smashes : CRUSHING <a ~ defeat> **2** : extraordinarily impressive or effective <a ~ performance> — **smash·ing·ly** \-iŋ-lē\ *adv*

smash·up \ˈsmash-ˌəp\ *n* **1** : a complete collapse **2** : a collision of motor vehicles

1**smat·ter** \ˈsmat-ər\ *vb* [ME *smateren*] *vt* **1** : to speak with spotty or superficial knowledge <~ French> **2** : to dabble in ~ *vi* : to talk superficially : BABBLE — **smat·ter·er** \-ər-ər\ *n*

2**smatter** *n* : SMATTERING

smat·ter·ing \ˈsmat-ə-riŋ\ *n* **1** : superficial piecemeal knowledge <a ~ of carpentry, house painting, bricklaying —Alva Johnston> **2** : a small scattered number or amount <a ~ of spectators>

smaze \ˈsmāz\ *n* [*sm*oke + h*aze*] : a combination of haze and smoke similar to smog in appearance but less damp in consistency

1**smear** \ˈsmi(ə)r\ *n* [ME *smere,* fr. OE *smeoru;* akin to OHG *smero* grease, Gk *smyris* emery, *myron* unguent] **1 a** : a viscous or sticky substance **b** : a spot made by or as if by an unctuous or adhesive substance **2** : material smeared on a surface (as of a microscopic slide); *also* : a preparation made by smearing material on a surface <a vaginal ~> **3** : a usu. unsubstantiated charge or accusation against a person or organization

2**smear** *vt* **1 a** : to overspread with something unctuous, viscous, or adhesive : DAUB **b** : to spread over a surface **2 a** : to stain, smudge, or dirty by or as if by smearing **b** : SULLY, BESMIRCH; *specif* : to vilify by applying an odious epithet or by secretly and maliciously spreading grave charges and imputations **3** : to obliterate, obscure, blur, blend, wipe out, or defeat by or as if by smearing — **smear·er** *n*

smear·case *or* **smier·case** \ˈsmi(ə)r-ˌkās\ *n* [modif. of G *schmierkäse,* fr. *schmieren* to smear + *käse* cheese] *chiefly Midland* : COTTAGE CHEESE

smear word *n* : an epithet intended to smear a person or group

smeary \ˈsmi(ə)r-ē\ *adj* **1** : marked by or covered with smears **2** : liable to cause smears <~ lipstick>

smec·tic \ˈsmek-tik\ *adj* [L *smecticus* cleansing, having the properties of soap, fr. Gk *smēktikos,* fr. *smēchein* to clean] : of, relating to, or being the phase of a liquid crystal characterized by the arrangement of the molecules in layers with the long axes of the molecules perpendicular to the plane of the layers — compare NEMATIC

smeg·ma \ˈsmeg-mə\ *n* [NL, fr. L, detergent, soap, fr. Gk *smēgma,* fr. *smēchein* to wash off, clean — more at SMITE] : the secretion of a sebaceous gland; *specif* : the cheesy sebaceous matter that collects between the glans penis and the foreskin or around the clitoris and labia minora

1**smell** \ˈsmel\ *vb* **smelled** \ˈsmeld\ *or* **smelt** \ˈsmelt\; **smell·ing** [ME *smellen;* akin to MD *smölen* to scorch, Russ *smalit'*] *vt* **1** : to perceive the odor or scent of through stimuli affecting the olfactory nerves : get the odor or scent of with the nose **2** : to detect or become aware of as if by the sense of smell **3** : to emit the odor of ~ *vi* **1** : to exercise the sense of smell **2 a** (1) : to have an odor or scent (2) : to have a characteristic aura or atmosphere : SUGGEST <the accounts . . . seemed to me to ~ of truth —R. S. Bourne> **b** (1) : to have an offensive odor : STINK (2) : to appear evil, dishonest, or ugly — **smell·er** *n* — **smell a rat** : to have a suspicion of something wrong

2**smell** *n* **1 a** : the process, function, or power of smelling **b** : the special sense concerned with the perception of odor **2** : the property of a thing that affects the olfactory organs : ODOR **3**

: a pervading quality : AURA <the ~ of affluence, of power —Harry Hervey> **4 :** an act or instance of smelling
syn SMELL, SCENT, ODOR, AROMA *shared meaning element* : a quality that makes a thing perceptible to the olfactory sense

smelling salts *n pl but sing or pl in constr* : a usu. scented aromatic preparation of ammonium carbonate and ammonia water used as a stimulant and restorative

smelly \ˈsmel-ē\ *adj* **smell·i·er; -est** : having a smell; *esp* : MALODOROUS

¹smelt \ˈsmelt\ *n, pl* **smelts** *or* **smelt** [ME, fr. OE; akin to Norw *smelte* whiting] : any of various small salmonoid fishes (family Osmeridae and esp. genus *Osmerus*) that closely resemble the trouts in general structure, live along coasts and ascend rivers to spawn or are landlocked, and have delicate oily flesh with a distinctive odor and taste

²smelt *vt* [D or LG *smelten;* akin to OHG *smelzan* to melt, OE *meltan*] **1 :** to melt or fuse (as ore) often with an accompanying chemical change usu. to separate the metal **2 :** REFINE, REDUCE

smelt·er \ˈsmel-tər\ *n* : one that smelts: **a :** a worker who smelts ore **b :** an owner or operator of a smeltery **c** *or* **smelt·ery** \-t(ə-)rē\ : an establishment for smelting

smew \ˈsmyü\ *n* [akin to MHG *smiehe* smew] : a merganser (*Mergus albellus*) of northern Europe and Asia the male of which is white-crested

smid·gen *or* **smid·geon** *or* **smid·gin** \ˈsmij-ən\ *n* [prob. alter. of E dial. *smitch* (soiling mark)] : a small amount : BIT

smi·lax \ˈsmī-ˌlaks\ *n* [L, bindweed, yew, fr. Gk] **1 :** GREENBRIER **2 :** a tender twining plant (*Asparagus asparagoides*) that has ovate bright green cladophylls and is often grown in greenhouses

¹smile \ˈsmī(ə)l\ *vb* **smiled; smil·ing** [ME *smilen;* akin to OE *smerian* to laugh, L *mirari* to wonder, Skt *smayate* he smiles] *vi* **1 :** to have, produce, or exhibit a smile **2 a :** to look or regard with amusement or ridicule <*smiled* at his own folly —Martin Gardner> **b :** to bestow approval <feeling that Heaven *smiled* on his labors —Sheila Rowlands> **c :** to appear pleasant or agreeable ~ *vt* **1 :** to affect with or by smiling **2 :** to express by a smile — **smil·er** *n* — **smil·ing·ly** \ˈsmī-liŋ-lē\ *adv*

²smile *n* **1 :** a change of facial expression in which the eyes brighten and the corners of the mouth curve slightly upward and which expresses esp. amusement, pleasure, approval, or sometimes scorn **2 :** a pleasant or encouraging appearance

smile·less \ˈsmī(ə)l-ləs\ *adj* : exhibiting no smile : SOLEMN — **smile·less·ly** *adv*

smirch \ˈsmərch\ *vt* [ME *smorchen*] **1 a :** to make dirty, stained, or discolored : SULLY **b :** to smear with something that stains or dirties **2 :** to bring discredit or disgrace on — **smirch** *n*

smirk \ˈsmərk\ *vi* [ME *smirken,* fr. OE *smearcian* to smile; akin to OE *smerian* to laugh] : to smile in an affected or smug manner : SIMPER — **smirk** *n*

smirky \ˈsmər-kē\ *adj* : that smirks : SMIRKING

smite \ˈsmīt\ *vb* **smote** \ˈsmōt\; **smit·ten** \ˈsmit-ᵊn\ *or* **smote; smit·ing** \ˈsmīt-iŋ\ [ME *smiten,* fr. OE *smītan;* akin to OHG *bismīzan* to defile and perh. to L *mittere* to let go, send] *vt* **1** : to strike sharply or heavily esp. with the hand or an implement held in the hand **2 a :** to kill or severely injure by smiting **b** : to attack or afflict suddenly and injuriously <*smitten* by disease> **3 :** to cause to strike **4 :** to affect as if by striking <children *smitten* with the fear of hell —V. L. Parrington> ~ *vi* : to deliver or deal a blow with or as if with the hand or something held ***syn*** see STRIKE — **smit·er** \ˈsmīt-ər\ *n*

smith \ˈsmith\ *n* [ME, fr. OE; akin to OHG *smid* smith, Gk *smilē* wood-carving knife] **1 :** a worker in metals : BLACKSMITH **2** : MAKER — often used in combination <gun*smith*> <tune*smith*>

smith·er·eens \ˌsmith-ə-ˈrēnz\ *n pl* [IrGael *smidirin*] : FRAGMENTS, BITS <the house was blown to ~ by the explosion>

smith·ery \ˈsmith-ə-rē\ *n, pl* **-er·ies** **1 :** the work, art, or trade of a smith **2 :** SMITHY 1

smith·son·ite \ˈsmith-sə-ˌnīt\ *n* [James *Smithson* †1829 Brit chemist] **1 :** a usu. white or nearly white native zinc carbonate $ZnCO_3$ **2 :** a mineral $Zn_4Si_2O_7OH.H_2O$ that is a silicate of zinc and constitutes an ore of zinc

smithy \ˈsmith-ē *also* ˈsmith-\ *n, pl* **smith·ies** **1 :** the workshop of a smith **2 :** BLACKSMITH

¹smock \ˈsmäk\ *n* [ME *smok,* fr. OE *smoc;* akin to OHG *smocco* adornment] **1** *archaic* : a woman's undergarment; *esp* : CHEMISE **2 :** a light loose garment worn esp. for protection of clothing while working

²smock *vt* : to embroider or shirr with smocking

smock frock *n* : a loose outer garment worn by workmen esp. in Europe

smock·ing \ˈsmäk-iŋ\ *n* : a decorative embroidery or shirring made by gathering cloth in regularly spaced round tucks

smog \ˈsmäg *also* ˈsmȯg\ *n* [blend of *smoke* and *fog*] : a fog made heavier and darker by smoke and chemical fumes ***syn*** see HAZE — **smog·less** \-ləs\ *adj*

smog·gy \-ē\ *adj* **smog·gi·er; -est** : characterized by or abounding in smog

smok·able *or* **smoke·able** \ˈsmō-kə-bəl\ *adj* : fit for smoking

¹smoke \ˈsmōk\ *n* [ME, fr. OE *smoca;* akin to MHG *smouch* smoke, Gk *smychein* to smolder] **1 a :** the gaseous products of burning carbonaceous materials made visible by the presence of small particles of carbon **b :** a suspension of particles in a gas **2 a :** a mass or column of smoke **b :** SMUDGE **3 :** fume or vapor often resulting from the action of heat on moisture **4 :** something of little substance, permanence, or value **5 :** something that obscures **6 a :** something (as a cigarette) to smoke : TOBACCO **b** : an act or spell of smoking tobacco **7 a :** a pale blue **b :** any of the colors of smoke **8 :** pitches consisting exclusively of fastballs <if a guy's going to hit you . . . he certainly isn't going to throw a spitter — he gives you ~ —Tony Conigliaro> — **smoke·less** \ˈsmō-kləs\ *adj* — **smoke·like** \-ˌklīk\ *adj*

²smoke *vb* **smoked; smok·ing** *vi* **1 a :** to emit or exhale smoke **b :** to emit excessive smoke **2** *archaic* : to undergo punishment : SUFFER **3 :** to spread or rise like smoke **4 :** to inhale and exhale the fumes of burning plant material and esp. tobacco; *esp* : to smoke tobacco habitually ~ *vt* **1 a :** FUMIGATE **b :** to drive (as mosquitoes) away by smoke **c :** to blacken or discolor with smoke <*smoked* glasses> **d :** to cure by exposure to smoke **e** : to stupefy (as bees) by smoke **2** *archaic* : SUSPECT **3 :** to inhale and exhale the smoke of **4** *archaic* : RIDICULE

smoke·chas·er \ˈsmōk-ˌchā-sər\ *n* : a forest fire fighter; *esp* : one with light equipment that enables him to get to fires quickly

smoke–filled room \ˌsmōk-ˌfil-ˈdrüm\ *n* : a room (as in a hotel) in which a small group of politicians carry on negotiations

smoke·house \ˈsmōk-ˌhau̇s\ *n* : a building where meat or fish is cured by means of dense smoke

smoke·jack \-ˌjak\ *n* : a device for turning a spit by a fly or wheel moved by rising gases in a chimney

smoke jumper *n* : a forest fire fighter who parachutes to locations otherwise difficult to reach

smokeless powder *n* : any of a class of explosive propellants that produce comparatively little smoke on explosion and consist mostly of gelatinized cellulose nitrates

smoke out *vt* **1 :** to drive out by or as if by smoke **2 :** to bring to public view or knowledge

smoke pipe *n* : a usu. thin metal pipe that connects a source of smoke to a chimney

smoke·proof \ˈsmōk-ˈprüf\ *adj* : impermeable to smoke; *specif* : designed to restrict the spread of smoke through a building

smok·er \ˈsmō-kər\ *n* **1 :** one that smokes **2 :** a railroad car or compartment in which smoking is allowed **3 :** an informal social gathering for men

smoke screen *n* **1 :** a screen of smoke to hinder enemy observation of a military force, area, or activity **2 :** something designed to obscure, confuse, or mislead

smoke·stack \ˈsmōk-ˌstak\ *n* : a chimney or funnel through which smoke and gases are discharged

smoke tree *n* : either of two small shrubby trees (genus *Cotinus*) of the sumac family often grown for their large panicles of minute flowers that suggest a cloud of smoke

smoking jacket *n* : a man's loose-fitting jacket for wear at home

smoking lamp *n* : a lamp on a ship kept lighted during the hours when smoking is allowed

smoking–room *adj* : marked by indecency or obscenity : SMUTTY

smoking room *n* : a room (as in a hotel or club) set apart for smokers

smoky *also* **smok·ey** \ˈsmō-kē\ *adj* **smok·i·er; -est** **1 :** emitting smoke esp. in large quantities **2 a :** having the characteristics of or resembling smoke **b :** suggestive of smoke esp. in flavor or odor **3 a :** filled with smoke **b :** made dark or black by smoke — **smok·i·ly** \-kə-lē\ *adv* — **smok·i·ness** \-kē-nəs\ *n*

smoky quartz *n* : CAIRNGORM

smoky topaz *n* : CAIRNGORM

¹smol·der *or* **smoul·der** \ˈsmōl-dər\ *n* [ME *smolder;* akin to ME *smellen* to smell] **1 :** SMOKE, SMUDGE **2 :** a smoldering fire

²smolder *or* **smoulder** *vi* **smol·dered** *or* **smoul·dered; smol·der·ing** *or* **smoul·der·ing** \-d(ə-)riŋ\ **1 a :** to burn sluggishly, without flame, and often with much smoke **b :** to be consumed by smoldering — often used with *out* **2 :** to exist in a state of suppressed activity <resentment ~*ed* in her> **3 :** to show suppressed anger, hate, or jealousy <eyes ~*ing* with hate>

smolt \ˈsmōlt\ *n* [ME (Sc)] : a young salmon or sea trout that is about two years old and that is at the stage of development when it assumes the silvery color of the adult

¹smooch \ˈsmüch\ *vt* [prob. alter. of *smutch,* vb.] : SMUDGE, SMEAR

²smooch *n* : SMUDGE, SMEAR — **smoochy** \ˈsmü-chē\ *adj*

³smooch *vi* [alter. of *smouch* (to kiss loudly)] : KISS, PET

⁴smooch *n* : KISS

¹smooth \ˈsmüth\ *adj* [ME *smothe,* fr. OE *smōth;* akin to OS *smōthi* smooth] **1 a :** having a continuous even surface **b :** being without hair **c :** GLABROUS <a ~ leaf> **d :** causing no resistance to sliding **2 :** free from obstructions or impediments <the ~ course of his life> **3 :** even and uninterrupted in flow or flight **4 :** excessively and often artfully suave : INGRATIATING **5 a :** SERENE, EQUABLE <a ~ disposition> **b :** AMIABLE, COURTEOUS **6** : not sharp or acid : BLAND <a ~ sherry> ***syn*** **1** see LEVEL **2** see SUAVE ***ant*** bluff — **smooth** *adv* — **smooth·ly** *adv* — **smooth·ness** *n*

²smooth *vt* **1 :** to make smooth **2 a :** to free from what is harsh or disagreeable : POLISH <~*ed* out his style> **b :** SOOTHE **3** : to minimize (as a fault) in order to allay anger or ill will : PALLIATE <his main job is to ~ over the friction that so often arises —Brian Crozier> **4 :** to free from obstruction or difficulty **5 a :** to press flat **b :** to remove expression from (one's face) : COMPOSE **6 :** to cause to lie evenly and in order : PREEN **7** : to free (as a graph or data) from irregularities by ignoring random variations ~ *vi* : to become smooth — **smooth·er** *n*

³smooth *n* **1 :** a smooth part **2 :** the act of smoothing **3 :** a smoothing implement

smooth·bore \ˈsmüth-ˈbō(ə)r, -ˈbȯ(ə)r\ *adj, of a firearm* : having a smooth-surfaced bore — **smoothbore** \-ˌbō(ə)r, -ˌbȯ(ə)r\ *n*

smooth breathing *n* **1 :** a mark ʼ placed over some initial vowels in Greek to show that they are not aspirated (as in ἐκεῖ pronounced \e-ˈkā\) **2 :** the absence of aspiration indicated by a mark ʼ

smooth·en \ˈsmü-thən\ *vb* **smooth·ened; smooth·en·ing** \ˈsmüth-(ə-)niŋ\ *vt* : to make smooth ~ *vi* : to become smooth

smooth hound *n* [fr. the absence of a spine in front of the dorsal fin] : any of various dogfishes (genus *Mustelus*)

smooth muscle *n* **:** muscle tissue that lacks cross striations, that is made up of elongated spindle-shaped cells having a central nucleus, and that is found in vertebrate visceral structures (as the stomach and bladder) as thin sheets performing functions not under direct voluntary control and in all or most of the musculature of invertebrates other than arthropods — compare STRIATED MUSCLE
smooth–tongued \ˈsmüt͟h-ˈtəŋd\ *adj* **:** ingratiating in speech
smoothy *or* **smooth·ie** \ˈsmü-t͟hē\ *n, pl* **smooth·ies** **1 a :** a person with polished manners **b :** one who behaves or performs with deftness, assurance, and easy competence; *esp* **:** a man with an ingratiating manner toward women **2 :** a smooth-tongued person
smor·gas·bord \ˈsmȯr-gəs-ˌbō(ə)rd, -ˌbȯ(ə)rd\ *n* [Sw *smörgåsbord,* fr. *smörgas* open sandwich + *bord* table] **1 :** a luncheon or supper buffet offering a variety of foods and dishes (as hors d'oeuvres, hot and cold meats, smoked and pickled fish, cheeses, salads, and relishes) **2 :** a heterogeneous mixture **:** MÉLANGE
smote *past of* SMITE
¹smoth·er \ˈsmət͟h-ər\ *n* [ME, alter. of *smorther,* fr. *smoren* to smother, fr. OE *smorian* to suffocate; akin to MD *smoren* to suffocate] **1 a :** thick stifling smoke or smudge **b :** a state of being stifled or suppressed **2 :** a dense cloud of fog, foam, spray, snow, or dust **3 :** a confused multitude of things **:** WELTER — **smoth·ery** \-(ə-)rē\ *adj*
²smother *vb* **smoth·ered; smoth·er·ing** \-(ə-)riŋ\ *vt* **1 :** to overcome or kill with smoke or fumes **2 a :** to destroy the life of by depriving of air **b :** to overcome or discomfit through or as if through lack of air **c :** to suppress (a fire) by excluding oxygen **3 a :** to cause to smolder **b :** to suppress expression or knowledge of <~ a yawn> <~*ed* his rage> **c :** to stop or prevent the growth or activity of <~ a child with too much care> **d :** to cover thickly **:** BLANKET <snow ~*ed* the trails> **e :** OVERCOME, VANQUISH **4 :** to cook in a covered pan or pot with little liquid over low heat ~ *vi* **:** to become smothered
SMSgt *abbr* senior master sergeant
¹smudge \ˈsməj\ *vb* **smudged; smudg·ing** [ME *smogen*] *vt* **1 a :** to make a smudge on **b :** to soil as if by smudging **2 a :** to rub, daub, or wipe in a smeary manner **b :** to make indistinct **:** BLUR **3 :** to smoke or protect by means of a smudge ~ *vi* **1 :** to make a smudge **2 :** to become smudged
²smudge *n* **1 a :** a blurry spot or streak **b :** an immaterial stain <cleanse him of every last ~ of impropriety —Richard Hanser> **c :** an indistinct mass **:** BLUR **2 :** a smoldering mass placed on the windward side (as to protect from frost) **3 :** a bid of 4 in pitch that if made wins the game — **smudg·i·ly** \ˈsməj-ə-lē\ *adv* — **smudg·i·ness** \ˈsməj-ē-nəs\ *n* — **smudgy** \-ē\ *adj*
smug \ˈsməg\ *adj* **smug·ger; smug·gest** [prob. modif. of LG *smuck* neat, fr. MLG, fr. *smucken* to dress; akin to OE *smoc* smock] **1 :** trim or smart in dress **:** SPRUCE **2 :** scrupulously clean, neat, or correct **:** TIDY **3 :** highly self-satisfied <~, self-righteous moralists —Edison Marshall> — **smug·ness** *n*
smug·gle \ˈsməg-əl\ *vb* **smug·gled; smug·gling** \-(ə-)liŋ\ [LG *smuggeln* & D *smokkelen;* akin to OE *smoc* smock] *vt* **1 :** to import or export secretly contrary to the law and esp. without paying duties imposed by law **2 :** to convey or introduce surreptitiously ~ *vi* **:** to import or export something in violation of the customs laws — **smug·gler** \ˈsməg-lər\ *n*
smug·ly \ˈsməg-lē\ *adv* **:** in a smug manner
¹smut \ˈsmət\ *vb* **smut·ted; smut·ting** [prob. alter. of earlier *smot* to stain, fr. ME *smotten;* akin to MHG *smutzen* to stain] *vt* **1 :** to stain or taint with smut **2 :** to affect (a crop or plant) with smut ~ *vi* **:** to become affected by smut
²smut *n* **1 :** matter that soils or blackens; *specif* **:** a particle of soot **2 :** any of various destructive diseases esp. of cereal grasses caused by parasitic fungi (order Ustilaginales) and marked by transformation of plant organs into dark masses of spores; *also* **:** a fungus causing a smut **3 :** obscene language or matter
smutch \ˈsməch\ *n* [prob. irreg. fr. ¹*smudge*] **:** a dark stain **:** SMUDGE — **smutch** *vt* — **smutchy** \-ē\ *adj*
smut·ty \ˈsmət-ē\ *adj* **smut·ti·er; -est** **1 :** soiled or tainted with smut; *esp* **:** affected with smut fungus **2 :** OBSCENE, INDECENT **3 :** resembling smut in appearance **:** SOOTY — **smut·ti·ly** \ˈsmət-ᵊl-ē\ *adv* — **smut·ti·ness** \ˈsmət-ē-nəs\ *n*
SMV *abbr* slow-moving vehicle
Sn *symbol* [LL *stannum*] tin
¹snack \ˈsnak\ *vi* [ME *snaken* to bite] **:** to eat a snack **:** LUNCH
²snack *n* **:** a light meal **:** food eaten between regular meals
snack bar *n* **:** a public eating place where snacks are served usu. at a counter
¹snaf·fle \ˈsnaf-əl\ *n* [origin unknown] **:** a simple usu. jointed bit for a bridle — see BIT illustration
²snaffle *vt* **snaf·fled; snaf·fling** \ˈsnaf-(ə-)liŋ\ [origin unknown] **:** to obtain esp. by devious or irregular means
¹sna·fu \sna-ˈfü\ *adj* [*s*ituation *n*ormal *a*ll *f*ucked *u*p (fouled up)] **:** snarled or stalled in confusion **:** AWRY
²snafu *n* **:** CONFUSION, MUDDLE
³snafu *vt* **:** to bring into a state of confusion
¹snag \ˈsnag\ *n* [of Scand origin; akin to ON *snagi* clothes peg] **1 a :** a stub or stump remaining after a branch has been lopped or torn off **b :** a tree or branch embedded in a lake or stream bed and constituting a hazard to navigation **2 :** a rough sharp or jagged projecting part **:** PROTUBERANCE: as **a :** a projecting tooth; *also* **:** a stump of a tooth **b :** one of the secondary branches of an antler **3 :** a concealed or unexpected difficulty or obstacle **4 :** a jagged tear made by or as if by catching on a snag <a ~ in her stocking> — **snag·gy** \ˈsnag-ē\ *adj*
²snag *vt* **snagged; snag·ging** **1 :** to hew, trim, or cut roughly or jaggedly **2 a :** to catch and usu. damage on or as if on a snag **b :** to halt or impede as if by catching on a snag **3 :** to clear (as a river) of snags **4 :** to catch or obtain by quick action
snag·gle·tooth \ˈsnag-əl-ˌtüth\ *n* [E dial. *snaggle* (irregularly shaped tooth) + E *tooth*] **:** an irregular, broken, or projecting tooth — **snag·gle·toothed** \ˌsnag-əl-ˈtütht\ *adj*
¹snail \ˈsnā(ə)l\ *n* [ME, fr. OE *snægl;* akin to OHG *snecko* snail, *snahhan* to creep, Lith *snāke* snail] **1 :** a gastropod mollusk esp. when having an external enclosing spiral shell **2 :** a slow-moving or sluggish person or thing — **snail·like** \ˈsnā(ə)l-ˌlīk\ *adj*
²snail *vi* **:** to move, act, or go slowly or lazily
snail fever *n* [fr. the snails which serve as intermediate hosts to the schistosomes causing the disease] **:** SCHISTOSOMIASIS
snail–paced \ˈsnā(ə)l-ˈpāst\ *adj* **:** moving very slowly

snail 1

¹snake \ˈsnāk\ *n* [ME, fr. OE *snaca;* akin to OE *snægl* snail] **1 :** any of numerous limbless scaled reptiles (suborder Serpentes or Ophidia) with a long tapering body and with salivary glands often modified to produce venom which is injected through grooved or tubular fangs **2 :** a worthless or treacherous fellow — **snake·like** \ˈsnā-ˌklīk\ *adj*
²snake *vb* **snaked; snak·ing** *vt* **1 :** to wind (as one's way) in the manner of a snake **2 :** to move (as logs) by dragging ~ *vi* **:** to crawl, move, or extend silently, secretly, or sinuously
snake·bird \ˈsnāk-ˌbərd\ *n* **:** any of several fish-eating birds (genus *Anhinga*) related to the cormorants but distinguished by a long slender neck and sharp-pointed bill
snake·bite \-ˌbīt\ *n* **:** the bite of a snake and esp. a venomous snake
snake charmer *n* **:** an entertainer who exhibits his professed power to charm or fascinate venomous snakes
snake–dance *vi* **:** to engage in a snake dance
snake dance *n* **1 :** a ceremonial dance in which snakes or their images are handled, invoked, or symbolically imitated by individual sinuous actions **2 :** a group progression in a single-file serpentine path (as in celebration of an athletic victory)
snake doctor *n* **1 :** HELLGRAMMITE **2 :** DRAGONFLY
snake fence *n* **:** WORM FENCE
snake in the grass : a secretly faithless friend
snake·mouth \ˈsnāk-ˌmau̇th\ *n* **:** a bog orchid (*Pogonia ophioglossoides*) of eastern No. America and Japan with showy pink flowers
snake oil *n* **:** any of various substances or mixtures sold (as by a traveling medicine show) as medicine usu. without regard to their medical worth or properties
snake pit *n* **:** a place of chaotic disorder and distress; *esp* **:** a hospital for mental diseases
snake·root \ˈsnā-ˌkrüt, -ˌkru̇t\ *n* **:** any of numerous plants most of which have roots sometimes believed to cure snakebites; *also* **:** the root of such a plant
snake·skin \ˈsnāk-ˌskin\ *n* **:** leather prepared from the skin of a snake
snake·weed \ˈsnā-ˌkwēd\ *n* **:** any of several plants associated with snakes (as in appearance, habitat, or use in treatment of snakebite)
snaky \ˈsnā-kē\ *adj* **1 :** of, formed of, or entwined with snakes <the Gorgon with ~ hair —Joseph Addison> **2 :** SERPENTINE, SNAKELIKE <the ~ arms of an octopus> **3 :** suggestive of a snake <the oiliness and ~ insinuation of his demeanor — Thomas DeQuincy> **4 :** abounding in snakes — **snak·i·ly** \-kə-lē\ *adv*
¹snap \ˈsnap\ *vb* **snapped; snap·ping** [D or LG *snappen;* akin to MHG *snappen* to snap] *vi* **1 a :** to make a sudden closing of the jaws **:** seize something sharply with the mouth <fish *snapping* at the bait> **b :** to grasp at something eagerly **:** make a pounce or snatch <~ at any chance> **2 :** to utter sharp biting words **:** bark out irritable or peevish retorts **3 a :** to break suddenly with a sharp sound <the twig *snapped*> **b :** to give way suddenly under strain **4 :** to make a sharp or crackling sound **5 :** to close or fit in place with an abrupt movement or sharp sound <the lock *snapped* shut> **6 :** to move briskly or sharply <~*s* to attention> **7 :** to open and close rapidly <eyes *snapping* with fury> ~ *vt* **1 :** to seize with or as if with a snap of the jaws <*snapped* the food right out of his hand> **2 :** to take possession or advantage of suddenly or eagerly — usu. used with *up* <shoppers *snapping* up bargains> **3 a :** to retort to or interrupt curtly and irritably **b :** to utter curtly or abruptly **4 :** to break suddenly **:** break short or in two **5 a :** to cause to make a snapping sound <~ a whip> **b :** to put into or remove from a particular position by a sudden movement or with a sharp sound <~ the lock shut> **6 a :** to project with a snap **b :** to put (a football) in play with a snap **c** (1) **:** to take photographically <*snapping* exclusive news pictures — *Current Biog.*> (2) **:** to take a snapshot of ***syn*** see JERK — **snap out of it :** to free oneself from something (as a mood or habit) by an effort of will
²snap *n* **1 :** an abrupt closing (as of the mouth in biting or of scissors in cutting) **2 a** *archaic* **:** a share of profits or booty **b :** something that brings quick and easy profit or advantage **c :** something that is easy and presents no problems **:** CINCH **3 :** a small amount **:** BIT **4 a :** an act or instance of seizing abruptly **:** a sudden snatching at something **b :** a quick short movement <lithe ~*s* of its body —Barbara Taylor> **c :** a sudden sharp breaking <the ~ of a twig> **5 a :** a sound made by snapping something <shut the book with a ~> **b :** a brief sharp and usu. irritable speech or retort **6 :** a sudden spell of weather <a cold ~> **7 :** a catch or fastening that closes or locks with a click <the ~ of a bracelet> **8 :** a flat brittle cookie — compare GINGERSNAP **9 :** SNAPSHOT **10 a :** the condition of being vigorous in body, mind, or spirit **:** ALERTNESS, ENERGY **b :** a pleasing vigorous quality **11 :** the act of a center's putting the football in play from its position on the ground by quickly passing it between his legs to a teammate (as a quarterback) standing behind him
³snap *adv* **:** with a snap <the sail went ~ in the wind>
⁴snap *adj* **1 :** done or carried through suddenly or without deliberation <a ~ judgment> **2 :** called or taken without prior warning <a ~ test> **3 :** shutting or fastening with a click or by means of a device that snaps <a ~ lock> **4 :** unusually easy or simple <a ~ course>
snap·back \ˈsnap-ˌbak\ *n* **1 :** a football snap **2 :** a sudden rebound or recovery <a ~ of prices on the stock exchange>

snap back \(ˈ)snap-ˈbak\ *vi* **:** to make a quick or vigorous recovery
snap bean *n* **:** a bean grown primarily for its pods that are usu. broken in pieces and cooked as a vegetable while young and tender and before the seeds have become enlarged — compare SHELL BEAN
snap–brim \ˌsnap-ˌbrim\ *n* **:** a usu. felt hat with brim turned up in back and down in front and with a dented crown
snap·drag·on \ˈsnap-ˌdrag-ən\ *n* [fr. the fancied resemblance of the flowers to the face of a dragon] **:** any of several garden plants (genus *Antirrhinum* and esp. *A. majus*) of the figwort family having showy white, crimson, or yellow bilabiate flowers
snap fastener *n* **:** a metal fastener consisting essentially of a ball and a socket attached to opposed parts of an article and used to hold meeting edges together
snap–on \ˈsnap-ˌȯn, -ˌän\ *adj* **:** designed to snap into position and fit tightly <~ cuffs>
snap·per \ˈsnap-ər\ *n, pl* **snappers** **1 a :** one that snaps **b** (1) **:** SNAPPING TURTLE (2) **:** CLICK BEETLE **2** *pl also* **snapper** **a :** any of numerous active carnivorous fishes (family Lutjanidae) of warm seas important as food and often as sport fishes **b :** any of several immature fishes (as the young of the bluefish) that resemble a snapper

snapdragon

snap·per–back \-ər-ˌbak\ *n* **:** a football center
snapping turtle *n* **:** either of two large edible American aquatic turtles (family Chelydridae) with powerful jaws and a strong musky odor: **a :** a turtle (*Chelydra serpentina*) that has the head covered with smooth skin, has large plates in a double row on the underside of the tail, and is distributed from eastern Canada to Central America and Ecuador **b :** ALLIGATOR SNAPPER
snap·pish \ˈsnap-ish\ *adj* **1 a :** given to curt irritable speech **b :** arising from annoyance or irascibility **2 :** inclined to bite <a ~ dog> — **snap·pish·ly** *adv* — **snap·pish·ness** *n*
snap·py \ˈsnap-ē\ *adj* **snap·pi·er; -est** **1 :** SNAPPISH 1 **2 a :** quickly made or done **b :** marked by vigor and movement **c :** briskly cold <a ~ day> **d :** STYLISH, SMART <a ~ dresser> — **snap·pi·ly** \ˈsnap-ə-lē\ *adv* — **snap·pi·ness** \ˈsnap-ē-nəs\ *n*
snap roll *n* **:** a maneuver in which an airplane is made by quick movement of the controls to complete a full revolution about its longitudinal axis while maintaining an approximately level line of flight
snap·shoot \ˈsnap-ˌshüt\ *vt* [back-formation fr. *snapshot*] **:** to take a snapshot of — **snap·shoot·er** *n*
snap·shot \ˈsnap-ˌshät\ *n* **1 :** a casual photograph made typically by an amateur with a small hand-held camera and without regard to technique **2 :** a brief or transitory impression or view
snap shot *n* **:** a quick shot (as with a rifle) made without deliberately taking aim
[1]**snare** \ˈsna(ə)r, ˈsne(ə)r\ *n* [ME, fr. OE *sneare,* fr. ON *snara;* akin to Gk *narkē* numbness, OHG *snuor* cord — more at NARROW] **1 a** (1) **:** a contrivance often consisting of a noose for entangling birds or mammals (2) **:** TRAP, GIN **b** (1) **:** something by which one is entangled, involved in difficulties, or impeded (2) **:** something deceptively attractive **2** [prob. fr. D *snaar,* lit., cord; akin to OHG *snuor*] **:** one of the catgut strings or metal spirals of a snare drum **3 :** a surgical instrument consisting usu. of a wire loop constricted by a mechanism in the handle and used for removing tissue masses (as tonsils)
[2]**snare** *vt* **snared; snar·ing** **1 a :** to capture by or as if by use of a snare **b :** to win or attain by artful or skillful maneuvers **2 :** to entangle or hold as if in a snare <any object that *snared* his eye —*Current Biog.*> ***syn*** see CATCH — **snar·er** *n*
snare drum *n* **:** a small double-headed drum with one or more snares stretched across its lower head — see DRUM illustration
[1]**snarl** \ˈsnär(ə)l\ *n* [ME *snarle,* prob. dim. of *snare*] **1 :** a tangle esp. of hairs or thread **:** KNOT **2 :** a tangled situation <traffic ~*s*> — **snarly** \ˈsnär-lē\ *adj*
[2]**snarl** *vt* **1 :** to cause to become knotted and intertwined **:** TANGLE **2 :** to make excessively complicated ~ *vi* **:** to become snarled — **snarl·er** *n*
[3]**snarl** *vb* [freq. of obs. E *snar* (to growl)] *vi* **1 :** to growl with a snapping or gnashing of teeth **2 :** to give vent to anger in surly language ~ *vt* **:** to utter or express with a snarl or by snarling — **snarl·er** *n*
[4]**snarl** *n* **:** a surly angry growl — **snarly** \ˈsnär-lē\ *adj*
snash \ˈsnash\ *n* [origin unknown] *chiefly Scot* **:** INSOLENCE, ABUSE
[1]**snatch** \ˈsnach\ *vb* [ME *snacchen* to give a sudden snap, seize; akin to MD *snacken* to snap at] *vi* **:** to attempt to seize something suddenly ~ *vt* **1 :** to grasp abruptly or hastily **2 :** to seize or grab suddenly without permission, ceremony, or right ***syn*** see TAKE — **snatch·er** *n*
[2]**snatch** *n* **1 a :** a snatching at or of something **b** *slang* **:** an act or instance of kidnapping **2 a :** a brief period <caught ~*es* of sleep> **b :** something brief, fragmentary, or hurried <caught ~*es* of the conversation> **3 :** a lift in weight lifting in which the weight is raised from the floor directly to an overhead position usu. with a lunge or squat under the weight — compare CLEAN AND JERK, PRESS
snatch block *n* **:** a block that can be opened on one side to receive the bight of a rope
snatchy \ˈsnach-ē\ *adj* **:** marked by breaks in continuity
snath \ˈsnath, ˈsneth\ *or* **snathe** \ˈsnāth, ˈsnāth\ *n* [ME *snede,* fr. OE *snǣd;* akin to OHG *snīdan* to cut, Czech *snět* branch] **:** the handle of a scythe
snaz·zy \ˈsnaz-ē\ *adj* **snaz·zi·er; -est** [origin unknown] **:** conspicuously or flashily attractive
SNCC \ˈsnik\ *abbr* Student Nonviolent Coordinating Committee
[1]**sneak** \ˈsnēk\ *vb* **sneaked** \ˈsnēkt\ *also* **snuck** \ˈsnək\; **sneak·ing** [akin to OE *snīcan* to sneak along, OHG *snahhan* to creep — more at SNAIL] *vi* **1 :** to go stealthily or furtively **:** SLINK **2 :** to behave in a furtive or servile manner **3 :** to carry the football on a quarterback sneak ~ *vt* **:** to put, bring, or take in a furtive or artful manner <~ a smoke> ***syn*** see LURK — **sneak up on :** to approach or act on stealthily
[2]**sneak** *n* **1 :** a person who acts in a stealthy, furtive, or shifty manner **2 a :** a stealthy or furtive move **b :** an unobserved departure or escape **3 :** SNEAKER 2 — usu. used in pl. **4 :** QUARTERBACK SNEAK
[3]**sneak** *adj* **1 :** carried on secretly **:** CLANDESTINE **2 :** occurring without warning **:** SURPRISE <a ~ attack>
sneak·er \ˈsnē-kər\ *n* **1 :** one that sneaks **2 :** a usu. canvas sports shoe with a pliable rubber sole — used usu. in pl. — **sneak·ered** \-kərd\ *adj*
sneak·ing \ˈsnē-kiŋ\ *adj* **1 :** characteristic of a sneak **:** FURTIVE, UNDERHAND **2 :** MEAN, CONTEMPTIBLE **3 a :** not openly expressed or acknowledged <he has a ~ respect for culture —H. A. Burton> **b :** that is a persistent conjecture <a ~ suspicion> — **sneak·ing·ly** \-kiŋ-lē\ *adv*
sneak preview *n* **:** a special advanced showing of a motion picture usu. announced but not named
sneak thief *n* **:** a thief who steals whatever he can without using violence or forcibly breaking into buildings
sneaky \ˈsnē-kē\ *adj* **sneak·i·er; -est** **:** marked by stealth, furtiveness, or shiftiness — **sneak·i·ly** \-kə-lē\ *adv* — **sneak·i·ness** \-kē-nəs\ *n*
[1]**sneap** \ˈsnēp\ *vt* [ME *snaipen,* prob. of Scand origin; akin to Icel *sneypa* to scold — more at SNUB] **1** *dial Eng* **:** CHIDE **2** *archaic* **:** to blast or blight with cold **:** NIP
[2]**sneap** *n, archaic* **:** REBUKE, SNUB
sneck \ˈsnek\ *n* [ME *snekke*] *chiefly dial* **:** LATCH
[1]**sneer** \ˈsni(ə)r\ *vb* [prob. akin to MHG *snerren* to chatter, gossip — more at SNORE] *vi* **1 :** to smile or laugh with facial contortions that express scorn or contempt **2 :** to speak or write in a scornfully jeering manner ~ *vt* **:** to utter with a sneer ***syn*** see SCOFF — **sneer·er** *n*
[2]**sneer** *n* **:** the act of sneering **:** a sneering expression or remark
sneesh \ˈsnēsh\ *n* [short for E dial. *sneeshing,* alter. of obs. E *sneezing,* fr. E, gerund of *sneeze*] *dial Brit* **:** [5]SNUFF 1
[1]**sneeze** \ˈsnēz\ *vi* **sneezed; sneez·ing** [ME *snesen,* alter. of *fnesen,* fr. OE *fnēosan;* akin to MHG *pfnūsen* to snort, sneeze, Gk *pnein* to breathe] **:** to make a sudden violent spasmodic audible expiration of breath — **sneez·er** *n* — **sneeze at :** to make light of
[2]**sneeze** *n* **:** an act or fact of sneezing
sneeze·weed \ˈsnēz-ˌwēd\ *n* **1 :** any of several composite plants; *esp* **:** a No. American yellow-flowered perennial herb (*Helenium autumnale*) whose odor is held to cause sneezing **2 :** SNEEZEWORT
sneeze·wort \-ˌwərt, -ˌwȯ(ə)rt\ *n* **:** a strong-scented Eurasian composite perennial herb (*Achillea ptarmica*) resembling yarrow
sneezy \ˈsnē-zē\ *adj* **:** given to or causing sneezing
[1]**snell** \ˈsnel\ *adj* [ME, fr. OE; akin to OHG *snel* bold, agile] **1** *chiefly Scot* **:** QUICK, ACUTE **2** *chiefly Scot* **:** KEEN, PIERCING <a ~ wind smote us —*Scotsman*> **3** *chiefly Scot* **:** GRIEVOUS, SEVERE
[2]**snell** *n* [origin unknown] **:** a short line (as of gut) by which a fishhook is attached to a longer line
[1]**snick** \ˈsnik\ *vb* [prob. fr. obs. *snick or snee* to engage in cut-and-thrust fighting — more at SNICKERSNEE] *vt* **1** *archaic* **:** to cut through **2 :** to cut slightly **:** NICK ~ *vi* **:** to perform a light cutting action
[2]**snick** *n* **:** a small cut **:** NICK
[3]**snick** *vb* [imit.] **:** CLICK
[4]**snick** *n* **:** a slight often metallic sound **:** CLICK
[1]**snick·er** \ˈsnik-ər\ *vi* **snick·ered; snick·er·ing** \-(ə-)riŋ\ [imit.] **:** to laugh in a covert or partly suppressed manner **:** TITTER — **snick·er·er** \-ər-ər\ *n* — **snick·ery** \-(ə-)rē\ *adj*
[2]**snicker** *n* **:** an act or sound of snickering
snick·er·snee *or* **snick–a–snee** *or* **snick–or–snee** \ˈsnik-ə(r)-ˌsnē\ *n* [obs. *snick or snee* to engage in cut-and-thrust fighting, alter. of earlier *steake or snye,* fr. D *steken of snijden* to thrust or cut] **:** a large knife
snide \ˈsnīd\ *adj* [origin unknown] **1 a :** FALSE, COUNTERFEIT **b :** practicing deception **:** DISHONEST <a ~ merchant> **2 :** unworthy of esteem **:** LOW <a ~ trick> **3 :** slyly disparaging **:** INSINUATING <~ remarks> — **snide·ly** *adv* — **snide·ness** *n*
[1]**sniff** \ˈsnif\ *vb* [ME *sniffen*] *vi* **1 :** to draw air audibly up the nose esp. for smelling <~*ed* at the flowers> **2 :** to show or express disdain or scorn ~ *vt* **1 :** to smell or take by inhalation through the nose **2 :** to utter contemptuously **3 :** to recognize or detect by or as if by smelling <~ out trouble>
[2]**sniff** *n* **1 :** an act or sound of sniffing **2 :** a quantity that is sniffed
sniff·er *n* **:** one that sniffs; *esp* **:** one who takes drugs illicitly by sniffing
sniff·ish \ˈsnif-ish\ *adj* **:** having or expressing a haughty attitude **:** DISDAINFUL, SUPERCILIOUS — **sniff·ish·ly** *adv* — **sniff·ish·ness** *n*
[1]**snif·fle** \ˈsnif-əl\ *vi* **snif·fled; snif·fling** \-(ə-)liŋ\ [freq. of *sniff*] **1 :** to sniff repeatedly **:** SNUFFLE **2 :** to speak with or as if with sniffling — **snif·fler** \-(ə-)lər\ *n*
[2]**sniffle** *n* **1 :** an act or sound of sniffling **2** *pl* **:** a head cold marked by nasal discharge
sniffy \ˈsnif-ē\ *adj* **:** SNIFFISH, SUPERCILIOUS — **sniff·i·ly** \ˈsnif-ə-lē\ *adv* — **sniff·i·ness** \ˈsnif-ē-nəs\ *n*
snif·ter \ˈsnif-tər\ *n* [E dial., sniff, snort, fr. ME *snifteren* to sniff, snort] **1 :** a small drink of distilled liquor **2 :** a large short-stemmed goblet with a bowl narrowing toward the top
[1]**snig·ger** \ˈsnig-ər\ *vi* **snig·gered; snig·ger·ing** \-(ə-)riŋ\ [by alter.] **:** SNICKER — **snig·ger·er** \-ər-ər\ *n*
[2]**snigger** *n* **:** SNICKER
snig·gle \ˈsnig-əl\ *vb* **snig·gled; snig·gling** \-(ə-)liŋ\ [E dial. *snig* small eel, fr. ME *snygge*] *vi* **:** to fish for eels by thrusting a baited

hook or needle into their hiding places ~ *vt* : to catch (an eel) by sniggling

[1]**snip** \'snip\ *n* [fr. or akin to D&LG *snip*] **1 a :** a small piece that is snipped off; *also* : FRAGMENT, BIT **b :** a cut or notch made by snipping **c :** an act or sound of snipping **2 :** a white or light mark (as on a horse) **3 :** a presumptuous or impertinent person; *esp* : an impertinent or saucy girl **4** *Brit* : BARGAIN, BUY

[2]**snip** *vb* **snipped; snip·ping** *vt* : to cut or cut off with or as if with shears or scissors; *specif* : to clip suddenly or by bits ~ *vi* : to make a short quick cut with or as if with shears or scissors — **snip·per** *n*

[1]**snipe** \'snīp\ *n, pl* **snipes** [ME, of Scand origin; akin to ON *snīpa* snipe; akin to OHG *snepfa* snipe] **1** *or pl* **snipe :** any of various usu. slender-billed birds (suborder Charadrii); *esp* : any of several game birds (genus *Capella*) that occur esp. in marshy areas and resemble the related woodcocks **2 :** a contemptible person

[2]**snipe** *vi* **sniped; snip·ing 1 :** to shoot or hunt snipe **2 a :** to shoot at exposed individuals of an enemy's forces esp. when not in action from a usu. concealed point of vantage **b :** to aim a carping or snide attack — **snip·er** *n*

snip·er·scope \'snī-pər-ˌskōp\ *n* : a snooperscope for use on a rifle or carbine

snip·per·snap·per \'snip-ər-ˌsnap-ər\ *n* [origin unknown] : WHIPPERSNAPPER

snip·pet \'snip-ət\ *n* [[1]*snip*] : a small part, piece, or thing; *esp* : a brief quotable passage

snip·pety \-ət-ē\ *adj* **1 :** made up of snippets **2** [prob. fr. [2]*snip* + *-ety* (as in *pernickety*)] : SNIPPY

snip·py \'snip-ē\ *adj* **snip·pi·er; -est** [[2]*snip*] **1 :** SHORT-TEMPERED, SNAPPISH **2 :** unduly brief or curt **3 :** putting on airs : SNIFFY

snips \'snips\ *n pl but sing or pl in constr* : hand shears used esp. for cutting sheet metal

snip–snap \'snip-ˌsnap\ *n, archaic* : clever quick repartee

snit \'snit\ *n* [origin unknown] : a state of agitation

snitch \'snich\ *vi* [origin unknown] : INFORM, TATTLE ~ *vt* [prob. alter. of *snatch*] : to take by stealth; : PILFER — **snitch·er** *n*

[1]**sniv·el** \'sniv-əl\ *vi* **sniv·eled** *or* **sniv·elled; sniv·el·ing** *or* **sniv·el·ling** \-(ə-)liŋ\ [ME *snivelen*, fr. (assumed) OE *snyflan;* akin to D *snuffelen* to snuffle, *snuffen* to sniff, Gk *nan* to flow — more at NOURISH] **1 :** to run at the nose **2 :** to snuff mucus up the nose audibly : SNUFFLE **3 :** to cry or whine with snuffling **4 :** to speak or act in a whining, sniffling, tearful, or weakly emotional manner — **sniv·el·er** \-(ə-)lər\ *n*

[2]**snivel** *n* **1** *pl, dial* : HEAD COLD **2 :** an act or instance of sniveling

snob \'snäb\ *n* [obs. *snob* member of the lower classes, fr. E dial., shoemaker] **1** *archaic* : COBBLER **2 :** one who blatantly imitates, fawningly admires, or vulgarly seeks association with those he regards as his superiors **3 a :** one who tends to rebuff, avoid, or ignore those he regards as inferior **b :** one who has an offensive air of superiority in matters of knowledge or taste <a cultural ~>

snob appeal *n* : qualities in a product (as high price, rarity, or foreign origin) that appeal to the snobbery in a purchaser

snob·bery \'snäb-(ə-)rē\ *n, pl* **-ber·ies 1 :** snobbish conduct or character : SNOBBISHNESS **2 :** an instance of snobbery

snob·bish \'snäb-ish\ *adj* : being, characteristic of, or befitting a snob — **snob·bish·ly** *adv* — **snob·bish·ness** *n*

snob·bism \'snäb-ˌiz-əm\ *n* : SNOBBERY

snob·by \'snäb-ē\ *adj* : characterized by snobbery

SNO·BOL \'snō-ˌbȯl\ *n* [*Str*ing *O*riented *Sym*bo*l*ic *L*anguage] : a computer programming language for manipulating strings of symbols

Sno–Cat \'snō-ˌkat\ *trademark* — used for a tracklaying vehicle designed for travel on snow

snol·ly·gos·ter \'snäl-ē-ˌgäs-tər\ *n* [prob. alter. of *snallygaster* (a mythical creature that preys on poultry and children)] : an unprincipled but shrewd person

[1]**snood** \'snüd\ *n* [(assumed) ME, fr. OE *snōd;* akin to OIr *snāth* thread, OE *nǣdl* needle] **1 a** *Scot* : a fillet or band for a woman's hair **b :** a net or fabric bag pinned or tied on at the back of a woman's head for holding the hair **2 :** SNELL

[2]**snood** *vt* : to secure with a snood

[1]**snook** \'snu̇k, 'snük\ *n, pl* **snook** *or* **snooks** [D *snoek* pike, snook] **1 :** a large vigorous percoid sport and food fish (*Centropomus undecimalis*) of warm seas resembling a pike **2 :** any of various marine fishes similar to the snook

[2]**snook** *n* [origin unknown] : a gesture of derision made by thumbing the nose

snook·er \'snu̇k-ər\ *n* [origin unknown] : a variation of pool played with 15 red balls and 6 variously colored balls

[1]**snoop** \'snüp\ *vi* [D *snoepen* to buy or eat on the sly; akin to D *snappen* to snap] : to look or pry in a sneaking or meddlesome manner — **snoop·er** *n*

[2]**snoop** *n* : one that snoops

snoop·er·scope \'snü-pər-ˌskōp\ *n* : a device utilizing infrared radiation for enabling a person to see an object obscured (as by darkness)

snoopy \'snü-pē\ *adj* : given to snooping esp. for personal information about others — **snoop·i·ly** \-pə-lē\ *adv*

[1]**snoot** \'snüt\ *n* [ME *snute*] **1 a :** SNOUT **b :** NOSE **2 :** a grimace expressive of contempt **3 :** a snooty person : SNOB

[2]**snoot** *vt* : to treat with disdain : look down one's nose at

snooty \'snüt-ē\ *adj* **snoot·i·er; -est 1 :** looking down the nose : showing disdain <~ people who won't speak to their neighbors> **2 :** characterized by snobbery <a ~ store> — **snoot·i·ly** \'snüt-ᵊl-ē\ *adv* — **snoot·i·ness** \'snüt-ē-nəs\ *n*

[1]**snooze** \'snüz\ *vi* **snoozed; snooz·ing** [origin unknown] : to take a nap : DOZE — **snooz·er** *n*

[2]**snooze** *n* : NAP

snoo·zle \'snü-zəl\ *vb* **snoo·zled; snoo·zling** \'snüz-(ə-)liŋ\ [perh. blend of *snooze* and *nuzzle*] *chiefly dial* : NUZZLE

[1]**snore** \'snō(ə)r, 'snȯ(ə)r\ *vb* **snored; snor·ing** [ME *snoren;* akin to MLG *snorren* to drone, MHG *snerren* to chatter] *vi* : to breathe during sleep with a rough hoarse noise due to vibration of the soft palate ~ *vt* : to spend in sleeping — **snor·er** *n*

[2]**snore** *n* **1 :** an act of snoring **2 :** a noise of or as if of snoring

[1]**snor·kel** \'snȯr-kəl\ *n* [G *schnorchel*] **1 :** a tube housing air intake and exhaust pipes protrusible above the surface of the water for operating submerged submarines **2 :** any of various devices (as for an underwater swimmer) resembling a snorkel in function

[2]**snorkel** *vi* **snor·keled; snor·kel·ing** \-k(ə-)liŋ\ : to operate or swim submerged with only a snorkel above water — **snor·kel·er** \-k(ə-)lər\ *n*

[1]**snort** \'snȯ(ə)rt\ *vb* [ME *snorten*] *vi* **1 a :** to force air violently through the nose with a rough harsh sound **b :** to express scorn, anger, indignation, or surprise by a snort **2 :** to emit explosive sounds resembling snorts **3 :** to take in a drug by inhalation ~ *vt* **1 :** to utter with or express by a snort **2 :** to expel or emit with or as if with snorts **3 :** to take in (a drug) by inhalation

[2]**snort** *n* **1 :** an act or sound of snorting **2 :** a drink of usu. straight liquor taken in one draft

snort·er \'snȯrt-ər\ *n* **1 :** one that snorts **2 :** something that is extraordinary or prominent : HUMDINGER **3 :** SNORT 2

snot \'snät\ *n* [ME, fr. OE *gesnot;* akin to OHG *snuzza* nasal mucus, Gk *nan* to flow — more at NOURISH] **1 :** nasal mucus **2 :** a snotty person

snot·ty \'snät-ē\ *adj* **1 :** foul with nasal mucus **2 :** annoyingly or spitefully unpleasant

snout \'snau̇t\ *n* [ME *snute;* akin to G *schnauze* snout] **1 a** (1) : a long projecting nose (as of a swine) (2) : an anterior prolongation of the head of various animals (as a weevil) : ROSTRUM **b :** the human nose esp. when large or grotesque **2 :** something resembling an animal's snout in position, function, or shape: as **a** : PROW **b :** NOZZLE — **snout·ed** \-əd\ *adj* — **snout·ish** \-ish\ *adj* — **snouty** \-ē\ *adj*

snout beetle *n* : any of a group (Rhynchophora) of beetles comprising the true weevils and usu. having the head produced into a snout or beak

[1]**snow** \'snō\ *n, often attrib* [ME, fr. OE *snāw;* akin to OHG *snēo* snow, L *niv-, nix*, Gk *nipha* (acc.)] **1 a :** precipitation in the form of small tabular and columnar white ice crystals formed directly from the water vapor of the air at a temperature of less than 32°F **b** (1) : a descent or shower of snow crystals (2) : a mass of fallen snow crystals **2 :** something resembling snow: as **a :** a dessert made of stiffly beaten whites of eggs, sugar, and fruit pulp <apple ~> **b :** any of various congealed or crystallized substances resembling snow in appearance **c** (1) : COCAINE (2) : HEROIN **d :** small transient light or dark spots on a television or radar screen — **snow·less** \-ləs\ *adj*

[2]**snow** *vi* : to fall in or as snow ~ *vt* **1 :** to cause to fall like or as snow **2 a :** to cover, shut in, or imprison with or as if with snow <found themselves ~*ed* in after the blizzard> **b :** to deceive, persuade, or charm glibly **3 :** to whiten like snow

[1]**snow·ball** \'snō-ˌbȯl\ *n* **1 a :** a round mass of snow pressed or rolled together **b :** shaved ice molded into a ball and flavored with a syrup **2 :** any of several cultivated shrubs (genus *Viburnum*) with clusters of white sterile flowers

[2]**snowball** *vt* **1 :** to throw snowballs at **2 :** to cause to increase or multiply at a rapidly accelerating rate ~ *vi* **1 :** to engage in throwing snowballs **2 :** to increase, accumulate, expand, or multiply at a rapidly accelerating rate

snow·bank \'snō-ˌbaŋk\ *n* : a mound or slope of snow

snow·ber·ry \-ˌber-ē\ *n* : any of several white-berried shrubs (esp. genus *Symphoricarpos* of the honeysuckle family); *esp* : a low-growing No. American shrub (*S. albus*) with pink flowers in small axillary clusters

snow·bird \-ˌbərd\ *n* : any of several small birds (as a junco or fieldfare) seen chiefly in winter

snow–blind \-ˌblīnd\ *or* **snow–blind·ed** \-ˌblīn-dəd\ *adj* : affected with snow blindness

snow blindness *n* : inflammation and photophobia caused by exposure of the eyes to ultraviolet rays reflected from snow or ice

snow·blink \'snō-ˌbliŋk\ *n* : a white glare in the sky over a snowfield

snow·bound \-'bau̇nd\ *adj* : shut in or blockaded by snow

snow–broth \-ˌbrȯth\ *n* : newly melted snow esp. when mixed with stream water

snow·brush \'snō-ˌbrəsh\ *n* : any of several white-flowered shrubs (genus *Ceanothus*) of the buckthorn family; *esp* : a spreading western No. American shrub (*C. velutina*) with scented leaves and panicles of small flowers

snow·cap \-ˌkap\ *n* : a covering cap of snow (as on a mountain peak) — **snow·capped** \-'kapt\ *adj*

snow·drift \-ˌdrift\ *n* : a bank of drifted snow

snow·drop \-ˌdräp\ *n* : a bulbous European herb (*Galanthus nivalis*) of the amaryllis family bearing nodding white flowers that often appear while the snow is on the ground

snow·fall \-ˌfȯl\ *n* : a fall of snow; *specif* : the amount of snow that falls in a single storm or in a given period

snow fence *n* : a usu. slatted fence placed across the path of prevailing winds to protect (as a building, road, or railroad track) from drifting snow by disrupting the flow of wind and causing the snow to be deposited on the lee side of the fence

snow·field \'snō-ˌfēld\ *n* : a broad level expanse of snow; *esp* : a mass of perennial snow at the head of a glacier

snow·flake \-ˌflāk\ *n* **1 :** a flake or crystal of snow **2 :** any of a genus (*Leucojum*) of bulbous plants of the amaryllis family; *esp* : one (*L. vernum*) resembling the snowdrop

snow job *n* : an intensive effort at persuasion or deception

snow leopard *n* : a showily marked large cat (*Felis uncia*) of upland central Asia with a long heavy pelt that is grayish white irregularly blotched with brownish black in summer and almost pure white in winter

snow lily *n* : a Rocky Mountain dogtooth violet (*Erythronium grandiflorum*) with showy yellow or white flowers

snow line *n* : the lower margin of a perennial snowfield

snow·mak·er \-ˌmā-kər\ *n* : a device for making snow artificially
snow·mak·ing \ˈsnō-ˌmā-kiŋ\ *adj* : used for the production of artificial snow usu. for ski slopes <~ machines>
snow·man \-ˌman, -ˈman\ *n* : snow shaped to resemble a human figure
snow·melt \-ˌmelt\ *n* : runoff produced by the melting of snow
snow·mo·bile \ˈsnō-mō-ˌbēl\ *n* [*snow* + auto*mobile*] : any of various automotive vehicles for travel on snow
snow·mo·bil·er \-ˌbē-lər\ *n* : one that operates a snowmobile — **snow·mo·bil·ing** \-liŋ\ *n*
snow–on–the–mountain *n* : a spurge (*Euphorbia marginata*) of the western U.S. that has showy white-bracted flower clusters and is grown as an ornamental
snow·pack \ˈsnō-ˌpak\ *n* : a seasonal accumulation of slow-melting packed snow
snow plant *n* : a fleshy bright-red saprophytic California herb (*Sarcodes sanguinea*) of the wintergreen family that grows in coniferous woods at high altitudes and often appears before the snow melts
1snow·plow \ˈsnō-ˌplau̇\ *n* **1** : any of various devices used for clearing away snow **2** : a stemming with both skis used for coming to a stop, slowing down, or descending slowly
2snowplow *vi* : to execute a snowplow <~*ed* to a stop>
snow pudding *n* : a pudding made very fluffy and light by the addition of whipped egg whites and gelatin
snow·scape \ˈsnō-ˌskāp\ *n* : a landscape covered with snow
snow·shed \-ˌshed\ *n* **1** : a shelter against snowslides **2** : a watershed supplied largely by snowfalls
1snow·shoe \-ˌshü\ *n* : a light oval wooden frame that is strengthened by two crosspieces, strung with thongs, and attached to the foot and that is used to enable a person to walk on soft snow without sinking
2snowshoe *vi* **snow·shoed; snow·shoe·ing** : to travel on snowshoes — **snow·sho·er** \-ˌshü-ər\ *n*
snow·slide \ˈsnō-ˌslīd\ *n* : an avalanche of snow
snow·storm \-ˌstȯrm\ *n* **1** : a storm of or with snow **2** : something that resembles a snowstorm
snow·suit \-ˌsüt\ *n* : a one-piece or two-piece lined garment for winter wear by children
snow tire *n* : an automotive tire with a tread designed to give added traction on snow or ice
snow under *vt* **1** : to overwhelm esp. in excess of capacity to absorb or deal with something **2** : to defeat by a large margin
snow–white \ˈsnō-ˈhwīt, -ˈwīt\ *adj* : white as snow
snowy \ˈsnō-ē\ *adj* **snow·i·er; -est** **1 a** : composed of snow or melted snow **b** : marked by or covered with snow **2 a** : whitened by snow **b** : SNOW-WHITE — **snow·i·ly** \ˈsnō-ə-lē\ *adv* — **snow·i·ness** \ˈsnō-ē-nəs\ *n*
1snub \ˈsnəb\ *vt* **snubbed; snub·bing** [ME *snubben*, of Scand origin; akin to ON *snubba* to scold; akin to Icel *sneypa* to scold] **1** : to check or stop with a cutting retort : REBUKE **2 a** : to check (as a line) suddenly while running out esp. by turning around a fixed object (as a post); *also* : to check the motion of by snubbing a line **b** : to restrain the action of : SUPPRESS <~ a vibration> **3** : to treat with contempt or neglect **4** : to extinguish by stubbing <~ out a cigarette>
2snub *n* : an act or an instance of snubbing; *esp* : SLIGHT
3snub *adj* **1** : used in snubbing <~ line> **2** *or* **snubbed** \ˈsnəbd\ : BLUNT, STUBBY <a ~ nose> — **snub·ness** *n*
snub·ber \ˈsnəb-ər\ *n* **1** : one that snubs **2** : SHOCK ABSORBER
snub·by \ˈsnəb-ē\ *adj* **1** : SNUB **2** : SNUB-NOSED — **snub·bi·ness** *n*
snub–nosed \ˈsnəb-ˈnōzd\ *adj* **1** : having a stubby and usu. slightly turned-up nose **2** : having a very short barrel <a ~ revolver>
1snuff \ˈsnəf\ *n* [ME *snoffe*] **1** : the charred part of a candlewick **2 a** *obs* : UMBRAGE, OFFENSE **b** *chiefly Scot* : HUFF
2snuff *vt* **1** : to crop the snuff of (a candle) by pinching or by the use of snuffers so as to brighten the light **2 a** : to extinguish by the use of snuffers **b** : to make extinct : put an end to — usu. used with *out* <an accident that ~*ed* out a life>
3snuff *vb* [akin to D *snuffen* to sniff, snuff — more at SNIVEL] *vt* **1** : to draw forcibly through or into the nostrils **2** : SCENT, SMELL **3** : to sniff at in order to examine — used of an animal ~ *vi* **1** : to inhale through the nose noisily and forcibly; *also* : to sniff or smell inquiringly **2** *obs* : to sniff loudly in or as if in disgust **3** : to take snuff
4snuff *n* : the act of snuffing : SNIFF
5snuff *n* [D *snuf*, short for *snuftabak*, fr. *snuffen* to snuff + *tabak* tobacco] **1** : a preparation of pulverized tobacco to be inhaled through the nostrils, chewed, or placed against the gums **2** : the amount of snuff taken at one time — **up to snuff** : of sufficient quality : meeting an applicable standard
snuff·box \ˈsnəf-ˌbäks\ *n* : a small box for holding snuff usu. carried about the person
1snuff·er \ˈsnəf-ər\ *n* **1** : a device somewhat like a pair of scissors for cropping and holding the snuff of a candle — usu. used in pl. but sing. or pl. in constr. **2** : a device for extinguishing candles
2snuffer *n* : one that snuffs or sniffs
1snuf·fle \ˈsnəf-əl\ *vb* **snuf·fled; snuf·fling** \-(ə-)liŋ\ [akin to D *snuffelen* to snuffle — more at SNIVEL] *vi* **1** : to snuff or sniff usu. audibly and repeatedly **2** : to breathe through an obstructed nose with a sniffing sound **3** : to speak through or as if through the nose : WHINE ~ *vt* : to seek or test by or as if by repeated sniffs — **snuf·fler** \-(ə-)lər\ *n*
2snuffle *n* **1** : the act or sound of snuffling **2** : a nasal twang **3** *pl* : SNIFFLES
1snuffy \ˈsnəf-ē\ *adj* [*3snuff*] **1** : quick to become annoyed or take offense **2** : marked by snobbery
2snuffy *adj* [*5snuff*] **1** : resembling snuff **2 a** : addicted to the use of snuff **b** : having unpleasant habits **3** : soiled with snuff
1snug \ˈsnəg\ *adj* **snug·ger; snug·gest** [perh. of Scand origin; akin to Sw *snygg* tidy; akin to ON *snöggr* shorn, bald, L *novacula* razor] **1 a** *of a ship* : manifesting seaworthiness : TAUT **b** : TRIM, NEAT **c** : fitting closely and comfortably <a ~ coat> **2 a** : enjoying or affording warm secure shelter or cover and opportunity for ease and contentment **b** : marked by cordiality and secure privacy **3** : affording a degree of comfort and ease **4** : offering safe concealment <a ~ hideout> *syn* see COMFORTABLE — **snug** *adv* — **snug·ly** *adv* — **snug·ness** *n*
2snug *vb* **snugged; snug·ging** *vi* : SNUGGLE ~ *vt* **1** : to cause to fit closely **2** : to make snug <~ the place for winter —Hal Borland> **3** : HIDE **4** : to secure by fastening or lashing down
3snug *n, Brit* [short for *snuggery*] : a small private room in a pub
snug·gery \ˈsnəg-(ə-)rē\ *n, pl* **-ger·ies** *chiefly Brit* : a snug cozy place; *esp* : a small room
snug·gle \ˈsnəg-əl\ *vb* **snug·gled; snug·gling** \-(ə-)liŋ\ [freq. of *2snug*] *vi* : to curl up comfortably or cozily : CUDDLE ~ *vt* **1** : to draw close esp. for comfort or in affection **2** : to make snug
1so \(ˈ)sō, *esp before adj or adv followed by "that"* sə\ *adv* [ME, fr. OE *swā*; akin to OHG *sō* so, L *sic* so, thus, *si* if, Gk *hōs* so, thus, L *suus* one's own — more at SUICIDE] **1 a** : in a manner or way that is indicated or suggested <do you really think ~> — often used as a substitute for an entire preceding clause <are you ready? if ~, let's go> **b** : in the same manner or way : ALSO <worked hard and ~ did she> **c** : THUS <for ~ the Lord said —Isa 18:4 (AV)> **d** : THEN, SUBSEQUENTLY <and ~ home and to bed> **2 a** : to an indicated or suggested extent or degree <had never been ~ happy> **b** : to a great extent or degree : VERY, EXTREMELY <left her because he loved her ~> **c** : to a definite but unspecified extent or degree <can only do ~ much in a day> **d** : most certainly : INDEED <you did ~ do it> **3** : THEREFORE, CONSEQUENTLY <the witness is biased and ~ unreliable>
2so \(ˈ)sō\ *conj* **1 a** : with the result that <her diction is good, ~ every word is clear> **b** : in order that <be quiet ~ he can sleep> **2** *archaic* : provided that **3 a** : for that reason : THEREFORE <don't want to go, ~ I won't> **b (1)** — used as an introductory particle <~ here we are> often to belittle a point under discussion <~ what?> **(2)** — used interjectionally to indicate awareness of a discovery <~, that's who did it> or surprised dissent
3so \ˈsō\ *adj* **1** : conforming with actual facts : TRUE <said things that were not ~> **2** : marked by a definite order <his books are always just ~>
4so \ˌsō, ˈsō\ *pron* **1** : such as has been specified or suggested : the same <became chairman and remained ~> **2** — used in the phrase *or so* to indicate an estimate, approximation, or conjecture <I've known him 20 years or ~>
5so \ˈsō\ *var of* SOL
6so *abbr* south; southern
SO *abbr* **1** seller's option **2** strikeout
1soak \ˈsōk\ *vb* [ME *soken*, fr. OE *socian*; akin to OE *sūcan* to suck] *vi* **1** : to lie immersed in liquid (as water) **2 a** : to enter or pass through something by or as if by pores or interstices : PERMEATE **b** : to penetrate or affect the mind or feelings — usu. used with *in* or *into* **3** : to drink alcoholic beverages intemperately ~ *vt* **1** : to permeate so as to wet, soften, or fill thoroughly **2 a** : to place in a surrounding element (as liquid) to wet or permeate thoroughly **b** : to engross the full attention of : IMMERSE **3** : to extract by or as if by steeping <~ the dirt out> **4 a** : to draw in by or as if by suction or absorption <~*ed* up the sunshine> **b** : to intoxicate (oneself) by drinking alcoholic beverages **5 a** : to levy an exorbitant charge against <~*ed* the taxpayers> **b** : to punish severely — **soak·er** *n*

syn SOAK, SATURATE, DRENCH, STEEP, IMPREGNATE *shared meaning element* : to permeate or be permeated with or as if with water. SOAK implies a usually prolonged exposure or immersion that results in thorough wetting, softening, or dissolving <*soak* a sponge> <they were caught in the storm and got *soaked*> and in extended use stresses completeness of permeation <old ladies *soaked* in religion —J. T. Farrell> SATURATE stresses absorption to the point where no more can be held <the air was *saturated* with moisture> <the city . . . was *saturated* with fear —*Kerner Report*> DRENCH basically implies thorough wetting (as with rainwater) and in extended use suggests a soaking or saturation with something that pours down <woodland glades *drenched* with sunlight> <*drenched* the rebel towns with bombs —*Atlanta (Ga.) Jour.*> STEEP implies immersion and soaking usually to extract an essence <*steep* tea in boiling water> or, in extended use, thorough saturation <a man *steeped* in classic lore> IMPREGNATE implies thorough interpenetration of one thing by another <*impregnate* posts with creosote to prevent decay> <this poem, everywhere *impregnated* with original excellence —William Wordsworth>

2soak *n* **1 a** : the act or process of soaking : the state of being soaked **b** : that (as liquid) in which something is soaked **2** : DRUNKARD **3** *slang* : 1PAWN 2
soak·age \ˈsō-kij\ *n* **1** : liquid gained by absorption or lost by seepage **2** : the act or process of soaking : the state of being soaked
1so–and–so \ˈsō-ən-ˌsō\ *n, pl* **so–and–sos** *or* **so–and–so's** \-ˌsōz\ **1** : an unnamed or unspecified person, thing, or action **2** : BASTARD 3
2so–and–so *adv* **1** : in an unspecified manner or fashion **2** : to an unspecified amount or degree
1soap \ˈsōp\ *n* [ME *sope*, fr. OE *sāpe*; akin to OHG *seifa* soap, L *sebum* tallow] **1 a** : a cleansing and emulsifying agent made usu. by action of alkali on fat or fatty acids and consisting essentially of sodium or potassium salts of such acids **b** : a salt of a fatty acid and a metal **2** : SOAP OPERA
2soap *vt* **1** : to rub soap over or into **2** : FLATTER

soap·bark \'sōp-ˌbärk\ *n* **1 :** a Chilean tree (*Quillaja saponaria*) of the rose family with shining leaves and terminal white flowers; *also* **:** its saponin-rich bark used in cleaning and in emulsifying oils **2 :** any of several tropical American trees or leguminous shrubs (genus *Pithecolobium*) with saponaceous bark

soap·ber·ry \-ˌber-ē\ *n* **:** any of a genus (*Sapindus* of the family Sapindaceae, the soapberry family) of chiefly tropical woody plants; *also* **:** the fruit of a soapberry and esp. of a tree (*S. saponaria*) that is saponin-rich and used as a soap substitute

soap·box \-ˌbäks\ *n* **:** an improvised platform used by a self-appointed, spontaneous, or informal orator — **soapbox** *adj*

Soap Box Derby *service mark* — used for a downhill race for children's homemade racing cars without pedals or motors

soap bubble *n* **:** a hollow iridescent globe formed by blowing a film of soapsuds (as from a pipe)

soap·less \'sō-pləs\ *adj* **1 :** having or containing no soap <~ detergents> **2 :** UNWASHED, DIRTY

soap·mak·ing \'sōp-ˌmā-kiŋ\ *n* **:** the act, process, or occupation of making soap

soap opera *n* [fr. its frequently being sponsored by soap manufacturers] **:** a radio or television serial drama performed usu. on a daytime commercial program and chiefly characterized by stock domestic situations and melodramatic or sentimental treatment

soap plant *n* **:** a plant having a part (as a root or fruit) that may be used in place of soap; *esp* **:** a California plant (*Chlorogalum pomeridianum*) of the lily family

soap·stone \'sōp-ˌstōn\ *n* **:** a soft stone having a soapy feel and composed essentially of talc, chlorite, and often some magnetite

soap·suds \-ˌsədz\ *n pl* **:** SUDS 1

soap·wort \-ˌwərt, -ˌwȯ(ə)rt\ *n* **:** BOUNCING BET

soapy \'sō-pē\ *adj* **soap·i·er; -est 1 :** smeared with soap **:** LATHERED **2 :** containing or combined with soap or saponin **3 a :** resembling or having the qualities of soap; *esp* **:** being smooth and slippery **b :** UNCTUOUS, SUAVE **4 :** of, relating to, or having the characteristics of soap opera <~ drama> — **soap·i·ly** \-pə-lē\ *adv* — **soap·i·ness** \-pē-nəs\ *n*

[1]**soar** \'sō(ə)r, 'sȯ(ə)r\ *vi* [ME *soren,* fr. MF *essorer* to air, soar, fr. (assumed) VL *exaurare* to air, fr. L *ex-* + *aura* air — more at AURA] **1 a :** to fly aloft or about **b** (1) **:** to sail or hover in the air often at a great height **:** GLIDE (2) *of a glider* **:** to fly without engine power and without loss of altitude **2 :** to go or move upward in position or status **:** RISE **3 :** to ascend to a higher or more exalted level **4 :** to rise to majestic stature **:** TOWER — **soar·er** *n*

[2]**soar** *n* **1 :** the range, distance, or height attained in soaring **2 :** the act of soaring **:** upward flight

soar·ing *n* **:** the act or process of soaring; *specif* **:** the act or sport of flying a heavier-than-air craft without power by utilizing ascending air currents

[1]**sob** \'säb\ *vb* **sobbed; sob·bing** [ME *sobben*] *vi* **1 a :** to catch the breath audibly in a spasmodic contraction of the throat **b :** to cry or weep with convulsive catching of the breath **2 :** to make a sound like that of a sob or sobbing ~ *vt* **1 :** to bring (as oneself) to a specified state by sobbing <*sobbed* himself to sleep> **2 :** to utter with sobs <*sobbed* out her grief>

[2]**sob** *n* **1 :** an act of sobbing **2 :** a sound like that of a sob

[3]**SOB** \ˌes-ˌō-'bē\ *n* [*s*on *o*f a *b*itch] **:** SON OF A BITCH, BASTARD 3

[1]**so·ber** \'sō-bər\ *adj* **so·ber·er** \-bər-ər\; **so·ber·est** \-b(ə-)rəst\ [ME *sobre,* fr. MF, fr. L *sobrius;* akin to L *ebrius* drunk] **1 a :** sparing in the use of food and drink **:** ABSTEMIOUS **b :** not addicted to intoxicating drink **c :** not drunk **2 :** marked by sedate or gravely or earnestly thoughtful character or demeanor **3** *archaic* **:** UNHURRIED, CALM **4 :** marked by temperance, moderation, or seriousness **5 :** subdued in tone or color **6 :** showing no excessive or extreme qualities of fancy, emotion, or prejudice: as **a :** REALISTIC **b :** well balanced **:** RESTRAINED **c :** RATIONAL — **so·ber·ly** \-bər-lē\ *adv* — **so·ber·ness** *n*

syn **1** SOBER, TEMPERATE, CONTINENT, UNIMPASSIONED *shared meaning element* **:** having or manifesting mastery of oneself and one's appetites *ant* excited, drunk

2 see SERIOUS *ant* gay

[2]**sober** *vb* **so·bered; so·ber·ing** \-b(ə-)riŋ\ *vt* **:** to make sober ~ *vi* **:** to become sober — usu. used with *up*

so·ber·ize \'sō-bə-ˌrīz\ *vt* **-ized; -iz·ing** *archaic* **:** to make sober

so·ber·sid·ed \ˌsō-bər-'sīd-əd\ *adj* **:** solemn or serious in nature or appearance

so·ber·sides \'sō-bər-ˌsīdz\ *n pl but sing or pl in constr* **:** one who is sobersided

so·bri·ety \sə-'brī-ət-ē, sō-\ *n* [ME *sobrietie,* fr. MF *sobrieté,* fr. L *sobrietat-, sobrietas,* fr. *sobrius*] **:** the quality or state of being sober

so·bri·quet \'sō-bri-ˌkā, -ˌket, ˌsō-bri-'\ *n* [F] **:** a fanciful name or epithet **:** NICKNAME

sob sister *n* **1 :** a journalist who specializes in writing or editing sob stories or other material of a sentimental type **2 :** a sentimental and often impractical person usu. engaged in good works

sob story *n* **:** a sentimental story or account designed chiefly to evoke sympathy or sadness

soc *abbr* **1** social **2** society

so·cage \'säk-ij, 'sōk-\ *or* **soc·cage** \'säk-\ *n* [ME, fr. *soc* soke] **:** a tenure of land by agricultural service fixed in amount and kind or by payment of money rent only and not burdened with any military service — **so·cag·er** \-ij-ər\ *n*

so–called \'sō-'kȯld\ *adj* **1 :** commonly named **:** popularly so termed <the ~ pocket veto> **2 :** falsely or improperly so named <deceived by his ~ friend>

soc·cer \'säk-ər\ *n* [by shortening & alter. fr. *association football*] **:** a game played on a field between two teams of 11 players each with the object to propel a round ball into the opponent's goal by kicking or by hitting it with any part of the body except the hands and arms — called also *association football*

so·cia·bil·i·ty \ˌsō-shə-'bil-ət-ē\ *n, pl* **-ties :** the quality or state of being sociable; *also* **:** the act or an instance of being sociable

[1]**so·cia·ble** \'sō-shə-bəl\ *adj* [MF or L; MF, fr. L *sociabilis,* fr. *sociare* to join, associate, fr. *socius*] **1 :** inclined by nature to companionship with others of the same species **:** SOCIAL **2 a :** inclined to seek or enjoy companionship **b :** conducive to friendliness or pleasant social relations *syn* see GRACIOUS *ant* unsociable — **so·cia·ble·ness** *n* — **so·cia·bly** \-blē\ *adv*

[2]**sociable** *n* **:** an informal social gathering frequently involving a special activity or interest

[1]**so·cial** \'sō-shəl\ *adj* [L *socialis,* fr. *socius* companion, ally, associate; akin to L *sequi* to follow — more at SUE] **1 :** involving allies or confederates <the *Social* War between the Athenians and their allies> **2 a :** marked by or passed in pleasant companionship with one's friends or associates <leads a very full ~ life> **b :** SOCIABLE **c :** of, relating to, or designed for sociability <a ~ club> **3 a :** tending to form cooperative and interdependent relationships with one's fellows **:** GREGARIOUS <man is a ~ being> **b :** living and breeding in more or less organized communities <~ insects> **c** *of a plant* **:** tending to grow in groups or masses so as to form a pure stand **4 :** of or relating to human society, the interaction of the individual and the group, or the welfare of human beings as members of society <~ institutions> **5 a :** of, relating to, or based on rank or status in a particular society <a member of his ~ set> **b :** of, relating to, or characteristic of the upper classes **c :** FORMAL

[2]**social** *n* **:** SOCIABLE

social climber *n* **:** one who attempts to gain a higher social position or acceptance in fashionable society — **social climbing** *n*

social contract *n* [trans. of F *contrat social*] **:** an actual or hypothetical agreement among individuals forming an organized society or between the community and the ruler that defines and limits the rights and duties of each

social Darwinism *n* **:** an extension of Darwinism to social phenomena; *specif* **:** a theory in sociology: sociocultural advance is the product of intergroup conflict and competition and the socially elite classes (as those possessing wealth and power) possess biological superiority in the struggle for existence

social democracy *n* **:** a political movement advocating a gradual and peaceful transition from capitalism to socialism by democratic means — **social democrat** *n* — **social democratic** *adj*

social disease *n* **1 :** VENEREAL DISEASE **2 :** a disease (as tuberculosis) whose incidence is directly related to social and economic factors

social engineering *n* **:** management of human beings in accordance with their place and function in society **:** applied social science — **social engineer** *n*

social gospel *n* **1 :** the application of Christian principles to social problems **2** *cap S&G* **:** a movement in American Protestant Christianity esp. in the first part of the 20th century to bring the social order into conformity with Christian principles

social insurance *n* **:** protection of the individual against economic hazards (as unemployment, old age, or disability) in which the government participates or enforces the participation of employers and affected individuals

so·cial·ism \'sō-shə-ˌliz-əm\ *n* **1 :** any of various economic and political theories advocating collective or governmental ownership and administration of the means of production and distribution of goods **2 a :** a system of society or group living in which there is no private property **b :** a system or condition of society in which the means of production are owned and controlled by the state **3 :** a stage of society in Marxist theory transitional between capitalism and communism and distinguished by unequal distribution of goods and pay according to work done

[1]**so·cial·ist** \'sōsh-(ə-)ləst\ *n* **1 :** one who advocates or practices socialism **2** *cap* **:** a member of a socialist party or political group

[2]**socialist** *adj* **1 :** of, relating to, or promoting socialism <~ theory> <a ~ state> <~ tendencies> **2** *cap* **:** of, relating to, or constituting a political party advocating socialism

so·cial·is·tic \ˌsō-shə-'lis-tik\ *adj* **:** of, relating to, or tending toward socialism — **so·cial·is·ti·cal·ly** \-ti-k(ə-)lē\ *adv*

socialist realism *n* **:** a Marxist aesthetic theory calling for the didactic use of literature, art, and music to develop social consciousness in an evolving socialist state — **social realist** *n*

so·cial·ite \'sō-shə-ˌlīt\ *n* **:** a socially prominent person

so·ci·al·i·ty \ˌsō-shē-'al-ət-ē\ *n* **1 a :** SOCIABILITY **b :** an instance of social intercourse or sociability **2 :** the tendency to associate in or form social groups

so·cial·ize \'sō-shə-ˌlīz\ *vb* **-ized; -iz·ing** *vt* **1 :** to make social; *esp* **:** to fit or train for a social environment **2 a :** to constitute on a socialistic basis <~ industry> **b :** to adapt to social needs or uses <~ science> **3 :** to organize group participation in <~ a recitation> ~ *vi* **:** to participate actively in a social group — **so·cial·iza·tion** \ˌsōsh-(ə-)lə-'zā-shən\ *n* — **so·cial·iz·er** \'sō-shə-ˌlī-zər\ *n*

socialized medicine *n* **:** medical and hospital services for the members of a class or population administered by an organized group (as a state agency) and paid for from funds obtained usu. by assessments, philanthropy, or taxation

so·cial·ly \'sōsh-(ə-)lē\ *adv* **1 :** in a social manner **2 :** with respect to society **3 :** by or through society

so·cial–mind·ed \ˌsō-shəl-'mīn-dəd\ *adj* **:** having an interest in society; *specif* **:** actively interested in social welfare or the well-being of society as a whole

social psychology *n* **:** the study of the manner in which the personality, attitudes, motivations, and behavior of the individual influence and are influenced by social groups — **social psychologist** *n*

social science *n* **1 :** a branch of science that deals with the institutions and functioning of human society and with the interpersonal relationships of individuals as members of society **2 :** a science (as economics or political science) dealing with a particular phase or aspect of human society — **social scientist** *n*

social secretary *n* **:** a personal secretary employed to handle social correspondence and appointments

social security *n* **:** the principle or practice or a program of public provision (as through social insurance or assistance) for the economic security and social welfare of the individual and his family; *specif, often cap* : a U.S. government program established in 1935 to include old-age and survivors insurance, contributions to state unemployment insurance, and old-age assistance

social service *n* : an activity designed to promote social welfare; *specif* : organized philanthropic assistance of the sick, destitute, or unfortunate : WELFARE WORK

social studies *n pl* : a part of a school or college curriculum concerned with the study of social relationships and the functioning of society and usu. made up of courses in history, government, economics, civics, sociology, geography, and anthropology

social welfare *n* : organized public or private social services for the assistance of disadvantaged groups; *specif* : SOCIAL WORK

social work *n* : any of various professional services, activities, or methods concretely concerned with the investigation, treatment, and material aid of the economically underprivileged and socially maladjusted — **social worker** *n*

so·ci·etal \sə-ˈsī-ət-ᵊl\ *adj* : of or relating to society : SOCIAL <~ forces> — **so·ci·etal·ly** \-ᵊl-ē\ *adv*

[1]**so·ci·ety** \sə-ˈsī-ət-ē\ *n, pl* **-et·ies** [MF *societé*, fr. L *societat-, societas*, fr. *socius* companion — more at SOCIAL] **1** : companionship or association with one's fellows : friendly or intimate intercourse : COMPANY **2** : a voluntary association of individuals for common ends; *esp* : an organized group working together or periodically meeting because of common interests, beliefs, or profession **3 a** : an enduring and cooperating social group whose members have developed organized patterns of relationships through interaction with one another **b** : a community, nation, or broad grouping of people having common traditions, institutions, and collective activities and interests **4 a** : a part of a community that is a unit distinguishable by particular aims or standards of living or conduct : a social circle or a group of social circles having a clearly marked identity <move in polite ~> <literary ~> **b** : a part of the community that sets itself apart as a leisure class and that regards itself as the arbiter of fashion and manners **5 a** (1) : a natural group of plants usu. of a single species or habit within an association (2) : ASSOCIATION 6 **b** : the progeny of a pair of insects when constituting a social unit (as a hive of bees); *broadly* : an interdependent system of organisms or biological units

[2]**society** *adj* : of, relating to, or characteristic of fashionable society

society verse *n* : VERS DE SOCIÉTÉ

So·cin·i·an \sə-ˈsin-ē-ən, sō-\ *n* [NL *socinianus*, fr. Faustus *Socinus* (Fausto Sozzini) †1604 It theologian] : an adherent of a 16th and 17th century theological movement professing belief in God and adherence to the Christian Scriptures but denying the divinity of Christ and consequently denying the Trinity — **Socinian** *adj* — **So·cin·i·an·ism** \-ē-ə-ˌniz-əm\ *n*

socio- *comb form* [F, fr. L *socius* companion] **1** : society <*socio*graphy> : social <*socio*gram> **2** : social and <*socio*political> **3** : sociological and <*socio*psychiatric>

so·cio·cul·tur·al \ˌsō-sē-ō-ˈkəlch(-ə)-rəl, ˌsō-shē-\ *adj* : of, relating to, or involving a combination of social and cultural factors — **so·cio·cul·tur·al·ly** \-rə-lē\ *adv*

so·cio·eco·nom·ic \-ˌek-ə-ˈnäm-ik, -ˌē-kə-\ *adj* : of, relating to, or involving a combination of social and economic factors

sociol *abbr* sociologist; sociology

so·cio·lin·guis·tic \ˌsō-sē-ō-liŋ-ˈgwis-tik, ˌsō-shē-\ *adj* **1** : of or relating to the social aspects of language **2** : of or relating to sociolinguistics

so·cio·lin·guis·tics \-tiks\ *n pl but sing in constr* : the study of linguistic behavior as determined by sociocultural factors

so·cio·log·i·cal \ˌsō-se-ə-ˈläj-i-kəl, ˌsō-sh(ē-)ə-\ *also* **so·cio·log·ic** \-ik\ *adj* **1** : of or relating to sociology or to the methodological approach of sociology **2** : oriented or directed toward social needs and problems — **so·cio·log·i·cal·ly** \-i-k(ə-)lē\ *adv*

so·ci·ol·o·gy \ˌsō-sē-ˈäl-ə-jē, ˌsō-shē-\ *n* [F *sociologie*, fr. *socio-* + *-logie* -logy] **1** : the science of society, social institutions, and social relationships; *specif* : the systematic study of the development, structure, interaction, and collective behavior of organized groups of human beings **2** : the scientific analysis of a social institution as a functioning whole and as it relates to the rest of society **3** : SYNECOLOGY — **so·ci·ol·o·gist** \-jəst\ *n*

so·ci·om·e·try \-ˈäm-ə-trē\ *n* [ISV] : the study and measurement of interpersonal relationships in a group of people — **so·cio·met·ric** \ˌsō-sē-ə-ˈme-trik, ˌsō-shē-\ *adj*

so·cio·path \ˈsō-sē-ə-ˌpath, ˈsō-sh(ē-)ə-\ *n* : a sociopathic person

so·cio·path·ic \ˌsō-sē-ə-ˈpath-ik, ˌsō-sh(ē-)ə-\ *adj* : of, relating to, or characterized by asocial or antisocial behavior

so·cio·po·lit·i·cal \ˌsō-sē-ō-pə-ˈlit-i-kəl, ˌsō-shē-\ *adj* : of, relating to, or involving a combination of social and political factors

so·cio·re·li·gious \-ri-ˈlij-əs\ *adj* : involving a combination of social and religious factors

so·cio·sex·u·al \-ˈseksh-(ə-)wəl, -ˈsek-shəl\ *adj* : of or relating to the interpersonal aspects of sexuality — **so·cio·sex·u·al·i·ty** \-ˌsek-shə-ˈwal-ət-ē\ *n*

[1]**sock** \ˈsäk\ *n, pl* **socks** [ME *socke*, fr. OE *socc*, fr. L *soccus*] **1** *archaic* : a low shoe or slipper **2** *or pl* **sox** \ˈsäks\ : a knitted or woven covering for the foot usu. extending above the ankle and sometimes to the knee **3 a** : a shoe worn by actors in Greek and Roman comedy **b** : comic drama

[2]**sock** *vb* [prob. of Scand origin; akin to ON *sökkva* to cause to sink; akin to OE *sincan* to sink] *vt* : to hit, strike, or apply forcefully ~ *vi* : to deliver a blow : HIT — **sock it to one** *slang* : to subject to vigorous assault <they may let you off the first time . . . but the second time they'll *sock it to you* —James Jones>

[3]**sock** *n* : a vigorous or violent blow : PUNCH

sock away *vt* [fr. the practice of concealing savings in the toe of a sock] : to put away (money) as savings or investment

sock·dol·a·ger *or* **sock·dol·o·ger** \säk-ˈdäl-i-jər\ *n* [perh. alter. of *doxology*] **1** : something that settles a matter : a decisive blow or answer : FINISHER **2** : something outstanding or exceptional

[1]**sock·et** \ˈsäk-ət\ *n* [ME *soket*, fr. AF, dim. of OF *soc* plowshare, of Celt origin; akin to MIr *soc* plowshare, lit., snout of a hog; akin to OE *sugu* sow — more at SOW] : an opening or hollow that forms a holder for something <an electric bulb ~> <the eye ~>

[2]**socket** *vt* : to provide with or support in or by a socket

sock·eye \ˈsäk-ˌī\ *n* [by folk etymology fr. Salish dial. *suk-kegh*] : a small but commercially important Pacific salmon (*Oncorhynchus nerka*) that ascends rivers chiefly from the Columbia northward to spawn in spring — called also *red salmon*

sockeye

sock in *vt* [(*wind*) *sock*] **1** : to close to takeoffs or landings by aircraft **2** : to restrict from flying

so·cle \ˈsō-kəl, ˈsäk-əl\ *n* [F, fr. It *zoccolo* sock, socle, fr. L *socculus*, dim. of *soccus* sock] : a projecting usu. molded member at the foot of a wall or pier or beneath the base of a column, pedestal, or superstructure

[1]**So·crat·ic** \sə-ˈkrat-ik, sō-\ *adj* : of or relating to Socrates, his followers, or his philosophical method of systematic doubt and questioning of another to reveal his hidden ignorance or to elicit a clear expression of a truth supposed to be implicitly known by all rational beings — **So·crat·i·cal·ly** \-i-k(ə-)lē\ *adv*

[2]**Socratic** *n* : a follower of Socrates

Socratic irony *n* : IRONY 1

[1]**sod** \ˈsäd\ *n* [ME, fr. MD or MLG *sode*; akin to OFris *sātha* sod] **1** : TURF 1; *also* : the grass and forb covered surface of the ground **2** : one's native land

[2]**sod** *vt* **sod·ded; sod·ding** : to cover with sod or turfs

SOD *abbr* seller's option to double

so·da \ˈsōd-ə\ *n* [It, barilla plant, soda, fr. (assumed) ML, barilla plant] **1 a** : SODIUM CARBONATE **b** : SODIUM BICARBONATE **c** : SODIUM HYDROXIDE **d** : sodium oxide Na_2O **e** : SODIUM — used in combination <~ alum> **2 a** : SODA WATER 2a **b** : SODA POP **c** : a sweet drink consisting of soda water, flavoring, and often ice cream **3** : the faro card that shows face up in the dealing box before play begins

soda ash *n* : commercial anhydrous sodium carbonate

soda biscuit *n* **1** : a biscuit leavened with baking soda and sour milk or buttermilk **2** : SODA CRACKER

soda cracker *n* : a cracker leavened with bicarbonate of soda and cream of tartar

soda fountain *n* **1** : an apparatus with delivery tube and faucets for drawing soda water **2** : the equipment and counter for the preparation and serving of sodas, sundaes, and ice cream

soda jerk \-ˌjərk\ *n* : a counterman who dispenses carbonated drinks and ice cream at a soda fountain — called also *soda jerker*

soda lime *n* : a mixture of sodium hydroxide and slaked lime used esp. to absorb moisture and gases

so·da·list \ˈsōd-ᵊl-əst, sō-ˈdal-\ *n* : a member of a Roman Catholic sodality

so·da·lite \ˈsōd-ᵊl-ˌīt\ *n* [*soda*] : a transparent to translucent mineral $Na_4Al_3Si_3O_{12}Cl$ that consists of a sodium aluminum silicate with some chlorine, has a vitreous or greasy luster, and is found in various igneous rocks

so·dal·i·ty \sō-ˈdal-ət-ē\ *n, pl* **-ties** [L *sodalitat-, sodalitas* comradeship, club, fr. *sodalis* comrade — more at ETHICAL] **1** : BROTHERHOOD, COMMUNITY **2** : an organized society or fellowship; *specif* : a devotional or charitable association of Roman Catholic laity

soda pop *n* : a beverage consisting of soda water, flavoring, and a sweet syrup

soda water *n* **1** : a weak solution of sodium bicarbonate with some acid added to cause effervescence **2 a** : a beverage consisting of water highly charged with carbonic acid gas **b** : SODA POP

sod·bust·er \ˈsäd-ˌbəs-tər\ *n* : one (as a farmer or a plow) that breaks the sod

[1]**sod·den** \ˈsäd-ᵊn\ *adj* [ME *soden*, fr. pp. of *sethen* to seethe] **1 a** : dull or expressionless esp. from continued indulgence in alcoholic beverages <his ~ features> **b** : TORPID, UNIMAGINATIVE <~ minds> **2 a** : heavy with moisture or water <the ~ ground> **b** : heavy or doughy because of imperfect cooking <~ biscuits> — **sod·den·ly** *adv* — **sod·den·ness** \-ᵊn-(n)əs\ *n*

[2]**sodden** *vb* **sod·dened; sod·den·ing** \ˈsäd-niŋ, -ᵊn-iŋ\ *vt* : to make sodden ~ *vi* : to become soaked or saturated

so·dic \ˈsōd-ik\ *adj* : of, relating to, or containing sodium

so·di·um \ˈsōd-ē-əm\ *n* [NL, fr. E *soda*] : a silver white soft waxy ductile element of the alkali metal group that occurs abundantly in nature in combined form and is very active chemically — see ELEMENT table

sodium benzoate *n* : a crystalline or granular salt $C_7H_5O_2Na$ used chiefly as a food preservative

sodium bicarbonate *n* : a white crystalline weakly alkaline salt $NaHCO_3$ used esp. in baking powders, fire extinguishers, and medicine — called also *baking soda, saleratus*

sodium carbonate *n* : a sodium salt of carbonic acid used esp. in making soaps and chemicals, in water softening, in cleaning and bleaching, and in photography: as **a** : a hygroscopic crystalline anhydrous strongly alkaline salt Na_2CO_3 **b** : SAL SODA

sodium chlorate *n* : a colorless crystalline salt $NaClO_3$ used esp. as an oxidizing agent and weed killer

sodium chloride *n* : SALT 1a

sodium cyanide *n* : a white deliquescent poisonous salt NaCN used esp. in electroplating, in fumigating, and in treating steel

sodium dichromate *n* : a red crystalline salt $Na_2Cr_2O_7$ used esp. in tanning and processing leather, in cleaning metals, and as an oxidizing agent

sodium fluoride *n* : a poisonous crystalline salt NaF that is used in trace amounts in the fluoridation of water, in metallurgy, as a flux, as an antiseptic, and as a pesticide
sodium fluoroacetate *n* : a poisonous powdery compound $C_2H_2FO_2Na$ used as a rodent poison
sodium hydroxide *n* : a white brittle solid NaOH that is a strong caustic base used esp. in making soap, rayon, and paper
sodium hypochlorite *n* : an unstable salt NaOCl produced usu. in aqueous solution and used as a bleaching and disinfecting agent
sodium hyposulfite *n* **1** : SODIUM THIOSULFATE **2** : a crystalline water-soluble salt $Na_2S_2O_4$ used esp. in dyeing and bleaching
sodium meta·sil·i·cate \-ˌmet-ə-ˈsil-ə-ˌkāt, -ˈsil-i-kət\ *n* : a toxic corrosive crystalline salt Na_2SiO_3 used esp. as a detergent or as a substitute for phosphates in detergent formulations
sodium nitrate *n* : a deliquescent crystalline salt $NaNO_3$ found in crude form in Chile and used as a fertilizer and an oxidizing agent and in curing meat
sodium nitrite *n* : a salt $NaNO_2$ used esp. in dye manufacture and as a meat preservative
sodium pump *n* : the process by which sodium ions are actively transported across a cell membrane; *esp* : the process by which the appropriate internal and external concentrations of sodium and potassium ions are maintained in a nerve fiber and which involves the active transport of sodium ions outward with movement of potassium ions to the interior
sodium salicylate *n* : a crystalline salt $NaC_7H_5O_3$ that has a sweetish saline taste and is used chiefly as an analgesic, antipyretic, and antirheumatic
sodium sulfate *n* : a bitter salt $NaSO_4$ used esp. in detergents, in the manufacture of wood pulp and rayon, in dyeing and finishing textiles, and in its hydrated form as a cathartic — compare GLAUBER'S SALT
sodium thiosulfate *n* : a hygroscopic crystalline salt $Na_2S_2O_3$ used esp. as a photographic fixing agent and a reducing or bleaching agent — called also *hypo, sodium hyposulfite*
sodium tri·poly·phos·phate \-ˌtrī-ˌpäl-i-ˈfäs-ˌfāt\ *n* : a crystalline salt $Na_5P_3O_{10}$ that is a major component of many detergents and a major contributor to water pollution
sodium–vapor lamp *n* : an electric lamp that contains sodium vapor and electrodes between which a luminous discharge takes place and that is used esp. for lighting highways
Sod·om \ˈsäd-əm\ *n* [*Sodom,* city of ancient Palestine destroyed by God for its wickedness (Gen 18:20, 21; 19:24–28)] : a place notorious for vice or corruption
sod·om·ite \ˈsäd-ə-ˌmīt\ *n* : one who practices sodomy
sod·omy \ˈsäd-ə-mē\ *n* [ME, fr. OF *sodomie,* fr. LL *Sodoma* Sodom; fr. the homosexual proclivities of the men of the city (Gen 19:1–11)] **1** : copulation with a member of the same sex or with an animal **2** : noncoital and esp. anal or oral copulation with a member of the opposite sex
so·ev·er \sō-ˈev-ər\ *adv* [*-soever* (as in *howsoever*)] **1** : to any possible or known extent — used after an adjective preceded by *how* or a superlative preceded by *the* <how fair ~ she may be > <the most selfish ~ in this world> **2** : of any or every kind that may be specified — used after a noun modified esp. by *any, no,* or *what* <he gives no information ~>
SOF *abbr* sound on film
so·fa \ˈsō-fə\ *n* [Ar *ṣuffah* long bench] : a long upholstered seat usu. with arms and a back and often convertible into a bed
sofa bed *n* : an upholstered sofa that can be made to serve as a bed by lowering its hinged upholstered back to horizontal position
so·far \ˈsō-ˌfär\ *n* [*so*und *f*ixing *a*nd *r*anging] : a system for locating an underwater explosion at sea by triangulation based on the reception of the sound by three widely separated shore stations
so far as *conj* : insofar as
sof·fit \ˈsäf-ət\ *n* [F *soffite,* fr. It *soffitto,* fr. (assumed) VL *suffictus,* pp. of L *suffigere* to fasten underneath — more at SUFFIX] : the underside of a part or member of a building (as of an overhang or staircase); *esp* : the intrados of an arch
[1]**soft** \ˈsȯft\ *adj* [ME, fr. OE *sōfte,* alter. of *sēfte;* akin to OHG *semfti* soft] **1 a** : pleasing or agreeable to the senses : bringing ease, comfort, or quiet <the ~ influences of home> **b** : having a bland or mellow rather than a sharp or acid taste or flavor **c** (1) : not bright or glaring : SUBDUED (2) : having or producing little contrast or a relatively short range of tones <a ~ photographic print> **d** : quiet in pitch or volume **e** *of the eyes* : having a liquid or gentle appearance **f** : smooth or delicate in texture, grain, or fiber <~ cashmere> <~ fur> **g** (1) : balmy, mild, or clement in weather or temperature (2) : moving or falling with slight force or impact : not violent <~ breezes> **2** : demanding little work or effort : EASY, IDLE <a ~ job> **3 a** : sounding as in *ace* and *gem* respectively — used of *c* and *g* or their sound **b** *of a consonant* : VOICED **c** : constituting a vowel before which there is a \y\ sound or a \y\-like modification of a consonant or constituting a consonant in whose articulation there is a \y\-like modification or which is followed by a \y\ sound (as in Russian) **4** *archaic* : moving in a leisurely manner **5** : rising gradually <a ~ slope> **6** : having curved or rounded outline : not harsh or jagged <~ hills against the horizon> **7** : marked by a gentleness, kindness, or tenderness: as **a** (1) : not being or involving harsh or onerous terms : EASY <a policy of ~ competition> (2) : based on negotiation and conciliation rather than on a show of power or on threats <took a ~ line towards the enemy> **b** : tending to ingratiate or disarm : ENGAGING, KIND <a ~ answer turns away wrath —Prov 15:1 (RSV)> **c** : marked by mildness : UNASSUMING, LOW-KEYED **8 a** : emotionally suggestible or responsive : IMPRESSIONABLE **b** : unduly susceptible to influence : COMPLIANT **c** (1) : lacking firmness or strength of character : FEEBLE, UNMANLY (2) : marked by a gradually declining trend : not firm <wool prices are increasingly ~> **d** : amorously attracted or emotionally involved — used with *on* <has been ~ on her for years> **9 a** : lacking robust strength, stamina, or endurance esp. because of living in ease or luxury **b** : weak or deficient mentally **10 a** : yielding to physical pressure **b** : permitting someone or something to sink in — used of wet ground **c** (1) : of a consistency that may be shaped or molded (2) *of cheese* : capable of being spread **d** : easily magnetized and demagnetized **e** : lacking relatively or comparatively in hardness <~ iron> **11** : deficient in or free from substances (as calcium and magnesium salts) that prevent lathering of soap <~ water> **12** : having relatively low energy <~ X rays> **13** : occurring at such a speed and under such circumstances as to avoid destructive impact <~ landing of a spacecraft on the moon> **14** : not protected against enemy attack <a ~ aboveground launching site> **15** *of a detergent* : BIODEGRADABLE **16** *of a drug* : considered less detrimental than a hard narcotic <marijuana is usually regarded as a ~ drug> **17** : easily polarized — used of acids and bases — **soft·ish** \ˈsȯf-tish\ *adj* — **soft·ly** \ˈsȯft-lē\ *adv* — **soft·ness** \ˈsȯf(t)-nəs\ *n*
syn SOFT, BLAND, MILD, GENTLE, LENIENT *shared meaning element* : devoid of harshness, roughness, or intensity ***ant*** hard, stern
[2]**soft** *n* : a soft object, material, or part <the ~ of the thumb>
[3]**soft** *adv* : in a soft or gentle manner : SOFTLY
soft·back \ˈsȯf(t)-ˌbak\ *adj* : SOFT-COVER — **softback** *n*
soft·ball \-ˌbȯl\ *n* : baseball played on a small diamond with a ball that is larger than a baseball and that is pitched underhand; *also* : the ball used in this game
soft–bill\-ˌbil\ *n* : a bird with a weak bill adapted to feeding esp. on insects — compare HARD-BILL
soft–boiled \-ˈbȯi(ə)ld\ *adj* **1** *of an egg* : boiled to a soft consistency **2** : SENTIMENTAL
soft·bound \-ˌbau̇nd\ *adj* : SOFT-COVER
soft chancre *n* : CHANCROID
soft coal *n* : BITUMINOUS COAL
soft–cov·er \ˈsȯft-ˈkəv-ər\ *adj* : bound in flexible covers : not bound in hard covers; *specif* : PAPERBACK <~ books>
soft drink *n* : SODA POP
soft·en \ˈsȯ-fən\ *vb* **soft·ened; soft·en·ing** \ˈsȯf-(ə-)niŋ\ *vt* **1** : to make soft or softer **2 a** : to weaken the military resistance or the morale of esp. by harassment (as preliminary bombardment) — often used with *up* **b** : to impair the strength or resistance of — often used with *up* <~ up a sales prospect> ~ *vi* : to become soft or softer — **soft·en·er** \ˈsȯf-(ə-)nər\ *n*
soft–finned \ˈsȯf(t)-ˈfind\ *adj* : having fins in which the membrane is supported entirely or mostly by soft or articulated rays — used of higher teleost fishes; compare SPINY-FINNED
soft goods *n pl* : goods that are not durable — used esp. of textile products
soft hail *n* : GRAUPEL
soft·head \ˈsȯft-ˌhed\ *n* : a silly or feebleminded person
soft·head·ed \-ˈhed-əd\ *adj* : having a weak, unrealistic, or uncritical mind — **soft·head·ed·ly** *adv* — **soft·head·ed·ness** *n*
soft·heart·ed \-ˈhärt-əd\ *adj* : emotionally responsive : SYMPATHETIC — **soft·heart·ed·ly** *adv* — **soft·heart·ed·ness** *n*
soft–land \-ˈland\ *vb* [back-formation fr. *soft landing*] *vi* : to make a soft landing on a celestial body (as the moon) ~ *vt* : to cause to soft-land — **soft–land·er** *n*
soft palate *n* : the fold at the back of the hard palate that partially separates the mouth and pharynx
soft–ped·al \ˈsȯf(t)-ˈped-ᵊl\ *vt* **1** : to use the soft pedal in playing **2** : to play down : OBSCURE, MUFFLE <~ the issue>
soft pedal *n* **1** : a foot pedal on a piano that reduces the volume of sound **2** : something that muffles, deadens, or reduces effect
soft rot *n* : a mushy, watery, or slimy decay of plants or their parts caused by bacteria or fungi
soft scale *n* : a scale insect more or less active in all stages
soft sell *n* : the use of suggestion or gentle persuasion in selling rather than aggressive pressure — compare HARD SELL
soft–shell \ˈsȯf(t)-ˌshel\ *or* **soft–shelled** \-ˈsheld\ *adj* : having a soft or fragile shell esp. as a result of recent shedding
soft–shell clam *n* : an elongated clam (*Mya arenaria*) of the east coast of No. America that has a thin friable shell and long siphons and is used esp. for steaming — called also *soft-shelled clam, steamer*
soft–shelled turtle *n* : any of numerous aquatic turtles (family Trionychidae) that have sharp claws and mandibles and a flat shell covered with soft leathery skin instead of with horny plates
soft–shoe \ˈsȯf(t)-ˈshü\ *adj* : of or relating to tap dancing done in soft-soled shoes without metal taps
soft–soap \ˈsȯf(t)-ˈsōp\ *vt* : to soothe or persuade with flattery or blarney — **soft–soap·er** \-ˈsō-pər\ *n*
soft soap *n* **1** : a semifluid soap **2** : FLATTERY
soft–spo·ken \-ˈspō-kən\ *adj* : having a mild or gentle voice; *also* : SUAVE
soft spot *n* **1** : a sentimental weakness <has a *soft spot* for him> **2** : a vulnerable point <a *soft spot* in the defense system>
soft touch *n* : one who is easily imposed on or taken advantage of
soft·ware \ˈsȯf-ˌtwa(ə)r, -ˌtwe(ə)r\ *n* **1** : the entire set of programs, procedures, and related documentation associated with a system and esp. a computer system; *specif* : computer programs **2** : something used or associated with and usu. contrasted with hardware; *esp* : materials for use with audiovisual equipment
soft wheat *n* : a wheat with soft starchy kernels high in starch but usu. low in gluten
[1]**soft·wood** \ˈsȯf-ˌtwu̇d\ *n* **1** : the wood of a coniferous tree including both soft and hard woods **2** : a tree that yields softwood
[2]**softwood** *adj* **1** : having or made of softwood **2** : consisting of immature still pliable tissue <~ cuttings for propagating plants>
soft–wood·ed \ˈsȯf-ˈtwu̇d-əd\ *adj* **1** : having soft wood that is easy to work or finish **2** : SOFTWOOD 1
softy *or* **soft·ie** \ˈsȯf-tē\ *n, pl* **soft·ies** [[1]*soft*] **1** : an excessively sentimental or susceptible person **2** : a weak, effeminate, or foolish person
Sog·di·an \ˈsäg-dē-ən\ *n* [L *Sogdiani,* pl., fr. pl. of *sogdianus* adj., Sogdian, fr. OPers *Sughuda* Sogdiana] **1** : a native or inhabitant of Sogdiana **2** : an Iranian language of the Sogdians — see INDO-EUROPEAN LANGUAGES table — **Sogdian** *adj*

sog·gy \'säg-ē, 'sȯg-\ *adj* **sog·gier; -est** [E dial. *sog* (to soak)] **1** : saturated or heavy with water or moisture: as **a** : WATERLOGGED, SOAKED <a ~ lawn> **b** : heavy or doughy because of imperfect cooking <~ bread> **2** : heavily dull <~ prose> — **sog·gi·ly** \'säg-ə-lē, 'sȯg-\ *adv* — **sog·gi·ness** \'säg-ē-nəs, 'sȯg-\ *n*

soi–di·sant \ˌswäd-ē-'zäⁿ\ *adj* [F, lit., saying oneself] : SELF-STYLED, SO-CALLED — usu. used disparagingly <a ~ artist>

soi·gné *or* **soi·gnée** \swän-'yā\ *adj* [F, fr. pp. of *soigner* to take care of, fr. ML *soniare*] **1** : elegantly maintained : MODISH <a ~ restaurant> **2** : WELL-GROOMED, SLEEK

[1]**soil** \'sȯi(ə)l\ *vb* [ME *soilen*, fr. OF *soiller* to wallow, soil, fr. *soil* pigsty, prob. fr. L *suile*, fr. *sus* pig — more at SOW] *vt* **1** : to stain or defile morally : CORRUPT, POLLUTE **2** : to make unclean esp. superficially : DIRTY **3** : to blacken or besmirch (as a person's reputation) by word or deed ~ *vi* : to become soiled or dirty

[2]**soil** *n* **1 a** : SOILAGE 1, STAIN <protect a dress from ~> **b** : moral defilement : CORRUPTION **2** : something that spoils or pollutes: as **a** : REFUSE **b** : SEWAGE **c** : DUNG, EXCREMENT

[3]**soil** *n* [ME, fr. AF, fr. L *solium* seat; prob. akin to L *sedēre* to sit — more at SIT] **1** : firm land : EARTH **2 a** : the upper layer of earth that may be dug or plowed and in which plants grow **b** : the superficial unconsolidated and usu. weathered part of the mantle of a planet and esp. of the earth **3** : COUNTRY, LAND <his native ~> **4** : the agricultural life or calling **5** : a medium in which something takes hold and develops

[4]**soil** *vt* [origin unknown] : to feed (livestock) in the barn or an enclosure with fresh grass or green food; *also* : to purge (livestock) by feeding on green food

soil·age \'sȯi-lij\ *n* **1** [[1]*soil*] : the act of soiling : the condition of being soiled **2** [[4]*soil*] : green crops for feeding confined animals

soil bank *n* : acreage retired from crop cultivation and planted with soil-building plants under a plan sponsored by the U.S. government that provides subsidies to farmers for the retired land

soil·borne \'sȯil-ˌbō(ə)rn, -ˌbȯ(ə)rn\ *adj* : transmitted by or in soil <~ fungi>

soil conservation *n* : management of soil so as to obtain optimum yields while improving and protecting the soil

soil·less \'sȯi(ə)l-ləs\ *adj* : carried on without soil <~ agriculture>

soil pipe *n* : a pipe for carrying off wastes from toilets

soil science *n* : [2]PEDOLOGY

soil series *n* : a collection of soils with similar profiles developed from similar parent materials under comparable climatic and vegetational conditions

soil·ure \'sȯil-yər\ *n* **1** : the act of soiling : the condition of being soiled **2** : STAIN, SMUDGE

soi·ree *or* **soi·rée** \swä-'rā\ *n* [F *soirée* evening period, evening party, fr. MF, fr *soir* evening, fr. L *sero* at a late hour, fr. *serus* late — more at SINCE] : a party or reception held in the evening

soi·xante–neuf \swȧ-säⁿt-nœf\ *n* [F] : SIXTY-NINE 2

[1]**so·journ** \'sō-ˌjərn, sō-'\ *n* [ME *sojorn*, fr. OF, fr. *sojorner*] : a temporary stay <a ~ in the country>

[2]**sojourn** *vi* [ME *sojornen*, fr. OF *sojorner*, fr. (assumed) VL *subdiurnare*, fr. L *sub* under, during + LL *diurnum* day — more at SUB-, JOURNEY] : to stay as a temporary resident : STOP <~*ed* for a month at a resort> *syn* see RESIDE — **so·journ·er** *n*

soke \'sōk\ *n* [ME *soc, soke*, fr. ML *soca*, fr. OE *sōcn* inquiry, jurisdiction; akin to OE *sēcan* to seek] **1** : the right in Anglo-Saxon and early English law to hold court and administer justice with the franchise to receive certain fees or fines arising from it : jurisdiction over a territory or over people **2** : the district included in a soke jurisdiction or franchise

soke·man \'sōk-mən\ *n* : a man who is under the soke of another : a tenant by socage

[1]**sol** \'sōl\ *also* **so** \'sō\ *n* [ML, *sol*, fr. the syllable sung to this note in a medieval hymn to St. John the Baptist] : the 5th tone of the diatonic scale in solmization

[2]**sol** \'säl, 'sȯl\ *n* [ME, fr. MF — more at SOU] : an old French coin equal to 12 deniers; *also* : a corresponding unit of value

[3]**sol** \'säl, 'sȯl\ *n, pl* **so·les** \'sō-(ˌ)lās\ [AmerSp, fr. Sp, sun, fr. L] — see MONEY table

[4]**sol** \'säl, 'sȯl\ *n* [*-sol* (as in *hydrosol*), fr. *solution*] : a fluid colloidal system; *esp* : one in which the continuous phase is a liquid

[5]**sol** *abbr* **1** solicitor **2** soluble **3** solution

Sol \'säl\ *n* [ME, fr. L] : SUN

sola *pl of* SOLUM

[1]**so·lace** \'säl-əs *also* 'sōl-\ *n* [ME *solas*, fr. OF, fr. L *solacium*, fr. *solari* to console — more at SILLY] **1** : alleviation of grief or anxiety **2** : a source of relief or consolation

[2]**solace** *vt* **so·laced; so·lac·ing** **1** : to give solace to : CONSOLE **2 a** : to make cheerful **b** : AMUSE **3** : ALLAY, SOOTHE <~ grief> *syn* see COMFORT — **so·lace·ment** \-ə-smənt\ *n* — **so·lac·er** *n*

so·la·na·ceous \ˌsō-lə-'nā-shəs\ *adj* [NL *Solanaceae*, group name, fr. *Solanum*] : of or relating to the nightshade family of plants

so·lan goose \ˌsō-lən-\ *n* [ME *soland*, fr. ON *sūla* pillar, gannet + *önd* duck; akin to OE *sȳl* pillar and to OHG *anut* duck, L *anas*] : a very large white gannet (*Sula bassana* or *Moris bassana*) with black wing tips

so·la·nine *or* **so·la·nin** \'sō-lə-ˌnēn, -nən\ *n* [F *solanine*, fr. L *solanum* nightshade] : a bitter poisonous crystalline alkaloid $C_{45}H_{72}NO_{15}$ from several plants (as some potatoes or tomatoes) of the nightshade family

so·la·num \sə-'lān-əm, -'län-, -'lan-\ *n* [NL, genus name, fr. L, nightshade] : any of a genus (*Solanum*) of herbs, shrubs, or trees of the nightshade family that have often prickly-veined leaves, cymose white, purple, or yellow flowers, and a fruit that is a berry

so·lar \'sō-lər, -ˌlär\ *adj* [ME, fr. L *solaris*, fr. *sol* sun; akin to OE & ON *sōl* sun, Gk *hēlios*] **1** : of, derived from, or relating to the sun esp. as affecting the earth **2** : measured by the earth's course in relation to the sun <~ time> <~ year>; *also* : relating to or reckoned by solar time **3** : produced or operated by the action of the sun's light or heat; *also* : utilizing the sun's rays

solar battery *n* : a device of one or more units for converting the energy of sunlight into electrical energy

solar cell *n* : a photovoltaic cell (as one including a junction between two types of silicon semiconductors) that is able to convert sunlight into electrical energy and is used as a power source

solar constant *n* : the quantity of radiant solar heat received normally at the outer layer of the earth's atmosphere and having an average value of about 1.94 gram calories per square centimeter per minute

solar day *n* : the interval between transits of the apparent or mean sun across the meridian at any place

solar flare *n* : a sudden temporary outburst of energy from a small area of the sun's surface

solar house *n* : a house equipped with glass areas and so planned as to utilize the sun's rays extensively in heating

so·lar·i·um \sō-'lar-ē-əm, sə-, -'ler-\ *n, pl* **-ia** \-ē-ə\ *also* **-ums** [L, fr. *sol*] : a room (as in a hospital) exposed to the sun and used esp. for treatment of illness by administration of sunbaths or therapeutic light

so·lar·iza·tion \ˌsō-lə-rə-'zā-shən\ *n* **1** : an act or process of solarizing **2** : a reversal of gradation in a photographic image obtained by intense or continued exposure

so·lar·ize \'sō-lə-ˌrīz\ *vt* **-ized; -iz·ing** **1 a** : to expose to sunlight **b** : to affect by the action of the sun's rays **2** : to subject (photographic materials) to solarization

solar panel *n* : a battery of solar cells (as in a spacecraft)

solar plexus \'sō-lər-\ *n* [fr. the radiating nerve fibers] **1** : a nerve plexus in the abdomen that is situated behind the stomach and in front of the aorta and the crura of the diaphragm and contains several ganglia distributing nerve fibers to the viscera **2** : the pit of the stomach

solar system *n* : the sun with the group of celestial bodies that are held by its attraction and revolve around it

solar wind *n* : the continuous ejection of plasma from the sun's surface into and through interplanetary space

sol·ate \'säl-ˌāt, 'sȯl-\ *vi* **sol·at·ed; sol·a·ting** [[4]*sol*] : to change to a sol — **sol·ation** \sä-lā-shən, sȯ-\ *n*

so·la·ti·um \sō-'lā-shē-əm\ *n, pl* **-tia** \-shē-ə\ [LL *solacium, solatium*, fr. L, solace] : a compensation (as money) given as solace for suffering, loss, or injured feelings

sold *past of* SELL

sol·dan \'säl-dən, 'sōl-\ *n* [ME, fr. MF, fr. Ar *sulṭān*] *archaic* : SULTAN; *esp* : the sultan of Egypt

[1]**sol·der** \'säd-ər, 'sȯd-, *Brit also* 'säl-dər, 'sōl-\ *n* [ME *soudure*, fr. MF, fr. *souder* to solder, fr. L *solidare* to make solid, fr. *solidus* solid] **1** : a metal or metallic alloy used when melted to join metallic surfaces; *esp* : an alloy of lead and tin so used **2** : something that unites or cements

[2]**solder** *vb* **soldered; sol·der·ing** \-(ə-)riŋ\ *vt* **1** : to unite or make whole by solder **2** : to bring into or restore to firm union <a friendship ~*ed* by common interests> ~ *vi* **1** : to use solder **2** : to become united or repaired by or as if by solder — **sol·der·abil·i·ty** \ˌsäd-ə-rə-'bil-ət-ē, ˌsȯd-\ *n* — **sol·der·er** \'säd-ər-ər, 'sȯd-\ *n*

soldering iron *n* : a pointed or wedge-shaped device that is usu. electrically heated and that is used for soldering

[1]**sol·dier** \'sōl-jər\ *n* [ME *soudier*, fr. OF, fr. *soulde* pay, fr. LL *solidus* solidus] **1 a** : one engaged in military service and esp. in the army **b** : an enlisted man or woman **c** : a skilled warrior **2** : a militant leader, follower, or worker **3 a** : one of a caste of wingless sterile termites usu. differing from workers in larger size and head and long jaws **b** : one of a type of worker ants distinguished by exceptionally large head and jaws **4** : one who shirks his work — **sol·dier·ly** \-lē\ *adj or adv* — **sol·dier·ship** \-ˌship\ *n*

[2]**soldier** *vi* **sol·diered; sol·dier·ing** \ˌsōlj-(ə-)riŋ\ **1 a** : to serve as a soldier **b** : to behave in a soldierly manner **c** : to push doggedly forward — usu. used with *on* <didn't know whether to quit or ~ on> **2** : to make a pretense of working while really loafing

sol·dier·ing *n* : the life, service, or practice of one who soldiers

soldier of fortune : one who follows a military career wherever there is promise of profit, adventure, or pleasure

soldiers' home *n* : an institution maintained (as by the federal or a state government) for the care and relief of military veterans

soldier's medal *n* : a U.S. military decoration awarded for heroism not involving combat

sol·diery \'sōlj-(ə-)rē\ *n* **1 a** : a body of soldiers **b** : SOLDIERS, MILITARY **2** : the profession or technique of soldiering

sol·do \'sȯl-(ˌ)dō\ *n, pl* **sol·di** \-(ˌ)dē\ [It, fr. LL *solidus*] : an old Italian coin worth five centesimi

sold–out \'sōl-'dau̇t\ *adj* : having all available tickets or accommodations sold completely and esp. in advance

[1]**sole** \'sōl\ *n* [ME, fr. MF, fr. L *solea* sandal; akin to L *solum* base, ground, soil] **1 a** : the undersurface of a foot **b** : the part of an item of footwear on which the sole rests **2** : the usu. flat or flattened bottom or lower part of something or the base on which something rests — **soled** \'sōld\ *adj*

[2]**sole** *vt* **soled; sol·ing** **1** : to furnish with a sole <~ a shoe> **2** : to place the sole of (a golf club) on the ground

[3]**sole** *n* [ME, fr. MF, L *solea* sandal, a flatfish] : a flatfish (family Soleidae) having a small mouth, small or rudimentary fins, and small eyes placed close together and including superior food fishes (as *Solea solea* of Europe); *also* : any of various mostly market flatfishes of other families

[4]**sole** *adj* [ME, alone, fr. MF *seul*, fr. L *solus*] **1** : not married — used chiefly of women **2** : having no companion : SOLITARY **3 a** : having no sharer **b** : being the only one <she was her mother's ~ confidant> **4** : functioning independently and without assist-

ance or interference <let conscience be the ~ judge> **5 :** belonging exclusively or otherwise limited to one usu. specified individual, unit, or group ***syn*** see SINGLE — **sole·ness** \ˈsōl-nəs\ *n*

so·le·cism \ˈsäl-ə-ˌsiz-əm, ˈsō-lə-\ *n* [L *soloecismus,* fr. Gk *soloikismos,* fr. *soloikos* speaking incorrectly, lit., inhabitant of Soloi, fr. *Soloi,* city in ancient Cilicia where a substandard form of Attic was spoken] **1 :** an ungrammatical combination of words in a sentence; *also* **:** a minor blunder in speech **2 :** something deviating from the proper, normal, or accepted order **3 :** a breach of etiquette or decorum — **so·le·cis·tic** \ˌsäl-ə-ˈsis-tik, ˌsō-lə-\ *adj*

sole·ly \ˈsō(l)-lē\ *adv* **1 :** without another **:** SINGLY <went ~ on her way> **2 :** to the exclusion of all else <done ~ for money>

sol·emn \ˈsäl-əm\ *adj* [ME *solemne,* fr. MF, fr. L *sollemnis* regularly appointed, solemn] **1 :** marked by the invocation of a religious sanction <a ~ oath> **2 :** marked by the observance of established form or ceremony; *specif* **:** celebrated with full liturgical ceremony **3 a :** awe-inspiring **:** SUBLIME **b :** marked by grave sedateness and earnest serious sobriety **c :** SOMBER, GLOOMY ***syn*** see SERIOUS — **sol·emn·ly** *adv* — **sol·emn·ness** *n*

solemn high mass *n* **:** a high mass following the ceremonial prescriptions of a solemn mass

so·lem·ni·fy \sə-ˈlem-nə-ˌfī\ *vt* **-fied; -fy·ing :** to make solemn

so·lem·ni·ty \sə-ˈlem-nət-ē\ *n, pl* **-ties 1 :** formal or ceremonious observance of an occasion or event **2 :** a solemn event or occasion **3 :** a solemn condition or quality <the ~ of his words>

sol·em·nize \ˈsäl-əm-ˌnīz\ *vb* **-nized; -niz·ing** *vt* **1 :** to observe or honor with solemnity **2 :** to perform with pomp or ceremony; *esp* **:** to celebrate (a marriage) with religious rites **3 :** to make solemn **:** DIGNIFY ~ *vi* **:** to speak or act with solemnity — **sol·em·ni·za·tion** \ˌsäl-əm-nə-ˈzā-shən\ *n*

solemn mass *n* **:** a mass marked by the use of incense and by the presence of a deacon and a subdeacon in attendance on the celebrant

solemn vow *n* **:** an absolute and irrevocable public vow taken by a religious in the Roman Catholic Church under which ownership of property by the individual is prohibited and marriage is invalid under canon law

so·le·noid \ˈsō-lə-ˌnȯid\ *n* [F *solénoïde,* fr. Gk *sōlēnoeidēs* pipe-shaped, fr. Gk, *sōlēn* pipe — more at SYRINGE] **:** a coil of wire commonly in the form of a long cylinder that when carrying a current resembles a bar magnet so that a movable core is drawn into the coil when a current flows — **so·le·noi·dal** \ˌsō-lə-ˈnȯid-ᵊl\ *adj*

sole·plate \ˈsōl-ˌplāt\ *n* **1 :** the lower plate of a studded partition on which the bases of the studs butt **2 :** the undersurface of a flatiron

sole·print \-ˌprint\ *n* **:** a print of the sole of the foot; *esp* **:** one made in the manner of a fingerprint and used for the identification of an infant

soles *pl of* SOL

[1]sol–fa \(ˈ)sōl-ˈfä\ *n* **1 :** SOL-FA SYLLABLES **2 :** SOLMIZATION; *also* **:** an exercise thus sung **3 :** TONIC SOL-FA — **sol–fa·ist** \-ˈfä(-ə)st, -ˈfä-ˌist\ *n*

[2]sol–fa *vi* **:** to sing the sol-fa syllables ~ *vt* **:** to sing (as a melody) to sol-fa syllables

sol–fa syllables *n pl* **:** the syllables *do, re, mi, fa, sol, la, ti,* used in singing the tones of the scale

sol·fa·ta·ra \ˌsōl-fə-ˈtär-ə\ *n* [It, sulfur mine, fr. *solfo* sulfur, fr. L *sulfur*] **:** a volcanic area or vent that yields only hot vapors and gases in part sulfurous

sol·fège \säl-ˈfezh\ *n* [F, fr. It *solfeggio*] **1 :** the application of the sol-fa syllables to a musical scale or to a melody **2 :** a singing exercise esp. using sol-fa syllables; *also* **:** practice in sight-reading vocal music using the sol-fa syllables

sol·feg·gio \säl-ˈfej-(ē-ˌ)ō\ *n* [It, fr. *sol-fa*] **:** SOLFÈGE

sol·gel \ˈsäl-ˌjel, ˈsōl-\ *adj* **:** involving alternation between sol and gel states

soli *pl of* SOLO

so·lic·it \sə-ˈlis-ət\ *vb* [ME *soliciten* to disturb, take charge of, fr. MF *solliciter,* fr. L *sollicitare* to disturb, fr. *sollicitus* anxious, fr. *sollus* whole (fr. Oscan; akin to Gk *holos* whole) + *citus,* pp. of *ciēre* to move — more at SAFE, HIGHT] *vt* **1 a :** to make petition to **:** ENTREAT **b :** to approach with a request or plea **2 :** to strongly urge (as one's cause) **3 a :** to entice or lure esp. into evil **b** *obs* **:** to attempt to seduce **c :** to proposition (a man) esp. as or in the character of a prostitute **4 :** to try to obtain by usu. urgent requests or pleas ~ *vi* **1 :** to make solicitation **:** IMPORTUNE **2** *of a prostitute* **:** to offer intercourse to a man ***syn*** see ASK, INVITE

so·lic·i·tant \sə-ˈlis-ət-ənt\ *n* **:** one who solicits

so·lic·i·ta·tion \sə-ˌlis-ə-ˈtā-shən\ *n* **1 :** the practice or act or an instance of soliciting; *esp* **:** ENTREATY, IMPORTUNITY **2 :** a moving or drawing force **:** INCITEMENT, ALLUREMENT

so·lic·i·tor \sə-ˈlis-ət-ər, -ˈlis-tər\ *n* **1 :** one that solicits; *esp* **:** an agent that solicits (as contributions to charity) **2 :** a counsel who advises clients, represents them in the lower courts, and prepares cases for barristers to try in higher courts **3 :** the chief law officer of a municipality, county, or government department

solicitor general *n, pl* **solicitors general :** a law officer appointed primarily to assist an attorney general

so·lic·i·tor·ship \sə-ˈlis-ət-ər-ˌship, -ˈlis-tər-\ *n* **:** the position or status of a solicitor

so·lic·i·tous \sə-ˈlis-ət-əs, -ˈlis-təs\ *adj* [L *sollicitus*] **1 :** full of concern or fears **:** APPREHENSIVE <~ about the future> **2 :** full of desire **:** EAGER **3 :** meticulously careful <~ in matters of dress> **4 :** manifesting or expressing solicitude <a ~ inquiry about his health> — **so·lic·i·tous·ly** *adv* — **so·lic·i·tous·ness** *n*

so·lic·i·tude \sə-ˈlis-ə-ˌt(y)üd\ *n* **1 a :** the state of being solicitous **:** ANXIETY **b :** attentive care and protectiveness; *also* **:** an attitude of solicitous concern or attention **2 :** a cause of care or concern — usu. used in pl. ***syn*** see CARE ***ant*** negligence

[1]sol·id \ˈsäl-əd\ *adj* [ME *solide,* fr. MF, fr. L *solidus;* akin to Gk *holos* whole — more at SAFE] **1 a :** being without an internal cavity <a ~ ball of rubber> **b (1) :** printed with minimum space between lines **(2) :** joined without a hyphen <a ~ compound> **c :** not interrupted by a break or opening <a ~ wall> **2 :** having, involving, or dealing with three dimensions or with solids <~ configuration> **3 a :** of uniformly close and coherent texture **:** not loose or spongy **:** COMPACT **b :** neither gaseous nor liquid **4 :** of good substantial quality or kind <~ comfort>: as **a :** SOUND <~ reasons> **b :** made firmly and well <~ furniture> **5 a :** having no break or interruption <waited three ~ hours> **b :** UNANIMOUS <had the ~ support of his party> **c :** intimately friendly or associated <~ with his boss> **6 a :** PRUDENT; *also* **:** well-established financially **b :** serious in purpose or character **7 :** of one substance or character: as **a :** entirely of one metal or containing the minimum of alloy necessary to impart hardness <~ gold> **b :** of a single color or tone ***syn*** see FIRM ***ant*** fluid, liquid — **sol·id·ly** *adv* — **sol·id·ness** *n*

[2]solid *adv* **:** in a solid manner; *also* **:** UNANIMOUSLY

[3]solid *n* **1 :** a geometrical figure or element (as a cube or sphere) having three dimensions **2 a :** a substance that does not flow perceptibly under moderate stress **b :** the part of a solution or suspension that when freed from solvent or suspending medium has the qualities of a solid — usu. used in pl. <milk ~*s*> **3 :** something that is solid: as **a :** a solid color **b :** a compound word whose members are joined together without a hyphen

sol·i·da·go \ˌsäl-ə-ˈdā-(ˌ)gō, -ˈdäg-(ˌ)ō\ *n, pl* **-gos** [NL, genus name, fr. ML *soldago,* an herb reputed to heal wounds, fr. *soldare* to make whole, fr. L *solidare,* fr. *solidus* solid] **:** any of a genus (*Solidago*) of chiefly No. American composite herbs including the typical goldenrods

solid angle *n* **:** the three-dimensional angular spread at the vertex of a cone measured by the area intercepted by the cone on a unit sphere whose center is the vertex of the cone

sol·i·da·rism \ˈsäl-əd-ə-ˌriz-əm\ *n* [*solidar*ity + *-ism*] **1 :** SOLIDARITY **2 :** a sociological theory maintaining that the mutual interdependence of members of society offers a basis for a social organization based upon solidarity of interests — **sol·i·da·rist** \-rəst\ *n* — **sol·i·da·ris·tic** \ˌsäl-əd-ə-ˈris-tik\ *adj*

sol·i·dar·i·ty \ˌsäl-ə-ˈdar-ət-ē\ *n* [F *solidarité,* fr. *solidaire* characterized by solidarity, fr. L *solidum* whole sum, fr. neut. of *solidus* solid] **:** unity (as of a group or class) that produces or is based on community of interests, objectives, and standards ***syn*** see UNITY

solid geometry *n* **:** a branch of geometry that deals with figures of three-dimensional space

so·lid·i·fy \sə-ˈlid-ə-ˌfī\ *vb* **-fied; -fy·ing** *vt* **1 :** to make solid, compact, or hard **2 :** to make secure, substantial, or firmly fixed <factors that ~ public opinion> ~ *vi* **:** to become solid, compact, or hard — **so·lid·i·fi·ca·tion** \-ˌlid-ə-fə-ˈkā-shən\ *n*

so·lid·i·ty \sə-ˈlid-ət-ē\ *n, pl* **-ties 1 :** the quality or state of being solid **2 :** moral, mental, or financial soundness **3 :** something solid

sol·id–look·ing \ˌsäl-əd-ˈlu̇k-iŋ\ *adj* **:** giving an impression of solid worth or substance <~ well-fed citizens>

solid of revolution : a mathematical solid conceived as formed by the revolution of a plane figure about an axis in its plane

solid–state *adj* **1 :** relating to the properties, structure, or reactivity of solid material; *esp* **:** relating to the arrangement or behavior of ions, molecules, nucleons, electrons, and holes in the crystals of a substance (as a semiconductor) or to the effect of crystal imperfections on the properties of a solid substance <~ physics> **2 :** utilizing the electric, magnetic, or photic properties of solid materials **:** not utilizing electron tubes <a ~ stereo system>

sol·i·dus \ˈsäl-əd-əs\ *n, pl* **-i·di** \-ə-ˌdī, -ˌdē\ [ME, fr. LL, fr. L, solid] **1 :** an ancient Roman gold coin introduced by Constantine and used to the fall of the Byzantine Empire **2** [ML, shilling, fr. LL; fr. its use as a symbol for shillings] **:** DIAGONAL 3

so·li·fluc·tion \ˈsō-lə-ˌflək-shən\ *n* [L *solum* soil + *-i-* + *fluction-, fluctio* act of flowing, fr. *fluctus,* pp. of *fluere* to flow — more at FLUID] **:** the slow creeping of saturated fragmental material (as soil) down a slope that usu. occurs in regions of perennial frost

so·lil·o·quist \sə-ˈlil-ə-kwəst\ *n* **:** one who soliloquizes

so·lil·o·quize \-ˌkwīz\ *vi* **-quized; -quiz·ing :** to utter a soliloquy **:** talk to oneself — **so·lil·o·quiz·er** *n*

so·lil·o·quy \sə-ˈlil-ə-kwē\ *n, pl* **-quies** [LL *soliloquium,* fr. L *solus* alone + *loqui* to speak] **1 :** the act of talking to oneself **2 :** a dramatic monologue that gives the illusion of being a series of unspoken reflections

so·lip·sism \ˈsō-ləp-ˌsiz-əm, ˈsäl-əp-\ *n* [L *solus* alone + *ipse* self] **:** a theory holding that the self can know nothing but its own modifications and that the self is the only existent thing — **so·lip·sist** \ˈsō-ləp-səst, ˈsäl-əp-, sə-ˈlip-\ *n* — **so·lip·sis·tic** \ˌsō-ləp-ˈsis-tik, ˌsäl-əp-\ *adj*

sol·i·taire \ˈsäl-ə-ˌta(ə)r, -ˌte(ə)r\ *n* [F, fr. *solitaire,* adj., solitary, fr. L *solitarius*] **1 :** a single gem (as a diamond) set alone **2 :** any of various card games that can be played by one person

[1]sol·i·tary \ˈsäl-ə-ˌter-ē\ *adj* [ME, fr. L *solitarius,* fr. *solitas* aloneness, fr. *solus* alone] **1 a :** being, living, or going alone or without companions **b :** saddened by isolation **2 :** UNFREQUENTED, DESOLATE **3 :** taken, passed, or performed without companions <a ~ ramble> **4 :** being at once single and isolated <a ~ example> **5 a :** occurring singly and not as part of a group or cluster <flowers terminal and ~> **b :** not gregarious, colonial, social, or compound <~ bees> ***syn*** see ALONE, SINGLE — **sol·i·tari·ly** \ˌsäl-ə-ˈter-ə-lē\ *adv* — **sol·i·tari·ness** \ˈsäl-ə-ˌter-ē-nəs\ *n*

[2]solitary *n, pl* **-tar·ies 1 :** one who lives or seeks to live a solitary life **:** RECLUSE **2 :** solitary confinement in prison

sol·i·tude \ˈsäl-ə-ˌt(y)üd\ *n* [ME, fr. MF, fr. L *solitudin-, solitudo,* fr. *solus*] **1 :** the quality or state of being alone or remote from society **:** SECLUSION **2 :** a lonely place (as a desert)
syn SOLITUDE, ISOLATION, SECLUSION *shared meaning element* **:** the state of one who is alone

sol·i·tu·di·nar·i·an \ˌsäl-ə-ˌt(y)üd-ᵊn-ˈer-ē-ən\ *n* [L *solitudin-, solitudo* + E *-arian*] **:** RECLUSE

sol·ler·et \ˌsäl-ə-ˈret\ *n* [F] **:** a flexible steel shoe forming part of a medieval suit of armor — see ARMOR illustration

sol·mi·za·tion \ˌsäl-mə-ˈzā-shən\ *n* [F *solmisation,* fr. *solmiser* to sol-fa, fr. *sol* (fr. ML) + *mi* (fr. ML) + *-iser* -ize] **:** the act, practice, or system of using syllables to denote the tones of a musical scale

soln *abbr* solution

[1]**so·lo** \ˈsō-(ˌ)lō\ *n, pl* **solos** [It, fr. *solo* alone, fr. L *solus*] **1** *or pl* **so·li** \ˈsō-(ˌ)lē\ **a :** a musical composition for a single voice or instrument with or without accompaniment **b :** the featured part of a concerto or similar work **2 :** a performance in which the performer has no partner or associate **3 :** any of several card games in which a player elects to play without a partner against the other players

[2]**solo** *adv* **:** without a companion **:** ALONE <fly ~>

[3]**solo** *adj* **:** of, relating to, or being a solo <a ~ performance>

[4]**solo** *vi* **so·loed; so·lo·ing** \-(ˌ)lō-iŋ, -lə-wiŋ\ **:** to perform by oneself; *esp* **:** to fly an airplane without one's instructor

so·lo·ist \ˈsō-lə-wəst, -(ˌ)lō-əst\ *n* **:** one who performs a solo

Sol·o·mon \ˈsäl-ə-mən\ *n* [LL, fr. Heb *Shĕlōmōh*] **:** a son of David and 10th-century B.C. king of Israel proverbial for his wisdom

Sol·o·mon·ic \ˌsäl-ə-ˈmän-ik\ *adj* **:** marked by notable wisdom, reasonableness, or discretion esp. under trying circumstances

Solomon's seal *n* **1 :** an emblem consisting of two interlaced triangles forming a 6-pointed star and formerly used as an amulet esp. against fever **2 :** any of a genus (*Polygonatum*) of perennial herbs of the lily family with gnarled rhizomes

Solomon's seal 1

so·lon \ˈsō-lən, -ˌlän\ *n* [*Solon,* Athenian lawgiver] **1 :** a wise and skillful lawgiver **2 :** a member of a legislative body

sol·on·chak \ˌsäl-ən-ˈchak\ *n* [Russ, salt marsh] **:** any of an intrazonal group of strongly saline usu. pale soils found esp. in poorly drained arid or semiarid areas

sol·o·netz *also* **sol·o·nets** \ˌsäl-ə-ˈnets\ *n* [Russ *solonets* salt not extracted by decoction] **:** any of an intrazonal group of dark hard alkaline soils evolved by leaching and alkalizing from solonchak — **sol·o·netz·ic** \-ˈnet-sik\ *adj*

so long \sō-ˈlȯŋ, sə-\ *interj* [prob. by folk etymology fr. Gael *slán* lit., health, security, fr. OIr *slán;* prob. akin to L *salvus* safe — more at SAFE] — used to express farewell

so long as *conj* **1 :** during and up to the end of the time that **:** WHILE **2 :** provided that

sol·stice \ˈsäl-stəs, ˈsōl-, ˈsȯl-\ *n* [ME, fr. OF, fr. L *solstitium,* fr. *sol* sun + *status,* pp. of *sistere* to come to a stop, cause to stand; akin to L *stare* to stand — more at SOLAR, STAND] **1 :** one of the two points on the ecliptic at which its distance from the celestial equator is greatest and which is reached by the sun each year about June 22d and December 22d **2 :** the time of the sun's passing a solstice which occurs on June 22d to begin summer in the northern hemisphere and on December 22d to begin winter in the northern hemisphere

sol·sti·tial \säl-ˈstish-əl, sōl-, sȯl-\ *adj* [L *solstitialis,* fr. *solstitium*] **1 :** of, relating to, or characteristic of a solstice and esp. the summer solstice **2 :** happening or appearing at or associated with a solstice

sol·u·bil·i·ty \ˌsäl-yə-ˈbil-ət-ē\ *n* **1 :** the quality or state of being soluble **2 :** the amount of a substance that will dissolve in a given amount of another substance

sol·u·bi·lize \ˈsäl-yə-bə-ˌlīz\ *vt* **-lized; -liz·ing :** to make soluble or increase the solubility of — **sol·u·bi·li·za·tion** \ˌsäl-yə-bə-lə-ˈzā-shən\ *n*

sol·u·ble \ˈsäl-yə-bəl\ *adj* [ME, fr. MF, capable of being loosened or dissolved, fr. LL *solubilis,* fr. L *solvere* to loosen, dissolve — more at SOLVE] **1 a :** susceptible of being dissolved in or as if in a fluid **b :** capable of being emulsified **:** EMULSIFIABLE <a ~ oil> **2 :** subject to being solved or explained <~ questions> — **sol·u·ble·ness** *n* — **sol·u·bly** \-blē\ *adv*

soluble glass *n* **:** WATER GLASS 4

soluble RNA *n* **:** TRANSFER RNA

so·lum \ˈsō-ləm\ *n, pl* **so·la** \-lə\ *or* **solums** [NL, fr. L, ground, soil] **:** the altered layer of soil above the parent material that includes the A- and B-horizons

so·lus \ˈsō-ləs\ *adv or adj* [L] **:** ALONE — often used in stage directions

sol·ute \ˈsäl-ˌyüt\ *n* [L *solutus,* pp.] **:** a dissolved substance

so·lu·tion \sə-ˈlü-shən\ *n* [ME, fr. MF, fr. L *solution-, solutio,* fr. *solutus,* pp. of *solvere* to loosen, solve] **1 a :** an action or process of solving a problem **b :** an answer to a problem **:** EXPLANATION; *specif* **:** a set of values of the variables that satisfies an equation **2 a :** an act or the process by which a solid, liquid, or gaseous substance is homogeneously mixed with a liquid or sometimes a gas or solid **b :** a typically liquid homogeneous mixture formed by this process **c :** the condition of being dissolved **d :** a liquid containing a dissolved substance **3 :** a bringing or coming to an end or into a state of discontinuity

solution set *n* **:** the set of values that satisfy an equation; *also* **:** TRUTH SET

So·lu·tre·an *or* **So·lu·tri·an** \sə-ˈlü-trē-ən\ *adj* [*Solutré,* village in France] **:** of or relating to an upper Paleolithic culture characterized by leaf-shaped finely flaked stone implements

solv·able \ˈsäl-və-bəl, ˈsȯl-\ *adj* **:** susceptible of solution or of being solved, resolved, or explained — **solv·abil·i·ty** \ˌsäl-və-ˈbil-ət-ē, ˌsȯl-\ *n*

[1]**sol·vate** \ˈsäl-ˌvāt, ˈsȯl-\ *n* [*solv*ent + *-ate*] **:** a complex ion formed by the chemical or physical combination of a solute ion or molecule with a solvent molecule; *also* **:** a substance (as a hydrate) containing such ions

[2]**solvate** *vb* **sol·vat·ed; sol·vat·ing** *vt* **:** to convert into a solvate ~ *vi* **:** to become or behave as a solvate — **sol·va·tion** \säl-ˈvā-shən, sȯl-\ *n*

Sol·vay process \ˈsäl-ˌvā-\ *n* [Ernest *Solvay* †1922 Belg chemist] **:** a process for making soda from common salt by passing carbon dioxide into ammoniacal brine resulting in precipitation of sodium bicarbonate which is then calcined to carbonate

solve \ˈsälv, ˈsȯlv\ *vb* **solved; solv·ing** [ME *solven* to loosen, fr. L *solvere* to loosen, solve, dissolve, fr. *sed-, se-* apart + *luere* to release — more at SECEDE, LOSE] *vt* **1 :** to find a solution for <~ a problem> **2 :** to pay (as a debt) in full ~ *vi* **:** to solve something <substitute the known values of the constants and ~ for *x*> — **solv·er** *n*

sol·ven·cy \ˈsäl-vən-sē, ˈsȯl-\ *n* **:** the quality or state of being solvent

[1]**sol·vent** \-vənt\ *adj* [L *solvent-, solvens,* prp. of *solvere* to dissolve, pay] **1 :** able to pay all legal debts **2 :** that dissolves or can dissolve <~ fluids> <~ action of water> — **sol·vent·ly** *adv*

[2]**solvent** *n* **1 :** a usu. liquid substance capable of dissolving or dispersing one or more other substances **2 :** something that provides a solution **3 :** something that eliminates or attenuates something esp. unwanted — **sol·vent·less** \-ləs\ *adj*

sol·vol·y·sis \säl-ˈväl-ə-səs, sȯl-\ *n* [NL, fr. E *solv*ent + *-o-* + NL *-lysis*] **:** a chemical reaction (as hydrolysis) of a solvent and solute that results in the formation of new compounds — **sol·vo·lyt·ic** \ˌsäl-və-ˈlit-ik, ˌsȯl-\ *adj*

[1]**so·ma** \ˈsō-mə\ *n* [Skt; akin to Av *haoma,* a Zoroastrian ritual drink, Gk *hyein* to rain — more at SUCK] **1 :** an East Indian leafless vine (*Sarcostemma acidum*) of the milkweed family with a milky acid juice **2 :** an intoxicating plant juice of ancient India used as an offering to the gods and as a drink of immortality by worshipers in Vedic ritual and worshiped as a Vedic god

[2]**soma** *n* [NL *somat-, soma,* fr. Gk *sōmat-, sōma* body] **1 :** all of an organism except the germ cells **2 :** the body of an organism

So·ma·li \sō-ˈmäl-ē, sə-\ *n, pl* **Somali** *or* **Somalis** **1 :** a member of a people of Somaliland apparently of mixed Mediterranean and Negroid stock **2 :** the Cushitic language of the Somali people

Somali shilling *n* **:** the shilling of Somalia

so many *adj* **1 :** constituting an unspecified number <read *so many* chapters each night> **2 :** constituting a group or pack <behaved like *so many* animals>

somat- *or* **somato-** *comb form* [NL, fr. Gk *sōmat-, sōmato-,* fr. *sōmat-, sōma* body; akin to L *tumēre* to swell — more at THUMB] **1 :** body <*somato*logy> **2 :** soma <*somato*plasm>

so·mat·ic \sō-ˈmat-ik, sə-\ *adj* [Gk *sōmatikos,* fr. *sōmat-, sōma*] **1 :** of, relating to, or affecting the body esp. as distinguished from the germ plasm or the psyche **2 :** of or relating to the wall of the body **:** PARIETAL **3 :** MESOMORPHIC *syn* see BODILY — **so·mat·i·cal·ly** \-i-k(ə-)lē\ *adv*

somatic cell *n* **:** one of the cells of the body that compose the tissues, organs, and parts of that individual other than the germ cells

so·mato·gen·ic \sō-ˌmat-ə-ˈjen-ik\ *adj* **:** originating in, affecting, or acting through the body — compare PSYCHOGENIC

so·ma·tol·o·gy \ˌsō-mə-ˈtäl-ə-jē\ *n* [NL *somatologia,* fr. *somat-* + *-logia* -logy] **:** a branch of anthropology primarily concerned with the comparative study of human evolution, variation, and classification esp. through measurement and observation — **so·ma·to·log·i·cal** \ˌsō-mət-ᵊl-ˈäj-i-kəl, sō-ˌmat-\ *adj*

so·mato·plasm \sō-ˈmat-ə-ˌplaz-əm\ *n* **1 :** protoplasm of somatic cells **2 :** somatic cells as distinguished from germ cells — **so·mato·plas·tic** \-ˌmat-ə-ˈplas-tik\ *adj*

so·mato·pleure \sō-ˈmat-ə-ˌplu̇(ə)r\ *n* [NL *somatopleura,* fr. *somat-* + Gk *pleura* side] **:** a complex layer in the embryo of a craniate vertebrate consisting of the outer of the two layers into which the lateral plate of the mesoderm splits together with the ectoderm that sheathes it externally and giving rise to the body wall — **so·mato·pleu·ric** \-ˌmat-ə-ˈplu̇r-ik\ *adj*

so·mato·sen·so·ry \sō-ˌmat-ə-ˈsen(t)s-(ə-)rē\ *adj* **:** of, relating to, or being sensory activity having its origin elsewhere than in the special sense organs (as eyes and ears) and conveying information about the state of the body proper and its immediate environment

so·mato·tro·phic hormone \-ˌtrō-fik-\ *n* [*somat-* + *-trophic*] **:** GROWTH HORMONE 1

so·mato·tro·pin \-ˈtrō-pən\ *or* **so·mato·tro·phin** \-fən\ *n* [*somatotropic, somatotrophic* + *-in*] **:** GROWTH HORMONE 1

so·mato·type \sō-ˈmat-ə-ˌtīp\ *n* **:** body type **:** PHYSIQUE — **so·mato·typ·ic** \sō-ˌmat-ə-ˈtip-ik\ *adj* — **so·mato·typ·i·cal·ly** \-i-k(ə-)lē\ *adv*

som·ber *or* **som·bre** \ˈsäm-bər\ *adj* [F *sombre*] **1 :** so shaded as to be dark and gloomy **2 a :** of a serious mien **:** GRAVE **b :** of a dismal or depressing character **:** MELANCHOLY **c :** conveying gloomy suggestions or ideas **3 :** of a dull or heavy cast or shade **:** dark colored — **som·ber·ly** *adv* — **som·ber·ness** *n*

som·bre·ro \səm-ˈbre(ə)r-(ˌ)ō, säm-\ *n, pl* **-ros** [Sp, fr. *sombra* shade] **:** a high-crowned hat of felt or straw with a very wide brim worn esp. in the Southwest and Mexico

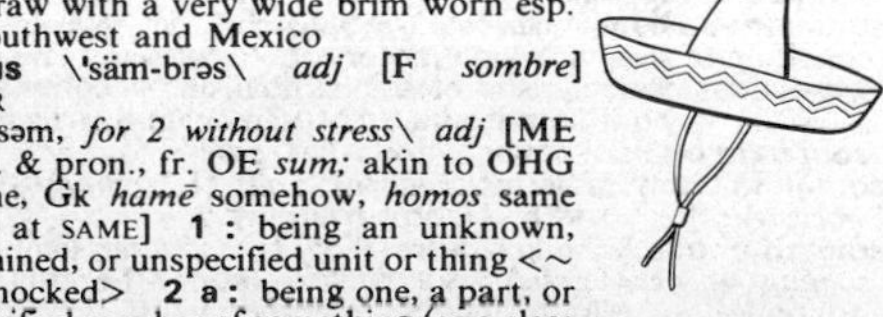

sombrero

som·brous \ˈsäm-brəs\ *adj* [F *sombre*] **:** SOMBER

[1]**some** \ˈsəm, *for 2 without stress*\ *adj* [ME *som,* adj. & pron., fr. OE *sum;* akin to OHG *sum* some, Gk *hamē* somehow, *homos* same — more at SAME] **1 :** being an unknown, undetermined, or unspecified unit or thing <~ person knocked> **2 a :** being one, a part, or an unspecified number of something (as a class or group) named or implied <~ gems are hard> **b :** being of an unspecified amount or number <give me ~ water> <have ~ apples> **3 :** IMPORTANT, STRIKING <that was ~ party> **4 :** being at least one — used to indicate that a logical proposition is asserted only of a subclass or certain members of the class denoted by the term which it modifies

2some \ˈsəm\ *pron, sing or pl in constr* **1 :** one indeterminate quantity, portion, or number as distinguished from the rest **2 :** an indefinite additional amount <ran a mile and then ~>

3some \ˈsəm, ˌsəm\ *adv* **1 :** ABOUT <~ eighty houses> **2 :** SOMEWHAT <felt ~ better>

1-some \səm\ *adj suffix* [ME *-som,* fr. OE *-sum;* akin to OHG *-sam* -some, OE *sum* some] **:** characterized by a (specified) thing, quality, state, or action <awe*some*> <burden*some*> <cuddle*some*>

2-some *n suffix* [ME (northern dial.) *-sum,* fr. ME *sum,* pron., one, some] **:** group of (so many) members and esp. persons <four*some*>

3-some \ˌsōm\ *n comb form* [NL *-somat-, -soma,* fr. Gk *sōmat-, soma* — more at SOMAT-] **1 :** body <chromo*some*> **2 :** chromosome <mono*some*>

1some·body \ˈsəm-ˌbäd-ē, -bəd-\ *pron* **:** one or some person of unspecified or indefinite identity <~ will come in>

2somebody *n* **:** a person of position or importance

some·day \ˈsəm-ˌdā\ *adv* **:** at some future time

some·deal \ˈsəm-ˌdēl\ *adv, archaic* **:** SOMEWHAT

some·how \ˈsəm-ˌhau̇\ *adv* **:** in one way or another not known or designated **:** by some means

some·one \-(ˌ)wən\ *pron* **:** some person **:** SOMEBODY

some·place \-ˌplās\ *adv* **:** SOMEWHERE

som·er·sault \ˈsəm-ər-ˌsȯlt\ *n* [MF *sombresaut* leap, deriv. of L *super* over + *saltus* leap, fr. *saltus,* pp. of *salire* to jump — more at OVER, SALLY] **:** a leap or roll in which a person turns forward or backward in a complete revolution bringing the feet over the head and finally landing on the feet — **somersault** *vi*

som·er·set \-ˌset\ *n or vi* [by alter.] **:** SOMERSAULT

1some·thing \ˈsəm(p)-thiŋ, *esp rapid or for 2* ˈsəmp-ᵊm\ *pron* **1 :** some indeterminate or unspecified thing **2 :** a person or thing of consequence

2something *adv* **1 :** in some degree **:** SOMEWHAT **2 :** to an extreme degree <swears ~ awful>

1some·time \ˈsəm-ˌtīm\ *adv* **1** *archaic* **:** in the past **:** FORMERLY **2** *archaic* **:** once in a while **:** OCCASIONALLY **3 :** at some time in the future <I'll do it ~> **4 :** at some not specified or definitely known point of time <~ last night>

2sometime *adj* **:** having been formerly **:** FORMER, LATE

1some·times \ˈsəm-ˌtīmz *also* (ˌ)səm-ˈ\ *adv* **:** at times **:** now and then **:** OCCASIONALLY

2sometimes *adj, archaic* **:** FORMER

some·way \ˈsəm-ˌwā\ *also* **some·ways** \-ˌwāz\ *adv* **:** SOMEHOW

1some·what \-ˌ(h)wät, -ˌ(h)wət, (ˌ)səm-ˈ\ *pron* **:** SOMETHING

2somewhat *adv* **:** in some degree or measure **:** SLIGHTLY

some·when \ˈsəm-ˌ(h)wen\ *adv* **:** SOMETIME

1some·where \-ˌ(h)we(ə)r, -ˌ(h)wa(ə)r, -(ˌ)(h)wər\ *adv* **1 :** in, at, from, or to a place unknown or unspecified <makes reference to it ~> **2 :** to a place symbolizing positive accomplishment or progress <at last we're getting ~> **3 :** in the vicinity of **:** APPROXIMATELY <~ about nine o'clock>

2somewhere *n* **:** an undetermined or unnamed place

some·wheres \-ˌ(h)we(ə)rz, -ˌ(h)wa(ə)rz, -(ˌ)(h)wərz\ *adv* **:** SOMEWHERE

some·whith·er \-ˌ(h)wit͟h-ər\ *adv* **:** to some place **:** SOMEWHERE

-so·mic \ˈsō-mik\ *adj comb form* [ISV 3*-some* + *-ic*] **:** having or being a body of chromosomes of which one or more but not all members exhibit (such) a degree of reduplication of chromosomes or genomes <mono*somic*>

so·mite \ˈsō-ˌmīt\ *n* [ISV, fr. Gk *sōma* body — more at SOMAT-] **:** one of the longitudinal series of segments into which the body of many animals (as articulate animals and vertebrates) is divided **:** METAMERE — **so·mit·ic** \sō-ˈmit-ik\ *adj*

som·me·lier \ˌsəm-əl-ˈyā\ *n, pl* **sommeliers** \-ˈyā(z)\ [F, fr. MF, court official charged with transportation of supplies, pack animal driver, fr. OProv *saumalier* pack animal driver, fr. *sauma* pack animal, load of a pack animal, fr. LL *sagma* packsaddle — more at SUMPTER] **:** a waiter in a restaurant who has charge of wines and their service **:** a wine steward

somnambul- *comb form* [NL, fr. *somnambulus* somnambulist, fr. L *somnus* sleep + *-ambulus* (as in *funambulus* funambulist) — more at SOMNOLENT] **:** somnambulism **:** somnambulist <somnambul*ant*>

som·nam·bu·lant \säm-ˈnam-byə-lənt\ *adj* **:** walking or addicted to walking while asleep

som·nam·bu·lar \-lər\ *adj* **:** of, relating to, or characterized by somnambulism

som·nam·bu·late \-ˌlāt\ *vi* **-lat·ed; -lat·ing :** to walk when asleep — **som·nam·bu·la·tion** \(ˌ)säm-ˌnam-byə-ˈlā-shən\ *n* — **som·nam·bu·la·tor** \säm-ˈnam-byə-ˌlāt-ər\ *n*

som·nam·bu·lism \säm-ˈnam-byə-ˌliz-əm\ *n* **1 :** an abnormal condition of sleep in which motor acts (as walking) are performed **2 :** actions characteristic of somnambulism — **som·nam·bu·list** \-ləst\ *n* — **som·nam·bu·lis·tic** \(ˌ)säm-ˌnam-byə-ˈlis-tik\ *adj* — **som·nam·bu·lis·ti·cal·ly** \-ti-k(ə-)lē\ *adv*

som·ni·fa·cient \ˌsäm-nə-ˈfā-shənt\ *adj* [L *somnus* sleep + E *-facient*] **:** HYPNOTIC 1 — **somnifacient** *n*

som·nif·er·ous \säm-ˈnif-(ə-)rəs\ *adj* [L *somnifer* somniferous, fr. *somnus* + *-fer* -ferous] **:** SOPORIFIC — **som·nif·er·ous·ly** *adv*

som·no·lence \ˈsäm-nə-lən(t)s\ *n* **:** the quality or state of being drowsy **:** SLEEPINESS

som·no·len·cy \-lən-sē\ *n* **:** SOMNOLENCE

som·no·lent \-lənt\ *adj* [ME *sompnolent,* fr. MF, fr. L *somnolentus,* fr. *somnus* sleep; akin to OE *swefn* sleep, Gk *hypnos*] **1 :** of a kind likely to induce sleep <a ~ sermon> **2 :** inclined to or heavy with sleep **:** DROWSY ***syn*** see SLEEPY — **som·no·lent·ly** *adv*

Soms *abbr* Somersetshire

1so much *adv* **:** by the amount indicated or suggested <if they lose their way, *so much* the better for us>

2so much *adj* — used as an intensive <the house burned like *so much* paper> <sounded like *so much* nonsense>

3so much *pron* **1 :** something (as an amount or price) unspecified or undetermined <charge *so much* a mile> **2 :** all that can be or is to be said or done <*so much* for the history of the case>

so much as *adv* **:** EVEN

son \ˈsən\ *n* [ME *sone,* fr. OE *sunu;* akin to OHG *sun* son, Gk *hyios*] **1 a :** a male offspring esp. of human beings **b :** a male adopted child **c :** a male descendant — usu. used in pl. **2** *cap* **:** the second person of the Trinity **3 :** a person closely associated with or deriving from a formative agent (as a nation, school, or race)

so·nance \ˈsō-nən(t)s\ *n* [L *sonare* to sound + E *-ance*] **:** SOUND

so·nant \-nənt\ *adj* [L *sonant-, sonans,* prp. of *sonare* to sound — more at SOUND] **1** *of a speech sound* **:** VOICED **2** *of a consonant* **:** SYLLABIC — **sonant** *n*

so·nar \ˈsō-ˌnär\ *n* [*so*und *na*vigation *r*anging] **:** an apparatus that detects the presence and location of a submerged object (as a submarine) by means of sonic and supersonic waves reflected back to it from the object

so·nar·man \-mən, -ˌman\ *n* **:** an enlisted man in the navy who operates sonar equipment

so·na·ta \sə-ˈnät-ə\ *n* [It, fr. *sonare* to sound, fr. L] **:** an instrumental musical composition typically of three or four movements in contrasting forms and keys

sonata form *n* **:** a musical form that consists basically of an exposition, a development, and a recapitulation and that is used esp. for the first movement of a sonata

son·a·ti·na \ˌsän-ə-ˈtē-nə\ *n* [It, dim. of *sonata*] **:** a short usu. simplified sonata

sonde \ˈsänd\ *n* [F, lit., sounding line — more at SOUND] **:** any of various devices for testing physical conditions (as at high altitudes or inside the body)

sone \ˈsōn\ *n* [ISV, fr. L *sonus* sound — more at SOUND] **:** a subjective unit of loudness for an average listener equal to the loudness of a 1000-cycle sound that has an intensity 40 decibels above the listener's own threshold of hearing

song \ˈsȯŋ\ *n* [ME, fr. OE *sang;* akin to OE *singan* to sing] **1 :** the act or art of singing **2 :** poetical composition **3 a :** a short musical composition of words and music **b :** a collection of such compositions **4 a :** a melody for a lyric poem or ballad **b :** a poem easily set to music **5 a :** a habitual or characteristic manner **b :** a violent, abusive, or noisy reaction <put up quite a ~> **6 :** a small amount <sold for a ~>

song and dance *n* **1 :** a theatrical performance (as a vaudeville performance) combining singing and dancing **2 :** a long and often familiar statement or explanation that is not necessarily true or pertinent

song·bird \ˈsȯŋ-ˌbərd\ *n* **1 a :** a bird that utters a succession of musical tones **b :** a passerine bird **2 :** a female singer

song·book \-ˈbu̇k\ *n* **:** a collection of songs; *specif* **:** a book containing vocal music (as hymns)

song cycle *n* **:** a group of related songs designed to form a musical entity

song·fest \ˈsȯŋ-fest\ *n* **:** an informal session of group singing of popular or folk songs

song·ful \-fəl\ *adj* **:** given to or suggestive of singing **:** MELODIOUS — **song·ful·ly** \-fə-lē\ *adv* — **song·ful·ness** *n*

song·less \-ləs\ *adj* **:** lacking in, incapable of, or not given to song — **song·less·ly** *adv*

Song of Sol·o·mon \-ˈsäl-ə-mən\ [fr. the opening verse: "The song of songs, which is Solomon's"] **:** a collection of love poems forming a book in the Protestant canon of the Old Testament

Song of Songs [trans of Heb *shīr hashshīrīm*] **:** a collection of love poems forming a book in the canonical Jewish Scriptures and corresponding to the Song of Solomon in the Protestant canon of the Old Testament — see BIBLE table

song·smith \ˈsȯŋ-ˌsmith\ *n* **:** a composer of songs

song sparrow *n* **:** a common No. American sparrow (*Melospiza melodia*) that is brownish above and white below and that is noted for its melodious song

song·ster \ˈsȯŋ(k)-stər\ *n* **1 :** one skilled in song **2 :** SONGBOOK — **song·stress** \-strəs\ *n*

song thrush *n* **:** an Old World thrush (*Turdus ericetorum*) largely brown above and white below — called also *mavis, throstle*

song·writ·er \ˈsȯŋ-ˌrīt-ər\ *n* **:** a person who composes words or music or both esp. for popular songs — **song·writ·ing** \-ˌrīt-iŋ\ *n*

son·ic \ˈsän-ik\ *adj* [L *sonus* sound — more at SOUND] **1 :** having a frequency within the audibility range of the human ear — used of waves and vibrations **2 :** utilizing, produced by, or relating to sound waves <~ altimeter> **3 :** of, relating to, or being the speed of sound in air or about 741 miles per hour at sea level **4 :** capable of uttering sounds — **son·i·cal·ly** \-i-k(ə-)lē\ *adv*

son·i·cate \ˈsän-ə-ˌkāt\ *vt* **-cat·ed; -cat·ing** [*sonic* + *-ate*] **:** to disrupt (as bacteria) by treatment with high-frequency sound waves — **son·i·ca·tion** \ˌsän-ə-ˈkā-shən\ *n* — **son·i·ca·tor** \ˈsän-ə-ˌkāt-ər\ *n*

sonic barrier *n* **:** a sudden large increase in aerodynamic drag that occurs as the speed of an aircraft approaches the speed of sound

sonic boom *n* **:** a sound resembling an explosion produced when a shock wave formed at the nose of an aircraft traveling at supersonic speed reaches the ground — called also *sonic bang*

son-in-law \ˈsən-ən-ˌlȯ\ *n, pl* **sons-in-law :** the husband of one's daughter

son·less \ˈsən-ləs\ *adj* **:** not possessing or never having had a son

son·ly \-lē\ *adj* **:** FILIAL

son·net \ˈsän-ət\ *n* [It *sonetto,* fr. OProv *sonet* little song, fr. *son* sound, song, fr. L *sonus* sound] **:** a fixed verse form of Italian origin consisting of fourteen lines that are typically five-foot iambics rhyming according to a prescribed scheme; *also* **:** a poem in this pattern

son·ne·teer \ˌsän-ə-ˈti(ə)r\ *n* **1 :** a composer of sonnets **2 :** a minor or insignificant poet

son·net·ize \ˈsän-ə-ˌtīz\ *vb* **-ized; -iz·ing** *vi* **:** to compose a sonnet ~ *vt* **:** to compose a sonnet on or to

sonnet sequence *n* **:** a series of sonnets often having a unifying theme

son·ny \ˈsən-ē\ *n* **:** a young boy — usu. used in address

so·no·buoy \'sō-nō-ˌbü-ē, 'sän-ō-, -ˌbȯi\ *n* [L *sonus* sound + E *-o-* + *buoy* — more at SOUND] : a buoy equipped for detecting underwater sounds and transmitting them by radio

son of a bitch \'sən-ə-və-ˌbich; *as an interj* ˌsən-ə-və-'bich\ *n, pl* **sons of bitch·es** \ˌsən-zə-'bich-əz\ : BASTARD 3 — sometimes considered vulgar; sometimes used interjectionally to express surprise or disappointment

son of God **1** *often cap S* : a superhuman or divine being (as an angel) **2** *cap S* : MESSIAH 1 **3** : a person established in the love of God by divine promise

son of man **1** : a human being **2** *often cap S* : God's messiah destined to preside over the final judgment of mankind

so·nor·i·ty \sə-'nȯr-ət-ē, -'när-\ *n, pl* **-ties** **1** : the quality or state of being sonorous : RESONANCE **2** : a sonorous tone or speech

so·no·rous \sə-'nōr-əs, -'nȯr-; 'sän-ə-rəs\ *adj* [L *sonorus;* akin to L *sonus* sound] **1** : producing sound (as when struck) **2** : full or loud in sound **3** : imposing or impressive in effect or style **4** : having a high or an indicated degree of sonority <~ sounds like \ä\ and \ȯ\> — **so·no·rous·ly** *adv* — **so·no·rous·ness** *n*

so·no·vox \'sō-nə-ˌväks, 'sän-ə-\ *n* [L *sonus* + *vox* voice — more at VOICE] : an electronic sound effects device held against the throat to give the effect of speech to recorded nonhuman sounds (as of a waterfall or train whistle) that are transmitted through the larynx and formed into words by the mouth

son·ship \'sən-ˌship\ *n* : the relationship of son to father

sonsy *or* **sons·ie** \'sän(t)-sē\ *adj* [Sc *sons* health] *chiefly dial* : BUXOM, COMELY

soon \'sün, *esp New Eng* 'sůn\ *adv* [ME *soone,* fr. OE *sōna;* akin to OHG *sān* immediately] **1 a** *obs* : at once : IMMEDIATELY **b** : before long : without undue time lapse <~ after sunrise> **2** : in a prompt manner : SPEEDILY <as ~ as possible> <the ~*er* the better> **3** *archaic* : before the usual time **4** : in agreement with one's choice or preference : WILLINGLY <I'd ~*er* walk than drive> ***syn*** see PRESENTLY

soon·er \'sü-nər\ *n* [*sooner,* compar. of *soon*] **1** : a person settling on land in the early West before its official opening to settlement in order to gain the prior claim allowed by law to the first settler after official opening **2** *cap* : a native or resident of Oklahoma — used as a nickname

sooner or later *adv* : at some uncertain future time : SOMETIME

[1]**soot** \'sůt, 'sət, 'süt\ *n* [ME, fr. OE *sōt;* akin to OIr *súide* soot, OE *sittan* to sit] : a black substance formed by combustion or separated from fuel during combustion, rising in fine particles, and adhering to the sides of the chimney or pipe conveying the smoke; *esp* : the fine powder consisting chiefly of carbon that colors smoke

[2]**soot** *vt* : to coat or cover with soot

[1]**sooth** \'süth\ *adj* [ME, fr. OE *sōth;* akin to OHG *sand* true, Gk *eteos,* L *esse* to be] **1** *archaic* : TRUE **2** *archaic* : SOFT, SWEET

[2]**sooth** *n* **1** *archaic* : TRUTH, REALITY **2** *obs* : BLANDISHMENT

soothe \'süth\ *vb* **soothed; sooth·ing** [ME *sothen* to prove the truth, fr. OE *sōthian,* fr. *sōth*] *vt* **1** : to please by or as if by attention or concern : PLACATE **2** : RELIEVE, ALLEVIATE **3** : to bring comfort, solace, or reassurance to ~ *vi* : to bring peace, composure, or quietude — **sooth·er** *n*

sooth·fast \'süth-ˌfast\ *adj* **1** *archaic* : TRUE **2** *archaic* : TRUTHFUL

sooth·ing \'sü-thiŋ\ *adj* : tending to soothe; *also* : having a sedative effect <~ syrup> — **sooth·ing·ly** \-thiŋ-lē\ *adv* — **sooth·ing·ness** *n*

sooth·ly \'süth-lē\ *adv, archaic* : in truth : TRULY

sooth·say \-ˌsā\ *vi* : to practice soothsaying — **sooth·say·er** *n*

sooth·say·ing \-ˌsā-iŋ\ *n* **1** : the act of foretelling events **2** : PREDICTION, PROPHECY

sooty \'sůt-ē, 'sət-, 'süt-\ *adj* **soot·i·er; -est** **1 a** : of, relating to, or producing soot **b** : soiled with soot **2** : of the color of soot — **soot·i·ly** \-ᵊl-ē\ *adv* — **soot·i·ness** \-ē-nəs\ *n*

sooty mold *n* : a dark growth of fungus mycelium growing in insect honeydew on plants; *also* : a fungus producing such growth

[1]**sop** \'säp\ *n* [ME *soppe,* fr. OE *sopp;* akin to OE *sūpan* to swallow — more at SUP] **1** *chiefly dial* : a piece of food dipped or steeped in a liquid **2** : a conciliatory or propitiatory bribe, gift, or advance

[2]**sop** *vt* **sopped; sop·ping** **1 a** : to steep or dip in or as if in liquid **b** : to wet thoroughly : SOAK **2** : to mop up (as water) **3** : to give a bribe or conciliatory gift to

SOP *abbr* standard operating procedure; standing operating procedure

soph *abbr* sophomore

soph·ism \'säf-ˌiz-əm\ *n* **1** : an argument apparently correct in form but actually invalid; *esp* : such an argument used to deceive **2** : SOPHISTRY 1

soph·ist \'säf-əst\ *n* [L *sophista,* fr. Gk *sophistēs,* lit., expert, wise man, fr. *sophizesthai* to become wise, deceive, fr. *sophos* clever, wise] **1** *cap* : one of a class of ancient Greek teachers of rhetoric, philosophy, and the art of successful living prominent about the middle of the 5th century B.C. for their adroit subtle and allegedly often specious reasoning **2** : PHILOSOPHER, THINKER **3** : a captious or fallacious reasoner

so·phis·tic \sä-'fis-tik, sə-\ *or* **so·phis·ti·cal** \-ti-kəl\ *adj* **1** : of or relating to sophists, sophistry, or the ancient Sophists <~ rhetoric> <~ subtleties> **2** : plausible but fallacious <~ reasoning> — **so·phis·ti·cal·ly** \-ti-k(ə-)lē\ *adv*

[1]**so·phis·ti·cate** \sə-'fis-tə-ˌkāt\ *vt* **-cat·ed; -cat·ing** [ME *sophisticaten,* fr. ML *sophisticatus,* pp. of *sophisticare,* fr. L *sophisticus* sophistic, fr. Gk *sophistikos,* fr. *sophistēs* sophist] **1** : to alter deceptively; *esp* : ADULTERATE **2** : to deprive of genuineness, naturalness, or simplicity; *esp* : to deprive of naiveté and make worldly-wise : DISILLUSION **3** : to make complicated or complex

[2]**so·phis·ti·cate** \-ti-kət, -tə-ˌkāt\ *n* : a sophisticated person

so·phis·ti·cat·ed \-tə-ˌkāt-əd\ *adj* [ML *sophisticatus*] **1** : not in a natural, pure, or original state : ADULTERATED <a ~ oil> **2** : deprived of native or original simplicity: as **a** : highly complicated or developed : COMPLEX <~ electronic devices> **b** : WORLDLY-WISE, KNOWING <a ~ adolescent> **3** : devoid of grossness: as **a** : finely experienced and aware <a ~ columnist> **b** : intellectually appealing <a ~ novel> — **so·phis·ti·cat·ed·ly** *adv*

so·phis·ti·ca·tion \sə-ˌfis-tə-'kā-shən\ *n* **1 a** : the use of sophistry : sophistic reasoning **b** : SOPHISM, QUIBBLE **2** : the process of making impure or weak : ADULTERATION **3** : the process or result of becoming cultured, knowledgeable, or disillusioned; *esp* : CULTIVATION, URBANITY **4** : the process or result of becoming more complex, developed, or subtle

soph·ist·ry \'säf-ə-strē\ *n* **1** : deceptively subtle reasoning or argumentation **2** : SOPHISM 1

soph·o·more \'säf-ᵊm-ˌō(ə)r, -ˌȯ(ə)r; 'säf-ˌmō(ə)r, -ˌmȯ(ə)r\ *n* [prob. fr. Gk *sophos* wise + *mōros* foolish — more at MORON] : a student in his second year at college or secondary school

soph·o·mor·ic \ˌsäf-ə-'mōr-ik, -'mȯr-, -'mär-\ *adj* **1** : of, relating to, or characteristic of a sophomore **2** : conceited and overconfident of knowledge but poorly informed and immature

So·pho·ni·as \ˌsäf-ə-'nī-əs, ˌsō-fə-\ *n* [LL, fr. Gk, fr. Heb *Sĕphanyāh*] : ZEPHANIAH

so·phy \'sō-fē\ *n* [Per *Safī*] *archaic* : a sovereign of Persia

-so·phy \sə-fē\ *n comb form* [ME *-sophie,* fr. OF, fr. L *-sophia,* fr. Gk, fr. *sophia* wisdom, fr. *sophos*] : knowledge : wisdom : science <anthropo*sophy*>

so·pite \sō-'pīt\ *vt* **so·pit·ed; so·pit·ing** [L *sopitus,* pp. of *sopire* to put to sleep, fr. *sopor*] **1** *archaic* : to put to sleep : LULL **2** *archaic* : to put an end to (as a claim) : SETTLE

so·por \'sō-pər, -ˌpȯ(ə)r\ *n* [L] : profound or lethargic sleep

so·po·rif·er·ous \ˌsäp-ə-'rif-(ə-)rəs, ˌsō-pə-\ *adj* [L *soporifer* soporiferous, fr. *sopor* + *-fer* -ferous] : SOPORIFIC — **so·po·rif·er·ous·ness** *n*

[1]**so·po·rif·ic** \-'rif-ik\ *adj* [prob. fr. F *soporifique,* fr. L *sopor* deep sleep; akin to L *somnus* sleep — more at SOMNOLENT] **1 a** : causing or tending to cause sleep **b** : tending to dull awareness or alertness **2** : of, relating to, or marked by sleepiness or lethargy

[2]**soporific** *n* : a soporific agent; *specif* : HYPNOTIC 1

[1]**sop·ping** \'säp-iŋ\ *adj* : wet through : SOAKING

[2]**sopping** *adv* : VERY, EXTREMELY <~ wet>

sop·py \'säp-ē\ *adj* **sop·pi·er; -est** **1 a** : soaked through : SATURATED **b** : very wet **2** : SENTIMENTAL, MAWKISH

so·pra·ni·no \ˌsō-prə-'nē-(ˌ)nō, ˌsäp-rə-\ *n, pl* **-nos** [It, dim. of *soprano*] : a musical instrument (as a recorder or saxophone) higher in pitch than the soprano

[1]**so·pra·no** \sə-'pran-(ˌ)ō, -'prän-\ *n, pl* **-nos** [It, adj. & n., fr. *sopra* above, fr. L *supra* — more at SUPRA-] **1** : the highest part in 4-part harmony **2** : the highest singing voice of women, boys, or castrati; *also* : a person having this voice **3** : a member of a family of instruments having the highest range

[2]**soprano** *adj* : relating to or having the range or part of a soprano

so·ra \'sōr-ə, 'sȯr-\ *n* [origin unknown] : a small short-billed No. American rail (*Porzana carolina*) common in marshes

[1]**sorb** \'sȯ(ə)rb\ *n* [F *sorbe* fruit of the service tree, fr. L *sorbum*] **1** : any of several Old World trees related to the apples and pears (as a service or rowan tree) **2** : the fruit of a sorb

[2]**sorb** *vt* [back-formation fr. *absorb* & *adsorb*] : to take up and hold by either adsorption or absorption — **sorb·abil·i·ty** \ˌsȯrb-ə-'bil-ət-ē\ *n* — **sorb·able** \'sȯrb-ə-bəl\ *adj*

Sorb \'sȯ(ə)rb\ *n* [G *Sorbe,* fr. Sorbian *Serb*] **1** : a member of a Slavic people whose present representatives are the Wends living in Saxony and Brandenburg **2** : WENDISH — **Sor·bi·an** \'sȯr-bē-ən\ *adj or n*

sor·bate \'sȯ(ə)r-ˌbāt, 'sȯr-bət\ *n* : a sorbed substance

sor·bent \'sȯr-bənt\ *n* [L *sorbent-, sorbens,* prp. of *sorbēre* to suck up — more at ABSORB] : a substance that sorbs

sor·bic acid \ˌsȯr-bik-\ *n* [[1]*sorb*] : a crystalline acid $C_6H_8O_2$ obtained from the unripe fruits of the mountain ash or synthesized and used as a fungicide and food preservative

Sor·bon·ist \sȯr-'bän-əst *also* -'bən-\ *n* [F *sorboniste,* fr. *Sorbonne*] : a doctor of or student at the Sorbonne

sor·cer·er \'sȯrs-(ə-)rər\ *n* : a person who practices sorcery : WIZARD — **sor·cer·ess** \-(ə-)rəs\ *n*

sor·cer·ous \'sȯrs-(ə-)rəs\ *adj* : of or relating to sorcery : MAGICAL

sor·cery \'sȯrs-(ə-)rē\ *n* [ME *sorcerie,* fr. OF, fr. *sorcier* sorcerer, fr. (assumed) VL *sortiarius,* fr. L *sort-, sors* chance, lot] : the use of power gained from the assistance or control of evil spirits esp. for divining : NECROMANCY

sor·did \'sȯrd-əd\ *adj* [L *sordidus,* fr. *sordes* dirt — more at SWART] **1 a** : DIRTY, FILTHY **b** : WRETCHED, SQUALID **2** : marked by baseness or grossness : VILE <~ motives> **3** : meanly avaricious : COVETOUS **4** : of a dull or muddy color ***syn*** see MEAN — **sor·did·ly** *adv* — **sor·did·ness** *n*

sor·di·no \sȯr-'dē-(ˌ)nō\ *n, pl* **-di·ni** \-(ˌ)nē\ [It, fr. *sordo* silent, fr. L *surdus* — more at SURD] : [2]MUTE 3

[1]**sore** \'sō(ə)r, 'sȯ(ə)r\ *adj* **sor·er; sor·est** [ME *sor,* fr. OE *sār;* akin to OHG *sēr* sore, L *saevus* fierce] **1 a** : causing pain or distress **b** : painfully sensitive : TENDER <~ muscles> **c** : hurt or inflamed so as to be or seem painful <~ runny eyes> <a dog limping on a ~ leg> **2** : attended by difficulties, hardship, or exertion **3** : ANGRY, VEXED — **sore·ness** *n*

[2]**sore** *n* **1** : a localized sore spot on the body; *esp* : one (as an ulcer) with the tissues ruptured or abraded and usu. with infection **2** : a source of pain or vexation : AFFLICTION

[3]**sore** *adv* : SORELY

sore·head \'sō(ə)r-ˌhed, 'sȯ(ə)r-\ *n* : a person easily angered or disgruntled — **sorehead** *or* **sore·head·ed** \-'hed-əd\ *adj*

sore·ly \'sō(ə)r-lē, 'sȯ(ə)r-\ *adv* **1** : in a sore manner : PAINFULLY **2** : VERY, EXTREMELY <~ needed changes>

sore throat *n* : painful throat due to inflammation of the fauces and pharynx

---

sor·ghum \'sȯr-gəm\ *n* [NL, genus name, fr. It *sorgo*] **1 :** any of an economically important genus (*Sorghum*) of Old World tropical grasses similar to Indian corn in habit but with the spikelets in pairs on a hairy rachis; *esp* **:** a cultivated plant (as a grain sorghum or sorgo) derived from a common species (*S. vulgare*) **2 :** syrup from the juice of a sorgo that resembles cane syrup **3 :** something cloyingly sentimental

sor·go \'sȯ(ə)r-(,)gō\ *n* [It] **:** a sorghum cultivated primarily for the sweet juice in its stems from which sugar and syrup are made but also used for fodder and silage — called also *sweet sorghum*

sor·i·cine \'sȯr-ə-,sīn, 'sär-, 'sōr-\ *adj* [L *soricinus*, fr. *soric-, sorex* shrew; akin to L *susurrus* hum — more at SWARM] **:** resembling a shrew <~ bats>

so·ri·tes \sə-'rīt-(,)ēz\ *n, pl* **sorites** [L, fr. Gk *sōritēs*, fr. *sōros* heap — more at SORUS] **:** an argument consisting of propositions so arranged that the predicate of any one forms the subject of the next and the conclusion unites the subject of the first proposition with the predicate of the last

So·rop·ti·mist \sə-'räp-tə-məst, sȯ-\ *n* [*Soroptomist* (club)] **:** a member of a service club composed of professional women and women business executives

so·ro·ral \sə-'rōr-əl, -'rȯr-\ *adj* [L *soror* sister — more at SISTER] **:** of, relating to, or characteristic of a sister **:** SISTERLY

so·ro·rate \sə-'rōr-ət, -'rȯr-\ *n* [L *soror* sister] **:** the marriage of one man with two or more sisters usu. successively and after the first wife has been found to be barren or after her death

so·ror·i·ty \sə-'rȯr-ət-ē, -'rär-\ *n, pl* **-ties** [ML *sororitas* sisterhood, fr. L *soror* sister] **:** a club of girls or women esp. at a college

sorp·tion \'sȯrp-shən\ *n* [back-formation fr. *absorption* & *adsorption*] **:** the process of sorbing **:** the state of being sorbed — **sorp·tive** \'sȯrp-tiv\ *adj*

[1]**sor·rel** \'sȯr-əl, 'sär-\ *n* [ME *sorelle*, fr. MF *sorel*, n. & adj., fr. *sor* reddish brown] **1 :** a sorrel-colored animal: as **a :** a light bright chestnut horse often with white mane and tail — compare [1]CHESTNUT 4, [2]BAY 1 **b :** a dark red roan horse **2 :** a brownish orange to light brown

[2]**sorrel** *n* [ME *sorel*, fr. MF *surele*, fr. OF, fr. *sur* sour, of Gmc origin; akin to OHG *sūr* sour — more at SOUR] **:** any of various plants with sour juice: as **a :** [1]DOCK 1 **b :** WOOD SORREL

sorrel tree *n* **:** SOURWOOD

[1]**sor·row** \'sär-(,)ō, 'sȯr-, -ə(-w)\ *n* [ME *sorow*, fr. OE *sorg*; akin to OHG *sorga* sorrow, OSlav *sraga* sickness] **1 :** deep distress and regret (as over the loss of something loved) **2 :** a cause of grief or sadness **3 :** a display of grief or sadness
syn SORROW, GRIEF, ANGUISH, WOE, REGRET *shared meaning element* **:** distress of mind *ant* joy

[2]**sorrow** *vi* **:** to feel or express sorrow *syn* see GRIEVE — **sor·row·er** \-ə-wər\ *n*

sor·row·ful \-ō-fəl, -ə-fəl\ *adj* **1 :** full of or marked by sorrow **2 :** expressive of or inducing sorrow — **sor·row·ful·ly** \-f(ə-)lē\ *adv* — **sor·row·ful·ness** \-fəl-nəs\ *n*

sor·ry \'sär-ē, 'sȯr-\ *adj* **sor·ri·er; -est** [ME *sory*, fr. OE *sārig*, fr. *sār* sore] **1 :** feeling sorrow, regret, or penitence **2 :** MOURNFUL, SAD **3 :** inspiring sorrow, pity, scorn, or ridicule *syn* see CONTEMPTIBLE — **sor·ri·ly** \-ə-lē\ *adv* — **sor·ri·ness** \-ē-nəs\ *n*

[1]**sort** \'sȯ(ə)rt\ *n* [ME, fr. MF *sorte*, prob. fr. ML *sort-, sors*, fr. L, chance, lot] **1 a :** a group set up on the basis of any characteristic in common **:** CLASS, KIND **b :** an instance of a kind <a ~ of black Paul Bunyan, towering 6′10″ —Jack Olsen> **c :** PERSON, INDIVIDUAL <he's not a bad ~> **2** *archaic* **:** GROUP, COMPANY **3 a :** method or manner of acting **:** WAY, MANNER **b :** CHARACTER, NATURE <people of an evil ~> **4 a :** a letter or character that is one element of a font **b :** a character or piece of type that is not part of a regular font *syn* see TYPE — **after a sort :** in a rough or haphazard way — **of sorts** *or* **of a sort :** of an inconsequential or mediocre quality <a poet *of sorts*> — **out of sorts 1 :** somewhat ill **2 :** GROUCHY, IRRITABLE

[2]**sort** *vt* **1 a :** to put in a certain place or rank according to kind, class, or nature <~ the good apples from the bad> **b :** to arrange according to characteristics **:** CLASSIFY <~ out colors> **2** *chiefly Scot* **:** to put to rights **:** put in order **3 :** to go over mentally in order to clarify <~*ing* out his problems> ~ *vi* **1 :** to join or associate with others esp. of the same kind <~ with thieves> **2** *archaic* **:** SUIT, AGREE — **sort·able** \'sȯrt-ə-bəl\ *adj* — **sort·er** *n*

sor·tie \'sȯrt-ē, sȯr-'tē\ *n* [F, fr. MF, fr. *sortir* to escape] **1 :** a sudden issuing of troops from a defensive position against the enemy **2 :** one mission or attack by a single plane — **sortie** *vi*

sor·ti·lege \'sȯrt-ᵊl-ij, -,ej\ *n* [ME, fr. ML *sortilegium*, fr. L *sortilegus* foretelling, fr. *sort-, sors* lot + *-i-* + *legere* to gather — more at LEGEND] **1 :** divination by lots **2 :** SORCERY

sor·ti·tion \sȯr-'tish-ən\ *n* [L *sortition-, sortitio*, fr. *sortitus*, pp. of *sortiri* to cast or draw lots, fr. *sort-, sors* lot] **:** the act or an instance of casting lots

sort of \,sȯrt-ə(v), -ər\ *adv* **:** to a moderate degree **:** RATHER

so·rus \'sōr-əs, 'sȯr-\ *n, pl* **so·ri** \'sō(ə)r-,ī, 'sȯ(ə)r-, -,ē\ [NL, fr. Gk *sōros* heap; akin to L *tumēre* to swell — more at THUMB] **:** a cluster of plant reproductive bodies: as **a :** one of the dots on the underside of a fertile fern frond consisting of a cluster of spores **b :** a mass of spores bursting through the epidermis of the host plant of a parasitic fungus **c :** a cluster of gemmae on the thallus of a lichen

SOS \,es-(,)ō-'es, ,es-ə-'wes\ *n* **1 :** an internationally recognized signal of distress in radio code · · · − − − · · · used esp. by ships calling for help **2 :** a call or request for help or rescue

[1]**so–so** \'sō-'sō\ *adv* **:** moderately well **:** TOLERABLY, PASSABLY

[2]**so–so** *adj* **:** neither very good nor very bad **:** MIDDLING

[1]**so·ste·nu·to** \,sō-stə-'nüt-(,)ō, ,sȯ-\ *adj or adv* [It, fr. pp. of *sostenere* to sustain, fr. L *sustinēre*] **:** sustained to or beyond the note's full value — used as a direction in music

[2]**sostenuto** *n* **:** a movement or passage whose notes are markedly prolonged

sot \'sät\ *n* [ME, fool, fr. OE *sott*] **:** an habitual drunkard

so·te·ri·ol·o·gy \sō-,tir-ē-'äl-ə-jē\ *n* [Gk *sōtērion* salvation (fr. *sōtēr* savior, fr. *sōzein* to save) + E *-logy*; akin to Gk *sōma* body — more at SOMAT-] **:** theology dealing with salvation esp. as effected by Jesus Christ — **so·te·ri·o·log·i·cal** \-ē-ə-'läj-i-kəl\ *adj*

so that *conj* **:** THAT 2a(1)

So·thic cycle \,sō-thik-, ,säth-ik-\ *n* **:** a cycle of 1460 Sothic years

Sothic year *n* [Gk *Sōthis* the star Sirius] **:** an ancient Egyptian year of 365¼ days

So·tho \'sō-(,)tō\ *n* **1 :** a group of closely related Bantu languages of Lesotho, Botswana, and northern So. Africa **2 :** any one of the Sotho languages and esp. the language of Lesotho

so·tol \'sō-,tōl\ *n* [AmerSp, fr. Nahuatl *tzotolli*] **:** a plant (genus *Dasylirion*) of the lily family of the southwestern U.S. and Mexico that resembles a yucca

sot·tish \'sät-ish\ *adj* **:** resembling a sot **:** DRUNKEN; *also* **:** DULL, STUPID — **sot·tish·ly** *adv* — **sot·tish·ness** *n*

sot·to vo·ce \,sät-ō-'vō-chē\ *adv or adj* [It *sottovoce*, lit., under the voice] **1 :** under the breath **:** in an undertone; *also* **:** in a private manner **2 :** very softly — used as a direction in music

sou \'sü\ *n, pl* **sous** \'süz\ [F, fr. OF *sol*, fr. LL *solidus* solidus] **1 :** [2]SOL **2 :** a 5-centime piece

sou·a·ri nut \sü-'är-ē-\ *n* [F *saouari* tree producing souari nuts, fr. Galibi *sawarra*] **:** the large edible oil-yielding seed of a So. American tree (genus *Caryocar* of the family Caryocaraceae, esp. *C. nuciferum*)

sou·bise \sü-'bēz\ *n* [F, fr. Charles de Rohan, Prince de *Soubise* †1787 F nobleman] **:** a white or brown sauce containing onions or onion purée

sou·brette \sü-'bret\ *n* [F, fr. Prov *soubreto*, fem. of *soubret* coy, fr. *soubra* to surmount, exceed, fr. L *superare* — more at SUPERABLE] **1 a :** a coquettish maid or frivolous young woman in comedies **b :** an actress who plays such a part **2 :** a soprano who sings supporting roles in comic opera

sou·bri·quet \'sō-, ,sō-, 'sü-, ,sü-\ *var of* SOBRIQUET

sou·chong \'sü-,chȯŋ, -,shȯŋ\ *n* [Chin (Pek) *hsiao*[3] *chung*[3], lit., small sort] **:** a large-leaved black tea esp. from China

[1]**souf·flé** \sü-'flā, 'sü-,\ *n* [F, fr. *soufflé*, pp. of *souffler* to blow, puff up, fr. L *sufflare*, fr. *sub-* + *flare* to blow — more at BLOW] **:** an entrée or dessert made with a sauce, egg yolks and stiffly whipped egg whites, and seasonings

[2]**soufflé** *or* **souf·fléed** \-'flād, -,flād\ *adj* **:** puffed by or in cooking

sough \'saů, 'səf\ *vi* [ME *swoughen*, fr. OE *swōgan*; akin to Goth *gaswogjan* to groan, Lith *svagěti* to sound] **:** to make a moaning or sighing sound — **sough** *n*

sought *past of* SEEK

[1]**soul** \'sōl\ *n* [ME *soule*, fr. OE *sāwol*; akin to OHG *sēula* soul] **1 :** the immaterial essence, animating principle, or actuating cause of an individual life **2 a :** the spiritual principle embodied in human beings, all rational and spiritual beings, or the universe **b** *cap, Christian Science* **:** GOD 1b **3 :** a person's total self **4 a :** an active or essential part **b :** a moving spirit **:** LEADER **5 a :** man's moral and emotional nature **b :** the quality that arouses emotion and sentiment **c :** spiritual or moral force **:** FERVOR **6 :** PERSON **7 :** EXEMPLIFICATION, PERSONIFICATION <he is the ~ of integrity> **8 a :** a strong positive feeling (as of intense sensitivity and emotional fervor) conveyed esp. by American Negro performers **b :** NEGRITUDE **c :** SOUL MUSIC **d :** SOUL FOOD **e :** SOUL BROTHER

[2]**soul** *adj* **1 :** of, relating to, or characteristic of American Negroes or their culture **2 :** designed for or controlled by Negroes <~ radio stations>

soul brother *n* **:** a male Negro — used esp. by other Negroes

souled \'sōld\ *adj* **:** having a soul **:** possessing soul and feeling — usu. used in combination <whole-*souled* repentance>

soul food *n* **:** food (as chitterlings, ham hocks, and collard greens) traditionally eaten by southern American Negroes

soul·ful \'sōl-fəl\ *adj* **:** full of or expressing feeling or emotion — **soul·ful·ly** \-fə-lē\ *adv* — **soul·ful·ness** *n*

soul kiss *n* **:** FRENCH KISS

soul·less \'sōl-ləs\ *adj* **:** having no soul or no greatness or warmth of mind or feeling — **soul·less·ly** *adv* — **soul·less·ness** *n*

soul mate *n* **:** one of two persons esp. of opposite sex temperamentally suited to each other; *esp* **:** LOVER, MISTRESS

soul music *n* **:** music that originated in American Negro gospel singing, is closely related to rhythm and blues, and is characterized by intensity of feeling and earthiness

soul–search·ing \'sōl-,sər-chiŋ\ *n* **:** examination of one's conscience esp. with regard to motives and values

[1]**sound** \'saůnd\ *adj* [ME, fr. OE *gesund*; akin to OHG *gisunt* healthy] **1 a :** free from injury or disease **:** exhibiting normal health **b :** free from flaw, defect, or decay <~ timber> **2 :** SOLID, FIRM; *also* **:** STABLE **3 a :** free from error, fallacy, or misapprehension <~ reasoning> **b :** exhibiting or based on thorough knowledge and experience <~ scholarship> **c :** legally valid <a ~ title> **d :** logically valid and having true premises **e :** agreeing with accepted views **:** ORTHODOX **4 a :** THOROUGH **b :** deep and undisturbed <a ~ sleep> **c :** HARD, SEVERE <a ~ whipping> **5 :** showing good judgment or sense *syn* **1** see HEALTHY *ant* unsound **2** see VALID *ant* unsound, fallacious — **sound·ly** \'saůn-(d)lē\ *adv* — **sound·ness** \'saůn(d)-nəs\ *n*

[2]**sound** *adv* **:** to the full extent **:** THOROUGHLY <~ asleep>

[3]**sound** *n* [ME *soun*, fr. OF *son*, fr. L *sonus*; akin to OE *swinn* melody, L *sonare* to sound, Skt *svanati* it sounds] **1 a :** the sensation perceived by the sense of hearing **b :** a particular auditory impression **:** TONE **c :** mechanical radiant energy that is transmitted by longitudinal pressure waves in a material medium (as air) and is the objective cause of hearing **2 a :** a speech sound <a peculiar *r-sound*> **b :** value in terms of speech sounds <*-cher* of *teacher* and *-ture* of *creature* have the same ~> **3** *archaic* **:** RUMOR, FAME **4 a :** meaningless noise **b** *obs* **:** MEANING **c :** the impression conveyed **:** IMPORT **5 :** hearing distance **:** EARSHOT **6 :** recorded auditory material **7 :** a particular musical style characteristic of an individual, a group, or an area <the Nashville ~>
syn SOUND, NOISE *shared meaning element* **:** a sensation or effect resulting from stimulation of the auditory receptors

4sound *vi* **1 a :** to make a sound **b :** RESOUND **c :** to give a summons by sound <the bugle ~*s* to battle> **2 :** to make or convey an impression **:** SEEM <his story ~*s* incredible> ~ *vt* **1 :** to cause to sound <~ a trumpet> **2 :** to put into words **:** VOICE **3 a :** to make known **:** PROCLAIM **b :** to order, signal, or indicate by a sound <~ the alarm> **4 :** to examine by causing to emit sounds <~ the lungs> — **sound·able** \'saun-də-bəl\ *adj*

5sound *n* [ME, fr. OE *sund* swimming, sea & ON *sund* swimming, strait; akin to OE *swimman* to swim] **1 a :** a long broad inlet of the ocean generally parallel to the coast **b :** a long passage of water connecting two larger bodies (as a sea with the ocean) or separating a mainland and an island **2 :** the air bladder of a fish

6sound *vb* [ME *sounden,* fr. MF *sonder,* fr. *sonde* sounding line, prob. of Gmc origin; akin to OE *sundline* sounding line, *sund* sea] *vt* **1 :** to measure the depth of **:** FATHOM **2 :** to try to find out the views or intentions of **:** PROBE **3 :** to explore or examine (a body cavity) with a sound ~ *vi* **1 a :** to ascertain the depth of water esp. with a sounding line **b :** to look into or investigate the possibility <sent commissioners . . . to ~ for peace —Thomas Jefferson> **2 :** to dive down suddenly — used of a fish or whale

7sound *n* [F *sonde,* fr. MF, lit., sounding line] **:** an elongated instrument for exploring or sounding body cavities

sound barrier *n* **:** SONIC BARRIER

sound·board \'saun(d)-ˌbō(ə)rd, -ˌbȯ(ə)rd\ *n* **1 :** a thin resonant board (as the belly of a violin) so placed in an instrument as to reinforce its tones by sympathetic vibration — see VIOLIN illustration **2 :** SOUNDING BOARD 1a

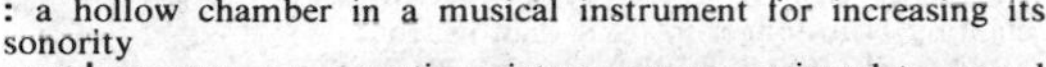
1, soundboard 1 (of a piano)

sound bow *n* **:** the thick part of a bell against which the clapper strikes — see BELL illustration

sound box *n* **1 :** a device in a phonograph using vibrating needle and thin diaphragm to convert phonograph record groove undulations into sound **2 :** a hollow chamber in a musical instrument for increasing its sonority

sound camera *n* **:** a motion-picture camera equipped to record sound simultaneously with the picture on a single film

sound effects *n pl* **:** effects that are imitative of sounds called for in the script of a play, radio or television program, or motion picture and are produced by various means

sound·er \'saun-dər\ *n* **:** one that sounds; *specif* **:** a device for making soundings

1sound·ing \'saun-diŋ\ *n* **1 a :** measurement by sounding **b :** the depth so ascertained **c** *pl* **:** a place or part of a body of water where a hand sounding line will reach bottom **2 :** measurement of atmospheric conditions at various heights **3 :** a probe, test, or sampling of opinion or intention

2sounding *adj* **1 :** RESONANT, SONOROUS **2 a :** POMPOUS **b :** IMPOSING — **sound·ing·ly** \-diŋ-lē\ *adv*

sounding board *n* **1 a :** a structure behind or over a pulpit, rostrum, or platform to give distinctness and sonority to sound **b :** a device or agency that helps propagate opinions or utterances **2 :** SOUNDBOARD 1

sounding line *n* **:** a line or wire weighted at one end for sounding

sounding rocket *n* **:** a rocket used to obtain information concerning atmospheric conditions at various altitudes

1sound·less \'saun-(d)ləs\ *adj* [6*sound*] **:** incapable of being sounded **:** UNFATHOMABLE

2soundless *adj* [3*sound*] **:** making no sound **:** SILENT — **sound·less·ly** *adv*

sound motion picture *n* **:** a motion picture accompanied by synchronized recorded sound

sound off *vi* **1 :** to play three chords before and after marching up and down a line of troops during a ceremonial parade or formal guard mount **2 :** to count cadence while marching **3 a :** to speak up in a loud voice **b :** to voice one's opinions freely and vigorously

sound pollution *n* **:** NOISE POLLUTION

sound pressure *n* **:** the difference between the actual pressure at any point in the field of a sound wave at any instant and the average pressure at that point

1sound·proof \'saun(d)-'prüf\ *adj* **:** impervious to sound

2soundproof *vt* **:** to insulate so as to obstruct the passage of sound

sound track *n* **:** the area on a motion-picture film that carries the sound record

sound truck *n* **:** a truck equipped with a loudspeaker

sound wave *n* **1 :** 3SOUND 1b **2** *pl* **:** longitudinal pressure waves in any material medium regardless of whether they constitute audible sound <earthquake waves and ultrasonic waves are sometimes called *sound waves*>

1soup \'süp\ *n* [F *soupe* sop, soup, of Gmc origin; akin to ON *soppa* soup, OE *sopp* sop] **1 :** a liquid food esp. with a meat, fish, or vegetable stock as a base and often containing pieces of solid food **2 :** something having or suggesting the consistency of soup (as a heavy fog or nitroglycerine) **3 :** an unfortunate predicament

2soup *vt* [E slang *soup* (dope injected into a racehorse to improve its performance)] **:** to increase the power or efficiency of <~ up an engine>

soup·çon \süp-'sōⁿ, 'süp-ˌsän\ *n* [F, lit., suspicion, fr. (assumed) VL *suspection-, suspectio,* fr. L *suspectus,* pp. of *suspicere* to suspect — more at SUSPECT] **:** a little bit **:** TRACE

soup du jour \ˌsüp-də-'zhu̇(ə)r\ *n* [part trans. of F *soupe du jour* soup of the day] **:** a soup that is offered by a restaurant on a particular day

soup kitchen *n* **:** an establishment dispensing minimum dietary essentials (as soup and bread) to the needy

soup·spoon \'süp-ˌspün\ *n* **:** a spoon with a large or rounded bowl for eating soup

soupy \'sü-pē\ *adj* **soup·i·er; -est 1 :** having the consistency of soup **2 :** densely foggy or cloudy

1sour \'sau̇(ə)r\ *adj* [ME, fr. OE *sūr;* akin to OHG *sūr* sour, Lith *suras* salty] **1 :** causing or characterized by the one of the four basic taste sensations that is produced chiefly by acids <~ pickles> — compare BITTER, SALT, SWEET **2 a (1) :** having the acid taste or smell of or as if of fermentation **:** TURNED <~ milk> **(2) :** of or relating to fermentation **b :** smelling or tasting of decay **:** RANCID, ROTTEN <~ breath> **c (1) :** BAD, WRONG <a project gone ~> **(2) :** HOSTILE, DISENCHANTED <went ~ on Marxism> **3 a :** UNPLEASANT, DISTASTEFUL **b :** CROSS, SULLEN **c :** not up to the usual, expected, or standard quality or pitch **4 :** acid in reaction — used esp. of soil **5 :** containing malodorous sulfur compounds — used esp. of petroleum products — **sour·ish** \'sau̇(ə)r-ish\ *adj* — **sour·ly** *adv* — **sour·ness** *n*

syn SOUR, ACID, ACIDULOUS, TART *shared meaning element* **:** having a taste devoid of sweetness

2sour *n* **1 a :** something sour **b :** the primary taste sensation produced by acid stimuli **2 :** a cocktail made with a liquor (as whiskey), lemon or lime juice, sugar, and sometimes soda water

3sour *vi* **:** to become sour ~ *vt* **:** to make sour

sour ball *n* **:** a spherical piece of hard candy having a tart flavor

source \'sō(ə)rs, 'sȯ(ə)rs\ *n* [ME *sours,* fr. MF *sors, sourse,* fr. OF, fr. pp. of *sourdre* to rise, spring forth, fr. L *surgere* — more at SURGE] **1 a :** the point of origin of a stream of water **:** FOUNTAINHEAD **b** *archaic* **:** SPRING, FOUNT **2 a :** a generative force **:** CAUSE **b (1) :** a point of origin **:** BEGINNING **(2) :** one that initiates **:** AUTHOR; *also* **:** PROTOTYPE, MODEL **(3) :** one that supplies information **3 :** a firsthand document or primary reference work ***syn*** see ORIGIN — **source·less** \-ləs\ *adj*

source book *n* **:** a fundamental document or record (as of history, literature, art, or religion) upon which subsequent writings, compositions, opinions, beliefs, or practices are based; *also* **:** a collection of such documents

source language *n* **:** a language which is to be translated into another language — compare TARGET LANGUAGE

sour cherry *n* **:** a round-headed Eurasian tree (*Prunus cerasus*) widely grown for its bright red to almost black soft-fleshed acid fruits; *also* **:** its fruit

sour cream *n* **:** a commercial cream product produced by the use of lactobacilli

sour·dough \'sau̇(ə)r-ˌdō, *1 is also* -'dō\ *n* **1 :** a leaven consisting of dough in which fermentation is active **2** [fr. the use of sourdough for making bread in prospectors' camps] **:** a veteran inhabitant and esp. an old-time prospector of Alaska or northwestern Canada

sour grapes *n pl* [fr. the fable ascribed to Aesop of the fox who after finding himself unable to reach some grapes he had desired disparaged them as sour] **:** disparagement of something that has proven unattainable

sour gum *n* **:** BLACK GUM

sour mash *n* **:** grain mash for brewing or distilling whose initial acidity has been adjusted to optimum condition for yeast fermentation by mash from a previous run

sour orange *n* **:** a citrus tree (*Citrus aurantium*) that is used esp. as an understock in grafting citrus; *also* **:** its bitter fruit

sour·puss \'sau̇(ə)r-ˌpu̇s\ *n* [2*puss*] **:** GROUCH, KILLJOY

sour salt *n* **:** CITRIC ACID

sour·sop \'sau̇(ə)r-ˌsäp\ *n* **1 :** a small tropical American tree (*Annona muricata*) of the custard-apple family that has spicy odoriferous leaves **2 :** the large edible fruit of the soursop that has fleshy spines and a slightly acid fibrous pulp

sour·wood \-ˌwu̇d\ *n* **:** a small tree (*Oxydendrum arboreum*) of the heath family with white flowers and sour-tasting leaves

sou·sa·phone \'sü-zə-ˌfōn, -sə-\ *n* [John Philip *Sousa*] **:** a large circular tuba that has a flared adjustable bell, that is designed to rest on the player's left shoulder, and that is used primarily in marching bands

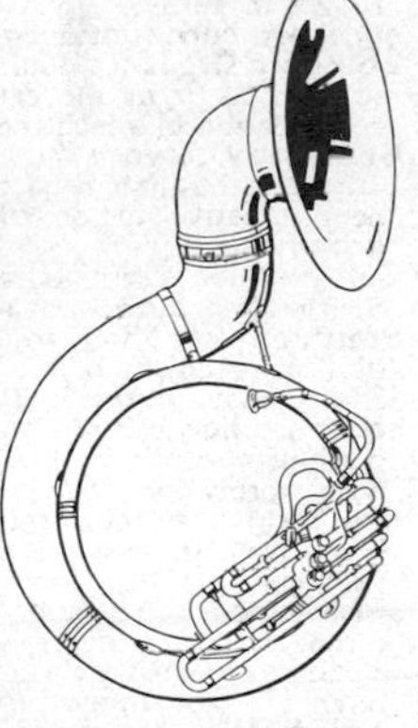
sousaphone

1souse \'sau̇s\ *vb* **soused; sous·ing** [ME *sousen,* fr. MF *souz, souce* pickling solution, of Gmc origin; akin to OHG *sulza* brine, OE *sealt* salt] *vt* **1 :** PICKLE **2 a :** to plunge in liquid **:** IMMERSE **b :** DRENCH, SATURATE **3 :** to make drunk **:** INEBRIATE ~ *vi* **:** to become immersed or drenched

2souse *n* **1 :** something pickled; *esp* **:** seasoned and chopped pork trimmings, fish, or shellfish **2 :** an act of sousing **:** WETTING **3 a :** an habitual drunkard **b :** a drinking spree **:** BINGE

3souse *n* [ME *souce* start of a bird's flight, alter. of *sours,* fr. MF *sourse,* fr. *sourdre* to rise] *obs* **:** the stoop of a hawk intercepting a bird

4souse *vb* **soused; sous·ing** *vi, archaic* **:** to swoop down **:** PLUNGE ~ *vt, archaic* **:** to swoop down upon

sou·tache \sü-'tash\ *n* [F, fr. Hung *sujtás*] **:** a narrow braid with herringbone pattern used as trimming

sou·tane \sü-'tän, -'tan\ *n* [F, fr. It *sottana,* lit., undergarment, fr. fem. of *sottano* being underneath, fr. ML *subtanus,* fr. L *subtus* underneath; akin to L *sub* under — more at UP] **:** CASSOCK

sou·ter \'süt-ər\ *n* [ME, fr. OE *sūtere,* fr. L *sutor,* fr. *sutus,* pp. of *suere* to sew — more at SEW] *chiefly Scot* **:** SHOEMAKER

[1]**south** \'sau̇th\ *adv* [ME, fr. OE *sūth;* akin to OHG *sund-* south, OE *sunne* sun] : to, toward, or in the south : SOUTHWARD
[2]**south** *adj* **1 :** situated toward or at the south <the ~ entrance> **2 :** coming from the south <a ~ wind>
[3]**south** *n* **1 a :** the direction of the south terrestrial pole : the direction to the right of one facing east **b :** the compass point directly opposite to north **2** *cap* **:** regions or countries lying to the south of a specified or implied point of orientation **3 :** the right side of a church looking toward the altar from the nave **4** *often cap* **a :** the one of four positions at 90-degree intervals that lies to the south or at the bottom of a diagram **b :** a person (as a bridge player) occupying this position in the course of a specified activity; *specif* **:** the declarer in bridge
South African *n* **:** a native or inhabitant of the Republic of South Africa; *esp* **:** AFRIKANER — **South African** *adj*
south·bound \'sau̇th-ˌbau̇nd\ *adj* **:** traveling or headed south
south by east : a compass point that is one point east of due south : S11°15′E
south by west : a compass point that is one point west of due south : S11°15′W
South·down \'sau̇th-ˌdau̇n\ *n* [*South Downs,* England]**:** any of an English breed of small medium-wooled hornless mutton-type sheep
[1]**south·east** \sau̇-'thēst, *naut* sau̇-'ēst\ *adv* **:** to, toward, or in the southeast
[2]**southeast** *n* **1 a :** the general direction between south and east **b :** the point midway between the south and east compass points **2** *cap* **:** regions or countries lying to the southeast of a specified or implied point of orientation
[3]**southeast** *adj* **1 :** coming from the southeast <a ~ wind> **2 :** situated toward or at the southeast <~ corner>
southeast by east : a compass point that is one point east of due southeast : S56°15′E
southeast by south : a compass point that is one point south of due southeast : S33°45′E
south·east·er \sau̇-'thē-stər, sau̇-'ē-\ *n* **1 :** a strong southeast wind **2 :** a storm with southeast winds
south·east·er·ly \-stər-lē\ *adv or adj* [[2]*southeast* + *-erly* (as in *easterly*)] **1 :** from the southeast **2 :** toward the southeast
south·east·ern \-stərn\ *adj* [[2]*southeast* + *-ern* (as in *eastern*)] **1** *often cap* **:** of, relating to, or characteristic of a region conventionally designated southeast **2 :** lying toward or coming from the southeast — **south·east·ern·most** \-ˌmōst\ *adj*
South·east·ern·er \-stə(r)-nər\ *n* **:** a native or inhabitant of the Southeast; *esp* **:** a native or resident of the southeastern part of the U.S.
[1]**south·east·ward** \sau̇-'thēs-twərd, sau̇-'ēs-\ *adv or adj* **:** toward the southeast — **south·east·wards** \-twərdz\ *adv*
[2]**southeastward** *n* **:** SOUTHEAST
south·er \'sau̇-t͟hər\ *n* **:** a southerly wind
[1]**south·er·ly** \'sət͟h-ər-lē\ *adj or adv* [[3]*south* + *-erly* (as in *easterly*)] **1 :** situated toward or belonging to the south <the ~ shore of the lake> **2 :** coming from the south <a ~ wind>
[2]**southerly** *n, pl* **-lies :** a wind from the south
south·ern \'sət͟h-ərn\ *adj* [ME *southern, southren,* fr. OE *sūtherne;* akin to OHG *sundrōni* southern, OE *sūth* south] **1** *cap* **:** of, relating to, or characteristic of a region conventionally designated South **2 a :** lying toward the south **b :** coming from the south <a ~ breeze> — **south·ern·ly** *adj* — **south·ern·most** \-ˌmōst\ *adj* — **south·ern·ness** \-ərn-nəs\ *n*
Southern *n* **:** the dialect of English spoken in most of the Chesapeake Bay area, the coastal plain and the greater part of the upland plateau in Virginia, North Carolina, South Carolina, and Georgia, and the Gulf states at least as far west as the valley of the Brazos in Texas
southern corn rootworm *n* **:** SPOTTED CUCUMBER BEETLE
Southern Cross *n* **:** four bright stars in the southern hemisphere, situated as if at the extremities of a Latin cross; *also* **:** the constellation of which these four stars are the brightest
Southern Crown *n* **:** CORONA AUSTRALIS
Southern English *n* **1 :** the English spoken esp. by cultivated people native to or educated in the South of England **2 :** SOUTHERN
South·ern·er \'sət͟h-ə(r)-nər\ *n* **:** a native or inhabitant of the South; *esp* **:** a native or resident of the southern part of the U.S.
South·ern·ism \'sət͟h-ər-ˌniz-əm\ *n* **1 :** a locution or pronunciation characteristic of the southern U.S. **2 :** an attitude or trait characteristic of the South or Southerners esp. in the U.S.
southern lights *n pl* **:** AURORA AUSTRALIS
south·ern·wood \'sət͟h-ərn-ˌwu̇d\ *n* **:** a shrubby fragrant European wormwood (*Artemisia abrotanum*) with bitter foliage
south·ing \'sau̇-thiŋ, -t͟hiŋ\ *n* **1 :** difference in latitude to the south from the last preceding point of reckoning **2 :** southerly progress
south·land \'sau̇th-ˌland, -lənd\ *n, often cap* **:** land in the south : the south of a country
south·paw \-ˌpȯ\ *n* **:** LEFT-HANDER; *specif* **:** a left-handed baseball pitcher — **southpaw** *adj*
south pole *n* **1 a** *often cap S & P* **:** the southernmost point of the earth **b :** the zenith of the heavens as viewed from the south terrestrial pole **2** *of a magnet* **:** the pole that points toward the south
[1]**South·ron** \'sət͟h-rən\ *adj* [ME (Sc), fr. ME *southren*] *chiefly Scot* **:** SOUTHERN; *specif* **:** ENGLISH
[2]**Southron** *n* **:** SOUTHERNER: as **a** *chiefly Scot* **:** ENGLISHMAN **b** *chiefly South* **:** a native or inhabitant of the southern U.S.
south–southeast *n* **:** a compass point two points east of due south : S22°30′E
south–southwest *n* **:** a compass point two points west of due south : S22°30′W
[1]**south·ward** \'sau̇th-wərd\ *adv or adj* **:** toward the south — **south·wards** \-wərdz\ *adv*
[2]**southward** *n* **:** southward direction or part <sail to the ~>
[1]**south·west** \sau̇th-'west, *naut* sau̇-'west\ *adv* **:** to, toward, or in the southwest
[2]**southwest** *n* **1 a :** the general direction between south and west **b :** the point midway between the south and west compass points **2** *cap* **:** regions or countries lying to the southwest of a specified or implied point of orientation
[3]**southwest** *adj* **1 :** coming from the southwest <a ~ wind> **2 :** situated toward or at the southwest
southwest by south : a compass point that is one point south of due southwest : S33°45′W
southwest by west : a compass point that is one point west of due southwest : S56°15′W
south·west·er \sau̇(th)-'wes-tər\ *n* **1 :** a strong southwest wind **2 :** a storm with southwest winds
south·west·er·ly \-tər-lē\ *adv or adj* [[2]*southwest* + *-erly* (as in *westerly*)] **1 :** from the southwest **2 :** toward the southwest
south·west·ern \-tərn\ *adj* [[2]*southwest* + *-ern* (as in *western*)] **1** *often cap* **:** of, relating to, or characteristic of a region conventionally designated Southwest **2 :** lying toward or coming from the southwest — **south·west·ern·most** \-ˌmōst\ *adj*
southwestern corn borer *n* **:** a pyralid moth (*Diatraea grandiosella*) whose larva causes serious damage esp. to corn crops by boring in the stalks
South·west·ern·er \sau̇(th)-'wes-tə(r)-nər\ *n* **:** a native or inhabitant of the Southwest; *esp* **:** a native or resident of the southwestern U.S.
[1]**south·west·ward** \sau̇(th)-'wes-twərd\ *adv or adj* **:** toward the southwest — **south·west·wards** \-wərdz\ *adv*
[2]**southwestward** *n* **:** SOUTHWEST
sou·ve·nir \'sü-və-ˌni(ə)r, ˌsü-və-'\ *n* [F, lit., act of remembering, fr. MF, fr. (*se*) *souvenir* to remember, fr. L *subvenire* to come up, come to mind] **:** something that serves as a reminder : MEMENTO
souvenir sheet *n* **:** a block or set of postage stamps or a single stamp printed on a single sheet of paper often without gum or perforations and with margins containing lettering or design that identifies some notable event being commemorated
sou'·west·er \sau̇-'wes-tər\ *n* **1 :** SOUTHWESTER **2 a :** a long oilskin coat worn esp. at sea during stormy weather **b :** a waterproof hat with wide slanting brim longer in back than in front
[1]**sov·er·eign** *also* **sov·ran** \'säv-(ə-)rən, 'säv-ərn, 'səv-\ *n* [ME *soverain,* fr. OF, fr. *soverain,* adj.] **1 a :** one possessing or held to possess sovereignty **b :** one that exercises supreme authority within a limited sphere **c :** an acknowledged leader : ARBITER **2 :** a gold coin of Great Britain containing 113 grains of fine gold

sou'wester 2b

[2]**sovereign** *also* **sovran** *adj* [ME *soverain,* fr. MF, fr. OF, fr. (assumed) VL *superanus,* fr. L *super* over, above — more at OVER] **1 a :** possessed of supreme power <~ ruler> **b :** unlimited in extent : ABSOLUTE **c :** enjoying autonomy : INDEPENDENT <a ~ state> **2 a :** of the most exalted kind : SUPREME <~ virtue> **b :** superlative in quality : EXCELLENT **c :** having generalized curative powers : POTENT <a ~ remedy> **d :** of an unqualified nature : UNMITIGATED <~ contempt> **e :** having undisputed ascendancy : PARAMOUNT **3 :** relating to, characteristic of, or befitting a sovereign *syn* see DOMINANT, FREE — **sov·er·eign·ly** *adv*
sov·er·eign·ty *also* **sov·ran·ty** \-tē\ *n, pl* **-ties** [ME *soverainte,* fr. MF *souveraineté,* fr. OF, fr. *soverain*] **1** *obs* **:** supreme excellence or an example of it **2 a :** supreme power esp. over a body politic **b :** freedom from external control : AUTONOMY **c :** controlling influence **3 :** one that is sovereign; *esp* **:** an autonomous state
so·vi·et \'sōv-ē-ˌet, 'säv-, -ē-ət-\ *n* [Russ *sovet*] **1 :** an elected governmental council in a Communist country **2** *pl, cap* **a :** BOLSHEVIKS **b :** the people and esp. the political and military leaders of the U.S.S.R. — **soviet** *adj, often cap* — **so·vi·et·ism** \-ˌiz-əm\ *n, often cap*
so·vi·et·ize \'sōv-ē-ˌet-ˌīz, 'säv-, -ē-ət-\ *vt* **-ized; -iz·ing** *often cap* **1 :** to bring under Soviet control **2 :** to force into conformity with Soviet cultural patterns or governmental policies — **so·vi·et·iza·tion** \ˌsōv-ē-ˌet-ə-'zā-shən, -ē-ət-\ *n, often cap*
sov·khoz \säf-'kȯz, -'kȯs\ *n, pl* **sov·kho·zy** \-'kȯ-zē\ *or* **sov·khoz·es** [Russ, short for *sovetskoe khozyaĭstvo* soviet farm] **:** a state-owned farm of the U.S.S.R. paying wages to the workers
[1]**sow** \'sau̇\ *n* [ME *sowe,* fr. OE *sugu;* akin to OE & OHG *sū* sow, L *sus* pig, swine, hog, Gk *hys*] **1 :** an adult female swine; *also* **:** the adult female of various other animals (as the grizzly bear) **2 a :** a channel that conducts molten metal to molds in a pig bed **b :** a mass of metal solidified in such a mold : INGOT
[2]**sow** \'sō\ *vb* **sowed; sown** \'sōn\ *or* **sowed; sow·ing** [ME *sowen,* fr. OE *sāwan;* akin to OHG *sāwen* to sow, L *serere*] *vi* **1 :** to plant seed for growth esp. by scattering **2 :** to set something in motion : begin an enterprise ~ *vt* **1 a :** to scatter (as seed) upon the earth for growth; *broadly* **:** PLANT 1a **b :** to strew with or as if with seed **c :** to introduce into a selected environment : IMPLANT **2 :** to set in motion : FOMENT <~ suspicion> **3 :** to spread abroad : DISPERSE — **sow·er** \'sō(-ə)r\ *n*
sow·bel·ly \'sau̇-ˌbel-ē\ *n* **:** fat salt pork or bacon
sow bug *n* **:** WOOD LOUSE 1
sow·ens \'sü-ənz, 'sō-\ *n pl but sing or pl in constr* [ScGael *sūghan*] **:** porridge from oat husks and siftings
sow thistle \'sau̇-\ *n* **:** any of a genus (*Sonchus*) of spiny weedy European composite herbs widely naturalized
sox *pl of* SOCK
soy \'sȯi\ *n* [Jap *shōyu,* fr. Chin (Cant) *shī-yaū,* lit., soybean oil] **1 :** an oriental brown liquid sauce made by subjecting beans (as soybeans) to long fermentation and to digestion in brine **2 :** SOYBEAN
soya \'sȯi-(y)ə\ *n* [D *soja,* fr. Jap *shōyu* soy] **:** SOYBEAN
soy·bean \'sȯi-'bēn, -ˌbēn\ *n* **:** a hairy annual Asiatic legume (*Glycine max*) widely grown for its oil-rich proteinaceous seeds and for forage and soil improvement; *also* **:** its seed
soybean oil *or* **soya–bean oil** *n* **:** a pale yellow drying or semidrying oil that is obtained from soybeans and is used chiefly as a food, in paints, varnishes, linoleum, printing ink, and soap, and

as a source of phospholipids, fatty acids, and sterols

sp *abbr* **1** special **2** species **3** specific **4** specimen **5** spelling **6** spirit

Sp *abbr* Spain; Spanish

SP *abbr* **1** self-propelled **2** shore patrol; shore patrolman **3** shore police **4** [L *sine prole*] without issue **5** single pole **6** specialist

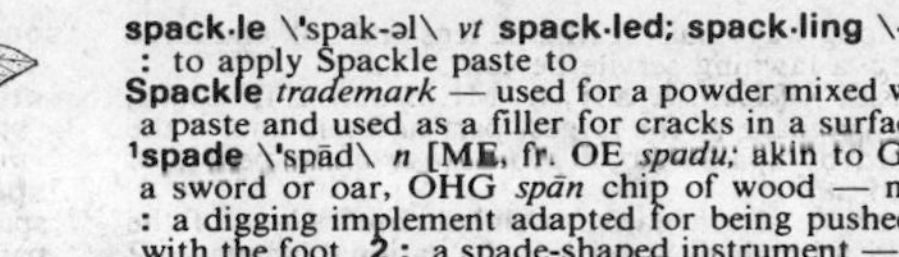

soybean: *1* stems and leaves, *2* seedpods, *3* flower

spa \'spä, 'spȯ\ *n* [*Spa,* watering place in Belgium] **1 a :** a mineral spring **b :** a resort with mineral springs **2 :** a fashionable resort or hotel **3** *NewEng* **:** SODA FOUNTAIN

¹space \'spās\ *n, often attrib* [ME, fr. OF *espace,* fr. L *spatium* area, room, interval of space or time — more at SPEED] **1 :** a period of time; *also* **:** its duration **2 a :** a limited extent in one, two, or three dimensions **:** DISTANCE, AREA, VOLUME **b :** an extent set apart or available <parking ~> <floor ~> **3 :** one of the degrees between or above or below the lines of a musical staff **4 a :** a boundless three-dimensional extent in which objects and events occur and have relative position and direction **b :** physical space independent of what occupies it — called also *absolute space* **5 :** the region beyond the earth's atmosphere or beyond the solar system **6 a :** a blank area separating words or lines **b :** material used to produce such blank area; *specif* **:** a piece of type less than one en in width **7 :** a set of mathematical elements and esp. of abstractions of all the points on a line, in a plane, or in physical space; *esp* **:** a set of mathematical entities with a set of axioms of geometric character — compare METRIC SPACE, TOPOLOGICAL SPACE, VECTOR SPACE **8 :** an interval in operation during which a telegraph key is not in contact **9 a :** LINAGE 1 **b :** broadcast time available esp. to advertisers **10 :** accommodations on a public vehicle

²space *vb* **spaced; spac·ing** *vt* **:** to place at intervals or arrange with space between — often used with *out* ~ *vi* **:** to leave one or more blank spaces (as in a line of typing) — **spac·er** *n*

space·band \'spās-ˌband\ *n* **:** a device on a linecaster that provides variable but even spacing between words in a justified line

space charge *n* **:** an electric charge (as the electrons in the region near the filament of a vacuum tube) distributed throughout a three-dimensional region

space·craft \'spā-ˌskraft\ *n* **:** a manned or unmanned device that is designed to orbit the earth or to travel beyond the earth's atmosphere

space·flight \'spās-ˌflīt\ *n* **:** flight beyond the earth's atmosphere

space heater *n* **:** a device for heating an enclosed space; *esp* **:** an often portable device that heats the space in which it is located and has no external heating ducts or connection to a chimney

space heating *n* **:** heating of spaces esp. for human comfort by any means (as fuel, electricity, or solar radiation) with the heater either within the space or external to it

space lattice *n* **:** the geometrical arrangement of the atoms in a crystal

space·less \'spā-sləs\ *adj* **1 :** having no limits **:** BOUNDLESS **2 :** occupying no space

space·man \'spā-ˌsman, -smən\ *n* **1 a :** one who travels outside the earth's atmosphere **b :** one engaged in any of various fields bearing on flight through outer space **2 :** a visitor to earth from outer space

space mark *n* **:** the symbol #

space medicine *n* **:** a branch of medicine that deals with the physiological and biological effects on the human body of rocket or jet flight beyond the earth's atmosphere

space·port \'spā-ˌspō(ə)rt, -ˌspȯ(ə)rt\ *n* **:** an installation for testing and launching spacecraft

space·ship \'spās(h)-ˌship\ *n* **:** a vehicle designed to operate in free space outside the earth's atmosphere

space shuttle *n* **:** a usu. two-stage vehicle that is designed to serve as transportation between the earth and an orbiting space station

space station *n* **:** a usu. manned artificial satellite designed for a fixed orbit about the earth and to serve as a base (as for scientific observation) — called also *space platform*

space suit *n* **1 :** a suit equipped with life supporting provisions to make life in space possible for its wearer **2 :** G SUIT

space–time \'spā-'stīm, 'spā-ˌ\ *n* **1 :** a system of one temporal and three spatial coordinates by which any physical object or event can be located — called also *space-time continuum* **2 :** the whole or a portion of physical reality determinable by a four-dimensional coordinate system; *also* **:** the properties characteristic of such an order

space walk *n* **:** an extravehicular venture made by an astronaut in space — **space walk** *vi* — **space·walk·er** \'spā-ˌswȯ-kər\ *n* — **space·walk·ing** \-kiŋ\ *n*

space·ward \'spā-swərd\ *adv* **:** toward space

space writer *n* **:** a writer paid according to the space his matter fills in print

spa·cial *var of* SPATIAL

spac·ing \'spā-siŋ\ *n* **1 a :** the act of providing with spaces or placing at intervals **b :** an arrangement in space **2 a :** a limited extent **:** SPACE **b :** the distance between any two objects in a usu. regularly arranged series

spa·cious \'spā-shəs\ *adj* [ME, fr. MF *spacieux,* fr. L *spatiosus,* fr. *spatium* space, room] **1 :** vast or ample in extent **:** ROOMY <a ~ residence> **2 :** large or magnificent in scale **:** EXPANSIVE <a more ~ and stimulating existence than the farm could offer —H. L. Mencken> — **spa·cious·ly** *adv* — **spa·cious·ness** *n*

syn SPACIOUS, COMMODIOUS, CAPACIOUS, AMPLE *shared meaning element* **:** larger in extent or capacity than the average

spack·le \'spak-əl\ *vt* **spack·led; spack·ling** \-(ə-)liŋ\ [*Spackle*] **:** to apply Spackle paste to

Spackle *trademark* — used for a powder mixed with water to form a paste and used as a filler for cracks in a surface before painting

¹spade \'spād\ *n* [ME, fr. OE *spadu;* akin to Gk *spathē* blade of a sword or oar, OHG *spān* chip of wood — more at SPOON] **1 :** a digging implement adapted for being pushed into the ground with the foot **2 :** a spade-shaped instrument — **spade·ful** \-ˌfu̇l\ *n* — **call a spade a spade 1 :** to call a thing by its right name however coarse **2 :** to speak frankly

²spade *vb* **spad·ed; spad·ing** *vt* **:** to dig up or out or shape with or as if with a spade ~ *vi* **:** to use a spade — **spad·er** *n*

³spade *n* [It *spada* or Sp *espada* broad sword; both fr. L *spatha,* fr. Gk *spathē* blade] **1 a :** a black figure that resembles a stylized spearhead on each playing card of one of the four suits; *also* **:** a card marked with this figure **b** *pl but sing or pl in constr* **:** the suit comprising cards marked with a spade **2 :** NEGRO — usu. taken to be offensive — **in spades :** to an unusually great degree **:** in the extreme

spade beard *n* **1 :** an oblong beard with square ends **2 :** a beard rounded off at the top and pointed at the bottom — **spade-beard·ed** \'spād-'bird-əd\ *adj*

spade·fish \'spād-ˌfish\ *n* **:** a deep-bodied spiny-finned food fish (*Chaetodipterus faber*) found in the warmer parts of the western Atlantic

spade·work \-ˌwərk\ *n* **1 :** work done with the spade **2 :** the hard plain preliminary drudgery in an undertaking

spa·dille \spə-'dil, -'dē\ *n* [F, fr. Sp *espadilla,* dim. of *espada* broad sword, spade (in cards) — more at SPADE] **:** the highest trump in various card games (as ombre)

spa·dix \'spād-iks\ *n, pl* **spa·di·ces** \'spād-ə-ˌsēz\ [NL *spadic-, spadix,* fr. L, frond torn from a palm tree, fr. Gk *spadik-, spadix,* fr. *span* to draw, pull — more at SPAN] **:** a floral spike with a fleshy or succulent axis usu. enclosed in a spathe

spae \'spā\ *vt* **spaed; spae·ing** [ME *span,* fr. ON *spā;* akin to OHG *spehōn* to watch, spy — more at SPY] *chiefly Scot* **:** FORETELL, PROPHESY

spa·ghet·ti \spə-'get-ē\ *n* [It, fr. pl. of *spaghetto,* dim. of *spago* cord, string] **1 :** pasta made in thin solid strings **2 :** electrically insulating tubing typically of varnished cloth or of plastic for covering bare wire or holding insulated wires together

spa·hi \'spä-ˌhē\ *n* [MF, fr. Turk *sipahi,* fr. Per *sipāhī* cavalryman] **1 :** one of a former corps of irregular Turkish cavalry **2 :** one of a former corps of Algerian native cavalry in the French Army

spake \'spāk\ *archaic past of* SPEAK

¹spall \'spȯl\ *n* [ME *spalle*] **:** a small fragment or chip esp. of stone

²spall *vt* **:** to break up or reduce by chipping with a hammer ~ *vi* **1 :** to break off chips, scales, or slabs **:** EXFOLIATE **2 :** to undergo spallation — **spall·able** \'spȯ-lə-bəl\ *adj*

spall·ation \spȯ-'lā-shən\ *n* [²*spall*] **:** a nuclear reaction in which light particles are ejected as the result of bombardment (as by high-energy protons)

spal·peen \spal-'pēn, spȯl-\ *n* [IrGael *spailpīn* migratory laborer, rascal] *chiefly Irish* **:** RASCAL

¹span \'span\ *archaic past of* SPIN

²span *n* [ME, fr. OE *spann;* akin to OHG *spanna* span, MD *spannen* to stretch, hitch up, L *pendere* to weigh, Gk *span* to draw, pull] **1 :** the distance from the end of the thumb to the end of the little finger of a spread hand; *also* **:** an English unit of length equal to 9 inches **2 :** an extent, stretch, reach, or spread between two limits: as **a :** a limited space (as of time); *esp* **:** an individual's lifetime **b :** spread or extent between abutments or supports (as of a bridge); *also* **:** a portion thus supported **c :** the maximum distance laterally from tip to tip of an airplane

³span *vt* **spanned; span·ning 1 a :** to measure by or as if by the hand with fingers and thumb extended **b :** MEASURE **2 a :** to extend across <his career *spanned* four decades> **b :** to form an arch over <a small bridge *spanned* the pond> **c :** to place or construct a span over **3 :** to be capable of forming any element of under given operations <a set of vectors that ~*s* a vector space>

⁴span *n* [D, fr. MD, fr. *spannen* to hitch up] **:** a pair of animals (as mules) usu. matched in appearance and action and driven together

Span *abbr* Spanish

span·drel *or* **span·dril** \'span-drəl\ *n* [ME *spandrell,* fr. AF *spaundre,* fr. OF *espandre* to spread out — more at SPAWN] **1 :** the sometimes ornamented space between the right or left exterior curve of an arch and an enclosing right angle **2 :** the triangular space beneath the string of a stair

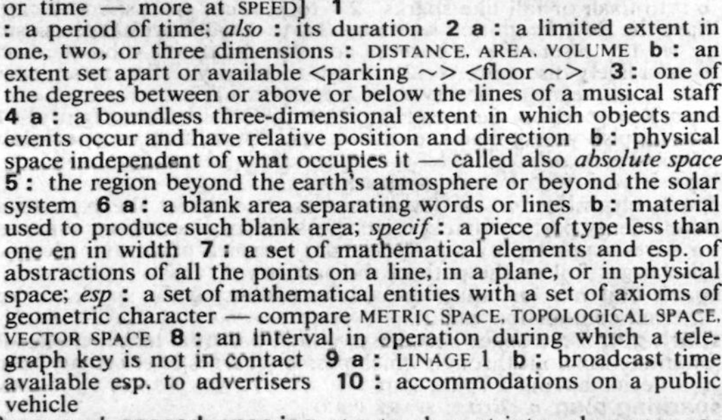

1, spandrels 1

spang \'spaŋ\ *adv* [Sc *spang* to leap, cast, bang] **1 :** to a complete degree **2 :** in an exact or direct manner **:** SQUARELY

¹span·gle \'spaŋ-gəl\ *n* [ME *spangel,* dim. of *spang* shiny ornament, prob. of Scand origin; akin to ON *spöng* spangle; akin to OE *spang* buckle, MD *spannen* to stretch] **1 :** a small plate of shining metal or plastic used for ornamentation esp. on clothing **2 :** a small glittering object or particle

²spangle *vb* **span·gled; span·gling** \'spaŋ-g(ə-)liŋ\ *vt* **:** to set or sprinkle with or as if with spangles ~ *vi* **:** to glitter as if covered with spangles **:** SPARKLE

Span·iard \'span-yərd\ *n* [ME *Spaignard,* fr. MF *Espaignart,* fr. *Espaigne* Spain, fr. L *Hispania*] **:** a native or inhabitant of Spain

span·iel \'span-yəl *also* 'span-ᵊl\ *n* [ME *spaniell,* fr. MF *espaignol,* lit., Spaniard, fr. (assumed) VL *Hispaniolus,* fr. L *Hispania* Spain] **1 :** any of numerous small or medium-sized mostly short-legged dogs usu. having long wavy hair, feathered legs and tail, and large drooping ears **2 :** a fawning servile person

Span·ish \'span-ish\ *n* [*Spanish*, adj., fr. ME *Spainish*, fr. *Spain*] **1 :** the Romance language of the largest part of Spain and of the countries colonized by Spaniards **2** *pl in constr* **:** the people of Spain — **Spanish** *adj*

Spanish American *n* **1 :** a native or inhabitant of one of the countries of America in which Spanish is the national language **2 :** a resident of the U.S. whose native language is Spanish and whose culture is of Spanish origin — **Spanish-American** *adj*

Spanish bayonet *n* **:** any of several yuccas; *esp* **:** one (*Yucca aloifolia*) with a short trunk and rigid spine-tipped leaves

Spanish chestnut *n* **:** MARRON

Spanish fly *n* **1 :** a green blister beetle (*Lytta vesicatoria*) of southern Europe **2 :** CANTHARIS 2

Spanish guitar *n* **:** GUITAR

Spanish heel *n* **:** a high covered wooden heel having a straight forepart

Spanish influenza *n* **:** pandemic influenza

Spanish mackerel *n* **:** any of various usu. large fishes (esp. genus *Scomberomorus*) chiefly of warm seas that resemble or are related to the common mackerel; *esp* **:** one (*S. maculatus*) that is bluish above with oval brown spots on the sides and is found off the American Atlantic coast from Cape Ann to Brazil

Spanish moss *n* **:** an epiphytic plant (*Tillandsia usneoides*) of the pineapple family forming pendent tufts of grayish green filaments on trees in the southern U.S. and the West Indies

Spanish moss on a tree

Spanish needles *n pl but sing or pl in constr* **:** a bur marigold (esp. *Bidens bipinnata*) of the eastern U.S.

Spanish omelet *n* **:** an omelet served with a sauce containing chopped green pepper, onion, and tomato

Spanish paprika *n* **1 :** PIMIENTO 1 **2 :** a paprika produced from pimientos usu. grown in Spain

Spanish rice *n* **:** rice cooked with onions, green pepper, and tomatoes

[1]**spank** \'spaŋk\ *vt* [imit.] **:** to strike esp. on the buttocks with the open hand — **spank** *n*

[2]**spank** *vi* [back-formation fr. *spanking*] **:** to move quickly, dashingly, or spiritedly <~*ing* along in his new car>

span·ker \'spaŋ-kər\ *n* [origin unknown] **1 :** the fore-and-aft sail on the mast nearest the stern of a square-rigged ship **2 :** the sail on the sternmost mast in a schooner of four or more masts

[1]**spank·ing** \'spaŋ-kiŋ\ *adj* [origin unknown] **1 :** remarkable of its kind **2 :** being fresh and strong **:** BRISK

[2]**spanking** *adv* **:** VERY <a ~ clean floor> <a ~ new car>

span·ner \'span-ər\ *n* [G, instrument for winding springs, fr. *spannen* to stretch; akin to MD *spannen* to stretch — more at SPAN] **1** *chiefly Brit* **:** WRENCH **2 :** a wrench that has a hole, projection, or hook at one or both ends of the head for engaging with a corresponding device on the object that is to be turned

span–new \'span-'n(y)ü\ *adj* [ME, part trans. of ON *spānnȳr*, fr. *spānn* chip of wood + *nȳr* new] **:** BRAND-NEW

span·worm \'span-,wərm\ *n* [[3]*span*] **:** LOOPER 1

[1]**spar** \'spär\ *n* [ME *sparre*; akin to OE *spere* spear] **1 :** a stout pole **2 a :** a stout rounded wood or metal piece (as a mast, boom, gaff, or yard) used to support rigging **b (1) :** one of the main longitudinal members of the wing of an airplane that carry the ribs **(2) :** LONGERON

[2]**spar** *vi* **sparred; spar·ring** [prob. alter. of [2]*spur*] **1 :** to strike or fight with feet or spurs in the manner of a gamecock **2 a :** BOX; *esp* **:** to gesture without landing a blow to draw one's opponent or create an opening **b :** to engage in a practice or exhibition bout of boxing **3 :** SKIRMISH, WRANGLE

[3]**spar** *n* **1 :** a movement of offense or defense in boxing **2 :** a sparring match or session

[4]**spar** *n* [LG; akin to OE *spærstān* gypsum, *spæren* of plaster] **:** any of various nonmetallic usu. cleavable and lustrous minerals

Spar \'spär\ *n* [*S*emper *Par*atus, motto of the U.S. Coast Guard, fr. NL, always ready] **:** a member of the women's reserve of the U.S. Coast Guard

[1]**spare** \'spa(ə)r, 'spe(ə)r\ *vb* **spared; spar·ing** [ME *sparen*, fr. OE *sparian*; akin to OHG *sparōn* to spare, OE *spær*, adj., spare] *vt* **1 :** to forbear to destroy, punish, or harm **2 :** to refrain from attacking or reprimanding with necessary or salutary severity **3 :** to relieve of the necessity of doing or undergoing something <~ yourself the trouble> **4 :** to refrain from **:** AVOID <*spared* no expense> **5 :** to use or dispense frugally — used chiefly in the negative <don't ~ the syrup> **6 a :** to give up as not strictly needed <do you have any cash to ~> **b :** to have left over or as margin <time to ~> ~ *vi* **1 :** to be frugal **2 :** to refrain from doing harm **:** be lenient — **spare·able** \-ə-bəl\ *adj* — **spar·er** *n*

[2]**spare** *adj* **spar·er; spar·est** [ME, fr. OE *spær*; akin to OSlav *sporŭ* abundant, OE *spēd* prosperity — more at SPEED] **1 :** not being used; *esp* **:** held for emergency use <a ~ tire> **2 :** being over and above what is needed **:** SUPERFLUOUS <~ time> **3 :** not liberal or profuse **:** SPARING <a ~ prose style> **4 :** healthily lean **5 :** not abundant or plentiful ***syn* 1** see LEAN ***ant*** corpulent **2** see MEAGER ***ant*** profuse — **spare·ly** *adv* — **spare·ness** *n*

[3]**spare** *n* **1 a :** a spare tire **b :** a duplicate (as a key or shirt) kept in reserve **2 :** the knocking down of all 10 pins with the first 2 balls in a frame in bowling

spare·ribs \'spa(ə)r-,(r)ibz, 'spe(ə)r-, -əbz\ *n pl* [by folk etymology fr. LG *ribbesper* pickled pork ribs roasted on a spit, fr. MLG, fr. *ribbe* rib + *sper* spear, spit] **:** a cut of pork ribs separated from the bacon strip

sparge \'spärj\ *vt* **sparged; sparg·ing** [prob. fr. MF *espargier*, fr. L *spargere* to scatter] **1 :** SPRINKLE, BESPATTER; *esp* **:** SPRAY **2 :** to agitate (a liquid) by means of compressed air or gas entering through a pipe — **sparge** *n* — **sparg·er** *n*

spar·ing \'spa(ə)r-iŋ, 'spe(ə)r-\ *adj* **1 :** marked by or practicing careful restraint (as in the use of resources) **2 :** MEAGER, BARE <the map is ~ of information> — **spar·ing·ly** \-iŋ-lē\ *adv*

syn SPARING, FRUGAL, THRIFTY, ECONOMICAL *shared meaning element* **:** careful in the use of money or resources ***ant*** lavish

[1]**spark** \'spärk\ *n* [ME *sparke*, fr. OE *spearca*; akin to MD *sparke* spark, L *spargere* to scatter, Gk *spargan* to swell] **1 a :** a small particle of a burning substance thrown out by a body in combustion or remaining when combustion is nearly completed **b :** a hot glowing particle struck from a larger mass; *esp* **:** one heated by friction <produce a ~ by striking flint with steel> **2 a :** a luminous disruptive electrical discharge of very short duration between two conductors separated by a gas (as air) **b :** the discharge in a spark plug **c :** the mechanism controlling the discharge in a spark plug **3 :** SPARKLE, FLASH **4 :** something that sets off a sudden force <provided the ~ that helped the team to rally> **5 :** a latent particle capable of growth or developing **:** GERM <still retains a ~ of decency> **6** *pl but sing in constr* **:** a radio operator on a ship

[2]**spark** *vb* [ME *sparken*, fr. *sparke*] *vi* **1 a :** to throw out sparks **b :** to flash or fall like sparks **2 :** to produce sparks; *specif* **:** to have the electric ignition working **3 :** to respond with enthusiasm ~ *vt* **1 :** to set off in a burst of activity **:** ACTIVATE <the question ~*ed* a lively discussion> **2 :** to stir to activity **:** INCITE <a player can ~ his team to victory> — **spark·er** *n*

[3]**spark** *n* [perh. of Scand origin; akin to ON *sparkr* sprightly] **1 :** a foppish young man **:** GALLANT **2 :** LOVER, BEAU — **spark·ish** \'spär-kish\ *adj*

[4]**spark** *vb* **:** WOO, COURT — **spark·er** *n*

spark chamber *n* **:** a device usu. used to detect the path of a high-energy particle that consists of a series of charged metal plates or wires separated by a gas (as neon) in which observable electric discharges follow the path of the particle

spark coil *n* **:** an induction coil for producing the spark for an internal-combustion engine

spark gap *n* **:** a space between two high-potential terminals (as of an induction coil) through which pass discharges of electricity; *also* **:** a device having a spark gap

sparking plug *n, Brit* **:** SPARK PLUG

[1]**spar·kle** \'spär-kəl\ *vb* **spar·kled; spar·kling** \-k(ə-)liŋ\ [ME *sparklen*, freq. of *sparken* to spark] *vi* **1 a :** to throw out sparks **b :** to give off or reflect bright moving points of light **c :** to perform brilliantly **2 :** EFFERVESCE <wine that ~*s*> **3 :** to become lively or animated <the dialogue ~*s* with wit> <eyes *sparkling* with anger> ~ *vt* **:** to cause to glitter or shine ***syn*** see FLASH

[2]**sparkle** *n* [ME, dim. of *sparke*] **1 :** a little spark **:** SCINTILLATION **2 :** the quality of sparkling **3 a :** ANIMATION, LIVELINESS **b :** the quality or state of being effervescent

spar·kler \'spär-klər\ *n* **:** one that sparkles: as **a :** DIAMOND **b :** a firework that throws off brilliant sparks on burning

sparkling wine *n* **:** an effervescent red or white table wine containing on the average 12 percent alcohol by volume

spark plug *n* **1 :** a part that fits into the cylinder head of an internal-combustion engine and carries two electrodes separated by an air gap across which the current from the ignition system discharges to form the spark for combustion **2 :** one that initiates or gives impetus to an undertaking — **spark·plug** \'spärk-,pləg\ *vt*

spark transmitter *n* **:** a radio transmitter that utilizes the discharge of a condenser through a spark gap as a source of its alternating-current power

sparky \'spär-kē\ *adj* **spark·i·er; -est :** marked by animation **:** LIVELY — **spark·i·ly** \-kə-lē\ *adv*

spar·ling \'spär-liŋ, -lən\ *n, pl* **sparling** *or* **sparlings** [ME *sperling*, fr. MF *esperling*, fr. MD *spierlinc*, fr. *spier* shoot, blade of grass] **:** a European smelt (*Osmerus eperlanus*)

sparring partner *n* **:** a boxer's companion for practice in sparring during training

spar·row \'spar-(,)ō, -ə(-w)\ *n* [ME *sparow*, fr. OE *spearwa*; akin to OHG *sparo* sparrow, Gk *psar* starling] **1 :** any of several small dull singing birds (genus *Passer* of the family Ploceidae) related to the finches; *esp* **:** ENGLISH SPARROW **2 :** any of various finches (as of the genera *Spezilla* or *Melospiza*) resembling the true sparrows

spar·row·grass \'spar-ə-,gras, -grəs\ *n* [by folk etymology fr. *asparagus*] *chiefly dial* **:** ASPARAGUS

sparrow hawk *n* **:** any of various small hawks or falcons (as the Old World *Accipiter nisus* or the No. American *Falco sparverius*)

sparse \'spärs\ *adj* **spars·er; spars·est** [L *sparsus* spread out, fr. pp. of *spargere* to scatter — more at SPARK] **:** of few and scattered elements; *esp* **:** not thickly grown or settled ***syn*** see MEAGER ***ant*** dense — **sparse·ly** *adv* — **sparse·ness** *n* — **spar·si·ty** \'spär-sət-ē, -stē\ *n*

Spar·ta·cist \'spärt-ə-səst\ *n* [G *Spartakist*, fr. *Spartakusbund*, lit., league of Spartakus, a revolutionary organization, fr. *Spartakus*, pen name of Karl Liebknecht, its cofounder] **:** a member of a revolutionary political group organized in Germany in 1918 and advocating extreme socialistic doctrines

[1]**Spar·tan** \'spärt-ᵊn\ *n* **1 :** a native or inhabitant of ancient Sparta **2 :** a person of great courage and fortitude — **Spar·tan·ism** \-,iz-əm\ *n*

[2]**Spartan** *adj* **1 :** of or relating to Sparta in ancient Greece **2 a :** marked by strict self-discipline or self-denial <a ~ athlete> **b :** marked by simplicity, frugality, or avoidance of luxury and comfort **c :** LACONIC **d :** undaunted by pain or danger

spar·te·ine \'spärt-ē-ən, 'spär-,tēn\ *n* [L *spartum* esparto, broom + ISV *-eine* — more at ESPARTO] **:** a liquid alkaloid $C_{15}H_{26}N_2$ extracted from the common broom and used in medicine in the form of its sulfate

spar varnish *n* [[1]*spar*] **:** an exterior waterproof varnish

spasm \'spaz-əm\ *n* [ME *spasme*, fr. MF, fr. L *spasmus*, fr. Gk *spasmos*, fr. *span* to draw, pull — more at SPAN] **1 :** an involuntary and abnormal muscular contraction **2 :** a sudden violent and temporary effort or emotion <a ~ of creativity>

spas·mod·ic \spaz-ˈmäd-ik\ *adj* [NL *spasmodicus,* fr. Gk *spasmōdēs,* fr. *spasmos*] **1 a :** relating to or affected or characterized by spasm **b :** resembling a spasm esp. in sudden violence <a ~ jerk> **2 :** acting or proceeding fitfully : INTERMITTENT **3 :** subject to outbursts of emotional excitement : EXCITABLE ***syn*** see FITFUL — **spas·mod·i·cal** \-i-kəl\ *adj* — **spas·mod·i·cal·ly** \-i-k(ə-)lē\ *adv*

[1]**spas·mo·lyt·ic** \ˌspaz-mə-ˈlit-ik\ *adj* [ISV *spasmo-* (fr. Gk *spasmos* spasm) + *-lytic* (fr. Gk *lytikos* able to loose) — more at LYTIC] : tending or having the power to relieve spasms or convulsions — **spas·mo·lyt·i·cal·ly** \-i-k(ə-)lē\ *adv*

[2]**spasmolytic** *n* : a spasmolytic agent

[1]**spas·tic** \ˈspas-tik\ *adj* [L *spasticus,* fr. Gk *spastikos* drawing in, fr. *span*] **1 :** of, relating to, or characterized by spasm <a ~ colon> **2 :** suffering from spastic paralysis <a ~ child> **3 :** SPASMODIC <a ~ influx of data> — **spas·ti·cal·ly** \-ti-k(ə-)lē\ *adv* — **spas·tic·i·ty** \spa-ˈstis-ət-ē\ *n*

[2]**spastic** *n* : one suffering from spastic paralysis

spastic paralysis *n* : paralysis with tonic spasm of the affected muscles and with increased tendon reflexes — compare CEREBRAL PALSY

[1]**spat** \ˈspat\ *past of* SPIT

[2]**spat** *n, pl* **spat** *or* **spats** [origin unknown] : a young oyster or other bivalve

[3]**spat** *n* [short for *spatterdash* (legging)] : a cloth or leather gaiter covering the instep and ankle

[4]**spat** *n* [prob. imit.] **1 :** a brief petty quarrel or angry outburst **2** *chiefly dial* : SLAP **3 :** a sound like that of rain falling in large drops <the ~ of bullets> ***syn*** see QUARREL

[5]**spat** *vb* **spat·ted; spat·ting** *vt, chiefly dial* : SLAP ~ *vi* **1 :** to quarrel pettily or briefly **2 :** to strike with a sound like that of rain falling in large drops

spate \ˈspāt\ *n* [ME] **1 :** FRESHET, FLOOD **2 a :** a large number or amount <a ~ of books on gardening> **b :** a sudden or strong outburst : RUSH <a ~ of anger>

spathe \ˈspāth\ *n* [NL *spatha,* fr. L, broad sword — more at SPADE] : a sheathing bract or pair of bracts enclosing an inflorescence and esp. a spadix on the same axis <the ~ of the calla>

spath·ic \ˈspath-ik\ *adj* [G *spath, spat* spar; akin to OHG *spān* chip — more at SPOON] : resembling spar : FOLIATED

spath·u·late \ˈspath-yə-lət\ *adj* [LL *spathula, spatula* spatula] : SPATULATE <~ petals of a flower>

spa·tial \ˈspā-shəl\ *adj* [L *spatium* space — more at SPEED] : relating to, occupying, or having the character of space — **spa·ti·al·i·ty** \ˌspā-shē-ˈal-ət-ē\ *n* — **spa·tial·ly** \ˈspāsh-(ə-)lē\ *adv*

spatial summation *n* : sensory summation that involves stimulation of several spatially separated neurons at the same time

spa·tio·tem·po·ral \ˌspā-shē-ō-ˈtem-p(ə-)rəl\ *adj* [L *spatium* + *tempor-, tempus* time — more at TEMPORAL] **1 :** having both spatial and temporal qualities **2 :** of or relating to space-time — **spa·tio·tem·po·ral·ly** \-ē\ *adv*

[1]**spat·ter** \ˈspat-ər\ *vb* [akin to Flem *spetteren* to spatter] *vt* **1 :** to splash with or as if with a liquid; *also* : to soil in this way <his coat was ~*ed* with mud> **2 :** to scatter by splashing <~ water> **3 :** to injure by aspersion : DEFAME <~ his good reputation> ~ *vi* : to spurt forth in scattered drops <blood ~*ing* everywhere>

[2]**spatter** *n* **1 a :** the act or process of spattering : the state of being spattered **b :** the noise of spattering **2 a :** a drop or splash spattered on something or a spot or stain due to spattering **b :** a small amount or number : SPRINKLE <a ~ of applause>

spat·ter·dock \ˈspat-ər-ˌdäk\ *n* : a common yellow No. American water lily (*Nuphar advenum*); *also* : a congeneric plant

spat·u·la \ˈspach-(ə-)lə\ *n* [LL, spoon, spatula — more at EPAULET] : a flat thin usu. metal implement used esp. for spreading or mixing soft substances, scooping, or lifting

spat·u·late \ˈspach-ə-lət\ *adj* : shaped like a spatula <a ~ leaf> <~ spines of a caterpillar>

spav·in \ˈspav-ən\ *n* [ME *spavayne,* fr. MF *espavain*] : SWELLING; *esp* : a bony enlargement of the hock of a horse associated with strain — **spav·ined** \-ənd\ *adj*

[1]**spawn** \ˈspón, ˈspän\ *vb* [ME *spawnen,* fr. AF *espaundre,* fr. OF *espandre* to spread out, expand; fr. L *expandere*] *vt* **1 a :** to produce or deposit (eggs) — used of an aquatic animal **b :** to induce (fish) to spawn **c :** to plant with mushroom spawn **2 :** to bring forth : GENERATE ~ *vi* **1 :** to deposit spawn **2 :** to produce young esp. in large numbers — **spawn·er** *n*

[2]**spawn** *n* **1 :** the eggs of aquatic animals (as fishes or oysters) that lay many small eggs **2 :** PRODUCT, OFFSPRING; *also* : numerous issue **3 :** the seed, germ, or source of something **4 :** mycelium esp. prepared (as in bricks) for propagating mushrooms

spay \ˈspā, *substand* \ˈspād\ *vt* **spayed** \ˈspād, *substand* ˈspād-əd\; **spay·ing** \ˈspā-iŋ, *substand* ˈspād-iŋ\ [ME *spayen,* fr. MF *espeer* to cut with a sword, fr. OF, fr. *espee* sword, fr. L *spatha* sword — more at SPADE] : to remove the ovaries of (a female animal)

SPCA *abbr* Society for the Prevention of Cruelty to Animals

SPCC *abbr* Society for the Prevention of Cruelty to Children

speak \ˈspēk\ *vb* **spoke** \ˈspōk\; **spo·ken** \ˈspō-kən\; **speak·ing** [ME *speken,* fr. OE *sprecan, specan;* akin to OHG *sprehhan* to speak, Gk *spharageisthai* to crackle] *vi* **1 a :** to utter words or articulate sounds with the ordinary voice : TALK **b (1) :** to express thoughts, opinions, or feelings orally **(2) :** to extend a greeting **(3) :** to be on speaking terms <still were not ~*ing* after the dispute> **c (1) :** to express oneself before a group **(2) :** to address one's remarks <~ to the issue> **2 a :** to make a written statement <his diaries . . . *spoke* . . . of his entrancement with death —Sy Kahn> **b :** to express oneself — often used in the phrase *so to speak* **c :** to serve as spokesman <*spoke* for the whole group> **3 a :** to express feelings by other than verbal means <actions ~ louder than words> **b :** SIGNAL **c :** to be interesting or attractive : APPEAL <great music . . . ~*s* directly to the emotions —A. N. Whitehead> **4 :** to make a request : ASK <*spoke* for the remaining piece of pie> **5 :** to make a characteristic or natural sound <all at once the thunder *spoke* —George Meredith> **6 a :** TESTIFY **b :** to be indicative or suggestive <his gold . . . *spoke* of riches in the land —Julian Dana> ~ *vt* **1 a (1) :** to utter with the speaking voice : PRONOUNCE **(2) :** to give a recitation of : DECLAIM **b :** to express orally : DECLARE <free to ~ their minds> **c :** ADDRESS, ACCOST; *esp* : HAIL **2 :** to make known in writing : STATE **3 :** to use or be able to use in speaking <~*s* Spanish> **4 :** to indicate by other than verbal means **5** *archaic* : DESCRIBE, DEPICT — **speak·able** \ˈspē-kə-bəl\ *adj*

syn SPEAK, TALK, CONVERSE *shared meaning element* : to articulate words so as to express one's thoughts

— **to speak of** : worthy of mention or notice — usu. used in negative constructions

speak·easy \ˈspē-ˌkē-zē\ *n, pl* **-eas·ies** : a place where alcoholic beverages are illegally sold

speak·er \ˈspē-kər\ *n* **1 a :** one that speaks **b :** one who makes a public speech **c :** one who acts as a spokesman **2 :** the presiding officer of a deliberative assembly <*Speaker* of the House of Representatives> **3 :** LOUDSPEAKER

speak·er·phone \ˈspē-kər-ˌfōn\ *n* : a combination microphone and loudspeaker device for two-way communication by telephone lines

speak·er·ship \-ˌship\ *n* : the position of speaker esp. of a legislative body

speak·ing \ˈspē-kiŋ\ *adj* **1 a :** that speaks : capable of speech **b :** containing chiefly native speakers of a (specified) language — usu. used in combination <English-*speaking* countries> **2 :** highly significant or expressive : ELOQUENT **3 :** resembling a living being or a real object

speaking tube *n* : a pipe through which conversation may be conducted (as between different parts of a building)

speak out *vi* **1 :** to speak loud enough to be heard **2 :** to speak boldly : express an opinion frankly <*spoke out* on the issues>

speak up *vi* **1 :** to speak loudly and distinctly **2 :** to express an opinion freely <*speak up* for truth and justice —Clive Bell>

spean \ˈspēn\ *vt* [MD *spenen*] *chiefly Scot* : WEAN

[1]**spear** \ˈspi(ə)r\ *n* [ME *spere,* fr. OE; akin to OHG *sper* spear, L *sparus,* Gk *sparos* gilthead] **1 :** a thrusting or throwing weapon with long shaft and sharp head or blade **2 :** a sharp-pointed instrument with barbs used in spearing fish **3 :** SPEARMAN

[2]**spear** *adj* [[1]*spear*] : PATERNAL, MALE <the ~ side of the family> — compare DISTAFF

[3]**spear** *vt* **1 :** to pierce, strike, or take with or as if with a spear <~ salmon> <~*ed* a chop from the platter> **2 :** to catch (as a baseball) with a sudden thrust of the arm ~ *vi* : to thrust at or wound something with or as if with a spear — **spear·er** *n*

[4]**spear** *n* [alter. of [1]*spire*] : a usu. young blade, shoot, or sprout (as of grass)

[5]**spear** *vi, of a plant* : to thrust a spear upward

[1]**spear·fish** \ˈspi(ə)r-ˌfish\ *n* : any of several large powerful pelagic fishes (genus *Tetrapturus*) related to the marlins and sailfishes

[2]**spearfish** *vi* : to fish with a spear

[1]**spear·head** \ˈspi(ə)r-ˌhed\ *n* **1 :** the sharp-pointed head of a spear **2 :** a leading element, force, or influence in an undertaking or development

[2]**spearhead** *vt* : to serve as leader or leading element of

spear·man \ˈspi(ə)r-mən\ *n* : one armed with a spear

spear·mint \-ˌmint, -mənt\ *n* : a common mint (*Mentha spicata*) grown for flavoring and esp. for its aromatic oil

spear·wort \-ˌwərt, -ˌwó(ə)rt\ *n* : any of several crowfoots (esp. *Ranunculus flammula*) with spear-shaped leaves

spec *abbr* **1** special **2** specifically

[1]**spe·cial** \ˈspesh-əl\ *adj* [ME, fr. OF or L; OF *especial,* fr. L *specialis* individual, particular, fr. *species* species] **1 :** distinguished by some unusual quality; *esp* : being in some way superior **2 :** held in particular esteem <a ~ friend> **3 a :** readily distinguishable from others of the same category : UNIQUE <they set it apart as a ~ day of thanksgiving> **b :** of, relating to, or constituting a species : SPECIFIC **4 :** being other than the usual : ADDITIONAL, EXTRA **5 :** designed for a particular purpose or occasion — **spe·cial·ly** \-(ə-)lē\ *adv* — **spe·cial·ness** *n*

syn SPECIAL, ESPECIAL, SPECIFIC, PARTICULAR, INDIVIDUAL *shared meaning element* : of or relating to one thing or class. SPECIAL implies differences that give the thing modified its distinctive quality, character, identity, or use <a *special* soap for dry skins> and may add a notion of superiority and then come close to *uncommon* or *exceptional* in meaning <a hereditary aristocracy with *special* privileges> ESPECIAL may add implications of preeminence or preference <his *especial* friend in that group> <a matter of *especial* importance> SPECIFIC basically implies unique and peculiar relationship to a kind or category or individual <*specific* nutritional needs of the aged> but in much of its use so stresses the notion of uniqueness as to obscure that of relationship <whether the *specific* freedoms we know and cherish . . . can be maintained —Sidney Hook> or even mean little more than explicitly mentioned or brought to attention <the policy covers only the *specific* losses mentioned above> PARTICULAR can replace *specific* in the last use and then stresses the distinctness of the thing as an individual; thus, one gives a *specific* illustration of a word's use but describes the *particular* applications of the word. In much of its use *particular* stands in opposition to *general* or *universal* in its stress on individuality <one is apt to amplify a *particular* judgment into a general opinion —Compton Mackenzie> INDIVIDUAL unequivocally refers to one of a class or group as distinct <it was not the magnitude or multiplicity of burdens that created martyrs and saints; it was the *individual* capacity to bear suffering —Harry Hervey>

2**special** *n* **1 :** something (as a television program) that is not part of a regular series **2 :** one that is used for a special service or occasion <caught the commuter ~ to work>

special act *n* **:** a legislative act applying only to particular persons or to a particular area

special assessment *n* **:** a specific tax levied on private property to meet the cost of public improvements that enhance the value of the property

special delivery *n* **:** expedited messenger delivery of mail matter for an extra fee

special district *n* **:** a political subdivision of a state established to provide a single public service (as water supply or sanitation) within a specific geographical area

special effects *n pl* **:** visual or acoustic effects introduced into a motion picture or a taped television production during laboratory processing

Special Forces *n pl* **:** a branch of the army composed of men specially trained in guerrilla warfare

special handling *n* **:** the handling of parcel-post or fourth-class mail as first-class but not as special-delivery matter for an extra postal fee

special interest *n* **:** a person or group having an interest in a particular part of the economy and receiving or seeking special advantages therein often to the detriment of the general public

spe·cial·ism \'spesh-ə-ˌliz-əm\ *n* **1 :** specialization in an occupation or branch of learning **2 :** a field of specialization **:** SPECIALTY

spe·cial·ist \'spesh-(ə-)ləst\ *n* **1 :** one who devotes himself to a special occupation or branch of learning **2 :** any of four enlisted ranks in the army corresponding to the grades of corporal through sergeant first class — **specialist** *or* **spe·cial·is·tic** \ˌspesh-ə-'lis-tik\ *adj*

spe·ci·al·i·ty \ˌspesh-ē-'al-ət-ē\ *n, pl* **-ties 1 :** a special mark or quality **2 :** a special object or class of objects **3 a :** a special aptitude or skill **b :** a particular occupation or branch of learning

spe·cial·iza·tion \ˌspesh-(ə-)lə-'zā-shən\ *n* **1 :** a making or becoming specialized **2 a :** structural adaptation of a body part to a particular function or of an organism for life in a particular environment **b :** a body part or an organism adapted by specialization

spe·cial·ize \'spesh-ə-ˌlīz\ *vb* **-ized; -iz·ing** *vt* **1 :** to make particular mention of **:** PARTICULARIZE **2 :** to apply or direct to a specific end or use <*specialized* his study> ~ *vi* **1 :** to concentrate one's efforts in a special activity or field **2 :** to undergo specialization; *esp* **:** to change adaptively <the sloth became highly *specialized* in the course of evolution>

specialized *adj* **1 :** designed or fitted for one particular purpose or occupation <~ personnel> **2 :** characterized by or exhibiting biological specialization; *esp* **:** highly differentiated esp. in a particular direction or for a particular end

special jury *n* **:** a jury chosen by the court upon request from a list of better educated or presumably more intelligent prospective jurors for a case involving complicated issues of fact or serious felonies — called also *blue-ribbon jury*

special pleading *n* **1 :** the allegation of special or new matter to offset the effect of matter pleaded by the opposite side and admitted, as distinguished from a direct denial of the matter pleaded **2 :** misleading argument that presents one point or phase as if it covered the entire question at issue

special privilege *n* **:** a privilege granted esp. by a law or constitution to an individual or group to the exclusion of others and in derogation of common right

special session *n* **:** an extraordinary session of a legislative body or a court

special theory of relativity : RELATIVITY 3a

spe·cial·ty \'spesh-əl-tē\ *n, pl* **-ties** [ME *specialte,* fr. MF *especialté,* fr. LL *specialitat-, specialitas,* fr. L *specialis* special] **1 :** a distinctive mark or quality **2 a :** a special object or class of objects: as **(1) :** a legal agreement embodied in a sealed instrument **(2) :** a product of a special kind or of special excellence <fried chicken was mother's ~> **b :** the state of being special, distinctive, or peculiar **3 :** something in which one specializes

spe·ci·ate \'spē-s(h)ē-ˌāt\ *vi* **-at·ed; -at·ing** [back-formation fr. *speciation,* fr. *species*] **:** to differentiate into new biological species — **spe·ci·a·tion** \ˌspē-s(h)ē-'ā-shən\ *n* — **spe·ci·a·tion·al** \-shnəl, -shən-ᵊl\ *adj*

1**spe·cie** \'spē-shē, -sē\ *n* [fr. *in specie,* fr. L, in kind] **:** money in coin — **in specie :** in the same or like form or kind <ready to return insult *in specie*>; *also* **:** in coin

2**specie** *n* [back-formation fr. *species* (taken as a pl.)] *substand* **:** SPECIES

1**spe·cies** \'spē-(ˌ)shēz, -(ˌ)sēz\ *n, pl* **species** [L, appearance, kind, species — more at SPY] **1 a :** a class of individuals having common attributes and designated by a common name; *specif* **:** a logical division of a genus or more comprehensive class **b :** KIND, SORT **c (1) :** a category of biological classification ranking immediately below the genus or subgenus, comprising related organisms or populations potentially capable of interbreeding, and being designated by a binomial that consists of the name of a genus followed by a Latin or latinized uncapitalized noun or adjective agreeing grammatically with the genus name **(2) :** an individual or kind belonging to a biological species **d :** a particular kind of atomic nucleus, atom, molecule, or ion **2 :** the consecrated eucharistic elements of the Roman Catholic or Eastern Orthodox eucharist **3 a :** a mental image; *also* **:** a sensible object **b :** an object of thought correlative with a natural object

2**species** *adj* **:** belonging to a biological species as distinguished from a horticultural variety <a ~ rose>

specif *abbr* specific; specifically

1**spe·cif·ic** \spi-'sif-ik\ *adj* [LL *specificus,* fr. L *species*] **1 a :** constituting or falling into a specifiable category **b :** sharing or being those properties of something that allow it to be referred to a particular category **2 a :** restricted by nature to a particular individual, situation, relation, or effect <a disease ~ to horses> **b :** exerting a distinctive influence (as on a body part or a disease) <~ antibodies> **3 :** free from ambiguity **:** ACCURATE <a ~ statement of faith> **4 :** of, relating to, or constituting a species and esp. a biologic species **5 a :** being any of various arbitrary physical constants and esp. one relating a quantitative attribute to unit mass, volume, or area **b :** imposed at a fixed rate per unit (as of weight or count) <~ import duties> — compare AD VALOREM *syn* **1** see SPECIAL *ant* generic **2** see EXPLICIT *ant* vague — **spe·cif·i·cal·ly** \-i-k(ə-)lē\ *adv*

2**specific** *n* **1 a :** something peculiarly adapted to a purpose or use **b :** a drug or remedy having a specific mitigating effect on a disease **2 a :** a characteristic quality or trait **b :** DETAILS, PARTICULARS — usu. used in pl. <haggling over the legal and financial ~*s* of independence —*Time*> **c** *pl* **:** SPECIFICATION 2a

spec·i·fi·ca·tion \ˌspes-(ə-)fə-'kā-shən\ *n* **1 :** the act or process of specifying **2 a :** a detailed precise presentation of something or of a plan or proposal for something — usu. used in pl. **b :** a statement of legal particulars (as of charges or of contract terms); *also* **:** a single item of such statement **c :** a written description of an invention for which a patent is sought

specific character *n* **:** a character distinguishing one species from another or from every other species of the same genus

specific epithet *n* **:** the Latin or latinized noun or adjective that follows the genus name in a taxonomic binomial

specific gravity *n* **:** the ratio of the density of a substance to the density of a substance (as pure water or hydrogen) taken as a standard when both densities are obtained by weighing in air

specific heat *n* **1 :** the ratio of the quantity of heat required to raise the temperature of a body one degree to that required to raise the temperature of an equal mass of water one degree **2 :** the heat in calories required to raise the temperature of one gram of a substance one degree centigrade

specific impulse *n* **:** the thrust produced per unit rate of consumption of the propellant that is usu. expressed in pounds of thrust per pound of propellant used per second and that is a measure of the efficiency of a rocket engine

spec·i·fic·i·ty \ˌspes-ə-'fis-ət-ē\ *n* **:** the quality or condition of being specific: as **a :** the condition of being peculiar to a particular individual or group of organisms <host ~ of a parasite> **b :** the condition of participating in or catalyzing only one or a few chemical reactions <the ~ of an enzyme>

specific performance *n* **1 :** the performance of a legal contract strictly or substantially according to its terms **2 :** an equitable remedy enjoining specific performance

spec·i·fy \'spes-ə-ˌfī\ *vt* **-fied; -fy·ing** [ME *specifien,* fr. OF *specifier,* fr. LL *specificare,* fr. *specificus*] **1 :** to name or state explicitly or in detail **2 :** to include as an item in a specification *syn* see MENTION — **spec·i·fi·able** \-ˌfī-ə-bəl\ *adj* — **spec·i·fi·er** \-ˌfī(-ə)r\ *n*

spec·i·men \'spes-(ə-)mən\ *n* [L, fr. *specere* to look at, look] **1 :** an item or part typical of a group or whole **2 a :** something that obviously belongs to a particular category but is noticed by reason of an individual distinguishing characteristic <a snub-nosed scraggly yellowish ~ of canine —*Boys' Life*> **b :** PERSON, INDIVIDUAL <he's a tough ~> *syn* see INSTANCE

spe·ci·os·i·ty \ˌspē-shē-'äs-ət-ē\ *n* **:** the quality or state of being specious **:** SPECIOUSNESS

spe·cious \'spē-shəs\ *adj* [ME, fr. L *speciosus* beautiful, plausible, fr. *species*] **1** *obs* **:** SHOWY **2 :** having deceptive attraction or allure **3 :** having a false look of truth or genuineness **:** SOPHISTICAL *syn* see PLAUSIBLE — **spe·cious·ly** *adv* — **spe·cious·ness** *n*

1**speck** \'spek\ *n* [ME *specke,* fr. OE *specca*] **1 :** a small discoloration or spot esp. from stain or decay **2 :** a very small amount **:** BIT **3 :** something marked or marred with specks

2**speck** *vt* **:** to produce specks on or in

1**speck·le** \'spek-əl\ *n* [ME; akin to OE *specca*] **:** a little speck (as of color)

2**speckle** *vt* **speck·led; speck·ling** \-(ə-)liŋ\ **1 :** to mark with speckles **2 :** to be distributed in or on like speckles

speckled perch *n* **:** BLACK CRAPPIE

specs \'speks\ *n pl* **1** [contr. of *spectacles*] **:** EYEGLASSES **2** [by contr.] **:** SPECIFICATIONS

spec·ta·cle \'spek-ti-kəl; *oftenest for 2, 3* -ˌtik-əl\ *n* [ME, fr. MF, fr. L *spectaculum,* fr. *spectare* to watch, fr. *spectus,* pp. of *specere* to look, look at — more at SPY] **1 a :** something exhibited to view as unusual, notable, or entertaining; *esp* **:** an eye-catching or dramatic public display **b :** an object of curiosity or contempt <made a ~ of herself> **2** *pl* **:** EYEGLASSES **3 :** something (as natural markings on an animal) suggesting a pair of glasses

spec·ta·cled \-ti-kəld, -ˌtik-əld\ *adj* **1 :** having or wearing spectacles **2 :** having markings suggesting a pair of spectacles <a ~ alligator>

1**spec·tac·u·lar** \spek-'tak-yə-lər, spək-\ *adj* [L *spectaculum*] **:** of, relating to, or constituting a spectacle **:** STRIKING, SENSATIONAL <a ~ display of fireworks> — **spec·tac·u·lar·ly** *adv*

2**spectacular** *n* **:** something that is spectacular

spec·tate \'spek-ˌtāt\ *vi* **spec·tat·ed; spec·tat·ing** [back-formation fr. *spectator*] **:** to be present as a spectator (as at a sports event)

spec·ta·tor \'spek-ˌtāt-ər, spek-'\ *n* [L, fr. *spectatus,* pp. of *spectare* to watch] **:** one who looks on or watches **:** ONLOOKER — **spectator** *adj* — **spec·ta·tress** \spek-'tā-trəs, 'spek-ˌ\ *n*

spec·ter *or* **spec·tre** \'spek-tər\ *n* [F *spectre,* fr. L *spectrum* appearance, specter, fr. *specere* to look, look at — more at SPY] **1 :** a visible disembodied spirit **:** GHOST **2 :** something that haunts or perturbs the mind **:** PHANTASM <the ~ of hunger>

spec·tral \'spek-trəl\ *adj* **1 :** of, relating to, or suggesting a specter **:** GHOSTLY **2 :** of, relating to, or made by a spectrum — **spec·tral·i·ty** \spek-'tral-ət-ē\ *n* — **spec·tral·ly** \'spek-trə-lē\ *adv* — **spec·tral·ness** *n*

spectral line *n* **:** one of a series of linear images of the narrow slit of a spectrograph or similar instrument corresponding to a component of the spectrum of the radiation emitted by a particular source

spectro- *comb form* [NL *spectrum*] **:** spectrum <*spectro*scope>

spec·tro·flu·o·rom·e·ter \ˈspek-(ˌ)trō-ˌflu̇(-ə)r-ˈäm-ət-ər\ *or* **spec·tro·flu·o·rim·e·ter** \-ˈim-\ *n* [*spectr-* + *fluorometer*] : a device for measuring and recording fluorescence spectra — **spec·tro·flu·o·ro·met·ric** \-ˌflu̇(-ə)r-ə-ˈme-trik\ *adj* — **spec·tro·flu·o·rom·e·try** \-ˌflu̇(-ə)r-ˈäm-ə-trē\ *n*

spec·tro·gram \ˈspek-t(r)ə-ˌgram\ *n* [ISV] : a photograph or diagram of a spectrum

spec·tro·graph \-ˌgraf\ *n* [ISV] : an instrument for dispersing radiation (as electromagnetic radiation or sound waves) into a spectrum and photographing or mapping the spectrum — **spec·tro·graph·ic** \ˌspek-t(r)ə-ˈgraf-ik\ *adj* — **spec·tro·graph·i·cal·ly** \-i-k(ə-)lē\ *adv* — **spec·trog·ra·phy** \spek-ˈträg-rə-fē\ *n*

spec·tro·he·lio·gram \ˌspek-trō-ˈhē-lē-ə-ˌgram\ *n* : a photograph of the sun that is made by monochromatic light and shows the sun's faculae and prominences

spec·tro·he·lio·graph \-ˌgraf\ *n* [ISV] : an apparatus for making spectroheliograms — **spec·tro·he·li·og·ra·phy** \-ˌhē-lē-ˈäg-rə-fē\ *n*

spec·tro·he·lio·scope \-ˈhē-lē-ə-ˌskōp\ *n* [ISV] **1** : SPECTROHELIOGRAPH **2** : an instrument similar to a spectroheliograph used for visual as distinguished from photographic observations

spec·trom·e·ter \spek-ˈträm-ət-ər\ *n* [ISV] **1** : an instrument used in determining the index of refraction **2** : a spectroscope fitted for measurements of the spectra observed with it — **spec·tro·met·ric** \ˌspek-trə-ˈme-trik\ *adj* — **spec·trom·e·try** \spek-ˈträm-ə-trē\ *n*

spec·tro·pho·tom·e·ter \ˌspek-trō-fə-ˈtäm-ət-ər\ *n* [ISV] : a photometer for measuring the relative intensities of the light in different parts of a spectrum — **spec·tro·pho·to·met·ric** \-trə-ˌfōt-ə-ˈme-trik\ *or* **spec·tro·pho·to·met·ri·cal** \-tri-kəl\ *adj* — **spec·tro·pho·to·met·ri·cal·ly** \-tri-k(ə-)lē\ *adv* — **spec·tro·pho·tom·e·try** \ˌspek-(ˌ)trō-fə-ˈtäm-ə-trē\ *n*

spec·tro·scope \ˈspek-trə-ˌskōp\ *n* [ISV] : an instrument for forming and examining optical spectra — **spec·tro·scop·ic** \ˌspek-trə-ˈskäp-ik\ *or* **spec·tro·scop·i·cal** \-i-kəl\ *adj* — **spec·tro·scop·i·cal·ly** \-i-k(ə-)lē\ *adv* — **spec·tros·co·pist** \spek-ˈträs-kə-pəst\ *n*

spec·tros·co·py \spek-ˈträs-kə-pē\ *n* **1** : physics that deals with the theory and interpretation of interactions between matter and radiation (as electromagnetic radiation) **2** : the action of using a spectroscope

spec·trum \ˈspek-trəm\ *n, pl* **spec·tra** \-trə\ *or* **spectrums** [NL, fr. L, appearance — more at SPECTER] **1** : an array of the components of an emission or wave separated and arranged in the order of some varying characteristic (as wavelength, mass, or energy): as **a** : a series of images formed when a beam of radiant energy is subjected to dispersion and brought to focus so that the component waves are arranged in the order of their wavelengths (as when a beam of sunlight that is refracted and dispersed by a prism forms a display of colors) **b** : ELECTROMAGNETIC SPECTRUM **c** : RADIO SPECTRUM **d** : the range of frequencies of sound waves **2** : a continuous sequence or range <a wide ~ of interests>

spec·u·lar \ˈspek-yə-lər\ *adj* [L *specularis* of a mirror, fr. *speculum*] **1** : of, relating to, or having the qualities of a mirror **2** : conducted with the aid of a medical speculum — **spec·u·lar·i·ty** \ˌspek-yə-ˈlar-ət-ē\ *n* — **spec·u·lar·ly** \ˈspek-yə-lər-lē\ *adv*

spec·u·late \ˈspek-yə-ˌlāt\ *vi* **-lat·ed; -lat·ing** [L *speculatus*, pp. of *speculari* to spy out, examine, fr. *specula* watchtower, fr. *specere* to look, look at] **1 a** : to meditate on or ponder a subject : REFLECT **b** : to review something idly or casually and often inconclusively **2** : to assume a business risk in hope of gain; *esp* : to buy or sell in expectation of profiting from market fluctuations ***syn*** see THINK — **spec·u·la·tor** \-ˌlāt-ər\ *n*

spec·u·la·tion \ˌspek-yə-ˈlā-shən\ *n* : an act or instance of speculating: as **a** : assumption of unusual business risk in hopes of obtaining commensurate gain **b** : a transaction involving such speculation

spec·u·la·tive \ˈspek-yə-lət-iv, -ˌlāt-\ *adj* **1** : involving, based on, or constituting intellectual speculation; *also* : theoretical rather than demonstrable <~ knowledge> **2** : marked by questioning curiosity <gave him a ~ glance> ***syn*** see THEORETICAL

spec·u·lum \ˈspek-yə-ləm\ *n, pl* **-la** \-lə\ *also* **-lums** [L, mirror, fr. *specere*] **1** : an instrument inserted into a body passage for inspection or medication **2 a** : an ancient mirror usu. of bronze or silver **b** : a reflector in an optical instrument **3** : a medieval compendium of all knowledge **4** : a drawing or table showing the relative positions of all the planets (as in an astrological nativity) **5** : a patch of color on the secondaries of most ducks and some other birds

speech \ˈspēch\ *n* [ME *speche*, fr. OE *sprǣc*, *spǣc*; akin to OE *sprecan* to speak — more at SPEAK] **1 a** : the communication or expression of thoughts in spoken words **b** : exchange of spoken words : CONVERSATION **2 a** : something that is spoken : UTTERANCE **b** : a public discourse : ADDRESS **3 a** : LANGUAGE, DIALECT **b** : an individual manner or style of speaking **4** : the power of expressing or communicating thoughts by speaking

speech community *n* : a group of people sharing characteristic patterns of vocabulary, grammar, and pronunciation

speech form *n* : LINGUISTIC FORM

speech·ify \ˈspē-chə-ˌfī\ *vi* **-ified; -ify·ing** : to make a speech

speech·less \ˈspēch-ləs\ *adj* **1** : unable to speak : DUMB **2** : not speaking : SILENT **3** : not capable of being expressed in words — **speech·less·ly** *adv* — **speech·less·ness** *n*

[1]**speed** \ˈspēd\ *n* [ME *spede*, fr. OE *spēd*; akin to OHG *spuot* prosperity, speed, L *spes* hope, *spatium* space] **1** *archaic* : prosperity in an undertaking : SUCCESS **2 a** : the act or state of moving swiftly : SWIFTNESS **b** : rate of motion: as (1) : VELOCITY (2) : the magnitude of a velocity irrespective of direction **c** : IMPETUS **3** : swiftness or rate of performance or action **4 a** : the sensitivity of a photographic film, plate, or paper expressed numerically **b** : the light-gathering power of a lens or optical system **c** : the time during which a camera shutter is open **5** : a transmission gear in automotive vehicles **6** : someone or something that appeals to one's taste **7** : METHAMPHETAMINE; *also* : a related drug ***syn*** see HASTE

[2]**speed** *vb* **sped** \ˈsped\ *or* **speed·ed; speed·ing** *vi* **1 a** : to prosper in an undertaking **b** : to get along : FARE **2 a** : to make haste <*sped* to her bedside> **b** : to go or drive at excessive or illegal speed **3** : to move, work, or take place faster : ACCELERATE <the heart ~*s* up> ~ *vt* **1 a** *archaic* : to cause or help to prosper : AID **b** : to further the success of **2 a** : to cause to move quickly : HASTEN **b** : to wish Godspeed to **c** : to increase the speed of : ACCELERATE <~*ed* up the engine> **3** : to send out <~ an arrow> — **speed·er** *n* — **speed·ster** \ˈspēd-stər\ *n*

[1]**speed·ball** \ˈspēd-ˌbȯl\ *n* : a game which resembles soccer but in which a ball that is caught in the air may be passed with the hands and in which scoring is accomplished by kicking or heading the ball between the goalposts or by a successful forward pass over the goal line

[2]**speedball** *n, slang* : cocaine mixed with heroin or morphine or an amphetamine and usu. taken by injection

speed·boat \-ˌbōt\ *n* : a fast launch or motorboat

speed·boat·ing \-iŋ\ *n* : the act, art, or sport of managing a speedboat — **speed·boat·er** \-ər\ *n*

speed freak *n* : one who habitually misuses amphetamines and esp. methamphetamine

speed·light \ˈspēd-ˌlīt\ *n* : STROBOTRON

speed limit *n* : the maximum speed permitted by law in a given area under specified circumstances

speed·om·e·ter \spi-ˈdäm-ət-ər\ *n* **1** : an instrument for indicating speed : TACHOMETER **2** : an instrument for indicating distance traversed as well as speed of travel; *also* : ODOMETER

speed–read·ing \ˈspēd-ˌrēd-iŋ\ *n* : a method of reading rapidly by skimming — **speed–read** *vt*

speed shop *n* : a shop that sells custom automotive equipment esp. to hot-rodders

speed trap *n* : a stretch of road policed by often concealed officers or devices (as radar) so as to catch speeders

speed·up \ˈspēd-ˌəp\ *n* **1** : ACCELERATION **2** : an employer's demand for accelerated output without increased pay

speed·way \ˈspēd-ˌwā\ *n* **1** : a public road on which fast driving is allowed; *specif* : EXPRESSWAY **2** : a racecourse for automobiles or motorcycles **3** : a sprint race for motorcycles limited to a few contestants at one time

speed·well \ˈspēd-ˌwel\ *n* **1** : a perennial European herb (*Veronica officinalis*) of the figwort family with small bluish flowers in axillary racemes **2** : a plant congeneric with the speedwell

speedy \ˈspēd-ē\ *adj* **speed·i·er; -est** : marked by swiftness of motion or action ***syn*** see FAST ***ant*** dilatory — **speed·i·ly** \ˈspēd-ᵊl-ē\ *adv* — **speed·i·ness** \ˈspēd-ē-nəs\ *n*

speel \ˈspē(ə)l\ *vb, chiefly Scot* [origin unknown] : CLIMB

speer *or* **speir** \ˈspi(ə)r\ *vb* [ME (Sc) *speren*, fr. OE *spyrian* to seek after; akin to OE *spor* spoor] *chiefly Scot* : ASK, INQUIRE

speiss \ˈspīs\ *n* [G *speise*, lit., food, fr. (assumed) VL *spesa*, fr. LL *expensa* expense] : a mixture of impure metallic arsenides produced as a regulus in smelting certain ores

spe·le·ol·o·gy \ˌspē-lē-ˈäl-ə-jē, ˌspel-ē-\ *n* [L *speleum* cave (fr. Gk *spēlaion*) + ISV *-o-* + *-logy*] : the scientific study or exploration of caves — **spe·le·o·log·i·cal** \ˌspē-lē-ə-ˈläj-i-kəl, ˌspel-ē-\ *adj* — **spe·le·ol·o·gist** \ˌspē-lē-ˈäl-ə-jəst, ˌspel-ē-\ *n*

[1]**spell** \ˈspel\ *n* [ME, talk, tale, fr. OE; akin to OHG *spel* talk, tale, Gk *apeilē* boast] **1 a** : a spoken word or form of words held to have magic power : INCANTATION **b** : a state of enchantment **2** : a strong compelling influence or attraction

[2]**spell** *vt* : to put under a spell : BEWITCH

[3]**spell** *vb* **spelled** \ˈspeld, ˈspelt\; **spell·ing** [ME *spellen*, fr. OF *espeller*, of Gmc origin; akin to OE *spell* talk] *vt* **1** : to read slowly and with difficulty — often used with *out* **2 a** : to find out by study : come to understand <it requires some pains to ~ out those decorations —F. J. Mather> **b** : to present in detail : make comprehensible by careful elaboration <no one ~*ed* out the answer for all to read —Irving Kolodin> **3 a** : to name the letters of in order; *also* : to write or print the letters of in order **b** : to make up (a word) <what word do these letters ~> **4** : to add up to : MEAN <crop failure was likely to ~ stark famine —Stringfellow Barr> ~ *vi* : to form words with letters

[4]**spell** *vb* **spelled** \ˈspeld\; **spell·ing** [ME *spelen*, fr. OE *spelian*; akin to OE *spala* substitute] *vt* **1** : to take the place of for a time : RELIEVE <he and the other assistant . . . ~*ed* each other —Mary McCarthy> **2** : REST ~ *vi* **1** : to work in turns **2** *chiefly Austral* : to rest from work or activity for a time

[5]**spell** *n* **1 a** *archaic* : a shift of workers **b** : one's turn at work **2 a** : a period spent in a job or occupation **b** *chiefly Austral* : a period of rest from work, activity, or use **3 a** : an indeterminate period of time <waited a ~ before advancing> **b** : a stretch of a specified type of weather **4** : a period of bodily or mental distress or disorder <a ~ of coughing> <fainting ~*s*>

spell·bind \ˈspel-ˌbīnd\ *vt* **-bound** \-ˌbau̇nd\; **-bind·ing** [back-formation fr. *spellbound*] : to bind or hold by or as if by a spell or charm : FASCINATE

spell·bind·er \-ˌbīn-dər\ *n* : a speaker of compelling eloquence

spell·bound \-ˈbau̇nd\ *adj* : held by or as if by a spell

spell·down \ˈspel-ˌdau̇n\ *n* : a spelling contest in which each contestant is eliminated as soon as he misspells a word

spell down \(ˈ)spel-ˈdau̇n\ *vt* : to defeat in a spelldown

spell·er \ˈspel-ər\ *n* **1** : one who spells words **2** : a book with exercises for teaching spelling

spell·ing \ˈspel-iŋ\ *n* **1** : the forming of words from letters according to accepted usage : ORTHOGRAPHY **2** : a sequence of letters composing a word

spelling bee *n* : SPELLDOWN

spell out *vt* : to make plain <*spelled out* his orders in detail>
[1]**spelt** \'spelt\ *n* [ME, fr. OE, fr. LL *spelta,* of Gmc origin; akin to MHG *spelte* split piece of wood, OHG *spaltan* to split — more at SPILL] : a wheat (*Triticum spelta*) with lax spikes and spikelets containing two light red kernels — called also *speltz*
[2]**spelt** \'spelt\ *chiefly Brit past of* SPELL
spel·ter \'spel-tər\ *n* [prob. alter. of MD *speauter*] : ZINC; *esp* : zinc cast in slabs for commercial use
speltz \'spelts\ *n* [G *spelz,* fr. OHG *spelza,* fr. LL *spelta*] : SPELT
spe·lunk·er \spi-'ləŋ-kər, 'spē-,\ *n* [L *spelunca* cave, fr. Gk *spēlynx;* akin to Gk *spēlaion* cave] : one who makes a hobby of exploring and studying caves
spe·lunk·ing \-kiŋ\ *n* : the hobby or practice of exploring caves
spence \'spen(t)s\ *n* [ME, fr. MF *despense,* fr. ML *dispensa,* fr. L, fem. of *dispensus,* pp. of *dispendere* to weigh out — more at DISPENSE] *dial Brit* : PANTRY
[1]**spen·cer** \'spen(t)-sər\ *n* [George John, 2d earl *Spencer* †1834 E politician] : a short waist-length jacket
[2]**spencer** *n* [prob. fr. the name *Spencer*] : a trysail abaft the foremast or mainmast
[1]**Spen·ce·ri·an** \spen-'sir-ē-ən\ *adj* : of or relating to Herbert Spencer or Spencerianism
[2]**Spencerian** *adj* [Platt R. *Spencer* †1864 Am calligrapher] : of or relating to a form of slanting handwriting
Spen·ce·ri·an·ism \spen-'sir-ē-ə-,niz-əm\ *n* : the synthetic philosophy of Herbert Spencer that has as its central idea the mechanistic evolution of the cosmos from relative simplicity to relative complexity
spend \'spend\ *vb* **spent** \'spent\; **spend·ing** [ME *spenden,* fr. OE & OF; OE *spendan,* fr. L *expendere* to expend; OF *despendre,* fr. L *dispendere* to weigh out — more at DISPENSE] *vt* **1** : to use up or pay out : EXPEND **2 a** : to wear out : EXHAUST <the hurricane gradually *spent* itself> **b** : to consume wastefully : SQUANDER <the waters are not ours to ~ —J. R. Ellis> **3** : to cause or permit to elapse : PASS <*spent* the summer at the beach> **4** : to give up : SACRIFICE ~ *vi* **1** : to expend or waste wealth or strength **2** : to become expended or consumed — **spend·er** *n*
spend·able \'spen-də-bəl\ *adj* : available for spending
spending money *n* : POCKET MONEY
spend·thrift \'spen(d)-,thrift\ *n* : one who spends improvidently or wastefully — **spendthrift** *adj*
syn SPENDTHRIFT, PRODIGAL, PROFLIGATE, WASTER, WASTREL *shared meaning element* : a person who dissipates his resources foolishly and wastefully
Speng·le·ri·an \s(h)peŋ-'(g)lir-ē-ən\ *adj* : of or relating to the theory of world history developed by Oswald Spengler which holds that all major cultures undergo similar cyclical developments from birth to maturity to decay — **Spenglerian** *n*
Spen·se·ri·an sonnet \spen-,sir-ē-ən-\ *n* [Edmund *Spenser*] : a sonnet consisting of three interlocked quatrains and a couplet with a rhyme scheme *abab bcbc cdcd ee*
Spenserian stanza *n* : a stanza consisting of eight verses of iambic pentameter and an alexandrine with a rhyme scheme *ababbcbcc*
spent \'spent\ *adj* [ME, fr. pp. of *spenden* to spend] **1 a** : used up : CONSUMED **b** : exhausted of active or required components or qualities often for a particular purpose <~ grain that remains from wort production is a useful livestock feed> **2** : drained of energy or effectiveness : EXHAUSTED **3** : exhausted of spawn or sperm <a ~ salmon>
sperm \'spərm\ *n, pl* **sperm** *or* **sperms** [ME, fr. MF *esperme,* fr. LL *spermat-, sperma,* fr. Gk, lit., seed; akin to Gk *speirein* to sow — more at SPROUT] **1 a** : the male fecundating fluid : SEMEN **b** : a male gamete **2** : a product (as spermaceti or oil) of the sperm whale
sperm- *or* **spermo-** *or* **sperma-** *or* **spermi-** *comb form* [Gk *sperm-, spermo-,* fr. *sperma*] : seed : germ : sperm <*sperma*theca> <*sperm*ary> <*spermi*cidal>
sper·ma·ce·ti \,spər-mə-'sēt-ē, -'set-\ *n* [ME *sperma cete,* fr. ML *sperma ceti* whale sperm] : a waxy solid obtained from the oil of cetaceans and esp. sperm whales and used in ointments, cosmetics, and candles
sper·ma·go·ni·um \,spər-mə-'gō-nē-əm\ *n, pl* **-nia** \-nē-ə\ [NL] : a flask-shaped or depressed receptacle in which spermatia are produced in some fungi and lichens
sper·ma·ry \'spərm-(ə-)rē\ *n, pl* **-ries** [NL *spermarium,* fr. Gk *sperma*] : an organ in which male gametes are developed
spermat- *or* **spermato-** *comb form* [MF, fr. LL, fr. Gk, fr. *spermat-, sperma*] : seed : spermatozoon <*spermat*id> <*spermato*cyte>
sper·ma·the·ca \,spər-mə-'thē-kə\ *n* [NL] : a sac for sperm storage in the female reproductive tract of many lower animals — **sper·ma·the·cal** \-kəl\ *adj*
sper·mat·ic \(,)spər-'mat-ik\ *adj* **1** : relating to sperm or a spermary **2** : resembling, carrying, or full of sperm
spermatic cord *n* : a cord that suspends the testis within the scrotum and contains the vas deferens and vessels and nerves of the testis
sper·ma·tid \'spər-mət-əd\ *n* : one of the cells that are formed by division of the secondary spermatocytes and that differentiate into spermatozoa
sper·ma·ti·um \(,)spər-'mā-sh(e-ə)m\ *n, pl* **-tia** \-sh(ē-)ə\ [NL, fr. Gk *spermation,* dim. of *spermat-, sperma*] : a nonmotile cell functioning or held to function as a male gamete in some lower plants — **sper·ma·tial** \-sh(ē-)əl\ *adj*
sper·mato·cide \(,)spər-'mat-ə-,sīd\ *n* : an agent that kills sperm — **sper·mato·cid·al** \(,)spər-,mat-ə-'sīd-ᵊl\ *adj*
sper·mato·cyte \(,)spər-'mat-ə-,sīt\ *n* : a cell giving rise to sperm cells; *esp* : a cell of the last generation or next to the last generation preceding the spermatozoon
sper·mato·gen·e·sis \(,)spər-,mat-ə-'jen-ə-səs\ *n* [NL] : the process of male gamete formation including meiosis and transformation of the four resulting spermatids into spermatozoa — **sper·mato·ge·net·ic** \-jə-'net-ik\ *adj*
sper·mato·gen·ic \-'jen-ik\ *adj* : of, relating to, or constituting spermatogenesis
sper·mato·go·ni·um \-'gō-nē-əm\ *n, pl* **-nia** \-nē-ə\ [NL] : a primitive male germ cell — **sper·mato·go·ni·al** \-nē-əl\ *adj*
sper·mato·phore \(,)spər-'mat-ə-,fō(ə)r, -,fȯ(ə)r\ *n* [ISV] : a capsule, packet, or mass enclosing spermatozoa extruded by the male and conveyed to the female in the insemination of various lower animals
sper·mato·phyte \-,fīt\ *n* [deriv. of NL *spermat-* + Gk *phyton* plant — more at PHYT-] : any of a group (Spermatophyta) of higher plants comprising those that produce seeds and including the gymnosperms and angiosperms — **sper·mato·phyt·ic** \-,mat-ə-'fit-ik\ *adj*
sper·ma·to·zo·an \(,)spər-,mat-ə-'zō-ən, ,spər-mət-\ *n* : SPERMATOZOON — **spermatozoan** *adj*
sper·ma·to·zo·id \-'zō-əd\ *n* [ISV, fr. NL *spermatozoa*] : a male gamete of a plant motile by anterior cilia and usu. produced in an antheridium
sper·ma·to·zo·on \-'zō-,än, -'zō-ən\ *n, pl* **-zoa** \-'zō-ə\ [NL] **1** : a motile male gamete of an animal usu. with rounded or elongate head and a long posterior flagellum **2** : SPERMATOZOID — **sper·ma·to·zo·al** \-'zō-əl\ *adj*
sperm cell *n* : a male gamete : a male germ cell
sper·mi·cide \'spər-mə-,sīd\ *n* : SPERMATOCIDE — **sper·mi·cid·al** \,spər-mə-'sīd-ᵊl\ *adj*
sper·mi·dine \'spər-mə-,dēn\ *n* : a crystalline aliphatic amine $C_7H_{19}N_3$ which is found esp. in semen
sper·mio·gen·e·sis \,spər-mē-ō-'jen-ə-səs\ *n* [NL, fr. *spermium* spermatozoon + *-o-* + L *genesis*] **1** : transformation of a spermatid into a spermatozoon **2** : SPERMATOGENESIS
sperm nucleus *n* : either of two nuclei that derive from the generative nucleus of a pollen grain and function in the fertilization of a seed plant
sperm oil *n* : a pale yellow oil from the sperm whale
sper·mo·phile \'spər-mə-,fīl\ *n* [deriv. of Gk *sperma* seed + *philos* loving] : any of various burrowing rodents (as of the genus *Citellus*) that are related to the squirrels and live in colonies esp. in open areas, often damage crops, and include vectors of plague
sperm whale \'spərm-\ *n* [short for *spermaceti whale*] : a large toothed whale (*Physeter catodon*) with a large closed cavity in the head containing a fluid mixture of spermaceti and oil

sperm whale

-sper·my \,spər-mē\ *n comb form* [Gk *sperma* seed, sperm] : state of exhibiting or resulting from (such) a fertilization <agamo*spermy*>
sper·ry·lite \'sper-i-,līt\ *n* [Francis L. *Sperry,* 19th cent. Can chemist + E *-lite*] : a mineral $PtAs_2$ consisting of a platinum arsenide occurring near Sudbury, Ontario, in grains and minute isometric crystals of a bluish white color
spes·sar·tite \'spes-ər-,tīt\ *also* **spec·sar·tine** \-,tēn\ *n* [F, fr. *Spessart* mountain range, Germany] : a manganese aluminum garnet usu. containing other elements (as iron and magnesium) in minor amounts
[1]**spew** \'spyü\ *vb* [ME *spewen,* fr. OE *spīwan;* akin to OHG *spīwan* to spit, L *spuere,* Gk *ptyein*] *vi* **1** : VOMIT **2** : to come forth in a flood or gush <pornography ~*ing* from the presses> **3** : to ooze out as if under pressure : EXUDE ~ *vt* **1** : VOMIT **2** : to send or cast forth with vigor or violence or in great quantity <glaciers that ~*ed* crashing bergs into the ocean —Jean Potter> — **spew·er** *n*
[2]**spew** *n* **1** : matter that is vomited : VOMIT **2** : material that exudes or is extruded
sp gr *abbr* specific gravity
sphag·nous \'sfag-nəs\ *adj* : of, relating to, or abounding in sphagnum
sphag·num \'sfag-nəm\ *n* [NL, genus name, fr. L *sphagnos,* a moss, fr. Gk] **1** : any of a large genus (*Sphagnum,* coextensive with the order Sphagnales) of atypical mosses that grow only in wet acid areas where their remains become compacted with other plant debris to form peat **2** : a mass of sphagnum plants
sphal·er·ite \'sfal-ə-,rīt\ *n* [G *sphalerit,* fr. Gk *sphaleros* deceitful, fr. *sphallein* to cause to fall; fr. its often being mistaken for galeria — more at SPILL] : a widely distributed ore of zinc composed essentially of zinc sulfide ZnS

sphagnum 1

sphene \'sfēn\ *n* [F *sphène,* fr. Gk *sphēn* wedge — more at SPOON] : a mineral $CaTiSiO_5$ that is a silicate of calcium and titanium and often contains other elements
sphen·odon \'sfē-nə-,dän, 'sfen-ə-\ *n* [NL, deriv. of Gk *sphēn* wedge + *odōn* tooth — more at TOOTH] : TUATARA — **sphen·odont** \-,dänt\ *adj*
[1]**sphe·noid** \'sfē-,nȯid\ *or* **sphe·noi·dal** \sfi-'nȯid-ᵊl\ *adj* [NL *sphenoides,* fr. Gk *sphēnoeidēs* wedge-shaped, fr. *sphēn* wedge] **1** : of, relating to, or being a winged compound bone of the base of the cranium **2** *usu sphenoidal* : wedge-shaped
[2]**sphenoid** *n* : a sphenoid bone
sphe·nop·sid \sfi-'näp-səd\ *n* [deriv. of Gk *sphēn* wedge + NL *-opsis*] : any of a subdivision (Sphenopsida) of the tracheophytes characterized by jointed stems, small leaves usu. in whorls at distinct stem nodes, and sporangia in sporangiophores and made up of the equisetums and extinct related forms

spher- *or* **sphero-** *also* **sphaer-** *or* **sphaero-** *comb form* [L *sphaer-*, fr. Gk *sphair-*, *sphairo-*, fr. *sphaira* sphere] : sphere <*spher*ule> <*sphero*meter>

spher·al \'sfir-əl\ *adj* **1 :** SPHERICAL **2 :** SYMMETRICAL, HARMONIOUS

1sphere \'sfi(ə)r\ *n* [ME *spere* globe, celestial sphere, fr. MF *espere*, fr. L *sphaera*, fr. Gk *sphaira*, lit., ball] **1 a** (1) **:** the apparent surface of the heavens of which half forms the dome of the visible sky (2) **:** one of the concentric and eccentric revolving spherical transparent shells in which according to ancient astronomy stars, sun, planets, and moon are set **b :** a globe depicting such a sphere; *broadly* **:** GLOBE a **2 a :** a globular body **:** BALL **b :** PLANET, STAR **c** (1) **:** a solid that is bounded by a surface consisting of all points at a given distance from a point constituting its center — see VOLUME table (2) **:** the bounding surface of a sphere **3 :** natural, normal, or proper place; *esp* **:** social order or rank **4 a** *obs* **:** ORBIT **b :** a field or range of influence or significance — **spher·ic** \'sfi(ə)r-ik, 'sfer-\ *adj* — **sphe·ric·i·ty** \sfir-'is-ət-ē\ *n*

2sphere *vt* **sphered; spher·ing 1 :** to place in a sphere or among the spheres **:** ENSPHERE **2 :** to form into a sphere

sphere of influence : a territorial area within which the political influence or the interests of one nation are held to be more or less paramount

spher·i·cal \'sfir-i-kəl, 'sfer-\ *adj* **1 :** having the form of a sphere or of one of its segments **2 :** relating to or dealing with a sphere or its properties — **spher·i·cal·ly** \-k(ə-)lē\ *adv*

spherical aberration *n* **:** aberration that is caused by the spherical form of a lens or mirror and that gives different foci for central and marginal rays

spherical angle *n* **:** the angle between two intersecting arcs of great circles of a sphere measured by the plane angle formed by the tangents to the arcs at the point of intersection

spherical coordinate *n* **:** one of three coordinates that are used to locate a point in space and that comprise the radius of the sphere on which the point lies in a system of concentric spheres, the angle formed by the point, the center, and a given axis of the sphere, and the angle between the plane of the first angle and a given reference plane through the axis of the sphere

spherical geometry : the geometry of figures on a sphere

spherical polygon *n* **:** a figure analogous to a plane polygon that is formed on a sphere by arcs of great circles

spherical triangle *n* **:** a spherical polygon of three sides

spherical trigonometry *n* **:** trigonometry applied to spherical triangles and polygons

spherics *var of* SFERICS

spher·oid \'sfi(ə)r-,ȯid, 'sfe(ə)r-\ *n* **:** a figure resembling a sphere — **sphe·roi·dal** \sfir-'ȯid-ᵊl\ *adj* — **sphe·roi·dal·ly** \-ᵊl-ē\ *adv*

sphe·rom·e·ter \sfir-'äm-ət-ər\ *n* [ISV] **:** an instrument for measuring the curvature of a surface

sphe·ro·plast \'sfir-ə-,plast, 'sfer-\ *n* **:** a modified gram-negative bacterium that is characterized by major alteration and partial loss of the cell wall and by increased osmotic sensitivity and that can result from various nutritional or environmental factors or be induced artificially by use of a lysozyme

spher·ule \'sfi(ə)r-(,)(y)ü(ə)l, 'sfe(ə)r-\ *n* **:** a little sphere or spherical body

spher·u·lite \'sfir-(y)ə-,līt, 'sfer-\ *n* **:** a usu. spherical crystalline body of radiating crystal fibers often found in vitreous volcanic rocks — **spher·u·lit·ic** \,sfir-(y)ə-'lit-ik, ,sfer-\ *adj*

sphery \'sfi(ə)r-ē\ *adj* **1 :** of, relating to, or suggestive of the celestial bodies **2 :** ROUND, SPHERICAL

sphinc·ter \'sfiŋ(k)-tər\ *n* [LL, fr. Gk *sphinktēr*, lit., band, fr. *sphingein* to bind tight] **:** an annular muscle surrounding and able to contract or close a bodily opening — **sphinc·ter·al** \-t(ə-)rəl\ *adj*

sphin·gid \'sfin-jəd\ *n* [deriv. of Gk *sphing-*, *sphinx* sphinx] **:** HAWKMOTH

sphin·go·sine \'sfiŋ-gə-,sēn\ *n* [Gk *sphingos* (gen. of *sphinx*) + E *-ine*; fr. riddles it posed to its first investigators] **:** a long chain unsaturated amino alcohol $C_{18}H_{37}O_2N$ found esp. in nervous tissue and cell membranes

sphinx \'sfiŋ(k)s\ *n, pl* **sphinx·es** *or* **sphin·ges** \'sfin-,jēz\ [L, fr. Gk; akin to Gk *sphinktēr* sphincter] **1 a** *cap* **:** a female monster having according to Greek mythology a lion's body and a human head and having the habit of asking a riddle and killing anyone who failed to answer it **b :** an enigmatic or mysterious person **2 :** an ancient Egyptian image in the form of a recumbent lion having a man's head, a ram's head, or a hawk's head **3 :** HAWKMOTH

sphinx 2

sp ht *abbr* specific heat

sphyg·mo·graph \'sfig-mə-,graf\ *n* [Gk *sphygmos* pulse + ISV *-graph*] **:** an instrument that records graphically the movements or character of the pulse — **sphyg·mo·graph·ic** \,sfig-mə-'graf-ik\ *adj* — **sphyg·mog·ra·phy** \sfig-'mäg-rə-fē\ *n*

sphyg·mo·ma·nom·e·ter \,sfig-mō-mə-'näm-ət-ər\ *n* [Gk *sphygmos* pulse + ISV *manometer*; akin to Gk *asphyxia* stopping of the pulse — more at ASPHYXIA] **:** an instrument for measuring blood pressure and esp. arterial blood pressure — **sphyg·mo·mano·met·ric** \-,man-ə-'me-trik\ *adj* — **sphyg·mo·mano·met·ri·cal·ly** \-tri-k(ə-)lē\ *adv* — **sphyg·mo·ma·nom·e·try** \-mə-'näm-ə-trē\ *n*

spi·ca \'spī-kə\ *n, pl* **spi·cae** \-,kē\ *or* **spicas** [L, spike of grain — more at SPIKE] **:** a spiral reverse plain or plaster bandage used to immobilize a limb esp. at a joint

Spi·ca \'spī-kə\ *n* [L, lit., spike of grain] **:** a star of the first magnitude in the constellation Virgo

spi·cate \'spī-,kāt\ *adj* [L *spicatus*, pp. of *spicare* to arrange in the shape of heads of grain, fr. *spica*] **:** POINTED, SPIKED; *specif* **:** arranged in the form of a spike <a ~ inflorescence>

1spic·ca·to \spi-'kät-(,)ō\ *adj* [It, pp. of *spiccare* to detach, pick off] **:** performed with springing bow — used as a direction in music for stringed instruments

2spiccato *n, pl* **-tos :** a spiccato technique, performance, or passage

1spice \'spīs\ *n* [ME, fr. OF *espice*, fr. LL *species* spices, fr. L, species] **1 :** any of various aromatic vegetable products (as pepper or nutmeg) used to season or flavor foods **2 a** *archaic* **:** a small portion, quantity, or admixture **:** DASH **b :** something that gives zest or relish <variety's the very ~ of life —William Cowper> **3 :** a pungent or fragrant odor **:** PERFUME

2spice *vt* **spiced; spic·ing 1 :** to season with spices **2 :** to add zest or relish to <cynicism *spiced* with humor —J. W. Dawson>

spice·ber·ry \'spīs-,ber-ē\ *n* **:** any of several spicy plants; *esp* **:** WINTERGREEN 2

spice box *n* **:** a box holding or designed to hold spices; *esp* **:** a box fitted with smaller boxes for holding spices

spice·bush \'spīs-,bu̇sh\ *n* **1 :** an aromatic shrub (*Lindera benzoin*) of the laurel family that bears dense clusters of small yellow flowers followed by scarlet or yellow berries **2 :** a tall upright strawberry shrub (*Calycanthus occidentalis*) with slightly fragrant brown flowers

spicebush swallowtail *n* **:** a large American black butterfly (*Papilio troilus*) that has yellow submarginal spots on the fore wings and the outer half of the upperside of the hind wings greenish or greenish blue

spic·ery \'spīs-(ə-)rē\ *n, pl* **-er·ies 1 :** SPICES **2** *archaic* **:** a repository of spices **3 :** a spicy quality

spick-and-span *or* **spic-and-span** \,spik-ən-'span, ,spik-ᵊŋ-\ *adj* [short for *spick-and-span-new*, fr. obs. E *spick* (spike) + E *and* + *span-new* (brand-new)] **1 :** FRESH, BRAND-NEW **2 :** spotlessly clean **:** SPRUCE

spic·u·la \'spik-yə-lə\ *n, pl* **-lae** \-,lē, -,lī\ [NL, fr. ML, arrowhead, alter. of L *spiculum*, dim. of *spica*] **:** SPICULE, PRICKLE — **spic·u·lar** \-lər\ *adj*

spic·u·late \'spik-yə-lət, -,lāt\ *adj* **:** covered with or having spicules — **spic·u·la·tion** \,spik-yə-'lā-shən\ *n*

spic·ule \,spik-(,)yü(ə)l\ *n* [NL *spicula* & L *spiculum*] **1 :** a minute slender pointed usu. hard body; *esp* **:** one of the minute calcareous or siliceous bodies that support the tissue of various invertebrates (as a sponge) **2 :** a small spikelike short-lived prominence appearing close to the chromosphere of the solar atmosphere — **spic·u·lif·er·ous** \,spik-yu̇-'lif-(ə-)rəs\ *adj*

spic·u·lum \,spik-yə-ləm\ *n, pl* **-la** \-lə\ [L, small sharp organ, arrowhead] **:** an organ having the form of a spicule; *broadly* **:** SPICULE 1

spicy \'spī-sē\ *adj* **spic·i·er; -est 1 :** having the quality, flavor, or fragrance of spice **2 :** producing or abounding in spices **3 :** LIVELY, SPIRITED <a ~ temper> **4 :** PIQUANT, RACY; *esp* **:** somewhat scandalous or salacious <~ gossip> — **spic·i·ly** \-sə-lē\ *adv* — **spic·i·ness** \-sē-nəs\ *n*

spi·der \'spīd-ər\ *n* [ME, alter. of *spithre*; akin to OE *spinnan* to spin] **1 :** any of an order (Araneida) of arachnids having a body with two main divisions, four pairs of walking legs, and two or more pairs of abdominal spinnerets for spinning threads of silk used in making cocoons for their eggs, nests for themselves, or webs for entangling their prey **2 :** a cast-iron frying pan orig. made with short feet to stand among coals on the hearth **3 :** any of various devices consisting of a frame or skeleton with radiating arm or members

spider crab *n* **:** any of numerous crabs (esp. family Majidae) with extremely long legs and nearly triangular bodies which they often cover with kelp

spider mite *n* **:** RED SPIDER

spider monkey *n* **:** any of a genus (*Ateles*) of New World monkeys with long slender limbs, the thumb absent or rudimentary, and a very long prehensile tail

spi·der·web \'spīd-ər-,web\ *n* **:** the silken web spun by most spiders and used as a resting place and a trap for small prey

spi·der·wort \-,wərt, -,wȯ(ə)rt\ *n* **:** any of a genus (*Tradescantia* of the family Commelinaceae) of monocotyledonous plants with ephemeral usu. blue or violet flowers

spi·dery \'spīd-ə-rē\ *adj* **1 a :** resembling a spider in form or manner **b :** resembling a spider web; *esp* **:** composed of fine threads or lines in a weblike arrangement <~ lace> **2 :** infested with spiders

spie·gel·ei·sen \'spē-gə-,līz-ᵊn\ *also* **spie·gel** \'spē-gəl\ *n* [G *spiegeleisen*, fr. *spiegel* mirror + *eisen* iron] **:** a composition of iron that contains 15 to 30 percent manganese and 4.5 to 6.5 percent carbon

1spiel \'spē(ə)l\ *vb* [G *spielen* to play, fr. OHG *spilōn*; akin to OE *spilian* to revel] *vi* **1 :** to play music **2 :** to talk volubly or extravagantly ~ *vt* **:** to utter, express, or describe volubly or extravagantly — **spiel·er** \'spē-lər\ *n*

2spiel *n* **:** a voluble line of often extravagant talk **:** PITCH

1spi·er \,spī(-ə)r\ *n* **:** SPY

2spier \'spi(ə)r\ *chiefly Scot var of* SPEER

spiffy \'spif-ē\ *adj* **spiff·i·er; -est** [E dial. *spiff* dandified] **:** fine looking **:** SMART <a ~ sports jacket>

spig·ot \'spig-ət, 'spik-ət\ *n* [ME] **1 :** SPILE 2 **2 :** the plug of a faucet or cock **3 :** FAUCET

1spike \'spīk\ *n* [ME, prob. fr. MD; akin to L *spina* thorn — more at SPINE] **1 :** a very large nail **2 a :** one of a row of pointed irons placed (as on the top of a wall) to prevent passage **b** (1) **:** one of several metal projections set in the sole and heel of a shoe to improve traction (2) *pl* **:** a pair of shoes having spikes attached to the soles or soles and heels **3 :** something resembling a spike: as **a :** a young mackerel not over six inches long **b :** an unbranched antler of a young deer **4** *pl* **:** shoes with spike heels **5 :** the act or an instance of spiking in volleyball **6 a :** a pointed element in a graph or tracing **b :** an unusually high and sharply defined maximum (as of amplitude in a wave train) **7** *slang* **:** HYPODERMIC NEEDLE **8 :** ACTION POTENTIAL

²spike *vt* **spiked; spik·ing 1 :** to fasten or furnish with spikes **2 a :** to disable (a muzzle-loading cannon) temporarily by driving a spike into the vent **b :** to suppress or block completely <*spiked* the rumor> **3 :** to pierce or impale with or on a spike **4 a :** to add alcohol or liquor to (a drink) **b :** to add something highly reactive (as a radioactive tracer) to **5 :** to drive (a volleyball) into an opponent's court at a sharp angle with a hard downward blow delivered from a front-line position — **spik·er** *n*

³spike *n* [ME *spik* head of grain, fr. L *spica;* akin to L *spina* thorn] **1 :** an ear of grain **2 :** an elongated inflorescence similar to a raceme but having the flowers sessile on the main axis — see INFLORESCENCE illustration

spiked \ˈspīkt, ˈspī-kəd\ *adj* **1 :** having an inflorescence that is a spike **2 :** having a sharp projecting point

spike heel *n* **:** a very high tapering heel used on women's shoes

spike lavender \ˈspīk-\ *n* [alter. of E dial. *spick* (lavender)] **:** a European mint (*Lavandula latifolia*) related to true lavender

spike·let \ˈspī-klət\ *n* **:** a small or secondary spike; *specif* **:** one of the small few-flowered bracted spikes that make up the compound inflorescence of a grass or sedge

spike·like \ˈspī-ˌklīk\ *adj* **:** resembling a spike

spike·nard \ˈspīk-ˌnärd\ *n* [ME, fr. MF or ML; MF *spicanarde,* fr. ML *spica nardi,* lit., spike of nard] **1 a :** a fragrant ointment of the ancients **b :** an East Indian aromatic plant (*Nardostachys jatamansi*) of the valerian family from which spikenard is believed to have been derived **2 :** an American herb (*Aralia racemosa*) of the ginseng family with aromatic root and panicled umbels

spike–tooth harrow \ˌspīk-ˌtüth-\ *n* **:** a harrow with straight steel teeth set in horizontal bars

spiky \ˈspī-kē\ *adj* **spik·i·er; -est 1 :** having a sharp projecting point **2** [fr. the alleged harshness of such views] *Brit* **:** strongly favoring Anglo-Catholic teaching or practice

¹spile \ˈspī(ə)l\ *n* [prob. fr. D *spijl* stake; akin to L *spina* thorn — more at SPINE] **1 :** ¹PILE **2 :** a small plug used to stop the vent of a cask **:** BUNG **3 :** a spout inserted in a tree to draw off sap

²spile *vt* **spiled; spil·ing 1 :** to plug with a spile **2 :** to supply with a spile

spil·ing \ˈspī-liŋ\ *n* **:** a set of piles **:** PILING

¹spill \ˈspil\ *vb* **spilled** \ˈspild, ˈspilt\ *also* **spilt** \ˈspilt\; **spill·ing** [ME *spillen,* fr. OE *spillan;* akin to OHG *spaltan* to split, L *spolia* spoils, Gk *sphallein* to cause to fall] *vt* **1 a** *archaic* **:** KILL, DESTROY **b :** to cause (blood) to flow **2 :** to cause or allow accidentally or unintentionally to fall, flow, or run out so as to be lost or wasted **3 a :** to relieve (a sail) from the pressure of the wind so as to reef or furl it **b :** to relieve the pressure of (wind) on a sail by coming about or by adjusting the sail with lines **4 :** to throw off or out <a horse ~*ed* him> **5 :** to let out **:** DIVULGE <~ a secret> ~ *vi* **1 a :** to flow, run, or fall out, over, or off and become wasted, scattered, or lost **b :** to cause or allow something to spill **2 :** to spread profusely or beyond bounds <crowds ~*ed* into the streets> **3 :** to fall from one's place (as on a horse) — **spill·able** \ˈspil-ə-bəl\ *adj* — **spill·er** *n* — **spill the beans :** to divulge information indiscreetly

²spill *n* **1 :** the act or an instance of spilling; *esp* **:** a fall from a horse or vehicle or an erect position **2 :** something spilled **3 :** SPILLWAY

³spill *n* [ME *spille*] **1 :** a wooden splinter **2 :** a slender piece: as **a :** a metallic rod or pin **b** (1) **:** a small roll or twist of paper or slip of wood for lighting a fire (2) **:** a roll or cone of paper serving as a container **c :** a peg or pin for plugging a hole **:** SPILE

spill·age \ˈspil-ij\ *n* **1 :** the act or process of spilling **2 :** the quantity that spills **:** material lost or scattered by spilling

spil·li·kin \ˈspil-i-kən\ *n* [prob. alter. of obs. D *spelleken* small peg] **1 :** JACKSTRAW 1 **2** *pl* **:** JACKSTRAW 2

spill·over \ˈspil-ˌō-vər\ *n* **1 :** the act or an instance of spilling over **2 :** a quantity that spills over

spill·way \-ˌwā\ *n* **:** a passage for surplus water to run over or around an obstruction (as a dam)

spi·lo·site \ˈspī-lə-ˌsīt\ *n* [G *spilosit,* fr. Gk *spilos* spot] **:** a spotted schistose rock produced by the metamorphism of clay slate by magma

spilth \ˈspilth\ *n* **1 :** the act or an instance of spilling **2 a :** something spilled **b :** REFUSE, RUBBISH

¹spin \ˈspin\ *vb* **spun** \ˈspən\; **spin·ning** [ME *spinnen,* fr. OE *spinnan;* akin to OHG *spinnan* to spin, L *sponte* voluntarily, Gk *span* to draw — more at SPAN] *vi* **1 :** to draw out and twist fiber into yarn or thread **2 :** to form a thread by extruding a viscous rapidly hardening fluid — used esp. of a spider or insect **3 a :** to revolve rapidly **:** GYRATE **b :** to feel as if in a whirl **:** REEL <my head is *spinning*> **4 :** to move swiftly esp. on wheels or in a vehicle **5 :** to fish with spinning bait **:** TROLL **6 a** *of an airplane* **:** to fall in a spin **b :** to plunge helplessly and out of control ~ *vt* **1 a :** to draw out and twist into yarns or threads **b :** to produce by drawing out and twisting a fibrous material **2 :** to form (as a web or cocoon) by spinning **3 a :** to stretch out or extend (as a story) lengthily **:** PROTRACT — usu. used with *out* **b :** to evolve, express, or fabricate by processes of mind or imagination <~ a yarn> **4 :** to cause to whirl **:** TWIRL <~ a top> **5 :** to shape into threadlike form in manufacture; *also* **:** to manufacture by a whirling process

²spin *n* **1 a :** the act of spinning or twirling something **b :** the whirling motion imparted (as to a ball or top) by spinning **c :** an excursion in a vehicle esp. on wheels **2 a :** an aerial maneuver or flight condition consisting of a combination of roll and yaw with the longitudinal axis of the airplane inclined steeply downward **b :** a plunging descent or downward spiral **c :** a state of mental confusion <in a ~> **3 a :** the rotation of an elementary particle on its axis or of a system of such particles in orbital motion that is responsible for measurable angular momentum and magnetic moment **b :** the angular momentum associated with such rotation — **spin·less** \ˈspin-ləs\ *adj*

spin·ach \ˈspin-ich\ *n* [MF *espinache, espinage,* fr. OSp *espinaca,* fr. Ar *isfānākh,* fr. Per] **1 :** a potherb (*Spinacia oleracea*) of the goosefoot family cultivated for its edible leaves **2 a :** something unwanted, insubstantial, or spurious **b :** an untidy overgrowth

¹spi·nal \ˈspīn-ᵊl\ *adj* **1 :** of, relating to, or situated near the backbone **2 a :** of, relating to, or affecting the spinal cord <~ reflexes> **b :** having the spinal cord functionally isolated (as by surgical section) from the brain <experiments on ~ animals> **3 :** of, relating to, or resembling a spine

²spinal *n* **:** a spinal anesthetic

spinal canal *n* **:** a canal that lodges the spinal cord and is delimited by the arches on the dorsal side of the vertebrae

spinal column *n* **:** the axial skeleton of the trunk and tail of a vertebrate consisting of an articulated series of vertebrae and protecting the spinal cord — called also *backbone*

spinal cord *n* **:** the longitudinal cord of nervous tissue extending from the brain along the back in the spinal canal — see BRAIN illustration

spinal ganglion *n* **:** a ganglion on the dorsal root of each spinal nerve that is one of a series of ganglia lodging cell bodies of sensory neurons

spi·nal·ly \ˈspīn-ᵊl-ē\ *adv* **:** with respect to or along the spine

spinal nerve *n* **:** any of the paired nerves which leave the spinal cord of a craniate vertebrate, supply muscles of the trunk and limbs, and connect with the nerves of the sympathetic nervous system, which arise by a short motor ventral root and a short sensory dorsal root, and of which there are 31 pairs in man classified according to the part of the spinal cord from which they arise into 8 cervical pairs, 12 thoracic pairs, 5 lumbar pairs, 5 sacral pairs, and one coccygeal pair

¹spin·dle \ˈspin-dᵊl\ *n* [ME *spindel,* fr. OE *spinel;* akin to OE *spinnan* to spin] **1 a :** a round stick with tapered ends used to form and twist the yarn in hand spinning **b :** the long slender pin by which the thread is twisted in a spinning wheel **c :** any of various rods or pins holding a bobbin in a textile machine (as a spinning frame) **d :** the pin in a loom shuttle **2 :** something shaped like a spindle: as **a :** a spindle-shaped achromatic figure along which the chromosomes are distributed during mitosis and meiosis **b :** MUSCLE SPINDLE **3 a :** the bar or shaft usu. of square section that carries the knobs and actuates the latch or bolt of a lock **b** (1) **:** a turned often decorative piece (as in a baluster) (2) **:** NEWEL **c** (1) **:** a revolving piece esp. if less in size than a shaft (2) **:** a horizontal or vertical axle revolving on pin or pivot ends (3) **:** a rod attached to a valve to move or guide it **d :** the part of an axle on which a vehicle wheel turns

²spindle *vb* **spin·dled; spin·dling** \-(d)liŋ, -dᵊl-iŋ\ *vi* **1 :** to shoot or grow into a long slender stalk **2 :** to grow to stalk or stem rather than to flower or fruit ~ *vt* **1 :** to impale, thrust, or perforate on the spike of a spindle file **2 :** to make or equip (as a piece of furniture) with spindles — **spin·dler** \-(d)lər, -dᵊl-ər\ *n*

spindle cell *n* **:** a fusiform cell; *esp* **:** a slender nucleated element that is the thrombocyte of a lower vertebrate and is equivalent in function to the blood platelet of higher forms

spindle file *n* **:** a device with a projecting spike, nail, or hook on which to stick papers

spin·dle–legged \ˌspin-dᵊl-ˈ(l)eg(-ə)d, -ˈ(l)āg(-ə)d\ *adj* **:** having long slender legs

spin·dle–shanked \-ˈshaŋ(k)t\ *adj* **:** SPINDLE-LEGGED

spindle tree *n* **:** EUONYMUS

spin·dling \ˈspin-(d)liŋ, -(d)lən, -dᵊl-iŋ, -dᵊl-ən\ *adj* **:** SPINDLY

spin·dly \ˈspin-(d)lē, -dᵊl-ē\ *adj* **1 :** of a disproportionately tall or long and thin appearance that often suggests physical weakness <~ legs> **2 :** frail or flimsy in appearance or structure

spin·drift \ˈspin-ˌdrift\ *n* [alter. of Sc *speendrift,* fr. *speen* to drive before a strong wind + E *drift*] **:** sea spray **:** SPOONDRIFT

spine \ˈspīn\ *n* [ME, thorn, spinal column, fr. L *spina;* akin to Latvian *spina* twig] **1 a :** SPINAL COLUMN **b :** something resembling a spinal column or constituting a central axis or chief support **c :** the backbone of a book **2 :** a stiff pointed plant process; *esp* **:** one that is a modified leaf or leaf part **3 :** a sharp rigid process on an animal: as **a :** SPICULE **b :** a stiff unsegmented fin ray of a fish **c :** a pointed prominence on a bone

spi·nel *or* **spi·nelle** \spə-ˈnel\ *n* [It *spinella,* dim. of *spina* thorn, fr. L] **1 :** a hard crystalline mineral $MgAl_2O_4$ consisting of an oxide of magnesium and aluminum that varies from colorless to ruby-red to black and is used as a gem **2 :** any of a group of minerals that are essentially oxides of magnesium, ferrous iron, zinc, or manganese

spine·less \ˈspīn-ləs\ *adj* **1 :** free from spines, thorns, or prickles **2 a :** having no spinal column **:** INVERTEBRATE **b :** lacking strength of character — **spine·less·ly** *adv* — **spine·less·ness** *n*

spi·nes·cent \spī-ˈnes-ᵊnt\ *adj* [NL *spinescent-, spinescens,* fr. LL, prp. of *spinescere* to become thorny, fr. L *spina*] **:** SPINY; *also* **:** tending toward spininess

spin·et \ˈspin-ət *also* spin-ˈet\ *n* [It *spinetta*] **1 :** an early harpsichord having a single keyboard and only one string for each note **2 a :** a compactly built small upright piano **b :** a small electronic organ

spin fishing *n* **:** SPINNING

spi·ni·fex \ˈspī-nə-ˌfeks\ *n* [NL, genus name, fr. L *spina* + *facere* to make — more at DO] **:** any of several Australian grasses (genera *Spinifex* or *Triodia*) with spiny seeds or stiff sharp leaves

spin·na·ker \ˈspin-i-kər\ *n* [origin unknown] **:** a large triangular sail set on a long light pole and used when running before the wind

spin·ner \ˈspin-ər\ *n* **1 :** one that spins **2 :** a fisherman's lure consisting of a spoon, blade, or set of wings that revolves when drawn through the water **3 :** a conical sheet metal fairing which is attached to an airplane propeller boss and revolves with it **4** : a movable arrow that is spun on its dial to indicate the number or kind of moves a player may make in a board game

spin·ner·et \ˌspin-ə-ˈret\ *n* **1** : an organ (as of a spider or caterpillar) for producing threads of silk from the secretion of silk glands **2** *or* **spin·ner·ette** : a small metal plate, thimble, or cap with fine holes through which a chemical solution (as of cellulose) is forced in the spinning of man-made filaments (as of rayon or nylon)

spin·ney \ˈspin-ē\ *n, pl* **spinneys** [MF *espinaye* thorny thicket, fr. *espine* thorn, fr. L *spina*] *Brit* : a small wood with undergrowth

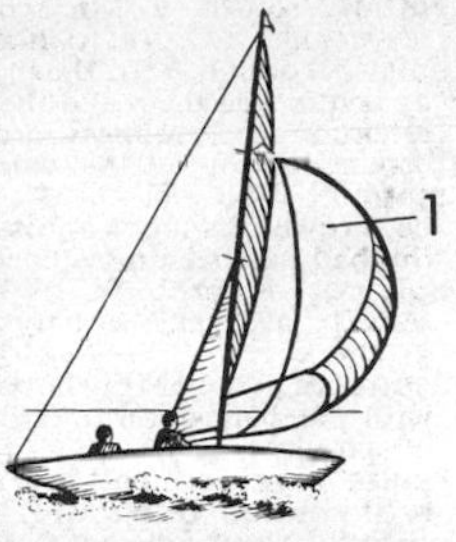

1 spinnaker

spin·ning \ˈspin-iŋ\ *n* : a method of fishing in which a lure is cast by use of a light flexible rod, a spinning reel, and a light line

spinning frame *n* : a machine that draws, twists, and winds yarn

spinning jen·ny \-ˌjen-ē\ *n* [*Jenny,* nickname for *Jane*] : an early multiple-spindle machine for spinning wool or cotton

spinning reel *n* : a fishing reel with a nonmoving spool on which the line is wound by means of a revolving arm which can be disengaged to allow the line to spiral freely off the spool during casting

spinning rod *n* : a light flexible fishing rod used with a spinning reel

spinning wheel *n* : a small domestic hand-driven or foot-driven machine for spinning yarn or thread

spin–off \ˈspin-ˌȯf\ *n* **1** : the distribution by a business to its stockholders of particular assets and esp. of stock of another company **2** : a collateral or derived product or effect : BY-PRODUCT <household products that are ~*s* of missile research>

spin·or \ˈspin-ər, -ˌȯ(ə)r\ *n* [ISV *spin* + *-or* (as in *vector*)] : a vector whose components are complex numbers in a two-dimensional or four-dimensional space and which is used esp. in the mathematics of the theory of relativity

spi·nose \ˈspī-ˌnōs\ *adj* : SPINY 1 <a fly with black ~ legs> — **spi·nose·ly** *adv*

spi·nos·i·ty \spī-ˈnäs-ət-ē\ *n, pl* **-ties** **1** : the quality or state of being spinose **2** : something that is nettlesome or difficult

spi·nous \ˈspī-nəs\ *adj* **1** : difficult or unpleasant to handle or meet : THORNY **2** : SPINY 1, 3 <~ appendages> <a ~ larva>

spin·out \ˈspin-ˌau̇t\ *n* : a rotational skid by an automobile that usu. causes it to leave the roadway

spin out \spin-ˈau̇t\ *vi* : to make a rotational skid in an automobile

Spi·no·zism \spin-ˈō-ˌziz-əm\ *n* : the philosophy of Spinoza who taught that reality is one substance with an infinite number of attributes of which only thought and extension are capable of being apprehended by the human mind — **Spi·no·zist** \-zəst\ *n* — **Spi·no·zis·tic** \ˌspin-ō-ˈzis-tik, spin-ˌō-\ *adj*

spin·ster \ˈspin(t)-stər\ *n* **1** : a woman whose occupation is to spin **2 a** *archaic* : an unmarried woman of gentle family **b** : an unmarried woman **3** : a woman past the common age for marrying or one who seems unlikely to marry — **spin·ster·hood** \-ˌhu̇d\ *n* — **spin·ster·ish** \-st(ə-)rish\ *adj*

spin·thari·scope \spin-ˈthar-ə-ˌskōp\ *n* [Gk *spintharis* spark + E *-scope*] : an instrument for visual detection of alpha rays that consists of a fluorescent screen and a magnifying lens system

spin the bottle *n* **1** : the game spin the plate when played with a bottle **2** : a method of choosing a performer (as a partner in a kissing game) according to whom the mouth of a bottle points to when it stops spinning; *also* : a kissing game

spin the plate *n* : a game in which something round (as a plate) is spun on edge and the name of a player is called upon which the named player must catch the spinning object before it falls or pay a forfeit — called also *spin the platter*

spi·nule \ˈspī-(ˌ)nyü(ə)l\ *n* [L *spinula,* dim. of *spina* thorn — more at SPINE] : a minute spine — **spi·nu·lose** \ˈspī-nyə-ˌlōs\ *adj*

spiny \ˈspī-nē\ *adj* **spin·i·er; -est** **1** : covered or armed with spines; *broadly* : bearing spines, prickles, or thorns **2** : abounding with difficulties, obstacles, or annoyances : THORNY <~ problems> **3** : slender and pointed like a spine — **spin·i·ness** *n*

spiny anteater *n* : ECHIDNA

spiny–finned \ˌspī-nē-ˈfind\ *adj* : having fins with one or more stiff unbranched rays without transverse segmentation — used of acanthopterygian fishes; compare SOFT-FINNED

spiny–head·ed worm \ˌspī-nē-ˌhed-əd-\ *n* : any of a small phylum (Acanthocephala) of unsegmented parasitic worms that have a proboscis bearing hooks by which attachment is made to the intestinal wall of the host

spiny lobster *n* : an edible crustacean (family Palinuridae) distinguished from the true lobster by the simple unenlarged first pair of legs and the spiny carapace

spi·ra·cle \ˈspir-i-kəl, ˈspī-ri-\ *n* [L *spiraculum,* fr. *spirare* to breathe — more at SPIRIT] **1** : a breathing hole : VENT **2** : a breathing orifice: as **a** : BLOWHOLE 2 **b** : an external tracheal aperture of a terrestrial arthropod that in an insect is usu. one of a series of small apertures located along each side of the thorax and abdomen — see INSECT illustration — **spi·rac·u·lar** \spə-ˈrak-yə-lər, spī-\ *adj*

[1]**spi·ral** \ˈspī-rəl\ *adj* [ML *spiralis,* fr. L *spira* coil] **1 a** : winding around a center or pole and gradually receding from or approaching it <the ~ curve of a watch spring> **b** : HELICAL **2** : of or relating to the advancement to higher levels through a series of cyclical movements — **spi·ral·ly** \-rə-lē\ *adv*

[2]**spiral** *n* **1 a** : the path of a point in a plane moving around an axis while continuously receding from or approaching it **b** : a three-dimensional curve (as a helix) with one or more turns about an axis **2** : a single turn or coil in a spiral object **3 a** : something having a spiral form **b (1)** : a spiral flight **(2)** : a kick or pass in which a football rotates on its long axis while moving through the air **4** : a continuously spreading and accelerating increase or decrease <wage ~*s*>

[3]**spiral** *vb* **-raled** *or* **-ralled; -ral·ing** *or* **-ral·ling** *vi* : to go and esp. to rise or fall in a spiral course <costs ~*ed* upward> ~ *vt* **1** : to form into a spiral **2** : to cause to spiral

spiral binding *n* : a book or notebook binding in which a continuous spiral wire or plastic strip is passed through holes along one edge

spi·ral–bound \ˌspī-rəl-ˈbau̇nd\ *adj* : having a spiral binding

spiral galaxy *n* : a galaxy exhibiting a central nucleus or barred structure from which extend concentrations of matter forming curved arms — called also *spiral nebula*

spiral of Ar·chi·me·des \-ˌär-kə-ˈmēd-ēz\ [*Archimedes,* Gk mathematician] : a plane curve that is generated by a point moving away from or toward a fixed point at a constant rate while the radius vector from the fixed point rotates at a constant rate and that has the equation $\rho = a\,\theta$ in polar coordinates

spiral spring *n* : a spring consisting of a wire coiled usu. in a flat spiral or in a helix

spi·rant \ˈspī-rənt\ *n* [ISV, fr. L *spirant-, spirans,* prp. of *spirare* to breathe — more at SPIRIT] : a consonant (as \f\, \s\, \sh\) uttered with friction of the breath against some part of the oral passage : FRICATIVE — **spirant** *adj*

[1]**spire** \ˈspī(ə)r\ *n* [ME, fr. OE *spīr;* akin to MD *spier* blade of grass, L *spina* thorn — more at SPINE] **1** : a slender tapering blade or stalk (as of grass) **2** : the upper tapering part of something (as a tree or antler) : PINNACLE **3 a** : a tapering roof or analogous pyramidal construction surmounting a tower **b** : STEEPLE

[2]**spire** *vi* **spired; spir·ing** : to rise taperingly like a spire

[3]**spire** *n* [L *spira* coil, fr. Gk *speira;* akin to Gk *sparton* rope, esparto, Lith *springti* to choke in swallowing] **1 a** : SPIRAL **b** : COIL **2** : the inner or upper part of a spiral gastropod shell consisting of all the whorls except the whorl in contact with the body

[4]**spire** *vi* **spired; spir·ing** : to rise in or as if in a spiral

spi·rea *or* **spi·raea** \spī-ˈrē-ə\ *n* [NL *Spiraea,* genus name, fr. L, a plant, fr. Gk *speiraia*] **1** : any of a genus (*Spiraea*) of shrubs of the rose family with small perfect white or pink flowers in dense racemes, corymbs, cymes, or panicles **2** : any of several garden plants resembling spireas; *esp* : a shrub (*Astilbe japonica*) of the saxifrage family

spired \ˈspī(ə)rd\ *adj* **1** : having a spire <a ~ church> **2** : tapering usu. to a sharp point <~ cedars>

spi·reme \ˈspī-ˌrēm\ *n* [G *spirem,* fr. Gk *speirama, speirēma* convolution, fr. *speirasthai* to be coiled, fr. *speira*] : a continuous thread observed in fixed preparations of the prophase of mitosis that appears to be a strand of chromatin but is generally held to be an artifact

spi·ril·lum \spī-ˈril-əm\ *n, pl* **-ril·la** \-ˈril-ə\ [NL, genus name, fr. dim. of L *spira* coil] : any of a genus (*Spirillum*) of long curved flagellate bacteria; *broadly* : a spiral filamentous bacterium (as a spirochete)

[1]**spir·it** \ˈspir-ət\ *n* [ME, fr. OF or L; OF, fr. L *spiritus,* lit., breath; akin to L *spirare* to blow, breathe, ON *fīsa* to break wind] **1** : an animating or vital principle held to give life to physical organisms **2** : a supernatural being or essence: as **a** *cap* : HOLY SPIRIT **b** : SOUL 2a **c** : an often malevolent being that is bodiless but can become visible; *specif* : GHOST 2 **d** : a malevolent being that enters and possesses a human being **3** : temper or disposition of mind esp. when vigorous or animated <in high ~*s*> **4** : the immaterial intelligent or sentient part of a person **5 a** : the activating or essential principle influencing a person <acted in a ~ of helpfulness> **b** : an inclination, impulse, or tendency of a specified kind : MOOD **6 a** : a special attitude or frame of mind <the money-making ~ was for a time driven back —J. A. Froude> **b** : the feeling, quality, or disposition characterizing something <undertaken in a ~ of fun> **7** : a lively or brisk quality in a person or his actions **8** : a person having a character or disposition of a specified nature **9** : a mental disposition characterized by firmness or assertiveness <denied the charge with ~> **10 a** : DISTILLATE 1: as **(1)** : the liquid containing ethyl alcohol and water that is distilled from an alcoholic liquid or mash — often used in pl. **(2)** : any of various volatile liquids obtained by distillation or cracking (as of petroleum, shale, or wood) — often used in pl. **(3)** : ALCOHOL 1 **b** : a usu. volatile organic solvent (as an alcohol, ester, or hydrocarbon) **11 a** : prevailing tone or tendency <~ of the age> **b** : general intent or real meaning <~ of the law> **12** : an alcoholic solution of a volatile substance <~ of camphor> **13** : enthusiastic loyalty <school ~> **14** *cap, Christian Science* : GOD 1b ***syn*** see COURAGE — **in spirits** : in a cheerful or lively frame of mind — **out of spirits** : in a gloomy or depressed frame of mind

[2]**spirit** *vt* **1** : to infuse with spirit; *esp* : ANIMATE <hope and apprehension of feasibleness ~*s* all industry —John Goodman> **2** : to carry off usu. secretly or mysteriously <was hustled into a . . . motorcar and ~*ed* off to the country —W.L. Shirer>

spir·it·ed \ˈspir-ət-əd\ *adj* : full of energy, animation, or courage <a ~ discussion> — **spir·it·ed·ly** *adv* — **spir·it·ed·ness** *n*

spirit gum *n* : a solution (as of gum arabic in ether) used esp. for attaching false hair to the skin

spir·it·ism \ˈspir-ət-ˌiz-əm\ *n* : SPIRITUALISM 2a — **spir·it·ist** \-ət-əst\ *n* — **spir·it·is·tic** \ˌspir-ət-ˈis-tik\ *adj*

spir·it·less \ˈspir-ət-ləs\ *adj* : lacking animation, cheerfulness, or courage — **spir·it·less·ly** *adv* — **spir·it·less·ness** *n*

spirit level *n* : LEVEL 1

spirit of hartshorn *or* **spirits of hartshorn** : AMMONIA WATER
spir·i·to·so \ˌspir-ə-ˈtō-(ˌ)sō, -(ˌ)zō\ *adj* [It, fr. *spirito* spirit, fr. L *spiritus*] : ANIMATED — used as a direction in music
spir·it·ous \ˈspir-ət-əs\ *adj* **1** *archaic* : PURE, REFINED **2** : SPIRITUOUS
spirit rapping *n* : communication by raps held to be from the spirits of the dead
spirits of turpentine : TURPENTINE 2a — called also *spirit of turpentine*
spirits of wine : rectified spirit : ALCOHOL 1 — called also *spirit of wine*
[1]**spir·i·tu·al** \ˈspir-ich-(ə-)wəl, -ich-əl\ *adj* [ME, fr. MF & LL; MF *spirituel,* fr. LL *spiritualis,* fr. L, of breathing, of wind, fr. *spiritus*] **1** : of, relating to, or consisting of spirit : INCORPOREAL <man's ~ needs> **2 a** : of or relating to sacred matters <~ songs> **b** : ecclesiastical rather than lay or temporal <lords ~> <~ authority> **3** : concerned with religious values **4** : spiritually akin or related <our ~ home> <his ~ heir> **5 a** : of or relating to supernatural beings or phenomena **b** : of, relating to, or involving spiritualism : SPIRITUALISTIC — **spir·i·tu·al·ly** \-ē\ *adv* — **spir·i·tu·al·ness** *n*
[2]**spiritual** *n* **1** *pl* : things of a spiritual, ecclesiastical, or religious nature **2** : a religious song usu. of a deeply emotional character that was developed esp. among Negroes in the southern U.S. **3** *cap* : any of a party of 13th and 14th century Franciscans advocating strict observance of a rule of poverty for their order
spiritual bouquet *n* : a card notifying the recipient of a number of devotional acts undertaken by a Roman Catholic on behalf of a person on special occasions (as name days or anniversaries) or of someone recently deceased esp. as an expression of sympathy
spir·i·tu·al·ism \ˈspir-ich-(ə-)wə-ˌliz-əm, -ich-ə-ˌliz-\ *n* **1** : the view that spirit is a prime element of reality **2 a** : a belief that spirits of the dead communicate with the living usu. through a medium **b** *cap* : a movement comprising religious organizations emphasizing spiritualism — **spir·i·tu·al·ist** \-ləst\ *n, often cap* — **spir·i·tu·al·is·tic** \ˌspir-ich-(ə-)wə-ˈlis-tik, -ich-ə-ˈlis-\ *adj*
spir·i·tu·al·i·ty \ˌspir-ich-ə-ˈwal-ət-ē\ *n, pl* **-ties** **1** : something that in ecclesiastical law belongs to the church or to a cleric as such **2** : CLERGY **3** : sensitivity or attachment to religious values **4** : the quality or state of being spiritual
spir·i·tu·al·ize \ˈspir-ich-(ə-)wə-ˌlīz, -ich-ə-ˌlīz\ *vt* **-ized; -iz·ing** **1** : to make spiritual; *esp* : to purify from the corrupting influences of the world **2** : to give a spiritual meaning to or understand in a spiritual sense — **spir·i·tu·al·iza·tion** \ˌspir-ich-(ə-)wə-lə-ˈzā-shən, -ich-ə-lə-\ *n*
spir·i·tu·al·ty \ˈspir-ich-(ə-)wəl-tē, -ich-əl-\ *n* [ME *spiritualte,* fr. MF *spiritualté,* fr. ML *spiritualitat-, spiritualitas,* fr. LL *spiritualis* spiritual] : SPIRITUALITY 1, 2
spi·ri·tu·el *or* **spi·ri·tu·elle** \ˌspir-i-chə-ˈwel, spē-rē-tw(ʸ)el\ *adj* [*spirituel* fr. F, lit., spiritual; *spirituelle* fr. F, fem. of *spirituel*] : having or marked by a refined and esp. sprightly or witty nature
spir·i·tu·ous \ˈspir-ich-(ə-)wəs, -ich-əs, ˈspir-ət-əs\ *adj* [prob. fr. F *spiritueux,* fr. L *spiritus* spirit] : containing or impregnated with alcohol obtained by distillation <~ liquors>
spirit varnish *n* : a varnish in which a volatile liquid (as alcohol) is the solvent
spirit writing *n* : automatic writing held to be produced under the influence of spirits
spiro- *comb form* [ISV, fr. L *spirare* to breathe — more at SPIRIT] : respiration <*spiro*graph>
spi·ro·chet·al \ˌspī-rə-ˈkēt-ᵊl\ *adj* : caused by spirochetes
spi·ro·chete *or* **spi·ro·chaete** \ˈspī-rə-ˌkēt\ *n* [NL *Spirochaeta,* genus of bacteria, fr. L *spira* coil + Gk *chaitē* long hair — more at SPIRE, CHAETA] : any of an order (Spirochaetales) of slender spirally undulating bacteria including those causing syphilis and relapsing fever
spi·ro·chet·osis \ˌspī-rə-ˌkēt-ˈō-səs\ *n, pl* **-oses** \-ˌsēz\ : infection with or a disease caused by spirochetes
spi·ro·graph \ˈspī-rə-ˌgraf\ *n* [ISV] : an instrument recording respiratory movements — **spi·ro·graph·ic** \ˌspī-rə-ˈgraf-ik\ *adj* — **spi·rog·ra·phy** \spī-ˈräg-rə-fē\ *n*
spi·ro·gy·ra \ˌspī-rə-ˈjī-rə\ *n* [NL, genus name, fr. Gk *speira* coil + *gyros* ring, circle — more at SPIRE, COWER] : any of a genus (*Spirogyra*) of freshwater green algae with spiral chlorophyll bands
spi·rom·e·ter \spī-ˈräm-ət-ər\ *n* [ISV] : an instrument for measuring the air entering and leaving the lungs — **spi·ro·met·ric** \ˌspī-rə-ˈme-trik\ *adj* — **spi·rom·e·try** \spī-ˈräm-ə-trē\ *n*
spirt *var of* SPURT
spi·ru·la \ˈspir-(y)ə-lə, ˈspīr-\ *n* [NL, genus name, fr. dim. of L *spira* coil] : any of a genus (*Spirula*) of small dibranchiate cephalopods having a many-chambered shell in a flat spiral
spiry \ˈspī(ə)r-ē\ *adj* : resembling a spire; *esp* : being tall, slender, and tapering <~ trees>
[1]**spit** \ˈspit\ n [ME, fr. OE *spitu;* akin to L *spina* thorn, spine] **1** : a slender pointed rod for holding meat over a fire **2** : a small point of land esp. of sand or gravel running into a body of water
[2]**spit** *vt* **spit·ted; spit·ting** : to fix on or as if on a spit : IMPALE
[3]**spit** *vb* **spit** *or* **spat** \ˈspat\; **spit·ting** [ME *spitten, fr. OE spittan,* of imit. origin] *vt* **1 a** : to eject (as saliva) from the mouth : EXPECTORATE **b** (1) : to express (unpleasant or malicious feelings) by or as if by spitting (2) : to utter with a spitting sound or scornful expression <*spat* out his words> **c** : to emit as if by spitting; *esp* : to emit (precipitation) in driving particles or in flurries <~ rain> **2** : to set to burning <~ a fuse> ~ *vi* **1 a** (1) : to eject saliva as an expression of aversion or contempt (2) : to exhibit contempt **b** : to eject saliva from the mouth : EXPECTORATE **2** : to rain or snow slightly or in flurries **3** : to make a noise suggesting expectoration : SPUTTER — **spit it out** : to say what is in the mind without further delay
[4]**spit** *n* **1 a** (1) : SPITTLE, SALIVA (2) : the act or an instance of spitting **b** (1) : a frothy secretion exuded by spittlebugs (2) : SPITTLEBUG **2** : perfect likeness **3** : a sprinkle of rain or flurry of snow
spit·al \ˈspit-ᵊl\ *n* [ME *spitel,* modif. of ML *hospitale* — more at HOSPITAL] : LAZARETTO, HOSPITAL
spit and polish *n* [fr. the practice of polishing objects such as shoes by spitting on them and then rubbing them with a cloth] : extreme attention to cleanliness, orderliness, smartness of appearance, and ceremonial esp. at the expense of operational efficiency
spit·ball \ˈspit-ˌbȯl\ *n* **1** : paper chewed and rolled into a ball to be thrown or shot as a missile **2** : a baseball pitch delivered after the ball has been moistened with saliva or sweat
spit curl *n* [prob. fr. its being sometimes plastered down with saliva] : a spiral curl that is usu. plastered on the forehead, temple, or cheek
[1]**spite** \ˈspīt\ *n* [ME, short for *despite*] **1** : petty ill will or hatred with the disposition to irritate, annoy, or thwart **2** : an instance of spite *syn* see MALICE — **in spite of** : in defiance or contempt of
[2]**spite** *vt* **spit·ed; spit·ing** **1** : to treat maliciously (as by shaming or thwarting) **2 a** : to fill with spite **b** : ANNOY, OFFEND
spite·ful \ˈspīt-fəl\ *adj* : filled with or showing spite : MALICIOUS — **spite·ful·ly** \-fə-lē\ *adv* — **spite·ful·ness** *n*
spit·fire \ˈspit-ˌfī(ə)r\ *n* : a quick-tempered or highly emotional person
[1]**spit·ter** \ˈspit-ər\ *n* : one that spits
[2]**spitter** *n* : SPITBALL 2
spitting cobra *n* : either of two venomous African elapid snakes (*Naja nigricollis* and *Haemachates haemachatus*) that eject their venom toward the victim without striking
spitting image *n* [by alter.] : spit and image : [4]SPIT 2
spit·tle \ˈspit-ᵊl\ *n* [ME *spetil,* fr. OE *spǣtl;* akin to OE *spittan*] **1** : SALIVA **2** : [4]SPIT 1b(1)
spit·tle·bug \-ˌbəg\ *n* : any of numerous leaping homopterous insects (family Cercopidae) whose larvae secrete froth
spittle insect *n* : SPITTLEBUG
spit·toon \spi-ˈtün, spə-\ *n* [[4]*spit* + *-oon* (as in *balloon*)] : a receptacle for spit — called also *cuspidor*
spit up *vb* : REGURGITATE, VOMIT
spitz \ˈspits\ *n* [G, fr. *spitz* pointed; akin to OE *spitu* spit; fr. the shape of its ears and muzzle] : any of several stocky heavy-coated dogs of northern origin with erect ears and a heavily furred tail tightly recurved over the back; *esp* : a medium-sized white dog descended from Pomeranian ancestors and often considered a separate breed

spitz

spiv \ˈspiv\ *n* [alter. of E dial. *spiff* flashy dresser, fr. *spiff* dandified] **1** *Brit* : one who lives by his wits without regular employment **2** *Brit* : SLACKER
splanch·nic \ˈsplaŋk-nik\ *adj* [NL *splanchnicus,* fr. Gk *splanchnikos,* fr. *splanchna,* pl., viscera; akin to Gk *splēn* spleen] : of or relating to the viscera : VISCERAL
[1]**splash** \ˈsplash\ *vb* [alter. of *plash*] *vi* **1 a** : to strike and dash about a liquid or semiliquid substance **b** : to move in or into a liquid or semiliquid substance and cause it to spatter **2 a** (1) : to become spattered about (2) : to spread or scatter in the manner of splashed liquid **b** : to fall, strike, or move with a splashing sound <a brook ~*ing* over rocks> ~ *vt* **1 a** (1) : to dash a liquid or thinly viscous substance upon or against (2) : to soil or stain with splashed liquid **b** : to mark or overlay with patches of contrasting color or texture **c** : to display prominently **2 a** : to cause (a liquid or thinly viscous substance) to spatter about esp. with force **b** : to scatter in the manner of a splashed liquid — **splash·er** *n*
[2]**splash** *n* **1 a** (1) : splashed liquid or semiliquid substance; *also* : impounded water released suddenly (2) : a spot or daub from or as if from splashed liquid <a mud ~ on the fender> **b** : a colored patch **2 a** : the action of splashing **b** : a short plunge **3** : a sound produced by or as if by a liquid falling, moving, being hurled, or oscillating **4 a** : a vivid impression created esp. by ostentatious activity or appearance **b** : ostentatious display
splash·board \ˈsplash-ˌbō(ə)rd, -ˌbȯ(ə)rd\ *n* **1 a** : DASHBOARD 1 **b** : a panel to protect against splashes **2** : a plank used to close a sluice or spillway of a dam
splash·down \ˈsplash-ˌdau̇n\ *n* : the landing of a manned spacecraft in the ocean — **splash down** \(ˈ)splash-ˈdau̇n\ *vi*
splash guard *n* : a flap suspended behind a rear wheel to prevent tire splash from muddying windshields of following vehicles
splashy \ˈsplash-ē\ *adj* **splash·i·er; -est** **1** : that can be easily splashed about **2** : moving or being moved with a splash or splashing sounds **3** : tending to or exhibiting ostentatious display **4** : consisting of, being, or covered with colored splashes — **splash·i·ly** \ˈsplash-ə-lē\ *adv* — **splash·i·ness** \ˈsplash-ē-nəs\ *n*
[1]**splat** \ˈsplat\ *n* [obs. *splat* (to spread flat)] : a single flat thin often ornamental member of a back of a chair
[2]**splat** *n* [imit.] : a splattering or slapping sound
[1]**splat·ter** \ˈsplat-ər\ *vb* [prob. blend of *splash* and *spatter*] *vt* : SPATTER ~ *vi* : to scatter or fall in or as if in drops
[2]**splatter** *n* : SPATTER, SPLASH
[1]**splay** \ˈsplā\ *vb* [ME *splayen,* short for *displayen* — more at DISPLAY] *vt* **1** : to spread out **2** : to make (as the jamb of a door) oblique : BEVEL ~ *vi* **1** : to become splayed **2** : SLOPE, SLANT
[2]**splay** *n* **1** : a slope or bevel esp. of the sides of a door or window **2** : SPREAD, EXPANSION
[3]**splay** *adj* **1** : turned outward <~ knees> **2** : AWKWARD, UNGAINLY
splay·foot \ˈsplā-ˌfu̇t, -ˈfu̇t\ *n* : a foot abnormally flattened and spread out; *specif* : FLATFOOT — **splayfoot** *or* **splay·foot·ed** \-ˈfu̇t-əd\ *adj*
spleen \ˈsplēn\ *n* [ME *splen,* fr. MF or L; MF *esplen,* fr. L *splen,* fr. Gk *splēn;* akin to L *lien* spleen] **1** : a highly vascular ductless organ near the stomach or intestine of most vertebrates concerned

with final destruction of blood cells, storage of blood, and production of lymphocytes **2** *obs* **:** the seat of emotions or passions **3** *archaic* **:** MELANCHOLY **4 :** mingled ill will and bad temper **5** *obs* **:** a sudden impulse or whim **:** CAPRICE ***syn*** see MALICE

spleen·ful \-fəl\ *adj* **:** full of or affected with spleen **:** SPLENETIC

spleen·wort \-ˌwərt, -ˌwȯ(ə)rt\ *n* [fr. the belief in its power to cure disorders of the spleen] **:** any of a genus (*Asplenium*) of ferns having linear or oblong sori borne obliquely on the upper side of a veinlet

spleeny \ˈsplē-nē\ *adj* **1 :** full of or displaying spleen **2** *New Eng* **:** peevish and irritable with hypochondriac inclinations

splen- *or* **spleno-** *comb form* [L, fr. Gk *splēn-, splēno-,* fr. *splēn*] **:** spleen <*splen*ectomy> <*spleno*megaly>

splen·dent \ˈsplen-dənt\ *adj* [ME, fr. LL *splendent-, splendens,* fr. L, prp. of *splendēre*] **1 :** SHINING, GLOSSY <~ luster> **2 :** ILLUSTRIOUS, BRILLIANT <~ genius>

splen·did \ˈsplen-dəd\ *adj* [L *splendidus,* fr. *splendēre* to shine; akin to Gk *splēdos* ashes, Skt *sphuliṅga* spark] **1 :** possessing or displaying splendor **:** as **a :** SHINING, BRILLIANT **b :** SHOWY, MAGNIFICENT **2 :** ILLUSTRIOUS, GRAND **3 :** EXCELLENT <~ motives> — **splen·did·ly** *adv* — **splen·did·ness** *n*

syn SPLENDID, RESPLENDENT, GORGEOUS, GLORIOUS, SUBLIME, SUPERB *shared meaning element* **:** extraordinarily or transcendently impressive

splen·dif·er·ous \splen-ˈdif-(ə-)rəs\ *adj* [*splendor* + *-i-* + *-ferous*] **1 :** SPLENDID **2 :** deceptively splendid — **splen·dif·er·ous·ly** *adv* — **splen·dif·er·ous·ness** *n*

splen·dor \ˈsplen-dər\ *n* [ME *splendure,* fr. AF *splendur,* fr. L *splendor,* fr. *splendēre*] **1 a :** great brightness or luster **:** BRILLIANCY **b :** MAGNIFICENCE, POMP **2 :** something splendid — **splen·dor·ous** *also* **splen·drous** \-d(ə-)rəs\ *adj*

splen·dour \-dər\ *chiefly Brit var of* SPLENDOR

sple·nec·to·my \spli-ˈnek-tə-mē\ *n, pl* **-mies** [ISV] **:** surgical removal of the spleen — **sple·nec·to·mized** \-ˌmīzd\ *adj*

sple·net·ic \spli-ˈnet-ik, *archaic* ˈsplen-ə-(ˌ)tik\ *adj* [LL *spleneticus,* fr. L *splen* spleen] **1** *archaic* **:** given to melancholy **2 :** marked by bad temper, malevolence, or spite ***syn*** see IRASCIBLE — **splenetic** *n* — **sple·net·i·cal·ly** \spli-ˈnet-i-k(ə-)lē\ *adv*

splen·ic \ˈsplen-ik\ *adj* [L *splenicus,* fr. Gk *splēnikos,* fr. *splēn* spleen] **:** of, relating to, or located in the spleen <~ blood flow>

sple·ni·us \ˈsplē-nē-əs\ *n, pl* **-nii** \-nē-ˌī\ [NL, fr. L *splenium* plaster, compress, fr. Gk *splēnion,* fr. *splēn*] **:** a flat oblique muscle of each side of the back of the neck

spleno·meg·a·ly \ˌsplen-ō-ˈmeg-ə-lē\ *n, pl* **-lies** [ISV *splen-* + Gk *megal-, megas* large — more at MUCH] **:** enlargement of the spleen

spleu·chan \ˈsplük-ən, ˈsplüek-\ *n* [ScGael *spliùcan* + IrGael *spliùchān*] *Scot & Irish* **:** a pouch esp. for tobacco or money

[1]splice \ˈsplīs\ *vt* **spliced; splic·ing** [obs. D *splissen;* akin to MD *splitten* to split] **1 a :** to unite (as two ropes) by interweaving the strands **b :** to unite (as spars, timbers, or rails) by lapping two ends together or by applying a piece that laps upon two ends and making fast **2 :** to unite in marriage **:** MARRY — **splic·er** *n*

[2]splice *n* **1 :** a joining or joint made by splicing **2 :** MARRIAGE, WEDDING

splice 1

spline \ˈsplīn\ *n* [origin unknown] **1 :** a thin wood or metal strip used in building construction **2 :** a key that is fixed to one of two connected mechanical parts and fits into a keyway in the other; *also* **:** a keyway for such a key

[1]splint \ˈsplint\ *or* **splent** \ˈsplent\ *n* [ME, fr. MLG *splinte, splente;* akin to OHG *spaltan* to split — more at SPILL] **1 :** a small plate or strip of metal used in making armor **2 a :** a thin strip of wood suitable for interweaving (as into baskets) **b :** SPLINTER **c :** material or a device used to protect and immobilize a body part (as a broken arm) **3 :** a bony enlargement on the upper part of the cannon bone of a horse usu. on the inside of the leg

[2]splint *vt* **1 :** to support and immobilize (as a broken bone) with a splint **2 :** to brace with or as if with splints

splint bone *n* **:** one of the slender rudimentary metacarpal or metatarsal bones on either side of the cannon bone in the limbs of the horse and related animals

[1]splin·ter \ˈsplint-ər\ *n* [ME, fr. MD; akin to MLG *splinte* splint] **1 :** a thin piece split or rent off lengthwise **:** SLIVER **2 :** a group or faction broken away from a parent body — **splinter** *adj* — **splin·tery** \ˈsplint-ə-rē, ˈsplin-trē\ *adj*

[2]splinter *vb* **splint·ered; splin·ter·ing** \ˈsplint-ə-riŋ, ˈsplin-triŋ\ *vt* **1 :** to split or rend into long thin pieces **:** SHIVER **2 :** to split into fragments, parts, or factions ~ *vi* **:** to become splintered

[1]split \ˈsplit\ *vb* **split; split·ting** [D *splitten,* fr. MD; akin to OHG *spaltan* to split — more at SPILL] *vt* **1 a :** to divide lengthwise usu. along a grain or seam or by layers **b :** to affect as if by cleaving or forcing apart <the river ~*s* the town in two> **2 a (1) :** to tear or rend apart **:** BURST(2) **:** to subject (an atom or atomic nucleus) to artificial disintegration esp. by fission **b :** to affect as if by breaking up or tearing apart **:** SHATTER <a roar that ~ the air> **3 :** to divide into parts or portions: as **a :** to divide between persons **:** SHARE **b :** to divide into factions, parties, or groups **c :** to mark (a ballot) or cast or register (a vote) so as to vote for candidates of different parties **d (1) :** to divide or break down (a chemical compound) into constituents <~ a fat into glycerol and fatty acids> **(2) :** to remove by such separation <~ off carbon dioxide> **e :** to divide (stock) by issuing a larger number of shares to existing shareholders usu. without increase in total par value **4 :** to separate (the parts of a whole) by interposing something <~ an infinitive> **5 :** LEAVE <~ the fraternity party after a few drinks> ~ *vi* **1 a :** to become split lengthwise or into layers **b :** to break apart **:** BURST **2 a :** to become divided up or separated off <~ into factions> **b :** to sever relations or connections **c :** LEAVE; *esp* **:** to leave without delay **3 :** to apportion shares ***syn*** see TEAR — **split·ter** *n* — **split hairs :** to make oversubtle or trivial distinctions — **split one's sides :** to laugh heartily

[2]split *n* **1 a :** a narrow break made by or as if by splitting **b :** a position of bowling pins left standing with space for pins between them **2 :** a piece split off or made thin by splitting **3 a :** a division into or between divergent or antagonistic elements or forces **b :** a faction formed in this way **4 a :** the act or process of splitting **b :** the act of lowering oneself to the floor or leaping into the air with legs extended at right angles to the trunk **5 :** a product of division by or as if by splitting **6 :** a bottle of half the size of the usual small bottle for a drink **7 :** a sweet composed of sliced fruit (as banana), ice cream, syrup, and often nuts and whipped cream

[3]split *adj* **1 :** DIVIDED, FRACTURED **2 :** prepared for use by splitting <~ bamboo> <~ hides> **3 :** HETEROZYGOUS — used esp. by breeders of cage birds sometimes with *for* **4 :** widely spaced

split decision *n* **:** a decision in a boxing match reflecting a division of opinion among the referee and judges

split end *n* **:** an offensive football end who lines up usu. several yards to the side of the formation

split infinitive *n* **:** an infinitive with *to* having a modifier between the *to* and the verbal (as in "to really start")

split–level \ˈsplit-ˈlev-əl\ *adj* **:** divided vertically so that the floor level of rooms in one part is approximately midway between the levels of two successive stories in an adjoining part <a ~ house> — **split–lev·el** \-ˌlev-əl\ *n*

split pea *n* **:** a dried hulled pea in which the cotyledons usu. split apart

split personality *n* **:** a personality structure composed of two or more internally consistent groups of behavior tendencies and attitudes each acting independently of and apparently dissociated from the other

split rail *n* **:** a fence rail split from a log

split second *n* **:** a fractional part of a second **:** FLASH

split shift *n* **:** a shift of working hours divided into two or more working periods at times (as mornings and evening) separated by more than normal periods of time off (as for lunch or rest)

split ticket *n* **:** a ballot cast by a voter who votes for candidates of more than one party

split·ting \ˈsplit-iŋ\ *adj* **:** that splits or causes to split: as **a :** causing a piercing sensation <a ~ headache> **b :** very fast or quick **c :** SIDESPLITTING <a ~ laugh>

splore \ˈsplō(ə)r, ˈsplȯ(ə)r\ *n* [origin unknown] **1** *Scot* **:** FROLIC, CAROUSAL **2** *Scot* **:** COMMOTION

[1]splotch \ˈspläch\ *n* [perh. blend of *spot* and *blotch*] **:** BLOTCH, SPOT — **splotchy** \-ē\ *adj*

[2]splotch *vt* **:** to mark with a splotch **:** cover with splotches

[1]splurge \ˈsplərj\ *n* [perh. blend of *splash* and *surge*] **:** an ostentatious demonstration or effort

[2]splurge *vb* **splurged; splurg·ing** *vi* **1 :** to make a splurge **2 :** to indulge oneself extravagantly — often used with *on* <~ on a new dress> ~ *vt* **:** to spend extravagantly or ostentatiously

[1]splut·ter \ˈsplət-ər\ *n* [prob. alter. of *sputter*] **1 :** a confused noise (as of hasty speaking) **2 :** a splashing or sputtering sound

[2]splutter *vi* **1 :** to make a noise as if spitting **2 :** to speak hastily and confusedly ~ *vt* **:** to utter hastily or confusedly **:** STAMMER — **splut·ter·er** \ˈsplət-ər-ər\ *n*

splut·tery \ˈsplət-ə-rē\ *adj* **:** marked by spluttering

Spode \ˈspōd\ *n* **:** ceramic ware (as bone china, stone china, or Parian ware) made at the works established by Josiah Spode in 1770 at Stoke in Staffordshire, England

spod·u·mene \ˈspäj-ə-ˌmēn\ *n* [prob. fr. F *spodumène,* fr. G *spodumen,* fr. Gk *spodoumenos,* prp. of *spodousthai* to be burnt to ashes, fr. *spodos* ashes] **:** a white to yellowish, purplish, or emerald-green monoclinic mineral $LiAlSi_2O_6$ that is a lithium aluminum silicate and occurs in prismatic crystals often of great size

[1]spoil \ˈspȯi(ə)l\ *n* [ME *spoile,* fr. MF *espoille,* fr. L *spolia,* pl. of *spolium* — more at SPILL] **1 a :** plunder taken from an enemy in war or a victim in robbery **:** LOOT **b :** public offices made the property of a successful party — usu. used in pl. **c :** something gained by special effort — usu. used in pl. **2 a :** SPOLIATION, PLUNDERING **b :** the act of damaging **:** HARM, IMPAIRMENT **3 :** an object of plundering **:** PREY **4 :** earth and rock excavated or dredged **5 :** an object damaged or flawed in the making

syn SPOIL, PILLAGE, PLUNDER, BOOTY, PRIZE, LOOT *shared meaning element* **:** something taken from another by force or craft

[2]spoil *vb* **spoiled** \ˈspȯi(ə)ld, ˈspȯi(ə)lt\ *or* **spoilt** \ˈspȯi(ə)lt\; **spoil·ing** [ME *spoilen,* fr. MF *espoillier,* fr. L *spoilare,* fr. *spolium*] *vt* **1 a :** DESPOIL, STRIP **b :** PILLAGE, ROB **2** *archaic* **:** to seize by force **3 a :** to damage seriously **:** RUIN **b :** to impair the quality or effect of <a quarrel ~*ed* the celebration> **4 a :** to impair the disposition or character of by overindulgence or excessive praise **b :** to pamper excessively **:** CODDLE ~ *vi* **1 :** to practice plunder and robbery **2 :** to lose valuable or useful qualities usu. as a result of decay **3 :** to have an eager desire <~*ing* for a fight> ***syn*** see INDULGE, DECAY — **spoil·able** \ˈspȯi-lə-bəl\ *adj*

spoil·age \ˈspȯi-lij\ *n* **1 :** the act or process of spoiling **2 :** something spoiled or wasted **3 :** loss by spoilage

spoil·er \ˈspȯi-lər\ *n* **1 :** one that spoils **2 :** a long narrow plate along the upper surface of an airplane wing that may be raised for reducing lift and increasing drag — see AIRPLANE illustration **3 :** an air deflector on the front or on the rear deck of an automobile and esp. a racer to reduce the tendency to lift off the road at high speeds

spoils·man \'spȯi(ə)lz-mən\ *n* **:** one who serves a party for a share of the spoils; *also* **:** one who sanctions such practice

spoil·sport \'spȯi(ə)l-ˌspō(ə)rt, -ˌspȯ(ə)rt\ *n* **:** one who spoils the sport or pleasure of others

spoils system *n* **:** a practice of regarding public offices and their emoluments as plunder to be distributed to members of the victorious party

[1]spoke \'spōk\ *past & archaic past part of* SPEAK

[2]spoke *n* [ME, fr. OE *spāca;* akin to MD *spike* spike] **1 a :** one of the small radiating bars inserted in the hub of a wheel to support the rim **b :** something resembling the spoke of a wheel **2 :** a rung of a ladder **3 :** one of the projecting handles of a steering wheel of a boat

[3]spoke *vt* **spoked; spok·ing :** to furnish with or as if with spokes

spo·ken \'spō-kən\ *adj* [pp. of *speak*] **1 a :** delivered by word of mouth **:** ORAL **b :** used in speaking **:** UTTERED <the ~ word> **2 :** characterized by speaking in (such) a manner — used in combination <soft-*spoken*> <plain*spoken*>

spoke·shave \'spōk-ˌshāv\ *n* [[2]*spoke*] **:** a draw knife or small transverse plane with end handles for planing convex or concave surfaces

spokes·man \'spōk-smən\ *n* [prob. irreg. fr. *spoke,* obs. pp. of *speak*] **:** one who speaks as the representative of another or others

spokes·wom·an \-ˌswu̇m-ən\ *n* **:** a female spokesman

spo·li·ate \'spō-lē-ˌāt\ *vt* **-at·ed; -at·ing** [L *spoliatus,* pp.] **:** DESPOIL

spo·li·a·tion \ˌspō-lē-'ā-shən\ *n* [ME, fr. L *spoliation-, spoliatio,* fr. *spoliatus* pp. of *spoliare* to plunder — more at SPOIL] **1 a :** the act of plundering **b :** the state of having been plundered esp. in war **2 :** the act of injuring esp. beyond reclaim — **spo·li·a·tor** \'spō-lē-ˌāt-ər\ *n*

spon·dee \'spän-ˌdē\ *n* [ME *sponde,* fr. MF or L; MF *spondee,* fr. L *spondeum,* fr. Gk *spondeios,* fr. *spondeios* of a libation, fr. *spondē* libation; fr. its use in music accompanying libations — more at SPOUSE] **:** a metrical foot consisting of two long or stressed syllables — **spon·da·ic** \spän-'dā-ik\ *adj or n*

spon·dy·li·tis \ˌspän-də-'līt-əs\ *n* [NL, fr. Gk *sphondylos, spondylos* vertebra, lit., whorl; akin to Gk *sphadazein* to jerk, *sphendonē* sling] **:** inflammation of the vertebrae

[1]sponge \'spənj\ *n* [ME, fr. OE, fr. L *spongia,* fr. Gk] **1 a (1) :** an elastic porous mass of interlacing horny fibers that forms the internal skeleton of various marine animals (phylum Porifera) and is able when wetted to absorb water **(2) :** a piece of sponge (as for scrubbing and cleaning) **(3) :** a porous rubber or cellulose product used similarly to a sponge **b :** any of a phylum (Porifera) of aquatic lower invertebrate animals that are essentially double-walled cell colonies and permanently attached as adults **2 a** *archaic* **:** something that effaces or blots out existing impressions, memories, or emotions **b** *obs* **:** a process or method of cancelling or wiping off indebtedness without making payment **3 :** a pad (as of folded gauze) used in surgery and medicine (as to remove discharge or apply medication) **4 :** one who lives on others **:** SPONGER **5 a :** raised dough (as for yeast bread) **b :** a whipped dessert usu. containing whites of eggs or gelatin **c :** a metal (as platinum) obtained in porous form usu. by reduction without fusion <titanium ~> **d :** the egg mass of a crab

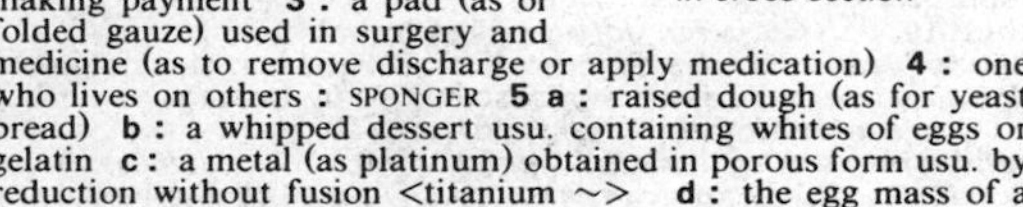

sponge 1b: right branch in cross section

[2]sponge *vb* **sponged; spong·ing** *vt* **1 :** to cleanse, wipe, or moisten with or as if with a sponge **2 :** to erase or destroy with or as if with a sponge — often used with *out* <whole paragraphs had been *sponged* out> **3 :** to get by sponging on another **4 :** to absorb with or as if with or in the manner of a sponge ~ *vi* **1 :** to absorb, soak up, or imbibe like a sponge **2 :** to get something from or live on another by imposing on hospitality or good nature **3 :** to dive or dredge for sponges — **spong·er** *n*

sponge cake *n* **:** a light cake made without shortening

sponge cloth *n* **:** any of various soft porous fabrics esp. in a loose honeycomb weave

sponge rubber *n* **:** cellular rubber resembling a natural sponge in structure used esp. for cushions, vibration dampeners, weather stripping, and gaskets

spon·gin \'spən-jən\ *n* [G, fr. L *spongia* sponge] **:** a scleroprotein that is the chief constituent of flexible fibers in sponge skeletons

spongy \'spən-jē\ *adj* **spong·i·er; -est 1 :** resembling a sponge: **a :** soft and full of cavities <~ ice> **b :** elastic, porous, and absorbent **2 a :** not firm or solid **b :** being in the form of a metallic sponge <~ iron> **3 :** moist and soft like a sponge full of water <a ~ moor> — **spong·i·ness** *n*

spongy parenchyma *n* **:** a spongy layer that is composed of irregular chlorophyll-bearing cells interspersed with air spaces and that fills the part of a leaf between the palisade parenchyma and the lower epidermis — called also *spongy layer, spongy tissue*

spon·son \'spän(t)-sən\ *n* [prob. by shortening & alter. fr. *expansion*] **1 a :** a projection (as a gun platform) from the side of a ship or a tank **b :** an air chamber along a canoe to increase stability and buoyancy **2 :** a light air-filled structure protruding from the hull of a seaplane to steady it on water

[1]spon·sor \'spän(t)-sər\ *n* [LL, fr. L, guarantor, surety, fr. *sponsus,* pp. of *spondēre* to promise — more at SPOUSE] **1 :** one who presents a candidate for baptism or confirmation and undertakes responsibility for his religious education or spiritual welfare **2 :** one who assumes responsibility for some other person or thing **3 :** a person or an organization that pays for or plans and carries out a project or activity; *esp* **:** one that pays the cost of a radio or television program usu. in return for limited advertising time during its course — **spon·so·ri·al** \spän-'sōr-ē-əl, -'sȯr-\ *adj* — **spon·sor·ship** \'spän(t)-sər-ˌship\ *n*

[2]sponsor *vt* **spon·sored; spon·sor·ing** \'spän(t)s-(ə-)riŋ\ **:** to be or stand sponsor for

spon·ta·ne·ity \ˌspänt-ən-'ē-ət-ē, ˌspänt-ᵊn-, -'ā-ət-\ *n* **1 :** the quality or state of being spontaneous **2 :** voluntary or undetermined action or movement; *also* **:** its source ***syn*** see UNCONSTRAINT

spon·ta·ne·ous \spän-'tā-nē-əs\ *adj* [LL *spontaneus,* fr. L *sponte* of one's free will, voluntarily — more at SPIN] **1 :** proceeding from natural feeling or native tendency without external constraint **2 :** arising from a momentary impulse **3 :** controlled and directed internally **:** SELF-ACTING <~ movement characteristic of living things> **4 :** produced without being planted or without human labor **:** INDIGENOUS **5 :** developing without apparent external influence, force, cause, or treatment <~ recovery from a severe illness> **6 :** not apparently contrived or manipulated **:** NATURAL — **spon·ta·ne·ous·ly** *adv* — **spon·ta·ne·ous·ness** *n*

syn SPONTANEOUS, IMPULSIVE, INSTINCTIVE, AUTOMATIC, MECHANICAL *shared meaning element* **:** acting or activated without deliberation ***ant*** studied

spontaneous combustion *n* **:** self-ignition of combustible material through chemical action (as oxidation) of its constituents

spontaneous generation *n* **:** ABIOGENESIS

spontaneous recovery *n* **:** reappearance of an extinguished conditioned response without positive reinforcement

spon·toon \spän-'tün\ *n* [F *sponton,* fr. It *spuntone,* fr. *punta* sharp point, fr. (assumed) VL *puncta* — more at POINT] **:** a short pike formerly borne by subordinate officers of infantry

[1]spoof \'spüf\ *vt* [*Spoof,* a hoaxing game invented by Arthur Roberts †1933 E comedian] **1 :** DECEIVE, HOAX **2 :** to make good-natured fun of

[2]spoof *n* **1 :** HOAX, DECEPTION **2 :** a light humorous parody

[1]spook \'spük\ *n* [D; akin to MLG *spōk* ghost] **:** GHOST, SPECTER — **spook·ish** \'spü-kish\ *adj*

[2]spook *vt* **1 :** HAUNT 3 **2 :** to make frightened or frantic **:** SCARE; *esp* **:** to startle into violent activity (as stampeding) <~*ed* the herd of horses> ~ *vi* **:** to become spooked <cattle ~*ing* at shadows>

spooky \'spü-kē\ *adj* **spook·i·er; -est 1 :** relating to, resembling, or suggesting spooks **2 :** NERVOUS, SKITTISH <a ~ horse> — **spook·i·ly** \-kə-lē\ *adv* — **spook·i·ness** \-kē-nəs\ *n*

[1]spool \'spül\ *n* [ME *spole,* fr. MF or MD; MF *espole,* fr. MD *spoele;* akin to OHG *spuola* spool] **1 :** a cylindrical device which has a rim or ridge at each end and an axial hole for a pin or spindle and on which material (as thread, wire, or tape) is wound **2 :** material or the amount of material wound on a spool

[2]spool *vt* **1 :** to wind on a spool **2 :** WIND <~ the thread off the bobbin> ~ *vi* **1 :** to wind itself on a spool **2 :** WIND

[1]spoon \'spün\ *n* [ME, fr. OE *spōn* splinter, chip; akin to OHG *spān* splinter, chip, Gk *sphēn* wedge] **1 :** an eating or cooking implement consisting of a small shallow bowl with a handle **2 :** something that resembles a spoon in shape (as a usu. metal or shell fishing lure)

[2]spoon *vt* **1 :** to take up and usu. transfer in a spoon **2 :** to propel (a ball) by a weak lifting stroke ~ *vi* **1** [prob. fr. the Welsh custom of an engaged man's presenting his fiancée with a spoon] **:** to make love by caressing, kissing, and talking amorously **:** NECK **2 :** to spoon a ball

spoon·bill \'spün-ˌbil\ *n* **1 :** any of several wading birds (family Plataleidae) related to the ibises that have the bill greatly expanded and flattened at the tip **2 :** any of several broad-billed ducks (as the shoveler)

spoonbill cat *n* **:** PADDLEFISH

spoon–billed \'spün-'bild\ *adj* **:** having the bill or snout expanded and spatulate at the end

spoon bread *n, chiefly South & Midland* **:** soft bread made of cornmeal mixed with milk, eggs, and shortening and served with a spoon

spoon·drift \'spün-ˌdrift\ *n* [alter. of Sc *speendrift* — more at SPINDRIFT] **:** spray blown from waves during a gale at sea

spoo·ner·ism \'spü-nə-ˌriz-əm\ *n* [William A. *Spooner* †1930 E clergyman & educator] **:** a transposition of usu. initial sounds of two or more words (as in *tons of soil* for *sons of toil*)

spoon–feed \'spün-ˌfēd\ *vt* **-fed** \-ˌfed\; **-feed·ing 1 :** to feed by means of a spoon **2 a :** to present (information) so completely as to preclude independent thought <~ material to students> **b :** to present information to in this manner

spoon·ful \'spün-ˌfu̇l\ *n, pl* **spoonfuls** \-ˌfu̇lz\ *also* **spoons·ful** \'spünz-ˌfu̇l\ **:** as much as a spoon will hold; *specif* **:** TEASPOONFUL

spoony *or* **spoon·ey** \'spü-nē\ *adj* **spoon·i·er; -est** [E slang *spoon* (simpleton)] **1 :** SILLY, FOOLISH *esp* **:** unduly sentimental **2:** sentimentally in love

[1]spoor \'spu̇(ə)r, 'spō(ə)r, 'spȯ(ə)r\ *n* [Afrik, fr. MD; akin to OE *spor* footprint, spoor, *spurnan* to kick — more at SPURN] **:** a track, a trail, or droppings esp. of a wild animal

[2]spoor *vt* **:** to track by a spoor ~ *vi* **:** to track something by its spoor

spor- *or* **spori-** *or* **sporo-** *comb form* [NL *spora*] **:** seed **:** spore <*sporo*cyst> <*spor*angium> <*spori*cidal>

spo·rad·ic \spə-'rad-ik\ *adj* [ML *sporadicus,* fr. Gk *sporadikos,* fr. *sporadēn* here and there, fr. *sporad-, sporas* scattered; akin to Gk *speirein* to sow] **:** occurring occasionally, singly, or in scattered instances ***syn*** see INFREQUENT — **spo·rad·i·cal·ly** \-i-k(ə-)lē\ *adv*

sporadic E layer *n* **:** a layer of ionization occurring irregularly within the E region of the ionosphere

spo·ran·gio·phore \spə-'ran-jē-ə-ˌfō(ə)r, -ˌfȯ(ə)r\ *n* **:** a stalk or receptacle bearing sporangia

spo·ran·gi·um \spə-'ran-jē-əm\ *n, pl* **-gia** \-jē-ə\ [NL, fr. *spor-* + Gk *angeion* vessel — more at ANGI-] **:** a case within which usu. asexual spores are produced whether a cell (as in bacteria or algae) producing spores endogenously or a complex structure (as in a fern) — **spo·ran·gial** \-j(ē-)əl\ *adj*

[1]spore \'spō(ə)r, 'spȯ(ə)r\ *n* [NL *spora* seed, spore, fr. Gk, act of sowing, seed, fr. *speirein* to sow — more at SPROUT] **:** a primitive usu. unicellular resistant or reproductive body produced by plants and some invertebrates and capable of development into a new individual in some cases unlike the parent either directly or after fusion with another spore — **spored** \'spō(ə)rd, 'spȯ(ə)rd\ *adj*

[2]**spore** *vi* **spored; spor·ing** : to produce or reproduce by spores

spore case *n* : a case containing spores : SPORANGIUM

spore fruit *n* : a specialized structure (as an ascocarp) that produces spores : FRUITING BODY

spo·ri·cid·al \ˌspōr-ə-'sīd-ᵊl, ˌspȯr-\ *adj* : tending to kill spores — **spo·ri·cide** \'spōr-ə-ˌsīd, 'spȯr-\ *n*

spo·rif·er·ous \spə-'rif-(ə-)rəs; spȯr-'if-, spōr-\ *adj* : bearing or producing spores

spo·ro·carp \'spōr-ə-ˌkärp, 'spȯr-\ *n* [ISV *spor-* + Gk *karpos* fruit — more at HARVEST] : a structure (as in red algae, fungi, or mosses) in or on which spores are produced

spo·ro·cyst \-ˌsist\ *n* [ISV] **1** : a unicellular resting cell (as in slime molds and algae) that may give rise to asexual spores **2 a** : a case or cyst secreted by some sporozoans preliminary to sporogony; *also* : a sporozoan encysted in such a case **b** : a saccular body that is the first asexual reproductive form of a digenetic trematode and buds off cells from its inner surface which develop into rediae — **spo·ro·cys·tic** \ˌspōr-ə-'sis-tik, ˌspȯr-\ *adj*

spo·ro·gen·e·sis \ˌspōr-ə-'jen-ə-səs, ˌspȯr-\ *n* [NL] **1** : reproduction by spores **2** : spore formation

spo·ro·gen·ic \ˌspōr-ə-'jen-ik, ˌspȯr-\ *adj* : SPOROGENOUS

spo·rog·e·nous \spə-'räj-ə-nəs, spȯ-\ *adj* : of, relating to, involving, or reproducing by sporogenesis

spo·ro·go·ni·um \ˌspōr-ə-'gō-nē-əm, ˌspȯr-\ *n, pl* **-nia** \-nē-ə\ [NL, fr. *spor-* + *-gonium* (as in *archegonium*)] : the sporophyte of a moss or liverwort consisting typically of a stalk bearing a capsule in which spores are produced and remaining permanently attached to the gametophyte

spo·rog·o·ny \spə-'räg-ə-nē, spȯ-\ *n* [ISV] : reproduction by spores; *specif* : spore formation in a sporozoan by encystment and subsequent division of a zygote — **spo·ro·gon·ic** \ˌspōr-ə-'gän-ik, ˌspȯr-\ *or* **spo·rog·o·nous** \spə-'räg-ə-nəs, spȯ-\ *adj*

spo·ro·phore \ˌspōr-ə-ˌfō(ə)r, 'spȯr-ə-ˌfȯ(ə)r\ *n* [ISV] : the part (as a spore fruit of a fungus or the placenta of a seed plant) of a sporophyte that develops spores

spo·ro·phyll \-ˌfil\ *n* [ISV] : a spore-bearing and usu. greatly modified leaf

spo·ro·phyte \-ˌfīt\ *n* [ISV] : the individual or generation of a plant exhibiting alternation of generations that bears asexual spores — compare GAMETOPHYTE — **spo·ro·phyt·ic** \ˌspōr-ə-'fit-ik, spȯr-\ *adj*

spo·ro·pol·len·in \ˌspōr-ə-'päl-ə-nən, ˌspȯr-\ *n* [ISV *spor-* + *pollen* + *-in*] : a relatively chemically inert polymer that makes up the outer layer of pollen grains and spores of higher plants

spo·ro·tri·cho·sis \spə-ˌrä-trik-'ō-səs; ˌspōr-ə-trik-, ˌspȯr-\ *n* [NL, fr. *sporotrichum,* genus name] : infection with or disease caused by fungi (genus *Sporotrichum*) that is characterized by nodules and abscesses in the superficial lymph nodes, skin, and subcutaneous tissues, that occurs esp. in man and horses, and that is usu. transmitted by entry of the fungus through a skin abrasion or wound (as from the prick of a thorn)

-spo·rous \'spōr-əs, 'spȯr-; s-pə-rəs\ *adj comb form* [NL *spora* spore] : having (such or so many) spores <homo*sporous*>

spo·ro·zo·an \ˌspōr-ə-'zō-ən, ˌspȯr-\ *n* [NL *Sporozoa,* class name, fr. *spor-* + *-zoa*] : any of a large class (Sporozoa) of strictly parasitic protozoans that have a complicated life cycle usu. involving both asexual and sexual generations often in different hosts and include important pathogens (as malaria parasites, coccidia, and piroplasms) — **sporozoan** *adj*

spo·ro·zo·ite \-'zō-ˌīt\ *n* [NL *Sporozoa* + ISV *-ite*] : a usu. motile infective form of some sporozoans that is a product of sporogony and initiates an asexual cycle in the new host

spor·ran \'spȯr-ən, 'spär-\ *n* [ScGael *sporan*] : a pouch of skin with the hair or fur on that is worn in front of the kilt with Scots Highland dress

1 sporran

[1]**sport** \'spō(ə)rt, 'spȯ(ə)rt\ *vb* [ME *sporten* to divert, disport, short for *disporten*] *vt* **1** : to make usu. ostentatious display of : show off <~ a new hat> **2** [[2]*sport*] : to put forth as a sport or bud variation ~ *vi* **1 a** : to amuse oneself : FROLIC <lambs ~*ing* in the meadow> **b** : to engage in a sport **2 a** : to mock or ridicule something **b** : to speak or act in jest : TRIFLE **3** [[2]*sport*] : to deviate or vary abruptly from type (as by bud variation) : MUTATE

[2]**sport** *n* **1 a** : a source of diversion : RECREATION **b** : sexual play **c (1)** : physical activity engaged in for pleasure **(2)** : a particular activity (as hunting or an athletic game) so engaged in **2 a** : PLEASANTRY, JEST **b** : MOCKERY, DERISION **3 a** : something tossed or driven about in or as if in play **b** : LAUGHINGSTOCK **4 a** : SPORTSMAN **b** : a person living up to the ideals of sportsmanship <he's a good ~ about losing> **c** : a companionable person **5** : an individual exhibiting a sudden deviation from type beyond the normal limits of individual variation usu. as a result of mutation esp. of somatic tissue ***syn*** see FUN

[3]**sport** *or* **sports** *adj* : of, relating to, or suitable for sports <~ equipment>; *esp* : styled in a manner suitable for casual or informal wear <~ coats>

sport fish *n* : a fish important for the sport it affords anglers

sport·fish·er·man \'spōrt-ˌfish-ər-mən, 'spȯrt-\ *n* : a powerboat equipped for sportfishing

sport·fish·ing \-ˌfish-iŋ\ *n* : fishing done with a rod and reel for sport or recreation

sport·ful \-fəl\ *adj* **1 a** : productive of sport or amusement : ENTERTAINING, DIVERTING **b** : PLAYFUL, FROLICSOME **2** : done in sport — **sport·ful·ly** \-fə-lē\ *adv* — **sport·ful·ness** *n*

sport·ing \'spōrt-iŋ, 'spȯrt-\ *adj* **1 a** : used or suitable for sport **b** : marked by or calling for sportsmanship **c** : involving such risk as a sports contender may expect to take or encounter <a ~ chance> **2** : of or relating to dissipation and esp. gambling **3** : tending to mutate freely — **sport·ing·ly** \-iŋ-lē\ *adv*

sport·ive \-iv\ *adj* **1 a** : FROLICSOME, PLAYFUL **b** : ARDENT, WANTON **2** : relating to sports and esp. field sports — **sport·ive·ly** *adv* — **sport·ive·ness** *n*

sports car *also* **sport car** *n* : a low comparatively small usu. 2-passenger automobile designed for quick response, easy maneuverability, and high-speed driving

sports·cast \'spō(ə)rt-ˌskast, 'spȯ(ə)rt-\ *n* [*sport* + broad*cast*] : a radio or television broadcast of a sports event or of information about sports — **sports·cast·er** \-ˌskas-tər\ *n*

sports·man \'spō(ə)rt-smən, 'spȯ(ə)rt-\ *n* **1** : one who engages in sports and esp. in hunting and fishing **2** : a person who is fair, generous, and a good loser, and a graceful winner — **sports·man·like** \-ˌlīk\ *adj* — **sports·man·ly** \-lē\ *adj*

sports·man·ship \-ˌship\ *n* : conduct becoming to a sportsman

sports·wear \'spō(ə)rt-ˌswa(ə)r, 'spȯ(ə)rt-, -ˌswe(ə)r\ *n* : clothing suitable for recreation

sports·wom·an \-ˌswu̇m-ən\ *n* : a female sportsman

sports·writ·er \'spō(ə)rts-ˌrīt-ər, 'spȯ(ə)rts-\ *n* : one who writes about sports esp. for a newspaper

sports·writ·ing \-iŋ\ *n* : writing that relates to sports

sporty \'spōrt-ē, 'spȯrt-\ *adj* **sport·i·er; -est** **1** : characteristic of a sport or sportsman : SPORTSMANLIKE **2 a** : notably loose or dissipated : FAST **b** : FLASHY, SHOWY <~ clothes> **3** : capable of giving good sport <a ~ boat> — **sport·i·ly** \'spōrt-ᵊl-ē, 'spȯrt-\ *adv* — **sport·i·ness** \'spōrt-ē-nəs, 'spȯrt-\ *n*

spor·u·late \'spȯr-(y)ə-ˌlāt, 'spȯr-\ *vi* **-lat·ed; -lat·ing** [back-formation fr. *sporulation*] : to undergo sporulation

spor·u·la·tion \ˌspōr-(y)ə-'lā-shən, ˌspȯr-\ *n* [ISV, fr. NL *sporula,* dim. of *spora* spore] : the formation of spores; *esp* : division into many small spores (as after encystment) — **spor·u·la·tive** \'spōr-(y)ə-ˌlāt-iv, 'spȯr-\ *adj*

-spo·ry \ˌspōr-ē, ˌspȯr-; s-pə-rē\ *n comb form* [*-sporous* + *-y*] : quality or state of having (such) spores <homo*spory*>

[1]**spot** \'spät\ *n* [ME; akin to MD *spotte* stain, speck, ON *spotti* small piece] **1** : a taint on character or reputation : FAULT <the only ~ on the family name> **2 a** : a small area visibly different (as in color, finish, or material) from the surrounding area **b (1)** : an area marred or marked (as by dirt) **(2)** : a circumscribed surface lesion of disease (as measles) or decay <~*s* of rot> <rust ~*s* on a leaf> **c** : a conventionalized design used on playing cards to distinguish suits and indicate values **3** : an object having a specified number of spots or a specified numeral on its surface **4** : a small quantity or amount : BIT **5 a** : a particular place or area **b** : a small extent of space **6** : a small croaker (*Leiostomus xanthurus*) of the Atlantic coast with a black spot behind the shoulders **7 a** : a particular position (as in an organization or a hierarchy) **b** : a place on an entertainment program **8** : SPOTLIGHT **9** : a position usu. of difficulty or embarrassment **10** : a brief announcement or advertisement broadcast between scheduled radio or television programs — **on the spot** *or* **upon the spot** **1** : at once : IMMEDIATELY **2** : at the place of action **3 a** : in a responsible or accountable position **b** : in difficulty or danger <their opposition put him *on the spot*>

[2]**spot** *vb* **spot·ted; spot·ting** *vt* **1** : to stain the character or reputation of : DISGRACE **2** : to mark in or with a spot : STAIN **3** : to locate or identify by a spot **4 a** : to single out : IDENTIFY; *specif* : to note as a known criminal or a suspicious person **b** : DETECT, NOTICE <~ a mistake> **c (1)** : to locate accurately <~ an enemy position> **(2)** : to cause to strike accurately <~ the battery's fire> **5 a** : to lie at intervals in or over : STUD **b** : to place at intervals or in a desired spot <~ field telephones> **c** : to fix in or as if in the beam of a spotlight **d** : to schedule in a particular spot or at a particular time **6** : to remove a spot from **7** : to allow as a handicap ~ *vi* **1** : to become stained or discolored in spots **2** : to cause a spot **3** : to act as a spotter; *esp* : to locate targets — **spot·ta·ble** \'spät-ə-bəl\ *adj*

[3]**spot** *adj* **1 a** : being, originating, or done on the spot or in or for a particular spot <~ coverage of the news> **b** : available for immediate delivery after sale <~ commodities> **c (1)** : paid out upon delivery <~ cash> **(2)** : involving immediate cash payment <~ transaction> **d (1)** : broadcast between scheduled programs <~ announcements> **(2)** : originating in a local station for a national advertiser **e** : performing occasionally when needed <chance of making the . . . varsity as a ~ starter and relief pitcher —*N.Y. Times*> **2** : made at random or restricted to a few places or instances <a ~ check>; *also* : selected at random or as a sample

SPOT \'spät\ *abbr* satellite positioning and tracking

spot–check \'spät-ˌchek\ *vt* : to sample or investigate quickly or at random ~ *vi* : to make a spot check

spot·less \'spät-ləs\ *adj* : having no spot: **a** : free from impurity : IMMACULATE <~ kitchens> **b** : PURE, UNBLEMISHED <~ reputation> — **spot·less·ly** *adv* — **spot·less·ness** *n*

[1]**spot·light** \'spät-ˌlīt\ *n* **1 a** : a projected spot of light used to illuminate brilliantly a person, object, or group on a stage **b** : conspicuous public notice <held the political ~> **2 a** : a light designed to direct a narrow intense beam of light on a small area **b** : something that illuminates brilliantly

[2]**spotlight** *vt* : to illuminate with or as if with a spotlight

---

ə abut	**ᵊ** kitten	**ər** further	**a** back	**ā** bake	**ä** cot, cart
au̇ out	**ch** chin	**e** less	**ē** easy	**g** gift	**i** trip **ī** life
j joke	**ŋ** sing	**ō** flow	**ȯ** flaw	**ȯi** coin	**th** thin **th** this
ü loot	**u̇** foot	**y** yet	**yü** few	**yu̇** furious	**zh** vision

spot pass *n* : a pass (as in football or basketball) made to a predetermined spot on the field or court rather than directly to a player
spot·ted \'spät-əd\ *adj* **1 :** marked with spots **2 :** being sullied : TARNISHED **3 :** characterized by the appearance of spots
spotted adder *n* **1 :** MILK SNAKE **2 :** HOGNOSE SNAKE
spotted alfalfa aphid *n* : a highly destructive Old World aphid (*Therioaphis maculata*) that is established in the U.S. from coast to coast in warmer areas and that injects a toxic saliva in feeding esp. on alfalfa and causes yellowing and stunting of affected plants
spotted cucumber beetle *n* : a rather slender greenish yellow beetle (*Diabrotica undecimpunctata howardi*) that feeds as an adult on various ornamental and crop plants and is a vector of wilt disease esp. of cucumbers and melons
spotted fever *n* : any of various eruptive fevers: as **a :** TYPHUS **b :** ROCKY MOUNTAIN SPOTTED FEVER
spotted sea trout *n* : a weakfish (*Cynoscion nebulosus*) that is a valuable food and sport fish of the south Atlantic and Gulf coasts of the U.S. — called also *sea trout, spotted weakfish*
spot·ter \'spät-ər\ *n* **1 :** one that makes or applies a spot (as for identification) **2 :** one that looks or keeps watch: as **a :** one that locates enemy targets **b :** a civilian who watches for approaching airplanes **3 :** one that removes spots **4 :** one that places something on or in a desired spot
spot test *n* **1 :** a test conducted on the spot to yield immediate results **2 :** a test limited to a few key or sample points or a relatively small percentage of random spots
spot·ty \'spät-ē\ *adj* **spot·ti·er; -est 1 :** marked with spots : SPOTTED **2 :** lacking uniformity esp. in quality <~ attendance> — **spot·ti·ly** \'spät-ᵊl-ē\ *adv* — **spot·ti·ness** \'spät-ē-nəs\ *n*
spou·sal \'spau̇-zəl, -səl\ *n* [ME *spousaille,* fr. MF *espousailles* espousal] : NUPTIALS — usu. used in pl. — **spousal** *adj*
[1]**spouse** \'spau̇s *also* 'spau̇z\ *n* [ME, fr. OF *espous* (masc.) & *espouse* (fem.), fr. L *sponsus* betrothed man, groom & *sponsa* betrothed woman, bride, fr. *sponsus,* pp. of *spondēre* to promise, betroth; akin to Gk *spendein* to make a libation, promise, *spondē* libation (pl., treaty)] : married person : HUSBAND, WIFE
[2]**spouse** \'spau̇z, 'spau̇s\ *vt* **spoused; spous·ing** *archaic* : WED
[1]**spout** \'spau̇t\ *vb* [ME *spouten;* akin to MD *spoiten* to spout, OE *spīwan* to spew] *vt* **1 :** to eject (as liquid) in a stream <wells ~*ing* oil> **2 a :** to speak or utter readily, volubly, and at length **b :** to speak or utter in a pompous or oratorical manner : DECLAIM ~ *vi* **1 :** to issue with force or in a jet : SPURT **2 :** to eject material (as liquid) in a jet **3 :** DECLAIM — **spout·er** *n*
[2]**spout** *n* **1 :** a pipe or conductor through which a liquid is discharged or conveyed in a stream: as **a :** a pipe for carrying rainwater from a roof **b :** a projecting tube or lip from which water issues **2 :** a discharge or jet of liquid from or as if from a pipe; *esp* : WATERSPOUT **3** *archaic* : PAWNSHOP — **spout·ed** \'spau̇t-əd\ *adj*
spp *abbr* species
SPQR *abbr* **1** [L *senatus populusque Romanus*] the senate and the people of Rome **2** small profits, quick returns
SPR *abbr* Society for Psychical Research
sprach·ge·fühl \'shpräk-kə-ˌfu̇ēl\ *n* [G, fr. *sprache* language + *gefühl* feeling] **1 :** sensibility to conformance with or divergence from the established usage of a language **2 :** a feeling for what is linguistically effective or appropriate
sprag \'sprag\ *n* [perh. of Scand origin; akin to Sw dial. *spragge* branch] : a pointed stake or steel bar let down from a halted vehicle (as a wagon) to prevent it from rolling
[1]**sprain** \'sprān\ *n* [origin unknown] **1 :** a sudden or violent twist or wrench of a joint with stretching or tearing of ligaments **2 :** a sprained condition
[2]**sprain** *vt* : to subject to sprain
sprat \'sprat\ *n* [alter. of ME *sprot,* fr. OE *sprott*] **1 :** a small European herring (*Clupea sprattus*) closely related to the common herring; *also* : a small or young herring or similar fish (as an anchovy) **2 :** a young, small, or insignificant person
sprawl \'sprȯl\ *vb* [ME *sprawlen,* fr. OE *sprēawlian*] *vi* **1 a** *archaic* : to lie thrashing or tossing about **b :** to creep or clamber awkwardly **2 :** to lie or sit with arms and legs spread out **3 :** to spread or develop irregularly ~ *vt* : to cause to spread out carelessly or awkwardly — **sprawl** *n*
[1]**spray** \'sprā\ *n* [ME] **1 :** a usu. flowering branch or shoot **2 :** a decorative flat arrangement of flowers and foliage (as on a coffin) **3 :** something (as a jeweled pin) resembling a spray
[2]**spray** *n* [obs. E *spray* (to sprinkle), fr. MD *sprayen;* akin to Gk *speirein* to scatter — more at SPROUT] **1 :** water flying in small drops or particles blown from waves or thrown up by a waterfall **2 a :** a jet of vapor or finely divided liquid **b :** a device (as an atomizer or sprayer) by which a spray is dispersed or applied **c** (1) : an application of a spray or by spraying (2) : a substance (as paint or insecticide) so applied
[3]**spray** *vt* **1 :** to disperse or apply as a spray **2 :** to project spray on or into ~ *vi* **1 :** to break up into spray **2 :** to disperse or apply a spray — **spray·er** *n*
spray gun *n* : an apparatus resembling a gun for applying a substance (as paint or insecticide) in the form of a spray
[1]**spread** \'spred\ *vb* **spread; spread·ing** [ME *spreden,* fr. OE *sprǣdan;* akin to OHG *spreiten* to spread, OE *-sprūtan* to sprout — more at SPROUT] *vt* **1 a :** to open or expand over a larger area <~ out the map> **b :** to stretch out : EXTEND <~ its wings for flight> **2 a :** to distribute over an area <~ fertilizer> **b :** to distribute over a period or among a group <~ the work over a few weeks> **c :** to apply on a surface <~ butter on bread> **d** (1) : to cover or overlay with <~ the cloth on the table> (2) *archaic* : to cover completely **e** (1) : to prepare or furnish for dining : SET <~ the table> (2) : SERVE <~ the afternoon tea> **3 a :** to make widely known <~ the news> **b :** to extend the range or incidence of <~ a disease> **c :** DIFFUSE, EMIT <flowers ~*ing* their fragrance> **4 :** to push apart by weight or force ~ *vi* **1 a :** to become dispersed, distributed, or scattered **b :** to become known or disseminated <panic ~ rapidly> **2 :** to grow in length or breadth : EXPAND **3 :** to move apart (as from pressure or weight) : SEPARATE — **spread·abil·i·ty** \ˌspred-ə-'bil-ət-ē\ *n* — **spread·able** \'spred-ə-bəl\ *adj*
[2]**spread** *n* **1 a :** the act or process of spreading **b :** extent of spreading **2 :** something spread out: as **a :** a surface area : EXPANSE **b** *West* (1) : RANCH (2) : a herd of animals **c** (1) : a prominent display in a periodical (2) : two facing pages (as of a newspaper) usu. with matter running across the fold; *also* : the matter occupying these pages **3 :** something spread on or over a surface: as **a :** a food to be spread (as on bread or crackers) <a cheese ~> **b :** a sumptuous meal : FEAST **c :** a cloth cover for a table or bed **4 :** distance between two points : GAP
[1]**spread–ea·gle** \'spred-ˌē-gəl\ *vb* **spread–ea·gled; spread–ea·gling** \-ˌē-g(ə-)liŋ\ *vi* **1 :** to execute a spread eagle (as in skating) **2 :** to stand or move with arms and legs stretched out : SPRAWL ~ *vt* **1 :** to stretch out into the position of a spread eagle **2 :** to spread over : stretch across
[2]**spread–eagle** *adj* [fr. the spread eagle on the Great Seal of the U.S.] : marked by bombast and boastful exaggeration esp. of the greatness of the U.S. <~ oratory>
spread eagle *n* **1 :** a representation of an eagle with wings raised and legs extended **2 :** something resembling or suggestive of a spread eagle; *specif* : a skating figure executed with the skates heel to heel in a straight line
spread end *n* : SPLIT END
spread·er \'spred-ər\ *n* : one that spreads: as **a :** an implement for scattering material **b :** a small knife for spreading butter **c** : WETTING AGENT **d :** a device (as a bar) holding two linear elements (as lines, guys, rails) apart and usu. taut
spread formation *n* : an offensive football formation in which the ends are positioned three to five yards outside the tackles, the tailback plays seven to eight yards behind the line, and the other three backs are in flanking position close to the line
spreading factor *n* : HYALURONIDASE
spree \'sprē\ *n* [perh. alter. of Sc *spreath* cattle raid, foray, fr. ScGael *sprēidh* cattle, fr. L *praeda* booty — more at PREY] : an unrestrained indulgence in or outburst of an activity <went on a buying ~> ; *esp* : BINGE, CAROUSAL
sprent \'sprent\ *adj* [fr. pp. of obs. *sprenge* (to sprinkle)] *archaic* : sprinkled over
[1]**sprig** \'sprig\ *n* [ME *sprigge*] **1 a :** a small shoot : TWIG **b** : a small division of grass used for propagation **2 a :** HEIR **b** : YOUTH **c :** a small specimen **3 :** an ornament resembling a sprig, stemmed flower, or leaf **4 :** a small headless nail : BRAD
[2]**sprig** *vt* **sprigged; sprig·ging 1 :** to drive sprigs or brads into **2 :** to mark or adorn with the representation of plant sprigs **3** : to propagate (a grass) by means of stolons or small divisions
spright·ful \'sprīt-fəl\ *adj* [obs. *spright*] : full of life or spirit : SPRIGHTLY — **spright·ful·ly** \-fə-lē\ *adv* — **spright·ful·ness** *n*
spright·ly \-lē\ *adj* **spright·li·er; -est** [obs. *spright* (sprite), alter. of *sprite*] : marked by a gay lightness and vivacity : SPIRITED ***syn*** see LIVELY — **spright·li·ness** *n*
sprig·tail \'sprig-ˌtāl\ *n* : any of several birds with pointed tails; *esp* : PINTAIL a
[1]**spring** \'spriŋ\ *vb* **sprang** \'spraŋ\ *or* **sprung** \'sprəŋ\; **sprung; spring·ing** \'spriŋ-iŋ\ [ME *springen,* fr. OE *springan;* akin to OHG *springan* to jump, Gk *sperchesthai* to hasten] *vi* **1 a** (1) : DART, SHOOT (2) : to be resilient or elastic; *also* : to move by elastic force <the lid *sprang* shut> **b :** to become warped **2** : to issue with speed and force or as a stream **3 a :** to grow as a plant **b :** to issue by birth or descent **c :** to come into being : ARISE **d** *archaic* : DAWN **e :** to begin to blow — used with *up* <a breeze quickly *sprang* up> **4 a :** to make a leap or series of leaps **b :** to leap or jump up suddenly **5 :** to stretch out in height : RISE ~ *vt* **1 :** to cause to spring **2 a :** to undergo or bring about the splitting or cracking of <wind *sprang* the mast> **b** : to undergo the opening of (a leak) **3 a :** to cause to operate suddenly <~ a trap> **b :** to apply or insert by bending **c :** to bend by force **4 :** to leap over **5 :** to produce or disclose suddenly or unexpectedly **6 :** to make lame : STRAIN **7 :** to release or cause to be released from confinement or custody
syn SPRING, ARISE, RISE, ORIGINATE, DERIVE, FLOW, ISSUE, EMANATE, PROCEED, STEM *shared meaning element* : to come up or out of something into existence
[2]**spring** *n, often attrib* **1 a :** a source of supply; *esp* : a source of water issuing from the ground **b :** an ultimate source esp. of action or motion **2 :** SPRING TIDE **3 :** a time or season of growth or development; *specif* : the season between winter and summer comprising in the northern hemisphere usu. the months of March, April, and May or as reckoned astronomically extending from the March equinox to the June solstice **4 :** an elastic body or device that recovers its original shape when released after being distorted **5 a :** the act or an instance of leaping up or forward : BOUND **b** (1) : capacity for springing : RESILIENCE (2) : BOUNCE, ENERGY **6** : the point or plane at which an arch or vault curve springs from its impost ***syn*** see MOTIVE
[3]**spring** *vt* **sprung** \'sprəŋ\; **spring·ing** \'spriŋ-iŋ\ : to fit with springs
spring·ald \'spriŋ-əld\ *or* **spring·al** \-əl\ *n* [prob. fr. ME, a kind of catapult, fr. MF *espringale*] : a young man : STRIPLING
spring beauty *n* : any of a genus (*Claytonia*) of plants of the purslane family; *esp* : one (*C. virginica*) that sends up in early spring a 2-leaved stem bearing delicate pink flowers
spring·board \'spriŋ-ˌbō(ə)rd, -ˌbȯ(ə)rd\ *n* **1 :** a flexible board usu. secured at one end and used for gymnastic stunts or diving **2 :** a point of departure : JUMPING-OFF PLACE
spring·bok \'spriŋ-ˌbäk\ *n, pl* **springbok** *or* **springboks** [Afrik, fr. *spring* to jump + *bok* male goat] : a swift and graceful southern African gazelle (*Antidorcas euchore*) noted for its habit of springing lightly and suddenly into the air
spring catch *n* : a catch (as for a door) with a bolt that can be retracted by pressure and is shot by a spring when the pressure is released
spring chicken *n* : a young person

spring–clean·ing \'spriŋ-'klē-niŋ\ *n* [2*spring*] : the act or process of doing a thorough cleaning of a place

springe \'sprinj\ *n* [ME *sprenge, springe;* akin to OE *springan* to spring] **1** : a noose fastened to an elastic body to catch small game **2** : SNARE, TRAP

spring·er \'spriŋ-ər\ *n* **1** : a stone or other solid laid at the impost of an arch — see ARCH illustration **2** : one that springs; *esp* : SPRINGER SPANIEL **3** : a cow nearly ready to calve

springer spaniel *n* : a medium-sized sporting dog of either of two breeds that is used chiefly for finding and flushing small game: **a** : ENGLISH SPRINGER SPANIEL **b** : WELSH SPRINGER SPANIEL

spring fever *n* : a lazy or restless feeling often associated with the onset of spring

Spring·field rifle \ˌspriŋ-ˌfēl(d)-\ *n* [*Springfield,* Mass.] : a .30 caliber bolt-operated repeating rifle used by U.S. troops esp. in World War I

spring·form pan \ˌspriŋ-ˌfȯrm-\ *n* [fr. the spring by which the rim is attached to the bottom] : a pan or mold with an upright detachable rim fastened to the bottom of the pan with a clamp or spring

spring·head \'spriŋ-ˌhed\ *n* : FOUNTAINHEAD

spring·house \-ˌhau̇s\ *n* : a small building situated over a spring and used for cool storage (as of dairy products or meat)

spring·ing \'spriŋ-iŋ\ *n* **1** : SPRING 5 **2** : SPRINGING LINE

springing bow *n* : a method of bowing a stringed instrument so that the bow rebounds from the string

springing line *n* : the usu. horizontal line connecting the two opposite points at which the curve of an arch or vault begins

spring load *vt* : to load or secure by means of spring tension or compression

spring peeper *n* : a small brown tree toad (*Hyla crucifer*) of the eastern U.S. and Canada that has a shrill piping call and breeds in ponds and streams in the spring

spring peeper

spring·tail \'spriŋ-ˌtāl\ *n* : COLLEMBOLAN

spring·tide \-ˌtīd\ *n* : SPRINGTIME

spring tide *n* : a tide of greater-than-average range around the times of new and full moon

spring·time \'spriŋ-ˌtīm\ *n* **1** : the season of spring **2** : YOUTH **3** : an early or flourishing stage of development

spring tooth *n* : a flat curved springy steel tooth (as on a cultivator)

spring wagon *n* : a light farm wagon equipped with springs

spring·wood \'spriŋ-ˌwu̇d\ *n* : the softer more porous portion of an annual ring of wood that develops early in the growing season — compare SUMMERWOOD

springy \'spriŋ-ē\ *adj* **spring·i·er; -est** **1** : abounding with springs : SPONGY **2** : having an elastic quality : RESILIENT — **spring·i·ly** \'spriŋ-ə-lē\ *adv* — **spring·i·ness** \'spriŋ-ē-nəs\ *n*

1**sprin·kle** \'spriŋ-kəl\ *vb* **sprin·kled; sprin·kling** \-k(ə-)liŋ\ [ME *sprenklen, sprinclen;* akin to MHG *spreckel, sprenkel* spot, OE *spearca* spark] *vt* **1** : to scatter in drops or particles **2 a** : to scatter over **b** : to scatter at intervals in or among : DOT **c** : to wet lightly ~ *vi* **1** : to scatter a liquid in fine drops **2** : to rain lightly in scattered drops — **sprin·kler** \-k(ə-)lər\ *n*

2**sprinkle** *n* **1** : the act or an instance of sprinkling; *specif* : a light rain **2** : SPRINKLING

sprin·klered \'spriŋ-klərd\ *adj* : having an automatic sprinkler system

sprinkler system *n* : a system for protecting a building against fire by means of overhead pipes which convey an extinguishing fluid (as water) to heat-activated outlets

sprin·kling \'spriŋ-kliŋ\ *n* **1** : a limited quantity or amount : MODICUM **2** : a small quantity falling in scattered drops or particles **3** : a small number distributed at random : SCATTERING

1**sprint** \'sprint\ *vi* [of Scand origin; akin to Sw dial. *sprinta* to jump, hop; akin to OHG *sprinzan* to jump up, Gk *spyrthizein*] : to run at top speed esp. for a short distance — **sprint·er** *n*

2**sprint** *n* **1** : the act or an instance of sprinting **2 a** : DASH 6b **b** : a burst of speed

sprint car *n* : a front-engined open wheel racing car used esp. on short dirt tracks

sprit \'sprit\ *n* [ME *spret, sprit,* fr. OE *sprēot* pole, spear; akin to OE *-sprūtan* to sprout] : a spar that crosses a fore-and-aft sail diagonally

sprite \'sprīt\ *n* [ME *sprit,* fr. OF *esprit,* fr. L *spiritus* spirit] **1 a** *archaic* : SOUL **b** : a disembodied spirit : GHOST **2 a** : ELF, FAIRY **b** : an elfish person

sprit·sail \'sprit-ˌsāl, -səl\ *n* : a sail extended by a sprit

sprock·et \'spräk-ət\ *n* [origin unknown] **1** : a tooth or projection (as on a wheel) shaped so as to engage with a chain **2** : a toothed cylinder or wheel that engages the perforations of something (as motion-picture film) to move it through a mechanism (as a projector)

sprocket wheel *n* : a wheel with cogs or sprockets to engage with the links of a chain

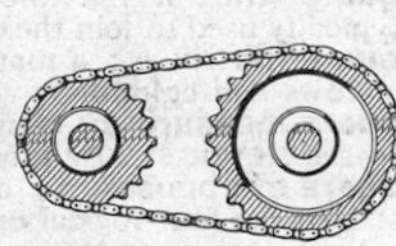
sprocket wheel

1**sprout** \'sprau̇t\ *vb* [ME *sprouten,* fr. OE *-sprūtan;* akin to OHG *spriozan* to sprout, Gk *speirein* to scatter, sow] *vi* **1** : to grow, spring up, or come forth as or as if a sprout **2** : to send out new growth <potatoes kept too warm will ~ prematurely> ~ *vt* : to send forth or up : cause to develop : GROW

2**sprout** *n* **1 a** : SHOOT 1a; *esp* : a young shoot (as from a seed or root) **b** *pl* (1) : edible shoots esp. of a crucifer (2) : a plant (as brussels sprouts) producing sprouts **2** : something resembling a sprout: as **a** : a young person **b** : SCION

sprouting broccoli *n* : BROCCOLI 2

1**spruce** \'sprüs\ *n* [obs. *Spruce* Prussia, fr. ME, alter. of *Pruce,* fr. OF] : any of a genus (*Picea*) of evergreen trees of the pine family with a conical head of dense foliage and soft light wood; *also* : any of several coniferous trees (as Douglas fir) of similar habit

2**spruce** *adj* **spruc·er; spruc·est** [perh. fr. obs. E *Spruce leather* leather imported from Prussia] : neat or smart in appearance : TRIM — **spruce·ly** *adv* — **spruce·ness** *n*

3**spruce** *vb* **spruced; spruc·ing** *vt* : to make spruce — often used with *up* ~ *vi* : to make oneself spruce <~ up a bit>

spruce beer *n* : a beverage flavored with spruce; *esp* : one made from spruce twigs and leaves boiled with molasses or sugar and fermented with yeast

spruce budworm *n* : a tortricid moth (*Choristoneura fumiferana*) whose larva feeds on evergreen trees (as spruce and balsam fir) in the northern U.S. and Canada

spruce pine *n* : an American tree (as some pines and spruces or the common eastern hemlock) of the pine family with light, soft, or weak wood

sprucy \'sprü-sē\ *adj* **spruc·i·er; -est** : SPRUCE

1**sprue** \'sprü\ *n* [D *spruw;* akin to MLG *sprūwe,* a kind of tumor] : a chronic disease marked esp. by fatty diarrhea and deficiency symptoms

2**sprue** *n* [origin unknown] **1** : the hole through which metal or plastic is poured into the gate and thence into a mold **2** : the waste piece cast in a sprue

sprung *past of* SPRING

sprung rhythm *n* : a poetic rhythm designed to approximate the natural rhythm of speech and characterized by the frequent juxtaposition of single accented syllables and the occurrence of mixed types of feet

spry \'sprī\ *adj* **spri·er** *or* **spry·er** \'sprī(-ə)r\; **spri·est** *or* **spry·est** \'sprī-əst\ [perh. of Scand origin; akin to Sw dial. *sprygg* spry] : vigorously active : BRISK ***syn*** see AGILE ***ant*** doddering — **spry·ly** *adv* — **spry·ness** *n*

sps *abbr* [L *sine prole superstite*] without surviving issue

1**spud** \'spəd\ *n* [ME *spudde* dagger] **1** : a tool or device (as for digging, lifting, or cutting) having the characteristics of a spade and a chisel **2** : POTATO

2**spud** *vb* **spud·ded; spud·ding** *vt* **1** : to dig with a spud **2** : to begin to drill (an oil well) ~ *vi* : to use a spud

1**spume** \'spyüm\ *n* [ME, fr. MF, fr. L *spuma* — more at FOAM] : frothy matter on liquids : FOAM, SCUM — **spu·mous** \'spyü-məs\ *adj* — **spumy** \-mē\ *adj*

2**spume** *vi* **spumed; spum·ing** : FROTH, FOAM

spu·mo·ni *or* **spu·mo·ne** \spu̇-'mō-nē\ *n* [It *spumone,* aug. of *spuma* foam, fr. L] : ice cream in layers of different colors, flavors, and textures often with candied fruits and nuts

spun *past of* SPIN

spun glass *n* **1** : FIBERGLASS **2** : blown glass that has slender threads of glass incorporated in it

1**spunk** \'spəŋk\ *n* [ScGael *spong* sponge, tinder, fr. L *spongia* sponge] **1 a** : a woody tinder : PUNK **b** : any of various fungi used to make tinder **2** : METTLE, PLUCK **3** : SPIRIT, LIVELINESS

2**spunk** *vi, dial* : to show spirit — usu. used with *up*

spunk·ie \'spəŋ-kē\ *n* **1** *Scot* : IGNIS FATUUS **2** *Scot* : LIQUOR, SPIRITS

spunky \'spəŋ-kē\ *adj* **spunk·i·er; -est** : full of spunk : SPIRITED — **spunk·i·ly** \-kə-lē\ *adv* — **spunk·i·ness** \-kē-nəs\ *n*

spun rayon *n* : a rayon-staple yarn or fabric

spun sugar *n* : sugar boiled to long threads and gathered up and shaped or heaped on a stick as a candy

spun yarn *n* **1** : a textile yarn spun from staple-length fiber **2** : a small rope or stuff formed of two or more rope yarns loosely twisted and used for seizings esp. on board ship

1**spur** \'spər\ *n* [ME *spure,* fr. OE *spura;* akin to OE *spurnan* to kick — more at SPURN] **1 a** : a pointed device secured to a rider's heel and used to urge on the horse **b** [fr. the acquisition of spurs by a person achieving knighthood] *pl* : recognition and reward for achievement <won his academic ~*s* as the holder of a chair in a university —James Mountford> **2** : a goad to action : STIMULUS **3** : something projecting like or suggesting a spur: as **a** : a projecting root or branch of a tree **b** (1) : a stiff sharp spine (as on the wings or legs of a bird or insect); *esp* : one on a cock's leg — see COCK illustration (2) : a gaff for a gamecock **c** : a hollow projecting appendage of a corolla or calyx (as in larkspur or columbine) **d** : CLIMBING IRON **4** : a ridge or lesser elevation that extends laterally from a mountain or mountain range **5** : a short wooden brace of a post **6** : a reinforcing buttress of masonry in a fortification ***syn*** see MOTIVE — **on the spur of the moment** : on impulse : SUDDENLY

2**spur** *vb* **spurred; spur·ring** *vt* **1** : to urge (a horse) on with spurs **2** : to incite to action or accelerated growth or development : STIMULATE **3** : to put spurs on ~ *vi* : to spur one's horse on

spurge \'spərj\ *n* [ME, fr. MF, purge, spurge, fr. *espurgier* to purge, fr. L *expurgare* — more at EXPURGATE] : any of various mostly shrubby plants (family Euphorbiaceae, the spurge family, and esp. genus *Euphorbia*) with a bitter milky juice

spur gear *n* : a gear wheel with radial teeth parallel to its axis — called also *spur wheel*

spurge laurel *n* : a low Eurasian shrub (*Daphne laureola*) with oblong evergreen leaves and axillary racemes of yellowish flowers

spu·ri·ous \'spyu̇r-ē-əs\ *adj* [LL & L; LL *spurius* false, fr. L, of illegitimate birth, fr. *spurius,* n., bastard] **1** : of illegitimate birth : BASTARD **2 a** : outwardly similar or corresponding to something without having its genuine qualities : FALSE **b** : superficially like but morphologically unlike <a ~ fruit> **3 a** : of falsified or erroneously attributed origin : FORGED **b :** of a deceitful nature or quality — **spu·ri·ous·ly** *adv* — **spu·ri·ous·ness** *n*

1spurn \'spərn\ *vb* [ME *spurnen,* fr. OE *spurnan;* akin to OHG *spurnan* to kick, L *spernere* to spurn, Gk *spairein* to quiver] *vi* **1** *obs* **a :** STUMBLE **b :** KICK **2 :** to reject something disdainfully — usu. used with *at* <~ at danger> ~ *vt* **1 :** to tread sharply or heavily upon : TRAMPLE **2 :** to reject with disdain or contempt : SCORN ***syn*** see DECLINE ***ant*** crave, embrace — **spurn·er** *n*

2spurn *n* **1 a :** KICK **b** *obs* **:** STUMBLE **2 a :** disdainful rejection **b :** contemptuous treatment

spur–of–the–moment *adj* **:** occurring or developing without premeditation : hastily extemporized <a ~ decision >

spurred \'spərd\ *adj* **1 :** wearing spurs **2 :** having one or more spurs <a ~ violet>

spur·ri·er \'spər-ē-ər, 'spə-rē-\ *n* **:** one who makes spurs

spur·ry *or* **spur·rey** \'spər-ē, 'spə-rē\ *n, pl* **spurries** *or* **spurreys** [D *spurrie,* fr. ML *spergula*] **:** a small white-flowered European weed (*Spergula arvensis*) of the pink family with whorled filiform leaves; *also* **:** any of several related and similar herbs

1spurt \'spərt\ *n* [origin unknown] **1 :** a short period of time : MOMENT **2 a :** a sudden brief burst of effort or activity **b :** a sharp or sudden increase in business activity

2spurt *vi* **:** to make a spurt

3spurt *vb* [perh. akin to MHG *spürzen* to spit, OE *-sprūtan* to sprout — more at SPROUT] *vi* **:** to gush forth : SPOUT ~ *vt* **:** to expel in a stream or jet : SQUIRT

4spurt *n* **:** a sudden gush : JET

spur·tle \'spərt-ᵊl\ *n* [origin unknown] *chiefly Scot* **:** a wooden stick for stirring porridge

spur track *n* **:** a track that diverges from a main line : SIDING

spur–winged \'spər-'wiŋd\ *adj* **:** having one or more horny spurs on the bend of the wings

sput·nik \'spu̇t-nik, 'spət-, 'spüt-\ *n* [Russ, lit., traveling companion, fr. *s, so* with + *put'* path; akin to Gk *hama* together and to Skt *patha* way — more at SAME, FIND] **:** SATELLITE 2b

1sput·ter \'spət-ər\ *vb* [akin to D *sputteren* to sputter, OE *-sprūtan* to sprout] *vt* **1 :** to spit or squirt from the mouth with explosive sounds : SPLUTTER **2 :** to utter hastily or explosively in confusion or excitement **3 :** to dislodge (atoms) from the surface of a material by collision with high energy particles; *also* **:** to deposit (a metallic film) by such a process ~ *vi* **1 :** to spit or squirt particles of food or saliva noisily from the mouth **2 :** to speak explosively or confusedly in anger or excitement **3 :** to make explosive popping sounds — **sput·ter·er** \-ər-ər\ *n*

2sputter *n* **1 :** confused and excited speech or discussion **2 :** the act or sound of sputtering

spu·tum \'sp(y)üt-əm\ *n, pl* **spu·ta** \-ə\ [L, fr. neut. of *sputus,* pp. of *spuere* to spit — more at SPEW] **:** expectorated matter made up of saliva and often discharges from the respiratory passages

1spy \'spī\ *vb* **spied; spy·ing** [ME *spien,* fr. OF *espier,* of Gmc origin; akin to OHG *spehōn* to spy; akin to L *specere* to look, look at, *species* appearance, species, Gk *skeptesthai* & *skopein* to watch, look at, consider] *vt* **1 :** to watch secretly usu. for hostile purposes **2 :** to catch sight of : SEE **3 :** to search or look for intensively ~ *vi* **1 :** to observe or search for something : LOOK **2 :** to watch secretly as a spy

2spy *n, pl* **spies** **1 :** one that spies: **a :** one who keeps secret watch on a person or thing to obtain information **b :** one who acts in a clandestine manner or on false pretenses to obtain information in the zone of operations of a belligerent with the intention of communicating it to the hostile party **2 :** an act of spying

spy·glass \'spī-ˌglas\ *n* **:** a small telescope

sq *abbr* **1** squadron **2** square

squab \'skwäb\ *n, pl* **squabs** [prob. of Scand origin; akin to Sw dial. *skvabb* anything soft and thick] **1** *or pl* **squab :** a fledgling bird; *specif* **:** a fledgling pigeon about four weeks old **2 :** a short fat person **3 a :** COUCH **b :** a cushion for a chair or couch — **squab** *adj*

1squab·ble \'skwäb-əl\ *n* [prob. of Scand origin; akin to Sw dial. *skvabbel* dispute] **:** a noisy altercation or quarrel usu. over trifles : WRANGLE ***syn*** see QUARREL

2squabble *vi* **squab·bled; squab·bling** \-(ə-)liŋ\ **:** to quarrel noisily and to no purpose : WRANGLE — **squab·bler** \-(ə-)lər\ *n*

1squad \'skwäd\ *n* [MF *esquade,* fr. OSp & OIt; OSp *escuadra* & OIt *squadra* derivs. of (assumed) VL *exquadrare* to make square — more at SQUARE] **1 :** a small organized group of military personnel; *esp* **:** a tactical unit that can be easily directed in the field **2 :** a small group engaged in a common effort or occupation

2squad *vt* **squad·ded; squad·ding :** to arrange in squads

squad car *n* **:** a police automobile connected by shortwave radiotelephone with headquarters — called also *cruiser, prowl car*

squad·ron \'skwäd-rən\ *n* [It *squadrone,* aug. of *squadra* squad] **:** a unit of military organization: **a :** a cavalry unit higher than a troop and lower than a regiment **b :** a naval unit consisting of two or more divisions and sometimes additional vessels **c** (1) **:** a unit of the U.S. Air Force higher than a flight and lower than a group (2) **:** a military flight formation

squadron leader *n* **:** a commissioned officer in the British air force who ranks with a major in the army

squad room *n* **1 :** a room in a barracks used to billet soldiers **2 :** a room in a police station where members of the force assemble

squa·lene \'skwā-ˌlēn\ *n* [ISV, fr. L *squalus,* a sea fish] **:** an acyclic hydrocarbon $C_{30}H_{50}$ that is widely distributed in nature (as in seeds and esp. in shark-liver oils) and is a precursor of sterols (as cholesterol)

squal·id \'skwäl-əd\ *adj* [L *squalidus* — more at SQUALOR] **1 :** marked by filthiness and degradation from neglect or poverty **2 :** SORDID ***syn*** see DIRTY — **squal·id·ly** *adv* — **squal·id·ness** *n*

1squall \'skwȯl\ *vb* [of Scand origin; akin to ON *skval* useless chatter] *vi* **:** to cry out raucously : SCREAM ~ *vt* **:** to utter in a strident voice — **squall·er** *n*

2squall *n* **:** a raucous cry

3squall *n* [prob. of Scand origin; akin to Sw *skval* rushing water] **1 :** a sudden violent wind often with rain or snow **2 :** a short-lived commotion

4squall *vi* **:** to blow a squall

squally \'skwȯ-lē\ *adj* **squall·i·er; -est** **1 :** marked by squalls **2 :** GUSTY

squa·lor \'skwäl-ər *also* 'skwāl-\ *n* [L; akin to L *squalidus* squalid, *squama* scale] **:** the quality or state of being squalid

squam- *or* **squamo-** *comb form* [NL, fr. L *squama*] **:** scale : squama <*squam*ation>

squa·ma \'skwā-mə, 'skwä-\ *n, pl* **squa·mae** \'skwā-ˌmē, 'skwä-ˌmī\ [L] **:** SCALE; *also* **:** a structure resembling a scale

squa·mate \-ˌmāt\ *adj* **:** SCALY <~ reptiles>

squa·ma·tion \skwə-'mā-shən\ *n* **1 :** the state of being scaly **2 :** the arrangement of scales on an animal

1squa·mo·sal \skwə-'mō-səl, -zəl\ *adj* **1 :** SQUAMOUS **2 :** of, relating to, or being a membrane bone of the skull of many vertebrates corresponding to the squamous portion of the temporal bone of man

2squamosal *n* **:** a squamosal bone

squa·mose \'skwā-ˌmōs, 'skwä-\ *adj* **:** SQUAMOUS

squa·mous \-məs\ *adj* [L *squamosus,* fr. *squama* scale] **1 a :** covered with or consisting of scales : SCALY **b :** of, relating to, or being a stratified epithelium that consists at least in its outer layers of small scalelike cells **2 :** of, relating to, or being the anterior upper portion of the temporal bone of various mammals (as man) — **squa·mous·ly** *adv*

squamous cell *n* **:** a cell of or derived from squamous epithelium

squa·mu·lose \'skwā-myə-ˌlōs, 'skwä-\ *adj* [L *squamula,* dim. of *squama*] **:** minutely squamous

1squan·der \'skwän-dər\ *vb* **squan·dered; squan·der·ing** \-d(ə-)riŋ\ [origin unknown] *vt* **1 :** to cause to disperse : SCATTER **2 :** to spend extravagantly or foolishly : DISSIPATE ~ *vi* **:** DISPERSE, SCATTER ***syn*** see WASTE — **squan·der·er** \-dər-ər\ *n*

2squander *n* **:** an act of squandering

1square \'skwa(ə)r, 'skwe(ə)r\ *n* [ME, fr. MF *esquarre,* fr. (assumed) VL *exquadra,* fr. *exquadrare* to square, fr. L *ex-* + *quadrare* to square — more at QUADRATE] **1 :** an instrument having at least one right angle and two straight edges used to lay out or test right angles **2 :** a rectangle with all four sides equal **3 :** any of the quadrilateral spaces marked out on a board for playing games **4 :** the product of a number multiplied by itself **5 a :** an open place or area formed at the meeting of two or more streets **b :** BLOCK 6c **6 :** a solid object or piece approximating a cube or having a square as its largest face **7 :** an unopened cotton flower with its enclosing bracts **8 :** a person who is overly conventional or conservative in taste or way of life — **on the square 1 :** at right angles **2 :** in a fair open manner : HONESTLY — **out of square :** not at an exact right angle

2square *adj* **squar·er; squar·est** **1 a :** having four equal sides and four right angles **b :** forming a right angle <~ corner> **2 :** raised to the second power **3 a :** being approximately a cube <~ cabinet> **b :** of a shape suggesting strength and solidity <~ shoulders> <a ~, thick, hard-working man —Maria Edgeworth> **c :** rectangular and equilateral in section <~ tower> **4 a :** converted from a linear unit into a square unit having the same length of side — see METRIC SYSTEM table, WEIGHT table **b :** being of a specified length in each of two equal dimensions <10 feet ~> **5 a :** exactly adjusted : precisely constructed or aligned **b :** JUST, FAIR <~ in all his dealings> **c :** leaving no balance : SETTLED **d :** EVEN, TIED **e :** SUBSTANTIAL, SATISFYING <~ meal> **f :** being unsophisticated, conservative, or conventional **6 :** set at right angles with the mast and keel — used of the yards of a square-rigged ship — **square·ly** *adv* — **square·ness** *n*

3square *vb* **squared; squar·ing** *vt* **1 a :** to make square or rectangular <~ a building stone> **b :** to test for deviation from a right angle, straight line, or plane surface **2 :** to bring approximately to a right angle <*squared* his shoulders> **3 a :** to multiply (a number) by itself : raise to the second power **b :** to find a square equal in area to <~ a circle> **4 :** to regulate or adjust by or to some standard or principle <~ our actions by the opinions of others —John Milton> **5 a :** BALANCE, SETTLE <~ an account> **b :** to even the score of **6 :** to mark off into squares **7 a :** to set right : bring into agreement **b :** BRIBE, FIX ~ *vi* **1 :** to agree with exactness : match precisely **2 :** to settle matters; *esp* **:** to pay the bill **3 :** to take a fighting stance ***syn*** see AGREE

4square *adv* **1 :** in a straightforward or honest manner **2 a :** so as to face or be face to face **b :** at right angles **3 :** with nothing intervening : DIRECTLY <ran ~ into him> **4 :** in a firm manner <looked him ~ in the eye> **5 :** in a square shape

square away *vi* **1 :** to square the yards so as to sail before the wind **2 :** to put everything in order or in readiness **3 :** to take up a fighting stance ~ *vt* **:** to put in order or in readiness

square bracket *n* **:** BRACKET 3a

square dance *n* **:** a dance for four couples who form a hollow square — **square dancer** *n* — **square dancing** *n*

square deal *n* **:** an honest and fair transaction or trade

square knot *n* **:** a knot made of two reverse half-knots and typically used to join the ends of two cords — see KNOT illustration

square matrix *n* **:** a mathematical matrix with the same number of rows and columns

square measure *n* **:** a unit or system of units for measuring area — see METRIC SYSTEM table, WEIGHT table

square of opposition : a square figure on which may be demonstrated the four logical oppositions of contrariety, subcontrariety, subalternation, and contradiction

squar·er \'skwar-ər, 'skwer-\ *n* **:** one who squares; *esp* **:** a workman who squares timber or stone

square rig *n* **:** a sailing-ship rig in which the principal sails are extended on yards fastened to the masts horizontally and at their center

square–rigged \'skwa(ə)r-'rigd, 'skwe(ə)r-\ *adj* **:** having or equipped with a square rig

square–rig·ger \-'rig-ər\ *n* **:** a square-rigged craft

square root *n* : a factor of a number that when squared gives the number <the *square root* of 9 is ± 3>

square sail \ˈskwa(ə)r-ˌsāl, ˈskwe(ə)r-səl\ *n* : a 4-sided sail extended on a yard suspended at the middle from a mast

square shooter *n* : a just or honest person

square–shoul·dered \ˈskwa(ə)r-ˈshōl-dərd, ˈskwe(ə)r-\ *adj* : having shoulders that are high and well braced back

square–toed \-ˈtōd\ *adj* **1** : having a toe that is square **2** : OLD-FASHIONED, CONSERVATIVE — **square–toed·ness** *n*

square wave *n* : the rectangular wave form of a quantity that varies periodically and abruptly from one to the other of two uniform values

squar·ish \ˈskwa(ə)r-ish, ˈskwe(ə)r-\ *adj* : somewhat square in form or appearance — **squar·ish·ly** *adv* — **squar·ish·ness** *n*

[1]**squash** \ˈskwäsh, ˈskwȯsh\ *vb* [MF *esquasser,* fr. (assumed) VL *exquassare,* fr. L *ex-* + *quassare* to shake — more at QUASH] *vt* **1** : to press or beat into a pulp or a flat mass : CRUSH **2** : to put down : SUPPRESS <~ a revolt> ~ *vi* **1** : to flatten out under pressure or impact **2** : to proceed with a splashing or squelching sound **3** : SQUEEZE, PRESS — **squash·er** *n*

[2]**squash** *n* **1** *obs* : something soft and easily crushed; *specif* : an unripe pod of peas **2** : the sudden fall of a heavy soft body or the sound of such a fall **3** : a squelching sound made by walking on oozy ground or in water-soaked boots **4** : a crushed mass **5** *Brit* : sweetened citrus fruit juice usu. with added soda water **6** : SQUASH RACQUETS

[3]**squash** *adv* : with a squash or a squashing sound

[4]**squash** *n, pl* **squash·es** *or* **squash** [by shortening & alter. fr. earlier *isquoutersquash,* fr. Natick & Narraganset *askútasquash*] : any of various fruits of plants (genus *Cucurbita*) of the gourd family widely cultivated as vegetables and for livestock feed; *also* : a plant and esp. a vine that bears squashes

squash bug *n* : a large black American bug (*Anasa tristis* of the family Coreidae) injurious to squash vines

squash racquets *n pl but sing in constr* : a singles or doubles game played in a 4-wall court with a long-handled racket and a rubber ball that can be caromed off any number of walls

squash tennis *n* : a singles racket game resembling squash racquets played with an inflated ball the size of a tennis ball

squashy \ˈskwäsh-ē, ˈskwȯsh-\ *adj* **squash·i·er; -est** **1** : easily squashed : very soft <~ cushions> **2** : softly wet : BOGGY **3** : soft because overripe <~ melons> — **squash·i·ly** \-ə-lē\ *adv* — **squash·i·ness** \-ē-nəs\ *n*

[1]**squat** \ˈskwät\ *vb* **squat·ted; squat·ting** [ME *squatten,* fr. MF *esquatir,* fr. *es-* ex- (fr. L *ex-*) + *quatir* to press, fr. (assumed) VL *coactire* to press together, fr. L *coactus,* pp. of *cogere* to drive together — more at COGENT] *vt* **1** : to cause (oneself) to crouch or sit on the ground **2** : to occupy as a squatter ~ *vi* **1** : to crouch close to the ground as if to escape observation <*squatting* hare> **2** : to assume or maintain a position in which the body is supported on the feet and the knees are bent so that the buttocks rest on or near the heels **3** : to become a squatter

[2]**squat** *n* **1 a** : the act of squatting **b** : the posture of one that squats **2 a** : a place where one squats **b** : the lair of a small animal <~ of a hare>

[3]**squat** *adj* **squat·ter; squat·test** **1** : sitting with the haunches close above the heels **2 a** : low to the ground **b** : marked by disproportionate shortness or thickness — **squat·ly** *adv* — **squat·ness** *n*

[1]**squat·ter** \ˈskwät-ər\ *vi* [prob. of Scand origin; akin to Dan *skvatte* to sprinkle] : to go along through or as if through water

[2]**squatter** *n* : one that squats: as **a** : one that settles on property without right or title or payment of rent **b** : one that settles on public land under government regulation with the purpose of acquiring title

squatter sovereignty *n* : POPULAR SOVEREIGNTY 2

squat·ty \ˈskwät-ē\ *adj* **squat·ti·er; -est** **1** : low to the ground **2** : DUMPY, THICKSET

squaw \ˈskwȯ\ *n* [of Algonquian origin; akin to Natick *squáas* woman] **1** : an American Indian woman **2** : WOMAN, WIFE — usu. used disparagingly

squaw·fish \-ˌfish\ *n* : any of several large cyprinid fishes (genus *Ptychocheilus*) of western No. America

[1]**squawk** \ˈskwȯk\ *vi* [prob. blend of *squall* and *squeak*] **1** : to utter a harsh abrupt scream **2** : to complain or protest loudly or vehemently — **squawk·er** *n*

[2]**squawk** *n* **1** : a harsh abrupt scream **2** : a noisy complaint

squawk box *n* : an intercom speaker

squaw man *n* : a white man married to an Indian woman and usu. living as one of her tribe

squaw·root \ˈskwȯ-ˌrüt, -ˌru̇t\ *n* : a No. American scaly herb (*Conopholis americana*) of the broomrape family parasitic on oak and hemlock roots

[1]**squeak** \ˈskwēk\ *vb* [ME *squeken*] *vi* **1** : to utter or make a short shrill cry or noise **2** : SQUEAL 2a **3** : to pass, succeed, or win by a narrow margin ~ *vt* : to utter in a shrill piping tone

[2]**squeak** *n* **1** : a sharp shrill cry or sound **2** : ESCAPE <a close ~> — **squeaky** \ˈskwē-kē\ *adj*

squeak·er \ˈskwē-kər\ *n* **1** : one that squeaks **2** : a contest (as an election) won by a small margin

[1]**squeal** \ˈskwē(ə)l\ *vb* [ME *squelen*] *vi* **1** : to make a shrill cry or noise **2 a** : to turn informer **b** : COMPLAIN, PROTEST ~ *vt* **1** : to utter or express with or as if with a squeal **2** : to cause to make a loud shrill noise <~*ing* the tires> — **squeal·er** *n*

[2]**squeal** *n* : a shrill sharp cry or noise

squea·mish \ˈskwē-mish\ *adj* [ME *squaymisch,* modif. of AF *escoymous*] **1 a** : easily nauseated : QUEASY **b** : affected with nausea : NAUSEATED **2 a** : excessively fastidious or scrupulous in conduct or belief **b** : easily offended or disgusted ***syn*** see NICE — **squea·mish·ly** *adv*

squea·mish·ness *n* : the quality or state of being squeamish

[1]**squee·gee** \ˈskwē-ˌjē\ *n* [prob. imit.] : a blade of leather or rubber set on a handle and used for spreading, pushing, or wiping liquid material on, across, or off a surface (as a window); *also* : a smaller similar device or a small rubber roller with handle used by a photographer or lithographer

[2]**squeegee** *vt* **squee·geed; squee·gee·ing** : to smooth, wipe, or treat with a squeegee

[1]**squeeze** \ˈskwēz\ *vb* **squeezed; squeez·ing** [alter. of obs. E *quease,* fr. ME *queysen,* fr. OE *cwӯsan;* akin to Icel *kveisa* stomach cramps] *vt* **1 a** : to exert pressure esp. on opposite sides of : COMPRESS **b** : to extract or emit under pressure **c** : to force or thrust by compression **2 a** (1) : to get by extortion (2) : to deprive by extortion **b** : to cause economic hardship to **c** : to reduce the amount of <~*s* profits> **3** : to crowd into a limited area **4** : to gain or win by a narrow margin **5** : to force (another player) to discard in bridge so as to unguard a suit **6** : to score by means of a squeeze play ~ *vi* **1** : to give way before pressure **2** : to exert pressure; *also* : to practice extortion or oppression **3** : to force one's way <~ through a door> **4** : to pass, win, or get by narrowly — **squeez·abil·i·ty** \ˌskwē-zə-ˈbil-ət-ē\ *n* — **squeez·able** \ˈskwē-zə-bəl\ *adj* — **squeez·er** *n*

[2]**squeeze** *n* **1 a** : an act or instance of squeezing : COMPRESSION **b** : HANDCLASP; *also* : EMBRACE **2 a** : a quantity squeezed out from something <a ~ of lemon> **b** : a group crowded together : CROWD **3 a** : a commission charged by an oriental servant for service **b** : a profit taken by a middleman on goods or transactions **4** : a financial pressure caused by narrowing margins or by shortages **5** : a forced discard in bridge **6** : SQUEEZE PLAY

squeeze bottle *n* : a bottle of flexible plastic that dispenses its contents by being pressed

squeeze off *vt* : to fire (a round) by squeezing the trigger ~ *vi* : to fire a weapon by squeezing the trigger

squeeze play *n* **1** : a baseball play in which a runner on third base starts for home plate as the ball is being pitched and the batter attempts to bunt to give the runner a chance to score **2** : the exertion of pressure in order to extort a concession or gain a goal

squeg \ˈskweg\ *vi* **squegged; squeg·ging** [back-formation fr. *squegger* (tube in which the valve oscillates)] : to oscillate in a highly irregular fashion — used of an electronic system

[1]**squelch** \ˈskwelch\ *n* [imit.] **1** : a sound of or as if of semiliquid matter under suction <the ~ of mud> **2** : the act of suppressing; *esp* : a retort that silences an opponent — **squelchy** *adj*

[2]**squelch** *vt* **1 a** : to fall or stamp on so as to crush **b** (1) : to completely suppress : QUELL (2) : SILENCE **2** : to emit or move with a sucking sound ~ *vi* **1** : to emit a sucking sound like that of an object being withdrawn from mire **2** : to splash through water, slush, or mire — **squelch·er** *n*

sque·teague \skwi-ˈtēg\ *n, pl* **squeteague** [Narraganset *pesukwiteaug,* pl.] : any of various weakfishes (esp. *Cynoscion regalis*)

[1]**squib** \ˈskwib\ *n* [origin unknown] **1 a** : a small firecracker **b** : a broken firecracker in which the powder burns with a fizz **2** : a small electric or pyrotechnic device used to ignite a charge; *also* a similar device used to fire an igniter in a rocket **3 a** : a short humorous or satiric writing or speech **b** : a short news item; *esp* : FILLER

[2]**squib** *vb* **squibbed; squib·bing** *vi* **1** : to speak, write, or publish squibs **2** : to fire a squib ~ *vt* **1 a** : to utter in an offhand manner **b** : to make squibs against : LAMPOON **2** : to shoot off : FIRE **3** : to kick (a football) just far enough on a kickoff to be legally recoverable by the kicking team

squib kick *n* : ONSIDE KICK

[1]**squid** \ˈskwid\ *n, pl* **squid** *or* **squids** [origin unknown] : any of numerous 10-armed cephalopods (esp. of the genera *Loligo* and *Ommastrephes*) having a long tapered body, a caudal fin on each side, and usu. a slender internal chitinous support

[2]**squid** *vi* **squid·ded; squid·ding** : to fish with or for squid

squiffed \ˈskwift\ *or* **squif·fy** \ˈskwif-ē\ *adj* [origin unknown] : INTOXICATED, DRUNK

[1]**squig·gle** \ˈskwig-əl\ *vb* **squig·gled; squig·gling** \-(ə-)liŋ\ [blend of *squirm* and *wriggle*] *vi* **1** : SQUIRM, WRIGGLE **2** : to write or paint hastily : SCRIBBLE ~ *vt* **1** : SCRIBBLE **2** : to form or cause to form in squiggles

[2]**squiggle** *n* : a short wavy twist or line : CURLICUE; *esp* : an illegible scrawl — **squig·gly** \-(ə-)lē\ *adj*

squil·gee \ˈskwē-ˌjē, ˈskwil-ˌjē\ *var of* SQUEEGEE

squill \ˈskwil\ *n* [ME, fr. L *squilla* sea onion, fr. Gk *skilla*] **1 a** : a Mediterranean bulbous herb (*Urginea maritima*) of the lily family — called also *sea onion* **b** (1) *usu pl* : the dried sliced bulb scales of a squill used as an expectorant, cardiac stimulant, and diuretic (2) : the bulb of a red-bulbed form of squill used in rat poison **2** : SCILLA **3** [NL *Squilla*] : SQUILLA

squil·la \ˈskwil-ə\ *n, pl* **squillas** *or* **squil·lae** \ˈskwil-ˌē, -ˌī\ [NL, genus name, fr. L, squill, prawn] : any of various stomatopod crustaceans (esp. genus *Squilla*) that burrow in mud or beneath stones in shallow water along the seashore

[1]**squinch** \ˈskwinch\ *n* [alter. of earlier *scunch* (back part of the side of an opening)] : a support (as an arch, lintel, or corbeling) carried across the corner of a room under a superimposed mass

[2]**squinch** *vb* [prob. blend of *squint* and *pinch*] *vt* **1** : to screw up (the eyes or face) : SQUINT **2 a** : to make more compact **b** : to cause to crouch down or draw together ~ *vi* **1** : FLINCH **2** : to crouch down or draw together **3** : SQUINT

[1]**squin·ny** \ˈskwin-ē\ *vb* **squin·nied; squin·ny·ing** [prob. fr. obs. E *squin* asquint, fr. ME *skuin*] : SQUINT

[2]**squinny** *n* : SQUINT — **squinny** *adj*

[1]**squint** \ˈskwint\ *adj* [short for *asquint*] **1** *of an eye* : looking or tending to look obliquely or askance (as with envy or disdain) **2** *of the eyes* : not having the visual axes parallel : CROSSED

2squint *vi* **1 a :** to have an indirect bearing, reference, or aim **b :** to deviate from a true line **2 a :** to look in a squint-eyed manner **b :** to be cross-eyed **c :** to look or peer with eyes partly closed ~ *vt* **:** to cause (an eye) to squint — **squint·er** *n* — **squint·ing·ly** \-iŋ-lē\ *adv*

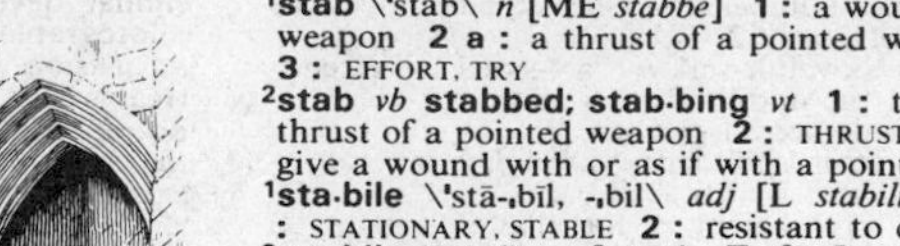
squinch

3squint *n* **1 :** STRABISMUS **2 :** an instance of squinting **3 :** HAGIOSCOPE — **squinty** \'skwint-ē\ *adj*

squint–eyed \'skwint-'īd\ *adj* **1 :** having eyes that squint; *specif* **:** affected with cross-eye **2 :** looking askance (as in envy)

squinting construction *n* **:** an ambiguous grammatical construction that contains a word or phrase (as *often* in "getting dressed often is a nuisance") interpretable as modifying either what precedes or what follows

1squire \'skwī(ə)r\ *n* [ME *squier,* fr. OF *esquier* — more at ESQUIRE] **1 :** a shield bearer or armor-bearer of a knight **2 a :** a male attendant esp. on a great personage **b :** a man who devotedly attends a lady **:** GALLANT **3 a :** a member of the British gentry ranking below a knight and above a gentleman **b :** an owner of a country estate; *esp* **:** the principal landowner in a village or district **c** (1) **:** JUSTICE OF THE PEACE (2) **:** LAWYER (3) **:** JUDGE — **squir·ish** \'skwī(ə)r-ish\ *adj*

2squire *vt* **squired; squir·ing :** to attend as a squire **:** ESCORT

squire·ar·chy *or* **squir·ar·chy** \'skwī(ə)r-ˌär-kē\ *n, pl* **-chies 1 :** the gentry or landed-proprietor class **2 :** government by a landed gentry

squirm \'skwərm\ *vi* [perh. imit.] **:** to twist about like a worm **:** FIDGET — **squirm** *n* — **squirmy** \'skwər-mē\ *adj*

1squir·rel \'skwər(-ə)l, 'skwə-rəl, *chiefly Brit* 'skwir-əl\ *n, pl* **squirrels** *also* **squirrel** [ME *squirel,* fr. MF *esquireul,* fr. (assumed) VL *scuriolus,* dim. of *scurius,* alter. of L *sciurus,* fr. Gk *skiouros,* fr. *skia* shadow + *oura* tail; akin to OHG *ars* buttocks, OIr *err* tail — more at SHINE] **1 :** any of various small or medium-sized rodents (family Sciuridae): as **a :** any of numerous New or Old World arboreal forms having a long bushy tail and strong hind legs **b :** GROUND SQUIRREL **2 :** the fur of a squirrel

2squirrel *vt* **-reled** *or* **-relled; -rel·ing** *or* **-rel·ling** [fr. the squirrel's habit of storing up gathered nuts and seeds for winter use] **:** to store up for future use — often used with *away*

squirrel cage *n* **1 :** a cage for a small animal (as a squirrel) that contains a rotatable cylinder for exercising **2 :** something resembling the working of a squirrel cage in repetitiveness or endlessness

squirrel corn *n* **:** a No. American herb (*Dicentra canadensis*) of the fumitory family with much-divided leaves and a scapose raceme of cream-colored flowers

squir·rel·ly \'skwər(-ə)-lē, 'skwə-rə-\ *adj* **:** extremely odd **:** CRAZY

squirrel monkey *n* **:** a small soft-haired So. American monkey (*Saimiri sciureus*) that has a long prehensile tail and is colored chiefly yellowish gray with a white face and black nose

squirrel rifle *n* [fr. its being suitable only for small game] **:** a small-bore rifle — called also *squirrel gun*

1squirt \'skwərt\ *vb* [ME *squirten;* akin to LG *swirtjen* to squirt] *vi* **:** to come forth in a sudden rapid stream from a narrow opening **:** SPURT ~ *vt* **:** to cause to squirt — **squirt·er** *n*

2squirt *n* **1 a :** an instrument (as a syringe) for squirting a liquid **b :** a small quick stream **:** JET **c :** the action or an instance of squirting **2 a :** an impudent youngster **b :** KID

squirt gun *n* **:** WATER PISTOL

squirting cucumber *n* **:** a Mediterranean plant (*Ecballium elaterium*) of the gourd family with oblong fruit that bursts from the peduncle when ripe and forcibly ejects the seeds

squish \'skwish\ *vb* [alter. of *squash*] *vt* **1 :** SQUASH **2 :** SQUELCH, SUCK ~ *vi* **:** SQUELCH, SUCK — **squish** *n*

squishy \-ē\ *adj* **squish·i·er; -est :** being soft, yielding, and damp — **squish·i·ness** *n*

squoosh \'skwu̇sh, 'skwüsh\ *vb* [by alter.] **:** SQUASH

squush \'skwəsh\ *vb* [by alter.] **:** SQUASH

1Sr *abbr* **1** senior **2** sister

2Sr *symbol* strontium

SR *abbr* **1** seaman recruit **2** sedimentation rate **3** shipping receipt

sri \'s(h)rē\ *n* [Skt *śrī,* lit., majesty, holiness; akin to Gk *kreiōn* ruler, master] — used as a conventional title of respect when addressing or speaking of a distinguished Indian

sRNA \'es-ˌär-ˌen-'ā\ *n* [*s*oluble *RNA*] **:** TRANSFER RNA

SRO *abbr* **1** single-room occupancy **2** standing room only

SRV *abbr* space rescue vehicle

ss *abbr* [L *semis*] one half

1SS \(')es-'es\ *n* [G, abbr. for *Schutzstaffel* elite guard] **:** a unit of Nazis created to serve as bodyguard to Hitler and later expanded to take charge of intelligence, central security, policing action, and extermination of undesirables

2SS *abbr* **1** saints **2** same size **3** steamship **4** Sunday school **5** sworn statement

SSA *abbr* Social Security Administration

SSE *abbr* south-southeast

SSG *abbr* staff sergeant

SSgt *abbr* staff sergeant

SSM *abbr* staff sergeant major

ssp *abbr* subspecies

SSR *abbr* Soviet Socialist Republic

SSRC *abbr* Social Science Research Council

SSS *abbr* Selective Service System

SST *abbr* supersonic transport

SSW *abbr* south-southwest

st *abbr* **1** stanza **2** state **3** stitch **4** stone **5** street

St *abbr* **1** saint **2** stratus

ST *abbr* **1** short ton **2** single throw

-st — see -EST

sta *abbr* station; stationary

1stab \'stab\ *n* [ME *stabbe*] **1 :** a wound produced by a pointed weapon **2 a :** a thrust of a pointed weapon **b :** a jerky thrust **3 :** EFFORT, TRY

2stab *vb* **stabbed; stab·bing** *vt* **1 :** to wound or pierce by the thrust of a pointed weapon **2 :** THRUST, DRIVE ~ *vi* **:** to thrust or give a wound with or as if with a pointed weapon — **stab·ber** *n*

1sta·bile \'stā-ˌbīl, -ˌbil\ *adj* [L *stabilis* — more at STABLE] **1 :** STATIONARY, STABLE **2 :** resistant to chemical change

2sta·bile \-ˌbēl\ *n* [prob. F, fr. L *stabilis,* adj.] **:** an abstract sculpture or construction similar in appearance to a mobile but made to be stationary

sta·bil·i·ty \stə-'bil-ət-ē\ *n, pl* **-ties 1 :** the quality, state, or degree of being stable: as **a :** the strength to stand or endure **:** FIRMNESS **b :** the property of a body that causes it when disturbed from a condition of equilibrium or steady motion to develop forces or moments that restore the original condition **c :** resistance to chemical change or to physical disintegration **2 :** residence for life in one monastery <monks that have taken a vow of ~>

sta·bi·lize \'stā-bə-ˌlīz\ *vb* **-lized; -liz·ing** *vt* **1 :** to make stable, steadfast, or firm **2 :** to hold steady: as **a :** to maintain the stability of (as an airplane) by means of a stabilizer **b :** to limit fluctuations of (as prices) **c :** to establish a minimum price for ~ *vi* **:** to become stable, firm, or steadfast — **sta·bi·li·za·tion** \ˌstā-bə-lə-'zā-shən\ *n*

sta·bi·liz·er \'stā-bə-ˌlī-zər\ *n* **:** one that stabilizes something: as **a :** a substance added to another substance (as an explosive or plastic) or to a system (as an emulsion) to prevent or retard an unwanted alteration of physical state **b :** a gyroscope device to keep ships steady in a heavy sea **c :** an airfoil providing stability for an airplane; *specif* **:** the fixed horizontal member of the tail assembly — see AIRPLANE illustration

1sta·ble \'stā-bəl\ *n* [ME, fr. OF *estable,* fr. L *stabulum,* fr. *stare* to stand — more at STAND] **1 :** a building in which domestic animals are sheltered and fed; *esp* **:** such a building having stalls or compartments <horse ~> **2 a :** the racehorses of one owner **b :** a group of athletes (as boxers) or performers under one management **c :** the racing cars of one owner **d :** GROUP, COLLECTION — **sta·ble·man** \-mən, -ˌman\ *n*

2stable *vb* **sta·bled; sta·bling** \-b(ə-)liŋ\ *vt* **:** to put or keep in a stable ~ *vi* **:** to dwell in or as if in a stable

3stable *adj* **sta·bler** \-b(ə-)lər\; **sta·blest** \-b(ə-)ləst\ [ME, fr. OF *estable,* fr. L *stabilis,* fr. *stare* to stand] **1 a :** firmly established **:** FIXED, STEADFAST **b :** not changing or fluctuating **:** UNVARYING **c :** PERMANENT, ENDURING **2 a :** steady in purpose **:** firm in resolution **b :** not subject to insecurity or emotional illness **:** SANE, RATIONAL <a ~ personality> **3 a** (1) **:** placed so as to resist forces tending to cause motion or change of motion (2) **:** designed so as to develop forces that restore the original condition when disturbed from a condition of equilibrium or steady motion **b** (1) **:** not readily altering in chemical makeup or physical state <~ emulsions> (2) **:** not spontaneously radioactive — **sta·ble·ness** \-bəl-nəs\ *n* — **sta·bly** \-b(ə-)lē\ *adv*

stable fly *n* **:** a two-winged fly (*Stomoxys calcitrans*) that bites severely, is abundant about stables, and often enters dwellings esp. in autumn

sta·ble·mate \'stā-bəl-ˌmāt\ *n* **1 :** a horse stabled with another **2 :** one of two or more boxers having the same manager

sta·bler \-b(ə-)lər\ *n* **:** one that keeps a stable

sta·bling \-b(ə-)liŋ\ *n* **:** accommodation for animals in a building; *also* **:** the building for this

stab·lish \'stab-lish\ *vb* [by shortening] *archaic* **:** ESTABLISH — **stab·lish·ment** \-mənt\ *n, archaic*

stac·ca·to \stə-'kät-(ˌ)ō\ *adj* [It, fr. pp. of *staccare* to detach, deriv. of OF *destachier* — more at DETACH] **1 a :** cut short or apart in performing **:** DISCONNECTED <~ notes> **b :** marked by short clear-cut playing or singing of tones or chords <a ~ style> **2 :** ABRUPT, DISJOINTED — **staccato** *adv* — **staccato** *n*

staccato mark *n* **:** a pointed vertical stroke or a dot placed over or under a musical note to be produced staccato

staccato marks

1stack \'stak\ *n* [ME *stak,* fr. ON *stakkr;* akin to OE *staca* stake] **1 :** a large usu. conical pile (as of hay, straw, or grain in the sheaf) left standing in the field for storage **2 a :** an orderly pile or heap **b :** a large quantity or number **3 :** an English unit of measure esp. for firewood that is equal to 108 cubic feet **4 a :** a number of flues embodied in one structure rising above a roof **b :** a vertical pipe (as to carry off smoke) **c :** the exhaust pipe of an internal-combustion engine **5 :** a pyramid of three rifles interlocked **6 :** a structure of bookshelves for compact storage of books — usu. used in pl. **7 :** a pile of chips sold to or won by a poker player **8 a :** a memory or a section of memory in a computer for temporary storage <a push-down ~> **b :** a computer memory consisting of arrays of memory elements stacked one on top of another

2stack *vt* **1 :** to arrange in a stack **:** PILE **2 :** to arrange secretly for cheating <the cards were ~*ed*> **3 :** to assign (an airplane) by radio to a particular altitude and position within a group circling before landing ~ *vi* **:** to form a stack — **stack·er** *n*

stack·able \'stak-ə-bəl\ *adj* **:** easily stacked

stacked \'stakt\ *adj, slang, of a woman* **:** well developed esp. in the breasts

stack up *vi* **1 :** to add up **:** TOTAL **2 :** to measure up **:** COMPARE — usu. used with *against*

stac·te \'stak-tē\ *n* [L, fr. Gk *staktē,* fr. fem. of *staktos* oozing out in drops, fr. *stazein* to drip — more at STAGNATE] **:** a sweet spice used by the ancient Jews in preparing incense

stad·dle \'stad-ᵊl\ *n* [ME *stathel* base, support, fr. OE *stathol;* akin to OE *stede* place — more at STEAD] **1 :** a base (as of piling) for a stack of hay or straw **2 :** a supporting framework

stade \'stād\ *n* [MF *estade,* fr. L *stadium*] **:** STADIUM 1a

sta·dia \'stād-ē-ə\ *n* [It, prob. fr. L, pl. of *stadium*] **:** a surveying method for determination of distances and differences of elevation by means of a telescopic instrument having two horizontal lines through which the marks on a graduated rod are observed; *also* : the instrument or rod

sta·di·um \ˈstād-ē-əm\ *n, pl* **-dia** \-ē-ə\ *or* **-di·ums** [ME, fr. L, fr. Gk *stadion,* alter. of *spadion,* fr. *span* to pull — more at SPAN] **1 a :** any of various ancient Greek units of length ranging in value from 607 to 738 English feet **b :** an ancient Roman unit of length equal to 606.95 English feet **2 a :** a course for footraces in ancient Greece orig. one stadium in length **b :** a tiered structure with seats for spectators surrounding an ancient Greek running track **c :** a large usu. unroofed building with tiers of seats for spectators at sports events **3** [NL, fr. L] **:** a stage in a life history; *esp* **:** one between successive molts

stadt·hold·er \ˈstat-ˌhōl-dər\ *n* [part trans. of D *stadhouder,* fr. *stad* place + *houder* holder] **1 :** a viceroy in a province of the Netherlands **2 :** a chief executive officer of the United Provinces of the Netherlands — **stadt·hold·er·ate** \-də-rət\ *n* — **stadt·hold·er·ship** \-dər-ˌship\ *n*

[1]**staff** \ˈstaf\ *n, pl* **staffs** \ˈstafs, ˈstavz\ *or* **staves** \ˈstavz, ˈstāvz\ [ME *staf,* fr. OE *stæf;* akin to OHG *stab* staff, *stampfōn* to stamp — more at STAMP] **1 a :** a long stick carried in the hand for support in walking **b :** a supporting rod: as (1) *archaic* **:** SHAFT 1a(1) (2) **:** a crosspiece in a ladder or chair **:** RUNG (3) **:** FLAGSTAFF (4) **:** a pivoted arbor **c :** CLUB, CUDGEL **2 a :** CROSIER **b :** a rod carried as a symbol of office or authority **3 :** the horizontal lines with their spaces on which music is written — called also *stave* **4 :** any of various graduated sticks or rules used for measuring **:** ROD **5** *pl staffs* **a :** the officers chiefly responsible for the internal operations of an institution or business **b :** a group of officers appointed to assist a civil executive or commanding officer **c :** military or naval officers not eligible for operational command **d :** the personnel who assist a director in carrying out an assigned task **e** *pl* **staff :** a member of a staff — **staff** *adj*

[2]**staff** *vt* **1 :** to supply with a staff or with workers **2 :** to serve as a staff member of

[3]**staff** *n* [prob. fr. G *staffieren* to trim] **:** a building material having a plaster of Paris base and used in exterior wall coverings of temporary buildings

staff·er \ˈstaf-ər\ *n* **:** a member of a staff (as of a newspaper)

staff officer *n* **:** a commissioned officer assigned to a military commander's staff — compare LINE OFFICER

staff of life : a staple of diet; *esp* **:** BREAD

Staf·ford·shire terrier \ˌstaf-ərd-ˌshi(ə)r-, -shər-\ *n* [*Staffordshire,* England] **:** any of a breed of strong, stocky, alert terriers that have a short, stiff glossy coat

Staffs *abbr* Staffordshire

staff sergeant *n* **:** a noncommissioned officer ranking in the army above a sergeant and below a platoon sergeant or sergeant first class, in the air force above a sergeant and below a technical sergeant, and in the marine corps above a sergeant and below a gunnery sergeant

staff sergeant major *n* **:** a noncommissioned officer in the army ranking above a master sergeant

staff tree *n* **:** any of a genus (*Celastrus* of the family Celastraceae, the staff-tree family) of mostly twining shrubby plants including the common bittersweet

[1]**stag** \ˈstag\ *n, pl* **stags** [ME *stagge,* fr. OE *stagga;* akin to ON *andarsteggi* drake, OE *stingan* to sting] **1** *or pl* **stag :** an adult male red deer; *broadly* **:** the male of various deer (esp. genus *Cervus*) **2** *chiefly Scot* **:** a young horse; *esp* **:** a young unbroken stallion **3 :** a male animal castrated after maturity — compare STEER 1 **4 :** a young adult male domestic fowl **5 a :** a social gathering of men only **b :** a man who attends a dance or party unaccompanied by a woman

[2]**stag** *vb* **stagged; stag·ging** *vt* [*stag* (informer)] *Brit* **:** to spy on ~ *vi* **:** to attend a dance or party without a woman companion

[3]**stag** *adj* **1 a :** restricted to men <a ~ party> **b :** intended or suitable for a gathering of men only; *esp* **:** PORNOGRAPHIC <~ movies> **2 :** unaccompanied by someone of the opposite sex <~ women> — **stag** *adv*

stag beetle *n* **:** any of numerous mostly large lamellicorn beetles (family Lucanidae) having males with long and often branched mandibles suggesting the antlers of a stag

[1]**stage** \ˈstāj\ *n* [ME, fr. OF *estage,* fr. (assumed) VL *staticum,* fr. L *stare* to stand — more at STAND] **1 a :** one of a series of positions or stations one above the other **:** STEP **b :** the height of the surface of a river above an arbitrary zero point **2 a** (1) **:** a raised platform (2) **:** the part of a theater between the proscenium and the rear wall including the acting area, wings, and storage space (3) **:** the acting profession **:** the theater as an occupation or activity **b :** a center of attention or scene of action **3 a :** a scaffold for workmen **b :** the small platform of a microscope on which an object is placed for examination **4 a :** a place of rest formerly provided for those traveling by stagecoach **:** STATION **b :** the distance between two stopping places on a road **c :** STAGECOACH **5 a :** a period or step in a progress, activity, or development; *esp* **:** one of the distinguishable periods of growth and development of a plant or animal <the larval ~ of an insect> **b :** one passing through a (specified) stage **6 :** an element or part in a complex electronic contrivance; *specif* **:** a single tube with its associated components in an amplifier **7 :** a propulsion unit of a rocket with its own fuel and container — **on the stage :** in or into the acting profession

[2]**stage** *vt* **staged; stag·ing 1 :** to produce (as a play) on a stage **2 :** to produce for public view <~ a track meet>

stage business *n* **:** BUSINESS 5

stage·coach \ˈstāj-ˌkōch\ *n* **:** a horse-drawn passenger and mail coach running on a regular schedule between established stops

stage·craft \-ˌkraft\ *n* **:** the effective management of theatrical devices or techniques

stage direction *n* **:** a description (as of a character or setting) or direction (as to indicate stage business) provided in the text of a play

stage director *n* **1 :** DIRECTOR c **2 :** STAGE MANAGER

stage fright *n* **:** nervousness felt at appearing before an audience

stage·hand \ˈstāj-ˌhand\ *n* **:** a stage worker who handles scenery, properties, or lights

stage–man·age \-ˌman-ij\ *vt* [back-formation fr. *stage manager*] **1 a :** to arrange or exhibit so as to achieve a desired effect **b :** to arrange or direct from behind the scenes **2 :** to act as stage manager for — **stage management** *n*

stage manager *n* **:** one who supervises the physical aspects of a stage production, assists the director during rehearsals, and is in charge of the stage during a performance

stag·er \ˈstā-jər\ *n* **:** an experienced person **:** VETERAN

stage set *n* **:** scenery and properties designed and arranged for a particular scene in a play

stage·struck \ˈstāj-ˌstrək\ *adj* **:** fascinated by the stage; *esp* **:** having an ardent desire to become an actor

stage whisper *n* **1 :** a loud whisper by an actor that is audible to the spectators but is supposed for dramatic effect not to be heard by one or more of the actors **2 :** an audible whisper

[1]**stag·ger** \ˈstag-ər\ *vb* **stag·gered; stag·ger·ing** \-(ə-)riŋ\ [alter. of earlier *stacker,* fr. ME *stakeren,* fr. ON *stakra,* freq. of *staka* to push; akin to OE *staca* stake] *vi* **1 a :** to reel from side to side **:** TOTTER **b :** to move on unsteadily **2 :** to rock violently **:** SHAKE <the ship ~*ed*> **3 :** to waver in purpose or action **:** HESITATE ~ *vt* **1 :** to cause to doubt or hesitate **:** PERPLEX **2 :** to cause to reel or totter **3 :** to arrange in any of various zigzags, alternations, or overlappings of position or time <~ work shifts> <~ teeth on a cutter> **4 :** to adjust (as the wings of a biplane) so that the leading edge of one wing projects beyond the leading edge of another wing — **stag·ger·er** \-ər-ər\ *n*

[2]**stagger** *n* **1** *pl but sing or pl in constr* **:** an abnormal condition of domestic mammals and birds associated with damage to the central nervous system and marked by incoordination and a reeling unsteady gait **2 :** a reeling or unsteady gait or stance **3 :** the amount by which the leading edge of an upper wing of a biplane is advanced over that of a lower expressed as percentage of gap

[3]**stagger** *adj* **:** marked by an alternating or overlapping arrangement

stag·ger·bush \ˈstag-ər-ˌbu̇sh\ *n* **:** a shrubby heath (*Lyonia mariana*) of the eastern U.S. that is poisonous to livestock

stag·ger·ing *adj* **:** tending to stagger **:** ASTONISHING, OVERWHELMING — **stag·ger·ing·ly** \ˈstag-(ə-)riŋ-lē\ *adv*

stag·gery \ˈstag-(ə-)rē\ *adj* **:** UNSTEADY

stag·gy \ˈstag-ē\ *adj* **:** having the appearance of a mature male — used of female or castrated male domestic animals

stag·horn sumac \ˌstag-ˌhȯrn-\ *n* **:** a small tree or shrub (*Rhus typhina*) of eastern No. America with velvety-pubescent branches and flower stalks, leaves that turn brilliant red in fall, and dense panicles of greenish yellow flowers followed by bright crimson fruits

stag·hound \ˈstag-ˌhau̇nd\ *n* **:** a hound formerly used in hunting the stag and other large animals; *specif* **:** a large heavy hound resembling the English foxhound

stag·ing \ˈstā-jiŋ\ *n* **1 :** SCAFFOLDING **2 a :** the business of running stagecoaches **b :** the act of journeying in stagecoaches **3 :** the putting of a play on the stage **4 a :** the moving of troops or matériel forward in several stages **b :** the assembling of troops or matériel in transit in a particular place **5 :** the disengaging and discarding of a burned-out rocket unit from a space vehicle during flight

staging area *n* **:** an area in which troops are assembled and readied prior to a new operation or mission

Stag·i·rite \ˈstaj-ə-ˌrīt\ *n* [Gk *Stagiritēs,* fr. *Stagira,* city in ancient Macedonia] **:** a native or resident of Stagira <Aristotle the ~>

stag·nant \ˈstag-nənt\ *adj* **1 a :** not flowing in a current or stream **:** MOTIONLESS <~ water> **b :** STALE <long disuse had made the air ~ and foul —Bram Stoker> **2 :** DULL, INACTIVE — **stag·nan·cy** \-nən-sē\ *n* — **stag·nant·ly** *adv*

stag·nate \ˈstag-ˌnāt\ *vi* **stag·nat·ed; stag·nat·ing** [L *stagnatus,* pp. of *stagnare,* fr. *stagnum* body of standing water; akin to Gk *stazein* to drip] **:** to become or remain stagnant — **stag·na·tion** \stag-ˈnā-shən\ *n*

stagy \ˈstā-jē\ *or* **stag·ey** *adj* **stag·i·er; -est :** of or resembling the stage; *esp* **:** marked by pretense or artificiality **:** THEATRICAL — **stag·i·ly** \-jə-lē\ *adv* — **stag·i·ness** \-jē-nəs\ *n*

[1]**staid** \ˈstād\ *adj* [fr. pp. of [3]*stay*] **:** marked by settled sedateness and often prim self-restraint **:** SOBER, GRAVE ***syn*** see SERIOUS ***ant*** jaunty — **staid·ly** *adv* — **staid·ness** *n*

[2]**staid** *past of* STAY

[1]**stain** \ˈstān\ *vb* [ME *steynen,* partly fr. MF *desteindre* to discolor & partly of Scand origin; akin to ON *steina* to paint — more at DISTAIN] *vt* **1 :** DISCOLOR, SOIL **2 :** to suffuse with color **3 a :** to taint with guilt, vice, or corruption **b :** to bring reproach on **4 :** to color (as wood, glass, or cloth) by processes affecting chemically or otherwise the material itself ~ *vi* **:** to receive a stain — **stain·able** \ˈstā-nə-bəl\ *adj*

[2]**stain** *n* **1 a :** a soiled or discolored spot **b :** a natural spot of color contrasting with the ground **2 :** a taint of guilt **:** STIGMA **3 a :** a preparation (as of dye or pigment) used in staining; *esp* **:** one capable of penetrating the pores of wood **b :** a dye or mixture of dyes used in microscopy to make visible minute and transparent structures, to differentiate tissue elements, or to produce specific chemical reactions

stain·abil·i·ty \ˌstā-nə-ˈbil-ət-ē\ *n* **:** the capacity of cells and cell parts to stain specifically and consistently with particular dyes and stains

---

ə abut	ᵊ kitten	ər further	a back	ā bake	ä cot, cart
au̇ out	ch chin	e less	ē easy	g gift	i trip	ī life
j joke	ŋ sing	ō flow	ȯ flaw	ȯi coin	th thin	t͟h this
ü loot	u̇ foot	y yet	yü few	yu̇ furious	zh vision

stained glass *n* : glass colored or stained for use in windows: **a** : glass colored throughout by metallic oxides fused into it **b** : clear glass cased with colored glass **c** : clear glass into whose surface the pigments have been burned
stain·er \'stā-nər\ *n* : one that stains: as **a** : a worker who applies a coloring or finishing stain to wood or leather **b** : a pigment used merely to give color to a paint as distinguished from the base **c** : an insect that stains the material on which it feeds
1stain·less \'stān-ləs\ *adj* **1 a** : free from stain or stigma **b** : highly resistant to stain **2** : made from materials resistant to stain — **stain·less·ly** *adv*
2stainless *n* : tableware made of stainless steel
stainless steel *n* : an alloy of iron with chromium and sometimes nickel or manganese that is practically immune to rusting and ordinary corrosion
stair \'sta(ə)r, 'ste(ə)r\ *n* [ME *steir*, fr. OE *stǣger;* akin to OE & OHG *stīgan* to rise, Gk *steichein* to walk] **1** : a series of steps or flights of steps for passing from one level to another — often used in pl. but sing. or pl. in constr. <a narrow private ~*s* —Lewis Mumford> **2** : a single step of a stairway
stair·case \-ˌkās\ *n* **1** : the structure containing a stairway **2** : a flight of stairs with the supporting framework, casing, and balusters
stair·way \-ˌwā\ *n* : one or more flights of stairs usu. with landings to pass from one level to another
stair·well \-ˌwel\ *n* : a vertical shaft in which stairs are located
1stake \'stāk\ *n* [ME, fr. OE *staca;* akin to MLG *stake* stake, L *tignum* beam] **1** : a pointed piece of wood or other material driven or to be driven into the ground as a marker or support **2 a** : a post to which a person is bound for execution by burning **b** : execution by burning at a stake **3 a** : something that is staked for gain or loss **b** : the prize in a contest **c** : an interest or share in an undertaking (as a commercial venture) **4** : a Mormon territorial jurisdiction comprising a group of wards **5** : an upright stick at the side or end of a vehicle to retain the load **6** : GRUBSTAKE — **at stake** : at issue : in jeopardy
2stake *vt* **staked; stak·ing 1** : to mark the limits of by or as if by stakes **2** : to tether to a stake **3** : BET, HAZARD **4** : to fasten up or support (as plants) with stakes **5** : to back financially **6** : GRUBSTAKE — **stake a claim** : to assert a title or right to something by or as if by placing stakes to satisfy a legal requirement
stake body *n* : an open motortruck body consisting of a platform with stakes inserted along the outside edges to retain a load
stake·hold·er \'stāk-ˌhōl-dər\ *n* : a person entrusted with the stakes of bettors
stake·out \'stā-ˌkau̇t\ *n* : a surveillance maintained by the police of an area or a person suspected of criminal activity
stake out \stā-'kau̇t\ *vt* **1** : to assign (as a policeman) to an area usu. to conduct a surveillance **2** : to maintain a stakeout of
stake race *n* : a horse race in which the prize offered is made up at least in part of money (as entry fees) put up by the owners of the horses entered
stake truck *n* : a truck having a stake body
Sta·kha·nov·ite \stə-'kän-ə-ˌvīt\ *n* [Alexei G. *Stakhanov b*1905 Russ miner] : a Soviet industrial worker awarded recognition and special privileges for output beyond production norms — **Sta·kha·nov·ism** \-ˌviz-əm\ *n*
sta·lac·tite \stə-'lak-ˌtīt *also* 'stal-ək-\ *n* [NL *stalactites*, fr. Gk *stalaktos* dripping, fr. *stalassein* to let drip — more at STALE] : a deposit of calcium carbonate (as calcite) resembling an icicle hanging from the roof or sides of a cavern — **sta·lac·tit·ic** \ˌstal-ˌak-'tit-ik, -ək-; stə-ˌlak-\ *adj*
sta·lag \'stäl-ˌäg\ *n* [G, short for *stammlager* base camp, fr. *stamm* base + *lager* camp] : a German prison camp for noncommissioned officers or enlisted men
sta·lag·mite \stə-'lag-ˌmīt *also* 'stal-əg-\ *n* [NL *stalagmites*, fr. Gk *stalagma* drop or *stalagmos* dripping; akin to Gk *stalassein* to let drip] : a deposit of calcium carbonate like an inverted stalactite formed on the floor of a cave by the drip of calcareous water — **sta·lag·mit·ic** \ˌstal-ˌag-'mit-ik, -əg-; stə-, lag-\ *adj*
1stale \'stā(ə)l\ *adj* **stal·er; stal·est** [ME, aged (of ale); akin to MD *stel* stale] **1** : tasteless or unpalatable from age **2** : tedious from familiarity **3** : impaired in legal force or effect by reason of being allowed to rest without timely use, action, or demand <a ~ affidavit> <a ~ debt> **4** : impaired in vigor or effectiveness — **stale·ly** \'stā(ə)l-lē\ *adv* — **stale·ness** *n*
2stale *vb* **staled; stal·ing** *vt* **1** : to make stale **2** *archaic* : to make common : CHEAPEN ~ *vi* : to become stale
3stale *n* [ME; akin to MLG *stal* horse urine, Gk *stalassein* to let drip] : urine of a domestic animal (as a horse)
4stale *vi* **staled; stal·ing** : URINATE — used chiefly of camels and horses
1stale·mate \'stā(ə)l-ˌmāt\ *n* [obs. E *stale* (stalemate) + E *mate*] **1** : a drawing position in chess in which only the king can move and although not in check can move only into check **2** : a drawn contest : DEADLOCK: *also* : the state of being stalemated
2stalemate *vt* : to bring into a stalemate
Sta·lin·ism \'stäl-ə-ˌniz-əm, 'stal-\ *n* : the political, economic, and social principles and policies associated with Stalin; *esp* : the theory and practice of communism developed by Stalin from Marxism-Leninism and characterized esp. by rigid authoritarianism, widespread use of terror, and often by emphasis on Russian nationalism — **Sta·lin·ist** \-nəst\ *n or adj* — **Sta·lin·ize** \-ˌnīz\ *vt* — **Sta·lin·oid** \-ˌnȯid\ *n or adj*
1stalk \'stȯk\ *vb* [ME *stalken*, fr. OE be*stealcian;* akin to OE *stealc* lofty, *stelan* to steal — more at STEAL] *vi* **1** : to pursue quarry or prey stealthily **2** : to walk stiffly or haughtily ~ *vt* **1** : to pursue by stalking **2** : to go through (an area) in search of prey or quarry <~ the woods for deer> — **stalk·er** *n*
2stalk *n* **1** : the act of stalking **2** : a stalking gait
3stalk *n* [ME *stalke;* akin to OE *stealc* lofty] **1 a** : the main stem of an herbaceous plant often with its dependent parts **b** : a part of a plant (as a petiole, stipe, or peduncle) that supports another **2** : a slender upright object or supporting or connecting part; *esp* : PEDUNCLE <the ~ of a crinoid> — **stalked** \'stȯkt\ *adj* — **stalk·less** \'stȯ-kləs\ *adj* — **stalky** \'stȯ-kē\ *adj*
stalk–eyed \'stȯ-'kīd\ *adj* : having the eyes raised on stalks — used chiefly of crustaceans
stalk·ing–horse \'stȯ-kiŋ-ˌhȯ(ə)rs\ *n* **1** : a horse or a figure like a horse behind which a hunter stalks game **2** : something used to mask a purpose **3** : a candidate put forward to divide the opposition or to conceal someone's real candidacy
1stall \'stȯl\ *n* [ME, fr. OE *steall;* akin to OHG *stal* place, stall, L *locus* (OL *stlocus*) place, Gk *stellein* to set up, place, send] **1 a** : a compartment for a domestic animal in a stable or barn **b** : a space marked off for parking a motor vehicle **2 a** : a seat in the chancel of a church with back and sides wholly or partly enclosed **b** : a church pew **c** *Brit* : a front orchestra seat in a theater **3** : a booth, stand, or counter at which articles are displayed for sale **4** : a protective sheath for a finger or toe : COT **5** : a small compartment <a shower ~>
2stall *vt* **1** : to put into or keep in a stall **2** *obs* : to install in office **3 a** : to bring to a standstill : BLOCK; *esp* : MIRE **b** : to cause (an engine) to stop usu. inadvertently **c** : to cause (an airplane or airfoil) to go into a stall ~ *vi* **1** : to come to a standstill (as from mired wheels or engine failure) **2** : to experience a stall in flying
3stall *n* : the condition of an airfoil or airplane operating so that there is a flow breakdown and loss of lift with a tendency to drop
4stall *n* [alter. of *stale* (lure)] : a ruse to deceive or delay
5stall *vi* : to play for time : DELAY ~ *vt* : to hold off, divert, or delay by evasion or deception
stall–feed \'stȯl-ˌfēd\ *vt* **-fed** \-ˌfed\; **-feed·ing** : to feed in a stall esp. so as to fatten <~ an ox>
stal·lion \'stal-yən\ *n* [ME *stalion*, fr. MF *estalon*, of Gmc origin; akin to OHG *stal* stall] : an uncastrated male horse : a male horse kept for breeding; *also* : a male animal (as a dog or a sheep) kept primarily as a stud
1stal·wart \'stȯl-wərt\ *adj* [ME, alter. of *stalworth*, fr. OE *stǣlwierthe* serviceable] : marked by outstanding strength and vigor of body, mind, or spirit <~ common sense> ***syn*** see STRONG — **stal·wart·ly** *adv* — **stal·wart·ness** *n*
2stalwart *n* **1** : a stalwart person **2** : an unwavering partisan
stal·worth \'stȯl-(ˌ)wərth\ *archaic var of* STALWART
sta·men \'stā-mən\ *n, pl* **stamens** *also* **sta·mi·na** \'stā-mə-nə, 'stam-ə-\ [L, warp, thread; akin to Gk *stēmōn* thread, *histanai* to cause to stand — more at STAND] : a microsporophyll of a seed plant; *specif* : the organ of a flower that produces the male gamete, consists of an anther and a filament, and is morphologically a spore-bearing leaf — see FLOWER illustration
stamin- *or* **stamini-** *comb form* [L *stamin-*, *stamen*] : stamen <*stamin*ody> <*stamini*ferous>
stam·i·na \'stam-ə-nə\ *n* [L, pl. of *stamen* warp, thread of life spun by the Fates] : STAYING POWER, ENDURANCE
sta·mi·nal \'stā-mən-ᵊl, 'stam-ən-\ *adj* : of, relating to, or consisting of a stamen
sta·mi·nate \'stā-mə-nət, 'stam-ə-, -ˌnāt\ *adj* **1** : having or producing stamens **2** *of a diclinous flower* : having stamens but no pistils
sta·mi·no·di·um \ˌstā-mə-'nōd-ē-əm, ˌstam-ə-\ *n pl* **-dia** \-ē-ə\ [NL, fr. *stamin-* + *-odium* thing resembling, fr. Gk *-ōdēs* like] : an abortive or sterile stamen
sta·mi·no·dy \'stā-mə-ˌnōd-ē, 'stam-ə-\ *n* [*stamin-* + Gk *-ōdēs* like] : the metamorphosis of other floral organs into stamens
stam·mel \'stam-əl\ *n* [prob. fr. *stamin* (a woolen fabric)] **1** *obs* : a coarse woolen clothing fabric usu. dyed red and used sometimes for undershirts of penitents **2** *archaic* : the bright red color of stammel
stam·mer \'stam-ər\ *vb* **stam·mered; stam·mer·ing** \-(ə-)riŋ\ [ME *stameren*, fr. OE *stamerian;* akin to OHG *stamalōn* to stammer, Lith *stumti* to push] *vi* : to make involuntary stops and repetitions in speaking : HALT — compare STUTTER ~ *vt* : to utter with involuntary stops or repetitions — **stammer** *n* — **stam·mer·er** \-ər-ər\ *n*
syn STAMMER, STUTTER *shared meaning element* : to speak or utter stumblingly
1stamp \'stamp; *vt2a & vi2 are also* 'stämp *or* 'stȯmp\ *vb* [ME *stampen;* akin to OHG *stampfōn* to stamp, L *temnere* to despise, Gk *stembein* to shake up] *vt* **1** : to pound or crush with a pestle or a heavy instrument **2 a** (1) : to strike or beat forcibly with the bottom of the foot (2) : to bring down (the foot) forcibly **b** : to extinguish or destroy by or as if by stamping with the foot — usu. used with *out* <~ out cancer> **3 a** : IMPRESS, IMPRINT <~ "paid" on the bill> **b** : to attach a stamp to **4** : to cut out, bend, or form with a stamp or die **5 a** : to provide with a distinctive character <~*ed* with a dreary, institutionalized look —Bernard Taper> **b** : CHARACTERIZE ~ *vi* **1** : POUND **2** : to strike or thrust the foot forcibly or noisily downward
2stamp *n* **1** : a device or instrument for stamping **2** : the impression or mark made by stamping or imprinting **3 a** : a distinctive character, indication, or mark **b** : a lasting imprint **4** : the act of stamping **5** : a stamped or printed paper affixed in evidence that a tax has been paid; *also* : POSTAGE STAMP
1stam·pede \stam-'pēd\ *n* [AmerSp *estampida*, fr. Sp, crash, fr. *estampar* to stamp, of Gmc origin; akin to OHG *stampfōn* to stamp] **1** : a wild headlong rush or flight of frightened animals **2** : a mass movement of people at a common impulse
2stampede *vb* **stam·ped·ed; stam·ped·ing** *vt* **1** : to cause to run away in headlong panic **2** : to cause (a group of people) to act on mass impulse ~ *vi* **1** : to flee headlong in panic **2** : to act on mass impulse — **stam·ped·er** *n*
stamp·er \'stam-pər, 'stäm-, 'stȯm-; *compare* 1STAMP\ *n* : one that stamps: as **a** : a worker who performs an industrial stamping operation **b** : an inplement for pounding or stamping **c** : any of various stamping machines
stamping ground \'stamp-, 'stämp-, 'stȯmp-\ *n* : a favorite or habitual resort

stamp mill \ˈstamp-\ *or* **stamping mill** \ˈstam-piŋ-\ *n* **:** a mill in which ore is crushed with stamps; *also* **:** a machine for stamping ore — called also *quartz battery*

stamp tax *n* **:** a tax collected by means of a stamp purchased and affixed (as to a deck of playing cards); *specif* **:** such a tax on a document (as a deed or promissory note) — called also *stamp duty*

stance \ˈstan(t)s\ *n* [MF *estance* position, posture, stay, fr. (assumed) VL *stantia*, fr. L *stant-, stans*, prp. of *stare* to stand] **1** *chiefly Scot* **a :** STATION **b :** SITE **2 a :** a way of standing or being placed **:** POSTURE **b :** intellectual or emotional attitude <took an anti-war ~> **3 a :** the position of the feet of a golfer or batter preparatory to making a swing **b :** the position of both body and feet from which an athlete starts or operates

[1]**stanch** \ˈstȯnch, ˈstänch\ *vt* [ME *staunchen*, fr. MF *estancher*, fr. (assumed) VL *stanticare*, fr. L *stant-, stans*, prp.] **1 :** to check or stop the flowing of <~*ed* her tears>; *also* **:** to stop the flow of blood from (a wound) **2** *archaic* **:** ALLAY, EXTINGUISH **3 a :** to stop or check in its course <trying to ~ the crime wave> **b :** to make watertight **:** stop up — **stanch·er** *n*

[2]**stanch** *var of* STAUNCH

[1]**stan·chion** \ˈstan-chən\ *n* [ME *stanchon*, fr. MF *estanchon*, fr. OF, aug. of *estance* stay, prop] **1 :** an upright bar, post, or support (as for a roof) **2 :** a device that fits loosely around a cow's neck and limits forward and backward motion (as in a stall)

[2]**stanchion** *vt* **stan·chioned; stan·chion·ing** \ˈstanch-(ə-)niŋ\ **1 a :** to provide with stanchions **b :** to support or brace with or as if with a stanchion **2 :** to secure (as a cow) by a stanchion

[1]**stand** \ˈstand\ *vb* **stood** \ˈstu̇d\; **stand·ing** [ME *standen*, fr. OE *standan*; akin to OHG *stantan, stān* to stand, L *stare*, Gk *histanai* to cause to stand, set, *histasthai* to stand, be standing] *vi* **1 a :** to support oneself on the feet in an erect position **b :** to be a specified height when fully erect <~*s* six feet two> **c :** to rise to an erect position **2 a :** to take up or maintain a specified position or posture <~ aside> **b :** to maintain one's position <~ firm> **3 :** to be in a particular state or situation <~*s* accused> **4 :** to hold a course at sea **5** *obs* **:** HESITATE **6 a :** to have or maintain a relative position in or as if in a graded scale <~*s* first in his class> **b :** to be in a position to gain or lose because of an action taken or a commitment made <~*s* to make quite a profit> **7** *chiefly Brit* **:** to be a candidate **:** RUN **8 a :** to rest or remain upright on a base or lower end <a clock *stood* on the mantle> **b :** to occupy a place or location <the house ~*s* on a knoll> **9 a :** to remain stationary or inactive <the car *stood* in the garage for a week> **b :** to gather slowly and remain <tears ~*ing* in her eyes> **10 :** AGREE, ACCORD — used chiefly in the expression *it stands to reason* **11 a :** to exist in a definite written or printed form <copy a passage exactly as it ~*s*> **b :** to remain valid or efficacious <the order given last week still ~*s*> **12** *of a male animal* **:** to be available as a sire — used esp. of horses ~ *vt* **1 a :** to endure or undergo successfully <this book will ~ the test of time> **b :** to tolerate without flinching **:** bear courageously <he ~*s* pain well> **c :** to endure the presence or personality of <can't ~ his boss> **d :** to afford to accept or have <looks like he could ~ a drink> **2 :** to remain firm in the face of <~ a siege> **3 :** to submit to <~ trial> **4 a :** to perform the duty of <~ guard> **b :** to participate in (a military formation) **5 :** to pay the cost of (a treat) **:** pay for <I'll ~ you a dinner> <~ drinks> **6 :** to cause to stand **:** set upright ***syn*** see BEAR — **stand·er** *n* — **stand a chance :** to have a chance — **stand for 1 :** to be a symbol for **:** REPRESENT **2 :** to put up with **:** PERMIT — **stand on 1 :** to depend upon **2 :** to insist on <never *stands on* ceremony> — **stand one's ground :** to maintain one's position — **stand on one's own feet :** to think or act independently — **stand treat :** to pay the cost of food, drink, or entertainment for others in a group

[2]**stand** *n* **1 :** an act of stopping or staying in one place **2 a :** a halt for defense or resistance **b :** an often defensive effort of some duration or degree of success <a goal-line ~> **c (1) :** a stop made to give a performance <a one-night ~> **(2) :** a town where such a stop is made **3 a :** a place or post where one stands **b :** a strongly or aggressively held position esp. on a debatable issue **4 a :** the place taken by a witness for testifying in court **b** *pl* **(1) :** a section of the tiered seats for spectators of a sport or spectacle **(2) :** the occupants of such seats **c :** a raised platform (as for a speaker) serving as a point of vantage **5 a :** a small often open-air structure for a small retail business <a vegetable ~> <a hot dog ~> **b :** a site fit for business opportunity **6 :** a place where a passenger vehicle stops or parks <a taxi ~> **7 :** [1]HIVE 2 **8 :** a frame on or in which something may be placed for support **9 :** a group of plants growing in a continuous area **10 :** a standing posture ***syn*** see POSITION

[1]**stan·dard** \ˈstan-dərd\ *n* [ME, fr. MF *estandard* rallying point, standard, of Gmc origin; akin to OE *standan* to stand and to OE *ord* point — more at ODD] **1 :** a conspicuous object (as a banner) formerly carried at the top of a pole and used to mark a rallying point esp. in battle or to serve as an emblem **2 a :** a long narrow tapering flag that is personal to an individual or corporation and bears heraldic devices **b :** the personal flag of the head of a state or of a member of a royal family **c :** an organization flag carried by a mounted or motorized military unit **d :** BANNER **3 :** something established by authority, custom, or general consent as a model or example **:** CRITERION **4 :** something set up and established by authority as a rule for the measure of quantity, weight, extent, value, or quality **5 a :** the fineness and legally fixed weight of the metal used in coins **b :** the basis of value in a monetary system **6 :** a structure built for or serving as a base or support **7 a :** a shrub or herb grown with an erect main stem so that it forms or resembles a tree **b :** a fruit tree grafted on a stock that does not induce dwarfing **8 a :** the large odd upper petal of a papilionaceous flower (as the pea) **b :** one of the three inner usu. erect and incurved petals of an iris **9 :** a musical composition (as a song) that has become a part of the standard repertoire
syn STANDARD, CRITERION, GAUGE, YARDSTICK, TOUCHSTONE *shared meaning element* **:** a means of determining what a thing should be

[2]**standard** *adj* **1 a :** constituting or conforming to a standard esp. as established by law or custom <~ weight> **b :** sound and usable but not of top quality <~ beef> **2 a :** regularly and widely used, available, or supplied <~ automobile equipment> **b :** well established and very familiar <the ~ opera> **3 :** having recognized and permanent value <a ~ reference work> **4 :** substantially uniform and well established by usage in the speech and writing of the educated and widely recognized as acceptable <~ pronunciation is subject to regional variations>

stan·dard–bear·er \ˈstan-dərd-ˌbar-ər, -ˌber-\ *n* **1 :** one that bears a standard or banner **2 :** the leader of an organization, movement, or party

stan·dard·bred \-ˌbred\ *n, often cap* **:** any of an American breed of light trotting and pacing horses bred for speed and noted for endurance

standard candle *n* **:** CANDLE 3

standard deviation *n* **1 :** a measure of the dispersion of a frequency distribution that is the square root of the arithmetic mean of the squares of the deviation of each of the class frequencies from the arithmetic mean of the frequency distribution; *also* **:** a similar quantity found by dividing by one less than the number of squares in the sum of squares instead of taking the arithmetic mean **2 :** a parameter that indicates the way in which a probability function or a probability density function is centered around its mean and that is equal to the square root of the moment in which the deviation from the mean is squared

Standard English *n* **:** the English that with respect to spelling, grammar, pronunciation, and vocabulary is substantially uniform though not devoid of regional differences, that is well established by usage in the formal and informal speech and writing of the educated, and that is widely recognized as acceptable wherever English is spoken and understood

standard error *n* **:** the standard deviation of the probability function or probability density function of a random variable and esp. of a statistic; *specif* **:** the standard error of the mean of a sample from a population with a normal distribution that is equal to the standard deviation of the normal distribution divided by the square root of the sample size

standard gauge *n* **:** a railroad gauge of 4 feet $8\frac{1}{2}$ inches

stan·dard·ize \ˈstan-dərd-ˌīz\ *vt* **-ized; -iz·ing 1 :** to compare with a standard **2 :** to bring into conformity with a standard — **stan·dard·iza·tion** \ˌstan-dərd-ə-ˈzā-shən\ *n*

standard of living 1 : the necessities, comforts, and luxuries enjoyed or aspired to by an individual or group **2 :** a minimum of necessities, comforts, or luxuries held essential to maintaining a person or group in customary or proper status or circumstances

standard operating procedure *n* **:** established or prescribed methods to be followed routinely for the performance of designated operations or in designated situations — called also *standing operating procedure*

standard position *n* **:** the position of an angle with its vertex at the origin of a rectangular-coordinate system and its initial side coinciding with the positive x-axis

standard schnauzer *n* **:** a schnauzer of a breed that attains a height at the highest point of the shoulder blades of 18 to 20 inches in the male and 17 to 19 inches in the female

standard score *n* **:** an individual test score expressed as the deviation from the mean score of the group in units of standard deviation

standard time *n* **:** the time of a region or country that is established by law or general usage as civil time; *specif* **:** the mean solar time of a meridian that is a multiple of 15 arbitrarily applied to a local area or to one of the 24 time zones and designated as a number of hours earlier or later than Greenwich time

stand·away \ˌstan-də-ˌwā\ *adj* **:** standing out from the body <a ~ skirt>

[1]**stand·by** \ˈstan(d)-ˌbī\ *n, pl* **stand·bys** \-ˌbīz\ **1 a :** one to be relied upon esp. in emergencies **b :** a favorite or reliable choice or resource **2 :** one that is held in reserve ready for use **:** SUBSTITUTE — **on standby :** ready or available for immediate action or use

[2]**stand·by** \ˌstan(d)-ˌbī\ *adj* **1 :** held near at hand and ready for use <a ~ power plant> <~ equipment> **2 :** relating to the act or condition of standing by <~ duty> <a ~ period>

stand by \(ˈ)stan(d)-ˈbī\ *vi* **1 :** to be present; *also* **:** to remain apart or aloof **2 :** to be or to get ready to act ~ *vt* **:** to remain loyal or faithful to **:** DEFEND

stand down *vi* **:** to leave the witness stand

stand·ee \stan-ˈdē\ *n* **:** one who occupies standing room

stand–in \ˈstan-ˌdin\ *n* **1 :** someone employed to occupy an actor's place while lights and camera are readied **2 :** SUBSTITUTE

stand in \(ˈ)stan-ˈdin\ *vi* **:** to act as a stand-in — **stand in with :** to be in a specially favored position with

[1]**stand·ing** \ˈstan-diŋ\ *adj* **1 a :** upright on the feet or base **:** ERECT <the ~ audience> **b :** not yet cut or harvested <~ timber> <~ grain> **2 a :** not being used or operated <a ~ factory> **b :** not flowing **:** STAGNANT <~ water> **3 a :** remaining at the same level, degree, or amount for an indeterminate period <a ~ offer> **b :** continuing in existence or use indefinitely **4 :** established by law or custom **5 :** not movable **6 :** done from a standing position <a ~ jump> <a ~ ovation>

[2]**standing** *n* **1 a :** a place to stand in **:** LOCATION **b :** a position from which one may assert or enforce legal rights and duties **2 a :** length of service or experience esp. as determining rank, pay, or privilege **b :** position or condition in society or in a profession; *esp* **:** good reputation **c :** position relative to a standard of achieve-

ment or to achievements of competitors **3 :** maintenance of position or condition **:** DURATION <a custom of long ~>

standing army *n* **:** a permanent army of paid soldiers

standing committee *n* **:** a permanent committee esp. of a legislative body

standing crop *n* **:** the total amount or number of living things or of one kind of living thing (as an uncut farm crop, the fish in a pond, or organisms in an ecosystem) in a particular situation at any given time

standing order *n* **:** an instruction or prescribed procedure in force permanently or until specifically changed or canceled; *esp* **:** any of the rules for the guidance and government of parliamentary procedure which endure through successive sessions until vacated or repealed

standing room *n* **:** space for standing; *esp* **:** accommodation available for spectators or passengers after all seats are filled

standing wave *n* **:** a single-frequency mode of vibration of a body or physical system in which the amplitude varies from place to place, is constantly zero at fixed points, and has maxima at other points

stan·dish \ˈstan-dish\ *n* [origin unknown] **:** a stand for writing materials **:** INKSTAND

1stand·off \ˈstan-ˌdȯf\ *adj* **1 :** STANDOFFISH **2 :** used for holding something at a distance from a surface <a ~ insulator>

2standoff *n* **1 :** the act of standing off **2 a :** a counterbalancing effect **b :** TIE, DRAW <the two teams played to a ~>

stand off \(ˈ)stan-ˈdȯf\ *vi* **1 :** to stay at a distance in social intercourse **2 :** to sail away from the shore ~ *vt* **1 :** to keep from advancing **:** REPEL **2 :** to put off **:** STALL

stand·off·ish \stan-ˈdȯ-fish\ *adj* **:** somewhat cold and reserved — **stand·off·ish·ly** *adv* — **stand·off·ish·ness** *n*

stand oil *n* **:** a thickened drying oil; *esp* **:** linseed oil heated to about 600° F

stand·out \ˈstan-ˌdau̇t\ *n* **:** one that is prominent or conspicuous esp. because of excellence

stand out \(ˈ)stan-ˈdau̇t\ *vi* **1 a :** to appear as if in relief **:** PROJECT **b :** to be prominent or conspicuous **2 :** to steer away from shore **3 :** to be stubborn in resolution or resistance

stand·pat \ˌstan(d)-ˌpat\ *adj* [*stand pat*] **:** stubbornly conservative **:** resisting or opposing change

stand pat \ˈstan(d)-ˈpat\ *vi* [4*pat*] **1 :** to play one's hand as dealt in draw poker without drawing **2 :** to oppose or resist change — **stand·pat·ter** \ˈstan(d)-ˌpat-ər, -ˈpat-\ *n* — **stand·pat·tism** \-ˌpat-ˌiz-əm\ *n*

stand·pipe \ˈstan(d)-ˌpīp\ *n* **:** a high vertical pipe or reservoir that is used to secure a uniform pressure in a water-supply system

stand·point \-ˌpȯint\ *n* **:** a position from which objects or principles are viewed and according to which they are compared and judged

stand·still \-ˌstil\ *n* **:** a state characterized by absence of motion or of progress **:** STOP

stand–up \ˌstan-ˌdəp\ *adj* **1 a :** ERECT, UPRIGHT **b :** stiffened to stay upright without folding over <a ~ collar> **2 :** performed in or requiring a standing position <a ~ bar>

stand up \(ˈ)stan-ˈdəp\ *vi* **1 :** to rise to a standing position **2 :** to remain sound and intact under stress, attack, or close scrutiny ~ *vt* **:** to fail to keep an appointment with — **stand up for :** to defend against attack or criticism — **stand up to 1 :** to meet fairly and fully **2 :** to face boldly — **stand up with :** to be best man or maid of honor for at a wedding ceremony

stand–up comedian *n* **:** a comedian whose act consists of a monologue of jokes, gags, or satirical comments performed usu. while standing alone on a stage or in front of a camera

stane \ˈstān\ *Scot var of* STONE

Stan·ford–Bi·net test \ˌstan-fərd-bi-ˈnā-\ *n* [*Stanford* University, Calif.] **:** an intelligence test prepared at Stanford University as a revision of the Binet-Simon scale and commonly employed with children — called also *Stanford-Binet*

1stang \ˈstaŋ\ *vt* [ME *stangen,* fr. ON *stanga* to prick; akin to ON *stinga* to sting] *chiefly Scot* **:** STING

2stang *n, chiefly Scot* **:** PANG

stan·hope \ˈstan-əp\ *n* [Fitzroy *Stanhope* †1864 Brit clergyman] **:** a gig, buggy, or phaeton typically having a high seat and closed back

Sta·ni·slav·ski method \ˌstan-ə-ˈslaf-skē-, -ˈslav-\ *n* [Konstantin *Stanislavski*] **:** a technique in acting by which an actor strives to empathize with the character he is portraying so as to effect a realistic interpretation

1stank \ˈstaŋk\ *past of* STINK

2stank *n* [ME, fr. OF *estanc*] **1** *dial Brit* **a :** POND, POOL **b :** a ditch containing water **2** *Brit* **:** a small dam **:** WEIR

stan·na·ry \ˈstan-ə-rē\ *n, pl* **-ries** [ML *stannaria* tin mine, fr. LL *stannum* tin] **:** one of the regions in England containing tinworks — usu. used in pl.

stan·nic \ˈstan-ik\ *adj* [prob. fr. F *stannique,* fr. LL *stannum* tin, fr. L, an alloy of silver and lead, prob. of Celt origin; akin to Corn *stēn* tin] **:** of, relating to, or containing tin esp. with a valence of four

stan·nite \ˈstan-ˌīt\ *n* [LL *stannum* tin] **:** a mineral Cu_2FeSnS that is a steel-gray or iron-black sulfide of copper, iron, and tin with a metallic luster and occurs in granular masses

stan·nous \ˈstan-əs\ *adj* [ISV, fr. LL *stannum*] **:** of, relating to, or containing tin esp. when bivalent

stan·za \ˈstan-zə\ *n* [It, stay, abode, room, stanza, fr. (assumed) VL *stantia* stay — more at STANCE] **:** a division of a poem consisting of a series of lines arranged together in a usu. recurring pattern of meter and rhyme **:** STROPHE — **stan·za·ic** \stan-ˈzā-ik\ *adj*

sta·pe·dec·to·my \ˌstā-pi-ˈdek-tə-mē\ *n, pl* **-mies** [ISV, fr. NL *staped-, stapes*] **:** surgical removal and prosthetic replacement of the stapes to relieve deafness — **sta·pe·dec·to·mized** \-ˌmīzd\ *adj*

sta·pe·di·al \stā-ˈpēd-ē-əl, stə-\ *adj* **:** of, relating to, or located near the stapes

sta·pe·lia \stə-ˈpēl-yə\ *n* [NL, genus name, fr. J. B. van *Stapel* †1636 D botanist] **:** any of a genus (*Stapelia*) of African plants of the milkweed family with succulent leafless toothed stems like cactus joints and showy but putrid-smelling flowers

sta·pes \ˈstā-(ˌ)pēz\ *n, pl* **stapes** *or* **sta·pe·des** \ˈstā-pə-ˌdēz\ [NL *staped-, stapes,* fr. ML, stirrup, alter. of LL *stapia*] **:** the innermost ossicle of the ear of mammals — see EAR illustration

staph \ˈstaf\ *n* **:** STAPHYLOCOCCUS

staph·y·li·nid \ˌstaf-ə-ˈlī-nəd\ *n* [NL *Staphylinidae,* deriv. of Gk *staphylē* bunch of grapes] **:** any of a family (Staphylinidae) of beetles that have a long body and very short wing covers beneath which the wings are folded transversely — **staphylinid** *adj*

staph·y·lo·coc·cal \ˌstaf-(ə-)lō-ˈkäk-əl\ *adj* **:** of, relating to, or being a staphylococcus

staph·y·lo·coc·cic \-ˈkäk-(s)ik\ *adj* **:** caused by a staphylococcus

staph·y·lo·coc·cus \-ˈkäk-əs\ *n, pl* **-coc·ci** \-ˈkäk-ˌ(s)ī, -(ˌ)(s)ē\ [NL, genus name, fr. Gk *staphylē* bunch of grapes + NL *-coccus;* akin to OE *stæf* staff] **:** any of various nonmotile gram-positive spherical bacteria (esp. genus *Staphylococcus*) that occur singly, in pairs or tetrads, or in irregular clusters and include parasites of skin and mucous membranes

1sta·ple \ˈstā-pəl\ *n* [ME *stapel* post, staple, fr. OE *stapol* post; akin to MD *stapel* step, heap, emporium, OE *steppan* to step] **1 :** a U-shaped metal loop both ends of which are driven into a surface to hold the hook, hasp, or bolt of a lock, secure a rope, or fix a wire in place **2 :** a small U-shaped wire both ends of which are driven through layers of thin and easily penetrable material (as paper) and usu. clinched to hold the layers together

2staple *vt* **sta·pled; sta·pling** \-p(ə-)liŋ\ **:** to provide with or secure by staples

3staple *n* [ME, fr. MD *stapel* emporium] **1 :** a town used as a center for the sale or exportation of commodities in bulk **2 :** a place of supply **:** SOURCE **3 :** a chief commodity or production of a place **4 a :** a commodity for which the demand is constant **b :** something having widespread and constant use or appeal **c :** the sustaining or principal element **:** SUBSTANCE **5 :** RAW MATERIAL **6 a :** textile fiber (as wool or rayon) of relatively short length that when spun and twisted forms a yarn rather than a filament **b :** the length of a piece of such textile fiber

4staple *adj* **1 :** used, needed, or enjoyed constantly usu. by many individuals **2 :** produced regularly or in large quantities <~ crops such as wheat and rice> **3 :** PRINCIPAL, CHIEF

1sta·pler \ˈstā-p(ə-)lər\ *n* **:** one that deals in staple goods or in staple fiber

2stapler *n* **:** one that inserts staples; *esp* **:** a small usu. hand-operated device for inserting wire staples

1star \ˈstär\ *n, often attrib* [ME *sterre,* fr. OE *steorra;* akin to OHG *sterno* star, L *stella,* Gk *astēr, astron*] **1 a :** a natural luminous body visible in the sky esp. at night **b :** a self-luminous gaseous celestial body of great mass whose shape is usu. spheroidal and whose size may be as small as the earth or larger than the earth's orbit **2 a** (1) **:** a planet or a configuration of the planets that is held in astrology to influence one's destiny or fortune — usu. used in pl. (2) **:** a waxing or waning fortune or fame <her ~ was rising> **b** *obs* **:** DESTINY **3 a :** a conventional figure with five or more points that represents a star; *esp* **:** ASTERISK **b :** an often star-shaped ornament or medal worn as a badge of honor, authority, or rank or as the insignia of an order **c :** one of a group of conventional stars used to place something in a scale of value **4 :** something resembling a star <was hit on the head and saw ~*s*> **5 a :** the principal member of a theatrical or operatic company who usu. plays the chief roles **b :** a highly publicized theatrical or motion-picture performer **c :** an outstandingly talented performer <a track ~> **d :** a person who stands out among his fellows — **star·less** \-ləs\ *adj* — **star·like** \-ˌlīk\ *adj*

2star *vb* **starred; star·ring** *vt* **1 :** to sprinkle or adorn with stars **2 a :** to mark with a star as being preeminent **b :** to mark with an asterisk **3 :** to advertise or display prominently **:** FEATURE <the movie ~*s* a famous stage personality> ~ *vi* **1 :** to play the most prominent or important role **2 :** to perform outstandingly

3star *adj* **1 :** of, relating to, or being a star <received ~ billing> **2 :** of outstanding excellence **:** PREEMINENT <a ~ athlete>

star apple *n* **:** a tropical American tree (*Chrysophyllum cainito*) of the sapodilla family grown in warm regions for ornament or fruit; *also* **:** the apple-shaped edible fruit

1star·board \ˈstär-bərd\ *n* [ME *sterbord,* fr. OE *stēorbord,* fr. *stēor-* steering oar + *bord* ship's side — more at STEER, BOARD] **:** the right side of a ship or aircraft looking forward — compare PORT

2starboard *vt* **:** to turn or put (a helm or rudder) to the right

3starboard *adj* **:** of, relating to, or situated to starboard

1starch \ˈstärch\ *vt* [ME *sterchen,* prob. fr. (assumed) OE *stercan* to stiffen; akin to OE *stearc* stiff — more at STARK] **:** to stiffen with or as if with starch

2starch *n* **1 :** a white odorless tasteless granular or powdery complex carbohydrate $(C_6H_{10}O_5)_x$ that is the chief storage form of carbohydrate in plants, is an important foodstuff, and is used also in adhesives and sizes, in laundering, and in pharmacy and medicine **2 :** a stiff formal manner **:** FORMALITY **3 :** resolute vigor

star–cham·ber \ˈstär-ˌchām-bər\ *adj* [*Star Chamber,* a court existing in England from the 15th century until 1641] **:** characterized by secrecy and often being irresponsibly arbitrary and oppressive

starchy \ˈstär-chē\ *adj* **starch·i·er; -est 1 :** containing, consisting of, or resembling starch **2 :** consisting of or marked by formality or stiffness — **starch·i·ly** \-chə-lē\ *adv* — **starch·i·ness** \-chē-nəs\ *n*

star–crossed \ˈstär-ˌkrȯst\ *adj* **:** not favored by the stars **:** ILL-FATED <a pair of ~ lovers take their life —Shak.>

star·dom \ˈstärd-əm\ *n* **1 :** the status or position of a star <the actress quickly reached ~> **2 :** a body of stars

star·dust \ˈstär-ˌdəst\ *n* **:** a feeling or impression of romance, magic, or ethereality

1stare \ˈsta(ə)r, ˈste(ə)r\ *vb* **stared; star·ing** [ME *staren,* fr. OE *starian;* akin to OHG *starēn* to stare, L *strenuus* strenuous, Gk *stereos* solid, Lith *starinti* to stiffen] *vi* **1 :** to look fixedly often with wide-open eyes **2 :** to show oneself conspicuously <the error

stared from the page> **3** *of hair* **:** to stand on end **:** BRISTLE; *also* **:** to appear rough and lusterless ~ *vt* **1 :** to have an effect upon by staring **2 :** to look at with a searching or earnest gaze ***syn*** see GAZE — **star·er** *n* — **stare one in the face :** to be undeniably and forcefully evident or apparent

²stare *n* **:** the act or an instance of staring <a blank ~>

sta·re de·ci·sis \ˌster-ē-di-ˈsī-səs, ˌstar-\ *n* [L, to stand by decided matters] **:** a doctrine or policy of following rules or principles laid down in previous judicial decisions unless they contravene the ordinary principles of justice

stare down *vt* **:** to come to waver or submit by or as if by staring

sta·rets \ˈstär-(y)əts\ *n, pl* **star·tsy** \ˈstärt-sē\ [Russ, lit., old man, fr. *staryĭ* old — more at STOUR] **:** a spiritual director or religious teacher in the Eastern Orthodox Church; *specif* **:** a spiritual adviser who is not necessarily a priest, who is recognized for his piety, and who is turned to by monks or laymen for spiritual guidance

star facet *n* **:** one of the eight small triangular facets which abut on the table in the bezel of a brilliant — see BRILLIANT illustration

star·fish \ˈstär-ˌfish\ *n* **:** any of a class (Asteroidea) of echinoderms having a body of usu. five radially disposed arms about a central disk and feeding largely on mollusks (as oysters)

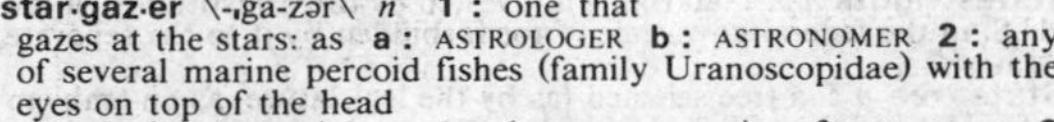
starfish

star·flow·er \-ˌflau̇(-ə)r\ *n* **:** any of several plants having star-shaped pentamerous flowers; *esp* **:** any of a genus (*Trientalis,* esp. *T. americana*) of plants of the primrose family

star·gaze \-ˌgāz\ *vi* [back-formation fr. *stargazer*] **1 :** to gaze at stars **2 :** to gaze raptly or contemplatively

star·gaz·er \-ˌgā-zər\ *n* **1 :** one that gazes at the stars: as **a :** ASTROLOGER **b :** ASTRONOMER **2 :** any of several marine percoid fishes (family Uranoscopidae) with the eyes on top of the head

star·gaz·ing \-ˌgā-ziŋ\ *n* **1 :** the act or practice of a stargazer **2 a :** absorption in chimerical or impractical ideas **:** WOOLGATHERING **b :** the quality or state of being absentminded

star grass *n* **:** any of various grassy plants with stellate flowers or arrangement of leaves: as **a :** any of a genus (*Hypoxis*) of herbs of the amaryllis family **b :** COLICROOT a **c :** a perennial grass (*Cynodon plectostachyum*) that has stems attaining a height of 3 to 4 feet and that is used esp. in Africa and India for pasture and hay

¹stark \ˈstärk\ *adj* [ME, stiff, strong, fr. OE *stearc;* akin to OHG *starc* strong, Lith *starinti* to stiffen — more at STARE] **1** *archaic* **:** STRONG, ROBUST **2 a :** rigid in or as if in death **b :** rigidly conforming (as to a pattern or doctrine) **:** ABSOLUTE <~ discipline> **3 :** SHEER, UTTER <~ nonsense> **4 a :** BARREN, DESOLATE **b (1) :** having few or no ornaments **:** BARE <a ~ white room> **(2) :** HARSH, BLUNT <the ~ realities of death> **5 :** sharply delineated ***syn*** see STIFF — **stark·ly** *adv* — **stark·ness** *n*

²stark *adv* **1 :** in a stark manner **2 :** to an absolute or complete degree **:** WHOLLY <~ naked> <~ mad>

star·let \ˈstär-lət\ *n* **:** a young movie actress being coached and publicized for starring roles

star·light \-ˌlīt\ *n* **:** the light given by the stars

star·ling \ˈstär-liŋ\ *n* [ME, fr. OE *stærlinc,* fr. *stær* starling + *-ling, -linc* -ling; akin to OHG *stara* starling, L *sturnus*] **:** any of a family (Sturnidae, esp. genus *Sturnus*) of usu. dark gregarious passerine birds; *esp* **:** a dark brown or in summer glossy greenish black European bird (*S. vulgaris*) naturalized and often a pest in the U.S., Australia, and New Zealand

star·lit \ˈstär-ˌlit\ *adj* **:** lighted by the stars

star–nosed mole \ˌstär-ˌnōz(d)-\ *n* **:** a common black long-tailed semiaquatic No. American mole (*Condylura cristata*) distinguished by a series of pink fleshy projections surrounding the nostrils

star–of–Bethlehem *n* **:** any of a genus (*Ornithogalum*) of bulbous herbs (as the chincherinchee) of the lily family with basal leaves resembling grass; *esp* **:** one (*O. umbellatum*) with greenish flowers that is naturalized in the eastern U.S.

star of Beth·le·hem \-ˈbeth-li-ˌhem, -lē-(h)əm\ **:** a star which according to Christian tradition guided the Magi to the infant Jesus in Bethlehem

Star of Da·vid \-ˈdā-vəd\ **:** MAGEN DAVID

star route *n* [so called fr. the asterisk used to designate such routes in postal publications] **:** a mail-delivery route in a rural or thinly populated area served by a private carrier under contract who takes mail from one post office to another or from a railroad station to a post office and usu. also delivers mail to private mailboxes along the route

star·ry \ˈstär-ē\ *adj* **star·ri·er; -est 1 a :** adorned or studded with stars **b :** of, relating to, or consisting of the stars **:** STELLAR **c :** shining like stars **:** SPARKLING **d :** having parts arranged like the rays of a star **:** STELLATE **2 :** as high as or seemingly as high as the stars <~ speculations> **3 :** STARRY-EYED

star·ry–eyed \ˌstär-ē-ˈīd\ *adj* **:** regarding an object or a prospect in an overly favorable light; *specif* **:** characterized by dreamy, impracticable, or utopian thinking **:** VISIONARY

Stars and Bars *n pl but sing in constr* **:** the first flag of the Confederate States of America having three bars of red, white, and red respectively and a blue union with white stars in a circle representing the seceded states

Stars and Stripes *n pl but sing in constr* **:** the flag of the United States having 13 alternately red and white horizontal stripes and a blue union with white stars representing the states

star sapphire *n* **:** a sapphire that when cut with a convex surface and polished exhibits asterism

star shell *n* **1 :** a shell that on bursting releases a shower of brilliant stars and is used for signaling **2 :** a shell with an illuminating projectile

star–span·gled \ˈstär-ˌspaŋ-gəld\ *adj* **:** studded with stars

star–stud·ded \ˈstär-ˌstəd-əd\ *adj* **:** abounding in or covered with stars <a ~ cast> <a ~ uniform>

star system *n* **:** the practice of casting famous performers in motion-picture and theatrical roles esp. in order to exploit their popular appeal

¹start \ˈstärt\ *vb* [ME *sterten;* akin to MHG *sterzen* to stand up stiffly, move quickly, Lith *starinti* to stiffen — more at STARE] *vi* **1 a :** to move suddenly and violently **:** SPRING <~*ed* angrily to his feet> **b :** to react with a sudden brief involuntary movement <~*ed* when a shot rang out> **2 a :** to issue with sudden force <blood ~*ing* from the wound> **b :** to come into being, activity, or operation <when does the movie ~> **3 :** to protrude or seem to protrude <his eyes ~*ing* from their sockets> **4 :** to become loosened or forced out of place <one of the planks has ~*ed*> **5 a :** to begin a course or journey <~*ed* towards the door> <~*ed* north> **b :** to range from a specified initial point <the rates ~ at $10> **6 :** to begin an activity or undertaking; *esp* **:** to begin work **7 :** to be a participant in a game or contest; *esp* **:** to be in the starting lineup ~ *vt* **1 :** to cause to leave a place of concealment **:** FLUSH <~ a rabbit> **2** *archaic* **:** STARTLE, ALARM **3 :** to bring up for consideration or discussion **4 :** to bring into being <~ a rumor> **5 :** to cause to become loosened or displaced **6 :** to begin the use or employment of <~ a fresh loaf of bread> **7 a :** to cause to move, act, or operate <~ the motor> **b :** to cause to enter a game or contest; *esp* **:** to put in the starting lineup **c :** to care for during early stages **8 :** to perform the first stages or actions of <~*ed* studying music at the age of five> ***syn*** see BEGIN — **start something :** to make trouble — **to start with 1 :** at the beginning **:** INITIALLY **2 :** in any event

²start *n* **1 a :** a sudden involuntary bodily movement or reaction **b :** a brief and sudden action or movement **c :** a sudden capricious impulse or outburst **2 :** a beginning of movement, activity, or development **3 :** a lead or handicap at the beginning of a race or competition **4 :** a place of beginning **5 :** the act or an instance of being a competitor in a race or a member of a starting lineup in a game <undefeated in six ~*s* —*Current Biog.*>

start·er \ˈstärt-ər\ *n* **1 :** one who initiates or sets going: as **a :** an official who gives the signal to begin a race **b :** one who dispatches vehicles **2 a :** one that enters a competition; *esp* **:** a member of a starting lineup **b :** one that begins to engage in an activity or process **3 :** one that causes something to begin operating: as **a :** SELF-STARTER **b :** material containing microorganisms used to induce a desired fermentation **c :** a compound used to start a chemical reaction **4 :** something that is the beginning of a process, activity, or series

star thistle *n* **1 :** a widely naturalized spiny European weed (*Centaurea calcitrapa*) with purple flowers — called also *caltrops* **2 :** any of various knapweeds related to the star thistle

starting block *n* **:** a device that consists of two blocks mounted on either side of an adjustable frame which is usu. anchored to the ground and that provides a runner with a rigid surface against which to brace his feet at the start of a race

starting gate *n* **1 :** a mechanically operated barrier used as a starting device for a race **2 :** a barrier that when knocked aside by a competitor (as a skier) starts an electronic timing device

¹star·tle \ˈstärt-ᵊl\ *vb* **star·tled; star·tling** \ˈstärt-liŋ, -ᵊl-iŋ\ [ME *stertlen,* freq. of *sterten* to start] *vi* **:** to move or jump suddenly (as in surprise or alarm) <the baby ~*s* easily> ~ *vt* **:** to frighten or surprise suddenly and usu. not seriously

²startle *n* **:** a sudden mild shock (as of surprise or alarm)

star·tling *adj* **:** causing momentary fright, surprise, or astonishment — **star·tling·ly** \ˈstärt-liŋ-lē, ᵊl-iŋ-\ *adv* — **star·tling·ness** \-nəs\ *n*

start–up \ˈstärt-ˌəp\ *n* **:** the act or an instance of setting in operation or motion

star turn *n, chiefly Brit* **:** the featured skit or number in a theatrical production; *broadly* **:** the most widely publicized person or item in a group

star·va·tion \stär-ˈvā-shən\ *n* **1 :** the act or an instance of starving **2 :** the state of being starved

starvation wages *n* **:** wages insufficient to provide the ordinary necessities of life

starve \ˈstärv\ *vb* **starved; starv·ing** [ME *sterven* to die, fr. OE *steorfan;* akin to OHG *sterban* to die, Lith *starinti* to stiffen — more at STARE] *vi* **1 a :** to perish from lack of food **b :** to suffer extreme hunger **2** *archaic* **a :** to die of cold **b :** to suffer greatly from cold **3 :** to suffer or perish from deprivation <*starved* for affection> ~ *vt* **1 a :** to kill with hunger **b :** to deprive of nourishment **c :** to cause to capitulate by or as if by depriving of nourishment **2 :** to destroy by or cause to suffer from deprivation **3** *archaic* **:** to kill with cold

starve·ling \ˈstärv-liŋ\ *n* **:** one that is thin from or as if from lack of food

¹stash \ˈstash\ *vt* [origin unknown] **1** *chiefly Brit* **:** to put an end to **:** STOP, QUIT **2 :** to store in a usu. secret place for future use

²stash *n* **1 :** hiding place **:** CACHE **2 :** something stored or hidden away <a ~ of narcotics>

sta·sis \ˈstā-səs, ˈstas-əs\ *n, pl* **sta·ses** \ˈstā-ˌsēz, ˈstas-ˌēz\ [NL, fr. Gk, act or condition of standing, stopping, fr. *histasthai* to stand — more at STAND] **1 :** a slowing or stoppage of the normal flow of body fluids: as **a :** slowing of the current of circulating blood **b :** reduced motility of the intestines with retention of feces **2 :** a state of static balance or equilibrium **:** STAGNATION

-sta·sis \ˈstā-səs\ *n comb form, pl* **-sta·ses** \ˈstā-ˌsēz\ [NL, fr. Gk *stasis* standing, stopping] **1 :** stoppage **:** slowing <hemo*stasis*> <bacterio*stasis*> **2 :** stable state <homeo*stasis*>

stat *abbr* **1** [L *statim*] immediately **2** statute

ə abut	ᵊ kitten	ər further	a back	ā bake	ä cot, cart
au̇ out	ch chin	e less	ē easy	g gift	i trip ī life
j joke	ŋ sing	ō flow	ȯ flaw	ȯi coin	th thin t͟h this
ü loot	u̇ foot	y yet	yü few	yu̇ furious	zh vision

-stat \ˌstat\ *n comb form* [NL *-stata,* fr. Gk *-statēs* one that stops or steadies, fr. *histanai* to cause to stand — more at STAND] **1** : stabilizing agent or device <gyro*stat*> <thermo*stat*> **2** : instrument for reflecting (something specified) constantly in one direction <helio*stat*> **3** : agent causing inhibition of growth without destruction <bacterio*stat*>

sta·tant \ˈstāt-ᵊnt\ *adj* [L *status,* pp. of *stare* to stand + E *-ant*] : standing in profile with all feet on the ground — used of a heraldic animal

[1]state \ˈstāt\ *n, often attrib* [ME *stat,* fr. OF & L; OF *estat,* fr. L *status,* fr. *status,* pp. of *stare* to stand — more at STAND] **1 a** : mode or condition of being <a ~ of readiness> **b (1)** : condition of mind or temperament <in a highly nervous ~> **(2)** : a condition of abnormal tension or excitement **2 a** : a condition or stage in the physical being of something <insects in the larval ~> <the gaseous ~ of water> **b** : any of various conditions characterized by definite quantities (as of energy, angular momentum, or magnetic moment) in which an atomic system may exist **3 a** : social position; *esp* : high rank **b (1)** : elaborate or luxurious style of living **(2)** : formal dignity : POMP — usu. used with *in* **4 a** : a body of persons constituting a special class in a society : ESTATE 3 **b** *pl* : the members or representatives of the governing classes assembled in a legislative body **c** *obs* : a person of high rank (as a noble) **5 a** : a politically organized body of people usu. occupying a definite territory; *esp* : one that is sovereign **b** : the political organization of such a body of people **6** : the operations or concerns of the government of a country **7** : one of the constituent units of a nation having a federal government <the United *States* of America> **8** : the territory of a state

syn STATE, CONDITION, SITUATION, STATUS *shared meaning element* : the way in which one manifests existence or the circumstances under which one exists or by which one is given distinctive character. STATE may imply a mode of existence <Hell is not a place but a *state* —T. S. Eliot> but more often implies the sum of the qualities involved in a particular kind of existence or existence at a particular time and place <he remained in a weakened *state* for many months> <the present *state* of the art allows no final conclusion> CONDITION more distinctly imputes the effect of immediate or temporary influences as a ruling factor <under the best *conditions,* a voyage is one of the severest tests to try a man —R. W. Emerson> SITUATION applies to a state or condition that is the resultant of a combination of definite circumstances; it implies arrangement of these circumstances that makes for a particular condition (as of embarrassment, advantage, or difficulty) <there was a dizzy succession of events and of constantly changing *situations* for a politician to watch —W. L. Shirer> <ready to exploit any favorable *situation*> STATUS applies to one's state or condition as determined with some definiteness especially for legal administrative purposes or by social or economic considerations <his *status* as executive assistant gave him access to confidential reports>

[2]state *vt* **stat·ed; stat·ing** **1** : to set by regulation or authority **2** : to express the particulars of esp. in words : REPORT; *broadly* : to express in words — **stat·able** *or* **state·able** \ˈstāt-ə-bəl\ *adj*

state aid *n* : public monies appropriated by a state government for the partial support or improvement of a public local institution

State attorney *or* **State's attorney** *n* : a legal officer appointed to represent a state in the courts : PROSECUTING ATTORNEY

state bank *n* **1** : NATIONAL BANK 1 **2** : a bank chartered by and operating under the laws of a state of the U.S.

State bird *n* : a bird selected (as by the legislature) as an emblem of a state of the U.S.

state capitalism *n* : an economic system in which private capitalism is modified by a varying degree of government ownership and control

state church *n, often cap S&C* : ESTABLISHED CHURCH

state college *n* : a college that is financially supported by a state government, often specializes in a branch of technical or professional education, and often forms part of the state university

state·craft \ˈstāt-ˌkraft\ *n* : the art of conducting state affairs

stat·ed \ˈstāt-əd\ *adj* **1** : FIXED, REGULAR <the president shall, at ~ times, receive . . . a compensation —*U.S. Constitution*> **2** : set down explicitly : DECLARED — **stat·ed·ly** *adv*

stated clerk *n* : an executive officer of a Presbyterian general assembly, synod, or presbytery ranking below the moderator

State flower *n* : a flowering plant selected (as by the legislature) as an emblem of a state of the U.S.

state·hood \ˈstāt-ˌhu̇d\ *n* : the condition of being a state; *esp* : the condition or status of one of the states of the U.S.

state·house \-ˌhau̇s\ *n* : the building in which a state legislature sits

state·less \ˈstāt-ləs\ *adj* **1** : having no state **2** : lacking the status of a national <a ~ person> — **state·less·ness** *n*

state·ly \ˈstāt-lē\ *adj* **state·li·er; -est** **1 a** : HAUGHTY, UNAPPROACHABLE **b** : marked by lofty or imposing dignity **2** : impressive in size or proportions ***syn*** see GRAND — **state·li·ness** *n* — **stately** *adv*

state medicine *n* : administration and control by the national government of medical and hospital services provided to the whole population and paid for out of funds raised by taxation

state·ment \ˈstāt-mənt\ *n* **1** : the act or process of stating or presenting orally or on paper **2** : something stated: as **a** : a report of facts or opinions **b** : a single declaration or remark : ASSERTION **3** : PROPOSITION 2a **4** : the presentation of a theme in a musical composition **5** : a summary of a financial account showing the balance due

state of the art : the level of development (as of a device, procedure, process, technique, or science) reached at any particular time usu. as a result of modern methods

state of war **1 a** : a state of actual armed hostilities regardless of a formal declaration of war **b** : a legal state created and ended by official declaration regardless of actual armed hostilities and usu. characterized by operation of the rules of war **2** : the period of time during which a state of war is in effect

state prison *n* : a prison maintained by a state of the U.S. for the imprisonment of persons convicted of the more serious crimes (as felonies)

sta·ter \ˈstāt-ər, stä-ˈte(ə)r\ *n* [ME, fr. LL, fr. Gk *statēr,* lit., a unit of weight, fr. *histanai* to cause to stand, weigh — more at STAND] : an ancient gold or silver coin of the Greek city-states of any of numerous standards

state·room \ˈstāt-ˌrüm, -ˌru̇m\ *n* **1** : CABIN 1a **2** : a private room on a railroad car with one or more berths and a toilet

state's evidence *n, often cap S* **1** : one who gives evidence for the prosecution in U.S. state or federal criminal proceedings **2** : evidence for the prosecution in a criminal proceeding

States General *n pl* **1** : the assembly of the three orders of clergy, nobility, and third estate in France before the Revolution **2** : the legislature of the Netherlands from the 15th century to 1796

[1]state·side \ˈstāt-ˌsīd\ *adj* [(*United*) *States* + *side*] : being in, going to, coming from, or characteristic of the 48 conterminous states of the U.S. <transferred from Europe to ~ duty>

[2]stateside *adv* : in or to the continental U.S.

states·man \ˈstāt-smən\ *n* **1** : one versed in the principles or art of government; *esp* : one actively engaged in conducting the business of a government or in shaping its policies **2** : one who exercises political leadership wisely and without narrow partisanship — **states·man·like** \-ˌlīk\ *adj* — **states·man·ly** \-lē\ *adj* — **states·man·ship** \-ˌship\ *n*

state socialism *n* : an economic system with limited socialist characteristics introduced by usu. gradual political action

states' right·er \ˈstāts-ˈrīt-ər\ *n* : one who advocates strict interpretation of the U.S. constitutional guarantee of states' rights

states' rights *n pl* : all rights not vested by the Constitution of the U.S. in the federal government nor forbidden by it to the separate states

State tree *n* : a tree selected (as by the legislature) as an emblem of a state of the U.S.

state university *n* : a university maintained and administered by one of the states of the U.S. as part of the state public educational system

[1]state·wide \ˈstāt-ˈwīd\ *adj* : including all parts of a state

[2]statewide *adv* : throughout the state

[1]stat·ic \ˈstat-ik\ *adj* [NL *staticus,* fr. Gk *statikos* causing to stand, skilled in weighing, fr. *histanai* to cause to stand, weigh — more at STAND] **1** : exerting force by reason of weight alone without motion **2** : of or relating to bodies at rest or forces in equilibrium **3** : showing little change <a ~ population> **4 a** : characterized by a lack of movement, animation, or progression **b** : producing an effect of repose or quiescence <a ~ design> **5 a** : standing or fixed in one place : STATIONARY **b** *of water* : stored in a tank but not under pressure **6** : of, relating to, or producing stationary charges of electricity : ELECTROSTATIC **7** : of, relating to, or caused by radio static — **stat·i·cal** \-i-kəl\ *adj* — **stat·i·cal·ly** \-i-k(ə-)lē\ *adv*

[2]static *n* [*static electricity*] **1** : disturbing effects produced in a radio or television receiver by atmospheric or various natural or manmade electrical disturbances; *also* : the electrical disturbances producing these effects **2** : OPPOSITION <don't give me any ~>

stat·i·ce \ˈstat-ə-(ˌ)sē\ *n* [NL, genus of herbs, fr. L, an astringent plant, fr. Gk *statikē,* fr. fem. of *statikos* causing to stand, astringent] : SEA LAVENDER, THRIFT

static line *n* : a cord attached to a parachute pack and to an airplane to open the parachute after a jumper clears the plane

stat·ics \ˈstat-iks\ *n pl but sing or pl in constr* : mechanics dealing with the relations of forces that produce equilibrium among material bodies

static tube *n* : a tube used for indicating static as distinct from impact pressure in a stream of fluid

[1]sta·tion \ˈstā-shən\ *n* [ME *stacioun,* fr. MF *station,* fr. L *station-, statio,* fr. *status,* pp. of *stare* to stand — more at STAND] **1** : the place or position in which something or someone stands or is assigned to stand or remain **2** : the act or manner of standing : POSTURE **3** : a stopping place: as **a (1)** : a regular stopping place in a transportation route **(2)** : the building connected with such a stopping place : DEPOT 3 **b** : one of the stations of the cross **4 a** : a post or sphere of duty or occupation **b** : a stock farm or ranch of Australia or New Zealand **5** : STANDING, RANK <a woman of high ~> **6** : a place for specialized observation and study of scientific phenomena <a seismological ~> <a marine biological ~> **7** : a place established to provide a public service: as **a** : FIRE STATION **b** : a branch post office **8 a** : a complete assemblage of radio or television equipment for transmitting or receiving **b** : the place in which such a station is located

[2]station *vt* **sta·tioned; sta·tion·ing** \ˈstā-sh(ə-)niŋ\ : to assign to or set in a station or position : POST

sta·tion·al \ˈstā-shnəl, -shən-ᵊl\ *adj* : of, relating to, or being a mass formerly celebrated by the pope at designated churches in Rome on appointed holy days

sta·tion·ary \ˈstā-shə-ˌner-ē\ *adj* **1** : fixed in a station, course, or mode : IMMOBILE **2** : unchanging in condition

stationary front *n* : the boundary between two air masses neither of which is replacing the other

stationary wave *n* : STANDING WAVE — called also *stationary vibration*

station break *n* : a pause in a radio or television broadcast for announcement of the identity of the network or station; *also* : an announcement or advertisement during this pause

sta·tio·ner \ˈstā-sh(ə-)nər\ *n* [ME *staciouner,* fr. ML *stationarius,* fr. *station-, statio* shop, fr. L, station] **1** *archaic* **a** : BOOKSELLER **b** : PUBLISHER **2** : one that sells stationery

sta·tio·nery \ˈstā-shə-ˌner-ē\ *n* [*stationer*] **1** : materials (as paper, pens, and ink) for writing or typing **2** : letter paper usu. accompanied with matching envelopes

station house *n* : a house at a post or station; *specif* : a police station

sta·tion·mas·ter \ˈstā-shən-ˌmas-tər\ *n* **:** an official in charge of the operation of a railroad station
stations of the cross *often cap S&C* **1 :** a series of usu. 14 images or pictures esp. in a church that represent the stages of Christ's passion **2 :** a devotion involving commemorative meditation before the stations of the cross
station wagon *n* **:** an automobile that has an interior longer than a sedan's, has one or more rear seats readily lifted out or folded to facilitate light trucking, has no separate luggage compartment, and often has an adjustable rear window and a tailgate
stat·ism \ˈstāt-ˌiz-əm\ *n* **:** concentration of economic controls and planning in the hands of a highly centralized government
stat·ist \ˈstāt-əst\ *n* **:** an advocate of statism — **statist** *adj*
sta·tis·tic \stə-ˈtis-tik\ *n* [back-formation fr. *statistics*] **1 :** a single term or datum in a collection of statistics **2 a :** a quantity (as the mean of a sample) that is computed from a sample; *specif* **:** ESTIMATE 3b **b :** a random variable that takes on the possible values of a statistic
sta·tis·ti·cal \-ti-kəl\ *adj* **:** of, relating to, or employing the principles of statistics — **sta·tis·ti·cal·ly** \-k(ə-)lē\ *adv*
statistical mechanics *n pl but usu sing in constr* **:** a branch of mechanics dealing with the application of the principles of statistics to the mechanics of a system consisting of a large number of parts having motions that differ by small steps over a large range
stat·is·ti·cian \ˌstat-ə-ˈstish-ən\ *n* **:** one versed in or engaged in compiling statistics
sta·tis·tics \stə-ˈtis-tiks\ *n pl but sing or pl in constr* [G *statistik* study of political facts and figures, fr. NL *statisticus* of politics, fr. L *status* state] **1 :** a branch of mathematics dealing with the collection, analysis, interpretation, and presentation of masses of numerical data **2 :** a collection of quantitative data
sta·tive \ˈstāt-iv\ *adj* **:** expressing a bodily or mental state — compare ACTIVE 3b
stato- *comb form* [ISV, fr. Gk *statos* stationary, fr. *histasthai* to stand — more at STAND] **1 :** resting <*stato*blast> **2 :** equilibrium <*stato*cyst>
stato·blast \ˈstat-ə-ˌblast\ *n* [ISV] **1 :** a bud in a freshwater bryozoan that overwinters in a chitinous envelope and develops into a new individual in spring **2 :** GEMMULE b
stato·cyst \-ˌsist\ *n* [ISV] **:** an organ of equilibrium occurring esp. among invertebrate animals and consisting usu. of a fluid-filled vesicle in which are suspended calcareous particles
stat·ol·a·try \stāt-ˈäl-ə-trē\ *n* [[1]*state* + *-o-* + *-latry*] **:** advocacy of a highly centralized and all-powerful national government
stato·lith \ˈstat-ᵊl-ˌith\ *n* [ISV] **1 :** the calcareous body in a statocyst **2 :** any of various starch grains or other solid bodies in the plant cytoplasm that are held to be responsible by changes in their position for changes in orientation of a part or organ
sta·tor \ˈstāt-ər\ *n* [NL, fr. L, one that stands, fr. *status,* pp. of *stare* to stand — more at STAND] **:** a stationary part in a machine in or about which a rotor revolves
stato·scope \ˈstat-ə-ˌskōp\ *n* [ISV] **1 :** a sensitive aneroid barometer for recording small changes in atmospheric pressure **2 :** an instrument for indicating small changes in the altitude of an airplane
[1]stat·u·ary \ˈstach-ə-ˌwer-ē\ *n, pl* **-ar·ies 1 a :** the art of making statues **b :** a collection of statues **2 :** SCULPTOR
[2]statuary *adj* **:** of, relating to, or suitable for statues
stat·ue \ˈstach-(ˌ)ü, ˈstach-ə(-w)\ *n* [ME, fr. MF, fr. L *statua,* fr. *statuere* to set up — more at STATUTE] **:** a three-dimensional representation usu. of a person, animal, or mythical being that is produced by sculpturing, modeling, or casting
Statue of Liberty 1 : a large copper statue of a woman holding a torch aloft in her right hand located on Liberty Island in New York harbor **2 :** an offensive football play in which a back raises his arm as if to throw a pass and the ball is taken from his hand by a teammate who runs by him
stat·u·esque \ˌstach-ə-ˈwesk\ *adj* **:** resembling a statue esp. in massive dignity or shapeliness — **stat·u·esque·ly** *adv* — **stat·u·esque·ness** *n*
stat·u·ette \ˌstach-ə-ˈwet\ *n* **:** a small statue
stat·ure \ˈstach-ər\ *n* [ME, fr. OF, fr. L *statura,* fr. *status,* pp. of *stare* to stand — more at STAND] **1 :** natural height (as of a person) in an upright position **2 :** quality or status gained by growth, development, or achievement ***syn*** see QUALITY
sta·tus \ˈstāt-əs, ˈstat-\ *n, often attrib* [L — more at STATE] **1 :** the condition of a person or thing in the eyes of the law **2 a :** position or rank in relation to others <the ~ of a father> **b :** relative rank in a hierarchy of prestige; *esp* **:** high prestige **3 :** state of affairs **:** SITUATION ***syn*** see STATE
sta·tus quo \ˌstāt-ə-ˈskwō, ˌstat-\ *n* [L, state in which] **:** the existing state of affairs <seeks to preserve the *status quo*>
stat·ut·able \ˈstach-ət-ə-bəl, ˈstach-ˌüt-\ *adj* **:** made, regulated, or imposed by or in conformity to statute **:** STATUTORY <~ tonnage>
stat·ute \ˈstach-(ˌ)üt, -ət\ *n* [ME, fr. OF *statut,* fr. LL *statutum* law, regulation, fr. L, neut. of *statutus,* pp. of *statuere* to set up, station, fr. *status* position, condition, state] **1 :** a law enacted by the legislative branch of a government **2 :** an act of a corporation or of its founder intended as a permanent rule **3 :** an international instrument setting up an agency and regulating its scope or authority
statute book *n* **:** the whole body of legislation of a given jurisdiction whether or not published as a whole — usu. used in pl.
statute mile *n* **:** MILE 1a
statute of limitations : a statute assigning a certain time after which rights cannot be enforced by legal action or offenses cannot be punished
stat·u·to·ry \ˈstach-ə-ˌtōr-ē, -ˌtȯr-\ *adj* **1 :** of or relating to statutes **2 :** enacted, created, or regulated by statute <a ~ age limit>
statutory offense *n* **:** a crime created by statute; *esp* **:** STATUTORY RAPE
statutory rape *n* **:** sexual intercourse with a female who is below the statutory age of consent

[1]staunch \ˈstȯnch, ˈstänch\ *var of* STANCH
[2]staunch \ˈstȯnch, ˈstänch\ *adj* [ME, fr. MF *estanche,* fem. of *estanc,* fr. OF, fr. *estancher* to stanch] **1 a :** WATERTIGHT, SOUND **b :** strongly built **:** SUBSTANTIAL **2 :** steadfast in loyalty or principle ***syn*** see FAITHFUL — **staunch·ly** *adv* — **staunch·ness** *n*
stau·ro·lite \ˈstȯr-ə-ˌlīt\ *n* [F, fr. Gk *stauros* cross + F *-lite* — more at STEER] **:** a mineral $(Fe,Mg)_2Al_9Si_4O_{23}(OH)$ consisting of basic iron aluminum silicate in prismatic orthorhombic crystals often twinned so as to resemble a cross — **stau·ro·lit·ic** \ˌstȯr-ə-ˈlit-ik\ *adj*
[1]stave \ˈstāv\ *n* [back-formation fr. *staves*] **1 :** [1]STAFF 1, 2 **2 :** any of the narrow strips of wood or narrow iron plates placed edge to edge to form the sides, covering, or lining of a vessel (as a barrel) or structure **3 :** RUNG 3b **4 :** STANZA **5 :** [1]STAFF 3
[2]stave *vb* **staved** *or* **stove** \ˈstōv\; **stav·ing** *vt* **1 :** to break in the staves of (a cask) **2 :** to smash a hole in <~ in a boat>; *also* **:** to crush or break inward <*staved* in several ribs> **3 :** to drive or thrust away ~ *vi* **1 :** to become stove in — used of a boat or ship **2 :** to walk or move rapidly
stave off *vt* **:** to ward or fend off
staves *pl of* STAFF
staves·acre \ˈstāv-ˌzā-kər\ *n* [by folk etymology fr. ME *staphisagre,* fr. ML *staphis agria,* fr. Gk, lit., wild raisin] **:** a Eurasian larkspur (*Delphinium staphisagria*); *also* **:** its violently emetic and cathartic seeds
[1]stay \ˈstā\ *n* [ME, fr. OE *stæg;* akin to ON *stag* stay, OE *stēle* steel] **1 :** a large strong rope usu. of wire used to support a mast **2 :** a guy rope — **in stays :** in process of going about from one tack to another
[2]stay *vt* **1 :** to fasten (as a smokestack) with or as if with stays **2 :** to incline (a mast) forward, aft, or to one side by the stays ~ *vi* **:** to go about **:** TACK
[3]stay *vb* **stayed** \ˈstād\ *or* **staid** \ˈstād\; **stay·ing** [ME *stayen,* fr. MF *ester* to stand, stay, fr. L *stare* — more at STAND] *vi* **1 :** to stop going forward **:** PAUSE **2 :** to stop doing something **:** CEASE **3 :** to continue in a place or condition **:** REMAIN **4 :** to stand firm **5 :** to take up residence **:** LODGE **6 :** to keep even in a contest or rivalry <~ with the leaders> **7 :** to call a poker bet without raising **8** *obs* **:** to be in waiting or attendance ~ *vt* **1 :** to wait for **:** AWAIT **2 :** to last out (as a race) **3 :** to remain during <~*ed* the whole time> **4 a :** to stop or delay the proceeding or advance of by or as if by interposing an obstacle **:** HALT <~ an execution> **b :** to check the course of (as a disease) **c :** ALLAY, PACIFY <~*ed* the civil war> **d :** to quiet the hunger of temporarily
syn **1** STAY, REMAIN, WAIT, ABIDE, TARRY, LINGER *shared meaning element* **:** to continue in a place
2 see DEFER
— **stay put :** to be firmly fixed, attached, or established
[4]stay *n* **1 a :** the action of halting **:** the state of being stopped **b :** a stopping or suspension of procedure or execution by judicial or executive order **2** *obs* **:** MODERATION, SELF-CONTROL **3 :** a residence or sojourn in a place **4 :** capacity for endurance
[5]stay *n* [MF *estaie,* of Gmc origin; akin to OHG *stān* to stand — more at STAND] **1 :** one that serves as a prop **:** SUPPORT **2 :** a corset stiffened with bones — usu. used in pl.
[6]stay *vt* **1 :** to provide physical or moral support for **:** SUSTAIN **2 :** to fix on as a foundation
stay–at–home \ˌstā-ət-ˌhōm\ *adj* **:** remaining habitually in one's residence, locality, or country — **stay–at–home** \ˈstā-\ *n*
stay·er \ˈstā-ər\ *n* **:** one that stays; *esp* **:** one that upholds or supports
staying power *n* **:** capacity for endurance **:** STAMINA
stay–in strike \ˈstā-ˌin-\ *n* **:** a slowdown or stoppage of work intended to bring pressure on an employer and concerted by workers who remain in their work place — compare SIT-DOWN
stay·sail \ˈstā-ˌsāl, -səl\ *n* **:** a fore-and-aft sail hoisted on a stay — see SAIL illustration
STB *abbr* **1** [L *sacrae theologiae baccalaureus*] bachelor of sacred theology **2** [L *scientiae theologicae baccalaureus*] bachelor of theology
stbd *abbr* starboard
std *abbr* standard
STD *abbr* [L *sacrae theologiae doctor*] doctor of sacred theology
Ste *abbr* [F *sainte*] saint (female)
[1]stead \ˈsted\ *n* [ME *stede,* fr. OE; akin to OHG *stat* place, *stān* to stand] **1** *obs* **:** LOCALITY, PLACE **2 :** ADVANTAGE, SERVICE — used chiefly in the phrase *to stand one in good stead* **3 :** the office, place, or function ordinarily occupied or carried out by someone or something else <acted in his brother's ~>
[2]stead *vt* **:** to be of avail to **:** HELP
stead·fast \ˈsted-ˌfast *also* -fəst\ *adj* **1 a :** firmly fixed in place **:** IMMOVABLE **b :** not subject to change <the ~ doctrine of original sin —Ellen Glasgow> **2 :** firm in belief, determination, or adherence **:** LOYAL ***syn*** see FAITHFUL ***ant*** capricious — **stead·fast·ly** *adv* — **stead·fast·ness** \-ˌfas(t)-nəs, -fəs(t)-\ *n*
stead·ing \ˈsted-ᵊn, ˈstēd-, -iŋ\ *n* [ME *steding,* fr. *stede* place, farm] **1 :** a small farm **2** *chiefly Scot* **:** the service buildings or area of a farm
[1]steady \ˈsted-ē\ *adj* **steadi·er; -est** [[1]*stead*] **1 a :** firm in position **:** FIXED **b :** direct or sure in movement **:** UNFALTERING **c :** keeping nearly upright in a seaway <a ~ ship> **2 :** showing little variation or fluctuation **:** STABLE, UNIFORM <a ~ breeze> <~ prices> **3 a :** not easily moved or upset **:** RESOLUTE <~ nerves> **b** (1) **:** constant in feeling, principle, purpose, or attachment (2) **:** DEPENDABLE **c :** not given to dissipation **:** SOBER — **steadi·ly** \ˈsted-ᵊl-ē\ *adv* — **steadi·ness** \ˈsted-ē-nəs\ *n*

ə abut ᵊ kitten ər further a back ā bake ä cot, cart
aù out ch chin e less ē easy g gift i trip ī life
j joke ŋ sing ō flow ȯ flaw ȯi coin th thin t͟h this
ü loot u̇ foot y yet yü few yu̇ furious zh vision

syn STEADY, EVEN, EQUABLE *shared meaning element* : not varying throughout a course or extent *ant* unsteady, nervous, jumpy

[2]**steady** *vb* **stead·ied; steady·ing** *vt* : to make or keep steady ~ *vi* : to become steady — **steadi·er** *n*

[3]**steady** *adv* **1** : in a steady manner : STEADILY **2** : on the course set — used as a direction to the helmsman of a ship

[4]**steady** *n, pl* **stead·ies** : one that is steady; *specif* : a boyfriend or girl friend with whom one goes steady

steady state *n* : a state or condition of a system or process (as one of the energy states of an atom) that does not change in time

steady state theory *n* : a theory in astronomy: the universe has always existed and has always been expanding with hydrogen being created continuously — compare BIG BANG THEORY

steak \'stāk\ *n* [ME *steke,* fr. ON *steik;* akin to ON *steikja* to roast on a stake, *stik,* stick, stake — more at STICK] **1 a** : a slice of meat cut from a fleshy part of a beef carcass **b** : a similar slice of a specified meat other than beef <ham ~> **c** : a cross-section slice of a large fish <swordfish ~> **2** : ground beef prepared for cooking or for serving in the manner of a steak <hamburg ~>

steak house *n* : a restaurant whose specialty is beefsteak

steak knife *n* : a table knife with an often serrated steel blade

[1]**steal** \'stē(ə)l\ *vb* **stole** \'stōl\; **sto·len** \'stō-lən\; **steal·ing** [ME *stelen,* fr. OE *stelan;* akin to OHG *stelan* to steal] *vi* **1** : to take the property of another **2** : to come or go secretly, unobtrusively, gradually, or unexpectedly **3** : to steal a base ~ *vt* **1 a** : to take or appropriate without right or leave and with intent to keep or make use of wrongfully **b** : to take away by force or unjust means **c** : to take secretly or without permission **d** : to appropriate entirely to oneself or beyond one's proper share <~ the show> **2 a** : to move, convey, or introduce secretly : SMUGGLE **b** : to accomplish in a concealed or unobserved manner <~ a visit> **3 a** : to seize, gain, or win by trickery, skill, or daring <a basketball player adept at ~*ing* the ball> **b** *of a base runner* : to gain (a base) by running without the aid of a hit or an error — **steal·er** *n*

syn STEAL, PILFER, FILCH, PURLOIN *shared meaning element* : to take another's possession without right and without his knowledge or permission

— **steal a march** : to gain an advantage unobserved — **steal one's thunder** : to appropriate or adapt for one's own ends something devised by another

[2]**steal** *n* **1** : the act or an instance of stealing **2** : a fraudulent or questionable political deal **3** : BARGAIN 2 <it's a ~ at that price>

steal·ing *n* : the act of one who steals

stealth \'stelth\ *n* [ME *stelthe;* akin to OE *stelan* to steal] **1 a** *archaic* : THEFT **b** *obs* : something stolen **2** : the act or action of proceeding furtively, secretly, or imperceptibly <the state moves by ~ to gather information —Nat Hentoff> **3** : the state of being furtive or unobtrusive <his leopard ~ and grace —James Purdy>

stealthy \'stel-thē\ *adj* **stealth·i·er; -est** **1** : slow, deliberate, and secret in action or character **2** : intended to escape observation : FURTIVE *syn* see SECRET — **stealth·i·ly** \-thə-lē\ *adv* — **stealth·i·ness** \-thē-nəs\ *n*

[1]**steam** \'stēm\ *n* [ME *stem,* fr. OE *stēam;* akin to D *stoom* steam] **1** : a vapor arising from a heated substance **2 a** : the invisible vapor into which water is converted when heated to the boiling point **b** : the mist formed by the condensation on cooling of water vapor **3 a** : water vapor kept under pressure so as to supply energy for heating, cooking, or mechanical work; *also* : the power so generated **b** : driving force : POWER <got there under his own ~> **c** : emotional tension <needed to let off a little ~ after exams> **4 a** : STEAMER 2a **b** : travel by or a trip in a steamer

[2]**steam** *vi* **1** : to rise or pass off as vapor **2** : to give off steam or vapor **3** : to move or travel by or as if by the agency of steam **4** : to be angry : BOIL <~*ing* over the insult he had received> ~ *vt* **1** : to give out as fumes : EXHALE **2** : to apply steam to; *esp* : to expose to the action of steam (as for softening or cooking)

steam beer *n* : a highly effervescent beer brewed in the western U.S.

steam·boat \'stēm-ˌbōt\ *n* : a boat propelled by steam power

steamboat Gothic *n* [fr. its use in homes of retired steamboat captains in imitation of the style of river steamboats] : an elaborately ornamented architectural style used in homes built in the middle 19th century in the Ohio and Mississippi river valleys

steam boiler *n* : a boiler for producing steam

steam chest *n* : the chamber from which steam is distributed to a cylinder of a steam engine

steam engine *n* : an engine driven or worked by steam; *specif* : a reciprocating engine having a piston driven in a closed cylinder by steam

steam·er \'stē-mər\ *n* **1** : a vessel in which articles are subjected to steam **2 a** : a ship propelled by steam **b** : an engine, machine, or vehicle operated or propelled by steam **3** : one that steams **4** : SOFT-SHELL CLAM

steamer rug *n* : a warm covering for the lap and feet esp. of a person sitting on a ship's deck

steamer trunk *n* : a trunk suitable for use in a stateroom of a steamer; *esp* : a shallow trunk that may be stowed beneath a berth

steam fitter *n* : one that installs or repairs equipment (as steam pipes) for heating, ventilating, or refrigerating systems — **steam fitting** *n*

steam heating *n* : a system of heating (as for a building) in which steam generated in a boiler is piped to radiators

steam iron *n* : a pressing iron with a compartment holding water that is converted to steam by the iron's heat and emitted through the soleplate onto the fabric being pressed

[1]**steam·roll·er** \'stēm-'rō-lər\ *n* **1** : a steam-driven road roller; *broadly* : ROAD ROLLER **2** : a crushing force esp. when ruthlessly applied to overcome opposition

[2]**steam·roll·er** \-'rō-lər\ *also* **steam·roll** \-ˌrōl\ *vt* **1** : to crush or consolidate with a steamroller **2 a** : to overwhelm by greatly superior force <~ the opposition> **b** : to bring by overwhelming force or pressure <~*ed* the bill through the legislature> ~ *vi* : to move or proceed with irresistible force

steam·ship \'stēm-ˌship\ *n* : STEAMER 2a

steam shovel *n* : a power shovel operated by steam; *broadly* : POWER SHOVEL

steam table *n* : a table having openings to hold containers of cooked food over steam or hot water circulating beneath them

steam turbine *n* : a turbine that is driven by the pressure of steam discharged at high velocity against the turbine vanes

steam up *vt* : to make angry or excited : AROUSE

steamy \'stē-mē\ *adj* **steam·i·er; -est** **1** : consisting of, characterized by, or full of steam **2** : EROTIC <a ~ love scene> — **steam·i·ly** \-mə-lē\ *adv* — **steam·i·ness** \-mē-nəs\ *n*

ste·ap·sin \stē-'ap-sən\ *n* [Gk *stear* fat + E *-psin* (as in *pepsin*)] : the lipase in pancreatic juice

stea·rate \'stē-ə-ˌrāt, 'sti(-ə)r-ˌāt\ *n* : a salt or ester of stearic acid

stea·ric \stē-'ar-ik, 'sti(ə)r-ik\ *adj* [F *stéarique,* fr. Gk *stear*] **1** : of, relating to, obtained from, or resembling stearin or tallow **2** : of or relating to stearic acid <~ esters>

stearic acid *n* : a white crystalline fatty acid $C_{18}H_{36}O_2$ obtained by saponifying tallow or other hard fats containing stearin; *also* : a commercial mixture of stearic and palmitic acids

stea·rin \'stē-ə-rən, 'sti(-ə)r-ən\ *n* [F *stéarine,* fr. Gk *stear*] **1** : an ester of glycerol and stearic acid **2** *also* **stea·rine** *same or* 'stē-ə-ˌrēn, 'sti(-ə)r-ˌēn\ : the solid portion of a fat **3** *usu* **stearine** : commercial stearic acid

steat- *or* **steato-** *comb form* [Gk, fr. *steat-, stear* — more at STONE] : fat <*steato*lysis>

ste·atite \'stē-ə-ˌtīt\ *n* [L *steatitis,* a precious stone, fr. Gk, fr. *steat-*] **1** : a massive talc having a grayish green or brown color : SOAPSTONE **2** : an electrically insulating porcelain composed largely of steatite — **ste·atit·ic** \ˌstē-ə-'tit-ik\ *adj*

ste·atol·y·sis \ˌstē-ə-'täl-ə-səs\ *n* [NL] : breakdown of neutral fats into glycerol and free fatty acids

ste·ato·py·gia \(ˌ)stē-ˌat-ə-'pī-j(ē-)ə\ *n* [NL, fr. *steat-* + Gk *pygē* rump, buttocks; akin to Latvian *pauga* cushion, Gk *physan* to blow — more at FOG] : an excessive development of fat on the buttocks esp. of females that is common among the Hottentots and some Negro peoples — **ste·ato·py·gic** \-'pī-jik\ *or* **ste·ato·py·gous** \-'pī-gəs\ *adj*

ste·at·or·rhea \(ˌ)stē-ˌat-ə-'rē-ə\ *n* [NL] : an excess of fat in the stools

stedfast *var of* STEADFAST

steed \'stēd\ *n* [ME *stede,* fr. OE *stēda* stallion; akin to OE *stōd* stud — more at STUD] : HORSE; *esp* : a spirited horse for state or war

steek \'stēk\ *vb* [ME *steken* to pierce, fix, enclose; akin to OE *stician* to pierce — more at STICK] *chiefly Scot* : SHUT, CLOSE

[1]**steel** \'stē(ə)l\ *n* [ME *stele,* fr. OE *style, stēle;* akin to OHG *stahal* steel, Skt *stakati* he resists] **1** : commercial iron that contains carbon in any amount up to about 1.7 percent as an essential alloying constituent, is malleable when under suitable conditions, and is distinguished from cast iron by its malleability and lower carbon content **2** : an instrument or implement of or characteristically of steel: as **a** : a thrusting or cutting weapon **b** : an instrument (as a fluted round rod with a handle) for sharpening knives **c** : a piece of steel for striking sparks from flint **d** : a strip of steel used for stiffening **3** : a quality (as of mind or spirit) that suggests steel <nerves of ~> **4 a** : the steel manufacturing industry **b** *pl* : shares of stock in steel companies

[2]**steel** *vt* **1** : to overlay, point, or edge with steel **2 a** : to cause to resemble steel (as in looks or hardness) **b** : to fill with resolution or determination

[3]**steel** *adj* **1** : made of steel **2** : of or relating to the production of steel **3** : resembling steel

steel band *n* : a band orig. developed in Trinidad and composed of tuned percussion instruments cut out of oil barrels

steel blue *n* **1** : a variable color averaging a grayish blue **2** : any of the blue colors assumed by steel at various temperatures in tempering

steel engraving *n* **1** : the art or process of engraving on steel **2** : an impression taken from an engraved steel plate

steel guitar *n* : HAWAIIAN GUITAR

steel·head \'stē(ə)l-ˌhed\ *n* : a large-sized western No. American silvery anadromous trout usu. held to be a race of the rainbow trout (*Salmo gairdneri*)

steel·ie *also* **steely** \'stē-lē\ *n, pl* **steel·ies** : a steel playing marble

steel–trap \ˌstē(ə)l-ˌtrap\ *adj* : extremely quick and incisive

steel wool *n* : an abrasive material composed of long fine steel shavings and used esp. for scouring and burnishing

steel·work \'stē(ə)l-ˌwərk\ *n* **1** : work in steel **2** *pl but sing or pl in constr* : an establishment where steel is made

steel·work·er \-ˌwər-kər\ *n* : one that works in steel and esp. in the manufacturing of it

steely \'stē-lē\ *adj* **steel·i·er; -est** **1** : made of steel **2** : resembling steel — **steel·i·ness** *n*

steel·yard \'stē(ə)l-ˌyärd, 'stil-yərd\ *n* [prob. fr. [1]*steel* + *yard* (rod)] : a balance in which an object to be weighed is suspended from the shorter arm of a lever and the weight determined by moving a counterpoise along a graduated scale on the longer arm until equilibrium is attained

steen·bok \'stēn-ˌbäk, 'stān-\ *or* **stein·bok** \'stīn-, 'stān-\ *n* [Afrik *steenbok;* akin to OE *stānbucca* ibex; both fr. a prehistoric WGmc compound whose elements are represented respectively by OE *stān* stone and OE *bucca* buck] : any of a genus (*Raphicerus*) of small plains antelopes of southern and eastern Africa

[1]**steep** \'stēp\ *adj* [ME *stepe,* fr. OE *stēap* high, steep, deep; akin to MHG *stief* steep, ON *staup* lump, knoll, cup] **1** : LOFTY, HIGH — used chiefly of a sea **2** : making a large angle with the plane of the horizon **3 a** : mounting or falling precipitously <the stairs were very ~> **b** : being or characterized by a rapid and intensive decline or increase **4** : difficult to accept, meet, or perform : EXCESSIVE — **steep·ly** *adv* — **steep·ness** *n*

syn STEEP, ABRUPT, PRECIPITOUS, SHEER *shared meaning element* : having an incline approaching the perpendicular

[2]**steep** *n* : a precipitous place

[3]**steep** *vb* [ME *stepen;* akin to Sw *stöpa* to steep, and prob. to ON *staup* cup] *vt* **1 :** to soak in a liquid at a temperature under the boiling point (as for softening, bleaching, or extracting an essence) **2 :** to cover with or plunge into a liquid (as in bathing, rinsing, or soaking) **3 :** to saturate with or subject thoroughly to (some strong or pervading influence) ~ *vi* **:** to undergo the process of soaking in a liquid ***syn*** see SOAK — **steep·er** *n*

[4]**steep** *n* **1 :** the state or process of being steeped **2 :** a bath or solution in which something is steeped **3 :** a tank in which a material is steeped

steep·en \'stē-pən, 'stēp-ᵊm\ *vb* **steep·ened; steep·en·ing** \'stēp-(ə-)niŋ\ *vt* **:** to make steeper ~ *vi* **:** to become steeper

stee·ple \'stē-pəl\ *n* [ME *stepel,* fr. OE *stēpel* tower; akin to OE *stēap* steep] **:** a tall structure usu. having a small spire at the top and surmounting a church tower; *broadly* **:** a whole church tower

stee·ple·bush \'stē-pəl-ˌbu̇sh\ *n* **:** HARDHACK

stee·ple·chase \-ˌchās\ *n* [fr. the use of church steeples as landmarks to guide the riders] **:** a race across country by horsemen; *also* **:** a race over a course obstructed by obstacles (as hedges, walls, or hurdles) — **stee·ple·chas·er** \-ˌchā-sər\ *n*

stee·ple·jack \-ˌjak\ *n* **:** one whose work is building smokestacks, towers, or steeples or climbing up the outside of such structures to paint and make repairs

[1]**steer** \'sti(ə)r\ *n* [ME, fr. OE *stēor* young ox; akin to OHG *stior* young ox, Skt *sthavira, sthūra* stout, thick, broad] **1 :** a male bovine animal castrated before sexual maturity — compare STAG 3 **2 :** an ox less than four years old

[2]**steer** *vb* [ME *steren,* fr. OE *stīeran;* akin to OE *stēor-* steering oar, Gk *stauros* stake, cross, *stylos* pillar, Skt *sthavira, sthūra* stout, thick, L *stare* to stand — more at STAND] *vt* **1 :** to direct the course of; *esp* **:** to guide by mechanical means (as a rudder) **2 :** to set and hold to (a course) ~ *vi* **1 :** to direct the course (as of a ship or automobile) **2 :** to pursue a course of action **3 :** to be subject to guidance or direction <an automobile that ~*s* well> ***syn*** see GUIDE — **steer·able** \'stir-ə-bəl\ *adj* — **steer·er** *n* — **steer clear :** to keep entirely away — often used with *of*

[3]**steer** *n* **:** a hint as to procedure **:** TIP

[4]**steer** *dial Brit var of* STIR

steer·age \'sti(ə)r-ij\ *n* **1 :** the act or practice of steering; *broadly* **:** DIRECTION **2** [fr. its orig. being located near the rudder] **:** a section in a passenger ship for passengers paying the lowest fares and given inferior accommodations

steer·age·way \-ˌwā\ *n* **:** a rate of motion sufficient to make a ship or boat answer the helm

steering column *n* **:** the column that encloses the connections to the steering gear of a vehicle (as an automobile)

steering committee *n* **:** a managing or directing committee; *specif* **:** a committee that determines the order in which business will be taken up in a U.S. legislative body

steering gear *n* **:** a mechanism by which something is steered

steering wheel *n* **:** a handwheel by means of which one steers

steers·man \'sti(ə)rz-mən\ *n* **:** one who steers **:** HELMSMAN

[1]**steeve** \'stēv\ *vt* **steeved; steev·ing** [ME *steven,* prob. fr. Sp *estibar* or Pg *estivar* to pack tightly, fr. L *stipare* to press together — more at STIFF] **:** to stow esp. in a ship's hold

[2]**steeve** *vb* **steeved; steev·ing** [origin unknown] *vi, of a bowsprit* **:** to incline upward at an angle with the horizon or the line of the keel ~ *vt* **:** to set (a bowsprit) at an upward inclination

[3]**steeve** *n* **:** the angle that a bowsprit makes with the horizon or with the keel

stego·saur \'steg-ə-ˌsȯr\ *n* [NL *Stegosauria,* group name, fr. *Stegosaurus,* genus name] **:** any of a suborder (Stegosauria) of dinosaurs with strongly developed dorsal bony armor

stego·sau·rus \ˌsteg-ə-'sȯr-əs\ *n* [NL, genus name, fr. Gk *stegos* roof + *sauros* lizard — more at THATCH, SAURIA] **:** any of a genus (*Stegosaurus*) of large armored dinosaurs of the Upper Jurassic rocks of Colorado and Wyoming

stein \'stīn\ *n* [prob. fr. G *steingut* stoneware, fr. *stein* stone + *gut* goods] **:** an earthenware mug esp. for beer often holding about a pint; *also* **:** the quantity of beer that a stein holds

ste·la \'stē-lə\ *or* **ste·le** \'stē-lē\ *n, pl* **ste·lae** \-(ˌ)lē\ [L & Gk; L *stela,* fr. Gk *stēlē;* akin to Gk *stellein* to set up — more at STALL] **:** a usu. carved or inscribed stone slab or pillar used for commemorative purposes

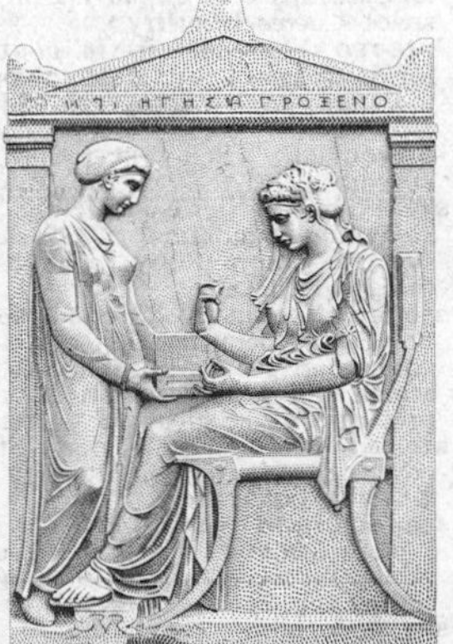

Greek grave stela

ste·lar \'stē-lər, -ˌlär\ *adj* **:** of, relating to, or constituting a stele

stele \'stē(ə)l, 'stē-lē\ *n* [NL, fr. Gk *stēlē* stela, pillar] **:** the usu. cylindrical central vascular portion of the axis of a vascular plant

stel·la \'stel-ə\ *n* [L, star; fr. the star on the reverse] **:** an experimental coin worth about four dollars that was issued by the U.S. in 1879 and 1880 and was designed to serve as an international coin based on the metric system

stel·lar \'stel-ər\ *adj* [LL *stellaris,* fr. L *stella* star — more at STAR] **1 a :** of or relating to the stars **:** ASTRAL **b :** composed of stars **2 :** of or relating to a theatrical or film star <~ names> **3 a :** PRINCIPAL, LEADING <a ~ role> **b :** OUTSTANDING

stel·late \'stel-ˌāt\ *adj* [L *stella*] **:** resembling a star (as in shape) <a ~ leaf>

stel·li·form \'stel-ə-ˌfȯrm\ *adj* [NL *stelliformis,* fr. L *stella* + *-iformis* -iform] **:** shaped like a star <a starfish is a ~ echinoderm>

stel·li·fy \-ˌfī\ *vt* **-fied; -fy·ing** [ME *stellifien,* fr. MF *stellifier,* fr. ML *stellificare,* fr. L *stella* star] **:** to turn into a star **:** place among the stars **:** GLORIFY

[1]**stem** \'stem\ *n* [ME, fr. OE *stefn, stemn* stem of a plant or ship; OE *stefn* akin to OE *stæf* staff; OE *stemn* akin to OE *standan* to stand] **1 a :** the main trunk of a plant; *specif* **:** a primary plant axis that develops buds and shoots instead of roots **b :** a plant part (as a branch, petiole, or stipe) that supports another (as a leaf or fruit) **c :** a bunch of bananas **2 :** the bow or prow of a ship — compare STERN **3 :** a line of ancestry **:** STOCK; *esp* **:** a fundamental line from which others have arisen **4 :** the part of an inflected word that remains unchanged except by phonetic changes or variations throughout an inflection **5 :** something held to resemble a plant stem: as **a :** a main or heavy stroke of a letter; *also* **:** BODY 7 **b :** the short perpendicular line extending from the head of a musical note **c :** the part of a tobacco pipe from the bowl outward **d :** the cylindrical support of a piece of stemware (as a goblet) **e :** a shaft of a watch used for winding — **from stem to stern :** THROUGHOUT, THOROUGHLY

[2]**stem** *vt* **stemmed; stem·ming 1 :** to make headway against (as an adverse tide, current, or wind) **2 :** to check or go counter to (something adverse) — **stem·mer** *n*

[3]**stem** *vb* **stemmed; stem·ming** *vi* **:** to have or trace an origin or development ~ *vt* **1 :** to remove the stem from **2 :** to make stems for (as artificial flowers) ***syn*** see SPRING — **stem·mer** *n*

[4]**stem** *vb* **stemmed; stem·ming** [ME *stemmen* to dam up, fr. ON *stemma;* akin to OE *stamerian* to stammer] *vt* **1 a :** to stop or dam up (as a river) **b :** to stop or check by or as if by damming; *esp* **:** STANCH <~ a flow of blood> **2 :** to turn (skis) in stemming ~ *vi* **1 :** to restrain or check oneself; *also* **:** to become checked or stanched **2 :** to retard oneself by forcing the heel of one ski or of both skis outward from the line of progress

[5]**stem** *n* **1 :** CHECK, DAM **2 :** an act or instance of stemming on skis

stem cell *n* **:** an unspecialized and usu. embryonic cell ancestral to one or more specialized cells (as a blood cell); *esp* **:** an embryonic cell destined to give rise to germ cells and often identifiable in early cleavage

stem christie *n, often cap C* **:** a turn in skiing begun by stemming one ski and completed by bringing the skis parallel into a christie

stem·less \'stem-ləs\ *adj* **:** having no stem **:** ACAULESCENT

stem·ma \'stem-ə\ *n, pl* **stem·ma·ta** \-ət-ə\ [L, wreath, pedigree (fr. the wreaths placed on ancestral images), fr. Gk, wreath, fr. *stephein* to crown, enwreathe] **1 :** a simple eye present in some insects **2 :** a scroll (as among the ancient Romans) containing a genealogical list **3 :** a tree showing the relationships of the manuscripts of a literary work

[1]**stemmed** \'stemd\ *adj* **:** having a stem — usu. used in combination <long-*stemmed* roses>

[2]**stemmed** *adj* **:** having the stem removed <~ berries>

stem·my \'stem-ē\ *adj* **stem·mi·er; -est :** abounding in stems

stem rust *n* **1 :** a rust attacking the stem of a plant; *esp* **:** a destructive disease esp. of wheat caused by a rust fungus (*Puccinia graminis*) which produces reddish brown lesions in the uredostage and black lesions in the teliospore stage and has any of several plants of the barberry family as an alternate host **2 :** the fungus causing stem rust

stem·son \'stem(p)-sən\ *n* [*stem* + *-son* (as in *keelson*)] **:** a piece of curved timber bolted to the stem, keelson, and apron in a ship's frame near the bow

stem turn *n* **:** a skiing turn executed by stemming an outside ski

stem·ware \'stem-ˌwa(ə)r, -ˌwe(ə)r\ *n* **:** glass hollow ware mounted on a stem

stem–wind·er \-'wīn-dər\ *n* **1 :** a stem-winding watch **2** [fr. the superiority of the stem-winding watch over the older key-wound watch] **:** one that is first-rate of its kind

stem–wind·ing \-diŋ\ *adj* **:** wound by an inside mechanism turned by the knurled knob at the outside end of the stem <a ~ watch>

Sten \'sten\ *n* [Major *S*heppard, 20th cent. E army officer + Mr. *T*urpin, 20th cent. E civil servant + *En*gland] **:** a light simple 9-millimeter British machine carbine

sten- *or* **steno-** *comb form* [Gk, fr. *stenos*] **:** close **:** narrow **:** little <*steno*bathic>

stench \'stench\ *n* [ME, fr. OE *stenc;* akin to OE *stincan* to emit a smell — more at STINK] **:** STINK — **stench·ful** \-fəl\ *adj* — **stenchy** \'sten-chē\ *adj*

[1]**sten·cil** \'sten(t)-səl\ *n* [ME *stanselen* to ornament with sparkling colors, fr. MF *estanceler,* fr. *estancele* spark, fr. (assumed) VL *stincilla,* fr. L *scintilla*] **1 :** an impervious material (as a sheet of paper, thin wax, or woven fabric) perforated with lettering or a design through which a substance (as ink, paint, or metallic powder) is forced onto a surface to be printed **2 :** something (as a pattern, design, or print) that is produced by means of a stencil **3 :** a printing process that uses a stencil

FRAGILE

stencil 1

[2]**stencil** *vt* **sten·ciled** *or* **sten·cilled; sten·cil·ing** *or* **sten·cil·ling** \-s(ə-)liŋ\ **1 :** to produce by stencil **2 :** to mark or paint with a stencil — **sten·cil·er** *or* **sten·cil·ler** \-s(ə-)lər\ *n*

sten·cil·ize \-sə-ˌlīz\ *vt* **-ized; -iz·ing 1 :** STENCIL 2 **2 :** to cut into a stencil

stencil paper *n* **:** strong tissue paper impregnated or coated (as with paraffin) for stencils

steno \'sten-(,)ō\ *n, pl* **sten·os** **1 :** STENOGRAPHER **2 :** STENOGRAPHY

steno·bath·ic \,sten-ə-'bath-ik\ *adj* [*sten-* + Gk *bathos* depth — more at BATH-] *of a pelagic organism* **:** living within narrow limits of depth

steno·graph \'sten-ə-,graf\ *vt* [back-formation fr. *stenographer*] **:** to write or report in stenographic characters

ste·nog·ra·pher \stə-'näg-rə-fər\ *n* **1 :** a writer of shorthand **2 :** one employed chiefly to take and transcribe dictation

ste·nog·ra·phy \-fē\ *n* **1 :** the art or process of writing in shorthand **2 :** shorthand esp. written from dictation or oral discourse **3 :** the making of shorthand notes and subsequent transcription of them — **steno·graph·ic** \,sten-ə-'graf-ik\ *adj* — **steno·graph·i·cal·ly** \-i-k(ə-)lē\ *adv*

steno·ha·line \,sten-ō-'hā-,līn, -'hal-,īn\ *adj* [ISV *sten-* + Gk *halinos* of salt, fr. *hals* salt — more at SALT] *of an aquatic organism* **:** unable to withstand wide variation in salinity of the surrounding water

ste·noph·a·gous \ste-'näf-ə-gəs\ *adj* [ISV] **:** eating few kinds of foods <~ insects>

ste·nosed \stə-'nōzd, -'nōst\ *adj* [fr. pp. of *stenose* (to affect with stenosis)] **:** affected with stenosis

ste·no·sis \stə-'nō-səs\ *n, pl* **-no·ses** \-,sēz\ [NL, fr. Gk *stenōsis* act of narrowing, fr. *stenoun* to narrow, fr. *stenos* narrow] **:** a narrowing or constriction of the diameter of a bodily passage or orifice — **ste·not·ic** \-'nät-ik\ *adj*

steno·therm \'sten-ə-,thərm\ *n* [back-formation fr. *stenothermal*] **:** an organism only slightly resistant to change in temperature — **steno·ther·mal** \,sten-ə-'thər-məl\ *adj* — **steno·ther·my** \'sten-ə-,thər-mē\ *n*

steno·top·ic \,sten-ə-'täp-ik\ *adj* [prob. fr. G *stenotop* stenotopic, fr. *sten-* + Gk *topos* place — more at TOPIC] **:** having a narrow range of adaptability to changes in environmental conditions

steno·type \'sten-ə-,tīp\ *n* [*steno-* (as in *stenography*) + *type*] **:** a small machine somewhat like a typewriter used to record speech by means of phonograms — **stenotype** *vt* — **steno·typ·ist** \-,tī-pəst\ *n* — **ste·no·ty·py** \'sten-ə-,tī-pē, stə-'nät-ə-pē\ *n*

sten·tor \'sten-,tȯ(ə)r, 'stent-ər\ *n* [L, fr. Gk *Stentōr* Stentor, a Greek herald in the Trojan War noted for his loud voice] **1 :** a person having a loud voice **2 :** any of a widely distributed genus (*Stentor*) of ciliate protozoans that have a trumpet-shaped body attached to the substrate by the smaller end with the mouth at the larger end

sten·to·ri·an \sten-'tōr-ē-ən, -'tȯr-\ *adj* **:** extremely loud

sten·to·ro·phon·ic \,stent-ə-rə-'fän-ik\ *adj* [NL *stentorophonicus,* fr. Gk *Stentōr* Stentor + *-o-* + *phōnē* voice — more at BAN] **:** speaking or sounding very loud **:** STENTORIAN

[1]**step** \'step\ *n* [ME, fr. OE *stæpe;* akin to OHG *stapfo* step, *stampfōn* to stamp] **1 :** a rest for the foot in ascending or descending: as **a :** STAIR **b :** a ladder rung **2 a** (1)**:** an advance or movement made by raising the foot and bringing it down elsewhere (2)**:** a combination of foot or foot and body movements constituting a unit or a repeated pattern <a dance ~> (3) **:** manner of walking **:** STRIDE **b :** FOOTPRINT **c :** the sound of a footstep <heard his ~*s* in the hall> **3 a :** the space passed over in one step **b :** a short distance <a store located just a ~ from the bank> **c :** the height of one stair **4** *pl* **:** COURSE, WAY <directed his ~*s* toward the river> **5 a :** a degree, grade, or rank in a scale **b :** a stage in a process <was guided through every ~ of her career> **6 :** a frame on a ship designed to receive an upright shaft; *esp* **:** a block supporting the heel of a mast **7 :** an action, proceeding, or measure often occurring as one in a series <is taking ~*s* to improve the situation> **8 :** a steplike offset or part usu. occurring in a series **9 :** a musical scale degree — **step·like** \-,līk\ *adj* — **stepped** \'stept\ *adj* — **in step 1 :** with each foot moving to the same time as the corresponding foot of others or in time to music **2 :** in harmony or agreement — **out of step :** not in step

[2]**step** *vb* **stepped; step·ping** *vi* **1 a :** to move by raising the foot and bringing it down elsewhere or by moving each foot in succession **b :** DANCE **2 a :** to go on foot **:** WALK **b** *obs* **:** ADVANCE, PROCEED **c :** to be on one's way **:** LEAVE — often used with *along* **d :** to move briskly <kept us *stepping*> **3 :** to press down with the foot <~ on the brake> **4 :** to come as if at a single step <*stepped* into a good job> ~ *vt* **1 :** to take by moving the feet in succession <~ three paces> **2 a :** to move (the foot) in any direction **:** SET <the first man to ~ foot on the moon> **b :** to traverse on foot **3 :** to go through the steps of **:** PERFORM <~ a minuet> **4 :** to make erect by fixing the lower end in a step **5 :** to measure by steps <~ off 50 yards> **6 a :** to provide with steps **b :** to make steps in <~ a key> **7 :** to construct or arrange in or as if in steps <craggy peaks with terraces *stepped* up the sides —*Time*> — **step on it :** to increase one's speed **:** hurry up

step- *comb form* [ME, fr. OE *stēop-;* akin to OHG *stiof-* step-] **:** related by virtue of a remarriage (as of a parent) and not by blood <*step*parent> <*step*sister>

step·broth·er \'step-,brəth-ər\ *n* **:** a son of one's stepparent by a former marriage

step–by–step \,step-bə-'step\ *adj* **:** marked by successive degrees usu. of limited extent **:** GRADUAL

step·child \'step-,chīld\ *n* **1 :** a child of one's wife or husband by a former marriage **2 :** one that fails to receive proper care or attention <is no longer a ~ in the family of nations —F. R. Smith>

step dance *n* **:** a dance in which steps are emphasized rather than gesture or posture

step·daugh·ter \'step-,dȯt-ər\ *n* **:** a daughter of one's wife or husband by a former marriage

step–down \'step-,daůn\ *n* **:** a decrease or reduction in size or amount <a ~ in dosage>

step down \(')step-'daůn\ *vt* **:** to lower the voltage of (a current) by means of a transformer ~ *vi* **:** RETIRE, RESIGN <*stepped down* as chairman of the board —*Current Biog.*>

step·fa·ther \'step-,fäth-ər\ *n* **:** the husband of one's mother by a subsequent marriage

steph·a·no·tis \,stef-ə-'nōt-əs\ *n* [NL, genus name, fr. Gk *stephanōtis* fit for a crown, fr. *stephanos* crown, fr. *stephein* to crown] **:** any of a genus (*Stephanotis*) of Old World tropical woody vines of the milkweed family with fragrant white flowers the corolla of which has a cylindrical dilated tube and spreading limb

[1]**step–in** \'step-,in\ *adj* **:** put on by being stepped into

[2]**step–in** *n* **:** an article of step-in clothing: as **a :** a shoe resembling but usu. having a higher vamp than a pump and concealed elastic to adjust the fit **b :** a woman's short panties — usu. used in pl.

step in \(')step-'in\ *vi* **1 :** to make a brief informal visit **2 :** to intervene in an affair or dispute

step·lad·der \'step-,lad-ər\ *n* **:** a portable set of steps with a hinged frame for steadying

step·moth·er \-,məth-ər\ *n* **:** the wife of one's father by a subsequent marriage

step out \(')step-'aůt\ *vi* **1 :** to go away from a place usu. for a short distance and for a short time <*stepped out* for a smoke> **2 :** to go or march at a vigorous or increased pace **3 :** DIE **4 :** to lead an active social life **5 :** to be unfaithful — usu. used with *on* <hadn't been married two months before I knew he was *stepping out* on me —James Jones>

step·par·ent \'step-,par-ənt, -,per-\ *n* **:** the husband or wife of one's mother or father by a subsequent marriage

steppe \'step\ *n* [Russ *step'*] **1 :** one of the vast usu. level and treeless tracts in southeastern Europe or Asia **2 :** arid land with xerophilous vegetation found usu. in regions of extreme temperature range and loess soil

stepped–up \'step-'təp\ *adj* **:** increased in intensity **:** ACCELERATED, INTENSIFIED <a ~ advertising program>

step·per \'step-ər\ *n* **:** one (as a fast horse or a dancer) that steps

step·ping–off place \,step-iŋ-'ȯf-\ *n* **1 :** the outbound end of a transportation line **2 :** a place from which one departs for unknown territory

step·ping–stone \'step-iŋ-,stōn\ *n* **1 :** a stone on which to step (as in crossing a stream) **2 :** a means of progress or advancement

step rocket *n* **:** a multistage rocket whose sections are fired successively

step·sis·ter \'step-,sis-tər\ *n* **:** a daughter of one's stepparent by a former marriage

step·son \-,sən\ *n* **:** a son of one's husband or wife by a former marriage

step stool *n* **:** a stool with one or two steps that often fold away beneath the seat

step turn *n* **:** a skiing turn executed in a downhill traverse by lifting the upper ski from the ground, placing it in the desired direction, weighting it, and bringing the other ski parallel

step–up \'step-,əp\ *n* **:** an increase or advance in size or amount

step up \(')step-'əp\ *vt* **1 :** to increase the voltage of (a current) by means of a transformer **2 :** to increase, augment, or advance by one or more steps <*step up* production> ~ *vi* **1 :** to come forward **2 :** to undergo an increase <business is *stepping up*> **3 :** to receive a promotion — **step–up** \'step-,əp\ *adj*

step·wise \-,wīz\ *adj* **1 :** marked by or proceeding in steps **2 :** moving by step to adjacent musical tones

ster *abbr* sterling

-ster \stər\ *n comb form* [ME, fr. OE *-estre* female agent; akin to MD *-ster*] **1 :** one that does or handles or operates <spin*ster*> <tap*ster*> <team*ster*> **2 :** one that makes or uses <song*ster*> <pun*ster*> **3 :** one that is associated with or participates in <game*ster*> <gang*ster*> **4 :** one that is <young*ster*>

ster·co·ra·ceous \,stər-kə-'rā-shəs\ *adj* [L *stercor-, stercus* excrement; akin to MHG *drec* filth] **:** relating to, being, or containing feces

ster·cu·lia gum \,stər-,k(y)ül-yə-\ *n* [NL *Sterculia,* genus of trees] **:** any of several vegetable gums similar to tragacanth and often used as substitutes for it that are obtained from tropical Asiatic trees (genera *Cochlospermum* and *Sterculia* and esp. *S. urens* and *C. gossypium*)

stere \'sti(ə)r, 'ste(ə)r\ *n* [F *stère,* fr. Gk *stereos*] — see METRIC SYSTEM table

stere- *or* **stereo-** *comb form* [NL, fr. Gk, fr. *stereos* solid — more at STARE] **1 :** solid **:** solid body <*stereo*taxis> **2 a :** stereoscopic <*stereo*psis> **b :** having or dealing with three dimensions of space <*stereo*chemistry>

[1]**ste·reo** \'ster-ē-,ō, 'stir-\ *n, pl* **ste·re·os** **1 :** STEREOTYPE **2** [short for *stereoscopy*] **a :** a stereoscopic method, system, or effect **b :** a stereoscopic photograph **3** [by shortening] **a :** stereophonic reproduction **b :** a stereophonic sound system

[2]**stereo** *adj* **1 a :** STEREOSCOPIC **b :** STEREOTYPED **2 :** STEREOPHONIC

ste·reo·bate \'ster-ē-ə-,bāt, 'stir-\ *n* [F or L; F *stéréobate,* fr. L *stereobata* foundation, fr. Gk *stereobatēs,* fr. *stere-* + *bainein* to step, go — more at COME] **:** a substructure of masonry visible above the ground level

ste·reo·chem·is·try \,ster-ē-ō-'kem-ə-strē, ,stir-\ *n* [ISV] **1 :** a branch of chemistry that deals with the spatial arrangement of atoms and groups in molecules **2 :** the spatial arrangement of atoms and groups within a substance and its relation to the properties of the substance — **ste·reo·chem·i·cal** \-'kem-i-kəl\ *adj*

ste·reo·gram \'ster-ē-ə-,gram, 'stir-\ *n* [ISV] **1 :** a diagram or picture representing objects with an impression of solidity or relief **2 :** STEREOGRAPH

ste·reo·graph \-,graf\ *n* [ISV] **:** a pair of stereoscopic pictures or a picture composed of two superposed stereoscopic images that gives a three-dimensional effect when viewed with a stereoscope or special spectacles — **stereograph** *vt*

ste·re·og·ra·phy \,ster-ē-'äg-rə-fē, ,stir-\ *n* **1 :** the art, process, or technique of delineating the forms of solid bodies on a plane **2 :** stereoscopic photography — **ste·reo·graph·ic** \,ster-ē-ə-'graf-ik\ *adj* — **ste·reo·graph·i·cal·ly** \-i-k(ə-)lē\ *adv*

ste·reo·iso·mer \,ster-ē-ō-'ī-sə-mər, ,stir-\ *n* [ISV] **:** any of a group of isomers in which atoms are linked in the same order but differ in their spatial arrangement — **ste·reo·iso·mer·ic** \-,ī-sə-'mer-ik\ *adj* — **ste·reo·isom·er·ism** \-ī-'säm-ə-,riz-əm\ *n*

ste·re·ol·o·gy \ˌster-ē-ˈäl-ə-jē, ˌstir-\ *n* [ISV] **:** a branch of science concerned with the development and testing of inferences about the three-dimensional properties and reactions of objects or matter ordinarily observed or observable from a two-dimensional point of view — **ste·reo·log·i·cal** \-ē-ə-ˈläj-i-kəl\ *adj* — **ste·reo·log·i·cal·ly** \-i-k(ə-)lē\ *adv*

ste·reo·met·ric \ˌster-ē-ō-ˈme-trik, ˌstir-\ *adj* [NL *stereometricus,* fr. Gk *stereometrikos,* fr. *stereometria* measurement of solids, fr. *stere-* + *-metria* -metry] **:** having or representing a simple readily measurable solid form

ste·reo·mi·cro·scope \-ˈmī-krə-ˌskōp\ *n* **:** a microscope having a set of optics for each eye to make an object appear in three dimensions — **ste·reo·mi·cro·scop·ic** \-ˌmī-krə-ˈskäp-ik\ *adj* — **ste·reo·mi·cro·scop·i·cal·ly** \-i-k(ə-)lē\ *adv*

ste·reo·phon·ic \ˌster-ē-ə-ˈfän-ik, ˌstir-\ *adj* [ISV] **:** giving, relating to, or constituting a three-dimensional effect of auditory perspective — **ste·reo·phon·i·cal·ly** \-i-k(ə-)lē\ *adv* — **ste·reo·pho·ny** \ˌster-ē-ˈäf-ə-nē, ˌstir-; ˈster-ē-ə-ˌfō-nē, ˈstir-\ *n*

ste·reo·pho·tog·ra·phy \ˌster-ē-ō-fə-ˈtäg-rə-fē, ˌstir-\ *n* [ISV] **:** stereoscopic photography — **ste·reo·pho·to·graph·ic** \-ˌfōt-ə-ˈgraf-ik\ *adj*

ste·re·op·sis \ˌster-ē-ˈäp-səs, ˌstir-\ *n* [NL, fr. *stere-* + Gk *opsis* vision — more at OPTIC] **:** stereoscopic vision

ste·re·op·ti·con \-ˈäp-ti-kən\ *n* [NL, fr. *stere-* + Gk *optikon,* neut. of *optikos* optic] **:** a projector for transparent slides often made double so as to produce dissolving views

ste·reo·reg·u·lar \ˌster-ē-ō-ˈreg-yə-lər, ˌstir-\ *adj* **:** of, relating to, or involving stereochemical regularity in the repeating units of a polymeric structure — **ste·reo·reg·u·lar·i·ty** \-ˌreg-yə-ˈlar-ət-ē\ *n*

ste·reo·scope \ˈster-ē-ə-ˌskōp, ˈstir-\ *n* **:** an optical instrument with two eyeglasses for helping the observer to combine the images of two pictures taken from points of view a little way apart and thus to get the effect of solidity or depth

ste·reo·scop·ic \ˌster-ē-ə-ˈskäp-ik, ˌstir-\ *adj* **1 :** of or relating to stereoscopy or the stereoscope **2 :** characterized by stereoscopy <~ vision> — **ste·reo·scop·i·cal·ly** \-i-k(ə-)lē\ *adv*

ste·re·os·co·py \ˌster-ē-ˈäs-kə-pē, ˌstir-; ˈster-ē-ə-ˌskō-pē, ˈstir-\ *n* [ISV] **1 :** a science that deals with stereoscopic effects and methods **2 :** the seeing of objects in three dimensions

ste·reo·spe·cif·ic \ˌster-ē-ō-spi-ˈsif-ik, ˌstir-\ *adj* **:** being, produced by, or involved in a stereochemically specific process <many enzymes act as ~ catalysts in biological reactions> <~ plastics> — **ste·reo·spe·cif·i·cal·ly** \-i-k(ə-)lē\ *adv* — **ste·reo·spec·i·fic·i·ty** \-ˌspes-ə-ˈfis-ət-ē\ *n*

ste·reo·tape \ˈster-ē-ō-ˌtāp, ˈstir-\ *n* **:** a stereophonic magnetic tape

ste·reo·tax·ic \ˌster-ē-ə-ˈtak-sik, ˌstir-\ *adj* [NL *stereotaxis* stereotaxic technique (fr. *stere-* + *taxis*) + E *-ic*] **:** of, relating to, or being a technique or apparatus used in neurological research or surgery for directing the tip of a delicate instrument (as a needle or an electrode) in three planes in attempting to reach a predetermined locus in the nervous system — **ste·reo·tax·i·cal·ly** \-si-k(ə-)lē\ *adv*

ste·re·ot·ro·pism \ˌster-ē-ˈä-trə-ˌpiz-əm, ˌstir-\ *n* [ISV] **:** THIGMOTROPISM

[1]**ste·reo·type** \ˈster-ē-ə-ˌtīp, ˈstir-\ *n* [F *stéréotype,* fr. *stéré-* stere- + *type*] **1 :** a plate made by molding a matrix of a printing surface and making from this a cast in type metal **2 :** something conforming to a fixed or general pattern; *esp* **:** a standardized mental picture that is held in common by members of a group and that represents an oversimplified opinion, affective attitude, or uncritical judgment — **ste·reo·typ·i·cal** \ˌster-ē-ə-ˈtip-i-kəl\ *also* **ste·reo·typ·ic** \-ik\ *adj*

[2]**stereotype** *vt* **1 :** to make a stereotype from **2 a :** to repeat without variation **:** make hackneyed **b :** to develop a mental stereotype about — **ste·reo·typ·er** *n*

ste·reo·typed *adj* **:** lacking originality or individuality

ste·reo·ty·py \ˈster-ē-ə-ˌtī-pē, ˈstir-\ *n, pl* **-pies 1 :** the art or process of making or of printing from stereotype plates **2 :** frequent almost mechanical repetition of the same posture, movement, or form of speech (as in schizophrenia)

ste·ric \ˈster-ik, ˈsti(ə)r-\ *adj* [ISV *stere-* + *-ic*] **:** relating to or involving the arrangement of atoms in space **:** SPATIAL — **ste·ri·cal·ly** \ˈster-i-k(ə-)lē, ˈstir-\ *adv*

ste·rig·ma \stə-ˈrig-mə\ *n, pl* **-ma·ta** \-mət-ə\ *also* **-mas** [NL, fr. Gk *stērigma* support, fr. *stērizein* to prop] **:** one of the slender stalks at the top of the basidium of some fungi from the tips of which the basidiospores are abstricted; *broadly* **:** a stalk or filament that bears conidia or spermatidia

ster·il·ant \ˈster-ə-lənt\ *n* **:** a sterilizing agent

ster·ile \ˈster-əl, *chiefly Brit* -ˌīl\ *adj* [L *sterilis;* akin to Goth *stairo* sterile, Gk *steira*] **1 a :** failing to produce or incapable of producing offspring <a ~ hybrid> **b :** failing to bear or incapable of producing fruit or spores **c :** incapable of germinating <~ spores> **d** *of a flower* **:** neither perfect nor pistillate **2 a :** unproductive of vegetation <a ~ arid region> **b :** deficient in ideas or originality **c :** free from living organisms and esp. microorganisms — **ste·ril·i·ty** \stə-ˈril-ət-ē\ *n*

syn STERILE, BARREN, IMPOTENT, UNFRUITFUL, INFERTILE *shared meaning element* **:** lacking the power to bear offspring or produce fruit ***ant*** fertile

ster·il·ize \ˈster-ə-ˌlīz\ *vt* **-ized; -iz·ing :** to make sterile: as **a :** to cause (land) to become unfruitful **b** (1) **:** to deprive of the power of reproducing (2) **:** to make incapable of germination **c :** to make powerless or useless usu. by restraining from a normal function, relation, or participation <capital *sterilized* by hoarders> **d :** to free from living microorganisms — **ster·il·iza·tion** \ˌster-ə-lə-ˈzā-shən\ *n* — **ster·il·iz·er** \ˈster-ə-ˌlī-zər\ *n*

ster·let \ˈstər-lət\ *n* [Russ *sterlyad'*] **:** a small sturgeon (*Acipenser ruthenus*) that is found in the Caspian sea and its rivers and is a source of caviar

[1]**ster·ling** \ˈstər-liŋ\ *n* [ME, silver penny] **1 :** British money **2 :** sterling silver or articles of it

[2]**sterling** *adj* **1 a :** of, relating to, or calculated in terms of British sterling **b :** payable in sterling **2 a** *of silver* **:** having a fixed standard of purity usu. defined legally as represented by an alloy of 925 parts of silver with 75 parts of copper **b :** made of sterling silver **3 :** conforming to the highest standard <~ character> — **ster·ling·ly** \-liŋ-lē\ *adv* — **ster·ling·ness** *n*

sterling area *n* **:** a group of countries whose currencies are tied to the British pound sterling — called also *sterling bloc*

[1]**stern** \ˈstərn\ *adj* [ME *sterne,* fr. OE *styrne;* akin to OE *starian* to stare] **1 a :** having a definite hardness or severity of nature or manner **:** AUSTERE **b :** expressive of severe displeasure **:** HARSH **2 :** forbidding or gloomy in appearance **3 :** INEXORABLE <~ necessity> **4 :** STURDY, STOUT <a ~ resolve> ***syn*** see SEVERE ***ant*** soft, lenient — **stern·ly** *adv* — **stern·ness** \ˈstərn-nəs\ *n*

[2]**stern** *n* [ME, rudder, prob. of Scand origin; akin to ON *stjōrn* act of steering; akin to OE *stīeran* to steer — more at STEER] **1 :** the rear end of a boat **2 :** a hinder or rear part **:** the last or latter part

ster·nal \ˈstərn-ᵊl\ *adj* **:** of or relating to the sternum

stern chase *n* [[2]*stern*] **:** a chase in which a pursuing ship follows in the path of another

stern chaser *n* **:** a gun so placed as to be able to fire astern at a pursuing ship

stern·fore·most \ˈstərn-ˈfō(ə)r-ˌmōst, -ˈfȯ(ə)r-\ *adv* **:** with the stern in advance **:** BACKWARD

ster·nite \ˈstər-ˌnīt\ *n* [ISV, fr. Gk *sternon* chest] **:** the ventral part or shield of a somite of an arthropod; *esp* **:** the chitinous plate that forms the ventral surface of an abdominal or occas. a thoracic segment of an insect

stern·most \ˈstərn-ˌmōst\ *adj* **:** farthest astern

ster·no·cos·tal \ˌstər-nō-ˈkäs-tᵊl\ *adj* [NL *sternum* + E *-o-* + *costal*] **:** of, relating to, or situated between the sternum and ribs

stern·post \ˈstərn-ˌpōst\ *n* **:** the principal member at the stern of a ship extending from keel to deck

stern sheets *n pl* **:** the space in the stern of an open boat not occupied by the thwarts

stern·son \ˈstərn(t)-sən\ *n* [*stern* + *keelson*] **:** the end of a keelson to which the sternpost is bolted

ster·num \ˈstər-nəm\ *n, pl* **sternums** *or* **ster·na** \-nə\ [NL, fr. Gk *sternon* chest, breastbone; akin to OHG *stirna* forehead, L *sternere* to spread out — more at STREW] **:** a compound ventral bone or cartilage connecting the ribs or the shoulder girdle or both — called also *breastbone*

ster·nu·ta·tion \ˌstər-nyə-ˈtā-shən\ *n* [L *sternutation-, sternutatio,* fr. *sternutatus,* pp. of *sternutare* to sneeze, fr. *sternutus,* pp. of *sternuere* to sneeze; akin to Gk *ptarnysthai* to sneeze] **:** the act, fact, or noise of sneezing — **ster·nu·ta·to·ry** \ˌstər-ˈn(y)üt-ə-ˌtōr-ē, -ˌtȯr-\ *adj*

ster·nu·ta·tor \ˈstər-nyə-ˌtāt-ər\ *n* **:** an agent that induces sneezing and often lacrimation and vomiting

stern·ward \ˈstərn-wərd\ *or* **stern·wards** \-wərdz\ *adv* **:** AFT, ASTERN

stern·way \ˈstərn-ˌwā\ *n* **:** movement of a ship backward or with stern foremost

stern–wheel·er \-ˈhwē-lər, -ˈwē-\ *n* **:** a paddle-wheel steamer having a stern wheel instead of side wheels

ste·roid \ˈsti(ə)r-ˌȯid *also* ˈste(ə)r-\ *n* [ISV *sterol* + *-oid*] **:** any of numerous compounds containing the carbon ring system of the sterols and including the sterols and various hormones and glycosides — **steroid** *or* **ste·roi·dal** \stə-ˈrȯid-ᵊl\ *adj*

ste·roido·gen·e·sis \stə-ˌrȯid-ə-ˈjen-ə-səs; ˌstir-ˌȯid- *also* ˌster-\ *n* [NL] **:** synthesis of steroids

ste·roido·gen·ic \-ˈjen-ik\ *adj* **:** of, relating to, or involved in steroidogenesis <~ cells> <~ response of ovarian tissue>

ste·rol \ˈsti(ə)r-ˌȯl, ˈste(ə)r-, -ˌōl\ *n* [ISV, fr. *-sterol* (as in *cholesterol*)] **:** any of various solid cyclic alcohols (as cholesterol) widely distributed in animal and plant lipides

ster·tor \ˈstərt-ər, ˈstər-ˌtȯ(ə)r\ *n* [NL, fr. L *stertere* to snore; akin to *sternuere* to sneeze] **:** the act or fact of producing a snoring sound **:** SNORING

ster·to·rous \ˈstərt-ə-rəs\ *adj* **:** characterized by a harsh snoring or gasping sound — **ster·to·rous·ly** *adv*

stet \ˈstet\ *vt* **stet·ted; stet·ting** [L, let it stand, fr. *stare* to stand — more at STAND] **:** to direct retention of (a word or passage previously ordered to be deleted or omitted from a manuscript or printer's proof) by annotating usu. with the word *stet*

stetho·scope \ˈsteth-ə-ˌskōp, *also* ˈsteth-\ *n* [F *stéthoscope,* fr. Gk *stēthos* chest + F *-scope*] **:** an instrument used to detect and study sounds produced in the body — **stetho·scop·ic** \ˌsteth-ə-ˈskäp-ik *also* ˌsteth-\ *adj* — **stetho·scop·i·cal·ly** \-i-k(ə-)lē\ *adv*

stet·son \ˈstet-sən\ *n, often cap* [fr. *Stetson,* a trademark] **:** a broad-brimmed high-crowned felt hat

[1]**ste·ve·dore** \ˈstē-v(-ə)-ˌdō(ə)r, -ˌdȯ(ə)r\ *n* [Sp *estibador,* fr. *estibar* to pack, fr. L *stipare* to press together — more at STIFF] **:** one who works at or is responsible for loading and unloading ships in port

[2]**stevedore** *vb* **-dored; -dor·ing** *vt* **:** to handle (cargo) as a stevedore; *also* **:** to load or unload the cargo of (a ship) in port ~ *vi* **:** to work as a stevedore

stevedore knot *n* **:** a stopper knot similar to a figure eight knot but with one or more extra turns — called also *stevedore's knot;* see KNOT illustration

Ste·ven·graph \ˈstē-vən-ˌgraf\ *or* **Ste·vens·graph** \-vənz-\ *n* [Thomas *Stevens,* 19th cent. Am weaver] **:** a woven silk picture

[1]**stew** \ˈst(y)ü\ *n* [ME *stu,* fr. MF *estuve,* fr. (assumed) VL *extufa,* fr. *extufare* to stew] **1** *obs* **:** a utensil used for boiling **2 :** a hot bath **3 a :** BROTHEL **b :** a district of brothels — usu. used in pl. **4 a :** fish or meat usu. with vegetables prepared by stewing **b** (1) **:** a heterogeneous mixture (2) **:** a state of heat and congestion **5 :** a state of excitement, worry, or confusion

[2]stew *vt* **:** to boil slowly or with simmering heat ~ *vi* **1 :** to become cooked by stewing **2 :** to swelter esp. from confinement in a hot or stuffy atmosphere **3 :** to become agitated or worried
[1]stew·ard \ˈst(y)ü-ərd, ˈst(y)u̇(-ə)rd\ *n* [ME, fr. OE *stiweard*, fr. *stī* hall, sty + *weard* ward] **1 :** one employed in a large household or estate to manage domestic concerns (as the supervision of servants, collection of rents, and keeping of accounts) **2 :** SHOP STEWARD **3 :** a fiscal agent **4 a :** an employee on a ship, airplane, bus, or train who manages the provisioning of food and attends passengers **b :** one appointed to supervise the provision and distribution of food and drink in an institution **5 :** one who actively directs affairs **:** MANAGER
[2]steward *vt* **:** to act as a steward for **:** MANAGE ~ *vi* **:** to perform the duties of a steward
stew·ard·ess \-əs\ *n* **:** a woman who performs the duties of a steward; *esp* **:** one who attends passengers (as on an airplane)
stew·ard·ship \-ˌship\ *n* **:** the office, duties, and obligations of a steward; *also* **:** the individual's responsibility to manage his life and property with proper regard to the rights of others
stewed \ˈst(y)üd\ *adj* **:** DRUNK
stew·pan \ˈst(y)ü-ˌpan\ *n* **:** a saucepan used for stewing
stg *abbr* sterling
stge *abbr* storage
sthen·ic \ˈsthen-ik\ *adj* [NL *sthenicus*, fr. Gk *sthenos* strength] **1 :** notably or excessively vigorous or energetic <~ fever> <~ emotions> **2 :** PYKNIC
stib·ine \ˈstib-ˌēn\ *n* [ISV, fr. L *stibium* antimony] **:** a colorless poisonous flammable gas SbH_3 of antimony and hydrogen with a disagreeable odor
stib·nite \ˈstib-ˌnīt\ *n* [alter. of obs. E *stibine* stibnite, fr. F, fr. L *stibium* antimony, fr. Gk *stibi*, fr. Egypt *stm*] **:** a mineral Sb_2S_3 consisting of antimony trisulfide that occurs in orthorhombic lead-gray crystals of metallic luster and that is also massive in form
sticho·myth·ia \ˌstik-ə-ˈmith-ē-ə\ *also* **sti·chom·y·thy** \stik-ˈäm-ə-thē\ *n* [Gk *stichomythia*, fr. *stichomythein* to speak dialogue in alternate lines, fr. *stichos* row, verse + *mythos* speech, myth; akin to Gk *steichein* to walk, go — more at STAIR] **:** dialogue esp. of altercation or dispute delivered by two actors in alternating lines (as in classical Greek drama) — **sticho·myth·ic** \ˌstik-ə-ˈmith-ik\ *adj*
[1]stick \ˈstik\ *n* [ME *stik*, fr. OE *sticca*; akin to ON *stik* stick, OE *stician* to stick] **1 :** a woody piece or part of a tree or shrub: as **a :** a usu. dry or dead severed shoot, twig, or slender branch **b :** a cut or broken branch or piece of wood gathered for fuel or construction material **2 a :** a long slender piece of wood: as **(1) :** a club or staff used as a weapon **(2) :** WALKING STICK **b :** an implement used for striking or propelling an object in a game **c :** something used to force compliance **d :** a baton symbolizing an office or dignity; *also* **:** a person entitled to bear such a baton **3 :** a piece of the materials composing something (as a building) **4 a :** any of various implements resembling a stick in shape, origin, or use: as **(1) :** COMPOSING STICK **(2) :** an airplane lever operating the elevators and ailerons **(3) :** the gearshift lever of an automobile **b :** STICKFUL **5 :** something prepared (as by cutting, molding, or rolling) in a relatively long and slender often cylindrical form <a ~ of candy> <a ~ of butter> **6 a :** PERSON, CHAP **b :** a dull, inert, stiff, or spiritless person **7** *pl* **:** wooded or rural districts **8 :** an herbaceous stalk resembling a woody stick <celery ~*s*> **9 :** MAST; *also* **:** YARD **10 :** a piece of furniture **11 a :** a number of bombs arranged for release from a bombing plane in a series across a target **b :** a number of parachutists dropping together **12** *slang* **:** a marijuana cigarette **13** *slang* **:** SURFBOARD
[2]stick *vt* **1 :** to arrange (lumber) in stacks **2 :** to provide a stick as a support for **3 :** to set (type) in a composing stick **:** COMPOSE
[3]stick *vb* **stuck** \ˈstək\; **stick·ing** [ME *stikken*, fr. OE *stician*; akin to OHG *sticken* to prick, L in*stigare* to urge on, goad, Gk *stizein* to tattoo] *vt* **1 a :** to pierce with something pointed **:** STAB **b :** to kill by piercing **2 :** to push or thrust so as or as if to pierce **3 a :** to fasten by thrusting in **b :** IMPALE **c :** PUSH, THRUST **4 :** to put or set in a specified place or position **5 :** to furnish with things fastened on by or as if by piercing **6 :** to attach by or as if by causing to adhere to a surface **7 a :** to compel to pay esp. by trickery **b :** OVERCHARGE **8 a :** to halt the movement or action of **b :** BAFFLE, STUMP **9 a :** CHEAT, DEFRAUD **b :** to saddle with something disadvantageous or disagreeable ~ *vi* **1 :** to hold to something firmly by or as if by adhesion: **a :** to become fixed in place by means of a pointed end **b :** to become fast by or as if by miring or by gluing or plastering <*stuck* in the mud> **2 a :** to remain in a place, situation, or environment **b :** to hold fast or adhere resolutely **:** CLING **c :** to remain effective **d :** to keep close in a chase or competition **3 :** to become blocked, wedged, or jammed **4 a :** BALK, SCRUPLE **b :** to find oneself baffled **c :** to be unable to proceed **5 :** PROJECT, PROTRUDE
syn STICK, ADHERE, COHERE, CLING, CLEAVE *shared meaning element* **:** to become closely attached
— **stick one's neck out :** to make oneself vulnerable unnecessarily (as by taking another's part) — **stick to one's knitting :** to mind one's own business — **stuck on :** infatuated with
[4]stick *n* **1 :** a thrust with a pointed instrument **:** STAB **2 a :** DELAY, STOP **b :** IMPEDIMENT **3 :** adhesive quality or substance
stick around *vi* **:** to stay or wait about **:** LINGER
stick·ball \ˈstik-ˌbȯl\ *n* **:** baseball adapted for play in streets or small areas and using a broomstick and a lightweight ball
stick·er \ˈstik-ər\ *n* **1 :** one that pierces with a point **2 a :** one that adheres or causes adhesion **b :** a slip of paper with gummed back that when moistened adheres to a surface
stick figure *n* **:** a drawing showing the head of a human being or animal as a circle and all other parts as straight lines
stick·ful \ˈstik-ˌfu̇l\ *n* **:** as much set type as fills a composing stick
stick·han·dler \-ˌhan-(d)lər, -dᵊl-ər\ *n* **:** a lacrosse or hockey player
sticking plaster *n* **:** an adhesive plaster esp. for closing superficial wounds
sticking point *n* **:** an item resulting or likely to result in an impasse
stick insect *n* **:** any of various usu. wingless insects (esp. family Phasmatidae) with a long round body resembling a stick
stick–in–the–mud \ˈstik-ən-t͟hə-ˌməd\ *n* **:** one who is slow, old-fashioned, or unprogressive; *esp* **:** an old fogy
stick·it \ˈstik-ət\ *adj* [Sc, fr. pp. of E [3]*stick*] **1** *Scot* **:** UNFINISHED **2** *chiefly Scot* **:** having failed esp. in an intended profession
stick·le \ˈstik-əl\ *vi* **stick·led; stick·ling** \-(ə-)liŋ\ [ME *stightlen*, freq. of *stighten* to arrange, fr. OE *stihtan*; akin to OE *stǣger* stair — more at STAIR] **1 :** to contend esp. stubbornly and usu. on insufficient grounds **2 :** to feel scruples **:** SCRUPLE
stick·le·back \ˈstik-əl-ˌbak\ *n* [ME *stykylbak*, fr. OE *sticel* goad + ME *bak* back; akin to OE *stician* to stick] **:** any of numerous small scaleless fishes (family Gasterosteidae) having two or more free spines in front of the dorsal fin
stick·ler \ˈstik-(ə-)lər\ *n* **1 :** one who insists on exactness or completeness in the observance of something <a ~ for obedience> **2 :** something that baffles or puzzles **:** POSER, STICKER
stick·man \ˈstik-ˌman, -mən\ *n* **:** one who handles a stick: as **a :** one who supervises the play at a dice table, calls the decisions, and retrieves the dice **b :** a player in any of various games (as hockey or lacrosse) played with a stick
stick out *vi* **1 a :** to jut out **:** PROJECT **b :** to be prominent or conspicuous **2 :** to be persistent (as in a demand or an opinion) ~ *vt* **:** to endure to the end — often used with *it*
stick·pin \ˈstik-ˌpin\ *n* **:** an ornamental pin; *esp* **:** one worn in a necktie
stick·seed \-ˌsēd\ *n* **:** any of a genus (*Lappula*) of weedy herbs of the borage family with bristly adhesive fruit
stick shift *n* **:** a manually operated gearshift mounted on the steering column or floor of an automobile
stick·tight \ˈstik-ˌtīt\ *n* **:** BUR MARIGOLD
stick–to–it·ive·ness \stik-ˈtü-ət-iv-nəs\ *n* [fr. the phrase *stick to it*] **:** dogged perseverance **:** TENACITY
stick·um \ˈstik-əm\ *n* [[3]*stick* + *-um* (prob. alter. of *them*)] **:** a substance that adheres or causes adhesion
stick·up \ˈstik-ˌəp\ *n* **:** a robbery at the point of a gun **:** HOLDUP
stick up \(ˈ)stik-ˈəp\ *vi* **:** to stand upright or on end **:** PROTRUDE ~ *vt* **:** to rob at the point of a gun — **stick up for :** to speak or act in defense of **:** SUPPORT
stick·weed \ˈstik-ˌwēd\ *n* **:** any of several plants (as a beggar's-lice) with adhesive seeds
stick·work \-ˌwərk\ *n* **1 :** the use (as in hockey) of one's stick in offensive and defensive techniques **2 :** batting ability in baseball
sticky \ˈstik-ē\ *adj* **stick·i·er; -est 1 a :** ADHESIVE **b (1) :** VISCOUS, GLUEY **(2) :** coated with a sticky substance **2 :** HUMID, MUGGY; *also* **:** CLAMMY **3 :** tending to stick **4 a :** DISAGREEABLE, UNPLEASANT **b :** AWKWARD, STIFF **c :** DIFFICULT, PROBLEMATIC — **stick·i·ly** \ˈstik-ə-lē\ *adv* — **stick·i·ness** \ˈstik-ē-nəs\ *n*
[1]stiff \ˈstif\ *adj* [ME *stif*, fr. OE *stīf*; akin to MD *stijf* stiff, L *stipare* to press together, Gk *steibein* to tread on] **1 a :** not easily bent **:** RIGID **b :** lacking in suppleness <~ muscles> **c :** impeded in movement — used of a mechanism **d :** DRUNK **e :** incapable of normal alert response <scared ~> **2 a :** FIRM, RESOLUTE **b :** STUBBORN, UNYIELDING **c :** PROUD **d (1) :** marked by reserve or decorum **(2) :** lacking in ease or grace **:** STILTED **3 :** hard fought **:** PUGNACIOUS, SHARP **4 a (1) :** exerting great force <a ~ wind> **(2) :** FORCEFUL, VIGOROUS **b :** POTENT <a ~ dose> **5 :** of a dense or glutinous consistency **:** THICK **6 a :** HARSH, SEVERE <a ~ penalty> **b :** ARDUOUS, RUGGED <~ terrain> **7 :** not easily heeled over by an external force (as the wind) <a ~ ship> **8 :** EXPENSIVE, STEEP <paid a ~ price> — **stiff·ly** *adv*
syn STIFF, RIGID, INFLEXIBLE, TENSE, STARK *shared meaning element* **:** difficult or impossible to bend or enliven ***ant*** relaxed, supple
[2]stiff *adv* **:** in a stiff manner **:** STIFFLY
[3]stiff *n* **1 :** CORPSE **2 a :** BUM, TRAMP **b :** HAND, LABORER
stiff–arm \ˈstif-ˌärm\ *vb or n* **:** STRAIGHT-ARM
stiff·en \ˈstif-ən\ *vb* **stiff·ened; stiff·en·ing** \-(ə-)niŋ\ **:** to make or become stiff or stiffer — **stiff·en·er** \-(ə-)nər\ *n*
stiff·ish \ˈstif-ish\ *adj* **:** moderately stiff
stiff–necked \-ˈnekt\ *adj* **1 :** HAUGHTY, STUBBORN **2 :** STILTED
stiff·ness \-nəs\ *n* **:** the quality or state of being stiff
[1]sti·fle \ˈstī-fəl\ *n* [ME] **:** the joint next above the hock in the hind leg of a quadruped (as a horse) corresponding to the knee in man — see HORSE illustration
[2]stifle *vb* **sti·fled; sti·fling** \-f(ə-)liŋ\ [alter. of ME *stuflen*] *vt* **1 a :** to kill by depriving of oxygen **:** SUFFOCATE **b (1) :** SMOTHER **(2) :** MUFFLE **2 a :** to cut off (as the voice or breath) **b :** to withhold from circulation or expression **:** REPRESS <~ his anger> **c :** DETER, DISCOURAGE ~ *vi* **:** to become suffocated by or as if by lack of oxygen **:** SMOTHER — **sti·fler** \-f(ə-)lər\ *n* — **sti·fling·ly** \-f(ə-)liŋ-lē\ *adv*
stig·ma \ˈstig-mə\ *n, pl* **stig·ma·ta** \stig-ˈmät-ə, ˈstig-mət-ə\ *or* **stigmas** [L *stigmat-, stigma* mark, brand, fr. Gk, fr. *stizein* to tattoo — more at STICK] **1 a** *archaic* **:** a scar left by a hot iron **:** BRAND **b :** a mark of shame or discredit **:** STAIN **c :** an identifying mark or characteristic; *specif* **:** a specific diagnostic sign of a disease **2 a** *stigmata pl* **:** bodily marks or pains resembling the wounds of the crucified Christ and sometimes accompanying religious ecstasy **b :** PETECHIA **3 a :** a small spot, scar, or opening on a plant or animal **b :** the part of the pistil of a flower which receives the pollen grains and on which they germinate —see FLOWER illustration — **stig·mal** \ˈstig-məl\ *adj*
stig·mas·ter·ol \stig-ˈmas-tə-ˌrōl, -ˌrȯl\ *n* [NL Physo*stigma* (genus including the Calabar bean) + ISV *sterol*] **:** a crystalline sterol $C_{29}H_{48}O$ obtained esp. from the oils of Calabar beans and soybeans
[1]stig·mat·ic \stig-ˈmat-ik\ *adj* **1 :** having or conveying a social stigma **2 :** of or relating to supernatural stigmata **3 :** ANASTIGMATIC — used esp. of a bundle of light rays intersecting at a single point — **stig·mat·i·cal·ly** \-i-k(ə-)lē\ *adv*
[2]stigmatic *n* **:** one marked with stigmata
stig·ma·tism \ˈstig-mə-ˌtiz-əm\ *n* [L *stigmat-, stigma*] **:** the condition of an optical system (as a lens) in which rays of light from a single point converge in a single focal point — compare ASTIGMATISM

stig·ma·tist \'stig-mət-əst, stig-'mät-\ *n* : STIGMATIC
stig·ma·tize \'stig-mə-ˌtīz\ *vt* **-tized; -tiz·ing** **1 a** *archaic* : BRAND **b** : to describe or identify in opprobrious terms **2** : to mark with stigmata — **stig·ma·ti·za·tion** \ˌstig-mət-ə-'zā-shən\ *n*
stil·bene \'stil-ˌbēn\ *n* [ISV, fr. Gk *stilbein* to glitter] : an aromatic hydrocarbon $C_{14}H_{12}$ used as a phosphor and in making dyes
stil·bes·trol \stil-'bes-ˌtrōl, -ˌtrȯl\ *n* [*stilbene* + *estrus* + *-ol*] **1** : a crystalline synthetic derivative $C_{14}H_{12}O_2$ of stilbene that differs from the related diethylstilbestrol in lack of the ethyl groups and in possession of but slight estrogenic activity **2** : DIETHYLSTILBESTROL
stil·bite \'stil-ˌbīt\ *n* [F, fr. Gk *stilbein*] : a mineral $NaCa_2Al_5Si_{13}O_{36}\cdot14H_2O$ consisting of a hydrous silicate of aluminum, calcium, and sodium and often occurring in sheaflike aggregations of crystals
[1]**stile** \'stī(ə)l\ *n* [ME, fr. OE *stigel;* akin to OE *stǣger* stair — more at STAIR] : a step or set of steps for passing over a fence or wall; *also* : TURNSTILE
[2]**stile** *n* [prob. fr. D *stijl* post] : one of the vertical members in a frame or panel into which the secondary members are fitted
sti·let·to \stə-'let-(ˌ)ō\ *n, pl* **-tos** *or* **-toes** [It, dim. of *stilo* stylus, dagger, fr. L *stilus* stylus — more at STYLE] **1** : a slender dagger with a blade thick in proportion to its breadth **2** : a pointed instrument for piercing holes for eyelets or embroidery
[1]**still** \'stil\ *adj* [ME *stille,* fr. OE; akin to OHG *stilli* still, OE *steall* stall] **1 a** : devoid of or abstaining from motion **b** *archaic* : SEDENTARY **c** : not carbonated <~ wine> **d (1)** : of, relating to, or being a static photograph as contrasted with a motion picture **(2)** : engaged in taking still photographs <a ~ photographer> **2 a** : uttering no sound : QUIET **b** : SUBDUED, MUTED **3 a** : CALM, TRANQUIL **b** : free from noise or turbulence — **still·ness** *n*
[2]**still** *vt* **1 a** : ALLAY, CALM **b** : to put an end to : SETTLE **2** : to arrest the motion of **3** : SILENCE ~ *vi* : to become motionless or silent : QUIET
[3]**still** *adv* **1** : without motion <sit ~> **2** *archaic* **a** : ALWAYS, CONTINUALLY **b** : in a progressive manner : INCREASINGLY **3** — used as a function word to indicate the continuance of an action or condition <~ lived there> <drink it while it's ~ hot> <will ~ be rich> **4** : in spite of that : NEVERTHELESS <those who take the greatest care ~ make mistakes> **5 a** : EVEN 2c <a ~ more difficult problem> **b** : YET 1a
[4]**still** *n* **1** : QUIET, SILENCE **2** : a static photograph; *specif* : a photograph of actors or scenes of a motion picture for publicity or documentary purposes
[5]**still** *vb* [ME *stillen,* short for *distillen* to distill] : DISTILL
[6]**still** *n* **1** : DISTILLERY **2** : apparatus used in distillation comprising either the chamber in which the vaporization is carried out or the entire equipment
still alarm *n* : a fire alarm transmitted (as by telephone call) without sounding the signal apparatus
still·birth \'stil-ˌbərth, -'bərth\ *n* : the birth of a dead fetus
still·born \-'bȯ(ə)rn\ *adj* **1** : dead at birth — compare LIVE-BORN **2** : failing from the start : ABORTIVE — **stillborn** \-ˌbȯ(ə)rn\ *n*
still–hunt \-ˌhənt\ *vi* : to ambush or stalk a quarry; *esp* : to pursue game noiselessly usu. without a dog ~ *vt* : to lie in wait for : approach by stealth
still hunt *n* : a quiet pursuing or ambushing of game
still life *n, pl* **still lifes** **1** : a picture consisting predominantly of inanimate objects **2** : the category of graphic arts concerned with inanimate subject matter
still·man \'stil-mən\ *n* **1** : one who owns or operates a still **2** : one who tends distillation equipment (as in an oil refinery)
still·room \'stil-ˌrüm, -ˌrum\ *n* [[6]*still*] *Brit* : a room connected with the kitchen where liqueurs, preserves, and cakes are kept and beverages (as tea) are prepared
still water *n* : a part of a stream where the gradient is so gentle that no current is visible
[1]**stil·ly** \'stil-lē\ *adv* : in a calm manner : QUIETLY
[2]**stilly** \'stil-ē\ *adj* [[4]*still* + *-y*] : STILL, QUIET
[1]**stilt** \'stilt\ *n* [ME *stilte;* akin to OHG *stelza* stilt, OE *steall* position, stall — more at STALL] **1 a** : one of two poles each with a rest or strap for the foot used to elevate the wearer above the ground in walking **b** : a pile or post serving as one of the supports of a structure above ground or water level **2** *pl also* **stilt** : any of various notably long-legged 3-toed limicoline birds (genera *Himantopus* and *Cladorhynchus*) that are related to the avocets, frequent inland ponds and marshes, and nest in small colonies
[2]**stilt** *vt* : to raise on or as if on stilts
stilt·ed \'stil-təd\ *adj* **1** : having the springing line higher than the apparent level of the impost <a ~ arch> **2 a** : POMPOUS, LOFTY **b** : FORMAL, STIFF — **stilt·ed·ly** *adv* — **stilt·ed·ness** *n*
Stil·ton \'stilt-ᵊn\ *n* [*Stilton,* Huntingdonshire, England] : a blue-veined cheese with wrinkled rind made of whole cows' milk enriched with cream
stime \'stīm\ *n* [ME (northern dial.)] *chiefly Scot & Irish* : GLIMMER; *also* : GLIMPSE
stim·u·lant \'stim-yə-lənt\ *n* **1** : an agent (as a drug) that produces a temporary increase of the functional activity or efficiency of an organism or any of its parts **2** : STIMULUS **3** : an alcoholic beverage — not used technically — **stimulant** *adj*
stim·u·late \-ˌlāt\ *vb* **-lat·ed; -lat·ing** [L *stimulatus,* pp. of *stimulare,* fr. *stimulus* goad; akin to L *stilus* stake, stylus — more at STYLE] *vt* **1** : to excite to activity or growth or to greater activity : ANIMATE, AROUSE **2 a** : to function as a physiological stimulus to **b** : to arouse or affect by a stimulant (as a drug) ~ *vi* : to act as a stimulant or stimulus ***syn*** see PROVOKE ***ant*** unnerve, deaden — **stim·u·la·tion** \ˌstim-yə-'lā-shən\ *n* — **stim·u·la·tive** \'stim-yə-ˌlāt-iv\ *adj* — **stim·u·la·tor** \-ˌlāt-ər\ *n* — **stim·u·la·to·ry** \-lə-ˌtōr-ē, -ˌtȯr-\ *adj*
stim·u·lus \'stim-yə-ləs\ *n, pl* **-li** \-ˌlī, -ˌlē\ [L] : something that rouses or incites to activity: as **a** : INCENTIVE **b** : STIMULANT 1 **c** : an agent (as an environmental change) that directly influences the activity of living protoplasm (as by exciting a sensory organ or evoking muscular contraction or glandular secretion)

[1]**sting** \'stiŋ\ *vb* **stung** \'stəŋ\; **sting·ing** \'stiŋ-iŋ\ [ME *stingen,* fr. OE *stingan;* akin to ON *stinga* to sting, Gk *stachys* spike of grain, *stochos* target, aim] *vt* **1** : to prick painfully: as **a** : to pierce or wound with a poisonous or irritating process **b** : to affect with sharp quick pain or smart <hail *stung* their faces> **2** : to cause to suffer acutely <*stung* with remorse> **3** : OVERCHARGE, CHEAT ~ *vi* **1** : to use a sting **2** : to feel a keen burning pain or smart — **sting·ing·ly** \-iŋ-lē\ *adv*
[2]**sting** *n* **1 a** : the act of stinging; *specif* : the thrust of a stinger into the flesh **b** : a wound or pain caused by or as if by stinging **2** : STINGER 2 **3** : a stinging element, force, or quality
sting·a·ree \'stiŋ-ə-rē *also* 'stiŋ-rē\ *n* [by alter.] : STINGRAY
sting·er \'stiŋ-ər\ *n* **1** : one that stings; *specif* : a sharp blow or remark **2** : a sharp organ (as of a bee, scorpion, or stingray) of offense and defense usu. connected with a poison gland or otherwise adapted to wound by piercing and inoculating a poisonous secretion **3** : a cocktail of equal parts of white crème de menthe and brandy
sting·ing hair \ˌstiŋ-iŋ-\ *n* : a glandular hair (as of a nettle) whose base secretes a stinging fluid
sting·less \'stiŋ-ləs\ *adj* : having no sting or stinger
sting·ray \-ˌrā *also* -rē\ *n* : any of numerous rays (as of the family Dasyatidae) with one or more large sharp barbed dorsal spines near the base of the whiplike tail capable of inflicting severe wounds

stingray

stin·gy \'stin-jē\ *adj* **stin·gi·er; -est** [prob. fr. (assumed) E dial. *stinge,* n., sting; akin to OE *stingan* to sting] **1** : not generous or liberal : sparing or scant in giving or spending **2** : meanly scanty or small — **stin·gi·ly** \-jə-lē\ *adv* — **stin·gi·ness** \-jē-nəs\ *n*
syn STINGY, CLOSE, NIGGARDLY, PARSIMONIOUS, PENURIOUS, MISERLY *shared meaning element* : being unwilling or showing unwillingness to share with others ***ant*** generous
[1]**stink** \'stiŋk\ *vi* **stank** \'staŋk\ *or* **stunk** \'stəŋk\; **stunk; stink·ing** [ME *stinken,* fr. OE *stincan;* akin to OHG *stinkan* to emit a smell] **1** : to emit a strong offensive odor **2** : to be offensive; *also* : to be in bad repute **3** : to possess something to an offensive degree <~*ing* with wealth> **4** : to be extremely bad in quality — **stinky** \'stiŋ-kē\ *adj*
[2]**stink** *n* **1** : a strong offensive odor : STENCH **2** : a public outcry against something offensive
stink·ard \'stiŋ-kərd\ *n* : a mean or contemptible person
stink·bug \'stiŋk-ˌbəg\ *n* : any of various true bugs (order Hemiptera) that emit a disagreeable odor
stink·er \'stiŋ-kər\ *n* **1 a** : one that stinks **b** : an offensive or contemptible person **c** : something of very poor quality **2** : any of several large petrels that have an offensive odor **3** *slang* : something extremely difficult <the examination was a real ~>
stink·horn \'stiŋk-ˌhȯ(ə)rn\ *n* : an ill-smelling fungus (order Phallales, esp. *Phallus impudicus*)
[1]**stink·ing** *adj* **1** : strong and offensive to the sense of smell **2** *slang* : offensively drunk ***syn*** see MALODOROUS — **stink·ing·ly** \'stiŋ-kiŋ-lē\ *adv*
[2]**stinking** *adv* : to an extreme degree <got ~ drunk>
stink·ing rog·er \ˌstiŋ-kiŋ-'räj-ər, -kən-\ *n* [fr. the name *Roger*] : any of various fetid plants (as a figwort or henbane)
stinking smut *n* : [2]BUNT
stink·pot \'stiŋk-ˌpät\ *n* **1** : an earthen jar charged with materials of an offensive and suffocating smell formerly sometimes thrown upon an enemy's deck **2** : STINKER 1
stink·stone \-ˌstōn\ *n* : a stone that emits a fetid smell on being struck or rubbed owing to decomposition of organic matter
stink up *vt* : to cause to stink or be filled with a stench
stink·weed \'stiŋ-ˌkwēd\ *n* : any of various strong-scented or fetid plants; *esp* : PENNYCRESS
stink·wood \-ˌkwu̇d\ *n* **1** : any of several trees with a wood of unpleasant odor; *esp* : a southern African tree (*Ocotia bullata*) of the laurel family yielding a valued cabinet wood **2** : the wood of a stinkwood
[1]**stint** \'stint\ *vb* [ME *stinten,* fr. OE *styntan* to blunt, dull; akin to ON *stuttr* scant, L *tundere* to beat, OE *stocc* stock] *vt* **1** *archaic* : to put an end to : STOP **2 a** : to restrain within certain limits : CONFINE **b** : to restrict with respect to a share or allowance **3** : to assign a task to (a person) ~ *vi* **1** *archaic* : STOP, DESIST **2** : to be sparing or frugal — **stint·er** *n*
[2]**stint** *n* **1** : RESTRAINT, LIMITATION **2** : a definite quantity of work assigned ***syn*** see TASK
[3]**stint** *n, pl* **stints** *also* **stint** [ME *stynte*] : any of several small sandpipers
stipe \'stīp\ *n* [NL *stipes,* fr. L, tree trunk; akin to L *stipare* to press together — more at STIFF] : a usu. short plant stalk: as **a** : the stem supporting the cap of a fungus **b** : a part that is similar to a stipe and connects the holdfast and blade of a frondose alga **c** : the petiole of a fern frond **d** : a prolongation of the receptacle beneath the ovary of a seed plant — **stiped** \'stīpt\ *adj*
sti·pel \'stī-pəl, stī-'pel\ *n* [NL *stipella,* dim. of *stipula* stipule] : the stipule of a leaflet — **sti·pel·late** \'stī-pə-ˌlāt, stī-'pel-ət\ *adj*
sti·pend \'stī-ˌpend, -pənd\ *n* [alter. of ME *stipendy,* fr. L *stipendium,* fr. *stip-, stips* gift + *pendere* to weigh, pay — more at PENDANT] : a fixed sum of money paid periodically for services or to defray expenses ***syn*** see WAGE

1sti·pen·di·ary \stī-'pen-dē-,er-ē\ *adj* **1 :** receiving or compensated by wages or salary <a ~ curate> **2 :** of or relating to a stipend
2stipendiary *n, pl* **-ar·ies :** one who receives a stipend
sti·pes \'stī-,pēz\ *n, pl* **stip·i·tes** \'stip-ə-,tēz\ [NL *stipit-, stipes,* fr. L, tree trunk — more at STIPE] **:** PEDUNCLE *esp* **:** the second basal segment of a maxilla of an insect or crustacean — **stip·i·tate** \'stip-ə-,tāt\ *adj*
1stip·ple \'stip-əl\ *vt* **stip·pled; stip·pling** \-(ə-)liŋ\ [D *stippelen* to spot, dot; akin to L *stipare* to press together] **1 :** to engrave by means of dots and flicks **2 a :** to make (as in paint or ink) by small short touches that together produce an even or softly graded shadow **b :** to apply (as paint) by repeated small touches **3 :** SPECKLE, FLECK — **stip·pler** \-(ə-)lər\ *n*
2stipple *n* **:** production of gradation of light and shade in graphic art by stippling small points, larger dots, or longer strokes; *also* **:** an effect produced by or as if by stippling
stip·u·lar \'stip-yə-lər\ *adj* **:** of, resembling, or provided with stipules <~ glands>
1stip·u·late \'stip-yə-,lāt\ *vb* **-lat·ed; -lat·ing** [L *stipulatus,* pp. of *stipulari* to demand some term in an agreement] *vi* **1 :** to make an agreement or covenant to do or forbear something **:** CONTRACT **2 :** to demand an express term in an agreement — used with *for* ~ *vt* **1 :** to specify as a condition or requirement of an agreement or offer **2 :** to give a guarantee of — **stip·u·la·tor** \-,lāt-ər\ *n*
2stip·u·late \'stip-yə-lət\ *adj* **:** having stipules
stip·u·la·tion \,stip-yə-'lā-shən\ *n* **1 :** an act of stipulating **2 :** something stipulated; *esp* **:** a condition, requirement, or item specified in a legal instrument — **stip·u·la·to·ry** \'stip-yə-lə-,tōr-ē, -,tȯr-\ *adj*
stip·ule \'stip-(,)yü(ə)l\ *n* [NL *stipula,* fr. L, stalk; akin to L *stipes* tree trunk] **:** either of a pair of appendages borne at the base of the leaf in many plants — **stip·uled** \-,yü(ə)ld\ *adj*
1stir \'stər\ *vb* **stirred; stir·ring** [ME *stiren,* fr. OE *styrian;* akin to MHG *stürn* to incite] *vt* **1 a :** to cause an esp. slight movement or change of position of **b :** to disturb the quiet of **:** AGITATE **2 a :** to disturb the relative position of the particles or parts of esp. by a continued circular movement **b :** to mix by or as if by stirring **3 :** BESTIR, EXERT **4 :** to bring into notice or debate **:** RAISE **5 a :** to rouse to activity **:** stir strong feelings in **b :** to call forth (as a memory) **:** EVOKE **c :** PROVOKE ~ *vi* **1 a :** to make a slight movement **b :** to begin to move (as in rousing) **2 :** to begin to be active **3 :** to be active or busy **4 :** to pass an implement through a substance with a circular movement **5 :** to be able to be stirred — **stir·rer** *n*
2stir *n* **1 a :** a state of disturbance, agitation, or brisk activity **b :** widespread notice and discussion **:** IMPRESSION **2 :** a slight movement **3 :** a stirring movement
syn STIR, BUSTLE, FLURRY, POTHER, FUSS, ADO *shared meaning element* **:** signs of excitement or hurry *ant* tranquillity
3stir *n* [origin unknown] *slang* **:** PRISON
Stir *abbr* Stirling
stir·about \'stər-ə-,bau̇t\ *n* **:** a porridge of Irish origin consisting of oatmeal or cornmeal boiled in water or milk and stirred
stirk \'stərk\ *n* [ME, fr. OE *stirc;* akin to L *sterilis* sterile] *Brit* **:** a young bull or cow esp. between one and two years old
Stir·ling's formula \'stər-liŋz-\ *n* [James *Stirling* †1770 Sc mathematician] **:** the formula

$$\sqrt{2\pi n}\, n^n e^{-n}$$

that gives the approximate value of the factorial of a very large number *n*
stirp \'stərp\ *n* [L *stirp-, stirps* — more at TORPID] **:** a line descending from a common ancestor **:** STOCK, LINEAGE
stirps \'sti(ə)rps, 'stərps\ *n, pl* **stir·pes** \'sti(ə)r-,pās, 'stər-(,)pēz\ [L, lit., stem, stock — more at TORPID] **1 :** a branch of a family or the person from whom it is descended **2 a :** a group of animals equivalent to a superfamily **b :** a race or fixed variety of plants
stir·ring \'stər-iŋ\ *adj* **1 :** ACTIVE, BUSTLING **2 :** ROUSING, INSPIRING
stir·rup \'stər-əp *also* 'stir-əp *or* 'stə-rəp\ *n* [ME *stirop,* fr. OE *stigrāp;* akin to OHG *stegareif* stirrup; both fr. a prehistoric NGmc-WGmc compound whose first element is akin to OHG *stīgan* to go up and whose second element is represented by OE *rāp* rope — more at STAIR] **1 :** either of a pair of small light frames or rings for receiving the foot of a rider that are attached by a strap to a saddle and used to aid in mounting and as a support while riding **2 :** a piece resembling a stirrup (as a support or clamp in carpentry and machinery) **3 :** a rope secured to a yard and attached to a thimble in its lower end for supporting a footrope
stirrup cup *n* **1 :** a cup of drink (as wine) taken by a rider about to depart **2 :** a farewell cup
stirrup leather *n* **:** the strap suspending a stirrup
stirrup pump *n* **:** a portable hand pump held in position by a foot bracket and used for throwing a jet or spray of liquid
1stitch \'stich\ *n* [ME *stiche,* fr. OE *stice;* akin to OE *stician* to stick] **1 :** a local sharp and sudden pain esp. in the side **2 a :** one in-and-out movement of a threaded needle in sewing, embroidering, or suturing **b :** a portion of thread left in the material after one stitch **3 :** a least part esp. of clothing **4 :** a single loop of thread or yarn around an implement (as a knitting needle or crochet hook) **5 :** a series of stitches **6 :** a method of stitching — **in stitches :** in a state of uncontrollable laughter
2stitch *vt* **1 a :** to fasten, join, or close with or as if with stitches **b :** to make, mend, or decorate with or as if with stitches **2 :** to unite by means of staples ~ *vi* **:** SEW — **stitch·er** *n*
stitch·ery \'stich-(ə-)rē\ *n* **:** NEEDLEWORK
stitch·wort \'stich-,wərt, -,wȯ(ə)rt\ *n* **:** any of several chickweeds (genus *Stellaria*)
stithy \'stit͟h-ē, 'stith-\ *n, pl* **stith·ies** [ME, fr. ON *stethi;* akin to OE *stede* stead] **1 :** ANVIL **2 :** SMITHY
sti·ver \'stī-vər\ *n* [D *stuiver*] **1 a :** a unit of value of the Netherlands equal to $\frac{1}{20}$ gulden **b :** a coin representing one stiver **2 :** something of little value
stk *abbr* stock
STL *abbr* [NL *sacrae theologiae licentiatus*] licentiate of sacred theology
STM *abbr* **1** [NL *sacrae theologiae magister*] master of sacred theology **2** master of theology
stoa \'stō-ə\ *n* [Gk; akin to Gk *stylos* pillar — more at STEER] **:** an ancient Greek portico usu. walled at the back with a front colonnade designed to afford a sheltered promenade
stoat \'stōt\ *n, pl* **stoats** *also* **stoat** [ME *stote*] **:** ERMINE 1a; *broadly* **:** a weasel with a black-tipped tail — used esp. of an animal in the brown summer coat
stob \'stäb\ *n* [ME, stump; akin to ME *stubb* stub] *chiefly dial* **:** STAKE, POST
stoc·ca·do \stə-'käd-(,)ō\ *n, pl* **-dos** [It *stoccata*] *archaic* **:** a thrust with a rapier
sto·chas·tic \stə-'kas-tik, stō-\ *adj* [Gk *stochastikos* skillful in aiming, fr. *stochazesthai* to aim at, guess at, fr. *stochos* target, aim, guess — more at STING] **1 :** RANDOM; *specif* **:** involving a random variable <a ~ process> **2 :** involving chance or probability **:** PROBABILISTIC <a ~ model of radiation-induced mutation> — **sto·chas·ti·cal·ly** \-ti-k(ə-)lē\ *adv*
1stock \'stäk\ *n* [ME *stok,* fr. OE *stocc;* akin to OHG *stoc* stick, MIr *tūag* bow] **1 a :** STUMP **b** *archaic* **:** a log or block of wood **c (1) :** something without life or consciousness **(2) :** a dull, stupid, or lifeless person **2 :** a supporting framework or structure: as **a** *pl* **:** the frame or timbers holding a ship during construction **b** *pl* **:** a device for publicly punishing offenders consisting of a wooden frame with holes in which the feet or feet and hands can be locked **c (1) :** the wooden part by which a rifle or shotgun is held during firing **(2) :** the butt of an implement (as a whip or fishing rod) **(3) :** BITSTOCK, BRACE **d (1) :** a long beam on a field gun forming the third support point in firing **(2) :** the beam of a plow to which handles, share, colter, and moldboard are secured **3 a :** the main stem of a plant **:** TRUNK **b (1) :** a plant or plant part united with a scion in grafting and supplying mostly underground parts to a graft **(2) :** a plant from which slips or cuttings are taken **4 :** the crosspiece of an anchor **5 a :** the original (as a man, race, or language) from which others derive **:** SOURCE **b (1) :** the descendants of one individual **:** FAMILY, LINEAGE **(2) :** a compound organism — compare CLONE **c :** an infraspecific group usu. having unity of descent **d (1) :** a related group of languages **(2) :** a language family **6 a (1) :** the equipment, materials, or supplies of an establishment **(2) :** LIVESTOCK **b :** a store or supply accumulated; *esp* **:** the inventory of goods of a merchant or manufacturer **7 a** *archaic* **:** a supply of capital **:** FUNDS; *esp* **:** money or capital invested or available for investment or trading **b (1) :** the part of a tally formerly given to the creditor in a transaction **(2) :** a debt or fund due (as from a government) for money loaned at interest; *also, Brit* **:** capital or a debt or fund bearing interest in perpetuity and not ordinarily redeemable as to principal **c (1) :** the proprietorship element in a corporation usu. divided into shares and represented by transferable certificates **(2) :** a portion of such stock of one or more companies **(3) :** STOCK CERTIFICATE **8 :** any of a genus (Matthiola) of herbs or subshrubs of the mustard family with racemes of usu. sweet-scented flowers **9 :** a wide band or scarf worn about the neck esp. by some clergymen **10 a :** liquid in which meat, fish, or vegetables have been simmered that is used as a basis for soup, gravy, or sauce **b :** raw material from which something is manufactured **c :** the portion of a pack of cards not distributed to the players at the beginning of a game **11 a (1) :** an estimate or evaluation of something <take ~ of the situation> **(2) :** the estimation in which someone or something is held <his ~ with the electorate remains high —*Newsweek*> **b :** confidence or faith placed in someone or something <put little ~ in his testimony> **12 :** the production and presentation of plays by a stock company **13 :** STOCK CAR 2 — **in stock :** on hand **:** in the store and ready for delivery — **out of stock :** having no more on hand **:** sold out
2stock *vt* **1 :** to make (a domestic animal) pregnant **2 :** to fit to or with a stock **3 :** to provide with stock or a stock **:** SUPPLY <~ a stream with trout> **4 :** to procure or keep a stock of **5 :** to graze (livestock) on land ~ *vi* **1 :** to send out new shoots **2 :** to put in stock or supplies <~ up on canned goods>
3stock *adj* **1 a :** kept regularly in stock <comes in ~ sizes> <a ~ model> **b :** commonly used or brought forward **:** STANDARD <the ~ answer> **2 a :** kept for breeding purposes **:** BROOD <a ~ mare> **b :** devoted to the breeding and rearing of livestock <a ~ farm> **c :** used or intended for livestock <a ~ train> **3 :** of or relating to a stock company **4 :** employed in handling, checking, or taking care of the stock of merchandise on hand <a ~ boy>
1stock·ade \stä-'kād\ *n* [Sp *estacada,* fr. *estaca* stake, pale, of Gmc origin; akin to OE *staca* stake] **1 :** a line of stout posts set firmly to form a defense **2 a :** an enclosure or pen made with posts and stakes **b :** an enclosure in which prisoners are kept
2stockade *vt* **stock·ad·ed; stock·ad·ing :** to fortify or surround with a stockade
stock·breed·er \'stäk-,brēd-ər\ *n* **:** one who is engaged in the breeding and care of livestock for the market, for show purposes, or for racing
stock·bro·ker \-,brō-kər\ *n* **:** a broker who executes orders to buy and sell securities and often also acts as a security dealer — **stock·brok·ing** \-,brō-kiŋ\ *or* **stock·bro·ker·age** \-k(ə-)rij\ *n*
stock·car \-,kär\ *n* **:** a latticed railroad boxcar for carrying livestock
stock car *n* **1 :** an automotive vehicle of a model and type kept in stock for regular sales **2 :** a racing car having the basic chassis of a commercially produced assembly-line model
stock certificate *n* **:** an instrument evidencing ownership of one or more shares of the capital stock of a corporation
stock company *n* **1 :** a corporation or joint-stock company of which the capital is represented by stock **2 :** a theatrical company attached to a repertory theater; *esp* **:** one without outstanding stars
stock dividend *n* **1 :** the payment by a corporation of a dividend in the form of shares usu. of its own stock without change in par

value — compare STOCK SPLIT **2 :** the stock distributed in a stock dividend

stock·er \'stäk-ər\ *n* **1 :** a young animal (as a steer or heifer) suitable for being fed and fattened for market **2 :** an animal (as a heifer) suitable for use in a breeding establishment **3 :** STOCK CAR 2

stock exchange *n* **1 :** a place where security trading is conducted on an organized system **2 :** an association of people organized to provide an auction market among themselves for the purchase and sale of securities

stock·fish \-ˌfish\ *n* [ME *stokfish,* fr. MD *stocvisch,* fr. *stoc* stick + *visch* fish] **:** fish (as cod, haddock, or hake) dried hard in the open air without salt

stock·hold·er \'stäk-ˌhōl-dər\ *n* **:** an owner of stocks **:** SHAREHOLDER

stock·i·nette *or* **stock·i·net** \ˌstäk-ə-'net\ *n* [alter. of earlier *stocking net*] **:** a soft elastic usu. cotton fabric used esp. for bandages and infants' wear

stock·ing \'stäk-iŋ\ *n* [obs. *stock* to cover with a stocking] **1 a :** a usu. knit close-fitting covering for the foot and leg **b :** SOCK **2 :** something resembling a stocking; *esp* **:** a ring of distinctive color on the lower part of the leg of an animal — **stock·inged** \-iŋd\ *adj* — **in one's stocking feet :** having on stockings but no shoes

stocking cap *n* **:** a long knitted cone-shaped cap with a tassel or pom-pom worn esp. for winter sports or play

stock–in–trade \ˌstäk-ən-'trād, 'stäk-ən-ˌ\ *n* **1 :** the equipment necessary to or used in a trade or business **2 :** something that resembles the standard equipment of a tradesman or business <the light and frivolous charm which was her stage ~ —S. H. Adams>

stock·ish \'stäk-ish\ *adj* **:** like a stock **:** STUPID

stock·ist \'stäk-əst\ *n, Brit* **:** one (as a retailer) that stocks goods

stock·job·ber \'stäk-ˌjäb-ər\ *n* **:** STOCKBROKER — usu. used disparagingly

stock·job·bing \-ˌjäb-iŋ\ *n* **:** speculative exchange dealings

stock·keep·er \'stäk-ˌkē-pər\ *n* **1 :** one (as a herdsman or shepherd) having the charge or care of livestock **2 :** one that keeps and records stock (as in a warehouse) **:** one that keeps an inventory of goods on hand, shipped, or received

stock·man \-mən, -ˌman\ *n* **:** one occupied as an owner or worker in the raising of livestock (as cattle or sheep)

stock market *n* **1 :** STOCK EXCHANGE 1 **2 a :** a market for particular stocks **b :** the market for stocks throughout a country

¹stock·pile \'stäk-ˌpīl\ *n* **:** a storage pile: as **a :** a reserve supply of something essential accumulated within a country for use during a shortage **b :** a gradually accumulated reserve of something <avert ~*s* of unsold cars —Bert Pierce>

²stockpile *vt* **1 :** to place or store in or on a stockpile **2 :** to accumulate a stockpile of <~ war materials in Europe —A. O. Wolfers> — **stock·pil·er** *n*

stock·pot \'stäk-ˌpät\ *n* **1 :** a pot in which soup stock is prepared **2 :** an abundant supply **:** REPOSITORY

stock·proof \-ˌprüf\ *adj* **:** proof against livestock

stock·room \-ˌrüm, -ˌrum\ *n* **1 :** a storage place for supplies or goods used in a business **2 :** a room (as in a hotel) where traveling salesmen may exhibit their goods

stock saddle *n* **:** a deep-seated saddle with a high pommel and broad skirts and fenders used orig. by cattlemen — called also *western saddle*

stock split *n* **:** a division of corporate stock by the issuance to existing shareholders of a specified number of new shares with a corresponding lowering of par value for each outstanding share — compare STOCK DIVIDEND

stock–still \'stäk-'stil\ *adj* **:** very still **:** MOTIONLESS <stood ~>

stock·tak·ing \'stäk-ˌtā-kiŋ\ *n* **1 :** the action of checking or taking an inventory of goods or supplies on hand (as in a store) **2 :** the action of estimating a situation at a given moment

stocky \'stäk-ē\ *adj* **stock·i·er; -est :** compact, sturdy, and relatively thick in build — **stock·i·ly** \'stäk-ə-lē\ *adv* — **stock·i·ness** \'stäk-ē-nəs\ *n*

stock·yard \'stäk-ˌyärd\ *n* **:** a yard for stock; *specif* **:** one in which transient cattle, sheep, swine, or horses are kept temporarily for slaughter, market, or shipping

¹stodge \'stäj\ *vt* **stodged; stodg·ing** [origin unknown] **:** to stuff full esp. with food

²stodge *n* **:** a thick filling food (as oatmeal or stew)

stodgy \'stäj-ē\ *adj* **stodg·i·er; -est** [²*stodge*] **1 :** having a thick gluey consistency **:** HEAVY <~ bread> **2 :** moving in a slow plodding way esp. as a result of physical bulkiness **3 :** DULL, BORING <out on a peaceful rather ~ Sunday boat trip —Edna Ferber> **4 :** extremely old-fashioned **:** HIDEBOUND **5 a :** DRAB **b :** DOWDY — **stodg·i·ly** \'stäj-ə-lē\ *adv* — **stodg·i·ness** \'stäj-ē-nəs\ *n*

sto·gie *or* **sto·gy** \'stō-gē\ *n, pl* **stogies** [*Conestoga,* Pa.] **1 :** a stout coarse shoe **:** BROGAN **2 :** an inexpensive slender cylindrical cigar; *broadly* **:** CIGAR

¹sto·ic \'stō-ik\ *n* [ME, fr. L *stoicus,* fr. Gk *stōïkos,* lit., of the portico, fr. *Stoa* (*Poikilē*) the Painted Portico, portico at Athens where Zeno taught] **1** *cap* **:** a member of a school of philosophy founded by Zeno of Citium about 300 B.C. holding that the wise man should be free from passion, unmoved by joy or grief, and submissive to natural law **2 :** one apparently or professedly indifferent to pleasure or pain

²stoic *or* **sto·i·cal** \-i-kəl\ *adj* **1** *cap* **:** of, relating to, or resembling the Stoics or their doctrines <*Stoic* logic> **2 :** not affected by or showing passion or feeling; *esp* **:** firmly restraining response to pain or distress <a ~ indifference to cold> ***syn*** see IMPASSIVE — **sto·ical·ly** \-i-k(ə-)lē\ *adv*

stoi·chio·met·ric \ˌstȯi-kē-ō-'me-trik\ *adj* **:** of, relating to, used in, or marked by stoichiometry — **stoi·chio·met·ri·cal·ly** \-tri-k(ə-)lē\ *adv*

stoi·chi·om·e·try \ˌstȯi-kē-'äm-ə-trē\ *n* [Gk *stoicheion* element + E *-metry;* akin to Gk *stichos* row, *steichein* to walk, go — more at STAIR] **1 :** a branch of science that deals with the application of the laws of definite proportions and of the conservation of matter and energy to chemical activity **2 :** quantitative chemical properties and composition esp. as a factor in processes of chemical or physical change

sto·icism \'stō-ə-ˌsiz-əm\ *n* **1** *cap* **:** the philosophy of the Stoics **2 :** indifference to pleasure or pain **:** IMPASSIVENESS

stoke \'stōk\ *vb* **stoked; stok·ing** [D *stoken;* akin to MD *stuken* to push] *vt* **1 :** to poke or stir up (as a fire) **:** supply with fuel **2 :** to feed abundantly ~ *vi* **:** to stir up or tend a fire (as in a furnace) **:** supply a furnace with fuel

stoke·hold \'stōk-ˌhōld\ *n* **1 :** one of the spaces in front of the boilers of a ship from which the furnaces are fed **2 :** a room containing a ship's boilers — called also *fireroom*

stoke·hole \-ˌhōl\ *n* **1 :** the mouth to the grate of a furnace **2 :** STOKEHOLD

stok·er \'stō-kər\ *n* **1 :** one employed to tend a furnace and supply it with fuel; *specif* **:** one that tends a marine steam boiler **2 :** a machine for feeding a fire

Stokes' aster \'stōk-ˌsas-tər, ˌstōk-sə-'zas-\ *n* [Jonathan *Stokes*] **:** STOKESIA

stoke·sia \stō-'kē-zh(ē-)ə, 'stōk-sē-ə\ *n* [NL, genus name, fr. Jonathan *Stokes* †1831 E botanist] **:** a perennial composite herb (*Stokesia laevis*) of the southern U.S. often grown for its large showy heads of blue flowers

STOL *abbr* short takeoff and landing

¹stole \'stōl\ *past of* STEAL

²stole *n* [ME, fr. OE, fr. L *stola,* fr. Gk *stolē* equipment, robe, fr. *stellein* to set up, make ready — more at STALL] **1 :** a long loose garment **:** ROBE **2 :** an ecclesiastical vestment consisting of a long usu. silk band worn traditionally around the neck by bishops and priests and over the left shoulder by deacons — see VESTMENT illustration **3 :** a long wide scarf or similar covering worn by women usu. across the shoulders

stoled \'stōld\ *adj* **:** having or wearing a stole

stolen *past part of* STEAL

stol·id \'stäl-əd\ *adj* [L *stolidus* dull, stupid; akin to OHG *stal* place — more at STALL] **:** having or expressing little or no sensibility **:** UNEMOTIONAL ***syn*** see IMPASSIVE ***ant*** adroit — **sto·lid·i·ty** \stä-'lid-ət-ē, stə-\ *n* — **stol·id·ly** \'stäl-əd-lē\ *adv*

stol·len \'s(h)tō-lən, 's(h)tō-; 'stəl-ə(n)\ *n, pl* **stollen** *or* **stollens** [G] **:** a sweet yeast bread of German origin containing fruit and nuts

sto·lon \'stō-lən, -ˌlän\ *n* [NL *stolon-, stolo,* fr. L, branch, sucker; akin to Arm *steln* branch, OHG *stal* place — more at STALL] **1 a :** a horizontal branch from the base of a plant that produces new plants from buds at its tip or nodes (as in the strawberry) — called also *runner* **b :** a hypha (as of rhizopus) produced on the surface and connecting a group of conidiophores **2 :** an extension of the body wall (as of a hydrozoan) that develops buds giving rise to new zooids which usu. remain united by the stolon — **sto·lon·ate** \-lə-ˌnāt\ *adj*

sto·lon·if·er·ous \ˌstō-lə-'nif-(ə-)rəs\ *adj* **:** bearing or developing stolons — **sto·lon·if·er·ous·ly** *adv*

stom- *or* **stomo-** *comb form* [Gk & NL *stoma*] **:** mouth **:** stoma <*stom*odaeum>

sto·ma \'stō-mə\ *n, pl* **sto·ma·ta** \-mət-ə\ *also* **stomas** [NL, fr. Gk *stomat-, stoma* mouth] **1 :** any of various small simple bodily openings esp. in a lower animal **2 :** one of the minute openings in the epidermis of a plant organ (as a leaf) through which gaseous interchange takes place; *also* **:** the opening with its associated cellular structures **3 :** an artificial permanent opening esp. in the abdominal wall made in surgical procedures

¹stom·ach \'stəm-ək, -ik\ *n* [ME *stomak,* fr. MF *estomac,* fr. L *stomachus* gullet, esophagus, stomach, fr. Gk *stomachos,* fr. *stoma* mouth; akin to MBret *staffu* mouth, Av *staman-*] **1 a :** a dilatation of the alimentary canal of a vertebrate communicating anteriorly with the esophagus and posteriorly with the duodenum **b :** a cavity in an invertebrate animal that is analogous to a stomach **c :** the part of the body that contains the stomach **:** BELLY, ABDOMEN **2 a :** desire for food caused by hunger **:** APPETITE **b :** INCLINATION, DESIRE <had no ~ for an argument> **3** *obs* **a :** SPIRIT, VALOR **b :** PRIDE **c :** SPLEEN, RESENTMENT

²stomach *vt* **1** *archaic* **:** to take offense at **2 :** to bear without overt reaction or resentment **:** BROOK <couldn't ~ her attitude>

stom·ach·ache \-ˌāk\ *n* **:** pain in or in the region of the stomach

stom·ach·er \'stəm-i-kər, -i-chər\ *n* **:** the center front section of a waist or underwaist or a usu. heavily embroidered or jeweled separate piece for the center front of a bodice worn by men and women in the 15th and 16th centuries

sto·mach·ic \stə-'mak-ik\ *adj* **1 :** of or relating to the stomach <~ vessels> **2 :** stimulating the function of the stomach — **stomachic** *n* — **sto·mach·i·cal·ly** \-i-k(ə-)lē\ *adv*

stom·achy \'stəm-ək-ē, -ik-\ *adj* **1** *dial Brit* **:** IRASCIBLE, IRRITABLE **2 :** having a large stomach

sto·mal \'stō-məl\ *adj* **:** STOMATAL

stomat- *or* **stomato-** *comb form* [NL, fr. Gk, fr. *stomat-, stoma*] **:** mouth **:** stoma <*stomat*itis> <*stomato*logy>

sto·ma·tal \'stōm-ət-ᵊl\ *adj* **:** of, relating to, or constituting a stoma <~ openings> <~ behavior of bean plants>

sto·mate \'stō-ˌmāt\ *n* [irreg. fr. NL *stomat-, stoma*] **:** STOMA 2

sto·ma·ti·tis \ˌstō-mə-'tīt-əs\ *n, pl* **-tit·i·des** \-'tit-ə-ˌdēz\ *or* **-ti·tises** \-'tīt-ə-səz\ [NL] **:** any of numerous inflammatory diseases of the mouth

sto·ma·tol·o·gy \ˌstō-mə-'täl-ə-jē\ *n* [ISV] **:** a branch of medical science dealing with the mouth and its disorders — **sto·ma·to·log·i-**

ə abut	ᵊ kitten	ər further	a back	ā bake	ä cot, cart
aù out	ch chin	e less	ē easy	g gift	i trip	ī life
j joke	ŋ sing	ō flow	ȯ flaw	ȯi coin	th thin	t͟h this
ü loot	ù foot	y yet	yü few	yù furious	zh vision

cal \ˌstō-mət-ᵊl-ˈäj-i-kəl\ *also* **sto·ma·to·log·ic** \-ik\ *adj* — **sto·ma·tol·o·gist** \ˌstō-mə-ˈtäl-ə-jəst\ *n*

sto·mato·pod \stō-ˈmat-ə-ˌpäd\ *n* [NL *Stomatopoda,* order name, fr. *stomat-* + *-poda*] **:** any of an order (Stomatopoda) of marine crustaceans (as a squilla) that have gills on the abdominal appendages — **stomatopod** *adj*

sto·mo·dae·um *or* **sto·mo·de·um** \ˌstō-mə-ˈdē-əm\ *n, pl* **-daea** \-ˈdē-ə\ *also* **-dae·ums** *or* **-dea** *also* **-de·ums** [NL, fr. *stom-* + Gk *hodaion,* neut. of *hodaios* being on the way, fr. *hodos* way — more at CEDE] **:** the anterior ectodermal part of the alimentary canal or tract — **sto·mo·dae·al** *or* **sto·mo·de·al** \-ˈdē-əl\ *adj*

[1]stomp \ˈstämp, ˈstȯmp\ *vb* **:** STAMP

[2]stomp *n* **1 :** STAMP 4 **2 :** a jazz dance characterized by heavy stamping

-s·to·my \s-tə-mē\ *n comb form* [ISV, fr. Gk *stoma* mouth, opening] **:** surgical operation establishing a usu. permanent opening into (such) a part <entero*stomy*> or between (such) parts <gastroduodeno*stomy*>

[1]stone \ˈstōn\ *n* [ME, fr. OE *stān;* akin to OHG *stein* stone, Gk *stear* hard fat] **1 :** a concretion of earthy or mineral matter: **a** (1) **:** such a concretion of indeterminate size or shape (2) **:** ROCK **b :** a piece of rock for a specified function: as (1) **:** a building block (2) **:** a paving block (3) **:** a precious stone **:** GEM (4) **:** GRAVESTONE (5) **:** GRINDSTONE (6) **:** WHETSTONE (7) **:** a stand or table with a smooth flat top on which to impose or set type (8) **:** a surface upon which a drawing, text, or design to be lithographed is drawn or transferred **c :** CALCULUS 1 **2 :** something resembling a small stone: as **a :** the hard central portion of a drupaceous fruit (as a peach) **b :** a hard stony seed (as of a date) **3** *pl usu* **stone :** any of various units of weight; *esp* **:** an official British unit equal to 14 pounds **4 a :** CURLING STONE **b :** a round playing piece used in various games (as backgammon or go)

[2]stone *vt* **stoned; ston·ing 1 :** to hurl stones at; *esp* **:** to kill by pelting with stones **2** *obs* **:** to make hard or insensitive to feeling **3 :** to face, pave, or fortify with stones **4 :** to remove the stones or seeds of (a fruit) **5 a :** to rub, scour, or polish with a stone **b :** to sharpen with a whetstone — **ston·er** *n*

[3]stone *adj* **:** of, relating to, or made of stone

stone- *comb form* [[1]*stone* (in such combinations as *stone-blind*)] **:** completely <*stone*-broke>

Stone Age *n* **:** the first known period of prehistoric human culture characterized by the use of stone tools

stone–blind \ˈstōn-ˈblīnd\ *adj* **:** totally blind — **stone–blind·ness** \-ˈblīn(d)-nəs\ *n*

stone–broke \-ˈbrōk\ *adj* **:** completely broke **:** lacking funds

stone canal *n* **:** a tube in many echinoderms that contains calcareous deposits and leads from the ring of the water-vascular system surrounding the mouth to the madreporite

stone cell *n* **:** a more or less spherical sclereid <*stone cells* provide the gritty texture of pears>

stone·chat \-ˌchat\ *n* **:** a common European songbird (*Saxicola torquata*); *also* **:** any of various related birds (genus *Saxicola*)

stone china *n* **:** a hard dense opaque feldspathic pottery developed in England; *broadly* **:** IRONSTONE CHINA

stone–cold \ˈstōn-ˈkōld\ *adj* **:** completely cold **:** lacking warmth

stone·crop \ˈstōn-ˌkräp\ *n* **1 :** SEDUM; *esp* **:** a mossy evergreen creeping sedum (*Sedum acre*) with pungent fleshy leaves **2 :** any of various plants of the orpine family related to the sedums

stone·cut·ter \-ˌkət-ər\ *n* **1 :** one that cuts, carves, or dresses stone **2 :** a machine for dressing stone — **stone·cut·ting** \-ˌkət-iŋ\ *n*

stoned \ˈstōnd\ *adj* **1 :** DRUNK **2 :** being under the influence of a drug taken esp. for pleasure

stone–dead \ˈstōn-ˈded\ *adj* **:** LIFELESS

stone–deaf \-ˈdef\ *adj* **:** totally deaf — **stone–deaf·ness** *n*

stone·fish \ˈstōn-ˌfish\ *n* **:** any of several small spiny venomous scorpion fishes (esp. genus *Synanceja*) common about coral reefs of the tropical Indo-Pacific

stone fly *n* **:** an insect (order Plecoptera) with an aquatic carnivorous nymph having gills and an adult used by anglers for bait

stone fruit *n* **:** a fruit with a stony endocarp **:** DRUPE

stone–ground \ˈstōn-ˈgrau̇nd\ *adj* **:** ground in a buhrstone mill <~ flour>

stone lily *n* **:** a fossil crinoid

stone·ma·son \ˈstōn-ˌmās-ᵊn\ *n* **:** a mason who builds with stone — **stone·ma·son·ry** \-rē\ *n*

stone parsley *n* **:** a slender herb (*Sison amomum*) of the carrot family with aromatic seeds that are used as a condiment

stone roller *n* **1 :** HOG SUCKER **2 :** a common American cyprinid fish (*Campostoma anomalum*) found chiefly in clear streams of the central U.S.

stone·wall \ˈstōn-ˈwȯl\ *vi, chiefly Brit* **:** to engage in obstructive parliamentary debate or delaying tactics — **stone·wall·er** *n*

stone wall *n* **1** *chiefly North* **:** a fence made of stones; *esp* **:** one built of rough stones without mortar to enclose a field **2 :** an immovable block or obstruction (as in public affairs)

stone·ware \-ˌwa(ə)r, -ˌwe(ə)r\ *n* **:** a strong opaque ceramic ware that is high-fired, well vitrified, and nonporous

stone·work \-ˌwərk\ *n* **1 :** a structure or part built of stone **:** MASONRY **2 :** the shaping, preparation, or setting of stone

stone·work·er \-ˌwər-kər\ *n* **:** STONECUTTER 1

stone·wort \-ˌwərt, -ˌwȯ(ə)rt\ *n* **:** any of a family (Characeae) of freshwater green algae resembling the horsetails and often encrusted with calcareous deposits

stony *also* **ston·ey** \ˈstō-nē\ *adj* **ston·i·er; -est 1 :** abounding in or having the nature of stone **:** ROCKY **2 a :** insensitive to pity or human feeling **b :** manifesting no movement or reaction **:** DUMB, EXPRESSIONLESS **c :** fearfully gripping **:** PETRIFYING **3** *archaic* **:** consisting of or made of stones **4 :** STONE-BROKE — **ston·i·ly** \ˈstōn-ᵊl-ē\ *adv* — **ston·i·ness** \ˈstō-nē-nəs\ *n*

stony·heart·ed \ˌstō-nē-ˈhärt-əd\ *adj* **:** UNFEELING, CRUEL — **stony·heart·ed·ness** *n*

stood *past of* STAND

[1]stooge \ˈstüj\ *n* [origin unknown] **1 :** STRAIGHT MAN **2 a :** one who plays a subordinate or compliant role to a principal **b :** PUPPET 3 **3 :** STOOL PIGEON

[2]stooge *vi* **stooged; stoog·ing :** to act as a stooge <congressmen who ~ for the oil and mineral interests —*New Republic*>

[1]stool \ˈstül\ *n* [ME, fr. OE *stōl;* akin to OHG *stuol* chair, OSlav *stolŭ* seat, throne, OE *standan* to stand] **1 a :** a seat usu. without back or arms supported by three or four legs or by a central pedestal **b :** a low bench or portable support for the feet or knees **:** FOOTSTOOL **2 :** a seat used as a symbol of office or authority; *also* **:** the rank, dignity, office, or rule of a chieftain **3 a :** a seat used while defecating or urinating **b :** a discharge of fecal matter **4 a :** a stump or group of stumps of a tree esp. when producing suckers **b :** a plant crown from which shoots grow out **c :** a shoot or growth from a stool **5 :** STOOL PIGEON — **fall between two stools :** to fail because of inability to choose between or reconcile two alternative or conflicting courses of action

[2]stool *vi* **:** to throw out shoots in the manner of a stool

stool·ie \ˈstü-lē\ *n* **:** STOOL PIGEON

stool pigeon *n* [prob. fr. the early practice of fastening the decoy bird to a stool] **1 :** a pigeon used as a decoy to draw others within a net **2 :** a person acting as a decoy or informer; *esp* **:** a spy sent into a group to report (as to the police) on its activities

[1]stoop \ˈstüp\ *vb* [ME *stoupen,* fr. OE *stūpian;* akin to OE *stēap* steep, deep — more at STEEP] *vi* **1 a :** to bend the body forward and downward sometimes simultaneously bending the knees **b :** to stand or walk with a temporary or habitual forward inclination of the head, body, or shoulders **2 :** YIELD, SUBMIT **3 a :** to descend from a superior rank, dignity, or status **b :** to lower oneself morally **4 a** *archaic* **:** to move down from a height **:** ALIGHT **b :** to fly or dive down swiftly usu. to attack prey ~ *vt* **1 :** DEBASE, DEGRADE **2 :** to bend (a part of the body) forward and downward

syn STOOP, CONDESCEND, DEIGN *shared meaning element* **:** to descend from one's level (as of rank or dignity) usu. to do something

[2]stoop *n* **1 a :** an act of bending the body forward **b :** a temporary or habitual forward bend of the back and shoulders **2 :** the descent of a bird esp. on its prey **3 :** a lowering of oneself

[3]stoop *n* [D *stoep;* akin to OE *stæpe* step — more at STEP] **:** a porch, platform, entrance stairway, or small veranda at a house door

stoop·ball \ˈstüp-ˌbȯl\ *n* **:** a variation of baseball in which a player throws a ball against a stoop or building and runs to base while other players attempt to retrieve the rebound and put him out

stoop crop *n* **:** a crop (as of a vegetable) that requires extensive hand labor and stooping in cultivating and harvesting

stoop labor *n* **1 :** the work required or done in cultivating or harvesting a stoop crop **2 :** workers employed to cultivate or harvest stoop crops

[1]stop \ˈstäp\ *vb* **stopped; stop·ping** [ME *stoppen,* fr. OE *-stoppian;* akin to OHG *stopfōn* to stop, stuff; both fr. a prehistoric WGmc word borrowed fr. (assumed) VL *stuppare* to stop with tow, fr. L *stuppa* tow, fr. Gk *styppē*] *vt* **1 a :** to close by filling or obstructing **b :** to hinder or prevent the passage of **c :** to get in the way of **:** be wounded or killed by <easy to ~ a bullet along a lonely . . . road —Harvey Fergusson> **2 a :** to close up or block off (an opening) **:** PLUG **b :** to make impassable **:** CHOKE, OBSTRUCT **c :** to cover over or fill in (a hole or crevice) **3 a :** to cause to give up or change a course of action **b :** to hold back **:** RESTRAIN, PREVENT **4 a :** to cause to cease **:** CHECK, SUPPRESS **b :** DISCONTINUE **5 a :** to deduct or withhold (a sum due) **b :** to instruct one's bank not to honor or pay **6 a :** to arrest the progress or motion of **:** cause to halt <*stopped* the car> **b :** PARRY **c :** to check by means of a weapon **:** bring down **:** KILL **d :** to beat in a prizefight by a knockout; *broadly* **:** DEFEAT **e :** BAFFLE, NONPLUS **7 :** to change the pitch of (as a violin string) by pressing with the finger or (as a wind instrument) by closing one or more finger holes or by thrusting the hand or a mute into the bell **8 :** to hold an honor card and enough protecting cards to be able to block (a bridge suit) before an opponent can run many tricks ~ *vi* **1 a :** to cease activity or operation **b :** to come to an end esp. suddenly **:** CLOSE, FINISH **2 a :** to cease to move on **:** HALT **b :** PAUSE, HESITATE **3 a :** to break one's journey **:** STAY **b** *chiefly Brit* **:** REMAIN **c :** to make a brief call **:** drop in **4 :** to become choked **:** CLOG — **stop·pa·ble** \ˈstäp-ə-bəl\ *adj*

syn STOP, CEASE, QUIT, DISCONTINUE, DESIST *shared meaning element* **:** to suspend or cause to suspend activity

[2]stop *n* **1 a :** CESSATION, END **b :** a pause or breaking off in speech **2 a** (1) **:** a graduated set of organ pipes of similar design and tone quality (2) **:** a corresponding set of vibrators or reeds of a reed organ (3) **:** STOP KNOB **b :** a means of regulating the pitch of a musical instrument **3 a :** something that impedes, obstructs, or brings to a halt **:** IMPEDIMENT, OBSTACLE **b :** the aperture of a camera lens; *also* **:** a marking of a series (as of f-numbers) on a camera for indicating settings of the diaphragm **c :** a drain plug **:** STOPPER **4 :** a device for arresting or limiting motion **5 :** the act of stopping **:** the state of being stopped **:** CHECK **6 a :** a halt in a journey **:** STAY <made a brief ~ to refuel> **b :** a stopping place <a bus ~> **7 a** *chiefly Brit* **:** any of several punctuation marks **b** — used in telegrams and cables to indicate a period **c :** a pause or break in a verse that marks the end of a grammatical unit **8 a :** an order stopping payment (as of a check or note) by a bank **b :** STOP ORDER **9 :** a consonant in the articulation of which there is a stage (as in the *p* of *apt* or the *g* of *tiger*) when the breath passage is completely closed **10 :** a depression in the face of an animal at the junction of forehead and foreface — see DOG illustration

[3]stop *adj* **:** serving to stop **:** designed to stop <~ line> <~ signal>

stop–and–go \ˌstäp-ən-ˈgō, -ᵊm-, *attrib* -ˌgō\ *adj* **:** of, relating to, or involving frequent stops; *esp* **:** controlled or regulated by traffic lights <~ driving>

stop bath *n* **:** an acid bath used to check photographic development of a negative or print

stop·cock \ˈstäp-ˌkäk\ *n* **:** a cock for stopping or regulating flow (as through a pipe)

stop down *vt* : to reduce the effective aperture of (a lens) by means of a diaphragm

1stope \ˈstōp\ *n* [prob. fr. LG *stope,* lit., step; akin to OE *stæpe* step — more at STEP] : a usu. steplike excavation underground for the removal of ore that is formed as the ore is mined in successive layers

2stope *vb* **stoped; stop·ing** *vi* : to mine by means of a stope ~ *vt* : to extract (ore) from a stope — **stop·er** *n*

stop·gap \ˈstäp-ˌgap\ *n* : something that serves as a temporary expedient : MAKESHIFT ***syn*** see RESOURCE

stop knob *n* : one of the handles by which an organist draws or shuts off a particular stop

stop·light \ˈstäp-ˌlīt\ *n* **1** : a light on the rear of a motor vehicle that is illuminated when the driver presses the brake pedal **2** : TRAFFIC SIGNAL

stop order *n* : an order to a broker to buy or sell respectively at the market when the price of a security advances or declines to a designated level

stop·over \ˈstäp-ˌō-vər\ *n* **1** : a stop at an intermediate point in one's journey **2** : a stopping place on a journey

stop·page \ˈstäp-ij\ *n* : the act of stopping : the state of being stopped : HALT, OBSTRUCTION

stop payment *n* : a depositor's order to a bank to refuse to honor a specified check drawn by him

1stop·per \ˈstäp-ər\ *n* **1** : one that brings to a halt or causes to stop operating or functioning : CHECK: as **a** : a playing card that will stop the run of a suit **b** : a baseball pitcher depended on to win important games or to stop a losing streak; *also* : an effective relief pitcher **2** : one that closes, shuts, or fills up; *specif* : something (as a bung or cork) used to plug an opening

2stopper *vt* **stop·pered; stop·per·ing** \-(ə-)riŋ\ : to close or secure with or as if with a stopper

stopper knot *n* : a knot used to prevent a rope from passing through a hole or opening

1stop·ple \ˈstäp-əl\ *n* [ME *stoppell,* fr. *stoppen* to stop] : something that closes an aperture : STOPPER, PLUG

2stopple *vt* **stop·pled; stop·pling** \-(ə-)liŋ\ : STOPPER

stop street *n* : a street on which a vehicle must stop just before entering a through street

stop·watch \ˈstäp-ˌwäch\ *n* : a watch having a hand that can be started and stopped at will for exact timing (as of a race)

stor *abbr* storage

stor·age \ˈstōr-ij, ˈstȯr-\ *n* **1 a** : space or a place for storing **b** : an amount stored **c** : MEMORY 4 **2 a** : the act of storing : the state of being stored; *specif* : the safekeeping of goods in a depository (as a warehouse) **b** : the price charged for keeping goods in a storehouse **3** : the production by means of electric energy of chemical reactions that when allowed to reverse themselves generate electricity again without serious loss

storage cell *n* : a cell or connected group of cells that converts chemical energy into electrical energy by reversible chemical reactions and that may be recharged by passing a current through it in the direction opposite to that of its discharge — called also *storage battery*

sto·rax \ˈstō(ə)r-ˌaks, ˈstȯ(ə)r-\ *n* [ME, fr. LL, alter. of L *styrax,* fr. Gk] **1 a** : a fragrant balsam obtained from the bark of an Asiatic tree (*Liquidambar orientalis*) of the witch-hazel family that is used as an expectorant and sometimes in perfumery — called also *Levant storax* **b** : a balsam from the sweet gum that is similar to storax **2** : any of a genus (*Styrax* of the family Styracaceae, the storax family) of trees or shrubs with usu. hairy leaves and flowers in drooping racemes — compare BENZOIN

1store \ˈstō(ə)r, ˈstȯ(ə)r\ *vt* **stored; stor·ing** [ME *storen,* fr. OF *estorer* to construct, restore, store, fr. L *instaurare* to renew, restore, fr. *in-* + *-staurare* (akin to Gk *stauros* stake) — more at STEER] **1** : FURNISH, SUPPLY; *esp* : to stock against a future time <~ a ship with provisions> **2** : to lay away : ACCUMULATE <~ vegetables for winter use> <an organism that absorbs and ~*s* DDT> **3** : to place or leave in a location (as a warehouse, library, or computer memory) for preservation or later use or disposal **4** : to provide storage room for : HOLD <elevators for *storing* surplus wheat> — **stor·able** \ˈstōr-ə-bəl, ˈstȯr-\ *adj*

2store *n* **1 a** : something that is stored or kept for future use **b** *pl* : articles (as of food) accumulated for some specific object and drawn upon as needed : STOCK, SUPPLIES **c** : something that is accumulated **d** : a source from which things may be drawn as needed : a reserve fund **2** : STORAGE — usu. used with *in* <when placing eggs in ~ —*Dublin Sunday Independent*> **3** : a large quantity, supply, or number : ABUNDANCE **4 a** : STOREHOUSE, WAREHOUSE **b** *chiefly Brit* : MEMORY 4 **5** : a business establishment where usu. diversified goods are kept for retail sale <grocery ~> — compare SHOP — **in store** : in a state of imminence

3store *adj* **1** *or* **stores** : of, relating to, kept in, or used for a store **2** : purchased from a store as opposed to natural or homemade : MANUFACTURED, READY-MADE <~ clothes> <~ bread>

store–bought \ˈstō(ə)r-ˌbȯt, ˈstȯ(ə)r-\ *adj* : STORE 2 <~ clothes>

store cheese *n* [fr. its being a staple article stocked in grocery stores] : CHEDDAR

1store·front \ˈstō(ə)r-ˌfrənt, ˈstȯ(ə)r-\ *n* **1** : the front side of a store or store building facing a street **2** : a building, room, or suite of rooms having a storefront

2storefront *adj* **1** : occupying a room or suite of rooms in a store building at street level and immediately behind a storefront <a ~ school> **2** : of, relating to, or characteristic of a storefront church <a ~ evangelist>

storefront church *n* : a city church that utilizes storefront quarters as a meeting place and that usu. holds services of a highly emotional nature

store·house \ˈstō(ə)r-ˌhau̇s, ˈstȯ(ə)r-\ *n* **1** : a building for storing goods (as provisions) : MAGAZINE, WAREHOUSE **2** : an abundant supply or source : REPOSITORY

store·keep·er \-ˌkē-pər\ *n* **1** : one that has charge of supplies (as military stores) **2** : one that operates a retail store

store·room \-ˌrüm, -ˌru̇m\ *n* **1** : a room or space for the storing of goods or supplies **2** : STOREHOUSE 2

store·ship \-ˌship\ *n* : a ship used to carry supplies

store·wide \-ˈwīd\ *adj* : including all or most merchandise in a store <a ~ sale>

1sto·ried \ˈstōr-ēd, ˈstȯr-\ *adj* **1** : decorated with designs representing scenes from story or history <a ~ frieze> <a ~ tapestry> **2** : having an interesting history : celebrated in story or history

2storied *or* **sto·reyed** \ˈstōr-ēd, ˈstȯr-\ *adj* : having stories <a two-*storied* house>

stork \ˈstȯ(ə)rk\ *n* [ME, fr. OE *storc;* akin to OHG *storah* stork, OE *stearc* stiff — more at STARK] : any of various large mostly Old World wading birds (family Ciconiidae) that have long stout bills and are related to the ibises and herons

storks·bill \ˈstȯrks-ˌbil\ *n* : any of several plants of the geranium family with elongate beaked fruits; *esp* : PELARGONIUM

1storm \ˈstȯ(ə)rm\ *n, often attrib* [ME, fr. OE; akin to OHG *sturm* storm, OE *styrian* to stir] **1 a** : a disturbance of the atmosphere marked by wind and usu. by rain, snow, hail, sleet, or thunder and lightning **b** : a heavy fall of rain, snow, or hail **c (1)** : wind having a speed of 64 to 72 miles per hour **(2)** : WHOLE GALE — see BEAUFORT SCALE table **d** : a serious disturbance of any element of nature **2** : a disturbed or agitated state : a sudden or violent commotion **3 a** : PAROXYSM, CRISIS **b** : a sudden heavy influx or onset **4** : a heavy discharge of objects (as missiles) **5** : a tumultuous outburst **6** : a violent assault on a defended position — **by storm** : by or as if by employing a bold swift frontal movement esp. with the intent of defeating or winning over quickly

2storm *vi* **1 a** : to blow with violence **b** : to rain, hail, snow, or sleet **2** : to attack by storm <~*ed* ashore at zero hour> **3** : to be in or to exhibit a violent passion : RAGE <~*ing* at the unusual delay> **4** : to rush about or move impetuously, violently, or angrily <the mob ~*ed* through the streets> ~ *vt* : to attack, take, or win over by storm <~ a fort> ***syn*** see ATTACK

storm and stress *n, often cap both Ss* : STURM UND DRANG

storm boat *n* : a light fast craft used to transport attacking troops across streams

storm·bound \ˈstȯ(ə)rm-ˈbau̇nd\ *adj* : cut off from outside communication by a storm or its effects : stopped or delayed by storms

storm cellar *n* : CYCLONE CELLAR

storm door *n* : an additional door placed outside an ordinary outside door for protection against severe weather

storm petrel *n* : any of various small petrels; *esp* : a small sooty black white-marked petrel (*Hydrobates pelagicus*) frequenting the north Atlantic and Mediterranean

storm trooper *n* **1** : a member of a private Nazi army notorious for aggressiveness, violence, and brutality **2** : one that resembles a Nazi storm trooper

storm window *n* : a sash placed outside an ordinary window as a protection against severe weather — called also *storm sash*

stormy \ˈstȯr-mē\ *adj* **storm·i·er; -est** **1** : relating to, characterized by, or indicative of a storm <a ~ day> <a ~ autumn> **2** : marked by turmoil or fury <a ~ life> <a ~ conference> — **storm·i·ly** \ˈstȯr-mə-lē\ *adv* — **storm·i·ness** \-mē-nəs\ *n*

stormy petrel *n* **1** : STORM PETREL **2 a** : one fond of strife **b** : a harbinger of trouble

1sto·ry \ˈstōr-ē, ˈstȯr-\ *n, pl* **stories** [ME *storie,* fr. OF *estorie,* fr. L *historia*] **1** *archaic* : HISTORY 1,3 **2 a** : an account of incidents or events **b** : a statement regarding the facts pertinent to a situation in question **c** : ANECDOTE; *esp* : an amusing one **3 a** : a fictional narrative shorter than a novel; *specif* : SHORT STORY **b** : the intrigue or plot of a narrative or dramatic work **4** : a widely circulated rumor **5** : LIE, FALSEHOOD **6** : LEGEND, ROMANCE **7** : a news article or broadcast

2story *vt* **sto·ried; sto·ry·ing** **1** *archaic* : to narrate or describe in story **2** : to adorn with a story or a scene from history

3story *also* **sto·rey** \ˈstōr-ē, ˈstȯr-ē\ *n, pl* **stories** *also* **storeys** [ME *storie,* fr. ML *historia* picture, story of a building, fr. L, history, tale; prob. fr. pictures adorning the windows of medieval buildings] **1** : a set of rooms on one floor level of a building **2** : a horizontal division of a building's exterior not necessarily corresponding exactly with the stories within

sto·ry·board \-ˌbō(ə)rd, -ˌbȯ(ə)rd\ *n* : a panel or series of panels on which is tacked a set of small rough drawings depicting consecutively the important changes of scene and action in a planned film or television show or act

1sto·ry·book \-ˌbu̇k\ *n* : a book of stories <~*s* for children>

2storybook *adj* : FAIRY-TALE

story line *n* : the plot of a story or play

sto·ry·tell·er \ˈstōr-ē-ˌtel-ər, ˈstȯr-\ *n* : a teller of stories: as **a** : a relator of anecdotes **b** : a reciter of tales (as in a children's library) **c** : LIAR, FIBBER **d** : a writer of stories

sto·ry·writ·er \-ˌrīt-ər\ *n* : a writer of stories

stoss \ˈstäs, ˈstȯs, ˈs(h)tōs\ *adj* [G *stoss-,* fr. *stossen* to push; akin to L *tundere* to beat — more at STINT] : facing toward the direction from which an overriding glacier impinges <the ~ slope of a hill>

sto·tin·ka \stō-ˈtiŋ-kə, stə-\ *n, pl* **-tin·ki** \-kē\ [Bulg] — see *lev* at MONEY table

stound \ˈstau̇nd, ˈstünd\ *n* [ME, fr. OE *stund;* akin to OHG *stunta* time, hour, OE *standan* to stand] *archaic* : TIME, WHILE

stoup \ˈstüp\ *n* [ME *stowp,* prob. of Scand origin; akin to ON *staup* cup — more at STEEP] **1** : a container for beverages: as **a** : a large glass **b** : TANKARD **c** : FLAGON **2** : a basin at the entrance of a church for holy water

1stour \ˈstu̇(ə)r\ *adj* [ME *stor,* fr. OE *stōr;* akin to OHG *stuori* large, Russ *staryĭ* old, OE *standan* to stand] **1** *chiefly Scot* : STRONG, HARDY **2** *chiefly Scot* : STERN, HARSH

[2]**stour** *n* [ME, fr. OF *estour*, of Gmc origin; akin to OHG *sturm* storm, battle — more at STORM] 1 a *archaic* : BATTLE, CONFLICT b *dial Brit* : TUMULT, UPROAR 2 *chiefly Scot* : DUST, POWDER

[1]**stout** \'stau̇t\ *adj* [ME, fr. OF *estout*, of Gmc origin; akin to OHG *stolz* proud] 1 : strong of character: as a : BRAVE, BOLD b : FIRM, DETERMINED; *also* : OBSTINATE, UNCOMPROMISING 2 : physically or materially strong: a : STURDY, VIGOROUS b : STAUNCH, ENDURING c : SOLID, SUBSTANTIAL 3 : FORCEFUL <a ~ attack>; *also* : VIOLENT <a ~ wind> 4 : bulky in body : FAT ***syn*** see STRONG — **stout·ish** \-ish\ *adj* — **stout·ly** *adv* — **stout·ness** *n*

[2]**stout** *n* 1 : a heavy-bodied brew that is darker and sweeter than porter and is made with roasted malt and a relatively high percentage of hops 2 a : a fat person b : a clothing size designed for the large figure

stout·en \'stau̇t-ᵊn\ *vb* **stout·ened; stout·en·ing** \'stau̇t-niŋ, -ᵊn-iŋ\ *vt* : to make stout <~ a resolve> ~ *vi* : to become stout

stout·heart·ed \'stau̇t-'härt-əd\ *adj* : having a stout heart or spirit: a : COURAGEOUS b : STUBBORN <hearken unto me, ye ~, that are far from righteousness —Isa 46:12 (AV)> — **stout·heart·ed·ly** *adv* — **stout·heart·ed·ness** *n*

[1]**stove** \'stōv\ *n* [ME, fr. MD or MLG, heated room, steam room; akin to OHG *stuba* heated room, steam room; both fr. a prehistoric WGmc-NGmc word borrowed fr. (assumed) VL *extufa*, deriv. of L *ex-* + Gk *typhein* to smoke — more at DEAF] 1 a : a portable or fixed apparatus that burns fuel or uses electricity to provide heat (as for cooking or heating) b : a device that generates heat for special purposes (as for heating tools or heating air for a hot blast) c : KILN 2 *chiefly Brit* : a hothouse esp. for the cultivation of tropical exotics; *broadly* : GREENHOUSE

[2]**stove** *past of* STAVE

stove·pipe \'stōv-ˌpīp\ *n* 1 : pipe of large diameter usu. of sheet steel used as a stove chimney or to connect a stove with a flue 2 : a tall silk hat

sto·ver \'stō-vər\ *n* [ME, modif. of AF *estovers* necessary supplies, fr. OF *estoveir* to be necessary, fr. L *est opus* there is need] 1 *chiefly dial Eng* : FODDER 2 : mature cured stalks of grain with the ears removed that are used as feed for livestock

stow \'stō\ *vt* [ME *stowen* to place, fr. *stowe* place, fr. OE *stōw*; akin to OFris *stō* place, Gk *stylos* pillar — more at STEER] 1 : HOUSE, LODGE 2 a : to put away : STORE b *obs* : to lock up for safekeeping : CONFINE 3 a : to dispose in an orderly fashion : ARRANGE, PACK b : LOAD 4 *slang* : to put aside : STOP 5 a *archaic* : CROWD b : to cram in (food) — usu. used with *away* <~*ed* away a huge dinner>

stow·age \-ij\ *n* 1 a : an act or process of stowing b : goods in storage or to be stowed 2 a : storage capacity b : a place or receptacle for storage 3 : the state of being stored

stow·away \'stō-ə-ˌwā\ *n* : one that stows away

stow away \ˌstō-ə-'wā\ *vi* : to secrete oneself aboard a vehicle as a means of obtaining transportation

[1]**STP** \ˌes-ˌtē-'pē\ *n* [fr. *STP*, a trademark for a motor fuel additive to which it is likened in its effects] : a psychedelic drug chemically related to mescaline and amphetamine

[2]**STP** *abbr* standard temperature and pressure

str *abbr* 1 steamer 2 strophe

STR *abbr* submarine thermal reactor

stra·bis·mus \strə-'biz-məs\ *n* [NL, fr. Gk *strabismos* condition of squinting, fr. *strabizein* to squint, fr. *strabos* squint-eyed; akin to Gk *strephein* to twist — more at STROPHE] : inability of one eye to attain binocular vision with the other because of imbalance of the muscles of the eyeball — called also *squint* — **stra·bis·mic** \-mik\ *adj*

[1]**strad·dle** \'strad-ᵊl\ *vb* **strad·dled; strad·dling** \'strad-liŋ, -ᵊl-iŋ\ [irreg. fr. *stride*] *vi* 1 : to stand, sit, or walk with the legs wide apart; *esp* : to sit astride 2 : to spread out irregularly : SPRAWL 3 : to be noncommittal : favor or seem to favor two apparently opposite sides 4 : to buy in one market and sell short in another ~ *vt* 1 : to stand, sit, or be astride of <~ a horse> 2 : to be noncommittal in regard to <~ an issue> — **strad·dler** \-lər, -ᵊl-ər\ *n* — **straddle the fence** : to be in a position of neutrality or indecision

[2]**straddle** *n* 1 : the act or position of one who straddles 2 : a noncommittal or equivocal position 3 a : an option giving the holder the double privilege of a put and a call b : the state of being long in one market and short in another

Stra·di·va·ri \ˌstrad-ə-'vär-ē, -'var-, -'ver-\ *n* : STRADIVARIUS

Strad·i·var·i·us \ˌstrad-ə-'var-ē-əs, -'ver-\ *n, pl* **-var·ii** \-ē-ˌī\ [latinized form of Stradivari] : a stringed instrument (as a violin) made by Antonio Stradivari of Cremona

strafe \'strāf, *esp Brit* 'sträf\ *vt* **strafed; straf·ing** [G *Gott strafe England* God punish England, slogan of the Germans in World War I] : to rake (as ground troops) with fire at close range and esp. with machine-gun fire from low-flying aircraft — **strafe** *n* — **straf·er** *n*

[1]**strag·gle** \'strag-əl\ *vi* **strag·gled; strag·gling** \-(ə-)liŋ\ [ME *straglen*] 1 : to wander from the direct course or way : ROVE, STRAY 2 : to trail off from others of its kind <little cabins *straggling* off into the woods> — **strag·gler** \-(ə-)lər\ *n*

[2]**straggle** *n* : a straggling group (as of persons or objects)

strag·gly \'strag-(ə-)lē\ *adj* **strag·gli·er; -est** : spread out or scattered irregularly <a ~ beard>

[1]**straight** \'strāt\ *adj* [ME *streght, straight*, fr. pp. of *strecchen* to stretch] 1 a : free from curves, bends, angles, or irregularities <~ hair> <~ timber> <a ~ stream> b : generated by a point moving continuously in the same direction and expressed by a linear equation <a ~ line> <the ~ segment of a curve> 2 : DIRECT, UNINTERRUPTED: as a : lying along or holding to a direct or proper course or method <a ~ thinker> b : CANDID, FRANK <gave me a ~ answer> c : coming directly from a trustworthy source <a ~ tip on the horses> d (1) : having the elements in an order <the ~ sequence of events> (2) : CONSECUTIVE <12 ~ days> e : having the cylinders arranged in a single straight line <a ~ eight-cylinder engine> f : UPRIGHT, VERTICAL <the picture isn't quite ~> 3 a : exhibiting honesty and fairness <~ dealing> b : properly ordered or arranged <set the kitchen ~> <set us ~ on that issue>; *also* : CORRECT <get the facts ~> c : free from extraneous matter : UNMIXED <~ gin> d : marked by no exceptions or deviations in support of a principle or party <a ~ Republican> <a ~ ballot> e : having a fixed price for each regardless of the number sold <cigars 20 cents ~> f : not deviating from the general norm or prescribed pattern <preferred acting in ~ dramas to musicals or comedies> g (1) : exhibiting no deviation from what is established or accepted as usual, normal, or proper : CONVENTIONAL; *also* : SQUARE 5f (2) : not using or under the influence of drugs h : HETEROSEXUAL 4 : being the only form of remuneration <a salesman on ~ commission> — **straight·ish** \-ish\ *adj* — **straight·ly** *adv* — **straight·ness** *n*

[2]**straight** *adv* : in a straight manner

[3]**straight** *vt, chiefly Scot* : STRAIGHTEN

[4]**straight** *n* 1 : something that is straight: as a : a straight line or arrangement b : STRAIGHTAWAY; *esp* : HOMESTRETCH c : a true or honest report or course 2 a : a sequence (as of shots, strokes, or moves) resulting in a perfect score in a game or contest b : first place at the finish of a horse race : WIN 3 : a poker hand containing five cards in sequence but not of the same suit — see POKER illustration 4 : a conventional person; *esp* : a person who is not a member of the hippie culture

straight A \ˌstrāt-ˌā\ *adj* : having or constituting a first-class record of achievement <a *straight A* student>

straight and narrow *n* [prob. alter. of *strait and narrow*; fr. the admonition of Mt 7:14 (AV), "strait is the gate and narrow is the way which leadeth unto life"] : the way of propriety and rectitude — used with *the*

straight angle *n* : an angle whose sides lie in opposite directions from the vertex in the same straight line and which equals two right angles

[1]**straight–arm** \'strāt-ˌärm\ *n* : an act or instance of warding off a football tackler with the arm fully extended from the shoulder, elbow locked, and the palm of the hand placed firmly against any part of his body — called also *stiff-arm*

[2]**straight–arm** *vt* : to ward off with or as if with a straight-arm ~ *vi* : to use a straight-arm in warding off an opponent

[1]**straight·away** \'strāt-ə-ˌwā\ *adj* 1 : proceeding in a straight line : continuous in direction 2 : IMMEDIATE

[2]**straightaway** *n* : a straight course: as a : the straight part of a closed racecourse : STRETCH b : a straight and unimpeded stretch of road or way

[3]**straight·away** \ˌstrāt-ə-'wā\ *adv* : without hesitation or delay

straight·bred \'strāt-'bred\ *adj* : produced by breeding a single breed, strain, or type <a ~ Angus heifer> — compare CROSSBRED — **straight·bred** \-ˌbred\ *n*

straight chain *n* : an open chain of atoms having no side chains

straight·edge \'strāt-ˌej\ *n* : a bar or piece of material (as of wood, metal, or plastic) with a straight edge for testing straight lines and surfaces or drawing straight lines

straight·en \'strāt-ᵊn\ *vb* **straight·ened; straight·en·ing** \'strāt-niŋ, -ᵊn-iŋ\ *vt* : to make straight — usu. used with *up* or *out* ~ *vi* : to become straight — usu. used with *up* or *out* — **straight·en·er** \'strāt-nər, -ᵊn-ər\ *n*

straight face *n* : a face giving no evidence of emotion and esp. of merriment — **straight–faced** \'strāt-'fāst\ *adj* — **straight–faced·ly** \-'fā-səd-lē, -'fās-tlē\ *adv*

straight flush *n* : a poker hand containing five cards of the same suit in sequence — see POKER illustration

[1]**straight·for·ward** \(')strāt-'fȯr-wərd\ *also* **straight·for·wards** \-wərdz\ *adv* : in a straightforward manner

[2]**straightforward** *adj* 1 : proceeding in a straight course or manner : DIRECT, UNDEVIATING 2 a : free from evasiveness or obscurity : EXACT, CANDID <a ~ account> b : CLEAR-CUT, PRECISE — **straight·for·ward·ly** *adv* — **straight·for·ward·ness** *n*
syn STRAIGHTFORWARD, FORTHRIGHT, ABOVEBOARD *shared meaning element* : free from all that is dishonest or secretive ***ant*** devious, indirect

straight–line \ˌstrāt-ˌlīn\ *adj* 1 : being a mechanical linkage or equivalent device designed to produce or copy motion in a straight line 2 : having the principal parts arranged in a straight line <a ~ compressor having the steam and air cylinders in a straight line> 3 : marked by a uniform spread and esp. in equal segments over a given term <~ amortization> <~ depreciation>

straight man *n* : a member of a comedy team who feeds lines to his partner who in turn replies with usu. humorous quips

straight off *adv* : at once : IMMEDIATELY

straight–out \ˌstrāt-ˌau̇t\ *adj* 1 : FORTHRIGHT, BLUNT <gave him a ~ answer> 2 : OUTRIGHT, THOROUGHGOING

straight poker *n* : poker in which the players bet on the five cards dealt to them and then have a showdown without drawing — compare DRAW POKER, STUD POKER

straight razor *n* : a razor with a rigid steel cutting blade hinged to a case that forms a handle when the razor is open for use

straight ticket *n* : a ballot cast for all the candidates of one party

[1]**straight·way** \'strāt-'wā, -ˌwā\ *adv* 1 : in a direct course : DIRECTLY <fell ~ to the bottom of the stairs> 2 : right away : IMMEDIATELY, FORTHWITH <~ the clouds began to part>

[2]**straight·way** \ˌstrāt-ˌwā\ *adj* : having or affording a straight way <a ~ valve>

[1]**strain** \'strān\ *n* [ME *streen* progeny, lineage, fr. OE *strēon* gain, acquisition; akin to OHG *gistriuni* gain, L *struere* to heap up — more at STRUCTURE] 1 a : LINEAGE, ANCESTRY b : a group of presumed common ancestry with clear-cut physiological but usu. not morphological distinctions <a high-yielding ~ of winter wheat>; *broadly* : a specified infraspecific group (as a stock, line, or ecotype) c : KIND, SORT <discussions of a lofty ~> 2 a : inherited or inherent character, quality, or disposition <a ~ of madness in the family> b : TRACE, STREAK <a ~ of fanaticism> 3 a : TUNE, AIR b : a passage of verbal or musical expression c : a stream or outburst of forceful or impassioned speech 4 a

: the tenor, pervading note, burden, or tone of an utterance or of a course of action or conduct **b** : MOOD, TEMPER

2strain *vb* [ME *strainen,* fr. MF *estraindre,* fr. L *stringere* to bind or draw tight, press together; akin to Gk *strang-, stranx* drop squeezed out, *strangalē* halter] *vt* **1 a** : to draw tight : cause to clasp firmly <~ the bandage over the wound> **b** : to stretch to maximum extension and tautness <~ a canvas over a frame> **2 a** : to exert (as oneself) to the utmost **b** : to injure by overuse, misuse, or excessive pressure <~*ed* his heart by overwork> **c** : to cause a change of form or size in (a body) by application of external force **3** : to squeeze or clasp tightly: as **a** : HUG **b** : to compress painfully : CONSTRICT **4 a** : to cause to pass through a strainer : FILTER **b** : to remove by straining <~ lumps out of the gravy> **5** : to stretch beyond a proper limit <that story ~*s* my credulity> **6** *obs* : to squeeze out : EXTORT ~ *vi* **1 a** : to make violent efforts : STRIVE <has to ~ to reach the high notes> **b** : to sustain a strain, wrench, or distortion **c** : to contract the muscles forcefully in attempting to defecate — often used in the phrase *strain at stool* **2** : to pass through or as if through a strainer <the liquid ~*s* readily> **3** : to make great difficulty or resistance : BALK — **strain a point** : to go beyond a usual, accepted, or proper limit or rule

3strain *n* **1** : an act of straining or the condition of being strained: as **a** : excessive physical or mental tension; *also* : a force, influence, or factor causing such tension <her responsibilities were a constant ~> **b** : excessive or difficult exertion or labor **c** : bodily injury from excessive tension, effort, or use <heart ~>; *esp* : one resulting from a wrench or twist and involving undue stretching of muscles or ligaments <back ~> **d** : deformation of a material body under the action of applied forces **2** : an unusual reach, degree, or intensity : PITCH **3** *archaic* : a strained interpretation of something said or written

strained \'strānd\ *adj* **1** : done or produced with excessive effort **2** : pushed by antagonism near to open conflict <~ relations>

strain·er \'strā-nər\ *n* : one that strains: as **a** : a device (as a sieve) to retain solid pieces while a liquid passes through **b** : any of various devices for stretching or tightening something

strain gauge *n* : EXTENSOMETER

straining beam *n* : a short piece of timber in a truss used to hold the ends of struts or rafters in place — see QUEEN POST illustration

strain·om·e·ter \strā-'näm-ət-ər\ *n* : EXTENSOMETER

1strait \'strāt\ *adj* [ME, fr. OF *estreit,* fr. L *strictus* strait, strict — more at STRICT] **1** *archaic* **a** : NARROW **b** : limited in space or time **c** : closely fitting : CONSTRICTED, TIGHT **2** *archaic* : STRICT, RIGOROUS **3 a** : causing distress : DIFFICULT **b** : limited as to means or resources — **strait·ly** *adv* — **strait·ness** *n*

2strait *adv, obs* : in a close or tight manner

3strait *n* **1 a** *archaic* : a narrow space or passage **b** : a comparatively narrow passageway connecting two large bodies of water — often used in pl. but sing. in constr. **c** : ISTHMUS **2** : a situation of perplexity or distress — often used in pl. ***syn*** see JUNCTURE

strait·en \'strāt-ᵊn\ *vt* **strait·ened; strait·en·ing** \'strāt-niŋ, -ᵊn-iŋ\ **1 a** : to make strait or narrow **b** : to hem in : CONFINE **2** *archaic* : to restrict in freedom or scope : HAMPER **3** : to subject to distress, privation, or deficiency <in ~*ed* circumstances>

1strait·jack·et *or* **straight·jack·et** \'strāt-ˌjak-ət\ *n* **1** : a cover or overgarment of strong material (as canvas) used to bind the body and esp. the arms closely in restraining a violent prisoner or patient **2** : something that restricts or confines like a straitjacket

2straitjacket *or* **straightjacket** *vt* : to confine in or as if in a straitjacket

strait·laced *or* **straight·laced** \'strāt-'lāst\ *adj* **1** : wearing or having a bodice or stays tightly laced **2** : excessively strict in manners, morals, or opinion — **strait·laced·ly** \-'lā-səd-lē, -'lāst-lē\ *adv* — **strait·laced·ness** \-'lās(t)-nəs, -'lā-səd-nəs\ *n*

Straits dollar \'strāts-\ *n* [*Straits* Settlements, former British crown colony] : a dollar formerly issued by British Malaya and used in much of southern and eastern Asia and the East Indies

strake \'strāk\ *n* [ME; akin to OE *streccan* to stretch — more at STRETCH] **1** : a continuous band of hull planking or plates on a ship; *also* : the width of such a band **2** : STREAK, STRIPE

stra·mash \strə-'mash\ *n* [prob. imit.] *chiefly Scot* **1** : DISTURBANCE, RACKET **2** : CRASH, SMASHUP

stra·mo·ni·um \strə-'mō-nē-əm\ *n* [NL] **1** : JIMSONWEED **2** : the dried leaves of the jimsonweed or of a related plant (genus *Datura*) used in medicine similarly to belladonna esp. in the treatment of asthma

1strand \'strand\ *n* [ME, fr. OE; akin to ON *strönd* strand, L *sternere* to spread out — more at STREW] : the land bordering a body of water : SHORE, BEACH

2strand *vt* **1** : to run, drive, or cause to drift onto a strand : run aground **2** : to leave in a strange or an unfavorable place esp. without funds or means to depart **3** : to leave (a base runner) on base at the end of an inning in baseball ~ *vi* : to become stranded

3strand *n* [ME *stronde, strande*] *Scot & dial Eng* **1** : STREAM **2** : SEA

4strand *n* [ME *strond*] **1 a** : fibers or filaments twisted, plaited, or laid parallel to form a unit for further twisting or plaiting into yarn, thread, rope, or cordage **b** : one of the wires twisted together or laid parallel to form a wire rope or cable **c** : something (as a molecular chain) resembling a strand **2** : an element (as a yarn or thread) of a woven or plaited material **3** : an elongated or twisted and plaited body resembling a rope <a ~ of pearls> **4** : one of the elements interwoven in a complex whole

5strand *vt* **1** : to break a strand of (a rope) accidentally **2 a** : to form (as a rope) from strands **b** : to play out, twist, or arrange in a strand

strand·ed \'stran-dəd\ *adj* : having a strand or strands esp. of a specified kind or number — usu. used in combination <the double-*stranded* molecule of DNA> — **strand·ed·ness** *n*

strand·er \'stran-dər\ *n* : a machine that makes strands into cable or rope

strand·line \'stran-ˌ(d)līn\ *n* : SHORELINE; *esp* : a shoreline above the present water level

strange \'strānj\ *adj* **strang·er; strang·est** [ME, fr. OF *estrange,* fr. L *extraneus,* lit., external, fr. *extra* outside — more at EXTRA-] **1 a** *archaic* : of, relating to, or characteristic of another country : FOREIGN **b** : not native to or naturally belonging in a place : of external origin, kind, or character **2 a** : not before known, heard, or seen : NEW, UNFAMILIAR **b** : exciting wonder or awe : EXTRAORDINARY, QUEER **3 a** : discouraging familiarities : RESERVED, DISTANT **b** : ill at ease **4** : UNACCUSTOMED, UNVERSED <she was ~ to his ways> — **strange·ly** *adv*

syn STRANGE, SINGULAR, UNIQUE, UNPARALLELED, PECULIAR *shared meaning element* : deviating from what is ordinary, usual, or to be expected ***ant*** familiar

strange·ness \'strānj-nəs\ *n* **1** : the quality or state of being strange **2** : the quantum characteristic of a strongly interacting elementary particle that indicates the possible transformations upon strong interaction with other elementary particles

strange particle *n* : a short-lived unstable elementary particle (as a kaon or a sigma) that is created in high-energy particle collisions and has a strangeness quantum number different from zero

1strang·er \'strān-jər\ *n* [ME, fr. MF *estrangier* foreign, foreigner, fr. *estrange*] **1** : one who is strange: as **a (1)** : FOREIGNER **(2)** : a resident alien **b** : one in the house of another as a guest, visitor, or intruder **c** : a person or thing that is unknown or with whom one is unacquainted **d** : one who does not belong to or is kept from the activities of a group **e** : one not privy or party to an act, contract, or title : one that interferes without right **2** : one ignorant of or unacquainted with someone or something

2stranger *adj* : of, relating to, or being a stranger : FOREIGN

3stranger *vt, obs* : ESTRANGE, ALIENATE

strange woman *n* [fr. the expression frequently used in Prov (AV)] : PROSTITUTE

stran·gle \'straŋ-gəl\ *vb* **stran·gled; stran·gling** \-g(ə-)liŋ\ [ME *stranglen,* fr. MF *estrangler,* fr. Gk *strangalan,* fr. *strangalē* halter — more at STRAIN] *vt* **1 a** : to choke to death by compressing the throat with something (as a hand or rope) : THROTTLE **b** : to obstruct seriously or fatally the normal breathing of <the bone wedged in his throat and *strangled* him> **c** : STIFLE **2** : to suppress or hinder the rise, expression, or growth of ~ *vi* **1** : to become strangled **2** : to die from or as if from interference with breathing — **stran·gler** \-g(ə-)lər\ *n*

stran·gle·hold \'straŋ-gəl-ˌhōld\ *n* **1** : an illegal wrestling hold by which one's opponent is choked **2** : a force or influence that chokes or suppresses freedom of movement or expression

stran·gles \'straŋ-gəlz\ *n pl but sing or pl in constr* [pl. of obs. *strangle* (act of strangling)] : an infectious febrile disease of horses caused by a bacterium (*Streptococcus equi*) and marked by inflammation and congestion of mucous membranes

stran·gu·late \'straŋ-gyə-ˌlāt\ *vb* **-lat·ed; -lat·ing** [L *strangulatus,* pp. of *strangulare*] *vt* : STRANGLE, CONSTRICT ~ *vi* : to become constricted so as to stop circulation <the hernia will ~ and become necrotic>

stran·gu·la·tion \ˌstraŋ-gyə-'lā-shən\ *n* **1** : the action or process of strangling or strangulating **2** : the state of being strangled or strangulated; *esp* : excessive or pathological constriction or compression of a bodily tube (as a blood vessel or a loop of intestine) that interrupts its ability to act as a passage

stran·gu·ry \'straŋ-gyə-rē, -ˌgyu̇r-ē\ *n, pl* **-ries** [ME, fr. L *stranguria,* fr. Gk *strangouria,* fr. *strang-, stranx* drop squeezed out + *ourein* to urinate, fr. *ouron* urine — more at STRAIN, URINE] : a slow and painful discharge of urine drop by drop

1strap \'strap\ *n* [alter. of *strop,* fr. ME, band or loop of leather or rope, fr. OE, thong for securing an oar; akin to MHG *strupfe* strap; all fr. a prehistoric WGmc word borrowed fr. L *struppus* band, strap, fr. Gk *strophos* twisted band; akin to Gk *strephein* to twist — more at STROPHE] **1** : a band, plate, or loop of metal for binding objects together or for clamping an object in position **2 a** : a narrow usu. flat strip or thong of a flexible material and esp. leather used for securing, holding together, or wrapping **b** : something made of a strap forming a loop <a boot ~> **c** : a strip of leather used for flogging **d** : STROP **3** : a shoe fastened with a usu. buckled strap **4** *Irish* : TROLLOP

2strap *vt* **strapped; strap·ping** **1 a (1)** : to secure with or attach by means of a strap **(2)** : to support (as a sprained joint) with overlapping strips of adhesive plaster **b** : BIND, CONSTRICT **2** : to beat or punish with a strap **3** : STROP **4** : to cause to suffer from an extreme scarcity <is often *strapped* for cash>

strap·hang·er \'strap-ˌhaŋ-ər\ *n* : a standing passenger in a subway, streetcar, bus, or train who clings for support to one of the short straps or similar devices placed along the aisle — **strap·hang** \-ˌhaŋ\ *vi*

strap·less \-ləs\ *adj* : having no strap; *specif* : made or worn without shoulder straps <a ~ evening gown>

strap·pa·do \strə-'pād-(ˌ)ō, -'päd-\ *n* [modif. of It *strappata,* lit., sharp pull] : a former punishment or torture consisting of hoisting the subject by a rope and letting him fall to the length of the rope; *also* : a machine used to inflict this torture

strap·per \'strap-ər\ *n* : one that is unusually large or robust

strap·ping \'strap-iŋ\ *adj* : having a vigorously sturdy constitution

strass \'stras\ *n* [F *stras, strass*] : PASTE 3

strat·a·gem \'strat-ə-jəm, -ˌjem\ *n* [It *stratagemma,* fr. L *strategema,* fr. Gk *stratēgēma,* fr. *stratēgein* to be a general, maneuver, fr. *stratēgos* general, fr. *stratos* army (akin to L *stratus,* pp. of *sternere* to spread out) + *agein* to lead — more at STRATUM, AGENT] **1 a** : an artifice or trick in war for deceiving and outwitting the enemy

b : a cleverly contrived trick or scheme for gaining an end **2** : skill in ruses or trickery ***syn*** see TRICK

stra·te·gic \strə-ˈtē-jik\ *adj* **1** : of, relating to, or marked by strategy <a ~ retreat> **2 a** : necessary to or important in the initiation, conduct, or completion of a strategic plan **b** : required for the conduct of war <~ materials> **c** : of great importance within an integrated whole or to a planned effect <emphasized ~ points> **3** : designed or trained to strike an enemy at the sources of his military, economic, or political power <a ~ bomber> — **stra·te·gi·cal** \-ji-kəl\ *adj* — **stra·te·gi·cal·ly** \-ji-k(ə-)lē\ *adv*

strat·e·gist \ˈstrat-ə-jəst\ *n* : one skilled in strategy

strat·e·gy \-jē\ *n, pl* **-gies** [Gk *stratēgia* generalship, fr. *stratēgos*] **1 a (1)** : the science and art of employing the political, economic, psychological, and military forces of a nation or group of nations to afford the maximum support to adopted policies in peace or war **(2)** : the science and art of military command exercised to meet the enemy in combat under advantageous conditions **b** : a variety of or instance of the use of strategy **2 a** : a careful plan or method : a clever stratagem **b** : the art of devising or employing plans or stratagems toward a goal

syn STRATEGY, TACTICS, LOGISTICS *shared meaning element* : an aspect of military science

strath \ˈstrath\ *n* [ScGael *srath*] : a flat wide river valley or the low-lying grassland along it

strath·spey \(ˈ)strath-ˈspā\ *n, pl* **strathspeys** [*Strath Spey*, district of Scotland] : a Scottish dance that is similar to but slower than the reel; *also* : the music for this dance

strati- *comb form* [NL *stratum*] : stratum <*strati*form>

stra·tic·u·late \strə-ˈtik-yə-lət, stra-\ *adj* [(assumed) NL *straticulum*, dim. of *stratum*] : characterized by thin parallel strata

strat·i·fi·ca·tion \ˌstrat-ə-fə-ˈkā-shən\ *n* **1 a** : the act or process of stratifying **b** : the state of being stratified **2** : a stratified formation

strat·i·fi·ca·tion·al grammar \ˌstrat-ə-fə-ˈkā-shnəl-, -shən-ᵊl-\ *n* : a grammar based on the theory that language consists of a series of hierarchically related strata linked together by representational rules

strat·i·form \ˈstrat-ə-ˌfȯrm\ *adj* : having a stratified formation

strat·i·fy \ˈstrat-ə-ˌfī\ *vb* **-fied; -fy·ing** [NL *stratificare*, fr. *stratum* + L *-ificare* -ify] *vt* **1 a** : to form, deposit, or arrange in strata **b (1)** : to divide or arrange into classes, castes, or social strata **(2)** : to divide into a series of graded statuses **2** : to store (seeds) in layers alternating with moisture-holding material (as earth or peat) ~ *vi* : to become arranged in strata

strati·graph·ic \ˌstrat-ə-ˈgraf-ik\ *adj* : of, relating to, or determined by stratigraphy

stra·tig·ra·phy \strə-ˈtig-rə-fē, stə-\ *n* [ISV] **1** : the arrangement of strata **2** : geology that deals with the origin, composition, distribution, and succession of strata

strato- *comb form* [NL *stratus*] : stratus and <*strato*cumulus>

stra·toc·ra·cy \strə-ˈtäk-rə-sē\ *n, pl* **-cies** [Gk *stratos* army — more at STRATAGEM] : a military government

stra·to·cu·mu·lus \ˌstrāt-ō-ˈkyü-myə-ləs, ˌstrat-\ *n* [NL] : stratified cumulus consisting of large balls or rolls of dark cloud which often cover the whole sky esp. in winter — see CLOUD illustration

strato·sphere \ˈstrat-ə-ˌsfi(ə)r\ *n* [F *stratosphère*, fr. NL *stratum* + *-o-* + F *sphère* sphere, fr. L *sphaera*] **1** : an upper portion of the atmosphere which is above approximately seven miles depending on latitude, season, and weather and in which temperature changes little with changing altitude and clouds of water are rare **2** : a very high or the highest region on a graded scale <the ~ of English society —*New Yorker*> — **strato·spher·ic** \ˌstrat-ə-ˈsfi(ə)r-ik, -ˈsfer-\ *adj*

stra·tum \ˈstrāt-əm ˈstrat-\ *n, pl* **stra·ta** \ˈstrāt-ə, ˈstrat-\ [NL, fr. L, spread, bed, fr. neut. of *stratus*, pp. of *sternere* to spread out — more at STREW] **1** : a bed or layer artificially made **2 a** : a sheetlike mass of sedimentary rock or earth of one kind lying between beds of other kinds **b** : a region of the sea or atmosphere that is analogous to a stratum of the earth **c** : a layer of tissue <deep ~ of the skin> **d** : a layer in which archaeological material (as artifacts, skeletons, and dwelling remains) is found on excavation **3 a** : a part of a historical or sociological series representing a period or a stage of development **b** : a socioeconomic level of society comprised of persons of the same or similar status esp. with regard to education or culture **4** : one of the sets considered as an integrated whole that make up an ordered, layered, or superimposed group of sets <a statistical sampling of population *strata*>

stra·tus \ˈstrāt-əs, ˈstrat-\ *n, pl* **stra·ti** \ˈstrāt-ˌī, ˈstrat-\ [NL, fr. L, pp. of *sternere*] : a cloud form of greater horizontal extension and comparatively lower altitude (2000 to 7000 feet) than the cumulostratus or cirrostratus — see CLOUD illustration

stra·vage *or* **stra·vaig** \strə-ˈvāg\ *vi* [prob. by shortening and alter. fr. *extravagate*] *chiefly Scot* : ROAM

¹straw \ˈstrȯ\ *n* [ME, fr. OE *strēaw*; akin to OHG *strō* straw, OE *strewian* to strew] **1 a** : stalks of grain after threshing; *broadly* : dry stalky plant residue used like grain straw (as for bedding or packing) **b** : a natural or artificial heavy fiber used for weaving, plaiting, or braiding **2** : a dry coarse stem esp. of a cereal grass **3 a (1)** : something of small worth or significance **(2)** : something too insubstantial to provide support or help in a desperate situation <clutching at ~*s*> **b** : CHAFF 2 **4 a** : something (as a hat) made of straw **b** : a tube (as of paper, plastic, or glass) for sucking up a beverage — **strawy** \ˈstrȯ(-)i\ *adj* — **straw in the wind** : a slight fact that is an indication of a coming event

²straw *adj* **1** : made of straw <a ~ rug> **2** : of, relating to, or used for straw <a ~ barn> **3** : of the color of straw <~ hair> **4** : of little or no value : WORTHLESS **5** : of, relating to, resembling, or being a man of straw **6** : of, relating to, or concerned with the discovery of preferences by means of a straw vote

straw·ber·ry \ˈstrȯ-ˌber-ē, -b(ə-)rē\ *n, often attrib* [fr. the appearance of the achenes on the surface] : the juicy edible usu. red fruit of a plant (genus *Fragaria*) of the rose family that is technically an enlarged pulpy receptacle bearing numerous achenes; *also* : a plant whose fruits are strawberries

strawberry

strawberry bush *n* **1** : a No. American euonymus (*Euonymus americanus*) with crimson pods and seeds with a scarlet aril **2** : ²WAHOO

strawberry mark *n* : a usu. red and elevated birthmark that is a small vascular tumor

strawberry roan *n* : a roan horse with a decidedly red ground color

strawberry shrub *n* : any of a genus (*Calycanthus* of the family Calycanthaceae, the strawberry-shrub family) of shrubs with fragrant brownish red flowers

strawberry tomato *n* : GROUND-CHERRY; *esp* : a stout hairy annual herb (*Physalis pruinosa*) of eastern No. America with sweet globular yellow fruits

strawberry tree *n* : a European evergreen tree (*Arbutus unedo*) of the heath family with racemose white flowers and fruits like strawberries

straw·board \ˈstrȯ-ˌbō(ə)rd, -ˌbȯ(ə)rd\ *n* : board made of straw pulp and used esp. for packing

straw boss *n* **1** : an assistant to a foreman in charge of supervising and expediting the work of a small gang of workmen **2** : a member of a group of workers who supervises the work of the others in addition to doing his own job

straw·flow·er \ˈstrȯ-ˌflau̇(-ə)r\ *n* : any of several everlasting flowers; *esp* : an Australian annual herb (*Helichrysum bracteatum*) that is much grown for its heads of chaffy brightly colored long-keeping flowers

straw-hat theater \ˌstrȯ-ˌhat-\ *n* [fr. the former fashion of wearing straw hats in summer] : SUMMER THEATER

straw man *n* **1** : a weak or imaginary opposition (as an argument or adversary) set up only to be easily confuted **2** : a person set up to serve as a cover for a usu. questionable transaction

straw vote *n* : an unofficial vote taken (as at a chance gathering) to indicate the relative strength of opposing candidates or issues

straw wine *n* : a sweet dessert wine produced from grapes partially dried in the sun often on straw before fermentation

straw·worm \ˈstrȯ-ˌwərm\ *n* : any of several larval chalcid flies that injure the straw of cereal grasses (as wheat)

straw yellow *n* : a pale yellow

¹stray \ˈstrā\ *vi* [ME *straien*, fr. MF *estraier*, fr. (assumed) VL *extragare*, fr. L *extra-* outside + *vagari* to wander — more at EXTRA-, VAGARY] : WANDER: as **a** : to wander from company, restraint, or proper limits **b** : to roam about without fixed direction or purpose **c** : to move in a winding course : MEANDER **d** : to move without voluntary control <eyes ~*ing* absently around the room> **e** : to become distracted from an argument or chain of thought <~*ed* from the point> **f** : to wander accidentally from a fixed or chosen route **g** : ERR, SIN — **stray·er** *n*

²stray *n* [ME, fr. OF *estraié*, pp. of *estraier*] **1 a** : a domestic animal that is wandering at large or is lost **b** : a person or thing that strays **2** [ME, fr. *straien* to stray] *archaic* : the act of going astray **3** : a disturbing electrical effect in radio reception not produced by a transmitting station **4** : an unexpected formation encountered in drilling an oil or gas well

³stray *adj* **1** : having strayed : WANDERING <a ~ cow> **2** : occurring at random or sporadically <a few ~ hairs> **3** : not serving any useful purpose : UNWANTED <~ light>

¹streak \ˈstrēk\ *n* [ME *streke*, fr. OE *strica*; akin to OHG *strich* line, L *striga* row — more at STRIKE] **1** : a line or mark of a different color or texture from the ground : STRIPE **2 a** : the color of the fine powder of a mineral obtained by scratching or rubbing against a hard white surface and constituting an important distinguishing character **b** : inoculum implanted in a line on a solid medium **c** : any of several virus diseases of plants (as the potato, tomato, or raspberry) resembling mosaic but usu. producing at least some linear markings **3 a** : a narrow band of light **b** : a lightning bolt **4 a** : a slight admixture : TRACE <had a mean ~ in him> **b** : a brief run (as of luck) **c** : a consecutive series <was on a winning ~> **5** : a narrow layer (as of ore)

²streak *vt* : to make streaks on or in <tears ~*ing* her face> ~ *vi* **1** : to move swiftly : RUSH <a jet ~*ing* across the sky> **2** : to have a streak (as of winning or outstanding performances)

streaked \ˈstrēkt, ˈstrē-kəd\ *adj* **1** : marked with stripes or linear discolorations **2** : physically or mentally disturbed : UPSET

streak·ing \ˈstrē-kiŋ\ *n* : the lightening (as by chemicals) of a few long strands of hair to produce a streaked effect

streaky \ˈstrē-kē\ *adj* **streak·i·er; -est** **1** : marked with streaks <~ bacon> **2** : APPREHENSIVE <nervous and ~> **3** : apt to vary (as in effectiveness) : UNRELIABLE — **streak·i·ness** *n*

¹stream \ˈstrēm\ *n* [ME *streme*, fr. OE *strēam*; akin to OHG *stroum* stream, Gk *rhein* to flow, Skt *sarati* it flows — more at SERUM] **1** : a body of running water (as a river or brook) flowing on the earth; *also* : any body of flowing fluid (as water or gas) **2 a** : a steady succession (as of words or events) <kept up an endless ~ of chatter> **b** : a constantly renewed supply **c** : a continuous moving procession <a ~ of traffic> **3** : an unbroken flow (as of gas or particles of matter) **4** : a ray of light **5 a** : a prevailing attitude or group <has always run against the ~ of current fashion> **b** : a dominant influence or line of development **6** *Brit* : TRACK 3b — **on stream** : in or into production

²stream *vi* **1 a** : to flow in or as if in a stream **b** : to leave a bright trail <a meteor ~*ed* through the sky> **2 a** : to exude a bodily fluid profusely <her eyes were ~*ing* from the onions> **b** : to become wet with a discharge of bodily fluid <~*ing* with perspiration> **3** : to trail out at full length <her hair ~*ing* back as she ran> **4** : to pour in large numbers <complaints came ~*ing*

in> ~ *vt* **1 :** to emit freely or in a stream <his eyes ~*ed* tears> **2 :** to display fully extended ***syn*** see POUR

stream·bed \ˈstrēm-ˌbed\ *n* **:** the channel occupied or formerly occupied by a stream

stream·er \ˈstrē-mər\ *n* **1 a :** a flag that streams in the wind; *esp* **:** PENNANT **b :** any long narrow wavy strip resembling or suggesting a banner floating in the wind **c :** BANNER 2 **2 a :** a long extension of the solar corona visible only during a total solar eclipse **b** *pl* **:** AURORA BOREALIS

stream·ing \ˈstrē-miŋ\ *n* **1 :** an act or instance of flowing; *specif* **:** CYCLOSIS **2** *Brit* **:** TRACKING

stream·let \ˈstrēm-lət\ *n* **:** a small stream

1stream·line \ˈstrēm-ˌlīn, -ˈlīn\ *n* **1 :** the path of a fluid particle relative to a solid body past which the fluid is moving in smooth flow without turbulence **2 a :** a contour designed to minimize resistance to motion through a fluid (as air) **b :** a smooth or flowing line designed as if for decreasing air resistance

2streamline *vt* **1 :** to design or construct with a streamline **2 :** to bring up to date **:** MODERNIZE **3 a :** ORGANIZE **b :** to make simpler or more efficient

stream·lined \-ˌlīnd, -ˈlīnd\ *adj* **1 a :** contoured to reduce resistance to motion through a fluid (as air) **b :** stripped of nonessentials **:** COMPACT **c :** effectively integrated **:** ORGANIZED **2 :** having flowing lines **3 :** brought up to date **:** MODERNIZED **4 :** of or relating to streamline flow

streamline flow *n* **:** an uninterrupted flow (as of air) past a solid body in which the direction at every point remains unchanged with the passage of time

stream·lin·er \ˈstrēm-ˈlī-nər\ *n* **:** one that is streamlined; *esp* **:** a streamlined train

stream of consciousness **1 :** individual conscious experience considered as a series of processes or experiences continuously moving forward in time **2 :** INTERIOR MONOLOGUE

streek \ˈstrēk\ *vt* [ME (northern dial.) *streken;* akin to OE *streccan* to stretch] **1** *chiefly Scot* **:** STRETCH, EXTEND **2** *chiefly Scot* **:** to lay out (a dead body)

1street \ˈstrēt\ *n* [ME *strete,* fr. OE *strǣt;* akin to OHG *strāza* street; both fr. a prehistoric WGmc word borrowed fr. LL *strata* paved road, fr. L, fem. of *stratus,* pp. of *sternere* to spread out — more at STREW] **1 a :** a thoroughfare esp. in a city, town, or village that is wider than an alley or lane and that usu. includes sidewalks **b :** the part of a street reserved for vehicles **c :** a thoroughfare with abutting property <lives on a fashionable ~> **2 :** the people occupying property on a street <the whole ~ knew about the accident> **3 :** a promising line of development or a channeling of effort **4** *cap* **:** a district (as Wall Street or Fleet Street) identified with a particular profession **5 :** an environment (as in a depressed neighborhood or section of a city) of prostitution, poverty, dereliction, or crime — **on the street** *or* **in the street 1 :** idle, homeless, or out of a job **2 :** out of prison **:** at liberty — **up one's street** *or* **down one's street :** suited to one's abilities or taste

2street *adj* **1 a :** adjoining or giving access to a street <the ~ door> **b :** carried on or taking place in the street <~ fighting> **c :** living or working on the streets <a ~ peddler> **d :** located in, used for, or serving as a guide to the streets <a ~ map> **e :** performing in or heard on the street <a ~ band> **f :** suitable for wear or use on the street <~ clothes> **g :** not touching the ground — used of a woman's dress in lengths reaching the knee, calf, or ankle **2 :** caused by a street virus <~ distemper>

street arab \-ˈar-əb, -ˈā-ˌrab\ *n, often cap A* **:** a homeless vagabond and esp. an outcast boy or girl in the streets of a city **:** GAMIN

street·car \ˈstrēt-ˌkär\ *n* **:** a vehicle on rails used primarily for transporting passengers and typically operating on city streets

street·light \-ˌlīt\ *n* **:** a light usu. mounted on a pole and constituting one of a series spaced at intervals along a public street or highway

street railway *n* **:** a line operating streetcars or buses

streets \ˈstrēts\ *adv, chiefly Brit* **:** far and away <a nice woman, ~ above these other callers —Katherine Mansfield>

street theater *n* **:** GUERRILLA THEATER

street virus *n* **:** virulent or natural virus (as that causing rabies) as distinguished from virus attenuated in the laboratory

street·walk·er \ˈstrēt-ˌwȯ-kər\ *n* **:** PROSTITUTE; *esp* **:** one who solicits in the streets — compare CALL GIRL — **street·walk·ing** \-kiŋ\ *n*

strength \ˈstreŋ(k)th\ *n* [ME *strengthe,* fr. OE *strengthu;* akin to OHG *strengi* strong — more at STRONG] **1 :** the quality or state of being strong **:** capacity for exertion or endurance **2 :** power to resist force **:** SOLIDITY, TOUGHNESS **3 :** power of resisting attack **:** IMPREGNABILITY **4 a :** legal, logical, or moral force **b :** a strong attribute or inherent asset <the ~*s* and the weaknesses of the book are evident> **5 a :** degree of potency of effect or of concentration **b :** intensity of light, color, sound, or odor **c :** vigor of expression **6 :** force as measured in numbers **:** effective numbers of any body or organization <an army at full ~> **7 :** one regarded as embodying or affording force or firmness **:** SUPPORT **8 :** maintenance of or a rising tendency in a price level **:** firmness of prices **9 :** BASIS — used in the phrase *on the strength of* — **from strength to strength :** vigorously forward **:** from one high point to the next

strength·en \ˈstreŋ(k)-thən\ *vb* **strength·ened; strength·en·ing** \ˈstreŋ(k)th-(ə-)niŋ\ *vt* **:** to make stronger ~ *vi* **:** to become stronger — **strength·en·er** \ˈstreŋ(k)th-(ə-)nər\ *n*

strength·less \ˈstreŋ(k)th-ləs\ *adj* [ME *strentheles,* fr. *strenthe* strength + *-les* -less] **:** having no strength — **strength·less·ness** *n*

stren·u·ous \ˈstren-yə-wəs\ *adj* [L *strenuus* — more at STARE] **1 a :** vigorously active **:** ENERGETIC **b :** FERVENT, ZEALOUS **2 :** marked by or calling for energy or stamina **:** ARDUOUS — **stren·u·os·i·ty** \ˌstren-yə-ˈwäs-ət-ē\ *n* — **stren·u·ous·ly** \ˈstren-yə-wəs-lē\ *adv* — **stren·u·ous·ness** *n*

strep \ˈstrep\ *adj* **:** STREPTOCOCCAL

strep throat *n* **:** SEPTIC SORE THROAT

strepto- *comb form* [NL, fr. Gk, fr. *streptos* twisted, fr. *strephein* to twist — more at STROPHE] **1 :** twisted **:** twisted chain <*strepto*coccus> **2 :** streptococcus <*strepto*kinase>

strep·to·ba·cil·lus \ˌstrep-tō-bə-ˈsil-əs\ *n* [NL] **:** any of various bacilli in which the individual cells are joined in a chain; *esp* **:** one (*Streptobacillus moniliformis*) that is the causative agent of one form of rat-bite fever

strep·to·coc·cal \ˌstrep-tə-ˈkäk-əl\ *also* **strep·to·coc·cic** \-ˈkäk-(s)ik\ *adj* **:** of, relating to, or caused by streptococci <a ~ sore throat> <~ organisms>

strep·to·coc·cus \-ˈkäk-əs\ *n, pl* **-coc·ci** \-ˈkäk-ˌ(s)ī, -ˈkäk-(ˌ)(s)ē\ [NL, genus name] **:** any of a genus (*Streptococcus*) of nonmotile chiefly parasitic gram-positive bacteria that divide only in one plane, occur in pairs or chains but not in packets, and include important pathogens of man and domestic animals; *broadly* **:** a coccus occurring in chains

strep·to·ki·nase \ˌstrep-tō-ˈkī-ˌnās, -ˌnāz\ *n* **:** a proteolytic enzyme from hemolytic streptococci active in promoting dissolution of blood clots

strep·to·ly·sin \ˌstrep-tə-ˈlīs-ᵊn\ *n* **:** an antigenic hemolysin produced by streptococci

strep·to·my·ces \-ˈmī-ˌsēz\ *n, pl* **streptomyces** [NL, fr. *strepto-* + Gk *mykēs* fungus; akin to L *mucus* mucus] **:** any of a genus (*Streptomyces*) of mostly soil actinomycetes including some that form antibiotics as by-products of their metabolism

strep·to·my·cete \-ˈmī-ˌsēt, -ˌmī-ˈsēt\ *n* [NL *Streptomycet-, Streptomyces,* genus name] **:** any of a family (Streptomycetaceae) of actinomycetes (as a streptomyces) that form vegetative mycelia which rarely break up into bacillary forms, have conidia borne on sporophores, and are typically aerobic soil saprophytes but include a few parasites of plants and animals

strep·to·my·cin \-ˈmīs-ᵊn\ *n* **:** an antibiotic organic base $C_{21}H_{39}H_7O_{12}$ produced by a soil actinomycete (*Streptomyces griseus*), active against many bacteria, and used esp. in the treatment of infections (as tuberculosis) by gram-negative bacteria

strep·to·thri·cin \-ˈthrīs-ᵊn, -ˈthris-\ *n* [NL *Streptothric-, Streptothrix,* genus of bacteria, fr. *strepto-* + Gk *trich-, thrix* hair — more at TRICH-] **:** a basic antibiotic produced by a soil actinomycete (*Streptomyces lavendulae*) and active against bacteria and to some degree against fungi

1stress \ˈstres\ *n* [ME *stresse* stress, distress, fr. *destresse* — more at DISTRESS] **1 :** constraining force or influence: as **a :** a force exerted when one body or body part presses on, pulls on, pushes against, or tends to compress or twist another body or body part; *esp* **:** the intensity of this mutual force commonly expressed in pounds per square inch **b :** the deformation caused in a body by such a force **c :** a physical, chemical, or emotional factor that causes bodily or mental tension and may be a factor in disease causation **d :** a state resulting from a stress; *esp* **:** one of bodily or mental tension resulting from factors that tend to alter an existent equilibrium **e :** STRAIN, PRESSURE <the environment is under ~ to the point of collapse —Joseph Shoben> **2 :** EMPHASIS, WEIGHT <lay ~ on a point> **3** *archaic* **:** intense effort or exertion **4 :** intensity of utterance given to a speech sound, syllable, or word producing relative loudness **5 a :** relative force or prominence of sound in verse **b :** a syllable having relative force or prominence **6 :** ACCENT 6a, 6b(2)

2stress *vt* **1 :** to subject to phonetic stress **:** ACCENT **2 :** to subject to physical stress **3 :** to lay stress on **:** EMPHASIZE

stress·ful \ˈstres-fəl\ *adj* **:** full of or subject to stress — **stress·ful·ly** \-fə-lē\ *adv*

stress·less \-ləs\ *adj* **:** having no stress; *specif* **:** having no accent <a ~ syllable> — **stress·less·ness** *n*

stress mark *n* **:** a mark used with (as before, after, or over) a written syllable in the respelling of a word to show that this syllable is to be stressed when spoken **:** ACCENT MARK

stress·or \ˈstres-ər, -ˌȯ(ə)r\ *n* **:** a stimulus that causes stress

stress–verse \ˈstres-ˌvərs\ *n* **:** verse whose rhythm is produced by recurrence of stresses without regard to number of syllables or any fixed distribution of unstressed elements

1stretch \ˈstrech\ *vb* [ME *strecchen,* fr. OE *streccan;* akin to OHG *strecchan* to stretch, OE *starian* to stare] *vt* **1 :** to extend (as one's limbs or body) in a reclining position **2 :** to reach out **:** EXTEND <~*ed* forth his arm> **3 :** to extend in length <~*ed* her neck to see what was going on> **4 :** to fell with or as if with a blow **5 :** to cause the limbs of (a person) to be pulled esp. in torture **6 :** to draw up (one's body) from a cramped, stooping, or relaxed position **7 :** to pull taut <canvas ~*ed* on a frame> **8 a :** to enlarge or distend esp. by force **b :** to extend or expand as if by physical force <~ one's mind with a good book> **c :** STRAIN <~*ed* his already thin patience> **9 :** to cause to reach or continue (as from one point to another or across a space) <~ a wire between two posts> **10 a :** to amplify or enlarge beyond natural or proper limits <the rules can be ~*ed* this once> **b :** to expand (as by improvisation) to fulfill a larger function <~*ing* a dollar> ~ *vi* **1 a :** to become extended in length or breadth or both **:** SPREAD <broad plains ~*ing* to the sea> **b :** to extend over a continuous period **2 :** to become extended without breaking **3 a :** to extend one's body or limbs **b :** to lie down at full length — **stretch·abil·i·ty** \ˌstrech-ə-ˈbil-ət-ē\ *n* — **stretch·able** \ˈstrech-ə-bəl\ *adj* — **stretch a point :** to go beyond what is strictly warranted in making a claim or concession — **stretch one's legs 1 :** to extend the legs **2 :** to take a walk in order to relieve stiffness caused by prolonged sitting

2stretch *n* **1 a :** an exercise of something (as the understanding or the imagination) beyond ordinary or normal limits **b :** an extension of the scope or application of something <a ~ of language> **2 :** the extent to which something may be stretched **3 :** the act of stretching : the state of being stretched **4 a :** an extent in length or area <a ~ of woods> **b :** a continuous period of time <can write for eight hours at a ~> **5 :** a walk to relieve fatigue **6 :** a term of imprisonment **7 a :** either of the straight sides of a racecourse; *esp* : HOMESTRETCH **b :** a final stage **8 :** the capacity for being stretched : ELASTICITY

³stretch *adj* : easily stretched : ELASTIC <a ~ wig>

stretch·er \ˈstrech-ər\ *n* **1 :** one that stretches; *esp* : a device or machine for stretching or expanding something **2 a :** a brick or stone laid with its length parallel to the face of the wall **b :** a timber or rod used esp. when horizontal as a tie in framed work **3 :** a litter (as of canvas) for carrying a disabled or dead person **4 :** a rod or bar extending between two legs of a chair or table

stretch·er–bear·er \-ˌbar-ər, -ˌber-\ *n* : one who carries one end of a stretcher

stretch–out \ˈstrech-ˌau̇t\ *n* **1 :** a system of industrial operation in which workers are required to do extra work and esp. to operate more machines than formerly either with slight or with no additional pay **2 a :** the act of stretching out : the state of being stretched out **b :** an economizing measure that spreads a limited quantity over a larger field than orig. intended

stretch receptor *n* : MUSCLE SPINDLE

stretch runner *n* : a racehorse that makes a strong bid in the homestretch

stret·to \ˈstret-(ˌ)ō\ *also* **stret·ta** \-ə\ *n, pl* **stret·ti** \-(ˌ)ē\ *or* **strettos** [*stretto* fr. It, fr. *stretto* narrow, close; *stretta* fr. It, fr. fem. of *stretto*] **1 a :** the overlapping of answer with subject in a musical fugue **b :** the part of a fugue characterized by this overlapping **2 :** a concluding passage performed in a quicker tempo

strew \ˈstrü\ *vt* **strewed; strewed** *or* **strewn** \ˈstrün\; **strew·ing** [ME *strewen, strowen,* fr. OE *strewian, strēowian;* akin to OHG *strewen* to strew, L *sternere* to spread out, Gk *stornynai*] **1 :** to spread by scattering **2 :** to cover by or as if by scattering something <~*ing* the highways with litter> **3 :** to become dispersed over as if scattered **4 :** to spread abroad : DISSEMINATE

strew·ment \ˈstrü-mənt\ *n, archaic* : something (as flowers) strewed or designed for strewing

stria \ˈstrī-ə\ *n, pl* **stri·ae** \ˈstrī-ˌē\ [L, furrow, channel — more at STRIKE] **1 :** a minute groove or channel **2 :** a narrow line or band (as of color) esp. when one of a series of parallel grooves or lines

¹stri·ate \ˈstrī-ət, -ˌāt\ *adj* : STRIATED

²stri·ate \-ˌāt\ *vt* **stri·at·ed; stri·at·ing :** to mark with striae

stri·at·ed \ˈstrī-ˌāt-əd\ *adj* **1 :** marked with striae **2 :** of, relating to, or being striated muscle

striated muscle *n* : muscle tissue that is marked by transverse dark and light bands, that is made up of elongated multinuclear fibers, and that is found in the muscles under voluntary control clothing the vertebrate skeleton and in all or most of the musculature of arthropods — compare SMOOTH MUSCLE

stri·a·tion \strī-ˈā-shən\ *n* **1 a :** the fact or state of being striated **b :** arrangement of striae **2 :** STRIA **3 :** one of the alternate dark and light cross bands of a myofibril of striated muscle

strick \ˈstrik\ *n* [ME *stric, strik,* prob. of LG or D origin; akin to MLG *strik* rope, MD *stric*] : a bunch of hackled flax, jute, or hemp

strick·en \ˈstrik-ən\ *adj* [fr. pp. of *strike*] **1 :** having the contents leveled off even with the top <a ~ measure of grain> **2 :** hit or wounded by or as if by a missile **3 a :** afflicted or overwhelmed by or as if by disease, misfortune, or sorrow **b :** made incapable or unfit : INCAPACITATED

¹strick·le \ˈstrik-əl\ *n* [ME *strikell;* akin to OE *strican* to stroke — more at STRIKE] **1 :** an instrument for leveling off measures of grain **2 :** an instrument for whetting scythes **3 :** a foundry tool for smoothing the surface of a core or mold

²strickle *vt* **strick·led; strick·ling** \-(ə-)liŋ\ **:** to smooth or form with a strickle

strict \ˈstrikt\ *adj* [L *strictus,* fr. pp. of *stringere* to bind tight — more at STRAIN] **1 a :** stringent in requirement or control <under ~ orders> **b :** severe in discipline <a ~ teacher> **2 a :** inflexibly maintained or adhered to : COMPLETE <~ secrecy> **b :** rigorously conforming to principle or a norm <a ~ Catholic> **3** *archaic* **a :** TIGHT, CLOSE; *also* : INTIMATE **b :** NARROW **4 :** EXACT, PRECISE <in the ~ sense of the word> **5 :** of narrow erect habit of growth <a ~ inflorescence> ***syn*** see RIGID ***ant*** lenient, indulgent — **strict·ly** \ˈstrik-(t)lē\ *adv* — **strict·ness** \ˈstrik(t)-nəs\ *n*

stric·ture \ˈstrik-chər\ *n* [ME, fr. LL *strictura,* fr. L *strictus,* pp. of *stringere* to bind tight] **1 :** an abnormal narrowing of a bodily passage; *also* : the narrowed part **2 :** something that closely restrains or limits : RESTRICTION <moral ~*s*> **3 :** an adverse criticism : CENSURE ***syn*** see ANIMADVERSION ***ant*** commendation

¹stride \ˈstrīd\ *vb* **strode** \ˈstrōd\; **strid·den** \ˈstrid-ᵊn\; **strid·ing** \ˈstrīd-iŋ\ [ME *striden,* fr. OE *stridan;* akin to MLG *striden* to straddle, OE *starian* to stare] *vi* **1 :** to stand astride **2 :** to move with or as if with long steps **3 :** to take a very long step ~ *vt* **1 :** BESTRIDE, STRADDLE **2 :** to step over **3 :** to move over or along with or as if with long measured steps — **strid·er** \ˈstrīd-ər\ *n*

²stride *n* **1 :** a long step **2 :** an act of striding **3 :** a stage of progress : ADVANCE **4 a :** a cycle of locomotor movements (as of a horse) completed when the feet regain the initial relative positions; *also* : the distance traversed in a stride **b :** the most effective natural pace : maximum competence or capability **5 :** a manner of striding — **in stride 1 :** without interference with regular activities **2 :** without becoming upset

stri·dence \ˈstrīd-ᵊn(t)s\ *n* : STRIDENCY

stri·den·cy \ˈstrīd-ᵊn-sē\ *n* : the quality or state of being strident

stri·dent \ˈstrīd-ᵊnt\ *adj* [L *strident-, stridens,* prp. of *stridere, stridēre* to make a harsh noise; akin to Gk & L *strix* owl] : characterized by harsh, insistent, and discordant sound <a ~ voice>; *also* : commanding attention by a loud or obtrusive quality <~ slogans> ***syn*** see VOCIFEROUS — **stri·dent·ly** *adv*

stride piano *n* [fr. the repeated strides taken by the left hand] : a style of jazz piano playing in which the right hand plays the melody while the left hand alternates between a single note and a chord played an octave or more higher

stri·dor \ˈstrīd-ər, ˈstrī-ˌdȯ(ə)r\ *n* [L, fr. *stridere, stridēre*] **1 :** a harsh, shrill, or creaking noise **2 :** a harsh vibrating sound heard during expiration in cases of obstruction of the air passages

strid·u·late \ˈstrij-ə-ˌlāt\ *vi* **-lat·ed; -lat·ing** [back-formation fr. *stridulation*] : to make a shrill creaking noise by rubbing together special bodily structures — used esp. of male insects (as crickets or grasshoppers) — **strid·u·la·tion** \ˌstrij-ə-ˈlā-shən\ *n* — **strid·u·la·to·ry** \ˈstrij-ə-lə-ˌtōr-ē, -ˌtȯr-\ *adj*

strid·u·lous \ˈstrij-ə-ləs\ *adj* [L *stridulus,* fr. *stridere, stridēre*] : making a shrill creaking sound — **strid·u·lous·ly** *adv*

strife \ˈstrīf\ *n* [ME *strif,* fr. OF *estrif*] **1 a :** bitter sometimes violent conflict or dissension <political ~> **b :** an act of contention : FIGHT, STRUGGLE **2 :** exertion or contention for superiority **3** *archaic* : earnest endeavor ***syn*** see DISCORD ***ant*** peace, accord — **strife·less** \ˈstrī-fləs\ *adj*

strig·il \ˈstrij-əl\ *n* [L *strigilis;* akin to L *stringere* to touch lightly — more at STRIKE] : an instrument used by ancient Greeks and Romans for scraping moisture off the skin after a bath or exercising

stri·gose \ˈstrī-ˌgōs\ *adj* [NL *strigosus,* fr. *striga* bristle, fr. L, furrow] : having appressed bristles or scales <a ~ leaf>

¹strike \ˈstrīk\ *vb* **struck** \ˈstrək\; **struck** *also* **strick·en** \ˈstrik-ən\; **strik·ing** \ˈstrī-kiŋ\ [ME *striken,* fr. OE *strican* to stroke, go; akin to OHG *strīhhan* to stroke, L *stringere* to touch lightly, *striga, stria* furrow] *vi* **1 :** to take a course : GO <*struck* off through the brush> **2 :** to aim and usu. deliver a blow or thrust (as with the hand, a weapon, or a tool) **3 :** to come into contact forcefully <the two ships *struck* in mid channel> **4 :** DELETE, CANCEL **5 :** to lower a flag usu. in surrender **6 a :** to become indicated by a clock, bell, or chime <the hour had just *struck*> **b :** to make known the time by sounding <the clock *struck* as they entered> **7 :** PIERCE, PENETRATE <the wind seemed to ~ through our clothes> **8 a :** to engage in battle **b :** to make a military attack **9 :** to become ignited **10 :** to discover something <he *struck* on a new plan of attack> **11 a :** to pull on a fishing rod in order to set the hook **b** *of a fish* **:** to seize the bait **12 :** DART, SHOOT **13 a** *of a plant cutting* **:** to take root **b** *of a seed* **:** GERMINATE **14 :** to make an impression **15 :** to stop work in order to force an employer to comply with demands **16 :** to make a beginning <the need to ~ vigorously for success> **17 :** to thrust oneself forward <he *struck* into the midst of the argument> **18 :** to work diligently : STRIVE ~ *vt* **1 a :** to strike at : HIT **b :** to drive or remove by or as if by a blow **c :** to attack or seize with a sharp blow (as of fangs or claws) <*struck* by a snake> **d :** INFLICT <~ a blow> **e :** to produce by or as if by a blow or stroke <Moses *struck* water from the rock> **f :** to separate by a sharp blow <~ off flints> **2 a :** to haul down : LOWER <~ a flag> **b :** to dismantle and take away **c :** to strike the tents of (a camp) **3 :** to afflict suddenly <*stricken* by a heart attack> **4 a :** to engage in (a battle) : FIGHT **b :** to make a military attack on **5 :** DELETE, CANCEL <~ the last paragraph> **6 a :** to penetrate painfully : PIERCE **b :** to cause to penetrate **c :** to send down or out <trees *struck* roots deep into the soil> **7 a :** to level (as a measure of grain) by scraping off what is above the rim **b :** STRICKLE **8 :** to indicate by sounding **9 a** (1) **:** to bring into forceful contact (2) **:** to shake (hands) in confirming an agreement (3) **:** to thrust suddenly **b :** to come into contact or collision with **c** *of light* **:** to fall on **d** *of a sound* **:** to become audible to **10 a :** to affect with a mental or emotional state or a strong emotion <*struck* with horror at the sight> **b :** to affect a person with (a strong emotion) <his words *struck* fear in the listeners> **c :** to cause to become by or as if by a sudden blow <*struck* him dead> **11 a :** to produce by stamping **b** (1) **:** to produce (as fire) by or as if by striking (2) **:** to cause to ignite by friction **12 :** to make and ratify the terms of <~ a bargain> **13 a :** to play or produce by stroking keys or strings <*struck* a series of chords on the piano> **b :** to produce as if by playing an instrument <his voice *struck* a note of concern> **14 a :** to hook (a fish) by a sharp pull on the line **b** *of a fish* **:** to snatch at (a bait) **15 a :** to occur to <the answer *struck* him suddenly> **b :** to appear to esp. as a revelation or as remarkable : IMPRESS **16 :** BEWITCH **17 :** to arrive at by computation <~ a balance> **18 a :** to come to : ATTAIN **b :** to come upon : DISCOVER <~ gold> **19 :** to engage in a strike against (an employer) **20 :** to take on : ASSUME <~ a pose> **21 a :** to place (a plant cutting) in a medium for growth and rooting **b :** to so propagate (a plant) **22 :** to make one's way along **23 :** to cause (an arc) to form (as between electrodes of an arc lamp) **24** *of an insect* **:** to oviposit on or in

***syn* 1** STRIKE, HIT, SMITE, SLAP, SWAT, PUNCH *shared meaning element* : to come or bring into contact with a sharp blow
2 see AFFECT

²strike *n* **1 :** STRICKLE **2 :** an act or instance of striking **3 a :** a work stoppage by a body of workers to enforce compliance with demands made on an employer **b :** a temporary stoppage of activities in protest against an act or condition **4 :** the direction of the line of intersection of a horizontal plane with an uptilted geological stratum **5 a :** a pull on a fishing rod to strike a fish **b :** a pull on a line by a fish in striking **6 :** a stroke of good luck; *esp* : a discovery of a valuable mineral deposit **7 a :** a pitched ball that is in the strike zone or is swung at and is not hit fair **b :** a perfectly thrown ball **8 :** DISADVANTAGE, HANDICAP <his racial background was a second ~ against him —K. D. Miller> **9 :** an act or instance of knocking down all the bowling pins with the first bowl **10 :** establishment of roots and plant growth **11 :** cutaneous myiasis (as of sheep) <body ~> **12 a :** a military attack; *esp* : an air attack on a single objective **b :** a group of airplanes taking part in such an attack

strike·bound \ˈstrīk-ˌbau̇nd\ *adj* : subjected to a strike

strike·break·er \-ˌbrā-kər\ *n* : one hired to replace a striking worker

strike·break·ing \-kiŋ\ *n* : action designed to break up a strike

strike·less \ˈstrī-kləs\ *adj* : marked by the absence of strikes

strike off *vt* **1 :** to produce in an effortless manner **2 :** to depict clearly and exactly

strike·out \'strī-ˌkau̇t\ *n* **:** an out in baseball resulting from a batter's being charged with three strikes

strike out \(ˈ)strī-'kau̇t\ *vt, of a baseball pitcher* **:** to retire (a batter) by a strikeout ~ *vi* **1 :** to enter upon a course of action **2 :** to set out vigorously **3 :** to make an out in baseball by a strikeout **4 :** to finish bowling a string with consecutive strikes; *specif* **:** to bowl three strikes in the last frame

strike·over \'strī-ˌkō-vər\ *n* **:** an act or instance of striking a typewriter character on a spot occupied by another character

strik·er \'strī-kər\ *n* **1 :** one that strikes: as **a :** a player in any of several games who strikes **b :** the hammer of the striking mechanism of a clock or watch **c :** BLACKSMITH **d :** a worker on strike **2 :** an enlisted man working for a petty officer's rate

strike up *vi* **:** to begin to sing or play or to be sung or played <a march *struck up* and the parade began> ~ *vt* **1 :** to cause to begin singing or playing <*strike up* the band> **2 :** to cause to begin <*strike up* a conversation>

strike zone *n* **:** the area (as between the armpits and tops of the knees of a batter in his natural stance) over home plate through which a pitched baseball must pass to be called a strike

strik·ing \'strī-kiŋ\ *adj* **:** attracting attention or notice through unusual or conspicuous qualities <a woman of ~ beauty> ***syn*** see NOTICEABLE — **strik·ing·ly** \-kiŋ-lē\ *adv*

¹string \'striŋ\ *n* [ME, fr. OE *streng;* akin to L *stringere* to bind tight — more at STRAIN] **1 :** a small cord used to bind, fasten, or tie **2 a** *archaic* **:** a cord (as a tendon or ligament) of an animal body **b :** a plant fiber (as a leaf vein) **3 a :** the gut or wire cord of a musical instrument **b** *pl* **(1) :** the stringed instruments of an orchestra **(2) :** the players of such instruments **4 a :** a group of objects threaded on a string <a ~ of fish> **b (1) :** a series of things arranged in or as if in a line <a ~ of cars> **(2) :** a sequence of like items (as bits, characters, or words) **c :** a group of business properties scattered geographically <a ~ of newspapers> **d :** the animals and esp. horses belonging to or used by one individual **5 a :** a means of recourse **:** EXPEDIENT **b :** a group of players ranked according to skill or proficiency **6 :** SUCCESSION, SEQUENCE <a ~ of successes> **7 a :** one of the inclined sides of a stair supporting the treads and risers **b :** STRINGCOURSE **8 a :** BALKLINE 1 **b :** the action of lagging for break in billiards **9 :** LINE 13 **10** *pl* **a :** contingent conditions or obligations **b :** CONTROL, DOMINATION — **string·less** \'striŋ-ləs\ *adj* — **on the string :** subject to one's influences

²string *vb* **strung** \'strəŋ\; **string·ing** \'striŋ-iŋ\ *vt* **1 a :** to equip with strings **b :** to tune the strings of **2 :** to make tense **:** key up **3 a :** to thread on or as if on a string **b :** to thread with objects **c :** to tie, hang, or fasten with string **4 :** to hang by the neck **5 :** to remove the strings of <~ beans> **6 a :** to extend or stretch like a string <~ wires from tree to tree> **b :** to set out in a line or series **7 :** FOOL, HOAX <cowboys ~*ing* tenderfeet with tall tales —Carl Van Doren> ~ *vi* **1 :** to move, progress, or lie in a string **2 :** to form into strings **3 :** LAG 3

string along *vi* **:** to go along **:** AGREE ~ *vt* **1 :** to keep dangling or waiting **2 :** DECEIVE, FOOL

string bass *n* **:** DOUBLE BASS

string bean *n* **1 :** a bean of one of the older varieties of kidney bean that have stringy fibers on the lines of separation of the pods; *broadly* **:** SNAP BEAN **2 :** a very tall thin person

string·board \'striŋ-ˌbō(ə)rd, -ˌbȯ(ə)rd\ *n* **:** a board or built-up facing used in stair building to cover the ends of the steps and hide the true string

string·course \-ˌkō(ə)rs, -ˌkȯ(ə)rs\ *n* **:** a horizontal band (as of bricks) in a building forming a part of the design

stringed \'striŋd\ *adj* **1 :** having strings **2 :** produced by strings

stringed instrument *n* **:** a musical instrument (as a violin, harp, or piano) sounded by plucking, striking, or drawing a bow across tense strings

strin·gen·cy \'strin-jən-sē\ *n* **:** the quality or state of being stringent

strin·gen·do \strin-'jen-(ˌ)dō\ *adv* [It, verbal of *stringere* to press, fr. L, to bind tight] **:** with quickening of tempo (as to a climax) — used as a direction in music

strin·gent \'strin-jənt\ *adj* [L *stringent-, stringens,* prp. of *stringere* to bind tight] **1 :** TIGHT, CONSTRICTED **2 :** marked by rigor, strictness, or severity esp. with regard to rule or standard **3 :** marked by money scarcity and credit strictness ***syn*** see RIGID — **strin·gent·ly** *adv*

string·er \'striŋ-ər\ *n* **1 :** one that strings **2 :** a string, wire, or chain often with snaps on which fish are strung by a fisherman **3 :** a narrow vein or irregular filament of mineral traversing a rock mass of different material **4 a :** a long horizontal timber to connect uprights in a frame or to support a floor **b :** STRING 7a **c :** a tie in a truss **5 a :** a longitudinal member extending from bent to bent of a railroad bridge and carrying the track **b :** a longitudinal member (as in an airplane fuselage or wing) to reinforce the skin **6 a :** a news correspondent who is paid space rates **b :** a newsman who works for a publication or news agency on a part-time basis; *broadly* **:** CORRESPONDENT **7 :** one estimated to be of specified excellence or efficiency — usu. used in combination <first-*stringer*> <second-*stringer*>

string·halt \'striŋ-ˌhȯlt\ *n* **:** a condition of lameness in the hind legs of a horse caused by muscular spasms — **string·halt·ed** \-ˌhȯl-təd\ *adj*

string·ing \'striŋ-iŋ\ *n* **:** the gut, silk, or nylon with which a racket is strung

string line *n* **:** BALKLINE 1

string·piece \'striŋ-ˌpēs\ *n* **:** the heavy squared timber lying along the top of the piles forming a dock front or timber pier

string quartet *n* **1 :** a quartet of performers on stringed instruments usu. including a first and second violin, a viola, and a cello **2 :** a composition for string quartet

string tie *n* **:** a narrow necktie

stringy \'striŋ-ē\ *adj* **string·i·er; -est** **1 a :** containing, consisting of, or resembling fibrous matter or string <~ hair> **b :** lean and sinewy in build **:** WIRY **2 :** capable of being drawn out to form a string **:** ROPY <a ~ precipitate> — **string·i·ness** *n*

stringy·bark \'striŋ-ē-ˌbärk\ *n* **1 :** any of several Australian eucalypti with fibrous inner bark **2 :** the bark of a stringybark

¹strip \'strip\ *vb* **stripped** \'stript\ *also* **stript; strip·ping** [ME *strippen,* fr. OE *-stripan;* akin to OHG *stroufen* to strip] *vt* **1 a :** to remove clothing, covering, or surface matter from **b :** to deprive of possessions **c :** to divest of honors, privileges, or functions **2 a :** to remove extraneous or superficial matter from <a prose style *stripped* to the bones> **b :** to remove furniture, equipment, or accessories from <~ a ship for action> **3 :** to make bare or clear (as by cutting or grazing) **4 :** to finish a milking of by pressing the last available milk from the teats <~ a cow> **5 a :** to remove cured leaves from the stalks of (tobacco) **b :** to remove the midrib from (tobacco leaves) **6 :** to tear or damage the thread of (a separable part or fitting) **7 :** to separate (components) from a mixture or solution **8 :** to press eggs or milt out of (a fish) ~ *vi* **1 a :** to take off clothes **b :** to perform a striptease **2 :** PEEL 1 — **strip·pa·ble** \'strip-ə-bəl\ *adj*

²strip *n* [perh. fr. MLG *strippe* strap] **1 a :** a long narrow piece of material **b :** a long narrow area of land or water **2 :** AIRSTRIP

strip chart *n* **:** a device used for the continuous graphic recording of time-dependent data

strip–crop \'strip-ˌkräp\ *vt* **:** to practice strip-cropping on ~ *vi* **:** to practice strip-cropping

strip–crop·ping *n* **:** the growing of a cultivated crop (as corn) in strips alternating with strips of a sod-forming crop (as hay) arranged to follow an approximate contour of the land and minimize erosion

¹stripe \'strīp\ *n* [ME; akin to MD *stripe*] **:** a stroke or blow with a rod or lash

²stripe *n* [prob. fr. MD; akin to OE *strica* streak — more at STREAK] **1 a :** a line or long narrow section differing in color or texture from parts adjoining **b (1) :** a textile design consisting of lines or bands against a plain background **(2) :** a fabric with a striped design **2 :** a narrow strip of braid or embroidery usu. in the shape of a bar, arc, or chevron that is worn (as on the sleeve of a military uniform) to indicate rank or length of service **3 :** a distinct variety or sort **:** TYPE <men of the same political ~> — **stripe·less** \'strī-pləs\ *adj*

³stripe *vt* **striped** \'strīpt; *see* STRIPED *adj*\; **strip·ing :** to make stripes on or variegate with stripes

striped \'strīpt, 'strī-pəd\ *adj* **:** having stripes or streaks

striped bass *n* **:** a large anadromous food and sport fish (*Morone saxatilis* of the family Percichthyidae) that occurs along the Atlantic coast of the U.S. and has been introduced along the Pacific coast

striped skunk *n* **:** a common No. American skunk (*Mephitis mephitis*) usu. with white on the top of the head that extends posteriorly in two narrowly separated stripes

strip·er \'strī-pər\ *n* **1 :** one that wears stripes (as on a sleeve) to indicate rank or length of service **2 :** STRIPED BASS

strip·film \'strip-ˌfilm\ *n* **:** FILMSTRIP

strip·ing \'strī-piŋ\ *n* **1 :** the act or process of marking with stripes **2 a :** the stripes marked or painted on something **b :** a design of stripes

strip·ling \'strip-liŋ\ *n* [ME] **:** an adolescent boy

strip mine *n* **:** a mine that is worked from the earth's surface by the stripping of overburden; *esp* **:** a coal mine situated along the outcrop of a flat dipping bed — **strip–mine** *vt* — **strip miner** *n*

strip·per \'strip-ər\ *n* **1 :** one that strips **2 :** STRIPTEASER **3 :** a machine that separates a desired part of an agricultural crop

strip poker *n* **:** a poker game in which a player pays his losses by removing articles of clothing

strip·tease \'strip-ˌtēz\ *n* **:** a burlesque act in which a female performer removes her clothing piece by piece in view of the audience

strip·teas·er \-ˌtē-zər\ *n* **:** one who performs a striptease

stripy \'strī-pē\ *adj* **strip·i·er; -est :** marked by stripes or streaks

strive \'strīv\ *vi* **strove** \'strōv\ *also* **strived** \'strīvd\; **striv·en** \'striv-ən\ *or* **strived; striv·ing** \'strī-viŋ\ [ME *striven,* fr. OF *estriver,* of Gmc origin; akin to MHG *streben* to endeavor, OE *strīdan* to stride] **1 :** to struggle in opposition **:** CONTEND **2 :** to devote serious effort or energy **:** ENDEAVOR ***syn*** see ATTEMPT — **striv·er** \'strī-vər\ *n*

strobe \'strōb\ *n* [by shortening & alter.] **1 :** STROBOSCOPE **2 :** a device that utilizes a flashtube for high-speed illumination (as in a stroboscope or in photography)

strobe light *n* **:** STROBE

stro·bi·la \strō-'bī-lə, 'strō-bə-\ *n, pl* **-lae** \-(ˌ)lē\ [NL, fr. Gk *strobilē* plug of lint shaped like a pinecone, fr. *strobilos* pinecone] **:** a linear series of similar animal structures (as the segmented body of a tapeworm) produced by budding — **stro·bi·lar** \-'bī-lər; -bə-lər, -ˌlär\ *adj*

stro·bi·la·tion \ˌstrō-bə-'lā-shən\ *n* [NL *strobila*] **:** asexual reproduction by transverse division of the body into segments which develop into separate individuals, zooids, or proglottids in many coelenterates and worms

stro·bile \'strō-ˌbīl, -bəl\ *n* [NL *strobilus*] **1 :** STROBILUS 1 **2 :** a spike with persistent overlapping bracts that resembles a cone and is the pistillate inflorescence of the hop

stro·bi·li·za·tion \ˌstrō-bə-lə-'zā-shən\ *n* **:** STROBILATION

stro·bi·lus \strō-'bī-ləs, 'strō-bə-\ *n, pl* **-li** \-ˌlī\ [NL, fr. LL, pinecone, fr. Gk *strobilos* twisted object, top, pinecone, fr. *strobos*

ə abut	ᵊ kitten	ər further	a back	ā bake	ä cot, cart
au̇ out	ch chin	e less	ē easy	g gift	i trip	ī life
j joke	ŋ sing	ō flow	ȯ flaw	ȯi coin	th thin	t͟h this
ü loot	u̇ foot	y yet	yü few	yu̇ furious	zh vision

action of whirling — more at STROPHE] **1 :** an aggregation of sporophylls resembling a cone (as in the club mosses and horsetails) **2 :** the cone of a gymnosperm

stro·bo·scope \'strō-bə-ˌskōp\ *n* [Gk *strobos* whirling + ISV *-scope*] **:** an instrument for determining the speed of cyclic motion (as rotation or vibration) that causes the motion to appear slowed or stopped: as **a :** a revolving disk with holes around the edge through which an object is viewed **b :** a flashtube that intermittently illuminates a moving object **c :** a cardboard disk with marks to be viewed under intermittent light

stro·bo·scop·ic \ˌstrō-bə-'skäp-ik\ *adj* **:** of, utilizing, or relating to a stroboscope or a strobe — **stro·bo·scop·i·cal·ly** \-i-k(ə-)lē\ *adv*

stro·bo·tron \'strō-bə-ˌträn\ *n* [*strobo*scope + *-tron*] **:** a gas-filled electron tube used esp. as a source of bright flashes of light for a stroboscope

strode *past of* STRIDE

[1]**stroke** \'strōk\ *vt* **stroked; strok·ing** [ME *stroken,* fr. OE *strācian;* akin to OHG *strīhhan* to stroke — more at STRIKE] **:** to rub gently in one direction; *also* **:** CARESS — **strok·er** *n*

[2]**stroke** *n* [ME; akin to OE *strīcan* to stroke — more at STRIKE] **1 :** the act of striking; *esp* **:** a blow with a weapon or implement **2 :** a single unbroken movement; *esp* **:** one of a series of repeated or to-and-fro movements **3 :** a striking of the ball in a game (as tennis); *specif* **:** a striking or attempt to strike the ball that constitutes the scoring unit in golf **4 a :** a sudden action or process producing an impact <~ of lightning> **b :** an unexpected result <~ of luck> **5 :** APOPLEXY **6 a :** one of a series of propelling beats or movements against a resisting medium <a ~ of the oar> **b :** an oarsman who sets the tempo for a crew **7 a :** a vigorous or energetic effort <a ~ of genius> **b :** a delicate or clever touch in a narrative, description, or construction **8 :** HEARTBEAT **9 :** the movement or the distance of the movement in either direction of a mechanical part (as a piston rod) having a reciprocating motion **10 :** the sound of a bell being struck <at the ~ of twelve> **11** [[1]*stroke*] **:** an act of stroking or caressing **12 a :** a mark or dash made by a single movement of an implement **b :** one of the lines of a letter of the alphabet

[3]**stroke** *vb* **stroked; strok·ing** *vt* **1 a :** to mark with a short line <~ the *t's*> **b :** to cancel by drawing a line through <*stroked* out his name> **2 :** to set the stroke for (a rowing crew); *also* **:** to set the stroke for the crew of (a rowing boat) **3 :** HIT; *esp* **:** to propel (a ball) with a controlled swinging blow ~ *vi* **:** to row at a certain number of strokes a minute

stroke play *n* **:** golf competition scored by total number of strokes

stroll \'strōl\ *vb* [prob. fr. G dial. *strollen*] *vi* **1 :** to walk in a leisurely or idle manner **:** RAMBLE **2 :** to go from place to place in search of occupation or profit <~*ing* players> <~*ing* musicians> ~ *vt* **:** to walk at leisure along or about — **stroll** *n*

stroll·er \'strō-lər\ *n* **1 :** one that strolls **2 a :** VAGRANT, TRAMP **b :** an itinerant actor **3 :** a carriage designed as a chair in which a baby may be pushed

stro·ma \'strō-mə\ *n, pl* **stro·ma·ta** \-mət-ə\ [NL *stromat-, stroma,* fr. L, bed covering, fr. Gk *strōmat-, strōma,* fr. *stornynai* to spread out — more at STREW] **1 a :** the supporting framework of an animal organ typically consisting of connective tissue **b :** the spongy protoplasmic framework of some cells (as a red blood cell) **2 a :** a compact mass of fungous hyphae producing perithecia or pycnidia **b :** the colorless proteinaceous matrix of a chloroplast in which the chlorophyll-containing lamellae are embedded — **stro·mal** \-məl\ *adj* — **stro·ma·tal** \-mət-ᵊl\ *adj* — **stro·mat·ic** \strō-'mat-ik\ *adj*

stro·mat·o·lite \strō-'mat-ᵊl-ˌīt\ *n* [L *stromat-, stroma* bed covering + E *-o-* + *-lite*] **:** a laminated sedimentary fossil formed from layers of blue-green algae — **stro·mat·o·lit·ic** \-ˌmat-ᵊl-'it-ik\ *adj*

stro·mey·er·ite \'strō-ˌmī(ə)r-ˌīt, strō-'\ *n* [G *stromeyerit,* fr. Friedrich *Strohmeyer* †1835 G chemist] **:** a steel-gray mineral CuAgS consisting of silver copper sulfide of metallic luster

strong \'strȯŋ\ *adj* **stron·ger** \'strȯŋ-gər\; **stron·gest** \'strȯŋ-gəst\ [ME, fr. OE *strang;* akin to OHG *strengi* strong, L *stringere* to bind tight — more at STRAIN] **1 :** having or marked by great physical power **:** ROBUST **2 :** having moral or intellectual power **3 :** having great resources (as of wealth or talent) **4 :** of a specified number <an army ten thousand ~> **5 a :** striking or superior of its kind <a ~ resemblance> **b :** effective or efficient esp. in a specified direction **6 :** FORCEFUL, COGENT <~ evidence> **7 :** not mild or weak **:** EXTREME, INTENSE: as **a :** rich in some active agent <~ beer> **b** *of a color* **:** high in chroma **c :** ionizing freely in solution <~ acids and bases> **d :** magnifying by refracting greatly <~ lens> **8** *obs* **:** FLAGRANT **9 :** moving with rapidity or force <~ wind> **10 :** ARDENT, ZEALOUS <a ~ supporter> **11 a :** not easily injured **:** SOLID **b :** not easily subdued or taken <a ~ fort> **12 :** well established **:** FIRM <~ beliefs> **13 :** not easily upset or nauseated <a ~ stomach> **14 :** having an offensive or intense odor or flavor **:** RANK **15 :** tending to steady or higher prices <a ~ market> **16 :** of, relating to, or constituting a verb or verb conjugation that forms the past tense by a change in the root vowel and the past participle usu. by the addition of *-en* with or without change of the root vowel (as *strive, strove, striven* or *drink, drank, drunk*) — **strong** *adv* — **strong·ish** \'strȯŋ-ish\ *adj* — **strong·ly** \'strȯŋ-lē\ *adv*

syn STRONG, STOUT, STURDY, STALWART, TOUGH, TENACIOUS *shared meaning element* **:** showing power to resist or endure *ant* weak

[1]**strong–arm** \'strȯŋ-'ärm\ *adj* **:** having or using undue force

[2]**strong–arm** *vt* **1 :** to use force on **:** ASSAULT **2 :** to rob by force

strong·box \'strȯŋ-ˌbäks\ *n* **:** a strongly made chest or case for money or valuables

strong breeze *n* **:** wind having a speed of 25 to 31 miles per hour

strong drink *n* **:** intoxicating liquor

strong gale *n* **:** wind having a speed of 47 to 54 miles per hour

strong·hold \'strȯŋ-ˌhōld\ *n* **1 :** a fortified place **2 a :** a place of security or survival <one of the last ~*s* of the ancient Gaelic language —George Holmes> **b :** a place dominated by a particular group or marked by a particular characteristic <a Republican ~> <~*s* of snobbery —Lionel Trilling>

strong interaction *n* **:** a fundamental interaction experienced by elementary particles (as hadrons) that is more powerful than any other known force and is responsible for the binding together of neutrons and protons in the atomic nucleus and for processes of particle creation in high-energy collisions

strong–mind·ed \'strȯŋ-'mīn-dəd\ *adj* **:** having a vigorous mind; *esp* **:** marked by independence of thought and judgment — **strong–mind·ed·ly** *adv* — **strong–mind·ed·ness** *n*

strong room *n* **:** a room for money or valuables specially constructed to be fireproof and burglarproof

strong side *n* **:** the side of a football formation having the greater number of players; *specif* **:** the side on which the tight end plays

strong suit *n* **1 :** a long suit containing high cards **2 :** something in which one excels **:** FORTE

stron·gyle \'strän-ˌjīl, -jəl\ *n* [deriv. of Gk *strongylos* round, compact; akin to L *stringere* to bind tight — more at STRAIN] **:** any of various roundworms (family Strongylidae) related to the hookworms and mostly parasitic in the alimentary tract and tissues of the horse

stron·gy·lo·sis \ˌsträn-jə-'lō-səs\ *n* [NL] **:** infestation with or disease caused by strongyles

stron·tia \'strän-ch(ē-)ə, 'stränt-ē-ə\ *n* [NL, fr. obs. E *strontian,* fr. *Strontian,* village in Scotland] **1 :** a white solid monoxide SrO of strontium resembling lime and baryta **2 :** strontium hydroxide $Sr(OH)_2$

stron·tian·ite \'strän-chə-ˌnīt\ *n* **:** a mineral $SrCO_3$ consisting of strontium carbonate and occurring in various forms and colors

stron·tic \'stränt-ik\ *adj* **:** of or relating to strontium

stron·tium \'strän-ch(ē-)əm, 'stränt-ē-əm\ *n* [NL, fr. *strontia*] **:** a soft malleable ductile bivalent metallic element of the alkaline-earth group occurring only in combination and used esp. in color TV tubes, in crimson fireworks, and in the production of some ferrites — see ELEMENT table

strontium 90 *n* **:** a heavy radioactive isotope of strontium having the mass number 90 that is present in the fallout from nuclear explosions and is hazardous because like calcium it can be assimilated in biological processes and deposited in the bones of human beings and animals — called also *radiostrontium*

[1]**strop** \'sträp\ *n* [ME — more at STRAP] **:** STRAP: **a :** a short rope with its ends spliced to form a circle **b :** a usu. leather band for sharpening a razor

[2]**strop** *vt* **stropped; strop·ping :** to sharpen (a razor) on a strop

stro·phan·thin \strō-'fan(t)-thən\ *n* [ISV, fr. NL *Strophanthus* (genus of tropical trees or vines)] **:** any of several glycosides or mixtures of glycosides from African plants (genera *Strophanthus* and *Acocanthera*) of the dogbane family; *esp* **:** a bitter toxic glycoside $C_{36}H_{54}O_{14}$ from a woody vine (*Strophanthus kombé*) used similarly to digitalis

stro·phe \'strō-fē, -ˌfē\ *n* [Gk *strophē,* lit., act of turning, fr. *strephein* to turn, twist; akin to Gk *strobos* action of whirling] **1 :** the movement of the classical Greek chorus while turning from one side to the other of the orchestra **2 a :** a rhythmic system composed of two or more lines repeated as a unit; *esp* **:** such a unit recurring in a series of strophic units **b :** STANZA **c :** the part of a Greek choral ode sung during the strophe of the dance

stro·phic \'strō-fik, 'sträf-ik\ *adj* **1 :** relating to, containing, or consisting of strophes **2** *of a song* **:** using the same music for successive stanzas — compare THROUGH-COMPOSED

stro·phoid \'strō-ˌfȯid\ *n* [F *strophoïde,* fr. Gk *strophos* twisted band (fr. *strephein* to twist) + *-oïde* -oid] **:** a plane curve that is generated by a point whose distance from the y-axis along a variable straight line which always passes through a fixed point is equal to the y-intercept and that has the equation $\rho = a\ (\sec\theta \pm \tan\theta)$ in polar coordinates

stroud \'strau̇d\ *n* [prob. fr. *Stroud,* town in England] **1** *also* **stroud·ing** \-iŋ\ **:** a coarse woolen cloth formerly used in trade with No. American Indians **2 :** a blanket or garment of stroud

strove *past & chiefly dial past part of* STRIVE

strow \'strō\ *vt* **strowed; strown** \'strōn\ *or* **strowed; strow·ing** [ME *strowen* — more at STREW] *archaic* **:** SCATTER

stroy *vb* [ME *stroyen,* short for *destroyen*] *obs* **:** DESTROY

struck \'strək\ *adj* [pp. of *strike*] **:** closed or affected by a labor strike <a ~ factory> <a ~ employer>

struc·tur·al \'strək-chə-rəl, 'strək-shrəl\ *adj* **1 a :** of, relating to, or affecting structure <~ stability> **b :** used in building structures <~ clay> **c :** involved in or caused by structure esp. of the economy <~ unemployment> **2 :** of or relating to the physical makeup of a plant or animal body **3 :** of, relating to, or resulting from the effects of folding or faulting of the earth's crust **:** TECTONIC **4 :** concerned with or relating to structure rather than history or comparison <~ linguistics> — **struc·tur·al·ly** \-ē\ *adv*

structural formula *n* **:** an expanded molecular formula showing the arrangement within the molecule of atoms and of bonds

structural gene *n* **:** a gene that determines the amino acid sequence of a protein (as an enzyme) through a specific messenger RNA

structural iron *n* **:** iron worked or cast in structural shapes

struc·tur·al·ism \'strək-chə-rə-ˌliz-əm, 'strək-shrə-\ *n* **1 :** structural linguistics **2 :** an anthropological movement associated esp. with Claude Lévi-Strauss that seeks to analyze social relationships in terms of highly abstract relational structures often expressed in a logical symbolism — **struc·tur·al·ist** \-ləst\ *n or adj*

structural isomerism *n* **:** isomerism in which atoms are linked in a different order

struc·tur·al·ize \'strək-chə-rə-ˌlīz, 'strək-shrə-ˌlīz\ *vt* **-ized; -iz·ing :** to organize or incorporate into a structure — **struc·tur·al·iza·tion** \ˌstrək-chə-rə-lə-'zā-shən, ˌstrək-shrə-\ *n*

structural steel *n* **1 :** rolled steel in structural shapes **2 :** steel suitable for structural shapes

[1]**struc·ture** \'strək-chər\ *n* [ME, fr. L *structura,* fr. *structus,* pp. of *struere* to heap up, build; akin to L *sternere* to spread out — more at STREW] **1 :** the action of building **:** CONSTRUCTION **2 a :** something (as a building) that is constructed **b :** something arranged in a definite pattern of organization <a rigid totalitarian

~ —J. L. Hess> **3 :** manner of construction **:** MAKEUP <Gothic in ~> **4 a :** the arrangement of particles or parts in a substance or body <soil ~> <molecular ~> **b :** arrangement or interrelation of parts as dominated by the general character of the whole <economic ~> **5 a :** the aggregate of elements of an entity in their relationships to each other **b** (1) **:** the composition of conscious experience with its elements and their combinations (2) **:** GESTALT

[2]structure *vt* **struc·tured; struc·tur·ing** \ˈstrək-chə-riŋ, ˈstrək-shriŋ\ **1 :** to form into a structure **2 :** BUILD, CONSTRUCT

struc·ture·less \ˈstrək-chər-ləs\ *adj* **:** lacking structure; *esp* **:** devoid of cells <a ~ membrane> — **struc·ture·less·ness** *n*

stru·del \ˈs(h)trüd-ᵊl\ *n* [G, lit., whirlpool] **:** a pastry made from a thin sheet of dough rolled up with filling and baked <apple ~>

[1]strug·gle \ˈstrəg-əl\ *vi* **strug·gled; strug·gling** \-(ə-)liŋ\ [ME *struglen*] **1 :** to make violent strenuous efforts against opposition **2 :** to proceed with difficulty or with great effort <*struggling* to maintain his composure> — **strug·gler** \-(ə-)lər\ *n*

[2]struggle *n* **1 :** a violent effort or exertion **:** a strong and strongly motivated attempt **2 :** CONTEST, STRIFE ***syn*** see ATTEMPT

struggle for existence : the automatic competition (as for food, space, or light) of members of a natural population that tends to eliminate less efficient individuals and thereby increase the chance of the more efficient to pass on inherited adaptive traits

[1]strum \ˈstrəm\ *vb* **strummed; strum·ming** [imit.] *vt* **1 a :** to brush the fingers lightly over the strings of (a musical instrument) in playing <~ a guitar>; *also* **:** [3]THRUM 1 **b :** to play (music) on a guitar <~ a tune> **2 :** to cause to sound vibrantly <winds *strummed* the rigging — H.A. Chippendale> ~ *vi* **1 :** to strum a stringed instrument **2 :** to sound vibrantly — **strum·mer** *n*

[2]strum *n* **:** an act, instance, or sound of strumming

stru·ma \ˈstrü-mə\ *n, pl* **stru·mae** \-(ˌ)mē, -ˌmī\ *or* **strumas 1** [L — more at STRUT] **a** *archaic* **:** SCROFULA **b :** GOITER **2** [NL, fr. L] **:** a swelling at the base of the capsule in many mosses — **stru·mose** \-ˌmōs\ *adj*

strum·pet \ˈstrəm-pət\ *n* [ME] **:** PROSTITUTE

strung \ˈstrəŋ\ *past of* STRING

strung out *adj* **1 :** addicted to a drug **2 :** physically debilitated from or as if from long-term drug addiction

[1]strunt \ˈstrənt\ *vi* [by alter.] *Scot* **:** STRUT

[2]strunt *n* [origin unknown] *Scot* **:** LIQUOR

[1]strut \ˈstrət\ *vb* **strut·ted; strut·ting** [ME *strouten,* fr. OE *strūtian* to exert oneself; akin to L *struma* goiter, OE *starian* to stare] *vi* **1 :** to become turgid **:** SWELL **2 a :** to walk with a high gait **b :** to walk with a pompous and affected air ~ *vt* **:** to parade (as clothes) with a show of pride — **strut·ter** *n*

syn STRUT, SWAGGER, BRISTLE, BRIDLE *shared meaning element* **:** to assume an air of dignity or importance

[2]strut *n* **1 :** a structural piece designed to resist pressure in the direction of its length **2 :** a pompous step or walk

[3]strut *vt* **strut·ted; strut·ting :** to provide, stiffen, support, or hold apart with or as if with a strut

stru·thi·ous \ˈstrü-thē-əs, -t͟hē-\ *adj* [LL *struthio* ostrich, irreg. fr. Gk *strouthos*] **:** of or relating to the ostriches and related birds **:** RATITE

strych·nine \ˈstrik-ˌnīn, -nən, -ˌnēn\ *n* [F, fr. NL *Strychnos,* genus name, fr. L, nightshade, fr. Gk] **:** a bitter poisonous alkaloid $C_{21}H_{22}N_2O_2$ that is obtained from nux vomica and related plants (genus *Strychnos*) and acts as a stimulant to the central nervous system

strych·nin·ism \-ˌiz-əm\ *n* **:** chronic strychnine poisoning

Stu·art \ˈst(y)ü-ərt, ˈst(y)u̇(-ə)rt\ *adj* [Robert *Stewart* (Robert II of Scotland) †1390] **:** of or relating to the Scottish royal house to which belonged the rulers of Scotland from 1371 to 1603 and of Great Britain from 1603 to 1649 and from 1660 to 1714 — **Stuart** *n*

[1]stub \ˈstəb\ *n* [ME *stubb,* fr. OE *stybb;* akin to Gk *stypos* stem, *typtein* to beat — more at TYPE] **1 a :** STUMP 2 **b :** a short piece remaining on a stem or trunk where a branch has been lost **2 :** something made or worn to a short or blunt shape; *esp* **:** a pen with a short blunt nib **3 :** a short blunt part left after a larger part has been broken off or used up <pencil ~> **4 :** something cut short or stunted **5 a :** a small part of a leaf (as of a checkbook) attached to the backbone for memoranda of the contents of the part torn away **b :** the part of a ticket returned to the user

[2]stub *vt* **stubbed; stub·bing 1 a :** to grub up by the roots **b :** to clear (land) by grubbing out rooted growth **c :** to hew or cut down (a tree) close to the ground **2 :** to extinguish (as a cigarette) by crushing **3 :** to strike (one's foot or toe) against an object

stub·ble \ˈstəb-əl\ *n, often attrib* [ME *stuble,* fr. OF *estuble,* fr. L *stupula* stalk, straw, alter. of *stipula* — more at STIPULE] **1 :** the basal part of herbaceous plants and esp. cereal grasses remaining attached to the soil after harvest **2 :** a rough surface or growth resembling stubble; *esp* **:** a short growth of beard — **stub·bly** \-(ə-)lē\ *adj*

stubble mulch *n* **:** a lightly tilled mulch of plant residue used to prevent erosion, conserve moisture, and add organic matter to the soil

stub·born \ˈstəb-ərn\ *adj* [ME *stuborn*] **1 a** (1) **:** unreasonably or perversely unyielding **:** MULISH (2) **:** justifiably unyielding **:** RESOLUTE **b :** suggestive or typical of a strong stubborn nature <a ~ jaw> **2 :** performed or carried on in an unyielding, obstinate, or persistent manner <~ strife> **3 :** difficult to handle, manage, or treat **:** REFRACTORY <a ~ cold> ***syn*** see OBSTINATE — **stub·born·ly** *adv* — **stub·born·ness** \-ərn-(n)əs\ *n*

stub·by \ˈstəb-ē\ *adj* **1 a :** resembling a stub **:** being short and thick <~ fingers> **b :** being short and thickset **:** SQUAT **c :** being short, broad, or blunt (as from use or wear) **2 :** abounding with stubs **:** BRISTLY

[1]stuc·co \ˈstək-(ˌ)ō\ *n, pl* **stuccos** *or* **stuccoes** [It, of Gmc origin; akin to OHG *stucki* piece, crust, OE *stocc* stock] **1 a :** a material usu. made of portland cement, sand, and a small percentage of lime and applied in a plastic state to form a hard covering for exterior walls **b :** a fine plaster used in the decoration and ornamentation of interior walls **2 :** STUCCOWORK

[2]stucco *vt* **:** to coat or decorate with stucco

stuc·co·work \ˈstək-ō-ˌwərk\ *n* **:** work done in stucco

stuck *past of* STICK

stuck–up \ˈstək-ˈəp\ *adj* **:** superciliously self-important

[1]stud \ˈstəd\ *n, often attrib* [ME *stod,* fr. OE *stōd;* akin to OE *standan* to stand] **1 a :** a group of animals and esp. horses kept primarily for breeding **b :** a place (as a farm) where a stud is kept **2 :** STUDHORSE; *broadly* **:** a male animal kept for breeding — **at stud :** for breeding as a stud <retired racers standing *at stud*>

[2]stud *n* [ME *stode,* fr. OE *studu;* akin to OE *stōw* place — more at STOW] **1 a :** one of the smaller uprights in the framing of the walls of a building to which sheathing, paneling, or laths are fastened **:** SCANTLING **b :** height from floor to ceiling **2 a :** a boss, rivet, or nail with a large head used (as on a shield or belt) for ornament or protection **b :** a solid button with a shank or eye on the back inserted through an eyelet in a garment as a fastener or ornament **3 a :** any of various infixed pieces (as a rod or pin) projecting from a machine and serving chiefly as a support or axis **b :** one of the metal cleats inserted in a snow tire to increase traction

[3]stud *vt* **stud·ded; stud·ding 1 :** to furnish (as a building or wall) with studs **2 :** to adorn, cover, or protect with studs **3 :** to set (a place or thing) with a number of prominent objects

[4]stud *abbr* student

stud·book \ˈstəd-ˌbu̇k\ *n* **:** an official record (as in a book) of the pedigree of purebred animals (as horses or dogs)

stud·ding \ˈstəd-iŋ\ *n* **1 :** material for studs **2 :** STUDS

stud·ding sail \ˈstəd-iŋ-ˌsāl, ˈstən(t)-səl\ *n* [origin unknown] **:** a light sail set at the side of a principal square sail of a ship in free winds

stu·dent \ˈst(y)üd-ᵊnt, *oftenest in South* -ənt\ *n, often attrib* [ME, fr. L *student-, studens,* fr. prp. of *studēre* to study — more at STUDY] **1 :** SCHOLAR, LEARNER; *esp* **:** one who attends a school **2 :** one who studies **:** an attentive and systematic observer

student body *n* **:** the aggregate of students at an educational institution

student government *n* **:** the organization and management of student life, activities, or discipline by various student organizations in a school or college

student lamp *n* **:** a desk reading lamp with a tubular shaft, one or two arms for a shaded light, and originally an oil reservoir

stu·dent·ship \ˈst(y)üd-ᵊnt-ˌship, -ənt-\ *n* **1 :** the state of being a student **2** *Brit* **:** a grant for university study

stu·dent's t distribution \ˈst(y)üd-ᵊn(t)s-, -ən(t)s-\ *n, often cap S* [*Student,* pen name of W. S. Gossett †1937 Brit statistician] **:** T DISTRIBUTION

student teacher *n* **:** a student who is engaged in practice teaching

student teaching *n* **:** PRACTICE TEACHING

student union *n* **:** a building on a college campus that is devoted to student activities and that usu. contains lounges, auditoriums, offices, and game rooms

stud·horse \ˈstəd-ˌhȯ(ə)rs\ *n* **:** a stallion kept esp. for breeding

stud·ied \ˈstəd-ēd\ *adj* **1 :** KNOWLEDGEABLE, LEARNED **2 :** carefully considered or prepared **:** THOUGHTFUL **3 :** produced or marked by conscious design or premeditation <~ indifference> — **stud·ied·ly** *adv* — **stud·ied·ness** *n*

stu·dio \ˈst(y)üd-ē-ˌō\ *n, pl* **-dios** [It, lit., study, fr. L *studium*] **1 a :** the working place of a painter, sculptor, or photographer **b :** a place for the study of an art (as dancing, singing, or acting) **2 :** a place where motion pictures are made **3 :** a place maintained and equipped for the transmission of radio or television programs

studio apartment *n* **:** a small apartment consisting typically of a main room, kitchenette, and bathroom

studio couch *n* **:** an upholstered usu. backless couch that can be made to serve as a double bed by sliding from underneath it the frame of a single cot

stu·di·ous \ˈst(y)üd-ē-əs\ *adj* **1 :** given to study <~ of Japanese art —J.G. Huneker> **2 a :** of, relating to, or concerned with study **b :** favorable to study **3 a :** diligent or earnest in intent <made a ~ effort> **b :** marked by or suggesting purposefulness or diligence <a ~ expression on his face> **c :** deliberately or consciously planned **:** STUDIED <spoke with a ~ accent> — **stu·di·ous·ly** *adv* — **stu·di·ous·ness** *n*

stud poker *n* [[1]*stud*] **:** poker in which each player is dealt his first card facedown and his other four cards faceup with a round of betting taking place after each of the last four rounds of dealing

[1]study \ˈstəd-ē\ *n, pl* **stud·ies** [ME *studie,* fr. OF *estudie,* fr. L *studium;* akin to L *studēre* to study] **1 :** a state of contemplation **:** REVERIE **2 a :** application of the mental faculties to the acquisition of knowledge <years of ~> **b :** such application in a particular field or to a specific subject <the ~ of Latin> **c :** careful or extended consideration <the proposal is under ~> **d** (1) **:** a careful examination or analysis of a phenomenon, development, or question (2) **:** a paper in which such a study is published **3 :** a building or room devoted to study or literary pursuits **4 :** PURPOSE, INTENT **5 a :** a branch or department of learning **:** SUBJECT **b :** the activity or work of a student <returning to his *studies* after vacation> **c :** an object of study or deliberation <every gesture a careful ~ —Marcia Davenport> **d :** something attracting close attention or examination **6 :** a literary or artistic production intended as a preliminary outline or an experimental interpretation of specific features or characteristics **7 :** a musical composition for the practice of a point of technique

[2]study *vb* **stud·ied; study·ing** *vi* **1 a :** to engage in study **b**

: to undertake formal study of a subject **2** *dial* : MEDITATE, REFLECT **3** : ENDEAVOR, TRY ~ *vt* **1** : to read in detail esp. with the intention of learning **2** : to engage in the study of <~ biology> <~ medicine> **3** : PLOT, DESIGN **4** : to consider attentively or in detail ***syn*** see CONSIDER — **studi·er** \ˈstəd-ē-ər\ *n*

study hall *n* **1** : a room in a school set aside for study **2** : a period in a student's day set aside for study and homework

[1]**stuff** \ˈstəf\ *n* [ME, fr. MF *estoffe,* fr. OF, fr. *estoffer* to equip, stock] **1** : materials, supplies, or equipment used in various activities: as **a** *obs* : military baggage **b** : bullets or shells fired from a gun **c** : PERSONAL PROPERTY, POSSESSIONS **2** : material to be manufactured, wrought, or used in construction <clear half-inch pine ~ —Emily Holt> **3** : a finished textile suitable for clothing; *esp* : wood or worsted material **4 a** : literary or artistic production **b** : writing, discourse, or ideas of little value : TRASH **5 a** : an aggregate of matter <volcanic rock is curious ~> **b** (1) : matter of a particular and often unspecified kind <sold tons of the ~> (2) : something (as a drug or food) consumed by man <he used to drink but is now off the ~> **c** : a group or scattering of miscellaneous objects or articles <pick that ~ up off the floor> **6 a** : fundamental material : SUBSTANCE <~ of greatness> <~ of manhood> **b** : subject matter <a teacher who knows his ~> **7 a** : actions or talk in specific circumstances <don't give me any of that ~> **b** : special knowledge or capability <showing their ~> **8 a** : spin imparted to a thrown or hit ball to make it curve or change course **b** : variety of breaking pitches as distinguished from fastballs <greatest pitcher of my time . . . had tremendous ~ —Ted Williams>

[2]**stuff** *vt* **1 a** : to fill by packing things in : CRAM <when offered candy, the child ~*ed* his pockets> **b** : to fill to satiety : SURFEIT <~*ed* himself with turkey> **c** : to prepare (meat or vegetables) by filling or lining with a stuffing **d** : to fill (as a cushion) with a soft material or padding **e** : to fill out the skin of (an animal) for mounting **f** : to fill (a hole) by packing in material **2** : to fill by intellectual effort <~*ing* their heads with facts> **3** : to choke or block up (the nasal passages) **4 a** : to cause to enter or fill : THRUST <~*ed* a lot of clothing into a laundry bag> **b** : to put (as a ball or puck) into a goal forcefully from close range

stuffed shirt *n* : a smug, conceited, and usu. pompous person with an inflexibly conservative or reactionary attitude

stuff·er \ˈstəf-ər\ *n* **1** : one that stuffs **2** : an enclosure (as a leaflet) inserted in an envelope in addition to a bill, statement, or notice **3** : a series of extra threads or yarn running lengthwise in a fabric to add weight and bulk and to form a backing esp. for carpets

stuff·ing \ˈstəf-iŋ\ *n* : material used to stuff; *esp* : a seasoned mixture used to stuff food (as meat, vegetables, or eggs)

stuffing box *n* : a device that prevents leakage along a moving part (as a piston rod) passing through a hole in a vessel (as a cylinder) containing steam, water, or oil and that consists of a box or chamber made by enlarging the hole and a gland to compress the contained packing

stuff·less \ˈstəf-ləs\ *adj* : lacking stuff or substance

stuff shot *n* : DUNK SHOT

stuffy \ˈstəf-ē\ *adj* **stuff·i·er; -est** **1** : ILL-NATURED, ILL-HUMORED **2 a** : oppressive to the breathing : CLOSE **b** : stuffed up <a ~ nose> **3** : lacking in vitality or interest : STODGY, DULL **4** : narrowly inflexible in standards of conduct : SELF-RIGHTEOUS — **stuff·i·ly** \ˈstəf-ə-lē\ *adv* — **stuff·i·ness** \ˈstəf-ē-nəs\ *n*

stull \ˈstəl\ *n* [perh. modif. of G *stollen* post, support] **1** : a round timber used to support the sides or back of a mine **2** : one of a series of props wedged between the walls of a stope to hold up a platform

stul·ti·fi·ca·tion \ˌstəl-tə-fə-ˈkā-shən\ *n* : the act or process of stultifying : the state of being stultified

stul·ti·fy \ˈstəl-tə-ˌfī\ *vt* **-fied; -fy·ing** [LL *stultificare* to make foolish, fr. L *stultus* foolish; akin to L *stolidus* stolid] **1** : to allege or prove to be of unsound mind and hence not responsible **2 a** : to cause to appear or be stupid, foolish, or absurdly illogical **b** : to impair, invalidate, or reduce to futility esp. through enfeebling or repressive influence <what provokes interest and what *stultifies* it —Jeanne S. Chall>

[1]**stum** \ˈstəm\ *vt* **stummed; stum·ming** [D *stommen,* fr. *stom,* n.] *archaic* : to renew (wine) by mixing with must and reviving fermentation

[2]**stum** *n* [D *stom*] *archaic* : unfermented or partly fermented grape juice; *esp* : must in which fermentation has been artificially arrested

[1]**stum·ble** \ˈstəm-bəl\ *vb* **stum·bled; stum·bling** \-b(ə-)liŋ\ [ME *stumblen,* prob. of Scand origin; akin to Norw dial. *stumle* to stumble; akin to OE *stamerian* to stammer] *vi* **1 a** : to fall into sin or waywardness **b** : to make an error : BLUNDER **c** : to come to an obstacle to belief **2** : to trip in walking or running **3 a** : to walk unsteadily or clumsily **b** : to speak or act in a hesitant or faltering manner **4 a** : to come unexpectedly or by chance <~ onto the truth> **b** : to fall or move carelessly ~ *vt* **1** : to cause to stumble : TRIP **2** : BEWILDER, CONFOUND — **stum·bler** \-b(ə-)lər\ *n* — **stum·bling·ly** \-b(ə-)liŋ-lē\ *adv*

[2]**stumble** *n* : an act or instance of stumbling

stum·ble·bum \ˈstəm-bəl-ˌbəm\ *n* : a clumsy or inept person; *specif* : an inept boxer

stumbling block \ˈstəm-bliŋ-\ *n* **1** : an impediment to belief or understanding : PERPLEXITY **2** : an obstacle to progress

[1]**stump** \ˈstəmp\ *n* [ME *stumpe;* akin to OHG *stumpf* stump, ME *stampen* to stamp] **1 a** : the basal portion of a bodily part remaining after the rest is removed **b** : a rudimentary or vestigial bodily part **2** : the part of a plant and esp. a tree remaining attached to the root after the trunk is cut **3** : a remaining part : STUB **4** : a place or occasion for political public speaking

[2]**stump** *vt* **1** : to reduce to a stump : TRIM **2 a** : DARE, CHALLENGE **b** : to frustrate the progress or efforts of : BAFFLE **3** : to clear (land) of stumps **4** : to travel over (a region) making political speeches or supporting a cause **5 a** : to walk over heavily or clumsily **b** : STUB 3 ~ *vi* **1** : to walk heavily or noisily **2** : to go about making political speeches or supporting a cause — **stump·er** *n*

[3]**stump** *n* [F or Flem; F *estompe,* fr. Flem *stomp,* lit., stub, fr. MD; akin to OHG *stumpf* stump] : a short thick roll of leather, felt, or paper usu. pointed at both ends and used for shading or blending a drawing in crayon, pencil, charcoal, pastel, or chalk

[4]**stump** *vt* : to tone or treat (a drawing) with a stump

stump·age \ˈstəm-pij\ *n* **1** : the value of standing timber **2** : uncut marketable timber; *also* : the right to cut it

stumpy \ˈstəm-pē\ *adj* **1** : full of stumps **2** : being short and thick : STUBBY

[1]**stun** \ˈstən\ *vt* **stunned; stun·ning** [ME *stunen,* modif. of OF *estoner* — more at ASTONISH] **1** : to make senseless, groggy, or dizzy by or as if by a blow : DAZE **2** : to bewilder with noise **3** : to overcome esp. with astonishment or disbelief : ASTONISH

[2]**stun** *n* : the effect of something that stuns : SHOCK

stung *past of* STING

stunk *past of* STINK

stun·ner \ˈstən-ər\ *n* **1** : one that stuns **2** : an unusually beautiful or attractive person or thing

stun·ning \ˈstən-iŋ\ *adj* : strikingly beautiful or attractive — **stun·ning·ly** \-iŋ-lē\ *adv*

stun·sail *or* **stun·s'l** \ˈstən(t)-səl\ *n* [by contr.] : STUDDING SAIL

[1]**stunt** \ˈstənt\ *vt* [E dial. *stunt* stubborn, stunted, abrupt, prob. of Scand origin; akin to ON *stuttr* scant — more at STINT] : to hinder the normal growth of : DWARF — **stunt·ed·ness** *n*

[2]**stunt** *n* **1** : a check in growth **2** : one (as an animal) that is stunted **3** : a plant disease in which dwarfing occurs

[3]**stunt** *n* [prob. alter. of *stump* (challenge)] **1** : an unusual or difficult feat performed or undertaken chiefly to gain attention or publicity **2** : a shifting or switching of the positions of the defensive players in football intended to confuse the blocking assignments of the opponents

[4]**stunt** *vi* **1** : to perform stunts **2** : to engage in a stunt in football

stu·pa \ˈstü-pə\ *n* [Skt *stūpa*] : a hemispherical or cylindrical mound or tower serving as a Buddhist shrine

stupa

[1]**stupe** \ˈst(y)üp\ *n* [ME, fr. L *stuppa* coarse part of flax, tow, fr. Gk *styppē*] : a hot wet often medicated cloth applied externally (as to stimulate circulation)

[2]**stupe** *n* [short for *stupid*] : a stupid person : DOLT

stu·pe·fa·cient \ˌst(y)ü-pə-ˈfā-shənt\ *n* [L *stupefacient-, stupefaciens,* prp. of *stupefacere* to stupefy] : something promoting stupefaction : NARCOTIC

stu·pe·fac·tion \-ˈfak-shən\ *n* [NL *stupefaction-, stupefactio,* fr. L *stupefactus,* pp. of *stupefacere*] : the act of stupefying : the state of being stupefied

stu·pe·fy \-ˌfī\ *vt* **-fied; -fy·ing** [MF *stupefier,* modif. of L *stupefacere,* fr. *stupēre* to be astonished + *facere* to make, do — more at DO] **1** : to make stupid, groggy, or insensible **2** : ASTONISH

stu·pen·dous \st(y)u̇-ˈpen-dəs\ *adj* [L *stupendus,* gerundive of *stupēre*] **1** : causing astonishment or wonder : AWESOME, MARVELOUS **2** : of amazing size or greatness : TREMENDOUS ***syn*** see MONSTROUS — **stu·pen·dous·ly** *adv* — **stu·pen·dous·ness** *n*

[1]**stu·pid** \ˈst(y)ü-pəd\ *adj* [MF *stupide,* fr. L *stupidus,* fr. *stupēre* to be benumbed, be astonished; akin to Gk *typtein* to beat — more at TYPE] **1 a** : slow of mind : OBTUSE **b** : given to unintelligent decisions or acts **c** : lacking intelligence or reason : BRUTISH **2** : dulled in feeling or sensation : TORPID <still ~ from the sedative> **3** : marked by or resulting from dullness : SENSELESS **4 a** : lacking interest or point **b** : VEXATIOUS, EXASPERATING <this ~ flashlight won't work> — **stu·pid·ly** *adv* — **stu·pid·ness** *n*

syn STUPID, DULL, DENSE, CRASS, DUMB ***shared meaning element*** : lacking in or exhibiting a lack of power to absorb ideas or impressions ***ant*** intelligent

[2]**stupid** *n* : a stupid person

stu·pid·i·ty \st(y)u̇-ˈpid-ət-ē\ *n, pl* **-ties** **1** : the quality or state of being stupid **2** : a stupid idea or act

stu·por \ˈst(y)ü-pər\ *n* [ME, fr. L, fr. *stupēre*] **1** : a condition characterized by great diminution or suspension of sense or feeling <drunken ~> **2** : a state of extreme apathy or torpor resulting often from stress or shock : DAZE

stu·por·ous \ˈst(y)ü-p(ə-)rəs\ *adj* : marked or affected by or as if by stupor

stur·dy \ˈstərd-ē\ *adj* **stur·di·er; -est** [ME, brave, stubborn, fr. OF *estourdi* stunned, fr. pp. of *estourdir* to stun, fr. (assumed) VL *exturdire* to be dizzy as a thrush that is drunk from eating grapes, fr. L *ex-* + *turdus* thrush — more at THRUSH] **1 a** : firmly built or constituted : STOUT **b** : HARDY **c** : sound in design or execution : SUBSTANTIAL **2 a** : marked by or reflecting physical strength or vigor **b** : FIRM, RESOLUTE ***syn*** see STRONG ***ant*** decrepit — **stur·di·ly** \ˈstərd-ᵊl-ē\ *adv* — **stur·di·ness** \ˈstərd-ē-nəs\ *n*

stur·geon \ˈstər-jən\ *n* [ME, fr. OF *estourjon,* of Gmc origin; akin to OE *styria* sturgeon] : any of various usu. large elongate edible ganoid fishes (as of the genus *Acipenser*) which are widely distributed in the north temperate zone and whose roe is made into caviar

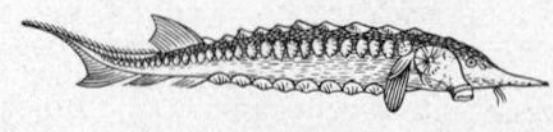

sturgeon

Sturm und Drang \ˌs(h)tu̇r-mu̇nt-ˈdräŋ, -mənt-\ *n* [G, fr. *Sturm und Drang* (*Storm and Stress*), drama by Friedrich von Klinger] **1** : a late 18th century German literary movement characterized by works containing rousing action and high emotionalism that often deal with the individual's revolt against society **2** : TURMOIL

sturt \'stərt\ *n* [ME, contention, alter. of *strut;* akin to OE *strūtian* to exert oneself — more at STRUT] *chiefly Scot* : CONTENTION

[1]**stut·ter** \'stət-ər\ *vb* [freq. of E dial. *stut* to stutter, fr. ME *stutten;* akin to D *stotteren* to stutter, L *tundere* to beat — more at STINT] *vi* **1** : to speak with involuntary disruption or blocking of speech (as by spasmodic repetition or prolongation of vocal sounds) **2** : to move or act in a halting or spasmodic manner <the old jalopy bucks and ~*s* uphill — William Cleary> ~ *vt* : to say, speak, or sound with or as if with a stutter ***syn*** see STAMMER — **stut·ter·er** \-ər-ər\ *n*

[2]**stutter** *n* **1** : an act or instance of stuttering **2** : a speech disorder involving stuttering accompanied by fear and anxiety

[1]**sty** \'stī\ *n, pl* **sties** *also* **styes** [ME, fr. OE *stig;* akin to ON *-stī* sty] **1** : a pen or enclosed housing for swine **2** : an unkempt filthy dwelling or abode <her house was a perfect ~>

[2]**sty** *vb* **stied** *or* **styed; sty·ing** *vt* : to lodge or keep in a sty ~ *vi* : to live in a sty

[3]**sty** *or* **stye** \'stī\ *n, pl* **sties** *or* **styes** [short for obs. E *styan,* fr. (assumed) ME, alter. of OE *stigend,* fr. *stīgan* to go up, rise — more at STAIR] : an inflamed swelling of a sebaceous gland at the margin of an eyelid

sty·gian \'stij-(ē-)ən\ *adj, often cap* [L *stygius,* fr. Gk *stygios,* fr. *Styg-, Styx* Styx] **1** : of or relating to the river Styx **2 a** : extremely dark **b** : having a gloomy or forbidding aspect <the expression on her heavy features . . . was ~ —Nancy Hale>

[1]**styl-** *or* **stylo-** *comb form* [L, fr. Gk, fr. *stylos* — more at STEER] : pillar <*stylo*lite>

[2]**styl-** *or* **styli-** *or* **stylo-** *comb form* [L *stilus* stake, stalk — more at STYLE] : style : styloid process <*styl*ate> <*styli*ferous><*stylo*graphic>

sty·lar \'stī-lər, -ˌlär\ *adj* [[1]*style*] **1** : of, relating to, or constituting an elongated process **2** : of or relating to the style of a plant ovary

-sty·lar \'stī-lər, -ˌlär\ *adj comb form* [Gk *stylos* pillar — more at STEER] : having (such or so many) pillars : having (such) columniation <amphi*stylar*>

[1]**style** \'stī(ə)l\ *n* [ME *stile, style,* fr. L *stilus* stake, stylus, style of writing; akin to OE *stician* to stick] **1 a** : STYLUS **b** : the shadow-producing pin of a sundial **c** : a filiform prolongation of a plant ovary bearing a stigma at its apex — see FLOWER illustration **d** : a slender bristle or other elongated process on an animal **2 a** : mode of expressing thought in language; *esp* : a manner of expression characteristic of an individual, period, school, or nation <a classic ~> **b** : manner or tone assumed in discourse **c** : the custom or plan followed in spelling, capitalization, punctuation, and typographic arrangement and display **3** : mode of address : TITLE **4 a** (1) : manner or method of acting or performing esp. as sanctioned by some standard (2) : a distinctive or characteristic manner **b** : a fashionable luxurious mode of life <lived in ~> **c** : overall excellence, skill, or grace in performance, manner, or appearance ***syn*** see FASHION — **style·less** \'stī(ə)l-ləs\ *adj* — **style·less·ness** *n*

[2]**style** *vt* **styled; styl·ing 1** : to designate by an identifying term : NAME <*styled* themselves pro-Marxists —John Womack *b*1937> **2 a** : to cause to conform to a customary style **b** : to design and make in accord with the prevailing mode — **styl·er** *n*

[1]**-style** \ˌstīl\ *adj comb form* : exhibiting the style of <ranch-*style*>

[2]**-style** *adv comb form* : in the style or manner of <cowboy-*style*>

style·book *n* : a book explaining, describing, or illustrating a prevailing, accepted, or authorized style

sty·let \stī-'let, 'stī-lət\ *n* [F, fr. MF *stilet* stiletto, fr. OIt *stiletto*] **1 a** : a slender surgical probe **b** : a thin wire inserted into a catheter to maintain rigidity or into a hollow needle to maintain patency **c** : a pointed instrument (as for graving) **2** : a relatively rigid elongated organ or appendage (as a piercing mouthpart) of an animal **3** : STILETTO

sty·li·form \'stī-lə-ˌfȯrm\ *adj* [NL *stiliformis,* fr. L *stilus* + *-formis* -form] : resembling a style : bristle-shaped <a ~ copulatory organ>

styl·ing \'stī-liŋ\ *n* : the way in which something is styled

styl·ish \'stī-lish\ *adj* : having style; *specif* : conforming to current fashion — **styl·ish·ly** *adv* — **styl·ish·ness** *n*

styl·ist \'stī-ləst\ *n* **1** : a master or model of style; *esp* : a writer or speaker in matters of style **2** : one who develops, designs, or advises on styles

sty·lis·tic \stī-'lis-tik\ *adj* : of or relating esp. to literary or artistic style — **sty·lis·ti·cal·ly** \-ti-k(ə-)lē\ *adv*

sty·lis·tics \stī-'lis-tiks\ *n pl but sing or pl in constr* **1** : an aspect of literary study that emphasizes the analysis of various elements of style (as metaphor and diction) **2** : the study of the devices in a language that produce expressive value

sty·lite \'stī-ˌlīt\ *n* [LGk *stylitēs,* fr. Gk *stylos* pillar — more at STEER] : a Christian ascetic living atop a pillar — **sty·lit·ic** \stī-'lit-ik\ *adj*

styl·ize \'stī(ə)l-ˌīz\ *vt* **styl·ized; styl·iz·ing** : to conform to a conventional style; *specif* : to represent or design according to a style or stylistic pattern rather than according to nature — **styl·i·za·tion** \ˌstī-lə-'zā-shən\ *n*

sty·lo·bate \'stī-lə-ˌbāt\ *n* [L *stylobates,* fr. Gk, *stylobatēs,* fr. *stylos* pillar + *bainein* to walk, go — more at COME] : a continuous flat coping or pavement on which a row of architectural columns is supported

sty·lo·graph \-ˌgraf\ *n* : a stylographic pen

sty·lo·graph·ic \ˌstī-lə-'graf-ik\ *adj* **1** : of or relating to stylography **2** : of, relating to, or being a fountain pen that has a fine point fitted with a needle which by pressure of the point on a surface is pushed back to release the flow of ink — **sty·lo·graph·i·cal** \-i-kəl\ *adj* — **sty·lo·graph·i·cal·ly** \-i-k(ə-)lē\ *adv*

sty·log·ra·phy \stī-'läg-rə-fē\ *n* : a mode of writing or tracing lines by means of a style or similar instrument

sty·loid \'stī(ə)l-ˌȯid\ *adj* : resembling a style : STYLIFORM — used esp. of slender pointed skeletal processes (as on the ulna)

sty·lo·lite \'stī-lə-ˌlīt\ *n* [ISV] : a small longitudinally grooved column of the same material as the rock in which it occurs

sty·lo·po·di·um \ˌstī-lə-'pōd-ē-əm\ *n, pl* **-dia** \-ē-ə\ [NL, fr. [2]*styl-* + Gk *podion* small foot, base — more at PEW] : a disk-shaped or conical expansion at the base of the style in plants of the carrot family

-sty·lous \'stī-ləs\ *adj comb form* [[1]*style*] : having (such or so many) floral styles <mono*stylous*>

sty·lus \'stī-ləs\ *n, pl* **sty·li** \'stī(ə)l-ˌī\ *also* **sty·lus·es** \'stī-lə-səz\ [modif. of L *stilus* stake, stylus — more at STYLE] : an instrument for writing, marking, or incising: as **a** : an instrument used by the ancients in writing on clay or waxed tablets **b** : a hard-pointed pen-shaped instrument for marking on stencils used in a reproducing machine **c** (1) : NEEDLE 3c (2) : a cutting tool used to produce an original record groove during disc recording

[1]**sty·mie** \'stī-mē\ *n* [perh. fr. Sc *stymie* person with poor eyesight] **1** : a condition existing on a golf putting green when the ball nearer the hole lies in the line of play of another ball **2** : OBSTACLE

[2]**stymie** *vt* **sty·mied; sty·mie·ing** : to present an obstacle to : stand in the way of

styp·tic \'stip-tik\ *adj* [ME *stiptik,* fr. L *stypticus,* fr. Gk *styptikos,* fr. *styphein* to contract] : tending to contract or bind : ASTRINGENT; *esp* : tending to check bleeding — **styptic** *n*

styptic pencil *n* : a cylindrical stick of a medicated styptic substance used esp. in shaving to stop the bleeding from small cuts

sty·rax \'stī-ˌraks\ *n* [L] : STORAX

sty·rene \'stī-ˌrēn\ *n* [ISV, fr. L *styrax*] : a fragrant liquid unsaturated hydrocarbon C_8H_8 used chiefly in making synthetic rubber, resins, and plastics and in improving drying oils

Sty·ro·foam \'stī-rə-ˌfōm\ *trademark* — used for an expanded rigid polystyrene plastic

Styx \'stiks\ *n* [L *Styg-, Styx,* fr. Gk] : a river of the underworld over which shades of the dead are ferried on their way to Hades

su·able \'sü-ə-bəl\ *adj* : liable to be sued in court — **su·abil·i·ty** \ˌsü-ə-'bil-ət-ē\ *n* — **su·ably** \-blē\ *adv*

sua·sion \'swā-zhən\ *n* [ME, fr. L *suasion-, suasio,* fr. *suasus,* pp. of *suadēre* to urge, persuade; akin to L *suavis*] : the act of influencing or persuading — **sua·sive** \'swā-siv, -ziv\ *adj* — **sua·sive·ly** *adv* — **sua·sive·ness** *n*

suave \'swäv\ *adj* [MF, pleasant, sweet, fr. L *suavis* — more at SWEET] **1** : smoothly though often superficially affable and polite **2** : smooth in performance or finish — **suave·ly** *adv* — **suave·ness** *n* — **sua·vi·ty** \'swäv-ət-ē\ *n*

syn SUAVE, URBANE, DIPLOMATIC, BLAND, SMOOTH, POLITIC *shared meaning element* : ingratiatingly tactful and well-mannered ***ant*** bluff

[1]**sub** \'səb\ *n* : SUBSTITUTE

[2]**sub** *vb* **subbed; sub·bing** *vi* : to act as a substitute ~ *vt* **1** : SUBEDIT **2** : to apply a substratum to (as a photographic film) **3** : SUBCONTRACT 1

[3]**sub** *n* : SUBMARINE

[4]**sub** *n* [short for *substratum*] : a photographic substratum

[5]**sub** *abbr* **1** subaltern **2** subtract **3** suburb

sub- *prefix* [ME, fr. L, under, below, secretly, from below, up, near, fr. *sub* under, close to — more at UP] **1** : under : beneath : below <*sub*soil> <*sub*aqueous> **2 a** : subordinate : secondary : next lower than or inferior to <*sub*station> <*sub*editor> **b** : subordinate portion of : subdivision of <*sub*committee><*sub*species> **c** : with repetition (as of a process) so as to form, stress, or deal with subordinate parts or relations <*sub*let> <*sub*contract> **3 a** : less than completely, perfectly, or normally : somewhat <*sub*dominant> <*sub*ovate> **b** (1) : containing less than the usual or normal amount of (such) an element or radical <*sub*oxide> (2) : basic — in names of salts <*sub*acetate> **4 a** : almost : nearly <*sub*erect> **b** : falling nearly in the category of and often adjoining : bordering upon <*sub*arctic>

sub·ac·id \ˌsəb-'as-əd, 'səb-\ *adj* [L *subacidus,* fr. *sub-* + *acidus* acid] **1** : moderately acid <~ fruit juices> **2** : rather tart <~ comments> — **sub·ac·id·ly** *adv* — **sub·ac·id·ness** *n*

sub·acute \ˌsəb-ə-'kyüt\ *adj* : moderately acute <a ~ angle> <a ~ flower petal> <~ inflammation> — **sub·acute·ly** *adv*

sub·adult \ˌsəb-ə-'dəlt; ˌsəb-'ad-ˌəlt, 'səb-\ *n* : an individual that has passed through the juvenile period but not yet attained typical adult characteristics — **subadult** *adj*

sub·aer·i·al \ˌsəb-'ar-ē-əl, 'səb-, -'er-; ˌsəb-ā-'ir-ē-əl\ *adj* : situated, formed, or occurring on or adjacent to the surface of the earth <~ erosion> <~ roots> — **sub·aer·i·al·ly** \-ē-ə-lē\ *adv*

sub·agen·cy \ˌsəb-'ā-jən-sē, 'səb-', 'səb-ˌ\ *n* : a subordinate agency

sub·agent \'səb-ˌā-jənt\ *n* : a subordinate agent; *specif* : a person employed by an agent to assist him in transacting the affairs of his principal

su·bah·dar *or* **su·ba·dar** \ˌsü-bə-'där\ *n* [Per *sūbadār*] **1** : a governor of a province **2** : the chief native officer of a native company in the former British Indian army

sub·al·pine \ˌsəb-'al-ˌpīn, 'səb-\ *adj* **1** : of or relating to the region about the foot and lower slopes of the Alps **2** *cap* : of, relating to, or growing on high upland slopes

[1]**sub·al·tern** \sə-'bȯl-tərn, *esp Brit* 'səb-əl-tərn\ *adj* [LL *subalternus,* fr. L *sub-* + *alternus* alternate, fr. *alter* other (of two) — more at ALTER] **1** : inferior in quality or status : SUBORDINATE **2** : particular with reference to a related universal proposition <"some S is P" is a ~ proposition to "all S is P">

[2]**subaltern** *n* **1** : a person holding a subordinate position **2** : SUBALTERNATE

[1]**sub·al·ter·nate** \sə-'bȯl-tər-nət\ *adj* : SUBALTERN 1 — **sub·al·ter·nate·ly** *adv*

[2]subalternate *n* **:** a particular proposition that follows immediately from a universal

sub·al·ter·na·tion \sə-ˌbȯl-tər-ˈnā-shən\ *n* **:** the relation of a subalternate to a universal

sub·ant·arc·tic \ˌsəb-ant-ˈärk-tik, -ˈärt-ik\ *adj* **:** of, relating to, characteristic of, or being a region just outside the antarctic circle

sub·api·cal \ˌsəb-ˈā-pi-kəl, ˈsəb- *also* -ˈap-i-\ *adj* **:** situated below or near an apex — **sub·api·cal·ly** \-k(ə-)lē\ *adv*

sub·aquat·ic \ˌsəb-ə-ˈkwät-ik, -ˈkwat-\ *adj* [ISV] **:** somewhat aquatic <a marginal ~ flora>

sub·aque·ous \ˌsəb-ˈā-kwē-əs, ˈsəb-, -ˈak-wē-\ *adj* **:** existing, formed, or taking place in or under water

sub·arc·tic \ˌsəb-ˈärk-tik, ˈsəb-ˈärt-ik\ *adj* [ISV] **:** of, relating to, characteristic of, or being regions immediately outside of the arctic circle or regions similar to these in climate or conditions of life — **subarctic** *n*

sub·ar·ea \ˈsəb-ˌar-ē-ə, -ˌer-\ *n* **:** a subdivision of an area

sub·as·sem·bly \ˌsəb-ə-ˈsem-blē\ *n* **:** an assembled unit designed to be incorporated with other units in a finished product

sub·at·mo·spher·ic \ˌsəb-ˌat-mə-ˈsfi(ə)r-ik, ˈsəb-, -ˈsfer-\ *adj* **:** less or lower than that of the atmosphere <~ temperatures>

sub·atom·ic \ˌsəb-ə-ˈtäm-ik\ *adj* **:** of or relating to the inside of the atom or to particles smaller than atoms

sub·au·di·ble \ˌsəb-ˈȯd-ə-bəl, ˈsəb-\ *adj* **:** having a frequency or intensity below the limit of hearing

sub·au·di·tion \ˌsəb-ȯ-ˈdish-ən\ *n* [LL *subaudition-, subauditio,* fr. *subauditus,* pp. of *subaudire* to understand, fr. L *sub-* + *audire* to hear — more at AUDIBLE] **1 :** the act of understanding or supplying something not expressed **2 :** something that is understood or supplied in comprehending a text

sub·av·er·age \ˌsəb-ˈav-(ə-)rij, ˈsəb-\ *adj* **:** of a lower level or quality than some norm <~ minds> <~ education>

sub·base \ˈsəb-ˌbās\ *n* **:** underlying support placed below what is normally construed as a base: as **a :** the lowest member horizontally of an architectural base or of a baseboard or pedestal **b :** pervious fill (as crushed stone) placed under a roadbed

sub·base·ment \ˈsəb-ˌbā-smənt\ *n* **:** a basement located below the true basement of a building

sub·bing \ˈsəb-iŋ\ *n* [[4]*sub*] **:** SUBSTRATUM e

sub·cab·i·net \ˌsəb-ˈkab-(ə-)nət, ˈsəb-\ *adj* **:** of, relating to, or being a high administrative position in the U.S. government that ranks below the cabinet level

sub·cap·su·lar \ˌsəb-ˈkap-sə-lər, ˈsəb-\ *adj* **:** situated or occurring beneath or within a capsule <~ cataracts>

sub·ce·les·tial \ˌsəb-sə-ˈles(h)-chəl\ *adj* **:** situated beneath the heavens; *specif* **:** MUNDANE

sub·cel·lu·lar \ˌsəb-ˈsel-yə-lər, ˈsəb-\ *adj* **:** of less than cellular scope or level of organization <~ particles>

sub·cen·ter \ˌsəb-ˌsent-ər\ *n* **:** a secondary center; *esp* **:** a center (as for shopping) located outside the main business area of a city

sub·cen·tral \ˌsəb-ˈsen-trəl, ˈsəb-\ *adj* **1 :** located under a center **2 :** nearly but not quite central — **sub·cen·tral·ly** \-trə-lē\ *adv*

sub·chas·er \ˈsəb-ˌchā-sər\ *n* **:** SUBMARINE CHASER

sub·chlo·ride \ˌsəb-ˈklō(ə)r-ˌīd, ˈsəb-, -ˈklȯ(ə)r-\ *n* [ISV] **1 :** a binary chloride containing a relatively small proportion of chlorine **2 :** a basic chloride

sub·class \ˈsəb-ˌklas\ *n* **:** a primary division of a class: as **a :** a biological taxonomic category below a class and above an order **b :** SUBSET

[1]sub·cla·vi·an \ˌsəb-ˈklā-vē-ən\ *adj* [NL *subclavius,* fr. *sub-* + *clavicula* clavicle] **1 :** located under the clavicle **2 :** of or relating to a subclavian part (as an artery, vein, or nerve)

[2]subclavian *n* **:** a subclavian part (as an artery, vein, or nerve)

subclavian artery *n* **:** the proximal part of the main artery of the arm or forelimb

subclavian vein *n* **:** the proximal part of the main vein of the arm or forelimb

sub·cli·max \ˌsəb-ˈklī-ˌmaks, ˈsəb-\ *n* **:** a stage or community in an ecological succession immediately preceding a climax; *esp* **:** one held in relative stability throughout edaphic or biotic influences or by fire

sub·clin·i·cal \-ˈklin-i-kəl\ *adj* **:** only slightly abnormal and not detectable by the usual clinical tests <a ~ infection> — **sub·clin·i·cal·ly** \-k(ə-)lē\ *adv*

sub·col·le·giate \ˌsəb-kə-ˈlē-j(ē-)ət\ *adj* **:** designed for students who are not adequately prepared to take college-level courses

sub·com·mit·tee \ˈsəb-kə-ˌmit-ē, ˌsəb-kə-ˈ\ *n* **:** a subdivision of a committee usu. organized for a specific purpose

sub·com·mu·ni·ty \ˌsəb-kə-ˈmyü-nət-ē\ *n* **:** a distinct community existing within a large urban area

sub·com·pact \ˈsəb-ˈkäm-ˌpakt\ *n* **:** an automobile smaller than a compact

[1]sub·con·scious \ˌsəb-ˈkän-chəs, ˈsəb-\ *adj* **1 :** existing in the mind but not immediately available to consciousness <his ~ motive> **2 :** imperfectly or incompletely conscious <a ~ state> — **sub·con·scious·ly** *adv* — **sub·con·scious·ness** *n*

[2]subconscious *n* **:** the mental activities just below the threshold of consciousness

sub·con·ti·nent \ˈsəb-ˈkänt-ᵊn-ənt, -ˈkänt-nənt, -ˌkänt-\ *n* **1 :** a landmass (as Greenland) of great size but smaller than any of the usu. recognized continents **2 :** a vast subdivision of a continent — **sub·con·ti·nen·tal** \ˌsəb-ˌkänt-ᵊn-ˈent-ᵊl\ *adj*

[1]sub·con·tract \ˌsəb-ˈkän-ˌtrakt, ˈsəb-; ˌsəb-kən-ˈ\ *vt* **1 :** to engage a third party to perform under a subcontract all or part of (work included in an original contract) **2 :** to undertake (work) under a subcontract ~ *vi* **:** to let out or undertake work under a subcontract

[2]sub·con·tract \ˈsəb-ˈkän-ˌtrakt, -ˌkän-\ *n* **:** a contract between a party to an original contract and a third party; *esp* **:** one to provide all or a specified part of the work or materials required in the original contract

sub·con·trac·tor \ˌsəb-ˈkän-ˌtrak-tər, ˈsəb-; ˌsəb-kən-ˈ\ *n* **:** an individual or business firm contracting to perform part or all of another's contract

sub·con·tra·oc·tave \ˌsəb-ˌkän-trə-ˈäk-tiv, ˈsəb-, -təv, -ˌtāv\ *n* **:** the musical octave that begins on the fourth C below middle C — see PITCH illustration

sub·con·tra·ri·ety \ˌsəb-ˌkän-trə-ˈrī-ət-ē\ *n* **:** the relation existing between subcontrary propositions in logic

[1]sub·con·trary \ˌsəb-ˈkän-ˌtrer-ē, ˈsəb-\ *adj* [LL *subcontrarius,* fr. L *sub-* + *contrarius* contrary — more at CONTRARY] **:** being one of two subcontraries

[2]subcontrary *n* **:** a proposition so related to another that both may be true but both cannot be false

sub·cool \-ˈkül\ *vt* **:** SUPERCOOL

sub·cor·date \-ˈkȯ(ə)r-ˌdāt\ *adj* **:** incompletely cordate <a ~ leaf>

sub·cor·tex \ˌsəb-ˈkȯr-ˌteks, ˈsəb-\ *n* [NL] **:** the parts of the brain immediately beneath the cerebral cortex

sub·cor·ti·cal \-ˈkȯrt-i-kəl\ *adj* **:** of, relating to, involving, or being nerve centers below the cerebral cortex <~ lesions>

sub·crit·i·cal \-ˈkrit-i-kəl\ *adj* **1 :** less or lower than critical in respect to a specified factor **2 a :** of insufficient size to sustain a chain reaction <a ~ mass of fissionable material> **b :** designed for use with fissionable material of subcritical mass <a ~ reactor>

sub·crust·al \-ˈkrəs-tᵊl\ *adj* **:** situated or occurring below a crust and esp. the crust of the earth

sub·cul·ture \ˈsəb-ˌkəl-chər\ *n* **1 a :** a culture (as of bacteria) derived from another culture **b :** an act or instance of producing a subculture **2 :** an ethnic, regional, economic, or social group exhibiting characteristic patterns of behavior sufficient to distinguish it from others within an embracing culture or society <a criminal ~> — **sub·cul·tur·al** \-ˈkəlch-(ə-)rəl\ *adj*

sub·cu·ta·ne·ous \ˌsəb-kyu̇-ˈtā-nē-əs\ *adj* [LL *subcutaneus,* fr. L *sub-* + *cutis* skin — more at HIDE] **:** being, living, used, or made under the skin <~ parasites> — **sub·cu·ta·ne·ous·ly** *adv*

sub·cu·tis \ˌsəb-ˈkyüt-əs, ˈsəb-\ *n* [NL, fr. LL, beneath the skin, fr. L *sub-* + *cutis*] **:** the deeper part of the dermis

sub·dea·con \-ˈdē-kən\ *n* [ME *subdecon,* fr. LL *subdiaconus,* fr. L *sub-* + LL *diaconus* deacon] **:** a cleric ranking below a deacon: as **a :** a cleric in the lowest of the former major orders of the Roman Catholic church **b :** an Eastern Orthodox or Armenian cleric in minor orders **c :** a clergyman performing the liturgical duties of a subdeacon

sub·deb \ˈsəb-ˌdeb\ *n* **:** SUBDEBUTANTE

sub·deb·u·tante \ˌsəb-ˈdeb-yu̇-ˌtänt, ˈsəb-\ *n* **:** a young girl who is about to become a debutante; *broadly* **:** a girl in her middle teens

sub·de·pot \-ˈdep-(ˌ)ō *also* -ˈdēp-\ *n* **:** a military depot that operates under the jurisdiction of another depot

sub·di·ac·o·nate \ˌsəb-dī-ˈak-ə-nət\ *n* **:** the office or rank of a subdeacon

sub·dis·ci·pline \-ˈdis-ə-plən\ *n* **:** a subdivision of a branch of learning

sub·di·vide \ˌsəb-də-ˈvīd, ˈsəb-də-ˌ\ *vb* [ME *subdividen,* fr. LL *subdividere,* fr. L *sub-* + *dividere* to divide] *vt* **1 :** to divide the parts of into more parts **2 :** to divide into several parts; *esp* **:** to divide (a tract of land) into building lots ~ *vi* **:** to separate or become separated into subdivisions — **sub·di·vid·able** \-ˈvīd-ə-bəl, -ˌvīd-\ *adj* — **sub·di·vid·er** *n* — **sub·di·vi·sion** \-ˈvizh-ən, -ˌvizh-\ *n*

sub·dom·i·nant \ˌsəb-ˈdäm(-ə)-nənt, ˈsəb-\ *n* **:** something dominant to an inferior or partial degree: as **a :** the fourth tone of a diatonic scale **b :** an ecologically important life form subordinate in influence to the dominants of a community — **sub·dom·i·nance** \-nən(t)s\ *n* — **subdominant** *adj*

sub·due \səb-ˈd(y)ü\ *vt* **sub·dued; sub·du·ing** [ME *sodewen, subduen* (influenced in form and meaning by L *subdere* to subject), fr. MF *soduire* to seduce (influenced in meaning by L *seducere* to seduce), fr. L *subducere* to withdraw] **1 :** to conquer and bring into subjection **:** VANQUISH **2 :** to bring under control esp. by an exertion of the will **:** CURB <*subdued* her foolish fears> **3 :** to bring under cultivation **4 :** to reduce the intensity or degree of <~ unwanted sound —Melvin Beck> — **sub·du·er** *n*

sub·dued \-ˈd(y)üd\ *adj* **1 :** brought under control by or as if by military conquest **2 :** reduced or lacking in force, intensity, or strength ***syn*** see TAME — **sub·dued·ly** \-ˈd(y)ü(-ə)d-lē\ *adv*

sub·ed·it \ˌsəb-ˈed-ət, ˈsəb-\ *vt* [back-formation fr. *subeditor*] **1 :** to act as subeditor of **2** *chiefly Brit* **:** COPYREAD

sub·ed·i·tor \-ˈed-ət-ər\ *n* **1 :** an assistant editor **2** *chiefly Brit* **:** COPYREADER — **sub·ed·i·to·ri·al** \ˌsəb-ˌed-ə-ˈtōr-ē-əl, -ˈtȯr-\ *adj*

sub·em·ployed \ˌsəb-im-ˈplȯid\ *adj* **:** subjected to subemployment

sub·em·ploy·ment \-ˈplȯi-mənt\ *n* **:** inadequate employment including unemployment, part-time employment, and full-time employment that does not provide a living wage — compare UNDEREMPLOYMENT

sub·en·try \ˈsəb-ˌen-trē\ *n* **:** an entry (as in a catalog or an account) made under a more general entry

sub·epi·der·mal \ˌsəb-ˌep-ə-ˈdər-məl\ *adj* **:** lying beneath or constituting the innermost part of the epidermis

su·ber \ˈsü-bər\ *n* [NL, fr. L, cork tree, cork] **:** corky plant tissue **:** PHELLEM

sub·erect \ˌsəb-i-ˈrekt\ *adj* **:** standing or growing in a nearly erect position <a ~ shrub>

su·ber·in \ˈsü-bə-rən\ *n* [F *subérine,* fr. L *suber*] **:** a complex fatty substance that is the basis of cork

su·ber·iza·tion \ˌsü-bə-rə-ˈzā-shən\ *n* **:** conversion of the cell walls into corky tissue by infiltration with suberin

su·ber·ized \ˈsü-bə-ˌrīzd\ *adj* **:** characterized by or having undergone suberization

sub·fam·i·ly \ˈsəb-ˌfam-(ə-)lē\ *n* [ISV] **1 :** a taxonomic category next below a family **2 :** a subgroup of languages within a language family

sub·field \-ˌfēld\ *n* **:** a subset of a mathematical field that is itself a field

sub·fix \-ˌfiks\ *n* [*sub-* + *-fix* (as in *prefix*)] **:** a subscript sign, letter, or character

sub·fos·sil \-ˌfäs-əl\ *adj* [ISV] **:** of less than typical fossil age but partially fossilized — **subfossil** *n*

sub·freez·ing \-ˈfrē-ziŋ\ *adj* : lower than is required to produce freezing <~ temperature>; *also* : marked by subfreezing temperature <~ weather>

sub·fusc \(ˌ)səb-ˈfəsk, ˈsəb-ˌ\ *adj* [L *subfuscus* brownish, dusky, fr. *sub-* + *fuscus* dark brown — more at DUSK] : DRAB, DUSKY <that gray, impoverished, ~ community —Marguerite Steen>

subg *abbr* subgenus

sub·ge·nus \ˈsəb-ˌjē-nəs\ *n* [NL] : a category in biological taxonomy below a genus and above a species

sub·gla·cial \ˌsəb-ˈglā-shəl, ˈsəb-\ *adj* : of or relating to the bottom of a glacier or the area immediately underlying a glacier — **sub·gla·cial·ly** \-shə-lē\ *adv*

sub·grade \ˈsəb-ˌgrād\ *n* : a surface of earth or rock leveled off to receive a foundation (as of a road)

sub·group \-ˌgrüp\ *n* **1** : a subordinate group whose members usu. share some common differential quality **2** : a subset of a mathematical group that is itself a group

sub·head \-ˌhed\ *n* **1** : a heading of a subdivision (as in an outline) **2** : a subordinate caption, title, or headline

sub·head·ing \-ˌhed-iŋ\ *n* : SUBHEAD

¹sub·hu·man \ˌsəb-ˈhyü-mən, ˈsəb-, -ˈyü-\ *adj* : less than human: as **a** : failing to attain the level (as of morality or intelligence) associated with normal human beings **b** : unsuitable to or unfit for human beings <~ living conditions> **c** : of or relating to an infrahuman group <the ~ primates>

²subhuman *n* : a subhuman individual

sub·in·dex \ˌsəb-ˈin-ˌdeks, ˈsəb-\ *n* : an index to a division of a main classification

sub·in·feu·date \ˌsəb-in-ˈfyü-ˌdāt\ *also* **sub·in·feud** \-ˈfyüd\ *vt* **-feu·dat·ed** *also* **-feud·ed; -feu·dat·ing** *also* **-feud·ing** [back-formation fr. *subinfeudation*] : to make subinfeudation of

sub·in·feu·da·tion \ˌsəb-ˌin-fyü-ˈdā-shən\ *n* [*sub-* + *infeudation* (enfeoffment)] : the granting of feudal lands by a vassal lord to another to hold as vassal of himself rather than of his own superior; *also* : the relation or tenure of a vassal so holding land — **sub·in·feu·da·to·ry** \ˌsəb-in-ˈfyüd-ə-ˌtōr-ē, -ˌtȯr-\ *adj*

sub·in·ter·val \ˌsəb-ˈint-ər-vəl, ˈsəb-\ *n* : an interval that is a subdivision of a larger or major interval (as in music)

sub·ir·ri·gate \ˌsəb-ˈir-ə-ˌgāt, ˈsəb-\ *vt* : to water from beneath (as by the periodic rise of a water table); *also* : to irrigate below the surface (as by a system of underground porous pipes) — **sub·ir·ri·ga·tion** \ˌsəb-ˌir-ə-ˈgā-shən\ *n*

su·bi·to \ˈsü-bi-ˌtō\ *adv* [It, fr. L, suddenly, fr. *subitus* sudden — more at SUDDEN] : IMMEDIATELY, SUDDENLY — used as a direction in music

subj *abbr* **1** subject **2** subjunctive

sub·ja·cen·cy \ˌsəb-ˈjās-ᵊn-sē\ *n* : the quality or state of being subjacent

sub·ja·cent \-ᵊnt\ *adj* [L *subjacent-, subjacens,* prp. of *subjacēre* to lie under, fr. *sub-* + *jacēre* to lie — more at ADJACENT] : lying under or below; *also* : lower than though not directly below <hills and ~ valleys> — **sub·ja·cent·ly** *adv*

¹sub·ject \ˈsəb-jikt\ *n* [ME, fr. MF, fr. L *subjectus* one under authority & *subjectum* subject of a proposition, fr. masc. & neut. respectively of *subjectus,* pp. of *subicere* to subject, lit., to throw under, fr. *sub-* + *jacere* to throw — more at JET] **1** : one that is placed under authority or control: as **a** : VASSAL **b (1)** : one subject to a monarch and governed by his law **(2)** : one who lives in the territory of, enjoys the protection of, and owes allegiance to a sovereign power or state **2 a** : that of which a quality, attribute, or relation may be affirmed or in which it may inhere **b** : SUBSTRATUM; *esp* : material or essential substance **c** : the mind, ego, or agent of whatever sort that sustains or assumes the form of thought or consciousness **3 a** : a department of knowledge or learning **b** : MOTIVE, CAUSE **c (1)** : one that is acted upon <the helpless ~ of his cruelty> **(2)** : an individual whose reactions or responses are studied **(3)** : a dead body for anatomical study and dissection **d (1)** : something concerning which something is said or done **(2)** : something represented or indicated in a work of art **e (1)** : the term of a logical proposition that denotes the entity of which something is affirmed or denied; *also* : the entity denoted **(2)** : a word or word group denoting that of which something is predicated **f** : the principal melodic phrase on which a musical composition or movement is based ***syn*** see CITIZEN — **sub·ject·less** \-ləs\ *adj*

²subject *adj* **1** : owing obedience or allegiance to the power or dominion of another **2 a** : suffering a particular liability or exposure <~ to temptation> **b** : having a tendency or inclination : PRONE <~ to colds> **3** : dependent upon or exposed to esp. as a prelude to finalization <the plan is ~ to discussion>

³sub·ject \səb-ˈjekt\ *vt* **1 a** : to bring under control or dominion : SUBJUGATE **b** : to make (as oneself) amenable to the discipline and control of a superior **2 a** : to make liable : PREDISPOSE **b** : to make accountable <refused to ~ himself to their judgment> **3** : to cause to undergo or submit to <unwilling to ~ himself to any inconvenience> — **sub·jec·tion** \-ˈjek-shən\ *n*

¹sub·jec·tive \(ˌ)səb-ˈjek-tiv\ *adj* **1** : of, relating to, or constituting a subject: as **a** *obs* : of, relating to, or characteristic of one that is subject esp. in lack of freedom of action or in submissiveness **b** : being or relating to a grammatical subject; *esp* : NOMINATIVE **2 a** : of or relating to the essential being of that which supports attributes or relations : SUBSTANTIAL **b (1)** : relating to or determined by the mind as the subject of experience <~ reality> **(2)** : characteristic of or belonging to reality as perceived rather than as independent of mind : PHENOMENAL **c** : relating to or being experience or knowledge as conditioned by personal mental characteristics or states **3 a** : peculiar to a particular individual : PERSONAL <~ judgments> **b** : arising from conditions within the brain or sense organs and not directly caused by external stimuli <~ sensations> **c** : arising out of or identified by means of one's awareness of his own states and processes <a ~ symptom of disease> **d** : lacking in reality or substance : ILLUSORY — **sub·jec·tive·ly** *adv* — **sub·jec·tive·ness** *n* — **sub·jec·tiv·i·ty** \-ˌjek-ˈtiv-ət-ē\ *n*

²subjective *n* : something that is subjective; *also* : NOMINATIVE

subjective complement *n* : a grammatical complement relating to the subject of an intransitive verb <in "he had fallen sick" *sick* is a *subjective complement*>

sub·jec·tiv·ism \(ˌ)səb-ˈjek-tiv-ˌiz-əm\ *n* **1 a** : a theory that limits knowledge to conscious states and elements **b** : a theory that stresses the subjective elements in experience **2 a** : a doctrine that the supreme good is a subjective experience or feeling (as pleasure) **b** : a doctrine that individual feeling or apprehension is the ultimate criterion of the good and the right — **sub·jec·tiv·ist** \-əst\ *n* — **sub·jec·tiv·is·tic** \-ˌjek-tiv-ˈis-tik\ *adj*

sub·jec·tiv·ize \-tiv-ˌīz\ *vt* **-ized; -iz·ing** : to make subjective — **sub·jec·tiv·iza·tion** \-jek-tiv-ə-ˈzā-shən\ *n*

subject matter *n* : matter presented for consideration in discussion, thought, or study

sub·join \(ˌ)səb-ˈjȯin\ *vt* [MF *subjoindre,* fr. L *subjungere* to join beneath, add, fr. *sub-* + *jungere* to join — more at YOKE] : ANNEX, APPEND <~*ed* a statement of expenses to his report>

sub ju·di·ce \(ˈ)sùb-ˈyüd-i-ˌkā, ˈsəb-ˈjüd-ə-(ˌ)sē\ *adv* [L] : before a judge or court : not yet judicially decided

sub·ju·gate \ˈsəb-ji-ˌgāt\ *vt* **-gat·ed; -gat·ing** [ME *subjugaten,* fr. L *subjugatus,* pp. of *subjugare,* lit., to bring under the yoke, fr. *sub-* + *jugum* yoke — more at YOKE] **1** : to force to submit to control and governance **2** : to bring into servitude — **sub·ju·ga·tion** \ˌsəb-ji-ˈgā-shən\ *n* — **sub·ju·ga·tor** \ˈsəb-ji-ˌgāt-ər\ *n*

sub·junc·tion \(ˌ)səb-ˈjəŋ(k)-shən\ *n* **1** : an act of subjoining or the state of being subjoined **2** : something subjoined

¹sub·junc·tive \səb-ˈjəŋ(k)-tiv\ *adj* [LL *subjunctivus,* fr. L *subjunctus,* pp. of *subjungere* to join beneath, subordinate] : of, relating to, or constituting a verb form or set of verb forms that represents a denoted act or state not as fact but as contingent or possible or viewed emotionally (as with doubt or desire) <the ~ mood>

²subjunctive *n* **1** : the subjunctive mood of a language **2** : a form in the subjunctive mood

sub·king·dom \ˈsəb-ˌkiŋ-dəm\ *n* : a primary division of a taxonomic kingdom

sub·late \ˌsəb-ˈlāt\ *vt* **sub·lat·ed; sub·lat·ing** [L *sublatus* (pp. of *tollere* to take away, lift up), fr. *sub-* up + *latus,* pp. of *ferre* to carry — more at SUB-, TOLERATE, BEAR] **1 a** : NEGATE, DENY **b** : CANCEL, ELIMINATE **2** : to cancel but also preserve and elevate (an element in a dialectic process) as a partial element in a synthesis — **sub·la·tion** \-ˈlā-shən\ *n*

¹sub·lease \ˈsəb-ˈlēs, -ˌlēs\ *n* : a lease by a tenant or lessee of part or all of leased premises to another person for a shorter term than his own and under which he retains some right or interest under the original lease

²sublease *vt* : to make or obtain a sublease of

¹sub·let \ˈsəb-ˈlet\ *vb* **-let; -let·ting** *vt* **1 a** : to lease or rent all or part of (a leased or rented property) to another person **b** : to lease or rent all or part of (a leased or rented property) from the original lessee or tenant **2** : SUBCONTRACT 1 ~ *vi* : to lease or rent all or part of a leased or rented property

²sub·let \-ˌlet\ *n* : property and esp. housing obtained by or available for subletting

sub·le·thal \ˌsəb-ˈlē-thəl, ˈsəb-\ *adj* : less than but usu. only slightly less than lethal <~ pollution> — **sub·le·thal·ly** \-thə-lē\ *adv*

sub·lev·el \ˈsəb-ˌlev-əl\ *n* : a level that is lower than another express or implied level

sub·lieu·ten·ant \ˌsəb-lü-ˈten-ənt, *Brit* le(f)-ˈten-\ *n* : a commissioned officer in the British navy ranking immediately below lieutenant

¹sub·li·mate \ˈsəb-lə-ˌmāt\ *vt* **-mat·ed; -mat·ing** [ML *sublimatus,* pp. of *sublimare*] **1 a** : SUBLIME 1 **b** *archaic* : to improve or refine as if by subliming **2** : to divert the expression of (an instinctual desire or impulse) from its primitive form to one that is considered more socially or culturally acceptable — **sub·li·ma·tion** \ˌsəb-lə-ˈmā-shən\ *n*

²sub·li·mate \ˈsəb-lə-ˌmāt, -mət\ *n* **1** : MERCURIC CHLORIDE **2** : a chemical product obtained by sublimation

¹sub·lime \sə-ˈblīm\ *vb* **sub·limed; sub·lim·ing** [ME *sublimen,* fr. MF *sublimer,* fr. ML *sublimare* to refine, sublime, fr. L, to elevate, fr. *sublimis*] *vt* **1** : to cause to pass from the solid to the vapor state by heating and again condense to solid form **2** [F *sublimer,* fr. L *sublimare*] **a (1)** : to elevate or exalt esp. in dignity or honor **(2)** : to render finer (as in purity or excellence) **b** : to convert (something inferior) into something of higher worth ~ *vi* : to pass directly from the solid to the vapor state — **sub·lim·able** \-ˈblī-mə-bəl\ *adj* — **sub·lim·er** *n*

²sublime *adj* [L *sublimis,* lit., to or in a high position, fr. *sub* under, up to + *limen* threshold, lintel — more at UP, LIMB] **1 a** : lofty, grand, or exalted in thought, expression, or manner **b** : of outstanding spiritual, intellectual, or moral worth **c** : tending to inspire awe usu. because of elevated quality (as of beauty, nobility, or grandeur) **2 a** *archaic* : high in place **b** *obs* : lofty of mien : HAUGHTY **c** *cap* : SUPREME — used in a style of address ***syn*** see SPLENDID — **sub·lime·ly** *adv* — **sub·lime·ness** *n*

sub·lim·i·nal \(ˌ)səb-ˈlim-ən-ᵊl, ˈsəb-\ *adj* [*sub-* + L *limin-, limen* threshold] **1** : inadequate to produce a sensation or a perception **2** : existing or functioning outside the area of conscious awareness <the ~ mind> <~ advertising> — **sub·lim·i·nal·ly** \-ē\ *adv*

sub·lim·i·ty \sə-ˈblim-ət-ē\ *n, pl* **-ties** **1** : something sublime or exalted **2** : the quality or state of being sublime

sub·lin·gual \ˌsəb-ˈliŋ-g(yə-)wəl, ˈsəb-\ *adj* [NL *sublingualis,* fr. L *sub-* + *lingua* tongue — more at TONGUE] : situated or occurring under the tongue

---

ə abut ᵊ kitten ər further a back ā bake ä cot, cart
aù out ch chin e less ē easy g gift i trip ī life
j joke ŋ sing ō flow ȯ flaw ȯi coin th thin th this
ü loot ù foot y yet yü few yù furious zh vision

sub·lit·er·ary \-'lit-ə-ˌrer-ē\ *adj* **:** of or relating to subliterature

sub·lit·er·a·ture \(ˈ)səb-'lit-ə-rə-ˌchu̇(ə)r, 'li-trə-ˌchu̇(ə)r, 'lit-ə(r)-ˌchu̇(ə)r, -chər, -ˌt(y)u̇(ə)r\ *n* **:** literature that is inferior to or less important than standard literature

1**sub·lit·to·ral** \(ˈ)səb-'lit-ə-rəl; ˌsəb-ˌlit-ə-'ral, -'räl\ *adj* **1 :** situated, occurring, or formed on the aquatic side of a shoreline or littoral zone **2 :** constituting the sublittoral

2**sublittoral** *n* **:** the deeper part of the littoral portion of a body of water: **a :** the region in an ocean between the lowest point exposed by a low-low tide and the margin of the continental shelf **b :** the region in a lake between the deepest-growing rooted vegetation and the part of the lake below the thermocline

sub·lu·na·ry \ˌsəb-'lü-nə-rē, 'səb-; 'səb-lü-ˌner-ē\ *also* **sub·lu·nar** \ˌsəb-'lü-nər, 'səb- *also* -ˌnär\ *adj* [modif. of LL *sublunaris,* fr. L *sub-* + *luna* moon — more at LUNAR] **:** situated beneath the moon **:** TERRESTRIAL <dull ~ lovers —John Donne>

sub·lux·a·tion \ˌsəb-ˌlək-'sā-shən\ *n* **:** partial dislocation (as of one of the bones in a joint)

sub·ma·chine gun \ˌsəb-mə-'shēn-ˌgən\ *n* **:** a lightweight automatic or semiautomatic portable firearm that uses pistol-type ammunition and is fired from the shoulder or hip

sub·man·dib·u·lar \ˌsəb-man-'dib-yə-lər\ *adj* **:** SUBMAXILLARY

sub·mar·gin·al \ˌsəb-'märj-nəl, 'səb-, -ən-ᵊl\ *adj* **1 :** adjacent to a margin or a marginal part or structure <~ spots on an insect wing> **2 :** falling below a necessary minimum <~ economic conditions> — **sub·mar·gin·al·ly** \-ē\ *adv*

1**sub·ma·rine** \'səb-mə-ˌrēn, ˌsəb-mə-'\ *adj* **:** being, acting, or growing under water esp. in the sea <~ plants>

2**submarine** *n* **1 :** something (as an explosive mine) that functions or operates underwater; *specif* **:** a warship designed for undersea operations **2 :** a large sandwich made from a long roll split and generously filled (as with cold cuts, cheese, onion, lettuce, and tomato) — called also *grinder, hero, hoagie, Italian sandwich, poor boy, sub, torpedo*

3**submarine** *vt* **-rined; -rin·ing :** to make an attack upon or to sink by means of a submarine

submarine chaser *n* **:** a boat fitted to operate offensively against submarines

sub·ma·ri·ner \'səb-mə-ˌrē-nər, ˌsəb-mə-' *also* ˌsəb-'mar-ə-\ *n* **:** a crewman of a submarine

sub·max·il·la \ˌsəb-mak-'sil-ə\ *n, pl* **-lae** \-(ˌ)ē, -ˌī\ *also* **-las** [NL] **:** the lower jaw or inferior maxillary bone; *specif* **:** the human mandible

1**sub·max·il·lary** \ˌsəb-'mak-sə-ˌler-ē, 'səb-, *chiefly Brit* ˌsəb-mak-'sil-ə-rē\ *adj* **1 :** of, relating to, or situated below the lower jaw **2 :** of, relating to, or associated with the submaxillary salivary gland of either side

2**submaxillary** *n, pl* **-lar·ies :** a submaxillary part (as an artery or bone)

sub·me·di·ant \ˌsəb-'mēd-ē-ənt, 'səb-\ *n* **:** the sixth tone of a diatonic scale midway between the subdominant and the upper tonic

sub·merge \səb-'mərj\ *vb* **sub·merged; sub·merg·ing** [L *submergere,* fr. *sub-* + *mergere* to plunge — more at MERGE] *vt* **1 :** to put under water **2 :** to cover or overflow with water **:** INUNDATE <*submerged* the town> **3 :** to make obscure or subordinate <personal lives *submerged* by professional responsibilities> ~ *vi* **:** to go under water — **sub·mer·gence** \-'mər-jən(t)s\ *n* — **sub·merg·ible** \-'mər-jə-bəl\ *adj*

sub·merged *adj* **1 :** covered with water **2 :** SUBMERSED b **3 :** sunk in poverty and misery **4 :** CRYPTIC, HIDDEN <a ~ gene effect>

sub·merse \səb-'mərs\ *vt* **sub·mersed; sub·mers·ing** [L *submersus,* pp. of *submergere*] **:** SUBMERGE — **sub·mer·sion** \-'mər-zhən, -shən\ *n*

sub·mersed *adj* **:** SUBMERGED as: **a :** covered with water **b :** growing or adapted to grow under water <~ weeds>

1**sub·mers·ible** \səb-'mər-sə-bəl\ *adj* **:** capable of being submerged

2**submersible** *n* **:** something that is submersible; *esp* **:** SUBMARINE

sub·mi·cro·gram \ˌsəb-'mī-krə-ˌgram, 'səb-\ *adj* **:** relating to or having a mass of less than one microgram <~ quantities of a chemical>

sub·mi·cron \-ˌkrän\ *adj* **1 :** being less than a micron in a (specified) measurement and esp. in diameter <a ~ particle> **2 :** having or consisting of submicron particles <a ~ metal powder>

sub·mi·cro·scop·ic \ˌsəb-ˌmī-krə-'skäp-ik\ *adj* [ISV] **1 :** too small to be seen in an ordinary light microscope **2 :** of, relating to, or dealing with the very minute <the ~ world> — **sub·mi·cro·scop·i·cal·ly** \-i-k(ə-)lē\ *adv*

sub·min·ia·ture \ˌsəb-'min-ē-ə-ˌchu̇(ə)r, 'səb-, -'min-i-ˌchu̇(ə)r, -'min-yə-, -chər, -ˌt(y)u̇(ə)r\ *adj* [ISV] **:** very small — used esp. of a very compact assembly of electronic equipment

sub·miss \səb-'mis\ *adj* [L *submissus,* fr. pp. of *submittere*] **1** *archaic* **:** SUBMISSIVE, HUMBLE **2** *archaic* **:** low in tone **:** SUBDUED

sub·mis·sion \səb-'mish-ən\ *n* [ME, fr. MF, fr. L *submission-, submissio* act of lowering, fr. *submissus,* pp. of *submittere*] **1 a :** a legal agreement to submit to the decision of arbitrators **b :** an act of submitting something (as for consideration, inspection, or comment) **2 :** the condition of being submissive, humble, or compliant **3 :** an act of submitting to the authority or control of another ***syn*** see SURRENDER

sub·mis·sive \-'mis-iv\ *adj* **:** submitting to others ***syn*** see TAME ***ant*** rebellious — **sub·mis·sive·ly** *adv* — **sub·mis·sive·ness** *n*

sub·mit \səb-'mit\ *vb* **sub·mit·ted; sub·mit·ting** [ME *submitten,* fr. L *submittere* to lower, submit, fr. *sub-* + *mittere* to send — more at SMITE] *vt* **1 a :** to yield to governance or authority **b :** to subject to a regime, condition, or practice <the metal was *submitted* to analysis> **2 a :** to commit to another (as for decision or judgment) <~ a question to the court> **b :** to make available **:** OFFER <~ a bid on a contract> <~ a report> **c :** to put forward as an opinion **:** AFFIRM <we ~ that the charge is not proved> ~ *vi* **1 a :** to yield oneself to the authority or will of another **b :** to permit oneself to be subjected to something <had to ~ to surgery> **2 :** to defer to the opinion or authority of another ***syn*** see YIELD ***ant*** resist, withstand

sub·mi·to·chon·dri·al \ˌsəb-ˌmit-ə-'kän-drē-əl\ *adj* **:** relating to, composed of, or being parts and esp. fragments of mitochondria <~ membranes> <~ particles>

sub·mon·tane \ˌsəb-'män-ˌtān, 'səb-; ˌsəb-(ˌ)män-'tān\ *adj* [LL *submontanus* lying under a mountain, fr. L *sub-* + *mont-, mons* mountain — more at MOUNT] **:** situated at the foot or near the base of a mountain or mountains

sub·mu·co·sa \ˌsəb-myü-'kō-zə\ *n* [NL] **:** a supporting layer of loose connective tissue directly under a mucous membrane — **sub·mu·co·sal** \-zəl\ *adj* — **sub·mu·co·sal·ly** \-zə-lē\ *adv*

sub·mu·cous \ˌsəb-'myü-kəs, 'səb-\ *adj* **:** lying under or involving the tissues under a mucous membrane

sub·mul·ti·ple \-'məl-tə-pəl\ *n* **:** an exact divisor of a number <8 is a ~ of 72>

sub·nor·mal \-'nȯr-məl\ *adj* [ISV] **1 :** lower or smaller than normal **2 :** having less of something and esp. of intelligence than is normal — **sub·nor·mal·i·ty** \ˌsəb-nȯr-'mal-ət-ē\ *n* — **sub·nor·mal·ly** \ˌsəb-'nȯr-mə-lē, 'səb-\ *adv*

sub·oce·an·ic \ˌsəb-ˌō-shē-'an-ik\ *adj* **:** situated, taking place, or formed beneath the ocean or its bottom <~ oil resources>

sub·op·po·site \ˌsəb-'äp-ə-zət, 'səb-, -'äp-sət\ *adj* **:** nearly opposite <~ flowers>

sub·op·ti·mal \-'äp-tə-məl\ *adj* **:** SUBOPTIMUM

sub·op·ti·mum \-məm\ *adj* **:** less than optimum

sub·or·bic·u·lar \ˌsəb-ȯr-'bik-yə-lər\ *adj* [ISV] **:** approximately circular <~ leaves>

sub·or·bit·al \ˌsəb-'ȯr-bət-ᵊl, 'səb-\ *adj* **1 :** situated beneath the orbit of the eye; *also* **:** SUBOCULAR **2 :** being or involving less than one complete orbit (as of the earth or moon) <a spacecraft's ~ flight>; *also* **:** intended for suborbital flight <a ~ rocket>

sub·or·der \'səb-ˌȯrd-ər\ *n* **:** a subdivision of an order <a soil ~>; *esp* **:** a taxonomic category ranking between an order and a family

1**sub·or·di·nate** \sə-'bȯrd-ᵊn-ət, -'bȯrd-nət\ *adj* [ME *subordinat,* fr. ML *subordinatus,* pp. of *subordinare* to subordinate, fr. L *sub-* + *ordinare* to order — more at ORDAIN] **1 :** placed in or occupying a lower class or rank **:** INFERIOR **2 :** submissive to or controlled by authority **3 a :** of, relating to, or constituting a clause that functions as a noun, adjective, or adverb **b :** grammatically subordinating — **sub·or·di·nate·ly** *adv* — **sub·or·di·nate·ness** *n*

2**subordinate** *n* **:** one that is subordinate

3**sub·or·di·nate** \sə-'bȯrd-ᵊn-ˌāt\ *vt* **-nat·ed; -nat·ing 1 :** to place in a lower order or class **2 :** to make subject or subservient **:** SUBDUE — **sub·or·di·na·tion** \-ˌbȯrd-ᵊn-'ā-shən\ *n* — **sub·or·di·na·tive** \-'bȯrd-ᵊn-ˌāt-iv\ *adj*

sub·orn \sə-'bȯ(ə)rn\ *vt* [MF *suborner,* fr. L *subornare,* fr. *sub-* secretly + *ornare* to furnish, equip — more at ORNATE] **1 :** to induce secretly to do an unlawful thing **2 :** to induce to commit perjury; *also* **:** to obtain (perjured testimony) from a witness — **sub·orn·er** *n*

sub·or·na·tion \ˌsəb-ˌȯr-'nā-shən\ *n* **:** the procuring (as by bribes or persuasion) of an improper or unlawful act; *esp* **:** the crime of procuring perjury

sub·ovate \ˌsəb-'ō-ˌvāt, 'səb-\ *adj* **:** approximately ovate

sub·ox·ide \-'äk-ˌsīd\ *n* [ISV] **:** an oxide containing a relatively small proportion of oxygen

sub·par \'səb-'pär\ *adj* **:** being below par

sub·par·al·lel \ˌsəb-'par-ə-ˌlel, 'səb-\ *adj* **:** nearly parallel **:** not quite parallel

sub·phy·lum \'səb-ˌfī-ləm\ *n* [NL] **:** a primary division of a phylum

sub·plot \'səb-ˌplät\ *n* **1 :** a subordinate plot in fiction or drama **2 :** a subdivision of an experimental plot of land

1**sub·poe·na** \sə-'pē-nə, *substand* -nē\ *n* [ME *suppena,* fr. L *sub poena* under penalty] **:** a writ commanding a person designated in it to appear in court under a penalty for failure

2**subpoena** *vt* **-naed; -na·ing :** to serve or summon with a writ of subpoena

subpoena ad tes·ti·fi·can·dum \-ˌad-ˌtes-tə-fi-'kan-dəm\ *n* [NL, under penalty to give testimony] **:** a writ commanding a person to appear in court for testifying as a witness

subpoena du·ces te·cum \-ˌdü-sə-'stē-kəm\ *n* [NL, under penalty you shall bring with you] **:** a writ commanding a person to produce in court certain designated documents or other evidence

sub·po·lar \ˌsəb-'pō-lər, 'səb-\ *adj* **:** SUBANTARCTIC, SUBARCTIC

sub·pop·u·la·tion \'səb-ˌpäp-yə-'lā-shən\ *n* **:** an identifiable fraction or subdivision of a population

sub·po·ten·cy \ˌsəb-'pōt-ᵊn-sē, 'səb-\ *n* **:** the quality or state of being subpotent

sub·po·tent \-'pōt-ᵊnt\ *adj* **:** of less than usu. or normal potency <recalled a drug because it was ~>

sub·prin·ci·pal \-'prin(t)-s(ə-)pəl, 'səb-, -sə-bəl\ *n* **1 :** an assistant principal (as of a school) **2 :** a secondary or bracing rafter

sub·prob·lem \'səb-ˌpräb-ləm\ *n* **:** a problem that is contingent on or forms a part of another more inclusive problem

sub·pro·fes·sion·al \ˌsəb-prə-'fesh-nəl, -ən-ᵊl\ *adj* **:** functioning or qualified to function below the professional level but distinctly above the clerical or labor level and usu. under the supervision of a professionally trained person — **subprofessional** *n*

sub·pro·gram \'səb-'prō-ˌgram, -grəm\ *n* **:** a semi-independent portion of a program (as for a computer)

sub·re·gion \'səb-ˌrē-jən\ *n* [ISV] **:** a subdivision of a region; *esp* **:** one of the primary divisions of a biogeographic region — **sub·re·gion·al** \-ˌrēj-nəl, -ən-ᵊl\ *adj*

sub·rep·tion \(ˌ)səb-'rep-shən\ *n* [LL *subreption-, subreptio,* fr. L, act of stealing, fr. *subreptus,* pp. of *subripere, surripere* to take away secretly — more at SURREPTITIOUS] **:** a deliberate misrepresentation; *also* **:** an inference drawn from it — **sub·rep·ti·tious** \ˌsəb-ˌrep-'tish-əs\ *adj* — **sub·rep·ti·tious·ly** *adv*

sub·ring \'səb-ˌriŋ\ *n* **:** a subset of a mathematical ring which is itself a ring

sub·ro·gate \'səb-rō-ˌgāt\ *vt* **-gat·ed; -gat·ing** [L *subrogatus,* pp. of *subrogare, surrogare* — more at SURROGATE] **:** to put in the place of another **:** SUBSTITUTE

sub·ro·ga·tion \ˌsəb-rō-'gā-shən\ *n* **:** the substitution of one for another as a creditor so that the new creditor succeeds to the former's rights

sub–rosa *adj* **:** designed to be secret or confidential **:** SECRETIVE

sub ro·sa \ˌsəb-'rō-zə\ *adv* [NL, lit., under the rose; fr. the ancient custom of hanging a rose over the council table to indicate that all present were sworn to secrecy] **:** in confidence **:** SECRETLY

sub·rou·tine \ˌsəb-(ˌ)rü-'tēn\ *n* [ISV] **:** a subordinate routine; *esp* **:** a sequence of computer instructions for performing a specified task that can be used repeatedly in a program or in different programs

sub·sa·line \ˌsəb-'sā-ˌlēn, 'səb-, -ˌlīn\ *adj* **:** somewhat salty

[1]**sub·sam·ple** \'səb-ˌsam-pəl, -'sam-\ *vt* **:** to draw samples from (a previously selected group or population) **:** sample a sample of

[2]**subsample** *n* **:** a sample or specimen obtained by subsampling

sub·sat·el·lite \'səb-'sat-ᵊl-ˌīt\ *n* **:** an object carried into orbit in and subsequently released from a satellite or spacecraft

sub·sat·u·rat·ed \ˌsəb-'sach-ə-ˌrāt-əd, 'səb-\ *adj* **:** nearly but not fully saturated — **sub·sat·u·ra·tion** \ˌsəb-ˌsach-ə-'rā-shən\ *n*

sub·scribe \səb-'skrīb\ *vb* **sub·scribed; sub·scrib·ing** [ME *subscriben,* fr. L *subscribere,* lit., to write beneath, fr. *sub-* + *scribere* to write — more at SCRIBE] *vt* **1 :** to write (one's name) underneath **:** SIGN **2 a :** to sign with one's own hand in token of consent or obligation **b :** to attest by signing **c :** to pledge (a gift or contribution) by writing one's name with the amount **3 :** to assent to **:** SUPPORT ~ *vi* **1 :** to sign one's name to a document **2 a :** to give consent or approval to something written by signing <found him unwilling to ~ to the agreement> **b :** to set one's name to a paper in token of promise to give something (as a sum of money); *also* **:** to give something in accordance with such a promise **c :** to enter one's name for a publication or service; *also* **:** to receive a periodical or service regularly on order **d :** to agree to purchase and pay for securities esp. of a new offering <*subscribed* for 1000 shares> **3 :** to feel favorably disposed <I ~ to your sentiments> ***syn*** see ASSENT ***ant*** boggle — **sub·scrib·er** *n*

sub·script \'səb-ˌskript\ *n* [L *subscriptus,* pp. of *subscribere*] **:** a distinguishing symbol or letter written immediately below or below and to the right or left of another character — **subscript** *adj*

sub·scrip·tion \səb-'skrip-shən\ *n* [ME *subscripcioun* signature, fr. L *subscription-, subscriptio,* fr. *subscriptus,* pp. of *subscribere*] **1 a :** the acceptance (as of ecclesiastical articles of faith) attested by the signing of one's name **b :** the act of signing one's name (as in attesting or witnessing a document) **2 :** something that is subscribed: as **a :** an autograph signature; *also* **:** a paper to which a signature is attached **b :** a sum subscribed **c** (1) **:** a purchase by prepayment for a certain number of issues (as of a periodical) (2) **:** application to purchase securities of a new issue **d :** a method of offering or presenting a series of public performances

sub·sec·tion \'səb-ˌsek-shən\ *n* **1 :** a subdivision or a subordinate division of a section **2 :** a subordinate part or branch

[1]**sub·se·quence** \'səb-sə-ˌkwen(t)s, -si-kwən(t)s\ *n* **:** the quality or state of being subsequent; *also* **:** a subsequent event

[2]**sub·se·quence** \'səb-'sē-kwən(t)s, -ˌsē-, -ˌkwen(t)s\ *n* **:** a mathematical sequence that is part of another sequence

sub·se·quent \'səb-si-kwənt, -sə-ˌkwent\ *adj* [ME, fr. L *subsequent-, subsequens,* prp. of *subsequi* to follow close, fr. *sub-* near + *sequi* to follow — more at SUB-, SUE] **:** following in time, order, or place **:** SUCCEEDING — **subsequent** *n* — **sub·se·quent·ly** \-ˌkwent-lē, -kwənt-\ *adv* — **sub·se·quent·ness** \-ˌkwent-, -kwənt-\ *n*

sub·sere \'səb-ˌsi(ə)r\ *n* **:** a secondary succession arising after an ecological climax community has been interrupted (as by fire)

sub·serve \(ˌ)səb-'sərv\ *vt* [L *subservire* to serve, be subservient, fr. *sub-* + *servire* to serve] **1 :** to serve as an instrument or means in carrying out **2 :** to promote the welfare or purposes of

sub·ser·vi·ence \səb-'sər-vē-ən(t)s\ *n* **1 :** a subservient or subordinate place or function **2 :** obsequious servility

sub·ser·vi·en·cy \-ən-sē\ *n* **:** SUBSERVIENCE

sub·ser·vi·ent \-ənt\ *adj* [L *subservient-, subserviens,* prp. of *subservire*] **1 :** useful in an inferior capacity **:** SUBORDINATE **2 :** serving to promote some end **3 :** obsequiously submissive **:** TRUCKLING — **sub·ser·vi·ent·ly** *adv*

syn SUBSERVIENT, SERVILE, SLAVISH, MENIAL, OBSEQUIOUS *shared meaning element* **:** showing extreme compliance or abject obedience ***ant*** domineering, overbearing

sub·set \'səb-ˌset\ *n* **:** a set each of whose elements is an element of an inclusive set

sub·shrub \-ˌshrəb, *esp South* -ˌsrəb\ *n* **1 :** a perennial plant having woody stems except for the terminal part of the new growth which is killed back annually **2 :** UNDERSHRUB 2 — **sub·shrub·by** \-ē\ *adj*

sub·side \səb-'sīd\ *vi* **sub·sid·ed; sub·sid·ing** [L *subsidere,* fr. *sub-* + *sidere* to sit down, sink; akin to L *sedēre* to sit — more at SIT] **1 :** to sink or fall to the bottom **:** SETTLE **2 :** to tend downward **:** DESCEND; *esp* **:** to flatten out so as to form a depression **3 :** to let oneself settle down **:** SINK <*subsided* into a chair> **4 :** to become quiet or less <as the fever ~*s*> <his anger *subsided*> ***syn*** see ABATE — **sub·si·dence** \səb-'sīd-ᵊn(t)s, 'səb-səd-ən(t)s\ *n*

[1]**sub·sid·iary** \səb-'sid-ē-ˌer-ē, -'sid-ə-rē\ *adj* [L *subsidiarius,* fr. *subsidium* reserve troops] **1 a :** furnishing aid or support; **:** AUXILIARY <~ details> **b :** of secondary importance **:** TRIBUTARY <a ~ stream> **2 :** of, relating to, or constituting a subsidy <a ~ payment to an ally> — **sub·sid·iari·ly** \-ˌsid-ē-'er-ə-lē\ *adv*

[2]**subsidiary** *n, pl* **-iar·ies :** one that is subsidiary; *esp* **:** a company wholly controlled by another

sub·si·di·za·tion \ˌsəb-səd-ə-'zā-shən, -zəd-\ *n* **:** the act of subsidizing

sub·si·dize \'səb-sə-ˌdīz, -zə-\ *vt* **-dized; -diz·ing :** to furnish with a subsidy: as **a :** to purchase the assistance of by payment of a subsidy **b :** to aid or promote (as a private enterprise) with public money <~ a steamship line> — **sub·si·diz·er** *n*

sub·si·dy \'səb-səd-ē, -zəd-\ *n, pl* **-dies** [ME, fr. L *subsidium* reserve troops, support, assistance, fr. *sub-* near + *sedēre* to sit — more at SUB-] **:** a grant or gift of money: as **a :** a sum of money formerly granted by the British Parliament to the crown and raised by special taxation **b :** money granted by one state to another **c :** a grant by a government to a private person or company to assist an enterprise deemed advantageous to the public

sub·sist \səb-'sist\ *vb* [LL *subsistere* to exist, fr. L, to come to a halt, remain, fr. *sub-* + *sistere* to come to a stand; akin to L *stare* to stand — more at STAND] *vi* **1 a :** to have existence **:** BE **b :** PERSIST, CONTINUE **2 :** to receive maintenance (as food and clothing) **:** LIVE **3 a :** to hold true **b :** to be logically conceivable as the subject of true statements ~ *vt* **:** to support with provisions

sub·sis·tence \səb-'sis-tən(t)s\ *n* [ME, fr. LL *subsistentia,* fr. *subsistent-, subsistens,* prp. of *subsistere*] **1 a** (1) **:** real being **:** EXISTENCE <an abstraction without real ~> (2) **:** the condition of remaining in existence **:** CONTINUATION, PERSISTENCE (3) **:** INHERENCE <~ of a quality in a body> **b :** something by which an individual is what it is **c :** the character possessed by whatever is logically conceivable **2 :** means of subsisting: as **a :** the minimum (as of food and shelter) necessary to support life **b :** a source or means of obtaining the necessities of life — **sub·sis·tent** \-tənt\ *adj*

subsistence farming *n* **1 :** farming or a system of farming that provides all or almost all the goods required by the farm family usu. without any significant surplus for sale **2 :** farming or a system of farming that produces a minimum and often inadequate return to the farmer — called also *subsistence agriculture*

[1]**sub·soil** \'səb-ˌsȯil\ *n* **:** the stratum of weathered material that underlies the surface soil

[2]**subsoil** *vt* **:** to turn, break, or stir the subsoil of — **sub·soil·er** *n*

sub·so·lar point \ˌsəb-ˌsō-lər-\ *n* **:** the point on the earth's surface at which the sun is at the zenith

sub·son·ic \ˌsəb-'sän-ik, 'səb-\ *adj* [ISV] **1 :** of, relating to, or being a speed less than that of sound in air **2 :** moving, capable of moving, or utilizing air currents moving at a subsonic speed **3 :** INFRASONIC 1 — **sub·son·i·cal·ly** \-i-k(ə-)lē\ *adv*

sub·space \'səb-ˌspās\ *n* **:** a subset of a space; *esp* **:** one that has the essential properties (as those of a vector space or topological space) of the including space

sub spe·cie ae·ter·ni·ta·tis \sůb-'spek-ē-ˌā-ˌī-ˌter-nə-'tät-əs\ *adv* [NL, lit., under the aspect of eternity] **:** in its essential or universal form or nature

sub·spe·cies \'səb-ˌspē-shēz, -sēz\ *n* [NL] **:** a subdivision of a species: as **a :** a taxonomic category that ranks immediately below a species and designates a morphologically or physiologically distinguishable and geographically isolated group whose members interbreed successfully with those of other subspecies of the same species where their ranges overlap **b :** a named subdivision (as a race or variety) of a taxonomic species — **sub·spe·cif·ic** \ˌsəb-spi-'sif-ik\ *adj*

sub·stage \'səb-ˌstāj\ *n* **:** an attachment to a microscope by means of which accessories (as mirrors, diaphragms, or condensers) are held in place beneath the stage of the instrument

sub·stance \'səb-stən(t)s\ *n* [ME, fr. OF, fr. L *substantia,* fr. *substant-, substans,* prp. of *substare* to stand under, fr. *sub-* + *stare* to stand — more at STAND] **1 a :** essential nature **:** ESSENCE **b :** a fundamental or characteristic part or quality **c** *Christian Science* **:** SPIRIT 14 **2 :** ultimate reality that underlies all outward manifestations and change **3 a :** physical material from which something is made or which has discrete existence **b :** matter of particular or definite chemical constitution **4 :** material possessions **:** PROPERTY <a man of ~> — **sub·stance·less** \-ləs\ *adj* — **in substance :** in respect to essentials **:** FUNDAMENTALLY

sub·stan·dard \ˌsəb-'stan-dərd, 'səb-\ *adj* **:** deviating from or falling short of a standard or norm: as **a :** of a quality lower than that prescribed by law **b :** conforming to a pattern of linguistic usage existing within a speech community but not that of the prestige group in that community — compare NONSTANDARD **c :** constituting a greater than normal risk to an insurer

sub·stan·tial \səb-'stan-chəl\ *adj* **1 a :** consisting of or relating to substance **b :** not imaginary or illusory **:** REAL, TRUE **c :** IMPORTANT, ESSENTIAL **2 :** ample to satisfy and nourish **:** FULL <a ~ meal> **3 a :** possessed of means **:** WELL-TO-DO **b :** considerable in quantity **:** significantly large <earned a ~ wage> **4 :** firmly constructed **:** STURDY **5 :** being largely but not wholly that which is specified <a ~ lie> — **substantial** *n* — **sub·stan·ti·al·i·ty** \-ˌstan-chē-'al-ət-ē\ *n* — **sub·stan·tial·ly** \-'stanch-(ə-)lē\ *adv* — **sub·stan·tial·ness** \-'stan-chəl-nəs\ *n*

sub·stan·ti·ate \səb-'stan-chē-ˌāt\ *vt* **-at·ed; -at·ing 1 :** to impart substance to **2 :** to put into concrete form **:** EMBODY **3 :** to establish by proof or competent evidence **:** VERIFY <~ a charge> ***syn*** see CONFIRM — **sub·stan·ti·a·tion** \-ˌstan-chē-'ā-shən\ *n* — **sub·stan·ti·a·tive** \-'stan-chē-ˌāt-iv\ *adj*

sub·stan·ti·val \ˌsəb-stən-'tī-vəl\ *adj* **:** of, relating to, or serving as a substantive — **sub·stan·ti·val·ly** \-və-lē\ *adv*

[1]**sub·stan·tive** \'səb-stən-tiv\ *n* [ME *substantif,* fr. MF, fr. *substantif,* adj., having or expressing substance, fr. LL *substantivus*] **:** NOUN; *broadly* **:** a word or word group functioning syntactically as a noun — **sub·stan·tiv·ize** \-tiv-ˌīz\ *vt*

[2]**sub·stan·tive** \'səb-stən-tiv; *except 2c & 3 also* səb-'stant-iv\ *adj* [ME, fr. LL *substantivus* having substance, fr. L *substantia*] **1 :** being a totally independent entity **2 a :** real rather than apparent **:** FIRM; *also* **:** ENDURING, PERMANENT **b :** belonging to the substance of a thing **:** ESSENTIAL **c :** betokening or expressing existence <the ~ verb is the verb *to be*> **d :** requiring or

involving no mordant <a ~ dyeing process> **3 a :** having the nature or function of a grammatical substantive <a ~ phrase> **b :** relating to or having the character of a noun or pronominal term in logic **4 :** considerable in amount or numbers : SUBSTANTIAL **5 :** creating and defining rights and duties <~ law> — **sub·stan·tive·ly** *adv* — **sub·stan·tive·ness** *n*

substantive right *n* **:** a right (as of life, liberty, property, or reputation) held to exist for its own sake and to constitute part of the normal legal order of society

sub·sta·tion \'səb-ˌstā-shən\ *n* **1 :** a subsidiary station in which electric current is transformed **2 :** a branch post office

sub·stit·u·ent \səb-'stich-(ə-)wənt\ *n* [L *substituent-, substituens,* prp. of *substituere*] **:** an atom or group that replaces another atom or group in a molecule — **substituent** *adj*

sub·sti·tut·able \'səb-stə-ˌt(y)üt-ə-bəl\ *adj* **:** capable of being substituted — **sub·sti·tut·abil·i·ty** \ˌsəb-stə-ˌt(y)üt-ə-'bil-ət-ē\ *n*

¹sub·sti·tute \'səb-stə-ˌt(y)üt\ *n* [ME, fr. L *substitutus,* pp. of *substituere* to put in place of, fr. *sub-* + *statuere* to set up, place — more at STATUTE] **1 :** a person or thing that takes the place of another **2 :** a word that replaces another word, phrase, or clause in a context — **substitute** *adj*

²substitute *vb* **-tut·ed; -tut·ing** *vt* **1 a :** to put in the place of another : EXCHANGE **b :** to introduce (an atom or group) as a substituent; *also* **:** to alter (as a compound) by introduction of a substituent <a *substituted* benzene ring> **2 :** to take the place of : REPLACE ~ *vi* **:** to serve as a substitute

sub·sti·tu·tion \ˌsəb-stə-'t(y)ü-shən\ *n* **1 :** the substituting of one person or thing (as a mathematical quantity) for another **2 :** something that functions as a substitute or exists in a particular relation as a result of an act of substituting — **sub·sti·tu·tion·al** \-shnəl, -shən-ᵊl\ *adj* — **sub·sti·tu·tion·al·ly** \-ē\ *adv* — **sub·sti·tu·tion·ary** \-shə-ˌner-ē\ *adj*

substitution cipher *n* **:** a cipher in which the letters of the plaintext are systematically replaced by substitute letters — compare TRANSPOSITION CIPHER

sub·sti·tu·tive \'səb-stə-ˌt(y)üt-iv\ *adj* **:** serving or suitable as a substitute — **sub·sti·tu·tive·ly** *adv*

sub·strate \'səb-ˌstrāt\ *n* [ML *substratum*] **1 :** SUBSTRATUM **2 :** the base on which an organism lives <the soil is the ~ of most seed plants> **3 :** a substance acted upon (as by an enzyme)

sub·strato·sphere \ˌsəb-'strat-ə-ˌsfi(ə)r, 'səb-\ *n* [ISV] **:** the region of the atmosphere just below the stratosphere — **sub·strato·spher·ic** \-ˌstrat-ə-'sfi(ə)r-ik, -'sfer-\ *adj*

sub·stra·tum \'səb-ˌstrāt-əm, -ˌstrat-, ˌsəb-'\ *n, pl* **-stra·ta** \-ə\ [ML, fr. L, neut. of *substratus,* pp. of *substernere* to spread under, fr. *sub-* + *sternere* to spread — more at STREW] **:** an underlying support : FOUNDATION: as **a :** substance that is a permanent subject of qualities or phenomena **b :** the material of which something is made and from which it derives its special qualities **c :** a layer beneath the surface soil; *specif* **:** SUBSOIL **d :** SUBSTRATE 2, 3 **e :** a thin coating (as of hardened gelatin) on the support of a photographic film or plate to facilitate the adhesion of the sensitive emulsion

sub·struc·ture \'səb-ˌstrək-chər\ *n* [*sub-* + *structure*] **:** FOUNDATION, GROUNDWORK — **sub·struc·tur·al** \-chə-rəl, -shrəl\ *adj*

sub·sume \səb-'süm\ *vt* **sub·sumed; sub·sum·ing** [NL *subsumere,* fr. L *sub-* + *sumere* to take up — more at CONSUME] **:** to classify within a larger category or under a general principle

sub·sump·tion \səb-'səm(p)-shən\ *n* [NL *subsumption-, subsumptio,* fr. *subsumptus,* pp. of *subsumere*] **1 :** MINOR PREMISE **2 :** something that is subsumed **3 :** the act or process of subsuming **4 :** the condition of something that is subsumed

sub·sur·face \'səb-ˌsər-fəs\ *n* **:** earth material (as rock) near but not exposed at the surface of the ground — **subsurface** *adj*

sub·sys·tem \-ˌsis-təm\ *n* **:** a secondary or subordinate system

sub·teen \'səb-'tēn\ *n* **:** a preadolescent child; *esp* **:** a girl under 13 years of age for whom clothing in sizes 8–14 is designed

sub·tem·per·ate \ˌsəb-'tem-p(ə-)rət, 'səb-\ *adj* **:** less than typically temperate <a ~ climate>; *also* **:** of or relating to the colder parts of the temperate zones

sub·ten·an·cy \-'ten-ən-sē\ *n* **:** the state of being a subtenant

sub·ten·ant \-'ten-ənt\ *n* **:** one who rents from a tenant

sub·tend \səb-'tend\ *vt* [L *subtendere* to stretch beneath, fr. *sub-* + *tendere* to stretch — more at THIN] **1 a :** to be opposite to and extend from one side to the other of <a hypotenuse ~*s* a right angle> **b :** to fix the angular extent of with respect to a fixed point or object taken as the vertex <the angle ~*ed* at the eye by an object of given width and a fixed distance away> <a central angle ~*ed* by an arc> **c :** to determine the measure of by marking off the endpoints of <a chord ~*s* an arc> **2 a :** to underlie so as to include **b :** to occupy an adjacent and usu. lower position to and often so as to embrace or enclose <a bract that ~*s* a flower>

sub·ter·fuge \'səb-tər-ˌfyüj\ *n* [LL *subterfugium,* fr. L *subterfugere* to escape, evade, fr. *subter-* secretly (fr. *subter* underneath) + *fugere* to flee; akin to L *sub* under — more at UP, FUGITIVE] **1 :** deception by artifice or stratagem in order to conceal, escape, or evade <employing ~ to get her own way> **2 :** a deceptive device or strategem <malingering or some other ~ is resorted to in order to save face —H. G. Armstrong>

sub·ter·mi·nal \ˌsəb-'tərm-nəl, -ən-ᵊl, 'səb-\ *adj* **:** situated or occurring near but not precisely at an end <a ~ band of color on the tail feathers> <a ~ collapse>

sub·ter·ra·nean \ˌsəb-tə-'rā-nē-ən, -nyən\ *or* **sub·ter·ra·neous** \-nē-əs, -nyəs\ *adj* [L *subterraneus,* fr. *sub* under + *terra* earth — more at UP, TERRACE] **1 :** being, lying, or operating under the surface of the earth **2 :** existing or working in secret : HIDDEN — **sub·ter·ra·nean·ly** *adv*

sub·te·tan·ic \ˌsəb-te-'tan-ik\ *adj* **:** approaching tetany or tetanus esp. in form or degree of contraction

sub·thresh·old \ˌsəb-'thresh-ˌ(h)ōld, 'səb-\ *adj* **:** inadequate to produce a response <~ dosage> <a ~ stimulus>

sub·tile \'sət-ᵊl, 'səb-tᵊl\ *adj* **sub·til·er** \'sət-lər, -ᵊl-ər; 'səb-tə-lər\; **sub·til·est** \'sət-ləst, -ᵊl-əst; 'səb-tə-ləst\ [ME, fr. L *subtilis*] **1 :** SUBTLE, ELUSIVE <a ~ aroma> **2 :** CUNNING, CRAFTY — **sub·tile·ly** \'sət-ᵊl-ē, -ᵊl-(l)ē; 'səb-tə-lē\ *adv* — **sub·tile·ness** \'sət-ᵊl-nəs, 'səb-tᵊl-\ *n*

sub·til·i·sin \ˌsəb-'til-ə-sən\ *n* [NL *subtilis,* specific epithet of *Bacillus subtilis,* species to which *Bacillus amyloliquefaciens* was once thought to belong] **:** an extracellular protease produced by a soil bacillus (*Bacillus amyloliquefaciens*)

sub·til·iza·tion \ˌsət-ᵊl-ə-'zā-shən, ˌsəb-tə-lə-\ *n* **:** an act of subtilizing; *also* **:** something subtilized

sub·til·ize \'sət-ᵊl-ˌīz, 'səb-tə-ˌlīz\ *vb* **-ized; -iz·ing** *vt* **:** to make subtile ~ *vi* **:** to act or think subtly

sub·til·ty \'sət-ᵊl-tē, 'səb-tᵊl-\ *n, pl* **-ties :** SUBTLETY

¹sub·ti·tle \'səb-ˌtīt-ᵊl\ *n* **1 :** a secondary or explanatory title **2 :** a printed statement or fragment of dialogue appearing on the screen between the scenes of a silent motion picture or appearing as a translation at the bottom of the screen during the scenes

²subtitle *vt* **:** to give a subtitle to

sub·tle \'sət-ᵊl\ *adj* **sub·tler** \'sət-lər, -ᵊl-ər\; **sub·tlest** \'sət-ləst, -ᵊl-əst\ [ME *sutil, sotil,* fr. OF *soutil,* fr. L *subtilis,* lit., finely woven, fr. *sub-* + *tela* web; akin to L *texere* to weave — more at TECHNICAL] **1 a :** DELICATE, ELUSIVE <a ~ fragrance> **b :** difficult to understand or distinguish : OBSCURE <~ differences in sound> **2 a :** PERCEPTIVE, REFINED <the artist's ~ awareness of color values> **b :** having or marked by keen insight and ability to penetrate deeply and thoroughly <a ~ scholar> **3 a :** highly skillful : EXPERT <~ workmanship> **b :** cunningly made or contrived : INGENIOUS **4 :** ARTFUL, CRAFTY <a ~ rogue> **5 :** operating insidiously <~ poisons> ***syn*** see LOGICAL ***ant*** dense (*in mind*), blunt (*in speech*) — **sub·tle·ness** \'sət-ᵊl-nəs\ *n* — **sub·tly** \'sət-lē, 'sət-ᵊl-(l)ē\ *adv*

sub·tle·ty \'sət-ᵊl-tē\ *n, pl* **-ties** [ME *sutilte,* fr. OF *sutilté,* fr. L *subtilitat-, subtilitas,* fr. *subtilis*] **1 :** the quality or state of being subtle: as **a :** the quality of being tenuous **b :** acuteness of mind **2 :** something subtle; *esp* **:** a fine distinction

sub·ton·ic \ˌsəb-'tän-ik, 'səb-\ *n* [fr. its being a half tone below the upper tonic] **:** LEADING TONE

sub·top·ic \'səb-ˌtäp-ik\ *n* **:** a secondary topic **:** one of the subdivisions into which a topic may be divided

¹sub·to·tal \ˌsəb-'tōt-ᵊl\ *adj* **:** somewhat less than complete **:** nearly total — **sub·to·tal·ly** \-ᵊl-ē\ *adv*

²sub·to·tal \'səb-ˌtōt-ᵊl\ *n* **:** the sum of part of a series of figures

³sub·to·tal \'səb-'tōt-ᵊl\ *vt* **:** to determine a subtotal for ~ *vi* **:** to determine a subtotal

sub·tract \səb-'trakt\ *vb* [L *subtractus,* pp. of *subtrahere* to draw from beneath, withdraw, fr. *sub-* + *trahere* to draw — more at DRAW] *vt* **:** to take away by deducting <~ 5 from 9> ~ *vi* **:** to perform a subtraction — **sub·tract·er** *n*

sub·trac·tion \səb-'trak-shən\ *n* **:** an act, operation, or instance of subtracting: as **a :** the withdrawing or withholding from one of a right to which he is entitled **b :** the operation of deducting one number from another

sub·trac·tive \-'trak-tiv\ *adj* **1 :** tending to subtract **2 :** constituting or involving subtraction

sub·tra·hend \'səb-trə-ˌhend\ *n* [L *subtrahendus,* gerundive of *subtrahere*] **:** a number that is to be subtracted from a minuend

sub·trop·i·cal \ˌsəb-'träp-i-kəl, 'səb-\ *also* **sub·trop·ic** \-ik\ *adj* [ISV] **:** of, relating to, or being the regions bordering on the tropical zone

sub·trop·ics \-iks\ *n pl* **:** subtropical regions

su·bu·late \'sü-byə-lət, 'səb-yə-, -ˌlāt\ *adj* [NL *subulatus,* fr. L *subula* awl; akin to OHG *siula* awl, L *suere* to sew — more at SEW] **:** linear and tapering to a fine point <a ~ leaf>

sub·um·brel·la \ˌsəb-(ˌ)əm-'brel-ə\ *n* **:** the concave undersurface of a jellyfish

sub·unit \'səb-ˌyü-nət\ *n* **:** a unit that forms a discrete part of a more comprehensive unit <~*s* of a protein>

sub·urb \'səb-ˌərb\ *n* [ME, fr. L *suburbium,* fr. *sub-* near + *urbs* city — more at SUB-] **1 a :** an outlying part of a city or town **b :** a smaller community adjacent to or within commuting distance of a city **c** *pl* **:** the residential area on the outskirts of a city or large town **2** *pl* **:** the near vicinity : ENVIRONS — **sub·ur·ban** \sə-'bər-bən\ *adj or n*

sub·ur·ban·ite \sə-'bər-bə-ˌnīt\ *n* **:** one who lives in the suburbs

sub·ur·ban·iza·tion \sə-ˌbərb-ə-nə-'zā-shən\ *n* **1 :** the quality or state of being suburbanized **2 :** the act of suburbanizing

sub·ur·ban·ize \sə-'bər-bə-ˌnīz\ *vt* **-ized; -iz·ing :** to make suburban : give a suburban character to

sub·ur·bia \sə-'bər-bē-ə\ *n* [NL, fr. E *suburb* + L *-ia* -y] **1 :** the suburbs of a city **2 :** suburbanites as a distinctive social element **3 :** the manners, styles, and customs typical of suburban life

sub·ven·tion \səb-'ven-chən\ *n* [LL *subvention-, subventio* assistance, fr. L *subventus,* pp. of *subvenire* to come up, come to the rescue, fr. *sub-* up + *venire* to come — more at SUB-, COME] **:** the provision of assistance or financial support: as **a :** ENDOWMENT **b :** a subsidy from a government or foundation — **sub·ven·tion·ary** \-chə-ˌner-ē\ *adj*

sub·ver·sion \səb-'vər-zhən, -shən\ *n* [ME, fr. MF, fr. LL *subversion-, subversio,* fr. L *subversus,* pp. of *subvertere*] **1 :** the act of subverting : the state of being subverted : OVERTHROW; *esp* **:** a systematic attempt to overthrow or undermine a government or political system by persons working secretly within the country involved **2** *obs* **:** a cause of overthrow or destruction — **sub·ver·sion·ary** \-zhə-ˌner-ē, -shə-\ *adj* — **sub·ver·sive** \-'vər-siv, -ziv\ *adj or n* — **sub·ver·sive·ly** *adv* — **sub·ver·sive·ness** *n*

sub·vert \səb-'vərt\ *vt* [ME *subverten,* fr. MF *subvertir,* fr. L *subvertere,* lit., to turn from beneath, fr. *sub-* + *vertere* to turn — more at WORTH] **1 :** to overturn or overthrow from the foundation : RUIN **2 :** to pervert or corrupt by an undermining of morals, allegiance, or faith — **sub·vert·er** *n*

sub·vi·ral \ˌsəb-'vī-rəl, 'səb-\ *adj* **:** relating to, being, or caused by a piece or a structural part (as a protein) of a virus <~ infection>

sub·vo·cal \-ˈvō-kəl\ *adj* **:** characterized by the occurrence in the mind of words in speech order with or without inaudible articulation of the speech organs — **sub·vo·cal·ly** \-kə-lē\ *adv*

sub·way \ˈsəb-ˌwā\ *n* **:** an underground way: as **a :** a passage under a street (as for pedestrians, power cables, or water or gas mains) **b :** a usu. electric underground railway **c :** UNDERPASS

suc·ce·da·ne·ous \ˌsək-sə-ˈdā-nē-əs\ *adj* **:** serving as a succedaneum **:** SUBSTITUTED

suc·ce·da·ne·um \-nē-əm\ *n, pl* **-ne·ums** *or* **-nea** \-nē-ə\ [NL, fr. L, neut. of *succedaneus* substituted, fr. *succedere* to follow after] **:** SUBSTITUTE

suc·ce·dent \sək-ˈsēd-ᵊnt\ *adj* [L *succedent-, succedens,* prp. of *succedere*] **:** coming next **:** SUCCEEDING, SUBSEQUENT

suc·ceed \sək-ˈsēd\ *vb* [ME *succeden,* fr. L *succedere* to go up, follow after, succeed, fr. *sub-* near + *cedere* to go — more at SUB-, CEDE] *vi* **1 a :** to come next after another in or in possession of an estate; *specif* **:** to inherit sovereignty, rank, or title **b :** to follow after another in order **2 a :** to turn out well **b :** to attain a desired object or end **3** *obs* **:** to devolve upon a person by inheritance ~ *vt* **1 :** to follow in sequence and esp. immediately **2 :** to come after as heir or successor — **suc·ceed·er** *n*
syn **1** see FOLLOW *ant* precede
2 SUCCEED, PROSPER, THRIVE, FLOURISH *shared meaning element* **:** to attain or be attaining a desired end *ant* fail, attempt

suc·cès de scan·dale \sək-ˌsā-də-skäⁿ-ˈdäl, (ˌ)sük-\ *n* [F, lit., success of scandal] **:** something (as a work of art) that wins popularity or notoriety because of its scandalous nature; *also* **:** the reception accorded such a piece

suc·cès d'es·time \-ˌdes-ˈtēm\ *n* [F, lit., success of esteem] **:** something (as a work of art) that wins critical respect but not popular success; *also* **:** the reception accorded such a piece

suc·cès fou \-ˈfü\ *n* [F, lit., mad success] **:** an extraordinary success

suc·cess \sək-ˈses\ *n* [L *successus,* fr. *successus,* pp. of *succedere*] **1** *obs* **:** OUTCOME, RESULT **2 a :** degree or measure of succeeding **b :** a favorable termination of a venture; *specif* **:** the attainment of wealth, favor, or eminence **3 :** one that succeeds

suc·cess·ful \-fəl\ *adj* **1 :** resulting or terminating in success **2 :** gaining or having gained success — **suc·cess·ful·ly** \-fə-lē\ *adv* — **suc·cess·ful·ness** *n*

suc·ces·sion \sək-ˈsesh-ən\ *n* [ME, fr. MF or L; MF, fr. L *succession-, successio,* fr. *successus,* pp.] **1 a :** the order in which or the conditions under which one person after another succeeds to a property, dignity, title, or throne **b :** the right of a person or line to succeed **c :** the line having such a right **2 a :** the act or process of following in order **:** SEQUENCE **b (1) :** the act or process of one person's taking the place of another in the enjoyment of or liability for his rights or duties or both **(2) :** the act or process of a person's becoming beneficially entitled to a property or property interest of a deceased person **c :** the continuance of corporate personality **d :** unidirectional change in the composition of an ecosystem and esp. the plants as the available competing organisms and esp. the plants respond to and modify the environment <the highlights of the ~ were the weed, grass, and forest communities developed in that order> **3 a :** a number of persons or things that follow each other in sequence **b :** a group, type, or series that succeeds or displaces another — **suc·ces·sion·al** \-ˈsesh-nəl, -ən-ᵊl\ *adj* — **suc·ces·sion·al·ly** \-ē\ *adv*

succession duty *n, chiefly Brit* **:** INHERITANCE TAX

succession state *n* **:** one of a number of states that succeed a former state in sovereignty over a certain territory

suc·ces·sive \sək-ˈses-iv\ *adj* **1 :** following in succession or serial order **:** following each other without interruption **2 :** characterized by or produced in succession *syn* see CONSECUTIVE — **suc·ces·sive·ly** *adv* — **suc·ces·sive·ness** *n*

suc·ces·sor \sək-ˈses-ər\ *n* [ME *successour,* fr. OF, fr. L *successor,* fr. *successus,* pp.] **:** one that follows; *esp* **:** one who succeeds to a throne, title, estate, or office

successor state *n* **:** SUCCESSION STATE

success story *n* **:** a real or fictitious account of a poor or unknown person who rises to fortune, acclaim, or brilliant achievement

suc·ci·nate \ˈsək-sə-ˌnāt\ *n* **:** a salt or ester of succinic acid

suc·cinct \(ˌ)sək-ˈsiŋ(k)t, sə-ˈsiŋ(k)t\ *adj* [ME, fr. L *succinctus,* pp. of *succingere* to gird from below, tuck up, fr. *sub-* + *cingere* to gird — more at CINCTURE] **1** *archaic* **a :** being girded **b :** close-fitting **2 :** marked by compact precise expression without wasted words *syn* see CONCISE *ant* discursive — **suc·cinct·ly** \-ˈsiŋ(k)-tlē, -ˈsiŋ-klē\ *adv* — **suc·cinct·ness** \-ˈsiŋt-nəs, -ˈsiŋk-nəs\ *n*

suc·cin·ic acid \(ˌ)sək-ˌsin-ik-\ *n* [F *succinique,* fr. L *succinum* amber] **:** a crystalline dicarboxylic acid $C_4H_6O_4$ found widely in nature and active in energy-yielding metabolic reactions

succinic dehydrogenase *n* **:** an iron-containing flavoprotein enzyme that catalyzes often reversibly the dehydrogenation of succinic acid to fumaric acid in the presence of a hydrogen acceptor and that is widely distributed esp. in animal tissues, bacteria, and yeast

suc·ci·nyl \ˈsək-sən-ᵊl, -sə-ˌnil\ *n* [ISV] **:** either of two radicals of succinic acid: **a :** a bivalent radical $C_4H_4O_2$ **b :** a univalent radical $C_3H_5O_3$

suc·ci·nyl·cho·line \ˌsək-sən-ᵊl-ˈkō-ˌlēn, -sə-ˌnil-\ *n* [*succinyl* + *choline*] **:** a basic compound that acts similarly to curare and is used intravenously chiefly in the form of a hydrated chloride $C_{14}H_{30}Cl_2N_2O_4.2H_2O$ as a muscle relaxant in surgery

¹suc·cor \ˈsək-ər\ *n* [ME *succur,* fr. earlier *sucurs,* taken as pl., fr. OF *sucors,* fr. ML *succursus,* fr. L *succursus,* pp. of *succurrere* to run up, run to help, fr. *sub-* up + *currere* to run — more at CURRENT] **1 :** RELIEF; *also* **:** AID, HELP **2 :** something that furnishes relief

²succor *vt* **suc·cored; suc·cor·ing** \ˈsək-(ə-)riŋ\ **:** to go to the aid of (one in want or distress) **:** RELIEVE — **suc·cor·er** \ˈsək-ər-ər\ *n*

suc·co·ry \ˈsək-(ə-)rē\ *n* [alter. of ME *cicoree*] **:** CHICORY

suc·co·tash \ˈsək-ə-ˌtash\ *n* [of Algonquian origin; akin to Narraganset *msakwatas̆* succotash] **:** lima or shell beans and green corn cooked together

suc·cour \ˈsək-ər\ *chiefly Brit var of* SUCCOR

suc·cu·ba \ˈsək-yə-bə\ *n, pl* **-bae** \-ˌbē, -ˌbī\ [LL, prostitute] **:** SUCCUBUS

suc·cu·bus \-bəs\ *n, pl* **suc·cu·bi** \-ˌbī, -ˌbē\ [ME, fr. ML, alter. of LL *succuba* prostitute, fr. L *succubare* to lie under, fr. *sub-* + *cubare* to lie, recline — more at HIP] **:** a demon assuming female form to have sexual intercourse with men in their sleep — compare INCUBUS

suc·cu·lence \ˈsək-yə-lən(t)s\ *n* **1 :** the state of being succulent **2 :** succulent feed <wild game subsisting on ~>

¹suc·cu·lent \-lənt\ *adj* [L *suculentus,* fr. *sucus* juice, sap; akin to L *sugere* to suck — more at SUCK] **1 a :** full of juice **:** JUICY **b :** TOOTHSOME **c** *of a plant* **:** having fleshy tissues designed to conserve moisture **2 :** full of vitality, freshness, or richness — **suc·cu·lent·ly** *adv*

²succulent *n* **:** a succulent plant (as a cactus)

suc·cumb \sə-ˈkəm\ *vi* [F & L; F *succomber,* fr. L *succumbere,* fr. *sub-* + *-cumbere* to lie down; akin to L *cubare* to lie — more at HIP] **1 :** to yield to superior strength or force or overpowering appeal or desire **2 :** to be brought to an end (as death) by the effect of destructive or disruptive forces *syn* see YIELD

¹such \(ˈ)səch, (ˌ)sich\ *adj* [ME, fr. OE *swilc;* akin to OHG *sulīh* such; both fr. a prehistoric Gmc compound whose constituents are respectively represented by OE *swā* so and by OE *gelīc* like — more at SO, LIKE] **1 a :** of a kind or character to be indicated or suggested <a bag ~ as a doctor carries> **b :** having a quality to a degree to be indicated <his excitement was ~ that he shouted> **2 a :** having a quality already or just specified <deeply moved by ~ acts of kindness> **b :** of the character, quality, or extent previously indicated or implied **3 :** of so extreme a degree or quality <never heard ~ a hubbub> **4 :** of the same class, type, or sort <other ~ clinics throughout the state> **5 :** not specified

²such *pron* **1 :** such a person or thing **2 :** someone or something stated, implied, or exemplified <~ was the result> **3 :** someone or something similar <tin and glass and ~> — **as such :** intrinsically considered **:** in itself <*as such* the gift was worth little>

³such *adv* **1 a :** to such a degree **:** SO <~ tall buildings> <~ a fine person> **b :** VERY, ESPECIALLY <hasn't been in ~ good spirits lately> **2 :** in such a way

such and such *adj* **:** not named or specified <said he went to *such and such* a place>

¹such·like \ˈsəch-ˌlīk\ *adj* **:** of like kind **:** SIMILAR

²suchlike *pron* **:** someone or something of the same sort **:** a similar person or thing

¹suck \ˈsək\ *vb* [ME *souken,* fr. OE *sūcan;* akin to OHG *sūgan* to suck, L *sugere,* Gk *hyein* to rain] *vt* **1 a :** to draw (as liquid) into the mouth through a suction force produced by movements of the lips and tongue <~*ed* milk from his mother's breast> **b :** to draw something (as liquid) from or consume by such movements <~ an orange> <~ a lollipop> **c :** to apply the mouth to as if sucking out a liquid <~*ed* his burned finger> **2 :** to draw by or as if by suction <plants ~*ing* moisture from the soil> **3 :** to involve in an enterprise by compulsion or deceit <inadvertently ~*ed* into the . . . intrigue —Martin Levin> ~ *vi* **1 :** to draw something in by or as if by exerting a suction force; *esp* **:** to draw milk from a breast or udder with the mouth **2 :** to make a sound or motion associated with or caused by suction <his pipe ~*ed* wetly> <flanks ~*ed* in and out, the long nose resting on his paws —Virginia Woolf> **3 :** to act in an obsequious manner <when they want votes . . . the candidates come ~*ing* around —W. G. Hardy> **4** *slang* **:** to be extremely or disgustingly unpleasant or objectionable — usu. considered vulgar

²suck *n* **1 :** the act of sucking **2 :** a sucking movement or force

¹suck·er \ˈsək-ər\ *n* **1 a :** one that sucks esp. a breast or udder **:** SUCKLING **b :** a device for creating or regulating suction (as a piston or valve in a pump) **c :** a pipe or tube through which something is drawn by suction **d (1) :** an organ in various animals for adhering or holding **(2) :** a mouth (as of a leech) adapted for sucking or adhering **2 :** a shoot from the roots or lower part of the stem of a plant **3 :** any of numerous freshwater fishes (family Catostomidae) closely related to the carps but distinguished from them esp. by the structure of the mouth which usu. has thick soft lips **4 :** LOLLIPOP **5 a :** a person easily cheated or deceived **b :** a person irresistibly attracted by a specific type of object

²sucker *vb* **suck·ered; suck·er·ing** \ˈsək-(ə-)riŋ\ *vt* **1 :** to remove suckers from <~ tobacco> **2 :** CHEAT, SWINDLE <got ~*ed* out of six grand —Gerald Hughes> ~ *vi* **:** to send out suckers

suck in *vt* **:** to contract, flatten, and tighten (the abdomen) esp. by inhaling deeply

suck·ing *adj* **:** not yet weaned; *broadly* **:** very young

sucking louse *n* **:** any of an order (Anoplura) of wingless insects comprising the true lice with mouthparts adapted to sucking body fluids

suck·le \ˈsək-əl\ *vt* **suck·led; suck·ling** \-(ə-)liŋ\ [prob. back-formation fr. *suckling*] **1 a :** to give milk to from the breast or udder <a mother *suckling* her child> **b :** to bring up <a pagan *suckled* in a creed outworn —William Wordsworth> **2 :** to draw milk from the breast or udder of <lambs *suckling* the ewes>

suck·ling \ˈsək-liŋ\ *n* **:** a young unweaned animal

su·crase \ˈsü-ˌkrās, -ˌkrāz\ *n* [ISV, fr. F *sucre* sugar — more at SUGAR] **:** INVERTASE

su·cre \ˈsü-(ˌ)krā\ *n* [Sp, fr. Antonio José de *Sucre* †1830 So. American liberator] — see MONEY table

su·crose \ˈsü-ˌkrōs, -ˌkrōz\ *n* [ISV, fr. F *sucre* sugar] **:** a sweet crystalline dextrorotatory nonreducing disaccharide sugar

$C_{12}H_{22}O_{11}$ that occurs naturally in most land plants and is the sugar obtained from sugarcane or sugar beets

suc·tion \ˈsək-shən\ *n* [LL *suction-, suctio,* fr. L *suctus,* pp. of *sugere* to suck — more at SUCK] **1 :** the act or process of sucking **2 a :** the act or process of exerting a force upon a solid, liquid, or gaseous body by reason of reduced air pressure over part of its surface **b :** force so exerted **3 :** a device (as a pipe or fitting) used in a machine that operates by suction — **suc·tion·al** \-shən-ᵊl, -shnəl\ *adj*

suction pump *n* **:** a common pump in which the liquid to be raised is pushed by atmospheric pressure into the partial vacuum under a retreating valved piston on the upstroke and reflux is prevented by a check valve in the pipe

suction stop *n* **:** a voice stop in the formation of which air behind the articulation is rarefied with consequent inrush of air when articulation is broken

suc·to·ri·al \ˌsək-ˈtōr-ē-əl, -ˈtȯr-\ *adj* [NL *suctorius,* fr. L *suctus,* pp.] **:** adapted for sucking; *esp* **:** serving to draw up fluid or to adhere by suction <~ mouths>

suc·to·ri·an \-ē-ən\ *n* [NL *Suctoria,* group name, fr. neut. pl. of *suctorius* suctorial] **:** any of a class (Suctoria) of complex protozoans which have cilia only early in development and in which the mature form is fixed to the substrate, lacks locomotor organelles or a mouth, and obtains food through specialized suctorial tentacles

Su·dan grass \sü-ˈdan-, -ˈdän-\ *n* [the *Sudan,* region in Africa] **:** a vigorous tall-growing annual grass (*Sorghum vulgare sudanensis*) widely grown for hay and fodder

Su·dan·ic \sü-ˈdan-ik\ *n* [the *Sudan*] **:** the languages neither Bantu nor Hamitic spoken in a belt extending from Senegal to southern Sudan — **Sudanic** *adj*

su·da·to·ri·um \ˌsüd-ə-ˈtōr-ē-əm, -ˈtȯr-\ *n* [L, fr. *sudatus,* pp. of *sudare* to sweat — more at SWEAT] **:** a sweat room in a bath

su·da·to·ry \ˈsüd-ə-ˌtōr-ē, -ˌtȯr-\ *n, pl* **-ries :** SUDATORIUM

sudd \ˈsəd\ *n* [Ar, lit., obstruction] **:** floating vegetable matter that forms obstructive masses in the upper White Nile

[1]**sud·den** \ˈsəd-ᵊn\ *adj* [ME *sodain,* fr. MF, fr. L *subitaneus,* fr. *subitus* sudden, fr. pp. of *subire* to come up, fr. *sub-* up + *ire* to go — more at SUB-, ISSUE] **1 a :** happening or coming unexpectedly <a ~ shower> **b :** changing angle or character all at once **2 :** marked by or manifesting abruptness or haste **3 :** made or brought about in a short time **:** PROMPT ***syn*** see PRECIPITATE — **sud·den·ly** *adv* — **sud·den·ness** \ˈsəd-ᵊn-(n)əs\ *n*

[2]**sudden** *n, obs* **:** an unexpected occurrence **:** EMERGENCY — **all of a sudden** *or* **on a sudden :** sooner than was expected **:** at once

sudden death *n* **1 :** unexpected death that is instantaneous or occurs within minutes from any cause other than violence <*sudden death* following coronary occlusion> **2 a :** a single full game played to break a tie **b :** an extra period of play to break a tie that terminates the moment one side scores or gains the lead

su·do·rif·er·ous \ˌsüd-ə-ˈrif-(ə-)rəs\ *adj* [LL *sudorifer,* fr. L *sudor* sweat + *-ifer* -iferous — more at SWEAT] **:** producing or conveying sweat <~ glands> <a ~ duct>

su·do·rif·ic \-ˈrif-ik\ *adj* [NL *sudorificus,* fr. L *sudor*] **:** causing or inducing sweat **:** DIAPHORETIC <~ herbs> — **sudorific** *n*

Su·dra \ˈs(h)ü-drə\ *n* [Skt *śūdra*] **:** a Hindu of a lower caste traditionally assigned to menial occupations — **Sudra** *adj*

[1]**suds** \ˈsədz\ *n pl but sing or pl in constr* [prob. fr. MD *sudse* marsh; akin to OE *sēothan* to seethe — more at SEETHE] **1 :** water impregnated with soap or a synthetic detergent compound and worked up into froth; *also* **:** the lather or froth on such water **2 a :** FOAM, FROTH **b :** BEER — **suds·less** \-ləs\ *adj*

[2]**suds** *vt* **:** to wash in suds ~ *vi* **:** to form suds — **suds·er** *n*

sudsy \ˈsəd-zē\ *adj* **suds·i·er; -est 1 :** full of suds **:** FROTHY, FOAMY **2 :** SOAPY 4

sue \ˈsü\ *vb* **sued; su·ing** [ME *suen,* fr. OF *suivre,* fr. (assumed) VL *sequere,* fr. L *sequi* to follow, come or go after; akin to Gk *hepesthai* to follow] *vt* **1** *obs* **:** to make petition to or for **2 :** to pay court or suit to **:** WOO **3 a :** to seek justice or right from (a person) by legal process; *specif* **:** to bring an action against **b :** to proceed with and follow up (a legal action) to proper termination ~ *vi* **1 :** to make a request or application **:** PLEAD — usu. used with *for* or *to* **2 :** to pay court **:** WOO **3 :** to take legal proceedings in court — **su·er** *n*

[1]**suede** *or* **suède** \ˈswād\ *n* [F *gants de Suède* Swedish gloves] **1 :** leather with a napped surface **2 :** a fabric finished with a nap to simulate suede

[2]**suede** *vb* **sued·ed; sued·ing** *vt* **:** to give a suede finish or nap to (a fabric or leather) ~ *vi* **:** to give cloth or leather a suede finish

su·et \ˈsü-ət\ *n* [ME *sewet,* fr. (assumed) AF, dim. of AF *sue,* fr. L *sebum* tallow, suet — more at SOAP] **:** the hard fat about the kidneys and loins in beef and mutton that yields tallow

suff *abbr* **1** sufficient **2** suffix

suf·fer \ˈsəf-ər\ *vb* **suf·fered; suf·fer·ing** \-(ə-)riŋ\ [ME *suffren,* fr. OF *souffrir,* fr. (assumed) VL *sufferire,* fr. L *sufferre,* fr. *sub-* up + *ferre* to bear — more at SUB-, BEAR] *vt* **1 a :** to submit to or be forced to endure <~ martyrdom> **b :** to feel keenly **:** labor under <~ thirst> **2 :** UNDERGO, EXPERIENCE **3 :** to put up with esp. as inevitable or unavoidable **4 :** to allow esp. by reason of indifference <the eagle ~*s* little birds to sing —Shak.> ~ *vi* **1 :** to endure death, pain, or distress **2 :** to sustain loss or damage **3 :** to be subject to disability or handicap ***syn*** see BEAR, LET — **suf·fer·able** \ˈsəf-(ə-)rə-bəl\ *adj* — **suf·fer·able·ness** *n* — **suf·fer·ably** \-blē\ *adv* — **suf·fer·er** \ˈsəf-ər-ər\ *n*

suf·fer·ance \ˈsəf-(ə-)rən(t)s\ *n* **1 :** patient endurance **:** LONGSUFFERING **2 :** PAIN, MISERY **3 :** consent or sanction implied by a lack of interference or failure to enforce a prohibition **4 :** power or ability to withstand **:** ENDURANCE ***syn*** see PERMISSION

suf·fer·ing *n* **1 :** the state or experience of one that suffers **2 :** PAIN ***syn*** see DISTRESS

suf·fice \sə-ˈfīs *also* -ˈfīz\ *vb* **suf·ficed; suf·fic·ing** [ME *sufficen,* fr. MF *suffis-,* stem of *suffire,* fr. L *sufficere,* lit., to put under, fr. *sub-* + *facere* to make, do — more at DO] *vi* **1 :** to meet or satisfy a need **:** be sufficient <a brief note will ~> — often used with an impersonal *it* <~ it to say that they are dedicated, serious personalities —Cheryl Aldridge> **2 :** to be competent or capable ~ *vt* **:** to be enough for — **suf·fic·er** *n*

suf·fi·cien·cy \sə-ˈfish-ən-sē\ *n* **1 :** sufficient means to meet one's needs **:** COMPETENCY; *also* **:** a modest but adequate scale of living **2 :** the quality or state of being sufficient **:** ADEQUACY

suf·fi·cient \sə-ˈfish-ənt\ *adj* [ME, fr. L *sufficient-, sufficiens,* fr. prp. of *sufficere*] **1 a :** enough to meet the needs of a situation or a proposed end <~ provisions for a month> **b :** being a sufficient condition **2** *archaic* **:** QUALIFIED, COMPETENT — **suf·fi·cient·ly** *adv*

syn SUFFICIENT, ENOUGH, ADEQUATE, COMPETENT *shared meaning element* **:** being what is requisite or desirable ***ant*** insufficient

sufficient condition *n* **1 :** a proposition whose truth assures the truth of another proposition **2 :** a state of affairs whose existence assures the existence of another state of affairs

[1]**suf·fix** \ˈsəf-ˌiks\ *n* [NL *suffixum,* fr. L, neut. of *suffixus,* pp. of *suffigere* to fasten underneath, fr. *sub-* + *figere* to fasten — more at DIKE] **:** an affix occurring at the end of a word, base, or phrase — compare PREFIX — **suf·fix·al** \ˈsəf-ˌik-səl, (ˌ)sə-ˈfik-səl\ *adj*

[2]**suf·fix** \ˈsəf-iks, (ˌ)sə-ˈfiks\ *vt* **:** to attach as a suffix — **suf·fix·ation** \ˌsəf-ˌik-ˈsā-shən\ *n*

suf·fo·cate \ˈsəf-ə-ˌkāt\ *vb* **-cat·ed; -cat·ing** [L *suffocatus,* pp. of *suffocare* to choke, stifle, fr. *sub-* + *fauces* throat] *vt* **1 a :** to stop the respiration of (as by strangling or asphyxiation) **b :** to deprive of oxygen **c :** to make uncomfortable by want of cool fresh air **2 :** to impede or stop the development of ~ *vi* **1 :** to become suffocated: **a :** to die from being unable to breathe **b :** to be uncomfortable through lack of air **2 :** to become checked in development — **suf·fo·cat·ing·ly** \-ˌkāt-iŋ-lē\ *adv* — **suf·fo·ca·tion** \ˌsəf-ə-ˈkā-shən\ *n* — **suf·fo·ca·tive** \ˈsəf-ə-ˌkāt-iv\ *adj*

Suf·folk \ˈsəf-ək, -ˌȯk\ *n* [*Suffolk,* England] **1 :** any of an English breed of black-faced hornless mutton-type sheep **2 :** any of an English breed of chestnut-colored draft horses

[1]**suf·fra·gan** \ˈsəf-ri-gən, ˈsəf-ri-jən\ *n* [ME, fr. MF, fr. ML *suffraganeus,* fr. *suffragium* support, prayer] **1 :** a diocesan bishop (as in the Roman Catholic Church and the Church of England) subordinate to a metropolitan **2 :** an Anglican or Episcopal bishop assisting a diocesan bishop and not having the right of succession

[2]**suffragan** *adj* **1 :** of or being a suffragan **2 :** subordinate to a metropolitan or archiepiscopal see

suf·frage \ˈsəf-rij, *substand* -ə-rij\ *n* [in sense 1, fr. ME, fr. MF, fr. ML *suffragium,* fr. L, vote, political support; in other senses, fr. L *suffragium*] **1 :** a short intercessory prayer usu. in a series **2 :** a vote given in deciding a controverted question or in the choice of a person for an office or trust **3 :** the right of voting **:** FRANCHISE; *also* **:** the exercise of such right

suf·frag·ette \ˌsəf-ri-ˈjet\ *n* **:** a woman who advocates suffrage for her sex

suf·frag·ist \ˈsəf-ri-jəst\ *n* **:** one who advocates extension of suffrage esp. to women

suf·fuse \sə-ˈfyüz\ *vt* **suf·fused; suf·fus·ing** [L *suffusus,* pp. of *suffundere,* lit., to pour beneath, fr. *sub-* + *fundere* to pour — more at FOUND] **:** to spread over or through in the manner of fluid or light **:** FLUSH, FILL ***syn*** see INFUSE — **suf·fu·sion** \-ˈfyü-zhən\ *n* — **suf·fu·sive** \-ˈfyü-siv, -ziv\ *adj*

Su·fi \ˈsü-(ˌ)fē\ *n* [Ar *ṣūfīy,* lit., (man) of wool] **:** a Muslim mystic — **Sufi** *adj* — **Su·fic** \-fik\ *adj* — **Su·fism** \-ˌfiz-əm\ *n*

[1]**sug·ar** \ˈshu̇g-ər\ *n* [ME *sucre,* fr. MF, fr. ML *zuccarum,* fr. OIt *zucchero,* fr. Ar *sukkar,* fr. Per *shakar,* fr. Skt *śarkarā;* akin to Skt *śarkara* pebble] **1 a :** a sweet crystallizable material that consists wholly or essentially of sucrose, is colorless or white when pure tending to brown when less refined, is obtained commercially from sugarcane or sugar beet and less extensively from sorghum, maples, and palms, and is nutritionally important as a source of dietary carbohydrate and as a sweetener and preservative of other foods **b :** any of various water-soluble compounds that vary widely in sweetness and comprise the oligosaccharides including sucrose **2 :** a unit (as a spoonful, cube, or lump) of sugar **3 :** a sugar bowl

[2]**sugar** *vb* **sug·ared; sug·ar·ing** \ˈshu̇g-(ə-)riŋ\ *vt* **1 :** to make palatable or attractive **:** SWEETEN **2 :** to sprinkle or mix with sugar ~ *vi* **1 :** to form or be converted into sugar **2 :** to become granular **:** GRANULATE

sugar apple *n* **:** the fruit of the sweetsop

sugar beet *n* **:** a white-rooted beet grown for the sugar in its roots

sugar beet

sug·ar·ber·ry \ˈshu̇g-ər-ˌber-ē\ *n* **:** a hackberry with sweet edible fruits

sugar bush *n* **:** a woods in which sugar maples predominate

sug·ar·cane \ˈshu̇g-ər-ˌkān\ *n* **:** a stout tall perennial grass (*Saccharum officinarum*) that has a large terminal panicle and is widely grown in warm regions as a source of sugar

sug·ar·coat \ˌshu̇g-ər-ˈkōt\ *vt* [back-formation fr. *sugarcoated*] **1 :** to coat with sugar **2 :** to make superficially attractive or palatable <tried to ~ an unpleasant truth>

sug·ar·house \ˈshu̇g-ər-ˌhau̇s\ *n* **:** a building where sugar is made or refined; *specif* **:** one where maple sap is boiled and maple syrup and maple sugar are made

sugaring off *n* **1 :** the act or process of converting maple syrup into sugar **2 :** a party held at the time of sugaring off

sug·ar·loaf \ˈshu̇g-ər-ˌlōf\ *n* **1 :** refined sugar molded into a cone **2 :** a hill or mountain shaped like a sugarloaf — **sugar–loaf** *adj*

sugar maple *n* **:** a maple with a sweet sap; *specif* **:** one (*Acer saccharum*) of eastern No. America with 3- to 5-lobed leaves, hard close-grained wood much used for cabinetwork, and sap that is the chief source of maple syrup and maple sugar

sugar off *vi* **:** to complete the process of boiling down the syrup in making maple sugar until it is thick enough to crystallize **:** approach or reach the state of granulation

sugar of lead : LEAD ACETATE

sugar orchard *n, chiefly NewEng* **:** SUGAR BUSH

sug·ar·plum \ˈshu̇g-ər-ˌpləm\ *n* **1 :** a small candy in a ball or disk **:** SWEETMEAT **2 :** SERVICEBERRY 2

sug·ary \ˈshu̇g-(ə-)rē\ *adj* **1 :** containing, resembling, or tasting of sugar **2 a :** exaggeratedly sweet **:** HONEYED <his ~ deprecating voice —D. H. Lawrence> **b :** cloyingly sweet **:** SENTIMENTAL

sug·gest \sə(g)-ˈjest\ *vt* [L *suggestus,* pp. of *suggerere* to put under, furnish, suggest, fr. *sub-* + *gerere* to carry — more at CAST] **1 a** *obs* **:** to seek to influence **:** SEDUCE **b :** to call forth **:** EVOKE **c :** to mention or imply as a possibility <~*ed* that he might bring his family> **d :** to propose as desirable or fitting <~ a stroll> **e :** to offer for consideration or as a hypothesis <~ a solution to a problem> **2 a :** to call to mind by thought or association <the explosion . . . ~*ed* sabotage —F. L. Paxson> **b :** to serve as a motive or inspiration for <a play ~*ed* by a historic incident> — **sug·gest·er** *n*

syn SUGGEST, IMPLY, HINT, INTIMATE, INSINUATE *shared meaning element* **:** to convey an idea indirectly. SUGGEST may stress putting into the mind by association of ideas, awakening of a desire, or initiating a train of thought <he can *suggest* in his work the immobility of a plain or the extreme action of a bolt of lightning, without showing either —Dale Nichols> IMPLY is close to *suggest* but may indicate a more definite or logical relation of the unexpressed idea to the expressed <the philosophy of Nature which is *implied* in Chinese art —Laurence Binyon> HINT implies the use of slight or remote suggestion with a minimum of overt statement <the soft *hinted* green in the branches —Shirley Jackson> <as thou with wary speech . . . hast *hinted* —John Keats> INTIMATE stresses delicacy of suggestion without connoting any lack of candor <quietly *intimated* that she could not entertain such a proposal> INSINUATE applies to the conveying of a usually unpleasant idea in a sly underhanded manner <the *insinuated* scoff of coward tongues —William Wordsworth> ***ant*** express

sug·gest·ible \sə(g)-ˈjes-tə-bəl\ *adj* **:** easily influenced by suggestion — **sug·gest·ibil·i·ty** \-ˌjes-tə-ˈbil-ət-ē\ *n*

sug·ges·tion \sə(g)-ˈjes(h)-chən\ *n* **1 a :** the act or process of suggesting **b :** something suggested **2 a :** the process by which one thought leads to another esp. through association of ideas **b :** a means or process of influencing attitudes and behavior hypnotically **3 :** a slight indication **:** TRACE <a ~ of a smile>

sug·ges·tive \sə(g)-ˈjes-tiv\ *adj* **1 a :** giving a suggestion **:** INDICATIVE <~ of a past era> **b :** full of suggestions **:** stimulating thought <provided a ~ . . . commentary on the era —Lloyd Morris> **c :** stirring mental associations **:** EVOCATIVE **2 :** suggesting or tending to suggest something improper or indecent **:** RISQUÉ — **sug·ges·tive·ly** *adv* — **sug·ges·tive·ness** *n*

sui·cid·al \ˌsü-ə-ˈsīd-ᵊl\ *adj* **1 :** relating to or of the nature of suicide **2 :** marked by an impulse to commit suicide **3 a :** dangerous esp. to life **b :** destructive to one's own interests — **sui·cid·al·ly** \-ᵊl-ē\ *adv*

¹sui·cide \ˈsü-ə-ˌsīd\ *n* [L *sui* (gen.) of oneself + E *-cide;* akin to OE & OHG *sīn* his, L *suus* one's own, Skt *sva* oneself, one's own] **1 a :** the act or an instance of taking one's own life voluntarily and intentionally esp. by a person of years of discretion and of sound mind **b :** ruin of one's own interests <political ~> **2 :** one that commits or attempts suicide

²suicide *vb* **sui·cid·ed; sui·cid·ing** *vi* **:** to commit suicide ~ *vt* **:** to put (oneself) to death **:** KILL

suicide squad *n* [fr. their use to spare the regular players from the danger of injuries] **:** a special squad used on kickoffs in football

sui ge·ner·is \ˌsü-ˌī-ˈjen-ə-rəs; ˌsü-ē-ˈjen-, -ˈgen-\ *adj* [L, of its own kind] **:** constituting a class alone **:** UNIQUE, PECULIAR

sui ju·ris \ˌsü-ˌī-ˈju̇r-əs, ˌsü-ē-ˈyu̇r-\ *adj* [L, of one's own right] **:** having full legal rights or capacity

su·int \ˈsü-ənt, ˈswint\ *n* [F, fr. MF, fr. *suer* to sweat, fr. L *sudare* — more at SWEAT] **:** dried perspiration of sheep deposited in the wool and rich in potassium salts

¹suit \ˈsüt\ *n* [ME *siute* act of following, retinue, sequence, set, fr. OF, act of following, retinue, fr. (assumed) VL *sequita,* fr. fem. of *sequitus,* pp. of *sequere* to follow — more at SUE] **1** *archaic* **:** SUITE 1 **2 a :** recourse or appeal to a feudal superior for justice or redress **b :** an action or process in a court for the recovery of a right or claim **3 :** an act or instance of suing or seeking by entreaty **:** APPEAL; *specif* **:** COURTSHIP **4 :** SUITE 2 — used chiefly of armor, sails, and counters in games **5 :** a set of garments: as **a :** an outer costume of two or more pieces **b :** a costume to be worn for a special purpose or under particular conditions <gym ~> **6 a :** all the playing cards in a pack bearing the same symbol **b :** all the dominoes bearing the same number **c :** all the cards or counters in a particular suit held by one player <a 5-card ~> **d :** the suit led <follow ~>

²suit *vi* **1 :** to be in accordance **:** AGREE <the position ~*s* with his abilities> **2 :** to be appropriate or satisfactory <these prices don't ~> **3 :** to put on specially required clothing (as a uniform or protective garb) — usu. used with *up* ~ *vt* **1 :** to outfit with clothes **:** DRESS **2 :** ACCOMMODATE, ADAPT <~ the action to the word> **3 a :** to be proper for **:** BEFIT **b :** to be becoming to <a lipstick that ~*ed* her coloring> **4 :** to meet the needs or desires of **:** PLEASE <~*s* me fine>

suit·able \ˈsüt-ə-bəl\ *adj* **1** *obs* **:** SIMILAR, MATCHING **2 a :** adapted to a use or purpose **b :** satisfying propriety **:** PROPER **c :** ABLE, QUALIFIED ***syn*** see FIT ***ant*** unsuitable, unbecoming — **suit·abil·i·ty** \ˌsüt-ə-ˈbil-ət-ē\ *n* — **suit·able·ness** *n* — **suit·ably** \-blē\ *adv*

suit·case \ˈsüt-ˌkās\ *n* **:** TRAVELING BAG; *esp* **:** a rigid flat rectangular one

suite \ˈswēt, *2d is also* ˈsüt\ *n* [F, alter. of OF *siute* — more at SUIT] **1 :** RETINUE; *esp* **:** the personal staff accompanying a ruler, diplomat, or dignitary on official business **2 :** a group of things forming a unit or constituting a collection **:** SET: as **a :** a group of rooms occupied as a unit **:** APARTMENT **b (1) :** a 17th and 18th century instrumental musical form consisting of a series of dances in the same or related keys **(2) :** a modern instrumental composition in several movements of different character **(3) :** a long orchestral concert arrangement in suite form of material drawn from a longer work (as a ballet) **c :** a collection of minerals or rocks having some characteristic in common (as type or origin) **d :** a set of matched furniture for a room

suit·ing \ˈsüt-iŋ\ *n* **:** fabric for suits

suit·or \ˈsüt-ər\ *n* [ME, follower, pleader, fr. AF, fr. L *secutor* follower, fr. *secutus,* pp. of *sequi* to follow — more at SUE] **1 :** one that petitions or entreats **:** PETITIONER **2 :** a party to a suit at law **3 :** one who courts a woman or seeks to marry her

su·ki·ya·ki \skē-ˈ(y)äk-ē; ˌsu̇k-ē-ˈ, ˌsük-\ *n* [Jap] **:** a dish consisting of thin slices of meat, soybean curd, and vegetables cooked in soy sauce, sake, and sugar

suk·kah \ˈsu̇k-ə\ *n* [Heb *sukkāh*] **:** a booth or shelter with a roof of branches and leaves that is used esp. for meals during the Sukkoth

Suk·koth \ˈsu̇k-əs, -ˌōt(h), -ˌōs\ *n* [Heb *sukkōth,* pl. of *sukkāh*] **:** a Jewish harvest festival beginning on the 15th of Tishri and commemorating the temporary shelters used by the Jews during their wandering in the wilderness

sul·cate \ˈsəl-ˌkāt\ *adj* [L *sulcatus,* pp. of *sulcare* to furrow, fr. *sulcus*] **:** scored with usu. longitudinal furrows <a ~ seedpod>

sul·cus \ˈsəl-kəs\ *n, pl* **sul·ci** \-ˌkī, -ˌkē, -ˌsī\ [L; akin to OE *sulh* plow, Gk *holkos* furrow, *helkein* to pull] **:** FURROW, GROOVE; *esp* **:** a shallow furrow on the surface of the brain separating adjacent convolutions

sulf- *or* **sulfo-** *or* **sulph-** *or* **sulpho-** *comb form* [F *sulf-, sulfo-,* fr. L *sulfur*] **:** sulfur **:** containing sulfur <*sulfo*chloride>

sul·fa \ˈsəl-fə\ *adj* [short for *sulfanilamide*] **1 :** related chemically to sulfanilamide **2 :** of, relating to, or containing sulfa drugs

sul·fa·di·a·zine \ˌsəl-fə-ˈdī-ə-ˌzēn\ *n* **:** a sulfa drug $C_{10}H_{10}N_4O_2S$ that is used esp. in the treatment of meningitis, pneumonia, and intestinal infections

sulfa drug *n* **:** any of various synthetic organic bacteria-inhibiting drugs that are sulfonamides closely related chemically to sulfanilamide

sul·fa·nil·amide \ˌsəl-fə-ˈnil-ə-ˌmīd, -məd\ *n* [*sulfanil*ic + *amide*] **:** a crystalline sulfonamide $C_6H_8N_2O_2S$ that is the amide of sulfanilic acid and the parent compound of most of the sulfa drugs

sul·fa·nil·ic acid \ˌsəl-fə-ˌnil-ik-\ *n* [ISV *sulf-* + *anil*ine + *-ic*] **:** a crystalline acid $C_6H_7NO_3S$ obtained from aniline and used esp. in making dyes

sul·fa·tase \ˈsəl-fə-ˌtās, -ˌtāz\ *n* [¹*sulfate*] **:** any of various esterases that accelerate the hydrolysis of sulfuric esters and that are found in animal tissues and in microorganisms

¹sul·fate \ˈsəl-ˌfāt\ *n* [F, fr. L *sulfur*] **1 :** a salt or ester of sulfuric acid **2 :** a bivalent group or anion SO_4 characteristic of sulfuric acid and the sulfates

²sulfate *vb* **sul·fat·ed; sul·fat·ing** *vt* **1 a :** to treat or combine with sulfuric acid or a sulfate **b :** to convert into a sulfate **2 :** to form a deposit of a whitish scale of sulfate of lead on (the plates of a storage battery) ~ *vi* **:** to become sulfated

sulf·hy·dryl \ˌsəlf-ˈ(h)ī-drəl\ *n* [ISV *sulf-* + *hydr-* + *-yl*] **:** a highly reactive group SH that is characteristic of mercaptans and is present in many biologically active compounds (as various proteins, coenzymes, and enzyme inhibitors)

sul·fide \ˈsəl-ˌfīd\ *n* **:** a compound of sulfur analogous to an oxide or ether with sulfur in place of oxygen **:** a salt or ester of hydrogen sulfide

sul·fi·nyl \ˈsəl-fə-ˌnil\ *n* [*sulfin*ic acid (RSO_2H) + *-yl*] **:** the bivalent group or radical SO

sul·fite \ˈsəl-ˌfīt\ *n* [F *sulfite,* alter. of *sulfate*] **:** a salt or ester of sulfurous acid — **sul·fit·ic** \ˌsəl-ˈfit-ik\ *adj*

sulfon- *comb form* [ISV *sulfonic*] **1 :** sulfonic <*sulfon*amide> **2 :** sulfonyl <*sulfon*methane>

sul·fon·amide \ˌsəl-ˈfän-ə-ˌmīd, -məd; -ˈfō-nə-ˌmīd\ *n* **:** an amide (as sulfanilamide) of a sulfonic acid; *also* **:** SULFA DRUG

¹sul·fo·nate \ˈsəl-fə-ˌnāt\ *n* **:** a salt or ester of a sulfonic acid

²sulfonate *vt* **-nat·ed; -nat·ing :** to introduce the sulfonic group into; *broadly* **:** to treat (an organic substance) with sulfuric acid — **sul·fo·na·tion** \ˌsəl-fə-ˈnā-shən\ *n*

sul·fone \ˈsəl-ˌfōn\ *n* **:** any of various compounds containing the sulfonyl group doubly united by its sulfur usu. with carbon

sul·fon·ic \ˌsəl-ˈfän-ik, -ˈfōn-\ *adj* **:** of, relating to, being, or derived from the univalent acid group SO_3H

sulfonic acid *n* **:** any of numerous acids that contain the sulfonic group and may be derived from sulfuric acid by replacement of a hydroxyl group by either an inorganic anion or a univalent organic radical

sul·fo·ni·um \ˌsəl-ˈfō-nē-əm\ *n* [NL, fr. *sulf-* + amm*onium*] **:** a univalent radical or cation SH_3 analogous to oxonium

sul·fon·meth·ane \ˌsəl-ˌfōn-ˈmeth-ˌān\ *n* **:** a crystalline hypnotic sulfone $C_5H_{10}O_4S_2$

sul·fo·nyl \ˈsəl-fə-ˌnil\ *n* **:** the bivalent group or radical SO_2

sul·fo·nyl·urea \ˌsəl-fə-ˌnil-ˈ(y)u̇r-ē-ə\ *n* [NL, fr. ISV *sulfonyl* + NL *urea*] **:** any of several hypoglycemic compounds related to the sulfonamides and used in the oral treatment of diabetes

sulf·ox·ide \ˌsəl-ˈfäk-ˌsīd\ *n* [ISV] **:** any of a class of organic compounds characterized by a sulfinyl group with its sulfur atom doubly united to carbon

¹sul·fur *or* **sul·phur** \ˈsəl-fər\ *n* [ME *sulphur* brimstone, fr. L *sulpur, sulphur, sulfur*] **1 :** a nonmetallic element that occurs either free or combined esp. in sulfides and sulfates, is a constituent of proteins, exists in several allotropic forms including yellow orthorhombic crystals, resembles oxygen chemically but is less active and more acidic, and is used esp. in the chemical and paper industries, in rubber vulcanization, and in medicine for treating skin diseases — see ELEMENT table **2 :** something (as scathing language) that suggests sulfur

2**sulfur** *vt* **sul·fured; sul·fur·ing** \-f(ə-)riŋ\ **:** to treat with sulfur or a sulfur compound

sulfur bacterium *n* **:** a bacterium (as many members of the suborder Rhodobacteriinae) capable of reducing sulfur compounds

sulfur dioxide *n* **:** a heavy pungent toxic gas SO_2 that is easily condensed to a colorless liquid, is used esp. in making sulfuric acid, in bleaching, as a preservative, and as a refrigerant, and is a major air pollutant esp. in industrial areas

sul·fu·re·ous \ˌsəl-ˈfyu̇r-ē-əs\ *adj* **:** SULFUROUS — **sul·fu·re·ous·ly** *adv* — **sul·fu·re·ous·ness** *n*

1**sul·fu·ret** \ˈsəl-f(y)ə-ˌret\ *n* [NL *sulfuretum,* fr. L *sulfur*] **:** SULFIDE

2**sulfuret** *vt* **-ret·ed** *or* **-ret·ted; -ret·ing** *or* **-ret·ting :** to combine or impregnate with sulfur

sul·fu·ric \ˌsəl-ˈfyu̇(ə)r-ik\ *adj* **:** of, relating to, or containing sulfur esp. with a higher valence than sulfurous compounds <~ esters>

sulfuric acid *n* **:** a heavy corrosive oily dibasic strong acid H_2SO_4 that is colorless when pure and is a vigorous oxidizing and dehydrating agent — called also *oil of vitriol*

sul·fu·rize \ˈsəl-f(y)ə-ˌrīz\ *vt* **-rized; -riz·ing :** SULFUR

sul·fu·rous \ˈsəl-f(y)ə-rəs, *also esp for 1b* ˌsəl-ˈfyu̇r-əs\ *adj* **1 a :** resembling or emanating from sulfur and esp. burning sulfur **b :** of, relating to, or containing sulfur esp. with a lower valence than sulfuric compounds <~ esters> **2** *or* **sul·phu·rous a :** of, relating to, or dealing with the fire of hell **:** INFERNAL **b :** SCATHING, VIRULENT <~ denunciations> **c :** PROFANE, BLASPHEMOUS <~ language> — **sul·fu·rous·ly** *adv* — **sul·fu·rous·ness** *n*

sulfurous acid *n* **:** a weak unstable dibasic acid H_2SO_3 known in solution and through its salts and used as a reducing and bleaching agent

sul·fu·ryl \ˈsəl-f(y)ə-ˌril\ *n* [ISV] **:** SULFONYL — used esp. in names of inorganic compounds

1**sulk** \ˈsəlk\ *vi* [back-formation fr. *sulky*] **:** to be moodily silent

2**sulk** *n* **1 :** the state of one sulking — often used in pl. <had a case of the ~*s*> **2 :** a sulky mood or spell <in a ~>

1**sulky** \ˈsəl-kē\ *adj* [prob. alter. of obs. *sulke* (sluggish)] **1 :** sulking or given to spells of sulking **2** [2*sulky*] **:** having wheels and usu. a seat for the driver <a ~ plow> ***syn*** see SULLEN — **sulk·i·ly** \-kə-lē\ *adv* — **sulk·i·ness** \-kē-nəs\ *n*

2**sulky** *n, pl* **sulkies** [prob. fr. 1*sulky;* fr. its having room for only one person] **:** a light 2-wheeled vehicle having a seat for the driver only and usu. no body

sul·lage \ˈsəl-ij\ *n* [prob. fr. MF *soiller, souiller* to soil — more at SOIL] **1 :** REFUSE, SEWAGE **2 :** mud deposited by water **:** SILT

sul·len \ˈsəl-ən\ *adj* [ME *solain* sullen, solitary, prob. fr. (assumed) MF, fr. L *solus* alone] **1 a :** gloomily or resentfully silent or repressed **b :** suggesting a sullen state **:** LOWERING **2 :** dull or somber in sound or color **3 :** DISMAL, GLOOMY **4 :** moving sluggishly — **sul·len·ly** *adv* — **sul·len·ness** \ˈsəl-ən-(n)əs\ *n*

syn SULLEN, GLUM, MOROSE, SURLY, SULKY *shared meaning element* **:** showing a forbidding or disagreeable mood

1**sul·ly** \ˈsəl-ē\ *vt* **sul·lied; sul·ly·ing** [prob. fr. MF *soiller* to soil] **:** to make soiled or tarnished **:** DEFILE

2**sully** *n, pl* **sullies** *archaic* **:** SOIL, STAIN

sulph- *or* **sulpho-** — see SULF-

sulphur butterfly *n* **:** any of numerous butterflies (family Pieridae) having the wings usu. yellow or orange with a black border — called also *sulphur*

sulphur yellow *n* **:** a variable color averaging a brilliant greenish yellow

Sul·pi·cian \ˌsəl-ˈpish-ən\ *n* [F *sulpicien,* fr. Compagnie de Saint-*Sulpice* Society of St. Sulpice] **:** a member of the Society of Priests of St. Sulpice founded by Jean Jacques Olier in Paris, France, in 1642 and dedicated to the teaching of seminarians

sul·tan \ˈsəlt-ᵊn\ *n* [MF, fr. Ar *sulṭān*] **:** a king or sovereign esp. of a Muslim state

sul·ta·na \(ˌ)səl-ˈtan-ə\ *n* [It, fem. of *sultano* sultan, fr. Ar *sulṭān*] **1 :** a female member of a sultan's family; *esp* **:** a sultan's wife **2 a :** a pale yellow seedless grape grown for raisins and wine **b :** the raisin of a sultana

sul·tan·ate \ˈsəlt-ᵊn-ˌāt\ *n* **1 :** the office, dignity, or power of a sultan **2 :** a state or country governed by a sultan

sul·tan·ess \ˈsəlt-ᵊn-əs\ *n, archaic* **:** SULTANA

sul·try \ˈsəl-trē\ *adj* **sul·tri·er; -est** [obs. E *sulter* to swelter, alter. of E *swelter*] **1 a :** very hot and humid **:** SWELTERING <a ~ day> **b :** burning hot **:** TORRID **2 a :** hot with passion or anger **b :** exciting or capable of exciting strong sexual desire <~ glances> — **sul·tri·ly** \-trə-lē\ *adv* — **sul·tri·ness** \-trē-nəs\ *n*

1**sum** \ˈsəm\ *n* [ME *summe,* fr. OF, fr. L *summa,* fr. fem. of *summus* highest; akin to L *super* over — more at OVER] **1 :** an indefinite or specified amount of money **2 :** the whole amount **:** AGGREGATE **3 :** the utmost degree **:** SUMMIT <reached the ~ of human happiness> **4 a :** a summary of the chief points or thoughts **:** SUMMATION <the ~ of this criticism follows —C. W. Hendel> **b :** GIST <the ~ and substance of an argument> **5 a** (1) **:** the result of adding numbers <~ of 5 and 7 is 12> (2) **:** the limit of the sum of the first *n* terms of an infinite series as *n* increases indefinitely **b :** numbers to be added; *broadly* **:** a problem in arithmetic **c** (1) **:** DISJUNCTION 2 (2) **:** UNION 2d — **sum·ma·bil·i·ty** \ˌsəm-ə-ˈbil-ət-ē\ *n* — **sum·ma·ble** \ˈsəm-ə-bəl\ *adj* — **in sum :** in short **:** BRIEFLY

2**sum** *vb* **summed; sum·ming** *vt* **1 :** to calculate the sum of **:** COUNT **2 :** SUMMARIZE ~ *vi* **:** to reach a sum **:** AMOUNT

su·mac *or* **su·mach** \ˈs(h)ü-ˌmak\ *n* [ME *sumac,* fr. MF, fr. Ar *summāq*] **1 :** any of a genus (*Rhus* of the family Anacardiaceae, the sumac family) of trees, shrubs, and woody vines that have feathery compound leaves turning to brilliant colors in the autumn, dioecious flowers, spikes or loose clusters of red or whitish berries, and in some cases foliage poisonous to the touch — compare POISON IVY, POISON OAK **2 :** a material used in tanning and dyeing that consists of dried powdered leaves and flowers of various sumacs

Su·me·ri·an \sü-ˈmer-ē-ən, -ˈmir-\ *n* **1 :** a native of Sumer **2 :** the agglutinative language of the Sumerians that has no known linguistic affinities — **Sumerian** *adj*

sum·ma \ˈsu̇m-ə, ˈsüm-, ˈsəm-\ *n, pl* **sum·mae** \ˈsu̇m-ˌī, ˈsüm-, -ˌā; ˈsəm-ˌē, -ˌī\ [ML, fr. L, sum] **:** a comprehensive treatise; *esp* **:** one by a scholastic philosopher

sum·ma cum lau·de \ˌsu̇m-ə-(ˌ)ku̇m-ˈlau̇d-ə, ˌsüm-, -ˈlau̇d-ē; ˌsəm-ə-ˌkəm-ˈlȯd-ē\ *adv or adj* [L, with highest praise] **:** with highest distinction <graduated *summa cum laude*> — compare CUM LAUDE, MAGNA CUM LAUDE

sum·mand \ˈsəm-ˌand, ˌsə-ˈmand\ *n* [ML *summandus,* gerund of *summare* to sum, fr. *summa*] **:** a term in a summation **:** ADDEND

sum·ma·ri·za·tion \ˌsəm-(ə-)rə-ˈzā-shən\ *n* **1 :** the act of summarizing **2 :** SUMMARY

sum·ma·rize \ˈsəm-ə-ˌrīz\ *vb* **-rized; -riz·ing** *vt* **:** to tell in or reduce to a summary ~ *vi* **:** to make a summary — **sum·ma·riz·er** *n*

1**sum·ma·ry** \ˈsəm-ə-rē *also* ˈsəm-rē *or* -ˌer-ē\ *adj* [ME, fr. ML *summarius,* fr. L *summa* sum] **1 :** COMPREHENSIVE; *esp* **:** covering the main points succinctly **2 a :** done without delay or formality **:** quickly executed <a ~ dismissal> **b :** of, relating to, or using a summary proceeding <a ~ trial> ***syn*** see CONCISE ***ant*** circumstantial — **sum·mari·ly** \(ˌ)sə-ˈmer-ə-lē\ *adv*

2**sum·ma·ry** \ˈsəm-ə-rē *also* ˈsəm-rē\ *n, pl* **-ries :** an abstract, abridgment, or compendium esp. of a preceding discourse

sum·mate \ˈsəm-ˌāt\ *vt* **sum·mat·ed; sum·mat·ing** [back-formation fr. *summation*] **:** to add together **:** sum up

sum·ma·tion \(ˌ)sə-ˈmā-shən\ *n* **1 :** the act or process of forming a sum **:** ADDITION **2 :** SUM, TOTAL **3 :** cumulative action or effect; *esp* **:** the process by which a sequence of stimuli that are individually inadequate to produce a response are cumulatively able to induce a nerve impulse **4 :** a final part of an argument reviewing points made and expressing conclusions — **sum·ma·tion·al** \-shnəl, -shən-ᵊl\ *adj*

sum·ma·tive \ˈsəm-ət-iv, -ˌāt-\ *adj* **:** ADDITIVE, CUMULATIVE

1**sum·mer** \ˈsəm-ər\ *n* [ME *sumer,* fr. OE *sumor;* akin to OHG & ON *sumer* summer, Skt *samā* year, season] **1 :** the season between spring and autumn comprising in the northern hemisphere usu. the months of June, July, and August or as reckoned astronomically extending from the June solstice to the September equinox **2 :** the warmer half of the year **3 :** YEAR <a girl of seventeen ~*s*> **4 :** a period of maturing powers

2**summer** *adj* **:** sown in the spring and harvested in the same year as sown <~ wheat> — compare WINTER

3**summer** *vb* **sum·mered; sum·mer·ing** \ˈsəm-(ə-)riŋ\ *vi* **:** to pass the summer ~ *vt* **:** to keep or carry through the summer; *esp* **:** to provide (as cattle or sheep) with pasture during the summer

4**summer** *n* [ME, packhorse, beam, fr. MF *somier,* fr. (assumed) VL *sagmarius,* fr. LL *sagma* packsaddle, fr. Gk] **:** a large horizontal beam or stone used esp. in building: as **a :** the lintel of a door or window **b :** a stone forming the cap of a pier (as to support a lintel or arch)

summer cypress *n* **:** a densely branched Eurasian herb (*Kochia scoparia*) of the goosefoot family grown for its foliage which turns red in autumn

sum·mer·house \ˈsəm-ər-ˌhau̇s\ *n* **:** a covered structure in a garden or park designed to provide a shady resting place in summer

summer kitchen *n* **:** a small building or shed that is adjacent to a house and is used as a kitchen in warm weather

sum·mer·sault *var of* SOMERSAULT

summer savory *n* **:** a European herb (*Satureia hortensis*) used in cookery

summer school *n* **:** a school or school session conducted in summer enabling students to accelerate progress toward a degree, to make up credits lost through absence or failure, or to round out professional education

summer squash *n* **:** any of various garden squashes derived from a variety (*Cucurbita pepo* var. *melopepo*) and used as a vegetable while immature and before hardening of the seeds and rind

summer stock *n* **:** theatrical productions of stock companies presented during the summer

summer theater *n* **:** a theater that presents several different plays or musicals during the summer

sum·mer·time \ˈsəm-ər-ˌtīm\ *n* **:** the summer season or a period like summer

summer time *n, chiefly Brit* **:** DAYLIGHT SAVING TIME

sum·mer·wood \ˈsəm-ər-ˌwu̇d\ *n* **:** the harder less porous portion of an annual ring of wood that develops late in the growing season — compare SPRINGWOOD

sum·mery \ˈsəm-(ə-)rē\ *adj* **:** of, resembling, or fit for summer

sum·mit \ˈsəm-ət\ *n* [ME *somete,* fr. MF, fr. OF, dim. of *sum* top, fr. L *summum,* neut. of *summus* highest — more at SUM] **1 :** TOP, APEX; *esp* **:** the highest point **:** PEAK **2 :** the topmost level attainable <the ~ of human fame> **3 a :** the highest level of officials; *esp* **:** the diplomatic level of heads of government **b :** a conference of highest-level officials (as heads of government)

syn SUMMIT, PEAK, PINNACLE, CLIMAX, APEX, ACME, CULMINATION *shared meaning element* **:** the highest point attained or attainable

sum·mon \ˈsəm-ən\ *vt* **sum·moned; sum·mon·ing** \-(ə-)niŋ\ [ME *somonen,* fr. OF *somondre,* fr. (assumed) VL *summonere,* alter. of L *summonēre* to remind secretly, fr. *sub-* secretly + *monēre* to warn — more at SUB-, MIND] **1 :** to issue a call to convene **:** CONVOKE **2 :** to command by service of a summons to appear in court **3 :** to call upon for specified action <~ one to be in readiness> **4 :** to bid to come **:** send for <~ a physician> **5 :** to call forth **:** EVOKE — **sum·mon·er** \-(ə-)nər\ *n*

syn SUMMON, CALL, CITE, CONVOKE, CONVENE, MUSTER *shared meaning element* **:** to demand the presence of

1**sum·mons** \ˈsəm-ənz\ *n, pl* **sum·mons·es** [ME *somouns,* fr. OF *somonse,* fr. pp. of *somondre*] **1 :** the act of summoning; *esp* **:** a call by authority to appear at a place named or to attend to a duty **2 :** a warning or citation to appear in court: as **a :** a written notification to be served on a person warning him to appear in court at a day specified to answer to the plaintiff **b :** a subpoena to appear as a witness **3 :** something (as a call) that summons

²summons *vt* **:** SUMMON 2

sum·mum bo·num \ˌsu̇m-əm-ˈbō-nəm, ˌsüm-, ˌsəm-\ *n* [L] **:** the supreme good from which all others are derived

summum ge·nus \-ˈgen-əs, -ˈgā-nəs; -ˈjē-nəs\ *n, pl* **sum·ma ge·nera** \ˌsu̇m-ə-ˈgen-ə-rə, ˌsüm-, -ˈgän-; ˌsəm-ə-ˈjen-ə-rə\ [NL, lit., highest genus] **:** a logical genus that cannot be classed as a species of a higher genus

su·mo \ˈsü-(ˌ)mō\ *n* [Jap *sumō*] **:** a Japanese form of wrestling in which a contestant loses if he is forced out of the ring or if any part of his body except the soles of his feet touches the ground

sump \ˈsəmp\ *n* [ME *sompe* swamp — more at SWAMP] **1 :** a pit or reservoir serving as a drain or receptacle for liquids: as **a :** CESSPOOL **b :** a pit at the lowest point in a circulating or drainage system (as the oil-circulating system of an internal-combustion engine) **c** *chiefly Brit* **:** OIL PAN **2** *Brit* **:** CRANKCASE **3** [G *sumpf,* lit., marsh, fr. MHG — more at SWAMP] **a :** the lowest part of a mine shaft into which water drains **b :** an excavation ahead of regular work in driving a mine tunnel or sinking a mine shaft

sump pump *n* **:** a pump to remove accumulations of liquid from a sump pit

sump·ter \ˈsəm(p)-tər\ *n* [short for *sumpter horse,* fr. ME *sumpter* driver of a packhorse, fr. MF *sometier,* fr. (assumed) VL *sagmatarius,* fr. LL *sagmat-, sagma* packsaddle, fr. Gk] **:** a pack animal

sump·tu·ary \ˈsəm(p)-chə-ˌwer-ē\ *adj* [L *sumptuarius,* fr. *sumptus* expense, fr. *sumptus,* pp. of *sumere* to take, spend — more at CONSUME] **1 :** designed to regulate personal expenditures and esp. to prevent extravagance and luxury <conservative ~ tastes —John Cheever> **2 :** designed to regulate habits on moral or religious grounds <~ laws> <~ tax>

sump·tu·ous \ˈsəm(p)-ch(ə-w)əs, ˈsəm(p)sh-wəs\ *adj* [MF *sumptueux,* fr. L *sumptuosus,* fr. *sumptus*] **:** excessively costly, rich, luxurious, or magnificent <~ banquets> ***syn*** see LUXURIOUS — **sump·tu·ous·ly** *adv* — **sump·tu·ous·ness** *n*

sum total *n* **1 :** a total arrived at through the counting of sums **2 :** total result **:** TOTALITY

sum–up \ˈsəm-ˌəp\ *n* **:** SUMMARY

sum up \ˌsəm-ˈəp\ *vt* **1 :** to be the sum of **:** bring to a total <10 victories *summed up* his record> **2 :** to state succinctly **:** SUMMARIZE <*sum up* the evidence presented> **~** *vi* **1 :** to present a summary or recapitulation **2 :** to be expressed or summarized <it *sums up* in exactly three words —W. A. Johnston>

¹sun \ˈsən\ *n* [ME *sunne,* fr. OE; akin to OHG *sunna* sun, L *sol* — more at SOLAR] **1 a :** the luminous celestial body around which the earth and other planets revolve, from which they receive heat and light, and which has a mean distance from earth of 93,000,000 miles, a linear diameter of 864,000 miles, a mass 332,000 times greater than earth, and a mean density about one fourth that of earth **b :** a celestial body like the sun **2 :** the heat or light radiated from the sun **3 :** one resembling the sun usu. in brilliance **4 :** the rising or setting of the sun <from ~ to ~> **5 :** GLORY, SPLENDOR — **in the sun :** in the public eye — **under the sun :** in the world **:** on earth

²sun *vb* **sunned; sun·ning** *vt* **:** to expose to or as if to the rays of the sun **~** *vi* **:** to sun oneself

Sun *abbr* Sunday

sun·baked \ˈsən-ˌbākt\ *adj* **1 :** baked by exposure to sunshine **2 :** heated, parched, or compacted esp. by excessive sunlight

sun·bath \ˈsən-ˌbath, -ˌbáth\ *n* **:** an exposure to sunlight or a sunlamp

sun·bathe \-ˌbāth\ *vi* [back-formation fr. *sunbather*] **:** to take a sunbath — **sun·bath·er** \-ˌbā-thər\ *n*

sun·beam \-ˌbēm\ *n* **:** a ray of sunlight

sun·bird \-ˌbərd\ *n* **:** any of numerous small brilliantly colored singing birds (family Nectariniidae) of the tropical Old World somewhat resembling hummingbirds

sun·bon·net \-ˌbän-ət\ *n* **:** a woman's bonnet with a wide brim framing the face and usu. having a ruffle at the back to protect the neck from the sun

sun·bow \-ˌbō\ *n* **:** an arch resembling a rainbow made by the sun shining through vapor or mist

¹sun·burn \-ˌbərn\ *vb* **-burned** \-ˌbərnd\ *or* **-burnt** \-ˌbərnt\; **-burn·ing** [back-formation fr. *sunburned,* fr. *sun* + *burned*] *vt* **:** to burn or discolor by the sun **~** *vi* **:** to become sunburned

²sunburn *n* **:** inflammation of the skin caused by overexposure to sunlight

sun·burst \ˈsən-ˌbərst\ *n* **1 :** a flash of sunlight esp. through a break in clouds **2 :** a jeweled brooch representing a sun surrounded by rays

sun·dae \ˈsən-dē\ *n* [prob. alter. of *Sunday*] **:** ice cream served with topping (as crushed fruit, syrups, nuts, or whipped cream)

sun dance *n* **:** a solo or group solstice rite of American Indians

¹Sun·day \ˈsən-dē\ *n* [ME, fr. OE *sunnandæg;* akin to OHG *sunnūntag* Sunday; both fr. a prehistoric WGmc-NGmc compound whose components are represented by OE *sunne* sun and by OE *dæg* day] **:** the first day of the week **:** the Christian analogue of the Jewish Sabbath — **Sun·days** \-dēz\ *adv*

²Sunday *adj* **1 :** of, relating to, or associated with Sunday **2** [fr. the practice of wearing one's best clothes on Sunday to attend church] **:** BEST <~ suit> **3 :** AMATEUR <~ painters>

³Sunday *vi* **:** to spend Sunday <was ~*ing* in the country>

Sun·day–go–to–meet·ing \ˈsən-de-ˌgōt-ə-ˈmēt-iŋ\ *adj* **:** appropriate for Sunday churchgoing

Sunday punch *n* **1 :** a powerful or devastating blow; *esp* **:** a knockout punch **2 :** something capable of delivering a powerful or devastating blow to the opposition <saving his *Sunday punch* for the end of the campaign —*Newsweek*>

Sunday school *n* **:** a school held on Sunday for religious education; *also* **:** the teachers and pupils of such a school

sun deck *n* **1 :** the usu. upper deck of a ship that is exposed to the most sun **2 :** a roof or terrace used for sunning

sun·der \ˈsən-dər\ *vt* **sun·dered; sun·der·ing** \-d(ə-)riŋ\ [ME *sunderen,* fr. OE *gesundrian, syndrian;* akin to OHG *suntarōn* to sunder, L *sine* without] **:** to break apart or in two **:** sever finally and completely or with violence ***syn*** see SEPARATE ***ant*** link

sun·dew \ˈsən-(ˌ)d(y)ü\ *n* **:** any of a genus (*Drosera* of the family Droseraceae, the sundew family) of bog-inhabiting insectivorous herbs having viscid glands on the leaves

sun·di·al \-ˌdī(-ə)l\ *n* **:** an instrument to show the time of day by the shadow of a gnomon on a usu. horizontal plate or on a cylindrical surface

sundial

sun disk *n* **:** an ancient Near Eastern symbol consisting of a disk with conventionalized wings emblematic of the sun-god (as Ra in Egypt)

sun disk

sun dog *n* **1 :** PARHELION **2 :** a small nearly round halo on the parhelic circle most frequently just outside the halo of 22 degrees

sun·down \ˈsən-ˌdau̇n\ *n* **:** SUNSET 2

sun·down·er \-ˌdau̇-nər\ *n* **1** [fr. his habit of arriving at a place where he hopes to obtain food and lodging too late to do any work] *Austral* **:** HOBO, TRAMP **2** *chiefly Brit* **:** a drink taken at sundown

sun·dries \ˈsən-drēz\ *n pl* [¹*sundry*] **:** miscellaneous small articles, details, or items

sun·drops \ˈsən-ˌdräps\ *n pl but sing or pl in constr* **:** any of several day-flowering herbs (genus *Oenothera*) — compare EVENING PRIMROSE

¹sun·dry \ˈsən-drē\ *adj* [ME, different for each, fr. OE *syndrig;* akin to OHG *suntarig* sundry, OE *syndrian* to sunder, L *sine* without] **:** MISCELLANEOUS, VARIOUS <~ articles>

²sundry *pron, pl in constr* **:** an indeterminate number <recommended for reading by all and ~ —Edward Huberman>

sun·fast \ˈsən-ˌfast\ *adj* **:** resistant to fading by sunlight <~ dyes>

sun·fish \-ˌfish\ *n* **1 :** a large marine plectognath fish (*Mola mola*) having high dorsal and anal fins and a body nearly oval in outline due to a sharply truncated posterior extremity and attaining a length of 10 feet and a weight in excess of 2 tons **2 :** any of numerous American percoid freshwater fishes (family Centrarchidae) usu. with a deep compressed body and metallic luster

sun·flow·er \-ˌflau̇(-ə)r\ *n* **:** any of a genus (*Helianthus*) of composite plants with large yellow-rayed flower heads bearing seeds that serve as stock food and yield an edible oil

sung \ˈsəŋ\ *past of* SING

Sung \ˈsu̇ŋ\ *n* [Chin (Pek) *Sung⁴*] **:** a Chinese dynasty dated A.D. 960–1280 and marked by cultural refinement and achievements in philosophy, literature, and art

sun·glass \ˈsən-ˌglas\ *n* **1 :** a convex lens for converging the sun's rays **2** *pl* **:** glasses to protect the eyes from the sun

sung mass *n* **:** HIGH MASS

sun–god \ˈsən-ˌgäd\ *n* **:** a god that represents or personifies the sun in various religions — **sun–god·dess** \-ˌgäd-əs\ *n*

sun–grebe \-ˌgrēb\ *n* **:** any of several tropical American and African birds (family Heliornithidae) related to the cranes and herons — called also *sun bittern*

sunk *past of* SINK

sunk·en \ˈsəŋ-kən\ *adj* [fr. obs. pp. of *sink*] **1 :** SUBMERGED; *esp* **:** lying at the bottom of a body of water **2 a :** HOLLOW, RECESSED <~ cheeks> **b :** lying in a depression <a ~ garden> **c :** settled below the normal level **d :** constructed below the normal floor level <a ~ living room>

sunk fence *n* **:** a ditch with a retaining wall used to divide lands without defacing a landscape — called also *ha-ha*

sun·lamp \ˈsən-ˌlamp\ *n* **:** an electric lamp designed to emit radiation of wavelengths from ultraviolet to infrared and used esp. for therapeutic purposes

sun·less \-ləs\ *adj* **:** lacking sunshine **:** DARK, CHEERLESS

sun·light \-ˌlīt\ *n* **:** the light of the sun **:** SUNSHINE

sun·lit \-ˌlit\ *adj* **:** lighted by or as if by the sun

sunn \ˈsən\ *n* [Hindi *san,* fr. Skt *śaṇa*] **:** an East Indian leguminous plant (*Crotalaria juncea*) with slender branches, simple leaves, and yellow flowers; *also* **:** its valuable fiber resembling hemp and lighter and stronger than jute

sun·na \ˈsu̇n-ə, ˈsən-\ *n, often cap* [Ar *sunnah*] **:** the body of Islamic custom and practice based on Muhammad's words and deeds

sunn hemp *n* **:** SUNN

Sun·ni \ˈsu̇n-(ˌ)(n)ē, ˈsu̇n-yē\ *n* [Ar *sunnīy,* fr. *sunnah*] **1 :** the Muslims of the branch of Islam that adheres to the orthodox tradition and acknowledges the first four caliphs as rightful successors of Muhammad — compare SHIA **2 :** SUNNITE — **Sunni** *adj*

Sun·nism \ˈsu̇n-(n)iz-əm\ *n* **:** the religious system or distinctive tenets of the Sunni

Sun·nite \-ˌ(n)īt\ *n* **:** a Sunni Muslim

sun·ny \ˈsən-ē\ *adj* **sun·ni·er; -est** **1 :** marked by brilliant sunlight **:** full of sunshine **2 :** MERRY, OPTIMISTIC <a ~ disposition> **3 :** exposed to, brightened, or warmed by the sun <a ~ room> — **sun·ni·ly** \ˈsən-ᵊl-ē\ *adv* — **sun·ni·ness** \ˈsən-ē-nəs\ *n*

sun·ny–side up \ˌsən-ē-ˌsīd-ˈəp\ *adj, of an egg* **:** fried on one side only

---

ə abut ᵊ kitten ər further a back ā bake ä cot, cart
au̇ out ch chin e less ē easy g gift i trip ī life
j joke ŋ sing ō flow ȯ flaw ȯi coin th thin t͟h this
ü loot u̇ foot y yet yü few yu̇ furious zh vision

sun parlor *n* **:** a glass enclosed porch or living room with a sunny exposure — called also *sun porch, sun-room*

sun·rise \ˈsən-ˌrīz\ *n* **1 :** the apparent rising of the sun above the horizon; *also* **:** the accompanying atmospheric effects **2 :** the time when the upper limb of the sun appears above the sensible horizon as a result of the diurnal rotation of the earth

sun·roof \-ˌrüf, -ˌru̇f\ *n* **:** an automobile roof having a panel that is openable

sun·scald \-ˌskȯld\ *n* **:** an injury of woody plants (as fruit or forest trees) characterized by localized death of the tissues and sometimes by cankers and caused when it occurs in the summer by the combined action of both the heat and light of the sun and in the winter by the combined action of sun and low temperature to produce freezing of bark and underlying tissues

sun·screen \-ˌskrēn\ *n* **:** a screen to protect against sun; *esp* **:** a substance used in suntan preparations to protect the skin from excessive ultraviolet radiation — **sunscreening** *adj*

sun·seek·er \-ˌsē-kər\ *n* **:** a person who travels to an area of warmth and sun esp. in winter

sun·set \-ˌset\ *n* **1 :** the apparent descent of the sun below the horizon; *also* **:** the accompanying atmospheric effects **2 :** the time when the upper limb of the sun disappears below the sensible horizon as a result of the diurnal rotation of the earth **3 :** a period of decline; *esp* **:** old age

sun·shade \ˈsən-ˌshād\ *n* **:** something used as a protection from the sun's rays: as **a :** PARASOL **b :** AWNING

sun·shine \-ˌshīn\ *n* **1 a :** the sun's light or direct rays **b :** the warmth and light given by the sun's rays **c :** a spot or surface on which the sun's light shines **2 :** something (as a person, condition, or influence) that radiates warmth, cheer, or happiness — **sun·shiny** \-ˌshī-nē\ *adj*

sun·spot \-ˌspät\ *n* **:** one of the dark spots that appear from time to time on the sun's surface consisting commonly of a blue-black umbra with a surrounding penumbra of lighter shade and usu. visible only with the telescope

sun·stroke \-ˌstrōk\ *n* **:** heatstroke caused by direct exposure to the sun

sun·struck \-ˌstrək\ *adj* **:** affected or touched by the sun

sun·suit \-ˌsüt\ *n* **:** an outfit (as of halter and shorts) worn usu. for sunbathing and play

sun·tan \-ˌtan\ *n* **1 :** a browning of the skin from exposure to the rays of the sun **2** *pl* **:** a tan-colored summer uniform

sun·up \-ˌəp\ *n* **:** SUNRISE

1sun·ward \ˈsən-wərd\ *or* **sun·wards** \-wərdz\ *adv* **:** toward the sun

2sunward *adj* **:** facing the sun

sun·wise \ˈsən-ˌwīz\ *adv* **:** CLOCKWISE

1sup \ˈsəp\ *vb* **supped; sup·ping** [ME *suppen,* fr. OE *sūpan, suppan;* akin to OHG *sūfan* to drink, sip, OE *sūcan* to suck — more at SUCK] *vt* **:** to take or drink in swallows or gulps ~ *vi, chiefly dial* **:** to take food and esp. liquid food into the mouth a little at a time either by drinking or with a spoon

2sup *n* **:** a mouthful esp. of liquor or broth **:** SIP; *also* **:** a small quantity of liquid <a ~ of tea>

3sup *vi* **supped; sup·ping** [ME *soupen, suppen,* fr. OF *souper,* fr. *soupe* sop, soup — more at SOUP] **1 :** to eat the evening meal **2 :** to make one's supper — used with *on* or *off* <~ on roast beef>

4sup *abbr* **1** superior **2** supplement; supplementary **3** supply **4** supra

1su·per \ˈsü-pər\ *n* **1** [by shortening] **a :** SUPERNUMERARY; *esp* **:** a supernumerary actor **b :** SUPERINTENDENT, SUPERVISOR; *esp* **:** the superintendent of an apartment building **2** [short for obs. *superhive*] **:** a removable upper story of a beehive **3** [3*super*] **:** a superfine grade or extra large size **4** [origin unknown] **:** a thin loosely woven open-meshed starched cotton fabric used esp. for reinforcing books

2super *vt* **su·pered; su·per·ing** \-p(ə-)riŋ\ **:** to reinforce (as a book backbone) with super

3super *adj* [short for *superfine*] **1 a :** SUPERFINE **b :** of great value, excellence, or superiority <is a ~ cook> **2 :** very large or powerful <a ~ atomic bomb> **3 :** exhibiting the characteristics of its type to an extreme or excessive degree <~ secrecy> **4 :** including in its structure or authority complexes of its own nature

4super *adv* [*super-*] **1 :** VERY, EXTREMELY <a ~ special car> **2 :** to an excessive degree

super- *prefix* [L, over, above, in addition, fr. *super* over, above, on top of — more at OVER] **1 a (1) :** over and above **:** higher in quantity, quality, or degree than **:** more than <*super*human> **(2) :** in addition **:** extra <*super*tax> **b (1) :** exceeding or so as to exceed a norm <*super*heat> **(2) :** in excessive degree or intensity <*super*subtle> **c :** surpassing all or most others of its kind <*super*highway> **2 a :** situated or placed above, on, or at the top of <*super*lunary>; *specif* **:** situated on the dorsal side of **b :** next above or higher <*super*tonic> **3 :** having the (specified) ingredient present in a large or unusually large proportion <*super*phosphate> **4 :** constituting a more inclusive category than that specified <*super*family> **5 :** superior in status, title, or position <*super*power>

su·per·a·ble \ˈsü-p(ə-)rə-bəl\ *adj* [L *superabilis,* fr. *superare* to surmount — more at INSUPERABLE] **:** capable of being overcome or conquered — **su·per·a·ble·ness** *n* — **su·per·a·bly** \-blē\ *adv*

su·per·abound \ˌsü-pə-rə-ˈbau̇nd\ *vi* [ME *superabounden,* fr. LL *superabundare,* fr. L *super-* + *abundare* to abound] **:** to abound or prevail in greater measure or to excess

su·per·abun·dant \-ˈbən-dənt\ *adj* [ME, fr. LL *superabundant-, superabundans,* fr. prp. of *superabundare*] **:** more than ample **:** EXCESSIVE — **su·per·abun·dance** \-dən(t)s\ *n* — **su·per·abun·dant·ly** *adv*

su·per·add \ˌsü-pə-ˈrad\ *vt* [ME *superadden,* fr. L *superaddere,* fr. *super-* + *addere* to add] **:** to add over and above something or in extra or superfluous amount — **su·per·ad·di·tion** \-pə-rə-ˈdish-ən\ *n*

su·per·agen·cy \ˈsü-pə-ˌrā-jən-sē\ *n* **:** a large complex governmental agency esp. when set up to supervise and coordinate a group of other agencies

su·per·al·tern \ˌsü-pə-ˈrȯl-tərn\ *n* [*super-* + *-altern* (as in *subaltern*)] **:** a universal proposition in traditional logic that is a ground for the immediate inference of a corresponding subalternate

su·per·an·nu·ate \ˌsü-pə-ˈran-yə-ˌwāt\ *vb* **-at·ed; -at·ing** [back-formation fr. *superannuated*] *vt* **1 :** to make, declare, or prove obsolete or out-of-date **2 :** to retire and pension because of age or infirmity ~ *vi* **1 :** to become retired **2 :** to become antiquated — **su·per·an·nu·a·tion** \-ˌran-yə-ˈwā-shən\ *n*

su·per·an·nu·at·ed *adj* [ML *superannuatus,* pp. of *superannuari* to be too old, fr. L *super-* + *annus* year — more at ANNUAL] **:** incapacitated or disqualified for active duty by advanced age

su·perb \su̇-ˈpərb\ *adj* [L *superbus* excellent, proud, fr. *super* above + *-bus* (akin to OE *bēon* to be) — more at OVER, BE] **:** marked to the highest degree by grandeur, excellence, brilliance, or competence ***syn*** see SPLENDID — **su·perb·ly** *adv* — **su·perb·ness** *n*

su·per·block \ˈsü-pər-ˌbläk\ *n* **:** a very large commercial or residential block barred to through traffic, crossed by pedestrian walks and sometimes access roads, and often spotted with grassed malls

1su·per·cal·en·der \-ˌkal-ən-dər\ *n* **:** a calender stack of highly polished rolls used to give an extra finish to paper

2supercalender *vt* **:** to process (paper) in a supercalender

su·per·car·go \ˌsü-pər-ˈkär-(ˌ)gō, ˈsü-pər-ˌ\ *n* [Sp *sobrecargo,* fr. *sobre-* over (fr. L *super-*) + *cargo*] **:** an officer in a merchant ship in charge of the commercial concerns of the voyage

supercede *var of* SUPERSEDE

1su·per·charge \ˈsü-pər-ˌchärj\ *vt* **1 :** to charge greatly or excessively (as with vigor or tension) <~*ed* rhetoric> **2 :** to supply a charge to the intake of (as an engine) at a pressure higher than that of the surrounding atmosphere **3 :** PRESSURIZE 1

2supercharge *n* **:** a great or excessive charge

su·per·charg·er \-ˌchär-jər\ *n* **:** a device (as a blower or compressor) for pressurizing the cabin of an airplane or for increasing the volume air charge of an internal-combustion engine over that which would normally be drawn in through the pumping action of the pistons

su·per·cil·i·ary \ˌsü-pər-ˈsil-ē-ˌer-ē\ *adj* [NL *superciliaris,* fr. L *supercilium*] **:** of, relating to, or adjoining the eyebrow **:** SUPRAORBITAL — **superciliary** *n*

su·per·cil·ious \-ˈsil-ē-əs, -ˈsil-yəs\ *adj* [L *superciliosus,* fr. *supercilium* eyebrow, haughtiness, fr. *super-* + *-cilium* (akin to *celare* to hide) — more at HELL] **:** coolly and patronizingly haughty ***syn*** see PROUD — **su·per·cil·ious·ly** *adv* — **su·per·cil·ious·ness** *n*

su·per·city \ˈsü-pər-ˌsit-ē\ *n* **:** MEGALOPOLIS

su·per·class \-ˌklas\ *n* **:** a category in taxonomy ranking between a phylum or division and a class

su·per·con·duct \ˌsü-pər-kən-ˈdəkt\ *vt* **:** to exhibit superconductivity

su·per·con·duc·tive \-ˈdək-tiv\ *adj* **:** exhibiting superconductivity

su·per·con·duc·tiv·i·ty \-ˌkän-ˌdək-ˈtiv-ət-ē, -kən-\ *n* **:** a complete disappearance of electrical resistance in various metals at temperatures near absolute zero — **su·per·con·duc·tor** \-kən-ˈdək-tər\ *n*

su·per·cool \ˌsü-pər-ˈkül\ *vt* **:** to cool below the freezing point without solidification or crystallization ~ *vi* **:** to become supercooled

su·per·dom·i·nant \-ˈdäm-(ə-)nənt\ *n* **:** SUBMEDIANT

su·per·ego \ˌsü-pə-ˈrē-(ˌ)gō *also* -ˈreg-(ˌ)ō\ *n* [*super-* + *ego*] **:** the one of the three divisions of the psyche in psychoanalytic theory that is only partly conscious, represents internalization of parental conscience and the rules of society, and functions to reward and punish through a system of moral attitudes, conscience, and a sense of guilt — compare EGO, ID

su·per·el·e·vate \ˌsü-pə-ˈrel-ə-ˌvāt\ *vt* **:** BANK 1c

su·per·el·e·va·tion \-ˌrel-ə-ˈvā-shən\ *n* **1 :** the vertical distance between the heights of inner and outer edges of highway pavement or railroad rails **2 :** additional elevation

su·per·em·i·nent \ˌsü-pə-ˈrem-ə-nənt\ *adj* [LL *supereminent-, supereminens,* fr. L, prp. of *supereminēre* to stand out above, fr. *super-* + *eminēre* to stand out — more at EMINENT] **:** extremely high, distinguished, or conspicuous — **su·per·em·i·nence** \-nən(t)s\ *n* — **su·per·em·i·nent·ly** *adv*

su·per·em·pir·i·cal \ˌsü-pə-rim-ˈpir-i-kəl, -(ˌ)rem-\ *adj* **:** experienced or experiencing by more than empirical means **:** TRANSCENDENT, TRANSCENDENTAL

su·per·en·ci·pher \-rin-ˈsī-fər\ *vt* **:** to encipher what is already a cryptogram — **su·per·en·ci·pher·ment** \-mənt\ *n*

su·per·er·o·ga·tion \ˌsü-pə-ˌrer-ə-ˈgā-shən\ *n* [ML *supererogation-, supererogatio,* fr. *supererogatus,* pp. of *supererogare* to perform beyond the call of duty, fr. LL, to expend in addition, fr. L *super-* + *erogare* to expend public funds after asking the consent of the people, fr. *e-* + *rogare* to ask — more at RIGHT] **:** the act of performing more than is required by duty, obligation, or need

su·per·erog·a·to·ry \ˌsü-pə-ri-ˈräg-ə-ˌtōr-ē, -ˌtȯr-\ *adj* **1 :** observed or performed to an extent not enjoined or required **2 :** SUPERFLUOUS, NONESSENTIAL

syn SUPEREROGATORY, GRATUITOUS, UNCALLED-FOR, WANTON *shared meaning element* **:** given or done without compulsion, need, or warrant

su·per·fam·i·ly \ˈsü-pər-ˌfam-(ə-)lē\ *n* **:** a category of taxonomic classification ranking next above a family

su·per·fe·cun·da·tion \ˌsü-pər-ˌfek-ən-ˈdā-shən, -ˌfē-kən-\ *n* **1 :** successive fertilization of two or more ova from the same ovulation esp. by different sires **2 :** fertilization at one time of a number of ova excessive for the species

su·per·fe·ta·tion \-fē-ˈtā-shən\ *n* [ML *superfetation-, superfetatio,* fr. L *superfetatus,* pp. of *superfetare* to conceive while already pregnant, fr. *super-* + *fetus* act of bearing young, offspring — more at FETUS] **1 :** successive fertilization of two or more ova of different ovulations resulting in the presence of embryos of unlike ages in the same uterus **2 :** a progressive accumulation or accretion reaching an extreme or excessive degree

su·per·fi·cial \ˌsü-pər-ˈfish-əl\ *adj* [ME, fr. LL *superficialis,* fr. L *superficies*] **1 a** (1) **:** of or relating to a surface (2) **:** lying on, not penetrating below, or affecting only the surface <~ wounds> **b** *of a unit of measure* **:** SQUARE <~ foot> **2 a :** concerned only with the obvious or apparent **:** SHALLOW **b :** lying on the surface **:** EXTERNAL **c :** presenting only an appearance without substance or significance — **su·per·fi·cial·ly** \-ˈfish-(ə-)lē\ *adv* — **su·per·fi·cial·ness** \-ˈfish-əl-nəs\ *n*

syn SUPERFICIAL, SHALLOW, CURSORY, UNCRITICAL *shared meaning element* **:** lacking in depth, solidity, and comprehensiveness *ant* radical

superficial fascia *n* **:** the thin layer of loose fatty connective tissue underlying the skin and binding it to the parts beneath — called also *hypodermis*

su·per·fi·ci·al·i·ty \ˌsü-pər-ˌfish-ē-ˈal-ət-ē\ *n, pl* **-ties 1 :** the quality or state of being superficial **2 :** something superficial

su·per·fi·cies \-ˈfish-(ˌ)ēz, -ē-ˌēz\ *n, pl* **superficies** [L, surface, fr. *super-* + *facies* face, aspect — more at FACE] **1 :** a surface of a body or a region of space **2 :** the external aspects or appearance of a thing

su·per·fine \ˌsü-pər-ˈfīn\ *adj* **1 :** overly refined or nice **2 :** of extremely fine size or texture <~ toothbrush bristles> <~ sugar> **3 :** of high quality or grade — used esp. of merchandise

su·per·fix \ˈsü-pər-ˌfiks\ *n* [*super-* + *-fix* (as in *prefix*)] **:** a recurrent predictable pattern of stress that characterizes small stretches of speech whose constituents are parallel in relationship

su·per·flu·id \ˌsü-pər-ˈflü-əd\ *n* **:** matter in a unique state characterized by extraordinarily large thermal conductivity and capillarity — **su·per·flu·id·i·ty** \-flü-ˈid-ət-ē\ *n*

su·per·flu·ity \ˌsü-pər-ˈflü-ət-ē\ *n, pl* **-ities** [ME *superfluitee,* fr. MF *superfluité,* fr. LL *superfluitat-, superfluitas,* fr. L *superfluus*] **1 a :** EXCESS, OVERSUPPLY **b :** something unnecessary or superfluous **2 :** immoderate and esp. luxurious living, habits, or desires

su·per·flu·ous \sü-ˈpər-flə-wəs\ *adj* [ME, fr. L *superfluus,* lit., running over, fr. *superfluere* to overflow, fr. *super-* + *fluere* to flow — more at FLUID] **1 :** exceeding what is sufficient or necessary **:** EXTRA **2** *obs* **:** marked by wastefulness **:** EXTRAVAGANT — **su·per·flu·ous·ly** *adv* — **su·per·flu·ous·ness** *n*

su·per·gal·axy \ˈsü-pər-ˌgal-ək-sē\ *n* **:** a large cluster of galaxies

su·per·gene \ˈsü-pər-ˌjēn\ *n* **:** a group of linked genes acting as an allelomorphic unit esp. when due to the suppression of crossing over

su·per·gi·ant \-ˌjī-ənt\ *n* **:** a star of very great intrinsic luminosity and enormous size

[1]su·per·heat \ˌsü-pər-ˈhēt\ *vt* **1 a :** to heat (a liquid) above the boiling point without converting into vapor **b :** to heat (a vapor not in contact with its own liquid) so as to cause to remain free from suspended liquid droplets <~*ed* steam> **2 :** OVERHEAT <~*ed* protest> — **su·per·heat·er** *n*

[2]su·per·heat \ˈsü-pər-ˌhēt, ˌsü-pər-ˈ\ *n* **:** the extra heat imparted to a vapor in superheating it from a dry and saturated condition; *also* **:** the corresponding rise of temperature

[1]su·per·het·ero·dyne \ˌsü-pər-ˈhet-ə-rə-ˌdīn, -ˈhe-trə-\ *adj* [*supersonic* + *heterodyne*] **:** of or relating to a form of beat reception in which beats are produced of a frequency above audibility but below that of the received signals and the current of the beat frequency is then rectified, amplified, and finally rectified again so as to reproduce the sound

[2]superheterodyne *n* **:** a radio set for superheterodyne reception

su·per·high frequency \ˈsü-pər-ˌhī-\ *n* **:** a radio frequency in the next to the highest range of the radio spectrum — see RADIO FREQUENCY table

su·per·high·way \ˌsü-pər-ˈhī-ˌwā\ *n* **:** a broad arterial highway (as an expressway or turnpike) designed for high-speed traffic

su·per·hu·man \ˌsü-pər-ˈhyü-mən, -ˈyü-\ *adj* **1 :** being above the human **:** DIVINE <~ beings> **2 :** exceeding normal human power, size, or capability **:** HERCULEAN <a ~ effort> — **su·per·hu·man·i·ty** \-hyü-ˈman-ət-ē, -yü-\ *n* — **su·per·hu·man·ly** \-ˈhyü-mən-lē, -ˈyü-\ *adv* — **su·per·hu·man·ness** \-mən-nəs\ *n*

su·per·im·pose \ˌsü-pə-rim-ˈpōz\ *vt* **:** to place or lay over or above something — **su·per·im·pos·able** \-ˈpō-zə-bəl\ *adj* — **su·per·im·po·si·tion** \-ˌrim-pə-ˈzish-ən\ *n*

su·per·in·cum·bent \-rin-ˈkəm-bənt\ *adj* [L *superincumbent-, superincumbens,* prp. of *superincumbere* to lie on top of, fr. *super-* + *incumbere* to lie down on — more at INCUMBENT] **:** lying or resting and usu. exerting pressure on something else — **su·per·in·cum·bent·ly** *adv*

su·per·in·di·vid·u·al \ˌsü-pə-ˌrin-də-ˈvij-(ə-)wəl, -ˈvij-əl\ *adj* **:** of, relating to, or being an organism, entity, or complex of more than individual complexity or nature

su·per·in·duce \-rin-ˈd(y)üs\ *vt* [L *superinducere,* fr. *super-* + *inducere* to lead in — more at INDUCE] **1 :** to introduce as an addition over or above something already existing **2 :** to bring on **:** INDUCE — **su·per·in·duc·tion** \-ˈdək-shən\ *n*

su·per·in·fec·tion \-rin-ˈfek-shən\ *n* **:** reinfection or a second infection with the same type of parasite (as a bacterium or virus)

su·per·in·tend \ˌsü-p(ə-)rin-ˈtend, ˌsü-pərn-\ *vt* [LL *superintendere,* fr. L *super-* + *intendere* to attend, direct attention to — more at INTEND] **:** to have or exercise the charge and oversight of **:** DIRECT

su·per·in·ten·dence \-ˈten-dən(t)s\ *n* **:** the act or function of superintending or directing **:** SUPERVISION

su·per·in·ten·den·cy \-dən-sē\ *n, pl* **-cies :** the office, post, or jurisdiction of a superintendent; *also* **:** SUPERINTENDENCE

su·per·in·ten·dent \-dənt\ *n* [ML *superintendent-, superintendens,* fr. LL, prp. of *superintendere*] **:** one who has executive oversight and charge — **superintendent** *adj*

[1]su·pe·ri·or \sü-ˈpir-ē-ər\ *adj* [ME, fr. MF *superieur,* fr. L *superior,* compar. of *superus* upper, fr. *super* over, above — more at OVER] **1 :** situated higher up **:** UPPER **2 :** of higher rank, quality, or importance **3 :** courageously or serenely indifferent (as to something painful or disheartening) **4 a :** greater in quantity or numbers <escaped by ~ speed> **b :** excellent of its kind **:** BETTER <her ~ memory> **5 :** being a superscript **6 a** *of an animal structure* **:** situated above or anterior or dorsal to another and esp. a corresponding part <a ~ artery> **b** *of a plant structure* **:** situated above or near the top of another part: as (1) *of a calyx* **:** attached to and apparently arising from the ovary (2) *of an ovary* **:** free from the calyx or other floral envelope **7 :** more comprehensive <a genus is ~ to a species> **8 :** affecting or assuming an air of superiority **:** SUPERCILIOUS

[2]superior *n* **1 :** one who is above another in rank, station, or office; *esp* **:** the head of a religious house or order **2 :** one that surpasses another in quality or merit **3 :** SUPERSCRIPT

superior conjunction *n* **:** a conjunction in which a lesser or secondary celestial body passes farther from the observer than the primary body around which it revolves

superior court *n* **1 :** a court of general jurisdiction intermediate between the inferior courts (as a justice of the peace court) and the higher appellate courts **2 :** a court with juries having original jurisdiction

superior general *n, pl* **superiors general :** the superior of a religious order or congregation

su·pe·ri·or·i·ty \sü-ˌpir-ē-ˈȯr-ət-ē, ˌsü-, -ˈär-\ *n, pl* **-ties :** the quality or state of being superior; *also* **:** a superior characteristic

superiority complex *n* **:** an exaggerated opinion of oneself

su·pe·ri·or·ly \sü-ˈpir-ē-ər-lē\ *adv* **1 :** in or to a higher position or direction **2 :** in a higher or better manner or degree; *also* **:** in a haughty or condescending manner

superior planet *n* **:** a planet whose orbit lies outside that of the earth

superior vena cava *n* **:** the branch of the vena cava of a vertebrate that brings blood back from the head and anterior part of the body to the heart

su·per·ja·cent \ˌsü-pər-ˈjās-ᵊnt\ *adj* [L *superjacent-, superjacens,* prp. of *superjacēre* to lie over or upon, fr. *super-* + *jacēre* to lie; akin to L *jacere* to throw — more at JET] **:** lying above or upon **:** OVERLYING <~ rocks>

su·per·jet \ˈsü-pər-ˌjet\ *n* **:** a supersonic jet airplane

[1]su·per·la·tive \sü-ˈpər-lət-iv\ *adj* [ME *superlatif,* fr. MF, fr. LL *superlativus,* fr. L *superlatus* (pp. of *superferre* to carry over, raise high), fr. *super-* + *latus,* pp. of *ferre* to carry — more at TOLERATE, BEAR] **1 :** of, relating to, or constituting the degree of grammatical comparison that denotes an extreme or unsurpassed level or extent **2 :** surpassing all others **:** SUPREME **3 :** EXCESSIVE, EXAGGERATED — **su·per·la·tive·ly** *adv* — **su·per·la·tive·ness** *n*

[2]superlative *n* **1 a :** the superlative degree of comparison in a language **b :** a superlative form of an adjective or adverb **2 :** the superlative or utmost degree of something **:** ACME **3 :** a superlative person or thing **4 :** an exaggerated expression esp. of praise

su·per·lin·er \ˈsü-pər-ˌlī-nər\ *n* **:** a fast luxurious passenger liner of great size

su·per·lu·na·ry \ˌsü-pər-ˈlü-nə-rē\ *also* **su·per·lu·nar** \-nər, -ˌnär\ *adj* [L *super-* + *luna* moon — more at LUNAR] **:** being above the moon **:** CELESTIAL

su·per·man \ˈsü-pər-ˌman\ *n* [trans. of G *übermensch*] **1 :** a superior man that according to Nietzsche has learned to forgo fleeting pleasures and attain happiness and dominance through the exercise of creative power **2 :** a person of extraordinary or superhuman power or achievements

su·per·mar·ket \-ˌmär-kət\ *n* **:** a self-service retail market selling foods and household merchandise

su·per·nal \sü-ˈpərn-ᵊl\ *adj* [ME, fr. MF, fr. L *supernus,* fr. *super* over, above — more at OVER] **1 a :** being or coming from on high **b :** ETHEREAL, HEAVENLY <~ melodies> **2 :** located in or belonging to the sky — **su·per·nal·ly** \-ᵊl-ē\ *adv*

su·per·na·tant \ˌsü-pər-ˈnāt-ᵊnt\ *adj* [L *supernatant-, supernatans,* prp. of *supernatare* to float, fr. *super-* + *natare* to swim — more at NATANT] **:** floating on the surface — **supernatant** *n*

su·per·nat·u·ral \ˌsü-pər-ˈnach-(ə-)rəl\ *adj* [ML *supernaturalis,* fr. L *super-* + *natura* nature] **1 :** of or relating to an order of existence beyond the visible observable universe; *esp* **:** of or relating to God or a god, demigod, spirit, or devil **2 a :** departing from what is usual or normal esp. so as to appear to transcend the laws of nature **b :** attributed to an invisible agent (as a ghost or spirit) — **supernatural** *n* — **su·per·nat·u·ral·ly** \-ˈnach-(ə-)rə-lē, -ˈnach-ər-lē\ *adv* — **su·per·nat·u·ral·ness** \-ˈnach-(ə-)rəl-nəs\ *n*

su·per·nat·u·ral·ism \-ˈnach-(ə-)rə-ˌliz-əm\ *n* **1 :** the quality or state of being supernatural **2 :** belief in a supernatural power and order of existence — **su·per·nat·u·ral·ist** \-ləst\ *n or adj* — **su·per·nat·u·ral·is·tic** \-ˌnach-(ə-)rə-ˈlis-tik\ *adj*

su·per·nor·mal \ˌsü-pər-ˈnȯr-məl\ *adj* **1 :** exceeding the normal or average **2 :** being beyond normal human powers **:** PARANORMAL — **su·per·nor·mal·i·ty** \-nȯr-ˈmal-ət-ē\ *n* — **su·per·nor·mal·ly** \-ˈnȯr-mə-lē\ *adv*

su·per·no·va \ˌsü-pər-ˈnō-və\ *n* [NL] **:** one of the rarely observed nova outbursts in which the maximum intrinsic luminosity may reach 100 million times that of the sun

[1]su·per·nu·mer·ary \ˌsü-pər-ˈn(y)ü-mə-ˌrer-ē, -ˈn(y)üm-(ə-)rē\ *adj* [LL *supernumerarius,* fr. L *super-* + *numerus* number — more at NIMBLE] **1 a :** exceeding the usual, stated, or prescribed number <a ~ tooth> **b :** not enumerated among the regular components of a group and esp. of a military organization **2 :** exceeding what is necessary, required, or desired **3 :** more numerous

[2]supernumerary *n, pl* **-ar·ies 1 :** a supernumerary person or thing: as **a :** a person employed not for regular service but for use in case of need **b :** an individual in excess of the number authorized for a given military or naval unit **c :** a person serving no apparent function **2 :** an actor employed to play a walk-on

su·per·or·der \'sü-pə-ˌrȯrd-ər\ *n* **:** a taxonomic category between an order and a class or a subclass

su·per·or·di·nate \ˌsü-pə-'rȯrd-nət, -ᵊn-ət, -ᵊn-ˌāt\ *adj* [*super-* + *-ordinate* (as in *subordinate*)] **:** superior in rank, class, or status

su·per·or·gan·ism \-'rȯr-gə-ˌniz-əm\ *n* **:** an organized society (as of a social insect) that functions as an organic whole

su·per·ovu·la·tion \-ˌräv-yə-'lā-shən, -ˌrōv-\ *n* **:** production of exceptional numbers of eggs at one time

su·per·par·a·sit·ism \ˌsü-pər-'par-ə-ˌsīt-ˌiz-əm, -sə-ˌtiz-\ *n* **:** parasitization of a host by more than one parasitic individual usu. of one kind — used esp. of parasitic insects

su·per·pa·tri·ot \-'pā-trē-ət, -trē-ˌät, *chiefly Brit* -'pa-\ *n* **:** an excessively patriotic individual — **su·per·pa·tri·ot·ic** \-ˌpā-trē-'ät-ik, *chiefly Brit* -ˌpa-\ *adj* — **su·per·pa·tri·o·tism** \-'pā-trē-ə-ˌtiz-əm, *chiefly Brit* -'pa-\ *n*

su·per·phos·phate \ˌsü-pər-'fäs-ˌfāt\ *n* **1 :** an acid phosphate **2 :** a soluble mixture of phosphates used as fertilizer and made from insoluble mineral phosphates by treatment with sulfuric acid

su·per·phys·i·cal \-'fiz-i-kəl\ *adj* **:** being above or beyond the physical world or explanation on physical principles

su·per·pose \ˌsü-pər-'pōz\ *vt* **-posed; -pos·ing** [prob. fr. F *superposer,* back-formation fr. *superposition,* fr. LL *superposition-, superpositio,* fr. L *superpositus,* pp. of *superponere* to superpose, fr. *super-* + *ponere* to place — more at POSITION] **1 :** to place or lay over or above whether in or not in contact **:** SUPERIMPOSE **2 :** to lay (as a geometric figure) upon another so as to make all like parts coincide — **su·per·pos·able** \-'pō-zə-bəl\ *adj* — **su·per·po·si·tion** \-pə-'zish-ən\ *n*

su·per·posed \-'pōzd\ *adj* **:** situated vertically over another layer or part

su·per·pow·er \'sü-pər-ˌpau̇(-ə)r\ *n* **1 :** excessive or superior power **2 a :** an extremely powerful nation; *specif* **:** one of a very few dominant states in an era when the world is divided politically into these states and their satellites **b :** an international governing body able to enforce its will upon the most powerful states — **su·per·pow·ered** \-ˌpau̇(-ə)rd\ *adj*

su·per·sat·u·rate \ˌsü-pər-'sach-ə-ˌrāt\ *vt* **:** to add to beyond saturation — **su·per·sat·u·ra·tion** \-ˌsach-ə-'rā-shən\ *n*

su·per·scribe \'sü-pər-ˌskrīb, ˌsü-pər-'\ *vt* **-scribed; -scrib·ing** [L *superscribere,* fr. *super-* + *scribere* to write — more at SCRIBE] **1 :** to write or engrave on the top or outside **2 :** to write (as a name or address) on the outside or cover of **:** ADDRESS

su·per·script \'sü-pər-ˌskript\ *n* [L *superscriptus,* pp. of *superscribere*] **:** a distinguishing symbol or letter written immediately above or above and to the right or left of another character — **superscript** *adj*

su·per·scrip·tion \ˌsü-pər-'skrip-shən\ *n* [ME, fr. MF, fr. LL *superscription-, superscriptio,* fr. L *superscriptus*] **1 :** the act of superscribing **2 :** something written or engraved on the surface of, outside, or above something else **:** INSCRIPTION; *also* **:** ADDRESS

su·per·sede \ˌsü-pər-'sēd\ *vt* **-sed·ed; -sed·ing** [MF *superseder* to refrain from, fr. L *supersedēre* to be superior to, refrain from, fr. *super-* + *sedēre* to sit — more at SIT] **1 a :** to cause to be set aside **b :** to force out of use as inferior **2 :** to take the place, room, or position of **3 :** to displace in favor of another **:** SUPPLANT ***syn*** see REPLACE — **su·per·sed·er** *n*

su·per·se·de·as \-'sēd-ē-əs\ *n, pl* **supersedeas** [ME, fr. L, you shall refrain, fr. *supersedēre*] **1 :** a common-law writ commanding a stay of legal proceedings issued under various conditions and esp. to stay an officer from proceeding under another writ **2 :** an order staying proceedings of an inferior court

su·per·se·dure \-'sē-jər\ *n* **:** the act or process of superseding; *esp* **:** the replacement of an old or inferior queen bee by a young or superior queen

su·per·sen·si·ble \ˌsü-pər-'sen(t)-sə-bəl\ *adj* **:** being above or beyond that which is apparent to the senses **:** SPIRITUAL

su·per·sen·si·tive \-'sen(t)-sət-iv, -'sen(t)-stiv\ *adj* **1 :** HYPERSENSITIVE <a ~ palate> **2 :** specially treated to increase sensitivity <a ~ photographic emulsion> — **su·per·sen·si·tive·ness** *n* — **su·per·sen·si·tiv·i·ty** \-ˌsen(t)-sə-'tiv-ət-ē\ *n*

su·per·sen·so·ry \-'sen(t)s-(ə-)rē\ *adj* **:** SUPERSENSIBLE

su·per·ser·vice·able \-'sər-və-sə-bəl\ *adj* **:** offering unwanted services **:** OFFICIOUS

su·per·ses·sion \ˌsü-pər-'sesh-ən\ *n* [ML *supersession-, supersessio,* fr. L *supersessus,* pp. of *supersedēre*] **:** the act of superseding **:** the state of being superseded — **su·per·ses·sive** \-'ses-iv\ *adj*

[1]**su·per·son·ic** \-'sän-ik\ *adj* [L *super-* + *sonus* sound — more at SOUND] **1 :** having a frequency above the human ear's audibility limit of about 20,000 cycles per second — used of waves and vibrations; compare SONIC **2 :** utilizing, produced by, or relating to supersonic waves or vibrations **3 :** of, being, or relating to speeds from one to five times the speed of sound in air — compare SONIC **4 :** moving, capable of moving, or utilizing air currents moving at supersonic speed **5 :** relating to supersonic airplanes or missiles <the ~ age> — **su·per·son·i·cal·ly** \-i-k(ə-)lē\ *adv*

[2]**supersonic** *n* **1 :** a supersonic wave or frequency **2 :** a supersonic airplane

su·per·son·ics \ˌsü-pər-'sän-iks\ *n pl but sing in constr* **1 :** the science of supersonic phenomena **2 :** the industry involved in the manufacture of supersonic airplanes

supersonic transport *n* **:** a supersonic transport airplane

su·per·star \'sü-pər-ˌstär\ *n* **:** a star (as in sports or the movies) who is considered extremely talented, has great public appeal, and who can usu. command a high salary

su·per·sti·tion \ˌsü-pər-'stish-ən\ *n* [ME *supersticion,* fr. MF, fr. L *superstition-, superstitio,* fr. *superstit-, superstes* standing over (as witness or survivor), fr. *super-* + *stare* to stand — more at STAND] **1 a :** a belief or practice resulting from ignorance, fear of the unknown, trust in magic or chance, or a false conception of causation **b :** an irrational abject attitude of mind toward the supernatural, nature, or God resulting from superstition **2 :** a notion maintained despite evidence to the contrary

su·per·sti·tious \-'stish-əs\ *adj* **:** of, relating to, or manifesting superstition — **su·per·sti·tious·ly** *adv* — **su·per·sti·tious·ness** *n*

su·per·stra·tum \'sü-pər-ˌstrāt-əm, -ˌstrat-\ *n* [*super-* + *-stratum* (as in *substratum*)] **:** an overlying stratum or layer

su·per·struc·ture \-ˌstrək-chər\ *n* **1 :** a structure built as a vertical extension of something else: as **a :** all of a building above the basement **b :** the structural part of a ship above the main deck **c :** the ties, rails, and fastenings of a railroad track as distinct from the roadbed **2 :** an entity, concept, or complex based on a more fundamental one; *specif* **:** social institutions (as the law or politics) that are in Marxist theory erected upon the economic base — **su·per·struc·tur·al** \ˌsü-pər-'strək-chə-rəl, -'strək-shrəl\ *adj*

su·per·sub·stan·tial \ˌsü-pər-səb-'stan-chəl\ *adj* [LL *supersubstantialis,* fr. L *super-* + *substantia* substance] **:** being above material substance **:** of a transcending substance

su·per·sub·tle \ˌsü-pər-'sət-ᵊl\ *adj* **:** extremely or excessively subtle — **su·per·sub·tle·ty** \-tē\ *n*

su·per·sys·tem \'sü-pər-ˌsis-təm\ *n* **:** a system that is made up of systems

su·per·tank·er \-ˌtaŋ-kər\ *n* **:** an exceptionally large and fast tanker

su·per·tax \-ˌtaks\ *n* **1 :** SURTAX **2 :** a graduated income tax imposed in the United Kingdom in addition to the normal income tax

su·per·ton·ic \ˌsü-pər-'tän-ik\ *n* **:** the second tone of a diatonic scale

su·per·vene \ˌsü-pər-'vēn\ *vi* **-vened; -ven·ing** [L *supervenire,* fr. *super-* + *venire* to come — more at COME] **:** to follow or result as an additional, adventitious, or unlooked-for development ***syn*** see FOLLOW — **su·per·ven·tion** \-'ven-chən\ *n*

su·per·ve·nient \-'vē-nyənt\ *adj* [L *supervenient-, superveniens,* prp. of *supervenire*] **:** coming or occurring as something additional, extraneous, or unexpected — **su·per·ve·nience** \-nyən(t)s\ *n*

su·per·vise \'sü-pər-ˌvīz\ *vt* **-vised; -vis·ing** [ML *supervisus,* pp. of *supervidēre,* fr. L *super-* + *vidēre* to see — more at WIT] **:** SUPERINTEND, OVERSEE

su·per·vi·sion \ˌsü-pər-'vizh-ən\ *n* **:** the action, process, or occupation of supervising; *esp* **:** a critical watching and directing (as of activities or a course of action) ***syn*** see OVERSIGHT

su·per·vi·sor \'sü-pər-ˌvī-zər\ *n* **:** one that supervises; *esp* **:** an administrative officer in charge of a business, government, or school unit or operation — **su·per·vi·so·ry** \ˌsü-pər-'vīz-(ə-)rē\ *adj*

su·pi·nate \'sü-pə-ˌnāt\ *vb* **-nat·ed; -nat·ing** [L *supinatus,* pp. of *supinare* to lay backward or on the back, fr. *supinus*] *vt* **:** to cause to assume a position of supination ~ *vi* **:** to assume a position of supination

su·pi·na·tion \ˌsü-pə-'nā-shən\ *n* **1 :** rotation of the forearm and hand so that the palm faces forward or upward and the radius lies parallel to the ulna; *also* **:** a corresponding movement of the foot and leg **2 :** the position resulting from supination

su·pi·na·tor \'sü-pə-ˌnāt-ər\ *n* [NL, fr. L *supinatus,* pp.] **:** a muscle that produces the motion of supination

[1]**su·pine** \su̇-'pīn, *attrib also* ˌsü-ˌpīn\ *adj* [L *supinus;* akin to L *sub* under, up to — more at UP] **1 a :** lying on the back or with the face upward **b :** marked by supination **2 :** exhibiting indolent or apathetic inertia or passivity; *esp* **:** mentally or morally slack **3** *archaic* **:** leaning or sloping backward ***syn*** see INACTIVE, PRONE — **su·pine·ly** \su̇-'pīn-lē\ *adv* — **su·pine·ness** \-'pīn-nəs\ *n*

[2]**su·pine** \'sü-ˌpīn\ *n* [ME *supyn,* fr. LL *supinum,* fr. L, neut. of *supinus,* adj.] **1 :** a Latin verbal noun having an accusative of purpose in *-um* and an ablative of specification in *-u* **2 :** an English infinitive with *to*

supp *or* **suppl** *abbr* supplement; supplementary

sup·per \'səp-ər\ *n* [ME, fr. OF *souper,* fr. *souper* to sup — more at SUP] **1 a :** the evening meal when dinner is taken at midday **b :** a social affair featuring a supper; *esp* **:** an evening social esp. for raising funds <a church ~> **2 :** the food served as a supper <eat your ~> **3 :** a light meal served late in the evening

supper club *n* **:** NIGHTCLUB

sup·plant \sə-'plant\ *vt* [ME *supplanten,* fr. MF *supplanter,* fr. L *supplantare* to overthrow by tripping up, fr. *sub-* + *planta* sole of the foot — more at PLACE] **1 :** to supersede (another) esp. by force or treachery **2 a** (1) *obs* **:** UPROOT (2) **:** to eradicate and supply a substitute for <efforts to ~ the vernacular> **b :** to take the place of and serve as a substitute for esp. by reason of superior excellence or power ***syn*** see REPLACE — **sup·plan·ta·tion** \(ˌ)sə-ˌplan-'tā-shən\ *n* — **sup·plant·er** \sə-'plant-ər\ *n*

[1]**sup·ple** \'səp-əl *also* 'süp-\ *adj* **sup·pler** \-(ə-)lər\; **sup·plest** \-(ə-)ləst\ [ME *souple,* fr. OF, fr. L *supplic-, supplex* submissive, suppliant, lit., bending under, fr. *sub-* + *plic-* (akin to *plicare* to fold) — more at PLY] **1 a :** compliant often to the point of obsequiousness **b :** readily adaptable or responsive to new situations **2 a :** capable of being bent or folded without creases, cracks, or breaks **:** PLIANT <~ leather> **b :** able to perform bending or twisting movements with ease and grace **:** LIMBER <~ legs of a dancer> **c :** easy and fluent without stiffness or awkwardness <sang with a lively, ~ voice —Douglas Watt> — **sup·ple·ly** \-ə(l)-lē\ *or* **sup·ply** \-(ə-)lē\ *adv* — **sup·ple·ness** \-əl-nəs\ *n*

[2]**supple** *vb* **sup·pled; sup·pling** \-(ə-)liŋ\ *vt* **1 :** to make pacific or complaisant <~ the tempers of your race —Laurence Sterne> **2 :** to alleviate with a salve **3 :** to make flexible or pliant ~ *vi* **:** to become soft and pliant

sup·ple·jack \'səp-əl-ˌjak *also* 'süp-\ *n* **:** any of various woody climbers having tough pliant stems; *esp* **:** a southern U.S. vine (*Berchemia scandens*) of the buckthorn family

[1]**sup·ple·ment** \'səp-lə-mənt\ *n* [ME, fr. L *supplementum,* fr. *supplēre* to fill up, complete — more at SUPPLY] **1 :** something that completes or makes an addition <dietary ~*s*> **2 :** a part added to or issued as a continuation of a book or periodical to correct errors or make additions **3 :** an angle or arc that when added to a given angle or arc equals 180°

[2]**sup·ple·ment** \'səp-lə-ˌment\ *vt* **:** to add a supplement to <~*s* his income by doing odd jobs> — **sup·ple·men·ta·tion** \ˌsəp-lə-ˌmen-'tā-shən, -mən-\ *n* — **sup·ple·ment·er** \'səp-lə-ˌment-ər\ *n*

sup·ple·men·tal \ˌsəp-lə-ˈment-ᵊl\ *adj* **1 :** serving to supplement **2 :** NONSCHEDULED <a ~ airline> — **supplemental** *n*
sup·ple·men·ta·ry \ˌsəp-lə-ˈment-ə-rē, -ˈmen-trē\ *adj* **1 :** added as a supplement : ADDITIONAL <a ~ power source> **2 :** being or relating to a supplement or a supplementary angle
supplementary angle *n* **:** one of two angles or arcs whose sum is 180° — usu. used in pl.
sup·ple·tion \sə-ˈplē-shən\ *n* [ML *suppletion-, suppletio* act of supplementing, fr. L *suppletus,* pp. of *supplēre*] **:** the occurrence of phonemically unrelated allomorphs of the same morpheme (as *go,* past tense *went* or *better* as the comparative form of *good*) — **sup·ple·tive** \sə-ˈplēt-iv, ˈsəp-lət-\ *adj*
sup·ple·to·ry \sə-ˈplēt-ə-rē; ˈsəp-lə-ˌtōr-ē, -ˌtȯr-\ *adj* [L *suppletus,* pp.] **:** supplying deficiencies : SUPPLEMENTARY
sup·pli·ance \ˈsəp-lē-ən(t)s\ *n* **:** ENTREATY, SUPPLICATION
[1]**sup·pli·ant** \-ənt\ *n* [ME, fr. MF, fr. prp. of *supplier* to supplicate, fr. L *supplicare*] **:** one who supplicates
[2]**suppliant** *adj* [MF, prp.] **1 :** humbly imploring : ENTREATING <a ~ sinner seeking forgiveness —O. J. Baab> **2 :** expressing supplication <upraised to the heavens . . . ~ arms —William Styron> — **sup·pli·ant·ly** *adv*
[1]**sup·pli·cant** \ˈsəp-li-kənt\ *adj* **:** SUPPLIANT — **sup·pli·cant·ly** *adv*
[2]**supplicant** *n* **:** SUPPLIANT
sup·pli·cate \ˈsəp-lə-ˌkāt\ *vb* **-cat·ed; -cat·ing** [ME *supplicaten,* fr. L *supplicatus,* pp. of *supplicare,* fr. *supplic-, supplex* suppliant — more at SUPPLE] *vi* **:** to make a humble entreaty; *esp* **:** to pray to God ~ *vt* **1 :** to ask humbly and earnestly of **2 :** to ask for earnestly and humbly ***syn*** see BEG — **sup·pli·ca·tion** \ˌsəp-lə-ˈkā-shən\ *n*
sup·pli·ca·to·ry \ˈsəp-li-kə-ˌtōr-ē, -ˌtȯr-\ *adj* **:** expressing supplication : SUPPLIANT <a ~ prayer>
[1]**sup·ply** \sə-ˈplī\ *vb* **sup·plied; sup·ply·ing** [ME *supplien,* fr. MF *soupleier,* fr. L *supplēre* to fill up, supplement, supply, fr. *sub-* up + *plēre* to fill — more at SUB-, FULL] *vt* **1 :** to add as a supplement **2 a :** to provide for : SATISFY <laws by which the material wants of men are *supplied* —*Bull. of Bates Coll.*> **b :** to provide or furnish with <*supplied* him with the details> **c :** to satisfy the needs or wishes of **3 :** to substitute for another in; *specif* **:** to serve as a supply in (a church or pulpit) ~ *vi* **:** to serve as a supply or substitute — **sup·pli·er** \-ˈplī(-ə)r\ *n*
[2]**supply** *n, pl* **supplies 1** *obs* **:** ASSISTANCE, SUCCOR **2 a** *obs* **:** REINFORCEMENTS — often used in pl. **b :** a clergyman filling a vacant pulpit temporarily **c :** the quantity or amount (as of a commodity) needed or available <beer was in short ~ in that hot weather —Nevil Shute> **d :** PROVISIONS, STORES — usu. used in pl. **3 :** the act or process of filling a want or need **4 :** the quantities of goods or services offered for sale at a particular time or at one price **5 :** something that maintains or constitutes a supply
[1]**sup·port** \sə-ˈpō(ə)rt, -ˈpȯ(ə)rt\ *vt* [ME *supporten,* fr. MF *supporter,* fr. LL *supportare,* fr. L, to carry, fr. *sub-* + *portare* to carry — more at FARE] **1 :** to endure bravely or quietly : BEAR **2 a** (1) **:** to promote the interests or cause of (2) **:** to uphold or defend as valid or right : ADVOCATE (3) **:** to argue or vote for **b** (1) **:** ASSIST, HELP (2) **:** to act with (a star actor) (3) **:** to bid in bridge so as to show support for **c :** to provide with substantiation : CORROBORATE <~ an alibi> **3 a :** to pay the costs of : MAINTAIN **b :** to provide a basis for the existence or subsistence of <the island could probably ~ three —A. B. C. Whipple> **4 a :** to hold up or serve as a foundation or prop for **b :** to maintain (a price) at a desired level by purchases or loans; *also* **:** to maintain the price of by purchases or loans **5 :** to keep from fainting, yielding, or losing courage : COMFORT <her indomitable pride ~*ed* her —Ellen Glasgow> **6 :** to keep (something) going
syn SUPPORT, UPHOLD, ADVOCATE, BACK, CHAMPION *shared meaning element* **:** to favor actively in the face of opposition
[2]**support** *n* **1 :** the act or process of supporting : the condition of being supported **2 :** one that supports
sup·port·able \sə-ˈpōrt-ə-bəl, -ˈpȯrt-\ *adj* **:** capable of being supported — **sup·port·abil·i·ty** \-ˌpōrt-ə-ˈbil-ət-ē\ *n* — **sup·port·able·ness** *n* — **sup·port·ably** \-blē\ *adv*
sup·port·er *n* **:** one that supports or acts as a support: as **a :** ADHERENT, PARTISAN **b :** one of two figures (as of men or animals) placed one on each side of an escutcheon and exterior to it **c :** GARTER 1 **d :** ATHLETIC SUPPORTER
sup·port·ive \sə-ˈpōrt-iv, -ˈpȯrt-\ *adj* **:** furnishing or intended to furnish support <~ evidence for the charge>
support level *n* **:** a price level on a declining market at which a security resists further decline due to increased attractiveness to traders and investors — called also *support area*
support mission *n* **:** an air attack in close support of ground forces against enemy ground forces
sup·pos·able \sə-ˈpō-zə-bəl\ *adj* **:** capable of being supposed : CONCEIVABLE — **sup·pos·ably** \-blē\ *adv*
sup·pos·al \-ˈpō-zəl\ *n* **1 :** the act or process of supposing **2 :** something supposed : HYPOTHESIS, SUPPOSITION
sup·pose \sə-ˈpōz, *oftenest after* "*I*" ˈspōz\ *vb* **sup·posed; sup·pos·ing** [ME *supposen,* fr. MF *supposer,* fr. ML *supponere* (perf. indic. *supposui*), fr. L, to put under, substitute, fr. *sub-* + *ponere* to put — more at POSITION] *vt* **1 a :** to lay down tentatively as a hypothesis or assumption <~ a fire broke out> **b** (1) **:** to hold as an opinion : BELIEVE <they *supposed* they were early> (2) **:** to think probable or in keeping with the facts <seems reasonable to ~ that he would profit> **2 a :** CONCEIVE, IMAGINE **b :** to have a suspicion of **3 :** PRESUPPOSE ~ *vi* **:** CONJECTURE, OPINE
sup·posed \sə-ˈpōz(-ə)d\ *adj* **1 a :** held as an opinion : BELIEVED; *also* **:** mistakenly believed : IMAGINED <the sight which makes ~ terror true —Shak.> **b :** considered probable or certain : EXPECTED <it was not ~ that everybody could master the technical aspects —J. C. Murray> **c :** UNDERSTOOD <you will be ~ to refer to my grandaunt —G. B. Shaw> **2 a :** PRETENDED <twelve hours are ~ to elapse between Acts I and II —A. S. Sullivan> **b :** ALLEGED <stupid things they may be ~ to have said —James Stoller> **3 a :** INTENDED <pills that are ~ to kill pain> **b :** made or fashioned by design <what's that button ~ to do> **4 a :** required by authority <soldiers are ~ to obey their commanding officers> **b :** given permission : PERMITTED <was not ~ to have visitors> — **sup·pos·ed·ly** \-ˈpō-zəd-lē *also* -ˈpōz-dlē\ *adv*
sup·pos·ing \sə-ˈpō-ziŋ\ *conj* **:** if by way of hypothesis : on the assumption that
sup·po·si·tion \ˌsəp-ə-ˈzish-ən\ *n* [ME, fr. LL *supposition-, suppositio,* fr. L, act of placing beneath, fr. *suppositus,* pp. of *supponere*] **1 :** something that is supposed : HYPOTHESIS **2 :** the act of supposing — **sup·po·si·tion·al** \-ˈzish-nəl, -ən-ᵊl\ *adj* — **sup·po·si·tion·al·ly** \-ē\ *adv*
sup·po·si·tious \-ˈzish-əs\ *adj* [by contr.] **:** SUPPOSITITIOUS
sup·pos·i·ti·tious \sə-ˌpäz-ə-ˈtish-əs\ *adj* [L *suppositicius,* fr. *suppositus,* pp. of *supponere* to substitute] **1 a :** fraudulently substituted : SPURIOUS **b** *of a child* (1) **:** falsely presented as a genuine heir (2) **:** ILLEGITIMATE **2** [influenced in meaning by *supposition*] **:** of the nature of or based on a supposition : HYPOTHETICAL <whether the anticipation be mine or that of a ~ observer —Victor Lowe> — **sup·pos·i·ti·tious·ly** *adv* — **sup·pos·i·ti·tious·ness** *n*
sup·pos·i·tive \sə-ˈpäz-ət-iv, -ˈpäz-tiv\ *adj* **:** characterized by, involving, or implying supposition — **sup·pos·i·tive·ly** *adv*
sup·pos·i·to·ry \sə-ˈpäz-ə-ˌtōr-ē, -ˌtȯr-\ *n, pl* **-ries** [ML *suppositorium,* fr. LL, neut. of *suppositorius* placed beneath, fr. L *suppositus,* pp. of *supponere* to put under] **:** a solid but readily meltable cone or cylinder of usu. medicated material for insertion into a bodily passage or cavity (as the rectum)
sup·press \sə-ˈpres\ *vt* [ME *suppressen,* fr. L *suppressus,* pp. of *supprimere,* fr. *sub-* + *premere* to press — more at PRESS] **1 :** to put down by authority or force : SUBDUE **2 :** to keep from public knowledge: as **a :** to keep secret **b :** to stop or prohibit the publication or revelation of **3 a :** to exclude from consciousness **b :** to keep from giving vent to : CHECK **4** *obs* **:** to press down **5 a :** to restrain from a usual course or action : ARREST <~ a cough> **b :** to inhibit the growth or development of : STUNT **6 :** to inhibit the genetic expression of — **sup·press·ibil·i·ty** \-ˌpres-ə-ˈbil-ət-ē\ *n* — **sup·press·ible** \-ˈpres-ə-bəl\ *adj*
***syn* 1** see CRUSH
2 SUPPRESS, REPRESS *shared meaning element* **:** to hold back more or less forcefully one that seeks an outlet
sup·pres·sant \sə-ˈpres-ᵊnt\ *n* **:** an agent (as a drug) that tends to suppress rather than eliminate something undesirable
sup·pres·sion \sə-ˈpresh-ən\ *n* **1 :** an act or instance of suppressing : the state of being suppressed **2 :** the conscious intentional exclusion from consciousness of a thought or feeling
sup·pres·sive \-ˈpres-iv\ *adj* **:** tending or serving to suppress — **sup·pres·sive·ness** *n*
sup·pres·sor \-ˈpres-ər\ *n* **:** one that suppresses; *esp* **:** a gene that suppresses the expression of another nonallelic gene when both are present
sup·pu·rate \ˈsəp-yə-ˌrāt\ *vi* **-rat·ed; -rat·ing** [L *suppuratus,* pp. of *suppurare,* fr. *sub-* + *pur-, pus* pus — more at FOUL] **:** to form or discharge pus — **sup·pu·ra·tion** \ˌsəp-yə-ˈrā-shən\ *n* — **sup·pu·ra·tive** \ˈsəp-yə-rət-iv, -ˌrāt-; ˈsəp-rət-iv\ *adj*
supr *abbr* supreme
su·pra \ˈsü-prə, -ˌprä\ *adv* [L] **:** ABOVE **:** earlier in this writing
supra- *prefix* [L, fr. *supra* above, beyond, earlier; akin to L *super* over — more at OVER] **1 :** SUPER- 2a <*supra*orbital> **2 :** transcending <*supra*molecular>
su·pra·lim·i·nal \ˌsü-prə-ˈlim-ən-ᵊl, -ˌprä-\ *adj* [*supra-* + L *limin-, limen* threshold — more at LIMB] **1 :** existing above the threshold of consciousness **2** *of a stimulus* **:** adequate to evoke or be distinguishable as a sensation — **su·pra·lim·i·nal·ly** \-ᵊl-ē\ *adv*
su·pra·mo·lec·u·lar \-mə-ˈlek-yə-lər\ *adj* **:** more complex than a molecule; *also* **:** composed of many molecules
su·pra·na·tion·al \-ˈnash-nəl, -ən-ᵊl\ *adj* **:** transcending national boundaries, authority, or interests <a ~ authority, regulating ocean usage —N. H. Jacoby> <taking a ~ view of economic problems> — **su·pra·na·tion·al·ism** \-ˌiz-əm\ *n* — **su·pra·na·tion·al·ist** \-əst\ *n* — **su·pra·na·tion·al·i·ty** \-ˌnash-ə-ˈnal-ət-ē\ *n*
su·pra·or·bit·al \-ˈȯr-bət-ᵊl\ *adj* [NL *supraorbitalis,* fr. L *supra-* + ML *orbita* orbit] **:** situated or occurring above the orbit of the eye
su·pra·pro·test \-ˈprō-ˌtest\ *n* [modif. of It *sopra protesto* upon protest] **:** an acceptance or payment of a bill by a third person for the honor of the drawer after protest for nonacceptance or nonpayment by the drawee
su·pra·ra·tio·nal \-ˈrash-nəl, -ən-ᵊl\ *adj* **:** transcending the rational **:** based on or involving factors not to be comprehended by reason alone <the stars inspire ~ dreams —R. J. Dubos>
[1]**su·pra·re·nal** \-ˈrēn-ᵊl\ *adj* [NL *suprarenalis,* fr. L *supra-* + *renes* kidneys] **:** situated above or anterior to the kidneys; *specif* **:** ADRENAL
[2]**suprarenal** *n* **:** a suprarenal part; *esp* **:** ADRENAL GLAND
suprarenal gland *n* **:** ADRENAL GLAND
su·pra·seg·men·tal \ˌsü-prə-seg-ˈment-ᵊl, -ˌprä-\ *adj* **:** of or relating to significant features (as stress, pitch, or juncture) that occur simultaneously with vowels and consonants in an utterance
su·pra·vi·tal \-ˈvīt-ᵊl\ *adj* [ISV] **:** constituting or relating to the staining of living tissues or cells surviving after removal from a living body by dyes that penetrate living substance but induce more or less rapid degenerative changes — compare INTRAVITAM 2 — **su·pra·vi·tal·ly** \-ᵊl-ē\ *adv*
su·prem·a·cist \sü-ˈprem-ə-səst\ *n* **:** an advocate or adherent of group supremacy; *esp* **:** WHITE SUPREMACIST
su·prem·a·cy \sü-ˈprem-ə-sē\ *n, pl* **-cies** [*supreme* + *-acy* (as in *primacy*)] **:** the quality or state of being supreme; *also* **:** supreme authority or power

syn SUPREMACY, ASCENDANCY *shared meaning element* : the position of being first (as in rank, power, or influence)

su·preme \sü-ˈprēm\ *adj* [L *supremus,* superl. of *superus* upper — more at SUPERIOR] **1 :** highest in rank or authority <the ~ commander> **2 :** highest in degree or quality <~ endurance in war and in labour —R. W. Emerson> **3 :** ULTIMATE, FINAL <the ~ sacrifice> — **su·preme·ly** *adv* — **su·preme·ness** *n*

Supreme Being *n* **:** GOD 1

supreme court *n* **1 :** the highest judicial tribunal in a political unit (as a nation or state) **2 :** a court of original jurisdiction in New York state that is subordinate to a final court of appeals

Supreme Søviet *n* **:** the highest legislative body of the Soviet Union consisting of two chambers one of which represents the overall population and the other the constituent republics

supt *abbr* superintendent

supvr *abbr* supervisor

sur *abbr* surface

sur- *prefix* [ME, fr. OF, fr. L *super-*] **1 :** over **:** SUPER- <*sur*print> <*sur*tax> **2 :** above **:** up <*sur*base>

su·ra \ˈsu̇r-ə\ *n* [Ar *sūrah,* lit., row] **:** a chapter of the Koran

su·rah \ˈsu̇r-ə\ *n* [prob. alter. of *surat* (a cotton produced in Surat, India)] **:** a soft twilled fabric of silk or rayon

sur·base \ˈsər-ˌbās\ *n* **:** a molding just above the base of a wall, pedestal, or podium

sur·based \-ˌbāst\ *adj* [F *surbaissé*] **1 :** having the curve center below the springing line of imposts <a ~ arch> **2 :** having a surbase

1**sur·cease** \(ˌ)sər-ˈsēs, ˈsər-ˌ\ *vb* **sur·ceased; sur·ceas·ing** [ME *sursesen, surcesen,* fr. MF *sursis,* pp. of *surseoir,* fr. L *supersedēre* — more at SUPERSEDE] *vi* **:** to desist from action; *also* **:** to come to an end **:** CEASE ~ *vt* **:** to put an end to **:** DISCONTINUE

2**sur·cease** \ˈsər-ˌsēs, (ˌ)sər-ˈ\ *n* **:** CESSATION; *esp* **:** a temporary respite or end

1**sur·charge** \ˈsər-ˌchärj\ *vt* [ME *surchargen,* fr. MF *surchargier,* fr. *sur-* + *chargier* to charge] **1 a :** OVERCHARGE **b :** to charge an extra fee **c :** to show an omission in (an account) for which credit ought to have been given **2** *Brit* **:** OVERSTOCK **3 :** to fill or load to excess <the atmosphere . . . was *surcharged* with war hysteria —H. A. Chippendale> **4 a :** to mark a new denomination figure or a surcharge on (a stamp) **b :** OVERPRINT <~ a banknote>

2**surcharge** *n* **1 a :** an additional tax, cost, or impost **b :** an extra fare <a sleeping car ~> **c :** an instance of surcharging an account **2 :** an excessive load or burden **3 :** the action of surcharging **:** the state of being surcharged **4 a (1) :** an overprint on a stamp; *specif* **:** one that alters the denomination **(2) :** a stamp bearing such an overprint **b :** an overprint on a currency note

sur·cin·gle \ˈsər-ˌsiŋ-gəl\ *n* [ME *sursengle,* fr. MF *surcengle,* fr. *sur-* + *cengle* girdle, fr. L *cingulum* — more at CINGULUM] **1 :** a belt, band, or girth passing around the body of a horse to bind a saddle or pack fast to the horse's back **2** *archaic* **:** the girdle or cincture of a cassock

sur·coat \ˈsər-ˌkōt\ *n* [ME *surcote,* fr. MF, fr. *sur-* + *cote* coat] **:** an outer coat or cloak; *specif* **:** a tunic worn over armor

1**surd** \ˈsərd\ *adj* [L *surdus* deaf, silent, stupid; akin to L *susurrus* hum — more at SWARM] **1 :** lacking sense **:** IRRATIONAL <the ~ mystery and the strange forces of existence —D. C. Williams> **2 :** VOICELESS — used of speech sounds

2**surd** *n* **1 a :** an irrational root (as $\sqrt{3}$) **b :** IRRATIONAL NUMBER **2 :** a surd speech sound

1**sure** \ˈshu̇(ə)r, *esp South* ˈshō(ə)r\ *adj* **sur·er; sur·est** [ME, fr. MF *sur,* fr. L *securus* secure] **1** *obs* **:** safe from danger or harm **2 :** firmly established **:** STEADFAST <a ~ hold> **3 :** RELIABLE, TRUSTWORTHY **4 :** marked by or given to feelings of confident certainty <he was ~ he was right> **5 :** admitting of no doubt **:** CERTAIN, INDISPUTABLE <spoke from ~ knowledge> **6 a :** bound to happen **:** INEVITABLE <~ disaster> **b :** BOUND, DESTINED <he is ~ to win> — **sure·ness** *n*

syn SURE, CERTAIN, POSITIVE, COCKSURE *shared meaning element* **:** having no doubt or uncertainty *ant* unsure

— **for sure :** as a certainty **:** ASSUREDLY — **to be sure :** it must be acknowledged **:** ADMITTEDLY

2**sure** *adv* **:** SURELY

sure–enough \ˌshu̇r-ə-ˌnəf\ *adj* **:** ACTUAL, GENUINE, REAL

sure enough *adv* **:** as one might confidently expect **:** CERTAINLY

sure·fire \ˌshu̇r-ˌfī(ə)r\ *adj* **:** certain to get results <a ~ recipe>

sure·foot·ed \ˈshu̇(ə)r-ˈfu̇t-əd\ *adj* **:** not liable to stumble, fall, or err — **sure·foot·ed·ly** *adv* — **sure·foot·ed·ness** *n*

sure–hand·ed \-ˈhan-dəd\ *adj* **:** having hands that are sure in performing some action **:** PROFICIENT — **sure–hand·ed·ness** *n*

sure·ly \ˈshu̇(ə)r-lē, *esp South* ˈshō(ə)r-\ *adv* **1 :** in a sure manner: **a** *archaic* **:** without danger or risk of injury or loss **:** SAFELY **b (1) :** with assurance **:** CONFIDENTLY <walked slowly but ~> **(2) :** without doubt **:** CERTAINLY <they will ~ be heard from in the future —R. J. Lifton> **2 :** INDEED, REALLY — often used as an intensive <you ~ don't believe that>

sure·ty \ˈshu̇r-ət-ē, ˈshu̇(ə)rt-ē\ *n, pl* **-ties** [ME *surte,* fr. MF *surté,* fr. L *securitat-, securitas* security, fr. *securus*] **1 :** the state of being sure: as **a :** sure knowledge **:** CERTAINTY **b :** confidence in manner or behavior **:** ASSURANCE **2 a :** a formal engagement (as a pledge) given for the fulfillment of an undertaking **:** GUARANTEE **b :** ground of confidence or security **3 :** one who has become legally liable for the debt, default, or failure in duty (as appearance in court) of another — **sure·ty·ship** \-ˌship\ *n*

surety bond *n* **:** a bond guaranteeing performance of a contract or obligation

1**surf** \ˈsərf\ *n* [origin unknown] **1 :** the swell of the sea that breaks upon the shore **2 :** the foam, splash, and sound of breaking waves

2**surf** *vi* **:** to ride the surf (as on a surfboard) — **surf·er** *n*

surf·able \ˈsər-fə-bəl\ *adj* **:** suitable for surfing — used esp. of a wave or a beach

1**sur·face** \ˈsər-fəs\ *n* [F, fr. *sur-* + *face*] **1 :** the exterior or upper boundary of an object or body **2 :** a plane or curved two-dimensional locus of points (as the boundary of a three-dimensional region) <plane ~> <~ of a sphere> **3 a :** the external or superficial aspect of something **b :** an external part or layer <sand down the damaged ~> **4 :** a complete airfoil used for sustentation or control or to increase stability — **on the surface :** to all outward appearances

2**surface** *vb* **sur·faced; sur·fac·ing** *vt* **1 :** to give a surface to: as **a :** to plane or make smooth **b :** to apply the surface layer to <~ a highway> **2 :** to bring to the surface ~ *vi* **1 :** to work on or at the surface **2 :** to come to the surface — **sur·fac·er** *n*

3**surface** *adj* **1 a :** of, located on, or designed for use at the surface of something **b :** situated or employed on the surface of the earth <~ transportation> **2 a :** appearing on the surface only **:** lacking depth <~ realism> **b :** SUPERFICIAL <~ friendships>

surface–active *adj* **:** altering the properties and esp. lowering the tension at the surface of contact between phases <soaps and wetting agents are typical ~ substances>

surface feeder *n* **:** DABBLER b

surface of revolution : a surface formed by the revolution of a plane curve about a line in its plane

sur·face–rip·ened \ˈsər-fəs-ˌrī-pənd, -ˌrīp-ᵊmd\ *adj, of cheese* **:** ripened by the action of microorganisms (as molds or bacteria) on the surface

surface structure *n* **:** a formal representation of the phonetic form of a sentence; *also* **:** the structure which such a representation describes

surface tension *n* **:** a condition that exists at the free surface of a body (as a liquid) by reason of intermolecular forces about the individual surface molecules and is manifested by properties resembling those of an elastic skin under tension

surface–to–air missile *n* **:** a usu. guided missile launched from the ground against a target in the air

sur·fac·ing *n* **:** material forming or used to form a surface

sur·fac·tant \(ˌ)sər-ˈfak-tənt, ˈsər-ˌ\ *n* [*surf*ace-*act*ive + *-ant*] **:** a surface-active substance (as a detergent) — **surfactant** *adj*

surf·bird \ˈsərf-ˌbərd\ *n* **:** a shorebird (*Aphriza virgata*) of the Pacific coasts of America that is related to the turnstones and has the tail blackish at the tip and white at the base

surf·board \-ˌbō(ə)rd, -ˌbȯ(ə)rd\ *n* **:** a long narrow buoyant board (as of lightweight wood or fiber glass covered foam) used in the sport of surfing — **surfboard** *vi* — **surf·board·er** *n*

surf·boat \-ˌbōt\ *n* **:** a boat for use in heavy surf

surf caster *n* **:** one that engages in surf casting

surf casting *n* **:** a method of fishing in which artificial or natural bait is cast into the open ocean or in a bay where waves break on a beach

surf clam *n* **:** any of various typically rather large surf-dwelling edible clams (family Mactridae)

1**sur·feit** \ˈsər-fət\ *n* [ME *surfait,* fr. MF, fr. *surfaire* to overdo, fr. *sur-* + *faire* to do, fr. L *facere* — more at DO] **1 :** an overabundant supply **:** EXCESS **2 :** an intemperate or immoderate indulgence in something (as food or drink) **3 :** disgust caused by excess

2**surfeit** *vt* **:** to feed, supply, or give to surfeit **:** CLOY ~ *vi, archaic* **:** to indulge to satiety in a gratification (as indulgence of the appetite or senses) *syn* see SATIATE — **sur·feit·er** *n*

surf fish *n* **1 :** any of a family (Embiotocidae) of small or medium-sized viviparous fishes of shallow water along the Pacific coast of No. America **2 :** any of several croakers of the same region as the surf fishes

sur·fi·cial \sər-ˈfish-əl\ *adj* [*surf*ace + *-icial* (as in *superficial*)] **:** of or relating to a surface

surf·ing \ˈsər-fiŋ\ *n* **:** the sport of riding the surf esp. on a surfboard

surf·perch \ˈsərf-ˌpərch\ *n* **:** SURF FISH 1

surg *abbr* **1** surgeon **2** surgery **3** surgical

1**surge** \ˈsərj\ *vb* **surged; surg·ing** [MF *sourge-,* stem of *sourdre* to rise, surge, fr. L *surgere* to go straight up, rise, fr. *sub-* up + *regere* to lead straight — more at SUB-, RIGHT] *vi* **1 :** to rise and fall actively **:** TOSS <a ship *surging* in heavy seas> **2 :** to rise and move in waves or billows **:** SWELL **3 :** to slip around a windlass, capstan, or bitts — used esp. of a rope **4 :** to rise suddenly to an excessive or abnormal value — used esp. of current or voltage **5 :** to move with a surge or in surges <felt the blood *surging* into his face —Harry Hervey> ~ *vt* **:** to let go or slacken gradually (as a rope) <~ a hawser to prevent its parting>

2**surge** *n* **1 :** a swelling, rolling, or sweeping forward like that of a wave or series of waves <a ~ of interest> **2 a :** a large wave or billow **:** SWELL **b (1) :** a series of such swells or billows **(2) :** the resulting elevation of water level **3 :** the tapered part of a windlass barrel or a capstan **4 a :** a movement (as a slipping or slackening) of a rope or cable **b :** a sudden jerk or strain caused by such a movement **5 :** a transient sudden rise of current in an electrical circuit

sur·geon \ˈsər-jən\ *n* [ME *surgien,* fr. AF, fr. OF *cirurgien,* fr. *cirurgie* surgery] **:** a medical specialist who practices surgery

surgeon general *n, pl* **surgeons general :** the chief medical officer of a branch of the armed services or of a federal or state public health service

surgeon's knot *n* **:** any of several knots used in tying ligatures or surgical stitches — see KNOT illustration

sur·gery \ˈsərj-(ə-)rē\ *n, pl* **-ger·ies** [ME *surgerie,* fr. OF *cirurgie, surgerie,* fr. L *chirurgia,* fr. Gk *cheirourgia,* fr. *cheirourgos* surgeon, fr. *cheirourgos* working with the hand, fr. *cheir* hand + *ergon* work — more at CHIR-, WORK] **1 :** a branch of medicine concerned with diseases and conditions requiring or amenable to operative or manual procedures **2 a** *Brit* **:** a physician's or dentist's office **b :** a room or area where surgery is performed **3 a :** the work done by a surgeon **b :** OPERATION

sur·gi·cal \ˈsər-ji-kəl\ *adj* [*surg*eon + *-ical*] **1 a :** of or relating to surgeons or surgery <~ skills> **b :** used in or in connection with surgery <a ~ stocking> **2 :** following or resulting from surgery <~ fevers> — **sur·gi·cal·ly** \-k(ə-)lē\ *adv*

sur·jec·tion \(ˌ)sər-ˈjek-shən\ *n* [prob. fr. F *sur* over, on, onto + E *-jection* (as in *projection*) — more at SUR-] : a mathematical function that is an onto mapping
sur·jec·tive \-ˈjek-tiv\ *adj* : ONTO
sur·ly \ˈsər-lē\ *adj* **sur·li·er; -est** [alter. of ME *sirly* lordly, imperious, fr. *sir*] **1** *obs* : ARROGANT, IMPERIOUS **2** : irritably sullen and churlish in mood or manner : CRABBED **3** : menacing or threatening in appearance <~ weather> ***syn*** see SULLEN ***ant*** amiable — **sur·li·ly** \-lə-lē\ *adv* — **sur·li·ness** \-lē-nəs\ *n* — **surly** *adv*
¹sur·mise \sər-ˈmīz\ *vt* **sur·mised; sur·mis·ing** [ME *surmisen* to accuse, fr. MF *surmis*, pp. of *surmetre*, fr. L *supermittere* to throw on, fr. *super-* + *mittere* to send — more at SMITE] : to imagine or infer on slight grounds ***syn*** see CONJECTURE — **sur·mis·er** *n*
²sur·mise \sər-ˈmīz, ˈsər-ˌ\ *n* : a thought or idea based on scanty evidence : CONJECTURE
sur·mount \sər-ˈmau̇nt\ *vt* [ME *surmounten*, fr. MF *surmonter*, fr. *sur-* + *monter* to mount] **1** *obs* : to surpass in quality or attainment : EXCEL **2** : to rise superior to : OVERCOME <~ an obstacle> **3** : to get to the top of : CLIMB **4** : to stand or lie at the top of — **sur·mount·able** \-ə-bəl\ *adj*
sur·mul·let \ˌsər-ˈməl-ət, ˈsər-ˌ\ *n, pl* **surmullets** *also* **surmullet** [F *surmulet*] : MULLET 2
¹sur·name \ˈsər-ˌnām\ *n* **1** : an added name derived from occupation or other circumstance : NICKNAME 1 **2** : the name borne in common by members of a family
²surname *vt* : to give a surname to
sur·pass \sər-ˈpas\ *vt* [MF *surpasser*, fr. *sur-* + *passer* to pass] **1** : to become better, greater, or stronger than : EXCEED **2** : to go beyond : OVERSTEP **3** : to transcend the reach, capacity, or powers of ***syn*** see EXCEED — **sur·pass·able** \-ə-bəl\ *adj*
sur·pass·ing *adj* : greatly exceeding others : of a very high degree — **sur·pass·ing·ly** \-iŋ-lē\ *adv*
¹sur·plice \ˈsər-pləs\ *n* [ME *surplis*, fr. OF *surpliz*, fr. ML *superpellicium*, fr. *super-* + *pellicium* coat of skins, fr. L, neut. of *pellicius* made of skins, fr. *pellis* skin — more at FELL] : a loose white outer ecclesiastical vestment usu. of knee length with large open sleeves
²surplice *adj* : having a diagonally overlapping neckline or closing <a ~ collar> <~ sweaters>
sur·plus \ˈsər-(ˌ)pləs\ *n* [ME, fr. MF, fr. ML *superplus*, fr. L *super-* + *plus* more — more at PLUS] **1 a** : the amount that remains when use or need is satisfied **b** : an excess of receipts over disbursements **2** : the excess of a corporation's net worth over the par or stated value of its capital stock — **surplus** *adj*
sur·plus·age \-(ˌ)pləs-ij\ *n* **1** : SURPLUS 1a **2 a** : excessive or nonessential matter **b** : matter introduced in legal pleading which is not necessary or relevant to the case
surplus value *n* : the difference in Marxist theory between the value of work done or of commodities produced by labor and the usu. subsistence wages paid by the employer
sur·print \ˈsər-ˌprint\ *vt or n* : OVERPRINT
sur·pris·al \sə(r)-ˈprī-zəl\ *n* : the action of surprising : the state of being surprised
¹sur·prise \sə(r)-ˈprīz\ *n* [ME, fr. MF, fr. fem. of *surpris*, pp. of *surprendre* to take over, surprise, fr. *sur-* + *prendre* to take — more at PRIZE] **1 a** : an attack made without warning **b** : a taking unawares **2** : something that surprises **3** : the state of being surprised : ASTONISHMENT
²surprise *also* **sur·prize** *vt* **sur·prised; sur·pris·ing** **1** : to attack unexpectedly; *also* : to capture by an unexpected attack **2 a** : to take unawares **b** : to detect or elicit by a taking unawares **3** : to strike with wonder or amazement esp. because unexpected — **sur·pris·er** *n*
syn **1** SURPRISE, WAYLAY, AMBUSH *shared meaning element* : to attack unawares
2 SURPRISE, ASTONISH, ASTOUND, AMAZE, FLABBERGAST *shared meaning element* : to impress forcibly through unexpectedness, startlingness, or unusualness
sur·pris·ing *adj* : of a nature that excites surprise — **sur·pris·ing·ly** \-ˈprī-ziŋ-lē\ *adv*
sur·ra \ˈsu̇r-ə\ *n* [Marathi *sūra* wheezing sound] : a severe Old World febrile and hemorrhagic disease of domestic animals that is caused by a flagellate protozoan (*Trypanosoma evansi*) and is transmitted by biting insects
sur·re·al \sə-ˈrē(-ə)l, -ˈri-əl *also* -ˈrā-əl\ *adj* [back-formation fr. *surrealism*] **1** : having the intense irrational reality of a dream **2** : SURREALISTIC
sur·re·al·ism \sə-ˈrē-ə-ˌliz-əm, -ˈri- *also* -ˈrā-\ *n* [F *surréalisme*, fr. *sur-* + *réalisme* realism] : the principles, ideals, or practice of producing fantastic or incongruous imagery or effects in art, literature, or theater by means of unnatural juxtapositions and combinations — **sur·re·al·ist** \-ləst\ *n or adj*
sur·re·al·is·tic \-ˌrē-ə-ˈlis-tik, -ˌri- *also* -ˌrā-\ *adj* **1** : of or relating to surrealism **2** : having a strange dreamlike atmosphere or quality like that of a surrealist painting <the ~ quality of Chinese politics —*Newsweek*> — **sur·re·al·is·ti·cal·ly** \-ti-k(ə-)lē\ *adv*
sur·re·but·ter \ˌsər-(r)i-ˈbət-ər\ *n* : the reply in common law pleading of a plaintiff to a defendant's rebutter
sur·re·join·der \-(r)i-ˈjȯin-dər\ *n* : the reply in common law pleading of a plaintiff to a defendant's rejoinder
¹sur·ren·der \sə-ˈren-dər\ *vb* **sur·ren·dered; sur·ren·der·ing** \-d(ə-)riŋ\ [ME *surrenderen*, fr. MF *surrendre*, fr. *sur-* + *rendre* to give back, yield — more at RENDER] *vt* **1 a** : to yield to the power, control, or possession of another upon compulsion or demand <~*ed* the fort> **b** : to give up completely or agree to forgo esp. in favor of another **2 a** : to give (oneself) up into the power of another esp. as a prisoner **b** : to give (oneself) over to something (as an influence or course of action) ~ *vi* : to give oneself up into the power of another : YIELD ***syn*** see RELINQUISH
²surrender *n* **1 a** : the action of yielding one's person or giving up the possession of something into the power of another **b** : the relinquishment by a patentee of his rights or claims under a patent **c** : the delivery of a principal into lawful custody by his bail — called also *surrender by bail* **d** : the voluntary cancellation of the legal liability of an insurance company by the insured and beneficiary for a consideration **e** : the delivery of a fugitive from justice by one government to another **2** : an instance of surrendering
syn SURRENDER, SUBMISSION, CAPITULATION *shared meaning element* : the yielding of one's person, forces, or possessions to another
sur·rep·ti·tious \ˌsər-əp-ˈtish-əs, ˌsə-rəp-, sə-ˌrep-\ *adj* [ME, fr. L *surrepticius*, fr. *surreptus*, pp. of *surripere* to snatch secretly, fr. *sub-* + *rapere* to seize — more at RAPID] **1** : done, made, or acquired by stealth : CLANDESTINE **2** : acting or doing something clandestinely : STEALTHY ***syn*** see SECRET — **sur·rep·ti·tious·ly** *adv* — **sur·rep·ti·tious·ness** *n*
sur·rey \ˈsər-ē, ˈsə-rē\ *n, pl* **surreys** [*Surrey*, England] : a four-wheel two-seated horse-drawn pleasure carriage

surrey

¹sur·ro·gate \ˈsər-ə-ˌgāt, ˈsə-rə-\ *vt* **-gat·ed; -gat·ing** [L *surrogatus*, pp. of *surrogare* to choose in place of another, substitute, fr. *sub-* + *rogare* to ask — more at RIGHT] : to put in the place of another: **a** : to appoint as successor, deputy, or substitute for oneself **b** : SUBSTITUTE
²sur·ro·gate \-ˌgāt, -gət\ *n, often attrib* **1 a** : a person appointed to act in place of another : DEPUTY **b** : a local judicial officer in some states (as New York) who has jurisdiction over the probate of wills, the settlement of estates, and the appointment and supervision of guardians **2** : something that serves as a substitute
sur·ro·ga·tion \ˌsər-ə-ˈgā-shən, ˌsə-rə-\ *n* : the use of surrogates (as abstracts) in place of longer items (as documents) in an information retrieval system
¹sur·round \sə-ˈrau̇nd\ *vt* [ME *surrounden* to overflow, fr. MF *suronder*, fr. LL *superundare*, fr. L *super-* + *unda* wave; influenced in meaning by ⁶*round* — more at WATER] **1 a** (1) : to enclose on all sides : ENVELOP <was ~*ed* by a crowd of people —Jonathan Swift> (2) : to enclose so as to cut off communication or retreat : INVEST **b** : to form or be a member of the entourage of <flatterers who ~ the king> **c** : to constitute part of the environment of <~*ed* by luxury> **d** : to extend around the margin or edge of : ENCIRCLE <a wall ~*s* the old city> **2** : to cause to be surrounded by something <he ~*ed* himself with able advisers>
²surround *n* : something (as a border) that surrounds <from urban centre to rural ~ —Emrys Jones>
sur·round·ings \sə-ˈrau̇n-diŋz\ *n pl* : the circumstances, conditions, or objects by which one is surrounded : ENVIRONMENT
sur·roy·al \ˈsər-ˌrȯi(-ə)l\ *n* [ME *surryal*, fr. *sur-* + *royal* royal antler] : one of the terminal tines above the royal antler of a large deer (as a stag) usu. attained at the age of four years — see ANTLER illustration
sur·sum cor·da \ˌsu̇(ə)r-səm-ˈkȯrd-ə, -ˈkȯ(ə)r-ˌdä\ *n* [LL, (lift) up (your) hearts] **1** *often cap S&C* : a versicle that in traditional eucharistic liturgies exhorts the faithful to enthusiastic worship **2** : something inspiriting
sur·tax \ˈsər-ˌtaks\ *n* **1** : an extra tax or charge **2** : a graduated income tax in addition to the normal income tax imposed on the amount by which one's net income exceeds a specified sum
sur·tout \(ˌ)sər-ˈtü, ˈsər-ˌ\ *n* [F, fr. *sur* over (fr. L *super*) + *tout* all, fr. L *totus* whole — more at OVER] : a man's long close-fitting overcoat
surv *abbr* survey; surveying; surveyor
sur·veil·lance \sər-ˈvā-lən(t)s *also* -ˈvāl-yən(t)s *or* -ˈvā-ən(t)s\ *n* [F, fr. *surveiller* to watch over, fr. *sur-* + *veiller* to watch, fr. L *vigilare*, fr. *vigil* watchful — more at VIGIL] : close watch kept over someone or something (as by a detective); *also* : SUPERVISION ***syn*** see OVERSIGHT — **sur·veil** \-ˈvā(ə)l\ *vt*
sur·veil·lant \-ˈvā-lənt *also* -ˈvāl-yənt *or* -ˈvā-ənt\ *n* : one that exercises surveillance
¹sur·vey \sər-ˈvā, ˈsər-ˌ\ *vb* **sur·veyed; sur·vey·ing** [ME *surveyen*, fr. MF *surveeir* to look over, fr. *sur-* + *veeir* to see — more at VIEW] *vt* **1 a** : to examine as to condition, situation, or value : APPRAISE **b** : to make a survey of **2** : to determine and delineate the form, extent, and position of (as a tract of land) by taking linear and angular measurements and by applying the principles of geometry and trigonometry **3** : to view or consider comprehensively **4** : INSPECT, SCRUTINIZE <he ~*ed* us in a lordly way —Alan Harrington> ~ *vi* : to make a survey
²sur·vey \ˈsər-ˌvā, sər-ˈ\ *n, pl* **surveys** : the act or an instance of surveying; *also* : something that is surveyed
survey course \ˈsər-ˌvā-\ *n* : a course treating briefly the chief topics of a broad field of knowledge
sur·vey·ing \sər-ˈvā-iŋ\ *n* : a branch of applied mathematics that teaches the art of determining the area of any portion of the earth's surface, the lengths and directions of the bounding lines, and the contour of the surface and of accurately delineating the whole on paper
sur·vey·or \sər-ˈvā-ər\ *n* : one that surveys; *esp* : one whose occupation is surveying land
surveyor's level *n* : a level consisting of a telescope and a spirit level mounted on a tripod and revolving on a vertical axis
sur·viv·able \sər-ˈvī-və-bəl\ *adj* : resulting in or permitting survival — **sur·viv·abil·i·ty** \-ˌvī-və-ˈbil-ət-ē\ *n*

sur·viv·al \sər-ˈvī-vəl\ *n* **1 a :** a living or continuing longer than another person or thing **b :** the continuation of life or existence <problems of ~ in arctic conditions> **2 :** one that survives

survival of the fittest : NATURAL SELECTION

survival value *n* **:** utility in the struggle for existence

sur·viv·ance \sər-ˈvī-vən(t)s\ *n* **:** SURVIVAL

sur·vive \sər-ˈvīv\ *vb* **sur·vived; sur·viv·ing** [ME *surviven,* fr. MF *survivre* to outlive, fr. L *supervivere,* fr. *super-* + *vivere* to live — more at QUICK] *vi* **:** to remain alive or in existence **:** live on <managed to ~ on bread and water> ~ *vt* **1 :** to remain alive after the death of <his son *survived* him> **2 :** to continue to exist or live after <*survived* the earthquake> — **sur·vi·vor** \-ˈvī-vər\ *n*

sur·viv·er \-ˈvī-vər\ *n, archaic* **:** one that survives **:** SURVIVOR

sur·vi·vor·ship \-ˈvī-vər-ˌship\ *n* **1 :** the legal right of the survivor of persons having joint interests in property (as an estate) to take the interest of the person who has died **2 :** the state of being a survivor

Su·san B. An·tho·ny Day \ˌsüz-ᵊn-ˌbē-ˈan(t)-thə-nē-\ *n* **:** February 15 observed in commemoration of the birthday of Susan B. Anthony

sus·cep·ti·bil·i·ty \sə-ˌsep-tə-ˈbil-ət-ē\ *n, pl* **-ties 1 :** the quality or state of being susceptible; *esp* **:** lack of ability to resist some extraneous agent (as a pathogen or drug) **:** SENSITIVITY **2 a :** a susceptible temperament or constitution **b** *pl* **:** FEELINGS, SENSIBILITIES **3 a :** the ratio of the magnetization in a substance to the corresponding magnetizing force **b :** the ratio of the electric polarization to the electric intensity in a polarized dielectric

sus·cep·ti·ble \sə-ˈsep-tə-bəl\ *adj* [LL *susceptibilis,* fr. L *susceptus,* pp. of *suscipere* to take up, admit, fr. *sub-, sus-* up + *capere* to take — more at SUB-, HEAVE] **1 :** capable of submitting to an action, process, or operation <a theory ~ to proof> **2 :** open, subject, or unresistant to some stimulus, influence, or agency <the foibles of the health faddists are particularly ~ to satire —Arthur Knight> **3 :** IMPRESSIONABLE, RESPONSIVE — **sus·cep·ti·ble·ness** *n* — **sus·cep·ti·bly** \-blē\ *adv*

sus·cep·tive \-tiv\ *adj* **1 :** RECEPTIVE **2 :** SUSCEPTIBLE — **sus·cep·tive·ness** *n* — **sus·cep·tiv·i·ty** \sə-ˌsep-ˈtiv-ət-ē\ *n*

su·slik \ˈsü-slik\ *n* [Russ] **1 :** any of several rather large short-tailed ground squirrels (genus *Citellus*) of eastern Europe or northern Asia **2 :** the mottled grayish black fur of a suslik

[1]**sus·pect** \ˈsəs-ˌpekt, sə-ˈspekt\ *adj* [ME, fr. MF, fr. L *suspectus,* fr. pp. of *suspicere*] **:** regarded or deserving to be regarded with suspicion **:** SUSPECTED

[2]**sus·pect** \ˈsəs-ˌpekt\ *n* **:** one who is suspected; *esp* **:** one suspected of a crime

[3]**sus·pect** \sə-ˈspekt\ *vb* [ME *suspecten,* fr. L *suspectare,* fr. *suspectus,* pp. of *suspicere* to look up at, regard with awe, suspect, fr. *sub-, sus-* up, secretly + *specere* to look at — more at SUB-, SPY] *vt* **1 :** to have doubts of **:** DISTRUST **2 :** to imagine (one) to be guilty or culpable on slight evidence or without proof <~ him of giving false information> **3 :** to imagine to be or be true, likely, or probable <I know that he is honest and ~ that he is right —H. L. Mencken> ~ *vi* **:** to imagine something to be true or likely

sus·pend \sə-ˈspend\ *vb* [ME *suspenden,* fr. OF *suspendre* to hang up, interrupt, fr. L *suspendere,* fr. *sub-, sus-* up + *pendere* to cause to hang, weigh — more at PENDANT] *vt* **1 :** to debar temporarily from a privilege, office, or function <~ a student from school> **2 a :** to cause to stop temporarily <~ bus service> **b :** to set aside or make temporarily inoperative <~ the rules> **3 :** to defer till later on specified conditions <~ sentence> **4 :** to hold in an undetermined or undecided state awaiting fuller information <~ judgment> **5 a :** HANG; *esp* **:** to hang so as to be free on all sides except at the point of support <~ a ball by a thread> **b :** to keep from falling or sinking by some invisible support (as buoyancy) <dust ~*ed* in the air> **6 a :** to keep fixed or lost (as in wonder or contemplation) **b :** to keep waiting in suspense or indecision **7 :** to hold (a musical note) over into the following chord ~ *vi* **1 :** to cease temporarily from operation **2 :** to stop payment or fail to meet obligations **3 :** HANG ***syn*** see EXCLUDE, DEFER

suspended animation *n* **:** temporary suspension of the vital functions (as in persons nearly drowned)

sus·pend·er \sə-ˈspen-dər\ *n* **1 :** one that suspends **2 :** a device by which something may be suspended: as **a :** one of two supporting bands worn across the shoulders to support trousers, skirt, or belt — usu. used in pl. and often with *pair* **b** *Brit* **:** GARTER

sus·pense \sə-ˈspen(t)s\ *n* [ME, fr. MF, fr. *suspendre*] **1 :** the state of being suspended **:** SUSPENSION **2 a :** mental uncertainty **:** ANXIETY **b :** pleasant excitement as to a decision or outcome <a novel of ~> **3 :** the state or character of being undecided or doubtful **:** INDECISIVENESS — **sus·pense·ful** \-fəl\ *adj*

suspense account *n* **:** an account for the temporary entry of charges or credits or esp. of doubtful accounts receivable pending determination of their ultimate disposition

sus·pen·sion \sə-ˈspen-chən\ *n* [LL *suspension-, suspensio,* fr. L *suspensus,* pp. of *suspendere*] **1 :** the act of suspending **:** the state or period of being suspended: as **a :** temporary removal from office or privileges **b :** temporary withholding (as of belief or decision) **c :** temporary abrogation of a law or rule **d** (1) **:** the holding over of one or more musical tones of a chord into the following chord producing a momentary discord and suspending the concord which the ear expects; *specif* **:** such a dissonance which resolves downward — compare RETARDATION (2) **:** the tone thus held over **e :** stoppage of payment of business obligations **:** FAILURE — used esp. of a business or a bank **f :** a rhetorical device whereby the principal idea is deferred to the end of a sentence or longer unit **2 a :** the act of hanging **:** the state of being hung **b** (1) **:** the state of a substance when its particles are mixed with but undissolved in a fluid or solid (2) **:** a substance in this state (3) **:** a system consisting of a solid dispersed in a solid, liquid, or gas usu. in particles of larger than colloidal size — compare EMULSION **3 :** something suspended **4 a :** a device by which something (as a magnetic needle) is suspended **b :** the system of devices (as springs) supporting the upper part of a vehicle on the axles **c :** the act, process, or manner in which the pendulum or torsion balance of a timepiece is suspended

suspension bridge *n* **:** a bridge that has its roadway suspended from two or more cables usu. passing over towers and securely anchored at the ends — see BRIDGE illustration

suspension points *n pl* **:** usu. three spaced periods used to show the omission of a word or word group from a written context

sus·pen·sive \sə-ˈspen(t)-siv\ *adj* **1 :** stopping temporarily **:** SUSPENDING **2 :** characterized by suspense, suspended judgment, or indecisiveness **3 :** characterized by suspension — **sus·pen·sive·ly** *adv*

sus·pen·soid \sə-ˈspen(t)-ˌsȯid\ *n* [ISV *suspens*ion + coll*oid*] **1 :** a colloidal system in which the dispersed particles are solid **2 :** a lyophobic sol (as a gold sol)

sus·pen·sor \sə-ˈspen(t)-sər\ *n* [NL, fr. *suspensus,* pp.] **:** a suspending part or structure: as **a :** a group or chain of cells that is produced from the zygote of a heterosporous plant and serves to push the embryo which arises at its extremity deeper into the embryo sac and into contact with the food supply of the megaspore **b :** one of the two hyphae in fungi (order Mucorales) that bear gametangia at their tips and later support the zygospore

[1]**sus·pen·so·ry** \sə-ˈspen(t)s-(ə-)rē\ *adj* **1 :** held in suspension; *also* **:** fitted or serving to suspend **2 :** temporarily leaving undetermined **:** SUSPENSIVE 1

[2]**suspensory** *n, pl* **-ries :** something that suspends or holds up; *esp* **:** a fabric supporter for the scrotum

suspensory ligament *n* **1 :** an annular fibrous membrane holding the lens of the eye in place — see EYE illustration **2 :** the falciform ligament of the liver

[1]**sus·pi·cion** \sə-ˈspish-ən\ *n* [ME, fr. L *suspicion-, suspicio,* fr. *suspicere* to suspect — more at SUSPECT] **1 a :** the act or an instance of suspecting something wrong without proof or on slight evidence **:** MISTRUST **b :** a state of mental uneasiness and uncertainty **:** DOUBT **2 :** a slight touch or trace <just a ~ of garlic> ***syn*** see UNCERTAINTY

[2]**suspicion** *vt* **sus·pi·cioned; sus·pi·cion·ing** \-ˈspish-(ə-)niŋ\ *chiefly substand* **:** SUSPECT

sus·pi·cious \sə-ˈspish-əs\ *adj* **1 :** tending to arouse suspicion **:** QUESTIONABLE **2 :** disposed to suspect **:** DISTRUSTFUL <~ of strangers> **3 :** expressing or indicative of suspicion <a ~ glance> — **sus·pi·cious·ly** *adv* — **sus·pi·cious·ness** *n*

sus·pi·ra·tion \ˌsəs-pə-ˈrā-shən\ *n* **:** a long deep breath **:** SIGH

sus·pire \sə-ˈspī(ə)r\ *vi* **sus·pired; sus·pir·ing** [ME *suspiren,* fr. L *suspirare,* fr. *sub-* + *spirare* to breathe — more at SPIRIT] **:** to draw a long deep breath **:** SIGH

Suss *abbr* Sussex

Sus·sex spaniel \ˌsəs-ik(s)-, -ˌek(s)-\ *n* [*Sussex,* England] **:** any of a British breed of short-legged short-necked long-bodied spaniels with a flat or slightly wavy golden liver-colored coat

sus·tain \sə-ˈstān\ *vt* [ME *sustenen,* fr. OF *sustenir,* fr. L *sustinēre* to hold up, sustain, fr. *sub-, sus-* up + *tenēre* to hold — more at SUB-, THIN] **1 :** to give support or relief to **2 :** to supply with sustenance **:** NOURISH **3 :** to keep up **:** PROLONG **4 :** to support the weight of **:** PROP; *also* **:** to carry or withstand (a weight or pressure) **5 :** to buoy up **6 a :** to bear up under **b :** SUFFER, UNDERGO <~*ed* heavy losses> <~*ed* a concussion of the brain —Allan Nevins> **7 a :** to support as true, legal, or just **b :** to allow or admit as valid <the court ~*ed* the motion> **8 :** to support by adequate proof **:** CONFIRM <testimony that ~*s* our contention> — **sus·tain·able** \-ˈstā-nə-bəl\ *adj* — **sus·tain·er** *n*

sus·tain·ing *adj* **1 a :** serving to sustain **b :** aiding in the support of an organization through a special fee <a ~ member> **2 :** of or relating to a sustaining program

sustaining program *n* **:** a radio or television program that is paid for by a station or network and has no commercial sponsor

sus·te·nance \ˈsəs-tə-nən(t)s\ *n* [ME, fr. OF, fr. *sustenir*] **1 a :** means of support, maintenance, or subsistence **:** LIVING **b :** FOOD, PROVISIONS; *also* **:** NOURISHMENT **2 a :** the act of sustaining **:** the state of being sustained **b :** a supplying or being supplied with the necessaries of life **3 :** something that gives support, endurance, or strength

sus·ten·tac·u·lar \ˌsəs-tən-ˈtak-yə-lər, -ˌten-\ *adj* [NL *sustentaculum* supporting part, fr. L, prop, fr. *sustentare*] **:** serving to support or sustain

sus·ten·ta·tion \-ˈtā-shən\ *n* [ME, fr. MF, fr. L *sustentation-, sustentatio* act of holding up, fr. *sustentatus,* pp. of *sustentare* to hold up, fr. *sustentus,* pp. of *sustinēre*] **1 :** the act of sustaining **:** the state of being sustained: as **a :** MAINTENANCE, UPKEEP **b :** PRESERVATION, CONSERVATION **c :** maintenance of life, growth, or morale **d :** provision with sustenance **2 :** something that sustains **:** SUPPORT — **sus·ten·ta·tive** \ˈsəs-tən-ˌtāt-iv, sə-ˈstent-ət-\ *adj*

sus·ten·tion \sə-ˈsten-chən\ *n* [fr. *sustain,* after such pairs as E *retain* : *retention*] **:** SUSTENTATION

Su·su \ˈsü-(ˌ)sü\ *n, pl* **Susu** *or* **Susus 1 :** a member of a West African people of Mali, Guinea, and the area along the northern border of Sierra Leone **2 :** the language of the Susu people

su·sur·ra·tion \ˌsü-sə-ˈrā-shən\ *n* **:** a whispering sound **:** MURMUR

su·sur·rous \sů-ˈsər-əs, -ˈsə-rəs\ *adj* **:** full of whispering sounds

su·sur·rus \sů-ˈsər-əs, -ˈsə-rəs\ *n* [L, hum, whisper — more at SWARM] **:** a whispering or rustling sound — **su·sur·rant** \-ˈsər-ənt, -ˈsə-rənt\ *adj*

Suth *abbr* Sutherlandshire

sut·ler \ˈsət-lər\ *n* [obs. D *soeteler,* fr. LG *suteler* sloppy worker, camp cook; akin to OE be*sūtian* to dirty, Gk *hyein* to rain — more at SUCK] **:** a provisioner to an army post often established in a shop on the post

su·tra \ˈsü-trə\ *n* [Skt *sūtra* thread, string of precepts, sutra; akin to L *suere* to sew — more at SEW] **1 :** a precept summarizing Vedic teaching; *also* **:** a collection of these precepts **2 :** a discourse of the Buddha

sut·tee \(ˌ)sə-ˈtē, ˈsə-ˌtē\ *n* [Skt *satī* wife who performs suttee, lit., good woman, fr. fem. of *sat* true, good; akin to OE *sōth* true — more at SOOTH] **:** the act or custom of a Hindu widow willingly being cremated on the funeral pile of her husband as an indication of her devotion to him; *also* **:** a woman cremated in this way

[1]**su·ture** \ˈsü-chər\ *n* [MF & L; MF, fr. L *sutura* seam, suture, fr. *sutus*, pp. of *suere* to sew — more at SEW] **1 a :** a strand or fiber used to sew parts of the living body **b :** a stitch made with a suture **c :** the act or process of sewing with sutures **2 a :** a uniting of parts **b :** the seam or seamlike line along which two things or parts are sewed or united **3 a :** the line of union in an immovable articulation (as between the bones of the skull); *also* **:** such an articulation **b :** a furrow at the junction of adjacent bodily parts; *esp* **:** a line of dehiscence (as on a fruit) — **su·tur·al** \ˈsüch(-ə)-rəl\ *adj* — **su·tur·al·ly** \-rə-lē\ *adv*

[2]**suture** *vt* **su·tured; su·tur·ing** \ˈsüch-(ə-)riŋ\ **:** to unite, close, or secure with sutures <~ a wound>

su·zer·ain \ˈsüz-(ə-)rən, -ə-ˌrān\ *n* [F, fr. (assumed) MF *suserain*, fr. MF *sus* up (fr. L *sursum*, fr. *sub-* up + *versum* -ward, fr. neut. of *versus*, pp. of *vertere* to turn) + *-erain* (as in *soverain* sovereign) — more at SUB-, WORTH] **1 :** a superior feudal lord to whom fealty is due **:** OVERLORD **2 :** a dominant state controlling the foreign relations of a vassal state but allowing it sovereign authority in its internal affairs

su·zer·ain·ty \-tē\ *n* [F *suzeraineté*, fr. MF *susereneté*, fr. (assumed) MF *suserain*] **:** the dominion of a suzerain **:** OVERLORDSHIP

sv *abbr* **1** sailing vessel **2** saves **3** [L *sub verbo* or *sub voce*] under the word

svc *or* **svce** *abbr* service

sved·berg \ˈsfed-ˌbərg, -ˌber-ē\ *n* [The *Svedberg* †1971 Sw chemist] **:** a unit of time amounting to 10^{-13} second that is used to measure the sedimentation velocity of a colloidal solution (as of a protein) in an ultracentrifuge and to determine molecular weight by substitution in an equation — called also *svedberg unit*

svelte \ˈsfelt\ *adj* [F, fr. It *svelto*, fr. pp. of *svellere* to pluck out, modif. of L *evellere*, fr. *e-* + *vellere* to pluck — more at VULNERABLE] **1 a :** SLENDER, LITHE **b :** having clean lines **:** SLEEK **2 :** URBANE, SUAVE — **svelte·ly** *adv* — **svelte·ness** *n*

Sven·ga·li \sfen-ˈgäl-ē\ *n* [*Svengali*, maleficent hypnotist in the novel *Trilby* (1894) by George du Maurier] **:** one who attempts usu. with evil intentions to persuade or force another to do his bidding

svgs *abbr* savings

sw *abbr* switch

Sw *abbr* Sweden; Swedish

SW *abbr* **1** seawater **2** shipper's weight **3** shortwave **4** southwest

SWA *abbr* South-West Africa

[1]**swab** \ˈswäb\ *n* [prob. fr. obs. D *swabbe*; akin to LG *swabber* mop] **1 a :** MOP; *esp* **:** a yarn mop **b (1) :** a wad of absorbent material usu. wound around one end of a small stick and used for applying medication or for removing material from an area **(2) :** a specimen taken with a swab **c :** a sponge attached to a long handle and used to clean the bore of a firearm **2 a :** a useless or contemptible person **b :** SAILOR, GOB

[2]**swab** *vt* **swabbed; swab·bing** [back-formation fr. *swabber*] **1 :** to clean with or as if with a swab **2 :** to apply medication to with a swab <*swabbed* the wound with iodine>

swab·ber \ˈswäb-ər\ *n* [akin to LG *swabber* mop, ME *swabben* to sway] **1 :** one that swabs **2 :** SWAB 2a

swab·bie *also* **swab·by** \-ē\ *n, pl* **swabbies** *slang* **:** SWAB 2b

swad·dle \ˈswäd-ᵊl\ *vt* **swad·dled; swad·dling** \ˈswäd-liŋ, -ᵊl-iŋ\ [ME *swadelen, swathelen*, prob. alter. of *swedelen, swethelen*, fr. *swethel* swaddling band, fr. OE; akin to OE *swathian* to swathe] **1 a :** to wrap (an infant) with swaddling clothes **b :** SWATHE, ENVELOP **2 :** RESTRAIN, RESTRICT

swaddling clothes *n pl* **1 :** narrow strips of cloth wrapped around an infant to restrict movement **2 :** limitations or restrictions imposed upon the immature or inexperienced

[1]**swag** \ˈswag\ *vi* **swagged; swag·ging** [prob. of Scand origin; akin to ON *sveggja* to cause to sway; akin to OHG *swingan* to swing] **1 :** SWAY, LURCH **2 :** SAG

[2]**swag** *n* **1 :** SWAY **2 a :** something (as a decoration) hanging in a curve between two points **:** FESTOON **b :** a suspended cluster (as of evergreen branches) **3 a :** goods acquired by unlawful means **:** LOOT **b :** SPOILS, PROFITS **4 :** a depression in the earth **5** *chiefly Austral* **:** a pack of personal belongings

[1]**swage** \ˈswāj, ˈswej\ *n* [ME, ornamental border, fr. MF *souage*] **:** a tool used by workers in metals for shaping their work by holding it on the work, or the work on it and striking with a hammer or sledge

[2]**swage** *vt* **swaged; swag·ing :** to shape by or as if by means of a swage

swage block *n* **:** a perforated cast-iron or steel block with grooved sides that is used in heading bolts and swaging bars by hand

[1]**swag·ger** \ˈswag-ər\ *vb* **swag·gered; swag·ger·ing** \-(ə-)riŋ\ [prob. fr. [1]*swag* + *-er* (as in *chatter*)] *vi* **1 :** to conduct oneself in an arrogant or superciliously pompous manner; *esp* **:** to walk with an air of overbearing self-confidence **2 :** BOAST, BRAG ~ *vt* **:** to force by argument or threat **:** BULLY *syn* see STRUT — **swag·ger·er** \-ər-ər\ *n* — **swag·ger·ing·ly** \-(ə-)riŋ-lē\ *adv*

[2]**swagger** *n* **1 a :** an act or instance of swaggering **b :** arrogant or conceitedly self-assured behavior **c :** ostentatious display or bravado **2 :** a self-confident outlook **:** COCKINESS

[3]**swagger** *adj* **:** marked by elegance or showiness **:** POSH

swagger stick *n* **:** a short light stick usu. covered with leather and tipped with metal at each end and intended for carrying in the hand (as by military officers)

swag·man \ˈswag-mən\ *n, chiefly Austral* **:** VAGRANT 2; *esp* **:** one who carries a swag when traveling

Swa·hi·li \swä-ˈhē-lē\ *n, pl* **Swahili** *or* **Swahilis** [Ar *sawāhil*, pl. of *sāhil* coast] **1 :** a member of a Bantu-speaking people of Zanzibar and the adjacent coast **2 :** a Bantu language that is a trade and governmental language over much of East Africa and in the Congo region

swain \ˈswān\ *n* [ME *swein* boy, servant, fr. ON *sveinn*; akin to OE *swān* swain, L *suus* one's own — more at SUICIDE] **1 :** RUSTIC, PEASANT; *specif* **:** SHEPHERD **2 :** a male admirer or suitor — **swain·ish** \ˈswā-nish\ *adj* — **swain·ish·ness** *n*

swale \ˈswā(ə)l\ *n* [ME, shade, prob. of Scand origin; akin to ON *svalr* cool; akin to OE *swelan* to burn — more at SWELTER] **:** a low-lying or depressed and often wet stretch of land

[1]**swal·low** \ˈswäl-(ˌ)ō, -ə(-w)\ *n* [ME *swalowe*, fr. OE *swealwe*; akin to OHG *swalawa* swallow, Russ *soloveĭ* nightingale] **1 :** any of numerous small long-winged passerine birds (family Hirundinidae) that are noted for their graceful flight and regular migrations, have a short bill with a wide gape, small weak feet, and often a deeply forked tail, occur in all parts of the world except New Zealand and polar regions, and feed on insects caught on the wing **2 :** any of several swifts that superficially resemble swallows

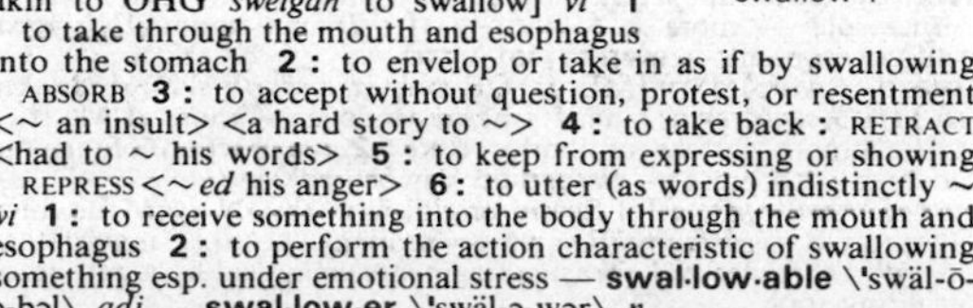
swallow 1

[2]**swallow** *vb* [ME *swalowen*, fr. OE *swelgan*; akin to OHG *swelgan* to swallow] *vt* **1 :** to take through the mouth and esophagus into the stomach **2 :** to envelop or take in as if by swallowing **:** ABSORB **3 :** to accept without question, protest, or resentment <~ an insult> <a hard story to ~> **4 :** to take back **:** RETRACT <had to ~ his words> **5 :** to keep from expressing or showing **:** REPRESS <~*ed* his anger> **6 :** to utter (as words) indistinctly ~ *vi* **1 :** to receive something into the body through the mouth and esophagus **2 :** to perform the action characteristic of swallowing something esp. under emotional stress — **swal·low·able** \ˈswäl-ō-ə-bəl\ *adj* — **swal·low·er** \ˈswäl-ə-wər\ *n*

[3]**swallow** *n* **1 :** the passage connecting the mouth to the stomach **2 :** a capacity for swallowing **3 a :** an act of swallowing **b :** an amount that can be swallowed at one time **4 :** an aperture in a block on a ship between the sheave and frame through which the rope reeves

swal·low·tail \ˈswäl-ō-ˌtāl, -ə-\ *n* **1 :** a deeply forked and tapering tail (as of a swallow) **2 :** TAILCOAT **3 :** any of various large butterflies (esp. genus *Papilio*) with the hind wing produced into a process resembling a tail — **swal·low–tailed** \ˌswäl-ō-ˈtāld, -ə-\ *adj*

swal·low·wort \ˈswäl-ō-ˌwərt, -ə-, -ˌwȯ(ə)rt\ *n* [fr. the shape of the pods] **1 :** CELANDINE 1 **2 :** any of several plants of the milkweed family; *specif* **:** a European twining vine (*Cynanchum nigrum*) whose root has been used as an emetic, cathartic, and diuretic

swam *past of* SWIM

swa·mi \ˈswäm-ē\ *n* [Hindi *svāmī*, fr. Skt *svāmin* owner, lord, fr. *sva* one's own — more at SUICIDE] **1 :** a Hindu ascetic or religious teacher; *specif* **:** a senior member of a religious order — used as a title **2 :** one that resembles or emulates a swami **:** PUNDIT, SEER

[1]**swamp** \ˈswämp, ˈswȯmp\ *n* [alter. of ME *sompe*, fr. MD *somp* morass; akin to MHG *sumpf* marsh, Gk *somphos* spongy] **1 :** wet spongy land saturated and sometimes partially or intermittently covered with water **2 :** a tract of swamp — **swamp** *adj*

[2]**swamp** *vt* **1 a :** to fill with or as if with water **:** INUNDATE, SUBMERGE **b :** to overwhelm numerically or by an excess of something **:** FLOOD <~*ed* with work> **2 :** to open by removing underbrush and debris ~ *vi* **:** to become submerged

swamp buggy *n* **:** a vehicle used to negotiate swampy terrain: as **a :** an amphibious tractor **b :** a flat-bottomed boat driven by an airplane propeller

swamp·er \ˈswäm-pər, ˈswȯm-\ *n* **1 a :** an inhabitant of swamps or lowlands **b :** one familiar with swampy terrain **2 :** a general assistant **:** HANDYMAN, HELPER

swamp·land \-ˌpland\ *n* **:** SWAMP 1

swampy \ˈswäm-pē, ˈswȯm-\ *adj* **swamp·i·er; -est :** consisting of or resembling swamp **:** MARSHY — **swamp·i·ness** *n*

[1]**swan** \ˈswän\ *n, pl* **swans** [ME, fr. OE; akin to MHG *swan*, L *sonus* sound — more at SOUND] **1** *pl also* **swan :** any of various heavy-bodied long-necked mostly pure white aquatic birds (family Anatidae) that are related to but larger than the geese, walk awkwardly, fly strongly when once started, and are graceful swimmers **2 :** a person or thing suggesting a swan because of its grace, whiteness, or fabled power of melody when dying **3** *cap* **:** the constellation Cygnus

[2]**swan** *vi* **swanned; swan·ning :** to wander aimlessly **:** DALLY

[3]**swan** *vi* **swanned; swan·ning** [perh. euphemism for *swear*] *dial* **:** DECLARE, SWEAR

swan boat *n* **:** a small boat usu. for children or sightseers pedaled by an operator who sits aft in a large model of a swan

swan dive *n* **:** a front dive executed with the head back, back arched, and arms spread sideways and then brought together above the head to form a straight line with the body as the diver enters the water

swan·herd \ˈswän-ˌhərd\ *n* **:** one that tends swans

[1]**swank** \ˈswaŋk\ *adj* [MLG or MD *swanc* supple; akin to OHG *swingan* to swing] *Scot* **:** full of life or energy **:** ACTIVE

[2]**swank** *vi* [perh. fr. MHG *swanken* to sway; akin to MD *swanc* supple] **:** to show off **:** SWAGGER <he ~*ed* around . . . in white suits —Saul Bellow>

[3]**swank** *n* **1 :** arrogance or ostentation of dress or manner **:** PRETENTIOUSNESS, SWAGGER **2 :** ELEGANCE

[4]**swank** *or* **swanky** \ˈswaŋ-kē\ *adj* **swank·er** *or* **swank·i·er; -est 1 :** characterized by showy display **:** OSTENTATIOUS <a ~ limousine> **2 :** fashionably elegant **:** SMART <a ~ restaurant> — **swank·i·ly** \-kə-lē\ *adv* — **swank·i·ness** \-kē-nəs\ *n*

ə abut	ᵊ kitten	ər further	a back	ā bake	ä cot, cart
au̇ out	ch chin	e less	ē easy	g gift	i trip	ī life
j joke	ŋ sing	ō flow	ȯ flaw	ȯi coin	th thin	th this
ü loot	u̇ foot	y yet	yü few	yu̇ furious	zh vision

swan·nery \'swän-(ə-)rē\ *n, pl* **-ner·ies :** a place where swans are bred or kept

swans·down \'swänz-ˌdau̇n\ *n* **1 :** the soft downy feathers of the swan often used as trimming on articles of dress **2 :** a heavy cotton flannel that has a thick nap on the face and is made with sateen weave

swan·skin \'swän-ˌskin\ *n* **1 :** the skin of a swan with the down or feathers on it **2 :** fabric resembling flannel and having a soft nap or surface

swan song *n* **1 :** a song of great sweetness said to be sung by a dying swan **2 :** a farewell appearance or final act or pronouncement

[1]**swap** \'swäp\ *vb* **swapped; swap·ping** [ME *swappen* to strike; fr. the practice of striking hands in closing a business deal] *vt* **:** to give in exchange **:** BARTER ~ *vi* **:** to make an exchange — **swap·per** *n*

[2]**swap** *n* **:** the act or process of exchanging one thing for another

swap meet *n* **:** a gathering for the sale or barter of secondhand objects

swa·raj \swə-'räj\ *n* [Skt *svarāj* self-ruling, fr. *sva* one's self + *rājya* rule — more at SUICIDE, RAJ] **:** Indian national or local self-government — **swa·raj·ist** \-əst\ *n*

sward \'swȯ(ə)rd\ *n* [ME, fr. OE *sweard, swearth* skin, rind; akin to MHG *swart* skin, hide, L *operire* to cover — more at WEIR] **1 :** the grassy surface of land **:** TURF **2 :** a portion of ground covered with grass — **sward·ed** \'swȯrd-əd\ *adj*

swarf \'swȯ(ə)rf\ *n* [of Scand origin; akin to ON *svarf* file dust; akin to OE *sweorfan* to file away — more at SWERVE] **:** material (as metallic particles and abrasive fragments) removed by a cutting or grinding tool

[1]**swarm** \'swȯ(ə)rm\ *n* [ME, fr. OE *swearm;* akin to OHG *swaram* swarm and prob. to L *susurrus* hum] **1 a** (1) **:** a great number of honeybees emigrating together from a hive in company with a queen to start a new colony elsewhere (2) **:** a colony of honeybees settled in a hive **b :** an aggregation of free-floating or free-swimming unicellular organisms — usu. used of zoospores **2 a :** a large number of animate or inanimate things massed together and usu. in motion **:** THRONG <~*s* of sightseers> <a ~ of meteors> **b :** a number of similar geological features or phenomena close together in space or time <a ~ of dikes> <an earthquake ~>

[2]**swarm** *vi* **1 a :** to form and depart from a hive in a swarm **b :** to escape in a swarm (as from a sporangium) **2 a :** to move or assemble in a crowd **:** THRONG **b :** to hover about in the manner of a bee in a swarm **3 :** to contain a swarm **:** TEEM ~ *vt* **:** to fill with a swarm — **swarm·er** *n*

[3]**swarm** *vb* [origin unknown] *vi* **:** to climb with the hands and feet; *specif* **:** SHIN <~ up a pole> ~ *vt* **:** to climb up **:** MOUNT

swarm spore *n* **:** any of various minute motile sexual or asexual spores; *esp* **:** ZOOSPORE

swart \'swȯ(ə)rt\ *adj* [ME, fr. OE *sweart;* akin to OHG *swarz* black, L *sordes* dirt] **1 a :** SWARTHY **b** *archaic* **:** producing a swarthy complexion **2 :** BANEFUL, MALIGNANT — **swart·ness** *n*

swar·thy \'swȯr-thē, -thē\ *adj* **swar·thi·er; -est** [alter. of obs. *swarty,* fr. *swart*] **:** being of a dark color, complexion, or cast *syn* see DUSKY — **swar·thi·ness** *n*

Swart·krans man \'swȯrt-ˌkranz-, 'sfärt-ˌkrän(t)s-\ *n* [*Swartkrans,* region in So. Africa] **:** an australopithecine (*Homo erectus capensis*) with a distinctly human jaw and teeth — called also *Swartkrans ape-man*

[1]**swash** \'swäsh, 'swȯsh\ *n* [prob. imit.] **1 a :** a body of splashing water **b :** a narrow channel of water lying within a sandbank or between a sandbank and the shore **2 :** a dashing of water against or on something **3 :** SWAGGER

[2]**swash** *vi* **1 :** BLUSTER, SWAGGER **2 :** to make violent noisy movements **3 :** to move with a splashing sound ~ *vt* **:** to cause to splash

[3]**swash** *adj* [obs. E *swash* slanting] **:** having one or more strokes ending in an extended flourish <~ capitals>

swash·buck·le \'swäsh-ˌbək-əl, 'swȯsh-\ *vi* **-led; -ling** \-ˌbək-(ə-)liŋ\ [back-formation fr. *swashbuckler*] **:** to act the part of a swashbuckler

swash·buck·ler \-ˌbək-lər\ *n* [[2]*swash* + *buckler*] **1 :** a boasting soldier or blustering daredevil **:** BRAVO **2 :** a novel or drama dealing with a swashbuckler

swash·buck·ling \-ˌbək-(ə-)liŋ\ *adj* [*swashbuckler*] **1 :** acting in the manner of a swashbuckler **2 :** characteristic of, marked by, or done by swashbucklers

swash·er \'swäsh-ər, 'swȯsh-\ *n* **:** SWASHBUCKLER

swas·ti·ka \'swäs-ti-kə *also* swä-'stē-\ *n* [Skt *svastika,* fr. *svasti* welfare, fr. *su-* well + *asti* he is; akin to OE *is;* fr. its being regarded as a good luck symbol] **:** a symbol or ornament in the form of a Greek cross with the ends of the arms extended at right angles all in the same rotary direction

[1]**swat** \'swät\ *vt* **swat·ted; swat·ting** [E dial., to squat, alter. of E *squat*] **:** to hit with a sharp slapping blow usu. with an instrument (as a bat or swatter) *syn* see STRIKE

[2]**swat** *n* **1 :** a powerful or crushing blow **2 :** a long hit in baseball; *esp* **:** HOME RUN

swatch \'swäch\ *n* [origin unknown] **1 a :** a sample piece (as of fabric) or a collection of samples **b :** a characteristic specimen **2 :** PATCH **3 :** a small collection

swath \'swäth, 'swȯth\ *or* **swathe** \'swäth, 'swȯth, 'swāth\ *n* [ME, fr. OE *swæth* footstep, trace; akin to MHG *swade* swath] **1 a :** the sweep of a scythe or a machine in mowing or the path cut in one course **b :** a row of cut grain or grass left by a scythe or mowing machine **2 :** a long broad strip or belt **3 :** a stroke of or as if of a scythe **4 :** a space devastated as if by a scythe

[1]**swathe** \'swäth, 'swȯth, 'swāth\ *vt* **swathed; swath·ing** [ME *swathen,* fr. OE *swathian;* akin to ON *svatha* to swathe, Lith *svaigti* to become dizzy] **1 :** to bind, wrap, or swaddle with or as if with a bandage **2 :** ENVELOP — **swath·er** *n*

[2]**swathe** \'swäth, 'swȯth, 'swāth\ *or* **swath** \'swäth, 'swäth, 'swȯth, 'swȯth\ *n* **1 :** a band used in swathing **2 :** an enveloping medium

swathing clothes *n pl* [ME] *obs* **:** SWADDLING CLOTHES

swats \'swäts\ *n pl* [prob. fr. OE *swātan,* pl., beer] *Scot* **:** DRINK; *esp* **:** new ale

swat·ter \'swät-ər\ *n* **:** one that swats; *esp* **:** FLYSWATTER

[1]**sway** \'swā\ *vb* [alter. of earlier *swey* to fall, swoon, fr. ME *sweyen,* prob. of Scand origin; akin to ON *sveigja* to sway; akin to OE *swathian* to swathe] *vi* **1 a :** to swing slowly and rhythmically back and forth from a base or pivot **b :** to move gently from an upright to a leaning position **2 :** to hold sway **:** act as ruler or governor **3 :** to fluctuate or veer between one point, position, or opinion and another ~ *vt* **1 a :** to cause to sway **:** set to swinging, rocking, or oscillating **b :** to cause to bend downward to one side **c :** to cause to turn aside **:** DEFLECT, DIVERT **2** *archaic* **a :** WIELD **b :** GOVERN, RULE **3 a :** to cause to vacillate **b :** to exert a guiding or controlling influence upon **4 :** to hoist in place <~ up a mast> *syn* see SWING, AFFECT — **sway·er** *n*

[2]**sway** *n* **1 :** the action or an instance of swaying or of being swayed **:** an oscillating, fluctuating, or sweeping motion **2 :** an inclination or deflection caused by or as if by swaying **3 a :** a controlling influence <scientists . . . under the ~ of a naturalistic optimism —W. R. Inge> **b :** sovereign power **:** DOMINION **c :** the ability to exercise influence or authority **:** DOMINANCE <classicism . . . held ~ —Carl Bridenbaugh>

sway·back \'swā-'bak, -ˌbak\ *n* **1 :** an abnormally hollow condition or sagging of the back found esp. in horses **2 :** a sagging back — **sway·backed** \-'bakt\ *adj*

Swa·zi \'swäz-ē\ *n, pl* **Swazi** *or* **Swazis** **1 :** a member of a Bantu people of Swaziland **2 :** a Bantu language of the Swazi people

[1]**swear** \'swa(ə)r, 'swe(ə)r\ *vb* **swore** \'swō(ə)r, 'swȯ(ə)r\; **sworn** \'swō(ə)rn, 'swȯ(ə)rn\; **swear·ing** [ME *sweren,* fr. OE *swerian;* akin to OHG *swerien* to swear, Russ *svara* altercation] *vt* **1 :** to utter or take solemnly (an oath) **2 a :** to assert as true or promise under oath <a *sworn* affidavit> **b :** to assert or promise emphatically or earnestly <*swore* to uphold the Constitution> **3 a :** to put to an oath **:** administer an oath to **b :** to bind by an oath <*swore* him to secrecy> **4** *obs* **:** to invoke the name of (a sacred being) in an oath **5 :** to bring into a specified state by swearing <*swore* his life away> ~ *vi* **1 :** to take an oath **2 :** to use profane or obscene language **:** CURSE — **swear·er** *n* — **swear by :** to place great confidence in — **swear for :** to answer for **:** GUARANTEE — **swear off :** to vow to abstain from **:** RENOUNCE <*swear off* smoking>

[2]**swear** *n* **:** OATH, SWEARWORD

swear in *vt* **:** to induct into office by administration of an oath

swear out *vt* **:** to procure (a warrant for arrest) by making a sworn accusation

swear·word \'swa(ə)r-ˌwərd, 'swe(ə)r-\ *n* **:** a profane or obscene oath or word

[1]**sweat** \'swet\ *vb* **sweat** *or* **sweat·ed; sweat·ing** [ME *sweten,* fr. OE *swǣtan,* fr. *swāt* sweat; akin to OHG *sweiz* sweat, L *sudor* sweat, *sudare* to sweat] *vi* **1 a :** to excrete moisture in visible quantities through the openings of the sweat glands **:** PERSPIRE **b :** to labor so as to cause perspiration **:** work hard **2 a :** to emit or exude moisture <cheese ~*s* in ripening> **b :** to gather surface moisture in beads as a result of condensation <stones ~ at night> **c** (1) **:** FERMENT (2) **:** PUTREFY **3 :** to undergo anxiety or mental or emotional distress **4 :** to become exuded through pores or a porous surface **:** OOZE ~ *vt* **1 :** to emit or seem to emit from pores **:** EXUDE **2 :** to manipulate or produce by hard work or drudgery **3 :** to get rid of or lose (weight) by or as if by sweating or being sweated **4 :** to make wet with perspiration **5 a :** to cause to excrete moisture from the skin **b :** to drive hard **:** OVERWORK **c :** to exact work from at low wages and under unfair or unhealthful conditions **d** *slang* **:** to give the third degree to **6 :** to cause to exude or lose moisture; *esp* **:** to subject (as tobacco leaves) to fermentation **7 a :** to extract something valuable from by unfair or dishonest means **:** FLEECE **b :** to remove particles of metal from (a coin) by abrasion **8 a :** to heat (as solder) so as to melt and cause to run esp. between surfaces to unite them; *also* **:** to unite by such means <~ a pipe joint> **b :** to heat so as to extract an easily fusible constituent <~ bismuth ore> **c :** to apply heat to **:** STEAM — **sweat blood :** to work or worry intensely

[2]**sweat** *n* **1 :** hard work **:** DRUDGERY **2 :** the fluid excreted from the sweat glands of the skin **:** PERSPIRATION **3 :** moisture issuing from or gathering in drops on a surface **4 a :** the condition of one sweating or sweated **b :** a spell of sweating **5 :** a state of anxiety or impatience — **no sweat** *slang* **:** with little or no difficulty

sweat·band \'swet-ˌband\ *n* **1 :** a usu. leather band lining the inner edge of a hat or cap to prevent sweat damage **2 :** a band of material tied around the head or wrist to absorb sweat

sweat·box \-ˌbäks\ *n* **1 :** a device for sweating something (as hides in tanning or dried figs) **2 :** a place in which one is made to sweat; *esp* **:** a narrow box in which a prisoner is placed for punishment

sweat·ed \'swet-əd\ *adj* **:** of, subjected to, or produced under a sweating system <~ labor> <~ goods>

sweat·er \'swet-ər\ *n* **1 :** one that sweats or causes sweating **2 :** a knitted or crocheted jacket or pullover

sweater girl *n* **:** a girl with a shapely bust

sweat gland *n* **:** a simple tubular gland of the skin that secretes perspiration, in man is widely distributed in nearly all parts of the skin, and consists typically of an epithelial tube extending spirally from a minute pore on the surface of the skin into the dermis or subcutaneous tissues where it ends in a convoluted tuft

sweating sickness *n* **:** an epidemic febrile disease characterized by profuse sweating and early high mortality

sweat out *vt* **1 :** to endure or wait through the course of **2 :** to work one's way painfully through or to

sweat pants *n pl* **:** pants having a drawstring waist and elastic cuffs at the ankle that are worn esp. by athletes in warming up

sweat shirt *n* **:** a loose collarless pullover of heavy cotton jersey

sweat·shop \'swet-ˌshäp\ *n* **:** a shop or factory in which workers are employed for long hours at low wages and under unhealthy conditions

sweat suit *n* : an exercise suit that consists of a sweat shirt and sweat pants
sweaty \ˈswet-ē\ *adj* **sweat·i·er; -est** **1** : wet or stained with or smelling of sweat **2** : causing sweat <a ~ day> <~ work> — **sweat·i·ly** \ˈswet-ᵊl-ē\ *adv* — **sweat·i·ness** \ˈswet-ē-nəs\ *n*
Swed *abbr* Sweden; Swedish
swede \ˈswēd\ *n* [LG or obs. D] **1** *cap* **a** : a native or inhabitant of Sweden **b** : a person of Swedish descent **2** : RUTABAGA
Swe·den·bor·gian \ˌswēd-ᵊn-ˈbȯr-j(ē-)ən, -ˈbȯr-gē-ən\ *adj* : of or relating to the teachings of Emanuel Swedenborg or the Church of the New Jerusalem based on his teachings — **Swedenborgian** *n* — **Swe·den·bor·gian·ism** \-ˌiz-əm\ *n*
Swed·ish \ˈswēd-ish\ *n* **1** : the North Germanic language spoken in Sweden and a part of Finland **2** *pl in constr* : the people of Sweden — **Swedish** *adj*
Swedish massage *n* : massage with Swedish movements
Swedish movements *n pl* : a system of active and passive exercise of muscles and joints
1**sweep** \ˈswēp\ *vb* **swept** \ˈswept\; **sweep·ing** [ME *swepen;* akin to OE *swāpan* to sweep — more at SWOOP] *vt* **1 a** : to remove from a surface with or as if with a broom or brush <*swept* the crumbs from the table> **b** : to destroy completely : wipe out — usu. used with *away* <everything she cherished, might be *swept* away overnight —Louis Bromfield> **c** : to remove or take with a single continuous forceful action <*swept* the books off the desk> **d** : to drive or carry along with irresistible force <a wave of protest that *swept* the opposition into office> **2 a** : to clean with or as if with a broom or brush **b** : to clear by repeated and forcible action **c** : to move across or along swiftly, violently, or overwhelmingly <fire *swept* the business district —*Amer. Guide Series: Md.*> **d** : to win an overwhelming victory in or on <~ the elections> **e** : to win all the games of <~ a double-header> <~ a series> **3** : to touch in passing with a swift continuous movement **4** : to trace or describe the locus or extent of (as a line, circle, or angle) **5** : to cover the entire range of <his eyes *swept* the horizon> ~ *vi* **1 a** : to clean a surface with or as if with a broom **b** : to move swiftly, forcefully, or devastatingly <the wind *swept* through the treetops> **2** : to go with stately or sweeping movements <his formidable wife *swept* past him to greet us —Maurice Cranston> **3** : to move or extend in a wide curve or range — **sweep·er** *n* — **sweep one off one's feet** : to gain immediate and unquestioning support, approval, or acceptance by a person — **sweep the board** *or* **sweep the table** **1** : to win all the bets on the table **2** : to win everything : excel all competitors
2**sweep** *n* **1** : something that sweeps or works with a sweeping motion: as **a** : a long pole or timber pivoted on a tall post and used to raise and lower a bucket in a well **b** : a triangular cultivator blade that cuts off weeds under the soil surface **c** : a windmill sail **2 a** : an instance of sweeping; *specif* : a clearing out or away with or as if with a broom **b** : the removal from the table in one play in casino of all the cards by pairing or combining **c** : an overwhelming victory **d** : a winning of all the contests or prizes in a competition **3 a** : a movement of great range and force **b** : a curving or circular course or line **c** : the compass of a sweeping movement : SCOPE **d** : a broad extent **e** : an end run in football in which one or more linemen pull back and run interference for the ballcarrier **4** : CHIMNEY SWEEP **5** : SWEEPSTAKES **6** : obliquity with respect to a reference line <~ of an airplane wing>; *esp* : SWEEPBACK
sweep·back \ˈswēp-ˌbak\ *n* : the backward slant of an airplane wing in which the outer portion of the wing is downstream from the inner portion
sweep hand *n* : SWEEP-SECOND
1**sweep·ing** *n* **1** : the act or action of one that sweeps <gave the room a good ~> **2** *pl* : things collected by sweeping : REFUSE
2**sweeping** *adj* **1 a** : moving or extending in a wide curve or over a wide area **b** : having a curving line or form **2 a** : EXTENSIVE <~ reforms> **b** : marked by wholesale and indiscriminate inclusion <~ generalities> *syn* see INDISCRIMINATE — **sweep·ing·ly** \ˈswē-piŋ-lē\ *adv* — **sweep·ing·ness** *n*
sweep–sec·ond \ˈswēp-ˌsek-ənd, -ənt\ *n* : a hand marking seconds on a timepiece mounted concentrically with the other hands and read on the minute dial
sweep·stakes \-ˌstāks\ *n pl but sing or pl in constr, also* **sweepstake** \-ˌstāk\ [ME *swepestake* one who wins all the stakes in a game, fr. *swepen* to sweep + *stake*] **1 a** : a race or contest in which the entire prize may be awarded to the winner; *specif* : STAKE RACE **b** : CONTEST, COMPETITION **2** : any of various lotteries
sweepy \ˈswē-pē\ *adj* **sweep·i·er; -est** : sweeping in motion, line, or force
1**sweet** \ˈswēt\ *adj* [ME *swete,* fr. OE *swēte;* akin to OHG *suozi* sweet, L *suavis,* Gk *hēdys*] **1 a (1)** : pleasing to the taste **(2)** : being or inducing the one of the four basic taste sensations that is typically induced by disaccharides and is mediated esp. by receptors in taste buds at the front of the tongue — compare BITTER, SALT, SOUR **b (1)** *of a beverage* : containing a sweetening ingredient : not dry **(2)** *of wine* : retaining a portion of natural sugar **2 a** : pleasing to the mind or feelings : AGREEABLE — often used as a generalized term of approval **b** : marked by gentle good humor or kindliness **c** : FRAGRANT **d (1)** : delicately pleasing to the ear or eye **(2)** : played in a straightforward melodic style <~ jazz> **e** : SACCHARINE, CLOYING **3** : much loved : DEAR **4 a** : not sour, rancid, decaying, or stale : WHOLESOME <~ milk> **b** : not salt or salted : FRESH <~ butter> **c** *of land* : free from excessive acidity **d** : free from noxious gases and odors **e** : free from excess of acid, sulfur, or corrosive salts **5** : FINE, GREAT — used as an intensive — **sweet·ly** *adv* — **sweet·ness** *n*
syn SWEET, ENGAGING, WINNING, WINSOME *shared meaning element* : distinctly pleasing or charming ***ant*** sour, bitter
— **sweet on** : in love with
2**sweet** *adv* : in a sweet manner
3**sweet** *n* **1** : something that is sweet to the taste: as **a** : a food (as a candy or preserve) having a high sugar content <fill up on ~*s*> **b** *Brit* : DESSERT **c** *Brit* : HARD CANDY **2** : a sweet taste sensation **3** : a pleasant or gratifying experience, possession, or state **4** : DARLING, SWEETHEART **5 a** *archaic* : FRAGRANCE **b** *pl, archaic* : things having a sweet smell
sweet alyssum *n* : a perennial European herb (*Lobularia maritima*) of the mustard family having clusters of small fragrant usu. white flowers
sweet–and–sour \ˌswēt-ᵊn-ˈsau̇(ə)r\ *adj* : seasoned with a sauce containing sugar and vinegar or lemon juice <~ shrimp>
sweet basil *n* : a common basil (*Ocimum basilicum*) that has white flowers tinged with purple and is used esp. in seasoning
sweet bay *n* **1** : LAUREL 1 **2** : an American magnolia (*Magnolia virginiana*) abundant along the Atlantic coast and in the southern states that has glaucous leaves and rather small globose fragrant white flowers
sweet birch *n* : a common birch (*Betula lenta*) of the eastern U.S. that has hard dark-colored wood and spicy brown bark containing a volatile oil
sweet·bread \ˈswēt-ˌbred\ *n* : the thymus of a young animal (as a calf) used for food
sweet·bri·er \-ˌbrī(-ə)r\ *n* : an Old World rose (esp. *Rosa eglanteria*) with stout recurved prickles and white to deep rosy pink single flowers — called also *eglantine*
sweet cherry *n* : a white-flowered Eurasian cherry (*Prunus avium*) widely grown for its large sweet-flavored fruits; *also* : its fruit
sweet chocolate *n* : chocolate that contains added sugar
sweet cicely *n* : any of various herbs of an American genus (*Osmorhiza*) that typically have thick fleshy roots and grow in moist woodlands
sweet clover *n* : any of a genus (*Melilotus*) of erect legumes widely grown for soil improvement or hay
sweet corn *n* : an Indian corn (esp. *Zea mays saccharata*) with kernels containing a high percentage of sugar and adapted for table use when in the milk stage
sweet·en \ˈswēt-ᵊn\ *vb* **sweet·ened; sweet·en·ing** \ˈswēt-niŋ, -ᵊn-iŋ\ *vt* **1** : to make sweet **2** : to soften the mood or attitude of **3** : to make less painful or trying **4** : to free from a harmful or undesirable quality or substance; *esp* : to remove sulfur compounds from <~ natural gas> **5** : to make more valuable or attractive: as **a** : to increase (a pot not won on the previous deal) by anteing prior to another deal **b** : to place additional securities as collateral for (a loan) ~ *vi* : to become sweet — **sweet·en·er** \ˈswēt-nər, -ᵊn-ər\ *n*
sweet·en·ing *n* : something that sweetens
sweet fern *n* : a small No. American shrub (*Comptonia peregrina*) of the wax-myrtle family with sweet-scented or aromatic leaves
sweet flag *n* : a perennial marsh herb (*Acorus calamus*) of the arum family with long leaves and a pungent rootstock — called also *calamus*
sweet gum *n* **1** : a No. American tree (*Liquidambar styraciflua*) with palmately lobed leaves, corky branches, and hard wood **2** : heartwood of the sweet gum or reddish brown lumber sawed from it

sweet gum 1: leaves and fruit

sweet·heart \ˈswēt-ˌhärt\ *n* **1** : DARLING **2** : LOVER
sweetheart contract *n* : an agreement between an employer and a labor union on terms favorable to the employer and often arranged by a union official without the participation or approval of the union members — called also *sweetheart agreement*
sweetheart neckline *n* : a neckline for women's clothing that is high in back and low in front where it is scalloped to resemble the top of a heart
sweet·ie \ˈswēt-ē\ *n* **1** *pl, Brit* : SWEET 1a **2** : SWEETHEART
sweetie pie *n* : SWEETHEART
sweet·ing \ˈswēt-iŋ\ *n* **1** *archaic* : SWEETHEART **2** : a sweet apple
sweet·ish \-ish\ *adj* **1** : somewhat sweet **2** : unpleasantly sweet — **sweet·ish·ly** *adv*
sweet marjoram *n* : an aromatic European herb (*Majorana hortensis*) with dense spikelike flower clusters
sweet·meat \ˈswēt-ˌmēt\ *n* : a food rich in sugar: as **a** : a candied or crystallized fruit **b** : CANDY, CONFECTION
sweetness and light *n* **1** : a harmonious combination of beauty and intelligence **2** : AMIABILITY, CONGENIALITY
sweet orange *n* : an orange (*Citrus sinensis*) that is prob. native to southeastern Asia, has a fruit with a pithy central axis, and is the source of the widely cultivated oranges of commerce; *also* : a cultivated orange derived from the sweet orange and usu. having fruit with a relatively thin skin and sweet juicy edible pulp
sweet pea *n* **1** : a garden plant (*Lathyrus odoratus*) having slender climbing stems and large fragrant flowers **2** : the flower of a sweet pea
sweet pepper *n* : a large mild thick-walled capsicum fruit; *also* : a pepper plant bearing this fruit
sweet potato *n* **1** : a tropical vine (*Ipomoea batatas*) related to the morning glory with variously shaped leaves and purplish flowers; *also* : its large thick sweet and nutritious tuberous root that is cooked and eaten as a vegetable **2** : OCARINA
sweet·shop \ˈswēt-ˌshäp\ *n, chiefly Brit* : a candy store

sweet·sop \-ˌsäp\ *n* **:** a tropical American tree (*Annona squamosa*) of the custard-apple family; *also* **:** its edible sweet pulpy fruit with thick green scaly rind and shining black seeds

sweet sorghum *n* **:** SORGO

sweet–talk \ˈswēt-ˌtȯk\ *vt* **:** BLANDISH, COAX ~ *vi* **:** to use flattery

sweet talk *n* **:** FLATTERY

sweet tooth *n* **:** a craving or fondness for sweet food

sweet wil·liam \swēt-ˈwil-yəm\ *n, often cap W* [fr. the name *William*] **:** a widely cultivated Eurasian pink (*Dianthus barbatus*) with small white to deep red or purple flowers often showily spotted, banded, or mottled and borne in flat bracteate heads on erect stalks

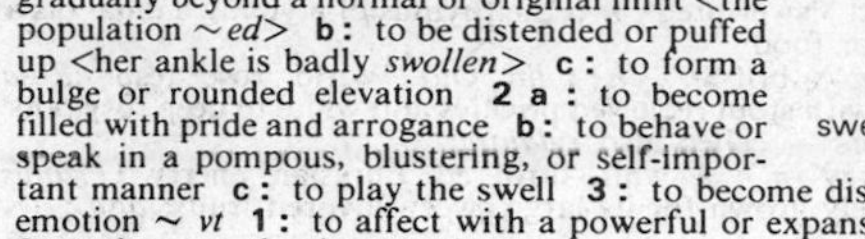

sweet william

[1]swell \ˈswel\ *vb* **swelled; swelled** *or* **swol·len** \ˈswō-lən\; **swell·ing** [ME *swellen,* fr. OE *swellan;* akin to OHG *swellan* to swell] *vi* **1 a :** to expand (as in size, volume, or numbers) gradually beyond a normal or original limit <the population ~*ed*> **b :** to be distended or puffed up <her ankle is badly *swollen*> **c :** to form a bulge or rounded elevation **2 a :** to become filled with pride and arrogance **b :** to behave or speak in a pompous, blustering, or self-important manner **c :** to play the swell **3 :** to become distended with emotion ~ *vt* **1 :** to affect with a powerful or expansive emotion **2 :** to increase the size, number, or intensity of ***syn*** see EXPAND ***ant*** shrink

[2]swell *n* **1 a :** the condition of being protuberant **b :** a rounded elevation **2 :** a long often massive and crestless wave or succession of waves often continuing beyond or after its cause (as a gale) **3 a :** the act or process of swelling **b** (1) **:** a gradual increase and decrease of the loudness of a musical sound; *also* **:** a sign < > indicating a swell (2) **:** a device used in an organ for governing loudness **4 a** *archaic* **:** an impressive, pompous, or fashionable air or display **b :** a person dressed in the height of fashion **c :** a person of high social position or outstanding competence

[3]swell *adj* **1 a :** STYLISH **b :** socially prominent **2 :** EXCELLENT — used as a generalized term of enthusiasm

swell box *n* **:** a chamber in an organ containing a set of pipes and having shutters that open or shut to regulate the volume of tone

swell–but·ted \ˈswel-ˈbət-əd\ *adj, of a tree* **:** greatly enlarged at the base

swelled head *n* **:** an exaggerated opinion of oneself **:** SELF-CONCEIT — **swelled–head·ed** \ˈsweld-ˈhed-əd\ *adj* — **swelled–head·ed·ness** *n*

swell·fish \ˈswel-ˌfish\ *n* **:** GLOBEFISH

swell–front \ˈswel-ˌfrənt\ *adj* **:** BOWFRONT 1

swell·head \-ˌhed\ *n* **:** one who has a swelled head — **swell·head·ed** \-ˈhed-əd\ *adj* — **swell·head·ed·ness** *n*

swell·ing \ˈswel-iŋ\ *n* **1 :** something that is swollen; *specif* **:** an abnormal bodily protuberance or localized enlargement **2 :** the condition of being swollen

[1]swel·ter \ˈswel-tər\ *vb* **swel·tered; swel·ter·ing** \-t(ə-)riŋ\ [ME *sweltren,* freq. of *swelten* to die, be overcome by heat, fr. OE *sweltan* to die; akin to OHG *swelzan* to burn up and prob. to OE *swelan* to burn] *vi* **:** to suffer, sweat, or be faint from heat ~ *vt* **1 :** to oppress with heat **2** *archaic* **:** EXUDE <~*ed* venom —Shak.>

[2]swelter *n* **1 :** a state of oppressive heat **2 :** WELTER **3 :** an excited or overwrought state of mind **:** SWEAT <in a ~>

swel·ter·ing *adj* **:** oppressively hot — **swel·ter·ing·ly** \-t(ə-)riŋ-lē\ *adv*

swept \ˈswept\ *adj* [*swept,* pp. of *sweep*] **:** slanted backward

swept–back \ˈswep(t)-ˈbak\ *adj* **:** possessing sweepback

[1]swerve \ˈswərv\ *vb* **swerved; swerv·ing** [ME *swerven,* fr. OE *sweorfan* to wipe, file away; akin to OHG *swerban* to wipe off, Gk *syrein* to drag] *vi* **:** to turn aside abruptly from a straight line or course **:** DEVIATE ~ *vt* **:** to cause to turn aside or deviate
syn SWERVE, VEER, DEVIATE, DEPART, DIGRESS, DIVERGE *shared meaning element* **:** to turn aside from a straight course

[2]swerve *n* **:** an act or instance of swerving

swev·en \ˈswev-ən\ *n* [ME, fr. OE *swefn* sleep, dream, vision — more at SOMNOLENT] *archaic* **:** DREAM, VISION

SWG *abbr* standard wire gauge

[1]swift \ˈswift\ *adj* [ME, fr. OE; akin to OE *swifan* to revolve — more at SWIVEL] **1 :** moving or capable of moving with great speed **2 :** occurring suddenly or within a very short time **3 :** quick to respond **:** READY ***syn*** see FAST

[2]swift *adv* **:** SWIFTLY <*swift*-flowing>

[3]swift *n* **1 :** any of several lizards (esp. of the genus *Sceloporus*) that run swiftly **2 a :** a reel for winding yarn or thread **b :** one of the large cylinders that carry forward the material in a carding machine; *also* **:** a comparable cylinder in another machine **3 :** any of numerous small plainly colored birds (family Apodidae) that are related to the hummingbirds and goatsuckers but superficially much resemble swallows

swift·ly *adv* **:** in a swift manner **:** with speed **:** QUICKLY

swift·ness \ˈswif(t)-nəs\ *n* **1 :** the quality or state of being swift **:** CELERITY **2 :** the fact of being swift

[1]swig \ˈswig\ *n* [origin unknown] **:** a quantity drunk at one time

[2]swig *vb* **swigged; swig·ging** *vt* **:** to drink in long drafts <~ cider> ~ *vi* **:** to take a swig **:** DRINK — **swig·ger** *n*

[1]swill \ˈswil\ *vb* [ME *swilen,* fr. OE *swillan*] *vt* **1 :** WASH, DRENCH **2 :** to drink great drafts of **:** GUZZLE **3 :** to feed (as a pig) with swill ~ *vi* **1 :** to drink or eat freely, greedily, or to excess **2 :** SWASH — **swill·er** *n*

[2]swill *n* **1 a :** a semiliquid food for animals (as swine) composed of edible refuse mixed with water or skimmmed or sour milk **b :** GARBAGE **2 :** something suggestive of slop or garbage **:** REFUSE **3 :** a draft of liquor

[1]swim \ˈswim\ *vb* **swam** \ˈswam\; **swum** \ˈswəm\; **swim·ming** [ME *swimmen,* fr. OE *swimman;* akin to OHG *swimman* to swim] *vi* **1 a :** to propel oneself in water by natural means (as movements of the limbs, fins, or tail) **b :** to frolic in the water (as at a beach or swimming pool) **2 :** to move with a motion like that of swimming **:** GLIDE <a cloud *swam* slowly across the moon> **3 a :** to float on a liquid **:** not sink **b :** to surmount difficulties **:** not go under <sink or ~, live or die, survive or perish —Daniel Webster> **4 :** to become immersed or flooded with or as if with a liquid **5 :** to have a floating or reeling appearance or sensation ~ *vt* **1 a :** to cross by propelling oneself through water <~ a stream> **b :** to execute in swimming **2 :** to cause to swim or float — **swim·mer** *n* — **swim against the stream :** to move counter to or work against the prevailing or popular trend

[2]swim *n* **1 :** a smooth gliding motion **2 :** an act or period of swimming **3 :** a temporary dizziness or unconsciousness **4 a :** an area frequented by fish **b :** the main current of activity <be in the ~>

[3]swim *adj* **:** of, relating to, or used in or for swimming <a ~ meet>

swim bladder *n* **:** the air bladder of a fish

swim fin *n* **:** FLIPPER 1b

swim·ma·ble \ˈswim-ə-bəl\ *adj* **:** that can be swum

swim·mer·et \ˌswim-ə-ˈret, ˈswim-ə-ˌ\ *n* **:** one of a series of small unspecialized appendages under the abdomen of many crustaceans that are best developed in some decapods and are used in some cases for swimming but usu. for carrying eggs

swimmer's itch *n* **:** a severe urticarial reaction to the presence in the skin of schistosomes that are not normally parasites of man

[1]swim·ming *n* **:** the act, art, or sport of one that swims and dives

[2]swimming *adj* **1** [prp. of *swim*] **:** that swims <a ~ bird> **2** [gerund of *swim*] **:** adapted to or used in or for swimming

swim·ming·ly \ˈswim-iŋ-lē\ *adv* **:** very well **:** SPLENDIDLY

swimming pool *n* **:** a pool suitable for swimming; *esp* **:** a tank (as of concrete or plastic) made for swimming

swim·my \ˈswim-ē\ *adj* **swim·mi·er; -est 1 :** verging on, causing, or affected by dizziness or giddiness **2** *of vision* **:** BLURRED, UNSTEADY — **swim·mi·ly** \ˈswim-ə-lē\ *adv* — **swim·mi·ness** \ˈswim-ē-nəs\ *n*

swim·suit \ˈswim-ˌsüt\ *n* **:** a suit for swimming or bathing

[1]swin·dle \ˈswin-dᵊl\ *vb* **swin·dled; swin·dling** \-(d)liŋ, -dᵊl-iŋ\ [back-formation fr. *swindler,* fr. G *schwindler* giddy person, fr. *schwindeln* to be dizzy, fr. OHG *swintilōn,* freq. of *swintan* to diminish, vanish; akin to OE *swindan* to vanish, OIr *a-sennad* finally] *vi* **:** to obtain money or property by fraud or deceit ~ *vt* **:** to take money or property from by fraud or deceit ***syn*** see CHEAT — **swin·dler** \-(d)lər, -dᵊl-ər\ *n*

[2]swindle *n* **:** an act or instance of swindling **:** FRAUD

swine \ˈswīn\ *n, pl* **swine** [ME, fr. OE *swīn;* akin to OHG *swīn* swine, L *sus* — more at SOW] **1 :** any of various stout-bodied short-legged omnivorous mammals (family Suidae) with a thick bristly skin and a long mobile snout; *esp* **:** a domesticated member of the species (*Sus scrofa*) that includes the European wild boar **2 :** a contemptible person

swine·herd \-ˌhərd\ *n* **:** one who tends swine

[1]swing \ˈswiŋ\ *vb* **swung** \ˈswəŋ\; **swing·ing** \ˈswiŋ-iŋ\ [ME *swingen* to beat, fling, hurl, rush, fr. OE *swingan* to beat, fling oneself, rush; akin to OHG *swingan* to fling, rush] *vt* **1 a :** to cause to move vigorously through a wide arc or circle <~ an ax> **b :** to cause to sway to and fro **c** (1) **:** to cause to turn on an axis (2) **:** to cause to face or move in another direction <~ the car into a side road> **2 :** to suspend so as to permit swaying or turning **3 :** to convey by suspension <huge cranes that ~ cargo up over the ship's side and into the hold> **4 a** (1) **:** to influence decisively <~ a lot of votes> (2) **:** to bring around by influence **b :** to handle successfully **:** MANAGE <wasn't able to ~ a new car on his income> **5 :** to play or sing (as a melody) in the style of swing music ~ *vi* **1 :** to move freely to and fro esp. in suspension from an overhead support **2 a :** to die by hanging **b :** to hang freely from a support **3 :** to move in or describe a circle or arc: **a :** to turn on a hinge or pivot **b :** to turn in place **c :** to convey oneself by grasping a fixed support <~ aboard the train> **4 a :** to have a steady pulsing rhythm **b :** to play or sing with a lively compelling rhythm; *specif* **:** to play swing music **5 :** to shift or fluctuate from one condition, form, position, or object of attention or favor to another <~ constantly from optimism to pessimism and back —Sinclair Lewis> **6 a :** to move along rhythmically **b :** to start up in a smooth vigorous manner <ready to ~ into action> **7 :** to hit or aim at something with a sweeping arm movement **8 a :** to be lively and up-to-date **b :** to engage freely in sex — **swing·able** \ˈswiŋ-ə-bəl\ *adj* — **swing·ably** \-blē\ *adv*
***syn* 1** SWING, WAVE, FLOURISH, BRANDISH, THRASH *shared meaning element* **:** to move or move something repetitively or in an orderly pattern
2 SWING, SWAY, OSCILLATE, VIBRATE, FLUCTUATE, WAVER, UNDULATE *shared meaning element* **:** to move to and fro, up and down, or back and forth

[2]swing *n* **1 :** an act or instance of swinging **:** swinging movement: as **a** (1) **:** a stroke or blow delivered with a sweeping arm movement <a batter with a powerful ~> (2) **:** a sweeping or rhythmic movement of the body or a bodily part (3) **:** a dance figure in which two dancers revolve with joined arms or hands (4) **:** jazz dancing in moderate tempo with a lilting syncopation **b** (1) **:** the regular movement of a freely suspended object (as a pendulum) along an arc and back (2) **:** back and forth sweep <the ~ of the tides> **c** (1) **:** steady pulsing rhythm (as in poetry or music) (2) **:** a steady vigorous movement characterizing an activity or creative work **d** (1) **:** a trend toward a high or low point in a fluctuating cycle (as of business activity) (2) **:** an often periodic shift from one condition, form, position, or object of attention or favor to another **2 a :** liberty of action **:** free scope **b** (1) **:** the driving power of something swung or hurled (2) **:** steady vigorous advance **:** driving speed <a train approaching at full ~> **3 :** the progression of an activity, process, or phase of existence <the work is in full ~> **4 :** the arc or range through which something swings **5 :** something that swings freely from or on a support; *esp* **:** a seat suspended by a rope or chains for swinging to and fro on for pleasure **6 a :** a curving course or outline **b :** a course from and back to a point **:** a circular tour **7 :** jazz played usu. by a large dance band and characterized by a steady lively rhythm, simple harmony, and a basic melody often submerged in improvisation **8 :** a short pass in football thrown to a back running to the outside **:** FLARE — **swing** *adj*

1swinge \ˈswinj\ *vt* **swinged; swinge·ing** [ME *swengen* to shake, fr. OE *swengan;* akin to OE *swingan*] *chiefly dial* **:** BEAT, SCOURGE

2swinge *vt* **swinged; swinge·ing** [alter. of *singe*] *dial* **:** SINGE, SCORCH

1swinge·ing *or* **swing·ing** \ˈswin-jiŋ\ *adj* [fr. prp. of 1*swinge*] *chiefly Brit* **:** superlative in size, amount, or character

2swingeing *or* **swinging** *adv, chiefly Brit* **:** VERY, SUPERLATIVELY

1swing·er \ˈswiŋ-ər\ *n* **:** one that swings: as **a :** a lively up-to-date person who indulges in what is considered fashionable **b :** one who engages freely in sex

2swing·er \ˈswin-jər\ *n* [1*swinge*] **:** WHOPPER 1

swing·ing \ˈswiŋ-iŋ\ *adj* [prp. of 1*swing*] **:** being lively and up-to-date <~ moderns>; *also* **:** abounding in swingers and swinging entertainment <a ~ coffeehouse>

1swing·ing·ly \ˈswin-jiŋ-lē\ *adv, chiefly Brit* **:** VERY, EXTREMELY

2swing·ing·ly \ˈswiŋ-iŋ-lē\ *adv* **:** in a swinging manner **:** with a swinging movement

swin·gle·tree \ˈswiŋ-gəl-(ˌ)trē\ *n* [*swingle* (cudgel) + *tree*] **:** WHIFFLETREE

swing shift *n* **1 :** the work shift between the day and night shifts (as from 4 P.M. to midnight) **2 :** a group of workers in a factory operating seven days a week that man the place as needed to permit the regular shift workers to have one or more free days per week

swingy \ˈswiŋ-ē\ *adj* **swing·i·er; -est :** marked by swing

swin·ish \ˈswī-nish\ *adj* **:** of, suggesting, or characteristic of swine **:** BEASTLY — **swin·ish·ly** *adv* — **swin·ish·ness** *n*

1swink \ˈswiŋk\ *vi* [ME *swinken,* fr. OE *swincan;* akin to OHG *swingan* to rush — more at SWING] *archaic* **:** TOIL, SLAVE

2swink *n, archaic* **:** LABOR, DRUDGERY

1swipe \ˈswīp\ *n* [prob. alter. of *sweep*] **1 :** a strong sweeping blow **2 :** one who takes care of horses **:** GROOM

2swipe *vb* **swiped; swip·ing** *vi* **:** to strike or move with a sweeping motion ~ *vt* **1 :** to strike or wipe with a sweeping motion **2 :** STEAL, PILFER

swipes \ˈswīps\ *n pl* [origin unknown] *Brit* **:** poor, thin, or spoiled beer; *also* **:** BEER

1swirl \ˈswər(-ə)l\ *n* [ME (Sc)] **1 a :** a whirling mass or motion **:** EDDY **b :** whirling confusion <a ~ of events> **2 :** a twisting shape, mark, or pattern **3 :** an act or instance of swirling

2swirl *vi* **1 a :** to move with an eddying or whirling motion **b :** to pass in whirling confusion **2 :** to have a twist or convolution ~ *vt* **:** to cause to swirl — **swirl·ing·ly** \ˈswər-liŋ-lē\ *adv*

swirly \ˈswər-lē\ *adj* **swirl·i·er; -est 1** *Scot* **:** KNOTTED, TWISTED **2 :** that swirls **:** SWIRLING <the ~ water of the rapids>

1swish \ˈswish\ *vb* [imit.] *vi* **:** to move, pass, swing, or whirl with the sound of a swish <windshield wipers ~*ing* —John McCarten> ~ *vt* **:** to move, cut, or strike with a swish <the horse ~*ed* its tail> — **swish·er** *n* — **swish·ing·ly** \-iŋ-lē\ *adv*

2swish *n* **1 a :** a prolonged hissing sound (as of a whip cutting the air) **b :** a light sweeping or brushing sound (as of a full silk skirt in motion) **2 :** a swishing movement **3** *slang* **:** HOMOSEXUAL

3swish *adj* [origin unknown] **:** SMART, FASHIONABLE

swishy \ˈswish-ē\ *adj* **swish·i·er; -est 1 :** producing a swishing sound **2** *slang* **:** characterized by effeminate behavior

1Swiss \ˈswis\ *n* [MF *Suisse,* fr. MHG *Swizer,* fr. *Swiz* Switzerland] **1** *pl* **Swiss a :** a native or inhabitant of Switzerland **b :** one that is of Swiss descent **2** *often not cap* **:** any of various fine sheer fabrics of cotton orig. made in Switzerland; *esp* **:** DOTTED SWISS **3 :** SWISS CHEESE

2Swiss *adj* **:** of, relating to, or characteristic of Switzerland or the Swiss

Swiss chard *n* **:** CHARD

Swiss cheese *n* **:** a hard cheese characterized by elastic texture, mild nutlike flavor, and large holes that form during ripening

Swiss steak *n* **:** a slice of steak pounded with flour and braised usu. with vegetables and seasonings

1switch \ˈswich\ *n* [perh. fr. MD *swijch* twig] **1 :** a slender flexible whip, rod, or twig <a riding ~> **2 :** an act of switching: as **a :** a blow with a switch **b :** a shift from one to another **3 :** a tuft of long hairs at the end of the tail of an animal (as a cow) — see COW illustration **4 a :** a device made usu. of two movable rails and necessary connections and designed to turn a locomotive or train from one track to another **b :** a railroad siding **5 :** a device for making, breaking, or changing the connections in an electrical circuit **6 :** a heavy strand of hair used in addition to a person's own hair for some coiffures

2switch *vt* **1 :** to strike or beat with or as if with a switch **2 :** WHISK, LASH <a cat ~*ing* his tail> **3 a** (1) **:** to turn from one railroad track to another **:** SHUNT (2) **:** to move (cars) to different positions on the same track within terminal areas **b :** to make a shift in or exchange of <~ the talk to another subject> **4 a :** to shift to another electrical circuit by means of a switch **b :** to operate an electrical switch so as to turn (as a light) off or on ~ *vi* **1 :** to lash from side to side **2 :** to make a shift or exchange — **switch·able** \-ə-bəl\ *adj* — **switch·er** *n*

switch·back \ˈswich-ˌbak\ *n* **:** a zigzag road in a mountainous region; *esp* **:** an arrangement of zigzag railroad tracks for surmounting the grade of a steep hill

switch·blade \-ˌblād\ *n* **:** a pocketknife having the blade spring-operated so that pressure on a release catch causes it to fly open — called also *switchblade knife*

switch·board \-ˌbō(ə)rd, -ˌbȯ(ə)rd\ *n* **:** an apparatus consisting of a panel or a frame on which are mounted insulated switching, measuring, controlling, and protective devices with connections so arranged that a number of circuits may be connected, combined, controlled, measured, and protected

switch cane *n* **:** an important forage grass (*Arundinaria tecta*) of moist locations esp. in the southern U.S.

switch engine *n* **:** a railroad engine used in switching cars (as in making up trains)

switch·er·oo \ˌswich-ə-ˈrü\ *n, pl* **-oos** [alter. of *switch*] *slang* **:** a surprising variation **:** REVERSAL

switch·grass \ˈswich-ˌgras\ *n* **:** a panic grass (*Panicum virgatum*) of the western U.S. that is used for hay

switch–hit \-ˈhit\ *vi* **-hit; -hit·ting** [back-formation fr. *switch-hitter*] *of a baseball player* **:** to bat either left-handed or right-handed

switch–hit·ter \-ˈhit-ər\ *n* **:** a baseball player who switch-hits

switch knife *n* **:** SWITCHBLADE

switch·man \ˈswich-mən\ *n* **:** one who attends a switch (as in a railroad yard)

switch·yard \-ˌyärd\ *n* **1 :** a place where railroad cars are switched from one track to another and trains are made up **2 :** a usu. enclosed area for the switching facilities of a power station

swith \ˈswith\ *adv* [ME, strongly, quickly, fr. OE *swīthe* strongly, fr. *swīth* strong; akin to OE *gesund* sound — more at SOUND] *chiefly dial* **:** INSTANTLY, QUICKLY

1swith·er \ˈswit͟h-ər\ *vi* [origin unknown] *dial chiefly Brit* **:** DOUBT, WAVER

2swither *n, dial chiefly Brit* **:** DOUBT, AGITATION

Switz *abbr* Switzerland

Swit·zer \ˈswit-sər\ *n* [MHG *Swizer*] **:** SWISS

1swiv·el \ˈswiv-əl\ *n, often attrib* [ME; akin to OE *swīfan* to revolve, ON *sveigja* to sway — more at SWAY] **:** a device joining two parts so that one or both can pivot freely (as on a bolt or pin)

2swivel *vb* **-eled** *or* **-elled; -el·ing** *or* **-el·ling** \-(ə-)liŋ\ *vt* **:** to turn on or as if on a swivel <~*ed* his eyes in various directions> ~ *vi* **:** to swing or turn on or as if on a swivel

swivel chair *n* **:** a chair that swivels on its base

swiv·el–hipped \ˌswiv-əl-ˈhipt\ *adj* **:** moving with or characterized by movement with a twisting motion of the hips

swiv·et \ˈswiv-ət\ *n* [origin unknown] **:** a state of extreme agitation <are in a ~ again over campaign strategy —*Newsweek*>

1swiz·zle \ˈswiz-əl\ *n* [origin unknown] **:** a cocktail consisting of liquor, lime or lemon juice, bitters, and sugar stirred vigorously in ice in a pitcher until the surface is frothed

2swizzle *vb* **swiz·zled; swiz·zling** \-(ə-)liŋ\ *vi* **:** to drink esp. to excess **:** GUZZLE ~ *vt* **:** to mix or stir with or as if with a swizzle stick — **swiz·zler** \-(ə-)lər\ *n*

swizzle stick *n* **:** a stick used to stir mixed drinks

swob *var of* SWAB

swollen *past part of* SWELL

1swoon \ˈswün\ *vi* [ME *swounen*] **1 a :** FAINT **b :** to become enraptured <the ladies were ~*ing* with joy —Frederick Way> **2 :** FLOAT, FADE — **swoon·er** *n* — **swoon·ing·ly** \ˈswü-niŋ-lē\ *adv*

2swoon *n* **1 a :** a partial or total loss of consciousness **b :** a state of bewilderment or ecstasy **:** DAZE, RAPTURE **2 :** a state of suspended animation **:** TORPOR

1swoop \ˈswüp\ *vb* [alter. of ME *swopen* to sweep, fr. OE *swāpan;* akin to ON *svatha* to swathe — more at SWATHE] *vi* **:** to move with a sweep; *specif* **:** to make a sudden attack — usu. used with *down* <the eagle ~*ed* down on its prey> ~ *vt* **:** to carry off abruptly **:** SWEEP, SNATCH <~*ed* her off the swing into his arms —Helen Howe> — **swoop·er** *n*

2swoop *n* **:** an act or instance of swooping

swoop·stake \ˈswüp-ˌstāk\ *adv* [fr. alter. of *sweepstake*] *obs* **:** in an indiscriminate manner

1swoosh \ˈswüsh, ˈswu̇sh\ *vb* [imit.] *vi* **1 :** to make or move with a rushing sound <a car ~*ed* by> **2 :** GUSH, SWIRL ~ *vt* **:** to discharge or transport with a rushing sound

2swoosh *n* **:** an act or instance of swooshing

swop *var of* SWAP

sword \ˈsō(ə)rd, ˈsȯ(ə)rd\ *n, often attrib* [ME, fr. OE *sweord;* akin to OHG *swert* sword, Av *xvara* wound] **1 :** a weapon (as a cutlass or rapier) with a long blade for cutting or thrusting often used as a symbol of honor or authority **2 a :** an agency or instrument of destruction or combat **b :** the use of force (as in war) <the pen is mightier than the ~ —E. G. Bulwer-Lytton> **3 :** coercive power **4 :** something (as the beak of a swordfish) that resembles a sword — **sword·like** \-ˌlīk\ *adj* — **at swords' points :** mutually antagonistic **:** ready to fight

sword cane *n* **:** a cane in which a sword blade is concealed

sword dance *n* **1 :** a dance performed by men in a circle holding a sword in the right hand and grasping the tip of a neighbor's sword in the left hand **2 :** a dance performed over or around swords — **sword dancer** *n*

sword fern *n* **:** any of several ferns with long narrow more or less sword-shaped fronds: as **a :** a tropical fern (*Nephrolepis exaltata*) from which the Boston fern has been developed **b :** a fern (*Polystichum munitum*) of western No. America with a large fleshy rhizome

sword·fish \ˈsō(ə)rd-ˌfish, ˈsȯ(ə)rd-\ *n* **:** a very large oceanic food fish (*Xiphias gladius*) having a long swordlike beak formed by the bones of the upper jaw

sword grass *n* **:** any of various grasses or sedges having leaves with a sharp or toothed edge

sword knot *n* **:** an ornamental cord or tassel tied to the hilt of a sword

sword of Dam·o·cles \-ˈdam-ə-ˌklēz\ *often cap S* **:** an impending disaster

sword·play \ˈsō(ə)rd-ˌplā, ˈsȯ(ə)rd-\ *n* **1 :** the art or skill of wielding a sword esp. in fencing **2 :** an exhibition of swordplay — **sword·play·er** *n*

swords·man \ˈsō(ə)rdz-mən, ˈsȯ(ə)rdz-\ *n* **1 :** one skilled in swordplay; *esp* **:** a saber fencer **2** *archaic* **:** a soldier armed with a sword

swords·man·ship \-ˌship\ *n* **:** SWORDPLAY

sword·tail \'sō(ə)rd-ˌtāl, 'sȯ(ə)rd-\ *n* **:** a small brightly marked Central American topminnow (*Xiphophorus helleri*) often kept in the tropical aquarium and bred in many colors
swore *past of* SWEAR
sworn *past part of* SWEAR
[1]**swot** \'swät\ *n* [alter. of *sweat*] *Brit* **:** GRIND 2b
[2]**swot** *vi* **swot·ted; swot·ting** *Brit* **:** GRIND 4
[1]**swound** \'swau̇nd, 'swünd\ *n* [ME, alter. of *swoun* swoon, fr. *swounen* to swoon] *archaic* **:** SWOON 1a
[2]**swound** *vi, archaic* **:** SWOON
swum *past part of* SWIM
swung *past of* SWING
swung dash *n* **:** a character ~ used in printing to conserve space by representing part or all of a previously spelled out word
Syb·a·rite \'sib-ə-ˌrīt\ *n* **1 :** a native or resident of the ancient city of Sybaris **2** [fr. the notorious luxury of the Sybarites] *often not cap* **:** VOLUPTUARY, SENSUALIST — **Syb·a·rit·ic** \ˌsib-ə-'rit-ik\ *adj* — **syb·a·rit·i·cal·ly** \-i-k(ə-)lē\ *adv* — **Syb·a·rit·ism** \'sib-ə-ˌrīt-ˌiz-əm\ *n*
syc·a·mine \'sik-ə-ˌmīn, -mən\ *n* [L *sycaminus,* fr. Gk *sykaminos,* of Sem origin; akin to Heb *shiqmāh* mulberry tree, sycamore] **:** MULBERRY 1
syc·a·more \'sik-ə-ˌmō(ə)r, -ˌmȯ(ə)r\ *n* [ME *sicamour,* fr. MF *sicamor,* fr. L *sycomorus,* fr. Gk *sykomoros,* prob. modif. of a Sem word akin to Heb *shiqmāh* sycamore] **1 :** a tree (*Ficus sycomorus*) of Egypt and Asia Minor that is the sycamore of Scripture, is useful as a shade tree, and has sweet and edible fruit similar but inferior to the common fig **2 :** a Eurasian maple (*Acer pseudo-platanus*) with long racemes of showy yellow flowers that is widely planted as a shade tree **3 :** [2]PLANE; *esp* **:** a very large spreading tree (*Platanus occidentalis*) of eastern and central No. America with 3- to 5-lobed broadly ovate leaves

sycamore 3: leaves and fruit

syce \'sīs\ *n* [Hindi *sā'is,* fr. Ar] **:** an attendant (as a groom) esp. in India
sy·cee \'sī-ˌsē\ *n* [Chin (Cant) *saì sz,* lit., fine silk] **:** silver money formerly used in China and made in the form of ingots measured by weight and usu. stamped
sy·co·ni·um \sī-'kō-nē-əm\ *n, pl* **-nia** \-nē-ə\ [NL, fr. Gk *sykon* fig + NL *-ium*] **:** a collective fleshy fruit in which the ovaries are borne within an enlarged succulent concave or hollow receptacle
sy·co·phan·cy \'sik-ə-fən-sē *also* 'sīk- *&* -ˌfan(t)-sē\ *n* **:** obsequious flattery; *also* **:** the character or behavior of a sycophant
sy·co·phant \-fənt *also* -ˌfant\ *n* [L *sycophanta* informer, swindler, sycophant, fr. Gk *sykophantēs* informer] **:** a servile self-seeking flatterer **:** PARASITE — **sycophant** *adj*
sy·co·phan·tic \ˌsik-ə-'fant-ik *also* ˌsīk-\ *adj* **:** of, relating to, or characteristic of a sycophant **:** FAWNING, OBSEQUIOUS — **sy·co·phan·ti·cal·ly** \-'fant-i-k(ə-)lē\ *adv*
sy·co·phant·ish \ˌsik-ə-'fant-ish *also* ˌsīk-\ *adj* **:** SYCOPHANTIC — **sy·co·phant·ish·ly** *adv*
sy·co·phant·ism \'sik-ə-fənt-ˌiz-əm *also* 'sīk- *&* -ˌfant-\ *n* **:** SYCOPHANCY
sy·co·phant·ly \-lē\ *adv* **:** in a sycophantic manner
sy·co·sis \sī-'kō-səs\ *n* [NL, fr. Gk *sykōsis,* fr. *sykon* fig] **:** a chronic inflammatory disorder of the hair follicles marked by papules, pustules, and tubercles with crusting
sy·enite \'sī-ə-ˌnīt\ *n* [L *Syenites* (*lapis*) stone of Syene, fr. *Syene,* ancient city in Egypt] **:** an igneous rock composed chiefly of feldspar — **sy·enit·ic** \ˌsī-ə-'nit-ik\ *adj*
syl *or* **syll** *abbr* syllable
syl·la·bar·i·um \ˌsil-ə-'ber-ē-əm\ *n, pl* **-ia** \-ē-ə\ [NL] **:** SYLLABARY
syl·la·bary \'sil-ə-ˌber-ē\ *n, pl* **-bar·ies** [NL *syllabarium,* fr. L *syllaba* syllable] **:** a table or listing of syllables; *specif* **:** a series or set of written characters each one of which is used to represent a syllable
[1]**syl·lab·ic** \sə-'lab-ik\ *adj* [LL *syllabicus,* fr. Gk *syllabikos,* fr. *syllabē* syllable] **1 :** of, relating to, or denoting syllables <~ accent> **2 :** constituting a syllable or the nucleus of a syllable: **a :** not accompanied in the same syllable by a vowel <\n\ is ~ in \bätᵊnē\ *botany,* nonsyllabic in \bätnē\> **b :** having vowel quality more prominent than that of another vowel in the syllable <the first vowel of a falling diphthong, as \ȯ\ in \ȯi\, is ~> **3 :** characterized by distinct enunciation or separation of syllables **4 :** of, relating to, or constituting a type of verse distinguished primarily by count of syllables rather than by rhythmical arrangement of accents or quantities — **syl·lab·i·cal·ly** \-i-k(ə-)lē\ *adv*
[2]**syllabic** *n* **:** a syllabic character or sound
syl·lab·i·cate \sə-'lab-ə-ˌkāt\ *vt* **-cat·ed; -cat·ing :** SYLLABIFY
syl·lab·i·ca·tion \sə-ˌlab-ə-'kā-shən\ *n* **:** the act, process, or method of forming or dividing words into syllables
syl·la·bic·i·ty \ˌsil-ə-'bis-ət-ē\ *n* **:** the state of being or the power of forming a syllable
syl·lab·i·fi·ca·tion \sə-ˌlab-ə-fə-'kā-shən\ *n* **:** SYLLABICATION
syl·lab·i·fy \sə-'lab-ə-ˌfī\ *vt* **-fied; -fy·ing** [L *syllaba* syllable] **:** to form or divide into syllables
[1]**syl·la·ble** \'sil-ə-bəl\ *n* [ME, fr. MF *sillabe,* fr. L *syllaba,* fr. Gk *syllabē,* fr. *syllambanein* to gather together, fr. *syn-* + *lambanein* to take — more at LATCH] **1 :** a unit of spoken language that is next bigger than a speech sound and consists of one or more vowel sounds alone or of a syllabic consonant alone or of either with one or more consonant sounds preceding or following **2 :** one or more letters (as *syl, la,* and *ble*) in a word (as *syl-la-ble*) usu. set off from the rest of the word by a centered dot or a hyphen and roughly corresponding to the syllables of spoken language and treated as helps to pronunciation or as guides to hyphenation at the end of a line **3 :** the smallest conceivable expression or unit of something **:** JOT **4 :** SOL-FA SYLLABLES
[2]**syllable** *vt* **syl·la·bled; syl·la·bling** \-b(ə-)liŋ\ **1 :** to give a number or arrangement of syllables to (a word or verse) **2 :** to express or utter in or as if in syllables
syl·la·bub \'sil-ə-ˌbəb\ *n* [origin unknown] **1 :** a drink or dessert made by curdling milk or cream with acid (as wine or cider) **2 :** a dessert of sweetened milk or cream beaten to a froth and flavored with wine or liquor
syl·la·bus \-bəs\ *n, pl* **-bi** \-ˌbī, -ˌbē\ *or* **-bus·es** [LL, alter. of L *sillybus* label for a book, fr. Gk *sillybos*] **1 :** a summary outline of a discourse, treatise, or course of study or of examination requirements **2 :** HEADNOTE 2
syl·lep·sis \sə-'lep-səs\ *n, pl* **-lep·ses** \-ˌsēz\ [L, fr. Gk *syllēpsis,* fr. *syllambanein*] **1 :** the use of a word to modify or govern syntactically two or sometimes more words with only one of which it formally agrees in gender, number, or case **2 :** the use of a word in the same grammatical relation to two adjacent words in the context with one literal and the other metaphorical in sense — **syl·lep·tic** \-'lep-tik\ *adj*
syl·lo·gism \'sil-ə-ˌjiz-əm\ *n* [ME *silogisme,* fr. MF, fr. L *syllogismus,* fr. Gk *syllogismos,* fr. *syllogizesthai* to syllogize, fr. *syn-* + *logizesthai* to calculate, fr. *logos* reckoning, word — more at LEGEND] **1 :** a deductive scheme of a formal argument consisting of a major and a minor premise and a conclusion (as in "every virtue is laudable; kindness is a virtue; therefore kindness is laudable") **2 :** deductive reasoning **3 :** a subtle, specious, or crafty argument — **syl·lo·gis·tic** \ˌsil-ə-'jis-tik\ *adj* — **syl·lo·gis·ti·cal·ly** \-ti-k(ə-)lē\ *adv*
syl·lo·gist \'sil-ə-jəst\ *n* **:** one who applies or is skilled in syllogistic reasoning
syl·lo·gize \'sil-ə-ˌjīz\ *vb* **-gized; -giz·ing** [ME *sylogysen,* fr. LL *syllogizare,* fr. Gk *syllogizesthai*] *vi* **:** to reason by means of syllogisms ~ *vt* **:** to deduce by syllogism <~*s* his moral laws>
sylph \'silf\ *n* [NL *sylphus*] **1 :** an elemental being in the theory of Paracelsus that inhabits air **2 :** a slender graceful woman or girl — **sylph·like** \'sil-ˌflīk\ *adj*
sylph·id \'sil-fəd\ *n* **:** a young or diminutive sylph
sylva, sylviculture *var of* SILVA, SILVICULTURE
[1]**syl·van** \'sil-vən\ *adj* [ML *silvanus, sylvanus,* fr. L *silva, sylva* wood] **1 a :** living or located in the woods or forest **b :** of, relating to, or characteristic of the woods or forest **2 a :** made, shaped, or formed of woods or trees **b :** abounding in woods, groves, or trees **:** WOODED
[2]**sylvan** *n* **:** one that frequents groves or woods
syl·va·nite \'sil-və-ˌnīt\ *n* [F *sylvanite,* fr. NL *sylvanium* tellurium, fr. *Transylvania,* region in Rumania] **:** a mineral (Au, Ag)Te_2 that is a gold silver telluride and often occurs in crystals resembling written characters
syl·vat·ic \sil-'vat-ik\ *adj* [L *silvaticus* of the woods, wild — more at SAVAGE] **1 :** SYLVAN <~ rodents> **2 :** occurring in or affecting wild animals <~ diseases>
syl·vite \'sil-ˌvīt\ *also* **syl·vine** \-ˌvēn\ *n* [F *sylvine,* fr. NL *sal digestivus Sylvii* digestive salt of Sylvius, fr. *Sylvius* latinized name of Jacques Dubois †1555 F physician] **:** a mineral KCl that is a natural potassium chloride and occurs in colorless cubes or crystalline masses
sym *abbr* **1** symbol **2** symmetrical
sym- — see SYN-
sym·bi·ont \'sim-ˌbī-ˌänt, -bē-\ *n* [prob. fr. G, modif. of Gk *symbiount-, symbiōn,* prp. of *symbioun*] **:** an organism living in symbiosis; *esp* **:** the smaller member of a symbiotic pair — **sym·bi·on·tic** \ˌsim-ˌbī-'änt-ik, -bē-\ *adj*
sym·bi·o·sis \ˌsim-ˌbī-'ō-səs, -bē-\ *n, pl* **-bi·o·ses** \-ˌsēz\ [NL, fr. G *symbiose,* fr. Gk *symbiōsis* state of living together, fr. *symbioun* to live together, fr. *symbios* living together, fr. *sym-* + *bios* life — more at QUICK] **1 :** the living together in more or less intimate association or close union of two dissimilar organisms **2 :** the intimate living together of two dissimilar organisms in a mutually beneficial relationship; *esp* **:** MUTUALISM — **sym·bi·ot·ic** \-'ät-ik\ *adj* — **sym·bi·ot·i·cal·ly** \-i-k(ə-)lē\ *adv*
sym·bi·ote \'sim-ˌbī-ˌōt, -bē-\ *n* [F, fr. Gk *symbiōtēs* companion, fr. *symbioun* to live together] **:** SYMBIONT
[1]**sym·bol** \'sim-bəl\ *n* [in sense 1, fr. LL *symbolum,* fr. LGk *symbolon,* fr. Gk, token, sign; in other senses fr. L *symbolum* token, sign, symbol, fr. Gk *symbolon,* lit., token of identity verified by comparing its other half, fr. *symballein* to throw together, compare, fr. *syn-* + *ballein* to throw — more at DEVIL] **1 :** an authoritative summary of faith or doctrine **:** CREED **2 :** something that stands for or suggests something else by reason of relationship, association, convention, or accidental resemblance; *esp* **:** a visible sign of something invisible <the lion is a ~ of courage> **3 :** an arbitrary or conventional sign used in writing or printing relating to a particular field to represent operations, quantities, elements, relations, or qualities **4 :** an object or act that represents a repressed complex through unconscious association <phallic ~*s*> **5 :** an act, sound, or object having cultural significance and the capacity to excite or objectify a response
[2]**symbol** *vb* **-boled** *or* **-bolled; -bol·ing** *or* **-bol·ling :** SYMBOLIZE
sym·bol·ic \sim-'bäl-ik\ *or* **sym·bol·i·cal** \-i-kəl\ *adj* **1 :** of, relating to, or constituting a symbol **2 a :** using, employing, or exhibiting a symbol **b :** consisting of or proceeding by means of symbols **3 :** characterized by or terminating in symbols <~ thinking> **4 :** characterized by symbolism <a ~ dance> — **sym·bol·i·cal·ly** \-i-k(ə-)lē\ *adv*
symbolic logic *n* **:** a science of developing and representing logical principles by means of a formalized system consisting of primitive symbols, combinations of these symbols, axioms, and rules of inference
sym·bol·ism \'sim-bə-ˌliz-əm\ *n* **1 :** the art or practice of using symbols esp. by investing things with a symbolic meaning or by expressing the invisible or intangible by means of visible or sensuous representations: as **a :** the use of conventional or traditional signs in the representation of divine beings and spirits **b :** artistic imitation or invention that is a method of revealing or suggesting immaterial, ideal, or otherwise intangible truth or states **2 :** a system of symbols or representations
sym·bol·ist \'sim-bə-ləst\ *n* **1 :** one who employs symbols or symbolism **2 :** one skilled in the interpretation or explication of

symbols **3 :** one of a group of writers and artists in France after 1880 reacting against realism, concerning themselves with general truths instead of actualities, exalting the metaphysical and the mysterious, and aiming to unify and blend the arts and the functions of the senses — **symbolist** *adj*

sym·bol·is·tic \ˌsim-bə-ˈlis-tik\ *adj* **:** SYMBOLIC

sym·bol·iza·tion \ˌsim-bə-lə-ˈzā-shən\ *n* **1 :** an act or instance of symbolizing **2 :** man's capacity to develop a system of meaningful symbols

sym·bol·ize \ˈsim-bə-ˌlīz\ *vb* **-ized; -iz·ing** *vi* **:** to use symbols or symbolism ~ *vt* **1 :** to serve as a symbol of **2 :** to represent, express, or identify by a symbol — **sym·bol·iz·er** *n*

sym·bol·o·gy \sim-ˈbäl-ə-jē\ *n, pl* **-gies** [*symbol* + *-logy*] **1 :** the art of expression by symbols **2 :** the study or interpretation of symbols **3 :** a system of symbols

sym·met·al·lism \(ˈ)sim-ˈ(m)et-ᵊl-ˌiz-əm\ *n* [*syn-* + *-metallism* (as in *bimetallism*)] **:** a system of coinage in which the unit of currency consists of a particular weight of an alloy of two or more metals (as gold and silver)

sym·met·ri·cal \sə-ˈme-tri-kəl\ *or* **sym·met·ric** \-trik\ *adj* **1 :** having, involving, or exhibiting symmetry **2 :** having corresponding points whose connecting lines are bisected by a given point or perpendicularly bisected by a given line or plane <~ curves> **3** *symmetric* **:** being such that the terms may be interchanged without altering the value, character, or truth <*symmetric* equations> <R is a *symmetric* relation if *a*R*b* implies *b*R*a*> **4 a :** capable of division by a longitudinal plane into similar halves <~ plant parts> **b :** having the same number of members in each whorl of floral leaves <~ flowers> **5 :** affecting corresponding parts simultaneously and similarly <~ rash> **6 :** exhibiting symmetry in a structural formula; *esp* **:** being a derivative with groups substituted symmetrically in the molecule — **sym·met·ri·cal·ly** \-tri-k(ə-)lē\ *adv* — **sym·met·ri·cal·ness** \-kəl-nəs\ *n*

symmetric group *n* **:** a permutation group that is composed of all of the permutations of *n* things

symmetric matrix *n* **:** a matrix that is its own transpose

sym·me·trize \ˈsim-ə-ˌtrīz\ *vt* **-trized; -triz·ing :** to make symmetrical — **sym·me·tri·za·tion** \ˌsim-ə-trə-ˈzā-shən\ *n*

sym·me·try \ˈsim-ə-trē\ *n, pl* **-tries** [L *symmetria,* fr. Gk, fr. *symmetros* symmetrical, fr. *syn-* + *metron* measure — more at MEASURE] **1 :** balanced proportions; *also* **:** beauty of form arising from balanced proportions **2 :** the property of being symmetrical; *esp* **:** correspondence in size, shape, and relative position of parts on opposite sides of a dividing line or median plane or about a center or axis — compare BILATERAL SYMMETRY, RADIAL SYMMETRY **3 :** a rigid motion of a geometric figure that determines a one-to-one mapping onto itself **4 :** the property of remaining invariant under certain changes (as of orientation in space, of the sign of the electric charge, of parity, or of the direction of time flow) — used of physical phenomena and of equations describing them

¹sym·pa·thet·ic \ˌsim-pə-ˈthet-ik\ *adj* [NL *sympatheticus,* fr. L *sympathia* sympathy] **1 :** existing or operating through an affinity, interdependence, or mutual association **2 a :** not discordant or antagonistic **b :** appropriate to one's mood, inclinations, or disposition **c :** marked by kindly or pleased appreciation **3 :** given to, marked by, or arising from sympathy, compassion, friendliness, and sensitivity to others' emotions <a ~ gesture> **4 :** favorably inclined **:** APPROVING <not ~ to the idea> **5 :** showing empathy **6 a :** of or relating to the sympathetic nervous system **b :** mediated by or acting on the sympathetic nerves **7 :** relating to musical tones produced by sympathetic vibration or to strings so tuned as to sound by sympathetic vibration ***syn*** see CONSONANT — **sym·pa·thet·i·cal·ly** \-i-k(ə-)lē\ *adv*

²sympathetic *n* **:** a sympathetic structure; *esp* **:** SYMPATHETIC NERVOUS SYSTEM

sympathetic nervous system *n* **:** the part of the autonomic nervous system that contains chiefly adrenergic fibers and tends to depress secretion, decrease the tone and contractility of smooth muscle, and cause the contraction of blood vessels

sympathetic strike *n* **:** SYMPATHY STRIKE

sympathetic vibration *n* **:** a vibration produced in one body by the vibrations of exactly the same period in a neighboring body

sym·pa·thin \ˈsim-pə-thən\ *n* [ISV, fr. ²*sympathetic*] **:** a substance that is secreted by sympathetic nerve endings and acts as a chemical mediator

sym·pa·thize \ˈsim-pə-ˌthīz\ *vi* **-thized; -thiz·ing 1 :** to react or respond in sympathy **2 :** to be in keeping, accord, or harmony **3 :** to share in suffering or grief **:** COMMISERATE <~ with a friend in trouble>; *also* **:** to express such sympathy **4 :** to be in sympathy intellectually <~ with a proposal> — **sym·pa·thiz·er** *n*

sym·pa·tho·lyt·ic \ˌsim-pə-thō-ˈlit-ik\ *adj* [ISV *sympath*etic + *-o-* + *-lytic*] **:** tending to oppose the physiological results of sympathetic nervous activity or of sympathomimetic drugs — **sympatholytic** *n*

sym·pa·tho·mi·met·ic \-mə-ˈmet-ik, -(ˌ)mī-\ *adj* [ISV *sympath*etic + *-o-* + *mimetic*] **:** simulating sympathetic nervous action in physiological effect — **sympathomimetic** *n*

sym·pa·thy \ˈsim-pə-thē\ *n, pl* **-thies** [L *sympathia,* fr. Gk *sympatheia,* fr. *sympathēs* having common feelings, sympathetic, fr. *syn-* + *pathos* feelings, emotion, experience — more at PATHOS] **1 a :** an affinity, association, or relationship between persons or things wherein whatever affects one similarly affects the other **b :** mutual or parallel susceptibility or a condition brought about by it **c :** unity or harmony in action or effect **2 a :** inclination to think or feel alike **:** emotional or intellectual accord **b :** feeling of loyalty **:** tendency to favor or support <republican *sympathies*> **3 a :** the act or capacity of entering into or sharing the feelings or interests of another **b :** the feeling or mental state brought about by such sensitivity <have ~ for the poor> **4 :** the correlation existing between bodies capable of communicating their vibrational energy to one another through some medium

syn* 1** see ATTRACTION ***ant antipathy

2 SYMPATHY, PITY, COMPASSION, RUTH, EMPATHY *shared meaning element* **:** a feeling for or a capacity for sharing in the interests or distress of another

sympathy strike *n* **:** a strike in which the strikers have no direct grievance against their own employer but attempt to support or aid usu. another group of workers on strike

sym·pat·ric \sim-ˈpa-trik\ *adj* [*syn-* + Gk *patra* fatherland, fr. *patēr* father — more at FATHER] **:** occurring in the same area; *specif* **:** occupying the same range without loss of identity from interbreeding <~ species> — compare ALLOPATRIC — **sym·pat·ri·cal·ly** \-tri-k(ə-)lē\ *adv* — **sym·pat·ry** \ˈsim-ˌpa-trē\ *n*

sym·pet·al·ous \(ˈ)sim-ˈpet-ᵊl-əs\ *adj* **:** GAMOPETALOUS — **sym·pet·aly** \-ᵊl-ē, ˈsim-ˌ\ *n*

sym·phon·ic \sim-ˈfän-ik\ *adj* **1 :** HARMONIOUS, SYMPHONIOUS **2 :** relating to or having the form or character of a symphony <~ music> **3 :** suggestive of a symphony esp. in form, interweaving of themes, or harmonious arrangement <a ~ drama> — **sym·phon·i·cal·ly** \-i-k(ə-)lē\ *adv*

symphonic poem *n* **:** an extended programmatic composition for symphony orchestra usu. freer in form than a symphony

sym·pho·ni·ous \sim-ˈfō-nē-əs\ *adj* **:** agreeing esp. in sound **:** HARMONIOUS — **sym·pho·ni·ous·ly** *adv*

sym·pho·nist \ˈsim(p)-fə-nəst\ *n* **1 :** a composer of symphonies **2 :** a member of a symphony orchestra

sym·pho·ny \-nē\ *n, pl* **-nies** [ME *symphonie,* fr. OF, fr. L *symphonia,* fr. Gk *symphōnia,* fr. *symphōnos* concordant in sound, fr. *syn-* + *phōnē* voice, sound — more at BAN] **1 :** consonance of sounds **2 a :** RITORNELLO 1 **b :** SINFONIA 1 **c** (1) **:** a usu. long and complex sonata for symphony orchestra (2) **:** a musical composition (as for organ) resembling such a symphony in complexity or variety **3 :** consonance or harmony of color (as in a painting) **4 a :** SYMPHONY ORCHESTRA **b :** a symphony orchestra concert **5 :** something that in its harmonious complexity or variety suggests a symphonic composition

symphony orchestra *n* **:** a large orchestra of winds, strings, and percussion that plays symphonic works

sym·phy·se·al \ˌsim(p)-fə-ˈsē-əl\ *also* **sym·phys·i·al** \sim-ˈfiz-ē-əl\ *adj* [Gk *symphyse-, symphysis* symphysis] **:** of, relating to, or constituting a symphysis

sym·phy·sis \ˈsim(p)-fə-səs\ *n, pl* **-phy·ses** \-ˌsēz\ [NL, fr. Gk, state of growing together, fr. *symphyesthai* to grow together, fr. *syn-* + *phyein* to make grow, bring forth — more at BE] **1 :** an immovable or more or less movable articulation of various bones in the median plane of the body **2 :** an articulation in which the bony surfaces are connected by pads of fibrous cartilage without a synovial membrane

sym·po·di·al \sim-ˈpōd-ē-əl\ *adj* [NL *sympodium* apparent main axis formed from secondary axes, fr. Gk *syn-* + *podion* base — more at -PODIUM] **:** having or involving the formation of an apparent main axis from successive secondary axes <~ branching of a cyme> — **sym·po·di·al·ly** \-ə-lē\ *adv*

sym·po·si·arch \sim-ˈpō-zē-ˌärk\ *n* [Gk *symposiarchos,* fr. *symposion* symposium + *-archos* -arch] **:** one who presides over a symposium

sym·po·si·ast \-zē-ˌast, -əst\ *n* [Gk *symposiazein* to take part in a symposium, fr. *symposion*] **:** one who contributes to a symposium

sym·po·sium \sim-ˈpō-zē-əm *also* -zh(ē-)əm\ *n, pl* **-sia** \-zē-ə, -zh(ē-)ə\ *or* **-siums** [L, fr. Gk *symposion,* fr. *sympinein* to drink together, fr. *syn-* + *pinein* to drink — more at POTABLE] **1 a :** a convivial party (as after a banquet in ancient Greece) with music and conversation **b :** a social gathering at which there is free interchange of ideas **2 a :** a formal meeting at which several specialists deliver short addresses on a topic or on related topics — compare COLLOQUIUM **b :** a collection of opinions on a subject; *esp* **:** one published by a periodical **c :** DISCUSSION

symp·tom \ˈsim(p)-təm\ *n* [LL *symptomat-, symptoma,* fr. Gk *symptōmat-, symptōma* happening, attribute, symptom, fr. *sympiptein* to happen, fr. *syn-* + *piptein* to fall — more at FEATHER] **1 a :** subjective evidence of disease or physical disturbance; *broadly* **:** something that indicates the presence of bodily disorder **b :** an evident reaction by a plant to a pathogen **2 a :** something that indicates the existence of something else <imagination is thought to be a ~ of indirection —Richard Poirier> **b :** a slight indication **:** TRACE — **symp·tom·less** \-ləs\ *adj*

symp·tom·at·ic \ˌsim(p)-tə-ˈmat-ik\ *adj* **1 a :** being a symptom of a disease **b :** having the characteristics of a particular disease but arising from another cause **2 :** concerned with or affecting symptoms **3 :** CHARACTERISTIC, INDICATIVE <his behavior was ~ of his character> — **symp·tom·at·i·cal·ly** \-i-k(ə-)lē\ *adv*

symp·tom·atol·o·gy \ˌsim(p)-tə-mə-ˈtäl-ə-jē\ *n* **1 :** a branch of medical science concerned with symptoms of diseases **2 :** the symptom complex of a disease — **symp·tom·at·o·log·i·cal** \-ˌmat-ᵊl-ˈäj-i-kəl\ *or* **symp·tom·at·o·log·ic** \-ˈäj-ik\ *adj* — **symp·tom·at·o·log·i·cal·ly** \-i-k(ə-)lē\ *adv*

syn *abbr* synonym; synonymous; synonymy

syn- *or* **sym-** *prefix* [ME, fr. OF, fr. L, fr. Gk, fr. *syn* with, together with] **1 :** with **:** along with **:** together <*syn*clinal> <*sym*petalous> **2 :** at the same time <*syn*esthesia>

syn·ae·re·sis *var of* SYNERESIS

syn·aes·the·sia, syn·aes·thet·ic *var of* SYNETHESIA, SYNESTHETIC

syn·aes·the·sis \ˌsin-əs-ˈthē-səs\ *n* [Gk *synaisthēsis* joint perception, fr. *synaisthanesthai* to perceive simultaneously, fr. *syn-* + *aisthanesthai* to perceive — more at AUDIBLE] **:** harmony of different or opposing impulses produced by a work of art

syn·a·gogue *or* **syn·a·gog** \ˈsin-ə-ˌgäg\ *n* [ME *synagoge,* fr. OF, fr. LL *synagoga,* fr. Gk *synagōgē* assembly, synagogue, fr. *synagein* to bring together, fr. *syn-* + *agein* to lead — more at AGENT] **1** : a Jewish congregation **2** : the house of worship and communal center of a Jewish congregation — **syn·a·gog·al** \ˌsin-ə-ˈgäg-əl\ *adj*

syn·a·loe·pha *or* **syn·a·le·pha** \ˌsin-ə-ˈlē-fə\ *n* [NL, fr. Gk *synaloiphē*, fr. *synaleiphein* to clog up, coalesce, unite two syllables into one, fr. *syn-* + *aleiphein* to anoint, besmear]: the reduction to one syllable of two vowels of adjacent syllables (as in *th' army* for *the army*)

[1]**synapse** \ˈsin-ˌaps, sə-ˈnaps\ *n* [NL *synapsis*, fr. Gk, juncture, fr. *synaptein* to fasten together, fr. *syn-* + *haptein* to fasten] : the point at which a nervous impulse passes from one neuron to another

[2]**synapse** *vi* **syn·apsed; syn·aps·ing** : to form a synapse or come together in synapsis

syn·ap·sis \sə-ˈnap-səs\ *n, pl* **-ap·ses** \-ˌsēz\ [NL, fr. Gk, juncture] **1** : the association of homologous chromosomes with chiasma formation that is characteristic of the first meiotic prophase and is held to be the mechanism for genetic crossing-over **2** : SYNAPSE — **syn·ap·tic** \-ˈnap-tik\ *adj* — **syn·ap·ti·cal·ly** \-ti-k(ə-)lē\ *adv*

syn·ap·to·some \sə-ˈnap-tə-ˈsōm\ *n* [*synaptic* + *-o-* + [3]*-some*] : a structure that is recovered from homogenized nerve tissue and prob. represents pinched off nerve endings — **syn·ap·to·som·al** \-ˌnap-tə-ˈsō-məl\ *adj*

syn·ar·thro·di·al \ˌsin-är-ˈthrōd-ē-əl\ *adj* [NL *synarthrodia* synarthrosis] : of, relating to, or being a synarthrosis — **syn·ar·thro·di·al·ly** \-ē-ə-lē\ *adv*

syn·ar·thro·sis \-ˈthrō-səs\ *n, pl* **-thro·ses** \-ˌsēz\ [Gk *synarthrōsis*, fr. *syn-* + *arthrōsis* arthrosis]: an immovable articulation in which the bones are united by intervening fibrous connective tissues

[1]**sync** *also* **synch** \ˈsiŋk\ *n* : SYNCHRONIZATION, SYNCHRONISM — **sync** *adj*

[2]**sync** *also* **synch** *vt* **synced** *also* **synched** \ˈsiŋ(k)t\; **sync·ing** *also* **synch·ing** \ˈsiŋ-kiŋ\ : SYNCHRONIZE

syn·car·pous \(ˈ)sin-ˈkär-pəs\ *adj* : having the carpels of the gynoecium united in a compound ovary — **syn·car·py** \ˈsin-ˌkär-pē\ *n*

[1]**syn·chro** \ˈsiŋ-(ˌ)krō, ˈsin-\ *n, pl* **synchros** [*synchronous*] : SELSYN

[2]**synchro** *adj* [*synchro-*] : adapted to synchronization

synchro- *comb form* [*synchronized* & *synchronous*] : synchronized : synchronous <*synchro*flash> <*synchro*mesh>

syn·chro–cy·clo·tron \ˌsiŋ-(ˌ)krō-ˈsī-klə-ˌträn, ˌsin-\ *n* : a modified cyclotron that achieves greater energies for the charged particles by compensating for the variation in mass that the particles experience with increasing velocity

syn·chro·flash \ˈsiŋ-krō-ˌflash, ˈsin-\ *adj* : employing or produced with a mechanism for synchronizing the firing or peak brilliance of a flash lamp with the opening of a camera shutter

syn·chro·mesh \-ˌmesh\ *adj* : designed for effecting synchronized shifting of gears — **synchromesh** *n*

syn·chro·nal \ˈsiŋ-krən-ᵊl, ˈsin-\ *adj* : SYNCHRONOUS

syn·chro·ne·ity \ˌsiŋ-krə-ˈnē-ət-ē, ˌsin-, -ˈnā-\ *n* [*synchronous* + *-eity* (as in *spontaneity*)] : the state of being synchronous

syn·chron·ic \sin-ˈkrän-ik, siŋ-\ *adj* **1** : SYNCHRONOUS **2 a** : DESCRIPTIVE 4 <~ linguistics> **b** : concerned with the complex of events existing in a limited time period and ignoring historical antecedents — **syn·chron·i·cal** \-i-kəl\ *adj* — **syn·chron·i·cal·ly** \-i-k(ə-)lē\ *adv*

syn·chro·nism \ˈsiŋ-krə-ˌniz-əm, ˈsin-\ *n* **1** : the quality or state of being synchronous : SIMULTANEOUSNESS **2** : chronological arrangement of historical events and personages so as to indicate coincidence or coexistence; *also* : a table showing such concurrences — **syn·chro·nis·tic** \ˌsiŋ-krə-ˈnis-tik, ˌsin-\ *adj*

syn·chro·ni·za·tion \ˌsiŋ-krə-nə-ˈzā-shən, ˌsin-\ *n* **1** : the act or result of synchronizing **2** : the state of being synchronous

syn·chro·nize \ˈsiŋ-krə-ˌnīz, ˈsin-\ *vb* **-nized; -niz·ing** *vi* : to happen at the same time ~ *vt* **1** : to represent or arrange (events) to indicate coincidence or coexistence **2** : to make synchronous in operation **3** : to make (motion picture sound) exactly simultaneous with the action — **syn·chro·niz·er** *n*

synchronized swimming *n* : exhibition swimming in which the movements of one or more swimmers are synchronized with a musical accompaniment so as to form changing patterns

syn·chro·nous \ˈsiŋ-krə-nəs, ˈsin-\ *adj* [LL *synchronos*, fr. Gk, fr. *syn-* + *chronos* time] **1** : happening, existing, or arising at precisely the same time **2** : recurring or operating at exactly the same periods **3** : involving or indicating synchronism **4 a** : having the same period; *also* : having the same period and phase **b** : GEOSTATIONARY ***syn*** see CONTEMPORARY — **syn·chro·nous·ly** *adv* — **syn·chro·nous·ness** *n*

synchronous motor *n* : an electric motor having a speed strictly proportional to the frequency of the operating current

syn·chro·ny \ˈsiŋ-krə-nē, ˈsin-\ *n, pl* **-nies** : synchronistic occurrence, arrangement, or treatment

syn·chro·scope \-ˌskōp\ *n* : any of several devices for showing whether two associated machines or moving parts are operating in synchronism with each other

syn·chro·tron \ˈsiŋ-k(r)ə-ˌträn, ˈsin-\ *n* **1** : an apparatus for imparting very high speeds to charged particles by means of a combination of a high-frequency electric field and a low-frequency magnetic field **2** : SYNCHROTRON RADIATION

synchrotron radiation *n* [fr. its having been first observed in a synchrotron] : radiation emitted by high-energy charged relativistic particles (as electrons) when they are accelerated by a magnetic field (as in a nebula)

syn·cli·nal \(ˈ)sin-ˈklīn-ᵊl\ *adj* [Gk *syn-* + *klinein* to lean — more at LEAN] **1** : inclined down from opposite directions so as to meet **2** : having or relating to a folded rock structure in which the sides dip toward a common line or plane

syn·cline \ˈsin-ˌklīn\ *n* [back-formation fr. *synclinal*] : a trough of stratified rock in which the beds dip toward each other from either side — compare ANTICLINE

syn·co·pate \ˈsiŋ-kə-ˌpāt, ˈsin-\ *vt* **-pat·ed; -pat·ing** **1 a** : to shorten or produce by syncope <~ *suppose* to *s'pose*> **b** : to cut short : CLIP, ABBREVIATE **2** : to modify or affect (musical rhythm) by syncopation — **syn·co·pa·tor** \-ˌpāt-ər\ *n*

syn·co·pat·ed *adj* **1** : marked by or exhibiting syncopation <~ rhythm> **2** : cut short : ABBREVIATED

syn·co·pa·tion \ˌsiŋ-kə-ˈpā-shən, ˌsin-\ *n* **1** : a temporary displacement of the regular metrical accent in music caused typically by stressing the weak beat **2** : a syncopated rhythm, passage, or dance step — **syn·co·pa·tive** \ˈsiŋ-kə-ˌpāt-iv, ˈsin-\ *adj*

syncopation

syn·co·pe \ˈsiŋ-kə-(ˌ)pē, ˈsin-\ *n* [LL, fr. Gk *synkopē*, lit., cutting short, fr. *synkoptein* to cut short, fr. *syn-* + *koptein* to cut — more at CAPON] **1** : a partial or complete temporary suspension of respiration and circulation due to cerebral ischemia : FAINT **2** : the loss of one or more sounds or letters in the interior of a word (as in *fo'c'sle* for *forecastle*) — **syn·co·pal** \-kə-pəl\ *adj*

syn·cret·ic \sin-ˈkret-ik, siŋ-\ *adj* : characterized or brought about by syncretism : SYNCRETISTIC

syn·cre·tism \ˈsiŋ-krə-ˌtiz-əm, ˈsin-\ *n* [NL *syncretismus*, fr. Gk *synkrētismos* federation of Cretan cities, fr. *syn-* + *Krēt-*, *Krēs* Cretan] **1** : the combination of different forms of belief or practice **2** : the fusion of two or more orig. different inflectional forms — **syn·cre·tist** \-təst\ *n or adj* — **syn·cre·tis·tic** \ˌsiŋ-krə-ˈtis-tik, ˌsin-\ *adj*

syn·cy·tium \sin-ˈsish-(ē-)əm\ *n, pl* **-tia** \-(ē-)ə\ [NL, fr. *syn-* + *cyt-*] **1** : a multinucleate mass of protoplasm resulting from fusion of cells **2** : COENOCYTE 1 — **syn·cy·tial** \-ˈsish-(ē-)əl\ *adj*

syn·dac·ty·lism \(ˈ)sin-ˈdak-tə-ˌliz-əm\ *n* : SYNDACTYLY

syn·dac·ty·ly \-lē\ *n* [NL *syndactylia*, fr. *syn-* + Gk *daktylos* finger] : a union of two or more digits that is normal in many birds (as kingfishers) and in some lower mammals (as the kangaroos) and occurs in man as a familial anomaly marked by webbing of two or more fingers or toes

syn·de·sis \ˈsin-də-səs\ *n* [NL, fr. Gk, action of binding together, fr. *syndein* to bind together — more at ASYNDETON] : SYNAPSIS

syn·des·mo·sis \ˌsin-ˌdez-ˈmō-səs, -ˌdes-\ *n, pl* **-mo·ses** \-ˌsēz\ [NL, fr. Gk *syndesmos* fastening, ligament, fr. *syndein*] : an articulation in which the contiguous surfaces of the bones are rough and are bound together by a ligament — **syn·des·mot·ic** \-ˈmät-ik\ *adj*

syn·det·ic \sin-ˈdet-ik\ *adj* [Gk *syndetikos*, fr. *syndein*] : CONNECTIVE, CONNECTING <~ pronoun>; *also* : marked by a conjunctive <~ relative clause> — **syn·det·i·cal·ly** \-i-k(ə-)lē\ *adv*

syn·dic \ˈsin-dik\ *n* [F, fr. LL *syndicus* representative of a corporation, fr. Gk *syndikos* assistant at law, advocate, representative of a state, fr. *syn-* + *dikē* judgment, case at law — more at DICTION] **1** : a municipal magistrate in some countries **2** : an agent of a university or corporation

syn·di·cal \-di-kəl\ *adj* **1** : of or relating to a syndic or to a committee that assumes the powers of a syndic **2** : of or relating to syndicalism

syn·di·cal·ism \ˈsin-di-kə-ˌliz-əm\ *n* [F *syndicalisme*, fr. *chambre syndicale* trade union] **1** : a revolutionary doctrine by which workers seize control of the economy and the government by direct means (as a general strike) **2** : a system of economic organization in which industries are owned and managed by the workers **3** : a theory of government based on functional rather than territorial representation — **syn·di·cal·ist** \-ləst\ *adj or n*

[1]**syn·di·cate** \ˈsin-di-kət\ *n* [F *syndicat*, fr. *syndic*] **1 a** : the office or jurisdiction of a syndic **b** : a council or body of syndics **2** : an association of persons officially authorized to undertake a duty or negotiate business **3 a** : a group of persons or concerns who combine to carry out a particular transaction **b** : CARTEL 2 **c** : a loose association of racketeers in control of organized crime **4** : a business concern that sells materials for publication in a number of newspapers or periodicals simultaneously **5** : a group of newspapers under one management

[2]**syn·di·cate** \ˈsin-də-ˌkāt\ *vb* **-cat·ed; -cat·ing** *vt* **1** : to subject to or manage as a syndicate **2** : to sell (as a cartoon) to a syndicate or for publication in many newspapers or periodicals at once ~ *vi* : to unite to form a syndicate — **syn·di·ca·tion** \ˌsin-də-ˈkā-shən\ *n* — **syn·di·ca·tor** \ˈsin-də-ˌkāt-ər\ *n*

syn·drome \ˈsin-ˌdrōm *also* -drəm\ *n* [NL, fr. Gk *syndromē* combination, syndrome, fr. *syn-* + *dramein* to run — more at DROMEDARY] : a group of signs and symptoms that occur together and characterize a particular abnormality

[1]**syne** \(ˈ)sīn\ *adv* [ME (northern), prob. fr. ON *sīthan*; akin to OE *siththan* since — more at SINCE] *chiefly Scot* : since then : AGO

[2]**syne** *conj, Scot* : SINCE

[3]**syne** *prep, Scot* : SINCE

syn·ec·do·che \sə-ˈnek-də-(ˌ)kē\ *n* [L, fr. Gk *synekdochē*, fr. *syn-* + *ekdochē* sense, interpretation, fr. *ekdechesthai* to receive, understand, fr. *ex* from + *dechesthai* to receive; akin to Gk *dokein* to seem good — more at EX-, DECENT] : a figure of speech by which a part is put for the whole (as *fifty sail* for *fifty ships*), the whole for a part (as *the smiling year* for *spring*), the species for the genus (as *cutthroat* for *assassin*), the genus for the species (as *a creature* for *a man*), or the name of the material for the thing made (as *boards* for *stage*) — **syn·ec·doch·ic** \ˌsin-ˌek-ˈdäk-ik\ *adj* — **syn·ec·doch·i·cal** \-ˈdäk-i-kəl\ *adj* — **syn·ec·doch·i·cal·ly** \-i-k(ə-)lē\ *adv*

syn·ecol·o·gy \ˌsin-i-ˈkäl-ə-jē, ˌsin-e-ˈkäl-\ *n* [G *synökologie*, fr. *syn* + *ökologie* ecology] : a branch of ecology that deals with the structure, development, and distribution of ecological communities — **syn·eco·log·i·cal** \ˌsin-ˌē-kə-ˈläj-i-kəl, -ˌek-ə-\ *or* **syn·eco·log·ic** \-ik\ *adj* — **syn·eco·log·i·cal·ly** \-i-k(ə-)lē\ *adv*

syn·ec·tics \sə-ˈnek-tiks\ *n pl but usu sing in constr* [perh. fr. Gk *synektik*tein to bring forth together (fr. *syn-* + *ektiktein* to bring forth, fr. *ex-* out + *tiktein* to beget) + E *-s* (as in *dialectics*) — more at EX-, THANE] : a theory or system of problem-stating and problem-solution based on creative thinking that involves free use of metaphor and analogy in informal interchange within a carefully

selected small group of individuals of diverse personality and areas of specialization — **syn·ec·tic** \-tik\ *adj* — **syn·ec·ti·cal·ly** \-ti-k(ə-)lē\ *adv*
syn·eph·rine \sə-ˈnef-rən\ *n* [*syn-* + epin*ephrine*] : a crystalline sympathomimetic amine $C_9H_{13}NO_2$
syn·ere·sis \sə-ˈner-ə-səs, -ˈnir-, *esp for 2* ˌsin-ə-ˈrē-\ *n* [LL *synaeresis*, fr. Gk *synairesis*, fr. *synairein* to contract, fr. *syn-* + *hairein* to take] **1 :** SYNIZESIS 1 **2 :** the separation of liquid from a gel caused by contraction
syn·er·get·ic \ˌsin-ər-ˈjet-ik\ *adj* [Gk *synergētikos*, fr. *synergein* to work with, cooperate, fr. *synergos* working together, fr. *syn-* + *ergon* work — more at WORK] : SYNERGIC
syn·er·gic \sə-ˈnər-jik\ *adj* **:** working together **:** COOPERATING — **syn·er·gi·cal·ly** \-ji-k(ə-)lē\ *adv*
syn·er·gid \sə-ˈnər-jəd, ˈsin-ər-\ *n* [NL *synergida*, fr. Gk *synergos* working together] **:** one of two small cells lying near the micropyle of the embryo sac of a seed plant
syn·er·gism \ˈsin-ər-ˌjiz-əm\ *n* [NL *synergismus*, fr. Gk *synergos*] **:** cooperative action of discrete agencies such that the total effect is greater than the sum of the effects taken independently
syn·er·gist \-jəst\ *n* **:** something (as a chemical or a muscle) that enhances the effectiveness of an active agent; *broadly* **:** either member of a synergistic pair
syn·er·gis·tic \ˌsin-ər-ˈjis-tik\ *adj* **1 :** having the capacity to act in synergism <~ drugs> <the effects on science of decisions in . . . industry or wherever there is a ~ or abrasive interface —*Science News*> **2 :** of, relating to, or resembling synergism <a ~ reaction> <a ~ effect> — **syn·er·gis·ti·cal·ly** \-ti-k(ə-)lē\ *adv*
syn·er·gy \ˈsin-ər-jē\ *n* [NL *synergia*, fr. Gk *synergos* working together] **:** combined action or operation (as of muscles); *specif* **:** SYNERGISM
syn·e·sis \ˈsin-ə-səs\ *n* [NL, fr. Gk, understanding, sense, fr. *synienai* to bring together, understand, fr. *syn-* + *hienai* to send — more at JET] **:** a grammatical construction in which agreement or reference is according to sense rather than strict syntax (as *anyone* and *them* in "if anyone calls, tell them I am out")
syn·es·the·sia \ˌsin-əs-ˈthē-zh(ē-)ə\ *n* [NL, fr. *syn-* + *-esthesia* (as in *anesthesia*)] **:** a concomitant sensation; *esp* **:** a subjective sensation or image of a sense (as of color) other than the one (as of sound) being stimulated — **syn·es·thet·ic** \-ˈthet-ik\ *adj*
syn·ga·my \ˈsiŋ-gə-mē\ *n* [ISV] **:** sexual reproduction by union of gametes
syn·ge·ne·ic \ˌsin-jə-ˈnē-ik\ *adj* [Gk *syngeneia* kinship (fr. *syn-* + *genos* kind, kin) + E *-ic* — more at KIN] **:** genetically identical <~ grafts between members of an inbred strain>
syn·i·ze·sis \ˌsin-ə-ˈzē-səs\ *n* [LL, fr. Gk *synizēsis*, fr. *synizein* to sit down together, collapse, blend, fr. *syn-* + *hizein* to sit down; akin to L *sidere* to sit down — more at SUBSIDE] **1 :** contraction of two syllables into one by uniting in pronunciation two adjacent vowels **2 a :** the massing of the chromatin of the nucleus preceding the maturation division **b :** SYNAPSIS 1
syn·kary·on \sin-ˈkar-ē-ˌän, -ē-ən\ *n* [NL, fr. Gk *syn-* + *karyon* nut — more at CAREEN] **:** a cell nucleus formed by the fusion of two preexisting nuclei
syn·od \ˈsin-əd *also* -ˌäd\ *n* [LL *synodus*, fr. LGk *synodos*, fr. Gk, meeting, assembly, fr. *syn-* + *hodos* way, journey — more at CEDE] **1 :** an ecclesiastical governing or advisory council: as **a :** the governing assembly of an Episcopal province **b :** a Presbyterian governing body ranking between the presbytery and the general assembly **c :** a regional or national organization of Lutheran congregations **2 :** the ecclesiastical district governed by a synod — **syn·od·al** \-əd-ᵊl *also* -ˌäd-ᵊl\ *adj*
syn·od·i·cal \sə-ˈnäd-i-kəl\ *or* **syn·od·ic** \-ik\ *adj* **1 :** of or relating to a synod **:** SYNODAL **2** *usu synodic* [Gk *synodikos*, fr. *synodos* meeting, conjunction] **:** relating to conjunction; *esp* **:** relating to the period between two successive conjunctions of the same celestial bodies
synodic month *n* **:** a lunar month
syn·onym \ˈsin-ə-ˌnim\ *n* [ME *sinonyme*, fr. L *synonymum*, fr. Gk *synōnymon*, fr. neut. of *synōnymos* synonymous, fr. *syn-* + *onyma* name — more at NAME] **1 :** one of two or more words or expressions of the same language that have the same or nearly the same meaning in some or all senses **2 :** a symbolic or figurative name **:** METONYM **3 :** a taxonomic name rejected as being incorrectly applied or incorrect in form — compare HOMONYM — **syn·onym·ic** \ˌsin-ə-ˈnim-ik\ *or* **syn·onym·i·cal** \-i-kəl\ *adj* — **syn·onym·i·ty** \-ˈnim-ət-ē\ *n*
syn·on·y·mist \sə-ˈnän-ə-məst\ *n* **:** one who lists, studies, or discriminates synonyms
syn·on·y·mize \-ˌmīz\ *vt* **-mized; -miz·ing 1 a :** to give or analyze the synonyms of (a word) **b :** to provide (as a dictionary) with synonymies **2 :** to demonstrate (a taxonomic name) to be a synonym
syn·on·y·mous \-məs\ *adj* **:** having the character of a synonym; *also* **:** alike in meaning or significance — **syn·on·y·mous·ly** *adv*
syn·on·y·my \-mē\ *n, pl* **-mies 1 a :** the study or discrimination of synonyms **b :** a list or collection of synonyms often defined and discriminated from each other **2 :** the scientific names that have been used in different publications to designate a taxonomic group (as a species); *also* **:** a list of these **3 :** the quality or state of being synonymous
syn·op·sis \sə-ˈnäp-səs\ *n, pl* **-op·ses** \-ˌsēz\ [LL, fr. Gk, lit., comprehensive view, fr. *synopsesthai* to be going to see together, fr. *syn-* + *opsesthai* to be going to see — more at OPTIC] **1 :** a condensed statement or outline (as of a narrative or treatise) **:** ABSTRACT **2 :** the abbreviated conjugation of a verb in one person only ***syn*** see ABRIDGMENT
syn·op·size \-ˌsīz\ *vt* **-sized; -siz·ing 1 :** to make a synopsis of (as a novel) **2 :** EPITOMIZE
syn·op·tic \sə-ˈnäp-tik\ *also* **syn·op·ti·cal** \-ti-kəl\ *adj* [Gk *synoptikos*, fr. *synopsesthai*] **1 :** affording a general view of a whole **2 :** manifesting or characterized by comprehensiveness or breadth of view **3 :** presenting or taking the same or common view; *specif, often cap* **:** of or relating to the first three Gospels of the New Testament **4 :** relating to or displaying conditions (as atmospheric or weather) as they exist simultaneously over a broad area — **syn·op·ti·cal·ly** \-ti-k(ə-)lē\ *adv*
syn·os·to·sis \ˌsin-ˌäs-ˈtō-səs\ *n, pl* **-to·ses** \-ˌsēz\ [NL] **:** union of two or more separate bones to form a single bone
sy·no·via \sə-ˈnō-vē-ə, sī-\ *n* [NL] **:** a transparent viscid lubricating fluid secreted by a membrane of an articulation, bursa, or tendon sheath
sy·no·vi·al \-vē-əl\ *adj* **:** of, relating to, or secreting synovia
sy·no·vi·tis \ˌsī-nə-ˈvīt-əs\ *n* **:** inflammation of a synovial membrane
syn·sep·al·ous \(ˈ)sin-ˈsep-ə-ləs\ *adj* **:** GAMOSEPALOUS
syn·tac·tic \sin-ˈtak-tik\ *or* **syn·tac·ti·cal** \-ti-kəl\ *adj* [NL *syntacticus*, fr. Gk *syntaktikos* arranging together, fr. *syntassein*] **:** of, relating to, or according to the rules of syntax or syntactics — **syn·tac·ti·cal·ly** \-ti-k(ə-)lē\ *adv*
syn·tac·tics \-tiks\ *n pl but sing or pl in constr* **:** a branch of semiotic that deals with the formal relations between signs or expressions in abstraction from their signification and their interpreters
syn·tax \ˈsin-ˌtaks\ *n* [F or LL; F *syntaxe*, fr. LL *syntaxis*, fr. Gk, fr. *syntassein* to arrange together, fr. *syn-* + *tassein* to arrange — more at TACTICS] **1 :** a connected or orderly system **:** harmonious arrangement of parts or elements **2 a :** the way in which words are put together to form phrases, clauses, or sentences **b :** the part of grammar dealing with this **3 :** syntactics esp. as dealing with the formal properties of languages or calculi
syn·the·sis \ˈsin(t)-thə-səs\ *n, pl* **-the·ses** \-ˌsēz\ [Gk, fr. *syntithenai* to put together, fr. *syn-* + *tithenai* to put, place — more at DO] **1 a :** the composition or combination of parts or elements so as to form a whole **b :** the production of a substance by the union of chemical elements, groups, or simpler compounds or by the degradation of a complex compound **c :** the combining of often diverse conceptions into a coherent whole; *also* **:** the complex so formed **2 a :** deductive reasoning **b :** the dialectic combination of thesis and antithesis into a higher stage of truth — **syn·the·sist** \-səst\ *n*
syn·the·size \-ˌsīz\ *vb* **-sized; -siz·ing** *vt* **1 :** to combine or produce by synthesis **2 :** to make a synthesis of ~ *vi* **:** to make a synthesis
syn·the·siz·er \-ˌsī-zər\ *n* **1 :** one that synthesizes <he is an expert ~ of diverse views> **2 :** an electronic apparatus for the production and control of sound (as for producing music)
syn·the·tase \ˈsin-thə-ˌtās, -ˌtāz\ *n* [*synthet*ic + *-ase*] **:** an enzyme that catalyzes the linking together of two molecules usu. with concurrent splitting off of a pyrophosphate group from ATP — called also *ligase*
[1]**syn·thet·ic** \sin-ˈthet-ik\ *also* **syn·thet·i·cal** \-i-kəl\ *adj* [Gk *synthetikos* of composition, component, fr. *syntithenai* to put together] **1 :** relating to or involving synthesis **:** not analytic **2 a :** attributing to a subject a predicate that is not part of the meaning of that subject **b :** EMPIRICAL **c :** not resulting in a contradiction upon being negated **3 :** characterized by frequent and systematic use of inflected forms to express grammatical relationships **4 a :** produced artificially **:** MAN-MADE <~ dyes> <~ drugs> <~ silk> **b :** devised, arranged, or fabricated for special situations to imitate or replace usual realities **c :** FACTITIOUS, BOGUS ***syn*** see ARTIFICIAL — **syn·thet·i·cal·ly** \-i-k(ə-)lē\ *adv*
[2]**synthetic** *n* **:** something resulting from synthesis rather than occurring naturally; *esp* **:** a product (as a drug or plastic) of chemical synthesis
synthetic division *n* **:** a simplified method for dividing a polynomial by another polynomial of the first degree by writing down only the coefficients of the several powers of the variable and changing the sign of the constant term in the divisor so as to replace the usual subtractions by additions
synthetic geometry *n* **:** elementary euclidean geometry or projective geometry as distinguished from analytic geometry
synthetic resin *n* **:** RESIN 2
synthetic rubber *n* **:** RUBBER 2b
syn·ton·ic \sin-ˈtän-ik\ *adj* [Gk *syntonos* being in harmony, fr. *syn-* + *tonos* tone] **:** normally responsive and adaptive to the social or interpersonal environment — **syn·ton·i·cal·ly** \-i-k(ə-)lē\ *adv*
syphil- *or* **syphilo-** *comb form* [NL, fr. *syphilis*] **:** syphilis <*syphilo*logy> <*syphil*oma>
syph·i·lis \ˈsif-(ə-)ləs\ *n* [NL, fr. *Syphilus*, hero of the poem *Syphilis sive Morbus Gallicus* (*Syphilis or the French disease*) (1530) by Girolamo Fracastoro] **:** a chronic contagious usu. venereal and often congenital disease caused by a spirochete (*Treponema pallidum*) and characterized by a clinical course in three stages continued over many years — **syph·i·lit·ic** \ˌsif-ə-ˈlit-ik\ *adj or n*
syph·i·lol·o·gist \ˌsif-ə-ˈläl-ə-jəst\ *n* **:** a physician who specializes in the diagnosis and treatment of syphilis
syph·i·lol·o·gy \-jē\ *n* **:** a branch of medicine that deals with syphilis
sy·phon *var of* SIPHON
sy·ren *chiefly Brit var of* SIREN
Sy·rette \sə-ˈret\ *trademark* — used for a small collapsible tube fitted with a hypodermic needle for injecting a single dose of a medicinal agent
Syr·i·ac \ˈsir-ē-ˌak\ *n* [L *syriacus* Syrian, fr. Gk *syriakos*, fr. *Syria*, ancient country in Asia] **1 :** a literary language based on an eastern Aramaic dialect and used as the literary and liturgical language by several eastern Christian churches **2 :** Aramaic spoken by Christian communities — **Syriac** *adj*

Syr·i·an hamster \ˌsir-ē-ən-\ *n* : GOLDEN HAMSTER

sy·rin·ga \sə-ˈriŋ-gə\ *n* [NL, genus name, fr. Gk *syring-, syrinx* panpipe] : PHILADELPHUS

[1]**sy·ringe** \sə-ˈrinj *also* ˈsir-inj\ *n* [ME *syring,* fr. ML *syringa,* fr. LL, injection, fr. Gk *syring-, syrinx* panpipe, tube; akin to Gk *sōlēn* pipe, Skt *tūṇava* flute] : a device used to inject fluids into or withdraw them from something (as the body or its cavities): as **a** : a device that consists of a nozzle of varying length and a compressible rubber bulb and is used for injection or irrigation **b** : an instrument (as for the injection of medicine or the withdrawal of bodily fluids) that consists of a hollow barrel fitted with a plunger and a hollow needle **c** : a gravity device consisting of a reservoir fitted with a long rubber tube ending with an exchangeable nozzle that is used for irrigation of the vagina or bowel

[2]**syringe** *vt* **sy·ringed; sy·ring·ing** : to irrigate or spray with or as if with a syringe

sy·rin·go·my·elia \sə-ˌriŋ-gō-mī-ˈē-lē-ə\ *n* [NL, fr. Gk *syring-, syrinx* tube, fistula + NL *-myelia*] : a chronic progressive disease of the spinal cord associated with sensory disturbances, muscle atrophy, and spasticity — **sy·rin·go·my·el·ic** \-ˈel-ik\ *adj*

syr·inx \ˈsir-iŋ(k)s\ *n, pl* **sy·rin·ges** \sə-ˈriŋ-ˌgēz, -ˈrin-ˌjēz\ *or* **syr·inx·es 1** [LL, fr. Gk] : PANPIPE **2** [NL, fr. Gk, panpipe] : the vocal organ of birds that is a special modification of the lower part of the trachea or of the bronchi or of both

Syr·inx \ˈsir-iŋ(k)s\ *n* [NL, fr. Gk] : an Arcadian maiden pursued by Pan and changed into a bunch of reeds which became Pan's musical pipes

syr·phid \ˈsər-fəd, ˈsir-\ *n* [NL *Syrphidae,* group name, fr. *Syrphus,* type genus] : any of a family (Syrphidae) of dipterous flies which frequent flowers and some of whose larvae prey on plant lice

syr·phus fly \ˈsər-fəs-, ˈsir-\ *n* [NL *Syrphus,* genus of flies, fr. Gk *syrphos* gnat] : SYRPHID

syr·up \ˈsər-əp, ˈsir-əp, ˈsə-rəp\ *n* [ME *sirup,* fr. MF *sirop,* fr. ML *syrupus,* fr. Ar *sharāb*] **1 a** : a thick sticky solution of sugar and water often flavored or medicated **b** : the concentrated juice of a fruit or plant **2** : cloying sweetness or sentimentality — **syr·upy** \-ē\ *adj*

syst *abbr* system

sys·tal·tic \sis-ˈtȯl-tik, -ˈtal-\ *adj* [Gk *systaltos,* (assumed) verbal of *systellein* to contract — more at SYSTOLE] : marked by regular contraction and dilatation : PULSING

sys·tem \ˈsis-təm\ *n* [LL *systemat-, systema,* fr. Gk *systēmat-, systēma,* fr. *synistanai* to combine, fr. *syn-* + *histanai* to cause to stand — more at STAND] **1** : a regularly interacting or interdependent group of items forming a unified whole <a number ~>: as **a** (1) : a group of interacting bodies under the influence of related forces <a gravitational ~> (2) : an assemblage of substances that is in or tends to equilibrium <a thermodynamic ~> **b** (1) : a group of body organs that together perform one or more vital functions <the digestive ~> (2) : the body considered as a functional unit **c** : a group of related natural objects or forces <a river ~> **d** : a group of devices or artificial objects or an organization forming a network esp. for distributing something or serving a common purpose <a telephone ~> <a heating ~> <a highway ~> <a data processing ~> **e** : a major division of rocks usu. larger than a series and including all formed during a period or era **f** : a form of social, economic, or political organization or practice <the capitalist ~> **2** : an organized set of doctrines, ideas, or principles usu. intended to explain the arrangement or working of a systematic whole <the Newtonian ~ of mechanics> **3 a** : an organized or established procedure <the touch ~ of typing> **b** : a manner of classifying, symbolizing, or schematizing <a taxonomic ~> <the decimal ~> **4** : harmonious arrangement or pattern : ORDER <bring ~ out of confusion —Ellen Glasgow> **5** : an organized society or social situation regarded as stultifying : ESTABLISHMENT 2 *syn* see METHOD — **sys·tem·less** \-ləs\ *adj*

sys·tem·at·ic \ˌsis-tə-ˈmat-ik\ *also* **sys·tem·at·i·cal** \-i-kəl\ *adj* [LL *systematicus,* fr. Gk *systēmatikos,* fr. *systēmat-, systēma*] **1** : relating to or consisting of a system <~ thought> **2** : presented or formulated as a system : SYSTEMATIZED **3 a** : methodical in procedure or plan <~ investigation> <a ~ scholar> **b** : marked by thoroughness and regularity <~ efforts> **4** : of, relating to, or concerned with classification; *specif* : TAXONOMIC — **sys·tem·at·i·cal·ly** \-i-k(ə-)lē\ *adv* — **sys·tem·at·ic·ness** \-ik-nəs\ *n*

systematic error *n* : an error that is not determined by chance but by a bias

sys·tem·at·ics \ˌsis-tə-ˈmat-iks\ *n pl but sing in constr* **1** : the science of classification **2 a** : a system of classification **b** : the classification and study of organisms with regard to their natural relationships : TAXONOMY

systematic theology *n* : a branch of theology concerned with summarizing the doctrinal traditions of a religion (as Christianity) esp. with a view to relating the traditions convincingly to the religion's present-day setting

sys·tem·atism \ˈsis-tə-mə-ˌtiz-əm, sis-ˈtem-ə-\ *n* : the practice of forming intellectual systems

sys·tem·atist \ˈsis-tə-mət-əst, sis-ˈtem-ət-\ *n* **1** : a maker or follower of a system **2** : a specialist in taxonomy : TAXONOMIST

sys·tem·atize \ˈsis-tə-mə-ˌtīz\ *vt* **-atized; -atiz·ing** : to arrange in accord with a definite plan or scheme : order systematically <the need to ~ his work> *syn* see ORDER — **sys·tem·ati·za·tion** \ˌsis-tə-mət-ə-ˈzā-shən, sis-ˌtem-ət-\ *n* — **sys·tem·atiz·er** *n*

[1]**sys·tem·ic** \sis-ˈtem-ik\ *adj* : of, relating to, or common to a system: as **a** : affecting the body generally **b** : supplying those parts of the body that receive blood through the aorta rather than through the pulmonary artery **c** : acting through the bodily systems after absorption or ingestion by making the organism toxic to a pest (as a mite or insect) — **sys·tem·i·cal·ly** \-i-k(ə-)lē\ *adv*

[2]**systemic** *n* : a systemic pesticide

sys·tem·ize \ˈsis-tə-ˌmīz\ *vt* **-ized; -iz·ing** : SYSTEMATIZE — **sys·tem·iza·tion** \ˌsis-tə-mə-ˈzā-shən\ *n*

systems analysis *n* : the act, process, or profession of studying an activity (as a procedure, a business, or a physiological function) typically by mathematical means in order to define its goals or purposes and to discover operations and procedures for accomplishing them most efficiently

systems analyst *n* : a specialist in systems analysis

sys·to·le \ˈsis-tə-(ˌ)lē\ *n* [Gk *systolē,* fr. *systellein* to contract, fr. *syn-* + *stellein* to send — more at STALL] : a rhythmically recurrent contraction; *esp* : the contraction of the heart by which the blood is forced onward and the circulation kept up — **sys·tol·ic** \sis-ˈtäl-ik\ *adj*

sy·zy·gial \sə-ˈzij-(ē-)əl\ *adj* : of or relating to a syzygy

syz·y·gy \ˈsiz-ə-jē\ *n, pl* **-gies** [LL *syzygia* conjunction, fr. Gk, fr. *syzygos* yoked together, fr. *syn-* + *zygon* yoke — more at YOKE] : the nearly straight-line configuration of three celestial bodies (as the sun, moon, and earth during a solar or lunar eclipse) in a gravitational system

¹t \ˈtē\ *n, pl* **t's** *or* **ts** \ˈtēz\ *often cap, often attrib* **1 a :** the 20th letter of the English alphabet **b :** a graphic representation of this letter **c :** a speech counterpart of orthographic *t* **2 :** a graphic device for reproducing the letter *t* **3 :** one designated *t* esp. as the 20th in order or class **4 :** something shaped like the letter T **5 :** T FORMATION — **to a T** [short for *to a tittle*] **:** to perfection

²t *abbr, often cap* **1** tablespoon **2** target **3** teaspoon **4** technical **5** temperature **6** [L *tempore*] in the time of **7** tense **8** tension **9** tera- **10** tertiary **11** time **12** ton **13** township **14** transitive **15** troy **16** true

T *symbol* **1** absolute temperature **2** kinetic energy **3** period **4** tritium

't \t\ *pron* **:** IT <my country, *'tis* of thee —S. F. Smith>

ta \ˈtä\ *n* [baby talk] *Brit* **:** THANKS

Ta *symbol* tantalum

Taal \ˈtäl\ *n* [Afrik, fr. D, language; akin to OE *talu* talk — more at TALE] **:** AFRIKAANS — usu. used with *the*

¹tab \ˈtab\ *n, often attrib* [origin unknown] **1 a :** a short projecting device (as a flap or loop): as (1) **:** a small hand grip (2) **:** a projection from a card used as an aid in filing **b :** a small insert, addition, or remnant <license plate ~> **c :** APPENDAGE, EXTENSION; *esp* **:** one of a series of small pendants forming a decorative border or edge of a garment **d :** a small auxiliary airfoil hinged to a control surface (as a trailing edge) to help stabilize an airplane in flight — see AIRPLANE illustration **2** [partly short for ¹*table;* partly fr. sense 1] **a :** close surveillance **:** WATCH <keep ~*s* on him> **b :** a creditor's statement **:** BILL, CHECK **3** [by shortening] **a :** TABLOID **b :** TABULATOR **c :** TABLET

²tab *vt* **tabbed; tab·bing 1 :** to furnish or ornament with tabs **2 :** to single out **:** DESIGNATE **3 :** TABULATE

ta·ba·nid \tə-ˈbā-nəd, -ˈban-əd\ *n* [deriv. of L *tabanus* horsefly] **:** HORSEFLY

tab·ard \ˈtab-ərd *also* -ˌärd\ *n* [ME, fr. OF *tabart*] **:** a short loose-fitting sleeveless or short-sleeved coat or cape: as **a :** a tunic worn by a knight over his armor and emblazoned with his arms **b :** a herald's official cape or coat emblazoned with his lord's arms

tabard b

Ta·bas·co \tə-ˈbas-(ˌ)kō\ *trademark* — used for a pungent condiment sauce made from hot peppers

¹tab·by \ˈtab-ē\ *n, pl* **tabbies** [F *tabis,* fr. ML *attabi,* fr. Ar *'attābī,* fr. Al-*'Attābīya,* quarter in Baghdad] **1 a** *archaic* **:** a plain silk taffeta esp. with moiré finish **b :** a plain-weave fabric **2** [²*tabby*] **a :** a domestic cat with a striped and mottled coat **b :** a domestic cat; *esp* **:** a female cat

²tabby *adj* **1 :** of, relating to, or made of tabby **2 :** striped and mottled with darker color **:** BRINDLED <a ~ cat>

¹tab·er·na·cle \ˈtab-ər-ˌnak-əl\ *n* [ME, fr. OF, fr. LL *tabernaculum,* fr. L, tent, dim. of *taberna* hut — more at TAVERN] **1 a** *often cap* **:** a tent sanctuary used by the Israelites during the Exodus **b** *archaic* **:** a dwelling place **c** *archaic* **:** a temporary shelter **:** TENT **2 :** a receptacle for the consecrated elements of the Eucharist; *esp* **:** an ornamental locked box fixed to the middle of the altar and used for reserving the host **3 :** a house of worship; *specif* **:** a large building or tent used for evangelistic services — **tab·er·nac·u·lar** \ˌtab-ər-ˈnak-yə-lər\ *adj*

²tabernacle *vi* **tab·er·na·cled; tab·er·na·cling** \-ˌnak-(ə-)liŋ\ **:** to take up temporary residence; *esp* **:** to inhabit a physical body

ta·bes \ˈtā-(ˌ)bēz\ *n, pl* **tabes** [L — more at THAW] **:** wasting accompanying a chronic disease — **ta·bet·ic** \tə-ˈbet-ik\ *adj or n*

tabes dor·sa·lis \-dȯr-ˈsal-əs, -ˈsāl-, -ˈsäl-\ *n* [NL, dorsal tabes] **:** a syphilitic disorder of the nervous system marked by wasting, pain, incoordination of voluntary movements and reflexes, and disorders of sensation, nutrition, and vision

ta·bla \ˈtäb-lə\ *n* [Hindi *tabla,* fr. Ar *tabla*] **:** a pair of small different-sized hand drums used esp. in Hindu music

tab·la·ture \ˈtab-lə-ˌchu̇(ə)r, -chər, -ˌt(y)u̇(ə)r\ *n* [MF, fr. ML *tabulatus* tablet, fr. L *tabula*] **:** an instrumental notation indicating the string, fret, key, or finger to be used instead of the tone to be sounded

¹ta·ble \ˈtā-bəl\ *n, often attrib* [ME, fr. OE *tabule* & OF *table;* both fr. L *tabula* board, tablet, list] **1 :** TABLET 1a **2 a** *pl* **:** BACKGAMMON **b :** one of the two leaves of a backgammon board or either half of a leaf **3 a :** a piece of furniture consisting of a smooth flat slab fixed on legs **b** (1) **:** a supply or source of food (2) **:** an act or instance of assembling to eat **:** MEAL <sit down to ~> <father mentioned the matter at ~> **c** (1) **:** a group of people assembled at or as if at a table <a famous poker ~, which challenged all comers —Harvey Fergusson> (2) **:** a legislative or negotiating session <bring the warring nations to the peace ~> **4 :** STRINGCOURSE **5 a :** a systematic arrangement of data usu. in rows and columns for ready reference **b :** a condensed enumeration **:** LIST <a ~ of contents> **6 a :** the upper flat surface of a precious stone — see BRILLIANT illustration **b** (1) **:** TABLELAND (2) **:** a horizontal stratum **7 :** something that resembles a table esp. in having a plane surface — **under the table 1 :** into a stupor <can drink you *under the table*> **2 :** not aboveboard

²table *adj* **:** suitable for a table or for table use <a ~ radio>

³table *vt* **ta·bled; ta·bling** \-b(ə-)liŋ\ **1 :** to enter in a table **2 a** *Brit* **:** to place on the agenda **b :** to remove (a parliamentary motion) from consideration indefinitely **c :** to put on a table

tab·leau \ˈtab-ˌlō, ta-ˈblō\ *n, pl* **tab·leaux** \-ˌlōz, -ˈblōz\ *also* **tableaus** [F, fr. MF *tablel* dim. of *table*] **1 :** a graphic description or representation **:** PICTURE <winsome *tableaux* of old-fashioned literary days —J. D. Hart> **2 :** a striking or artistic grouping **3** [short for *tableau vivant* (fr. F, lit., living picture)] **:** a depiction of a scene usu. presented on a stage by silent and motionless costumed participants

tableau curtain *n* **:** a stage curtain that opens in the center and has its sections drawn upward as well as to the side in order to produce a draped effect

ta·ble·cloth \ˈtā-bəl-ˌklȯth\ *n* **:** a covering spread over a dining table before the places are set

ta·ble d'hôte \ˌtäb-əl-ˈdōt, ˌtab-\ *n* [F, lit., host's table] **1 :** a meal served to all guests at a stated hour and fixed price **2 :** a complete meal of several courses offered at a fixed price

ta·ble·ful \ˈtā-bəl-ˌfu̇l\ *n* **:** as much or as many as a table can hold or accommodate

ta·ble–hop \ˈtā-bəl-ˌhäp\ *vi* **:** to move from table to table (as in a restaurant) in order to chat with friends — **ta·ble–hop·per** *n*

ta·ble·land \-bəl-ˌ(l)and\ *n* **:** a broad level elevated area **:** PLATEAU

table linen *n* **:** linen (as tablecloths and napkins) for the table

table of organization : a table listing the number and duties of personnel and the major items of equipment authorized for a military unit

table salt *n* **:** salt suitable for use at the table and in cooking **:** refined sodium chloride

ta·ble·spoon \ˈtā-bəl-ˌspün\ *n* **1 :** a large spoon used for serving **2 :** TABLESPOONFUL

ta·ble·spoon·ful \ˌtā-bəl-ˈspün-ˌfu̇l, ˈtā-bəl-ˌ\ *n, pl* **tablespoonfuls** \-ˌfu̇lz\ *also* **ta·ble·spoons·ful** \-ˈspünz-ˌfu̇l, -ˌspünz-\ **1 :** enough to fill a tablespoon **2 :** a unit of measure used esp. in cookery equal to 4 fluidrams

table sugar *n* **:** SUGAR 1a; *esp* **:** granulated white sugar

tab·let \ˈtab-lət\ *n* [ME *tablett,* fr. MF *tablete,* dim. of *table*] **1 a :** a flat slab or plaque suited for or bearing an inscription **b :** a thin slab or one of a set of portable sheets used for writing **c :** a collection of sheets of paper glued together at one edge **2 a :** a compressed or molded block of a solid material **b :** a small mass of medicated material (as in the shape of a disk)

table talk *n* **:** informal conversation at or as if at a dining table; *esp* **:** the social talk of a celebrity recorded for publication

table tennis *n* **:** a game resembling lawn tennis that is played on a tabletop with wooden paddles and a small hollow plastic ball

ta·ble·top \ˈtā-bəl-ˌtäp\ *n* **1 :** the top of a table **2 :** a photograph of small objects or a miniature scene arranged on a table — **table·top** *adj*

ta·ble·ware \-ˌwa(ə)r, -ˌwe(ə)r\ *n* **:** utensils (as of china, glass, or silver) for table use

table wine *n* **:** a still wine of not more than 14 percent alcohol by volume usu. served with food

¹tab·loid \ˈtab-ˌlȯid\ *adj* [fr. *Tabloid,* a trademark] **1 :** compressed or condensed into small scope <~ criticism> **2 :** of, relating to, or characteristic of tabloids <~ journalism>

²tabloid *n* **1 :** a newspaper that is about half the page size of an ordinary newspaper and that contains news in condensed form and much photographic matter **2 :** DIGEST, SUMMARY

¹ta·boo *also* **ta·bu** \tə-ˈbü, ta-\ *adj* [Tongan *tabu*] **1 :** forbidden to profane use or contact because of supposedly dangerous supernatural powers **2 a :** banned on grounds of morality or taste **b :** banned as constituting a risk <the area beyond is ~, still alive with explosives —Robert Leckie>

²taboo *also* **tabu** *n, pl* **taboos** *also* **tabus 1 :** a prohibition against touching, saying, or doing something for fear of immediate harm from a mysterious superhuman force **2 :** a prohibition imposed by social custom or as a protective measure **3 :** belief in taboos

³taboo *also* **tabu** *vt* **1 :** to set apart as taboo esp. by marking with a ritualistic symbol **2 :** to avoid or ban as taboo

ta·bor *also* **ta·bour** \ˈtā-bər\ *n* [ME, fr. OF] **:** a small drum with one head of soft calfskin used to accompany a pipe or fife played by the same person

tabor

ta·bor·er *also* **ta·bour·er** \-bər-ər\ *n* **:** one that plays on the tabor

tab·o·ret *or* **tab·ou·ret** \ˌtab-ə-ˈret, -ˈrā\ *n* [F *tabouret,* lit., small drum, fr. MF, dim. of *tabor, tabour* drum] **1 :** a cylindrical seat or stool without arms or back **2 :** a small portable stand

tab·u·lar \ˈtab-yə-lər\ *adj* [L *tabularis* of boards, fr. *tabula* board, tablet] **1 :** having a flat surface **:** LAMINAR <a ~ crystal> **2 a :** of, relating to, or arranged in a table; *specif* **:** set up in rows and columns **b :** computed by means of a table — **tab·u·lar·ly** *adv*

ta·bu·la ra·sa \ˌtab-yə-lə-ˈräz-ə, -ˈräs-\ *n, pl* **ta·bu·lae ra·sae** \-lī-ˈräz-ˌī, -ˈräs-\ [L, smoothed or erased tablet] **:** the mind in its hypothetical primary blank or empty state before receiving outside impressions

tab·u·late \ˈtab-yə-ˌlāt\ *vt* **-lat·ed; -lat·ing** [L *tabula* tablet] **:** to put into tabular form — **tab·u·la·tion** \ˌtab-yə-ˈlā-shən\ *n*

tab·u·la·tor \ˈtab-yə-ˌlāt-ər\ *n* **:** one that tabulates: as **a :** a business machine that sorts and selects information from marked or perforated cards **b :** a device on a typewriter or biller for arranging data in columns

TAC \ˈtak\ *abbr* Tactical Air Command

tac·a·ma·hac \ˈtak-ə-mə-ˌhak\ *n* [Sp *tacamahaca,* fr. Nahuatl *tecamaca*] **1 :** any of several aromatic oleoresins used in ointments and plasters and for incense **2 :** BALSAM POPLAR

tace \ˈtas, ˈtās\ *var of* TASSE

ə abut ᵊ kitten ər further a back ā bake ä cot, cart
au̇ out ch chin e less ē easy g gift i trip ī life
j joke ŋ sing ō flow ȯ flaw ȯi coin th thin t͟h this
ü loot u̇ foot y yet yü few yu̇ furious zh vision

ta·cet \ˈtäk-ˌet; ˈtās-ət, ˈtas-\ [L, lit., (it) is silent, fr. *tacēre* to be silent — more at TACIT] — used as a direction in music to indicate that a particular instrument is not to play during a movement or long section

tach \ˈtak\ *n* : TACHOMETER

tach·i·na fly \ˌtak-ə-nə-\ *n* [NL *Tachina,* genus of flies, fr. Gk *tachinos* fleet, fr. *tachos* speed; akin to Gk *tachys* swift] : TACHINID

tach·i·nid \ˈtak-ə-nəd, -ˌnid\ *n* [NL *Tachinidae,* group name, fr. *Tachina,* type genus] : any of a family (Tachinidae) of bristly usu. grayish or black flies whose parasitic larvae are often important in the biological control of insect pests — **tachinid** *adj*

tach·ism \ˈtash-ˌiz-əm\ *n, often cap* [F *tachisme,* fr. *tache* stain, spot, blob, fr. MF *teche, tache,* of Gmc origin; akin to OS *tēkan* sign — more at TOKEN] : ACTION PAINTING — **tach·ist** \ˈtash-əst\ *also* **ta·chiste** \ta-ˈshēst\ *adj or n, often cap*

ta·chis·to·scope \tə-ˈkis-tə-ˌskōp, ta-\ *n* [Gk *tachistos* (superl. of *tachys* swift) + ISV *-scope*] : an apparatus for the brief exposure of visual stimuli that is used in the study of learning, attention, and perception — **ta·chis·to·scop·ic** \-ˌkis-tə-ˈskäp-ik\ *adj* — **ta·chis·to·scop·i·cal·ly** \-i-k(ə-)lē\ *adv*

ta·chom·e·ter \ta-ˈkäm-ət-ər, tə-\ *n* [Gk *tachos* speed + E *-meter*] : a device for indicating speed of rotation

tachy- *comb form* [Gk, fr. *tachys*] : rapid : accelerated <*tachy*cardia>

tachy·car·dia \ˌtak-i-ˈkärd-ē-ə\ *n* [NL] : relatively rapid heart action whether physiological (as after exercise) or pathological — compare BRADYCARDIA

ta·chyg·ra·phy \ta-ˈkig-rə-fē, tə-\ *n* [Gk *tachygraphos* stenographer, fr. *tachy-* + *graphein* to write — more at CARVE] **1 :** the art or practice of rapid writing; *esp* : the shorthand of the ancient Greeks and Romans **2 :** the abbreviated form of writing Greek and Latin used in manuscripts of the Middle Ages — **tachy·graph·ic** \ˌtak-ə-ˈgraf-ik\ *also* **tachy·graph·i·cal** \-i-kəl\ *adj*

tachy·lyte *also* **tachy·lite** \ˈtak-ə-ˌlīt\ *n* [G *tachylyt,* fr. Gk *tachy-* + *lyein* to dissolve — more at LOSE] : black glossy basalt

ta·chym·e·ter \ta-ˈkim-ət-ər, tə-\ *n* [ISV] **1 :** a surveying instrument (as a transit) for determining quickly the distances, bearings, and elevations of distant objects **2 :** a speed indicator

tac·it \ˈtas-ət\ *adj* [F or L; F *tacite,* fr. L *tacitus* silent, fr. pp. of *tacēre* to be silent; akin to OHG *dagēn* to be silent] **1 :** expressed or carried on without words or speech **2 a :** implied or indicated but not actually expressed <~ consent> **b** (1) **:** arising without express contract or agreement (2) **:** arising by operation of law <~ mortgage> — **tac·it·ly** *adv* — **tac·it·ness** *n*

tac·i·turn \ˈtas-ə-ˌtərn\ *adj* [F or L; F *taciturne,* fr. L *taciturnus,* fr. *tacitus*] : temperamentally disinclined to talk **syn** see SILENT **ant** garrulous, clamorous — **tac·i·tur·ni·ty** \ˌtas-ə-ˈtər-nət-ē\ *n*

[1]**tack** \ˈtak\ *n, often attrib* [ME *tak* something that attaches; akin to MD *tac* sharp point] **1 :** a small short sharp-pointed nail usu. having a broad flat head **2 a :** a rope to hold in place the forward lower corner of a course on a sailing ship **b :** a rope for hauling the outer lower corner of a studding sail to the end of the boom **c :** the lower forward corner of a fore-and-aft sail **d :** the corner of a sail to which a tack is fastened **3 a :** the direction of a ship with respect to the trim of her sails <starboard ~> **b :** the run of a sailing ship on one tack **c :** a change when close-hauled from the starboard to the port tack or vice versa **d :** a zigzag movement on land **e :** a course or method of action; *esp* : one sharply divergent from that previously followed **4 :** any of various usu. temporary stitches **5 :** a sticky or adhesive quality or condition **6 :** stable gear; *esp* : articles of harness (as saddle and bridle) for use on a saddle horse

[2]**tack** *vt* **1 :** ATTACH; *esp* : to fasten or affix with tacks **2 :** to join in a slight or hasty manner **3 a :** to add as a supplement **b :** to add (a rider) to a parliamentary bill **4 :** to change the direction of (a sailing ship) when sailing close-hauled by turning the bow to the wind and shifting the sails so as to fall off on the other side at about the same angle as before ~ *vi* **1 a :** to tack a sailing ship **b** *of a ship* **:** to change to an opposite tack by turning the bow to the wind **2 a :** to follow a zigzag course **b :** to modify one's policy or attitude abruptly — **tack·er** *n*

[3]**tack** *n* [origin unknown] : HARDTACK 1

tack·board \ˈtak-ˌbō(ə)rd, -ˌbȯ(ə)rd\ *n* : a board (as of cork) for tacking up notices and display materials

tack claw *n* : a small hand tool for removing tacks

tacki·fy \ˈtak-ə-ˌfī\ *vt* **-fied; -fy·ing :** to make (as a resin adhesive) tacky or more tacky — **tacki·fi·er** \-ˌfī(-ə)r\ *n*

tacki·ly \ˈtak-ə-lē\ *adv* : in a tacky manner : so as to be tacky

tacki·ness \ˈtak-ē-nəs\ *n* : the quality or state of being tacky

[1]**tack·le** \ˈtak-əl, *naut often* ˈtāk-\ *n* [ME *takel;* akin to MD *takel* ship's rigging] **1 :** a set of the equipment used in a particular activity : GEAR <fishing ~> **2 a :** a ship's rigging **b :** an assemblage of ropes and pulleys arranged to gain mechanical advantage for hoisting and pulling **3 a :** the act or an instance of tackling **b** (1) **:** one of two offensive football players positioned on each side of the center and between guard and end (2) **:** one of two football players positioned on the inside of a defensive line

tackle 2b

[2]**tackle** *vb* **tack·led; tack·ling** \-(ə-)liŋ\ *vt* **1 :** to attach or secure with or as if with tackle **2 a :** to seize, take hold of, or grapple with esp. with the intention of stopping or subduing **b :** to seize and throw down or stop (an opposing player with the ball) in football **3 :** to set about dealing with <~ the problem> ~ *vi* **:** to tackle an opposing player in football — **tack·ler** \-(ə-)lər\ *n*

tack·ling \ˈtak-liŋ, *naut often* ˈtāk-\ *n* : GEAR, TACKLE

[1]**tacky** \ˈtak-ē\ *adj* **tack·i·er; -est** [[2]*tack*] : somewhat sticky to the touch <~ varnish>; *also* : characterized by tack : ADHESIVE

[2]**tacky** *adj* **tack·i·er; -est** [*tacky* (a low-class person)] **1 a :** characterized by lack of good breeding : COMMON <a poor-white and untidy person . . . he, in short, was ~ —J. B. Cabell> **b :** SHABBY, SEEDY **2 a :** marked by lack of style or good taste : DOWDY **b :** marked by cheap showiness : GAUDY

ta·co \ˈtäk-(ˌ)ō\ *n, pl* **tacos** \-(ˌ)ōz, -(ˌ)ōs\ [MexSp] : a sandwich made of a tortilla rolled up with or folded over a filling

tac·o·nite \ˈtak-ə-ˌnīt\ *n* [*Taconic* mountain range, U.S.] : a flintlike rock high enough in iron content to constitute a low-grade iron ore

tact \ˈtakt\ *n* [F, sense of touch, fr. L *tactus,* fr. *tactus,* pp. of *tangere* to touch — more at TANGENT] **1 :** sensitive mental or aesthetic perception <converted the novel into a play with remarkable skill and ~> **2 :** a keen sense of what to do or say in order to maintain good relations with others or avoid offense **syn** TACT, ADDRESS, POISE, SAVOIR FAIRE *shared meaning element* : skill and grace in dealing with others. TACT implies delicate and considerate perception of what is appropriate <without the *tact* to perceive when remarks were untimely —Thomas Hardy> ADDRESS stresses dexterity and grace in dealing with new and trying situations and may imply success in attaining one's ends <to bring the thing off as well as Mike has done requires *address* —Herman Wouk> POISE may imply both tact and address but stresses self-possession and ease in meeting difficult situations <the . . . *poise* that comes from an habitual attention to what is graceful and becoming —D. C. Hodges> SAVOIR FAIRE is likely to stress worldly experience and a sure awareness of what is proper or expedient <the inexperience and want of *savoir faire* in high matters of diplomacy —C. C. F. Greville> **ant** awkwardness

tact·ful \ˈtakt-fəl\ *adj* : having or showing tact — **tact·ful·ly** \-fə-lē\ *adv* — **tact·ful·ness** *n*

[1]**tac·tic** \ˈtak-tik\ *adj* [NL *tacticus,* fr. Gk *taktikos* — more at TACTICS] : of or relating to arrangement or order

[2]**tactic** *n* [NL *tactica,* fr. Gk *taktikē,* fr. fem. of *taktikos*] **1 :** a method of employing forces in combat **2 :** a device for accomplishing an end

-tac·tic \ˈtak-tik\ *adj comb form* [Gk *taktikos*] **1 :** of, relating to, or having (such) an arrangement or pattern <para*tactic*> **2 :** showing orientation or movement directed by a (specified) force or agent <geo*tactic*>

tac·ti·cal \ˈtak-ti-kəl\ *adj* **1 :** of or relating to combat tactics: as **a :** involving actions or means of less magnitude or at a shorter distance from a base of operations than those of strategy **b** *of an air force* : of, relating to, or designed for air attack in close support of friendly ground forces **2 a :** of or relating to tactics: as (1) **:** of or relating to small-scale actions serving a larger purpose (2) **:** made or carried out with only a limited or immediate end in view **b :** adroit in planning or maneuvering to accomplish a purpose — **tac·ti·cal·ly** \-k(ə-)lē\ *adv*

tac·ti·cian \tak-ˈtish-ən\ *n* : one versed in tactics

tac·tics \ˈtak-tiks\ *n pl but sing or pl in constr* [NL *tactica,* pl., fr. Gk *taktika,* fr. neut. pl. of *taktikos* of order, of tactics, fit for arranging, fr. *tassein* to arrange, place in battle formation; akin to Lith pa*togus* comfortable] **1 a :** the science and art of disposing and maneuvering forces in combat **b :** the art or skill of employing available means to accomplish an end **2 :** a system or mode of procedure **3 :** the study of the grammatical relations within a language including morphology and syntax **syn** see STRATEGY

tac·tile \ˈtak-tᵊl, -ˌtīl\ *adj* [F or L; F, fr. L *tactilis,* fr. *tactus,* pp. of *tangere* to touch — more at TANGENT] **1 :** perceptible by touch : TANGIBLE **2 :** of or relating to the sense of touch — **tac·tile·ly** \-tə-lē, -ˌtīl-lē\ *adv*

tactile corpuscle *n* : an end organ of touch

tac·til·i·ty \tak-ˈtil-ət-ē\ *n* **1 :** the capability of being felt or touched **2 :** responsiveness to stimulation of the sense of touch

tac·tion \ˈtak-shən\ *n* [L *taction-, tactio,* fr. *tactus,* pp.] : TOUCH

tact·less \ˈtakt-ləs\ *adj* : marked by lack of tact — **tact·less·ly** *adv* — **tact·less·ness** *n*

tac·tu·al \ˈtak-ch(ə-w)əl\ *adj* [L *tactus* sense of touch — more at TACT] : TACTILE 2 — **tac·tu·al·ly** \-ē\ *adv*

[1]**tad** \ˈtad\ *n* [prob. fr. E dial., toad, fr. ME *tode* — more at TOAD] : BOY

[2]**tad** *n* [perh. fr. E dial., toad] : a small or insignificant amount or degree : BIT <looked a ~ bigger than me —Larry Hodgson>

tad·pole \ˈtad-ˌpōl\ *n* [ME *taddepol,* fr. *tode* toad + *polle* head — more at POLL] : a larval amphibian; *specif* : a frog or toad larva that has a rounded body with a long tail bordered by fins and external gills soon replaced by internal gills and that undergoes a metamorphosis to the adult

tadpole in successive stages of development

tae·di·um vi·tae \ˌtēd-ē-əm-ˈvī-ˌtē, ˌtīd-ē-əm-ˈwē-ˌtī\ *n* [L] : weariness or loathing of life

tael \ˈtā(ə)l\ *n* [Pg, fr. Malay *tahil*] **1 :** any of various units of weight of eastern Asia; *esp* : LIANG **2 :** any of various Chinese units of value based on the value of a tael weight of silver

tae·nia \ˈtē-nē-ə\ *n, pl* **-ni·ae** \-nē-ˌī, -ˌē\ *or* **-nias** [L, fr. Gk *tainia;* akin to Gk *teinein* to stretch — more at THIN] **1 :** an ancient Greek fillet **2 :** a band on a Doric order separating the frieze from the architrave **3** [NL, fr. L, fillet, band] : a band of nervous tissue or muscle **4 :** TAPEWORM

tae·nia·cide *also* **te·nia·cide** \ˈtē-nē-ə-ˌsīd\ *n* : an agent that destroys tapeworms

tae·ni·a·sis \tē-ˈnī-ə-səs\ *n* [NL, fr. L *taenia* tapeworm] : infestation with or disease caused by tapeworms

taf·fe·ta \ˈtaf-ət-ə\ *n* [ME, fr. MF *taffetas,* fr. OIt *taffettà,* fr. Turk *tafta,* fr. Per *tāftah* woven] : a crisp plain-woven lustrous fabric of various fibers used esp. for women's clothing

taf·fe·tized \ˈtaf-ə-ˌtīzd\ *adj, of cloth* : having a crisp finish

taff·rail \ˈtaf-ˌrāl, -rəl\ *n* [modif. of D *tafereel,* fr. MD, picture, fr. OF *tablel* — more at TABLEAU] **1 :** the upper part of the stern of a wooden ship **2 :** a rail around the stern of a ship

taf·fy \ˈtaf-ē\ *n, pl* **taffies** [origin unknown] **1 :** a boiled candy usu. of molasses or brown sugar that is pulled until porous and light-colored **2 :** insincere flattery

taf·ia \ˈtaf-ē-ə\ *n* [F, fr. West Indian Creole, alter. of *ratafia*] **:** a West Indian rum made esp. from distilled sugarcane juice

[1]**tag** \ˈtag\ *n* [ME *tagge,* prob. of Scand origin; akin to Sw *tagg* barb] **1 :** a loose hanging piece of cloth **:** TATTER **2 :** a metal or plastic binding on an end of a shoelace **3 :** a piece of hanging or attached material; *specif* **:** a loop, knot, or tassel on a garment **4 a :** a brief quotation used for rhetorical emphasis or sententious effect **b :** a recurrent or characteristic verbal expression **c :** TAG LINE 1 **5 a :** a cardboard, plastic, or metal marker used for identification or classification <license ~*s*> **b :** a descriptive or identifying epithet **c :** something used for identification or location **:** FLAG **d :** LABEL 3d **6 :** a small piece of tinsel or other bright material around the shank of the hook at the end of the body of an artificial fly **7 :** a detached fragmentary piece **:** BIT

[2]**tag** *vb* **tagged; tag·ging** *vt* **1 :** to provide or mark with or as if with a tag: as **a :** to supply with an identifying marker <*tagged* every item in his store> **b :** to provide with a name or epithet **:** LABEL, BRAND <one might ~ this book traditional —William Nicoll> <the trick is . . . to ~ the other fellow as . . . left-wing —T. H. White *b*1915> **c :** to put a ticket on (a motor vehicle) for a traffic violation **2 :** to attach as an addition **:** APPEND **3 :** to follow closely and persistently **4 :** to hold to account; *esp* **:** to charge with violating the law <was *tagged* for . . . assault —Burt Woolis> **5 :** LABEL 2 ~ *vi* **:** to keep close <*tagging* at their heels —Corey Ford>

[3]**tag** *n* [origin unknown] **1 :** a game in which one player chases others and tries to make one of them it by touching him **2 :** an act or instance of tagging a runner in baseball

[4]**tag** *vt* **tagged; tag·ging 1 a :** to touch in or as if in a game of tag **b :** to put out (a runner) in baseball by a touch with the ball or the gloved hand containing the ball **2 :** to hit solidly <got *tagged* . . . with a brick —Henry Allen> **3 :** to choose usu. for a special purpose **:** SELECT **4 :** to make a hit or run off (a pitcher) in baseball <was *tagged* for three runs in the second inning>

TAG *abbr* the adjutant general

Ta·ga·log \tə-ˈgäl-əg, -ˌȯg\ *n, pl* **Tagalog** *or* **Tagalogs** [Tag] **1 :** a member of a people of central Luzon **2 :** an Austronesian language of the Tagalog people

tag·along \ˈtag-ə-ˌlȯŋ\ *n* **:** one that persistently and often annoyingly follows the lead of another

tag along \ˌtag-ə-ˈlȯŋ\ *vi* **:** to follow another's lead esp. in going from one place to another <the biggest first and the smallest *tagging along* —Alan Moorehead>

tag·board \ˈtag-ˌbō(ə)rd, -ˌbȯ(ə)rd\ *n* **:** strong cardboard used esp. for making shipping tags

tag day *n* **:** a day on which contributions are solicited (as for a charity) and small tags are given in return

tag end *n* **1 :** the last part **2 :** a miscellaneous or random bit

tag line *n* **1 :** a final line (as in a play or joke); *esp* **:** one that serves to clarify a point or create a dramatic effect **2 :** a reiterated phrase identified with an individual, group, or product **:** SLOGAN

tag, rag, and bobtail *or* **tagrag and bobtail** \ˌtag-ˌrag-ən-ˈbäb-ˌtāl, ˌrag-ᵊŋ-\ *n* **:** RABBLE

tag sale *n* [fr. the tag on each item indicating its price] **:** GARAGE SALE

tag team *n* [[4]*tag*] **:** a team of two or more professional wrestlers who spell each other during a match

tag up *vi* **:** to touch a base in baseball before running after a fly ball is caught

Ta·hi·tian \tə-ˈhē-shən\ *n* **1 :** a native or inhabitant of Tahiti **2 :** the Polynesian language of the Tahitians — **Tahitian** *adj*

tah·sil \tä-ˈsē(ə)l\ *n* [Hindi *taḥsīl,* fr. Ar, collection of revenue] **:** a district administration or revenue subdivision in India

tah·sil·dar \tä-ˈsē(ə)l-ˌdär\ *n* [Hindi *taḥsīldār*] **:** a revenue officer in India

Tai \ˈtī\ *n, pl* **Tai :** a widespread group of peoples in southeast Asia associated ethnically with valley paddy-rice culture

tai·ga \ˈtī-gə\ *n* [Russ *taĭga*] **:** moist subarctic coniferous forest that begins where the tundra ends and is dominated by spruces and firs

[1]**tail** \ˈtā(ə)l\ *n, often attrib* [ME, fr. OE *tægel;* akin to OHG *zagal* tail, OIr *dúal* lock of hair] **1 :** the rear end or a process or prolongation of the rear end of the body of an animal **2 :** something resembling an animal's tail (as the luminous train of a comet) in shape or position **3 :** RETINUE **4** *pl* **a :** TAILCOAT **b :** full evening dress for men **5 a :** BUTTOCKS **b :** SEXUAL INTERCOURSE — usu. considered vulgar **6 :** the back, last, lower, or inferior part of something **7 :** the reverse of a coin — usu. used in pl. <~*s,* I win> **8 :** one (as a detective) who follows or keeps watch on someone **9 :** a group of lines of verse added to a recognized prosodic form **10 :** the blank space at the bottom of a page **11 :** the rear part of an airplane consisting of horizontal and vertical stabilizing surfaces with attached control surfaces **12 :** the trail of a fugitive in flight <had a posse on his ~> — **tailed** \ˈtā(ə)ld\ *adj* — **tail·less** \ˈtā(ə)l-ləs\ *adj* — **tail·like** \-ˌlīk\ *adj*

[2]**tail** *vt* **1 :** to connect end to end **2 :** to remove the tail of (an animal) **:** DOCK **3 a :** to make or furnish with a tail **b :** to follow or be drawn behind like a tail **4 :** to fasten an end of (a tile, brick, or timber) into a wall or other support **5 :** to follow for purposes of surveillance ~ *vi* **1 :** to form or move in a straggling line **2 :** to grow progressively smaller, fainter, or more scattered **:** ABATE — usu. used with *off* <productivity is ~*ing* off —Tom Nicholson> **3 :** to hold by the end — used of a timber, tile, or brick built into a support **4 :** to swing or lie with the stern in a named direction — used of a ship at anchor **5 :** [2]TAG

[3]**tail** *adj* [ME *taille,* fr. AF *taylé,* fr. OF *taillié,* pp. of *taillier* to cut, limit — more at TAILOR] **:** limited as to tenure **:** ENTAILED

[4]**tail** *n* **:** ENTAIL 1a

tail·back \ˈtā(ə)l-ˌbak\ *n* **:** the offensive football back farthest from the line of scrimmage

tail·board \-ˌbō(ə)rd, -ˌbȯ(ə)rd\ *n* **:** TAILGATE 1

tail·bone \-ˈbōn, -ˌbōn\ *n* **1 :** a caudal vertebra **2 :** COCCYX

tail·coat \-ˈkōt\ *n* **:** a coat with tails; *esp* **:** a man's full-dress coat with two long tapering skirts at the back — **tail·coat·ed** \-əd\ *adj*

tail covert *n* **:** one of the coverts of the tail quills

tailed sonnet *n* **:** a sonnet augmented by additional systematically arranged lines

tail end *n* **1 :** RUMP, BUTTOCKS **2 :** the hindmost end **3 :** the concluding period <the *tail end* of the session>

tail·er \ˈtā-lər\ *n* **:** one that tails; *specif* **:** SHADOW 10b

tail fin *n* **1 :** the terminal fin of a fish **2 :** FIN 2b

[1]**tail·gate** \ˈtā(ə)l-ˌgāt\ *n* **1 :** a board or gate at the rear of a vehicle that can be removed or let down (as for loading) **2** [fr. the custom of seating trombonists at the rear of trucks carrying jazz bands in parades] **:** a jazz trombone style marked by much use of slides to and from long sustained tones

[2]**tailgate** \ˈtā(ə)l-ˌgāt\ *vi* **tail·gat·ed; tail·gat·ing :** to drive dangerously close behind another vehicle — **tail·gat·er** *n*

tail·ing \ˈtā-liŋ\ *n* **1 :** residue separated in the preparation of various products (as grain or ores) — usu. used in pl. **2 :** the part of a projecting stone or brick inserted in a wall

tail lamp *n* **:** TAILLIGHT

taille \ˈtä-yə, ˈtī-, ˈtā(ə)l\ *n* [F, fr. OF, fr. *taillier* to cut, tax] **:** a tax formerly levied by a French king or seigneur on his subjects or on lands held of him

tail·light \ˈtā(ə)l-ˌlīt\ *n* **:** a usu. red warning light mounted at the rear of a vehicle

[1]**tai·lor** \ˈtā-lər\ *n* [ME *taillour,* fr. OF *tailleur,* fr. *taillier* to cut, fr. LL *taliare,* fr. L *talea* twig, cutting; akin to Gk *tēlis* fenugreek] **:** one whose occupation is making or altering outer garments — **tai·lor·ess** \-lə-rəs\ *n*

[2]**tailor** *vi* **:** to do the work of a tailor ~ *vt* **1 a :** to make or fashion as the work of a tailor **b :** to make or adapt to suit a special need or purpose **2 :** to fit with clothes **3 :** to style with trim straight lines and finished handwork

tai·lor·bird \ˈtā-lər-ˌbərd\ *n* **:** any of numerous Asiatic, East Indian, and African warblers (family Sylviidae) that stitch leaves together to support and hide their nests

tai·lored \ˈtā-lərd\ *adj* **1 :** made by a tailor **2 :** fashioned or fitted to resemble a tailor's work **3 :** CUSTOM-MADE **4 a :** having the look of one fitted by a custom tailor <a slim, smartly ~ man —*Current Biog.*> **b :** appearing well cared for

tai·lor·ing \ˈtā-lə-riŋ\ *n* **1 a :** the business or occupation of a tailor **b :** the work or workmanship of a tailor **2 :** the making or adapting of something to suit a particular purpose

[1]**tai·lor–made** \ˌtā-lər-ˈmād\ *adj* **1 a :** made by a tailor or with a tailor's care and style **b :** finely trim in fit and simple in line, ornament, and finish — used of women's garments **c :** appearing like one turned out by a good tailor **2 :** made or fitted esp. to a particular use or purpose

[2]**tailor–made** *n* **:** one that is tailor-made; *specif* **:** a woman's garment styled for a trim fit and with stiff straight lines

tailor's chalk *n* **:** a thin flat piece of hard chalk or soapstone used by tailors and sewers to make temporary marks on cloth

tail·piece \ˈtā(ə)l-ˌpēs\ *n* **1 :** a piece added at the end **:** APPENDAGE **2 :** a triangular piece from which the strings of a stringed instrument are stretched to the pegs — see VIOLIN illustration **3 :** a short beam or rafter tailed in a wall and supported by a header **4 :** an ornament placed below the text matter of a page (as at the end of a chapter)

tail pipe *n* **1 :** the pipe discharging the exhaust gases from the muffler of an automotive engine **2 :** the part of a jet engine that carries the exhaust gases rearward and discharges them through a nozzle

tail plane *n* **:** the horizontal tail surfaces of an airplane including the stabilizer and the elevator

tail·race \ˈtā(ə)l-ˌrās\ *n* **1 :** a lower millrace **2 :** a channel in which mine tailings are floated off

tail rhyme *n* **:** a verse form in which a rhymed couplet or triplet is followed by a line of different and usu. shorter length that does not rhyme with the couplet or triplet — called also *tailed rhyme*

tail·spin \ˈtā(ə)l-ˌspin\ *n* **1 :** SPIN 2a **2 :** a mental or emotional collapse **:** loss of capacity to cope or react **3 :** a sharp financial depression <may tip the economy into a ~ —*Newsweek*>

tail·wa·ter \-ˌwȯt-ər, -ˌwät-\ *n* **1 :** water below a dam or waterpower development **2 :** excess surface water draining esp. from a field under cultivation

tail wind *n* **:** a wind having the same general direction as the course of a moving airplane or ship

Tai·no \ˈtī-(ˌ)nō\ *n, pl* **Taino** *or* **Tainos** [Sp] **1 :** a member of an extinct aboriginal Arawakan people of the Greater Antilles and the Bahamas **2 :** the language of the Taino people

[1]**taint** \ˈtānt\ *vb* [ME *tainten* to color & *taynten* to attaint; ME *tainten,* fr. AF *teinter,* fr. MF *teint,* pp. of *teindre,* fr. L *tingere;* ME *taynten,* fr. MF *ataint,* pp. of *ataindre* — more at TINGE, ATTAIN] *vt* **1 :** to touch or affect slightly with something bad <persons ~*ed* with prejudice> **2 :** to affect with putrefaction **:** SPOIL **3 :** to contaminate morally **:** CORRUPT <scholarship ~*ed* by envy> ~ *vi* **1** *obs* **:** to become weak **2 :** to become affected with putrefaction **:** SPOIL ***syn*** see CONTAMINATE

[2]**taint** *n* **:** a contaminating mark or influence <free from every ~ but that of vice —William Cowper> — **taint·less** \-ləs\ *adj*

[1]**tai·pan** \ˈtī-ˌpan, ˈtī-ˈpän\ *n* [Chin (Pek) *tai*[4] *pan*[1]] **:** a foreigner living in China and wielding economic power (as through control of a business house) there

[2]**tai·pan** \'tī-ˌpan\ *n* [native name in Australia] **:** an exceedingly venomous elapid snake (*Oxyuranus scutellatus*) of northern Australia and the Pacific islands

Tai·ping \'tī-'piŋ\ *n* [Chin (Pek) *t'ai*[4] *ping*[2] peaceful] **:** a Chinese insurgent taking part in a rebellion (1848–65) against the Manchu dynasty

Ta·jik \tä-'jik, tə-, -'jēk\ *n* **:** a member of a people of Iranian blood and speech who resemble Europeans and are dispersed among the populations of Afghanistan and Turkestan

ta·ka \'täk-ə, -(ˌ)ä\ *n* [Bengali *tākā* rupee, *ṭaka,* fr. Skt *ṭaṅka,* a stamped coin] — see MONEY table

Ta·jiki \-'jik-ē, -'jē-kē\ *n* **:** the Iranian language of the Tajik people

[1]**take** \'tāk\ *vb* **took** \'tu̇k\; **tak·en** \'tā-kən\; **tak·ing** [ME *taken,* fr. OE *tacan,* fr. ON *taka;* akin to MD *taken* to take] *vt* **1 :** to get into one's hands or into one's possession, power, or control: as **a :** to seize or capture physically **b :** to get possession of (as fish or game) by killing or capturing **c (1) :** to move against (as an opponent's piece in chess) and remove from play **:** CAPTURE **(2) :** to win in a card game <able to ~ 12 tricks with that hand> **d :** to acquire property by eminent domain **e :** to catch (a batted ball) in baseball or cricket <~ it on the fly> **2 :** GRASP, GRIP <~ the ax by the handle> **3 a :** to catch or attack through the effect of a sudden force or influence <*taken* with a fit of laughing> <*taken* ill> **b :** to catch or come upon in a particular situation or action <was *taken* unawares> **c :** to strike or hit in or on a specified part <*took* the boy a smart box on the ear> **d :** to gain the approval or liking of **:** CAPTIVATE, DELIGHT <was quite *taken* with her at their first meeting> **4 a :** to receive into one's body (as by eating, drinking, or inhaling) <~ a glass of water> **b :** to expose oneself to (as sun or air) for pleasure or physical benefit **c :** to partake of **:** EAT <~*s* dinner about seven> **5 a :** to bring or receive into a relation or connection <reduced to *taking* lodgers> <it's time he *took* a wife> **b :** to copulate with **6 :** to transfer into one's own keeping: **a :** APPROPRIATE **b (1) :** to obtain or secure for use (as by lease or contract) <~ a cottage for the summer> **(2) :** BUY <the salesman persuaded him to ~ the station wagon> **7 a :** ASSUME <gods often *took* the likeness of a human being> **b :** to charge oneself with (as a duty, obligation, or task) **:** UNDERTAKE <~ office> **c :** to subject oneself to **:** bind oneself by <~ a vow> **d :** to impose upon oneself <~ the trouble to do good work> **e :** to adopt as one's own **:** align or ally oneself with <his mother *took* his side> **f :** to adopt or advance as one's fundamental point of argument or defense <a point well *taken*> **g :** to assume as if rightfully one's own or as if granted <~ the credit> **h :** to have or assume as a proper part of or accompaniment to itself <transitive verbs ~ an object> **8 a :** to secure by winning in competition <*took* first place> **b :** DEFEAT **9 :** to pick out **:** CHOOSE, SELECT **10 :** to adopt, choose, or avail oneself of for use: as **a :** to have recourse to as an instrument for doing something <~ a scythe to the weeds> **b :** to use as a means of transportation or progression <*took* a freighter to Europe> **c :** to have recourse to for safety or refuge <~ shelter> **d (1) :** to proceed to occupy <~ a seat in the rear> **(2) :** to use up (as space or time) <~*s* a long time to dry> **(3) :** NEED, REQUIRE <~*s* a size nine shoe> **11 a :** to obtain by deriving from a source **:** DRAW <~*s* its title from the name of the hero> **b (1) :** to obtain as the result of a special procedure **:** ASCERTAIN <~ the temperature> <~ a census> **(2) :** to get in writing **:** write down <~ notes> <~ an inventory> **(3) :** to get by drawing or painting or by photography <~ a snapshot> **(4) :** to get by transference from one surface to another <~ a proof> <~ fingerprints> **12 :** to receive or accept whether willingly or reluctantly <~ a bribe> <~ a bet> **:** as **a :** to receive when bestowed or tendered <~ an honorary degree> **b (1) :** to submit to **:** ENDURE, UNDERGO <*took* his punishment like a man> **(2) :** WITHSTAND <~*s* a punch well> **c (1) :** to accept as true **:** BELIEVE <*took* his word for it> **(2) :** FOLLOW <~ a suggestion> **(3) :** to accept with the mind in a specified way <~ things as they come> **d :** to indulge in and enjoy <was *taking* his ease on the porch> **e :** to receive or accept as a return (as in payment, compensation, or reparation) **f :** to refrain from hitting at (a pitched ball) **13 a (1) :** to let in **:** ADMIT <the boat was ~*ing* water fast> **(2) :** ACCOMMODATE <the suitcase wouldn't ~ another thing> **b :** to be affected injuriously by (as a disease) **:** CONTRACT <~ cold> **:** be seized by <~ a fit> **c :** to absorb or become impregnated with (as dye) **:** be affected by (as polish) **14 a :** APPREHEND, UNDERSTAND <slow to ~ his meaning> **b :** CONSIDER, SUPPOSE <~ it as settled> **c :** to accept or reckon as being or as equal to <*taking* a stride at 30 inches> <*took* the report at face value> **d :** FEEL, EXPERIENCE <~ pleasure> **15 :** to lead, carry, or cause to go along to another place <this bus will ~ you into town> **16 a :** to remove or obtain by removing <~ eggs from a nest> **b :** to remove by death <was *taken* in his prime> **c :** SUBTRACT <~ two from four> **17 :** to undertake and make, do, or perform <~ a walk> <~ aim> <~ legal action> **18 a :** to deal with <~ first things first> **b :** to consider or view in a particular relation <*taken* together, the details were significant> **c :** to apply oneself to the study of <~ music lessons> **19 :** CHEAT, SWINDLE <was *taken* for $5000 by a confidence man> ~ *vi* **1 :** to obtain possession: as **a :** CAPTURE **b :** to receive property under law as one's own **2 :** to lay hold **:** CATCH, HOLD **3 :** to establish a take esp. by uniting or growing <90 percent of the grafts ~> **4 a :** to betake oneself **:** set out **:** GO <~ after a purse snatcher> **b** *chiefly dial* — used as an intensifier or redundantly with a following verb <*took* and swung at the ball> **5 a :** to take effect **:** ACT, OPERATE <hoped the lesson he taught would ~> **b :** to show the natural or intended effect <dry fuel ~*s* readily> **6 :** CHARM, CAPTIVATE: **a :** to exert a spell <no planets strike, no fairy ~*s,* nor witch hath power to charm —Shak.> **b :** to prove attractive **:** win popular favor <nothing ~*s* . . . like a romance —Henry Vaughan> **7 :** DETRACT <irritations that *took* from their general satisfaction> **8 a :** to be seized or attacked in a specified way **:** BECOME <*took* sick> **b :** to be capable of being moved in a specified way <the table ~*s* apart for packing> **c :** to adhere or become absorbed <ink that ~*s* well on cloth> **d :** to admit of being photographed — **tak·er** *n*

syn **1** TAKE, SEIZE, GRASP, CLUTCH, SNATCH, GRAB *shared meaning element* **:** to get hold of by or as if by catching up with the hand **2** see RECEIVE

— **take account of :** to take into account — **take advantage of 1 :** to use to advantage **:** profit by **2 :** to impose upon **:** EXPLOIT — **take after 1 :** to take as an example **:** FOLLOW **2 :** to resemble in features, build, character, or disposition — **take amiss :** to impute a wrong motive or a bad meaning or intention to **:** take offense at — **take apart 1 :** DISASSEMBLE, DISMANTLE **2 :** to analyze or dissect esp. in order to discover or reveal a weakness, flaw, or fallacy **3 :** to treat roughly or harshly **:** tear into — **take a powder :** to leave hurriedly — **take care :** to be careful **:** exercise caution or prudence **:** be watchful — **take care of :** to attend to or provide for the needs, operation, or treatment of — **take charge :** to assume care, custody, command, or control — **take effect 1 :** to become operative **2 :** to be effective — **take exception :** OBJECT, DEMUR <*took exception* to his critic's remarks> — **take five** *or* **take ten :** to take a brief intermission — **take for :** to suppose to be; *esp* **:** to suppose mistakenly to be — **take for granted 1 :** to assume as true, real, or expected **2 :** to value too lightly — **take heart :** to gain courage or confidence — **take hold 1 :** GRASP, GRIP, SEIZE **2 :** to become attached or established **:** take effect — **take into account :** to make allowances for <*took* the boy's age *into account*> — **take in vain :** to use (a name) profanely or without proper respect — **take issue :** to take up the opposite side — **take notice of :** to observe or treat with special attention — **take one's time :** to be leisurely about doing something — **take part :** JOIN, PARTICIPATE, SHARE — **take place :** HAPPEN, OCCUR — **take root 1 :** to become rooted **2 :** to become fixed or established — **take shape :** to assume a definite or distinctive form — **take stock :** INVENTORY, ASSESS — **take the cake :** to carry off the prize **:** rank first — **take the count 1** *of a boxer* **:** to be counted out **2 :** to go down in defeat — **take the field 1 :** to go upon the playing field **2 :** to enter upon a military campaign — **take the floor :** to rise (as in a meeting or a legislative assembly) to make a formal address — **take to 1 :** to take in hand **:** take care of **2 :** to betake oneself to <*take to* the woods> **3 :** to apply or devote oneself to (as a practice, habit, or occupation) <*take to* begging> **4 :** to adapt oneself to **:** respond to <*takes to* water lake a duck> **5 :** to conceive a liking for — **take to task :** to call to account for a shortcoming

[2]**take** *n* **1 :** an act or the action of taking (as by seizing, accepting, or otherwise coming into possession): as **a :** the action of killing, capturing, or catching (as game or fish) **b (1) :** the uninterrupted photographing or televising of a scene **(2) :** the making of a sound recording **2 :** something that is taken: **a :** the amount of money received (as from a business venture, sale, or admission charge) **:** PROCEEDS, RECEIPTS, INCOME **b :** SHARE, CUT <wanted a bigger ~> **c :** the number or quantity (as of animals, fish, or pelts) taken at one time **:** CATCH, HAUL **d :** a section or installment (as of an article or a speech) arbitrarily chosen (as for convenience in reading, recording, or translation) **e (1) :** a scene filmed or televised at one time without stopping the camera **(2) :** a sound recording made during a single recording period; *esp* **:** a trial recording **3 a :** a local or systemic reaction indicative of successful vaccination against smallpox **b :** a successful union (as of a graft) **4 :** mental response or reaction <a delayed ~> — **on the take :** alert to an opportunity to take or take advantage of another

take back *vt* **:** to make a retraction of **:** WITHDRAW

[1]**take·down** \'tāk-ˌdau̇n\ *adj* **:** constructed so as to be readily taken apart <a ~ rifle>

[2]**take·down** \'tāk-ˌdau̇n\ *n* **1 :** the action or an act of taking down: as **a :** the action of humiliating **b :** the action of taking apart **c :** the act of bringing one's opponent in amateur wrestling to the mat and under control from a standing position **2 :** something (as a rifle or shotgun) having takedown construction

take down \(ˈ)tāk-'dau̇n\ *vt* **1 a :** to pull to pieces <*take down* a building> **b :** DISASSEMBLE <*take* a rifle *down*> **2 :** to lower the spirit or vanity of **:** HUMBLE **3 a :** to write down **b :** to record by mechanical means **4 :** to lower without removing <*took down* his pants> ~ *vi* **:** to become seized or attacked esp. by illness

take–home pay \ˌtāk-ˌhōm-\ *n* **:** the part of gross salary or wages remaining after deductions (as for income-tax withholding)

take–in \'tā-ˌkin\ *n* **:** an act of taking in esp. by deceiving

take in \(ˈ)tā-'kin\ *vt* **1 :** to draw into a smaller compass <*take in* the slack of a line>: **a :** FURL **b :** to make (a garment) smaller by enlarging seams or tucks **2 a :** to receive as a guest or lodger **b :** to give shelter to **c :** to take to a police station as a prisoner **3 :** to receive as payment or proceeds <the store *took in* a lot of money today> **4 :** to receive (work) into one's house to be done for pay <*take in* washing> **5 :** to encompass within its limits **6 a :** to include in an itinerary **b :** ATTEND <*take in* a movie> **7 :** to receive into the mind **:** PERCEIVE **8 :** DECEIVE, DUPE

taken *past part of* TAKE

take·off \'tā-ˌkȯf\ *n* **1 :** an imitation esp. in the way of caricature **2 a :** a rise or leap from a surface in making a jump or flight or an ascent in an aircraft or in the launching of a rocket **b :** an action of starting out **3 a :** a spot at which one takes off **b :** a starting point **:** point of departure **4 :** an action of removing something **5 :** the action of estimating or measuring an amount of material needed **6 :** a mechanism for transmission of the power of an engine or vehicle to operate some other mechanism

take off \(ˈ)tā-'kȯf\ *vt* **1 :** REMOVE <*take* your shoes *off*> **2 a :** RELEASE <*take* the brake *off*> **b :** DISCONTINUE, WITHDRAW <*took off* the morning train> **c :** to take or allow as a discount **:** DEDUCT <*took* 10 percent *off*> **3 :** to omit or withhold from service owed or from time being spent (as at one's occupation) <*took* two weeks *off* in August> **4 :** to take the life of <*taken off* by pneumonia> **5 a :** to copy from an original **:** REPRODUCE **b :** to make a likeness of **:** PORTRAY **c :** MIMIC <mannerisms that his critics delighted in *taking off*> ~ *vi* **1 :** to take away

: DETRACT **2 a** : to start off or away : set out : DEPART <*took off* without delay> **b (1)** : to branch off (as from a main stream or stem) **(2)** : to have as a point of origin **c** : to begin a leap or spring **d** : to leave the surface : begin flight

take on *vt* **1 a** : to begin to perform or deal with : UNDERTAKE <*took on* new responsibilities> **b** : to contend with as an opponent <*took on* the neighborhood bully> **2 a** : ENGAGE, HIRE **b** : to accept in a relationship <*taking* me *on* as a client> **3** : to assume or acquire (as an appearance or quality) as or as if one's own <the city's plaza *takes on* a carnival air —W. T. LeViness> ~ *vi* **1** : to show one's feelings esp. of grief or anger in a demonstrative way <they cried and *took on* something terrible —Bob Hope> **2** : to behave in a proud or haughty manner

take·out \ˈtā-ˌkau̇t\ *n* **1** : the action or an act of taking out; *esp* : a bridge bid that takes a partner out of a bid, double, or redouble **2** : something taken out or prepared to be taken out

take out \(ˈ)tā-ˈkau̇t\ *vt* **1 a (1)** : DEDUCT, SEPARATE **(2)** : EXCLUDE, OMIT **(3)** : WITHDRAW, WITHHOLD **b** : to draw out by cleansing <*took* the stain *out*> **c** : to find release for : VENT <*take out* their resentments on one another —J. W. Aldridge> **d** : ELIMINATE **2** : to conduct or escort into the open or to a public entertainment **3** : to take as an equivalent in another form <*took* the debt *out* in goods> **4 a** : to obtain from the proper authority <*take out* a charter> **b** : to arrange for (insurance) **5** : to overcall (a bridge partner) in a different suit ~ *vi* : to start on a course : set out — **take it out on** : to expend anger, vexation, or frustration in harassment of

take·out double \ˌtā-ˌkau̇t-\ *n* : a double made in bridge to convey information to one's partner and to invite a bid from him

take·over \ˈtā-ˌkō-vər\ *n* : the action or an act of taking over

take over \(ˈ)tā-ˈkō-vər\ *vt* : to assume control or possession of or responsibility for <military leaders *took over* the government> ~ *vi* **1** : to assume control or possession **2** : to become dominant

take–up \ˈtā-ˌkəp\ *n* **1** : the action of taking up (as by gathering, contraction, absorption, or adjustment) **2** : UPTAKE 2 **3** : any of various devices for tightening or drawing in

take up \(ˈ)tā-ˈkəp\ *vt* **1 a** : to pick up : LIFT **b** : to remove by lifting or pulling up **2 a** : to begin to occupy (land) **b** : to buy up **c** : to pay the amount of (as a loan) **d** : to gather from a number of sources <*took up* a collection> **3** : to accept or adopt for the purpose of assisting **4 a** : to take or accept (as a belief, idea, or practice) as one's own <*took up* smoking> **b** : ASSUME <*take up* a hostile attitude> **c** : to receive into itself or upon its surface and hold : SORB <plants *take up* nutrients> **5 a** : to enter upon (as a business, profession, or subject of study) <*took up* teaching as a profession> **b** : to proceed to deal with <*take up* one problem at a time> **6** : REBUKE, REPRIMAND **7** : to establish oneself in <*took up* residence in town> **8** : to occupy (as space, time, or attention) entirely or exclusively : fill up <outside activities *took up* too much of his time> **9** : to make tighter or shorter (as by adjusting parts or pulling up or in extensions) **10** : ARREST, SEIZE **11** : to respond favorably to (as a bet, challenge, or proposal) **12** : to begin again or take over from another ~ *vi* **1** : to make a beginning where another has left off **2** : to become shortened : draw together : SHRINK — **take up for** : to take the part or side of — **take up the cudgels** : to engage vigorously in a defense — **take up with 1** : to become interested or absorbed in **2** : to begin to associate with : CONSORT

ta·kin \ˈtäk-ēn\ *n* [Mishmi] : a large heavily built ruminant (*Budorcas taxicolor*) of Tibet that is related to the goats but in some respects resembles the antelopes

¹tak·ing \ˈtā-kiŋ\ *n* **1** : SEIZURE **2 a** *chiefly Scot* : an unhappy state : PLIGHT **b** : a state of violent agitation and distress **3 a** *pl* : receipts esp. of money **b** : a take of fish or animals

²taking *adj* : ATTRACTIVE, CAPTIVATING

¹ta·la \ˈtäl-ə\ *n* [Skt *tāla*, lit., hand-clapping]: one of the ancient traditional rhythmic patterns of Indian music — compare RAGA

²ta·la \ˈtäl-ə, -(ˌ)ä\ *n* [Samoan, fr. E *dollar*] — see MONEY table

Tal·bot \ˈtȯl-bət, ˈtal-\ *n* [prob. fr. *Talbot*, name of a Norman family in England] : a large heavy mostly white hound with pendulous ears and drooping flews held to be ancestral to the bloodhound

talc \ˈtalk\ *n* [MF *talc* mica, fr. ML *talk*, fr. Ar *talq*] : a soft mineral $Mg_3Si_4O_{10}(OH)_2$ that is a basic magnesium silicate, is usu. whitish, greenish, or grayish with a soapy feel, and occurs in foliated, granular, or fibrous masses (hardness 1, sp. gr. 2.6–2.9) — **talc·ose** \ˈtal-ˌkōs\ *adj*

tal·cum powder \ˈtal-kəm-\ *n* [ML *talcum* mica, alter. of earlier *talk*] **1** : powdered talc **2** : a toilet powder composed of perfumed talc or talc and a mild antiseptic

tale \ˈtā(ə)l\ *n* [ME, fr. OE *talu*; akin to ON *tala* talk, and prob. to L *dolus* guile, deceit, Gk *dolos*] **1** *obs* : DISCOURSE, TALK **2 a** : a series of events or facts told or presented : ACCOUNT **b (1)** : a report of a private or confidential matter <dead men tell no ~*s*> **(2)** : a libelous report or piece of gossip **3 a** : a usu. imaginative narrative of an event : STORY **b** : an intentionally untrue relation : FALSEHOOD <always preferred the ~ to the truth —Sir Winston Churchill> **4 a** : COUNT, TALLY **b** : TOTAL

tale·bear·er \-ˌbar-ər, -ˌber-\ *n* : one that spreads gossip, scandal, or idle rumors : GOSSIP — **tale·bear·ing** \-iŋ\ *adj or n*

tal·ent \ˈtal-ənt\ *n* [ME, fr. OE *talente*, fr. L *talenta*, pl. of *talentum* unit of weight or money, fr. Gk *talanton*; akin to L *tollere* to lift up; in senses 2–5, fr. the parable of the talents in Mt 25:14–30 — more at TOLERATE] **1 a** : any of several ancient units of weight (as a unit of Palestine and Syria equal to 3000 shekels or a Greek unit equal to 6000 drachmas) **b** : a unit of value equal to the value of a talent of gold or silver **2** *archaic* : a characteristic feature, aptitude, or disposition of a person or animal **3** : the natural endowments of a person **4 a** : a special often creative or artistic aptitude **b** : general intelligence or mental power : ABILITY **5** : a person of talent or a group of persons of talent in a field or activity ***syn*** see GIFT — **tal·ent·ed** \-ən-təd\ *adj* — **tal·ent·less** \-ənt-ləs\ *adj*

talent scout *n* : a person engaged in discovering and recruiting people of talent for a specialized field or activity

talent show *n* : a show consisting of a series of individual performances (as singing) by amateurs who may be selected for special recognition as performing talent

ta·ler \ˈtäl-ər\ *n* [G — more at DOLLAR] : any of numerous silver coins issued by various German states from the 15th to the 19th centuries

tales·man \ˈtā(ə)lz-mən, ˈtā-lēz-\ *n* [ME *tales* talesmen, fr. ML *tales de circumstantibus* such (persons) of the bystanders; fr. the wording of the writ summoning them] **1** : a person added to a jury usu. from among bystanders to make up a deficiency in the available number of jurors **2** : a member of a large pool of persons called for jury duty from which jurors are selected

tale–tell·er \ˈtā(ə)l-ˌtel-ər\ *n* **1** : one who tells tales or stories **2** : TALEBEARER — **tale–tell·ing** \-ˌtel-iŋ\ *adj or n*

tali *pl of* TALUS

tali·pes \ˈtal-ə-ˌpēz\ *n* [NL, fr. L *talus* ankle + *pes* foot — more at FOOT] : CLUBFOOT

tal·i·pot \ˈtal-ə-ˌpät\ *n* [Bengali *tālipōt* palm leaf] : a tall showy fan-leaved palm (*Corypha umbraculifera*) of Ceylon, the Philippines, and the Malabar coast bearing a crown of huge leaves that are used as umbrellas and fans and are cut into strips for writing paper

tal·is·man \ˈtal-ə-smən, -əz-mən\ *n, pl* **-mans** [F *talisman* or Sp *talismán* or It *talismano*, fr. Ar *ṭilsam*, fr. MGk *telesma*, fr. Gk, consecration, fr. *telein* to initiate into the mysteries, complete, fr. *telos* end — more at WHEEL] **1** : an object bearing a sign or character engraved under astrological influences and held to act as a charm to avert evil and bring good fortune **2** : something producing apparently magical or miraculous effects ***syn*** see FETISH — **tal·is·man·ic** \ˌtal-ə-ˈsman-ik, -əz-ˈman-\ *adj* — **tal·is·man·i·cal·ly** \-i-k(ə-)lē\ *adv*

¹talk \ˈtȯk\ *vb* [ME *talken*; akin to OE *talu* tale] *vt* **1** : to deliver or express in speech : UTTER **2** : to make the subject of conversation or discourse : DISCUSS <~ business> **3** : to influence, affect, or cause by talking <~*ed* them into agreeing> **4** : to use (a language) for conversing or communicating : SPEAK ~ *vi* **1 a** : to express or exchange ideas by means of spoken words **b** : to convey information or communicate in any way (as with signs or sounds) <can make a trumpet ~> **2** : to use speech : SPEAK **3 a** : to speak idly : PRATE **b** : GOSSIP **c** : to reveal secret or confidential information **4** : to give a talk : LECTURE ***syn*** see SPEAK — **talk·er** *n* — **talk back** : to answer impertinently — **talk sense** : to voice rational, logical, or sensible thoughts — **talk through one's hat** : to voice irrational, illogical, or erroneous ideas — **talk turkey** : to speak frankly or bluntly

²talk *n* **1** : the act or an instance of talking : SPEECH **2** : a way of speaking : LANGUAGE **3** : pointless or fruitless discussion : VERBIAGE **4** : a formal discussion, negotiation, or exchange of views : CONFERENCE **5 a** : MENTION, REPORT **b** : RUMOR, GOSSIP **6** : the topic of interested comment, conversation, or gossip **7 a** : ADDRESS, LECTURE **b** : written analysis or discussion presented in an informal or conversational manner **8** : communicative sounds or signs resembling or functioning as talk <bird ~>

talk·athon \ˈtȯ-kə-ˌthän\ *n* [*talk* + mar*athon*] : a long session of discussion or speech-making

talk·ative \ˈtȯ-kət-iv\ *adj* : given to talking — **talk·ative·ly** *adv* — **talk·ative·ness** *n*

syn TALKATIVE, LOQUACIOUS, GARRULOUS, VOLUBLE *shared meaning element* : given to talk or talking ***ant*** silent

talk down *vt* **1** : to overcome or silence by argument or by loud talking **2** : to disparage or belittle by talking ~ *vi* : to speak in a condescending or oversimplified fashion

talk·ie \ˈtȯ-kē\ *n* [*talk* + mov*ie*] : a motion picture with a synchronized sound track

talking book *n* : a phonograph or tape recording of a reading of a book or magazine designed chiefly for the use of the blind

talking machine *n* : PHONOGRAPH

talking point *n* : something that lends support to an argument

talk·ing–to \ˈtȯ-kiŋ-ˌtü\ *n* : REPRIMAND, LECTURE <gave the boys . . . a firm ~ on just how fortunate they were —Ken Graham>

talk out *vt* : to clarify or settle by oral discussion

talk over *vt* : to review or consider in conversation : DISCUSS

talk show *n* : a radio or television program in which usu. well-known persons engage in discussions or are interviewed

talk up *vt* : to discuss favorably : ADVOCATE, PROMOTE <a book which was *talked up* by the . . . editor — V. S. Navasky> ~ *vi* : to speak up plainly or directly

talky \ˈtȯ-kē\ *adj* **1** : TALKATIVE **2** : containing too much talk

tall \ˈtȯl\ *adj* [ME, prob. fr. OE *getæl* quick, ready; akin to OHG *gizal* quick, OE *talu* tale] **1** *obs* : BRAVE, COURAGEOUS **2 a** : high in stature **b** : of a specified height <five feet ~> **3 a** : of considerable height <~ trees> **b** : long from bottom to top <a ~ book> **c** : of a higher growing variety or species of plant **4 a** : large or formidable in amount, extent, or degree <a ~ order to fill> **b** : POMPOUS, HIGH-FLOWN <~ talk about the vast mysteries of life —W. A. White> **c** : highly exaggerated : INCREDIBLE, IMPROBABLE <a ~ story> ***syn*** see HIGH ***ant*** short — **tall** *adv* — **tall·ish** \ˈtȯ-lish\ *adj* — **tall·ness** \ˈtȯl-nəs\ *n*

tal·lage \ˈtal-ij\ *n* [ME *taillage, tallage*, fr. OF *taillage*, fr. *taillier* to cut, limit, tax — more at TAILOR] **1** : a toll, fee, or render paid by a feudal tenant to his lord **2** : an impost or due levied by a lord upon his tenants

---

ə abut ᵊ kitten ər further a back ā bake ä cot, cart
au̇ out ch chin e less ē easy g gift i trip ī life
j joke ŋ sing ō flow ȯ flaw ȯi coin th thin t͟h this
ü loot u̇ foot y yet yü few yu̇ furious zh vision

tall·boy \'tȯl-,bȯi\ *n* **1 a :** HIGHBOY **b :** a double chest of drawers usu. with the upper section slightly smaller than the lower **2** *Brit* **:** CLOTHESPRESS

tal·lith \'täl-əs, 'tal-, -ət(h)\ *n, pl* **tal·li·thim** \,täl-ə-'sēm, -'t(h)ēm\ *or* **ta·ley·sim** \tə-'lā-səm\ [Heb *ṭallīth* cover, cloak] **:** a shawl with fringed corners traditionally worn over the head or shoulders by Jewish men during morning prayers

tall oil \'täl-, 'tȯl-\ *n* [part trans. of G *tallöl,* part trans. of Sw *tallolja,* fr. *tall* pine + *olja* oil] **:** a resinous by-product from the manufacture of chemical wood pulp used esp. in making soaps, coatings, and oils

1**tal·low** \'tal-(,)ō, -ə(-w)\ *n, often attrib* [ME *talgh, talow;* akin to MD *talch* tallow] **:** the white nearly tasteless solid rendered fat of cattle and sheep used chiefly in soap, margarine, candles, and lubricants — **tal·lowy** \'tal-ə-wē\ *adj*

2**tallow** *vt* **:** to grease or smear with tallow

1**tal·ly** \'tal-ē\ *n, pl* **tallies** [ME *talye,* fr. ML *talea, tallia* fr. L *talea* twig, cutting — more at TAILOR] **1 :** a device for visibly recording or accounting esp. business transactions: as **a :** a wooden rod notched with marks representing numbers and split lengthwise through the notches so that each of two parties may have a record of a transaction and of the amount due or paid **b :** any of various bookkeeping forms or sheets **c :** a mechanical counter held in the hand and operated with a button or lever **2 a :** a recorded reckoning or account (as of items or charges) <keep a daily ~ of accidents> **b :** a score or point made (as in a game) **3 a :** a part that corresponds to an opposite or companion member **:** COMPLEMENT **b :** a state of correspondence or agreement

2**tally** *vb* **tal·lied; tal·ly·ing** *vt* **1 a :** to mark on or as if on a tally **:** TABULATE **b :** to list or check off (as a cargo) by items **c :** to register (as a score) in a contest **2 :** to make a count of **:** RECKON **3 :** to cause to correspond ~ *vi* **1 a :** to make a tally by or as if by tabulating **b :** to register a point in a contest **:** SCORE **2 :** CORRESPOND, MATCH

tal·ly·ho \,tal-ē-'hō\ *n, pl* **-hos** [prob. fr. F *taïaut,* a cry used to excite hounds in deer hunting] **1 :** a call of a huntsman at sight of the fox **2** [*Tally-ho,* name of a coach formerly plying between London and Birmingham] **:** a four-in-hand coach

tal·ly·man \'tal-ē-mən, -,man\ *n* **1** *Brit* **:** one who sells goods on the installment plan **2 :** one who tallies, checks, or keeps an account or record (as of receipt of goods)

Tal·mud \'täl-,mu̇d, 'tal-məd\ *n* [LHeb *talmūdh,* lit., instruction] **:** the authoritative body of Jewish tradition comprising the Mishnah and Gemara — **tal·mu·dic** \tal-'m(y)üd-ik, -'məd-; täl-'mu̇d-\ *also* **tal·mu·di·cal** \-i-kəl\ *adj, often cap* — **tal·mud·ism** \'täl-,mu̇d-,iz-əm, 'tal-məd-\ *n, often cap*

Tal·mud·ist \'täl-,mu̇d-əst, 'tal-məd-\ *n* **:** a specialist in talmudic studies

tal·on \'tal-ən\ *n* [ME, fr. MF, heel, spur, fr. (assumed) VL *talon-, talo,* fr. L *talus* ankle, anklebone] **1 a :** the claw of an animal and esp. of a bird of prey **b :** a finger or hand of a human being **2 :** a part or object shaped like or suggestive of a heel or claw: as **a :** an ogee molding **b :** the shoulder of the bolt of a lock on which the key acts to shoot the bolt **3 a :** cards laid aside in a pile in solitaire **b :** STOCK 10c — **tal·oned** \-ənd\ *adj*

1**ta·lus** \'tā-ləs, 'tal-əs\ *n* [F, fr. L *talutium* slope indicating presence of gold under the soil] **1 :** a slope formed esp. by an accumulation of rock debris **2 :** rock debris at the base of a cliff

2**ta·lus** \'tā-ləs\ *n, pl* **ta·li** \'tā-,lī\ [NL, fr. L] **1 :** the astragalus of man bearing the weight of the body and with the tibia and fibula forming the ankle joint **2 :** the entire ankle

tam \'tam\ *n* **:** TAM-O'-SHANTER

ta·ma·le \tə-'mäl-ē\ *n* [MexSp *tamales,* pl. of *tamal* tamale, fr. Nahuatl *tamalli*] **:** ground meat seasoned usu. with chili, rolled in cornmeal dough, wrapped in corn husks, and steamed

ta·man·dua \tə-'man-də-wə, -,man-də-'wä\ *n* [Pg *tamanduá,* fr. Tupi] **:** an arboreal anteater (*Tamandua tetradactyla*) of Central and So. America

tam·a·rack \'tam-(ə-),rak\ *n* [origin unknown] **1 :** any of several American larches; *esp* **:** a larch (*Larix laricina*) of the northern U.S., Canada, and Alaska **2 :** the wood of a tamarack

tam·a·rau \,tam-ə-'rau̇\ *n* [Tag *tamaráw*] **:** a small dark sturdily built buffalo (*Bubalus mindorensis*) native to Mindoro

tam·a·rin \'tam-ə-rən, -,ran\ *n* [F, fr. Galibi] **:** any of numerous small So. American marmosets (genus *Leontocebus*) with silky fur and long tail

tam·a·rind \'tam-ə-rənd, -,rind\ *n* [Sp & Pg *tamarindo,* fr. Ar *tamr hindī,* lit., Indian date] **:** a tropical leguminous tree (*Tamarindus indica*) with hard yellowish wood, pinnate leaves, and red-striped yellow flowers; *also* **:** its fruit which has an acid pulp used for preserves or in a cooling laxative drink

tam·a·risk \'tam-ə-,risk\ *n* [ME *tamarisc,* fr. LL *tamariscus,* fr. L *tamaric-, tamarix*] **:** any of a genus (*Tamarix* of the family Tamaricaceae, the tamarisk family) of chiefly desert shrubs and trees having tiny narrow leaves and masses of minute flowers with five stamens and a one-celled ovary

tam·ba·la \täm-'bäl-ə\ *n, pl* **-la** *or* **-las** [native name in Malawi, lit., cockerel] — see *kwacha* at MONEY table

1**tam·bour** \'tam-,bu̇(ə)r, tam-'\ *n* [F, drum, fr. Ar *ṭanbūr,* modif. of Per *tabīr*] **1 :** 1DRUM 1 **2 a :** an embroidery frame; *esp* **:** a set of two interlocking hoops between which cloth is stretched before stitching **b :** embroidery made on a tambour frame **3 :** a shallow metallic cup or drum with a thin elastic membrane supporting a writing lever used to transmit and register slight motions (as arterial pulsations) **4 :** a rolling top or front (as of a desk) of narrow strips of wood glued on canvas

2**tambour** *vt* **:** to embroider (cloth) with tambour ~ *vi* **:** to work at a tambour frame — **tam·bour·er** *n*

tam·bou·ra *or* **tam·bu·ra** \tam-'bu̇r-ə\ *n* [Per *ṭambūra*] **:** an Asian musical instrument resembling a lute in construction but without frets and used to produce a drone accompaniment to singing

tam·bou·rine \,tam-bə-'rēn\ *n* [MF *tambourin,* dim. of *tambour*] **:** a small drum; *esp* **:** a shallow one-headed drum with loose metallic disks at the sides played by shaking, striking with the hand, or rubbing with the thumb

tambourine

tam·bu·rit·za \,tam-bə-'rit-sə\ *n* [Serb *tamburica,* prob. fr. Turk *tambur, tambura* tamboura, fr. Per *ṭambūra*] **:** one of a family of plucked stringed instruments of Yugoslavia similar to the guitar in shape and the mandolin in sound

1**tame** \'tām\ *adj* **tam·er; tam·est** [ME, fr. OE *tam;* akin to OHG *zam* tame, L *domare* to tame, Gk *damnanai*] **1 :** reduced from a state of native wildness esp. so as to be tractable and useful to man **:** DOMESTICATED <~ animals> **2 :** made docile and submissive **:** SUBDUED **3 :** lacking spirit, zest, or interest **:** INSIPID <a ~ campaign> — **tame·ly** *adv* — **tame·ness** *n*

syn TAME, SUBDUED, SUBMISSIVE *shared meaning element* **:** docilely tractable ***ant*** fierce

2**tame** *vb* **tamed; tam·ing** *vt* **1 a :** to reduce from a wild to a domestic state **b :** to subject to cultivation **2 :** to deprive of spirit **:** HUMBLE, SUBDUE <the once revolutionary . . . party, long since tamed —*Times Lit. Supp.*> **3 :** to tone down **:** SOFTEN <*tamed* the language in the play> ~ *vi* **:** to become tame — **tam·able** *or* **tame·able** \'tā-mə-bəl\ *adj* — **tam·er** *n*

tame·less \'tām-ləs\ *adj* **:** not tamed or not capable of being tamed

Tam·il \'tam-əl\ *n* **1 :** a Dravidian language of Tamil Nadu state and of northern and eastern Ceylon **2 :** a Tamil-speaking person or a descendant of Tamil-speaking ancestors

Tam·ma·ny \'tam-ə-nē\ *adj* [*Tammany Hall,* headquarters of the Tammany Society, political organization in New York City] **:** of, relating to, or constituting a group or organization exercising or seeking municipal political control by methods often associated with corruption and bossism — **Tam·ma·ny·ism** \-,iz-əm\ *n*

Tam·muz \'täm-,u̇z\ *n* [Heb *Tammūz*] **:** the 10th month of the civil year or the 4th month of the ecclesiastical year in the Jewish calendar — see MONTH table

Tam o' Shan·ter *n* **1** \,tam-ə-'shant-ər\ **:** the hero of Burns's poem *Tam o' Shanter* **2** *usu* **tam–o'–shanter** \'tam-ə-,\ **:** a woolen cap of Scottish origin with a tight headband, wide flat circular crown, and usu. a pompon in the center

1**tamp** \'tamp\ *vt* [prob. back-formation fr. obs. *tampion, tampin* (plug), fr. ME, fr. MF *tapon, tampon,* fr. (assumed) OF *taper* to plug, of Gmc origin; akin to OE *tæppa* tap] **1 :** to fill up (a drill hole above a blasting charge) with material (as clay) to confine the force of the explosion **2 :** to drive in or down by a succession of light or medium blows <~ wet concrete> — **tamp·er** *n*

2**tamp** *n* **:** a tool for tamping

tam·pala \tam-'pal-ə\ *n* [native name in India] **:** an annual amaranth (*Amaranthus tricolor*) cultivated as a potherb

tam·per \'tam-pər\ *vb* **tam·pered; tam·per·ing** \-p(ə-)riŋ\ [prob. fr. MF *temprer* to temper, mix, meddle — more at TEMPER] *vi* **1 :** to carry on underhand or improper negotiations (as by bribery) **2 a :** to interfere so as to weaken or change for the worse **b :** to try foolish or dangerous experiments ~ *vt* **:** to alter for an improper purpose or in an improper way ***syn*** see MEDDLE — **tam·per·er** \-pər-ər\ *n* — **tam·per·proof** \,tam-pər-'prüf\ *adj*

tam·pi·on \'tam-pē-ən, 'täm-\ *n* [obs. *tampion, tampin* plug — more at TAMP] **:** a wooden plug or a metal or canvas cover for the muzzle of a gun

1**tam·pon** \'tam-,pän\ *n* [F, lit., plug — more at TAMP] **:** a plug (as of cotton) introduced into a cavity usu. to arrest hemorrhage or absorb secretions

2**tampon** *vt* **:** to plug with a tampon

tam–tam \'tam-,tam, 'täm-,täm\ *n* [Hindi *ṭamṭam*] **1 :** TOM-TOM **2 :** GONG; *esp* **:** one of a tuned set in a gamelan orchestra

1**tan** \'tan\ *vb* **tanned; tan·ning** [ME *tannen,* fr. MF *tanner,* fr. ML *tannare,* fr. *tanum, tannum* tanbark] *vt* **1 a :** to convert (hide) into leather by treatment with an infusion of tannin-rich bark or other agent of similar effect **b :** to convert (protein) to leather or a similar substance **2 :** to make (skin) tan esp. by exposure to the sun **3 :** THRASH, WHIP ~ *vi* **:** to get or become tanned

2**tan** *n* [F, tanbark, fr. OF, fr. ML *tanum*] **1 :** a tanning material or its active agent (as tannin) **2 :** a brown color imparted to the skin by exposure to the sun or wind **3 :** a variable color averaging a light yellowish brown **4** *pl* **:** tan-colored articles of clothing

3**tan** *adj* **tan·ner; tan·nest** **1 :** of, relating to, or used for tan or tanning **2 :** of the color of tan

4**tan** *symbol* tangent

tan·a·ger \'tan-i-jər\ *n* [NL *tanagra,* fr. Pg *tangará,* fr. Tupi] **:** any of numerous American passerine birds (family Thraupidae) having brightly colored males, being mainly unmusical, and chiefly inhabiting woodlands

tan·bark \'tan-,bärk\ *n* **1 :** a bark rich in tannin bruised or cut into small pieces and used in tanning **2 :** a surface (as a circus ring) covered with spent tanbark

1**tan·dem** \'tan-dəm\ *n* [L, at last, at length (taken to mean "lengthwise"), fr. *tam* so; akin to OE *thæt* that] **1 a** (1) **:** a 2-seated carriage drawn by horses harnessed one before the other (2) **:** a team so harnessed **b :** TANDEM BICYCLE **c :** a vehicle (as a motortruck) having close-coupled pairs of axles **2 :** a group of two or more arranged one behind the other or used or acting in conjunction — **in tandem** **1 :** in a tandem arrangement **2 :** in partnership or conjunction

2**tandem** *adv* **:** one after or behind another <ride ~>

3**tandem** *adj* **1 :** consisting of things or having parts arranged one behind the other **2 :** working in conjunction with each other

tandem bicycle *n* **:** a bicycle for two or more persons sitting tandem

1**tang** \'taŋ\ *n* [ME, of Scand origin; akin to ON *tangi* point of land, tang] **1 :** a projecting shank, prong, fang, or tongue (as on a knife, file, or sword) to connect with the handle **2 a :** a sharp distinctive often lingering flavor **b :** a pungent odor **c :** something having the effect of a tang (as in stimulation of the senses) <treated murder as a joke with a ~ to it —Graham Greene> **3 a :** a faint suggestion : TRACE **b :** a distinguishing characteristic that sets apart or gives a special individuality — **tanged** \ˈtaŋd\ *adj*

²tang *vt* **1 :** to furnish with a tang **2 :** to affect with a tang

³tang *n* [of Scand origin; akin to Dan & Norw *tang* seaweed] : any of various large coarse seaweeds (esp. genus *Fucus*)

⁴tang *vb* [imit.] **:** CLANG, RING

⁵tang *n* **:** a sharp twanging sound

Tang \ˈtäŋ\ *n* [Chin (Pek) *tʻang²*] **:** a Chinese dynasty dated A.D. 618–907 and marked by wide contacts with other cultures and by the development of printing and the flourishing of poetry and art

tan·ge·lo \ˈtan-jə-ˌlō\ *n, pl* **-los** [blend of *tangerine* and *pomelo*] : a hybrid between a tangerine or mandarin orange and either a grapefruit or pomelo; *also* **:** its fruit

tan·gen·cy \ˈtan-jən-sē\ *n* **:** the quality or state of being tangent

¹tan·gent \-jənt\ *adj* [L *tangent-, tangens,* prp. of *tangere* to touch; akin to OE *thaccian* to touch gently, stroke] **1 a :** meeting a curve or surface in a single point if a sufficiently small interval is considered <straight line ~ to a curve> **b (1) :** having a common tangent line at a point <~ curves> **(2) :** having a common tangent plane at a point <~ surfaces> **2 :** diverging from an original purpose or course **:** IRRELEVANT <~ remarks>

²tangent *n* [NL *tangent-, tangens,* fr. *linea tangens* tangent line] **1** : the trigonometric function that for an acute angle is the ratio between the side opposite to the angle when it is considered part of a right triangle and the side adjacent **2 a :** a tangent line; *specif* : a straight line that is the limiting position of a secant of a curve through a fixed point and a variable point on the curve as the variable point approaches the fixed point **b :** the part of a tangent to a plane curve between the point of tangency and the x-axis **3** : an abrupt change of course **:** DIGRESSION <the speaker went off on a ~> **4 :** a small upright flat-ended metal pin at the inner end of a clavichord key that strikes the string to produce the tone **5** : a straight section of a road or railroad

tan·gen·tial \tan-ˈjen-chəl\ *adj* **1 :** of, relating to, or of the nature of a tangent **2 :** acting along or lying in a tangent <~ forces> **3 a :** DIVERGENT, DIGRESSIVE **b :** touching lightly **:** INCIDENTAL, PERIPHERAL <~ comment> — **tan·gen·tial·ly** \-ˈjench-(ə-)lē\ *adv*

tangent plane *n* **:** the plane through a point of a surface that contains the tangent lines to all the curves on the surface through the same point

tan·ger·ine \ˈtan-jə-ˌrēn, ˌtan-jə-ˈ\ *n* [F *Tanger* Tangier, Morocco] **1 a :** any of various mandarins that have deep orange to almost scarlet skin and pulp and are grown in the U.S. and southern Africa; *broadly* **:** MANDARIN 3b **b :** a tree producing tangerines **2 :** a moderate to strong reddish orange

¹tan·gi·ble \ˈtan-jə-bəl\ *adj* [LL *tangibilis,* fr. L *tangere* to touch] **1 a :** capable of being perceived esp. by the sense of touch : PALPABLE **b :** substantially real **:** MATERIAL **2 :** capable of being precisely realized by the mind **3 :** capable of being appraised at an actual or approximate value <~ assets> ***syn*** see PERCEPTIBLE ***ant*** intangible — **tan·gi·bil·i·ty** \ˌtan-jə-ˈbil-ət-ē\ *n* — **tan·gi·ble·ness** \ˈtan-jə-bəl-nəs\ *n* — **tan·gi·bly** \-blē\ *adv*

²tangible *n* **:** something tangible; *esp* **:** a tangible asset

¹tan·gle \ˈtaŋ-gəl\ *vb* **tan·gled; tan·gling** \-g(ə-)liŋ\ [ME *tangilen,* prob. of Scand origin; akin to Sw dial. *taggla* to tangle] *vt* **1** : to involve so as to hamper, obstruct, or embarrass **2 :** to seize and hold in or as if in a snare **:** ENTRAP **3 :** to unite or knit together in intricate confusion ~ *vi* **1 :** to engage in conflict **2** : to become entangled

²tangle *n* **1 :** a tangled twisted mass (as of vines) confusedly interwoven**:** SNARL **2 a :** a complicated or confused state or condition **b :** a state of perplexity or complete bewilderment **3** : a serious altercation **:** DISPUTE

³tangle *n* [of Scand origin; akin to ON *thöngull* tangle, *thang* kelp] : a large seaweed

tan·gled \ˈtaŋ-gəld\ *adj* **1 :** existing in or giving the appearance of a state of utter disorder **2 :** very involved <~ relationships>

tan·gle·ment \-gəl-mənt\ *n* **:** ENTANGLEMENT

tan·gly \ˈtaŋ-g(ə-)lē\ *adj* **:** full of tangles or knots **:** INTRICATE

¹tan·go \ˈtaŋ-(ˌ)gō\ *n, pl* **tangos** [AmerSp] **:** a ballroom dance of Latin-American origin in $^2/_4$ time with a basic pattern of step-step-step-step-close and characterized by long pauses and stylized body positions; *also* **:** the music for this dance

²tango *vi* **:** to dance the tango

Tango — a communications code word for the letter *t*

tan·gram \ˈtaŋ-grəm, ˈtan-\ *n* [perh. fr. Chin (Pek) *tʻang²* Chinese + E *-gram*] **:** a Chinese puzzle made by cutting a square of thin material into five triangles, a square, and a rhomboid which are capable of being recombined in many different figures

tangy \ˈtaŋ-ē\ *adj* **tang·i·er; -est :** having or suggestive of a tang

¹tank \ˈtaŋk\ *n* [Pg *tanque,* alter. of *estanque,* fr. *estancar* to stanch, fr. (assumed) VL *stanticare* — more at STANCH] **1** *dial* : POND, POOL; *esp* **:** one built as a water supply **2 :** a usu. large receptacle for holding, transporting, or storing liquids **3 :** an enclosed heavily armed and armored combat vehicle that moves on two endless metal belts **4 :** a prison cell or enclosure used esp. for receiving prisoners — **tank·ful** \-ˌfu̇l\ *n*

²tank *vt* **:** to place, store, or treat in a tank

tan·ka \ˈtäŋ-kə\ *n* [Jap]**:** an unrhymed Japanese verse form of five lines containing 5, 7, 5, 7, and 7 syllables respectively; *also* **:** a poem in this form — compare HAIKU

tank·age \ˈtaŋ-kij\ *n* **1 a :** the capacity or contents of a tank **b** : the aggregate of tanks required for a purpose **2 :** dried animal residues usu. freed from the fat and gelatin and used as fertilizer and feedstuff **3 a :** the act or process of putting or storing in tanks **b :** fees charged for storage in tanks

tan·kard \ˈtaŋ-kərd\ *n* [ME] **:** a tall one-handled drinking vessel; *esp* **:** a silver or pewter mug with a lid

tank destroyer *n* **:** a highly mobile lightly armored vehicle usu. on a half-track or a tank chassis and mounting a cannon

tanked \ˈtaŋ(k)t\ *adj, slang* **:** DRUNK

tank·er \ˈtaŋ-kər\ *n* **1 a :** a cargo boat fitted with tanks for carrying liquid in bulk **b :** a vehicle on which a tank is mounted to carry fluids; *also* **:** a cargo airplane for transporting fuel **2** : a member of a military tank crew

tank farm *n* **:** an area with tanks for storage of oil

tank town *n* [fr. the fact that formerly trains stopped at such towns only to take on water] **:** a small town

tank trailer *n* **:** a truck-drawn trailer equipped as a tanker

tan·nage \ˈtan-ij\ *n* **:** the act, process, or result of tanning

tan·nate \ˈtan-ˌāt\ *n* [F, fr. *tannin*]**:** a compound of a tannin

¹tan·ner \ˈtan-ər\ *n* **:** one that tans hides

tankard

²tanner *n* [origin unknown] *Brit* **:** SIXPENCE

tan·nery \ˈtan-(ə-)rē\ *n, pl* **-ner·ies :** a place where tanning is carried on

tan·nic \ˈtan-ik\ *adj* [F *tannique,* fr. *tannin*] **:** of, resembling, or derived from tan or a tannin

tannic acid *n* **:** TANNIN 1

tan·nin \ˈtan-ən\ *n* [F, fr. *tanner* to tan] **1 :** any of various soluble astringent complex phenolic substances of plant origin used in tanning, dyeing, the making of ink, and in medicine **2 :** a substance that has a tanning effect

tan·ning \ˈtan-iŋ\ *n* **1 :** the art or process by which a skin is tanned **2 :** a browning of the skin by exposure to sun **3 :** a sound spanking **4 :** a natural darkening and hardening of the cuticle of an insect immediately after molting

tan·nish \ˈtan-ish\ *adj* **:** somewhat tan

tan oak *n* **:** an evergreen oak (*Lithocarpus densiflora*) of the Pacific coast area that yields tanbark and differs from the typical oaks esp. in having erect staminate catkins

Ta·no·an \ˈtän-ə-wən\ *n* [*Tano,* a group of former pueblos in New Mexico] **:** a language family of New Mexico — **Tanoan** *adj*

tan·sy \ˈtan-zē\ *n, pl* **tansies** [ME *tanesey,* fr. OF *tanesie,* fr. ML *athanasia,* fr. Gk, immortality, fr. *athanatos* immortal, fr. *a-* + *thanatos* death — more at THANATOS] **:** a common weedy composite herb (*Tanacetum vulgare*) with an aromatic odor, very bitter taste, and finely divided leaves; *broadly* **:** a plant of the same genus

tansy ragwort *n* **:** a common ragwort (*Senecio jacobaea*) that has yellow flower heads, is a troublesome weed in some areas, and is toxic to cattle

tan·ta·late \ˈtant-ᵊl-ˌāt\ *n* **:** a salt of a tantalic acid

tan·tal·ic \tan-ˈtal-ik\ *adj* **:** of, relating to, or derived from tantalum; *esp* **:** being one of the weak acids derived from the pentoxide of tantalum and known chiefly in salts

tan·ta·lite \ˈtant-ᵊl-ˌīt\ *n* **:** a mineral (FeMn) $(TaCb)_2O_6$ consisting of a heavy dark lustrous oxide of iron, manganese, tantalum, and columbium

tan·ta·lize \ˈtant-ᵊl-ˌīz\ *vb* **-lized; -liz·ing** [*Tantalus*] *vt* **:** to tease or torment by or as if by presenting something desirable to the view but continually keeping it out of reach ~ *vi* **:** to cause one to be tantalized ***syn*** see WORRY — **tan·ta·liz·er** *n*

tan·ta·liz·ing *adj* **:** possessing a quality that arouses or stimulates desire or interest; *also* **:** mockingly or teasingly out of reach — **tan·ta·liz·ing·ly** \-ˌī-ziŋ-lē\ *adv*

tan·ta·lum \ˈtant-ᵊl-əm\ *n* [NL, fr. L *Tantalus;* fr. its inability to absorb acid] **:** a hard ductile gray-white acid-resisting metallic element of the vanadium family found combined in rare minerals (as tantalite and columbite) — see ELEMENT table

Tan·ta·lus \ˈtant-ᵊl-əs\ *n* [L, fr. Gk *Tantalos*] **1 :** a legendary king of Lydia condemned to stand up to the chin in a pool of water in Hades and beneath fruit-laden boughs only to have the water or fruit recede at each attempt to drink or eat **2** *not cap* **:** a locked cellarette with contents visible but not obtainable without a key

tan·ta·mount \ˈtant-ə-ˌmau̇nt\ *adj* [obs. *tantamount,* n. (equivalent), fr. AF *tant amunter* to amount to as much]**:** equivalent in value, significance, or effect

tan·ta·ra \tan-ˈtar-ə, -ˈtär-\ *n* [L *taratantara,* of imit. origin]**:** the blare of a trumpet or horn

¹tan·tivy \tan-ˈtiv-ē\ *adv* [origin unknown] **:** at a gallop

²tantivy *n, pl* **-tiv·ies 1 :** a rapid gallop or ride **2 :** TANTARA

tan·tra \ˈtən-trə, ˈtän-\ *n, often cap* [Skt, lit., warp, fr. *tanoti* he stretches, weaves; akin to Gk *teinein* to stretch — more at THIN] : one of the later Hindu or Buddhist scriptures marked by mysticism and magic and used esp. in the worship of Shakti — **tan·tric** \-trik\ *adj, often cap* — **Tan·trism** \-ˌtriz-əm\ *n* — **Tan·trist** \-trəst\ *n*

tan·trum \ˈtan-trəm\ *n* [origin unknown] **:** a fit of bad temper

tan·yard \ˈtan-ˌyärd\ *n* **:** the section or part of a tannery housing tanning vats

tan·za·nite \ˈtan-zə-ˌnīt\ *n* [*Tanzania,* Africa] **:** a mineral that is a deep blue variety of zoisite and is used as a gemstone

Tao \ˈdau̇, ˈtau̇\ *n* [Chin (Pek) *tao⁴*, lit., way] **1 :** the creative principle that orders the universe as conceived by Taoists **2** *often not cap* **:** the path of virtuous conduct as conceived by Confucians

Tao·ism \-ˌiz-əm\ *n* [*Tao*] **1 :** a Chinese mystical philosophy traditionally founded by Lao-tzu in the 6th century B.C. that teaches conformity to the Tao by unassertive action and simplicity **2 :** a religion developed from Taoist philosophy and folk and Buddhist religion and concerned with obtaining long life and good fortune often by magical means — **Tao·ist** \-əst\ *adj or n* — **Tao·is·tic** \dau̇-ˈis-tik, tau̇-\ *adj*

¹tap \ˈtap\ *n* [ME *tappe,* fr. OE *tæppa;* akin to OHG *zapho* tap] **1 a :** a plug for a hole (as in a cask) **:** SPIGOT **b :** a device consisting of a spout and valve attached to the end of a pipe to control the flow of a fluid **:** COCK **2 a :** liquor drawn through a tap **b :** the procedure of removing fluid (as from a body cavity)

3 : a tool for forming an internal screw thread 4 : an intermediate point in an electric circuit where a connection may be made 5 : the action or an instance of wiretapping — **on tap** 1 : ready to be drawn from a large container (as a cask or keg) <ale *on tap*> 2 : broached or furnished with a tap 3 : on hand : AVAILABLE

[2]tap *vt* **tapped; tap·ping** 1 : to let out or cause to flow by piercing or by drawing a plug from the containing vessel <~ wine from a cask> 2 **a** : to pierce so as to let out or draw off a fluid <~ maple trees> **b** : to draw from or upon <~ new sources of revenue>: as (1) : to cut in on (a telephone or telegraph wire) to get information (2) : to cut in (an electrical circuit) on another circuit 3 : to form a female screw in by means of a tap 4 : to get money from as a loan or gift 5 : to connect (a street gas or water main) with a local supply — **tap·per** *n*

[3]tap *vb* **tapped; tap·ping** [ME *tappen,* fr. MF *taper* to strike with the flat of the hand, of Gmc origin; akin to MHG *tāpe* paw, blow dealt with the paw] *vt* 1 : to strike lightly esp. with a slight sound 2 : to give a light blow with <~ a pencil on the table> 3 : to bring about by repeated light blows <*tapped* out his by-line on the typewriter> 4 : to repair by putting a tap on 5 : SELECT, DESIGNATE; *specif* : to elect to membership (as in a fraternity) ~ *vi* 1 : to strike a light audible blow : RAP 2 : to walk with light audible steps 3 : TAP-DANCE — **tap·per** *n*

[4]tap *n* 1 **a** : a light usu. audible blow; *also* : its sound **b** : one of several usu. rapid drumbeats on a snare drum 2 : HALF SOLE 3 : a small metal plate for the sole or heel of a shoe

ta·pa \'täp-ə, 'tap-\ *n* [Marquesan & Tahitian] 1 : the bark of the paper mulberry or of an Hawaiian tree (*Pipturus albidus*) 2 : a coarse cloth made in the Pacific islands from the pounded bark of the paper mulberry, breadfruit, and other plants and usu. decorated with geometric patterns

tap dance *n* : a step dance tapped out audibly by means of shoes with hard soles or soles and heels to which taps have been added — **tap–dance** *vi* — **tap dancer** *n* — **tap dancing** *n*

[1]tape \'tāp\ *n* [ME, fr. OE *tæppe*] 1 : a narrow woven fabric 2 : a string stretched breast-high above the finishing line of a race 3 : a narrow flexible strip or band; *esp* : MAGNETIC TAPE 4 : TAPE RECORDING

[2]tape *vb* **taped; tap·ing** *vt* 1 : to fasten, tie, bind, cover, or support with tape 2 : to measure with a tape measure 3 : to record on tape and esp. magnetic tape <~ an interview> ~ *vi* : to record something on tape and esp. magnetic tape

[3]tape *adj* 1 : recorded on tape <~ music> 2 : intended for use with recording (as magnetic) tape <a ~ cartridge>

tape deck *n* 1 **a** : a mechanism that moves a tape past a magnetic head (as of a tape recorder) **b** : a device that contains such a mechanism and provisions usu. for the recording as well as the playback of magnetic tapes and that usu. has to be connected to a separate audio system 2 : TAPE PLAYER

tape grass *n* : a submerged aquatic plant (*Vallisneria spiralis* of the family Vallisneriaceae) with long ribbonlike leaves

tape·line \'tā-ˌplīn\ *n* : TAPE MEASURE

tape measure *n* : a narrow strip (as of a limp cloth or steel tape) marked off in units (as inches or centimeters) for measuring

tape player *n* : a self-contained device for the playback of recorded magnetic tapes

[1]ta·per \'tā-pər\ *n* [ME, fr. OE *tapor, taper*] 1 **a** : a slender candle **b** : a long waxed wick used esp. for lighting candles, lamps, pipes, or fires **c** : a feeble light 2 **a** : a tapering form or figure **b** : gradual diminution of thickness, diameter, or width in an elongated object **c** : a gradual decrease

[2]taper *adj* 1 : progressively narrowed toward one end 2 : furnished with or adjusted to a scale : GRADUATED <~ freight rates>

[3]taper *vb* **ta·pered; ta·per·ing** \'tā-p(ə-)riŋ\ *vi* 1 : to become progressively smaller toward one end 2 : to diminish gradually ~ *vt* : to cause to taper

[4]tap·er \'tā-pər\ *n* : one that applies or dispenses tape

tape–re·cord \ˌtā-pri-'kȯ(ə)rd\ *vt* [back-formation fr. *tape recording*] : to make a recording of on magnetic tape

tape recorder *n* : a device for recording on magnetic tape; *esp* : a combination of such a device and a playback device including a built-in power amplifier and a loudspeaker

tape recording *n* : magnetic recording on magnetic tape; *also* : a recording made by this process

ta·per·er \'tā-pər-ər\ *n* : one who bears a taper in a religious procession

taper off *vb* : TAPER

tap·es·tried \'tap-ə-strēd\ *adj* 1 : covered or decorated with or as if with tapestry 2 : woven or depicted in tapestry

tap·es·try \'tap-ə-strē\ *n, pl* **-tries** [ME *tapistry,* modif. of MF *tapisserie,* fr. *tapisser* to carpet, cover with tapestry, fr. OF *tapis* carpet, fr. Gk *tapēs* rug, carpet] 1 : a heavy handwoven reversible textile used for hangings, curtains, and upholstery and characterized by complicated pictorial designs 2 : a nonreversible imitation of tapestry used chiefly for upholstery 3 : embroidery on canvas resembling woven tapestry <needlepoint ~> 4 : something resembling tapestry (as in complexity or richness of design)

tapestry carpet *n* : a carpet in which the designs are printed in colors on the threads before the fabric is woven

ta·pe·tum \tə-'pēt-əm\ *n, pl* **ta·pe·ta** \-'pēt-ə\ [NL, fr. L *tapete* carpet, tapestry, fr. Gk *tapēt-, tapēs* rug, carpet] 1 : a layer of nutritive cells that invests the sporogenous tissue in the sporangium of higher plants 2 : any of various membranous layers or areas esp. of the choroid coat and retina of the eye

tape·worm \'tāp-ˌwərm\ *n* [fr. its shape] : any of numerous cestode worms (as of the genus *Taenia*) parasitic when adult in the intestine of man or other vertebrates

tap·hole \'tap-ˌhōl\ *n* : a hole for a tap; *specif* : a hole at or near the bottom of a furnace or ladle through which molten metal, matte, or slag can be tapped

tap·i·o·ca \ˌtap-ē-'ō-kə\ *n* [Sp & Pg, fr. Tupi *typyóca*] 1 : a usu. granular preparation of cassava starch used esp. in puddings and as a thickening in liquid food; *also* : a dish (as pudding) containing tapioca 2 : a cassava plant — called also *tapioca plant*

ta·pir \'tā-pər *also* tə-'pi(ə)r *or* 'ta-ˌpi(ə)r\ *n, pl* **tapir** *or* **tapirs** [Tupi *tapiira*] : any of several large inoffensive chiefly nocturnal ungulates (family Tapiridae) of tropical America, Malaya, and Sumatra related to the horses and rhinoceroses

ta·pis \'tap-ˌē\ *n* [MF — more at TAPESTRY] *obs* : tapestry or similar material used for hangings and floor and table coverings — **on the tapis** : under consideration <two more large jobs *on the tapis* —J. D. Beresford>

tapeworm

tap–off \'tap-ˌȯf\ *n* : [2]TIP-OFF

tap·pet \'tap-ət\ *n* [irreg. fr. [3]*tap*] : a lever or projection moved by some other piece (as a cam) or intended to tap or touch something else to cause a particular motion

tap·ping *n* : the act, process, or means by which something is tapped

tap·pit hen \'tap-ət-\ *n* [Sc *tappit,* alter. of E *topped*] 1 *Scot* : a crested hen 2 *Scot* : a drinking vessel with a knob on the lid

tap·room \'tap-ˌrüm, -ˌru̇m\ *n* : BARROOM

tap·root \-ˌrüt, -ˌru̇t\ *n* [[1]*tap*] 1 : a primary root that grows vertically downward and gives off small lateral roots 2 : one that has a deep central position in a line of growth or development

taps \'taps\ *n pl but sing or pl in constr* [prob. alter. of earlier *taptoo* tattoo — more at TATTOO] : the last bugle call at night blown as a signal that lights are to be put out; *also* : a similar call blown at military funerals and memorial services

tap·sal–tee·rie \ˌtap-səl-'tē-rē\ *adv* [by alter.] *Scot* : TOPSY-TURVY

tap·ster \'tap-stər\ *n* : one employed to dispense liquors in a barroom

[1]tar \'tär\ *n* [ME *terr, tarr,* fr. OE *teoru;* akin to OE *trēow* tree — more at TREE] 1 **a** : a dark brown or black bituminous usu. odorous viscous liquid obtained by destructive distillation of organic material (as wood, coal, or peat) **b** : a substance in some respects resembling tar; *esp* : a condensable residue present in smoke from burning tobacco that contains combustion by-products (as resins, acids, phenols, and essential oils) 2 [short for *tarpaulin*] : SAILOR

taproot 1

[2]tar *vt* **tarred; tar·ring** : to smear with or as if with tar — **tar and feather** : to smear (a person) with tar and cover with feathers as a punishment or indignity

[3]tar *or* **tarre** \'tär\ *vt* **tarred; tar·ring; tars** *or* **tarres** [ME *terren, tarren,* fr. OE *tyrwan*] : to urge to action — usu. used with *on*

Tar·a·ca·hi·tian \ˌtar-ə-kə-'hē-shən\ *adj* [*Tara*humara (a Mexican people) + *Cahita* (a Mexican people)] : of, relating to, or constituting a language family of the Uto-Aztecan phylum

tar·a·did·dle *or* **tar·ra·did·dle** \ˌtar-ə-'did-ᵊl, 'tar-ə-ˌ\ *n* [origin unknown] 1 : a minor falsehood : FIB 2 : pretentious nonsense

tar·an·tel·la \ˌtar-ən-'tel-ə\ *n* [It, fr. *Taranto,* Italy] : a vivacious folk dance of southern Italy in 6/8 time

tar·an·tism \'tar-ən-ˌtiz-əm\ *n* [NL *tarantismus,* fr. *Taranto,* Italy] : a dancing mania or malady of late medieval Europe

ta·ran·tu·la \tə-'ranch-(ə-)lə, -'rant-ᵊl-ə\ *n, pl* **ta·ran·tu·las** *also* **ta·ran·tu·lae** \-'ran-chə-ˌlē, -'rant-ᵊl-ˌē\ [ML, fr. OIt *tarantola,* fr. *Taranto*] 1 : a European wolf spider (*Lycosa tarentula*) popularly held to be the cause of tarantism 2 : any of various large hairy spiders (family Theraphosidae) that are typically rather sluggish and though capable of biting sharply are not significantly poisonous to man

ta·rax·a·cum \tə-'rak-si-kəm\ *n* [NL, genus name, fr. Ar *tarakhshaqūn* wild chicory] : the dried rhizome and roots of the dandelion (*Taraxacum officinale*) used as a diuretic, a tonic, and an aperient

tarantula 2

tar·boosh *also* **tar·bush** \tär-'büsh, 'tär-ˌ\ *n* [Ar *ṭarbūsh*] : a red hat similar to the fez worn esp. by Muslim men

tar·di·grade \'tärd-ə-ˌgrād\ *n* [deriv. of L *tardigradus* slow-moving, fr. *tardus* slow + *gradi* to step, go — more at GRADE] : any of a division (Tardigrada) of microscopic arthropods with four pairs of legs that live usu. in water or damp moss — **tardigrade** *adj*

tar·di·ly \'tärd-ᵊl-ē\ *adv* 1 : at a slow pace 2 : LATE

tar·do \'tärd-(ˌ)ō\ *adj* [It, fr. L *tardus*] : SLOW — used as a direction in music

[1]tar·dy \'tärd-ē\ *adj* **tar·di·er; -est** [alter. of earlier *tardif,* fr. MF, fr. (assumed) VL *tardivus,* fr. L *tardus*] 1 : moving slowly : SLUGGISH 2 : delayed beyond the expected or proper time : LATE — **tar·di·ly** \'tärd-ᵊl-ē\ *adv* — **tar·di·ness** \'tärd-ē-nəs\ *n*

syn TARDY, LATE, BEHINDHAND, OVERDUE *shared meaning element* : not arriving, occurring, or done at the set, due, or expected time ***ant*** prompt, punctual

[2]tardy *n, pl* **tardies** : an instance of being tardy (as to a class)

[1]tare \'ta(ə)r, 'te(ə)r\ *n* [ME] 1 **a** : the seed of a vetch **b** : any of several vetches (esp. *Vicia sativa* and *V. hirsuta*) 2 *pl* : a weed of grainfields usu. held to be the darnel 3 *pl* : an undesirable element

[2]tare *n* [ME, fr. MF, fr. OIt *tara,* fr. Ar *ṭarḥa,* lit., that which is removed] 1 : a deduction from the gross weight of a substance and its container made in allowance for the weight of the container 2 : COUNTERWEIGHT; *esp* : an empty vessel similar to a container used to counterpoise change in weight of the container due to conditions (as temperature or moisture)

[3]tare *vt* **tared; tar·ing** : to ascertain or mark the tare of; *esp*

: to weigh so as to determine the tare
targe \'tärj\ *n* [ME, fr. OF] *archaic* : a light shield
[1]**tar·get** \'tär-gət\ *n* [ME, fr. MF *targette,* dim. of *targe* light shield, of Gmc origin; akin to ON *targa* shield] **1** : a small round shield : BUCKLER **2 a** : a mark to shoot at **b** : a target marked by shots fired at it **c** : something fired at **3 a** : an object of ridicule or criticism **b** : something to be affected by an action or development **c** : a goal to be achieved **4 a** : a railroad day signal that is attached to a switch stand and indicates whether the switch is open or closed **b** : a sliding sight on a surveyor's leveling rod **5 a** : the metallic surface usu. of platinum or tungsten upon which the stream of cathode rays within an X-ray tube is focused and from which the X rays are emitted **b** : a body, surface, or material bombarded with nuclear particles or electrons; *esp* : fluorescent material on which desired visual effects are produced in electronic devices (as in radar and television)
[2]**target** *vt* : to make a target of; *esp* : to set as a goal
target date *n* : the date set for an event or for the completion of a project, goal, or quota
target language *n* : a language into which another language is to be translated — compare SOURCE LANGUAGE
Tar·gum \'tär-ˌgüm, -ˌgüm\ *n* [LHeb *targūm,* fr. Aram, translation] : an Aramaic translation or paraphrase of a portion of the Old Testament
Tar·heel \'tär-ˌhēl\ *n* : a native or resident of North Carolina — used as a nickname
[1]**tar·iff** \'tar-əf\ *n* [It *tariffa,* fr. Ar *ta'rīf* notification] **1 a** : a schedule of duties imposed by a government on imported or in some countries exported goods **b** : a duty or rate of duty imposed in such a schedule **2** : a schedule of rates or charges of a business or public utility
[2]**tariff** *vt* : to subject to a tariff
tar·la·tan \'tär-lət-ᵊn\ *n* [F *tarlatane*] : a sheer cotton fabric in open plain weave usu. heavily sized for stiffness
tar·mac \'tär-ˌmak\ *n* [fr. *Tarmac,* a trademark] : a tarmacadam road, apron, or runway
Tarmac *trademark* — used for a bituminous binder for roads
tar·mac·ad·am \ˌtär-mə-'kad-əm\ *n* **1** : a pavement constructed by spraying or pouring a tar binder over layers of crushed stone and then rolling **2** : a material of tar and aggregates mixed in a plant and shaped on the roadway
tarn \'tärn\ *n* [ME *tarne,* of Scand origin; akin to ON *tjörn* small lake; akin to OE *teran* to tear] : a small steep-banked mountain lake or pool
[1]**tar·nish** \'tär-nish\ *vb* [MF *terniss-,* stem of *ternir*] *vt* **1** : to dull or destroy the luster of by or as if by air, dust, or dirt : SOIL, STAIN **2 a** : to detract from the good quality of : VITIATE <his fine dreams now slightly ~*ed*> **b** : to bring disgrace on : SULLY ~ *vi* : to become tarnished — **tar·nish·able** \-ə-bəl\ *adj*
[2]**tarnish** *n* : something that tarnishes; *esp* : a film of chemically altered material on the surface of a metal (as silver)
tarnished plant bug *n* : a common and widespread destructive bug (*Lygus oblineatus*) that causes decline and disfigurement of plants by sucking sap from buds, leaves, and fruits and that carries plant diseases
ta·ro \'tär-(ˌ)ō, 'tar-, 'ter-\ *n, pl* **taros** [Tahitian & Maori] : a plant (*Colocasia esculenta*) of the arum family grown throughout the tropics for its edible starchy tuberous rootstocks and in temperate regions for ornament; *also* : its rootstock
tar·ok \'tar-ˌäk\ *n* [It *tarocchi* tarots] : an old card game popular in central Europe and played with a pack containing 40, 52, or 56 cards equivalent to modern playing cards plus the 22 tarots
tar·ot \'tar-(ˌ)ō\ *n* [MF, fr. It *tarocchi* (pl.)] : any of a set of 22 pictorial playing cards used for fortune-telling and serving as trumps in tarok
tarp \'tärp\ *n* : TARPAULIN
tar paper *n* : a heavy paper coated or impregnated with tar for use esp. in building
tar·pau·lin \tär-'pȯ-lən, 'tär-pə-; *nonstand* tär-'pōl-yən\ *n* [prob. fr. [1]*tar* + *-palling, -pauling* (fr. *pall*)] **1** : material (as waterproofed canvas) used for protecting exposed objects **2** : SAILOR
Tar·pe·ian \tär-'pē-(y)ən\ *adj* [L *tarpeius*] : of, relating to, or being a cliff of the Capitoline hill in Rome from which condemned criminals were hurled to their deaths in ancient times
tar·pon \'tär-pən\ *n, pl* **tarpon** *or* **tarpons** [origin unknown] : a large silvery elongate isospondylous marine sport fish (*Tarpon atlanticus*) that is common off the coast of Florida and reaches a length of about six feet
tar·ra·gon \'tar-ə-gən\ *n* [MF *targon,* fr. ML *tarchon,* fr. Ar *ṭarkhūn*] : a small European perennial wormwood (*Artemisia dracunculus*) grown for its pungent aromatic foliage which is used as a flavoring (as in making pickles and vinegar); *also* : its foliage
tarre *var of* TAR
tar·ri·ance \'tar-ē-ən(t)s\ *n* : the act or an instance of tarrying
[1]**tar·ry** \'tar-ē\ *vi* **tar·ried; tar·ry·ing** [ME *tarien*] **1 a** : to delay or be tardy in acting or doing **b** : to linger in expectation : WAIT **2** : to abide or stay in or at a place ***syn*** see STAY
[2]**tarry** *n, pl* **tarries** : STAY, SOJOURN
[3]**tar·ry** \'tär-ē\ *adj* : of, resembling, or covered with tar
[1]**tar·sal** \'tär-səl\ *adj* **1** : of or relating to the tarsus **2** : being or relating to plates of dense connective tissue that serve to stiffen the eyelids
[2]**tarsal** *n* : a tarsal part (as a bone or cartilage)
tar·si·er \'tär-sē-ˌā, -sē-ər\ *n* [F, fr. *tarse* tarsus, fr. NL *tarsus*] : any of several small nocturnal arboreal East Indian mammals (genus *Tarsius*) related to the lemurs
tar·so·meta·tar·sus \'tär-(ˌ)sō-'met-ə-ˌtär-səs\ *n* [NL, fr. *tarsus* + *-o-* + *metatarsus*] : the large compound bone of the tarsus of a bird; *also* : the segment of the limb it supports
tar·sus \'tär-səs\ *n, pl* **tar·si** \-ˌsī, -ˌsē\ [NL, fr. Gk *tarsos* wickerwork mat, flat of the foot, ankle, edge of the eyelid; akin to Gk *tersesthai* to become dry — more at THIRST] **1** : the part of the foot of a vertebrate between the metatarsus and the leg; *also* : the small bones that support this part of the limb **2** : TARSOMETATARSUS **3** : the distal part of the limb of an arthropod **4** : the tarsal plate of the eyelid
[1]**tart** \'tärt\ *adj* [ME, fr. OE *teart* sharp, severe; akin to MHG *traz* spite] **1** : agreeably sharp or acid to the taste **2** : marked by a biting, acrimonious, or cutting quality ***syn*** see SOUR — **tart·ish** \'tärt-ish\ *adj* — **tart·ish·ly** *adv* — **tart·ly** *adv* — **tart·ness** *n*
[2]**tart** *n* [ME *tarte,* fr. MF] **1** : a small pie or pastry shell containing jelly, custard, or fruit **2** : PROSTITUTE
[3]**tart** *vt, chiefly Brit* : to dress up : fancy up — usu. used with *up* <~*ed* up pubs and restaurants for the spenders —Arnold Ehrlich>
tar·tan \'tärt-ᵊn\ *n* [prob. fr. MF *tiretaine* linsey-woolsey] **1** : a plaid textile design of Scottish origin consisting of stripes of varying width and color usu. patterned to designate a distinctive clan **2 a** : a twilled woolen fabric with tartan design **b** : a fabric with tartan design **3** : a garment of tartan design
[1]**tar·tar** \'tärt-ər\ *n* [ME, fr. ML *tartarum*] **1** : a substance consisting essentially of cream of tartar that is derived from the juice of grapes and deposited in wine casks together with yeast and other suspended matters as a pale or dark reddish crust or sediment; *esp* : a recrystallized product yielding cream of tartar on further purification **2** : an incrustation on the teeth consisting of salivary secretion, food residue, and various salts (as calcium carbonate)
[2]**tartar** *n* [ME *Tartre,* fr. MF *Tartare,* prob. fr. ML *Tartarus,* modif. of Per *Tātār* — more at TATAR] **1** *cap* : a native or inhabitant of Tatary **2** *cap* : TATAR 2 **3** *often cap* : a person of irritable or violent temper **4** : one that proves to be unexpectedly formidable — **Tartar** *adj* — **Tar·tar·i·an** \tär-'tar-ē-ən, -'ter-\ *adj*
Tar·tar·e·an \tär-'tar-ē-ən, -'ter-\ *adj* [L *tartareus,* fr. Gk *tartareios,* fr. *Tartaros*] : of, relating to, or resembling Tartarus : INFERNAL
tartar emetic *n* : a poisonous efflorescent crystalline salt $KSbOC_4H_4O_6 \cdot \frac{1}{2}H_2O$ of sweetish metallic taste that is used in dyeing as a mordant and in medicine esp. in the treatment of amebiasis
tar·tar·ic acid \(ˌ)tär-ˌtar-ik-\ *n* : a strong dicarboxylic acid $C_4H_6O_6$ of plant origin that occurs in four optically isomeric crystalline forms, is usu. obtained from tartar, and is used esp. in food and medicines, in photography, and in making salts and esters
tar·tar sauce *or* **tar·tare sauce** \ˌtärt-ər-\ *n* [F *sauce tartare*] : mayonnaise with chopped pickles, olives, capers, and parsley
Tar·ta·rus \'tärt-ə-rəs\ *n* [L, fr. Gk *Tartaros*] : a section of Hades reserved for punishment of the worst offenders
tart·let \'tärt-lət\ *n* : a small tart
tar·trate \'tär-ˌtrāt\ *n* [ISV, fr. F *tartre* tartar, fr. ML *tartarum*] : a salt or ester of tartaric acid
Tar·tuffe \tär-'tu̇f, -'tüf\ *n* [F *Tartufe*] **1** : a religious hypocrite and protagonist in Molière's play *Tartuffe* **2** : HYPOCRITE
Tar·tuf·fery *or* **Tar·tuf·fer·ie** \-'tu̇f-ə-rē, -'tüf-\ *n, pl* **-fer·ies** : the character or behavior of a Tartuffe : HYPOCRISY
Tar·via \'tär-vē-ə\ *trademark* — used for a viscid surfacing and binding material for roads
Tar·zan \'tärz-ᵊn, 'tär-ˌzan\ *n* [*Tarzan,* hero of adventure stories by Edgar Rice Burroughs] : a well-built, agile, and very strong person
TAS *abbr* **1** telephone answering service **2** true airspeed
[1]**task** \'task\ *n* [ME *taske,* fr. ONF *tasque,* fr. ML *tasca* tax or service imposed by a feudal superior, fr. *taxare* to tax] **1 a** : a usu. assigned piece of work often to be finished within a certain time **b** : something hard or unpleasant that has to be done **c** : DUTY, FUNCTION **2** : subjection to adverse criticism : REPRIMAND —used in the expressions *to take, call,* or *bring to task*
syn TASK, DUTY, JOB, CHORE, STINT, ASSIGNMENT *shared meaning element* : a piece of work assigned or to be done
[2]**task** *vt* **1** *obs* : to impose a tax on **2** : to assign a task to **3** : to oppress with great labor <~*s* his mind with petty details>
task force *n* : a temporary grouping under one leader for the purpose of accomplishing a definite objective
task·mas·ter \'task-ˌmas-tər\ *n* : one that imposes a task or burdens another with labor
task·mis·tress \-ˌmis-trəs\ *n* : a female taskmaster
task·work \-ˌwərk\ *n* **1** : PIECEWORK **2** : hard work
Tas·ma·nian devil \(ˌ)taz-ˌmā-nē-ən-, -nyən-\ *n* : a powerful carnivorous burrowing Tasmanian marsupial (*Sarcophilus ursinus*) that is about the size of a large cat or badger and has a black coat marked with white on the chest

Tasmanian devil

Tasmanian wolf *n* : a carnivorous marsupial (*Thylacinus cynocephalus*) that was formerly common in Australia but is now limited to the remoter parts of Tasmania and that somewhat resembles a dog — called also *Tasmanian tiger*
tasse \'tas\ *n* [perh. fr. MF *tasse* purse, pouch] : one of a series of overlapping metal plates in a suit of armor that form a short skirt over the body below the waist
[1]**tas·sel** \'tas-əl, *oftenest of corn* 'täs-, 'tȯs-\ *n* [ME, clasp, tassel, fr. OF, fr. (assumed) VL *tassellus,* fr. L *taxillus* small die; akin to L *talus* anklebone, die] **1** : a dangling ornament made by laying parallel a bunch of cords or threads of even length and fastening them at one end **2** : something resembling a tassel; *esp* : the terminal male inflorescence of some plants and esp. Indian corn
[2]**tassel** *vb* **-seled** *or* **-selled; -sel·ing** *or* **-sel·ling** \-(ə-)liŋ\ *vt* : to adorn with tassels ~ *vi* : to put forth tassel inflorescences
[1]**taste** \'tāst\ *vb* **tast·ed; tast·ing** [ME *tasten* to touch, test, taste, fr. OF *taster,* fr. (assumed) VL *taxitare,* freq. of L *taxare* to touch — more at TAX] *vt* **1** : to become acquainted with by experience

<has *tasted* the frustration of defeat> **2 :** to ascertain the flavor of by taking a little into the mouth **3 :** to eat or drink esp. in small quantities <the first food he has *tasted* in two days> **4 :** to perceive or recognize as if by the sense of taste **5** *archaic* **:** APPRECIATE, ENJOY ~ *vi* **1 :** to eat or drink a little **2 :** to test the flavor of something by taking a small part into the mouth **3 :** to have perception, experience, or enjoyment **:** PARTAKE — often used with *of* **4 :** to have a specific flavor <the milk ~*s* sour>

tassel 1

[2]taste *n* **1** *obs* **:** TEST **2 a** *obs* **:** the act of tasting **b :** a small amount tasted **c :** a small amount **:** BIT; *esp* **:** a sample of experience <her first ~ of success> **3 :** the one of the special senses that perceives and distinguishes the sweet, sour, bitter, or salty quality of a dissolved substance and is mediated by taste buds on the tongue **4 :** the objective sweet, sour, bitter, or salty quality of a dissolved substance as perceived by the sense of taste **5 a :** a sensation produced by the stimulation of the sense of taste usu. together with that of touch and smell **:** FLAVOR **b :** the distinctive quality of an experience <his attempt to cheat left a bad ~ in my mouth> **6 :** individual preference **:** INCLINATION **7 a :** critical judgment, discernment, or appreciation **b :** manner or aesthetic quality indicative of such discernment or appreciation ***syn*** TASTE, PALATE, RELISH, GUSTO, ZEST *shared meaning element* **:** a liking for or enjoyment of something because of the pleasure it gives

taste bud *n* **:** an end organ mediating the sensation of taste and lying chiefly in the epithelium of the tongue

taste·ful \ˈtāst-fəl\ *adj* **1 :** TASTY 1a **2 :** having, exhibiting, or conforming to good taste — **taste·ful·ly** \-fə-lē\ *adv* — **taste·ful·ness** *n*

taste·less \ˈtāst-ləs\ *adj* **1 a :** having no taste **:** INSIPID <~ vegetables> **b :** arousing no interest **:** DULL **2 :** not having or exhibiting good taste — **taste·less·ly** *adv* — **taste·less·ness** *n*

taste·mak·er \-ˌmā-kər\ *n* **:** one who sets the standards of what is currently popular or fashionable

tast·er \ˈtā-stər\ *n* **1 :** one that tastes; *esp* **:** one that tests (as tea) for quality by tasting **2 :** a device for tasting or sampling; *esp* **:** a shallow metal cup used in testing wine

tasty \ˈtā-stē\ *adj* **tast·i·er; -est 1 a :** having a marked and appetizing flavor **b :** strikingly attractive or interesting <stopped to listen to a ~ bit of gossip> **2 :** TASTEFUL ***syn*** see PALATABLE ***ant*** bland — **tast·i·ly** \-stə-lē\ *adv* — **tast·i·ness** \-stē-nəs\ *n*

tat \ˈtat\ *vb* **tat·ted; tat·ting** [back-formation fr. *tatting*] *vi* **:** to work at tatting ~ *vt* **:** to make by tatting

TAT *abbr* thematic apperception test

ta·ta·mi \tä-ˈtäm-ē, ta-\ *n, pl* **-mi** *or* **-mis** [Jap] **:** straw matting used as a floor covering in a Japanese home

Ta·tar \ˈtät-ər\ *n* [Per *Tātār,* of Turkic origin; akin to Turk *Tatar*] **1 :** a member of any of numerous chiefly Turkic peoples found mainly in the Tatar Republic of the U.S.S.R., the north Caucasus, Crimea, and parts of Siberia **2 :** the Turkic language of any of the Tatar peoples

ta·ter \ˈtāt-ər\ *n* [by shortening & alter.] *dial* **:** POTATO

[1]tat·ter \ˈtat-ər\ *n* [ME, of Scand origin; akin to ON *tötturr* tatter; akin to OHG *zotta* matted hair, tuft] **1 :** a part torn and left hanging **:** SHRED **2** *pl* **:** tattered clothing **:** RAGS

[2]tatter *vt* **:** to make ragged ~ *vi* **:** to become ragged

[1]tat·ter·de·ma·lion \ˌtat-ərd-i-ˈmāl-yən, -ˈmal-, -ē-ən\ *n* [origin unknown] **:** a person dressed in ragged clothing **:** RAGAMUFFIN

[2]tatterdemalion *adj* **1 a :** ragged or disreputable in appearance **b :** being in a decayed state or condition **:** DILAPIDATED **2 :** BEGGARLY, DISREPUTABLE

tat·tered \ˈtat-ərd\ *adj* **1 :** wearing ragged clothes <a ~ barefoot boy> **2 :** torn into shreds **:** RAGGED **3 a :** broken down **:** DILAPIDATED **b :** being in a shattered condition **:** DISRUPTED

tat·ter·sall \ˈtat-ər-ˌsȯl, -səl\ *n* [*Tattersall's* horse market, London, England] **1 :** a pattern of colored lines forming squares of solid background **2 :** a fabric woven or printed in a tattersall pattern

tat·ting \ˈtat-iŋ\ *n* [origin unknown] **1 :** a delicate handmade lace formed usu. by looping and knotting with a single cotton thread and a small shuttle **2 :** the act or process of making tatting

[1]tat·tle \ˈtat-ᵊl\ *vb* **tat·tled; tat·tling** \ˈtat-liŋ, -ᵊl-iŋ\ [MD *tatelen;* akin to ME *tateren* to tattle] *vi* **1 :** CHATTER, PRATE **2 :** to tell secrets **:** BLAB ~ *vt* **:** to utter or disclose in gossip or chatter

[2]tattle *n* **1 :** idle talk **:** CHATTER **2 :** GOSSIP

tat·tler \ˈtat-lər, -ᵊl-ər\ *n* **1 :** TATTLETALE **2 :** any of various slender long-legged shorebirds (as the willet, yellowlegs, and redshank) with a loud and frequent call

tat·tle·tale \ˈtat-ᵊl-ˌtāl\ *n* **:** one that tattles **:** INFORMER

tattletale gray *n* [fr. the suggestion made by a soap advertiser that such a color observed in clothes hanging out to dry betrays inefficient laundering] **:** a grayish white

[1]tat·too \ta-ˈtü\ *n, pl* **tattoos** [alter. of earlier *taptoo,* fr. D *taptoe,* fr. the phrase *tap toe!* taps shut!] **1 a :** a call sounded shortly before taps as notice to go to quarters **b :** outdoor military exercise given by troops as evening entertainment **2 :** a rapid rhythmic rapping

[2]tattoo *vt* **:** to beat or rap rhythmically on **:** drum on ~ *vi* **:** to give a series of rhythmic taps

[3]tattoo *n, pl* **tattoos** [Tahitian *tatau*] **1 :** the act of tattooing **:** the fact of being tattooed **2 :** an indelible mark or figure fixed upon the body by insertion of pigment under the skin or by production of scars

[4]tattoo *vt* **1 :** to mark or color (the skin) with tattoos **2 :** to mark the skin with (a tattoo) <~*ed* a flag on his chest> — **tat·too·er** *n* — **tat·too·ist** \-ˈtü-əst\ *n*

tat·ty \ˈtat-ē\ *adj* **tat·ti·er; -est** [perh. akin to OE *tætteca* rag, ON *tötturr* tatter — more at TATTER] **:** rather worn or frayed **:** SHABBY

tau \ˈtau̇, ˈtȯ\ *n* [Gk, of Sem origin; akin to Heb *tāw* taw] **:** the 19th letter of the Greek alphabet — see ALPHABET table

tau cross *n* **:** a T-shaped cross sometimes having expanded ends and foot — see CROSS illustration

taught *past of* TEACH

[1]taunt \ˈtȯnt, ˈtänt\ *vt* [perh. fr. MF *tenter* to try, tempt — more at TEMPT] **:** to reproach or challenge in a mocking or insulting manner **:** jeer at ***syn*** see RIDICULE — **taunt·er** *n* — **taunt·ing·ly** \-iŋ-lē\ *adv*

[2]taunt *n* **:** a sarcastic challenge or insult

[3]taunt *adj* [origin unknown] **:** very tall — used of a ship's mast

taupe \ˈtōp\ *n* [F, lit., mole, fr. L *talpa*] **:** a brownish gray

[1]tau·rine \ˈtȯ-ˌrīn\ *adj* [L *taurinus,* fr. *taurus* bull; akin to Gk *tauros* bull, MIr *tarb*] **1 :** of or relating to a bull **:** BOVINE **2 :** of or relating to the common ox (*Bos taurus*) as distinguished from the zebu (*B. indicus*)

[2]tau·rine \ˈtȯ-ˌrēn\ *n* [ISV, fr. L *taurus;* fr. its having been discovered in ox bile] **:** a colorless crystalline compound $C_2H_7NO_3S$ of neutral reaction found in the juices of muscle esp. in invertebrates and obtained as a cleavage product of taurocholic acid

tau·ro·cho·lic \ˌtȯr-ə-ˈkō-lik, -ˈkäl-ik\ *adj* [L *taurus* + ISV *-o-* + *cholic* (*acid*)] **:** of, relating to, or being a deliquescent acid $C_{26}H_{45}NO_7S$ occurring as the sodium salt in the bile of man, the ox, and various carnivores

Tau·rus \ˈtȯr-əs\ *n* [ME, fr. L (gen. *Tauri*), lit., bull] **1 :** a zodiacal constellation that contains the Pleiades and Hyades and is represented pictorially by a bull's forequarters **2 a :** the 2d sign of the zodiac in astrology — see ZODIAC table **b :** one born under this sign

[1]taut \ˈtȯt\ *adj* [ME *tought*] **1 a :** having no give or slack **:** tightly drawn **b :** HIGH-STRUNG, TENSE <~ nerves> **2 a :** kept in proper order or condition <a ~ ship> **b** (1) **:** not loose or flabby (2) **:** marked by economy of structure and detail <a ~ story> ***syn*** see TIGHT ***ant*** slack — **taut·ly** *adv* — **taut·ness** *n*

[2]taut *vt* [origin unknown] *Scot* **:** MAT, TANGLE

taut- *or* **tauto-** *comb form* [LL, fr. Gk, fr. *tauto* the same, contr. of *to auto*] **:** same <*tauto*merism> <*taut*onym>

taut·en \ˈtȯt-ᵊn\ *vb* **taut·ened; taut·en·ing** \ˈtȯt-niŋ, -ᵊn-iŋ\ *vt* **:** to make taut ~ *vi* **:** to become taut

tau·tog \ˈtȯ-ˌtȯg, -ˌtäg, tȯ-ˈ\ *n* [Narraganset *tautauog,* pl.] **:** an edible fish (*Tautoga onitis*) of the wrasse family found along the Atlantic coast of the U.S. — called also *blackfish*

tau·to·log·i·cal \ˌtȯt-ᵊl-ˈäj-i-kəl\ *adj* **:** TAUTOLOGOUS — **tau·to·log·i·cal·ly** \-k(ə-)lē\ *adv*

tau·tol·o·gous \tȯ-ˈtäl-ə-gəs\ *adj* [Gk *tautologos,* fr. *taut-* + *legein* to say — more at LEGEND] **1 :** involving or containing rhetorical tautology **:** REDUNDANT **2 :** true by virtue of its logical form alone **:** ANALYTIC — **tau·tol·o·gous·ly** *adv*

tau·tol·o·gy \tȯ-ˈtäl-ə-jē\ *n, pl* **-gies** [LL *tautologia,* fr. Gk, fr. *tautologos*] **1 a :** needless repetition of an idea, statement, or word **b :** an instance of tautology **2 :** a tautologous statement

tau·to·mer \ˈtȯt-ə-mər\ *n* [ISV, fr. *tautomeric*] **:** one of the forms of a tautomeric compound

tau·to·mer·ic \ˌtȯt-ə-ˈmer-ik\ *adj* [ISV] **:** of, relating to, or marked by tautomerism

tau·tom·er·ism \tȯ-ˈtäm-ə-ˌriz-əm\ *n* **:** isomerism in which the isomers change into one another with great ease so that they ordinarily exist together in equilibrium

taut·onym \ˈtȯt-ə-ˌnim\ *n* [*taut-* + *-onym*] **:** a taxonomic binomial in which the generic name and specific epithet are alike and which is common in zoology esp. to designate a typical form but is forbidden to botany under the International Code of Botanical Nomenclature — **taut·onym·ic** \ˌtȯt-ə-ˈnim-ik\ *or* **tau·ton·y·mous** \tȯ-ˈtän-ə-məs\ *adj* — **tau·ton·y·my** \-mē\ *n*

tav·ern \ˈtav-ərn\ *n* [ME *taverne,* fr. OF, fr. L *taberna,* lit., shed, hut, shop, fr. *trabs* beam] **1 :** an establishment where alcoholic liquors are sold to be drunk on the premises **2 :** INN

tav·ern·er \ˈtav-ə(r)-nər\ *n* **:** one who keeps a tavern

[1]taw \ˈtȯ\ *vt* [ME *tawen* to prepare for use, fr. OE *tawian;* akin to L *bonus* good] **:** to dress (skins) usu. by a dry process (as with alum or salt)

[2]taw *n* [origin unknown] **1 a :** a marble used as a shooter **b :** RINGTAW **2 :** the line from which players shoot at marbles **3 :** a square-dance partner

[3]taw *vi* **:** to shoot a marble

[4]taw \ˈtäf, ˈtȯf, ˈtäv, ˈtȯv\ *n* [Heb *tāw,* lit., mark, cross] **:** the 23d letter of the Hebrew alphabet — see ALPHABET table

[1]taw·dry \ˈtȯd-rē, ˈtäd-\ *n* [*tawdry lace* (a tie of lace for the neck), fr. *St. Audrey* (St. Etheldreda) †679 queen of Northumbria] **:** cheap showy finery

[2]tawdry *adj* **taw·dri·er; -est :** cheap and gaudy in appearance and quality ***syn*** see GAUDY — **taw·dri·ly** \-rə-lē\ *adv* — **taw·dri·ness** \-rē-nəs\ *n*

taw·ie \ˈtȯ-ē\ *adj* [prob. fr. [1]*taw*] *Scot* **:** TRACTABLE

[1]taw·ny \ˈtȯ-nē, ˈtän-ē\ *adj* **taw·ni·er; -est** [ME, fr. MF *tanné,* pp. of *tanner* to tan] **1 :** of the color tawny **2 :** of a warm sandy color like that of well-tanned skin <the lion's ~ coat> ***syn*** see DUSKY — **taw·ni·ness** *n*

[2]tawny *n, pl* **tawnies :** a brownish orange to light brown that is slightly redder than sorrel

taw·pie \ˈtȯ-pē\ *n* [of Scand origin; akin to Norw *tåpe* simpleton] *chiefly Scot* **:** a foolish or awkward young person

taws *also* **tawse** \ˈtȯz\ *n pl but sing or pl in constr* [prob. fr. pl. of obs. *taw* (tawed leather)] *Brit* **:** a leather strap slit into strips at the end

[1]tax \ˈtaks\ *vt* [ME *taxen* to estimate, assess, tax, fr. MF *taxer,* fr. ML *taxare,* fr. L, to feel, estimate, censure, freq. of *tangere* to touch — more at TANGENT] **1 :** to assess or determine judicially the amount of (costs in a court action) **2 :** to levy a tax on **3** *obs* **:** to enter (a name) in a list <there went out a decree . . . that all the world should be ~*ed* —Lk 2:1 (AV)> **4 :** CHARGE, ACCUSE; *also* **:** CENSURE <~*ed* him with neglect of his duty> **5 :** to make onerous and rigorous demands upon <the job ~*ed* his strength> — **tax·abil·i·ty** \ˌtak-sə-ˈbil-ət-ē\ *n* — **tax·able** \ˈtak-sə-bəl\ *adj* — **tax·er** *n*

[2]tax *n* **1 a :** a charge usu. of money imposed by authority upon persons or property for public purposes **b :** a sum levied on members of an organization to defray expenses **2 :** a heavy demand

tax- *or* **taxo-** *also* **taxi-** *comb form* [Gk *taxi-,* fr. *taxis*] **:** arrangement <*taxeme*> <*taxi*dermy>
taxa *pl of* TAXON
tax·a·tion \tak-ˈsā-shən\ *n* **1 :** the action of taxing; *esp* **:** the imposition of taxes **2 :** revenue obtained from taxes **3 :** the amount assessed as a tax
tax·eme \ˈtak-ˌsēm\ *n* [*tax-*] **:** a minimum grammatical feature of selection, order, stress, pitch, or phonetic modification — **tax·e·mic** \tak-ˈsē-mik\ *adj*
tax evasion *n* **:** deliberate failure to pay taxes usu. by falsely reporting taxable income or property
tax–ex·empt \ˌtak-sig-ˈzem(p)t\ *adj* **1 :** exempted from a tax **2 :** bearing interest that is free from federal or state income tax
¹taxi \ˈtak-sē\ *n, pl* **tax·is** \-sēz\ *also* **tax·ies :** TAXICAB; *also* **:** a similarly operated boat or airplane
²taxi *vb* **tax·ied; taxi·ing** *or* **taxy·ing; tax·is** *or* **tax·ies** *vi* **1 :** to ride in a taxicab **2 a** *of an airplane* **:** to go at low speed along the surface of the ground or water **b :** to operate an airplane on the ground under its own power ~ *vt* **1 :** to transport by taxi **2 :** to cause (an airplane) to taxi
taxi·cab \ˈtak-sē-ˌkab\ *n* [*taxi*meter *cab*] **:** an automobile that carries passengers for a fare usu. determined by the distance traveled
taxi dancer *n* **:** a girl employed by a dance hall, café, or cabaret to dance with patrons who pay a certain amount for each dance
taxi·der·my \ˈtak-sə-ˌdər-mē\ *n* [*tax-* + *derm-* + *-y*] **:** the art of preparing, stuffing, and mounting the skins of animals and esp. vertebrates — **taxi·der·mic** \ˌtak-sə-ˈdər-mik\ *adj* — **taxi·der·mist** \ˈtak-sə-ˌdər-məst\ *n*
taxi·man \ˈtak-sē-mən\ *n, chiefly Brit* **:** the operator of a taxi
taxi·me·ter \ˈtak-sē-ˌmēt-ər\ *n* [F *taximètre,* modif. of G *taxameter,* fr. ML *taxa* tax, charge (fr. *taxare* to tax) + *-meter*] **:** an instrument for use in a hired vehicle (as a taxicab) for automatically showing the fare due
tax·ing \ˈtak-siŋ\ *adj* **:** ONEROUS, WEARING <a ~ operatic role> — **tax·ing·ly** \-siŋ-lē\ *adv*
tax·is \ˈtak-səs\ *n, pl* **tax·es** \-ˌsēz\ [Gk, lit., arrangement, order, fr. *tassein* to arrange — more at TACTICS] **1 :** the manual restoration of a displaced body part; *specif* **:** manual reduction of a hernia **2 a :** reflex translational or orientational movement by a freely motile and usu. simple organism in relation to a source of stimulation (as a light or a temperature or chemical gradient) **b :** a reflex reaction involving a taxis
-tax·is \ˈtak-səs\ *n comb form, pl* **-tax·es** \-ˌsēz\ [NL, fr. Gk, fr. *taxis*] **1 :** arrangement **:** order <homo*taxis*> **2 :** physiological taxis <chemo*taxis*>
taxi squad *n* **:** a group of professional football players under contract who practice with a team but are ineligible to participate in official games
taxi stand *n* **:** a place where taxis may park while awaiting hire
taxi·way \ˈtak-sē-ˌwā\ *n* **:** a usu. paved strip for taxiing (as from the terminal to a runway) at an airport
¹tax·on \ˈtak-ˌsän\ *n, pl* **taxa** \-sə\ *also* **tax·ons** [NL, back-formation fr. ISV *taxonomy*] **1 :** a taxonomic group or entity **2 :** the name applied to a taxonomic group in a formal system of nomenclature
²taxon *abbr* taxonomic; taxonomy
tax·on·o·my \tak-ˈsän-ə-mē\ *n* [F *taxonomie,* fr. *tax-* + *-nomie* -nomy] **1 :** the study of the general principles of scientific classification **:** SYSTEMATICS **2 :** CLASSIFICATION; *specif* **:** orderly classification of plants and animals according to their presumed natural relationships — **tax·o·nom·ic** \ˌtak-sə-ˈnäm-ik\ *adj* — **tax·o·nom·i·cal·ly** \-i-k(ə-)lē\ *adv* — **tax·on·o·mist** \tak-ˈsän-ə-məst\ *n*
tax·pay·er \ˈtak-ˌspā-ər\ *n* **:** one that pays or is liable for a tax
tax·pay·ing \-ˌspā-iŋ\ *adj* **:** of, relating to, or subject to the paying of a tax
tax selling *n* **:** concerted selling of securities late in the year to establish gains and losses for income-tax purposes
tax shelter *n* **:** a factor (as special depreciation allowances) that reduces the taxes on current earnings either to a corporation or to its stockholders — **tax–shel·tered** \ˈtaks-ˌshel-tərd, ˈtaksh-ˌshel-\ *adj*
tax stamp *n* **:** a stamp marked on or affixed to a taxable item as evidence that the tax has been paid
tax·us \ˈtak-səs\ *n, pl* **tax·us** \-səs\ [NL, genus comprising the yews, fr. L, yew] **:** YEW 1a
Tay·lor's series \ˈtā-lərz-\ *n* [Brook *Taylor* †1731 E mathematician] **:** a power series that gives the expansion of a function $f(x)$ in the neighborhood of a point a provided all derivatives exist and the series converges and that has the form

$$f(x) = f(a) + \frac{f^{[1]}(a)}{1!}(x-a) + \frac{f^{[2]}(a)}{2!}(x-a)^2 + \ldots + \frac{f^{[n]}(a)}{n!}(x-a)^n + \ldots$$

where $f^{[n]}(a)$ is the derivative of *n*th order of $f(x)$ evaluated at a — called also *Taylor series*
taz·za \ˈtät-sə\ *n* [It, cup, fr. Ar *ṭassah*] **:** a shallow cup or vase on a pedestal
tb *abbr* tablespoon; tablespoonful
Tb *symbol* terbium
¹TB \(ˈ)tē-ˈbē\ *n* [*TB* (abbr. for *tubercle bacillus*)] **:** TUBERCULOSIS
²TB *abbr* **1** trial balance **2** tubercle bacillus
TBA *abbr, often not cap* to be announced
T–bar lift \ˌtē-ˌbär-\ *n* **:** a ski lift having a series of T-shaped bars each of which pulls two skiers
T–bone \ˈtē-ˌbōn\ *n* **:** a small beefsteak from the thin end of the short loin containing a T-shaped bone and a small piece of tenderloin — see BEEF illustration
tbs *or* **tbsp** *abbr* **1** tablespoon **2** tablespoonful
TBS *abbr* talk between ships
tc *abbr* tierce
Tc *symbol* technetium
TC *abbr* **1** teachers college **2** terra-cotta **3** till countermanded
tchr *abbr* teacher
TD *abbr* **1** tank destroyer **2** touchdown **3** treasury department
t distribution *n* **:** a probability density function that is used esp. in testing hypotheses concerning means of normal distributions whose standard deviations are unknown and that is the distribution of a random variable

$$t = \frac{u}{\frac{v}{\sqrt{n}}}$$

where u and v are themselves independent random variables and u has a normal distribution with mean 0 and a standard deviation of 1 and v^2 has a chi-square distribution with n degrees of freedom — called also *student's t distribution*
TDN *abbr* total digestible nutrients
TDY *abbr* temporary duty
Te *symbol* tellurium
TE *abbr* **1** table of equipment **2** trailing edge
tea \ˈtē\ *n* [Chin (Amoy) *t'e*] **1 a :** a shrub (*Camellia sinensis* of the family Theaceae, the tea family) cultivated esp. in China, Japan, and the East Indies **b :** the leaves, leaf buds, and internodes of the tea plant prepared and cured for the market, classed according to method of manufacture (as green tea, black tea, or oolong), and graded according to leaf size (as congou, orange pekoe, pekoe, or souchong) **2 :** an aromatic beverage prepared from tea leaves by infusion with boiling water **3 :** any of various plants somewhat resembling tea in properties; *also* **:** an infusion of their leaves used medicinally or as a beverage **4 a :** refreshments usu. including tea with sandwiches, crackers, or cookies served in late afternoon **b :** a reception at which tea is served **5** *slang* **:** MARIJUANA
tea bag *n* **:** a cloth or filter paper bag holding enough tea for an individual serving
tea ball *n* **:** a perforated metal ball for making tea
tea·ber·ry \ˈtē-ˌber-ē\ *n* [fr. the use of its leaves as a substitute for tea] **:** CHECKERBERRY
tea biscuit *n, Brit* **:** CRACKER, COOKIE
tea·board \ˈtē-ˌbō(ə)rd, -ˌbȯ(ə)rd\ *n* **:** a tray for serving tea
tea·bowl \-ˌbōl\ *n* **:** a teacup having no handle
tea caddy *n* **:** CADDY
tea cake *n* **1** *Brit* **:** a light flat cake **2 :** COOKIE
tea cart *n* **:** TEA WAGON
teach \ˈtēch\ *vb* **taught** \ˈtȯt\; **teach·ing** [ME *techen* to show, instruct, fr. OE *tǣcan;* akin to OE *tācn* sign — more at TOKEN] *vt* **1 a :** to cause to know a subject <*taught* his sons a trade> **b :** to cause to know how <is ~*ing* me to drive> **c :** to accustom to some action or attitude <~ students to think for themselves> **d :** to make to know the disagreeable consequences of some action <I'll ~ you to come home late> **2 :** to guide the studies of **3 :** to impart the knowledge of <~ algebra> **4 a :** to instruct by precept, example, or experience **b :** to seek to make known and accepted <experience ~*es* us our limitations> ~ *vi* **:** to provide instruction **;** act as a teacher
syn TEACH, INSTRUCT, EDUCATE, TRAIN, DISCIPLINE, SCHOOL *shared meaning element* **:** to cause to acquire knowledge or skill
teach·abil·i·ty \ˌtē-chə-ˈbil-ət-ē\ *n* **1 :** suitability for use in teaching **2 :** ability to learn by instruction
teach·able \ˈtē-chə-bəl\ *adj* **1 a :** capable of being taught **b :** apt and willing to learn **2 :** favorable to teaching — **teach·able·ness** *n* — **teach·ably** \-blē\ *adv*
teach·er \ˈtē-chər\ *n* **1 :** one that teaches; *esp* **:** one whose occupation is to instruct **2 :** a Mormon ranking above a deacon in the Aaronic priesthood
teachers college *n* **:** a college for the training of teachers usu. offering a full four-year course and granting a bachelor's degree
teach·er·ship \ˈtē-chər-ˌship\ *n* **:** a teaching position
teacher's pet *n* **1 :** a pupil who has won his teacher's special favor **2 :** one who has ingratiated himself with an authority
teach–in \ˈtē-ˌchin\ *n* [*teach* + *-in* (as in *sit-in*)] **:** an extended and often nightlong meeting esp. of college students and faculty members for lectures, debates, and discussions on an important and often controversial topic (as U.S. foreign policy)
¹teach·ing *n* **1 :** the act, practice, or profession of a teacher **2 :** something taught; *esp* **:** DOCTRINE <the ~*s* of Confucius>
²teaching *adj* **:** that teaches <a ~ doctor>
teaching aid *n* **:** a device (as a record player, map, or picture) used by a teacher to reinforce or supplement classroom instruction
teaching fellow *n* **:** a resident student at a graduate school who holds a fellowship that involves teaching or laboratory duties
teaching hospital *n* **:** a hospital that is affiliated with a medical school and provides the means for medical education to students, interns, residents, and sometimes postgraduates
teaching machine *n* **:** any of various mechanical devices for presenting a program of instructional material
tea·cup \ˈtē-ˌkəp\ *n* **:** a cup usu. of less than 8-ounce capacity used with a saucer for hot beverages — **teacupful** *n*
tea dance *n* **:** a dance held in the late afternoon
tea garden *n* **1 :** a public garden where tea and light refreshments are served **2 :** a tea plantation
tea gown *n* **:** a semiformal gown of fine materials in graceful flowing lines worn esp. for afternoon entertaining at home
tea·house \ˈtē-ˌhau̇s\ *n* **:** a public house or restaurant where tea and light refreshments are sold
teak \ˈtēk\ *n* [Pg *teca,* fr. Malayalam *tēkka*] **1 :** a tall East Indian timber tree (*Tectona grandis*) of the vervain family **2 :** the hard yellowish brown wood of teak used esp. for shipbuilding
tea·ket·tle \ˈtē-ˌket-ᵊl, -ˌkit-\ *n* **:** a covered kettle with a handle and spout for boiling water
teak·wood \ˈtē-ˌkwu̇d\ *n* **:** TEAK 2

ə abut	ᵊ kitten	ər further	a back	ā bake	ä cot, cart
au̇ out	ch chin	e less	ē easy	g gift	i trip ī life
j joke	ŋ sing	ō flow	ȯ flaw	ȯi coin	th thin th this
ü loot	u̇ foot	y yet	yü few	yu̇ furious	zh vision

teal \ˈtē(ə)l\ *n, pl* **teal** *or* **teals** [ME *tele;* akin to MD *teling* teal] : any of several small short-necked river ducks (esp. genus *Anas*) of Europe and America
teal blue *n* : a variable color averaging a dark greenish blue
[1]**team** \ˈtēm\ *n* [ME *teme,* fr. OE *tēam* offspring, lineage, group of draft animals; akin to OE *tēon* to draw, pull — more at TOW] **1 a :** two or more draft animals harnessed to the same vehicle or implement; *also* : these with their harness and attached vehicle **b** : a draft animal often with harness and vehicle **c :** a drawn vehicle (as a wagon) **2** *obs* : LINEAGE, RACE **3 :** a group of animals: as **a :** a brood esp. of young pigs or ducks **b :** a matched group of animals for exhibition **4 :** a number of persons associated together in work or activity: as **a :** a group on one side (as in football or a debate) **b :** CREW, GANG
[2]**team** *vt* **1 :** to yoke or join in a team **2 :** to convey or haul with a team ~ *vi* **1 :** to drive a team or motortruck **2 :** to form a team
[3]**team** *adj* : of or performed by a team <a ~ effort>
tea maker *n* : a perforated covered spoon that holds tea leaves and is used in brewing tea in a cup
team foul *n* : one of a designated number of personal fouls the players on a basketball team may commit during a given period of play before the opposing team begins receiving bonus free throws
team handball *n* : a game developed from soccer which is played between two teams of seven players each and in which the ball is thrown, caught, and dribbled with the hands
team·mate \ˈtēm-ˌmāt\ *n* : a fellow member of a team
team play *n* **1 :** collective play with mutual assistance of team members <skillful *team play* in hockey> **2 :** cooperative effort <need for *team play* in time of war —Christopher La Farge>
team·ster \ˈtēm(p)-stər\ *n* : one who drives a team or motortruck esp. as an occupation
team·work \ˈtēm-ˌwərk\ *n* : work done by several associates with each doing a part but all subordinating personal prominence to the efficiency of the whole
tea party *n* **1 :** an afternoon social gathering at which tea is served **2** [fr. the Boston Tea Party, name facetiously applied to the occasion in 1773 when a group of citizens threw a shipment of tea into Boston harbor in protest against the tax on imports] : an exciting disturbance or proceeding
tea·pot \ˈtē-ˌpät\ *n* : a vessel with a spout in which tea is brewed and from which it is served
tea·poy \ˈtē-ˌpȯi\ *n* [Hindi *tipāī*] **1 :** a 3-legged ornamental stand **2 :** a stand for a tea service
[1]**tear** \ˈti(ə)r\ *n* [ME, fr. OE *tæhher, tēar;* akin to OHG *zahar* tear, L *dacruma, lacrima,* Gk *dakry*] **1 a :** a drop of clear saline fluid secreted by the lacrimal gland and diffused between the eye and eyelids to moisten the parts and facilitate their motion **b** *pl* : a secretion of profuse tears that overflow the eyelids and dampen the face **2** *pl* : an act of weeping or grieving <broke into ~*s*> **3** : a transparent drop of fluid or hardened fluid matter (as resin)
[2]**tear** *vi* : to fill with tears : shed tears <eyes ~*ing* in the November wind —Saul Bellow>
[3]**tear** \ˈta(ə)r, ˈte(ə)r\ *vb* **tore** \ˈtō(ə)r, ˈtȯ(ə)r\; **torn** \ˈtō(ə)rn, ˈtȯ(ə)rn\; **tear·ing** [ME *teren,* fr. OE *teran;* akin to OHG *zeran* to destroy, Gk *derein* to skin] *vt* **1 a :** to separate parts of or pull apart by force : REND **b :** to wound by tearing : LACERATE <~ the skin> **2 :** to divide or disrupt by the pull of contrary forces <a mind *torn* with doubts> **3 :** to remove by force : WRENCH <~ a cover off a box> **4 :** to make or effect by or as if by tearing <~ a hole in the wall> ~ *vi* **1 :** to separate on being pulled : REND <this cloth ~*s* easily> **2 :** to move or act with violence, haste, or force <went ~*ing* down the street> — **tear·er** *n*
syn TEAR, RIP, REND, SPLIT, CLEAVE, RIVE *shared meaning element* : to separate forcibly
— **tear at :** LACERATE <the sight of her grief *tore at* his heart> — **tear into :** to attack without restraint or caution — **tear one's hair :** to pull one's hair as an expression of grief, rage, frustration, desperation, or anxiety
[4]**tear** \ˈta(ə)r, ˈte(ə)r\ *n* **1 a :** the act of tearing **b :** damage from being torn; *esp* : a hole or flaw made by tearing **2 a :** a tearing pace : HURRY **b :** SPREE <go on a ~>
tear around *vi* **1 :** to go about in excited or angry haste **2** : to lead a wild or disorderly life
tear away *vt* : to remove (as oneself) reluctantly
tear·down \ˈta(ə)r-ˌdau̇n, ˈte(ə)r-\ *n* : the act or process of disassembling
tear down \(ˈ)ta(ə)r-ˈdau̇n, (ˌ)te(ə)r-\ *vt* **1 a :** to cause to decompose or disintegrate **b :** VILIFY, DENIGRATE **2 :** to take apart : DISASSEMBLE <*tear* an engine *down* for an overhaul>
tear·drop \ˈti(ə)r-ˌdräp\ *n* **1 :** [1]TEAR 1a **2 :** something shaped like a dropping tear; *specif* : a pendent gem (as on an earring)
tear·ful \ˈti(ə)r-fəl\ *adj* **1 :** flowing with or accompanied by tears <~ entreaties> **2 :** causing tears : TEARY — **tear·ful·ly** \-fə-lē\ *adv* — **tear·ful·ness** *n*
tear·gas \-ˌgas\ *vt* : to use tear gas on
tear gas *n* : a solid, liquid, or gaseous substance that on dispersion in the atmosphere blinds the eyes with tears and is used chiefly in dispelling mobs
tear·ing \ˈta(ə)r-iŋ, ˈte(ə)r-\ *adj* **1 :** causing continued or repeated pain or distress **2 :** HASTY, VIOLENT **3** *chiefly Brit* : SPLENDID
tear·jerk·er \ˈti(ə)r-ˌjər-kər\ *n* : an extravagantly pathetic story, play, film, or broadcast — **tear–jerk·ing** \-kiŋ\ *adj*
tear·less \ˈti(ə)r-ləs\ *adj* : shedding no tears : free from tears — **tear·less·ly** *adv* — **tear·less·ness** *n*
tear–off \ˈta(ə)r-ˌȯf, ˈte(ə)r-\ *n* : part of a piece of paper intended to be removed by tearing usu. along a marked line
tear off \(ˈ)ta(ə)r-ˈȯf, (ˈ)te(ə)r-\ *vt* : to compose rapidly <*tore off* two letters before dinner>
tea·room \ˈtē-ˌrüm, -ˌru̇m\ *n* : a small restaurant with service and decor designed primarily for a female clientele
tea rose *n* : any of numerous tender or half-hardy hybrid garden bush roses descended chiefly from a Chinese rose (*Rosa odorata*) and valued esp. for their abundant large usu. tea-scented blossoms — compare HYBRID TEA ROSE
tear sheet *n* : a sheet torn from a publication usu. to prove insertion of an advertisement to an advertiser
tear·stain \ˈti(ə)r-ˌstān\ *n* : a spot or streak left by tears — **tear-stained** \-ˌstānd\ *adj*
tear strip *n* : the scored band in a can or added narrow ribbon in a wrapper or on a fiber box that provides an easy and defined way of opening
tear tape *n* : a strong tape glued to the inside of a shipping container with one end protruding so that the container is readily opened by pulling out the tape
tear up *vt* **1 :** to damage, remove, or effect an opening in <*tore up* the street to lay a new water main> **2 :** to tear into pieces
teary \ˈti(ə)r-ē\ *adj* **tear·i·er; -est** **1 a :** wet or stained with tears : TEARFUL **b :** consisting of tears or drops resembling tears **2** : causing tears : PATHETIC <a ~ story> — **tear·i·ly** \ˈtir-ə-lē\ *adv*
[1]**tease** \ˈtēz\ *vt* **teased; teas·ing** [ME *tesen,* fr. OE *tǣsan;* akin to OHG *zeisan* to tease] **1 a :** to disentangle and lay parallel by combing or carding <~ wool> **b :** TEASEL **2 :** to tear in pieces; *esp* : to shred (a tissue or specimen) for microscopic examination **3 a :** to disturb or annoy by persistent irritating or provoking **b** : to attempt to provoke to anger, resentment, or confusion : GOAD **c :** to annoy with petty persistent requests : PESTER; *also* : to obtain by repeated coaxing **d :** to persuade to acquiesce esp. by persistent small efforts : COAX **4 :** to comb (hair) by taking hold of a strand and pushing the short hairs toward the scalp with the comb ***syn*** see WORRY — **teas·er** *n* — **teas·ing·ly** \ˈtē-ziŋ-lē\ *adv*
[2]**tease** *n* **1 :** the act of teasing : the state of being teased **2** : one that teases
[1]**tea·sel** *or* **tea·zel** *or* **tea·zle** \ˈtē-zəl\ *n* [ME *tesel,* fr. OE *tǣsel;* akin to OE *tǣsan* to tease] **1 a :** an Old World prickly herb (*Dipsacus fullonum* of the family Dipsacaceae, the teasel family) with flower heads that are covered with stiff hooked bracts and are used in the woolen industry — called also *fuller's teasel* **b :** a plant of the same genus as the teasel **2 a :** a flower head of the fuller's teasel used when dried to raise a nap on woolen cloth **b :** a wire substitute for the teasel

teasel 1a

[2]**teasel** *vt* **tea·seled** *or* **tea·selled; tea·sel·ing** *or* **tea·sel·ling** \ˈtēz-(ə-)liŋ\ : to nap (cloth) with teasels
tease out *vt* : to obtain by disentangling or freeing with a pointed instrument
tea service *n* : a set of china or metalware for service at table: **a** : a set of china consisting of a teapot, sugar bowl, creamer, sometimes a coffeepot, and usu. plates, cups, and saucers **b :** a set of metalware consisting of a teapot, sugar bowl, creamer, sometimes a coffeepot, and usu. waste bowl, kettle, and tray
tea set *n* **1 :** TEA SERVICE b **2 :** a china set consisting of a teapot, sugar bowl, creamer, cups and saucers, and plates
tea shop *n* **1** *chiefly Brit* : TEAROOM **2** *Brit* : RESTAURANT
tea·spoon \ˈtē-ˌspün, -ˈspün\ *n* **1 :** a small spoon that is used esp. for eating soft foods and stirring beverages and that holds one third of a tablespoon **2 :** TEASPOONFUL
tea·spoon·ful \-ˌfu̇l\ *n, pl* **teaspoonfuls** \-ˌfu̇lz\ *also* **tea·spoons·ful** \-ˌspünz-ˌfu̇l, -ˈspünz-\ **1 :** as much as a teaspoon can hold **2 :** a unit of measure equal to $1\frac{1}{3}$ fluidrams
teat \ˈtit, ˈtēt\ *n* [ME *tete,* fr. OF, of Gmc origin; akin to OE *tit* teat, MHG *zitze*] **1 :** the protuberance through which milk is drawn from an udder or breast : NIPPLE **2 :** a small projection or a nib (as on a mechanical part) — **teat·ed** \-əd\ *adj*
tea table *n* : a table used or spread for tea; *specif* : a small table for serving afternoon tea
tea·time \ˈtē-ˌtīm\ *n* : the customary time for tea : late afternoon or early evening
tea towel *n* : DISH TOWEL
tea tray *n* : a tray that accommodates a tea service
tea wagon *n* : a small table on wheels used in serving tea
Te·bet \tā-ˈvāt(h), ˈtā-ˌves\ *n* [Heb *Ṭēbhēth*]: the 4th month of the civil year or the 10th month of the ecclesiastical year in the Jewish calendar — see MONTH table
tec *abbr* technical; technician
tech *abbr* **1** technical; technically; technician **2** technological; technology
teched \ˈtecht\ *adj* [alter. of *touched*] : mentally unbalanced
tech·ne·tium \tek-ˈnē-sh(ē-)əm\ *n* [NL, fr. Gk *technētos* artificial, fr. *technasthai* to devise by art, fr. *technē*] : a metallic element obtained by bombarding molybdenum with deuterons or neutrons and in the fission of uranium — see ELEMENT table
tech·ne·tron·ic \ˌtek-nə-ˈträn-ik\ *adj* [*techn*ological + elec*tronic*] : of, relating to, or being a society shaped by the impact of technology and electronics and esp. by the impact of computers and communications on its structure, culture, psychology, and economics
tech·nic \ˈtek-nik, *for 1 also* tek-ˈnēk\ *n* **1 :** TECHNIQUE 1 **2** *pl but sing or pl in constr* : TECHNOLOGY 2a
tech·ni·cal \ˈtek-ni-kəl\ *adj* [Gk *technikos* of art, skillful, fr. *technē* art, craft, skill; akin to Gk *tektōn* builder, carpenter, L *texere* to weave, OHG *dahs* badger] **1 a :** having special and usu. practical knowledge esp. of a mechanical or scientific subject **b :** marked by or characteristic of specialization **2 :** of or relating to a particular subject; esp : of or relating to a practical subject organized on scientific principles **3 a :** marked by a strict legal interpretation **b :** LEGAL 6 **4 :** of or relating to technique **5 :** of, relating to, or produced by ordinary commercial processes without being subjected to special purification <~ sulfuric acid> **6 :** resulting chiefly from internal market factors rather than external influences <~ reaction of the stock market> — **tech·ni·cal·ly** \-k(ə-)lē\ *adv* — **tech·ni·cal·ness** \-kəl-nəs\ *n*
technical foul *n* : a foul (as in basketball) that involves no physical contact with an opponent and that usu. is incurred by unsportsmanlike conduct —compare PERSONAL FOUL

tech·ni·cal·i·ty \ˌtek-nə-ˈkal-ət-ē\ *n, pl* **-ties** **1 :** the quality or state of being technical **2 :** something technical; *esp* **:** a detail meaningful only to a specialist <a legal ~>
tech·ni·cal·ize \ˈtek-ni-kə-ˌlīz\ *vt* **-ized; -iz·ing :** to give a technical slant to — **tech·ni·cal·iza·tion** \ˌtek-ni-kə-lə-ˈzā-shən\ *n*
technical knockout *n* **:** the termination of a boxing match when a boxer is unable or is declared by the referee to be unable (as because of injuries) to continue the fight
technical sergeant *n* **:** a noncommissioned officer in the air force ranking above a staff sergeant and below a master sergeant
tech·ni·cian \tek-ˈnish-ən\ *n* **1 :** a specialist in the technical details of a subject or occupation <a medical ~> **2 :** one who has acquired the technique of an art or other area of specialization <a superb ~ and a musician of integrity —Irving Kolodin>
tech·nique \tek-ˈnēk\ *n* [F, fr. *technique* technical, fr. Gk *technikos*] **1 :** the manner in which technical details are treated (as by a writer) or basic physical movements are used (as by a dancer); *also* **:** ability to treat such details or use such movements <good piano ~> **2 a :** a body of technical methods (as in a craft or in scientific research) **b :** a method of accomplishing a desired aim
techno- *comb form* [Gk, fr. *technē*] **1 :** art **:** craft <*techno*graphy> **2 :** technical **:** technological <*techno*cracy>
tech·noc·ra·cy \tek-ˈnäk-rə-sē\ *n* **:** government by technicians; *specif* **:** management of society by technical experts
tech·no·crat \ˈtek-nə-ˌkrat\ *n* **1 :** an adherent of technocracy **2 :** a member of a technocracy
tech·no·crat·ic \ˌtek-nə-ˈkrat-ik\ *adj* **:** of, relating to, or resembling a technocrat or a technocracy
technol *abbr* technological; technology
tech·no·log·i·cal \ˌtek-nə-ˈläj-i-kəl\ *or* **tech·no·log·ic** \-ˈläj-ik\ *adj* **1 :** of, relating to, or characterized by technology <~ advances> **2 :** resulting from improvements in technical processes that increases productivity of machines and eliminates manual operations or operations done by older machines <~ unemployment> — **tech·no·log·i·cal·ly** \-i-k(ə-)lē\ *adv*
tech·nol·o·gist \tek-ˈnäl-ə-jəst\ *n* **:** a specialist in technology
tech·nol·o·gize \-ˌjīz\ *vt* **-gized; -giz·ing :** to make technological
tech·nol·o·gy \-jē\ *n, pl* **-gies** [Gk *technologia* systematic treatment of an art, fr. *techno-* + *-logia* -logy] **1 :** technical language **2 a :** applied science **b :** a technical method of achieving a practical purpose **3 :** the totality of the means employed to provide objects necessary for human sustenance and comfort
tech·no·struc·ture \ˈtek-nō-ˌstrək-chər\ *n* **:** the network of professionally skilled managers (as scientists, engineers, and administrators) that increasingly tends to control the economy both within and beyond individual corporate groups
techy *var of* TETCHY
tec·ton·ic \tek-ˈtän-ik\ *adj* [LL *tectonicus*, fr. Gk *tektonikos* of a builder, fr. *tektōn* builder — more at TECHNICAL] **:** of or relating to tectonics: as **a :** ARCHITECTURAL **b :** of or relating to the deformation of the earth's crust, the forces involved in or producing such deformation, and the resulting forms — **tec·ton·i·cal·ly** \-i-k(ə-)lē\ *adv*
tec·ton·ics \-iks\ *n pl but sing or pl in constr* **1 :** the science or art of construction (as of a building) **2 :** geological structural features **3 a :** a branch of geology concerned with structure esp. with folding and faulting **b :** DIASTROPHISM
tec·to·nism \ˈtek-tə-ˌniz-əm\ *n* [ISV *tecton-* (fr. *tectonic*) + *-ism*] **:** DIASTROPHISM
tec·tum \ˈtek-təm\ *n, pl* **tec·ta** \-tə\ [NL, fr. L, roof, dwelling, fr. neut. of *tectus*, pp. of *tegere* to cover — more at THATCH] **:** a bodily structure resembling or serving as a roof; *esp* **:** the dorsal part of the midbrain — **tec·tal** \ˈtek-tᵊl\ *adj*
ted \ˈted\ *vt* **ted·ded; ted·ding** [(assumed) ME *tedden*; akin to Gk *daiesthai* to divide, distribute — more at TIDE] **:** to spread or turn from the swath and scatter (as new-mown grass) for drying
ted·der \ˈted-ər\ *n* **:** one that teds; *specif* **:** a machine for stirring and spreading hay to hasten drying and curing
ted·dy bear \ˈted-ē-, ˌted-ē-ˈ\ *n* [*Teddy*, nickname of Theodore Roosevelt †1919 26th U.S. president; fr. a cartoon depicting the president sparing the life of a bear cub while hunting] **:** a stuffed toy bear
ted·dy boy \ˈted-ē-ˌ\ *n* [*Teddy*, nickname for Edward] **:** a young British hoodlum who affects Edwardian dress
Te De·um \(ˈ)tā-ˈdā-əm, (ˌ)tē-ˈdē-\ *n, pl* **Te Deums** [ME, fr. LL *te deum laudamus* thee, God, we praise; fr. the opening words of the hymn] **:** a liturgical Christian hymn of praise to God
te·dious \ˈtēd-ē-əs, ˈtē-jəs\ *adj* [ME, fr. LL *taediosus*, fr. L *taedium*] **:** tiresome because of length or dullness **:** BORING <a ~ public ceremony> — **te·dious·ly** *adv* — **te·dious·ness** *n*
te·di·um \ˈtēd-ē-əm\ *n* [L *taedium* disgust, irksomeness, fr. *taedēre* to disgust, weary] **1 :** the quality or state of being tedious **:** TEDIOUSNESS; *also* **:** BOREDOM **2 :** a tedious period of time <long ~*s* of strained anxiety —H. G. Wells>
[1]**tee** \ˈtē\ *n* [ME] **1 :** the letter *t* **2 :** something shaped like a capital T **3 :** a mark aimed at in various games (as curling) — **to a tee :** EXACTLY, PRECISELY
[2]**tee** *n* [of unknown origin] **1 a :** a small mound or a peg on which a golf ball is placed before the beginning of play on a hole **b :** a device for holding a football in position for kicking **2 :** the area from which a golf ball is struck at the beginning of play on a hole
[3]**tee** *vt* **teed; tee·ing :** to place (a ball) on a tee — often used with *up*
teed off \(ˈ)tēd-ˈȯf\ *adj* [prob. alter. of earlier *pee'd off, peed off*] **:** ANGRY, ANNOYED
[1]**teem** \ˈtēm\ *vb* [ME temen, fr. OE *tīman, tȳman*; akin to OE *tēam* offspring — more at TEAM] *vt, archaic* **:** to bring forth **:** give birth to **:** PRODUCE ~ *vi* **1** *obs* **:** to become pregnant **:** CONCEIVE **2 a :** to become filled to overflowing **:** ABOUND <lakes ~ with fish> **b :** to be present in large quantity — **teem·ing·ly** \ˈtē-miŋ-lē\ *adv* — **teem·ing·ness** *n*
[2]**teem** *vt* [ME *temen*, fr. ON *tœma*; akin to OE *tōm* empty] **:** EMPTY, POUR <~ molten metal into a mold>

[1]**teen** \ˈtēn\ *n* [ME *tene*, fr. OE *tēona*, injury, grief; akin to ON *tjōn* loss, damage] *archaic* **:** MISERY, AFFLICTION
[2]**teen** *adj* **:** TEENAGE
teen·age \ˈtē-ˌnāj\ *or* **teen·aged** \-ˌnājd\ *adj* **:** of, being, or relating to people in their teens
teen·ag·er \-ˌnā-jər\ *n* **:** a person in his teens
teen·er \ˈtē-nər\ *n* **:** TEENAGER
teens \ˈtēnz\ *n pl* [*-teen* (as in *thirteen*)] **1 :** the numbers 13 to 19 inclusive; *specif* **:** the years 13 to 19 in a lifetime or century **2 :** TEENAGERS
teen·sy *also* **teent·sy** \ˈtēn(t)-sē\ *adj* **teen·si·er** *also* **teent·si·er; -est** [baby-talk alter. of *teeny*] **:** TINY
teen·sy–ween·sy *also* **teent·sy–weent·sy** *or* **teen·sie–ween·sie** \ˌtēn(t)-sē-ˈwēn(t)-sē\ *adj* [baby-talk alter. of *teeny-weeny*] **:** TINY
tee·ny \ˈtē-nē\ *adj* **tee·ni·er; -est** [by alter. (influenced by *weeny*)] **:** TINY
teeny·bop·per \ˈtē-nē-ˌbäp-ər\ *n* [[2]*teen* + *-y* + *bopper*] **1 :** a teenage girl **2 :** a young teenager who rejects middle-class mores, dresses in mod styles, is addicted to rock 'n' roll music, and is interested in the use of drugs (as LSD and marijuana)
tee·ny–wee·ny *also* **tee·nie–wee·nie** \ˌtē-nē-ˈwē-nē\ *adj* [*teeny* + *weeny*] **:** TINY
tee off *vi* **1 :** to drive from a tee **2 :** BEGIN, START **3 :** to hit hard **4 :** to make an angry denunciation — often used with *on*
tee·pee *var of* TEPEE
tee shirt *var of* T-SHIRT
[1]**tee·ter** \ˈtēt-ər\ *vi* [ME *titeren* to totter, reel; akin to OHG *zittarōn* to shiver, Gk *dramein* to run] **1 a :** to move unsteadily **:** WOBBLE **b :** WAVER, VACILLATE <a passive type who ~*s* between conformity and revolt —R. N. Denney> **2 :** SEESAW
[2]**teeter** *n* **:** SEESAW 2b
tee·ter·board \-ˌbō(ə)rd, -ˌbȯ(ə)rd\ *n* **1 :** SEESAW 2b **2 :** a board placed on a raised support in such a way that a person standing on one end of the board is thrown into the air if another person jumps on the opposite end
tee·ter–tot·ter \ˈtēt-ər-ˌtät-ər\ *n* **:** SEESAW 2b
teeth *pl of* TOOTH
teethe \ˈtēth\ *vi* **teethed; teeth·ing** [back-formation fr. *teething*] **:** to cut one's teeth **:** grow teeth
teeth·er \ˈtē-thər\ *n* **:** an object (as a teething ring) designed for a baby to bite on during teething
teeth·ing \ˈtē-thiŋ\ *n* [*teeth*] **1 :** the first growth of teeth **2 :** the phenomena accompanying growth of teeth through the gums
teething ring *n* **:** a usu. rubber or plastic ring for a teething infant to bite on
teeth·ridge \ˈtē-ˌthrij\ *n* **:** the inner surface of the gums of the upper front teeth
tee·to·tal \ˈtē-ˈtōt-ᵊl, -ˌtōt-\ *adj* [*total* + *total* (abstinence)] **1 :** of, relating to, or practicing teetotalism **2 :** TOTAL, COMPLETE — **tee·to·tal·ly** \-ᵊl-ē\ *adv*
tee·to·tal·er *or* **tee·to·tal·ler** \-ˈtōt-ᵊl-ər\ *n* **:** one who practices or advocates teetotalism
tee·to·tal·ism \-ᵊl-ˌiz-əm\ *n* **:** the principle or practice of complete abstinence from alcoholic drinks — **tee·to·tal·ist** \-ᵊl-əst\ *n*
tee·to·tum \ˈtē-ˈtōt-əm\ *n* [[1]*tee* + L *totum* all, fr. neut. of *totus* whole; fr. the letter *T* inscribed on one side as an abbr. of *totum* (take) all] **:** a small top usu. inscribed with letters and used in put-and-take
teff \ˈtef\ *n* [Amharic *ṭēf*] **:** an economically important African cereal grass (*Eragrostis abyssinica*) that is grown for its grain which yields a white flour and as a forage and hay crop — called also *teff grass*
TEFL \ˈtef-əl\ *abbr* teaching English as a foreign language
Tef·lon \ˈtef-ˌlän\ *trademark* — used for synthetic fluorine-containing resins used esp. for molding articles and for coatings to prevent sticking (as of food in cooking utensils)
teg·men \ˈteg-mən\ *n, pl* **teg·mi·na** \-mə-nə\ [NL *tegmin-, tegmen*, fr. L, covering, fr. *tegere* to cover — more at THATCH] **:** a superficial layer or cover usu. of a plant or animal part
teg·men·tal \teg-ˈment-ᵊl\ *adj* **:** of, relating to, or associated with an integument or a tegmentum
teg·men·tum \teg-ˈment-əm\ *n, pl* **-men·ta** \-ˈment-ə\ [NL, fr. L *tegumentum, tegmentum*, covering, fr. *tegere*] **:** an anatomical covering **:** TEGMEN
teg·u·ment \ˈteg-yə-mənt\ *n* [ME, fr. L *tegumentum*] **:** INTEGUMENT — **teg·u·men·tal** \ˌteg-yə-ˈment-ᵊl\ *adj*
teg·u·men·ta·ry \ˌteg-yə-ˈment-ə-rē\ *adj* **:** of, relating to, or consisting of an integument **:** serving as a covering
te·iid \ˈtē-(y)əd, ˈtī-əd\ *n* [NL *Teiidae*, group name, fr. *Teius*, genus of lizards, fr. Pg *teiu*, a lizard, fr. Tupi *tejú*] **:** any of a family (Teiidae) of mostly tropical American lizards (as the race runner) with a flat elongate scaly tongue that ends in two long smooth points — **teiid** *adj*
teil tree \ˈtē(ə)l-\ *n* [F dial. *teil*, fr. OF, fr. L *tilia*] **:** LINDEN 1a
tek·tite \ˈtek-ˌtīt\ *n* [ISV, fr. Gk *tēktos* molten, fr. *tēkein* to melt — more at THAW] **:** a glassy body of probably meteoritic origin and of rounded but indefinite shape found esp. in Czechoslovakia, Indonesia, and Australia — **tek·tit·ic** \tek-ˈtit-ik\ *adj*
tel *abbr* **1** telegram **2** telegraph **3** telephone
tel- *or* **telo-** *comb form* [ISV, fr. Gk *telos* — more at WHEEL] **:** end <*tel*angiectasia>
tel·a·mon \ˈtel-ə-ˌmän\ *n, pl* **tel·a·mo·nes** \ˌtel-ə-ˈmō-(ˌ)nēz\ [L, fr. Gk *telamōn* bearer, supporter; akin to Gk *tlēnai* to bear — more at TOLERATE] **:** a male figure used like a caryatid as a supporting column or pilaster

tel·an·gi·ec·ta·sia \ˌtel-ˌan-jē-ˌek-ˈtā-zh(ē-)ə, ˌtēl-, təl-\ *or* **tel·an·gi·ec·ta·sis** \-ˈek-tə-səs\ *n* [NL, fr. *tel-* + *angi-* + *ectasia, ectasis* dilatation, fr. Gk *ektasis* extension, fr. *ekteinein* to stretch out, fr. *ex-* + *teinein* to stretch — more at THIN] **:** an abnormal dilatation of capillary vessels and arterioles that often forms an angioma — **tel·an·gi·ec·tat·ic** \-ˌek-ˈtat-ik\ *adj*

tele \ˈtel-ē\ *n* **:** TELEVISION

tele- *or* **tel-** *comb form* [NL, fr. Gk *tēle-, tēl-,* fr. *tēle* far off — more at PALE-] **1 :** distant **:** at a distance **:** over a distance <*tele*gram> <*tel*esthesia> **2 a :** telegraph <*tele*typewriter> **b :** television <*tele*cast> **c :** telecommunication <*tele*man>

tele·cam·era \ˈtel-i-ˌkam-(ə-)rə\ *n* **:** a television camera

tele·cast \ˈtel-i-ˌkast\ *vb* **-cast** *also* **-cast·ed; -cast·ing** [*tele-* + broad*cast*] *vt* **:** to broadcast by television ~ *vi* **:** to broadcast a television program — **telecast** *n* — **tele·cast·er** *n*

tele·com·mu·ni·ca·tion \ˌtel-i-kə-ˌmyü-nə-ˈkā-shən\ *n* [ISV] **1 :** communication at a distance (as by telegraph) **2 :** a science that deals with telecommunication — usu. used in pl.

tele·course \ˈtel-i-ˌkō(ə)rs, -ˌkȯ(ə)rs\ *n* **:** a course of study conducted over television

te·le·du \ˈtel-ə-ˌdü, tə-ˈled-(ˌ)ü\ *n* [Malay *tēledu*] **:** a small short-tailed blackish brown carnivorous mammal (*Mydaus meliceps*) of the mountains of Java and Sumatra that like the related skunk secretes and expels offensive fluid

tele·fac·sim·i·le \ˌtel-i-fak-ˈsim-ə-(ˌ)lē\ *n* **:** a system of transmitting and reproducing fixed graphic material (as printing) by means of signals transmitted over telephone lines

tele·film \ˈtel-i-ˌfilm\ *n* **:** a motion picture produced for televising

teleg *abbr* telegraphy

tele·ge·nic \ˌtel-ə-ˈjen-ik, -ˈjēn-\ *n* **:** having an appearance and manner that are markedly attractive to television viewers

te·leg·o·ny \tə-ˈleg-ə-nē\ *n* [ISV] **:** the supposed carrying over of the influence of a sire to the offspring of subsequent matings of the dam with other males

¹tele·gram \ˈtel-ə-ˌgram, *South also* -grəm\ *n* **:** a telegraphic dispatch

²tele·gram \-ˌgram\ *vb* **-grammed; -gram·ming :** TELEGRAPH

¹tele·graph \-ˌgraf\ *n* [F *télégraphe,* fr. *télé-* tele- (fr. Gk *tēle-*) + *-graphe* -graph] **1 :** an apparatus for communication at a distance by coded signals; *esp* **:** an apparatus, system, or process for communication at a distance by electric transmission over wire **2 :** TELEGRAM

²telegraph *vt* **1 a :** to send or communicate by or as if by telegraph **b :** to send a telegram to **c :** to send by means of a telegraphic order <~ flowers to a sick friend> **2 :** to make known by signs esp. unknowingly and in advance <~ a punch> — **te·leg·ra·pher** \tə-ˈleg-rə-fər\ *n* — **te·leg·ra·phist** \-fəst\ *n*

tele·graph·ese \ˌtel-ə-graf-ˈēz, -ˈēs\ *n* **:** language characterized by the terseness and ellipses that are common in telegrams

tele·graph·ic \ˌtel-ə-ˈgraf-ik\ *adj* **1 :** of or relating to the telegraph **2 :** CONCISE, TERSE <with ~ economy of words —F. S. Mitchell> — **tele·graph·i·cal·ly** \-i-k(ə-)lē\ *adv*

telegraph plant *n* **:** an East Indian tick trefoil (*Desmodium gyrans*) whose lateral leaflets jerk up and down like the arms of a semaphore and also rotate on their axes

te·leg·ra·phy \tə-ˈleg-rə-fē\ *n* **:** the use or operation of a telegraph apparatus or system for transmitting or receiving communications

tele·ki·ne·sis \ˌtel-i-kə-ˈnē-səs, -kī-\ *n* [NL, fr. Gk *tēle-* + *kinēsis* motion — more at -KINESIS] **:** the apparent production of motion in objects (as by a spiritualistic medium) without contact or other physical means — **tele·ki·net·ic** \-ˈnet-ik\ *adj* — **tele·ki·net·i·cal·ly** \-i-k(ə-)lē\ *adv*

Te·lem·a·chus \tə-ˈlem-ə-kəs\ *n* [L, fr. Gk *Tēlemachos*] **:** the son of Odysseus and Penelope who contrived with his father to slay his mother's suitors

tele·man \ˈtel-ē-ˌman\ *n* [*tele-* + *man*] **:** a petty officer in the navy who performs clerical, coding, and communications duties

tel·e·mark \ˈtel-ə-ˌmärk\ *n, often cap* [Norw, fr. *Telemark,* region in Norway] **:** a turn in skiing in which the outside ski is advanced considerably ahead of the other ski and then turned inward at a steadily widening angle until the turn is completed

¹tele·me·ter \ˈtel-ə-ˌmēt-ər\ *n* [ISV] **1 :** an instrument for measuring the distance of an object from an observer **2 :** an electrical apparatus for measuring a quantity (as pressure, speed, or temperature), transmitting the result esp. by radio to a distant station, and there indicating or recording the quantity measured

²telemeter *vt* **:** to transmit (as the measurement of a quantity) by telemeter ~ *vi* **:** to telemeter the measurement of a quantity

te·lem·e·try \tə-ˈlem-ə-trē\ *n* **1 :** the science or process of telemetering data **2 :** data transmitted by telemetry **3 :** BIOTELEMETRY — **tele·met·ric** \ˌtel-ə-ˈme-trik\ *adj* — **tele·met·ri·cal·ly** \-tri-k(ə-)lē\ *adv*

tel·en·ceph·a·lon \ˌtel-en-ˈsef-ə-ˌlän, -lən\ *n* [NL, fr. *tel-* + *encephalon*] **:** the anterior subdivision of the forebrain comprising the cerebral hemispheres and associated structures — **tel·en·ce·phal·ic** \-ˌen-sə-ˈfal-ik\ *adj*

te·le·o·log·i·cal \ˌtel-ē-ə-ˈläj-i-kəl, ˌtēl-\ *also* **te·le·o·log·ic** \-ˈläj-ik\ *adj* **:** exhibiting or relating to design or purpose esp. in nature — **te·le·o·log·i·cal·ly** \-i-k(ə-)lē\ *adv*

te·le·ol·o·gist \-ˈäl-ə-jəst\ *n* **:** a specialist or believer in teleology

te·le·ol·o·gy \-jē\ *n* [NL *teleologia,* fr. Gk *tele-, telos* end, purpose + *-logia* -logy — more at WHEEL] **1 a :** the study of evidences of design in nature **b :** a doctrine (as in vitalism) that ends are immanent in nature **c :** a doctrine explaining phenomena by final causes **2 :** the fact or character attributed to nature or natural processes of being directed toward an end or shaped by a purpose **3 :** the use of design or purpose as an explanation of natural phenomena

te·le·ost \ˈtel-ē-ˌäst, ˈtē-lē-\ *n* [deriv. of Gk *teleios* complete, perfect (fr. *telos* end) + *osteon* bone — more at OSSEOUS] **:** any of a group (Teleostei or Teleostomi) of fishes comprising the fishes with a bony rather than a cartilaginous skeleton and including all jawed fishes with the exception of the elasmobranchs and sometimes the ganoids and dipnoans — **teleost** *adj* — **te·le·os·te·an** \ˌtel-ē-ˈäs-tē-ən, ˌtēl-\ *adj or n*

tel·eo·stome \ˈtel-ē-ə-ˌstōm, ˈtēl-\ *n* [deriv. of Gk *teleios* + *stoma* mouth — more at STOMACH] **:** TELEOST

te·lep·a·thy \tə-ˈlep-ə-thē\ *n* **:** apparent communication from one mind to another otherwise than through the channels of sense — **tele·path·ic** \ˌtel-ə-ˈpath-ik\ *adj* — **tele·path·i·cal·ly** \-i-k(ə-)lē\ *adv*

¹tele·phone \ˈtel-ə-ˌfōn\ *n, often attrib* **:** an instrument for reproducing sounds at a distance; *specif* **:** one in which sound is converted into electrical impulses for transmission by wire

²telephone *vb* **-phoned; -phon·ing** *vi* **:** to communicate by telephone ~ *vt* **1 :** to send by telephone **2 :** to speak to by telephone — **tele·phon·er** *n*

telephone booth *n* **:** an enclosure within which one may stand or sit while making a telephone call

telephone box *n, Brit* **:** a public telephone booth

telephone directory *n* **:** a book listing names, addresses, and telephone numbers of telephone subscribers — called also *telephone book*

telephone number *n* **:** a number assigned to a telephone and used by a person to call that telephone

telephone receiver *n* **:** a device (as in a telephone) for converting electric impulses or varying current into sound

tele·phon·ic \ˌtel-ə-ˈfän-ik\ *adj* **1 :** conveying sound to a distance **2 :** of, relating to, or conveyed by telephone — **tele·phon·i·cal·ly** \-i-k(ə-)lē\ *adv*

te·le·pho·nist \tə-ˈlef-ə-nist, ˈtel-ə-ˌfō-nist\ *n, Brit* **:** a telephone switchboard operator

te·le·pho·ny \tə-ˈlef-ə-nē *also* ˈtel-ə-ˌfō-\ *n* **:** the use or operation of an apparatus for transmission of sounds between widely removed points with or without connecting wires

¹tele·pho·to \ˌtel-ə-ˈfōt-(ˌ)ō\ *adj* **1 :** TELEPHOTOGRAPHIC <a ~ effect> **2 :** being a camera lens system designed to give a usu. large image of a distant object

²telephoto *n, pl* **-tos 1 :** a telephoto lens **2 :** a photograph taken with a camera having a telephoto lens

Telephoto *trademark* — used for an apparatus for transmitting photographs electrically or for a photograph so transmitted

tele·pho·to·graph·ic \ˌtel-ə-ˌfōt-ə-ˈgraf-ik\ *adj* **:** of, relating to, or being the photographic process of telephotography

tele·pho·tog·ra·phy \-fə-ˈtäg-rə-fē\ *n* [ISV] **1 :** FACSIMILE 2 **2 :** the photography of distant objects (as by a camera provided with a telephoto lens)

tele·play \ˈtel-i-ˌplā\ *n* **:** a play written for television

tele·print·er \ˈtel-ə-ˌprint-ər\ *n* **:** a device capable of producing hard copy from signals received over a communications circuit; *esp* **:** TELETYPEWRITER

tele·pro·cess·ing \-ˈpräs-ˌes-iŋ, -ˈprōs-, -əs-\ *n* **:** computer processing via remote terminals

Tele·Promp·Ter \ˈtel-ə-ˌpräm(p)-tər\ *trademark* — used for a device for unrolling a magnified script in front of a speaker on television

tele·ran \ˈtel-ə-ˌran\ *n* [*tele*vision-*ra*dar *n*avigation] **:** a system of aerial navigation that utilizes a combination of television and radar for the guidance of aircraft

¹tele·scope \ˈtel-ə-ˌskōp\ *n, often attrib* [NL *telescopium,* fr. Gk *tēleskopos* farseeing, fr. *tēle-* tele- + *skopein* to look — more at SPY] **1 :** a usu. tubular optical instrument for viewing distant objects by means of the refraction of light rays through a lens or the reflection of light rays by a concave mirror — compare REFLECTOR, REFRACTOR **2 :** any of various tubular magnifying optical instruments **3 :** RADIO TELESCOPE **4 :** an expandable traveling bag having an unhinged top half that slips over the bottom half and is fastened with straps — called also *telescope bag*

²telescope *vb* **-scoped; -scop·ing** *vi* **1 :** to slide or pass one within another like the cylindrical sections of a hand telescope **2 :** to force a way into or enter another lengthwise as the result of collision **3 :** to become telescoped ~ *vt* **1 :** to cause to telescope **2 :** COMPRESS, CONDENSE <he's got . . . history all *telescoped* into a few years —Ray Russell>

telescope box *n* **:** a two-piece box in which the sides of one part fit over those of the other

tele·scop·ic \ˌtel-ə-ˈskäp-ik\ *adj* **1 a :** of, relating to, or performed with a telescope **b :** suitable for seeing or magnifying distant objects **2 :** seen or discoverable only by a telescope <~ stars> **3 :** able to discern objects at a distance **4 :** having parts that telescope — **tele·scop·i·cal·ly** \-i-k(ə-)lē\ *adv*

tel·e·sis \ˈtel-ə-səs\ *n, pl* **-e·ses** \-ˌsēz\ [NL, fr. Gk, fulfillment, fr. *telein* to complete, fr. *telos* end — more at WHEEL] **:** progress that is intelligently planned and directed **:** the attainment of desired ends by the application of intelligent human effort to the means

tel·es·the·sia \ˌtel-əs-ˈthē-zh(ē-)ə\ *n* [NL, fr. *tele-* + *esthesia*] **:** an impression supposedly received at a distance without the normal operation of the organs of sense — **tel·es·thet·ic** \-ˈthet-ik\ *adj*

tele·ther·mo·scope \ˌtel-ə-ˈthər-mə-ˌskōp\ *n* **:** an apparatus for indicating the temperature at a distant point (as by a thermoelectric circuit and a galvanometer)

tele·thon \ˈtel-ə-ˌthän\ *n* [*tele-* + *-thon* (as in *marathon*)] **:** a long television program usu. to solicit funds for a charity

Tele·type \ˈtel-ə-ˌtīp\ *trademark* — used for a teletypewriter

Tele·type·set·ter \ˌtel-ə-ˈtīp-ˌset-ər\ *trademark* — used for a telegraphic apparatus for the automatic operation of a keyboard typesetting machine

tele·type·writ·er \-ˈrīt-ər\ *n* **:** a device capable of being used over most telephonic communications systems to send and receive signals and produce hard copy from them

tele·typ·ist \ˈtel-ə-ˌtī-pəst\ *n* **:** one that operates a teletypewriter

te·leu·to·spore \tə-ˈlüt-ə-ˌspō(ə)r, -ˌspȯ(ə)r\ *n* [Gk *teleutē* end + ISV *spore;* akin to Gk *telos* end — more at WHEEL] **:** TELIOSPORE — **te·leu·to·spor·ic** \-ˌlüt-ə-ˈspōr-ik, -ˈspȯr-\ *adj*

tele·view \ˈtel-i-ˌvyü\ *vi* **:** to observe or watch by means of a television receiver — **tele·view·er** *n*

tele·vise \'tel-ə-ˌvīz\ *vb* **-vised; -vis·ing** [back-formation fr. *television*] *vt* : to pick up and usu. broadcast (as a baseball game) by television ~ *vi* : to broadcast by television

tele·vi·sion \'tel-ə-ˌvizh-ən *esp Brit* ˌtel-ə-'\ *n* [F *télévision*, fr. *télé-* tele- (fr. Gk *tēle*) + *vision*] **1 :** an electronic system of transmitting transient images of fixed or moving objects together with sound over a wire or through space by apparatus that converts light and sound into electrical waves and reconverts them into visible light rays and audible sound **2 :** a television receiving set **3 a :** the television broadcasting industry **b :** television as a medium of communication — **tele·vi·sion·al·ly** \ˌtel-ə-'vizh-nə-lē, -'vizh-ən-ᵊl-ē\ *adv* — **tele·vi·sion·ary** \-'vizh-ə-ˌner-ē\ *adj*

television tube *n* : PICTURE TUBE

tele·vi·sor \'tel-ə-ˌvī-zər\ *n* **1 :** a transmitting or receiving apparatus for television **2 :** a television broadcaster : TELECASTER

tele·vi·su·al \ˌtel-ə-'vizh-(ə-)wəl, -'vizh-əl\ *adj, chiefly Brit* : of, relating to, or suitable for broadcast by television

tel·ex \'tel-ˌeks\ *n* [*tel*eprinter + *ex*change] : a communication service involving teletypewriters connected by wire through automatic exchanges — **telex** *vt*

te·li·al \'tē-lē-əl\ *adj* : of or relating to a telium

te·lic \'tel-ik, 'tēl-\ *adj* [Gk *telikos*, fr. *telos* end — more at WHEEL] : tending toward an end — **te·li·cal·ly** \-i-k(ə-)lē\ *adv*

te·lio·spore \'tē-lē-ə-ˌspō(ə)r, -ˌspȯ(ə)r\ *n* [Gk *teleios* complete (fr. *telos* end) + E *spore*] : a thick-walled chlamydospore that is the final stage in the life cycle of a rust fungus and that after nuclear fusion gives rise to the basidium — **te·lio·spor·ic** \ˌtē-lē-ə-'spōr-ik, -'spȯr-\ *adj*

te·li·um \'tē-lē-əm\ *n, pl* **te·lia** \-lē-ə\ [NL, fr. Gk *teleios* complete] : a teliospore-containing sorus or pustule on the host plant of a rust fungus

tell \'tel\ *vb* **told** \'tōld\; **tell·ing** [ME *tellen*, fr. OE *tellan*; akin to OHG *zellen* to count, tell, OE *talu* tale] *vt* **1 :** COUNT, ENUMERATE <all *told* there were 27 public schools —C. L. Jones> **2 a :** to relate in detail : NARRATE **b :** to give utterance to : SAY <who dares think one thing, and another ~ —Alexander Pope> **3 a :** to make known : DIVULGE, REVEAL **b :** to express in words <she never *told* her love —Shak.> **4 a :** to report to : INFORM **b :** to assure emphatically <he did not do it, I ~ you> **5 :** ORDER, DIRECT <*told* her to wait> **6 :** to ascertain by observing : find out ~ *vi* **1 :** to give an account **2 :** to act as an informer — often used with *on* <the sister *told* on him, though he tried to shush her —John Dollard> **3 :** to take effect : have a marked effect **4 :** to serve as evidence or indication ***syn*** see REVEAL

tell·er \'tel-ər\ *n* **1 :** one that relates or communicates <a ~ of stories> **2 :** one that reckons or counts: as **a :** one appointed to count votes **b :** a member of a bank's staff concerned with the direct handling of money received or paid out

tell·ing \'tel-iŋ\ *adj* : carrying great weight and producing a marked effect : IMPRESSIVE, EFFECTIVE <the most ~ evidence against him> ***syn*** see VALID — **tell·ing·ly** \-iŋ-lē\ *adv*

tell off *vt* **1 :** to number and set apart; *esp* **:** to assign to a special duty <*told off* a detail and put them to opening a trench —J. F. Dobie> **2 :** REPRIMAND, SCOLD <when she increases her nagging, I . . . *tell* her *off* quite brutally —Rex Ingamells>

tell·tale \'tel-ˌtāl\ *n* **1 a :** TALEBEARER, INFORMER **b :** an outward sign : INDICATION **2 :** a device for indicating or recording something: as **a :** a device for keeping a check on employees; *esp* : TIME CLOCK **b :** a device that shows the position of the helm or rudder **c :** a strip of metal on the front wall of a racquets or squash court to a height of from 2 to 2½ feet above the ground over which the ball must be hit **d :** a railroad warning device (as a row of long strips hanging over tracks at the approach to a low overhead bridge) — **telltale** *adj*

tellur- *or* **telluro-** *comb form* [L *tellur-*, *tellus* — more at THILL] **1 :** earth <*tellur*ian> **2** [NL *tellurium*] : tellurium <*tellur*ic>

¹tel·lu·ri·an \tə-'lu̇r-ē-ən, te-\ *adj* : of, relating to, or characteristic of the earth

²tellurian *n* : a dweller on the earth

tel·lu·ric \tə-'lu̇(ə)r-ik, te-\ *adj* **1 :** of, relating to, or containing tellurium esp. with a higher valence than in tellurous compounds **2 :** of or relating to the earth : TERRESTRIAL **3 :** being or relating to a usu. natural electric current flowing near the earth's surface

tel·lu·ride \'tel-yə-ˌrīd\ *n* [ISV] : a binary compound of tellurium usu. with a more electropositive element or radical

tel·lu·rite \-ˌrīt\ *n* : a mineral TeO_2 that consists of the dioxide of tellurium and occurs sparingly in tufts of white or yellowish crystals

tel·lu·ri·um \tə-'lu̇r-ē-əm, te-\ *n* [NL, fr. L *tellur-*, *tellus* earth] : a semimetallic element related to selenium and sulfur that occurs in a silvery white brittle crystalline form of metallic luster, in a dark amorphous form, or combined with metals and that is used esp. in alloys — see ELEMENT table

tel·lu·rom·e·ter \ˌtel-yə-'räm-ət-ər\ *n* : a device that measures distance by means of microwaves

tel·lu·rous \'tel-yə-rəs; tə-'lu̇r-əs, te-\ *adj* [ISV] : of, relating to, or containing tellurium esp. with a lower valence than in telluric compounds

tel·ly \'tel-ē\ *n* [by shortening & alter.] *chiefly Brit* : TELEVISION

telo- — see TEL-

telo·cen·tric \ˌtel-ə-'sen-trik, ˌtēl-\ *adj* [ISV *tel-* + *centro*mere + *-ic*] : having the form of a straight rod due to the terminal position of the centromere <a ~ chromosome> — **telocentric** *n*

te·lome \'tē-ˌlōm\ *n* [ISV *tel-* + *-ome*] : a basic structural unit of the vascular plant consisting typically of a terminal branchlet with distal sporangium and vascular supply — **te·lo·mic** \tē-'lōm-ik, -'läm-\ *adj*

telo·phase \'tel-ə-ˌfāz, 'tēl-\ *n* [ISV] **1 :** the final stage of mitosis in which the spindle disappears and two new nuclei appear each with a set of chromosomes **2 :** a stage in meiosis that is usu. the final stage in the first and second meiotic divisions but may be missing in the first and that is characterized by formation of the nuclear membrane and by changes in coiling and arrangement of the chromosomes

te·los \'tel-ˌäs, 'tē-ˌläs\ *n* [Gk — more at WHEEL] : an ultimate end

telo·tax·is \ˌtel-ə-'tak-səs, ˌtēl-\ *n* [NL] : a taxis in which an organism orients itself in respect to a stimulus (as a light source) as though that were the only stimulus acting on it

tel·pher \'tel-fər\ *n* [irreg. fr. Gk *tēle-* tele- + *pherein* to bear — more at BEAR] : a light car suspended from and running on aerial cables; *esp* : one propelled by electricity

tel·son \'tel-sən\ *n* [NL, fr. Gk, end of a plowed field; prob. akin to Gk *telos* end] : the terminal segment of the body of an arthropod or segmented worm; *esp* : that of a crustacean forming the middle lobe of the tail

Tel·u·gu \'tel-ə-ˌgü\ *n, pl* **Telugu** *or* **Telugus** **1 :** a member of the largest group of people in Andhra Pradesh, India **2 :** the Dravidian language of the Telugu people

tem·blor \'tem-blər; 'tem-ˌblō(ə)r, -ˌblȯ(ə)r, tem-'\ *n* [Sp, lit., trembling, fr. *temblar* to tremble, fr. ML *tremulare* — more at TREMBLE] : EARTHQUAKE

tem·er·ar·i·ous \ˌtem-ə-'rer-ē-əs, -'rar-\ *adj* [L *temerarius*, fr. *temere*] : marked by temerity : rashly or presumptuously daring — **tem·er·ar·i·ous·ly** *adv* — **tem·er·ar·i·ous·ness** *n*

te·mer·i·ty \tə-'mer-ət-ē\ *n, pl* **-ties** [ME *temeryte*, fr. L *temeritas*, fr. *temere* at random, rashly, lit., in the dark; akin to OHG *demar* darkness, L *tenebrae*, Skt *tamas*] **1 :** unreasonable or foolhardy contempt of danger or opposition : RASHNESS, RECKLESSNESS **2 :** an act or instance of temerity
syn TEMERITY, AUDACITY, HARDIHOOD, EFFRONTERY, NERVE, CHEEK, GALL *shared meaning element* : conspicuous or flagrant boldness
ant caution

temp *abbr* **1** temperance **2** temperature **3** template **4** temporal **5** temporary **6** [L *tempore*] in the time of

tem·peh \'tem-ˌpā\ *n* [Indonesian *tempé*] : an Asiatic food prepared by fermenting soybeans with a rhizopus

¹tem·per \'tem-pər\ *vb* **tem·pered; tem·per·ing** \-p(ə-)riŋ\ [ME *temperen*, fr. OE & OF; OE *temprian* & OF *temprer*, fr. L *temperare* to moderate, mix, temper; prob. akin to L *tempor-*, *tempus* time — more at TEMPORAL] *vt* **1 :** to adjust to the needs of a situation by a counterbalancing or mitigating addition <~ justice with mercy> **2** *archaic* **a :** to exercise control over : GOVERN, RESTRAIN **b :** to cause to be well disposed : MOLLIFY <~*ed* and reconciled them both —Richard Steele> **3 :** to bring to a suitable state by mixing in or adding a usu. liquid ingredient: as **a :** to mix (clay) with water or a modifier (as grog) and knead to a uniform texture **b :** to mix oil with (colors) in making paint ready for use **4 a** (1) **:** to soften (hardened steel or cast iron) by reheating at a lower temperature (2) **:** to harden (steel) by reheating and cooling in oil **b :** to anneal or toughen (glass) by a process of gradually heating and cooling **5 :** to make stronger and more resilient through hardship : TOUGHEN <troops ~*ed* in battle> **6 a :** to put in tune with something : ATTUNE **b :** to adjust the pitch of (a note, chord, or instrument) to a temperament ~ *vi* **:** to produce satisfactory temper (as in a metal) ***syn*** see MODERATE — **tem·per·able** \-p(ə-)rə-bəl\ *adj* — **tem·per·er** \-pər-ər\ *n*

²temper *n* **1 a** *archaic* **:** a suitable proportion or balance of qualities : a middle state between extremes : MEAN, MEDIUM <virtue is . . . a just ~ between propensities —T. B. Macaulay> **b** *archaic* **:** CHARACTER, QUALITY <the ~ of the land you design to sow —John Mortimer> **c :** characteristic tone : TREND, TENDENCY <the ~ of the times> **d :** high quality of mind or spirit : COURAGE, METTLE **2 :** the state of a substance with respect to certain desired qualities (as hardness, elasticity, or workability): as **a** (1) **:** the degree of hardness or resiliency given steel by tempering (2) **:** the color of steel after tempering **b :** the feel and relative solidity of leather **3 :** a substance added to or mixed with something else to modify the properties of the latter: as **a :** any of various mixtures of metals added to another metal in making an alloy **b :** the carbon content of steel that affects its hardening properties **4 a :** a characteristic cast of mind or state of feeling : DISPOSITION **b :** calmness of mind : COMPOSURE, EQUANIMITY **c :** state of feeling or frame of mind at a particular time usu. dominated by a single strong emotion **d :** heat of mind or emotion : proneness to anger : PASSION ***syn*** see DISPOSITION, MOOD

tem·pera \'tem-pə-rə\ *n* [It *tempera*, lit., temper, fr. *temperare* to temper, fr. L] **1 :** a process of painting in which an albuminous or colloidal medium (as egg yolk) is employed as a vehicle instead of oil; *also* **:** a painting done in tempera **2 :** POSTER COLOR

tem·per·a·ment \'tem-p(ə-)rə-mənt, -pər-mənt\ *n* [ME, fr. L *temperamentum*, fr. *temperare* to mix, temper] **1** *obs* **a :** constitution of a substance, body, or organism with respect to the mixture or balance of its elements, qualities, or parts : MAKEUP **b :** COMPLEXION 1 **2 a :** the peculiar or distinguishing mental or physical character determined by the relative proportions of the humors according to medieval physiology **b :** characteristic or habitual inclination or mode of emotional response <he is of a nervous ~> **c :** extremely high sensibility; *esp* **:** excessive sensitiveness or irritability **3** *obs* **a :** CLIMATE **b :** TEMPERATURE 2 **4 a :** the act or process of tempering or modifying : ADJUSTMENT, COMPROMISE **b :** middle course : MEAN **5 :** the process of slightly modifying the musical intervals of the pure scale to produce a set of 12 equally spaced tones to the octave which enables a keyboard instrument to play in all keys ***syn*** see DISPOSITION

tem·per·a·men·tal \ˌtem-p(ə-)rə-'ment-ᵊl\ *adj* **1 :** of, relating to, or arising from temperament : CONSTITUTIONAL <~ peculiarities> **2 a :** marked by excessive sensitivity and impulsive changes of mood <a ~ opera singer> **b :** unpredictable in behavior or performance — **tem·per·a·men·tal·ly** \-ᵊl-ē\ *adv*

ə abut	ᵊ kitten	ər further	a back	ā bake	ä cot, cart
au̇ out	ch chin	e less	ē easy	g gift	i trip	ī life
j joke	ŋ sing	ō flow	ȯ flaw	ȯi coin	th thin	t͟h this
ü loot	u̇ foot	y yet	yü few	yu̇ furious	zh vision

tem·per·ance \'tem-p(ə-)rən(t)s, -pərn(t)s\ *n* [ME, fr. L *temperantia,* fr. *temperant-, temperans,* prp. of *temperare* to moderate, be moderate] **1 :** moderation in action, thought, or feeling : RESTRAINT **2 :** habitual moderation in the indulgence of the appetites or passions; *specif* **:** moderation in or abstinence from the use of intoxicating drink

tem·per·ate \'tem-p(ə-)rət\ *adj* [ME *temperat,* fr. L *temperatus,* fr. pp. of *temperare*] **1 :** marked by moderation: as **a :** keeping or held within limits : not extreme or excessive : MILD **b :** moderate in indulgence of appetite or desire **c :** moderate in the use of intoxicating liquors **d :** marked by an absence or avoidance of extravagance, violence, or extreme partisanship : RESTRAINED **2 a :** having a moderate climate **b :** found in or associated with a moderate climate <~ insects> **3 :** existing as a prophage in infected cells and rarely causing lysis <~ phages> ***syn*** see SOBER ***ant*** intemperate — **tem·per·ate·ly** *adv* — **tem·per·ate·ness** *n*

temperate zone *n, often cap T&Z* **:** the area or region between the tropic of Cancer and the arctic circle or between the tropic of Capricorn and the antarctic circle

tem·per·a·ture \'tem-pə(r)-ˌchu̇(ə)r, -p(ə-)rə-, -chər, -ˌt(y)u̇(ə)r; *rapid* 'tem(p)-chər\ *n* [L *temperatura* mixture, moderation, fr. *temperatus,* pp. of *temperare*] **1** *archaic* **a :** COMPLEXION 1 **b :** TEMPERAMENT 2b **2 a :** degree of hotness or coldness measured on a definite scale — compare THERMOMETER **b :** the degree of heat that is natural to the body of a living being **c :** abnormally high body heat **d :** relative state of emotional warmth <aware of a change in the ~ of our friendship —Christopher Isherwood>

temperature gradient *n* **:** the rate of change of temperature with displacement in a given direction (as with increase of height)

tem·pered \'tem-pərd\ *adj* **1 a :** having the elements mixed in satisfying proportions : TEMPERATE **b :** qualified, lessened, or diluted by the mixture or influence of an additional ingredient : MODERATED <a pale gleam of ~ sunlight fell through the leaves —W. H. Hudson †1922> **2 :** treated by tempering **3 :** having a specified temper — used in combination <short-*tempered*> **4 :** conforming to esp. equal temperament — used of a musical interval, intonation, semitone, or scale

1**tem·pest** \'tem-pəst\ *n* [ME, fr. OF *tempeste,* fr. (assumed) VL *tempesta,* alter. of L *tempestas* season, weather, storm, fr. *tempus* time — more at TEMPORAL] **1 :** an extensive violent wind esp. when accompanied by rain, hail, or snow **2 :** TUMULT, UPROAR

2**tempest** *vt* **:** to raise a tempest in or around

tem·pes·tu·ous \tem-'pes(h)-chə-wəs\ *adj* [LL *tempestuosus,* fr. OL *tempestus* season, weather, storm, fr. *tempus*] **:** of, relating to, or resembling a tempest : TURBULENT, STORMY <~ weather> <a ~ debate> — **tem·pes·tu·ous·ly** *adv* — **tem·pes·tu·ous·ness** *n*

Tem·plar \'tem-plər\ *n* [ME *templer,* fr. OF *templier,* fr. ML *templarius,* fr. L *templum* temple] **1 :** a knight of a religious military order established in the early 12th century in Jerusalem for the protection of pilgrims and the Holy Sepulcher **2** *not cap* **:** a barrister or student of law in London **3 :** KNIGHT TEMPLAR 2

tem·plate *or* **tem·plet** \'tem-plət\ *n* [prob. fr. F *templet,* dim. of *temple* temple of a loom] **1 :** a short piece or block placed horizontally in a wall under a beam to distribute its weight or pressure (as over a door) **2 a** (1) **:** a gauge, pattern, or mold (as a thin plate or board) used as a guide to the form of a piece being made (2) **:** a molecule (as of RNA) in a biological system that carries the genetic code for another macromolecule **b :** OVERLAY d

1**tem·ple** \'tem-pəl\ *n* [ME, fr. OE & OF; OE *tempel* & OF *temple,* fr. L *templum* space marked out for observation of auguries, temple; prob. akin to L *tempus* time] **1 :** an edifice for religious exercises: as **a** *often cap* **:** one of three successive national sanctuaries in ancient Jerusalem **b :** a building for Mormon sacred ordinances **c :** a Reform or Conservative synagogue **2 :** a local lodge of any of various fraternal orders; *also* **:** the building housing it **3 :** a place devoted to a special purpose — **tem·pled** \-pəld\ *adj*

2**temple** *n* [ME, fr. MF, fr. (assumed) VL *tempula,* alter. of L *tempora* (pl.) temples; prob. akin to L *tempor-, tempus* time] **1 :** the flattened space on each side of the forehead of some mammals (as man) **2 :** one of the side supports of a pair of glasses jointed to the bows and passing on each side of the head

tem·po \'tem-(ˌ)pō\ *n, pl* **tem·pi** \-(ˌ)pē\ *or* **tempos** [It, lit., time, fr. L *tempus*] **1 :** the rate of speed of a musical piece or passage indicated by one of a series of directions (as largo, presto, or allegro) and often by an exact metronome marking **2 :** rate of motion or activity : PACE **3 :** a turn to move in chess in relation to the number of moves required to gain an objective

1**tem·po·ral** \'tem-p(ə-)rəl\ *adj* [ME, fr. L *temporalis,* fr. *tempor-, tempus* time; akin to Lith *tempti* to stretch, and prob. to L *tendere* to stretch — more at THIN] **1 a :** of or relating to time as opposed to eternity **b :** of or relating to earthly life **c :** of or relating to lay or secular concerns **2 :** of or relating to grammatical tense or a distinction of time **3 a :** of or relating to time as distinguished from space **b :** of or relating to the sequence of time or to a particular time : CHRONOLOGICAL — **tem·po·ral·ly** \-ē\ *adv*

2**temporal** *adj* [MF, fr. LL *temporalis,* fr. L *tempora* temples] **:** of or relating to the temples or the sides of the skull behind the orbits

3**temporal** *n* **:** a temporal part (as a bone or muscle)

temporal bone *n* **:** a compound bone of the side of the human skull

tem·po·ral·i·ty \ˌtem-pə-'ral-ət-ē\ *n, pl* **-ties 1 a :** civil or political as distinguished from spiritual or ecclesiastical power or authority **b :** an ecclesiastical property or revenue — often used in pl. **2 :** the quality or state of being temporal

tem·po·ral·ize \'tem-p(ə-)rə-ˌlīz\ *vt* **-ized; -iz·ing 1 :** to place or define in time relations **2 :** SECULARIZE

temporal lobe *n* **:** a large lobe of each cerebral hemisphere that is situated in front of the occipital lobe and contains a sensory area associated with the organ of hearing

temporal summation *n* **:** sensory summation that involves the addition of single stimuli over a period of time

tem·po·rar·i·ly \ˌtem-pə-'rer-ə-lē\ *adv* **:** during a limited time

1**tem·po·rary** \'tem-pə-ˌrer-ē\ *adj* [L *temporarius,* fr. *tempor-, tempus* time] **:** lasting for a limited time — **tem·po·rari·ness** *n*

2**temporary** *n, pl* **-rar·ies :** one serving for a limited time <adding several *temporaries* as typists during the summer>

temporary duty *n* **:** temporary military service away from one's permanent duty station

tem·po·ri·za·tion \ˌtem-pə-rə-'zā-shən\ *n* **:** the act, policy, or practice of temporizing

tem·po·rize \'tem-pə-ˌrīz\ *vi* **-rized; -riz·ing** [MF *temporiser,* fr. ML *temporizare* to pass the time, fr. L *tempor-, tempus*] **1 :** to act to suit the time or occasion : yield to current or dominant opinion : COMPROMISE **2 :** to draw out discussions or negotiations so as to gain time <you'd have to ~ until you found out how she wanted to be advised —Mary Austin> — **tem·po·riz·er** *n*

tempt \'tem(p)t\ *vt* [ME *tempten,* fr. OF *tempter, tenter,* fr. L *temptare, tentare* to feel, try, tempt; akin to L *tendere* to stretch — more at THIN] **1 :** to entice to do wrong by promise of pleasure or gain **2 a** *obs* **:** to make trial of : TEST **b :** to try presumptuously : PROVOKE **c :** to risk the dangers of **3 a :** to induce to do something **b :** to cause to be strongly inclined <he was ~*ed* to call it quits> ***syn*** see LURE — **tempt·able** \'tem(p)-tə-bəl\ *adj*

temp·ta·tion \tem(p)-'tā-shən\ *n* **1 :** the act of tempting or the state of being tempted esp. to evil : ENTICEMENT **2 :** something tempting : a cause or occasion of enticement

tempt·er \'tem(p)-tər\ *n* **:** one that tempts or entices — **tempt·ress** \-trəs\ *n*

tempt·ing *adj* **:** having an appeal : ENTICING <a ~ offer> — **tempt·ing·ly** \-tiŋ-lē\ *adv*

tem·pu·ra \'tem-pə-rə, -ˌrä; tem-'pu̇r-ə\ *n* [Jap *tenpura*] **:** seafood or vegetables dipped in batter and fried

ten \'ten\ *n* [ME, fr. OE *tīene,* fr. *tīen,* adj., ten; akin to OHG *zehan* ten, L *decem,* Gk *deka*] **1** — see NUMBER table **2 :** the tenth in a set or series <wears a ~> **3 :** something having ten units or members **4 :** the number occupying the position two to the left of the decimal point in the Arabic notation — usu. used in pl. **5 :** a 10-dollar bill — **ten** *adj or pron* — **tenth** \'ten(t)th\ *adj or adv* — **tenth** *n*

ten·a·ble \'ten-ə-bəl\ *adj* [F, fr. OF, fr. *tenir* to hold, fr. L *tenēre* — more at THIN] **:** capable of being held, maintained, or defended : DEFENSIBLE, REASONABLE — **ten·a·bil·i·ty** \ˌten-ə-'bil-ət-ē\ *n* — **ten·a·ble·ness** *n* — **ten·a·bly** \'ten-ə-blē\ *adv*

ten·ace \'ten-ˌās, te-'nās, 'ten-əs\ *n* [modif. of Sp *tenaza,* lit., forceps, prob. fr. L *tenacia,* neut. pl. of *tenax*] **:** a combination of two high or relatively high cards (as ace and queen) of the same suit in one hand with one ranking two degrees below the other

te·na·cious \tə-'nā-shəs\ *adj* [L *tenac-, tenax* tending to hold fast, fr. *tenēre* to hold] **1 a :** not easily pulled apart : COHESIVE, TOUGH <a ~ metal> **b :** tending to adhere or cling esp. to another substance : STICKY <~ burs> <~ clay> **2 a :** persistent in maintaining or adhering to something valued as habitual <a man very ~ of his rights> **b :** RETENTIVE <a ~ memory> ***syn*** see STRONG — **te·na·cious·ly** *adv* — **te·na·cious·ness** *n*

te·nac·i·ty \tə-'nas-ət-ē\ *n* **:** the quality or state of being tenacious ***syn*** see COURAGE

te·nac·u·lum \tə-'nak-yə-ləm\ *n, pl* **-la** \-lə\ *or* **-lums** [NL, fr. LL, instrument for holding, fr. L *tenēre*] **1 :** a slender sharp-pointed hook attached to a handle and used mainly in surgery for seizing and holding parts (as arteries) **2 :** an adhesive animal structure

ten·an·cy \'ten-ən-sē\ *n, pl* **-cies :** a holding of an estate or a mode of holding an estate : the temporary possession or occupancy of something (as a house) that belongs to another; *also* **:** the period of a tenant's occupancy or possession

1**ten·ant** \'ten-ənt\ *n* [ME, fr. MF, fr. prp. of *tenir* to hold] **1 a :** one who holds or possesses real estate or sometimes personal property (as an annuity) by any kind of right **b :** one who has the occupation or temporary possession of lands or tenements of another; *specif* **:** one who rents or leases (as a house) from a landlord **2 :** OCCUPANT, DWELLER — **ten·ant·less** \-ləs\ *adj*

2**tenant** *vt* **:** to hold or occupy as a tenant : INHABIT — **ten·ant·able** \-ən-tə-bəl\ *adj*

tenant farmer *n* **:** a farmer who works land owned by another and pays rent either in cash or in shares of produce

ten·ant·ry \'ten-ən-trē\ *n, pl* **-ries 1 :** TENANCY **2 :** a body of tenants

ten–cent store \ten-'sent-\ *n* **:** FIVE-AND-TEN

tench \'tench\ *n, pl* **tench** *or* **tench·es** [ME, fr. MF *tenche,* fr. LL *tinca*] **:** a Eurasian freshwater fish (*Tinca tinca*) related to the dace and noted for its ability to survive outside water

Ten Commandments *n pl* **:** the ethical commandments of God given according to Biblical accounts to Moses by voice and by writing on stone tablets on Mount Sinai

1**tend** \'tend\ *vb* [ME *tenden,* short for *attenden* to attend] *vi* **1** *archaic* **:** to give ear : LISTEN **2 :** to pay attention : apply oneself <~ to your own affairs> **3 :** to act as an attendant : SERVE **4** *obs* **:** AWAIT ~ *vt* **1** *archaic* **:** to attend as a servant **2 a :** to apply oneself to the care of : watch over **b :** to have or take charge of as a caretaker or overseer **c :** CULTIVATE, FOSTER **d :** to manage the operations of : MIND <~ a store> **3 :** to stand by (as a rope) in readiness to prevent mischance (as fouling) ***syn*** TEND, ATTEND, MIND, WATCH *shared meaning element* **:** to take charge of or look after

2**tend** *vi* [ME *tenden,* fr. MF *tendre* to stretch, fr. L *tendere* — more at THIN] **1 :** to move, direct, or develop one's course in a particular direction **2 :** to exhibit an inclination or tendency : CONDUCE

ten·dance \'ten-dən(t)s\ *n* [short for *attendance*] **1 :** watchful care **2** *archaic* **:** persons in attendance : RETINUE

ten·den·cy \'ten-dən-sē\ *n, pl* **-cies** [ML *tendentia,* fr. L *tendent-, tendens,* prp. of *tendere*] **1 a :** direction or approach toward a place, object, effect, or limit **b :** a proneness to a particular kind of thought or action **2 a :** the purposeful trend of something written or said : AIM **b :** deliberate but indirect advocacy ***syn*** TENDENCY, TREND, DRIFT, TENOR, CURRENT *shared meaning element* **:** a movement or course having a particular direction and character. TENDENCY implies an inclination sometimes amounting to an impelling force <had a *tendency* to be absentminded> <the whole *tendency* of evolution is towards a diminishing birthrate —Havelock Ellis> TREND applies to the general direction maintained by a winding or irregular course <the long-term *trend* of the market is upward> DRIFT may apply to a tendency determined by external influences (as a wind, a fashion, or a state of public feeling) <the *drift* of young people towards social action> or, specifically, to an underlying or obscure trend of meaning or argument <I see the whole *drift* of your argument —Oliver Goldsmith> TENOR, often close to *drift* in this latter usage, carries a stronger implication of clearness of meaning or purport. In this, as in its more common application to a course with clearly perceptible direction, the word stresses continuity and absence of divagation <his answer was bellicose in *tenor*> <along the cool sequestered vale of life they kept the noiseless *tenor* of their way —Thomas Gray> CURRENT implies a clearly defined but not necessarily unalterable course <no *current* should be yielded to merely because it is strong —R. M. Hutchins> <he has not . . . changed the *current* of our constitutional law —M. R. Cohen>

ten·den·tious *also* **ten·den·cious** \ten-ˈden-chəs\ *adj* **:** marked by a tendency in favor of a particular point of view **:** BIASED — **ten·den·tious·ly** *adv* — **ten·den·tious·ness** *n*

¹ten·der \ˈten-dər\ *adj* [ME, fr. OF *tendre,* fr. L *tener*] **1 a :** having a soft or yielding texture **:** easily broken, cut, or damaged **:** DELICATE, FRAGILE <~ feet> **b :** easily chewed **:** SUCCULENT **2 a :** physically weak **:** not able to endure hardship **b :** IMMATURE, YOUNG <children of ~ years> **c :** incapable of resisting cold **:** not hardy **3 :** marked by, responding to, or expressing the softer emotions **:** FOND, LOVING <a ~ lover> **4 a :** showing care **:** CONSIDERATE, SOLICITOUS <~ regard> **b :** highly susceptible to impressions or emotions **:** IMPRESSIONABLE <a ~ conscience> **5 a :** appropriate or conducive to a delicate or sensitive constitution or character **:** GENTLE, MILD <~ breeding> <~ irony> **b :** delicate or soft in quality or tone <never before heard the piano sound so ~ —Elva S. Daniels> **6** *obs* **:** DEAR, PRECIOUS **7 a :** sensitive to touch or palpation <~ skin> **b :** sensitive to injury or insult **:** TOUCHY <~ pride> **c :** demanding careful and sensitive handling **:** TICKLISH <a ~ situation> **d** *of a ship* **:** inclined to heel over easily under sail — **ten·der·ly** *adv* — **ten·der·ness** *n*

²tender *vb* **ten·dered; ten·der·ing** \-d(ə-)riŋ\ *vt* **1 :** to make tender **:** SOFTEN, WEAKEN **2** *archaic* **:** to regard or treat with tenderness ~ *vi* **:** to become tender

³tender *n* [¹*tender*] *obs* **:** CONSIDERATION, REGARD

⁴tend·er \ˈten-dər\ *n* **:** one that tends: as **a (1) :** a ship employed to attend other ships (as to supply provisions) **(2) :** a boat or small steamer for communication between shore and a larger ship **(3) :** a warship that provides logistic support **b :** a vehicle attached to a locomotive for carrying a supply of fuel and water

⁵ten·der *n* [MF *tendre* to stretch, stretch out, offer — more at TEND] **1 :** an unconditional offer of money or service in satisfaction of a debt or obligation made to save a penalty or forfeiture for nonpayment or nonperformance **2 :** an offer or proposal made for acceptance: as **a :** an offer of a bid for a contract **b :** a public expression of willingness to buy not less than a specified number of shares of a stock at a fixed price from stockholders usu. in an attempt to gain control of the issuing company — called also *tender offer* **3 :** something that may be offered in payment; *specif* **:** MONEY

⁶ten·der *vb* **ten·dered; ten·der·ing** \-d(ə-)riŋ\ *vt* **1 :** to make a tender of **2 :** to present for acceptance **:** PROFFER <~*ed* his resignation> ~ *vi* **:** to make a bid <the nuclear consortia ~ for and build . . . power stations —Christopher Hinton>

ten·der·foot \ˈten-dər-ˌfu̇t\ *n, pl* **ten·der·feet** \-ˌfēt\ *also* **ten·der·foots** \-ˌfu̇ts\ **1 :** a newcomer in a comparatively rough or newly settled region; *esp* **:** one not hardened to frontier or outdoor life **2 :** an inexperienced beginner **:** NOVICE <a political ~>

ten·der·heart·ed \ˌten-dər-ˈhärt-əd\ *adj* **:** easily moved to love, pity, or sorrow **:** COMPASSIONATE, IMPRESSIONABLE — **ten·der·heart·ed·ly** *adv* — **ten·der·heart·ed·ness** *n*

ten·der–heft·ed \-ˈhef-təd\ *adj* [¹*tender* + *heft,* alter. of *haft* handle] *archaic* **:** TENDERHEARTED

ten·der·ize \ˈten-də-ˌrīz\ *vt* **-ized; -iz·ing :** to make (meat or meat products) tender by applying a process or substance that breaks down connective tissue — **ten·der·iza·tion** \ˌten-d(ə-)rə-ˈzā-shən\ *n* — **ten·der·iz·er** \ˈten-də-ˌrī-zər\ *n*

ten·der·loin \ˈten-dər-ˌlȯin\ *n* **1 :** a strip of tender meat consisting of a large internal muscle of the loin on each side of the vertebral column **2** [fr. its making possible a luxurious diet for a corrupt policeman] **:** a district of a city largely devoted to vice

ten·der–mind·ed \ˌten-dər-ˈmīn-dəd\ *adj* **:** marked by idealism, optimism, and dogmatism; *esp* **:** reluctant to test assumptions by facts

ten·der·om·e·ter \ˌten-də-ˈräm-ət-ər\ *n* **:** a device for determining the maturity and tenderness of samples of fruits and vegetables

ten·di·nous \ˈten-də-nəs\ *adj* [NL *tendinosus,* fr. *tendin-, tendo* tendon, alter. of ML *tendon-, tendo*] **1 :** of, relating to, or resembling a tendon **2 :** consisting of tendons **:** SINEWY <~ tissue>

ten·don \ˈten-dən\ *n* [ML *tendon-, tendo,* fr. L *tendere* to stretch — more at THIN] **:** a tough cord or band of dense white fibrous connective tissue that unites a muscle with some other part and transmits the force which the muscle exerts

tendon of Achil·les \-ə-ˈkil-ēz\ **:** ACHILLES TENDON

ten·dresse \tän-dres\ *n* [F, fr. MF, fr. *tendre* tender] **:** FONDNESS

ten·dril \ˈten-drəl\ *n* [perh. modif. of MF *tendron,* alter. of *tendon,* lit., tendon, fr. ML *tendon-, tendo*] **1 :** a leaf, stipule, or stem modified into a slender spirally coiling sensitive organ serving to attach a plant to its support **2 :** something (as a ringlet of hair) that curls like a tendril — **ten·driled** *or* **ten·drilled** \-drəld\ *adj* — **ten·dril·ous** \-drə-ləs\ *adj*

¹-tene \ˌtēn\ *adj comb form* [L *taenia* ribbon, band — more at TAENIA] **:** having (such or so many) chromosomal filaments <poly*tene*> <pachy*tene*>

²-tene *n comb form* **:** stage of meiotic prophase characterized by (such) chromosomal filaments <diplo*tene*> <pachy*tene*>

Ten·e·brae \ˈten-ə-ˌbrā, -ˌbrī, -ˌbrē\ *n pl but sing or pl in constr* [ML, fr. L, darkness — more at TEMERITY] **:** the office of matins and lauds for the last three days of Holy Week commemorating the sufferings and death of Christ

ten·e·brif·ic \ˌten-ə-ˈbrif-ik\ *adj* [L *tenebrae* darkness] **1 :** GLOOMY **2 :** causing gloom or darkness

1, tendril 1

te·ne·bri·o·nid \tə-ˈneb-rē-ə-nəd, ˌten-ə-ˈbrī-ə-nəd\ *n* [NL *Tenebrionidae,* group name, fr. *Tenebrion-, Tenebrio,* type genus, fr. L, one that shuns the light, fr. *tenebrae* darkness] **:** any of a family (Tenebrionidae) of firm-bodied mostly dark-colored vegetable-feeding beetles which often have the hind wings vestigial and functionless and whose larvae are usu. hard cylindrical worms — **tenebrionid** *adj*

te·neb·ri·ous \tə-ˈneb-rē-əs\ *adj* [by alter.] **:** TENEBROUS

ten·e·brism \ˈten-ə-ˌbriz-əm\ *n, often cap* [L *tenebrae* darkness] **:** a style of painting esp. associated with the Italian painter Caravaggio and his followers in which most of the figures are engulfed in shadow but some are dramatically illuminated by a concentrated beam of light usu. from an identifiable source — **ten·e·brist** \-brəst\ *n or adj, often cap*

ten·e·brous \ˈten-ə-brəs\ *adj* [ME, fr. MF *tenebreus,* fr. L *tenebrosus,* fr. *tenebrae*] **1 :** shut off from the light **:** DARK, MURKY **2 :** hard to understand **:** OBSCURE **3 :** causing gloom

1080 *also* **ten-eighty** \te-ˈnāt-ē\ *n* [fr. its laboratory serial number] **:** a poisonous substance that is chemically sodium fluoroacetate $C_2H_2FNaO_2$ and is used as a rodenticide

ten·e·ment \ˈten-ə-mənt\ *n* [ME, fr. MF, fr. ML *tenementum,* fr. L *tenēre* to hold — more at THIN] **1 :** land or any of various forms of incorporeal property treated like land that is held by one person from another **:** HOLDING **2 a :** a house used as a dwelling **:** RESIDENCE **b :** APARTMENT, FLAT **c :** TENEMENT HOUSE **3 :** DWELLING

ten·e·men·ta·ry \ˌten-ə-ˈment-ə-rē, -ˈmen-trē\ *adj* **:** consisting of tenements

tenement house *n* **:** APARTMENT HOUSE; *esp* **:** one meeting minimum standards of sanitation, safety, and comfort and occupied by poorer families usu. in a city

te·nes·mus \tə-ˈnez-məs\ *n* [L, fr. Gk *teinesmos,* fr. *teinein* to stretch, strain — more at THIN] **:** a distressing but ineffectual urge to evacuate the rectum or bladder

te·net \ˈten-ət *also* ˈtē-nət\ *n* [L, he holds, fr. *tenēre* to hold] **:** a principle, belief, or doctrine generally held to be true; *esp* **:** one held in common by members of an organization, group, movement, or profession ***syn*** see DOCTRINE

ten·fold \ˈten-ˌfōld, -ˈfōld\ *adj* **1 :** having 10 units or members **2 :** being 10 times as great or as many — **ten·fold** \-ˈfōld\ *adv*

ten-gallon hat *n* [fr. its great size] **:** COWBOY HAT

te·nia *var of* TAENIA

te·ni·a·sis *var of* TAENIASIS

Tenn *abbr* Tennessee

Ten·nes·see walking horse \ˈten-ə-ˌsē-\ *n* [*Tennessee,* U.S.] **:** any of an American breed of large easy-gaited saddle horses largely of Standardbred and Morgan ancestry — called also *Tennessee walker*

ten·nis \ˈten-əs\ *n, often attrib* [ME *tenetz, tenys*] **1 :** COURT TENNIS **2 :** a typically outdoor game that is played with rackets and a light elastic ball by two players or pairs of players on a level court (as of clay or grass) divided by a low net

tennis shoe *n* **:** SNEAKER

ten·nist \ˈten-əst\ *n* [blend of *tennis* and *-ist*] **:** a tennis player

¹ten·on \ˈten-ən\ *n* [ME, fr. OF, fr. *tenir* to hold — more at TENABLE] **:** a projecting member in a piece of wood or other material for insertion into a mortise to make a joint — see DOVETAIL illustration

²tenon *vt* **1 :** to unite by a tenon **2 :** to cut or fit for insertion in a mortise

¹ten·or \ˈten-ər\ *n* [ME, fr. OF, fr. L *tenor* uninterrupted course, fr. *tenēre* to hold — more at THIN] **1 a :** the drift of something spoken or written **:** PURPORT **b :** an exact copy of a writing **:** TRANSCRIPT **c :** the concept, object, or person meant in a metaphor **2 a :** the melodic line usu. forming the cantus firmus in medieval music **b :** the next to the lowest part in 4-part harmony **c :** the highest natural adult male singing voice; *also* **:** a person having this voice **d :** a member of a family of instruments having a range next higher than that of the bass **3 :** a continuance in a course, movement, or activity ***syn*** see TENDENCY

²tenor *adj* **:** relating to or having the range or part of a tenor

te·no·syn·o·vi·tis \ˈten-ō-ˌsin-ə-ˈvīt-əs, ˌtē-nō-\ *n* [NL, fr. Gk *tenōn* tendon + NL *synovitis;* akin to Gk *teinein* to stretch — more at THIN] **:** inflammation of a tendon sheath

ten·our \ˈten-ər\ *chiefly Brit var of* TENOR

ten·pen·ny \ˌten-ˌpen-ē, *Brit* -pə-nē-\ *adj* **:** amounting to, worth, or costing ten pennies

tenpenny nail *n* [fr. its original price per hundred] **:** a nail 3 inches long

ten·pin \ˈten-ˌpin\ *n* **1 :** a bottle-shaped bowling pin 15 inches high **2** *pl but sing in constr* **:** a bowling game using 10 tenpins and a large ball 27 inches in circumference and allowing each player to bowl 2 balls in each of 10 frames

ten·pound·er \ˈten-ˈpau̇n-dər\ *n* **:** LADYFISH 2

ten·rec \'ten-ˌrek\ *n* [F, fr. Malagasy *tàndraka*] **:** any of numerous small often spiny insectivorous mammals (family Tenrecidae) of Madagascar

[1]**tense** \'ten(t)s\ *n* [ME *tens* time, tense, fr. MF, fr. L *tempus* — more at TEMPORAL] **1 :** a distinction of form in a verb to express distinctions of time or duration of the action or state it denotes **2 a :** a set of inflectional forms of a verb that express distinctions of time **b :** a particular inflectional form of a verb expressing a specific time distinction

[2]**tense** *adj* **tens·er; tens·est** [L *tensus,* fr. pp. of *tendere* to stretch — more at THIN] **1 :** stretched tight **:** made taut **:** RIGID **2 a :** feeling or showing nervous tension **b :** marked by strain or suspense **3 :** produced with the muscles involved in a relatively tense state <the vowels \ē\ and \ü\ in contrast with the vowels \i\ and \u̇\ are ~> ***syn* 1** see TIGHT ***ant*** relaxed **2** see STIFF ***ant*** expansive — **tense·ly** *adv* — **tense·ness** *n*

[3]**tense** *vb* **tensed; tens·ing** *vt* **:** to make tense ~ *vi* **:** to become tense

ten·sile \'ten(t)-səl *also* 'ten-ˌsīl\ *adj* **1 :** capable of tension **:** DUCTILE **2 :** of, relating to, or involving tension <~ stress> — **ten·sil·i·ty** \ten-'sil-ət-ē\ *n*

tensile strength *n* **:** the greatest longitudinal stress a substance can bear without tearing apart

ten·sim·e·ter \ten-'sim-ət-ər\ *n* [*tension* + *-meter*] **:** an instrument for measuring differences of vapor pressure

ten·si·om·e·ter \ˌten(t)-sē-'äm-ət-ər\ *n* [*tension*] **1** *or* **ten·som·e·ter** \ten-'säm-\ [[2]*tense*] **:** a device for measuring tension (as of fabric, yarn, or structural material) **2 :** an instrument for determining the moisture content of soil **3 :** an instrument for measuring the surface tension of liquids — **ten·sio·met·ric** \-sē-ō-'me-trik\ *adj* — **ten·si·om·e·try** \-sē-'äm-ə-trē\ *n*

[1]**ten·sion** \'ten-chən\ *n* [MF or L; MF, fr. L *tension-, tensio,* fr. *tensus,* pp.] **1 a :** the act or action of stretching or the condition or degree of being stretched to stiffness **:** TAUTNESS **b :** STRESS 1b **2 a :** either of two balancing forces causing or tending to cause extension **b :** the stress resulting from the elongation of an elastic body **c** *archaic* **:** PRESSURE **3 a :** inner striving, unrest, or imbalance often with physiological indication of emotion **b :** a state of latent hostility or opposition between individuals or groups **c :** a balance maintained in an artistic work between opposing forces or elements **4 :** electrical potential **5 :** a device to produce a desired tension (as in a loom) — **ten·sion·al** \'tench-nəl, -ən-ᵊl\ *adj* — **ten·sion·less** \'ten-chən-ləs\ *adj*

[2]**tension** *vt* **ten·sioned; ten·sion·ing** \'tench-(ə-)niŋ\ **:** to subject to tension; *esp* **:** to tighten to a desired or appropriate degree — **ten·sion·er** \-(ə-)nər\ *n*

ten·si·ty \'ten(t)-sət-ē\ *n, pl* **-ties :** the quality or state of being tense **:** TENSENESS

ten·sive \'ten(t)-siv\ *adj* **:** of, relating to, or causing tension

ten·sor \'ten(t)-sər, 'ten-ˌsȯ(ə)r\ *n* [NL, fr. L *tensus,* pp.] **1 :** a muscle that stretches a part **2 :** a generalized vector with more than three components each of which is a function of the coordinates of an arbitrary point in space of an appropriate number of dimensions

ten–strike \'ten-ˌstrīk\ *n* **1 :** a strike in tenpins **2 :** a highly successful stroke or achievement

[1]**tent** \'tent\ *n* [ME *tente,* fr. OF, fr. L *tenta,* fem. of *tentus,* pp. of *tendere* to stretch — more at THIN] **1 :** a collapsible shelter of canvas or other material stretched and sustained by poles and used for camping outdoors or as a temporary building **2 :** DWELLING **3 a :** something that resembles a tent or that serves as a shelter; *esp* **:** a canopy or enclosure placed over the head and shoulders to retain vapors or oxygen during medical administration **b :** the web of a tent caterpillar — **tent·less** \'tent-ləs\ *adj*

[2]**tent** *vi* **1 :** to reside for the time being **:** LODGE **2 :** to live in a tent ~ *vt* **1 :** to cover with or as if with a tent **2 :** to lodge in tents

[3]**tent** *vt* [ME *tenten,* fr. *tent* attention, short for *attent,* fr OF *attente,* fr. *attendre* to attend] *chiefly Scot* **:** to attend to

ten·ta·cle \'tent-i-kəl\ *n* [NL *tentaculum* fr. L *tentare* to feel, touch — more at TEMPT] **1 :** any of various elongate flexible usu. tactile or prehensile processes borne by animals chiefly on the head or about the mouth **2 a :** something that functions like a tentacle in grasping or feeling out **b :** a sensitive hair or emergence on a plant (as the sundew) — **ten·ta·cled** \-kəld\ *adj*

ten·tac·u·lar \ten-'tak-yə-lər\ *adj* [NL *tentaculum*] **1 :** of, relating to, or resembling tentacles **2 :** equipped with tentacles

tent·age \'tent-ij\ *n* **:** a collection of tents **:** tent equipment

ten·ta·tive \'tent-ət-iv\ *adj* [ML *tentativus,* fr. L *tentatus,* pp. of *tentare* to feel, try — more at TEMPT] **1 :** not fully worked out or developed <~ plans> **2 :** HESITANT, UNCERTAIN <a ~ smile> — **tentative** *n* — **ten·ta·tive·ly** *adv* — **ten·ta·tive·ness** *n*

tent caterpillar *n* **:** any of several destructive gregarious caterpillars (genus *Malacosoma* and esp. *M. americanum* of the family Lasiocampidae) that construct large silken webs on trees

tent·ed \'tent-əd\ *adj* **1 :** covered with a tent or tents **2 :** shaped like a tent

ten·ter \'tent-ər\ *n* [ME *teyntur, tentowre*] **1 :** a frame or endless track with hooks or clips along two sides that is used for drying and stretching cloth **2** *archaic* **:** TENTERHOOK

ten·ter·hook \'tent-ər-ˌhu̇k\ *n* **:** a sharp hooked nail used esp. for fastening cloth on a tenter — **on tenterhooks :** in a state of uneasiness, strain, or suspense

tenth–rate \'ten-'thrāt\ *adj* **:** of the lowest character or quality

tent·mak·er \'tent-ˌmā-kər\ *n* **:** one that makes tents

tent stitch *n* **:** a short stitch slanting to the right that is used in embroidery and canvas work to form even lines of solid background

tenty *also* **tent·ie** \'tent-ē\ *adj* [[3]*tent*] *Scot* **:** ATTENTIVE, WATCHFUL

ten·u·is \'ten-yə-wəs\ *n, pl* **-u·es** \-yə-ˌwēz, -ˌwās\ [ML, fr. L, thin, slight] **:** an unaspirated voiceless stop

te·nu·ity \te-'n(y)ü-ət-ē, tə-\ *n* [L *tenuitas,* fr. *tenuis* thin, tenuous] **1 :** lack of substance or strength **2 :** lack of thickness **:** SLENDERNESS, THINNESS **3 :** lack of density **:** rarefied quality or state

ten·u·ous \'ten-yə-wəs\ *adj* [L *tenuis* thin, slight, tenuous — more at THIN] **1 :** not dense **:** RARE <a ~ fluid> **2 :** not thick **:** SLENDER <a ~ rope> **3 :** having little substance or strength **:** FLIMSY, WEAK <~ influences> <a ~ hold on reality> ***syn*** see THIN ***ant*** dense — **ten·u·ous·ly** *adv* — **ten·u·ous·ness** *n*

ten·ure \'ten-yər *also* -ˌyu̇(ə)r\ *n* [ME, fr. OF *teneüre, tenure,* fr. ML *tenitura,* fr. (assumed) VL *tenitus,* pp. of L *tenēre* to hold — more at THIN] **1 :** the act, right, manner, or term of holding something (as a landed property, a position, or an office); *esp* **:** a status granted after a trial period to a teacher protecting him from summary dismissal **2 :** GRASP, HOLD — **te·nur·ial** \te-'nyu̇r-ē-əl\ *adj* — **te·nur·ial·ly** \-ə-lē\ *adv*

ten·ured \'ten-yərd\ *adj* **:** having tenure <~ faculty members>

te·nu·to \tā-'nüt-(ˌ)ō\ *adv or adj* [It, fr. pp. of *tenere* to hold, fr. L *tenēre*] **:** in a manner so as to hold a tone or chord to its full value — used as a direction in music

te·o·cal·li \ˌtē-ə-'kal-ē, ˌtā-ə-'käl-\ *n* [Nahuatl, fr. *teotl* god + *calli* house] **:** an ancient temple of Mexico or Central America usu. built upon the summit of a truncated pyramidal mound; *also* **:** the mound itself

teo·na·na·catl \ˌtā-ō-ˌnän-ə-'kät-ᵊl\ *n* [Nahuatl, fr. *teotl* god + *nanacatl* mushroom] **:** any of several New World mushrooms (*Psilocybe* and related genera of the family Agaricaceae) that are sources of hallucinogens

te·o·sin·te \ˌtā-ō-'sint-ē\ *n* [MexSp, fr. Nahuatl *teocentli,* fr. *teotl* god + *centli* ear of corn] **:** a large annual fodder grass (*Euchlaena mexicana*) of Mexico and Central America closely related to and possibly ancestral to maize

te·pa \'tē-pə\ *n* [*t*ri- + *e*thylene + *p*hosphor- + *a*mide] **:** a soluble crystalline compound $C_6H_{12}N_3OP$ that is used esp. as a chemosterilant of insects, an alleviant in some kinds of cancer, and in finishing and flame-proofing textiles

te·pa·ry bean \'tep-ə-rē-\ *n* [origin unknown] **:** an annual twining bean (*Phaseolus acutifolius* var. *latifolius*) that is native to the southwestern U.S. and Mexico and is cultivated for its roundish white, yellow, brown, or bluish black edible seeds

te·pee \'tē-(ˌ)pē\ *n* [Dakota *tipi,* fr. *ti* to dwell + *pi* to use for] **:** an American Indian conical tent usu. consisting of skins and used esp. by the Plains peoples

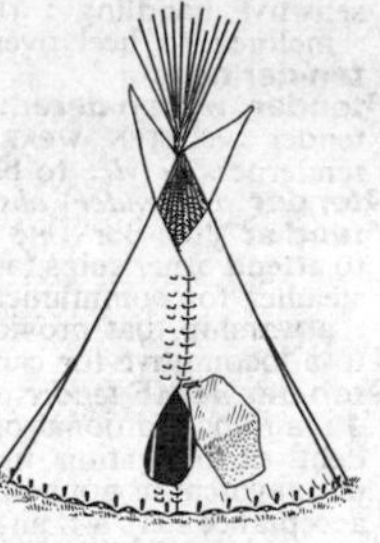
tepee

teph·ra \'tef-rə\ *n* [NL, fr. Gk, ashes] **:** solid material ejected during the eruption of a volcano and transported through the air

tep·id \'tep-əd\ *adj* [L *tepidus,* fr. *tepēre* to be moderately warm; akin to Skt *tapati* it gives out heat, OIr *tess* heat] **1 :** moderately warm **:** LUKEWARM <a ~ bath> **2 :** marked by an absence of enthusiasm or conviction <a ~ interest> — **te·pid·i·ty** \tə-'pid-ət-ē, te-\ *n* — **tep·id·ly** \'tep-əd-lē\ *adv* — **tep·id·ness** *n*

TEPP \ˌtē-ˌē-ˌpē-'pē\ *n* [*te*tra*e*thyl *py*ro*p*hosphate] **:** a mobile hygroscopic corrosive liquid organophosphate $C_8H_{20}O_7P_2$ that is a powerful anticholinesterase and is used as an insecticide and parasympathomimetic agent

te·qui·la \tə-'kē-lə, tā-\ *n* [Sp, fr. *Tequila,* district of Mexico] **1 :** a Mexican century plant (*Agave tequilana*) much cultivated as a source of mescal **2 :** a Mexican liquor made by redistilling mescal

ter *abbr* **1** terrace **2** territory

ter- *comb form* [L, fr. *ter;* akin to Gk & Skt *tris* three times, L *tres* three — more at THREE] **:** three times **:** threefold **:** three <*ter*centenary>

tera- \'ter-ə\ *comb form* [ISV, fr. Gk *teras* monster — more at TERATOLOGY] **:** TRILLION <*tera*ton> <*tera*hertz>

te·rai \tə-'rī\ *n* [*Tarai,* lowland belt of India] **:** a wide-brimmed double felt sun hat worn esp. in subtropical regions

ter·aph \'ter-əf\ *n, pl* **ter·a·phim** \'ter-ə-ˌfim\ [Heb *tərāphīm* (pl. in form but sing. in meaning)] **:** an image of a Semitic household god

te·rato·gen \tə-'rat-ə-jən\ *n* **:** a teratogenic agent

ter·a·to·gen·e·sis \ˌter-ət-ə-'jen-ə-səs\ *n* [NL, fr. Gk *terat-, teras* monster + *genesis*] **:** production of monstrous growths or fetuses

ter·a·to·gen·ic \-'jen-ik\ *adj* **:** tending to cause developmental malformations and monstrosities — **ter·a·to·ge·nic·i·ty** \-jə-'nis-ət-ē\ *n*

ter·a·to·log·i·cal \ˌter-ət-ᵊl-'äj-i-kəl\ *or* **ter·a·to·log·ic** \-ik\ *adj* **1 :** abnormal in growth or structure **2 :** of or relating to teratology

ter·a·tol·o·gy \ˌter-ə-'täl-ə-jē\ *n* [Gk *terat-, teras* marvel, monster + ISV *-logy;* akin to Lith *keras* enchantment] **:** the study of malformations, monstrosities, or serious deviations from the normal type in organisms — **ter·a·tol·o·gist** \-jəst\ *n*

ter·a·to·ma \ˌter-ə-'tō-mə\ *n* [NL, fr. Gk *terat-, teras* monster] **:** a tumor made up of a heterogeneous mixture of tissues — **ter·a·to·ma·tous** \-mət-əs\ *adj*

ter·bi·um \'tər-bē-əm\ *n* [NL, fr. *Ytterby,* Sweden] **:** a usu. trivalent metallic element of the rare-earth group — see ELEMENT table

terbium metal *n* **:** any of several rare-earth metals separable as a group from other metals and including terbium, europium, gadolinium, and sometimes dysprosium

terce \'tərs\ *n* [ME, third, terce — more at TIERCE] *often cap* **:** the third of the canonical hours

ter·cel \'tər-səl\ *var of* TIERCEL

ter·cen·te·na·ry \ˌtər-(ˌ)sen-'ten-ə-rē, (ˈ)tər-'sent-ᵊn-ˌer-ē\ *n, pl* **-ries :** a 300th anniversary or its celebration — **tercentenary** *adj*

ter·cen·ten·ni·al \ˌtər-(ˌ)sen-'ten-ē-əl\ *adj or n* **:** TERCENTENARY

ter·cet \'tər-sət, ˌtər-'set\ *n* [It *terzetto,* fr. dim. of *terzo* third, fr. L *tertius* — more at THIRD] **:** a unit or group of three lines of verse: **a :** one of the 3-line stanzas in terza rima **b :** one of the two groups of three lines forming the sestet in an Italian sonnet

ter·e·bene \'ter-ə-ˌbēn\ *n* [F *térébène,* fr. *térébinthe* terebinth] : a mixture of terpenes from oil of turpentine
te·re·bic \tə-'reb-ik, -'rēb-\ *adj* [L *terebinthus* terebinth] : of, relating to, or constituting a white crystalline acid $C_7H_{10}O_4$ obtained esp. by the oxidation of oil of turpentine
ter·e·binth \'ter-ə-ˌbin(t)th\ *n* [ME *terebynt,* fr. MF *terebinthe,* fr. L *terebinthus* — more at TURPENTINE] : a small European tree (*Pistacia terebinthus*) of the sumac family yielding Chian turpentine
ter·e·bin·thine \ˌter-ə-'bin(t)-thən, -'bin-ˌthīn\ *adj* [L *terebinthinus* of the terebinth] : consisting of or resembling turpentine
te·re·do \tə-'rēd-(ˌ)ō, -'rād-\ *n, pl* **teredos** *or* **te·red·i·nes** \-'red-ᵊn-ˌēz\ [L *teredin-, teredo,* fr. Gk *terēdōn;* akin to Gk *tetrainein* to bore — more at THROW] : SHIPWORM
tere·phthal·ate \ˌter-ə(f)-'thal-ˌāt\ *n* : a salt or ester of terephthalic acid; *esp* : a dimethyl ester that is a major starting material for polyester fibers and coatings
tere·phthal·ic acid \ˌter-ə(f)-ˌthal-ik-\ *n* [ISV *tere*bene + *phthalic acid*] : a *p*-dicarboxylic acid $C_8H_6O_2$ that is obtained esp. by oxidation of turpentine and is used chiefly in the synthesis of polyesters
te·rete \tə-'rēt, te-\ *adj* [L *teret-, teres* well turned, rounded; akin to L *terere* to rub — more at THROW] : approximately cylindrical but usu. tapering at both ends <a ~ seedpod>
Te·reus \'tir-ˌyüs, 'tē-ˌrüs\ *n* [L, fr. Gk *Tēreus*] : the husband of Procne who violates his sister-in-law Philomela
ter·gite \'tər-ˌgīt\ *n* [ISV *terg-* (fr. L *tergum* back) + *-ite*] : the dorsal plate or dorsal portion of the covering of a metameric segment of an articulate animal; *esp* : one on the abdomen
ter·gi·ver·sate \ˌtər-'jiv-ər-ˌsāt, -'giv-; ˌtər-jə-'vər-\ *vi* **-sat·ed; -sat·ing** [L *tergiversatus,* pp. of *tergiversari* to turn the back, shuffle, fr. *tergum* back + *versare* to turn, fr. *versus,* pp. of *vertere* to turn — more at WORTH] **1** : to become a renegade : APOSTATIZE **2** : to use subterfuges : EQUIVOCATE — **ter·gi·ver·sa·tor** \-ˌsāt-ər\ *n*
ter·gi·ver·sa·tion \ˌtər-ˌjiv-ər-'sā-shən, -ˌgiv-; ˌtər-ji-(ˌ)vər-\ *n* **1** : desertion of a cause, party, or faith **2** : evasion of straightforward action or clear-cut statement : EQUIVOCATION
ter·gum \'tər-gəm\ *n, pl* **ter·ga** \-gə\ [NL, fr. L, back] : the dorsal part or plate of a segment of an arthropod : TERGITE, NOTUM — **ter·gal** \-gəl\ *adj*
ter·i·ya·ki \ˌter-ē-'(y)äk-ē\ *n* [Jap] : a Japanese dish of meat, chicken, or shellfish that is grilled or broiled after being soaked in a spicy soy sauce marinade
[1]**term** \'tərm\ *n* [ME *terme* boundary, end, fr. OF, fr. L *terminus;* akin to Gk *termōn* boundary, end, Skt *tarati* he crosses over — more at THROUGH] **1 a** : END, TERMINATION; *also* : a point in time assigned to something (as a payment) **b** : the time at which a pregnancy of normal length terminates <had her baby at full ~> **2 a** : a limited or definite extent of time; *esp* : the time for which something lasts : DURATION, TENURE **b** : the whole period for which an estate is granted; *also* : the estate or interest held by one for a term **c** : the time during which a court is in session **3** : division in a school year during which instruction is regularly given to students **4 a** : a unitary or compound expression connected with another by a plus or minus sign **b** : an element of a fraction or proportion or of a series or sequence **5** : one of the three substantive elements of a syllogism **6 a** : a word or expression that has a precise meaning in some uses or is peculiar to a science, art, profession, or subject <legal ~*s*> **b** *pl* : diction of a specified kind **7** *pl* : provisions that are stated or offered for acceptance and that determine the nature and scope of an agreement : CONDITIONS <~*s* of sale> <liberal credit ~*s*> **8** *pl* **a** : mutual relationship **b** : AGREEMENT, CONCORD **9** : a boundary post or stone; *esp* : a quadrangular pillar often tapering downward and adorned with a head or upper body — **in terms of** : with respect to or in relation to <thinks of everything *in terms of* money>
[2]**term** *vt* : to apply a term to : CALL, NAME
[1]**ter·ma·gant** \'tər-mə-gənt\ *n* [ME] **1** *cap* : a legendary Muslim deity represented in early English drama as a boisterous character **2** : an overbearing or nagging woman : SHREW
[2]**termagant** *adj* : OVERBEARING, SHREWISH <life . . . wrecked by a ~ mother —*Newsweek*> — **ter·ma·gant·ly** *adv*
term·er \'tər-mər\ *n* : a person serving for a specified term (as in a political office or in prison) <a first ~>
ter·mi·na·ble \'tərm-(ə-)nə-bəl\ *adj* [ME, fr. *terminen* to terminate, fr. OF *terminer,* fr. L *terminare*] : capable of being terminated — **ter·mi·na·ble·ness** *n* — **ter·mi·na·bly** \-blē\ *adv*
[1]**ter·mi·nal** \'tərm-nəl, -ən-ᵊl\ *adj* [L *terminalis,* fr. *terminus*] **1 a** : of or relating to an end, extremity, boundary, or terminus <a ~ pillar> **b** : growing at the end of a branch or stem <a ~ bud> **2 a** : of, relating to, or occurring in a term or each term <~ payments> **b** : occurring at or contributing to the end of life <~ cancer> **3 a** : occurring at or constituting the end of a period or series : CONCLUDING <the ~ moments of life> **b** : not intended as preparation for further academic work <a ~ curriculum> ***syn*** see LAST ***ant*** initial — **ter·mi·nal·ly** \-ē\ *adv*
[2]**terminal** *n* **1** : a part that forms the end : EXTREMITY, TERMINATION **2** : a terminating usu. ornamental detail : FINIAL **3** : a device attached to the end of a wire or cable or to an electrical apparatus for convenience in making connections **4 a** : either end of a carrier line (as a railroad, trucking or shipping line, or airline) with classifying yards, dock and lighterage facilities, management offices, storage sheds, and freight and passenger stations **b** : a freight or passenger station that is central to a considerable area or serves as a junction at any point with other lines **c** : a town or city at the end of a carrier line : TERMINUS **5** : a device (as a teletypewriter) through which a user can communicate with a computer
terminal leave *n* : a final leave consisting of accumulated unused leave granted to a member of the armed forces just prior to his separation or discharge from service
[1]**ter·mi·nate** \'tər-mə-ˌnāt\ *vb* **-nat·ed; -nat·ing** [L *terminatus,* pp. of *terminare,* fr. *terminus*] *vt* **1 a** : to bring to an end : CLOSE <~ a marriage by divorce> **b** : to form the conclusion of <review questions ~ each chapter> **c** : to discontinue the employment of <workers *terminated* because of slow business> **2** : to serve as an ending, limit, or boundary of ~ *vi* **1** : to extend only to a limit (as a point or line); *esp* : to reach a terminus **2** : to come to an end in time **3** : to form an ending ***syn*** see CLOSE
[2]**ter·mi·nate** \-nət\ *adj* : coming to an end or capable of ending
terminating decimal *n* : a decimal that can be expressed in a finite number of figures — compare REPEATING DECIMAL
ter·mi·na·tion \ˌtər-mə-'nā-shən\ *n* **1** : end in time or existence : CONCLUSION <the ~ of life> **2** : a limit in space or extent : BOUND **3** : the last part of a word; *esp* : an inflectional ending **4** : the act of terminating **5** : OUTCOME, RESULT ***syn*** see END ***ant*** inception, source — **ter·mi·na·tion·al** \-shnəl, -shən-ᵊl\ *adj*
ter·mi·na·tive \'tər-mə-ˌnāt-iv\ *adj* : tending or serving to terminate : ENDING — **ter·mi·na·tive·ly** *adv*
ter·mi·na·tor \-ˌnāt-ər\ *n* **1** : one that terminates **2** : the dividing line between the illuminated and the unilluminated part of the moon's or a planet's disk
ter·mi·nol·o·gy \ˌtər-mə-'näl-ə-jē\ *n* [ML *terminus* term, expression (fr. L, boundary, limit) + E *-o-* + *-logy*] **1** : the technical or special terms used in a business, art, science, or special subject **2** : nomenclature as a field of study — **ter·mi·no·log·i·cal** \-mən-ᵊl-'äj-i-kəl\ *adj* — **ter·mi·no·log·i·cal·ly** \-i-k(ə-)lē\ *adv*
term insurance *n* : insurance for a specified period that provides for no payment to the insured except on losses during the period and that becomes void upon its expiration
ter·mi·nus \'tər-mə-nəs\ *n, pl* **-ni** \-ˌnī, -ˌnē\ *or* **-nus·es** [L, boundary, end — more at TERM] **1** : a final goal : a finishing point **2** : a post or stone marking a boundary **3** : either end of a transportation line or travel route; *also* : the station, town, or city at such a place : TERMINAL **4** : an extreme point or element : TIP <the ~ of a glacier> ***syn*** see END ***ant*** starting point
terminus ad quem \-ˌäd-'kwem\ *n* [NL, lit., limit to which] **1** : a goal, object, or course of action : DESTINATION, PURPOSE **2** : a final limiting point in time
terminus a quo \-ˌä-'kwō\ *n* [NL, lit., limit from which] **1** : a point of origin **2** : the first of two limiting points in time
ter·mi·tar·i·um \ˌtər-mə-'ter-ē-əm, -ˌmī-\ *n, pl* **-ia** \-ē-ə\ [NL] : a termites' nest
ter·mite \'tər-ˌmīt\ *n* [NL *Termit-, Termes,* genus of termites, fr. LL, a worm that eats wood, alter. of L *tarmit-, tarmes;* akin to Gk *tetrainein* to bore — more at THROW] : any of numerous pale-colored soft-bodied social insects (order Isoptera) that live in colonies consisting of winged sexual forms, wingless sterile workers, and often soldiers, feed on wood, and include some which are very destructive to wooden structures and trees — called also *white ant*

termite

term·less \'tərm-ləs\ *adj* **1** : having no term or end : BOUNDLESS, UNENDING **2** : UNCONDITIONED, UNCONDITIONAL
term paper *n* : a major written assignment in a school or college course representative of a student's achievement during a term
term·time \'tərm-ˌtīm\ *n* : the time during an academic or legal term
tern \'tərn\ *n* [of Scand origin; akin to Dan *terne* tern] : any of numerous sea gulls (*Sterna* and related genera) that are smaller and slenderer in body and bill than typical gulls and have narrower wings, often forked tails, black cap, and white body
ter·na·ry \'tər-nə-rē\ *adj* [ME, fr. L *ternarius,* fr. *terni* three each; akin to L *tres* three — more at THREE] **1 a** : of, relating to, or proceeding by threes **b** : having three elements, parts, or divisions : THREEFOLD **c** : arranged in threes <~ petals> **2** : using three as the base <a ~ logarithm> **3 a** : being or consisting of an alloy of three elements **b** : of, relating to, or containing three different elements, atoms, radicals, or groups <sulfuric acid is a ~ acid> **4** : third in order or rank
ter·nate \'tər-ˌnāt, -nət\ *adj* [NL *ternatus,* fr. ML, pp. of *ternare* to treble, fr. L *terni*] : arranged in threes or in subdivisions so arranged <a ~ leaf> — **ter·nate·ly** *adv*
terne \'tərn\ *n* [*terneplate*] **1** : an alloy of lead and tin typically in a ratio of four to one that is used as a coating in producing terneplate **2** : TERNEPLATE
terne·plate \-ˌplāt\ *n* [prob. fr. F *terne* dull (fr. MF, fr. *ternir* to tarnish) + E *plate*] : sheet iron or steel coated with an alloy of about four parts lead to one part tin
ter·pene \'tər-ˌpēn\ *n* [ISV *terp-* (fr. G *terpentin* turpentine, fr. ML *terbentina*) + *-ene* — more at TURPENTINE] : any of various isomeric hydrocarbons $C_{10}H_{16}$ found present in essential oils (as from conifers) and used esp. as solvents and in organic synthesis; *broadly* : any of numerous hydrocarbons $(C_5H_8)_n$ found esp. in essential oils, resins, and balsams — **ter·pene·less** \-ləs\ *adj* — **ter·pe·nic** \ˌtər-'pē-nik, -'pen-ik\ *adj* — **ter·pe·noid** \'tər-pə-ˌnȯid, ˌtər-'pē-\ *adj or n*
ter·pin·e·ol \ˌtər-'pin-ē-ˌȯl, -ˌōl\ *n* [ISV, fr. *terpine* $(C_{10}H_{18}(OH)_2)$] : any of three fragrant isomeric alcohols $C_{10}H_{17}OH$ found in essential oils or made artificially and used esp. in perfume or as solvents
ter·poly·mer \ˌtər-'päl-ə-mər\ *n* : a polymer (as a complex resin) that results from copolymerization of three discrete monomers
Terp·sich·o·re \ˌtərp-'sik-ə-(ˌ)rē\ *n* [L, fr. Gk *Terpsichorē*] : the Greek Muse of dancing and choral song
terp·si·cho·re·an \ˌtərp-(ˌ)sik-ə-'rē-ən; -sə-'kōr-ē-, -'kȯr-\ *adj* : of or relating to dancing
terr *abbr* territory

---

ter·ra \'ter-ə\ *n, pl* **ter·rae** \-(ˌ)ē, -ˌī\ [NL, fr. L, land] **:** any of the areas on the surface of the moon other than the maria

ter·ra al·ba \ˌter-ə-'al-bə, -'ȯl-\ *n* [NL, lit., white earth] **:** any of several white mineral substances: as **a :** a pigment consisting of ground gypsum; *broadly* **:** GYPSUM **b :** kaolin used esp. as an adulterant of paints

¹ter·race \'ter-əs\ *n* [MF, pile of earth, platform, terrace, fr. OProv *terrassa,* fr. *terra* earth, fr. L, earth, land; akin to L *torrēre* to parch — more at THIRST] **1 a :** a colonnaded porch or promenade **b :** a flat roof or open platform **c :** a relatively level paved or planted area adjoining a building **2 :** a raised embankment with the top leveled **3 :** a level ordinarily narrow plain usu. with steep front bordering a river, lake, or sea; *also* **:** a similar undersea feature **4 a :** a row of houses or apartments on raised ground or a sloping site **b :** a group of row houses **c :** a strip of park in the middle of a street often planted with trees or shrubs **d :** STREET

²terrace *vt* **ter·raced; ter·rac·ing 1 :** to make into a terrace **2 :** to provide (as a building) with a terrace

ter·ra–cot·ta \ˌter-ə-'kät-ə\ *n* [It *terra cotta,* lit., baked earth] **1 :** a glazed or unglazed fired clay used esp. for statuettes and vases and architectural purposes (as roofing, facing, and relief ornamentation) **2 :** a brownish orange

terra fir·ma \-'fər-mə *also* -'fir-\ *n* [NL, lit., solid land] **:** dry land **:** solid ground

ter·rain \tə-'rān *also* te-\ *n* [F, land, ground, fr. L *terrenum,* fr. neut. of *terrenus* of earth — more at TERRENE] **1 a (1) :** a geographical area **(2) :** a piece of earth **b :** the physical features of a tract of land **2 :** TERRANE 1 **3 :** ENVIRONMENT, MILIEU

ter·ra in·cog·ni·ta \ˌter-ə-ˌin-ˌkäg-'nēt-ə, -in-'käg-nət-ə\ *n, pl* **ter·rae in·cog·ni·tae** \'te(ə)r-ˌī-ˌin-ˌkäg-'nē-ti, -in-'käg-nə-ˌtī\ [L] **:** unknown territory **:** an unexplored country or field of knowledge

Ter·ra·my·cin \ˌter-ə-'mīs-ᵊn\ *trademark* — used for oxytetracycline

ter·rane \tə-'rān, te-\ *n* [alter. of *terrain*] **1 :** the area or surface over which a particular rock or group of rocks is prevalent **2 :** TERRAIN 1a

ter·ra·pin \'ter-ə-pən, 'tar-\ *n* [of Algonquian origin; akin to Delaware *torope* turtle] **:** any of various edible No. American turtles (family Testudinidae) living in fresh or brackish water

terr·aque·ous \te-'rā-kwē-əs, tə-, -'rak-wē-\ *adj* [L *terra* land + E *aqueous*] **:** consisting of land and water

ter·rar·i·um \tə-'rar-ē-əm, -'rer-\ *n, pl* **-ia** \-ē-ə\ *or* **-i·ums** [NL, fr. L *terra* + *-arium* (as in *aquarium*)] **:** a vivarium without standing water

ter·raz·zo \tə-'raz-(ˌ)ō, -'rät-(ˌ)sō\ *n* [It, lit., terrace, perh. fr. OProv *terrassa*] **:** a mosaic flooring made by embedding small pieces of marble or granite in mortar and polishing

¹ter·rene \te-'rēn, tə-; 'te(ə)r-ˌēn\ *adj* [ME, fr. L *terrenus* of earth, fr. *terra* earth] **:** MUNDANE, EARTHLY

²terrene *n* **:** a land area **:** EARTH, TERRAIN

ter·re·plein \'ter-ə-ˌplān\ *n* [MF, fr. OIt *terrapieno,* fr. ML *terraplenum,* fr. *terra plenus* filled with earth] **:** the level space behind a parapet of a rampart where guns are mounted

ter·res·tri·al \tə-'res-t(r)ē-əl, -'res(h)-chəl\ *adj* [ME, fr. L *terrestris,* fr. *terra* earth — more at TERRACE] **1 a :** of or relating to the earth or its inhabitants <~ magnetism> **b :** mundane in scope or character **:** PROSAIC **2 a :** of or relating to land as distinct from air or water <~ transportation> **b (1) :** living on or in or growing from land <~ plants> **(2) :** of or relating to terrestrial organisms <~ habits> **3 :** belonging to the class of planets that are like the earth (as in density and composition) ***syn*** see EARTHLY — ***terrestrial*** *n* — **ter·res·tri·al·ly** \-ē\ *adv*

ter·ret \'ter-ət\ *n* [ME *teret,* alter. of *toret,* fr. MF, fr. OF, dim. of *tour* circuit, ring — more at TURN] **:** one of the rings on the top of a harness pad through which the reins pass

ter·ri·ble \'ter-ə-bəl\ *adj* [ME, fr. MF, fr. L *terribilis,* fr. *terrēre* to frighten — more at TERROR] **1 a :** exciting extreme alarm or intense fear **:** TERRIFYING **b :** formidable in nature **:** AWESOME <a ~ responsibility> **c :** DIFFICULT **2 :** EXTREME, GREAT **3 a :** strongly repulsive **:** OBNOXIOUS <a ~ smell> **b :** notably unattractive or objectionable <~ sentimentality> **4 :** of very poor quality ***syn*** see FEARFUL — **ter·ri·ble·ness** *n* — **ter·ri·bly** \-blē\ *adv*

ter·ric·o·lous \te-'rik-ə-ləs, tə-\ *adj* [L *terricola* earth dweller, fr. *terra* earth + *colere* to inhabit — more at WHEEL] **:** living on or in the ground

ter·ri·er \'ter-ē-ər\ *n* [F (*chien*) *terrier,* lit., earth dog, fr. *terrier* of earth, fr. ML *terrarius,* fr. L *terra*] **:** any of various usu. small dogs orig. used by hunters to dig for small furred game and engage the quarry underground or drive it out

terrier

ter·rif·ic \tə-'rif-ik\ *adj* [L *terrificus,* fr. *terrēre* to frighten] **1 a :** exciting or fit to excite fear or awe **b :** very bad **:** FRIGHTFUL **2 :** EXTRAORDINARY <~ speed> **3 :** unusually fine **:** MAGNIFICENT ***syn*** see FEARFUL — **ter·rif·i·cal·ly** \-i-k(ə-)lē\ *adv*

ter·ri·fy \'ter-ə-ˌfī\ *vt* **-fied; -fy·ing** [L *terrificare,* fr. *terrificus*] **1 :** to fill with terror **2 a :** to drive or impel by menacing **:** SCARE **b :** DETER, INTIMIDATE

ter·ri·fy·ing \-ˌfī-iŋ\ *adj* **1 :** causing terror or apprehension **2 :** of a formidable nature — **ter·ri·fy·ing·ly** \-iŋ-lē\ *adv*

ter·rig·e·nous \te-'rij-ə-nəs, tə-\ *adj* [L *terrigena* earthborn, fr. *terra* earth + *gignere* to beget — more at KIN] **:** being or relating to oceanic sediment derived directly from the destruction of rocks on the earth's surface

¹ter·ri·to·ri·al \ˌter-ə-'tōr-ē-əl, -'tȯr-\ *adj* **1 a :** NEARBY, LOCAL **b :** serving outlying areas **:** REGIONAL **2 a :** of or relating to a territory <~ government> **b :** of or relating to or organized chiefly for home defense <a ~ army> **c :** of or relating to private property <the soil of Italy was . . . passing into the hands of . . . ~ magnates —J. A. Froude> **3 a :** of or relating to an assigned or preempted area <~ commanders> **b :** exhibiting territoriality <~ birds> — **ter·ri·to·ri·al·ly** \-ē-ə-lē\ *adv*

²territorial *n* **:** a member of a territorial military unit

territorial court *n* **:** a court in a U.S. territory that has jurisdiction over local and federal cases

ter·ri·to·ri·al·ism \ˌter-ə-'tōr-ē-ə-ˌliz-əm, -'tȯr-\ *n* **1 :** LANDLORDISM **2 :** the principle established in 1555 requiring the inhabitants of a territory of the Holy Roman Empire to conform to the religion of their ruler or to emigrate **3** *often cap* **:** a theory or movement proposing an autonomous territory for the Jews — **ter·ri·to·ri·al·ist** \-ləst\ *n*

ter·ri·to·ri·al·i·ty \-ˌtōr-ē-'al-ət-ē, -ˌtȯr-\ *n* **1 :** territorial status **2 a :** persistent attachment to a specific territory **b :** the pattern of behavior associated with the defense of a territory

ter·ri·to·ri·al·ize \-'tōr-ē-ə-ˌlīz, -'tȯr-\ *vt* **-ized; -iz·ing :** to organize on a territorial basis — **ter·ri·to·ri·al·iza·tion** \-ˌtōr-ē-ə-lə-'zā-shən, -ˌtȯr-\ *n*

territorial waters *n pl* **:** the waters under the sovereign jurisdiction of a nation or state including both marginal sea and inland waters

ter·ri·to·ry \'ter-ə-ˌtōr-ē, -ˌtȯr-\ *n, pl* **-ries** [ME, fr. L *territorium,* lit., land around a town, prob. fr. *terra* land + *-torium* (as in *praetorium*) — more at TERRACE] **1 a :** a geographical area belonging to or under the jurisdiction of a governmental authority **b :** an administrative subdivision of a country **c :** a part of the U.S. not included within any state but organized with a separate legislature **d :** a geographical area (as a colonial possession) dependent upon an external government but having some degree of autonomy **2 a :** an indeterminate geographical area **b :** a field of knowledge or interest **3 a :** an assigned area; *esp* **:** one in which a salesman or distributor operates **b :** an area often including a nesting or denning site and a variable foraging range that is preempted and defended by an animal or group of animals

ter·ror \'ter-ər\ *n* [ME, fr. MF *terreur,* fr. L *terror,* fr. *terrēre* to frighten; akin to Gk *trein* to be afraid, flee, *tremein* to tremble — more at TREMBLE] **1 :** a state of intense fear **2 a :** one that inspires fear **:** SCOURGE **b :** a frightening aspect <the ~s of invasion> **c :** a cause of anxiety **:** WORRY **d :** an appalling person or thing; *esp* **:** BRAT **3 :** REIGN OF TERROR **4 :** violence (as bomb-throwing) committed by groups in order to intimidate a population or government into granting their demands <insurrection and revolutionary ~> — **ter·ror·less** \-ləs\ *adj*

ter·ror·ism \'ter-ər-ˌiz-əm\ *n* **:** the systematic use of terror esp. as a means of coercion — **ter·ror·ist** \-ər-əst\ *adj or n* — **ter·ror·is·tic** \ˌter-ər-'is-tik\ *adj*

ter·ror·ize \'ter-ər-ˌīz\ *vt* **-ized; -iz·ing 1 :** to fill with terror or anxiety **:** SCARE **2 :** to coerce by threat or violence — **ter·ror·iza·tion** \ˌter-ər-ə-'zā-shən\ *n*

ter·ry \'ter-ē\ *n, pl* **terries** [perh. modif. of F *tiré,* pp. of *tirer* to draw — more at TIRADE] **1 :** the loop forming the pile in uncut pile fabrics **2 :** an absorbent fabric with such loops — called also *terry cloth*

terse \'tərs\ *adj* **ters·er; ters·est** [L *tersus* clean, neat, fr. pp. of *tergēre* to wipe off; akin to Gk *trōgein* to gnaw, L *terere* to rub — more at THROW] **1 :** smoothly elegant **:** POLISHED **2 :** devoid of superfluity <a ~ reply> ***syn*** see CONCISE — **terse·ly** *adv* — **terse·ness** *n*

¹ter·tian \'tər-shən\ *adj* [ME *tercian,* fr. L *tertianus,* lit., of the third, fr. *tertius* third — more at THIRD] **:** recurring at approximately 48-hour intervals — used of malaria

²tertian *n* **:** a tertian fever; *specif* **:** malaria caused by a malaria parasite (*Plasmodium vivax*) and marked by recurrence of paroxysms at 48-hour intervals — called also *vivax malaria*

¹ter·tia·ry \'tər-shē-ˌer-ē, -shə-rē\ *n, pl* **-ries 1** [ML *tertiarius,* fr. L, of a third] **:** a member of a monastic third order esp. of lay people **2** *cap* **:** the Tertiary period or system of rocks

²tertiary *adj* [L *tertiarius* of or containing a third, fr. *tertius* third] **1 a :** of third rank, importance, or value **b :** of, relating to, or constituting the third strongest of the three or four degrees of stress recognized by most linguists <the third syllable of *basketball team* carries ~ stress> **2** *cap* **:** of, relating to, or being the first period of the Cenozoic era or the corresponding system of rocks marked by the formation of high mountains (as the Alps, Caucasus, and Himalayas) and the dominance of mammals on land **3 a :** involving or resulting from the substitution of three atoms or groups <a ~ salt> **b :** being or containing a carbon atom with 3 valences linked to other carbon atoms <an acid containing a ~ carbon> <~ alcohols> **4 :** occurring in or being a third stage

tertiary color *n* **:** a color produced by mixing two secondary colors

tertiary syphilis *n* **:** the third stage of syphilis that develops after the disappearance of the secondary symptoms and is marked by ulcers in and gummas under the skin and commonly by involvement of the skeletal, cardiovascular, and nervous systems

ter·ti·um quid \ˌtər-shē-əm-'kwid, ˌtərt-ē-\ *n* [LL, lit., third something; fr. its failing to fit into a dichotomy] **1 :** a middle course or an intermediate component <where there are two systems of law and two orders of courts, there must . . . be some *tertium quid* to deal with conflicts of law and jurisdiction —Ernest Baker> **2 :** a third party of ambiguous status <there was a man and his wife and a *tertium quid* —Rudyard Kipling>

ter·va·lent \ˌtər-'vā-lənt, 'tər-\ *adj* **:** TRIVALENT

ter·za ri·ma \ˌtert-sə-'rē-mə\ *n* [It, lit., third rhyme] **:** a verse form consisting of tercets usu. in iambic pentameter in English poetry with an interlaced rhyme scheme (as *aba, bcb, cdc*)

TESL \'tes-əl\ *abbr* teaching English as a second language

tes·la \'tes-lə\ *n* [Nikola *Tesla*] **:** a unit of magnetic flux density in the mks system equivalent to one weber per square meter

TE·SOL \'tē-ˌsȯl\ *abbr* Teachers of English to Speakers of Other Languages

tes·sel·late \'tes-ə-ˌlāt\ *vt* **-lat·ed; -lat·ing** [LL *tessellatus,* pp. of *tessellare* to pave with tesserae, fr. L *tessella,* dim. of *tessera*] **:** to form into or adorn with mosaic

tes·sel·lat·ed \-ˌlāt-əd\ *adj* **:** having a checkered appearance

tes·sel·la·tion \ˌtes-ə-ˈlā-shən\ *n* **1 :** an act of tessellating **:** the state of being tessellated **2 :** a careful juxtaposition of elements into a coherent pattern **:** MOSAIC

tes·sera \ˈtes-ə-rə\ *n, pl* **-ser·ae** \-ˌrē, -ˌrī\ [L; prob. deriv. of Gk *tessares* four; fr. its having four corners — more at FOUR] **1 :** a small tablet (as of wood, bone, or ivory) used by the ancient Romans as a ticket, tally, voucher, or means of identification **2 :** a small piece (as of marble, glass, or tile) used in mosaic work

tes·ser·act \ˈtes-ə-ˌrakt\ *n* [Gk *tessares* four + *aktis* ray — more at ACTIN-] **:** the four-dimensional analogue of a cube

tes·si·tu·ra \ˌtes-ə-ˈtu̇r-ə\ *n* [It, lit., texture, fr. L *textura*] **:** the general range of a melody or voice part; *specif* **:** the part of the register in which most of the tones of a melody or voice part lie

1test \ˈtest\ *n* [ME, vessel in which metals were assayed, cupel, fr. MF, fr. L *testum* earthen vessel; akin to L *testa* earthen pot, shell, *texere* to weave — more at TECHNICAL] **1 a** *chiefly Brit* **:** CUPEL **b** (1) **:** a critical examination, observation, or evaluation **:** TRIAL; *specif* **:** the procedure of submitting a statement to such conditions or operations as will lead to its proof or disproof or to its acceptance or rejection <a ~ of a statistical hypothesis> (2) **:** a basis for evaluation **:** CRITERION **c :** an ordeal or oath required as proof of conformity with a set of beliefs **2 a :** a means of testing: as (1) **:** a procedure, reaction, or reagent used to identify or characterize a substance or constituent (2) **:** something (as a series of questions or exercises) for measuring the skill, knowledge, intelligence, capacities, or aptitudes of an individual or group **b :** a positive result in such a test **3 :** a result or value determined by testing

2test *vt* **1 :** to put to test or proof **:** TRY **2 :** to require a doctrinal oath of ~ *vi* **1 a :** to undergo a test **b :** to achieve a rating on the basis of tests **2 :** to apply a test as a means of analysis or diagnosis — used with *for* <~ for mechanical aptitude> — **test·abil·i·ty** \ˌtes-tə-ˈbil-ət-ē\ *n* — **test·able** \ˈtes-tə-bəl\ *adj*

3test *n* [L *testa* shell] **:** an external hard or firm covering (as a shell) of many invertebrates (as a foraminifer or a mollusk)

tes·ta \ˈtes-tə\ *n, pl* **tes·tae** \-ˌtē, -ˌtī\ [NL, fr. L, shell] **:** the hard external coating or integument of a seed

tes·ta·cean \tes-ˈtā-shən\ *n* [deriv. of L *testaceus*] **:** any of an order (Testacea) of shelled rhizopods — **testacean** *adj*

tes·ta·ceous \-shəs\ *adj* [L *testaceus*, fr. *testa* shell, earthen pot, brick] **1 a :** having a shell <a ~ protozoan> **b :** consisting of shell or calcareous material <stone of ~ composition> **2 :** of any of the several light colors of bricks

tes·ta·cy \ˈtes-tə-sē\ *n, pl* **-cies :** the state of being testate

tes·ta·ment \ˈtes-tə-mənt\ *n* [ME, fr. LL & L; LL *testamentum* covenant with God, holy scripture, fr. L, last will, fr. *testari* to be a witness, call to witness, make a will, fr. *testis* witness; akin to L *tres* three & to L *stare* to stand; fr. the witness's standing by as a third party in a litigation — more at THREE, STAND] **1 a** *archaic* **:** a covenant between God and man **b** *cap* **:** either of two main divisions of the Bible **2 a :** a tangible proof or tribute **b :** an expression of conviction **:** CREDO **3 a :** an act by which a person determines the disposition of his property after his death **b :** WILL — **tes·ta·men·ta·ry** \ˌtes-tə-ˈment-ə-rē, -ˈmen-trē\ *adj*

tes·tate \ˈtes-ˌtāt, -tət\ *adj* [ME, fr. L *testatus*, pp. of *testari* to make a will] **:** having made a valid will <he died ~>

tes·ta·tor \ˈtes-ˌtāt-ər, tes-ˈ\ *n* [ME *testatour*, fr. AF, fr. LL *testator*, fr. L *testatus*, pp.] **:** a person who leaves a will or testament in force at his death — **tes·ta·trix** \tes-ˈtā-triks\ *n*

test ban *n* **:** a self-imposed ban on the atmospheric testing of nuclear weapons that is mutually agreed to by countries possessing such weapons

test case *n* **1 :** a representative case whose outcome is likely to serve as a precedent **2 :** a proceeding brought by agreement or on an understanding of the parties to obtain a decision as to the constitutionality of a statute

1test·cross \ˈtes(t)-ˌkrȯs\ *n* **:** a genetic cross between a homozygous recessive individual and a corresponding suspected heterozygote to determine the genotype of the latter

2testcross *vt* **:** to subject to a testcross

test–drive \ˈtes(t)-ˌdrīv\ *vt* **-drove** \-ˌdrōv\; **-driv·en** \-ˌdriv-ən\; **-driv·ing** \-ˌdrī-viŋ\ **:** to drive (a motor vehicle) before buying in order to evaluate performance

test·ed \ˈtes-təd\ *adj* **:** subjected to or qualified through testing — often used in combination <time-*tested* principles>

1tes·ter \ˈtē-stər, ˈtes-\ *n* [ME, fr. MF *testiere* headpiece, head covering, fr. *teste* head, fr. LL *testa* skull, fr. L, shell — more at TEST] **:** the canopy over a bed, pulpit, or altar

tester

2tes·ter \ˈtes-tər\ *n* [modif. of MF *testart*, fr. *teston*] **:** TESTON b

3test·er \ˈtes-tər\ *n* **:** one that tests

test–fire \ˈtest-ˌfī(ə)r\ *vt* **:** to subject to a firing test <~ a gun>

test–fly \-ˌflī\ *vt* **-flew** \-ˌflü\; **-flown** \-ˌflōn\; **-fly·ing :** to subject to a flight test <~ an experimental plane>

tes·ti·cle \ˈtes-ti-kəl\ *n* [ME *testicule*, fr. L *testiculus*, dim. of *testis*] **:** a male genital gland usu. with its enclosing structures **:** TESTIS — **tes·tic·u·lar** \tes-ˈtik-yə-lər\ *adj*

tes·ti·fi·er \ˈtes-tə-ˌfī(-ə)r\ *n* **:** one that testifies **:** WITNESS

tes·ti·fy \ˈtes-tə-ˌfī\ *vb* **-fied; -fy·ing** [ME *testifien*, fr. L *testificari*, fr. *testis* witness] *vi* **1 a :** to make a statement based on personal knowledge or belief **:** bear witness **b :** to serve as evidence or proof **2 :** to express a personal conviction **3 :** to make a solemn declaration under oath for the purpose of establishing a fact (as in a court) ~ *vt* **1 a :** to bear witness to **:** ATTEST **b :** to serve as evidence of **:** PROVE **2** *archaic* **a :** to make known (a personal conviction) **b :** to give evidence of **:** SHOW **3 :** to declare under oath before a tribunal or officially constituted public body

1tes·ti·mo·ni·al \ˌtes-tə-ˈmō-nē-əl, -nyəl\ *adj* **1 :** of, relating to, or constituting testimony **2 :** expressive of appreciation or esteem <a ~ dinner>

2testimonial *n* **1 :** EVIDENCE, TESTIMONY **2 a :** a statement testifying to benefits received **b :** a character reference **:** letter of recommendation **3 :** an expression of appreciation **:** TRIBUTE

tes·ti·mo·ny \ˈtes-tə-ˌmō-nē\ *n, pl* **-nies** [ME, fr. LL & L; LL *testimonium* Decalogue, fr. L, evidence, witness, fr. *testis* witness — more at TESTAMENT] **1 a** (1) **:** the tablets inscribed with the Mosaic law (2) **:** the ark containing the tablets **b :** a divine decree attested in the Scriptures **2 a :** firsthand authentication of a fact **:** EVIDENCE **b :** an outward sign **c :** a solemn declaration usu. made orally by a witness under oath in response to interrogation by a lawyer or authorized public official **3 a :** an open acknowledgment **b :** a public profession of religious experience

test·ing *adj* **:** requiring maximum effort or ability <a most difficult and ~ problem —Ernest Bevin>

tes·tis \ˈtes-təs\ *n, pl* **tes·tes** \ˈtes-ˌtēz\ [L, witness, testis] **:** a male reproductive gland

test match *n* **1 :** any of a series of championship cricket matches played between teams representing Australia and England **2 :** a championship game or series (as of cricket) played between teams representing different countries

tes·ton \ˈtes-ˌtän\ *or* **tes·toon** \tes-ˈtün\ *n* [MF, fr. OIt *testone*, aug. of *testa* head, fr. LL, skull — more at TESTER] **:** any of several old European coins: as **a :** a French silver coin of the 16th century worth between 10 and 14½ sous **b :** a shilling of Henry VIII of England decreasing in value to ninepence and then to sixpence in Shakespeare's time

tes·tos·ter·one \te-ˈstäs-tə-ˌrōn\ *n* [*testis* + *-o-* + *sterol* + *-one*] **:** a male hormone that is produced by the testes or made synthetically, is responsible for inducing and maintaining male secondary sex characters, and is a crystalline hydroxy steroid ketone $C_{19}H_{28}O_2$

test pattern *n* **:** a fixed picture broadcast by a television station to assist viewers in adjusting their receivers

test pilot *n* **:** a pilot who specializes in putting new or experimental airplanes through maneuvers designed to test them (as for strength) by producing strains in excess of normal

test–tube *adj* **:** produced by artificial insemination <~ babies>

test tube *n* **:** a plain or lipped tube of thin glass closed at one end and used esp. in chemistry and biology

tes·tu·do \tes-ˈt(y)üd-(ˌ)ō\ *n, pl* **-dos** [L *testudin-, testudo*, lit., tortoise, tortoise shell; akin to L *testa* shell — more at TEST] **:** a cover of overlapping shields or a shed wheeled up to a wall used by the ancient Romans to protect an attacking force

tes·ty \ˈtes-tē\ *adj* **tes·ti·er; -est** [ME *testif*, fr. AF, headstrong, fr. OF *teste* head — more at TESTER] **1 :** easily annoyed **:** IRRITABLE **2 :** marked by impatience or ill humor <~ remarks> ***syn*** see IRASCIBLE — **tes·ti·ly** \-tə-lē\ *adv* — **tes·ti·ness** \-tē-nəs\ *n*

Tet \ˈtet\ *n* [Vietnamese *tết*] **:** the Vietnamese New Year observed for three days beginning at the first new moon after January 20

tet·a·nal \ˈtet-ᵊn-əl\ *adj* **:** of, relating to, or derived from tetanus

te·tan·ic \te-ˈtan-ik\ *adj* **:** of, relating to, being, or tending to produce tetanus or tetany — **te·tan·i·cal·ly** \-i-k(ə-)lē\ *adv*

tet·a·nize \ˈtet-ᵊn-ˌīz\ *vt* **-nized; -niz·ing :** to induce tetanus in <~ a muscle> — **tet·a·ni·za·tion** \ˌtet-ᵊn-ə-ˈzā-shən, ˌtet-nə-\ *n*

tet·a·nus \ˈtet-ᵊn-əs, ˈtet-nəs\ *n* [ME, fr. L, fr. Gk *tetanos*, fr. *tetanos* stretched, rigid; akin to Gk *teinein* to stretch — more at THIN] **1 a :** an acute infectious disease characterized by tonic spasm of voluntary muscles esp. of the jaw and caused by the specific toxin of a bacillus (*Clostridium tetani*) which is usu. introduced through a wound **b :** the bacterium that causes tetanus **2 :** prolonged contraction of a muscle resulting from rapidly repeated motor impulses

tet·a·ny \ˈtet-ᵊn-ē, ˈtet-nē\ *n* [ISV, fr. L *tetanus*] **:** a condition of physiologic mineral imbalance marked by tonic spasm of muscles and associated usu. with deficient parathyroid secretion

te·tar·to·he·dral \te-ˌtärt-ə-ˈhē-drəl\ *adj* [Gk *tetartos* fourth; akin to Gk *tettares* four — more at FOUR] *of a crystal* **:** having one fourth the number of planes required by complete symmetry — compare HEMIHEDRAL, HOLOHEDRAL

tetched *var of* TECHED

tetchy \ˈtech-ē\ *adj* **tetchi·er; -est** [perh. fr. obs. *tetch* (habit)] **:** irritably or peevishly sensitive **:** TOUCHY <the ~ manner of two women living in the same house —Elizabeth Taylor>

1tête–à–tête \ˌtāt-ə-ˈtāt\ *adv* [F, lit., head to head] **:** in private

2tête–à–tête \ˈtāt-ə-ˌtāt, *2 is also* ˈtet-ə-ˌtet\ *n* **1 :** a private conversation between two persons **2 :** a short piece of furniture (as a sofa) intended to seat two persons esp. facing each other

3tête–à–tête \ˌtāt-ə-ˌtāt\ *adj* **:** FACE-TO-FACE, PRIVATE

tête–bêche \ˈtāt-ˈbāsh, ˈtet-ˈbesh\ *adj* [F, n., pair of inverted stamps, fr. *tête* head + *-bêche*, alter. of MF *bechevet* head against foot] **:** of or relating to a pair of stamps inverted in relation to one another either through a printing error or intentionally

teth \ˈtāt(h), ˈtās\ *n* [Heb *ṭēth*] **:** the 9th letter of the Hebrew alphabet — see ALPHABET table

1teth·er \ˈteth-ər\ *n* [ME *tethir*, prob. of Scand origin; akin to ON *tjōthr* tether; akin to OHG *zeotar* pole of a wagon] **1 :** something (as a rope or chain) by which an animal is fastened so that it can range only within a set radius **2 :** the limit of one's strength or resources **:** SCOPE <the end of his ~>

2tether *vt* **teth·ered; teth·er·ing** \-(ə-)riŋ\ **:** to fasten or restrain by or as if by a tether

teth·er·ball \ˈteth-ər-ˌbȯl\ *n* **:** a game played with a ball suspended by a string from an upright pole with the object for each contestant

ə abut ᵊ kitten ər further a back ā bake ä cot, cart
au̇ out ch chin e less ē easy g gift i trip ī life
j joke ŋ sing ō flow ȯ flaw ȯi coin th thin th this
ü loot u̇ foot y yet yü few yu̇ furious zh vision

to wrap the string around the pole by striking the ball in a direction opposite to that of the other contestant

Te·thys \ˈtē-thəs\ *n* [L, fr. Gk *Tēthys*] **:** a Titaness and wife of Oceanus

tet·ra \ˈte-trə\ *n* [by shortening fr. NL *Tetragonopterus,* former genus name, fr. LL *tetragonum* quadrangle + Gk *pteron* wing — more at TETRAGONAL, FEATHER] **:** any of numerous small brightly colored So. American characin fishes often bred in the tropical aquarium

tetra- *or* **tetr-** *comb form* [ME, fr. L, fr. Gk; akin to Gk *tettares* four — more at FOUR] **1 :** four **:** having four **:** having four parts <*tetra*atomic> **2 :** containing four atoms, radicals, or groups (of a specified kind) <*tetra*basic> <*tetr*acid>

tet·ra·ba·sic \ˌte-trə-ˈbā-sik\ *adj* [ISV] **1 :** having four hydrogen atoms capable of replacement by basic atoms or radicals <a ~ acid> **2 :** containing four atoms of a univalent metal or their equivalent **3 :** having four basic hydroxyl groups **:** able to react with four molecules of a monoacid — **tet·ra·ba·sic·i·ty** \-bā-ˈsis-ət-ē\ *n*

tet·ra·caine \ˈte-trə-ˌkān\ *n* [*tetra-* + pro*caine*] **:** a crystalline basic ester $C_{15}H_{24}N_2O_2$ that is closely related chemically to procaine and is used chiefly in the form of its hydrochloride as a local anesthetic

tet·ra·chlo·ride \ˌte-trə-ˈklō(ə)r-ˌīd, -ˈklȯ(ə)r-\ *n* **:** a chloride containing four atoms of chlorine

tet·ra·chord \ˈte-trə-ˌkȯ(ə)rd\ *n* [Gk *tetrachordon,* fr. neut. of *tetrachordos* of four strings, fr. *tetra-* + *chordē* string — more at YARN] **:** a diatonic series of four tones with an interval of a perfect fourth between the first and last

te·trac·id \te-ˈtras-əd\ *adj* **1 :** able to react with four molecules of a monoacid or two of a diacid to form a salt or ester **2 :** TETRABASIC 1

tet·ra·cy·cline \ˌte-trə-ˈsī-ˌklēn\ *n* [ISV *tetracyclic* + *-ine*] **:** a yellow crystalline broad-spectrum antibiotic $C_{22}H_{24}N_2O_8$ produced by a soil actinomycete (*Streptomyces viridifaciens*) or synthetically

tet·rad \ˈte-ˌtrad\ *n* [Gk *tetrad-, tetras,* fr. *tetra-*] **:** a group or arrangement of four: as **a :** a tetravalent element, atom, or radical **b :** a group of four cells arranged usu. in the form of a tetrahedron and produced by the successive divisions of a mother cell <a ~ of spores> **c :** a group of four synapsed chromatids that become visibly evident in the pachytene stage of meiotic prophase and are produced by the longitudinal splitting of each of two paired homologous chromosomes — **te·trad·ic** \te-ˈtrad-ik\ *adj*

tet·ra·drachm \ˈte-trə-ˌdram\ *n* [Gk *tetradrachmon,* fr. *tetra-* + *drachmē* drachma] **:** an ancient Greek silver coin worth four drachmas

te·trad·y·mite \te-ˈtrad-ə-ˌmīt\ *n* [LGk *tetradymos* fourfold, fr. Gk *tetra-* + *-dymos* (as in *didymos* didymous); fr. its occurrence in compound twin crystals] **:** a pale steel-gray mineral Bi_2Te_2S consisting essentially of a telluride and sulfide of bismuth and having a metallic luster

tet·ra·dy·na·mous \ˌte-trə-ˈdī-nə-məs\ *adj* [ISV *tetra-* + Gk *dynamis* power — more at DYNAMIC] **:** having six stamens four of which are longer than the others <~ plants of the mustard family>

tet·ra·eth·yl \ˌte-trə-ˈeth-əl\ *adj* [ISV] **:** containing four ethyl groups in the molecule

tet·ra·eth·yl·lead \-ˌeth-əl-ˈled\ *n* **:** a heavy oily poisonous liquid $Pb(C_2H_5)_4$ used as an antiknock agent

tet·ra·flu·o·ride \ˌte-trə-ˈflü(-ə)r-ˌīd\ *n* **:** a fluoride containing four atoms of fluorine

te·trag·o·nal \te-ˈtrag-ən-ᵊl\ *adj* [LL *tetragonalis* having four angles and four sides, fr. *tetragonum* quadrangle, fr. Gk *tetragōnon,* fr. neut. of *tetragōnos* tetragonal, fr. *tetra-* + *gōnia* angle — more at -GON] **:** of, relating to, or characteristic of the tetragonal system — **te·trag·o·nal·ly** \-ᵊl-ē\ *adv*

tetragonal system *n* **:** a crystal system characterized by three axes at right angles of which only the two lateral axes are equal

tet·ra·gram·ma·ton \ˌte-trə-ˈgram-ə-ˌtän\ *n* [ME, fr. Gk, fr. neut. of *tetragrammatos* having four letters, fr. *tetra-* + *grammat-, gramma* letter — more at GRAM] **:** the four Hebrew letters usu. transliterated YHWH or JHVH that form a biblical proper name of God — compare YAHWEH

tet·ra·he·dral \ˌte-trə-ˈhē-drəl\ *adj* **1 :** relating to, forming, or having the form of a tetrahedron **2 :** having four faces <~ angle> — **tet·ra·he·dral·ly** \-drə-lē\ *adv*

tet·ra·he·drite \-ˌdrīt\ *n* [G *tetraëdrit,* fr. L Gk *tetraedros* having four faces] **:** a fine-grained gray mineral $(Cu,Fe)_{12}Sb_4S_{13}$ that consists essentially of a sulfide of copper, iron, and antimony, often contains other elements (as silver), occurs in tetrahedral crystals and also massive, and is often a valuable ore of silver

tet·ra·he·dron \ˌte-trə-ˈhē-drən\ *n, pl* **-drons** *or* **-dra** \-drə\ [NL, fr. LGk *tetraedron,* neut. of *tetraedros* having four faces, fr. Gk *tetra-* + *hedra* seat, face — more at SIT] **:** a polyhedron of four faces

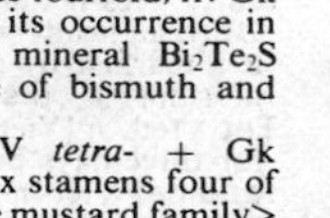

tetrahedron

tet·ra·hy·drate \-ˈhī-drət, -ˌdrāt\ *n* **:** a chemical compound hydrated with four molecules of water — **tet·ra·hy·drat·ed** \-ˌdrāt-əd\ *adj*

tet·ra·hy·dro·can·nab·i·nol \-ˌhī-drə-kə-ˈnab-ə-ˌnȯl, -ˌnōl\ *n* [*tetrahydro-* (combined with four atoms of hydrogen) + *cannabin* + *-ol*] **:** THC

tet·ra·hy·dro·fu·ran \-ˈfyu̇(ə)r-ˌan, -fyu̇-ˈran\ *n* [*tetrahydro-* + *furan*] **:** a flammable liquid heterocyclic ether C_4H_8O that is derived from furan and used as a solvent and as an intermediate in the production of nylon

tet·ra·hy·droxy \-hī-ˈdräk-sē\ *adj* [*tetra-* + *hydroxyl*] **:** containing four hydroxyl groups in the molecule

tet·ra·hy·me·na \ˌte-trə-ˈhī-mə-nə\ *n* [NL, genus name, fr. *tetra-* + Gk *hymēn* membrane] **:** any of a genus (*Tetrahymena*) of ciliate protozoans

te·tral·o·gy \te-ˈträl-ə-jē, -ˈtral-\ *n, pl* **-gies** [Gk *tetralogia,* fr. *tetra-* + *-logia* -logy] **1 :** a group of four dramatic pieces presented consecutively on the Attic stage at the Dionysiac festival **2 :** a series of four connected works (as operas or novels)

tet·ra·mer \ˈte-trə-mər\ *n* [*tetra-* + poly*mer*] **:** a polymer formed from four molecules of a monomer — **tet·ra·mer·ic** \ˌte-trə-ˈmer-ik\ *adj*

te·tram·er·ous \te-ˈtram-ə-rəs\ *adj* [NL *tetramerus,* fr. Gk *tetramerēs,* fr. *tetra-* + *meros* part — more at MERIT] **:** having or characterized by the presence of four parts or of parts arranged in sets or multiples of four <~ flowers>

te·tram·e·ter \te-ˈtram-ət-ər\ *n* [Gk *tetrametron,* fr. neut. of *tetrametros* having four measures, fr. *tetra-* + *metron* measure — more at MEASURE] **:** a line of verse consisting either of four dipodies (as in classical iambic, trochaic, and anapestic verse) or four metrical feet (as in modern English verse)

tet·ra·meth·yl \ˌte-trə-ˈmeth-əl\ *adj* [ISV] **:** containing four methyl groups in the molecule

tet·ra·meth·yl·lead \-ˌmeth-əl-ˈled\ *n* **:** a volatile poisonous liquid $Pb(CH_3)_4$ used as an antiknock agent

[1]**tet·ra·ploid** \ˈte-trə-ˌplȯid\ *adj* [ISV] **:** having or being a chromosome number four times the monoploid number <a ~ cell> — **tet·ra·ploi·dy** \-ˌplȯid-ē\ *n*

[2]**tetraploid** *n* **:** a tetraploid individual

tet·ra·pod \ˈte-trə-ˌpäd\ *n* [NL *tetrapodus,* fr. Gk *tetrapod-, tetrapous* four-footed, fr. *tetra-* + *pod-, pous* foot — more at FOOT] **:** a vertebrate (as a frog, bird, or cat) with two pairs of limbs

tet·ra·pyr·role \ˌte-trə-ˈpi(ə)r-ˌōl\ *n* **:** a chemical group consisting of four pyrrole rings joined either in a straight chain (as in phycobilins) or in a ring (as in chlorophyll)

te·trarch \ˈte-ˌträrk, ˈtē-\ *n* [ME, fr. L *tetrarcha,* fr. Gk *tetrarchēs,* fr. *tetra-* + *-archēs* -arch] **1 :** a governor of the fourth part of a province **2 :** a subordinate prince — **te·trar·chic** \te-ˈträr-kik, tē-\ *adj*

te·trar·chy \ˈte-ˌträr-kē, ˈtē-\ *n, pl* **-chies :** government by four persons ruling jointly

tet·ra·spore \ˈte-trə-ˌspō(ə)r, -ˌspȯ(ə)r\ *n* [ISV] **:** one of the haploid asexual spores developed meiotically in the red algae usu. in groups of four — **tet·ra·spor·ic** \ˌte-trə-ˈspōr-ik, -ˈspȯr-\ *adj*

tet·ra·tom·ic \ˌte-trə-ˈtäm-ik\ *adj* [ISV] **1 :** consisting of four atoms **:** having four atoms in the molecule **2 :** having four replaceable atoms or radicals

[1]**tet·ra·va·lent** \ˌte-trə-ˈvā-lənt\ *adj* [ISV] **1 :** having a valence of four **2 :** QUADRIVALENT 2

[2]**tetravalent** *n* **:** QUADRIVALENT

tet·ra·zo·li·um \ˌte-trə-ˈzō-lē-əm\ *n* [NL, fr. ISV *tetrazole* (CH_2N_4) + NL *-ium* (as in *ammonium*)] **:** a univalent cation or radical CH_3N_4 that is analogous to ammonium; *also* **:** any of several of its derivatives used esp. as electron acceptors to test for metabolic activity in living cells

tet·rode \ˈte-ˌtrōd\ *n* **:** a vacuum tube with four electrodes, a cathode, an anode, a control grid, and an additional grid or other electrode

te·tro·do·tox·in \te-ˌtrōd-ə-ˈtäk-sən\ *n* [ISV *tetrodo-* (fr. NL *Tetrodon,* genus of tropical marine fishes) + *toxin*] **:** a poisonous compound $C_{11}H_{17}N_3O_8$ that has been isolated from a Japanese globefish and a newt and that blocks nerve conduction by suppressing permeability of the nerve fiber to sodium ions

te·trox·ide \te-ˈträk-ˌsīd\ *n* [ISV] **:** a compound of an element or radical with four atoms of oxygen

tet·ryl \ˈte-trəl\ *n* [ISV *tetra-* + *-yl*] **:** a pale yellow crystalline explosive $C_7H_5N_5O_8$ used esp. as a detonator

tet·ter \ˈtet-ər\ *n* [ME *teter,* fr. OE; akin to OE *teran* to tear] **:** any of various vesicular skin diseases (as ringworm, eczema, and herpes)

Teu·ton \ˈt(y)üt-ᵊn\ *n* [L *Teutoni,* pl.] **1 :** a member of an ancient prob. Germanic or Celtic people **2 :** a member of a people speaking a language of the Germanic branch of the Indo-European language family; *esp* **:** GERMAN

[1]**Teu·ton·ic** \t(y)ü-ˈtän-ik\ *adj* **:** of, relating to, or characteristic of the Teutons — **Teu·ton·i·cal·ly** \-i-k(ə-)lē\ *adv*

[2]**Teutonic** *n* **:** GERMANIC

Teu·ton·ism \ˈt(y)üt-ᵊn-ˌiz-əm\ *n* **:** GERMANISM

Teu·ton·ist \-ᵊn-əst\ *n* **:** GERMANIST

teu·ton·ize \-ᵊn-ˌīz\ *vt* **-ized; -iz·ing** *often cap* **:** GERMANIZE

Tex *abbr* Texas

tex·as \ˈtek-səs, -siz\ *n* [*Texas,* state of U.S.; fr. the naming of cabins on Mississippi steamboats after states, the officers' cabins being the largest] **:** a structure on the awning deck of a steamer containing the officers' cabins and having the pilothouse in front or on top

Texas citrus mite *n* **:** a red spider (*Eutetrarychus banksi*) that causes leaf injury to citrus trees

Texas fever *n* **:** an infectious disease of cattle transmitted by the cattle tick and caused by a protozoan (*Babesia bigemina*) that multiplies in the blood and destroys the red blood cells

Texas Independence Day *n* **:** March 2 observed as the anniversary of the declaration of independence of Texas from Mexico in 1836 and also as the birthday of Sam Houston

texas leaguer *n* [*Texas League,* a baseball minor league] **:** a fly in baseball that falls too far out to be caught by an infielder and too close in to be caught by an outfielder

Texas Ranger *n* **:** a member of a mounted police force in Texas

text \ˈtekst\ *n* [ME, fr. MF *texte,* fr. ML *textus,* fr. L, texture, context, fr. *textus,* pp. of *texere* to weave — more at TECHNICAL] **1 a** (1) **:** the original written or printed words and form of a literary work (2) **:** an edited or emended copy of an original work **b :** a work containing such text **2 a :** the main body of printed or written matter on a page **b :** the principal part of a book exclusive of front and back matter **c :** the printed score of a musical composition **3 a** (1) **:** a verse or passage of Scripture chosen esp. for the subject of a sermon or for authoritative support (as for a doctrine) (2) **:** a passage from an authoritative source providing an introduction or basis (as for a speech) **b :** a source of information or authority **4 :** TEXTBOOK **5 :** a type suitable for printing running text **6 :** THEME, TOPIC **7 :** the words of something (as a poem) set to music

text·book \ˈteks(t)-ˌbu̇k\ *n* **:** a book used in the study of a subject: as **a :** one containing a presentation of the principles of a subject **b :** a literary work relevant to the study of a subject

text·book·ish \-ish\ *adj* **:** of, relating to, or having the characteristics of a textbook <except for a few all too brief interludes, the style is heavy and ~ —*Nation*>

text edition *n* **:** an edition of a book prepared for use esp. in schools and colleges — compare TRADE EDITION

text hand *n* **:** a style of handwriting marked by use of large letters

tex·tile \ˈtek-ˌstīl, ˈteks-tᵊl\ *n* [L, fr. neut. of *textilis* woven, fr. *textus,* pp. of *texere*] **1 :** CLOTH 1a; *esp* **:** a woven or knit cloth **2 :** a fiber, filament, or yarn used in making cloth

tex·tu·al \ˈteks-chə(-wə)l\ *adj* [ME, fr. ML *textus* text] **:** of, relating to, or based on a text — **tex·tu·al·ly** \-ē\ *adv*

textual critic *n* **:** a practitioner of textual criticism

textual criticism *n* **1 :** the study of a literary work that aims to establish the original text **2 :** a critical study of literature emphasizing a close reading and analysis of the text

¹tex·tu·ary \ˈteks-chə-ˌwer-ē\ *n, pl* **-ar·ies** [ML *textus*] **:** one who is well informed in the Bible or in biblical scholarship

²textuary *adj* **:** TEXTUAL

¹tex·ture \ˈteks-chər\ *n* [L *textura,* fr. *textus,* pp. of *texere* to weave — more at TECHNICAL] **1 a :** something composed of closely interwoven elements; *specif* **:** a woven cloth **b :** the structure formed by the threads of a fabric **2 a :** essential part **:** SUBSTANCE **b :** identifying quality **:** CHARACTER **3 a :** the disposition or manner of union of the particles of a body or substance **b :** the visual or tactile surface characteristics and appearance of something <the ~ of an oil painting> **4 a :** a composite of the elements of prose or poetry <all these words . . . meet violently to form a ~ impressive and exciting —John Berryman> **b :** a pattern of musical sound created by tones or lines played or sung together **5 a :** basic scheme or structure **b :** overall structure — **tex·tur·al** \-chə-rəl\ *adj* — **tex·tur·al·ly** \-ē\ *adv* — **tex·tured** \-chərd\ *adj*

²texture *vt* **tex·tured; tex·tur·ing :** to give a particular texture to

tex·tus re·cep·tus \ˌtek-stəs-ri-ˈsep-təs\ *n* [NL, lit., received text] **:** the generally accepted text of a literary work (as the Greek New Testament)

TF *abbr* **1** task force **2** territorial force **3** till forbidden

T formation *n* **:** an offensive football formation in which the fullback lines up behind the center and quarterback with one halfback stationed on each side of the fullback

tfr *abbr* transfer

TG *abbr* type genus

TGIF *abbr* thank God it's Friday

T–group \ˈtē-ˌgrüp\ *n* [*training group*] **:** a group of people under the leadership of a trainer who seek to develop self-awareness and sensitivity to others by verbalizing feelings uninhibitedly at group sessions — compare ENCOUNTER GROUP

tgt *abbr* target

¹Th *abbr* Thursday

²Th *symbol* thorium

TH *abbr* true heading

¹-th — see -ETH

²-th *or* **-eth** *adj suffix* [ME *-the, -te,* fr. OE *-tha, -ta;* akin to OHG *-do* -th, L *-tus,* Gk *-tos,* Skt *-tha*] — used in forming ordinal numbers <hundred*th*> <forti*eth*>

³-th *n suffix* [ME, fr. OE; akin to OHG *-ida,* suffix forming abstract nouns, L *-ta,* Gk *-tē,* Skt *-tā*] **1 :** act or process <spil*th*> **2 :** state or condition <dear*th*>

¹Thai \ˈtī\ *n* **1 a :** a native or inhabitant of Thailand **b :** one who is descended from a Thai **2 :** the official language of Thailand **3 :** a group of languages including Thai held by some to belong to the Sino-Tibetan language group

²Thai *abbr* Thailand

thal·am·en·ceph·a·lon \ˌthal-ə-ˌmen-ˈsef-ə-ˌlän, -lən\ *n* [NL, fr. *thalamus* + *encephalon*] **:** DIENCEPHALON

tha·lam·ic \thə-ˈlam-ik\ *adj* **:** of, relating to, or involving the thalamus — **tha·lam·i·cal·ly** \-i-k(ə-)lē\ *adv*

thal·a·mus \ˈthal-ə-məs\ *n, pl* **-mi** \-ˌmī, -ˌmē\ [NL, fr. Gk *thalamos* chamber] **1 :** the largest subdivision of the diencephalon consisting chiefly of an ovoid mass of nuclei in each lateral wall of the third ventricle — see BRAIN illustration **2 :** RECEPTACLE 2b

thal·as·se·mia \ˌthal-ə-ˈsē-mē-ə\ *n* [NL, fr. Gk *thalassa* sea + NL *-emia*] **:** a familial hypochromic anemia that is characterized by the presence of microcytes, by splenomegaly, and by changes in the bones and skin and that occurs esp. in children of Mediterranean parents — **thal·as·se·mic** \-mik\ *adj*

tha·las·sic \thə-ˈlas-ik\ *adj* [F *thalassique,* fr. Gk *thalassa* sea] **1 :** of or relating to deep seas or the depths of the sea <~ fishes with luminous organs> **2 :** of, relating to, or situated or developed about inland seas <~ civilizations of the Aegean>

thal·as·soc·ra·cy \ˌthal-ə-ˈsäk-rə-sē\ *n* [Gk *thalassokratia,* fr. *thalassa* + *-kratia* -cracy] **:** maritime supremacy

tha·las·so·crat \thə-ˈlas-ə-ˌkrat\ *n* **:** one who has maritime supremacy

tha·ler \ˈtäl-ər\ *var of* TALER

Tha·lia \thə-ˈlī-ə\ *n* [L, fr. Gk *Thaleia*] **1 :** the Greek Muse of comedy **2 :** one of the three Graces

tha·lid·o·mide \thə-ˈlid-ə-ˌmīd, -məd\ *n* [ph*thal*ic acid + *-id-* (fr. *imide*) + *-o-* + i*mide*] **:** a sedative and hypnotic drug $C_{13}H_{10}N_2O_4$ that was found to cause malformation of infants born to mothers using it during pregnancy

thall- *or* **thallo-** *comb form* [NL, fr. Gk, fr. *thallos* — more at THALLUS] **1 a :** a young shoot <*thall*ium> **b :** thallus <*thall*oid> **2 :** thallium <*thall*ic>

thal·lic \ˈthal-ik\ *adj* **:** of, relating to, or containing thallium esp. with a valence of three

thal·li·um \ˈthal-ē-əm\ *n* [NL; so called from the bright green line in its spectrum] **:** a sparsely but widely distributed poisonous metallic element that resembles lead in physical properties and is used chiefly in the form of compounds in photoelectric cells or as a pesticide — see ELEMENT table

thal·loid \ˈthal-ˌȯid\ *adj* **:** of, relating to, resembling, or consisting of a thallus

thal·lo·phyte \ˈthal-ə-ˌfīt\ *n* [deriv. of Gk *thallos* + *phyton* plant — more at PHYT-] **:** any of a primary division (Thallophyta) of the plant kingdom comprising plants with single-celled sex organs or with many-celled sex organs of which all cells give rise to gametes, including the algae, fungi, and lichens, and usu. held to be a heterogeneous assemblage — **thal·lo·phyt·ic** \ˌthal-ə-ˈfit-ik\ *adj*

thal·lous \ˈthal-əs\ *adj* **:** of, relating to, or containing thallium with a valence of one

thal·lus \ˈthal-əs\ *n, pl* **thal·li** \ˈthal-ˌī, -ˌē\ *or* **thal·lus·es** [NL, fr. Gk *thallos,* fr. *thallein* to sprout; akin to Alb *dal* I come forth] **:** a plant body that is characteristic of thallophytes, lacks differentiation into distinct members (as stem, leaves, and roots), and does not grow from an apical point

¹than \t͟hən, (ˈ)t͟han\ *conj* [ME *than, then* then, than — more at THEN] **1 a** — used as a function word to indicate the second member or the member taken as the point of departure in a comparison expressive of inequality; used with comparative adjectives and comparative adverbs <older ~ I am> <easier said ~ done> **b** — used as a function word to indicate difference of kind, manner, or identity; used esp. with some adjectives and adverbs that express diversity <anywhere else ~ at home> **2 :** rather than — usu. used only after *prefer, preferable,* and *preferably* **3 :** other than **4 :** WHEN — used esp. after *scarcely* and *hardly*

²than *prep* **:** in comparison with <he is older ~ me>

Than·a·tos \ˈthan-ə-ˌtäs\ *n* [Gk, death; akin to Skt *adhvanīt* it vanished, L *fumus* smoke] **:** instinctual desire for death — compare EROS 2

thane \ˈthān\ *n* [ME *theyn,* fr. OE *thegn;* akin to OHG *thegan* thane, Gk *tiktein* to bear, beget] **1 :** a free retainer of an Anglo-Saxon lord; *esp* **:** one resembling a feudal baron by holding lands of and performing military service for the king **2 :** a Scottish feudal lord — **thane·ship** \-ˌship\ *n*

thank \ˈthaŋk\ *vt* [ME *thanken,* fr. OE *thancian;* akin to OE *thanc* gratitude — more at THANKS] **1 :** to express gratitude to <~*ed* her for the present> — used in the phrase *thank you* usu. without a subject to politely express gratitude <~ you for the loan>; used in such phrases as *thank God, thank heaven* usu. without a subject to express gratitude or more often only the speaker's or writer's pleasure or satisfaction in something **2 :** to hold responsible <had only himself to ~ for his loss> — **thank·er** *n*

thank·ful \ˈthaŋk-fəl\ *adj* **1 :** conscious of benefit received <for what we are about to receive make us truly ~> **2 :** expressive of thanks <~ service> **3 :** well pleased **:** GLAD <he was ~ that the room was dark> ***syn*** see GRATEFUL ***ant*** thankless — **thank·ful·ly** \-fə-lē\ *adv* — **thank·ful·ness** *n*

thank·less \ˈthaŋ-kləs\ *adj* **1 :** not expressing or feeling gratitude **:** UNGRATEFUL <~ children> **2 :** not likely to obtain thanks **:** UNAPPRECIATED <a ~ task> — **thank·less·ly** *adv* — **thank·less·ness** *n*

thanks \ˈthaŋ(k)s\ *n pl* [pl. of ME *thank,* fr. OE *thanc* thought, gratitude; akin to OHG *dank* gratitude, L *tongēre* to know] **1 :** kindly or grateful thoughts **:** GRATITUDE **2 :** an expression of gratitude <return ~ before the meal> — often used in an utterance containing no verb and serving as a courteous and somewhat informal expression of gratitude <many ~> — **no thanks to :** not as a result of any benefit conferred by <he feels better now, *no thanks to* you> — **thanks to 1 :** with the help of <*thanks to* modern medicine, man's life span is growing longer> **2 :** owing to <our arrival was delayed, *thanks to* the fog>

thanks·giv·ing \thaŋ(k)s-ˈgiv-iŋ\ *n* **1 :** the act of giving thanks **2 :** a prayer expressing gratitude **3 a :** a public acknowledgment or celebration of divine goodness **b** *cap* **:** THANKSGIVING DAY

Thanksgiving Day *n* **:** a day appointed for giving thanks for divine goodness: as **a :** the fourth Thursday in November observed as a legal holiday in the U.S. **b :** the second Monday in October observed as a legal holiday in Canada

thank·wor·thy \ˈthaŋ-ˌkwər-t͟hē\ *adj* **:** worthy of thanks or gratitude **:** MERITORIOUS

thank–you \ˈthaŋ-ˌkyü\ *n* [fr. the phrase *thank you* used in expressing gratitude, short for *I thank you*] **:** a polite expression of one's gratitude

thank–you–ma'am \ˈthaŋk-yu̇-ˌmam, -(y)ē-\ *n* [prob. fr. its causing a nodding of the head] **:** a bump or depression in a road; *esp* **:** a ridge or hollow made across a road on a hillside to cause water to run off

¹that \(ˈ)t͟hat\ *pron, pl* **those** \(ˈ)t͟hōz\ [ME, fr. OE *thæt,* neut. demonstrative pron. & definite article; akin to OHG *daz,* neuter demonstrative pron. & definite article, Gk *to,* L is*tud* neut. demonstrative pron.] **1 a :** the person, thing, or idea indicated, mentioned, or understood from the situation <~ is my father> **b :** the time, action, or event specified <after ~ he went to bed> **c :** the kind or thing specified as follows <the purest water is ~ produced by distillation> **d :** one or a group of the indicated kind <~'s a fox — wily and destructive> **2 a :** the one farther away or less immediately under observation or discussion <*those* are maples and these are elms> **b :** the former one **3 a** — used as a function word after *and* to indicate emphatic repetition of the idea expressed by a previous word or phrase <he was helpful, and ~ to an unusual degree> **b** — used as a function word immediately before or after a word group consisting of a verbal auxiliary or a form of the verb *be* preceded by *there* or a personal pronoun subject to indicate emphatic repetition of the idea expressed by a previous verb or predicate noun or predicate adjective <is he capable? He is ~> **4 a :** the one **:** the thing **:** the kind **:** SOMETHING, ANYTHING

<the truth of ~ which is true> <the senses are ~ whereby we experience the world> <what's ~ you say> **b** *pl* : some persons <*those* who think the time has come> — **all that** : everything of the kind indicated <tact, discretion, and *all that*> — **at that 1** : in spite of what has been said or implied **2** : in addition : BESIDES

[2]**that** *adj* **1 a :** being the person, thing, or idea specified, mentioned, or understood **b :** so great a : SUCH **2 :** the farther away or less immediately under observation or discussion <this chair or ~ one>

[3]**that** \th̲ət, (ˌ)th̲at\ *conj* **1 a** (1) — used as a function word to introduce a noun clause that is usu. the subject or object of a verb or a predicate nominative <said ~ he was afraid> (2) — used as a function word to introduce a subordinate clause that is anticipated by the expletive *it* occurring as subject of the verb <it is unlikely ~ he'll be in> (3) — used as a function word to introduce a subordinate clause that is joined as complement to a noun or adjective <we are certain ~ this is true> <the certainty ~ this is true> <the fact ~ you are here> (4) — used as a function word to introduce a subordinate clause modifying an adverb or adverbial expression <will go anywhere ~ he is invited> **b** — used as a function word to introduce an exclamatory clause expressing a strong emotion esp. of surprise, sorrow, or indignation <~ it should come to this!> **2 a** (1) — used as a function word to introduce a subordinate clause expressing purpose or desired result <cutting down expenses ~ her son might inherit an unencumbered estate —W. B. Yeats> (2) — used as a function word to introduce a subordinate clause expressing a reason or cause <rejoice ~ you are lightened of a load —Robert Browning> (3) — used as a function word to introduce a subordinate clause expressing consequence, result, or effect <are of sufficient importance ~ they cannot be neglected —Hannah Wormington> **b** — used as a function word to introduce an exclamatory clause expressing a wish <oh, ~ he would come> **3** — used as a function word after a subordinating conjunction without modifying its meaning <if ~ thy bent of love be honorable —Shak.>

[4]**that** \th̲ət, (ˌ)th̲at\ *pron* **1** — used as a function word to introduce a restrictive relative clause and to serve as a substitute within that clause for the substantive modified by that clause <the house ~ Jack built> **2 a :** at which : in which : on which : by which : with which : to which <each year ~ the lectures are given> **b :** according to what : to the extent of what — used after a negative <has never been here ~ I know of> **3 a** *archaic* : that which **b** *obs* : the person who

[5]**that** \ˈth̲at\ *adv* **1 :** to such an extent <a nail about ~ long> **2 :** VERY, EXTREMELY — usu. used with the negative <did not take the festival ~ seriously —Eric Goldman>

[1]**thatch** \ˈthach\ *vt* [ME *thecchen,* fr. OE *theccan* to cover; akin to OHG *decchen* to cover, L *tegere,* Gk *stegein* to cover, *stegos* roof, Skt *sthagati* he covers] : to cover with or as if with thatch — **thatch·er** *n*

[2]**thatch** *n* **1 a :** a plant material (as straw) used as a sheltering cover esp. of a house **b :** a sheltering cover (as a house roof) made of such material **2 :** something resembling the thatch of a house; *esp* : the hair of one's head

thau·ma·turge \ˈthȯ-mə-ˌtərj\ *n* [F, fr. NL *thaumaturgus,* fr. Gk *thaumatourgos* working miracles, fr. *thaumat-, thauma* miracle + *ergon* work — more at THEATER, WORK] : THAUMATURGIST

thau·ma·tur·gic \ˌthȯ-mə-ˈtər-jik\ *adj* **1 :** performing miracles **2 :** of, relating to, or dependent on thaumaturgy

thau·ma·tur·gist \ˈthȯ-mə-ˌtər-jəst\ *n* : a performer of miracles; *esp* : MAGICIAN

thau·ma·tur·gy \-jē\ *n* : the performance of miracles; *specif* : MAGIC

[1]**thaw** \ˈthȯ\ *vb* [ME *thawen,* fr. OE *thawian;* akin to OHG *douwen* to thaw, Gk *tēkein* to melt, L *tabes* wasting disease] *vt* : to cause to thaw ~ *vi* **1 a :** to go from a frozen to a liquid state : MELT **b :** to become free of the effect (as stiffness, numbness, or hardness) of cold as a result of exposure to warmth **2 :** to be warm enough to melt ice and snow — used with *it* in reference to the weather **3 :** to abandon aloofness, reserve, or hostility : UNBEND **4 :** to become mobile, active, or susceptible to change

[2]**thaw** *n* **1 :** the action, fact, or process of thawing **2 :** a warmth of weather sufficient to thaw ice **3 :** the action or process of becoming less aloof, less hostile, or more genial

ThB *abbr* [NL *theologiae baccalaureus*] bachelor of theology

THC \ˌtē-ˌāch-ˈsē\ *n* [*tetrahydrocannabinol*] : a physiologically active liquid from hemp plant resin that is the chief intoxicant in marijuana

ThD *abbr* [NL *theologiae doctor*] doctor of theology

[1]**the** \th̲ə (*before consonant & esp South sometimes vowel sounds*), th̲ē (*before vowel sounds*); *1k is often* ˈth̲ē\ *definite article* [ME, fr. OE *thē,* masc. demonstrative pron. & definite article, alter. (influenced by oblique cases — as *thæs,* gen. — & neut., *thæt*) of *sē;* akin to Gk *ho,* masc. demonstrative pron. & definite article — more at THAT] **1 a** — used as a function word to indicate that a following noun or noun equivalent is definite or has been previously specified by context or by circumstance <put ~ cat out> **b** — used as a function word to indicate that a following noun or noun equivalent is a unique or a particular member of its class <~ President> <~ Lord> **c** — used as a function word before nouns that designate natural phenomena or points of the compass <~ night is cold> **d** — used as a function word before a noun denoting time to indicate reference to what is present or immediate or is under consideration <in ~ future> **e** — used as a function word before names of some parts of the body or of the clothing as an equivalent of a possessive adjective <how's ~ arm today> **f** — used as a function word before the name of a branch of human endeavor or proficiency <~ law> **g** — used as a function word in prepositional phrases to indicate that the noun in the phrase serves as a basis for computation <sold by ~ dozen> **h** — used as a function word before a proper name (as of a ship or a well-known building) <~ Mayflower> **i** — used as a function word before the plural form of a numeral that is a multiple of ten to denote a particular decade of a century or of a person's life <life in ~ twenties> **j** — used as a function word before the name of a commodity or any familiar appurtenance of daily life to indicate reference to the individual thing, part, or supply thought of as at hand <talked on ~ telephone> **k** — used as a function word to designate one of a class as the best, most typical, or most worth singling out <this is ~ life> **2 a** (1) — used as a function word with a noun modified by an adjective or by an attributive noun to limit the application of the modified noun to that specified by the adjective or by the attributive noun <~ right answer> <Peter ~ Great> (2) — used as a function word before an absolute adjective <nothing but ~ best> **b** — used as a function word before a noun to limit its application to that specified by a succeeding element in the sentence <~ poet Wordsworth> <~ days of our youth> <didn't have ~ time to write> **3 a** — used as a function word before a singular noun to indicate that the noun is to be understood generically <~ dog is a domestic animal> **b** — used as a function word before a singular substantivized adjective to indicate an abstract idea <an essay on ~ sublime> **4** — used as a function word before a noun or a substantivized adjective to indicate reference to a group as a whole <~ elite>

[2]**the** *adv* [ME, fr. OE *thȳ* by that, instrumental of *thæt* that] **1 :** than before : than otherwise — used before a comparative <none ~ wiser for attending> **2 a :** to what extent <~ sooner the better> **b :** to that extent <the sooner ~ better> **3 :** beyond all others <likes this ~ best>

[3]**the** *prep* [[1]*the*] : PER 2

the- *or* **theo-** *comb form* [ME *theo-,* fr. L, fr. Gk *the-, theo-,* fr. *theos*] : god : God <*the*ism> <*theo*centric>

theat *abbr* theater; theatrical

the·ater *or* **the·atre** \ˈthē-ət-ər, *oftenest in South* ˈthē-ˌāt-\ *n* [ME *theatre,* fr. MF, fr. L *theatrum,* fr. Gk *theatron,* fr. *theasthai* to view, fr. *thea* act of seeing; akin to Gk *thauma* miracle] **1 a :** an outdoor structure for dramatic performances or spectacles in ancient Greece and Rome **b :** a building for dramatic performances **c :** a building or area for showing motion pictures **2 a :** a place rising by steps or gradations <a woody ~ of stateliest view —John Milton> **b :** a room often with rising tiers of seats for assemblies (as for lectures or surgical demonstrations) **3 :** a place of enactment of significant events or action <the ~ of public life> **4 a :** dramatic literature or performance **b :** dramatic effectiveness <the play makes lively ~> **5 :** the theatrical world

the·ater·go·er \ˈthē-ət-ər-ˌgō(-ə)r\ *n* : one who frequently goes to the theater

the·ater·go·ing \-ˌgō-iŋ, -ˌgȯ(-)iŋ\ *n* : attendance at the theater

theater-in-the-round *n* : ARENA THEATER

theater of cruelty : theater that seeks to heighten the audience's awareness and sensibility by depicting realistically acts of sadism and extreme suffering

theater of operations : the part of a theater of war in which active operations are conducted and that includes a combat zone and a communications zone

theater of the absurd : theater that seeks to represent the absurdity of man's existence in a meaningless universe by bizarre or fantastic means

theater of war : the entire land, sea, and air area that is or may become involved directly in war operations

The·atine \ˈthē-ə-ˌtin, -ˌtēn\ *n* [NL *Theatinus,* fr. L *Teatinus* inhabitant of Chieti, fr. *Teate* Chieti, Italy] : a priest of the Order of Clerks Regular founded in 1524 in Italy by St. Cajetan and Gian Pietro Caraffa to reform Catholic morality and combat Lutheranism — **Theatine** *adj*

[1]**the·at·ri·cal** \thē-ˈa-tri-kəl\ *adj* **1 :** of or relating to the theater or the presentation of plays <a ~ costume> **2 :** marked by pretense or artificiality of emotion **3 a :** HISTRIONIC <a ~ gesture> **b :** marked by extravagant display or exhibitionism — **the·at·ri·cal·ism** \-kə-ˌliz-əm\ *n* — **the·at·ri·cal·i·ty** \-ˌa-trə-ˈkal-ət-ē\ *n* — **the·at·ri·cal·ly** \-ˈa-tri-k(ə-)lē\ *adv*

[2]**theatrical** *n* **1** *pl* **a :** the performance of plays <amateur ~*s*> **b :** DRAMATICS **2 :** a professional actor **3** *pl* **:** showy or extravagant gestures

the·at·ri·cal·ize \thē-ˈa-tri-kə-ˌlīz\ *vt* **-ized; -iz·ing 1 :** to adapt to the theater : DRAMATIZE **2 :** to display in showy fashion — **the·at·ri·cal·iza·tion** \-ˌa-tri-kə-lə-ˈzā-shən\ *n*

the·at·rics \thē-ˈa-triks\ *n pl* **1 :** THEATRICAL 1 **2 :** staged or contrived effects

the·ca \ˈthē-kə\ *n, pl* **the·cae** \ˈthē-ˌsē, -ˌkē\ [NL, fr. Gk *thēkē* case — more at TICK] **1 :** an urn-shaped spore-containing upper part of the capsule of a moss **2 :** an enveloping sheath or case of an animal or animal part — **the·cal** \ˈthē-kəl\ *or* **the·cate** \-ˌkāt\ *adj*

-the·ci·um \ˈthē-s(h)ē-əm\ *n comb form, pl* **-the·cia** \-s(h)ē-ə\ [NL, fr. Gk *thēkion,* dim. of *thēkē* case — more at TICK] : small containing structure <endo*thecium*>

[1]**thec·odont** \ˈthē-kə-ˌdänt\ *adj* [ISV *thec-* (fr. NL *theca*) + *-odont*] : having the teeth inserted in sockets

[2]**thecodont** *n* : a thecodont animal; *esp* : any of an order (Thecodontia) of Triassic diapsid thecodont reptiles that were presumably on the common ancestral line of the dinosaurs, birds, and crocodiles

thé dan·sant \tā-dä^n-sä^n\ *n, pl* **thés dansants** *same*\ [F] : TEA DANCE

thee \(ˈ)th̲ē\ *pron, objective case of* THOU **1 a** — used esp. in ecclesiastical or literary language and by Friends esp. among themselves in contexts where the objective case form would be expected **b** — used by Friends esp. among themselves in contexts where the subjective case form would be expected **2** *archaic* : THYSELF

thee·lin \ˈthē(-ə)-lən\ *n* [irreg. fr. Gk *thēlys* female — more at FEMININE] : ESTRONE

thee·lol \-ˌlȯl, -ˌlōl\ *n* [ISV, fr. *theelin*] : ESTRIOL

theft \ˈtheft\ *n* [ME *thiefthe,* fr. OE *thiefth;* akin to OE *thēof* thief] **1 a :** the act of stealing; *specif* : the felonious taking and removing of personal property with intent to deprive the rightful owner of it **b :** an unlawful taking (as by embezzlement or burglary) of property **2** *obs* **:** something stolen **3 :** a stolen base in baseball

thegn \'thān\ *n* [OE — more at THANE] **:** THANE 1

thegn·ly \-lē\ *adj* **:** of, relating to, or befitting a thegn

the·ine \'thē-ən\ *n* [NL *theina,* fr. *thea* tea, fr. Chin (Amoy) *t'e*] **:** CAFFEINE

their \thər, (,)the(ə)r, (,)tha(ə)r\ *adj* [ME, fr. *their,* pron., fr. ON *theirra,* gen. pl. demonstrative & personal pron.; akin to OE *thæt* that] **1 :** of or relating to them or themselves esp. as possessors, agents, or objects of an action <~ furniture> <~ verses> <~ being seen> **2 :** his or her **:** HIS, HER, ITS — used with an indefinite third person singular antecedent <anyone in ~ senses —W. H. Auden>

theirs \'the(ə)rz, 'tha(ə)rz\ *pron, sing or pl in constr* **1 :** that which belongs to them — used without a following noun as a pronoun equivalent in meaning to the adjective *their* **2 :** his or hers **:** HIS, HERS — used with an indefinite third person singular antecedent <I will do my part if everybody else will do ~>

the·ism \'thē-,iz-əm\ *n* **:** belief in the existence of a god or gods; *specif* **:** belief in the existence of one God viewed as the creative source of man and the world who transcends yet is immanent in the world — **the·ist** \-əst\ *n or adj* — **the·is·tic** \thē-'is-tik\ *adj* — **the·is·ti·cal** \-ti-kəl\ *adj* — **the·is·ti·cal·ly** \-ti-k(ə-)lē\ *adv*

-theism *n comb form* [MF *-théisme,* fr. Gk *theos* god] **:** belief in (such) a god or (such or so many) gods <mono*theism*>

-theist *n comb form* **:** believer in (such) a god or (such or so many) gods <pan*theist*>

them \(th)əm, (')them, *after* p, b, v, f, *also* ᵊm\ *pron, objective case of* THEY

the·mat·ic \thi-'mat-ik\ *adj* [Gk *thematikos,* fr. *themat-, thema* theme] **1 a :** of or relating to the stem of a word **b** *of a vowel* **:** being the last part of a word stem before an inflectional ending **2 :** of, relating to, or constituting a theme — **the·mat·i·cal·ly** \-i-k(ə-)lē\ *adv*

thematic apperception test *n* **:** a projective technique that is widely used in clinical psychology to make personality, psychodynamic, and diagnostic assessments based on the subject's verbal responses to a series of black and white pictures — abbr. *TAT*

theme \'thēm\ *n* [ME *teme, theme,* fr. OF & L; OF *teme,* fr. L *thema,* fr. Gk, lit., something laid down, fr. *tithenai* to place — more at DO] **1 :** a subject or topic of discourse or of artistic representation **2 :** STEM 4 **3 :** a written exercise **:** COMPOSITION **4 :** a melodic subject of a musical composition or movement

theme song *n* **1 :** a melody recurring so often in a musical play that it characterizes the production or one of its characters **2 :** SIGNATURE 6

them·selves \th̲əm-'selvz, th̲em-\ *pron pl* **1 a :** those identical ones that are they — compare THEY 1a; used reflexively, for emphasis, or in absolute constructions <nations that govern ~> <they ~ were present> <~ busy, they disliked idleness in others> **b :** himself or herself **:** HIMSELF, HERSELF — used with an indefinite third person singular antecedent <nobody can call ~ oppressed —Leonard Wibberley> **2 :** their normal, healthy, or sane condition <were ~ again after a night's rest>

¹then \(')th̲en\ *adv* [ME *than, then* then, than, fr. OE *thonne, thænne;* akin to OHG *denne* then, than, OE *thæt* that] **1 :** at that time **2 a :** soon after that **:** next in order of time <walked to the door, ~ turned> **b :** following next after in order of position, narration, or enumeration **:** being next in a series <first came the clowns, ~ came the elephants> **c :** in addition **:** BESIDES <~ there is the interest to be paid> **3 a** (1) **:** in that case <take it, ~, if you want it so much> (2) — used after *but* to qualify or offset a preceding statement <he lost the race, but ~ he never really expected to win> **b :** according to that **:** as may be inferred <your mind is made up, ~> **c :** as it appears **:** by way of summing up <the cause of the accident, ~, is established> **d :** as a necessary consequence <if the angles are equal, ~ the complements are equal> — **and then some :** with much more in addition <would require all his strength *and then some*>

²then \'th̲en\ *n* **:** that time <since ~, he's been more cautious>

³then \'th̲en\ *adj* **:** existing or acting at or belonging to the time mentioned <the ~ secretary of state>

then and there *adv* **:** on the spot **:** IMMEDIATELY <wanted the money right *then and there*>

the·nar \'thē-,när, -nər\ *n* [NL, fr. Gk — more at DEN] **1 :** the ball of the thumb **2 :** ²PALM 1; *also* **:** ¹SOLE 1a — **thenar** *adj*

thence \'th̲en(t)s *also* 'then(t)s\ *adv* [ME *thannes,* fr. *thanne* from that place, fr. OE *thanon;* akin to OHG *thanan* from that place, OE *thænne* then — more at THEN] **1 :** from that place **2** *archaic* **:** from that time **:** THENCEFORTH **3 :** from that fact or circumstance **:** THEREFROM

thence·forth \-,fō(ə)rth, -,fȯ(ə)rth\ *adv* **:** from that time forward

thence·for·ward \th̲en(t)s-'fȯr-wərd *also* then(t)s-\ *also* **thence·for·wards** \-wərdz\ *adv* **:** onward from that place or time

theo- — see THE-

theo·bro·mine \,thē-ə-'brō-,mēn, -mən\ *n* [NL *Theobroma,* genus of trees, fr. *the-* + Gk *brōma* food, fr. *bibrōskein* to devour — more at VORACIOUS] **:** a bitter alkaloid $C_7H_8N_4O_2$ closely related to caffeine that occurs esp. in cacao beans and has stimulant and diuretic properties

theo·cen·tric \-'sen-trik\ *adj* **:** having God as the central interest and ultimate concern <a ~ culture> — **theo·cen·tric·i·ty** \-,sen-'tris-ət-ē\ *n* — **theo·cen·trism** \-'sen-,triz-əm\ *n*

the·oc·ra·cy \thē-'äk-rə-sē\ *n, pl* **-cies** [Gk *theokratia,* fr. *the-* + *-kratia* -cracy] **1 :** government of a state by immediate divine guidance or by officials who are regarded as divinely guided **2 :** a state governed by a theocracy

theo·crat \'thē-ə-,krat\ *n* **1 :** one who rules in or lives under a theocratic form of government **2 :** one who favors a theocratic form of government

theo·crat·ic \,thē-ə-'krat-ik\ *also* **theo·crat·i·cal** \-i-kəl\ *adj* **:** of, relating to, or being a theocracy — **theo·crat·i·cal·ly** \-i-k(ə-)lē\ *adv*

the·od·i·cy \thē-'äd-ə-sē\ *n, pl* **-cies** [modif. of F *théodicée,* fr. *théo-* the- (fr. L *theo-*) + Gk *dikē* judgment, right — more at DICTION] **:** defense of God's goodness and omnipotence in view of the existence of evil

the·od·o·lite \thē-'äd-ᵊl-,īt\ *n* [NL *theodolitus*] **:** a surveyor's instrument for measuring horizontal and usu. also vertical angles — **the·od·o·lit·ic** \-,äd-ᵊl-'it-ik\ *adj*

the·og·o·ny \thē-'äg-ə-nē\ *n, pl* **-nies** [Gk *theogonia,* fr. *the-* + *-gonia* -gony] **:** an account of the origin and descent of the gods — **theo·gon·ic** \,thē-ə-'gän-ik\ *adj*

theol *abbr* theological; theology

theo·lo·gian \,thē-ə-'lō-jən\ *n* **:** a specialist in theology

theo·log·i·cal \-'läj-i-kəl\ *also* **theo·log·ic** \-ik\ *adj* **1 :** of or relating to theology **2 :** preparing for a religious vocation <a ~ student> — **theo·log·i·cal·ly** \-i-k(ə-)lē\ *adv*

theological virtue *n* **:** one of the three spiritual graces faith, hope, and charity drawing the soul to God according to scholastic theology

the·ol·o·gize \thē-'äl-ə-,jīz\ *vb* **-gized; -giz·ing** *vi* **:** to theorize theologically ~ *vt* **:** to make theological **:** give a religious significance to — **the·ol·o·giz·er** *n*

theo·logue *or* **theo·log** \'thē-ə-,lȯg, -,läg\ *n* [L *theologus* theologian, fr. Gk *theologos,* fr. *the-* + *legein* to speak — more at LEGEND] **:** a theological student or specialist

the·ol·o·gy \thē-'äl-ə-jē\ *n, pl* **-gies** [ME *theologie,* fr. L *theologia,* fr. Gk, fr. *the-* + *-logia* -logy] **1 :** the study of God and his relation to the world esp. by analysis of the origins and teachings of an organized religious community (as the Christian Church) **2 a :** a theological theory or system <Thomist ~> <a ~ of atonement> **b :** a distinctive body of theological opinion <Catholic ~> **3 :** a usu. four-year course of specialized religious training in a Roman Catholic major seminary

the·on·o·mous \thē-'än-ə-məs\ *adj* [*the-* + *-nomous* (as in *autonomous*)] **:** governed by God **:** subject to God's authority — **the·on·o·mous·ly** *adv*

the·on·o·my \-mē\ *n* [G *theonomie,* fr. *theo-* the- (fr. L) + *-nomie* -nomy] **:** the state of being theonomous **:** government by God

the·oph·a·ny \thē-'äf-ə-nē\ *n, pl* **-nies** [ML *theophania,* fr. LGk *theophaneia,* fr. Gk *the-* + *-phaneia* (as in *epiphaneia* appearance) — more at EPIPHANY] **:** a visible manifestation of a deity — **theo·phan·ic** \,thē-ə-'fan-ik\ *adj*

the·oph·yl·line \thē-'äf-ə-lən\ *n* [ISV *theo-* (fr. NL *thea* tea) + *phyll-* + *-ine* — more at THEINE] **:** a feebly basic bitter crystalline compound $C_7H_8N_4O_2$ from tea leaves that is isomeric with theobromine and is used in medicine esp. as a muscle relaxant and vasodilator

the·o·rem \'thē-ə-rəm, 'thi(-ə)r-əm\ *n* [LL *theorema,* fr. Gk *theōrēma,* fr. *theōrein* to look at, fr. *theōros* spectator, fr. *thea* act of seeing — more at THEATER] **1 :** a formula, proposition, or statement in mathematics or logic deduced or to be deduced from other formulas or propositions **2 :** an idea accepted or proposed as a demonstrable truth often as a part of a general theory **:** PROPOSITION <the ~ that the best defense is offense> — **the·o·rem·at·ic** \,thē-ə-rə-'mat-ik, ,thi(-ə)r-ə-\ *adj*

the·o·ret·i·cal \,thē-ə-'ret-i-kəl, ,thi(-ə)r-'et-\ *also* **the·o·ret·ic** \-ik\ *adj* [LL *theoreticus,* fr. Gk *theōrētikos,* fr. *theōrein*] **1 a :** relating to or having the character of theory **:** ABSTRACT **b :** confined to theory or speculation **:** SPECULATIVE <~ mechanics> **2 :** given to or skilled in theorizing <a brilliant ~ physicist> **3 :** existing only in theory **:** HYPOTHETICAL <gave as an example a ~ situation> — **the·o·ret·i·cal·ly** \-i-k(ə-)lē\ *adv*

syn THEORETICAL, SPECULATIVE, ACADEMIC *shared meaning element* **:** concerned principally with abstractions and theories

the·o·re·ti·cian \,thē-ə-rə-'tish-ən, -re-; ,thi(-ə)r-ə-\ *n* **:** THEORIST

the·o·rist \'thē-ə-rəst, 'thi(-ə)r-əst\ *n* **:** a person that theorizes

the·o·ri·za·tion \,thē-ə-rə-'zā-shən, ,thi(-ə)r-ə-\ *n* **:** an act or product of theorizing

the·o·rize \'thē-ə-,rīz\ *vb* **-rized; -riz·ing** *vi* **:** to form a theory **:** SPECULATE ~ *vt* **:** to form a theory about — **the·o·riz·er** *n*

the·o·ry \'thē-ə-rē, 'thi(-ə)r-ē\ *n, pl* **-ries** [LL *theoria,* fr. Gk *theōria,* fr. *theōrein*] **1 :** the analysis of a set of facts in their relation to one another **2 a :** a belief, policy, or procedure proposed or followed as the basis of action <her method is based on the ~ that all children want to learn> **b :** an ideal or hypothetical set of facts, principles, or circumstances — often used in the phrase *in theory* <in ~, we have always advocated freedom for all> **3 :** the general or abstract principles of a body of fact, a science, or an art <music ~> **4 :** a plausible or scientifically acceptable general principle or body of principles offered to explain phenomena <wave ~ of light> **5 a :** a hypothesis assumed for the sake of argument or investigation **b :** an unproved assumption **:** CONJECTURE **c :** a body of theorems presenting a concise systematic view of a subject <~ of equations> **6 :** abstract thought **:** SPECULATION *syn* see HYPOTHESIS

theory of games : the analysis of a situation involving conflicting interests (as in business or military strategy) in terms of gains and losses among opposing players

theory of numbers : NUMBER THEORY

the·os·o·phist \thē-'äs-ə-fəst\ *n* **1 :** an adherent of theosophy **2** *cap* **:** a member of a theosophical society

the·os·o·phy \-fē\ *n* [ML *theosophia,* fr. LGk, fr. Gk *the-* + *sophia* wisdom — more at -SOPHY] **1 :** teaching about God and the world based on mystical insight **2** *often cap* **:** the teachings of a modern movement originating in the U.S. in 1875 and following chiefly Buddhist and Brahmanic theories esp. of pantheistic evolution and reincarnation — **theo·soph·i·cal** \ˌthē-ə-ˈsäf-i-kəl\ *adj* — **theo·soph·i·cal·ly** \-k(ə-)lē\ *adv*

therap *abbr* therapeutics

ther·a·peu·sis \ˌther-ə-ˈpyü-səs\ *n* [NL, fr. Gk, treatment, fr. *therapeuein*] : THERAPEUTICS

ther·a·peu·tic \-ˈpyüt-ik\ *adj* [Gk *therapeutikos*, fr. *therapeuein* to attend, treat, fr. *theraps* attendant] : of or relating to the treatment of disease or disorders by remedial agents or methods : MEDICINAL <~ diets> — **ther·a·peu·ti·cal·ly** \-i-k(ə-)lē\ *adv*

therapeutic index *n* : a measure of the relative desirability of a drug for the attaining of a particular medical end that is usu. expressed as the ratio of the largest dose producing no toxic symptoms to the smallest dose routinely producing cures

ther·a·peu·tics \ˌther-ə-ˈpyüt-iks\ *n pl but sing or pl in constr* : a branch of medical science dealing with the application of remedies to diseases

ther·a·peu·tist \-ˈpyüt-əst\ *n* : one skilled in therapeutics

ther·a·pist \ˈther-ə-pəst\ *n* : one specializing in therapy; *esp* : a person trained in methods of treatment and rehabilitation other than the use of drugs or surgery <a speech ~>

the·rap·sid \thə-ˈrap-səd\ *n* [NL *Therapsida*, group name, perh. fr. Gk *theraps* attendant] : any of an order (Therapsida) of Permian and Triassic reptiles that walked upright rather than crawled and are held to be ancestral to the mammals — **therapsid** *adj*

ther·a·py \ˈther-ə-pē\ *n, pl* **-pies** [NL *therapia*, fr. Gk *therapeia*, fr. *therapeuein*] : therapeutic treatment: as **a** : remedial treatment of bodily disorder **b** : PSYCHOTHERAPY **c** : an agency (as treatment) designed or serving to bring about social adjustment

Ther·a·va·da \ˌther-ə-ˈväd-ə\ *n* [Pali *theravāda*, lit., doctrine of the elders] : a conservative branch of Buddhism comprising sects chiefly in Ceylon, Burma, Thailand, Laos, and Cambodia and adhering to the original Pali scriptures alone and to the nontheistic ideal of nirvana for a limited select number — compare MAHAYANA

[1]there \ˈtha(ə)r, ˈthe(ə)r\ *adv* [ME, fr. OE *thǣr*; akin to OHG *dār* there, OE *thæt* that] **1** : in or at that place <stand over ~> — often used interjectionally **2** : to or into that place : THITHER <went ~ after church> **3** : at that point or stage <stop right ~ before you say something you'll regret> **4** : in that matter, respect, or relation <~ is where I disagree with you> **5** — used interjectionally to express satisfaction, approval, encouragement or sympathy, or defiance <~, it's finished at last>

[2]there \(ˌ)tha(ə)r, (ˌ)the(ə)r, *1 is also* thər\ *pron* **1** — used as a function word to introduce a sentence or clause <~ shall come a time> **2** — used as an indefinite substitute for a name <hi ~>

[3]there *like* [1]\ *n* **1** : that place or position <there is no here and no ~ . . . in pure space —James Ward> **2** : that point <you take it from ~>

[4]there *like* [1]\ *adj* **1** — used for emphasis esp. after a demonstrative pronoun or a noun modified by a demonstrative adjective <those men ~ can tell you> **2** *substand* — used for emphasis after a demonstrative adjective but before the noun modified <I bet I cussed that ~ blamed mule five hundred times if I cussed once today —Elizabeth M. Roberts>

there·abouts *or* **there·about** \ˌthar-ə-ˈbau̇t(s), ˈthar-ə-ˌ, ˌther-ə-ˈbau̇t(s), ˈther-ə-ˌ\ *adv* **1** : near that place or time **2** : near that number, degree, or quantity <a boy of 18 or ~>

there·af·ter \tha-ˈraf-tər, the-\ *adv* **1** : after that **2** *archaic* : according to that : ACCORDINGLY

there·at \-ˈrat\ *adv* **1** : at that place **2** : at that occurrence

there·by \tha(ə)r-ˈbī, the(ə)r-, ˈtha(ə)r-ˌ, ˈthe(ə)r-ˌ\ *adv* **1** : by that : by that means <~ lost his chance to win> **2** : connected with or with reference to that <~ hangs a tale —Shak.>

there·for \tha(ə)r-ˈfō(ə)r, the(ə)r-\ *adv* : for or in return for that <ordered a change and gave his reasons ~>

there·fore \ˈtha(ə)r-ˌfō(ə)r, ˈthe(ə)r-, -ˌfȯ(ə)r\ *adv* **1 a** : for that reason : CONSEQUENTLY **b** : because of that **c** : on that ground **2** : to that end

there·from \tha(ə)r-ˈfrəm, the(ə)r-, -ˈfräm\ *adv* : from that or it

there·in \tha-ˈrin, the-\ *adv* **1** : in or into that place, time, or thing **2** : in that particular or respect <~ lies the problem>

there·in·af·ter \ˌthar-in-ˈaf-tər, ˌther-\ *adv* : in the following part of that matter (as writing, document, or speech)

there·in·to \tha-ˈrin-(ˌ)tü, the-\ *adv, archaic* : into that or it

there·of \-ˈrəv, -ˈräv\ *adv* **1** : of that or it **2** : from that cause or particular : THEREFROM <more good ~ shall spring —John Milton>

there·on \-ˈrȯn, -ˈrän\ *adv* **1** : on that <a text with a commentary ~> **2** *archaic* : THEREUPON

there·to \tha(ə)r-ˈtü, the(ə)r-\ *adv* : to that <a text and the notes ~>

there·to·fore \ˈthart-ə-ˌfō(ə)r, ˈthert-, -ˌfȯ(ə)r; ˌthart-ə-ˈ, ˌthert-\ *adv* : up to that time <a ~ unknown author>

there·un·der \tha-ˈrən-dər, the-\ *adv* : under that <acreage with . . . mineral wealth lying ~ —*U.S. Code*>

there·un·to \-ˈrən-(ˌ)tü; ˌthar-ən-ˈtü, ˌther-\ *adv, archaic* : THERETO

there·upon \ˈthar-ə-ˌpȯn, ˈther-, -ˌpän; ˌthar-ə-ˈ, ˌther-\ *adv* **1** : on that matter **2** : THEREFORE **3** : immediately after that

there·with \tha(ə)r-ˈwith, the(ə)r-, -ˈwith\ *adv* **1** : with that **2** *archaic* : THEREUPON, FORTHWITH

there·with·al \ˈtha(ə)r-with-ˌȯl, ˈthe(ə)r-, -with-\ *adv* **1** *archaic* : BESIDES **2** : THEREWITH

the·ri·ac \ˈthir-ē-ˌak\ *n* [NL *theriaca*] **1** : THERIACA **2** : CURE-ALL

the·ri·a·ca \thi-ˈrī-ə-kə\ *n* [NL, fr. L, antidote against poison — more at TREACLE] : a mixture of many drugs and honey formerly held to be an antidote to poison — **the·ri·a·cal** \-kəl\ *adj*

the·rio·mor·phic \ˌthir-ē-ō-ˈmȯr-fik\ *adj* [Gk *thēriomorphos*, fr. *thērion* beast + *morphē* form — more at TREACLE] : having an animal form <~ gods>

[1]therm \ˈthərm\ *n* [Gk *thermē* heat; akin to Gk *thermos* hot — more at WARM] : any of several units of quantity of heat: as **a** : CALORIE 1b **b** : CALORIE 1a **c** : 1000 kilogram calories **d** : 100,000 British thermal units

[2]therm *abbr* thermometer

therm- *or* **thermo-** *comb form* [Gk, fr. *thermē*] **1** : heat <*therm*ion> <*thermo*stat> **2** : thermoelectric <*thermo*pile>

-therm \ˌthərm\ *n comb form* [Gk *thermē* heat] : animal having a (specified) body temperature <ecto*therm*>

ther·mae \ˈthər-ˌmē, -ˌmī\ *n pl* [L, fr. Gk *thermai*, fr. pl. of *thermē* heat] : a public bathing establishment esp. in ancient Greece or Rome

[1]ther·mal \ˈthər-məl\ *adj* [Gk *thermē*] **1** [*thermae*] : of, relating to, or marked by the presence of hot springs <~ waters> **2 a** : of, relating to, or caused by heat <~ stress> <~ insulation> **b** : being or involving a state of matter dependent upon temperature <~ conductivity> <~ agitation of molecular structure> **3** : designed (as with insulating air spaces) to prevent the dissipation of body heat <~ underwear> — **ther·mal·ly** \-mə-lē\ *adv*

[2]thermal *n* : a rising body of warm air

thermal barrier *n* : a limit to unlimited increase in aircraft or rocket speeds imposed by aerodynamic heating

thermal pollution *n* : the discharge of heated liquid (as water) into natural waters at a temperature detrimental to existent ecosystems

thermal spring *n* : a spring whose water issues at a temperature higher than the mean temperature of the locality where the spring is situated

ther·mic \ˈthər-mik\ *adj* : THERMAL 2 <~ energy> — **ther·mi·cal·ly** \-mi-k(ə-)lē\ *adv*

therm·ion \ˈthər-ˌmī-ən, -ˌmī-ˌän\ *n* [ISV *therm-* + *ion*] : an electrically charged particle emitted by an incandescent substance — **therm·ion·ic** \ˌthər-(ˌ)mī-ˈän-ik\ *adj*

thermionic current *n* : an electric current due to the directed movements of thermions (as in the electric discharge through a vacuum tube with the cathode incandescent)

therm·ion·ics \ˌthər-(ˌ)mī-ˈän-iks\ *n pl but sing in constr* : physics dealing with thermionic phenomena

thermionic tube *n* : an electron tube in which electron emission is produced by the heating of an electrode

therm·is·tor \ˈthər-ˌmis-tər\ *n* [*therm*al res*istor*] : an electrical resistor making use of a semiconductor whose resistance varies sharply in a known manner with the temperature

Ther·mit \ˈthər-mət, -ˌmit\ *trademark* —used for thermite

ther·mite \ˈthər-ˌmīt\ *n* [*therm-* + *-ite*] : a mixture of aluminum powder and iron oxide that when ignited evolves a great deal of heat and is used in welding and in incendiary bombs

ther·mo·chem·is·try \ˌthər-mō-ˈkem-ə-strē\ *n* : a branch of chemistry that deals with the interrelation of heat with chemical reaction or physical change of state — **ther·mo·chem·i·cal** \-ˈkem-i-kəl\ *adj* — **ther·mo·chem·ist** \-ˈkem-əst\ *n*

ther·mo·cline \ˈthər-mə-ˌklīn\ *n* : a layer in a thermally stratified body of water that separates an upper warmer lighter oxygen-rich zone from a lower colder heavier oxygen-poor zone; *specif* : a stratum in which temperature declines at least one degree centigrade with each meter increase in depth

ther·mo·co·ag·u·la·tion \ˌthər-mō-kō-ˌag-yə-ˈlā-shən\ *n* : surgical coagulation of tissue by the application of heat

ther·mo·cou·ple \ˈthər-mə-ˌkəp-əl\ *n* : a thermoelectric couple used to measure temperature differences

ther·mo·du·ric \ˌthər-mō-ˈd(y)u̇(ə)r-ik\ *adj* [*therm-* + L *durare* to last — more at DURING] : able to survive high temperatures; *specif* : able to survive pasteurization — used of microorganisms

ther·mo·dy·nam·ic \ˌthər-mō-dī-ˈnam-ik, -də-\ *also* **ther·mo·dy·nam·i·cal** \-i-kəl\ *adj* **1** : of or relating to thermodynamics **2** : being or relating to a system of atoms, molecules, colloidal particles, or larger bodies considered as an isolated group in the study of thermodynamic processes — **ther·mo·dy·nam·i·cal·ly** \-i-k(ə-)lē\ *adv*

ther·mo·dy·nam·ics \-iks\ *n pl but sing or pl in constr* **1** : physics that deals with the mechanical action or relations of heat **2** : thermodynamic processes and phenomena — **ther·mo·dy·nam·i·cist** \-ˈnam-ə-səst\ *n*

ther·mo·elec·tric \ˌthər-mō-i-ˈlek-trik\ *adj* : of, relating to, or dependent on phenomena that involve relations between the temperature and the electrical condition in a metal or in contacting metals

thermoelectric couple *n* : a union of two conductors (as bars or wires of dissimilar metals joined at their extremities) for producing a thermoelectric current

ther·mo·elec·tric·i·ty \ˌthər-mō-i-ˌlek-ˈtris-ət-ē, -ˈtris-tē\ *n* : electricity produced by the direct action of heat (as by the unequal heating of a circuit composed of two dissimilar metals)

ther·mo·elec·tron \-i-ˈlek-ˌträn\ *n* : an electron released in thermionic emission

ther·mo·el·e·ment \-ˈel-ə-mənt\ *n* [*thermo*couple + *element*] : a device for measuring small currents consisting of a wire heating element and a thermocouple in electrical contact with it

ther·mo·form \ˈthər-mə-ˌfȯrm\ *vt* : to give a final shape to (as a plastic) with the aid of heat and usu. pressure — **ther·mo·form·able** \-ˌfȯr-mə-bəl\ *adj*

ther·mo·gram \-ˌgram\ *n* **1** : the record made by a thermograph **2** : a photographic record made by thermography

ther·mo·graph \-ˌgraf\ *n* [ISV] **1** : a self-recording thermometer **2** : THERMOGRAM **3** : the apparatus used in thermography

ther·mog·ra·phy \(ˌ)thər-ˈmäg-rə-fē\ *n* **1** : a process of writing or printing involving the use of heat; *esp* : a raised-printing process in which matter printed by letterpress is dusted with powder and heated to make the lettering rise **2** : a technique for detecting and measuring variations in the heat emitted by various regions of the body and transforming them into visible signals that can be recorded photographically (as for diagnosing abnormal or diseased underlying conditions); *also* : a similar technique used elsewhere (as on engines) — **ther·mo·graph·ic** \ˌthər-mə-ˈgraf-ik\ *adj* — **ther·mo·graph·i·cal·ly** \-i-k(ə-)lē\ *adv*

ther·mo·ha·line \ˌthər-mō-ˈhā-ˌlīn, -ˈhal-ˌīn\ *adj* [*therm-* + Gk *hal-*, *hals* salt — more at SALT] : involving or dependent upon the conjoint effect of temperature and salinity <a trans-equatorial ~ circulation in the eastern Pacific>

ther·mo·junc·tion \ˌthər-mō-ˈjəŋ(k)-shən\ *n* : a junction of two dissimilar conductors used to produce a thermoelectric current
ther·mo·la·bile \-ˈlā-ˌbīl, -bəl\ *adj* [ISV] : unstable when heated; *specif* : subject to loss of characteristic properties on being heated to or above 55°C <many immune bodies, enzymes, and vitamins are ~> — **ther·mo·la·bil·i·ty** \-lā-ˈbil-ət-ē\ *n*
ther·mo·lu·mi·nes·cence \-ˌlü-mə-ˈnes-ᵊn(t)s\ *n* [ISV] : phosphorescence developed in a previously excited substance upon gentle heating — **ther·mo·lu·mi·nes·cent** \-ᵊnt\ *adj*
ther·mol·y·sis \(ˌ)thər-ˈmäl-ə-səs\ *n* [NL] : the dissipation of heat from the living body — **ther·mo·lyt·ic** \ˌthər-mə-ˈlit-ik\ *adj*
ther·mo·mag·net·ic \ˌthər-mō-mag-ˈnet-ik\ *adj* : of or relating to the effects of heat upon the magnetic properties of substances or to the effects of a magnetic field upon thermal conduction — **ther·mo·mag·net·i·cal·ly** \-i-k(ə-)lē\ *adv*
ther·mom·e·ter \thə(r)-ˈmäm-ət-ər\ *n* [F *thermomètre,* fr. Gk *thermē* heat + F *-o-* + *-mètre* -meter — more at THERM] : an instrument for determining temperature consisting typically of a glass bulb attached to a fine tube of glass with a numbered scale and containing a liquid (as mercury or colored alcohol) that is sealed in and rises and falls with changes of temperature
ther·mo·met·ric \ˌthər-mə-ˈme-trik\ *adj* — **ther·mo·met·ri·cal·ly** \-tri-k(ə-)lē\ *adv*
ther·mom·e·try \thə(r)-ˈmäm-ə-trē\ *n* [ISV] : the measurement of temperature
ther·mo·nu·cle·ar \ˌthər-mō-ˈn(y)ü-klē-ər\ *adj* [ISV] **1** : of or relating to the transformations in the nucleus of atoms of low atomic weight (as hydrogen) that require a very high temperature for their inception (as in the hydrogen bomb or in the sun) <~ reaction> <~ weapon> **2** : of, utilizing, or relating to a thermonuclear bomb <~ war> <~ attack>
ther·mo·pe·ri·od·ic·i·ty \-ˌpir-ē-ə-ˈdis-ət-ē\ *n* : THERMOPERIODISM
ther·mo·pe·ri·od·ism \ˌthər-mō-ˈpir-ē-ə-ˌdiz-əm\ *n* : the sum of the responses of an organism and esp. a plant to appropriately fluctuating temperatures
ther·mo·phile \ˈthər-mə-ˌfīl\ *n* : an organism growing at a high temperature — **ther·mo·phil·ic** \ˌthər-mə-ˈfil-ik\ *also* **thermophile** *or* **ther·moph·i·lous** \(ˌ)thər-ˈmäf-ə-ləs\ *adj*
ther·mo·pile \ˈthər-mə-ˌpīl\ *n* [³*pile*] : an apparatus that consists of a number of thermoelectric couples combined so as to multiply the effect and is used for generating electric currents or for determining intensities of radiation
ther·mo·plas·tic \ˌthər-mə-ˈplas-tik\ *adj* : capable of softening or fusing when heated and of hardening again when cooled <~ synthetic resins> — compare THERMOSETTING — **thermoplastic** *n* — **ther·mo·plas·tic·i·ty** \-ˌplas-ˈtis-ət-ē\ *n*
ther·mo·re·cep·tor \ˌthər-mō-ri-ˈsep-tər\ *n* : a sensory end organ that is stimulated by heat or cold
ther·mo·reg·u·la·tion \-ˌreg-yə-ˈlā-shən\ *n* [ISV] : the maintenance or regulation of temperature; *specif* : the maintenance of a particular temperature of the living body
ther·mo·reg·u·la·tor \-ˌlāt-ər\ *n* [ISV] : a device (as a thermostat) for the regulation of temperature

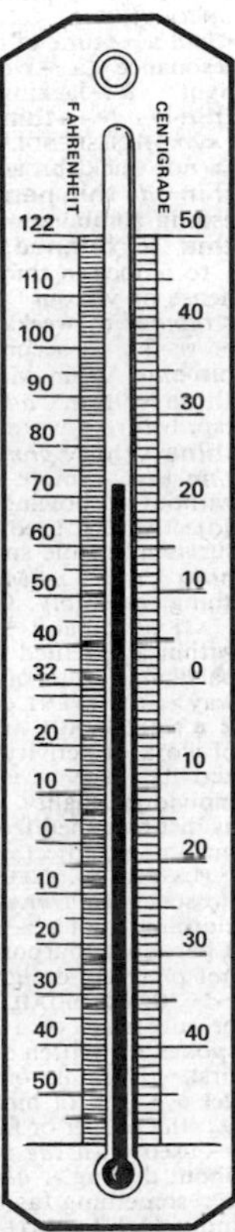

thermometer

ther·mo·reg·u·la·to·ry \-ˈreg-yə-lə-ˌtōr-ē, -ˌtȯr-\ *adj* : tending to maintain a body at a particular temperature whatever its environmental temperature
ther·mo·rem·a·nent \-ˈrem-ə-nənt\ *adj* : being or relating to magnetic remanence (as in a rock cooled from a molten state or in a baked clay object containing magnetic minerals) that indicates the strength and direction of the earth's magnetic field at a former time — **ther·mo·rem·a·nence** \-nən(t)s\ *n*
ther·mos \ˈthər-məs\ *n* [fr. *Thermos,* a trademark] : VACUUM BOTTLE
ther·mo·scope \ˈthər-mə-ˌskōp\ *n* [NL *thermoscopium,* fr. *therm-* + *-scopium* -scope] : an instrument for indicating changes of temperature by accompanying changes in volume (as of a gas)
ther·mo·set \ˈthər-mō-ˌset\ *n* : a thermosetting resin or plastic
ther·mo·set·ting \-ˌset-iŋ\ *adj* : capable of becoming permanently rigid when heated or cured <a ~ resin> — compare THERMOPLASTIC
ther·mo·sphere \ˈthər-mə-ˌsfi(ə)r\ *n* [ISV] : the part of the earth's atmosphere that begins at about 50 miles above the earth's surface, extends to outer space, and is characterized by steadily increasing temperature with height — **ther·mo·spher·ic** \ˌthər-mə-ˈsfi(ə)r-ik, -ˈsfe(ə)r-\ *adj*
ther·mo·sta·ble \ˌthər-mō-ˈstā-bəl\ *adj* : stable when heated; *specif* : retaining characteristic properties on being moderately heated <a ~ bacterial proteinase> — **ther·mo·sta·bil·i·ty** \-stə-ˈbil-ət-ē\ *n*
¹**ther·mo·stat** \ˈthər-mə-ˌstat\ *n* : an automatic device for regulating temperature (as by controlling the supply of gas or electricity to a heating apparatus); *also* : a similar device for actuating fire alarms or for controlling automatic sprinklers — **ther·mo·stat·ic** \ˌthər-mə-ˈstat-ik\ *adj* — **ther·mo·stat·i·cal·ly** \-i-k(ə-)lē\ *adv*
²**thermostat** *vt* **-stat·ed** \-ˌstat-əd\ *or* **-stat·ted; -stat·ing** *or* **-stat·ting** : to provide with or control by a thermostat
ther·mo·tac·tic \ˌthər-mə-ˈtak-tik\ *adj* : of, relating to, or exhibiting thermotaxis
ther·mo·tax·is \-ˈtak-səs\ *n* [NL] **1** : a taxis in which a temperature gradient constitutes the directive factor **2** : the regulation of body temperature
ther·mo·trop·ic \-ˈträp-ik\ *adj* [ISV] : of, relating to, or exhibiting thermotropism
ther·mot·ro·pism \(ˌ)thər-ˈmä-trə-ˌpiz-əm\ *n* [ISV] : a tropism in which a temperature gradient determines the orientation
-ther·my \ˌthər-mē\ *n comb form* [NL *-thermia,* fr. Gk *thermē* heat — more at THERM] **1** : state of heat <homoio*thermy*> **2** : generation of heat <dia*thermy*>
Ther·si·tes \(ˌ)thər-ˈsīt-(ˌ)ēz\ *n* [L, fr. Gk *Thersitēs*] : a Greek warrior at Troy known as a carping critic and slain by Achilles for mocking him
the·sau·rus \thi-ˈsȯr-əs\ *n, pl* **-sau·ri** \-ˈsȯ(ə)r-ˌī, -ˌē\ *or* **-sau·rus·es** \-ˈsȯr-ə-səz\ [NL, fr. L, treasure, collection, fr. Gk *thēsauros*] **1 a** : a book of words or of information about a particular field or set of concepts; *esp* : a book of words and their synonyms **b** : a list of subject headings or descriptors usu. with a cross-reference system for use in the organization of a collection of documents for reference and retrieval **2** : TREASURY, STOREHOUSE — **the·sau·ral** \-ˈsȯr-əl\ *adj*
these *pl of* THIS
The·seus \ˈthē-ˌsüs, -sē-əs\ *n* [L, fr. Gk *Thēseus*] : a king of Athens who according to Greek mythology killed Procrustes and the Minotaur before defeating the Amazons and marrying their queen
the·sis \ˈthē-səs, *Brit esp for 4* ˈthes-is\ *n, pl* **the·ses** \ˈthē-ˌsēz\ [L, fr. Gk, lit., act of laying down, fr. *tithenai* to put, lay down — more at DO] **1 a** : a position or proposition that a person (as a candidate for scholastic honors) advances and offers to maintain by argument **b** : a proposition to be proved or one advanced without proof : HYPOTHESIS **2** : the first and least adequate stage of dialectic — compare SYNTHESIS **3** : a dissertation embodying results of original research and esp. substantiating a specific view; *esp* : one written by a candidate for an academic degree **4** [LL & Gk; LL, lowering of the voice, fr. Gk, downbeat, more important part of foot, lit., act of laying down] **a** (1) : the unstressed part of a poetic foot esp. in accentual verse (2) : the longer part of a poetic foot esp. in quantitative verse **b** : the accented part of a musical measure : DOWNBEAT — compare ARSIS
¹**thes·pi·an** \ˈthes-pē-ən\ *adj* **1** *cap* : of or relating to Thespis **2** *often cap* [fr. the tradition that Thespis was the originator of the actor's role] : relating to the drama : DRAMATIC
²**thespian** *n* : ACTOR
Thess *abbr* Thessalonians
Thes·sa·lo·nians \ˌthes-ə-ˈlō-nyənz, -nē-ənz\ *n pl but sing in constr* [*Thessalonian* (inhabitant of ancient Thessalonica), irreg. fr. *Thessalonica*] : either of two letters written by St. Paul to the Christians of Thessalonica and included as books in the New Testament — see BIBLE table
the·ta \ˈthāt-ə, ˈthēt-\ *n* [Gk *thēta,* of Sem origin; akin to Heb *ṭēth* teth] **:** the 8th letter of the Greek alphabet — see ALPHABET table
thet·ic \ˈthet-ik, ˈthēt-\ *adj* [Gk *thetikos* of a proposition, fr. *tithenai* to lay down] : constituting or beginning with a poetic thesis <a ~ syllable> — **thet·i·cal·ly** \-i-k(ə-)lē\ *adv*
The·tis \ˈthēt-əs\ *n* [L, fr. Gk] : a sea goddess who marries Peleus and becomes the mother of Achilles
the·ur·gist \ˈthē-(ˌ)ər-jəst\ *n* : WONDER-WORKER, MAGICIAN
the·ur·gy \ˈthē-(ˌ)ər-jē\ *n* [LL *theurgia,* fr. LGk *theourgia,* fr. *theourgos* miracle worker, fr. Gk *the-* + *ergon* work — more at WORK] : the art or technique of compelling or persuading a god or beneficent or supernatural power to do or refrain from doing something — **the·ur·gic** \thē-ˈər-jik\ *or* **the·ur·gi·cal** \-ji-kəl\ *adj*
thew \ˈth(y)ü\ *n* [ME, personal quality, virtue, fr. OE *thēaw;* akin to OHG *kathau* discipline] **1** : MUSCLE, SINEW — usu. used in pl. <by the . . . sheer hard labour of our ~*s* we struggled on —J. R. Fethney> **2 a** : muscular power or development **b** : STRENGTH, VITALITY <the naked ~ and sinew of the English language —G. M. Hopkins>
they \(ˈ)t͟hā\ *pron, pl in constr* [ME, fr. ON *their,* masc. pl. demonstrative & personal pron.; akin to OE *thæt* that] **1 a** : those ones — used as third person pronoun serving as the plural of *he, she,* or *it* or referring to a group of two or more individuals not all of the same sex <~ dance well> **b** : ¹HE 2 — often used with an indefinite third person singular antecedent **2** : PEOPLE 1a — used in a generic sense <as lazy as ~ come> <~ say we'll have a hard winter>
they'd \(ˌ)t͟hād\ : they had : they would
they'll \(ˌ)t͟hā(ə)l, t͟hel\ : they will : they shall
they're \t͟hər, (ˌ)t͟he(ə)r\ : they are
they've \(ˌ)t͟hāv\ : they have
thi- *or* **thio-** *comb form* [ISV, fr. Gk *thei-, theio-* sulfur, fr. *theion*] : containing sulfur <*thi*amin> <*thio*phosphate>
thia·ben·da·zole \ˌthī-ə-ˈben-də-ˌzōl\ *n* [*thia*zole + *benz-* + imi*de* + *azole*] : a drug $C_{10}H_7N_3S$ used in the control of parasitic roundworms and in the treatment of fungus infections
thi·ami·nase \thī-ˈam-ə-ˌnās, ˈthī-ə-mə-, -ˌnāz\ *n* [ISV] : an enzyme that promotes the breakdown of thiamine
thi·a·mine \ˈthī-ə-mən, -ˌmēn\ *also* **thi·a·min** \-mən\ *n* [*thiamine* alter. of *thiamin,* fr. *thi-* + *-amin* (as in *vitamin*)] : a vitamin $(C_{12}H_{17}N_4OS)Cl$ of the B complex that is essential to normal metabolism and nerve function and is widespread in plants and animals — called also *vitamin B_1*
thi·a·zide \ˈthī-ə-ˌzīd, -zəd\ *n* [*thia-* + *diazine* + diox*ide*] : any of several drugs used as oral diuretics esp. in the control of high blood pressure

ə abut	ᵊ kitten	ər further	a back	ā bake	ä cot, cart
au̇ out	ch chin	e less	ē easy	g gift	i trip	ī life
j joke	ŋ sing	ō flow	ȯ flaw	ȯi coin	th thin	t͟h this
ü loot	u̇ foot	y yet	yü few	yu̇ furious	zh vision

thi·a·zine \ˈthī-ə-ˌzēn\ *n* [ISV] **:** any of various compounds that are characterized by a ring composed of four carbon atoms, one sulfur atom, and one nitrogen atom and include some important as dyes and others as tranquilizers

thi·a·zole \ˈthī-ə-ˌzōl\ *n* [ISV] **1 :** a colorless basic liquid C_3H_3NS consisting of a five-membered ring and having an odor like pyridine **2 :** any of various thiazole derivatives including some used in the treatment of inflammation and others important as chemical accelerators

[1]thick \ˈthik\ *adj* [ME *thikke,* fr. OE *thicce;* akin to OHG *dicki* thick, OIr *tiug*] **1 a :** having or being of relatively great depth or extent from one surface to its opposite <a ~ plank> **b :** heavily built **:** THICKSET **2 a :** close-packed with units or individuals <the air was ~ with snow> **b :** occurring in large numbers **:** NUMEROUS **c :** viscous in consistency <~ syrup> **d :** SULTRY, STUFFY **e :** marked by haze, fog, or mist <~ weather> **f :** impenetrable to the eye **:** PROFOUND <~ darkness> **g :** extremely intense <~ silence> **3 :** measuring in thickness <12 inches ~> **4 a :** imperfectly articulated **:** INDISTINCT <~ speech> **b :** plainly apparent **:** DECIDED <a ~ French accent> **c :** producing inarticulate speech <a ~ tongue> **5 :** OBTUSE, STUPID **6 :** associated on close terms **:** INTIMATE <was quite ~ with his pastor> **7 :** exceeding bounds of propriety or fitness **:** EXCESSIVE <called it a bit ~ to be fired without warning> ***syn*** see CLOSE — **thick·ish** \-ish\ *adj* — **thick·ly** *adv*

[2]thick *n* **1 :** the most crowded or active part <in the ~ of the battle> **2 :** the part of greatest thickness <the ~ of the thumb>

[3]thick *adv* **:** in a thick manner **:** THICKLY

thick and thin *n* **:** every difficulty and obstacle — used esp. in the phrase *through thick and thin*

thick·en \ˈthik-ən\ *vb* **thick·ened; thick·en·ing** \-(ə-)niŋ\ *vt* **1 a :** to make thick, dense, or viscous in consistency <~ gravy with flour> **b :** to make close or compact **2 :** to increase the depth or diameter of **3 :** to make inarticulate **:** BLUR <alcohol ~*ed* his speech> ~ *vi* **1 a :** to become dense <the mist ~*ed*> **b :** to become concentrated in numbers, mass, or frequency **2 :** to grow blurred or obscure **3 :** to grow broader or bulkier **4 :** to grow complicated or keen <the plot ~*s*> — **thick·en·er** \-(ə-)nər\ *n*

thick·en·ing *n* **1 :** the act of making or becoming thick **2 :** something used to thicken (as flour in a gravy) **3 :** a thickened part or place

thick·et \ˈthik-ət\ *n* [(assumed) ME *thikket,* fr. OE *thiccet,* fr. *thicce* thick] **1 :** a dense growth of shrubbery or small trees **:** COPPICE **2 :** something resembling a thicket in density or impenetrability **:** TANGLE <minds, existing in a ~ of practicalities and contingencies —Richard Todd> — **thick·ety** \-ē\ *adj*

thick·et·ed \ˈthik-ət-əd\ *adj* **:** dotted or covered with thickets

thick·head \ˈthik-ˌhed\ *n* **:** a stupid person **:** BLOCKHEAD

thick·head·ed \-ˈhed-əd\ *adj* **1 :** having a thick head **2 :** sluggish and obtuse of mind

thick·ness \-nəs\ *n* **1 :** the quality or state of being thick **2 :** the smallest of three dimensions <length, width, and ~> **3 a :** viscous consistency <boiled to the ~ of honey> **b :** the condition of being smoky, foul, or foggy **4 :** the thick part of something **5 :** CONCENTRATION, DENSITY **6 :** STUPIDITY, DULLNESS **7 :** LAYER, PLY, SHEET <a single ~ of canvas>

thick·set \-ˈset\ *adj* **1 :** closely placed; *also* **:** growing thickly <a ~ wood> **2 :** having a thick body **:** BURLY

thick–skinned \-ˈskind\ *adj* **1 :** having a thick skin **:** PACHYDERMATOUS **2 :** CALLOUS, INSENSITIVE

thick–wit·ted \-ˈwit-əd\ *adj* **:** dull or slow of mind **:** STUPID

thief \ˈthēf\ *n, pl* **thieves** \ˈthēvz\ [ME *theef,* fr. OE *thēof;* akin to OHG *diob* thief, Lith *tupėti* to crouch] **:** one that steals esp. stealthily or secretly; *also* **:** one who commits theft or larceny

thieve \ˈthēv\ *vb* **thieved; thiev·ing** [fr. *thief*] **:** STEAL, ROB

thiev·ery \ˈthēv-(ə-)rē\ *n, pl* **-er·ies :** the act or practice or an instance of stealing **:** THEFT

thiev·ish \ˈthē-vish\ *adj* **1 :** given to stealing **2 :** of, relating to, or characteristic of a thief — **thiev·ish·ly** *adv* — **thiev·ish·ness** *n*

thigh \ˈthī\ *n* [ME, fr. OE *thēoh;* akin to OHG *dioh* thigh, L *tumēre* to swell — more at THUMB] **1 a :** the proximal segment of the vertebrate hind limb extending from the hip to the knee and supported by a single large bone **b :** the segment of the leg immediately distal to the thigh in a bird or in a quadruped in which the true thigh is obscured **c :** the femur of an insect **2 :** something resembling or covering a thigh — **thighed** \ˈthīd\ *adj*

thigh·bone \ˈthī-ˈbōn, -ˌbōn\ *n* **:** FEMUR

thig·mo·tax·is \ˌthig-mə-ˈtak-səs\ *n* [NL, fr. Gk *thigma* touch (fr. *thinganein* to touch) + NL *-taxis;* akin to L *fingere* to shape — more at DOUGH] **:** a taxis in which contact esp. with a solid body is the directive factor

thig·mot·ro·pism \thig-ˈmä-trə-ˌpiz-əm\ *n* [Gk *thigma* + ISV *-o-* + *-tropism*] **:** a tropism in which contact esp. with a solid or a rigid surface is the orienting factor

thill \ˈthil\ *n* [ME *thille,* perh. fr. OE, plank; akin to OHG *dili* plank, L *tellus* earth] **:** a shaft of a vehicle

thim·ble \ˈthim-bəl\ *n* [ME *thymbyl,* prob. alter. of OE *thȳmel* thumbstall, fr. *thūma* thumb] **1 :** a pitted cap or cover worn on the finger to push the needle in sewing **2 :** a thimble-shaped cup, appendage, or fixture: as **a :** a grooved ring of thin metal used to fit in a spliced loop in a rope as protection from chafing **b :** a fixed or movable ring, tube, or lining in a hole

thim·ble·ber·ry \-ˌber-ē\ *n* **:** any of several American raspberries or blackberries (esp. *Rubus occidentalis, R. parviflorus,* and *R. argutus*) having thimble-shaped fruit

thim·ble·ful \-ˌfu̇l\ *n* **1 :** as much as a thimble will hold **2 :** a very small quantity

[1]thim·ble·rig \-ˌrig\ *n* **1 :** a swindling trick in which a small ball or pea is quickly shifted from under one to another of three small cups to fool the spectator guessing its location **2 :** one who manipulates the cup in thimblerig **:** THIMBLERIGGER

[2]thimblerig *vt* **1 :** to swindle by thimblerig **2 :** to cheat by trickery — **thim·ble·rig·ger** *n*

thim·ble·weed \ˈthim-bəl-ˌwēd\ *n* **:** any of various anemones (as *Anemone virginiana*)

thi·mer·o·sal \thī-ˈmer-ə-ˌsal\ *n* [prob. fr. *thi-* + *mercury* + *-o-* + *salicylate*] **:** a crystalline organic mercurial $C_9H_9HgNaO_2S$ used as an antiseptic and germicide

[1]thin \ˈthin\ *adj* **thin·ner; thin·nest** [ME *thinne,* fr. OE *thynne;* akin to OHG *dunni* thin, L *tenuis* thin, *tenēre* to hold, *tendere* to stretch, Gk *teinein*] **1 a :** having little extent from one surface to its opposite <~ paper> **b :** measuring little in cross section or diameter <~ rope> **2 :** not dense in arrangement or distribution <~ hair> **3 :** not well fleshed **:** LEAN **4 a :** more fluid or rarefied than normal <~ air> **b :** having less than the usual number **:** SCANTY <~ attendance> **c :** few in number **:** SCARCE **d :** scantily supplied **e :** characterized by a paucity of bids or offerings <a ~ market> **5 a :** lacking substance or strength <~ broth> <a ~ plot> **b** *of a soil* **:** POOR, INFERTILE **6 a :** FLIMSY, UNCONVINCING <a ~ disguise> **b :** disappointingly poor or hard <had a ~ time of it> **7 :** somewhat feeble, shrill, and lacking in resonance <a ~ voice> **8 :** lacking in intensity or brilliance <~ light> **9 :** lacking sufficient photographic density or contrast — **thin·ly** *adv* — **thin·ness** \ˈthin-nəs\ *n* — **thin·nish** \ˈthin-ish\ *adj*
syn THIN, SLENDER, SLIM, SLIGHT, TENUOUS *shared meaning element* **:** not thick, broad, abundant, or dense ***ant*** thick

[2]thin *adv* **thin·ner; thin·nest :** in a thin manner **:** THINLY — used esp. in combinations <*thin*-clad>

[3]thin *vb* **thinned; thin·ning** *vt* **:** to make thin or thinner: **a :** to reduce in thickness or depth **:** ATTENUATE **b :** to make less dense or viscous **c :** DILUTE, WEAKEN **d :** to cause to lose flesh <*thinned* by weeks of privation> **e :** to reduce in number or bulk ~ *vi* **1 :** to become thin or thinner **2 :** to become weak

thin·clad \ˈthin-ˌklad\ *n* **:** a runner on a track team

[1]thine \(ˈ)t͟hīn\ *adj* [ME *thin,* fr. OE *thīn*] *archaic* **:** THY — used esp. before a word beginning with a vowel or *h*

[2]thine \ˈt͟hīn\ *pron, sing or pl in constr* [ME *thin,* fr. OE *thīn,* fr. *thū* thy — more at THY] **:** that which belongs to thee — used without a following noun as a pronoun equivalent in meaning to the adjective *thy;* used esp. in ecclesiastical or poetic language and still surviving in the speech of Friends esp. among themselves

thing \ˈthiŋ\ *n* [ME, fr. OE, thing, assembly; akin to OHG *ding* thing, assembly, Goth *theihs* time] **1 a :** a matter of concern **:** AFFAIR <many ~*s* to do> **b** *pl* **:** state of affairs in general or within a specified or implied sphere <~*s* are improving> **c :** a particular state of affairs **:** SITUATION <look at this ~ another way> **d :** EVENT, CIRCUMSTANCE <that shooting was a terrible ~> **2 a :** DEED, ACT, ACCOMPLISHMENT <do great ~*s*> **b :** a product of work or activity <likes to build ~*s*> **c :** the aim of effort or activity <the ~ is to get well> **3 a :** a separate and distinct individual quality, fact, idea, or usu. entity **b :** the concrete entity as distinguished from its appearances **c :** a spatial entity **d :** an inanimate object distinguished from a living being **4 a** *pl* **:** POSSESSIONS, EFFECTS <pack your ~*s*> **b :** whatever may be possessed or owned or be the object of a right **c :** an article of clothing <not a ~ to wear> **d** *pl* **:** equipment or utensils esp. for a particular purpose <bring the tea ~*s*> **5 :** an object or entity not precisely designated or capable of being designated <use this ~> **6 a :** DETAIL, POINT <checks every little ~> **b :** a material or substance of a specified kind <avoid starchy ~*s*> **7 a :** a spoken or written observation or point **b :** IDEA, NOTION <says the first ~ he thinks of> **c :** a piece of news or information <couldn't get a ~ out of him> **8 :** INDIVIDUAL <not a living ~ in sight> **9 :** the proper or fashionable way of behaving, talking, or dressing — used with *the* **10 a :** a mild obsession or phobia <has a ~ about driving>; *also* **:** the object of such an obsession or phobia **b :** something (as an activity) that makes a strong appeal to the individual **:** FORTE <letting students do their own ~ —*Newsweek*>

thing·am·a·bob \ˈthiŋ-ə-mə-ˌbäb\ *n* **:** THINGAMAJIG

thing·am·a·jig *or* **thing·um·a·jig** \ˈthiŋ-ə-mə-ˌjig\ *n* [alter. of earlier *thingum,* fr. *thing*] **:** something that is hard to classify or whose name is unknown or forgotten

thing–in–itself *n, pl* **things–in–themselves** [trans. of G *ding an sich*] **:** NOUMENON

thing·ness \ˈthiŋ-nəs\ *n* **:** the quality or state of objective existence or reality

thing·um·my \ˈthiŋ-ə-mē\ *n, pl* **-mies** [alter. of earlier *thingum*] **:** THINGAMAJIG

[1]think \ˈthiŋk\ *vb* **thought** \ˈthȯt\; **think·ing** [ME *thenken,* fr. OE *thencan;* akin to OHG *denken* to think, L *tongēre* to know — more at THANK] *vt* **1 :** to form or have in the mind **2 :** to have as an intention <*thought* to return early> **3 a :** to have as an opinion <~ it's so> **b :** to regard as **:** CONSIDER <~ the rule unfair> **4 a :** to reflect on **:** PONDER <~ the matter over> **b :** to determine by reflecting <~ what to do next> **5 :** to call to mind **:** REMEMBER <he never ~*s* to ask how we do> **6 :** to devise by thinking — usu. used with *up* <*thought* up a plan to escape> **7 :** to have as an expectation **:** ANTICIPATE <we didn't ~ we'd have any trouble> **8 a :** to center one's thoughts on <talks and ~*s* business> **b :** to form a mental picture of **9 :** to subject to the processes of logical thought <~ things out> ~ *vi* **1 a :** to exercise the powers of judgment, conception, or inference **:** REASON **b :** to have in or call to mind a thought **2 a :** to have the mind engaged in reflection **:** MEDITATE **b :** to consider the suitability <*thought* of him for president> **3 :** to have a view or opinion **:** REGARD <~*s* of himself as a poet> **4 :** to have concern — usu. used with *of* <a man must ~ first of his family> **5 :** EXPECT, SUSPECT <better than he ~*s* possible> — **think·er** *n*
syn **1** THINK, CONCEIVE, IMAGINE, FANCY, REALIZE, ENVISAGE, ENVISION *shared meaning element* **:** to form an idea of something in the mind
2 THINK, COGITATE, REFLECT, REASON, SPECULATE, DELIBERATE *shared meaning element* **:** to use one's powers of conception, judgment, or inference
3 see KNOW

— **think better of :** to reconsider and make a wiser decision — **think much of :** to view with satisfaction : APPROVE — usu. used in negative constructions <he didn't *think much of* the new car>

²think *n* : an act of thinking <has another ~ coming>

³think *adj* : of or relating to thinking

think·able \'thiŋ-kə-bəl\ *adj* **1 :** capable of being comprehended or reasoned about <the ultimate nature of Deity is scarcely ~> **2 :** conceivably possible — **think·able·ness** *n* — **think·ably** \-blē\ *adv*

¹think·ing *n* **1 :** the action of using one's mind to produce thoughts **2 a :** OPINION, JUDGMENT **b :** thought that is characteristic (as of a period, group, or person) <the current student ~ on fraternities>

²thinking *adj* : marked by use of the intellect : RATIONAL <~ citizens> — **think·ing·ly** \'thiŋ-kiŋ-lē\ *adv* — **think·ing·ness** *n*

thinking cap *n* : a state or mood in which one thinks

think piece *n* : a news article consisting chiefly of background material and personal opinion and analysis

think tank *n* : an institute, corporation, or group organized for interdisciplinary research (as in technological and social problems) — called also *think factory*

thin–layer chromatography *n* : chromatography in which the absorbent medium is a thin layer (as of siliceous fibers) — **thin–layer chromatographic** *adj*

thin·ner \'thin-ər\ *n* : one that thins; *specif* : a volatile liquid (as turpentine) used esp. to thin paint

thin–skinned \'thin-'skind\ *adj* **1 :** having a thin skin or rind **2 :** unduly susceptible to criticism or insult : TOUCHY

thio- — see THI-

thio·ace·tic acid \ˌthī-ō-ə-ˌsēt-ik-\ *n* [ISV] : a pungent liquid acid C_2H_4OS made by heating acetic acid with a phosphorus sulfide and used as a chemical reagent

thio acid \'thī-ō-\ *n* [ISV, fr. *thi-*] : an acid in which oxygen is partly or wholly replaced by sulfur

thio·car·ba·mide \ˌthī-ō-'kär-bə-ˌmīd, -kär-'bam-ˌīd\ *n* [ISV] : THIOUREA

thio·cy·a·nate \-'sī-ə-ˌnāt, -nət\ *n* [ISV] : a salt or ester of thiocyanic acid

thio·cy·an·ic \-sī-'an-ik\ *adj* [ISV] : of, relating to, or being a colorless unstable liquid acid HSCN of strong odor

thio·gua·nine \-'gwän-ˌēn\ *n* : a crystalline compound $C_5H_5N_5S$ that is an antimetabolite and has been used in the treatment of leukemia

Thi·o·kol \'thī-ə-ˌkȯl, -ˌkōl\ *trademark* — used for polysulfide polymers or water-dispersed latices

thi·ol \'thī-ˌȯl, -ˌōl\ *n* [ISV *thi-* + ¹*-ol*] **1 :** MERCAPTAN **2 :** the group SH characteristic of mercaptans — **thi·o·lic** \thī-'ō-lik\ *adj*

thion- *comb form* [ISV, fr. Gk *theion*] : sulfur <*thion*ic>

thi·o·nate \'thī-ə-ˌnāt\ *n* [ISV] : a salt or ester of a thionic acid

thi·on·ic \thī-'än-ik\ *adj* [ISV] : relating to or containing sulfur

thionic acid *n* **1 :** any of various unstable acids of the general formula $H_2S_xO_6$ **2 :** a thio acid in which sulfur is doubly bonded to another atom

thio·pen·tal \ˌthī-ō-'pen-ˌtal, -ˌtȯl\ *n* [*thio-* + *pento*barbit*al*] : a barbiturate $C_{11}H_{18}N_2O_2S$ used as the sodium derivative in intravenous anesthesia and psychotherapy

thio·phene \'thī-ə-ˌfēn\ *n* [ISV *thi-* + *phene* (benzene)] : a heterocyclic liquid C_4H_4S from coal tar that resembles benzene

thio·phos·phate \ˌthī-ō-'fäs-ˌfāt\ *n* [ISV] : a salt or ester of a thiophosphoric acid

thio·phos·pho·ric acid \-ˌfäs-ˌfȯr-ik-, -ˌfär-; -ˌfäs-f(ə-)rik-\ *n* : an acid derived from a phosphoric acid by replacement of one or more atoms of oxygen with sulfur

thio·sul·fate \-'səl-ˌfāt\ *n* [ISV] : a salt or ester of thiosulfuric acid

thio·sul·fu·ric \-ˌsəl-'fyu̇(ə)r-ik\ *adj* : of, relating to, or being an unstable acid $H_2S_2O_3$ derived from sulfuric acid by replacement of one oxygen atom by sulfur and known only in solution or in salts and esters

thio·te·pa \ˌthī-ə-'tē-pə\ *n* [*thi-* + *tepa*] : a sulfur analogue of tepa $C_6H_{12}N_3PS$ that is used esp. as an antineoplastic agent and is less toxic than tepa

thio·ura·cil \ˌthī-ō-'yu̇r-ə-ˌsil\ *n* [ISV *thi-* + *uracil*] : a bitter crystalline compound $C_4H_4N_2OS$ that depresses the function of the thyroid gland

thio·urea \-yu̇-'rē-ə\ *n* [NL, fr. *thi-* + *urea*] : a colorless crystalline bitter compound $CS(NH_2)_2$ analogous to and resembling urea that is used esp. as a photographic and organic chemical reagent; *also* : a substituted derivative of this compound

thir \t͟hər, (ˈ)t͟hi(ə)r, (ˈ)t͟hu̇(ə)r\ *pron* [ME (northern), perh. irreg. fr. ME *this*] *dial Brit* : THESE

thi·ram \'thī-ˌram\ *n* [prob. by alter. fr. *thiuram* (the chemical radical NH_2CS)] : a compound $C_6H_{12}N_2S_4$ used as a fungicide and seed disinfectant

¹third \'thərd\ *adj* [ME *thridde, thirde*, fr. OE *thridda, thirdda;* akin to L *tertius* third, Gk *tritos, treis* three — more at THREE] **1 a :** being next to the second in place or time <the ~ man in line> **b :** ranking next to the second of a grade or degree in authority or precedence <~ mate> **c :** being the forward speed or gear next higher than second in a motor vehicle **2 a :** being one of three equal parts into which something is divisible **b :** being the last in each group of three in a series <take out every ~ card> — **third** *or* **third·ly** *adv*

²third *n* **1 a** — see NUMBER table **b :** one that is next after second in rank, position, authority, or precedence <the ~ in line> **2 :** one of three equal parts of something **3 a :** the musical interval embracing three diatonic degrees **b :** a tone at this interval; *specif* : MEDIANT **c :** the harmonic combination of two tones a third apart **4** *pl* : merchandise whose quality falls below the manufacturer's standard for seconds **5 :** THIRD BASE **6 :** the third forward gear or speed of a motor vehicle

third base *n* **1 :** the base that must be touched third by a base runner in baseball **2 :** the player position for defending the area around third base — **third baseman** *n*

third–class *adj* : of or relating to a class, rank, or grade next below the second — **third–class** *adv*

third class *n* **1 :** the third and usu. next below second class in a classification **2 :** the least expensive class of accommodations (as on a passenger ship) **3 a :** a class of U.S. mail comprising printed matter exclusive of regularly issued periodicals and merchandise less than 16 ounces in weight and not sealed against inspection **b :** a similar class of Canadian mail with different weight limits

third degree *n* : the subjection of a prisoner to mental or physical torture to wring a confession from him

third–degree burn *n* : a burn characterized by destruction of the skin through the depth of the derma and possibly into underlying tissues, loss of fluid, and sometimes shock

third dimension *n* **1 :** THICKNESS, DEPTH; *also* : a dimension that adds the effect of solidity to a two-dimensional system **2 :** a quality that confers reality or lifelikeness <night sounds that stick in the mind and give a *third dimension* to the memory —Adie Suehsdorf> — **third–di·men·sion·al** \ˌthərd-də-'mench-nəl, -(ˌ)dī-, -ən-ᵊl\ *adj*

third estate *n, often cap T & E* : the third of the traditional political orders; *specif* : the commons

third force *n* : a grouping (as of political parties or international powers) intermediate between two opposing political forces

third·hand \'thərd-'hand\ *adj* **1 :** received from or through two intermediaries <~ information> **2 a :** acquired after being used by two previous owners **b :** dealing in thirdhand merchandise

third house *n* : a legislative lobby

third market *n* : the over-the-counter market in listed securities

third order *n, often cap T & O* **1 :** an organization composed of lay people living in secular society under a religious rule and directed by a religious order **2 :** a congregation esp. of teaching or nursing sisters affiliated with a religious order

third party *n* **1 :** a person other than the principals <a *third party* to a divorce proceeding> **2 a :** a major political party operating over a limited period of time in addition to two other major parties in a nation or state normally characterized by a two-party system **b :** MINOR PARTY

third person *n* **1 a :** a set of linguistic forms (as verb forms, pronouns, and inflectional affixes) referring to one that is neither the speaker or writer of the utterance in which they occur nor the one to whom that utterance is addressed **b :** a linguistic form belonging to such a set **2 :** reference of a linguistic form to one that is neither the speaker or writer of the utterance in which it occurs nor the one to whom that utterance is addressed

third rail *n* : a metal rail through which electric current is led to the motors of an electric locomotive

third–rate \'thər-'drāt\ *adj* : of third quality or value; *specif* : worse than second-rate — **third–rat·er** \-'drāt-ər\ *n*

third reading *n* : the final stage of the consideration of a legislative bill before a vote on its final disposition

third sex *n* : HOMOSEXUALS

third–stream *adj* : of, relating to, or being music that incorporates elements of classical music and jazz

third ventricle *n* : the median unpaired ventricle of the brain bounded by parts of the telencephalon and diencephalon

third world *n, often cap T&W* **1 :** a group of nations esp. in Africa and Asia that are not aligned with either the Communist or the non-Communist blocs **2 :** an aggregate of minority groups within a larger predominant culture **3 :** the aggregate of the underdeveloped nations of the world

¹thirl \'thər(-ə)l\ *n* [ME, fr. OE *thyrel*, fr. *thurh* through — more at THROUGH] *dial* : HOLE, PERFORATION, OPENING

²thirl *vt* **1** *dial Brit* : PIERCE, PERFORATE **2** *dial Brit* : THRILL

¹thirst \'thərst\ *n* [ME, fr. OE *thurst;* akin to OHG *durst* thirst, L *torrēre* to dry, parch, Gk *tersesthai* to become dry] **1 a :** a sensation of dryness in the mouth and throat associated with a desire for liquids; *also* : the bodily condition (as of dehydration) that induces this sensation **b :** a desire or need to drink **2 :** an ardent desire : CRAVING, LONGING

²thirst *vi* **1 :** to feel thirsty : suffer thirst **2 :** to crave vehemently and urgently ***syn*** see LONG — **thirst·er** *n*

thirst·i·ly \'thər-stə-lē\ *adv* : with or on account of thirst

thirsty \'thər-stē\ *adj* **thirst·i·er; -est** **1 a :** feeling thirst **b :** deficient in moisture : PARCHED <~ land> **c :** highly absorbent <~ towels> **2 :** having a strong desire : AVID <~ for knowledge> — **thirst·i·ness** \-stē-nəs\ *n*

thir·teen \ˌthər(t)-'tēn, 'thər(t)-ˌ\ *n* [ME *thrittene*, fr. *thrittene*, adj., fr. OE *thrēotīne;* akin to OE *tīen* ten — more at TEN] — see NUMBER table — **thirteen** *adj or pron* — **thir·teenth** \-'tēn(t)th\ *adj or n*

thir·ty \'thərt-ē\ *n, pl* **thirties** [ME *thritty*, fr. *thritty*, adj., fr. OE *thrītig*, fr. *thrītig* group of 30, fr. *thrie* three + *-tig* group of ten — more at EIGHTY] **1** — see NUMBER table **2** *pl* : the numbers 30 to 39; *specif* : the years 30 to 39 in a lifetime or century **3 :** a sign of completion : END — usu. written 30 <wrote ~ on the last page of his story> **4 :** the second point scored by a side in a game of tennis **5 :** a .30 caliber machine gun — usu. written .30 — **thir·ti·eth** \-ē-əth\ *adj or n* — **thirty** *adj or pron*

thir·ty–eight \ˌthərt-ē-'āt\ *n* **1** — see NUMBER table **2 :** a .38 caliber pistol — usu. written .38 — **thirty–eight** *adj or pron*

thir·ty–sec·ond note \-'sek-ən-ˌnōt\ *n* : a musical note with the time value of $^1/_{32}$ of a whole note — see NOTE illustration

thir·ty–sec·ond rest \-ˌsek-ən-'(d)rest\ *n* : a musical rest corresponding in time value to a thirty-second note

thir·ty–thir·ty \ˌthərt-ē-'thərt-ē\ *n* : a rifle that fires a .30 caliber cartridge having a 30 grain powder charge — usu. written .30-30

thir·ty–three \ˌthərt-ē-ˈthrē\ *n* **1** — see NUMBER table **2 :** a microgroove phonograph record designed to be played at 33⅓ revolutions per minute — usu. written 33 — **thirty–three** *adj or pron*

thir·ty–two \-ˈtü\ *n* **1** — see NUMBER table **2 :** a .32 caliber pistol — usu. written .32 — **thirty–two** *adj or pron*

thir·ty–two·mo \-(ˌ)mō\ *n, pl* **-mos :** the size of a piece of paper cut 32 from a sheet; *also* **:** a book, a page, or paper of this size

1this \(ˈ)t͟his, t͟həs\ *pron, pl* **these** \(ˈ)t͟hēz\ [ME, pron. & adj., fr. OE *thes* (masc.), *this* (neut.); akin to OHG *dese* this; akin to OE *thæt* that] **1 a (1) :** the person, thing, or idea that is present or near in place, time, or thought or that has just been mentioned <*these* are my hands> **(2) :** what is stated in the following phrase, clause, or discourse <I can only say ~: he wasn't here yesterday> **b :** this time or place <expected to return before ~> **2 a :** the one nearer or more immediately under observation or discussion <~ is iron and that is tin> **b :** the latter one

2this *adj* **1 a :** being the person, thing, or idea that is present or near in place, time, or thought or that has just been mentioned <~ book is mine> <early ~ morning> **b :** constituting the immediately following part of the present discourse **c :** constituting the immediate past or future <friends all *these* years> **d :** being one not previously mentioned — used esp. in narrative to give a sense of immediacy or vividness <she had on ~ big hat, pulled down low around her face —Berry Morgan> **2 :** being the nearer at hand or more immediately under observation or discussion <~ car or that one>

3this \ˈt͟his\ *adv* **:** to the degree or extent indicated by something in the immediate context or situation <didn't expect to wait ~ long>

This·be \ˈthiz-bē\ *n* [L, fr. Gk *Thisbē*] **:** a legendary young woman of Babylon who dies for love of Pyramus

this·tle \ˈthis-əl\ *n* [ME *thistel,* fr. OE; akin to OHG *distill* thistle] **:** any of various prickly composite plants (esp. genera *Carduus, Circium,* and *Onopordon*) with often showy heads of mostly tubular flowers; *also* **:** any of various other prickly plants — **this·tly** \ˈthis-(ə-)lē\ *adj*

thistle

this·tle·down \ˈthis-əl-ˌdau̇n\ *n* **:** the pappus from the ripe flower head of a thistle

thistle tube *n* **:** a funnel tube usu. of glass with a bulging top and flaring mouth

this–world·li·ness \ˈt͟his-ˈwərld-lē-nəs\ *n* **:** interest in, concern with, or devotion to things of this world

this–world·ly \-lē\ *adj* **:** characterized by or manifesting this-worldliness <the struggle between ~ and otherworldly values —George Orwell>

1thith·er \ˈthit͟h-ər *also* ˈt͟hit͟h-\ *adv* [ME, fr. OE *thider;* akin to ON *thathra* there, OE *thæt* that] **:** to that place **:** THERE

2thither *adj* **:** being on the other and farther side **:** more remote

thith·er·to \-ˌtü; ˌthit͟h-ər-ˈ, ˌt͟hit͟h-\ *adv* **:** until that time

thith·er·ward \ˈthit͟h-ər-wərd, ˈt͟hit͟h-\ *also* **thith·er·wards** \-wərdz\ *adv* **:** toward that place **:** THITHER

thix·ot·ro·py \thik-ˈsä-trə-pē\ *n* [ISV *thixo-* (fr. Gk *thixis* act of touching, fr. *thinganein* to touch) + *-tropy* — more at THIGMOTAXIS] **:** the property of various gels of becoming fluid when disturbed (as by shaking) — **thixo·tro·pic** \ˌthik-sə-ˈtrō-pik, -ˈträp-ik\ *adj*

ThM *abbr* [NL *theologiae magister*] master of theology

tho *var of* THOUGH

1thole \ˈthōl\ *vb* **tholed; thol·ing** [ME *tholen,* fr. OE *tholian*] *chiefly dial* **:** ENDURE

2thole *n* [ME *tholle,* fr. OE *thol;* akin to Gk *tylos* knob, callus, L *tumēre* to swell — more at THUMB] **1 :** PEG, PIN **2 :** one of a pair of pins set in the gunwale of a boat to serve as oarlocks

tho·lei·ite \ˈt(h)ō-lə-ˌīt\ *n* [G *tholeiit,* fr. *Tholey,* village in Saarland, Germany + G *-it* -ite] **:** a basaltic rock that is rich in aluminum and low in potassium, typically underlies the depths of the sea, and is prob. derived from the earth's mantle — **tho·lei·it·ic** \ˌt(h)ō-lə-ˈit-ik\ *adj*

thole·pin \ˈthōl-ˌpin\ *n* **:** THOLE 2

Thom·as \ˈtäm-əs\ *n* [Gk *Thōmas,* fr. Heb *tʼōm* twin] **:** an apostle who demanded proof of Christ's resurrection

Thom·as Jef·fer·son's Birthday \ˌtäm-əs-ˌjef-ər-sənz-\ *n* **:** April 13 observed as a legal holiday in Alabama, Missouri, Oklahoma, and Virginia

Tho·mism \ˈtō-ˌmiz-əm\ *n* [prob. fr. (assumed) NL *thomismus,* fr. St. *Thomas* Aquinas] **:** the scholastic philosophical and theological system of St. Thomas Aquinas — **Tho·mist** \-məst\ *n or adj* — **Tho·mis·tic** \tō-ˈmis-tik\ *adj*

Thomp·son submachine gun \ˈtäm(p)-sən-\ *n* [John T. *Thompson* †1940 Am army officer] **:** a .45 caliber submachine gun with a magazine or drum feed, a pistol grip, and a buttstock — called also *tommy gun*

thong \ˈthȯŋ\ *n* [ME, fr. OE *thwong;* akin ON *thvengr* thong, Av *thwazjaiti* he is distressed] **1 :** a strip esp. of leather or hide **2 :** a sandal held on the foot by a thong fitting between the toes and connected to a strap across the top or around the sides of the foot — **thonged** \ˈthȯŋd\ *adj*

Thor \ˈthō(ə)r\ *n* [ON *Thōrr*] **:** the Norse god of thunder, weather, and crops

tho·rac·ic \thə-ˈras-ik\ *adj* **:** of, relating to, located within, or involving the thorax — **tho·rac·i·cal·ly** \-i-k(ə-)lē\ *adv*

thoracic duct *n* **:** the main trunk of the system of lymphatic vessels that lies along the front of the spinal column and opens into the left subclavian vein

tho·ra·cot·o·my \ˌthōr-ə-ˈkät-ə-mē, ˌthȯr-\ *n, pl* **-mies** [L *thorac-, thorax* + ISV *-tomy*] **:** surgical incision of the chest wall

tho·rax \ˈthō(ə)r-ˌaks, ˈthȯ(ə)r-\ *n, pl* **tho·rax·es** *or* **tho·ra·ces** \ˈthōr-ə-ˌsēz, ˈthȯr-\ [ME, fr. L *thorac-, thorax* breastplate, thorax, fr. Gk *thōrak-, thōrax*] **1 :** the part of the mammalian body between the neck and the abdomen; *also* **:** its cavity in which the heart and lungs lie **2 :** the middle of the three chief divisions of the body of an insect; *also* **:** the corresponding part of a crustacean or an arachnid

tho·ria \ˈthōr-ē-ə, ˈthȯr-\ *n* [NL, fr. *thorium* + *-a*] **:** a powdery white oxide of thorium ThO_2 used esp. as a catalyst and in crucibles and refractories and optical glass

tho·ri·a·nite \-ē-ə-ˌnīt\ *n* [irreg. fr. *thoria*] **:** a strongly radioactive mineral ThO_2 that is an oxide of thorium and often contains rare-earth metals

tho·ric \ˈthȯr-ik, ˈthär-, ˈthōr-\ *adj* **:** of, relating to, or containing thorium

tho·rite \ˈthō(ə)r-ˌīt, ˈthȯ(ə)r-\ *n* [Sw *thorit,* fr. NL *thorium*] **:** a rare mineral $ThSiO_4$ that is a brown to black or sometimes orange-yellow thorium silicate resembling zircon

tho·ri·um \ˈthōr-ē-əm, ˈthȯr-\ *n* [NL, fr. ON *Thōrr* Thor] **:** a radioactive tetravalent metallic element that occurs combined in minerals and is usu. associated with rare earths — see ELEMENT table

thorn \ˈthȯ(ə)rn\ *n, often attrib* [ME, fr. OE; akin to OHG *dorn* thorn, Skt *tṛṇa* grass, blade of grass] **1 :** a woody plant bearing sharp impeding processes (as briers, prickles, or spines); *esp* **:** any of a genus (*Crataegus*) of the rose family **2 a :** a sharp rigid process on a plant; *specif* **:** a short, indurated, sharp-pointed, and leafless branch **b :** any of various sharp spinose structures on an animal **3 :** something that causes distress or irritation **4 :** the runic letter þ used in Old English and Middle English for either of the sounds of Modern English *th* (as in *thin, then*) — **thorned** \ˈthȯ(ə)rnd\ *adj* — **thorn·less** \ˈthȯ(ə)rn-ləs\ *adj* — **thorn·like** \-ˌlīk\ *adj*

thorn apple *n* **1 :** the fruit of a hawthorn; *also* **:** HAWTHORN **2 :** JIMSONWEED; *also* **:** any plant of the same genus

thorn·back \ˈthȯ(ə)rn-ˌbak\ *n* **1 :** any of various rays having spines on the back **2 :** a large European spider crab (*Maja squinado*)

thorn·bush \-ˌbu̇sh\ *n* **1 :** any of various spiny or thorny shrubs or small trees **2 :** a low growth of thorny shrubs esp. of dry tropical regions

thorny \ˈthȯr-nē\ *adj* **thorn·i·er; -est 1 :** full of thorns **2 :** full of difficulties or controversial points **:** TICKLISH <a ~ problem> — **thorn·i·ness** *n*

thoro *nonstand var of* THOROUGH

tho·ron \ˈthō(ə)r-ˌän, ˈthȯ(ə)r-\ *n* [NL, fr. *thorium*] **:** a gaseous radioactive isotope of radon that has a half-life of about 55 seconds

1thor·ough \ˈthər-(ˌ)ō, -ə(-w), *sporadically* ˈthȯr-; ˈthə-(ˌ)rō, -rə(-w)\ *prep* [ME *thorow,* fr. OE *thurh, thuruh,* prep. & adv.] *archaic* **:** THROUGH

2thorough *adv, archaic* **:** THROUGH

3thorough *adj* **1 :** carried through to completion **:** EXHAUSTIVE <a ~ search> **2 a :** marked by full detail <a ~ description> **b :** careful about detail **:** PAINSTAKING <a ~ scholar> **c :** complete in all respects <~ pleasure> **d :** having full mastery (as of an art) <a ~ musician> **3 :** passing through — **thor·ough·ly** *adv* — **thor·ough·ness** *n*

thor·ough·bass \ˈthər-ə-ˌbās, ˈthə-rə-\ *n* **:** CONTINUO

thor·ough·brace \-ˌbrās\ *n* **:** one of several leather straps supporting the body of a carriage and serving as springs

1thor·ough·bred \-ˌbred\ *adj* **1 :** thoroughly trained or skilled **2 :** bred from the best blood through a long line **:** PUREBRED <~ dogs> **3 a** *cap* **:** of, relating to, or being a member of the Thoroughbred breed of horses **b (1) :** having characteristics resembling those of a Thoroughbred **:** ELEGANT **(2) :** FIRST-CLASS

2thoroughbred *n* **1** *cap* **:** any of an English breed of light speedy horses kept chiefly for racing that originated from crosses between English mares of uncertain ancestry and Arabian stallions **2 :** a purebred or pedigreed animal **3 :** one that has characteristics resembling those of a Thoroughbred

thor·ough·fare \-ˌfa(ə)r, -ˌfe(ə)r\ *n* **1 :** a way or place for passage: as **a :** a street open at both ends **b :** a main road **2 a :** PASSAGE, TRANSIT **b :** the conditions necessary for passing through

thor·ough·go·ing \ˌthər-ə-ˈgō-iŋ, ˌthə-rə-, -ˈgō(-)iŋ\ *adj* **:** marked by thoroughness or zeal

thor·ough–paced \-ˈpāst\ *adj* **1 :** thoroughly trained **:** ACCOMPLISHED **2 :** THOROUGH, COMPLETE

thor·ough·pin \ˈthər-ə-ˌpin, ˈthə-rə-\ *n* **:** a synovial dilatation just above the hock of a horse on both sides of the leg and slightly anterior to the hamstring tendon that is often associated with lameness

thor·ough·wort \-ˌwərt, -ˌwȯ(ə)rt\ *n* **:** BONESET

thorp \ˈthȯ(ə)rp\ *n* [ME, fr. OE; akin to OHG *dorf* village, L *trabs* beam, roof] *archaic* **:** VILLAGE, HAMLET

those [ME, fr. *those* these, fr. OE *thās,* pl. of *thes* this — more at THIS] *pl of* THAT

1thou \(ˈ)t͟hau̇\ *pron* [ME, fr. OE *thū;* akin to OHG *dū* thou, L *tu,* Gk *sy*] **:** the one addressed <~ shalt have no other gods before me —Exod 20:3 (AV)> — used esp. in ecclesiastical or literary language and by Friends as the universal form of address to one person; compare THEE, THINE, THY, YE, YOU

2thou \ˈt͟hau̇\ *vt* **:** to address as *thou*

3thou \ˈthau̇\ *n, pl* **thou** *or* **thous** \ˈthau̇z\ [short for *thousand*] **:** a thousand of something (as dollars)

1though \ˈt͟hō\ *adv* [ME, adv. & conj., of Scand origin; akin to ON *thō* nevertheless; akin to OE *thēah* nevertheless, OHG *doh*] **:** HOWEVER, NEVERTHELESS <It's hard work. I enjoy it ~>

2though \(ˌ)t͟hō\ *conj* **1 :** in spite of the fact that **:** WHILE <~ they know the war is lost, they continue to fight —Bruce Bliven *b* 1889> **2 :** in spite of the possibility that **:** even if <~ they all may fail, they all will try>

syn THOUGH, ALTHOUGH, ALBEIT *shared meaning element* **:** in spite of the fact that. All introduce subordinate clauses stating something that is or may be true notwithstanding what is asserted in the main clause. THOUGH, the most widely used of these words, can introduce a clause that states an established fact <*though* philology was Bede's chief interest . . . , he by no means stopped there —Kemp Malone> or one that offers a hypothesis or admission (as of probability) <they decided to go on *though* rain

seemed likely> and is the usual term to introduce a contrary-to-fact or imaginary condition <*though* he slay me, yet will I trust in him —Job 13:15 (AV)> It is also likely to be preferred when inverted order is chosen for effect <modest *though* his needs were, he found it hard to get by on his income> ALTHOUGH, in most uses interchangeable with *though*, may be chosen to introduce an assertion of especially unexpected fact <has lived in England almost continuously . . . , *although* he has remained an American citizen —*Current Biog.*> ALBEIT is especially appropriate when the notion of concession or of admitting something that seems or suggests a contradiction is to be stressed <a worthy fellow, *albeit* he comes on angry purpose now —Shak.> <try . . . to see economics as a great and continuing, *albeit* constantly altering, concern of mankind —R. L. Heilbroner>

[1]**thought** \ˈthȯt\ *past of* THINK

[2]**thought** *n* [ME, fr. OE *thōht;* akin to OE *thencan* to think — more at THINK] **1 a :** the action or process of thinking : COGITATION **b :** serious consideration : REGARD **c** *archaic* : RECOLLECTION, REMEMBRANCE **2 a :** reasoning power **b :** the power to imagine : CONCEPTION **3 :** something that is thought: as **a :** an individual act or product of thinking **b :** a developed intention or plan <he had no ~ of leaving home> **c :** something (as an opinion or belief) in the mind <he spoke his ~*s* freely> **d :** the intellectual product or the organized views and principles of a period, place, group, or individual **4 :** a slight amount : BIT — used in the adverbial phrase *a thought* <there's a ~ too much seasoning in the stew> ***syn*** see IDEA

thought·ful \ˈthȯt-fəl\ *adj* **1 a :** absorbed in thought : MEDITATIVE **b :** characterized by careful reasoned thinking **2 a :** having thoughts : HEEDFUL <became ~ about his parents> **b :** given to heedful anticipation of the needs and wants of others : SOLICITOUS — **thought·ful·ly** \-fə-lē\ *adv* — **thought·ful·ness** *n*

syn THOUGHTFUL, CONSIDERATE, ATTENTIVE *shared meaning element* : mindful of others ***ant*** thoughtless

thought·less \-ləs\ *adj* **1 a :** insufficiently alert : CARELESS **b :** RECKLESS, RASH **2 :** devoid of thought : INSENSATE **3 :** lacking concern for others : INCONSIDERATE — **thought·less·ly** *adv* — **thought·less·ness** *n*

thought–out \-ˈau̇t\ *adj* **:** produced or arrived at through mental effort and esp. through careful and thorough consideration

thought·way \-ˌwā\ *n* **:** a way of thinking that is characteristic of a particular group, time, or culture

thou·sand \ˈthau̇z-ᵊn(d)\ *n, pl* **thousands** *or* **thousand** [ME, fr. OE *thūsend;* akin to OHG *dūsunt* thousand; both fr. a prehistoric Gmc compound whose constituents are respectively akin to Russ *tys*yacha thousand, Skt *tavas* strong, L *tumēre* to swell and to OE *hund* hundred — more at THUMB] **1** — see NUMBER table **2 :** the number occupying the position four to the left of the decimal point in the Arabic notation **3 :** a very large number <~*s* of ants> — **thousand** *adj* — **thou·sandth** \-ᵊn(t)th\ *adj or n*

thou·sand–head·ed kale \ˌthau̇z-ᵊn(d)-ˌhed-əd-\ *n* **:** a tall branched leafy kale (*Brassica oleracea fruticosa*) used as green feed for livestock

Thousand Island dressing *n* [prob. fr. *Thousand Islands,* islands in the St. Lawrence river] **:** mayonnaise with chili sauce and seasonings (as chopped pimientos and green peppers)

thou·sand–leg·ger \ˌthau̇z-ᵊn-ˈ(d)leg-ər, -ˈ(d)lāg-\ *n* **:** MILLIPEDE

thp *abbr* thrust horsepower

Thra·cian \ˈthrā-shən\ *n* **1 :** a native or inhabitant of Thrace **2 :** the language of the Thracians generally assumed to be Indo-European — see INDO-EUROPEAN LANGUAGES table — **Thracian** *adj*

Thra·co–Il·lyr·i·an \ˌthrā-(ˌ)kō-il-ˈir-ē-ən\ *adj* **:** of, relating to, or constituting a supposed subfamily of Indo-European languages comprising Thracian, Illyrian, and Albanian

Thra·co–Phry·gian \-ˈfrij-(ē-)ən\ *adj* **:** of, relating to, or constituting a tentative branch of the Indo-European language family to which are sometimes assigned various languages of the Balkans and Asia Minor

[1]**thrall** \ˈthrȯl\ *n* [ME *thral,* fr. OE *thræl,* fr. ON *thræll*] **1 a :** a servant slave : BONDMAN; *also* : SERF **b :** a person in moral or mental servitude **2 a :** the state of a thrall : SLAVERY **b :** a state of complete absorption <mountains could hold me in ~ with a subtle attraction of their own —Elyne Mitchell> — **thrall** *adj*

[2]**thrall** *vt, archaic* **:** ENTHRALL, ENSLAVE

thrall·dom *or* **thral·dom** \ˈthrȯl-dəm\ *n* **:** the condition of a thrall

[1]**thrash** \ˈthrash\ *vb* [alter. of *thresh*] *vt* **1 :** to separate the seeds of from the husks and straw by beating : THRESH 1 **2 a :** to beat soundly with or as if with a stick or whip : FLOG **b :** to defeat decisively or severely <~*ed* the visiting team> **3 :** to swing, beat, or strike in the manner of a rapidly moving flail <~*ing* his arms> **4 a :** to go over again and again <~ the matter over inconclusively> **b :** to hammer out : FORGE <~ out a plan> ~ *vi* **1 :** THRESH 1 **2 :** to deal blows or strokes like one using a flail or whip **3 :** to move or stir about violently : toss about <~ in bed with a fever> ***syn*** see SWING

[2]**thrash** *n* **:** an act of thrashing esp. in swimming

[1]**thrash·er** \ˈthrash-ər\ *n* **:** one that thrashes or threshes

[2]**thrash·er** \ˈthrash-ər\ *n* [prob. alter. of *thrush*] **:** any of numerous long-tailed American singing birds (family Mimidae and esp. genus *Toxostoma*) that resemble thrushes and include notable singers and mimics

thra·son·i·cal \thrā-ˈsän-i-kəl, thrə-\ *adj* [L *Thrason-, Thraso* Thraso, braggart soldier in the comedy *Eunuchus* by Terence] **:** of, relating to, resembling, or characteristic of Thraso : BRAGGING, BOASTFUL — **thra·son·i·cal·ly** \-k(ə-)lē\ *adv*

[1]**thraw** \ˈthrä\ *vb* [ME *thrawen,* fr. OE *thrāwan*] *vt* **1** *chiefly Scot* **:** to cause to twist or turn **2** *chiefly Scot* **:** CROSS, THWART ~ *vi* **1** *chiefly Scot* **:** TWIST, TURN **2** *chiefly Scot* **:** to be in disagreement

[2]**thraw** *n* **1** *chiefly Scot* **:** TWIST, TURN **2** *chiefly Scot* **:** ill humor

thra·wart \ˈthrä-wərt\ *adj* [ME (Sc), alter. of ME *fraward, froward* froward] **1** *chiefly Scot* **:** STUBBORN **2** *Scot* **:** CROOKED

thrawn \ˈthrän\ *adj* [ME (Sc) *thrawin,* fr. pp. of ME *thrawen* to twist] *chiefly Scot* **:** lacking in pleasing or attractive qualities: as **a :** PERVERSE, RECALCITRANT **b :** CROOKED, MISSHAPEN — **thrawn·ly** *adv, chiefly Scot*

[1]**thread** \ˈthred\ *n* [ME *thred,* fr. OE *thrǣd;* akin to OHG *drāt* wire, OE *thrāwan* to cause to twist or turn — more at THROW] **1 a :** a filament, a group of filaments twisted together, or a filamentous length formed by spinning and twisting short textile fibers into a continuous strand **b :** a piece of thread **2 a :** any of various natural filaments <the ~*s* of a spider web> **b :** a slender stream (as of water) **c :** a streak of light or color **d :** a projecting helical rib (as in a fitting or on a pipe) by which parts can be screwed together : SCREW THREAD **3 :** something continuous or drawn out: as **a :** a train of thought **b :** a continuing element <a ~ of melancholy marked all his writing> **4 :** a tenuous or feeble support — **thread·less** \-ləs\ *adj* — **thread·like** \-ˌlīk\ *adj*

[2]**thread** *vt* **1 a :** to pass a thread through the eye of (a needle) **b :** to arrange a thread, yarn, or lead-in piece in working position for use in (a machine) **2 a (1) :** to pass something through in the manner of a thread <~ a pipe with wire> **(2) :** to pass (as a tape, line, or film) into or through something <~*ed* a fresh film into the camera> **b :** to make one's way through or between <~*ing* narrow alleys> **3 :** to put together on or as if on a thread : STRING <~ beads> **4 :** to interweave with or as if with threads : INTERSPERSE <dark hair ~*ed* with silver> **5 :** to form a screw thread on or in ~ *vi* **1 :** to make one's way **2 :** to form a thread when poured from a spoon — **thread·er** *n*

thread·bare \ˈthred-ˌba(ə)r, -ˌbe(ə)r\ *adj* **1 :** having the nap worn off so that the thread shows : SHABBY **2 :** HACKNEYED <~ phrases> — **thread·bare·ness** *n*

thread·fin \-ˌfin\ *n* **:** any of a family (Polynemidae) of fishes related to the mullets and having filamentous rays on the lower part of the pectoral fin

thread·worm \-ˌwərm\ *n* **:** a long slender nematode worm

thready \-ē\ *adj* **1 :** consisting of or bearing fibers or filaments <a ~ bark> **2 a :** resembling a thread : FILAMENTOUS **b :** tending to form or draw out into strands : ROPY **3 :** lacking in fullness, body, or vigor : THIN <a ~ voice> — **thread·i·ness** *n*

threap \ˈthrēp\ *vt* [ME *threpen,* fr. OE *thrēapian*] **1** *chiefly Scot* **:** SCOLD, CHIDE **2** *chiefly Scot* **:** to maintain persistently

[1]**threat** \ˈthret\ *n* [ME *thret* coercion, threat, fr. OE *thrēat* coercion; akin to MHG *drōz* annoyance, L *trudere* to push, thrust] **1 :** an indication of something impending <the air held a ~ of rain> **2 :** an expression of intention to inflict evil, injury, or damage **3 :** something that threatens

[2]**threat** *vb, archaic* **:** THREATEN

threat·en \ˈthret-ᵊn\ *vb* **threat·ened; threat·en·ing** \ˈthret-niŋ, -ᵊn-iŋ\ *vt* **1 :** to utter threats against **2 a :** to give signs or warning of : PORTEND **b :** to hang over dangerously : MENACE **3 :** to announce as intended or possible <the workers ~*ed* a strike> ~ *vi* **1 :** to utter threats **2 :** to portend evil — **threat·en·er** \ˈthret-nər, -ᵊn-ər\ *n* — **threat·en·ing·ly** \ˈthret-niŋ-lē, -ᵊn-iŋ-\ *adv*

syn THREATEN, MENACE *shared meaning element* : to announce or forecast impending danger or evil

three \ˈthrē\ *n* [ME, fr. *three,* adj., fr. OE *thrīe* (masc.), *thrēo* (fem. & neut.); akin to OHG *drī* three, L *tres,* Gk *treis*] **1** — see NUMBER table **2 :** the third in a set or series <the ~ of hearts> **3 :** something having three units or members — **three** *adj or pron*

three–bag·ger \-ˈbag-ər\ *n* **:** TRIPLE

three–ball \-ˌbȯl\ *adj* **:** relating to or being a golf match in which three players compete against one another with each playing his own ball

three–card monte \ˌthrē-ˌkärd-\ *n* **:** a gambling game in which the dealer shows three cards, shuffles them, places them face down, and invites spectators to bet they can identify the location of a particular card

three–col·or \ˈthrē-ˈkəl-ər\ *adj* **:** being or relating to a printing or photographic process wherein three primary colors are used to reproduce all the colors of the subject

3–D \ˈthrē-ˈdē\ *n* [*D,* abbr. of *dimensional*] **:** the three-dimensional form; *also* : an image or a picture produced in it

three–deck·er \ˈthrē-ˈdek-ər\ *n* **1 a :** a warship carrying guns on three decks **b :** a cargo or passenger ship with three full decks **2 :** something made with three floors, tiers, or layers; *esp* **:** a sandwich made of three slices of bread and two fillings

three–dimensional *adj* **1 :** of or relating to three dimensions **2 :** giving the illusion of depth or varying distances — used of an image or a pictorial representation esp. when this illusion is enhanced by stereoscopic means **3 :** describing or being described in well-rounded completeness <a ~ analysis of multiple historical processes —L. L. Snyder> **4 :** true to life : LIFELIKE

three·fold \ˈthrē-ˌfōld, -ˈfōld\ *adj* **1 :** having three units or members : TRIPLE **2 :** being three times as great or as many — **three·fold** \-ˈfōld\ *adv*

three–gait·ed \-ˈgāt-əd\ *adj, of a horse* **:** trained to use the walk, trot, and canter

three–hand·ed \-ˈhan-dəd\ *adj* **:** played by three players <~ bridge>

Three Hours *n* **:** a service of devotion between noon and three o'clock on Good Friday

three–legged \ˈthrē-ˈleg(-ə)d, -ˈlāg(-ə)d\ *adj* **:** having three legs <a ~ stool>

three–legged race *n* **:** a race between contestants who run in pairs with their adjacent legs bound together

three–line octave *n* **:** the musical octave that begins on the second C above middle C — see PITCH illustration

three–mast·er \ˈthrē-ˈmas-tər\ *n* **:** a ship having three masts

three–mile limit *n* : the limit of the marginal sea of three miles included in the territorial waters of a state
three of a kind : three cards of the same rank in one hand — see POKER illustration
three·pence \'threp-ən(t)s, 'thrip-, 'thrəp-, *US also* 'thrē-pen(t)s\ *n* **1** : the sum of three British pennies **2** *pl* **threepence** *or* **three·penc·es** : a coin worth threepence
three·pen·ny \'threp-(ə-)nē, 'thrip-, 'thrəp-, *US also* 'thrē-ˌpen-ē\ *adj* **1** : costing or worth threepence **2** : POOR
three–phase *adj* : of, relating to, or operating by means of a combination of three circuits energized by alternating electromotive forces that differ in phase by one third of a cycle
three–piece *adj* : consisting of or made in three pieces
three–point landing *n* : an airplane landing in which the two main wheels of the landing gear and the tail wheel or skid or nose wheel touch the ground simultaneously
three–quarter *adj* : extending to three-quarters of the normal full length <a ~ sleeve>
three–quarter–bound *adj, of a book* : bound like a half-bound book but having the material on the spine extended to cover about one third of the boards — **three–quarter binding** *n*
three–ring circus *n* **1** : a circus with simultaneous performances in three rings **2** : something confusing, engrossing, or entertaining
three R's *n pl* [fr. the facetiously used phrase *reading, 'riting, and 'rithmetic*] **1** : the fundamentals taught in elementary school; *esp* : reading, writing, and arithmetic **2** : the fundamental skills in a field or endeavor
three·score \'thrē-'skō(ə)r, -'skȯ(ə)r\ *adj* : being three times twenty : SIXTY
three·some \'thrē-səm\ *n* **1** : a group of three persons or things : TRIO **2** : a golf match in which one person plays his ball against the ball of two others playing each stroke alternately
three–spined stickleback \ˌthrē-ˌspīn(d)-\ *n* : a stickleback (*Gasterosteus aculeatus*) of fresh and brackish waters that typically has three dorsal spines
three–val·ued \-'val-(ˌ)yüd, -yəd\ *adj* : possessing three truth= values instead of the customary two of truth and falsehood <~ logic>
threm·ma·tol·o·gy \ˌthrem-ə-'täl-ə-jē\ *n* [Gk *thremmat-, thremma* nursling + E *-o-* + *-logy;* akin to Gk *trephein* to nourish — more at ATROPHY] : the science of breeding animals and plants under domestication
thre·node \'thrē-ˌnōd, 'thren-ˌōd\ *n* : THRENODY — **thre·nod·ic** \thri-'näd-ik\ *adj* — **thren·o·dist** \'thren-əd-əst\ *n*
thren·o·dy \'thren-əd-ē\ *n, pl* **-dies** [Gk *thrēnōidia,* fr. *thrēnos* dirge + *aeidein* to sing; akin to Skt *dhraṇati* it sounds — more at ODE] : a song of lamentation for the dead : ELEGY
thre·o·nine \'thrē-ə-ˌnēn\ *n* [prob. fr. *threonic acid* ($C_4H_8O_5$)] : a colorless crystalline amino acid $C_4H_9NO_3$ that is essential to normal nutrition
thresh \'thrash, 'thresh\ *vb* [ME *thresshen,* fr. OE *threscan;* akin to OHG *dreskan* to thresh, L *terere* to rub — more at THROW] *vt* **1** : to separate seed from (a harvested plant) mechanically; *also* : to separate (seed) in this way **2** : THRASH 4 **3** : to strike repeatedly ~ *vi* **1** : to thresh grain **2** : to strike with or as if with a flail or whip **3** : to toss about
thresh·er *n* **1** : one that threshes **2** : a large nearly cosmopolitan shark (*Alopias vulpinus*) having a greatly elongated curved upper lobe of its tail with which it is said to thresh the water to round up the fish on which it feeds

thresher 2

threshing machine *n* : a machine for separating grain crops into grain or seeds and straw
thresh·old \'thresh-ˌ(h)ōld\ *n* [ME *thresshold,* fr. OE *threscwald;* akin to ON *threskjöldr* threshold, OE *threscan* to thresh] **1** : the plank, stone, or piece of timber that lies under a door : SILL **2 a** : GATE, DOOR **b** (1) : END, BOUNDARY; *specif* : the end of a runway (2) : the place or point of entering or beginning : OUTSET **3 a** : the point at which a physiological or psychological effect begins to be produced **b** : a level, point, or value above which something is true or will take place and below which it is not or will not
threw *past of* THROW
thrice \'thrīs\ *adv* [ME *thrie, thries,* fr. OE *thriga;* akin to OFris *thria* three times, OE *thrie* three] **1** : three times **2 a** : in a threefold manner or degree **b** : to a high degree
thrift \'thrift\ *n* [ME, fr. ON, prosperity, fr. *thrifask* to thrive] **1** : healthy and vigorous growth **2** : careful management esp. of money **3** *chiefly Scot* : gainful occupation **4** : any of a genus (*Armeria*) of the plumbago family of tufted acaulescent herbs; *esp* : a scapose herb (*A. maritima*) with pink or white flower heads
thrift·less \'thrift-ləs\ *adj* **1** : lacking usefulness or worth **2** : careless, wasteful, or incompetent in handling money or resources : IMPROVIDENT — **thrift·less·ly** *adv* — **thrift·less·ness** *n*
thrift shop *n* : a shop that sells secondhand articles and esp. clothes and is often run (as by Junior Leaguers) for charitable purposes
thrifty \'thrif-tē\ *adj* **thrift·i·er; -est** **1** : thriving by industry and frugality : PROSPEROUS **2** : growing vigorously **3** : practicing economy and good management : PROVIDENT ***syn*** see SPARING ***ant*** wasteful — **thrift·i·ly** \-tə-lē\ *adv* — **thrift·i·ness** \-tē-nəs\ *n*
thrill \'thril\ *vb* [ME *thirlen, thrillen* to pierce, fr. OE *thyrlian,* fr. *thyrel* hole, fr. *thurh* through — more at THROUGH] *vt* **1 a** : to cause to experience a sudden sharp feeling of excitement **b** : to cause to have a shivering or tingling sensation **2** : to cause to vibrate or tremble perceptibly ~ *vi* **1** : to move or pass so as to cause thrills **2** : to become thrilled: **a** : to experience a sudden sharp excitement **b** : TINGLE, THROB **3** : TREMBLE, VIBRATE — **thrill** *n* — **thrill·ing·ly** \-iŋ-lē\ *adv*
syn THRILL, ELECTRIFY, ENTHUSE *shared meaning element* : to fill with emotions that stir or excite or to be so stirred

thril·ler \'thril-ər\ *n* : one that thrills; *esp* : a work of fiction or drama designed to hold the interest by the use of a high degree of intrigue, adventure, or suspense
thrips \'thrips\ *n, pl* **thrips** [L, woodworm, fr. Gk] : any of an order (Thysanoptera) of small to minute sucking insects most of which feed often destructively on plant juices
thrive \'thrīv\ *vi* **throve** \'thrōv\ *or* **thrived; thriv·en** \'thriv-ən\ *also* **thrived; thriv·ing** \'thrī-viŋ\ [ME *thriven,* fr. ON *thrīfask,* prob. reflexive of *thrīfa* to grasp] **1** : to grow vigorously : FLOURISH **2** : to gain in wealth or possessions : PROSPER **3** : to progress toward or realize a goal ***syn*** see SUCCEED ***ant*** languish — **thriv·er** \'thrī-vər\ *n*
thriv·ing *adj* : PROSPEROUS — **thriv·ing·ly** \'thrī-viŋ-lē\ *adv*
thro \(ˈ)thrü\ *prep, archaic* : THROUGH
[1]**throat** \'thrōt\ *n* [ME *throte,* fr. OE; akin to OHG *drozza* throat] **1 a** (1) : the part of the neck in front of the spinal column (2) : the passage through the neck to the stomach and lungs **b** (1) : VOICE (2) : the seat of the voice **2** : something resembling the throat esp. in being an entrance, a passageway, a constriction, or a narrowed part: as **a** : the orifice of a tubular organ esp. of a plant **b** : the opening in the vamp of a shoe at the instep **c** : the part of a tennis racket between the head and the handle **3** : the curved part of an anchor's arm where it joins the shank
[2]**throat** *vt* **1** : to utter in the throat : MUTTER **2** : to sing or enunciate in a throaty voice
throat·ed \'thrōt-əd\ *adj* : having a throat esp. of a specified kind — usu. used in combination <white-*throated*>
throat·latch \-ˌlach\ *n* **1** : a strap of a bridle or halter passing under a horse's throat **2** : the part of a horse's throat around which the throatlatch passes — see HORSE illustration
throaty \'thrōt-ē\ *adj* **throat·i·er; -est** **1** : uttered or produced from low in the throat <a ~ voice> **2** : heavy, thick, and deep as if from the throat <~ notes of a horn> — **throat·i·ly** \'thrōt-ᵊl-ē\ *adv* — **throat·i·ness** \'thrōt-ē-nəs\ *n*
[1]**throb** \'thräb\ *vi* **throbbed; throb·bing** [ME *throbben,* prob. of imit. origin] **1** : to pulsate or pound with abnormal force or rapidity **2** : to beat or vibrate rhythmically — **throb·ber** *n*
[2]**throb** *n* : BEAT, PULSE
throe \'thrō\ *n* [ME *thrawe, throwe,* fr. OE *thrawu, thrēa* threat, pang; akin to OHG *drawa* threat, Gk *trauma* wound, *tetrainein* to bore — more at THROW] **1** : PANG, SPASM <death ~*s*> <~*s* of childbirth> **2** *pl* : a hard or painful struggle <the ~*s* of revolutionary social change —M. D. Geismar>
thromb- *or* **thrombo-** *comb form* [Gk *thrombos* clot] : blood clot : clotting of blood <*thromb*in> <*thrombo*plastic>
throm·bin \'thräm-bən\ *n* [ISV] : a proteolytic enzyme that is formed from prothrombin and facilitates the clotting of blood by catalyzing conversion of fibrinogen to fibrin
throm·bo·cyte \-bə-ˌsīt\ *n* [ISV] : BLOOD PLATELET; *also* : an invertebrate cell with similar function — **throm·bo·cyt·ic** \ˌthräm-bə-'sit-ik\ *adj*
throm·bo·cy·to·pe·nia \ˌthräm-bə-ˌsīt-ə-'pē-nē-ə, -nyə\ *n* [NL, fr. ISV *thrombocyte* + Gk *penia* poverty, lack] : persistent decrease in the number of blood platelets that is usu. associated with hemorrhagic conditions — **throm·bo·cy·to·pe·nic** \-nik\ *adj*
throm·bo·em·bo·lism \ˌthräm-bō-'em-bə-ˌliz-əm\ *n* : the blocking of a blood vessel by an embolus that has broken away from a thrombus at its site of formation — **throm·bo·em·bol·ic** \-em-'bäl-ik\ *adj*
throm·bo·ki·nase \ˌthräm-bō-'kī-ˌnās, -ˌnāz\ *n* [ISV] : THROMBOPLASTIN
throm·bo·phle·bi·tis \-fli-'bīt-əs\ *n* [NL] : inflammation of a vein with formation of a thrombus
throm·bo·plas·tic \ˌthräm-bō-'plas-tik\ *adj* [ISV] : initiating or accelerating the clotting of blood — **throm·bo·plas·ti·cal·ly** \-ti-k(ə-)lē\ *adv*
throm·bo·plas·tin \-'plas-tən\ *n* [ISV, fr. *thromboplastic*] : a complex enzyme found esp. in blood platelets that functions in the clotting of blood
throm·bo·sis \thräm-'bō-səs, thrəm-\ *n, pl* **-bo·ses** \-ˌsēz\ [NL, fr. Gk *thrombōsis* clotting, deriv. of *thrombos* clot] : the formation or presence of a blood clot within a blood vessel during life — **throm·bot·ic** \-'bät-ik\ *adj*
throm·bus \'thräm-bəs\ *n, pl* **throm·bi** \-ˌbī, -ˌbē\ [NL, fr. Gk *thrombos* clot] : a clot of blood formed within a blood vessel and remaining attached to its place of origin — compare EMBOLUS
[1]**throne** \'thrōn\ *n* [ME *trone, throne,* fr. OF *trone,* fr. L *thronus,* fr. Gk *thronos* — more at FIRM] **1 a** : the chair of state of a king, prince, or bishop **b** : the seat of a deity **2** : royal power and dignity : SOVEREIGNTY **3** *pl* : an order of angels — see CELESTIAL HIERARCHY
[2]**throne** *vb* **throned; thron·ing** *vt* **1** : to seat on a throne **2** : to invest with kingly rank or power ~ *vi* **1** : to sit on a throne **2** : to hold kingly power
throne room *n* : a formal audience room containing the throne of a sovereign
[1]**throng** \'thrȯŋ\ *n* [ME *thrang, throng,* fr. OE *thrang, gethrang;* akin to OE *thringan* to press, crowd, OHG *dringan,* Lith *trenkti* to jolt] **1 a** : a multitude of assembled persons **b** : a large number : HOST **2 a** : a crowding together of many persons **b** : PRESSURE <this ~ of business —S. R. Crockett> ***syn*** see CROWD
[2]**throng** *vb* **thronged; throng·ing** \'thrȯŋ-iŋ\ *vt* **1** : to crowd upon : PRESS **2** : to crowd into : PACK <shoppers ~*ing* the streets> ~ *vi* : to crowd together in great numbers
thros·tle \'thräs-əl\ *n* [ME, fr. OE — more at THRUSH] : [1]THRUSH 1; *specif* : SONG THRUSH
[1]**throt·tle** \'thrät-ᵊl\ *vb* **throt·tled; throt·tling** \'thrät-liŋ, -ᵊl-iŋ\ [ME *throtlen,* fr. *throte* throat] *vt* **1 a** (1) : to compress the throat of : CHOKE (2) : to kill by such action **b** : to prevent or check expression or activity of : SUPPRESS **2 a** : to decrease the flow of (as steam or fuel to an engine) by a valve **b** : to regulate and esp. to reduce the speed of (as an engine) by such means **c** : to vary the thrust of (a rocket engine) during flight ~ *vi* : CHOKE — **throt·tler** \-lər, -ᵊl-ər\ *n*

[2]**throttle** *n* [perh. alter. of E dial. *thropple* (throat)] **1 a :** THROAT 1a **b :** TRACHEA 1 **2 a :** a valve for regulating the supply of a fluid (as steam) to an engine; *esp* **:** the valve controlling the volume of vaporized fuel charge delivered to the cylinders of an internal-combustion engine **b :** the lever controlling this valve **c :** the condition of being throttled — **at full throttle :** at full speed

throt·tle·able \ˈthrät-ᵊl-ə-bəl\ *adj* **:** capable of having the thrust varied — used of a rocket engine

throt·tle·hold \ˈthrät-ᵊl-ˌhōld\ *n* **:** a vicious, strangling, or stultifying control

[1]**through** \(ˈ)thrü\ *prep* [ME *thurh, thruh, through,* fr. OE *thurh;* akin to OHG *durh* through, L *trans* across, beyond, Skt *tarati* he crosses over] **1 a (1)** — used as a function word to indicate movement into at one side or point and out at another and esp. the opposite side of <drove a nail ~ the board> <a path ~ the woods> **(2) :** by way of <left ~ the door> **(3)** — used as a function word to indicate passage from one end or boundary to another <a highway ~ the forest> <a road ~ the desert> **(4) :** PAST <drove ~ a red light> **b** — used as a function word to indicate passage into and out of a treatment, handling, or process <the matter has already passed ~ his hands> **2** — used as a function word to indicate means, agency, or intermediacy: as **a :** by means of **:** by the agency of **b :** because of <failed ~ ignorance> **c :** by common descent from or relationship with <related ~ their grandfather> **3 a :** over the whole surface or extent of <homes scattered ~ the valley> **b** — used as a function word to indicate movement within a large expanse <flew ~ the air> **c** — used as a function word to indicate exposure to a specified set of conditions <put her ~ hell> **4** — used as a function word to indicate a period of time: as **a :** during the entire period of <all ~ her life> **b :** from the beginning to the end of <the tower stood ~ the earthquake> **c :** to and including <Monday ~ Friday> **5 a** — used as a function word to indicate completion or exhaustion <got ~ the book> <went ~ a fortune in a year> **b** — used as a function word to indicate acceptance or approval esp. by an official body <got the bill ~ the legislature> ***syn*** see BY

[2]**through** \ˈthrü\ *adv* **1 :** from one end or side to the other **2 a :** from beginning to end **b :** to completion, conclusion, or accomplishment <see it ~> **3 :** to the core **:** COMPLETELY **4 :** into the open **:** OUT <break ~>

[3]**through** \ˈthrü\ *adj* **1 a :** extending from one surface to another <a ~ mortise> **b :** admitting free or continuous passage **:** DIRECT <a ~ road> **2 a (1) :** going from point of origin to destination without change or reshipment <a ~ train> **(2) :** of or relating to such movement <a ~ ticket> **b :** initiated at and destined for points outside a local zone <~ traffic> **3 a :** arrived at completion or accomplishment <he is ~ with the job> **b :** WASHED-UP, FINISHED <you're ~ — that was your last chance>

through and through *adv* **:** in every way **:** THOROUGHLY

through–com·posed \ˌthrü-kəm-ˈpōzd\ *adj* [trans. of G *durchkomponiert*] *of a song* **:** having new music provided for each stanza — compare STROPHIC

through·ith·er *or* **through·oth·er** \ˈthrü-(ə-)thər\ *adv* [[1]*through* + *other*] *chiefly Scot* **:** in confusion **:** PROMISCUOUSLY

through·ly \ˈthrü-lē\ *adv, archaic* **:** in a thorough manner

[1]**through·out** \thrü-ˈau̇t\ *adv* **1 :** in or to every part **:** EVERYWHERE <of one color ~> **2 :** during the whole time or action **:** from beginning to end <remained loyal ~>

[2]**throughout** *prep* **1 :** all the way from one end to the other of **:** in or to every part of <cities ~ the United States> **2 :** during the whole course or period of <troubled him ~ his life>

through·put \ˈthrü-ˌpu̇t\ *n* **:** OUTPUT, PRODUCTION <the ~ of a computer>

through street *n* **:** a street on which the through movement of traffic is given preference

through·way *var of* THRUWAY

throve *past of* THRIVE

[1]**throw** \ˈthrō\ *vb* **threw** \ˈthrü\; **thrown** \ˈthrōn\; **throw·ing** [ME *thrawen, throwen* to cause to twist, throw, fr. OE *thrāwan* to cause to twist or turn; akin to OHG *drāen* to turn, L *terere* to rub, Gk *tetrainein* to bore, pierce] *vt* **1 a :** to propel through the air by a forward motion of the hand and arm <~ a baseball> **b :** to propel through the air in any manner <a rifle that can ~ a bullet five miles> **2 a :** to cause to fall <*threw* his opponent> **b :** to cause to fall off **:** UNSEAT <the horse *threw* his rider> **c :** to get the better of **:** OVERCOME <the problem didn't ~ her> **3 a :** to fling (oneself) precipitately <*threw* himself down on the sofa> **b :** to drive or impel violently **:** DASH <the ship was *thrown* on a reef> **4 a (1) :** to put in a particular position or condition **(2) :** to put on or off hastily or carelessly <*threw* on a coat> **b :** to bring to bear **:** EXERT <*threw* all his influence into the boy's defense> **c :** BUILD, CONSTRUCT <*threw* a pontoon bridge over the river> **5 :** to form or shape on a potter's wheel **6 :** to deliver (a blow) in or as if in boxing **7 :** to twist two or more filaments of into a thread or yarn **8 :** to make a cast of (dice or a specified number on dice) **9 :** to give up **:** ABANDON **10 :** to send forth **:** PROJECT <the setting sun *threw* long shadows> **11 :** to make (oneself) dependent **:** commit (oneself) for help, support, or protection <*threw* himself on the mercy of the court> **12 :** to give oneself up to unrestrainedly **:** give way to <*threw* a temper tantrum> **13 :** to bring forth **:** PRODUCE <~*s* a good crop> <*threw* large litters> **14 :** to lose intentionally <~ a game> **15 :** to move (a lever) so as to connect or disconnect parts of a clutch or switch; *also* **:** to make or break (a connection) with a lever **16 :** to give by way of entertainment <~ a party> ~ *vi* **:** CAST, HURL — **throw·er** \ˈthrō(-ə)r\ *n*

syn THROW, CAST, TOSS, FLING, HURL, PITCH, SLING *shared meaning element* **:** to cause to move swiftly through space by a propulsive movement or a propelling force

— **throw one's weight around** *or* **throw one's weight about :** to exercise influence or authority esp. to an excessive degree or in an objectionable manner — **throw together 1 :** to put together in a hurried and usu. careless manner <a bookshelf hastily *thrown together*> **2 :** to bring into casual association <different kinds of people are *thrown together* — Richard Sennett>

[2]**throw** *n* **1 a :** an act of throwing, hurling, or flinging **b (1) :** an act of throwing dice **(2) :** the number thrown with a cast of dice **c :** a method of throwing an opponent in wrestling or judo **2 :** the distance a missile may be thrown <lived within a stone's ~ from school> **3 :** an undertaking involving chance or danger **:** RISK, VENTURE **4 :** the amount of vertical displacement produced by a geological fault **5 a :** the extreme movement given to a pivoted or reciprocating piece by a cam, crank, or eccentric **:** STROKE **b :** the length of the radius of a crank or the virtual crank radius of an eccentric or cam **6 a :** a light coverlet (as for a bed) **b :** a woman's scarf or light wrap **7 :** an object or individual regarded as a distinct member of a kind or class **:** UNIT <copies are to be sold at $5 a ~ —Harvey Breit>

[1]**throw·away** \ˈthrō-ə-ˌwā\ *n* **1 :** a free handbill or circular **2 :** a line of dialogue (as in a play) de-emphasized by casual delivery

[2]**throw·away** \ˌthrō-ə-ˌwā\ *adj* **1 :** designed to be thrown away **:** DISPOSABLE <~ containers> **2 :** written or spoken (as in a play) in a low-key or unemphasized manner <~ lines>

throw away \ˌthrō-ə-ˈwā\ *vt* **1 a :** to get rid of as worthless or unnecessary **b :** DISCARD 1b **2 a :** to use in a foolish or wasteful manner **:** SQUANDER **b :** to fail to take advantage of **:** WASTE **3 :** to make (as a line in a play) unemphatic by casual delivery

throw·back \ˈthrō-ˌbak\ *n* **1 a :** reversion to an earlier type or phase **:** ATAVISM **b :** an instance or product of atavistic reversion **2 :** FLASHBACK

throw back \(ˈ)thrō-ˈbak\ *vt* **1 :** to delay the progress or advance of **:** CHECK **2 :** to cause to rely **:** make dependent <won't let the publishers have paper to print . . . textbooks, so everybody is *thrown back* upon the . . . library —S. P. B. Mais> **3 :** REFLECT ~ *vi* **:** to revert to an earlier type or phase

throw down *vt* **1 :** to cause to fail **:** OVERTHROW **2 :** PRECIPITATE **3 :** to cast off **:** DISCARD

throw–in \ˈthrō-ˌin\ *n* **:** an act or instance of throwing a ball in: as **a :** a throw made from the touchline in soccer to put the ball back in play after it has gone into touch **b :** a throw made by an outfielder to the infield in baseball **c :** a throw made from outside the boundaries in basketball to put the ball back in play after it has gone out of bounds

throw in \(ˈ)thrō-ˈin\ *vt* **1 :** to add as a gratuity or supplement **2 :** to introduce or interject in the course of something **:** CONTRIBUTE <they *throw in* some . . . sound effects on several songs —Tom Phillips> **3 :** DISTRIBUTE 3b **4 a :** to cause (as gears) to mesh **b :** ENGAGE <*throw in* the clutch> ~ *vi* **:** to enter into association or partnership **:** JOIN <agrees to *throw in* with a crooked ex-cop —*Newsweek*> — **throw in the sponge** *or* **throw in the towel :** to abandon a struggle or contest **:** acknowledge defeat **:** give up

throw off *vt* **1 a :** to free oneself from **:** get rid of <*throw off* his political masters and start a revolution —T. P. Whitney> **b :** to cast off often in a hurried or vigorous manner **:** ABANDON <*threw off* all restraint> **c :** DIVERT, DISTRACT <dogs *thrown off* by a false scent> **2 :** to give off **:** EMIT <stacks *throwing off* plumes of smoke> **3 :** to produce in an offhand manner **:** execute with speed or facility <some little . . . tune that the composer had *thrown off* —James Hilton> **4 a :** to cause to depart from an expected or desired course <mistakes *threw* his calculations *off* a bit> **b :** to cause to make a mistake **:** MISLEAD ~ *vi* **1 :** to begin hunting **2 :** to make derogatory comments

throw out \(ˈ)thrō-ˈau̇t\ *vt* **1 a :** to remove from a place, office, or employment usu. in a sudden or unexpected manner **b :** to get rid of as worthless or unnecessary **2 :** to give expression to **:** UTTER <*threw out* a remark . . . that utterly confounded him —Jean Stafford> **3 :** to dismiss from acceptance or consideration **:** REJECT <a coerced confession . . . is sure to be *thrown out* —Charles Oldfather> **4** to make visible or manifest **:** DISPLAY <the signal was *thrown out* for the . . . fleet to prepare for action —Archibald Duncan> **5 :** to leave behind **:** OUTDISTANCE **6 :** to give forth from within **:** EMIT **7 a :** to send out **b :** to cause to project **:** EXTEND **8 :** CONFUSE, DISCONCERT <automobiles in line blocking the road . . . *threw* the whole schedule *out* . . . F. D. Roosevelt> **9 :** to cause to stand out **:** make prominent **10 :** to make a throw that enables a teammate to put out (a base runner) **11 :** DISENGAGE <*throw out* the clutch>

throw over *vt* **1 :** to forsake despite bonds of attachment or duty **2 :** to refuse to accept **:** REJECT

throw rug *n* **:** SCATTER RUG

throw·ster \ˈthrō-stər\ *n* **:** one who throws textile filaments

throw up *vt* **1 :** to raise quickly **2 :** to give up **:** QUIT <the urge . . . to *throw up* all intellectual work —Norman Mailer> **3 :** to build hurriedly <new houses *thrown up* almost overnight> **4 :** VOMIT **5 :** to bring forth **:** PRODUCE <science . . . will continue to *throw up* discoveries which threaten . . . society —*Times Lit. Supp.*> **6 :** to make distinct esp. by contrast **:** cause to stand out **7 :** to mention repeatedly by way of reproach ~ *vi* **:** VOMIT — **throw up one's hands :** to admit defeat <in the end *throws up his hands* in despair —Frank Conroy>

thru *var of* THROUGH

[1]**thrum** \ˈthrəm\ *n* [ME, fr. OE *-thrum* (in *tungethrum* ligament of the tongue); akin to OHG *drum* fragment, L *terminus* boundary, end — more at TERM] **1 a (1) :** a fringe of warp threads left on the loom after the cloth has been removed **(2) :** one of these warp threads **b :** a tuft or short piece of rope yarn used in thrumming canvas — usu. used in pl. **c :** BIT, PARTICLE **2 :** a hair, fiber, or

threadlike leaf on a plant; *also* : a tuft or fringe of such structures — **thrum** *adj*

2thrum *vt* **thrummed; thrum·ming** **1** : to furnish with thrums : FRINGE **2** : to insert short pieces of rope yarn or spun yarn in (a piece of canvas) to make a rough surface or a mat which can be wrapped about rigging to prevent chafing

3thrum *vb* **thrummed; thrum·ming** [imit.] *vi* **1** : to play or pluck a stringed instrument idly : STRUM **2** : to sound with a monotonous hum ~ *vt* **1** : to play (as a stringed instrument) in an idle or relaxed manner **2** : to recite tiresomely or monotonously

4thrum *n* : the monotonous sound of thrumming

1thrush \'thrəsh\ *n* [ME *thrusche,* fr. OE *thrysce;* akin to OE *throstle* thrush, OHG *droscala,* L *turdus*] **1** : any of numerous small or medium-sized passerine birds (family Turdidae) which are mostly of a plain color often with spotted underparts and many of which are excellent singers **2** : a bird held to resemble a thrush

2thrush *n* [prob. of Scand origin; akin to Dan & Norw *trøske* thrush] **1** : a disease that is caused by a fungus (*Candida albicans*), occurs esp. in infants, and is marked by white patches in the oral cavity **2** : a suppurative disorder of the feet in various animals

1thrust \'thrəst\ *vb* **thrust; thrust·ing** [ME *thrusten, thristen,* fr. ON *thrȳsta*] *vt* **1** : to push or drive with force : SHOVE **2** : to cause to enter or pierce something by or as if by pushing <~ a dagger into her heart> **3** : EXTEND, SPREAD **4** : STAB, PIERCE **5 a** : to put (as an unwilling person) forcibly into a course of action or position <was *thrust* into power> **b** : to introduce often improperly into a position : INTERPOLATE **6** : to press, force, or impose the acceptance of upon someone <~ new responsibilities upon him> ~ *vi* **1 a** : to force an entrance or passage **b** : to push forward : press onward **c** : to push upward : PROJECT **2** : to make a thrust, stab, or lunge with or as if with a pointed weapon <~ at her with a knife> ***syn*** see PUSH

2thrust *n* **1 a** : a push or lunge with a pointed weapon **b** (1) : a verbal attack (2) : a military assault **2 a** : a strong continued pressure **b** : the sideways force or pressure of one part of a structure against another part (as of an arch against an abutment) **c** (1) : the force exerted endwise through a propeller shaft to give forward motion (2) : the forward directed reaction force produced by a high-speed jet of fluid discharged rearward from a nozzle (as in a jet airplane) **d** : a nearly horizontal geological fault **3 a** : a forward or upward push **b** : a movement (as by a group of people) in a specified direction **4** : salient or essential meaning

thrust·er *also* **thrust·or** \'thrəs-tər\ *n* : one that thrusts; *esp* : a rocket engine <~*s* for maneuvering a spacecraft>

thrust·ful \'thrəst-fəl\ *adj, Brit* : characterized by thrusting or an ability to thrust : AGGRESSIVE, PUSHY <~ young man on the make —*Current Literature*> — **thrust·ful·ness** *n, Brit*

thrust stage *n* [*thrust,* pp. of 1*thrust*] : a stage surrounded on three sides by the audience; *also* : a forestage that is extended into the auditorium to increase the stage area

thru·way \'thrü-ˌwā\ *n* : EXPRESSWAY

1thud \'thəd\ *vi* **thud·ded; thud·ding** [prob. fr. ME *thudden* to thrust, fr. OE *thyddan*] : to move or strike so as to make a thud

2thud *n* **1** : BLOW **2** : a dull sound : THUMP

thug \'thəg\ *n* [Hindi *ṭhag,* lit., thief, fr. Skt *sthaga* rogue, fr. *sthagati* he covers, conceals — more at THATCH] : a brutal ruffian or assassin : GANGSTER, KILLER

thu·ja \'th(y)ü-jə\ *n* [NL *Thuja,* genus name, fr. ML *thuia,* a cedar, fr. Gk *thyia*] : any of a genus (*Thuja*) of evergreen shrubs and trees of the pine family; *esp* : ARBORVITAE

Thu·le \'th(y)ü-lē\ *n* [L *Thule, Thyle,* fr. Gk *Thoulē, Thylē*] : the northernmost part of the habitable ancient world

thu·li·um \'th(y)ü-lē-əm\ *n* [NL, fr. L *Thule*] : a trivalent metallic element of the rare-earth group — see ELEMENT table

1thumb \'thəm\ *n* [ME *thoume, thoumbe,* fr. OE *thūma;* akin to OHG *thūmo* thumb, L *tumēre* to swell, Gk *sōs* safe, whole] **1** : the digit of the human hand that is closest to the trunk when the hand extends forward with the palm down; *also* : the corresponding digit in lower animals **2** : the part of a glove or mitten that covers the thumb **3** : a convex molding : OVOLO — **all thumbs** : extremely awkward or clumsy <dropped everything he picked up and was *all thumbs*> — **under one's thumb** *or* **under the thumb** : under control : in a state of subservience <her father did not have her that much *under his thumb* —Hamilton Basso>

2thumb *vt* **1 a** : to leaf through (pages) with the thumb : TURN **b** : to soil or wear by or as if by repeated thumbing <a badly ~*ed* book> **2** : to request or obtain (a ride) in a passing automobile by signaling with the thumb ~ *vi* **1** : to turn over pages <~ through a book> **2** : to travel by thumbing rides : HITCH-HIKE <~*ed* across the country> — **thumb one's nose 1** : to place the thumb at one's nose and extend the fingers as a gesture of scorn or defiance **2** : to react with disdain or defiance <*thumb their nose* at opulence —*Sales Management*>

thumb·hole \'thəm-ˌhōl\ *n* **1** : an opening in which to insert the thumb **2** : a hole in a wind musical instrument opened or closed by the thumb

thumb index *n* : a series of notches cut in the fore edge of a book to facilitate reference

1thumb·nail \'thəm-ˌnāl, -'nā(ə)l\ *n* : the nail of the thumb

2thumb·nail \ˌthəm-ˌnāl\ *adj* : BRIEF, CONCISE <a ~ sketch>

thumb piano *n* : MBIRA

thumb·print \'thəm-ˌprint\ *n* : an impression made by the thumb; *esp* : a print made by the inside of the first joint

thumb·screw \-ˌskrü\ *n* **1** : a screw having a flat-sided or knurled head so that it may be turned by the thumb and forefinger **2** : an instrument of torture for compressing the thumb by a screw

thumb·tack \-ˌtak\ *n* : a tack with a broad flat head for pressing into a surface with the thumb

1thump \'thəmp\ *vb* [imit.] *vt* **1** : to strike or beat with or as if with something thick or heavy so as to cause a dull sound **2** : POUND, KNOCK **3** : WHIP, THRASH **4** : to produce (music) mechanically or in a mechanical manner — usu. used with *out* <~*ed* out a tune on the piano> ~ *vi* **1** : to inflict or emit a thump **2** : to make a vigorous endorsement <got a couple of . . . senators to ~ for him —*N.Y. Herald Tribune*> — **thump·er** *n*

2thump *n* : a blow or knock with or as if with something blunt or heavy; *also* : the sound made by such a blow

thump·ing *adj* [*thumping,* prp. of 1*thump*] : impressively large, great, or excellent <a ~ majority>

1thun·der \'thən-dər\ *n* [ME *thoner, thunder,* fr. OE *thunor;* akin to OHG *thonar* thunder, L *tonare* to thunder] **1** : the sound that follows a flash of lightning and is caused by sudden expansion of the air in the path of the electrical discharge **2** : a loud utterance or threat **3** : BANG, RUMBLE <the ~ of big guns>

2thunder *vb* **thun·dered; thun·der·ing** \-d(ə-)riŋ\ *vi* **1 a** : to produce thunder — usu. used impersonally <it ~*ed*> **b** : to give forth a sound that resembles thunder <horses ~*ed* down the road> **2** : ROAR, SHOUT ~ *vt* **1** : to utter loudly : ROAR **2** : to strike with a sound likened to thunder — **thun·der·er** \-dər-ər\ *n*

thun·der·bird \'thən-dər-ˌbərd\ *n* : a mythical bird believed by American Indians to cause lightning and thunder

thun·der·bolt \-ˌbōlt\ *n* **1 a** : a single discharge of lightning with the accompanying thunder **b** : an imaginary elongated mass cast as a missile to earth in the lightning flash **2 a** : a person or thing that resembles lightning in suddenness, effectiveness, or destructive power **b** : a vehement threat or censure

thun·der·clap \-ˌklap\ *n* **1** : a clap of thunder **2** : something sharp, loud, or sudden like a clap of thunder

thun·der·cloud \-ˌklau̇d\ *n* : a cloud charged with electricity and producing lightning and thunder

thun·der·head \-ˌhed\ *n* : a rounded mass of cumulus cloud often appearing before a thunderstorm

thun·der·ing *adj* [*thundering,* prp. of 2*thunder*] : awesomely great, intense, or unusual — **thun·der·ing·ly** \-d(ə-)riŋ-lē\ *adv*

thunder lizard *n* [trans. of NL *brontosaurus*] : BRONTOSAUR

thun·der·ous \'thən-d(ə-)rəs\ *adj* : producing thunder; *also* : making or accompanied by a noise like thunder <~ applause> — **thun·der·ous·ly** *adv*

thun·der·peal \'thən-dər-ˌpēl\ *n* : THUNDERCLAP

thun·der·show·er \-ˌshau̇(-ə)r\ *n* : a shower accompanied by lightning and thunder

thun·der·stone \-ˌstōn\ *n* **1** *archaic* : THUNDERBOLT 1b **2** : any of various stones (as a meteorite or an ancient artifact) that are the probable source of the imaginary thunderbolt

thun·der·storm \-ˌstȯ(ə)rm\ *n* : a storm accompanied by lightning and thunder

thun·der·strike \-ˌstrīk\ *vt* **-struck** \-ˌstrək\; **-struck** *also* **-strick·en** \-ˌstrik-ən\; **-strik·ing** \-ˌstrī-kiŋ\ **1** *archaic* : to strike, blast, or injure by or as if by lightning **2** : to strike dumb : ASTONISH

thun·der·stroke \-ˌstrōk\ *n* : a stroke of or as if of lightning with the attendant thunder

thu·ri·ble \'th(y)u̇r-ə-bəl, 'thər-\ *n* [ME *turrible,* fr. MF *thurible,* fr. L *thuribulum,* fr. *thur-, thus* incense, fr. Gk *thyos* incense, sacrifice, fr. *thyein* to sacrifice — more at THYME] : CENSER

thu·ri·fer \-ə-fər\ *n* [NL, fr. L *thurifer,* adj., incense-bearing, fr. *thur-, thus* + *-ifer* -iferous] : one who carries a censer in a liturgical service

Thu·rin·ger \'th(y)u̇r-ən-jər\ *n* [G *thüringerwurst,* fr. *thüringer* Thuringian + *wurst* sausage] : a mildly seasoned fresh or smoked sausage

Thu·rin·gian \th(y)u̇-'rin-j(ē-)ən\ *n* **1** : a member of an ancient Germanic people whose kingdom was overthrown by the Franks in the 6th century **2** : a native or inhabitant of Thuringia — **Thuringian** *adj*

thurl \'thər(-ə)l\ *n* [perh. fr. E dial., gaunt] : the hip joint in cattle — see COW illustration

Thurs *or* **Thu** *abbr* Thursday

Thurs·day \'thərz-dē\ *n* [ME, fr. OE *thursdæg,* fr. ON *thōrsdagr;* akin to OE *thunresdæg* Thursday, OHG *Donares tag;* all fr. a prehistoric NGmc-WGmc compound whose components are represented by OHG *Donar,* Germanic god of the sky (fr. *thonar, donar* thunder) and by OHG *tag* day — more at THUNDER, DAY] : the fifth day of the week — **Thurs·days** \-dēz\ *adv*

thus \'t͟həs\ *adv* [ME, fr. OE; akin to MD *dus* thus, OE *thæt,* neut. demonstrative pron. — more at THAT] **1** : in this or that manner or way **2** : to this degree or extent : SO **3** : because of this or that : HENCE, CONSEQUENTLY **4** : as an example

1thwack \'thwak\ *vt* [imit.] : to strike with or as if with something flat or heavy : WHACK

2thwack *n* : a heavy blow : WHACK

1thwart \'thwȯ(ə)rt, *naut often* 'thȯ(ə)rt\ *adv* [ME *thwert,* fr. ON *thvert,* fr. neut. of *thverr* transverse, oblique; akin to OHG *dwerah* transverse, oblique, L *torquēre* to twist — more at TORTURE] : ATHWART

2thwart *adj* : situated or placed across something else : TRANSVERSE — **thwart·ly** *adv*

3thwart *vt* **1 a** : to run counter to so as to effectively oppose or baffle : CONTRAVENE **b** : to oppose successfully : defeat the hopes or aspirations of **2** : to pass through or across ***syn*** see FRUSTRATE — **thwart·er** *n*

4thwart *n* : a rower's seat extending athwart a boat

thwart·wise \-ˌwīz\ *adv or adj* : CROSSWISE

thy \(ˌ)t͟hī\ *adj* [ME *thin, thy,* fr. OE *thīn,* gen. of *thū* thou — more at THOU] *archaic* : of or relating to thee or thyself esp. as possessor or agent or as object of an action — used esp. in ecclesiastical or literary language and sometimes by Friends esp. among themselves

Thy·es·te·an \thī-'es-tē-ən\ *adj* [*Thyestes,* brother of Atreus who unwittingly ate the flesh of his children] : of or relating to the eating of human flesh : CANNIBAL

thy·la·cine \'thī-lə-ˌsīn\ *n* [NL *Thylacinus,* genus of marsupials, fr. Gk *thylakos* sack, pouch] : TASMANIAN WOLF

thy·la·koid \'thī-lə-ˌkȯid\ *n* [ISV *thylak-* (fr. Gk *thylakos* sack) + *-oid;* prob. orig. formed in G] : a membranous lamella of protein and lipid in plant chloroplasts where the photochemical reactions of photosynthesis take place

[1]**thym-** *or* **thymo-** *comb form* [ISV, fr. L *thymum*] : thyme <*thym*ol>
[2]**thym-** *or* **thymo-** *comb form* [NL *thymus*] : thymus <*thym*ic> <*thymo*cyte>
thyme \'tīm *also* 'thīm\ *n* [ME, fr. MF *thym*, fr. L *thymum*, fr. Gk *thymon*, fr. *thyein* to make a burnt offering, sacrifice; akin to L *fumus* smoke — more at FUME] : any of a genus (*Thymus*) of mints with small pungent aromatic leaves; *esp* : a garden herb (*T. vulgaris*) used in seasoning and formerly in medicine
thy·mec·to·my \thī-'mek-tə-mē\ *n, pl* **-mies** : excision of the thymus — **thy·mec·to·mize** \-ˌmīz\ *vt*
-thy·mia \'thī-mē-ə\ *n comb form* [NL, fr. Gk, fr. *thymos* mind — more at FUME] : condition of mind and will <schizo*thymia*>
thy·mic \'thī-mik\ *adj* : of or relating to the thymus
thy·mi·dine \'thī-mə-ˌdēn\ *n* [*thymine* + *-idine*] : a nucleoside $C_{10}H_{14}N_2O_5$ that is composed of thymine and deoxyribose and occurs as a structural part of DNA
thy·mine \'thī-ˌmēn\ *n* [G *thymin*, fr. *thym-* [2]thym- + *-in* -ine] : a pyrimidine base $C_5H_6N_2O_2$ that is one of the four bases coding genetic information in the polynucleotide chain of DNA — compare ADENINE, CYTOSINE, GUANINE, URACIL
thy·mo·cyte \'thī-mə-ˌsīt\ *n* [ISV] : a cell of the thymus; *esp* : a thymic lymphocyte
thy·mol \'thī-ˌmȯl, -ˌmōl\ *n* [ISV] : a crystalline phenol $C_{10}H_{14}O$ of aromatic odor and antiseptic properties found esp. in thyme oil or made synthetically and used chiefly as a fungicide and preservative
thy·mus \'thī-məs\ *n* [NL, fr. Gk *thymos* warty excrescence, thymus] : a glandular structure of largely lymphoid tissue that is held to function esp. in the development of the body's immune system, is present in the young of most vertebrates typically in the upper anterior chest or at the base of the neck, and tends to disappear or become rudimentary in the adult
thymy *or* **thym·ey** \'tī-mē *also* 'thē-\ *adj* : abounding in or fragrant with thyme
thyr- *or* **thyro-** *comb form* [*thyroid*] : thyroid <*thyro*toxicosis> <*thyro*xine>
thy·ra·tron \'thī-rə-ˌträn\ *n* [fr. *Thyratron*, a trademark] : a gas-filled 3-element hot-cathode electron tube in which the grid controls only the start of a continuous current thus giving the tube a trigger effect
thy·ro·cal·ci·to·nin \ˌthī-rō-ˌkal-sə-'tō-nən\ *n* [*thyr-* + *calcitonin*] : a polypeptide hormone from the thyroid gland that tends to lower the level of calcium in the blood plasma
thy·ro·glob·u·lin \-'gläb-yə-lən\ *n* [ISV] : an iodine-containing protein of the thyroid gland that is the form in which hormones of the thyroid are stored
[1]**thy·roid** \'thī-ˌrȯid\ *or* **thy·roi·dal** \thī-'rȯid-ᵊl\ *adj* [NL *thyroides*, fr. Gk *thyreoeidēs* shield-shaped, thyroid, fr. *thyreos* shield shaped like a door, fr. *thyra* door — more at DOOR] **1 a** : of, relating to, or being a large endocrine of craniate vertebrates lying at the base of the neck and producing esp. the hormone thyroxine **b** : suggestive of a disordered thyroid <a ~ personality> **2** : of, relating to, or being the chief cartilage of the larynx
[2]**thyroid** *n* **1** : a thyroid gland or cartilage; *also* : a part (as an artery or nerve) associated with either of these **2** : a preparation of mammalian thyroid gland used in treating thyroid disorders
thy·roid·ec·to·my \ˌthī-ˌrȯid-'ek-tə-mē, -rəd-\ *n, pl* **-mies** : surgical removal of thyroid gland tissue — **thy·roid·ec·to·mized** \-ˌmīzd\ *adj*
thy·roid·itis \ˌthī-ˌrȯid-'īt-əs, -rəd-\ *n* [NL] : inflammation of the thyroid gland
thyroid–stimulating hormone *n* : THYROTROPHIN
thy·ro·tox·i·co·sis \'thī-rō-ˌtäk-sə-'kō-səs\ *n* [NL] : HYPERTHYROIDISM
thy·ro·tro·phic \ˌthī-rə-'trō-fik\ *or* **thy·ro·tro·pic** \-'trō-pik, -'träp-ik\ *adj* : exerting or characterized by a direct influence on the secretory activity of the thyroid gland <~ functions>
thy·ro·tro·phin \ˌthī-rə-'trō-fən\ *or* **thy·ro·tro·pin** \-pən\ *n* [*thyrotrophic*, *thyrotropic*] : a hormone secreted by the anterior pituitary that regulates the formation and secretion of thyroid hormone — called also *thyroid-stimulating hormone, thyrotrophic hormone, thyrotropic hormone*
thy·rox·ine *or* **thy·rox·in** \thī-'räk-ˌsēn, -sən\ *n* [ISV] : an iron-containing amino acid $C_{15}H_{11}I_4NO_4$ that is the active principle of the thyroid gland, is a product of the cleavage of thyroglobulin, is made synthetically or obtained from animal thyroid glands, and is used to treat thyroid disorders
thyrse \'thərs\ *n* [NL *thyrsus*, fr. L, thyrsus] : an inflorescence (as in the lilac and horse chestnut) in which the main axis is racemose and the secondary and later axes are cymose
thyr·sus \'thər-səs\ *n, pl* **thyr·si** \-ˌsī, -ˌsē\ [L, fr. Gk *thyrsos*] : a staff surmounted by a pine cone or by a bunch of vine or ivy leaves with grapes or berries that is an attribute of Bacchus and of satyrs and others engaging in bacchic rites
thy·sa·nop·ter·an \ˌthī-sə-'näp-tə-rən\ *n* [deriv. of Gk *thysanos* tassel + *pteron* wing — more at FEATHER] : any of an order (Thysanoptera) of winged insects comprising the thrips — **thysanopteran** *adj*
thy·sa·nu·ran \ˌthī-sə-'n(y)u̇r-ən\ *n* [deriv. of Gk *thysanos* tassel + *oura* tail — more at SQUIRREL] : any of an order (Thysanura) of wingless insects having projecting caudal bristles and comprising the bristletails — **thysanuran** *adj*
thy·self \t͟hī-'self\ *pron, archaic* : YOURSELF — used esp. in ecclesiastical or literary language and sometimes by Friends esp. among themselves
[1]**ti** \'tē\ *n* [Tahitian, Marquesan, Samoan, & Maori] : any of several Asiatic and Pacific trees or shrubs (genus *Cordyline*) of the lily family with leaves in terminal tufts
[2]**ti** *n* [alter. of *si*] : the seventh tone of the diatonic scale in solmization
Ti *symbol* titanium
ti·ara \tē-'ar-ə, -'er-, -'är-\ *n* [L, royal Persian headdress, fr. Gk] **1** : a 3-tiered crown worn by the pope **2** : a decorative jeweled or flowered headband or semicircle for formal wear by women
Ti·bet·an \tə-'bet-ᵊn\ *n* **1 a** : a member of the Mongoloid native race of Tibet modified in the west and south by intermixture with Indian peoples and in the east with Chinese **b** : a native or inhabitant of Tibet **2** : the Tibeto-Burman language of the Tibetan people — **Tibetan** *adj*
Tibetan terrier *n* : any of a breed of terriers resembling Old English sheepdogs but having a curled well-feathered tail
Ti·beto–Bur·man \tə-ˌbet-ō-'bər-mən\ *n* **1** : a language family of Asia by some included in Sino-Tibetan **2** : a member of a people speaking a Tibeto-Burman language
tib·ia \'tib-ē-ə\ *n, pl* **-i·ae** \-ē-ˌē, -ē-ˌī\ *also* **-i·as** [L] **1** : the inner and usu. larger of the two bones of the vertebrate hind limb between the knee and ankle **2** : the fourth joint of the leg of an insect between the femur and tarsus — **tib·i·al** \-ē-əl\ *adj*
tib·io·fib·u·la \ˌtib-ē-ō-'fib-yə-lə\ *n* [NL] : a bone esp. in frogs and toads that is formed by fusion of the tibia and fibula
tic \'tik\ *n* [F] **1** : local and habitual spasmodic motion of particular muscles esp. of the face : TWITCHING **2** : a persistent trait of character or behavior <"you know" is a verbal ~ of many inexperienced speakers>
ti·cal \ti-'käl, 'tik-əl\ *n, pl* **ticals** *or* **tical** [Thai, fr. Malay *tikal*, a monetary unit] : BAHT
tic dou·lou·reux \'tik-ˌdü-lə-'rü, -'rə(r)\ *n* [F, painful twitch] : TRIGEMINAL NEURALGIA
[1]**tick** \'tik\ *n* [ME *tyke, teke*; akin to MHG *zeche* tick, Arm *tiz*] **1** : any of numerous bloodsucking arachnids that form a superfamily (Ixodoidea of the order Acarina), are larger than the related mites, attach themselves to warm-blooded vertebrates to feed, and include important vectors of infectious diseases **2** : any of various usu. wingless parasitic dipterous insects — compare SHEEP KED
[2]**tick** *n* [ME *tek*; akin to MHG *zic* light push] **1 a** : a light rhythmic audible tap or beat; *also* : a series of such ticks **b** *chiefly Brit* : the time taken by the tick of a clock : MOMENT **2** : a small spot or mark; *esp* : one used to direct attention to something, to check an item on a list, or to represent a point on a scale
[3]**tick** *vi* **1** to make the sound of a tick or a series of ticks **2** : to operate as a functioning mechanism : RUN <tried to understand what made him ~> <the motor was ~*ing* over quietly> ~ *vt* **1** : to mark with a written tick : CHECK — usu. used with *off* <~*ed* off each item in the list> **2** : to mark, count, or announce by or as if by ticking beats <a meter ~*ing* off his cab fare>
[4]**tick** *n* [ME *tike*, prob. fr. MD; akin to OHG *ziahha* tick; both fr. a prehistoric WGmc word borrowed fr. L *theca* cover, fr. Gk *thēkē* case; akin to Gk *tithenai* to place — more at DO] **1** : the fabric case of a mattress, pillow, or bolster; *also* : a mattress consisting of a tick and its filling **2** : TICKING
[5]**tick** *n* [short for [1]*ticket*] : CREDIT, TRUST; *also* : a credit account
tick–borne \'tik-ˌbō(ə)rn, -ˌbȯ(ə)rn\ *adj* : capable of being transmitted by the bites of ticks <a ~ disease>
ticked \'tikt\ *adj* **1** : marked with ticks : FLECKED **2** *of a hair* : banded with two or more colors
tick·er \'tik-ər\ *n* : something that ticks or produces a ticking sound: as **a** : WATCH **b** : a telegraphic receiving instrument that automatically prints off information (as stock quotations or news) on a paper ribbon **c** *slang* : HEART
ticker tape *n* : the paper ribbon on which a telegraphic ticker prints off its information
[1]**tick·et** \'tik-ət\ *n* [obs. F *etiquet* (now *étiquette*), notice attached to something, fr. MF *estiquet*, fr. *estiquier* to attach, fr. MD *steken* to stick; akin to OHG *sticken* to prick — more at STICK] **1 a** : a document that serves as a certificate, license, or permit; *esp* : a mariner's or airman's certificate **b** : TAG, LABEL **2** : a summons or warning issued to a traffic-law violator **3** : a certificate or token showing that a fare or admission fee has been paid **4** : a list of candidates for nomination or election : SLATE **5** : a slip or card recording a transaction or undertaking or giving instructions <a savings deposit ~> **6** : the correct or desirable thing <cooperation, that's the ~ —K. E. Trombley>
[2]**ticket** *vt* **1** : to attach a ticket to : LABEL; *also* : DESIGNATE **2** : to furnish or serve with a ticket <~*ed* for illegal parking>
ticket agency *n* : an agency selling transportation or theater and entertainment tickets
ticket agent *n* **1** : one who acts as an agent of a transportation company to sell tickets for travel by train, boat, airplane, or bus **2** : one who sells theater and entertainment tickets
ticket office *n* : an office of a transportation company, theatrical or entertainment enterprise, or ticket agency where tickets are sold and reservations made
tick·et–of–leave \ˌtik-ət-ə(v)-'lēv\ *n, pl* **tickets–of–leave** : a license or permit formerly given in the United Kingdom and the British Commonwealth to a convict under imprisonment to go at large and to labor for himself subject to certain specific conditions
tick fever *n* **1** : a febrile disease (as Rocky Mountain spotted fever) transmitted by the bites of ticks **2** : TEXAS FEVER
tick·icide \'tik-ə-ˌsīd\ *n* : an agent used to kill ticks
[1]**tick·ing** \'tik-iŋ\ *n* [[4]*tick*] : a strong linen or cotton fabric used in upholstering and as a covering for a mattress or pillow
[2]**ticking** *n* [[2]*tick*] : ticked marking on a bird or mammal or on individual hairs
[1]**tick·le** \'tik-əl\ *vb* **tick·led**; **tick·ling** \-(ə-)liŋ\ [ME *tikelen*; akin to OE *tinclian* to tickle] *vi* **1** : to have a tingling or prickling sensation <my back ~*s*> **2** : to excite the surface nerves to prickle ~ *vt* **1 a** : to excite or stir up agreeably : PLEASE <music . . . does more than ~ our sense of rhythm —Edward Sapir> **b** : to provoke to laughter or merriment : AMUSE <were *tickled* by the clown's antics> **2** : to touch (as a body part) lightly so as to

excite the surface nerves and cause uneasiness, laughter, or spasmodic movements

2tickle *n* **1 :** something that tickles **2 :** a tickling sensation **3 :** the act of tickling

tick·ler \ˈtik-(ə-)lər\ *n* **1 :** a person or device that tickles **2 :** a device for jogging the memory; *specif* **:** a file that serves as a reminder and is arranged to bring matters to timely attention

tickler coil *n* **:** small coil connected in series with the plate circuit of an electron tube and inductively coupled with its grid circuit to return a part of the amplified signal for repeated amplification

tick·lish \ˈtik-(ə-)lish\ *adj* **1 :** sensitive to tickling **2 a :** TOUCHY, OVERSENSITIVE <~ about his baldness> **b :** easily overturned <a canoe is a ~ craft> **3 :** requiring delicate handling **:** CRITICAL <a ~ subject> — **tick·lish·ly** *adv* — **tick·lish·ness** *n*

tick off *vt* [3*tick*] **1 :** REPRIMAND, REBUKE <his father *ticked* him *off* for his impudence> **2 :** to make angry or indignant <the cancellation really *ticked* me *off*>

tick·seed \ˈtik-ˌsēd\ *n* [1*tick*] **:** COREOPSIS

tick·tack *or* **tic·tac** \ˈtik-ˌtak\ *n* [imit.] **1 :** a ticking or tapping beat like that of a clock or watch **2 :** a contrivance used by children to tap on a window from a distance

tick·tack·toe *also* **tic–tac–toe** \ˌtik-ˌtak-ˈtō\ *n* [*tic-tac-toe* (former game in which players with eyes shut brought a pencil down on a slate marked with numbers and scored the number hit)] **:** a game in which two players alternately put Xs and Os in compartments of a figure formed by two vertical lines crossing two horizontal lines and each tries to get a row of three Xs or three Os before the opponent does

tick·tock \ˈtik-ˈtäk, -ˌtäk\ *n* [imit.] **:** the ticking sound of a clock

tick trefoil *n* [1*tick*] **:** any of various leguminous plants (genus *Desmodium*) with trifoliolate leaves and rough sticky loments

ticky–tacky \ˌtik-ē-ˈtak-ē\ *n* [coined by Malvina Reynolds *b*1900 Am songwriter] **:** sleazy or shoddy material

TID *abbr* [L *ter in die*] three times a day

tid·al \ˈtīd-ᵊl\ *adj* **1 a :** of, relating to, caused by, or having tides <~ cycles> <~ erosion> **b :** periodically rising and falling or flowing and ebbing <~ waters> **2 :** dependent (as to the time of arrival or departure) upon the state of the tide <a ~ steamer> — **tid·al·ly** \-ᵊl-ē\ *adv*

tid·al wave *n* **1 a :** an unusually high sea wave that sometimes follows an earthquake **b :** an unusual rise of water alongshore due to strong winds **2 :** something overwhelming (as a sweeping majority vote or an irresistible impulse)

tid·bit \ˈtid-ˌbit\ *n* [perh. fr. *tit-* (as in *titmouse*) + *bit*] **1 :** a choice morsel of food **2 :** a choice or pleasing bit (as of news)

tid·dle·dy·winks *or* **tid·dly·winks** \ˈtid-ᵊl-(d)ē-ˌwiŋ(k)s, ˈtid-lē-ˌwiŋ(k)s\ *n pl but sing in constr* [prob. fr. E dial. *tiddly* little] **:** a game whose object is to snap small disks from a flat surface into a small container

1tide \ˈtīd\ *n* [ME, time, fr. OE *tīd;* akin to OHG *zīt* time, Gk *daiesthai* to divide] **1 a** *obs* **:** a space of time **:** PERIOD **b :** a fit or opportune time **:** OPPORTUNITY **c :** an ecclesiastical anniversary or festival; also **:** its season — usu. used in combination <Easter*tide*> <Kingdom*tide*> **2 a** (1) **:** the alternate rising and falling of the surface of the ocean and of water bodies (as gulfs and bays) connected with the ocean that occurs twice a day and is caused by the gravitational attraction of the sun and moon occurring unequally on different parts of the earth (2) **:** a less marked rising and falling of an inland body of water (3) **:** a periodic movement in the earth's crust caused by the same forces that produce ocean tides (4) **:** a tidal distortion on one celestial body caused by the gravitational attraction of another (5) **:** one of the tidal movements of the atmosphere resembling those of the ocean but produced by diurnal temperature changes — called also *atmospheric tide* **b :** FLOOD TIDE **3 :** something that fluctuates like the tides of the sea <the ~ of public opinion> **4 a :** a flowing stream **:** CURRENT **b :** the waters of the ocean **:** the overflow of a flooding stream — **tide·less** \-ləs\ *adj*

2tide *vb* **tid·ed; tid·ing** *vi* **1 :** to flow as or in a tide **:** SURGE **2 :** to drift with the tide esp. in navigating a ship into or out of an anchorage, harbor, or river ~ *vt* **1 :** to cause to float with or as if with the tide **2 :** to proceed along (one's way) by taking advantage of tides

3tide *vi* **tid·ed; tid·ing** [ME *tiden,* fr. OE *tīdan;* akin to MD *tiden* to go, come, OE *tīd* time] *archaic* **:** BETIDE, BEFALL

tide·land \ˈtīd-ˌland, -lənd\ *n* **1 :** land overflowed during flood tide **2 :** land underlying the ocean and lying beyond the low-water limit of the tide but being within the territorial waters of a nation — often used in pl.

tide·mark \-ˌmärk\ *n* **1 a :** a high-water or sometimes low-water mark left by tidal water or a flood **b :** a mark placed to indicate this point **2 :** the point to which something has attained or below which it has receded <the ~ of tolerance has risen —*New Republic*>

tide over *vt* [2*tide*] **:** to enable to surmount or endure a difficulty <money to *tide* him *over* the emergency>

tide table *n* **:** a table that indicates the height of the tide at one place at different times of day throughout one year

tide·wait·er \ˈtīd-ˌwāt-ər\ *n* **:** a customs inspector working on the docks or aboard ships

tide·wa·ter \-ˌwȯt-ər, -ˌwät-\ *n* **1 :** water overflowing land at flood tide; *also* **:** water affected by the ebb and flow of the tide **2 :** low-lying coastal land

tide·way \-ˌwā\ *n* **:** a channel in which the tide runs

tid·ing \ˈtīd-iŋ\ *n* [ME, fr. OE *tīdung,* fr. *tīdan* to betide] **:** a piece of news — usu. used in pl. <good ~*s*>

1ti·dy \ˈtīd-ē\ *adj* **ti·di·er; -est** [ME, timely, in good condition, fr. *tide* time] **1 :** properly filled out **:** PLUMP **2 :** adequately satisfactory **:** ACCEPTABLE, FAIR <a ~ solution to their problem> **3 a :** neat and orderly in appearance or habits **:** well ordered and cared for **b :** METHODICAL, PRECISE <a ~ mind> **4 :** LARGE, SUBSTANTIAL <a ~ profit> ***syn*** see NEAT ***ant*** untidy — **ti·di·ly** \ˈtīd-ᵊl-ē\ *adv* — **ti·di·ness** \ˈtīd-ē-nəs\ *n*

2tidy *vb* **ti·died; ti·dy·ing** *vt* **:** to put in order <~ up a room> ~ *vi* **:** to make things tidy <~*ing* up after supper> — **ti·di·er** *n*

3tidy *n, pl* **tidies** **1 :** a piece of fancywork used to protect the back, arms, or headrest of a chair or sofa from wear or soil **2 :** a receptacle for sewing materials or odds and ends

ti·dy·tips \ˈtīd-ē-ˌtips\ *n pl but sing or pl in constr* **:** an annual California composite herb (*Layia platyglossa*) having yellow-rayed flower heads often tipped with white

1tie \ˈtī\ *n* [ME *teg, tye,* fr. OE *tēag;* akin to ON *taug* rope, OE *tēon* to pull — more at TOW] **1 a :** a line, ribbon, or cord used for fastening, uniting, or drawing something closed; *esp* **:** SHOELACE **b** (1) **:** a structural element (as a rod or angle iron) holding two pieces together **:** a tension member in a construction (2) **:** one of the transverse supports to which railroad rails are fastened to keep them to line **2 :** something that serves as a connecting link: as **a :** a moral or legal obligation to someone or something typically constituting a restraining power, influence, or duty **b :** a bond of kinship or affection **3 :** a curved line that joins two musical notes of the same pitch to denote a single tone sustained through the time value of the two **4 a :** an equality in number (as of votes or scores) **b :** equality in a contest; *also* **:** a contest that ends in a draw **5 :** a method or style of tying or knotting **6 :** something that is knotted or is to be knotted when worn: as **a :** NECKTIE **b :** a low laced shoe **:** OXFORD — **tie·less** \-ləs\ *adj*

tie 3

2tie *vb* **tied; ty·ing** \ˈtī-iŋ\ *or* **tie·ing** *vt* **1 a :** to fasten, attach, or close by means of a tie **b :** to form a knot or bow in <~ your scarf> **c :** to make by tying constituent elements <*tied* a wreath> <~ a fishing fly> **2 a :** to unite in marriage **b :** to unite (musical notes) by a tie **c :** to join electrically (power systems) **3 :** to restrain from independence or freedom of action or choice **:** constrain by or as if by authority, influence, agreement, or obligation **4 a** (1) **:** to make or have an equal score with in a contest (2) **:** to equalize (the score) in a game or contest (3) **:** to equalize the score of (a game) **b :** to provide or offer something equal to **:** EQUAL ~ *vi* **:** to make a tie: as **a :** to make a bond or connection **b :** to make an equal score **c :** to become attached **d :** to close by means of a tie — **tie into :** to attack with vigor — **tie one on** *slang* **:** to get drunk — **tie the knot :** to perform a marriage ceremony; *also* **:** to get married

tie–and–dye \ˈtī-ən-ˌdī\ *n* **:** TIE-DYEING

tie·back \ˈtī-ˌbak\ *n* **1 :** a decorative strip or device of cloth, cord, or metal for draping a curtain to the side of a window **2 :** a curtain with a tieback — usu. used in pl.

tie breaker *n* **:** a contest used to select a winner from among contestants with tied scores at the end of a previous contest

tie–dye \ˈtī-ˌdī\ *n* **:** TIE-DYEING

tie–dyed *adj* **:** having patterns produced by tie-dyeing <~ jeans>

tie–dye·ing *n* **:** a hand method of producing patterns in textiles by tying portions of the fabric or yarn so that they will not absorb the dye

tie–in \ˈtī-ˌin\ *n* **:** something that ties in, relates, or connects

tie in \(ˈ)tī-ˈin\ *vt* **:** to bring into connection with something relevant: as **a :** to make the final connection of <*tied in* the new branch pipeline> **b :** to coordinate in such a manner as to produce balance and unity <the illustrations were cleverly *tied in* with the text> **c :** to use as a tie-in esp. in advertising ~ *vi* **:** to become tied in

tie·mann·ite \ˈtē-mə-ˌnīt\ *n* [G *tiemannit,* fr. W. *Tiemann,* 19th cent. G scientist who discovered it] **:** a mineral HgSe that consists of mercuric selenide and occurs in dark gray or nearly black masses of metallic luster

tie·pin \ˈtī-ˌpin\ *n* **:** an ornamental straight pin that has usu. an ornamental head and a sheath for the point and is used to hold the ends of a necktie in place

1tier \ˈti(ə)r\ *n* [MF *tire* rank] **:** a row, rank, or layer of articles; *esp* **:** one of two or more rows or ranks arranged one above another

2tier *vt* **:** to place or arrange in tiers ~ *vi* **:** to rise in tiers

3ti·er \ˈtī(-ə)r\ *n* **:** one that ties

1tierce \ˈti(ə)rs\ *var of* TERCE

2tierce *n* [ME *terce, tierce,* fr. MF, fr. fem. of *terz,* adj., third, fr. L *tertius* — more at THIRD] **1** *obs* **:** THIRD 1 **2 :** any of various units of liquid capacity equal to ⅓ pipe; *esp* **:** a unit equal to 42 gallons **3 :** a sequence of three playing cards of the same suit

tier·cel \ˈti(ə)r-səl\ *n* [ME *tercel,* fr. MF, fr. (assumed) VL *tertiolus,* fr. dim. of L *tertius* third] **:** a male hawk

tiered \ˈti(ə)rd\ *adj* **:** having or arranged in tiers, rows, or layers — often used in combination <triple-*tiered*>

tie–rod \ˈtī-ˌräd\ *n* **:** a rod (as of steel) used as a connecting member or brace

tier table *n* **:** a small table or stand with two or more usu. round tops arranged one above another

tie silk *n* **:** a silk fabric of firm resilient pliable texture used for neckties and for blouses and accessories

tie tack *or* **tie tac** \-ˌtak\ *n* **:** an ornamented pin with a receiving button or clasp that is used to attach the two ends of a necktie together or to attach a necktie to a shirt

tie–up \ˈtī-ˌəp\ *n* **1 a :** a mooring place for a boat **b :** a cow stable; *also* **:** a space for a single cow in a stable **2 :** a suspension of traffic, business, or operation (as by a mechanical breakdown) **3 :** CONNECTION, ASSOCIATION <a helpful financial ~>

tie up \(ˈ)tī-ˈəp\ *vt* **1 :** to attach, fasten, or bind securely; *also* **:** to wrap up and fasten **2 a :** to connect closely **:** JOIN <*tie up* the loose ends> **b :** to cause to be linked so as to depend on something **3 a :** to place or invest in such a manner as to make unavailable for other purposes <his money was *tied up* in stocks> **b :** to restrain from operation or progress <traffic was *tied up* for miles> **4 a :** to keep busy <was *tied up* in conference all day> **b :** to preempt the use of <*tied up* the phone for an hour> ~ *vi* **1 :** DOCK <the ferry *ties up* at the south slip> **2 :** to assume a definite relationship <this *ties up* with what you were told before>

[1]tiff \ˈtif\ *n* [origin unknown] **:** a petty quarrel ***syn*** see QUARREL
[2]tiff *vi* **:** to have a minor quarrel
tif·fa·ny \ˈtif-ə-nē\ *n, pl* **-nies** [prob. fr. obs. F *tiphanie* Epiphany, fr. LL *theophania,* fr. LGk, deriv. of Gk *theos* god + *phainein* to show] **1 :** a sheer silk gauze formerly used for clothing and trimmings **2 :** a plain-weave open-mesh cotton fabric (as cheesecloth)
tif·fin \ˈtif-ən\ *n, chiefly Brit* [prob. alter. of *tiffing,* gerund of obs. E *tiff* (to eat between meals)] **:** a midday meal **:** LUNCHEON
ti·ger \ˈtī-gər\ *n, pl* **tigers** [ME *tigre,* fr. OE *tiger* & OF *tigre,* both fr. L *tigris,* fr. Gk, of Iranian origin; akin to Av *tighra-* pointed; akin to Gk *stizein* to tattoo — more at STICK] **1** *pl also* **tiger a :** a large Asiatic carnivorous mammal (*Felis tigris*) of the cat family having a tawny coat transversely striped with black **b :** any of several large wildcats (as the jaguar or cougar) **c :** a domestic cat with striped pattern **d** *Austral* **:** TASMANIAN WOLF **2 a :** a fierce and bloodthirsty person or quality <aroused the ~ in him> **b :** a vigorously aggressive person <he's a ~ for work> **3** *Brit* **:** a groom in livery; *esp* **:** a young or small groom — **ti·ger·ish** \-g(ə-)rish\ *adj* — **ti·ger·ish·ly** *adv* — **ti·ger·ish·ness** *n* — **ti·ger·like** \-gər-ˌlīk\ *adj*
tiger beetle *n* **:** any of numerous active carnivorous beetles (family Cicindelidae) having larvae that tunnel in the soil
tiger cat *n* **1 :** any of various wildcats (as the serval, ocelot, or margay) of moderate size and variegated coloration **2 :** a striped or sometimes blotched tabby cat
ti·ger·eye \ˈtī-gə-ˌrī\ *or* **ti·ger's-eye** \-gər-ˌzī\ *n* **:** a usu. yellowish to grayish brown chatoyant stone that is much used for ornament and is a silicified crocidolite
tiger lily *n* **:** a common Asiatic garden lily (*Lillium tigrinum*) having nodding orange-colored flowers densely spotted with black; *also* **:** any of various lilies with similar flowers
tiger moth *n* **:** any of a family (Arctiidae) of stout-bodied moths usu. with broad striped or spotted wings
tiger salamander *n* **:** a widely distributed No. American salamander (*Ambystoma tigrinum*) that is brown or black above with vertical yellowish lateral blotches often running together ventrally
tiger shark *n* **:** a large gray or brown stocky-bodied shark (*Galeocerdo cuvieri* or *G. arcticus*) that is a man-eater and is nearly cosmopolitan esp. in warm seas
tiger swallowtail *n* **:** a large widely distributed swallowtail (*Papilio glaucus*) of eastern No. America that is largely yellow with black margins and striped on the wings
[1]tight \ˈtīt\ *adj* [ME, alter. of *thight,* of Scand origin; akin to ON *théttr* tight; akin to MHG *dihte* thick, Skt *tanakti* it causes to coagulate] **1 :** so close or substantial in structure as not to permit passage (as of a liquid or gas or light) <a ~ roof> — often used in combination <a hog*tight* fence> **2 a :** fixed very firmly in place <loosen a ~ jar cover> **b :** firmly stretched, drawn, or set <a ~ drumhead> <a ~ knot> **c :** fitting usu. too closely (as for comfort) <~ shoes> **3 :** set close together **:** COMPACT <a ~ defensive formation in football> **4 a :** CAPABLE, ALERT, READY **b** (1) **:** trim and tidy in dress (2) **:** neat and orderly in arrangement or design **:** SNUG **5 :** difficult to get through or out of **:** TRYING, EXACTING <in a ~ situation> **6 a :** firm in control <kept a ~ hand on all his affairs> **b :** characterized by firmness of control <ran a ~ courtroom> **c :** STINGY, MISERLY **7 :** evenly contested **:** CLOSE <a ~ tennis match> **8 :** packed or compressed to the limit **:** entirely full <a ~ bale> **9 :** INTOXICATED, DRUNK **10 a :** highly condensed <a ~ literary style> **b :** closely spaced <a ~ line of print> **11 :** scantily supplied or obtainable in proportion to demand <~ money>; *also* **:** characterized by such a scarcity <a ~ labor market> **12** *of lumber* **:** sound and free from checks <logs with ~ hearts> **13** *slang* **:** FRIENDLY — **tight·ly** *adv* — **tight·ness** *n*
syn TIGHT, TAUT, TENSE ***shared meaning element*** **:** drawn or stretched to the limit ***ant*** loose
[2]tight *adv* **1 :** FAST, TIGHTLY, FIRMLY <the door was shut ~> **2 :** in a sound manner **:** SOUNDLY <sleep ~>
tight·en \ˈtīt-ᵊn\ *vb* **tight·ened; tight·en·ing** \ˈtīt-niŋ, -ᵊn-iŋ\ *vt* **:** to make tight or tighter ~ *vi* **:** to become tight or tighter — **tight·en·er** \-nər, -ᵊn-ər\ *n*
tight end *n* **:** an offensive football end who lines up within two yards of the tackle
tight·fist·ed \ˈtīt-ˈfis-təd\ *adj* **:** reluctant to part with money
tight-lipped \-ˈlipt\ *adj* **1 :** having the lips closed tight (as in determination) **2 :** reluctant to speak **:** TACITURN
tight-mouthed \-ˈmau̇thd, -ˈmau̇tht\ *adj* **:** CLOSEMOUTHED
tight·rope \ˈtīt-ˌrōp\ *n* **1 :** a rope or wire stretched taut for acrobats to perform on **2 :** a dangerously precarious situation
tights \ˈtīts\ *n pl* **:** a skintight garment covering the body from the neck down or from the waist down
tight·wad \ˈtīt-ˌwäd\ *n* **:** a close or miserly person
tight·wire \-ˌwī(ə)r\ *n* **:** a tightrope made of wire
ti·glon \ˈtī-glən\ *n* [*tiger* + *lion*] **:** a hybrid between a male tiger and a female lion
ti·gon \ˈtī-gən\ *n* [*tiger* + *lion*] **:** TIGLON
Ti·gre \ti-ˈgrā\ *n* **:** a Semitic language of northern Ethiopia
ti·gress \ˈtī-grəs\ *n* **:** a female tiger; *also* **:** a tigerish woman
Ti·gri·nya \tə-ˈgrē-nyə\ *n* **:** a Semitic language of northern Ethiopia
tike *var of* TYKE
ti·ki \ˈtē-kē\ *n* [Maori & Marquesan fr. *Tiki,* first man or creator of first man] **:** a wood or stone image of a Polynesian supernatural power
til \ˈtil\ *n* [Hindi, fr. Skt *tila*] **:** SESAME
ti·la·pia \tə-ˈläp-ē-ə, -ˈläp-\ *n* [NL, genus name] **:** any of a genus (*Tilapia*) of African freshwater cichlid food fishes
til·bury \ˈtil-ˌber-ē, -b(ə-)rē\ *n, pl* **-bur·ies** [*Tilbury,* 19th cent. E coach builder] **:** a light 2-wheeled carriage **:** GIG
til·de \ˈtil-də\ *n* [Sp, fr. ML *titulus* tittle] **1 :** a mark ~ placed esp. over the letter *n* (as in Spanish *señor* sir) to denote the sound \nʸ\ or over vowels (as in Portuguese *irmã* sister) to indicate nasality **2 :** the mark ~ used in logic and mathematics to indicate negation

[1]tile \ˈtī(ə)l\ *n, often attrib* [ME, fr. OE *tigele;* akin to ON *tigl* tile; both fr. a prehistoric WGmc-NGmc word borrowed fr. L *tegula* tile; akin to L *tegere* to cover — more at THATCH] **1** *pl* **tiles** *or* **tile a :** a flat or curved piece of fired clay, stone, or concrete used esp. for roofs, floors, or walls and often for ornamental work **b :** a hollow or a semicircular and open earthenware or concrete piece used in constructing a drain **c :** a hollow building unit made of fired clay or of shale or gypsum **2 :** TILING **3 :** HAT; *esp* **:** a high silk hat **4 :** a thin piece of resilient material (as cork, linoleum, or rubber) used esp. for covering floors or walls

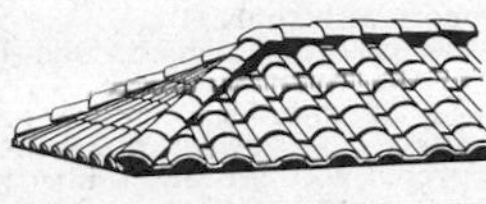
tiles 1a

[2]tile *vt* **tiled; til·ing 1 :** to cover with tiles **2 :** to install drainage tile in — **til·er** *n*
tile·fish \ˈtī(ə)l-ˌfish\ *n* [*tile-* modif. of NL *Lopholatilus,* genus name] **:** a large violet marine percoid food fish (*Lopholatilus chamaeleonticeps*) of deep waters with a fleshy appendage on the head and large round yellow spots
til·ing \ˈtī-liŋ\ *n* **1 :** the action or work of one who tiles **2 a :** TILES **b :** a surface of tiles
[1]till \tᵊl, təl, (ˌ)til\ *prep* [ME, fr. OE *til;* akin to ON *til* to, till, OE *til* good] **1** *chiefly Scot* **:** TO **2 :** UNTIL
[2]till *conj* **:** UNTIL
[3]till \ˈtil\ *vt* [ME *tilien, tillen,* fr. OE *tilian;* akin to OE *til* good, suitable, OHG *zil* goal] **:** to work by plowing, sowing, and raising crops **:** CULTIVATE — **till·able** \-ə-bəl\ *adj*
[4]till \ˈtil\ *n* [AF *tylle*] **1 a :** a box, drawer, or tray in a receptacle (as a cabinet or chest) used esp. for valuables **b :** a money drawer in a store or bank **2 a :** the money contained in a till **b :** a supply of esp. ready money
[5]till \ˈtil\ *n* [origin unknown] **:** unstratified glacial drift consisting of clay, sand, gravel, and boulders intermingled
till·age \ˈtil-ij\ *n* **1 :** the operation of tilling land **2 :** cultivated land
til·land·sia \tə-ˈlan(d)-zē-ə\ *n* [NL, genus name, fr. Elias *Tillands* †1693 Finn botanist] **:** any of a very large genus (*Tillandsia*) of chiefly epiphytic plants of the pineapple family native to tropical and subtropical America
[1]till·er \ˈtil-ər\ *n* **:** one that tills **:** CULTIVATOR
[2]til·ler \ˈtil-ər\ *n* [ME *tiler* stock of a crossbow, fr. MF *telier,* lit., beam of a loom, fr. ML *telarium,* fr. L *tela* web — more at TOIL] **:** a lever used to turn the rudder of a boat from side to side; *broadly* **:** a device or system that plays a part in steering something
[3]til·ler *n* [fr. (assumed) ME, fr. OE *telgor, telgra* twig, shoot; akin to OHG *zelga* twig, Gk *daidalos* ingeniously formed — more at CONDOLE] **:** SPROUT, STALK; *esp* **:** one from the base of a plant or from the axils of its lower leaves
[4]til·ler *vi* **til·lered; til·ler·ing** \ˈtil-(ə-)riŋ\ *of a plant* **:** to put forth tillers
til·ler·man \ˈtil-ər-mən\ *n* **:** one in charge of a tiller **:** STEERSMAN
[1]tilt \ˈtilt\ *vb* [ME *tulten, tilten;* akin to Sw *tulta* to waddle] *vt* **1 :** to cause to slope **:** INCLINE <don't ~ the boat> **2 a :** to point or thrust in or as if in a tilt <~ a lance> **b :** to charge against <~ an adversary> ~ *vi* **1 :** to move or shift so as to lean or incline **:** SLANT **2 a :** to engage in a combat with lances **:** JOUST **b :** to make an impetuous attack <~ at wrongs> — **tilt·able** \ˈtil-tə-bəl\ *adj* — **tilt·er** *n*
[2]tilt *n* **1 a :** a contest on horseback in which two combatants charging with lances or similar weapons try to unhorse each other **:** JOUST **b :** a tournament of tilts **2 a :** a verbal contest between disputants **:** CONTENTION **b :** SPEED — used in the phrase *at full tilt* **3 a :** the act of tilting **:** the state or position of being tilted **b :** a sloping surface **4 :** any of various sports resembling or suggesting tilting with lances; *esp* **:** a water sport in which the contestants stand on logs or in canoes or boats and thrust with poles — **tilt** *adj*
[3]tilt *n* [ME *teld, telte* tent, canopy, fr. OE *teld;* akin to OHG *zelt* tent] **:** a canopy for a wagon, boat, or stall
[4]tilt *vt* **:** to cover or provide with a tilt
tilth \ˈtilth\ *n* [ME, fr. OE, fr. *tilian* to till] **1 :** cultivation of the soil **2 :** cultivated land **:** TILLAGE **3 :** the state of being tilled **4 :** the state of aggregation of a soil
tilt·me·ter \ˈtilt-ˌmēt-ər\ *n* **:** an instrument to measure the tilting of the earth's surface
tilt·yard \ˈtilt-ˌyärd\ *n* **:** a yard or place for tilting contests
Tim *abbr* Timothy
tim·bal \ˈtim-bəl\ *n* [F *timbale,* fr. MF, alter. of *tamballe,* modif. of OSp *atabal,* fr. Ar *at-tabl* the drum] **:** KETTLEDRUM
tim·bale \ˈtim-bəl; tim-ˈbäl, tam-\ *n* [F, lit., kettledrum] **1 :** a creamy mixture (as of meat or vegetables) baked in a mold; *also* **:** the mold in which it is baked **2 :** a small pastry shell filled with a cooked timbale mixture
[1]tim·ber \ˈtim-bər\ *n* [ME, fr. OE, building, wood; akin to OHG *zimbar* wood, room, L *domus* house, Gk *demein* to build] **1 a :** growing trees or their wood **b** — used interjectionally to warn of a falling tree **2 :** wood suitable for building or for carpentry **3 :** MATERIAL, STUFF; *esp* **:** personal qualification for a particular position or status **4 a :** a large squared or dressed piece of wood ready for use or forming part of a structure **b** *Brit* **:** [2]LUMBER 2a **c :** a curving frame branching outward from the keel of a ship and bending upward in a vertical direction that is usu. composed of several pieces united **:** RIB — **timber** *adj* — **tim·ber·man** \-mən, -ˌman\ *n*

ə abut	ᵊ kitten	ər further	a back	ā bake	ä cot, cart
au̇ out	ch chin	e less	ē easy	g gift	i trip	ī life
j joke	ŋ sing	ō flow	ȯ flaw	ȯi coin	th thin	t͟h this
ü loot	u̇ foot	y yet	yü few	yu̇ furious	zh vision

²**timber** *vt* **tim·bered; tim·ber·ing** \-b(ə-)riŋ\ **:** to frame, cover, or support with timbers
tim·ber·doo·dle \ˌtim-bər-ˈdüd-ᵊl\ *n* [¹*timber* + *doodle* (cock)] **:** the American woodcock
tim·bered \ˈtim-bərd\ *adj* **1 :** having walls framed by exposed timbers **2 :** having a specified structure or constitution **3 :** covered with growing timber **:** WOODED
tim·ber·head \ˈtim-bər-ˌhed\ *n* **1 :** the top end of a ship's timber used above the gunwale (as for belaying ropes) **2 :** a bollard bolted to the deck where the end of a timber would come
timber hitch *n* **:** a knot used to secure a line to a log or spar — see KNOT illustration
tim·ber·ing \ˈtim-b(ə-)riŋ\ *n* **:** a set or arrangement of timbers
tim·ber·land \-bər-ˌland\ *n* **:** wooded land esp. with marketable timber
tim·ber·line \-ˌlīn\ *n* **:** the upper limit of arboreal growth in mountains or high latitudes — called also *tree line*
tim·ber·man \-mən\ *n* **:** LUMBERMAN
timber rattlesnake *n* **:** a moderate-sized rattlesnake (*Crotalus horridus horridus*) that is widely distributed through the eastern half of the U.S.
timber right *n* **:** ownership of standing timber without ownership of the land
timber wolf *n* **:** a wolf (*Canis lupus lycaon*) formerly common over much of eastern No. America — called also *lobo*

timber wolf

tim·ber·work \ˈtim-bər-ˌwərk\ *n* **:** timber construction
tim·bre *also* **tim·ber** \ˈtam-bər, ˈtim-\ *n* [F, fr. MF, bell struck by a hammer, fr. OF, drum, fr. MGk *tymbanon* kettledrum, fr. Gk *tympanon* — more at TYMPANUM] **:** the quality given to a sound by its overtones: as **a :** the resonance by which the ear recognizes and identifies a voiced speech sound **b :** the quality of tone distinctive of a particular singing voice or musical instrument
tim·brel \ˈtim-brəl\ *n* [dim. of obs. E *timbre* tambourine, fr. ME, fr. OF, drum] **:** a small hand drum or tambourine — **tim·brelled** \-brəld\ *adj*
¹**time** \ˈtīm\ *n* [ME, fr. OE *tīma;* akin to ON *tīmi* time, OE *tīd* — more at TIDE] **1 a :** the measured or measurable period during which an action, process, or condition exists or continues **:** DURATION **b :** a continuum which lacks spatial dimensions and in which events succeed one another from past through present to future **c :** LEISURE <~ for reading> **2 :** the point or period when something occurs **:** OCCASION **3 :** an appointed, fixed, or customary moment or hour for something to happen, begin, or end <arrived ahead of ~> **4 a :** an historical period **:** AGE **b :** a division of geologic chronology **c :** conditions at present or at some specified period <~*s* are hard> <move with the ~*s*> **d :** the present time <issues of the ~> **5 a :** LIFETIME **b :** a period of apprenticeship **c :** a term of military service **d :** a prison sentence **6 :** SEASON <very hot for this ~ of year> **7 a :** rate of speed **:** TEMPO **b :** the grouping of the beats of music **:** RHYTHM **8 a :** a moment, hour, day, or year as indicated by a clock or calendar <what ~ is it> **b :** any of various systems (as sidereal or solar) of reckoning time **9 a :** one of a series of recurring instances or repeated actions <you've been told many ~*s*> **b** *pl* (1) **:** multiplied instances <five ~*s* greater> (2) **:** equal fractional parts of which an indicated number equal a comparatively greater quantity <seven ~*s* smaller> <three ~*s* closer> **c :** TURN <three ~*s* at bat> **10 :** finite as contrasted with infinite duration **11 :** a person's experience during a specified period or on a particular occasion <a good ~> **12 a :** the hours or days occupied by one's work <make up ~> **b :** an hourly pay rate <straight ~> **c :** wages paid at discharge or resignation <pick up your ~ and get out> **13 a :** the playing time of a game **b :** TIME-OUT — **at the same time :** HOWEVER, NEVERTHELESS <glorify the equalitarian ideal and *at the same time* keep woman in the subordinate role —Vance Packard> — **at times :** at intervals **:** OCCASIONALLY — **for the time being :** for the present — **from time to time :** once in a while **:** OCCASIONALLY — **in no time :** in the shortest possible time — **in time 1 :** sufficiently early **2 :** in the course of time **:** EVENTUALLY **3 :** in correct tempo <learn to play *in time*> — **on time 1 a :** at the appointed time **b :** on schedule **2 :** on the installment plan — **time and again :** FREQUENTLY, REPEATEDLY

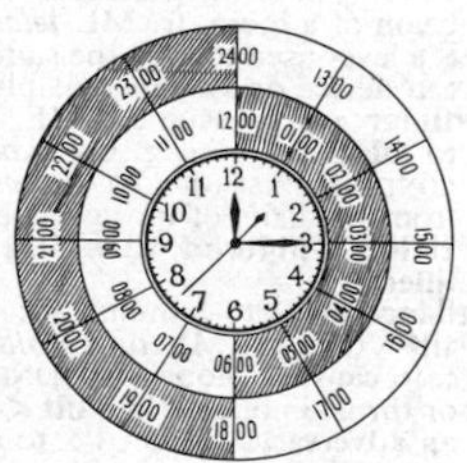
time 8b: a standard 12-hour dial surrounded by bands to show equivalent 24-hour time

²**time** *vb* **timed; tim·ing** *vt* **1 a :** to arrange or set the time of **:** SCHEDULE **b :** to regulate (a watch) to keep correct time **2 :** to set the tempo, speed, or duration of <*timed* his leap perfectly —Neil Amdur> **3 :** to cause to keep time with something **4 :** to determine or record the time, duration, or rate of <~ a horse> **5 :** to dispose (as a mechanical part) so that an action occurs at a desired instant or in a desired way ~ *vi* **:** to keep or beat time
³**time** *adj* **1 a :** of or relating to time **b :** recording time **2 :** timed to ignite or explode at a specific moment <a ~ bomb> **3 a :** payable on a specified future day or a certain length of time after presentation for acceptance **b :** based on installment payments <a ~ sale>
time and a half *n* **:** payment of a worker (as for overtime or holiday work) at one and a half times his regular wage rate
time bill *n* **:** a bill of exchange payable at a definite future time
time capsule *n* **:** a container holding historical records or objects representative of current culture that is deposited (as in a cornerstone) for preservation until discovery by some future age
time card *n* **:** a card used with a time clock to record an employee's starting and quitting times each day or on each job
time chart *n* **1 :** a chart showing the standard times in various parts of the world with reference to a specified time at a specified place **2 :** a table listing important events for successive years within a particular historical period
time clock *n* **:** a clock that stamps an employee's starting and quitting times on his time card
time–con·sum·ing \ˈtīm-kən-ˈsü-miŋ\ *adj* **1 :** using or taking up a great deal of time <~ chores> **2 :** wasteful of time <~ tactics>
timed \ˈtīmd\ *adj* **1 :** made to occur at or in a set time <a ~ explosion> **2 :** done or taking place at a time of a specified sort <an ill-*timed* arrival>
time deposit *n* **:** a bank deposit payable a specified number of days after deposit or on advance notice to the bank
time dilation *n* **:** a slowing of time on a system moving at a velocity approaching that of light relative to an observer as predicted by the theory of relativity — called also *time dilatation*
time draft *n* **:** a draft payable a specified number of days after date of the draft or presentation to the drawee
time exposure *n* **:** exposure of a photographic film for a definite time usu. of more than one half second; *also* **:** a photograph taken by such exposure
time–hon·ored \ˈtī-ˌmän-ərd\ *adj* **:** honored because of age or long usage <~ traditions>
time immemorial *n* **1 :** a time antedating a period legally fixed as the basis for a custom or right **2 :** time so long past as to be indefinite in history or tradition — called also *time out of mind*
time·keep·er \ˈtīm-ˌkē-pər\ *n* **1 :** TIMEPIECE **2 :** a clerk who keeps records of the time worked by employees **3 :** one appointed to mark and announce the time in an athletic game or contest — **time·keep·ing** \-piŋ\ *n*
time killer *n* **1 :** a person with time on his hands **2 :** something that passes the time **:** DIVERSION
time lag *n* **:** an interval of time between two related phenomena (as a cause and its effect)
time–lapse \ˈtīm-ˌlaps\ *adj* **:** of, relating to, or constituting a motion picture made so that when projected a slow action (as the opening of a flower bud) appears to be speeded up
time·less \ˈtīm-ləs\ *adj* **1** *archaic* **:** PREMATURE, UNTIMELY **2 a :** having no beginning or end **:** ETERNAL **b :** not restricted to a particular time or date **:** DATELESS <the ~ themes of love, solitude, joy, and nature —*Writer*> **3 :** not affected by time **:** AGELESS — **time·less·ly** *adv* — **time·less·ness** *n*
time loan *n* **:** a loan with a definite maturity date
time lock *n* **:** a lock controlled by clockwork to prevent its being opened before a set time
¹**time·ly** \ˈtīm-lē\ *adv* **1** *archaic* **:** EARLY, SOON **2 :** in time **:** OPPORTUNELY <the question was not . . . ~ raised in the state court —W. O. Douglas>
²**timely** *adj* **time·li·er; -est 1 :** coming early or at the right time **:** OPPORTUNE **2 :** appropriate or adapted to the times or the occasion <a ~ book> ***syn*** see SEASONABLE ***ant*** untimely — **time·li·ness** *n*
time machine *n* **:** a hypothetical device that permits travel into the past and future
time money *n* **:** money loaned or available to be loaned for a specified period of time
time note *n* **:** a note payable at a specified time
time·ous \ˈtī-məs\ *adj* **:** TIMELY — **time·ous·ly** *adv*
time–out \ˈtī-ˈmau̇t\ *n* **:** a brief suspension of activity **:** BREAK; *esp* **:** a suspension of play in an athletic game
time out of mind : TIME IMMEMORIAL 2
time·piece \ˈtīm-ˌpēs\ *n* **:** a device (as a clock or watch) to measure or show progress of time
time·pleas·er \-ˌplē-zər\ *n, obs* **:** TIMESERVER
tim·er \ˈtī-mər\ *n* **:** one that times: as **a :** TIMEPIECE; *esp* **:** a stopwatch for timing races **b :** TIMEKEEPER **c :** a device in the ignition system of an internal-combustion engine that causes the spark to be produced in the cylinder at the correct time **d :** a device (as a clock) that indicates by a sound the end of an interval of time or that starts or stops a device at predetermined times
time reversal *n* **:** a formal operation in mathematical physics that reverses the order in which a sequence of events occurs
times \ˌtīmz, təmz\ *prep* **:** multiplied by <two ~ two is four>
time–sav·er \ˈtīm-ˌsā-vər\ *n* **:** something that saves time
time·sav·ing \-viŋ\ *adj* **:** intended or serving to expedite something <~ kitchen appliances>
time·serv·er \-ˌsər-vər\ *n* **:** a person who fits his behavior and ideas to the pattern of his time or his superiors **:** TEMPORIZER
¹**time·serv·ing** \-viŋ\ *n* **:** the behavior or practice of a timeserver
²**timeserving** *adj* **:** marked by or revealing a lack of independence or integrity <a mean, ~ little man, grovelling odiously before the wealthy people —Peter Forster>
time–shar·ing \ˈtīm-ˌshe(ə)r-iŋ, -ˌsha(ə)r-\ *n* **:** simultaneous access to a computer by many users whose programs are interleaved
time sheet *n* **1 :** a sheet for recording the time of arrival and departure of workers and for recording the amount of time spent on each job **2 :** a sheet for summarizing hours worked by each worker during a pay period
time signature *n* **:** a fractional sign placed just after the key signature whose denominator indicates the kind of note (as a quarter note) taken as the time unit for the beat and whose numerator indicates the number of these to the measure
times sign *n* **:** the symbol x used to indicate multiplication
time stamp *n* **:** a device for recording the date and time of day that letters or papers are received or sent out — **time–stamp** *vt*
time·ta·ble \ˈtīm-ˌtā-bəl\ *n* **1 :** a table of departure and arrival times of trains, buses, or airplanes **2 :** a schedule showing a planned order or sequence

time–test·ed \-ˌtes-təd\ *adj* : having effectiveness that has been proved over a long period of time <~ methods>
time trial *n* : a competitive event (as in auto racing) in which individuals are successively timed over a set course or distance
time·work \'tīm-ˌwərk\ *n* : work paid for at a standard rate for the hour or the day — **time·work·er** \-ˌwər-kər\ *n*
time·worn \-ˌwō(ə)rn, -ˌwȯ(ə)rn\ *adj* **1** : worn or impaired by time <~mansions> **2 a** : AGE-OLD, ANCIENT <~ procedures> **b** : HACKNEYED, STALE <a ~ joke>
time zone *n* : a geographical region within which the same standard time is used
tim·id \'tim-əd\ *adj* [L *timidus,* fr. *timēre* to fear] **1** : lacking in courage or self-confidence <a ~ person> **2** : lacking in boldness or determination <a ~ policy> — **ti·mid·i·ty** \tə-'mid-ət-ē\ *n* — **tim·id·ly** \'tim-əd-lē\ *adv* — **tim·id·ness** *n*

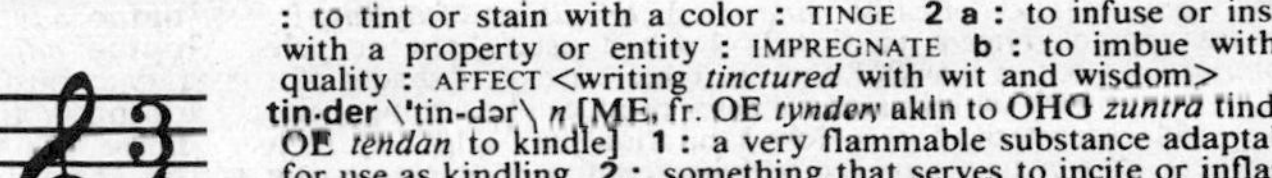

time signatures: *1* ¾ time, *2* common time

tim·ing \'tī-miŋ\ *n* **1** : selection for maximum effect of the precise moment for beginning or doing something **2** : observation and recording (as by a stopwatch) of the elapsed time of an act, action, or process

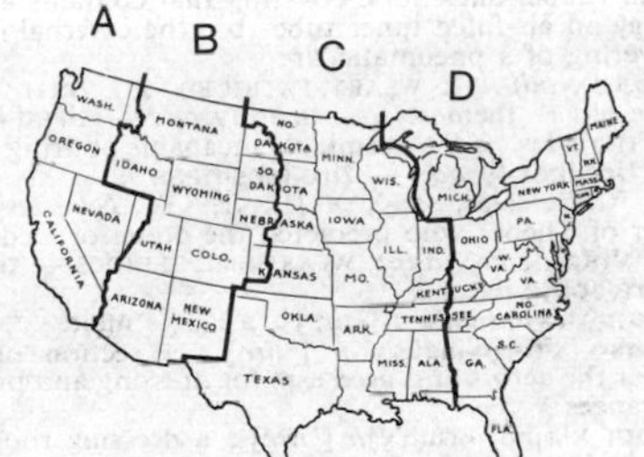

time zones in the United States; *A* Pacific time, *B* mountain time, *C* central time, *D* eastern time

ti·moc·ra·cy \tī-'mäk-rə-sē\ *n* [MF *tymocracie,* fr. ML *timocratia,* fr. Gk *timokratia,* fr. *timē* price, value, honor + *-kratia* -cracy — more at PAIN] **1** : government in which political and civil honors are distributed according to wealth **2** : government in which love of honor is the ruling principle — **ti·mo·crat·ic** \ˌtī-mə-'krat-ik\ *or* **ti·mo·crat·i·cal** \-i-kəl\ *adj*
tim·o·rous \'tim-(ə-)rəs\ *adj* [ME, fr. MF *timoureus,* fr. ML *timorosus,* fr. L *timor* fear, fr. *timēre* to fear] **1** : of a timid disposition : FEARFUL **2** : expressing or suggesting timidity <proceed with doubtful and ~ steps —Edward Gibbon> — **tim·o·rous·ly** *adv* — **tim·o·rous·ness** *n*
tim·o·thy \'tim-ə-thē\ *n* [prob. after *Timothy* Hanson, 18th cent. Am farmer said to have introduced it from New England to the southern states] : a European grass (*Phleum pratense*) that has long cylindrical spikes and is widely grown for hay
Tim·o·thy \'tim-ə-thē\ *n* [L *Timotheus,* fr. Gk *Timotheos*] **1** : a disciple of the apostle Paul **2** : either of two letters written with regard to pastoral care in the early Church and included as books in the New Testament — see BIBLE table
tim·pa·ni \'tim-pə-nē\ *n pl but sing or pl in constr* [It, pl. of *timpano* kettledrum, fr. L *tympanum* drum — more at TYMPANUM] : a set of two or three kettledrums played by one performer in an orchestra or band
tim·pa·nist \-nəst\ *n* : a member of an orchestra or band who plays the timpani
Tim·u·cua \ˌtim-ə-'kü-ə\ *n* : an extinct American Indian language of northeastern Florida
¹tin \'tin\ *n* [ME, fr. OE; akin to OHG *zin* tin] **1** : a soft faintly bluish white lustrous low-melting crystalline metallic element that is malleable and ductile at ordinary temperatures and that is used as a protective coating, in tinfoil, and in soft solders and alloys — see ELEMENT table **2 a** : a box, can, pan, vessel, or a sheet made of tinplate **b** : a tinplate container and its contents <a ~ of tomatoes> — **tin·ful** \-ˌfu̇l\ *n*
²tin *vt* **tinned; tin·ning** **1** : to cover or plate with tin or a tin alloy **2** *chiefly Brit* : to put up or pack in tins : CAN
tin·a·mou \'tin-ə-ˌmü\ *n* [F, fr. Galibi *tinamu*] : any of a family (Tinamidae) of So. American game birds that have a deeply keeled sternum and a rudimentary tail and that produce eggs with a surface resembling enamel
tinc *abbr* tincture
tin·cal \'tiŋ-kəl\ *n* [Malay *tingkal*] : crude native borax
tin can *n* **1** : a can made of tinplate; *broadly* : CAN 1c **2** *slang* : DESTROYER 2
¹tinct \'tiŋ(k)t\ *adj* [L *tinctus,* pp.] : COLORED, TINGED
²tinct *n* : TINCTURE, TINGE
tinc·to·ri·al \tiŋ(k)-'tōr-ē-əl, -'tȯr-\ *adj* [L *tinctorius,* fr. *tinctus,* pp.] : of or relating to colors or to dyeing or staining; *also* : imparting color — **tinc·to·ri·al·ly** \-ē-ə-lē\ *adv*
¹tinc·ture \'tiŋ(k)-chər\ *n* [ME, fr. L *tinctura* act of dyeing, fr. *tinctus,* pp. of *tingere* to tinge] **1 a** : a substance that colors, dyes, or stains **b** : COLOR, TINT **2 a** : a characteristic quality : CAST **b** : a slight admixture : TRACE **3** *obs* : an active principle or extract **4** : a heraldic metal, color, or fur **5** : a solution of a medicinal substance in an alcoholic menstruum
²tincture *vt* **tinc·tured; tinc·tur·ing** \'tiŋ(k)-chə-riŋ, -shriŋ\ **1** : to tint or stain with a color : TINGE **2 a** : to infuse or instill with a property or entity : IMPREGNATE **b** : to imbue with a quality : AFFECT <writing *tinctured* with wit and wisdom>
tin·der \'tin-dər\ *n* [ME, fr. OE *tynder;* akin to OHG *zuntra* tinder, OE *tendan* to kindle] **1** : a very flammable substance adaptable for use as kindling **2** : something that serves to incite or inflame <the . . . agreement could not possibly be more loaded with ~ —*Life*>
tin·der·box \'tin-dər-ˌbäks\ *n* **1 a** : a metal box for holding tinder and usu. a flint and steel for striking a spark **b** : a highly inflammable object or place **2** : a potentially explosive place or situation
¹tine \'tīn\ *n* [ME *tind,* fr. OE; akin to OHG *zint* point, tine] **1** : a slender pointed projecting part : PRONG **2** : a pointed branch of an antler — **tined** \'tīnd\ *adj*
²tine *vb* **tined** \'tīnd\ *or* **tint** \'tint\; **tin·ing** \'tī-niŋ\ [ME *tinen,* of Scand origin; akin to ON *tȳna* to lose, destroy; akin to ON *tjōn* injury — more at TEEN] *vt, dial Brit* : LOSE ~ *vi, dial Brit* : to become lost
tin·ea \'tin-ē-ə\ *n* [ME, fr. ML, fr. L, worm, moth] : any of several fungous diseases of the skin; *esp* : RINGWORM — **tin·e·al** \-ē-əl\ *adj*
tinea cru·ris \-'krůr-əs\ *n* [NL, lit., tinea of the leg] : a fungous infection involving esp. the groin and perineum
tin ear *n* **1** : CAULIFLOWER EAR **2** : a deafened or insensitive ear
tin fish *n, slang* : TORPEDO
tin·foil \'tin-ˌfȯil\ *n* **1** : a thin metal sheeting usu. of aluminum or tin-lead alloy **2** : SILVER PAPER
ting *n* [*ting,* vb., fr. ME *tingen,* of imit. origin] : a high-pitched sound like that made by a light stroke on a crystal goblet — **ting** *vi*
¹tinge \'tinj\ *vt* **tinged; tinge·ing** *or* **ting·ing** \'tin-jiŋ\ [ME *tingen,* fr. L *tingere* to dip, moisten, tinge; akin to OHG *dunkōn* to dip, Gk *tengein* to moisten] **1 a** : to color with a slight shade or stain : TINT **b** : to affect or modify with a slight odor or taste **2** : to affect or modify in character
²tinge *n* **1** : a slight staining or suffusing shade or color **2** : an affective or modifying property or influence : TOUCH
tin·gle \'tiŋ-gəl\ *vi* **tin·gled; tin·gling** \-g(ə-)liŋ\ [ME *tinglen,* alter. of *tinklen* to tinkle, tingle] **1 a** : to feel a ringing, stinging, prickling, or thrilling sensation **b** : to cause such a sensation **2** : TINKLE — **tingle** *n* — **tin·gling·ly** \-g(ə-)liŋ-lē\ *adv* — **tin·gly** \-g(ə-)lē\ *adj*
tin hat *n* : a metal helmet
tin·horn \'tin-ˌhȯ(ə)rn\ *n* : one (as a gambler) who pretends to have money, ability, or influence
¹tin·ker \'tiŋ-kər\ *n* [ME *tinkere*] **1 a** : a usu. itinerant mender of household utensils **b** : an unskillful mender : BUNGLER **2** : *chiefly Irish* : GYPSY
²tinker *vb* **tin·kered; tin·ker·ing** \-k(ə-)riŋ\ *vi* : to work in the manner of a tinker; *esp* : to repair, adjust, or work with something in an unskilled or experimental manner : FIDDLE ~ *vt* **:** to repair, adjust, or experiment with — **tin·ker·er** \-kər-ər\ *n*
tinker's damn *or* **tinker's dam** \-'dam\ *n* [prob. fr. the tinkers' reputation for blasphemy] : a minimum amount or degree (as of care or consideration) : the least bit <didn't give a *tinker's damn* about poetry —James Blish>
¹tin·kle \'tiŋ-kəl\ *vb* **tin·kled; tin·kling** \-k(ə-)liŋ\ [ME *tinklen,* freq. of *tinken* to tinkle, of imit. origin] *vi* : to make or emit a tinkle or a sound suggestive of a tinkle ~ *vt* **1** : to sound or make known (the time) by a tinkle **2 a** : to cause to make a tinkle **b** : to produce by tinkling <~ a tune>
²tinkle *n* **1** : a series of short high ringing or clinking sounds **2** : a jingling effect in verse or prose
tin·kly \'tiŋ-k(ə-)lē\ *adj* : that tinkles : TINKLING
tin·man \'tin-mən\ *n* : TINSMITH
tin·ner \'tin-ər\ *n* **1** : a tin miner **2** : TINSMITH
tin·ni·tus \'tin-ət-əs\ *n* [L, ringing, tinnitus, fr. *tinnitus,* pp. of *tinnire* to ring, of imit. origin] : a sensation of noise (as a ringing or roaring) that is purely subjective
tin·ny \'tin-ē\ *adj* **tin·ni·er; -est** **1** : of, abounding in, or yielding tin **2 a** : resembling tin **b** : LIGHT, CHEAP **3** : thin in tone <a ~ voice> — **tin·ni·ly** \'tin-ᵊl-ē\ *adv* — **tin·ni·ness** \'tin-ē-nəs\ *n*
Tin Pan Alley *n* : a district that is a center for composers and publishers of popular music; *also* : the body of such composers and publishers
tin·plate \'tin-'plāt\ *n* : thin sheet iron or steel coated with tin
tin–plate *vt* : to plate or coat (as a metal sheet) with tin
¹tin·sel \'tin(t)-səl *also* 'tin-zəl\ *n* [MF *estincelle, etincelle* spark, glitter, spangle — more at STENCIL] **1** : a thread, strip, or sheet of metal, paper, or plastic used to produce a glittering and sparkling appearance in fabrics, yarns, or decorations **2** : something superficially attractive or glamorous but of little real worth <disfigured by no gaudy ~ of rhetoric or declamation —Thomas Jefferson>
²tinsel *adj* **1** : made of or covered with tinsel **2 a** : cheaply gaudy : TAWDRY **b** : SPECIOUS <spent his life chasing ~ promises —Ved Mehta>
³tinsel *vt* **tin·seled** *or* **tin·selled; tin·sel·ing** *or* **tin·sel·ling** \'tin(t)-s(ə-)liŋ, 'tin-zə-liŋ\ **1** : to interweave, overlay, or adorn with or as if with tinsel **2** : to impart a specious brightness to
tin·sel·ly \'tin(t)-s(ə-)lē, 'tin-zə-lē\ *adj* : TINSEL
tin·smith \'tin-ˌsmith\ *n* : a worker who makes or repairs things of sheet metal (as tinplate)
tin spirit *n* : a solution of various tin compounds used as a mordant
tin·stone \'tin-ˌstōn\ *n* : CASSITERITE

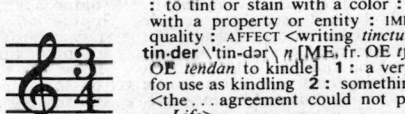

1tint \'tint\ *n* [alter. of earlier *tinct,* fr. L *tinctus* act of dyeing, fr. *tinctus,* pp. of *tingere* to tinge] **1 a :** a usu. slight or pale coloration : HUE **b :** any of various lighter or darker shades of a color : TINGE **2 :** a variation of a color produced by adding white to it and characterized by a low saturation with relatively high lightness **3 :** a usu. slight modifying quality or characteristic : TOUCH **4 :** a shaded effect in engraving produced by fine parallel lines close together **5 :** a panel of light color serving as background **6 :** dye for the hair — **tint·er** *n*

2tint *vt* **:** to impart or apply a tint to : COLOR

tint·ing *n* **1 :** the act or process of one that tints **2 :** the engraved or colored tint produced by tinting

tin·tin·nab·u·lary \,tin-tə-'nab-yə-,ler-ē\ *adj* [L *tintinnabulum* bell] **:** of, relating to, or characterized by bells or their sounds

tin·tin·nab·u·la·tion \,tin-tə-,nab-yə-'lā-shən\ *n* [L *tintinnabulum* bell, fr. *tintinnare* to ring, jingle, of imit. origin] **1 :** the ringing or sounding of bells **2 :** a jingling or tinkling sound as if of bells

tint·less \'tint-ləs\ *adj* **:** having no tints : lacking color

tin·type \-,tīp\ *n* **:** FERROTYPE 1

tin·ware \'tin-,wa(ə)r, -,we(ə)r\ *n* **:** articles and esp. utensils made of tinplate

tin·work \-,wərk\ *n* **1 :** work in tin **2** *pl but sing or pl in constr* **:** an establishment where tin is smelted, rolled, or otherwise worked

ti·ny \'tī-nē\ *adj* **ti·ni·er; -est** [alter. of ME *tine*] **:** very small or diminutive : MINUTE ***syn*** see SMALL — **ti·ni·ly** \'tīn-ᵊl-ē\ *adv* — **ti·ni·ness** \'tī-nē-nəs\ *n*

1tip \'tip\ *n* [ME; akin to MHG *zipf* tip, OE *tæppa* tap — more at TAP] **1 :** the usu. pointed end of something **2 :** a small piece or part serving as an end, cap, or point — **tipped** \'tipt\ *adj*

2tip *vt* **tipped; tip·ping 1 a :** to furnish with a tip **b** (1) **:** to cover or adorn the tip of (2) **:** to blend (furs) for improved appearance by brushing the tips of the hair with dye **2 :** to affix (an insert) in a book — often used with *in* **3 :** to remove the ends of <~ raspberries>

3tip *vb* **tipped; tip·ping** [ME *tipen*] *vt* **1 :** OVERTURN, UPSET — usu. used with *over* **2 a :** CANT, TILT **b :** to raise and tilt forward in salute <*tipped* his hat> ~ *vi* **1 :** to become tipped : TOPPLE **2 :** LEAN, SLANT — **tip the scales 1 :** to register weight <*tips the scales* at 285 pounds> **2 :** to shift the balance of power or influence <*tipped the scales* in favor of a declaration of war —S. F. Bemis>

4tip *n* **1 :** the act or an instance of tipping : TILT **2 :** a place for depositing something (as rubbish) by dumping

5tip *n* [ME *tippe;* akin to LG *tippen* to tap] **:** a light touch or blow

6tip *vb* **tipped; tip·ping** *vt* **1 :** to strike lightly : TAP **2 :** to give (a baseball) a glancing blow ~ *vi* **:** TIPTOE

7tip *vb* **tipped; tip·ping** [perh. fr. ⁶*tip*] *vt* **1 :** GIVE, PRESENT **2 :** to give a gratuity to ~ *vi* **:** to bestow a gratuity

8tip *n* **:** a gift or a sum of money tendered for a service performed or anticipated : GRATUITY

9tip *n* [perh. fr. ⁷*tip*] **1 :** an item of expert or authoritative information **2 :** a piece of advance or confidential information given by one thought to have access to special or inside sources

10tip *vt* **tipped; tip·ping 1 :** to impart a piece of information or advice about or to **2 :** to mention as a prospective winner or profitable investment <industrials are being *tipped* in the forecasts> — **tip one's hand** *also* **tip one's mitt :** to declare one's intentions or reveal one's resources <the Justice Department wouldn't *tip its hand* by saying what its next move . . . would be —*Newsweek*>

Tip *abbr* Tipperary

tip·cart \'tip-,kärt\ *n* **:** a cart whose body can be tipped on the frame to empty its contents

tip·cat \-,kat\ *n* [⁶*tip*] **:** a game in which one player using a bat strikes lightly a tapered wooden peg and as it flies up strikes it again to drive it as far as possible while fielders try to recover it; *also* **:** the peg used in this game

ti·pi \'tē-(,)pē\ *var of* TEPEE

tip–in \'tip-,in\ *n* [⁶*tip*] **:** a goal in basketball made by deflecting a rebound into the basket with the fingertips

1tip–off \'tip-,ȯf\ *n* [¹⁰*tip*] **:** WARNING, TIP

2tip–off *n* [⁶*tip*] **:** the act or an instance of putting the ball in play in basketball by a jump ball

tip·per \'tip-ər\ *n* **:** one that tips

tip·pet \'tip-ət\ *n* [ME *tipet*] **1 :** a long hanging end of cloth attached to a sleeve, cap, or hood **2 :** a shoulder cape of fur or cloth often with hanging ends **3 :** a long black scarf worn over the robe by Anglican clergymen during morning and evening prayer

1tip·ple \'tip-əl\ *vb* **tip·pled; tip·pling** \-(ə-)liŋ\ [back-formation fr. obs. *tippler* (barkeeper)] *vt* **:** to drink (liquor) esp. continuously in small amounts ~ *vi* **:** to drink liquor esp. by habit or to excess — **tip·pler** \-(ə-)lər\ *n*

2tipple *n* **:** an intoxicating beverage : DRINK

3tipple *n* [E dial. *tipple* to tip over, freq. of E *tip*] **1 a :** a place where or an apparatus by which cars (as for coal) are loaded or emptied **b :** a coal-screening plant **2 :** a place where tipping is done

tip·py \'tip-ē\ *adj* **tip·pi·er; -est :** liable to tip <a ~ boat>

tip·staff \'tip-,staf\ *n, pl* **tip·staves** \-,stavz, -,stāvz\ [obs. *tipstaff* (staff tipped with metal)] **:** an officer (as a constable or bailiff) who bears a staff

tip·ster \'tip-stər\ *n* **:** one who gives or sells tips esp. for gambling or speculation

tip·stock \'tip-,stäk\ *n* [¹*tip*] **:** the detachable or movable forepart of the stock of a gun that lies beneath the barrel and forms a hold for the left hand

tip·sy \'tip-sē\ *adj* **tip·si·er; -est** [³*tip* + *-sy* (as in *tricksy*)] **1 :** unsteady, staggering, or foolish from the effects of liquor : FUDDLED **2 :** UNSTEADY, ASKEW <a ~ angle> — **tip·si·ly** \-sə-lē\ *adv* — **tip·si·ness** \-sē-nəs\ *n*

1tip·toe \'tip-,tō, -'tō\ *n* **:** the tip of a toe; *also* **:** the ends of the toes — **on tiptoe :** ALERT, AROUSED <the contest of skill that puts one *on tiptoe* to win —*Deerfield (Wisc.) Independent*>

2tiptoe *adv* **:** on or as if on tiptoe

3tiptoe *adj* **1 :** standing or walking on or as if on tiptoe **2 :** CAUTIOUS, STEALTHY

4tiptoe *vi* **tip·toed; tip·toe·ing 1 :** to stand or raise oneself on tiptoe **2 :** to walk or proceed on or as if on tiptoe

1tip–top \'tip-'täp, -,täp\ *n* [¹*tip* + *top*] **:** the highest point

2tip–top *adj* **:** EXCELLENT, FIRST-RATE <~ working conditions>

3tip–top *adv* **:** very well

ti·rade \tī-'rād, 'tī-,\ *n* [F, shot, tirade, fr. MF, fr. OIt *tirata,* fr. *tirare* to draw, shoot; akin to Sp & Pg *tirar* to draw, shoot, OF *tirer*] **:** a protracted speech usu. marked by intemperate, vituperative, or harshly censorious language

1tire \'tī(ə)r\ *vb* **tired; tir·ing** [ME *tyren,* fr. OE *tēorian, tȳrian*] *vi* **:** to become weary ~ *vt* **1 :** to exhaust or greatly decrease the physical strength of : FATIGUE **2 :** to wear out the patience of : bore completely

syn TIRE, WEARY, FATIGUE, EXHAUST, JADE, FAG *shared meaning element* **:** to make or become unwilling to proceed because of loss of strength or endurance

2tire *n* [ME, short for *attire*] **1** *obs* **:** ATTIRE **2 :** a woman's headband or hair ornament

3tire *vt* **tired; tir·ing 1** *obs* **:** ATTIRE **2 :** to adorn (the hair) with an ornament

4tire *n, often attrib* [ME, prob. fr. ²*tire*] **1 :** a metal hoop forming the tread of a wheel **2 a :** a continuous solid or pneumatic rubber cushion encircling a wheel and usu. consisting when pneumatic of an external rubber-and-fabric covering that contains and protects from injury an air-filled inner tube **b :** the external rubber-and-fabric covering of a pneumatic tire

tired \'tī(ə)rd\ *adj* **1 :** WEARY, FATIGUED **2 :** TRITE, HACKNEYED <the same old ~ themes> — **tired·ly** *adv* — **tired·ness** *n*

tire·less \'tī(ə)r-ləs\ *adj* **:** seemingly incapable of tiring : INDEFATIGABLE — **tire·less·ly** *adv* — **tire·less·ness** *n*

Ti·re·si·as \tī-'rē-sē-əs, -zē-\ *n* [L, fr. Gk *Teiresias*] **:** a blind soothsayer of Thebes who predicted the doom of Oedipus

tire·some \'tī(ə)r-səm\ *adj* **:** WEARISOME, TEDIOUS — **tire·some·ly** *adv* — **tire·some·ness** *n*

tire·wom·an \-,wu̇m-ən\ *n* [²*tire*] **:** a lady's maid

tir·ing–house \'tī-riŋ-,hau̇s\ *n* [³*tire*] **:** a section of a theater reserved for the actors and used esp. for dressing and preparing for stage entrances

tir·ing–room \-,rüm, -,ru̇m\ *n* [³*tire*] **:** a dressing room esp. in a theater

tirl \'tərl\ *vb* [alter. of ¹*trill*] *vi, chiefly Scot* **:** to make a rattling sound (as with a door latch) ~ *vt, chiefly Scot* **:** TWIRL

tiro *var of* TYRO

ti·sane \ti-'zan, -'zän\ *n* [ME, fr. MF, fr. L *ptisana,* fr. Gk *ptisanē,* lit., crushed barley] **:** an infusion (as of dried herbs) used as a beverage or for medicinal effects

Tish·ah–b'Ab \'tish-ə-,bäv, -,bȯv\ *n* [Heb *tish'āh bē Ābh* ninth in Ab] **:** a Jewish holiday observed with fasting on the 9th of Ab in commemoration of the destruction of the temples at Jerusalem

Tish·ri \'tish-rē\ *n* [Heb *tishrī*] **:** the 1st month of the civil year or the 7th month of the ecclesiastical year in the Jewish calendar — see MONTH table

tis·sue \'tish-(,)ü, 'tish-ə(-w), *chiefly Brit* 'tis-(,)yü\ *n* [ME *tissu,* a rich fabric, fr. OF, fr. pp. of *tistre* to weave, fr. L *texere* — more at TECHNICAL] **1 a :** a fine lightweight often sheer fabric **b :** MESH, NETWORK, WEB <a ~ of lies> **2 :** a piece of soft absorbent tissue paper used esp. as a handkerchief or for removing cosmetics **3 :** an aggregate of cells usu. of a particular kind together with their intercellular substance that form one of the structural materials of a plant or an animal — **tis·su·ey** \'tish-ə-wē\ *adj*

tissue culture *n* **:** the process or technique of making body tissue grow in a culture medium outside the organism; *also* **:** a culture of tissue (as epithelium)

tissue fluid *n* **:** a fluid that permeates the spaces between individual cells, that is in osmotic contact with the blood and lymph, and that serves in interstitial transport of nutrients and waste

tissue paper *n* **:** a thin gauzy paper used esp. for protecting something (as by covering or wrapping)

1tit \'tit\ *n* [ME, fr. OE] **:** TEAT

2tit *n* [*tit-* (as in *titmouse*)] **:** a small or inferior horse

3tit *n* **:** TITMOUSE; *broadly* **:** any of various small plump often long-tailed birds

4tit *abbr* title

Tit *abbr* Titus

ti·tan \'tīt-ᵊn\ *n* [Gk] **1** *cap* **:** one of a family of giants born of Uranus and Gaea and ruling the earth until overthrown by the Olympian gods **2 :** one that is gigantic in size or power : one that stands out for greatness of achievement — **ti·tan·ess** \-əs\ *n*

titan- *or* **titano-** *comb form* [NL *titanium*] **:** titanium <*titan*ate>

ti·ta·nate \'tīt-ᵊn-,āt\ *n* **1 :** any of various multiple oxides of titanium dioxide with other metallic oxides **2 :** a titanium ester of the general formula $Ti(OR)_4$

ti·ta·nia \tī-'tān-ē-ə, tə-, -'tān-yə *also* -'tan-\ *n* **:** TITANIUM DIOXIDE; *esp* **:** a clear transparent rutile cut as a gemstone

Ti·ta·nia \tə-'tān-yə, -'tän-; tī-'tān-\ *n* **:** the wife of Oberon and queen of the fairies in Shakespeare's *A Midsummer Night's Dream*

1ti·tan·ic \tī-'tan-ik *also* tə-\ *adj* [Gk *titanikos* of the Titans] **:** having great magnitude, force, or power : COLOSSAL — **ti·tan·i·cal·ly** \-i-k(ə-)lē\ *adv*

2ti·ta·nic \tī-'tan-ik, tə-, -'tān-\ *adj* [NL *titanium*] **:** of, relating to, or containing titanium esp. when tetravalent

ti·ta·nif·er·ous \,tīt-ᵊn-'if-(ə-)rəs\ *adj* **:** containing or yielding titanium <~ minerals>

ti·tan·ism \'tīt-ᵊn-,iz-əm\ *n, often cap* [fr. the charge of presumption laid upon the Titans by their father Uranus for their part in a plot against him] **:** defiance of and revolt against social or artistic conventions

ti·ta·ni·um \tī-'tān-ē-əm, tə- *also* -'tan-\ *n* [NL, fr. Gk *Titan*] **:** a silvery gray light strong metallic element found combined in ilmenite and rutile and used esp. in alloys (as steel) and combined in refractory materials and in coatings — see ELEMENT table

titanium dioxide *n* **:** an oxide TiO_2 of titanium that occurs in rutile or ilmenite and is used esp. as a pigment

titanium white *n* **:** TITANIUM DIOXIDE; *also* **:** a brilliant white lead-free pigment consisting of titanium dioxide often together with barium sulfate and zinc oxide

ti·ta·nous \tī-ˈtan-əs, tə-, -ˈtān-; ˈtīt-ᵊn-\ *adj* [ISV] **:** of, relating to, or containing titanium esp. when trivalent

tit·bit \ˈtit-ˌbit\ *var of* TIDBIT

ti·ter \ˈtīt-ər\ *n* [F *titre* title, proportion of gold or silver in a coin, fr. OF *title* inscription, title] **:** the strength of a solution or the concentration of a substance in solution as determined by titration

tit for tat \ˌtit-fər-ˈtat\ [alter. of earlier *tip for tap,* fr. *tip* (blow) + *for* + *tap*] **:** an equivalent given in return (as for an injury)

tith·able \ˈtī-t͟hə-bəl\ *adj* **:** subject or liable to payment of tithes

¹tithe \ˈtīt͟h\ *vb* **tithed; tith·ing** [ME *tithen,* fr. OE *teogothian,* fr. *teogotha* tenth] *vt* **1 :** to pay or give a tenth part of esp. for the support of the church **2 :** to levy a tithe on ~ *vi* **:** to give a tenth of one's income as a tithe

²tithe *n* [ME, fr. OE *teogotha* tenth; akin to MLG *tegede* tenth; both fr. a prehistoric WGmc derivative of the word represented by OE *tien* ten — more at TEN] **1 :** a tenth part of something paid as a voluntary contribution or as a tax esp. for the support of a religious establishment **2 :** the obligation represented by individual tithes **3 :** TENTH; *broadly* **:** a small part **4 :** a small tax or levy

tith·er \ˈtī-t͟hər\ *n* **1 :** one that pays tithes **2 :** one that collects or advocates the payment of tithes

tith·ing \ˈtī-t͟hiŋ\ *n* [ME, fr. OE *tēothung,* fr. *teogothian, tēothian* to tithe, take one tenth] **:** a small administrative division preserved in parts of England apparently orig. consisting of ten men with their families

ti·tho·nia \tə-ˈthō-nyə, ti-, -nē-ə\ *n* [NL, genus name, prob. fr. L *Tithonia,* poetical name of Aurora] **:** any of a genus (*Tithonia*) of tall composite herbs that have alternate leaves and flower heads resembling sunflowers and that are sometimes grown as annual ornamentals

¹ti·ti \ˈtī-ˌtī\ *n* [prob. fr. Timucua] **:** a tree (*Cliftonia monophylla* of the family Cyrillaceae) of the southern U.S. with glossy leaves and racemes of fragrant white flowers; *also* **:** any of several trees of a related genus (*Cyrilla*)

²ti·ti \ti-ˈtē\ *n* [Sp *tití,* fr. Aymara *titi,* lit., little cat] **:** any of various small So. American monkeys (genus *Callicebus*) resembling squirrel monkeys

ti·tian \ˈtish-ən\ *adj, often cap* [*Titian,* It painter] **:** of a brownish orange color

tit·il·late \ˈtit-ᵊl-ˌāt\ *vt* **-lat·ed; -lat·ing** [L *titillatus,* pp. of *titillare*] **1 :** TICKLE **2 :** to excite pleasurably **:** arouse by stimulation — **tit·il·la·tion** \ˌtit-ᵊl-ˈā-shən\ *n* — **tit·il·la·tive** \ˈtit-ᵊl-ˌāt-iv\ *adj*

tit·il·lat·ing \ˈtit-ᵊl-ˌāt-iŋ\ *adj* **:** pleasantly stimulating or exciting <~ reading> — **tit·il·lat·ing·ly** \-iŋ-lē\ *adv*

tit·i·vate *or* **tit·ti·vate** \ˈtit-ə-ˌvāt\ *vb* **-vat·ed; -vat·ing** [perh. fr. ¹*tidy* + *-vate* (as in *renovate*)] *vt* **:** to make smart or spruce ~ *vi* **:** SMARTEN, SPRUCE — **tit·i·va·tion** \ˌtit-ə-ˈvā-shən\ *n*

tit·lark \ˈtit-ˌlärk\ *n* [*tit-* (as in *titmouse*) + *lark*] **:** PIPIT

¹ti·tle \ˈtīt-ᵊl\ *n* [ME, fr. OF, fr. L *titulus* inscription, title] **1 a** *obs* **:** INSCRIPTION **b :** written material introduced into a motion picture or television program to give credits, explain an action, or represent dialogue — usu. used in pl. **2 a :** the union of all the elements constituting legal ownership **b :** something that constitutes a legally just cause of exclusive possession **c :** the instrument (as a deed) that is evidence of a right **3 a :** something that justifies or substantiates a claim **b :** an alleged or recognized right **4 a :** a descriptive or general heading (as of a chapter in a book) **b :** the heading which names an act or statute **c :** the heading of a legal action or proceeding **5 a :** the distinguishing name of a written, printed, or filmed production **b :** a similar distinguishing name of a musical composition or a work of art **6 :** a descriptive name **:** APPELLATION **7 :** a division of an instrument, book, or bill; *esp* **:** one larger than a section or article **8 a :** an appellation of dignity, honor, distinction, or preeminence attached to a person or family by virtue of rank, office, precedent, privilege, attainment, or lands **b :** a person holding a title esp. of nobility **9 :** a literary work as distinguished from a particular copy <published 25 ~*s* last year> **10 :** CHAMPIONSHIP 1 <won the batting ~>

²title *vt* **ti·tled; ti·tling** \ˈtīt-liŋ, -ᵊl-iŋ\ **1 :** to provide a title for **2 :** to designate or call by a title **:** TERM, STYLE

³title *adj* **:** of or relating to a title: as **a :** having the same name as the title of a production <did the ~ role in *Hamlet*> **b :** having the same title as or providing the title for the collection or production of which it forms a part <the ~ story> <the ~ song> **c :** of, relating to, or involving a championship <a ~ match> **d :** of, relating to, or used with the titles which introduce a motion picture or television program <~ music>

ti·tled \ˈtīt-ᵊld\ *adj* **:** having a title esp. of nobility

title deed *n* **:** the deed constituting the evidence of a person's legal ownership

ti·tle·hold·er \ˈtīt-ᵊl-ˌhōl-dər\ *n* **:** one that holds a title; *specif* **:** CHAMPION

title page *n* **:** a page of a book bearing the title and usu. the names of the author and publisher and the place and sometimes date of publication

ti·tlist \ˈtīt-ᵊl-əst, ˈtīt-ləst\ *n* **:** TITLEHOLDER

tit·mouse \ˈtit-ˌmau̇s\ *n, pl* **tit·mice** \-ˌmīs\ [ME *titmose,* fr. (assumed) ME *tit* any small object or creature + ME *mose* titmouse, fr. OE *māse;* akin to OHG *meisa* titmouse] **:** any of numerous small arboreal and insectivorous passerine birds (family Paridae and esp. genus *Parus*) that are related to the nuthatches but have longer tails

Ti·to·ism \ˈtēt-(ˌ)ō-ˌiz-əm\ *n* **:** the political, economic, and social policies associated with Tito; *specif* **:** nationalistic policies and practices followed by a communist state or group independently of and often in opposition to the U.S.S.R. — **Ti·to·ist** \-ō-əst\ *n or adj*

ti·trant \ˈtī-trənt\ *n* **:** a material (as a reagent solution of precisely known strength) that is added in titration

ti·trate \ˈtī-ˌtrāt\ *vb* **ti·trat·ed; ti·trat·ing** [*titer*] *vt* **:** to subject to titration ~ *vi* **:** to perform titration — **ti·trat·able** \-ˌtrāt-ə-bəl\ *adj* — **ti·tra·tor** \-ˌtrāt-ər\ *n*

ti·tra·tion \tī-ˈtrā-shən\ *n* **:** a method or the process of determining the strength of a solution or the concentration of a substance in solution in terms of the smallest amount of a reagent of known concentration required to bring about a given effect in reaction with a known volume of the test solution

ti·tre \ˈtīt-ər\ *var of* TITER

ti·tri·met·ric \ˌtī-trə-ˈme-trik\ *adj* [*titration* + *-i-* + *-metric*] **:** employing or determined by titration — **ti·tri·met·ri·cal·ly** \-tri-k(ə-)lē\ *adv*

tit–tat–toe \ˌti-ˌta(t)-ˈtō\ *var of* TICKTACKTOE

tit·ter \ˈtit-ər\ *vi* [imit.] **:** to laugh in a nervous, affected, or partly suppressed manner **:** GIGGLE, SNICKER — **titter** *n*

tit·tie \ˈtit-ē\ *n* [prob. baby talk alter. of *sister*] *chiefly Scot* **:** SISTER

tit·tle \ˈtit-ᵊl\ *n* [ME *titel,* fr. ML *titulus,* fr. L, title] **1 :** a point or small sign used as a diacritical mark in writing or printing **2 :** a very small part

tit·tle–tat·tle \ˈtit-ᵊl-ˌtat-ᵊl\ *n* [redupl. of ²*tattle*] **:** GOSSIP, PRATTLE — **tittle–tattle** *vi*

¹tit·tup \ˈtit-əp\ *n* [imit. of the sound of a horse's hooves] **:** lively, gay, or restless behavior **:** PRANCE, CAPER

²tittup *vi* **-tupped** *or* **-tuped; -tup·ping** *or* **-tup·ing :** to move in a lively manner often with an exaggerated or affected action

¹tit·u·lar \ˈtich-(ə-)lər\ *adj* [L *titulus* title] **1 a :** existing in title only; *esp* **:** bearing a title derived from a defunct ecclesiastical jurisdiction (as an episcopal see) <a ~ bishop> **b :** having the title and usu. the honors belonging to an office or dignity without the duties, functions, or responsibilities <the ~ head of a political party> **2 :** bearing a title **:** TITLED **3 :** of, relating to, or constituting a title <the ~ hero of the play> — **tit·u·lar·ly** *adv*

²titular *n* **:** a person holding a title

Ti·tus \ˈtīt-əs\ *n* [LL, fr. Gk *Titos*] **1 :** an early Christian convert who assisted Paul in his missionary work **2 :** a letter written on the subject of pastoral care in the early Church and included as a book in the New Testament — see BIBLE table

Tiu \ˈtē-(ˌ)ü\ *n* [OE *Tīw* — more at DEITY] **:** the Norse god of war

tiz·zy \ˈtiz-ē\ *n, pl* **tizzies** [origin unknown] **:** a highly excited and distracted state of mind

tk *abbr* **1** tank **2** truck

TKO \ˌtē-ˌkā-ˈō\ *n* [*t*echnical *k*nock*o*ut] **:** TECHNICAL KNOCKOUT

tkt *abbr* ticket

Tl *symbol* thallium

TL *abbr* **1** total loss **2** truckload

TLC *abbr* **1** tender loving care **2** thin-layer chromatography

Tlin·git \ˈtliŋ-(g)ət, ˈtliŋ-kət\ *n, pl* **Tlingit** *or* **Tlingits 1 :** a member of a group of Indian peoples of the islands and coast of southern Alaska **2 :** a language stock of the Na-dene phylum

TLO *abbr* total loss only

tlr *abbr* **1** tailor **2** trailer

Tm *symbol* thulium

TM *abbr* **1** technical manual **2** trademark

T–man \ˈtē-ˌman\ *n* [*T*reasury *man*] **:** a special agent of the U.S. Treasury Department

tme·sis \(tə-)ˈmē-səs\ *n* [LL, fr. Gk *tmēsis* act of cutting, fr. *temnein* to cut — more at TOME] **:** separation of parts of a compound word by the intervention of one or more words (as *what place soever* for *whatsoever place*)

TMO *abbr* telegraph money order

TMV *abbr* tobacco mosaic virus

tn *abbr* **1** ton **2** town **3** train

TN *abbr* **1** Tennessee **2** true north

tng *abbr* training

tnpk *abbr* turnpike

TNT \ˌtē-ˌen-ˈtē\ *n* [*t*ri*n*itro*t*oluene] **:** TRINITROTOLUENE

¹to *sentence-final* (ˈ)tü; *before vowels* tə *also* təw *in US speech, usu* təw *in Brit speech; after* -t (*as in* "*want*") *often* ə\ *prep* [ME, fr. OE *tō;* akin to OHG *zuo* to, L *donec* as long as, until] **1 a** — used as a function word to indicate movement or an action or condition suggestive of movement toward a place, person, or thing reached <drove ~ the city> <went back ~ his original idea> **b** — used as a function word to indicate direction <a mile ~ the south> <turned his back ~ the door> <a tendency ~ silliness> **c** — used as a function word to indicate contact or proximity <applied polish ~ the table> <stood there with her hands ~ her eyes> **d** (1) — used as a function word to indicate the place or point that is the far limit <100 miles ~ the nearest town> (2) — used as a function word to indicate the limit of extent <stripped ~ the waist> **e** — used as a function word to indicate relative position <perpendicular ~ the floor> **2 a** — used as a function word to indicate purpose, intention, tendency, result, or end <came ~ our aid> <drink ~ his health> **b** — used as a function word to indicate the result of an action or a process <broken all ~ pieces> <go ~ seed> <~ their surprise, the train left on time> **c** — used as a function word to indicate a determined condition or end <sentenced ~ death> **3** — used as a function word to indicate position or relation in time: as **a :** BEFORE <five minutes ~ five> **b :** TILL <from eight ~ five> **4** — used as a function word to indicate addition, attachment, connection, belonging, possession, accompaniment, or response <the key ~ the door> <danced ~ live music> <comes ~ his call> **5** — used as a function word (1) to indicate the extent or degree (as of completeness or accuracy) <loyal ~ a man> or the extent and result (as of an action or a condition) <beaten ~ death>

(2) to indicate the last or an intermediate point of a series <moderate ~ cool temperatures> **6 a** — used as a function word (1) to indicate a relation to one that serves as a standard <inferior ~ his earlier works> (2) to indicate similarity, correspondence, dissimilarity, or proportion <compared him ~ a god> **b** — used as a function word to indicate agreement or conformity <add salt ~ taste> <~ my knowledge> **c** — used as a function word to indicate a proportion in terms of numbers or quantities <400 ~ the box> **7 a** — used as a function word (1) to indicate the application of an adjective or a noun <agreeable ~ everyone> <attitude ~ friends> <title ~ the property> (2) to indicate the relation of a verb to its complement or to a complementary element <refers ~ the traditions > <refers him ~ the traditions> (3) to indicate the receiver of an action or the one for which something is done or exists <spoke ~ his father> <gives a dollar ~ the man> <the total effect was a gain ~ reading —Joseph Trenaman> and often used with a reflexive pronoun to indicate exclusiveness (as of possession) or separateness <had the house ~ themselves> <thought ~ himself> **b** — used as a function word to indicate agency <falls ~ his opponent's blows> **8** — used as a function word to indicate that the following verb is an infinitive <wants ~ go> and often used by itself at the end of a clause in place of an infinitive suggested by the preceding context <knows more than he seems ~>

2**to** \'tü\ *adv* **1 a** — used as a function word to indicate direction toward <feathers wrong end ~> <run ~ and fro> **b** : close to the wind <the gale having gone over, we came ~ —R. H. Dana> **2 a** : into contact esp. with the frame — used of a door or a window <the door snapped ~> **b** — used as a function word to indicate physical application or attachment <set ~ his seal> **3** — used as a function word to indicate application or attention <were hungry and fell ~ with a vengeance> **4** : to a state of consciousness or awareness <brings her ~ with smelling salts> **5** : at hand : BY <get to see 'em close ~ —Richard Llewellyn>

TO *abbr* **1** table of organization **2** telegraph office **3** traditional orthography **4** turn over

toad \'tōd\ *n* [ME *tode,* fr. OE *tāde, tādige*] **1** : any of numerous tailless leaping amphibians (esp. family Bufonidae) that as compared with the related frogs are generally more terrestrial in habit though returning to water to lay their eggs, squatter and shorter in build and with weaker hind limbs, and rough, dry, and warty rather than smooth and moist of skin **2** : a contemptible person or thing

toad 1

toad·eat·er \-ˌēt-ər\ *n, archaic* : TOADY

toad·fish \-ˌfish\ *n* : any of various marine fishes (family Batrachoididae) with jugular pelvic fins, a large thick head, a wide mouth, and scaleless slimy skin

toad·flax \-ˌflaks\ *n* **1** : BUTTER-AND-EGGS **2** : any of numerous plants similar to or related to toadflax

toad·stone \-ˌstōn\ *n* : a stone or similar object held to have formed in the head or body of a toad and formerly often worn as a charm or antidote to poison

toad·stool \-ˌstül\ *n* : a fungus having an umbrella-shaped pileus : MUSHROOM; *esp* : a poisonous or inedible one as distinguished from an edible mushroom

1**toady** \'tōd-ē\ *n, pl* **toad·ies** : one who flatters in the hope of gaining favors : SYCOPHANT

2**toady** *vi* **toad·ied; toady·ing** : to behave as a toady : engage in sycophancy *syn* see FAWN — **toady·ism** \-ē-ˌiz-əm\ *n*

1**to–and–fro** \ˌtü-ən-'frō\ *n* : activity involving alternating movement in opposite directions <the busy ~ of the holiday shoppers>

2**to–and–fro** *adj* : forward and backward <~ motion>

to and fro *adv* : from one place to another

1**toast** \'tōst\ *vb* [ME *tosten,* fr. MF *toster,* fr. LL *tostare* to roast, fr. L *tostus,* pp. of *torrēre* to dry, parch — more at THIRST] *vt* **1** : to make (as bread) crisp, hot, and brown by heat **2** : to warm thoroughly ~ *vi* : to become toasted; *esp* : to warm thoroughly

2**toast** *n* **1 a** : sliced bread browned on both sides by heat **b** : food prepared with toasted or recooked bread **2** [fr. the use of pieces of spiced toast to flavor drinks] **a** (1) : a person whose health is drunk (2) : something in honor of which persons drink **b** : a highly admired person <she's the ~ of society> **3** [[3]*toast*] : an act of proposing or of drinking in honor of a toast

3**toast** *vt* [[2]*toast*] : to propose or drink to as a toast

toast·er \'tō-stər\ *n* : one that toasts; *esp* : an electrical appliance for toasting

toast·mas·ter \'tōs(t)-ˌmas-tər\ *n* : one that presides at a banquet and introduces the after-dinner speakers

toast·mis·tress \-ˌmis-trəs\ *n* : a female toastmaster

toasty \'tō-stē\ *adj* **toast·i·er; -est** : pleasantly or comfortably warm <felt snug and ~ by the fire>

to·bac·co \tə-'bak-(ˌ)ō, -'bak-ə(-w)\ *n, pl* **-cos** [Sp *tabaco,* prob. fr. Taino, roll of tobacco leaves smoked by the Indians of the Antilles at the time of Columbus] **1** : any of a genus (*Nicotiana*) of chiefly American plants of the nightshade family with viscid foliage and tubular flowers; *esp* : a tall erect annual So. American herb (*N. tabacum*) cultivated for its leaves **2** : the leaves of cultivated tobacco prepared for use in smoking or chewing or as snuff **3** : manufactured products of tobacco (as cigars or cigarettes); *also* : smoking as a practice <has sworn off ~>

tobacco budworm *n* : a noctuid moth (*Heliothis virescens*) whose small rusty often green-striped caterpillar feeds on buds and young leaves esp. of tobacco and cotton

tobacco heart *n* : a functional disorder of the heart marked by irregularity of action and caused by excessive use of tobacco

tobacco hornworm *n* **1** : a hawkmoth (*Manduca sexta*) whose large usu. green larva is a hornworm feeding on plants of the nightshade family and esp. tobacco **2** : TOMATO HORNWORM

tobacco juice *n* : saliva colored brown by the use of tobacco or snuff

tobacco mosaic *n* : any of a complex of virus diseases of plants of the nightshade family and esp. of tobacco

to·bac·co·nist \tə-'bak-ə-nəst\ *n* [irreg. fr. *tobacco* + *-ist*] : a dealer in tobacco esp. at retail

to–be \tə-'bē\ *adj* : that is to be : FUTURE — usu. used postpositively and often in combination <a bride-*to-be*>

To·bi·as \tə-'bī-əs\ *n* [Gk *Tobias*] **1** : a Jewish hero who with divine aid marries his kinswoman Sarah in spite of a jealous evil spirit and restores his father Tobit's sight **2** : a book of Scripture included in the Roman Catholic canon of the Old Testament and corresponding to the Book of Tobit in the Protestant Apocrypha — see BIBLE table

To·bit \'tō-bət\ *n* [Gk *Tōbit*] **1** : the elderly father of Tobias **2** : a book of Scripture in the Protestant Apocrypha — see BIBLE table

1**to·bog·gan** \tə-'bäg-ən\ *n* [CanF *tobogan,* of Algonquian origin; akin to Micmac *tobâgun* drag made of skin] **1** : a long flat-bottomed light sled made of thin boards curved up at one end with usu. low handrails at the sides **2** : a downward course or a sharp decline

2**toboggan** *vi* **1** : to coast on a toboggan **2** : to decline suddenly and sharply (as in value) — **to·bog·gan·er** *n* — **to·bog·gan·ist** \-ə-nəst\ *n*

to·bog·gan·ing *n* : the act, art, or sport of riding a toboggan

to·by \'tō-bē\ *n, pl* **tobies** *often cap* [*Toby,* nickname fr. the name *Tobias*] : a small jug, pitcher, or mug generally used for ale and shaped somewhat like a stout man with a cocked hat for the brim — called also *toby jug*

toc·ca·ta \tə-'kät-ə\ *n* [It, fr. *toccare* to touch, fr. (assumed) VL] : a musical composition usu. for organ or harpsichord in a free style and characterized by full chords, rapid runs, and high harmonies

To·char·i·an \tō-'kar-ē-ən, -'ker-, -'kär-\ *n* [L *Tochari* (pl.), fr. Gk *Tocharoi*] **1** : a member of a people of presumably European origin dwelling in central Asia during the first millennium of the Christian era **2 a** : a language of central Asia known from documents from the seventh century A.D. **b** : a branch of the Indo-European language family containing Tocharian — see INDO-EUROPEAN LANGUAGES table

Tocharian A *n* : the eastern dialect of Tocharian — see INDO-EUROPEAN LANGUAGES table

Tocharian B *n* : the western dialect of Tocharian — see INDO-EUROPEAN LANGUAGES table

toch·er \'täk-ər\ *n* [ScGael *tochar*] *chiefly Scot* : marriage portion

to·coph·er·ol \tō-'käf-ə-ˌrōl, -ˌrȯl\ *n* [ISV, deriv. of Gk *tokos* childbirth, offspring + *pherein* to carry, bear — more at BEAR] : any of several fat-soluble oily phenolic compounds with varying degrees of antioxidant vitamin E activity; *esp* : one $C_{29}H_{50}O_2$ of high vitamin E potency obtained from germ oils or by synthesis

toc·sin \'täk-sən\ *n* [MF *toquassen,* fr. OProv *tocasenh,* fr. *tocar* to touch, ring a bell (fr. assumed VL *toccare*) + *senh* sign, bell, fr. ML & L *signum;* ML, bell, fr. LL, ringing of a bell, fr. L, mark, sign — more at TOUCH, SIGN] **1** : an alarm bell or the ringing of it **2** : a warning signal

1**tod** \'täd\ *n* [ME] *chiefly Scot* : FOX

2**tod** *n* [ME *todd, todde;* prob. akin to OHG *zotta* tuft of hair] **1** : any of various units of weight for wool; *esp* : one equal to 28 pounds **2** *Brit* : a bushy clump (as of ivy)

1**to·day** \tə-'dā\ *adv* **1** : on or for this day **2** : at the present time

2**today** *n* : the present day, time, or age <the youth of ~>

1**tod·dle** \'täd-ᵊl\ *vi* **tod·dled; tod·dling** \'täd-liŋ, -ᵊl-iŋ\ [origin unknown] **1** : to walk with short tottering steps in the manner of a young child **2** : to take a stroll : SAUNTER — **toddle** *n*

tod·dler \'täd-lər, -ᵊl-ər\ *n* : one that toddles; *esp* : a young child

tod·dy \'täd-ē\ *n, pl* **toddies** [Hindi *tāṛī* juice of the palmyra palm, fr. *tāṛ* palmyra palm, fr. Skt *tāla*] **1** : the fresh or fermented sap of various chiefly East Indian palms **2** : a usu. hot drink consisting of an alcoholic liquor, water, sugar, and spices

to–do \tə-'dü\ *n, pl* **to–dos** \-'düz\ : BUSTLE, STIR

to·dy \'tōd-ē\ *n, pl* **todies** [modif. of F *todier,* fr. L *todus,* a small bird] : any of several tiny nonpasserine insectivorous West Indian birds (genus *Todus*) closely related to the kingfishers

1**toe** \'tō\ *n* [ME *to,* fr. OE *tā;* akin to OHG *zēha* toe, L *digitus* finger, toe] **1 a** (1) : one of the terminal members of a vertebrate's foot (2) : the fore end of a foot or hoof **b** : a terminal segment of a limb of an invertebrate **c** : the forepart of something worn on the foot <the ~ of a boot> **2** : a part that by its position or form is felt to resemble a toe <the ~ of Italy>: as **a** : a journal or pivot supported in a bearing **b** : a lateral projection at one end or between the ends of a piece (as a rod or bolt) by which it is moved **c** : the lowest part (as of an embankment, dam, or cliff) — **on one's toes** : alert and ready to seize any advantage — **toe to toe** : facing one another

2**toe** *vb* **toed; toe·ing** *vt* **1** : to furnish with a toe <~ a sock> **2** : to touch, reach, or drive with the toe <~ a football> **3** : to drive (as a nail) obliquely; *also* : to clinch or fasten by or with nails or rods so driven ~ *vi* **1** : TIPTOE **2** : to stand, walk, or be placed so that the toes assume an indicated position or direction <~ in> — **toe the line** *or* **toe the mark** : to conform rigorously to a rule or standard

toe box *n* : a piece of material (as leather) placed between the toe cap and lining of a shoe and treated with a substance (as a gum) that hardens after the shoe is lasted permanently

toe cap *n* : a piece of leather covering the toe of a shoe and reinforcing or decorating it

toe crack *n* : a sand crack in the front wall of a horse's hoof

toed \'tōd\ *adj* [[1]*toe*] **1** : having a toe or toes esp. of a specified kind or number — usu. used in combination <five-*toed*> <round-*toed* shoes> **2** [fr. pp. of [2]*toe*] : driven obliquely <a ~ nail>; *also* : secured by diagonal or oblique nailing

toe dance *n* : a dance executed on the tips of the toes by means of a ballet slipper with a reinforced toe — **toe–dance** *vi* — **toe dancer** *n* — **toe dancing** *n*

toe·hold \'tō-ˌhōld\ *n* **1 a** : a hold or place of support for the toes (as in climbing) **b** (1) : a means of progressing (as in surmounting

barriers) (2) : a slight footing **2 :** a wrestling hold in which the aggressor bends or twists his opponent's foot
toe–in \'tō-ˌin\ *n* **1 :** CAMBER 3 **2 :** adjustment of the front wheels of an automotive vehicle so that they are closer together at the front than at the back
toe·less \'tō-ləs\ *adj* : lacking a toe <a ~ shoe>
[1]toe·nail \'tō-ˌnāl, -'nā(ə)l\ *n* : a nail of a toe
[2]toenail *vt* : to fasten by toed nails : TOE
toe·piece \'tō-ˌpēs\ *n* : a piece designed to form a toe (as of a shoe) or cover the toes of the foot
toe·plate \-ˌplāt\ *n* : a metal tab attached to the toe of a shoe (as to prevent wear due to heavy use)
toff \'täf\ *n* [prob. alter. of *tuft* (titled college student)] *chiefly Brit* : DANDY, SWELL
tof·fee *or* **tof·fy** \'täf-ē\ *n, pl* **toffees** *or* **toffies** [alter. of *taffy*] : candy of brittle but tender texture made by boiling sugar and butter together
tof·fee–nosed \ˌtäf-ē-'nōzd\ *adj, Brit* : STUCK-UP
toft \'tȯft, 'täft\ *n* [ME, fr. OE, fr. ON *topt*] *Brit* : a site for a dwelling and its outbuildings; *also* : an entire holding comprising a homestead and additional land
to·fu \'tō-(ˌ)fü\ *n* [Jap *tōfu*] : BEAN CURD
tog \'täg, 'tȯg\ *vt* **togged; tog·ging** [*togs*] : to dress esp. in fine clothing — usu. used with *up* or *out*
to·ga \'tō-gə\ *n* [L; akin to L *tegere* to cover — more at THATCH] : the loose outer garment worn in public by citizens of ancient Rome; *also* : a similar loose wrap or a professional, official, or academic gown — **to·gaed** \-gəd\ *adj*
to·ga vi·ri·lis \ˌtō-gə-və-'rēl-əs, -'ril-\ *n, pl* **to·gae vi·ri·les** \'tō-ˌgī-və-'rēl-ˌās, -'ril-\ [L, men's toga] : the white toga of manhood assumed by boys of ancient Rome at age 15
to·geth·er \tə-'geth-ər\ *adv* [ME *togedere*, fr. OE *togædere*, fr. *tō* to + *gædere* together; akin to MHG *gater* together, OE *gaderian* to gather] **1 a :** in or into one place, mass, collection, or group <the men get ~ every Thursday for poker> **b :** in a body : as a group <students and faculty ~ presented the petition> **2 a :** in or into contact (as connection, collision, or union) <mix these ingredients ~> **b :** in or into association or relationship <colors that go well ~> <went to school ~> **3 a :** at one time : SIMULTANEOUSLY <events that happened ~> **b :** in succession : without intermission <was depressed for days ~> **4 a :** by combined action : JOINTLY <~ we forced the door> **b :** in or into agreement or harmony <the soloist and the orchestra weren't quite ~> **c :** in or into a unified or coherent structure or an integrated whole <can't even put a simple sentence ~> <pull yourself ~> **5 a :** with each other — used pleonastically and as an intensive after certain verbs <join ~> <add ~> **b :** as a unit : in the aggregate <these arguments taken ~ make a convincing case> **c :** considered as a whole : counted or summed up <all ~, there were 21 entries> — **to·geth·er·ness** *n* — **together with** : in addition to

toga

tog·gery \'täg-(ə-)rē, 'tȯg-\ *n* [*togs*] : CLOTHING
[1]tog·gle \'täg-əl\ *n* [origin unknown] **1 :** a piece or device for holding or securing: as **a :** a pin inserted in a nautical knot to make it more secure or easier to slip **b :** a crosspiece attached to the end of or to a loop in something (as a chain, rope, line, strap, or belt) usu. to prevent slipping, to serve in twisting or tightening, or to hold something attached **2 :** a device having a toggle joint
[2]toggle *vt* **tog·gled; tog·gling** \-(ə-)liŋ\ **1 :** to fasten with or as if with a toggle **2 :** to furnish with a toggle
toggle joint *n* : a device consisting of two bars jointed together end to end but not in line so that when a force is applied to the knee tending to straighten the arrangement the parts abutting or jointed to the ends of the bars will receive an endways pressure
toggle switch *n* : an electric switch that depends on a toggle joint with a spring to open or close the circuit when a projecting lever is pushed through a small arc
togs \'tägz, 'tȯgz\ *n pl* [pl. of E slang *tog* (coat), short for obs. E cant *togeman, togman*] : CLOTHING; *esp* : a set of clothes and accessories for a specified use <riding ~>

toggle joint

togue \'tōg\ *n* [CanF] : LAKE TROUT
[1]toil \'tȯi(ə)l\ *n* [ME *toile*, fr. AF *toyl*, fr. OF *toeil* battle, confusion, fr. *toeillier*] **1** *archaic* **a :** STRUGGLE, BATTLE **b :** laborious effort **2 :** long strenuous fatiguing labor *syn* see WORK *ant* leisure
[2]toil *vb* [ME *toilen* to argue, struggle, fr. AF *toiller*, fr. OF *toeillier* to stir, disturb, dispute, fr. L *tudiculare* to crush, grind, fr. *tudicula* machine for crushing olives, dim. of *tudes* hammer; akin to L *tundere* to beat — more at STINT] *vi* **1 :** to work hard and long : LABOR **2 :** to proceed with laborious effort : PLOD <~*ing* wearily up the hill> ~ *vt* **1** *archaic* : OVERWORK **2** *archaic* : to get or accomplish with great effort — **toil·er** \'tȯi-lər\ *n*
[3]toil *n* [MF *toile* cloth, net, fr. L *tela* web, fr. *texere* to weave, construct — more at TECHNICAL] **1 :** a net to trap game **2 :** something by which one is held fast or inextricably involved : SNARE, TRAP — usu. used in pl. <caught in the ~*s* of the law>
toile \'twäl\ *n* [F, cloth, linen] **1 :** any of many plain or simple twill weave fabrics; *esp* : LINEN **2 :** a muslin model of a garment
toile de Jouy \ˌtwäl-dəzh-'wē\ *n* [F, lit., cloth of Jouy, fr. *Jouy*-en-Josar, France] : an 18th century French scenic pattern usu. printed on cotton, linen, or silk in one color on a light ground; *broadly* : a similar printed fabric
[1]toi·let \'tȯi-lət\ *n* [MF *toilette* cloth put over the shoulders while dressing the hair or shaving, dim. of *toile* cloth] **1** *archaic* : DRESSING TABLE **2 :** the act or process of dressing and grooming oneself **3 a** (1) : BATHROOM, LAVATORY 2 (2) : PRIVY **b :** a fixture for defecation and urination; *esp* : WATER CLOSET **4 :** cleansing in preparation for or in association with a medical or surgical procedure
[2]toilet *vi* **1 :** to dress and groom oneself **2 :** to use the toilet — usu. used of a child ~ *vt* **1 :** DRESS, GARB **2 :** to help (a child) use the toilet
toilet paper *n* : a thin sanitary absorbent paper for bathroom use chiefly after evacuation
toilet powder *n* : a fine powder usu. with soothing or antiseptic ingredients for sprinkling or rubbing (as after bathing) over the skin
toi·let·ry \'tȯi-lə-trē\ *n, pl* **-ries** : an article or preparation (as toothpaste, shaving cream, or cologne) used in making one's toilet — usu. used in pl.
toilet soap *n* : a mild soap that is often perfumed and colored and stabilized with preservatives
toi·lette \twä-'let\ *n* [F, fr. MF] **1 :** TOILET 2 **2 a :** formal or fashionable attire or style of dressing **b :** a particular costume or outfit
toilet training *n* : the process of training a child to control bladder and bowel movements and to use the toilet — **toilet train** *vt*
toilet water *n* : a perfumed liquid containing a high percentage of alcohol for use in or after a bath or as a skin freshener
toil·ful \'tȯi(ə)l-fəl\ *adj* : marked by or demanding toil : LABORIOUS — **toil·ful·ly** \-fə-lē\ *adv*
toil·some \-səm\ *adj* : marked by or full of toil or fatigue : LABORIOUS — **toil·some·ly** *adv* — **toil·some·ness** *n*
toil·worn \-ˌwō(ə)rn, -ˌwȯ(ə)rn\ *adj* : showing the effects of or worn out with toil <~ hands>
to–ing and fro–ing \'tü-iŋ-ən(d)-'frō-iŋ\ *n, pl* **to–ings and fro–ings** [*to and fro*] : a passing back and forth
To·kay \tō-'kā\ *n* **1 :** a sweet usu. dark gold dessert wine made near Tokaj, Hungary **2 :** a blend of Angelica, port, and sherry
toke \'tōk\ *n* [origin unknown] *slang* : a puff on a marijuana cigarette
[1]to·ken \'tō-kən\ *n* [ME, fr. OE *tācen, tācn* sign, token; akin to OHG *zeihhan* sign, Gk *deiknynai* to show — more at DICTION] **1 :** an outward sign or expression <his tears were ~*s* of his grief> **2 a :** SYMBOL, EMBLEM <a white flag is a ~ of surrender> **b :** an instance of a linguistic expression **3 :** a distinguishing feature : CHARACTERISTIC **4 a :** SOUVENIR, KEEPSAKE **b :** a small part representing the whole : INDICATION <this is only a ~ of what he hopes to accomplish> **c :** something given or shown as a guarantee (as of authority, right, or identity) **5 a :** a piece resembling a coin issued as money by some person or body other than a de jure government **b :** a piece resembling a coin issued for use (as for fare on a bus) by a particular group on specified terms — **by the same token** : for the same reason
[2]token *adj* **1 :** done or given as a token esp. in partial fulfillment of an obligation or engagement <a ~ payment> **2 :** MINIMAL, PERFUNCTORY <~ resistance> <~ integration>
to·ken·ism \'tō-kə-ˌniz-əm\ *n* : the policy or practice of making only a token effort; *esp* : the policy or practice of accepting token integration : minimal desegregation
token money *n* **1 :** money of regular government issue (as paper currency or coins) having a greater face value than intrinsic value **2 :** a medium of exchange consisting of privately issued tokens
To·khar·i·an *var of* TOCHARIAN
to·ko·no·ma \ˌtō-kə-'nō-mə\ *n* [Jap] : a niche or recess opening from the living room of a Japanese house in which a kakemono may be hung
tol- *or* **tolu-** *comb form* [ISV, fr. *tolu*] **1 :** tolu <*tolu*ol> **2 :** toluene <*tolu*ic> <*tolyl*> : toluic <*tolu*ate>
to·la \'tō-lə, tō-'lä\ *n* [Hindi *tolā*, fr. Skt *tulā* weight; akin to L *tollere* to lift up] : a unit of weight of India equal to 180 grains troy or 0.4114 ounce
tol·booth \'tō(l)-ˌbüth, 'täl-, 'tȯl-\ *n* [ME *tolbothe, tollbothe* tollbooth, town hall, jail] **1** *Scot* : a town or market hall **2** *Scot* : JAIL, PRISON
tol·bu·ta·mide \täl-'byüt-ə-ˌmīd\ *n* [*tol-* + *but*yric + *amide*] : a sulfonamide $C_{12}H_{18}N_2O_3S$ that lowers blood sugar level and is used in the treatment of diabetes
told *past of* TELL
tole \'tōl\ *n* [F *tôle* sheet metal (esp. iron), fr. F dial. (Bordeaux area), table, slab, fr. L *tabula* board, tablet] : sheet metal and esp. tinplate for use in domestic and ornamental wares in which it is usu. japanned or painted and often elaborately decorated; *also* : objects made of tole
To·le·do \tə-'lēd-(ˌ)ō\ *n, pl* **-dos** : a finely tempered sword of a kind made in Toledo, Spain
tol·er·a·ble \'täl-(ə-)rə-bəl, 'täl-ər-bəl\ *adj* **1 :** capable of being borne or endured <~ pain> **2 :** moderately good or agreeable : PASSABLE <a ~ singing voice> — **tol·er·a·bil·i·ty** \ˌtäl-(ə-)rə-'bil-ət-ē\ *n* — **tol·er·a·bly** \'täl-(ə-)rə-blē, -ər-blē\ *adv*
tol·er·ance \'täl(-ə)-rən(t)s\ *n* **1 :** capacity to endure pain or hardship : ENDURANCE, FORTITUDE, STAMINA **2 a** (1) : the ability to endure the effects of a drug or food or of a physiologic insult without exhibiting the usu. unfavorable effects <immunological ~ to a virus> <an addict's increasing ~ for a drug> (2) : relative capacity of an organism to grow or thrive when subjected to an unfavorable environmental factor **b :** the maximum amount of a pesticide residue that may lawfully remain on or in food **3 a :** sympathy or indulgence for beliefs or practices differing from or

conflicting with one's own **b :** the act of allowing something **:** TOLERATION <has a large ~ for uncertainty> **4 :** the allowable deviation from a standard; *esp* **:** the range of variation permitted in maintaining a specified dimension in machining a piece

tol·er·ant \-rənt\ *adj* **1 :** inclined to tolerate; *esp* **:** marked by forbearance or endurance **2 :** exhibiting tolerance (as for an environmental factor) — **tol·er·ant·ly** *adv*

tol·er·ate \ˈtäl-ə-ˌrāt\ *vt* **-at·ed; -at·ing** [L *toleratus,* pp. of *tolerare* to endure, put up with; akin to OE *tholian* to bear, L *tollere* to lift up, *latus* carried (suppletive pp. of *ferre*), Gk *tlēnai* to bear] **1 :** to endure or resist the action of (as a drug) without grave or lasting injury **2 :** to suffer to be or to be done without prohibition, hindrance, or contradiction ***syn*** see BEAR — **tol·er·a·tive** \-ˌrāt-iv\ *adj* — **tol·er·a·tor** \-ˌrāt-ər\ *n*

tol·er·a·tion \ˌtäl-ə-ˈrā-shən\ *n* **1 a :** the act or practice of tolerating something **b :** a government policy of permitting forms of religious belief and worship not officially established **2 :** TOLERANCE 2b

tol·i·dine \ˈtäl-ə-ˌdēn\ *n* [ISV *tol-* + *-idine*] **:** any of several isomeric aromatic diamines $C_{14}H_{16}N_2$ that are homologues of benzidine and used esp. as dye intermediates

[1]**toll** \ˈtōl\ *n* [ME, fr. OE; akin to ON *tollr* toll; both fr. a prehistoric WGmc-NGmc word borrowed fr. (assumed) VL *tolonium,* alter. of LL *telonium* customhouse, fr. Gk *telōnion,* fr. *telōnēs* collector of tolls, fr. *telos* tax, toll; akin to Gk *tlēnai* to bear] **1 :** a tax or fee paid for some liberty or privilege (as of passing over a highway or bridge) **2 :** compensation for services rendered: as **a :** a charge for transportation **b :** a charge for a long-distance telephone call **3 :** a grievous or ruinous price; *esp* **:** cost in life or health <fever had taken a heavy ~ of her —L. C. Douglas>

[2]**toll** *vi* **:** to take or levy toll ~ *vt* **1 a :** to exact part of as a toll **b :** to take as toll **2 :** to exact a toll from (someone)

[3]**toll** *or* **tole** \ˈtōl\ *vt* **tolled** *or* **toled; toll·ing** *or* **tol·ing** [ME *tollen, tolen;* akin to OE *talu* talk, narrative — more at TALE] **1 :** ALLURE, ENTICE **2 a :** to entice (game) to approach **b :** to attract (fish) with scattered bait **c :** to lead or attract (domestic animals) to a desired point

[4]**toll** *vb* [ME *tollen,* perh. fr. *tollen* to entice] *vt* **1 :** to sound (a bell) by pulling the rope **2 a :** to give signal or announcement of <the clock ~*ed* each hour> **b :** to announce by tolling <church bells ~*ed* the death of the bishop> **c :** to call to or from a place or occasion <bells ~*ed* the congregation to church> ~ *vi* **:** to sound with slow measured strokes <the bell ~*s* solemnly>

[5]**toll** *n* **:** the sound of a tolling bell

toll·booth \ˈtōl-ˌbüth\ *n* [ME *tolbothe, tollbothe* tollbooth, town hall, jail, fr. *tol, toll* toll + *bothe* booth] **:** a booth (as on a highway or bridge) where tolls are paid

toll bridge *n* **:** a bridge at which a toll is charged for crossing

toll call *n* **:** a long-distance telephone call at charges above a local rate

toll·gate \ˈtōl-ˌgāt\ *n* **:** a point where the driver of a vehicle must pay a toll

toll·house \-ˌhau̇s\ *n* **:** a house or booth where tolls are taken

toll·man \-mən\ *n* **:** a collector of tolls (as on a highway or bridge)

toll·way \-ˌwā\ *n* **:** a road for the use of which tolls are collected

Tol·tec \ˈtōl-ˌtek, ˈtäl-\ *n* [Sp *tolteca,* of AmerInd origin] **:** a member of a Nahuatlan people of central and southern Mexico — **Tol·tec·an** \-ən\ *adj*

tolu *n* [Sp *tolú,* fr. Santiago de *Tolú,* Colombia] **:** BALSAM OF TOLU

tol·u·ate \ˈtäl-yə-ˌwāt\ *n* [ISV] **:** a salt or ester of a toluic acid

tol·u·ene \-yə-ˌwēn\ *n* [ISV] **:** a liquid aromatic hydrocarbon C_7H_8 that resembles benzene but is less volatile, flammable, and toxic, is produced commercially from light oils from coke-oven gas and coal tar and from petroleum, and is used as a solvent, in organic synthesis, and as an antiknock agent for gasoline

to·lu·ic \tə-ˈlü-ik\ *adj* [ISV] **:** of, relating to, or being any of four isomeric acids $C_8H_8O_2$ derived from toluene

to·lu·idine \tə-ˈlü-ə-ˌdēn\ *n* [ISV *tol-* + *-idine*] **:** any of three isomeric amino derivatives of toluene C_7H_9N that are analogous to aniline and are used as dye intermediates

toluidine blue *n* **:** a basic thiazine dye that is related to methylene blue and is used as a biological stain and in medicine to treat hemorrhage

tol·u·ol \ˈtäl-yə-ˌwȯl, -ˌwōl\ *n* **:** toluene esp. of commercial grade

tol·yl \ˈtäl-əl\ *n* [ISV] **:** any of three univalent radicals $CH_3C_6H_4$ derived from toluene

tom \ˈtäm\ *n* [*Tom,* nickname for *Thomas*] **1 :** the male of various animals; *esp* **:** TOMCAT **2** *cap* **:** UNCLE TOM 2

[1]**tom·a·hawk** \ˈtäm-i-ˌhȯk\ *n* [*tomahack* (in some Algonquian language of Virginia)] **:** a light ax used as a missile and as a hand weapon esp. by No. American Indians

[2]**tomahawk** *vt* **:** to cut, strike, or kill with a tomahawk

to·mal·ley \tə-ˈmal-ē, ˈtäm-ˌal-ē\ *n, pl* **-leys** [of Cariban origin; akin to Galibi *tumali* sauce of lobster livers] **:** the liver of the lobster

Tom and Jer·ry \ˌtäm-ən-ˈjer-ē\ *n* [Corinthian *Tom* & *Jerry* Hawthorne, characters in *Life in London* (1821) by Pierce Egan] **:** a hot sweetened drink of rum, water, spices, and beaten egg

to·ma·to \tə-ˈmāt-(ˌ)ō, -ə(-w), -ˈmät-\ *n, pl* **-toes** [alter. of earlier *tomate,* fr. Sp, fr. Nahuatl *tomatl*] **1 :** any of a genus (*Lycopersicon*) of So. American herbs of the nightshade family; *esp* **:** a perennial plant (*L. esculentum*) widely cultivated for its edible fruits **2 :** the usu. large rounded and red or yellow pulpy berry of a tomato

tomato fruitworm *n* **:** CORN EARWORM

tomato hornworm *n* **:** a hawkmoth (*Manduca quinquemaculata*) whose larva is a hornworm feeding on plants of the nightshade family and esp. tobacco and tomato

[1]**tomb** \ˈtüm\ *n* [ME *tombe,* fr. AF *tumbe,* fr. LL *tumba* sepulchral mound, fr. Gk *tymbos;* akin to L *tumēre* to be swollen — more at THUMB] **1 a :** an excavation in which a corpse is buried **:** GRAVE **b :** a place of interment **2 :** a house, chamber, or vault for the dead formed wholly or partly in the earth or entirely above ground **3 :** a building or structure resembling a tomb in form or appearance — **tomb·less** \-ləs\ *adj*

[2]**tomb** *vt* **:** BURY, ENTOMB

tom·bac \ˈtäm-ˌbak\ *n* [F, fr. D *tombak,* fr. Malay *tĕmbaga* copper] **:** an alloy essentially of copper and zinc and sometimes tin or arsenic that is used esp. for cheap jewelry and gilding

tom·bo·lo \ˈtōm-bə-ˌlō, ˈtäm-\ *n, pl* **-los** [It] **:** a sand or gravel bar connecting an island with the mainland or another island

tom·boy \ˈtäm-ˌbȯi\ *n* **:** a girl of boyish behavior **:** HOYDEN — **tom·boy·ish** \-ish\ *adj* — **tom·boy·ish·ness** *n*

tomb·stone \ˈtüm-ˌstōn\ *n* **:** GRAVESTONE

tom·cat \ˈtäm-ˌkat\ *n* **:** a male cat

tom·cod \-ˌkäd\ *n* **1 :** any of several small fishes (genus *Microgadus*) resembling the related common codfish **2 :** any of several croakers of the Pacific coast

Tom Col·lins \ˈtäm-ˈkäl-ənz\ *n* [fr. the name *Tom Collins*] **:** a collins with a base of gin

Tom, Dick, and Har·ry \ˌtäm-ˌdik-ən-ˈhar-ē\ *n* **:** the common man **:** ANYONE — often used with *every* <helps every *Tom, Dick, and Harry* in need>

tome \ˈtōm\ *n* [MF or L; MF, fr. L *tomus,* fr. Gk *tomos* section, roll of papyrus, tome, fr. *temnein* to cut; akin to L *tondēre* to shear, Gk *tendein* to gnaw] **1 :** a volume forming part of a larger work **2 :** BOOK; *esp* **:** a large or scholarly book

-tome \ˌtōm\ *n comb form* [Gk *tomos*] **1 :** part **:** segment <myo*tome*> **2 :** cutting instrument <pharyngo*tome*>

to·men·tose \tō-ˈmen-ˌtōs, ˈtō-mən-\ *adj* [NL *tomentosus,* fr. *tomentum*] **:** covered with densely matted hairs <a ~ leaf>

to·men·tum \tō-ˈment-əm\ *n, pl* **-ta** \-ə\ [NL, fr. L, cushion stuffing; akin to L *tumēre* to be swollen — more at THUMB] **:** pubescence composed of densely matted woolly hairs

[1]**tom·fool** \ˈtäm-ˈfül\ *n* **:** a great fool **:** BLOCKHEAD

[2]**tom·fool** \ˌtäm-ˌfül\ *adj* **:** extremely foolish, stupid, or doltish

tom·fool·ery \täm-ˈfül-(ə-)rē\ *n* **:** foolish trifling **:** NONSENSE

Tom·my \ˈtäm-ē\ *n, pl* **Tommies** [*Thomas* Atkins, name used as model in official army forms] **:** a British soldier

Tommy At·kins \-ˈat-kənz\ *n* **:** TOMMY

tommy–gun *vt* **:** to shoot with a tommy gun

tom·my gun \ˈtäm-ē-ˌgən\ *n* [by shortening & alter.] **:** THOMPSON SUBMACHINE GUN; *broadly* **:** SUBMACHINE GUN

tom·my·rot \ˈtäm-ē-ˌrät\ *n* [E dial. *tommy* fool + E *rot*] **:** utter foolishness or nonsense

to·mo·gram \ˈtō-mə-ˌgram\ *n* **:** a roentgenogram made by tomography

to·mog·ra·phy \tō-ˈmäg-rə-fē\ *n* [Gk *tomos* section + ISV *-graphy* — more at TOME] **:** a diagnostic technique using X-ray photographs in which the shadows of structures before and behind the section under scrutiny do not show

[1]**to·mor·row** \tə-ˈmär-(ˌ)ō, -ˈmȯr-, -ə(-w)\ *adv* [ME *to morgen,* fr. OE *tō morgen,* fr. *tō* to + *morgen* morrow, morning — more at MORN] **:** on or for the day after today <will do it ~>

[2]**tomorrow** *n* **1 :** the day after the present <the court will recess until ~> **2 :** FUTURE 1a <the world of ~>

tom·pi·on \ˈtäm-pē-ən\ *var of* TAMPION

Tom Thumb \ˈtäm-ˈthəm\ *n* **1 :** a legendary English dwarf **2 :** a dwarf type, race, or individual

tom·tit \ˈtäm-ˌtit, täm-ˈ\ *n* [prob. short for *tomtitmouse,* fr. the name *Tom* + *titmouse*] **:** any of various small active birds

tom–tom \ˈtäm-ˌtäm, ˈtəm-ˌtəm\ *n* [Hindi *tamtam*] **1 :** a usu. long and narrow small-headed drum commonly beaten with the hands **2 :** a monotonous beating, rhythm, or rhythmical sound

-t·o·my \t-ə-mē\ *n comb form* [NL *-tomia,* fr. Gk, fr. *-tomos* that cuts, fr. *temnein* to cut — more at TOME] **:** incision **:** section <laparo*tomy*>

[1]**ton** \ˈtən\ *n, pl* **tons** *also* **ton** [ME *tunne* unit of weight or capacity — more at TUN] **1 :** any of various units of weight: **a —** see WEIGHT table **b :** METRIC TON **2 a :** a unit of internal capacity for ships equal to 100 cubic feet — called also *register ton* **b :** a unit approximately equal to the volume of a long ton weight of seawater used in reckoning the displacement of ships and equal to 35 cubic feet **c :** a unit of volume for cargo freight usu. reckoned at 40 cubic feet — called also *freight ton, measurement ton* **3 :** a great quantity **:** LOT — often used in pl. <ate ~*s* of hamburgers> <has ~*s* of money>

[2]**ton** \ˈtōⁿ\ *n* [F, lit., tone, fr. L *tonus*] **1 :** the prevailing fashion **:** VOGUE **2 :** the quality or state of being smart or fashionable

ton·al \ˈtōn-ᵊl\ *adj* **1 :** of or relating to tone, tonality, or tonicity **2 :** having tonality — **ton·al·ly** \-ᵊl-ē\ *adv*

to·nal·i·ty \tō-ˈnal-ət-ē\ *n, pl* **-ties** **1 :** tonal quality **2 a :** KEY 8 **b :** the organization of all the tones and chords of a piece of music in relation to a tonic **3 :** the arrangement or interrelation of the tones of a picture

ton·do \ˈtän-(ˌ)dō\ *n, pl* **ton·di** \-(ˌ)dē\ [It, fr. *tondo* round, short for *rotondo,* fr. L *rotundus* — more at ROUND] **1 :** a circular painting **2 :** a sculptured medallion

[1]**tone** \ˈtōn\ *n* [ME, fr. L *tonus* tension, tone, fr. Gk *tonos,* lit., act of stretching; akin to Gk *teinein* to stretch — more at THIN] **1 :** vocal or musical sound; *esp* **:** sound of a specific quality <spoke in low ~*s*> <masculine ~*s*> **2 a :** a sound of definite pitch and vibration **b :** WHOLE STEP **3 :** accent or inflection expressive of a mood or emotion **4 :** the pitch of a word often used to express differences of meaning **5 :** a particular pitch or change of pitch constituting an element in the intonation of a phrase or sentence <high ~> <low ~> <mid ~> <low-rising ~> <falling ~> **6 :** style or manner of expression in speaking or writing <seemed wise to adopt a conciliatory ~> **7 a** (1) **:** color quality or value (2) **:** a tint or shade of color **b :** the color that appreciably modifies a hue or white or black <gray walls of greenish ~> **8 :** the effect in painting of light and shade together with color **9 a :** the state of a living body or of any of its organs or parts in which the functions are healthy and performed with due vigor **b :** normal tension or responsiveness to stimuli; *specif* **:** muscular tonus **10 a :** healthy elasticity **:** RESILIENCY **b :** general character, quality, or trend <a city's low moral ~> **c :** frame of mind **:** MOOD

[2]tone *vb* **toned; ton·ing** *vt* **1 :** INTONE **2 :** to give a particular intonation or inflection to **3 a :** to impart tone to : STRENGTHEN <medicine to ~ up the system> **b :** to soften in color, appearance, or sound : MELLOW **c :** to change the normal silver image of (as a photographic print) into a colored image ~ *vi* **1 :** to assume a pleasing color quality or tint **2 :** to blend or harmonize in color

tone arm *n* **:** the movable part of a phonograph or record player that carries the pickup and permits the needle to follow the record groove

toned \ˈtōnd\ *adj* **1 :** having tone or a specified tone : characterized or distinguished by a tone **2** *of paper* **:** having a slight tint

tone–deaf \ˈtōn-ˌdef\ *adj* **:** relatively insensitive to differences in musical pitch — **tone deafness** *n*

tone language *n* **:** a language (as Chinese, Sudanic, or Bantu) in which variations in tone distinguish words of different meaning that otherwise would sound alike

tone·less \ˈtōn-ləs\ *adj* **:** lacking in tone, modulation, or expression — **tone·less·ly** *adv* — **tone·less·ness** *n*

to·neme \ˈtō-ˌnēm\ *n* **:** an intonation phoneme in a tone language — **to·ne·mic** \tō-ˈnē-mik\ *adj*

tone poem *n* **:** SYMPHONIC POEM — **tone poet** *n*

ton·er \ˈtō-nər\ *n* **:** one that tones or is a source of tones: as **a :** a pure organic pigment **b :** a solution used to impart color to a silver photographic image **c :** a substance used to develop a latent xerographic image

to·net·ic \tō-ˈnet-ik\ *adj* **1 :** relating to linguistic tones or to tone languages **2 :** of or relating to intonation <~ notation> — **to·net·i·cal·ly** \-i-k(ə-)lē\ *adv*

to·net·ics \-iks\ *n pl but sing in constr* **:** the use or study of linguistic tones

to·nette \tō-ˈnet\ *n* [[1]*tone* + *-ette*] **:** a simple fipple flute with a range somewhat larger than an octave that is often used in elementary music education

[1]tong \ˈtäŋ, ˈtȯŋ\ *vt* **:** to take, gather, hold, or handle with tongs <~ oysters> ~ *vi* **:** to use tongs esp. in taking or gathering something — **tong·er** \ˈtäŋ-ər, ˈtȯŋ-\ *n*

[2]tong *n* [Chin (Cant) *t'ong* hall] **:** a secret society or fraternal organization esp. of Chinese in the U.S. formerly notorious for gang warfare

ton·ga \ˈtäŋ-gə\ *n* [Hindi *tāṅgā*] **:** a light 2-wheeled vehicle for two or four persons drawn by one horse and common in India

Ton·gan \ˈtäŋ-(g)ən\ *n* **1 :** a member of a Polynesian people of the Tonga islands **2 :** the Polynesian language of the Tongans — **Tongan** *adj*

tongs \ˈtäŋz, ˈtȯŋz\ *n pl but sing or pl in constr* [ME *tonges*, pl. of *tonge*, fr. OE *tang*; akin to OHG *zanga* tongs, Gk *daknein* to bite] **:** any of numerous grasping devices consisting commonly of two pieces joined at one end by a pivot or hinged like scissors

[1]tongue \ˈtəŋ\ *n* [ME *tunge*, fr. OE; akin to OHG *zunga* tongue, L *lingua*] **1 a :** a fleshy movable process of the floor of the mouths of most vertebrates that bears sensory end organs and small glands and functions esp. in taking and swallowing food and in man as a speech organ — see LARYNX illustration **b :** a part of various invertebrate animals that is analogous to the tongue **2 :** the flesh of a tongue (as of the ox or sheep) used as food **3 :** the power of communication through speech **4 a :** LANGUAGE; *esp* **:** a spoken language **b :** manner or quality of utterance with respect to tone or sound, the sense of what is expressed, or the intention of the speaker <she has a clever ~> <a sharp ~> **c** (1) **:** ecstatic usu. unintelligible utterance accompanying religious excitation (2) **:** the charismatic gift of ecstatic speech **d :** the cry of or as if of a hound pursuing or in sight of game — used esp. in the phrase *to give tongue* **5 :** a long narrow strip of land projecting into a body of water **6 :** something resembling an animal's tongue in being elongated and fastened at one end only: as **a :** a movable pin in a buckle **b :** a metal ball suspended inside a bell so as to strike against the sides as the bell is swung **c :** the pole of a vehicle **d :** the flap under the lacing or buckles of a shoe at the throat of the vamp **7 a :** the rib on one edge of a board that fits into a corresponding groove in an edge of another board to make a flush joint **b :** FEATHER 4 — **tongue·like** \-ˌlīk\ *adj* — **on the tip of one's tongue 1 :** about to be uttered <it was *on the tip of my tongue* to tell him exactly what I thought> **2 :** just eluding recall

[2]tongue *vb* **tongued; tongu·ing** \ˈtəŋ-iŋ\ *vt* **1** *archaic* **:** SCOLD **2 :** to touch or lick with or as if with the tongue **3 a :** to cut a tongue on <~ a board> **b :** to join (as boards) by means of a tongue and groove <~ flooring together> **4 :** to articulate (notes) by tonguing ~ *vi* **1 :** to project in a tongue **2 :** to articulate notes on a wind instrument by successively interrupting the stream of wind with the action of the tongue

tongue and groove *n* **:** a joint made by a tongue on one edge of a board fitting into a corresponding groove on the edge of another board

tongued \ˈtəŋd\ *adj* **:** having a tongue esp. of a specified kind — often used in combination <sharp-*tongued*>

tongue–in–cheek *adj* **:** characterized by insincerity, irony, or whimsical exaggeration

tongue in cheek *adv* **:** with insincerity, irony, or whimsical exaggeration

tongue–lash \ˈtəŋ-ˌlash\ *vb* [back-formation fr. *tongue-lashing*] **:** CHIDE, SCOLD — **tongue–lash·ing** *n*

tongue·less \ˈtəŋ-ləs\ *adj* **1 :** having no tongue **2 :** lacking power of speech : MUTE

[1]tongue–tie \ˈtəŋ-ˌtī\ *vt* [back-formation fr. *tongue-tied*] **:** to deprive of speech or the power of distinct articulation

[2]tongue–tie *n* **:** limited mobility of the tongue due to shortness of its frenum

tongue–tied \ˈtəŋ-ˌtīd\ *adj* **1 :** affected with tongue-tie **2 :** unable or disinclined to speak freely (as from shyness)

tongue twister *n* **:** a word, phrase, or sentence difficult to articulate because of a succession of similar consonantal sounds (as in "twin-screw steel cruiser")

tongu·ing \ˈtəŋ-iŋ\ *n* **:** use of the tongue in attacking or articulating notes on a wind instrument

-to·nia \ˈtō-nē-ə\ *n comb form* [NL, fr. *tonus*] **:** condition or degree of tonus <myo*tonia*>

[1]ton·ic \ˈtän-ik\ *adj* [Gk *tonikos*, fr. *tonos* tension, tone] **1 a :** characterized by tonus <~ contraction of muscle>; *also* **:** marked by prolonged muscular contraction <~ convulsions> **b :** producing or adapted to produce healthy muscular condition and reaction of organs (as muscles) **2 a :** increasing or restoring physical or mental tone **b :** yielding a tonic substance **3 :** relating to or based on the first tone of a scale <~ harmony> **4** *of a syllable* **:** bearing a principal stress or accent **5 :** of or relating to speech tones or to languages using them to distinguish words otherwise identical — **ton·i·cal·ly** \ˈtän-i-k(ə-)lē\ *adv*

[2]tonic *n* **1 a :** an agent (as a drug) that increases body tone **b :** something that invigorates, restores, refreshes, or stimulates <a day in the country was a ~ for him> **c :** a liquid preparation for the scalp or hair **d** *chiefly NewEng* **:** a carbonated flavored beverage **e :** QUININE WATER **2 :** the first tone of a diatonic scale : KEYNOTE **3 :** a voiced sound

tonic accent *n* **1 :** relative phonetic prominence (as from greater stress or higher pitch) of a spoken syllable or word **2 :** accent depending on pitch rather than stress

to·nic·i·ty \tō-ˈnis-ət-ē\ *n* **1 :** the property of possessing tone; *esp* **:** healthy vigor of body or mind **2 :** muscular tonus

tonic sol–fa *n* **:** a system of solmization based on key relationships that replaces the normal notation with sol-fa syllables or their initials

[1]to·night \tə-ˈnīt\ *adv* **:** on this present night or the night following this present day <will do it ~>

[2]tonight *n* **:** the present night or the night following this present day

ton·ka bean \ˈtäŋ-kə-\ *n* [prob. fr. Tupi *tonka*] **:** the seed of any of several leguminous trees (genus *Dipteryx*) that contains coumarin and is used in perfumes and as a flavoring; *also* **:** a tree bearing tonka beans

tonn *abbr* tonnage

ton·nage \ˈtən-ij\ *n* **1** [ME, fr. OF *tonne* tun — more at TUNNEL] **:** a duty formerly levied on every tun of wine imported into England **2 a :** a duty or impost on vessels based on cargo capacity **b :** a duty on goods per ton transported **3 :** ships in terms of the total number of tons registered or carried or of their carrying capacity **4 a :** the cubical content of a merchant ship in units of 100 cubic feet **b :** the displacement of a warship **5 :** total weight in tons shipped, carried, or produced

tonne \ˈtən\ *n* [F, fr. *tonne* tun, fr. OF — more at TUNNEL] **:** METRIC TON

ton·neau \ˈtän-ˌō, tə-ˈnō\ *n, pl* **tonneaus** [F, lit., tun, fr. OF *tonel* — more at TUNNEL] **1 :** the rear seating compartment of an automobile; *also* **:** the entire seating compartment **2 :** a shape of watch case or dial resembling a barrel in profile

ton·ner \ˈtən-ər\ *n* **:** an object (as a ship) having a specified tonnage — used in combination <a thousand-*tonner*>

to·nom·e·ter \tō-ˈnäm-ət-ər\ *n* [Gk *tonos* tone + E *-meter*] **1 :** an instrument or device for determining the exact pitch or the vibration rate of tones **2 :** an instrument for measuring tension (as of the eyeball) or pressure (as of blood or a gas) **3 :** a device for measuring vapor pressure — **to·no·met·ric** \ˌtō-nə-ˈme-trik\ *adj* — **to·nom·e·try** \tō-ˈnäm-ə-trē\ *n*

to·no·plast \ˈtō-nə-ˌplast\ *n* [ISV *tono-* (fr. Gk *tonos* tension) + *-plast* — more at TONE] **:** a semipermeable protoplasmic membrane surrounding a plant-cell vacuole

ton·sil \ˈtän(t)-səl\ *n* [L *tonsillae*, pl., tonsils] **1 :** either of a pair of prominent masses of lymphoid tissue that lie one on each side of the throat between the anterior and posterior pillars of the fauces **2 :** any of various masses of lymphoid tissue that are similar to tonsils — **ton·sil·lar** \ˈtän(t)-s(ə-)lər\ *adj*

tonsill- *or* **tonsillo-** *comb form* [L *tonsillae*] **:** tonsil <*tonsill*ectomy> <*tonsillo*tomy>

ton·sil·lec·to·my \ˌtän(t)-sə-ˈlek-tə-mē\ *n, pl* **-mies :** the surgical removal of the tonsils

ton·sil·li·tis \-ˈlīt-əs\ *n* [NL] **:** inflammation of the tonsils

ton·so·ri·al \tän-ˈsōr-ē-əl, -ˈsȯr-\ *adj* [L *tonsorius*, fr. *tonsus*, pp.] **:** of or relating to a barber or his work

[1]ton·sure \ˈtän-chər\ *n* [ME, fr. ML *tonsura*, fr. L, act of shearing, fr. *tonsus*, pp. of *tondēre* to shear — more at TOME] **1 :** the Roman Catholic or Eastern rite of admission to the clerical state by the clipping or shaving of a portion of the head **2 :** the shaven crown or patch worn by monks and other clerics **3 :** a bald spot resembling a tonsure

[2]tonsure *vt* **ton·sured; ton·sur·ing** \ˈtänch-(ə-)riŋ\ **:** to shave the head of; *esp* **:** to confer the tonsure upon

ton·tine \ˈtän-ˌtēn, tän-ˈ\ *n* [F, fr. Lorenzo *Tonti* †1695 It banker] **:** a financial arrangement whereby a group of participants share various advantages on such terms that upon the death or default of any member his advantages are distributed among the remaining members until on the death of all but one the whole goes to him or on the expiration of an agreed period the whole goes to those remaining; *also* **:** the share or right of each individual

to·nus \ˈtō-nəs\ *n* [NL, fr. L, tension, tone] **:** TONE 9a; *esp* **:** a state of partial contraction characteristic of normal muscle

tony \ˈtō-nē\ *adj* **ton·i·er; -est :** marked by an aristocratic or high-toned manner or style <~ private schools>

To·ny \ˈtō-nē\ *n, pl* **Tonys** [*Tony*, nickname of Antoinette Perry †1946 Am actress & producer] **:** a medallion awarded annually by a professional organization for notable achievement in the theater

too \(ˈ)tü\ *adv* [ME, fr. OE *tō* to, too — more at TO] **1 :** ALSO, BESIDES <sell the house and furniture ~> **2 a :** to an excessive

degree : EXCESSIVELY <~ large a house for us> **b** : to such a degree as to be regrettable <this time he has gone ~ far> **c** : VERY **3** : SO 2d <"I didn't do it." "You did ~.">
took *past of* TAKE
[1]tool \'tül\ *n* [ME, fr. OE *tōl;* akin to OE *tawian* to prepare for use — more at TAW] **1 a** : an instrument (as a hammer) used or worked by hand : IMPLEMENT **b** (1) : the cutting or shaping part in a machine or machine tool (2) : a machine for shaping metal : MACHINE TOOL **2 a** : something (as an instrument or apparatus) used in performing an operation or necessary in the practice of a vocation or profession <a scholar's books are his ~*s*> **b** : a means to an end **3** : one that is used or manipulated by another
[2]tool *vt* **1 a** : to cause (a vehicle) to go : DRIVE **b** : to convey in a vehicle **2** : to shape, form, or finish with a tool; *esp* : to letter or ornament (as leather) by means of hand tools **3** : to equip (as a plant or industry) with tools, machines, and instruments for production ~ *vi* **1** : DRIVE, RIDE <~*ed* about the countryside in a small automobile —R. G. Tugwell> **2** : to equip a plant or industry with the means (as machines, machine tools, and instruments) of production — often used with *up* <the necessary time it takes to ~ up for new models —*Ethyl News*>
[3]tool *n* : a design (as on the binding of a book) made by tooling
tool·box \'tül-ˌbäks\ *n* : a chest for tools
tool·head \'tül-ˌhed\ *n* : a part of a machine in which a tool or toolholder is clamped and which is provided with adjustments to bring the tool into the desired position
tool·hold·er \-ˌhōl-dər\ *n* : a short steel bar having a shank at one end to fit into the toolhead of a machine and a clamp at the other end to hold small interchangeable cutting bits
tool·house \-ˌhau̇s\ *n* : a building (as in a garden) for storing tools
tool·mak·er \'tül-ˌmā-kər\ *n* : a machinist who specializes in the construction, repair, maintenance, and calibration of the tools, jigs, fixtures, and instruments of a machine shop
tool·mak·ing \-kiŋ\ *n* : the action, process, or art of making tools; *also* : the trade of a toolmaker
tool·room \'tül-ˌrüm, -ˌru̇m\ *n* : a room where tools are kept; *esp* : a room in a machine shop in which tools are made, stored, and issued for use by workmen
tool·shed \-ˌshed\ *n* : TOOLHOUSE
tool subject *n* : a subject studied to gain competence in a skill used in other subjects
toom \'tüm\ *adj* [ME, fr. OE *tōm* — more at TEEM] *chiefly Scot* : EMPTY
toon \'tün\ *n* [Hindi *tūn,* fr. Skt *tunna*] : an East Indian and Australian tree (*Cedrela toona*) of the mahogany family with fragrant dark red wood and flowers that yield a dye; *also* : its wood
[1]toot \'tüt\ *vb* [prob. imit.] *vi* **1 a** : to sound a short blast <the horn ~*ed*> **b** : to sound a note or call suggesting the short blast of a wind instrument **2** : to blow or sound an instrument (as a horn) esp. so as to produce short blasts ~ *vt* : to cause to sound <~ a whistle> — **toot·er** *n*
[2]toot *n* : a short blast (as on a horn); *also* : a sound resembling such a blast
[3]toot *n* [Sc *toot* to drink heavily] : a drinking bout : SPREE
[1]tooth \'tüth\ *n, pl* **teeth** \'tēth\ [ME, fr. OE *tōth;* akin to OHG *zand* tooth, L *dent-, dens,* Gk *odont-, odous*] **1 a** : one of the hard bony appendages that are borne on the jaws or in many of the lower vertebrates on other bones in the walls of the mouth or pharynx and serve esp. for the prehension and mastication of food and as weapons of offense and defense **b** : any of various usu. hard and sharp processes esp. about the mouth of an invertebrate **2** : TASTE, LIKING **3** : a projection resembling or suggesting the tooth of an animal in shape, arrangement, or action <saw ~>: as **a** : one of the regular projections on the circumference or sometimes the face of a wheel that engage with corresponding projections on another wheel esp. to transmit force : COG **b** : a small sharp-pointed marginal lobe or process on a plant **4 a** : something that injures, tortures, devours, or destroys **b** *pl* : effective means of enforcement **5** : a roughness of surface produced by mechanical or artificial means — **tooth·like** \'tüth-ˌlīk\ *adj* — **in the teeth of 1** : in or into direct contact or collision with <found themselves sailing *in the teeth of* a hurricane —*Current Biog.*> **2** : in direct opposition to <rule had . . . been imposed by conquest *in the teeth of* obstinate resistance —A. J. Toynbee> — **to the teeth** : FULLY, COMPLETELY <armed *to the teeth*>

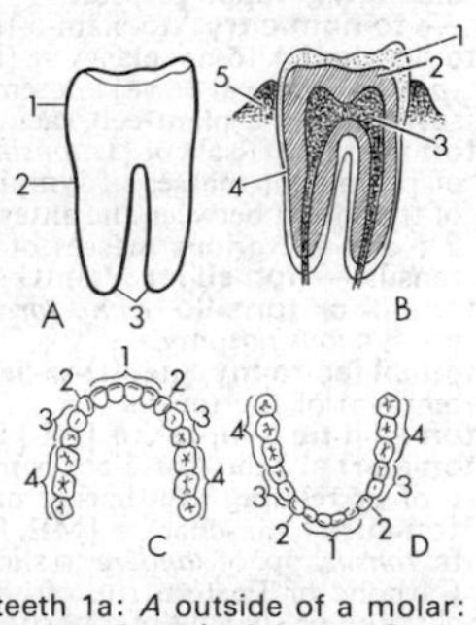

teeth 1a: *A* outside of a molar: *1* crown, *2* neck, *3* roots; *B* cross section of a molar: *1* enamel, *2* neck, *3* roots, *4* cementum, *5* gum; *C* dentition of adult human, upper; *D* dentition of adult human, lower: *1* incisors, *2* canines, *3* bicuspids, *4* molars

[2]tooth \'tüth, 'tüt͟h\ *vt* **1** : to furnish with teeth esp. by cutting notches <~ a saw> **2** : to roughen the surface of <~ a cement floor to prevent slipping>
tooth·ache \'tü-ˌthāk\ *n* : pain in or about a tooth
tooth and nail *adv* : with every available means : all out <fight *tooth and nail*>
tooth–billed \'tüth-'bild\ *adj* : having a notched bill
tooth·brush \-ˌbrəsh\ *n* : a brush for cleaning the teeth
tooth·brush·ing \-iŋ\ *n* : the action of using a toothbrush to clean teeth
toothed \'tütht, *uncompounded also* 'tü-t͟həd\ *adj* : having teeth esp. of a specified kind or number — often used in combination <buck*toothed*>
toothed whale \'tütht-, ˌtü-t͟həd-\ *n* : any of various whales (suborder Odontoceti) with numerous simple conical teeth — compare WHALEBONE WHALE
tooth·less \'tüth-ləs\ *adj* **1** : having no teeth **2 a** : lacking in sharpness or bite <spoke in ~ generalities —Arthur Hepner> **b** : lacking in means of enforcement or coercion : INEFFECTUAL
tooth·paste \-ˌpāst\ *n* : a paste for cleaning the teeth
tooth·pick \-ˌpik\ *n* : a pointed instrument (as a small tapering piece of wood) used for removing food particles lodged between the teeth
tooth powder *n* : a powder for cleaning the teeth
tooth shell *n* : any of a class (Scaphopoda) of marine mollusks with a tapering tubular shell; *also* : this shell
tooth·some \'tüth-səm\ *adj* **1** : of palatable flavor and pleasing texture : DELICIOUS <crisp ~ fried chicken> **2 a** : AGREEABLE, ATTRACTIVE **b** : sexually attractive <a ~ blonde> ***syn*** see PALATABLE — **tooth·some·ly** *adv* — **tooth·some·ness** *n*
tooth·wort \-ˌwərt, -ˌwȯ(ə)rt\ *n* **1** : a European parasitic plant (*Lathraea squamaria*) of the broomrape family having a rootstock covered with tooth-shaped scales **2** : any of various cresses (genus *Dentaria*) including several cultivated for their showy flowers
toothy \'tü-thē\ *adj* **tooth·i·er; -est 1** : having or showing prominent teeth <~ grin> **2** : TOOTHSOME 1 — **tooth·i·ly** \-thə-lē\ *adv*
too·tle \'tüt-ᵊl\ *vb* **too·tled; too·tling** \'tüt-liŋ, -ᵊl-iŋ\ [freq. of [1]*toot*] *vi* **1** : to toot gently, repeatedly, or continuously **2** : to drive or move along in a leisurely manner ~ *vt* : to toot continuously on — **tootle** *n* — **too·tler** \'tüt-lər, -ᵊl-ər\ *n*
too–too \'tü-'tü\ *adj* **1** : going beyond the bounds of convention, good taste, or common sense : EXTREME **2** : LA-DI-DA
toot·sie \'tu̇t-sē\ *n* [origin unknown] **1** : DEAR, SWEETHEART **2** : PROSTITUTE
toot·sy *also* **toot·sie** \'tu̇t-sē\ *n, pl* **tootsies** [baby-talk alter. of *foot*] : FOOT
[1]top \'täp\ *n* [ME, fr. OE; akin to OHG *zopf* tip, tuft of hair] **1 a** (1) : the highest point, level, or part of something : SUMMIT, CROWN (2) : the head or top of the head — used esp. in the phrase *top to toe* (3) : the head of a plant and esp. one with edible roots <beet ~*s*> (4) : a garment worn on the upper body **b** (1) : the highest or uppermost region or part (2) : the upper end, edge, or surface **2** : a fitted, integral, or attached part or unit serving as an upper piece, lid, or covering **3 a** : a platform surrounding the head of a lower mast that serves to spread the topmast rigging, strengthen the mast, and furnish a standing place for men aloft **b** : a comparable part of the superstructure; *esp* : such a part on a warship used as a fire-control station or antiaircraft gun platform **4** : the highest degree or pitch conceivable or attained : ACME, PINNACLE **5 a** : the part that is nearest in space or time to the source or beginning **b** : the first half of an inning in baseball **6 a** (1) : the highest position (as in rank or achievement) (2) : a person or thing at the top **b** *pl* : aces and kings in a hand or the three highest honors in a suit **7** : the choicest part : CREAM, PICK **8** : a forward spin given to a ball (as in golf, tennis, or billiards) by striking it on or near the top or above the center; *also* : the stroke so given — **topped** \'täpt\ *adj* — **off the top of one's head** : in an impromptu manner <sat down and wrote the . . . story *off the top of his head* — Jerome Beatty, Jr.> — **on top of 1 a** : in control of <acted like a man *on top of* his job —*Newsweek*> **b** : informed about <a teacher trying to keep *on top of* developments in his field —Frank Ross> **2** : in sudden and unexpected proximity to <the situation was *on top of* them now . . . they couldn't evade it —Frank O'Connor> **3** : in addition to <a bad idea to get chilled *on top of* getting wet —Sylvia T. Warner> — **on top of the world** : in a position of eminent success, happiness, or fame
[2]top *vb* **topped; top·ping** *vt* **1** : to remove or cut the top of: as **a** : to shorten or remove the top of (a plant) : PINCH 1b **b** : to remove the most volatile parts from (as crude petroleum) **2 a** : to cover with a top or on the top : provide, form, or serve as a top for **b** : to supply with a decorative or protective finish or final touch **c** : REFUEL, RESUPPLY — usu. used with *off* or *up* **d** : to complete the basic structure of (as a high-rise building) by putting on a cap or uppermost section — usu. used with *out* or *off* <the tallest commercial building in the state . . . was *topped* off . . . yesterday —John Okai> **3 a** : to be or become higher than : OVERTOP <~*s* the previous record> **b** : to be superior to : EXCEL, SURPASS <~*s* everything of the kind in print —Alfred Frankenstein> **c** : to gain ascendancy over : DOMINATE **4 a** : to rise to, reach, or be at the top of **b** : to go over the top of : CLEAR, SURMOUNT **5** : to strike (a ball) above the center thereby imparting top spin ~ *vi* **1** : to make an end, finish, or conclusion **2** : to reach a summit or crest — usu. used with *off* or *out* <the business-investment boom . . . has *topped* out —*Newsweek*>
[3]top *adj* **1** : of, relating to, or being at the top : UPPERMOST **2** : CHIEF, LEADING <one of the world's ~ journalists> **3** : of the highest quality, amount, or degree <~ value> <~ form>
[4]top *n* [ME, fr. OE] : a commonly cylindrical or conoidal device that has a tapering usu. steel-shod point on which it is made to spin and that is used esp. as a toy
top- *or* **topo-** *comb form* [ME, fr. LL, fr. Gk, fr. *topos* — more at TOPIC] : place : locality <*topo*logy> <*top*onymy>
to·paz \'tō-ˌpaz\ *n* [ME *topace,* fr. OF, fr. L *topazus,* fr. Gk *topazos*] **1 a** : a mineral $Al_2SiO_4(F,OH)_2$ that is essentially a silicate of aluminum and usu. occurs in orthorhombic translucent or transparent crystals or in white translucent masses **b** : a usu. yellow to brownish yellow transparent mineral topaz used as a gem **c** : a yellow sapphire **d** : a yellow quartz (as cairngorm or altered citrine) **2** : either of two large brilliantly colored So. American hummingbirds (*Topaza pella* and *T. pyra*)
top banana *n* [fr. a burlesque routine involving three comedians in which the one that gets the punch line also gets a banana] : the leading comedian in a burlesque show; *broadly* : KINGPIN 2

top billing *n* **1 :** the position at the top of a theatrical bill usu. featuring the star's name **2 :** prominent emphasis, featuring, or advertising
top boot *n* **:** a high boot often with light-colored leather bands around the upper part
top·coat \'täp-ˌkōt\ *n* **:** a lightweight overcoat
top·cross \-ˌkrȯs\ *n* **:** a cross between a superior or purebred male and inferior female stock to improve the average quality of the progeny; *also* **:** the product of such a cross
top dog *n* **:** a person or group in a position of authority esp. through victory in a hard-fought competition
top–down \ˌtäp-ˌdau̇n\ *adj* [fr. the phrase *from the top down*] **:** closely organized, controlled, and directed
top drawer *n* **:** the highest level of society, authority, or excellence
top–dress \'täp-ˌdres\ *vt* [back-formation fr. *topdressing*] **:** to apply material to (as land or a road) without working it in; *esp* **:** to scatter fertilizer over (land)
top·dress·ing \-iŋ\ *n* **:** a material used to top-dress soil
[1]tope \'tōp\ *vi* **toped; top·ing** [obs. E *tope* (interj. used to wish good health before drinking)] **:** to drink liquor to excess
[2]tope *n* [origin unknown] **:** a small cosmopolitan shark (*Galeorhinus galeus*) with a liver very rich in vitamin A
[3]tope *n* [Hindi *top,* perh. fr. Skt *stūpa*] **:** STUPA
to·pee *or* **to·pi** \tō-'pē, 'tō-(ˌ)pē\ *n* [Hindi *topī*] **:** a lightweight helmet-shaped hat made of pith or cork
top·er \'tō-pər\ *n* **:** one that topes; *esp* **:** DRUNKARD
top flight *n* **:** the highest level of achievement, excellence, or eminence — **top·flight** *adj*
[1]Top 40 *n pl* **:** the forty best-selling phonograph records for a given period
[2]Top 40 *adj* **:** constituting, playing, listing, or relating to the Top 40 <*Top 40* hits> <*Top 40* stations> <*Top 40* charts>
top·ful *or* **top·full** \'täp-'fu̇l\ *adj* **:** BRIMFUL
[1]top·gal·lant \(ˈ)täp-'gal-ənt, tə-'gal-\ *adj* [[1]*top* + *gallant*, adj.] **1 :** of, relating to, or being a part next above the topmast and below the royal mast <~ sails> <the ~ mast> **2 :** raised above adjoining parts or structures
[2]topgallant *n* **1 :** a topgallant mast or sail **2 :** the topmost point **:** SUMMIT <the high ~ of my joy —Shak.>
top–ham·per \'täp-'ham-pər\ *n* **1 :** matter or weight (as spars or rigging) in the upper part of a ship **2 :** unnecessary cumbersome matter
top hat *n* **:** a man's tall-crowned hat usu. of beaver or silk
top–heavy \'täp-ˌhev-ē\ *adj* **1 :** having the top part too heavy for the lower part **2 :** capitalized beyond what is prudent or safe
To·phet \'tō-fət\ *n* [ME, shrine south of ancient Jerusalem where human sacrifices were performed to Moloch (Jer 7:31), Gehenna, fr. Heb *tōpheth*] **:** HELL, GEHENNA
top–hole \'täp-'hōl\ *adj, chiefly Brit* **:** EXCELLENT, FIRST-CLASS
to·phus \'tō-fəs\ *n, pl* **to·phi** \'tō-ˌfī, -ˌfē\ [L, tufa] **:** a deposit of urates in tissues (as cartilage) characteristic of gout
[1]to·pi·ary \'tō-pē-ˌer-ē\ *adj* [L *topiarius,* fr. *topia* ornamental gardening, irreg. fr. Gk *topos* place] **:** of, relating to, or being the practice or art of training, cutting, and trimming trees or shrubs into odd or ornamental shapes; *also* **:** characterized by such work
[2]topiary *n, pl* **-ar·ies :** topiary art or gardening; *also* **:** a topiary garden
top·ic \'täp-ik\ *n* [L *Topica* Topics (work by Aristotle), fr. Gk *Topika,* fr. *topika,* neut. pl. of *topikos* of a place, of a topos, fr. *topos* place, topos; akin to OE *thafian* to agree] **1 a :** one of the general forms of argument employed in probable reasoning **b :** ARGUMENT, REASON **2 a :** a heading in an outlined argument or exposition **b :** the subject of a discourse or of a section of a discourse
top·i·cal \-i-kəl\ *adj* **1 a :** of or relating to a place **b :** local or designed for local application <a ~ remedy> <a ~ anesthetic> **2 a :** of, relating to, or arranged by topics <set down in ~ form> **b :** referring to the topics of the day or place **:** of local or temporary interest — **top·i·cal·ly** \-k(ə-)lē\ *adv*
top·i·cal·i·ty \ˌtäp-ə-'kal-ət-ē\ *n, pl* **-ties 1 :** the quality or state of being topical **2 :** an item of merely topical interest
topic sentence *n* **:** a sentence that states the main thought of a paragraph or of a larger unit of discourse and is usu. placed at or near the beginning
top·kick \'täp-'kik\ *n* **:** FIRST SERGEANT 1
top·knot \-ˌnät\ *n* **1 :** an ornament (as a knot of ribbons or a pompom) forming a headdress or worn as part of a coiffure **2 :** a crest of feathers or hair on the top of the head
top·less \-ləs\ *adj* **1 :** being without a top **2** *archaic* **:** so high as to reach up beyond sight <and burnt the ~ towers of Ilium —Christopher Marlowe> **3 a :** wearing no clothing on the upper body **b :** featuring topless waitresses or entertainers
top–lev·el \-'lev-əl\ *adj* **:** very high or highest in level of authority, importance, or quality <~ management>
top lift *n* **:** the bottom layer of a heel
top·lofty \'täp-ˌlȯf-tē\ *also* **top·loft·i·cal** \täp-'lȯf-ti-kəl\ *adj* [prob. fr. the phrase *top loft*] **:** very superior in air or attitude — **top·loft·i·ly** \täp-'lȯf-tə-lē\ *adv* — **top·loft·i·ness** \'täp-ˌlȯf-tē-nəs\ *n*
top·mast \'täp-ˌmast, -məst\ *n* **:** the mast that is next above the lower mast and is topmost in a fore-and-aft rig
top milk *n* **:** the upper layer of milk in a container enriched by whatever cream has risen
top·min·now \'täp-ˌmin-(ˌ)ō, -ə(-w)\ *n* **1 :** any of numerous small viviparous surface-feeding fishes constituting a family (Poeciliidae) **2 :** KILLIFISH 1
top·most \'täp-ˌmōst\ *adj* **:** highest of all **:** UPPERMOST
top–notch \-'näch\ *adj* **:** of the highest quality **:** FIRST-RATE — **top·notch·er** \-'näch-ər\ *n*
to·po·cen·tric \ˌtäp-ə-'sen-trik, ˌtōp-\ *adj* [*top-* + *-centric*] **:** relating to, measured from, or as if observed from a particular point on the earth's surface **:** having or relating to such a point as origin <~ coordinates> — compare GEOCENTRIC
topog *abbr* topography
to·po·graph \'täp-ə-ˌgraf, 'tōp-\ *n* [back-formation fr. *topography*] **:** a detailed photograph of the surface of an object
to·pog·ra·pher \tə-'päg-rə-fər\ *n* **:** one skilled in topography
to·po·graph·ic \ˌtäp-ə-'graf-ik, ˌtōp-ə-\ *adj* **:** TOPOGRAPHICAL 1
to·po·graph·i·cal \-i-kəl\ *adj* **1 :** of, relating to, or concerned with topography <a ~ engineer> **2 :** of, relating to, or concerned with the artistic representation of a particular locality <a ~ poem> <~ painting> — **to·po·graph·i·cal·ly** \-k(ə-)lē\ *adv*
to·pog·ra·phy \tə-'päg-rə-fē\ *n* [ME *topographie,* fr. LL *topographia,* fr. Gk, fr. *topographein* to describe a place, fr. *topos* place + *graphein* to write — more at CARVE] **1 a :** the art or practice of graphic delineation in detail usu. on maps or charts of natural and man-made features of a place or region esp. in a way to show their relative positions and elevations; *also* **:** the practice of making topographs **b :** topographical surveying **2 a :** the configuration of a surface including its relief and the position of its natural and man-made features **b :** the physical or natural features of an object or entity and their structural relationships
to·po·log·i·cal \ˌtäp-ə-'läj-i-kəl, ˌtōp-\ *adj* **1 :** of or relating to topology **2 :** being or involving properties unaltered under a homeomorphism <continuity and connectedness are ~ properties> — **to·po·log·i·cal·ly** \-k(ə-)lē\ *adv*
topological group *n* **:** a mathematical group which is also a topological space, whose multiplicative operation is continuous such that given any neighborhood of a product there exist neighborhoods of the elements composing the product with the property that any pair of elements representing each of these neighborhoods form a product belonging to the given neighborhood, and whose operation of taking inverses is continuous such that for any neighborhood of the inverse of an element there exists a neighborhood of the element itself in which every element has its inverse in the other neighborhood
topologically equivalent *adj* **:** related by a homeomorphism
topological space *n* **:** a set with a collection of subsets satisfying the conditions that both the empty set and the set itself belong to the collection, the union of any number of the subsets is also an element of the collection, and the intersection of a finite number of the subsets is an element of the collection
topological transformation *n* **:** HOMEOMORPHISM
to·pol·o·gist \tə-'päl-ə-jəst, tō-\ *n* **:** a student of or specialist in topology
to·pol·o·gy \-jē\ *n, pl* **-gies** [ISV] **1 :** topographical study of a particular place; *specif* **:** the history of a region as indicated by its topography **2 a :** a branch of mathematics concerned with those properties of geometric configurations (as point sets) which are unaltered by elastic deformations (as a stretching or a twisting) that are homeomorphisms **b :** CONFIGURATION <~ of a molecule> <~ of a magnetic field>
top·onym \'täp-ə-ˌnim, 'tōp-\ *n* [ISV, back-formation fr. *toponymy*] **:** PLACE-NAME
top·onym·ic \ˌtäp-ə-'nim-ik, ˌtōp-\ *adj* **:** of or relating to toponyms or toponymy — **top·onym·i·cal** \-i-kəl\ *adj*
to·pon·y·my \tə-'pän-ə-mē, tō-\ *n* [ISV, fr. *top-* + Gk *onyma, onoma* name — more at NAME] **:** the place-names of a region or language or esp. the etymological study of them
to·pos \'tōp-ˌäs, 'täp-\ *n, pl* **to·poi** \-ˌȯi\ [Gk, short for *koinos topos,* lit., common place —more at TOPIC] **:** a stock rhetorical theme or topic
top·per \'täp-ər\ *n* **1 :** one that puts on or takes off tops **2 :** one that is at or on the top **3 a :** SILK HAT **b :** OPERA HAT **4 :** something (as a joke) that caps everything preceding **5 :** a woman's usu. short and loose-fitting lightweight outer coat
[1]top·ping \'täp-iŋ\ *n* **1 :** something that forms a top: as **a :** a garnish (as a sauce, bread crumbs, or whipped cream) placed on top of a food for flavor or decoration **b :** a finishing layer of mortar on concrete **2 :** the action of one that tops **3 :** something removed by topping
[2]topping *adj* **1 :** highest in rank or eminence **2** *NewEng* **:** PROUD **3** *chiefly Brit* **:** EXCELLENT
top·ple \'täp-əl\ *vb* **top·pled; top·pling** \-(ə-)liŋ\ [freq. of [2]*top*] *vi* **1 :** to fall from or as if from being top-heavy **2 :** to be or seem unsteady **:** TOTTER ~ *vt* **1 :** to cause to topple **2 :** OVERTHROW
top round *n* **:** meat (as steak) from the inner part of a round of beef
tops \'täps\ *adj* [pl. of [1]*top*] **:** topmost in quality, ability, popularity, or eminence — used predicatively <is ~ in his field>
top·sail \'täp-ˌsāl, -səl\ *also* **top·s'l** \-səl\ *n* **1 :** the sail next above the lowermost sail on a mast in a square-rigged ship **2 :** the sail set above and sometimes on the gaff in a fore-and-aft rigged ship
top secret *adj* **1 :** demanding inviolate secrecy among those concerned **2 :** containing information whose unauthorized disclosure could result in exceptionally grave danger to the nation — compare CONFIDENTIAL, SECRET
top sergeant *n* **:** FIRST SERGEANT 1
[1]top·side \'täp-'sīd\ *n* **1** *pl* **:** the top portion of the outer surface of a ship on each side above the waterline **2 :** the highest level of authority **3 :** the upper portion of the ionosphere
[2]topside *adv or adj* **1 :** on deck **2 :** to or on the top or surface **3 :** in a position of authority
top·soil \'täp-ˌsȯil\ *n* **:** surface soil usu. including the organic layer in which plants have most of their roots and which the farmer turns over in plowing
top spin *n* [[1]*top*] **:** a rotary motion imparted to a ball that causes it to rotate forward in the direction of its flight
top·stitch \'täp-ˌstich\ *vt* **:** to make a line of stitching on the outside of (a garment) close to a seam

top·sy–tur·vi·ness \ˌtäp-sē-ˈtər-vē-nəs\ *n* **:** the quality or state of being topsy-turvy

1**top·sy–tur·vy** \ˌtäp-sē-ˈtər-vē\ *adv* [prob. deriv. of *tops* (pl. of 1*top*) + obs. E *terve* (to turn upside down)] **1 :** with the top or head downward **:** upside down **2 :** in utter confusion or disorder

2**topsy–turvy** *adj* **:** turned topsy-turvy **:** totally disordered — **top·sy–tur·vi·ly** \-ˈtər-və-lē\ *adv* — **top·sy–tur·vy·dom** \-vēd-əm\ *n*

3**topsy–turvy** *n* **:** TOPSY-TURVINESS

top·work \ˈtäp-ˌwərk\ *vt* **:** to graft scions of another variety on the main branches of (as fruit trees) usu. to obtain more desirable fruit

toque \ˈtōk\ *n* [MF, soft hat with a narrow brim worn esp. in the 16th cent., fr. OSp *toca* headdress] **1 :** a woman's small hat without a brim made in any of various soft close-fitting shapes **2 :** TUQUE

tor \ˈtȯ(ə)r\ *n* [ME, fr. OE *torr*] **:** a high craggy hill

To·rah \ˈtōr-ə, ˈtȯr-; ˈtȯi-rə\ *n* [Heb *tōrāh*] **1 :** LAW 2b **2 :** the body of wisdom and law contained in Jewish Scripture and other sacred literature and oral tradition **3 :** a leather or parchment scroll of the Pentateuch used in a synagogue for liturgical purposes

1**torch** \ˈtȯ(ə)rch\ *n, often attrib* [ME *torche*, fr. OF, bundle of twisted straw or tow, torch, fr. (assumed) VL *torca;* akin to L *torquēre* to twist — more at TORTURE] **1 :** a burning stick of resinous wood or twist of tow used to give light and usu. carried in the hand **:** FLAMBEAU **2 :** something (as wisdom or knowledge) likened to a torch as giving light or guidance **3 :** any of various portable devices for emitting an unusually hot flame —compare BLOWTORCH **4** *chiefly Brit* **:** FLASHLIGHT

2**torch** *vt* **:** to set fire to with or as if with a torch

torch·bear·er \-ˌbar-ər, -ˌber-\ *n* **1 :** one that carries a torch **2 :** someone in the forefront of a campaign, crusade, or movement

torch·light \-ˌlīt\ *n* **1 :** light given by torches **2 :** TORCH

tor·chon \ˈtȯr-ˌshän\ *n* [F, duster, fr. OF, bundle of twisted straw, fr. *torche*] **:** a coarse bobbin or machine-made lace made with fan-shaped designs forming a scalloped edge

torch singer *n* **:** a singer of torch songs

torch song *n* **:** a popular sentimental song of unrequited love

torch·wood \ˈtȯrch-ˌwu̇d\ *n* **1 :** a notably resinous or oily wood suitable for torches **2 a :** any of a genus (*Amyris*) usu. placed in the rue family of tropical American trees and shrubs with hard heavy fragrant resinous streaky yellowish brown wood **b :** the wood of a torchwood

tore *past of* TEAR

to·re·ador \ˈtȯr-ē-ə-ˌdȯ(ə)r, ˈtōr-, ˈtär-\ *n* [Sp, fr. *toreado*, pp. of *torear* to fight bulls, fr. *toro* bull, fr. L *taurus* — more at TAURINE] **:** TORERO, BULLFIGHTER

to·re·ro \tə-ˈre(ə)r-(ˌ)ō\ *n, pl* **-ros** [Sp, fr. LL *taurarius*, fr. L *taurus* bull] **:** a matador or a member of his cuadrilla

to·reu·tics \tə-ˈrüt-iks\ *n pl but sing in constr* [*toreutic*, adj., fr. Gk *toreutikos*, fr. *toreuein* to bore through, chase, fr. *toreus* boring tool; akin to Gk *tetrainein* to bore — more at THROW] **:** the art or process of working in metal esp. by embossing or chasing — **to·reu·tic** \-ˈrüt-ik\ *adj*

tori *pl of* TORUS

to·ric \ˈtōr-ik, ˈtȯr-\ *adj* **:** of, relating to, or shaped like a torus or segment of a torus

to·rii \ˈtōr-ē-ˌē, ˈtȯr-\ *n, pl* **torii** [Jap] **:** a Japanese gateway of light construction commonly built at the approach to a Shinto shrine

torii

1**tor·ment** \ˈtȯr-ˌment\ *n* [ME, fr. OF, fr. L *tormentum* torture, fr. *torquēre* to twist — more at TORTURE] **1 :** the infliction of torture (as by rack or wheel) **2 :** extreme pain or anguish of body or mind **:** AGONY **3 :** a source of vexation or pain

2**tor·ment** \tȯr-ˈment, ˈtȯr-ˌ\ *vt* **1 :** to cause severe usu. persistent or recurrent distress of body or mind to <cattle ~*ed* by flies> **2 :** DISTORT, TWIST ***syn*** see AFFLICT

tor·men·til \ˈtȯr-mən-ˌtil\ *n* [ME *tur-mentill*, fr. ML *tormentilla*, fr. L *tormentum;* fr. its use in allaying pain] **:** a yellow-flowered Eurasian potentilla (*Potentilla tormentilla*) with a root used in tanning and dyeing

tor·men·tor *also* **tor·ment·er** \tȯr-ˈment-ər, ˈtȯr-ˌ\ *n* **1 :** one that torments **2 :** a fixed curtain or flat on each side of a theater stage that prevents the audience from seeing into the wings **3 :** a covered screen used to prevent echo during the filming of motion-picture scenes

torn *past part of* TEAR

tor·na·dic \tȯr-ˈnād-ik, -ˈnad-\ *adj* **:** relating to, characteristic of, or constituting a tornado

tor·na·do \tȯr-ˈnād-(ˌ)ō\ *n, pl* **-does** *or* **-dos** [modif. of Sp *tronada* thunderstorm, fr. *tronar* to thunder, fr. L *tonare* — more at THUNDER] **1** *archaic* **:** a tropical thunderstorm **2 a :** a squall accompanying a thunderstorm in Africa **b :** a violent destructive whirling wind accompanied by a funnel-shaped cloud that progresses in a narrow path over the land **3 :** a violent or destructive windstorm **:** WHIRLWIND

tor·nil·lo \tȯr-ˈnē-(ˌ)(y)ō, -ˈnil-(ˌ)ō\ *n, pl* **-los** [Sp, lit., small lathe, screw, dim. of *torno* lathe, fr. L *tornus* — more at TURN] **:** SCREW BEAN 1

to·roid \ˈtō(ə)r-ˌȯid, ˈtȯ(ə)r-\ *n* [NL *torus*] **1 :** a surface generated by a plane closed curve rotated about a line that lies in the same plane as the curve but does not intersect it **2 :** a body whose surface has the form of a toroid

to·roi·dal \tō-ˈrȯid-ᵊl\ *adj* **:** of, relating to, or shaped like a torus or toroid **:** doughnut-shaped <a ~ resistance coil> — **to·roi·dal·ly** \-ᵊl-ē\ *adv*

1**tor·pe·do** \tȯr-ˈpēd-(ˌ)ō\ *n, pl* **-does** [L, lit., stiffness, numbness, fr. *torpēre* to be stiff or numb] **1 :** ELECTRIC RAY **2 :** an engine or machine for destroying ships by blowing them up: as **a :** a submarine mine **b :** a dirigible self-propelling cigar-shaped submarine projectile filled with an explosive charge **3 a :** a charge of explosive enclosed in a container or case **b :** a small firework that explodes when thrown against a hard object **4 :** a professional gunman or assassin **5 :** SUBMARINE 2

2**torpedo** *vt* **tor·pe·doed; tor·pe·do·ing** \-ˈpēd-ə-wiŋ\ **1 :** to hit or sink (a ship) with a naval torpedo **:** strike or destroy by torpedo **2 :** to destroy or nullify altogether **:** WRECK <~ a plan>

torpedo boat *n* **:** a boat designed for firing torpedoes; *specif* **:** a small very fast thinly plated boat with one or more torpedo tubes

torpedo–boat destroyer *n* **:** a large, swift, and powerfully armed torpedo boat orig. intended principally for the destruction of torpedo boats but later used also as a formidable torpedo boat

torpedo bomber *n* **:** a military airplane designed to carry torpedoes

torpedo plane *n* **:** TORPEDO BOMBER

tor·pid \ˈtȯr-pəd\ *adj* [L *torpidus*, fr. *torpēre* to be stiff or numb; akin to L *stirps* trunk, stock, lineage, OE *starian* to stare — more at STARE] **1 a :** having lost motion or the power of exertion or feeling **:** DORMANT, NUMB **b :** sluggish in functioning or acting <a ~ frog> <a ~ mind> **2 :** lacking in energy or vigor **:** APATHETIC, DULL ***syn*** see LETHARGIC — **tor·pid·i·ty** \tȯr-ˈpid-ət-ē\ *n* — **tor·pid·ly** \ˈtȯr-pəd-lē\ *adv*

tor·por \ˈtȯr-pər\ *n* [L, fr. *torpēre*] **1 :** a state of mental and motor inactivity with partial or total insensibility **:** extreme sluggishness or stagnation of function **2 :** APATHY, DULLNESS

1**torque** \ˈtȯ(ə)rk\ *n* [F, fr. L *torques*, fr. *torquēre* to twist — more at TORTURE] **:** a usu. metal collar or neck chain worn by the ancient Gauls, Germans, and Britons

2**torque** *n* [L *torquēre* to twist] **1 :** a force that produces or tends to produce rotation or torsion <an automobile engine delivers ~ to the drive shaft>; *also* **:** a measure of the effectiveness of such a force that consists of the product of the force and the perpendicular distance from the line of action of the force to the axis of rotation **2 :** a turning or twisting force

3**torque** *vt* **torqued; torqu·ing :** to impart torque to **:** cause to twist (as about an axis) — **torqu·er** *n*

torque converter *n* **:** a device for transmitting and amplifying torque esp. by hydraulic means

torr \ˈtȯ(ə)r\ *n, pl* **torr** [Evangelista *Torricelli*] **:** a unit of pressure equal to $\frac{1}{760}$ of an atmosphere

1**tor·rent** \ˈtȯr-ənt, ˈtär-\ *n* [F, fr. L *torrent-*, *torrens*, fr. *torrent-*, *torrens* burning, seething, rushing, fr. prp. of *torrēre* to parch, burn — more at THIRST] **1 :** a violent stream of a liquid (as water or lava) **2 :** a channel of a mountain stream **3 :** a raging flood **:** a tumultuous outpouring **:** FLUX, RUSH

2**torrent** *adj* **:** TORRENTIAL

tor·ren·tial \tȯ-ˈren-chəl, tə-\ *adj* **1 a :** relating to or having the character of a torrent <~ rains> **b :** caused by or resulting from action of rapid streams <~ gravel> **2 :** resembling a torrent in violence or rapidity of flow — **tor·ren·tial·ly** \-ˈrench-(ə-)lē\ *adv*

tor·rid \ˈtȯr-əd, ˈtär-\ *adj* [L *torridus*, fr. *torrēre*] **1 a :** parched with heat esp. of the sun **:** HOT <~ sands> **b :** giving off intense heat **:** SCORCHING **2 :** ARDENT, PASSIONATE <~ love letters> — **tor·rid·i·ty** \tȯ-ˈrid-ət-ē\ *n* — **tor·rid·ly** \ˈtȯr-əd-lē, ˈtär-\ *adv* — **tor·rid·ness** *n*

torrid zone *n* **:** the belt of the earth between the tropics over which the sun is vertical at some period of the year

tor·sade \tȯr-ˈsäd, -ˈsād\ *n* [F, fr. obs. F *tors* twisted, fr. LL *torsus*] **:** a twisted cord or ribbon used esp. as a hat ornament

tor·sion \ˈtȯr-shən\ *n* [LL *torsus*, pp. of L *torquēre* to twist] **1 :** the twisting or wrenching of a body by the exertion of forces tending to turn one end or part about a longitudinal axis while the other is held fast or turned in the opposite direction; *also* **:** the state of being twisted **2 :** the reactive torque that an elastic solid exerts by reason of being under torsion **3 :** the twisting of a bodily organ on its own axis — **tor·sion·al** \ˈtȯr-shnəl, -shən-ᵊl\ *adj* — **tor·sion·al·ly** \-ē\ *adv*

torsion balance *n* **:** an instrument used to measure minute forces (as electrostatic or magnetic attraction and repulsion) by the torsion of a wire or filament

torsion bar *n* **:** a long metal element in an automobile suspension that has one end held rigidly to the frame end and the other twisted and connected to the axle and that acts as a spring

tor·so \ˈtȯr-(ˌ)sō\ *n, pl* **torsos** *or* **tor·si** \ˈtȯr-ˌsē\ [It, lit., stalk, fr. L *thyrsus* stalk, thyrsus] **1 :** the trunk of a sculptured representation of a human body; *esp* **:** the trunk of a statue whose head and limbs are mutilated **2 :** something (as a piece of writing) that is mutilated or left unfinished **3 :** the human trunk

tort \ˈtȯ(ə)rt\ *n* [ME, fr. MF, fr. ML *tortum*, fr. L, neut. of *tortus* twisted, fr. pp. of *torquēre*] **:** a wrongful act for which a civil action will lie except one involving a breach of contract

torte \ˈtȯrt-ə, ˈtȯ(ə)rt\ *n, pl* **tor·ten** \ˈtȯrt-ᵊn\ *or* **tortes** [G, prob. fr. It *torta*, fr. LL, round loaf of bread] **:** a cake made of many eggs and often grated nuts or dry bread crumbs and usu. covered with a rich frosting

tor·tel·li·ni \ˌtȯrt-ᵊl-ˈē-nē\ *n* [It] **:** pasta cut in rounds, filled, and boiled

tor·ti·col·lis \ˌtȯrt-ə-ˈkäl-əs\ *n* [NL, fr. L *tortus* twisted + *-i-* + *collum* neck — more at COLLAR] **:** a more-or-less fixed twisting of the neck resulting in an abnormal carriage of the head — called also *wryneck*

tor·ti·lla \tȯr-ˈtē-(y)ə\ *n* [AmerSp, dim. of Sp *torta* cake, fr. LL, round loaf of bread] **:** a round thin cake of unleavened cornmeal bread usu. eaten hot with a topping or filling of ground meat or cheese

tor·tious \ˈtȯr-shəs\ *adj* **:** implying or involving tort — **tor·tious·ly** *adv*

tor·toise \ˈtȯrt-əs\ *n* [ME *tortu*, *tortuce*, fr. MF *tortue* — more at TURTLE] **1 :** any of an order (Testudinata) of reptiles that have a trunk more or less enclosed in a shell of bony dermal plates usu. covered externally with horny shields and jaws that are toothless and sheathed : TURTLE; *esp* : a land turtle **2** : someone or something regarded as slow or laggard

tortoise beetle *n* : any of a family (Chrysomelidae) of small tortoise-shaped beetles with larvae that feed on leaves

[1]**tor·toise·shell** \ˈtȯrt-ə-ˌshel, -əs(h)-ˌshel\ *n* **1** : the mottled horny substance of the shell of some turtles (as the hawksbill turtle) used in inlaying and in making various ornamental articles **2** : any of several showy nymphalid butterflies (genus *Nymphalis*)

[2]**tortoiseshell** *adj* : made of or resembling tortoiseshell esp. in spotted brown and yellow coloring

tor·to·ni \tȯr-ˈtō-nē\ *n* [prob. fr. *Tortoni,* 19th cent. It restaurateur in Paris] : ice cream made of heavy cream often with minced almonds and chopped maraschino cherries and often flavored with rum

tor·tri·cid \ˈtȯr-trə-səd\ *n* [NL *Tortricidae,* group name, fr. *Tortric-, Tortrix*] : any of a family (Tortricidae) of small stout-bodied moths many of whose larvae feed in fruits — **tortricid** *adj*

tor·trix \ˈtȯr-ˌtriks\ *n* [NL *Tortric-, Tortrix,* genus of moths, fr. L *tortus,* pp. of *torquēre* to twist; fr. the habit of twisting or rolling leaves to make a nest] : a tortricid moth

tor·tu·os·i·ty \ˌtȯr-chə-ˈwäs-ət-ē\ *n, pl* **-ties 1** : the quality or state of being tortuous **2** : something winding or twisted : BEND

tor·tu·ous \ˈtȯrch-(ə-)wəs\ *adj* [ME, fr. MF *tortueux,* fr. L *tortuosus,* fr. *tortus* twist, fr. *tortus,* pp. of *torquēre*] **1** : marked by repeated twists, bends, or turns : WINDING **2 a** : marked by devious or indirect tactics : CROOKED, TRICKY **b** : CIRCUITOUS, INVOLVED — **tor·tu·ous·ly** *adv* — **tor·tu·ous·ness** *n*

[1]**tor·ture** \ˈtȯr-chər\ *n* [F, fr. LL *tortura,* fr. L *tortus,* pp. of *torquēre* to twist; akin to OHG *drāhsil* turner, Gk *atraktos* spindle] **1** : the infliction of intense pain (as from burning, crushing, or wounding) to punish, coerce, or afford sadistic pleasure **2 a** : anguish of body or mind : AGONY **b** : something that causes agony or pain **3** : distortion or overrefinement of a meaning or an argument : STRAINING

[2]**torture** *vt* **tor·tured; tor·tur·ing** \ˈtȯrch-(ə-)riŋ\ **1** : to punish or coerce by inflicting excruciating pain **2** : to cause intense suffering to : TORMENT **3** : to twist or wrench out of shape : DISTORT, WARP *syn* see AFFLICT — **tor·tur·er** \ˈtȯr-chər-ər\ *n*

tor·tur·ous \ˈtȯrch-(ə-)rəs\ *adj* : causing torture : cruelly painful — **tor·tur·ous·ly** *adv*

tor·u·la \ˈtȯr-(y)ə-lə, ˈtär-\ *n, pl* **-lae** \-ˌlē, -ˌlī\ *also* **-las** [NL, fr. L *torus* protuberance] : any of various fungi and esp. yeasts that lack sexual spores, do not produce alcoholic fermentations, and are typically acid formers

to·rus \ˈtōr-əs, ˈtȯr-\ *n, pl* **to·ri** \ˈtō(ə)r-ˌī, ˈtȯ(ə)r-, -ˌē\ [NL, fr. L, protuberance, bulge, torus molding] **1** : a smooth rounded anatomical protuberance **2** : a large molding of convex profile commonly occurring as the lowest molding in the base of a column — see BASE illustration, MOLDING illustration **3 a** : RECEPTACLE 2b **b** : the thickening of a membrane closing a wood-cell pit (as of gymnosperm tracheids) having the secondary cell wall arched over the pit cavity **4** : a doughnut-shaped surface generated by a circle rotated about an axis in its plane that does not intersect the circle; *broadly* : TOROID

To·ry \ˈtōr-ē, ˈtȯr-\ *n, pl* **Tories** [IrGael *tōraidhe* pursued man, robber, fr. MIr *tōir* pursuit] **1** : an Irish papist or royalist outlaw chiefly of the 17th century **2** *obs* : BANDIT, OUTLAW **3 a** : a member or supporter of a major British political group of the 18th and early 19th centuries favoring at first the Stuarts and later royal authority and the established church and seeking to preserve the traditional political structure and defeat parliamentary reform — compare WHIG **b** : CONSERVATIVE 1b **4** : an American upholding the cause of the British Crown against the supporters of colonial independence during the American Revolution : LOYALIST **5** *often not cap* : an extreme conservative esp. in political and economic principles — **Tory** *adj*

Tory Democracy *n* : a political philosophy advocating preservation of established institutions and traditional principles combined with political democracy and a social and economic program designed to benefit the common man

To·ry·ism \ˈtōr-ē-ˌiz-əm, ˈtȯr-\ *n* **1** : the principles and practices of or associated with Tories **2** : the British Tory party or its members

tory–rory *adj* [origin unknown] *obs* : UPROARIOUS, ROISTERING

tosh \ˈtäsh\ *n* [origin unknown] : sheer nonsense : BOSH, TWADDLE

[1]**toss** \ˈtȯs, ˈtäs\ *vb* [prob. of Scand origin; akin to Sw dial. *tossa* to spread, scatter] *vt* **1 a** : to fling or heave continuously about, to and fro, or up and down <a ship ~*ed* by waves> **b** : BANDY 2c **c** : to mix lightly until well coated with a dressing <~ a salad> **2** : to make uneasy : stir up : DISTURB **3 a** : to throw with a quick, light, or careless motion or with a sudden jerk <~ a ball around> **b** : to throw up in the air <~*ed* by a bull> **c** : [2]MATCH 5a **4 a** : to fling or lift with a sudden motion <~*es* her head angrily> **b** : to tilt suddenly so as to empty by drinking <~*ed* his glass> **5** : to accomplish, provide, or dispose of readily or easily <~ off a few verses> ~ *vi* **1 a** : to move restlessly or turbulently; *esp* : to twist and turn repeatedly <~*ed* sleeplessly all night> **b** : to move with a quick or spirited gesture **2** : to decide an issue by flipping a coin *syn* see THROW — **toss·er** *n*

[2]**toss** *n* **1** : the state or fact of being tossed **2** : an act or instance of tossing: as **a** : an abrupt tilting or upward fling **b** : a deciding by chance and esp. by flipping a coin **c** : THROW, PITCH

toss·pot \-ˌpät\ *n* : DRUNKARD, SOT

toss–up \-ˌəp\ *n* **1** : TOSS 2b **2** : an even chance

[1]**tot** \ˈtät\ *n* [origin unknown] **1** : a small child : TODDLER **2** : a small drink or allowance of liquor : SHOT

[2]**tot** *vb* **tot·ted; tot·ting** [*tot.,* abbr. of *total*] *vt* : to add together : TOTAL — usu. used with *up* <~*s* up the score> ~ *vi* : ADD

[3]**tot** *abbr* total

TOT *abbr* time on target

[1]**to·tal** \ˈtōt-ᵊl\ *adj* [ME, fr. MF, fr. ML *totalis,* fr. L *totus* whole, entire] **1** : comprising or constituting a whole : ENTIRE <the ~ amount> **2** : COMPLETE, UTTER <a ~ failure> **3** : concentrating all available personnel and resources on a single objective

[2]**total** *n* **1** : a product of addition : SUM **2** : an entire quantity : AMOUNT

[3]**total** *adv* : TOTALLY

[4]**total** *vt* **to·taled** *or* **to·talled; to·tal·ing** *or* **to·tal·ling 1** : to add up : COMPUTE **2** : to amount to : NUMBER **3** : to make a total wreck of (a car) : DEMOLISH

total depravity *n* : a state of corruption due to original sin held in Calvinism to infect every part of man's nature and to make the natural man unable to know or obey God

total eclipse *n* : an eclipse in which one celestial body is completely obscured by the shadow or body of another

to·tal·ism \ˈtōt-ᵊl-ˌiz-əm\ *n* : TOTALITARIANISM — **to·tal·is·tic** \ˌtōt-ᵊl-ˈis-tik\ *adj*

[1]**to·tal·i·tar·i·an** \(ˌ)tō-ˌtal-ə-ˈter-ē-ən\ *adj* [*total* + *-itarian* (as in *authoritarian*)] **1 a** : of or relating to centralized control by an autocratic leader or hierarchy : AUTHORITARIAN, DICTATORIAL; *esp* : DESPOTIC **b** : of or relating to a political regime based on subordination of the individual to the state and strict control of all aspects of the life and productive capacity of the nation esp. by coercive measures (as censorship and terrorism) **2 a** : advocating or characteristic of totalitarianism **b** : completely regulated by the state esp. as an aid to national mobilization in an emergency **c** : exercising autocratic powers : tending toward monopoly

[2]**totalitarian** *n* : an advocate or practitioner of totalitarianism

to·tal·i·tar·i·an·ism \(ˌ)tō-ˌtal-ə-ˈter-ē-ə-ˌniz-əm\ *n* **1** : centralized control by an autocratic authority **2** : the political concept that the citizen should be totally subject to an absolute state authority

to·tal·i·tar·i·an·ize \-ˌnīz\ *vt* **-ized; -iz·ing** : to make totalitarian <a society *totalitarianized* by the military-industrial complex —W. F. Buckley *b*1925>

to·tal·i·ty \tō-ˈtal-ət-ē\ *n, pl* **-ties 1** : an aggregate amount : SUM, WHOLE **2 a** : the quality or state of being total : WHOLENESS **b** : a period (as during an eclipse) during which totality exists

to·tal·iza·tor *or* **to·tal·isa·tor** \ˈtōt-ᵊl-ə-ˌzāt-ər\ *n* : a pari-mutuel machine

to·tal·ize \ˈtōt-ᵊl-ˌīz\ *vt* **-ized; -iz·ing 1** : to add up : TOTAL **2** : to express as a whole : SUMMARIZE

to·tal·iz·er \-ˌī-zər\ *n* : one that totalizes: as **a** : a pari-mutuel machine **b** : a device (as a meter) that records a remaining total (as of fuel)

to·tal·ly \ˈtōt-ᵊl-ē\ *adv* **1** : in a total manner : WHOLLY **2** : as a whole : in toto

total recall *n* : the faculty of remembering with complete clarity and in complete detail

total utility *n* : the degree of utility of an economic good (as an article or service) considered as a whole

to·ta·quine \ˈtōt-ə-ˌkwīn, -ˌk(w)ēn, -k(w)ən\ *or* **to·ta·qui·na** \ˌtōt-ə-ˈkwī-nə, -ˈk(w)ē-\ *n* [NL *totaquina,* fr. ML *totalis* total + Sp *quina* cinchona; fr. its containing all the alkaloids of cinchona bark — more at QUININE] : an antimalarial drug containing alkaloids and esp. quinine extracted from American cinchona bark

[1]**tote** \ˈtōt\ *vt* **toted; tot·ing** [origin unknown] **1** : to carry by hand : bear on the person : LUG, PACK **2** : HAUL, CONVEY

[2]**tote** *n* **1** : BURDEN, LOAD **2** : a large handbag — called also *tote bag*

[3]**tote** *vt* **toted; tot·ing** [E dial. *tote,* n. (total)] : ADD, TOTAL — usu. used with *up* <*toted* up his accomplishments —G. P. Morrill>

[4]**tote** *n* [short for *totalizator*] : a pari-mutuel machine

to·tem \ˈtōt-əm\ *n* [Ojibwa *ototeman* his totem] **1 a** : an object (as an animal or plant) serving as the emblem of a family or clan and often as a reminder of its ancestry; *also* : a usu. carved or painted representation of such an object **b** : a family or clan identified by a common totemic object **2** : something that serves as an emblem or revered symbol

to·tem·ic \tō-ˈtem-ik\ *adj* **1** : of, relating to, or characteristic of a totem or totemism <a ~ animal> **2** : based on or practicing totemism <~ clan structure> — **to·tem·i·cal·ly** \-i-k(ə-)lē\ *adv*

to·tem·ism \ˈtōt-ə-ˌmiz-əm\ *n* **1** : belief in kinship with or a mystical relationship between a group or an individual and a totem **2** : a system of social organization based on totemic affiliations

to·tem·ist \-məst\ *n* : a practitioner of or specialist in totemism

to·tem·is·tic \ˌtōt-ə-ˈmis-tik\ *adj* : of or relating to totemists or totemism : TOTEMIC

to·tem·ite \ˈtōt-ə-ˌmīt\ *n* : TOTEMIST

totem pole *n* **1** : a pole or pillar carved and painted with a series of totemic symbols representing family lineage and often mythical or historical incidents and erected before the houses of Indian tribes of the northwest coast of No. America **2** : an order of rank : HIERARCHY

tot·er \ˈtōt-ər\ *n* : one that totes

toth·er *or* **t'oth·er** \ˈtəth-ər\ *pron or adj* [ME *tother,* alter. (resulting from incorrect division of *thet other* the other, fr. *thet* the — fr. OE *thæt* — + *other*) of *other* — more at THAT] *chiefly dial* : the other

toti- *comb form* [L *totus* whole, entire] : whole : wholly <*toti*potent>

to·ti·po·ten·cy \tō-ˈtip-ət-ən-sē, ˌtōt-ə-ˈpōt-ᵊn-\ *n* : ability to generate or regenerate a whole organism from a part

to·ti·po·tent \-ənt, -ᵊnt\ *adj* : capable of development along any of the lines inherently possible to its kind <~ blastomeres each capable of developing into a complete embryo>

[1]**tot·ter** \ˈtät-ər\ *vi* [ME *toteren*] **1 a** : to tremble or rock as if about to fall : SWAY **b** : to become unstable : threaten to collapse **2** : to move unsteadily : STAGGER, WOBBLE

[2]**totter** *n* : an unsteady gait : WOBBLE

ə abut ᵊ kitten ər further a back ā bake ä cot, cart
au̇ out ch chin e less ē easy g gift i trip ī life
j joke ŋ sing ō flow ȯ flaw ȯi coin th thin t͟h this
ü loot u̇ foot y yet yü few yu̇ furious zh vision

tot·ter·ing *adj* **1 a :** being in an unstable condition <a ~ building> **b :** walking unsteadily **2 :** lacking firmness or stability : INSECURE <a ~ regime> — **tot·ter·ing·ly** \-ə-riŋ-lē\ *adv*

tot·tery \'tät-ə-rē\ *adj* **:** of an infirm or precarious nature

Toua·reg *var of* TUAREG

tou·can \'tü-ˌkan, -ˌkän, tü-'\ *n* [F, fr. Pg *tucano,* fr. Tupi] **:** any of a family (Ramphastidae) of fruit-eating birds of tropical America with brilliant coloring and a very large but light and thin-walled beak

toucan

[1]**touch** \'təch\ *vb* [ME *touchen,* fr. OF *tuchier,* fr. (assumed) VL *toccare* to knock, strike a bell, touch, of imit. origin] *vt* **1 :** to bring a bodily part into contact with esp. so as to perceive through the tactile sense : handle or feel gently usu. with the intent to understand or appreciate <loved to ~ the soft silk> **2 :** to strike or push lightly esp. with the hand or foot or an implement **3 :** to lay hands upon (one afflicted with scrofula) with intent to heal — compare KING'S EVIL **4** *archaic* **a :** to play on (a stringed instrument) **b :** to perform (a melody) by playing or singing **5 a :** to take into the hands or mouth <never ~*es* alcohol> **b :** to put hands upon in any way or degree <don't ~ anything before the police come>; *esp* **:** to commit violence upon <swears he never ~*ed* the child> **6 :** to concern oneself with **7 :** to induce to give or lend <~*ed* him for ten dollars> **8 :** to cause to be briefly in contact or conjunction with something <~*ed* his spurs to his horse> <~ a match to the wick> **9 a (1) :** to meet without overlapping or penetrating : ADJOIN **(2) :** to get to : REACH <the speedometer needle ~*ed* 80> **b :** to be tangent to **c :** to rival in quality or value <nothing can ~ that cloth for durability> **10 :** to speak or tell of esp. in passing <barely ~*ed* on the incident in his speech> **11 :** to affect the interest of : CONCERN **12 a :** to leave a mark or impression on <few reagents will ~ gold> **b :** to harm slightly by or as if by contact : TAINT, BLEMISH <fruit ~*ed* by frost> <a horse ~*ed* in the wind> **c :** to give a delicate tint, line, or expression to <a smile ~*ed* her lips> **13 :** to draw or delineate with light strokes **14 a :** to hurt the feelings of : WOUND **b :** to move to sympathetic feeling <~*ed* by the loyalty of his friends> ~ *vi* **1 a :** to feel something with a body part (as the hand or foot) **b :** to lay hand or finger on a person to cure disease (as scrofula) **2 :** to be in contact **3 :** to come close : VERGE <his actions ~ on treason> **4 :** to have a bearing : RELATE — used with *on* or *upon* **5 a :** to make a brief or incidental stop on shore during a trip by water <~*ed* at several ports> **b :** to treat a topic in a brief or casual manner — used with *on* or *upon* <~*ed* upon many points> — **touch·able** \-ə-bəl\ *adj* — **touch·er** *n*

***syn* 1** TOUCH, FEEL, PALPATE, HANDLE, PAW *shared meaning element* **:** to probe with a sensitive part of the body (as the fingers) so as to get or produce a sensation often in examination or exploration
2 see AFFECT
3 see MATCH

[2]**touch** *n* **1 :** a light stroke, tap, or push **2 :** the act or fact of touching **3 :** the special sense by which pressure or traction exerted on the skin or mucous membrane is perceived **4 :** mental or moral sensitiveness, responsiveness, or tact <has a wonderful ~ in dealing with children> **5 :** a specified sensation conveyed through the tactile receptors : FEEL <the velvety ~ of a fabric> **6 a :** the act of rubbing gold or silver on a touchstone to test its quality **b :** TEST, TRIAL — used chiefly in the phrase *put to the touch* **7 a :** a visible effect : MARK <a ~ of the tropical sun> **b :** WEAKNESS, DEFECT **8 :** something slight of its kind: as **a :** a light attack <a ~ of fever> **b :** a small quantity : TRACE <a ~ of spring in the air> **c :** a transient emotion <a momentary ~ of compunction> **d :** a near approach : a close call <beaten in the championships by a mere ~> **e :** BIT, LITTLE — used adverbially with *a* <aimed a ~ too low and missed> **9 a** *archaic* **:** the playing of an instrument (as a lute or piano) with the fingers; *also* **:** musical notes or strains so produced **b :** a manner or method of touching or striking esp. the keys of a keyboard instrument **c :** particular action of a keyboard instrument with reference to the resistance of its keys to pressure <piano with a stiff ~> **10 :** a set of changes in change ringing that is less than a peal **11 :** an effective and subtle detail in creating or improving an artistic composition <applies the finishing ~*es* to his story> **12 :** distinctive manner or method <the ~ of a master> **13 :** a characteristic or distinguishing trait or quality <this room needs a woman's ~> **14** *slang* **:** an act of soliciting or getting a gift or loan **15 :** the state or fact of being in contact or communication <lost ~ with her cousin> <let's keep in ~> <out of ~ with modern times> **16 :** the area outside of the touchlines in soccer or outside of and including the touchlines in rugby

touch and go *n* **1 :** rapid movement from point to point **2 :** a highly uncertain or precarious situation

touch·back \'təch-ˌbak\ *n* **:** a situation in football in which the ball is down behind the goal line after a kick or intercepted forward pass after which it is put in play by the team defending the goal on its own 20-yard line — compare SAFETY

touch·down \'təch-ˌdau̇n\ *n* **1 :** the act of touching a football to the ground behind an opponent's goal; *specif* **:** the act of scoring six points in American football by being lawfully in possession of the ball on, above, or behind an opponent's goal line when the ball is declared dead **2 :** the act or moment of touching down (as with an airplane or spacecraft)

touch down \(')təch-'dau̇n\ *vt* **:** to place (the ball in rugby) by hand on the ground on or over an opponent's goal line in scoring a try or behind one's own goal line as a defensive measure ~ *vi* **:** to reach the ground : LAND

tou·ché \tü-'shā\ *interj* [F, fr. pp. of *toucher* to touch, fr. OF *tuchier*] — used to acknowledge a hit in fencing or the success of an argument, an accusation, or a witty point

touched \'təcht\ *adj* **1 :** emotionally stirred (as with gratitude) **2 :** slightly unbalanced mentally

touch football *n* **:** football played informally and chiefly characterized by the substitution of touching for tackling

touch·hole \'təch-ˌhōl\ *n* **:** the vent in old-time cannons or firearms through which the charge was ignited

[1]**touch·ing** *prep* **:** in reference to : CONCERNING

[2]**touching** *adj* **:** capable of arousing emotions of tenderness or compassion ***syn*** see MOVING — **touch·ing·ly** \-iŋ-lē\ *adv*

touch·line \'təch-ˌlīn\ *n* **:** either of the lines that bound the sides of the field of play in rugby and soccer

touch·mark \-ˌmärk\ *n* **:** an identifying maker's mark impressed on pewter

touch–me–not \'təch-mē-ˌnät\ *n* [fr. the bursting of the ripe pods and scattering of their seeds when touched] **1 :** IMPATIENS **2 :** a haughty, aloof, or prudish person; *esp* **:** a girl or woman inclined to be distant or cold

touch off *vt* **1 :** to describe or characterize with precision **2 a :** to cause to explode by or as if by touching with fire **b :** to release or initiate with sudden intensity <the charges *touched off* a storm of protest —R. A. Billington>

touch·stone \'təch-ˌstōn\ *n* **1 :** a black siliceous stone related to flint and formerly used to test the purity of gold and silver by the streak left on the stone when rubbed by the metal **2 :** a test or criterion for determining the quality or genuineness of a thing ***syn*** see STANDARD

touch system *n* **:** a method of typewriting that assigns a particular finger to each key and makes it possible to type without looking at the keyboard

touch–type \'təch-ˌtīp\ *vi* **:** to type by the touch system

touch–up \'təch-ˌəp\ *n* **:** an act or instance of touching up

touch up \(')təch-'əp\ *vt* **1 :** to improve or perfect by small additional strokes or alterations : make good the minor and usu. visible defects or damages of **2 :** to stimulate by or as if by a flick of a whip

touch·wood \'təch-ˌwu̇d\ *n* **:** [3]PUNK

touchy \'təch-ē\ *adj* **touch·i·er; -est 1 :** marked by readiness to take offense on slight provocation **2 a** *of a body part* **:** acutely sensitive or irritable **b** *of a chemical* **:** highly explosive or inflammable **3 :** calling for tact, care, or caution in treatment <a ~ subject among the members of his family> ***syn*** see IRASCIBLE ***ant*** imperturbable — **touch·i·ly** \'təch-ə-lē\ *adv* — **touch·i·ness** \'təch-ē-nəs\ *n*

[1]**tough** \'təf\ *adj* [ME, fr. OE *tōh;* akin to OHG *zāhi* tough] **1 a :** strong or firm in texture but flexible and not brittle **b :** not easily chewed **2 :** GLUTINOUS, STICKY **3 :** characterized by severity or uncompromising determination <a ~ and inflexible foreign policy —*New Statesman & Nation*> **4 :** capable of enduring strain, hardship, or severe labor **5 :** very hard to influence : STUBBORN **6 :** extremely difficult to cope with <a ~ question to answer> **7 :** stubbornly fought <a ~ contest> **8 :** UNRULY, ROWDYISH **9 :** marked by absence of softness or sentimentality **10** *slang* **:** EXCELLENT, GREAT ***syn*** see STRONG ***ant*** fragile — **tough·ly** *adv* — **tough·ness** *n*

[2]**tough** *n* **:** a tough person; *esp* **:** ROWDY

[3]**tough** *adv* **:** in a tough manner <talks ~ and insensitively —A. E. Stevenson †1965>

tough·en \'təf-ən\ *vb* **tough·ened; tough·en·ing** \-(ə-)niŋ\ *vt* **:** to make tough ~ *vi* **:** to become tough

tough·ie *also* **toughy** \'təf-ē\ *n, pl* **tough·ies :** one that is tough: as **a :** a loud rough rowdy person **b :** a difficult problem

tough–mind·ed \'təf-'mīn-dəd\ *adj* **:** realistic or unsentimental in temper or habitual point of view — **tough–mind·ed·ness** *n*

tou·pee \tü-'pā\ *n* [F *toupet* forelock, fr. OF, dim. of *top, toup,* of Gmc origin; akin to OHG *zopf* tuft of hair — more at TOP] **1 :** a curl or lock of hair made into a topknot on a periwig or natural coiffure; *also* **:** a periwig with such a topknot **2 :** a wig or section of hair worn to cover a bald spot

[1]**tour** \'tu̇(ə)r, *1 is also* 'tau̇(ə)r\ *n* [ME, fr. MF, fr. OF *tourn, tour* lathe, circuit, turn — more at TURN] **1 a :** one's turn in an orderly schedule : SHIFT **b :** a period during which an individual or unit is on a specific duty or at one place <served a ~ of duty in Europe> **2 a :** a journey for business, pleasure, or education in which one returns to the starting point **b :** a brief turn : ROUND

[2]**tour** *vi* **:** to make a tour ~ *vt* **1 :** to make a tour of **2 :** to present (as a theatrical production) on a tour

tou·ra·co \'tu̇r-ə-ˌkō\ *n, pl* **-cos** [native name in western Africa] **:** any of a family (Musophagidae) of African birds that are related to the cuckoos and have a long tail, a short stout often colored bill, and red wing feathers

tour·bil·lion \tu̇r-'bil-yən\ *or* **tour·bil·lon** \tür-bē-(y)ōⁿ\ *n* [MF *tourbillon,* fr. L *turbin-, turbo* — more at TURBINE] **1 :** WHIRLWIND **2 :** a vortex esp. of a whirlwind or whirlpool **3 :** a firework having a spiral flight

tour de force \ˌtu̇(ə)rd-ə-'fō(ə)rs, -'fȯ(ə)rs\ *n, pl* **tours de force** *same*\ [F] **:** a feat of strength, skill, or ingenuity

tour·er \'tu̇r-ər\ *n* **:** TOURING CAR

tour·ing \'tu̇(ə)r-iŋ\ *n* **1 :** participation in a tour **2 :** cross-country skiing for pleasure

touring car *n* **:** an automobile suitable for distance driving: as **a :** a vintage automobile with two cross seats, usu. four doors, and a folding top **b :** a modern usu. 2-door sedan as distinguished from a sports car

tour·ism \'tu̇(ə)r-ˌiz-əm\ *n* **1 :** the practice of traveling for recreation **2 :** the guidance or management of tourists **3 a :** the promotion or encouragement of touring **b :** the accommodation of tourists

tour·ist \'tu̇r-əst\ *n* **1 :** one that makes a tour for pleasure or culture **2 :** TOURIST CLASS — **tourist** *adj*

tourist card *n* **:** a citizenship identity card issued to a tourist usu. for a stated period of time in lieu of a passport or a visa

tourist class *n* : economy accommodations (as on a ship)
tourist court *n* : MOTEL
tourist home *n* : a house in which rooms are available for rent to transients
tour·is·tic \tu̇r-'is-tik\ *adj* : of or relating to a tour, tourism, or tourists <~ sites and monuments —R. J. Clements> — **tour·is·ti·cal·ly** \-ti-k(ə-)lē\ *adv*
tour·ma·line \'tu̇r-mə-lən, -ˌlēn\ *n* [Sinhalese *toramalli* carnelian] : a mineral $(Na,Ca)(Li,Mg,Fe,Al)(Al,Fe)_6B_3Si_6O_{27}(O,OH,F)_4$ of variable color that consists of a complex silicate and makes a striking gem when transparent and cut
tour·na·ment \'tu̇r-nə-mənt *also* 'tər- *or* 'tȯr-\ *n* [ME *tornement,* fr. OF *torneiement,* fr. *torneier*] **1 a** : a knightly sport of the middle ages between mounted combatants armed with blunted lances or swords and divided into two parties contesting for a prize or favor bestowed by the lady of the tournament **b** : the whole series of knightly sports, jousts, and tilts occurring at one time and place **2** : a championship series of games or athletic contests
tour·ne·dos \ˌtu̇r-nə-'dō\ *n, pl* **tour·ne·dos** \-'dō(z)\ [F, fr. *tourner* to turn (fr. OF) + *dos* back, fr. L *dorsum* — more at TURN] : a small fillet of beef usu. cut from the tip of the tenderloin and encircled by a strip of suet, salt pork, or bacon for quick cooking
[1]**tour·ney** \'tu̇(ə)r-nē *also* 'tər- *or* 'tȯr-\ *vi* **tour·neyed; tour·ney·ing** [ME *tourneyen,* fr. MF *torneier,* fr. OF, fr. *torn, tourn* lathe, circuit] : to perform in a tournament
[2]**tourney** *n, pl* **tourneys** : TOURNAMENT
tour·ni·quet \'tu̇r-ni-kət, 'tər-\ *n* [F, turnstile, tourniquet, fr. *tourner* to turn, fr. OF — more at TURN] : a device (as a bandage twisted tight with a stick) to check bleeding or blood flow
[1]**touse** \'tau̇z\ *vt* **toused; tous·ing** [ME *-tousen;* akin to OHG *zirzūsōn* to pull to pieces] : RUMPLE, TOUSLE
[2]**touse** *n* : a noisy disturbance
[1]**tou·sle** \'tau̇-zəl\ *vt* **tou·sled; tou·sling** \'tau̇z-(ə-)liŋ\ [ME *touselen,* freq. of *-tousen*] : DISHEVEL, RUMPLE
[2]**tou·sle** \'tau̇-zəl, *1 is also* 'tü-\ *n* **1** *Scot* : rough dalliance : TUSSLE **2** : a tangled mass (as of hair)
[1]**tout** \'tau̇t\ *vb* [ME *tuten* to peer; akin to OE *tōtian* to stick out, Norw *tyte*] *vi* **1** : to canvass for customers **2 a** *chiefly Brit* : to spy on racehorse trials or stable secrets for betting purposes **b** : to give a tip or solicit bets on a racehorse ~ *vt* **1** : to spy on : WATCH **2 a** *Brit* : to spy out information about (as a racing stable or horse) **b** : to give a tip or solicit bets on (a racehorse) **3** : to solicit or peddle importunately
[2]**tout** *n* : one who touts: as **a** : one who solicits patronage **b** *chiefly Brit* : one who spies out racing information for betting purposes **c** : one who gives tips or solicits bets on a racehorse
[3]**tout** \'tau̇t, 'tüt\ *vt* [alter. of [1]*toot*] : to praise or publicize loudly or extravagantly : BALLYHOO <~*ed* as the . . . most elaborate suburban shopping development —*Wall Street Jour.*>
tout·er \'tau̇t-ər\ *n* : [2]TOUT
to·va·rich *or* **to·va·rish** \tə-'vär-ish, -ich\ *n* [Russ *tovarishch*] : COMRADE
[1]**tow** \'tō\ *vb* [ME *towen,* fr. OE *togian;* akin to OE *tēon* to draw, pull, OHG *ziohan* to draw, pull, L *ducere* to draw, lead] *vt* : to draw or pull along behind : HAUL ~ *vi* : to move in tow <trailers that ~ behind the family auto —Bob Munger>
[2]**tow** *n* **1** : a rope or chain for towing **2 a** : the act or an instance of towing **b** : the fact or state of being towed **3** : something towed (as a boat or car) **4 a** : something (as a towboat or tugboat) that tows **b** : SKI TOW — **in tow 1** : in the state of being towed <passed a wrecker with a car *in tow*> **2 a** : under guidance or protection <taken *in tow* by a friendly native> **b** : in the position of a dependent or devoted follower or admirer <a young man passed with a good-looking girl *in tow*>
[3]**tow** *n* [ME, fr. OE *tōw-* spinning; akin to ON *tō* tuft of wool for spinning, OE *tawian* to prepare for use — more at TAW] **1** : short or broken fiber (as of flax, hemp, or synthetic material) that is used esp. for yarn, twine, or stuffing **2 a** : yarn or cloth made of tow **b** : a loose essentially untwisted strand of synthetic fibers
[4]**tow** *n* [ME (Sc), prob. fr. OE *toh-* (in *tohline* towline); akin to OE *togian* to tow] *chiefly Scot & dial Eng* : ROPE
tow·age \'tō-ij\ *n* **1** : the act of towing **2** : the price paid for towing
[1]**to·ward** \'tō(-ə)rd, 'tȯ(-ə)rd\ *adj* [ME *toward,* fr. OE *tōweard* facing, imminent, fr. *tō,* prep., to + *-weard* -ward] **1** *also* **to·wards** \'tō(-ə)rdz, 'tȯ(-ə)rdz\ [ME *towardes,* fr. OE *tōweardes,* prep., toward, fr. *tōweard,* adj.] **a** : coming soon : IMMINENT **b** : happening at the moment : AFOOT **2 a** *obs* : quick to learn : APT **b** : PROPITIOUS, FAVORING <a ~ breeze>
[2]**to·ward** *or* **to·wards** \(ˈ)tō(-ə)rd(z), (ˈ)tȯ(-ə)rd(z), tə-'wȯrd(z), (ˈ)twȯrd(z), (ˈ)twōrd(z)\ *prep* **1** : in the direction of <driving ~ town> **2 a** : along a course leading to <a long stride ~ disarmament> **b** : in relation to <an attitude ~ life> **3 a** : at a point in the direction of : NEAR <a cottage somewhere up ~ the lake> **b** : in such a position as to be in the direction of <his back was ~ me> **4** : not long before <~ the end of the afternoon> **5 a** : in the way of help or assistance in <did all he could ~ raising campaign funds> **b** : for the partial payment of <proceeds go ~ the establishment of a scholarship>
to·ward·li·ness \'tōrd-lē-nəs, 'tȯrd-\ *n, archaic* : the quality or state of being toward or towardly
to·ward·ly \'tō(-ə)rd-lē, 'tȯ(-ə)rd-\ *adj, archaic* **1** : FAVORABLE, PROPITIOUS **2** : developing favorably : PROMISING **3** : PLEASANT, AFFABLE — **towardly** *adv*
tow·boat \'tō-ˌbōt\ *n* **1** : TUGBOAT **2** : a compact shallow-draft boat with a squared bow designed and fitted for pushing tows of barges on inland waterways
[1]**tow·el** \'tau̇(-ə)l\ *n* [ME *towaille,* fr. OF *toaille,* of Gmc origin; akin to OHG *dwahila* towel; akin to OHG *dwahan* to wash, OPruss *twaxtan* bath cloth] : an absorbent cloth or paper for wiping or drying
[2]**towel** *vb* **-eled** *or* **-elled; -el·ing** *or* **-el·ling** *vt* : to rub or dry (as the body) with a towel ~ *vi* : to use a towel

tow·el·ing *or* **tow·el·ling** \'tau̇-(ə-)liŋ\ *n* : a cotton or linen fabric often used for making towels
[1]**tow·er** \'tau̇(-ə)r\ *n* [ME *tour, tor,* fr. OE *torr* & OF *tor, tur,* both fr. L *turris,* fr. Gk *tyrsis*] **1** : a building or structure typically higher than its diameter and high relative to its surroundings that may stand apart (as a campanile), or be attached (as a church belfry) to a larger structure, and that may be fully walled in or of skeleton framework (as an observation or transmission tower) **2** : a towering citadel : FORTRESS **3** : one that provides support or protection : BULWARK <a ~ of strength> — **tow·ered** \'tau̇(-ə)rd\ *adj* — **tow·er·like** \'tau̇(-ə)r-ˌlīk\ *adj*
[2]**tower** *vi* : to reach or rise to a great height
tower house *n* : a medieval fortified castle (as in Scotland)
tow·er·ing *adj* **1** : impressively high or great : IMPOSING <~ pines> **2** : reaching a high point of intensity : OVERWHELMING <a ~ rage> **3** : going beyond proper bounds : EXCESSIVE <~ ambitions> — **tow·er·ing·ly** \'tau̇(-ə)r-iŋ-lē\ *adv*
tower wagon *n* : a wagon or motortruck with a high adjustable platform on which workmen can stand (as when repairing overhead wires)
tow·head \'tō-ˌhed\ *n* **1** : a head of hair resembling tow esp. in being flaxen or tousled; *also* : a person having such a head of hair **2** : a low alluvial island or shoal in a river : SANDBAR — **tow·head·ed** \-'hed-əd\ *adj*
to·whee \'tō-ˌhē, 'tō-(ˌ)ē, tō-'hē\ *n* [imit.] **1** : a common finch (*Pipilo erythrophthalmus*) of eastern No. America having the male black, white, and rufous — called also *chewink* **2** : any of numerous American finches (genera *Pipilo* and *Chlorura*) that are related to the towhee
tow·ie \'tau̇-ē\ *n* [origin unknown] : a form of contract bridge for three players
to wit \tə-'wit\ *adv* [ME *to witen,* lit., to know — more at WIT] : that is to say : NAMELY
tow·line \'tō-ˌlīn\ *n* : a line used in towing
tow·mond \'tō-ˌmänd\ *n* [ME *towlmonyth,* fr. OE *twelf mōnath,* fr. *twelf* twelve + *mōnath* month] *Scot* : TWELVEMONTH, YEAR
town \'tau̇n\ *n* [ME, fr. OE *tūn* enclosure, village, town; akin to OHG *zūn* enclosure, OIr *dūn* fortress] **1** *dial Eng* : a cluster or aggregation of houses recognized as a distinct place with a place-name : HAMLET **2 a** : a compactly settled area as distinguished from surrounding rural territory **b** : a compactly settled area usu. larger than a village but smaller than a city **c** : a large densely populated urban area : CITY **d** : an English village having a periodic fair or market **3** : a neighboring city, capital city, or metropolis **4** : the city or urban life as contrasted with the country **5** : a New England territorial and political unit usu. containing both rural and unincorporated urban areas under a single town government — called also *township; also* : a New England community governed by a town meeting — **town** *adj* — **on the town** : in usu. carefree pursuit of entertainment or amusement (as city nightlife) esp. as a relief from routine
town car *n* : a 4-door automobile with a permanently enclosed passenger compartment in the rear separated from the driver's compartment by a sliding glass partition
town clerk *n* : a public officer charged with recording the official proceedings and vital statistics of a town
town crier *n* : a town officer who makes public proclamations
town·ee \tau̇-'nē\ *n* : TOWNSMAN
town hall *n* : a public building used for town-government offices and meetings
town house *n* **1** : a house in town; *specif* : the city residence of one having a countryseat or having a chief residence elsewhere <stayed at their *town house* during the social season> **2** : a usu. single-family house of two or sometimes three stories that is usu. connected to a similar house by a common sidewall
town·let \'tau̇n-lət\ *n* : a very small town
town manager *n* : an appointed town official having the status and functions of a city manager
town meeting *n* : a meeting of inhabitants or taxpayers constituting the legislative authority of a town
towns·folk \'tau̇nz-ˌfōk\ *n pl* : TOWNSPEOPLE
town·ship \'tau̇n-ˌship\ *n* **1** : an ancient unit of administration in England identical in area with or a division of a parish **2 a** : TOWN 5 **b** : a unit of local government in some northeastern and north central states usu. having a chief administrative officer or board **c** : an unorganized subdivision of the county in Maine, New Hampshire, and Vermont **d** : an electoral and administrative district of the county in the southern U.S. **3** : a division of territory in surveys of U.S. public land containing 36 sections or 36 square miles
towns·man \'tau̇nz-mən\ *n* **1 a** : a native or resident of a town or city **b** : an urban or urbane person **2** : a fellow citizen of a town
towns·peo·ple \-ˌpē-pəl\ *n pl* **1** : the inhabitants of a town or city : TOWNSMEN **2** : town-dwelling or town-bred persons
towns·wom·an \-ˌwu̇m-ən\ *n* **1** : a female native or resident of a town or city **2** : a woman born or residing in the same town or city as another
town·wear \'tau̇n-ˌwa(ə)r, -ˌwe(ə)r\ *n* : apparel (as of dark color or tailored style) that is suitable for wear in the city or to business
towny \'tau̇-nē\ *n, pl* **town·ies** : TOWNSMAN
tow·path \'tō-ˌpath, -ˌpȧth\ *n* : a path (as along a canal) traveled by men or animals towing boats — called also *towing path*
tow·rope \-ˌrōp\ *n* : a line used in towing something (as a boat)
tow sack \'tō-ˌsak\ *n* [[3]*tow*] *Midland & South* : GUNNYSACK
tow truck *n* : WRECKER 2b

tox- *or* **toxi-** *or* **toxo-** *comb form* [LL, fr. L *toxicum* poison] : poisonous : poison <*tox*emia>
tox·a·phene \'täk-sə-,fēn\ *n* [fr. *Toxaphene,* a trademark] : a chlorinated camphene insecticide $C_{10}H_{10}Cl_8$
tox·emia \täk-'sē-mē-ə\ *n* [NL] : an abnormal condition associated with the presence of toxic substances in the blood — **tox·emic** \-mik\ *adj*
tox·ic \'täk-sik\ *adj* [LL *toxicus,* fr. L *toxicum* poison, fr. Gk *toxikon* arrow poison, fr. neut. of *toxikos* of a bow, fr. *toxon* bow, arrow] **1 :** of, relating to, or caused by a poison or toxin **2 :** affected by a poison or toxin <~ pregnant women> **3 :** POISONOUS — **tox·ic·i·ty** \täk-'sis-ət-ē\ *n*
toxic- *or* **toxico-** *comb form* [NL, fr. L *toxicum*] : poison <*toxico*logy> <*toxic*osis>
[1]**tox·i·cant** \'täk-si-kənt\ *n* [ML *toxicant-, toxicans,* prp. of *toxicare* to poison, fr. L *toxicum*] : a toxic agent; *esp* : one for insect control that kills rather than repels
[2]**toxicant** *adj* : producing a toxic effect : POISONOUS <~ diseases>
tox·i·co·gen·ic \,täk-si-kō-'jen-ik\ *adj* : producing toxic products <~ bacteria>
tox·i·co·log·i·cal \-kə-'läj-i-kəl\ *or* **tox·i·co·log·ic** \-ik\ *adj* : of or relating to toxicology or toxins — **tox·i·co·log·i·cal·ly** \-i-k(ə-)lē\ *adv*
tox·i·col·o·gy \-'käl-ə-jē\ *n* : a science that deals with poisons and their effect and with the problems involved (as clinical, industrial, or legal) — **tox·i·col·o·gist** \-jəst\ *n*
tox·i·co·sis \,täk-sə-'kō-səs\ *n, pl* **-co·ses** \-,sēz\ [NL] : a pathological condition caused by the action of a poison or toxin
toxi·gen·ic \,täk-sə-'jen-ik\ *adj* : producing toxin <~ bacteria and fungi> — **toxi·ge·nic·i·ty** \,täk-si-jə-'nis-ət-ē\ *n*
tox·in \'täk-sən\ *n* [ISV] : a colloidal proteinaceous poisonous substance that is a specific product of the metabolic activities of a living organism and is usu. very unstable, notably toxic when introduced into the tissues, and typically capable of inducing antibody formation
tox·in–an·ti·tox·in \'täk-sə-'nant-i-,täk-sən\ *n* : a mixture of toxin and antitoxin used esp. formerly in immunizing against a disease (as diphtheria) for which they are specific
tox·oid \'täk-,sȯid\ *n* [ISV] : a toxin of a pathogenic organism treated so as to destroy its toxicity but leave it capable of inducing the formation of antibodies on injection
tox·oph·i·lite \täk-'säf-ə-,līt\ *n* [Gk *toxon* bow, arrow + *philos* dear, loving] : one fond of or expert at archery — **toxophilite** *adj* — **tox·oph·i·ly** \-lē\ *n*
toxo·plas·ma \,täk-sə-'plaz-mə\ *n* [NL, genus name] : any of a genus (*Toxoplasma*) of parasitic microorganisms that are usu. held to be protozoans related to the sporozoans and that are typically serious pathogens of vertebrates — **toxo·plas·mic** \-mik\ *adj*
toxo·plas·mo·sis \-,plaz-'mō-səs\ *n, pl* **-mo·ses** \-,sēz\ [NL] : infection of man, other mammals, or birds with disease caused by toxoplasmas that invade the tissues and may seriously damage the central nervous system esp. of infants
[1]**toy** \'tȯi\ *n* [ME *toye* dalliance] **1** *obs* **a :** flirtatious or seductive behavior **b :** PASTIME; *also* : a sportive or amusing act : ANTIC **2 a :** something (as a preoccupation) that is paltry or trifling **b :** a literary or musical trifle or diversion **c :** TRINKET, BAUBLE **3 :** something for a child to play with **4 :** something diminutive; *esp* : a diminutive animal (as of a small breed or variety) **5 :** something that can be toyed with **6** *Scot* : a headdress of linen or woolen hanging down over the shoulders and formerly worn by old women of the lower classes — **toy-like** \-,līk\ *adj*
[2]**toy** *vi* **1 :** to engage in flirtation **2 :** to act or deal with something lightly or without vigor or purpose **3 :** to amuse oneself as if with a toy : PLAY ***syn*** see TRIFLE — **toy·er** \'tȯi-ər\ *n*
[3]**toy** *adj* **1 :** designed or made for use as a toy <a ~ stove> **2 :** resembling a toy esp. in diminutive size
toy Man·ches·ter terrier \-,man-,ches-tər-, -chə-stər-\ *n* : a Manchester terrier of a variety with erect ears of moderate size and weighing not more than 12 pounds — called also *toy Manchester*
toy·on \'tȯi-,än\ *n* [AmerSp *tollon*] : an ornamental evergreen shrub (*Photinia arbutifolia*) of the rose family of the No. American Pacific coast having white flowers succeeded by persistent bright red berries
toy poodle *n* : a toy dog that was developed from the standard poodle and is not more than 10 inches high at the withers
tp *abbr* **1** title page **2** township
tpk *or* **tpke** *abbr* turnpike
TPN \,tē-,pē-'en\ *n* [*t*ri*p*hosphopyridine *n*ucleotide] : NADP
tps *abbr* **1** townships **2** troops
tr *abbr* **1** translated; translation; translator **2** transpose **3** troop **4** trustee
TR *abbr* **1** tons registered **2** transmit-receive
tra·be·at·ed \'trā-bē-,āt-əd\ *also* **tra·be·ate** \-,āt\ *adj* [L *trabes* beam] : designed or constructed with horizontal beams or lintels — **tra·be·ation** \,trā-bē-'ā-shən\ *n*
tra·bec·u·la \trə-'bek-yə-lə\ *n, pl* **-lae** \-,lē, -,lī\ *also* **-las** [NL, fr. L, little beam, dim. of *trabs, trabes* beam — more at THORP] **1 :** a small bar, rod, bundle of fibers, or septal membrane in the framework of a body organ or part **2 :** a fold, ridge, or bar projecting into or extending from a plant part; *esp* : a row of cells bridging an intercellular space — **tra·bec·u·lar** \-lər\ *adj* — **tra·bec·u·late** \-lət\ *adj*
[1]**trace** \'trās\ *n* [ME, fr. MF, fr. *tracier* to trace] **1** *archaic* : a course or path that one follows : ROAD **2 a :** a mark or line left by something that has passed; *also* : FOOTPRINT **b :** a path beaten by or as if by feet : TRAIL **3 :** a sign or evidence of some past thing : VESTIGE; *esp* : ENGRAM **4 :** something (as a line) traced or drawn: as **a :** the marking made by a recording instrument (as a seismograph or kymograph) **b :** the ground plan of a military installation or position either on a map or on the ground **5 a :** the intersection of a line or plane with a plane **b :** the usu. bright line or spot that moves across the screen of a cathode-ray tube; *also* : the path taken by such a line or spot **6 :** a minute and often barely detectable amount or indication <a ~ of a smile>; esp. : an amount of a chemical constituent not quantitatively determined because of minuteness
syn TRACE, VESTIGE, TRACK *shared meaning element* : a perceptible sign left behind
[2]**trace** *vb* **traced; trac·ing** [ME *tracen,* fr. MF *tracier,* fr. (assumed) VL *tractiare* to drag, draw, fr. L *tractus,* pp. of *trahere* to pull, draw — more at DRAW] *vt* **1 a :** DELINEATE, SKETCH **b :** to form (as letters or figures) carefully or painstakingly **c :** to copy (as a drawing) by following the lines or letters as seen through a transparent superimposed sheet **d :** to impress or imprint (as a design or pattern) with a tracer **e :** to record a tracing of in the form of a curved, wavy, or broken line <~ the heart action> **f :** to adorn with linear ornamentation (as tracery or chasing) **2** *archaic* : to travel over : TRAVERSE **3 a :** to follow the footprints, track, or trail of **b :** to follow or study out in detail or step by step <~ the history of the labor movement> **c :** to discover by going backward over the evidence step by step <~ one's ancestry back to the crusaders —Curtis Cate> **d :** to discover signs, evidence, or remains of **4 :** to lay out the trace of (a military installation) ~ *vi* **1 :** to make one's way; *esp* : to follow a track or trail **2 :** to be traceable historically — **trace·abil·i·ty** \,trā-sə-'bil-ət-ē\ *n* — **trace·able** \'trā-sə-bəl\ *adj* — **trace·able·ness** *n* — **trace·ably** \-blē\ *adv*
[3]**trace** *n* [ME *trais,* pl., traces, fr. MF, pl. of *trait* pull, draft, trace — more at TRAIT] **1 :** either of two straps, chains, or lines of a harness for attaching a horse to something (as a vehicle) to be drawn **2 :** LEADER 1e(2) **3 :** one or more vascular bundles supplying a leaf or twig **4 :** a connecting bar or rod pivoted at each end to another piece and used for transmitting motion
trace element *n* : a chemical element present in minute quantities; *esp* : one used by organisms and held essential to their physiology
trace·less \'trā-sləs\ *adj* : having or leaving no trace — **trace·less·ly** *adv*
trac·er \'trā-sər\ *n* **1 :** one that traces, tracks down, or searches out: as **a :** a person who traces missing persons or property and esp. goods lost in transit **b :** an inquiry sent out in tracing a shipment lost in transit **2 :** one (as a draftsman) who traces designs, patterns, or markings **3 :** a device (as a stylus) used in tracing **4 a :** ammunition containing a chemical composition to mark the flight of projectiles by a trail of smoke or fire **b :** a substance and esp. a labeled element or atom used to trace the course of a chemical or biological process
trac·ery \'trās(-ə)-rē\ *n, pl* **-er·ies** **1 :** architectural ornamental work with branching lines; *esp* : decorative openwork in the head of a Gothic window **2 :** a decorative interlacing of lines suggestive of Gothic tracery — **trac·er·ied** \-rēd\ *adj*

tracery 1

trache- *or* **tracheo-** *comb form* [NL, fr. ML *trachea*] **1 :** trachea <*trache*itis> <*tracheo*tomy> **2 :** tracheal and <*tracheo*bronchial>
tra·chea \'trā-kē-ə\ *n, pl* **-che·ae** \-kē-,ē, -kē-,ī\ *also* **-che·as** [ME, fr. ML, fr. LL *trachia,* fr. Gk *tracheia* (*artēria*) rough (artery), fr. fem. of *trachys* rough; akin to Gk *thrassein* to trouble — more at DARK] **1 :** the main trunk of the system of tubes by which air passes to and from the lungs in vertebrates — see LARYNX illustration **2** [NL, fr. ML] : VESSEL 3b; *also* : one of its constituent cellular elements **3** [NL] : one of the air-conveying tubules forming the respiratory system of most insects and many other arthropods — **tra·che·al** \-kē-əl\ *adj*
tra·che·ary \'trā-kē-,er-ē\ *adj* : of, relating to, or being plant tracheae
tra·che·ate \-kē-,āt, -ət\ *also* **tra·che·at·ed** \-,āt-əd\ *adj* : having tracheae as breathing organs
tra·cheid \'trā-kē-əd, -,kēd\ *n* [ISV] : a long tubular cell that is peculiar to xylem, functions in conduction and support, and has tapering closed ends and thickened lignified walls — **tra·cheid·al** \trā-'kē-dᵊl, -'kēd-ᵊl\ *adj*
tra·che·itis \,trā-kē-'īt-əs\ *n* [NL] : inflammation of the trachea
tra·cheo·bron·chi·al \,trā-kē-ō-'bräŋ-kē-əl\ *adj* : of or relating to both trachea and bronchi <~ lesions>
tra·che·ole \'trā-kē-,ōl\ *n* [NL *tracheola,* dim. of *trachea*] : one of the minute delicate endings of a branched trachea of an insect — **tra·che·o·lar** \trā-'kē-ə-lər\ *adj*
tra·cheo·phyte \'trā-kē-ə-,fīt\ *n* [NL *Tracheophyta,* fr. *trache-* + Gk *phyton* plant; akin to Gk *phyein* to bring forth — more at BE] : any of a division (Tracheophyta) comprising green plants (as ferns and seed plants) with a vascular system that contains tracheids or tracheary elements
tra·che·ot·o·my \,trā-kē-'ät-ə-mē\ *n, pl* **-mies** : the surgical operation of cutting into the trachea esp. through the skin
tra·cho·ma \trə-'kō-mə\ *n* [NL, fr. Gk *trachōma,* fr. *trachys* rough] : a chronic contagious conjunctivitis marked by inflammatory granulations on the conjunctival surfaces and caused by a rickettsia (*Chlamydia trachomatis*) — **tra·cho·ma·tous** \trə-'kō-mət-əs\ *adj*
tra·chyte \'trak-,īt, 'trā-,kīt\ *n* [F, fr. Gk *trachys* rough] : a usu. light-colored volcanic rock consisting chiefly of potash feldspar
tra·chyt·ic \trə-'kit-ik\ *adj* : of or relating to a texture of igneous rocks in which lath-shaped feldspar crystals are in almost parallel lines
trac·ing \'trā-siŋ\ *n* **1 :** the act of one that traces **2 :** something that is traced: as **a :** a copy made on a superimposed transparent sheet **b :** a graphic record made by an instrument (as a seismograph) that registers some movement
tracing paper *n* : a semitransparent paper for tracing drawings
[1]**track** \'trak\ *n* [ME *trak,* fr. MF *trac,* perh. of Gmc origin; akin to MD *tracken, trecken* to pull, haul — more at TREK] **1 a :** detectable evidence (as the wake of a ship, a line of footprints, or a wheel rut) that something has passed **b :** a path made by repeated footfalls : TRAIL **c :** a course laid out esp. for racing **d :** the parallel rails of a railroad **e** (1) **:** one of a series of parallel or concentric paths along which material (as music or information)

is recorded (as on magnetic tape) (2) : BAND 7 **2 a :** a footprint whether recent or fossil <the huge ~ of a dinosaur> **b** *archaic* **:** a visible mark or sign **:** VESTIGE, TRACE **3 a :** the course along which something moves **b :** one of several curricula of study to which students are assigned according to their needs or levels of ability **c :** the projection on the earth's surface of the path along which something (as a missile or an airplane) has actually flown **4 a :** a sequence of events **:** a train of ideas **:** SUCCESSION **b :** a condition of being aware of a fact or progression <keep ~ of the costs> <lose ~ of the time> **5 a :** the width of a wheeled vehicle from wheel to wheel and usu. from the outside of the rims **b :** the tread of an automobile tire **c :** either of two endless metal belts on which a tracklaying vehicle travels **6 :** track-and-field sports; *esp* **:** those performed on a running track ***syn*** see TRACE — **track·less** \'trak-ləs\ *adj* — **in one's tracks :** where one stands or is at the moment **:** on the spot <was stopped *in his tracks*>

²track *vt* **1 a :** to follow the tracks or traces of **:** TRAIL **b :** to pursue until caught up with <~ down a criminal> **c :** to search for until found <~ down the source> **2 a :** to follow by vestiges **:** TRACE **b :** to observe or plot the moving path of (as a spacecraft or missile) instrumentally **3 :** to pass over **:** TRAVERSE <~ a desert> **4 a :** to make tracks upon **b :** to carry (as mud) on the feet and deposit ~ *vi* **1 a** *of a phonograph needle* **:** to follow the groove undulations of a recording **b** *of a pair of wheels* **(1) :** to maintain a constant distance apart on the straightaway **(2) :** to fit a track or rails **c** *of a rear wheel of a vehicle* **:** to follow accurately the corresponding fore wheel on a straightaway **2 :** to leave tracks (as on a floor) — **track·er** *n*

track·age \'trak-ij\ *n* **1 :** lines of railway track **2 a :** a right to use the tracks of another railroad line **b :** the charge for such right

track-and-field \ˌtrak-ən-'fē(ə)ld\ *adj* **:** of, relating to, or being any of various competitive athletic events (as running, jumping, and weight throwing) performed on a running track and on the adjacent field

tracked \'trakt\ *adj* **1 :** traveling on endless metal belts instead of wheels **2 :** moving along a rail <a ~ air-cushion vehicle>

track·ing \'trak-iŋ\ *n* **:** the assigning of students to a curricular track

track·lay·er \'trak-ˌlā-ər, -ˌle(-ə)r\ *n* **1 :** a workman engaged in tracklaying **2 :** a tracklaying vehicle

¹track·lay·ing \-ˌlā-iŋ\ *n* **:** the laying of tracks on a railway line

²tracklaying *adj* **:** of, relating to, or being a vehicle that travels on two or more endless usu. metal belts

trackless trolley *n* **:** TROLLEYBUS

track·man \'trak-mən, -ˌman\ *n* **:** a runner on a track team

track record *n* [¹*track* (track-and-field sports)] **:** a record of accomplishments

track·side \ˌtrak-ˌsīd\ *adj* **:** of, relating to, or situated in the area immediately adjacent to a track

track·walk·er \'trak-ˌwȯ-kər\ *n* **:** a worker employed to walk over and inspect a section of railroad tracks

¹tract \'trakt\ *n, often cap* [ME *tracte,* fr. ML *tractus,* fr. L, action of drawing, extension; fr. its being sung without a break by one voice] **:** verses of Scripture (as from the Psalms) used between the gradual and the Gospel at some masses (as during penitential seasons)

²tract *n* [ME, modif. of L *tractatus* tractate] **:** a pamphlet or leaflet of political or religious propaganda

³tract *n* [L *tractus* action of drawing, extension, fr. *tractus,* pp. of *trahere* to pull, draw — more at DRAW] **1** *archaic* **:** extent or lapse of time **2 :** an area either large or small: as **a :** an indefinite stretch of land **b :** a defined area of land **3 :** a system of body parts or organs that collectively serve some special purpose <the digestive ~>; *esp* **:** a bundle of nerve fibers having a common origin, termination, and function

trac·ta·ble \'trak-tə-bəl\ *adj* [L *tractabilis,* fr. *tractare* to handle, treat] **1 :** capable of being easily led, taught, or controlled **:** DOCILE <a ~ horse> **2 :** easily handled, managed, or wrought **:** MALLEABLE ***syn*** see OBEDIENT ***ant*** intractable, unruly — **trac·ta·bil·i·ty** \ˌtrak-tə-'bil-ət-ē\ *n* — **trac·ta·ble·ness** \'trak-tə-bəl-nəs\ *n* — **trac·ta·bly** \-blē\ *adv*

Trac·tar·i·an \trak-'ter-ē-ən\ *n* [fr. the fact that the Oxford movement was expounded in a series of pamphlets called *Tracts for the Times*] **:** a promoter or supporter of the Oxford movement

Trac·tar·i·an·ism \-ē-ə-ˌniz-əm\ *n* **:** a system of High Church principles set forth in a series of tracts at Oxford (1833–41)

trac·tate \'trak-ˌtāt\ *n* [L *tractatus,* fr. *tractatus,* pp. of *tractare* to draw out, handle, treat — more at TREAT] **:** TREATISE, DISSERTATION

trac·tion \'trak-shən\ *n* [ML *traction-, tractio,* fr. L *tractus,* pp.] **1 :** the act of drawing **:** the state of being drawn; *also* **:** the force exerted in drawing **2 :** the drawing of a vehicle by motive power; *also* **:** the motive power employed **3 a :** the adhesive friction of a body on a surface on which it moves <the ~ of a wheel on a rail> **b :** a pulling force exerted on a skeletal structure (as in a fracture) by means of a special device <a ~ splint>; *also* **:** a state of tension created by such a pulling force <a leg in ~> — **trac·tion·al** \-shnəl, -shən-ᵊl\ *adj*

trac·tive \'trak-tiv\ *adj* [L *tractus,* pp.] **1 :** serving to draw **2 :** of or relating to traction **:** TRACTIONAL

trac·tor \'trak-tər\ *n* [NL, fr. L *tractus,* pp.] **1 :** a steam-powered vehicle used to draw other vehicles or equipment (as a threshing rig) over roads or fields and sometimes to provide power (as for sawing or threshing) **2 a :** a 4-wheeled or tracklaying rider-controlled automotive vehicle used esp. for drawing implements (as agricultural) or for bearing and propelling such implements **b :** a smaller 2-wheeled apparatus controlled through handlebars by a walking operator **c :** a truck with short chassis and no body used in combination with a trailer for the highway hauling of freight **3 :** an airplane having the propeller forward of the main supporting surfaces

trad \'trad\ *adj, chiefly Brit* **:** TRADITIONAL

¹trade \'trād\ *n* [ME, fr. MLG; akin to OHG *trata* track, course, OE *tredan* to tread] **1 a** *obs* **:** a path traversed **:** WAY **b** *archaic* **:** a track or trail left by a man or animal **:** TREAD **1 2 :** a customary course of action **:** PRACTICE <thy sin's not accidental, but a ~ —Shak.> **3 a :** the business or work in which one engages regularly **:** OCCUPATION **b :** an occupation requiring manual or mechanical skill **:** CRAFT **c :** the persons engaged in an occupation, business, or industry **4 a** *obs* **:** dealings between persons or groups **b (1) :** the business of buying and selling or bartering commodities **:** COMMERCE **(2) :** BUSINESS, MARKET <novelties for the tourist ~> <did a good ~ in small appliances> **5 a :** an act or instance of trading **:** TRANSACTION; *also* **:** an exchange of property usu. without use of money **b :** a firm's customers **:** CLIENTELE **c :** the group of firms engaged in a business or industry **6 :** TRADE WIND ***syn*** see BUSINESS

²trade *vb* **trad·ed; trad·ing** *vt* **1** *archaic* **:** to do business with **2 a :** to give in exchange for another commodity **:** BARTER; *also* **:** to make an exchange of <*traded* places> **b :** to engage in frequent buying and selling of (as stocks or commodities) usu. in search of quick profits ~ *vi* **1** *obs* **:** to have dealings **:** NEGOTIATE **2 a :** to engage in the exchange, purchase, or sale of goods **b :** to make one's purchases **:** SHOP <~*s* at his store> **3 :** to give one thing in exchange for another — **trad·able** *also* **trade·able** \'trād-ə-bəl\ *adj* — **trade on :** to take often unscrupulous advantage of **:** EXPLOIT <*traded on* their influence . . . in securing special favors —T. C. Pease>

³trade *adj* **1 :** of, relating to, or used in trade **2 a :** intended for or limited to persons in a business or industry <a ~ publication> <~ sales> **b :** serving others in the same business rather than the ultimate user or consumer <a ~ printing house> **3** *also* **trades :** of, composed of, or representing the trades or trade unions <a ~ committee> **4 :** of or associated with a trade wind <the ~ belts>

trade acceptance *n* **:** a time draft or bill of exchange for the amount of a specific purchase drawn by the seller on the buyer, bearing the buyer's acceptance, and often noting the place of payment (as a bank)

trade agreement *n* **1 :** an international agreement on conditions of trade in goods and services **2 :** an agreement resulting from collective bargaining

trade book *n* **1 :** a book intended for general readership **2 :** TRADE EDITION

trade discount *n* **:** a deduction from the list price of goods allowed by a manufacturer or wholesaler to a retailer

trade dollar *n* **:** a U.S. silver dollar weighing 420 grains .900 fine issued 1873–85 for use in oriental trade

trade down *vi* **:** to trade something in (as an automobile) for something less expensive or valuable of its kind

trade edition *n* **:** an edition of a book in a standard format intended for general distribution — compare TEXT EDITION

trade-in \'trād-ˌin\ *n* **:** an item of merchandise (as an automobile or refrigerator) taken as payment or part payment for a purchase

trade in \(')trād-'in\ *vt* **:** to turn in as payment or part payment for a purchase or bill <*trade* an old car *in* for a new one>

trade language *n* **:** a mongrel language (as a lingua franca or pidgin) used esp. in commercial communication

trade-last \'trād-ˌlast\ *n* **:** a complimentary remark by a third person that a hearer offers to repeat to the person complimented if he will first report a compliment made about the hearer

¹trade·mark \-ˌmärk\ *n* **1 :** a device (as a word) pointing distinctly to the origin or ownership of merchandise to which it is applied and legally reserved to the exclusive use of the owner as maker or seller **2 :** a distinguishing characteristic or feature firmly associated with a person or thing <derringers . . . became almost a ~ of gamblers —Elmer Keith>

²trademark *vt* **:** to secure trademark rights for **:** register the trademark of

¹trade name *n* **1 a :** the name used for an article among traders **b :** an arbitrarily adopted name that is given by a manufacturer or merchant to an article or service to distinguish it as produced or sold by him and that may be used and protected as a trademark **2 :** the name or style under which a concern does business

²trade name *vt* **:** to designate with a trade name

trade-off \'trād-ˌȯf\ *n* **1 :** a balancing of factors all of which are not attainable at the same time <the education versus experience ~ which governs personnel practices —H. S. White> **2 :** a giving up of one thing in return for another **:** EXCHANGE

trad·er \'trād-ər\ *n* **1 :** a person whose business is buying and selling or barter: as **a :** MERCHANT **b :** a person who buys and sells (as securities) for his own account in search of short-term profits **2 :** a ship engaged in the coastal or foreign trade

trade route *n* **1 :** a route followed by traders (as in caravans) **2 :** one of the sea-lanes ordinarily used by merchant ships

trad·es·can·tia \ˌtrad-ə-'skan-ch(ē-)ə\ *n* [NL, genus name, fr. John *Tradescant* †1638 E traveler & gardener] **:** any of a genus (*Tradescantia* of the family Commelinaceae) of American herbs **:** SPIDERWORT

trade school *n* **:** a secondary school teaching the skilled trades

trade secret *n* **:** a formula, process, or device used in a business that is not published or divulged and that thereby gives an advantage over competitors

trades·man \'trādz-mən\ *n* **1 :** one who runs a retail store **:** SHOPKEEPER **2 :** a workman in a skilled trade **:** CRAFTSMAN

trades·peo·ple \-ˌpē-pəl\ *n pl* **:** people engaged in trade

trade union *also* **trades union** *n* **:** LABOR UNION — **trade unionism** *n* — **trade unionist** *n*

trade up *vi* **:** to trade something in (as an automobile) for something more expensive or valuable of its kind

tra·dev·man \trə-'dev-mən, 'trā-ˌ\ *n* [*tra*ining *dev*ices *man*] **:** a petty officer in charge of naval training equipment

---

ə abut	ᵊ kitten	ər further	a back	ā bake	ä cot, cart
au̇ out	ch chin	e less	ē easy	g gift	i trip	ī life
j joke	ŋ sing	ō flow	ȯ flaw	ȯi coin	th thin	t͟h this
ü loot	u̇ foot	y yet	yü few	yu̇ furious	zh vision

trade wind *n* **:** a wind blowing almost constantly in one direction; *esp* **:** a wind blowing almost continually toward the equator from the northeast in the belt between the northern horse latitudes and the doldrums and from the southeast in the belt between the southern horse latitudes and the doldrums

trading post *n* **1 :** a station of a trader or trading company established in a sparsely settled region where trade in products of local origin (as furs) is carried on **2 :** [6]POST 3b

trading stamp *n* **:** a printed stamp of value given as a premium to a retail customer to be accumulated and redeemed in merchandise

tra·di·tion \trə-'dish-ən\ *n* [ME *tradicioun,* fr. MF & L; MF *tradition,* fr. L *tradition-, traditio* action of handing over, tradition — more at TREASON] **1 :** the handing down of information, beliefs, and customs by word of mouth or by example from one generation to another without written instruction **2 :** an inherited pattern of thought or action (as a religious practice or a social custom) **3 :** cultural continuity in social attitudes and institutions — **tra·di·tion·al** \-'dish-nəl, -ən-ᵊl\ *adj* — **tra·di·tion·al·ly** \-ē\ *adv* — **tra·di·tion·less** \-'dish-ən-ləs\ *adj*

tra·di·tion·al·ism \trə-'dish-nə-ˌliz-əm, -ən-ᵊl-ˌiz-\ *n* **1 :** the doctrines or practices of those who follow or accept tradition **2 :** the beliefs of those opposed to modernism, liberalism, or radicalism — **tra·di·tion·al·ist** \-nə-ləst, -ən-ᵊl-əst\ *n or adj* — **tra·di·tion·al·is·tic** \-ˌdish-nə-'lis-tik, -ən-ᵊl-'is-\ *adj*

tra·di·tion·al·ize \trə-'dish-nə-ˌlīz, -ən-ᵊl-ˌīz\ *vt* **-ized; -iz·ing :** to make traditional **:** imbue with traditions or traditionalism

tra·di·tion·ary \trə-'dish-ə-ˌner-ē\ *adj* **:** TRADITIONAL

tra·duce \trə-'d(y)üs\ *vt* **tra·duced; tra·duc·ing** [L *traducere* to lead across, transfer, degrade, fr. *tra-, trans-* trans- + *ducere* to lead — more at TOW] **1 :** to expose to shame or blame by means of falsehood and misrepresentation **2 :** VIOLATE, BETRAY <~ a principle of law> ***syn*** see MALIGN — **tra·duce·ment** \-mənt\ *n* — **tra·duc·er** *n*

[1]**traf·fic** \'traf-ik\ *n, often attrib* [MF *trafique,* fr. OIt *traffico,* fr. *trafficare* to traffic] **1 a :** import and export trade **b :** the business of bartering or buying and selling **c :** illegal or disreputable commercial activity <the drug ~> **2 a :** communication or dealings between individuals or groups **b :** EXCHANGE <a lively ~ in ideas —F. L. Allen> **3** *archaic* **:** GOODS, WARES **4 a :** the movement (as of vehicles or pedestrians) through an area or along a route **b :** the vehicles, pedestrians, ships, or planes moving along a route **c :** the information or signals transmitted over a communications system **:** MESSAGES **5 a :** the passengers or cargo carried by a transportation system **b :** the business of transporting passengers or freight ***syn*** see BUSINESS

[2]**traffic** *vb* **traf·ficked; traf·fick·ing** *vi* **:** to carry on traffic ~ *vt* **1 :** to travel over <heavily *trafficked* highways> **2 :** TRADE, BARTER — **traf·fick·er** *n*

traf·fic·able \'traf-i-kə-bəl\ *adj* **1 :** suitable for trading **:** MARKETABLE **2 :** open to traffic <~ roads>

traffic circle *n* **:** ROTARY 2

traffic cone *n* **:** a conical marker used on a road or highway (as for indicating an area under repair)

traffic court *n* **:** a minor court for disposition of petty prosecutions for violations of statutes, ordinances, and local regulations governing the use of highways and motor vehicles

traffic engineering *n* **:** engineering dealing with the design of streets and control of traffic — **traffic engineer** *n*

traffic island *n* **:** a paved or planted island in a roadway designed to guide the flow of traffic

traffic light *n* **:** an electrically operated visual signal (as a system of colored lights) for controlling traffic

traffic manager *n* **1 :** a supervisor of the traffic functions of a commercial or industrial organization **2 :** the director of a large telegraph office

traffic signal *n* **:** a signal (as a traffic light) for controlling traffic

trag *abbr* tragedy; tragic

trag·a·canth \'traj-ə-ˌkan(t)th, 'trag-, -kən(t)th; *also* 'trag-ə-ˌsan(t)th\ *n* [MF *tragacanthe,* fr. L *tragacantha,* fr. Gk *tragakantha,* fr. *tragos* goat + *akantha* thorn — more at ACANTH-] **1 :** a gum obtained from various Asiatic or East European leguminous plants (genus *Astragalus,* esp. *A. gummifer*) that swells in water and is used in the arts and in pharmacy **2 :** a plant yielding tragacanth

tra·ge·di·an \trə-'jēd-ē-ən\ *n* **1 :** a writer of tragedies **2 :** an actor specializing in tragic roles

tra·ge·di·enne \trə-ˌjēd-ē-'en\ *n* [F *tragédienne,* fr. MF, fr. *tragedie*] **:** an actress who plays tragic roles

trag·e·dy \'traj-əd-ē\ *n, pl* **-dies** [ME *tragedie,* fr. MF, fr. L *tragoedia,* fr. Gk *tragōidia,* fr. *tragos* goat + *aeidein* to sing; prob. fr. the satyrs represented by the original chorus; akin to Gk *trōgein* to gnaw — more at TERSE, ODE] **1 a :** a medieval narrative poem or tale typically describing the downfall of a great man **b :** a serious drama typically describing a conflict between the protagonist and a superior force (as destiny) and having a sorrowful or disastrous conclusion that excites pity or terror **c :** the literary genre of tragic dramas **2 a :** a disastrous event **:** CALAMITY **b :** MISFORTUNE **3 :** tragic quality or element

trag·ic \'traj-ik\ *also* **trag·i·cal** \-i-kəl\ *adj* [L *tragicus,* fr. Gk *tragikos,* irreg. fr. *tragōidia* tragedy] **1 :** of, marked by, or expressive of tragedy <the ~ significance of the atomic bomb —H. S. Truman> **2 a :** dealing with or treated in tragedy <the ~ hero> **b :** appropriate to or typical of tragedy **3 a :** regrettably serious or unpleasant **:** DEPLORABLE, LAMENTABLE <the ~ disparity between the actual and the ideal —*Current Biog.*> **b :** marked by a sense of tragedy — **trag·i·cal·ly** \-i-k(ə-)lē\ *adv*

tragic flaw *n* **:** a flaw in the character of the hero of a tragedy that brings about his downfall

tragic irony *n* **:** IRONY 3b

tragi·com·e·dy \ˌtraj-i-'käm-əd-ē\ *n* [MF *tragicomedie,* fr. OIt *tragicomedia,* fr. OSp, fr. L *tragicomoedia,* fr. *tragicus* + *comoedia* comedy] **:** a drama or a situation blending tragic and comic elements — **tragi·com·ic** \-'käm-ik\ *also* **tragi·com·i·cal** \-i-kəl\ *adj*

trago·pan \'trag-ə-ˌpan\ *n* [NL, genus name, fr. L, an Ethiopian bird, fr. Gk, fr. *tragos* goat + *Pan* Pan] **:** any of several brilliantly colored Asiatic pheasants (genus *Tragopan*) having the back and breast usu. covered with white or buff ocelli

tra·gus \'trā-gəs\ *n, pl* **tra·gi** \-ˌgī, -ˌjī\ [NL, fr. Gk *tragos,* a part of the ear, lit., goat] **:** the prominence in front of the external opening of the ear

[1]**trail** \'trā(ə)l\ *vb* [ME *trailen,* fr. MF *trailler* to tow, fr. (assumed) VL *tragulare,* fr. L *tragula* sledge, dragnet] *vi* **1 a :** to hang down so as to drag along or sweep the ground **b :** to extend over a surface in a loose or straggling manner <a vine that ~*s* over the ground> **c :** to grow to such length as to droop over toward the ground <~*ing* branches of a weeping birch> **2 a :** to walk or proceed draggingly, heavily, or wearily **:** PLOD, TRUDGE **b :** to lag behind **:** do poorly in relation to others **3 :** to move, flow, or extend slowly in thin streams <smoke ~*ing* from chimneys> **4 a :** to extend in an erratic or uneven course or line **:** STRAGGLE **b :** DWINDLE <voice ~*ing* off> **5 :** to follow a trail **:** track game ~ *vt* **1 a :** to draw or drag loosely along a surface **:** allow to sweep the ground **b :** HAUL, TOW **2 a :** to drag (as a limb or the body) heavily or wearily **b :** to carry or bring along as an addition, burden, or encumbrance **c :** to draw along in one's wake **3 a :** to follow upon the scent or trace of **:** TRACK **b :** to follow in the footsteps of **:** PURSUE **c :** to follow along behind **d :** to lag behind (as competitor) ***syn*** see FOLLOW

[2]**trail** *n* **1 :** something that trails or is trailed: as **a :** a trailing plant **b :** the train of a gown **c :** a trailing arrangement (as of flowers) **:** SPRAY **d :** the part of a gun carriage that rests on the ground when the piece is unlimbered **2 a :** something that follows or moves along as if being drawn along **:** TRAIN <a ~ of admirers> **b** (1) **:** the streak produced by a meteor (2) **:** a continuous line produced photographically by permitting the image of a celestial body (as a star) to move over the plate **c :** a chain of consequences **:** AFTERMATH <the . . . movement left a ~ of bitterness and prejudice behind it —Paul Blanshard> **3 a :** a trace or mark left by something that has passed or been drawn along **:** SCENT, TRACK <a ~ of blood> **b** (1) **:** a track made by passage esp. through a wilderness (2) **:** a marked path through a forest or mountainous region **c :** a course followed or to be followed <hit the campaign ~> — **trail·less** \'trā(ə)l-ləs\ *adj*

trail bike *n* **:** a small motorcycle designed for uses other than on highways and for easy transport (as on an automobile bumper)

trail·blaz·er \'trā(ə)l-ˌblā-zər\ *n* **1 :** one that blazes a trail to guide others **:** PATHFINDER **2 :** PIONEER 2 <a ~ in astrophysics>

trail·blaz·ing \-ziŋ\ *adj* **:** making or pointing a new way <~ legislation>

trail·break·er \-ˌbrā-kər\ *n* **:** TRAILBLAZER

[1]**trail·er** \'trā-lər\ *n* **1 :** one that trails **2 :** a trailing plant **3 a :** a highway or industrial-plant vehicle designed to be hauled (as by a tractor) **b :** a usu. automobile-drawn highway vehicle designed to serve wherever parked as a dwelling or as a place of business **4 a :** PREVIEW 2 **b :** a short blank strip of film attached to the end of a reel

[2]**trailer** *vt* **:** to transport (as a boat) by means of a trailer ~ *vi* **1 :** to live or travel in a trailer **2 :** to be transportable by trailer <a light boat that ~*s* easily> — **trail·er·able** \-lə-rə-bəl\ *adj*

trail·er·ist \-ə-rəst\ *n* **1 :** a person traveling or vacationing with a trailer **2 :** TRAILERITE 1

trail·er·ite \-ˌrīt\ *n* **1 :** a person living in a mobile home **2 :** TRAILERIST 1

trailer park *n* **:** an area equipped to accommodate house trailers — called also *trailer camp, trailer court*

trail·er·ship \'trā-lər-ˌship\ *n* **:** a ship designed to carry trucks and trailers

trailing arbutus *n* **:** an arbutus (*Epigaea repens*)

trailing edge *n* **:** the rearmost edge of an object that moves and esp. of an airfoil

trail·side \ˌtrāl-ˌsīd\ *adj* **:** of, relating to, or situated in the area immediately adjacent to a trail

[1]**train** \'trān\ *n* [ME *traine,* fr. MF, fr. OF, fr. *traïr* to betray, fr. L *tradere* — more at TRAITOR] *obs* **:** SCHEME, TRICK

[2]**train** *n* [ME, fr. MF, fr. OF, fr. *trainer* to draw, drag] **1 :** a part of a gown that trails behind the wearer **2 a :** RETINUE, SUITE **b :** a moving file of persons, vehicles, or animals **3 :** the vehicles, men, and sometimes animals that furnish supply, maintenance, and evacuation services to a combat unit **4 a :** order designed to lead to some result **b :** an orderly succession <a ~ of thought> **c :** accompanying or resultant circumstances **:** AFTERMATH **5 :** a line of gunpowder laid to lead fire to a charge **6 :** a series of moving mechanical parts (as gears) that transmit and modify motion **7 a :** a connected line of railroad cars with or without a locomotive **b :** an automotive tractor with one or more trailer units **8 :** a series of parts or elements that together constitute a system for producing a result and esp. for carrying on a process (as of manufacture) automatically — **train·ful** \'trān-ˌfu̇l\ *n*

[3]**train** *vb* [ME *trainen,* fr. MF *trainer,* fr. OF, fr. (assumed) VL *traginare;* akin to L *trahere* to draw — more at DRAW] *vt* **1 :** TRAIL, DRAG **2 :** to direct the growth of (a plant) usu. by bending, pruning, and tying **3 a :** to form by instruction, discipline, or drill **b :** to teach so as to make fit, qualified, or proficient **4 :** to make prepared (as by exercise) for a test of skill **5 :** to aim at an object or objective **:** DIRECT <~*ed* his gaze at the deer> <~*ing* every effort toward success> ~ *vi* **1 :** to undergo instruction, discipline, or drill **2 :** to go by train ***syn*** see TEACH — **train·abil·i·ty** \ˌtrā-nə-'bil-ət-ē\ *n* — **train·able** \'trā-nə-bəl\ *adj* — **train·er** \'trā-nər\ *n*

train·band \'trān-ˌband\ *n* [alter. of *trained band*] **:** a 17th or 18th century militia company in England or America

train·bear·er \'trān-ˌbar-ər, -ˌber-\ *n* **:** an attendant who holds up (as on a ceremonial occasion) the train of a robe or gown

train case *n* **:** a small boxlike piece of luggage used esp. for toilet articles

train dispatcher *n* **:** a railroad employee who directs the movement of trains within a division and coordinates their movement from one division to another
train·ee \trā-ˈnē\ *n* **:** one who is being trained for a job — **train·ee·ship** \-ˈnē-ˌship\ *n*
train·ing *n* **1 :** the act, process, or method of one who trains **2 :** the state of being trained
training college *n, Brit* **:** TEACHERS COLLEGE
training school *n* **1 :** a school preparing students for a particular occupation **2 :** a correctional institution for the custody and reeducation of juvenile delinquents
training table *n* **:** a table where men under an athletic training regimen eat meals planned to help in their conditioning
train·load \ˈtrān-ˈlōd, -ˌlōd\ *n* **:** the full freight or passenger capacity of a railroad train
train·man \ˈtrān-mən, -ˌman\ *n* **:** a member of a train crew supervised by a conductor
train oil \ˈtrān-\ *n* [obs. *train* (train oil), fr. ME *trane,* fr. MD *trane* or MLG *trān*] **:** oil from a marine animal (as a whale)
train·sick \ˈtrān-ˌsik\ *adj* **:** affected with motion sickness induced by riding on a train — **train sickness** *n*
traipse \ˈtrāps\ *vb* **traipsed; traips·ing** [origin unknown] *vi* **:** to walk or tramp about **:** GAD ~ *vt* **:** TRAMP, WALK — **traipse** *n*
trait \ˈtrāt, *Brit usu* ˈtrā\ *n* [MF, lit., act of drawing, fr. L *tractus* — more at TRACT] **1 a :** a stroke of or as if of a pencil **b :** TOUCH, TRACE **2 a :** a distinguishing quality (as of personal character) **:** PECULIARITY **b :** an inherited characteristic
trai·tor \ˈtrāt-ər\ *n* [ME *traitre,* fr. OF, fr. L *traditor,* fr. *traditus,* pp. of *tradere* to hand over, deliver, betray, fr. *trans-, tra-* trans- + *dare* to give — more at DATE] **1 :** one who betrays another's trust or is false to an obligation or duty **2 :** one who commits treason
trai·tor·ous \ˈtrāt-ə-rəs, ˈtrā-trəs\ *adj* **1 :** guilty or capable of treason **2 :** constituting treason <~ activities> ***syn*** see FAITHLESS — **trai·tor·ous·ly** *adv*
trai·tress \ˈtrā-trəs\ *or* **trai·tor·ess** \ˈtrāt-ə-rəs, ˈtrā-trəs\ *n* **:** a female traitor
tra·ject \trə-ˈjekt\ *vt* [L *trajectus,* pp.] **:** TRANSMIT — **tra·jec·tion** \-ˈjek-shən\ *n*
tra·jec·to·ry \trə-ˈjek-t(ə-)rē\ *n, pl* **-ries** [NL *trajectoria,* fr. fem. of *trajectorius* of passing, fr. L *trajectus,* pp. of *traicere* to cause to cross, cross, fr. *trans-, tra-* trans- + *jacere* to throw — more at JET] **1 :** the curve that a body (as a planet or comet in its orbit or a rocket) describes in space **2 :** a path, progression, or line of development resembling a physical trajectory
[1]**tram** \ˈtram\ *n* [E dial., shaft of a wheelbarrow, prob. fr. LG *traam,* lit., beam] **1 :** any of various vehicles: as **a :** a boxlike wagon running on rails (as in a mine) **b** *chiefly Brit* **:** STREETCAR **c :** a carrier that travels on an overhead cable or rails **2 a** *pl, chiefly Brit* **:** a streetcar line **b :** TRAMROAD
[2]**tram** *vt* **trammed; tram·ming :** to haul in a tram or over a tramway
tram·car \ˈtram-ˌkär\ *n* **1** *chiefly Brit* **:** STREETCAR **2 :** TRAM 1a
tram·line \-ˌlīn\ *n, Brit* **:** a streetcar line
[1]**tram·mel** \ˈtram-əl\ *n* [ME *tramayle,* a kind of net, fr. MF *tremail,* fr. LL *tremaculum,* fr. L *tres* three + *macula* mesh, spot — more at THREE] **1 :** a net for catching birds or fish; *esp* **:** one having three layers with the middle one finer-meshed and slack so that fish passing through carry some of the center net through the coarser opposite net and are trapped **2 :** a shackle used for making a horse amble **3 :** something impeding activity, progress, or freedom **:** RESTRAINT — usu. used in pl. **4 :** an adjustable pothook for a fireplace crane **5 a :** an instrument for drawing ellipses **b :** a compass for drawing large circles that consists of a beam with two sliding parts — usu. used in pl. **c :** any of various gauges used for aligning or adjusting machine parts
[2]**trammel** *vt* **-meled** *or* **-melled; -mel·ing** *or* **-mel·ling** \-(ə-)liŋ\ **1 :** to catch or hold in or as if in a net **:** ENMESH **2 :** to prevent or impede the free play of **:** CONFINE ***syn*** see HAMPER
[1]**tra·mon·tane** \trə-ˈmän-ˌtān, ˌtram-ən-ˈ\ *adj* [It *tramontano,* fr. L *transmontanus,* fr. *trans-* + *mont-, mons* mountain — more at MOUNT] **1 :** TRANSALPINE **2 :** lying on or coming from the other side of a mountain range
[2]**tramontane** *n* **:** one dwelling in a tramontane region; *broadly* **:** FOREIGNER
[1]**tramp** \ˈtramp, *vi 1 & vt 1 are also* ˈträmp, ˈtrómp\ *vb* [ME *trampen;* akin to MLG *trampen* to stamp, OE *treppan* to tread — more at TRAP] *vi* **1 :** to walk, tread, or step esp. heavily **2 a :** to travel about on foot **:** HIKE **b :** to journey as a tramp ~ *vt* **1 :** to tread on forcibly and repeatedly **2 :** to travel or wander through on foot <has ~*ed* all the woods on his property> — **tramp·er** *n*
[2]**tramp** \ˈtramp, *3, 4 are also* ˈträmp, ˈtrómp\ *n* **1 a :** a foot traveler **b :** a begging or thieving vagrant **c :** a woman of loose morals; *specif* **:** PROSTITUTE **2 :** a walking trip **:** HIKE **3 :** the succession of sounds made by the beating of feet on a surface (as a road, pavement, or floor) **4 :** an iron plate to protect the sole of a shoe **5 :** a ship not making regular trips but taking cargo when and where it offers and to any port — called also *tramp steamer*
[3]**tramp** \ˈtramp\ *adj* **:** having no fixed abode, connection, or destination <a ~ dog>
tram·ple \ˈtram-pəl\ *vb* **tram·pled; tram·pling** \-p(ə-)liŋ\ [ME *tramplen,* freq. of *trampen* to tramp] *vi* **1 :** TRAMP; *esp* **:** to tread heavily so as to bruise, crush, or injure **2 :** to inflict injury or destruction esp. contemptuously or ruthlessly — usu. used with *on, over,* or *upon* <*trampling* on the rights of others> ~ *vt* **:** to press down, crush, or injure by or as if by treading **:** STAMP — **trample** *n* — **tram·pler** \-p(ə-)lər\ *n*
tram·po·line \ˌtram-pə-ˈlēn, ˈtram-pə-ˌ\ *n* [Sp *trampolín,* fr. It *trampolino,* of Gmc origin; akin to MLG *trampen* to stamp] **:** a resilient canvas sheet or web supported by springs in a metal frame and used as a springboard in tumbling — **tram·po·lin·er** \-ˈlē-nər, -ˌlē-\ *n* — **tram·po·lin·ist** \-nəst\ *n*
tram·po·lin·ing *n* **:** the sport of jumping and tumbling on a trampoline
tram·road \ˈtram-ˌrōd\ *n* **:** a roadway for trams consisting of parallel tracks made usu. of metal-faced wooden beams, stone blocks, metal plates, or rails; *esp* **:** a railway in a mine
tram·way \-ˌwā\ *n* **:** a way for trams: as **a :** TRAMROAD **b** *Brit* **:** a streetcar line **c :** an overhead cable or rails for trams
[1]**trance** \ˈtran(t)s\ *n* [ME, fr. MF *transe,* fr. *transir* to pass away, swoon, fr. L *transire* to pass, pass away — more at TRANSIENT] **1 :** a state of partly suspended animation or inability to function **2 :** a somnolent state (as of deep hypnosis) **3 :** a state of profound abstraction or absorption — **trance·like** \-ˌlīk\ *adj*
[2]**trance** *vt* **tranced; tranc·ing :** ENTRANCE, ENRAPTURE
tran·gam \ˈtraŋ-gəm\ *n* [origin unknown] *archaic* **:** TRINKET, GIMCRACK
tran·quil \ˈtraŋ-kwəl, ˈtran-\ *adj* [L *tranquillus*] **1 a :** free from agitation of mind or spirit <~ faith> **b :** free from disturbance or turmoil <a ~ scene> **2 :** unvarying in aspect **:** STEADY, STABLE ***syn*** see CALM ***ant*** troubled — **tran·quil·ly** \-kwə-lē\ *adv* — **tran·quil·ness** *n*
tran·quil·ize *or* **tran·quil·lize** \ˈtraŋ-kwə-ˌlīz, ˈtran-\ *vb* **-ized** *or* **-lized; -iz·ing** *or* **-liz·ing** *vt* **:** to make tranquil or calm **:** PACIFY; *esp* **:** to relieve of mental tension and anxiety by means of drugs ~ *vi* **1 :** to become tranquil **:** RELAX 2 **2 :** to make one tranquil
tran·quil·iz·er *also* **tran·quil·liz·er** \-ˌlī-zər\ *n* **1 :** one that tranquilizes **2 :** a drug used to reduce mental disturbance (as anxiety and tension) in people and animals
tran·quil·li·ty *or* **tran·quil·i·ty** \tran-ˈkwil-ət-ē, traŋ-\ *n* **:** the quality or state of being tranquil
trans *abbr* **1** transactions **2** transitive **3** translated; translation; translator **4** transportation **5** transverse
trans- *prefix* [L *trans-, tra-* across, beyond, through, so as to change, fr. *trans* across, beyond — more at THROUGH] **1 :** on or to the other side of **:** across **:** beyond <*trans*atlantic> **2 a :** beyond (a specified chemical element) in the periodic table <*trans*uranium> **b** *usu ital* **:** characterized by having such atoms or groups on opposite sides of the molecule <*trans*-dichloro-ethylene> <the isomer with *trans*-configuration> **3 :** through <*trans*cutaneous> **4 :** so or such as to change or transfer <*trans*literate> <*trans*location> <*trans*amination> <*trans*ship>
trans·act \tran(t)s-ˈakt, tranz-\ *vb* [L *transactus,* pp. of *transigere* to drive through, complete, transact, fr. *trans-* + *agere* to drive, do — more at AGENT] *vi* **:** to carry on business ~ *vt* **:** to carry out **:** PERFORM; *esp* **:** to carry on — **trans·ac·tor** \-ˈak-tər\ *n*
trans·ac·ti·nide \-ˈak-tə-ˌnīd\ *adj* **:** of, relating to, or being actual or hypothetical elements with atomic weights higher than those of the actinide series <~ chemistry>
trans·ac·tion \-ˈak-shən\ *n* **1 :** an act, process, or instance of transacting **2 a :** something transacted; *esp* **:** a business deal **b** *pl* **:** the often published record of the meeting of a society or association — **trans·ac·tion·al** \-shnəl, -shən-ᵊl\ *adj*
trans·al·pine \tran(t)s-ˈal-ˌpīn, tranz-\ *adj* [L *transalpinus,* fr. *trans-* + *Alpes* the Alps] **:** situated on the north side of the Alps <*Transalpine* Gaul> — compare CISALPINE
trans·am·i·nase \tran(t)s-ˈam-ə-ˌnās, tranz-, -ˌnāz\ *n* **:** an enzyme promoting transamination — called also *aminotransferase*
trans·am·i·na·tion \ˌtran(t)s-ˌam-ə-ˈnā-shən, ˌtranz-\ *n* **:** a reversible oxidation-reduction reaction in which an amino group is transferred typically from an alpha-amino acid to the carbonyl carbon atom of an alpha-keto acid
trans·at·lan·tic \ˌtran(t)s-ət-ˈlant-ik, ˌtranz-\ *adj* **1 a :** crossing or extending across the Atlantic ocean <a ~ cable> **b :** relating to or involving crossing the Atlantic ocean <~ air fares> **2 :** situated beyond the Atlantic ocean
trans·ax·le \tran(t)s-ˈak-səl, tranz-\ *n* [*trans*mission + *axle*] **:** a mechanical unit in an automotive vehicle that consists of a combined transmission and differential gear
trans·ceiv·er \tran(t)s-ˈē-vər, tranz-\ *n* [*trans*mitter + *receiver*] **:** a radio transmitter-receiver that uses many of the same components for both transmission and reception
tran·scend \tran(t)s-ˈend\ *vb* [L *transcendere* to climb across, transcend, fr. *trans-* + *scandere* to climb — more at SCAN] *vt* **1 a :** to rise above or go beyond the limits of **b :** to be prior to, beyond, and above (the universe or material existence) **2 :** to outstrip or outdo in some attribute, quality, or power ~ *vi* **:** to rise above or extend notably beyond ordinary limits ***syn*** see EXCEED
tran·scen·dence \-ˈen-dən(t)s\ *n* **:** the quality or state of being transcendent
tran·scen·den·cy \-dən-sē\ *n* **:** TRANSCENDENCE
tran·scen·dent \-dənt\ *adj* [L *transcendent-, transcendens,* prp. of *transcendere*] **1 a :** exceeding usual limits **:** SURPASSING **b :** extending or lying beyond the limits of ordinary experience **c** *Kantianism* **:** being beyond the limits of all possible experience and knowledge **2 :** being beyond comprehension **3 :** transcending the universe or material existence — **tran·scen·dent·ly** *adv*
tran·scen·den·tal \ˌtran(t)s-ˌen-ˈdent-ᵊl, -ən-\ *adj* **1** *Kantianism* **a :** of or relating to experience as determined by the mind's makeup **b :** transcending experience but not human knowledge **2 :** TRANSCENDENT 1a **3 a:** incapable of being the root of an algebraic equation with rational coefficients <π is a ~ number> **b :** being, involving, or representing a function (as sin x, log x, e^x) that cannot be expressed by a finite number of algebraic operations <~ curves> **4 a :** TRANSCENDENT 1b **b :** SUPERNATURAL **c :** ABSTRUSE, ABSTRACT **d :** of or relating to transcendentalism — **tran·scen·den·tal·ly** \-ᵊl-ē\ *adv*
tran·scen·den·tal·ism \-ᵊl-ˌiz-əm\ *n* **1 :** a philosophy that emphasizes the a priori conditions of knowledge and experience or the unknowable character of ultimate reality or that emphasizes the

transcendent as the fundamental reality **2 :** a philosophy that asserts the primacy of the spiritual and transcendental over the material and empirical **3 :** the quality or state of being transcendental; *esp* **:** visionary idealism — **tran·scen·den·tal·ist** \-ᵊl-əst\ *adj or n*

trans·con·ti·nen·tal \ˌtran(t)s-ˌkänt-ᵊn-ˈent-ᵊl\ *adj* **:** extending or going across a continent <a ~ railroad>

tran·scribe \tran(t)s-ˈkrīb\ *vt* **tran·scribed; tran·scrib·ing** [L *transcribere*, fr. *trans-* + *scribere* to write — more at SCRIBE] **1 a :** to make a written copy of **b :** to make a copy of (dictated or recorded matter) in longhand or on a typewriter **c :** to paraphrase or summarize in writing **d :** to write down **:** RECORD **2 a :** to represent (speech sounds) by means of phonetic symbols **b :** TRANSLATE 2a **c :** to transfer (data) from one recording form to another **d :** to record (as on magnetic tape) for later broadcast **3 :** to make a musical transcription of **4 :** to broadcast by electrical transcription **5 :** to cause (as DNA) to undergo genetic transcription — **tran·scrib·er** *n*

tran·script \ˈtran(t)s-ˌkript\ *n* [ME, fr. ML *transcriptum*, fr. L, neut. of *transcriptus*, pp. of *transcribere*] **1 a :** a written, printed, or typed copy; *esp* **:** a usu. typewritten copy of dictated or recorded material **b :** an official or legal and often published copy <a court reporter's ~>; *esp* **:** an official copy of a student's educational record **2 :** a representation (as of experience) in an art form

tran·scrip·tion \tran(t)s-ˈkrip-shən\ *n* **1 :** an act, process, or instance of transcribing **2 :** COPY, TRANSCRIPT: as **a :** an arrangement of a musical composition for some instrument or voice other than the original **b :** ELECTRICAL TRANSCRIPTION **3 :** the process of constructing a messenger RNA molecule using a DNA molecule as a template with resulting transfer of genetic information to the messenger RNA — compare TRANSLATION 2 — **tran·scrip·tion·al** \-shnəl, -shən-ᵊl\ *adj* — **tran·scrip·tion·al·ly** \-ē\ *adv*

trans·cu·ta·ne·ous \ˌtran(t)s-kyu̇-ˈtā-nē-əs\ *adj* **:** passing or entering through the skin <~ infection> <~ inoculation>

trans·duce \tran(t)s-ˈd(y)üs, tranz-\ *vt* **trans·duced; trans·duc·ing** [L *transducere* to lead across, transfer, fr. *trans-* + *ducere* to lead — more at TOW] **1 :** to convert (as energy or a message) into another form <essentially sense organs ~ physical energy into a nervous signal> **2 :** to bring about the transfer of (as a gene) from one microorganism to another by means of a viral agent

trans·duc·er \-ˈd(y)ü-sər\ *n* [L *transducere* to lead across, fr. *trans-* + *ducere* to lead — more at TOW] **:** a device that is actuated by power from one system and supplies power usu. in another form to a second system (as a telephone receiver that is actuated by electric power and supplies acoustic power to the surrounding air)

trans·duc·tion \-ˈdək-shən\ *n* [L *transductus*, pp. of *transducere*] **:** the action or process of transducing; *esp* **:** the transfer of genetic determinants from one microorganism to another by a viral agent (as a bacteriophage) — **trans·duc·tion·al** \-shnəl, -shən-ᵊl\ *adj*

[1]tran·sect \tran(t)s-ˈekt\ *vt* [*trans-* + *-sect*] **:** to cut transversely — **tran·sec·tion** \-ˈek-shən\ *n*

[2]tran·sect \ˈtran(t)s-ˌekt\ *n* **:** a sample area (as of vegetation) usu. in the form of a long continuous strip

tran·sept \ˈtran(t)s-ˌept\ *n* [NL *transeptum*, fr. L *trans-* + *septum*, *saeptum* enclosure, wall — more at SEPTUM] **:** the part of a cruciform church that crosses at right angles to the greatest length between the nave and the apse or choir; *also* **:** either of the projecting ends of a transept — see BASILICA illustration — **tran·sep·tal** \tran(t)s-ˈep-tᵊl\ *adj*

transf *abbr* transfer; transferred

[1]trans·fer \tran(t)s-ˈfər, ˈtran(t)s-ˌ\ *vb* **trans·ferred; trans·fer·ring** [ME *transferren*, fr. L *transferre*, fr. *trans-* + *ferre* to carry — more at BEAR] *vt* **1 a :** to convey from one person, place, or situation to another **:** TRANSPORT **b :** to cause to pass from one to another **:** TRANSMIT **c :** TRANSFORM, CHANGE **2 :** to make over the possession or control of **:** CONVEY **3 :** to print or otherwise copy from one surface to another by contact ~ *vi* **1 :** to move to a different place, region, or situation; *esp* **:** to withdraw from one educational institution to enroll at another **2 :** to change from one vehicle or transportation line to another — **trans·fer·abil·i·ty** \(ˌ)tran(t)s-ˌfər-ə-ˈbil-ət-ē\ *n* — **trans·fer·able** \-ə-bəl\ *adj* — **trans·fer·al** \-əl\ *n* — **trans·fer·rer** \-ər\ *n*

syn TRANSFER, CONVEY, ALIENATE, DEED *shared meaning element* **:** to make over (property) from one owner to another

[2]trans·fer \ˈtran(t)s-ˌfər\ *n* **1 a :** conveyance of right, title, or interest in real or personal property from one person to another **b :** removal or acquisition of property by mere delivery with intent to transfer title **2 a :** an act, process, or instance of transferring **:** TRANSFERENCE 2 **b :** the carry-over or generalization of learned responses from one type of situation to another **3 :** one that transfers or is transferred; *esp* **:** a graphic image transferred by contact from one surface to another **4 :** a place where a transfer is made (as of trains to ferries or as where one form of power is changed to another) **5 :** a ticket entitling a passenger on a public conveyance to continue his journey on another route

trans·fer·ase \ˈtran(t)s-(ˌ)fər-ˌās, -ˌāz\ *n* **:** an enzyme that promotes transfer of a group from one molecule to another

trans·fer·ee \ˌtran(t)s-(ˌ)fər-ˈē\ *n* **1 :** a person to whom a conveyance is made **2 :** one who is transferred

trans·fer·ence \tran(t)s-ˈfər-ən(t)s, ˈtran(t)s-(ˌ)\ *n* **1 :** an act, process, or instance of transferring **:** CONVEYANCE, TRANSFER **2 :** the redirection of feelings and desires and esp. of those unconsciously retained from childhood toward a new object (as a psychoanalyst conducting therapy) — **trans·fer·en·tial** \ˌtran(t)s-fə-ˈren-chəl\ *adj*

trans·fer·or \ˌtran(t)s-(ˌ)fər-ˈȯ(ə)r\ *n* **:** one that conveys a title, right, or property

transfer payment *n* **1 :** a public expenditure made for a purpose (as veterans' benefits or unemployment compensation) other than procuring goods or services — usu. used in pl. **2** *pl* **:** money (as welfare payments or pensions) that is received by individuals or families and that is neither compensation for goods or services currently supplied nor income from investments

trans·fer·rin \tran(t)s-ˈfer-ən\ *n* [*trans-* + L *ferrum* iron] **:** a beta globulin in blood plasma capable of combining with ferric ions and transporting iron in the body

transfer RNA \ˈtran(t)s-ˌfər-\ *n* **:** a relatively small RNA that transfers a particular amino acid to a growing polypeptide chain at the ribosomal site of protein synthesis during translation

trans·fig·u·ra·tion \(ˌ)tran(t)s-ˌfig-(y)ə-ˈrā-shən\ *n* **1 a :** a change in form or appearance **:** METAMORPHOSIS **b :** an exalting, glorifying, or spiritual change **2** *cap* **:** August 6 observed as a Christian feast in commemoration of the transfiguration of Christ on a mountaintop with three disciples looking on

trans·fig·ure \tran(t)s-ˈfig-yər, *esp Brit* -ˈfig-ər\ *vt* **-ured; -uring** [ME *transfiguren*, fr. L *transfigurare*, fr. *trans-* + *figurare* to shape, fashion, fr. *figura* figure] **:** to give a new and typically exalted or spiritual appearance to **:** transform outwardly and usu. for the better ***syn*** see TRANSFORM

trans·fi·nite \(ˈ)tran(t)s-ˈfī-ˌnīt\ *adj* [G *transfinit*, fr. *trans-* (fr. L) + *finit* finite, fr. L *finitus*] **1 :** going beyond or surpassing any finite number, group, or magnitude **2 :** being or relating to cardinal and ordinal numbers of sets with an infinite number of elements

trans·fix \tran(t)s-ˈfiks\ *vt* [L *transfixus*, pp. of *transfigere*, fr. *trans-* + *figere* to fasten, pierce — more at DIKE] **1 :** to pierce through with or as if with a pointed weapon **:** IMPALE **2 :** to hold motionless by or as if by piercing — **trans·fix·ion** \-ˈfik-shən\ *n*

[1]trans·form \tran(t)s-ˈfȯ(ə)rm\ *vb* [ME *transformen*, fr. L *transformare*, fr. *trans-* + *formare* to form, fr. *forma* form] *vt* **1 a :** to change in composition or structure **b :** to change the outward form or appearance of **c :** to change in character or condition **:** CONVERT **2 :** to subject to mathematical transformation **3 :** to change (a current) in potential (as from high voltage to low) or in type (as from alternating to direct) **4 :** to cause (a cell) to undergo genetic transformation ~ *vi* **:** to become transformed **:** CHANGE — **trans·form·able** \-ˈfȯr-mə-bəl\ *adj* — **trans·for·ma·tive** \-ˈfȯr-mət-iv\ *adj*

syn TRANSFORM, METAMORPHOSE, TRANSMUTE, CONVERT, TRANSMOGRIFY, TRANSFIGURE *shared meaning element* **:** to change a thing into another or from one form to another

[2]trans·form \ˈtran(t)s-ˌfȯrm\ *n* **1 :** a mathematical element obtained from another by transformation **2 :** TRANSFORMATION 2 **3 :** a linguistic structure (as a sentence) produced by means of a transformation <"the duckling is killed by the farmer" is a ~ of "the farmer kills the duckling">

trans·for·ma·tion \ˌtran(t)s-fər-ˈmā-shən, -fȯr-\ *n* **1 :** an act, process, or instance of transforming or being transformed **2 a** (1) **:** the operation of changing (as by rotation or mapping) one configuration or expression into another in accordance with a mathematical rule; *esp* **:** a change of variables or coordinates in which a function of new variables or coordinates is substituted for each original variable or coordinate (2) **:** the formula that effects a transformation **b :** FUNCTION 5a **3 :** one of an ordered set of rules that converts the deep structures of a language into surface structures **4 :** genetic modification of a cell and esp. of a bacterium by introduction of DNA from a genetically different source

trans·for·ma·tion·al \-shnəl, -shən-ᵊl\ *adj* **:** of, relating to, or characterized by linguistic transformation

transformational grammar *n* **:** a grammar that generates the deep structures of a language and converts these to the surface structures by means of transformations

trans·for·ma·tion·al·ist \ˌtran(t)s-fər-ˈmā-shnəl-əst, -shən-ᵊl-\ *n* **:** an exponent of transformational grammar

trans·form·er \tran(t)s-ˈfȯr-mər\ *n* **:** one that transforms; *specif* **:** a device employing the principle of mutual induction to convert variations of current in a primary circuit into variations of voltage and current in a secondary circuit

trans·fuse \tran(t)s-ˈfyüz\ *vt* **trans·fused; trans·fus·ing** [ME *transfusen*, fr. L *transfusus*, pp. of *transfundere*, fr. *trans-* + *fundere* to pour — more at FOUND] **1 a :** to cause to pass from one to another **:** TRANSMIT **b :** to diffuse into or through **:** PERMEATE <sunlight ~*s* the bay> **2 a :** to transfer (as blood) into a vein of a man or animal **b :** to subject (a patient) to transfusion — **trans·fus·ible** *or* **trans·fus·able** \-ˈfyü-zə-bəl\ *adj*

trans·fu·sion \tran(t)s-ˈfyü-zhən\ *n* **:** an act, process, or instance of transfusing; *esp* **:** the process of transfusing fluid into a vein or artery — **trans·fu·sion·al** \-ˈfyüzh-nəl, -ən-ᵊl\ *adj*

trans·gress \tran(t)s-ˈgres, tranz-\ *vb* [F *transgresser*, fr. L *transgressus*, pp. of *transgredi* to step beyond or across, fr. *trans-* + *gradi* to step — more at GRADE] *vt* **1 :** to go beyond limits set or prescribed by **:** VIOLATE <~ the divine law> **2 :** to pass beyond or go over (a limit or boundary) ~ *vi* **1 :** to violate a command or law **:** SIN **2 :** to go beyond a boundary or limit — **trans·gres·sive** \-ˈgres-iv\ *adj* — **trans·gres·sor** \-ˈgres-ər\ *n*

trans·gres·sion \-ˈgresh-ən\ *n* **:** an act, process, or instance of transgressing: as **a :** infringement or violation of a law, command, or duty **b :** the spread of the sea over land areas and the consequent unconformable deposit of sediments on older rocks

tran·ship *var of* TRANSSHIP

trans·hu·mance \tran(t)s-ˈ(h)yü-mən(t)s, tranz-\ *n* [F, fr. *transhumer* to practice transhumance, fr. Sp *trashumar*, fr. *tras-* trans- (fr. L *trans-*) + L *humus* earth — more at HUMBLE] **:** seasonal movement of livestock and esp. sheep between mountain and lowland pastures either under the care of herders or in company with the owners — **trans·hu·mant** \-mənt\ *adj or n*

tran·sience \ˈtranch-ən(t)s; ˈtranz-ē-ən(t)s, ˈtran(t)s-ē-, ˈtranch-ē-; ˈtranzh-ən(t)s, ˈtranj-\ *n* **:** the quality or state of being transient

tran·sien·cy \-ən-sē\ *n* **:** TRANSIENCE

[1]tran·sient \-ənt\ *adj* [L *transeunt-*, *transiens*, prp. of *transire* to go across, pass, fr. *trans-* + *ire* to go] **1 a :** passing esp. quickly into and out of existence **:** TRANSITORY **b :** passing through or by a place with only a brief stay or sojourn **2 :** affecting something or producing results beyond itself — **tran·sient·ly** *adv*

syn TRANSIENT, TRANSITORY, EPHEMERAL, MOMENTARY, FLEETING, FUGITIVE, EVANESCENT, SHORT-LIVED *shared meaning element* : lasting or staying only a short time ***ant*** perpetual

[2]**transient** *n* **1 :** one that is transient: as **a :** a transient guest **b :** a person traveling about usu. in search of work **2 a :** a temporary oscillation that occurs in a circuit because of a sudden change of voltage or of load **b :** a transient current or voltage

trans·il·lu·mi·nate \ˌtran(t)s-ə-ˈlü-mə-ˌnāt, ˌtranz-\ *vt* **:** to cause light to pass through; *esp* **:** to pass light through (a body part) for medical examination — **trans·il·lu·mi·na·tion** \-ˌlü-mə-ˈnā-shən\ *n* — **trans·il·lu·mi·na·tor** \-ˈlü-mə-ˌnāt-ər\ *n*

tran·sis·tor \tranz-ˈis-tər, tran(t)s-\ *n* [[1]*trans*fer + re*sistor;* fr. its transferring an electrical signal across a resistor] **1 :** an electronic device that is similar to the electron tube in use (as amplification and rectification) and consists of a small block of a semiconductor (as germanium) with at least three electrodes **2 :** a transistorized radio

tran·sis·tor·ize \-tə-ˌrīz\ *vt* **-ized; -iz·ing :** to equip (a device) with transistors — **tran·sis·tor·iza·tion** \-ˌis-tə-rə-ˈzā-shən\ *n*

[1]**tran·sit** \ˈtran(t)s-ət, ˈtranz-\ *n* [L *transitus,* fr. *transitus,* pp. of *transire* to go across, pass] **1 a :** an act, process, or instance of passing through or over **:** PASSAGE **b :** CHANGE, TRANSITION **c (1) :** conveyance of persons or things from one place to another **(2) :** usu. local transportation esp. of people by public conveyance; *also* **:** vehicles or a system engaged in such transportation **2 a :** passage of a celestial body over the meridian of a place or through the field of a telescope **b :** passage of a smaller body (as Venus) across the disk of a larger (as the sun) **3 :** a theodolite with the telescope mounted so that it can be transited — **in transit :** in passage

[2]**transit** *vi* **:** to make a transit ~ *vt* **1 a :** to pass over or through **:** TRAVERSE **b :** to cause to pass over or through **2 :** to pass across (a meridian, a celestial body, or the field of view of a telescope) **3 :** to turn (a telescope) over about the horizontal transverse axis in surveying

transit instrument *n* **1 :** a telescope at right angles to a horizontal east-west axis and used with a clock and chronograph for observing the time of transit of a celestial body over the meridian of a place **2 :** TRANSIT 3

tran·si·tion \tran(t)s-ˈish-ən, tranz-, *chiefly Brit* tran(t)s-ˈizh-\ *n* [L *transition-, transitio,* fr. *transitus,* pp. of *transire*] **1 a :** passage from one state, stage, or place to another **:** CHANGE **b :** a movement, development, or evolution from one form, stage, or style to another **2 a :** a musical modulation **b :** a musical passage leading from one section of a piece to another **3 :** an abrupt change in energy state or level (as of an atomic nucleus or a molecule) usu. accompanied by loss or gain of a single quantum of energy **4 :** a genetic mutation in RNA or DNA that results from the substitution of one purine base for the other or of one pyrimidine base for the other — **tran·si·tion·al** \-ˈish-nəl, -ˈizh-, -ən-ᵊl\ *adj* — **tran·si·tion·al·ly** \-ē\ *adv*

transition element *n* [fr. their being transitional between the more highly electropositive and the less highly electropositive elements] **:** any of various metallic elements (as chromium, iron, and nickel) that have valence electrons in two shells instead of only one — called also *transition metal*

tran·si·tive \ˈtran(t)s-ət-iv, ˈtranz-; ˈtran(t)s-tiv\ *adj* [LL *transitivus,* fr. L *transitus,* pp. of *transire*] **1 :** characterized by having or containing a direct object <a ~ verb> <a ~ construction> **2 :** being or relating to a relation with the property that if the relation holds between a first element and a second and between the second element and a third, it holds between the first and third elements <equality is a ~ relation> **3 :** of, relating to, or characterized by transition — **tran·si·tive·ly** *adv* — **tran·si·tive·ness** *n* — **tran·si·tiv·i·ty** \ˌtran(t)s-ə-ˈtiv-ət-ē, ˌtranz-\ *n*

tran·si·to·ry \ˈtran(t)s-ə-ˌtōr-ē, ˈtranz-, -ˌtȯr-\ *adj* [ME *transitorie,* fr. MF *transitoire,* fr. LL *transitorius,* fr. L, of or allowing passage, fr. *transitus,* pp. of *transire*] **1 :** tending to pass away **:** not persistent **2 :** of brief duration **:** TEMPORARY ***syn*** see TRANSIENT ***ant*** enduring — **tran·si·to·ri·ly** \ˌtran(t)s-ə-ˈtōr-ə-lē, ˌtranz-, -ˈtȯr-\ *adv* — **tran·si·to·ri·ness** \ˈtran(t)s-ə-ˌtōr-ē-nəs, ˈtran(z)-, -ˌtȯr-\ *n*

transl *abbr* translated; translation

trans·late \tran(t)s-ˈlāt, tranz-\ *vb* **trans·lat·ed; trans·lat·ing** [L *translatus* (pp. of *transferre* to transfer, translate), fr. *trans-* + *latus,* pp. of *ferre* to carry — more at TOLERATE, BEAR] *vt* **1 a :** to bear, remove, or change from one place, state, form, or appearance to another **:** TRANSFER, TRANSFORM <a country boy *translated* to the city> <~ ideas into action> **b :** to convey to heaven or to a nontemporal condition without death **c :** to transfer (a bishop) from one see to another **2 a :** to turn into one's own or another language **b :** to transfer or turn from one set of symbols into another **:** TRANSCRIBE **c (1) :** to express in different words **:** PARAPHRASE **(2) :** to express in more comprehensible terms **:** EXPLAIN **3 :** ENRAPTURE **4 :** to subject to mathematical translation **5 :** to subject (as genetic information) to translation in protein synthesis ~ *vi* **1 :** to practice translation or make a translation; *also* **:** to admit of or be adaptable to translation <a word that doesn't ~ easily> **2 :** to undergo a translation — **trans·lat·abil·i·ty** \(ˌ)tran(t)s-ˌlāt-ə-ˈbil-ət-ē, (ˌ)tranz-\ *n* — **trans·lat·able** \tran(t)s-ˈlāt-ə-bəl, tranz-\ *adj* — **trans·la·tor** \-ˈlāt-ər\ *n*

trans·la·tion \tran(t)s-ˈlā-shən, tranz-\ *n* **1 :** an act, process, or instance of translating: as **a :** a rendering from one language into another; *also* **:** the product of such a rendering **b :** a change to a different substance, form, or appearance **:** CONVERSION **c (1) :** a transformation of coordinates in which the new axes are parallel to the old ones **(2) :** uniform motion of a body in a straight line **2 :** the process of forming a protein molecule at a ribosomal site of protein synthesis from information contained in messenger RNA — compare TRANSCRIPTION 3 — **trans·la·tion·al** \-shnəl, -shən-ᵊl\ *adj*

trans·la·tive \-ˈlāt-iv\ *adj* **1 :** of, relating to, or involving removal or transference from one person or place to another **2 :** of, relating to, or serving to translate from one language or system into another

trans·la·to·ry \ˈtran(t)s-lə-ˌtōr-ē, ˈtranz-, -ˌtȯr-; tran(t)s-ˈlāt-ə-rē, tranz-\ *adj* **:** of, relating to, or involving uniform motion in one direction

trans·lit·er·ate \tran(t)s-ˈlit-ə-ˌrāt, tranz-\ *vt* **-at·ed; -at·ing** [*trans-* + L *littera* letter] **:** to represent or spell in the characters of another alphabet — **trans·lit·er·a·tion** \(ˌ)tran(t)s-ˌlit-ə-ˈrā-shən, (ˌ)tranz-\ *n*

trans·lo·cate \ˈtrans(t)s-lō-ˌkāt, ˈtranz-, (ˈ)tran(t)s-ˈ, (ˈ)tranz-ˈ\ *vt* [prob. back-formation fr. *translocation*] **:** to transfer (as food materials or products of metabolism) from one location to another in the plant body

trans·lo·ca·tion \ˌtrans(t)s-lō-ˈkā-shən, ˌtranz-\ *n* **:** a change of location **:** DISPLACEMENT: as **a :** the conduction of soluble material from one part of a plant to another **b :** the exchange of parts between nonhomologous chromosomes

trans·lu·cence \tran(t)s-ˈlüs-ᵊn(t)s, tranz-\ *n* **:** the quality or state of being translucent

trans·lu·cen·cy \-ᵊn-sē\ *n, pl* **-cies 1 :** TRANSLUCENCE **2 :** something that is translucent

trans·lu·cent \-ᵊnt\ *adj* [L *translucent-, translucens,* prp. of *translucēre* to shine through, fr. *trans-* + *lucēre* to shine — more at LIGHT] **1 :** permitting the passage of light: **a :** CLEAR, TRANSPARENT <the water was ~, and I could readily watch from the side of the canoe what was going on —V. G. Heiser> **b :** transmitting and diffusing light so that objects beyond cannot be seen clearly <which looks like honey, ~ and sunny, from clover-tops —Elinor Wylie> **2 :** free from disguise or falseness <his ~ patriotism —*Newsweek*> <gave one of her ~ performances of a dreaming, wounded . . . young girl —Stark Young> — **trans·lu·cent·ly** *adv*

trans·ma·rine \ˌtran(t)s-mə-ˈrēn, ˌtranz-\ *adj* [L *transmarinus,* fr. *trans-* + *mare* sea — more at MARINE] **1 :** being or coming from beyond or across the sea <a ~ people> **2 :** passing over or extending across the sea

trans·mem·brane \(ˈ)tran(t)s-ˈmem-ˌbrān, (ˈ)tranz-\ *adj* taking place or existing across a membrane <a ~ potential>

trans·mi·grate \(ˈ)tran(t)s-ˈmī-ˌgrāt, (ˈ)tranz-, ˈtran(t)s-ˌ, ˈtranz-ˌ\ *vb* [L *transmigratus,* pp. of *transmigrare* to migrate to another place, fr. *trans-* + *migrare* to migrate] *vi* **1** *of the soul* **:** to pass at death from one body or being to another **2 :** MIGRATE ~ *vt* **:** to cause to transmigrate — **trans·mi·gra·tion** \ˌtran(t)s-mī-ˈgrā-shen, ˌtranz-\ *n* — **trans·mi·gra·tor** \(ˈ)tran(t)s-ˈmī-ˌgrāt-ər, (ˈ)tranz-, ˈtran(t)s-ˌ, ˈtranz-ˌ\ *n* — **trans·mi·gra·to·ry** \tran(t)s-ˈmī-grə-ˌtōr-ē, tranz-, -ˌtȯr-\ *adj*

trans·mis·si·ble \tran(t)s-ˈmis-ə-bəl, tranz-\ *adj* **:** capable of being transmitted — **trans·mis·si·bil·i·ty** \(ˌ)tran(t)s-ˌmis-ə-ˈbil-ət-ē, (ˌ)tranz-\ *n*

trans·mis·sion \tran(t)s-ˈmish-ən, tranz-\ *n* [L *transmission-, transmissio,* fr. *transmissus,* pp. of *transmittere* to transmit] **1 :** an act, process, or instance of transmitting <~ of a nerve impulse across a synapse> **2 :** the passage of radio waves in the space between transmitting and receiving stations; *also* **:** the act or process of transmitting by radio or television **3 :** an assembly of parts including the speed-changing gears and the propeller shaft by which the power is transmitted from an automobile engine to a live axle; *also* **:** the speed-changing gears in such an assembly **4 :** something that is transmitted **:** MESSAGE — **trans·mis·sive** \-ˈmis-iv\ *adj* — **trans·mis·siv·i·ty** \ˌtran(t)s-(ˌ)mis-ˈiv-ət-ē, ˌtranz-\ *n*

trans·mis·som·e·ter \ˌtran(t)s-(ˌ)mis-ˈäm-ət-ər, ˌtranz-\ *n* **:** an instrument for measuring the transmission of light through a fluid (as the atmosphere)

trans·mit \tran(t)s-ˈmit, tranz-\ *vb* **trans·mit·ted; trans·mit·ting** [ME *transmitten,* fr. L *transmittere,* fr. *trans-* + *mittere* to send — more at SMITE] *vt* **1 a :** to send or transfer from one person or place to another **:** FORWARD **b :** to cause or allow to spread: as **(1) :** to convey by or as if by inheritance or heredity **:** hand down **(2) :** to convey (infection) abroad or to another **2 a (1) :** to cause (as light or force) to pass or be conveyed through space or a medium **(2) :** to admit the passage of **:** CONDUCT <glass ~*s* light> **b :** to send out (a signal) either by radio waves or over a wire ~ *vi* **:** to send out a signal either by radio waves or over a wire — **trans·mit·ta·ble** \-ˈmit-ə-bəl\ *adj* — **trans·mit·tal** \-ˈmit-ᵊl\ *n*

trans·mit·tance \-ˈmit-ᵊn(t)s\ *n* **1 :** TRANSMISSION **2 :** the fraction of radiant energy that having entered a layer of absorbing matter reaches its farther boundary

trans·mit·ter \-ˈmit-ər\ *n* **:** one that transmits: as **a (1) :** a part on a telephone into which one speaks and which contains a mechanism for converting sound waves into equivalent electric waves **(2) :** the portion of a telegraph instrument by which the message is sent **b :** a radio or television transmitting set **c :** NEUROTRANSMITTER

trans·mog·ri·fy \tran(t)s-ˈmäg-rə-ˌfī, tranz-\ *vt* **-fied; -fy·ing** [origin unknown] **:** to change or alter greatly and often with grotesque or humorous effect ***syn*** see TRANSFORM — **trans·mog·ri·fi·ca·tion** \(ˌ)tran(t)s-ˌmäg-rə-fə-ˈkā-shən, (ˌ)tranz-\ *n*

trans·mon·tane \(ˈ)tran(t)s-ˈmän-ˌtān, (ˈ)tranz-; ˌtran(t)s-(ˌ)män-ˈ, ˌtranz-\ *adj* [L *transmontanus*] **:** TRAMONTANE

trans·moun·tain \(ˈ)tran(t)s-ˈmau̇nt-ᵊn, (ˈ)tranz-\ *adj* **:** crossing or extending over or through a mountain <a ~ road> <a ~ tunnel>

trans·mu·ta·tion \ˌtran(t)s-myu̇-ˈtā-shən, ˌtranz-\ *n* **:** an act or instance of transmuting or being transmuted: as **a :** the conversion of base metals into gold or silver **b :** the conversion of one element or nuclide into another either naturally or artificially — **trans·mut·ative** \tran(t)s-ˈmyüt-ət-iv, tranz-\ *adj*

trans·mute \tran(t)s-ˈmyüt, tranz-\ *vb* **trans·mut·ed; trans·mut·ing** [ME *transmuten,* fr. L *transmutare,* fr. *trans-* + *mutare* to change — more at MISS] *vt* **1 :** to change or alter in form, appearance, or nature and esp. to a higher form **2 :** to subject (as an element) to transmutation ~ *vi* **:** to undergo transmutation ***syn*** see TRANSFORM — **trans·mut·able** \-ˈmyüt-ə-bəl\ *adj*

trans·na·tion·al \(ˌ)tran(t)s-ˈnash-nəl, (ˌ)tranz-, -ən-ᵊl\ *adj* **:** extending or going beyond national boundaries

trans·nat·u·ral \-ˈnach-(ə-)rəl\ *adj* **:** being above or beyond nature

trans·oce·an·ic \ˌtran(t)s-ˌō-shē-ˈan-ik, ˌtranz-\ *adj* **1 :** lying or dwelling beyond the ocean **2 :** crossing or extending across the ocean <a ~ telephone cable>

tran·som \ˈtran(t)-səm\ *n* [ME *traunsom,* prob. fr. L *transtrum,* fr. *trans* across — more at THROUGH] **1 :** a transverse piece in a structure **:** CROSSPIECE: as **a :** LINTEL **b :** a horizontal crossbar in a window, over a door, or between a door and a window or fanlight above it **c :** the horizontal bar or member of a cross or gallows **d :** any of several transverse timbers or beams secured to the sternpost of a boat; *also* **:** the planking forming the stern of a square-ended boat **2 :** a window above a door or other window built on and commonly hinged to a transom

tran·son·ic *also* **trans–son·ic** \tran(t)s-ˈsän-ik, tran-ˈsän-\ *adj* [*trans-* + *-sonic* (as in *supersonic*)] **1 :** being or relating to a speed approximating the speed of sound in air which is a speed of about 1087 feet per second or about 738 miles per hour at sea level — often used of aeronautical speeds between 600 and 900 miles per hour **2 :** moving, capable of moving, or utilizing air currents moving at a transonic speed

transp *abbr* transportation

trans·pa·cif·ic \ˌtran(t)s-pə-ˈsif-ik\ *adj* **1 a :** crossing or extending across the Pacific ocean <~ airlines> **b :** relating to or involving crossing the Pacific ocean <~ air fares> **2 :** situated beyond the Pacific ocean

trans·par·ence \tran(t)s-ˈpar-ən(t)s, -ˈper-\ *n* **:** TRANSPARENCY 1

trans·par·en·cy \-ən-sē\ *n, pl* **-cies 1 :** the quality or state of being transparent **2 :** something transparent: as **a :** a picture or design on glass, thin cloth, paper, or film designed to be viewed by light shining through it or by projection **b :** a framework covered with thin cloth or paper bearing a device for public display (as for advertisement) and lighted from within

trans·par·ent \-ənt\ *adj* [ME, fr. ML *transparent-, transparens,* prp. of *transparēre* to show through, fr. L *trans-* + *parēre* to show oneself — more at APPEAR] **1 a** (1) **:** having the property of transmitting light without appreciable scattering so that bodies lying beyond are entirely visible **:** PELLUCID (2) **:** pervious to a specified form of radiation (as X rays or ultraviolet light) **b :** fine or sheer enough to be seen through **:** DIAPHANOUS **2 a :** free from pretense or deceit **:** FRANK **b :** easily detected or seen through **:** OBVIOUS **c :** readily understood **:** CLEAR — **trans·par·ent·ly** *adv* — **trans·par·ent·ness** *n*

trans·par·ent·ize \-ən-ˌtīz\ *vt* **-ized; -iz·ing :** to make transparent or more nearly transparent <~ tracing paper>

trans·per·son·al \(ˌ)tran(t)s-ˈpərs-nəl, -ən-ᵊl\ *adj* **:** extending or going beyond the personal or individual

tran·spic·u·ous \tran(t)s-ˈpik-yə-wəs\ *adj* [NL *transpicuus,* fr. L *transpicere* to look through, fr. *trans-* + *specere* to look, see — more at SPY] **:** clearly seen through or understood

trans·pierce \tran(t)s-ˈpi(ə)rs\ *vt* [MF *transpercer,* fr. OF, fr. *trans-* (fr. L) + *percer* to pierce] **:** to pierce through **:** PENETRATE

tran·spi·ra·tion \ˌtran(t)s-pə-ˈrā-shən\ *n* **:** the act or process or an instance of transpiring; *esp* **:** the passage of watery vapor from a living body through a membrane or pores

tran·spire \tran(t)s-ˈpī(ə)r\ *vb* **trans·pired; trans·pir·ing** [MF *transpirer,* fr. L *trans-* + *spirare* to breathe — more at SPIRIT] *vt* **:** to pass off or give passage to (a fluid) through pores or interstices; *esp* **:** to excrete (as water) in the form of a vapor through a living membrane (as the skin) ~ *vi* **1 :** to give off vaporous material; *specif* **:** to give off or exude watery vapor esp. from the surfaces of leaves **2 :** to pass in the form of a vapor from a living body **3 a :** to become known or apparent **:** DEVELOP **b :** to be revealed **:** come to light **4 :** to come to pass **:** OCCUR ***syn*** see HAPPEN

trans·pla·cen·tal \ˌtran(t)s-plə-ˈsent-ᵊl\ *adj* [ISV] **:** passing through or occurring by way of the placenta <~ immunization> — **trans·pla·cen·tal·ly** \-ᵊl-ē\ *adv*

[1]**trans·plant** \tran(t)s-ˈplant\ *vb* [ME *transplaunten,* fr. LL *transplantare,* fr. L *trans-* + *plantare* to plant] *vt* **1 :** to lift and reset (a plant) in another soil or situation **2 :** to remove from one place and settle or introduce elsewhere **:** TRANSPORT **3 :** to transfer (an organ or tissue) from one part or individual to another ~ *vi* **:** to admit of being transplanted — **trans·plant·abil·i·ty** \ˌtran(t)s-ˌplant-ə-ˈbil-ət-ē\ *n* — **trans·plant·able** \tran(t)s-ˈplant-ə-bəl\ *adj* — **trans·plan·ta·tion** \ˌtran(t)s-ˌplan-ˈtā-shən\ *n* — **trans·plant·er** \tran(t)s-ˈplant-ər\ *n*

[2]**trans·plant** \ˈtran(t)s-ˌplant\ *n* **1 :** the act or process of transplanting **2 :** something transplanted

trans·po·lar \(ˌ)tran(t)s-ˈpō-lər\ *adj* **:** crossing or extending across either of the polar regions

tran·spon·der \tran(t)s-ˈpän-dər\ *n* [*trans*mitter + res*ponder*] **:** a radio or radar set that upon receiving a designated signal emits a radio signal of its own

trans·pon·tine \tran(t)s-ˈpän-ˌtīn\ *adj* [*trans-* + L *pont-, pons* bridge — more at FIND] **1 :** situated on the farther side of a bridge **2 :** resembling or characteristic of melodramas once popular in the theaters of London south of the Thames

[1]**trans·port** \tran(t)s-ˈpō(ə)rt, -ˈpȯ(ə)rt, ˈtran(t)s-ˌ\ *vt* [ME *transporten,* fr. MF or L; MF *transporter,* fr. L *transportare,* fr. *trans-* + *portare* to carry — more at FARE] **1 :** to transfer or convey from one place to another <mechanisms of ~*ing* ions across a living membrane> **2 :** to carry away with strong and often intensely pleasant emotion **3 :** to send to a penal colony overseas — **trans·port·abil·i·ty** \(ˌ)tran(t)s-ˌpōrt-ə-ˈbil-ət-ē, -ˌpȯrt-\ *n* — **trans·port·able** \tran(t)s-ˈpōrt-ə-bəl, -ˈpȯrt-\ *adj*

***syn* 1** see CARRY

2 TRANSPORT, RAVISH, ENRAPTURE, ENTRANCE *shared meaning element* **:** to carry away by strong and usu. pleasant emotion

3 see BANISH

[2]**trans·port** \ˈtran(t)s-ˌpō(ə)rt, -ˌpȯ(ə)rt\ *n* **1 :** an act or process of transporting **:** TRANSPORTATION **2 :** strong and often intensely pleasurable emotion <~*s* of joy> **3 a :** a ship for carrying soldiers or military equipment **b :** a vehicle (as a truck) used to transport persons or goods **c :** a system of public conveyance **4 :** a transported convict **5 :** a mechanism for moving tape and esp. magnetic tape past a sensing or recording head ***syn*** see ECSTASY

trans·por·ta·tion \ˌtran(t)s-pər-ˈtā-shən\ *n* **1 :** an act, process, or instance of transporting or being transported **2 :** banishment to a penal colony **3 a :** means of conveyance or travel from one place to another **b :** public conveyance of passengers or goods esp. as a commercial enterprise — **trans·por·ta·tion·al** \-shnəl, -shən-ᵊl\ *adj*

trans·port·er \tran(t)s-ˈpōrt-ər, -ˈpȯrt-, ˈtran(t)s-ˌ\ *n* **:** one that transports; *esp* **:** a vehicle for transporting large or heavy loads

[1]**trans·pose** \tran(t)s-ˈpōz\ *vt* **trans·posed; trans·pos·ing** [ME *transposen,* fr. MF *transposer,* fr. L *transponere* (perf. indic. *transposui*) to change the position of, fr. *trans-* + *ponere* to put, place — more at POSITION] **1 :** to change in form or nature **:** TRANSFORM **2 :** to render into another language, style, or manner of expression **:** TRANSLATE **3 :** to transfer from one place or period to another **:** SHIFT **4 :** to change the relative place or normal order of **:** alter the sequence of <~ letters to change the spelling> **5 :** to write or perform (a musical composition) in a different key **6 :** to bring (a term) from one side of an algebraic equation to the other with change of sign ***syn*** see REVERSE — **trans·pos·able** \-ˈpō-zə-bəl\ *adj*

[2]**trans·pose** \ˈtran(t)s-ˌpōz\ *n* **:** a matrix formed by interchanging the rows and columns of a given matrix

trans·po·si·tion \ˌtran(t)s-pə-ˈzish-ən\ *n* [ML *transposition-, transpositio,* fr. L *transpositus,* pp. of *transponere* to transpose] **1 :** an act, process, or instance of transposing or being transposed **2 a :** the transfer of any term of an equation from one side over to the other side with a corresponding change of the sign **b :** a mathematical permutation or interchange of two letters or symbols — **trans·po·si·tion·al** \-ˈzish-nəl, -ən-ᵊl\ *adj*

transposition cipher *n* **:** a cipher in which the letters of the plaintext are systematically rearranged into another sequence — compare SUBSTITUTION CIPHER

trans·sex·u·al \(ˌ)tran(t)s-ˈseksh-(ə-)wəl, -ˈsek-shəl\ *n* **:** a person genetically of one sex with a psychological urge to belong to the opposite sex that may be carried to the point of undergoing surgery to modify the sex organs to mimic the opposite sex — **trans·sex·u·al·ism** \-wə-ˌliz-əm, -shə-ˌliz-\ *n*

trans·shape \tran(ch)-ˈshāp, tran(t)s-\ *vt, archaic* **:** to change into another shape **:** TRANSFORM

trans·ship \tran(ch)-ˈship, tran(t)s-\ *vt* **:** to transfer for further transportation from one ship or conveyance to another ~ *vi* **:** to change from one ship or conveyance to another — **trans·ship·ment** \-mənt\ *n*

trans·tho·rac·ic \ˌtran(t)s-thə-ˈras-ik\ *adj* **:** done or made by way of the thoracic cavity — **trans·tho·rac·i·cal·ly** \-i-k(ə-)lē\ *adv*

tran·sub·stan·tial \ˌtran(t)s-əb-ˈstan-chəl\ *adj* **:** changed or capable of being changed from one substance to another

tran·sub·stan·ti·ate \ˌtran(t)s-əb-ˈstan-chē-ˌāt\ *vb* **-at·ed; -at·ing** [ML *transubstantiatus,* pp. of *transubstantiare,* fr. L *trans-* + *substantia* substance] *vt* **1 :** to change into another substance **:** TRANSMUTE **2 :** to effect transubstantiation in (sacramental bread and wine) ~ *vi* **:** to undergo transubstantiation

tran·sub·stan·ti·a·tion \-ˌstan-chē-ˈā-shən\ *n* **1 :** an act or instance of transubstantiating or being transubstantiated **2 :** the miraculous change by which according to Roman Catholic and Eastern Orthodox dogma the eucharistic elements at their consecration become the body and blood of Christ while keeping only the appearances of bread and wine

tran·su·date \tran(t)s-ˈ(y)üd-ət, tranz-, -ˌāt; ˈtran(t)s-(y)u̇-ˌdāt, ˈtranz-\ *n* **:** a product of transudation

tran·su·da·tion \ˌtran(t)s-(y)ü-ˈdā-shən, ˌtranz-\ *n* **1 :** the act or process of transuding or being transuded **2 :** TRANSUDATE

tran·sude \tran(t)s-ˈ(y)üd, tranz-\ *vb* **tran·sud·ed; tran·sud·ing** [NL *transudare,* fr. L *trans-* + *sudare* to sweat — more at SWEAT] *vi* **:** to pass through a membrane or permeable substance **:** EXUDE ~ *vt* **:** to permit passage of

trans·ura·nic \ˌtran-shə-ˈran-ik, -ˈrā-nik, ˌtran-zhə-, ˌtran(t)s-yu̇-, ˌtranz-yu̇-\ *n* **:** a transuranium element

trans·ura·ni·um \-ˈrā-nē-əm\ *or* **trans·ura·nic** \-ˈran-ik, -ˈrā-nik\ *adj* **:** of, relating to, or being an element with an atomic number greater than that of uranium

trans·val·u·ate \(ˌ)tran(t)s-ˈval-yə-ˌwāt, (ˌ)tranz-\ *vt* **-at·ed; -at·ing** [back-formation fr. *transvaluation*] **:** TRANSVALUE

trans·val·u·a·tion \ˌtran(t)s-ˌval-yə-ˈwā-shən, ˌtranz-\ *n* **:** the act or process of transvaluing

trans·val·ue \(ˌ)tran(t)s-ˈval-(ˌ)yü, (ˌ)tranz-, -ˈval-yə(-w)\ *vt* **-val·ued; -valu·ing :** to reevaluate esp. on a basis that repudiates accepted standards

[1]**trans·ver·sal** \tran(t)s-ˈvər-səl, tranz-\ *adj* **:** TRANSVERSE <~ line>

[2]**transversal** *n* **:** a line that intersects a system of lines

[1]**trans·verse** \tran(t)s-ˈvərs, tranz-, ˈtran(t)s-ˌ, ˈtranz-ˌ\ *adj* [L *transversus,* fr. pp. of *transvertere* to turn across, fr. *trans-* + *vertere* to turn — more at WORTH] **1 :** lying or being across **:** set crosswise **2 :** made at right angles to the anterior-posterior axis of the body <a ~ section> — **trans·verse·ly** *adv*

[2]**trans·verse** \ˈtran(t)s-ˌvərs, ˈtranz-\ *n* **:** something (as a piece, section, or part) that is transverse

transverse colon *n* **:** the middle portion of the colon that extends across the abdominal cavity

transverse process *n* **:** a lateral process of a vertebra — see VERTEBRA illustration

transverse wave *n* **:** a wave in which the vibrating element moves in a direction perpendicular to the direction of advance of the wave

trans·ves·tism \tran(t)s-ˈves-ˌtiz-əm, tranz-\ *n* [G *transvestismus,* fr. L *trans-* + *vestire* to clothe — more at VEST] **:** adoption of the dress and often the behavior of the opposite sex — **trans·ves·tite** \-ˌtīt\ *adj or n*

¹trap \ˈtrap\ *n* [ME, fr. OE *treppe* & OF *trape* (of Gmc origin); akin to MD *trappe* trap, stair, OE *treppan* to tread, Skt *dravati* he runs] **1 :** a device for taking game or other animals; *esp* **:** one that holds by springing shut suddenly **2 a :** something by which one is caught or stopped unawares **b :** a football play in which a defensive player is allowed to cross the line of scrimmage and then is blocked from the side while the ballcarrier advances through the spot vacated by the defensive player **3 a :** a device for hurling clay pigeons into the air **b :** SAND TRAP **c :** a piece of leather or section of interwoven leather straps between the thumb and forefinger of a baseball glove that forms an extension of the pocket **4** *slang* **:** MOUTH **5 :** a light usu. one-horse carriage with springs **6 :** any of various devices for preventing passage of something often while allowing other matter to proceed; *esp* **:** a device for drains or sewers consisting of a bend or partitioned chamber in which the liquid forms a seal to prevent the passage of sewer gas **7** *pl* **:** a group of percussion instruments (as a bass drum, snare drums, and cymbals) used esp. in a dance or jazz band **8** *pl* [*speed trap*] **:** a measured stretch of a course over which electronic timing devices measure the speed of a vehicle (as a racing car or dragster)

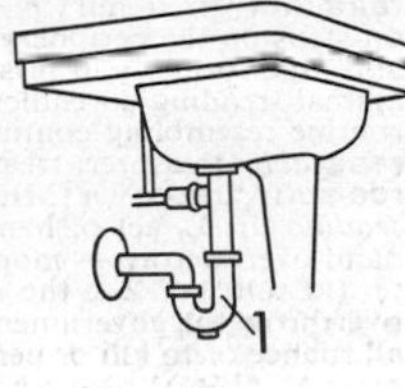

1, trap 6

²trap *vb* **trapped; trap·ping** *vt* **1 a :** to catch or take in or as if in a trap **:** ENTRAP **b :** to place in a restricted position **:** CONFINE <*trapped* in the burning wreck> **2 :** to provide or set (a place) with traps **3 a :** STOP, HOLD <these mountains ~ rains and fogs generated over the ocean —*Amer. Guide Series: Calif.*> **b :** to separate out (as water from steam) **4 a :** to catch (as a baseball) when or immediately after it hits the ground **b :** to block out (a defensive football player) by means of a trap ~ *vi* **:** to engage in trapping animals (as for furs) ***syn*** see CATCH — **trap·per** *n*

³trap *vt* **trapped; trap·ping** [ME *trappen,* fr. *trappe* cloth, modif. of MF *drap* — more at DRAB] **:** to adorn with or as if with trappings

⁴trap *n* [Sw *trapp,* fr. *trappa* stair, fr. MLG *trappe;* akin to MD *trappe* stair] **:** any of various dark-colored fine-grained igneous rocks (as basalt or amygdaloid) used esp. in road making

trap·door \ˈtrap-ˈdō(ə)r, -ˈdȯ(ə)r\ *n* **:** a lifting or sliding door covering an opening (as in a roof, ceiling, or floor)

trap–door spider *n* **:** any of various often large burrowing spiders (esp. family Ctenizidae) that construct a tubular subterranean silk-lined nest topped with a hinged lid

tra·peze \tra-ˈpēz *also* trə-\ *n* [F *trapèze,* fr. NL *trapezium*] **:** a gymnastic or acrobatic apparatus consisting of a short horizontal bar suspended by two parallel ropes

tra·pez·ist \-ˈpē-zəst\ *n* **:** a performer on the trapeze — called also *trapeze artist*

tra·pe·zi·um \trə-ˈpē-zē-əm, tra-\ *n, pl* **-zi·ums** *or* **-zia** \-zē-ə\ [NL, fr. Gk *trapezion,* lit., small table, dim. of *trapeza* table, fr. *tra-* four (akin to *tettares* four) + *peza* foot; akin to Gk *pod-, pous* foot — more at FOUR, FOOT] **1 a :** a quadrilateral having no two sides parallel **b** *Brit* **:** TRAPEZOID 1b **2 :** a bone in the wrist at the base of the thumb

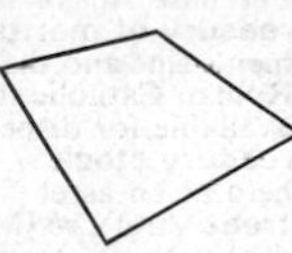

trapezium 1a

tra·pe·zi·us \-zē-əs\ *n* [NL, fr. *trapezium;* fr. the pair on the back forming together the figure of a trapezium] **:** a large flat triangular superficial muscle of each side of the back

tra·pe·zo·he·dron \trə-ˌpē-zō-ˈhē-drən, ˌtrap-ə-\ *n, pl* **-drons** *or* **-dra** \-drə\ [NL, fr. *trapezium* + *-o-* + *-hedron*] **:** a crystalline form whose faces are trapeziums

trap·e·zoid \ˈtrap-ə-ˌzȯid\ *n* [NL *trapezoïdes,* fr. Gk *trapezoeidēs* trapezium-shaped, fr. *trapeza* table] **1 a** *Brit* **:** TRAPEZIUM 1a **b :** a quadrilateral having only two sides parallel **2 :** a bone in the wrist at the base of the forefinger — **trap·e·zoi·dal** \ˌtrap-ə-ˈzȯid-ᵊl\ *adj*

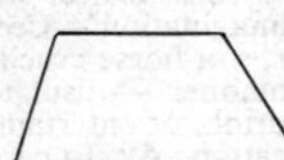

trapezoid 1b

¹trap·nest \ˈtrap-ˌnest\ *n* **:** a nest equipped with a hinged door designed to trap and confine a hen so that individual egg production may be determined

²trapnest *vt* **:** to determine the productivity of (individual domestic fowls) by means of a trapnest

trap·ping \ˈtrap-iŋ\ *n* [ME, fr. gerund of *trappen* to adorn] **1 :** CAPARISON 1 — usu. used in pl. **2** *pl* **:** outward decoration or dress **:** ornamental equipment; *also* **:** outward signs <conventional men with all the ~*s* . . . of banality —Robert Plank>

Trap·pist \ˈtrap-əst\ *n* [F *trappiste,* fr. La *Trappe,* France] **:** a member of a reformed branch of the Roman Catholic Cistercian Order established by the Abbot de Rancé in 1664 at the monastery of La Trappe in Normandy — **Trappist** *adj*

trap·rock \ˈtrap-ˈräk\ *n* **:** ⁴TRAP

traps \ˈtraps\ *n pl* [ME *trappe* cloth — more at TRAP] **:** personal belongings **:** LUGGAGE

trap·shoot·er \ˈtrap-ˌshüt-ər\ *n* **:** one who engages in trapshooting

trap·shoot·ing \-ˌshüt-iŋ\ *n* **:** shooting at clay pigeons sprung into the air from a trap

tra·pun·to \trə-ˈpün-(ˌ)tō, -ˈpu̇n-\ *n, pl* **-tos** [It] **:** a decorative quilted design in high relief worked through at least two layers of cloth by outlining the design in running stitch and padding it from the underside

trash \ˈtrash\ *n* [of Scand origin; akin to Norw *trask* trash; akin to OE *teran* to tear] **1 :** something worth little or nothing: as **a :** JUNK, RUBBISH **b** (1) **:** empty talk **:** NONSENSE (2) **:** inferior or worthless writing or artistic matter **2 :** something in a crumbled or broken condition or mass; *esp* **:** debris from pruning or processing plant material **3 :** a worthless person; *also* **:** such persons as a group **:** RIFFRAFF

trash farming *n* **:** a method of cultivation in which the soil is loosened by methods that leave vegetational residues (as stubble) on or near the surface to check erosion and serve as a mulch

trash fish *n* **1 :** ROUGH FISH **2 :** any of various sea fishes that have no market value as human food but are sometimes processed for oil or meal for domestic animals

trash·man \ˈtrash-ˌman, -mən\ *n* **:** one who collects and hauls away trash

trashy \ˈtrash-ē\ *adj* **trash·i·er; -est :** resembling or containing trash **:** of inferior quality — **trash·i·ness** *n*

trass \ˈtras\ *n* [D] **:** a light-colored volcanic tuff resembling pozzolana in composition sometimes ground for use in a hydraulic cement

trat·to·ria \ˌträt-ə-ˈrē-ə\ *n, pl* **-ri·as** *or* **-rie** \-ˈrē-ˌā\ [It] **:** RESTAURANT

trau·ma \ˈtrau̇-mə, ˈtrȯ-\ *n, pl* **trau·ma·ta** \-mət-ə\ *or* **traumas** [Gk *traumat-, trauma* wound — more at THROE] **1 a :** an injury (as a wound) to living tissue caused by an extrinsic agent <surgical ~> **b :** a disordered psychic or behavioral state resulting from mental or emotional stress or physical injury **2 :** an agent, force, or mechanism that causes trauma — **trau·mat·ic** \trə-ˈmat-ik, trȯ-, trau̇-\ *adj* — **trau·mat·i·cal·ly** \-i-k(ə-)lē\ *adv*

trau·ma·tism \ˈtrau̇-mə-ˌtiz-əm, ˈtrȯ-\ *n* **:** the development or occurrence of trauma; *also* **:** TRAUMA

trau·ma·tize \-ˌtīz\ *vt* **-tized; -tiz·ing :** to inflict a trauma upon — **trau·ma·ti·za·tion** \ˌtrau̇-mət-ə-ˈzā-shən, ˌtrȯ-\ *n*

trav *abbr* travel; traveler; travels

¹tra·vail \trə-ˈvā(ə)l, ˈtrav-ˌāl\ *n* [ME, fr. OF, fr. *travaillier* to torture, travail, fr. (assumed) VL *tripaliare* to torture, fr. *tripalium* instrument of torture, fr. L *tripalis* having three stakes, fr. *tri-* + *palus* stake — more at POLE] **1 a :** work esp. of a painful or laborious nature **:** TOIL **b :** a physical or mental exertion or piece of work **:** TASK, EFFORT **c :** AGONY, TORMENT **2 :** LABOR, PARTURITION ***syn*** see WORK

²travail *like* ¹; *in prayer-book communion service usu* ˈtrav-ˌāl\ *vi* [ME *travailen,* fr. OF *travaillier*] **1 :** to labor hard **:** TOIL **2 :** LABOR 3

trave \ˈtrāv\ *n* [ME, fr. MF, beam, fr. L *trabs* — more at THORP] **1 :** a traverse beam **2 :** a division or bay (as in a ceiling) made by or as if by traverse beams

¹trav·el \ˈtrav-əl\ *vb* **-eled** *or* **-elled; -el·ing** *or* **-el·ling** \-(ə-)liŋ\ [ME *travailen* to travail, journey, fr. OF *travaillier* to travail] *vi* **1 a :** to go on or as if on a trip or tour **:** JOURNEY **b** (1) **:** to go as if by traveling **:** PASS <the news ~*ed* fast> (2) **:** ASSOCIATE <~*s* with a sophisticated crowd> **c :** to go from place to place as a salesman or business agent **2 a :** to move or undergo transmission from one place to another <goods ~*ing* by plane> **b :** to move in a given direction or path or through a given distance <the stylus ~*s* in a groove> **c :** to move rapidly <a car that can really ~> **3 :** to walk or run with a basketball in violation of the rules ~ *vt* **1 a :** to journey through or over **b :** to follow (a course or path) as if by traveling **2 :** to traverse (a specified distance) **3 :** to cover (a place or region) as a commercial traveler — **travel light :** to travel with a minimum of equipment or baggage

²travel *n* **1 a :** the act of traveling **:** PASSAGE **b :** a journey esp. to a distant or unfamiliar place **:** TOUR, TRIP — often used in pl. **2** *pl* **:** an account of one's travels **3 :** the number traveling **:** TRAFFIC **4 a :** MOVEMENT, PROGRESSION <the ~ of satellites around the earth> **b :** the motion of a piece of machinery; *esp* **:** reciprocating motion

travel agency *n* **:** an agency engaged in selling and arranging personal transportation and accommodations for travelers — called also *travel bureau*

travel agent *n* **:** a person engaged in selling and arranging personal transportation, tours, or trips for travelers

trav·eled *or* **trav·elled** \ˈtrav-əld\ *adj* **1 :** experienced in travel <a widely ~ journalist> **2 :** used by travelers <a well-*traveled* highway>

trav·el·er *or* **trav·el·ler** \ˈtrav-(ə-)lər\ *n* **1 :** one that travels: as **a :** one that goes on a trip or journey **b :** TRAVELING SALESMAN **2 a :** an iron ring sliding along a rope, bar, or rod of a ship **b :** a rod on the deck on which such a ring slides **3 :** any of various devices for handling something that is being transported laterally

traveler's check *n* **:** a draft purchased from a bank or express company and signed by the purchaser at the time of purchase and again at the time of cashing as a precaution against forgery

trav·el·ing *or* **trav·el·ling** \ˈtrav-(ə-)liŋ\ *adj* **1 :** that travels <a ~ opera company> <a ~ executive> **2 :** carried, used by, or accompanying a traveler <a ~ alarm clock> <a ~ companion>

traveling bag *n* **:** a bag carried by hand and designed to hold a traveler's clothing and personal articles

traveling case *n* **:** a usu. stiff and box-shaped traveling bag

traveling fellowship *n* **:** a fellowship whose terms permit or direct the holder to travel or go abroad for study or research

traveling salesman *n* **:** a traveling representative of a business concern who solicits orders usu. in an assigned territory

trav·el·ogue *or* **trav·el·og** \ˈtrav-ə-ˌlȯg, -ˌläg\ *n* [*travel* + *-logue*] **1 :** a talk or lecture on travel usu. accompanied by a film or slides **2 :** a narrated motion picture about travel

tra·vers·al \trə-ˈvər-səl *also* tra-ˈ *or* ˈtra-ˌ\ *n* **:** the act or an instance of traversing

[1]tra·verse \ˈtra-vərs *also* -ˌvərs, *esp for 6 & 8 also* trə-ˈ*or* tra-ˈ\ *n* [ME *travers,* fr. MF *traverse,* fr. *traverser* to cross, fr. LL *transversare,* fr. L *transversus,* pp. of *transvertere* — more at TRANSVERSE] **1 :** something that crosses or lies across **2 :** OBSTACLE, ADVERSITY **3 :** a formal denial of a matter of fact alleged by the opposite party in a legal pleading **4 a :** a compartment or recess formed by a partition, curtain, or screen **b :** a gallery or loft of communication from side to side in a large building **5 :** a route or way across or over: as **a :** a zigzag course of a sailing ship with contrary winds **b :** a curving or zigzag way up a steep grade **c :** the course followed in traversing **6 :** the act or an instance of traversing : CROSSING **7 :** a protective projecting wall or bank of earth in a trench **8 a :** a lateral movement (as of the saddle of a lathe carriage); *also* **:** a device for imparting such movement **b :** the lateral movement of a gun about a pivot or on a carriage to change direction of fire **9 :** a line surveyed across a plot of ground

[2]tra·verse \trə-ˈvərs *also* tra-ˈ *or* ˈtra-(ˌ)\ *vb* **tra·versed; tra·vers·ing** *vt* **1 a :** to go against or act in opposition to : OPPOSE, THWART **b :** to deny (as an allegation of fact or an indictment) formally at law **2 :** to pass through : PENETRATE <light rays *traversing* a crystal> **3 a :** to go or travel across or over **b :** to move along or through **4 :** to make a study of : EXAMINE **5 :** to lie or extend across : CROSS <the bridge ~*s* a brook> **6 a :** to move to and fro over or along **b :** to ascend, descend, or cross (a slope or gap) at an angle **c :** to move (a gun) to right or left on a pivot **7 :** to make or carry out a traverse survey of ~ *vi* **1 :** to move back and forth or from side to side **2 :** to move or turn laterally : SWIVEL **3 a :** to climb at an angle or in a zigzag course **b :** to ski across rather than straight down a hill **4 :** to make a traverse survey — **tra·vers·able** \-ˈvər-sə-bəl, -(ˌ)vər-\ *adj* — **tra·vers·er** *n*

[3]tra·verse \ˈtra-(ˌ)vərs, trə-ˈ, tra-ˈ\ *adj* **:** lying across : TRANSVERSE

trav·erse jury \ˈtrav-ərs-\ *n* **:** PETIT JURY

traverse rod *n* **:** a metal rod or track with a pulley mechanism for drawing curtains

trav·er·tine \ˈtrav-ər-ˌtēn, -tən\ *n* [F *travertin*] **:** a mineral consisting of a massive usu. layered calcium carbonate (as aragonite or calcite) formed by deposition from spring waters or esp. from hot springs

[1]trav·es·ty \ˈtrav-ə-stē\ *n, pl* **-ties** [obs. E *travesty,* disguised, parodied, fr. F *travesti,* pp. of *travestir* to disguise, fr. It *travestire,* fr. *tra-* across (fr. L *trans-*) + *vestire* to dress, fr. L, fr. *vestis* garment — more at WEAR] **1 :** a burlesque translation or literary or artistic imitation usu. grotesquely incongruous in style, treatment, or subject matter **2 :** a debased, distorted, or grossly inferior imitation <a ~ of justice> ***syn*** see CARICATURE

[2]travesty *vt* **-tied; -ty·ing :** to make a travesty of : PARODY

tra·vois \trə-ˈvȯi, ˈtrav-ˌȯi\ *n, pl* **tra·vois** *also* **tra·voises** \-ˈvȯiz, -ˌȯiz\ [CanF *travois*] **:** a primitive vehicle used by Plains Indians consisting of two trailing poles serving as shafts and bearing a platform or net for the load

[1]trawl \ˈtrȯl\ *vb* [prob. fr. obs. D *tragelen*] *vi* **1 :** to fish with a trawl **2 :** TROLL 2 ~ *vt* **:** to catch (fish) with a trawl

[2]trawl *n* **1 :** a large conical net dragged along the sea bottom in gathering fish or other marine life **2 :** SETLINE

trawl·er \ˈtrȯ-lər\ *n* **1 :** a person who fishes by trawling **2 :** a boat used in trawling

trawl·er·man \-mən\ *n* **:** a fisherman who uses a trawl or mans a trawler

tray \ˈtrā\ *n* [ME, fr. OE *trīg, trēg;* akin to OE *trēow* tree — more at TREE] **:** an open receptacle with a flat bottom and a low rim for holding, carrying, or exhibiting articles — **tray·ful** \-ˌfu̇l\ *n*

treach·er·ous \ˈtrech-(ə-)rəs\ *adj* **1 :** characterized by or manifesting treachery : PERFIDIOUS **2 a :** likely to betray trust : UNRELIABLE <a ~ memory> **b :** providing insecure footing or support <~ quicksand> **c :** marked by hidden dangers, hazards, or perils ***syn*** see FAITHLESS — **treach·er·ous·ly** *adv* — **treach·er·ous·ness** *n*

treach·ery \ˈtrech-(ə-)rē\ *n, pl* **-er·ies** [ME *trecherie,* fr. OF, fr. *trechier* to deceive] **1 :** violation of allegiance or of faith and confidence : TREASON **2 :** an act of perfidy or treason

trea·cle \ˈtrē-kəl\ *n* [ME *triacle,* fr. MF, fr. L *theriaca,* fr. Gk *thēriakē* antidote against a poisonous bite, fr. fem. of *thēriakos* of a wild animal, fr. *thērion* wild animal, dim. of *thēr* wild animal — more at FIERCE] **1 :** a medicinal compound formerly in wide use as a remedy against poison **2** *chiefly Brit* **:** MOLASSES **3 :** something (as a tone of voice) heavily sweet and cloying

trea·cly \-k(ə-)lē\ *adj* **:** resembling treacle (as in quality or appearance) <~ sentimentality>

[1]tread \ˈtred\ *vb* **trod** \ˈträd\ *also* **tread·ed; trod·den** \ˈträd-ᵊn\ *or* **trod; tread·ing** [ME *treden,* fr. OE *tredan;* akin to OHG *tretan* to tread] *vt* **1 a :** to step or walk on or over **b :** to walk along : FOLLOW **2 a :** to beat or press with the feet : TRAMPLE **b :** to subdue or repress as if by trampling : CRUSH **3 :** to copulate with — used of a male bird **4 a :** to form by treading : BEAT <~ a path> **b :** to execute by stepping or dancing <~ a measure> ~ *vi* **1 :** to move on foot : WALK **2 a :** to set foot **b :** to put one's foot : STEP **3 :** COPULATE 1 — **tread·er** *n* — **tread on one's toes :** to give offense (as by encroaching on one's rights or feelings) — **tread water :** to keep the body nearly upright in the water and the head above water by a treading motion of the feet usu. aided by the hands

[2]tread *n* **1 :** a mark (as a footprint or the imprint of a tire) made by or as if by treading **2 a** (1) **:** the action of treading (2) **:** an act or instance of treading : STEP **b :** manner of stepping **c :** the sound of treading **3 a :** the part of a sole that touches the ground; *also* **:** the pattern on the bottom of a sole **b** (1) **:** the part of a wheel or tire that makes contact with a road or rail (2) **:** the pattern of ridges or grooves made or cut in the face of a tire **4 :** the distance between the points of contact with the ground of the two front wheels or the two rear wheels of a vehicle **5 a :** the upper horizontal part of a step **b :** the width of such a tread — **tread·less** \-ləs\ *adj*

[1]trea·dle \ˈtred-ᵊl\ *n* [ME *tredel* step of a stair, fr. OE, fr. *tredan*] **:** a swiveling or lever device pressed by the foot to drive a machine

[2]treadle *vb* **trea·dled; trea·dling** \ˈtred-liŋ, -ᵊl-iŋ\ *vi* **:** to operate a treadle ~ *vt* **:** to operate (as a machine) by a treadle

tread·mill \ˈtred-ˌmil\ *n* **1 a :** a mill worked by persons treading on steps on the periphery of a wide wheel having a horizontal axis and used formerly in prison punishment **b :** a mill worked by an animal treading an endless belt **2 :** a wearisome or monotonous routine resembling continued activity on a treadmill

treas *abbr* treasurer; treasury

trea·son \ˈtrēz-ᵊn\ *n* [ME *tresoun,* fr. OF *traison,* fr. ML *tradition-, traditio,* fr. L, act of handing over, fr. *traditus,* pp. of *tradere* to hand over, betray — more at TRAITOR] **1 :** the betrayal of a trust **:** TREACHERY **2 :** the offense of attempting by overt acts to overthrow the government of the state to which the offender owes allegiance or to kill or personally injure the sovereign or his family

trea·son·able \ˈtrēz-nə-bəl, -ᵊn-ə-bəl\ *adj* **:** relating to, consisting of, or involving treason — **trea·son·ably** \-blē\ *adv*

trea·son·ous \ˈtrēz-nəs, -ᵊn-əs\ *adj* **:** TREASONABLE

trea·sur·able \ˈtrezh-(ə-)rə-bəl, ˈtrāzh-\ *adj* **:** worthy of being treasured : PRECIOUS

[1]trea·sure \ˈtrezh-ər, ˈtrāzh-\ *n* [ME *tresor,* fr. OF, fr. L *thesaurus,* fr. Gk *thēsauros*] **1 a** (1) **:** wealth (as money, jewels, or precious metals) stored up or hoarded <buried ~> (2) **:** wealth of any kind or in any form : RICHES **b :** a store of money in reserve **2 :** something of great worth or value; *also* **:** a person esteemed as rare or precious **3 :** a collection of precious things

[2]treasure *vt* **trea·sured; trea·sur·ing** \-(ə-)riŋ\ **1 :** to collect and store up (something of value) for future use : HOARD **2 :** to hold or keep as precious : CHERISH, PRIZE <she *treasured* those memories> ***syn*** see APPRECIATE

treasure hunt *n* **:** a game in which each player or team tries to be first to find whatever has been hidden

trea·sur·er \ˈtrezh-rər, ˈtrezh-ər-ər, ˈtrāzh-\ *n* **1 :** a guardian of a collection of treasures : CURATOR **2 :** an officer entrusted with the receipt, care, and disbursement of funds: as **a :** a governmental officer charged with receiving, keeping, and disbursing public revenues **b :** the executive financial officer of a club, society, or business corporation — **trea·sur·er·ship** \-ˌship\ *n*

treasure trove \-ˌtrōv\ *n* [AF *tresor trové* lit., found treasure] **1 :** treasure that anyone finds; *specif* **:** gold or silver in the form of money, plate, or bullion which is found hidden and whose ownership is not known **2 :** a valuable or productive discovery

trea·sury \ˈtrezh-(ə-)rē, ˈtrāzh-\ *n, pl* **-sur·ies** **1 a :** a place in which stores of wealth are kept **b :** the place of deposit and disbursement of collected funds; *esp* **:** one where public revenues are deposited, kept, and disbursed **c :** funds kept in such a depository **2** *obs* **:** TREASURE **3** *cap* **a :** a governmental department in charge of finances and esp. the collection, management, and expenditure of public revenues **b :** the building in which the business of such a governmental department is transacted **4** *cap* **:** a government security (as a note or bill) issued by the Treasury **5 :** a repository for treasures <a ~ of poems>

treasury note *n* **:** a currency note issued by the U.S. Treasury in payment for silver bullion purchased under the Sherman Silver Purchase Act of 1890

treasury of merits : the superabundant satisfaction of Christ for men's sins and the excess of merit of the saints which according to Roman Catholic theology is effective for salvation of others and is available for dispensation through indulgences

treasury stock *n* **:** issued stock reacquired by a corporation and held as an asset

[1]treat \ˈtrēt\ *vb* [ME *treten,* fr. OF *traitier,* fr. L *tractare* to handle, deal with, fr. *tractus,* pp. of *trahere* to draw — more at DRAW] *vi* **1 :** to discuss terms of accommodation or settlement : NEGOTIATE **2 :** to deal with a matter esp. in writing : DISCOURSE — usu. used with *of* <a book ~*ing* of conservation> **3 :** to pay another's expenses (as for a meal or drink) esp. as a compliment or as an expression of regard or friendship ~ *vt* **1 a :** to deal with in speech or writing : EXPOUND **b :** to present or represent artistically **c :** to deal with : HANDLE <food is plentiful and ~*ed* with imagination —Cecil Beaton> **2 a :** to bear oneself toward : USE <~ a horse cruelly> **b :** to regard and deal with in a specified manner — usu. used with *as* **3 a :** to provide with free food, drink, or entertainment **b :** to provide with enjoyment or gratification **4 :** to care for or deal with medically or surgically <~ a disease> **5 :** to act upon with some agent esp. to improve or alter <~ a metal with acid> — **treat·er** *n*

syn TREAT, DEAL, HANDLE *shared meaning element* **:** to have to do with in a specified manner

[2]treat *n* **1 :** an entertainment given without expense to those invited **2 :** an esp. unexpected source of joy, delight, or amusement

treat·able \ˈtrēt-ə-bəl\ *adj* **:** capable of being treated : yielding or responsive to treatment — **treat·abil·i·ty** \ˌtrēt-ə-ˈbil-ət-ē\ *n*

trea·tise \ˈtrēt-əs *also* -əz\ *n* [ME *tretis,* fr. AF *tretiz,* fr. OF *traitier* to treat] **1 :** a systematic exposition or argument in writing including a methodical discussion of the facts and principles involved and conclusions reached <a ~ on higher education> **2** *obs* **:** ACCOUNT, TALE

treat·ment \ˈtrēt-mənt\ *n* **1 a :** the act or manner or an instance of treating someone or something : HANDLING, USAGE **b :** the techniques or actions customarily applied in a specified situation <the new recruit got the ~ from a sergeant> **2 a :** a substance or technique used in treating **b :** an experimental condition

trea·ty \ˈtrēt-ē\ *n, pl* **treaties** [ME *tretee,* fr. MF *traité,* fr. ML *tractatus,* fr. L, handling, treatment, fr. *tractatus,* pp. of *tractare* to treat] **1 :** the action of treating and esp. of negotiating **2 a :** an agreement or arrangement made by negotiation: (1) **:** PRIVATE TREATY (2) **:** a contract in writing between two or more political authorities (as states or sovereigns) formally signed by representatives duly authorized and usu. **ratified by the lawmaking** authority of the state **b :** a document in which such a contract is set down

treaty port *n* : any of numerous ports and inland cities in China, Japan, and Korea formerly open by treaty to foreign commerce

[1]tre·ble \ˈtreb-əl\ *n* [ME, perh. fr. MF, trio, fr. *treble,* adj.] **1 a** : the highest voice part in harmonic music : SOPRANO **b** : one that performs a treble part; *also* : a member of a family of instruments having the highest range **c** : a high-pitched or shrill voice, tone, or sound **d** : the upper half of the whole vocal or instrumental tonal range — compare BASS **e** : the higher portion of the audio frequency range in sound recording and broadcasting **2** : something treble in construction, uses, amount, number, or value

[2]treble *adj* [ME, fr. MF, fr. L *triplus* — more at TRIPLE] **1 a** : having three parts or uses : THREEFOLD **b** : triple in number or amount **2 a** : relating to or having the range or part of a treble **b** : high-pitched : SHRILL **c** : of, relating to, or having the range of treble in sound recording and broadcasting <~ frequencies> — **tre·bly** \ˈtreb-(ə-)lē\ *adv*

[3]treble *vb* **tre·bled; tre·bling** \ˈtreb-(ə-)liŋ\ *vt* : to increase threefold ~ *vi* **1** : to sing treble **2** : to grow to three times the size, amount, or number

treble clef *n* [fr. its use for the notation of treble parts] **1** : a clef that places G above middle C on the second line of the staff **2** : TREBLE STAFF

treble staff *n* : the musical staff carrying the treble clef

treb·u·chet \ˌtreb-(y)ə-ˈshet, -ˈchet\ *or* **treb·uc·ket** \ˌtreb-ə-ˈket\ *n* [ME *trebochet,* fr. MF *trebuchet*] : a medieval military engine for hurling missiles with great force

tre·cen·to \trā-ˈchen-(ˌ)tō\ *n, pl* **-tos** [It, lit., three hundred, fr. L *tres* three + *centum* hundred — more at THREE, HUNDRED] : the 14th century; *specif* : the 14th century in Italian literature and art

tre·de·cil·lion \ˌtrēd-i-ˈsil-yən\ *n, often attrib* [L *tredecim* thirteen (fr. *tres* three + *decem* ten) + E *-illion* (as in *million*) — more at THREE, TEN] — see NUMBER table

[1]tree \ˈtrē\ *n* [ME, fr. OE *trēow;* akin to ON *trē* tree, Gk *drys,* Skt *dāru* wood] **1 a** : a woody perennial plant having a single usu. elongate main stem generally with few or no branches on its lower part **b** : a shrub or herb of arborescent form <rose ~*s*> <a banana ~> **2 a** (1) : a piece of wood (as a post or pole) usu. adapted to a particular use or forming part of a structure or implement (2) *archaic* : the cross on which Jesus was crucified **b** *archaic* : GALLOWS **3** : something in the form of or felt to resemble a tree: as **a** : a diagram or graph that branches usu. from a simple stem without forming loops or polygons <genealogical ~> **b** : an arborescent aggregation of crystals **c** : a much-branched system of channels esp. in an animal body <the vascular ~> — **tree·less** \-ləs\ *adj* — **tree·like** \-ˌlīk\ *adj*

[2]tree *vt* **treed; tree·ing** **1 a** : to drive to or up a tree <*treed* by a bull> <dogs ~*ing* game> **b** : to put into a position of extreme disadvantage : CORNER; *esp* : to bring to bay **2** : to furnish or fit (as a shoe) with a tree

treed \ˈtrēd\ *adj* : planted or grown with trees : WOODED

tree farm *n* : an area of forest land managed to ensure continuous commercial production

tree fern *n* : a fern (chiefly of families Cyatheaceae and Marattiaceae) of arborescent habit with a woody caudex

tree frog *n* : any of numerous tailless amphibians (esp. family Hylidae) of arboreal habits

tree·hop·per \ˈtrē-ˌhäp-ər\ *n* : any of numerous small leaping homopterous insects (family Membracidae) living on a sap from branches and twigs

tree house *n* : a structure (as a playhouse) built among the branches of a tree

tree line *n* : TIMBERLINE

tree·nail *also* **tre·nail** \ˈtrē-ˌnāl, ˈtren-ᵊl, ˈtrən-ᵊl\ *n* : a wooden peg made usu. of dry compressed timber so as to swell in its hole when moistened

tree of heaven : an Asiatic ailanthus (*Ailanthus glandulosa*) that has foliage similar to that of the sumacs, has ill-scented staminate flowers, and is widely grown as a shade and ornamental tree

tree peony *n* : a shrubby Chinese peony (*Paeonia suffruticosa*) that has large showy flowers and is the source of many horticultural varieties

tree shrew *n* : any of a family (Tupaiidae) of arboreal insectivorous mammals sometimes classified as true insectivores and sometimes as primitive primates

tree sparrow *n* **1** : a European sparrow (*Passer montanus*) that has a black spot on the ear coverts **2** : an American sparrow (*Spizella arborea*) that breeds in northern No. America and winters in the U.S.

tree surgeon *n* : a specialist in tree surgery

tree surgery *n* : operative treatment of diseased trees esp. for control of decay; *broadly* : practices forming part of the professional care of specimen or shade trees

tree toad *n* : TREE FROG

tree·top \ˈtrē-ˌtäp\ *n* **1** : the topmost part of a tree **2** *pl* : the height or line marked by the tops of a group of trees

tre·foil \ˈtrē-ˌfȯil, ˈtref-ˌȯil\ *n* [ME, fr. MF *trefeuil,* fr. L *trifolium,* fr. *tri-* + *folium* leaf] **1 a** : CLOVER; *broadly* : any of several trifoliolate leguminous herbs **b** : a trifoliolate leaf **2** : an ornament or symbol in the form of a stylized trifoliolate leaf

tre·ha·lase \tri-ˈhäl-ˌās, -ˌāz\ *n* [ISV *trehalose* + *-ase*] : an enzyme that accelerates the hydrolysis of trehalose and is found in yeasts and molds

tre·ha·lose \-ˈhäl-ˌōs, -ˌōz\ *n* [ISV *trehala* (a sweet substance constituting the pupal covering of a beetle)] : a crystalline disaccharide $C_{12}H_{22}O_{11}$ stored instead of starch by many fungi and found in the blood of many insects

treil·lage \trē-ˈyäzh\ *n* [F, fr. MF, fr. *treille* vine arbor, fr. L *trichila*] : latticework for vines : TRELLIS

[1]trek \ˈtrek\ *n* [Afrik, fr. MD *treck* pull, haul, fr. *trecken*] **1** *chiefly So Afr* : a journey by ox wagon; *esp* : an organized migration by a group of settlers **2** : a trip or movement esp. when involving difficulties or complex organization

[2]trek *vi* **trekked; trek·king** [Afrik, fr. MD *trecken* to pull, haul, migrate; akin to OHG *trechan* to pull] **1** *chiefly So Afr* **a** : to travel by ox wagon **b** : to migrate by ox wagon or in a train of such **2** : to make one's way arduously; *broadly* : to go on a journey — **trek·ker** *n*

[1]trel·lis \ˈtrel-əs\ *n* [ME *trelis,* fr. MF *treliz* fabric of coarse weave, trellis, fr. (assumed) VL *trilicius* woven with triple thread, fr. L *tri-* + *liceum* thread] **1** : a frame of latticework used as a screen or as a support for climbing plants **2** : a construction (as a summerhouse) chiefly of latticework **3** : an arrangement that forms or gives the effect of a lattice <a ~ of interlacing streams>

[2]trellis *vt* **1** : to provide with a trellis; *esp* : to train (as a vine) on a trellis **2** : to cross or interlace on or through : INTERWEAVE

trel·lised \ˈtrel-əst\ *adj* : having or furnished with a trellis

trel·lis·work \ˈtrel-ə-ˌswərk\ *n* : LATTICEWORK

trem·a·tode \ˈtrem-ə-ˌtōd\ *n* [deriv. of Gk *trēmatōdēs* pierced with holes, fr. *trēmat-, trēma* hole, fr. *tetrainein* to bore — more at THROW] : any of a class (Trematoda) of parasitic flatworms including the flukes — **trematode** *adj*

[1]trem·ble \ˈtrem-bəl\ *vi* **trem·bled; trem·bling** \-b(ə-)liŋ\ [ME *tremblen,* fr. MF *trembler,* fr. ML *tremulare,* fr. L *tremulus* tremulous, fr. *tremere* to tremble; akin to Gk *tremein* to tremble] **1** : to shake involuntarily (as with fear or cold) : SHIVER **2** : to move, sound, pass, or come to pass as if shaken or tremulous <the building *trembled* from the blast> **3** : to be affected with fear or doubt <~ for the safety of another> — **trem·bler** \-b(ə-)lər\ *n*

[2]tremble *n* **1** : an act or instance of trembling: as **a** : a fit or spell of involuntary shaking or quivering **b** : a tremor or series of tremors **2** *pl but sing in constr* : severe poisoning of livestock and esp. cattle by a toxic alcohol present in a snakeroot and rayless goldenrod that is characterized by muscular tremors, weakness, and constipation

trem·bly \ˈtrem-b(ə-)lē\ *adj* : marked by trembling : TREMULOUS

tre·men·dous \tri-ˈmen-dəs\ *adj* [L *tremendus,* fr. gerundive of *tremere*] **1** : being such as may excite trembling or arouse dread, awe, or terror **2 a** : astonishing by reason of extreme size, power, greatness, or excellence **b** : unusually large : HUGE ***syn*** see MONSTROUS — **tre·men·dous·ly** *adv* — **tre·men·dous·ness** *n*

[1]trem·o·lant \ˈtrem-ə-lənt\ *n* [It *tremolante,* fr. *tremolante* tremulant, fr. ML *tremulant-, tremulans*] **1** : an organ pipe producing a tremolant tone **2** : a device to impart a vibration causing a tremolant sound

[2]tremolant *adj* : marked by tremolo

trem·o·lite \ˈtrem-ə-ˌlīt\ *n* [F *trémolite,* fr. *Tremola,* valley in Switzerland] : a white or gray mineral $Ca_2Mg_5Si_8O_{22}(OH)_2$ of the amphibole group that is a calcium magnesium silicate — **trem·o·lit·ic** \ˌtrem-ə-ˈlit-ik\ *adj*

trem·o·lo \ˈtrem-ə-ˌlō\ *n, pl* **-los** [It, fr. *tremolo* tremulous, fr. L *tremulus*] **1 a** : the rapid reiteration of a musical tone or of alternating tones to produce a tremulous effect **b** : a perceptible rapid variation of pitch in the voice esp. in singing similar to the vibrato of a stringed instrument **2** : a mechanical device in an organ for causing a tremulous effect

trem·or \ˈtrem-ər\ *n* [ME *tremour,* fr. MF, L *tremor,* fr. *tremere*] **1** : a trembling or shaking usu. from physical weakness, emotional stress, or disease **2** : a quivering or vibratory motion; *esp* : a discrete small movement following or preceding a major seismic event **3 a** : a feeling of uncertainty or insecurity **b** : a cause of such a feeling

trem·u·lant \ˈtrem-yə-lənt\ *adj* [ML *tremulant-, tremulans,* prp. of *tremulare* — more at TREMBLE] : TREMULOUS, TREMBLING

trem·u·lous \-ləs\ *adj* [L *tremulus* — more at TREMBLE] **1** : characterized by or affected with trembling or tremors **2** : affected with timidity : TIMOROUS **3** : such as is caused by a tremulous state <~ handwriting> **4** : exceedingly sensitive : easily shaken or disordered — **trem·u·lous·ly** *adv* — **trem·u·lous·ness** *n*

[1]trench \ˈtrench\ *n* [ME *trenche* track cut through a wood, fr. MF, act of cutting, fr. *trenchier* to cut] **1** : a long cut in the ground : DITCH; *esp* : one used for military defense often with the excavated dirt thrown up in front **2** : a long, narrow, and usu. steep-sided depression in the ocean floor — compare TROUGH

[2]trench *vt* **1** : to make a cut in : CARVE **2 a** : to protect with or as if with a trench **b** : to cut a trench in : DITCH ~ *vi* **1 a** : ENTRENCH, ENCROACH <~*ing* on other domains which were more vital —Sir Winston Churchill> **b** : to come close : VERGE **2** : to dig a trench

tren·chan·cy \ˈtren-chən-sē\ *n* : the quality or state of being trenchant

tren·chant \-chənt\ *adj* [ME, fr. MF, prp. of *trenchier*] **1** : KEEN, SHARP **2** : vigorously effective and articulate <a ~ analysis>; *also* : CAUSTIC <~ remarks> **3 a** : sharply perceptive : PENETRATING **b** : CLEAR-CUT, DISTINCT <the ~ divisions between right and wrong —Edith Wharton> ***syn*** see INCISIVE — **tren·chant·ly** *adv*

trench coat *n* **1** : a waterproof overcoat with a removable lining designed for wear in trenches **2** : a double-breasted raincoat with deep pockets, wide belt, and straps on the shoulders

trenched \ˈtrencht\ *adj* **1** : furrowed or drained by trenches **2** : provided with protective trenches

[1]tren·cher \ˈtren-chər\ *n* [ME, fr. MF *trencheoir,* fr. *trenchier* to cut] : a wooden platter for serving food

[2]trencher *adj* **1** : of or relating to a trencher or to meals **2** *archaic* : having the nature of a parasite : SYCOPHANTIC

[3]trench·er \ˈtren-chər\ *n* [[2]*trench*] : one that digs trenches

tren·cher·man \ˈtren-chər-mən\ *n* **1** : a hearty eater **2** *archaic* : HANGER-ON, SPONGER

trench fever *n* **:** a rickettsial disease marked by fever and pain in muscles, bones, and joints and transmitted by the body louse
trench foot *n* **:** a painful foot disorder resembling frostbite and resulting from exposure to cold and wet
trench knife *n* **:** a knife with a strong double-edged blade about 8 inches long suited for use in hand-to-hand fighting
trench mouth *n* **1 :** VINCENT'S ANGINA **2 :** VINCENT'S INFECTION
trench warfare *n* **:** warfare in which the opposing forces attack and counterattack from a relatively permanent system of trenches protected by barbed-wire entanglements
[1]trend \'trend\ *vi* [ME *trenden* to turn, revolve, fr. OE *trendan;* akin to MHG *trendel* disk, spinning top, OE *teran* to tear — more at TEAR] **1 a :** to extend in a general direction **:** follow a general course <mountain ranges ~*ing* north and south> **b :** to veer in a new direction **:** BEND <coastline that ~*s* westward> **2 a :** to show a tendency **:** INCLINE <prices ~*ing* upward> **b :** to become deflected **:** SHIFT <opinions ~*ing* toward conservatism>
[2]trend *n* **1 :** a line of general direction or movement <the ~ of the coast turned toward the west> **2 a :** a prevailing tendency or inclination **:** DRIFT **b :** a general movement **:** SWING <the ~ toward suburban living> **c :** a current style or preference **:** VOGUE <new fashion ~*s*> **d :** a line of development **:** APPROACH **3 :** the general movement in the course of time of a statistically detectable change; *also* **:** a statistical curve reflecting such a change ***syn*** see TENDENCY
trendy \'tren-dē\ *adj* **trend·i·er; -est** *chiefly Brit* **:** very fashionable **:** UP-TO-DATE <he's a ~ dresser —*Sunday Mirror*> — **trend·i·ly** \-də-lē\ *adv* — **trend·i·ness** \-dē-nəs\ *n*
[1]tre·pan \'trē-ˌpan, tri-'pan\ *n* [ME *trepane,* fr. ML *trepanum,* fr. Gk *trypanon* auger, fr. *trypan* to bore, fr. *trypa* hole; akin to Gk *tetrainein* to pierce — more at THROW] **1 :** TREPHINE **2 :** a heavy tool used in boring mine shafts
[2]tre·pan \tri-'pan\ *vt* **tre·panned; tre·pan·ning 1 :** to use a trephine on (the skull) **2 :** to remove a disk or cylindrical core (as from metal for testing) — **trep·a·na·tion** \ˌtrep-ə-'nā-shən\ *n*
[3]tre·pan \tri-'pan\ *n* [origin unknown] **1** *archaic* **:** TRICKSTER **2** *archaic* **:** a deceptive device **:** SNARE
[4]tre·pan \tri-'pan\ *vt* **tre·panned; tre·pan·ning** *archaic* **:** ENTRAP, LURE
tre·pang \tri-'paŋ, 'trē-ˌ\ *n* [Malay *tĕripang*] **:** any of several large sea cucumbers (esp. genera *Actinopyga* and *Holothuria*) that are taken mostly in northern Australia and the East Indies, boiled, dried, and used esp. by the Chinese for making soup — called also *bêche-de-mer*
treph·i·na·tion \ˌtref-ə-'nā-shən\ *n* **:** an act or instance of perforating the skull with a surgical instrument
[1]tre·phine \'trē-ˌfīn\ *n* [F *tréphine,* fr. obs. E *trefine, trafine,* fr. L *tres fines* three ends, fr. *tres* three + *fines,* pl. of *finis* end — more at THREE] **:** a surgical instrument for cutting out circular sections (as of bone or corneal tissue)
[2]tre·phine \'trē-ˌfīn, tri-'\ *vt* **tre·phined; tre·phin·ing :** to operate on with or extract by means of a trephine
trep·id \'trep-əd\ *adj* [L *trepidus*] **:** TIMOROUS
trep·i·dant \'trep-əd-ənt\ *adj* [L *trepidant-, trepidans,* prp. of *trepidare*] **:** TIMID, TREMBLING
trep·i·da·tion \ˌtrep-ə-'dā-shən\ *n* [L *trepidation-, trepidatio,* fr. *trepidatus,* pp. of *trepidare* to tremble, fr. *trepidus* agitated; akin to OE *thrafian* to urge, push, Gk *trapein* to press grapes] **1** *archaic* **:** a tremulous motion **:** TREMOR **2 :** timorous uncertain agitation **:** APPREHENSION ***syn*** see FEAR
trepo·ne·ma \ˌtrep-ə-'nē-mə\ *n, pl* **-ma·ta** \-mət-ə\ *or* **-mas** [NL *Treponemat-, Treponema,* genus name, deriv. of Gk *trepein* to turn + *nēma* thread, fr. *nēn* to spin — more at TROPE, NEEDLE] **:** any of a genus (*Treponema*) of spirochetes that parasitize man and other warm-blooded animals and include organisms causing syphilis and yaws — **trepo·ne·mal** \-məl\ *or* **trepo·nem·a·tous** \-'nem-ət-əs\ *adj*
trepo·ne·ma·to·sis \-ˌnē-mə-'tō-səs, -ˌnem-ə-\ *n, pl* **-to·ses** \-ˌsēz\ [NL] **:** infection with or disease caused by treponemata
trepo·neme \'trep-ə-ˌnēm\ *n* **:** TREPONEMA
[1]tres·pass \'tres-pəs, -ˌpas\ *n* [ME *trespas,* fr. OF, crossing, trespass, fr. *trespasser* to go across] **1 a :** a violation of moral or social ethics **:** TRANSGRESSION; *esp* **:** SIN **b :** an unwarranted infringement **2 a (1) :** an unlawful act committed on the person, property, or rights of another **(2) :** the action for injuries done by such an act **b :** the tort of wrongful entry on real property
[2]trespass *same;* -ˌpas *more often than for* [1]\ *vb* [ME *trespassen,* fr. MF *trespasser,* fr. OF, lit., to go across, fr. *tres* across (fr. L *trans*) + *passer* to pass — more at THROUGH, PASS] *vi* **1 a :** ERR, SIN **b :** to make an unwarranted or uninvited incursion **2 :** to commit a trespass; *esp* **:** to enter unlawfully upon the land of another ~ *vt* **:** VIOLATE <~ the bounds of good taste> — **tres·pass·er** *n*
syn TRESPASS, ENCROACH, ENTRENCH, INFRINGE, INVADE *shared meaning element* **:** to make inroads upon the property, territory, or rights of another
tress \'tres\ *n* [ME *tresse,* fr. OF *trece*] **1** *archaic* **:** a plait of hair **:** BRAID **2 :** a long lock of hair; *esp* **:** the long unbound hair of a woman — usu. used in pl.
tressed \'trest\ *adj* **1** *obs* **:** being braided **:** PLAITED **2 :** having tresses — usu. used in combination <golden-*tressed*>
tres–tine \'tres-ˌtīn\ *n* [prob. fr. L *tres* three + E *tine*] **:** ROYAL ANTLER
tres·tle *also* **tres·sel** \'tres-əl *also* 'trəs-\ *n* [ME *trestel,* fr. MF, modif. of (assumed) VL *transtellum,* fr. L *transtillum,* dim. of *transtrum* traverse beam, transom — more at TRANSOM] **1 :** HORSE 2b **2 :** a braced frame serving as a support (as for a table top) **3 :** a braced framework of timbers, piles, or steelwork for carrying a road or railroad over a depression
tres·tle·tree \-(ˌ)trē\ *n* **:** one of a pair of timber crosspieces fixed fore and aft on the masthead to support the crosstrees, top, and fid of the mast — usu. used in pl.
tres·tle·work \-ˌwərk\ *n* **:** a system of connected trestles supporting a structure (as a bridge)

trews \'trüz\ *n pl* [ScGael *triubhas*] **1 :** tight-fitting trousers usu. of tartan **2 :** close-cut tartan shorts worn under the kilt in Highland dress
trey \'trā\ *n, pl* **treys** [ME *treye, treis,* fr. MF *treie, treis,* fr. L *tres* three] **1 :** the side of a die or domino that has three spots **2 :** a card numbered three or having three main pips
TRF *abbr* tuned radio frequency
tri- *comb form* [ME, fr. L (fr. *tri-, tres*) & Gk, fr. *tri-, treis* — more at THREE] **1 :** three <*tri*costate> **:** having three elements or parts <*tri*graph> **2 :** into three <*tri*sect> **3 :** thrice <*tri*weekly> **:** every third <*tri*monthly>
tri·able \'trī-ə-bəl\ *adj* **:** liable or subject to judicial or quasi-judicial examination or trial <a case ~ without a jury> — **tri·able·ness** *n*
tri·ac·e·tate \(ˈ)trī-'as-ə-ˌtāt\ *n* [ISV] **1 :** an acetate containing three acetate groups **2 :** a textile fiber or fabric consisting of a triacetate of cellulose
[1]tri·ac·id \-'as-əd\ *adj* [ISV] **1 :** able to react with three molecules of a monobasic acid or one of a triacid to form a salt or ester — used esp. of bases **2 :** containing three hydrogen atoms replaceable by basic atoms or radicals — used esp. of acid salts
[2]triacid *n* **:** an acid having three acid hydrogen atoms
tri·ad \'trī-ˌad *also* -əd\ *n* [L *triad-, trias,* fr. Gk, fr. *treis* three] **1 :** a union or group of three and esp. of three closely related or associated persons, beings, or things **:** TRINITY **2 :** a chord of three tones consisting of a root with its third and fifth and constituting the harmonic basis of tonal music — called also *common chord* — **tri·ad·ic** \trī-'ad-ik\ *adj* — **tri·ad·i·cal·ly** \-i-k(ə-)lē\ *adv*
tri·age \trē-'äzh, 'trē-ˌ\ *n* [F, sorting, sifting, fr. *trier* to sort, fr. OF — more at TRY] **:** the sorting of and allocation of treatment to patients and esp. battle and disaster victims according to a system of priorities designed to maximize the number of survivors
[1]tri·al \'trī(-ə)l\ *n* [AF, fr. *trier* to try] **1 a :** the action or process of trying or putting to the proof **:** TEST **b :** a preliminary contest (as in a sport) **2 :** the formal examination before a competent tribunal of the matter in issue in a civil or criminal cause in order to determine such issue **3 :** a test of faith, patience, or stamina by suffering or temptation; *broadly* **:** a source of vexation or annoyance **4 a :** a tryout or experiment to test quality, value, or usefulness **b :** one of a number of repetitions of an experiment <what is the probability of getting *k* successes in *n* ~*s*> **5 :** ATTEMPT
[2]trial *adj* **1 :** of, relating to, or used in a trial **2 :** made or done as a test or experiment **3 :** used or tried out in a test or experiment
trial and error *n* **:** a finding out of the best way to reach a desired result or a correct solution by trying out one or more ways or means and by noting and eliminating errors or causes of failure; *also* **:** the trying of this and that until something succeeds
trial balance *n* **:** a list of the debit and credit balances of accounts in a double-entry ledger at a given date prepared primarily to test their equality
trial balloon *n* **1 :** a balloon sent up to test air currents and wind velocity **2 :** a project or scheme tentatively announced in order to test public opinion
trial court *n* **:** the court before which issues of fact and law are first determined as distinguished from an appellate court
trial examiner *n* **:** a person appointed to hold hearings and to investigate and report facts sometimes with recommendations to an administrative or quasi-judicial agency or tribunal
trial horse *n* **:** one set up as an opponent for a champion in trial competitions or workouts <he offered his 12-meter yacht . . . as a *trial horse* —*Life*>
trial jury *n* **:** a jury impaneled to try a cause **:** PETIT JURY
trial lawyer *n* **:** a lawyer who engages chiefly in the trial of cases before courts of original jurisdiction
tri·alogue \'trī-ə-ˌlȯg, -ˌläg\ *n* [*tri-* + *-alogue* (as in *dialogue*)] **:** a scene, discourse, or colloquy in which three persons share
trial run *n* **:** a testing exercise **:** EXPERIMENT
tri·am·cin·o·lone \ˌtrī-ˌam-'sin-ᵊl-ˌōn\ *n* [*tri-* + *-amcin-* (of unknown origin) + predniso*lone*] **:** a corticoid drug $C_{21}H_{27}FO_6$ used esp. in treating psoriasis and allergic skin and respiratory disorders
tri·an·gle \'trī-ˌaŋ-gəl\ *n* [ME, fr. L *triangulum,* fr. neut. of *triangulus* triangular, fr. *tri-* + *angulus* angle] **1 :** a polygon having three sides — compare SPHERICAL TRIANGLE **2 a :** a percussion instrument consisting of a rod of steel bent into the form of a triangle open at one angle and sounded by striking with a small metal rod **b :** a drafting instrument consisting of a thin flat right-angled triangle of wood or plastic with acute angles of 45 degrees or of 30 degrees and 60 degrees **3 :** a situation involving the love of two persons of one sex for one of the opposite sex with the resulting complications <the eternal ~>

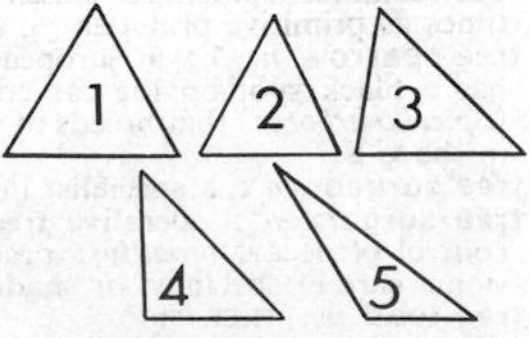

triangles: *1* equilateral, *2* isosceles, *3* scalene, *4* right-angled, *5* obtuse

triangle inequality *n* [fr. its application to the distances between three points in a coordinate system] **:** an inequality stating that the absolute value of a sum is less than or equal to the sum of the absolute value of the terms
tri·an·gu·lar \trī-'aŋ-gyə-lər\ *adj* [LL *triangularis,* fr. L *triangulum*] **1 a :** of, relating to, or having the form of a triangle <a ~ plot of land> **b :** having a triangular base or principal surface <a ~ table> <a ~ pyramid> **2 a (1) :** of, relating to, or involving three elements **(2)** *of a military group* **:** based primarily on three units <~ division> **b :** of or relating to a love triangle <a ~ love affair> — **tri·an·gu·lar·i·ty** \(ˌ)trī-ˌaŋ-gyə-'lar-ət-ē\ *n* — **tri·an·gu·lar·ly** \trī-'aŋ-gyə-lər-lē\ *adv*

[1]**tri·an·gu·late** \trī-ˈaŋ-gyə-lət\ *adj* [ML *triangulatus,* pp. of *triangulare* to make triangles, fr. L *triangulum*] **:** consisting of or marked with triangles — **tri·an·gu·late·ly** *adv*

[2]**tri·an·gu·late** \-ˌlāt\ *vt* **-lat·ed; -lat·ing** **1 a :** to divide into triangles **b :** to give triangular form to **2 :** to survey, map, or determine by triangulation

tri·an·gu·la·tion \(ˌ)trī-ˌaŋ-gyə-ˈlā-shən\ *n* **:** the measurement of the elements necessary to determine the network of triangles into which any part of the earth's surface is divided in surveying; *broadly* **:** any similar trigonometric operation for finding a position or location by means of bearings from two fixed points a known distance apart

tri·ar·chy \ˈtrī-ˌär-kē\ *n, pl* **-chies** [Gk *triarchia,* fr. *tri-* + *-archia* -archy] **1 :** government by three persons **:** TRIUMVIRATE **2 :** a country under three rulers

Tri·as·sic \trī-ˈas-ik\ *adj* [ISV, fr. L *trias* triad; fr. the three subdivisions of the European Triassic — more at TRIAD] **:** of, relating to, or being the earliest period of the Mesozoic era or the corresponding system of rocks — **Triassic** *n*

tri·at·ic stay \(ˌ)trī-ˌat-ik-\ *n* [origin unknown] **:** a stay running horizontally between the heads of the foremast and mainmast

tri·atom·ic \ˌtrī-ə-ˈtäm-ik\ *adj* [ISV] **1 :** having three atoms in the molecule <ozone is ~ oxygen> **2 :** having three replaceable atoms or radicals

tri·ax·i·al \(ˈ)trī-ˈak-sē-əl\ *adj* [ISV] **:** having or involving three axes — **tri·ax·i·al·i·ty** \(ˌ)trī-ˌak-sē-ˈal-ət-ē\ *n*

tri·azine \ˈtrī-ə-ˌzēn, trī-ˈaz-ˌēn\ *n* [ISV] **:** any of three compounds $C_3H_3N_3$ containing a ring composed of three carbon and three nitrogen atoms; *also* **:** any of various derivatives of these including several used as herbicides

trib *abbr* tributary

tri·bal \ˈtrī-bəl\ *adj* **:** of, relating to, or characteristic of a tribe <~ customs> — **trib·al·ly** \-bə-lē\ *adv*

trib·al·ism \-bə-ˌliz-əm\ *n* **1 :** tribal consciousness and loyalty; *esp* **:** exaltation of the tribe above other groups **2 :** strong ingroup loyalty

tri·ba·sic \(ˈ)trī-ˈbā-sik\ *adj* **1 :** having three hydrogen atoms capable of replacement by basic atoms or radicals — used of acids **2 :** containing three atoms of a univalent metal or their equivalent **3 :** having three basic hydroxyl groups and able to react with three molecules of a monobasic acid — used of bases and basic salts

tribe \ˈtrīb\ *n* [ME, fr. L *tribus,* a division of the Roman people, tribe] **1 a :** a social group comprising numerous families, clans, or generations together with slaves, dependents, or adopted strangers **b :** a political division of the Roman people orig. representing one of the three primitive tribes of ancient Rome **c :** PHYLE **2 :** a group of persons having a common character, occupation, or interest **3 a :** a category of taxonomic classification sometimes equivalent to or ranking just below a suborder or ranking below a subfamily; *also* **:** a natural group irrespective of taxonomic rank <the cat ~> <rose ~> **b :** a group of closely related animals or strains within a breed

tribes·man \ˈtrībz-mən\ *n* **:** a member of a tribe

tribo- *comb form* [F, fr. Gk *tribein* to rub; akin to L *terere* to rub — more at THROW] **:** friction <*tribo*luminescence>

tri·bo·elec·tric·i·ty \ˌtrī-bō-i-ˌlek-ˈtris-ət-ē, ˌtrib-ō-, -ˈtris-tē\ *n* **:** a charge of electricity generated by friction (as by rubbing glass with silk) — **tri·bo·elec·tric** \-ˈlek-trik\ *adj*

tri·bol·o·gy \trī-ˈbäl-ə-jē, trib-ˈäl-\ *n* [*tribo-*] *Brit* **:** a science that deals with the design, friction, wear, and lubrication of interacting surfaces in relative motion (as in bearings or gears) — **tri·bo·log·i·cal** \ˌtrī-bə-ˈläj-i-kəl, ˌtrib-ə-\ *adj, Brit* — **tri·bol·o·gist** \trī-ˈbäl-ə-jəst, trib-ˈäl-\ *n, Brit*

tri·bo·lu·mi·nes·cence \ˈtrī-bō-ˌlü-mə-ˈnes-ᵊn(t)s, ˈtrib-ō-\ *n* [ISV] **:** luminescence due to friction — **tri·bo·lu·mi·nes·cent** \-ᵊnt\ *adj*

tri·bo·phys·ics \ˈtrī-bō-ˌfiz-iks, ˈtrib-ō-\ *n pl but sing or pl in constr* **:** the physics of friction

tri·brach \ˈtrī-brak\ *n* [L *tribrachys,* fr. Gk, having three short syllables, fr. *tri-* + *brachys* short — more at BRIEF] **:** a metrical foot of three short syllables of which two belong to the thesis and one to the arsis — **tri·brach·ic** \trī-ˈbrak-ik\ *adj*

tri·bro·mide \(ˈ)trī-ˈbrō-ˌmīd\ *n* **:** a compound of an element or radical with three atoms of bromine

trib·u·late \ˈtrib-yə-ˌlāt\ *vt* **-lat·ed; -lat·ing** [LL *tribulatus,* pp. of *tribulare* to oppress, afflict] **:** to cause to endure tribulation

trib·u·la·tion \ˌtrib-yə-ˈlā-shən\ *n* [ME *tribulacion,* fr. OF, fr. L *tribulation-, tribulatio,* fr. *tribulatus,* pp. of *tribulare* to press, oppress, fr. *tribulum* drag used in threshing, fr. *terere* to rub — more at THROW] **:** distress or suffering resulting from oppression or persecution; *also* **:** a trying experience

tri·bu·nal \trī-ˈbyün-ᵊl, trib-ˈyün-\ *n* [L, platform for magistrates, fr. *tribunus* tribune] **1 :** the seat of a judge **:** TRIBUNE **2 :** a court or forum of justice **3 :** something that decides or determines <the ~ of public opinion>

tri·bu·nate \ˈtrib-yə-ˌnāt, trib-ˈyü-nət\ *n* **:** the office, function, or term of office of a tribune

[1]**tri·bune** \ˈtrib-ˌyün, trib-ˈ\ *n* [ME, fr. L *tribunus,* fr. *tribus* tribe] **1 :** a Roman official under the monarchy and the republic with the function of protecting the plebeian citizen from arbitrary action by the patrician magistrates **2 :** an unofficial defender of the rights of the individual — **tri·bune·ship** \-ˌship\ *n*

[2]**tribune** *n* [F, fr. It *tribuna,* fr. L *tribunal*] **:** a dais or platform from which an assembly is addressed

[1]**trib·u·tary** \ˈtrib-yə-ˌter-ē\ *adj* **1 :** paying tribute to another to acknowledge submission, to obtain protection, or to purchase peace **:** SUBJECT **2 :** paid or owed as tribute **3 :** channeling material or supplies into something more inclusive **:** CONTRIBUTORY

[2]**tributary** *n, pl* **-tar·ies** **1 :** a ruler or state that pays tribute to a conqueror **2 :** a stream feeding a larger stream or a lake

trib·ute \ˈtrib-(ˌ)yüt, -yət\ *n* [ME *tribut,* fr. L *tributum,* fr. neut. of *tributus,* pp. of *tribuere* to allot, bestow, grant, pay, fr. *tribus* tribe] **1 a :** a payment by one ruler or nation to another in acknowledgment of submission or as the price of protection; *also* **:** the tax levied for such a payment **b** (1) **:** an excessive tax, rental, or tariff imposed by a government, sovereign, lord or landlord (2) **:** an exorbitant charge levied by a person or group having the power of coercion **c :** the liability to pay tribute **2 a :** something given or contributed voluntarily as due or deserved; *esp* **:** a gift or service showing respect, gratitude, or affection <floral ~> **b :** something (as material evidence or a formal attestation) that bespeaks the worth, virtue, or effectiveness of the one in question <will receive so many ~*s* that it may seem unnecessary to add . . . to the general paean —Harold Nicolson> <the vote was a ~ to their good sense> ***syn*** see ENCOMIUM

tri·car·box·yl·ic \ˌtrī-ˌkär-ˌbäk-ˈsil-ik\ *adj* **:** containing three carboxyl groups in the molecule

tricarboxylic acid cycle *n* **:** KREBS CYCLE

tri·car·pel·late \(ˈ)trī-ˈkär-pə-ˌlāt, -lət\ *or* **tri·car·pel·lary** \-ˌler-ē\ *adj* **:** having or made up of three usu. fused carpels

[1]**trice** \ˈtrīs\ *vt* **triced; tric·ing** [ME *trisen, tricen* to pull, trice, fr. MD *trisen* to hoist] **:** to haul up or in and lash or secure (as a sail) with a small rope

[2]**trice** *n* [ME *trise,* lit., pull, fr. *trisen*] **:** a brief space of time **:** INSTANT — used chiefly in the phrase *in a trice*

tri·ceps \ˈtrī-ˌseps\ *n, pl* **tri·ceps·es** *also* **triceps** [NL *tricipit-, triceps,* fr. L, three-headed, fr. *tri-* + *capit-, caput* head — more at HEAD] **:** a muscle that arises from three heads; *esp* **:** the great extensor muscle along the back of the upper arm

tri·cer·a·tops \(ˈ)trī-ˈser-ə-ˌtäps\ *n* [NL, genus name, fr. *tri-* + *cerat-* + Gk *ōps* face — more at EYE] **:** any of a genus (*Triceratops*) of large herbivorous Cretaceous dinosaurs with three horns, a bony hood or crest on the neck, and hoofed toes

-trices *pl of* -TRIX

trich- *or* **tricho-** *comb form* [NL, fr. Gk, fr. *trich-, thrix* hair; akin to MIr gairb*driuch* bristle] **:** hair **:** filament <*tricho*gyne>

tri·chi·a·sis \trik-ˈī-ə-səs\ *n* [LL, fr. Gk, fr. *trich* + *-iasis*] **:** a turning inward of the eyelashes often causing irritation of the eyeball

tri·chi·na \trik-ˈī-nə\ *n, pl* **-nae** \-(ˌ)nē\ *also* **-nas** [NL, fr. Gk *trichinos* made of hair, fr. *trich-, thrix* hair] **1 :** a small slender nematode worm (*Trichinella spiralis*) that in the larval state is parasitic in the voluntary muscles of flesh-eating mammals (as man and swine) **2 :** TRICHINOSIS — **tri·chi·nal** \-ˈīn-ᵊl\ *adj*

trich·i·nize \ˈtrik-ə-ˌnīz\ *vt* **-nized; -niz·ing** **:** to infest with trichinae

trich·i·no·sis \ˌtrik-ə-ˈnō-səs\ *n* [NL] **:** infestation with or disease caused by trichinae and marked esp. by muscular pain, dyspnea, fever, and edema

tri·chi·nous \ˈtrik-ə-nəs, trik-ˈī-\ *adj* [ISV] **1 :** infested with trichinae <~ meat> **2 :** of, relating to, or involving trichinae or trichinosis <~ infection>

trich·ite \ˈtrik-ˌīt\ *n* [G *trichit,* fr. Gk *trich-, thrix* hair] **:** a minute acicular body

tri·chlor·fon \(ˈ)trī-ˈklō(ə)r-ˌfän, -ˈklȯ(ə)r-\ *n* [*tri-* + *chlor-* + *-fon* (irreg. fr. *phosphonate* — a salt derived from phosphine)] **:** a crystalline compound $C_4H_8Cl_3O_4P$ that is used as an insecticide and anthelmintic

tri·chlo·ride \(ˈ)trī-ˈklō(ə)r-ˌīd, -ˈklȯ(ə)r-\ *n* [ISV] **:** a compound of an element or radical with three atoms of chlorine

tri·chlo·ro·ace·tic acid \ˌtrī-ˌklōr-ō-ə-ˌsēt-ik-, -ˌklȯr-\ *n* [ISV] **:** a strong vesicant pungent acid $C_2Cl_3HO_2$ used in weed control and in medicine as a caustic and astringent

tricho·cyst \ˈtrik-ə-ˌsist\ *n* **:** any of the minute lassoing or stinging organs on the body of protozoans and esp. of many ciliates — **tricho·cys·tic** \ˌtrik-ə-ˈsis-tik\ *adj*

tricho·gyne \-ˌjīn, -ˌgīn\ *n* [ISV] **:** a slender terminal prolongation of the ascogonium of a fungus or lichen that may serve as a fertilization tube; *also* **:** a similar reproductive structure in a red alga

tri·choid \ˈtrik-ˌȯid, ˈtrī-ˌkȯid\ *adj* [Gk *trichoeidēs,* fr. *trich-, thrix*] **:** resembling a hair **:** CAPILLARY

tri·chome \ˈtrik-ˌōm, ˈtrī-ˌkōm\ *n* [G *trichom,* fr. Gk *trichōma* growth of hair, fr. *trichoun* to cover with hair, fr. *trich-, thrix* hair — more at TRICH-] **:** a filamentous outgrowth; *esp* **:** an epidermal hair structure on a plant — **tri·cho·mic** \trik-ˈäm-ik, -ˈōm-; trī-ˈkäm-, -ˈkōm-\ *adj*

tricho·mo·na·cide \ˌtrik-ə-ˈmō-nə-ˌsīd\ *n* [*trichomonad* + *-cide*] **:** an agent used to destroy trichomonads — **tricho·mo·na·cid·al** \-ˌmō-nə-ˈsīd-ᵊl\ *adj*

tricho·mo·nad \ˌtrik-ə-ˈmō-ˌnad, -nəd\ *n* [NL *Trichomonad-, Trichomonas,* genus name, fr. *trich-* + LL *monad-, monas* monad] **:** any of a genus (*Trichomonas*) of flagellated protozoans parasitic in many animals including man — **trichomonad** *or* **tricho·mo·nad·al** \-ˈmō-nəd-ᵊl\ *or* **tricho·mo·nal** \-ˈmōn-ᵊl\ *adj*

tricho·mo·ni·a·sis \ˌtrik-ə-mə-ˈnī-ə-səs\ *n, pl* **-a·ses** \-ˌsēz\ [NL, fr. *Trichomonas* + *-iasis*] **:** infection with or disease caused by trichomonads: as **a :** a human vaginitis characterized by a persistent discharge and caused by a trichomonad (*Trichomonas vaginalis*) that sometimes also invades the male urethra and bladder **b :** a venereal disease of domestic cattle marked by abortion and sterility **c :** one or more diseases of various birds resembling blackhead

tri·chop·ter·an \trik-ˈäp-tə-rən\ *n* [deriv. of Gk *trich-, thrix* hair + *pteron* wing — more at FEATHER] **:** any of an order (Trichoptera) of insects consisting of the caddis flies — **trichopteran** *adj*

tri·chot·o·mous \trī-ˈkät-ə-məs\ *adj* [LGk *trichotomein* to trisect, fr. Gk *tricha* in three (fr. *treis* three) + *-tomein* (akin to *temnein* to cut) — more at THREE, TOME] **:** divided or dividing into three parts or into threes <~ branching> — **tri·chot·o·mous·ly** *adv*

tri·chot·o·my \-mē\ *n, pl* **-mies** : division into three parts, elements, or classes

-tri·chous \tri-kəs\ *adj comb form* [Gk *-trichos,* fr. *trich-, thrix* hair — more at TRICH-] : having (such) hair <peri*trichous*>

tri·chro·mat \'trī-krō-ˌmat, (ˈ)trī-'\ *n* [back-formation fr. *trichromatic*] : a person with normal color vision requiring that three primary colors be mixed in order to match the spectrum as he sees it

tri·chro·mat·ic \ˌtrī-krō-'mat-ik\ *adj* **1** : of, relating to, or consisting of three colors <~ light> **2 a** : relating to or being the theory that human color vision involves three types of retinal sensory receptors **b** : characterized by trichromatism <~ vision>

tri·chro·ma·tism \(ˈ)trī-'krō-mə-ˌtiz-əm\ *n* **1** : the quality or state of being trichromatic : the use of three colors (as in photography) **2** : vision in which all of the fundamental colors are perceived though not necessarily with equal facility

trich·u·ri·a·sis \ˌtrik-yə-'rī-ə-səs\ *n, pl* **-a·ses** \-ˌsēz\ [NL, fr. *Trichuris,* genus of worms] : infestation with or disease caused by whipworms (genus *Trichuris*)

[1]**trick** \'trik\ *n* [ME *trik,* fr. ONF *trique,* fr. *trikier* to deceive, cheat] **1 a** : a crafty procedure or practice meant to deceive or defraud **b** : a mischievous act : PRANK **c** : an indiscreet or childish action **d** : a deceptive, dexterous, or ingenious feat designed to puzzle or amuse <a juggler's ~*s*> **2 a** : an habitual peculiarity of behavior or manner <a horse with the ~ of shying> **b** : a characteristic and identifying feature <a ~ of speech> **c** : a delusive appearance esp. when caused by art or legerdemain : an optical illusion <a mere ~ of the light> **3 a** : a quick or artful way of getting a result : KNACK **b** : a technical device (as of an art or craft) <the ~*s* of stage technique> **4** : the cards played in one round of a card game often used as a scoring unit **5 a** : a turn of duty at the helm usu. lasting for two hours **b** : SHIFT 4b(1) **c** : a trip taken as part of one's employment **6** : an attractive child or pretty young woman <a cute little ~>
syn TRICK, RUSE, STRATAGEM, MANEUVER, ARTIFICE, WILE, FEINT *shared meaning element* : an indirect means to gain an end

[2]**trick** *adj* **1 a** : of or relating to or involving tricks or trickery <~ photography> <~ dice> **b** : skilled in or used for tricks <a ~ horse> **2** : TRIG **3 a** : somewhat defective and unreliable <a ~ lock> **b** : inclined to give way unexpectedly <a ~ knee>

[3]**trick** *vt* **1** : to deceive by cunning or artifice : CHEAT **2** : to dress or adorn fancifully or ornately : ORNAMENT <~*ed* out in a gaudy uniform> ***syn*** see DUPE

trick·er \'trik-ər\ *n* : one that tricks : TRICKSTER

trick·ery \'trik-(ə-)rē\ *n* : the practice of crafty underhand ingenuity to deceive or cheat

trick·ish \'trik-ish\ *adj* : given to or characterized by tricks or trickery : TRICKY — **trick·ish·ly** *adv* — **trick·ish·ness** *n*

[1]**trick·le** \'trik-əl\ *vi* **trick·led; trick·ling** \-(ə-)liŋ\ [ME *triklen*] **1 a** : to issue or fall in drops **b** : to flow in a thin gentle stream **2 a** : to move or go one by one or little by little **b** : to dissipate slowly <his enthusiasm *trickled* away>

[2]**trickle** *n* : a thin, slow, or intermittent stream or movement

trick or treat *n* : a children's Halloween practice of asking for treats from door to door under threat of playing tricks on householders who refuse — **trick-or-treat** *vi*

trick·ster \'trik-stər\ *n* : one who tricks: as **a** : a dishonest person who defrauds others by trickery **b** : a person (as a stage magician) skilled in the use of tricks and illusion

tricksy \'trik-sē\ *adj* **tricks·i·er; -est** [*tricks,* pl. of *trick*] **1** *archaic* : smartly attired : SPRUCE **2** : full of tricks : PRANKISH **3 a** *archaic* : having the craftiness of a trickster **b** : difficult to cope with or handle : TRYING <a ~ job> — **tricks·i·ness** *n*

tricky \'trik-ē\ *adj* **trick·i·er; -est** **1** : inclined to or marked by trickery **2 a** : giving a deceptive impression of easiness, simplicity, or order : TICKLISH <a ~ path through the swamp> **b** : TRICK 3 **3** : requiring skill, knack, or caution (as in doing or handling); *also* : INGENIOUS <a ~ rhythm> ***syn*** see SLY — **trick·i·ly** \'trik-ə-lē\ *adv* — **trick·i·ness** \'trik-ē-nəs\ *n*

tri·clad \'trī-ˌklad\ *n* [NL *Tricladida,* group name, fr. *tri-* + Gk *klados* branch — more at GLADIATOR] : any of an order (Tricladida) of turbellarian flatworms (as a planarian) that have the intestine composed of a median anterior division and two lateral posterior divisions with side branches — **triclad** *adj*

tri·clin·ic \(ˈ)trī-'klin-ik\ *adj* [ISV] : having three unequal axes intersecting at oblique angles — used esp. of a crystal

tri·clin·i·um \trī-'klin-ē-əm\ *n, pl* **-ia** \-ē-ə\ [L, fr. Gk *triklinion,* fr. *tri-* + *klinein* to lean, recline — more at LEAN] **1** : a couch used by ancient Romans for reclining at meals, extending round three sides of a table, and usu. divided into three parts **2** : a dining room furnished with a triclinium

tric·o·lette \ˌtrik-ə-'let\ *n* [*tricot* + *-lette* (as in *flannelette*)] : a usu. silk or rayon knitted fabric used esp. for women's clothing

[1]**tri·col·or** \'trī-ˌkəl-ər *also* 'trē-, *esp Brit* 'trik-ə-lər\ *n* [F *tricolore,* fr. *tricolore* three-colored, fr. LL *tricolor,* fr. L *tri-* + *color*] : a flag of three colors <the French ~>

[2]**tricolor** *adj* [F *tricolore*] **1 a** *or* **tri·col·ored** \'trī-'kəl-ərd\ : having or using three colors **b** *of a dog* : having a coat of black, tan, and white **2** : of, relating to, or characteristic of a tricolor or a nation whose flag is a tricolor; *esp* : FRENCH

tri·corn \'trī-ˌkȯ(ə)rn\ *adj* [L *tricornis*] : having three horns or corners

tri·corne *or* **tri·corn** \'trī-ˌkȯ(ə)rn\ *n* [F *tricorne,* fr. *tricorne* three-cornered, fr. L *tricornis,* fr. *tri-* + *cornu* horn — more at HORN] : COCKED HAT 1

tri·cor·nered \'trī-'kȯ(r)-nərd\ *adj* : having three corners

tri·cot \'trē-(ˌ)kō, 'trī-kət\ *n* [F, fr. *tricoter* to knit] **1** : a plain warp-knitted fabric of nylon, wool, rayon, silk, or cotton with a close inelastic knit and used esp. in clothing (as underwear) **2** : a twilled clothing fabric of wool with fine warp ribs or of wool and cotton with fine weft ribs

tri·co·tine \ˌtrik-ə-'tēn, ˌtrē-kə-\ *n* [F, fr. *tricot*] : a sturdy suiting woven of tightly twisted yarns in a double twill

tri·cot·y·le·don·ous \ˌtrī-ˌkät-ᵊl-'ēd-nəs, -ᵊn-əs\ *adj* : having three cotyledons <a ~ seedling>

tric·trac \'trik-ˌtrak\ *n* [F, of imit. origin; fr. the sound made by the pegs] : an old form of backgammon played with pegs

[1]**tri·cus·pid** \(ˈ)trī-'kəs-pəd\ *adj* [L *tricuspid-, tricuspis,* fr. *tri-* + *cuspid-, cuspis* point] : having three cusps <a ~ molar>

[2]**tricuspid** *n* : a tricuspid anatomical structure; *esp* : a tooth having three cusps

tricuspid valve *n* : a valve of three flaps that prevents reflux of blood from the right ventricle to the right auricle

tri·cy·cle \'trī-ˌsik-əl\ *n* [F, fr. *tri-* + Gk *kyklos* wheel — more at WHEEL] : a 3-wheeled vehicle propelled by pedals, hand levers, or a motor

tri·cy·clic \(ˈ)trī-'sī-klik, -'sik-lik\ *adj* [*tri* + *cyclic*] : containing three usu. fused rings in the molecular structure

[1]**tri·dent** \'trīd-ᵊnt\ *n* [L *trident-, tridens,* fr. *trident-, tridens* having three teeth, fr. *tri-* + *dent-, dens* tooth — more at TOOTH] **1** : a 3-pronged spear serving in classical mythology as the attribute of a sea-god **2** : a 3-pronged spear used by ancient Roman retiarii **3** : a 3-pronged fish spear

[2]**trident** *adj* [L *trident-, tridens*] : having three teeth, processes, or points

Tri·den·tine \trī-'den-ˌtīn, -ˌtēn; 'trīd-ᵊn-, 'trid-\ *adj* [NL *Tridentinus,* fr. L *Tridentum* Trent] : of or relating to Trent, Italy, or to a Roman Catholic church council held there from 1545 to 1563

tri·di·men·sion·al \ˌtrīd-ə-'mench-nəl, ˌtrīd-ī-, -ən-ᵊl\ *adj* [ISV] : of, relating to, or concerned with three dimensions <~ space> — **tri·di·men·sion·al·i·ty** \-ˌmen-chə-'nal-ət-ē\ *n*

trid·u·um \'trij-ə-wəm, 'trid-yə-\ *n* [L, fr. *tri-* + *-duum* (akin to *dies* day) — more at DEITY] : a period of three days of prayer usu. preceding a Roman Catholic feast

tried \'trīd\ *adj* [ME, fr. pp. of *trien* to try, test] **1** : found good, faithful, or trustworthy through experience or testing <a ~ recipe> **2** : subjected to trials or distress <a kind but much-*tried* father>

tried and true *adj* : proved good, desirable, or feasible : shown or known to be worthy <a *tried and true* sales technique>

tri·ene \'trī-ˌēn\ *n* : a chemical compound containing three double bonds

tri·en·ni·al \(ˈ)trī-'en-ē-əl\ *adj* **1** : consisting of or lasting for three years **2** : occurring or being done every three years — **triennial** *n* — **tri·en·ni·al·ly** \-ē-ə-lē\ *adv*

tri·en·ni·um \trī-'en-ē-əm\ *n, pl* **-ni·ums** *or* **-nia** \-ē-ə\ [L, fr. *tri-* + *annus* year — more at ANNUAL] : a period of three years

tri·er \'trī(-ə)r\ *n* **1** : someone or something that tries **2** : an implement (as a tapered hollow tube) used in obtaining samples of bulk material for examination and testing

tri·er·arch \'trī(-ə)-ˌrärk\ *n* [L *trierarchus,* fr. Gk *triērarchos,* fr. *triērēs* trireme (fr. *tri-* + *-ērēs* — akin to L *rēmus* oar) + *-archos* -arch — more at ROW] **1** : the commander of a trireme **2** : an Athenian citizen who had to fit out a trireme for the public service

tri·er·ar·chy \-ˌrär-kē\ *n* : the ancient Athenian plan whereby individual citizens furnished and maintained triremes as part of their civic duty

tries *pl of* TRY

tri·eth·yl \(ˈ)trī-'eth-əl\ *adj* [ISV] : containing three ethyl groups in the molecule

tri·fa·cial \-'fā-shəl\ *adj* [ISV] : TRIGEMINAL

tri·fid \'trī-ˌfid, -fəd\ *adj* [L *trifidus* split into three, fr. *tri-* + *findere* to split — more at BITE] : being deeply and narrowly cleft into three teeth, processes, or points <a ~ tablespoon>

[1]**tri·fle** \'trī-fəl\ *n* [ME *trufle, trifle,* fr. OF *trufe, trufle* mockery] **1** : something of little value or importance; *esp* : an insignificant amount (as of money) **2** *chiefly Brit* : a dessert of sponge cake spread with jam or jelly, sprinkled with crumbled macaroons, soaked in wine, and served with custard and whipped cream **3** : a pewter of moderate hardness used esp. for small utensils — **a trifle** : to some small degree <*a trifle* annoyed at the delay>

[2]**trifle** *vb* **tri·fled; tri·fling** \-f(ə-)liŋ\ [ME *truflen, triflen,* fr. OF *trufer, trufler* to mock, trick] *vi* **1 a** : to talk in a jesting or mocking manner or with intent to delude or mislead **b** : to act heedlessly or frivolously : PLAY **2** : to waste time : DALLY **3** : to handle something idly : TOY ~ *vt* : to spend or waste in trifling or on trifles <*trifling* his time away> — **tri·fler** \-f(ə-)lər\ *n*
syn TRIFLE, TOY, DALLY, FLIRT, COQUET *shared meaning element* : to deal with or act toward without serious purpose

tri·fling \'trī-fliŋ\ *adj* : lacking in significance or solid worth: as **a** : FRIVOLOUS <~ talk> **b** : TRIVIAL <a ~ gift> **c** *chiefly dial* : LAZY, SHIFTLESS <a ~ fellow>

tri·flu·ra·lin \trī-'flu̇r-ə-lən\ *n* [*tri-* + *fluor-* + *ani*line] : an herbicide $C_{13}H_{16}F_3N_3O_4$ used in the control of weeds (as pigweed and annual grasses)

[1]**tri·fo·cal** \(ˈ)trī-'fō-kəl\ *adj* : having three focal lengths

[2]**trifocal** *n* **1** : a trifocal glass or lens **2** *pl* : eyeglasses with trifocal lenses

tri·fo·li·ate \(ˈ)trī-'fō-lē-ət\ *adj* **1** : having three leaves <a ~ plant> **2** : TRIFOLIOLATE

trifoliate orange *n* : a hardy deciduous Chinese orange (*Poncirus trifoliata*) with trifoliolate leaves that is widely grown for ornament and esp. as a stock for budding other oranges

tri·fo·li·o·late \(ˈ)trī-'fō-lē-ə-ˌlāt\ *adj* [ISV] : having three leaflets <a ~ leaf>

tri·fo·li·um \trī-'fō-lē-əm\ *n* [NL, genus name, fr. L, trefoil — more at TREFOIL] : any of a genus (*Trifolium*) of leguminous herbs comprising the typical clovers

tri·fo·ri·um \trī-'fōr-ē-əm, -'fȯr-\ *n, pl* **-ria** \-ē-ə\ [ML] : a gallery forming an upper story to the aisle of a church and typically an arcaded story between the nave arches and clerestory

tri·form \'trī-ˌfȯrm\ *adj* [L *triformis,* fr. *tri-* + *forma* form] : having a triple form or nature

tri·fur·cate \(ˈ)trī-'fər-kət, -ˌkāt; 'trī-(ˌ)fər-ˌkāt\ *adj* [L *trifurcus,* fr. *tri-* + *furca* fork] : having three branches or forks : TRICHOTOMOUS — **tri·fur·cate** \'trī-(ˌ)fər-ˌkāt, trī-'fər-\ *vi* — **tri·fur·ca·tion** \ˌtrī-(ˌ)fər-'kā-shən\ *n*

[1]trig \'trig\ *adj* [ME, trusty, nimble, of Scand origin; akin to ON *tryggr* faithful; akin to OE *trēowe* faithful — more at TRUE] **1** : stylishly or jauntily trim **2** : extremely precise : PRIM **3** *dial chiefly Brit* : FIRM, VIGOROUS *syn* see NEAT

[2]trig *vt* **trigged; trig·ging** *dial chiefly Brit* : to put in order : TIDY — usu. used with *up*

[3]trig *vt* **trigged; trig·ging** [perh. of Scand origin; akin to ON *tryggja* to make firm, *tryggr* faithful] *chiefly dial* : to restrain from moving or shifting: as **a** : to stop or slow the motion of (a wheel) usu. with a block **b** : to support with props or wedges

[4]trig *n, chiefly dial* : a stone or block used as a support in trigging

[5]trig *n* : TRIGONOMETRY

tri·gem·i·nal \trī-'jem-ən-ᵊl\ *adj* [NL *trigeminus* trigeminal nerve, fr. L, threefold, fr. *tri-* + *geminus* twin] : of or relating to the trigeminal nerve

trigeminal nerve *n* : either of a pair of large mixed nerves that are the fifth cranial nerves and supply motor and sensory fibers mostly to the face — called also *trigeminal*

trigeminal neuralgia *n* : an intense paroxysmal neuralgia involving one or more branches of the trigeminal nerve

[1]trig·ger \'trig-ər\ *n* [alter. of earlier *tricker*, fr. D *trekker*, fr. MD *trecker* one that pulls, fr. *trecken* to pull — more at TREK] **1** : a piece (as a lever) connected with a catch or detent as a means of releasing it; *esp* : the part of the action moved by the finger to fire a gun **2** : a stimulus that initiates a physiological or pathological process <the sight or odor of food may be a ~ for salivation> — **trigger** *adj* — **trig·gered** \-ərd\ *adj*

[2]trigger *vb* **trig·gered; trig·ger·ing** \'trig-(ə-)riŋ\ *vt* **1 a** : to release or activate by means of a trigger; *esp* : to fire by pulling a mechanical trigger <~ a rifle> **b** : to cause the explosion of <~ a missile with a proximity fuze> **2** : to initiate, actuate, or set off as if by pulling a trigger <an indiscreet remark that ~*ed* a fight> ~ *vi* : to release a mechanical trigger

trig·ger·fish \'trig-ər-ˌfish\ *n* : any of numerous deep-bodied plectognath fishes (as of the genus *Balistes*) of warm seas having an anterior dorsal fin with two or three stout erectile spines

trig·ger–hap·py \-ˌhap-ē\ *adj* **1** : irresponsible in the use of firearms; *esp* : inclined to shoot before clearly identifying the target **2 a** : inclined to be irresponsible in matters that might precipitate war **b** : aggressively belligerent in attitude

trig·ger·man \-mən, -ˌman\ *n* : a gunman who shoots the victim in a gangland murder; *also* : a gangster's personal bodyguard

tri·glyc·er·ide \(')trī-'glis-ə-ˌrīd\ *n* [ISV] : an ester of glycerol that contains three ester groups and involves one, two, or three acids

tri·glyph \'trī-ˌglif\ *n* [L *triglyphus*, fr. Gk *triglyphos*, fr. *tri-* + *glyphein* to carve — more at CLEAVE] : a slightly projecting rectangular tablet in a Doric frieze with two vertical channels of V section and two corresponding chamfers or half channels on the vertical sides — **tri·glyph·ic** \trī-'glif-ik\ *or* **tri·glyph·i·cal** \-i-kəl\ *adj*

tri·gon \'trī-ˌgän\ *n* [L *trigonum*, fr. Gk *trigōnon*, fr. neut. of *trigōnos* triangular, fr. *tri-* + *gōnia* angle — more at -GON] **1** : TRIANGLE **2 a** : TRIPLICITY 1 **b** : TRINE 2 **3** : an ancient triangular harp

tri·go·nal \tri-'gōn-ᵊl\ *adj* **1** : TRIANGULAR **2** : of, relating to, or being the division of the hexagonal crystal system or the forms belonging to it characterized by a vertical axis of threefold symmetry — **tri·go·nal·ly** \-ᵊl-ē\ *adv*

trig·o·no·met·ric \ˌtrig-ə-nə-'me-trik\ *also* **trig·o·no·met·ri·cal** \-tri-kəl\ *adj* : of, relating to, or being in accordance with trigonometry — **trig·o·no·met·ri·cal·ly** \-tri-k(ə-)lē\ *adv*

trigonometric function *n* **1** : a function (as the sine, cosine, tangent, cotangent, secant, or cosecant) of an arc or angle most simply expressed in terms of the ratios of pairs of sides of a right-angled triangle — called also *circular function* **2** : the inverse (as the arc sine, arc cosine, arc tangent, arc cotangent, arc secant, or arc cosecant) of a trigonometric function

trig·o·nom·e·try \ˌtrig-ə-'näm-ə-trē\ *n* [NL *trigonometria*, fr. Gk *trigōnon* + *-metria* -metry] : the study of the properties of triangles and trigonometric functions and of their applications

tri·go·nous \trī-'gō-nəs, 'trig-ə-\ *adj* [L *trigonus* triangular, fr. Gk *trigōnos*] : triangular in cross section <a ~ achene>

tri·graph \'trī-ˌgraf\ *n* **1** : three letters spelling a single consonant, vowel, or diphthong <*eau* of *beau* is a ~> **2** : a cluster of three successive letters <the letters *the* are a high frequency ~> — **tri·graph·ic** \(')trī-'graf-ik\ *adj*

tri·he·dral \-'hē-drəl\ *adj* **1** : having three faces <~ angle> **2** : of or relating to a trihedral angle — **trihedral** *n*

tri·hy·brid \-'hī-brəd\ *n* : an individual or strain that is heterozygous for three pairs of genes

tri·hy·droxy \ˌtrī-hī-'dräk-sē, -hə-\ *adj* [ISV *tri-* + *hydroxyl*] : containing three hydroxyl groups in the molecule

tri·io·do·thy·ro·nine \ˌtrī-ˌī-əd-ō-'thī-rə-ˌnēn\ *n* [*tri-* + *iod-* + *thyronine* (an amino acid of which thyroxine is a derivative)] : an iodine-containing amino acid $C_{15}H_{12}I_3NO_4$ that is made synthetically, may be formed naturally from thyroxine by loss of one iodine atom per molecule, and is used esp. in the treatment of hypothyroidism

tri·jet \ˌtrī-ˌjet\ *adj* : powered with three jet engines <a ~ airplane> — **tri·jet** \-ˌjet\ *n*

tri·lat·er·al \(')trī-'lat-ə-rəl, -'la-trəl\ *adj* [L *trilaterus*, fr. *tri-* + *later-, latus* side] : having three sides <a triangle is ~> — **tri·lat·er·al·i·ty** \ˌtrī-ˌlat-ə-'ral-ət-ē\ *n* — **tri·lat·er·al·ly** \(')trī-'lat-ə-rə-lē, -'la-trə-\ *adv*

tril·by \'tril-bē\ *n, pl* **trilbies** [fr. the fact that such a hat was worn in the London stage version of *Trilby*, novel by George du Maurier] *chiefly Brit* : a soft felt hat with indented crown

tri·lin·ear \(')trī-'lin-ē-ər\ *adj* : of, relating to, or involving three lines

tri·lin·gual \(')trī-'liŋ-g(yə-)wəl\ *adj* : consisting of, having, or expressed in three languages; *also* : familiar with or able to use three languages — **tri·lin·gual·ly** \-ē\ *adv*

[1]tri·lit·er·al \-'lit-ə-rəl, -'li-trəl\ *adj* [*tri-* + L *litera* letter] : consisting of three letters and esp. of three consonants <~ roots in Semitic languages> — **tri·lit·er·al·ism** \-ˌiz-əm\ *n*

[2]triliteral *n* : a root or word that is triliteral

[1]trill \'tril\ *vb* [ME *trillen*, prob. of Scand origin; akin to Sw *trilla* to roll; akin to MD *trillen* to vibrate] *vi* **1** : TWIRL, REVOLVE **2** : to flow in a small stream or in drops : TRICKLE ~ *vt* : to cause to flow in a small stream

[2]trill *n* [It *trillo*, fr. *trillare* to trill, prob. fr. D *trillen* to vibrate; akin to MD *trappe* step, trap] **1 a** : the alternation of two musical tones a diatonic second apart — called also *shake* **b** : VIBRATO **c** : a rapid reiteration of the same tone esp. on a percussion instrument **2** : a sound resembling a musical trill : WARBLE **3 a** : the rapid vibration of one speech organ against another (as of the tip of the tongue against the teethridge) **b** : a speech sound made by a trill

[3]trill *vt* : to utter as or with a trill <~ the *r*> ~ *vi* : to play or sing with a trill : QUAVER — **trill·er** *n*

tril·lion \'tril-yən\ *n* [F, fr. *tri-* + *-illion* (as in *million*)] **1** — see NUMBER table **2** : a very large number — **trillion** *adj* — **tril·lionth** \-yən(t)th\ *adj or n*

tril·li·um \'tril-ē-əm\ *n* [NL, genus name, fr. Sw *trilling* triplet; fr. its three leaves] : any of a genus (*Trillium*) of herbs of the lily family with short rootstocks and an erect stem bearing a whorl of three leaves and a large solitary flower

tri·lo·bate \(')trī-'lō-ˌbāt\ *adj* : TRILOBED — **tri·lo·ba·tion** \ˌtrī-lō-'bā-shən\ *n*

tri·lobed \'trī-'lōbd\ *adj* : having three lobes <a ~ leaf>

tri·lo·bite \'trī-lə-ˌbīt\ *n* [deriv. of Gk *trilobos* three-lobed, fr. *tri-* + *lobos* lobe] : any of numerous extinct Paleozoic marine arthropods (group Trilobita) having the segments of the body divided by furrows on the dorsal surface into three lobes

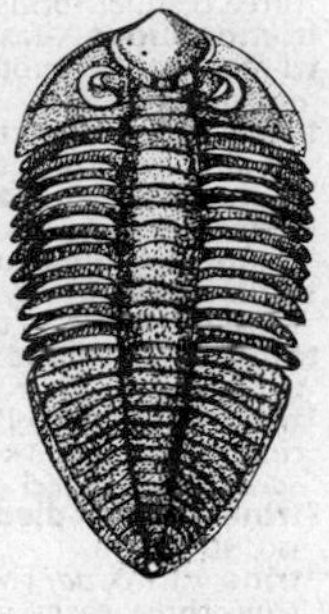

trilobite

tri·loc·u·lar \(')trī-'läk-yə-lər\ *adj* [ISV] : having three cells or cavities

tri·loc·u·late \-lət, -ˌlāt\ *adj* : TRILOCULAR

tril·o·gy \'tril-ə-jē\ *n, pl* **-gies** [Gk *trilogia*, fr. *tri-* + *-logia* -logy] : a series of three dramas or literary works or sometimes three musical compositions that are closely related and develop a single theme

[1]trim \'trim\ *vb* **trimmed; trim·ming** [(assumed) ME *trimmen* to prepare, put in order, fr. OE *trymian, trymman* to strengthen, arrange, fr. *trum* strong, firm; akin to Skt *dāru* wood — more at TREE] *vt* **1 a** : to embellish with ribbons, lace, or ornaments : ADORN **b** : to arrange a display of goods in (a shop window) **2 a** (1) : to administer a beating to : THRASH (2) : to defeat resoundingly <*trimmed* him at chess> **b** : CHEAT, SWINDLE **3 a** : to make trim and neat esp. by cutting or clipping **b** : to free of excess or extraneous matter by or as if by cutting <~ a tree> <~ a budget> **c** : to remove by or as if by cutting <*trimmed* thousands from federal payrolls —*Grit*> **4 a** (1) : to cause (as a ship) to assume a desirable position in the water by arrangement of ballast, cargo, or passengers (2) : to adjust (as an airplane or submarine) for horizontal movement or for motion upward or downward **b** : to adjust (as cargo or a sail) to a desired position ~ *vi* **1 a** : to maintain neutrality between opposing parties or to favor each equally **b** : to change one's views for reasons of expediency **2** : to assume or cause a boat to assume a desired position in the water <a boat that ~*s* badly>

[2]trim *adj* **trim·mer; trim·mest** **1** *obs* : EXCELLENT, FINE; *also* : PLEASANT **2** *archaic* : suitably adjusted, equipped, or prepared for service or use **3** : exhibiting neatness, good order, or compactness of line or structure <~ houses> <a ~ figure> *syn* see NEAT *ant* frowzy — **trim·ly** *adv* — **trim·ness** *n*

[3]trim *adv* : in a trim manner : TRIMLY — used chiefly in combination <the *trim*-cut forest vistas —W. M. Thackeray>

[4]trim *n* **1** : the readiness of a person or thing for action or use **2 a** : one's clothing or appearance **b** : material used for ornament or trimming **c** : the lighter woodwork in the finish of a building esp. around openings **d** : the interior furnishings of an automobile **e** : WINDOW DRESSING **3 a** : the position of a ship or boat esp. with reference to the horizontal; *also* : the difference between the draft of a ship forward and that aft **b** : the relation between the plane of a sail and the direction of the ship **c** : the buoyancy status of a submarine **d** : the attitude of a lighter-than-air craft relative to a fore-and-aft horizontal plane **e** : the attitude with respect to wind axes at which an airplane will continue in level flight with free controls **4** : something that is trimmed off or cut out

tri·ma·ran \'trī-mə-ˌran, ˌtrī-mə-'\ *n* [*tri-* + *-maran* (as in *catamaran*)] : a fast pleasure sailboat with three hulls side by side

tri·mer \'trī-mər\ *n* [ISV *tri-* + *-mer* (as in *polymer*)] : a polymer formed from three molecules of a monomer — **tri·mer·ic** \trī-'mer-ik\ *adj*

trim·er·ous \'trim-ə-rəs\ *adj* [NL *trimerus*, fr. Gk *tri-* + *meros* part — more at MERIT] : having the parts in threes — used of a flower and often written *3-merous*

tri·mes·ter \(')trī-'mes-tər, 'trī-ˌ\ *n* [F *trimestre*, fr. L *trimestris* of three months, fr. *tri-* + *mensis* month — more at MOON] **1** : a period of three or about three months **2** : one of three terms into which the academic year is sometimes divided — **tri·mes·tral** \trī-'mes-trəl\ *also* **tri·mes·tri·al** \-trē-əl\ *adj*

trim·e·ter \ˈtrim-ət-ər\ *n* [L *trimetrus*, fr. Gk *trimetros* having three measures, fr. *tri-* + *metron* measure — more at MEASURE] **:** a line of verse consisting of either three dipodies (as in classical iambic, trochaic, and anapestic verse) or three metrical feet (as in modern English verse)

tri·met·ro·gon \trī-ˈme-trə-ˌgän\ *n* [*tri-* + Gk *metron* measure + E *-gon*] **:** a system of aerial mapping involving the use of sets of one vertical and two oblique aerial photographs taken simultaneously over the area being mapped

trim·mer \ˈtrim-ər\ *n* **1 a :** one that trims articles; *esp* **:** one that stows coal or freight on a ship so as to distribute the weight properly **b :** an instrument or machine with which trimming is done **c :** a circuit element (as a condenser) used to tune a circuit to a desired frequency **2 :** a beam that receives the end of a header in floor framing — see HEADER illustration **3 :** a person who modifies his policy, position, or opinions out of expediency

trim·ming *n* **1 a :** the act of one who trims **b :** pieces cut off in trimming something **:** SCRAPS **2 a :** a decorative accessory or additional item that serves to finish or complete <~*s* for a hat> **b :** an additional garnishing that is not essential but adds to the interest or attractiveness of a main item <turkey and all the ~*s*> **3 :** DEFEAT, BEATING

tri·month·ly \(ˈ)trī-ˈmən(t)th-lē\ *adj* **:** occurring every three months

tri·morph \ˈtrī-ˌmȯrf\ *n* [ISV, back-formation fr. *trimorphous*] **:** any of the three crystalline forms of a trimorphous substance

tri·mor·phic \(ˈ)trī-ˈmȯr-fik\ *adj* [Gk *trimorphos* having three forms, fr. *tri-* + *-morphos* -morphous] **:** occurring in or having three distinct forms — **tri·mor·phism** \-ˌfiz-əm\ *n*

tri·mor·phous \-fəs\ *adj* **:** TRIMORPHIC

tri·mo·tor \ˈtrī-ˌmōt-ər, -ˈmōt-\ *n* **:** an airplane powered by three engines

trim size *n* **:** the actual size (as of a book page) after excess material required in production has been cut off

Tri·mur·ti \tri-ˈmu̇(ə)rt-ē\ *n* [Skt *-trimūrti*, fr. *trimūrti* having three forms, fr. *tri-* + *mūrti* body, form] **:** the great triad of Hindu gods comprising Brahma, Vishnu, and Siva

tri·nal \ˈtrīn-ᵊl\ *adj* [LL *trinalis*, fr. L *trini* three each — more at TRINE] **:** THREEFOLD

tri·na·ry \ˈtrī-nə-rē\ *adj* [LL *trinarius*, fr. L *trini* three each] **:** TERNARY

[1]trin·dle \ˈtrin-(d)ᵊl\ *n* [ME *trindel*, fr. OE *trendel, tryndel* circle, ring — more at TRUNDLE] *dial Eng* **:** a round or circular object; *specif* **:** the wheel of a wheelbarrow

[2]trindle *vi* **trin·dled; trin·dling** \ˈtrin-(d)liŋ, -(d)ᵊl-iŋ\ *dial* **:** ROLL, TRUNDLE

[1]trine \ˈtrīn\ *adj* [ME, fr. MF *trin*, fr. L *trinus*, back-formation fr. *trini* three each; akin to L *tres* three — more at THREE] **1 :** THREEFOLD, TRIPLE **2 :** of, relating to, or being the favorable astrological aspect of two celestial bodies 120 degrees apart

[2]trine *n* **1 :** a group of three **:** TRIAD **2 :** the trine astrological aspect of two celestial bodies

trine immersion *n* **:** the practice of immersing a candidate for baptism three times in the names of the members of the Trinity

trin·i·tar·i·an \ˌtrin-ə-ˈter-ē-ən\ *adj* **1** *cap* **:** of or relating to the Trinity, the doctrine of the Trinity, or adherents to that doctrine **2 :** having three parts or aspects **:** THREEFOLD

Trinitarian *n* **1 :** a member of a religious teaching and nursing order for men founded in France in 1198 by John of Matha and Philip of Valois **2 :** one who subscribes to the doctrine of the Trinity — **Trin·i·tar·i·an·ism** \-ē-ə-ˌniz-əm\ *n*

tri·ni·tro·tol·u·ene \-ˈtäl-yə-ˌwēn\ *n* [ISV] **:** a flammable toxic derivative $C_7H_5N_3O_6$ of toluene obtained by nitrating toluene and used as a high explosive and in chemical synthesis — called also *TNT*

Trin·i·ty \ˈtrin-ət-ē\ *n* [ME *trinite*, fr. OF *trinité*, fr. LL *trinitat-, trinitas* state of being threefold, fr. L *trinus* trine] **1 :** the unity of Father, Son, and Holy Spirit as three persons in one Godhead according to Christian dogma **2** *not cap* **:** a group of three closely related persons or things **3 :** the Sunday after Whitsunday observed as a feast in honor of the Trinity

Trin·i·ty·tide \-ˌtīd\ *n* **:** the season of the church year between Trinity Sunday and Advent

[1]trin·ket \ˈtriŋ-kət\ *n* [perh. fr. ME *trenket* small knife, fr. ONF *trenquet*] **1 :** a small article of equipment **2 :** a small ornament (as a jewel or ring) **3 :** a thing of little value **:** TRIFLE

[2]trinket *vi* [perh. fr. [1]*trinket*] **:** to deal clandestinely **:** INTRIGUE — **trin·ket·er** *n*

trin·ket·ry \-kə-trē\ *n* **:** small items of personal ornament

trin·kums \ˈtriŋ-kəmz\ *n pl* [alter. of *trinkets*] **:** TRINKETS

trin·oc·u·lar \(ˈ)trī-ˈnäk-yə-lər\ *adj* [alter. (influenced by *binocular*) of earlier *triocular*] **:** relating to or being a binocular microscope equipped with a lens for photographic recording during direct visual observation

[1]tri·no·mi·al \trī-ˈnō-mē-əl\ *n* [*tri-* + *-nomial* (as in *binomial*)] **1 :** a polynomial of three terms **2 :** a trinomial name

[2]trinomial *adj* **1 :** consisting of three mathematical terms **2 :** of, relating to, or being biological taxa of three terms of which the first designates the genus, the second the species, and the third the subspecies or variety

tri·nu·cle·o·tide \(ˈ)trī-ˈn(y)ü-klē-ə-ˌtīd\ *n* **:** a nucleotide consisting of three mononucleotides in combination **:** CODON

trio \ˈtrē-(ˌ)ō\ *n, pl* **tri·os** [F, fr. It, fr. *tri-* (fr. L)] **1 a :** a musical composition for three voice parts or three instruments **b :** the secondary or episodic division of a minuet or scherzo, a march, or of various dance forms **2 :** the performers of a musical or dance trio **3 :** a group or set of three

tri·ode \ˈtrī-ˌōd\ *n* **:** an electron tube with an anode, a cathode, and a controlling grid

tri·ol \ˈtrī-ˌȯl, -ˌōl\ *n* **:** a chemical compound containing three hydroxyl groups

tri·o·let \ˈtrī-ə-lət, ˈtrē-\ *n* [F] **:** a poem or stanza of eight lines in which the first line is repeated as the fourth and seventh and the second line as the eighth with a rhyme scheme of *ABaAabAB*

tri·ose \ˈtrī-ˌōs, -ˌōz\ *n* [ISV] **:** either of two simple sugars $C_3H_6O_3$ containing three carbon atoms

tri·ox·ide \(ˈ)trī-ˈäk-ˌsīd\ *n* [ISV] **:** an oxide containing three atoms of oxygen

[1]trip \ˈtrip\ *vb* **tripped; trip·ping** [ME *trippen*, fr. MF *triper*, of Gmc origin; akin to OE *treppan* to tread — more at TRAP] *vi* **1 a :** to dance, skip, or caper with light quick steps **b :** to walk with light quick steps **2 :** to catch the foot against something so as to stumble **3 :** to make a mistake or false step (as in morality or accuracy) **4 :** to stumble in articulation when speaking **5 :** to make a journey **6 :** to run past the pallet of an escapement without previously locking — used of a tooth of the escapement wheel of a watch **7 a :** to actuate a mechanism **b :** to become operative **8 :** to get high on a psychedelic drug (as LSD) **:** turn on — often used with *out* ~ *vt* **1 a :** to cause to stumble **b :** to cause to fail **:** OBSTRUCT **2 :** to detect in a misstep, fault, or blunder; *also* **:** EXPOSE **3** *archaic* **:** to perform (as a dance) lightly or nimbly **4 :** to raise (an anchor) from the bottom so as to hang free **5 a :** to pull (a yard) into a perpendicular position for lowering **b :** to hoist (a topmast) far enough to enable the fid to be withdrawn preparatory to housing or lowering **6 :** to release or operate (a mechanism) esp. by releasing a catch or detent

[2]trip *n* **1 :** a stroke or catch by which a wrestler is made to lose footing **2 a :** VOYAGE, JOURNEY **b :** a single round or tour on a business errand **3 :** ERROR, MISSTEP **4 :** a quick light step **5 :** a faltering step caused by stumbling **6 a :** the action of tripping mechanically **b (1) :** a device for tripping a mechanism (as a catch or detent) **(2) :** TUP 2 **7 :** an intense visionary experience undergone by a person who has taken a psychedelic drug (as LSD)

tri·pack \ˈtrī-ˌpak\ *n* **:** a combination of three superposed films or emulsions each sensitive to a different primary color for simultaneous exposure in one camera

tri·par·tite \(ˈ)trī-ˈpär-ˌtīt\ *adj* [ME, fr. L *tripartitus*, fr. *tri-* + *partitus* partite] **1 :** divided into or composed of three parts **2 :** having three corresponding parts or copies **3 :** made between or involving three parties <a ~ treaty> — **tri·par·tite·ly** *adv*

tri·par·ti·tion \ˌtrī-(ˌ)pär-ˈtish-ən\ *n* **:** a division by threes or into three parts; *also* **:** the taking of a third part

tripe \ˈtrīp\ *n* [ME, fr. OF] **1 :** stomach tissue of a ruminant and esp. of the ox for use as a food: **a :** that of the rumen wall **b :** that of the reticulum wall **2 :** something poor, worthless, or offensive **:** TRASH

trip–ham·mer \ˈtrip-ˌham-ər\ *n* **:** a massive power hammer having a helve that is tripped and allowed to fall by cam or lever action

tri·phe·nyl·meth·ane \ˌtrī-ˌfen-ᵊl-ˈmeth-ˌān, -ˌfēn-\ *n* [ISV] **:** a crystalline hydrocarbon $CH(C_6H_5)_3$ that is the parent compound of many dyes

[1]tri·phib·i·an \(ˈ)trī-ˈfib-ē-ən\ *n* [*tri-* + *-phibian* (as in *amphibian*)] **:** a triphibian airplane

[2]triphibian *adj* **1 :** designed for or equipped to operate from a solid surface (as of land or ice) or water as well as in the air <a ~ airplane> **2 :** TRIPHIBIOUS 1 <a ~ military operation>

tri·phib·i·ous \-ē-əs\ *adj* [*tri-* + *-phibious* (as in *amphibious*)] **1 :** employing, involving, or constituted by land, naval, and air forces and often including airborne troops in coordinated attack <~ operations> **2 :** TRIPHIBIAN 1 <~ marines>

tri·phos·phate \(ˈ)trī-ˈfäs-ˌfāt\ *n* **:** a salt or acid that contains three phosphate groups and is derived from a complex acid anhydride of orthophosphoric acid

tri·phos·pho·pyr·i·dine nucleotide \ˈtrī-ˈfäs-fō-ˌpir-ə-ˌdēn-\ *n* **:** NADP

triph·thong \ˈtrif-ˌthȯŋ, ˈtrip-\ *n* [*tri-* + *-phthong* (as in *diphthong*)] **1 :** a speech item consisting of three successive sounds that serves or is capable of serving as a monosyllable **2 :** TRIGRAPH — **triph·thon·gal** \trif-ˈthȯŋ-(g)əl, trip-\ *adj*

tri·pin·nate \(ˈ)trī-ˈpin-ˌāt\ *adj* **:** bipinnate with each division pinnate — **tri·pin·nate·ly** *adv*

tri·plane \ˈtrī-ˌplān\ *n* **:** an airplane with three main supporting surfaces superposed

[1]tri·ple \ˈtrip-əl\ *vb* **tri·pled; tri·pling** \-(ə-)liŋ\ [ME *triplen*, fr. LL *triplare*, fr. L *triplus*, adj.] *vt* **1 :** to make three times as great or as many **2 a :** to score (a base runner) by a triple **b :** to bring about the scoring of (a run) by a triple ~ *vi* **1 :** to become three times as great or as numerous **2 :** to make a triple in baseball

[2]triple *n* [ME, fr. L *triplus*, adj.] **1 a :** a triple sum, quantity, or number **b :** a combination, group, or series of three **2 :** a base hit that allows the batter to reach third base safely **3 :** a system of betting (as on horse races) in which the bettor must pick the first, second, and third place finishers in this sequence in a specified race in order to win — compare PERFECTA

[3]triple *adj* [MF or L; MF, fr. L *triplus*, fr. *tri-* + *-plus* multiplied by — more at DOUBLE] **1 :** having three units or members **2 :** being three times as great or as many **3 :** having a threefold relation or character <worked as a double or even ~ agent —*Time*> **4 :** three times repeated **:** TREBLE **5 :** marked by three beats per musical measure <~ meter> **6 a :** having units of three components <~ feet> **b** *of rhyme* **:** involving correspondence of three syllables (as in *unfortunate-importunate*)

triple counterpoint *n* **:** three-part musical counterpoint so written that any part may be transposed above or below any other

Triple Crown *n* **1 :** an unofficial title in horse racing representing the championship achieved by a horse that wins the three classic races for a designated category **2 :** the unofficial title representing the championship attained by a baseball player who at the end of a single season leads his league in batting average, home runs, and RBIs

tri·ple–head·er \ˌtrip-əl-ˈhed-ər\ *n* **:** a sports program consisting of three consecutive contests — compare DOUBLEHEADER

triple jump *n* **:** a jump for distance in track-and-field athletics usu. from a running start and combining a hop, a stride, and a jump in succession

triple play *n* **:** a play in baseball by which three players are put out

triple point *n* : the condition of temperature and pressure under which the gaseous, liquid, and solid phases of a substance can exist in equilibrium

tri·ple–space \ˌtrip-əl-ˈspās\ *vt* : to type (copy) leaving two blank lines between lines of copy ~ *vi* : to type on every third line

trip·let \ˈtrip-lət\ *n* [[2]*triple*] **1** : a unit of three lines of verse **2 a** : a combination, set, or group of three **b** : a group of three elementary particles (as positive, negative, and neutral pions) with different charge states but otherwise similar properties **c** *or* **triplet state** : any state of an elementary particle having one quantum unit of spin **3** : one of three children or offspring born at one birth **4** : a group of three musical notes or tones performed in the time of two of the same value

tri·ple·tail \ˈtrip-əl-ˌtāl\ *n* : a large edible marine percoid fish (*Lobotes surinamensis*) of the warm western Atlantic in which the long dorsal and anal fins extend backward and with the caudal fin appear like a 3-lobed tail

triple threat *n* : a football player adept at running, kicking, and passing

tri·ple–tongue \ˌtrip-əl-ˈtəŋ\ *vi* : to articulate the notes of triplets in fast tempo on a wind instrument by using the tongue positions for *t, t, k* for the notes of each successive triplet

[1]**tri·plex** \ˈtrip-ˌleks, ˈtrī-ˌpleks\ *adj* [L, fr. *tri-* + *-plex* -fold — more at SIMPLE] **1** : THREEFOLD, TRIPLE <~ windows> **2 a** : containing three apartments <~ buildings> **b** : having three floors <~ apartments>

[2]**triplex** *n* : something (as a building or apartment) that is triplex

[1]**trip·li·cate** \ˈtrip-li-kət\ *adj* [ME, fr. L *triplicatus*, pp. of *triplicare* to triple, fr. *triplic-*, *triplex* threefold] **1** : consisting of or existing in three corresponding or identical parts or examples <~ invoices> **2** : being the third of three things exactly alike <file the ~ copy>

[2]**trip·li·cate** \-lə-ˌkāt\ *vt* **-cat·ed; -cat·ing 1** : to make triple or threefold **2** : to prepare in triplicate

[3]**trip·li·cate** \-li-kət\ *n* **1** : one of three things exactly alike; *specif* : one of three identical copies **2** : three copies all alike — used with *in* <typed in ~>

trip·li·ca·tion \ˌtrip-lə-ˈkā-shən\ *n* : the action of tripling, making threefold, or adding three together; *also* : something that is triplicated or threefold

tri·plic·i·ty \trip-ˈlis-ət-ē, trī-ˈplis-\ *n, pl* **-ties** [ME *triplicite*, fr. LL *triplicitas* condition of being threefold, fr. L *triplic-*, *triplex*] **1** : one of the groups of three signs each distant 120 degrees from the other two into which the signs of the zodiac are divided — called also *trigon* **2** : the quality or state of being triple or threefold

trip·lite \ˈtrip-ˌlīt\ *n* [G *triplit*, fr. L *triplus* triple; fr. its threefold cleavage] : a dark brown monoclinic mineral that consists of a basic phosphate of manganese, iron, magnesium, and calcium

trip·lo·blas·tic \ˌtrip-lō-ˈblas-tik\ *adj* [L *triplus* + E *-o-* + *-blastic*] : having three primary germ layers

trip·loid \ˈtrip-ˌlȯid\ *adj* [ISV, fr. L *triplus* triple] : having or being a chromosome number three times the monoploid number — **trip·loid** *n* — **trip·loi·dy** \-ˌlȯid-ē\ *n*

tri·ply \ˈtrip-(ə-)lē\ *adv* : in a triple degree, amount, or manner

tri·pod \ˈtrī-ˌpäd\ *n* [L *tripod-*, *tripus*, fr. Gk *tripod-*, *tripous*, fr. *tripod-*, *tripous* three-footed, fr. *tri-* + *pod-*, *pous* foot — more at FOOT] **1** : a vessel (as a caldron) resting on three legs **2** : a stool, table, or altar with three legs **3** : a three-legged stand (as for a camera) — **tripod** *or* **tri·po·dal** \ˈtrip-əd-ᵊl, ˈtrī-ˌpäd-\ *adj*

trip·o·li \ˈtrip-ə-lē\ *n* [F, fr. *Tripoli*, region of Africa] **1** : an earth consisting of very friable soft schistose deposits of silica and including diatomite and kieselguhr **2** : an earth consisting of friable dustlike silica not of diatomaceous origin

tri·pos \ˈtrī-ˌpäs\ *n* [modif. of L *tripus*] **1** *archaic* : TRIPOD **2** [fr. the three-legged stool occupied by a participant in a disputation at the degree ceremonies] : a final honors examination at Cambridge university orig. in mathematics

trip·per \ˈtrip-ər\ *n* **1** *chiefly Brit* : one that takes a trip : EXCURSIONIST **2** : a tripping device (as for operating a railroad signal)

trip·pet \ˈtrip-ət\ *n* [ME *tripet* tipcat peg, fr. *trippen* to trip] : a cam, wiper, or projecting piece that strikes another piece at definite times

trip·ping·ly \ˈtrip-iŋ-lē\ *adv* : NIMBLY; *also* : FLUENTLY <speak the speech . . . ~ on the tongue —Shak.>

trip·tane \ˈtrip-ˌtān\ *n* [irreg. fr. *tri-* + *butane*] : a liquid hydrocarbon C_7H_{16} of high antiknock properties used esp. in aviation gasolines to increase their power

trip·tych \ˈtrip-(ˌ)tik\ *n* [Gk *triptychos* having three folds, fr. *tri-* + *ptychē* fold] **1** : an ancient Roman writing tablet with three waxed leaves hinged together **2** : a picture or carving in three panels side by side; *esp* : an altarpiece with a central panel and two flanking panels half its size that fold over it

tri·que·trous \trī-ˈkwē-trəs, -ˈkwe-\ *adj* [L *triquetrus* three-cornered, fr. *tri-*] : having three acute angles <~ stems>

tri·ra·di·ate \(ˈ)trī-ˈrād-ē-ət, -ē-ˌāt\ *adj* : having three rays or radiating branches <a ~ sponge spicule>

tri·reme \ˈtrī-ˌrēm\ *n* [L *triremis*, fr. *tri-* + *remus* oar — more at ROW] : an ancient galley having three banks of oars

tris- \tris\ *prefix* [Gk *tris* — more at TER-] : thrice : tripled — esp. in complex chemical expressions

tri·sac·cha·ride \(ˈ)trī-ˈsak-ə-ˌrīd\ *n* [ISV] : a sugar that yields on complete hydrolysis three monosaccharide molecules

tri·sect \ˈtrī-ˌsekt, trī-ˈ\ *vt* : to divide into three usu. equal parts — **tri·sec·tion** \ˈtrī-ˌsek-shən, trī-ˈ\ *n* — **tri·sec·tor** \ˈtrī-ˌsek-tər, trī-ˈ\ *n*

tri·skel·i·on \trī-ˈskel-ē-ən, tris-ˈkel-\ *or* **tri·skele** \ˈtrī-ˌskēl, ˈtris-ˌkēl\ *n* [*triskelion*, fr. NL, fr. Gk *triskelēs* three-legged, fr. *tri-* + *skelos* leg; *triskele* fr. Gk *triskelēs*] : a figure composed of three usu. curved or bent branches radiating from a center

tris·mus \ˈtriz-məs\ *n* [NL, fr. Gk *trismos* gnashing (of teeth), fr. *trizein* to squeak, gnash; akin to L *stridēre* to creak — more at STRIDENT] : spasm of the muscles of mastication : LOCKJAW

tris·oc·ta·he·dron \ˌtris-ˌäk-tə-ˈhē-drən\ *n* : a solid (as a crystal) having 24 congruent faces meeting on the edges of a regular octahedron

tri·so·di·um \ˌtrī-ˌsōd-ē-əm\ *adj* : containing three atoms of sodium in the molecule

tri·so·mic \(ˈ)trī-ˈsō-mik\ *adj* : having one or a few chromosomes triploid in an otherwise diploid set — **trisomic** *or* **tri·some** \ˈtrī-ˌsōm\ *n* — **tri·so·my** \-ˌsō-mē\ *n*

Tris·tan \ˈtris-tən, -ˌtän, -ˌtan\ *n* : TRISTRAM

triste \ˈtrēst\ *adj* [F, fr. L *tristis*] : SAD, MOURNFUL; *also* : WISTFUL

triskelion

tri·stea·rin \(ˈ)trī-ˈstē-ə-rən, -ˈsti(-ə)r-ən\ *n* [ISV] : the crystallizable triglyceride $C_{57}H_{110}O_6$ of stearic acid that is found esp. in hard fats

tris·te·za \tris-ˈtā-zə\ *n* [Pg, lit., sadness, fr. L *tristitia*, fr. *tristis* sad] : a highly infectious viral disease of citrus trees grafted on sour orange rootstocks that is characterized by rotting of the rootlets and eventually causes the death of the trees

trist·ful \ˈtrist-fəl\ *adj* [ME *trist* sad, fr. MF *triste*] : SAD, MELANCHOLY — **trist·ful·ly** \-fə-lē\ *adv* — **trist·ful·ness** *n*

tri·stim·u·lus \(ˈ)trī-ˈstim-yə-ləs\ *adj* : of or relating to values giving the amounts of the three colored lights red, green, and blue that when combined additively produce a match for the color being considered

Tris·tram \ˈtris-t(r)əm\ *n* [ME *Tristrem*, fr. AF *Tristan*, fr. OW *Trystan*] : the lover of Isolde of Ireland and husband of Isolde of Britanny in medieval legend

tri·sub·sti·tut·ed \ˈtrī-ˈsəb-stə-ˌt(y)üt-əd\ *adj* : having three substituent atoms or groups in the molecule

tri·sul·fide \(ˈ)trī-ˈsəl-ˌfīd\ *n* : a compound of an element or radical with three atoms of sulfur

tri·syl·lab·ic \ˌtrī-sə-ˈlab-ik\ *adj* [L *trisyllabus*, fr. Gk *trisyllabos*, fr. *tri-* + *syllabē* syllable] : having three syllables <a ~ word> — **tri·syl·lab·i·cal·ly** \-i-k(ə-)lē\ *adv*

tri·syl·la·ble \ˈtrī-ˌsil-ə-bəl, (ˈ)trī-ˈ\ *n* : a word of three syllables

trit *abbr* triturate

trite \ˈtrīt\ *adj* **trit·er; trit·est** [L *tritus*, fr. pp. of *terere* to rub, wear away — more at THROW] : hackneyed from much use : STALE — **trite·ly** *adv* — **trite·ness** *n*

tri·the·ism \ˈtrī-thē-ˌiz-əm\ *n* : the doctrine that the Father, Son, and Holy Spirit are three distinct Gods — **tri·the·ist** \-(ˌ)thē-əst\ *n or adj* — **tri·the·is·tic** \ˌtrī-thē-ˈis-tik\ *or* **tri·the·is·ti·cal** \-ˈis-ti-kəl\ *adj*

tri·thing \ˈtrī-thiŋ\ *n* [ME, alter. of (assumed) OE *thrithing*, *thriding*] *archaic* : [1]RIDING 1

tri·ti·at·ed \ˈtrit-ē-ˌāt-əd, ˈtrish-ē-\ *adj* : containing and esp. labeled with tritium

trit·i·ca·le \ˌtrit-ə-ˈkā-lē\ *n* [NL, blend of *Triticum*, genus of wheat + *Secale*, genus of rye] : an amphidiploid hybrid between wheat and rye that has a high yield and rich protein content

tri·ti·um \ˈtrit-ē-əm, ˈtrish-ē-\ *n* [NL, fr. Gk *tritos* third — more at THIRD] : a radioactive isotope of hydrogen with atoms of three times the mass of ordinary light hydrogen atoms

trit·o·ma \ˈtrit-ə-mə\ *n* [NL, genus name, fr. Gk *tritomos* cut thrice, fr. *tri-* + *temnein* to cut; fr. their trimerous flowers — more at TOME] : any of a genus (*Khiphofia*) of African herbs of the lily family that are often grown for their spikes of showy red or yellow flowers

[1]**tri·ton** \ˈtrīt-ᵊn\ *n* [L, fr. Gk *Tritōn*] **1** *cap* : a son of Poseidon and Amphitrite described as a demigod of the sea with the lower part of his body like that of a fish **2** [NL, genus name, fr. L *Triton*] **a** : any of various large marine gastropod mollusks (esp. family Cymatiidae) with a heavy elongated conical shell; *also* : this shell **b** : any of various aquatic salamanders : NEWT, EFT

[2]**tri·ton** \ˈtrī-ˌtän\ *n* [*tritium* + *-on*] : the nucleus of tritium

tri·tone \ˈtrī-ˌtōn\ *n* [Gk *tritonon*, fr. *tri-* + *tonos* tone] : a musical interval of three whole steps

[1]**trit·u·rate** \ˈtrich-ə-ˌrāt\ *vt* **-rat·ed; -rat·ing** [LL *trituratus*, pp. of *triturare* to thresh, fr. L *tritura* act of rubbing, threshing, fr. *tritus*, pp. of *terere* to rub — more at THROW] **1** : CRUSH, GRIND **2** : to pulverize and comminute thoroughly by rubbing or grinding — **trit·u·ra·ble** \ˈtrich-ə-rə-bəl\ *adj* — **trit·u·ra·tor** \-ˌrāt-ər\ *n*

[2]**trit·u·rate** \-rət\ *n* : a triturated substance : TRITURATION 2

trit·u·ra·tion \ˌtrich-ə-ˈrā-shən\ *n* **1** : the act or process of triturating : the state of being triturated : COMMINUTION **2** : a triturated powder; *esp* : one made by triturating a substance with lactose as a diluent

[1]**tri·umph** \ˈtrī-əm(p)f\ *n, pl* **tri·umphs** \-əm(p)fs, -əm(p)s\ [ME *triumphe*, fr. MF, fr. L *triumphus*] **1** : a ceremony attending the entering of Rome by a general who had won a decisive victory over a foreign enemy — compare OVATION 1 **2** : the joy or exultation of victory or success **3 a** : a military victory or conquest **b** : a notable success ***syn*** see VICTORY — **tri·um·phal** \trī-ˈəm(p)-fəl\ *adj*

[2]**triumph** *vi* **1 a** : to receive the honor of a triumph **b** : to celebrate victory or success boastfully or exultingly **2** : to obtain victory : PREVAIL

tri·um·phant \trī-ˈəm(p)-fənt\ *adj* **1** : VICTORIOUS, CONQUERING **2** *archaic* : of or relating to a triumph : TRIUMPHAL **3** : rejoicing for or celebrating victory : EXULTANT — **tri·um·phant·ly** *adv*

tri·um·vir \trī-ˈəm-vər\ *n, pl* **-virs** *also* **-vi·ri** \-və-ˌrī, -ˌrē\ [L, back-formation fr. *triumviri*, pl., commission of three men, fr. *trium virum* of three men] : one of a commission or ruling body of three — **tri·um·vi·ral** \-və-rəl\ *adj*

ə abut **ᵊ** kitten **ər** further **a** back **ā** bake **ä** cot, cart
au̇ out **ch** chin **e** less **ē** easy **g** gift **i** trip **ī** life
j joke **ŋ** sing **ō** flow **ȯ** flaw **ȯi** coin **th** thin **th** this
ü loot **u̇** foot **y** yet **yü** few **yu̇** furious **zh** vision

tri·um·vi·rate \-və-rət\ *n* **1 :** the office or government of triumvirs **2 :** a body of triumvirs **3 :** a group or association of three

1tri·une \ˈtrī-ˌ(y)ün\ *n* [L *tri-* + *unus* one — more at ONE] *often cap* **:** TRINITY 1

2triune *adj, often cap* **:** three in one; *esp* **:** of or relating to the Trinity <the ~ God>

1tri·va·lent \(ˈ)trī-ˈvā-lənt\ *adj* [ISV] **:** having a valence of three

2trivalent *n* **:** a group of three synapsed homologous chromosomes in meioses

tri·valve \ˈtrī-ˌvalv\ *adj* **:** having three valves

triv·et \ˈtriv-ət\ *n* [ME *trevet,* fr. OE *trefet,* prob. modif. of LL *triped-, tripes,* fr. L, three-footed, fr. *tri-* + *ped-, pes* foot — more at FOOT] **1 :** a three-legged stand **:** TRIPOD **2 :** a usu. metal stand with short feet for use under a hot dish at table

triv·ia \ˈtriv-ē-ə\ *n pl but sometimes sing in constr* [NL, back-formation fr. L *trivialis* trivial] **:** unimportant matters **:** TRIFLES

triv·i·al \ˈtriv-ē-əl\ *adj* [L *trivialis* found everywhere, commonplace, trivial, fr. *trivium* crossroads, fr. *tri-* + *via* way — more at VIA] **1 :** COMMONPLACE, ORDINARY **2 a :** of little worth or importance **b :** relating to or being the mathematically simplest case; *specif* **:** characterized by having all variables equal to zero <a ~ solution to an equation> **3 :** SPECIFIC 4 — **triv·i·al·ly** \-ə-lē\ *adv*

triv·i·al·i·ty \ˌtriv-ē-ˈal-ət-ē\ *n, pl* **-ties 1 :** the quality or state of being trivial **2 :** something trivial **:** TRIFLE

triv·i·al·ize \ˈtriv-ē-ə-ˌlīz\ *vt* **-ized; -iz·ing :** to make trivial **:** reduce to triviality — **triv·i·al·iza·tion** \ˌtriv-ē-ə-lə-ˈzā-shən\ *n*

trivial name *n* **1 :** SPECIFIC EPITHET **2 :** a common or vernacular name of an organism or chemical

triv·i·um \ˈtriv-ē-əm\ *n, pl* **triv·ia** \-ē-ə\ [ML, fr. L, meeting of three ways, crossroads] **:** a group of studies consisting of grammar, rhetoric, and logic and forming the lower division of the seven liberal arts in medieval universities — compare QUADRIVIUM

1tri·week·ly \(ˈ)trī-ˈwē-klē\ *adj* **1 :** occurring or appearing three times a week **2 :** occurring or appearing every three weeks — **triweekly** *adv*

2triweekly *n, pl* **-lies :** a triweekly publication

-trix \(ˌ)triks\ *n suffix, pl* **-tri·ces** \trə-ˌsēz, ˈtrī-(ˌ)sēz\ *or* **-trix·es** \(ˌ)trik-səz\ [ME, fr. L, fem. of *-tor,* suffix denoting an agent, fr. *-tus,* pp. ending + *-or* — more at -ED] **1 :** female that does or is associated with a (specified) thing <avia*trix*> **2 :** geometric line, point, or surface <genera*trix*>

tRNA \ˌtē-ˌär-ˌen-ˈā, ˈtē-ˌär-ˌen-ˌā\ *n* **:** TRANSFER RNA

tro·car *also* **tro·char** \ˈtrō-ˌkär\ *n* [F *trocart,* fr. *trois* three (fr. L *tres*) + *carre* side of a sword blade, fr. *carrer* to make square, fr. L *quadrare* — more at THREE, QUADRATE] **:** a sharp-pointed instrument fitted with a cannula and used esp. to insert the cannula into a body cavity as a drainage outlet

tro·cha·ic \trō-ˈkā-ik\ *adj* [MF *trochaïque,* fr. L *trochaicus,* fr. Gk *trochaikos,* fr. *trochaios* trochee] **:** of, relating to, or consisting of trochees — **trochaic** *n*

tro·chal \ˈtrō-kəl, ˈträk-əl\ *adj* [Gk *trochos* wheel] **:** resembling a wheel <the ~ disc at the anterior end of a rotifer's body>

tro·chan·ter \trō-ˈkant-ər\ *n* [Gk *trochantēr;* akin to Gk *trechein* to run] **1 :** a rough prominence at the upper part of the femur of many vertebrates **2 :** the second segment counting from the base of the leg of an insect — **tro·chan·ter·al** \-ə-rəl\ *or* **tro·chan·ter·ic** \ˌtrō-kən-ˈter-ik, -ˌkan-\ *adj*

tro·che \ˈtrō-kē, *Brit also* ˈtrōsh\ *n* [alter. of earlier *trochisk,* fr. LL *trochiscus,* fr. Gk *trochiskos,* fr. dim. of *trochos* wheel] **:** a usu. circular medicinal tablet or lozenge; *esp* **:** one used as a demulcent

tro·chee \ˈtrō-(ˌ)kē\ *n* [F *trochée,* fr. L *trochaeus,* fr. Gk *trochaios,* fr. *trochaios* running, fr. *trochē* run, course, fr. *trechein* to run; akin to Gk *trochos* wheel, OIr *droch*] **:** a metrical foot consisting of one long syllable followed by one short syllable or of one stressed syllable followed by one unstressed syllable (as in *apple*) — compare IAMB

troch·i·lus \ˈträk-ə-ləs\ *n, pl* **-li** \-ˌlī, -ˌlē\ [NL, genus name, fr. Gk *trochilos* crocodile bird; akin to Gk *trechein* to run] **:** CROCODILE BIRD

troch·lea \ˈträk-lē-ə\ *n* [NL, fr. L, block of pulleys, fr. Gk *trochileia,* akin to Gk *trechein* to run] **:** an anatomical structure that is held to resemble a pulley; *esp* **:** the articular surface on the medial condyle of the humerus that articulates with the ulna

troch·le·ar \-ər\ *adj* **1 a :** of, relating to, or being a trochlea **b :** of, relating to, or being a trochlear nerve **2 :** round and narrow in the middle like the wheel of a pulley <a ~ plant embryo>

trochlear nerve *n* **:** either of the fourth pair of cranial nerves that supply some of the eye muscles with motor fibers — called also *trochlear*

tro·choid \ˈtrō-ˌkȯid, ˈträk-ˌȯid\ *n* [Gk *trochoeidēs* like a wheel, fr. *trochos* wheel] **:** the curve generated by a point on the radius of a circle or the radius extended as the circle rolls on a fixed straight line — **tro·choi·dal** \trō-ˈkȯid-ᵊl, trä-\ *adj*

trocho·phore \ˈträk-ə-ˌfō(ə)r, -ˌfȯ(ə)r\ *n* [deriv. of Gk *trochos* wheel + *pherein* to carry — more at BEAR] **:** a free-swimming ciliate larva typical of marine annelid worms but occurring in several invertebrate groups

trod *past of* TREAD

trodden *past part of* TREAD

trof·fer \ˈträf-ər, ˈtrȯf-\ *n* [blend of *trough* and *coffer*] **:** an inverted trough serving as a support and reflector usu. for a fluorescent lighting unit

trog·lo·dyte \ˈträg-lə-ˌdīt\ *n* [L *troglodytae,* pl., fr. Gk *trōglodytai,* fr. *trōglē* hole, cave + *dyein* to enter; akin to Gk *trōgein* to gnaw] **1 :** a member of a primitive people dwelling in caves **2 :** a person felt to resemble a troglodyte; *esp* **:** an unsocial seclusive person **3 :** an anthropoid ape — **trog·lo·dyt·ic** \ˌträg-lə-ˈdit-ik\ *adj*

tro·gon \ˈtrō-ˌgän\ *n* [NL, genus name, fr. Gk *trōgōn,* prp. of *trōgein* to gnaw] **:** any of numerous nonpasserine tropical birds (family Trogonidae) with brilliant lustrous plumage

troi·ka \ˈtrȯi-kə\ *n* [Russ *troĭka,* fr. *troe* three; akin to OE *thrīe* three] **1 :** a Russian vehicle drawn by three horses abreast; *also* **:** a team for such a vehicle **2 :** a group of three closely related persons or things: as **a :** an administrative or ruling body of three <replaced by a ~ of three coequal secretaries-general —*Newsweek*> **b :** a group of three <astrology, yoga, and poetry are the ~ of humanities that most interest him —A. J. Liebling>

troi·lite \ˈtrō-ə-ˌlīt, ˈtrȯi-ˌlīt\ *n* [G *troilit,* fr. Domenico *Troili,* 18th cent. It scientist + G *-it* -ite] **:** a mineral FeS that is a widely but sparsely distributed (as on earth, in meteorites, and in lunar soil samples) variety of pyrrhotite

Troi·lus \ˈtrȯi-ləs, ˈtrō-ə-ləs\ *n* [ME, fr. L, fr. Gk *Trōïlos*] **:** a son of Priam who in medieval legend loved Cressida and lost her to Diomedes

1Tro·jan \ˈtrō-jən\ *n* [ME, fr. L *trojanus* of Troy, fr. *Troia, Troja* Troy, fr. Gk *Trōia*] **1 :** a native or inhabitant of Troy **2 :** one who shows qualities (as pluck, endurance, or determined energy) attributed to the defenders of ancient Troy **3 :** a gay, irresponsible, or disreputable companion

2Trojan *adj* **1 :** of, relating to, or resembling ancient Troy or its inhabitants **2 :** of, relating to, or constituting a Trojan horse

Trojan horse *n* [fr. the large hollow wooden horse filled with Greek soldiers and introduced within the walls of Troy by a stratagem during the Trojan War] **:** someone or something intended to undermine or subvert from within

Trojan War *n* **:** a 10-year war between the Greeks and Trojans brought on by the abduction of Helen by Paris and ended with the destruction of Troy

1troll \ˈtrōl\ *vb* [ME *trollen*] *vt* **1 :** to cause to move round and round **:** ROLL **2 a :** to sing the parts of (as a round or catch) in succession **b :** to sing loudly **c :** to celebrate in song **3 :** to speak or recite in a rolling voice **4** *obs* **:** to move rapidly **:** WAG **5 a :** to angle for with a hook and line drawn through the water **b :** to angle in <~ lakes> **c :** to pull through the water in angling <~ a lure> ~ *vi* **1 :** to move around **:** RAMBLE **2 :** to fish esp. by trolling a hook **3 :** to sing or play in a jovial manner **4 :** to speak rapidly — **troll·er** *n*

2troll *n* **1 :** a lure or a line with its lure and hook used in trolling **2 :** a song sung in parts successively **:** ROUND

3troll *n* [Norw *troll* & Dan *trold,* fr. ON *troll* giant, demon; akin to MHG *trolle* monster, OE *treppan* to tread — more at TRAP] **:** a dwarf or giant of Teutonic folklore inhabiting caves or hills

1trol·ley *or* **trol·ly** \ˈträl-ē\ *n, pl* **trolleys** *or* **trollies** [prob. fr. *1troll*] **1** *dial Eng* **:** a cart of any of various kinds **2 a :** a current collector operating in connection with a trolley wire **b :** TROLLEY CAR **3 :** a wheeled carriage running on an overhead rail or track (as of a parcel railway in a store) **4** *chiefly Brit* **:** a table or shelved stand equipped with wheels and usu. a handle and used for conveying something (as food or books)

2trolley *or* **trolly** *vb* **trol·leyed** *or* **trol·lied; trol·ley·ing** *or* **trol·ly·ing** *vt* **:** to convey by a trolley ~ *vi* **:** to ride on a trolley

trol·ley·bus \ˈträl-ē-ˌbəs\ *n* **:** a bus electrically propelled by power from two overhead wires and similar in appearance to a motor bus

trolley car *n* **:** a public conveyance for passengers that runs on tracks with motive power derived through a trolley

trol·lop \ˈträl-əp\ *n* [prob. irreg. fr. G dial. *trolle,* fr. MHG *trulle* prostitute — more at TRULL] **1 :** a slovenly woman **:** SLATTERN **2 :** a loose woman **:** WANTON

trom·bi·di·a·sis \ˌträm-bə-ˈdī-ə-səs\ *n* [NL, fr. *Trombidium,* genus of mites] **:** infestation with chiggers

trom·bone \träm-ˈbōn, (ˌ)trəm-ˈ, ˈträm-ˌ\ *n* [It, aug. of *tromba* trumpet, of Gmc origin; akin to OHG *trumba, trumpa* trumpet] **:** a brass instrument consisting of a long cylindrical metal tube with two turns and having a movable slide for varying the tone and a usual range one octave lower than that of the trumpet — **trom·bon·ist** \-ˈbō-nəst, -ˌbō-\ *n*

trombone

trom·mel \ˈträm-əl\ *n* [G, drum, fr. MHG *trummel,* dim. of *trumme* drum — more at DRUM] **:** a usu. cylindrical or conical revolving screen used esp. for screening or sizing rock, ore, or coal

tromp \ˈträmp, ˈtrȯmp\ *vb* [by alter.] *vi* **1 :** TRAMP 1 <a lot of knocking on doors, ~*ing* from room to room —Sara Davidson> **2 :** to step hard **:** STAMP <~*ed* on the brake> ~ *vt* **1 :** TRAMP 2 **:** STAMP <~*s* the accelerator to the floor —Jim Becker> **3 a :** to give a physical beating to **b :** to defeat decisively

trompe l'oeil \(ˈ)trȯmp-ˈləi, trōⁿp-lœ̄i\ *n* [F *trompe-l'oeil,* lit., deceive the eye] **1 :** a style of painting in which objects are depicted with photographically realistic detail; *also* **:** the use of similar technique in interior decorating **2 :** a trompe l'oeil painting or effect

-tron \ˌträn\ *n suffix* [Gk, suffix denoting an instrument; akin to OE *-thor,* suffix denoting an instrument, L *-trum*] **1 :** vacuum tube <magne*tron*> **2 :** device for the manipulation of subatomic particles <cyclo*tron*>

tro·na \ˈtrō-nə\ *n* [Sw] **:** a gray-white or yellowish white monoclinic mineral $Na_3H(CO_3)_2{\cdot}2H_2O$ consisting of a hydrous acid sodium carbonate

trone \ˈtrōn\ *n* [AF] *chiefly Scot* **:** a weighing machine for heavy wares

1troop \ˈtrüp\ *n* [MF *trope, troupe* company, herd, of Gmc origin; akin to OE *thorp, throp* village — more at THORP] **1 a :** a group of soldiers **b :** a cavalry unit corresponding to an infantry company **c :** armed forces **:** SOLDIERS — usu. used in pl. **2 :** a collection of people or things **:** COMPANY **3 :** a flock of mammals or birds **4 :** a unit of boy or girl scouts under a leader

2troop *vi* **1 :** to move or gather in crowds **:** ASSEMBLE **2 :** to consort in company **:** ASSOCIATE — usu. used with *with* **3 :** to move in large numbers **:** THRONG

troop carrier *n* **:** a transport airplane used to carry troops

troop·er \'trü-pər\ *n* **1 a** (1) : an enlisted cavalryman (2) : the horse of a cavalryman **b** : PARATROOPER **c** : SOLDIER **2 a** : a mounted policeman **b** : a state policeman

troop·ship \'trüp-,ship\ *n* : a ship for carrying troops : TRANSPORT

troost·ite \'trü-,stīt, 'trō-\ *n* [Gerard *Troost* †1850 Am geologist] : a variety of willemite occurring in large reddish crystals in which the zinc is partly replaced by manganese

trop *abbr* tropic; tropical

trop- *or* **tropo-** *comb form* [ISV, fr. Gk *tropos*] **1** : turn : turning : change <*tropo*sphere> **2** : tropism <*tropic*>

tro·pae·o·lum \trō-'pē-ə-ləm\ *n* [NL, genus name, dim. of L *tropaeum* trophy — more at TROPHY] : any of a genus (*Tropaeolum*) of tropical American diffuse or climbing pungent herbs (as a nasturtium) having lobed or dissected peltate leaves and showy flowers

trope \'trōp\ *n* [L *tropus*, fr. Gk *tropos* turn, way, manner, style, trope, fr. *trepein* to turn; akin to L *trepit* he turns] **1** : the use of a word or expression in a figurative sense : FIGURE OF SPEECH **2** : a phrase or verse added as an embellishment or interpolation to the sung parts of the Mass in the medieval period

troph- *or* **tropho-** *comb form* [F, fr. Gk, fr. *trophē* nourishment] : nutritive <*tropho*plasm>

troph·al·lax·is \,trō-fə-'lak-səs\ *n* [NL, fr. *troph-* + Gk *allaxis* exchange, fr. *allassein* to change, exchange, fr. *allos* other — more at ELSE] : exchange of food (as from special glands) between organisms; *also* : the association of different organisms and esp. social insects on the basis of such a unilateral or mutual exchange

tro·phic \'trō-fik\ *adj* [F *trophique*, fr. Gk *trophikos*, fr. *trophē* nourishment, fr. *trephein* to nourish — more at ATROPHY] **1** : of or relating to nutrition : NUTRITIONAL <~ disorders> **2** : [3]TROPIC — **tro·phi·cal·ly** \-fi-k(ə-)lē\ *adv*

-tro·phic \'trō-fik\ *adj comb form* [NL *-trophia* -trophy] **1 a** : of, relating to, or characterized by (such) nutrition <ecto*trophic*> **b** : requiring or utilizing (such) a kind of nutrition <poly*trophic*> **2** : -TROPIC <lipo*trophic*>

trophic level *n* : one of the hierarchical strata of a food web characterized by organisms which are the same number of steps removed from the primary producers

tro·pho·blast \'trō-fə-,blast\ *n* [ISV] : a layer of ectoderm that forms the outer surface of the blastodermic vesicle of many mammals and functions in the nutrition and implantation of the embryo — **tro·pho·blas·tic** \,trō-fə-'blas-tik\ *adj*

tro·pho·zo·ite \,trō-fə-'zō-,īt\ *n* : a vegetative protozoan as distinguished from a reproductive or resting form

[1]**tro·phy** \'trō-fē\ *n, pl* **trophies** [MF *trophee*, fr. L *tropaeum*, *trophaeum*, fr. Gk *tropaion*, fr. neut. of *tropaios* of a turning, of a rout, fr. *tropē* turn, rout, fr. *trepein* to turn — more at TROPE] **1 a** : a memorial of an ancient Greek or Roman victory raised on the field of battle or in case of a naval victory on the nearest land **b** : a representation of such a memorial (as on a medal); *also* : an architectural ornament representing a group of military weapons **2** : something gained or given in victory or conquest esp. when preserved or mounted as a memorial

[2]**trophy** *vt* **tro·phied; tro·phy·ing** : to honor or adorn with a trophy

-tro·phy \trə-fē\ *n comb form* [NL *-trophia*, fr. Gk, fr. *-trophos* nourishing, fr. *trephein*] : nutrition : nurture : growth <hypo*trophy*>

[1]**trop·ic** \'träp-ik\ *n* [ME *tropik*, fr. L *tropicus* of the solstice, fr. Gk *tropikos*, fr. *tropē* turn] **1** : either of the two small circles of the celestial sphere on each side of and parallel to the equator at a distance of 23½ degrees which the sun reaches at its greatest declination north or south **2 a** : either of the two parallels of terrestrial latitude corresponding to the celestial tropics — compare TROPIC OF CANCER, TROPIC OF CAPRICORN **b** *pl, often cap* : the region lying between these parallels of latitude

[2]**tropic** *adj* : of, relating to, or occurring in the tropics : TROPICAL

[3]**tro·pic** \'trō-pik\ *adj* [*trop-*] **1** : of, relating to, or characteristic of tropism or of a tropism **2** *of a hormone* : influencing the activity of a specified gland

-tro·pic \'trō-pik\ *adj comb form* [F *-tropique*, fr. Gk *-tropos* -tropous] **1** : turning, changing, or tending to turn or change in a (specified) manner or in response to a (specified) stimulus <geo*tropic*> **2** : attracted to or acting upon (something specified) <neuro*tropic*>

trop·i·cal *for 1* 'träp-i-kəl, *for 2* 'trōp- *also* 'träp-\ *adj* **1 a** : of, located in, or used in the tropics **b** *of a sign of the zodiac* : beginning at one of the tropics **2** [L *tropicus*, fr. Gk *tropikos*, fr. *tropos* trope] : FIGURATIVE 2 — **trop·i·cal·ly** \-i-k(ə-)lē\ *adv*

tropical aquarium *n* : an aquarium kept at a uniform warmth and used esp. for tropical fish

tropical cyclone *n* : a cyclone in the tropics characterized by winds rotating at the rate of 75 miles an hour or more

tropical fish *n* : any of various small usu. showy fishes of exotic origin often kept in the tropical aquarium

trop·i·cal·ize \'träp-i-kə-,līz\ *vt* **-ized; -iz·ing** **1** : to make tropical (as in character, conditions, or appearance) **2** : to fit or adapt for use in a tropical climate esp. by measures designed to combat the effects of fungi and moisture

tropical storm *n* : a tropical cyclone with strong winds of less than hurricane intensity

tropic bird *n* : any of several web-footed birds (genus *Phaëthon*) that are related to the gannets, are found chiefly in tropical seas often far from land, and are marked by mostly white satiny plumage with a little black, a greatly elongated central pair of tail feathers, and a bright-colored bill

tropic of Cancer [fr. the sign of the zodiac which its celestial projection intersects] : the parallel of latitude that is 23½ degrees north of the equator and that is the northernmost latitude reached by the overhead sun

tropic of Capricorn [fr. the sign of the zodiac which its celestial projection intersects] : the parallel of latitude that is 23½ degrees south of the equator and that is the southernmost latitude reached by the overhead sun

tro·pism \'trō-,piz-əm\ *n* [ISV *-tropism*] **1 a** : involuntary orientation by an organism or one of its parts that involves turning or curving and is a positive or negative response to a source of stimulation **b** : a reflex reaction involving a tropism **2** : an innate tendency to react in a definite manner to stimuli — **tro·pis·tic** \trō-'pis-tik\ *adj*

-tro·pism \trə-,piz-əm, -'trō-, -,trō-\ *n comb form* [ISV, fr. *trop-*] : tropism <helio*tropism*>

tropo- — see TROP-

tro·po·col·la·gen \,träp-ə-'käl-ə-jən, ,trōp-\ *n* [[1]*trop-*] : a soluble precursor of collagen with elongated molecules that form the elementary building units of collagen fibers

tro·po·log·i·cal \,trōp-ə-'läj-i-kəl, ,träp-\ *also* **tro·po·log·ic** \-ik\ *adj* **1** : characterized or varied by tropes : FIGURATIVE **2** : of, relating to, or involving tropology; *also* : MORAL — **tro·po·log·i·cal·ly** \-i-k(ə-)lē\ *adv*

tro·pol·o·gy \trō-'päl-ə-jē\ *n* [LL *tropologia*, fr. LGk, fr. Gk *tropos* trope + *-logia* -logy] **1** : a figurative mode of speech or writing **2** : a mode of biblical interpretation stressing moral metaphor

tropo·my·o·sin \,träp-ə-'mī-ə-sən, ,trōp-\ *n* [[1]*trop-*] : a crystallizable rod-shaped protein of muscle that is responsible in part for the calcium sensitivity of myofibrils

tro·po·pause \'trōp-ə-,pȯz, 'träp-\ *n* [ISV *tropo*sphere + *pause*] : the region at the top of the troposphere; *also* : a comparable layer of a celestial body

tro·poph·i·lous \trō-'päf-ə-ləs\ *adj* : physiologically adjusted to or thriving in an environment that undergoes marked periodic changes esp. in temperature, moisture, or light

tro·po·sphere \'trōp-ə-,sfi(ə)r, 'träp-\ *n* [ISV] : the portion of the atmosphere which is below the stratosphere, which extends outward about 7 to 10 miles from the earth's surface, and in which generally temperature decreases rapidly with altitude, clouds form, and convection is active — **tro·po·spher·ic** \,trōp-ə-'sfi(ə)r-ik, ,träp-, -'sfer-\ *adj*

tro·po·tax·is \,trōp-ə-'tak-səs, ,träp-\ *n* [NL] : a taxis in which an organism orients itself through a process of simultaneous comparison of stimuli of different intensity acting on separate end organs

-tro·pous \trə-pəs\ *adj comb form* [Gk *-tropos*, fr. *trepein* to turn — more at TROPE] : turning or curving in (such) a way : exhibiting (such) a tropism <ana*tropous*>

-tro·py \trə-pē\ *n comb form* [F *-tropie*, fr. Gk *-tropia*, fr. *-tropos*] : condition of turning or curving in (such) a way or of exhibiting (such) a tropism <photo*tropy*>

[1]**trot** \'trät\ *n* [ME, fr. MF, fr. *troter* to trot, of Gmc origin; akin to OHG *trottōn* to tread, OE *tredan*] **1 a** (1) : a moderately fast gait of a quadruped (as a horse) in which the legs move in diagonal pairs (2) : a jogging gait of man that falls between a walk and a run **b** : a ride on horseback **2 a** : a small child **b** : an old woman **3** : a literal translation of a foreign text

[2]**trot** *vb* **trot·ted; trot·ting** *vi* **1** : to ride, drive, or proceed at a trot <the fox *trotted* over the knoll> **2** : to proceed briskly : HURRY ~ *vt* **1** : to cause to go at a trot **2** : to traverse at a trot

[3]**trot** *n* : TROTLINE; *also* : one of the short lines with hooks that are attached to it at intervals

[1]**troth** \'träth, 'trȯth, 'trōth, *or with* th\ *n* [ME *trouth*, fr. OE *trēowth* — more at TRUTH] **1** : loyal or pledged faithfulness : FIDELITY **2** : one's pledged word; *also* : BETROTHAL

[2]**troth** *vt* : PLEDGE, BETROTH

[1]**troth·plight** \'träth-,plīt, 'trȯth-, 'trōth-\ *n, archaic* : BETROTHAL

[2]**trothplight** *vt, archaic* : BETROTH

trot·line \'trät-,līn\ *n* [prob. fr. [3]*trot*] : SETLINE; *esp* : a comparatively short setline used near shore or along streams

trot out *vt* **1** : to lead out and show the paces of (as a horse) **2** : to bring forward for display

Trots·ky·ism \'trät-skē-,iz-əm, 'trȯt-\ *n* : the political, economic, and social principles advocated by Trotsky; *esp* : the theory and practice of communism developed by or associated with Trotsky and usu. including adherence to the concept of worldwide revolution as opposed to socialism in one country — **Trots·ky·ist** \-skē-əst\ *n or adj* — **Trots·ky·ite** \-skē-,īt\ *n or adj*

trot·ter \'trät-ər\ *n* **1** : one that trots; *specif* : a standardbred horse trained for harness racing **2** : a pig's foot used as food

trou·ba·dour \'trü-bə-,dō(ə)r, -,dȯ(ə)r, -,dü(ə)r\ *n* [F, fr. OProv *trobador*, fr. *trobar* to compose, prob. fr. (assumed) VL *tropare*, fr. L *tropus* trope] : one of a class of lyric poets and poet-musicians often of knightly rank who flourished from the 11th to the end of the 13th century chiefly in the south of France and the north of Italy and whose major theme was courtly love — compare TROUVÈRE

[1]**trou·ble** \'trəb-əl\ *vb* **trou·bled; trou·bling** \'trəb-(ə-)liŋ\ [ME *troublen*, fr. OF *tourbler*, *troubler*, fr. (assumed) VL *turbulare*, alter. of L *turbidare*, fr. *turbidus* turbid, troubled] *vt* **1 a** : to agitate mentally or spiritually : WORRY, DISTURB **b** (1) *archaic* : MISTREAT, OPPRESS (2) : to produce physical disorder in : AFFLICT <*troubled* with deafness> **c** : to put to exertion or inconvenience **2** : to put into confused motion <the wind *troubled* the sea> ~ *vi* **1** : to become mentally agitated : WORRY <refused to ~ over trifles> **2** : to make an effort : be at pains <do not ~ to come> — **trou·bler** \-(ə-)lər\ *n*

syn TROUBLE, DISTRESS, AIL *shared meaning element* : to cause to be uneasy or upset

[2]**trouble** *n* **1 a** : the quality or state of being troubled : MISFORTUNE **b** : an instance of distress, annoyance, or perturbation **2** : a cause of disturbance, annoyance, or distress: as **a** : public unrest or demonstrations of dissatisfaction <labor ~> **b** : an effort made : EXERTION <went to some ~ to match the silk> **c** (1) : a condition of physical distress (2) : DISEASE,

AILMENT <heart ~> (3) : MALFUNCTION <engine ~> <~ with the plumbing> **d** : pregnancy out of wedlock — usu. used in the phrase *in trouble* **e** : a personal characteristic that is a handicap or a source of distress <his greatest ~ was his gullibility> **3** : SITUATION, FACT <the ~ is, the . . . war will be "lost" even if it is "won" —H. B. Hoffman> ***syn*** see EFFORT

trou·ble·mak·er \'trəb-əl-ˌmā-kər\ *n* : a person who consciously or unconsciously causes trouble

trou·ble·shoot \-ˌshüt\ *vb* **-shot** \-ˌshät\; **-shoot·ing** [back-formation fr. *troubleshooter*] *vi* : to operate or serve as a troubleshooter <is ~*ing* for an electronics firm> ~ *vt* : to investigate or deal with in the role of troubleshooter <~*s* TV receivers>

trou·ble·shoot·er \-ˌshüt-ər\ *n* **1** : a skilled workman employed to locate trouble and make repairs in machinery and technical equipment **2** : one who is expert in resolving diplomatic or political disputes : a mediator of disputes that are at an impasse

trou·ble·some \-səm\ *adj* **1** : giving trouble or anxiety : VEXATIOUS **2** *archaic* : characterized by disturbance : TURBULENT **3** *archaic* : full of trouble or distress **4** : DIFFICULT, BURDENSOME — **trou·ble·some·ly** *adv* — **trou·ble·some·ness** *n*

trou·blous \'trəb-(ə-)ləs\ *adj* **1** : full of trouble : AFFLICTED; *also* : STORMY, AGITATED **2** : causing trouble : TURBULENT — **trou·blous·ly** *adv* — **trou·blous·ness** *n*

trou–de–loup \ˌtrüd-ᵊl-'ü\ *n, pl* **trous–de–loup** \ˌtrüd-ᵊl-'ü(z)\ [F, lit., wolf's hole] : a sloping pit with a pointed stake in the middle to form one of a group constructed as obstacles to the movements of an enemy — usu. used in pl.

trough \'trȯf, 'trȯth, *by bakers often* 'trō\ *n, pl* **troughs** \'trȯfs, 'trȯvz; 'trȯths, 'trȯ(th)z; 'trōz\ [ME, fr. OE *trog;* akin to OE *trēow* tree, wood — more at TREE] **1 a** : a long shallow often V-shaped receptacle for the drinking water or feed of domestic animals **b** : any of various domestic or industrial containers **2 a** : a conduit, drain, or channel for water; *esp* : a gutter along the eaves of a building **b** : a long and narrow or shallow channel or depression (as between waves or hills); *esp* : a long but shallow depression in the bed of the sea — compare TRENCH **3** : the minimum point of a complete cycle of a periodic function: as **a** : an elongated area of low barometric pressure **b** : the low point in a business cycle

trounce \'traún(t)s\ *vt* **trounced; trounc·ing** [origin unknown] : to thrash or punish severely: as **a** : FLOG, CUDGEL **b** : to defeat decisively

[1]**troupe** \'trüp\ *n* [F, fr. MF — more at TROOP] : COMPANY, TROOP; *esp* : a group of theatrical performers

[2]**troupe** *vi* **trouped; troup·ing** : to travel in a troupe; *also* : to perform as a member of a theatrical troupe — **troup·er** *n*

trou·pi·al \'trü-pē-əl\ *n* [F *troupiale,* fr. *troupe;* fr. its living in flocks] : any of a family (Icteridae) of birds including the American blackbirds, grackles, and orioles; *specif* : one of the large showy orioles (as *Icterus icterus*) of Central and So. America

trou·ser \'traú-zər\ *adj* : of, relating to, or designed for trousers <~ pockets>

trou·sers \'traú-zərz\ *n pl* [alter. of earlier *trouse,* fr. ScGael *triubhas*] **1** *or* **trow·sers** : an outer garment extending from the waist to the ankle or sometimes only to the knee, covering each leg separately, and worn typically by men and boys **2** : baggy pantaloons worn by both sexes in the Near East

trous·seau \'trü-(ˌ)sō, trü-'\ *n, pl* **trous·seaux** \-(ˌ)sōz, -'sōz\ *or* **trousseaus** [F, fr. OF, dim. of *trousse* bundle, fr. *trousser* to truss] : the personal possessions of a bride usu. including clothes, accessories, and household linens and wares

trout \'traút\ *n, pl* **trout** *also* **trouts** [ME, fr. OE *trūht,* fr. LL *trocta, tructa,* a fish with sharp teeth, fr. Gk *trōktēs,* lit., gnawer, fr. *trōgein* to gnaw — more at TERSE] **1** : any of various food and sport fishes (family Salmonidae) mostly smaller than the typical salmons and restricted to cool clear fresh waters: **a** : any of various Old or New World fishes (genus *Salmo*) some of which are anadromous — compare RAINBOW TROUT **b** : any of various No. American fishes (genera *Salvelinus* or *Cristivomer*) : CHAR **2** : any of various fishes (as the largemouth bass) held to resemble the true trouts

trout lily *n* [prob. fr. its speckled leaves] : DOGTOOTH VIOLET

trout–perch \'traút-ˌpərch\ *n* : a small freshwater fish (*Percopsis omiscomaycus*) of the central and eastern U.S.

trouty \'traút-ē\ *adj* **trout·i·er; -est** : containing or likely to contain abundant trout

trou·vère \trü-'ve(ə)r\ *n* [F, fr. OF *troveor, troverre,* fr. *trover* to compose, find, fr. (assumed) VL *tropare* — more at TROUBADOUR] : one of a school of poets who flourished from the 11th to the 14th centuries and who composed mostly narrative works (as chansons de geste and fabliaux) — compare TROUBADOUR

trove \'trōv\ *n* [short for *treasure trove*] **1** : DISCOVERY, FIND **2** : a valuable collection : TREASURE; *also* : HAUL

tro·ver \'trō-vər\ *n* [MF *trover* to find] : a common law action to recover the value of goods wrongfully converted by another to his own use

trow \'trō\ *vb* [ME *trowen,* fr. OE *trēowan;* akin to OE *trēowe* faithful, true — more at TRUE] **1** *obs* : BELIEVE **2** *archaic* : THINK

[1]**trow·el** \'traú(-ə)l\ *n* [ME *truel,* fr. MF *truelle,* fr. LL *truella,* fr. L *trulla,* dim. of *trua* ladle; akin to L *turbare* to disturb — more at TURBID] : any of various hand tools used to apply, spread, shape, or smooth loose or plastic material; *also* : a scoop-shaped or flat-bladed garden tool for taking up and setting small plants

[2]**trowel** *vt* **-eled** *or* **-elled; -el·ing** *or* **-el·ling** : to smooth, mix, or apply with or as if with a trowel — **trow·el·er** *n*

troy \'trȯi\ *adj* [ME *troye,* fr. *Troyes,* France] : expressed in troy weight

troy weight *n* : a series of units of weight based on a pound of 12 ounces and the ounce of 20 pennyweights or 480 grains — see WEIGHT table

tru·an·cy \'trü-ən-sē\ *n, pl* **-cies** : an act or instance of playing truant : the state of being truant

[1]**tru·ant** \'trü-ənt\ *n* [ME, vagabond, idler, fr. OF, vagrant, of Celt origin; akin to ScGael *truaghan* wretch] : one who shirks duty; *esp* : one who stays out of school without permission

[2]**truant** *adj* : being, resembling, or characteristic of a truant

[3]**truant** *vi* : to idle away time esp. while playing truant

truant officer *n* : one employed by a public school system to investigate the continued absences of pupils

tru·ant·ry \'trü-ən-trē\ *n, pl* **-ries** : TRUANCY

trowels: *1* gardener's, *2* plasterer's, *3* bricklayer's

[1]**truce** \'trüs\ *n* [ME *trewes,* pl. of *trewe* agreement, fr. OE *trēow* fidelity; akin to OE *trēowe* faithful — more at TRUE] **1** : a suspension of fighting esp. of considerable duration by agreement of opposing forces : ARMISTICE, CEASE-FIRE **2** : a respite esp. from a disagreeable or painful state or action

[2]**truce** *vb* **truced; truc·ing** *vi* : to make a truce ~ *vt* : to end with a truce

[1]**truck** \'trək\ *vb* [ME *trukken,* fr. OF *troquer*] *vt* **1** : to give in exchange : SWAP **2** : to barter or dispose of by barter ~ *vi* **1** : to exchange commodities : BARTER **2** : to negotiate or traffic esp. in an underhanded way : have dealings

[2]**truck** *n* **1** : BARTER **2** : commodities appropriate for barter or for small trade **3** : close association : DEALINGS **4** : payment of wages in goods instead of cash **5** : vegetables grown for market **6** : heterogeneous small articles often of little value; *also* : RUBBISH

[3]**truck** *n* [prob. fr. L *trochus* iron hoop, fr. Gk *trochos* wheel — more at TROCHEE] **1** : a small wheel; *specif* : a small strong wheel for a gun carriage **2** : a small wooden cap at the top of a flagstaff or masthead usu. having holes for reeving flag or signal halyards **3** : a wheeled vehicle for moving heavy articles: as **a** : a strong horse-drawn or automotive vehicle for hauling; *also* : an automotive vehicle equipped with a swivel for hauling a trailer **b** : a small barrow consisting of a rectangular frame having at one end a pair of handles and at the other end a pair of small heavy wheels and a projecting edge to slide under a load — called also *hand truck* **c** : a small heavy rectangular frame supported on four wheels for moving heavy objects **d** : a small flat-topped car pushed or pulled by hand **e** : a shelved stand mounted on casters **4 a** *Brit* : an open railroad freight car **b** : a swiveling carriage consisting of a frame with one or more pairs of wheels and springs to carry and guide one end (as of a railroad car) in turning sharp curves

[4]**truck** *vt* : to load or transport on a truck ~ *vi* **1** : to transport goods by truck **2** : to be employed in driving a truck

truck·age \'trək-ij\ *n* **1** : money paid for conveyance on a truck **2** : conveyance by truck

[1]**truck·er** \'trək-ər\ *n* **1** : one that barters **2** *Scot* : PEDDLER

[2]**trucker** *n* **1** : one whose business is transporting goods by truck **2** : a truck driver

truck farm *n* [[2]*truck*] : a farm devoted to the production of vegetables for the market — **truck farmer** *n*

truck·ing *n* : the process or business of transporting goods on trucks

truck·le \'trək-əl\ *vi* **truck·led; truck·ling** \-(ə-)liŋ\ [fr. the lower position of the truckle bed] : to act in a subservient manner : SUBMIT ***syn*** see FAWN — **truck·ler** \-(ə-)lər\ *n*

truckle bed *n* : TRUNDLE BED

truck·line \'trək-ˌlīn\ *n* : a transportation line using trucks and related freight vehicles

truck·load \-'lōd, -ˌlōd\ *n* **1** : a load that fills a truck **2** : the minimum weight required for shipping at truckload rates

truck·man \-mən\ *n* **1** : [2]TRUCKER **2** : a member of a fire department unit that operates a hook and ladder truck

truck·mas·ter \-ˌmas-tər\ *n, archaic* : an officer in charge of trade with Indians esp. among the early settlers

truck system *n* : the system of paying wages in goods instead of cash

tru·cu·lence \'trək-yə-lən(t)s *also* 'trük-\ *n* : the quality or state of being truculent

tru·cu·len·cy \-lən-sē\ *n* : TRUCULENCE

tru·cu·lent \-lənt\ *adj* [L *truculentus,* fr. *truc-, trux* fierce] **1** : feeling or displaying ferocity : CRUEL, SAVAGE **2** : DEADLY, DESTRUCTIVE **3** : scathingly harsh : VITRIOLIC **4** : aggressively self-assertive : BELLIGERENT — **tru·cu·lent·ly** *adv*

[1]**trudge** \'trəj\ *vb* **trudged; trudg·ing** [origin unknown] *vi* : to walk or march steadily and usu. laboriously <*trudged* through deep snow> ~ *vt* : to trudge along or over — **trudg·er** *n*

[2]**trudge** *n* : a long tiring walk : TRAMP

trud·gen stroke \'trəj-ən-\ *n* [John *Trudgen,* 19th cent. E swimmer] : a swimming stroke consisting of alternating overarm strokes and a scissors kick

[1]**true** \'trü\ *adj* **tru·er; tru·est** [ME *trewe,* fr. OE *trēowe* faithful; akin to OHG *gitriuwi* faithful, Skt *dāruṇa* hard, *dāru* wood — more at TREE] **1 a** : STEADFAST, LOYAL **b** : HONEST, JUST **c** *archaic* : TRUTHFUL **2 a** (1) : being in accordance with the actual state of affairs <~ description> (2) : conformable to an essential reality **b** : IDEAL, ESSENTIAL **c** : being that which is the case rather than what is manifest or assumed <the ~ dimension of the problem> **d** : CONSISTENT <~ to expectations> **3 a** : properly so called <~ love> <the ~ faith> <the ~ stomach> **b** (1) : possessing the basic characters of and belonging to the same natural group as <a whale is a ~ but not a typical mammal> (2) : TYPICAL <the ~ cats> **4** : LEGITIMATE, RIGHTFUL <our ~ and lawful king> **5 a** : that is fitted or formed or that functions accurately **b** : conformable to a standard or pattern : ACCURATE **6** : determined with reference to the earth's axis rather than the magnetic poles <~ north> **7** : logically necessary **8** : NARROW, STRICT <in the *truest* sense> **9** : corrected for error ***syn*** see REAL ***ant*** false

[2]**true** *n* **1** : TRUTH, REALITY — usu. used with *the* **2** : the quality or state of being accurate (as in alignment or adjustment) — used in the phrases *in true* and *out of true*

[3]**true** *vt* **trued; true·ing** *also* **tru·ing** : to make level, square, balanced, or concentric : bring or restore to a desired mechanical accuracy or form <~ up a board> <~ up an engine cylinder>

⁴true *adv* [ME *trewe,* fr. *trewe,* adj., true] **1 :** in accordance with fact or reality **2 a :** without deviation <the bullet flew straight and ~> **b :** without variation from type <breed ~>

true bill *n* **:** a bill of indictment endorsed by a grand jury as warranting prosecution of the accused

true–blue *adj* **:** marked by unswerving loyalty (as to a party)

true blue *n* [fr. the old association of blue with constancy] **:** one who is true-blue

true·born \'trü-'bȯ(ə)rn\ *adj* **:** genuinely such by birth <a ~ Englishman —Shak.>

true–false test \'trü-'fȯls-\ *n* **:** a test consisting of a series of statements to be marked as true or false

true·heart·ed \-'härt-əd\ *adj* **:** FAITHFUL, LOYAL — **true·heart·ed·ness** *n*

true–life \ˌtrü-ˌlīf\ *adj* **:** true to life <a ~ story>

true·love \'trü-ˌləv\ *n* **:** one truly beloved or loving **:** SWEETHEART

true lover's knot *n* **:** a complicated ornamental knot not readily untied and symbolic of mutual love — called also *truelove knot;* see KNOT illustration

true·ness \'trü-nəs\ *n* **:** the quality or state of being true

true·pen·ny \'trü-ˌpen-ē\ *n* **:** an honest or trusty person

true rib *n* **:** one of the ribs having costal cartilages connected directly with the sternum and in man constituting the first seven pairs

truf·fle \'trəf-əl, 'trüf-\ *n* [modif. of MF *truffe,* fr. OProv *trufa,* fr. (assumed) VL *tufera,* alter. of L *tuber* — more at TUBER] **:** the usu. dark and rugose edible subterranean fruiting body of several European ascomycetous fungi (genus *Tuber*); *also* **:** one of these fungi

truf·fled \-əld\ *adj* **:** cooked, stuffed, or garnished with truffles

tru·ism \'trü-ˌiz-əm\ *n* **:** an undoubted or self-evident truth; *esp* **:** one too obvious or unimportant for mention — **tru·is·tic** \trü-'is-tik\ *adj*

trull \'trəl\ *n* [obs. G *trulle,* fr. MHG; akin to ON *troll* giant, demon — more at TROLL] **:** PROSTITUTE, STRUMPET

tru·ly \'trü-lē\ *adv* **1 :** SINCERELY — often used with *yours* as a complimentary close **2 :** in agreement with fact **:** TRUTHFULLY **3 :** with exactness of construction or operation **:** ACCURATELY **4 a :** INDEED — often used as an intensive <~, she is fair> or interjectionally to express astonishment or doubt **b :** without feigning, falsity, or inaccuracy in truth or fact **5 :** PROPERLY

¹trump \'trəmp\ *n* [ME *trompe,* fr. OF] **1 a :** TRUMPET **b** *chiefly Scot* **:** JEW'S HARP **2 :** a sound of or as if of trumpeting

²trump *n* [alter. of ¹*triumph*] **1 a :** a card of a suit any of whose cards will win over a card that is not a trump **b :** the suit whose cards are trumps for a particular hand — often used in pl. **2 :** an influential factor or final resource **3 :** a dependable and exemplary person

³trump *vt* **1 :** to play a trump on (a card or trick) when another suit was led **2 :** to get the better of **:** OUTDO ~ *vi* **:** to play a trump when another suit was led

trump card *n* **1 :** ²TRUMP 1a **2 :** a telling argument or decisive factor **:** CLINCHER

trumped–up \'trəm(p)-'təp\ *adj* **:** fraudulently concocted **:** SPURIOUS <~ charges>

trum·pery \'trəm-p(ə-)rē\ *n* [ME *tromperie* deceit, fr. MF, fr. *tromper* to deceive] **1 a :** trivial or useless articles <a wagon loaded with household ~ —Washington Irving> **b :** worthless nonsense **2** *archaic* **:** tawdry finery — **trumpery** *adj*

¹trum·pet \'trəm-pət\ *n* [ME *trompette,* fr. MF, fr. OF *trompe* trump] **1 a :** a wind instrument consisting of a conical or cylindrical usu. metal tube, a cup-shaped mouthpiece, and a flared bell; *specif* **:** a valved brass instrument having a cylindrical tube with two turns and a usual range from F sharp below middle C upward for 2½ octaves **b :** a musical instrument (as a cornet) resembling a trumpet **2 :** a trumpet player **3 :** something that resembles a trumpet or its tonal quality: as **a :** a funnel-shaped instrument (as a megaphone) for collecting, directing, or intensifying sound **b** (1) **:** a stentorian voice (2) **:** a penetrating cry (as of an elephant)

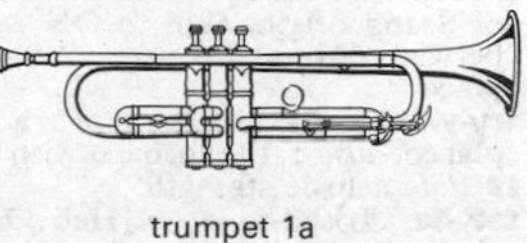

trumpet 1a

²trumpet *vi* **1 :** to blow a trumpet **2 :** to make a sound suggestive of that of a trumpet ~ *vt* **:** to sound or proclaim on or as if on a trumpet

trumpet creeper *n* **:** a No. American woody vine (*Campsis radicans* of the family Bignoniaceae, the trumpet-creeper family) having pinnate leaves and large red trumpet-shaped flowers

trum·pet·er \'trəm-pət-ər\ *n* **1 a :** a trumpet player; *specif* **:** one that gives signals with a trumpet **b :** one that praises or advocates **:** EULOGIST, SPOKESMAN **2 a :** any of several large gregarious long-legged long-necked So. American birds (genus *Psophia*) related to the cranes and often kept to protect poultry **b :** TRUMPETER SWAN **c :** any of an Asiatic breed of pigeons with a rounded crest and heavily feathered feet **3 :** any of several Australian and New Zealand marine spiny-finned food fishes (family Latrididae)

trumpeter swan *n* **:** a rare pure white No. American wild swan (*Olor buccinator*) noted for its sonorous voice

trumpet flower *n* **1 :** any of various plants (as a trumpet creeper or a datura) with trumpet-shaped flowers **2 :** the flower of a trumpet flower

trumpet honeysuckle *n* **:** a No. American honeysuckle (*Lonicera sempervirens*) with coral-red or orange flowers and a trumpet-shaped corolla

trum·pet·like \'trəm-pət-ˌlīk\ *adj* **:** resembling a trumpet in shape or sound

trumpet vine *n* **:** TRUMPET CREEPER

trum·pet·weed \'trəm-pət-ˌwēd\ *n* **:** any of several weedy herbs (esp. genus *Eupatorium*)

trump up *vt* **1 :** to concoct esp. with intent to deceive **:** FABRICATE, INVENT **2** *archaic* **:** to cite as support for an action or claim

¹trun·cate \'trəŋ-ˌkāt, 'trən-\ *vt* **trun·cat·ed; trun·cat·ing** [L *truncatus,* pp. of *truncare,* fr. *truncus* trunk] **1 :** to shorten by or as if by cutting off **2 :** to replace (an edge or corner of a crystal) by a plane

²truncate *adj* **:** having the end square or even <the ~ leaves of the tulip tree>

trun·cat·ed \-ˌkāt-əd\ *adj* **1 :** having the apex replaced by a plane section and esp. by one parallel to the base <~ cone> **2 a :** cut short **:** CURTAILED **b :** lacking an expected or normal element (as a syllable) at the beginning or end **:** CATALECTIC

trun·ca·tion \ˌtrəŋ-'kā-shən, ˌtrən-\ *n* **1 :** an act or instance of truncating **2 :** the quality or state of being truncated

¹trun·cheon \'trən-chən\ *n* [ME *tronchoun,* fr. MF *tronchon,* fr. (assumed) VL *truncion-, truncio,* fr. L *truncus* trunk] **1 :** a shattered spear or lance **2 a** *obs* **:** CLUB, BLUDGEON **b :** BATON 2 **c :** a policeman's billy

²truncheon *vt, archaic* **:** to beat with a truncheon

¹trun·dle \'trən-dᵊl\ *n* [alter. of earlier *trendle,* fr. ME, circle, ring, wheel, fr. OE *trendel;* akin to OE *trendan* to revolve — more at TREND] **1 :** a small wheel or roller **2 :** a round or oval wooden tub **3 a :** a low-wheeled cart or truck **b :** TRUNDLE BED **4 :** the motion or sound of something rolling

²trundle *vb* **trun·dled; trun·dling** \-(d)liŋ, -dᵊl-iŋ\ *vt* **1 a :** to propel by causing to rotate **:** ROLL **b** *archaic* **:** to cause to revolve **:** SPIN **2 :** to transport in a wheeled vehicle **:** HAUL, WHEEL ~ *vi* **1 :** to progress by revolving **2 :** to move on or as if on wheels **:** ROLL — **trun·dler** \-(d)lər, -dᵊl-ər\ *n*

trundle bed *n* **:** a low bed usu. on casters that can be slid under a higher bed — called also *truckle bed*

trun·dle–tail \'trən-dᵊl-ˌtāl\ *n, archaic* **:** a curly-tailed dog

trunk \'trəŋk\ *n* [ME *tronke* box, trunk, fr. MF *tronc,* fr. L *truncus* trunk, torso] **1 a :** the main stem of a tree apart from limbs and roots — called also *bole* **b** (1) **:** the human or animal body apart from the head and appendages **:** TORSO (2) **:** the thorax of an insect **c :** the central part of anything; *specif* **:** the shaft of a column or pilaster **2 a** (1) **:** a large rigid piece of luggage used usu. for transporting clothing and personal effects (2) **:** the luggage compartment of an automobile **b** (1) **:** a superstructure over a ship's hatches usu. level with the poop deck (2) **:** the part of the cabin of a boat projecting above the deck (3) **:** the housing for a centerboard or rudder **3 :** PROBOSCIS; *esp* **:** the long muscular proboscis of the elephant **4** *pl* **:** men's shorts worn chiefly for sports **5 a :** a usu. major channel or passage (as a chute or shaft) **b :** a circuit between two telephone exchanges for making connections between subscribers; *broadly* **:** a usu. electronic path over which information is transmitted (as between computer memories) **6 :** TRUNK LINE

trunked \'trəŋ(k)t\ *adj* **:** having a trunk esp. of a specified kind — usu. used in combination <a gray-*trunked* tree>

trunk·fish \'trəŋk-ˌfish\ *n* **:** any of numerous small bright-colored fishes (family Ostraciidae) of tropical seas with the body and head enclosed in a bony carapace

trunk hose \'trəŋk-\ *n pl* [prob. fr. obs. E *trunk* (to truncate)] **:** short full breeches reaching about halfway down the thigh that were worn chiefly in the late 16th and early 17th centuries

trunk line *n* **1 :** a system handling long-distance through traffic **2 a :** a main supply channel **b :** a direct link

trun·nel \'trən-ᵊl\ *var of* TREENAIL

trun·nion \'trən-yən\ *n* [F *trognon* core, stump] **:** a pin or pivot on which something can be rotated or tilted; *esp* **:** either of two opposite gudgeons on which a cannon is swiveled

¹truss \'trəs\ *vt* [ME *trussen,* fr. OF *trousser*] **1 a :** to secure tightly **:** BIND **b :** to arrange for cooking by binding close the wings or legs of (a fowl) **2 :** to support, strengthen, or stiffen by a truss — **truss·er** *n*

²truss *n* **1 :** an iron band around a lower mast **2 a :** BRACKET 1 **b :** an assemblage of members (as beams) forming a rigid framework **3 :** a device worn to reduce a hernia by pressure **4 :** a compact flower or fruit cluster

truss bridge *n* **:** a bridge supported mainly by trusses — see BRIDGE illustration

truss·ing \'trəs-iŋ\ *n* **1 :** the members forming a truss **2 :** the trusses and framework of a structure

¹trust \'trəst\ *n* [ME, prob. of Scand origin; akin to ON *traust* trust; akin to OE *trēowe* faithful — more at TRUE] **1 a :** assured reliance on the character, ability, strength, or truth of someone or something **b :** one in which confidence is placed **2 a :** dependence on something future or contingent **:** HOPE **b :** reliance on future payment for property (as merchandise) delivered **:** CREDIT **3 a :** a property interest held by one person for the benefit of another **b :** a combination of firms or corporations formed by a legal agreement; *esp* **:** one that reduces or threatens to reduce competition **4** *archaic* **:** TRUSTWORTHINESS **5 a** (1) **:** a charge or duty imposed in faith or confidence or as a condition of some relationship (2) **:** something committed or entrusted to one to be used or cared for in the interest of another **b :** responsible charge or office **c :** CARE, CUSTODY <child committed to his ~> — **in trust :** in the care or possession of a trustee

²trust *vi* **1 a :** to place confidence **:** DEPEND <~ in God> <~ to luck> **b :** to be confident **:** HOPE **2 :** to sell or deliver on credit ~ *vt* **1 a :** to commit or place in one's care or keeping **:** ENTRUST **b :** to permit to stay or go or to do something without fear or misgiving **2 a :** to rely on the truthfulness or accuracy of

: BELIEVE **b** : to place confidence in : rely on **c** : to hope or expect confidently **3** : to extend credit to ***syn*** see RELY — **trust·abil·i·ty** \ˌtrəs-tə-ˈbil-ət-ē\ *n* — **trust·able** \ˈtrəs-tə-bəl\ *adj* — **trust·er** *n* — **trust·ing·ly** \ˈtrəs-tiŋ-lē\ *adv*

trust·bust·er \ˈtrəs(t)-ˌbəs-tər\ *n* [[1]*trust* + *buster*] : one who seeks to break up business trusts; *specif* : a federal official who prosecutes trusts under the antitrust laws — **trust–bust·ing** \-tiŋ\ *n*

trust company *n* : an incorporated trustee; *broadly* : a corporation that functions as a corporate and personal trustee and usu. also engages in the normal activities of a commercial bank

[1]**trust·ee** \ˌtrəs-ˈtē\ *n* **1 a** : one to whom something is entrusted **b** : a country charged with the supervision of a trust territory **2 a** : a natural or legal person to whom property is legally committed to be administered for the benefit of a beneficiary (as a person or a charitable organization) **b** : one (as a corporate director) occupying a position of trust and performing functions comparable to those of a trustee

[2]**trustee** *vb* **trust·eed; trust·ee·ing** *vt* : to commit to the care of a trustee ~ *vi* : to serve as trustee

trust·ee·ship \ˌtrəs-ˈtē-ˌship\ *n* **1** : the office or function of a trustee **2** : supervisory control by one or more countries over a trust territory

trust·ful \ˈtrəst-fəl\ *adj* : full of trust : CONFIDING — **trust·ful·ly** \-fə-lē\ *adv* — **trust·ful·ness** *n*

trust fund *n* : property (as money or securities) settled or held in trust

trust·i·ness \ˈtrəs-tē-nəs\ *n* : the quality or state of being trusty

trust·less \ˈtrəst-ləs\ *adj* **1** : not deserving of trust : FAITHLESS **2** : DISTRUSTFUL

trust territory *n* : a non-self-governing territory placed under an administrative authority by the Trusteeship Council of the United Nations

trust·wor·thi·ness \ˈtrəst-ˌwər-t͟hē-nəs\ *n* : the quality or state of being trustworthy

trust·wor·thy \-t͟hē\ *adj* : worthy of confidence : DEPENDABLE — **trust·wor·thi·ly** \-t͟hə-lē\ *adv*

[1]**trusty** \ˈtrəs-tē\ *adj* **trust·i·er; -est** : TRUSTWORTHY, DEPENDABLE

[2]**trusty** \ˈtrəs-tē *also* ˌtrəs-ˈtē\ *n, pl* **trust·ies** : a trusty or trusted person; *specif* : a convict considered trustworthy and allowed special privileges

truth \ˈtrüth\ *n, pl* **truths** \ˈtrüt͟hz, ˈtrüths\ [ME *trouthe,* fr. OE *trēowth* fidelity; akin to OE *trēowe* faithful — more at TRUE] **1 a** *archaic* : FIDELITY, CONSTANCY **b** : sincerity in action, character, and utterance **2 a (1)** : the state of being the case : FACT **(2)** : the body of real things, events, and facts : ACTUALITY **(3)** *often cap* : a transcendent fundamental or spiritual reality **b** : a judgment, proposition, or idea that is true or accepted as true <~*s* of thermodynamics> **c** : the body of true statements and propositions **3 a** : the property (as of a statement) of being in accord with fact or reality **b** *chiefly Brit* : TRUE 2 **c** : fidelity to an original or to a standard **4** *cap, Christian Science* : GOD
syn TRUTH, VERACITY, VERITY, VERISIMILITUDE *shared meaning element* : the quality or property of keeping close to fact and avoiding distortion or misrepresentation ***ant*** untruth, lie, falsehood
— **in truth** : in accordance with fact : ACTUALLY

truth·ful \ˈtrüth-fəl\ *adj* : telling or disposed to tell the truth — **truth·ful·ly** \-fə-lē\ *adv* — **truth·ful·ness** *n*

truth serum *n* : a hypnotic or anesthetic held to induce a subject under questioning to talk freely

truth set *n* : a mathematical or logical set containing all the elements that make a given statement of relationships true when substituted in it <the equation x + 7 = 10 has as its *truth set* the single number 3>

truth table *n* : a table that shows the truth-value of a compound statement for every truth-value of its component statements; *also* : a similar table (as for a computer logic circuit) showing the value of the output for each value of each input

TRUTH TABLE

p a statement	q a statement	$\sim p$ not p denial	$p \cdot q$ p and q conjunction	$p \vee q$ p or q (inclusive) inclusive disjunction	$p + q$ p or q (exclusive) exclusive disjunction	$p \supset q$ if p then q conditional	$p \equiv q$ p if and only if q biconditional
T	T	F	T	T	F	T	T
T	F		F	T	T	F	F
F	T	T	F	T	T	T	F
F	F		F	F	F	T	T

T = true F = false

truth–value *n* : the truth or falsity of a proposition or statement

[1]**try** \ˈtrī\ *vb* **tried; try·ing** [ME *trien,* fr. AF *trier,* fr. OF, to pick out, sift, prob. fr. LL *tritare* to rub to pieces, fr. *tritus,* pp. of *terere* to rub — more at THROW] *vt* **1 a** : to examine or investigate judicially **b (1)** : to conduct the trial of **(2)** : to participate as counsel in the judicial examination of **2 a** : to put to test or trial **b** : to subject to something (as undue strain or excessive hardship or provocation) that tests the powers of endurance **c** : DEMONSTRATE, PROVE **3 a** *obs* : PURIFY, REFINE **b** : to melt down and procure in a pure state : RENDER <~ out whale oil from blubber> **4** : to fit or finish with accuracy **5** : to make an attempt at — often used with an infinitive ~ *vi* : to make an attempt ***syn*** see AFFLICT, ATTEMPT — **try conclusions** : to test one's skill or strength against opposition — **try one's hand** : to attempt something for the first time

[2]**try** *n, pl* **tries 1** : an experimental trial : ATTEMPT **2** : a play in rugby that is similar to a touchdown in football, scores three points, and entitles the scoring side to attempt a placekick at the goal for additional points; *also* : the score made on a try

try for point : an attempt made after scoring a touchdown in football to kick a goal so as to score an additional point or to again carry the ball across the opponents' goal line or complete a forward pass in the opponents' end zone so as to score two additional points

try·ing \ˈtrī-iŋ\ *adj* : severely straining the powers of endurance — **try·ing·ly** \-iŋ-lē\ *adv*

try on \(ˈ)trī-ˈȯn, -ˈän\ *vt* **1** : to put on (a garment) in order to test the fit **2** : to use or test experimentally — **try–on** \ˈtrī-ˌȯn, -ˌän\ *n*

try·out \ˈtrī-ˌau̇t\ *n* : an experimental performance or demonstration: as **a** : a test of the ability (as of an athlete or actor) to fill a part or meet standards **b** : a performance of a play prior to its official opening to determine response and discover weaknesses

try out *vi* : to compete for a position esp. on an athletic team or for a part in a play

try·pano·some \trip-ˈan-ə-ˌsōm\ *n* [NL *Trypanosoma,* genus name, fr. Gk *trypanon* auger + NL *-soma* -some — more at TREPAN] : any of a genus (*Trypanosoma*) of parasitic flagellate protozoans that infest the blood of various vertebrates including man, are usu. transmitted by the bite of an insect, and include some that cause serious disease (as sleeping sickness)

try·pano·so·mi·a·sis \trip-ˌan-ə-sə-ˈmī-ə-səs\ *n, pl* **-a·ses** \-ˌsēz\ : infection with or disease caused by trypanosomes

tryp·ars·amide \trip-ˈär-sə-ˌmīd\ *n* [fr. *Tryparsamide,* a trademark] : an organic arsenical $C_8H_{10}AsN_2O_4Na.½H_2O$ used in the treatment of African sleeping sickness and syphilis

try–pot \ˈtrī-ˌpät\ *n* : a metallic pot used on a whaler or on shore to try out whale oil from blubber

tryp·sin \ˈtrip-sən\ *n* [Gk *tryein* to wear down + ISV *-psin* (as in *pepsin*); akin to L *terere* to rub — more at THROW] : a proteolytic enzyme from pancreatic juice active in an alkaline medium; *also* : any of several similar enzymes

tryp·sin·o·gen \trip-ˈsin-ə-jən\ *n* [ISV] : the inactive precursor of trypsin present in the pancreas

trypt·amine \ˈtrip-tə-ˌmēn\ *n* [*tryptophan* + *amine*] : a crystalline amine $C_{10}H_{12}N_2$ derived from tryptophan; *also* : any of various substituted derivatives of this amine of which some are significantly hallucinogenic or neurotoxic

tryp·tic \ˈtrip-tik\ *adj* [ISV, fr. *trypsin,* after such pairs as ISV *pepsin: peptic*] **1** : of or relating to trypsin or its action **2** : produced by trypsin <~ digestion>

tryp·to·phan \ˈtrip-tə-ˌfan\ *or* **tryp·to·phane** \-ˌfān\ *n* [ISV *tryptic* + *-o-* + *-phane*] : a crystalline amino acid $C_{11}H_{12}N_2O_2$ that is widely distributed in proteins and is essential to animal life

try·sail \ˈtrī-ˌsāl, -səl\ *n* [obs. *at try* (lying to)] : a fore-and-aft sail bent to a gaff and hoisted on a lower mast or a small mast close abaft

try square *n* : an instrument used for laying off right angles and testing whether work is square

tryst \ˈtrist *esp Brit* ˈtrīst\ *n* [ME, fr. OF *triste* watch post, prob. of Scand origin; akin to ON *traust* trust] **1** : an agreement (as between lovers) to meet **2** : an appointed meeting or meeting place

try·works \ˈtrī-ˌwərks\ *n pl* : a brick furnace in which try-pots are placed; *also* : the furnace with the pots

ts *abbr* tensile strength

tsa·de \ˈ(t)säd-ə, -ē\ *n* [Heb *ṣādhē*] : SADHE

tsar \ˈzär, ˈ(t)sär\ *var of* CZAR

tset·se \ˈ(t)set-sē, ˈtet-, ˈ(t)sēt-, ˈtēt-\ *n, pl* **tsetse** *or* **tsetses** [Afrik, fr. Tswana *tsêtsê*] : any of several two-winged flies (genus *Glossina*) that occur in Africa south of the Sahara desert and include vectors of human and animal trypanosomes

TSgt *abbr* technical sergeant

TSH *abbr* thyroid-stimulating hormone

Tshi \ˈchwē, chə-ˈwē, ˈtwē, ˈchē\ *var of* TWI

Tshi·lu·ba \chi-ˈlü-bə\ *n* : one of the major trade languages of Congo esp. in the southern part

T–shirt \ˈtē-ˌshərt\ *n* [fr. its being shaped like a **T**] : a collarless short-sleeved or sleeveless cotton undershirt for men; *also* : a cotton or wool jersey outer shirt of similar design

tsp *abbr* teaspoon; teaspoonful

T square *n* : a ruler with a crosspiece or head at one end used in making parallel lines

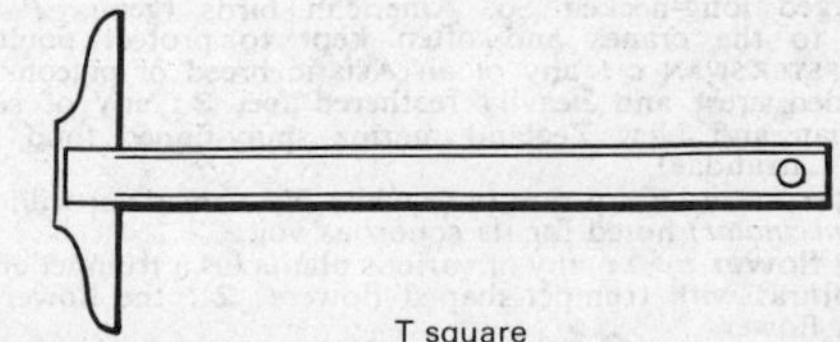

T square

tsu·na·mi \(t)sü-ˈnäm-ē\ *n* [Jap] : a great sea wave produced by submarine earth movement or volcanic eruption — **tsu·na·mic** \-ik\ *adj*

tsu·tsu·ga·mu·shi disease \ˌ(t)süt-sə-gə-ˈmü-shē-, ˌtüt-, -ˈgäm-ù-shē-\ *n* [Jap *tsutsugamushi* scrub typhus mite, fr. *tsutsuga* sickness + *mushi* insect] : an acute febrile rickettsial disease resembling louse-borne typhus that is widespread in the western Pacific area and is transmitted by mite larvae — called also *scrub typhus, tsutsugamushi*

TT *abbr* 1 telegraphic transfer 2 teletypewriter 3 tuberculin tested

Tu *abbr* Tuesday

TU *abbr* 1 trade union 2 transmission unit

Tu·a·mo·tu \ˌtü-ə-ˈmō-ˈ ˌü\ *n* : the Polynesian language of the Tuamotu archipelago

Tua·reg \ˈtwä-ˌreg\ *n, pl* **Tuareg** *or* **Tuaregs** [Ar *Tawāriq*] : a member of the dominant nomadic people of the central and western Sahara and along the Middle Niger from Timbuktu to Nigeria who have preserved their Hamitic speech but have adopted the Muslim religion

tu·a·ta·ra \ˌtü-ə-ˈtär-ə\ *n* [Maori *tuatàra*] : a large spiny quadrupedal reptile (*Sphenodon punctatum*) of islands off the coast of New Zealand that is the only surviving rhynchocephalian

[1]**tub** \ˈtəb\ *n* [ME *tubbe*, fr. MD; akin to MLG *tubbe* tub] **1** : a wide low vessel orig. formed with wooden staves, round bottom, and hoops **2** : an old or slow boat **3** : BATHTUB; *also* : BATH **4** : the amount that a tub will hold — **tub·ful** \-ˌfu̇l\ *n*

[2]**tub** *vb* **tubbed; tub·bing** *vt* **1** : to wash or bathe in a tub **2** : to put or store in a tub ~ *vi* **1** : BATHE **2** : to undergo washing — **tub·ba·ble** \ˈtəb-ə-bəl\ *adj* — **tub·ber** *n*

tu·ba \ˈt(y)ü-bə\ *n* [It, fr. L, trumpet] : a large low-pitched brass instrument usu. oval in shape and having a conical tube, a cup-shaped mouthpiece, and a usual range an octave lower than that of the euphonium

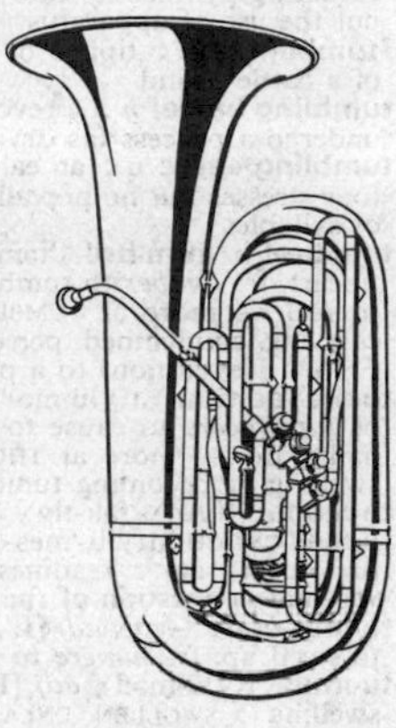

tuba

tu·bal \ˈt(y)ü-bəl\ *adj* : of, relating to, or involving a tube and esp. a fallopian tube

tub·by \ˈtəb-ē\ *adj* **tub·bi·er; -est** **1** : PUDGY, FAT **2** : sounding dull and without proper resonance or freedom of sound <a ~ violin>

tube \ˈt(y)üb\ *n* [F, fr. L *tubus*; akin to L *tuba* trumpet] **1 a** : a hollow elongated cylinder; *esp* : one to convey fluids **b** (1) : a slender channel within a plant or animal body : DUCT (2) : the narrow basal portion of a gamopetalous corolla or a gamosepalous calyx **2** : any of various usu. cylindrical structures or devices: as **a** : a round metal container from which a paste is dispensed by squeezing **b** (1) : TUNNEL (2) *Brit* : SUBWAY 6 **c** : the basically cylindrical section between the mouthpiece and bell that is the fundamental part of a wind instrument **3** : an airtight tube of rubber placed inside the casing of a pneumatic tire to hold air under pressure **4** : ELECTRON TUBE **5** : VACUUM TUBE **6** : TELEVISION TUBE; *broadly* : TELEVISION — **tubed** \ˈt(y)übd\ *adj* — **tube·like** \ˈt(y)ü-ˌblīk\ *adj*

tube foot *n* : one of the small flexible tubular processes of most echinoderms that are extensions of the water-vascular system and are used esp. in locomotion and grasping

tube·less \ˈt(y)ü-bləs\ *adj* : lacking a tube; *specif* : being a pneumatic tire that does not depend on an inner tube for airtightness

tube nucleus *n* : the one of the two nuclei formed by mitotic division of a microspore during the formation of a pollen grain that is held to control subsequent growth of the pollen tube and that does not divide again — compare GENERATIVE NUCLEUS

tu·ber \ˈt(y)ü-bər\ *n* [L, lump, tuber, truffle; akin to L *tumēre* to swell — more at THUMB] **1 a** : a short fleshy usu. underground stem bearing minute scale leaves each of which bears a bud in its axil and is potentially able to produce a new plant — compare BULB, CORM **b** : a fleshy root or rhizome resembling a tuber **2** : an anatomical prominence : TUBEROSITY

tu·ber·cle \ˈt(y)ü-bər-kəl\ *n* [L *tuberculum*, dim. of *tuber*] **1** : a small knobby prominence or excrescence esp. on a plant or animal : NODULE: as **a** : a protuberance near the head of a rib that articulates with the transverse process of a vertebra **b** : any of several prominences in the central nervous system **c** : NODULE b **2** : a small abnormal discrete lump in the substance of an organ or in the skin; *esp* : the specific lesion of tuberculosis

tubercle bacillus *n* : a bacterium (*Mycobacterium tuberculosis*) that is the cause of tuberculosis

tu·ber·cled \ˈt(y)ü-bər-kəld\ *adj* : TUBERCULATE

tubercul- *or* **tuberculo-** *comb form* [NL, fr. L *tuberculum*] **1** : tubercle <*tubercular*> **2** : tubercle bacillus <*tuberculin*> **3** : tuberculosis <*tuberculoid*>

[1]**tu·ber·cu·lar** \t(y)u̇-ˈbər-kyə-lər\ *adj* **1** : relating to, resembling, or constituting a tubercle : TUBERCULATE **2** : characterized by tubercular lesions <~ leprosy> **3 a** : of, relating to, or affected with tuberculosis : TUBERCULOUS **b** : caused by the tubercle bacillus <~ meningitis> — **tu·ber·cu·lar·ly** *adv*

[2]**tubercular** *n* : a person with tuberculosis

tu·ber·cu·late \t(y)u̇-ˈbər-kyə-lət\ *or* **tu·ber·cu·lat·ed** \-ˌlāt-əd\ *adj* **1** : having a tubercle : characterized by or beset with tubercles **2** : TUBERCULAR — **tu·ber·cu·la·tion** \-ˌbər-kyə-ˈlā-shən\ *n*

tu·ber·cu·lin \t(y)u̇-ˈbər-kyə-lən\ *n* [ISV] : a sterile liquid containing the growth products of or specific substances extracted from the tubercle bacillus and used in the diagnosis of tuberculosis esp. in children and cattle

tuberculin test *n* : a test for hypersensitivity to tuberculin as an indication of past or present tubercular infection

tu·ber·cu·loid \t(y)u̇-ˈbər-kyə-ˌlȯid\ *adj* [ISV] : resembling tuberculosis esp. in the presence of tubercles <~ leprosy>

tu·ber·cu·lo·sis \t(y)u̇-ˌbər-kyə-ˈlō-səs\ *n, pl* **-lo·ses** \-ˌsēz\ [NL] : a highly variable communicable disease of man and some other vertebrates caused by the tubercle bacillus and characterized by toxic symptoms or allergic manifestations which in man primarily affect the lungs

tu·ber·cu·lous \t(y)u̇-ˈbər-kyə-ləs\ *adj* **1** : constituting or affected with tuberculosis <a ~ process> **2** : caused by or resulting from the presence or products of the tubercle bacillus <~ peritonitis> — **tu·ber·cu·lous·ly** *adv*

tube·rose \ˈt(y)ü-ˌbrōz (*by folk etymology*), *also* -bə-ˌrōz, -bə-ˌrōs\ *n* [NL *tuberosa*, specific epithet, fr. L, fem. of *tuberosus* tuberous, fr. *tuber*] : a Mexican bulbous herb (*Polianthes tuberosa*) of the amaryllis family cultivated for its spike of fragrant white single or double flowers

tu·ber·os·i·ty \ˌt(y)ü-bə-ˈräs-ət-ē\ *n, pl* **-ties** : a rounded prominence; *esp* : a large prominence on a bone usu. serving for the attachment of muscles or ligaments

tu·ber·ous \ˈt(y)ü-b(ə-)rəs\ *adj* **1** : consisting of, bearing, or resembling a tuber **2** : of, relating to, or being a plant tuber or tuberous root of a plant

tuberous root *n* : a thick fleshy storage root like a tuber but lacking buds or scale leaves — **tu·ber·ous–root·ed** \ˌt(y)ü-b(ə-)rəs-ˈrüt-əd, -ˈru̇t-\ *adj*

tu·bi·fex \ˈt(y)ü-bə-ˌfeks\ *n, pl* **tubifex** *or* **tu·bi·fex·es** [NL *Tubific-, Tubifex*, genus name, fr. L *tubus* tube + *facere* to make — more at DO] : any of a genus (*Tubifex*) of slender reddish oligochaete worms that live in tubes in fresh or brackish water and are widely used as food for aquarium fish

tu·bif·i·cid \t(y)ü-ˈbif-ə-səd, ˌt(y)ü-bə-ˈfis-əd\ *n* [NL *Tubificidae*, group name, fr. *Tubific-, Tubifex*, type genus] : any of a family (Tubificidae) of aquatic oligochaete worms that do not reproduce asexually — **tubificid** *adj*

tub·ing \ˈt(y)ü-biŋ\ *n* **1** : material in the form of a tube; *also* : a length or piece of tube **2** : a series or system of tubes

tu·bo·cu·ra·rine \ˈt(y)ü-bō-kyu̇-ˈrär-ən, -ˌēn\ *n* [ISV *tubo-* (fr. L *tubus* tube) + *curare* + *-ine*; fr. its being shipped in sections of hollow bamboo] : a toxic alkaloid or its crystalline quaternary ammonium chloride $C_{38}H_{44}Cl_2N_2O_6.5H_2O$ that is obtained chiefly from the bark and stems of a So. American vine (*Chondrodendron tomentosum* of the family Menispermaceae) and in its dextrorotatory form constitutes the chief active constituent of curare and is used esp. as a skeletal muscle relaxant

tu·bu·lar \ˈt(y)ü-byə-lər\ *adj* **1 a** : having the form of or consisting of a tube <a ~ calyx> **b** : made or provided with tubes **2** : of, relating to, or sounding as if produced through tubes — **tu·bu·lar·i·ty** \ˌt(y)ü-byə-ˈlar-ət-ē\ *n* — **tu·bu·lar·ly** \ˈt(y)ü-byə-lər-lē\ *adv*

tu·bule \ˈt(y)ü-(ˌ)byü(ə)l\ *n* [L *tubulus*, dim. of *tubus*] : a small tube; *esp* : a slender elongated anatomical channel

tu·bu·lous \ˈt(y)ü-byə-ləs\ *adj* : having the form of a tube or containing tubular elements

TUC *abbr* Trades Union Congress

tu·chun \ˈdü-ˈjün, -ˈju̇en\ *n* [Chin (Pek) *tu*[1] *chün*[1]] **1** : a Chinese military governor (as of a province) **2** : a Chinese warlord

[1]**tuck** \ˈtək\ *vb* [ME *tuken* to pull up sharply, scold, fr. OE *tūcian* to ill-treat; akin to OE *togian* to pull — more at TOW] *vt* **1 a** : to pull up into a fold **b** : to make a tuck in **2** : to put into a snug often concealing or isolating place <cottage ~*ed* away in the hill> **3 a** : to push in the loose end of so as to hold tightly <~ in your shirt> **b** : to cover by tucking in bedclothes **4** : EAT —usu. used with *away* or *in* **5** : to put into a tuck position ~ *vi* **1** : to draw together into tucks or folds **2** : to eat heartily — usu. used with *into* **3** : to fit snugly

[2]**tuck** *n* **1** : a fold stitched into cloth to shorten, decorate, or control fullness **2** : the part of a vessel where the ends of the lower planks meet under the stern **3 a** : an act or instance of tucking **b** : something tucked or to be tucked in **4 a** : a body position (as in diving) in which the knees are bent, the thighs drawn tightly to the chest, and the hands clasped around the shins **b** : a skiing position in which the skier squats forward and holds his ski poles under his arms and parallel to the ground

[3]**tuck** *n* [obs. E *tuk* (to beat the drum)] : a sound of or as if of a drumbeat

[4]**tuck** *n* [MF *estoc*, fr. OF, tree trunk, sword point, of Gmc origin; akin to OE *stocc* stump of a tree — more at STOCK] *archaic* : RAPIER

[5]**tuck** *n* [prob. fr. [2]*tuck*] : VIGOR, ENERGY <seemed to kind of take the ~ all out of me —Mark Twain>

tuck·a·hoe \ˈtək-ə-ˌhō\ *n* [*tockawhoughe* (in some Algonquian language of Virginia)] **1** : either of two American arums (*Peltandra virginica* and *Orantium aquaticum*) with rootstocks used as food by the Indians **2** : the large edible sclerotium of a subterranean fungus (*Poria cocos*)

[1]**tuck·er** \ˈtək-ər\ *n* **1** : one that tucks **2** : a piece of lace or cloth in the neckline of a dress

[2]**tucker** *vt* **tuck·ered; tuck·er·ing** \ˈtək-(ə-)riŋ\ [obs. E *tuck* (to reproach) + *-er* (as in [1]*batter*)] : EXHAUST — often used with *out*

tuck·er–bag \ˈtək-ər-ˌbag\ *n* [Austral slang *tucker* (food, rations)] *chiefly Austral* : a bag used esp. by travelers in the bush to hold food

tuck·et \ˈtək-ət\ *n* [prob. fr. obs. E *tuk* (to beat the drum, sound the trumpet)] : a fanfare on a trumpet

tuck–point \-ˌpȯint\ *vt* : to finish (the mortar joints between bricks or stones) with a narrow ridge of putty or fine lime mortar

tuck–shop \-ˌshäp\ *n* [Brit slang *tuck* (food, confectionery)] *Brit* : confectioner's shop : CONFECTIONERY

-tude \ˌt(y)üd\ *n suffix* [MF or L; MF, fr. L *-tudin-, -tudo*] : -NESS <plenti*tude*>

ə abut   ᵊ kitten   ər further   a back   ā bake   ä cot, cart
au̇ out   ch chin   e less   ē easy   g gift   i trip   ī life
j joke   ŋ sing   ō flow   ȯ flaw   ȯi coin   th thin   th this
ü loot   u̇ foot   y yet   yü few   yu̇ furious   zh vision

Tu·dor \'t(y)üd-ər\ *adj* [Henry *Tudor* (Henry VII of England)] **1** : of or relating to the English royal house that ruled from 1485 to 1603 **2** : of, relating to, or characteristic of the Tudor period — **Tudor** *n*

Tudor arch *n* : a low elliptical or pointed arch drawn from three, four, or five centers; *esp* : a pointed arch drawn from four centers — see ARCH illustration

Tues *or* **Tue** *abbr* Tuesday

Tues·day \'t(y)üz-dē\ *n* [ME *tiwesday,* fr. OE *tīwesdæg;* akin to OHG *ziostag* Tuesday; both fr. a prehistoric WGmc-NGmc compound whose components are represented by OE *Tīw,* god of war and by OE *dæg* day — more at DEITY] : the 3d day of the week — **Tues·days** \-dēz\ *adv*

tu·fa \'t(y)ü-fə\ *n* [It *tufo,* fr. L *tophus*] **1** : TUFF **2** : a porous rock formed as a deposit from springs or streams — **tu·fa·ceous** \t(y)ü-'fā-shəs\ *adj*

tuff \'təf\ *n* [MF *tuf,* fr. OIt *tufo* tufa] : a rock composed of the finer kinds of volcanic detritus usu. fused together by heat — **tuff·a·ceous** \ˌtə-'fā-shəs\ *adj*

tuf·fet \'təf-ət\ *n* [alter. of 1*tuft*] **1** : TUFT 1a **2** : a low seat

1**tuft** \'təft\ *n* [ME, modif. of MF *tufe*] **1 a** : a small cluster of elongated flexible outgrowths attached or close together at the base and free at the opposite ends; *esp* : a growing bunch of grasses or close-set plants **b** : a bunch of soft fluffy threads cut off short and used as ornament **2** : CLUMP, CLUSTER **3** : MOUND — **tuft·ed** \'təf-təd\ *adj* — **tufty** \'təf-tē\ *adj*

2**tuft** *vt* **1** : to provide or adorn with a tuft **2** : to make (as a mattress) firm by stitching at intervals and sewing on tufts ~ *vi* : to form into or grow in tufts — **tuft·er** *n*

1**tug** \'təg\ *vb* **tugged; tug·ging** [ME *tuggen;* akin to OE *togian* to pull — more at TOW] *vi* **1** : to pull hard **2** : to struggle in opposition : CONTEND **3** : to exert oneself laboriously : LABOR ~ *vt* **1** : to pull or strain hard at **2 a** : to move by pulling hard : HAUL **b** : to carry with difficulty : LUG **3** : to tow with a tugboat ***syn*** see PULL — **tug·ger** *n*

2**tug** *n* **1 a** : 3TRACE 1 **b** : a short leather strap or loop **c** : a rope or chain used for pulling **2 a** : an act or instance of tugging : PULL **b** : a strong pulling force **3 a** : a straining effort **b** : a stuggle between two people or opposite forces **4** : TUGBOAT

tug·boat \'təg-ˌbōt\ *n* : a strongly built powerful boat used for towing and pushing — called also *towboat*

tug-of-war \ˌtəg-ə(v)-'wȯ(ə)r\ *n, pl* **tugs-of-war** **1** : a struggle for supremacy **2** : an athletic contest in which two teams pull against each other at opposite ends of a rope

tu·grik \'tü-grik\ *n* [Mongolian *dughurik,* lit., round thing, wheel] — see MONEY table

tui \'tü-ē\ *n* [Maori] : a predominantly glossy black New Zealand honey eater (*Prosthemadera novaeseelandiae*) with white markings on throat, neck, and wings that is a notable mimic and is often kept as a cage bird

tuille \'twē(ə)l\ *n* [ME *toile,* fr. MF *tuille* tile, fr. *tegula* — more at TILE] : one of the hinged plates before the thigh in plate armor — see ARMOR illustration

tu·ition \t(y)ü-'ish-ən\ *n* [ME *tuicioun* protection, fr. OF *tuicion,* fr. L *tuition-, tuitio,* fr. *tuitus,* pp. of *tueri* to look at, look after] **1** *archaic* : CUSTODY, GUARDIANSHIP **2** : the act or profession of teaching : INSTRUCTION <pursued his studies under private ~> **3** : the price of or payment for instruction — **tu·ition·al** \-'ish-nəl, -ən-ᵊl\ *adj*

tu·la·re·mia \ˌt(y)ü-lə-'rē-mē-ə\ *n* [NL, fr. *Tulare* county, Calif.] : an infectious disease of rodents, man, and some domestic animals that is caused by a bacterium (*Pasteurella tularensis*), is transmitted esp. by the bites of insects, and in man is marked by symptoms (as fever) of toxemia — **tu·la·re·mic** \-mik\ *adj*

tu·le \'tü-lē\ *n* [Sp, fr. Nahuatl *tullin*] : either of two large bulrushes (*Scirpus lacustris* and *S. acutus*) growing on overflowed land in the southwestern U.S.

tu·lip \'t(y)ü-ləp\ *n* [NL *tulipa,* fr. Turk *tülbend* turban] : any of a genus (*Tulipa*) of Eurasian bulbous herbs of the lily family that have linear or broadly lanceolate leaves and are widely grown for their showy flowers; *also* : the flower or bulb of a tulip

tulip tree *n* **1** : a tall No. American timber tree (*Liriodendron tulipifera*) of the magnolia family having large greenish yellow tulip-shaped flowers and soft white wood used esp. for cabinetwork and woodenware **2** : any of various trees other than the tulip tree with tulip-shaped flowers

tu·lip·wood \'t(y)ü-ləp-ˌwu̇d\ *n* **1** : wood of the No. American tulip tree : WHITEWOOD **2 a** : any of several showily striped or variegated woods; *esp* : the rose-colored wood of a Brazilian tree (*Physocalymma scabberimum* of the family Lythraceae) that is much used by cabinetmakers for inlaying **b** : a tree that yields tulipwood

tulle \'tül\ *n* [F, fr. *Tulle,* France] : a sheer often stiffened silk, rayon, or nylon net used chiefly for veils, evening dresses, or ballet costumes

tul·li·bee \'təl-ə-bē\ *n* [CanF *toulibi*] : any of several whitefishes of central and northern No. America; *esp* : a common cisco (*Leucichthys artedi*) that is a commercially important food fish

1**tum·ble** \'təm-bəl\ *vb* **tum·bled; tum·bling** \-b(ə-)liŋ\ [ME *tumblen,* freq. of *tumben* to dance, fr. OE *tumbian;* akin to OHG *tūmōn* to reel] *vi* **1 a** : to perform gymnastic feats in tumbling **b** : to turn end over end in falling or flight **2 a** : to fall suddenly and helplessly <~*s* to the ground> **b** : to suffer a sudden downfall, overthrow, or defeat **c** : to decline suddenly and sharply (as in price) : DROP <the stock market *tumbled*> **d** : to fall into ruin : COLLAPSE **3** : to roll over and over, to and fro, or end over end : TOSS **4** : to issue forth hurriedly and confusedly **5** : to come by chance : STUMBLE **6** : to come to understand : catch on ~ *vt* **1** : to cause to tumble (as by pushing, tossing, or toppling) **2 a** : to throw together in a confused mass **b** : RUMPLE, DISORDER **3** : to whirl in a tumbling barrel (as in drying clothes)

2**tumble** *n* **1 a** : a random collection : HEAP **b** : a disorderly state **2** : an act or instance of tumbling

tum·ble·bug \'təm-bəl-ˌbəg\ *n* : any of various scarabaeid beetles (esp. genera *Scarabaeus, Canthon, Copris,* or *Phanaeus*) that roll dung into small balls, bury them in the ground, and lay eggs in them

tum·ble·down \ˌtəm-bəl-ˌdau̇n\ *adj* : DILAPIDATED, RAMSHACKLE

tum·bler \'təm-blər\ *n* **1** : one that tumbles: as **a** : one that performs tumbling feats : ACROBAT **b** : any of various domestic pigeons that tumble or somersault backward in flight or on the ground **2** : a drinking glass without foot or stem and orig. with pointed or convex base **3 a** : a movable obstruction in a lock (as a lever, latch, wheel, slide, or pin) that must be adjusted to a particular position (as by a key) before the bolt can be thrown **b** : a piece on which the mainspring acts in a gunlock **c (1)** : a projecting piece on a revolving shaft or rockshaft for actuating another piece **(2)** : the movable part of a reversing or speed-changing gear **4** : a device or mechanism for tumbling (as a revolving cage in which clothes are dried) **5** : a worker that operates a tumbler — **tum·bler·ful** \-ˌfu̇l\ *n*

tum·ble·weed \'təm-bəl-ˌwēd\ *n* : a plant (as Russian thistle or any of several amaranths or pigweeds) that breaks away from its roots in the autumn and is driven about by the wind as a light rolling mass

1**tum·bling** \'təm-b(ə-)liŋ\ *n* : the skill, practice, or sport of executing gymnastic feats (as somersaults and handsprings) without the use of apparatus

2**tumbling** *adj* : tipped or slanted out of the vertical — used esp. of a cattle brand

tumbling barrel *n* : a revolving cask in which objects or materials undergo a process (as drying) by being whirled about

tumbling verse *n* : an early modern English type of verse having four stresses but no prevailing type of foot and no regular number of syllables

tum·brel *or* **tum·bril** \'təm-brəl\ *n* [ME *tombrel,* fr. OF *tumberel* tipcart, fr. *tomber* to tumble, of Gmc origin; akin to OHG *tūmōn* to reel — more at TUMBLE] **1** : a farm tipcart **2** : a vehicle carrying condemned persons (as political prisoners during the French Revolution) to a place of execution

tu·me·fac·tion \ˌt(y)ü-mə-'fak-shən\ *n* [MF, fr. L *tumefactus,* pp. of *tumefacere* to cause to swell, fr. *tumēre* to swell + *facere* to make, do — more at THUMB, DO] **1** : an action or process of swelling or becoming tumorous **2** : SWELLING

tu·me·fac·tive \-'fak-tiv\ *adj* : producing swelling

tu·mes·cence \t(y)ü-'mes-ᵊn(t)s\ *n* : the quality or state of being tumescent; *esp* : readiness for sexual activity marked esp. by vascular congestion of the sex organs

tu·mes·cent \-ᵊnt\ *adj* [L *tumescent-, tumescens,* prp. of *tumescere* to swell up, fr. *tumēre* to swell] : somewhat swollen <~ tissue>

tu·mid \'t(y)ü-məd\ *adj* [L *tumidus,* fr. *tumēre*] **1** : marked by swelling : SWOLLEN, ENLARGED <a badly infected ~ leg> **2** : PROTUBERANT, BULGING <sails ~ in the breeze> **3** : BOMBASTIC, TURGID — **tu·mid·i·ty** \t(y)ü-'mid-ət-ē\ *n* — **tu·mid·ly** \'t(y)ü-məd-lē\ *adv*

tum·my \'təm-ē\ *n, pl* **tummies** [baby-talk for *stomach*] : STOMACH 1c

tu·mor \'t(y)ü-mər\ *n* [L *tumor,* fr. *tumēre*] **1** : a swollen or distended part **2** : an abnormal mass of tissue that is not inflammatory, arises without obvious cause from cells of preexistent tissue, and possesses no physiologic function — **tu·mor·al** \-mə-rəl\ *adj* — **tu·mor·like** \-mər-ˌlīk\ *adj*

tu·mor·i·gen·ic \ˌt(y)ü-mə-rə-'jen-ik\ *adj* : producing or tending to produce tumors; *also* : CARCINOGENIC — **tu·mor·i·ge·nic·i·ty** \-jə-'nis-ət-ē\ *n*

tu·mor·ous \'t(y)üm-(ə-)rəs\ *adj* : of, relating to, or resembling a tumor

tu·mour \'tyü-mər\ *chiefly Brit var of* TUMOR

tump \'təmp\ *n* [origin unknown] **1** *chiefly dial Eng* : MOUND, HUMMOCK **2** : a clump of vegetation

tump·line \'təm-ˌplīn\ *n* [*tump,* of Algonquian origin; akin to Abnaki *mádûmbi* pack strap] : a sling formed by a strap slung over the forehead or chest and used for carrying or helping to support a pack on the back or in hauling loads

tu·mult \'t(y)ü-ˌməlt\ *n* [ME *tumulte,* fr. MF, fr. L *tumultus;* akin to Skt *tumula* noisy, L *tumēre* to swell] **1 a** : disorderly agitation or milling about of a crowd usu. with uproar and confusion of voices : COMMOTION **b** : a turbulent uprising : RIOT **2** : HUBBUB, DIN **3 a** : violent agitation of mind or feelings **b** : a violent outburst

tu·mul·tu·ary \t(y)u̇-'məl-chə-ˌwer-ē\ *adj* : attended or marked by tumult, riot, lawlessness, confusion, or impetuosity

tu·mul·tu·ous \t(y)u̇-'məlch-(ə-)wəs, -'məl-chəs\ *adj* **1** : marked by tumult **2** : tending or disposed to cause or incite a tumult **3** : marked by violent or overwhelming turbulence or upheaval — **tu·mul·tu·ous·ly** *adv* — **tu·mul·tu·ous·ness** *n*

tu·mu·lus \'t(y)ü-myə-ləs, 'təm-yə-\ *n, pl* **-li** \-ˌlī, -ˌlē\ [L; akin to L *tumēre* to swell — more at THUMB] : an artificial hillock or mound (as over a grave); *esp* : an ancient grave : BARROW

tun \'tən\ *n* [ME *tunne,* fr. OE] **1** : a large cask esp. for wine **2** : any of various units of liquid capacity; *esp* : one equal to 252 gallons

1**tu·na** \'tü-nə\ *n* [Sp, fr. Taino] **1** : any of various flat-jointed prickly pears (genus *Opuntia*); *esp* : one (*O. tuna*) common in tropical America **2** : the edible fruit of a tuna

2**tu·na** \'t(y)ü-nə\ *n, pl* **tuna** *or* **tunas** [AmerSp, alter. of Sp *atún,* modif. of Ar *tūn,* fr. L *thunnus,* fr. Gk *thynnos*] **1** : any of numerous large vigorous scombroid food and sport fishes (as an albacore or a bonito) **2** : the flesh of a tuna esp. when canned for use as food — called also *tuna fish*

tun·able *also* **tune·able** \'t(y)ü-nə-bəl\ *adj* **1** *archaic* **a** : TUNEFUL **b** : sounding in tune : CONCORDANT **2** : capable of being tuned — **tun·abil·i·ty** \ˌt(y)ü-nə-'bil-ət-ē\ *n* — **tun·able·ness** \'t(y)ü-nə-bəl-nəs\ *n* — **tun·ably** \-blē\ *adv*

tun·dish \'tən-ˌdish\ *n* [ME, funnel for filling a tun] : a reservoir in the top part of a mold into which molten metal is poured

tun·dra \'tən-drə *also* 'tu̇n-\ *n* [Russ, of Finno-Ugric origin; akin to Lapp *tundar* hill] : a level or undulating treeless plain that is characteristic of arctic and subarctic regions, consists of black mucky soil with a permanently frozen subsoil, and supports a dense growth of often conspicuously flowering dwarf herbs

¹tune \'t(y)ün\ *n* [ME, alter. of *tone*] **1 a** *archaic* **:** quality of sound **:** TONE **b :** manner of utterance **:** INTONATION; *specif* **:** phonetic modulation **2 a :** a succession of pleasing musical tones **:** MELODY **b :** a dominant theme **3 :** correct musical pitch or consonance — used chiefly in the phrases *in tune* and *out of tune* **4 a** *archaic* **:** a frame of mind **:** MOOD **b :** AGREEMENT, HARMONY <in ~ with the times> **c :** general attitude **:** APPROACH <changed his ~ when the going got rough> **5 :** AMOUNT, EXTENT <custom-made to the ~ of $40 to $50 apiece — *Amer. Fabrics*>

²tune *vb* **tuned; tun·ing** *vi* **1 :** to become attuned **2 :** to adjust a radio or television receiver to respond to waves of a particular frequency ~ *vt* **1 :** to adjust in musical pitch or cause to be in tune <*tuned* his guitar> **2 a :** to bring into harmony **:** ATTUNE **b :** to adjust for precise functioning — often used with *up* <~ up an engine> **3 :** to adjust with respect to resonance at a particular frequency: as **a :** to adjust (a radio or television receiver) to respond to waves of a particular frequency — often used with *in* **b :** to establish radio contact with <~ in a directional beacon>

tuned–in \'t(y)ün-'din\ *adj* **:** TURNED-ON

tune·ful \'t(y)ün-fəl\ *adj* **:** MELODIOUS, MUSICAL — **tune·ful·ly** \-fə-lē\ *adv* — **tune·ful·ness** *n*

tune·less \'t(y)ün-ləs\ *adj* **1 :** not tuneful **2 :** not producing music — **tune·less·ly** *adv*

tune out *vi* **:** to turn off ~ *vt* **:** to cause to turn off

tun·er \'t(y)ü-nər\ *n* **1 :** one that tunes <a piano ~> **2 :** something used for tuning; *specif* **:** the part of a receiving set that converts radio signals into audio or video signals

tune·smith \'t(y)ün-ˌsmith\ *n* **:** a composer esp. of popular songs

tune–up \'t(y)ü-ˌnəp\ *n* **1 :** a general adjustment to insure operation at peak efficiency **2 :** a preliminary trial **:** WARM-UP

tung \'təŋ\ *n* **:** TUNG TREE

tung oil *n* [part trans. of Chin (Pek) *yu*[2] *t'ung*[2]] **:** a pale yellow pungent drying oil obtained from the seeds of tung trees and used chiefly in quick-drying varnishes and paints and as a waterproofing agent

tungst- *or* **tungsto-** *comb form* [ISV, fr. *tungsten*] **:** tungsten <*tungstate*>

tung·state \'təŋ-ˌstāt\ *n* **:** a salt or ester of a tungstic acid and esp. H_2WO_4

tung·sten \'təŋ-stən\ *n* [Sw, fr. *tung* heavy + *sten* stone] **:** a gray-white heavy high-melting ductile hard polyvalent metallic element that resembles chromium and molybdenum in many of its properties and is used esp. for electrical purposes and in hardening alloys (as steel) — called also *wolfram;* see ELEMENT table

tung·stic \-stik\ *adj* [ISV] **:** of, relating to, or containing tungsten esp. with a valence of six

tungstic acid *n* **:** a yellow crystalline powder WO_3 that is the trioxide of tungsten; *also* **:** an acid (as H_2WO_4) derived from this

tung·stite \'təŋ-ˌstīt\ *n* **:** a mineral $WO_3.H_2O$(?) consisting of a hydrous tungsten trioxide and occurring in yellow or yellowish green pulverulent masses

tung tree *n* [Chin (Pek) *t'ung*[2]] **:** any of several trees (genus *Aleurites*) of the spurge family whose seeds yield a poisonous fixed drying oil; *esp* **:** a Chinese tree (*A. fordii*) widely grown in warm regions

Tun·gus \tủŋ-'güz, tən-\ *n, pl* **Tungus** *or* **Tun·gus·es** [Russ] **1 :** a member of a Mongoloid people widely spread over eastern Siberia **2 :** the Tungusic languages of the Tungus peoples

Tun·gu·sic \-'gü-zik\ *n* **:** a subfamily of Altaic languages spoken in Manchuria and northward — **Tungusic** *adj*

tu·nic \'t(y)ü-nik\ *n* [L *tunica,* of Sem origin; akin to Heb *kuttōneth* coat] **1 a :** a simple slip-on garment made with or without sleeves and usu. knee-length or longer, belted at the waist, and worn as an under or outer garment by men and women of ancient Greece and Rome **b :** SURCOAT **2 :** an enclosing or covering membrane or tissue <the ~ of a seed> **3 :** a long usu. plain close-fitting jacket with high collar worn esp. as part of a uniform **4 :** TUNICLE **5 a :** a short overskirt **b :** a hip-length or longer blouse or jacket

tu·ni·ca \'t(y)ü-ni-kə\ *n, pl* **tu·ni·cae** \-nə-ˌkē, -ˌkī, -ˌsē\ [L, tunic, membrane] **:** an enveloping membrane or layer of body tissue

¹tu·ni·cate \'t(y)ü-ni-kət, -nə-ˌkāt\ *also* **tu·ni·cat·ed** \-nə-ˌkāt-əd\ *adj* [L *tunicatus,* fr. *tunica*] **1 a :** having or covered with a tunic or tunica **b :** having, arranged in, or made up of concentric layers <a ~ bulb> **2 :** of or relating to the tunicates

²tu·ni·cate \-ni-kət, -nə-ˌkāt\ *n* [NL *Tunicata,* group name, fr. neut. pl. of L *tunicatus* tunicate] **:** any of a subphylum (Urochorda syn. Tunicata) of specialized or degenerate marine chordate animals that have clefts in the vascular walls of the pharyngeal gills, a thick secreted covering layer, a greatly reduced nervous system, and a heart able to reverse the direction of blood flow by changes of its contractions

tu·ni·cle \'t(y)ü-ni-kəl\ *n* [ME, fr. L *tunicula,* dim. of *tunica*] **:** a short vestment worn by a subdeacon over the alb during mass and by a bishop under the dalmatic at pontifical ceremonies — see VESTMENT illustration

tuning fork *n* **:** a 2-pronged metal implement that gives a fixed tone when struck and is useful for tuning musical instruments and ascertaining standard pitch

tuning fork

tuning pipe *n* **:** PITCH PIPE; *specif* **:** one of a set of pitch pipes used esp. for tuning stringed musical instruments

¹tun·nel \'tən-ᵊl\ *n* [ME *tonel* tube-shaped net, fr. MF, tun, fr. OF, fr. *tonne* tun, fr. ML *tunna,* of Celt origin; akin to MIr *tonn* skin, hide; akin to L *tondēre* to shear — more at TOME] **1 :** a hollow conduit or recess **:** TUBE, WELL **2 a :** a covered passageway; *specif* **:** a horizontal passageway through or under an obstruction **b :** a subterranean gallery (as in a mine) **c :** BURROW — **tun·nel·like** \-ᵊl-ˌ(l)īk\ *adj*

²tunnel *vb* **tun·neled** *or* **tun·nelled; tun·nel·ing** *or* **tun·nel·ling** \'tən-liŋ, -ᵊl-iŋ\ *vt* **:** to make a tunnel or similar opening through or under ~ *vi* **1 :** to make or use a tunnel **2** *physics* **:** to pass through a potential barrier <electrons ~*ing* through an insulator between semiconductors> — **tun·nel·er** \'tən-lər, -ᵊl-ər\ *n*

tunnel vision *n* **1 :** a field of vision of 70 percent or less from the straight-ahead position that results in elimination of the peripheral field **2 :** extreme narrowness of viewpoint **:** NARROWMINDEDNESS

tun·ny \'tən-ē\ *n, pl* **tunnies** *also* **tunny** [modif. of MF *thon* or OIt *tonno;* both fr. OProv *ton,* fr. L *thunnus,* fr. Gk *thynnos*] **:** TUNA; *esp* **:** BLUEFIN

¹tup \'təp\ *n* [ME *tupe*] **1** *chiefly Brit* **:** RAM 1a **2 :** a heavy metal body (as the weight of a pendulum)

²tup *vt* **tupped; tup·ping** *chiefly Brit* **:** to copulate with (a ewe)

tu·pe·lo \'t(y)ü-pə-ˌlō\ *n, pl* **-los** [Creek *ito opilwa* swamp tree] **1 :** any of a genus (*Nyssa*) of mostly No. American trees that have simple alternate leaves, small greenish dioecious stalked flowers, and a rounded drupe; *esp* **:** BLACK GUM **2 :** the pale soft easily worked wood of a tupelo

Tu·pi \tü-'pē, 'tü-(ˌ)\ *n, pl* **Tupi** *or* **Tupis 1 :** a member of a group of Tupi-Guaranian peoples of Brazil living esp. in the Amazon valley **2 :** the language of the Tupi people

Tu·pi·an \tü-'pē-ən, 'tü-(ˌ)\ *adj* **:** of, relating to, or constituting the Tupi or other Tupi-Guaranian peoples or their languages

Tu·pi–Gua·ra·ni \tü-ˌpē-ˌgwär-ə-'nē, 'tü-(ˌ)pē-\ *n* **1 :** a member of a So. American people spread over an area from eastern Brazil to the Peruvian Andes and from the Guianas to Uruguay **2 :** TUPI-GUARANIAN

Tupi–Gua·ra·ni·an \-'nē-ən\ *n* **:** a language stock widely distributed in tropical So. America

-tu·ple \ˌtəp-əl, ˌtüp-\ *n comb form* [quin*tuple,* sex*tuple*] **:** set of (so many) elements — usu. used of sets with ordered elements <the ordered 2-*tuple* (*a, b*)>

tup·pence *var of* TWOPENCE

tuque \'t(y)ük\ *n* [CanF, fr. F *toque* — more at TOQUE] **:** a warm knitted usu. pointed stocking cap

tu quo·que \'t(y)ü-'k(w)ō-kwē\ *n* [L, you too] **:** a retort charging an adversary with being or doing what he criticizes in others

Tu·ra·ni·an \t(y)ủ-'rā-nē-ən, -'rän-ē-\ *n* [Per *Tūrān* Turkestan, the region north of the Amu Darya] **1 :** a member of any of the peoples of Ural-Altaic stock **2 :** the total body of various language families of Asia — **Turanian** *adj*

tur·ban \'tər-bən\ *n* [MF *turbant,* fr. It *turbante,* fr. Turk *tülbend,* fr. Per *dulband*] **1 :** a headdress worn chiefly in countries of the eastern Mediterranean and southern Asia esp. by Muslims and made of a cap around which is wound a long cloth **2 :** a headdress resembling a Muslim turban; *specif* **:** a woman's close-fitting hat without a brim — **tur·baned** *or* **tur·banned** \-bənd\ *adj*

turban 1

tur·bel·lar·i·an \ˌtər-bə-'ler-ē-ən, -'lar-\ *n* [deriv. of L *turbellae* (pl.) bustle, stir, dim. of *turba* confusion, crowd; fr. the tiny eddies created in water by the cilia] **:** any of a class (Turbellaria) of mostly aquatic and free-living flatworms; *esp* **:** PLANARIAN — **turbellarian** *adj*

tur·bid \'tər-bəd\ *adj* [L *turbidus* confused, turbid, fr. *turba* confusion, crowd; akin to OHG *dweran* to stir, L *turbare* to throw into disorder, disturb, Gk *tyrbē* confusion] **1 a :** thick or opaque with or as if with roiled sediment <a ~ stream> **b :** heavy with smoke or mist **2 a :** deficient in clarity or purity **:** FOUL, MUDDY <~ depths of degradation and misery —C. I. Glicksberg> **b :** characterized by or producing obscurity (as of mind or emotions) <an emotionally ~ response> — **tur·bid·i·ty** \ˌtər-'bid-ət-ē\ *n* — **tur·bid·ly** \'tər-bəd-lē\ *adv* — **tur·bid·ness** *n*

syn TURBID, MUDDY, ROILY *shared meaning element* **:** not clear or translucent but clouded with or as if with sediment. TURBID describes something (as a liquid, an idea, or an affair) which is so stirred up and disturbed as to become opaque or obscured or confused <the *turbid* waters of a river in flood> <the *turbid* ebb and flow of human misery —Matthew Arnold> <*turbid* feelings, arising from ideas not fully mastered, had to clarify . . . themselves —H. O. Taylor> MUDDY describes something turbid as a result of being mixed with or as if with mud <*muddy* coffee> or something that suggests this state (as in color or in dull heavy quality) <a *muddy* complexion> <a *muddy* thinker, but a superb artist —J. D. Adams> ROILY describes something that is both turbid and agitated <where the *roily* Monongahela meets the clear Allegheny —J. M. Weed> <human rubble . . . washed up by the *roily* wake of the war —John Woodburn> ***ant*** clear, limpid

tur·bi·dim·e·ter \ˌtər-bə-'dim-ət-ər\ *n* [ISV *turbidi*ty + *-meter*] **1 :** an instrument for measuring and comparing the turbidity of liquids by viewing light through them and determining how much light is cut off **2 :** NEPHELOMETER — **tur·bi·di·met·ric** \ˌtər-bəd-ə-'me-trik, ˌtər-ˌbid-ə-\ *adj* — **tur·bi·di·met·ri·cal·ly** \-tri-k(ə-)lē\ *adv* — **tur·bi·dim·e·try** \ˌtər-bə-'dim-ə-trē\ *n*

tur·bi·dite \'tər-bə-ˌdīt\ *n* [*turbidi*ty current (a current flowing down a slope and spreading out on the ocean floor) + *-ite*] **:** a sedimentary deposit consisting of material that has moved down the steep slope at the end of a continental shelf; *also* **:** a rock formed from this deposit

¹tur·bi·nal \'tər-bən-ᵊl\ *adj* [L *turbin-, turbo* top, whirlwind, whirl] **:** of, relating to, or being one of usu. several thin plicated membrane-covered bony or cartilaginous plates on the walls of the nasal chambers

²**turbinal** *n* : a turbinal bone or cartilage

¹**tur·bi·nate** \'tər-bə-nət, -ˌnāt\ *also* **tur·bi·nat·ed** \-ˌnāt-əd\ *adj* [L *turbinatus,* fr. *turbin-, turbo*] **1** : shaped like a top or an inverted cone <~ seed capsule> **2** : TURBINAL

²**turbinate** *n* : a turbinal bone, process, or cartilage

tur·bine \'tər-bən, -ˌbīn\ *n* [F, fr. L *turbin-, turbo* top, whirlwind, whirl; akin to L *turbare* to disturb] : a rotary engine actuated by the reaction or impulse or both of a current of fluid (as water or steam) subject to pressure and usu. made with a series of curved vanes on a central rotating spindle

tur·bit \'tər-bət\ *n* [origin unknown] : a pigeon of a fancy breed having a short crested head, short beak, frilled breast, and mostly white plumage

tur·bo \'tər-(ˌ)bō\ *n, pl* **turbos** [*turbo-*] **1** : TURBINE **2** [by shortening] : TURBOSUPERCHARGER

turbo- *comb form* [*turbine*] **1** : coupled directly to a driving turbine <*turbo*fan> <*turbo*generator> **2** : consisting of or incorporating a turbine <*turbo*jet engine> <*turbo*machine>

tur·bo·car \'tər-bō-ˌkär\ *n* : an automotive vehicle propelled by a gas turbine

tur·bo·charge \-ˌchärj\ *vt* : to supercharge (an engine) by means of a turbine-driver compressor

tur·bo·charg·er \-ˌchär-jər\ *n* : a centrifugal blower driven by exhaust gas turbines and used to supercharge an engine

tur·bo·elec·tric \'tər-bō-i-'lek-trik\ *adj* : involving or depending as a power source on electricity produced by turbine generators <ships with ~ drive>

tur·bo·fan \-ˌfan\ *n* **1** : a fan that is directly connected to and driven by a turbine and is used to supply air for cooling, ventilation, or combustion **2** : a jet engine having a turbofan

tur·bo·jet \-ˌjet\ *n* **1** : an airplane powered by turbojet engines **2** : TURBOJET ENGINE

turbojet engine *n* : an airplane propulsion system in which the power developed by a turbine is used to drive a compressor that supplies air to a burner and hot gases from the burner pass through the turbine and thence to a rearward-directed thrust-producing exhaust nozzle

tur·bo·prop \'tər-bō-ˌpräp\ *n* **1** : TURBO-PROPELLER ENGINE **2** : an airplane powered by turbo-propeller engines

tur·bo–pro·pel·ler engine \ˌtər-bō-prə-'pel-ər-\ *n* : a jet engine having a turbine-driven propeller and designed to produce thrust principally by means of a propeller although additional thrust is usu. obtained from the hot exhaust gases which issue in a jet

tur·bo·prop–jet engine \-'präp-ˌjet-\ *n* : TURBO-PROPELLER ENGINE

tur·bo·ram·jet engine \-'ram-ˌjet-\ *n* : a jet engine consisting essentially of a turbojet engine with provisions for burning additional fuel in the tail pipe or the portion of the engine to the rear of the turbine

tur·bo·shaft \'tər-bō-ˌshaft\ *n* : a gas turbine engine that is similar in operation to a turboprop engine but instead of being used to power a propeller is used through a transmission system for powering other devices (as helicopter rotors and pumps)

tur·bo·su·per·charged \ˌtər-bō-'sü-pər-ˌchärjd\ *adj* : equipped with a turbosupercharger

tur·bo·su·per·charg·er \-ˌchär-jər\ *n* : a turbine compressor driven by hot exhaust gases of an airplane engine for feeding rarefied air at high altitudes into the carburetor of the engine at sea-level pressure so as to increase engine power

tur·bot \'tər-bət\ *n, pl* **turbot** *also* **turbots** [ME, fr. OF *tourbot*] **1** : a large European flatfish (*Psetta maxima*) that is a popular food fish and has a brownish upper surface marked with scattered tubercles and a white undersurface **2** : any of various flatfishes resembling the turbot

tur·bu·lence \'tər-byə-lən(t)s\ *n* : the quality or state of being turbulent: as **a** : wild commotion **b** : irregular atmospheric motion esp. when characterized by up and down currents **c** : departure in a fluid from a smooth flow

tur·bu·len·cy \-lən-sē\ *n, pl* **-cies** *archaic* : TURBULENCE

tur·bu·lent \-lənt\ *adj* [L *turbulentus,* fr. *turba* confusion, crowd] **1** : causing unrest, violence, or disturbance **2 a** : characterized by agitation or tumult : TEMPESTUOUS **b** : exhibiting physical turbulence — **tur·bu·lent·ly** *adv*

turbulent flow *n* : a fluid flow in which the velocity at a given point varies erratically in magnitude and direction — compare LAMINAR FLOW

Tur·co- *or* **Tur·ko-** *comb form* [*Turco-* fr. ML *Turcus* Turk; *Turko-* fr. *Turk*] **1** : Turkic : Turkish : Turk <*Turco*phil> **2** \'tər-(ˌ)kō\ : Turkish and <*Turco*-Greek>

turd \'tərd\ *n* [ME *tord, turd,* fr. OE *tord;* akin to MD *tort* dung, OE *teran* to tear — more at TEAR] : a piece of dung — sometimes considered vulgar

tu·reen \tə-'rēn, tyü-\ *n* [F *terrine,* fr. MF, fr. fem. of *terrin* of earth, fr. (assumed) VL *terrinus,* fr. L *terra* earth — more at TERRACE] **1** : a deep and usu. covered bowl from which foods (as soup) are served **2** : CASSEROLE 2

¹**turf** \'tərf\ *n, pl* **turfs** \'tərfs\ *or* **turves** \'tərvz\ [ME, fr. OE; akin to OHG *zurba* turf, Skt *darbha* tuft of grass] **1 a** : the upper stratum of soil bound by grass and plant roots into a thick mat; *also* : a piece of this : SOD **b** : an artificial substitute for this (as on a playing field) **2 a** : PEAT **b** : a piece of peat dried for fuel **3 a** : a track or course for horse racing **b** : the sport or business of horse racing **4 a** : territory considered by a teenage gang to be under its control **b** : TERRITORY 2a <looking for cheap thrills on strange ~ —*Playboy*> — **turfy** \'tər-fē\ *adj*

²**turf** *vt* **1** : to cover with turf **2** *chiefly Brit* : to eject forcefully : KICK — usu. used with *out*

turf accountant *n, Brit* : BOOKMAKER 2

turf·man \'tərf-mən\ *n* : a devotee of horse racing; *esp* : one who owns and races horses

turf·ski \-ˌskē\ *n* : a short ski with rollers on the bottom that can be used to ski down a grassy slope — **turf·ski·ing** *n*

tur·ges·cence \ˌtər-'jes-ᵊn(t)s\ *n* : TURGIDITY

tur·ges·cent \-ᵊnt\ *adj* [L *turgescent-, turgescens,* prp. of *turgescere* to swell, inchoative of *turgēre* to be swollen] : becoming turgid, distended, or inflated : SWELLING

tur·gid \'tər-jəd\ *adj* [L *turgidus,* fr. *turgēre* to be swollen] **1** : being in a state of distension : SWOLLEN, TUMID <~ limbs>; *esp* : exhibiting turgor **2** : excessively embellished in style or language : BOMBASTIC, POMPOUS — **tur·gid·i·ty** \ˌtər-'jid-ət-ē\ *n* — **tur·gid·ly** \'tər-jəd-lē\ *adv* — **tur·gid·ness** *n*

tur·gor \'tər-gər, -ˌgó(ə)r\ *n* [LL, turgidity, swelling, fr. L *turgēre*] : the normal state of turgidity and tension in living cells; *esp* : the distension of the protoplasmic layer and wall of a plant cell by the fluid contents

Tu·ring machine \'t(y)u̇(ə)r-iŋ-\ *n* [A. M. *Turing* †1954 E mathematician] : a hypothetical computing machine that has an unlimited amount of information storage and is not subject to malfunctioning

¹**Turk** \'tərk\ *n* [ME, fr. MF or Turk; MF *Turc,* fr. ML or Turk; ML *Turcus,* fr. Turk *Türk*] **1** : a member of any of numerous Asian peoples speaking Turkic languages who live in the region ranging from the Adriatic to the Okhotsk **2** : a native or inhabitant of Turkey **3** *archaic* : one who is cruel or tyrannical **4** : MUSLIM; *specif* : a Muslim subject of the Turkish sultan **5** : a Turkish horse; *specif* : a Turkish strain of Arab and crossbred horses

²**Turk** *abbr* Turkey; Turkish

tur·key \'tər-kē\ *n, pl* **turkeys** [*Turkey,* country in western Asia and southeastern Europe; fr. confusion with the guinea fowl, supposed to be imported from Turkish territory] **1** : a large American gallinaceous bird (*Meleagris gallopavo*) that is of wide range in No. America and is domesticated in most parts of the world **2** : FAILURE, FLOP; *esp* : a theatrical production that has failed **3** : three successive strikes in bowling

turkey buzzard *n* : an American vulture (*Cathartes aura*) common in So. and Central America and in the southern U.S.

tur·key–cock \'tər-kē-ˌkäk\ *n* **1** : a male turkey **2** : a strutting pompous person

tur·key–gob·bler \ˌtər-kē-'gäb-lər\ *n* : TURKEY-COCK 1

Tur·key red \ˌtər-kē-\ *n* [*Turkey*] **1 a** : a brilliant durable red produced on cotton by means of alizarin in connection with an aluminum mordant and fatty matter **b** : ALIZARIN 1 **2** : red iron oxide used as a pigment

turkey shoot \'tər-kē-\ *n* : a marksmanship contest using a moving target with a turkey offered as a prize

turkey trot \'tər-kē-\ *n* [*turkey*] : a ragtime dance danced with the feet well apart and with a characteristic rise on the ball of the foot followed by a drop upon the heel

Tur·ki \'tər-(ˌ)kē, 'tu̇(ə)r-\ *adj* [Per *turkī,* fr. *Turk* Turk, fr. Turk *Türk*] **1** : of or relating to the peoples of Turkic speech **2** : of or relating to any central Asian Turkic language particularly of the eastern group — **Turki** *n*

Turk·ic \'tər-kik\ *adj* **1 a** : of, relating to, or constituting a subfamily of Altaic languages including Turkish **b** : of or relating to the peoples speaking Turkic **2** : TURKISH 1 — **Turkic** *n*

¹**Turk·ish** \'tər-kish\ *adj* **1** : of, relating to, or characteristic of Turkey, the Turks, or Turkish **2** : TURKIC 1a

²**Turkish** *n* : the Turkic language of the Republic of Turkey

Turkish bath *n* : a bath in which the bather passes through a series of steam rooms of increasing temperature and then receives a rubdown, massage, and cold shower

Turkish coffee *n* : a sweetened decoction of pulverized coffee

Turkish delight *n* : a jellylike or gummy confection usu. cut in cubes and dusted with sugar — called also *Turkish paste*

Turkish tobacco *n* : a very aromatic tobacco of small leaf size grown chiefly in Turkey and Greece and used esp. in cigarettes

Turkish towel *n* : a towel made of cotton terry cloth

Turk·ism \'tər-ˌkiz-əm\ *n* : the customs, beliefs, institutions, and principles of the Turks

Tur·ko·man *or* **Tur·co·man** \'tər-kə-mən\ *n, pl* **Turkomans** *or* **Turcomans** [ML *Turcomannus,* fr. Per *Turkmān,* fr. *turkmān* resembling a Turk, fr. *Turk*] : a member of a group of peoples of East Turkic stock living chiefly in the Turkmen, Uzbek, and Kazakh republics of the U.S.S.R.

Turk's head *n* : a turban-shaped knot worked on a rope with a piece of small line — see KNOT illustration

tur·mer·ic \'tər-mə-rik *also* 't(y)ü-mə-\ *n* [modif. of MF *terre merite* saffron, fr. ML *terra merita,* lit., deserving or deserved earth] **1 a** : an East Indian perennial herb (*Curcuma longa*) with a large aromatic deep yellow rhizome **b** : the cleaned boiled dried and usu. pulverized rhizome of the turmeric plant used as a coloring agent, a condiment, or a stimulant **c** : a yellow to reddish brown dyestuff obtained from turmeric **2** : any of several plants that are closely related to turmeric and yield a similar product

tur·moil \'tər-ˌmói(ə)l\ *n* [origin unknown] : an utterly confused or extremely agitated state or condition

¹**turn** \'tərn\ *vb* [ME *turnen;* partly fr. OE *tyrnan* & *turnian* to turn, fr. ML *tornare,* fr. L, to turn on a lathe, fr. *tornus* lathe, fr. Gk *tornos;* partly fr. OF *torner, tourner* to turn, fr. ML *tornare;* akin to L *terere* to rub — more at THROW] *vt* **1 a** : to cause to move around an axis or a center : make rotate or revolve <~ a wheel> <~ a crank> **b** (1) : to cause to move around so as to effect a desired end (as of locking, opening, or shutting) <~ a key> (2) : to affect or alter the functioning of (as a mechanical device) by such movement <~*ed* the oven to a higher temperature> **c** : to execute or perform by rotating or revolving <~ handsprings> **d** : to twist out of line or shape : WRENCH <had ~*ed* his ankle> **2 a** (1) : to cause to change position by moving through an arc of a circle <~*ed* his chair to the fire> (2) : to cause to move around a center so as to show another side of <~ the page> (3) : to cause (as a scale) to move so as to register weight (4) : to cause to move or stir in any way <a fate she did not ~ a finger to escape —V. L. Parrington> **b** : to revolve mentally : think over : PONDER **3 a** : to reverse the sides or surfaces of : INVERT <~ pancakes> (1) : to dig or plow so as to bring the lower soil to the surface (2) : to make (as a garment) over by reversing the material and

resewing <~ a collar> (3) : to invert feet up and face down (as a character, rule, or slug) in setting type **b** : to reverse or upset the order or disposition of <everything *~ed* topsy-turvy> **c** : to disturb or upset the mental balance of : DERANGE, UNSETTLE <a mind *~ed* by grief> **d** : to set in another esp. contrary direction **4 a** : to bend or change the course of : DIVERT **b** : to cause to retreat <used fire hoses to ~ the mob> **c** : to alter the drift, tendency, or expected result of **d** : to bend a course around or about : ROUND <*~ed* the corner at full speed> **e** : to reach or go beyond (as an amount, age, or time) <he just *~ed* 21> **5 a** (1) : to direct or point (as the face) in a specified way or direction (2) : to present by a change in direction or position <*~ing* his back to his guests> **b** : to bring to bear (as by aiming, pointing, or focusing) : TRAIN <*~ed* his light into the dark doorway> **c** : to direct (as the attention or mind) toward or away from something **d** : to induce or influence (a person) to change his way of life **e** : to direct the employment of : APPLY, DEVOTE <*~ed* his skills to the service of mankind> **f** (1) : to cause to rebound or recoil <*~s* their argument against them> (2) : to make antagonistic : PREJUDICE <~ a child against its mother> **g** (1) : to cause to go in a particular direction <*~ed* his steps homeward> (2) : DRIVE, SEND <~ cows to pasture> <officers were *~ed* adrift by the mutineers> <*~ing* hunters off his land> (3) : to convey or direct into or out of a receptacle by inverting **6 a** (1) : to make acid or sour : CURDLE, FERMENT (2) : to change the color of (as foliage) **b** (1) : CONVERT, TRANSFORM <~ defeat into victory> (2) : TRANSLATE, PARAPHRASE **c** : to cause to become of a specified nature or appearance <*~ed* him into a fiend> <illness *~ed* his hair white> **d** : to exchange for something else <~ coins into paper money> **7 a** : to shape esp. in a rounded form by applying a cutting tool while revolving in a lathe **b** : to give a rounded form to by any means <~ the heel of a sock> **c** : to shape or mold artistically, gracefully, or neatly <well *~ed* ankles> <a knack for *~ing* a phrase> **8** : to make a fold, bend, or curve in: **a** : to form by bending <~ a lead pipe> **b** : to cause (the edge of a blade) to bend back or over : BLUNT, DULL **9 a** : to keep (as money or goods) moving; *specif* : to dispose of (a stock) to make room for another **b** : to gain in the course of business <*~ing* a quick profit> ~ *vi* **1 a** : to move around on an axis or through an arc of a circle : ROTATE **b** : to become giddy or dizzy : REEL <heights always made his head ~> **c** (1) : HINGE <argument *~s* upon a point not of ethics but logic —Gail Kennedy> (2) : to have a center (as of interest) in something specified **2 a** : to direct one's course **b** (1) : to reverse a course or direction (2) : to have a reactive usu. adverse effect : RECOIL **c** : to take a different course or direction <*~ed* toward home> <the main road *~s* sharply to the right> **3 a** : to change position so as to face another way **b** : to face toward or away from someone or something **c** : to change one's attitude or reverse one's course of action to one of opposition or hostility <felt the world had *~ed* against him> <*~ed* upon them with ferocity> **d** : to make a sudden violent assault esp. without evident cause <dogs *~ing* on their owners> **4 a** : to direct one's attention or thoughts to or away from someone or something **b** (1) : to change one's religion (2) : to go over to another side or party : DEFECT **c** : to have recourse : REFER, RESORT <*~ed* to a friend for help> <*~ed* to his notes for the exact figures> **d** : to direct one's efforts or interests : devote or apply oneself <*~ed* to the study of the law> **5 a** : to become changed, altered, or transformed: as (1) *archaic* : to become different (2) : to change color <the leaves have *~ed*> (3) : to become sour, rancid, or tainted <the milk had *~ed*> (4) : to be variable or inconstant (5) : to become mentally unbalanced : become deranged **b** (1) : to pass from one state to another : CHANGE <water had *~ed* to ice> (2) : GROW <his hair had *~ed* gray> <the weather *~ed* bad> (3) : to become someone or something specified by change from another state : change into <~ traitor> <doctors *~ed* authors> **6** : to become curved or bent (as from pressure); *esp* : to become blunted by bending <edge of the knife had *~ed*> **7** : to operate a lathe **8** *of merchandise* : to be stocked and disposed of : change hands ***syn*** see CURVE — **turn·able** \ˈtər-nə-bəl\ *adj* — **turn a blind eye** : to refuse to see : be oblivious <might *turn a blind eye* to the use of violence —Arthur Krock> — **turn a deaf ear** : to refuse to listen — **turn a hair** : to become upset or frightened <did not *turn a hair* when told of the savage murder —*Times Lit. Supp.*> — **turn color 1** : to become of a different color **2a** : BLUSH, FLUSH **b** : to grow pale — **turn loose 1a** : to set free <*turned loose* the captured animal> **b** : to free from all restraints <*turned* them *loose* with a pile of theme paper to write whatever they liked —Elizabeth P. Schafer> **2** : to fire off : DISCHARGE **3** : to open fire — **turn one's back on 1** : REJECT, DENY <would be *turning one's back on* history —Pius Walsh> **2** : FORSAKE <*turned his back on* his family —*Playboy*> — **turn one's hand** *or* **turn a hand** : to set to work : apply oneself — **turn one's head** : to cause to become infatuated or to harbor extravagant notions of pride or conceit <success had not *turned his head*> — **turn one's stomach 1** : to disgust completely <that sort of conduct *turns my stomach*> **2** : SICKEN, NAUSEATE <the foul smell *turned his stomach*> — **turn tail** : to run away : FLEE — **turn the other cheek** : to respond to injury or unkindness with patience : forgo retaliation — **turn the scale** : to tip the scales — **turn the tables** : to bring about a reversal of the relative conditions or fortunes of two contending parties — **turn the trick** : to bring about the desired result or effect — **turn turtle** : CAPSIZE, OVERTURN

²turn *n* [ME; partly fr. OF *tourn, tour* lathe, circuit, turn (partly fr. L *tornus* lathe; partly fr. OF *torner, tourner* to turn); partly fr. ME *turnen* to turn] **1 a** : the action or an act of turning about a center or axis : REVOLUTION, ROTATION **b** : any of various rotating or pivoting movements in dancing **2 a** : the action or an act of giving or taking a different direction : change of course or posture <illegal left ~>: as (1) : a drill maneuver in which troops in mass formation change direction without preserving alignment (2) : any of various shifts of direction in skiing (3) : an interruption of a curve in figure skating **b** : DEFLECTION, DEVIATION **c** : the action or an act of turning so as to face in the opposite direction : reversal of posture or course <an about ~> <~ of the tide> **d** : a change effected by turning over to another side <~ of the cards> **e** : a place at which something turns, turns off, or turns back : BEND, CURVE **3** : a short trip out and back or round about <took a ~ through the park> **4** : an act or deed affecting another esp. when incidental or unexpected <one good ~ deserves another> **5 a** : a period of action or activity : GO, SPELL; *specif* : a bout of wrestling **b** : a place, time, or opportunity accorded an individual or unit of a series in simple succession or in a scheduled order <waiting his ~ in a doctor's office> **c** : a period or tour of duty : SHIFT **d** : a short act (as for a variety show) **e** (1) : an event in any gambling game after which bets are settled (2) : the order of the last three cards in faro — used in the phrase *call the turn* **6** : something that revolves around a center: as **a** (1) : LATHE (2) : a catch or latch for a cupboard or cabinet door operated by turning a handle **b** : a musical ornament consisting of a group of four or more notes that wind about the principal note by including the notes next above and next below **7** : a special purpose or requirement — used chiefly in the phrase *serve one's turn* **8 a** : an act of changing : ALTERATION, MODIFICATION <a nasty ~ in the weather> **b** : a change in tendency, trend, or drift <hoped for a ~ in his luck> <a ~ for the better> **c** : the beginning of a new period of time <the ~ of the century> **9 a** : distinctive quality or character **b** (1) : a skillful fashioning of language or arrangement of words (2) : a particular form of expression or peculiarity of phrasing **c** : the shape or mold in which something is fashioned : CAST **10 a** : the state or manner of being coiled or twisted **b** : a single round (as of rope passed about an object or of wire wound on a core) **11** : natural or special ability or aptitude : BENT, INCLINATION <a ~ for logic> <an optimistic ~ of mind> **12** : a special twist, construction, or interpretation <gave the old yarn a new ~> **13 a** : a disordering spell or attack (as of illness, faintness, or dizziness) **b** : a nervous start or shock **14 a** : a complete transaction involving a purchase and sale of securities; *also* : a profit from such a transaction **b** : TURNOVER 7b **15** : something turned or to be turned: as **a** : a character or slug inverted in setting type **b** : a piece of type placed bottom up — **at every turn** : on every occasion : CONSTANTLY, CONTINUALLY — **by turns** : one after another in regular succession : ALTERNATELY, SUCCESSIVELY — **in turn** : in due order of succession : SUCCESSIVELY, ALTERNATELY — **on the turn** : at the point of turning <tide is *on the turn*> — **out of turn 1** : not in due order of succession <play *out of turn*> **2** : at a wrong time or place : IMPRUDENTLY, UNWISELY <talking *out of turn*> — **to a turn** : to perfection

turn 6b: *1* written, *2* played

turn·about \ˈtər-nə-ˌbau̇t\ *n* **1 a** : a change or reversal of direction, trend, policy, or role **b** : a changing from one allegiance to another **c** : TURNCOAT, RENEGADE **d** : an act or instance of retaliating <~ is fair play> **2** : MERRY-GO-ROUND

turn·around \-ˌrau̇nd\ *n* **1** : a space permitting the turning around of a vehicle **2** : TURNABOUT 1a, 1b **3** : the time required for a round trip (as of a ship) including loading, unloading, and maintenance

turn away *vt* **1** : DEFLECT, AVERT **2 a** : to send away : REJECT, DISMISS **b** : REPEL **c** : to refuse admittance or acceptance to ~ *vi* : to start to go away : DEPART

turn back *vi* **1 a** : to stop going forward **b** : to go in the reverse direction **2** : to refer to an earlier time or place ~ *vt* **1** : to drive back or away **2** : to stop the advance of **3** : to fold back — **turn back the clock** : to revert to a condition existing in the past

turn·buck·le \ˈtərn-ˌbək-əl\ *n* : a device that consists of a link with screw threads at both ends or a screw thread at one end and a swivel at the other, that is turned to bring the ends closer together, and that is used for tightening a rod or stay

turn·coat \-ˌkōt\ *n* : one who switches to an opposing side or party; *specif* : TRAITOR

¹turn·down \ˌtərn-ˌdau̇n\ *adj* : capable of being turned down; *esp* : worn turned down <~ collar>

²turn·down \ˈtərn-ˌdau̇n\ *n* **1** : REJECTION **2** : something turned down **3** : DOWNTURN

turn down \ˌtərn-ˈdau̇n, ˈtərn-\ *vi* : to be capable of being folded or doubled down <collar *turns down*> ~ *vt* **1** : to fold or double down **2** : to turn (a card) face downward **3** : to reduce the height or intensity of by turning a control <*turn down* the radio> **4** : to decline to accept : REJECT <*turned down* the offer>

turned–on \ˈtərn-ˈdȯn, -ˈdän\ *adj* : keenly aware of and responsive to what is new and smart

¹turn·er \ˈtər-nər\ *n* : one that turns or is used for turning <a pancake ~>; *esp* : one who forms articles with a lathe

²tur·ner \ˈtər-nər, ˈtu̇(ə)r-\ *n* [G, fr. *turnen* to perform gymnastic exercises, fr. OHG *turnēn* to turn, fr. ML *tornare* — more at TURN] : a member of a turnverein : GYMNAST

Tur·ner's syndrome \ˈtər-nərz-\ *n* [Henry Hubert *Turner b*1892 Am physician] : a genetically determined condition that is associated with the presence of one X chromosome and no Y chromosome and that is characterized by an outwardly female phenotype with incomplete and infertile gonads

turn·ery \'tər-nə-rē\ *n, pl* **-er·ies :** the work, products, or shop of a turner

turn–in \'tər-ˌnin\ *n* **:** something that turns in or is turned in

turn in \ˌtər-'nin, 'tər-\ *vt* **1 :** to deliver up **:** hand over <*turned in* his badge and quit> **2 a :** to inform on **:** BETRAY **b :** to deliver to an authority <urged the wanted man to *turn* himself *in*> **3 :** to acquit oneself of **:** put on **:** PRODUCE <*turned in* a good performance> ~ *vi* **1 :** to make an entrance by turning from a road or path **2 :** to go to bed <*turned in* early>

turn·ing *n* **1 :** the act or course of one that turns **2 :** a place of a change in direction **3 a :** a forming by use of a lathe; *broadly* **:** TURNERY **b** *pl* **:** waste produced in turning

turning chisel *n* **:** a chisel used for shaping or finishing work in a lathe — see CHISEL illustration

turning point *n* **:** a point at which a significant change occurs

tur·nip \'tər-nəp\ *n* [prob. fr. [1]*turn* + E dial. *neep* (turnip); fr. the well-rounded root] **1 :** either of two biennial herbs of the mustard family with thick roots eaten as a vegetable or fed to stock: **a :** one (*Brassica rapa*) with hairy leaves and usu. flattened roots **b :** RUTABAGA **2 :** a large pocket watch

[1]**turn·key** \'tərn-ˌkē\ *n, pl* **turnkeys :** one who has charge of a prison's keys

[2]**turnkey** *adj* **:** of, relating to, or being a job or project (as a housing development) in which a private contractor completes the work of building and installation to the point of readiness for operation or occupancy at which time it is then sold to the customer at a prearranged price

turn·off \'tər-ˌnȯf\ *n* **1 :** a turning off **2 :** a place where one turns off; *esp* **:** an exit ramp on a turnpike

turn off \ˌtər-'nȯf, 'tər-\ *vt* **1 a :** DISMISS, DISCHARGE **b :** to dispose of **:** SELL **2 :** DEFLECT, EVADE **3 :** PRODUCE, ACCOMPLISH **4 :** to stop the flow of or shut off by or as if by turning a control <*turn* the water *off*> **5 :** HANG 1b **6 a :** to remove (material) by the process of turning **b :** to shape or produce by turning **7 :** to cause to lose interest **:** BORE <a subject that *turned off* a number of students>; *also* **:** to evoke a negative feeling in ~ *vi* **1 :** to deviate from a straight course or from a main road <*turn off* into a side road> **2 a** *Brit* **:** to turn bad **:** SPOIL **b :** to change to a specified state **:** BECOME **3 :** to lose interest **:** WITHDRAW

turn on *vt* **1 :** to cause to flow or operate by or as if by turning a control <*turn* the water *on* full> **2 a :** to cause to undergo an intense often visionary experience by taking a drug; *broadly* **:** to cause to get high **b :** to move pleasurably <rock music *turns* her *on*>; *also* **:** to excite sexually ~ *vi* **:** to become turned on

turn·out \'tər-ˌnau̇t\ *n* **1 :** an act of turning out **2** *chiefly Brit* **a :** STRIKE 3a **b :** STRIKER 1d **3 :** a gathering of people for a special purpose **4 a :** a place where something (as a road) turns out or branches off **b :** a space adjacent to a highway in which vehicles may park or pull into to enable others to pass **c :** a railroad siding **5 :** a clearing out and cleaning **6 a :** a coach or carriage together with the horses, harness, and attendants **b :** EQUIPMENT, RIG **c :** manner of dress **:** GETUP **7 :** net quantity of produce yielded

turn out \ˌtər-'nau̇t, 'tər-\ *vt* **1 a :** EXPEL, EVICT **b :** to put (as a horse) to pasture **2 a :** to turn inside out <*turning out* his pockets> **b :** to empty the contents of esp. for cleaning or rearranging; *also* **:** CLEAN **3 :** to produce often rapidly or regularly by or as if by machine **4 :** to equip, dress, or finish in a careful or elaborate way **5 :** to put out by turning a switch <*turn out* the lights> **6 :** to call (as the guard or a company) out from rest or shelter and into formation ~ *vi* **1 a :** to come or go out from home in answer to a summons <voters *turned out* in droves> **b :** to get out of bed **2 a :** to prove to be in the result or end <the play *turned out* to be a flop> **b :** to become in maturity <nobody thought he'd *turn out* like this> **c :** END <stories that *turn out* happily>

[1]**turn·over** \'tər-ˌnō-vər\ *n* **1 :** an act or result of turning over **:** UPSET **2 :** a turning from one side, place, or direction to its opposite **:** SHIFT, REVERSAL **3 :** a reorganization with a view to a shift in personnel **:** SHAKE-UP **4 :** something that is turned over **5 :** a filled pastry made by folding half of the crust over the other half **6 :** the amount of business done; *esp* **:** the volume of shares traded on a stock exchange **7 a :** movement (as of goods or people) into, through, and out of a place **b :** a cycle of purchase, sale, and replacement of a stock of goods; *also* **:** the ratio of sales for a stated period to average inventory **c :** the number of persons hired within a period to replace those leaving or dropped from a working force; *also* **:** the ratio of this number to the number in the average force maintained **8 :** the act or an instance of a team's losing possession of a ball through error or a minor violation of the rules

[2]**turn·over** \ˌtər-ˌnō-vər\ *adj* **:** capable of being turned over

turn over \ˌtər-'nō-vər, 'tər-\ *vt* **1 a :** to turn from an upright position **:** OVERTURN **b :** ROTATE <*turn over* a stiff valve with a wrench>; *also* **:** to cause (an internal-combustion engine) to kick over **2 :** to search (as clothes or papers) by lifting or moving one by one **3 :** to think over **:** meditate on **4 :** to read or examine (as a book) slowly or idly **5 :** DELIVER, SURRENDER **6 a :** to receive and dispose of (a stock of merchandise) **b :** to do business to the amount of <*turning over* $1000 a week> ~ *vi* **1 :** UPSET, CAPSIZE **2 :** ROTATE **3 a** *of one's stomach* **:** to heave with nausea **b** *of one's heart* **:** to seem to leap or lurch convulsively with sudden fright — **turn over a new leaf :** to make a change for the better esp. in one's way of living

turn·pike \'tərn-ˌpīk\ *n* [ME *turnepike* revolving frame bearing spikes and serving as a barrier, fr. *turnen* to turn + *pike*] **1 :** TOLLGATE **2 a :** a toll road or one formerly maintained as such; *esp* **:** a toll expressway **b :** a main road; *esp* **:** a paved highway with crowned surface

turn·sole \'tərn-ˌsōl\ *n* [ME *turnesole,* fr. MF *tournesol,* fr. OIt *tornasole,* fr. *tornare* to turn (fr. ML) + *sole* sun, fr. L *sol* — more at SOLAR] **1 :** any of several plants whose flowers or stems are supposed to turn with the sun; *esp* **:** HELIOTROPE **2 :** a European herb (*Chrozophora tinctoria*) of the spurge family with juice that is turned blue by ammonia; *also* **:** a purple dye obtained from it

turn·spit \-ˌspit\ *n* **1 a :** one that turns a spit; *specif* **:** a small dog formerly used in a treadmill to turn a spit **b :** a roasting jack **2 :** a rotatable spit

turn·stile \-ˌstīl\ *n* **:** a post with arms pivoted on the top set in a passageway so that persons can pass through only on foot one by one

turn·stone \-ˌstōn\ *n* [fr. a habit of turning over stones to find food] **:** any of a genus (*Arenaria*) of various widely distributed migratory shorebirds resembling the related plovers and sandpipers; *esp* **:** a widely distributed bird (*A. interpres*) having the upper surfaces variegated with black and chestnut and a black breast

turn·ta·ble \-ˌtā-bəl\ *n* **:** a revolvable platform: as **a :** a platform with a track for turning wheeled vehicles **b :** LAZY SUSAN **c :** a rotating platform that carries a phonograph record

turn to \'tərn-'tü\ *vi* **:** to apply oneself to work **:** act vigorously

[1]**turn·up** \'tər-ˌnəp\ *n* **:** something that is turned up

[2]**turn·up** \ˌtər-ˌnəp\ *adj* **1 :** turned up <a ~ nose> **2 :** made or fitted to be turned up <a ~ collar>

turn up \ˌtər-'nəp, 'tər-\ *vt* **1 :** FIND, DISCOVER **2 :** to raise or increase by or as if by turning a control **3** *Brit* **a :** to look up (as a word or fact) in a book **b :** to refer to or consult (a book) **4 :** to turn (a card) face upward **5 :** to reach a rotational speed of **:** develop power to the extent of <engine *turns up* 101 horsepower> ~ *vi* **1 :** to appear or come to light unexpectedly or after being lost **2 a** (1) **:** to turn out to be <he *turned up* missing at roll call> (2) **:** to become evident <her name is always *turning up* in the newspapers> **b :** to arrive or show up at an appointed or expected time or place <*turned up* half an hour late> **3 :** to happen or occur unexpectedly <something always *turned up* to prevent their meeting> **4** *of a ship* **:** TACK 1b — **turn up one's nose :** to show scorn or disdain

turn·ver·ein \'tərn-və-ˌrīn, 'tu̇(ə)rn-\ *n* [G, fr. *turnen* to perform gymnastic exercises + *verein* club] **:** an athletic club

[1]**tur·pen·tine** \'tər-pən-ˌtīn, 'tərp-ᵊm-\ *n* [ME *terbentyne, turpentyne,* fr. MF & ML; MF *terbentine, tourbentine,* fr. ML *terbentina,* fr. L *terebinthina,* fem. of *terebinthinus* of terebinth, fr. *terebinthus* terebinth, fr. Gk *terebinthos*] **1 a :** a yellow to brown semifluid oleoresin obtained as an exudate from the terebinth — called also *Chian turpentine* **b :** an oleoresin obtained from various conifers (as some pines and firs) **2 a :** an essential oil obtained from turpentines by distillation and used esp. as a solvent and thinner — called also *gum turpentine, oil of turpentine* **b :** a similar oil obtained by distillation or carbonization of pinewood — called also *wood turpentine* — **tur·pen·tin·ic** \ˌtər-pən-'tin-ik, ˌtərp-ᵊm-\ *or* **tur·pen·tin·ous** \-'tī-nəs\ *adj*

[2]**turpentine** *vt* **1 :** to apply turpentine to **2 :** to extract turpentine from; *esp* **:** to tap (pine trees) in order to obtain turpentine ~ *vi* **:** to collect or make turpentine

tur·pi·tude \'tər-pə-ˌt(y)üd\ *n* [MF, fr. L *turpitudo,* fr. *turpis* vile, base] **:** inherent baseness **:** DEPRAVITY <moral ~>; *also* **:** a base act

turps \'tərps\ *n pl but sing in constr* [by shortening & alter.] **:** TURPENTINE

tur·quoise *also* **tur·quois** \'tər-ˌk(w)ȯiz\ *n* [ME *turkeis, turcas,* fr. MF *turquoyse,* fr. fem. of *turquoys* Turkish, fr. OF, fr. *Turc* Turk] **1 :** a mineral $CuAl_6(PO_4)_4(OH)_8 \cdot 5H_2O$ that is a blue, bluish green, or greenish gray hydrous basic copper aluminum phosphate, takes a high polish, changes sometimes to a green tint, but when sky blue is valued as a gem **2 :** a variable color averaging a light greenish blue

turquoise blue *n* **:** a variable color averaging a light greenish blue that is paler and slightly bluer than average turquoise

turquoise green *n* **:** a variable color averaging a light bluish green

tur·ret \'tər-ət, 'tə-rət, 'tu̇r-ət\ *n* [ME *touret,* fr. MF *torete, tourete,* fr. OF, dim. of *tor, tur* tower — more at TOWER] **1 :** a little tower; *specif* **:** an ornamental structure at an angle of a larger structure **2 a :** a pivoted and revolvable holder in a machine tool **b :** a device (as on a microscope or a television camera) holding several lenses **3 a :** a tall building usu. moved on wheels and formerly used for carrying soldiers and equipment for breaching or scaling a wall **b** (1) **:** a gunner's fixed or movable enclosure in an airplane (2) **:** a revolving armored structure on warships that protects one or more guns (3) **:** a similar upper structure usu. for one gun on tanks

tur·ret·ed \-əd\ *adj* **:** furnished with or as if with turrets

[1]**tur·tle** \'tərt-ᵊl\ *n* [ME, fr. OE *turtla,* fr. L *turtur,* of imit. origin] *archaic* **:** TURTLEDOVE

[2]**turtle** *n, pl* **turtles** *also* **turtle** *often attrib* [prob. by folk etymology fr. F *tortue,* prob. fr. (assumed) VL *tartaruca,* fr. LL *tartarucha,* fem of *tartaruchus* of Tartarus, fr. Gk *tartarouchos,* fr. *Tartaros* Tartarus] **:** any of an order (Testudinata) of land, freshwater, and marine reptiles with a toothless horny beak and a bony shell which encloses the trunk and into which the head, limbs, and tail usu. may be withdrawn

hawksbill turtle

[3]**turtle** *n* **:** TURTLENECK

tur·tle·back \'tərt-ᵊl-ˌbak\ *n* **:** a raised convex surface — **tur·tleback** *or* **tur·tle–backed** \ˌtərt-ᵊl-'bakt\ *adj*

tur·tle·dove \'tərt-ᵊl-ˌdəv\ *n* **:** any of several small wild pigeons esp. of an Old World genus (*Streptopelia*) noted for plaintive cooing

tur·tle·head \-ˌhed\ *n* **:** any of a genus (*Chelone*) of perennial herbs of the figwort family with spikes of showy white or purple flowers

tur·tle·neck \-ˌnek\ *n* **1 :** a high close-fitting turnover collar used esp. for sweaters

tur·tling \'tərt-liŋ, -ᵊl-iŋ\ *n* **:** the action or process of catching turtles

turves *pl of* TURF

[1]Tus·can \'təs-kən\ *n* [ME, fr. L *tuscanus*, adj., Etruscan, fr. *Tusci* Etruscans] **1 :** a native or inhabitant of Tuscany **2 a :** the Italian language spoken in Tuscany **b :** the standard literary dialect of Italian

[2]Tuscan *adj* **1 :** of, relating to, or characteristic of Tuscany, the Tuscans, or Tuscan **2** of or relating to one of the five classical orders of architecture that is of Roman origin and plain in style

Tus·ca·ro·ra \ˌtəs-kə-'rōr-ə, -'rȯr-\ *n, pl* **Tuscarora** *or* **Tuscaroras** [Tuscarora *Ska-ru-rĕⁿ*, lit., Indian hemp gatherers] **1 :** a member of an Amerindian people orig. of No. Carolina and later of New York and Ontario **2 :** the language of the Tuscarora people

tu·sche \'tu̇sh-ə\ *n* [G, back-formation fr. *tuschen* to lay on color, fr. F *toucher*, lit., to touch] **:** a black liquid used in lithography for drawing and painting and in etching and the silk-screen process as a resist

[1]tush \'təsh\ *n* [ME *tusch*, fr. OE *tūsc;* akin to OFris *tusk* tooth, OE *tōth* tooth] **:** a long pointed tooth; *esp* **:** a horse's canine

[2]tush *interj* [ME *tussch*] — used to express disdain or reproach

[1]tusk \'təsk\ *n* [ME, alter. of *tux*, fr. OE *tūx;* akin to OE *tūsc* tush] **1 :** an elongated greatly enlarged tooth that projects when the mouth is closed and serves for digging food or as a weapon; *broadly* **:** a long protruding tooth **2 :** one of the small projections on a tusk tenon — **tusked** \'təskt\ *adj* — **tusk·like** \'təs-ˌklīk\ *adj*

[2]tusk *vt* **:** to dig up with a tusk; *also* **:** to gash with a tusk

tusk·er \'təs-kər\ *n* **:** an animal with tusks; *esp* **:** a male elephant with two normally developed tusks

tusk tenon *n* **:** a tenon strengthened by one or more smaller tenons underneath forming a steplike outline

tus·sah \'təs-ə, -ˌō\ *or* **tus·sore** \-ˌō(ə)r, -ˌȯ(ə)r\ *n* [Hindi *tasar*] **1 :** any of several oriental silkworms that are larvae of saturniid moths (esp. *Antheraea paphia*) and that produce a brownish silk **2 :** silk or silk fabric from the tussah's filament

tus·sive \'təs-iv\ *adj* [L *tussis* cough] **:** of, relating to, or involved in coughing

[1]tus·sle \'təs-əl\ *vi* **tus·sled; tus·sling** \-(ə-)liŋ\ [ME *tussillen*, freq. of ME *-tusen, -tousen* to tousle — more at TOUSE] **:** to struggle roughly **:** SCUFFLE

[2]tussle *n* **1 :** a physical contest or struggle **:** SCUFFLE **2 :** an intense argument, controversy, or struggle

tus·sock \'təs-ək\ *n* [origin unknown] **:** a compact tuft esp. of grass or sedge; *also* **:** a hummock in marsh bound together by plant roots — **tus·socky** \-ə-kē\ *adj*

tussock grass *n* **:** a grass or sedge that typically grows in tussocks

tussock moth *n* **:** any of numerous dull-colored moths (esp. family Lymantriidae) that usu. have wingless females and larvae with long tufts or brushes of hair

tut *a t-sound made by suction rather than explosion; often read as* 'tət\ *interj* [origin unknown] — used to express disapproval or disbelief

tu·tee \t(y)ü-'tē\ *n* [*tut*or + *-ee*] **:** one who is being tutored

tu·te·lage \'t(y)üt-ᵊl-ij\ *n* [L *tutela* protection, guardian, fr. *tutus*, pp. of *tueri* to look at, guard] **1 a :** an act or process of serving as guardian or protector **:** GUARDIANSHIP **b :** hegemony over a foreign territory **:** TRUSTEESHIP 2 **2 :** the state of being under a guardian or tutor **3 a :** instruction esp. of an individual **b :** a guiding influence

tu·te·lar \'t(y)üt-ᵊl-ər, -ᵊl-ˌär\ *adj or n* **:** TUTELARY

[1]tu·te·lary \'t(y)üt-ᵊl-ˌer-ē\ *adj* **1 :** having the guardianship of a person or a thing <a ~ goddess> **2 :** of or relating to a guardian

[2]tutelary *n, pl* **-lar·ies :** a tutelary power (as a deity)

[1]tu·tor \'t(y)üt-ər\ *n* [ME, fr. MF & L; MF *tuteur*, fr. L *tutor*, fr. *tutus*, pp. of *tueri*] **:** a person charged with the instruction and guidance of another: as **a :** a private teacher **b :** a teacher in a British university who gives individual instruction to undergraduates — **tu·tor·ess** \-ə-rəs\ *n*

[2]tutor *vt* **1 :** to have the guardianship, tutelage, or care of **2 :** to teach or guide usu. individually in a special subject or for a particular purpose **:** COACH ~ *vi* **1 :** to do the work of a tutor **2 :** to receive instruction esp. privately

tu·tor·age \'t(y)üt-ə-rij\ *n* **:** the function or work of a tutor

[1]tu·to·ri·al \t(y)ü-'tōr-ē-əl, -'tȯr-\ *adj* **:** of, relating to, or involving a tutor

[2]tutorial *n* **1 :** a class conducted by a tutor for one student or a small number of students **2 :** a paper and esp. a technical paper written to give practical information about a specific subject

tu·tor·ship \'t(y)üt-ər-ˌship\ *n* **1 :** the office, function, or work of a tutor **2 :** TUTELAGE 3

tu·toy·er \tue-twà-yā\ *vt* [F, to address with the pronoun *tu* ("thou"), fr. MF, fr. *tu* thou (fr. L) + *toi* thee, fr. L *te* (acc. of *tu*) — more at THOU] **:** to address familiarly

[1]tut·ti \'tüt-ē, 'tu̇t-, 'tü-ˌtē, 'tu̇-\ *adj or adv* [It, masc. pl. of *tutto* all] **:** ALL — used as a direction in music for voices or instruments to perform together

[2]tutti *n* **:** a passage or section performed by all the performers

tut·ti-frut·ti \ˌtüt-i-'früt-ē, ˌtu̇t-\ *n* [It *tutti frutti*, lit., all fruits] **:** a confection or ice cream containing chopped usu. candied fruits

tut-tut \'tət-'tət\ *interj* **:** TUT

tu·tu \'tü-(ˌ)tü\ *n* [F, fr. (baby talk) *cucu, tutu* backside, alter. of *cul* — more at CULET] **:** a very short projecting skirt worn by a ballerina

tu-whit tu-whoo \tə-ˌ(h)wit-tə-'(h)wü\ *n* [imit.] **:** the cry of an owl

tux \'təks\ *n* **:** TUXEDO

tux·e·do \ˌtək-'sēd-(ˌ)ō\ *n, pl* **-dos** *or* **-does** [*Tuxedo* Park, N.Y.] **1 :** a single-breasted or double-breasted usu. black or blackish blue jacket **2 :** semiformal evening clothes for men

tu·yere \twē-'e(ə)r\ *n* [F *tuyère*, fr. MF, fr. *tuyau* pipe] **:** a nozzle through which an air blast is delivered to a forge or blast furnace

tv \'tē-'vē\ *n, often cap T & V* [*tele*vision] **:** TELEVISION

TV *abbr* terminal velocity

TVA *abbr* Tennessee Valley Authority

TV dinner \ˌtē-ˌvē-\ *n* [fr. its saving the television viewer from having to interrupt his viewing to prepare and serve a meal] **:** a quick-frozen packaged dinner (as of meat, potatoes, and a vegetable) that requires only heating before it is served

Tvl *abbr* Transvaal

twa \'twä\ *or* **twae** \'twā, 'twē\ *Scot var of* TWO

[1]twad·dle \'twäd-ᵊl\ *n* [prob. alter. of E dial. *twattle* (idle talk)] **1 :** silly idle talk **:** DRIVEL **2 :** one that twaddles **:** TWADDLER

[2]twaddle *vb* **twad·dled; twad·dling** \'twäd-liŋ, -ᵊl-iŋ\ **:** PRATE, BABBLE — **twad·dler** \-lər, -ᵊl-ər\ *n*

[1]twain \'twān\ *adj* [ME, fr. OE *twēgen* — more at TWO] *archaic* **:** TWO

[2]twain *pron* **:** TWO <mark ~>

[3]twain *n* **1 :** TWO **2 :** COUPLE, PAIR

[1]twang \'twaŋ\ *n* [imit.] **1 :** a harsh quick ringing sound like that of a plucked bowstring **2 a :** nasal speech or resonance **b :** the characteristic speech of a region, locality, or group of people **3 a :** an act of plucking **b :** PANG, TWINGE — **twangy** \'twaŋ-ē\ *adj*

[2]twang *vb* **twanged; twang·ing** \'twaŋ-iŋ\ *vi* **1 :** to sound with a twang <the catch of the gate ~*ed* and squealed> **2 :** to speak or sound with a nasal intonation **3 :** to throb or twitch with pain or tension ~ *vt* **1 :** to cause to sound with a twang **2 :** to utter or pronounce with a nasal twang **3 :** to pluck the string of

[3]twang *n* [alter. of *tang*] **1 :** a persisting flavor, taste, or odor **:** TANG **2 :** SUGGESTION, TRACE

twat \'twät\ *n* [origin unknown] **:** VULVA — usu. considered vulgar

tway·blade \'twā-ˌblād\ *n* [E dial. *tway* (two)] **:** any of several orchids (esp. genera *Listera* or *Liparis*) having a pair of opposite leaves

[1]tweak \'twēk\ *vb* [ME *twikken*, fr. OE *twiccian* to pluck — more at TWITCH] *vt* **1 :** to pinch and pull with a sudden jerk and twist **:** TWITCH <~*ed* a bud from the stem> **2 :** to pinch (a person or a body part) lightly or playfully <~*ed* the baby's ear affectionately> ~ *vi* **:** TWITCH 1

[2]tweak *n* **:** an act of tweaking **:** PINCH

tweed \'twēd\ *n* [alter. of Sc *tweel* twill, fr. ME *twyll*] **1 :** a rough woolen fabric made usu. in twill weaves and used esp. for suits and coats **2** *pl* **:** tweed clothing; *specif* **:** a tweed suit

Twee·dle·dum and Twee·dle·dee \ˌtwēd-ᵊl-'dəm-ən-ˌtwēd-ᵊl-'dē\ *n* [E *tweedle* (to chirp) + *dum* (imit. of a low musical note) *& dee* (imit. of a high musical note)] **:** two individuals or groups that are practically indistinguishable

tweedy \'twēd-ē\ *adj* **tweed·i·er; -est 1 :** of or resembling tweed **2 a :** given to wearing tweeds **b :** informal or suggestive of the outdoors in taste or habits — **tweed·i·ness** *n*

tween \(ˈ)twēn\ *prep* [ME *twene*, short for *betwene*] **:** BETWEEN

[1]tweet \'twēt\ *n* [imit.] **:** a chirping note

[2]tweet *vi* **:** CHIRP

tweet·er \'twēt-ər\ *n* **:** a small loudspeaker responsive only to the higher acoustic frequencies and reproducing sounds of high pitch

tweeze \'twēz\ *vt* **tweezed; tweez·ing** [back-formation fr. *tweezers*] **:** to pluck, remove, or handle with tweezers

twee·zer \'twē-zər\ *n* **:** TWEEZERS

twee·zers \-zərz\ *n pl but sing or pl in constr* [obs. E *tweeze*, n. (etui), short for obs. E *etweese*, fr. pl. of obs. E *etwee*, fr. F *étui*] **:** any of various small metal instruments that are usu. held between the thumb and forefinger, are used for plucking, holding, or manipulating, and consist of two legs joined at one end

Twelfth Day *n* [fr. its being the 12th day after Christmas] **:** EPIPHANY

Twelfth Night *n* **1 :** the eve preceding Epiphany **2 :** the evening of Epiphany

twelve \'twelv\ *n* [ME, fr. *twelve*, adj., fr. OE *twelf;* akin to OHG *zwelif* twelve; both fr. a prehistoric Gmc compound whose first element is represented by OE *twā* two, and whose second element is represented by OE *-leofan* (in *endleofan* eleven) — more at TWO, ELEVEN] **1** — see NUMBER table **2** *cap* **a :** the twelve original disciples of Jesus **b :** the books of the Minor Prophets in the Jewish Scriptures **3 :** the 12th in a set or series **4 :** something having 12 units or members **5** *pl* **:** TWELVEMO — **twelfth** \'twelf(t)th\ *adj or n* — **twelve** *adj or pron*

twelve·mo \'twelv-(ˌ)mō\ *n, pl* **-mos :** the size of a piece of paper cut 12 from a sheet; *also* **:** a book, a page, or paper of this size

twelve·month \-ˌmən(t)th\ *n* **:** YEAR

twelve-tone \-'tōn\ *adj* **:** of, relating to, or being serial music utilizing the 12 chromatic tones

twelve-tone row *n* **:** the 12 chromatic tones of the octave placed in a chosen fixed order and constituting with some permitted permutations and derivations the melodic and harmonic material of a musical piece

twen·ty \'twent-ē\ *n, pl* **twenties** [ME, fr. *twenty*, adj., fr. OE *twēntig*, n., group of 20, fr. *twēn-* (akin to OE *twā* two) + *-tig* group of 10 — more at TWO, EIGHTY] **1** — see NUMBER table **2** *pl* **:** the numbers 20 to 29; *specif* **:** the years 20 to 29 in a lifetime or century **3 :** a 20-dollar bill — **twen·ti·eth** \-ē-əth\ *adj or n* — **twenty** *adj or pron*

twen·ty-four·mo \ˌtwent-ē-'fō(ə)r-(ˌ)mō, -'fȯ(ə)r-\ *n, pl* **-mos :** the size of a piece of paper cut 24 from a sheet; *also* **:** a book, a page, or paper of this size

twen·ty-one \ˌtwent-ē-'wən\ *n* **1** — see NUMBER table **2** [trans. of F *vingt-et-un*] **:** BLACKJACK — **twenty-one** *adj or pron*

twenty-twenty *or* **20/20** \ˌtwent-ē-'twent-ē\ *adj* [fr. the testing of vision by reading letters at a distance of 20 feet] *of the human eye* **:** meeting a standard of normal visual acuity <~ vision>

twen·ty-two \ˌtwent-ē-'tü\ *n* **1** — see NUMBER table **2 :** a .22-caliber rifle or pistol — usu. written .22 — **twenty-two** *adj or pron*

twerp \ˈtwərp\ *n* [origin unknown] : a silly, insignificant, or contemptible person

Twi \ˈchwē, chə-ˈwē, ˈtwē, ˈchē\ *n* **1** : a dialect of Akan **2** : a literary language based on the Twi dialect and used by the Akan-speaking peoples (as the Ashanti)

twi- \ˈtwī\ *prefix* [ME, fr. OE; akin to OHG *zwi-* twi-, L *bi-*, Gk *di-*, OE *twā* TWO] : two : double : doubly : twice <*twi*-headed>

twice \ˈtwīs\ *adv* [ME *twiges, twies,* fr. OE *twiga;* akin to OE *twi-*] **1** : on two occasions <~ absent> **2** : two times : in doubled quantity or degree <~ two is four> <~ as much>

twice–born \-ˈbȯ(ə)rn\ *adj* **1** : born a second time **2** : having undergone a definite experience of fundamental moral and spiritual renewal : REGENERATE **3** : of or forming one of the three upper Hindu caste groups in which boys undergo an initiation symbolizing spiritual birth

twice–laid \-ˈlād\ *adj* : made from the ends of rope and strands of used rope <~ rope>

twice–told \-ˈtōld\ *adj* : well known from repeated telling — used chiefly in the phrase *a twice-told tale*

1twid·dle \ˈtwid-ᵊl\ *vb* **twid·dled; twid·dling** \ˈtwid-liŋ, -ᵊl-iŋ\ [origin unknown] *vi* **1** : to play negligently with something : FIDDLE **2** : to turn or jounce lightly <~*s* round and round in the water —J. B. S. Haldane> ~ *vt* : to rotate lightly or idly <*twiddled* his cigar —James Lord> — **twiddle one's thumbs** : to spend time idly : do nothing

2twiddle *n* : TURN, TWIST

1twig \ˈtwig\ *n* [ME *twigge,* fr. OE; akin to OHG *zwīg* twig, OE *twā* two] **1** : a small shoot or branch usu. without its leaves **2** : a minute branch of a nerve or artery — **twigged** \ˈtwigd\ *adj* — **twig·gy** \ˈtwig-ē\ *adj*

2twig *vb* **twigged; twig·ging** [perh. fr. ScGael *twig* I understand] *vt* **1** : NOTICE, OBSERVE **2** : to understand the meaning of : COMPREHEND ~ *vi* : to gain a grasp : UNDERSTAND <*twigged* instinctively about things —H. E. Bates>

3twig *n* [origin unknown] *Brit* : FASHION, STYLE

twig pruner *n* : a longicorn beetle (*Elaphidionoides villosus*) whose larva bores into the twigs of various American hardwood trees and cuts them off as if pruned

twi·light \ˈtwī-ˌlīt\ *n, often attrib* **1** : the light from the sky between full night and sunrise or between sunset and full night produced by diffusion of sunlight through the atmosphere and its dust **2 a** : an intermediate state that is not clearly defined <lived in the ~ of neutrality —*Newsweek*> **b** : a period of decline

twilight glow *n* : airglow seen at twilight

twilight sleep *n* : a state produced by injection of morphine and scopolamine in which awareness and memory of pain is dulled or effaced

twi·lit \ˈtwī-ˌlit\ *adj* [*twi*light + *lit*] : lighted by or as if by twilight

twill \ˈtwil\ *n* [ME *twyll,* fr. OE *twilic* having a double thread, modif. of L *bilic-, bilix,* fr. *bi-* + *licium* thread] **1** : a fabric with a twill weave **2** : a textile weave in which the filling threads pass over one and under two or more warp threads to give an appearance of diagonal lines

twilled \ˈtwild\ *adj* : made with a twill weave

twill·ing \ˈtwil-iŋ\ *n* : twilled fabric; *also* : the process of making it

1twin \ˈtwin\ *adj* [ME, fr. OE *twinn* twofold, two by two; akin to ON *tvinnr* two by two, OE *twā* two] **1** : born with one other or as a pair at one birth <~ brother> <~ girls> **2 a** : made up of two similar, related, or connected members or parts : DOUBLE **b** : paired in a close or necessary relationship : MATCHING **c** : having or consisting of two identical units **d** : being one of a pair

2twin *n* **1 a** : either of two offspring produced at a birth **b** *pl, cap* : GEMINI **2** : one of two persons or things closely related to or resembling each other **3** : a compound crystal composed of two or more crystals or parts of crystals of the same kind that are grown together in a specific manner — **twin·ship** \-ˌship\ *n*

3twin *vb* **twinned; twin·ning** *vt* **1** : to bring together in close association : COUPLE **2** : DUPLICATE, MATCH ~ *vi* **1** : to bring forth twins **2** : to grow as a twin crystal

twin bed *n* : one of a pair of matching single beds

twin·ber·ry \ˈtwin-ˌber-ē\ *n* [fr. the occurrence of the berries in pairs] **1** : a shrubby No. American honeysuckle (*Lonicera involucrata*) with purple involucrate flowers **2** : PARTRIDGEBERRY

twin bill *n* : DOUBLEHEADER

twin·born \ˈtwin-ˈbȯ(ə)rn\ *adj* : born at the same birth

twin double *n* : a system of betting (as on horse races) in which the bettor must pick the winners of four stipulated races in order to win — compare DAILY DOUBLE

1twine \ˈtwīn\ *n* [ME *twin,* fr. OE *twin;* akin to MD *twijn* twine, OE *twā* two] **1** : a strong string of two or more strands twisted together **2** : a twined or interlaced part or object **3** : an act of twining, interlacing, or embracing — **twiny** \ˈtwī-nē\ *adj*

2twine *vb* **twined; twin·ing** *vt* **1 a** : to twist together **b** : to form by twisting : WEAVE **2 a** : INTERLACE <the girl *twined* her hands —John Buchan> **b** : to cause to encircle or enfold something **c** : to cause to be encircled ~ *vi* **1** : to coil about a support **2** : to stretch or move in a sinuous manner : MEANDER <the river ~*s* through the valley> — **twin·er** *n*

3twine *vb* **twined; twin·ing** [alter. of Sc *twin,* fr. ME *twinnen,* fr. *twin* double] *vt, chiefly Scot* : to cause (one) to lose possession : DEPRIVE <*twined* him of his nose —J. C. Ransom> ~ *vi, chiefly Scot* : PART <you and me must ~ —R. L. Stevenson>

twin·flow·er \ˈtwin-ˌflau̇(-ə)r\ *n* : either of two low prostrate subshrubs (*Linnaea borealis* of northern Europe and Asia and *L. americana* of northern No. America) of the honeysuckle family with opposite leaves and fragrant usu. pink flowers in pairs

1twinge \ˈtwinj\ *vb* **twinged; twing·ing** \ˈtwin-jiŋ\ *or* **twinge·ing** [ME *twengen,* fr. OE *twengan*] *vt* **1** *dial* : PLUCK, TWEAK **2** : to affect with a sharp pain or pang ~ *vi* : to feel a sudden sharp local pain

2twinge *n* **1** : a sudden sharp stab of pain **2** : a moral or emotional pang <a ~ of conscience>

twi–night \ˈtwī-ˌnīt\ *adj* [*twi*light + *night*] : of, relating to, or being a baseball doubleheader in which the first game is played in the late afternoon and the second continues into the evening

1twin·kle \ˈtwiŋ-kəl\ *vb* **twin·kled; twin·kling** \-k(ə-)liŋ\ [ME *twinklen,* fr. OE *twinclian;* akin to MHG *zwinken* to blink] *vi* **1** : to shine with a flickering or sparkling light : SCINTILLATE **2 a** : to flutter the eyelids **b** : to appear bright with merriment or other usu. happy feeling <his eyes *twinkled*> **3** : to flutter or flit rapidly ~ *vt* **1** : to cause to shine with fluctuating light **2** : to flicker or flirt rapidly <*twinkled* the straight, red-lacquered toes —Glenway Wescott> — **twin·kler** \-k(ə-)lər\ *n*

2twinkle *n* **1** : a wink of the eyelids **2** : the instant's duration of a wink : TWINKLING **3** : an intermittent radiance : FLICKER **4** : a rapid flashing motion : FLIRT — **twin·kly** \-k(ə-)lē\ *adj*

twin·kling \ˈtwiŋ-kliŋ\ *n* : the time required for a wink : INSTANT <the kettle will boil in a ~ —*Punch*>

twin–size \ˈtwin-ˈsīz\ *adj* [*twin bed*] : having the dimensions 39 inches by 75 inches — used of a bed; compare FULL-SIZE, KING-SIZE, QUEEN-SIZE

1twirl \ˈtwər(-ə)l\ *vb* [perh. of Scand origin; akin to Norw dial. *tvirla* to twirl; akin to OHG *dweran* to stir — more at TURBID] *vi* **1** : to revolve rapidly **2** : to pitch in a baseball game ~ *vt* **1** : to cause to rotate rapidly **2** : PITCH 2a — **twirl·er** \ˈtwər-lər\ *n*

2twirl *n* **1** : an act of twirling **2** : COIL, WHORL — **twirly** \ˈtwər-lē\ *adj*

twirp *var of* TWERP

1twist \ˈtwist\ *vb* [ME *twisten,* fr. OE *-twist* rope; akin to MD *twist* quarrel, twine, OE *twā* two] *vt* **1 a** : to unite by winding <~*ing* strands together> **b** : to make by twisting strands together <~ thread from yarn> **c** : to mingle by interlacing **2** : TWINE, COIL **3 a** : to wring or wrench so as to dislocate or distort; *esp* : SPRAIN <~*ed* my ankle> **b** : to alter the meaning of : PERVERT <~*ed* the facts> **c** : CONTORT <~*ed* his face into a grin> **d** : to pull off, turn, or break by torsion **e** : to cause to move with a turning motion **f** : to form into a spiral shape **g** : to debase or falsify deviously : DISTORT **h** : to make (one's way) in a winding or devious manner to a destination or objective ~ *vi* **1** : to follow a winding course : SNAKE **2 a** : to turn or change shape under torsion **b** : to assume a spiral shape **c** : SQUIRM, WRITHE **d** : to dance the twist **3** *of a ball* : to rotate while taking a curving path or direction **4** : TURN 3a <~*ed* around to see behind him> ***syn*** see CURVE — **twist one's arm** : to bring strong pressure to bear on one

2twist *n* **1** : something formed by twisting or winding: as **a** : a thread, yarn, or cord formed by twisting two or more strands together **b** : a strong tightly twisted sewing silk **c** : a baked piece of twisted dough **d** : tobacco leaves twisted into a thick roll **e** : a strip of citrus peel used to flavor a drink **2** : the fleshing between the hind legs esp. of cattle or sheep **3 a** : an act of twisting : the state of being twisted **b** : a dance performed with strenuous gyrations esp. of the hips **c** : the spin given the ball in any of various games (as baseball) **d** : a spiral turn or curve **e** (1) : torque or torsional stress applied to a body (as a rod or shaft) (2) : torsional strain (3) : the angle through which a thing is twisted **4 a** : a turning off a straight course **b** : ECCENTRICITY, IDIOSYNCRASY **c** : a distortion of meaning or sense **5 a** : an unexpected turn or development <weird ~*s* of fate —W. L. Shirer> **b** : a clever device : TRICK <questions demanding special ~*s* of thinking —*New Yorker*> **c** : a variant approach or method : GIMMICK <a kind of ~ on the old triangle theme —Dave Fedo> **6** : a front or back dive in which the diver twists his body sideways a half or full turn before entering the water

twist drill *n* : a drill having deep helical grooves extending from the point to the smooth portion of the shank

twist·er \ˈtwis-tər\ *n* **1** : one that twists; *esp* : a ball with a forward and spinning motion **2** : a tornado, waterspout, or dust devil in which the rotatory ascending movement of a column of air is esp. apparent

twist·ing \ˈtwis-tiŋ\ *n* : the use of misrepresentation or trickery to get someone to lapse a life insurance policy and buy another usu. in another company

1twit \ˈtwit\ *vt* **twit·ted; twit·ting** [ME *atwiten* to reproach, fr. OE *ætwītan,* fr. *æt* at + *wītan* to reproach; akin to OHG *wīzan* to punish, OE *witan* to know] **1** : to subject to light ridicule or reproach : RALLY **2** : to make fun of as a fault ***syn*** see RIDICULE

2twit *n* **1** : an act of twitting : TAUNT **2** *Brit* : a silly annoying person : FOOL

1twitch \ˈtwich\ *vb* [ME *twicchen;* akin to OE *twiccian* to pluck, OHG *gizwickan* to pinch] *vt* : to move or pull with a sudden motion : JERK ~ *vi* **1** : PULL 1a, PLUCK <~*ed* at my sleeve> **2** : to move jerkily : QUIVER ***syn*** see JERK — **twitch·er** *n*

2twitch *n* **1** : an act of twitching; *esp* : a short sudden pull or jerk **2** : a physical or mental pang **3** : a loop of rope or strap that is tightened over a horse's lip as a restraining device **4 a** : a short spastic contraction of the muscle fibers **b** : a slight jerk of a body part — **twitch·i·ly** \ˈtwich-ə-lē\ *adv* — **twitchy** \ˈtwich-ē\ *adj*

3twitch *n* [alter. of *quitch*] : QUACK GRASS

1twit·ter \ˈtwit-ər\ *vb* [ME *twiteren;* akin to OHG *zwizzirōn* to twitter] *vi* **1** : to utter successive chirping noises **2 a** : to talk in a chattering fashion **b** : GIGGLE, TITTER **3** : to tremble with agitation : FLUTTER ~ *vt* **1** : to utter in chirps or twitters <the robin ~*ed* his morning song> **2** : to shake rapidly back and forth : FLUTTER — **twit·ter·er** \-ər-ər\ *n*

2twitter *n* **1** : a trembling agitation : QUIVER **2** : a small tremulous intermittent sound (as of birds) **3 a** : a light chattering **b** : a light silly laugh : GIGGLE — **twit·tery** \ˈtwit-ə-rē\ *adj*

twixt \(ˈ)twikst\ *prep* [ME *twix,* short for *betwix, betwixt*] : BETWEEN

1two \ˈtü\ *adj* [ME *twa, two,* fr. OE *twā* (fem. & neut.); akin to OE *twēgen* two (masc.), *tū* (neut.), OHG *zwēne,* L *duo,* Gk *dyo*] **1** : being one more than one in number **2** : being the second — used post-positively <section ~ of the instructions>

²two *pron, pl in constr* **1 :** two countable individuals not specified <only ~ were found> **2 :** a small approximate number of indicated things <only a shot or ~ were fired>
³two *n, pl* **twos** **1** — see NUMBER table **2 :** the second in a set or series <the ~ of spades> **3 :** a 2-dollar bill **4 :** something having two units or members
two–bag·ger \-'bag-ər\ *n* **:** DOUBLE
two–bit \ˌtü-ˌbit\ *adj* **1 :** of the value of two bits **2 :** cheap or trivial of its kind **:** PETTY, SMALL-TIME
two bits *n pl but sing or pl in constr* **1 :** the value of a quarter of a dollar **2 :** something of small worth or importance
¹two–by–four \ˌtü-bə-'fō(ə)r, -'fȯ(ə)r\ *adj* **1 :** measuring two units (as inches) by four **2 :** small or petty of its kind <this house and its ~ garden —Philip Barry>
²two–by–four *n* **:** a piece of lumber approximately 2 by 4 inches as sawed and usu. 1⅝ by 3⅝ inches if dressed
two cents worth *n* **:** an opinion or view on a topic under discussion <each speaker . . . is getting in his *two cents worth* —Dwight Macdonald>
two–cycle *adj, of an internal-combustion engine* **:** having a two-stroke cycle
two–dimensional *adj* **1 :** having two dimensions **2 :** lacking depth of characterization <~ fiction>
two–faced \'tü-'fāst\ *adj* **1 :** having two faces **2 :** DOUBLE-DEALING, FALSE — **two–faced·ness** \-'fāst-nəs, -'fā-səd-nəs\ *n*
two·fer \'tü-fər\ *n* [alter. of *two for (one)*] **1 :** a cheap item of merchandise; *esp* **:** a cigar selling at two for a nickel **2 :** a free coupon entitling the bearer to purchase two tickets to a specified theatrical production for the price of one
two–fist·ed \-'fis-təd\ *adj* **:** marked by vigorous energy **:** VIRILE
two–fold \'tü-ˌfōld, -'fōld\ *adj* **1 :** having two units or members **2 :** being twice as great or as many — **two·fold** \-'fōld\ *adv*
2, 4–D \ˌtü-ˌfōr-'dē, -ˌfȯr-\ *n* **:** a white crystalline compound $C_8H_6Cl_2O_3$ used as a weed killer
2, 4, 5–T \-ˌfīv-'tē\ *n* **:** an irritant compound $Cl_3C_8H_5O_3$ used in brush and weed control
two–hand·ed \'tü-'han-dəd\ *adj* **1 :** used with both hands <a ~ sword> **2 :** requiring two persons <a ~ saw> **3** *archaic* **:** STOUT, STRONG **4 a :** having two hands **b :** efficient with either hand — **two–hand·ed·ness** *n*
two–line octave *n* **:** the musical octave that begins on the first C above middle C — see PITCH illustration
two–party *adj* **:** characterized by two major political parties of comparable strength
two·pence \'təp-ən(t)s, *US also* 'tü-ˌpen(t)s\ *n* **1 :** the sum of two British pennies **2** *pl* **twopence** *or* **two·pen·ces :** a coin worth twopence
two·pen·ny \'təp-(ə-)nē, *US also* 'tü-ˌpen-ē\ *adj* **:** costing or worth twopence
two–phase *adj* **:** DIPHASE
¹two–piece \ˌtü-ˌpēs\ *adj* **:** forming a clothing ensemble with matching top and bottom parts
²two–piece \'tü-ˌpēs\ *n* **:** a garment (as a bathing suit) that is two-piece
two–piec·er \'tü-'pē-sər\ *n* **:** TWO-PIECE
two–ply \-'plī\ *adj* **1 :** consisting of two thicknesses **2 a :** woven with two sets of warp thread and two of filling <a ~ carpet> **b :** consisting of two strands <~ yarn>
two–sid·ed \-'sīd-əd\ *adj* **:** having two sides **:** BILATERAL
two·some \'tü-səm\ *n* **1 :** a group of two persons or things **:** COUPLE **2 :** a golf single
two–spot·ted spider mite \ˌtü-ˌspät-əd-\ *n* **:** a widely distributed plant-feeding mite (*Tetranychus urticae*) that feeds on various usu. herbaceous plants and is a serious pest in greenhouses
two–step \'tü-ˌstep\ *n* **1 :** a ballroom dance in ²⁄₄ or ⁴⁄₄ time having a basic pattern of step-close-step **2 :** a piece of music for the two-step — **two–step** *vi*
two–suit·er \-'süt-ər\ *n* **:** a man's traveling bag designed to hold two suits and accessories
two–tailed test \ˌtü-ˌtāl(d)-\ *n* **:** a statistical test for which the critical region consists of all values of the test statistic greater than a given value plus the values less than another given value — called also *two-sided test, two-tail test;* compare ONE-TAILED TEST
two–time \'tü-ˌtīm\ *vt* **1 :** to betray (a spouse or lover) by secret lovemaking with another **2 :** DOUBLE-CROSS — **two–tim·er** *n*
two–tone \ˌtü-ˌtōn\ *adj* **:** colored in two colors or in two shades of one color <~ shoes>
two–toned \'tü-'tōnd\ *adj* **:** TWO-TONE
two–way *adj* **1 :** being a cock or valve that will connect a pipe or channel with either of two others **2 :** moving or allowing movement in either direction <a ~ bridge> **3 a :** involving or allowing an exchange between two individuals or groups <there must be good ~ communication —Jerrold Orne>; *esp* **:** designed for both sending and receiving messages <~ radio> **b :** involving mutual responsibility or reciprocal relationships <political alliance is a ~ thing —T. H. White *b*1915> **4 :** involving two participants <a ~ race> **5 :** usable in either of two manners <a ~ lamp>
two–way street *n* **:** a situation or relationship requiring give-and-take <marriage is a *two-way street*>
two–winged fly \ˌtü-ˌwiŋ(d)-\ *n* **:** any of a large order (Diptera) of winged or rarely wingless insects (as the housefly, mosquito, or gnat) that have segmented often headless, eyeless, and legless larvae, the anterior wings functional, and the posterior wings reduced to balancers
twp *abbr* township
TWX *abbr* teletypewriter exchange
TX *abbr* Texas
-ty *n suffix* [ME *-te,* fr. OF *-té,* fr. L *-tat-, -tas* — more at -ITY] **:** quality **:** condition **:** degree <apriori*ty*>
y·coon \tī-'kün\ *n* [Jap *taikun,* fr. Chin (Pek) *ta*⁴ great + *chün*¹ ruler] **1 :** SHOGUN **2 a :** a businessman of exceptional wealth and power **:** MAGNATE **b :** a top leader (as in politics)
ng *pres part of* TIE
tyke \'tīk\ *n* [ME *tyke,* fr. ON *tík* bitch] **1 :** DOG; *esp* **:** an inferior or mongrel dog **2 a** *chiefly Brit* **:** a clumsy, churlish, or eccentric person **b :** a small child
¹tym·bal \'tim-bəl\ *var of* TIMBAL
²tym·bal *n* [alter. of *timbal*] **:** the vibrating membrane in the shrilling organ of a cicada
tym·pan \'tim-pən\ *n* [in sense 1, fr. ME, fr. OE *timpana,* fr. L *tympanum;* in other senses, fr. ML & L *tympanum*] **1 :** DRUM **2 :** a sheet (as of paper or cloth) placed between the impression surface of a press and the paper to be printed **3 :** TYMPANUM 2
tympani, tympanist *var of* TIMPANI, TIMPANIST
tym·pan·ic \tim-'pan-ik\ *adj* [L & NL *tympanum*] **:** of, relating to, or being a tympanum
tympanic bone *n* **:** a bone of the mammalian skull enclosing part of the middle ear and supporting the tympanic membrane
tympanic membrane *n* **:** a thin membrane that closes externally the cavity of the middle ear and functions in the mechanical reception of sound waves and in their transmission to the site of sensory reception — called also *eardrum;* see EAR illustration
tym·pa·ni·tes \ˌtim-pə-'nīt-ēz\ *n* [ME, fr. LL, fr. Gk *tympanitēs,* fr. *tympanon*] **:** a distension of the abdomen caused by accumulation of gas in the intestinal tract or peritoneal cavity — **tym·pa·nit·ic** \-'nit-ik\ *adj*
tym·pa·num \'tim-pə-nəm\ *n, pl* **-na** \-nə\ *also* **-nums** [ML & L; ML, eardrum, fr. L, drum, architectural panel, fr. Gk *tympanon* drum, kettledrum; akin to Gk *typtein* to beat] **1 a (1) :** TYMPANIC MEMBRANE **(2) :** the middle ear **b :** a thin tense membrane covering an organ of hearing of an insect — see INSECT illustration **c :** a membranous resonator in a sound-producing organ **2 a :** the recessed usu. triangular face of a pediment within the frame made by the upper and lower cornices **b :** the space within an arch and above a lintel or a subordinate arch **3 :** the diaphragm of a telephone
tym·pa·ny \-nē\ *n, pl* **-nies** [ML *tympanias,* fr. Gk, fr. *tympanon*] **1 :** TYMPANITES **2 :** BOMBAST, TURGIDITY
Tyn·dar·e·us \tin-'dar-ē-əs\ *n* [L, fr. Gk] **:** a king of Sparta who was father by Leda of Castor and Clytemnestra
tyne *var of* TINE
typ·al \'tī-pəl\ *adj* **1 :** of or relating to a type **2 :** serving as a type **:** TYPICAL
¹type \'tīp\ *n, often attrib* [LL *typus,* fr. L & Gk; L *typus* image, fr. Gk *typos* blow, impression, model, fr. *typtein* to strike, beat; akin to L *stuprum* defilement] **1 a :** a person or thing (as in the Old Testament) believed to foreshadow another (as in the New Testament) **b :** one having qualities of a higher category **:** MODEL **c :** a lower taxonomic category selected as a standard of reference for a higher category; *also* **:** a specimen or series of specimens on which a taxonomic species or subspecies is actually based **2 :** a distinctive mark or sign **3 a (1) :** a rectangular block usu. of metal bearing a relief character from which an inked print can be made **(2) :** a collection of such blocks <a font of ~> **(3) :** alphanumeric characters for printing <the ~ for this book has been photoset> **b :** TYPEFACE <italic ~> **c : printed letters d :** matter set in type **4 a :** qualities common to a number of individuals that distinguish them as an identifiable class: as **(1) :** the morphological, physiological, or ecological characters by which relationship between organisms may be recognized **(2) :** the form common to all instances of a word **b :** a typical and often superior specimen **c :** a member of an indicated class or variety of people <the guests were mostly urban ~*s* —Lucy Cook> **d :** a particular kind, class, or group: as **(1) :** a taxonomic category essentially equivalent to a division or phylum **(2) :** a group distinguishable on physiologic or serological bases **(3) :** one of a hierarchy of mutually exclusive classes in logic suggested to avoid paradoxes **e :** something distinguishable as a variety **:** SORT <what ~ of films to make —*Current Biog.*>
syn TYPE, KIND, SORT, NATURE, DESCRIPTION, CHARACTER *shared meaning element* **:** a number of individuals thought of as a group because of a common quality or qualities

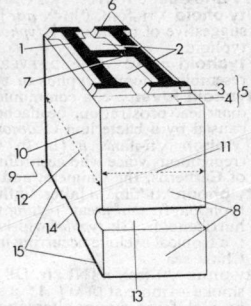

type 3a(1): *1* face, *2* counters, *3* bevel, *4* shoulder, *5* beard, *6* serifs, *7* crossbar, *8* belly, *9* back, *10* body, *11* set size, *12* point size, *13* nick, *14* groove, *15* feet

²type *vb* **typed; typ·ing** *vt* **1 :** to represent beforehand as a type **:** PREFIGURE **2 a :** to produce a copy of **b :** to represent in terms of typical characteristics **:** TYPIFY **3 :** TYPEWRITE **4 :** to identify as belonging to a type: as **a :** to determine the natural type of (as a blood sample) **b :** TYPECAST ~ *vi* **:** TYPEWRITE — **type·able** \'tī-pə-bəl\ *adj*
-type \ˌtīp\ *adj comb form* **:** of a specified type <cheddar-*type*>
type·case \'tīp-ˌkās\ *n* **:** ²CASE 3
type·cast \-ˌkast\ *vt* **-cast; -cast·ing 1 :** to cast (an actor) in a part calling for the same characteristics as those possessed by the actor himself **2 :** to cast (an actor) repeatedly in the same type of role
type·face \-ˌfās\ *n* **1 :** the face of printing type **2 :** all type of a single design

type·found·er \-ˌfau̇n-dər\ *n* **:** one engaged in the design and production of metal printing type for hand composition
type·found·ing \-diŋ\ *n* **:** the business or occupation of a typefounder
type·found·ry \-ˌfau̇n-drē\ *n* **:** the manufacturing establishment of a typefounder
type genus *n* **:** the genus of a taxonomic family or subfamily from which the name of the family or subfamily is formed
type–high \ˈtīp-ˈhī\ *adj or adv* **:** having the same foot-to-face height as printing type
type metal *n* **:** an alloy that consists essentially of lead, antimony, and tin and is used in making printing type
type I error \ˌtīp-ˈwən-\ *n* **:** rejection of the null hypothesis in statistical testing when it is true
type·script \ˈtīp-ˌskript\ *n* [*type* + manu*script*] **:** a typewritten manuscript; *esp* **:** one intended for use as printer's copy
type·set \-ˌset\ *vt* **-set; -set·ting :** to set in type **:** COMPOSE
type·set·ter \-ˌset-ər\ *n* **:** one that sets type — **type·set·ting** \-ˌset-iŋ\ *adj or n*
type species *n* **:** the species of a genus with which the generic name is permanently associated
type specimen *n* **:** a specimen or individual designated as type of a species or lesser group and serving as the final criterion of the characteristics of that group
type II error \ˌtīp-ˈtü-\ *n* **:** acceptance of the null hypothesis in statistical testing when it is false
type·write \ˈtī-ˌprīt\ *vb* **-wrote** \-ˌprōt\; **-writ·ten** \-ˌprit-ᵊn\ [back formation fr. *typewriter*] *vt* **:** to write with a typewriter ~ *vi* **:** to use a typewriter
type·writ·er \ˈtī-ˌprīt-ər\ *n* **1 :** a machine for writing in characters similar to those produced by printer's type by means of keyboard-operated types striking through an inked ribbon **2 :** TYPIST
type·writ·ing \-ˌprīt-iŋ\ *n* **1 :** the act or study of or skill in using a typewriter **2 :** the printing done with a typewriter
typh·lo·sole \ˈtif-lə-ˌsōl\ *n* [Gk *thpylos* blind + *sōlēn* pipe, channel — more at SYRINGE] **:** a longitudinal fold of the intestinal wall that projects into the cavity esp. in bivalve mollusks, annelids, and starfishes
Ty·phoe·an \tī-ˈfē-ən\ *adj* **:** suggestive of Typhoeus
Ty·pho·eus \-ˈfō-ˌyüs, -yəs\ *n* [L, fr. Gk *Typhōeus*] **:** TYPHON
[1]**ty·phoid** \ˈtī-ˌfȯid, (ˈ)tī-ˈ\ *adj* [NL *typhus*] **1 :** of, relating to, or suggestive of typhus **2** [[2]*typhoid*] **:** of, relating to, or constituting typhoid
[2]**typhoid** *n* **1 :** TYPHOID FEVER **2 :** a disease of domestic animals resembling human typhus or typhoid
typhoid fever *n* **:** a communicable disease marked esp. by fever, diarrhea, prostration, headache, and intestinal inflammation and caused by a bacterium (*Salmonella typhosa*)
Ty·phon \ˈtī-ˌfän\ *n* [L, fr. Gk *Typhōn*] **:** a monster with a tremendous voice who according to classical mythology was father of Cerberus, the Chimera, and the Sphinx
ty·phoon \tī-ˈfün\ *n* [alter. (influenced by Chin — Cant — *taaî fung* typhoon, fr. *taaî* great + *fung* wind) of earlier *touffon,* fr. Ar *ṭūfān* hurricane, fr. Gk *typhōn* whirlwind; akin to Gk *typhein* to smoke] **:** a tropical cyclone occurring in the region of the Philippines or the China sea
ty·phus \ˈtī-fəs\ *n* [NL, fr. Gk *typhos* fever; akin to Gk *typhein* to smoke — more at DEAF] **1 :** a severe human febrile disease marked by high fever, stupor alternating with delirium, intense headache, and a dark red rash, caused by a rickettsia (*Rickettsia prowazekii*), and transmitted esp. by body lice **2 :** MURINE TYPHUS **3 :** TSUTSUGAMUSHI DISEASE
typ·ic \ˈtip-ik\ *adj* **:** TYPICAL 1, 2b
typ·i·cal \ˈtip-i-kəl\ *adj* **1 :** constituting or having the nature of a type **:** SYMBOLIC **2 a :** combining or exhibiting the essential characteristics of a group <~ suburban houses> **b :** conforming to a type <a specimen ~ of the species> ***syn*** see REGULAR ***ant*** atypical, distinctive — **typ·i·cal·i·ty** \ˌtip-ə-ˈkal-ət-ē\ *n* — **typ·i·cal·ness** \ˈtip-i-kəl-nəs\ *n*
typ·i·cal·ly \ˈtip-i-k(ə-)lē\ *adv* **1 :** in a typical manner <~ American> **2 :** on a typical occasion **:** in typical circumstances
typ·i·fy \ˈtip-ə-ˌfī\ *vt* **-fied; -fy·ing 1 a :** to represent in typical fashion (as by an image, form, model, or resemblance) <the anthropologist has tried to ~ the various strata of society —*Times Lit. Supp.*> **b :** to constitute a typical mark or instance of <realism . . . that *typified* his earlier work —*Current Biog.*> **2 :** to embody the essential or salient characteristics of **:** be the type of — **typ·i·fi·ca·tion** \ˌtip-ə-fə-ˈkā-shən\ *n*
typ·ist \ˈtī-pəst\ *n* **:** one who typewrites
ty·po \ˈtī-(ˌ)pō\ *n, pl* **typos** [short for *typographical* (*error*)] **:** a typographical error
ty·po·graph \ˈtī-pə-ˌgraf\ *vt* **:** to produce (stamps) by letterpress
ty·pog·ra·pher \tī-ˈpäg-rə-fər\ *n* **1 :** COMPOSITOR **2 :** PRINTER **3 :** a specialist in the design, choice, and arrangement of type matter
ty·po·graph·ic \ˌtī-pə-ˈgraf-ik\ *adj* **:** of, relating to, or occurring or used in typography or typeset matter <a ~ character>
ty·po·graph·i·cal \-i-kəl\ *adj* **:** TYPOGRAPHIC <a ~ error> — **ty·po·graph·i·cal·ly** \-i-k(ə-)lē\ *adv*
ty·pog·ra·phy \tī-ˈpäg-rə-fē\ *n* [ML *typographia,* fr. Gk *typos* impression, cast + *-graphia* -graphy — more at TYPE] **:** the style, arrangement, or appearance of typeset matter
ty·po·log·i·cal \ˌtī-pə-ˈläj-i-kəl\ *adj* **:** of or relating to typology or types — **ty·po·log·i·cal·ly** \-i-k(ə-)lē\ *adv*
ty·pol·o·gy \tī-ˈpäl-ə-jē\ *n, pl* **-gies 1 :** a doctrine of theological types **2 :** study of or analysis or classification based on types — **ty·pol·o·gist** \-jəst\ *n*
typy *or* **typ·ey** \ˈtī-pē\ *adj* **typ·i·er; -est :** characterized by strict conformance to type; *also* **:** exhibiting superior bodily conformation
Tyr *abbr* Tyrone
ty·ra·mine \ˈtī-rə-ˌmēn\ *n* [ISV *tyrosine* + *amine*] **:** a phenolic amine $C_8H_{11}NO$ that has a sympathomimetic action and is derived from tyrosine
ty·ran·ni·cal \tə-ˈran-i-kəl, tī-\ *also* **ty·ran·nic** \-ik\ *adj* [L *tyrannicus,* fr. Gk *tyrannikos,* fr. *tyrannos* tyrant] **1 :** characteristic of a tyrant or tyranny <~ rule> **2 :** characterized by oppressive, unjust, or arbitrary behavior or control **:** DESPOTIC <a ~ ruler> — **ty·ran·ni·cal·ly** \-i-k(ə-)lē\ *adv* — **ty·ran·ni·cal·ness** \-kəl-nəs\ *n*
ty·ran·ni·cide \tə-ˈran-ə-ˌsīd, tī-\ *n* [in sense 1, fr. F, fr. L *tyrannicidium,* fr. *tyrannus* + *-i-* + *-cidium* -cide (killing); in sense 2, fr. F, fr. L *tyrannicida,* fr. *tyrannus* + *-i-* + *-cida*-cide (killer)] **1 :** the act of killing a tyrant **2 :** the killer of a tyrant
tyr·an·nize \ˈtir-ə-ˌnīz\ *vb* **-nized; -niz·ing** *vi* **:** to exercise arbitrary oppressive power or severity <some ways the living ~ over the dying —Thomas Powers> ~ *vt* **:** to treat tyrannically **:** OPPRESS — **tyr·an·niz·er** *n*
ty·ran·no·saur \tə-ˈran-ə-ˌsȯ(ə)r, tī-\ *n* [NL *Tyrannosaurus,* genus name, deriv. of Gk *tyrannos* tyrant + *sauros* lizard — more at SAURIAN] **:** a very large bipedal carnivorous dinosaur (*Tyrannosaurus rex*) with small forelegs that occurs in the Upper Cretaceous of No. America
ty·ran·no·sau·rus \tə-ˌran-ə-ˈsȯr-əs, (ˌ)tī-\ *n* [NL] **:** TYRANNOSAUR
tyr·an·nous \ˈtir-ə-nəs\ *adj* **:** marked by tyranny; *esp* **:** unjustly severe — **tyr·an·nous·ly** *adv*
tyr·an·ny \ˈtir-ə-nē\ *n, pl* **-nies** [ME *tyrannie,* fr. MF, *tyrannia,* fr. L *tyrannus* tyrant] **1 a :** a government in which absolute power is vested in a single ruler; *esp* **:** one characteristic of an ancient Greek city-state **b :** the office, authority, and administration of a tyrant **2 :** oppressive power <every form of ~ over the mind of man —Thomas Jefferson>; *specif* **:** oppressive power exerted by government <the ~ of a police state> **3 :** a severe condition or effect **:** RIGOR <living under the ~ of the clock —Dixon Wecter> **4 :** a tyrannical act
ty·rant \ˈtī-rənt\ *n* [ME *tirant,* fr. OF *tyran, tyrant,* fr. L *tyrannus,* fr. Gk *tyrannos*] **1 a :** an absolute ruler unrestrained by law or constitution **b :** a usurper of sovereignty **2 a :** a ruler who exercises absolute power oppressively or brutally **b :** one resembling such a tyrant in the harsh use of authority or power
tyrant flycatcher *n* **:** any of various large American flycatchers (family Tyrannidae) that are usu. strictly insectivorous, take their prey on the wing, and have a flattened bill often hooked at the tip and usu. bristly at the gape
tyre *chiefly Brit var of* TIRE
Tyr·i·an purple \ˌtir-ē-ən-\ *n* [*Tyre,* maritime city of ancient Phoenicia] **:** a crimson or purple dye that is related to indigo, obtained by the ancient Greeks and Romans from gastropod mollusks, and now made synthetically
ty·ro \ˈtī-(ˌ)rō\ *n, pl* **tyros** [ML, fr. L *tiro* young soldier, tyro] **:** a beginner in learning **:** NOVICE ***syn*** see AMATEUR ***ant*** expert
ty·ro·ci·dine *or* **ty·ro·ci·din** \tī-rə-ˈsīd-ᵊn \ *n* [*tyro-* (as in *tyrothricin*) + *-cid-* (as in *gramicidin*) + *-ine*] **:** a basic polypeptide antibiotic produced by a soil bacillus (*Bacillus brevis*)
Ty·ro·le·an \tə-ˈrō-lē-ən, tī-; ˌtir-ə-ˈlē-\ *also* **Ty·ro·li·an** \tə-ˈrō-lē-ən, tī-\ *adj* **1 :** of or relating to the Tirol **2** *of a hat* **:** of a style originating in the Tirol and marked by soft often green felt, a narrow brim and pointed crown, and an ornamental feather
ty·ros·i·nase \tə-ˈräs-ə-ˌnās, tī-, -ˌnāz\ *n* **:** an enzyme that promotes the oxidation of phenols (as tyrosine) and is widespread in plants and animals
ty·ro·sine \ˈtī-rə-ˌsēn\ *n* [ISV, irreg. fr. Gk *tyros* cheese — more at BUTTER] **:** a metabolically important phenolic amino acid $C_9H_{11}NO_3$ that is a precursor of various alkaloids
ty·ro·thri·cin \ˌtī-rə-ˈthrīs-ᵊn\ *n* [NL *Tyrothoric-, Tyrothrix,* generic name formerly applied to various bacteria including *Bacillus brevis*] **:** an antibiotic mixture that consists chiefly of tyrocidine and gramicidin, is usu. extracted from a soil bacillus (*Bacillus brevis*) as a gray to brown powder, and is used for local applications esp. for infection caused by gram-positive bacteria
tzaddik *n, pl* **tzaddikim** *var of* ZADDIK
tzar \ˈzär, ˈ(t)sär\ *var of* CZAR
tzi·gane \(t)sē-ˈgän\ *n* [F, fr. Hung *cigány*] **:** GYPSY 1, 2
tzim·mes \ˈtsim-əs\ *n* [Yiddish *tsimes*] **:** a sweetened combination of vegetables (as carrots and potatoes) or of meat and carrots often with dried fruits (as prunes) that is stewed or baked in a casserole
tzi·tzis *var of* ZIZITH

[1]u \'yü\ *n, pl* **u's** *or* **us** \'yüz\ *often cap, often attrib* **1 a** : the 21st letter of the English alphabet **b** : a graphic representation of this letter **c** : a speech counterpart of orthographic *u* **2** : a graphic device for reproducing the letter *u* **3** : one designated *u* esp. as the 21st in order or class **4** [abbr. for *unsatisfactory*] **a** : a grade rating a student's work as unsatisfactory **b** : one graded or rated with a U **5** : something shaped like the letter U

[2]u *abbr, often cap* **1** uncle **2** unit **3** unsymmetrical **4** upper

[1]U \'yü\ *adj* [*u*pper class] : characteristic of the upper classes

[2]U *abbr* university

[3]U *symbol* **1** [abbr. of *Union of Orthodox Hebrew Congregations*] kosher certification **2** uranium

UAPA *abbr* United Amateur Press Association

UAR *abbr* United Arab Republic

UAW *abbr* United Automobile Workers

Uban·gi \(y)ü-'baŋ-(g)ē\ *n* [*Ubangi-Shari,* Africa] : a woman of the district of Kyabé village in Africa with lips pierced and distended to unusual dimensions with wooden disks

ubi·qui·none \,yü-bə-kwin-'ōn, -'kwin-,ōn\ *n* [blend of L *ubique* everywhere and E *quinone;* fr. its widespread occurrence in nature] : a quinone that functions as an electron transfer agent between cytochromes in the Krebs cycle — called also *coenzyme Q*

ubiq·ui·tous \yü-'bik-wət-əs\ *adj* : existing or being everywhere at the same time : constantly encountered : WIDESPREAD — **ubiq·ui·tous·ly** *adv* — **ubiq·ui·tous·ness** *n*

ubiq·ui·ty \-wət-ē\ *n* [L *ubique* everywhere, fr. *ubi* where + *-que,* enclitic generalizing particle; akin to L *quis* who and to L *-que* and — more at WHO, SESQUI-] : presence everywhere or in many places esp. simultaneously : OMNIPRESENCE

U–boat \'yü-'bōt, -,bōt\ *n* [trans. of G *u-boot,* short for *unterseeboot,* lit., undersea boat] : a German submarine

UC *abbr* **1** undercharge **2** uppercase

UDC *abbr* universal decimal classification

ud·der \'əd-ər\ *n* [ME, fr. OE *ūder;* akin to OHG *ūtar* udder, L *uber,* Gk *outhar,* Skt *ūdhar*] **1** : a large pendulous organ consisting of two or more mammary glands enclosed in a common envelope and each provided with a single nipple — see COW illustration **2** : a mammary gland

UFO \,yü-(,)ef-'ō\ *n, pl* **UFO's** *or* **UFOs** \-'ōz\ [*u*nidentified *f*lying *o*bject] : an unidentified flying object; *esp* : FLYING SAUCER

UFT *abbr* United Federation of Teachers

UG *abbr* underground

[1]Uga·rit·ic \,(y)ü-gə-'rit-ik\ *adj* : of, relating to, or characteristic of the ancient city of Ugarit, its inhabitants, or Ugaritic

[2]Ugaritic *n* : the Semitic language of ancient Ugarit closely related to Phoenician and Hebrew

ugh *often read as* 'əg *or* 'ək\ *interj* — used to indicate the sound of a cough or grunt or to express disgust or horror

ug·li·fy \'əg-li-,fī\ *vt* **-fied; -fy·ing** : to make ugly — **ug·li·fi·ca·tion** \,əg-li-fə-'kā-shən\ *n*

ug·li·ness \'əg-lē-nəs\ *n* **1** : the quality or state of being ugly **2** : something that is ugly

ug·ly \'əg-lē\ *adj* **ug·li·er; -est** [ME, fr. ON *uggligr,* fr. *uggr* fear; akin to ON *ugga* to fear] **1** : FRIGHTFUL, DIRE **2 a** : offensive to the sight : HIDEOUS **b** : offensive or unpleasing to any sense **3** : morally offensive or objectionable : REPULSIVE **4 a** : likely to cause inconvenience or discomfort <the ~ truth> **b** : SURLY, QUARRELSOME <an ~ drunk> — **ug·li·ly** \-lə-lē\ *adv*

syn UGLY, HIDEOUS, ILL-FAVORED, UNSIGHTLY *shared meaning element* : neither pleasing nor beautiful, esp. to the eye ***ant*** beautiful

ugly duckling *n* [*The Ugly Duckling,* story by Hans Christian Andersen] : something that appears very unpromising but often has great potential

UGPA *abbr* undergraduate grade-point average

Ugri·an \'(y)ü-grē-ən\ *n* [ORuss *Ugre* Hungarians] : a member of the eastern division of the Finno-Ugric peoples — **Ugrian** *adj*

Ugric \-grik\ *adj* : of, relating to, or characteristic of the languages of the Ugrians

ug·some \'əg-səm\ *adj* [ME, fr. *uggen* to fear, inspire fear, fr. ON *ugga* to fear] *archaic* : FRIGHTFUL, LOATHSOME

ugt *abbr* urgent

UH *abbr* upper half

UHF *abbr* ultrahigh frequency

uh–huh *two* m*'s separated by the voiceless sound* h\ *interj* — used to indicate affirmation, agreement, or gratification

uh·lan \'ü-,län, ü-'; '(y)ü-lən\ *n* [G] : one of a body of Prussian light cavalry orig. modeled on Tatar lancers

Ui·ghur *or* **Ui·gur** \'wē-,gü(ə)r\ *n* [Uighur *Uighur*] **1** : a member of a Turkic people powerful in Mongolia and eastern Turkestan between the 8th and 12th centuries A.D. who constitute a majority of the population of Chinese Turkestan **2** : the Turkic language of the Uighur — **Uighur** *or* **Uigur** *adj*

uin·ta·ite *also* **uin·tah·ite** \yù-'int-ə-,īt\ *n* [*Uinta, Uintah,* mountains in Utah] : a black lustrous asphalt occurring esp. in Utah

Uit·land·er \'āt-,lan-dər\ *n* [Afrik] : FOREIGNER; *esp* : a British resident in the former republics of the Transvaal and Orange Free State

UK *abbr* United Kingdom

ukase \yü-'kās, -'kāz, 'yü-,; ü-'käz\ *n* [F & Russ; F, fr. Russ *ukaz,* fr. *ukazat'* to show, order; akin to OSlav *u-* away, L *au-,* Skt *ava-* and to OSlav *kazati* to show] **1** : a proclamation by a Russian emperor or government having the force of law **2** : EDICT

uke \'yük\ *n* : UKULELE

uki·yo–e *also* **uki·yo–ye** \ü-,kē-ō-'yā, -,kē-yō-'ā\ *n* [Jap *ukiyo-e* genre picture, fr. *ukiyo* world, life + *e* picture] : a Japanese art movement that flourished from the 17th to the 19th century and produced paintings and prints depicting the everyday life and interests of the common people; *also* : the paintings and prints themselves

Ukrai·ni·an \yü-'krā-nē-ən *also* -'krī-\ *n* **1** : a native or inhabitant of the Ukraine **2** : the Slavic language of the Ukrainian people — **Ukrainian** *adj*

uku·le·le \,yü-kə-'lā-lē, ,ü-\ *n* [Hawaiian *'ukulele,* fr. *'uku* small person + *lele* jumping] : a small guitar of Portuguese origin popularized in Hawaii in the 1880s and strung typically with four strings

ukulele

ula·ma *or* **ule·ma** \,ü-lə-'mä\ *n* [Ar, Turk, & Per; Turk & Per *'ulemā,* fr. Ar *'ulamā*] **1** *pl* : the body of mullahs **2** : MULLAH 1

-u·lar \(y)ə-lər\ *adj suffix* [L *-ularis,* fr. *-ulus, -ula, -ulum* -ule + *-aris* -ar] : of, relating to, or resembling <valv*ular*>

[1]ul·cer \'əl-sər\ *n* [ME, fr. L *ulcer-, ulcus;* akin to Gk *helkos* wound] **1** : a break in skin or mucous membrane with loss of surface tissue, disintegration and necrosis of epithelial tissue, and often pus **2** : something that festers and corrupts like an open sore

[2]ulcer *vb* **ul·cered; ul·cer·ing** \'əls-(ə-)riŋ\ : ULCERATE

ul·cer·ate \'əl-sə-,rāt\ *vb* **-at·ed; -at·ing** *vt* : to affect with or as if with an ulcer ~ *vi* : to undergo ulceration

ul·cer·ation \,əl-sə-'rā-shən\ *n* **1** : the process of becoming ulcerated : the state of being ulcerated **2** : ULCER — **ul·cer·ative** \'əl-sə-,rāt-iv, 'əls-(ə-)rət-\ *adj*

ul·cero·gen·ic \,əl-sə-rō-'jen-ik\ *adj* : tending to produce or develop into ulcers or ulceration

ul·cer·ous \'əls-(ə-)rəs\ *adj* **1** : being or marked by an ulceration <~ lesions> **2** : affected with an ulcer : ULCERATED

-ule \(,)(y)ü(ə)l\ *n suffix* [F & L; F, fr. L *-ulus,* masc. dim. suffix, *-ula,* fem. dim. suffix, *-ulum,* neut. dim. suffix] : little one <duct*ule*>

-u·lent \(y)ə-lənt\ *adj suffix* [L *-ulentus*] : that abounds in (a specified thing) <flocc*ulent*>

ulex·ite \'yü-lək-,sīt\ *n* [George L. *Ulex* †1883 G chemist] : a mineral $NaCaB_5O_9 \cdot 8H_2O$ consisting of a hydrous sodium calcium borate and usu. occurring in loosely packed white fibers that transmit light lengthwise with nearly undiminished intensity

ul·lage \'əl-ij\ *n* [ME *ulage,* fr. MF *eullage* act of filling a cask, fr. *eullier* to fill a cask, fr. OF *ouil* eye, bunghole, fr. L *oculus* eye] : the amount that a container (as a tank or cask) lacks of being full

ul·na \'əl-nə\ *n* [NL, fr. L, elbow — more at ELL] : the bone on the little-finger side of the human forearm; *also* : a corresponding part of the forelimb of vertebrates above fishes — **ul·nar** \-nər, -när\ *adj*

-u·lose \(y)ə-,lōs, -,lōz\ *n suffix* [lev*ulose*] : ketose sugar <hept*ulose*>

ulot·ri·chous \yü-'lä-tri-kəs\ *adj* [deriv. of Gk *oulotrich-, oulothrix,* fr. *oulos* curly + *trich-, thrix* hair; akin to Gk *eilyein* to roll — more at VOLUBLE, TRICH-] : having woolly or crisp hair — **ulot·ri·chy** \-trə-kē\ *n*

-u·lous \(y)ə-ləs\ *adj suffix* [L *-ulus,* dim. suffix] : being slightly or minutely (such) <hirsut*ulous*>

ul·ster \'əl-stər\ *n* [*Ulster,* Ireland] : a long loose overcoat of Irish origin made of heavy material (as frieze)

ult *abbr* **1** ultimate **2** ultimo

ul·te·ri·or \,əl-'tir-ē-ər\ *adj* [L, farther, further, compar. of (assumed) L *ulter* situated beyond, fr. *uls* beyond; akin to L *ollus, ille,* that one, OIr ind*oll* beyond] **1 a** : FURTHER, FUTURE **b** : more distant : REMOTER **c** : situated on the farther side : THITHER **2** : going beyond what is openly said or shown and esp. what is proper <~ motives> — **ul·te·ri·or·ly** *adv*

ul·ti·ma \'əl-tə-mə\ *n* [L, fem. of *ultimus* last] : the last syllable of a word

ul·ti·ma·cy \'əl-tə-mə-sē\ *n, pl* **-cies** **1** : the quality or state of being ultimate **2** : ULTIMATE 1

ul·ti·ma ra·tio \,ùl-tə-mə-'rät-ē-,ō\ *n* [NL] : the final argument; *also* : the last resort (as force)

[1]ul·ti·mate \'əl-tə-mət\ *adj* [ML *ultimatus* last, final, fr. LL, pp. of *ultimare* to come to an end, be last, fr. L *ultimus* farthest, last, final, superl. of (assumed) L *ulter* situated beyond — more at ULTERIOR] **1 a** : most remote in space or time : FARTHEST **b** : last in a progression or series <their ~ destination was Paris> **c** : EVENTUAL <they hoped for ~ success> **d** : EXTREME, UTMOST **2** : finally reckoned **3 a** : BASIC, FUNDAMENTAL **b** : incapable of further analysis, division, or separation : ELEMENTAL **4** : MAXIMUM ***syn*** see LAST — **ul·ti·mate·ness** *n*

[2]ultimate *n* **1** : something ultimate : FUNDAMENTAL **2** : ACME

ul·ti·mate·ly *adv* : in the end : at last : FINALLY

ul·ti·ma Thu·le \,əl-tə-mə-'th(y)ü-lē\ *n* [L, farthest Thule] : THULE

ul·ti·ma·tum \,əl-tə-'māt-əm, -'mät-\ *n, pl* **-tums** *or* **-ta** \-ə\ [NL, fr. ML, neut. of *ultimatus* final] : a final proposition, condition, or demand; *esp* : one whose rejection will end negotiations and cause a resort to force or other direct action

ul·ti·mo \'əl-tə-,mō\ *adj* [L *ultimo mense* in the last month] : of or occurring in the month preceding the present

ul·ti·mo·gen·i·ture \,əl-tə-mō-'jen-ə-,chù(ə)r, -i-chər, -ə-,t(y)ù(ə)r\ *n* [L *ultimus* last + E *-o-* + *-geniture* (as in *primogeniture*)] : a system of inheritance by which the youngest son succeeds to the estate

[1]ul·tra \'əl-trə\ *adj* [*ultra-*] : going beyond others or beyond due limit : EXTREME

[2]ultra *n* [*ultra-*] : EXTREMIST

ə abut   ᵊ kitten   ər further   a back   ā bake   ä cot, cart
aù out   ch chin   e less   ē easy   g gift   i trip   ī life
j joke   ŋ sing   ō flow   ȯ flaw   ȯi coin   th thin   th this
ü loot   ù foot   y yet   yü few   yù furious   zh vision

ul·tra- *prefix* [L, fr. *ultra* beyond, adv. & prep., fr. (assumed) L *ulter* situated beyond — more at ULTERIOR] **1 :** beyond in space **:** on the other side **:** TRANS- <*ultra*violet> **2 :** beyond the range or limits of **:** transcending **:** SUPER- <*ultra*microscopic> **3 :** beyond what is ordinary, proper, or moderate **:** excessively **:** extremely <*ultra*modern>

ul·tra·ba·sic \ˌəl-trə-ˈbā-sik\ *adj* [ISV] **:** extremely basic; *specif* **:** very low in silica and rich in iron and magnesium minerals — **ultrabasic** *n*

ul·tra·cen·trif·u·gal \-ˌsen-ˈtrif-yə-gəl, -ˈtrif-i-gəl\ *adj* **:** of, relating to, or obtained by means of an ultracentrifuge — **ul·tra·cen·trif·u·gal·ly** \-gə-lē\ *adv*

[1]ul·tra·cen·tri·fuge \-ˈsen-trə-ˌfyüj\ *n* **:** a high-speed centrifuge able to sediment colloidal and other small particles and used esp. in determining sizes of such particles and molecular weights of large molecules

[2]ultracentrifuge *vt* **:** to subject to an ultracentrifuge — **ul·tra·cen·tri·fu·ga·tion** \-ˌsen-trə-fyù-ˈgā-shən\ *n*

ul·tra·con·ser·va·tive \ˌəl-trə-kən-ˈsər-vət-iv\ *adj* **:** extremely conservative — **ultraconservative** *n*

ul·tra·fash·ion·able \-ˈfash-(ə-)nə-bəl\ *adj* **:** extremely fashionable

ul·tra·fiche \ˈəl-trə-ˌfēsh\ *n* **:** a microfiche whose microimages are of printed matter reduced 90 or more times

ul·tra·fil·tra·tion \ˌəl-trə-fil-ˈtrā-shən\ *n* **:** filtration through a medium (as a semipermeable capillary wall) which allows small molecules (as of water) to pass but holds back larger ones (as of protein)

ul·tra·high \-ˈhī\ *adj* **:** very high **:** exceedingly high <~ vacuum> <at ~ temperatures>

ultrahigh frequency *n* **:** a radio frequency between superhigh frequency and very high frequency — see RADIO FREQUENCY table

ul·tra·ism \ˈəl-trə-ˌiz-əm\ *n* **1 :** the principles of those who advocate extreme measures (as radicalism) **2 :** an instance or example of radicalism — **ul·tra·ist** \-trə-əst\ *adj or n* **ul·tra·is·tic** \ˌəl-trə-ˈis-tik\ *adj*

ul·tra·lib·er·al \ˌəl-trə-ˈlib-(ə-)rəl\ *adj* **:** extremely liberal — **ultraliberal** *n*

ul·tra·maf·ic \-ˈmaf-ik\ *adj* **:** ULTRABASIC

[1]ul·tra·ma·rine \ˌəl-trə-mə-ˈrēn\ *n* [ML *ultramarinus* coming from beyond the sea] **1 a (1) :** a blue pigment prepared by powdering lapis lazuli **(2) :** a similar pigment prepared from kaolin, soda ash, sulfur, and charcoal **b :** any of several related pigments **2 :** a vivid blue

[2]ultramarine *adj* [ML *ultramarinus*, fr. L *ultra-* + *mare* sea — more at MARINE] **:** situated beyond the sea

ul·tra·mi·cro \ˌəl-trə-ˈmī-(ˌ)krō\ *adj* **:** being or dealing with something smaller than micro

ul·tra·mi·cro·scope \ˌəl-trə-ˈmī-krə-ˌskōp\ *n* [back-formation fr. *ultramicroscopic*] **:** an apparatus for making visible by scattered light particles too small to be perceived by the ordinary microscope

ul·tra·mi·cro·scop·ic \-ˌmī-krə-ˈskäp-ik\ *adj* [ISV] **1 :** too small to be seen with an ordinary microscope **2 :** of or relating to an ultramicroscope — **ul·tra·mi·cro·scop·i·cal·ly** \-i-k(ə-)lē\ *adv*

ul·tra·mi·cro·tome \-ˈmī-krə-ˌtōm\ *n* **:** a microtome designed to cut extremely thin sections for examination with the electron microscope — **ul·tra·mi·crot·o·my** \-mī-ˈkrät-ə-mē\ *n*

ul·tra·mil·i·tant \-ˈmil-ə-tənt\ *adj* **:** extremely militant — **ultramilitant** *n*

ul·tra·min·ia·ture \-ˈmin-ē-ə-ˌchù(ə)r, -ˈmin-i-ˌchù(ə)r, -ˈmin-yə-, -chər, -ˌt(y)ù(ə)r\ *adj* **:** SUBMINIATURE — **ul·tra·min·ia·tur·iza·tion** \-ˌmin-ē-ə-ˌchùr-ə-ˈzā-shən, ˌmin-i-ˌchùr-, ˌmin-yə-ˌchùr-, -chər-, -ˌt(y)ùr-\ *n*

ul·tra·mod·ern \ˌəl-trə-ˈmäd-ərn\ *adj* **:** having the very latest ideas, styles, or tendencies — **ul·tra·mod·ern·ist** \-ər-nəst\ *n*

ul·tra·mon·tane \-ˈmän-ˌtān, -ˌmän-ˈ\ *adj* [ML *ultramontanus*, fr. L *ultra-* + *mont-*, *mons* mountain — more at MOUNT] **1 :** of or relating to countries or peoples beyond the mountains (as the Alps) **2 :** favoring greater or absolute supremacy of papal over national or diocesan authority in the Roman Catholic Church — **ultramontane** *n, often cap* — **ul·tra·mon·tan·ism** \-ˈmänt-ᵊn-ˌiz-əm\ *n*

ul·tra·na·tion·al·ism \-ˈnash-nə-ˌliz-əm, -ən-ᵊl-ˌiz-\ *n* **:** great or excessive devotion to or advocacy of national interests and rights esp. as opposed to international considerations — **ul·tra·na·tion·al·ist** \-nə-ləst, -ən-ᵊl-əst\ *adj or n*

ul·tra·pure \-ˈpyù(ə)r\ *adj* **:** of the utmost purity <the distinctive qualities of an ~ metal> — **ul·tra·pure·ly** *adv*

ul·tra·se·cret \ˌəl-trə-ˈsē-krət\ *adj* **:** highly secret

ul·tra·short \-ˈshò(ə)rt\ *adj* **1 :** very short in duration <an ~ pulse of light> **2 :** having a wavelength below 10 meters <~ radiation>

[1]ul·tra·son·ic \-ˈsän-ik\ *adj* **:** SUPERSONIC: **a :** having a frequency above the human ear's audibility limit of about 20,000 cycles per second — used of waves and vibrations **b :** utilizing, produced by, or relating to ultrasonic waves or vibrations <~ testing of metal> — **ul·tra·son·i·cal·ly** \-i-k(ə-)lē\ *adv*

[2]ultrasonic *n* **:** an ultrasonic wave or frequency

ul·tra·son·ics \ˌəl-trə-ˈsän-iks\ *n pl but sing in constr* **:** the science or technology of ultrasonic phenomena

ul·tra·so·phis·ti·cat·ed \-sə-ˈfis-tə-ˌkāt-əd\ *adj* **:** extremely sophisticated <~ machinery>

ul·tra·sound \ˈəl-trə-ˌsaùnd\ *n* **:** vibrations of the same physical nature as sound but with frequencies above the range of human hearing

ul·tra·struc·ture \ˈəl-trə-ˌstrək-chər\ *n* **:** the invisible ultimate physiochemical organization of protoplasm — **ul·tra·struc·tur·al** \ˌəl-trə-ˈstrək-chə-rəl, -ˈstrək-shrəl\ *adj* — **ul·tra·struc·tur·al·ly** \-ē\ *adv*

ul·tra·vi·o·let \ˌəl-trə-ˈvī-ə-lət\ *adj* **1 :** situated beyond the visible spectrum at its violet end — used of radiation having a wavelength shorter than wavelengths of visible light and longer than those of X rays **2 :** relating to, producing, or employing ultraviolet radiation — **ultraviolet** *n*

ultraviolet light *n* **:** ultraviolet radiation

ul·tra vi·res \ˌəl-trə-ˈvī-(ˌ)rēz\ *adv or adj* [NL, lit., beyond power] **:** beyond the scope or in excess of legal power or authority

ul·u·lant \ˈəl-yə-lənt\ *adj* **:** having a howling sound **:** WAILING

ul·u·late \-ˌlāt\ *vi* **-lat·ed; -lat·ing** [L *ululatus*, pp. of *ululare*, of imit. origin] **:** HOWL, WAIL — **ulu·la·tion** \ˌəl-yə-ˈlā-shən\ *n*

ul·va \ˈəl-və\ *n* [NL, genus name, fr. L, sedge] **:** SEA LETTUCE

Ulys·ses \yù-ˈlis-(ˌ)ēz\ *n* [L, modif. of Gk *Odysseus*] **:** ODYSSEUS

um·bel \ˈəm-bəl\ *n* [NL *umbella*, fr. L, umbrella] **:** a racemose inflorescence typical of the carrot family in which the axis is very much contracted so that the pedicels appear to spring from the same point to form a flat or rounded flower cluster — see INFLORESCENCE illustration — **um·beled** *or* **um·belled** \-bəld\ *adj*

um·bel·late \ˈəm-bə-ˌlāt, ˌəm-ˈbəl-ət\ *adj* **1 :** bearing, consisting of, or arranged in umbels **2 :** resembling an umbel in form

um·bel·li·fer \ˌəm-ˈbel-ə-fər\ *n* [NL *Umbelliferae*, group name, fem. pl. of *umbellifer* bearing umbels] **:** a plant of the carrot family

ulva

um·bel·lif·er·ous \ˌəm-bə-ˈlif-(ə-)rəs\ *adj* **:** of or relating to the carrot family

[1]um·ber \ˈəm-bər\ *n* [ME *umbre*, fr. MF, fr. L *umbra* shade, shadow, grayling] **:** a European grayling (*Thymallus thymallus*)

[2]umber *n* [prob. fr. obs. E, shade, color, fr. ME *umbre* shade, shadow, fr. MF, fr. L *umbra* — more at UMBRAGE] **1 :** a brown earth that is darker in color than ocher and sienna because of its content of manganese and iron oxides and is highly valued as a permanent pigment either in the raw or burnt state **2 a :** a moderate to dark yellowish brown **b :** a moderate brown

[3]umber *adj* **:** of, relating to, or having the characteristics of umber; *specif* **:** of the color of umber

[4]umber *vt* **um·bered; um·ber·ing** \-b(ə-)riŋ\ **:** to darken with or as if with umber

[1]um·bil·i·cal \ˌəm-ˈbil-i-kəl\ *adj* **1 :** of, relating to, or used at the navel **2 :** of or relating to the central region of the abdomen

[2]umbilical *n* **:** UMBILICAL CORD 2

umbilical cord *n* **1 :** a cord arising from the navel that connects the fetus with the placenta; *also* **:** YOLK STALK **2 :** a cable conveying power to a rocket or spacecraft before takeoff; *also* **:** a tethering or supply line (as for an astronaut outside a spacecraft or an aquanaut underwater)

um·bil·i·cate \ˌəm-ˈbil-i-kət\ *or* **um·bil·i·cat·ed** \-ə-ˌkāt-əd\ *adj* **1 :** depressed like a navel **2 :** having an umbilicus — **um·bil·i·ca·tion** \ˌəm-ˌbil-ə-ˈkā-shən\ *n*

um·bi·li·cus \ˌəm-bə-ˈlī-kəs, ˌəm-ˈbil-i-\ *n, pl* **um·bi·li·ci** \ˌəm-bə-ˈlī-ˌkī, -ˌsī; ˌəm-ˈbil-ə-ˌkī, -ˌkē\ *or* **um·bi·li·cus·es** [L — more at NAVEL] **1 a :** a small depression in the abdominal wall at the point of attachment of the umbilical cord to the embryo **b :** any of several morphological depressions; *esp* **:** HILUM 1a **2 :** a central point **:** CORE, HEART

um·bles \ˈəm-bəlz\ *n pl* [ME, alter. of *nombles*, fr. MF, pl. of *nomble* fillet of beef, pork loin, modif. of L *lumbulus*, dim. of *lumbus* loin — more at LOIN] **:** the entrails of an animal and esp. of a deer formerly used as food

um·bo \ˈəm-(ˌ)bō\ *n, pl* **um·bo·nes** \ˌəm-ˈbō-(ˌ)nēz\ *or* **umbos** [L; akin to L *umbilicus* — more at NAVEL] **1 :** the boss of a shield **2 :** a rounded elevation: as **a :** an elevation in the tympanic membrane of the ear **b :** one of the lateral prominences just above the hinge of a bivalve shell — **um·bo·nal** \ˈəm-bən-ᵊl, ˌəm-ˈbōn-\ *adj* — **um·bo·nate** \ˈəm-bə-ˌnāt, ˌəm-ˈbō-nət\ *adj*

um·bra \ˈəm-brə\ *n, pl* **umbras** *or* **um·brae** \-(ˌ)brē, -ˌbrī\ [L] **1 :** a shaded area **2 a :** a conical shadow excluding all light from a given source; *specif* **:** the conical part of the shadow of a celestial body excluding all light from the primary source **b (1) :** PENUMBRA 2 **(2) :** the central dark part of a sunspot — **um·bral** \-brəl\ *adj*

um·brage \ˈəm-brij\ *n* [ME, fr. MF, fr. L *umbraticum*, neut. of *umbraticus* of shade, fr. *umbratus*, pp. of *umbrare* to shade, fr. *umbra* shade, shadow; akin to Lith *unksna* shadow] **1 :** SHADE, SHADOW **2 :** shady branches **:** FOLIAGE **3 a :** an indistinct indication **:** vague suggestion **:** HINT **b :** a reason for doubt **:** SUSPICION **4 :** a feeling of pique or resentment often at some fancied slight or insult <took ~ at the chairman's comment> ***syn*** see OFFENSE

um·bra·geous \ˌəm-ˈbrā-jəs\ *adj* **1 a :** SHADY **b :** filled with shadows **2 :** inclined to take offense easily — **um·bra·geous·ly** *adv* — **um·bra·geous·ness** *n*

[1]um·brel·la \ˌəm-ˈbrel-ə, *esp South* ˈəm-ˌ\ *n* [It *ombrella*, modif. of L *umbella*, dim. of *umbra*] **1 :** a collapsible shade for protection against weather consisting of fabric stretched over hinged ribs radiating from a central pole; *esp* **:** a small one for carrying in the hand **2 :** the bell-shaped or saucer-shaped largely gelatinous structure that forms the chief part of the body of most jellyfishes **3 :** something which provides protection: as **a :** a defensive formation of planes maintained over surface operations or a landmass **b :** a heavy barrage **4 :** something which covers or embraces a broad range of elements or factors <decided to expand . . . by building new colleges under a federation ~ —Diane Ravitch>

[2]umbrella *vt* **:** to protect, cover, or provide with an umbrella

umbrella bird *n* **:** any of several tropical American birds (genus *Cephalopterus* and esp. *C. ornatus*) related to the tyrant flycatchers and noted for the black male with a radiating crest curving forward over the head

umbrella leaf *n* **:** a No. American herb (*Diphylleia cymosa*) of the barberry family with two large peltate stem leaves or a solitary lobed basal one

umbrella plant *n* **:** an African sedge (*Cyperus alternifolius*) that has large terminal whorls of slender leaves and is often grown as an ornamental

umbrella tree *n* **1 :** an American magnolia (*Magnolia tripetala*) having large leaves clustered at the ends of the branches **2 :** any of various trees or shrubs resembling an umbrella esp. in the arrangement of leaves or the shape of the crown

Um·bri·an \ˈəm-brē-ən\ *n* **1 a :** a member of a people of ancient Italy occupying Umbria **b :** a native or inhabitant of the Italian province of Umbria **2 :** the Italic language of ancient Umbria — see INDO-EUROPEAN LANGUAGES table — **Umbrian** *adj*

Um·bun·du \ˌəm-ˈbün-(ˌ)dü\ *n* **:** a Congo language of central Angola

umi·ak \ˈü-mē-ˌak\ *n* [Esk] **:** an open Eskimo boat made of a wooden frame covered with hide and usu. propelled with broad paddles

umiak

1um·laut \ˈüm-ˌlau̇t, ˈu̇m-\ *n* [G, fr. *um-* around, transformation + *laut* sound] **1 a :** the change of a vowel caused by partial assimilation to a succeeding sound; *esp* **:** the fronting or raising of a back or low vowel (as *a, o,* or *u*) caused by an *i* or *j* orig. standing in the following syllable but usu. lost or altered **b :** a vowel resulting from such partial assimilation **2 :** a diacritical mark ¨ placed esp. over a German vowel to indicate umlaut

2umlaut *vt* **1 :** to produce by umlaut **2 :** to write or print an umlaut over

1ump \ˈəmp\ *n* **:** UMPIRE 2

2ump *vi* **:** to act as umpire

um·pir·age \ˈəm-ˌpī(ə)r-ij\ *n* **1 :** the office or authority of an umpire **2 a :** an act or instance of umpiring **b :** a decision of an umpire

1um·pire \ˈəm-ˌpī(ə)r\ *n* [ME *oumpere,* alter. (resulting fr. incorrect division of *a noumpere*) of *noumpere,* fr. MF *nomper* not equal, not paired, fr. *non-* + *per* equal, fr. L *par*] **1 :** one having authority to decide finally a controversy or question between parties: as **a :** one appointed to decide between arbitrators who have disagreed **b :** an impartial third party chosen to arbitrate disputes arising under the terms of a labor agreement **2 :** an official in a sport who rules on plays **3 :** a military officer who evaluates maneuvers

2umpire *vb* **um·pired; um·pir·ing** *vt* **:** to supervise or decide as umpire ~ *vi* **:** to act as umpire

ump·teen \ˈəm(p)-ˈtēn, ˌəm(p)-\ *adj* [blend of *umpty* (such and such) + *-teen* (as in *thirteen*)] **:** very many **:** indefinitely numerous — **ump·teenth** \-ˈtēn(t)th\ *adj*

UMT *abbr* Universal Military Training

UMW *abbr* United Mine Workers

UN *abbr* United Nations

1un- \ˌən, ˈən *before* ˈ-*stressed syll,* ˌən *before* ˌ-*stressed or unstressed syll*\ *prefix* [ME, fr. OE; akin to OHG *un-* un-, L *in-*, Gk *a-, an-*, OE *ne* not — more at NO] **1 :** not **:** IN-, NON- — in adjectives formed from adjectives <*un*strenuous> <*un*skilled> or participles <*un*dressed>, in nouns formed from nouns <*un*ostentation>, and rarely in verbs formed from verbs <*un*be>; sometimes in words, that have a meaning that merely negates that of the base word and are thereby distinguished from words that prefix *in-* or a variant of it (as *im-*) to the same base word and have a meaning positively opposite to that of the base word <*un*artistic> <*un*moral> **2 :** opposite of **:** contrary to — in adjectives formed from adjectives <*un*constitutional> <*un*graceful> <*un*mannered> or participles <*un*believing> and in nouns formed from nouns <*un*rest>

2un- *prefix* [ME, fr. OE *un-, on-*, alter. of *and-* against — more at ANTE-] **1 :** do the opposite of **:** reverse (a specified action) **:** DE-1a, DIS-1a — in verbs formed from verbs <*un*bend> <*un*dress> <*un*fold> **2 a :** deprive of **:** remove (a specified thing) from **:** remove — in verbs formed from nouns <*un*frock> <*un*sex> **b :** release from **:** free from — in verbs formed from nouns <*un*hand> **c :** remove from **:** extract from **:** bring out of — in verbs formed from nouns <*un*bosom> **d :** cause to cease to be — in verbs formed from nouns <*un*man> **3 :** completely <*un*loose>

unabbreviated
unabsolved
unabsorbable
unabsorbed
unabsorbent
unacademic
unaccented
unaccentuated
unaccepted
unacclimated
unacclimatized
unaccommodating
unaccomplished
unaccredited
unachievable
unachieved
unacknowledged
unacquainted
unactable
unacted
unadaptable
unadapted
unadjusted
unadmirable
unadvantageous
unadventurous
unadvertised
unadvisable
unaesthetic
unaffiliated
unaffluent
unafraid
unaged
unaggressive
unagile
unaided
unaimed
unair-conditioned
unaired
unalienated
unalike
unalleviated
unallied
unallocated
unallowable
unaltered
unambitious
unamenable
unamiable
unamplified
unanalyzable
unanalyzed
unanimated
unannotated
unannounced
unanonymous
unanswered
unappalled
unapparent
unappeased
unappreciated
unappreciative
unapproached
unappropriated
unapproved
unaristocratic
unarmored
unarrested
unartistic
unaspirated
unaspiring
unassailed
unassigned
unassimilable
unassimilated
unassisted
unassociated
unassuaged
unastronomical
unathletic
unattainable
unattempted
unattended
unattested
unauspicious
unauthentic
unauthenticated
unauthorized
unavowed
unawakened
unawed
unbaked
unbaptized
unbeautified
unbefitting
unbemused
unbigoted
unblamable
unblamed
unbleached
unblemished
unblenching
unblended
unblotted
unboastful
unbookish
unborrowed
unbothered
unbought
unbowdlerized
unbracketed
unbranded
unbreakable
unbridgeable
unbridged
unbrotherly
unbruised
unbrushed
unbudgeted
unburned
unburnished
unburnt
uncalcified
uncalled
uncanceled
uncanonical
uncapitalized
uncaptured
uncared-for
uncaring
uncarpeted
uncashed
uncastrated
uncataloged
uncaught
uncensored
uncensured
unchallenged
unchanged
unchaperoned
uncharismatic
uncharming
unchary
unchastened
unchecked
unchic
unchristened
unciliated
unclad
unclaimed
unclassifiable
uncleaned
unclear
uncleared
unclimbed
uncluttered
uncoated
uncoerced
uncollected
uncollectible
uncolored
uncombed
uncombined
uncomely
uncomforted
uncomic
uncommanding
uncompanionable
uncompensated
uncompleted
uncompounded
uncomprehended
uncomprehensible
uncompromised
unconcealed
unconfessed
unconfined
unconfirmed
unconfused
uncongealed
unconnected
unconquered
unconscientious
unconsecrated
unconstrained
unconsumed
uncontainable
uncontaminated
uncontemporary
uncontested
uncontradicted
uncontrived
uncontrolled
uncontroversial
unconverted
unconvinced
uncooked
uncooperative
uncoordinated
uncordial
uncorrected
uncorroborated
uncorrupt
uncorrupted
uncountable
uncourteous
uncreative
uncredited
uncrippled
uncriticized
uncropped
uncrossable
uncrowded
uncultivable
uncultivated
uncultured
uncurbed
uncured
uncurious
uncurrent
uncurtained
uncustomary
undamaged
undamped
undaring
undated
undazzled
undecidable
undecided
undecipherable
undecked
undeclared
undeclinable
undecorated
undefeated
undefiled
undefinable
undefined
undeformed
undelayed
undeliverable
undelivered
undemanding
undenominational
undependable
undeserved
undeserving
undesired
undetachable
undetectable
undetected
undeterminable
undetermined
undeterred
undeveloped
undialectical
undifferentiated
undigested
undignified
undiluted
undiminished
undimmed
undiscerning
undischarged
undisciplined
undisclosed
undiscoverable
undiscovered
undiscriminating
undiscussed
undismayed
undisputed
undissolved
undistinguished
undistorted
undistracted
undistributed
undisturbed
undiversified
undivided
undivulged
undoctored
undoctrinaire
undocumented
undomestic
undomesticated
undoubtable
undoubting
undrained
undrinkable
undulled
undyed
uneager
uneatable
uneaten
unedifying
uneducable
uneducated
unembarrassed
unembellished
unenclosed
unendorsed
unenduring
unenforceable
unenforced
unengaged
unenjoyable
unenlarged
unenlightened
unenlightening
unenrolled
unenterprising
unentertaining
unenticing
unenviable
unenvied
unenvious
unequipped
unescapable
unesthetic
unethical
unevaluated
unexaggerated
unexamined
unexcavated
unexcelled
unexchangeable
unexcitable
unexcited
unexciting
unexecuted
unexhausted
unexotic
unexpanded
unexpectable
unexpended
unexpired
unexplainable
unexplained
unexploded
unexplored
unexposed
unexpressed
unexpressible
unexpurgated
unextended
unextinguished
unfaded
unfanatical
unfashioned
unfastidious
unfathomed
unfazed
unfeasible
unfed
unfeminine
unfenced
unfermentable
unfermented
unfertile
unfertilized
unfilled
unfired
unflamboyant
unflavored
unflexed
unflyable
unfond
unforced
unforeseeable
unforeseen
unforgivable
unforked
unformatted
unformulated
unfortified
unfossiliferous
unframed
unfrantic
unfree
unfrustrated
unfulfilled
unfunctional
unfurnished
unfused
ungarnished
ungathered
ungenteel
ungentle
ungentlemanly
ungerminated
ungifted
unglamorized

ə abut ᵊ kitten ər further a back ā bake ä cot, cart
au̇ out ch chin e less ē easy g gift i trip ī life
j joke ŋ sing ō flow ȯ flaw ȯi coin th thin th this
ü loot u̇ foot y yet yü few yu̇ furious zh vision

unglazed
ungodlike
ungoverned
ungraded
ungraspable
ungreedy
ungrounded
unguided
unhackneyed
unhampered
unhanged
unhardened
unharmed
unharmonious
unharvested
unhatched
unhealable
unhealed
unhealthful
unheated
unheeded
unheeding
unheralded
unheroic
unheroical
unhesitant
unhindered
unhip
unhired
unhistorical
unhonored
unhoped-for
unhumorous
unhurt
unhydrated
unhygienic
unideal
unidealized
unidentifiable
unidentified
unideological
unidiomatic
unilluminated
unimaginative
unimpaired
unimpeded
unimportance
unimportant
unimposing
unimpressed
unimpressible
unimpressionable
unimpressive
uninclined
unincorporated
unindexed
unindustrialized
uninfected
uninflammable
uninflected
uninfluenced
uninformed
uninhabitable
uninhabited
uninitiated
uninjured
uninoculated
uninspired
uninspiring
uninstructed
uninstructive
uninsulated
unintegrated
unintellectual
unintended
uninterested
uninteresting
unintermitted
unintermittent
unintimidated
uninvaded
uninventive
uninvested
uninvited
uninviting
uninvolved
unirradiated
unjointed
unjudged
unjustifiable
unjustified
unkept
unknowledgeable
unkosher
unlabeled
unlabored
unladylike
unlamented
unleavened
unlethal
unliberal
unlicensed
unlighted
unlikable
unlined
unlit
unliterary
unlivable
unlobed
unlovable
unloved
unloving
unmagnified
unmailable
unmalleable
unmanageable
unmanufactured
unmapped
unmarked
unmarketable
unmarried
unmasculine
unmastered
unmatchable
unmatched
unmatching
unmaterialistic
unmeasurable
unmeasured
unmechanical
unmediated
unmeditated
unmellow
unmelodious
unmelted
unmentioned
unmerchantable
unmerited
unmet
unmetabolized
unmethodical
unmetrical
unmilitary
unmilled
unmingled
unmitigable
unmixed
unmodernized
unmodified
unmodulated
unmolested
unmonitored
unmortgaged
unmotivated
unmounted
unmovable
unmoved
unmoving
unmusical
unnameable
unnamed
unnaturalized
unnavigable
unneeded
unneighborly
unnoisy
unnoticeable
unnoticed
unnourishing
unobjectionable
unobliging
unobscured
unobservable
unobservant
unobserved
unobserving
unobstructed
unobtainable
unobvious
unopen
unopened
unopposed
unordered
unorganizable
unoriginal
unostentatious
unowned
unoxygenated
unpainted
unparasitized
unpardonable
unpardoned
unparenthesized
unpartisan
unpartitioned
unpasteurized
unpastoral
unpatentable
unpatient
unpatriotic
unpatterned
unpaved
unpedantic
unpedigreed
unperceivable
unperceived
unperceiving
unperceptive
unperformed
unperplexed
unpersuadable
unpersuaded
unpersuasive
unperturbed
unphilosophic
unphilosophical
unphonetic
unphotogenic
unphotographed
unpicturesque
unpitied
unpitying
unplaced
unplanned
unplanted
unplausible
unplayable
unpleased
unpleasing
unpledged
unplowed
unplundered
unpoetic
unpoetical
unpointed
unpolemic
unpolemical
unpoliced
unpolished
unpolled
unpolluted
unpolymerized
unposed
unpossessing
unpowered
unpractical
unpracticed
unpremeditated
unprepossessing
unprescribed
unpresentable
unpressed
unpressured
unpretty
unprevailing
unpreventable
unprinted
unprivileged
unprocessed
unproductive
unprofessional
unprogrammed
unprogressive
unprohibited
unprompted
unpronounceable
unpropertied
unpropitious
unproportionate
unproportioned
unprosperous
unprotected
unprotesting
unproved
unproven
unprovided
unprovoked
unpruned
unpublished
unpunctual
unpunished
unpurchasable
unpure
unquantifiable
unquenchable
unquenched
unquestioned
unradical
unraised
unransomed
unranked
unratified
unrationed
unravished
unreachable
unreadable
unrealizable
unrealized
unreasoned
unreclaimable
unrecompensed
unreconcilable
unreconciled
unrecorded
unrecoverable
unredeemed
unredressed
unrefined
unreflecting
unreflective
unreformable
unreformed
unrefuted
unregarded
unregimented
unregistered
unregulated
unrehearsed
unreimbursed
unreinforced
unrelated
unrelaxed
unrelaxing
unreliable
unrelieved
unreligious
unreluctant
unremarkable
unremembered
unreminiscent
unremitted
unremovable
unremunerated
unremunerative
unrenowned
unrent
unrepaid
unrepaired
unrepealed
unrepentant
unreplaced
unreported
unrepresentative
unrepresented
unrepressed
unreproduced
unreproved
unrequited
unresistant
unresisted
unresisting
unresolvable
unresolved
unresonant
unrespectable
unrestful
unrestricted
unretentive
unretracted
unreturnable
unrevealed
unrevenged
unrevoked
unrevolutionary
unrewarded
unrewarding
unrhymed
unrhythmic
unrhythmical
unridable
unrightful
unrinsed
unripened
unromantic
unromanticized
unruled
unrushed
unsafe
unsaintly
unsalable
unsalaried
unsalted
unsalvageable
unsanctified
unsanctioned
unsanitary
unsaponified
unsated
unsatiated
unsatisfactory
unsatisfiable
unsatisfied
unsatisfying
unscalable
unscaled
unscanned
unscarred
unscented
unscheduled
unscholarly
unscorched
unscreened
unscriptural
unseasoned
unseaworthy
unseconded
unsectarian
unsecured
unseeded
unseeing
unsegmented
unselfconscious
unsensitive
unsensitized
unsensual
unsentimental
unseparated
unserious
unserved
unserviceable
unsexual
unshaded
unshadowed
unshakable
unshaken
unshapely
unshared
unsharp
unshaved
unshaven
unshed
unsheltered
unshielded
unshorn
unshrinkable
unshrinking
unshut
unsifted
unsigned
unsilent
unsingable
unsinkable
unsized
unslacked
unslaked
unsmiling
unsmokable
unsnuffed
unsoiled
unsold
unsoldierly
unsolicited
unsolicitous
unsolid
unsolvable
unsolved
unsorted
unsounded
unsoured
unsown
unspecialized
unspecific
unspecified
unspectacular
unspent
unspiritual
unsplit
unspoiled
unspoken
unsprayed
unspun
unsquared
unstained
unstandardized
unstatesmanlike
unsterile
unsterilized
unstinted
unstinting
unstintingly
unstrained
unstratified
unstrenuous
unstriped
unsubdued
unsubsidized
unsubstantiated
unsubtle
unsuggestible
unsuggestive
unsuited
unsullied
unsuperstitious
unsupervised
unsupportable
unsupported
unsuppressed
unsure
unsurfaced
unsurpassable
unsurpassed
unsurprised
unsurprising
unsusceptible
unsuspected
unsuspecting
unsuspenseful
unsuspicious
unsustainable
unsustained
unswayed
unsweetened
unsworn
unsympathetic
unsympathizing
unsynchronized
unsystematic
unsystematical
unsystematized
untactful
untagged
untainted
untalented
untalked-of
untamable
untamed
untanned
untapped
untarnishable
untarnished
untaxed
unteachable
untechnical
untempered
untenanted
untended
unterrified
untestable
untested
unthanked
unthankful
unthatched
unthawed
untheatrical
unthoughtful
unthreatened
unthrifty
untillable
untilled
untired
untiring
untraceable
untracked
untractable
untraditional
untrained
untrammeled
untransferable
untranslatable
untranslated
untraveled
untraversed
untreated
untrimmed
untroublesome
untrustworthy
untufted
untunable
untypical
ununderstandable
unusable
unuttered
unvaried
unvarying
unventilated
unveracious
unverifiable
unverified
unversed
unvexed
unviable
unvisited
unvulcanized
unwalled
unwanted
unwarlike
unwarranted
unwatched
unweaned
unwearable
unwearying
unweathered
unwed
unwedded
unweeded
unwelcome
unwelded
unwept
unwifely
unwinking
unwished
unwitnessed
unwomanly
unwon
unwooded
unworkable
unworked
unworkmanlike
unworried
unwounded
unwrinkled
unwrought
unyoung

un·abashed \ˌən-ə-ˈbasht\ *adj* : not abashed : UNDISGUISED — **un·abash·ed·ly** \-ˈbash-əd-lē\ *adv*

un·abat·ed \ˌən-ə-ˈbāt-əd\ *adj* : not abated : being at full strength or force — **un·abat·ed·ly** *adv*

un·able \ˌən-ˈā-bəl, ˈən-\ *adj* : not able : INCAPABLE as **a** : UNQUALIFIED, INCOMPETENT **b** : IMPOTENT, HELPLESS

un·abridged \ˌən-ə-ˈbrijd\ *adj* **1** : not abridged : COMPLETE <an ~ reprint of a novel> **2** : being the most complete of its class : not based on one larger <an ~ dictionary>

un·ac·cept·able \ˌən-ik-ˈsep-tə-bəl, -ak-\ *adj* : not acceptable : not pleasing or welcome — **un·ac·cept·abil·i·ty** \-ˌsep-tə-ˈbil-ət-ē\ *n* — **un·ac·cept·ably** \-ˈsep-tə-blē\ *adv*

un·ac·com·mo·dat·ed \ˌən-ə-ˈkäm-ə-ˌdāt-əd\ *adj* : not accommodated : UNPROVIDED

un·ac·com·pa·nied \ˌən-ə-ˈkəmp-(ə-)nēd\ *adj* : not accompanied; *specif* : being without instrumental accompaniment

un·ac·count·able \ˌən-ə-ˈkau̇nt-ə-bəl\ *adj* **1** : not to be accounted for : INEXPLICABLE, STRANGE **2** : not to be called to account : not responsible — **un·ac·count·abil·i·ty** \-ˌkau̇nt-ə-ˈbil-ət-ē\ *n* — **un·ac·count·ably** \-ˈkau̇nt-ə-blē\ *adv*

un·ac·count·ed \-ˈkau̇nt-əd\ *adj* : not accounted : UNEXPLAINED — often used with *for*

un·ac·cus·tomed \ˌən-ə-ˈkəs-təmd\ *adj* **1** : not customary : not usual or common **2** : not habituated — usu. used with *to* — **un·ac·cus·tomed·ly** \-təm-dlē\ *adv*

una cor·da \ˌü-nə-ˈkȯrd-ə, -ˈkȯr-(ˌ)dä\ *adv or adj* [It, lit., one string] : with soft pedal depressed — used as a direction in piano music

una corda pedal *n* : SOFT PEDAL

un·adorned \ˌən-ə-ˈdȯ(ə)rnd\ *adj* : not adorned : lacking embellishment or decoration : PLAIN, SIMPLE

un·adorn·ment \-ˈdȯ(ə)rn-mənt\ *n* : the quality or state of being unadorned

un·adul·ter·at·ed \ˌən-ə-ˈdəl-tə-ˌrāt-əd\ *adj* : PURE, UNMIXED — **un·adul·ter·at·ed·ly** *adv*

un·ad·vised \ˌən-əd-ˈvīzd\ *adj* **1** : done without due consideration : RASH <a cruel and ~ act> **2** : not prudent : INDISCREET <her ~ love of gossip> — **un·ad·vis·ed·ly** \-ˈvī-zəd-lē\ *adv*

un·af·fect·ed \ˌən-ə-ˈfek-təd\ *adj* **1** : not influenced or changed mentally, physically, or chemically **2** : free from affectation : GENUINE — **un·af·fect·ed·ly** *adv* — **un·af·fect·ed·ness** *n*

un·af·fec·tion·ate \-ˈfek-sh(ə-)nət\ *adj* : lacking affection : not affectionate — **un·af·fec·tion·ate·ly** *adv*

un·ag·ing *or* **un·age·ing** \ˌən-ˈā-jiŋ, ˈən-\ *adj* : AGELESS

un·alien·able \-ˈāl-yə-nə-bəl, -ˈā-lē-ə-\ *adj* : INALIENABLE

un·aligned \ˌən-ᵊl-ˈīnd\ *adj* : NONALIGNED

un·al·loyed \ˌən-ᵊl-ˈȯid\ *adj* : not alloyed : UNMIXED, UNQUALIFIED, PURE <~ metals> <~ happiness>

un·al·ter·able \ˌən-ˈȯl-t(ə-)rə-bəl, ˈən-\ *adj* : not capable of being altered or changed <an ~ resolve> <~ hatred> — **un·al·ter·abil·i·ty** \ˌən-ˌȯl-t(ə-)rə-ˈbil-ət-ē\ *n* — **un·al·ter·able·ness** \ˌən-ˈȯl-t(ə-)rə-bəl-nəs, ˈən-\ *n* — **un·al·ter·ably** \-blē\ *adv*

un·am·big·u·ous \ˌən-am-ˈbig-yə-wəs\ *adj* : not ambiguous : CLEAR, PRECISE — **un·am·big·u·ous·ly** *adv*

un·am·biv·a·lent \-ˈbiv-ə-lənt\ *adj* : not ambivalent : CLEAR-CUT, DEFINITE — **un·am·biv·a·lent·ly** *adv*

un–Amer·i·can \ˌən-ə-ˈmer-ə-kən\ *adj* : not American : not characteristic of or consistent with American customs, principles, or traditions

unan *abbr* unanimous

un·an·chor \ˌən-ˈaŋ-kər, ˈən-\ *vt* : to loosen from an anchor

un·aneled \ˌən-ə-ˈnē(ə)ld\ *adj, archaic* : not having received extreme unction

un·anes·the·tized \ˌən-ə-ˈnes-thə-ˌtīzd\ *adj* : not having been subjected to an anesthetic

una·nim·i·ty \ˌyü-nə-ˈnim-ət-ē\ *n* : the quality or state of being unanimous

unan·i·mous \yu̇-ˈnan-ə-məs\ *adj* [L *unanimus,* fr. *unus* one + *animus* mind — more at ONE, ANIMATE] **1** : being of one mind : AGREEING **2** : formed with or indicating unanimity : having the agreement and consent of all — **unan·i·mous·ly** *adv*

un·an·swer·able \ˌən-ˈan(t)s-(ə-)rə-bəl, ˈən-\ *adj* : not answerable; *esp* : IRREFUTABLE — **un·an·swer·abil·i·ty** \ˌən-ˌan(t)s-(ə-)rə-ˈbil-ət-ē\ *n* — **un·an·swer·ably** \ˌən-ˈan(t)s-(ə-)rə-blē, ˈən-\ *adv*

un·an·tic·i·pat·ed \ˌən-an-ˈtis-ə-ˌpāt-əd\ *adj* : not anticipated : UNEXPECTED, UNFORESEEN — **un·an·tic·i·pat·ed·ly** *adv*

un·apol·o·get·ic \ˌən-ə-ˌpäl-ə-ˈjet-ik\ *adj* : not apologetic : offered or put forward without apology — **un·apol·o·get·i·cal·ly** \-i-k(ə-)lē\ *adv*

un·ap·peal·able \ˌən-ə-ˈpē-lə-bəl\ *adj* : not appealable : not subject to appeal

un·ap·peal·ing \-ˈpē-liŋ\ *adj* : not appealing : UNATTRACTIVE — **un·ap·peal·ing·ly** \-liŋ-lē\ *adv*

un·ap·peas·able \-ˈpē-zə-bəl\ *adj* : not to be appeased : IMPLACABLE — **un·ap·peas·ably** \-blē\ *adv*

un·ap·pe·tiz·ing \ˌən-ˈap-ə-ˌtī-ziŋ, ˈən-\ *adj* : not appetizing : INSIPID, UNATTRACTIVE — **un·ap·pe·tiz·ing·ly** \-ziŋ-lē\ *adv*

un·ap·pre·ci·a·tion \ˌən-ə-ˌprē-shē-ˈā-shən\ *n* : failure to appreciate something

un·ap·proach·able \ˌən-ə-ˈprō-chə-bəl\ *adj* **1** : not approachable : physically inaccessible **2** : discouraging intimacies : RESERVED — **un·ap·proach·abil·i·ty** \-ˌprō-chə-ˈbil-ət-ē\ *n* — **un·ap·proach·ably** \-ˈprō-chə-blē\ *adv*

un·apt \ˌən-ˈapt, ˈən-\ *adj* **1** : UNSUITABLE, INAPPROPRIATE <an ~ quote> **2** : not accustomed and not likely <a man ~ to tolerate carelessness> **3** : DULL, BACKWARD <~ scholars> — **un·apt·ly** \-ˈap-(t)lē\ *adv* — **un·apt·ness** \-ˈap(t)-nəs\ *n*

un·ar·gu·able \ˌən-ˈär-gyə-wə-bəl, ˈən-\ *adj* : not arguable — **un·ar·gu·ably** \-blē\ *adv*

un·arm \ˌən-ˈärm, ˈən-\ *vt* : DISARM

un·armed \-ˈärmd\ *adj* **1** : not armed or armored **2** : having no hard and sharp projections (as spines, spurs, or claws)

un·ar·tic·u·lat·ed \ˌən-är-ˈtik-yə-ˌlāt-əd\ *adj* : not articulated; *esp* : not carefully reasoned or analyzed

una·ry \ˈyü-nə-rē\ *adj* [L *unus* one + E *-ary*] : having or consisting of a single element, item, or component : MONADIC

un·ashamed \ˌən-ə-ˈshāmd\ *adj* : not ashamed : being without guilt, self-consciousness, or doubt — **un·asham·ed·ly** \-ˈshā-məd-lē\ *adv*

un·asked \ˌən-ˈas(k)t, ˈən-\ *adj* **1** : not asked <~ questions> **2** : not being asked : UNINVITED **3** : not asked for <~ advice>

un·as·sail·able \ˌən-ə-ˈsā-lə-bəl\ *adj* : not assailable : not liable to doubt, attack, or question — **un·as·sail·abil·i·ty** \-ˌsā-lə-ˈbil-ət-ē\ *n* — **un·as·sail·able·ness** \-ˈsā-lə-bəl-nəs\ *n* — **un·as·sail·ably** \-blē\ *adv*

un·as·ser·tive \ˌən-ə-ˈsərt-iv\ *adj* : not assertive : MODEST, SHY

un·as·sist·ed \ˌən-ə-ˈsis-təd\ *adj* **1** : not assisted : lacking help **2** : made or performed without an assist <an ~ double play>

un·as·suage·able \ˌən-ə-ˈswā-jə-bəl\ *adj* : not capable of being assuaged

un·as·sum·ing \ˌən-ə-ˈsü-miŋ\ *adj* : not assuming : not arrogant or presuming : MODEST, RETIRING — **un·as·sum·ing·ness** *n*

un·at·tached \ˌən-ə-ˈtacht\ *adj* **1 a** : not assigned or committed (as to a particular task, organization, or person); *esp* : not married or engaged **b** : not seized as security for a legal judgment **2** : not joined or united <~ polyps> <~ buildings>

un·at·trac·tive \-ˈtrak-tiv\ *adj* : not attractive : PLAIN, DULL — **un·at·trac·tive·ly** *adv* — **un·at·trac·tive·ness** *n*

un·avail·able \ˌən-ə-ˈvā-lə-bəl\ *adj* : not available — **un·avail·abil·i·ty** \-ˌvā-lə-ˈbil-ət-ē\ *n*

un·avail·ing \-ˈvā-liŋ\ *adj* : not availing : FUTILE, USELESS — **un·avail·ing·ly** \-liŋ-lē\ *adv* — **un·avail·ing·ness** *n*

un·av·er·age \ˌən-ˈav-(ə-)rij, ˈən-\ *adj* : not average : UNUSUAL, OUTSTANDING

un·avoid·able \ˌən-ə-ˈvȯid-ə-bəl\ *adj* : not avoidable : INEVITABLE — **un·avoid·ably** \-blē\ *adv*

¹un·aware \-ə-ˈwa(ə)r, -ˈwe(ə)r\ *adv* : UNAWARES

²unaware *adj* : not aware : IGNORANT — **un·aware·ly** *adv* — **un·aware·ness** *n*

un·awares \-ˈwa(ə)rz, -ˈwe(ə)rz\ *adv* [*un-* + *aware* + *-s,* adv. suffix, fr. ME, fr. *-s,* gen. sing. ending of nouns — more at -s] **1** : without design, attention, preparation, or premeditation **2** : without warning : SUDDENLY, UNEXPECTEDLY

un·backed \ˌən-ˈbakt, ˈən-\ *adj* **1** : never mounted by a rider : not broken **2** : lacking support or aid **3** : having no back

¹un·bal·ance \-ˈbal-ən(t)s\ *vt* : to put out of balance; *esp* : to derange mentally

²unbalance *n* : lack of balance : IMBALANCE

un·bal·anced \-ən(t)st\ *adj* : not balanced: as **a** : not in equilibrium **b** : mentally disordered or deranged **c** : not adjusted so as to make credits equal to debts <an ~ account>

un·bal·last·ed \-ˈbal-ə-stəd\ *adj* : not furnished with or steadied by ballast : UNSTEADY

un·ban·dage \-ˈban-dij\ *vt* : to remove a bandage from

un·bar \ˌən-ˈbär, ˈən-\ *vt* : to remove a bar from : UNBOLT, OPEN

un·bar·bered \-ˈbär-bərd\ *adj* : having long and esp. unkempt hair

un·barred \-ˈbärd\ *adj* **1** : not secured by a bar : UNLOCKED **2** : not marked with bars

un·bat·ed \-ˈbāt-əd\ *adj* **1** : UNABATED **2** *archaic* : not blunted

un·be \-ˈbē\ *vi, archaic* : to lack or cease to have being

un·bear·able \ˌən-ˈbar-ə-bəl, ˈən-, -ˈber-\ *adj* : not bearable : UNENDURABLE — **un·bear·ably** \-blē\ *adv*

un·beat·able \-ˈbēt-ə-bəl\ *adj* **1** : not capable of being defeated **2** : possessing unsurpassable qualities — **un·beat·ably** \-blē\ *adv*

un·beat·en \-ˈbēt-ᵊn\ *adj* **1** : not pounded or beaten : not whipped **2** : not traversed : UNTROD **3** : not defeated

un·beau·ti·ful \-ˈbyüt-i-fəl\ *adj* : not beautiful : UNATTRACTIVE — **un·beau·ti·ful·ly** \-f(ə-)lē\ *adv*

un·be·com·ing \ˌən-bi-ˈkəm-iŋ\ *adj* : not becoming <an ~ dress>; *esp* : not according with the standards appropriate to one's position or condition of life <~ conduct> ***syn*** see INDECOROUS — **un·be·com·ing·ly** \-iŋ-lē\ *adv* — **un·be·com·ing·ness** *n*

un·be·known \ˌən-bi-ˈnōn\ *or* **un·be·knownst** \-ˈnōn(t)st\ *adj* [¹*un-* + obs. E *beknown* (known)] : happening without one's knowledge : UNKNOWN — usu. used with *to*

un·be·lief \ˌən-bə-ˈlēf\ *n* : incredulity or skepticism esp. in matters of religious faith

syn UNBELIEF, DISBELIEF, INCREDULITY *shared meaning element* : the attitude or state of mind of one who does not believe ***ant*** belief

un·be·liev·able \-ˈlē-və-bəl\ *adj* : too improbable for belief : INCREDIBLE — **un·be·liev·ably** \-blē\ *adv*

un·be·liev·er \-ˈlē-vər\ *n* **1** : one that does not believe : an incredulous person : DOUBTER, SKEPTIC **2** : one that does not believe in a particular religious faith ***syn*** see ATHEIST

un·be·liev·ing \-ˈlē-viŋ\ *adj* : marked by unbelief : INCREDULOUS, SKEPTICAL — **un·be·liev·ing·ly** \-viŋ-lē\ *adv*

un·belt·ed \ˌən-ˈbel-təd, ˈən-\ *adj* : not furnished with a belt

un·bend \-ˈbend\ *vb* **-bent** \-ˈbent\; **-bend·ing** *vt* **1** : to free from flexure : make or allow to become straight <~ a bow> **2** : to cause (as the mind) to relax **3 a** : to unfasten (as a sail) from a spar or stay **b** : to cast loose or untie (as a rope) ~ *vi* **1** : to relax one's severity, stiffness, or austerity **2** : to cease to be bent : become straight

un·bend·able \-ˈben-də-bəl\ *adj* : SINGLE-MINDED, FIRM

un·bend·ing \-ˈben-diŋ\ *adj* [¹*un-*] **1** : not bending : UNYIELDING, INFLEXIBLE <an ~ will> **2** : aloof or unsocial in manner : RESERVED

un·be·seem·ing \ˌən-bi-ˈsē-miŋ\ *adj* : not befitting : UNBECOMING

un·bi·ased \ˌən-ˈbī-əst, ˈən-\ *adj* **1** : free from bias; *esp* : free from all prejudice and favoritism : eminently fair **2** *of a statistic* : having an expected value equal to a population parameter being

---

ə abut ᵊ kitten ər further a back ā bake ä cot, cart
au̇ out ch chin e less ē easy g gift i trip ī life
j joke ŋ sing ō flow ȯ flaw ȯi coin th thin t͟h this
ü loot u̇ foot y yet yü few yu̇ furious zh vision

estimated — **un·bi·ased·ness** \-əs(t)-nəs\ *n* ***syn*** see FAIR ***ant*** biased

un·bib·li·cal \ˌən-ˈbib-li-kəl, ˈən-\ *adj* **:** contrary to or unsanctioned by the Bible

un·bid·den \-ˈbid-ᵊn\ *also* **un·bid** \-ˈbid\ *adj* **:** not bidden **:** UNASKED, UNINVITED

un·bind \-ˈbīnd\ *vt* **-bound** \-ˈbau̇nd\; **-bind·ing** **1 :** to remove a band from **:** free from fastenings **:** UNITE, UNFASTEN **2 :** to set free **:** RELEASE

un·bit·ted \-ˈbit-əd\ *adj* **:** UNBRIDLED, UNCONTROLLED

un·blenched \-ˈblencht\ *adj* **:** not disconcerted **:** UNDAUNTED

un·blessed *also* **un·blest** \ˌən-ˈblest, ˈən-\ *adj* **1 :** not blessed **2 :** EVIL, ACCURSED

un·blind·ed \-ˈblīn-dəd\ *adj* **:** not blinded; *esp* **:** free from illusion

un·blink·ing \-ˈbliŋ-kiŋ\ *adj* **1 :** not blinking **2 :** not showing signs of emotion, doubt, or confusion — **un·blink·ing·ly** \-kiŋ-lē\ *adv*

un·block \-ˈbläk\ *vt* **:** to free from being blocked ~ *vi* **:** to unblock something

un·blush·ing \-ˈbləsh-iŋ\ *adj* **1 :** not blushing **2 :** SHAMELESS, UNABASHED — **un·blush·ing·ly** \-iŋ-lē\ *adv*

un·bod·ied \-ˈbäd-ēd\ *adj* **1 :** having no body **:** INCORPOREAL; *also* **:** freed from the body <~ souls> **2 :** FORMLESS

un·bolt \ˌən-ˈbōlt, ˈən-\ *vt* **:** to open or unfasten by withdrawing a bolt

¹un·bolt·ed \-ˈbōl-təd\ *adj* **:** not sifted <~ flour>

²unbolted *adj* **:** not fastened by bolts

un·bon·net·ed \ˌən-ˈbän-ət-əd, ˈən-\ *adj* **:** BAREHEADED

un·born \-ˈbȯ(ə)rn\ *adj* **1 :** not born **:** not brought into life **2 :** still to appear **:** FUTURE **3 :** existing without birth

un·bo·som \-ˈbu̇z-əm *also* -ˈbüz-\ *vt* **1 :** to give expression to **:** DISCLOSE, REVEAL **2 :** to disclose the thoughts or feelings of (oneself) ~ *vi* **:** to unbosom oneself

un·bound \-ˈbau̇nd\ *adj* **:** not bound: as **a** (1) **:** not fastened (2) **:** not confined **b :** not having the leaves fastened together **c :** not bound together with other issues <~ periodicals> <an ~ book> **d :** not held in chemical or physical combination

un·bound·ed \-ˈbau̇n-dəd\ *adj* **1 :** having no limit **2 :** UNRESTRAINED, UNCONTROLLED — **un·bound·ed·ness** *n*

un·bowed \ˌən-ˈbau̇d, ˈən-\ *adj* **:** not bowed down; *esp* **:** not subdued

un·box \-ˈbäks\ *vt* **:** to remove from a box

un·brace \-ˈbrās\ *vt* **1 :** to free or detach by or as if by untying or removing a brace or bond **2 :** ENFEEBLE, WEAKEN

un·braid \-ˈbrād\ *vt* **:** to separate the strands of **:** UNRAVEL

un·branched \-ˈbrancht\ *adj* **1 :** having no branches <a straight ~ trunk> **2 :** not divided into branches <a leaf with ~ veins>

un·breath·able \-ˈbrē-t͟hə-bəl\ *adj* **:** not fit for being breathed

un·bred \-ˈbred\ *adj* **1** *obs* **:** ILL-BRED **2 :** not taught **:** UNTRAINED **3 :** not bred **:** never having been bred <an ~ heifer>

un·bri·dle \ˌən-ˈbrīd-ᵊl, ˈən-\ *vt* **:** to free or loose from a bridle; *broadly* **:** to set loose **:** free from restraint

un·bri·dled \-ˈbrīd-ᵊld\ *adj* **1 :** not confined by a bridle **2 :** UNRESTRAINED, UNGOVERNED

un·broke \-ˈbrōk\ *adj* **:** UNBROKEN

un·bro·ken \-ˈbrō-kən\ *adj* **:** not broken: as **a :** not violated **b :** WHOLE, INTACT **c :** not subdued **:** UNTAMED; *esp* **:** not trained for service or use <~ colts> **d :** UNINTERRUPTED <miles of ~ forest> **e :** not plowed **f :** not disorganized <advanced in ~ ranks>

un·buck·le \-ˈbək-əl\ *vt* **:** to loose the buckle of **:** UNFASTEN ~ *vi* **1 :** to loosen buckles **2 :** RELAX

un·budge·able \-ˈbəj-ə-bəl\ *adj* **:** not able to be budged or changed **:** INFLEXIBLE — **un·budge·ably** \-blē\ *adv*

un·budg·ing \-ˈbəj-iŋ\ *adj* **:** not budging **:** resisting movement or change — **un·budg·ing·ly** \-iŋ-lē\ *adv*

un·build \ˌən-ˈbild, ˈən-\ *vb* **-built** \-ˈbilt\; **-build·ing** *vt* **:** to pull down **:** DEMOLISH, RAZE ~ *vi* **:** to unbuild something

un·built \-ˈbilt\ *adj* **1 :** not built **:** not yet constructed **2 :** not built on <an ~ plot> <a forest which was ~ on>

un·bun·dle \-ˈbən-dᵊl\ *vi* **:** to give separate prices for equipment and supporting services <lifts price of computers; won't ~ —*Wall St. Jour.*> ~ *vt* **:** to price separately <the software is *unbundled* —*Datamation*>

un·bur·den \-ˈbərd-ᵊn\ *vt* **1 :** to free or relieve from a burden **2 :** to relieve oneself of (as cares, fears, or worries) **:** cast off

un·bur·dened \-ˈbərd-ᵊnd\ *adj* **:** not burdened **:** having no weight or load

un·bur·ied \-ˈber-ēd\ *adj* **:** not buried

un·but·tered \-ˈbət-ərd\ *adj* **:** not buttered **:** lacking butter

un·but·ton \-ˈbət-ᵊn\ *vt* **1 :** to loose the buttons of **2 :** to open as if by loosing buttons; *specif* **:** to open the hatches or apertures of (an armored vehicle) ~ *vi* **:** to undo buttons

un·but·toned \-ᵊnd\ *adj* **1 a :** not buttoned **b :** not provided with buttons **2 :** not under constraint **:** free and unrestricted in action and expression

un·cage \ˌən-ˈkāj, ˈən-\ *vt* **:** to release from or as if from a cage **:** free from restraint

un·cal·cu·lat·ed \-ˈkal-kyə-ˌlāt-əd\ *adj* **:** not planned or thought out beforehand **:** SPONTANEOUS

un·cal·cu·lat·ing \-ˌlāt-iŋ\ *adj* **:** not based on or marked by calculation

un·called–for \ˌən-ˈkȯl(d)-ˌfȯ(ə)r, ˈən-\ *adj* **1 :** not called for or needed **:** UNNECESSARY **2 :** being or offered without provocation or justification <an ~ display of temper> <~ insults> ***syn*** see SUPEREROGATORY

un·can·did \-ˈkan-dəd\ *adj* **:** not frank or honest — **un·can·did·ly** *adv*

un·can·ny \-ˈkan-ē\ *adj* **1 a :** seeming to have a supernatural character or origin **:** EERIE, MYSTERIOUS **b :** being beyond what is normal or expected **:** suggesting superhuman or supernatural powers <an ~ sense of direction> **2** *chiefly Scot* **:** SEVERE, PUNISHING **3** *chiefly Scot* **:** DANGEROUS ***syn*** see WEIRD — **un·can·ni·ly** \-ˈkan-ᵊl-ē\ *adv* — **un·can·ni·ness** \-ˈkan-ē-nəs\ *n*

un·cap \-ˈkap\ *vt* **:** to remove a cap or covering from

un·catch·able \-ˈkach-ə-bəl, -ˈkech-\ *adj* **:** not able to be caught

un·caused \-ˈkȯzd\ *adj* **:** having no antecedent cause

un·ceas·ing \-ˈsē-siŋ\ *adj* **:** never ceasing **:** CONTINUOUS, INCESSANT — **un·ceas·ing·ly** \-siŋ-lē\ *adv*

un·cel·e·brat·ed \-ˈsel-ə-ˌbrāt-əd\ *adj* **1 :** not formally honored or commemorated **2 :** not famous **:** OBSCURE

un·cer·e·mo·ni·ous \ˌən-ˌser-ə-ˈmō-nē-əs\ *adj* **1 :** not ceremonious **:** INFORMAL **2 :** ABRUPT, RUDE <an ~ dismissal> — **un·cer·e·mo·ni·ous·ly** *adv* — **un·cer·e·mo·ni·ous·ness** *n*

un·cer·tain \ˌən-ˈsərt-ᵊn, ˈən-\ *adj* **1 :** INDEFINITE, INDETERMINATE <the time of departure is ~> **2 :** not certain to occur **:** PROBLEMATICAL **3 :** not reliable **:** UNTRUSTWORTHY **4 a :** not known beyond doubt **:** DUBIOUS **b :** not having certain knowledge **:** DOUBTFUL **c :** not clearly identified or defined **5 :** not constant **:** VARIABLE, FITFUL — **un·cer·tain·ly** *adv* — **un·cer·tain·ness** \-ᵊn-(n)əs\ *n*

un·cer·tain·ty \-ᵊn-tē\ *n* **1 :** the quality or state of being uncertain **:** DOUBT **2 :** something that is uncertain

syn UNCERTAINTY, DOUBT, DUBIETY, SKEPTICISM, SUSPICION, MISTRUST *shared meaning element* **:** lack of sureness about someone or something ***ant*** certainty

uncertainty principle *n* **:** a principle in quantum mechanics: it is impossible to assert in terms of the ordinary conventions of geometrical position and of motion that a particle (as an electron) is at the same time at a specified point and moving with a specified velocity

un·chain \ˌən-ˈchān, ˈən-\ *vt* **:** to free by or as if by removing a chain **:** set loose

un·chal·lenge·able \-ˈchal-ən-jə-bəl\ *adj* **:** not able to be challenged or disputed

un·chancy \-ˈchan(t)-sē\ *adj* **1** *chiefly Scot* **:** ILL-FATED **2** *chiefly Scot* **:** DANGEROUS

un·change·able \-ˈchān-jə-bəl\ *adj* **:** not changing or to be changed **:** IMMUTABLE — **un·change·abil·i·ty** \ˌən-ˌchān-jə-ˈbil-ət-ē\ *n* — **un·change·able·ness** \ˌən-ˈchān-jə-bəl-nəs, ˈən-\ *n* — **un·change·ably** \-blē\ *adv*

un·chang·ing \-ˈchān-jiŋ\ *adj* **:** CONSTANT, INVARIABLE — **un·chang·ing·ly** \-jiŋ-lē\ *adv* — **un·chang·ing·ness** *n*

un·char·ac·ter·is·tic \ˌən-ˌkar-ik-tə-ˈris-tik\ *adj* **:** not characteristic **:** not typical or distinctive — **un·char·ac·ter·is·ti·cal·ly** \-ti-k(ə-)lē\ *adv*

un·charge \ˌən-ˈchärj, ˈən-\ *vt, obs* **:** ACQUIT

un·charged \-ˈchärjd\ *adj* **:** not charged; *specif* **:** having no electric charge

un·char·i·ta·ble \-ˈchar-ət-ə-bəl\ *adj* **:** lacking in charity **:** severe in judging **:** HARSH — **un·char·i·ta·ble·ness** *n* — **un·char·i·ta·bly** \-blē\ *adv*

un·chart·ed \-ˈchärt-əd\ *adj* **:** not recorded or plotted on a map, chart, or plan; *broadly* **:** UNKNOWN

un·chaste \-ˈchāst\ *adj* **:** not chaste **:** lacking in chastity — **un·chaste·ly** *adv* — **un·chaste·ness** \-ˈchās(t)-nəs\ *n*

un·chas·ti·ty \-ˈchas-tət-ē\ *n* **:** the quality or state of being unchaste

un·chiv·al·rous \-ˈshiv-əl-rəs\ *adj* **:** not chivalrous **:** lacking in chivalry — **un·chiv·al·rous·ly** *adv*

un·choke \-ˈchōk\ *vt* **:** to clear of obstruction

un·chris·tian \-ˈkris(h)-chən\ *adj* **1 :** not of the Christian faith **2 a :** contrary to the Christian spirit or character **b :** BARBAROUS, UNCIVILIZED

un·church \-ˈchərch\ *vt* **1 :** to expel from a church **:** EXCOMMUNICATE **2 :** to deprive of a church or of status as a church

un·churched \-ˈchərcht\ *adj* **:** not belonging to or connected with a church

unci *pl of* UNCUS

¹un·cial \ˈən-shəl, -chəl; ˈən(t)-sē-əl\ *adj* [L *uncialis* inch-high, fr. *uncia* twelfth part, ounce, inch] **:** written in the style or size of uncials — **un·cial·ly** \-ē\ *adv*

²uncial *n* **1 :** a handwriting used esp. in Greek and Latin manuscripts of the 4th to the 8th centuries A.D. and made with somewhat rounded separated majuscules but having cursive forms for some letters **2 :** an uncial letter **3 :** a manuscript written in uncial

ROMAN UNCIAL

uncials

¹un·ci·form \ˈən(t)-sə-ˌfȯrm\ *adj* [NL *unciformis*, fr. L *uncus* hook + *-formis* -form — more at ANGLE] **:** hook-shaped **:** UNCINATE

²unciform *n* [NL *unciforme*, fr. neut. of *unciformis*] **:** HAMATE

un·ci·nar·ia \ˌən(t)-sə-ˈnar-ē-ə, -ˈner-\ *n* [NL, fr. L *uncinus* hook] **:** HOOKWORM

un·ci·na·ri·a·sis \ˌən-ˌsin-ə-ˈrī-ə-səs\ *n* [NL] **:** ANCYLOSTOMIASIS

un·ci·nate \ˈən(t)-sə-ˌnāt\ *adj* **:** bent at the tip like a hook **:** HOOKED

un·ci·nus \ˌən-ˈsī-nəs\ *n, pl* **-ni** \-ˌnī\ [NL, fr. L, hook, fr. *uncus* — more at ANGLE] **:** a small uncinate structure or process

un·cir·cum·cised \ˌən-ˈsər-kəm-ˌsīzd, ˈən-\ *adj* **1 :** not circumcised **2 :** spiritually impure **:** HEATHEN — **un·cir·cum·ci·sion** \ˌən-ˌsər-kəm-ˈsizh-ən\ *n*

un·civ·il \ˌən-ˈsiv-əl, ˈən-\ *adj* **1 :** not civilized **:** BARBAROUS **2 :** lacking in courtesy **:** ILL-MANNERED, IMPOLITE **3 :** not conducive to civic harmony and welfare — **un·civ·il·ly** \-ə-lē\ *adv*

un·civ·i·lized \-ˈsiv-ə-ˌlīzd\ *adj* **1 :** not civilized **:** BARBAROUS **2 :** remote from settled areas **:** WILD

un·clamp \-ˈklamp\ *vt* **:** to loosen the clamp of **:** to free from a clamp

un·clar·i·ty \-ˈklar-ət-ē\ *n, pl* **-ties :** lack of clarity **:** AMBIGUITY, OBSCURITY

un·clasp \-ˈklasp\ *vt* **1 :** to open the clasp of **2 :** to open or cause to be opened (as a clenched hand) ~ *vi* **:** to loosen a hold

un·clas·si·cal \-ˈklas-i-kəl\ *adj* **:** not classical; *esp* **:** unconcerned with the classics

un·clas·si·fied \-ˈklas-ə-ˌfīd\ *adj* **1 :** not placed or belonging in a class **2 :** not subject to a security classification

un·cle \ˈəŋ-kəl\ *n* [ME, fr. OF, fr. L *avunculus* mother's brother; akin to OE *ēam* uncle, OIr *aue* grandson, L *avus* grandfather] **1 a :** the brother of one's father or mother **b :** the husband of one's aunt **2 :** one who helps, advises, or encourages **3** — used as a cry of surrender <was forced to cry ~> **4** *cap* **:** UNCLE SAM

un·clean \ˌən-ˈklēn, ˈən-\ *adj* **1 :** morally or spiritually impure **2 :** infected with a harmful supernatural contagion; *also* **:** prohibited by ritual law for use or contact **3 :** DIRTY, FILTHY **4 :** lacking in clarity and precision of conception or execution — **un·clean·ness** \-ˈklēn-nəs\ *n*

¹un·clean·ly \-ˈklen-lē\ *adj* **:** morally or physically unclean — **un·clean·li·ness** *n*

²un·clean·ly \-ˈklēn-lē\ *adv* **:** in an unclean manner

un·clench \-ˈklench\ *vt* **1 :** to open from a clenched position **2 :** to release from a grip ~ *vi* **:** to become unclasped or relaxed

Un·cle Sam \ˌəŋ-kəl-ˈsam\ *n* [expansion of *U.S.*, abbr. of *United States*] **1 :** the U.S. government **2 :** the American nation or people

¹Uncle Tom \-ˈtäm\ *n* **1 :** a pious and faithful elderly Negro slave in the novel *Uncle Tom's Cabin* by Harriet Beecher Stowe **2 :** a black eager to win the approval of whites and willing to cooperate with them

²Uncle Tom *vi* **Uncle Tommed; Uncle Tom·ming :** to behave like an Uncle Tom

Uncle Tom·ism \-ˈtäm-ˌiz-əm\ *n* **:** behavior characteristic of an Uncle Tom

un·climb·able \ˌən-ˈklī-mə-bəl, ˈən-\ *adj* **:** not able to be climbed — **un·climb·able·ness** *n*

un·clinch \ˌən-ˈklinch, ˈən-\ *vt* **:** UNCLENCH

un·cloak \-ˈklōk\ *vt* **1 :** to remove a cloak or cover from **2 :** REVEAL, UNMASK ~ *vi* **:** to take off a cloak

un·clog \-ˈkläg\ *vt* **:** to free from a difficulty or obstruction

un·close \-ˈklōz\ *vt* **1 :** OPEN **2 :** DISCLOSE, REVEAL ~ *vi* **:** to become opened

un·closed \-ˈklōzd\ *adj* **:** not closed or settled **:** not concluded

un·clothe \-ˈklōth\ *vt* **1 :** to strip of clothes **2 :** DIVEST, UNCOVER

un·clothed \-ˈklōthd\ *adj* **:** not clothed

un·cloud·ed \-ˈklau̇d-əd\ *adj* **:** not covered by clouds **:** not darkened **:** CLEAR — **un·cloud·ed·ly** *adv*

un·clut·ter \-ˈklət-ər\ *vt* **:** to remove clutter from **:** make neat and orderly

¹un·co \ˈəŋ-(ˌ)kō, -kə\ *adj* [ME (Sc) *unkow*, alter. of ME *uncouth*] **1** *chiefly Scot* **a :** STRANGE, UNKNOWN **b :** UNCANNY, WEIRD **2** *chiefly Scot* **:** EXTRAORDINARY

²unco *adv* **:** EXTREMELY, REMARKABLY, UNCOMMONLY

³unco *n, pl* **uncos 1** *pl, chiefly Scot* **:** NEWS, TIDINGS **2** *chiefly Scot* **:** STRANGER

un·cock \ˌən-ˈkäk, ˈən-\ *vt* **:** to remove the hammer of (a firearm) from a cocked position

un·cof·fin \-ˈkȯ-fən\ *vt* **:** to remove from or as if from a coffin

un·cof·fined \-ənd\ *adj* **:** not placed in a coffin

un·coil \ˌən-ˈkȯi(ə)l, ˈən-\ *vt* **:** to release from a coiled state **:** UNWIND ~ *vi* **:** to become uncoiled

un·coiled \-ˈkȯi(ə)ld\ *adj* **:** not coiled

un·coined \-ˈkȯind\ *adj* **1 :** not minted <~ metal> **2 :** not fabricated **:** NATURAL

un·com·fort·able \ˌən-ˈkəm(p)(f)-tə-bəl, ˈən-, -ˈkəm(p)-fərt-ə-\ *adj* **1 :** causing discomfort or annoyance <an ~ chair> <an ~ performance> **2 :** feeling discomfort **:** UNEASY <was ~ with them> — **un·com·fort·ably** \-blē\ *adv*

un·com·mer·cial \ˌən-kə-ˈmər-shəl\ *adj* **1 :** not engaged in or related to commerce **2 :** not based on commercial principles

un·com·mit·ted \-ˈmit-əd\ *adj* **:** not committed; *specif* **:** not pledged to a particular belief, allegiance, or program

un·com·mon \ˌən-ˈkäm-ən, ˈən-\ *adj* **1 :** not ordinarily encountered **:** UNUSUAL **2 :** REMARKABLE, EXCEPTIONAL ***syn*** see INFREQUENT ***ant*** common — **un·com·mon·ly** *adv* — **un·com·mon·ness** \-ən-nəs\ *n*

un·com·mu·ni·ca·ble \ˌən-kə-ˈmyü-ni-kə-bəl\ *adj* **:** INCOMMUNICABLE

un·com·mu·ni·ca·tive \-ˈmyü-nə-ˌkāt-iv, -ni-kət-\ *adj* **:** not disposed to talk or impart information **:** RESERVED

un·com·pas·sion·ate \ˌən-kəm-ˈpash-(ə-)nət\ *adj* **:** HARDHEARTED, UNFEELING

un·com·pet·i·tive \-ˈpet-ət-iv\ *adj* **:** not competitive **:** unable to compete — **un·com·pet·i·tive·ness** *n*

un·com·plain·ing \-ˈplā-niŋ\ *adj* **:** not complaining **:** PATIENT — **un·com·plain·ing·ly** \-niŋ-lē\ *adv*

un·com·pli·cat·ed \ˌən-ˈkäm-plə-ˌkāt-əd, ˈən-\ *adj* **1 :** not complicated by something outside itself; *specif* **:** not involving medical complications <~ peptic ulcer> **2 :** not complex **:** SIMPLE <~ machinery>

un·com·pli·men·ta·ry \ˌən-ˌkäm-plə-ˈment-ə-rē, -ˈmen-trē\ *adj* **:** not complimentary **:** DEROGATORY

un·com·pre·hend·ing \-pri-ˈhen-diŋ\ *adj* **:** not comprehending **:** lacking understanding — **un·com·pre·hend·ing·ly** \-diŋ-lē\ *adv*

un·com·pro·mis·able \ˌən-ˈkäm-prə-ˌmī-zə-bəl, ˈən-\ *adj* **:** not able to be compromised

un·com·pro·mis·ing \-ˌmī-ziŋ\ *adj* **:** not making or accepting a compromise **:** making no concessions **:** INFLEXIBLE, UNYIELDING — **un·com·pro·mis·ing·ly** \-ziŋ-lē\ *adv*

un·con·ceiv·able \ˌən-kən-ˈsē-və-bəl\ *adj* **:** INCONCEIVABLE

un·con·cern \ˌən-kən-ˈsərn \ *n* **1 :** lack of care or interest **:** INDIFFERENCE **2 :** freedom from excessive concern or anxiety

un·con·cerned \-ˈsərnd\ *adj* **1 :** not involved **:** not having any part or interest **2 :** not anxious or upset **:** free of worry ***syn*** see INDIFFERENT ***ant*** concerned — **un·con·cerned·ly** \-ˈsər-nəd-lē, -ˈsərn-dlē\ *adv* — **un·con·cerned·ness** \-ˈsər-nəd-nəs, -ˈsərn(d)-nəs\ *n*

un·con·di·tion·al \ˌən-kən-ˈdish-nəl, -ˈdish-ən-ᵊl\ *adj* **1 :** not limited **:** ABSOLUTE, UNQUALIFIED **2 :** UNCONDITIONED 2 — **un·con·di·tion·al·ly** \-ē\ *adv*

un·con·di·tioned \-ˈdish-ənd\ *adj* **1 :** not subject to conditions or limitations **2 a :** not dependent on or subjected to conditioning or learning **:** NATURAL **b :** producing an unconditioned response <~ stimuli>

un·con·form·able \-ˈfȯr-mə-bəl\ *adj* **1 :** not conforming **2 :** exhibiting geological unconformity — **un·con·form·ably** \-blē\ *adv*

un·con·for·mi·ty \-ˈfȯr-mət-ē\ *n* **1** *archaic* **:** lack of conformity **2 a :** lack of continuity in deposition between rock strata in contact corresponding to a period of nondeposition, weathering, or erosion **b :** the surface of contact between unconformable strata

un·con·ge·nial \-ˈjē-nyəl, -nē-əl\ *adj* **1 :** not sympathetic or compatible <~ roommates> **2 a :** not fitted **:** UNSUITABLE <a soil ~ to most crops> **b :** not to one's taste **:** DISAGREEABLE <an ~ task>

un·con·ge·nial·i·ty \-ˌjē-nē-ˈal-ət-ē, -ˌjēn-ˈyal-\ *n* **:** the quality or state of being uncongenial

un·con·quer·able \ˌən-ˈkäŋ-k(ə-)rə-bəl, ˈən-\ *adj* **1 :** incapable of being conquered **:** INDOMITABLE <an ~ will> **2 :** incapable of being surmounted <~ difficulties> — **un·con·quer·ably** \-blē\ *adv*

un·con·scio·na·ble \-ˈkänch-(ə-)nə-bəl\ *adj* **1 :** not guided or controlled by conscience **:** UNSCRUPULOUS <an ~ villain> **2 a :** EXCESSIVE, UNREASONABLE <found an ~ number of defects in the car> **b :** shockingly unfair or unjust <~ sales practices> — **un·con·scio·na·bil·i·ty** \ˌən-ˌkänch-(ə-)nə-ˈbil-ət-ē\ *n* — **un·con·scio·na·ble·ness** \ˌən-ˈkänch-(ə-)nə-bəl-nəs, ˈən-\ *n* — **un·con·scio·na·bly** \-blē\ *adv*

¹un·con·scious \ˌən-ˈkän-chəs, ˈən-\ *adj* **1 a :** not knowing or perceiving **:** not aware **b :** free from self-awareness **2 a :** not possessing mind or consciousness <~ matter> **b (1) :** not marked by conscious thought, sensation, or feeling <~ motivation> **(2) :** of or relating to the unconscious **c :** having lost consciousness <was ~ for three days> **3 :** not consciously held or deliberately planned or carried out <~ bias> — **un·con·scious·ly** *adv* — **un·con·scious·ness** *n*

²unconscious *n* **:** the part of the psychic apparatus that does not ordinarily enter the individual's awareness and that is manifested in overt behavior esp. by slips of the tongue or dissociated acts or in dreams

un·con·sid·ered \ˌən-kən-ˈsid-ərd\ *adj* **1 :** not considered or worth consideration **2 :** not resulting from consideration

un·con·sol·i·dat·ed \-ˈsäl-ə-ˌdāt-əd\ *adj* **:** loosely arranged **:** not stratified <~ soil>

un·con·sti·tu·tion·al \ˌən-ˌkän(t)-stə-ˈt(y)üsh-nəl, -ən-ᵊl\ *adj* **:** not according or consistent with the constitution of a body politic (as a nation) — **un·con·sti·tu·tion·al·i·ty** \-t(y)ü-shə-ˈnal-ət-ē\ *n* — **un·con·sti·tu·tion·al·ly** \-ˈt(y)üsh-nə-lē, -ən-ᵊl-ē\ *adv*

un·con·straint \ˌən-kən-ˈstrānt\ *n* **:** freedom from constraint **:** EASE

syn UNCONSTRAINT, ABANDON, SPONTANEITY ***shared meaning element*** **:** free and uninhibited expression or a mood or style marked by this

un·con·trol·la·ble \-ˈtrō-lə-bəl\ *adj* **1** *archaic* **:** free from control by a superior power **:** ABSOLUTE **2 :** incapable of being controlled **:** UNGOVERNABLE — **un·con·trol·la·bly** \-blē\ *adv*

un·con·ven·tion·al \-ˈvench-nəl, -ən-ᵊl\ *adj* **:** not conventional **:** not bound by or in accordance with convention **:** being out of the ordinary — **un·con·ven·tion·al·i·ty** \-ˌven-chə-ˈnal-ət-ē\ *n* — **un·con·ven·tion·al·ly** \-ˈvench-nə-lē, -ən-ᵊl-ē\ *adv*

un·con·vinc·ing \-ˈvin(t)-siŋ\ *adj* **:** not convincing **:** IMPLAUSIBLE — **un·con·vinc·ing·ly** \-siŋ-lē\ *adv* — **un·con·vinc·ing·ness** *n*

un·cool \ˌən-ˈkül, ˈən-\ *adj* **1 :** lacking in assurance **2 :** failing to accord with the mores of a particular group

un·cork \ˌən-ˈkȯ(ə)rk, ˈən-\ *vt* **1 :** to draw a cork from **2 a :** to release from a sealed or pent-up state <~ a surprise> **b :** to let go **:** RELEASE <~ a wild pitch>

un·corked \-ˈkȯ(ə)rkt\ *adj* **:** not provided with a cork

un·cor·set·ed \-ˈkȯr-sət-əd\ *adj* **1 :** not wearing a corset **2 :** not controlled or inhibited

un·count·ed \-ˈkau̇nt-əd\ *adj* **1 :** not counted **2 :** INNUMERABLE

un·cou·ple \-ˈkəp-əl\ *vt* **1 :** to release (dogs) from a couple **2 :** DETACH, DISCONNECT <~ railroad cars> — **un·cou·pler** \-(ə-)lər\ *n*

un·couth \-ˈküth\ *adj* [ME, fr. OE *uncūth*, fr. *un-* + *cūth* familiar, known; akin to OHG *kund* known, OE *can* know — more at CAN] **1 a** *archaic* **:** not known or not familiar to one **:** seldom experienced **:** UNCOMMON, RARE **b** *obs* **:** MYSTERIOUS, UNCANNY **2 a :** strange or clumsy in shape or appearance **:** OUTLANDISH **b :** lacking in polish and grace **:** RUGGED <~ verse> **c :** awkward and uncultivated in appearance, manner, or behavior — **un·couth·ly** *adv* — **un·couth·ness** *n*

un·cov·er \-ˈkəv-ər\ *vt* **1 :** to make known **:** bring to light **:** DISCLOSE, REVEAL **2 :** to expose to view by removing some covering **3 a :** to take the cover from **b :** to remove the hat from **4 :** to deprive of protection ~ *vi* **1 :** to remove a cover or covering **2 :** to take off the hat as a token of respect

un·cov·ered \-ərd\ *adj* **:** not covered: as **a :** not supplied with a covering **b :** not covered by insurance or included in a social insurance or welfare program **c :** not covered by collateral <an ~ note>

un·cre·at·ed \ˌən-krē-ˈāt-əd\ *adj* **1 :** not existing by creation **:** ETERNAL, SELF-EXISTENT **2 :** not yet created

un·crit·i·cal \ˌən-ˈkrit-i-kəl, ˈən-\ *adj* **1 :** not critical **:** lacking in discrimination **2 :** showing lack or improper use of critical standards or procedures ***syn*** see SUPERFICIAL ***ant*** critical — **un·crit·i·cal·ly** \-k(ə-)lē\ *adv*

un·cross \-ˈkrȯs\ *vt* **:** to change from a crossed position

un·crown \-ˈkrau̇n\ *vt* : to take the crown from : DEPOSE, DETHRONE

un·crum·ple \-ˈkrəm-pəl\ *vt* : to restore to an original smooth condition

un·crush·able \-ˈkrəsh-ə-bəl\ *adj* : not able to be crushed

un·crys·tal·lized \-ˈkris-tə-ˌlīzd\ *adj* : not crystallized; *also* : not finally or definitely formed

unc·tion \ˈəŋ(k)-shən\ *n* [ME *unctioun,* fr. L *unction-, unctio,* fr. *unctus,* pp. of *unguere* to anoint — more at OINTMENT] **1 :** the act of anointing as a rite of consecration or healing **2 :** something used for anointing : OINTMENT, UNGUENT **3 a :** religious or spiritual fervor or the expression of such fervor **b :** exaggerated, assumed, or superficial earnestness of language or manner : UNCTUOUSNESS

unc·tu·ous \ˈəŋ(k)-chə(-wə)s, ˈəŋ(k)sh-wəs\ *adj* [ME, fr. MF or ML; MF *unctueux,* fr. ML *unctuosus,* irreg. fr. L *unctum* ointment, fr. neut. of *unctus,* pp.] **1 a :** FATTY, OILY **b :** smooth and greasy in texture or appearance **2 a :** rich in organic matter and easily workable <~ soil> **b :** PLASTIC <fine ~ clay> **3 :** full of unction; *esp* : revealing or marked by a smug, ingratiating, and false earnestness or spirituality — **unc·tu·ous·ly** *adv* — **unc·tu·ous·ness** *n*

un·curl \ˌən-ˈkər(-ə)l, ˈən-\ *vi* : to become straightened out from a curled or coiled position ~ *vt* : to straighten the curls of : UNROLL

un·cus \ˈəŋ-kəs\ *n, pl* **un·ci** \ˈəŋ-ˌkī, -ˌkē; ˈən-ˌsī\ [NL, fr. L, hook — more at ANGLE] : a hooked anatomical part or process

un·cut \ˌən-ˈkət, ˈən-\ *adj* **1 :** not cut down or cut into **2 :** not shaped by cutting <an ~ diamond> **3** *of a book* : not having the folds of the leaves slit **4 :** not abridged or curtailed

un·cyn·i·cal \-ˈsin-i-kəl\ *adj* : not cynical — **un·cyn·i·cal·ly** \-k(ə-)lē\ *adv*

un·daunt·able \ˌən-ˈdȯnt-ə-bəl, -ˈdänt-\ *adj* : incapable of being daunted : FEARLESS

un·daunt·ed \-əd\ *adj* : courageously resolute esp. in the face of stress — **un·daunt·ed·ly** *adv*

un·de·bat·able \ˌən-di-ˈbāt-ə-bəl\ *adj* : not subject to debate : INDISPUTABLE — **un·de·bat·ably** \-blē\ *adv*

undec- *comb form* [L *undecim,* fr. *unus* one + *decem* ten — more at ONE, TEN] : eleven <*undec*illion>

un·de·ceive \ˌən-di-ˈsēv\ *vt* : to free from deception, illusion, or error

un·de·cil·lion \ˌən-di-ˈsil-yən\ *n, often attrib* [*undec-* + *-illion* (as in *million*)] — see NUMBER table

un·dec·y·le·nic acid \ˌən-ˌdes-ə-ˌlen-ik-, -ˌlēn-\ *n* [*undecylene* ($C_{11}H_{22}$)] : an acid $C_{11}H_{20}O_2$ found in perspiration, obtained commercially from castor oil, and used in the treatment of fungous infections of the skin

un·de·fend·ed \ˌən-di-ˈfen-dəd\ *adj* : not defended

un·dem·o·crat·ic \ˌən-ˌdem-ə-ˈkrat-ik\ *adj* : not democratic : not agreeing with democratic practice or ideals — **un·dem·o·crat·i·cal·ly** \-i-k(ə-)lē\ *adv*

un·de·mon·stra·tive \ˌən-di-ˈmän(t)-strət-iv\ *adj* : restrained in expression of feeling : RESERVED — **un·de·mon·stra·tive·ly** *adv* — **un·de·mon·stra·tive·ness** *n*

un·de·ni·able \ˌən-di-ˈnī-ə-bəl\ *adj* **1 :** plainly true : INCONTESTABLE **2 :** unquestionably excellent or genuine <an applicant with ~ references> — **un·de·ni·able·ness** *n* — **un·de·ni·ably** \-blē\ *adv*

¹un·der \ˈən-dər\ *adv* [ME, adv. & prep., fr. OE; akin to OHG *untar* under, L *inferus* situated beneath, lower, *infra* below, Skt *adha*] **1 :** in or into a position below or beneath something **2 :** below or short of some quantity or limit <$10 or ~> — often used in combination <*under*-staffed> **3 :** in or into a condition of subjection, subordination, or unconsciousness **4 :** so as to be covered

²un·der \ˌən-dər, ˈən-\ *prep* **1 :** below or beneath so as to be overhung, surmounted, covered, protected, or concealed by <~ sunny skies> <swims ~ water> <a soft heart ~ a stern exterior> <~ cover of darkness> **2 a :** subject to the authority, control, guidance, or instruction of <served ~ the general> <studied ~ the leading sculptor of that era> **b :** receiving or undergoing the action or effect of <~ pressure> <courage ~ fire > <~ ether> **3 :** within the group or designation of <~ this heading> **4 :** inferior to (as in size, amount, or rank); *esp* : falling short of a standard or required degree <~ the legal age> <~ par>

³under \ˈən-dər\ *adj* **1 a :** lying or placed below, beneath, or on the ventral side — often used in combination <*under*lip> **b :** facing or protruding downward **2 :** lower in rank or authority : SUBORDINATE **3 :** lower than usual, proper, or desired in amount, quality, or degree <an ~ dose of medicine>

un·der·achiev·er \ˌən-də-rə-ˈchē-vər\ *n* : a student who fails to achieve his scholastic potential

un·der·act \ˌən-də-ˈrakt\ *vt* **1 :** to perform (a dramatic part) with less than the requisite skill or vigor **2 :** to perform with restraint for greater dramatic impact or personal force ~ *vi* : to perform feebly or with restraint

un·der·ac·tiv·i·ty \-rak-ˈtiv-ət-ē\ *n* : an abnormally low level of activity

un·der·age \ˌən-də-ˈrāj\ *adj* : of less than mature or legal age

un·der·ap·pre·ci·at·ed \ˌən-də-rə-ˈprē-shē-ˌāt-əd\ *adj* : not duly appreciated

¹un·der·arm \ˌən-də-ˌrärm\ *adj* **1 :** placed under or on the underside of the arm <~ seams> **2 :** UNDERHAND 4

²un·der·arm \ˌən-də-ˈrärm\ *adv* : UNDERHAND

³un·der·arm \ˈən-də-ˌrärm\ *n* **1 :** ARMPIT **2 :** the part of a garment that covers the underside of the arm

un·der·bel·ly \ˈən-dər-ˌbel-ē\ *n* : the under surface of a body or mass; *esp* : a vulnerable area

un·der·bid \ˌən-dər-ˈbid\ *vb* **-bid; -bid·ding** *vt* **1 :** to bid less than (a competing bidder) **2 :** to bid (a hand of cards) at less than the strength of the hand warrants ~ *vi* : to bid too low — **un·der·bid·der** *n*

un·der·body \ˈən-dər-ˌbäd-ē\ *n* : the lower part of something: as **a :** the lower part of an animal's body : UNDERPARTS **b :** the lower parts of the body of a vehicle

un·der·bred \ˌən-dər-ˈbred\ *adj* **1 :** marked by lack of good breeding : ILL-BRED **2 :** of inferior or mixed breed <an ~ dog>

un·der·brim \ˈən-dər-ˌbrim\ *n* : a facing on the underside of a hat brim

un·der·brush \ˈən-dər-ˌbrəsh\ *n*: shrubs, bushes, or small trees growing beneath large trees in a wood or forest : BRUSH

un·der·bud·get·ed \ˌən-dər-ˈbəj-ət-əd\ *adj* : provided with an inadequate budget

un·der·cap·i·tal·ized \-ˈkap-ət-ᵊl-ˌīzd, -ˈkap-tᵊl-\ *adj* : having too little capital for efficient operation

un·der·car·riage \ˈən-dər-ˌkar-ij\ *n* **1 :** a supporting framework (as of an automobile) **2 :** the landing gear of an airplane

un·der·charge \ˌən-dər-ˈchärj\ *vt* : to charge (as a person) too little — **undercharge** \ˈən-dər-ˌ\ *n*

un·der·class \ˈən-dər-ˌklas\ *n* : LOWER CLASS

un·der·class·man \ˌən-dər-ˈklas-mən\ *n* : a member of the freshman or sophomore class in a school or college

un·der·clothes \ˈən-dər-ˌklō(th)z\ *n pl* : UNDERWEAR

un·der·cloth·ing \-ˌklō-thiŋ\ *n* : UNDERWEAR

un·der·coat \-ˌkōt\ *n* **1 :** a coat or jacket worn under another **2 :** a growth of short hair or fur partly concealed by a longer growth <a dog's ~> **3 a :** a coat (as of paint) applied as a base for another coat **b :** UNDERCOATING **4** *dial* : PETTICOAT

un·der·coat·ing \-ˌkōt-iŋ\ *n* : a usu. asphalt-based waterproof coating applied to the undersurfaces of a vehicle

un·der·col·ored \ˌən-dər-ˈkəl-ərd\ *adj* : having less color than needed or proper

un·der·cool \-ˈkül\ *vt* : SUPERCOOL

un·der·cov·er \-ˌkəv-ər\ *adj* : acting or executed in secret; *specif* : employed or engaged in spying or secret investigation <an ~ agent>

un·der·croft \ˈən-dər-ˌkrȯft\ *n* [ME, fr. *under* + *crofte* crypt, fr. MD, fr. ML *crupta,* fr. L *crypta*] : a subterranean room; *esp* : a vaulted chamber under a church

un·der·cur·rent \-ˌkər-ənt, -ˌkə-rənt\ *n* **1 :** a current below the upper currents or surface **2 :** a hidden opinion or feeling often contrary to the one publicly shown — **undercurrent** *adj*

¹un·der·cut \ˌən-dər-ˈkət\ *vb* **-cut; -cut·ting** *vt* **1 :** to cut away the underpart of <~ a vein of ore> **2 :** to cut away material from the under side of (an object) so as to leave an overhanging portion in relief **3 :** to offer to sell at lower prices than or to work for lower wages than (a competitor) **4 :** to cut obliquely into (a tree) below the main cut and on the side toward which the tree will fall **5 :** to strike (a ball) with a downward glancing blow so as to give a backspin or elevation to the shot **6 :** to undermine or destroy the force or effectiveness of <a technology that ~s democracy> ~ *vi* : to perform the action of cutting away beneath

²un·der·cut \ˈən-dər-ˌkət\ *n* **1 :** the action or result of cutting away from the underside or lower part of something **2** *Brit* : TENDERLOIN 1 **3 :** a notch cut before felling in the base of a tree to determine the direction of falling and to prevent splitting **4 :** a stroke (as in tennis) made with an underhand swing

un·der·de·vel·oped \ˌən-dər-di-ˈvel-əpt\ *adj* **1 :** not normally or adequately developed <~ muscles> <an ~ film> **2 :** failing to realize a potential economic level of industrial production and standard of living (as from lack of capital)

un·der·de·vel·op·ment \-əp-mənt\ *n* : the quality or state of being underdeveloped : lack of adequate development

un·der·do \ˌən-dər-ˈdü\ *vt* **-did** \-ˈdid\; **-done** \-ˈdən\; **-do·ing** \-ˈdü-iŋ\ : to do less thoroughly than one can

un·der·dog \ˈən-dər-ˌdȯg\ *n* **1 :** a loser or predicted loser in a struggle or contest **2 :** a victim of injustice or persecution

un·der·done \ˌən-dər-ˈdən\ *adj* : not thoroughly cooked : RARE

un·der·draw·ers \ˈən-dər-ˌdrȯ(-ə)rz\ *n pl* : an article of underwear for the lower body

un·der·dress \-ˌdres\ *n* : a woman's garment that is similar to a dress and that is designed to be worn under a sheer outer garment

un·der·ed·u·cat·ed \ˌən-də-ˈrej-ə-ˌkāt-əd\ *adj* : poorly educated

un·der·ed·u·ca·tion \-ˌrej-ə-ˈkā-shən\ *n* : the quality or state of being undereducated

un·der·em·pha·sis \ˌən-də-ˈrem(p)-fə-səs\ *n* : less emphasis than is possible or desirable

un·der·em·pha·size \-ˌsīz\ *vt* : to fail to emphasize adequately

un·der·em·ployed \ˌən-də-rim-ˈplȯid\ *adj* : having less than full-time or adequate employment

un·der·em·ploy·ment \-ˈplȯi-mənt\ *n* **1 :** less than full employment of the labor force in an economy **2 :** employment at less than full time : partial or inadequate employment

un·der·es·ti·mate \ˌən-də-ˈres-tə-ˌmāt\ *vt* **1 :** to estimate as being less than the actual size, quantity, or number **2 :** to place too low a value on : UNDERRATE — **un·der·es·ti·mate** \-mət\ *n* — **un·der·es·ti·ma·tion** \-ˌres-tə-ˈmā-shən\ *n*

un·der·ex·pose \ˌən-də-rik-ˈspōz\ *vt* : to expose insufficiently; *esp* : to expose (as film) to insufficient radiation (as light) — **un·der·ex·po·sure** \-ˈspō-zhər\ *n*

un·der·feed \ˌən-dər-ˈfēd\ *vt* **-fed** \-ˈfed\; **-feed·ing** **1 :** to feed with too little food **2 :** to feed with fuel from the underside

un·der·fi·nanced \-fə-ˈnan(t)st, -ˈfī-ˌ, -fī-ˈ\ *adj* : inadequately financed

un·der·foot \-ˈfu̇t\ *adv* **1 :** under the foot esp. against the ground <trampled the flowers ~> **2 :** below, at, or before one's feet <warm sand ~> **3 :** in the way <children always getting ~>

un·der·fur \ˈən-dər-ˌfər\ *n* : the thick soft undercoat of fur lying beneath the longer and coarser hair of a mammal

un·der·gar·ment \-ˌgär-mənt\ *n* : a garment to be worn under another

un·der·gird \ˌən-dər-ˈgərd\ *vt* **1 :** to make secure underneath <~ a ship> **2 :** to form the basis or foundation of : STRENGTHEN, SUPPORT <faith ~s morals>

un·der·glaze \ˈən-dər-ˌglāz\ *adj* : applied or suitable for applying before the glaze is put on <~ decorations> <~ colors> — **underglaze** *n*

un·der·go \ˌən-dər-ˈgō\ *vt* **-went** \-ˈwent\; **-gone** \-ˈgȯn *also* -ˈgän\; **-go·ing** \-ˈgō-iŋ, -ˈgȯ(-)iŋ\ **1** *obs* : UNDERTAKE **2** *obs* : to partake of **3** : to submit to : ENDURE **4** : to go through : EXPERIENCE

un·der·grad·u·ate \ˌən-dər-ˈgraj-(ə-)wət, -ə-ˌwāt\ *n* : a student at a college or university who has not taken a first and esp. a bachelor's degree

[1]**un·der·ground** \ˌən-dər-ˈgrau̇nd\ *adv* **1** : beneath the surface of the earth **2** : in or into hiding or secret operation

[2]**un·der·ground** \ˈən-dər-ˌgrau̇nd\ *adj* **1** : being, growing, operating, or situated below the surface of the ground **2 a** : conducted by secret means **b** (1) : existing outside the establishment <an ~ literary reputation> (2) : produced or published outside the establishment esp. by the avant-garde <~ movies> <~ newspapers>; *also* : of or relating to the avant-garde underground <an ~ moviemaker> <an ~ theater>

[3]**underground** \ˈən-dər-ˌ\ *n* **1** : a subterranean space or channel **2** : an underground city railway system **3 a** : a movement or group organized in strict secrecy among citizens esp. in an occupied country for maintaining communications, popular solidarity, and concerted resistive action pending liberation **b** : a clandestine conspiratorial organization set up for revolutionary or other disruptive purposes esp. against a civil order **c** : an unofficial, unsanctioned, or illegal but informal movement or group; *esp* : a usu. avant-garde group or movement that functions outside the establishment

un·der·ground·er \ˈən-dər-ˌgrau̇n-dər\ *n* : a member of the underground

Underground Railroad *n* : a system of cooperation among active antislavery people in the U.S. before 1863 by which fugitive slaves were secretly helped to reach the North or Canada — called also *Underground Railway*

un·der·growth \ˈən-dər-ˌgrōth\ *n* : low growth on the floor of a forest including seedlings and saplings, shrubs, and herbs

[1]**un·der·hand** \ˈən-dər-ˌhand\ *adv* **1 a** : in a clandestine manner **b** *archaic* : QUIETLY **2** : with the target seen below the hand holding the bow **3** : with an underhand motion <bowl ~> <pitch ~>

[2]**underhand** *adj* **1** : aimed so that the target is seen below the hand holding the bow <~ shooting at long range> **2** : marked by secrecy, chicanery, and deception : not honest and aboveboard : SLY **3** : done so as to evade notice **4** : made with the hand brought forward and up from below the shoulder level ***syn*** see SECRET ***ant*** aboveboard

[1]**un·der·hand·ed** \ˌən-dər-ˈhan-dəd\ *adj or adv* : UNDERHAND ***syn*** see SECRET ***ant*** aboveboard — **un·der·hand·ed·ly** *adv* — **un·der·hand·ed·ness** *n*

[2]**underhanded** *adj* : insufficiently provided with workers

un·der·hung \ˌən-dər-ˈhəŋ\ *adj* **1 a** *of a lower jaw* : projecting beyond the upper jaw **b** : having an underhung jaw **2** : UNDERSLUNG

un·der·in·sured \ˌən-də-rin-ˈshu̇(ə)rd\ *adj* : not sufficiently insured

un·der·laid \ˌən-dər-ˈlād\ *adj* **1** : laid or placed underneath **2** : having something laid or lying underneath

[1]**un·der·lay** \-ˈlā\ *vt* **-laid** \-ˈlād\; **-lay·ing** **1** : to cover, line, or traverse the bottom of : give support to on the underside or below **2** : to raise or support by something laid under

[2]**un·der·lay** \ˈən-dər-ˌlā\ *n* : something that is or is designed to be laid under

un·der·lay·ment \ˌən-dər-ˈlā-mənt\ *n* : UNDERLAY

un·der·let \ˌən-dər-ˈlet\ *vt* **-let**; **-let·ting** **1** : to let below the real value **2** : SUBLET

un·der·lie \-ˈlī\ *vt* **-lay** \-ˈlā\; **-lain** \-ˈlān\; **-ly·ing** \-ˈlī-iŋ\ **1** : to be subject or amenable to <~ a challenge> **2** : to lie or be situated under **3** : to be at the basis of : form the foundation of : SUPPORT <ideas *underlying* the revolution> **4** : to exist as a claim or security superior and prior to (another)

[1]**un·der·line** \ˈən-dər-ˌlīn, ˌən-dər-ˈ\ *vt* **1** : to mark (a word) with a line underneath **2** : to put emphasis upon : STRESS

[2]**un·der·line** \ˈən-dər-ˌlīn\ *n* **1** : a horizontal line placed underneath something **2** : the outline of an animal's underbody

un·der·ling \ˈən-dər-liŋ\ *n* : one who is under the orders of another : SUBORDINATE, INFERIOR

un·der·lip \ˌən-dər-ˈlip\ *n* : the lower lip

un·der·ly·ing \ˌən-dər-ˌlī-iŋ\ *adj* **1 a** : lying beneath or below <the ~ rock is shale> **b** : BASIC, FUNDAMENTAL <an investigation of the ~ issues> **2** : evident only on close inspection : IMPLICIT **3** : anterior and prior in claim <~ mortgage>

un·der·manned \ˌən-dər-ˈmand\ *adj* : inadequately staffed

un·der·mine \-ˈmīn\ *vt* **1** : to excavate the earth beneath : form a mine under : SAP **2** : to wash away supporting material from under **3** : to subvert or weaken insidiously or secretly **4** : to weaken or ruin by degrees ***syn*** see WEAKEN ***ant*** reinforce

un·der·most \ˈən-dər-ˌmōst\ *adj* : lowest in relative position — **undermost** *adv*

[1]**un·der·neath** \ˌən-dər-ˈnēth\ *prep* [ME *undernethe*, prep. & adv., fr. OE *underneothan*, fr. *under* + *neothan* below — more at BENEATH] **1 a** : directly beneath <write the date ~ the address> **b** : close under esp. so as to be hidden <treachery lying ~ a mask of friendliness> <wore a swimsuit ~ his slacks> **2** : under subjection to

[2]**underneath** *adv* **1** : under or below an object or a surface : BENEATH **2** : on the lower side

un·der·nour·ished \ˌən-dər-ˈnər-isht, -ˈnə-risht\ *adj* : supplied with less than the minimum amount of the foods essential for sound health and growth — **un·der·nour·ish·ment** \-ˈnər-ish-mənt, -ˈnə-rish-\ *n*

un·der·nu·tri·tion \-n(y)u̇-ˈtrish-ən\ *n* : deficient bodily nutrition due to inadequate food intake or faulty assimilation

un·der·paid \-ˈpād\ *adj* : receiving less than adequate or normal pay

un·der·pants \ˈən-dər-ˌpan(t)s\ *n pl* : short or long pants worn under an outer garment : DRAWERS

un·der·part \-ˌpärt\ *n* **1** : a part lying on the lower side esp. of a bird or mammal **2** : a subordinate or auxiliary part or role

un·der·pass \-ˌpas\ *n* : a crossing of two highways or of a highway and pedestrian path or railroad at different levels where clearance to traffic on the upper level is sometimes obtained by depressing the lower level; *also* : the lower level of such a crossing

un·der·pin \ˌən-dər-ˈpin\ *vt* **1** : to form part of, strengthen, or replace the foundation of <~ a structure> <~ a sagging building> **2** : SUPPORT, SUBSTANTIATE <~ a thesis with evidence>

un·der·pin·ning \ˈən-dər-ˌpin-iŋ\ *n* **1** : the material and construction (as a foundation) used for support of a structure **2** : something that serves as a foundation : BASIS, SUPPORT — often used in pl. <the philosophical ~*s* of psychoanalysis> **3** : a person's legs — usu. used in pl.

un·der·play \ˌən-dər-ˈplā\ *vt* **1** : to play a card lower than (a held high card) **2** : to act or present (as a role or a scene) with restraint : play down ~ *vi* : to play a role with subdued force

un·der·plot \ˈən-dər-ˌplät\ *n* : a dramatic plot that is subordinate to the main action

un·der·powered \ˌən-dər-ˈpau̇(-ə)rd\ *adj* : driven by an engine of insufficient power

un·der·priv·i·leged \-ˈpriv-(ə-)lijd\ *adj* **1** : deprived through social or economic condition of some of the fundamental rights of all members of a civilized society : POOR **2** : of or relating to underprivileged people <~ areas of the city>

un·der·pro·duc·tion \-ˈdək-shən\ *n* : the production of less than enough to satisfy the demand or of less than the usual supply

un·der·pro·duc·tive \-prə-ˈdək-tiv\ *adj* : not capable of adequate production <unskilled ~ workers>

un·der·proof \ˌən-dər-ˈprüf\ *adj* : containing less alcohol than proof spirit

un·der·rate \ˌən-də(r)-ˈrāt\ *vt* : to rate too low : UNDERVALUE

un·der·re·port \-ri-ˈpō(ə)rt, -ˈpȯ(ə)rt\ *vt* : to report (as income) to be less than is actually the case : UNDERSTATE

un·der·rep·re·sen·ta·tion \-ˌrep-ri-ˌzen-ˈtā-shən, -zən-\ *n* : the state of being underrepresented

un·der·rep·re·sent·ed \-ˈzent-əd\ *adj* : inadequately represented

un·der·ripe \ˌən-də(r)-ˈrīp\ *adj* : insufficiently ripe

[1]**un·der·run** \-ˈrən\ *vt* **-ran** \-ˈran\; **-run**; **-run·ning** **1** : to pass or extend under **2** : to pass along under in order to examine (a cable)

[2]**un·der·run** \ˈən-də(r)-ˌrən\ *n* : the amount by which something produced (as a cut of lumber) falls below an estimate

un·der·sat·u·rat·ed \ˌən-dər-ˈsach-ə-ˌrāt-əd\ *adj* : less than normally or adequately saturated

[1]**un·der·score** \ˈən-dər-ˌskō(ə)r, -ˌskȯ(ə)r\ *vt* **1** : to draw a line under : UNDERLINE **2** : EMPHASIZE, STRESS

[2]**underscore** *n* **1** : a line drawn under a word or line esp. for emphasis or to indicate intent to italicize **2** : music accompanying the action and dialogue of a film

[1]**un·der·sea** \ˌən-dər-ˌsē\ *adj* **1** : being or carried on under the sea or under the surface of the sea <~ oil deposits> <~ fighting> **2** : designed for use under the surface of the sea <an ~ fleet>

[2]**un·der·sea** \ˌən-dər-ˈsē\ *or* **un·der·seas** \-ˈsēz\ *adv* : under the sea : beneath the surface of the sea <photographs taken ~>

un·der·sec·re·tar·i·at \-ˌsek-rə-ˈter-ē-ət\ *n* : the office and staff of an under secretary : a subdivision of a ministry

under secretary *n* : a secretary immediately subordinate to a principal secretary <*under secretary* of state>

un·der·sell \ˌən-dər-ˈsel\ *vt* **-sold** \-ˈsōld\; **-sell·ing** **1** : to sell articles cheaper than <~ a competitor> **2** : to sell cheaper than <imported cars that ~ domestic ones>

un·der·sexed \-ˈsekst\ *adj* : deficient in sexual desire

un·der·shirt \ˈən-dər-ˌshərt\ *n* : a collarless undergarment with or without sleeves

un·der·shoot \ˌən-dər-ˈshüt\ *vt* **-shot** \-ˈshät\; **-shoot·ing** **1** : to shoot short of or below (a target) **2** : to fall short of (a runway) in landing an airplane

un·der·shorts \ˈən-dər-ˌshȯ(ə)rts\ *n pl* : [3]SHORT 4b

un·der·shot \ˌən-dər-ˌshät\ *adj* **1** : having the lower incisor teeth or lower jaw projecting beyond the upper when the mouth is closed **2** : moved by water passing beneath <an ~ wheel>

un·der·shrub \ˈən-dər-ˌshrəb, *esp South* -ˌsrəb\ *n* **1** : SUBSHRUB 1 **2** : a small low-growing shrub

un·der·side \ˈən-dər-ˌsīd, ˌən-dər-ˈ\ *n* **1** : the side or surface lying underneath **2** : the side usu. hidden from sight; *specif* : the worse side

un·der·signed \ˈən-dər-ˌsīnd\ *n, pl* **undersigned** : one who signs his name at the end of a document <the ~ testifies> <the ~ all agree>

un·der·sized \ˌən-dər-ˈsīzd\ *also* **un·der·size** \-ˈsīz\ *adj* : of a size less than is common, proper, normal, or average <~ trout>

un·der·skirt \ˈən-dər-ˌskərt\ *n* : a skirt worn under an outer skirt; *esp* : PETTICOAT

un·der·slung \ˌən-dər-ˈsləŋ\ *adj* **1 a** *of a vehicle frame* : suspended below the axles **b** : having a low center of gravity **2** : UNDERSHOT 1

un·der·song \ˈən-dər-ˌsȯŋ\ *n* : a subordinate melody or part

un·der·spin \-ˌspin\ *n* : BACKSPIN

un·der·staffed \-ˈstaft\ *adj* : UNDERMANNED

un·der·stand \ˌən-dər-ˈstand\ *vb* **-stood** \-ˈstu̇d\; **-stand·ing** [ME *understanden*, fr. OE *understandan*, fr. *under* + *standan* to stand] *vt* **1 a** : to grasp the meaning of <~ Russian> <~ a message in code> **b** : to grasp the reasonableness of <his behavior is hard to ~> **c** : to have thorough or technical acquaintance with or expertness in the practice of <~ finance> **d** : to be thoroughly familiar with the character and propensities of <~*s* children> **2**

ə abut ᵊ kitten ər further a back ā bake ä cot, cart
au̇ out ch chin e less ē easy g gift i trip ī life
j joke ŋ sing ō flow ȯ flaw ȯi coin th thin t͟h this
ü loot u̇ foot y yet yü few yu̇ furious zh vision

: to accept as a fact or truth or regard as plausible without utter certainty <we ~ that he is returning from abroad> **3** : to interpret in one of a number of possible ways **4** : to supply in thought as though expressed <"to be married" is commonly *understood* after the word *engaged*> ~ *vi* **1** : to have understanding : have the power of comprehension **2** : to achieve a grasp of the nature, significance, or explanation of something **3** : to believe or infer something to be the case **4** : to show a sympathetic or tolerant attitude toward something — **un·der·stand·abil·i·ty** \-ˌstan-də-ˈbil-ət-ē\ *n* — **un·der·stand·able** \-ˈstan-də-bəl\ *adj* — **un·der·stand·ably** \-blē\ *adv*
syn UNDERSTAND, COMPREHEND, APPRECIATE *shared meaning element* : to have a clear or complete idea of

[1]**un·der·stand·ing** \ˌən-dər-ˈstan-diŋ\ *n* **1** : a mental grasp : COMPREHENSION **2 a** : the power of comprehending; *esp* : the capacity to apprehend general relations of particulars **b** : the power to make experience intelligible by applying concepts and categories **3 a** : friendly or harmonious relationship **b** : an agreement of opinion or feeling : adjustment of differences **c** : a mutual agreement not formally entered into but in some degree binding on each side **4** : EXPLANATION, INTERPRETATION **5** : SYMPATHY 3a ***syn*** see REASON

[2]**understanding** *adj* **1** *archaic* : KNOWING, INTELLIGENT **2** : endowed with understanding : TOLERANT, SYMPATHETIC — **un·der·stand·ing·ly** \-ˈstan-diŋ-lē\ *adv*

un·der·state \ˌən-dər-ˈstāt\ *vt* **1** : to represent as less than is the case **2** : to state or present with restraint esp. for greater effect — **un·der·state·ment** \-mənt\ *n*

un·der·stat·ed \-ˈstāt-əd\ *adj* : avoiding obvious emphasis or embellishment

un·der·steer \ˈən-dər-ˌsti(ə)r\ *n* : the tendency of an automobile to go straight ahead and turn less sharply than the driver intends — **un·der·steer** \ˌən-dər-ˈ\ *vi*

un·der·stood \ˌən-dər-ˈstu̇d\ *adj* **1** : fully apprehended **2** : agreed upon **3** : IMPLICIT

un·der·sto·ry \ˈən-dər-ˌstōr-ē, -ˌstȯr-\ *n* : the plants of a forest undergrowth; *broadly* : an underlying layer of low vegetation

un·der·strap·per \-ˌstrap-ər\ *n* [[3]*under* + *strapper* (one who harnesses horses)] : a petty agent or subordinate : UNDERLING

un·der·strength \ˌən-dər-ˈstreŋ(k)th\ *adj* : deficient in strength; *esp* : lacking sufficient or prescribed personnel

[1]**un·der·study** \ˈən-dər-ˌstəd-ē, ˌən-dər-ˈ\ *vi* : to study another actor's part in order to be his substitute in an emergency ~ *vt* : to prepare (as a part) as understudy; *also* : to prepare as understudy to (as an actor)

[2]**un·der·study** \ˈən-dər-ˌstəd-ē\ *n* : one who is prepared to act another's part or take over another's duties

un·der·sup·ply \ˌən-dər-sə-ˈplī\ *n* : an inadequate supply or amount

[1]**un·der·sur·face** \ˈən-dər-ˌsər-fəs\ *n* : UNDERSIDE

[2]**un·der·sur·face** \ˌən-dər-ˌsər-fəs\ *adj* : existing or moving below the surface

un·der·take \ˌən-dər-ˈtāk\ *vb* **-took** \-ˈtu̇k\; **-tak·en** \-ˈtā-kən\; **-tak·ing** *vt* **1** : to take in hand : enter upon : set about : ATTEMPT <~ a task> **2** : to put oneself under obligation to perform : CONTRACT, COVENANT **3** : GUARANTEE, PROMISE **4** : to accept as a charge <the lawyer who *undertook* the case> ~ *vi, archaic* : to give surety or assume responsibility

un·der·tak·er \ˌən-dər-ˈtā-kər, *2 is* ˈən-dər-ˌ\ *n* **1** : one that undertakes : one that takes the risk and management of business : ENTREPRENEUR **2** : one whose business is to prepare the dead for burial and to arrange and manage funerals **3** : an Englishman taking over forfeited lands in Ireland in the 16th and 17th centuries

un·der·tak·ing \ˈən-dər-ˌtā-kiŋ, ˌən-dər-ˈ; *1b is* ˈən-dər-ˌ *only*\ *n* **1 a** : the act of one who undertakes or engages in a project or business **b** : the business of an undertaker **2** : something undertaken : ENTERPRISE **3** : PLEDGE, GUARANTEE

un·der·ten·ant \ˈən-dər-ˌten-ənt\ *n* : one who holds lands or tenements by a sublease

under–the–counter *adj* [fr. the hiding of illicit wares under the counter of stores where they are sold] : surreptitious and usu. irregular or illicit

un·der·tone \ˈən-dər-ˌtōn\ *n* **1** : a low or subdued utterance or accompanying sound **2 a** : a quality (as of emotion) underlying the surface of an utterance or action **b** : the underlying tendency of a market **3** : a subdued color; *specif* : a color seen through and modifying another color

un·der·tow \-ˌtō\ *n* : the current beneath the surface that sets seaward or along the beach when waves are breaking upon the shore

un·der·trick \-ˌtrik\ *n* : one of the tricks by which a declarer in bridge falls short of making his contract

un·der·used \ˌən-dər-ˈyüzd\ *adj* : not fully used

un·der·uti·lize \ˌən-dər-ˈyüt-ᵊl-ˌīz\ *vt* : to utilize less than fully or below the potential use — **un·der·uti·li·za·tion** \ˈən-dər-ˌyüt-ᵊl-ə-ˈzā-shən\ *n*

un·der·val·u·a·tion \ˌən-dər-ˌval-yə-ˈwā-shən\ *n* **1** : the act of undervaluing **2** : a value under the real worth

un·der·val·ue \-ˈval-(ˌ)yü, -yə(-w)\ *vt* **1** : to value, rate, or estimate below the real worth <~ stock> **2** : to treat as of little value : DEPRECIATE 2 <was *undervalued* as a poet>

un·der·waist \ˈən-dər-ˌwāst\ *n* : a waist for wear under another garment; *specif* : WAIST 3c

un·der·wa·ter \ˌən-dər-ˌwȯt-ər, -ˌwät-\ *adj* **1** : lying, growing, worn, or operating below the surface of the water **2** : being below the waterline of a ship — **un·der·wa·ter** \-ˈwȯt-, -ˈwät-\ *adv*

un·der·way \ˌən-dər-ˌwā\ *adj* : occurring, performed, or used while traveling or in motion <~ refueling>

under way \-ˈwā\ *adv* [prob. fr. D *onderweg,* fr. MD *onderwegen,* lit., under or among the ways] **1** : in motion : not at anchor or aground **2** : into motion from a standstill **3** : in progress : AFOOT <preparations were *under way*>

un·der·wear \ˈən-dər-ˌwa(ə)r, -ˌwe(ə)r\ *n* : clothing or an article of clothing worn next to the skin and under other clothing

under weigh *adv* [by folk etymology] : under way

[1]**un·der·weight** \ˌən-dər-ˈwāt\ *n* : weight below normal, average, or requisite weight

[2]**underweight** *adj* : weighing less than the normal or requisite amount

[1]**un·der·wing** \ˈən-dər-ˌwiŋ\ *n* **1** : one of the posterior wings of an insect **2** : any of various noctuid moths (esp. genus *Catocala*) that have the hind wings banded with contrasting colors (as red and black)

[2]**underwing** *adj* : placed or growing underneath the wing <~ coverts>

un·der·wood \ˈən-dər-ˌwu̇d\ *n* : UNDERGROWTH, UNDERBRUSH

un·der·wool \-ˌwu̇l\ *n* : short woolly underfur

un·der·world \-ˌwərld\ *n* **1** *archaic* : EARTH **2** : the place of departed souls : HADES **3** : the side of the earth opposite to one **4** : a social sphere below the level of ordinary life; *esp* : the world of organized crime

un·der·write \ˈən-də(r)-ˌrīt, ˌən-də(r)-ˈ\ *vb* **-wrote** \-ˌrōt, -ˈrōt\; **-writ·ten** \-ˌrit-ᵊn, -ˈrit-ᵊn\; **-writ·ing** \-ˌrīt-iŋ, -ˈrīt-\ *vt* **1** : to write under or at the end of something else **2** : to set one's name to (an insurance policy) for the purpose of thereby becoming answerable for a designated loss or damage on consideration of receiving a premium percent : insure on life or property; *also* : to assume (a sum or risk) by way of insurance **3** : to subscribe to : agree to **4 a** : to agree to purchase (a security issue) usu. on a fixed date at a fixed price with a view to public distribution **b** : to guarantee financial support of ~ *vi* : to carry on the business of an underwriter

un·der·writ·er \ˈən-də(r)-ˌrīt-ər\ *n* **1** : one that underwrites : GUARANTOR **2 a** : one that underwrites a policy of insurance : INSURER **b** : one who selects risks to be solicited or rates the acceptability of risks solicited **3** : one that underwrites a security issue

un·de·scend·ed \ˌən-di-ˈsen-dəd\ *adj* : not having descended; *specif* : retained within the inguinal region rather than descending into the scrotum <an ~ testis>

un·de·sign·ing \ˌən-di-ˈzī-niŋ\ *adj* : having no ulterior or fraudulent purpose : SINCERE

[1]**un·de·sir·able** \-ˈzī-rə-bəl\ *adj* : not desirable : UNWANTED — **un·de·sir·abil·i·ty** \-ˌzī-rə-ˈbil-ət-ē\ *n* — **un·de·sir·able·ness** \-ˈzī-rə-bəl-nəs\ *n* — **un·de·sir·ably** \-blē\ *adv*

[2]**undesirable** *n* : one that is undesirable

un·de·vi·at·ing \ˌən-ˈdē-vē-ˌāt-iŋ, ˈən-\ *adj* : keeping a true course : UNSWERVING — **un·de·vi·at·ing·ly** \-iŋ-lē\ *adv*

un·dies \ˈən-dēz\ *n pl* [by shortening & alter.] : UNDERWEAR; *esp* : women's underwear

un·dine \ˌən-ˈdēn, -ˈən-ˌ\ *n* [NL *undina,* fr. L *unda* wave — more at WATER] : an elemental being in the theory of Paracelsus inhabiting water : WATER NYMPH

un·dip·lo·mat·ic \ˌən-ˌdip-lə-ˈmat-ik, ˈən-\ *adj* : not diplomatic : TACTLESS — **un·dip·lo·mat·i·cal·ly** \-i-k(ə-)lē\ *adv*

un·di·rect·ed \ˌən-də-ˈrek-təd, -dī-\ *adj* : not directed : not planned or guided <~ efforts>

un·dis·guised \ˌən-dis-ˈgīzd\ *adj* : not disguised or concealed : FRANK, OPEN — **un·dis·guis·ed·ly** \-ˈgī-zəd-lē\ *adv*

un·dis·so·ci·at·ed \ˌən-dis-ˈō-s(h)ē-ˌāt-əd\ *adj* : not electrolytically dissociated

un·do \ˌən-ˈdü, ˈən-\ *vb* **-did** \-ˈdid\; **-done** \-ˈdən\; **-do·ing** \-ˈdü-iŋ\ *vt* **1** : to open or loose by releasing a fastening **2** : to make of no effect or as if not done : make null : REVERSE **3 a** : to ruin the worldly means, reputation, or hopes of **b** : to disturb the composure of : UPSET **c** : SEDUCE 3 ~ *vi* : to come open or apart — **un·do·er** \-ˈdü-ər\ *n*

un·dock \-ˈdäk\ *vi* : to move away from a dock (as at sailing time)

un·dog·mat·ic \ˌən-dȯg-ˈmat-ik, -däg-\ *adj* : not dogmatic : not committed to dogma — **un·dog·mat·i·cal·ly** \-i-kə-lē\ *adv*

un·do·ing \-ˈdü-iŋ\ *n* **1** : an act of loosening : UNFASTENING **2** : RUIN; *also* : a cause of ruin <a redhead was to prove his ~> **3** : ANNULMENT, REVERSAL

un·done \-ˈdən\ *adj* : not done : not performed or finished

un·dou·ble \ˌən-ˈdəb-əl, ˈən-\ *vb* : UNFOLD, UNCLENCH

un·dou·bled \-ˈdəb-əld\ *adj* : not doubled

un·doubt·ed \-ˈdau̇t-əd\ *adj* : not doubted : GENUINE, UNDISPUTED — **un·doubt·ed·ly** *adv*

un·dra·mat·ic \ˌən-drə-ˈmat-ik\ *adj* : lacking dramatic force or quality : UNSPECTACULAR — **un·dra·mat·i·cal·ly** \-i-k(ə-)lē\ *adv*

un·drape \ˌən-ˈdrāp, ˈən-\ *vt* : to strip of drapery : UNVEIL

un·draw \-ˈdrȯ\ *vt* **-drew** \-ˈdrü\; **-drawn** \-ˈdrȯn\; **-draw·ing** : to draw aside (as a curtain) : OPEN

un·dreamed \-ˈdrem(p)t, -ˈdrēmd\ *also* **undreamt** \-ˈdrem(p)t\ *adj* : not dreamed : not thought of : UNIMAGINED <technical advances ~ of a few years ago>

[1]**un·dress** \-ˈdres\ *vt* **1** : to remove the clothes or covering of : DIVEST, STRIP **2** : EXPOSE, REVEAL ~ *vi* : to take off one's clothes : DISROBE

[2]**undress** *n* **1** : informal dress: as **a** : a loose robe or dressing gown **b** : ordinary dress — compare FULL DRESS **2** : NUDITY

un·dressed \ˌən-ˈdrest, ˈən-\ *adj* : not dressed: as **a** : partially, improperly, or informally clothed **b** : not fully processed or finished <~ hides> **c** : not cared for or tended <an ~ wound> <~ fields>

un·drunk \-ˈdrəŋk\ *adj* : not swallowed

un·due \-ˈd(y)ü\ *adj* **1** : not due : not yet payable **2** : exceeding or violating propriety or fitness

un·du·lant \ˈən-jə-lənt, ˈən-d(y)ə-\ *adj* : rising and falling in waves : ROLLING

undulant fever *n* : a persistent human brucellosis marked by remittent fever, pain and swelling in the joints, and great weakness and contracted by contact with infected domestic animals or consumption of their products

[1]**un·du·late** \ˈən-jə-lət, ˈən-d(y)ə-, -ˌlāt\ *or* **un·du·lat·ed** \-ˌlāt-əd\ *adj* [L *undulatus,* fr. (assumed) L *undula,* dim. of L *unda* wave — more at WATER] : having a wavy surface, edge, or markings <the ~ margin of a leaf>

2un·du·late \-ˌlāt\ *vb* **-lated; -lating** [LL *undula* small wave, fr. (assumed) L] *vi* **1 :** to form or move in waves : FLUCTUATE **2 :** to rise and fall in volume, pitch, or cadence **3 :** to present a wavy appearance ~ *vt* : to move or cause to move in wavy, sinuous, or flowing manner *syn* see SWING

un·du·la·tion \ˌən-jə-ˈlā-shən, ˌən-d(y)ə-\ *n* **1 a :** a rising and falling in waves **b :** a wavelike motion to and fro in a fluid or elastic medium propagated continuously among its particles but with little or no permanent translation of the particles in the direction of the propagation : VIBRATION **2 :** the pulsation caused by the vibrating together of two tones not quite in unison **3 :** a wavy appearance, outline, or form : WAVINESS

un·du·la·to·ry \ˈən-jə-lə-ˌtōr-ē, ˈən-d(y)ə-, -ˌtȯr-\ *adj* : of or relating to undulation : moving in or resembling waves : UNDULATING

undulatory theory *n* : a theory in physics: light is transmitted from luminous bodies to the eye and other objects by an undulatory movement — called also *wave theory*

un·du·ly \ˌən-ˈd(y)ü-lē, ˈən-\ *adv* : in an undue manner : EXCESSIVELY

un·du·ti·ful \-ˈd(y)üt-i-fəl\ *adj* : not dutiful — **un·du·ti·ful·ly** \-fə-lē\ *adv* — **un·du·ti·ful·ness** *n*

un·dy·ing \-ˈdī-iŋ\ *adj* : not dying : IMMORTAL, PERPETUAL

un·earned \-ˈərnd\ *adj* **1 :** not gained by labor, service, or skill <~ income> **2 :** scored as a result of an error by the opposing team <~ run>

unearned increment *n* : an increase in the value of property (as land) that is due to no labor or expenditure of the owner but to natural causes (as the increase of population) that create an increased demand for it

un·earth \ˌən-ˈərth, ˈən-\ *vt* **1 :** to dig up out of the earth : EXHUME, DISINTER <~ a hidden treasure> **2 :** to make known or public : bring to light <~ a plot> *syn* see DISCOVER

un·earth·ly \-lē\ *adj* : not earthly: as **a :** not terrestrial <~ radio sources> **b :** PRETERNATURAL, SUPERNATURAL <an ~ light> **c :** WEIRD, EERIE <~ howls> **d :** not mundane : IDEAL <~ love> **e :** FANTASTIC, PREPOSTEROUS <getting up at an ~ hour> — **un·earth·li·ness** *n*

un·ease \ˌən-ˈēz, ˈən-\ *n* : mental or spiritual discomfort: as **a :** vague dissatisfaction : MISGIVING **b :** ANXIETY, DISQUIET **c :** lack of ease (as in social relations) : EMBARRASSMENT

un·eas·i·ly \-ˈēz-ə-lē\ *adv* : in an uneasy manner

1un·easy \-ˈē-zē\ *adj* **1** *archaic* : causing physical or mental discomfort **2 :** not easy : DIFFICULT **3 :** marked by lack of ease : AWKWARD, EMBARRASSED <gave an ~ laugh> **4 :** APPREHENSIVE, WORRIED **5 :** RESTLESS, UNQUIET **6 :** PRECARIOUS, UNSTABLE <an ~ truce> — **un·eas·i·ness** *n*

2uneasy *adv* : UNEASILY

un·eco·nom·ic \ˌən-ˌek-ə-ˈnäm-ik, -ˌē-kə-\ *also* **un·eco·nom·i·cal** \-i-kəl\ *adj* : not economically practicable : COSTLY, WASTEFUL

un·ed·it·ed \ˌən-ˈed-ət-əd, ˈən-\ *adj* : not edited: as **a :** left unrevised **b :** not yet edited : still unpublished

un·emo·tion·al \ˌən-i-ˈmō-shnəl, -shən-ᵊl\ *adj* : not emotional: as **a :** not easily aroused or excited : COLD **b :** involving a minimum of emotion : INTELLECTUAL — **un·emo·tion·al·ly** \-ē\ *adv*

un·em·phat·ic \ˌən-im-ˈfat-ik, -ˌem-\ *adj* : not emphatic : lacking emphasis — **un·em·phat·i·cal·ly** \-i-k(ə-)lē\ *adv*

un·em·ploy·able \ˌən-im-ˈplȯi-ə-bəl\ *adj* : not acceptable for employment — **un·em·ploy·abil·i·ty** \-ˌplȯi-ə-ˈbil-ət-ē\ *n* — **unemployable** *n*

un·em·ployed \-ˈplȯid\ *adj* : not employed: **a :** not being used **b :** not engaged in a gainful occupation **c :** not invested — **unemployed** *n*

un·em·ploy·ment \-ˈplȯi-mənt\ *n* : the state of being unemployed : involuntary idleness of workers

unemployment benefit *n* : a sum of money paid at regular intervals to an unemployed worker by his union, his employer, or a government agency

unemployment compensation *n* : compensation to unemployed workers provided under social security

unemployment insurance *n* : social insurance against involuntary unemployment that provides unemployment benefits for a limited period to unemployed workers

un·en·cum·bered \ˌən-in-ˈkəm-bərd\ *adj* : free of encumbrance

un·end·ing \ˌən-ˈen-diŋ, ˈən-\ *adj* : never ending : ENDLESS — **un·end·ing·ly** \-diŋ-lē\ *adv*

un·en·dur·able \ˌən-in-ˈd(y)u̇r-ə-bəl\ *adj* : not endurable : UNBEARABLE — **un·en·dur·able·ness** *n* — **un·en·dur·ably** \-blē\ *adv*

un–En·glish \ˌən-ˈiŋ-glish, ˈən- *also* -ˈiŋ-lish\ *adj* **1 :** not characteristically English **2 :** not agreeing with standard or generally accepted usage of the English language

un·en·thu·si·as·tic \ˌən-in-ˌth(y)ü-zē-ˈas-tik\ *adj* : not enthusiastic or excited — **un·en·thu·si·as·ti·cal·ly** \-ti-kə-lē\ *adv*

1un·equal \ˌən-ˈē-kwəl, ˈən-\ *adj* **1 a :** not of the same measurement, quantity, or number as another **b :** not like or not the same as another in degree, worth, or status **2 :** not uniform : VARIABLE, UNEVEN **3 a :** badly balanced or matched <an ~ contest> **b :** contracted between unequals <~ marriages> **c** *archaic* : not equable **4** *archaic* : not equitable : UNJUST **5 :** INADEQUATE, INSUFFICIENT <~ to the task> — **un·equal·ly** \-kwə-lē\ *adv*

2unequal *n* : one that is not equal to another

3unequal *adv, archaic* : in an unequal manner <~ match'd —Shak.>

un·equaled \-kwəld\ *adj* : not equaled : UNPARALLELED

un·equiv·o·ca·bly \ˌən-i-ˈkwiv-ə-kə-blē\ *adv* [by alter.] *nonstand* : UNEQUIVOCALLY

un·equiv·o·cal \ˌən-i-ˈkwiv-ə-kəl\ *adj* : leaving no doubt : CLEAR, UNAMBIGUOUS

un·equiv·o·cal·ly \-kə-lē\ *adv* : in an unequivocal manner

un·err·ing \ˌən-ˈe(ə)r-iŋ, ˌən-ˈər-, ˈən-\ *adj* : committing no error : FAULTLESS, UNFAILING — **un·err·ing·ly** \-iŋ-lē\ *adv*

UNES·CO \yu̇-ˈnes-(ˌ)kō\ *abbr* United Nations Educational, Scientific, and Cultural Organization

un·es·sen·tial \ˌən-ə-ˈsen-chəl\ *adj* **1 :** not essential : DISPENSABLE, UNIMPORTANT **2** *archaic* : void of essence : INSUBSTANTIAL

un–Eu·ro·pe·an \ˌən-ˌyu̇r-ə-ˈpē-ən\ *adj* : not characteristically European

un·even \ˌən-ˈē-vən, ˈən-\ *adj* **1 a** *archaic* : UNEQUAL 1a **b :** ODD 3a **2 a :** not even : not level or smooth : RUGGED, RAGGED <large ~ teeth> <~ handwriting> **b :** varying from the straight or parallel **c :** not uniform : IRREGULAR <~ combustion> **d :** varying in quality <an ~ performance> **3 :** UNEQUAL 3a <an ~ confrontation> *syn* see ROUGH *ant* even — **un·even·ly** *adv*

un·even·ness \ˌən-ˈē-vən-nəs, ˈən-\ *n* : the quality or state of being uneven

un·event·ful \ˌən-i-ˈvent-fəl\ *adj* : marked by no noteworthy or untoward incidents : PLACID — **un·event·ful·ly** \-fə-lē\ *adv*

un·ex·am·pled \ˌən-ig-ˈzam-pəld\ *adj* : having no example or parallel : UNPRECEDENTED

un·ex·cep·tion·able \ˌən-ik-ˈsep-sh(ə-)nə-bəl\ *adj* [*un-* + obs. *exception* (to take exception, object)] : not open to objection or criticism : beyond reproach : UNIMPEACHABLE — **un·ex·cep·tion·able·ness** *n* — **un·ex·cep·tion·ably** \-blē\ *adv*

un·ex·cep·tion·al \-shnəl, -shən-ᵊl\ *adj* : not out of the ordinary : COMMONPLACE

un·ex·cep·tion·al·ly \-shnə-lē, -shən-ᵊl-ē\ *adv* : without exception : in every case

un·ex·pect·ed \ˌən-ik-ˈspek-təd\ *adj* : not expected : UNFORESEEN — **un·ex·pect·ed·ly** *adv* — **un·ex·pect·ed·ness** *n*

un·ex·ploit·ed \ˌən-ik-ˈsplȯit-əd\ *adj* : not exploited : not taken advantage of; *esp* : UNDEVELOPED <~ lowland tropics>

un·ex·pres·sive \ˌən-ik-ˈspres-iv\ *adj* **1 :** not expressive : failing to convey the feeling or meaning intended **2** *obs* : INEFFABLE

un·fad·ing \ˌən-ˈfād-iŋ, ˈən-\ *adj* **1 :** not losing color or freshness **2 :** not losing value or effectiveness — **un·fad·ing·ly** \-iŋ-lē\ *adv*

un·fail·ing \ˌən-ˈfā-liŋ, ˈən-\ *adj* : not failing or liable to fail: **a :** CONSTANT, UNFLAGGING <~ courtesy> **b :** EVERLASTING, INEXHAUSTIBLE <a subject of ~ interest> **c :** INFALLIBLE, SURE <an ~ test> — **un·fail·ing·ly** \-liŋ-lē\ *adv*

un·fail·ing·ness *n* : the quality or state of being unfailing

un·fair \ˌən-ˈfa(ə)r, ˈən-, -ˈfe(ə)r\ *adj* **1 :** marked by injustice, partiality, or deception : UNJUST **2 :** not equitable in business dealings — **un·fair·ness** *n*

un·fair·ly *adv* : in an unfair manner

un·faith \ˌən-ˈfāth, ˈən-ˈ, ˈən-ˌ\ *n* : absence of faith : DISBELIEF

un·faith·ful \ˌən-ˈfāth-fəl, ˈən-\ *adj* : not faithful: **a :** not adhering to vows, allegiance, or duty : DISLOYAL **b :** not faithful to marriage vows **c :** INACCURATE, UNTRUSTWORTHY — **un·faith·ful·ly** \-fə-lē\ *adv* — **un·faith·ful·ness** *n*

un·fal·ter·ing \ˌən-ˈfȯl-t(ə-)riŋ\ *adj* : not wavering or weakening : FIRM — **un·fal·ter·ing·ly** \-t(ə-)riŋ-lē\ *adv*

un·fa·mil·iar \ˌən-fə-ˈmil-yər\ *adj* : not familiar: **a :** not well known : STRANGE <an ~ place> **b :** not well acquainted <~ with the subject> — **un·fa·mil·iar·i·ty** \-ˌmil-ˈyar-ət-ē, -ˌmil-ē-ˈ(y)ar-\ *n* — **un·fa·mil·iar·ly** \-ˈmil-yər-lē\ *adv*

un·fan·cy \ˌən-ˈfan(t)-sē, ˈən-\ *adj* : not fancy : SIMPLE, UNPRETENTIOUS

un·fash·ion·able \-ˈfash-(ə-)nə-bəl\ *adj* **1 :** not in keeping with the current fashion <~ clothes> **2 :** not favored socially <~ neighborhoods> — **un·fash·ion·ably** \-blē\ *adv*

un·fas·ten \-ˈfas-ᵊn\ *vt* : to make loose: as **a :** UNPIN, UNBUCKLE **b :** UNDO <~ a button> **c :** DETACH <~ a boat from its moorings>

un·fa·thered \-ˈfa͟th-ərd\ *adj* **1 :** having no father : ILLEGITIMATE, BASTARD **2 :** having no known origin <~ slanders>

un·fath·om·able \-ˈfa͟th-ə-mə-bəl\ *adj* : not capable of being fathomed: **a :** impossible to comprehend **b :** IMMEASURABLE

un·fa·vor·able \ˌən-ˈfāv-(ə-)rə-bəl, ˈən-, -ˈfā-vər-bəl\ *adj* **1 a :** OPPOSED, CONTRARY **b :** expressing disapproval : NEGATIVE <~ reviews> **2 :** not propitious : DISADVANTAGEOUS **3 :** not pleasing — **un·fa·vor·able·ness** *n* — **un·fa·vor·ably** \-blē\ *adv*

un·feath·ered \-ˈfe͟th-ərd\ *adj* : UNFLEDGED

un·feel·ing \-ˈfē-liŋ\ *adj* **1 :** devoid of feeling : INSENSATE <an ~ corpse> **2 :** devoid of kindness or sympathy : HARDHEARTED, CRUEL <an ~ wretch> — **un·feel·ing·ly** \-liŋ-lē\ *adv* — **un·feel·ing·ness** *n*

un·feigned \-ˈfānd\ *adj* : not feigned or hypocritical : GENUINE *syn* see SINCERE — **un·feigned·ly** \-ˈfā-nəd-lē, -ˈfān-dlē\ *adv*

un·fet·ter \-ˈfet-ər\ *vt* **1 :** to free from fetters <~ a prisoner> **2 :** EMANCIPATE, LIBERATE <~ the mind from prejudice>

un·fet·tered \-ərd\ *adj* : FREE, UNRESTRAINED

un·fil·ial \ˌən-ˈfil-ē-əl, ˈən-, -ˈfil-yəl\ *adj* : not observing the obligations of a child to a parent : UNDUTIFUL — **un·fil·ial·ly** \-ē\ *adv*

un·find·able \ˌən-ˈfīn-də-bəl, ˈən-\ *adj* : not capable of being found

un·fin·ished \-ˈfin-isht\ *adj* : not finished: **a :** not brought to an end or to the desired final state **b :** subjected to no other processes (as bleaching or dyeing) after coming from the loom

1un·fit \-ˈfit\ *adj* : not fit: **a :** not adapted to a purpose : UNSUITABLE **b :** not qualified : INCAPABLE, INCOMPETENT **c :** physically or mentally unsound — **un·fit·ly** *adv* — **un·fit·ness** *n*

2unfit *vt* : to make unfit : DISABLE, DISQUALIFY

un·fit·ted \ˌən-ˈfit-əd, ˈən-\ *adj* : not adapted : UNQUALIFIED

un·fit·ting \-ˈfit-iŋ\ *adj* : not fitting : UNSUITABLE

un·fix \-ˈfiks\ *vt* **1 :** to loosen from a fastening : DETACH, DISENGAGE **2 :** to make unstable : UNSETTLE

un·flag·ging \-ˈflag-iŋ\ *adj* : not flagging : TIRELESS — **un·flag·ging·ly** \-iŋ-lē\ *adv*

ə abut ᵊ kitten ər further a back ā bake ä cot, cart
au̇ out ch chin e less ē easy g gift i trip ī life
j joke ŋ sing ō flow ȯ flaw ȯi coin th thin t͟h this
ü loot u̇ foot y yet yü few yu̇ furious zh vision

un·flap·pa·ble \-ˈflap-ə-bəl\ *adj* [[1]*un-* + *flap* (state of excitement) + *-able*] : marked by assurance and self-control — **un·flap·pa·bil·i·ty** \-ˌflap-ə-ˈbil-ət-ē\ *n*
un·flat·ter·ing \-ˈflat-ə-riŋ\ *adj* : not flattering; *esp* : UNFAVORABLE — **un·flat·ter·ing·ly** \-riŋ-lē\ *adv*
un·fledged \ˌən-ˈflejd, ˈən-\ *adj* **1** : not feathered : not ready for flight **2** : not fully developed : IMMATURE, CALLOW <an ~ writer>
un·flinch·ing \-ˈflin-chiŋ\ *adj* : not flinching or shrinking : STEADFAST — **un·flinch·ing·ly** \-chiŋ-lē\ *adv*
un·fo·cused *also* **un·fo·cussed** \-ˈfō-kəst\ *adj* **1** : not adjusted to a focus **2** : not concentrated on one point or objective <~ rage>
un·fold \-ˈfōld\ *vt* **1 a** : to open the folds of : spread or straighten out : EXPAND <~*ed* the map> **b** : to remove (as a package) from the folds : UNWRAP **2** : to open to the view : REVEAL; *esp* : to make clear by gradual disclosure and often by recital ~ *vi* **1 a** : to open from a folded state : open out : EXPAND **b** : BLOSSOM **2** : DEVELOP, EVOLVE <as the story ~*s*> **3** : to open out gradually to the view or understanding : become known <a panorama ~*s* before their eyes>
un·fold·ment \-ˈfōl(d)-mənt\ *n* : the act or process of unfolding : DEVELOPMENT
un·for·get·ta·ble \ˌən-fər-ˈget-ə-bəl\ *adj* : incapable of being forgotten : MEMORABLE — **un·for·get·ta·bil·i·ty** \-ˌget-ə-ˈbil-ət-ē\ *n* — **un·for·get·ta·bly** \-ˈget-ə-blē\ *adv*
un·for·giv·ing \ˌən-fər-ˈgiv-iŋ\ *adj* : unwilling or unable to forgive — **un·for·giv·ing·ness** *n*
un·formed \-ˈfȯ(ə)rmd\ *adj* : not arranged in regular shape, order, or relations; *esp* : IMMATURE, UNDEVELOPED
[1]**un·for·tu·nate** \-ˈfȯrch-(ə-)nət\ *adj* **1 a** : not favored by fortune : UNSUCCESSFUL, UNLUCKY <an ~ young man> **b** : marked or accompanied by or resulting in misfortune <an ~ decision> **2 a** : UNSUITABLE, INFELICITOUS <an ~ choice of words> **b** : DEPLORABLE, REGRETTABLE <an ~ lack of taste>
[2]**unfortunate** *n* : an unfortunate person; *specif* : a social outcast
un·for·tu·nate·ly *adv* **1** : in an unfortunate manner **2** : it is unfortunate <the matter, ~, is not so simple>
un·found·ed \ˌən-ˈfau̇n-dəd, ˈən-\ *adj* : lacking a sound basis : GROUNDLESS, UNWARRANTED
un·freeze \-ˈfrēz\ *vt* **-froze** \-ˈfrōz\; **-fro·zen** \-ˈfrōz-ᵊn\; **-freez·ing** : to cause to thaw
un·fre·quent·ed \ˌən-frē-ˈkwent-əd; ˌən-ˈfrē-kwənt-, ˈən-\ *adj* : not often visited or traveled over
un·friend·ed \ˌən-ˈfren-dəd, ˈən-\ *adj* : having no friends : not befriended
un·friend·li·ness \-ˈfren-(d)lē-nəs\ *n* : the quality or state of being unfriendly : HOSTILITY
un·friend·ly \-ˈfren-(d)lē\ *adj* : not friendly: **a** : HOSTILE, UNSYMPATHETIC **b** : INHOSPITABLE, UNFAVORABLE
un·frock \-ˈfräk\ *vt* **1** : to deprive (as a priest) of the right to exercise the functions of office **2** : to remove from a position of honor or privilege
un·fruit·ful \-ˈfrüt-fəl\ *adj* : not fruitful: as **a** : not producing offspring : BARREN **b** : yielding no valuable result <an ~ conference> ***syn*** see STERILE ***ant*** fruitful, prolific — **un·fruit·ful·ly** \-fə-lē\ *adv* — **un·fruit·ful·ness** *n*
un·fund·ed \-ˈfən-dəd\ *adj* **1** : not funded : FLOATING <an ~ debt> **2** : not provided with funds <proposed but ~ schools>
un·furl \-ˈfər(-ə)l\ *vt* : to release from a furled state ~ *vi* : to become visible or known
un·fussy \-ˈfəs-ē\ *adj* : not fussy: as **a** : not particular : UNCONCERNED **b** : not cluttered with pretentious or nonessential matters : UNCOMPLICATED
un·gain·ly \-ˈgān-lē\ *adj* **1 a** : lacking in smoothness or dexterity : CLUMSY **b** : hard to handle : UNWIELDY **2** : having an awkward appearance : UGLY — **un·gain·li·ness** *n*
un·gal·lant \ˌən-ˈgal-ənt, ˈən-; ˌən-gə-ˈlant, -ˈlänt\ *adj* : not gallant — **un·gal·lant·ly** *adv*
un·gen·er·os·i·ty \ˌən-ˌjen-ə-ˈräs-ət-ē, -ˈräs-tē\ *n* : lack of generosity
un·gen·er·ous \ˌən-ˈjen-(ə-)rəs, ˈən-\ *adj* : not generous: **a** : PETTY, MEAN **b** : deficient in liberality : STINGY — **un·gen·er·ous·ly** *adv*
un·gird \-ˈgərd\ *vt* : to divest of a restraining band or girdle : UNBIND
un·girt \-ˈgərt\ *adj* **1** : having the belt or girdle off or loose **2** : lacking in discipline or compactness : LOOSE, SLACK
un·glue \-ˈglü\ *vt* : to separate by or as if by dissolving an adhesive
un·glued \-ˈglüd\ *adj* : UPSET, DISORDERED
un·god·li·ness \ˌən-ˈgäd-lē-nəs, ˈən- *also* -ˈgȯd-\ *n* : the quality or state of being ungodly
un·god·ly \-lē\ *adj* **1 a** : denying God or disobedient to him : IMPIOUS, IRRELIGIOUS **b** : contrary to moral law : SINFUL, WICKED **2** : INDECENT, OUTRAGEOUS <gets up at an ~ hour>
un·got·ten \-ˈgät-ᵊn\ *or* **un·got** \-ˈgät\ *adj* **1** *obs* : not begotten **2** : not obtained
un·gov·ern·able \-ˈgəv-ər-nə-bəl\ *adj* : not capable of being governed, guided, or restrained ***syn*** see UNRULY ***ant*** governable, docile
un·grace·ful \-ˈgrās-fəl\ *adj* : not graceful : AWKWARD, INELEGANT — **un·grace·ful·ly** \-fə-lē\ *adv* — **un·grace·ful·ness** *n*
un·gra·cious \-ˈgrā-shəs\ *adj* **1** *archaic* : WICKED **2** : not courteous : RUDE **3** : not pleasing : DISAGREEABLE — **un·gra·cious·ly** *adv* — **un·gra·cious·ness** *n*
un·gram·mat·i·cal \ˌən-grə-ˈmat-i-kəl\ *adj* : not following rules of grammar — **un·gram·mat·i·cal·i·ty** \-ˌmat-ə-ˈkal-ət-ē\ *n*
un·grate·ful \ˌən-ˈgrāt-fəl, ˈən-\ *adj* **1** : showing no gratitude : making a poor return : THANKLESS **2** : DISAGREEABLE, REPELLENT — **un·grate·ful·ly** \-fə-lē\ *adv* — **un·grate·ful·ness** *n*
un·grudg·ing \-ˈgrəj-iŋ\ *adj* : being without envy or reluctance
un·gual \ˈəŋ-gwəl, ˈən-\ *adj* [L *unguis* nail, claw, hoof — more at NAIL] : of, relating to, or resembling a nail, claw, or hoof
un·guard \ˌən-ˈgärd, ˈən-\ *vt* [back-formation fr. *unguarded*] : to leave unprotected
un·guard·ed \-ˈgärd-əd\ *adj* **1** : vulnerable to attack : UNPROTECTED **2** : free from guile or wariness : DIRECT, INCAUTIOUS — **un·guard·ed·ly** *adv* — **un·guard·ed·ness** *n*
un·guent \ˈəŋ-gwənt, ˈən-; ˈən-jənt\ *n* [L *unguentum* — more at OINTMENT] : a soothing or healing salve : OINTMENT
un·guis \ˈəŋ-gwəs, ˈən-\ *n, pl* **un·gues** \-ˌgwēz\ [L] **1** : a nail, claw, or hoof esp. on a digit of a vertebrate **2** : a narrow pointed base of a petal
[1]**un·gu·late** \ˈəŋ-gyə-lət, ˈən-, -ˌlāt\ *adj* [LL *ungulatus*, fr. L *ungula* hoof, fr. *unguis* nail, hoof] **1** : having hoofs **2** : of or relating to the ungulates
[2]**ungulate** *n* [deriv. of L *ungula*] : any of the group (Ungulata) consisting of the hoofed mammals (as a ruminant, swine, horse, tapir, rhinoceros, elephant, or hyrax) of which most are herbivorous and many horned
un·hair \ˌən-ˈha(ə)r, ˈən-, -ˈhe(ə)r\ *vt, archaic* : to deprive of hair
un·hal·low \-ˈhal-(ˌ)ō, -ˈhal-ə(-w)\ *vt, archaic* : to make profane
un·hal·lowed \-(ˌ)ōd, -əd\ *adj* **1** : not blessed : UNCONSECRATED, UNHOLY **2 a** : unsanctioned by or showing lack of reverence for religion : IMPIOUS, PROFANE **b** : contrary to accepted standards : IMMORAL
un·hand \ˌən-ˈhand, ˈən-\ *vt* : to remove the hand from : let go
un·hand·some \-ˈhan(t)-səm\ *adj* : not handsome: as **a** : not beautiful : HOMELY **b** : UNBECOMING, UNSEEMLY **c** : lacking in courtesy or taste : RUDE — **un·hand·some·ly** *adv*
un·handy \-ˈhan-dē\ *adj* **1** : hard to handle : INCONVENIENT **2** : lacking in skill or dexterity : AWKWARD — **un·handi·ly** \-də-lē\ *adv* — **un·handi·ness** \-dē-nəs\ *n*
un·hap·pi·ly \-ˈhap-ə-lē\ *adv* **1** : in an unhappy manner **2** : UNFORTUNATELY 2
un·hap·py \-ˈhap-ē\ *adj* **1** : not fortunate : UNLUCKY **2** : not cheerful or glad : SAD, WRETCHED **3 a** : causing or subject to misfortune : INAUSPICIOUS **b** : INFELICITOUS, INAPPROPRIATE — **un·hap·pi·ness** *n*
un·har·ness \-ˈhär-nəs\ *vt* : to divest of harness
un·healthy \-ˈhel-thē\ *adj* **1** : not conducive to health <an ~ climate> **2** : not in good health : SICKLY, DISEASED **3 a** : DANGEROUS, RISKY **b** : BAD, INJURIOUS **c** : morally contaminated : CORRUPT, UNWHOLESOME — **un·health·i·ly** \-thə-lē\ *adv* — **un·health·i·ness** \-thē-nəs\ *n*
un·heard \-ˈhərd\ *adj* **1 a** : not perceived by the ear **b** : not given a hearing **2** *archaic* : UNHEARD-OF
un·heard–of \-ˌəv, -ˌäv\ *adj* : previously unknown : UNPRECEDENTED
un·help·ful \ˌən-ˈhelp-fəl, ˈən-\ *adj* : not helpful : USELESS, UNCOOPERATIVE — **un·help·ful·ly** \-fə-lē\ *adv*
un·hes·i·tat·ing \-ˈhez-ə-ˌtāt-iŋ\ *adj* : not hesitating : not checked or qualified — **un·hes·i·tat·ing·ly** \-iŋ-lē\ *adv*
un·hinge \-ˈhinj\ *vt* **1** : to remove (as a door) from the hinges **2** : to make unstable : UNSETTLE, DISRUPT <~ the balance of world peace> <experiences that would ~ a lesser man>
un·hitch \-ˈhich\ *vt* : to free from or as if from being hitched
un·ho·ly \ˌən-ˈhō-lē, ˈən-\ *adj* **1** : showing disregard for what is holy : WICKED **2** : SHOCKING, OUTRAGEOUS — **un·ho·li·ness** *n*
un·hood \-ˈhu̇d\ *vt* : to remove a hood or covering from
un·hook \-ˈhu̇k\ *vt* **1** : to remove from a hook **2** : to unfasten by disengaging a hook
un·hoped \-ˈhōpt\ *adj, archaic* : not hoped for or expected
un·horse \-ˈhȯ(ə)rs\ *vt* : to dislodge from or as if from a horse
un·hou·seled \-ˈhau̇-zəld\ *adj, archaic* : not having received the Eucharist esp. shortly before death
un·hur·ried \-ˈhər-ēd, -ˈhə-rēd\ *adj* : not hurried : LEISURELY — **un·hur·ried·ly** *adv*
un·hys·ter·i·cal \ˌən-his-ˈter-i-kəl\ *adj* : not hysterical — **un·hys·ter·i·cal·ly** \-k(ə-)lē\ *adv*
uni- *prefix* [ME, fr. MF, fr. L, fr. *unus* — more at ONE] : one : single <*uni*cellular>
uni·al·gal \ˌyü-nē-ˈal-gəl\ *adj* : of, relating to, or derived from a single algal individual or cell <a ~ culture>
Uni·ate *or* **Uni·at** \ˈ(y)ü-nē-ˌat\ *n* [Russ *uniyat*] : a Christian of a church adhering to an Eastern rite and discipline but submitting to papal authority — **Uniate** *adj*
uni·ax·i·al \-ˈak-sē-əl\ *adj* **1** : having only one axis **2** : of or relating to only one axis — **uni·ax·i·al·ly** \-ə-lē\ *adv*
uni·cam·er·al \ˌyü-ni-kam-(ə-)rəl\ *adj* : having or consisting of a single legislative chamber — **uni·cam·er·al·ly** \-ē\ *adv*
UNI·CEF \ˈyü-nə-ˌsef\ *abbr* [*United Nations Children's Emergency Fund*, its former name] United Nations Children's Fund
uni·cel·lu·lar \ˌyü-ni-ˈsel-yə-lər\ *adj* : having or consisting of a single cell — **uni·cel·lu·lar·i·ty** \-ˌsel-yə-ˈlar-ət-ē\ *n*
uni·corn \ˈyü-nə-ˌkȯ(ə)rn\ *n* [ME *unicorne*, fr. OF, fr. LL *unicornis*, fr. L, having one horn, fr. *uni-* + *cornu* horn — more at HORN] : a fabulous animal generally depicted with the body and head of a horse, the hind legs of a stag, the tail of a lion, and a single horn in the middle of the forehead

unicorn

uni·cy·cle \ˈyü-ni-ˌsī-kəl\ *n* [*uni* + *-cycle* (as in *tricycle*)] : any of various vehicles that have a single wheel and are propelled usu. by pedals or applied draft — **uni·cy·clist** \-ˌsī-k(ə-)ləst\ *n*
uni·di·rec·tion·al \ˌyü-ni-də-ˈrek-shnəl, -dī-, -shən-ᵊl\ *adj* **1** : involving, functioning, moving, or responsive in a single direction **2** : not subject to change or reversal of direction — **uni·di·rec·tion·al·ly** \-ē\ *adv*
unidirectional current *n* : DIRECT CURRENT
uni·fac·to·ri·al \ˌyü-ni-fak-ˈtōr-ē-əl, -ˈtȯr-\ *adj* : relating to or controlled by a single gene
uni·fi·ca·tion \ˌyü-nə-fə-ˈkā-shən\ *n* : the act, process, or result of unifying : the state of being unified

uni·fi·lar \ˌyü-ni-ˈfī-lər\ *adj* : having or involving use of only one thread, wire, or fiber
uni·fo·li·ate \-ˈfō-lē-ət\ *adj* **1** : having only one leaf **2** : UNIFOLIOLATE
uni·fo·li·o·late \-ˈfō-lē-ə-ˌlāt\ *adj, of a leaf* : compound but having only a single leaflet and distinguishable from a simple leaf by the basal joint
[1]**uni·form** \ˈyü-nə-ˌfȯrm\ *adj* [MF *uniforme,* fr. L *uniformis,* fr. *uni-* + *-formis* -form] **1** : having always the same form, manner, or degree : not varying or variable **2** : of the same form with others : conforming to one rule or mode : CONSONANT **3** : presenting an undiversified appearance of surface, pattern, or color <~ brown clapboard houses> **4** : consistent in conduct or opinion <~ interpretation of laws> ***syn*** see SIMILAR ***ant*** various — **uni·form·ly** \ˈyü-nə-ˌfȯrm-lē, yü-nə-ˈ\ *adv* — **uni·form·ness** \ˈyü-nə-ˌfȯrm-nəs\ *n*
[2]**uniform** *vt* **1** : to bring into uniformity **2** : to clothe with a uniform
[3]**uniform** *n* : dress of a distinctive design or fashion worn by members of a particular group and serving as a means of identification
Uniform — a communications code word for the letter *u*
uni·for·mi·tar·i·an \ˌyü-nə-ˌfȯr-mə-ˈter-ē-ən\ *n* **1** : an adherent of the doctrine of uniformitarianism **2** : an advocate of uniformity — **uniformitarian** *adj*
uni·for·mi·tar·i·an·ism \-ē-ə-ˌniz-əm\ *n* : a geological doctrine that existing processes acting in the same manner as at present are sufficient to account for all geological changes
uni·for·mi·ty \ˌyü-nə-ˈfȯr-mət-ē\ *n, pl* **-ties** **1** : the quality or state of being uniform **2** : an instance of uniformity
uni·fy \ˈyü-nə-ˌfī\ *vt* **-fied; -fy·ing** [LL *unificare,* fr. L *uni-* + *-ficare* -fy] : to make into a unit or a coherent whole : UNITE — **uni·fi·able** \-ˌfī-ə-bəl\ *adj* — **uni·fi·er** \-ˌfī(-ə)r\ *n*
uni·ju·gate \yü-ˈnij-ə-ˌgāt, ˌyü-ni-ˈjü-gət\ *adj* : having but one pair of leaflets — used of a pinnate leaf
uni·lat·er·al \ˌyü-ni-ˈlat-ə-rəl, -ˈla-trəl\ *adj* **1 a** : done or undertaken by one person or party **b** : of, relating to, or affecting one side of a subject : ONE-SIDED **c** : constituting or relating to a contract or engagement by which an express obligation to do or forbear is imposed on only one party **2** : produced or arranged on or directed toward one side <a ~ raceme> **3** : tracing descent through either the maternal or paternal line only **4** : having only one side — **uni·lat·er·al·ly** \-ē\ *adv*
uni·lin·ear \ˌyü-ni-ˈlin-ē-ər\ *adj* : developing in or involving a series of stages usu. from the primitive to the more advanced <a ~ cultural sequence>
uni·lin·gual \ˌyü-ni-ˈliŋ-g(yə-)wəl\ *adj* [*uni-* + L *lingua* tongue, language — more at TONGUE] : composed in or using one language only
un·il·lu·sioned \ˌən-il-ˈü-zhənd, ˌən-ᵊl-\ *adj* : free from illusion
uni·loc·u·lar \ˌyü-ni-ˈläk-yə-lər\ *adj* : containing a single cavity
un·imag·in·able \ˌən-ə-ˈmaj-(ə-)nə-bəl\ *adj* : not imaginable or comprehensible — **un·imag·in·ably** \-blē\ *adv*
un·im·pas·sioned \ˌən-im-ˈpash-ənd\ *adj* : not impassioned; *esp* : marked by cool or sometimes frigid reasonableness and freedom from purely emotional appeal ***syn*** see SOBER ***ant*** impassioned
un·im·peach·able \-ˈpē-chə-bəl\ *adj* : not impeachable : not to be called in question : not liable to accusation : IRREPROACHABLE, BLAMELESS — **un·im·peach·ably** \-blē\ *adv*
[1]**un·im·proved** \-ˈprüvd\ *adj, obs* : UNREPROVED
[2]**unimproved** *adj* : not improved: as **a** : not tilled, built on, or otherwise improved for use <~ land> **b** : not used or employed advantageously <wasted time and ~ opportunities> **c** : not selectively bred for better quality or productiveness
un·in·for·ma·tive \ˌən-in-ˈfȯr-mət-iv\ *adj* : not informative — **un·in·for·ma·tive·ly** *adv*
un·in·hib·it·ed \-ˈhib-ət-əd\ *adj* : free from inhibition; *also* : boisterously informal — **un·in·hib·it·ed·ly** *adv* — **un·in·hib·it·ed·ness** *n*
un·ini·tiate \ˌən-ə-ˈnish-(ē-)ət\ *adj* : not initiated : INEXPERIENCED
un·in·tel·li·gence \ˌən-in-ˈtel-ə-jən(t)s\ *n* : the quality or state of being unintelligent
un·in·tel·li·gent \-jənt\ *adj* : lacking intelligence : UNWISE, IGNORANT — **un·in·tel·li·gent·ly** *adv*
un·in·tel·li·gi·ble \-ˈtel-ə-jə-bəl\ *adj* : not intelligible : OBSCURE — **un·in·tel·li·gi·bil·i·ty** \-ˌtel-ə-jə-ˈbil-ət-ē\ *n* — **un·in·tel·li·gi·ble·ness** \-ˈtel-ə-jə-bəl-nəs\ *n* — **un·in·tel·li·gi·bly** \-blē\ *adv*
un·in·ten·tion·al \ˌən-in-ˈtench-nəl, -ˈten-chən-ᵊl\ *adj* : not intentional — **un·in·ten·tion·al·ly** \-ē\ *adv*
un·in·ter·rupt·ed \ˌən-ˌint-ə-ˈrəp-təd\ *adj* : not interrupted : CONTINUOUS — **un·in·ter·rupt·ed·ly** *adv* — **un·in·ter·rupt·ed·ness** *n*
uni·nu·cle·ate \ˌyü-ni-ˈn(y)ü-klē-ət\ *adj* : having a single nucleus <a ~ yeast cell>
[1]**union** \ˈyü-nyən\ *n* [ME, fr. MF, fr. LL *union-, unio* oneness, union, fr. L *unus* one — more at ONE] **1 a** : an act or instance of uniting or joining two or more things into one: as (1) : the formation of a single political unit from two or more separate and independent units (2) : a uniting in marriage; *also* : SEXUAL INTERCOURSE (3) : the growing together of severed parts **b** : a unified condition : COMBINATION, JUNCTION <a gracious ~ of excellence and strength> **2** : something that is made one : something formed by a combining or coalition of parts or members: as **a** : a confederation of independent individuals (as nations or persons) for some common purpose **b** : a political unit constituting an organic whole formed usu. from previously independent units (as England and Scotland in 1707) which have surrendered their principal powers to the government of the whole or to a newly created government (as the U.S. in 1789) **c** *cap* : an organization on a college or university campus providing recreational, social, cultural, and sometimes dining facilities; *also* : the building housing such an organization **d** : the set of all elements belonging to one or more of a given collection of two or more sets — called also *join, sum* **e** : LABOR UNION **3 a** : a device emblematic of the union of two or more sovereignties borne on a national flag typically in the upper inner corner or constituting the whole design of the flag **b** : the upper inner corner of a flag **4** : any of various devices for connecting parts (as of a machine); *esp* : a coupling for pipes or pipes and fittings ***syn*** see UNITY

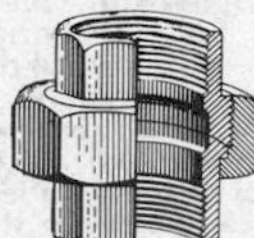
union 4, partly cut away

[2]**union** *adj* : of, relating to, dealing with, or constituting a union
union card *n* **1** : a card certifying personal membership in good standing in a labor union **2** : something that resembles a union card esp. in being necessary for employment or in providing evidence of in-group status
union church *n* : a local church uniting members of diverse denominational backgrounds in an interdenominational congregation
union·ism \ˈyü-nyə-ˌniz-əm\ *n* : the principle or policy of forming or adhering to a union: as **a** *cap* : adherence to the policy of a firm federal union between the states of the United States esp. during the Civil War period **b** : the principles, theory, or system of trade unions
union·ist \-nəst\ *n* : an advocate or supporter of union or unionism
union·iza·tion \ˌyü-nyə-nə-ˈzā-shən\ *n* **1** : the quality or state of being unionized **2** : the action of unionizing
union·ize \ˈyü-nyə-ˌnīz\ *vt* **-ized; -iz·ing** : to cause to become a member of or subject to the rules of a labor union : form into a labor union
union jack *n, often cap U&J* : a jack consisting of the union of a national ensign
union shop *n* : an establishment in which the employer by agreement is free to hire nonmembers as well as members of the union but retains nonmembers on the payroll only on condition of their becoming members of the union within a specified time
union suit *n* : an undergarment with shirt and drawers in one piece
uni·pa·ren·tal \ˌyü-ni-pə-ˈrent-ᵊl\ *adj* : having or involving a single parent; *esp* : PARTHENOGENETIC — **uni·pa·ren·tal·ly** \-ᵊl-ē\ *adv*
unip·a·rous \yü-ˈnip-ə-rəs\ *adj* **1 a** : producing but one egg or offspring at a time **b** : having produced but one offspring **2** : producing but one axis at each branching <a ~ cyme>
uni·pla·nar \ˌyü-ni-ˈplā-nər, -ˌnär\ *adj* : lying or occurring in one plane : PLANAR
uni·po·lar \ˌyü-ni-ˈpō-lər\ *adj* **1** : having, produced by, or acting by a single magnetic or electrical pole **2** : having but one process <~ ganglion cells> — **uni·po·lar·i·ty** \-pō-ˈlar-ət-ē, -pə-\ *n*
unique \yu̇-ˈnēk\ *adj* [F, fr. L *unicus,* fr. *unus* one — more at ONE] **1 a** : being the only one : SOLE <his ~ concern was his own comfort> **b** : producing only one result <the ~ factorization of a number into prime factors> **2** : being without a like or equal : UNEQUALED **3** : very rare or uncommon : very unusual ***syn*** see SINGLE, STRANGE — **unique·ly** *adv* — **unique·ness** *n*
uni·ra·mous \ˌyü-ni-ˈrā-məs\ *adj* : having only one branch
[1]**uni·sex** \ˈyü-nə-ˌseks\ *n* : the state or condition of not being distinguishable (as by hair or clothing) as to sex
[2]**unisex** *adj* : AMBISEXTROUS
uni·sex·u·al \-ˈseksh-(ə-)wəl, -ˈsek-shəl\ *adj* : of, relating to, or restricted to one sex: **a** : male or female but not hermaphroditic **b** : DICLINOUS <a ~ flower> — **uni·sex·u·al·i·ty** \-ˌsek-shə-ˈwal-ət-ē\ *n* — **uni·sex·u·al·ly** \-ˈseksh-(ə-)wə-lē, -ˈsek-shə-lē\ *adv*
uni·son \ˈyü-nə-sən, -nə-zən\ *n* [MF, fr. ML *unisonus* having the same sound, fr. L *uni-* + *sonus* sound — more at SOUND] **1 a** : identity in musical pitch; *specif* : the interval of a perfect prime **b** : the state of being so tuned or sounded **c** : the writing, playing, or singing of parts in a musical passage at the same pitch or in octaves **2** : a harmonious agreement or union : CONCORD — **unison** *adj* — **in unison** : in perfect agreement : so as to harmonize exactly
unit \ˈyü-nət\ *n* [back-formation fr. *unity*] **1 a** (1) : the first and least natural number : ONE (2) : a single quantity regarded as a whole in calculation **b** : the number occupying the position immediately to the left of the decimal point in the Arabic system of numerals **2** : a determinate quantity (as of length, time, heat, value, or housing) adopted as a standard of measurement: as **a** : an amount of work (as 120 hours in a completed course) used in education in calculating student credits **b** : an amount of a biologically active agent (as a drug or antigen) required to produce a specific result under strictly controlled conditions **3 a** : a single thing or person or group that is a constituent of a whole **b** : a part of a military establishment that has a prescribed organization (as of personnel and materiel) **c** : a piece or complex of apparatus serving to perform one particular function **d** : a part of a school course focusing on a central theme and making use of resources from numerous subject areas and the pupils' own experience **e** : a local congregation of Jehovah's Witnesses — **unit** *adj*
unit·age \ˈyü-nət-ij\ *n* **1** : specifications of the amount constituting a unit **2** : amount in units
uni·tar·i·an \ˌyü-nə-ˈter-ē-ən\ *n* [NL *unitarius,* fr. L *unitas* unity] **1 a** *often cap* : one who believes that the deity exists only in one person **b** *cap* : a member of a denomination that stresses individual freedom of belief, the free use of reason in religion, a united world community, and liberal social action **2** : an advocate of unity or a unitary system — **unitarian** *adj, often cap* — **uni·tar·i·an·ism** \-ē-ə-ˌniz-əm\ *n, often cap*
uni·tary \ˈyü-nə-ˌter-ē\ *adj* **1 a** : of or relating to a unit **b** : based on or characterized by unity or units **2** : having the

character of a unit : UNDIVIDED, WHOLE — **uni·tar·i·ly** \ˌyü-nə-ˈter-ə-lē\ *adv*
unit cell *n* : the simplest polyhedron that embodies all the structural characteristics of and by indefinite repetition makes up the lattice of a crystal
unit character *n* : a natural character inherited on an all or none basis; *esp* : one dependent on the presence or absence of a single gene
unit circle *n* : a circle whose radius is one unit of length long
[1]**unite** \yu̇-ˈnīt\ *vb* **unit·ed; unit·ing** [ME *uniten*, fr. LL *unitus*, pp. of *unire*, fr. L *unus* one — more at ONE] *vt* **1 a** : to put together to form a single unit **b** : to cause to adhere **c** : to link by a legal or moral bond **2** : to possess (as qualities) in combination ~ *vi* **1 a** : to become one or as if one **b** : to become combined by or as if by adhesion or mixture **2** : to act in concert ***syn*** see JOIN ***ant*** divide, alienate — **unit·er** *n*
[2]**unite** \ˈyü-ˌnīt\ *n* [obs. *unite* (united), fr. ME *unit*, fr. LL *unitus*, pp.] : an old British gold 20-shilling piece issued first by James I in 1604 for the newly united England and Scotland — called also *Jacobus*
unit·ed \yu̇-ˈnīt-əd\ *adj* **1** : made one : COMBINED **2** : relating to or produced by joint action **3** : being in agreement : HARMONIOUS — **unit·ed·ly** *adv*
United Nations Day *n* : October 24 observed in commemoration of the founding of the United Nations
Unit·ed States \yu̇-ˌnīt-əd-, *esp South* ˈyü-\ *n pl but sing or pl in constr* : a federation of states esp. when forming a nation in a usu. specified territory <advocating a *United States* of Europe>
uni·tive \ˈyü-nət-iv, yu̇-ˈnīt-\ *adj* : characterized by or tending to produce union
unit·ize \ˈyü-nət-ˌīz\ *vt* **-ized; -iz·ing 1** : to form or convert into a unit **2** : to divide into units <the added cost of *unitizing* bulk products> — **unit·iza·tion** \ˌyü-nət-ə-ˈzā-shən\ *n*
unit magnetic pole *n* : a magnetic pole that will repel an equal and like pole at a distance of one centimeter in a vacuum with a force of one dyne
unit membrane *n* [fr. its being the basic structural unit of the cell] : a 3-layered membrane that consists of an inner bimolecular lipid layer surrounded by a protein layer on each side
unit rule *n* : a rule under which a delegation to a Democratic national convention casts its entire vote as a unit as determined by a majority vote
unit train *n* : a railway train that transports a single commodity
uni·ty \ˈyü-nət-ē\ *n, pl* **-ties** [ME *unite*, fr. OF *unité*, fr. L *unitat-, unitas*, fr. *unus* one] **1 a** : the quality or state of not being multiple : ONENESS **b (1)** : a definite amount taken as one or for which 1 is made to stand in calculation <in a table of natural sines the radius of the circle is regarded as ~> **(2)** : a number multiplication by which leaves any element of a system unchanged **2 a** : a condition of harmony : ACCORD **b** : continuity without deviation or change (as in purpose or action) **3 a** : the quality or state of being made one : UNIFICATION **b** : a combination or ordering of parts in a literary or artistic production that constitutes a whole or promotes an undivided total effect; *also* : the resulting singleness of effect or symmetry and consistency of style and character **4** : a totality of related parts : an entity that is a complex or systematic whole **5** : any of three principles of dramatic structure derived by French classicists from Aristotle's *Poetics* and requiring a play to have a single action represented as occurring in one place and within one day **6** *cap* : a 20th century American religious movement for health and prosperity formerly affiliated with New Thought but closer to orthodox Christianity
syn UNITY, SOLIDARITY, INTEGRITY, UNION *shared meaning element* : the quality or character of a whole made up of intimately associated elements, parts, or individuals
univ *abbr* **1** universal **2** university
[1]**uni·va·lent** \ˌyü-ni-ˈvā-lənt\ *adj* [ISV] **1** : having a valence of one **2** *of a chromosome* : lacking a synaptic mate
[2]**univalent** *n* : a univalent chromosome
[1]**uni·valve** \ˈyü-ni-ˌvalv\ *adj* : having or consisting of one valve
[2]**univalve** *n* **1** : a mollusk with a univalve shell; *esp* : GASTROPOD **2** : a mollusk shell consisting of one piece
[1]**uni·ver·sal** \ˌyü-nə-ˈvər-səl\ *adj* [ME, fr. MF, fr. L *universalis*, fr. *universum* universe] **1** : including or covering all or a whole collectively or distributively without limit or exception **2 a** : present or occurring everywhere **b** : existent or operative everywhere or under all conditions <~ cultural patterns> **3 a** : embracing a major part or the greatest portion (as of mankind) <a ~ state> <~ practices> **b** : comprehensively broad and versatile <a ~ genius > **4 a** : affirming or denying something of all members of a class or of all values of a variable **b** : denoting every member of a class <a ~ term> **5** : adapted or adjustable to meet varied requirements (as of use, shape, or size) <a ~ gear cutter> — **uni·ver·sal·ly** \-s(ə-)lē\ *adv* — **uni·ver·sal·ness** \-səl-nəs\ *n*
syn UNIVERSAL, GENERAL, GENERIC *shared meaning element* : characteristic of, relating to, comprehending, or affecting all or the whole ***ant*** particular
[2]**universal** *n* **1 a** : a universal proposition in logic **b** : a predicable of traditional logic **c** : a general concept or term or something in reality to which it corresponds : ESSENCE **2 a** : a mode of behavior existing in all cultures **b** : a culture trait characteristic of all normal adult members of a particular society
uni·ver·sal·ism \ˌyü-nə-ˈvər-sə-ˌliz-əm\ *n* **1** *often cap* **a** : a theological doctrine that all men will eventually be saved **b** : the principles and practices of a liberal Christian denomination founded in the 18th century to uphold belief in universal salvation and now united with Unitarianism **2** : something that is universal in scope **3** : the state of being universal : UNIVERSALITY **4** : a social relationship in which behavior is determined by an impersonal code or standard — **uni·ver·sal·ist** \-s(ə-)ləst\ *n or adj, often cap*
uni·ver·sal·is·tic \-ˌvər-sə-ˈlis-tik\ *adj* : of or relating to the whole : universal in scope or nature
uni·ver·sal·i·ty \-(ˌ)vər-ˈsal-ət-ē\ *n* **1** : the quality or state of being universal **2** : universal comprehensiveness in range
uni·ver·sal·ize \-ˈvər-sə-ˌlīz\ *vt* **-ized; -iz·ing** : to make universal : GENERALIZE — **uni·ver·sal·iza·tion** \-ˌvər-sə-lə-ˈzā-shən\ *n*
universal joint *n* : a shaft coupling capable of transmitting rotation from one shaft to another not collinear with it — called also *universal coupling*
universal motor *n* : an electric motor that can be used on either an alternating or a direct current supply 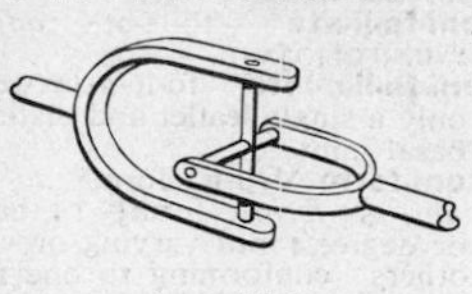

universal joint

Universal time *n* : GREENWICH TIME
uni·verse \ˈyü-nə-ˌvərs\ *n* [L *universum*, fr. neut. of *universus* entire, whole, fr. *uni-* + *versus* turned toward, fr. pp. of *vertere* to turn — more at WORTH] **1** : the whole body of things and phenomena observed or postulated : COSMOS **2 a** : a systematic whole held to arise by and persist through the direct intervention of divine power **b** : the world of human experience **c (1)** : the entire celestial cosmos **(2)** : MILKY WAY GALAXY **(3)** : an aggregate of stars comparable to the Milky Way galaxy **3** : a distinct field or province of thought or reality that forms a closed system or self-inclusive and independent organization **4** : POPULATION 4 **5** : a set that contains all elements relevant to a particular discussion or problem **6** : a great number or quantity ***syn*** see EARTH
universe of discourse : an inclusive class of entities that is tacitly implied or explicitly delineated as the subject of a statement, discourse, or theory
uni·ver·si·ty \ˌyü-nə-ˈvər-sət-ē, -ˈvər-stē\ *n, pl* **-ties** [ME *universite*, fr. OF *université*, fr. ML *universitat-, universitas*, fr. L *universus*] **1** : an institution of higher learning providing facilities for teaching and research and authorized to grant academic degrees; *specif* : one made up of an undergraduate division which confers bachelor's degrees and a graduate division which comprises a graduate school and professional schools each of which may confer master's degrees and doctorates **2** : the physical plant of a university
univ·o·cal \yü-ˈniv-ə-kəl\ *adj* [LL *univocus*, fr. L *uni-* + *voc-, vox* voice — more at VOICE] : having one meaning only — **univ·o·cal·ly** \-k(ə-)lē\ *adv*
un·just \ˌən-ˈjəst, ˈən-\ *adj* **1** : characterized by injustice : UNFAIR **2** *archaic* : DISHONEST, FAITHLESS — **un·just·ly** *adv* — **un·just·ness** \-ˈjəs(t)-nəs\ *n*
un·kempt \-ˈkem(p)t\ *adj* [*un-* + *kempt* (combed, neat)] **1** : not combed <~ hair> **2** : deficient in order or neatness <~ individuals> <~ hotel rooms>; *also* : ROUGH, UNPOLISHED <~ prose>
un·kenned \-ˈkend\ *adj, chiefly dial* : UNKNOWN, STRANGE
un·ken·nel \-ˈken-ᵊl\ *vt* **1 a** : to drive (as a fox) from a hiding place or den **b** : to free (dogs) from a kennel **2** : to bring out into the open : UNCOVER
un·kind \-ˈkīnd\ *adj* **1** : not pleasing or mild : INCLEMENT <an ~ climate> **2** : lacking in kindness or sympathy : HARSH, CRUEL — **un·kind·ness** \-ˈkīn(d)-nəs\ *n*
[1]**un·kind·ly** \-ˈkīn-(d)lē\ *adj* : not kindly — **un·kind·li·ness** *n*
[2]**unkindly** *adv* : in an unkind manner
un·kink \ˌən-ˈkiŋk, ˈən-\ *vt* : to free from kinks : STRAIGHTEN ~ *vi* : to become lax or loose : RELAX
un·knit \-ˈnit\ *vb* **-knit** *or* **-knit·ted; -knit·ting** : UNDO, UNRAVEL
un·know·able \ˌən-ˈnō-ə-bəl, ˈən-\ *adj* : not knowable; *esp* : lying beyond the limits of human experience or understanding
un·know·ing \-ˈnō-iŋ\ *adj* : not knowing — **un·know·ing·ly** \-iŋ-lē\ *adv*
[1]**un·known** \-ˈnōn\ *adj* : not known; *also* : having an unknown value <an ~ quantity>
[2]**unknown** *n* **1** : one that is not known or not well-known; *esp* : a person who is little known (as to the public) **2** : something that requires to be discovered, identified, or clarified: as **a** : a symbol in a mathematical equation representing an unknown quantity and often being one of the last letters of the alphabet **b** : a specimen (as of bacteria or mixed chemicals) required to be identified as an exercise in appropriate laboratory techniques
Unknown Soldier *n* : an unidentified soldier whose body is selected to receive national honors as a representative of all of the same nation who died in a war and esp. in one of the world wars
un·lace \ˌən-ˈlās, ˈən-\ *vt* **1** : to loose by undoing a lacing **2** *obs* : UNDO, DISGRACE
un·lade \-ˈlād\ *vb* **-lad·ed; -laded** *or* **-lad·en** \-ˈlād-ᵊn\; **-lad·ing** *vt* **1** : to take the load or cargo from **2** : DISCHARGE, UNLOAD ~ *vi* : to discharge cargo
un·lash \-ˈlash\ *vt* : to untie the lashing of
un·latch \-ˈlach\ *vt* : to open or loose by lifting the latch ~ *vi* : to become loosed or opened
un·law·ful \ˌən-ˈlȯ-fəl, ˈən-\ *adj* **1** : not lawful : ILLEGAL **2** : not morally right or conventional — **un·law·ful·ly** \-f(ə-)lē\ *adv* — **un·law·ful·ness** \-fəl-nəs\ *n*
un·lay \-ˈlā\ *vb* **-laid** \-ˈlād\; **-lay·ing** *vt* : to untwist the strands of (as a rope) ~ *vi* : UNTWIST
un·lead·ed \-ˈled-əd\ *adj* **1 a** : stripped of lead **b** : not treated or mixed with lead or lead compounds <~ fuels> **2** : not having leads between the lines in printing
un·learn \-ˈlərn\ *vt* **1** : to put out of one's knowledge or memory **2** : to undo the effect of : discard the habit of
un·learned \-ˈlər-nəd *for 1, 2,* -ˈlərnd *for 3*\ *adj* **1** : possessing inadequate learning or education; *esp* : deficient in scholarly attainments **2** : characterized by or revealing ignorance **3** : not gained by study or training ***syn*** see IGNORANT
un·leash \-ˈlēsh\ *vt* : to free from or as if from a leash : let loose
[1]**un·less** \ən-ˌles, ˌən-, *in some contexts* ᵊn-, ᵊm-, *or* ᵊŋ-\ *conj* [ME *unlesse*, alter. of *onlesse*, fr. *on* + *lesse* less] **1** : except on the condition that : under any other circumstance than **2** : without the accompanying circumstance or condition that : but that : BUT
[2]**unless** *prep* : except possibly : EXCEPT

un·let·tered \ˌən-ˈlet-ərd, ˈən-\ *adj* **1 a :** lacking facility in reading and writing and ignorant of the knowledge to be gained from books **b :** ILLITERATE **2 :** not marked with letters ***syn*** see IGNORANT

un·licked \-ˈlikt\ *adj* **1** *archaic* **:** not licked dry **2** *archaic* **:** lacking proper form or shape

[1]**un·like** \-ˈlīk\ *prep* **:** not like: as **a :** different from **b :** not characteristic of **c :** in a different manner from

[2]**unlike** *adj* **:** not like: as **a :** marked by dissimilarity **:** DIFFERENT <the two books are quite ~> **b :** marked by inequality **:** UNEQUAL <contributed ~ amounts> — **un·like·ness** *n*

un·like·li·hood \ˌən-ˈlī-klē-ˌhu̇d, ˈən-\ *n* **1 :** IMPROBABILITY **2 :** something unlikely

un·like·li·ness \-nəs\ *n* **:** IMPROBABILITY

un·like·ly \-ˈlī-klē\ *adj* **1 :** not likely **:** IMPROBABLE **2 :** likely to fail **:** UNPROMISING

un·lim·ber \ˌən-ˈlim-bər, ˈən-\ *vt* **1 :** to detach the limber from and so make ready <~ a gun for action> **2 :** to prepare for action <~*ed* his banjo and began to sing> ~ *vi* **:** to perform the task of preparing something for action

un·lim·it·ed \-ˈlim-ət-əd\ *adj* **1 :** lacking any controls **:** UNRESTRICTED **2 :** BOUNDLESS, INFINITE **3 :** not bounded by exceptions **:** UNDEFINED — **un·lim·it·ed·ly** *adv*

un·link \-ˈliŋk\ *vt* **:** to unfasten the links of **:** SEPARATE, DISCONNECT ~ *vi* **:** to become detached

un·linked \-ˈliŋ(k)t\ *adj* **:** not belonging to the same genetic linkage group <~ genes>

un·list·ed \-ˈlis-təd\ *adj* **1 :** not appearing on a list; *esp* **:** not appearing in a telephone book <~ numbers> **2 :** being or involving a security not listed formally on an organized exchange **:** OVER-THE-COUNTER

un·live \-ˈliv\ *vt* **:** to live down **:** ANNUL, REVERSE

un·load \ˌən-ˈlōd, ˈən-\ *vt* **1 a (1) :** to take off **:** DELIVER **(2) :** to take the cargo from **b :** to give outlet to **:** pour forth <~*ed* her bitter feelings> **2 :** to relieve of something burdensome, unwanted, or oppressive <~*ed* the pack animals> <~*ed* himself to his friend> **3 :** to draw the charge from <~*ed* the gun> **4 :** to sell esp. in large quantities **:** DUMP **5 :** to hit or propel with a great release of power <~*ed* his ninth homer> ~ *vi* **:** to perform the act of unloading — **un·load·er** *n*

un·lock \-ˈläk\ *vt* **1 :** to unfasten the lock of **2 :** OPEN, UNDO **3 :** to free from restraints or restrictions <the shock ~*ed* a flood of tears> **4 :** to furnish a key to **:** DISCLOSE ~ *vi* **:** to become unfastened or freed from restraints

un·looked–for \-ˈlu̇k-ˌtfȯ(ə)r\ *adj* **:** not foreseen **:** UNEXPECTED

un·loose \ˌən-ˈlüs, ˈən-\ *vt* **1 :** to relax the strain of <~ a grip> **2 :** to release from or as if from restraints **:** set free **3 :** to loosen the ties of <~ traditional social bonds>

un·loos·en \-ˈlüs-ᵊn\ *vt* **:** UNLOOSE

un·love·ly \-ˈləv-lē\ *adj* **:** not likable **:** DISAGREEABLE, UNPLEASANT — **un·love·li·ness** *n*

un·lucky \-ˈlək-ē\ *adj* **1 :** marked by adversity or failure <an ~ year> **2 :** likely to bring misfortune **:** INAUSPICIOUS **3 :** having or meeting with bad luck <~ people> **4 :** producing dissatisfaction **:** REGRETTABLE — **un·luck·i·ly** \-ˈlək-ə-lē\ *adv* — **un·luck·i·ness** \-ˈlək-ē-nəs\ *n*

un·made \ˌən-ˈmād, ˈən-\ *adj* **:** not made <an ~ bed>

un·make \-ˈmāk\ *vt* **-made** \-ˈmād\; **-mak·ing 1 :** to cause to disappear **:** DESTROY **2 :** to deprive of rank or office **:** DEPOSE **3 :** to deprive of essential characteristics **:** change the nature of

un·ma·li·cious \ˌən-mə-ˈlish-əs\ *adj* **:** not malicious — **un·ma·li·cious·ly** *adv*

un·man \ˌən-ˈman, ˈən-\ *vt* **1 :** to deprive of manly vigor, fortitude, or spirit **2 :** CASTRATE, EMASCULATE ***syn*** see UNNERVE

un·man·ly \-ˈman-lē\ *adj* **:** not manly: as **a :** being of weak character **:** COWARDLY **b :** EFFEMINATE — **un·man·li·ness** *n*

un·manned \-ˈmand\ *adj* **1 :** not manned <an ~ spaceflight> **2** *obs, of a hawk* **:** not trained

un·man·nered \-ˈman-ərd\ *adj* **1 :** marked by a lack of good manners **:** RUDE **2 :** characterized by an absence of artificiality **:** UNAFFECTED — **un·man·nered·ly** *adv*

[1]**un·man·ner·ly** \-ˈman-ər-lē\ *adv* **:** in an unmannerly fashion

[2]**unmannerly** *adj* **:** not mannerly **:** DISCOURTEOUS — **un·man·ner·li·ness** *n*

un·mask \ˌən-ˈmask, ˈən-\ *vt* **1 :** to remove a mask from **2 :** to reveal the true nature of **:** EXPOSE ~ *vi* **:** to remove one's mask

un·mean·ing \-ˈmē-niŋ\ *adj* **1 :** lacking intelligence **:** VAPID **2 :** having no meaning **:** SENSELESS

un·meant \-ˈment\ *adj* **:** not meant **:** UNINTENTIONAL

un·meet \-ˈmēt\ *adj* **:** not meet **:** UNSUITABLE, IMPROPER

un·mem·o·ra·ble \-ˈmem-(ə-)rə-bəl\ *adj* **:** not memorable **:** not worth remembering — **un·mem·o·ra·bly** \-blē\ *adv*

[1]**un·men·tion·able** \-ˈmench-(ə-)nə-bəl\ *adj* **:** not mentionable **:** UNSPEAKABLE

[2]**unmentionable** *n* **:** one that is not to be mentioned or discussed: as **a** *pl* **:** TROUSERS **b** *pl* **:** UNDERWEAR

un·mer·ci·ful \ˌən-ˈmər-si-fəl, ˈən-\ *adj* **1 :** not merciful **:** MERCILESS **2 :** EXCESSIVE, EXTREME <chatted for an ~ length of time> — **un·mer·ci·ful·ly** \-f(ə-)lē\ *adv*

un·mind·ful \-ˈmīn(d)-fəl\ *adj* **:** not carefully attentive or heedful **:** INATTENTIVE, CARELESS ***syn*** see FORGETFUL ***ant*** mindful, solicitous

un·mis·tak·able \ˌən-mə-ˈstā-kə-bəl\ *adj* **:** not capable of being mistaken or misunderstood **:** CLEAR — **un·mis·tak·ably** \-blē\ *adv*

un·mit·i·gat·ed \ˌən-ˈmit-ə-ˌgāt-əd, ˈən-\ *adj* **1 :** not lessened **:** UNRELIEVED <sufferings ~ by any hope of early relief> **2 :** being so definitely what is stated as to offer little chance of change or relief <an ~ evil> ***syn*** see OUTRIGHT — **un·mit·i·gat·ed·ly** *adv* — **un·mit·i·gat·ed·ness** *n*

un·moor \-ˈmu̇(ə)r\ *vt* **:** to loose from or as if from moorings ~ *vi* **:** to cast off moorings

un·mor·al \-ˈmȯr-əl, -ˈmär-\ *adj* **1 :** having no moral perception or quality; *also* **:** not influenced or guided by moral considerations **2 :** lying outside the bounds of morals or ethics ***syn*** see IMMORAL — **un·mo·ral·i·ty** \ˌən-mə-ˈral-ət-ē, -mȯ-\ *n*

un·muf·fle \ˌən-ˈməf-əl, ˈən-\ *vt* **:** to free from something that muffles

un·muz·zle \-ˈməz-əl\ *vt* **:** to free from or as if from a muzzle

un·my·elin·at·ed \-ˈmī-ə-lə-ˌnāt-əd\ *adj* **:** lacking a myelin sheath

un·nail \ˌən-ˈnā(ə)l, ˈən-\ *vt* **:** to unfasten by removing nails

un·nat·u·ral \ˌən-ˈnach-(ə-)rəl, ˈən-\ *adj* **1 :** not being in accordance with nature or consistent with a normal course of events **2 a :** not being in accordance with normal feelings or behavior **:** PERVERSE **b :** lacking ease and naturalness **:** CONTRIVED <her manner was forced and ~> **c :** inconsistent with what is reasonable or expected <an ~ alliance> ***syn*** see IRREGULAR ***ant*** natural — **un·nat·u·ral·ly** \-ˈnach-(ə-)rə-lē, -ˈnach-ər-lē\ *adv* — **un·nat·u·ral·ness** \-ˈnach-(ə-)rəl-nəs\ *n*

un·nec·es·sar·i·ly \ˌən-ˌnes-ə-ˈser-ə-lē\ *adv* **:** not by necessity **:** to an unnecessary degree

un·nec·es·sary \ˌən-ˈnes-ə-ˌser-ē, ˈən-\ *adj* **:** not necessary

un·nerve \-ˈnərv\ *vt* **1 :** to deprive of courage, strength, or steadiness **2 :** to cause to become nervous **:** UPSET — **un·nerv·ing·ly** \-ˈnər-viŋ-lē\ *adv*

syn UNNERVE, ENERVATE, UNMAN, EMASCULATE ***shared meaning element*** **:** to deprive of strength or vigor and the capacity for effective action

un·num·bered \-ˈnəm-bərd\ *adj* **1 :** INNUMERABLE **2 :** not having an identifying number <~ pages>

un·ob·tru·sive \ˌən-əb-ˈtrü-siv, -ziv\ *adj* **:** not obtrusive **:** not blatant or aggressive **:** INCONSPICUOUS — **un·ob·tru·sive·ly** *adv* — **un·ob·tru·sive·ness** *n*

un·oc·cu·pied \ˌən-ˈäk-yə-ˌpīd, ˈən-\ *adj* **:** not occupied: as **a :** not busy **:** UNEMPLOYED **b :** not lived in **:** EMPTY

un·of·fi·cial \ˌən-ə-ˈfish-əl\ *adj* **:** not official — **un·of·fi·cial·ly** \-ˈfish-(ə-)lē\ *adv*

un·open·able \ˌən-ˈōp-(ə-)nə-bəl\ *adj* **:** incapable of being opened

un·or·ga·nized \-ˈȯr-gə-ˌnīzd\ *adj* **1 a :** not brought into a coherent or well-ordered whole **b :** not belonging to a labor union **2 :** not having the characteristics of a living organism

un·or·tho·dox \-ˈȯr-thə-ˌdäks\ *adj* **:** not orthodox — **un·or·tho·dox·ly** *adv*

un·or·tho·doxy \-ˌdäk-sē\ *n* **1 :** the quality or state of being unorthodox **2 :** something (as an opinion or doctrine) that is unorthodox

unp *abbr* unpaged

un·pack \ˌən-ˈpak, ˈən-\ *vt* **1 a :** to remove the contents of <~ a trunk> **b :** UNBURDEN, REVEAL **2 :** to remove or undo from packing or a container <~*ed* his gear> ~ *vi* **:** to engage in unpacking a container — **un·pack·er** *n*

un·paged \-ˈpājd\ *adj* **:** having no page numbers

un·paid \-ˈpād\ *adj* **1 :** not paid **2 :** not paying a salary <an ~ position>

un·paired \-ˈpa(ə)rd, -ˈpe(ə)rd\ *adj* **1 a :** not paired; *esp* **:** not matched or mated **b :** characterized by the absence of pairing <electrons in the ~ state> **2 :** situated in the median plane of the body <an ~ fin>

un·pal·at·able \-ˈpal-ət-ə-bəl\ *adj* **1 :** not palatable **:** DISTASTEFUL **2 :** UNPLEASANT, DISAGREEABLE — **un·pal·at·abil·i·ty** \ˌən-ˌpal-ət-ə-ˈbil-ət-ē\ *n*

un·par·al·leled \ˌən-ˈpar-ə-ˌleld, ˈən-, -ləld\ *adj* **:** having no parallel; *esp* **:** having no equal or match **:** unique in kind or quality ***syn*** see STRANGE

un·par·lia·men·ta·ry \ˌən-ˌpär-lə-ˈment-ə-rē, -ˌpärl-yə-, -ˈmen-trē\ *adj* **:** contrary to the practice of parliamentary bodies

un·peg \ˌən-ˈpeg, ˈən-\ *vt* **:** to remove a peg from **:** UNFASTEN

un·peo·ple \-ˈpē-pəl\ *vt* **:** DEPOPULATE

un·per·fect \-ˈpər-fikt\ *adj* **:** IMPERFECT

un·per·son \ˈən-ˈpərs-ᵊn, -ˌpərs-\ *n* **:** an individual who usu. for political or ideological reasons is removed completely from recognition or consideration

un·pick \ˌən-ˈpik, ˈən-\ *vt* **:** to undo (as sewing) by taking out stitches

un·pile \-ˈpī(ə)l\ *vt* **:** to take or disentangle from a pile

un·pin \-ˈpin\ *vt* **1 :** to remove a pin from **2 :** to loosen, free, or unfasten by or as if by removing a pin

un·pleas·ant \-ˈplez-ᵊnt\ *adj* **:** not pleasant **:** not amiable or agreeable **:** DISPLEASING <~ odors> — **un·pleas·ant·ly** *adv*

un·pleas·ant·ness *n* **1 :** the quality or state of being unpleasant **2 :** an unpleasant situation, experience, or event

un·plug \ˌən-ˈpləg, ˈən-\ *vt* **1 a :** to take a plug out of **b :** to remove an obstruction from **2 a :** to remove (as an electric plug) from a socket or receptacle **b :** to disconnect from an electric circuit by removing a plug <~ the refrigerator>

un·plumbed \-ˈpləmd\ *adj* **1 :** not tested with a plumb line **2 a :** not measured with a plumb **b :** not thoroughly explored

un·po·lar·ized \-ˈpō-lə-ˌrīzd\ *adj* **:** not polarized; *specif* **:** having a random pattern of vibrations

un·po·lit·i·cal \ˌən-pə-ˈlit-i-kəl\ *adj* **:** not interested or engaged in politics <an ~ person>

un·pop·u·lar \ˌən-ˈpäp-yə-lər, ˈən-\ *adj* **:** not popular **:** viewed or received unfavorably by the public — **un·pop·u·lar·i·ty** \ˌən-ˌpäp-yə-ˈlar-ət-ē\ *n*

un·prec·e·dent·ed \ˌən-ˈpres-ə-ˌdent-əd, ˈən-\ *adj* **:** having no precedent **:** NOVEL, UNEXAMPLED — **un·prec·e·dent·ed·ly** *adv*

un·pre·dict·able \ˌən-pri-ˈdik-tə-bəl\ *adj* **:** not predictable — **un·pre·dict·abil·i·ty** \-ˌdik-tə-ˈbil-ət-ē\ *n* — **un·pre·dict·ably** \-blē\ *adv*

unpregnant *adj, obs* **:** INEPT 1

ə abut ᵊ kitten ər further a back ā bake ä cot, cart
au̇ out ch chin e less ē easy g gift i trip ī life
j joke ŋ sing ō flow ȯ flaw ȯi coin th thin t͟h this
ü loot u̇ foot y yet yü few yu̇ furious zh vision

un·prej·u·diced \ˌən-ˈprej-əd-əst, ˈən-\ *adj* : not prejudiced : IMPARTIAL
un·pre·pared \ˌən-pri-ˈpa(ə)rd, -ˈpe(ə)rd\ *adj* : not prepared
un·pre·tend·ing \-ˈten-diŋ\ *adj* : UNPRETENTIOUS
un·pre·ten·tious \-ˈten-chəs\ *adj* : free from ostentation, elegance, or affectation : MODEST <~ homes> ***syn*** see PLAIN ***ant*** pretentious — **un·pre·ten·tious·ly** *adv* — **un·pre·ten·tious·ness** *n*
un·prin·ci·pled \ˌən-ˈprin(t)-s(ə-)pəld, ˈən-, -sə-bəld\ *adj* : lacking moral principles : UNSCRUPULOUS — **un·prin·ci·pled·ness** *n*
un·print·able \-ˈprint-ə-bəl\ *adj* : unfit to be printed
un·pro·fessed \ˌən-prə-ˈfest\ *adj* : not professed <an ~ aim>
un·prof·it·able \ˌən-ˈpräf-ət-ə-bəl, ˈən-, -ˈpräf-tə-bəl\ *adj* : not profitable : USELESS, VAIN — **un·prof·it·able·ness** *n* — **un·prof·it·ably** \-blē\ *adv*
un·prom·is·ing \-ˈpräm-ə-siŋ\ *adj* : appearing unlikely to prove worthwhile or result favorably — **un·prom·is·ing·ly** \-siŋ-lē\ *adv*
un·pro·nounced \ˌən-prə-ˈnaủn(t)st\ *adj* : not pronounced; *esp* : MUTE
un·qual·i·fied \ˌən-ˈkwäl-ə-ˌfīd, ˈən-\ *adj* **1** : not fit : not having requisite qualifications **2** : not modified or restricted by reservations <an ~ denial> — **un·qual·i·fied·ly** \-ˌfī(-ə)d-lē\ *adv*
un·ques·tion·able \-ˈkwes(h)-chə-nə-bəl, *rapid* -ˈkwesh-nə-\ *adj* : not questionable : INDISPUTABLE <~ evidence> — **un·ques·tion·ably** \-blē\ *adv*
un·ques·tion·ing \-ˈkwes(h)-chə-niŋ\ *adj* : not questioning : not expressing or marked by doubt or hesitation <~ obedience> — **un·ques·tion·ing·ly** \-niŋ-lē\ *adv*
un·qui·et \-ˈkwī-ət\ *adj* **1** : not quiet : AGITATED, TURBULENT **2** : physically, emotionally, or mentally restless : UNEASY — **un·qui·et·ly** *adv* — **un·qui·et·ness** *n*
un·quote \ˈən-ˌkwōt *also* -ˌkōt\ *n* — used orally to indicate the end of a direct quotation
un·rav·el \ˌən-ˈrav-əl, ˈən-\ *vt* **1** : to disengage or separate the threads of : DISENTANGLE **2** : to resolve the intricacy, complexity, or obscurity of : clear up ~ *vi* : to become unraveled
un·read \-ˈred\ *adj* **1** : not read : left unexamined **2** : lacking the experience or the benefits of reading <~ in political science>
un·ready \-ˈred-ē\ *adj* : not ready : UNPREPARED — **un·readi·ness** *n*
un·re·al \-ˈrē(-ə)l, -ˈri(-ə)l\ *adj* : lacking in reality, substance, or genuineness : ARTIFICIAL, ILLUSORY
un·re·al·is·tic \ˌən-ˌrē-ə-ˈlis-tik, -ˌri-ə-\ *adj* : not realistic : inappropriate to reality or fact — **un·re·al·is·ti·cal·ly** \-ti-k(ə-)lē\ *adv*
un·re·al·i·ty \ˌən-rē-ˈal-ət-ē\ *n* **1 a** : the quality or state of being unreal : lack of substance or validity **b** : something unreal, insubstantial, or visionary : FIGMENT **2** : ineptitude in dealing with reality
un·rea·son \ˌən-ˈrēz-ᵊn, ˈən-ˈrēz-\ *n* : the absence of reason or sanity : IRRATIONALITY, MADNESS
un·rea·son·able \-ˈrēz-nə-bəl, -ᵊn-ə-\ *adj* **1 a** : not governed by or acting according to reason <~ people> **b** : not conformable to reason : ABSURD <~ beliefs> **2** : exceeding the bounds of reason or moderation <working under ~ pressure> ***syn*** see IRRATIONAL — **un·rea·son·ably** \-blē\ *adv*
un·rea·son·able·ness \-bəl-nəs\ *n* : the quality or state of being unreasonable
un·rea·son·ing \-ˈrēz-niŋ, -ᵊn-iŋ\ *adj* : not reasoning; *esp* : not moderated or controlled by reason <~ fear> — **un·rea·son·ing·ly** \-ˈrēz-niŋ-lē, -ᵊn-iŋ-\ *adv*
un·rec·og·nized \-ˈrek-ig-ˌnīzd, -əg-\ *adj* : not recognized
un·re·con·struct·ed \ˌən-ˌrē-kən-ˈstrək-təd\ *adj* : not reconciled to some political, economic, or social change; *esp* : holding stubbornly to principles, beliefs, or views that are outmoded
un·reel \ˌən-ˈrē(ə)l, ˈən-\ *vt* **1** : to unwind from a reel **2** : to carry out <~*ed* a 66-yard pass play> ~ *vi* **1** : to become unwound **2** : to be presented <the dress rehearsal ~*ed* flawlessly>
un·reeve \-ˈrēv\ *vt* **-rove** \-ˈrōv\ *or* **-reeved; -reev·ing** : to withdraw (a rope) from an opening (as a ship's block or thimble)
un·re·gen·er·ate \ˌən-ri-ˈjen-(ə-)rət\ *adj* **1** : not regenerated : UNREPENTANT **2 a** : not reformed : UNRECONSTRUCTED <~ revolutionaries> **b** : OBSTINATE, STUBBORN <struggling against ~ impulses>
un·re·lent·ing \-ˈlent-iŋ\ *adj* **1** : not softening or yielding in determination : HARD, STERN <an ~ leader> **2** : not letting up or weakening in vigor or pace <~ struggles> — **un·re·lent·ing·ly** \-iŋ-lē\ *adv*
un·re·marked \-ˈmärkt\ *adj* : not remarked : UNNOTICED
un·re·mit·ting \-ˈmit-iŋ\ *adj* : not remitting : CONSTANT, INCESSANT — **un·re·mit·ting·ly** \-iŋ-lē\ *adv*
un·re·serve \-ˈzərv\ *n* : absence of reserve : FRANKNESS
un·re·served \-ˈzərvd\ *adj* **1** : not limited or partial : ENTIRE, UNQUALIFIED <~ enthusiasm> **2** : not cautious or reticent : FRANK, OPEN **3** : not set aside for special use — **un·re·serv·ed·ly** \-ˈzər-vəd-lē\ *adv* — **un·re·served·ness** \-ˈzər-vəd-nəs, -ˈzərv(d)-nəs\ *n*
un·re·spon·sive \ˌən-ri-ˈspän(t)-siv\ *adj* : not responsive — **un·re·spon·sive·ly** *adv* — **un·re·spon·sive·ness** *n*
un·rest \ˌən-ˈrest, ˈən-\ *n* : a disturbed or uneasy state : TURMOIL <campus ~>
un·re·strained \ˌən-ri-ˈstrānd\ *adj* **1** : not restrained : IMMODERATE, UNCONTROLLED <~ proliferation of technology> **2** : free of constraint : SPONTANEOUS <felt happy and ~> — **un·re·strain·ed·ly** \-ˈstrā-nəd-lē\ *adv* — **un·re·strained·ness** \-ˈstrā-nəd-nəs, -ˈstrān(d)-nəs\ *n*
un·re·straint \-ˈstrānt\ *n* : freedom from or lack of restraint
un·rid·dle \ˌən-ˈrid-ᵊl, ˈən-\ *vt* : to find the explanation of : SOLVE
un·rig \-ˈrig\ *vt* : to strip of rigging <~ a ship>
un·righ·teous \-ˈrī-chəs\ *adj* **1** : not righteous : SINFUL, WICKED <an ~ man> **2** : UNJUST, UNMERITED <intolerable and ~ interference in their lives —W. W. Wagar> — **un·righ·teous·ly** *adv* — **un·righ·teous·ness** *n*
un·rip \-ˈrip\ *vt* : to rip or slit up : cut or tear open **2** : REVEAL
un·ripe \-ˈrīp\ *adj* **1** : not ripe : IMMATURE **2** : UNREADY, UNPREPARED — **un·ripe·ness** *n*

un·ri·valed *or* **un·ri·valled** \ˌən-ˈrī-vəld, ˈən-\ *adj* : having no rival : INCOMPARABLE, SUPREME
un·robe \-ˈrōb\ *vb* : UNDRESS, DISROBE
un·roll \-ˈrōl\ *vt* **1** : to unwind a roll of : open out : UNCOIL **2** : to spread out like a scroll for reading or inspection : UNFOLD, REVEAL ~ *vi* : to be unrolled : UNWIND
un·roof \-ˈrüf, -ˈrủf\ *vt* : to strip off the roof or covering of
un·root \-ˈrüt, -ˈrủt\ *vt* : to tear up by the roots : UPROOT
1un·round \ˌən-ˈraủnd, ˈən-\ *vt* **1** : to spread (the lips) laterally <necessary to ~ the lips in pronouncing \ē\> **2** : to pronounce (a sound) without lip rounding or with decreased lip rounding
2unround *adj* : pronounced with the lips not rounded : UNROUNDED
un·ruf·fled \ˌən-ˈrəf-əld, ˈən-\ *adj* **1** : poised and serene esp. in the face of setbacks or confusion <a man of ~ calm> **2** : not ruffled : SMOOTH <~ water> ***syn*** see COOL ***ant*** ruffled, excited
un·ruly \-ˈrü-lē\ *adj* [ME *unreuly*, fr. *un-* + *reuly* disciplined, fr. *reule* rule] : not readily ruled, disciplined, or managed : TURBULENT — **un·rul·i·ness** *n*
syn UNRULY, UNGOVERNABLE, INTRACTABLE, REFRACTORY, RECALCITRANT, WILLFUL, HEADSTRONG *shared meaning element* : not submissive to government or control ***ant*** tractable, docile
UNRWA *abbr* United Nations Relief and Works Agency
uns *abbr* unsymmetrical
un·sad·dle \ˌən-ˈsad-ᵊl, ˈən-\ *vt* **1** : to take the saddle from **2** : to throw from the saddle ~ *vi* : to remove the saddle from a horse
un·safe·ty \-ˈsāf-tē\ *n* : lack of safety : INSECURITY
un·said \-ˈsed\ *adj* : not said; *esp* : not spoken aloud
un·sat·u·rate \-ˈsach-(ə-)rət\ *n* : an unsaturated chemical compound
un·sat·u·rat·ed \-ˈsach-ə-ˌrāt-əd\ *adj* : not saturated: as **a** : capable of absorbing or dissolving more of something <an ~ solution> **b** : able to form products by chemical addition; *esp* : containing double or triple bonds between carbon atoms
un·saved \ˌən-ˈsāvd, ˈən-\ *adj* : not saved; *esp* : not absolved from eternal punishment : not regenerate
un·sa·vory \-ˈsāv-(ə-)rē\ *adj* **1** : INSIPID, TASTELESS **2 a** : unpleasant to taste or smell **b** : DISAGREEABLE, DISTASTEFUL <an ~ assignment>; *esp* : morally offensive
un·say \-ˈsā, *South also* -ˈse\ *vt* **-said** \-ˈsed\; **-say·ing** \-ˈsā-iŋ\ : to make as if not said : RECANT, RETRACT
un·say·able \-ˈsā-ə-bəl\ *adj* : not sayable : not easily expressed or related
un·scathed \-ˈskāthd\ *adj* : wholly unharmed : not injured
un·schooled \-ˈsküld\ *adj* **1** : not schooled : UNTAUGHT, UNTRAINED <an ~ woodsman> **2** : not artificial : NATURAL <~ talent>
un·sci·en·tif·ic \ˌən-ˌsī-ən-ˈtif-ik\ *adj* : not scientific: as **a** : not used in scientific work **b** : not being in accord with the principles and methods of science <~ management of woodlands> **c** : not showing scientific knowledge or familiarity with scientific methods — **un·sci·en·tif·i·cal·ly** \-i-k(ə-)lē\ *adv*
un·scram·ble \ˌən-ˈskram-bəl, ˈən-\ *vt* **1** : to separate (as a conglomeration or tangle) into original components : RESOLVE, CLARIFY **2** : to restore (scrambled communication) to intelligible form — **un·scram·bler** \-b(ə-)lər\ *n*
un·screw \-ˈskrü\ *vt* **1** : to draw the screws from **2** : to loosen or withdraw by turning ~ *vi* : to become or admit of being unscrewed
un·script·ed \-ˈskrip-təd\ *adj* : not following a prepared script
un·scru·pu·lous \-ˈskrü-pyə-ləs\ *adj* : not scrupulous : UNPRINCIPLED — **un·scru·pu·lous·ly** *adv* — **un·scru·pu·lous·ness** *n*
un·seal \-ˈsē(ə)l\ *vt* : to break or remove the seal of : OPEN
un·sealed \-ˈsē(ə)ld\ *adj* : not sealed
un·seam \ˌən-ˈsēm, ˈən-\ *vt* : to open the seams of
un·search·able \-ˈsər-chə-bəl\ *adj* : not capable of being searched or explored : INSCRUTABLE — **un·search·ably** \-blē\ *adv*
un·sea·son·able \-ˈsēz-nə-bəl, -ˈsēz-ᵊn-ə-\ *adj* **1** : occurring at other than the proper time : UNTIMELY **2** : not being in season **3 a** : not normal for the season of the year <~ weather> **b** : marked by unseasonable weather <an ~ summer> — **un·sea·son·able·ness** *n* — **un·sea·son·ably** \-blē\ *adv*
un·seat \-ˈsēt\ *vt* **1** : to dislodge from one's seat esp. on horseback **2** : to remove from a place or position; *esp* : to remove from political office
1un·seem·ly \-ˈsēm-lē\ *adj* : not seemly: as **a** : not according with established standards of good form or taste <~ bickering> **b** : not suitable for time or place : INAPPROPRIATE, UNSEASONABLE ***syn*** see INDECOROUS ***ant*** seemly
2unseemly *adv* : in an unseemly manner
un·seen \ˌən-ˈsēn, ˈən-\ *adj* **1** : not seen or perceived : INVISIBLE **2** : SIGHT 1 <an ~ translation>
un·seg·re·gat·ed \-ˈseg-ri-ˌgāt-əd\ *adj* : not segregated; *esp* : free from racial segregation
un·se·lect·ed \ˌən(t)-sə-ˈlek-təd\ *adj* : not selected : chosen at random
un·se·lec·tive \-ˈlek-tiv\ *adj* : not marked by selection : RANDOM, INDISCRIMINATE
un·self·ish \-ˈsel-fish\ *adj* : not selfish : GENEROUS — **un·self·ish·ly** *adv* — **un·self·ish·ness** *n*
un·set \-ˈset\ *adj* : not set: as **a** : not fixed in a setting : UNMOUNTED <~ diamonds> **b** : not firmed or solidified <~ concrete>
un·set·tle \ˌən-ˈset-ᵊl, ˈən-\ *vt* **1** : to loosen or move from a settled state or condition : make unstable : DISORDER **2** : to perturb or agitate mentally or emotionally : DISCOMPOSE ~ *vi* : to become unsettled — **un·set·tling·ly** \-ˈset-liŋ-lē, -ᵊl-iŋ-\ *adv*
un·set·tled \-ˈset-ᵊld\ *adj* : not settled: as **a** (1) : not calm or tranquil : DISTURBED <~ political conditions> (2) : likely to vary widely esp. in the near future : VARIABLE <~ weather> (3) : not settled down <~ dust> **b** (1) : not decided or determined : DOUBTFUL <an ~ state of mind> (2) : not resolved or worked out : UNDECIDED <an ~ question> **c** : characterized by ir-

regularity <an ~ life> **d** : not inhabited or populated <~ land> **e** : mentally unbalanced **f** (1) : not disposed of according to law <an ~ estate> (2) : not paid or discharged <~ debts> — **un·set·tled·ness** \-ᵊl(d)-nəs\ *n*

un·set·tle·ment \-ᵊl-mənt\ *n* **1** : an act, process, or instance of unsettling **2** : the quality or state of being unsettled

un·sew \-ˈsō\ *vt* **-sewed; -sewn** \-ˈsōn\ *or* **-sewed; -sew·ing** : to undo the sewing of

un·sex \-ˈseks\ *vt* **1** : to deprive of sex or sexual power **2** : to remove the qualities typical of one's sex

un·shack·le \-ˈshak-əl\ *vt* : to free from shackles

un·shaped \-ˈshāpt\ *adj* : not shaped: as **a** : not dressed or finished to final form <an ~ timber> **b** : imperfect in form or formulation <~ ideas>

un·shap·en \-ˈshā-pən\ *adj* [ME, fr. [1]*un-* + *shapen,* pp. of *shapen* to shape] : UNSHAPED

un·sheathe \ˌən-ˈshēth, ˈən-\ *vt* : to draw from or as if from a sheath or scabbard

un·shell \-ˈshel\ *vt* : SHELL 1a

un·shelled \-ˈsheld\ *adj* : not shelled

un·shift \-ˈshift\ *vi* : to release the shift key (as on a typewriter)

un·ship \-ˈship\ *vt* **1** : to take out of a ship : DISCHARGE, UNLOAD **2** : to remove (as an oar or tiller) from position : DETACH ~ *vi* : to become or admit of being detached or removed

un·shock·able \-ˈshäk-ə-bəl\ *adj* : incapable of being shocked — **un·shock·abil·i·ty** \ˌən-ˌshäk-ə-ˈbil-ət-ē\ *n*

un·shod \ˌən-ˈshäd, ˈən-\ *adj* : not wearing or provided with shoes

[1]**un·sight** \-ˈsīt\ *vt* : to prevent from seeing

[2]**unsight** *adj* : not sighted or examined

un·sight·ly \ˌən-ˈsīt-lē, ˈən-\ *adj* : not pleasing to the sight : not comely ***syn*** see UGLY ***ant*** sightly

un·skilled \-ˈskild\ *adj* **1** : not skilled in a specified branch of work : lacking technical training <an ~ worker> **2** : not requiring skill <~ jobs> **3** : marked by lack of skill <produced ~ poems>

un·skill·ful \-ˈskil-fəl\ *adj* : not skillful : lacking in skill or proficiency — **un·skill·ful·ly** \-fə-lē\ *adv* — **un·skill·ful·ness** *n*

un·sling \-ˈsliŋ\ *vt* **-slung** \-ˈsləŋ\; **-sling·ing** \-ˈsliŋ-iŋ\ **1** : to remove from being slung <*unslung* his carbine> **2** : to take off the slings of esp. aboard ship : release from slings

un·snap \-ˈsnap\ *vt* : to loosen or free by or as if by undoing a snap

un·snarl \-ˈsnär(ə)l\ *vt* : to disentangle a snarl in

un·so·cia·ble \ˌən-ˈsō-shə-bəl, ˈən-\ *adj* **1** : having or showing a disinclination for social activity : SOLITARY, RESERVED **2** : not conducive to sociability — **un·so·cia·bil·i·ty** \ˌən-ˌsō-shə-ˈbil-ət-ē\ *n* — **un·so·cia·ble·ness** \ˌən-ˈsō-shə-bəl-nəs, ˈən-\ *n* — **un·so·cia·bly** \-blē\ *adv*

un·so·cial \-ˈsō-shəl\ *adj* : lacking a taste or desire for society or close association; *also* : marked by or arising from such a lack <an ~ disposition> — **un·so·cial·ly** \-ˈsōsh-(ə-)lē\ *adv*

syn UNSOCIAL, ASOCIAL, ANTISOCIAL, NONSOCIAL *shared meaning element* : opposed to what is social. In spite of their common element of meaning the words are rarely interchangeable without loss of precision. UNSOCIAL implies a distaste for the society of others or an aversion to close association and interaction <a withdrawn *unsocial* person> <a very *unsocial* temperament> ASOCIAL applies more often to behavior, thoughts, or acts viewed objectively and implies a lack of all the qualities conveyed by the word *social.* Typically it stresses a self-centered individualistic orientation <dreaming is an *asocial* act> <his interests are predominantly *asocial*> ANTISOCIAL applies especially to things (as acts, ideas, or movements) that are felt as harmful to or destructive of society or the social order <anarchists are *asocial* in their thinking and *antisocial* in their propaganda> <crime is *antisocial* behavior detrimental to the whole community> or to persons more or less consciously alienated from society <an *antisocial* delinquent> NONSOCIAL denies the relevance of the concept *social* and may apply to whatever cannot be described as social in a relevant sense <*nonsocial* bees> <a man's *nonsocial* correspondence —Elizabeth L. Post> ***ant*** social

un·so·phis·ti·cat·ed \ˌən(t)-sə-ˈfis-tə-ˌkāt-əd\ *adj* : not sophisticated: as **a** : not changed or corrupted : GENUINE **b** (1) : not worldly-wise : lacking social or economic sophistication (2) : lacking complexity of structure : SIMPLE, STRAIGHTFORWARD <an ~ approach to a problem> ***syn*** see NATURAL ***ant*** sophisticated

un·so·phis·ti·ca·tion \-ˌfis-tə-ˈkā-shən\ *n* : lack of or freedom from sophistication

un·sought \ˌən-ˈsȯt, ˈən-\ *adj* : not searched for or sought out <~ compliments>

un·sound \-ˈsau̇nd\ *adj* : not sound: as **a** : not healthy or whole **b** : not mentally normal : not wholly sane **c** : not firmly made, placed, or fixed **d** : not valid or true : INVALID, SPECIOUS — **un·sound·ly** \-ˈsau̇n-(d)lē\ *adv*

un·sound·ness \-ˈsau̇n(d)-nəs\ *n* **1** : the quality or state of being unsound **2** : something (as a disease) that causes one to be unsound

un·spar·ing \-ˈspa(ə)r-iŋ, -ˈspe(ə)r-\ *adj* **1** : not merciful or forbearing : HARD, RUTHLESS **2** : not frugal : LIBERAL, PROFUSE — **un·spar·ing·ly** \-iŋ-lē\ *adv*

un·speak \-ˈspēk\ *vt, obs* : UNSAY

un·speak·able \-ˈspē-kə-bəl\ *adj* **1 a** : incapable of being expressed in words : UNUTTERABLE **b** : inexpressibly bad : HORRENDOUS **2** : that may not or cannot be spoken <the bawdy thoughts that come into one's head — the ~ words —L. P. Smith> <~ collections of consonants —Rosemary Jellis> — **un·speak·ably** \-blē\ *adv*

un·sphere \ˌən-ˈsfi(ə)r, ˈən-\ *vt* : to remove (as a planet) from a sphere

un·sports·man·like \-ˈspōrt-smən-ˌlīk, -ˈspȯrt-\ *adj* : not characteristic of or exhibiting good sportsmanship : not sportsmanlike

un·spot·ted \-ˈspät-əd\ *adj* : not spotted : free from spot or stain; *esp* : free from moral stain

un·sprung \-ˈsprəŋ\ *adj* : not sprung; *esp* : not equipped with springs

un·sta·ble \-ˈstā-bəl\ *adj* : not stable : not firm or fixed : not constant: as **a** : not steady in action or movement : IRREGULAR <an ~ pulse> **b** : wavering in purpose or intent : VACILLATING **c** : lacking steadiness : apt to move, sway, or fall <an ~ tower> **d** : readily decomposing or changing otherwise in chemical composition or biological activity **e** : characterized by inability to control the emotions ***syn*** see INCONSTANT ***ant*** stable — **un·sta·ble·ness** *n* — **un·sta·bly** \-b(ə-)lē\ *adv*

un·state \-ˈstāt\ *vt* : to deprive of state, dignity, or rank

un·stat·ed \-ˈstāt-əd\ *adj* : not stated or set forth

[1]**un·steady** \ˌən-ˈsted-ē, ˈən-\ *vt* : to make unsteady

[2]**unsteady** *adj* : not steady: as **a** : not firm or solid : not fixed in position : UNSTABLE **b** : marked by change or fluctuation : CHANGEABLE **c** : not uniform or even : IRREGULAR — **un·steadi·ly** \-ˈsted-ᵊl-ē\ *adv* — **un·steadi·ness** \-ˈsted-ē-nəs\ *n*

un·step \ˌən-ˈstep, ˈən-\ *vt* : to remove (a mast) from a step

un·stick \-ˈstik\ *vt* **-stuck** \-ˈstək\; **-stick·ing** : to release from a state of adhesion

un·stop \-ˈstäp\ *vt* **1** : to free from an obstruction : OPEN **2** : to remove a stopper from

un·stop·pa·ble \-ˈstäp-ə-bəl\ *adj* : incapable of being stopped — **un·stop·pa·bly** \-blē\ *adv*

un·strap \-ˈstrap\ *vt* : to remove or loose a strap from

un·stressed \ˌən-ˈstrest, ˈən-\ *adj* **1** : not bearing a stress or accent <~ syllables> **2** : not subjected to stress <~ wires>

un·string \-ˈstriŋ\ *vt* **-strung** \-ˈstrəŋ\; **-string·ing** \-ˈstriŋ-iŋ\ **1** : to loosen or remove the strings of **2** : to remove from a string **3** : to make weak, disordered, or unstable <was *unstrung* by the news>

un·struc·tured \-ˈstrək-chərd\ *adj* : not structured : as **a** : having few formal requirements <an ~ college course> **b** : not having a patterned social organization <in a neighborhood gang . . . with a relatively ~ system —*Jour. of Social Issues*>

un·stud·ied \-ˈstəd-ēd\ *adj* : not studied: as **a** : not acquired by study **b** : not forced : not done or planned for effect

un·sub·stan·tial \ˌən(t)-səb-ˈstan-chəl\ *adj* : not substantial : lacking substance, firmness, or strength — **un·sub·stan·ti·al·i·ty** \-ˌstan-chē-ˈal-ət-ē\ *n* — **un·sub·stan·tial·ly** \ˌən(t)-səb-ˈstanch-(ə-)lē\ *adv*

un·suc·cess \ˌən(t)-sək-ˈses\ *n* : lack of success : FAILURE

un·suc·cess·ful \-fəl\ *adj* : not successful : not meeting with or producing success — **un·suc·cess·ful·ly** \-fə-lē\ *adv*

un·suit·able \ˌən-ˈsüt-ə-bəl, ˈən-\ *adj* : not suitable or fitting : UNBECOMING, INAPPROPRIATE — **un·suit·abil·i·ty** \ˌən-ˌsüt-ə-ˈbil-ət-ē\ *n* — **un·suit·ably** \ˌən-ˈsüt-ə-blē, ˈən-\ *adv*

un·sung \ˌən-ˈsəŋ, ˈən-\ *adj* **1** : not sung **2** : not celebrated or praised (as in song or verse)

un·swathe \-ˈswäth, -ˈswȯth, -ˈswāth\ *vt* : to free from something that swathes

un·swear \-ˈswa(ə)r, -ˈswe(ə)r\ *vb* **-swore** \-ˈswō(ə)r, -ˈswȯ(ə)r\; **-sworn** \-ˈswō(ə)rn, -ˈswȯ(ə)rn\; **swear·ing** *vi, archaic* : to unsay or retract something sworn ~ *vt, archaic* : to recant or recall (as an oath) esp. by a second oath

un·swerv·ing \-ˈswər-viŋ\ *adj* **1** : not swerving or turning aside **2** : STEADY <~ loyalty>

un·sym·met·ri·cal \ˌən(t)-sə-ˈme-tri-kəl\ *adj* : ASYMMETRIC — **un·sym·met·ri·cal·ly** \-k(ə-)lē\ *adv*

un·tan·gle \ˌən-ˈtaŋ-gəl, ˈən-\ *vt* : to loose from tangles or entanglement : straighten out ***syn*** see EXTRICATE

un·tapped \-ˈtapt\ *adj* **1** : not subjected to tapping <an ~ keg> **2** : not drawn upon or utilized <as yet ~ markets>

un·taught \-ˈtȯt\ *adj* **1** : not instructed or trained : IGNORANT **2** : NATURAL, SPONTANEOUS <~ kindness>

un·teach \-ˈtēch\ *vt* **-taught** \-ˈtȯt\; **-teach·ing** **1** : to cause to unlearn something **2** : to teach the contrary of

un·ten·a·ble \-ˈten-ə-bəl\ *adj* **1** : not able to be defended **2** : not able to be occupied — **un·ten·a·bil·i·ty** \ˌən-ˌten-ə-ˈbil-ət-ē\ *n*

un·tent·ed \-ˈtent-əd\ *adj* [[1]*un-* + obs. E *tented,* pp. of *tent* (to probe)] : not probed or dressed <the ~ woundings of a father's curse —Shak.>

un·teth·er \-ˈteth-ər\ *vt* : to free from a tether

un·think \-ˈthiŋk\ *vb* **-thought** \-ˈthȯt\; **-think·ing** *vi* : to terminate or reverse a thought process ~ *vt* : to put out of mind

un·think·able \-ˈthiŋ-kə-bəl\ *adj* **1** : not capable of being grasped by the mind **2** : contrary to what is reasonable, desirable, or probable : out of the question — **un·think·abil·i·ty** \ˌən-ˌthiŋ-kə-ˈbil-ət-ē\ *n* — **un·think·ably** \ˌən-ˈthiŋ-kə-blē, ˈən-\ *adv*

un·think·ing \ˌən-ˈthiŋ-kiŋ, ˈən-\ *adj* **1** : not taking thought : HEEDLESS, UNMINDFUL **2** : not indicating thought or reflection **3** : not having the power of thought — **un·think·ing·ly** \-kiŋ-lē\ *adv*

un·thought \-ˈthȯt\ *adj* : not anticipated : UNEXPECTED — often used with *of* or *on*

un·thread \ˌən-ˈthred, ˈən-\ *vt* **1** : to draw or take out a thread from **2** : to loosen the threads or connections of **3** : to make one's way through <~ a maze>

un·throne \-ˈthrōn\ *vt* : to remove from or as if from a throne

un·ti·dy \-ˈtīd-ē\ *adj* **1** : not neat : CARELESS, SLOVENLY **2 a** : not neatly organized or carried out <an ~ manuscript> **b** : conducive to a lack of neatness <~ tasks like bathing the baby —*New Yorker*> — **un·ti·di·ly** \-ˈtīd-ᵊl-ē\ *adv* — **un·ti·di·ness** \-ˈtīd-ē-nəs\ *n*

un·tie \-ˈtī\ *vb* **-tied; -ty·ing** *or* **-tie·ing** *vt* **1** : to free from something that ties, fastens, or restrains : UNBIND **2 a** : to disengage the knotted parts of **b :** DISENTANGLE, RESOLVE <~ a traffic jam> ~ *vi* : to become loosened or unbound

1**un·til** \ˌən-ˌtil, -tᵊl, -ˌtel, ˌən-, *in some contexts* ᵊn-, ᵊm-, *or* ᵊŋ-\ *prep* [ME, fr. *un-* unto, until (akin to OE *oth* to, until, OHG *unt* unto, until, OE *ende* end) + *til, till* till] **1** *chiefly Scot* : TO **2** — used as a function word to indicate continuance (as of an action or condition) to a specified time <stayed ~ morning> **3 :** BEFORE <not available ~ tomorrow>

2**until** *conj* : up to the time that : till such time as <play continued ~ it got dark> <never able to relax ~ he took up fishing> <ran ~ he was breathless>

1**un·time·ly** \ˌən-'tīm-lē, 'ən-\ *adv* **1 :** at an inopportune time : UNSEASONABLY **2 :** before the due, natural, or proper time : PREMATURELY

2**untimely** *adj* **1 :** occurring or done before the due, natural, or proper time : too early : PREMATURE <~ death> **2 :** INOPPORTUNE, UNSEASONABLE <an ~ joke> <~ frost> — **un·time·li·ness** *n*

un·time·ous \-'tī-məs\ *adj, chiefly Scot* : UNTIMELY

un·ti·tled \-'tīt-ᵊld\ *adj* **1** *obs* : having no title or right to rule **2** : not named <an ~ novel> **3 :** not called by a title <~ nobility>

un·to \ˌən-tə(-w), 'ən-(ˌ)tü\ *prep* [ME, fr. *un-* unto, until + *to*] : TO

un·told \ˌən-'tōld, 'ən-\ *adj* **1 :** too great or numerous to count : INCALCULABLE, VAST **2 a :** not told or related **b :** kept secret

un·touch·abil·i·ty \ˌən-ˌtəch-ə-'bil-ət-ē\ *n* : the quality or state of being untouchable; *esp* : the state of being an untouchable

1**un·touch·able** \ˌən-'təch-ə-bəl, 'ən-\ *adj* **1 a :** forbidden to the touch : not to be handled **b :** exempt from criticism or control **2 :** lying beyond reach <~ mineral resources buried deep within the earth> **3 :** disagreeable or defiling to the touch

2**untouchable** *n* : one that is untouchable; *specif, often cap* : a member of a large formerly segregated hereditary group in India having in traditional Hindu belief the quality of defiling by contact a member of a higher caste

un·touched \ˌən-'təcht, 'ən-\ *adj* **1 :** not subjected to touching : not handled **2 :** not described or dealt with **3 a :** not tasted **b :** being in the first or a primeval state or condition **4 :** not influenced : UNAFFECTED

un·to·ward \ˌən-'tō(-ə)rd, 'ən-, -'tȯ(-ə)rd; ˌən-tə-'wȯ(ə)rd\ *adj* **1** : difficult to guide, manage, or work with : UNRULY, INTRACTABLE **2 a :** marked by trouble or unhappiness : UNLUCKY **b :** not favorable : ADVERSE, UNPROPITIOUS — **un·to·ward·ly** *adv* — **un·to·ward·ness** *n*

un·tread \ˌən-'tred, 'ən-\ *vt, archaic* : to tread back : RETRACE

un·tried \-'trīd\ *adj* **1 :** not tested or proved by experience or trial **2 :** not tried in court

un·trod \-'träd\ *or* **un·trod·den** \-'träd-ᵊn\ *adj* : not trod : UNTRAVERSED

un·trou·bled \-'trəb-əld\ *adj* **1 :** not given trouble : not made uneasy **2 :** CALM, TRANQUIL

un·true \-'trü\ *adj* **1 :** not faithful : DISLOYAL **2 :** not according with a standard of correctness : not level or exact **3 :** not according with the facts : FALSE — **un·tru·ly** \-'trü-lē\ *adv*

un·truss \-'trəs\ *vt* **1** *archaic* : UNTIE, UNFASTEN — used in the phrase *untruss one's points* **2** *archaic* : UNDRESS ~ *vi, archaic* : to unfasten or take off one's clothes and esp. one's breeches

un·truth \ˌən-'trüth, 'ən-\ *n* **1** *archaic* : DISLOYALTY **2 :** lack of truthfulness : FALSITY **3 :** something that is untrue : FALSEHOOD

un·truth·ful \-'trüth-fəl\ *adj* : not containing or telling the truth : FALSE, INACCURATE <~ report> ***syn*** see DISHONEST ***ant*** truthful — **un·truth·ful·ly** \-fə-lē\ *adv* — **un·truth·ful·ness** *n*

un·tuck \-'tək\ *vt* : to release from being tucked up

un·tune \-'t(y)ün\ *vt* **1 :** to put out of tune **2 :** DISARRANGE, DISCOMPOSE

un·tu·tored \-'t(y)üt-ərd\ *adj* **1 a :** having no formal learning or training **b :** NAIVE, UNSOPHISTICATED **2 :** not produced or developed by instruction : NATIVE <his ~ shrewdness> ***syn*** see IGNORANT

un·twine \-'twīn\ *vt* **1 :** to unwind the twisted or tangled parts of : DISENTANGLE **2 :** to remove by unwinding ~ *vi* : to become disentangled or unwound

un·twist \ˌən-'twist, 'ən-\ *vt* : to separate the twisted parts of : UNTWINE ~ *vi* : to become untwined

un·twist·ed \-'twis-təd\ *adj* : not twisted

un·used \-'yüzd, *in the phrase "unused to" usually* -'yüs(t)\ *adj* **1** : not habituated : UNACCUSTOMED <~ to crowds> **2 :** not used: as **a :** FRESH, NEW <set an ~ canvas on the easel> **b :** not put to use : IDLE <~ land> **c :** not consumed : ACCRUED <~ sick leave>

un·usu·al \-'yüzh-(ə-)wəl, -'yü-zhəl\ *adj* : not usual : UNCOMMON, RARE — **un·usu·al·ly** \-ē\ *adv* — **un·usu·al·ness** *n*

un·ut·ter·able \ˌən-'ət-ə-rə-bəl, 'ən-\ *adj* : being beyond the powers of description : INEXPRESSIBLE — **un·ut·ter·ably** \-blē\ *adv*

un·val·ued \-'val-(ˌ)yüd, -yəd\ *adj* **1** *obs* : INVALUABLE **2 a :** not important or prized : DISREGARDED **b :** not appraised

un·var·nished \-'vär-nisht\ *adj* **1 a :** not adorned or glossed : PLAIN, STRAIGHTFORWARD <told the ~ truth> **b :** ARTLESS, FRANK <the ~ candor of old people and children —Janet Flanner> **2 :** not coated with or as if with varnish : CRUDE, UNFINISHED

un·veil \ˌən-'vā(ə)l, 'ən-\ *vt* **1 :** to remove a veil or covering from **2 :** to make public : DIVULGE, REVEAL ~ *vi* : to throw off a veil or protective cloak

un·veiled \-'vā(ə)ld\ *adj* : not veiled : OPEN, REVEALED

un·ver·bal·ized \-'vər-bə-ˌlīzd\ *adj* : not put into words or given conscious expression

un·vo·cal \ˌən-'vō-kəl, 'ən-\ *adj* **1 :** not eloquent or outspoken : INARTICULATE **2 :** not musical : DISCORDANT

un·voice \-'vȯis\ *vt* : DEVOICE

un·voiced \-'vȯist\ *adj* **1 :** not verbally expressed **2 :** VOICELESS **2**

un·war·rant·able \-'wȯr-ənt-ə-bəl, -'wär-\ *adj* : not justifiable : INEXCUSABLE — **un·war·rant·ably** \-blē\ *adv*

un·wary \ˌən-'wa(ə)r-ē, 'ən-, -'we(ə)r-\ *adj* : not alert : easily fooled or surprised : HEEDLESS, GULLIBLE — **un·wari·ly** \-'war-ə-lē, -'wer-\ *adv* — **un·wari·ness** \-'war-ē-nəs, -'wer-\ *n*

1**un·washed** \-'wȯsht, -'wäsht\ *adj* **1 :** not cleaned with or as if with soap and water **2 :** IGNORANT, PLEBEIAN — **un·washed·ness** *n*

2**unwashed** *n* : an ignorant or underprivileged group : RABBLE

un·wa·ver·ing \ˌən-'wāv(-ə)-riŋ, 'ən-\ *adj* : not wavering : FIXED, STEADFAST — **un·wa·ver·ing·ly** \-riŋ-lē\ *adv*

un·wea·ried \-'wi(ə)r-ēd\ *adj* : not tired or jaded : FRESH — **un·wea·ried·ly** *adv*

un·weave \-'wēv\ *vt* **-wove** \-'wōv\; **-wo·ven** \-'wō-vən\; **-weav·ing** : DISENTANGLE, RAVEL

un·weet·ing \-'wēt-iŋ\ *adj, archaic* : UNWITTING — **un·weet·ing·ly** \-iŋ-lē\ *adv, archaic*

un·weight \-'wāt\ *vt* : to reduce momentarily the force exerted by (as a ski) upon a surface by shifting the weight or position of one's body ~ *vi* : to unweight something by shifting the weight or position of one's body

un·well \ˌən-'wel, 'ən-\ *adj* **1 :** being in poor health : AILING, SICK **2 :** undergoing menstruation

un·whole·some \-'hōl-səm\ *adj* **1 :** detrimental to physical, mental, or moral well-being : UNHEALTHY <~ food> <~ pastimes> **2 a :** CORRUPT, UNSOUND **b :** offensive to the senses : LOATHSOME — **un·whole·some·ly** *adv*

un·wieldy \-'wē(ə)l-dē\ *adj* : not easily managed or handled esp. because of bulk or weight : CUMBERSOME — **un·wield·i·ly** \-'wel-də-lē\ *adv* — **un·wield·i·ness** \-dē-nəs\ *n*

un·willed \-'wild\ *adj* : not willed : INVOLUNTARY

un·will·ing \-'wil-iŋ\ *adj* : not willing: **a :** LOATH, RELUCTANT <was ~ to learn> **b :** done or given reluctantly <his ~ approval> **c :** offering opposition : OBSTINATE <a hard, ~ man> — **un·will·ing·ly** \-iŋ-lē\ *adv* — **un·will·ing·ness** *n*

un·wind \-'wīnd\ *vb* **-wound** \-'waund\; **-wind·ing** *vt* **1 a :** to cause to uncoil : wind off : UNROLL **b :** to free from or as if from a binding or wrapping **c :** to release from tension : RELAX **2** *archaic* : RETRACE ~ *vi* **1 :** to become uncoiled or disentangled : UNFOLD **2 :** to become released from tension

un·win·na·ble \-'win-ə-bəl\ *adj* : incapable of being won

un·wis·dom \ˌən-'wiz-dəm, 'ən-\ *n* : lack of wisdom : FOOLISHNESS, FOLLY

un·wise \-'wīz\ *adj* : lacking wisdom or good sense : FOOLISH, IMPRUDENT — **un·wise·ly** *adv*

un·wish \-'wish\ *vt* **1 :** to take back (a wish) **2** *obs* : to wish away

un·wit·ting \-'wit-iŋ\ *adj* **1 :** not intended : INADVERTENT <an ~ mistake> **2 :** not knowing : UNAWARE <kept the truth from his ~ friends> — **un·wit·ting·ly** \-iŋ-lē\ *adv*

un·wont·ed \-'wȯnt-əd, -'wōnt- *also* -'wənt- *or* -'wänt-\ *adj* **1** : being out of the ordinary : RARE, UNUSUAL **2 :** not accustomed by experience — **un·wont·ed·ly** *adv* — **un·wont·ed·ness** *n*

un·world·ly \-'wər(-ə)l-dlē, -'wərl-lē\ *adj* **1 :** not of this world : UNEARTHLY; *specif* : SPIRITUAL **2 a :** not wise in the ways of the world : NAIVE **b :** not swayed by mundane considerations — **un·world·li·ness** \-'wərl-(d)lē-nəs\ *n*

un·worn \-'wō(ə)rn, -'wȯ(ə)rn\ *adj* **1 a :** not impaired by use : not worn away **b :** not worn : NEW **2 :** not jaded : FRESH, ORIGINAL

un·wor·thy \ˌən-'wər-thē, 'ən-\ *adj* **1 a :** lacking in excellence or value : POOR, WORTHLESS **b :** BASE, DISHONORABLE **2 :** not meritorious : UNDESERVING <~ of attention> **3 :** not deserved : UNMERITED <~ treatment> — **un·wor·thi·ly** \-thə-lē\ *adv* — **un·wor·thi·ness** \-thē-nəs\ *n*

un·wo·ven \-'wō-vən\ *adj* : not woven

un·wrap \-'rap\ *vt* : to remove the wrapping from : DISCLOSE <~ a package> <~ evidence in a criminal case>

un·wreathe \-'rēth\ *vt* : UNCOIL, UNTWIST

un·writ·ten \-'rit-ᵊn\ *adj* **1 :** not expressed in writing : ORAL, TRADITIONAL **2 :** containing no writing : BLANK

unwritten constitution *n* : a constitution not embodied in a single document but based chiefly on custom and precedent as expressed in statutes and judicial decisions

unwritten law *n* : law based chiefly on custom rather than legislative enactments

un·yield·ing \ˌən-'yē(ə)l-diŋ, 'ən-\ *adj* **1 :** characterized by lack of softness or flexibility **2 :** characterized by firmness or obduracy — **un·yield·ing·ly** \-diŋ-lē\ *adv*

un·yoke \-'yōk\ *vt* **1 :** to free from a yoke or harness **2 :** to take apart : DISJOIN ~ *vi* **1** *archaic* : to unharness a draft animal **2** *archaic* : to cease from work

un·zip \-'zip\ *vt* : to zip open ~ *vi* : to open by or as if by means of a zipper

1**up** \'əp\ *adv* [partly fr. ME *up* upward, fr. OE *ūp*; partly fr. ME *uppe* on high, fr. OE; both akin to OHG *ūf* up, L *sub* under, Gk *hypo* under, *hyper* over — more at OVER] **1 a** (1) : in or into a higher position or level; *specif* : away from the center of the earth (2) : from beneath the ground or water to the surface (3) : from below the horizon (4) : UPSTREAM (5) : in or into an upright position <sit ~>; *specif* : out of bed **b :** upward from the ground or surface <pull ~ a daisy> **c :** so as to expose a particular surface **2 :** with greater intensity <speak ~> **3 a :** in or into a better or more advanced state **b :** at an end <your time is ~> **c** : in or into a state of greater intensity or excitement **d :** in a continual sequence <from third grade ~> **4 a** (1) : into existence, evidence, prominence, or prevalence <put ~ several new buildings> (2) : into operation or practical form **b :** into consideration or attention <bring ~ for discussion> **5 :** into possession or custody **6 a :** ENTIRELY, COMPLETELY <button ~ your coat> **b** — used as an intensifier <clean ~ the house> **7** : in or into storage : BY <lay ~ supplies> **8 a :** so as to arrive or approach **b :** in a direction conventionally the opposite of down: (1) : to windward (2) : NORTHWARD (3) : to or at the top (4) : to or at the rear of a theatrical stage **9 :** in or into parts

10 : to a stop — usu. used with *draw, bring, fetch,* or *pull* **11** : for each side <the score is 15 ~>

2up *adj* **1 a** : risen above the horizon <the sun is ~> **b** : STANDING **c** : being out of bed **d** : relatively high <the river is ~> <was well ~ in his class> **e** : being in a raised position : LIFTED <windows are ~> **f** : being in a state of completion : CONSTRUCTED, BUILT **g** : having the face upward **h** : mounted on a horse <a new jockey ~> **i** : grown above a surface <the corn is ~> **j (1)** : moving, inclining, or directed upward <the ~ escalator> **(2)** : bound in a direction regarded as up **2 a** : marked by agitation, excitement, or activity **b** : being above a former or normal level (as of quantity or intensity) <attendance is ~> <the wind is ~> **c** : exerting enough power (as for operation) <sail when steam is ~> **d** : READY; *specif* : highly prepared **e** : going on : taking place <find out what is ~> **3 a** : risen from a lower position <men ~ from the ranks> **b** : being at the same level or point <did not feel ~ to par> **c (1)** : well informed : ABREAST <~ on the news> **(2)** : being on schedule <~ on his homework> **d** : being ahead of one's opponent **4 a** : presented for or undergoing consideration <contract ~ for negotiation>; *specif* : charged before a court <~ for robbery> **b** : BET, WAGERED — **up to 1** : capable of performing or dealing with <feels *up to* her role> **2** : engaged in <what is he *up to*> **3** : being the responsibility of <it's *up to* me>

3up *vb* **upped** *or in vi 1* **up; upped; up·ping; ups** *or in vi 1* **up** *vi* **1** — used with *and* and another verb to indicate that the action of the following verb was either surprisingly or abruptly initiated <he ~ and married a showgirl> **2 a** : to rise from a lying or sitting position **b** : to move upward : ASCEND ~ *vt* **1** : RAISE, LIFT **2 a** : to advance to a higher level: **(1)** : INCREASE **(2)** : PROMOTE 1a **b** : RAISE 8d, 8e

4up \(ˌ)əp, ˈəp\ *prep* **1 a** — used as a function word to indicate motion to or toward or situation at a higher point of **b** : up into or in the <went ~ attic> **2 a** : in a direction regarded as being toward or near the upper end or part of <journeyed ~ the valley> <lives a few miles ~ the coast> **b** : toward or near a point closer to the source or beginning of <sail ~ the river> **3** : in the direction opposite to : AGAINST <sailed ~ the wind>

5up \ˈəp\ *n* **1** : one in a high or advantageous position **2** : an upward slope **3** : a period or state of prosperity or success **4** : 3UPPER

UP *abbr* underproof

up–and–coming \ˌəp-ən-ˈkəm-iŋ\ *adj* : alertly active and likely to advance or succeed

up–and–down *adj* **1** : marked by alternate upward and downward movement, action, or surface **2** : PERPENDICULAR

up and down \ˌəp-ᵊm-ˈdau̇n, ˌəp-ən-\ *adv* **1** : to and fro **2** : here and there esp. throughout an area **3** : with regard to every particular : THOROUGHLY <knew the territory *up and down*>

up–and–up \ˈəp-ən-ˌəp\ *n* : an honest or respectable course — used chiefly in the phrase *on the up-and-up*

Upa·ni·shad \ü-ˈpän-i-ˌshäd, yü-ˈpan-ə-ˌshad\ *n* [Skt *upaniṣad*] : one of a class of Vedic treatises dealing with broad philosophic problems — **Upa·ni·shad·ic** \(ˌ)ü-ˌpän-i-ˈshäd-ik, (ˌ)yü-ˌpan-ə-ˈshad-ik\ *adj*

upas \ˈyü-pəs\ *n* [Malay *pohon upas* poison tree] **1 a** : a tall Asiatic and East Indian tree (*Antiaris toxicaria*) of the mulberry family with a latex that contains poisonous glucosides used as an arrow poison **b** : a shrub or tree (*Strychnos tieuté* of the family Loganiaceae) of the same region also yielding an arrow poison **2** : a poisonous concentrate of the juice or latex of a upas **3** : a poisonous or harmful influence or institution

1up·beat \ˈəp-ˌbēt\ *n* **1** : an unaccented beat in a musical measure; *specif* : the last beat of the measure **2** : an increase in activity or prosperity <business that is on the ~>

2upbeat *adj* : OPTIMISTIC, CHEERFUL

up–bow \ˈəp-ˌbō\ *n* : a stroke in playing a bowed instrument (as a violin) in which the bow is moved across the strings from the tip to the heel

up·braid \ˌəp-ˈbrād\ *vt* [ME *upbreyden,* fr. OE *ūpbregdan*] **1** : to criticize severely : find fault with **2** : to reproach severely : scold vehemently ***syn*** see SCOLD — **up·braid·er** *n*

up·bring·ing \ˈəp-ˌbriŋ-iŋ\ *n* : early training; *esp* : a particular way of bringing up a child <had a strict Protestant ~>

up·build \ˌəp-ˈbild\ *vt* **-built** \-ˈbilt\; **-build·ing** : to build up — **up·build·er** *n*

up·cast \ˈəp-ˌkast\ *n* : something cast up

up·chuck \ˈəp-ˌchək\ *vb* : VOMIT

up·com·ing \ˌəp-ˌkəm-iŋ\ *adj* : FORTHCOMING, APPROACHING

up–coun·try \ˌəp-ˌkən-trē\ *adj* : of, relating to, or characteristic of an inland, upland, or outlying region — **up–country** \ˈəp-ˌ\ *n* — **up–country** \ˌəp-ˈ\ *adv*

1up·date \ˌəp-ˈdāt\ *vt* : to bring up to date

2up·date \ˈəp-ˌdāt\ *n* : an act or instance of updating <a computer file ~>

up·do \ˈəp-(ˌ)dü\ *n, pl* **updos** [*up*swept hair*do*] : an upswept hairdo

up·draft \ˈəp-ˌdraft, -ˌdräft\ *n* : an upward movement of gas (as air)

up·end \ˌə-ˈpend\ *vt* **1** : to set or stand on end **2 a** : to affect to the point of being upset or flurried <a . . . literary shocker, designed to ~ the credulous matrons —Wolcott Gibbs> **b** : BEAT, DEFEAT ~ *vi* : to rise on an end

up·field \ˈəp-ˈfē(ə)ld\ *adv or adj* : in or into the part of the field toward which the offensive team is headed

1up·grade \ˈəp-ˌgrād\ *n* **1** : an upward grade or slope **2** : INCREASE, RISE

2up·grade \ˈəp-ˌgrād, ˌəp-ˈ\ *vt* : to raise or improve the grade of: as **a** : to improve (livestock) by use of purebred sires **b** : to advance to a job requiring a higher level of skill esp. as part of a training program **c** : to raise the classification and usu. the price of (a product) without improving the quality

up·growth \ˈəp-ˌgrōth\ *n* : the process of growing upward : DEVELOPMENT; *also* : a product or result of this

up·heav·al \ˌəp-ˈhē-vəl, (ˌ)ə-ˈpē-\ *n* **1** : the action or an instance of upheaving esp. of part of the earth's crust **2** : extreme agitation or disorder : radical change; *also* : an instance of this

up·heave \ˌəp-ˈhēv, (ˌ)ə-ˈpēv\ *vt* : to heave up : LIFT ~ *vi* : to move upward esp. with power — **up·heav·er** *n*

1up·hill \ˈəp-ˌhil\ *n* : rising ground : ASCENT

2up·hill \-ˈhil\ *adv* **1** : upward on a hill or incline **2** : against difficulties <seemed to be talking ~ —Willa Cather>

3up·hill \-ˌhil\ *adj* **1** : situated on elevated ground **2 a** : going up : ASCENDING **b** : being the higher one or part esp. of a set; *specif* : being nearer the top of an incline <keep the ~ ski far enough ahead to prevent the skis from crossing —Ernie McCulloch> **3** : DIFFICULT, LABORIOUS <the battle for the arts was still all ~ —Hubert Humphrey>

up·hold \(ˌ)əp-ˈhōld\ *vt* **-held** \-ˈheld\; **-hold·ing 1 a** : to give support to **b** : to support against an opponent **2 a** : to keep elevated **b** : to lift up ***syn*** see SUPPORT — **up·hold·er** *n*

up·hol·ster \(ˌ)əp-ˈhōl-stər, (ˌ)ə-ˈpōl-\ *vt* **up·hol·stered; up·hol·ster·ing** \-st(ə-)riŋ\ [back-formation fr. *upholstery*] : to furnish with or as if with upholstery — **up·hol·ster·er** \-stər-ər\ *n*

up·hol·stery \-st(ə-)rē\ *n, pl* **-ster·ies** [ME *upholdester* upholsterer, fr. *upholden* to uphold, fr. *up* + *holden* to hold] : materials (as fabric, padding, and springs) used to make a soft covering esp. for a seat

UPI *abbr* United Press International

up·keep \ˈəp-ˌkēp\ *n* **1** : the act of maintaining in good condition : the state of being maintained in good condition **2** : the cost of maintaining in good condition

up·land \ˈəp-lənd, -ˌland\ *n* **1** : high land esp. at some distance from the sea : PLATEAU **2** : ground elevated above the lowlands along rivers or between hills — **upland** *adj* — **up·land·er** \-lən-dər, -ˌlan-\ *n*

upland cotton *n* : any of various usu. short-staple cottons cultivated esp. in the U.S.

upland plover *n* : a large sandpiper (*Bartramia longicauda*) of eastern No. America that frequents fields and uplands

1up·lift \(ˌ)əp-ˈlift\ *vt* **1** : to lift up : ELEVATE; *esp* : to cause (a portion of the earth's surface) to rise above adjacent areas **2** : to improve the spiritual, social, or intellectual condition of ~ *vi* : RISE — **up·lift·er** *n*

2up·lift \ˈəp-ˌlift\ *n* **1** : an act, process, result, or cause of uplifting: as **a (1)** : the uplifting of a part of the earth's surface **(2)** : an uplifted mass of land **b** : a bettering of a condition esp. spiritually, socially, or intellectually **c (1)** : influences intended to uplift **(2)** : a social movement to improve esp. morally or culturally **2** : a brassiere designed to hold the breasts up

up·man·ship \ˈəp-mən-ˌship\ *n* : ONE-UPMANSHIP

up·most \ˈəp-ˌmōst\ *adj* : UPPERMOST

1up·on \ə-ˈpȯn, -ˈpän, -(ˌ)pən\ *prep* : ON

2up·on \ə-ˈpȯn, -ˈpän\ *adv* **1** *obs* : on the surface : on it **2** *obs* : THEREAFTER, THEREON

1up·per \ˈəp-ər\ *adj* **1 a** : higher in physical position, rank, or order **b** : farther inland <the ~ Mississippi> **2** : constituting the branch of a bicameral legislature that is usu. smaller and more restricted in membership and possesses greater traditional prestige than the lower house **3 a** : constituting a stratum relatively near the earth's surface **b** *cap* : being a later epoch or series of the period or series named <*Upper* Carboniferous> **4** : NORTHERN <~ Manhattan>

2upper *n* : one that is upper: as **a** : the parts of a shoe or boot above the sole **b** : an upper tooth or denture **c** : an upper berth — **on one's uppers** : in straitened circumstances : at the end of one's means

3upper *n* [*up* + 2*-er*] : a stimulant drug; *esp* : AMPHETAMINE

upper atmosphere *n* : the part of the atmosphere that lies exterior to the troposphere and usu. includes the stratosphere, mesosphere, and thermosphere

1up·per·case \ˌəp-ər-ˈkās\ *adj* [fr. the compositor's practice of keeping capital letters in the upper of a pair of type cases] : CAPITAL 2

2uppercase *n* : capital letters

3uppercase *vt* **-cased; -cas·ing** : to print or set in capital letters

upper case *n* : a type case containing capitals and usu. small capitals, fractions, symbols, and accents

upper–class *adj* : of, relating to, or characteristic of the upper class

upper class *n* : a social class occupying a position above the middle class and having the highest status in a society usu. by virtue of wealth, prestige, or education

up·per·class·man \ˌəp-ər-ˈklas-mən\ *n* : a member of the junior or senior class in a school or college

upper crust *n* : the highest social class or group; *esp* : the highest circle of the upper class

up·per·cut \ˈəp-ər-ˌkət\ *n* : a swinging blow (as in boxing) directed upward with a bent arm — **uppercut** *vb*

upper hand *n* : MASTERY, ADVANTAGE, CONTROL <was determined not to let his opponent get the *upper hand*>

up·per·most \ˈəp-ər-ˌmōst\ *adv* : in or into the highest or most prominent position — **uppermost** *adj*

up·per·part \-ˌpärt\ *n* : a part lying on the upper side (as of a bird)

upper partial *n* : OVERTONE 1a

up·pish \ˈəp-ish\ *adj* : UPPITY — **up·pish·ly** *adv* — **up·pish·ness** *n*

up·pi·ty \ˈəp-ət-ē\ *adj* [prob. fr. *up* + *-ity* (as in *persnickity,* var. of *persnickety*)] : putting on airs of superiority : ARROGANT, PRESUMPTUOUS — **up·pi·ty·ness** *n*

up·raise \(ˌ)ə-ˈprāz\ *vt* : to raise or lift up : ELEVATE

ə abut ᵊ kitten ər further a back ā bake ä cot, cart
au̇ out ch chin e less ē easy g gift i trip ī life
j joke ŋ sing ō flow ȯ flaw ȯi coin th thin th this
ü loot u̇ foot y yet yü few yu̇ furious zh vision

up·rear \(ˌ)ə-ˈpri(ə)r\ *vt* **1 :** to lift up **2 :** ERECT ~ *vi* **:** RISE
[1]**up·right** \ˈəp-ˌrīt\ *adj* **1 a :** PERPENDICULAR, VERTICAL **b :** erect in carriage or posture **c :** having the main axis or a main part perpendicular <~ freezer> **2 :** marked by strong moral rectitude — **up·right·ly** *adv* — **up·right·ness** *n*
syn UPRIGHT, HONEST, JUST, CONSCIENTIOUS, SCRUPULOUS, HONORABLE *shared meaning element* **:** having or exhibiting a strict regard for what is morally right
[2]**upright** *vt* **:** to make upright
[3]**upright** *adv* **:** vertically upward **:** in an upright position
[4]**upright** *n* **1 :** the state of being upright **:** PERPENDICULAR <a pillar out of ~> **2 :** something that stands upright **3 :** UPRIGHT PIANO
upright piano *n* **:** a piano with vertical frame and strings — compare GRAND PIANO

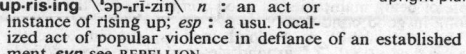

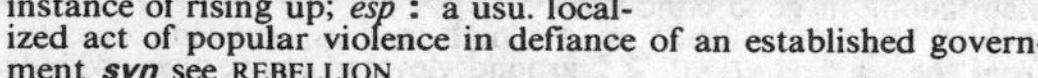
upright piano

[1]**up·rise** \ˌə-ˈprīz\ *vi* **up·rose** \-ˈprōz\; **up·ris·en** \-ˈpriz-ᵊn\; **up·ris·ing** \-ˈprī-ziŋ\ **1 a :** to rise to a higher position **b** (1) **:** to stand up (2) **:** to get out of bed **c :** to come into view esp. from below the horizon **2 :** to rise up in sound — **up·ris·er** \ˌə-ˈprī-zər, ˈəp-ˌrī-\ *n*
[2]**up·rise** \ˈəp-ˌrīz\ *n* **1 :** an act or instance of uprising **2 :** an upward slope
up·ris·ing \ˈəp-ˌrī-ziŋ\ *n* **:** an act or instance of rising up; *esp* **:** a usu. localized act of popular violence in defiance of an established government *syn* see REBELLION
up·riv·er \ˈəp-ˈriv-ər\ *adv or adj* **:** toward or at a point nearer the source of a river
up·roar \ˈəp-ˌrō(ə)r, -ˌrȯ(ə)r\ *n* [by folk etymology fr. D *oproer,* fr. MD, fr. *op* up + *roer* motion; akin to OE *ūp* up and to OE *hrēran* to stir] **:** a state of commotion, excitement, or violent disturbance
up·roar·i·ous \ˌə-ˈprōr-ē-əs, -ˈprȯr-\ *adj* **1 :** marked by uproar **2 :** very noisy and full **3 :** extremely funny <an ~ comedy> — **up·roar·i·ous·ly** *adv* — **up·roar·i·ous·ness** *n*
up·root \(ˌ)ə-ˈprüt, -ˈprůt\ *vt* **1 :** to pull up by the roots **2 :** to remove as if by pulling up **3 :** to displace from a country or traditional habitat *syn* see EXTERMINATE — **up·root·er** *n*
up·rush \ˈəp-ˌrəsh\ *n* **1 :** an upward rush (as of gas or liquid) **2 :** a sudden increase
UPS *abbr* **1** Underground Press Syndicate **2** United Parcel Service
ups and downs *n pl* **:** alternating rise and fall esp. in fortune
[1]**up·set** \(ˌ)əp-ˈset\ *vb* **-set; -set·ting** *vt* **1 :** to thicken and shorten (as a heated bar of iron) by hammering on the end **:** SWAGE **2 :** to force out of the usual upright, level, or proper position **:** OVERTURN **3 a :** to trouble mentally or emotionally **:** disturb the poise of **b :** to throw into disorder **c :** INVALIDATE **d :** to defeat unexpectedly **4 :** to cause a physical disorder in; *specif* **:** to make somewhat ill ~ *vi* **:** to become overturned *syn* see DISCOMPOSE — **up·set·ter** *n*
[2]**up·set** \ˈəp-ˌset\ *n* **1 :** an act of overturning **:** OVERTURN **2 a** (1) **:** an act of throwing into disorder **:** DERANGEMENT (2) **:** a state of disorder **:** CONFUSION **b :** an unexpected defeat **3 a :** a minor physical disorder <a stomach ~> **b :** an emotional disturbance <went through a big ~ after his father's death> **4 a :** a part of a rod (as the head on a bolt) that is upset **b :** the expansion of a bullet on striking **5 :** a swage used in upsetting
up·set price \ˌəp-ˌset-\ *n* **:** the minimum price set for property offered at auction or public sale
up·shift \ˈəp-ˌshift\ *vi* **:** to shift an automotive vehicle into a higher gear — **upshift** *n*
up·shot \ˈəp-ˌshät\ *n* **:** the final result **:** OUTCOME
up·side down \ˌəp-ˌsīd-ˈdau̇n\ *adv* [alter. of ME *up so doun,* fr. *up* + *so* + *doun* down] **1 :** in such a way that the upper and the lower parts are reversed in position **2 :** in or into great disorder — **upside–down** *adj*
upside–down cake *n* **:** a cake baked with its batter covering an arrangement of fruit (as pineapple) and served fruit side up
up·si·lon \ˈyüp-sə-ˌlän, ˈəp-, -lən, *Brit usu* yüp-ˈsī-lən\ *n* [MGk *y psilon,* lit., simple *y;* fr. the desire to distinguish it from *oi,* which was pronounced the same in later Greek] **:** the 20th letter of the Greek alphabet — see ALPHABET table
up·spring \ˌəp-ˈspriŋ\ *vi* **-sprang** \-ˈspraŋ\ *or* **-sprung** \-ˈsprəŋ\; **-spring·ing** \-ˈspriŋ-iŋ\ **1 :** to spring up **2 :** to come into being
[1]**up·stage** \ˈəp-ˈstāj\ *adv* **1 :** toward or at the rear of a theatrical stage **2 :** away from a motion-picture or television camera
[2]**upstage** *adj* **1 :** of or relating to the rear of a stage **2** [[4]*upstage*] **:** HAUGHTY
[3]**up·stage** \ˈəp-ˌstāj\ *n* **:** the part of a stage that is farthest from the audience or camera
[4]**up·stage** \ˌəp-ˈstāj\ *vt* **1 :** to force (an actor) to face away from the audience by staying upstage **2 :** to steal the show from **3 :** to treat snobbishly
[1]**up·stairs** \ˈəp-ˈsta(ə)rz, -ˈste(ə)rz\ *adv* **1 :** up the stairs **:** on or to a higher floor **2 :** to or at a high altitude or higher position <quietly moved him ~ to board chairman —*Newsweek*> **3 :** in the head <she's all vacant ~ —J. T. Farrell>
[2]**up·stairs** \ˌəp-ˌsta(ə)rz, -ˌste(ə)rz\ *adj* **:** situated above the stairs esp. on an upper floor <an ~ bedroom>
[3]**up·stairs** \ˈəp-ˈ, ˈəp-ˌ\ *n pl but sing or pl in constr* **:** the part of a building above the ground floor
up·stand·ing \ˌəp-ˈstan-diŋ, ˈəp-ˌ\ *adj* **1 :** ERECT, UPRIGHT **2 :** marked by integrity — **up·stand·ing·ness** *n*
[1]**up·start** \ˌəp-ˈstärt\ *vi* **:** to jump up (as to one's feet) suddenly
[2]**up·start** \ˈəp-ˌstärt\ *n* **:** one that has risen suddenly (as from a low position to wealth or power) **:** PARVENU; *esp* **:** one that claims more personal importance than he warrants — **up·start** \ˌəp-ˌ\ *adj*
up·state \ˈəp-ˌstāt\ *n* **:** the chiefly northerly sections of a state of the U.S. as distinguished from a southerly part and esp. a metropolitan region often designated as *downstate* — **up·state** \-ˈstāt\ *adv or adj* — **up·stat·er** \-ˈstāt-ər\ *n*
up·stream \ˈəp-ˈstrēm\ *adv or adj* **:** in the direction opposite to the flow of a stream
up·stroke \ˈəp-ˌstrōk\ *n* **:** a stroke made in an upward direction
up·surge \ˈəp-ˌsərj\ *n* **:** a rapid or sudden rise
[1]**up·sweep** \ˈəp-ˌswēp\ *vi* **-swept** \-ˌswept\; **-sweep·ing :** to sweep upward
[2]**upsweep** *n* **:** an upward sweep; *esp* **:** a hairdo in which the hair is brushed up to the top of the head
up·swept \ˈəp-ˌswept\ *adj* **:** swept upward; *specif* **:** brushed up to the top of the head <~ hairdo>
up·swing \ˈəp-ˌswiŋ\ *n* **1 :** an upward swing **2 :** a marked increase (as in activity)
up·take \ˈəp-ˌtāk\ *n* [Sc *uptake* to understand] **1 :** UNDERSTANDING, COMPREHENSION <quick on the ~> **2 :** a flue leading upward **3 :** an act or instance of absorbing and incorporating esp. into a living organism
up–tem·po \ˈəp-ˌtem-(ˌ)pō\ *n, often attrib* **:** a fast-moving tempo (as in jazz)
[1]**up·throw** \ˈəp-ˌthrō\ *vt* **-threw** \-ˌthrü\; **-thrown** \-ˌthrōn\; **-throw·ing :** to throw or thrust upward
[2]**upthrow** *n* **:** an upward displacement (as of a rock stratum) **:** UPHEAVAL, UPTHRUST
[1]**up·thrust** \ˈəp-ˌthrəst\ *vt* **:** to thrust up; *esp* **:** to elevate (a part of the earth's surface) in an upthrust ~ *vi* **:** to rise with an upward thrust
[2]**upthrust** *n* **:** an upward thrust; *specif* **:** an uplift of part of the earth's crust
up·tight \ˈəp-ˈtīt, (ˌ)əp-ˈ, ˌəp-ˌ\ *adj* **1 :** being in financial difficulties <the surtax was another blow to an industry already ~ —*Chem. & Engineering News*> **2 a :** being tense, nervous, or uneasy <the . . . community is understandably ~ about bombs —D. D. Darling> **b :** ANGRY, INDIGNANT <I've been doing that voice in Negro theaters for years . . . Nobody ever got ~ —Flip Wilson> **c :** rigidly conventional <the ~ and antiseptic white community —J. M. Culkin> — **up·tight·ness** \(ˌ)əp-ˈtīt-nəs\ *n*
up·tilt \ˌəp-ˈtilt\ *vt* **:** to tilt upward
up·time \ˈəp-ˌtīm\ *n* **:** time during which a piece of equipment is functioning or able to function
up to *prep* **1 —** used as a function word to indicate extension as far as a specified place <sank *up to* his knees in the mud> **2 —** used as a function word to indicate a limit or boundary <*up to* 50,000 copies a month> <worked *up to* the last minute>
up–to–date *adj* **1 :** extending up to the present time **:** including the latest information <~ maps> **2 :** abreast of the times **:** MODERN <~ methods> — **up–to–date·ly** *adv* — **up–to–date·ness** *n*
up–to–the–minute *adj* **1 :** extending up to the immediate present **:** including the very latest information **2 :** marked by complete up-to-dateness
[1]**up·town** \ˈəp-ˈtau̇n\ *adv* **:** to, toward, or in the upper part of a town or city; *esp* **:** to, toward, or in the residential district — **up·town** \ˌəp-ˌtau̇n\ *adj*
[2]**up·town** \ˈəp-ˌtau̇n\ *n* **:** the section of a town or city located uptown
up·trend \ˈəp-ˌtrend\ *n* **:** an upturn esp. in business or economic activity
[1]**up·turn** \ˈəp-ˌtərn, ˌəp-ˈ\ *vt* **1 :** to turn up or over **2 :** to direct upward ~ *vi* **:** to turn upward
[2]**up·turn** \ˈəp-ˌtərn\ *n* **:** an upward turn esp. toward better conditions or higher prices
[1]**up·ward** \ˈəp-wərd\ *or* **up·wards** \-wərdz\ *adv* **1 a :** in a direction from lower to higher <the kite rose ~> **b** (1) **:** toward the source (as of a river) (2) **:** toward the interior (as of a region) **c :** in a higher position <held out his hand, palm ~> **d :** in the upper parts **:** toward the head **:** ABOVE <from the waist ~> **2 :** toward a higher or better condition or level <young lawyers moving ~> **3 a :** to an indefinitely greater amount, figure, or rank <from $5 ~> **b :** toward a greater amount or higher number, degree, or rate <attendance figures have risen ~> **4 :** toward or into later years <from his youth ~>
[2]**upward** *adj* **1 :** directed toward or situated in a higher place or level **:** ASCENDING **2 :** rising to a higher pitch — **up·ward·ly** *adv* — **up·ward·ness** *n*
upwards of *also* **upward of** *adv* **:** more than **:** in excess of <they cost *upwards of* $25>
up·well \ˌəp-ˈwel\ *vi* **:** to well up; *specif* **:** to move or flow upward <lava ~*ing* from the depths of a fissure>
up·wind \ˈəp-ˈwind\ *adv or adj* **:** in the direction from which the wind is blowing
[1]**ur-** *or* **uro-** *comb form* [NL, fr. Gk *our-, ouro-,* fr. *ouron* urine — more at URINE] **1 :** urine <*ur*ic> **2 :** urinary tract <*uro*logy> **3 :** urinal and <*uro*genital> **4 :** urea <*ur*acil>
[2]**ur-** *or* **uro-** *comb form* [NL, fr. Gk *our-, ouro-,* fr. *oura* tail — more at SQUIRREL] **:** tail <*uro*chord>
Ur- \ˈu̇(ə)r\ *prefix* [G, fr. OHG *ir-, ur-* thoroughly (perfective prefix) — more at ABIDE] **1 :** original **:** primitive <*Ur*-form> **2 :** original version of <*Ur*-Hamlet>
ura·cil \ˈyu̇r-ə-ˌsil, -səl\ *n* [ISV [1]*ur-* + *ac*etic + *-il* (substance relating to)] **:** a pyrimidine base $C_4H_4N_2O_2$ that is one of the four bases coding genetic information in the polynucleotide chain of RNA — compare ADENINE, CYTOSINE, GUANINE, THYMINE
urae·mia *var of* UREMIA
urae·us \yu̇-ˈrē-əs\ *n, pl* **uraei** \-ˈrē-ˌī\ [NL, fr. LGk *ouraios,* a snake] **:** a representation of the sacred asp (*Naja haje*) on the headdress of ancient Egyptian rulers serving as a symbol of sovereignty
Ural–Al·ta·ic \ˌyu̇r-ə-lal-ˈtā-ik\ *n* **1 :** a postulated language group comprising the Uralic and Altaic languages **2 :** a language type showing agglutination and vowel harmony and occurring esp. in languages of Eurasia — **Ural–Altaic** *adj*
Ura·li·an \yu̇-ˈrā-lē-ən, -ˈral-ē-\ *adj* **1 :** of or relating to the Ural mountains **2 :** URALIC

[1]**Ural·ic** \yu̇-ˈral-ik\ *adj* **:** of, relating to, or constituting the Finno-Ugric and Samoyed languages

[2]**Uralic** *n* **:** a language family comprising the Finno-Ugric and Samoyed languages

ural·ite \ˈyu̇r-ə-ˌlīt\ *n* [G *uralit,* fr. *Ural* mountains] **:** a usu. fibrous and dark green amphibole resulting from alteration of pyroxene — **ural·it·ic** \ˌyu̇r-ə-ˈlit-ik\ *adj*

[1]**uran-** *or* **urano-** *comb form* [L, fr. Gk *ouran-, ourano-,* fr. *ouranos*] **:** sky **:** heaven <*urano*metry>

[2]**uran-** *or* **urano-** *comb form* [F, fr. NL *uranium*] **:** uranium <*uran*yl>

Ura·nia \yu̇-ˈrā-nē-ə, -nyə\ *n* [L, fr. Gk *Ourania*]**:** the Greek Muse of astronomy

ura·nic \yu̇-ˈran-ik, -ˈrā-nik\ *adj* [ISV] **:** of, relating to, or containing uranium esp. with a valence higher than in uranous compounds

ura·nide \ˈyu̇r-ə-ˌnīd\ *n* **1 :** URANIUM **2 :** a transuranium element

ura·ni·nite \yu̇-ˈrā-nə-ˌnīt\ *n* [G *uranin* uraninite (fr. NL *uranium*) + E *-ite*] **:** a mineral that is basically a black octahedral or cubic oxide UO_2 of uranium containing thorium, the cerium and yttrium metals, and lead, that often when heated yields a gas consisting chiefly of helium, and that is the chief ore of uranium

ura·ni·um \yu̇-ˈrā-nē-əm\ *n, often attrib* [NL, fr. *Uranus*] **:** a silvery heavy radioactive polyvalent metallic element that is found esp. in pitchblende and uraninite and exists naturally as a mixture of three isotopes of mass number 234, 235, and 238 in the proportions of 0.006 percent, 0.71 percent, and 99.28 percent respectively — see ELEMENT table

uranium hexa·flu·o·ride \-ˌhek-sə-ˈflu̇(-ə)r-ˌīd\ *n* **:** a volatile compound UF_6 of uranium and fluorine that is used in one major process of isolating uranium 235

uranium trioxide *n* **:** a brilliant orange compound UO_3 that is formed in the course of refining uranium and that has been used as a coloring agent for ceramic wares

uranium 238 *n* **:** an isotope of uranium of mass number 238 that absorbs fast neutrons to form a uranium isotope of mass number 239 which then decays through neptunium to form plutonium of mass number 239

uranium 235 *n* **:** a light isotope of uranium of mass number 235 that is physically separable from natural uranium, that when bombarded with slow neutrons undergoes rapid fission into smaller atoms with the release of neutrons and atomic energy, and that is used in power plants and atom bombs

ura·nog·ra·phy \ˌyu̇r-ə-ˈnäg-rə-fē\ *n* [Gk *ouranographia* description of the heavens, fr. *ouran-* uran- + *-graphia* -graphy] **1 :** a science dealing with the description of the heavens and the celestial bodies **2 :** the construction of celestial representations (as maps) — **ura·no·graph·ic** \ˌyu̇r-ə-nō-ˈgraf-ik\ *or* **ura·no·graph·i·cal** \-i-kəl\ *adj*

ura·nol·o·gy \ˌyu̇r-ə-ˈnäl-ə-jē\ *n* **1 :** ASTRONOMY **2 :** a treatise on the heavens and the celestial bodies — **ura·no·log·i·cal** \ˌyu̇r-ən-ᵊl-ˈäj-i-kəl\ *adj*

ura·nom·e·try \ˌyu̇r-ə-ˈnäm-ə-trē\ *n* [NL *uranometria,* fr. *uran-* + *-metria* -metry] **1 :** a chart or catalog of celestial bodies and esp. of visible fixed stars **2 :** the measurement of the heavens

ura·nous \yu̇-ˈrā-nəs, ˈyu̇r-ə-\ *adj* **:** of, relating to, or containing uranium esp. with a lower valence than in uranic compounds

Ura·nus \ˈyu̇r-ə-nəs, yu̇-ˈrā-\ *n* [LL, fr. Gk *Ouranos*] **1 :** the sky personified as a god in Greek mythology **2 :** the planet seventh in order from the sun — see PLANET table

ura·nyl \ˈyu̇r-ə-ˌnil, yu̇-ˈrān-ᵊl\ *n* [ISV] **:** a bivalent radical UO_2 formed by uranium trioxide in acid solution

urate \ˈyu̇(ə)r-ˌāt\ *n* [F, fr. *urique* uric, fr. E *uric*] **:** a salt of uric acid — **urat·ic** \yu̇-ˈrat-ik\ *adj*

ur·ban \ˈər-bən\ *adj* [L *urbanus,* fr. *urbs* city] **:** of, relating to, characteristic of, or constituting a city

ur·bane \ˌər-ˈbān\ *adj* [L *urbanus* urban, urbane] **:** notably polite or finished in manner **:** POLISHED ***syn*** see SUAVE ***ant*** rude, clownish, bucolic — **ur·bane·ly** *adv*

ur·ban·ism \ˈər-bə-ˌniz-əm\ *n* **1 :** the characteristic way of life of city dwellers **2 :** the study of the physical needs of urban societies **3 :** URBANIZATION

ur·ban·ist \ˈər-bə-nəst\ *n* **:** a specialist in city planning — **ur·ban·is·tic** \ˌər-bə-ˈnis-tik\ *adj* — **ur·ban·is·ti·cal·ly** \-ti-k(ə-)lē\ *adv*

ur·ban·ite \ˈər-bə-ˌnīt\ *n* **:** one living in a city

ur·ban·i·ty \ˌər-ˈban-ət-ē\ *n, pl* **-ties 1 :** the quality or state of being urbane **2** *pl* **:** urbane acts or conduct

ur·ban·iza·tion \ˌər-bə-nə-ˈzā-shən\ *n* **:** the quality or state of being or becoming urbanized

ur·ban·ize \ˈər-bə-ˌnīz\ *vt* **-ized; -iz·ing 1 :** to cause to take on urban characteristics <*urbanized* areas> **2 :** to impart an urban way of life to <~ migrants from rural areas>

ur·ban·ol·o·gy \ˌər-bə-ˈnäl-ə-jē\ *n* **:** a study dealing with specialized problems of cities (as planning, education, sociology, and politics) — **ur·ban·ol·o·gist** \-jəst\ *n*

urban renewal *n* **:** a construction program to replace or restore substandard buildings in an urban area

urban sprawl *n* **:** the spreading of urban developments (as houses and shopping centers) on undeveloped land near a city

ur·bi·cul·ture \ˈər-bə-ˌkəl-chər\ *n* [L *urb-, urbs* city + E *-i-* + *culture*] **:** practices and problems peculiar to cities or to urban life

ur·ce·o·late \ˌər-ˈsē-ə-lət, ˈər-sē-ə-ˌlāt\ *adj* [NL *urceolatus,* fr. L *urceolus,* dim. of *urceus* pitcher] **:** shaped like an urn <the ~ corolla of a blueberry>

ur·chin \ˈər-chən\ *n* [ME, fr. MF *herichon,* fr. L *ericius,* fr. *er;* akin to Gk *chēr* hedgehog, L *horrēre* to bristle, tremble — more at HORROR] **1 :** HEDGEHOG **2 :** a mischievous youngster **:** SCAMP **3 :** SEA URCHIN

urd \ˈu̇(ə)rd, ˈərd\ *n* [Hindi] **:** an annual bean (*Phaseolus mungo*) widely grown in warm regions for its edible blackish seed, for green manure, or for forage

Ur·du \ˈu̇(ə)r-(ˌ)dü, ˈər-\ *n* [Hindi *urdū-zabān,* lit., camp language] **:** an Indic language that is an official literary language of Pakistan and is widely used in India

-ure *n suffix* [ME, fr. OF, fr. L *-ura*] **1 :** act **:** process <expos*ure*> **2 :** office **:** function; *also* **:** body performing (such) a function <legislat*ure*>

urea \yu̇-ˈrē-ə\ *n* [NL, fr. F *urée,* fr. *urine*] **:** a soluble weakly basic nitrogenous compound $CO(NH_2)_2$ that is the chief solid component of mammalian urine and an end product of protein decomposition, is synthesized from carbon dioxide and ammonia, and is used esp. in synthesis (as of resins and plastics) and in fertilizers and animal rations

urea–formaldehyde resin *n* **:** a thermosetting synthetic resin made by condensing urea with formaldehyde

ure·ase \ˈyu̇r-ē-ˌās, -ˌāz\ *n* **:** an enzyme that promotes the hydrolysis of urea

ure·din·i·um \ˌyu̇r-ə-ˈdin-ē-əm\ *n, pl* **-ia** \-ē-ə\ [NL, fr. L *uredin-, uredo* burning, blight, fr. *urere* to burn — more at EMBER] **:** a crowded usu. brownish mass of hyphae and spores of a rust fungus forming pustules that rupture the host's cuticle — **ure·din·i·al** \-ē-əl\ *adj*

ure·dio·spore \yu̇-ˈrēd-ē-ə-ˌspō(ə)r, -ˌspȯ(ə)r\ *or* **ure·do·spore** \-ˈrēd-ə-\ *n* [NL *uredium* + E *-o-* + *spore*] **:** one of the thin-walled spores that are produced in repeated crops by the uredinial hyphae of rust fungi, spread the fungus vegetatively, and follow the aecial spores

ure·di·um \yu̇-ˈrēd-ē-əm\ *n, pl* **-dia** \-ē-ə\ [NL, fr. *uredo*] **:** UREDINIUM

ure·do·stage \yu̇-ˈrēd-ō-ˌstāj\ *n* **:** the uredinial stage of a rust

ure·ide \ˈyu̇r-ē-ˌīd\ *n* **:** a cyclic or acyclic acyl derivative of urea

ure·mia \yu̇-ˈrē-mē-ə\ *n* [NL] **:** accumulation in the blood usu. in severe kidney disease of constituents normally eliminated in the urine producing a severe toxic condition — **ure·mic** \-mik\ *adj*

ureo·tel·ic \yu̇-ˌrē-ə-ˈtel-ik, ˌyu̇r-ē-ō-\ *adj* [*urea* + *-o-* + *tel-* + *-ic;* fr. the fact that urea is the end product]**:** excreting nitrogen mostly in the form of urea <~ mammals> — **ureo·te·lism** \-ˈtel-ˌiz-əm, ˌyu̇r-ē-ˈät-ᵊl-ˌiz-əm\ *n*

ure·ter \ˈyu̇r-ət-ər\ *n* [NL, fr. Gk *ourētēr,* fr. *ourein* to urinate — more at URINE] **:** a duct that carries away the urine from a kidney to the bladder or cloaca — **ure·ter·al** \yu̇-ˈrēt-ə-rəl\ *or* **ure·ter·ic** \ˌyu̇r-ə-ˈter-ik\ *adj*

ure·thane \ˈyu̇r-ə-ˌthān\ *or* **ure·than** \-ˌthan\ *n* [F *uréthane,* fr. *ur-* + *éth-* eth- + *-ane*] **1 a :** a crystalline compound $C_3H_7NO_2$ that is the ethyl ester of carbamic acid and is used esp. as a solvent and medicinally as an antineoplastic agent **b :** an ester of carbamic acid other than the ethyl ester **2 :** POLYURETHANE

urethr- *or* **urethro-** *comb form* [NL, fr. LL *urethra*] **:** urethra <*urethr*itis> <*urethro*scope>

ure·thra \yu̇-ˈrē-thrə\ *n, pl* **-thras** *or* **-thrae** \-(ˌ)thrē\ [LL, fr. Gk *ourēthra,* fr. *ourein* to urinate] **:** the canal that in most mammals carries off the urine from the bladder and in the male serves also as a genital duct — **ure·thral** \-thrəl\ *adj*

ure·thri·tis \ˌyu̇r-i-ˈthrīt-əs\ *n* [NL] **:** inflammation of the urethra

ure·thro·scope \yu̇-ˈrē-thrə-ˌskōp\ *n* [ISV] **:** an instrument for viewing the interior of the urethra

[1]**urge** \ˈərj\ *vb* **urged; urg·ing** [L *urgēre* — more at WREAK] *vt* **1 :** to present, advocate, or demand earnestly or pressingly <his conviction was upheld on a theory never *urged* at his . . . trial —Leon Friedman> **2 :** to undertake the accomplishment of with energy, swiftness, or enthusiasm <~ the attack> **3 a :** SOLICIT, ENTREAT **b :** to serve as a motive or reason for **4 :** to force or impel in an indicated direction or into motion or greater speed <the dog *urged* the sheep toward the gate> **5 :** STIMULATE, PROVOKE ~ *vi* **:** to declare, advance, or press earnestly a statement, argument, charge, or claim — **urg·er** *n*

[2]**urge** *n* **1 :** the act or process of urging **2 :** a force or impulse that urges; *esp* **:** a continuing impulse toward an activity or goal

ur·gen·cy \ˈər-jən-sē\ *n, pl* **-cies 1 :** the quality or state of being urgent **:** INSISTENCE **2 :** a force or impulse that impels or constrains **:** URGE

ur·gent \ˈər-jənt\ *adj* [ME, fr. MF, fr. L *urgent-, urgens,* prp. of *urgēre*] **1 a :** calling for immediate attention **:** PRESSING <~ appeals> **b :** conveying a sense of urgency **2 :** urging insistently **:** IMPORTUNATE — **ur·gent·ly** *adv*

-ur·gy \(ˌ)ər-jē\ *n comb form* [NL *-urgia,* fr. Gk *-ourgia,* fr. *-ourgos* working, fr. *-o-* + *ergon* work — more at WORK]**:** technique or art of dealing or working with (such) a product, matter, or tool <chem*urgy*>

-uria \(y)u̇r-ē-ə\ *n comb form* [NL, fr. Gk *-ouria,* fr. *ouron* urine — more at URINE] **1 :** presence of (a specified substance) in urine <albumin*uria*> **2 :** condition of having (such) urine <poly*uria*>; *esp* **:** abnormal or diseased condition marked by the presence of (a specified substance) <py*uria*>

uric \ˈyu̇(ə)r-ik\ *adj* **:** of, relating to, or found in urine

uric acid *n* **:** a white odorless and tasteless nearly insoluble diacid $C_5H_4N_4O_3$ that is present in small quantity in mammalian urine, is present abundantly in the form of urates in the excreta of most lower vertebrates and in vertebrates as the chief nitrogenous waste, and occurs pathologically in renal calculi and the tophi of gout

uri·co·su·ric \ˌyu̇r-i-kə-ˈs(h)u̇r-ik\ *adj* [irreg. fr. *uric*] **:** relating to or promoting the excretion of uric acid in the urine

uri·co·tel·ic \ˌyu̇r-i-kō-ˈtel-ik\ *adj* [*uric* + *-o-* + *tel-* + *-ic;* fr. the fact that uric acid is the end product] **:** excreting nitrogen mostly in the form of uric acid <birds are typical ~ animals> — **uri·co·tel·ism** \-ˈtel-ˌiz-əm, -ˈkät-ᵊl-ˌiz-əm\ *n*

uri·dine \ˈyu̇r-ə-ˌdēn\ *n* [ISV [1]*ur-* + *-idine*] **:** a crystalline nucleoside $C_9H_{12}N_2O_6$ that is derived by hydrolysis from nucleic acids and in the form of phosphate derivatives and is important in carbohydrate metabolism

Uri·el \ˈyu̇r-ē-əl\ *n* [Heb *Ūrīʼēl*] **:** one of the four archangels named in Hebrew tradition

Urim and Thum·mim \ˌ(y)u̇r-ə-mən-ˈthəm-əm, ˌu̇(ə)r-ˌē-mən-ˈtüm-ˌēm\ *n pl* [part trans. of Heb *ūrīm wĕthummīm*] **:** sacred lots used in early times by the Hebrews

urin- *or* **urino-** *comb form* [ME, fr. OF, fr. L, fr. *urina* urine] **:** [1]UR- <*urino*genital> <*urin*ary>

uri·nal \ˈyu̇r-ən-ᵊl\ *n* [ME, fr. OF, fr. LL, fr. L *urina*] **1 :** a vessel for receiving urine **2 :** a building or enclosure with facilities for urinating; *also* **:** a fixture used for urinating

uri·nal·y·sis \ˌyu̇r-ə-ˈnal-ə-səs\ *n* [NL, irreg. fr. *urin-* + *analysis*] **:** chemical analysis of urine

uri·nary \ˈyu̇r-ə-ˌner-ē\ *adj* **1 :** relating to, occurring in, or constituting the organs concerned with the formation and discharge of urine **2 :** of, relating to, or for urine **3 :** excreted as or in urine

urinary bladder *n* **:** a membranous sac in many vertebrates that serves for the temporary retention of urine and discharges by the urethra

uri·nate \ˈyu̇r-ə-ˌnāt\ *vi* **-nat·ed; -nat·ing :** to discharge urine **:** MICTURATE — **uri·na·tion** \ˌyu̇r-ə-ˈnā-shən\ *n*

urine \ˈyu̇r-ən\ *n* [ME, fr. MF, fr. L *urina;* akin to Gk *ouron* urine, *ourein* to urinate, OE *wæter* water] **:** waste material that is secreted by the kidney in vertebrates, is rich in end products of protein metabolism together with salts and pigments, and forms a clear amber and usu. slightly acid fluid in mammals but is semisolid in birds and reptiles — **urin·ous** \ˈyu̇r-ə-nəs\ *adj*

uri·no·gen·i·tal \ˌyu̇r-ə-nō-ˈjen-ə-tᵊl\ *adj* **:** UROGENITAL

uri·nom·e·ter \ˌyu̇r-ə-ˈnäm-ət-ər\ *n* [ISV] **:** a small hydrometer for determining the specific gravity of urine

urn \ˈərn\ *n* [ME *urne,* fr. L *urna*] **1 :** a vessel that is typically an ornamental vase on a pedestal and that is used for various purposes (as preserving the ashes of the dead after cremation) **2 :** a closed vessel usu. with a spigot for serving a hot beverage <a coffee ~>

uro- — see UR-

uro·ca·nic acid \ˌyu̇r-ə-ˌkā-nik-, -ˈkan-ik-\ *n* [[1]*ur-* + *canine* + *-ic;* fr. its being first obtained from the urine of a dog] **:** a crystalline acid $C_6H_6N_2O_2$ that is normally present in human skin and is held to act as a screening agent for ultraviolet radiation

uro·chord \ˈyu̇r-ə-ˌkȯ(ə)rd\ *n* [[2]*ur-* + NL *chorda* notochord, fr. L, cord] **1 :** the notochord of a tunicate which is typically restricted to the tail region of the larva **2** [NL *Urochorda,* group name, fr. *ur-* + *chorda* notochord] **:** TUNICATE — **uro·chor·dal** \ˌyu̇r-ə-ˈkȯrd-ᵊl\ *adj*

uro·chor·date \ˌyu̇r-ə-ˈkȯrd-ət, -ˌāt\ *n* [NL *Urochordata,* former group name, fr. [2]*ur-* + *chordatus* having a notochord, fr. *chorda* notochord] **:** TUNICATE — **urochordate** *adj*

uro·chrome \ˈyu̇r-ə-ˌkrōm\ *n* **:** a yellow pigment to which the color of normal urine is principally due

uro·dele \ˈyu̇r-ə-ˌdēl\ *n* [F *urodèle,* deriv. of Gk *oura* tail + *dēlos* evident, showing — more at SQUIRREL] **:** any of an order (Caudata) of amphibians (as newts) that have a tail throughout life — **urodele** *adj*

uro·gen·i·tal \ˌyu̇r-ō-ˈjen-ə-tᵊl\ *adj* [ISV] **:** of, relating to, or being the organs or functions of excretion and reproduction

uro·ki·nase \ˌyu̇r-ō-ˈkī-ˌnās, -ˌnāz\ *n* **:** an enzyme similar to streptokinase that is found in human urine and is used to dissolve blood clots (as in the heart)

urol *abbr* urological; urology

uro·lith \ˈyu̇r-ə-ˌlith\ n [ISV] **:** a calculus in the urinary tract

uro·lith·ia·sis \ˌyu̇r-ə-lith-ˈī-ə-səs\ *n* [NL, fr. ISV *urolith*] **:** a condition that is characterized by the formation or presence of calculi in the urinary tract

uro·log·ic \ˌyu̇r-ə-ˈläj-ik\ *or* **uro·log·i·cal** \-i-kəl\ *adj* **:** of or relating to the urinary tract or to urology

urol·o·gist \yu̇-ˈräl-ə-jəst\ *n* **:** a physician who specializes in urology

urol·o·gy \-jē\ *n* **:** a branch of medicine dealing with the urinary or urogenital tract

-u·ron·ic \(y)u̇-ˈrän-ik\ *adj suffix* [Gk *ouron* urine] **:** connected with urine — in names of certain aldehyde-acids derived from sugars or compounds of such acids <hyal*uronic*>

uron·ic acid \yu̇-ˌrän-ik-\ *n* **:** any of a class of acidic compounds of the general formula $HOOC(CHOH)_nCHO$ that contain both carboxylic and aldehydic groups, are oxidation products of sugars, and occur combined in many polysaccharides and in urine

uro·pod \ˈyu̇r-ə-ˌpäd\ *n* [ISV [2]*ur-* + Gk *pod-, pous* foot — more at FOOT] **:** either of the flattened lateral appendages of the last abdominal segment of a crustacean; *broadly* **:** an abdominal appendage of a crustacean

[1]**uro·py·gi·al** \ˌyu̇r-ə-ˈpī-jē-əl\ *adj* **:** of or relating to the uropygium

[2]**uropygial** *n* **:** a tail feather

uropygial gland *n* **:** a large gland that occurs in most birds, opens dorsally at the base of the tail feathers, and usu. secretes an oily fluid which the bird uses in preening its feathers — called also *oil gland*

uro·py·gi·um \ˌyu̇r-ə-ˈpī-jē-əm\ *n* [NL, fr. Gk *ouropygion,* fr. *ouro-* [2]ur- + *pygē* rump — more at STEATOPYGIA] **:** the fleshy and bony prominence at the posterior extremity of a bird's body that supports the tail feathers

uro·style \ˈyu̇r-ə-ˌstīl\ *n* [ISV [2]*ur-* + Gk *stylos* pillar — more at STEER] **:** a long unsegmented bone that represents a number of fused vertebrae and forms the posterior part of the vertebral column of frogs and toads

-urous \ˈ(y)u̇r-əs\ *adj comb form* [NL *-urus,* fr. Gk *-ouros,* fr. *oura* tail — more at SQUIRREL] **:** -tailed <macr*urous*>

Ur·sa Ma·jor \ˌər-sə-ˈmā-jər\ *n* [L (gen. *Ursae Majoris*), lit., greater bear] **:** a constellation that is the most conspicuous of the northern constellations, is situated near the north pole of the heavens, and contains the stars forming the Big Dipper two of which are in a line indicating the direction of the North Star — called also *Great Bear*

Ursa Mi·nor \-ˈmī-nər\ *n* [L (gen. *Ursae Minoris*), lit., lesser bear] **:** a constellation that includes the north pole of the heavens and the stars which form the Little Dipper with the North Star at the tip of the handle — called also *Little Bear*

ur·sine \ˈər-ˌsīn\ *adj* [L *ursinus,* fr. *ursus* bear — more at ARCTIC] **:** of, relating to, or resembling a bear or the bear family (Ursidae)

Ur·spra·che \ˈu̇(ə)r-ˌshpräk-ə\ *n* [G, fr. *Ur-* Ur- + *sprache* language] **:** a parent language; *esp* **:** one reconstructed from the evidence of later languages

Ur·su·line \ˈər-sə-lən, -ˌlīn, -ˌlēn\ *n* [NL *Ursulina,* fr. *Ursula* St. Ursula, legendary Christian martyr] **:** a member of any of several Roman Catholic teaching orders of nuns; *esp* **:** a member of a teaching order founded by St. Angela Merici in Brescia, Italy, in 1535

ur·ti·car·ia \ˌərt-ə-ˈkar-ē-ə, -ˈker-\ *n* [NL, fr. L *urtica* nettle] **:** an allergic disorder marked by raised edematous patches of skin or mucous membrane and usu. intense itching and caused by contact with a specific precipitating factor either externally or internally (as by a food, drug, or inhalant) — **ur·ti·car·i·al** \-ē-əl\ *adj*

ur·ti·cate \ˈərt-ə-ˌkāt\ *vb* **-cat·ed; -cat·ing** *vi* [ML *urticatus,* pp. of *urticare* to sting, fr. L *urtica*] *vi* **:** to produce wheals or itching; *esp* **:** to induce urticaria — **ur·ti·ca·tion** \ˌərt-ə-ˈkā-shən\ *n*

urus \ˈyu̇r-əs\ *n* [L, of Gmc origin; akin to OHG *ūro* urus — more at AUROCHS] **:** an extinct large long-horned wild ox (*Bos primigenius*) of the German forests held to be a wild ancestor of domestic cattle

uru·shi·ol \(y)u̇-ˈrü-shē-ˌȯl, -ˌōl\ *n* [ISV, fr. Jap *urushi* lacquer] **:** an oily toxic irritant principle present in poison ivy and some related plants (genus *Rhus*) and in oriental lacquers derived from such plants that consists of one or more phenolic compounds with unsaturated side chains of 15 carbon atoms

us \(ˈ)əs\ *pron* [ME, fr. OE *ūs;* akin to OHG *uns* us, L *nos*] *objective case of* WE

US *abbr* **1** [L *ubi supra*] where above mentioned **2** United States **3** [L *ut supra*] as above

USA *abbr* **1** United States Army **2** United States of America

us·able *also* **use·able** \ˈyü-zə-bəl\ *adj* **1 :** capable of being used **2 :** convenient and practicable for use — **us·abil·i·ty** \ˌyü-zə-ˈbil-ət-ē\ *n* — **us·able·ness** \ˈyü-zə-bəl-nəs\ *n* — **us·ably** \-blē\ *adv*

USAC *abbr* United States Auto Club

USAF *abbr* United States Air Force

us·age \ˈyü-sij, -zij\ *n* **1 a :** firmly established and generally accepted practice or procedure **b :** a uniform certain reasonable lawful practice existing in a particular locality or occupation and binding persons entering into transactions chiefly on the basis of presumed familiarity **c :** the way in which words and phrases are actually used (as in a particular form or sense) in a language community **2 a :** the action, amount, or mode of using <parts subject to rough ~> **b :** manner of treating <suffered ill ~ at the hands of his captors> ***syn*** see HABIT

us·ance \ˈyüz-ᵊn(t)s\ *n* **1 :** USAGE 1a **2 :** USE, EMPLOYMENT **3 a** *obs* **:** USURY **b :** INTEREST **4 :** the time allowed by custom for payment of a bill of exchange in foreign commerce

USCF *abbr* United States Chess Federation

USCG *abbr* United States Coast Guard

USDA *abbr* United States Department of Agriculture

[1]**use** \ˈyüs\ *n* [ME *us,* fr. OF, fr. L *usus,* fr. *usus,* pp. of *uti* to use] **1 a :** the act or practice of employing something **:** EMPLOYMENT, APPLICATION <he made good ~ of his spare time> **b :** the fact or state of being used <a dish in daily ~> **c :** a method or manner of employing or applying something <gained practice in the ~ of his camera> **2 a** (1) **:** habitual or customary usage (2) **:** an individual habit or group custom **b :** a liturgical form or observance; *esp* **:** a liturgy having modifications peculiar to a local church or religious order **3 a :** the privilege or benefit of using something <gave him the ~ of her car> **b :** the ability or power to use something (as a limb or faculty) **c :** the legal enjoyment of property that consists in its employment, occupation, exercise, or practice <she had the ~ of the estate for life> **4 a :** a particular service or end <put learning to practical ~> **b :** the quality of being suitable for employment <saving things that might be of ~> **c :** the occasion or need to employ <took only what he had ~ for> **5 a :** the benefit in law of one or more persons; *specif* **:** the benefit or profit of property established in one other than the legal possessor **b :** a legal arrangement by which such benefits and profits are so established **6 :** a favorable attitude **:** LIKING <had no ~ for modern art>

***syn* 1** USE, USEFULNESS, UTILITY *shared meaning element* **:** capacity for serving an end or purpose **2** see HABIT

[2]**use** \ˈyüz\ *vb* **used** \ˈyüzd, *in the phrase "used to" usually* ˈyüs(t)\; **us·ing** \ˈyü-ziŋ\ *vt* **1 :** ACCUSTOM, HABITUATE **2 :** to put into action or service **:** avail oneself of **:** EMPLOY **3 :** to consume or take (as liquor or drugs) regularly **4 :** to carry out a purpose or action by means of **:** UTILIZE **5 :** to expend or consume by putting to use **6 :** to behave toward **:** act with regard to **:** TREAT <*used* the prisoners cruelly> ~ *vi* — used in the past with *to* to indicate a former fact or state <claims winters *used* to be harder>

syn USE, EMPLOY, UTILIZE *shared meaning element* **:** to put into service *esp.* to attain an end

used \ˈyüzd, *in the phrase "used to" usually* ˈyüs(t)\ *adj* **1 :** employed in accomplishing something **2 :** that has endured use; *specif* **:** SECONDHAND <a ~ car> **3 :** ACCUSTOMED, HABITUATED

use·ful \ˈyüs-fəl\ *adj* **:** capable of being put to use **:** SERVICEABLE; *esp* **:** having utility — **use·ful·ly** \-fə-lē\ *adv*

use·ful·ness *n* **:** the quality of having utility and esp. practical worth or applicability ***syn*** see USE

use·less \ˈyü-sləs\ *adj* **:** having or being of no use: **a :** INEFFECTUAL **b :** not able to give service or aid **:** INEPT — **use·less·ly** *adv* — **use·less·ness** *n*

us·er \ˈyü-zər\ *n* **:** one that uses

USES *abbr* United States Employment Service

use up *vt* **1 :** to consume completely <*used up* his supplies> **2 :** to leave no capacity of force or use in : EXHAUST <land that has been *used up*>

1ush·er \ˈəsh-ər\ *n* [ME *ussher,* fr. MF *ussier,* fr. (assumed) VL *ustiarius* doorkeeper, fr. L *ostium, ustium* door, **mouth of** a river; akin to L *or-, os* mouth — more at ORAL] **1 a :** an officer or servant who has the care of the door of a court, hall, or chamber **b :** an officer who walks before a person of rank **c :** one who escorts persons to their seats (as in a theater) **2** *archaic* **:** an assistant teacher

2usher *vt* **ush·ered; ush·er·ing** \ˈəsh-(ə-)riŋ\ **1 :** to conduct to a place **2 :** to precede as an usher, forerunner, or harbinger **3 :** INAUGURATE, INTRODUCE — often used with *in* <~ in a new era>

ush·er·ette \ˌəsh-ə-ˈret\ *n* **:** a woman who escorts persons to their seats (as in a **theater**) **:** a female usher

USIA *abbr* United States Information Agency

USLTA *abbr* United States Lawn Tennis Association

USM *abbr* United States Mail

USMC *abbr* United States Marine Corps

USN *abbr* United States Navy

us·nea \ˈəs-nē-ə, ˈəz-\ *n* [NL, genus name, fr. Ar *ushnah* moss] **:** any of a genus (*Usnea*) of widely distributed lichens (as old-man's beard) that have a grayish or yellow pendulous freely branched thallus

USO *abbr* United Service Organizations

USP *abbr* United States Pharmacopoeia

USPS *abbr* United States Postal Service

us·que·baugh \ˈəs-kwi-ˌbȯ, -ˌbä\ *n* [IrGael *uisce beathadh*] *Irish & Scot* **:** WHISKEY

USS *abbr* United States ship

USSR *abbr* Union of Soviet Socialist Republics

usu *abbr* usual; usually

usu·al \ˈyüzh-(ə-)wəl, ˈyüzh-əl\ *adj* [LL *usualis,* fr. L *usus* use] **1 :** accordant with usage, custom, or habit **:** NORMAL **2 :** commonly or ordinarily used <followed his ~ route> **3 :** found in ordinary practice or in the ordinary course of events **:** ORDINARY — **usu·al·ly** \ˈyüzh-(ə-)wə-lē, ˈyüzh-(ə-)lē *rapid* ˈyüz-lē\ *adv* — **usu·al·ness** \ˈyüzh-(ə-)wəl-nəs, -əl-nəs\ *n*

syn USUAL, CUSTOMARY, HABITUAL, WONTED, ACCUSTOMED *shared meaning element* **:** familiar through frequent or regular repetition — **as usual :** in the accustomed or habitual way <*as usual* he was late>

usu·fruct \ˈyü-zə-ˌfrəkt, -sə-\ *n* [L *ususfructus,* fr. *usus et fructus* use and enjoyment] **1 :** the legal right of using and enjoying the fruits or profits of something belonging to another **2 :** the right to use or enjoy something

1usu·fruc·tu·ary \ˌyü-zə-ˈfrək-chə-ˌwer-ē, -sə-\ *n* **1 :** one having the usufruct of property **2 :** one having the use or enjoyment of something

2usufructuary *adj* **:** of, relating to, or having the character of a usufruct

usu·rer \ˈyü-zhər-ər, ˈyüzh-rər\ *n* **:** one that lends money esp. at an exorbitant rate

usu·ri·ous \yu̇-ˈzh(h)u̇r-ē-əs\ *adj* **1 :** practicing usury **2 :** involving usury **:** of the character of usury — **usu·ri·ous·ly** *adv* — **usu·ri·ous·ness** *n*

usurp \yu̇-ˈsərp *also* -ˈzərp\ *vb* [ME *usurpen,* fr. MF *usurper,* fr. L *usurpare,* lit., to take possession of by use, fr. *usu* (abl. of *usus* use) + *rapere* to seize — more at RAPID] *vt* **:** to seize and hold (as office, place, or powers) in possession by force or without right <~ a throne> ~ *vi* **:** to seize or exercise authority or possession wrongfully — **usur·pa·tion** \ˌyü-sər-ˈpā-shən *also* ˌyü-zər-\ *n* — **usurp·er** \yu̇-ˈsər-pər *also* -ˈzər-\ *n*

usu·ry \ˈyüzh-(ə-)rē\ *n, pl* **-ries** [ME, fr. ML *usuria,* alter. of L *usura,* fr. *usus,* pp. of *uti* to use] **1** *archaic* **:** INTEREST **2 :** the lending of money with an interest charge for its use **3 :** an unconscionable or exorbitant rate or amount of interest; *specif* **:** interest in excess of a legal rate charged to a borrower for the use of money

ut \ˈət, ˈüt, ˈu̇t\ *n* [ME, first note in the diatonic scale, fr. ML, fr. the syllable sung to this note in a medieval hymn to St. John the Baptist] **:** the musical tone *C* in the French fixed-do system replaced in solmization by *do*

UT *abbr* **1** Universal time **2** Utah

ut dict *abbr* [L *ut dictum*] as directed

Ute \ˈyüt\ *n, pl* **Ute** *or* **Utes** [Ute *Yuta*] **:** a member of an Amerindian people orig. ranging through Utah, Colorado, Arizona, and New Mexico

uten·sil \yu̇-ˈten(t)-səl, ˈyu-ˌ\ *n* [ME, vessels for domestic use, fr. MF *utensile,* fr. L *utensilia,* fr. neut. pl. of *utensilis* useful, fr. *uti* to use] **1 :** an implement, instrument, or vessel used in a household and esp. a kitchen **2 :** a useful tool or implement

uter- *or* **utero-** *for 2,* ˌyüt-ə-rō\ *comb form* [L *uterus*] **1 :** uterus <*uter*ectomy> **2 :** uterine and <*utero*placental>

uter·ine \ˈyüt-ə-ˌrīn, -rən\ *adj* [ME, fr. LL *uterinus,* fr. L *uterus*] **1 :** born of the same mother but by a different father **2 :** of, relating to, or affecting the uterus

uter·us \ˈyüt-ə-rəs, ˈyü-trəs\ *n, pl* **uteri** \ˈyüt-ə-ˌrī\ *also* **uter·us·es** [L] **1 :** an organ of the female mammal for containing and usu. for nourishing the young during development previous to birth — called also *womb* **2 :** a structure in some lower animals analogous to the uterus in which eggs or young develop

Uther \ˈyü-thər\ *n* **:** the father of Arthur in Arthurian legend

utile \ˈyüt-ᵊl, ˈyü-ˌtīl\ *adj* [MF, fr. L *utilis*] **:** USEFUL

1util·i·tar·i·an \(ˌ)yü-ˌtil-ə-ˈter-ē-ən\ *n* **:** an advocate or adherent of utilitarianism

2utilitarian *adj* **1 :** of or relating to or advocating utilitarianism **2 :** marked by utilitarian views or practices **3 a :** of, relating to, or aiming at utility **b :** exhibiting or preferring mere utility <spare ~ furnishings>

util·i·tar·i·an·ism \-ē-ə-ˌniz-əm\ *n* **1 :** a doctrine that the useful is the good and that the determining consideration of right conduct should be the usefulness of its consequences; *specif* **:** a theory that the aim of action should be the largest possible balance of pleasure over pain or the greatest happiness of the greatest number **2 :** utilitarian character, spirit, or quality

1util·i·ty \yü-ˈtil-ət-ē\ *n, pl* **-ties** [ME *utilite,* fr. MF *utilité,* fr. L *utilitat-, utilitas,* fr. *utilis* useful, fr. *uti* to use] **1 :** fitness for some purpose or worth to some end **2 :** something useful or designed for use **3 a :** PUBLIC UTILITY **b (1) :** a service (as light, power, or water) provided by a public utility **(2) :** equipment or a piece of equipment to provide such service or a comparable service *syn* see USE

2utility *adj* **1 :** capable of serving as a substitute in various roles or positions <a ~ infielder> **2 a :** kept for the production of a useful product rather than for show or as pets <~ livestock> **b :** being of a usable but inferior grade <~ beef> **3 :** serving primarily for utility rather than beauty **:** UTILITARIAN **4 :** designed or adapted for general use <a ~ knife>

uti·lize \ˈyüt-ᵊl-ˌīz\ *vt* **-lized; -liz·ing** [F *utiliser,* fr. *utile*] **:** to make use of **:** turn to practical use or account <~ wasted skills> *syn* see USE — **uti·liz·able** \-ˌī-zə-bəl\ *adj* — **uti·li·za·tion** \ˌyüt-ᵊl-ə-ˈzā-shən\ *n* — **uti·liz·er** \ˈyüt-ᵊl-ˌī-zər\ *n*

1ut·most \ˈət-ˌmōst, *esp South* -məst\ *adj* [ME, alter. of *utmest,* fr. OE *ūtmest,* superl. adj., fr. *ūt* out, adv. — more at OUT] **1 :** situated at the farthest or most distant point **:** EXTREME <the ~ point of the earth —John Hunt> **2 :** of the greatest or highest degree, quantity, number, or amount <a matter of ~ concern>

2utmost *n* **1 :** the most possible **:** the extreme limit **:** the highest attainable point or degree <the ~ in reliability> **2 :** the highest, greatest, or best of one's abilities, powers, and resources <did his ~ to help>

Uto–Az·tec·an \ˌyüt-ō-ˈaz-ˌtek-ən\ *n* [*Ute* + *-o-* + *Aztec*] **:** a language phylum comprising the Nahuatlan, Taracahitian, Piman, and Shoshonean families — **Uto–Aztecan** *adj*

uto·pia \yu̇-ˈtō-pē-ə\ *n* [*Utopia,* imaginary and ideal country in *Utopia* (1516) by Sir Thomas More, fr. Gk *ou* not, no + *topos* place] **1 :** an imaginary and indefinitely remote place **2** *often cap* **:** a place of ideal perfection esp. in laws, government, and social conditions **3 :** an impractical scheme for social improvement

1uto·pi·an \-pē-ən\ *adj, often cap* **1 :** of, relating to, or having the characteristics of a utopia; *specif* **:** having impossibly ideal conditions esp. of social organization **2 :** proposing or advocating impractically ideal social and political schemes <~ idealists> **3 :** impossibly ideal **:** VISIONARY <recognised the ~ nature of his hopes —C. S. Kilby> **4 :** believing in, advocating, or having the characteristics of utopian socialism <~ doctrines> <~ novels>

2utopian *n* **1 :** one that believes in the perfectibility of human society **2 :** one that proposes or advocates utopian schemes

uto·pi·an·ism \-pē-ə-ˌniz-əm\ *n* **1 :** a utopian idea or theory **2** *often cap* **:** the body of ideas, views, or aims of a utopian

utopian socialism *n* **:** socialism based on a belief that social ownership of the means of production can be achieved by voluntary and peaceful surrender of their holdings by propertied groups — **utopian socialist** *n*

uto·pism \ˈyüt-ə-ˌpiz-əm, yu̇-ˈtō-\ *n* **:** UTOPIANISM 2 — **uto·pist** \yu̇-ˈtō-pəst\ *n* — **uto·pis·tic** \ˌyüt-ə-ˈpis-tik, yu̇-ˌtō-\ *adj*

utri·cle \ˈyü-tri-kəl\ *n* [L *utriculus,* dim. of *uter* leather bag] **:** any of various small pouches or saccate parts of an animal or plant body: as **a :** the part of the membranous labyrinth of the ear into which the semicircular canals open **b :** a small one-celled usu. indehiscent one-seeded or few-seeded achene with thin membranous pericarp

utric·u·lar \yu̇-ˈtrik-yə-lər\ *adj* **:** of, relating to, resembling, or containing a utricle

utric·u·lar·ia \yu̇-ˌtrik-yə-ˈlar-ē-ə, -ˈler-\ *n* [NL, genus name, fr. L *utriculus*] **:** BLADDERWORT

utric·u·lus \yu̇-ˈtrik-yə-ləs\ *n* [L, small bag] **:** UTRICLE; *esp* **:** that of the ear

1ut·ter \ˈət-ər\ *adj* [ME, remote, fr. OE *ūtera* outer, compar. adj. fr. *ūt* out, adv. — more at OUT] **:** ABSOLUTE, TOTAL <~ darkness> <~ strangers> — **ut·ter·ly** *adv*

2utter *vt* [ME *uttren,* fr. *utter* outside, adv., fr. OE *ūtor,* compar. of *ūt* out] **1** *obs* **:** to offer for sale **2 a :** to send forth as a sound **b :** to give utterance to **:** PRONOUNCE, SPEAK **c :** to give public expression to **:** express in words **3 :** to put (as currency) into circulation; *specif* **:** to circulate (as a counterfeit note) as if legal or genuine **4 :** to put forth or out **:** DISCHARGE *syn* see EXPRESS — **ut·ter·able** \ˈət-ə-rə-bəl\ *adj* — **ut·ter·er** \ˈət-ər-ər\ *n*

1ut·ter·ance \ˈət-ə-rən(t)s, ˈə-trən(t)s\ *n* [ME *uttraunce,* modif. of MF *outrance*] **:** the last extremity **:** BITTER END

2ut·ter·ance \ ˈət-ə-rən(t)s *also* ˈə-trən(t)s\ *n* **1 :** something uttered; *esp* **:** an oral or written statement **:** a stated or published expression **2 :** vocal expression **:** SPEECH **3 :** power, style, or manner of speaking

1ut·ter·most \ˈət-ər-ˌmōst\ *adj* [ME, alter. of *uttermest,* fr. 1*utter* + *-mest* (as in *utmest* utmost)] **1 :** OUTERMOST **2 :** EXTREME, UTMOST

2uttermost *n* **:** UTMOST <to the ~ of our capacity —H. S. Truman>

UV *abbr* ultraviolet

uva·rov·ite \(y)ü-ˈvär-ə-ˌvīt\ *n* [G *uwarowit,* fr. Count Sergei S. *Uvarov* †1855 Russ statesman] **:** an emerald green calcium-chromium garnet $Ca_3Cr_2(SiO_4)_3$

uvea \ˈyü-vē-ə\ *n* [ML, fr. L *uva* grape] **:** the posterior pigmented layer of the iris; *also* **:** the iris and ciliary body together with the choroid coat — **uve·al** \-vē-əl\ *adj*

uve·itis \ˌyü-vē-ˈīt-əs\ *n* [NL] **:** inflammation of the uvea of the eye

---

ə abut	ᵊ kitten	ər further	a back	ā bake	ä cot, cart
au̇ out	ch chin	e less	ē easy	g gift	i trip	ī life
j joke	ŋ sing	ō flow	ȯ flaw	ȯi coin	th thin	t͟h this
ü loot	u̇ foot	y yet	yü few	yu̇ furious	zh vision

uvu·la \'yü-vyə-lə\ *n, pl* **-las** *or* **-lae** \-ˌlē, -ˌlī\ [ML, dim. of L *uva* grape, uvula; akin to OE *īw* yew] **:** the pendent fleshy lobe in the middle of the posterior border of the soft palate

uvu·lar \-lər\ *adj* **1 :** of or relating to the uvula <~ glands> **2 :** produced with the aid of the uvula — **uvu·lar·ly** *adv*

UW *abbr* underwriter

ux *abbr* [L *uxor*] wife

UXB *abbr* unexploded bomb

ux·o·ri·al \ˌək-'sōr-ē-əl, -'sȯr-, ˌəg-'zōr-, -'zȯr-\ *adj* [L *uxorius*] **:** of, relating to, or characteristic of a wife

ux·or·i·cide \ˌək-'sȯr-ə-ˌsīd, -'sär-; ˌəg-'zȯr-, -'zär-\ *n* **1** [ML *uxoricidium,* fr. L *uxor* wife + *-i-* + *-cidium* -cide] **:** murder of a wife by her husband **2** [L *uxor* + E *-i-* + *-cide*] **:** a wife murderer

ux·o·ri·ous \ˌək-'sōr-ē-əs, -'sȯr-; ˌəg-'zōr-, -'zȯr-\ *adj* [L *uxorius* uxorious, uxorial, fr. *uxor* wife] **:** excessively fond of or submissive to a wife — **ux·o·ri·ous·ly** *adv* — **ux·o·ri·ous·ness** *n*

Uz·bek \'u̇z-ˌbek, 'əz-, u̇z-'\ *or* **Uz·beg** \-ˌbeg, -'beg\ *n* **1 :** a member of a Turkic people of Turkestan and esp. of the Uzbek Republic of the U.S.S.R. **2 :** the Turkic language of the Uzbek people

1v \'vē\ *n, pl* **v's** *or* **vs** \'vēz\ *often cap, often attrib* **1 a :** the 22d letter of the English alphabet **b :** a graphic representation of this letter **c :** a speech counterpart of orthographic *v* **2 :** FIVE — see NUMBER table **3 :** a graphic device for reproducing the letter *v* **4 :** one designated *v* esp. as the 22d in order or class **5 :** something shaped like the letter V

2v *abbr, often cap* **1** vector **2** velocity **3** verb **4** verse **5** versus **6** very **7** vice **8** victory **9** vide **10** voice **11** volt; voltage **12** volume **13** vowel

V *symbol* **1** electric potential **2** potential energy **3** vanadium

Va *abbr* Virginia

VA *abbr* **1** Veterans Administration **2** vicar apostolic **3** vice admiral **4** Virginia **5** visual aid **6** volt-ampere

vac *abbr* vacuum

va·can·cy \'vā-kən-sē\ *n, pl* **-cies** **1** *archaic* **:** an interval of leisure **2 :** physical or mental inactivity or relaxation **:** IDLENESS **3 a :** a vacating of an office, post, or piece of property **b :** the time such office or property is vacant **4 :** a vacant office, post, or tenancy **5 :** empty space **:** VOID **6 :** the state of being vacant **:** VACUITY

va·cant \'vā-kənt\ *adj* [ME, fr. OF, fr. L *vacant-, vacans,* prp. of *vacare* to be empty, be free — more at VACUUM] **1 :** not occupied by an incumbent, possessor, or officer <a ~ office> <~ thrones> **2 :** being without content or occupant <a ~ seat in a bus> <a ~ room> **3 :** free from activity or work **:** DISENGAGED <~ hours> **4 a :** STUPID, FOOLISH <a ~ mind> **b :** EXPRESSIONLESS <a ~ face> **c :** marked by a respite from reflection or care **5 :** not lived in <~ houses> **6 a :** not put to use <~ land> **b :** having no heir or claimant **:** ABANDONED <a ~ estate> ***syn*** see EMPTY — **va·cant·ly** *adv* — **va·cant·ness** *n*

va·cate \'vā-ˌkāt, vā-'\ *vb* **va·cat·ed; va·cat·ing** [L *vacatus,* pp. of *vacare*] *vt* **1 :** to make legally void **:** ANNUL **2 a :** to deprive of an incumbent or occupant **b :** to give up the incumbency or occupancy of ~ *vi* **:** to vacate an office, post, or tenancy

1va·ca·tion \vā-'kā-shən, və-\ *n, often attrib* [ME *vacacioun,* fr. MF *vacation,* fr. L *vacation-, vacatio* freedom, exemption, fr. *vacatus*] **1 :** a respite or a time of respite from something **:** INTERMISSION **2 a :** a scheduled period during which activity (as of a court or school) is suspended **b :** a period of exemption from work granted to an employee for rest and relaxation **3 :** a period spent away from home or business in travel or recreation <had a restful ~ at the beach> **4 :** an act or an instance of vacating

2vacation *vi* **va·ca·tioned; va·ca·tion·ing** \-sh(ə-)niŋ\ **:** to take or spend a vacation

va·ca·tion·er \-sh(ə-)nər\ *n* **:** VACATIONIST

va·ca·tion·ist \-sh(ə-)nəst\ *n* **:** a person taking a vacation

va·ca·tion·land \-shən-ˌland\ *n* **:** an area with recreational attractions and facilities for vacationists

vac·ci·nal \'vak-sən-ᵊl, vak-'sēn-\ *adj* **:** of or relating to vaccine or vaccination

1vac·ci·nate \'vak-sə-ˌnāt\ *vb* **-nat·ed; -nat·ing** *vt* **1 :** to inoculate (a person) with cowpox virus in order to produce immunity to smallpox **2 :** to administer a vaccine to usu. by injection ~ *vi* **:** to perform or practice vaccination — **vac·ci·na·tor** \-ˌnāt-ər\ *n*

2vac·ci·nate \'vak-sə-ˌnāt, -nət\ *n* **:** a vaccinated individual

vac·ci·na·tion \ˌvak-sə-'nā-shən\ *n* **1 :** the act of vaccinating **2 :** the scar left by vaccinating

1vac·cine \vak-'sēn, 'vak-ˌ\ *adj* [L *vaccinus* of or from cows, fr. *vacca* cow; akin to Skt *vaśa* cow] **1 :** derived from cows infected with cowpox or inoculated with its virus <~ lymph> **2** [NL *vaccinus,* fr. L] **:** of or relating to vaccinia or vaccination <a ~ pustule>

2vaccine *n* **1 :** matter or a preparation containing the virus of cowpox in a form used for vaccination **2 :** a preparation of killed microorganisms, living attenuated organisms, or living fully virulent organisms that is administered to produce or artificially increase immunity to a particular disease

vac·cin·ia \vak-'sin-ē-ə\ *n* [NL, fr. *vaccinus*] **:** COWPOX — **vac·cin·i·al** \-ē-əl\ *adj*

vac·il·late \'vas-ə-ˌlāt\ *vi* **-lat·ed; -lat·ing** [L *vacillatus,* pp. of *vacillare* to sway, waver — more at PREVARICATE] **1 a :** to sway through lack of equilibrium **b :** FLUCTUATE, OSCILLATE **2 :** to waver in mind, will, or feeling **:** hesitate in choice of opinions or courses ***syn*** see HESITATE — **vac·il·lat·ing·ly** \-ˌlāt-iŋ-lē\ *adv* — **vac·il·la·tor** \-ˌlāt-ər\ *n*

vac·il·la·tion \ˌvas-ə-'lā-shən\ *n* **1 :** an act or instance of vacillating **2 :** inability to take a stand **:** IRRESOLUTION, INDECISION

va·cu·ity \va-'kyü-ət-ē, və-\ *n, pl* **-ities** [L *vacuitas,* fr. *vacuus* empty] **1 :** an empty space **2 :** the state, fact, or quality of being vacuous **3 :** something (as an idea) that is vacuous or inane

vac·u·o·late \'vak-yə-(ˌ)wō-ˌlāt\ *or* **vac·u·o·lat·ed** \-ˌlāt-əd\ *adj* **:** containing one or more vacuoles <highly *vacuolated* cells>

vac·u·o·la·tion \ˌvak-yə-(ˌ)wō-'lā-shən\ *n* **:** the development or formation of vacuoles

vac·u·ole \'vak-yə-ˌwōl\ *n* [F, lit., small vacuum, fr. L *vacuum*] **1 :** a small cavity or space in the tissues of an organism containing air or fluid **2 :** a cavity or vesicle in the protoplasm of a cell containing fluid — see AMOEBA illustration — **vac·u·o·lar** \ˌvak-yə-'wō-lər, -ˌlär\ *adj*

vac·u·ous \'vak-yə-wəs\ *adj* [L *vacuus*] **1 :** emptied of or lacking content **2 :** marked by lack of ideas or intelligence **:** STUPID, INANE <~ mind> <~ expression> **3 :** devoid of serious occupation **:** IDLE ***syn*** see EMPTY — **vac·u·ous·ly** *adv* — **vac·u·ous·ness** *n*

1vac·u·um \'vak-yü-əm, -(ˌ)yüm, -yəm\ *n, pl* **vac·u·ums** *or* **vac·ua** \-yə-wə\ [L, fr. neut. of *vacuus* empty; akin to L *vacare* to be empty] **1 :** emptiness of space **2 a :** a space absolutely devoid of matter **b :** a space partially exhausted (as to the highest degree possible) by artificial means (as an air pump) **c :** a degree of rarefaction below atmospheric pressure **:** negative pressure **3 a :** a vacant space **:** VOID <his death has left a ~ in our lives> **b :** a state of isolation from outside influences <people who live in a ~ . . . so that the world outside them is of no moment —W. S. Maugham> **4 :** a device creating or utilizing a partial vacuum

2vacuum *adj* **1 :** of, containing, producing, or utilizing a partial vacuum <separated by means of ~ distillation> **2 :** of or relating to a vacuum device or system <expert at ~ repair>

3vacuum *vt* **:** to use a vacuum device (as a cleaner) on ~ *vi* **:** to operate a vacuum device

vacuum bottle *n* **:** a cylindrical container with a vacuum between an inner and an outer wall used to keep material and esp. liquids either hot or cold for considerable periods

vacuum cleaner *n* **:** an electrical appliance for cleaning (as floors, carpets, tapestry, or upholstered work) by suction — called also *vacuum sweeper*

vacuum gauge *n* **:** a gauge indicating degree of negative pressure

vac·u·um·ize \'vak-yü-(ə-)ˌmīz\ *vt* **-ized, -iz·ing** **1 :** to produce a vacuum in **2 a :** to clean or dry by a vacuum mechanism **b :** to pack in a vacuum container

vac·u·um–packed \ˌvak-yu̇-əm-'pakt, -(ˌ)yüm-, -yəm-\ *adj* **:** having much of the air removed before being hermetically sealed

vacuum pan *n* **:** a tank with a vacuum pump for rapid evaporation and condensation (as of sugar syrup) by boiling at a low temperature

vacuum pump *n* **:** a pump for exhausting gas from an enclosed space

vacuum tube *n* **:** an electron tube evacuated to a high degree of vacuum

va·de me·cum \ˌväd-ē-'mē-kəm, ˌväd-ē-'mā-\ *n, pl* **vade mecums** [L, go with me] **1 :** a book for ready reference **:** MANUAL **2 :** something regularly carried about by a person

VADM *abbr* vice admiral

va·dose \'vā-ˌdōs\ *adj* [L *vadosus* shallow, fr. *vadum,* n., shallow, ford; akin to L *vadere* to go — more at WADE] **:** of, relating to, or being water or solutions in the earth's crust above the permanent groundwater level

vag- *or* **vago-** *comb form* [ISV, fr. NL *vagus*] **:** vagus nerve <*vagal*> <*vagotomy*>

1vag·a·bond \'vag-ə-ˌbänd\ *adj* [ME, fr. MF, fr. L *vagabundus,* fr. *vagari* to wander] **1 :** moving from place to place without a fixed home **:** WANDERING **2 a :** of, relating to, or characteristic of a wanderer **b :** leading an unsettled, irresponsible, or disreputable life — **vag·a·bond·ish** \-ˌbän-dish\ *adj*

2vagabond *n* **:** one leading a vagabond life; *esp* **:** TRAMP — **vag·a·bond·ism** \-ˌbän-ˌdiz-əm\ *n*

3vagabond *vi* **:** to wander in the manner of a vagabond **:** roam about

vag·a·bond·age \'vag-ə-ˌbän-dij\ *n* **1 :** the act, condition, or practice of a vagabond **:** the state or habit of wandering about **2 :** VAGABONDS

va·gal \ˈvā-gəl\ *adj* [ISV] **:** of, relating to, mediated by, or being the vagus nerve — **va·gal·ly** \-gə-lē\ *adv*

va·gar·i·ous \vā-ˈger-ē-əs, və-, -ˈgar-\ *adj* **:** marked by vagaries **:** CAPRICIOUS, WHIMSICAL — **va·gar·i·ous·ly** *adv*

va·ga·ry \ˈvā-gə-rē; və-ˈge(ə)r-ē, -ˈgā(ə)r-, vā-; *also* ˈvag-ə-rē\ *n, pl* **-ries** [prob. fr. L *vagari* to wander; akin to L *vagus* wandering — more at PREVARICATE] **:** an erratic, unpredictable, or extravagant manifestation, action, or notion ***syn*** see CAPRICE

vag·ile \ˈvaj-əl, -ˌīl\ *adj* [ISV, fr. L *vagus* wandering] **:** free to move about — **va·gil·i·ty** \və-ˈjil-ət-ē, va-\ *n*

va·gi·na \və-ˈjī-nə\ *n, pl* **-nae** \-(ˌ)nē\ *or* **-nas** [L, lit., sheath] **1 a :** a canal in a female mammal that leads from the uterus to the external orifice of the genital canal **b :** a canal that is similar in function or location to the vagina and occurs in various animals other than mammals **2 :** SHEATH; *specif* **:** the expanded or ensheathing part of the base of a leaf

vag·i·nal \ˈvaj-ən-ᵊl\ *adj* **1 :** of or relating to a theca **2 :** of, relating to, or affecting the genital vagina — **vag·i·nal·ly** \-ᵊl-ē\ *adv*

vag·i·nis·mus \ˌvaj-ə-ˈniz-məs\ *n* [NL, fr. L *vagina*] **:** a painful spasmodic contraction of the vagina

vag·i·ni·tis \ˌvaj-ə-ˈnīt-əs\ *n* [NL] **:** inflammation of the vagina or of a sheath (as a tendon sheath)

va·got·o·my \vā-ˈgät-ə-mē\ *n, pl* **-mies** [ISV] **:** surgical division of the vagus nerve

va·go·to·nia \ˌvā-gə-ˈtō-nē-ə\ *n* [NL] **:** excessive excitability of the vagus nerve resulting typically in vasomotor instability, constipation, and sweating — **va·go·ton·ic** \-ˈtän-ik\ *adj*

va·go·tro·pic \-ˈtrō-pik\ *adj* **:** acting selectively upon the vagus nerve <~ drugs>

va·gran·cy \ˈvā-grən-sē\ *n, pl* **-cies 1 :** VAGARY **2 :** the state or action of being vagrant **3 :** the offense of being a vagrant

¹va·grant \ˈvā-grənt\ *n* [ME *vagraunt,* prob. modif. of MF *waucrant, wacrant* wandering, fr. OF, fr. prp. of *waucrer, wacrer* to roll, wander, of Gmc origin; akin to OE *wealcan* to roll — more at WALK] **1 a :** one who has no established residence and wanders idly from place to place without lawful or visible means of support **b :** one (as a common prostitute or drunkard) whose conduct constitutes statutory vagrancy **2 :** ROVER, WANDERER

²vagrant *adj* **1 :** wandering about from place to place usu. with no means of support **2 a :** having a fleeting, wayward, or inconstant quality **b :** having no fixed course **:** RANDOM — **va·grant·ly** *adv*

va·grom \ˈvā-grəm\ *adj* **:** VAGRANT

vague \ˈvāg\ *adj* **vagu·er; vagu·est** [MF, fr. L *vagus,* lit., wandering] **1 a :** not clearly expressed **:** stated in indefinite terms <~ accusation> **b :** not having a precise meaning <~ term of abuse> **2 a :** not clearly defined, grasped, or understood **:** INDISTINCT <~ idea> **b :** not clearly felt or sensed **:** somewhat subconscious <a ~ longing> **3 :** not thinking or expressing one's thoughts clearly or precisely <~ about dates and places> **4 :** lacking expression **:** VACANT **5 :** not sharply outlined **:** HAZY ***syn*** see OBSCURE ***ant*** definite, specific — **vague·ly** *adv*

vague·ness \ˈvāg-nəs\ *n* **1 :** the quality or state of being vague **2 :** something that is vague

va·gus \ˈvā-gəs\ *n, pl* **va·gi** \ˈvā-ˌgī, -ˌjī\ [NL *vagus nervus,* lit., wandering nerve] **:** either of the tenth pair of cranial nerves that arise from the medulla and supply chiefly the viscera esp. with autonomic sensory and motor fibers

vail \ˈvā(ə)l\ *vt* [ME *valen,* partly fr. MF *valer* (short for *avaler* to let fall) & partly short for ME *avalen* to let fall, fr. MF *avaler,* fr. OF, fr. *aval* downward, fr. *a* to (fr. L *ad*) + *val* valley — more at AT] **:** to lower often as a sign of respect or submission

vain \ˈvān\ *adj* [ME, fr. OF, fr. L *vanus* empty, vain — more at WANE] **1 :** having no real value **:** IDLE, WORTHLESS **2 :** marked by futility or ineffectualness **:** UNSUCCESSFUL, USELESS <~ efforts to escape> **3 :** FOOLISH, SILLY **4 :** having or showing undue or excessive pride in one's appearance or achievements **:** CONCEITED — **vain·ly** *adv* — **vain·ness** \ˈvān-nəs\ *n*

syn **1** VAIN, NUGATORY, OTIOSE, IDLE, EMPTY, HOLLOW *shared meaning element* **:** devoid of worth or significance
2 see FUTILE

— **in vain 1 :** to no end **:** without success or result **2 :** in an irreverent or blasphemous manner <you shall not take the name of the Lord your God *in vain* — Deut 5:11 (RSV)>

vain·glo·ri·ous \(ˈ)vān-ˈglōr-ē-əs, -ˈglȯr-\ *adj* **:** marked by vainglory **:** BOASTFUL — **vain·glo·ri·ous·ly** *adv* — **vain·glo·ri·ous·ness** *n*

vain·glo·ry \ˈvān-ˌglōr-ē, -ˌglȯr-, (ˈ)vān-ˈ\ *n* **1 :** excessive or ostentatious pride esp. in one's achievements **2 :** vain display or show **:** VANITY

vair \ˈva(ə)r, ˈve(ə)r\ *n* [ME *veir,* fr. OF *vair,* fr. *vair,* adj., variegated, fr. L *varius* variegated, various] **:** the bluish gray and white fur of a squirrel prized for ornamental use in medieval times

Vaish·na·va \ˈvīsh-nə-və\ *n* [Skt *vaiṣṇava* of Vishnu, fr. *Viṣṇu* Vishnu] **:** a member of a major Hindu sect devoted to the cult of Vishnu — **Vaishnava** *adj* — **Vaish·na·vism** \-ˌviz-əm\ *n*

Vais·ya \ˈvīsh-(y)ə\ *n* [Skt *vaiśya,* fr. *viś* settlement; akin to Gk *oikos* house — more at VICINITY] **:** a Hindu of an upper caste traditionally assigned to commercial and agricultural occupations

val *abbr* value; valued

va·lance \ˈval-ən(t)s, ˈvāl-\ *n* [ME *vallance,* perh. fr. *Valence,* France] **1 :** a drapery hung along the edge of a bed, table, altar, canopy, or shelf **2 :** a short drapery or wood or metal frame used as a decorative heading to conceal the top of curtains and fixtures — **va·lanced** \-ən(t)st\ *adj*

vale \ˈvā(ə)l\ *n* [ME, fr. OF *val,* fr. L *valles, vallis;* akin to L *volvere* to roll — more at VOLUBLE] **:** VALLEY, DALE

vale·dic·tion \ˌval-ə-ˈdik-shən\ *n* [L *valedictus,* pp. of *valedicere* to say farewell, fr. *vale* farewell + *dicere* to say — more at DICTION] **1 :** an act of bidding farewell **2 :** VALEDICTORY

vale·dic·to·ri·an \-ˌdik-ˈtōr-ē-ən, -ˈtȯr-\ *n* **:** the student usu. having the highest rank in a graduating class who delivers the valedictory address at the commencement exercises

¹vale·dic·to·ry \-ˈdik-t(ə-)rē\ *adj* [L *valedictus*] **:** of or relating to a valediction **:** expressing or containing a farewell

²valedictory *n, pl* **-ries :** an address or statement of farewell or leave-taking

va·lence \ˈvā-lən(t)s\ *n* [LL *valentia* power, capacity, fr. L *valent-, valens,* prp. of *valēre* to be strong] **1 a :** the degree of combining power of an element or radical as shown by the number of atomic weights of a univalent element (as hydrogen) with which the atomic weight of the element or the partial molecular weight of the radical will combine or for which it can be substituted or with which it can be compared **b :** a unit of valence <the four ~*s* of carbon> **2 a :** relative capacity to unite, react, or interact (as with antigens or a biological substrate) **b :** the degree of attractiveness an individual, activity, or object possesses as a behavioral goal

Va·len·ci·ennes \və-ˌlen(t)-sē-ˈen(z), ˌval-ən-sē-\ *n* [*Valenciennes,* France] **:** a fine bobbin lace

-va·lent \ˈvā-lənt\ *adj comb form* [ISV, fr. L *valent-, valens*] **1 :** having a (specified) valence or valences <bi*valent*> <multi*valent*> **2 :** having (so many) chromosomal strands or homologous chromosomes <uni*valent*>

val·en·tine \ˈval-ən-ˌtīn\ *n* **1 :** a sweetheart chosen or complimented on St. Valentine's Day **2 :** a gift or greeting sent or given esp. to a sweetheart on St. Valentine's Day; *esp* **:** a greeting card sent on this day

Valentine Day *or* **Valentine's Day** *n* **:** SAINT VALENTINE'S DAY

val·er·ate \ˈval-ə-ˌrāt\ *n* **:** a salt or ester of valeric acid

va·le·ri·an \və-ˈlir-ē-ən\ *n* [ME, fr. MF or ML; MF *valeriane,* fr. ML *valeriana,* prob. fr. fem. of *valerianus* of Valeria, fr. *Valeria,* Roman province formerly part of Pannonia] **1 :** any of a genus (*Valeriana* of the family Valerianaceae, the valerian family) of perennial herbs many of which possess medicinal properties **2 :** a drug consisting of the dried rootstock and roots of the garden heliotrope (*Valeriana officinalis*) formerly used as a carminative and sedative

va·le·ric acid \və-ˌlir-ik-, -ˌler-\ *n* [*valerian;* fr. its occurrence in the root of valerian] **:** any of four isomeric fatty acids $C_5H_{10}O_2$ or a mixture of these; *esp* **:** a liquid acid of disagreeable odor obtained from valerian or made synthetically and used esp. in organic synthesis

¹va·let \ˈval-ət, ˈval-(ˌ)ā, va-ˈlā\ *n* [MF *vaslet, varlet, valet* young nobleman, page, domestic servant, fr. (assumed) ML *vassellittus,* dim. of ML *vassus* servant — more at VASSAL] **1 a :** a man's male servant who performs personal services (as taking care of clothing) **b :** an employee (as of a hotel or a public facility) who performs personal services for customers **2 :** a device (as a rack or tray) for holding clothing or personal effects

²valet *vt* **:** to serve as a valet

va·let de cham·bre \(ˌ)va-ˌlād-ə-ˈshäⁿbrᵊ\ *n, pl* **va·lets de cham·bre** *same*\ [F, lit., chamber valet] **:** VALET 1a

¹val·e·tu·di·nar·i·an \ˌval-ə-ˌt(y)üd-ᵊn-ˈer-ē-ən\ *n* [L *valetudinarius* sickly, infirm, fr. *valetudin-, valetudo* state of health, sickness, fr. *valēre* to be strong, be well] **:** a person of a weak or sickly constitution; *esp* **:** one whose chief concern is his invalidism

²valetudinarian *adj* **:** of, relating to, or characteristic of a valetudinarian **:** SICKLY, WEAK

val·e·tu·di·nar·i·an·ism \-ē-ə-ˌniz-əm\ *n* **:** the condition or state of mind of a valetudinarian

¹val·e·tu·di·nary \-ˈt(y)üd-ᵊn-ˌer-ē\ *adj* [L *valetudinarius*] **:** VALETUDINARIAN

²valetudinary *n, pl* **-nar·ies :** VALETUDINARIAN

val·gus \ˈval-gəs\ *n* [NL, fr. L, bowlegged — more at WALK] **:** the position of a joint that is turned outward to an abnormal degree <the heel is in ~ — *Yr. Bk. of Orthopedics & Traumatic Surgery*>

Val·hal·la \val-ˈhal-ə *also* väl-ˈhäl-\ *n* [G & ON; G *Walhalla,* fr. ON *Valhöll,* lit., hall of the slain, fr. *valr* the slain + *höll* hall; akin to OE *wæl* slaughter, the slain, OIr *fuil* blood, and to OE *heall* hall] **:** the hall of Odin in Norse mythology where warriors who have died in battle are received

val·iance \ˈval-yən(t)s\ *n* **:** VALOR

val·ian·cy \-yən-sē\ *n* **:** VALOR

¹val·iant \ˈval-yənt\ *adj* [ME *valiaunt* fr. MF *vaillant,* fr. OF, fr. prp. of *valoir* to be of worth, fr. L *valēre* to be strong — more at WIELD] **1 :** possessing or exhibiting valor **:** COURAGEOUS <~ soldiers> **2 :** characterized by or performed with valor <~ feats> — **val·iant·ly** *adv* — **val·iant·ness** *n*

²valiant *n* **:** a valiant person

val·id \ˈval-əd\ *adj* [MF or ML; MF *valide,* fr. ML *validus,* fr. L strong, fr. *valēre*] **1 :** having legal efficacy or force; *esp* **:** executed with the proper legal authority and formalities <a ~ contract> **2 a :** well grounded or justifiable **:** being at once relevant and meaningful <a ~ theory> **b** (1) **:** having a conclusion correctly derived from premises <~ argument> (2) **:** correctly derived from premises <~ inference> **3 :** appropriate to the end in view **:** EFFECTIVE <every craft has its own ~ methods> **4** *of a taxon* **:** conforming to accepted principles of sound biological classification — **va·lid·i·ty** \və-ˈlid-ət-ē, va-\ *n* — **val·id·ly** \ˈval-əd-lē\ *adv* — **val·id·ness** *n*

syn VALID, SOUND, COGENT, CONVINCING, TELLING *shared meaning element* **:** having such force as to compel serious attention and usually acceptance. VALID implies being supported by objective truth or generally accepted authority <a *valid* conclusion> <a contract which satisfies all the requirements for enforceability by a court is termed a *valid* contract —L. B. Howard> SOUND implies a basis of flawless reasoning or of solid grounds <a *sound* objection> <he has a *sound* claim against the estate> COGENT

ə abut ᵊ kitten ər further a back ā bake ä cot, cart
aù out ch chin e less ē easy g gift i trip ī life
j joke ŋ sing ō flow ȯ flaw ȯi coin th thin t͟h this
ü loot ù foot y yet yü few yù furious zh vision

may stress either weight of sound argument and evidence or lucidity of presentation <a soul-searching melancholia through which he was to create a *cogent* universality of form and meaning —J. A. Dennis> <his argument is *cogent* and the conclusion he reaches sound> CONVINCING suggests a power to overcome doubt, opposition, or reluctance to accept <the very lack of planning . . . is *convincing* proof that there was nc conspiracy —Sylvan Fox> TELLING stresses an immediate and crucial effect striking at the heart of a matter and need not impute thereto soundness or validity <a *telling* attack, made with skill and shrewd insight —V. L. Parrington> ***ant*** invalid, fallacious, sophistic

val·i·date \ˈval-ə-ˌdāt\ *vt* **-dat·ed; -dat·ing** **1 a :** to make legally valid **b :** to grant official sanction to by marking **c :** to confirm the validity of (an election); *also* **:** to declare (a person) elected **2 :** to support or corroborate on a sound or authoritative basis <experiments designed to ~ his hypothesis> ***syn*** see CONFIRM ***ant*** invalidate

val·i·da·tion \ˌval-ə-ˈdā-shən\ *n* **:** an act, process, or instance of validating; *specif* **:** the determination of the degree of validity of a measuring device

va·line \ˈval-ˌēn, ˈvā-ˌlēn\ *n* [ISV, fr. *valeric (acid)*] **:** a crystalline essential amino acid $C_5H_{11}NO_2$ that occurs esp. in fibrous proteins

va·lise \və-ˈlēs\ *n* [F, fr. It *valigia*] **:** TRAVELING BAG

Val·ky·rie \val-ˈkir-ē *also* val-ˈkī-rē *&* ˈval-kə-rē\ *n* [G & ON; G *walküre,* fr. ON *valkyrja,* lit., chooser of the slain; akin to OE *wælcyrige* witch; both fr. a prehistoric WGmc-NGmc compound whose first constituent is represented by ON *valr* the slain and whose second constituent is akin to OE *cēosan* to choose — more at CHOOSE] **:** one of the maidens of Odin who choose the heroes to be slain in battle and conduct them to Valhalla

val·late \ˈval-ˌāt\ *adj* [L *vallatus,* pp. of *vallare* to surround with a wall, fr. *vallum* wall, rampart — more at WALL] **:** having a raised edge surrounding a depression

val·lec·u·la \va-ˈlek-yə-lə, və-\ *n, pl* **-u·lae** \-yə-ˌlē, -ˌlī\ [NL, fr. LL, little valley, dim. of L *valles* valley — more at VALE] **:** an anatomical groove, channel, or depression; *esp* **:** one between the base of the tongue and the epiglottis — **val·lec·u·lar** \-lər\ *adj*

val·ley \ˈval-ē\ *n, pl* **valleys** [ME *valey,* fr. OF *valee,* fr. *val* valley — more at VALE] **1 a :** an elongate depression of the earth's surface usu. between ranges of hills or mountains **b :** an area drained by a river and its tributaries **2 a :** HOLLOW, DEPRESSION **b :** the place of meeting of two slopes of a roof that form on the plan a reentrant angle

valley fever *n* [fr. its prevalence in the San Joaquin valley of California] **:** COCCIDIOIDOMYCOSIS

Va·lois \ˈval-ˌwä, val-ˈ\ *adj* [Philippe de *Valois* (Philip VI of France)] **:** of or relating to the French royal house that ruled from 1328 to 1589

va·lo·nia \və-ˈlō-nē-ə, -nyə\ *n* [It *vallonia,* fr. MGk *balanidia,* pl. of *balanidion,* dim. of Gk *balanos* acorn — more at GLAND] **:** dried acorn cups esp. from a Eurasian evergreen oak (*Quercus aegilops*) used in tanning or dressing leather

val·or \ˈval-ər\ *n* [ME, fr. MF *valour,* fr. ML *valor* value, valor, fr. L *valēre* to be strong] **:** strength of mind or spirit that enables a man to encounter danger with firmness **:** personal bravery ***syn*** see HEROISM

val·o·rize \ˈval-ə-ˌrīz\ *vt* **-rized; -riz·ing** [Pg *valorizare,* fr. *valor* value, price, fr. ML] **:** to enhance or try to enhance the price, value, or status of by organized and usu. governmental action <using subsidies to ~ coffee> — **val·o·ri·za·tion** \ˌval-ə-rə-ˈzā-shən\ *n*

val·or·ous \ˈval-ə-rəs\ *adj* **:** VALIANT — **val·or·ous·ly** *adv*

val·our \ˈval-ər\ *chiefly Brit var of* VALOR

Val·sal·va maneuver \val-ˌsal-və-\ *n* [Antonio Maria *Valsalva* †1723 It anatomist] **:** the process of making a forceful attempt at expiration while holding the nostrils closed and keeping the mouth shut for the purpose of testing the patency of the eustachian tubes or of adjusting middle ear pressure — called also *Valsalva*

valse \väls\ *n* [F, fr. G *walzer*] **:** WALTZ; *specif* **:** a concert waltz

¹valu·able \ˈval-yə-(wə-)bəl\ *adj* **1 a :** having monetary value **b :** worth a good price **2 a :** having desirable or esteemed characteristics or qualities <~ friendships> **b :** of great use or service <~ advice > ***syn*** see COSTLY — **valu·able·ness** *n* — **valu·ably** \-blē\ *adv*

²valuable *n* **:** a usu. personal possession (as jewelry) of relatively great monetary value — usu. used in pl.

valuable consideration *n* **:** an equivalent or compensation having value that is given for something acquired or promised (as money or marriage) and that may consist either in a benefit accruing to one party or a loss falling upon the other

val·u·ate \ˈval-yə-ˌwāt\ *vt* **-at·ed; -at·ing :** to place a value on **:** APPRAISE

val·u·a·tion \ˌval-yə-ˈwā-shən\ *n* **1 :** the act or process of valuing; *specif* **:** appraisal of property **2 :** the estimated or determined market value of a thing **3 :** judgment or appreciation of worth or character — **val·u·a·tion·al** \-shnəl, -shən-ᵊl\ *adj* — **val·u·a·tion·al·ly** \-ē\ *adv*

val·u·a·tor \ˈval-yə-ˌwāt-ər\ *n* **:** one that valuates; *specif* **:** one that appraises

¹val·ue \ˈval-(ˌ)yü, -yə(-w)\ *n* [ME, fr. MF, fr. (assumed) VL *valuta,* fr. fem. of *valutus,* pp. of L *valēre* to be worth, be strong] **1 :** a fair return or equivalent in goods, services, or money for something exchanged **2 :** the monetary worth of something **:** marketable price **3 :** relative worth, utility, or importance **:** degree of excellence <had nothing of ~ to say> **4 a :** a numerical quantity assigned or computed **b :** the amount or extent of a specified measurement of space, time, or quantity **c :** precise signification <~ of a word> **5 :** the relative duration of a musical note **6 a :** relative lightness or darkness of a color **:** LUMINOSITY **b :** the relation of one part in a picture to another with respect to lightness and darkness **7 :** something (as a principle or quality) intrinsically valuable or desirable <sought material ~*s* instead of human ~*s* —W. H. Jones> **8 :** DENOMINATION 4

²value *vt* **val·ued; valu·ing** **1 a :** to estimate or assign the monetary worth of **:** APPRAISE <~ a necklace> **b :** to rate or scale in usefulness, importance, or general worth **:** EVALUATE **2 :** to consider or rate highly **:** PRIZE, ESTEEM <*valued* his friendship> ***syn*** see ESTIMATE, APPRECIATE — **valu·er** \-yə-wər\ *n*

val·ue–add·ed tax \ˌval-yə-ˌwad-əd-\ *n* **:** an incremental excise that is levied on the value added at each stage of the processing of a raw material or the production and distribution of a commodity and that typically has the impact of a sales tax on the ultimate consumer

val·ued \ˈval-(ˌ)yüd, -yəd\ *adj* **:** having a value or values esp. of a specified kind or number — usu. used in combination <real-valued>

value judgment *n* **:** a judgment attributing a value (as good, evil, beautiful, or desirable) to a certain thing, action, or entity

val·ue·less \ˈval-yü-ləs, -yə-\ *adj* **:** of no value **:** WORTHLESS — **val·ue·less·ness** *n*

va·lu·ta \və-ˈlüt-ə, -ˈlü-(ˌ)tä\ *n* [It, value, fr. (assumed) VL *valuta*] **1 :** the agreed or exchange value of a currency **2 :** FOREIGN EXCHANGE 2

val·vate \ˈval-ˌvāt\ *adj* **:** having valves or parts resembling a valve: **a :** meeting at the edges without overlapping in the bud <~ leaves> **b :** opening as if by doors or valves <~ capsules> <~ anthers>

valve \ˈvalv\ *n* [L *valva;* akin to L *volvere* to roll — more at VOLUBLE] **1** *archaic* **:** a leaf of a folding or double door **2** [NL *valva,* fr. L] **:** a structure esp. in a vein or lymphatic that closes temporarily a passage or orifice or permits movement of fluid in one direction only **3 a :** any of numerous mechanical devices by which the flow of liquid, gas, or loose material in bulk may be started, stopped, or regulated by a movable part that opens, shuts, or partially obstructs one or more ports or passageways; *also* **:** the movable part of such a device **b :** a device in a brass instrument for quickly varying the tube length in order to change the fundamental tone by some definite interval **c** *chiefly Brit* **:** ELECTRON TUBE **4** [NL *valva,* fr. L] **:** one of the distinct and usu. movably articulated pieces of which the shell of some shell-bearing animals (as lamellibranch mollusks, brachiopods, and barnacles) consists **5** [NL *valva,* fr. L] **a :** one of the segments or pieces into which a dehiscing capsule or legume separates **b :** the portion of various anthers (as of the barberry) resembling a lid **c :** one of the two encasing membranes of a diatom — **valved** \ˈvalvd\ *adj* — **valve·less** \ˈvalv-ləs\ *adj*

valve–in–head engine *n* **:** an internal-combustion engine in which both inlet and exhaust valves are located in the cylinder head

val·vu·la \ˈval-vyə-lə\ *n, pl* **-lae** \-ˌlē, -ˌlī\ [NL] **:** a small valve or fold

val·vu·lar \ˈval-vyə-lər\ *adj* **1 :** resembling or functioning as a valve; *also* **:** opening by valves **2 :** of or relating to a valve esp. of the heart <~ disorders>

val·vu·li·tis \ˌval-vyə-ˈlīt-əs\ *n* [NL] **:** inflammation of a valve esp. of the heart

va·moose \və-ˈmüs, va-\ *vi* **va·moosed; va·moos·ing** [Sp *vamos* let us go, suppletive 1st pl. imper. (fr. L *vadere* to go) of *ir* to go, fr. L *ire* — more at WADE, ISSUE] *slang* **:** to depart quickly **:** DECAMP

¹vamp \ˈvamp\ *n* [ME *vampe* sock, fr. OF *avantpié,* fr. *avant-* fore- + *pié* foot, fr. L *ped-, pes* — more at VANGUARD, FOOT] **1 :** the part of a shoe upper or boot upper covering esp. the forepart of the foot and sometimes also extending forward over the toe or backward to the back seam of the upper **2** [²*vamp*] **:** an introductory musical passage of two or four measures often repeated several times (as in vaudeville) before a solo or between verses

²vamp *vt* **1 a :** to provide (a shoe) with a new vamp **b :** to piece (something old) with a new part **:** PATCH <~ up old sermons> **2 :** INVENT, FABRICATE <~ up an excuse> ~ *vi* **:** to play a musical vamp — **vamp·er** *n*

³vamp *n* [short for *vampire*] **:** a woman who uses her charm or wiles to seduce and exploit men — **vamp·ish** \ˈvam-pish\ *adj*

⁴vamp *vt* **:** to practice seductive wiles on

vam·pire \ˈvam-ˌpī(ə)r\ *n* [F, fr. G *vampir,* of Slav origin; akin to Serb *vampir* vampire] **1 :** the body of a dead person believed to come from the grave at night and suck the blood of persons asleep **2 a :** one who lives by preying on others **b :** a woman who exploits and ruins her lover **3 :** any of various So. American bats (genera *Desmodus* and *Diphylla* of the family Desmodontidae) structurally adapted for subsisting on blood and dangerous to man and domestic animals esp. as vectors of equine trypanosomiasis and of rabies; *also* **:** any of several other bats that do not feed on blood but are sometimes reputed to do so

vam·pir·ism \-ˌpī(ə)r-ˌiz-əm\ *n* **1 :** belief in vampires **2 :** the actions of a vampire

¹van \ˈvan\ *n* [ME, fr. MF, fr. L *vannus* — more at WINNOW] **1** *dial Eng* **:** a winnowing device (as a fan) **2 :** WING 1a

²van *n* [by shortening] **:** VANGUARD

³van *n* [short for *caravan*] **1 a :** a usu. enclosed wagon or motortruck used for transportation of goods or animals; *also* **:** CARAVAN 2a **b :** a detachable passenger cabin transportable by aircraft or truck **2** *chiefly Brit* **:** an enclosed railroad freight or baggage car

van·a·date \ˈvan-ə-ˌdāt\ *n* **:** a salt or ester of a vanadic acid

va·na·dic \və-ˈnād-ik, -ˈnad-\ *adj* **:** of, relating to, or containing vanadium esp. with a higher valence than in vanadous compounds

vanadic acid *n* **1 :** any of various acids that are hydrates of vanadium pentoxide or are known esp. in the form of salts and esters **2 :** VANADIUM PENTOXIDE

va·na·di·nite \və-ˈnād-ᵊn-ˌīt, ˌvan-ə-ˈdē-\ *n* [G *vanadinit,* fr. *vanadin* vanadium, fr. NL *vanadium*] **:** a mineral consisting of a lead vanadate and chloride and occurring in yellowish, brownish, or ruby-red hexagonal crystals

va·na·di·um \və-ˈnād-ē-əm\ *n* [NL, fr. ON *Vanadīs* Freya] **:** a grayish malleable ductile polyvalent metallic element found combined in minerals and used esp. to form alloys (as vanadium steel) — see ELEMENT table

vanadium pentoxide *n* : a yellowish red crystalline compound V_2O_5 used esp. in glass manufacture and as a catalyst

va·na·dous \və-ˈnād-əs, ˈvan-əd-\ *adj* : of, relating to, or containing vanadium esp. with a lower valence than in vanadic compounds

Van Al·len belt \va-ˈnal-ən-, və-\ *n* [James A. *Van Allen*] : a belt of intense ionizing radiation that surrounds the earth in the outer atmosphere

va·nas·pa·ti \və-ˈnəs-pət-ē, -ˈnäs-\ *n* [Skt, forest tree, soma plant, lit., lord of the forest, fr. *vana* forest + *pati* lord] : a hydrogenated vegetable fat used as a butter substitute in India

van·da \ˈvan-də\ *n* [NL, genus name, fr. Hindi *vandā* mistletoe, fr. Skt, a parasitic plant] : any of a large genus (*Vanda*) of Indo-Malayan epiphytic orchids often grown for their loose racemes of showy flowers

van·dal \ˈvan-dᵊl\ *n* [L *Vandalii* (pl.), of Gmc origin] **1** *cap* : a member of a Germanic people who lived in the area south of the Baltic between the Vistula and the Oder, overran Gaul, Spain, and northern Africa in the 4th and 5th centuries A.D. and in 455 sacked Rome **2** : one who willfully or ignorantly destroys, damages, or defaces property belonging to another or to the public — **vandal** *adj, often cap* — **Van·dal·ic** \van-ˈdal-ik\ *adj*

van·dal·ism \ˈvan-dᵊl-ˌiz-əm\ *n* : willful or malicious destruction or defacement of public or private property

van·dal·is·tic \ˌvan-dᵊl-ˈis-tik\ *adj* : of or relating to vandalism

van·dal·ize \ˈvan-dᵊl-ˌīz\ *vt* **-ized; -iz·ing** : to subject to vandalism : DAMAGE — **van·dal·iza·tion** \ˌvan-dᵊl-ə-ˈzā-shən\ *n*

Van de Graaff generator \ˌvan-də-ˌgraf-\ *n* [Robert J. *Van de Graaff* †1967 Am physicist] : ELECTROSTATIC GENERATOR

van der Waals forces \ˌvan-dər-ˌwȯlz-\ *n pl* [Johannes D. *van der Waals* †1923 D physicist] : the relatively weak attractive forces that are operative between neutral atoms and molecules and that arise because of the electric polarization induced in each of the particles by the presence of other particles

Van·dyke \van-ˈdīk, vən-\ *n* [Sir Anthony *Vandyke*] **1 a** : a wide collar with a deeply indented edge **b** : one of several V-shaped points forming a decorative edging **c** : a border of such points **2** : a trim pointed beard — **van·dyked** \-ˈdīkt\ *adj*

Vandyke 2

Vandyke brown *n* [fr. its use by the painter Vandyke] : a natural brown-black pigment of organic matter obtained from bog earth or peat or lignite deposits; *also* : any of various synthetic brown pigments

vane \ˈvān\ *n* [ME (southern dial.), fr. OE *fana* banner; akin to OHG *fano* cloth, L *pannus* cloth, rag] **1 a** : a movable device attached to an elevated object (as a spire) for showing the direction of the wind **b** : one that is changeable or inconstant **2** : a thin flat or curved object that is rotated about an axis by a flow of fluid or that rotates to cause a fluid to flow or that redirects a flow of fluid <the ~*s* of a windmill> **3** : the web or flat expanded part of a feather **4** : a feather fastened to the shaft near the nock of an arrow **5 a** : the target of a leveling rod **b** : one of the sights of a compass or quadrant — **vaned** \ˈvānd\ *adj*

van·guard \ˈvan-ˌgärd *also* ˈvaŋ-\ *n* [ME *vantgard*, fr. MF *avant-garde*, fr. OF, fr. *avant-* fore- (fr. *avant* before, fr. L *abante*) + *garde* guard — more at ADVANCE] **1** : the troops moving at the head of an army **2** : the forefront of an action or movement — **van·guard·ism** \-ˌiz-əm\ *n* — **van·guard·ist** \-əst\ *n*

va·nil·la \və-ˈnil-ə, -ˈnel-\ *n* [NL, genus name, fr. Sp. *vainilla* vanilla (plant and fruit), dim. of *vaina* sheath, fr. L *vagina* sheath, vagina] **1** : any of a genus (*Vanilla*) of tropical American climbing orchids **2 a** : VANILLA BEAN **b** : a commercially important extract of the vanilla bean that is used esp. as a flavoring

vanilla 1: *1* flowering stem and leaves, *2* pod

vanilla bean *n* : the long capsular fruit of a vanilla (esp. *Vanilla planifolia*) that is an important article of commerce

va·nil·lic \və-ˈnil-ik, -ˈnel-\ *adj* : of or derived from vanilla or vanillin

van·il·lin \ˈvan-ᵊl-ən\ *n* : a crystalline phenolic aldehyde $C_8H_8O_3$ that is the chief fragrant component of vanilla and is used esp. in flavoring and in perfumery

Va·nir \ˈvän-ˌi(ə)r\ *n pl* [ON] : a race of Norse gods who become united with the Aesir

van·ish \ˈvan-ish\ *vb* [ME *vanisshen*, fr. MF *evaniss-*, stem of *evanir*, fr. (assumed) VL *exvanire*, alter. of L *evanescere* to dissipate like vapor, vanish, fr. *e-* + *vanescere* to vanish, fr. *vanus* empty] *vi* **1 a** : to pass quickly from sight : DISAPPEAR **b** : to pass completely from existence **2** : to assume the value zero ~ *vt* : to cause to disappear — **van·ish·er** *n*

vanishing cream *n* : a cosmetic preparation less oily than cold cream that is used chiefly as a foundation for face powder

vanishing point *n* **1** : a point at which receding parallel lines seem to meet when represented in linear perspective — see LINEAR PERSPECTIVE illustration **2** : a point at which something disappears or ceases to exist

van·i·ty \ˈvan-ət-ē\ *n, pl* **-ties** [ME *vanite*, fr. OF *vanité*, fr. L *vanitat-, vanitas* quality of being empty or vain, fr. *vanus* empty, vain — more at WANE] **1** : something that is vain, empty, or valueless **2** : the quality or fact of being vain **3** : inflated pride in oneself or one's appearance : CONCEIT **4** : a fashionable trifle or knicknack **5 a** : ³COMPACT 1 **b** : a small case or handbag for toilet articles used by women **6** : DRESSING TABLE

vanity fair *n, often cap V&F* [*Vanity-Fair*, a fair held in the frivolous town of Vanity in John Bunyan's *Pilgrim's Progress* (1678)] : a scene or place characterized by frivolity and ostentation

vanity plate *n* : a license plate bearing letters or numbers or a combination of these as designated by the owner of the vehicle

vanity press *n* : a publishing house that publishes books at the author's expense — called also *vanity publisher*

van·quish \ˈvaŋ-kwish, ˈvan-\ *vt* [ME *venquissen* fr. MF *venquis*, preterit of *veintre* to conquer, fr. L *vincere* — more at VICTOR] **1** : to overcome in battle : subdue completely **2** : to defeat in a conflict or contest **3** : to gain mastery over (an emotion, passion, or temptation) — **van·quish·able** \-kwish-ə-bəl\ *adj* — **van·quish·er** *n*

van·tage \ˈvant-ij\ *n* [ME, fr. AF, fr. MF *avantage* — more at ADVANTAGE] **1** *archaic* : BENEFIT, GAIN **2** : superiority in a contest **3** : a position giving a strategic advantage, commanding perspective, or comprehensive view **4** : ADVANTAGE 4 — **to the vantage** *obs* : in addition

¹van·ward \ˈvan-wərd\ *adj* : located in the vanguard : ADVANCED

²vanward *adv* : to or toward the vanguard : FOREWARD

va·pid \ˈvap-əd, ˈvā-pəd\ *adj* [L *vapidus* flat tasting; akin to L *vappa* vapid wine and prob. to L *vapor steam*] : lacking liveliness, tang, briskness, or force : FLAT, UNINTERESTING *syn* see INSIPID — **va·pid·ly** *adv* — **va·pid·ness** *n*

va·pid·i·ty \va-ˈpid-ət-ē, vā-, və-\ *n, pl* **-ties** **1** : the quality or state of being vapid **2** : something vapid

¹va·por \ˈvā-pər\ *n* [ME *vapour*, fr. MF *vapeur*, fr. L *vapor* steam, vapor — more at COVET] **1** : diffused matter (as smoke or fog) suspended floating in the air and impairing its transparency **2 a** : a substance in the gaseous state as distinguished from the liquid or solid state **b** : a substance (as gasoline, alcohol, mercury, or benzoin) vaporized for industrial, therapeutic, or military uses; *also* : a mixture (as the explosive mixture in an internal-combustion engine) of such a vapor with air **3 a** : something unsubstantial or transitory : PHANTASM **b** : a foolish or fanciful idea **4** *pl* **a** *archaic* : exhalations of bodily organs (as the stomach) held to affect the physical or mental condition **b** : a depressed or hysterical nervous condition

²vapor *vi* **va·pored; va·por·ing** \-p(ə-)riŋ\ **1 a** : to rise or pass off in vapor **b** : to emit vapor **2** : to indulge in bragging, blustering, or idle talk — **va·por·er** \-pər-ər\ *n*

vapor barrier *n* : a layer of material (as roofing paper or polyethylene film) used to retard or prevent the absorption of moisture into a construction (as a wall or floor)

va·por·ing \ˈvā-p(ə-)riŋ\ *n* : the act or speech of one that vapors; *specif* : an idle, extravagant, or high-flown expression or speech — usu. used in pl.

va·por·ish \ˈvā-p(ə-)rish\ *adj* **1** : resembling or suggestive of vapor **2** : given to fits of depression or hysteria — **va·por·ish·ness** *n*

va·por·iza·tion \ˌvā-p(ə-)rə-ˈzā-shən\ *n* : the action or process of vaporizing : the state of being vaporized

va·por·ize \ˈvā-pə-ˌrīz\ *vb* **-ized; -iz·ing** *vt* **1** : to convert (as by the application of heat or by spraying) into vapor **2** : to cause to become ethereal or dissipated ~ *vi* **1** : to become vaporized **2** : VAPOR 2 — **va·por·iz·able** \-ˌrī-zə-bəl\ *adj*

va·por·iz·er \-ˌrī-zər\ *n* : one that vaporizes : as **a** : ATOMIZER **b** : an apparatus for vaporizing a heavy oil (as petroleum) for the explosive charge of an internal-combustion engine; *also* : a simple form of carburetor **c** : a device for converting water or a medicated liquid into a vapor for inhalation

vapor lock *n* : partial or complete interruption of flow of a fluid (as fuel in an internal-combustion engine) caused by the formation of bubbles of vapor in the feeding system

va·por·ous \ˈvā-p(ə-)rəs\ *adj* **1** : consisting or characteristic of vapor **2** : producing vapors : VOLATILE **3** : containing or obscured by vapors : MISTY **4 a** : ETHEREAL, UNSUBSTANTIAL **b** : consisting of or indulging in vaporings — **va·por·ous·ly** *adv* — **va·por·ous·ness** *n*

vapor pressure *n* : the pressure exerted by a vapor that is in equilibrium with its solid or liquid form — called also *vapor tension*

vapor trail *n* : CONTRAIL

va·pory \ˈvā-p(ə-)rē\ *adj* : VAPOROUS, MISTY

va·pour *chiefly Brit var of* VAPOR

va·que·ro \vä-ˈke(ə)r-(ˌ)ō\ *n, pl* **-ros** [Sp — more at BUCKAROO] : HERDSMAN, COWBOY

var *abbr* **1** variable **2** variant **3** variation **4** variety **5** various

VAR *abbr* **1** visual-aural range **2** volt-ampere reactive

va·ra \ˈvär-ə\ *n* [Sp & Pg, lit., pole, fr. L, forked pole, fr. fem. of *varus* bent, crooked — more at PREVARICATE] **1** : any of various Spanish, Portuguese, and Latin American units of length equal to between 31 and 34 inches **2** : a Texas unit of length equal to 33.33 inches

vari- *or* **vario-** *comb form* [L *varius* — more at VARIOUS] : varied : diverse <*vari*form> <*vario*coupler>

var·ia \ˈver-ē-ə, ˈvar-\ *n pl* [NL, fr. L, neut. pl. of *varius* various] : MISCELLANY; *esp* : a literary miscellany

¹vari·able \ˈver-ē-ə-bəl, ˈvar-\ *adj* **1 a** : able or apt to vary : subject to variation or changes <~ winds> **b** : FICKLE, INCONSTANT **2** : characterized by variations **3** : having the characteristics of a variable **4** : not true to type : ABERRANT — used of a biological group or character — **vari·abil·i·ty** \ˌver-ē-ə-ˈbil-ət-ē, ˌvar-\ *n* — **vari·able·ness** \ˈver-ē-ə-bəl-nəs, ˈvar-\ *n* — **vari·ably** \-blē\ *adv*

ə abut	ᵊ kitten	ər further	a back	ā bake	ä cot, cart	
aù out	ch chin	e less	ē easy	g gift	i trip	ī life
j joke	ŋ sing	ō flow	ȯ flaw	ȯi coin	th thin	t͟h this
ü loot	ù foot	y yet	yü few	yù furious	zh vision	

[2]variable *n* **1 :** something that is variable **2 a :** a quantity that may assume any one of a set of values **b :** a symbol representing a variable **3 :** VARIABLE STAR

variable cost *n* **:** a cost (as for labor or materials) that varies directly with the level of production

variable star *n* **:** a star whose brightness changes usu. in more or less regular periods

vari·ance \ˈver-ē-ən(t)s, ˈvar-\ *n* **1 :** the fact, quality, or state of being variable or variant **:** DIFFERENCE, VARIATION <yearly ~ in crops> **2 :** the fact or state of being in disagreement **:** DISSENSION, DISPUTE **3 :** a disagreement between two parts of the same legal proceeding that must be consonant **4 :** a license to do some act contrary to the usual rule <a zoning ~> **5 :** the square of the standard deviation ***syn*** see DISCORD — **at variance :** not in harmony or agreement

[1]vari·ant \ˈver-ē-ənt, ˈvar-\ *adj* **1** *obs* **:** VARIABLE **2 :** manifesting variety, deviation, or disagreement **3 :** varying usu. slightly from the standard form <~ readings>

[2]variant *n* **:** one of two or more persons or things exhibiting usu. slight differences: as **a :** one that exhibits variation from a type or norm **b :** one of two or more different spellings (as *labor* and *labour*) or pronunciations (as of *economics* \ek-, ēk-\) of the same word **c :** one of two or more words (as *geographic* and *geographical*) or word elements (as *mon-* and *mono-*) of essentially the same meaning differing only in the presence or absence of an affix

vari·ate \ˈver-ē-ˌāt, ˈvar-, -ət\ *n* **:** RANDOM VARIABLE

vari·a·tion \ˌver-ē-ˈā-shən, ˌvar-\ *n* **1 a :** the act or process of varying **:** the state or fact of being varied **b :** an instance of varying **c :** the extent to which or the range in which a thing varies **2 :** DECLINATION 6 **3 :** a change in the mean motion or mean orbit of a celestial body **4 a :** a change of algebraic sign between successive terms of a sequence **b :** a measure of the change in a variable or function **5 :** the repetition of a musical theme with modifications in rhythm, tune, harmony, or key **6 a :** divergence in qualities of an organism or biotype from those typical or usual to its group **b :** an individual or group exhibiting variation **7 a :** a solo dance in classic ballet **b :** a repetition in modern ballet of a movement sequence with changes — **vari·a·tion·al** \-shnəl, -shən-ᵊl\ *adj* — **vari·a·tion·al·ly** \-ē\ *adv*

var·i·cel·la \ˌvar-ə-ˈsel-ə\ *n* [NL, irreg. dim. of *variola*] **:** CHICKEN POX

var·i·co·cele \ˈvar-ə-kō-ˌsēl\ *n* [NL, fr. L *varic-, varix* + *-o-* + *-cele*] **:** a varicose enlargement of the veins of the spermatic cord

vari·col·ored \ˈver-i-ˌkəl-ərd, ˈvar-\ *adj* **:** having various colors **:** VARIEGATED <~ nuptial plumage of a bird>

var·i·cose \ˈvar-ə-ˌkōs\ *adj* [L *varicosus* full of dilated veins, fr. *varic-, varix* dilated vein] **1 a** *also* **var·i·cosed** \-ˌkōst, -ˌkōzd\ **:** abnormally swollen or dilated <~ veins> **b :** causing abnormal swelling <~ stasis> **2 :** of, relating to, or exhibiting varices <~ mollusks>

var·i·cos·i·ty \ˌvar-ə-ˈkäs-ət-ē\ *n, pl* **-ties 1 :** the quality or state of being varicose **2 :** VARIX

var·ied \ˈve(ə)r-ēd, ˈva(ə)r-\ *adj* **1 :** having numerous forms or types **:** DIVERSE **2 :** VARIEGATED 2 — **var·ied·ly** *adv*

var·ie·gate \ˈver-ē-ə-ˌgāt, ˈver-i-ˌgāt, ˈvar-\ *vt* **-gat·ed; -gat·ing** [L *variegatus,* pp. of *variegare,* fr. *varius* various + *-egare* (akin to L *agere* to drive) — more at AGENT] **1 :** to diversify in external appearance esp. with different colors **:** DAPPLE **2 :** to enliven or give interest to by means of variety — **var·ie·ga·tor** \-ˌgāt-ər\ *n*

var·ie·gat·ed \-ˌgāt-əd\ *adj* **1 :** VARIED 1 **2 :** having discrete markings of different colors <~ leaves>

variegated cutworm *n* **:** a widespread noctuid moth (*Peridroma saucia*) whose destructive larva is a cutworm attacking crops in most cultivated areas of the earth

var·ie·ga·tion \ˌver-ē-ə-ˈgā-shən, ˌver-i-ˈgā-, ˌvar-\ *n* **:** the act of variegating **:** the state of being variegated; *esp* **:** diversity of colors

vari·er \ˈver-ē-ər, ˈvar-\ *n* **:** one that varies

va·ri·etal \və-ˈrī-ət-ᵊl\ *adj* **:** of, relating to, or characterizing a variety <~ name>; *also* **:** being a variety in distinction from an individual or species — **va·ri·etal·ly** \-ᵊl-ē\ *adv*

va·ri·ety \və-ˈrī-ət-ē\ *n, pl* **-et·ies** [MF or L; MF *varieté,* fr. L *varietat-, varietas,* fr. *varius* various] **1 :** the quality or state of having different forms or types **:** MULTIFARIOUSNESS **2 :** a number or collection of different things esp. of a particular class **:** ASSORTMENT **3 a :** something differing from others of the same general kind **:** SORT **b :** any of various groups of plants or animals of less than specific rank **4 :** VARIETY SHOW

variety meat *n* **:** an edible part (as the liver or tongue) of a slaughter animal other than skeletal muscle

variety show *n* **:** a theatrical entertainment of successive separate performances (as of songs, dances, skits, acrobatic feats, and trained animal acts)

variety store *n* **:** a retail store that carries a large variety of merchandise esp. of low unit value

vari·form \ˈver-ə-ˌfȯrm, ˈvar-\ *adj* **:** having various forms **:** varied or different in form

var·io·cou·pler \ˈver-ē-ō-ˌkəp-lər, ˈvar-\ *n* **:** an inductive coupler the mutual inductance of which is adjustable by moving one coil with respect to the other

va·ri·o·la \ˌver-ē-ˈō-lə, ˌvar-; və-ˈrī-ə-lə\ *n* [NL, fr. ML, pustule, pox, fr. LL, pustule] **:** any of several virus diseases (as smallpox or cowpox) marked by a pustular eruption

va·ri·o·loid \ˌver-ē-ˈō-ˌlȯid, ˌvar-; və-ˈrī-ə-ˌlȯid\ *n* [NL *variola*] **:** a modified mild form of smallpox occurring in persons who have been vaccinated or who have had smallpox

va·ri·o·lous \ˌver-ē-ˈō-ləs, ˌvar-; və-ˈrī-ə-ləs\ *adj* **:** of or relating to smallpox

var·i·om·e·ter \ˌver-ē-ˈäm-ət-ər, ˌvar-\ *n* **1 :** VARIOCOUPLER **2 :** an instrument for measuring magnetic declination **3 :** an aeronautical instrument for indicating rate of climb

[1]var·i·o·rum \ˌver-ē-ˈōr-əm, ˌvar-, -ˈȯr-\ *n* [L *variorum* of various persons (gen. pl. masc. of *varius*), in the phrase *cum notis variorum* with the notes of various persons] **1 :** an edition or text with notes by different persons **2 :** an edition of a publication containing variant readings of the text

[2]variorum *adj* **1 :** relating to or being an edition or text containing notes by different persons **2 :** derived from various sources

var·i·ous \ˈver-ē-əs, ˈvar-\ *adj* [L *varius;* prob. akin to L *varus* bent, crooked — more at PREVARICATE] **1** *archaic* **:** VARIABLE, INCONSTANT **2 :** VARICOLORED <birds of ~ plumage> **3 a :** of differing kinds **:** MULTIFARIOUS **b :** dissimilar in nature or form **:** UNLIKE <animals as ~ as the jaguar and the sloth> **4 :** having a number of different aspects or characteristics <~ genius> **5 :** of an indefinite number greater than one <stop at ~ towns> **6 :** INDIVIDUAL, SEPARATE <refunds to the ~ club members> ***syn*** see DIFFERENT ***ant*** uniform, cognate — **var·i·ous·ness** *n*

var·i·ous·ly *adv* **1 :** in various ways **:** at various times <was ~ occupied teaching, farming, and clerking> **2 :** by various designations <known ~ as principal, headmaster, and rector>

vari·sized \ˈver-i-ˌsīzd, ˈvar-\ *adj* **:** of various sizes

va·ris·tor \va-ˈris-tər, ve-\ *n* [*vari-* + *resistor*] **:** an electrical resistor whose resistance depends on the applied voltage

var·ix \ˈvar-iks\ *n, pl* **var·i·ces** \ˈvar-ə-ˌsēz\ [L *varic-, varix*] **1 :** an abnormally dilated and lengthened vein, artery, or lymph vessel; *esp* **:** a varicose vein **2 :** one of the prominent ridges across each whorl of a gastropod shell

var·let \ˈvär-lət\ *n* [ME, fr. MF *vaslet, varlet* young nobleman, page — more at VALET] **1** *archaic* **a :** ATTENDANT, MENIAL **b :** a knight's page **2 :** a base unprincipled person **:** KNAVE

var·let·ry \-lə-trē\ *n, archaic* **:** a group of common people **:** RABBLE

var·mint \ˈvär-mənt\ *n* [alter. of *vermin*] **1 :** an animal or bird considered a pest; *specif* **:** an animal classed as vermin and unprotected by game law **2 :** a contemptible person **:** RASCAL; *broadly* **:** PERSON, FELLOW

[1]var·nish \ˈvär-nish\ *n* [ME, *vernisch,* fr. MF *vernis,* fr. OIt or ML; OIt *vernice,* fr. ML *veronic-, veronix* sandarac (resin)] **1 a :** a liquid preparation that when spread and allowed to dry on a surface forms a hard lustrous typically transparent coating **b :** the covering or glaze given by the application of varnish **c** (1) **:** something that suggests varnish by its gloss (2) **:** a coating (as of deposits in an internal-combustion engine) comparable to varnish **2 :** outside show **:** GLOSS **3** *chiefly Brit* **:** a liquid nail polish — **var·nishy** \-ē\ *adj*

[2]varnish *vt* **1 :** to apply varnish to **2 :** to cover or conceal (as something unpleasant) with something that gives a fair appearance **:** [2]GLOSS **3 :** ADORN, EMBELLISH — **var·nish·er** \-ər\ *n*

varnish tree *n* **:** any of various trees yielding a milky juice from which in some cases varnish or lacquer is prepared; *esp* **:** a Japanese sumac (*Rhus verniciflua*)

var·si·ty \ˈvär-sət-ē, -stē\ *n, pl* **-ties** [by shortening & alter. fr. *university*] **1** *Brit* **:** UNIVERSITY **2 a :** the principal squad representing a university, college, school, or club esp. in a sport **b :** [2]REGULAR 1d

Var·u·na \ˈvar-ə-nə\ *n* [Skt *Varuṇa*] **:** a chief Vedic god responsible for natural and moral order in the cosmos

var·us \ˈvar-əs, ˈver-\ *n* [NL, fr. L, bent, knock-kneed] **:** the position of a joint that is turned inward to an abnormal degree <the foot must turn into ~ to keep in line with the knee joint —*Yr. Bk. of Orthopedics & Traumatic Surgery*>

varve \ˈvärv\ *n* [Sw *varv* turn, layer; akin to OE *hweorfan* to turn — more at WHARF] **:** a pair of layers of alternately finer and coarser silt or clay believed to comprise an annual cycle of deposition in a body of still water — **varved** \ˈvärvd\ *adj*

vary \ˈve(ə)r-ē, ˈva(ə)r-\ *vb* **var·ied; vary·ing** [ME *varien,* fr. MF or L; MF *varier,* fr. L *variare,* fr. *varius* various] *vt* **1 a :** to make a partial change in **:** make different in some attribute or characteristic **b :** to make differences between items in **:** DIVERSIFY **2 :** to present under new aspects <~ the rhythm and harmonic treatment> ~ *vi* **1 :** to exhibit or undergo change <a constantly ~*ing* sky> **2 :** DEVIATE, DEPART **3 :** to take on successive values <*y varies* inversely with *x*> **4 :** to exhibit divergence in structural or physiological characters from those typical or usual in the group ***syn*** see CHANGE — **vary·ing·ly** \-iŋ-lē\ *adv*

varying hare *n* **:** any of several hares having white fur in winter

varying hare: *1* in winter coat, *2* in summer coat

vas \ˈvas\ *n, pl* **va·sa** \ˈvā-zə\ [NL, fr. L, vessel] **:** an anatomical vessel **:** DUCT — **va·sal** \-zəl\ *adj*

vas- *or* **vaso-** *comb form* [NL, fr. L *vas*] **1 :** vessel: as **a :** blood vessel <*vaso*motor> **b :** vas deferens <*vas*ectomy> **2 :** vascular and <*vaso*vagal> **3 :** vasomotor <*vaso*inhibitor>

va·sa ef·fer·en·tia \ˈvā-zə-ˌef-ə-ˈren-ch(ē-)ə\ *n pl* [NL, lit., efferent vessels] **:** the 12 to 20 tubes that lead from the rete of the testis to the vas deferens and except near their commencement are greatly convoluted and form the compact head of the epididymis

vas·cu·lar \ˈvas-kyə-lər\ *adj* [NL *vascularis,* fr. L *vasculum* small vessel, dim. of *vas*] **1 :** of or relating to a channel for the conveyance of a body fluid (as blood of an animal or sap of a plant) or to a system of such channels; *also* **:** supplied with or made up of such channels and esp. blood vessels <a ~ tumor> <a ~ system> **2 :** marked by vigor and ardor **:** SPIRITED, PASSIONATE — **vas·cu·lar·i·ty** \ˌvas-kyə-ˈlar-ət-ē\ *n*

vascular bundle *n* **:** a unit of the vascular system of a higher plant consisting usu. of vessels and sieve tubes together with parenchyma cells and fibers

vascular cylinder *n* **:** STELE

vas·cu·lar·iza·tion \ˌvas-kyə-lə-rə-ˈzā-shən\ *n* : the process of becoming vascular; *also* : abnormal or excessive formation of blood vessels (as in the retina or on the cornea)

vascular plant *n* : a plant having a specialized conducting system that includes xylem and phloem : TRACHEOPHYTE

vascular ray *n* : a ray of cambial origin that in the stele of many vascular plants separates the vascular bundles

vascular tissue *n* : plant tissue concerned mainly with conduction; *esp* : the specialized tissue of higher plants consisting essentially of phloem and xylem and forming a continuous system throughout the body

vas·cu·la·ture \ˈvas-kyə-lə-ˌchu̇(ə)r, -ˌt(y)u̇(ə)r\ *n* [L *vasculum* vessel + E *-ature* (as in *musculature*)] : the disposition or arrangement of blood vessels in an organ or part

vas·cu·lum \ˈvas-kyə-ləm\ *n, pl* **-la** \-lə\ [NL, fr. L, small vessel] : a usu. metal and commonly cylindrical or flattened covered box used in collecting plants

vas def·er·ens \ˈvas-ˈdef-ə-rənz, -ˌrenz\ *n, pl* **va·sa def·er·en·tia** \ˈvā-zə-ˌdef-ə-ˈren-ch(ē-)ə\ [NL, lit., deferent vessel] : a spermatic duct esp. of a higher vertebrate forming in man a small thick-walled tube about two feet long greatly convoluted in its proximal portion

vase \ *US oftenest* ˈvās; *Can usu & US also* ˈvāz; *Brit, Can also, & US sometimes* ˈväz\ *n* [F, fr. L *vas* vessel; akin to Umbrian *vasor* vessels] : a usu. round vessel of greater depth than width used chiefly as an ornament or for holding flowers — **vase·like** \-ˌlīk\ *adj*

va·sec·to·my \və-ˈsek-tə-mē, vā-ˈzek-\ *n, pl* **-mies** [ISV] : surgical excision of the vas deferens usu. to induce permanent sterility

Vas·e·line \ˈvas-ə-ˌlēn, ˌvas-ə-ˈ\ *trademark* — used for petrolatum

va·si·form \ˈvāz-ə-ˌfȯrm\ *adj* [NL *vasiformis*, fr. L *vas* + *-iformis* -iform] **1** : having the form of a hollow tube **2** \ˈvās-ə-, ˈvāz-, ˈväz- (*see* VASE)\ : having the form of a vase <a ~ lamp>

va·so·ac·tive \ˌvā-zō-ˈak-tiv\ *adj* : affecting the blood vessels esp. in respect to the degree of their relaxation or contraction — **va·so·ac·tiv·i·ty** \-ak-ˈtiv-ət-ē\ *n*

va·so·con·stric·tion \-kən-ˈstrik-shən\ *n* [ISV] : narrowing of the lumen of blood vessels esp. as a result of vasomotor action

va·so·con·stric·tive \-ˈstrik-tiv\ *adj* : inducing vasoconstriction

va·so·con·stric·tor \-tər\ *n* : an agent (as a sympathetic nerve fiber or a drug) that induces or initiates vasoconstriction

va·so·di·la·ta·tion \-ˌdil-ə-ˈtā-shən, -ˌdī-lə-\ *or* **va·so·di·la·tion** \-dī-ˈlā-shən, -də-\ *n* [ISV] : widening of the lumen of blood vessels

va·so·di·la·tor \-ˌlāt-ər\ *n* : an agent (as a parasympathetic nerve fiber or a drug) that induces or initiates vasodilatation

va·so·mo·tor \ˌvā-zə-ˈmōt-ər\ *adj* [ISV] : of, relating to, or being nerves or centers controlling the size of blood vessels

va·so·pres·sin \ˌvā-zō-ˈpres-ᵊn\ *n* [fr. *Vasopressin*, a trademark] : a polypeptide hormone secreted by the posterior lobe of the pituitary that increases blood pressure and decreases urine flow — called also *antidiuretic hormone*

va·so·pres·sor \-ˈpres-ər\ *adj* : causing a rise in blood pressure by exerting a vasoconstrictor effect — **vasopressor** *n*

va·so·spasm \ˈvā-zō-ˌspaz-əm\ *n* [ISV] : sharp and often persistent contraction of a blood vessel reducing its caliber and blood flow — **va·so·spas·tic** \ˌvā-zō-ˈspas-tik\ *adj*

va·so·to·cin \ˌvā-zə-ˈtōs-ᵊn\ *n* [*vaso-* + oxy*tocin*] : a polypeptide pituitary hormone of most lower vertebrates that is held to have an antidiuretic function

va·so·va·gal \ˌvā-zō-ˈvā-gəl\ *adj* : of, relating to, or involving both vascular and vagal factors

vas·sal \ˈvas-əl\ *n* [ME, fr. MF, fr. ML *vassallus*, fr. *vassus* servant, vassal, of Celt origin; akin to W *gwas* boy, servant] **1** : a person under the protection of another who is his feudal lord and to whom he has vowed homage and fealty : a feudal tenant **2** : one in a subservient or subordinate position — **vassal** *adj*

vas·sal·age \-ə-lij\ *n* **1** : the state of being a vassal **2** : the homage, fealty, or services due from a vassal **3** : a position of subordination or submission (as to a political power)

¹vast \ˈvast\ *adj* [L *vastus*; akin to OIr *fot* length] : very great in size, amount, degree, intensity, or esp. in extent or range ***syn*** see HUGE — **vast·ly** *adv* — **vast·ness** \ˈvas(t)-nəs\ *n*

²vast *n* : a boundless space <the ~ of heaven —John Milton>

vas·ti·tude \ˈvas-tə-ˌt(y)üd\ *n* : IMMENSITY, VASTNESS

vas·ti·ty \ˈvas-tət-ē\ *n, pl* **-ties** : VASTITUDE

vasty \ˈvas-tē\ *adj* : VAST <call spirits from the ~ deep —Shak.>

¹vat \ˈvat\ *n* [ME *fat, vat*, fr. OE *fæt*; akin to OHG *vaz* vessel, Lith *puodas* pot] **1** : a large vessel (as a cistern, tub, or barrel) esp. for holding liquors in an immature state or preparations for dyeing or tanning **2** : a liquor containing a dye converted into a soluble reduced colorless or weakly colored form that on textile material steeped in the liquor and exposed to the air is converted by oxidation to the original insoluble dye and precipitated in the fiber

²vat *vt* **vat·ted**; **vat·ting** : to put into or treat in a vat

VAT *abbr* value-added tax

vat dye *n* : a water-insoluble generally fast dye used in the form of a vat liquor — called also *vat color*

vat–dyed \ˈvat-ˈdīd\ *adj* : dyed with one or more vat dyes

vat·ic \ˈvat-ik\ *adj* [L *vates* seer, prophet; akin to OE *wōth* poetry, OHG *wuot* madness, OIr *fāith* seer, poet] : PROPHETIC, ORACULAR

Vat·i·can \ˈvat-i-kən\ *n* [L *Vaticanus* Vatican Hill (in Rome)] **1** : the papal headquarters in Rome **2** : the papal government — **Vatican** *adj*

va·tic·i·nal \və-ˈtis-ᵊn-əl, va-\ *adj* [L *vaticinus*, fr. *vaticinari*] : PROPHETIC

va·tic·i·nate \-ᵊn-ˌāt\ *vb* **-nat·ed**; **-nat·ing** [L *vaticinatus*, pp. of *vaticinari*, fr. *vates* + *-cinari* (akin to L *canere* to sing) — more at CHANT] : PROPHESY, PREDICT — **va·tic·i·na·tor** \-ˌāt-ər\ *n*

va·tic·i·na·tion \-ˌtis-ᵊn-ˈā-shən\ *n* **1** : something foretold : PREDICTION **2** : the act of prophesying

vaude·ville \ˈvȯd-(ə-)vəl, ˈväd-, ˈvōd-, -(ə-)ˌvil\ *n* [F, fr. MF, popular satirical song, alter. of *vaudevire*, fr. *vau-de-Vire* valley of Vire, fr. *vau, val* valley + *de* from, of (fr. L) + *Vire*, town in northwest France where such songs were composed — more at VALE, DE-] **1** : a light often comic theatrical piece frequently combining pantomime, dialogue, dancing, and song **2** : stage entertainment consisting of various unrelated acts (as performing animals, acrobats, comedians, dancers, or singers)

¹vaude·vil·lian \ˌvȯd-(ə-)ˈvil-yən, ˌväd-, ˌvōd-\ *n* : a vaudeville writer, actor, singer, or performer

²vaudevillian *adj* : of, relating to, or characteristic of vaudeville

Vau·dois \vō-ˈdwä, ˈvō-ˌ\ *n pl* [MF, fr. ML *Valdenses*] : WALDENSES

¹vault \ˈvȯlt\ *n* [ME *voute*, fr. MF, fr. (assumed) VL *volvita* turn, vault, prob. fr. *volvitare*] **1 a** : an arched structure of masonry usu. forming a ceiling or roof **b** : something (as the sky) resembling a vault **c** : an arched or dome-shaped anatomical structure **2 a** : a space covered by an arched structure; *esp* : an underground passage or room **b** : an underground storage compartment **c** : a room or compartment for the safekeeping of valuables **3 a** : a burial chamber **b** : a prefabricated container usu. of metal or concrete into which a casket is placed at burial — **vaulty** \ˈvȯl-tē\ *adj*

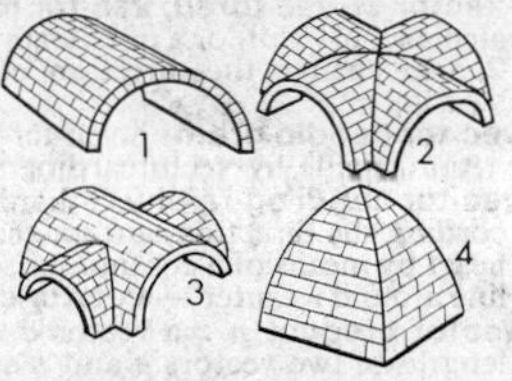

vaults 1a: *1* barrel, *2* cross, *3* Welsh, *4* cloister

²vault *vt* : to form or cover with or as if with a vault : ARCH

³vault *vb* [MF *volter*, fr. OIt *voltare*, fr. (assumed) VL *volvitare* to turn, leap, freq. of L *volvere* to roll — more at VOLUBLE] *vi* : to bound vigorously; *esp* : to execute a leap using the hands or a pole ~ *vt* : to leap over; *esp* : to leap over by aid of the hands or a pole

⁴vault *n* : an act of vaulting : LEAP

vault·ed \ˈvȯl-təd\ *adj* **1** : built in the form of a vault : ARCHED **2** : covered with a vault

vault·er \-tər\ *n* : one that vaults; *esp* : POLE-VAULTER

¹vault·ing \-tiŋ\ *n* : vaulted construction

²vaulting *adj* **1** : reaching or stretching for the heights **2** : designed for use in vaulting or in gymnastic exercises <a ~ block>

vaulting horse *n* : LONG HORSE

¹vaunt \ˈvȯnt, ˈvänt\ *vb* [ME *vaunten*, fr. MF *vanter*, fr. LL *vanitare*, fr. L *vanitas* vanity] *vi* : to make a vain display of one's own worth or attainments : BRAG ~ *vt* : to call attention to pridefully and often boastfully <our ~*ed* progress has its darker side> ***syn*** see BOAST — **vaunt·er** *n* — **vaunt·ing·ly** \-iŋ-lē\ *adv*

²vaunt *n* **1** : a vainglorious display of what one is or has or has done **2** : a bragging assertive statement

vaunt–cou·ri·er \vȯnt-ˈku̇r-ē-ər, vänt-, -ˈkər-ē-, -ˈkə-rē-\ *n* [MF *avant-courrier*, lit., advance courier] : one sent in advance : FORERUNNER

vaunt·ful \ˈvȯnt-fəl, ˈvänt-\ *adj* : VAINGLORIOUS, BOASTFUL

veal 2: *A* wholesale cuts: *1* leg, *2* loin, *3* flank, *4* rib, *5* breast, *6* shoulder, *7* shank *B* retail cuts: *1* hind shank, *2* heel of round, *3* round, *4* rump roast, *5* sirloin steak, *6* loin chops, *7* kidney chops, *8* flank, *9* breast, *10* rib roast, *11* blade steak, *12* arm steak, *13* shoulder roast, *14* fore shank

vaunty \ˈvȯnt-ē, ˈvänt-\ *adj, Scot* : PROUD, BOASTFUL, VAIN

vav *var of* WAW

vav·a·sor *or* **vav·a·sour** \ˈvav-ə-ˌsȯ(ə)r, -ˌsō(ə)r, -ˌsu̇(ə)r\ *n* [ME *vavasour*, fr. OF *vavassor*, prob. fr. ML *vassus vassorum* vassal of vassals] : a feudal tenant ranking directly below a baron

va·ward \ˈvau̇-ˌ(w)ō(ə)rd\ *n* [ME *vauntwarde, vaward*, fr. ONF *avantwarde*, fr. *avant* before (fr. L *abante*) + *warde* guard, fr. *warder* to guard — more at ADVANCE, REWARD] : the foremost part : FOREFRONT <the ~ of our youth —Shak.>

vb *abbr* verb; verbal

VC *abbr* **1** veterinary corps **2** vice-chancellor **3** vice-consul **4** Victoria Cross **5** Vietcong

VD *abbr* **1** vapor density **2** various dates **3** venereal disease

V–day \ˈvē-ˌdā\ *n* [*v*ictory *day*] : a day of victory

VDRL *abbr* venereal disease research laboratory

've \v, əv\ *vb* [by contr.] : HAVE <we'*ve* been there>

Ve·adar \ˈvā-ˌä-ˌdär, ˈvā-ə-\ *n* [Heb *wĕ-Adhār*, lit., and Adar (i.e., the second Adar)] : the intercalary month of the Jewish calendar following Adar in leap years

¹veal \ˈvē(ə)l\ *n* [ME *veel*, fr. MF, fr. L *vitellus* small calf, dim. of *vitulus* calf — more at WETHER] **1** : CALF; *esp* : VEALER **2** : the flesh of a young calf

²veal *vt* : to kill and dress (a calf) for veal

veal·er \ˈvē-lər\ *n* : a calf grown for or suitable for veal

vealy \ˈve-lē\ *adj* **1** : resembling or suggesting veal or a calf **2** : IMMATURE

vec·to·graph \ˈvek-tə-ˌgraf\ *n* [*vector* + *-graph*] : a picture composed of two superposed stereoscopic images that give a three-dimensional effect when viewed through polarizing spectacles — **vec·to·graph·ic** \ˌvek-tə-ˈgraf-ik\ *adj*

[1]**vec·tor** \'vek-tər\ *n* [NL, fr. L, carrier, fr. *vectus*, pp. of *vehere* to carry — more at WAY] **1 a :** a quantity that has magnitude and direction and that is commonly represented by a directed line segment whose length represents the magnitude and whose orientation in space represents the direction; *broadly* **:** an element of a vector space **b :** a course or compass direction esp. of an airplane **2 a :** an organism (as an insect) that transmits a pathogen **b :** POLLINATOR a **3 :** DRIVE 6 — **vec·to·ri·al** \vek-'tōr-ē-əl, -'tȯr-\ *adj*

[2]**vector** *vt* **vec·tored; vec·tor·ing** \-t(ə-)riŋ\ **1 :** to guide (as an airplane, its pilot, or a missile) in flight by means of a radioed vector **2 :** to change the direction of (the thrust of a jet engine) for steering

vec·tor·car·dio·gram \,vek-tər-'kärd-ē-ə-,gram\ *n* **:** a graphic record made by vectorcardiography

vec·tor·car·di·og·ra·phy \-,kärd-ē-'äg-rə-fē\ *n* **:** a method of recording the direction and magnitude of the electrical forces of the heart by means of a continuous series of vectors that form a curving line around a center — **vec·tor·car·dio·graph·ic** \-ē-ə-'graf-ik\ *adj*

vector product *n* **:** a vector *c* whose length is the product of the lengths of two vectors *a* and *b* and the sine of their included angle, whose direction is perpendicular to their plane, and whose sense is that of a right-handed screw with axis *c* when *a* is rotated into *b* — called also *cross product*

vector space *n* **:** a set representing a generalization of a system of vectors and consisting of elements which comprise a commutative group under addition, each of which is left unchanged under multiplication by the multiplicative identity of a field, and for which multiplication by the multiplicative operation of the field is commutative, closed, distributive such that both $c(A + B) = cA + cB$ and $(c + d)A = cA + dA$, and associative such that $(cd)A = c(dA)$ where *A*, *B* are vectors and *c*, *d* are elements of the field

vector sum *n* **:** the sum of a number of vectors that for the sum of two vectors is geometrically represented by the diagonal of a parallelogram whose sides represent the two vectors being added

Ve·da \'väd-ə\ *n* [Skt, lit., knowledge; akin to Gk *eidenai* to know — more at WIT] **:** any of four canonical collections of hymns, prayers, and liturgical formulas that comprise the earliest Hindu sacred writings

ve·da·lia \vi-'dāl-yə\ *n* [NL] **:** an Australian ladybug (*Rodolia cardinalis*) introduced to many countries to control scale insects

Ve·dan·ta \vā-'dänt-ə, və-, -'dant-\ *n* [Skt *Vedānta*, lit., end of the Veda, fr. *Veda* + *anta* end; akin to OE *ende* end] **:** an orthodox system of Hindu philosophy developing esp. in a qualified monism the speculations of the Upanishads on ultimate reality and the liberation of the soul — **Ve·dan·tism** \-'dän-,tiz-əm, -'dan-\ *n* — **Ve·dan·tist** \-'dänt-əst, -'dant-\ *n*

Ve·dan·tic \-'dänt-ik, -'dant-\ *adj* **1 :** of or relating to the Vedanta philosophy **2 :** VEDIC

Ved·da *or* **Ved·dah** \'ved-ə\ *n* [Sinhalese *vedda* hunter] **:** a member of an aboriginal people of Ceylon

Ved·doid \'ved-,ȯid\ *n* **:** a member of an ancient race of southern Asia characterized by wavy to curly hair, chocolate-brown skin color, slender body build, and fine features — **Veddoid** *adj*

ve·dette \vi-'det\ *n* [F, fr. It *vedetta*, alter. of *veletta*, prob. fr. Sp *vela* watch, fr. *velar* to keep watch, fr. L *vigilare* to wake, watch, fr. *vigil* awake] **:** a mounted sentinel stationed in advance of pickets

Ve·dic \'väd-ik\ *adj* **:** of or relating to the Vedas, the language in which they are written, or Hindu history and culture between 1500 B.C. and 500 B.C.

vee \'vē\ *n* **1 :** the letter *v* **2 :** something shaped like the letter V

vee·na *var of* VINA

veep \'vēp\ *n* [fr. *v. p.* (abbr. for *vice-president*)] **:** VICE-PRESIDENT

[1]**veer** \'vi(ə)r\ *vt* [ME *veren*, of LG or D origin; akin to MD *vieren* to slacken, MLG *vīren*] **:** to let or pay out (as a rope)

[2]**veer** *vb* [MF *virer*, prob. of Celt origin; akin to OIr *fiar* oblique; akin to OE *wīr* wire] *vi* **1 :** to change direction or course **2** *of the wind* **:** to shift in a clockwise direction **3 :** to wear ship ~ *vt* **:** to direct to a different course; *specif* **:** WEAR 7 ***syn*** see SWERVE — **veer·ing·ly** \-iŋ-lē\ *adv*

[3]**veer** *n* **:** a change in course or direction <a ~ to the right>

vee·ry \'vi(ə)r-ē\ *n, pl* **veeries** [perh. imit. of one of its notes] **:** a thrush (*Hylocichla fuscescens*) common in the eastern U.S.

veg \'vej\ *n, pl* **veg** *Brit* **:** VEGETABLE

Ve·ga \'vē-gə, 'vā-\ *n* [NL, fr. Ar (*al-Nasr*) *al-Wāqiʿ*, lit., the falling (vulture)] **:** a star of the first magnitude that is the brightest in the constellation Lyra

veg·an \'vej-ən, -,an\ *n* [by contr. fr. *vegetarian*] **:** an extreme vegetarian **:** one that consumes no animal food or dairy products — **veg·an·ism** \'vej-ə-,niz-əm\ *n*

[1]**veg·e·ta·ble** \'vej-tə-bəl, 'vej-ət-ə-\ *adj* [ME, fr. ML *vegetabilis* vegetative, fr. *vegetare* to grow, fr. L, to animate, fr. *vegetus* lively, fr. *vegēre* to rouse, excite — more at WAKE] **1 a :** of, relating to, constituting, or growing like plants **b :** consisting of plants **:** VEGETATIONAL **2 :** made or obtained from plants or plant products **3 :** resembling or suggesting a plant (as in monotony or passivity)

[2]**vegetable** *n* **1 :** PLANT 1b **2 :** a usu. herbaceous plant (as the cabbage, bean, or potato) grown for an edible part which is usu. eaten with the principal part of a meal; *also* **:** such edible part **3 :** a human being having a dull or merely physical existence

vegetable ivory *n* **1 :** the hard white opaque endosperm of the ivory nut that takes a high polish and is used as a substitute for ivory **2 :** IVORY NUT

vegetable marrow *n* **:** any of various smooth-skinned elongated summer squashes with creamy white to deep green skins

vegetable oil *n* **:** an oil of plant origin; *esp* **:** a fatty oil from seeds or fruits

vegetable oyster *n* **:** SALSIFY

vegetable plate *n* **:** a main course without meat consisting of several vegetables cooked separately and served on one plate

vegetable silk *n* **:** a cottony fibrous material obtained from the coating of tree seeds (as of a Brazilian tree, *Chorisia speciosa*, of the silk-cotton family) and used esp. for stuffing cushions

vegetable wax *n* **:** a wax of plant origin secreted commonly in thin flakes by the walls of epidermal cells

veg·e·ta·bly \'vej-tə-blē, 'vej-ət-ə-\ *adv* **:** in the manner of or like a vegetable

veg·e·tal \'vej-ət-ᵊl\ *adj* [ML *vegetare* to grow] **1 :** VEGETABLE **2 :** VEGETATIVE

vegetal pole *n* **:** the point on the surface of an egg that is diametrically opposite to the animal pole and usu. marks the center of the protoplasm containing more yolk, dividing more slowly and into larger blastomeres than that about the animal pole, and giving rise to the hypoblast of the embryo

[1]**veg·e·tar·i·an** \,vej-ə-'ter-ē-ən\ *n* [[2]*vegetable* + *-arian*] **1 :** one who believes in or practices vegetarianism **2 :** HERBIVORE

[2]**vegetarian** *adj* **1 :** of or relating to vegetarians **2 :** consisting wholly of vegetables <a ~ diet>

veg·e·tar·i·an·ism \-ē-ə-,niz-əm\ *n* **:** the theory or practice of living on a diet made up of vegetables, fruits, grains, nuts, and sometimes animal products (as milk and cheese)

veg·e·tate \'vej-ə-,tāt\ *vb* **-tat·ed; -tat·ing** [ML *vegetatus*, pp. of *vegetare* to grow] *vi* **1 a :** to grow in the manner of a plant; *also* **:** to grow exuberantly or with proliferation of fleshy or warty outgrowths **b :** to produce vegetation **2 :** to lead a passive existence without exertion of body or mind ~ *vt* **:** to establish vegetation in or on

veg·e·ta·tion \,vej-ə-'tā-shən\ *n* **1 :** the act or process of vegetating **2 :** inert existence **3 :** plant life or total plant cover (as of an area) **4 :** an abnormal outgrowth upon a body part — **veg·e·ta·tion·al** \-shnəl, -shən-ᵊl\ *adj* — **veg·e·ta·tion·al·ly** \-shnə-lē, -shən-ᵊl-ē\ *adv*

veg·e·ta·tive \'vej-ə-,tāt-iv\ *adj* **1 a** (1) **:** growing or having the power of growing (2) **:** of, relating to, or engaged in nutritive and growth functions as contrasted with reproductive functions <a ~ nucleus> **b :** promoting plant growth <the ~ properties of soil> **c :** of, relating to, or involving propagation by nonsexual processes or methods **2 :** relating to, composed of, or suggesting vegetation <~ cover> **3 :** of or relating to the division of nature comprising the plant kingdom **4 :** affecting, arising from, or relating to involuntary bodily functions **5 :** VEGETABLE 3 — **veg·e·ta·tive·ly** *adv* — **veg·e·ta·tive·ness** *n*

ve·gete \və-'jēt\ *adj* [L *vegetus* — more at VEGETABLE] *archaic* **:** LIVELY, HEALTHY

veg·e·tive \'vej-ət-iv\ *adj* [ML *vegetare* to grow] **1 :** VEGETABLE **2 :** VEGETATIVE

ve·he·mence \'vē-ə-mən(t)s\ *n* **:** the quality or state of being vehement **:** INTENSITY

ve·he·ment \-mənt\ *adj* [MF, fr. L *vehement-*, *vehemens*; akin to L *vehere*] **:** marked by forceful energy **:** POWERFUL <a ~ wind>: as **a :** intensely emotional **:** IMPASSIONED, FERVID <~ patriotism> **b** (1) **:** deeply felt <a ~ suspicion> (2) **:** forcibly expressed <~ denunciations> **c :** bitterly antagonistic <a ~ debate> — **ve·he·ment·ly** *adv*

ve·hi·cle \'vē-,(h)ik-əl, 'vē-ə-kəl\ *n* [F *véhicule*, fr. L *vehiculum* carriage, conveyance, fr. *vehere* to carry — more at WAY] **1 a :** an inert medium in which a medicinally active agent is administered **b :** any of various media acting usu. as solvents, carriers, or binders for active ingredients or pigments **2 :** an agent of transmission **:** CARRIER **3 :** a medium through which something is expressed, achieved, or displayed **4 :** a means of carrying or transporting something **:** CONVEYANCE: as **a :** MOTOR VEHICLE **b :** a piece of mechanized equipment

ve·hic·u·lar \vē-'hik-yə-lər\ *adj* **1 a :** of, relating to, or designed for vehicles and esp. motor vehicles **b :** transported by vehicle **2 :** serving as a vehicle

V–8 \'vē-'āt\ *n* **:** an internal-combustion engine having two banks of four cylinders each with the banks at an angle to each other; *also* **:** an automobile having such an engine

[1]**veil** \'vā(ə)l\ *n* [ME *veile*, fr. ONF, fr. L *vela*, pl. of *velum* veil] **1 a :** a length of cloth worn by women as a covering for the head and shoulders and often esp. in eastern countries the face; *specif* **:** the outer covering of a nun's headdress **b :** a length of veiling or netting worn over the head or face or attached for protection or ornament to a hat or headdress **c :** any of various liturgical cloths; *esp* **:** a cloth used to cover the chalice **2 :** the cloistered life of a nun **3 :** a concealing curtain or cover of cloth **4 :** something that hides or obscures like a veil **5 :** a covering body part or membrane: as **a :** VELUM **b :** CAUL

[2]**veil** *vt* **:** to cover, provide, obscure, or conceal with or as if with a veil ~ *vi* **:** to put on or wear a veil

veiled \'vā(ə)ld\ *adj* **1 a :** having or wearing a veil or a concealing cover <a ~ hat> **b :** characterized by a softening tonal distortion **2 :** obscured as if by a veil **:** DISGUISED <~ threats>

veil·ing \'vā-liŋ\ *n* **1 :** VEIL **2 :** any of various light sheer fabrics

[1]**vein** \'vān\ *n* [ME *veine*, fr. OF, fr. L *vena*] **1 a :** a narrow water channel in rock or earth, or ice **b** (1) **:** LODE 2, 3 (2) **:** a bed of useful mineral matter **2 a :** BLOOD VESSEL **b :** one of the tubular branching vessels that carry blood from the capillaries toward the heart **3 a :** one of the vascular bundles forming the framework of a leaf **b :** one of the thickened cuticular ribs that serve to stiffen the wings of an insect **4 :** something suggesting veins (as in reticulation); *specif* **:** a wavy variegation (as in marble) **5 a :** a distinctive mode of expression **:** STYLE **b :** a pervasive element or quality **:** STRAIN **c :** a line of thought or action **6 a :** a special aptitude **:** TALENT **b :** a usu. transitory and casually attained mood **c :** top form **:** FETTLE ***syn*** see MOOD — **vein·al** \-ᵊl\ *adj*

[2]**vein** *vt* **:** to pattern with or as if with veins

veined \'vānd\ *adj* **:** patterned with or as if with veins **:** having venation **:** STREAKED <a ~ leaf> <~ marble>

vein·er \'vā-nər\ *n* **:** a small V gouge used in wood carving

vein·ing \'vā-niŋ\ *n* **:** a pattern of veins **:** VENATION

vein·let \'vān-lət\ *n* : a small vein esp. of a leaf
veiny \'vā-nē\ *adj* : full of veins : VEINED
vel *abbr* **1** vellum **2** velocity
ve·la·men \və-'lā-mən\ *n, pl* **ve·lam·i·na** \-'lam-ə-nə\ [NL, fr. L, covering, fr. *velare* to cover, fr. *velum* veil] : the thick corky epidermis of aerial roots of an epiphytic orchid that absorbs water from the atmosphere
vel·a·men·tous \ˌvel-ə-'ment-əs\ *adj* [NL *velamentum* membrane, fr. L, covering, fr. *velare* to cover] : of, relating to, or resembling a thin membrane
ve·lar \'vē-lər\ *adj* [NL *velaris*, fr. *velum*] **1** : of, forming, or relating to a velum and esp. the soft palate **2** : formed with the back of the tongue touching or near the soft palate <the ~ \k\ of \'kül\ *cool*> — **velar** *n*
ve·lar·i·um \vi-'lar-ē-əm, -'ler-\ *n, pl* **-ia** \-ē-ə\ [L, fr. *velum* veil] : an awning over an ancient Roman theater or amphitheater
ve·lar·iza·tion \ˌvē-lə-rə-'zā-shən\ *n* **1** : the quality or state of being velarized **2** : an act or instance of velarizing
ve·lar·ize \'vē-lə-ˌrīz\ *vt* **-ized; -iz·ing** : to modify (as the \l\ of \'pül\ *pool*) by a simultaneous velar articulation
veld *or* **veldt** \'velt, 'felt\ *n* [Afrik *veld*, fr. MD, field; akin to OE *feld* field] : a grassland esp. of southern Africa usu. with scattered shrubs or trees
ve·li·ger \'vē-lə-jər, 'vel-ə-\ *n* [NL, fr. *velum* + *-ger* -gerous] : a larval mollusk in the stage when it has developed the velum
vel·i·ta·tion \ˌvel-ə-'tā-shən\ *n* [L *velitation-, velitatio*, fr. *velitatus*, pp. of *velitari* to skirmish, fr. *velit-, veles* light-armed foot soldier; akin to L *vehere* to carry] **1** : SKIRMISH **2** : DISPUTE
vel·le·ity \ve-'lē-ət-ē, və-\ *n, pl* **-ities** [NL *velleitas*, fr. L *velle* to wish, will — more at WILL] **1** : the lowest degree of volition **2** : a slight wish or tendency : INCLINATION
[1]**vel·lum** \'vel-əm\ *n* [ME *velim*, fr. MF *veelin*, fr. *veelin*, adj., of a calf, fr. *veel* calf — more at VEAL] **1** : a fine-grained unsplit lambskin, kidskin, or calfskin prepared esp. for writing on or for binding books **2** : a strong cream-colored paper
[2]**vellum** *adj* **1** : of, resembling, or bound in vellum **2** : slightly rough <paper with a ~ finish>
ve·lo·ce \vā-'lō-(ˌ)chā\ *adv or adj* [It, fr. L *veloc-, velox*] : in a rapid manner — used as a direction in music
ve·lo·cim·e·ter \ˌvē-lō-'sim-ət-ər, ˌvel-ō-\ *n* [*velocity* + *-meter*] : a device for measuring speed (as of machinery or sound)
ve·loc·i·pede \və-'läs-ə-ˌpēd\ *n* [F *vélocipède*, fr. L *veloc-, velox* + *ped-, pes* foot — more at FOOT] : a lightweight wheeled vehicle propelled by the rider: as **a** *archaic* : BICYCLE **b** : TRICYCLE **c** : a 3-wheeled railroad handcar
ve·loc·i·ty \və-'läs-ət-ē, -'läs-tē\ *n, pl* **-ties** [MF *velocité*, fr. L *velocitat-, velocitas*, fr. *veloc-, velox* quick; akin to L *vehere* to carry — more at WAY] **1** : quickness of motion : SPEED <the ~ of sound> **2** : time rate of linear motion in a given direction **3 a** : rate of occurrence or action : RAPIDITY <the ~ of historical change —R. J. Lifton> **b** : rate of turnover <the ~ of money>
ve·lo·drome \'vēl-ə-ˌdrōm, 'vel-, 'väl-\ *n* [F *vélodrome*, fr. *vélo* cycle (short for *vélocipède*) + *-drome*] : a track designed for cycling
ve·lour *or* **ve·lours** \və-'lu̇(ə)r\ *n, pl* **velours** \-'lu̇(ə)rz\ [F *velours* velvet, velour, fr. MF *velours, velour*, fr. OF *velous*, fr. L *villosus* shaggy, fr. *villus* shaggy hair] **1** : any of various fabrics with a pile or napped surface resembling velvet used in heavy weights for upholstery and curtains and in lighter weights esp. for coats and jackets **2** : a fur felt (as of rabbit or nutria) finished with a long velvety nap and used esp. for hats
ve·lum \'vē-ləm\ *n, pl* **ve·la** \-lə\ [NL, fr. L, curtain, veil] **1** : a membrane or membranous part resembling a veil or curtain: as **a** : SOFT PALATE **b** : an annular membrane projecting inward from the margin of the umbrella in some jellyfishes (as the hydromedusans) **2** : a swimming organ that is esp. well developed in the later larval stages of many marine gastropods
ve·lure \vel-'(y)u̇(ə)r, 'vel-yər\ *n* [modif. of MF *velour*] *obs* : VELVET; *also* : a fabric resembling velvet
ve·lu·ti·nous \və-'lüt-ᵊn-əs\ *adj* [NL *velutinus*, fr. ML *velutum* velvet, prob. fr. OIt *velluto* shaggy, fr. (assumed) VL *villutus*] : covered with a silky pubescence : VELVETY <a ~ rhizome>
[1]**vel·vet** \'vel-vət\ *n* [ME *veluet, velvet*, fr. MF *velu* shaggy, fr. (assumed) VL *villutus*, fr. L *villus* shaggy hair; akin to L *vellus* fleece — more at WOOL] **1** : a clothing and upholstery fabric (as of silk, rayon, or wool) characterized by a short soft dense pile **2 a** : something suggesting velvet **b** : a characteristic (as softness or smoothness) of velvet **3** : the soft vascular skin that envelops and nourishes the developing antlers of deer **4 a** : the cash or chips a player is ahead in a gambling game : WINNINGS **b** : a profit or gain beyond ordinary expectation
[2]**velvet** *adj* **1** : made of or covered with velvet; *also* : clad in velvet **2** : resembling or suggesting velvet : VELVETY <a ~ voice>
velvet ant *n* : any of various solitary usu. brightly colored and hairy fossorial wasps (family Mutillidae) with the female wingless
velvet bean *n* : an annual legume (*Stizolobium deeringianum*) grown esp. in the southern U.S. for green manure and grazing; *also* : its seed often used as stock feed
vel·ve·teen \ˌvel-və-'tēn\ *n* **1** : a clothing fabric usu. of cotton in twill or plain weaves made with a short close weft pile in imitation of velvet **2** *pl* : clothes made of velveteen
velvet sponge *n* : a fine soft usu. flat and rounded commercial sponge (*Hippiospongia equina meandriformis*) found in the Gulf of Mexico and off the West Indies
vel·vety \'vel-vət-ē\ *adj* **1** : soft and smooth like velvet <~ hair> **2** : smooth to the taste : MILD <~ rum>
Ven *abbr* venerable
ven- *or* **veni-** *or* **veno-** *comb form* [L *vena*] : vein <*venation*> <*veni*puncture> <*veno*stasis>
ve·na \'vē-nə\ *n, pl* **ve·nae** \-(ˌ)nē\ [ME, fr. L] : VEIN
ve·na ca·va \ˌvē-nə-'kā-və\ *n, pl* **ve·nae ca·vae** \-ni-kā-(ˌ)vē\ [NL, lit., hollow vein] : one of the large veins by which in air-breathing vertebrates the blood is returned to the right atrium of the heart — **vena ca·val** \-vəl\ *adj*
ve·nal \'vēn-ᵊl\ *adj* [L *venalis*, fr. *venum* (acc.) sale; akin to Gk *ōneisthai* to buy, Skt *vasna* price] : capable of being bought or obtained for money or other valuable consideration : PURCHASABLE; *esp* : open to corrupt influence and esp. bribery : MERCENARY <a ~ legislator> — **ve·nal·i·ty** \vi-'nal-ət-ē\ *n* — **ve·nal·ly** \'vēn-ᵊl-ē\ *adv*
ve·nat·ic \vi-'nat-ik\ *adj* [L *venaticus*, fr. *venatus*, pp. of *venari* to hunt — more at VENISON] **1** : of, relating to, or used in hunting <~ equipment> **2** : fond of or living by hunting
ve·na·tion \ve-'nā-shən, vē-\ *n* [L *vena* vein] : an arrangement or system of veins: as **a** : that in the tissue of a leaf blade **b** : that in the wing of an insect — **ve·na·tion·al** \-shnəl, -shən-ᵊl\ *adj*

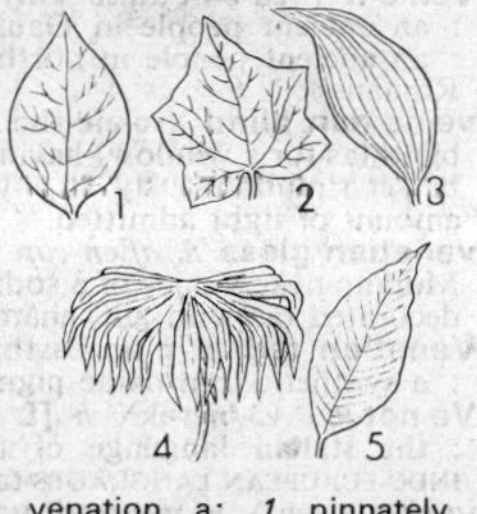

venation a: *1* pinnately veined, *2* palmately veined, *3* base to tip, *4* base to midrib, *5* midrib to margin

vend \'vend\ *vb* [L *vendere* to sell, v.t., contr. for *venum dare* to give for sale] *vi* : to dispose of something by sale : SELL; *also* : to engage in selling ~ *vt* **1 a** : to sell esp. as a hawker or peddler **b** : to sell by means of vending machines **2** : to utter publicly : PUBLISH
Ven·da \'ven-də\ *n* : a Bantu language of the northern Transvaal
ven·dace \'ven-dəs\ *n, pl* **vendace** *also* **ven·dac·es** [NL *vandesius*, fr. MF *vandoise*] : a whitefish (*Coregonus vandesius*) native to various lakes of Scotland and England
vend·ee \ven-'dē\ *n* : one to whom a thing is sold : BUYER
vend·er \'ven-dər\ *n* : VENDOR
ven·det·ta \ven-'det-ə\ *n* [It, lit., revenge, fr. L *vindicta* — more at VINDICTIVE] **1** : BLOOD FEUD **2** : a prolonged feud marked by bitter hostility
[1]**vend·ible** *or* **vend·able** \'ven-də-bəl\ *adj* **1** : capable of being vended : SALABLE **2** *obs* : VENAL — **vend·ibil·i·ty** \ˌven-də-'bil-ət-ē\ *n* — **vend·ibly** \'ven-də-blē\ *adv*
[2]**vendible** *n* : a vendible article — usu. used in pl.
vending machine *n* : a coin-operated machine for vending merchandise
ven·di·tion \ven-'dish-ən\ *n* [L *vendition-, venditio*, fr. *venditus*, pp. of *vendere* to vend] : the act of selling : SALE
ven·dor \'ven-dər, *for 1 also* ven-'dȯ(ə)r\ *n* **1** : one that vends : SELLER **2** : VENDING MACHINE
ven·due \'ven-ˌd(y)ü, 'vän-, 'fen-; ven-', vän-'\ *n* [obs. F, fr. MF, fr. *vendre* to sell, fr. L *vendere*] : a public sale at auction
[1]**ve·neer** \və-'ni(ə)r\ *n* [G *furnier*, fr. *furnieren* to veneer, fr. F *fournir* to furnish — more at FURNISH] **1** : a thin sheet of a material: as **a** : a layer of wood of superior value or excellent grain to be glued to an inferior wood **b** : any of the thin layers bonded together to form plywood **2** : a protective or ornamental facing (as of brick or stone) **3** : a superficial or deceptively attractive appearance or display : GLOSS
[2]**veneer** *vt* **1** : to overlay or plate (as a common wood) with a thin layer of finer wood for outer finish or decoration; *broadly* : to face with a material giving a superior surface **2** : to cover over with a veneer; *esp* : to conceal (as a defect of character) under a superficial and deceptive attractiveness — **ve·neer·er** *n*
ve·neer·ing *n* **1** : material for veneering **2** : a veneered surface
ven·e·nate \'ven-ə-ˌnāt\ *vb* **-nat·ed; -nat·ing** [L *venenatus*, pp. of *venenare* to poison, fr. *venenum* poison — more at VENOM] *vt* : POISON; *specif* : to inject a toxic substance into ~ *vi* : to use a toxic substance in preying or feeding — **ven·e·na·tion** \ˌven-ə-'nā-shən\ *n*
ven·er·a·ble \'ven-ər(-ə)-bəl, 'ven-rə-bəl\ *adj* **1** : deserving to be venerated — used as a title for an Anglican archdeacon or for a Roman Catholic who has been accorded the lowest of three degrees of recognition for sanctity **2** : made sacred esp. by religious or historical association **3 a** : calling forth respect through age, character, and attainments; *broadly* : conveying an impression of aged goodness and benevolence **b** : impressive by reason of age <under ~ pines> ***syn*** see OLD — **ven·er·a·bil·i·ty** \ˌven-(ə-)rə-'bil-ət-ē\ *n* — **ven·er·a·ble·ness** \'ven-ər(-ə)-bəl-nəs, 'ven-rə-\ *n* — **ven·er·a·bly** \-blē\ *adv*
ven·er·ate \'ven-ə-ˌrāt\ *vt* **-at·ed; -at·ing** [L *veneratus*, pp. of *venerari*, fr. *vener-, venus* love, charm — more at WIN] : to regard with reverential respect or with admiring deference ***syn*** see REVERE — **ven·er·a·tor** \-ˌrāt-ər\ *n*
ven·er·a·tion \ˌven-ə-'rā-shən\ *n* **1** : respect or awe inspired by the dignity, wisdom, dedication, or talent of a person **2** : the act of venerating **3** : the condition of one that is venerated
ve·ne·re·al \və-'nir-ē-əl\ *adj* [ME *venerealle*, fr. L *venereus*, fr. *vener-, venus* love, sexual desire] **1** : of or relating to sexual pleasure or indulgence **2 a** : resulting from or contracted during sexual intercourse <~ infections> **b** : of, relating to, or affected with venereal disease <a high ~ rate> **c** : involving the genital organs <~ sarcoma>
venereal disease *n* : a contagious disease (as gonorrhea or syphilis) that is typically acquired in sexual intercourse
ve·ne·re·ol·o·gy \və-ˌnir-ē-'äl-ə-jē\ *or* **ven·er·ol·o·gy** \ˌven-ə-'räl-ə-jē\ *n* [*venereology* ISV *venereal* + *-o-* + *-logy*; *venerology*, fr. G *venerologie*, fr. *venerisch* venereal (fr. L *vener-, venus*) + *-o-* + *-logie* -logy] : a branch of medical science concerned with venereal diseases — **ve·ne·re·o·log·i·cal** \və-ˌnir-ē-ə-'läj-i-kəl\ *adj* — **ve·ne·re·ol·o·gist** \-ē-'äl-ə-jəst\ *n*

1ven·ery \'ven-ə-rē\ *n* [ME *venerie*, fr. MF, fr. *vener* to hunt, fr. L *venari* — more at VENISON] **1 :** the art, act, or practice of hunting **2 :** animals that are hunted : GAME

2venery *n* [ME *venerie*, fr. ML *veneria*, fr. L *vener-*, *venus* sexual desire] **1 :** the pursuit of or indulgence in sexual pleasure **2 :** SEXUAL INTERCOURSE

vene·sec·tion *also* **veni·sec·tion** \'ven-ə-ˌsek-shən, 'vēn-\ *n* [NL *venae section-*, *venae sectio*, lit., cutting of a vein] **:** the operation of opening a vein for letting blood : PHLEBOTOMY

Ven·e·ti \'ven-ə-ˌtī\ *also* **Ven·e·tes** \'ven-ə-ˌtēz\ *n pl* [L *Veneti*] **1 :** an ancient people in Gaul conquered by Caesar in 56 B.C. **2 :** an ancient people in northeastern Italy allied politically to the Romans

ve·ne·tian blind \və-ˌnē-shən-\ *n* [*Venetian* of Venice, Italy] **:** a blind (as for a window) having numerous horizontal slats that may be set simultaneously at any of several angles so as to vary the amount of light admitted

venetian glass *n, often cap V* **:** often colored glassware made at Murano near Venice of a soda-lime metal and typically elaborately decorated (as with gilt, enamel, or engraving)

Venetian red *n* **:** an earthy hematite used as a pigment; *also* **:** a synthetic iron oxide pigment

Ve·net·ic \və-'net-ik\ *n* [L *veneticus* of the Veneti, fr. *Veneti*] **:** the Italian language of the ancient Veneti of Italy — see INDO-EUROPEAN LANGUAGES table — **Venetic** *adj*

venge \'venj\ *vt* **venged; veng·ing** [ME *vengen*, fr. OF *vengier*] **:** AVENGE

ven·geance \'ven-jən(t)s\ *n* [ME, fr. OF, fr. *vengier* to avenge, fr. L *vindicare* to lay claim to, avenge — more at VINDICATE] **:** punishment inflicted in retaliation for an injury or offense : RETRIBUTION — **with a vengeance 1 :** with great force or vehemence **2 :** to an extreme or excessive degree

venge·ful \'venj-fəl\ *adj* [obs. E *venge* (revenge)] **:** REVENGEFUL: as **a :** seeking to avenge **b :** serving to gain vengeance ***syn*** see VINDICTIVE — **venge·ful·ly** \-fə-lē\ *adv* — **venge·ful·ness** *n*

V–en·gine \'vē-\ *n* **:** an internal-combustion engine whose cylinders are arranged in two banks forming an acute angle or a 90-degree angle

veni- *or* **veno-** — see VEN-

ve·nial \'vē-nē-əl, -nyəl\ *adj* [ME, fr. OF, fr. LL *venialis*, fr. L *venia* favor, indulgence, pardon; akin to L *venus* love, charm — more at WIN] **:** of a kind that can be remitted : FORGIVABLE, PARDONABLE; *also* **:** meriting no particular censure or notice : EXCUSABLE <~ faults> — **ve·nial·ly** \-ē\ *adv* — **ve·nial·ness** *n*

venial sin *n* **:** a sin that is relatively slight or that is committed without full reflection or consent and so according to Thomist theology does not deprive the soul of sanctifying grace — compare MORTAL SIN

ven·in \'ven-ən\ *n* [*ven*om + *-in*] **:** any of various toxic substances in snake venom

ve·ni·punc·ture \'vēn-ə-ˌpəŋ(k)-chər, 'ven-ə-\ *n* **:** surgical puncture of a vein esp. for the withdrawal of blood or for intravenous medication

ve·ni·re \və-'nī-rē\ *n* [*venire facias*] **:** an entire panel from which a jury is drawn

ve·ni·re fa·ci·as \-ˌnī-rē-'fā-shē-əs\ *n* [ME, fr. ML, you should cause to come] **:** a judicial writ directing the sheriff to summon a specified number of qualified persons to serve as jurors

ve·ni·re·man \və-'nī-rē-mən, -'nir-ē-\ *n* **:** a member of a venire

ven·i·son \'ven-ə-sən *also* -ə-zən\ *n, pl* **venisons** *also* **venison** [ME, fr. OF *veneison* hunting, game, fr. L *venation-*, *venatio*, fr. *venatus*, pp. of *venari* to hunt, pursue; akin to OE *winnan* to struggle — more at WIN] **1 :** the edible flesh of a wild animal taken by hunting **2 :** the flesh of a deer

Ve·ni·te \və-'nīt-ē, -'nē-ˌtā\ *n* [L, O come, fr. *venire* to come; fr. the opening word of Ps 95:1 — more at COME] **:** a liturgical chant composed of parts of Psalms 95 and 96

Venn diagram \'ven-\ *n* [John *Venn* †1923 E logician] **:** a graph that employs circles to represent logical relations between and operations on sets and the terms of propositions by the inclusion, exclusion, or intersection of the circles

ve·nog·ra·phy \vi-'näg-rə-fē, vā-\ *n* [ISV] **:** roentgenography of a vein after injection of an opaque substance

1ven·om \'ven-əm\ *n* [ME *venim*, *venom*, fr. OF *venim*, fr. (assumed) VL *venimen*, alter. of L *venenum* magic charm, drug, poison; akin to L *venus* love, charm — more at WIN] **1 :** poisonous matter normally secreted by some animals (as snakes, scorpions, or bees) and transmitted to prey or an enemy chiefly by biting or stinging; *broadly* **:** material that is poisonous **2 :** ILL WILL, MALEVOLENCE

2venom *vt* **:** ENVENOM

ven·om·ous \'ven-ə-məs\ *adj* **1 :** full of venom: as **a :** POISONOUS, ENVENOMED **b :** NOXIOUS, PERNICIOUS <expose a ~ dope ring —Don Porter> **c :** SPITEFUL, MALEVOLENT <~ criticism> **2 :** having a venom-producing gland and able to inflict a poisoned wound <~ snakes> — **ven·om·ous·ly** *adv* — **ven·om·ous·ness** *n*

ve·no·sta·sis \ˌvē-nə-'stā-səs\ *n* [NL] **:** abnormal slowing or stoppage of the flow of blood in a vein

ve·nous \'vē-nəs\ *adj* [L *venosus*, fr. *vena* vein] **1 :** of, relating to or full of veins <a ~ rock> <a ~ system> **2** *of blood* **:** having passed through the capillaries and given up oxygen for the tissues and become charged with carbon dioxide — **ve·nous·ly** *adv*

1vent \'vent\ *vt* [ME *venten*, prob. fr. MF *esventer* to expose to the air, fr. *es-* ex- (fr. L *ex-*) + *vent* wind, fr. L *ventus* — more at WIND] **1 :** to provide with a vent **2 a :** to serve as a vent for <chimneys ~ smoke> **b :** DISCHARGE, EXPEL **c :** to give often vigorous or emotional expression to **3 :** to relieve by venting ***syn*** see EXPRESS

2vent *n* **1 :** an opportunity or means of escape, passage, or release **:** OUTLET <finally gave ~ to his pent-up hostility> **2 :** an opening for the escape of a gas or liquid or for the relief of pressure: as **a :** the external opening of the rectum or cloaca : ANUS **b :** PIPE 3c, FUMAROLE **c :** an opening at the breech of a gun through which fire is touched to the powder **d** *chiefly Scot* **:** CHIMNEY, FLUE — **vent·less** \-ləs\ *adj*

3vent *n* [ME *vente*, alter. of *fente*, fr. MF, slit, fissure, fr. *fendre* to split, fr. L *findere* — more at BITE] **:** a slit in a garment; *specif* **:** an opening in the lower part of a seam (as of a jacket or skirt)

vent·age \'vent-ij\ *n* **:** a small hole (as a flute stop)

ven·tail \'ven-ˌtāl\ *n* [ME, fr. MF *ventaille*, fr. *vent* wind] **:** the lower movable front of a medieval helmet

ven·ter \'vent-ər\ *n* [AF, fr. L, belly, womb; akin to OHG *wanast* paunch, L *vesica* bladder] **1 a :** a wife or mother that is a source of offspring **2 :** a protuberant and often hollow anatomical structure: as **a :** ABDOMEN **b :** BELLY 5b **c :** a broad shallow concavity esp. of a bone **d :** the swollen basal portion of an archegonium in which the egg of a vascular cryptogam is developed

ven·ti·late \'vent-əl-ˌāt\ *vt* **-lat·ed; -lat·ing** [LL *ventilatus*, pp. of *ventilare*, fr. L, to fan, winnow, fr. *ventulus*, dim. of *ventus* wind — more at WIND] **1 a :** to examine, discuss, or investigate freely and openly : EXPOSE <*ventilating* family quarrels in public> **b :** to make public : UTTER <*ventilated* his objections at length> **2** *archaic* **:** to free from chaff by winnowing **3 :** to expose to air and esp. to a current of fresh air for purifying, curing, or refreshing <~ stored grain>; *also* **:** OXYGENATE, AERATE <~ blood in the lungs> **4 a** *of a current of air* **:** to pass or circulate through so as to freshen **b :** to cause fresh air to circulate through (as a room or mine) **5 :** to provide an opening in (a burning structure) to permit escape of smoke and heat — **ven·ti·la·tive** \'vent-əl-ˌāt-iv\ *adj*

ven·ti·la·tion \ˌvent-əl-'ā-shən\ *n* **1 :** the act or process of ventilating **2 a :** circulation of air <a room with good ~> **b :** the circulation and exchange of gases in the lungs that is basic to respiration **3 :** a system or means of providing fresh air

ven·ti·la·tor \'vent-əl-ˌāt-ər\ *n* **:** one that ventilates; *esp* **:** a contrivance for introducing fresh air or expelling foul or stagnant air

ven·ti·la·to·ry \'vent-əl-ə-ˌtōr-ē, -ˌtȯr-\ *adj* **:** of, relating to, or provided with ventilation

ventr- *or* **ventro-** *comb form* [L *ventr-*, *venter* belly] **:** ventral and <*ventro*lateral>

1ven·tral \'ven-trəl\ *adj* [F, fr. L *ventralis*, fr. *ventr-*, *venter*] **1 a :** of or relating to the belly : ABDOMINAL **b :** being or located near or on the anterior or lower surface of an animal that is opposite the back **2 a :** AXIAL **b :** being or located on the lower surface of a dorsiventral plant structure — **ven·tral·ly** \-trə-lē\ *adv*

2ventral *n* **:** a ventral part (as a scale or fin)

ventral root *n* **:** the one of the two roots of a spinal nerve that passes ventrally from the spinal cord and consists of motor fibers — compare DORSAL ROOT

ven·tri·cle \'ven-tri-kəl\ *n* [ME, fr. L *ventriculus*, fr. dim. of *ventr-*, *venter* belly] **:** a cavity of a bodily part or organ: as **a :** a chamber of the heart which receives blood from a corresponding atrium and from which blood is forced into the arteries — see HEART illustration **b :** one of the system of communicating cavities in the brain that are continuous with the central canal of the spinal cord — see BRAIN illustration

ven·tri·cose \-ˌkōs\ *adj* [NL *ventricosus*, fr. L *ventr-*, *venter* + *-icosus* (as in *varicosus* varicose)] **:** markedly swollen, distended, or inflated esp. on one side <~ corollas>

ven·tric·u·lar \ven-'trik-yə-lər, vən-\ *adj* **:** of, relating to, or being a ventricle or ventriculus

ven·tric·u·lus \ven-'trik-yə-ləs, vən-\ *n, pl* **-li** \-ˌlī, -ˌlē\ [NL, fr. L, dim. of *venter*] **:** a digestive cavity: as **a :** STOMACH **b :** GIZZARD 1a **c :** the digestive part of an insect's stomach

ven·tril·o·quism \ven-'tril-ə-ˌkwiz-əm\ *n* [LL *ventriloquus* ventriloquist, fr. L *ventr-*, *venter* + *loqui* to speak; fr. the belief that the voice is produced from the ventriloquist's stomach] **:** the production of the voice in such a manner that the sound appears to come from a source other than the vocal organs of the speaker — **ven·tri·lo·qui·al** \ˌven-trə-'lō-kwē-əl\ *adj* — **ven·tri·lo·qui·al·ly** \-ə-lē\ *adv*

ven·tril·o·quist \ven-'tril-ə-kwəst\ *n* **:** one who uses or is skilled in ventriloquism; *esp* **:** one who entertains by using ventriloquism to carry on an apparent conversation with a hand-manipulated dummy — **ven·tril·o·quis·tic** \(ˌ)ven-ˌtril-ə-'kwis-tik\ *adj*

ven·tril·o·quize \ven-'tril-ə-ˌkwīz\ *vb* **-quized; -quiz·ing** *vi* **:** to use ventriloquism ~ *vt* **:** to utter in the manner of a ventriloquist

ven·tril·o·quy \-kwē\ *n* **:** VENTRILOQUISM

ven·tro·lat·er·al \ˌven-ˌtrō-'lat-ə-rəl, -'la-trəl\ *adj* **:** ventral and lateral

ven·tro·me·di·al \-'mēd-ē-əl\ *adj* **:** ventral and medial

1ven·ture \'ven-chər\ *vb* **ven·tured; ven·tur·ing** \'vench-(ə-)riŋ\ [ME *venteren*, by shortening & alter. fr. *aventuren*, fr. *aventure* adventure] *vt* **1 :** to expose to hazard : RISK, GAMBLE **2 :** to undertake the risks and dangers of : BRAVE <*ventured* the stormy sea> **3 :** to offer at the risk of rebuff, rejection, or censure <~ an opinion> ~ *vi* **:** to proceed despite danger : DARE

2venture *n* **1** *obs* **:** FORTUNE, CHANCE **2 a :** an undertaking involving chance, risk, or danger; *esp* **:** a speculative business enterprise **b :** a venturesome act **3 :** something (as money or property) at hazard in a speculative venture — **at a venture :** at random <a certain man drew a bow *at a venture*, and smote the king — 1 Kings 22:34 (AV)>

venture capital *n* **:** capital (as retained corporate earnings or individual savings) invested or available for investment in the ownership element of new or fresh enterprise — called also *risk capital*

ven·tur·er \'vench-(ə-)rər\ *n* **:** one that ventures; *specif* **:** a person who engages in business ventures

ven·ture·some \'ven-chər-səm\ *adj* **1 :** inclined to court or incur risk or danger : DARING <a ~ hunter> **2 :** involving risk : HAZARDOUS <a ~ journey> ***syn*** see ADVENTUROUS — **ven·ture·some·ly** *adv* — **ven·ture·some·ness** *n*

ven·tu·ri \ven-'tu̇(ə)r-ē\ *n* [G. B. *Venturi* †1822 It physicist] **:** a short tube that is inserted in a pipeline, that has flaring ends connected by a constricted middle, that depends for operation on the fact that as the velocity of flow of a fluid increases in the constricted part the pressure decreases, and that is used for measuring the quantity of a fluid flowing, in connection with other devices for measuring airspeed, and for producing suction esp. for driving aircraft instruments

ven·tur·ous \ˈvench-(ə-)rəs\ *adj* : VENTURESOME — **ven·tur·ous·ly** *adv* — **ven·tur·ous·ness** *n*

ven·ue \ˈven-ˌyü\ *n* [ME *venyw* action of coming, fr. MF *venue,* fr. *venir,* to come, fr. L *venire* — more at COME] **1 a :** the place or county in which alleged events from which a legal action arises take place **b :** the place from which the jury is drawn and in which trial is held in such an action **c :** a statement showing that a case is brought to the proper court or authority **2 :** the locale of a gathering (as for a sports event or a political conference)

ven·ule \ˈvēn-(ˌ)yü(ə)l, ˈven-\ *n* [L *venula,* dim. of *vena* vein] **:** a small vein; *esp* **:** one of the minute veins connecting the capillary bed with the larger systemic veins

Ve·nus \ˈvē-nəs\ *n* [ME, fr. L *Vener-, Venus*] **1 :** the Roman goddess of natural productivity and in later times of love and beauty — compare APHRODITE **2 :** the planet second in order from the sun — see PLANET table

Ve·nus·berg \-ˌbərg\ *n* **:** a mountain in central Germany containing a cavern in which according to medieval legend Venus held court

Ve·nus·hair \-ˌha(ə)r, -ˌhe(ə)r\ *n* **:** a delicate maidenhair fern (*Adiantum capillus-veneris*) with a slender black stipe and branches

Ve·nu·sian \vi-ˈn(y)ü-zhən\ *adj* **:** of or relating to the planet Venus

Ve·nus's–fly·trap \ˌvē-nəs(-əz)-ˈflī-ˌtrap\ *n* **:** an insectivorous plant (*Dionaea muscipula*) of the sundew family of the Carolina coast with the leaf apex modified into an insect trap

Venus's-flytrap

ver *abbr* verse

ve·ra·cious \və-ˈrā-shəs\ *adj* [L *verac-, verax* — more at VERY] **1 :** TRUTHFUL, HONEST **2 :** marked by truth **:** ACCURATE — **ve·ra·cious·ly** *adv* — **ve·ra·cious·ness** *n*

ve·rac·i·ty \və-ˈras-ət-ē\ *n, pl* **-ties 1 :** devotion to the truth **:** TRUTHFULNESS **2 :** power of conveying or perceiving truth **3 :** conformity with truth or fact **:** ACCURACY **4 :** something true <he can make lies sound like *veracities*> ***syn*** see TRUTH

ve·ran·da *or* **ve·ran·dah** \və-ˈran-də\ *n* [Hindi *varandā*] **:** a usu. roofed open gallery or portico attached to the exterior of a building

ve·ran·daed *also* **ve·ran·dahed** \-dəd\ *adj* **:** having a veranda

ve·rat·ri·dine \və-ˈra-trə-ˌdēn\ *n* [*veratrine* + *-idine*] **:** a poisonous amorphous alkaloid $C_{36}H_{51}NO_{11}$ occurring esp. in sabadilla seed

ve·ra·trine \ˈver-ə-ˌtrēn, və-ˈra-trən\ *n* [NL *veratrina,* fr. *Veratrum,* genus of herbs] **:** a poisonous irritant mixture of alkaloids from sabadilla seed that has been used as a counterirritant, insecticide, and c-mitotic agent

ve·ra·trum \və-ˈrā-trəm\ *n* [NL, genus name, fr. L, hellebore] **:** HELLEBORE 2

verb \ˈvərb\ *n* [ME *verbe,* fr. MF, fr. L *verbum* word, verb — more at WORD] **:** a word that characteristically is the grammatical center of a predicate and expresses an act, occurrence, or mode of being, that in various languages is inflected for agreement with the subject, for tense, for voice, for mood, or for aspect, and that typically has rather full descriptive meaning and characterizing quality but is sometimes nearly devoid of these esp. when used as an auxiliary or copula

[1]**ver·bal** \ˈvər-bəl\ *adj* [MF or LL; MF, fr. LL *verbalis,* fr. L *verbum* word] **1 a :** of, relating to, or consisting of words <~ instructions> **b :** of, relating to, or involving words rather than meaning or substance <a consistency that is merely ~ and scholastic —B. N. Cardozo> **c :** consisting of or using words only and not involving action <a ~ protest> **2 :** of, relating to, or formed from a verb <a ~ adjective> **3 :** spoken rather than written <a ~ contract> **4 :** VERBATIM, WORD-FOR-WORD <a ~ translation> **5 :** of or relating to facility in the use and comprehension of words <~ aptitude> — **ver·bal·ly** \-bə-lē\ *adv*

[2]**verbal** *n* **:** a word that combines characteristics of a verb with those of a noun or adjective — compare GERUND, INFINITIVE, PARTICIPLE

verbal auxiliary *n* **:** an auxiliary verb

ver·bal·ism \ˈvər-bə-ˌliz-əm\ *n* **1 a :** a verbal expression **:** TERM **b :** PHRASING, WORDING **2 :** words used as if they were more important than the realities they represent <the emancipation of science from ~ —G. A. L. Sarton> **3 a :** a wordy expression of little meaning **b :** VERBOSITY

ver·bal·ist \-ləst\ *n* **1 :** one who stresses words above substance or reality **2 :** a person who uses words skillfully — **ver·bal·is·tic** \ˌvər-bə-ˈlis-tik\ *adj*

ver·bal·ize \ˈvər-bə-ˌlīz\ *vb* **-ized; -iz·ing** *vi* **1 :** to speak or write verbosely **2 :** to express something in words ~ *vt* **1 :** to convert into a verb **2 :** to name or describe in words — **ver·bal·iza·tion** \ˌvər-bə-lə-ˈzā-shən\ *n* — **ver·bal·iz·er** \ˈvər-bə-ˌlī-zər\ *n*

verbal noun *n* **:** a noun derived directly from a verb or verb stem and in some uses having the sense and constructions of a verb

[1]**ver·ba·tim** \(ˌ)vər-ˈbāt-əm\ *adv* [ME, fr. ML, fr. L *verbum* word] **:** in the exact words **:** word for word

[2]**verbatim** *adj* **:** being in or following the exact words **:** WORD-FOR-WORD

ver·be·na \(ˌ)vər-ˈbē-nə\ *n* [NL, genus of herbs or subshrubs, fr. L, sing. of *verbenae* sacred boughs, certain medicinal plants — more at VERVAIN] **:** VERVAIN; *esp* **:** any of numerous garden plants of hybrid origin widely grown for their showy spikes of white, pink, red, or blue flowers which are borne in profusion over a long season

ver·biage \ˈvər-bē-ij *also* -bij\ *n* [F, fr. MF *verbier* to chatter, fr. *verbe* speech, fr. L *verbum* word] **1 :** superfluity of words in proportion to sense or content **:** WORDINESS **2 :** manner of expressing oneself in words **:** DICTION <concise military ~>

ver·bi·cide \ˈvər-bə-ˌsīd\ *n* [L *verbum* word + E *-cide*] **1 :** deliberate distortion of the sense of a word (as in punning) **2 :** one who distorts the sense of a word

ver·bid \ˈvər-bəd\ *n* **:** VERBAL

verb·ify \ˈvər-bə-ˌfī\ *vt* **-ified; -ify·ing :** to make into a verb

ver·big·er·a·tion \(ˌ)vər-ˌbij-ə-ˈrā-shən\ *n* [ISV, fr. L *verbigeratus,* pp. of *verbigerare* to talk, chat, fr. *verbum* word + *gerere* to carry, wield — more at WORD, CAST] **:** continual repetition of stereotyped phrases (as in some forms of mental illness)

verbena

ver·bile \ˈvər-ˌbīl\ *n* [L *verbum* word + E *-ile* (as in *audile*)] **:** one whose mental imagery consists of words

ver·bose \(ˌ)vər-ˈbōs\ *adj* **1 :** containing more words than necessary **:** WORDY <a ~ reply>; *also* **:** impaired by wordiness <a ~ style> **2 :** given to wordiness <a ~ orator> ***syn*** see WORDY ***ant*** laconic — **ver·bose·ly** *adv* — **ver·bose·ness** *n* — **ver·bos·i·ty** \-ˈbäs-ət-ē\ *n*

ver·bo·ten \vər-ˈbōt-ᵊn, fər-\ *adj* [G] **:** FORBIDDEN; *esp* **:** prohibited by dictate

verb sap \ˈvərb-ˈsap\ **:** verbum sap

ver·bum sap \ˌvər-bəm-ˈsap\ [short for NL *verbum sapienti* (*sat est*) a word to the wise (is sufficient)] **:** enough said — used to indicate that something left unsaid may or should be inferred

ver·dan·cy \ˈvərd-ᵊn-sē\ *n* **:** the quality or state of being verdant

ver·dant \ˈvərd-ᵊnt\ *adj* [modif. of MF *verdoyant,* fr. prp. of *verdoyer* to be green, fr. OF *verdoier,* fr. *verd, vert* green, fr. L *viridis,* fr. *virēre* to be green] **1 a :** green in tint or color <~ grass> **b :** green with growing plants <~ fields> **2 :** unripe in experience or judgment **:** GREEN — **ver·dant·ly** *adv*

verd an·tique *or* **verde an·tique** \ˌvər-ˌdan-ˈtēk\ *n* [It *verde antico,* lit., ancient green] **1 :** a green mottled or veined serpentine marble or calcareous serpentine much used for indoor decoration esp. by the ancient Romans **2 :** an andesite porphyry showing crystals of feldspar in a dark green groundmass

ver·der·er *or* **ver·der·or** \ˈvərd-ər-ər\ *n* [AF, fr. OF *verdier,* fr. *verd* green] **:** an English judicial officer having charge of the king's forest

ver·dict \ˈvər-(ˌ)dikt\ *n* [alter. of ME *verdit,* fr. AF, fr. OF *ver* true (fr. L *verus*) + *dit* saying, dictum, fr. L *dictum* — more at VERY] **1 :** the finding or decision of a jury on the matter submitted to them in trial **2 :** OPINION, JUDGMENT

ver·di·gris \ˈvərd-ə-ˌgrēs, -ˌgris, -grəs *also* -ˌgrē\ *n* [ME *vertegrez,* fr. OF *vert de Grice,* lit., green of Greece] **1 a :** a green or greenish blue poisonous pigment resulting from the action of acetic acid on copper and consisting of one or more basic copper acetates **b :** normal copper acetate $Cu(C_2H_3O_2)_2.H_2O$ **2 :** a green or bluish deposit esp. of copper carbonates formed on copper, brass, or bronze surfaces

ver·din \ˈvərd-ᵊn\ *n* [F, yellowhammer] **:** a very small yellow-headed titmouse (*Auriparus flaviceps*) found from Texas to California and southward

ver·dure \ˈvər-jər\ *n* [ME, fr. MF, fr. *verd* green] **1 :** the greenness of growing vegetation; *also* **:** such vegetation itself **2 :** a condition of health and vigor — **ver·dur·ous** \ˈvərj-(ə-)rəs\ *adj* — **ver·dur·ous·ness** *n*

ver·dured \ˈvər-jərd\ *adj* **:** covered with verdure

[1]**verge** \ˈvərj\ *n* [ME, fr. MF, fr. L *virga* rod, stripe — more at WHISK] **1 a (1) :** a rod or staff carried as an emblem of authority or symbol of office **(2)** *obs* **:** a stick or wand held by a person being admitted to tenancy while he swears fealty **b :** the spindle of a watch balance; *esp* **:** a spindle with pallets in an old vertical escapement **c :** the male intromittent organ of any of various invertebrates **2 a :** something that borders, limits, or bounds: as **(1) :** an outer margin of an object or structural part **(2) :** the edge of the tiling projecting over the gable of a roof **b :** BRINK, THRESHOLD ***syn*** see BORDER

[2]**verge** *vi* **verged; verg·ing 1 :** to be contiguous **2 :** to be on the verge or border

[3]**verge** *vi* **verged; verg·ing** [L *vergere* to bend, incline — more at WRENCH] **1 a** *of the sun* **:** to incline toward the horizon **:** SINK **b :** to move or extend in some direction or toward some condition **2 :** to be in transition or change

ver·gence \ˈvər-jən(t)s\ *n* [back-formation fr. *convergence* & *divergence*] **:** a movement of one eye in relation to the other

verg·er \ˈvər-jər\ *n* **1** *chiefly Brit* **:** an attendant that carries a verge (as before a bishop or justice) **2 :** a church official who keeps order during services or serves as an usher or a sacristan

ve·rid·i·cal \və-ˈrid-i-kəl\ *adj* [L *veridicus,* fr. *verus* true + *dicere* to say — more at VERY, DICTION] **1 :** TRUTHFUL, VERACIOUS **2 :** not illusory **:** GENUINE — **ve·rid·i·cal·i·ty** \-ˌrid-ə-ˈkal-ət-ē\ *n* — **ve·rid·i·cal·ly** \-k(ə-)lē\ *adv*

ver·i·fi·able \ˈver-ə-ˌfī-ə-bəl\ *adj* **:** capable of being verified — **ver·i·fi·abil·i·ty** \ˌver-ə-ˌfī-ə-ˈbil-ət-ē\ *n* — **ver·i·fi·able·ness** *n*

ver·i·fi·ca·tion \ˌver-ə-fə-ˈkā-shən\ *n* **:** the act or process of verifying **:** the state of being verified

ver·i·fy \ˈver-ə-ˌfī\ *vt* **-fied; -fy·ing** [ME *verifien,* fr. MF *verifier,* fr. ML *verificare,* fr. L *verus* true — more at VERY] **1 :** to confirm or substantiate in law by oath **2 :** to establish the truth, accuracy, or reality of ***syn*** see CONFIRM — **ver·i·fi·er** \-ˌfī(-ə)r\ *n*

ver·i·ly \ˈver-ə-lē\ *adv* [ME *verraily,* fr. *verray* very] **1 :** in truth **:** CERTAINLY **2 :** TRULY, CONFIDENTLY

ə abut ᵊ kitten ər further a back ā bake ä cot, cart
aü out ch chin e less ē easy g gift i trip ī life
j joke ŋ sing ō flow ȯ flaw ȯi coin th thin t͟h this
ü loot u̇ foot y yet yü few yu̇ furious zh vision

ver·i·sim·i·lar \ˌver-ə-ˈsim-(ə-)lər\ *adj* [L *verisimilis*] **:** having the appearance of truth **:** PROBABLE — **ver·i·sim·i·lar·ly** *adv*
ver·i·si·mil·i·tude \-sə-ˈmil-ə-ˌt(y)üd\ *n* [L *verisimilitudo,* fr. *verisimilis* verisimilar, fr. *veri similis* like the truth] **1 :** the quality or state of being verisimilar **2 :** something verisimilar ***syn*** see TRUTH — **ver·i·si·mil·i·tu·di·nous** \-ˌmil-ə-ˈt(y)üd-nəs, -ᵊn-əs\ *adj*
ve·rism \ˈvi(ə)r-ˌiz-əm, ˈve(ə)r-\ *n* [It *verismo,* fr. *vero* true, fr. L *verus*] **:** artistic use of contemporary everyday material in preference to the heroic or legendary esp. in grand opera — **ve·rist** \-əst\ *n or adj* — **ve·ris·tic** \vi(ə)r-ˈis-tik, ve(ə)r-\ *adj*
ve·ris·mo \vā-ˈrēz-(ˌ)mō\ *n* [It] **:** VERISM
ver·i·ta·ble \ˈver-ət-ə-bəl\ *adj* **:** being in fact the thing named and not false, unreal, or imaginary — often used to stress the aptness of a metaphor <a ~ mountain of references> ***syn*** see AUTHENTIC ***ant*** factitious — **ver·i·ta·ble·ness** *n* — **ver·i·ta·bly** \-blē\ *adv*
ver·i·ty \ˈver-ət-ē\ *n, pl* **-ties** [ME *verite,* fr. MF *verité,* fr. L *veritat-, veritas,* fr. *verus* true] **1 :** the quality or state of being true or real **2 :** something (as a statement) that is true; *esp* **:** a fundamental and inevitably true value esp. of an ethical, aesthetic, or religious nature <such eternal *verities* as honor, love, and patriotism> **3 :** the quality or state of being truthful or honest <the king-becoming graces, as justice, ~ —Shak.>
ver·juice \ˈvər-ˌjüs\ *n* [ME *verjus,* fr. MF, fr. *vert jus,* lit., green juice] **1 :** the sour juice of crab apples or of unripe fruit (as grapes or apples); *also* **:** an acid liquor made from verjuice **2 :** acidity of disposition or manner
ver·meil *n* [MF, fr. *vermeil,* adj. — more at VERMILION] **1** \ˈvər-məl, -ˌmāl\ **:** VERMILION **2** \ve(ə)r-ˈmā\ **:** gilded silver — **vermeil** *adj*
vermi- *comb form* [NL, fr. LL, fr. L *vermis* — more at WORM] **:** worm <*vermi*form>
ver·mi·an \ˈvər-mē-ən\ *adj* [ISV] **:** of, relating to, or resembling worms
ver·mi·cel·li \ˌvər-mə-ˈchel-ē, -ˈsel-\ *n* [It, fr. pl. of *vermicello,* dim. of *verme* worm, fr. L *vermis*] **:** pasta made in long solid strings smaller in diameter than spaghetti
ver·mi·cide \ˈvər-mə-ˌsīd\ *n* **:** an agent that destroys worms
ver·mic·u·lar \(ˌ)vər-ˈmik-yə-lər\ *adj* [NL *vermicularis,* fr. L *vermiculus,* dim. of *vermis*] **1 a :** resembling a worm in form or motion **b :** VERMICULATE **2 :** of, relating to, or caused by worms
ver·mic·u·late \-lət\ *or* **ver·mic·u·lat·ed** \-ˌlāt-əd\ *adj* [L *vermiculatus,* fr. *vermiculus*] **1 a :** VERMIFORM **b :** marked with irregular fine lines or with wavy impressed lines <a ~ nut> **2 :** TORTUOUS, INVOLUTE **3 :** full of worms **:** WORM-EATEN — **ver·mic·u·la·tion** \-ˌmik-yə-ˈlā-shən\ *n*
ver·mic·u·lite \(ˌ)vər-ˈmik-yə-ˌlīt\ *n* [L *vermiculus* little worm] **:** any of various micaceous minerals that are hydrous silicates resulting usu. from expansion of the granules of mica at high temperatures to give a lightweight highly water-absorbent material
ver·mi·form \ˈvər-mə-ˌfȯrm\ *adj* [NL *vermiformis,* fr. *vermi-* + *-formis* form] **:** resembling a worm in shape
vermiform appendix *n* **:** a narrow blind tube usu. about three or four inches long that extends from the cecum in the lower right-hand part of the abdomen
ver·mi·fuge \ˈvər-mə-ˌfyüj\ *adj* [prob. fr. (assumed) NL *vermifugus,* fr. *vermi-* + L *fugare* to put to flight — more at -FUGE] **:** serving to destroy or expel parasitic worms **:** ANTHELMINTIC — **vermifuge** *n*
ver·mil·ion *or* **ver·mil·lion** \vər-ˈmil-yən\ *n* [ME *vermilioun,* fr. OF *vermeillon,* fr. *vermeil,* adj., bright red, vermilion, fr. LL *vermiculus* kermes, fr. L, little worm] **1 :** a bright red pigment consisting of mercuric sulfide; *broadly* **:** any of various red pigments **2 :** a variable color averaging a vivid reddish orange
ver·min \ˈvər-mən\ *n, pl* **vermin** [ME, fr. MF, fr. (assumed) L *vermin-, vermen* worm; akin to L *vermis* worm — more at WORM] **1 a :** small common harmful or objectionable animals (as lice or fleas) that are difficult to control **b :** birds and mammals that prey on game **2 :** an offensive person
ver·min·osis \ˌvər-mə-ˈnō-səs\ *n, pl* **-oses** \-ˌsēz\ [NL, fr. (assumed) L *vermin-, vermen* worm] **:** infestation with or disease caused by parasitic worms
ver·min·ous \ˈvər-mə-nəs\ *adj* **1 :** consisting of or being vermin **:** NOXIOUS **2 :** forming a breeding place for or infested by vermin **:** FILTHY <~ garbage> **3 :** caused by vermin <~ disease> — **ver·min·ous·ly** *adv*
ver·mouth \vər-ˈmüth\ *n* [F *vermout,* fr. G *wermut* wormwood, fr. OHG *wermuota* — more at WORMWOOD] **:** a dry or sweet alcoholic beverage that has a white wine base, that is flavored with aromatic herbs, and that is used as an aperitif or in mixed drinks
[1]**ver·nac·u·lar** \və(r)-ˈnak-yə-lər\ *adj* [L *vernaculus* native, fr. *verna* slave born in his master's house, native] **1 a :** using a language or dialect native to a region or country rather than a literary, cultured, or foreign language **b :** of, relating to, or being a nonstandard or substandard language or dialect of a place, region, or country **c :** of, relating to, or being the normal spoken form of a language **2 :** applied to a plant or animal in the common native speech as distinguished from the Latin nomenclature of scientific classification **3 :** of, relating to, or characteristic of a period, place, or group; *esp* **:** of, relating to, or being the common building style of a period or place — **ver·nac·u·lar·ly** *adv*
[2]**vernacular** *n* **1 :** a vernacular language, expression, or mode of expression **2 :** the mode of expression of a group or class **3 :** a vernacular name of a plant or animal ***syn*** see DIALECT
ver·nac·u·lar·ism \və(r)-ˈnak-yə-lə-ˌriz-əm\ *n* **:** a vernacular word or idiom
ver·nal \ˈvərn-ᵊl\ *adj* [L *vernalis,* alter. of *vernus,* fr. *ver* spring; akin to Gk *ear* spring] **1 :** of, relating to, or occurring in the spring <~ equinox> <~ sunshine> **2 :** fresh or new like the spring; *also* **:** YOUTHFUL — **ver·nal·ly** \-ᵊl-ē\ *adv*
ver·nal·ize \ˈvərn-ᵊl-ˌīz\ *vt* **-ized; -iz·ing :** to hasten the flowering and fruiting of (plants) by treating seeds, bulbs, or seedlings so as to induce a shortening of the vegetative period — **ver·nal·iza·tion** \ˌvərn-ᵊl-ə-ˈzā-shən\ *n*
ver·na·tion \(ˌ)vər-ˈnā-shən\ *n* [NL *vernation-, vernatio,* fr. L *vernatus,* pp. of *vernare* to behave as in spring, fr. *vernus* vernal] **:** the arrangement of foliage leaves within the bud
Ver·ner's law \ˌve(ə)r-nərz-\ *n* [Karl A. *Verner*] **:** a statement in historical linguistics: in medial or final position in voiced environments and when the immediately preceding vowel did not bear the principal accent in Proto-Indo-European, the Proto-Germanic voiceless fricatives *f, þ,* and *χ* derived from the Proto-Indo-European voiceless stops *p, t,* and *k* and the Proto-Germanic voiceless fricative *s* derived from Proto-Indo-European *s* became the voiced fricatives ƀ, đ, ǥ, and *z* represented in various recorded Germanic languages by *b, d, g,* and *r*
ver·ni·cle *or* **ver·na·cle** \ˈvər-ni-kəl\ *n* [ME *vernicle,* fr. MF *veronique, vernicle,* fr. ML *veronica*] **:** VERONICA
[1]**ver·ni·er** \ˈvər-nē-ər\ *n* [Pierre *Vernier*] **1 :** a short scale made to slide along the divisions of a graduated instrument for indicating parts of divisions **2 a :** a small auxiliary device used with a main device to obtain fine adjustment **b :** any of two or more small supplementary rocket engines or gas nozzles on a missile or a rocket vehicle for making fine adjustments in the speed or course or controlling the attitude — called also *vernier engine*

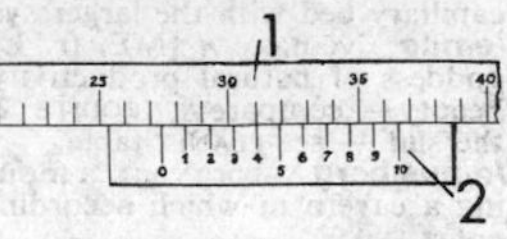

vernier 1: *1* regular scale, *2* vernier scale indicating measurement of 27.4

[2]**vernier** *adj* **:** having or comprising a vernier
vernier caliper *n* **:** a measuring device that consists of a main scale with a fixed jaw and a sliding jaw with an attached vernier
ver·nis·sage \ˌver-ni-ˈsäzh\ *n* [F, day before an exhibition opens reserved for artists to varnish and put finishing touches to their paintings, lit., varnishing, fr. *vernis* varnish — more at VARNISH] **:** a private showing or preview of an art exhibition
Ver·o·nal \ˈver-ə-ˌnȯl, -ən-ᵊl\ *trademark* — used for barbital
[1]**ve·ron·i·ca** \və-ˈrän-i-kə\ *n* [NL, genus of herbs] **:** SPEEDWELL
[2]**veronica** *n* [ML, fr. *Veronica* St. Veronica] **:** an image of Christ's face said to have been impressed on the cloth that St. Veronica gave him to wipe his face with on the way to his crucifixion; *also* **:** a cloth resembling the legendary one of St. Veronica
[3]**veronica** *n* [Sp *verónica,* fr. St. *Veronica*] **:** a pase in bullfighting in which the cape is swung slowly away from the charging bull while the matador keeps his feet in the same position
ver·ru·ca \və-ˈrü-kə\ *n, pl* **-cae** \-(ˌ)kē, -ˌkī, -ˌsī\ [L — more at WART] **1 :** a wart or warty skin lesion **2 :** a warty elevation on a plant or animal surface
verruca vul·ga·ris \-ˌvəl-ˈgar-əs, -ˈger-\ *n* [NL, lit., common verruca] **:** WART 1a
ver·ru·cose \və-ˈrü-ˌkōs\ *adj* **:** covered with warty elevations
vers *symbol* versed sine
ver·sal \ˈvər-səl, ˈvär-\ *adj* [short for *universal*] *archaic* **:** ENTIRE, WHOLE <as pale as any clout in the ~ world —Shak.>
[1]**ver·sant** \ˈvərs-ᵊnt\ *adj* [L *versant-, versans,* pres. part. of *versare, versari* to turn, occupy oneself, meditate] **1 :** mentally engaged or occupied **2 :** EXPERIENCED, PRACTICED **3 :** CONVERSANT
[2]**ver·sant** \ˈvərs-ᵊnt, ve(ə)r-ˈsäⁿ\ *n* [F, fr. MF, fr. prp. of *verser* to turn, pour, fr. L *versare* to turn; fr. its shedding of water] **1 :** the slope of a side of a mountain chain **2 :** the general slope of a country **:** INCLINATION
ver·sa·tile \ˈvər-sət-ᵊl, *esp Brit* -sə-ˌtīl\ *adj* [F or L; F, fr. L *versatilis* turning easily, fr. *versatus,* pp. of *versare* to turn, fr. *versus,* pp. of *vertere*] **1 :** changing or fluctuating readily **:** VARIABLE <a ~ disposition> **2 :** embracing a variety of subjects, fields, or skills; *also* **:** turning with ease from one thing to another **3 a (1) :** capable of turning forward or backward **:** REVERSIBLE <a ~ toe of a bird> **(2) :** capable of moving laterally and up and down <~ antennae> **b** *of an anther* **:** having the filaments attached at or near the middle so as to swing freely **4 :** having many uses or applications <~ building material> — **ver·sa·tile·ly** \-ᵊl-(l)ē, -ˌtīl-lē\ *adv* — **ver·sa·tile·ness** \-ᵊl-nəs, -ˌtīl-nəs\ *n*
syn VERSATILE, MANY-SIDED, ALL-AROUND *shared meaning element* **:** marked by or showing skill or ability or capacity or usefulness of many kinds
ver·sa·til·i·ty \ˌvər-sə-ˈtil-ət-ē\ *n* **:** the quality or state of being versatile <a writer of great ~>
vers de so·ci·é·té \ˌve(ə)r-də-ˌsō-sē-ə-ˈtā\ *n* [F, society verse] **:** witty and typically ironic light verse
[1]**verse** \ˈvərs\ *n* [ME *vers,* fr. OF, fr. L *versus,* lit., turning, fr. *versus,* pp. of *vertere* to turn — more at WORTH] **1 :** a line of metrical writing **2 a (1) :** metrical language **(2) :** metrical writing distinguished from poetry esp. by its lower level of intensity **(3) :** POETRY 2 **b :** POEM **c :** a body of metrical writing (as of a period or country) **3 :** STANZA **4 :** one of the short divisions into which a chapter of the Bible is traditionally divided
[2]**verse** *vb* **versed; vers·ing** *vi* **:** to make verse **:** VERSIFY ~ *vt* **1 :** to tell or celebrate in verse **2 :** to turn into verse
[3]**verse** *vt* **versed; vers·ing** [back-formation fr. *versed,* fr. L *versatus,* pp. of *versari* to be active, be occupied (in), pass. of *versare* to turn, fr. *versus,* pp.] **:** to familiarize by close association, study, or experience <*versed* himself in the theater>
versed sine \ˈvərs(t)-\ *n* [NL *versus* turned, fr. L, pp. of *vertere*] **:** 1 minus the cosine of an angle
verse·man \ˈvərs-mən\ *n* **:** a maker of verses **:** VERSIFIER
vers·er \ˈvər-sər\ *n* **:** VERSIFIER
vers·et \ˈvərs-ət, -ˌet; ˌvər-ˈset\ *n* [ME, fr. OF, dim. of *vers* verse] **:** a short verse esp. from a sacred book (as the Koran)
ver·si·cle \ˈvər-si-kəl\ *n* [ME, fr. L *versiculus,* dim. of *versus* verse] **1 :** a short verse or sentence (as from a psalm) said or sung by a leader in public worship and followed by a response from the people **2 :** a little verse
ver·si·col·or \ˈvər-si-ˌkəl-ər\ *or* **ver·si·col·ored** \-ərd\ *adj* [L *versicolor,* fr. *versus,* pp. of *vertere* to turn, change + *color*] **1**

: having various colors : VARIEGATED <~ flowers> **2** : changeable in color : IRIDESCENT <~ silk>
ver·sic·u·lar \vər-ˈsik-yə-lər\ *adj* [L *versiculus* little verse] : of or relating to verses or versicles
ver·si·fi·ca·tion \ˌvər-sə-fə-ˈkā-shən\ *n* **1** : the making of verses **2 a** : metrical structure : PROSODY **b** : a particular metrical structure or style **3** : a version in verse of something orig. in prose
ver·si·fi·er \ˈvər-sə-ˌfī(-ə)r\ *n* : one that versifies
ver·si·fy \-ˌfī\ *vb* **-fied; -fy·ing** *vi* : to compose verses ~ *vt* **1** : to relate or describe in verse **2** : to turn into verse
ver·sine \ˈvər-ˌsīn\ *n* [by contr.] : VERSED SINE
ver·sion \ˈvər-zhən, -shən\ *n* [MF, fr. ML *version-, versio* act of turning, fr. L *versus,* pp. of *vertere*] **1** : a translation from another language; *esp* : a translation of the Bible or a part of it **2 a** : an account or description from a particular point of view esp. as contrasted with another account **b** : an adaptation of a literary work <the movie ~ of the novel> **c** : an arrangement of a musical composition **3** : a form or variant of a type or original <an experimental ~ of the plane> **4 a** : a condition in which an organ and esp. the uterus is turned from its normal position **b** : manual turning of a fetus in the uterus to aid delivery — **ver·sion·al** \ˈvərzh-nəl, ˈvərsh-, -ən-ᵊl\ *adj*
vers li·bre \ve(ə)r-ˈlēbrᵊ\ *n, pl* **vers li·bres** *same*\ [F] : FREE VERSE
vers–li·brist \-ˈlē-brəst\ *n* [F *vers-libriste*] : a writer of free verse
ver·so \ˈvər-(ˌ)sō\ *n, pl* **versos** [NL *verso* (*folio*) the page being turned] **1** : the side of a leaf (as of a manuscript) that is to be read second **2** : a left-hand page — compare RECTO
verst \ˈvərst\ *n* [F *verste* & G *werst,* fr. Russ *versta;* akin to L *vertere* to turn] : a Russian unit of distance equal to 0.6629 miles
ver·sus \ˈvər-səs, -səz\ *prep* [ML, towards, against, fr. L, adv., so as to face, fr. pp. of *vertere* to turn] **1** : AGAINST **2** : in contrast to or as the alternative of <free trade ~ protection>
[1]**vert** \ˈvərt\ *n* [ME *verte,* fr. MF *vert,* fr. *vert* green — more at VERDANT] **1 a** : green forest vegetation esp. when forming cover or providing food for deer **b** : the right or privilege (as in England) of cutting living wood or sometimes of pasturing animals in a forest **2** : the heraldic color green
[2]**vert** *abbr* **1** vertebrate **2** vertical
ver·te·bra \ˈvərt-ə-brə, *nonstand* -ˌbrā\ *n, pl* **-brae** \-ˌbrā, -(ˌ)brē\ *or* **-bras** [L, joint, vertebra, fr. *vertere* to turn — more at WORTH] : one of the bony or cartilaginous segments composing the spinal column, consisting in some lower vertebrates of several distinct elements which never become united, and in higher vertebrates having a short more or less cylindrical body whose ends articulate by pads of elastic or cartilaginous tissue with those of adjacent vertebrae and a bony arch that encloses the spinal cord

sixth thoracic vertebra, seen from above: *1* neural spine, *2* neural arch, *3* transverse process, *4* spinal foramen, *5* centrum

ver·te·bral \(ˌ)vər-ˈtē-brəl *also* ˈvərt-ə-\ *adj* **1** : of, relating to, or being vertebrae or the vertebral column : SPINAL **2** : composed of or having vertebrae — **vertebral** *n* — **ver·te·bral·ly** \-ē\ *adv*
vertebral column *n* : SPINAL COLUMN
[1]**ver·te·brate** \ˈvərt-ə-brət, -ˌbrāt\ *adj* [NL *vertebratus,* fr. L, jointed, fr. *vertebra*] **1 a** : having a spinal column **b** : of or relating to the vertebrates **2** : organized or constructed in orderly or developed form
[2]**vertebrate** *n* [deriv. of NL *vertebratus*] : any of a comprehensive division (Vertebrata) usu. held to be a subphylum of chordates comprising animals (as mammals, birds, reptiles, amphibians, and fishes) with a segmented spinal column together with a few primitive forms in which the backbone is represented by a notochord
ver·te·bra·tion \ˌvərt-ə-ˈbrā-shən\ *n* : highly developed organization : FIRMNESS <the solid ~ of his logic>
ver·tex \ˈvər-ˌteks\ *n, pl* **ver·tex·es** *or* **ver·ti·ces** \ˈvərt-ə-ˌsēz\ [L *vertic-, vertex, vortic-, vortex* whirl, whirlpool, top of the head, summit, fr. *vertere* to turn] **1 a** (1) : the point opposite to and farthest from the base in a figure (2) : the termination or intersection of lines or curves <the ~ of an angle> (3) : a point where an axis of an ellipse, parabola, or hyperbola intersects the curve itself **b** : ZENITH 1 **2** : the top of the head **3** : a principal or highest point : SUMMIT <the ~ of the hill>
ver·ti·cal \ˈvərt-i-kəl\ *adj* [MF or LL; MF, fr. LL *verticalis,* fr. L *vertic-, vertex*] **1 a** : situated at the highest point : directly overhead or in the zenith **b** : being an aerial photograph taken with the camera pointing straight down or nearly so **2 a** : perpendicular to the plane of the horizon or to a primary axis : UPRIGHT **b** (1) : located at right angles to the plane of a supporting surface (2) : lying in the direction of an axis : LENGTHWISE **3** : relating to, involving, or integrating discrete elements (as from lowest to highest) <a ~ business organization> <the ~ arrangement of society> — **vertical** *n* — **ver·ti·cal·i·ty** \ˌvərt-ə-ˈkal-ət-ē\ *n* — **ver·ti·cal·ly** \ˈvərt-i-k(ə-)lē\ *adv* — **ver·ti·cal·ness** \-kəl-nəs\ *n*
syn VERTICAL, PERPENDICULAR, PLUMB *shared meaning element* : forming a right angle with the plane of the horizon ***ant*** horizontal
vertical angle *n* : either of two angles lying on opposite sides of two intersecting lines
vertical circle *n* : a great circle of the celestial sphere whose plane is perpendicular to that of the horizon
vertical file *n* : a collection of articles (as pamphlets and clippings) that is maintained (as in a library) to answer brief questions or to provide points of information not easily located
vertical union *n* : INDUSTRIAL UNION
ver·ti·cil \ˈvərt-ə-ˌsil\ *n* [NL *verticillus,* dim. of L *vertex* whirl] : a circle of similar parts (as flowers around a stem or sensory hairs around an antennal joint) about the same point on the axis : WHORL
ver·ti·cil·late \ˌvərt-ə-ˈsil-ət\ *adj* : arranged in verticils : WHORLED; *esp* : arranged in a transverse whorl like the spokes of a wheel <~ leaves> <a ~ shell>
ver·ti·cil·li·um wilt \ˌvərt-ə-ˌsil-ē-əm-\ *n* [NL *Verticillium,* genus of fungi, fr. *verticillus*] : a wilt disease of various plants that is caused by soil-borne imperfect fungi (genus *Verticillium*) having conidia borne singly at the apex of whorled branchlets
ver·tig·i·nous \(ˌ)vər-ˈtij-ə-nəs\ *adj* [L *vertiginosus,* fr. *vertigin-, vertigo*] **1** : characterized by or suffering from vertigo : DIZZY **2 a** : afflicted with dizziness : GIDDY **b** : inclined to frequent and often pointless change : INCONSTANT **3** : causing or tending to cause dizziness <the ~ heights> **4** : marked by turning : ROTARY <the ~ motion of the earth> — **ver·tig·i·nous·ly** *adv*
ver·ti·go \ˈvərt-i-ˌgō\ *n, pl* **-goes** *or* **-gos** [L *vertigin-, vertigo,* fr. *vertere* to turn] **1 a** : a disordered state in which the individual or his surroundings seem to whirl dizzily : GIDDINESS **b** : a dizzy confused state of mind **2** : disordered vertiginous movement as a symptom of disease in lower animals; *also* : a disease (as gid) causing this
ver·tu \ˌvər-ˈtü, ve(ə)r-\ *var of* VIRTU
ver·vain \ˈvər-ˌvān\ *n* [ME *verveine,* fr. MF, fr. L *verbena,* sing. of *verbenae* sacred boughs, certain medicinal plants; akin to L *verber* rod, Gk *rhabdos*] : any of a genus (*Verbena* of the family Verbenaceae, the vervain family) of plants that have bracted flowers in heads or spikes, a regular corolla with a 5-lobed limb, and four 1-seeded nutlets; *esp* : one with small spicate flowers
verve \ˈvərv\ *n* [F, fantasy, caprice, animation, fr. L *verba,* pl. of *verbum* word — more at WORD] **1** *archaic* : special ability or talent **2 a** : the spirit and enthusiasm animating artistic composition or performance : VIVACITY **b** : ENERGY, VITALITY
ver·vet monkey \ˌvər-vət-\ *n* [F] : a southern and eastern African guenon monkey (*Cercopithecus pygerythrus*) related to the grivet but having the face, chin, hands, and feet black — called also *vervet*
[1]**very** \ˈver-ē\ *adj* **veri·er; -est** [ME *verray, verry,* fr. OF *verai,* fr. (assumed) VL *veracus,* alter. of L *verac-, verax* truthful, fr. *verus* true; akin to OE *wǣr* true, OHG *wāra* trust, care, Gk *ēra* (acc.) favor] **1 a** : properly entitled to the name or designation : TRUE <the fierce hatred of a ~ woman —J. M. Barrie> **b** : ACTUAL, REAL <the ~ blood and bone of our grammar —H. L. Smith *b*1913> **c** : SIMPLE, PLAIN <in ~ truth> **2 a** : being exactly as stated <the ~ heart of the city> **b** : exactly suitable or necessary <the ~ thing for the purpose> **3 a** : ABSOLUTE, UTTER <the *veriest* fool alive> **b** : SHEER, UNQUALIFIED <the ~ shame of it> **4** : MERE, BARE <the ~ thought terrified him> **5** : being the same one : SELFSAME <the ~ man I saw> **6** : SPECIAL, PARTICULAR <the ~ essence of truth is plainness and brightness —John Milton> ***syn*** see SAME
[2]**very** *adv* **1** : to a high degree : EXCEEDINGLY <a ~ hot day> <~ much better> **2** : in actual fact : TRULY <the ~ best store in town> <told the ~ same story>
very hard *adj, of cheese* : suitable chiefly for grating
very high frequency *n* : a radio frequency between ultrahigh frequency and high frequency — see RADIO FREQUENCY table
Very light \ˌver-ē-, ˌvi(ə)r-ē-\ *n* [Edward W. *Very* †1910 Am naval officer] : a pyrotechnic signal in a system of signaling using white or colored balls of fire projected from a special pistol
very low frequency *n* : a radio frequency between low frequency and voice frequency — see RADIO FREQUENCY table
Very pistol *n* : a pistol for firing Very lights
Very Reverend — used as a title for various ecclesiastical officials (as cathedral deans and canons, rectors of Roman Catholic colleges and seminaries, and superiors of some religious houses)
ve·si·ca \və-ˈsē-kə, -ˈsī-; ˈves-i-kə\ *n, pl* **-cae** \-ˈsē-ˌkī; -ˈsī-(ˌ)kē, -(ˌ)sē; -i-ˌkī, -(ˌ)kē, -ˌsē\ [L, bladder — more at VENTER] **1** : a decorative form (as in architecture or heraldry) in the shape of a 2-pointed oval : a marquise shape **2** [NL, fr. L] : an internal sac or tube of an insect phallus
ves·i·cal \ˈves-i-kəl\ *adj* [L *vesica* bladder] : of or relating to a bladder and esp. to the urinary bladder
ves·i·cant \-kənt\ *n* [L *vesica* bladder, blister] : an agent (as a drug or a war gas) that induces blistering — **vesicant** *adj*
ves·i·cate \ˈves-ə-ˌkāt\ *vb* **-cat·ed; -cat·ing** [L *vesica* blister] : BLISTER
ves·i·ca·tion \ˌves-ə-ˈkā-shən\ *n* **1** : an instance or the process of blistering **2** : BLISTER
ves·i·cle \ˈves-i-kəl\ *n* [MF *vesicule,* fr. L *vesicula* small bladder, blister, fr. dim. of *vesica*] **1 a** : a membranous and usu. fluid-filled pouch (as a cyst, vacuole, or cell) in a plant or animal **b** : a small abnormal elevation of the outer layer of skin enclosing a watery liquid : BLISTER **c** : a pocket of embryonic tissue that is the beginning of an organ **2** : a small cavity in a mineral or rock
ve·sic·u·lar \və-ˈsik-yə-lər, ve-\ *adj* [NL *vesicula* vesicle, fr. L, small bladder] **1** : of or relating to vesicles and esp. to the alveoli of the lungs **2** : having the form of structure of a vesicle **3** : containing, composed of, or characterized by vesicles <~ lava> — **ve·sic·u·lar·i·ty** \-ˌsik-yə-ˈlar-ət-ē\ *n* — **ve·sic·u·lar·ly** \-ˈsik-yə-lər-lē\ *adv*
vesicular stomatitis *n* : an acute virus disease esp. of horses and mules that is marked by erosive blisters in and about the mouth and that much resembles foot-and-mouth disease
[1]**ve·sic·u·late** \və-ˈsik-yə-lət, ve-\ *adj* **1** : containing or covered with vesicles **2** : VESICULAR 2

2ve·sic·u·late \-ˌlāt\ *vb* **-lat·ed; -lat·ing** *vt* **:** to make vesicular ~ *vi* **:** to become vesicular — **ve·sic·u·la·tion** \-ˌsik-yə-ˈlā-shən\ *n*

1ves·per \ˈves-pər\ *n* [ME, fr. L, evening, evening star — more at WEST] **1** *cap* **:** EVENING STAR **2 :** a vesper bell **3** *archaic* **:** EVENING, EVENTIDE

2vesper *adj* **:** of or relating to vespers or the evening

ves·per·al \ˈves-p(ə-)rəl\ *adj* **:** VESPER <a ~ breeze>

ves·pers \ˈves-pərz\ *n pl but sing or pl in const, often cap* [F *vespres,* fr. ML *vesperae,* fr. L, pl. of *vespera* evening; akin to L *vesper* evening star] **1 :** the sixth of the canonical hours that is said or sung in the late afternoon **2 :** a service of evening worship

ves·per·til·ian \ˌves-pər-ˈtil-ē-ən, -ˈtil-yən\ *adj* [L *vespertilio* bat, fr. *vesper*] **:** of or relating to bats

ves·per·ti·nal \-ˈtīn-ᵊl\ *adj* **:** VESPERTINE

ves·per·tine \ˈves-pər-ˌtīn\ *adj* [L *vespertinus,* fr. *vesper*] **1 :** of, relating to, or occurring in the evening <~ shadows> **2 :** active or flourishing in the evening **:** CREPUSCULAR: as **a :** feeding or flying in early evening **b :** blossoming in the evening

ves·pi·ary \ˈves-pē-ˌer-ē\ *n, pl* **-ar·ies** [L *vespa* + E *-iary* (as in *apiary*)] **:** a nest of a social wasp; *also* **:** the colony inhabiting it

ves·pid \ˈves-pəd\ *n* [deriv. of L *vespa* wasp — more at WASP] **:** any of a cosmopolitan family (Vespidae) of hymenopterous insects comprising the social wasps that live in colonies like bees — **vespid** *adj*

ves·pine \ˈves-ˌpīn\ *adj* [L *vespa* wasp] **:** of, relating to, or resembling wasps and esp. vespid wasps

ves·sel \ˈves-əl\ *n* [ME, fr. OF *vaissel,* fr. LL *vascellum,* dim. of L *vas* vase, vessel — more at VASE] **1 a :** a hollow or concave utensil (as a hogshead, bottle, kettle, cup, or bowl) for holding something **b :** a person into whom some quality (as grace) is infused <a child of light, a true ~ of the Lord —H. J. Laski> **2 a :** a hollow structure designed for navigation on the water; *esp* **:** one bigger than a rowboat **b :** any of various aircraft **3 a :** a tube or canal (as an artery) in which a body fluid is contained and conveyed or circulated **b :** a conducting tube in a vascular plant formed by the fusion and loss of end walls of a series of cells

1vest \ˈvest\ *vb* [ME *vesten,* fr. MF *vestir* to clothe, invest, fr. L *vestire* to clothe, fr. *vestis* clothing, garment — more at WEAR] *vt* **1 a :** to place or give into the possession or discretion of some person or authority; *esp* **:** to give to a person a legally fixed immediate right of present or future enjoyment of (as an estate) **b :** to clothe with a particular authority, right, or property **2 :** to clothe with or as if with a garment; *esp* **:** to robe in ecclesiastical vestments ~ *vi* **1 :** to become legally vested **2 :** to put on garments; *esp* **:** to robe in ecclesiastical vestments

2vest *n* [F *veste,* fr. It, fr. L *vestis* garment] **1** *archaic* **a :** a loose outer garment **:** ROBE **b :** CLOTHING, GARB **2 a :** a man's sleeveless garment worn under a suit coat; *also* **:** a similar garment for women **b :** a protective usu. sleeveless garment (as a life preserver) that extends to the waist **3 a** *chiefly Brit* **:** a man's undershirt **b :** a knitted undershirt for women **4 :** a plain or decorative piece used to fill in the front neckline of a woman's outer garment (as a waist, coat, or gown) — **vest·ed** \ˈves-təd\ *adj* — **vest·like** \-ˌlīk\ *adj*

ves·ta \ˈves-tə\ *n* [L *Vesta*] **1** *cap* **:** the Roman goddess of the hearth fire and of the state — compare HESTIA **2 :** a short match with a shank of wax-coated threads; *also* **:** a short wooden match

1ves·tal \ˈves-tᵊl\ *adj* **1 :** of or relating to the Roman goddess Vesta **2 a :** of or relating to a vestal virgin **b :** CHASTE — **ves·tal·ly** \-tə-lē\ *adv*

2vestal *n* **:** VESTAL VIRGIN

vestal virgin *n* **1 :** a virgin consecrated to the Roman goddess Vesta and to the service of watching the sacred fire perpetually kept burning on her altar **2 :** a chaste woman

vested interest *n* **1 a :** an interest (as a title to an estate) carrying a legal right of present or future enjoyment and of present alienation **b :** an interest (as in an existing political, economic, or social arrangement) in which the holder has a strong personal commitment **2 :** one having a vested interest in something; *specif* **:** a group enjoying benefits from an existing economic or political privilege

vest·ee \ve-ˈstē\ *n* **1 :** DICKEY; *esp* **:** one made to resemble a vest and worn under a coat **2 :** VEST 4

ves·ti·ary \ˈves-tē-ˌer-ē, ˈves(h)-chē-\ *n* [ME *vestiarie,* fr. OF, vestry — more at VESTRY] **1 :** a room where clothing is kept **2 :** CLOTHING, RAIMENT

ves·tib·u·lar \ve-ˈstib-yə-lər\ *adj* **:** of, relating to, or functioning as a vestibule

ves·ti·bule \ˈves-tə-ˌbyü(ə)l\ *n* [L *vestibulum*] **1 a :** a passage, hall, or room between the outer door and the interior of a building **:** LOBBY **b :** an enclosed entrance at the end of a railway passenger car **2 :** a course that offers access (as to something new) <a ~ to reconstruction of . . . education —William Brandon> **3 :** any of various bodily cavities esp. when serving as or resembling an entrance to some other cavity or space: as **a :** the central cavity of the bony labyrinth of the ear or the parts of the membranous labyrinth that it contains **b :** the part of the left ventricle below the aortic orifice **c :** the space between the labia minora containing the orifice of the urethra **d :** the part of the mouth cavity outside the teeth and gums

ves·ti·buled \-ˌbyü(ə)ld\ *adj* **:** having a vestibule

vestibule school *n* **:** a school organized in an industrial plant to train new workers in specific skills

ves·tige \ˈves-tij\ *n* [F, fr. L *vestigium* footstep, footprint, track, vestige] **1 a (1) :** a trace or visible sign left by something vanished or lost **(2) :** a minute remaining amount **b :** the mark of a foot on the earth **:** TRACK **2 :** a bodily part or organ that is small and degenerate or imperfectly developed in comparison to one more fully developed in an earlier stage of the individual, in a past generation, or in closely related forms ***syn*** see TRACE — **ves·ti·gial** \ve-ˈstij-(ē-)əl\ *adj* — **ves·ti·gial·ly** \-ē\ *adv*

vest·ing \ˈves-tiŋ\ *n* **:** the conveying to an employee of inalienable rights to share in a pension fund esp. in the event of termination of employment prior to the normal retirement age; *also* **:** the right so conveyed

vest·ment \ˈves(t)-mənt\ *n* [ME *vestement,* fr. OF, fr. L *vestimentum,* fr. *vestire* to clothe] **1 a :** an outer garment; *esp* **:** a robe of ceremony or office **b** *pl* **:** CLOTHING, GARB **2 :** a covering resembling a garment **3 :** one of the articles of the ceremonial attire and insignia worn by ecclesiastical officiants and assistants as indicative of their rank and appropriate to the rite being celebrated — **vest·men·tal** \ves(t)-ˈment-ᵊl\ *adj*

vestments 3 of 16th century archbishop: *1* alb, *2* stole, *3* apparel on alb, *4* tunicle, *5* dalmatic, *6* chasuble, *7* maniple, *8* pallium, *9* amice, *10* miter, *11* lappet, *12* crosier

vest–pocket *adj* **1 :** adapted to fit into the vest pocket <a ~ edition of a book> **2 :** of very small size or scope

vest–pocket park *n* **:** a very small urban park

ves·try \ˈves-trē\ *n, pl* **vestries** [ME *vestrie,* prob. modif. of MF *vestiarie,* fr. ML *vestiarium,* fr. L *vestire;* fr. its use as a robing room for the clergy] **1 a :** SACRISTY **b :** a room used for church meetings and classes **2 a :** the business meeting of an English parish **b :** an elective body in an Episcopal parish composed of the rector and a group of elected parishioners administering the temporal affairs of the parish

ves·try·man \-trē-mən\ *n* **:** a member of a vestry

1ves·ture \ˈves(h)-chər\ *n* [ME, fr. MF, fr. *vestir* to clothe — more at VEST] **1 a :** a covering garment (as a robe or vestment) **b :** CLOTHING, APPAREL **2 :** something that covers like a garment

2vesture *vt* **ves·tured; ves·tur·ing :** to cover with vesture **:** CLOTHE

ve·su·vi·an \və-ˈsü-vē-ən\ *n* **1** [G, fr. *Vesuv* Vesuvius, volcano in Italy] **:** IDOCRASE **2** [*Vesuvian*] **:** a match or fusee used esp. formerly for lighting cigars

Ve·su·vi·an \və-ˈsü-vē-ən\ *adj* **1 :** of, relating to, or resembling the volcano Vesuvius **2 :** marked by sudden outbursts <has a ~ temper, but quickly controls himself —Sidney Shalett>

ve·su·vi·an·ite \-vē-ə-ˌnīt\ *n* **:** IDOCRASE

1vet \ˈvet\ *n* **:** VETERINARIAN, VETERINARY

2vet *vt* **vet·ted; vet·ting 1** *chiefly Brit* **a :** to provide veterinary care for (an animal) or medical care for (a person) **b :** to subject (a person or animal) to a physical examination or checkup **2** *chiefly Brit* **:** to subject to expert appraisal or correction

3vet *adj or n* **:** VETERAN

vetch \ˈvech\ *n* [ME *vecche,* fr. ONF *veche,* fr. L *vicia;* akin to OE *wicga* insect, L *vincire* to bind, OE *wīr* wire] **:** any of a genus (*Vicia*) of herbaceous twining leguminous plants including valuable fodder and soil-building plants

vetch·ling \-liŋ\ *n* **:** any of various small leguminous plants (genus *Lathyrus* and esp. *L. pratensis*)

vet·er·an \ˈvet-ə-rən, ˈve-trən\ *n* [L *veteranus,* fr. *veteranus* old, of long experience, fr. *veter-, vetus* old — more at WETHER] **1 a (1) :** an old soldier of long service **(2) :** a former member of the armed forces **b :** a person of long experience in some occupation or skill (as politics or the arts) **2 :** an old tree usu. over two feet in diameter breast high — **veteran** *adj*

Veterans Day *n* **:** a day set aside in commemoration of the end of hostilities in 1918 and 1945: **a :** November 11 formerly observed as a legal holiday in the U.S. **b :** the fourth Monday in October observed as a legal holiday in the U.S. **c :** November 11 observed as a legal holiday in Canada

veterans' preference *n* **:** preferential treatment given qualified veterans of the U.S. armed forces under federal or state law; *specif* **:** special consideration (as by allowance of points) on a civil service examination

vet·er·i·nar·i·an \ˌvet-ə-rən-ˈer-ē-ən, ˌve-trən-, ˌvet-ᵊn-\ *n* **:** one qualified and authorized to treat diseases and injuries of animals

1vet·er·i·nary \ˈvet-ə-rən-ˌer-ē, ˈve-trən-, ˈvet-ᵊn-\ *adj* [L *veterinarius* of beasts of burden, fr. *veterinae* beasts of burden, fr. fem. pl. of *veterinus* of beasts of burden; akin to L *veter-, vetus* old] **:** of, relating to, or being the science and art of prevention, cure, or alleviation of disease and injury in animals and esp. domestic animals

2veterinary *n, pl* **-nar·ies :** VETERINARIAN

veterinary surgeon *n, Brit* **:** VETERINARIAN

vet·i·ver \ˈvet-ə-vər\ *n* [F *vétiver,* fr. Tamil *veṭṭivēr*] **:** an East Indian grass (*Vetiveria zizanioides*) cultivated in warm regions esp. for its fragrant roots which are used for making mats and screens and in perfumes; *also* **:** its root

1ve·to \ˈvēt-(ˌ)ō\ *n, pl* **vetoes** [L, I forbid, fr. *vetare* to forbid] **1 :** an authoritative prohibition **:** INTERDICTION **2 a :** a power of one department or branch of a government to forbid or prohibit finally or provisionally the carrying out of projects attempted by another department; *esp* **:** a power vested in a chief executive to prevent permanently or temporarily the enactment of measures passed by a legislature **b (1) :** the exercise of such authority **(2) :** a message communicating the reasons of an executive and esp. the president of the U.S. for vetoing a proposed law

2veto *vt* **:** to refuse to admit or approve **:** PROHIBIT; *also* **:** to refuse assent to (a legislative bill) so as to prevent enactment or cause reconsideration — **ve·to·er** \-ˌō(-ə)r\ *n*

vex \ˈveks\ *vt* **vexed** *also* **vext; vex·ing** [ME *vexen,* fr. MF *vexer,* fr. L *vexare* to agitate, trouble, vex] **1 a :** to bring trouble, distress, or agitation to <~*ed* by a restless desire for change> **b :** to bring physical distress to <a headache ~*ed* him all morning> **c :** to irritate or annoy by petty provocations **:** HARASS <a father ~*ed* by his children> **d :** PUZZLE, BAFFLE <a problem to ~ the

keenest wit> **2 :** to debate or discuss at length <a *vexed* question> **3 :** to shake or toss about ***syn*** see ANNOY ***ant*** please, regale

vex·a·tion \vek-ˈsā-shən\ *n* **1 :** the quality or state of being vexed **:** IRRITATION **2 :** the act of harassing or vexing **:** TROUBLING **3 :** a cause of trouble **:** AFFLICTION

vex·a·tious \-shəs\ *adj* **1 a :** causing vexation **:** DISTRESSING **b :** intended to harass **2 :** full of disorder or stress **:** TROUBLED — **vex·a·tious·ly** *adv* — **vex·a·tious·ness** *n*

vexed·ly \ˈvek-səd-lē, ˈveks-tlē\ *adv* **:** in a vexed manner

[1]vex·il·lary \ˈvek-sə-ˌler-ē\ *n, pl* **-lar·ies** [L *vexillarius,* fr. *vexillum*] **1 :** a veteran under a special standard in an ancient Roman army **2 :** STANDARD-BEARER

[2]vexillary *adj* **1 :** of or relating to an ensign or standard **2 :** of, relating to, or being a vexillum

vex·il·lol·o·gy \ˌvek-sə-ˈläl-ə-jē\ *n* [L *vexillum*] **:** the study of flags — **vex·il·lo·log·ic** \(ˌ)vek-ˌsil-ə-ˈläj-ik\ *or* **vex·il·lo·log·i·cal** \-ˈläj-i-kəl\ *adj* — **vex·il·lol·o·gist** \ˌvek-sə-ˈläl-ə-jəst\ *n*

vex·il·lum \vek-ˈsil-əm\ *n, pl* **-la** \-ə\ [L] **1 :** a square flag of the ancient Roman cavalry **2 :** STANDARD 8a **3 :** the web or vane of a feather **4 :** a company of ancient Roman troops serving under one standard

VF *abbr* **1** very fair; very fine **2** video frequency **3** visual field **4** voice frequency

VFD *abbr* volunteer fire department

VFR *abbr* visual flight rules

VFW *abbr* Veterans of Foreign Wars

vg *abbr* vulgate

VG *abbr* **1** very good **2** vicar general

VHF *abbr* very high frequency

vi *abbr* **1** verb intransitive **2** [L *vide infra*] see below

VI *abbr* **1** Virgin Islands **2** viscosity index **3** volume indicator

via \ˌvī-ə, ˌvē-ə\ *prep* [L, abl. of *via* way; akin to Gk *hiesthai* to hurry — more at VIM] **1 :** by way of **2 :** through the medium of; *also* **:** by means of

vi·a·ble \ˈvī-ə-bəl\ *adj* [F, fr. MF, fr. *vie* life, fr. L *vita* — more at VITAL] **1 :** capable of living; *esp* **:** born alive with such form and development of organs as to be normally capable of living **2 :** capable of growing or developing <~ seeds> <~ eggs> **3 a :** capable of working, functioning, or developing adequately <~ alternatives> **b :** capable of existence and development as an independent unit <the colony is now a ~ state> — **vi·a·bil·i·ty** \ˌvī-ə-ˈbil-ət-ē\ *n* — **vi·a·bly** \ˈvī-ə-blē\ *adv*

via·duct \ˈvī-ə-ˌdəkt\ *n* [L *via* way, road + E *-duct* (as in *aqueduct*)] **1 :** a bridge esp. when resting on a series of narrow reinforced concrete or masonry arches, having high supporting towers or piers, and carrying a road or railroad over an obstruction (as a valley or highway) **2 :** a steel bridge made up of short spans carried on high steel towers

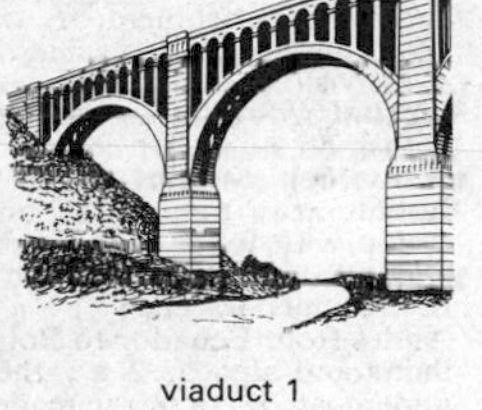

viaduct 1

vi·al \ˈvī(-ə)l\ *n* [ME *fiole, viole,* fr. MF *fiole,* fr. OProv *fiola,* fr. L *phiala* — more at PHIAL] **:** a small closed or closable vessel esp. for liquids

via me·dia \ˌvī-ə-ˈmēd-ē-ə; ˌvē-ə-ˈmäd-ē-ə, -ˈmed-\ *n* [L] **:** a middle way

vi·and \ˈvī-ənd\ *n* [ME, fr. MF *viande,* fr. ML *vivanda* food, alter. of L *vivenda,* neut. pl. of *vivendus,* gerundive of *vivere* to live — more at QUICK] **1 :** an item of food; *esp* **:** a choice or tasty dish **2** *pl* **:** PROVISIONS, FOOD

vi·at·i·cum \vī-ˈat-i-kəm, vē-\ *n, pl* **-cums** *or* **-ca** \-kə\ [L — more at VOYAGE] **1 a :** an allowance (as of transportation or supplies and money) for traveling expenses **b :** provisions for a journey **2 :** the Christian Eucharist given to a person in danger of death

vi·a·tor \vī-ˈāt-ər, vē-ˈä-ˌtȯ(ə)r\ *n* [L, fr. *via*] **:** TRAVELER

vibes \ˈvībz\ *n pl* **1** *usu sing in constr* **:** VIBRAPHONE **2 :** VIBRATIONS <the ~ were good there, and the film makers were able to show . . . the heightened rapport between performers and audience —Arthur Knight> — **vib·ist** \ˈvī-bəst\ *n*

vi·bra·harp \ˈvī-brə-ˌhärp\ *n* [fr. *Vibra-Harp,* a trademark] **:** VIBRAPHONE — **vi·bra·harp·ist** \-ˌhär-pəst\ *n*

vi·brance \ˈvī-brən(t)s\ *n* **:** VIBRANCY

vi·bran·cy \ˈvī-brən-sē\ *n* **:** the quality or state of being vibrant

vi·brant \-brənt\ *adj* **1 a** (1) **:** oscillating or pulsating rapidly (2) **:** pulsating with life, vigor, or activity <a ~ personality> **b** (1) **:** readily set in vibration (2) **:** RESPONSIVE, SENSITIVE **2 :** sounding as a result of vibration **:** RESONANT <a ~ voice> — **vi·brant·ly** *adv*

vi·bra·phone \ˈvī-brə-ˌfōn\ *n* [L *vibra*re + ISV *-phone*] **:** a percussion instrument resembling the xylophone but having metal bars and motor-driven resonators for sustaining the tone and producing a vibrato — **vi·bra·phon·ist** \-ˌfō-nəst\ *n*

vibraphone

vi·brate \ˈvī-ˌbrāt, *esp Brit* vī-ˈ\ *vb* **vi·brat·ed; vi·brat·ing** [L *vibratus,* pp. of *vibrare* to shake, vibrate — more at WIPE] *vt* **1 :** to swing or move to and fro **2 :** to emit with or as if with a vibratory motion **3 :** to mark or measure by oscillation <a pendulum *vibrating* seconds> **4 :** to set in vibration **~** *vi* **1 a :** to move to and fro or from side to side **:** OSCILLATE **b :** WAVER, FLUCTUATE <~ between two choices> **2 :** to have an effect as of vibration <music, when soft voices die, ~*s* in the memory —P. B. Shelley> **3 :** to be in a state of vibration **:** QUIVER **4 :** to respond sympathetically **:** THRILL <~ to the opportunity> ***syn*** see SWING

vi·bra·tile \ˈvī-brət-ᵊl, -brə-ˌtīl\ *adj* **1 :** characterized by vibration **2 :** adapted to or used in vibratory motion <the ~ organs of insects> — **vi·bra·til·i·ty** \ˌvī-brə-ˈtil-ət-ē\ *n*

vi·bra·tion \vī-ˈbrā-shən\ *n* **1 a :** a periodic motion of the particles of an elastic body or medium in alternately opposite directions from the position of equilibrium when that equilibrium has been disturbed (as when a stretched cord produces musical tones or particles of air transmit sounds to the ear) **b :** the action of vibrating **:** the state of being vibrated or in vibratory motion: as (1) **:** OSCILLATION (2) **:** a quivering or trembling motion **:** QUIVER **2 :** an instance of vibration **3 :** vacillation in opinion or action **:** WAVERING **4 a :** a characteristic emanation, aura, or spirit that infuses or vitalizes someone or something and that can be instinctively sensed or experienced **b :** a distinctive usu. emotional atmosphere capable of being sensed — usu. used in pl. — **vi·bra·tion·al** \-shnəl, -shən-ᵊl\ *adj* — **vi·bra·tion·less** \-shən-ləs\ *adj*

vi·bra·to \vē-ˈbrät-(ˌ)ō\ *n, pl* **-tos** [It, fr. pp. of *vibrare* to vibrate, fr. L] **1 :** a slightly tremulous effect imparted to vocal or instrumental tone for added warmth and expressiveness by slight and rapid variations in pitch **2 :** TREMOLO 1b

vi·bra·tor \ˈvī-ˌbrāt-ər\ *n* **1 :** one that vibrates or causes vibration: as **a :** a vibrating electrical apparatus used in massage **b :** a vibrating device (as in an electric bell or buzzer) **2 :** an electromagnetic device that converts low direct current to pulsating direct current or alternating current

vi·bra·to·ry \ˈvī-brə-ˌtōr-ē, -ˌtȯr-\ *adj* **1 :** consisting in, capable of, or causing vibration or oscillation **2 :** characterized by vibration **:** VIBRANT

vib·rio \ˈvib-rē-ˌō\ *n, pl* **-rios** [NL, *Vibrion-, Vibrio,* genus name, fr. L *vibrare* to vibrate] **:** any of a genus (*Vibrio*) of short rigid motile bacteria typically shaped like a comma or an S — **vib·ri·on·ic** \ˌvib-rē-ˈän-ik\ *adj*

vib·ri·on \ˈvib-rē-ˌän\ *n* [NL *Vibrion-, Vibrio*] **:** VIBRIO; *also* **:** a motile bacterium

vib·ri·o·sis \ˌvib-rē-ˈō-səs\ *n, pl* **-o·ses** \-ˌsēz\ [NL, fr. *Vibrio*] **:** infestation with or disease caused by vibrios

vi·bris·sa \vī-ˈbris-ə, və-\ *n, pl* **vi·bris·sae** \vī-ˈbris-(ˌ)ē; və-ˈbris-(ˌ)ē, -ˌī\ [L; akin to L *vibrare*] **1 :** one of the stiff hairs that are located esp. about the nostrils or on other parts of the face in many mammals and that often serve as tactile organs **2 :** one of the bristly feathers near the mouth of many and esp. insectivorous birds that may help to prevent the escape of insects

vi·bur·num \vī-ˈbər-nəm\ *n* [NL, genus name, fr. L, wayfaring tree] **:** any of a genus (*Viburnum*) of widely distributed shrubs or trees of the honeysuckle family with simple leaves and white or rarely pink cymose flowers

vic *abbr* vicinity

Vic *abbr* Victoria

vic·ar \ˈvik-ər\ *n* [ME, fr. L *vicarius,* fr. *vicarius* vicarious] **1 :** one serving as a substitute or agent; *specif* **:** an administrative deputy **2 :** an ecclesiastical agent: as **a :** a Church of England incumbent receiving a stipend but not the tithes of a parish **b :** an Episcopal clergyman or layman having charge of a mission or chapel **c :** a clergyman exercising a broad pastoral responsibility as the representative of a prelate <patriarchal ~ for all Syrian Orthodox people in North America —F. S. Mead> — **vic·ar·ship** \-ˌship\ *n*

vic·ar·age \ˈvik-(ə)rij\ *n* **1 :** the benefice of a vicar **2 :** the house of a vicar **3 :** VICARIATE 1

vicar apostolic *n, pl* **vicars apostolic :** a Roman Catholic titular bishop who governs a territory not organized as a diocese

vic·ar·ate \ˈvik-ə-rət, -ˌrāt\ *n* **:** VICARIATE

vicar–general *n, pl* **vicars–general :** an administrative deputy of a Roman Catholic or Anglican bishop or of the head of a religious order

vi·car·i·al \vī-ˈker-ē-əl, və-, -ˈkar-\ *adj* [L *vicarius*] **1 :** VICARIOUS 1 **2 :** of or relating to a vicar

vi·car·i·ate \-ē-ət\ *n* [ML *vicariatus,* fr. L *vicarius* vicar] **1 :** the office, jurisdiction, or tenure of a vicar **2 :** the office or district of a governmental administrative deputy

vi·car·i·ous \vī-ˈker-ē-əs, və-, -ˈkar-\ *adj* [L *vicarius,* fr. *vicis* change, alternation, stead — more at WEEK] **1 a :** serving instead of someone or something else <~ elements in a mineral> **b :** DELEGATED <~ authority> **2 :** performed or suffered by one person as a substitute for another or to the benefit or advantage of another **:** SUBSTITUTIONARY <a ~ sacrifice> **3 :** experienced or realized through imaginative or sympathetic participation in the experience of another **4 :** occurring in an unexpected or abnormal part of the body instead of the usual one <bleeding from the gums sometimes replaces the discharge from the uterus in ~ menstruation> — **vi·car·i·ous·ly** *adv* — **vi·car·i·ous·ness** *n*

Vicar of Christ : the Roman Catholic pope

[1]vice \ˈvīs\ *n* [ME, fr. OF, fr. L *vitium* fault, vice] **1 a :** moral depravity or corruption **:** WICKEDNESS **b :** a moral fault or failing **c :** a habitual and usu. trivial defect or shortcoming **:** FOIBLE <suffered from the ~ of curiosity> **2 :** BLEMISH, DEFECT **3 :** a physical imperfection, deformity, or taint **4 a** *often cap* **:** a character representing one of the vices in an English morality play **b :** BUFFOON, JESTER **5 :** an abnormal behavior pattern in a domestic animal detrimental to its health or usefulness **6 :** sexual immorality; *esp* **:** PROSTITUTION ***syn*** see FAULT, OFFENSE

[2]vice *n* [ME *vis, vice* screw, fr. MF *vis, viz* something winding] *chiefly Brit* **:** VISE

[3]vice *vt* **viced; vic·ing** *chiefly Brit* **:** VISE

[4]vi·ce \ˈvī-sē\ *prep* [L, abl. of *vicis* change, alternation, stead — more at WEEK] **:** in the place of **:** SUCCEEDING

vice- \(ˈ)vīs, ˌvīs\ *prefix* [ME *vis-, vice-,* fr. MF, fr. LL *vice-,* fr. L *vice,* abl. of *vicis*] **:** one that takes the place of <*vice*-president>

vice admiral *n* [MF *visamiral,* fr. *vis-* vice- + *amiral* admiral] : a commissioned officer in the navy or coast guard who ranks above a rear admiral and whose insignia is three stars

vice–chan·cel·lor \(ˌ)vīs-ˈchan(t)-s(ə-)lər\ *n* [ME *vichauncellor,* fr. MF *vischancelier,* fr. *vis-* + *chancelier* chancellor] : an officer ranking next below a chancellor and serving as his deputy; *esp* : a judge appointed to act for or to assist a chancellor

vice–con·sul \-ˈkän(t)-səl\ *n* : a consular officer subordinate to a consul general or to a consul

vice·ge·ren·cy \-ˈjir-ən-sē\ *n, pl* **-cies** : the office or jurisdiction of a vicegerent

vice·ge·rent \-ˈjir-ənt\ *n* [ML *vicegerent-, vicegerens,* fr. LL *vice-* + L *gerent-, gerens,* prp. of *gerere* to carry, carry on — more at CAST] : an administrative deputy of a king or magistrate

vi·cen·ni·al \vī-ˈsen-ē-əl\ *adj* [LL *vicennium* period of 20 years, fr. L *vicies* 20 times + *annus* year; akin to L *viginti* twenty — more at VIGESIMAL, ANNUAL] : occurring once every 20 years

vice–pres·i·den·cy \(ˈ)vīs-ˈprez-əd-ən-sē, -ˈprez-dən- *also* -ə-ˌden(t)-sē\ *n* : the office of vice-president

vice–pres·i·dent \-ˈprez-əd-ənt, -ˈprez-dənt *also* -ə-ˌdent\ *n* **1** : an officer next in rank to a president and usu. empowered to serve as president in that officer's absence or disability **2** : any of several officers serving as a president's deputies in charge of particular locations or functions — **vice–pres·i·den·tial** \ˌvīs-ˌprez-ə-ˈden-chəl\ *adj*

vice·re·gal \(ˈ)vīs-ˈrē-gəl\ *adj* : of or relating to a viceroy or viceroyalty — **vice·re·gal·ly** \-gə-lē\ *adv*

vice–re·gent \-ˈrē-jənt\ *n* : a regent's deputy

vice·reine \ˈvīs-ˌrān\ *n* [F, fr. *vice-* + *reine* queen, fr. L *regina,* fem. of *reg-, rex* king — more at ROYAL] **1** : the wife of a viceroy **2** : a woman viceroy

vice·roy \ˈvīs-ˌrȯi\ *n* [MF *vice-roi,* fr. *vice-* + *roi* king, fr. L *reg-, rex* — more at ROYAL] **1** : the governor of a country or province who rules as the representative of his king or sovereign **2** : a showy American butterfly (*Limenitis archippus*) closely mimicking the monarch in coloration but smaller

vice·roy·al·ty \ˈvīs-ˌrȯi(-ə)l-tē, vīs-ˈ\ *n* : the office, jurisdiction, or term of service of a viceroy

vice·roy·ship \ˈvīs-ˌrȯi-ˌship\ *n* : VICEROYALTY

vice squad *n* : a police squad charged with enforcement of laws concerning gambling, pornography, prostitution, and the illegal use of liquor and narcotics

vice ver·sa \ˌvī-si-ˈvər-sə, (ˈ)vīs-ˈvər-\ *adv* [L] : with the order changed : CONVERSELY

vi·chys·soise \ˌvish-ē-ˈswäz, ˌvē-shē-\ *n* [F, fr. fem. of *vichyssois* of Vichy, fr. *Vichy,* France] : a soup made of pureed leeks or onions and potatoes, cream, and chicken stock and usu. served cold

Vi·chy water \ˈvish-ē-\ *n* : a natural sparkling mineral water from Vichy, France; *also* : an imitation of or substitute for this

vic·i·nage \ˈvis-ᵊn-ij, ˈvis-nij\ *n* [ME *vesinage,* fr. MF, fr. *vesin* neighboring, fr. L *vicinus*] : a neighboring or surrounding district : VICINITY

vic·i·nal \ˈvis-ᵊn-əl, ˈvis-nəl\ *adj* [L *vicinalis,* fr. *vicinus* neighbor, fr. *vicinus* neighboring] **1** : of or relating to a limited district : LOCAL **2** : of, relating to, or being subordinate forms or faces on a crystal which sometimes take the place of fundamental ones **3** : of, relating to, or substituted in adjacent sites in a molecule <a ~ disulfide group>

vi·cin·i·ty \və-ˈsin-ət-ē\ *n, pl* **-ties** [MF *vicinité,* fr. L *vicinitat-, vicinitas,* fr. *vicinus* neighboring, fr. *vicus* row of houses, village; akin to Goth *weihs* village, Gk. *oikos, oikia* house] **1** : the quality or state of being near : PROXIMITY **2** : a surrounding area or district : NEIGHBORHOOD **3** : NEIGHBORHOOD 3b

vi·cious \ˈvish-əs\ *adj* **1** : having the nature or quality of vice or immorality : DEPRAVED **2** : DEFECTIVE, FAULTY; *also* : INVALID **3** : IMPURE, NOXIOUS **4 a** : dangerously aggressive : SAVAGE <a ~ dog> **b** : marked by violence or ferocity : FIERCE <a ~ fight> **5** : MALICIOUS, SPITEFUL <~ gossip> **6** : worsened by internal causes that reciprocally augment each other <a ~ wage-price spiral> — **vi·cious·ly** *adv* — **vi·cious·ness** *n*

syn VICIOUS, VILLAINOUS, INIQUITOUS, NEFARIOUS, FLAGITIOUS, INFAMOUS, CORRUPT, DEGENERATE *shared meaning element* : highly reprehensible or offensive in character, nature, or conduct ***ant*** virtuous

vicious circle *n* **1** : a chain of events in which the solution of one difficulty creates a new problem involving increased difficulty **2** : an argument or definition that assumes something that is to be proved or defined **3** : a chain of abnormal processes in which a primary disorder leads to a second which in turn aggravates the first

vi·cis·si·tude \və-ˈsis-ə-ˌt(y)üd, vī-\ *n* [MF, fr. L *vicissitudo,* fr. *vicissim* in turn, fr. *vicis* change, alternation — more at WEEK] **1 a** : the quality or state of being changeable : MUTABILITY **b** : natural change or mutation visible in nature or in human affairs **2 a** : a favorable or unfavorable event or situation that occurs by chance : a fluctuation of state or condition <the ~*s* of daily life> **b** : alternating change : SUCCESSION ***syn*** see CHANGE, DIFFICULTY

vi·cis·si·tu·di·nous \və-ˌsis-ə-ˈt(y)üd-nəs, (ˌ)vī-, -ᵊn-əs\ *adj* [L *vicissitudin-, vicissitudo*] : marked by or filled with vicissitudes

vic·tim \ˈvik-təm\ *n* [L *victima;* akin to OHG *wīh* holy, Skt *vinakti* he sets apart] **1** : a living being sacrificed to a deity or in the performance of a religious rite **2** : one that is acted upon and usu. adversely affected by a force or agent <the schools are ~*s* of the social system>: as **a (1)** : one that is injured, destroyed, or sacrificed under any of various conditions <a ~ of cancer> <a ~ of the auto crash> **(2)** : one that is subjected to oppression, hardship, or mistreatment <a frequent ~ of severe political attacks> **b** : one that is tricked or duped <a con man's ~>

vic·tim·ize \ˈvik-tə-ˌmīz\ *vt* **-ized; -iz·ing 1** : to make a victim of **2** : to subject to deception or fraud : CHEAT — **vic·tim·iza·tion** \ˌvik-tə-mə-ˈzā-shən\ *n* — **vic·tim·iz·er** \ˈvik-tə-ˌmī-zər\ *n*

vic·tor \ˈvik-tər\ *n* [ME, fr. L, fr. *victus,* pp. of *vincere* to conquer, win; akin to OE *wīgan* to fight, OSlav *vĕkŭ* strength] : one that defeats an enemy or opponent : WINNER — **victor** *adj*

Victor — a communications code word for the letter *v*

vic·to·ria \vik-ˈtōr-ē-ə, -ˈtȯr-\ *n* [*Victoria,* queen of England] **1** : a low four-wheeled pleasure carriage for two with a calash top and a raised seat in front for the driver **2** : an open passenger automobile with a calash top that usu. extends over the rear seat only **3** [NL, genus name, fr. Queen *Victoria*] : any of a genus (*Victoria*) of So. American aquatic plants of the water-lily family with large spreading leaves often over five feet in diameter and immense rose-white flowers

victoria 1

Victoria Cross *n* [Queen *Victoria*] : a bronze Maltese cross awarded to members of the British armed services for acts of remarkable valor

1**Vic·to·ri·an** \vik-ˈtōr-ē-ən, -ˈtȯr-\ *adj* **1** : of or relating to the reign of Queen Victoria of England or the art, letters, or taste of her time **2** : typical of the moral standards or conduct of the age of Victoria esp. when considered stuffy or hypocritical

2**Victorian** *n* : a person living during Queen Victoria's reign; *esp* : a representative figure of that time

Vic·to·ri·ana \(ˌ)vik-ˌtōr-ē-ˈan-ə, -ˌtȯr-, -ˈän-, -ˈān-\ *n* [NL, neut. pl. of *Victorianus* Victorian] : materials concerning or characteristic of the Victorian age; *also* : a collection of such materials

Vic·to·ri·an·ism \vik-ˈtōr-ē-ə-ˌniz-əm, -ˈtȯr-\ *n* **1** : the quality or state of being Victorian esp. in taste or conduct **2** : a typical instance or product of Victorian expression, taste, or conduct

Vic·to·ri·an·ize \-ə-ˌnīz\ *vt* **-ized; -iz·ing** : to make Victorian (as in style or taste) — **Vic·to·ri·an·iza·tion** \(ˌ)vik-ˌtōr-ē-ə-nə-ˈzā-shən, -ˌtȯr-\ *n*

vic·to·ri·ous \vik-ˈtōr-ē-əs, -ˈtȯr-\ *adj* **1 a** : having won a victory **b** : of, relating to, or characteristic of victory **2** : evincing moral harmony or a sense of fulfillment : FULFILLED — **vic·to·ri·ous·ly** *adv* — **vic·to·ri·ous·ness** *n*

vic·to·ry \ˈvik-t(ə-)rē\ *n, pl* **-ries** [ME, fr. MF *victorie,* fr. L *victoria,* fr. fem. of (assumed) L *victorius* of winning or conquest, fr. L *victus,* pp. of *vincere*] **1** : the overcoming of an enemy or antagonist **2** : achievement of mastery or success in a struggle or endeavor against odds or difficulties

syn VICTORY, CONQUEST, TRIUMPH *shared meaning element* : a successful outcome in a contest or struggle ***ant*** defeat

vic·tress \ˈvik-trəs\ *n* : a female victor

1**vict·ual** \ˈvit-ᵊl\ *n* [alter. of ME *vitaille,* fr. MF, fr. LL *victualia,* pl., provisions, victuals, fr. neut. pl. of *victualis* of nourishment, fr. L *victus* nourishment, fr. *victus,* pp. of *vivere* to live — more at QUICK] **1** : food usable by man **2** *pl* : supplies of food : PROVISIONS

2**victual** *vb* **-ualed** *or* **-ualled; -ual·ing** *or* **-ual·ling** *vt* : to supply with food ~ *vi* **1** : EAT **2** : to lay in provisions

vict·ual·ler *or* **vict·ual·er** \ˈvit-ᵊl-ər\ *n* **1** : the keeper of a restaurant or tavern **2** : one that provisions an army, a navy, or a ship with food **3** : an army or navy provision ship

vi·cu·ña *or* **vi·cu·na** \vi-ˈkün-yə, vī-; vī-ˈk(y)ü-nə, və-\ *n* [Sp *vicuña,* fr. Quechua *wikúña*] **1** : a wild ruminant (*Lama vicugna*) of the Andes from Ecuador to Bolivia that is related to the domesticated llama and alpaca **2 a** : the wool from the vicuña's fine lustrous undercoat **b** : a fabric made of vicuña wool; *also* : a sheep's wool imitation of this

vi·de \ˈvīd-ē, ˈvē-ˌdā\ *vb imper* [L, fr. *vidēre* to see — more at WIT] : SEE — used to direct a reader to another item

vi·de·li·cet \və-ˈdel-ə-ˌset, vī-; vi-ˈdā-li-ˌket\ *adv* [ME, fr. L, fr. *vidēre* to see + *licet* it is permitted, fr. *licēre* to be permitted — more at LICENSE] : that is to say : NAMELY

1**vid·eo** \ˈvid-ē-ˌō\ *adj* [L *vidēre* to see + E *-o* (as in *audio*)] : being, relating to, or used in the transmission or reception of the television image <~ channel> — compare AUDIO

2**video** *n* : TELEVISION <~ drama>

vid·eo·phone \ˈvid-ē-ə-ˌfōn\ *n* : a telephone equipped for transmission of video as well as audio signals so that users can see each other

vid·eo·tape \ˈvid-ē-ō-ˌtāp\ *vt* [*video tape*] : to make a recording of (a television production) on magnetic tape — **videotape** *n*

vi·dette *var of* VEDETTE

vid·icon \ˈvid-i-ˌkän\ *n, often cap* [*vid*eo + *icon*oscope] : a camera tube using the principle of photoconductivity

vi·du·ity \vid-ˈ(y)ü-ət-ē\ *n* [ME (Sc) *viduite,* fr. MF *viduite,* fr. L *viduitat-, viduitas,* fr. *vidua* widow — more at WIDOW] : WIDOWHOOD

vie \ˈvī\ *vb* **vied; vy·ing** \ˈvī-iŋ\ [modif. of MF *envier* to invite, challenge, wager, fr. L *invitare* to invite] *vi* : to strive for superiority : CONTEND ~ *vt* : HAZARD, WAGER <~ money on the turn of a card>; *also* : to exchange in rivalry : MATCH <~ accusation against accusation> ***syn*** see RIVAL — **vi·er** \ˈvī(-ə)r\ *n*

Vi·en·na sausage \vē-ˌen-ə-\ *n* [*Vienna,* Austria] : a short slender frankfurter

Viet·cong \vē-ˈet-ˈkäŋ, vyet-, ˌvē-ət-, vēt-, -ˈkȯŋ\ *n, pl* **Vietcong** [Vietnamese *Viêt Nam công-san* Vietnam communists] : an adherent of the Vietnamese communist movement supported by North Vietnam and engaged esp. in guerrilla warfare in South Vietnam

Viet·minh \-ˈmin\ *n, pl* **Vietminh** [Vietnamese *Viêt Nam Dôc-Lâp Dông-Minh* League for the Independence of Vietnam] : an adherent of the Vietnamese communist movement

Viet·nam·ese \vē-ˌet-nə-ˈmēz, ˌvyet-, ˌvē-ət-, ˌvēt-, -na-, -nä-, -ˈmēs\ *n, pl* **Vietnamese 1** : a native or inhabitant of Vietnam **2** : the language of the largest group in Vietnam and the official language of the country — **Vietnamese** *adj*

Viet·nam·iza·tion \-nə-mə-ˈzā-shən\ *n* : the act or process of transferring responsibility to the Vietnamese <~ of the war> — **Viet·nam·ize** \vē-ˈet-nə-ˌmīz, ˈvyet-, ˈvē-ət-, ˈvēt-\ *vt*

1**view** \ˈvyü\ *n* [ME *vewe,* fr. MF *veue, vue,* fr. OF, fr. *veeir, voir* to see, fr. L *vidēre* — more at WIT] **1** : the act of seeing or examining : INSPECTION; *also* : SURVEY <a ~ of English literature> **2** : an opinion or judgment colored by the feeling or bias of its holder <in my ~ the conference has no chance of success> **3** : SCENE, PROSPECT <the lovely ~ from the balcony> **4** : extent or range of vision : SIGHT <tried to keep the ship in ~> <sat high in the bleachers to get a good ~> **5** : something that is looked toward or kept in sight : OBJECT <studied hard with a ~ to getting an A> **6** : the foreseeable future <no hope in ~> **7** : a pictorial representation ***syn*** see OPINION — **in view of** : in regard to : in consideration of — **on view** : open to public inspection : on exhibition

[2]**view** *vt* **1 a** : SEE, WATCH <~ a film> **b** : to look on in a particular light : REGARD <doesn't ~ himself as a rebel> **2** : to look at attentively : SCRUTINIZE <~ an exhibit> **3** : to survey or examine mentally : CONSIDER <~ all sides of a question> — **view·able** \-ə-bəl\ *adj*

view·er \ˈvyü-ər\ *n* : one that views: as **a** : a person legally appointed to inspect and report on property **b** : an optical device used in viewing **c** : a person who watches television

view·find·er \ˈvyü-ˌfīn-dər\ *n* : FINDER 3

view hal·loo \ˌvyü-hə-ˈlü\ *n* : a shout given by a hunter on seeing a fox break cover

view·ing *n* : an act of seeing, watching, or taking a look; *esp* : an act of watching television

view·less \ˈvyü-ləs\ *adj* **1** : affording no view **2** : expressing no views or opinions — **view·less·ly** *adv*

view·point \-ˌpȯint\ *n* : POINT OF VIEW, STANDPOINT

viewy \ˈvyü-ē\ *adj* **1** : possessing visionary, impractical, or fantastic views **2** : spectacular or arresting in appearance : SHOWY

vi·ges·i·mal \vī-ˈjes-ə-məl\ *adj* [L *vicesimus, vigesimus* twentieth; akin to L *viginti* twenty, Gk *eikosi*] : based on the number 20

vig·il \ˈvij-əl\ *n* [ME *vigile*, fr. OF, fr. LL & L; LL *vigilia* watch on the eve of a feast, fr. L, wakefulness, watch, fr. *vigil* awake, watchful; akin to L *vigēre* to be vigorous, *vegēre* to be active, rouse — more at WAKE] **1 a** : a watch formerly kept on the night before a religious feast with prayer or other devotions **b** : the day before a religious feast observed as a day of spiritual preparation **c** : evening or nocturnal devotions or prayers — usu. used in pl. **2** : the act of keeping awake at times when sleep is customary; *also* : a period of wakefulness **3** : an act or period of watching or surveillance : WATCH

vig·i·lance \ˈvij-ə-lən(t)s\ *n* : the quality or state of being vigilant

vigilance committee *n* : a volunteer committee of citizens organized to suppress and punish crime summarily (as when the processes of law appear inadequate)

vig·i·lant \ˈvij-ə-lənt\ *adj* [ME, fr. MF, fr. L *vigilant-, vigilans*, fr. prp. of *vigilare* to keep watch, stay awake, fr. *vigil* awake] : alertly watchful esp. to avoid danger ***syn*** see WATCHFUL — **vig·i·lant·ly** *adv*

vig·i·lan·te \ˌvij-ə-ˈlant-ē\ *n* [Sp, watchman, guard, fr. *vigilante* vigilant, fr. L *vigilant-, vigilans*] : a member of a vigilance committee

vig·i·lan·tism \-ˈlan-ˌtiz-əm\ *n* : the summary action resorted to by vigilantes

vigil light *n* : a candle lighted devotionally (as in a Roman Catholic church) before a shrine or image — called also *vigil candle*

vi·gin·til·lion \ˌvī-jin-ˈtil-yən\ *n, often attrib* [L *viginti* twenty + E *-illion* (as in *million*) — more at VIGESIMAL] — see NUMBER table

[1]**vi·gnette** \vin-ˈyet\ *n* [F, fr. MF *vignete*, dim. of *vigne* vine — more at VINE] **1** : a running ornament (as of vine leaves, tendrils, and grapes) put on or just before a title page or at the beginning or end of a chapter; *also* : a small decorative design or picture so placed **2 a** : a picture (as an engraving or photograph) that shades off gradually into the surrounding ground or the unprinted paper **b** : the pictorial part of a postage stamp design as distinguished from the frame and lettering **3 a** : a short descriptive literary sketch **b** : a brief incident or scene (as in a play or movie) — **vi·gnett·ist** \-ˈyet-əst\ *n*

[2]**vignette** *vt* **vi·gnett·ed; vi·gnett·ing** **1** : to finish (as a photograph) in the manner of a vignette **2** : to describe briefly — **vi·gnett·er** *n*

vig·or \ˈvig-ər\ *n* [ME, fr. MF *vigor*, fr. L, fr. *vigēre* to be vigorous] **1** : active bodily or mental strength or force **2** : active healthy well-balanced growth esp. of plants **3** : intensity of action or effect : FORCE **4** : effective legal status

vig·o·rish \ˈvig-ə-rish\ *n* [prob. fr. Yiddish, fr. Russ *vyigrysh* winnings, profit] **1** : a charge taken (as by a bookie or a gambling house) on bets; *also* : the degree of such a charge <a ~ of five per cent> **2** : interest paid to a moneylender

vi·go·ro·so \ˌvig-ə-ˈrō-(ˌ)sō, ˌvē-gə-, -(ˌ)zō\ *adj or adv* [It, lit., vigorous, fr. MF *vigorous*] : energetic in style — used as a direction in music

vig·or·ous \ˈvig-(ə-)rəs\ *adj* [ME, fr. MF, fr. OF, fr. *vigor*] **1** : possessing vigor : full of physical or mental strength or active force : STRONG <a ~ youth> <a ~ plant> **2** : done with vigor : carried out forcefully and energetically <~ exercises> — **vig·or·ous·ly** *adv* — **vig·or·ous·ness** *n*

vig·our \ˈvig-ər\ *chiefly Brit var of* VIGOR

Vi·king \ˈvī-kiŋ\ *n* [ON *vikingr*] **1 a** : one of the pirate Norsemen plundering the coasts of Europe in the 8th to 10th centuries **b** *not cap* : SEA ROVER **2** : SCANDINAVIAN

vil *abbr* village

vile \ˈvī(ə)l\ *adj* **vil·er** \ˈvī-lər\; **vil·est** [ME, fr. OF *vil*, fr. L *vilis*] **1** : of small worth or account : COMMON; *also* : MEAN **2 a** : morally despicable or abhorrent <nothing is so ~ as intellectual dishonesty> **b** : physically repulsive : FOUL <a ~ slum> **3** : tending to degrade <~ employments> **4** : disgustingly or utterly bad : OBNOXIOUS, CONTEMPTIBLE <~ weather> <had a ~ temper> ***syn*** see BASE — **vile·ly** \ˈvī(ə)l-lē\ *adv* — **vile·ness** *n*

vil·i·fi·ca·tion \ˌvil-ə-fə-ˈkā-shən\ *n* **1** : the act of vilifying : ABUSE **2** : an instance of vilifying : a defamatory utterance

vil·i·fy \ˈvil-ə-ˌfī\ *vt* **-fied; -fy·ing** **1** : to lower in estimation or importance **2** : to utter slanderous and abusive statements against : DEFAME ***syn*** see MALIGN ***ant*** eulogize — **vil·i·fi·er** \-ˌfī(-ə)r\ *n*

vil·i·pend \ˈvil-ə-ˌpend\ *vt* [ME *vilipenden*, fr. MF *vilipender*, fr. ML *vilipendere*, fr. L *vilis* of small worth + *pendere* to weigh, estimate — more at PENDANT] **1** : to hold or treat as of small worth or account : CONTEMN **2** : to express a low opinion of : DISPARAGE

vill \ˈvil\ *n* [AF, fr. OF *ville* village] **1** : a division of a hundred : TOWNSHIP **2** : VILLAGE

vil·la \ˈvil-ə\ *n* [It, fr. L; akin to L *vicus* row of houses — more at VICINITY] **1** : a country estate **2** : the rural or suburban residence of a wealthy person **3** : an agricultural estate of ancient Rome or of early medieval times

vil·la·dom \ˈvil-əd-əm\ *n, Brit* : the world constituted by villas and their occupants

vil·lage \ˈvil-ij\ *n, often attrib* [ME, fr. MF, fr. OF, fr. *ville* farm, village, fr. L *villa* country estate] **1 a** : a settlement usu. larger than a hamlet and smaller than a town **b** : an incorporated minor municipality **2** : the residents of a village **3** : something (as an aggregation of burrows or nests) suggesting a village **4** : a territorial area having the status of a village esp. as a unit of local government

vil·lag·er \ˈvil-ij-ər\ *n* : an inhabitant of a village

vil·lage·ry \ˈvil-ij-(ə-)rē\ *n* : VILLAGES

vil·lain \ˈvil-ən\ *n* [ME *vilain, vilein*, fr. MF, fr. ML *villanus*, fr. L *villa* country estate] **1** : VILLEIN **2** : an uncouth person : BOOR **3** : a deliberate scoundrel or criminal **4** : a scoundrel in a story or play **5** : a person or thing blamed for a particular evil or difficulty <automation as the ~ in job . . . displacement —M. H. Goldberg>

vil·lain·ess \-ə-nəs\ *n* : a female villain

vil·lain·ous \-ə-nəs\ *adj* **1 a** : befitting a villain (as in evil, depraved, or vile character) <a ~ attack> **b** : being or having the character of a villain : DEPRAVED <the ~ foe> **2** : highly objectionable : WRETCHED ***syn*** see VICIOUS — **vil·lain·ous·ly** *adv* — **vil·lain·ous·ness** *n*

vil·lainy \-ə-nē\ *n, pl* **-lain·ies** **1** : villainous conduct; *also* : a villainous act **2** : the quality or state of being villainous : DEPRAVITY

vil·la·nel·la \ˌvil-ə-ˈnel-ə\ *n, pl* **-nel·le** \-ˈnel-ē\ [It, fr. *villano* villein, peasant, fr. ML *villanus*] **1** : a 16th century Italian rustic part-song unaccompanied and in free form **2** : an instrumental piece in the style of a rustic dance

vil·la·nelle \ˌvil-ə-ˈnel\ *n* [F, fr. It *villanella*] : a chiefly French verse form running on two rhymes and consisting typically of five tercets and a quatrain in which the first and third lines of the opening tercet recur alternately at the end of the other tercets and together as the last two lines of the quatrain

vil·lat·ic \vil-ˈat-ik\ *adj* [L *villaticus*, fr. *villa*] : RURAL

-ville \ˌvil, *esp South* -vəl\ *n suffix* [*-ville*, suffix occurring in names of towns, fr. F, fr. OF, fr. *ville* village] : place or category of a specified nature <dulls*ville*>

vil·lein \ˈvil-ən, ˈvil-ˌān, vil-ˈān\ *n* [ME *vilain, vilein* — more at VILLAIN] **1** : a free common villager or village peasant of any of the feudal classes lower in rank than the thane **2** : a free peasant of a feudal class lower than a sokeman and higher than a cotter **3** : an unfree peasant standing as the slave of his feudal lord but free in his legal relations with respect to all others

vil·len·age \ˈvil-ə-nij\ *n* [ME *vilenage*, fr. MF, fr. OF, fr. *vilein, vilain*] **1** : tenure at the will of a feudal lord by villein services **2** : the status of a villein

vil·li·form \ˈvil-ə-ˌfȯrm\ *adj* [ISV] : having the form or appearance of villi; *also* : resembling bristles or the pile of velvet <a fish with ~ teeth>

vil·los·i·ty \vil-ˈäs-ət-ē\ *n, pl* **-ties** **1** : the state of being villous **2** : a villous patch or area

vil·lous \ˈvil-əs\ *adj* **1** : covered or furnished with villi **2** : having soft long hairs <leaves ~ underneath> — compare PUBESCENT — **vil·lous·ly** *adv*

vil·lus \ˈvil-əs\ *n, pl* **vil·li** \ˈvil-ˌī, -(ˌ)ē\ [NL, fr. L, tuft of shaggy hair — more at VELVET] : a small slender often vascular process: as **a** : one of the minute finger-shaped processes of the mucous membrane of the small intestine that serve in the absorption of nutriment **b** : one of the branching processes of the surface of the chorion of the developing egg of most mammals that help to form the placenta

vim \ˈvim\ *n* [L, accus. of *vis* strength; akin to Gk *is* strength, *hiesthai* to hurry, OE *wāth* pursuit] : robust energy and enthusiasm

vi·na \ˈvē-nə\ *n* [Skt *vīṇā*] : a stringed instrument of India having usu. four strings on a long bamboo fingerboard with movable frets and a gourd resonator at each end

vi·na·ceous \vī-ˈnā-shəs, vin-ˈā-\ *adj* [L *vinaceus* of wine, fr. *vinum* wine — more at WINE] : of the color wine

vin·ai·grette \ˌvin-i-ˈgret\ *n* [F, fr. *vinaigre* vinegar] : a small ornamental box or bottle with perforated top used for holding an aromatic preparation (as smelling salts)

vinaigrette sauce *n* : a sauce made typically of oil and vinegar, onions, parsley, and herbs and used esp. on cold meats or fish

[1]**vi·nal** \ˈvīn-ᵊl\ *adj* [L *vinalis*, fr. *vinum* wine] : of or relating to wine : VINOUS

[2]**vi·nal** \ˈvī-ˌnal\ *n* [poly*vinyl* *al*cohol] : a synthetic textile fiber that is a long-chain polymer consisting largely of vinyl alcohol units

vin·blas·tine \(ˈ)vin-ˈblas-ˌtēn\ *n* [contr. of *vincaleukoblastine*, fr. *vinca* + *leukoblast* (developing leukocyte), fr. *leuk-* + *-blast*] : an alkaloid $C_{46}H_{58}N_4O_9$ from Madagascar periwinkle used to relieve human neoplastic diseases

vin·ca \ˈviŋ-kə\ *n* [NL, short for L *pervinca* periwinkle] : PERIWINKLE

ə abut **ᵊ** kitten **ər** further **a** back **ā** bake **ä** cot, cart
aú out **ch** chin **e** less **ē** easy **g** gift **i** trip **ī** life
j joke **ŋ** sing **ō** flow **ȯ** flaw **ȯi** coin **th** thin **t͟h** this
ü loot **ú** foot **y** yet **yü** few **yú** furious **zh** vision

Vin·cen·tian \vin-ˈsen-chən\ *n* **:** a member of the Roman Catholic Congregation of the Mission founded by St. Vincent de Paul in Paris, France, in 1625 and devoted to missions and seminaries — **Vincentian** *adj*
Vin·cent's angina \ˌvin(t)-sən(t)s-, (ˌ)va^{n}-ˌsä^{n}z-\ *n* [Jean Hyacinthe *Vincent* †1950 F bacteriologist] **:** a contagious disease marked by ulceration of the mucous membrane of the mouth and adjacent parts and caused by a bacterium (*Fusobacterium fusiforme*) often in association with a spirochete (*Borrelia vincentii*) — called also *trench mouth*
Vincent's infection *n* **:** a bacterial infection of the respiratory tract and mouth marked by destructive ulceration esp. of the mucous membranes
vin·ci·ble \ˈvin(t)-sə-bəl\ *adj* [L *vincibilis,* fr. *vincere* to conquer — more at VICTOR] **:** capable of being overcome or subdued
vin·cris·tine \(ˈ)vin-ˈkris-ˌtēn\ *n* [*vinca* + L *crista* crest + E *-ine*] **:** an alkaloid $C_{46}H_{56}N_4O_{10}$ from Madagascar periwinkle used to relieve human neoplastic diseases (as leukemias)
vin·cu·lum \ˈviŋ-kyə-ləm\ *n, pl* **-lums** *or* **-la** \-lə\ [L, fr. *vincire* to bind — more at VETCH] **1 :** a unifying bond **:** LINK, TIE **2 :** a straight horizontal mark placed over two or more members of a compound mathematical expression and equivalent to parentheses or brackets about them (as in $a-\overline{b-c}=a-[b-c]$)
vin·di·ca·ble \ˈvin-di-kə-bəl\ *adj* **:** capable of being vindicated
vin·di·cate \ˈvin-də-ˌkāt\ *vt* **-cat·ed; -cat·ing** [L *vindicatus,* pp. of *vindicare* to lay claim to, avenge, fr. *vindic-, vindex* claimant, avenger] **1** *obs* **:** to set free **:** DELIVER **2 :** AVENGE **3 a :** EXONERATE, ABSOLVE **b** (1) **:** CONFIRM, SUBSTANTIATE (2) **:** to provide justification or defense for **:** JUSTIFY **c :** to protect from attack or encroachment **:** DEFEND **4 :** to maintain a right to *syn* see MAINTAIN — **vin·di·ca·tor** \-ˌkāt-ər\ *n*
vin·di·ca·tion \ˌvin-də-ˈkā-shən\ *n* **:** an act of vindicating **:** the state of being vindicated; *specif* **:** justification against denial or censure **:** DEFENSE
vin·dic·a·tive \vin-ˈdik-ət-iv\ *adj* **1** *obs* **:** VINDICTIVE, VENGEFUL **2** *archaic* **:** PUNITIVE
vin·di·ca·to·ry *adj* **1** \ˈvin-di-kə-ˌtōr-ē, -ˌtȯr-\ **:** providing vindication **:** JUSTIFICATORY **2** \vin-ˈdik-ə-\ **:** PUNITIVE, RETRIBUTIVE
vin·dic·tive \vin-ˈdik-tiv\ *adj* [L *vindicta* revenge, vindication, fr. *vindicare*] **1 a :** disposed to seek revenge **:** VENGEFUL **b :** intended for or involving revenge **2 :** intended to cause anguish or hurt **:** SPITEFUL — **vin·dic·tive·ly** *adv* — **vin·dic·tive·ness** *n*
syn VINDICTIVE, REVENGEFUL, VENGEFUL *shared meaning element* **:** showing or motivated by a desire for vengeance
[1]**vine** \ˈvīn\ *n* [ME, fr. OF *vigne,* fr. L *vinea* vine, vineyard, fr. fem. of *vineus* of wine, fr. *vinum* wine — more at WINE] **1 :** GRAPE 2 **2 a :** a plant whose stem requires support and which climbs by tendrils or twining or creeps along the ground; *also* **:** the stem of such a plant **b :** any of various sprawling herbaceous plants (as a tomato or potato) that lack specialized adaptations for climbing
[2]**vine** *vi* **vined; vin·ing :** to form or grow in the manner of a vine
vin·eal \ˈvin-ē-əl, ˈvīn-\ *adj* [L *vinealis* of vines, fr. *vinea* vine] **:** of or relating to wine
vine·dress·er \ˈvīn-ˌdres-ər\ *n* **:** one that cultivates and prunes grapevines
vin·e·gar \ˈvin-i-gər\ *n* [ME *vinegre,* fr. OF *vinaigre,* fr. *vin* wine (fr. L *vinum*) + *aigre* keen, sour — more at EAGER] **1 :** a sour liquid obtained by acetic fermentation of dilute alcoholic liquids and used as a condiment or preservative **2 :** ill humor **:** SOURNESS **3 :** VIM
vinegar eel *n* **:** a minute nematode worm (*Turbatrix aceti*) often found in great numbers in vinegar or acid fermenting vegetable matter
vinegar fly *n* [fr. its breeding in pickles] **:** DROSOPHILA
vin·e·gar·ish \ˈvin-i-g(ə-)rish\ *adj* **:** VINEGARY 2
vin·e·gar·roon \ˌvin-i-gə-ˈrün\ *n* [MexSp *vinagrón,* aug. of Sp *vinagre* vinegar, fr. OF *vinaigre*] **:** a large harmless whip scorpion (*Mastigoproctus giganteus*) of the southern U.S. and Mexico that emits a vinegary odor when disturbed and is popularly held to be venomous
vin·e·gary \ˈvin-i-g(ə-)rē\ *adj* **1 :** resembling vinegar **:** SOUR **2 :** disagreeable, bitter, or irascible in character or manner
vin·ery \ˈvīn-(ə-)rē\ *n, pl* **-er·ies :** an area or building in which vines are grown
vine·yard \ˈvin-yərd\ *n* **1 :** a planting of grapevines **2 :** an area or category of physical or mental occupation
vine·yard·ist \-əst\ *n* **:** one who owns or cultivates a vineyard
vingt–et–un \ˌvan-ˌtā-ˈən\ *n* [F, lit., twenty-one] **:** BLACKJACK 5
vi·nic \ˈvī-nik\ *adj* [ISV, fr. L *vinum* wine — more at WINE] **:** of, relating to, or derived from wine or alcohol <~ ether>
vi·ni·cul·ture \ˈvin-ə-ˌkəl-chər, ˈvī-nə-\ *n* [L *vinum* + ISV *-i-* + *culture*] **:** VITICULTURE
vi·nif·er·ous \vī-ˈnif-(ə-)rəs, vin-ˈif-\ *adj* [L *vinifer,* fr. *vinum* + *-ifer* -iferous] **:** yielding or grown for the production of wine
vi·ni·fi·ca·tion \ˌvin-ə-fə-ˈkā-shən, ˌvīn-\ *n* [F, fr. *vin* wine + *-i-* + *-fication*] **:** the conversion of a sugar-containing solution (as a fruit juice) into wine by fermentation
vi·no \ˈvē-(ˌ)nō\ *n* [It & Sp, fr. L *vinum*] **:** WINE
vi·nos·i·ty \vī-ˈnäs-ət-ē\ *n, pl* **-ties :** the characteristic body, flavor, and color of a wine
vi·nous \ˈvī-nəs\ *adj* [L *vinosus,* fr. *vinum* wine] **1 :** of, relating to, or made with wine <~ medications> **2 :** showing the effects of the use of wine **3 :** VINACEOUS — **vi·nous·ly** *adv*
[1]**vin·tage** \ˈvint-ij\ *n* [ME, alter. of *vendage,* fr. MF *vendenge,* fr. L *vindemia,* fr. *vinum* wine, grapes + *demere* to take off, fr. *de-* + *emere* to take — more at WINE, REDEEM] **1 a** (1) **:** a season's yield of grapes or wine from a vineyard (2) **:** WINE; *specif* **:** a wine of a particular type, region, and year and usu. of superior quality that is dated and allowed to mature **b :** a collection of contemporaneous and similar persons or things **:** CROP **2 :** the act or time of harvesting grapes or making wine **3 a :** a period of origin or manufacture <a piano of 1845 ~> **b :** length of existence **:** AGE
[2]**vintage** *adj* **1 :** of or relating to a vintage **2 :** of old, recognized, and enduring interest, importance, or quality **:** CLASSIC **3 :** OLD-FASHIONED, OUTMODED **4 :** of the best and most characteristic — used with a proper noun <~ Shaw: a wise and winning comedy —*Time*>
vin·tag·er \-ij-ər\ *n* **:** one concerned with the production of grapes and wine
vintage year *n* **1 :** a year in which a vintage wine is produced **2 :** a year of outstanding distinction or success
vint·ner \ˈvint-nər\ *n* [ME *vineter,* fr. OF *vinetier,* fr. ML *vinetarius,* fr. L *vinetum* vineyard, fr. *vinum* wine] **1 :** a wine merchant **2 :** a person who makes wine
viny \ˈvī-nē\ *adj* **vin·i·er; -est 1 :** of, relating to, or resembling vines <~ plants> **2 :** covered with or abounding in vines
vi·nyl \ˈvīn-^{ə}l\ *n* [ISV, fr. L *vinum* wine] **1 :** a univalent radical $CH_2{=}CH$ derived from ethylene by removal of one hydrogen atom **2 :** a polymer of a vinyl compound or a product (as a resin or a textile fiber) made from one <~ upholstery> — **vi·nyl·ic** \vī-ˈnil-ik\ *adj*
vinyl alcohol *n* **:** an unstable compound $CH_2{=}CHOH$ known only in the form of its polymers or derivatives
vi·nyl·i·dene \vī-ˈnil-ə-ˌdēn\ *n* [ISV *vinyl* + *-ide* + *-ene*] **:** a bivalent radical $CH_2{=}C$ derived from ethylene by removal of two hydrogen atoms from one carbon atom
vinylidene resin *n* **:** any of a group of tough thermoplastic resins formed by polymerization of a vinylidene compound and used esp. for filaments, films, and molded articles
vinyl resin *n* **:** any of various thermoplastic resinous materials that are essentially polymers of vinyl compounds
vi·ol \ˈvī(-ə)l, ˈvī-(ˌ)ōl\ *n* [MF *viole* viol, viola, fr. OProv *viola* viol] **:** a bowed stringed instrument chiefly of the 16th and 17th centuries having a deep body, flat back, sloping shoulders, usu. six strings, fretted fingerboard, and low-arched bridge and made in treble, alto, tenor, and bass sizes
[1]**vi·o·la** \vē-ˈō-lə\ *n* [It & Sp, viol, viola, fr. OProv, viol] **:** a musical instrument of the violin family that is intermediate in size and compass between the violin and cello and is tuned a fifth below the violin — **vi·o·list** \-ləst\ *n*
[2]**vi·o·la** \vī-ˈō-lə, vē-; ˈvī-ə-\ *n* [L] **:** VIOLET 1a; *esp* **:** any of various garden hybrids with solitary white, yellow, or purple often variegated flowers resembling but smaller than typical pansies
vi·o·la·ble \ˈvī-ə-lə-bəl\ *adj* **:** capable of being or likely to be violated — **vi·o·la·bil·i·ty** \ˌvī-ə-lə-ˈbil-ət-ē\ *n* — **vi·o·la·ble·ness** \ˈvī-ə-lə-bəl-nəs\ *n* — **vi·o·la·bly** \-blē\ *adv*
vi·o·la·ceous \ˌvī-ə-ˈlā-shəs\ *adj* [L *violaceus,* fr. *viola* violet] **:** of the color violet — **vi·o·la·ceous·ly** *adv*
vi·o·la da brac·cio \vē-ˌō-ləd-ə-ˈbräch-(ē-ˌ)ō\ *n, pl* **vi·o·le da braccio** \-(ˌ)lād-\ [It, arm viol] **:** a viol having roughly the range of the viola
viola da gam·ba \-ləd-ə-ˈgäm-bə, -ˈgam-\ *n, pl* **viole da gamba** [It, leg viol] **:** a bass member of the viol family having a range approximating the cello
viola d'a·mo·re \-ləd-ə-ˈmōr-ē, -ˈmȯr-\ *n, pl* **viole d'amore** [It, viol of love] **:** a tenor viol having usu. seven gut and seven wire strings
[1]**vi·o·late** \ˈvī-ə-ˌlāt\ *vt* **-lat·ed; -lat·ing** [ME *violaten,* fr. L *violatus,* pp. of *violare;* akin to L *vis* strength — more at VIM] **1 :** BREAK, DISREGARD <~ the law> **2 :** to do harm to the person or esp. the chastity of; *specif* **:** RAPE **3 :** PROFANE, DESECRATE <~ a shrine> **4 :** INTERRUPT, DISTURB <~ the peace of a spring evening —Nancy Larter> — **vi·o·la·tive** \-ˌlāt-iv\ *adj* — **vi·o·la·tor** \-ˌlāt-ər\ *n*
[2]**vi·o·late** \ˈvī-ə-lət\ *adj, archaic* **:** subjected to violation
vi·o·la·tion \ˌvī-ə-ˈlā-shən\ *n* **:** the act of violating **:** the state of being violated: as **a :** INFRINGEMENT, TRANSGRESSION; *specif* **:** an infringement of the rules in sports that is less serious than a foul and usu. involves technicalities of play **b :** an act of irreverence or desecration **:** PROFANATION **c :** INTERRUPTION, DISTURBANCE **d :** RAPE, RAVISHMENT
vi·o·lence \ˈvī-ə-lən(t)s\ *n* **1 a :** exertion of physical force so as to injure or abuse (as in effecting illegal entry into a house) **b :** an instance of violent treatment or procedure **2 :** injury by or as if by distortion, infringement, or profanation **:** OUTRAGE **3 a :** intense, turbulent, or furious and often destructive action or force <the ~ of the storm> **b :** vehement feeling or expression **:** FERVOR; *also* **:** an instance of such action or feeling **c :** a clashing or jarring quality **:** DISCORDANCE **4 :** undue alteration (as of wording or sense in editing a text)
vi·o·lent \-lənt\ *adj* [ME, fr. MF, fr. L *violentus;* akin to L *violare* to violate] **1 :** marked by extreme force or sudden intense activity <a ~ attack> **2 a :** notably furious or vehement <a ~ denunciation>; *also* **:** excited or mentally disordered to the point of loss of self-control <the patient became ~ and had to be restrained> **b :** EXTREME, INTENSE <~ pain> **3 :** caused by force **:** not natural <a ~ death> — **vi·o·lent·ly** *adv*
violent storm *n* **:** STORM 1c(1) — see BEAUFORT SCALE table
vi·o·let \ˈvī-ə-lət\ *n* [ME, fr. MF *violete,* dim. of *viole* violet, fr. L *viola*] **1 a :** any of a genus (*Viola* of the family Violaceae, the violet family) of herbs or subshrubs with alternate stipulate leaves and both aerial and cleistogamous flowers; *esp* **:** one with smaller usu. solid-colored flowers as distinguished from the usu. larger-flowered violas and pansies **b :** any of several plants of genera other than that of the violet — compare DOGTOOTH VIOLET **2 :** any of a group of colors of reddish blue hue, low lightness, and medium saturation
vi·o·lin \ˌvī-ə-ˈlin\ *n* [It *violino,* dim. of *viola*] **:** a bowed stringed instrument having four strings tuned at intervals of a fifth and a usual range from G below middle C upwards for more than 4½ octaves and distinguished from the viol in having a shallower body, shoulders at right angles to the neck, a fingerboard without frets, and a more curved bridge — **vi·o·lin·ist** \-əst\ *n*
vi·o·lon·cel·lo \ˌvī-ə-lən-ˈchel-(ˌ)ō, ˌvē-\ *n* [It, dim. of *violone,* aug. of *viola*] **:** CELLO — **vi·o·lon·cel·list** \-ˈchel-əst\ *n*
vio·my·cin \ˌvī-ə-ˈmīs-^{ə}n\ *n* [*violet* + *-mycin,* fr. the color of the soil organism] **:** a polypeptide antibiotic $C_{23}H_{36}N_{12}O_8$ that is produced by a soil actinomycete (*Streptomyces puniceus*) and is administered in the form of its sulfate in the treatment of tuberculosis

vi·os·ter·ol \vī-ˈäs-tə-ˌrȯl, -ˌrōl\ *n* [ultra*vio*let + *sterol*] : vitamin D_2 esp. when dissolved in an edible vegetable oil

VIP \ˌvē-ˌī-ˈpē\ *n, pl* **VIPs** \-ˈpēz\ [*v*ery *i*mportant *p*erson] : a person of great influence or prestige; *esp* : a high official with special privileges

vi·per \ˈvī-pər\ *n* [MF *vipere,* fr. L *vipera*] **1 a** : a common European venomous snake (*Vipera berus*) that attains a length of two feet, varies in color from red, brown, or gray with dark markings to black, occurs across Eurasia from England to Sakhalin, and is rarely fatal to man; *broadly* : any of various Old World venomous snakes (family Viperidae) **b** : PIT VIPER **c** : a venomous or reputedly venomous snake **2** : a vicious or treacherous person

vi·per·ine \-pə-ˌrīn\ *adj* : of, relating to, or resembling a viper : VENOMOUS

vi·per·ish \-p(ə-)rish\ *adj* : spitefully vituperative : VENOMOUS

vi·per·ous \-p(ə-)rəs\ *adj* **1** : VIPERINE **2** : having the qualities attributed to a viper : MALIGNANT, VENOMOUS — **vi·per·ous·ly** *adv*

violin: *1* bridge, *2* sound hole, *3* soundboard, *4* fingerboard, *5* pegs, *6* scroll, *7* tailpiece, *g* G-string, *d* D-string, *a* A-string, *e* E-string

viper's bugloss *n* : a coarse bristly Old World weed (*Echium vulgare*) of the borage family that is naturalized in No. America and has showy blue tubular flowers with exserted stamens

vi·ra·go \və-ˈräg-(ˌ)ō, -ˈrāg-; ˈvir-ə-ˌgō\ *n, pl* **-goes** *or* **-gos** [L *viragin-, virago,* fr. *vir* man — more at VIRILE] **1** : a woman of great stature, strength, and courage **2** : a loud overbearing woman : TERMAGANT — **vi·rag·i·nous** \və-ˈraj-ə-nəs\ *adj*

vi·ral \ˈvī-rəl\ *adj* : of, relating to, or caused by a virus — **vi·ral·ly** \-rə-lē\ *adv*

vir·e·lay \ˈvir-ə-ˌlā\ *n* [ME, fr. MF *virelai*] : a chiefly French verse form consisting of stanzas of indeterminate length and number with alternating long and short lines and interlaced rhyme (as *abab bcbc cdcd dada*)

vi·re·mia \vī-ˈrē-mē-ə\ *n* [NL, fr. *virus* + *-emia*] : the presence of virus in the blood of a host — **vi·re·mic** \-mik\ *adj*

vir·eo \ˈvir-ē-ˌō\ *n, pl* **-e·os** [L, a small bird, fr. *virēre* to be green] : any of various small insectivorous American passerine birds (family Vireonidae) that are chiefly olivaceous and grayish in color

vires *pl of* VIS

vi·res·cence \və-ˈres-ᵊn(t)s, vī-\ *n* : the state or condition of becoming green; *esp* : such a condition due to the development of chloroplasts in plant organs (as petals) normally white or colored

vi·res·cent \-ᵊnt\ *adj* [L *virescent-, virescens,* prp. of *virescere* to become green, incho. of *virēre* to be green] **1** : beginning to be green : GREENISH **2** : developing or displaying virescence

vir·ga \ˈvər-gə\ *n* [NL, fr. L, branch, rod, streak in the sky suggesting rain — more at WHISK] : wisps of precipitation evaporating before reaching the ground

¹vir·gate \ˈvər-ˌgāt\ *n* [ML *virgata,* fr. *virga,* a land measure, fr. L, rod] : an old English unit of land area equal to one quarter of a hide or one quarter of an acre

²virgate *adj* [NL *virgatus,* fr. L, made of twigs, fr. *virga*] : shaped like a rod or wand <a ~ one-flowered branch>

¹vir·gin \ˈvər-jən\ *n* [ME, fr. OF *virgine,* fr. L *virgin-, virgo* young woman, virgin] **1 a** : an unmarried woman devoted to religion **b** *cap* : VIRGO **2 a** : an absolutely chaste young woman **b** : an unmarried girl or woman **3** *cap* : VIRGIN MARY **4** : a person who has not had sexual intercourse **5** : a female animal that has never copulated

²virgin *adj* **1** : free of impurity or stain : UNSULLIED **2** : CHASTE **3** : characteristic of or befitting a virgin : MODEST **4** : FRESH, UNSPOILED; *specif* : not altered by human activity <a ~ forest> **5 a** : being used or worked for the first time **b** : INITIAL, FIRST **6 a** : NATIVE 8b <~ sulfur> **b** *of a vegetable oil* : obtained from the first light pressing and without heating **7** : produced directly from ore or by primary smelting — used of metal

¹vir·gin·al \ˈvər-jən-ᵊl, ˈvərj-nəl\ *adj* **1** : of, relating to, or characteristic of a virgin or virginity; *esp* : PURE, CHASTE **2** : PRISTINE, UNSULLIED — **vir·gin·al·ly** \-ē\ *adv*

²virginal *n* [prob. fr. L *virginalis* of a virgin, fr. *virgin-, virgo*] : a small rectangular spinet having no legs and only one wire to a note and popular in the 16th and 17th centuries — often used in pl.; called also *pair of virginals*

virgin birth *n* **1** : birth from a virgin **2** *often cap V&B* : the theological doctrine that Jesus was miraculously begotten of God and born of a virgin mother

Vir·gin·ia cowslip \vər-ˌjin-yə-, -ˌjin-ē-ə-\ *n* [*Virginia,* state of the U.S.] : a smooth erect eastern No. American herb (*Mertensia virginica*) of the borage family with entire leaves and showy blue flowers pink in the bud — called also *Virginia bluebell*

Virginia creeper *n* : a common No. American tendril-climbing vine (*Parthenocissus quinquefolia*) of the grape family with palmately compound leaves and bluish black berries

Virginia fence *n* : WORM FENCE — called also *Virginia rail fence*

Virginia ham *n* : a flat lean hickory-smoked ham with dark red meat esp. from a peanut-fed razorback hog

Virginia pine *n* : a common often straggling pine (*Pinus virginiana*) of the eastern U.S. that has short needles occurring in pairs — called also *Jersey pine*

Virginia rail *n* : an American long-billed rail (*Rallus limicola*) that has gray cheeks

Virginia reel *n* : an American dance in which two lines of couples face each other and all couples in turn participate in a series of figures

Virginia snakeroot *n* : a birthwort (*Aristolochia serpentaria*) of the eastern U.S. with oblong leaves cordate at the base and a solitary basal very irregular flower

vir·gin·i·ty \(ˌ)vər-ˈjin-ət-ē\ *n, pl* **-ties** **1** : the quality or state of being virgin; *esp* : MAIDENHOOD **2** : the unmarried life : CELIBACY, SPINSTERHOOD

vir·gin·ium \vər-ˈjin-ē-əm, -ˈjin-yəm\ *n* [NL, fr. *Virginia*] : FRANCIUM

Virgin Mary *n* : the mother of Jesus

virgin's bower *n* : any of several usu. small-flowered and climbing clematises

virgin wool *n* : wool not used before in manufacture

Vir·go \ˈvər-(ˌ)gō, ˈvi(ə)r-\ *n* [L (gen. *Virginis*), lit., virgin] **1** : a zodiacal constellation on the celestial equator that lies due south of the handle of the Dipper and is pictured as a woman holding a spike of grain **2 a** : the 6th sign of the zodiac in astrology — see ZODIAC table **b** : one born under this sign

vir·gu·late \ˈvər-gyə-lət, -ˌlāt\ *adj* [L *virgula* little rod] : shaped like a rod <a ~ cercaria>

vir·gule \ˈvər-(ˌ)gyü(ə)l\ *n* [F, fr. L *virgula* small stripe, obelus, fr. dim. of *virga* rod — more at WHISK] : DIAGONAL 3

vi·ri·cide \ˈvī-rə-ˌsīd\ *n* [NL *virus* + E *-i-* + *-cide*] : an agent that destroys or inactivates viruses — **vi·ri·cid·al** \ˌvī-rə-ˈsīd-ᵊl\ *adj*

vir·id \ˈvir-əd\ *adj* [L *viridis* green — more at VERDANT] : vividly green : VERDANT

vir·i·des·cent \ˌvir-ə-ˈdes-ᵊnt\ *adj* [L *viridis* green — more at VERDANT] : slightly green : GREENISH

vi·rid·i·an \və-ˈrid-ē-ən\ *n* [L *viridis*] : a chrome green that is probably a hydrated oxide of chrome $Cr_2O_3{\cdot}2H_2O$

vi·rid·i·ty \və-ˈrid-ət-ē\ *n* [ME *viridite,* fr. MF *viridité,* fr. L *viriditat-, viriditas,* fr. *viridis*] **1 a** : the quality or state of being green **b** : the color of grass or foliage **2** : naive innocence

vir·ile \ˈvir-əl, ˈvi(ə)r-ˌīl, *Brit also* ˈvi(ə)r-ˌīl\ *adj* [MF or L; MF *viril,* fr. L *virilis,* fr. *vir* man, male; akin to OE & OHG *wer* man, Skt *vīra*] **1** : having the nature, properties, or qualities of a man; *specif* : capable of functioning as a male in copulation **2** : ENERGETIC, VIGOROUS **3** : characteristic of or associated with men : MASCULINE **4** : MASTERFUL, FORCEFUL

vir·il·ism \ˈvir-ə-ˌliz-əm\ *n* **1** : precocious development of secondary sex characters in the male **2** : the appearance of secondary male characters in the female

vi·ril·i·ty \və-ˈril-ət-ē, *Brit also* vī-\ *n* : the quality or state of being virile: **a** : MANHOOD **b** : manly vigor : MASCULINITY

vi·ri·on \ˈvī-rē-ˌän, ˈvir-ē-\ *n* [ISV *viri-* (fr. *virus*) + ²*-on*] : a complete virus particle with its outer coat intact : the extracellular infective form of a virus

virl \ˈvər(-ə)l\ *n* [ME *virole* — more at FERRULE] *Scot* : FERRULE 1

vi·rol·o·gy \vī-ˈräl-ə-jē\ *n* [NL *virus* + ISV *-logy*] : a branch of science that deals with viruses — **vi·ro·log·i·cal** \ˌvī-rə-ˈläj-i-kəl\ *or* **vi·ro·log·ic** \-ik\ *adj* — **vi·ro·log·i·cal·ly** \-i-k(ə-)lē\ *adv* — **vi·rol·o·gist** \vī-ˈräl-ə-jəst\ *n*

vi·ro·sis \vī-ˈrō-səs\ *n, pl* **vi·ro·ses** \-ˌsēz\ [NL] : infection with or disease caused by a virus

vir·tu \ˌvər-ˈtü, vi(ə)r-\ *n* [It *virtù,* lit., virtue, fr. L *virtut-, virtus*] **1** : a love of or taste for curios or objets d'art **2** : productions of art esp. of a curious or antique nature : OBJETS D'ART

vir·tu·al \ˈvərch-(ə-)wəl, ˈvər-chəl\ *adj* [ME, possessed of certain physical virtues, fr. ML *virtualis,* fr. L *virtus* strength, virtue] : being such in essence or effect though not formally recognized or admitted <a ~ dictator> <a ~ promise>

virtual focus *n* : a point from which divergent rays (as of light) seem to emanate but do not actually do so (as in the image of a point source seen in a plane mirror)

virtual image *n* : an image (as seen in a plane mirror) formed of virtual foci

vir·tu·al·i·ty \ˌvər-chə-ˈwal-ət-ē\ *n, pl* **-ties** **1** : ESSENCE **2** : potential existence : POTENTIALITY

vir·tu·al·ly \ˈvərch-(ə-)wə-lē, ˈvərch-(ə-)lē\ *adv* : almost entirely : for all practical purposes <unnoticed and ~ unknown —Philip Brady>

vir·tue \ˈvər-(ˌ)chü, -chə(-w)\ *n* [ME *virtu,* fr. OF, fr. L *virtut-, virtus* strength, manliness, virtue, fr. *vir* man — more at VIRILE] **1 a** : conformity to a standard of right : MORALITY **b** : a particular moral excellence **2** *pl* : an order of angels — see CELESTIAL HIERARCHY **3** : a beneficial quality or power of a thing **4** : manly strength or courage : VALOR **5** : a commendable quality or trait : MERIT **6** : a capacity to act : POTENCY **7** : chastity esp. in a woman — **by virture of** *or* **in virture of** : through the force of : by authority of

vir·tue·less \-(ˌ)chü-ləs, -chə-\ *adj* **1** : devoid of excellence or worth **2** : lacking in moral goodness

vir·tu·o·sa \ˌvər-chə-ˈwō-sə, -zə\ *n* [It, fem. of *virtuoso*] : a female virtuoso

vir·tu·os·i·ty \-ˈwäs-ət-ē\ *n, pl* **-ties** **1** : a taste for or interest in virtu **2** : great technical skill in the practice of a fine art

¹vir·tu·o·so \-ˈwō-(ˌ)sō, -(ˌ)zō\ *n, pl* **-sos** *or* **-si** \-(ˌ)sē, -(ˌ)zē\ [It, fr. *virtuoso,* adj., virtuous, skilled, fr. LL *virtuosus* virtuous, fr. L *virtus*] **1** : an experimenter or investigator esp. in the arts and sciences : SAVANT **2** : one skilled in or having a taste for the fine arts **3** : one who excels in the technique of an art; *esp* : a highly skilled musical performer (as on the violin) — **vir·tu·o·sic** \-ˈwō-sik, -zik\ *adj*

²virtuoso *adj* : of, relating to, or characteristic of a virtuoso : having the manner or style of a virtuoso

vir·tu·ous \ˈvərch-(ə-)wəs\ *adj* **1** : POTENT, EFFICACIOUS **2 a** : having or exhibiting virtue **b** : morally excellent : RIGHTEOUS **3** : CHASTE ***syn*** see MORAL ***ant*** vicious — **vir·tu·ous·ly** *adv* — **vir·tu·ous·ness** *n*

vi·ru·cide \'vī-rə-ˌsīd\ *n* [NL *virus* + E *-cide*] : VIRICIDE — **vi·ru·cid·al** \ˌvī-rə-'sīd-ᵊl\ *adj*
vir·u·lence \'vir-(y)ə-lən(t)s\ *n* : the quality or state of being virulent: as **a** : extreme bitterness or malignity of temper : RANCOR **b** : MALIGNANCY, VENOMOUSNESS <ameliorate the ~ of a disease> **c** : the relative capacity of a pathogen to overcome body defenses
vir·u·len·cy \-lən-sē\ *n* : VIRULENCE
vir·u·lent \-lənt\ *adj* [ME, fr. L *virulentus,* fr. *virus* poison] **1 a** : marked by a rapid, severe, and malignant course <a ~ infection> **b** : able to overcome bodily defensive mechanisms <a ~ pathogen> **2** : extremely poisonous or venomous : NOXIOUS **3** : full of malice : MALIGNANT <~ racists> **4** : objectionably harsh or strong — **vir·u·lent·ly** *adv*
vir·u·lif·er·ous \ˌvir-(y)ə-'lif-(ə-)rəs\ *adj* [*virul*ence + *-iferous*] : containing, producing, or conveying an agent of infection <offspring of ~ females>
vi·rus \'vī-rəs\ *n* [L, slimy liquid, poison, stench; akin to OE *wāse* marsh, Gk *ios* poison, Skt *viṣa;* in senses 2 & 4, fr. NL, fr. L] **1** *archaic* : VENOM 1 **2 a** : the causative agent of an infectious disease **b** : FILTERABLE VIRUS; *specif* : any of a large group of submicroscopic infective agents that are regarded either as the simplest microorganisms or as extremely complex molecules, that typically contain a protein coat surrounding an RNA or DNA core of genetic material, that are capable of growth and multiplication only in living cells, and that cause various important diseases in man, lower animals, or plants **c** : a disease caused by a filterable virus **3** : something that poisons the mind or soul <the force of this ~ of prejudice —V. S. Waters> **4** : an antigenic but not infective material (as vaccine lymph) obtainable from a case of an infectious disease
vi·ru·stat·ic \ˌvī-rə-'stat-ik\ *adj* [*virus* + Gk *statikos* causing to stand — more at STATIC] : tending to check the growth of viruses
1vis \'vis\ *n, pl* **vi·res** \'vī-ˌrēz\ [L — more at VIM] : FORCE, POWER
2vis *abbr* **1** visibility **2** visual
1vi·sa \'vē-zə *also* -sə\ *n* [F, fr. L, neut. pl. of *visus,* pp.] **1** : an endorsement made on a passport by the proper authorities denoting that it has been examined and that the bearer may proceed **2** : a signature of formal approval by a superior upon a document
2visa *vt* **vi·saed** \-zəd, -səd\; **vi·sa·ing** \-zə-iŋ, -sə-\ : to give a visa to (a passport)
vis·age \'viz-ij\ *n* [ME, fr. OF, fr. *vis* face, fr. L *visus* sight, fr. *visus,* pp. of *vidēre* to see — more at WIT] **1** : the face, countenance, or appearance of a person or sometimes an animal **2** : ASPECT, APPEARANCE <grimy ~ of a mining town> — **vis·aged** \-ijd\ *adj*
1vis-à-vis \ˌvēz-ə-'vē *also* ˌvēs- *or* -ä-'vē\ *n, pl* **vis-à-vis** \-ə-'vē(z), -ä-\ [F, lit., face to face] **1** : one that is face to face with another **2 a** : ESCORT, DATE **b** : COUNTERPART **3** : TÊTE-À-TÊTE 1
2vis-à-vis *prep* **1** : face to face with : OPPOSITE **2** : in relation to **3** : as compared with
3vis-à-vis *adv* : in company : TOGETHER
Vi·sa·yan \və-'sī-ən\ *var of* BISAYAN
vis·ca·cha *var of* VIZCACHA
viscera *pl of* VISCUS
vis·cer·al \'vis-ə-rəl\ *adj* **1** : felt in or as if in the viscera : DEEP <~ sensation> **2** : INSTINCTIVE, APPETITIVE <~ drives> **3** : dealing with crude or elemental emotions : EARTHY <a ~ novel> **4** : of, relating to, or located on or among the viscera : SPLANCHNIC — **vis·cer·al·ly** \-rə-lē\ *adv*
vis·cero·gen·ic \ˌvis-ə-rə-'jen-ik\ *adj* [L *viscera* + E *-genic*] : arising within the body <~ needs>
vis·cero·mo·tor \-'mōt-ər\ *adj* : causing or concerned in the functional activity of the viscera <~ nerves>
vis·cid \'vis-əd\ *adj* [LL *viscidus,* fr. L *viscum* birdlime — more at VISCOUS] **1 a** : having an adhesive quality : STICKY **b** : having a glutinous consistency : VISCOUS **2** : covered with a sticky layer — **vis·cid·i·ty** \vis-'id-ət-ē\ *n* — **vis·cid·ly** \'vis-əd-lē\ *adv*
vis·co·elas·tic \ˌvis-kō-ə-'las-tik\ *adj* [*viscous* + *elastic*] : having appreciable and conjoint viscous and elastic properties <such ~ materials as asphalt>; *also* : constituting or relating to the state of viscoelastic materials <~ data> <~ properties> — **vis·co·elas·tic·i·ty** \-ˌlas-'tis-ət-ē, -'tis-tē\ *n*
vis·com·e·ter \vis-'käm-ət-ər\ *n* [*viscosity* + *-meter*] : an instrument with which to measure viscosity — **vis·co·met·ric** \ˌvis-kə-'me-trik\ *adj* — **vis·com·e·try** \-ə-trē\ *n*
1vis·cose \'vis-ˌkōs, -ˌkōz\ *n* [obs. *viscose,* adj. (viscous)] **1** : a viscous golden-brown solution made by treating cellulose with caustic alkali solution and carbon disulfide and used in making rayon and films of regenerated cellulose **2** : viscose rayon
2viscose *adj* : of, relating to, or made from viscose
vis·co·sim·e·ter \ˌvis-kə-'sim-ət-ər\ *n* [ISV *viscosi*ty + *-meter*] : VISCOMETER — **vis·cosi·met·ric** \(ˌ)vis-ˌkäs-ə-'me-trik\ *adj*
vis·cos·i·ty \vis-'käs-ət-ē\ *n, pl* **-ties** **1** : the quality or state of being viscous **2** : the property of a fluid or semifluid that enables it to develop and maintain an amount of shearing stress dependent upon the velocity of flow and then to offer continued resistance to flow **3** : the ratio of the tangential frictional force per unit area to the velocity gradient perpendicular to the direction of flow of a liquid — called also *coefficient of viscosity* **4** : the capability possessed by a solid of yielding continually under stress
viscosity index *n* : an arbitrary number assigned as a measure of the constancy of the viscosity of a lubricating oil with change of temperature with higher numbers indicating viscosities that change little with temperature
vis·count \'vī-ˌkau̇nt\ *n* [ME *viscounte,* fr. MF *viscomte,* fr. ML *vicecomit-, vicecomes,* fr. LL *vice-* + *comit-, comes* count — more at COUNT] : a member of the peerage in Great Britain ranking below an earl and above a baron — **vis·count·cy** \-ˌkau̇n(t)-sē\ *n* — **vis·count·ess** \-ˌkau̇nt-əs\ *n* — **vis·county** \-ˌkau̇nt-ē\ *n*
vis·cous \'vis-kəs\ *adj* [ME *viscouse,* fr. LL *viscosus* full of birdlime, viscous, fr. L *viscum* mistletoe, birdlime; akin to OHG *wihsila* cherry, Gk *ixos* mistletoe] **1** : VISCID **2** : having or characterized by viscosity <~ flow> — **vis·cous·ly** *adv* — **vis·cous·ness** *n*
vis·cus \'vis-kəs\ *n, pl* **vis·cera** \'vis-ə-rə\ [L (pl. *viscera*)] : an internal organ of the body; *esp* : one (as the heart, liver, or intestine) located in the great cavity of the trunk proper
1vise \'vīs\ *n* [MF *vis* something winding, fr. L *vitis* vine — more at WITHY] : any of various tools with two jaws for holding work that close usu. by a screw, lever, or cam
2vise *vt* **vised; vis·ing** : to hold, force, or squeeze with or as if with a vise
1vi·sé \'vē-ˌzā, vē-'\ *vt* **vi·séd** *or* **vi·séed; vi·sé·ing** [F, pp. of *viser* to visa, fr. *visa*] : VISA
2visé *n* : VISA
vise·like \'vī-ˌslīk\ *adj* : acting like a vise <a ~ grip>

vise

Vish·nu \'vish-(ˌ)nü\ *n* [Skt *Viṣṇu*] : the preserver god of the Hindu sacred triad — compare BRAHMA, SIVA
vis·i·bil·i·ty \ˌviz-ə-'bil-ət-ē\ *n, pl* **-ties** **1** : the quality or state of being visible **2 a** : the degree of clearness of the atmosphere; *specif* : the greatest distance toward the horizon that prominent objects can be identified visually with the naked eye **b** : capability of affording an unobstructed view **3** : a measure of the ability of radiant energy to evoke visual sensation
vis·i·ble \'viz-ə-bəl\ *adj* [ME, fr. MF or L; MF, fr. L *visibilis,* fr. *visus,* pp.] **1** : capable of being seen : perceptible to vision <stars ~ to the naked eye> <~ light> **2 a** : exposed to view <the ~ horizon> **b** : MANIFEST, APPARENT **c** : CONSPICUOUS **3** : capable of being discovered or perceived : RECOGNIZABLE <no ~ means of support> **4** : AVAILABLE 4 **5** : devised to keep a particular part or item always in full view or readily seen or referred to <a ~ index> — **vis·i·ble·ness** *n* — **vis·i·bly** \-blē\ *adv*
visible speech *n* **1** : a set of phonetic symbols based on symbols for articulatory position **2** : speech reproduced spectrographically
Visi·goth \'viz-ə-ˌgäth\ *n* [LL *Visigothi,* pl.] : a member of the western division of the Goths — **Visi·goth·ic** \ˌviz-ə-'gäth-ik\ *adj*
1vi·sion \'vizh-ən\ *n* [ME, fr. OF, fr. L *vision-, visio,* fr. *visus,* pp. of *vidēre* to see — more at WIT] **1 a** : something seen in a dream, trance, or ecstasy; *specif* : a supernatural appearance that conveys a revelation **b** : an object of imagination **c** : a manifestation to the senses of something immaterial <look, not at ~*s,* but at realities —Edith Wharton> **2 a** : the act or power of imagination **b** (1) : mode of seeing or conceiving (2) : unusual discernment or foresight <a man of ~> **c** : direct mystical awareness of the supernatural usu. in visible form **3 a** : the act or power of seeing : SIGHT **b** : the special sense by which the qualities of an object (as color, luminosity, shape and size) constituting its appearance are perceived and which is mediated by the eye **4 a** : something seen **b** : a lovely or charming sight — **vi·sion·al** \'vizh-nəl, -ən-ᵊl\ *adj* — **vi·sion·al·ly** \-ē\ *adv*
2vision *vt* **vi·sioned; vi·sion·ing** \'vizh-(ə-)niŋ\ : ENVISION
1vi·sion·ary \'vizh-ə-ˌner-ē\ *adj* **1 a** : able or likely to see visions **b** : disposed to reverie or imagining : DREAMY **2 a** : of the nature of a vision : ILLUSORY **b** : IMPRACTICABLE, UTOPIAN <a ~ scheme> **c** : existing only in imagination : UNREAL **3** : of, relating to, or characterized by visions or the power of vision ***syn*** see IMAGINARY — **vi·sion·ari·ness** \-ē-nəs\ *n*
2visionary *n, pl* **-ar·ies** **1** : one who sees visions : SEER **2** : one whose ideas or projects are impractical : DREAMER
vi·sioned \'vizh-ənd\ *adj* **1** : seen in a vision <a ~ face> **2** : produced by or experienced in a vision <~ agony> **3** : endowed with vision : INSPIRED
vi·sion·less \'vizh-ən-ləs\ *adj* **1** : SIGHTLESS, BLIND <~ eyes> **2** : lacking vision or inspiration <a ~ leader>
1vis·it \'viz-ət\ *vb* **vis·it·ed** \'viz-ət-əd, 'viz-təd\; **vis·it·ing** \'viz-ət-iŋ, 'viz-tiŋ\ [ME *visiten,* fr. OF *visiter,* fr. L *visitare,* freq. of *visere* to go to see, fr. *vidēre* to see] *vt* **1 a** *archaic* : COMFORT — used of the Deity <~ us with Thy salvation —Charles Wesley> **b** (1) : AFFLICT <~*ed* his people with distempers —Tobias Smollett> (2) : INFLICT, IMPOSE <~*ed* his wrath upon them> **c** : AVENGE <~*ed* the sins of the fathers upon the children> **d** : to present itself to or come over momentarily <was ~*ed* by a strange notion> **2** : to go to see in order to comfort or help **3 a** : to pay a call upon as an act of friendship or courtesy **b** : to reside with temporarily as a guest **c** : to go to see or stay at (a place) for a particular purpose (as business or sightseeing) **d** : to go or come officially to inspect or oversee <a bishop ~*ing* his parish> ~ *vi* **1** : to make a visit; *also* : to make frequent or regular visits **2** : CHAT, CONVERSE
2visit *n* **1 a** : a short stay : CALL **b** : a brief residence as a guest **c** : an extended stay : SOJOURN **2** : a journey to and stay or short sojourn at a place **3** : an official or professional call or tour : VISITATION **4** : the act of a naval officer in boarding a merchant ship on the high seas in exercise of the right of search
syn VISIT, VISITATION, CALL *shared meaning element* : a coming to stay with another temporarily and usu. briefly
vis·it·able \'viz-ət-ə-bəl, 'viz-tə-\ *adj* **1** : subject to or allowing visitation or inspection **2** : socially eligible to receive visits
Vis·i·tan·dine \ˌviz-ə-'tan-ˌdēn\ *n* [F, fr. L *visitandum,* gerund of *visitare* to visit] : a nun of the Roman Catholic Order of the Visitation of the Blessed Virgin Mary founded by St. Francis de Sales and St. Jane de Chantal in Annecy, France, in 1610 and devoted to contemplation and education
vis·i·tant \'viz-ət-ənt, 'viz-tənt\ *n* **1** : VISITOR; *esp* : one thought to come from a spirit world **2** : a migratory bird that appears at intervals for a limited period — **visitant** *adj*
vis·i·ta·tion \ˌviz-ə-'tā-shən\ *n* **1** : an instance of visiting; *esp* : an official visit (as for inspection) **2 a** : a special dispensation of divine favor or wrath **b** : a severe trial : AFFLICTION **3** *cap* : the visit of the Virgin Mary to Elizabeth recounted in Luke and celebrated July 2 by a Christian feast ***syn*** see VISIT — **vis·i·ta·tion·al** \-shnəl, -shən-ᵊl\ *adj*
vis·i·ta·to·ri·al \ˌviz-ət-ə-'tōr-ē-əl, ˌviz-tə-, -'tȯr-\ *adj* : of or relating to visitation or to a judicial visitor or superintendent

visiting card *n* : a small card bearing the name and sometimes the address of a person or married couple that is presented when calling — called also *calling card*
visiting fireman *n* : a usu. important or influential visitor whom it is desirable or expedient to show about or entertain impressively
visiting nurse *n* : a nurse employed by a hospital or social-service agency to perform public health services and esp. to visit sick persons in a community
visiting professor *n* : a professor invited to join a college or university faculty for a limited time (as an academic year)
visiting teacher *n* : an educational officer employed by a public school system to visit the homes of pupils in order to bring about cooperation between school and family and to enforce attendance regulations or to instruct sick or handicapped pupils unable to attend school
vis·i·tor \ˈviz-ət-ər, ˈviz-tər\ *n* : one that visits; *specif* : one that makes formal visits of inspection
vi·sive \ˈviz-iv, ˈvī-siv\ *adj* [ML *visivus*, fr. L *visus*, pp. of *vidēre* to see — more at WIT] **1** *archaic* : of, relating to, or serving for vision **2** *archaic* : capable of seeing or of being seen
vi·sor \ˈvī-zər\ *n* [ME *viser*, fr. AF, fr. OF *visiere*, fr. *vis* face — more at VISAGE] **1** : the front piece of a helmet; *esp* : a movable upper piece **2 a** : a face mask **b** : DISGUISE **3 a** : a projecting front on a cap for shading the eyes **b** : a usu. movable flat sunshade attached at the top of an automobile windshield — **vi·sored** \-zərd\ *adj* — **vi·sor·less** \-zər-ləs\ *adj*
vis·ta \ˈvis-tə\ *n* [It, sight, fr. *visto*, pp. of *vedere* to see, fr. L *vidēre* — more at WIT] **1** : a distant view through or along an avenue or opening : PROSPECT **2** : an extensive mental view (as over a stretch of time or a series of events)
VISTA *abbr* Volunteers in Service to America
vis·taed \ˈvis-təd\ *adj* **1** : affording or made to form a vista **2** : seen in or as if in a vista
vi·su·al \ˈvizh-(ə-)wəl, ˈvizh-əl\ *adj* [ME, fr. LL *visualis*, fr. L *visus* sight, fr. *visus*, pp. of *vidēre* to see] **1** : of, relating to, or used in vision <~ organs> **2** : attained or maintained by sight <~ impressions> **3** : OPTICAL <the ~ focus of a lens> **4** : VISIBLE **5** : producing mental images : VIVID **6** : done or executed by sight only <~ navigation> **7** : of, relating to, or employing visual aids — **vi·su·al·ly** \ˈvizh-(ə-)wə-lē, ˈvizh-(ə-)lē\ *adv*
visual acuity *n* : the relative ability of the visual organ to resolve detail that is usu. expressed as the reciprocal of the minimum angular separation in minutes of two lines just resolvable as separate and that forms in the average human eye an angle of one minute
visual aid *n* : an instructional device (as a chart, map, or model) that appeals chiefly to vision; *esp* : an educational motion picture or filmstrip
visual–aural radio range *n* : a radio aid to air navigation by which a pilot determines if he is on course by an appropriate aural signal, a meter reading, or both — called also *visual-aural range*
visual field *n* : the entire expanse of space visible at a given instant without moving the eyes — called also *field of vision*
vi·su·al·iza·tion \ˌvizh-(ə-)wə-lə-ˈzā-shən, ˌvizh-ə-lə-\ *n* **1** : formation of mental visual images **2** : the act or process of interpreting in visual terms or of putting into visible form **3 a** : the process of exposing an organ to view by surgery **b** : the process of making a viscus visible by injection of a radiopaque substance followed by roentgenography
vi·su·al·ize \ˈvizh-(ə-)wə-ˌlīz, ˈvizh-ə-ˌlīz\ *vb* **-ized; -iz·ing** *vt* : to make visible: as **a** : to see or form a mental image of : ENVISAGE **b** : to make (an organ) visible by surgical or roentgenographic visualization ~ *vi* : to form a mental visual image
vi·su·al·iz·er \-ˌlī-zər\ *n* : one that visualizes; *esp* : one whose mental imagery is prevailingly visual
visual purple *n* : a photosensitive red or purple pigment in the retinal rods of various vertebrates; *esp* : RHODOPSIN
vi·ta \ˈwē-ˌtä, ˈvīt-ə\ *n*, *pl* **vi·tae** \ˈwē-ˌtī, ˈvīt-ē\ [L, lit., life] : a brief autobiographical sketch (as in a doctoral thesis)
VITA *abbr* Volunteers for International Technical Assistance
vi·tal \ˈvīt-ᵊl\ *adj* [ME, fr. MF, fr. L *vitalis* of life, fr. *vita* life; akin to L *vivere* to live — more at QUICK] **1 a** : existing as a manifestation of life **b** : concerned with or necessary to the maintenance of life <~ organs> <blood and other ~ fluids> **2** : full of life and vigor : ANIMATED **3** : characteristic of life or living beings **4 a** : fundamentally concerned with or affecting life or living beings: as (1) : tending to renew or refresh the living : INVIGORATING (2) : destructive to life : MORTAL **b** : of the utmost importance : essential to continued worth or well-being **5** : recording data relating to lives **6** : of, relating to, or constituting the staining of living tissues ***syn*** see LIVING, ESSENTIAL — **vi·tal·ly** \-ᵊl-ē\ *adv*
vital capacity *n* : the breathing capacity of the lungs expressed as the number of cubic inches or cubic centimeters of air that can be forcibly exhaled after a full inspiration
vi·tal·ism \ˈvīt-ᵊl-ˌiz-əm\ *n* **1** : a doctrine that the functions of a living organism are due to a vital principle distinct from physicochemical forces **2** : a doctrine that the processes of life are not explicable by the laws of physics and chemistry alone and that life is in some part self-determining — **vi·tal·ist** \-ᵊl-əst\ *n or adj* — **vi·tal·is·tic** \ˌvīt-ᵊl-ˈis-tik\ *adj*
vi·tal·i·ty \vī-ˈtal-ət-ē\ *n*, *pl* **-ties** **1 a** : the peculiarity distinguishing the living from the nonliving **b** : capacity to live and develop; *also* : physical or mental vigor esp. when highly developed **2 a** : power of enduring or continuing **b** : lively and animated character
vi·tal·iza·tion \ˌvīt-ᵊl-ə-ˈzā-shən\ *n* : the quality or state of being vitalized
vi·tal·ize \ˈvīt-ᵊl-ˌīz\ *vt* **-ized; -iz·ing** : to endow with vitality : ANIMATE
syn VITALIZE, ENERGIZE, ACTIVATE *shared meaning element* : to arouse to activity, animation, or life ***ant*** atrophy
vi·tals \ˈvīt-ᵊlz\ *n pl* **1** : vital organs (as the heart, liver, lungs, and brain) **2** : essential parts
vital signs *n pl* : the pulse rate, respiratory rate, body temperature, and sometimes blood pressure of a person
vital statistics *n pl* : statistics relating to births, deaths, marriages, health, and disease
vi·ta·mer \ˈvīt-ə-mər\ *n* [*vita*min + iso*mer*] : any of two or more compounds that relieve a particular vitamin deficiency; *also* : a structural analogue of a vitamin — **vi·ta·mer·ic** \ˌvīt-ə-ˈmer-ik\ *adj*
vi·ta·min \ˈvīt-ə-mən, *Brit also* ˈvit-\ *n* [L *vita* life + ISV *amine*] : any of various organic substances that are essential in minute quantities to the nutrition of most animals and some plants, act esp. as coenzymes and precursors of coenzymes in the regulation of metabolic processes but do not provide energy or serve as building units, and are present in natural foodstuffs or sometimes produced within the body
vitamin A *n* : any of several fat-soluble vitamins found esp. in animal products (as egg yolk, milk, or fish-liver oils) or a mixture of them whose lack in the animal body causes epithelial tissues to become keratinous (as in the eye with resulting visual defects)
vitamin B *n* **1** : VITAMIN B COMPLEX **2** *or* **vitamin B$_1$** \-ˈbē-ˈwən\ : THIAMINE
vitamin B$_c$ \-ˈbē-ˈsē\ *n* : FOLIC ACID
vitamin B complex *n* : a group of water-soluble vitamins found esp. in yeast, seed germs, eggs, liver and flesh, and vegetables that have varied metabolic functions and include coenzymes and growth factors — called also *B complex;* compare BIOTIN, CHOLINE, NICOTINIC ACID, PANTOTHENIC ACID
vitamin B$_6$ \-ˈbē-ˈsiks\ *n* : pyridoxine or a closely related compound found widely in combined form and considered essential to vertebrate nutrition
vitamin B$_{12}$ \-ˈbē-ˈtwelv\ *n* : a complex cobalt-containing compound $C_{63}H_{90}CoN_{14}O_{14}P$ that occurs esp. in liver, is essential to normal blood formation, neural function, and growth, and is used esp. in treating pernicious and related anemias and in animal rations; *also* : any of several compounds of similar action but different chemistry
vitamin B$_2$ \-ˈbē-ˈtü\ *n* : RIBOFLAVIN
vitamin C *n* : a water-soluble vitamin $C_6H_8O_6$ found in plants and esp. in fruits and leafy vegetables or made synthetically and used in the prevention and treatment of scurvy and as an antioxidant for foods — called also *ascorbic acid*
vitamin D *n* : any or all of several fat-soluble vitamins chemically related to steroids, essential for normal bone and tooth structure, and found esp. in fish-liver oils, egg yolk, and milk or produced by activation (as by ultraviolet irradiation) of sterols: as **a** *or* **vitamin D$_2$** \-ˈdē-ˈtü\: an alcohol $C_{28}H_{43}OH$ usu. prepared by irradiation of ergosterol and used as a dietary supplement in nutrition and medicinally in the control of rickets and related disorders — called also *calciferol* **b** *or* **vitamin D$_3$** \-ˈdē-ˈthrē\ : an alcohol $C_{27}H_{43}OH$ that is the predominating form of vitamin D in most fish-liver oils and is formed in the skin on exposure to sunlight or ultraviolet rays
vitamin E *n* : any of several fat-soluble vitamins that are chemically tocopherols, are essential in the nutrition of various vertebrates in which their absence is associated with infertility, degenerative changes in muscle, or vascular abnormalities, are found esp. in leaves and in seed germ oils, and are used chiefly in animal feeds and as antioxidants
vitamin G *n* : RIBOFLAVIN
vitamin H *n* : BIOTIN
vi·ta·min·ize \ˈvīt-ə-mə-ˌnīz\ *vt* **-ized; -iz·ing** **1** : to provide or supplement with vitamins **2** : to make vigorous as if by the feeding of vitamins — **vi·ta·min·iza·tion** \ˌvīt-ə-mə-nə-ˈzā-shən\ *n*
vitamin K *n* [Dan *k*oagulation coagulation] **1** : either of two naturally occurring fat-soluble vitamins $C_{31}H_{46}O_2$ and $C_{41}H_{56}O_2$ essential for the clotting of blood because of their role in the production of prothrombin — called also respectively *vitamin K_1*, *vitamin K_2* **2** : any of several synthetic compounds closely related chemically to natural vitamins K_1 and K_2 and of similar biological activity
vitamin P *n* [*p*aprika & *p*ermeability] : BIOFLAVONOID
vitamin PP \-ˈpē-ˈpē\ *n* [*p*ellagra-*p*reventive] : a pellagra-preventive vitamin (as nicotinamide or nicotinic acid)
vi·tel·lin \vī-ˈtel-ən, və-\ *n* [*vitellus*] : a phosphoprotein in egg yolk
vi·tel·line \-ˈtel-ən, -ˌēn, -ˌīn\ *adj* **1** : resembling the yolk of an egg esp. in yellow color **2** : of, relating to, or producing yolk
vitelline membrane *n* : a membrane enclosing the egg proper and corresponding to the cell wall of an ordinary cell; *esp* : a membrane separating from the surface of the egg in many invertebrates immediately after the egg is fertilized and thereby preventing other spermatozoa from entering
vi·tel·lo·gen·e·sis \vī-ˌtel-ō-ˈjen-ə-səs, və-\ *n* [NL, fr. L *vitellus* + NL *-o-* + *genesis*] : yolk formation
vi·tel·lus \-ˈtel-əs\ *n* [L, lit., small calf — more at VEAL] : YOLK 1c
vi·ti·ate \ˈvish-ē-ˌāt\ *vt* **-at·ed; -at·ing** [L *vitiatus*, pp. of *vitiare*, fr. *vitium* fault, vice] **1** : to make faulty or defective often by the addition of something that impairs **2** : to debase in moral or aesthetic status <a spirit *vitiated* by luxury> **3** : to make ineffective or weak : INVALIDATE ***syn*** see DEBASE — **vi·ti·a·tor** \ˈvish-ē-ˌāt-ər\ *n*
vi·ti·a·tion \ˌvish-ē-ˈā-shən\ *n* **1** : the quality or state of being vitiated **2** : the act of vitiating
vi·ti·cul·ture \ˈvit-ə-ˌkəl-chər, ˈvīt-\ *n* [L *vitis* vine + E *culture* — more at WITHY] : the cultivation or culture of grapes — **vi·ti·cul·tur·al** \ˌvit-ə-ˈkəlch(-ə)-rəl, ˌvīt-\ *adj* — **vi·ti·cul·tur·ist** \-rəst\ *n*
vit·i·li·go \ˌvit-ᵊl-ˈī-(ˌ)gō, -ˈē-\ *n* [NL, fr. L, tetter] : a skin disorder manifested by smooth white spots on various parts of the body

vi·ti·os·i·ty \ˌvish-ē-ˈäs-ət-ē\ *n* [L *vitiositat-, vitiositas,* fr. *vitiosus* vicious, fr. *vitium*] *archaic* : DEPRAVITY, VICIOUSNESS
vit·re·ous \ˈvi-trē-əs\ *adj* [L *vitreus,* fr. *vitrum* glass — more at WOAD] **1 :** of, relating to, derived from, or consisting of glass **2 a :** resembling glass (as in color, composition, brittleness, or luster) : GLASSY <~ rocks> **b :** characterized by low porosity and usu. translucence due to the presence of a glassy phase <~ china> **3 :** of, relating to, or constituting the vitreous humor — **vit·re·ous·ly** *adv* — **vit·re·ous·ness** *n*
vitreous enamel *n* **:** a fired-on opaque glassy coating on metal (as steel)
vitreous humor *n* **:** the clear colorless transparent jelly that fills the eyeball posterior to the lens — see EYE illustration
vitreous silica *n* **:** a chemically stable and refractory glass made from silica alone — compare QUARTZ GLASS
vit·ri·fy \ˈvi-trə-ˌfī\ *vb* **-fied; -fy·ing** [F *vitrifier,* fr. MF, fr. L *vitrum* glass] *vt* **:** to convert into glass or a glassy substance by heat and fusion ~ *vi* **:** to become vitrified — **vit·ri·fi·able** \-ˌfī-ə-bəl\ *adj* — **vit·ri·fi·ca·tion** \ˌvi-trə-fə-ˈkā-shən\ *n*
vi·trine \və-ˈtrēn\ *n* [F, fr. *vitre* pane of glass, fr. OF, fr. L *vitrum* glass] **:** a glass showcase or cabinet esp. for displaying fine wares or specimens
vit·ri·ol \ˈvi-trē-əl\ *n* [ME, fr. MF, fr. ML *vitriolum,* alter. of LL *vitreolum,* neut. of *vitreolus* glassy, fr. L *vitreus* vitreous] **1 a :** a sulfate of any of various metals (as copper, iron, or zinc); *esp* **:** a glassy hydrate of such a sulfate **b :** OIL OF VITRIOL **2 :** something felt to resemble vitriol esp. in caustic quality; *esp* **:** virulence of feeling or of speech — **vit·ri·ol·ic** \ˌvi-trē-ˈäl-ik\ *adj*
vit·ta \ˈvit-ə\ *n, pl* **vit·tae** \ˈvit-ē, ˈvi-ˌtē, ˈvi-ˌtī\ [NL, fr. L, fillet; akin to L *viēre* to plait — more at WIRE] **1 :** one of the oil tubes in the fruits of plants of the carrot family **2 :** STRIPE, STREAK
vit·tate \ˈvi-ˌtāt\ *adj* **1 :** bearing or containing vittae **2 :** striped longitudinally
vit·tles \ˈvit-ᵊlz\ *n pl* **:** VICTUALS
vi·tu·per·ate \vī-ˈt(y)ü-pə-ˌrāt, və-\ *vb* **-at·ed; -at·ing** [L *vituperatus,* pp. of *vituperare,* fr. *vitium* fault + *parare* to make — more at PARE] *vt* **:** to abuse or censure severely or abusively **:** BERATE ~ *vi* **:** to use harsh condemnatory language ***syn*** see SCOLD — **vi·tu·per·a·tor** \-ˌrāt-ər\ *n*
vi·tu·per·a·tion \(ˌ)vī-ˌt(y)ü-pə-ˈrā-shən, və-\ *n* **1 :** sustained and bitter railing and condemnation **:** vituperative utterance **2 :** an act or instance of vituperating ***syn*** see ABUSE ***ant*** acclaim, praise
vi·tu·per·a·tive \vī-ˈt(y)ü-p(ə-)rət-iv, -pə-ˌrāt-\ *adj* **:** uttering or given to censure **:** containing or characterized by verbal abuse — **vi·tu·per·a·tive·ly** *adv*
vi·tu·per·a·to·ry \-p(ə-)rə-ˌtōr-ē, -ˌtȯr-\ *adj* **:** VITUPERATIVE
vi·va \ˈvē-və, -ˌvä\ *interj* [It, long live, fr. 3d pers. sing. pres. subj. of *vivere* to live, fr. L — more at QUICK] — used to express goodwill or approval
vi·va·ce \vē-ˈväch-(ˌ)ā, -ē\ *adv or adj* [It, vivacious, fr. L *vivac-, vivax*] **:** in a brisk spirited manner — used as a direction in music
vi·va·cious \və-ˈvā-shəs *also* vī-\ *adj* [L *vivac-, vivax,* lit., long-lived, fr. *vivere* to live — more at QUICK] **:** lively in temper or conduct **:** SPRIGHTLY ***syn*** see LIVELY ***ant*** languid — **vi·va·cious·ly** *adv* — **vi·va·cious·ness** *n*
vi·vac·i·ty \-ˈvas-ət-ē\ *n* **:** the quality or state of being vivacious
vi·van·dière \ˌvē-ˌvän-ˈdye(ə)r\ *n* [F, fem. of MF *vivandier,* fr. ML *vivanda* food — more at VIAND] **:** a female sutler
vi·var·i·um \vī-ˈvar-ē-əm, -ˈver-\ *n, pl* **-ia** \-ē-ə\ *or* **-i·ums** [L, park, preserve, fr. *vivus* alive — more at QUICK] **:** an enclosure for keeping or raising and observing animals or plants indoors; *esp* **:** one for terrestrial animals — compare TERRARIUM
[1]**vi·va vo·ce** \ˌvī-və-ˈvō-(ˌ)sē *or (as if fr It)* ˌvē-və-ˈvō-(ˌ)chā\ *adv* [ML, with the living voice] **:** by word of mouth **:** ORALLY
[2]**viva voce** *adj* **:** expressed or conducted by word of mouth **:** ORAL
[3]**viva voce** *n* **:** an examination conducted viva voce
vi·vax malaria \ˈvī-ˌvaks-\ *n* [NL *vivax,* specific epithet of *Plasmodium vivax,* parasite causing tertian] **:** TERTIAN
vi·ver·rid \vī-ˈver-əd\ *n* [NL *Viverridae,* group name, fr. *Viverra,* type genus, fr. L *viverra* ferret] **:** any of a family (*Viverridae*) of carnivorous mammals (as a civet, a genet, or a mongoose) that are rarely larger than a domestic cat but are long, slender, and like a weasel in build with short more or less retractile claws and rounded feet — **viverrid** *adj*
vi·vers \ˈvē-vərz, ˈvī-\ *n pl* [MF *vivres,* pl. of *vivre* food, fr. *vivre* to live, fr. L *vivere*] *chiefly Scot* **:** VICTUALS, FOOD
Viv·i·an *or* **Viv·i·en** \ˈviv-ē-ən\ *n* **:** the mistress of Merlin in Arthurian legend — called also *Lady of the Lake*
viv·id \ˈviv-əd\ *adj* [L *vividus,* fr. *vivere* to live — more at QUICK] **1 :** having the appearance of vigorous life or freshness **:** LIVELY <~ sketch> **2** *of a color* **:** very strong **:** very high in chroma **3 :** producing a strong or clear impression on the senses **:** SHARP, INTENSE; *specif* **:** producing distinct mental images <a ~ description> **4 :** acting clearly and vigorously <a ~ imagination> ***syn*** see GRAPHIC — **viv·id·ly** *adv* — **viv·id·ness** *n*
vi·vif·ic \vī-ˈvif-ik\ *adj* [L *vivificus*] **:** imparting spirit or vivacity
viv·i·fi·ca·tion \ˌviv-ə-fə-ˈkā-shən\ *n* **:** the act of vivifying **:** the state of being vivified
viv·i·fi·er \ˈviv-ə-ˌfī(-ə)r\ *n* **:** one that vivifies
viv·i·fy \ˈviv-ə-ˌfī\ *vt* **-fied; -fy·ing** [MF *vivifier,* fr. LL *vivificare,* fr. L *vivificus* enlivening, fr. *vivus* alive — more at QUICK] **1 :** to endue with life or renewed life **:** ANIMATE <rains that ~ the barren hills> **2 :** to impart vitality or vividness to <concentrating this union of quality and meaning in a way which *vivifies* both — John Dewey> ***syn*** see QUICKEN
vi·vi·par·i·ty \ˌvī-və-ˈpar-ət-ē, ˌviv-ə-\ *n* **:** the quality or state of being viviparous
vi·vip·a·rous \vī-ˈvip-(ə-)rəs, və-\ *adj* [L *viviparus,* fr. *vivus* alive + *-parus* -parous] **1 :** producing living young instead of eggs from within the body in the manner of nearly all mammals, many reptiles, and a few fishes **2 :** germinating while still attached to the parent plant <the ~ seed of the mangrove> — **vi·vip·a·rous·ly** *adv* — **vi·vip·a·rous·ness** *n*
vivi·sect \ˈviv-ə-ˌsekt\ *vb* [back-formation fr. *vivisection*] *vt* **:** to perform vivisection on ~ *vi* **:** to practice vivisection — **vivi·sec·tor** \-ˌsek-tər\ *n*
vivi·sec·tion \ˌviv-ə-ˈsek-shən, ˈviv-ə-ˌ\ *n* [L *vivus* + E *section*] **:** the cutting of or operation on a living animal usu. for physiological or pathological investigation; *broadly* **:** animal experimentation esp. if considered to cause distress to the subject — **vivi·sec·tion·al** \ˌviv-ə-ˈsek-shnəl, -shən-ᵊl\ *adj* — **vivi·sec·tion·al·ly** \-ē\ *adv* — **vivi·sec·tion·ist** \-ˈsek-sh(ə-)nəst\ *n*
vix·en \ˈvik-sən\ *n* [(assumed) ME (southern dial.) *vixen,* alter. of ME *fixen,* fr. OE *fyxe,* fem. of *fox*] **1 :** a female fox **2 :** a shrewish ill-tempered woman — **vix·en·ish** \-s(ə-)nish\ *adj* — **vix·en·ish·ly** *adv* — **vix·en·ish·ness** *n*
viz \ˈnām-lē, ˈviz, və-ˈdel-ə-ˌset\ *abbr* videlicet
viz·ard \ˈviz-ərd, -ˌärd\ *n* [alter. of ME *viser* mask, visor] **1 :** a mask for disguise or protection **2 :** DISGUISE, GUISE
viz·ca·cha \vis-ˈkäch-ə\ *n* [Sp *vizcacha,* fr. Quechua *wiskácha*] **:** any of several So. American burrowing rodents (genera *Lagostomus* and *Lagidium*) closely related to the chinchilla
vi·zier \və-ˈzi(ə)r\ *n* [Turk *vezir,* fr. Ar *wazīr*] **:** a high executive officer of various Muslim countries and esp. of the former Turkish Empire — **vi·zier·ate** \-ˈzir-ət, -ˈzi(ə)r-ˌāt\ *n* — **vi·zier·ial** \-ˈzir-ē-əl\ *adj* — **vi·zier·ship** \-ˈzi(ə)r-ˌship\ *n*
vi·zor *var of* VISOR
vizs·la \ˈvizh-ˌlō\ *n* [*Vizsla,* Hungary] **:** any of a Hungarian breed of hunting dog resembling the weimaraner but having a rich deep red coat and brown eyes
VLF *abbr* very low frequency
V neck *n* **:** a V-shaped neck of a garment
VO *abbr* verbal order
VOA *abbr* Voice of America
voc *abbr* vocative
vocab *abbr* vocabulary
vo·ca·ble \ˈvō-kə-bəl\ *n* [MF, fr. L *vocabulum,* fr. *vocare* to call — more at VOICE] **:** TERM; *specif* **:** a word composed of various sounds or letters without regard to its meaning
vo·cab·u·lar \vō-ˈkab-yə-lər, və-\ *adj* [back-formation fr. *vocabulary*] **:** of or relating to words or phraseology **:** VERBAL
vo·cab·u·lary \vō-ˈkab-yə-ˌler-ē, və-\ *n, pl* **-lar·ies** [MF *vocabulaire,* prob. fr. ML *vocabularium,* fr. neut. of *vocabularius* verbal, fr. L *vocabulum*] **1 :** a list or collection of words or of words and phrases usu. alphabetically arranged and explained or defined **:** LEXICON **2 a :** a sum or stock of words employed by a language, group, individual, or work or in a field of knowledge **b :** a list or collection of terms or codes available for use (as in an indexing system) **3 :** a supply of expressive techniques or devices (as of an art form)
vocabulary entry *n* **:** a word (as the noun *book*), hyphened or open compound (as the verb *book-match* or the noun *book review*), word element (as the affix *pro-*), abbreviation (as *agt*), verbalized symbol (as *Na*), or term (as *man in the street*) entered alphabetically in a dictionary for the purpose of definition or identification or expressly included as an inflected form (as the noun *mice* or the verb *saw*) or as a derived form (as the noun *godlessness* or the adverb *globally*) or related phrase (as *one for the book*) run on at its base word and usu. set in a type (as boldface) readily distinguishable from that of the lightface running text which defines, explains, or identifies the entry
[1]**vo·cal** \ˈvō-kəl\ *adj* [ME, fr. L *vocalis,* fr. *voc-, vox* voice — more at VOICE] **1 a :** uttered by the voice **:** ORAL **b :** produced in the larynx **:** uttered with voice **2 :** relating to, composed or arranged for, or sung by the human voice <~ music> **3 :** VOCALIC **4 a :** having or exercising the power of producing voice, speech, or sound **b :** EXPRESSIVE **c :** full of voices **:** RESOUNDING **d :** given to expressing oneself freely or insistently **:** OUTSPOKEN **e :** expressed in words **5 :** of, relating to, or resembling the voice <~ impairment> — **vo·cal·i·ty** \vō-ˈkal-ət-ē\ *n* — **vo·cal·ly** \ˈvō-kə-lē\ *adv*
[2]**vocal** *n* **1 :** a vocal sound **2 :** a usu. accompanied musical composition for the human voice **:** SONG; *also* **:** a performance of such a composition
vocal cords *n pl* **:** either of two pairs of folds of mucous membranes that project into the cavity of the larynx and have free edges extending dorsoventrally toward the middle line — see LARYNX illustration
[1]**vo·cal·ic** \vō-ˈkal-ik, və-\ *adj* [L *vocalis* vowel, fr. *vocalis* vocal] **1 :** marked by or consisting of vowels **2 a :** being or functioning as a vowel **b :** of, relating to, or associated with a vowel — **vo·cal·i·cal·ly** \-i-k(ə-)lē\ *adv*
[2]**vocalic** *n* **:** a vowel sound or sequence in its function as the most sonorous part of a syllable
vo·cal·ism \ˈvō-kə-ˌliz-əm\ *n* **1 :** VOCALIZATION **2 :** vocal art or technique **:** SINGING **3 :** the vowel system of a language or dialect
vo·cal·ist \-kə-ləst\ *n* **:** [1]SINGER
vo·cal·iza·tion \ˌvō-kə-lə-ˈzā-shən\ *n* **:** an act, process, or instance of vocalizing
vo·cal·ize \ˈvō-kə-ˌlīz\ *vb* **-ized; -iz·ing** *vt* **1 :** to give voice to **:** UTTER; *specif* **:** SING **2 a :** to make voiced rather than voiceless **:** VOICE **b :** to convert to a vowel **3 :** to furnish (as a consonantal Hebrew or Arabic text) with vowels or vowel points ~ *vi* **1 :** to utter vocal sounds **2 :** SING; *specif* **:** to sing without words — **vo·cal·iz·er** *n*
vo·ca·tion \vō-ˈkā-shən\ *n* [ME *vocacioun,* fr. L *vocation-, vocatio* summons, fr. *vocatus,* pp. of *vocare* to call — more at VOICE] **1 a :** a summons or strong inclination to a particular state or course of action; *esp* **:** a divine call to the religious life **b :** an entry into the priesthood or a religious order **2 a :** the work in which a person is regularly employed **:** OCCUPATION **b :** the persons engaged in a particular occupation **3 :** the special function of an individual or group
vo·ca·tion·al \-shnəl, -shən-ᵊl\ *adj* **1 :** of, relating to, or concerned with a vocation **2 :** of, relating to, or being in training in a skill or trade to be pursued as a career — **vo·ca·tion·al·ly** \-ē\ *adv*

vo·ca·tion·al·ism \-ˌiz-əm\ *n* **:** emphasis on vocational training in education — **vo·ca·tion·al·ist** \-əst\ *n*

[1]**voc·a·tive** \ˈväk-ət-iv\ *adj* [ME *vocatif,* fr. MF, fr. L *vocativus,* fr. *vocatus,* pp.] **1 :** of, relating to, or being a grammatical case marking the one addressed <Latin *Domine* in *miserere, Domine* "have mercy, O Lord" is in the ~ case> **2** *of a word or word group* **:** marking the one addressed <*mother* in "mother, come here" is a ~ expression> — **voc·a·tive·ly** *adv*

[2]**vocative** *n* **1 :** the vocative case of a language **2 :** a form in the vocative case

vo·cif·er·ant \vō-ˈsif-ə-rənt\ *adj* **:** CLAMOROUS, VOCIFEROUS

vo·cif·er·ate \-ˌrāt\ *vb* **-at·ed; -at·ing** [L *vociferatus,* pp. of *vociferari,* fr. *voc-, vox* voice + *ferre* to bear — more at VOICE, BEAR] *vi* **:** to cry out loudly **:** CLAMOR ~ *vt* **:** to utter loudly **:** SHOUT — **vo·cif·er·a·tion** \-ˌsif-ə-ˈrā-shən\ *n* — **vo·cif·er·a·tor** \-ˈsif-ə-ˌrāt-ər\ *n*

vo·cif·er·ous \vō-ˈsif-(ə-)rəs\ *adj* **:** marked by or given to vehement insistent outcry — **vo·cif·er·ous·ly** *adv* — **vo·cif·er·ous·ness** *n* ***syn*** VOCIFEROUS, CLAMOROUS, BLATANT, STRIDENT, BOISTEROUS, OBSTREPEROUS *shared meaning element* **:** so loud or insistent as to compel attention

vo·cod·er \ˈvō-ˌkōd-ər\ *n* [*voice coder*] **:** an electronic mechanism that reduces speech signals to slowly varying signals which can be transmitted over communication systems of limited frequency bandwidth

vod·ka \ˈväd-kə\ *n* [Russ, fr. *voda* water; akin to OE *wæter* water] **:** a colorless and unaged liquor of neutral spirits distilled from a mash (as of rye or wheat)

vo·dun \vō-ˈdü^{n}\ *n* [Haitian Creole] **:** VOODOO 1

vo·gie \ˈvō-gē\ *adj* [origin unknown] *Scot* **:** PROUD, VAIN

vogue \ˈvōg\ *n* [MF, action of rowing, course, fashion, fr. OIt *voga,* fr. *vogare* to row; akin to OSp *bogar* to row] **1 :** the leading place in popularity or acceptance **2 a :** popular acceptation or favor **:** POPULARITY **b :** a period of popularity **3 :** one that is in fashion at a particular time ***syn*** see FASHION — **vogue** *adj*

vogu·ish \ˈvō-gish\ *adj* **1 :** FASHIONABLE, SMART **2 :** suddenly or temporarily popular — **vogu·ish·ness** *n*

[1]**voice** \ˈvȯis\ *n* [ME, fr. OF *vois,* fr. L *voc-, vox;* akin to OHG *giwahanen* to mention, L *vocare* to call, Gk *epos* word, speech] **1 a :** sound produced by vertebrates by means of lungs, larynx, or syrinx; *esp* **:** sound so produced by human beings **b (1) :** musical sound produced by the vocal cords and resonated by the cavities of head and throat **(2) :** the power or ability to produce musical tones **(3) :** SINGER **(4) :** one of the melodic parts in a vocal or instrumental composition **(5) :** condition of the vocal organs with respect to production of musical tones **(6) :** the use of the voice (as in singing or acting) <studying ~> **c :** expiration of air with the vocal cords drawn close so as to vibrate audibly (as in uttering vowels and consonant sounds as \v\ or \z\) **d :** the faculty of utterance **:** SPEECH **2 :** a sound resembling or suggesting vocal utterance **3 :** an instrument or medium of expression <the party became the ~ of the workers> **4 a :** wish, choice, or opinion openly or formally expressed <claimed to follow the ~ of the people> **b :** right of expression; *also* **:** influential power **5 :** distinction of form or a system of inflections of a verb to indicate the relation of the subject of the verb to the action which the verb expresses — **with one voice :** without dissent **:** UNANIMOUSLY

[2]**voice** *vt* **voiced; voic·ing 1 :** to express in words **:** UTTER <~ a complaint> **2 :** to adjust for producing the proper musical sounds **3 :** to pronounce (as a consonant) with voice ***syn*** see EXPRESS

voice box *n* **:** LARYNX

voiced \ˈvȯist\ *adj* **1 :** furnished with a voice — often used in combination <soft-*voiced*> **2 :** uttered with vocal cord vibration <a ~ consonant> — **voiced·ness** \ˈvȯis(t)-nəs, ˈvȯi-səd-nəs\ *n*

voice frequency *n* **:** a radio frequency in the next to the lowest range of the radio spectrum — see RADIO FREQUENCY table

voice·ful \ˈvȯis-fəl\ *adj* **:** having a voice or vocal quality; *also* **:** having a loud voice or many voices — **voice·ful·ness** *n*

voice·less \ˈvȯi-sləs\ *adj* **1 :** having no voice **:** MUTE **2 :** not voiced **:** SURD <a ~ consonant> — **voice·less·ly** *adv* — **voice·less·ness** *n*

voice–over \ˈvȯi-ˌsō-vər\ *n* **:** the voice of an unseen narrator heard in a motion picture or television program; *also* **:** the voice of a visible character indicating his thoughts but without motion of his lips

voice part *n* **:** VOICE 1b(4)

voice·print \ˈvȯi-ˌsprint\ *n* [*voice* + *-print* (as in *fingerprint*)] **:** an individually distinctive pattern of certain voice characteristics that is spectrographically produced

voic·er \ˈvȯi-sər\ *n* **:** one that voices; *specif* **:** one that voices organ pipes

voice vote *n* **:** a parliamentary vote taken by calling for ayes and noes and estimating which response is stronger

[1]**void** \ˈvȯid\ *adj* [ME *voide,* fr. OF, fr. (assumed) VL *vocitus,* deriv. of L *vacuus* — more at VACUUM] **1 :** containing nothing <~ space> **2 :** IDLE, LEISURE **3 a :** not occupied **:** VACANT <a ~ bishopric> **b :** not inhabited **:** DESERTED **4 a :** being without **:** DEVOID <a nature ~ of all malice> **b :** having no members or examples; *specif, of a suit* **:** having no cards represented in a particular hand <bid a ~ suit as a slam signal> **5 :** VAIN, USELESS **6 a :** of no legal force or effect **:** NULL <a ~ contract> **b :** VOIDABLE ***syn*** see EMPTY

[2]**void** *n* **1 a :** empty space **:** EMPTINESS, VACUUM **b :** OPENING, GAP **2 :** the quality or state of being without something **:** LACK, ABSENCE **3 :** a feeling of want or hollowness **4 :** absence of cards of a particular suit in a hand as dealt

[3]**void** *vb* [ME *voiden,* fr. MF *vuidier,* fr. (assumed) VL *vocitare,* fr. *vocitus*] *vt* **1 a :** to make empty or vacant **:** CLEAR **b :** VACATE, LEAVE **2 :** DISCHARGE, EMIT <~ excrement> **3 :** NULLIFY, ANNUL <~ a contract> ~ *vi* **:** to eliminate solid or liquid waste from the body — **void·er** *n*

void·able \ˈvȯid-ə-bəl\ *adj* **:** capable of being voided; *specif* **:** capable of being adjudged void — **void·able·ness** *n*

void·ance \ˈvȯid-^{ə}n(t)s\ *n* **1 :** the act of voiding **2** *of a benefice* **:** the state of being without an incumbent

void·ed \ˈvȯid-əd\ *adj* **:** having the inner part cut away or left vacant with a narrow border left at the sides — used of a heraldic charge

void·ness \-nəs\ *n* **:** the quality or state of being void **:** EMPTINESS

voile \ˈvȯi(ə)l\ *n* [F, veil, fr. L *vela,* neut. pl. of *velum*] **:** a fine soft sheer fabric used esp. for women's summer clothing or curtains

voir dire \(ˌ)(v)wä(r)-ˈdi(ə)r\ *n* [AF, fr. OF, to speak the truth] **:** a preliminary examination to determine the competency of a witness or juror

vol *abbr* **1** volcano **2** volume **3** volunteer

vo·lant \ˈvō-lənt\ *adj* [MF, fr. L *volant-, volans,* prp. of *volare* to fly] **1 :** having the wings extended as if in flight — used of a heraldic bird **2 :** flying or capable of flying **3 :** QUICK, NIMBLE

vo·lan·te \vō-ˈlän-(ˌ)tā\ *adj* [It, lit., flying, fr. L *volant-, volans,* prp.] **:** moving with light rapidity — used as a direction in music

Vo·la·pük \ˈvō-lə-ˌpu̇k, ˈväl-ə-\ *n* [Volapük, lit., world's speech, fr. *vola* of the world (gen. of *vol* world, modif. of E *world*) + *pük* speech, modif. of E *speak*] **:** an artificial international language based largely on English but with some root words from German, French, and Latin

vo·lar \ˈvō-lər, -ˌlär\ *adj* [L *vola* palm of the hand, sole of the foot] **:** relating to the palm of the hand or the sole of the foot; *specif* **:** located on the same side as the palm of the hand <the ~ part of the forearm>

[1]**vol·a·tile** \ˈväl-ət-^{ə}l, *esp Brit* -ə-ˌtīl\ *n* [ME *volatil,* fr. OF, fr. *volatilie* group of birds, fr. ML *volatilia,* fr. L, neut. pl. of *volatilis* winged, volatile] **1 :** a winged creature (as a bird or insect) **2 :** a volatile substance

[2]**volatile** *adj* [F, fr. L *volatilis,* fr. *volatus,* pp. of *volare* to fly] **1 :** flying or having the power to fly **2 :** readily vaporizable at a relatively low temperature **3 a :** LIGHTHEARTED, LIVELY **b :** easily aroused <~ suspicions> **c :** tending to erupt into violence **:** EXPLOSIVE **4 a :** unable to hold the attention fixed because of an inherent lightness or fickleness of disposition **:** CHANGEABLE **b :** characterized by rapid change **5 :** difficult to capture or hold permanently **:** EVANESCENT, TRANSITORY

vol·a·tile·ness \-nəs\ *n* **:** VOLATILITY

volatile oil *n* **:** an oil that vaporizes readily; *esp* **:** ESSENTIAL OIL

vol·a·til·i·ty \ˌväl-ə-ˈtil-ət-ē\ *n* **:** the quality or state of being volatile ***syn*** see LIGHTNESS

vol·a·til·ize \ˈväl-ət-^{ə}l-ˌīz, *Brit also* və-ˈlat-\ *vb* **-ized; -iz·ing** *vt* **:** to make volatile; *esp* **:** to cause to pass off in vapor ~ *vi* **:** to pass off in vapor — **vol·a·til·iz·able** \-ˌī-zə-bəl\ *adj* — **vol·a·til·iza·tion** \ˌväl-ət-^{ə}l-ə-ˈzā-shən, *Brit also* və-ˌlat-\ *n*

vol–au–vent \ˌvȯ-lō-ˈvä^{n}\ *n* [F, lit., flight in the wind] **:** a large baked patty shell filled with a ragout of meat, fowl, game, or fish

[1]**vol·ca·nic** \väl-ˈkan-ik, vȯl- *also* -ˈkān-\ *adj* **1 a :** of, relating to, or produced by a volcano **b :** characterized by volcanoes **c :** made of materials from volcanoes **2 :** explosively violent **:** VOLATILE <~ emotions> — **vol·ca·ni·cal·ly** \-i-k(ə-)lē\ *adv*

[2]**volcanic** *n* **:** a volcanic rock

volcanic glass *n* **:** natural glass produced by the cooling of molten lava too rapidly to permit crystallization

vol·ca·nic·i·ty \ˌväl-kə-ˈnis-ət-ē, ˌvȯl-\ *n* **:** VOLCANISM

vol·ca·nism \ˈväl-kə-ˌniz-əm, ˈvȯl-\ *n* **:** volcanic power or action

vol·ca·no \väl-ˈkā-(ˌ)nō, vȯl-\ *n, pl* **-noes** *or* **-nos** [It *vulcano,* fr. L *Volcanus, Vulcanus* Vulcan] **:** a vent in the planetary crust from which molten or hot rock and steam issue; *also* **:** a hill or mountain composed wholly or in part of the ejected material

vol·ca·no·log·ic \ˌväl-kən-^{ə}l-ˈäj-ik, ˌvȯl-\ *or* **vol·ca·no·log·i·cal** \-i-kəl\ *adj* **:** of, relating to, or involving volcanology or volcanic phenomena <~ processes that shape the planets>

vol·ca·nol·o·gist \ˌväl-kə-ˈnäl-ə-jəst, ˌvȯl-\ *n* **:** a specialist in volcanology

vol·ca·nol·o·gy \-kə-ˈnäl-ə-jē\ *n* **:** a branch of science that deals with volcanic phenomena

[1]**vole** \ˈvōl\ *n* [F, prob. fr. *voler* to fly — more at VOLLEY] **:** GRAND SLAM 1

[2]**vole** *n* [earlier *vole-mouse,* fr. *vole-* (of Scand origin; akin to ON *vǫllr* field) + *mouse*] **:** any of various small rodents (family Cricetidae and esp. genus *Microtus*) that typically have a stout body, rather blunt nose, and short ears, that inhabit both moist meadows and dry uplands and do much damage to crops, and that are closely related to muskrats and lemmings but in general resemble stocky mice or rats

vo·li·tion \vō-ˈlish-ən, və-\ *n* [F, fr. ML *volition-, volitio,* fr. L *vol-* (stem of *velle* to will, wish) + *-ition-, -itio* (as in L *position-, positio* position) — more at WILL] **1 :** an act of making a choice or decision; *also* **:** a choice or decision made **2 :** the power of choosing or determining **:** WILL — **vo·li·tion·al** \-ˈlish-nəl, -ən-^{ə}l\ *adj*

vol·i·tive \ˈväl-ət-iv\ *adj* **1 :** of or relating to the will **2 :** expressing a wish or permission

volks·lied \ˈfōk-ˌslēt, ˈfōlk-\ *n, pl* **volks·lie·der** \-ˌslēd-ər\ [G, fr. *volk* people + *lied* song] **:** a folk song

[1]**vol·ley** \ˈväl-ē\ *n, pl* **volleys** [MF *volee* flight, fr. *voler* to fly, fr. L *volare*] **1 a :** a flight of missiles (as arrows) **b :** simultaneous discharge of a number of missile weapons **c :** one round per gun in a battery fired as soon as a gun is ready without regard to order **d (1) :** the flight of the ball (as in volleyball or tennis) or its course before striking the ground; *also* **:** a return of the ball before it touches the ground **(2) :** a kick of the ball in soccer before it rebounds **(3) :** the exchange of the shuttlecock in badminton following the serve **2 a :** a burst or emission of many things at

once **b :** a burst of simultaneous or immediately sequential nerve impulses passing to an end organ, synapse, or center

2volley *vb* **vol·leyed; vol·ley·ing** *vt* **1 :** to discharge in or as if in a volley **2 :** to propel (an object) while in the air and before touching the ground; *esp* **:** to hit (a tennis ball) on the volley ~ *vi* **1 :** to become discharged in or as if in a volley **2 :** to make a volley; *specif* **:** to volley an object of play (as in tennis) — **vol·ley·er** *n*

vol·ley·ball \'väl-ē-ˌbȯl\ *n* **:** a game played by volleying a large inflated ball over a net

vol·plane \'väl-ˌplān, 'vȯl-\ *vi* **vol·planed; vol·plan·ing** [F *vol plané* gliding flight] **1 :** to glide in or as if in an airplane **2 :** GLIDE 3

Vol·sci \'vȯl-ˌskē, 'väl-ˌsī\ *n pl* [L] **:** a people of ancient Italy dwelling between the Latins and Samnites

Vol·scian \'väl-shən, 'vȯl-skē-ən\ *n, pl* **Volscians 1 :** a member of the Volsci **2 :** the Italic language of the Volsci — **Volscian** *adj*

1volt \'vōlt, 'vȯlt\ *n* [F *volte,* fr. It *volta* turn, fr. *voltare* to turn, fr. (assumed) VL *volvitare,* freq. of L *volvere* to roll — more at VOLUBLE] **1 a :** a tread or gait in which a horse going sideways makes a turn around a center **b :** a circle traced by a horse in this movement **2 :** a leaping movement in fencing to avoid a thrust

2volt \'vōlt\ *n* [Alessandro *Volta*] **1 :** the practical mks unit of electrical potential difference and electromotive force equal to the difference of potential between two points in a conducting wire carrying a constant current of one ampere when the power dissipated between these two points is equal to one watt and equivalent to the potential difference across a resistance of one ohm when one ampere is flowing through it **2 :** a unit of electrical potential difference and electromotive force equal to 1.00034 volts and formerly taken as the standard in the U. S. — called also *international volt*

volt·age \'vōl-tij\ *n* **:** electric potential or potential difference expressed in volts

voltage divider *n* **:** a resistor or series of resistors provided with taps at certain points and used to provide various potential differences from a single power source

vol·ta·ic \väl-'tā-ik, vōl-, vȯl-\ *adj* [Alessandro *Volta*]**:** of, relating to, or producing direct electric current by chemical action (as in a battery) **:** GALVANIC <~ cell>

voltaic couple *n* **:** GALVANIC COUPLE

voltaic pile *n* **:** 3PILE 4a

vol·ta·me·ter \vōl-'tam-ət-ər, 'vōl-tə-ˌmēt-\ *n* [ISV *volta*ic + *-meter*] **:** an apparatus for measuring the quantity of electricity passed through a conductor by the amount of electrolysis produced — **vol·ta·met·ric** \ˌvōl-tə-'me-trik\ *adj*

volt–am·me·ter \'vōl-'tam-ˌēt-ər\ *n* **:** an instrument for indicating one or more ranges of volts and amperes by changing terminal connections

volt–am·pere \-'tam-ˌpi(ə)r *also* -ˌpe(ə)r\ *n* **:** a unit of electric measurement equal to the product of a volt and an ampere that for direct current constitutes a measure of power equivalent to a watt

volte–face \ˌvȯlt-(ə-)'fäs\ *n* [F, fr. It *voltafaccia,* fr. *voltare* to turn + *faccia* face, fr. (assumed) VL *facia* — more at VOLT] **:** a reversal in policy **:** ABOUT-FACE

-vol·tine \'vōl-ˌtēn, 'vȯl-\ *adj comb form* [F, fr. It *volta* time, occasion, lit., turn — more at VOLT]**:** having (so many) generations or broods in a season or year <multi*voltine*>

volt·me·ter \'vōlt-ˌmēt-ər\ *n* [ISV]**:** an instrument (as a galvanometer) for measuring in volts the differences of potential between different points of an electrical circuit

vol·u·ble \'väl-yə-bəl\ *adj* [MF or L; MF, fr. L *volubilis,* fr. *volvere* to roll; akin to OE *wealwian* to roll, Gk *eilyein* to roll, wrap] **1 :** easily rolling or turning **:** ROTATING **2 :** characterized by ready or rapid speech **:** GLIB, FLUENT ***syn*** see TALKATIVE ***ant*** curt — **vol·u·bil·i·ty** \ˌväl-yə-'bil-ət-ē\ *n* — **vol·u·ble·ness** \'väl-yə-bəl-nəs\ *n* — **vol·u·bly** \-blē\ *adv*

1vol·ume \'väl-yəm, -(ˌ)yüm\ *n* [ME, fr. MF, fr. L *volumen* roll, scroll, fr. *volvere* to roll] **1 :** SCROLL 1a **2 a :** a series of printed sheets bound typically in book form **:** BOOK **b :** a series of issues of a periodical **c :** ALBUM 1c **3 :** space occupied as measured in cubic units (as inches, quarts, or pecks) **:** cubic capacity — see METRIC SYSTEM table, WEIGHT table **4 a (1) :** AMOUNT; *also* **:** BULK, MASS **(2) :** a considerable quantity **b :** the amount of a substance occupying a particular volume **c :** mass or the representation of mass in art or architecture **5 :** the degree of loudness or the intensity of a sound; *also* **:** LOUDNESS ***syn*** see BULK — **vol·umed** \-yəmd, -(ˌ)yümd\ *adj*

VOLUME FORMULAS

FIGURE	FORMULA	MEANING OF LETTERS
cube	$V = a^3$	a = length of one edge
rectangular prism	$V = abc$	a = length; b = width; c = depth
pyramid	$V = \frac{Ah}{3}$	A = area of base; h = height
cylinder	$V = \pi r^2 h$	$\pi = 3.14159^+$; r = radius of the base; h = height
cone	$V = \frac{\pi r^2 h}{3}$	$\pi = 3.1416$; r = radius of the base; h = height
sphere	$V = \frac{4\pi r^3}{3}$	$\pi = 3.1416$; r = radius

2volume *adj* **:** involving large quantities <did a ~ business in staples>

3volume *vb* **vol·umed; vol·um·ing** *vi* **:** to roll or rise in volume ~ *vt* **:** to send or give out in volume

vol·u·meter \'väl-yü-ˌmēt-ər\ *n* [ISV, blend of *volume* and *-meter*] **:** an instrument for measuring volumes (as of gases or liquids) directly or (as of solids) by displacement of a liquid

vol·u·met·ric \ˌväl-yü-'me-trik\ *adj* **:** of, relating to, or involving the measurement of volume — **vol·u·met·ri·cal·ly** \-tri-k(ə-)lē\ *adv*

volumetric analysis *n* **1 :** quantitative analysis by the use of definite volumes of standard solutions of reagents **2 :** analysis of gases by volume

volume unit *n* **:** a unit equal to a decibel for specifying the power level in audio equipment of a signal above a value of 1 milliwatt in a 500 ohm circuit

vo·lu·mi·nos·i·ty \və-ˌlü-mə-'näs-ət-ē\ *n* **:** the quality or state of being voluminous

vo·lu·mi·nous \və-'lü-mə-nəs\ *adj* [LL *voluminosus,* fr. L *volumin-, volumen*] **1 :** consisting of many folds, coils, or convolutions **:** WINDING **2 a :** having or marked by great volume or bulk **:** LARGE; *also* **:** FULL <a ~ skirt> **b :** NUMEROUS <trying to keep track of ~ white slips> **3 a :** filling or capable of filling a large volume or several volumes <a ~ literature on the subject> **b :** writing or speaking much or at great length — **vo·lu·mi·nous·ly** *adv* — **vo·lu·mi·nous·ness** *n*

vol·un·ta·rism \'väl-ən-tə-ˌriz-əm\ *n* **1 :** the principle or system of doing something by or relying on voluntary action **2 :** a theory that conceives will to be the dominant factor in experience or in the world — **vol·un·ta·rist** \-rəst\ *n* — **vol·un·ta·ris·tic** \ˌväl-ən-tə-'ris-tik\ *adj*

1vol·un·tary \'väl-ən-ˌter-ē\ *adj* [ME, fr. L *voluntarius,* fr. *voluntas* will, fr. *velle* to will, wish — more at WILL] **1 :** proceeding from the will or from one's own choice or consent **2 :** unconstrained by interference **:** SELF-DETERMINING **3 :** done by design or intention **:** INTENTIONAL <~ manslaughter> **4 :** of, relating to, subject to, or regulated by the will <~ behavior> **5 :** having power of free choice <man is a ~ agent> **6 :** provided or supported by voluntary action <a ~ hospital> **7 :** acting or done of one's own free will without valuable consideration or legal obligation — **vol·un·tari·ly** *adv* — **vol·un·tari·ness** *n*

syn VOLUNTARY, INTENTIONAL, DELIBERATE, WILLFUL *shared meaning element* **:** done or brought about of one's own will ***ant*** involuntary, instinctive

2voluntary *n, pl* **-tar·ies 1 a :** a prefatory often extemporized musical piece **b :** an improvisatory organ piece played before, during, or after a religious service **2 :** one who participates voluntarily **:** VOLUNTEER

vol·un·tary·ism \'väl-ən-ˌter-ē-ˌiz-əm\ *n* **:** VOLUNTARISM — **vol·un·tary·ist** \-ē-əst\ *n*

voluntary muscle *n* **:** muscle under voluntary control

1vol·un·teer \ˌväl-ən-'ti(ə)r\ *n* [obs. F *voluntaire* (now *volontaire*), fr. *voluntaire,* adj., voluntary, fr. L *voluntarius*] **1 :** one who enters into or offers himself for a service of his own free will: as **a :** one who enters into military service voluntarily **b (1) :** one who renders a service or takes part in a transaction while having no legal concern or interest **(2) :** one who receives a conveyance or transfer of property without giving valuable consideration **2 :** a volunteer plant **3** *cap* [*Volunteers of America*] **:** a member of a quasi-military religious and philanthropic organization founded in 1896 by Commander and Mrs. Ballington Booth

2volunteer *adj* **1 :** being, consisting of, or engaged in by volunteers <a ~ army> <~ activities to help the mentally handicapped> **2 :** growing spontaneously without direct human control or supervision esp. from seeds lost from a previous crop

3volunteer *vt* **:** to offer or bestow voluntarily <~ one's services> ~ *vi* **:** to offer oneself as a volunteer

vol·un·teer·ism \ˌväl-ən-'ti(ə)r-ˌiz-əm\ *n* **:** VOLUNTARISM 1

vo·lup·tu·ary \və-'ləp-chə-ˌwer-ē\ *n, pl* **-ar·ies :** one whose chief interest is luxury and the gratification of sensual appetites — **voluptuary** *adj*

vo·lup·tuous \-chə(-wə)s\ *adj* [ME, fr. L *voluptuosus,* fr. *voluptas* pleasure; akin to Gk *elpis* hope, L *velle* to wish — more at WILL] **1 :** full of delight or pleasure to the senses **:** conducive to or arising from sensuous or sensual gratification **:** LUXURIOUS <a ~ dance> <~ ornamentation> **2 :** given to or spent in enjoyments of luxury, pleasure, or sensual gratifications <a long and ~ holiday —Edmund Wilson> — **vo·lup·tuous·ly** *adv* — **vo·lup·tuous·ness** *n*

vo·lute \və-'lüt\ *n* [L *voluta,* fr. fem. of *volutus,* pp. of *volvere* to roll] **1 :** a spiral or scroll-shaped form **2 :** a spiral scroll-shaped ornament forming the chief feature of the Ionic capital **3 a :** any of numerous marine gastropod mollusks (family Volutidae) with a thick short-spired shell **b :** the shell of a volute — **volute** *or* **vo·lut·ed** \-'lüt-əd\ *adj*

vo·lu·tin \'väl-yə-ˌtin, və-'lüt-ᵊn\ *n* [G, fr. NL *volutans,* specific epithet of the bacterium *Spirillum volutans* in which it was first found] **:** a granular basophilic substance that is probably a nucleic acid compound and is common in microorganisms

vol·va \'väl-və, 'vȯl-\ *n* [NL, fr. L *volva, vulva* integument — more at VULVA] **:** a membranous sac or cup about the base of the stipe in many gill fungi

vol·vox \-ˌväks\ *n* [NL, genus name, fr. L, *volvere* to roll — more at VOLUBLE]**:** any of a genus (*Volvox*) of green flagellates that form spherical colonies

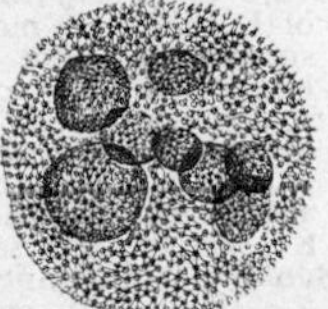
volvox colony

vol·vu·lus \'väl-vyə-ləs, 'vȯl-\ *n* [NL, fr. L *volvere*] **:** a twisting of the intestine upon itself that causes obstruction

vo·mer \'vō-mər\ *n* [NL, fr. L, plowshare] **:** a bone of the skull of most vertebrates that is situated below the ethmoid region and in man forms part of the nasal septum — **vo·mer·ine** \'vō-mə-ˌrin\ *adj*

1vom·it \'väm-ət\ *n* [ME, fr. MF, fr. L *vomitus,* fr. *vomitus,* pp. of *vomere* to vomit; akin to ON *vāma* nausea, Gk *emein* to vomit] **1 :** an act or instance of disgorging the contents of the stomach through the mouth; *also* **:** the disgorged matter **2 :** EMETIC

2vomit *vi* **1 :** to disgorge the stomach contents **2 :** to spew forth **:** BELCH, GUSH ~ *vt* **1 :** to disgorge (the contents of the stomach)

through the mouth **2 :** to eject violently or abundantly **:** SPEW **3 :** to cause to vomit — **vom·it·er** *n*

vom·i·to·ry \'väm-ə-ˌtōr-ē, -ˌtȯr-\ *n, pl* **-ries** [LL *vomitorium,* fr. L *vomitus,* pp.; fr. its disgorging the spectators] **:** an entrance piercing the banks of seats of a theater, amphitheater, or stadium

vom·i·tu·ri·tion \ˌväm-ə-chə-'rish-ən, -ə-tü-'\ *n* [*vomit* + *-urition* (as in *micturition*)] **:** repeated ineffectual attempts at vomiting

vom·i·tus \'väm-ət-əs\ *n* [L] **:** material discharged by vomiting

V-1 \'vē-'wən\ *n* [G, abbr. for *vergeltungswaffe 1,* lit., reprisal weapon 1] **:** ROBOT BOMB

¹voo·doo \'vüd-(ˌ)ü\ *n, pl* **voodoos** [LaF *voudou,* of African origin; akin to Ewe *vo¹du³* tutelary deity, demon] **1 :** a religion derived from African ancestor worship, practiced chiefly by Negroes of Haiti, and characterized by propitiatory rites and communication by trance with animistic deities **2 a :** one who deals in spells and necromancy **b (1) :** a sorcerer's spell **:** HEX **(2) :** a hexed object **:** CHARM — **voodoo** *adj*

²voodoo *vt* **:** to bewitch by or as if by means of voodoo **:** HEX

voo·doo·ism \'vüd-(ˌ)ü-ˌiz-əm\ *n* **1 :** VOODOO 1 **2 :** the practice of witchcraft — **voo·doo·ist** \-ü-əst\ *n* — **voo·doo·is·tic** \ˌvüd-(ˌ)ü-'is-tik\ *adj*

VOP *abbr* valued as in original policy

VOR *abbr* very-high-frequency omnirange

vo·ra·cious \vȯ-'rā-shəs, və-\ *adj* [L *vorac-, vorax,* fr. *vorare* to devour; akin to OHG *querdar* bait, L *gurges* whirlpool] **1 :** having a huge appetite **:** RAVENOUS **2 :** excessively eager **:** INSATIABLE <a ~ reader> — **vo·ra·cious·ly** *adv* — **vo·ra·cious·ness** *n*

vo·rac·i·ty \vȯ-'ras-ət-ē, və-\ *n* **:** the quality or state of being voracious

vor·la·ge \'fōr-ˌläg-ə, 'fȯr-\ *n* [G, lit., forward position, fr. *vor* fore + *lage* position] **:** the position of a skier leaning forward from the ankles usu. without lifting the heels from the skis

-v·o·rous \v-(ə-)rəs\ *adj comb form* [L *-vorus,* fr. *vorare* to devour] **:** eating **:** feeding on <frugi*vorous*>

vor·tex \'vȯ(ə)r-ˌteks\ *n, pl* **vor·ti·ces** \'vȯrt-ə-ˌsēz\ *also* **vor·tex·es** \'vȯr-ˌtek-səz\ [NL *vortic-, vortex,* fr. L *vertex, vortex* whirlpool — more at VERTEX] **1 a :** a mass of fluid and esp. of a liquid with a whirling or circular motion that tends to form a cavity or vacuum in the center of the circle and to draw toward this cavity or vacuum bodies subject to its action; *esp* **:** WHIRLPOOL, EDDY **b :** a region within a body of fluid in which the fluid elements have an angular velocity **2 :** something that resembles a whirlpool <the hellish ~ of battle —*Time*>

vor·ti·cal \'vȯrt-i-kəl\ *adj* **:** of, relating to, or resembling a vortex **:** SWIRLING — **vor·ti·cal·ly** \-k(ə-)lē\ *adv*

vor·ti·cel·la \ˌvȯrt-ə-'sel-ə\ *n, pl* **-cel·lae** \-'sel-(ˌ)ē\ *or* **-cellas** [NL, genus name, fr. L *vortic-, vortex*] **:** any of a genus (*Vorticella*) of stalked bell-shaped ciliates

vor·ti·cism \'vȯrt-ə-ˌsiz-əm\ *n* [L *vortic-, vortex*] **:** an English abstract art movement from about 1912-15 embracing cubist and futurist concepts — **vor·ti·cist** \-səst\ *n*

vor·tic·i·ty \vȯr-'tis-ət-ē\ *n* **1 :** the state of a fluid in vortical motion; *broadly* **:** vortical motion **2 :** a measure of vortical motion; *esp* **:** a vector measure of local rotation in a fluid flow

vor·ti·cose \'vȯrt-i-ˌkōs\ *adj* **:** VORTICAL

vor·tig·i·nous \vȯr-'tij-ə-nəs\ *adj* [L *vortigin-, vortigo, vertigin-, vertigo* action of whirling, vertigo] *archaic* **:** VORTICAL

vo·ta·ress \'vōt-ə-rəs\ *n* **:** a female votary

vo·ta·rist \-rəst\ *n* **:** VOTARY

vo·ta·ry \'vōt-ə-rē\ *n, pl* **-ries** [L *votum* vow] **1** *archaic* **:** a sworn adherent **2 a :** ENTHUSIAST, DEVOTEE **b :** a devoted admirer **3 a :** a devout or zealous worshiper **b :** a staunch believer or advocate

¹vote \'vōt\ *n* [ME (Sc), fr. L *votum* vow, wish — more at VOW] **1 a :** a usu. formal expression of opinion or will in response to a proposed decision; *esp* **:** one given as an indication of approval or disapproval of a proposal, motion, or candidate for office **b :** the total number of such expressions of opinion made known at a single time (as at an election) **c :** an expression of opinion or preference that resembles a vote **d :** BALLOT 1 **2 :** the collective opinion or verdict of a body of persons expressed by voting **3 :** the right to cast a vote; *specif* **:** the right of suffrage **:** FRANCHISE **4 a :** the act or process of voting <brought the question to a ~> **b :** a method of voting <a voice ~> **5 :** a formal expression of a wish, will, or choice voted by a meeting **6 a :** VOTER **b :** a group of voters with some common and identifying characteristics <the labor ~> **7** *chiefly Brit* **a :** a proposition to be voted upon; *esp* **:** a legislative money item **b :** APPROPRIATION **8** *often cap* **:** a daily record of proceedings in the House of Commons

²vote *vb* **vot·ed; vot·ing** *vi* **1 :** to express one's views in response to a poll; *esp* **:** to exercise a political franchise **2 :** to express an opinion <consumers . . . ~ with their dollars —Lucia Mouat> ~ *vt* **1 :** to choose, endorse, decide the disposition of, defeat, or authorize by vote **2 a :** to adjudge by general agreement **:** DECLARE **b :** to offer as a suggestion **:** PROPOSE <I ~ we all go home> **3 a :** to cause to vote in a given way **b :** to cause to be cast for or against a proposal

vote·less \'vōt-ləs\ *adj* **:** having no vote; *esp* **:** denied the political franchise

vot·er \'vōt-ər\ *n* **:** one that votes or has the legal right to vote

voting machine *n* **:** a mechanical device for recording and counting votes cast in an election

vo·tive \'vōt-iv\ *adj* [L *votivus,* fr. *votum* vow] **1 :** offered or performed in fulfillment of a vow or in gratitude or devotion **2 :** consisting of or expressing a vow, wish, or desire <a ~ prayer> — **vo·tive·ly** *adv* — **vo·tive·ness** *n*

votive mass *n* **:** a mass celebrated for a special intention (as for a wedding or funeral) in place of the mass of the day

vo·tress \'vō-trəs\ *n* [by alter.] *archaic* **:** VOTARESS

vou *abbr* voucher

¹vouch \'vau̇ch\ *vb* [ME *vochen, vouchen,* fr. MF *vocher,* fr. L *vocare* to call, summon, fr. *voc-, vox* voice — more at VOICE] *vt* **1 :** to summon into court to warrant or defend a title **2** *archaic* **a :** ASSERT, AFFIRM **b :** ATTEST **3** *archaic* **:** to cite or refer to as authority or supporting evidence **4 a :** PROVE, SUBSTANTIATE **b :** to verify (a business transaction) by examining documentary evidence ~ *vi* **1 :** to give a guarantee **:** become surety **2 a :** to supply supporting evidence or testimony **b :** to give personal assurance

²vouch *n, obs* **:** ALLEGATION, DECLARATION

vouch·ee \vau̇-'chē\ *n* **:** one for whom another vouches

¹vouch·er \'vau̇-chər\ *n* [MF *vocher, voucher* to vouch] **1 :** an act of vouching **2 a :** a piece of supporting evidence **:** PROOF **b :** a documentary record of a business transaction **c :** a written affidavit or authorization **:** CERTIFICATE

²voucher *vt* **1 :** to establish the authenticity of **2 :** to prepare a voucher for

³voucher *n* [¹*vouch* + *-er*] **:** one that guarantees **:** SURETY

vouch·safe \vau̇ch-'sāf, 'vau̇ch-ˌ\ *vt* **vouch·safed; vouch·saf·ing** **1 a :** to grant or furnish often in a gracious or condescending manner **b :** to give by way of reply <refused to ~ an explanation> **2 :** to grant as a privilege or special favor ***syn*** see GRANT — **vouch·safe·ment** \vau̇ch-'sāf-mənt\ *n*

vous·soir \vü-'swär, 'vü-ˌ\ *n* [F, fr. (assumed) VL *volsorium,* fr. *volsus,* pp. of L *volvere* to roll — more at VOLUBLE] **:** one of the wedge-shaped pieces forming an arch or vault — see ARCH illustration

¹vow \'vau̇\ *n* [ME *vowe,* fr. OF *vou,* fr. L *votum,* fr. neut. of *votus,* pp. of *vovēre* to vow; akin to Gk *euchesthai* to pray, vow] **:** a solemn promise or assertion; *specif* **:** one by which a person binds himself to an act, service, or condition

²vow *vt* **1 :** to promise solemnly **:** SWEAR **2 :** to bind or consecrate by a vow ~ *vi* **:** to make a vow — **vow·er** \'vau̇(-ə)r\ *n*

³vow *vt* [ME *vowen,* short for *avowen*] **:** AVOW, DECLARE

vow·el \'vau̇(-ə)l\ *n* [ME, fr. MF *vouel,* fr. L *vocalis* — more at VOCALIC] **1 :** one of a class of speech sounds in the articulation of which the oral part of the breath channel is not blocked and is not constricted enough to cause audible friction; *broadly* **:** the one most prominent sound in a syllable **2 :** a letter or other symbol representing a vowel — usu. used in English of *a, e, i, o, u,* and sometimes *y*

vow·el·ize \'vau̇-(ə-)ˌlīz\ *vt* **-ized; -iz·ing :** to furnish with vowel signs or points

vowel point *n* **:** a mark placed below or otherwise near a consonant in some languages (as Hebrew) and representing the vowel sound that precedes or follows the consonant sound

vowel rhyme *n* **:** ASSONANCE 2b

vox po·pu·li \'väk-'späp-yə-ˌlī, -'späp-(y)ə-(ˌ)lē\ *n* [L, voice of the people] **:** popular sentiment

¹voy·age \'vȯi-ij, 'vȯ(-)ij\ *n* [ME, fr. OF *voiage,* fr. LL *viaticum,* fr. L, traveling money, fr. neut. of *viaticus* of a journey, fr. *via* way — more at VIA] **1 :** an act or instance of traveling **:** JOURNEY **2 :** a course or period of traveling by other than land routes **3 :** an account of a journey esp. by sea

²voyage *vb* **voy·aged; voy·ag·ing** *vi* **:** to take a trip **:** TRAVEL ~ *vt* **:** SAIL, TRAVERSE — **voy·ag·er** *n*

voya·geur \ˌvȯi-ə-'zhər, ˌvwä-yä-\ *n* [CanF, fr. F, traveler, fr. *voyager* to travel, fr. *voyage* voyage, fr. OF *voiage*] **:** a man employed by a fur company to transport goods and men to and from remote stations esp. in the Canadian Northwest

voy·eur \vwä-'yər, vȯi-'ər\ *n* [F, lit., one who sees, fr. MF, fr. *voir* to see, fr. L *vidēre* — more at WIT] **1 :** one obtaining sexual gratification from seeing sex organs and sexual acts; *broadly* **:** one who habitually seeks sexual stimulation by visual means **2 :** a prying observer who is usu. seeking the sordid or the scandalous — **voy·eur·ism** \-ˌiz-əm\ *n* — **voy·eur·is·tic** \ˌvwä-(ˌ)yər-'is-tik, ˌvȯi-ər-\ *adj* — **voy·eur·is·ti·cal·ly** \-ti-k(ə-)lē\ *adv*

VP *abbr* **1** variable pitch **2** various places **3** verb phrase **4** vice-president

V-par·ti·cle \'vē-\ *n* [fr. the shape of its track in a cloud chamber] **:** a charged or uncharged short-lived elementary particle produced by collisions of very high-energy protons or neutrons with nuclei

vroom \'vrüm, və-'rüm\ *vi* [imit.] **:** to operate a motor vehicle at high speed or so as to create a great deal of engine noise

vrouw *or* **vrow** \'frō\ *n* [D *vrouw* & Afrik *vrou*] **:** a Dutch or Afrikaner woman

VS *abbr* **1** verse **2** versus **3** veterinary surgeon **4** [L *vide supra*] see above

V sign *n* **:** a sign made by raising the index and middle fingers in a V and used as a victory salute, a gesture of approval, or an okay

vss *abbr* **1** verses **2** versions

V/STOL *abbr* vertical short takeoff and landing

vt *abbr* verb transitive

Vt *abbr* Vermont

VT *abbr* **1** vacuum tube **2** variable time **3** Vermont **4** voice tube

VTOL *abbr* vertical takeoff and landing

VTR *abbr* video tape recorder

V-2 \'vē-'tü\ *n* [G, abbr. for *vergeltungswaffe 2,* lit., reprisal weapon 2] **:** a rocket-propelled bomb of German invention

VU *abbr* volume unit

vug *or* **vugg** *or* **vugh** \'vəg\ *n* [Corn dial. *vooga* underground chamber, fr. L *fovea* small pit] **:** a small unfilled cavity in a lode or in rock — **vug·gy** \'vəg-ē\ *adj*

Vul·can \'vəl-kən\ *n* [L *Volcanus, Vulcanus*] **:** the Roman god of fire and metalworking — compare HEPHAESTUS

vul·ca·ni·an \ˌvəl-'kā-nē-ən\ *adj* **1** *cap* **:** of or relating to Vulcan or to working in metals (as iron) **2 a :** VOLCANIC **b :** of or relating to a volcanic eruption in which highly viscous or solid lava is blown into fragments and dust

vul·ca·nic·i·ty \ˌvəl-kə-'nis-ət-ē\ *n* **:** VOLCANISM

vul·ca·nism \'vəl-kə-ˌniz-əm\ *n* : VOLCANISM

vul·ca·ni·zate \'vəl-kə-nə-ˌzāt, ˌvəl-kə-'nī-\ *n* [back-formation fr. *vulcanization*] : a vulcanized product

vul·ca·ni·za·tion \ˌvəl-kə-nə-'zā-shən\ *n* : the process of treating crude or synthetic rubber or similar plastic material chemically to give it useful properties (as elasticity, strength, and stability)

vul·ca·nize \'vəl-kə-ˌnīz\ *vb* **nized; -niz·ing** [ISV, fr. L *Vulcanus* Vulcan, fire] *vt* : to subject to vulcanization ~ *vi* : to undergo vulcanization — **vul·ca·niz·er** *n*

vulcanized fiber *n* [fr. *Vulcanized Fibre*, a trademark] : a tough substance made by treatment of cellulose (as paper from rags) and used for luggage and for electrical insulation

vul·ca·nol·o·gist \ˌvəl-kə-'näl-ə-jəst\ *n* : VOLCANOLOGIST

vul·ca·nol·o·gy \-jē\ *n* [ISV] : VOLCANOLOGY

V sign

Vulg *abbr* Vulgate

vul·gar \'vəl-gər\ *adj* [ME, fr. L *vulgaris* of the mob, vulgar, fr. *volgus, vulgus* mob, common people; akin to Skt *varga* group] **1 a** : generally used, applied, or accepted **b** : understood in or having the ordinary sense <they reject the ~ conception of miracle —W. R. Inge> **2** : VERNACULAR <the ~ name of a plant> **3 a** : of or relating to the common people : PLEBEIAN **b** : generally current : PUBLIC <the ~ opinion of that time> **c** : of the usual, typical, or ordinary kind **4 a** : lacking in cultivation, perception, or taste : COARSE **b** : morally crude, undeveloped, or unregenerate : GROSS **c** : ostentatious or excessive in expenditure or display : PRETENTIOUS **5 a** : offensive in language : EARTHY **b** : lewdly or profanely indecent : OBSCENE *syn* see COMMON, COARSE — **vul·gar·ly** *adv*

vulgar era *n* : CHRISTIAN ERA

vul·gar·i·an \ˌvəl-'gar-ē-ən, -'ger-\ *n* : a vulgar person

vul·gar·ism \'vəl-gə-ˌriz-əm\ *n* **1 a** : a word or expression originated or used chiefly by illiterate persons : a substandard use **b** : a coarse word or phrase : OBSCENITY **2** : VULGARITY

vul·gar·i·ty \ˌvəl-'gar-ət-ē\ *n, pl* **-ties** **1** : the quality or state of being vulgar **2** : something vulgar

vul·gar·ize \'vəl-gə-ˌrīz\ *vt* **-ized; -iz·ing** **1** : to diffuse generally : POPULARIZE **2** : to make vulgar : COARSEN — **vul·gar·iza·tion** \ˌvəl-gə-rə-'zā-shən\ *n* — **vul·gar·iz·er** \'vəl-gə-ˌrī-zər\ *n*

Vulgar Latin *n* : the nonclassical Latin of ancient Rome including the speech of plebeians and the informal speech of the educated established by comparative evidence as the chief source of the Romance languages

vul·gate \'vəl-ˌgāt, -gət\ *n* [ML *vulgata*, fr. LL *vulgata editio* edition in general circulation] **1** *cap* : a Latin version of the Bible authorized and used by the Roman Catholic Church **2** : a commonly accepted text or reading

vul·gus \'vəl-gəs\ *n* [prob. alter. of obs. *vulgars* (English sentences to be translated into Latin)] : a short composition in Latin verse formerly common as an exercise in some English public schools

vul·ner·a·ble \'vəln-(ə-)rə-bəl, 'vəl-nər-bəl\ *adj* [LL *vulnerabilis*, fr. L *vulnerare* to wound, fr. *vulner-, vulnus* wound; akin to Goth *wilwan* to rob, L *vellere* to pluck, Gk *oulē* wound] **1** : capable of being physically wounded **2** : open to attack or damage : ASSAILABLE **3** : liable to increased penalties but entitled to increased bonuses after winning a game in contract bridge — **vul·ner·a·bil·i·ty** \ˌvəln-(ə-)rə-'bil-ət-ē\ *n* — **vul·ner·a·ble·ness** \'vəln-(ə-)rə-bəl-nəs, 'vəl-nər-bəl-\ *n* — **vul·ner·a·bly** \-blē\ *adv*

[1]vul·ner·ary \'vəl-nə-ˌrer-ē\ *adj* [L *vulnerarius*, fr. *vulner-, vulnus*] : used for or useful in healing wounds <~ plants>

[2]vulnerary *n, pl* **-ar·ies** : a vulnerary remedy

vul·pine \'vəl-ˌpīn\ *adj* [L *vulpinus*, fr. *vulpes* fox; akin to Gk *alōpēx* fox] **1** : of, relating to, or resembling a fox **2** : FOXY, CRAFTY

vul·ture \'vəl-chər\ *n* [ME, fr. L *vultur*] **1** : any of various large raptorial birds (families Aegypiidae and Cathartidae) that are related to the hawks, eagles, and falcons but have weaker claws and the head usu. naked and that subsist chiefly or entirely on carrion **2** : a rapacious or predatory person

vul·tur·ine \-chə-ˌrīn\ *adj* **1 a** : of or relating to the vultures **b** : characteristic of a vulture **2** : RAPACIOUS, PREDATORY <~ legislators>

vul·tur·ous \'vəlch-(ə-)rəs\ *adj* : resembling a vulture esp. in rapacity or scavenging habits

vulture

vul·va \'vəl-və\ *n, pl* **vul·vae** \-ˌvē, -ˌvī\ [NL, fr. L *volva, vulva* integument, womb; akin to Skt *ulva* womb, L *volvere* to roll — more at VOLUBLE] : the external parts of the female genital organs; *also* : the opening between the projecting parts of the external organs — **vul·val** \'vəl-vəl\ *or* **vul·var** \-vər, -ˌvär\ *adj*

vul·vi·form \'vəl-və-ˌfȯrm\ *adj* [NL *vulva* + E *-iform*] **1** : having an oval shape with a middle cleft and projecting lips **2** : suggesting a cleft with projecting edges — used of plant forms

vul·vi·tis \ˌvəl-'vīt-əs\ *n* [NL] : inflammation of the vulva

vul·vo·vag·i·ni·tis \ˌvəl-(ˌ)vō-ˌvaj-ə-'nīt-əs\ *n* [NL] : coincident inflammation of the vulva and vagina

vv *abbr* **1** verses **2** vice versa

vying *pres part of* VIE

[1]w \'dəb-əl-(ˌ)yü, -yə(-w), *rapid* 'dəb(-ə)-yə(-w), 'dəb-yē\ *n, pl* **w's** *or* **ws** \-(ˌ)yüz, -yəz, -yēz\ *often cap, often attrib* **1 a** : the 23d letter of the English alphabet **b** : a graphic representation of this letter **c** : a speech counterpart of orthographic *w* **2** : a graphic device for reproducing the letter *w* **3** : one designated *w* esp. as the 23d in order or class **4** : something shaped like the letter W

[2]w *abbr, often cap* **1** warden **2** water **3** watt **4** week **5** weight **6** Welsh **7** west **8** western **9** white **10** wicket **11** wide **12** width **13** wife **14** with **15** withdrawal **16** work

W *symbol* **1** energy **2** [G *Wolfram*] tungsten

WA *abbr* **1** Washington **2** Western Australia **3** with average

wab·ble \'wäb-əl\ *var of* WOBBLE

Wac \'wak\ *n* [*W*omen's *A*rmy *C*orps] : a member of the Women's Army Corps

wacky \'wak-ē\ *adj* **wacki·er; -est** [perh. fr. E dial. *whacky* (fool)] : absurdly or amusingly eccentric or irrational : CRAZY — **wacki·ly** \'wak-ə-lē\ *adv* — **wacki·ness** \'wak-ē-nəs\ *n*

[1]wad \'wäd\ *n* [origin unknown] **1** : a small mass, bundle, or tuft: as **a** : a soft mass esp. of a loose fibrous material variously used (as to stop an aperture, pad a garment, or hold grease around an axle) **b** (1) : a soft plug used to retain a powder charge or to avoid windage esp. in a muzzle-loading cannon or gun (2) : a felt or paper disk used to separate the components of a shotgun cartridge **c** : a small mass of a chewing substance <a ~ of gum> **2** : a considerable amount (as of money) **3 a** : a roll of paper money **b** : MONEY

[2]wad *vt* **wad·ded; wad·ding** **1** : to form into a wad or wadding; *esp* : to roll or crush into a tight wad **2 a** : to insert a wad into <~ a gun> **b** : to hold in by a wad <~ a bullet in a gun> **3** : to stuff or line with some soft substance — **wad·der** *n*

wad·able *or* **wade·able** \'wād-ə-bəl\ *adj* : capable of being waded

wad·ding \'wäd-iŋ\ *n* **1** : wads or material for making wads **2** : a soft mass or sheet of short loose fibers used for stuffing or padding

[1]wad·dle \'wäd-ᵊl\ *vi* **wad·dled; wad·dling** \'wäd-liŋ, -ᵊl-iŋ\ [freq. of *wade*] **1** : to walk with short steps swinging the forepart of the body from side to side **2** : to move clumsily in a manner suggesting a waddle — **wad·dler** \-lər, -ᵊl-ər\ *n*

[2]waddle *n* : an awkward clumsy swaying gait

[1]wad·dy \'wäd-ē\ *n, pl* **waddies** [native name in Australia] *Austral* : CLUB 1a

[2]waddy *vt* **wad·died; wad·dy·ing** *Austral* : to attack or beat with a waddy

[3]wad·dy *or* **wad·die** \'wäd-ē\ *n, pl* **waddies** [origin unknown] *West* : COWBOY

[1]wade \'wād\ *vb* **wad·ed; wad·ing** [ME *waden*, fr. OE *wadan*; akin to OHG *watan* to go, wade, L *vadere* to go] *vi* **1** : to step in or through a medium (as water) offering more resistance than air **2** : to move or proceed with difficulty or labor <~ through a dull book> **3** : to set to work or attack with determination or vigor — used with *in* or *into* <~ into a task> ~ *vt* : to pass or cross by wading

[2]wade *n* : an act of wading <a ~ in the brook>

wad·er \'wād-ər\ *n* **1** : one that wades **2** : WADING BIRD **3** *pl* : high waterproof boots or trousers used for wading

wa·di \'wäd-ē\ *n* [Ar *wādiy*] **1** : the bed or valley of a stream in regions of southwestern Asia and northern Africa that is usu. dry except during the rainy season and that often forms an oasis : GULLY, WASH **2** : a shallow usu. sharply defined depression in a desert region

wading bird *n* : any of many long-legged birds including the shorebirds (as sandpipers and snipe) and the inland water birds (as cranes and herons) that wade in water in search of food

wading pool *n* : a shallow pool of portable or permanent construction used by children for wading

wad·mal *or* **wad·mol** *or* **wad·mel** \'wäd-məl\ *n* [ME *wadmale*, fr. ON *vathmāl*, lit., standard cloth, fr. *vāth* cloth, clothing + *māl* measure; akin to L *metiri* to measure — more at WEED, MEASURE]

: a coarse rough woolen fabric formerly used in the British Isles and Scandinavia for protective coverings and warm clothing
wae·sucks \'wā-ˌsəks\ *interj* [Sc *wae* woe (fr. ME *wa*) + *sucks*, alter. of E *sakes* — more at WOE] *Scot* — used to express pity
Waf \'waf\ *n* [*W*omen in the *A*ir *F*orce] : a member of the women's component of the air force formed after World War II
1wa·fer \'wā-fər\ *n* [ME, fr. ONF *waufre*, of Gmc origin; akin to MD *wafel*, *wafer* waffle] **1 a :** a thin crisp cake, candy, or cracker **b :** a round thin piece of unleavened bread used in the celebration of the Eucharist **2 :** an adhesive disk of dried paste with added coloring matter used as a seal **3 a :** a thin disk or ring resembling a wafer and variously used (as for a valve or diaphragm) **b :** a thin slice of material (as silicon or arsenide of gallium) used as a base for an electronic component or components (as an integrated circuit)
2wafer *vt* **wa·fered; wa·fer·ing** \-f(ə-)riŋ\ **1 :** to seal, close, or fasten with a wafer **2 :** to divide (as a silicon rod) into wafers
waff \'waf\ *n* [E dial. *waff* (to wave)] **1** *chiefly Scot* **:** a waving motion **2** *chiefly Scot* **:** PUFF, GUST
1waf·fle \'wäf-əl, 'wȯf-\ *n* [D *wafel*, fr. MD *wafel*, *wafer*; akin to OE *wefan* to weave] : a crisp cake of pancake batter baked in a waffle iron
2waffle *vi* **waf·fled; waf·fling** \-(ə-)liŋ\ [freq. of obs. *woff* to yelp, of imit. origin] **1 :** to talk or write foolishly **:** BLATHER <can ~ . . . tiresomely off the point —*Times Lit. Supp.*> **2 :** EQUIVOCATE
3waffle *n* **:** empty or pretentious words **:** TRIPE
waffle iron *n* **:** a cooking utensil having two hinged metal parts that shut upon each other and impress surface projections on waffles that are being cooked
1waft \'wäft, 'waft\ *vb* [(assumed) ME *waughten* to guard, convoy, fr. MD or MLG *wachten* to watch, guard; akin to OE *wæccan* to watch — more at WAKE] *vt* **:** to cause to move or go lightly by or as if by the impulse of wind or waves ~ *vi* **:** to become wafted on or as if on a buoyant medium — **waft·er** *n*
2waft *n* **1 :** something (as an odor) that is wafted **:** WHIFF **2 :** a slight breeze **:** PUFF **3 :** the act of waving **4 :** a pennant or flag used to signal or to show wind direction
waft·age \'wäf-tij, 'waf-\ *n* **:** the act of wafting or state of being wafted; *broadly* **:** CONVEYANCE
waf·ture \'wäf-chər, 'waf-\ *n* **:** the act of waving or a wavelike motion
1wag \'wag\ *vb* **wagged; wag·ging** [ME *waggen*; akin to MHG *wacken* to totter, OE *wegan* to move — more at WAY] *vi* **1 :** to be in motion **:** STIR **2 :** to move to and fro or up and down esp. with quick jerky motions **3 :** to move in chatter or gossip <scandal caused tongues to ~> **4** *archaic* **:** DEPART **5 :** WADDLE ~ *vt* **1 :** to swing to and fro or up and down esp. with quick jerky motions **:** SWITCH; *specif* **:** to nod (the head) or shake (a finger) at (as in assent or mild reproof) **2 :** to move (as the tongue) animatedly in conversation — **wag·ger** *n*
2wag *n* **:** an act of wagging **:** SHAKE
3wag *n* [prob. short for obs. E *waghalter* (gallows bird), fr. E 1*wag* + *halter*] **1** *obs* **:** a young man **:** CHAP **2 :** WIT, JOKER
1wage \'wāj\ *vb* **waged; wag·ing** [ME *wagen* to pledge, give as security, fr. ONF *wagier*, fr. *wage*] *vt* **:** to engage in or carry on <~ war> <~ a campaign> ~ *vi* **:** to be in process of occurring <the riot *waged* for several hours —*Amer. Guide Series: Md.*>
2wage *n* [ME, pledge, wage, fr. ONF, of Gmc origin; akin to Goth *wadi* pledge — more at WED] **1 a :** a payment usu. of money for labor or services usu. according to contract and on an hourly, daily, or piecework basis **b** *pl* **:** the share of the national product attributable to labor as a factor in production **2 :** RECOMPENSE, REWARD — usu. used in pl. but sing. or pl. in constr. <the ~*s* of sin is death — Rom 6:23 (RSV)> — **wage·less** \'wāj-ləs\ *adj*
syn WAGE, SALARY, STIPEND, PAY, FEE, HIRE, EMOLUMENT *shared meaning element* **:** the price paid for services or labor
wage earner *n* **:** one who works for wages or salary
wage level *n* **:** the approximate position of wages at any given time in any occupation or trade or esp. in industry at large
1wa·ger \'wā-jər\ *n* [ME, pledge, bet, fr. AF *wageure*, fr. ONF *wagier* to pledge] **1 a :** something (as a sum of money) risked on an uncertain event **:** STAKE **b :** something on which bets are laid **:** GAMBLE <do a stunt as a ~> **2** *archaic* **:** an act of giving a pledge to take and abide by the result of some action
2wager *vb* **wa·gered; wa·ger·ing** \'wāj-(ə-)riŋ\ *vt* **:** to risk or venture on a final outcome; *specif* **:** to lay as a gamble <~ $5 on a horse> ~ *vi* **:** to make a bet — **wa·ger·er** \'wā-jər-ər\ *n*
wage scale *n* **1 :** a schedule of rates of wages paid for related tasks **2 :** the level of wages paid by an employer
wage slave *n* **:** a person dependent on wages or a salary for his livelihood
wage·work·er \'wāj-ˌwər-kər\ *n* **:** WAGE EARNER
wag·gery \'wag-ə-rē\ *n, pl* **-ger·ies** **1 :** mischievous merriment **:** PLEASANTRY **2 :** JEST; *esp* **:** PRACTICAL JOKE
wag·gish \'wag-ish\ *adj* **1 :** resembling or characteristic of a wag <a ~ disposition> **2 :** done or made in waggery or for sport **:** HUMOROUS — **wag·gish·ly** *adv* — **wag·gish·ness** *n*
1wag·gle \'wag-əl\ *vb* **wag·gled; wag·gling** \-(ə-)liŋ\ [freq. of 1*wag*] *vi* **:** to reel, sway, or move from side to side **:** WAG ~ *vt* **:** to move frequently one way and the other **:** WAG — **wag·gly** \-(ə-)lē\ *adj*
2waggle *n* **1 :** an instance of waggling **:** a jerky motion back and forth or up and down **2 :** a preliminary swinging of a golf club head back and forth over the ball before the swing
wag·gon *chiefly Brit var of* WAGON
1Wag·ne·ri·an \väg-'nir-ē-ən, -'ner-\ *adj* [Richard *Wagner*] **:** of, relating to, or characteristic of Wagner or his music or theories
2Wagnerian *n* **:** an admirer of the musical theories and style of Wagner
Wag·ner·ite \'väg-nə-ˌrīt\ *n* **:** WAGNERIAN
1wag·on \'wag-ən\ *n* [D *wagen*, fr. MD — more at WAIN] **1 a :** a usu. four-wheel vehicle for transporting bulky commodities and drawn orig. by animals **b :** a lighter typically horse-drawn vehicle for transporting goods or passengers **c :** PATROL WAGON **2** *Brit* **:** a railway freight car **3 :** a low four-wheel vehicle with an open rectangular body and a retroflex tongue made for the play or use (as for carrying newspapers) of a child **4 :** a small wheeled table used for the service of a dining room **5 :** a delivery truck <milk ~> **6 :** STATION WAGON — **off the wagon :** no longer abstaining from alcoholic beverages — **on the wagon :** abstaining from alcoholic beverages
2wagon *vi* **:** to travel or transport goods by wagon ~ *vt* **:** to transport (goods) by wagon
wag·on·er \'wag-ə-nər\ *n* **1 :** the driver of a wagon **2** *cap* **a :** AURIGA **b :** CHARLES'S WAIN
wag·on·ette \ˌwag-ə-'net\ *n* **:** a light wagon with two facing seats along the sides back of a transverse front seat
wa·gon-lit \vȧ-gōⁿ-lē\ *n, pl* **wagons-lits** *or* **wagon-lits** \-gōⁿ-lē(z)\ [F, fr. *wagon* railroad car + *lit* bed] **:** a railroad sleeping car
wagon master *n* **:** a person in charge of one or more wagons esp. for transporting freight
wagon train *n* **:** a column of wagons (as of supplies for a group of settlers) traveling overland
wag·tail \'wag-ˌtāl\ *n* **1 :** any of numerous chiefly Old World birds (family Motacillidae) related to the pipits and having a trim slender body and a very long tail that they habitually jerk up and down **2 :** a bird (as an American water thrush) resembling a wagtail
Wah·habi *or* **Wa·habi** \wə-'häb-ē, wä-\ *n* [Ar *wahhābīy*, fr. Muḥammad b. ʽAbd al-*Wahhāb* (Abdul-Wahhab) †1787 Arab religious reformer] **:** a member of a puritanical Muslim sect founded in Arabia in the 18th century by Muhammad ibn-Abdul Wahhab and revived by ibn-Saud in the 20th century — **Wah·hab·ism** \-'häb-ˌiz-əm\ *n* — **Wah·hab·ite** \-ˌīt\ *adj or n*
wa·hi·ne \wä-'hē-nē, -(ˌ)nā\ *n* [Maori & Hawaiian] **1 :** a Polynesian woman **2 :** a girl surfer
1wa·hoo \'wä-ˌhü, 'wȯ-\ *n, pl* **wahoos** [Creek *ûhawhu*] **:** WINGED ELM
2wahoo *n, pl* **wahoos** [Dakota *wāhu*, lit., arrowwood] **:** a shrubby No. American spindle tree (*Euonymus atropurpureus*) having purple capsules which in dehiscence expose the scarlet-ariled seeds — called also *burning bush*
3wahoo *n, pl* **wahoos** [origin unknown] **:** a large vigorous mackerel (*Acanthocybium solandri*) that is common in warm seas and esteemed as a food and sport fish
4wa·hoo \'wä-ˌhü\ *interj, chiefly West* — used to express exuberance or enthusiasm or to attract attention
wah·wah pedal *var of* WAWA PEDAL
1waif \'wāf\ *n* [ME, fr. ONF, adj., lost, unclaimed] **1 a :** a piece of property found (as washed up by the sea) but unclaimed **b** *pl* **:** stolen goods thrown away by a thief in flight **2 a :** something found without an owner and esp. by chance **b :** a stray person or animal; *esp* **:** a homeless child
2waif *n* **:** WAFT 4
1wail \'wā(ə)l\ *vb* [ME *wailen*, of Scand origin; akin to ON *væla*, *vāla* to wail; akin to ON *vei* woe — more at WOE] *vi* **1 :** to express sorrow audibly **:** LAMENT **2 :** to make a sound suggestive of a mournful cry **3 :** to express dissatisfaction plaintively **:** COMPLAIN ~ *vt, archaic* **:** BEWAIL — **wail·er** \'wā-lər\ *n*
2wail *n* **1 :** the act or practice of wailing **:** loud lamentation **2 a :** a usu. prolonged cry or sound expressing grief or pain **b :** a sound suggestive of wailing <the ~ of an air-raid siren> **c :** a querulous expression of grievance **:** COMPLAINT
wail·ful \'wā(ə)l-fəl\ *adj* **1 :** expressing grief or pain **:** SORROWFUL, MOURNFUL **2 :** uttering a sound suggestive of wailing — **wail·ful·ly** \-fə-lē\ *adv*
wailing wall *n* **1** *cap* **:** a surviving section of the wall which in ancient times formed a part of the enclosure of Herod's temple near the Holy of Holies and at which Jews traditionally gather for prayer and religious lament **2 :** a source of comfort and consolation in misfortune <a soldier making the chaplain's office his *wailing wall*>
wain \'wān\ *n* [ME, wagon, chariot, fr. OE *wægn*; akin to MD *wagen* wagon, OE *wegan* to move — more at WAY] **1 :** a usu. large and heavy vehicle for farm use **2** *cap* **:** CHARLES'S WAIN
1wain·scot \'wān-skət, -ˌskōt, -ˌskät\ *n* [ME, fr. MD *wagenschot*] **1** *Brit* **:** a fine grade of oak imported for woodwork **2 a (1) :** a usu. paneled wooden lining of an interior wall **(2) :** a lining of an interior wall irrespective of material **b :** the lower three or four feet of an interior wall when finished differently from the remainder of the wall
2wainscot *vt* **-scot·ed** *or* **-scot·ted; -scot·ing** *or* **-scot·ting :** to line with or as if with boards or paneling
wain·scot·ing *or* **wain·scot·ting** \-ˌskōt-iŋ, -ˌskät-, -skət-\ *n* **1 :** material used to wainscot a surface **2 :** WAINSCOT 2
wain·wright \'wān-ˌrīt\ *n* **:** a maker and repairer of wagons
waist \'wāst\ *n* [ME *wast*; akin to OE *weaxan* to grow — more at WAX] **1 a :** the narrowed part of the body between the thorax and hips **b :** the greatly constricted basal part of the abdomen of some insects (as wasps and flies) **2 :** the part of something corresponding to or resembling the human waist: as **a (1) :** the part of a ship's deck between the poop and forecastle **(2) :** the middle part of a sailing ship between foremast and mainmast **b :** the middle section of the fuselage of an airplane **3 :** a garment or the part of a garment covering the body from the neck to the waistline or just below: **a :** BODICE 2 **b :** BLOUSE **c :** a child's undergarment to which other garments may be buttoned
waist·band \'wās(t)-ˌband\ *n* **:** a band (as of trousers or a skirt) fitting around the waist

waist·coat \'wes-kət, 'wās(t)-ˌkōt\ *n* **1 :** an ornamental garment worn under a doublet **2** *chiefly Brit* **:** VEST 2a — **waist·coat·ed** \-əd\ *adj*

waist·er \'wā-stər\ *n* **:** a usu. green or broken-down seaman stationed in the waist of a ship (as a whaling ship)

waist·line \'wāst-ˌlīn\ *n* **1 :** an arbitrary line encircling the narrowest part of the waist; *also* **:** the part of a garment that covers this line or may be above or below it as fashion dictates **2 :** body circumference at the waist

1**wait** \'wāt\ *vb* [ME *waiten*, fr. ONF *waitier* to watch, of Gmc origin; akin to OHG *wahta* watch, OE *wæccan* to watch — more at WAKE] *vt* **1 a :** to stay in place in expectation of **:** AWAIT **b :** to delay in hope of a favorable change in <~ out a storm> **2 :** to delay serving (a meal) **3 :** to serve as waiter for <~ table> ~ *vi* **1 a :** to remain stationary in readiness or expectation <~ for a train> **b :** to pause for another to catch up **2 a :** to look forward expectantly <just ~*ing* to see his rival lose> **b :** to hold back expectantly <~*ing* for his chance to strike> **3 :** to serve at meals — usu. used in the phrases *wait at table* or *wait on table* **4 a :** to be ready and available <slippers ~*ing* by the bed> **b :** to remain temporarily neglected or unrealized ***syn*** see STAY — **wait on** *or* **wait upon 1a :** to attend as a servant **b :** to supply the wants of **:** SERVE **2 :** to make a formal call on **3 :** to follow as a consequence — **wait up :** to delay going to bed

2**wait** *n* [ME *waite* watchman, public musician, wait, fr. ONF, watchman, watch, of Gmc origin; akin to OHG *wahta* watch] **1 a :** one of a band of public musicians in England employed to play for processions or public entertainments **b (1) :** one of a group who serenade for gratuities esp. at the Christmas season **(2) :** a piece of music by such a group **2 a :** a hidden or concealed position — used chiefly in the expression *lie in wait* **b :** a state or attitude of watchfulness and expectancy <anchored in ~ for early morning fishing —Fred Zimmer> **3 :** an act or period of waiting <a long ~ in line>

wait·er \'wāt-ər\ *n* **1 :** one that waits upon another; *esp* **:** a man who waits on table (as in a restaurant) **2 :** a tray on which something (as a tea service) is carried **:** SALVER

waiting game *n* **:** a strategy in which one or more participants withhold action temporarily in the hope of having a favorable opportunity for more effective action later

waiting list *n* **:** a list or roster of those waiting (as for election to a club or appointment to a position)

waiting room *n* **:** a room (as in a doctor's office) for the use of persons (as patients) who are waiting

wait·ress \'wā-trəs\ *n* **:** a girl or woman who waits on table (as in a hotel or restaurant) usu. as a means of livelihood

waive \'wāv\ *vt* **waived; waiv·ing** [ME *weiven*, fr. ONF *weyver*, fr. *waif* lost, unclaimed] **1** *archaic* **:** to give up **:** FORSAKE **2 :** to throw away (stolen goods) **3** *archaic* **:** to shunt aside (as a danger or duty) **:** EVADE **4 a :** to relinquish voluntarily (as a legal right) <~ a jury trial> **b :** to refrain from pressing or enforcing (as a claim or rule) **:** FORGO **5 :** to put off from immediate consideration **:** POSTPONE **6 :** to dismiss with or as if with a wave of the hand <*waived* the problem aside> ***syn*** see RELINQUISH

waiv·er \'wā-vər\ *n* [AF *weyver*, fr. ONF *weyver* to abandon, waive] **1 :** the act of intentionally relinquishing or abandoning a known right, claim, or privilege; *also* **:** the legal instrument evidencing such an act **2 :** the act of a club's waiving the right to claim a professional ball player who is being removed from another club's roster

Wa·kash·an \wó-'kash-ən, 'wó-ˌ\ *n* **:** a language family of the Mosan phylum

1**wake** \'wāk\ *vb* **waked** \'wākt\ *or* **woke** \'wōk\; **waked** *or* **wo·ken** \'wō-kən\ *or* **woke; wak·ing** [partly fr. ME *waken* (past *wook*, pp. *waken*), fr. OE *wacan* to awake (past *wōc*, pp. *wacen*) and partly fr. ME *wakien*, *waken* (past & pp. *waked*), fr. OE *wacian* to be awake (past *wacode*, pp. *wacod*); akin to OE *wæccan* to watch, L *vegēre* to rouse, excite] *vi* **1 a :** to be or remain awake **b :** to remain awake on watch esp. over a corpse **c** *obs* **:** to stay up late in revelry **2 :** AWAKE — often used with *up* ~ *vt* **1 :** to stand watch over (as a dead body); *esp* **:** to hold a wake over **2 a :** to rouse from or as if from sleep **:** AWAKE — often used with *up* **b :** STIR, EXCITE <*woke* up latent possibilities —Norman Douglas> **c :** to arouse conscious interest in **:** ALERT — usu. used with *to* <*woke* the publishers to the fact that there was an enormous . . . audience —Harrison Smith> — **wak·er** *n*

2**wake** *n* **1 :** the state of being awake **2 a (1) :** an annual English parish festival formerly held in commemoration of the church's patron saint **(2) :** VIGIL 1a **b :** the festivities orig. connected with the wake of an English parish church — usu. used in pl. but sing. or pl. in constr. **c** *Brit* **:** an annual holiday or vacation — usu. used in pl. but sing. or pl. in constr. **3 :** a watch held over the body of a dead person prior to burial and sometimes accompanied by festivity

3**wake** *n* [of Scand origin; akin to ON *vök* hole in ice; akin to ON *vökr* damp — more at HUMOR] **:** the track left by a moving body (as a ship) in a fluid (as water); *broadly* **:** a track or path left — **in the wake of 1 :** close behind and in the same path of travel <*in the wake of* trappers and . . . riflemen came . . . settlers —*Amer. Guide Series: Ind.*> **2 :** as a result of **:** as a consequence of <power vacuums left *in the wake of* the second world war —A. M. Schlesinger *b*1917>

wake·ful \'wāk-fəl\ *adj* **:** not sleeping or able to sleep **:** SLEEPLESS — **wake·ful·ly** \-fə-lē\ *adv* — **wake·ful·ness** *n*

wake·less \'wā-kləs\ *adj* **:** SOUND, UNBROKEN <~ sleep>

wak·en \'wā-kən\ *vb* **wak·ened; wak·en·ing** \'wāk-(ə-)niŋ\ [ME *waknen*, fr. OE *wæcnian*; akin to ON *vakna* to awaken, OE *wæccan* to watch] *vi* **:** AWAKE — often used with *up* ~ *vt* **:** to rouse out of sleep **:** WAKE

wak·en·er \'wāk-(ə-)nər\ *n*, *archaic* **:** one that causes to waken

wake·rife \'wā-ˌkrīf\ *adj* [ME (Sc) *walkryfe*, fr. *walk* awake (fr. *waken*, *walken* to wake) + *ryfe* rife] *Scot* **:** WAKEFUL, ALERT

wake–rob·in \'wā-ˌkräb-ən\ *n* **1** *Brit* **a :** any of various arums; *esp* **:** CUCKOOPINT **b :** a European orchid (*Orchis maculata*) **2 :** TRILLIUM **3 :** JACK-IN-THE-PULPIT

Wal·den·ses \wól-'den(t)-(ˌ)sēz, wäl-\ *n pl* [ME *Waldensis*, fr. ML *Waldenses*, *Valdenses*, fr. Peter *Waldo* (or *Valdo*), 12th cent. F heretic] **:** a Christian sect arising in southern France in the 12th century, adopting Calvinist doctrines in the 16th century, and later living chiefly in Piedmont — **Wal·den·sian** \-'den-chən, -'den(t)-sē-ən\ *adj or n*

Wal·dorf salad \ˌwól-ˌdórf-\ *n* [*Waldorf*-Astoria Hotel, New York City] **:** a salad made typically of diced apples, celery, nuts, and mayonnaise

1**wale** \'wā(ə)l\ *n* [ME, fr. OE *walu*; akin to ON *valr* round, L *volvere* to roll — more at VOLUBLE] **1 a :** a streak or ridge made on the skin esp. by the stroke of a whip **:** WEAL **b :** a narrow raised surface **:** RIDGE **2 :** one of a number of strakes usu. of extra thick and strong planks in the sides of a wooden ship — usu. used in pl. **3 a :** one of a series of even ribs in a fabric **b :** the texture esp. of a fabric

2**wale** *vt* **waled; wal·ing :** to mark (as the skin) with welts

3**wale** *n* [ME (Sc & northern dial.) *wal*, fr. ON *val*; akin to OHG *wala* choice, OE *wyllan* to wish — more at WILL] **1** *dial Brit* **:** CHOICE **2** *dial Brit* **:** the best part **:** PICK

4**wale** *vb*, *dial Brit* **:** CHOOSE

wal·er \'wā-lər\ *n*, *often cap* [New So. *Wales*, Australia] **:** a horse from New So. Wales; *esp* **:** a rather large rugged saddle horse of mixed ancestry formerly exported in quantity from Australia to British India for military use

Wal·hal·la \väl-'häl-ə\ *n* [G] **:** VALHALLA

1**walk** \'wók\ *vb* [partly fr. ME *walken* (past *welk*, pp. *walken*), fr. OE *wealcan* to roll, toss (past *wēolc*, pp. *wealcen*) and partly fr. ME *walkien* (past *walked*, pp. *walked*), fr. OE *wealcian* to roll up, muffle up; akin to MD *walken* to knead, press, full, L *valgus* bowlegged] *vi* **1 a** *obs* **:** ROAM, WANDER **b** *of a spirit* **:** to move about in visible form **:** APPEAR **c** *of a ship* **:** to make headway **2 a :** to move along on foot **:** advance by steps **b :** to go on foot for exercise or pleasure **c :** to go at a walk **3 a :** to pursue a course of action or way of life **:** conduct oneself **:** BEHAVE <~ in darkness — Jn 8:12 (AV)> **b :** to be or act in association **:** continue in union <the British and American peoples will . . . ~ together side by side . . . in peace —Sir Winston Churchill> **4 :** to go to first base as a result of a base on balls **5** *of an inanimate object* **a :** to move in a manner that is suggestive of walking **b :** to stand with an appearance suggestive of strides <pylons ~*ing* across the valley> **6** *of an astronaut* **:** to move about in space outside a spacecraft ~ *vt* **1 a :** to pass on foot or as if on foot through, along, over, or upon **:** TRAVERSE, PERAMBULATE <~ the streets> <~ a tightrope> **b :** to perform or accomplish by going on foot <~ guard> **2 a :** to cause (an animal) to go at a walk <~*ing* a dog> **b :** to cause to move by walking <~*ed* his bicycle up the hill>; *specif* **:** to haul (as an anchor) by walking round the capstan **3 :** to follow on foot for the purpose of measuring, surveying, or inspecting <~ a boundary> **4 a :** to accompany on foot **:** walk with <~*ed* her home> **b :** to compel to walk (as by a command) **c :** to bring to a specified condition by walking <~*ed* us off our feet> **5 :** to move (an object) in a manner suggestive of walking **6 :** to perform (a dance) at a walking pace <~ a quadrille> **7 :** to give a base on balls to — **walk away from 1 :** to outrun or get the better of without difficulty **2 :** to survive (an accident) with little or no injury — **walk into 1 a :** ATTACK **b :** to reprimand or criticize severely **2 a :** to eat or drink greedily **b :** to use up rapidly — **walk off with 1 a :** to steal and take away **b :** to take over unexpectedly from someone else **:** STEAL 1d <*walked off with* the show> **2 :** to win or gain esp. by outdoing one's competitors without difficulty — **walk over :** to treat contemptuously — **walk the plank 1 :** to walk under compulsion over the side of a ship into the sea **2 :** to resign an office or position under compulsion — **walk through 1 :** to go through (a play or acting part) perfunctorily (as in an early stage of rehearsal) **2 :** to deal with or carry out perfunctorily

2**walk** *n* **1 a :** an act or instance of going on foot esp. for exercise or pleasure <go for a ~> **b :** SPACE WALK **2 :** an accustomed place of walking **:** HAUNT **3 :** a place designed for walking: as **a :** a railed platform above the roof of a dwelling house **b (1) :** a path specially arranged or paved for walking **(2) :** SIDEWALK **c :** a public avenue for promenading **:** PROMENADE **d :** ROPEWALK **4 :** a place or area of land in which animals feed and exercise with minimal restraint **5 :** distance to be walked <a quarter mile ~ from here> **6** *Brit* **:** a ceremonial procession **7 :** manner of living **:** CONDUCT, BEHAVIOR **8 a :** the gait of a biped in which the feet are lifted alternately with one foot not clear of the ground before the other touches **b :** the gait of a quadruped in which there are always at least two feet on the ground; *specif* **:** a four-beat gait of a horse in which the feet strike the ground in the sequence near hind, near fore, off hind, off fore **c :** a low rate of speed <the shortage of raw materials slowed production to a ~> **9 :** a route regularly traversed by a person in the performance of a particular activity (as patrolling, begging, or vending) **10 :** characteristic manner of walking <his ~ is just like his father's> **11 a :** social or economic status <all ~*s* of life> **b (1) :** range or sphere of action **:** FIELD, PROVINCE **(2) :** VOCATION **12 :** BASE ON BALLS

walk·about \'wó-kə-ˌbaùt\ *n* **1 :** a short period of wandering bush life engaged in by an Australian aborigine as an occasional interruption of regular work **2 :** a walking tour **:** walking trip

walk·away \'wó-kə-ˌwā\ *n* **:** an easily won contest

walk·er \'wó-kər\ *n* **1 :** one that walks: as **a :** one who conducts himself in a specified way **b :** a competitor in a walking race **c :** a peddler going on foot **2 :** something used in walking: as **a :** a framework designed to support a baby learning to walk or a crippled or handicapped person learning to walk again **b :** a walking shoe

walk·ie–look·ie \ˌwó-kē-'lùk-ē\ *n* **:** a portable one-man television camera

walk·ie–talk·ie \-ˈtȯ-kē, ˈwȯ-kē-ˌ\ *n* : a compact easily transportable battery-operated radio transmitting and receiving set

[1]**walk–in** \ˌwȯ-ˌkin\ *adj* **1 :** large enough to be walked into <a ~ closet> **2 :** arranged so as to be entered directly rather than through a lobby <a ~ apartment> **3 a :** being a person who walks in without an appointment <a ~ blood donor> **b :** of or relating to such persons <~ clinics . . . find cases and help those in need —Donald Klein>

[2]**walk–in** \ˈwȯ-ˌkin\ *n* **1 :** a walk-in refrigerator or cold storage room **2 :** an easy election victory **3 :** one who walks in without an appointment

[1]**walk·ing** \ˈwȯ-kiŋ\ *n* **1 :** the action of one that walks <~ is good exercise> **2 :** the condition of a surface for one going on foot <the ~ is slippery>

[2]**walking** *adj* **1 a :** HUMAN <a ~ encyclopedia> **b :** able to walk : AMBULATORY **2 a :** used for or in walking <~ shoes> **b :** characterized by or consisting of the action of walking <a ~ tour> **3 :** that moves or appears to move in a manner suggestive of walking; *esp* **:** that swings or rocks back and forth <~ beam> **4 :** not requiring bed rest **5 :** guided or operated by a man on foot <a ~ plow>

walking catfish *n* : an Asiatic catfish (*Clarias batrachus*) that is able to scramble about on land and has been inadvertently introduced into Florida waters where it presents ecological problems

walking delegate *n* : a labor union representative appointed to visit members and their places of employment, to secure enforcement of union rules and agreements, and at times to represent the union in dealing with employers

walking leaf *n* **1 :** any of a genus (*Camptosorus*) of ferns — called also *walking fern;* see FERN illustration **2 :** any of a family (Phasmatidae) of insects with wings and legs resembling leaves

walking papers *n pl* : DISMISSAL, DISCHARGE — called also *walking ticket*

walking stick *n* **1 :** a stick used in walking **2** *usu* **walk·ing·stick :** STICK INSECT; *esp* **:** a phasmid (*Diapheromera femorata*) common in parts of the U.S.

walk–on \ˈwȯ-ˌkȯn, -ˌkän\ *n* : a small usu. nonspeaking part in a dramatic production

walk·out \ˈwȯ-ˌkau̇t\ *n* **1 :** STRIKE 3a **2 :** the action of leaving a meeting or organization as an expression of disapproval **3 :** a prospective customer that leaves a store without making a purchase

walk out \(ˈ)wȯ-ˈkau̇t\ *vi* **1 :** to go on strike **2 :** to leave suddenly often as an expression of disapproval — **walk out on :** to leave in the lurch : ABANDON, DESERT

walk·over \ˈwȯ-ˌkō-vər\ *n* **1 :** a horse race with only one starter **2 :** a one-sided contest : an easy or uncontested victory

walk–through \ˈwȯk-ˌthrü\ *n* **1 :** a perfunctory performance of a play or acting part (as in an early stage of rehearsal) **2 :** a television rehearsal without cameras

[1]**walk–up** \ˌwȯ-ˌkəp\ *adj* **1 :** located above the ground floor in a building with no elevator <a ~ apartment> **2 :** consisting of several stories and having no elevator <a ~ tenement> **3 :** designed to allow pedestrians to be served without entering a building <the ~ window of a bank>

[2]**walk–up** \ˈwȯ-ˌkəp\ *n* : a building or apartment house of several stories that has no elevator; *also* **:** an apartment or office in such a building

walk·way \ˈwȯ-ˌkwā\ *n* : a passage for walking : WALK

Wal·ky·rie \väl-ˈkir-ē *also* väl-ˈkī-rē *&* ˈväl-kə-rē\ *n* [G *walküre* & ON *valkyrja*] : VALKYRIE

[1]**wall** \ˈwȯl\ *n* [ME, fr. OE *weall;* akin to MHG *wall;* both fr. a prehistoric WGmc word borrowed fr. L *vallum* rampart, fr. *vallus* stake, palisade; akin to ON *völr* round stick, L *volvere* to roll — more at VOLUBLE] **1 a :** a high thick masonry structure forming a long rampart or an enclosure chiefly for defense — often used in pl. **b :** a masonry fence around a garden, park, or estate **c :** a structure that serves to hold back pressure (as of water or sliding earth) **2 :** one of the sides of a room or building connecting floor and ceiling or foundation and roof **3 :** the side of a footpath next to buildings **4 :** an extreme or desperate position or a state of defeat, failure, or ruin — usu. used in the phrase *to the wall* **5 :** a material layer enclosing space <the ~ of a container> <heart ~*s*> **6 :** something resembling a wall (as in appearance or effect); *esp* **:** something that acts as a barrier or defense <a ~ of reserve> <tariff ~> — **walled** \ˈwȯld\ *adj* — **wall–like** \ˈwȯl-ˌlīk\ *adj*

[2]**wall** *vt* **1 a :** to provide, cover with, or surround with or as if with a wall <~ in the garden> **b :** to separate by or as if by a wall <~*ed* off half the house> **2 a :** IMMURE **b :** to close (an opening) with or as if with a wall

[3]**wall** *vb* [ME (Sc) *wawlen,* prob. fr. ME *wawil-* (in *wawil-eghed* walleyed)] *vt* **:** to roll (one's eyes) in a dramatic manner ~ *vi, of the eyes* **:** to roll in a dramatic manner

wal·la·by \ˈwäl-ə-bē\ *n, pl* **wallabies** *also* **wallaby** [*wolabā,* native name in New So. Wales, Australia] : any of various small or medium-sized usu. brightly colored kangaroos (esp. genus *Macropus*)

Wal·lace's line \ˌwäl-ə-səz-\ *n* [Alfred Russel *Wallace* †1913 E naturalist] : a hypothetical boundary separating the characteristic Asiatic flora and fauna from that of Australasia and forming the common boundary of the Australian and Oriental biogeographic regions

wal·lah \ˈwäl-ə, *in combination usu* ˌwäl-ə\ *n* [Hindi *-wālā* man, one in charge, fr. Skt *pāla* protector; akin to Skt *pāti* he protects — more at FUR] : a person who is associated with a particular work or who performs a specific duty or service — usu. used in combination <the book ~ was an itinerant peddler —George Orwell>

wal·la·roo \ˌwäl-ə-ˈrü\ *n, pl* **-roos** [*wolarū,* native name in New So. Wales, Australia] : EURO

wall·board \ˈwȯl-ˌbō(ə)rd, -ˌbȯ(ə)rd\ *n* : a structural boarding of any of various materials (as wood pulp, gypsum, or plastic) made in large rigid sheets and used esp. for sheathing interior walls and ceilings

wal·let \ˈwäl-ət\ *n* [ME *walet*] **1 :** a bag for carrying miscellaneous articles while traveling **2 a :** BILLFOLD **b :** a pocketbook with compartments for change, photographs, cards, and keys **c :** a large pocketbook usu. carried in a breast pocket

wall·eye \ˈwȯ-ˌlī\ *n* [back-formation fr. *walleyed*] **1 a :** an eye with a whitish iris **b :** an eye with an opaque white cornea **c :** an eye that turns outward showing more than a normal amount of white **2 a :** LEUCOMA **b :** strabismus in which the eye turns outward **3** *pl* **:** eyes affected with divergent strabismus **4 :** a large vigorous American freshwater food and sport fish (*Stizostedion vitreum*) that has prominent eyes and is related to the perches but resembles the true pike — called also *walleyed pike*

wall·eyed \-ˈlīd\ *adj* [by folk etymology, fr. ME *wawil-eghed* part trans. of ON *vagl-eygr* walleyed, fr. *vagl* beam, roost + *eygr* eyed; akin to OE *wegan* to move, carry — more at WAY] **1 :** having walleyes or affected with walleye **2 :** marked by a wild irrational staring of the eyes

wall fern *n* : a low-growing mat-forming fern (*Polypodium vulgare*)

wall·flow·er \ˈwȯl-ˌflau̇(-ə)r\ *n* **1 a :** any of several Old World herbaceous or subshrubby perennial plants (genus *Cheiranthus*) of the mustard family; *esp* **:** a hardy erect herb (*C. cheiri*) widely cultivated for its showy fragrant flowers **b :** any of a related genus (*Erysimum*) with alternate leaves and yellow flowers **2 :** a person who from shyness or unpopularity remains on the sidelines of a social activity (as a dance)

wall hanging *n* : a drapery or tapestry hung against a wall for decoration

Wal·loon \wä-ˈlün\ *n* [MF *Wallon,* adj. & n., of Gmc origin; prob. akin to OHG *Walah* Celt, Roman, OE *Wealh* Celt, Welshman — more at WELSH] **1 :** a member of a chiefly Celtic people of southern and southeastern Belgium and adjacent parts of France **2 :** a French dialect of the Walloons — **Walloon** *adj*

[1]**wal·lop** \ˈwäl-əp\ *n* [ME, gallop, fr. ONF *walop,* fr. *waloper* to gallop] **1 a :** a powerful blow : [2]PUNCH 2 **b :** the ability (as of a boxer) to hit hard **2 a :** emotional or psychological force : IMPACT **b :** an exciting emotional response : THRILL **3** *Brit* **:** BEER

[2]**wallop** *vb* [ME *walopen* to gallop, fr. ONF *waloper*] *vi* **1 a :** to move with reckless or disorganized haste : advance in a headlong rush **b :** WALLOW, FLOUNDER **2 :** to boil noisily ~ *vt* **1 a :** to thrash soundly : LAMBASTE **b :** to beat by a wide margin : TROUNCE **2 :** to hit with force : SOCK — **wal·lop·er** *n*

wal·lop·ing *adj* **1 :** LARGE, WHOPPING **2 :** exceptionally fine or impressive : SMASHING

[1]**wal·low** \ˈwäl-(ˌ)ō, -ə(-w)\ *vi* [ME *walwen,* fr. OE *wealwian* to roll — more at VOLUBLE] **1 :** to roll oneself about in an indolent or ungainly manner **2 :** to billow forth : SURGE **3 :** to devote oneself entirely; *esp* **:** to take unrestrained pleasure : DELIGHT **4 a :** to become abundantly supplied : LUXURIATE <a family that ~*s* in money> **b :** to indulge oneself immoderately <~*ing* in self-pity> **5 :** to become or remain helpless <allowed them to ~ in their ignorance> — **wal·low·er** \ˈwäl-ə-wər\ *n*

[2]**wallow** *n* **1 :** an act or instance of wallowing **2 a :** a muddy area or one filled with dust used by animals for wallowing **b :** a depression formed by or as if by the wallowing of animals **3 :** a state of degradation or degeneracy

wall painting *n* : FRESCO

[1]**wall·pa·per** \ˈwȯl-ˌpā-pər\ *n* : decorative paper for the walls of a room

[2]**wallpaper** *vt* : to provide the walls of (a room) with wallpaper ~ *vi* **:** to put wallpaper on a wall

wall pellitory *n* : a European herb (*Parietaria officinalis*) of the nettle family that has diuretic properties and grows esp. on old walls

wall plate *n* : PLATE 5

wall plug *n* : an electric receptacle in a wall

wall rock *n* : a rock through which a fault or vein runs

wall rocket *n* : any of several plants (genus *Diplotaxis*) of the mustard family; *esp* **:** a yellow-flowered European weed (*D. tenuifolia*) adventive in No. America

wall rue *n* : a small delicate spleenwort (*Asplenium rutamuraria*) found esp. on walls or cliffs

Wall Street \ˈwȯl-\ *n* [*Wall Street,* New York City, on which is located the New York Stock Exchange] : the influential financial interests of the U.S. economy

Wall Street·er \-ˌstrēt-ər\ *n* : one who is involved in the activities of Wall Street

wal·ly \ˈwā-lē\ *adj* [prob. fr. [3]*wale*] *Scot* **:** FINE, STURDY

wal·ly·drai·gle \ˈwā-lē-ˌdrā-gəl, ˈwäl-ē-\ *n* [origin unknown] *chiefly Scot* **:** a feeble, imperfectly developed, or slovenly creature

wal·nut \ˈwȯl-(ˌ)nət\ *n* [ME *walnot,* fr. OE *wealhhnutu,* lit., foreign nut, fr. *Wealh* Welshman, foreigner + *hnutu* nut — more at WELSH, NUT] **1 a :** an edible nut of any of a genus (*Juglans* of the family Juglandaceae, the walnut family) of trees; *also* **:** one of these trees or its wood often valued for cabinetmaking and veneers **b :** a hickory tree or its nut — called also *white walnut* **2 :** a moderate reddish brown

Wal·pur·gis Night \väl-ˈpu̇r-gəs-\ *n* [part trans. of G *walpurgisnacht,* fr. *Walpurgis* St. Walburga †A.D. 777 E saint whose feast day falls on May Day + G *nacht* night] **1 :** the eve of May Day on which witches are held to ride to an appointed rendezvous **2 :** something (as an event or situation) having a nightmarish quality

wal·rus \ˈwȯl-rəs, ˈwäl-\ *n, pl* **walrus** *or* **wal·rus·es** [D, of Scand origin; akin to Dan & Norw *hvalros* walrus, ON *rosmhvalr*] : either of two large marine mammals (*Odobenus rosmarus* and *O. divergens* of the family Odobenidae) of northern seas related to the seals and hunted for the tough heavy hide, the ivory tusks, the oil yielded by the blubber, and locally for the flesh

walrus

Wal·ter Mit·ty \ˌwȯl-tər-ˈmit-ē\ *n* [*Walter Mitty*, daydreaming hero of stories by James Thurber] **:** a commonplace unadventurous person who seeks escape from reality through daydreaming — **Walter Mit·ty·ish** \-ē-ish\ *adj*

[1]**waltz** \ˈwȯl(t)s\ *n* [G *walzer*, fr. *walzen* to roll, dance, fr. OHG *walzan* to turn, roll — more at WELTER] **1 :** a ballroom dance in ¾ time with strong accent on the first beat and a basic pattern of step-step-close **2 :** music for a waltz or a concert composition in ¾ time

[2]**waltz** *vi* **1 :** to dance a waltz **2 :** to move or advance in a lively or conspicuous manner **:** FLOUNCE **3 a :** to advance easily and successfully **:** BREEZE — usu. used with *through* **b :** to approach boldly — used with *up* <can't just ~ up and introduce ourselves> ~ *vt* **1 :** to dance a waltz with **2 :** to grab and lead (as a person) unceremoniously **:** MARCH — **waltz·er** *n*

[1]**wam·ble** \ˈwäm-bəl\ *vi* **wam·bled; wam·bling** \-b(ə-)liŋ\ [ME *wamlen;* akin to Dan *vamle* to become nauseated, L *vomere* to vomit — more at VOMIT] **1 a :** to feel nausea **b** *of a stomach* **:** RUMBLE 1 **2 :** to move unsteadily or with a weaving or rolling motion

[2]**wamble** *n* **1 :** a wambling esp. of the stomach **2 :** a reeling or staggering gait or movement

wame \ˈwām\ *n* [ME, alter. of *wamb* — more at WOMB] *chiefly Scot* **:** BELLY

wam·pum \ˈwäm-pəm\ *n* [short for *wampumpeag*] **1 :** beads of polished shells strung in strands, belts, or sashes and used by No. American Indians as money, ceremonial pledges, and ornaments **2** *slang* **:** MONEY

wam·pum·peag \-ˌpēg\ *n* [Narraganset *wampompeag*, fr. *wampan* white + *api* string + *-ag*, pl. suffix] **:** WAMPUM; *esp* **:** that made of the less valuable white shell beads

[1]**wan** \ˈwän\ *adj* **wan·ner; wan·nest** [ME, fr. OE, dark, livid] **1 a :** suggestive of poor health **:** SICKLY, PALLID **b :** lacking vitality **:** FEEBLE **2 :** DIM, FAINT **3 :** LANGUID <a ~ smile> — **wan·ly** *adv* — **wan·ness** \ˈwän-nəs\ *n*

[2]**wan** *vi* **wanned; wan·ning :** to grow or become pale or sickly

wand \ˈwänd\ *n* [ME, slender stick, fr. ON *vǫndr;* akin to OE *windan* to wind, twist — more at WIND] **1 :** a slender staff carried in a procession **:** VERGE **2 :** a slender rod used by conjurers and magicians **3 :** a slat 6 feet by 2 inches used as a target in archery; *also* **:** a narrow strip of paper pasted vertically on a target face

wan·der \ˈwän-dər\ *vb* **wan·dered; wan·der·ing** \-d(ə-)riŋ\ [ME *wandren*, fr. OE *wandrian;* akin to MHG *wandern* to wander, OE *windan* to wind, twist] *vi* **1 a :** to move about without a fixed course, aim, or goal **b :** to go idly about **:** RAMBLE **2 :** to follow a winding course **:** MEANDER **3 a :** to deviate (as from a course) **:** STRAY **b :** to go astray morally **:** ERR **c :** to lose normal mental contact **:** stray in thought ~ *vt* **:** to roam over — **wander** *n*

wan·der·er \-dər-ər\ *n* **:** one that wanders

[1]**wan·der·ing** *n* **1 :** a going about from place to place — often used in pl. **2 :** movement away from the proper, normal, or usual course or place — often used in pl.

[2]**wandering** *adj* **:** characterized by aimless, slow, or pointless movement: as **a :** that winds or meanders <a ~ course> **b :** not keeping a rational or sensible course **:** VAGRANT **c :** NOMADIC <~ tribes> **d** *of a plant* **:** having long runners or tendrils

wandering jenny *n* **:** MONEYWORT

Wandering Jew *n* **1 :** a Jew of medieval legend condemned by Christ to wander over the earth till Christ's second coming **2** *not cap W* **:** any of several plants (genera *Zebrina* and *Tradescantia*) of the spiderwort family; *esp* **:** either of two trailing or creeping plants (*Z. pendula* and *T. fluminensis*) cultivated for their showy and often white-striped foliage

wan·der·lust \ˈwän-dər-ˌləst\ *n* [G, fr. *wandern* to wander + *lust* desire, pleasure] **:** strong or unconquerable longing for or impulse toward wandering

wan·de·roo \ˌwän-də-ˈrü\ *n, pl* **-roos** [Sinhalese *vanduru*, pl. of *vandurā*, fr. Skt *vānara* monkey, fr. *vanar-, vana* forest; akin to Av *vana* forest] **1 :** a purple-faced langur (*Presbytis cephalopterus*) of Ceylon **2 :** a macaque (*Macaca albibarbata*) of the Indian peninsula with a tufted tail

[1]**wane** \ˈwān\ *vi* **waned; wan·ing** [ME *wanen*, fr. OE *wanian;* akin to OHG *wanōn* to wane, OE *wan* wanting, deficient, L *vanus* empty, vain] **1 :** to decrease in size or extent **:** DWINDLE: as **a :** to diminish in phase or intensity — used chiefly of the moon **b :** to become less brilliant or powerful **:** DIM **c :** to flow out **:** EBB **2 :** to fall gradually from power, prosperity, or influence **:** DECLINE ***syn*** see ABATE ***ant*** wax

[2]**wane** *n* **1 a :** the act or process of waning <strength on the ~> **b :** a period or time of waning; *specif* **:** the period from full phase of the moon to the new moon **2** [ME, defect, fr. OE *wana;* akin to OE *wan* deficient] **:** a defect in lumber characterized by bark or a lack of wood at a corner or edge

wan·ey *or* **wany** \ˈwā-nē\ *adj* **wan·i·er; -est 1 :** waning or diminished in some parts **2** *of sawed timber* **:** marked by wane

wan·gle \ˈwaŋ-gəl\ *vb* **wan·gled; wan·gling** \-g(ə-)liŋ\ [perh. alter. of *waggle*] *vi* **1 :** to extricate oneself (as from difficulty) **:** WIGGLE **2 :** to resort to trickery or devious methods ~ *vt* **1 :** SHAKE, WIGGLE **2 :** to adjust or manipulate for personal or fraudulent ends **3 :** to make or get by devious means **:** FINAGLE <~ an invitation> — **wan·gler** \-g(ə-)lər\ *n*

wan·i·gan *or* **wan·ni·gan** \ˈwän-i-gən\ *n* [of Algonquian origin; akin to Abnaki *waniigan* trap, lit., that into which something strays] **:** a shelter (as for sleeping, eating, or storage) often mounted on wheels or tracks and towed by tractor or mounted on a raft or boat

wan·ion \ˈwän-yən\ *n* [fr. the obs. phrase *in the waniand* unluckily, lit., in the waning (moon), fr. ME, fr. *waniand*, northern pres. part. of *wanien, wanen* to wane] *archaic* **:** PLAGUE, VENGEANCE — used in the phrase *with a wanion*

Wan·kel engine \ˌväŋ-kəl-, ˌwäŋ-\ *n* [Felix *Wankel* b1902 G engineer] **:** an internal-combustion rotary engine that has a rounded triangular rotor functioning as a piston and rotating in a space in the engine and that has only two major moving parts

[1]**want** \ˈwȯnt *also* ˈwänt & ˈwənt\ *vb* [ME *wanten*, fr. ON *vanta;* akin to OE *wan* deficient] *vt* **1 :** to fail to possess esp. in customary or required amount **:** LACK <his answer ~*s* courtesy> **2 a :** to have a strong desire for <~*ed* a chance to rest> **b :** to have an inclination to **:** LIKE <say what you ~, he is efficient> **3 a :** to have need of **:** REQUIRE <the motor ~*s* a tune-up> **b :** to suffer from the lack of <thousands still ~ food and shelter> **4 :** to wish or demand the presence of **5 :** to hunt or seek in order to apprehend <he is ~*ed* for murder> ~ *vi* **1 :** to be deficient or short <it ~*s* three minutes to twelve> **2 :** to be needy or destitute **3 :** to have or feel need <never ~*s* for friends> **4 :** to be necessary or needed **5 :** to desire to come or go <the cat ~*s* in> <the dog ~*s* out> ***syn*** see LACK, DESIRE

[2]**want** *n* **1 a :** the quality or state of lacking a required or usual amount <he suffers from a ~ of good sense> **b :** grave and extreme poverty that deprives one of the necessities of life **2 :** something wanted **:** NEED, DESIRE **3 :** personal defect **:** FAULT ***syn*** see POVERTY

want ad *n* **:** a newspaper advertisement stating that something (as an employee, employment, or a specified item) is wanted

[1]**want·ing** *adj* **1 :** not present or in evidence **:** ABSENT **2 a :** not being up to standards or expectations **b :** lacking in ability or capacity **:** DEFICIENT

[2]**wanting** *prep* **1 :** WITHOUT <a book ~ a cover> **2 :** LESS, MINUS <a month ~ two days>

[1]**wan·ton** \ˈwȯnt-ᵊn, ˈwänt-\ *adj* [ME, fr. *wan-* deficient, wrong, mis- (fr. OE, fr. *wan* deficient) + *towen*, pp. of *teen* to draw, train, discipline, fr. OE *tēon* — more at TOW] **1 a** *archaic* **:** hard to control **:** UNDISCIPLINED, UNRULY **b :** playfully mean or cruel **:** MISCHIEVOUS **2 a :** LEWD, BAWDY **b :** causing sexual excitement **:** LUSTFUL, SENSUAL **3 a :** MERCILESS, INHUMANE <~ cruelty> **b :** having no just foundation or provocation **:** MALICIOUS <a ~ attack> **4 :** being without check or limitation: as **a :** luxuriantly rank <~ vegetation> **b :** unduly lavish **:** EXTRAVAGANT <~ complaints> ***syn*** see SUPEREROGATORY — **wan·ton·ly** *adv* — **wan·ton·ness** \-ən-nəs\ *n*

[2]**wanton** *n* **1 :** a pampered person or animal **:** PET; *esp* **:** a spoiled child **2 :** a frolicsome child or animal **3 a :** a person given to luxurious self-enjoyment **b :** a lewd or lascivious person

[3]**wanton** *vi* **:** to be wanton or act wantonly ~ *vt* **:** to pass or waste wantonly or in wantonness — **wan·ton·er** *n*

wa·pen·take \ˈwap-ən-ˌtāk, ˈwäp-\ *n* [ME, fr. OE *wǣpentæc*, fr. ON *vāpnatak* act of grasping weapons, fr. *vāpn* weapon + *tak* act of grasping, fr. *taka* to take; prob. fr. the brandishing of weapons as an expression of approval when the chief of the wapentake entered upon his office — more at WEAPON, TAKE] **:** a subdivision of some English shires corresponding to a hundred

wa·pi·ti \ˈwäp-ət-ē\ *n, pl* **wapiti** *or* **wapitis** [of Algonquian origin; akin to Cree *wapitew* white, whitish; fr. its white rump and tail] **:** an American elk (*Cervus canadensis* and related forms) similar to the European red deer but larger

wapiti

wap·pen·schaw·ing \ˈwap-ən-ˌshȯ(-)riŋ, ˈwäp-\ *n* [ME (northern dial.) *wapynschawing*, fr. *wapen* weapon (fr. ON *vāpn*) + *schawing*, gerund of *schawen* to show, fr. OE *scēawian* to look, look at — more at WEAPON, SHOW] **:** an inspection or muster of soldiers formerly held at various times in each district of Scotland

wap·per-jawed \ˌwäp-ər-ˈjȯd, ˌwäp-ē-ˈjȯd\ *adj* [origin unknown] **:** having a crooked, undershot, or wry jaw

[1]**war** \ˈwȯ(ə)r\ *n* [ME *werre*, fr. ONF, of Gmc origin; akin to OHG *werra* strife; akin to OHG *werran* to confuse, L *verrere* to sweep] **1 a (1) :** a state of usu. open and declared armed hostile conflict between states or nations **(2) :** a period of such armed conflict **(3) :** STATE OF WAR **b :** the art or science of warfare **c (1)** *obs* **:** weapons and equipment for war **(2)** *archaic* **:** soldiers armed and equipped for war **2 a :** a state of hostility, conflict, or antagonism **b :** a struggle between opposing forces or for a particular end <a class ~> <a ~ against disease>

[2]**war** *vi* **warred; war·ring 1 :** to engage in warfare **2 :** to be in active or vigorous conflict

[3]**war** \ˈwär\ *adv or adj* [ME *werre*, fr. ON *verri*, adj., *verr*, adv. — more at WORSE] *chiefly Scot* **:** WORSE

[4]**war** \ˈwär\ *vt* **warred; war·ring** *Scot* **:** WORST, OVERCOME

[5]**war** *abbr* warrant

War *abbr* Warwickshire

war baby *n* **:** a child born or conceived during a war

[1]**war·ble** \ˈwȯr-bəl\ *n* [ME *werble* tune, fr. ONF, of Gmc origin; akin to MHG *wirbel* whirl, tuning peg, OHG *wirbil* whirlwind — more at WHIRL] **1 :** a melodious succession of low pleasing sounds **2 :** a musical trill **3 :** the action of warbling

[2]**warble** *vb* **war·bled; war·bling** \-b(ə-)liŋ\ *vi* **1 :** to sing in a trilling manner or with many turns and variations **2 :** to become sounded with trills, quavers, and rapid modulations in pitch **3 :** SING ~ *vt* **:** to render with turns, runs, or rapid modulations **:** TRILL

[3]**warble** *n* [perh. of Scand origin; akin to obs. Sw *varbulde* boil, fr. *var* pus + *bulde* swelling] **1 :** a swelling under the hide esp. of the back of cattle, horses, and wild mammals caused by the maggot of a botfly or warble fly **2 :** the maggot of a warble fly — **war·bled** \-bəld\ *adj*

warble fly *n* **:** any of various two-winged flies (family Oestridae) whose larvae live under the skin of various mammals and cause warbles

war·bler \'wȯr-blər\ *n* **1 :** one that warbles **:** SINGER, SONGSTER **2 a :** any of numerous small Old World singing birds (family Sylviidae) many of which are noted songsters and are closely related to the thrushes **b :** any of numerous small brightly colored American songbirds (family Parulidae) with a usu. weak and unmusical song — called also *wood warbler*

war·bon·net \'wȯr-ˌbän-ət\ *n* **:** an American Indian ceremonial headdress with a feathered extension down the back

war bride *n* **1 :** a woman who marries a serviceman ordered into active service in time of war **2 :** a woman who marries a serviceman esp. of a foreign nation met during a time of war

war chest *n* **:** a fund accumulated to finance a war; *broadly* **:** a fund earmarked for a specific purpose, action, or campaign

war club *n* **:** a club-shaped implement used as a weapon esp. by American Indians

war correspondent *n* **:** a correspondent employed to report news concerning the conduct of a war and esp. of events at the scene of a battle

war crime *n* **:** a crime (as genocide or maltreatment of prisoners) committed during or in connection with war — usu. used in pl. — **war criminal** *n*

war cry *n* **1 :** a cry used by a body of fighters in war **2 :** a slogan used esp. to rally people to a cause

[1]**ward** \'wȯ(ə)rd\ *n* [ME, fr. OE *weard;* akin to OHG *warta* act of watching, OE *warian* to beware of, guard — more at WARE] **1 a :** the action or process of guarding **b :** a body of guards **2 :** the state of being under guard; *esp* **:** CUSTODY **3 a :** the inner court of a castle or fortress **b :** a division (as a cell or block) of a prison **c :** a division in a hospital; *esp* **:** a large room in a hospital where a number of patients often requiring similar treatment are accommodated **4 a :** a division of a city for representative, electoral, or administrative purposes **b :** a division of some English and Scottish counties corresponding to a hundred **c :** the Mormon local congregation having auxiliary organizations (as Sunday schools and relief societies) and one or more quorums of each office of the Aaronic priesthood **5 :** a projecting ridge of metal in a lock casing or keyhole permitting only the insertion of a key with a corresponding notch; *also* **:** a corresponding notch in a bit of a key **6 :** a person under guard, protection, or surveillance: as **a :** a minor subject to wardship **b :** a person who by reason of incapacity (as minority or lunacy) is under the protection of a court either directly or through a guardian appointed by the court — called also *ward of court* **c :** a person or body of persons under the protection or tutelage of a government **7 :** a means of defense **:** PROTECTION — **ward·ed** \'wȯrd-əd\ *adj*

[2]**ward** *vt* [ME *warden,* fr. OE *weardian;* akin to OHG *wartēn* to watch, ON *vartha* to guard, OE *weard* ward] **1 :** to keep watch over **:** GUARD **2 :** DEFLECT — usu. used with *off*

[1]**-ward** \wərd\ *also* **-wards** \wərdz\ *adj suffix* [*-ward* fr. ME, fr. OE *-weard;* akin to OHG *-wart, -wert* -ward, L *vertere* to turn; *-wards* fr. *-wards,* adv. suffix — more at WORTH] **1 :** that moves, tends, faces, or is directed toward <river*ward*> **2 :** that occurs or is situated in the direction of <left*ward*>

[2]**-ward** *or* **-wards** *adv suffix* [*-ward* fr. ME, fr. OE *-weard,* fr. *-weard,* adj. suffix; *-wards* fr. ME, fr. OE *-weardes,* gen. sing. neut. of *-weard,* adj. suffix] **1 :** in a (specified) spatial or temporal direction <up*ward*> <after*ward*> **2 :** toward a (specified) point, position, or area <earth*ward*>

war dance *n* **:** a dance performed by primitive peoples as preparation for battle or in celebration of victory

ward·ed \'wȯr-dəd\ *adj* **:** provided with a ward <a ~ lock>

war·den \'wȯrd-ᵊn\ *n* [ME *wardein,* fr. ONF, fr. *warder* to guard, of Gmc origin; akin to OHG *wartēn* to watch] **1 :** one having care or charge of something **:** GUARDIAN, KEEPER **2 a :** REGENT 2 **b :** the governor of a town, district, or fortress **c :** a member of the governing body of a guild **3 a :** an official charged with special supervisory duties or with the enforcement of specified laws or regulations <game ~> <air raid ~> **b :** an official in charge of the operation of a prison **c :** any of various British officials having designated administrative functions <~ of the mint> **4 a :** one of two ranking lay officers of an Episcopal parish **b :** any of various British college officials whose duties range from the administration of academic matters to the supervision of student discipline

war·den·ship \-ˌship\ *n* **:** the office, jurisdiction, or powers of a warden

[1]**ward·er** \'wȯrd-ər\ *n* [ME, fr. AF *wardere,* fr. *warde* act of guarding, of Gmc origin; akin to OHG *warta* act of watching] **1 :** WATCHMAN, PORTER **2** *Brit* **a :** WARDEN **b :** a prison guard

[2]**war·der** *n* [ME, perh. fr. *warden* to ward] **:** a truncheon used by a king or commander in chief to signal orders

ward·er·ship \-ˌship\ *n* **:** the office, position, or function of a warder

ward heeler *n* **:** a worker for a political boss in a ward or other local area

ward off *vt* [[2]*ward*] **:** to fend off (as an anticipated evil) **:** AVERT, PARRY *syn* see PREVENT *ant* conduce (*to*)

ward·ress \'wȯr-drəs\ *n* **:** a female warden in a prison

ward·robe \'wȯr-ˌdrōb\ *n* [ME *warderobe,* fr. ONF, fr. *warder* to guard + *robe* robe] **1 a :** a room or closet where clothes are kept **b :** CLOTHESPRESS **c :** a large trunk in which clothes may be hung upright **2 a :** a collection of wearing apparel (as of one person or for one activity) <a summer ~> **b :** a collection of stage costumes and accessories **3 :** the department of a royal or noble household entrusted with the care of wearing apparel, jewels, and personal articles

ward·room \'wȯr-ˌdrüm, -ˌdru̇m\ *n* **:** the space in a warship allotted for living quarters to the commissioned officers excepting the captain; *specif* **:** the messroom assigned to these officers

ward·ship \'wȯrd-ˌship\ *n* **1 a :** care and protection of a ward **b :** the right to the custody of an infant heir of a feudal tenant and of his property **2 :** the state of being under a guardian

[1]**ware** \'wa(ə)r, 'we(ə)r\ *adj* [ME *war, ware* careful, aware, fr. OE *wær* — more at WARY] **1 :** AWARE, CONSCIOUS <was ~ of black looks cast at me —Mary Webb> **2** *archaic* **:** WARY, VIGILANT

[2]**ware** *vt* **wared; war·ing** [ME *waren,* fr. OE *warian;* akin to OHG *biwarōn* to protect, OE *wær* aware] **:** to beware of **:** AVOID — used chiefly as a command to hunting animals

[3]**ware** *n* [ME, fr. OE *waru;* akin to MHG *ware* ware and prob. to OE *wær* aware] **1 a :** manufactured articles, products of art or craft, or farm produce **:** GOODS — often used in combination <tin*ware*> **b :** an article of merchandise **2 :** articles (as pottery or dishes) of fired clay <earthen*ware*> **3 :** an intangible item (as a service) that is a marketable commodity

[4]**ware** *vt* **wared; war·ing** [ME *waren,* fr. ON *verja* to clothe, invest, spend — more at WEAR] *Scot* **:** SPEND, EXPEND

[1]**ware·house** \'wa(ə)r-ˌhau̇s, 'we(ə)r-\ *n* **:** a structure or room for the storage of merchandise or commodities

[2]**ware·house** \-ˌhau̇z, -ˌhau̇s\ *vt* **:** to deposit, store, or stock in or as if in a warehouse

ware·house·man \-ˌhau̇-smən\ *n* **:** one who manages or works in a warehouse

ware·hous·er \-ˌhau̇-zər, -sər\ *n* **:** WAREHOUSEMAN

ware·room \'wa(ə)r-ˌrüm, 'we(ə)r-, -ˌru̇m\ *n* **:** a room in which goods are exhibited for sale

war·fare \'wȯr-ˌfa(ə)r, -ˌfe(ə)r\ *n* [ME, fr. *werre, warre* war + *fare* journey, passage — more at FARE] **1 :** military operations between enemies **:** HOSTILITIES, WAR; *also* **:** an activity undertaken by a political unit (as a nation) to weaken or destroy another <economic ~> **2 :** struggle between competing entities **:** CONFLICT

war·fa·rin \'wȯr-fə-rən\ *n* [*W*isconsin *A*lumni *R*esearch *F*oundation (its patentee) + coum*arin*] **:** a crystalline anticoagulant compound $C_{19}H_{16}O_4$ used as a rodent poison and in medicine

war footing *n* **:** the condition of being prepared to undertake or maintain war

war–game *vt* **:** to plan or conduct in the manner of a war game <*war-gamed* an invasion —*Newsweek*> ~ *vi* **:** to conduct a war game

war game *n* **1 :** a simulated battle or campaign to test military concepts and usu. conducted in conferences by officers acting as the opposing staffs **2 :** a two-sided umpired training maneuver with actual elements of the armed forces participating

war gas *n* **:** a gas for use in warfare

war hawk *n* **:** one who clamors for war; *esp* **:** an American jingo favoring war with Britain around 1812

war·head \'wȯ(ə)r-ˌhed\ *n* **:** the section of a missile containing the explosive, chemical, or incendiary charge

war–horse \-ˌhȯ(ə)rs\ *n* **1 :** a horse used in war **:** CHARGER **2 :** a veteran soldier or public person (as a politician) **3 :** a work of art (as a musical composition) that has become hackneyed due to much repetition in the standard repertoire

war·i·son \'war-ə-sən\ *n* [prob. a misunderstanding by Sir Walter Scott in the *Lay of the Last Minstrel* (1805) of ME *waryson* reward, fr. ONF *warison* defense, possessions, fr. *warir* to protect, provide, of Gmc origin; akin to OHG *werien* to defend — more at WEIR] **:** a bugle call to attack

war·less \'wȯr-ləs\ *adj* **:** free from war

war·like \'wȯ(ə)r-ˌlīk\ *adj* **1** *obs* **:** ready for war **:** equipped to fight **2 :** fit for, disposed to, or fond of war **:** BELLICOSE **3 :** of, relating to, or useful in war **4 :** befitting or characteristic of war or a soldier *syn* see MARTIAL

war·lock \-ˌläk\ *n* [ME *warloghe,* fr. OE *wǣrloga* one that breaks faith, the Devil, fr. *wǣr* faith, troth + *-loga* (fr. *lēogan* to lie); akin to OE *wǣr* true — more at VERY, LIE] **1 :** a man practicing the black arts **:** SORCERER — compare WITCH **2 :** CONJURER

war·lord \-ˌlȯ(ə)rd\ *n* **1 :** a supreme military leader **2 :** a military commander exercising civil power by force usu. in a limited area — **war·lord·ism** \-ˌiz-əm\ *n*

[1]**warm** \'wȯ(ə)rm\ *adj* [ME, fr. OE *wearm;* akin to OHG *warm* warm, L *formus,* Gk *thermos* warm, hot] **1 a :** having or giving out heat to a moderate or adequate degree **b :** serving to maintain or preserve heat esp. to a satisfactory degree <a ~ sweater> **c :** feeling or causing sensations of heat brought about by strenuous exertion **2 :** comfortably established **:** SECURE <a ~ existence in his old age> **3 a :** marked by strong feeling **:** ARDENT **b :** marked by excitement, disagreement, or anger <a ~ debate> **4 :** marked by or readily showing affection, gratitude, cordiality, or sympathy <a ~ welcome> <~ regards> **5 :** emphasizing or exploiting sexual imagery or incidents **6 :** accompanied or marked by extreme danger or duress **7 :** newly made **:** FRESH <a ~ scent> **8 :** having the color or tone of something that imparts heat; *specif* **:** of a hue in the range yellow through orange to red **9 :** near to a goal, object, or solution sought — **warm·ish** \'wȯr-mish\ *adj* — **warm·ness** \'wȯrm-nəs\ *n*

[2]**warm** *vt* **1 :** to make warm **2 a :** to infuse with a feeling of love, friendship, well-being, or pleasure **b :** to fill with anger, zeal, or passion **3 :** to reheat (cooked food) for eating — often used with *over* **4 :** to make ready for operation or performance by preliminary exercise or operation — often used with *up* ~ *vi* **1 :** to become warm **2 a :** to become ardent or interested **b :** to become filled with affection or love — used with *to* or *toward* **3 :** to experience feelings of pleasure **:** BASK **4 :** to become ready

for operation or performance by preliminary activity — often used with *up*
[3]warm *adv* : WARMLY — usu. used in combination <*warm*-clad>
warm–blood·ed \'wȯrm-'bləd-əd\ *adj* **1 :** having warm blood; *specif* : having a relatively high and constant body temperature relatively independent of the surroundings **2 :** fervent or ardent in spirit — **warm–blood·ed·ness** *n*
warmed–over \'wȯrm-'dō-vər\ *adj* **1 :** heated again <~ beans> **2 :** not fresh or new : STALE <~ ideas>
warm·er \'wȯr-mər\ *n* : one that warms; *esp* : a device for keeping something warm <a hand ~>
warm front *n* : an advancing edge of a warm air mass
warm·heart·ed \'wȯ(-ə)rm-'härt-əd\ *adj* : marked by ready affection, cordiality, generosity, or sympathy — **warm·heart·ed·ness** *n*
warming pan *n* : a long-handled covered pan filled with live coals that is used to warm a bed
warm·ly \'wȯ(ə)rm-lē\ *adv* **1 :** in a manner that causes or maintains warmth **2 :** in a manner characterized or accompanied by warmth of emotion
war·mon·ger \'wȯ(ə)r-,məŋ-gər, -,mäŋ-\ *n* : one who urges or attempts to stir up war : JINGO — **war·mon·ger·ing** \-g(ə-)riŋ\ *n*
war·mouth \'wȯ(ə)r-,mau̇th\ *n* [origin unknown] : a freshwater sunfish (*Lepomis gulosus*) of the eastern U.S. — called also *warmouth bass*
warm spot *n* **1 :** a cutaneous sensory end organ that is stimulated by an increase of temperature **2 :** a lasting affection for a particular person or object
warmth \'wȯ(ə)rm(p)th\ *n* **1 :** the quality or state of being warm in temperature **2 :** the quality or state of being warm in feeling <a child needing human ~ and family life> **3 :** a glowing effect that is often produced by the use of warm colors
warm–up \'wȯr-,məp\ *n* : the act or an instance of warming up; *also* : a procedure (as a set of exercises) used in warming up
warm up \(')wȯr-'məp\ *vi* **1 :** to engage in exercise or practice esp. before entering a game or contest; *broadly* : to get ready **2 :** to approach a state of violence, conflict, or danger
warn \'wȯ(ə)rn\ *vb* [ME *warnen*, fr. OE *warnian*; akin to OHG *warnōn* to take heed, OE *wær* careful, aware — more at WARY] *vt* **1 a :** to give notice to beforehand esp. of danger or evil **b :** to give admonishing advice to : COUNSEL **c :** to call to one's attention : INFORM **2 :** to order to go or stay away ~ *vi* : to give a warning — **warn·er** *n*
syn WARN, FOREWARN, CAUTION *shared meaning element* : to let one know of approaching or possible danger or risk
[1]warn·ing \'wȯr-niŋ\ *n* **1 :** the act of warning : the state of being warned <he had ~ of his illness> **2 :** something that warns or serves to warn
[2]warning *adj* : serving as an alarm, signal, summons, or admonition <~ bell> <~ shot> — **warn·ing·ly** \'wȯr-niŋ-lē\ *adv*
warning coloration *n* : conspicuous coloration possessed by an animal otherwise effectively but not obviously defended that serves to warn off potential enemies
warning track *n* : a usu. dirt or cinder strip around the outside edge of a baseball outfield to warn a fielder when running to make a catch that he is approaching the fence — called also *warning path*
war of nerves : a conflict characterized by psychological tactics (as bluff, threats, and intimidation) designed primarily to create confusion, indecision, or breakdown of morale
[1]warp \'wȯ(ə)rp\ *n* [ME, fr. OE *wearp*; akin to OHG *warf* warp, ON *verpa* to throw] **1 a (1) :** a series of yarns extended lengthwise in a loom and crossed by the woof **(2) :** the cords forming the carcass of a pneumatic tire **b :** FOUNDATION, BASE <the ~ of the economic structure is agriculture — *Amer. Guide Series: N.C.*> **2 :** a rope for warping a ship or boat **3** [[2]*warp*] **a :** a twist or curve that has developed in something orig. flat or straight <a ~ in a door panel> **b :** a mental twist or aberration — **war·page** \'wȯr-pij\ *n*
[2]warp *vb* [ME *warpen*, fr. OE *weorpan* to throw; akin to ON *verpa* to throw, Gk *rhembein* to whirl] *vt* **1 a :** to turn or twist out of shape; *esp* : to twist or bend out of a plane **b :** to cause to judge, choose, or act wrongly : PERVERT **c :** FALSIFY, DISTORT **d :** to deflect from a course **2** [ME *warpen*, fr. [1]*warp*] : to arrange (yarns) so as to form a warp **3** [[1]*warp*] : to move (as a ship) by hauling on a line attached to a fixed object ~ *vi* **1 :** to become warped **2 :** to move a ship by warping *syn* see DEFORM — **warp·er** *n*
war paint *n* **1 :** paint put on parts of the body (as the face) by American Indians as a sign of going to war **2 :** ceremonial dress : REGALIA **3 :** MAKEUP 3a
warp and woof *n* : FOUNDATION, BASE <the vigorous Anglo-Saxon base had become the *warp and woof* of English speech —H. R. Warfel>
war party *n* **1 :** a group of American Indians on the warpath **2 :** a usu. jingoistic political party advocating or upholding a war
war·path \'wȯ(ə)r-,path, -,päth\ *n* **1 :** the route taken by a party of American Indians going on a warlike expedition or to a war **2 :** a hostile course of action or frame of mind
warp beam *n* : a roll on which warp is wound for a loom
warp–knit·ted \-'nit-əd\ *adj* : produced in machine knitting with the yarns running in a lengthwise direction
war·plane \'wȯ(ə)r-,plān\ *n* : a military airplane; *esp* : one armed for combat
war power *n* : the power to make war; *specif* : an extraordinary power exercised usu. by the executive branch of a government in the prosecution of a war
[1]war·rant \'wȯr-ənt, 'wär-\ *n* [ME, protector, warrant, fr. ONF *warant*, modif. of a Gmc noun represented by OHG *werēnto* guarantor, fr. prp. of *werēn* to warrant; akin to OHG *wāra* trust, care — more at VERY] **1 a (1) :** SANCTION, AUTHORIZATION; *also* : evidence for or token of authorization **(2) :** GUARANTEE, SECURITY **b (1) :** GROUND, JUSTIFICATION **(2) :** CONFIRMATION, PROOF **2 a :** a commission or document giving authority to do something; *specif* : a writing that authorizes a person to pay or deliver to another and the other to receive money or other consideration **b :** a precept or writ issued by a competent magistrate authorizing an officer to make an arrest, a seizure, or a search or to do other acts incident to the administration of justice **c :** an official certificate of appointment issued to an officer of lower rank than a commissioned officer **d (1) :** a short-term obligation of a governmental body (as a municipality) issued in anticipation of revenue **(2) :** an instrument issued by a corporation giving to the holder the right to purchase the capital stock of the corporation at a stated price either prior to a stipulated date or at any future time — **war·rant·less** \-ləs\ *adj*
[2]warrant *vt* [ME *warranten*, fr. ONF *warantir*, fr. *warant*] **1 a :** to declare or maintain with certainty : be sure that <I'll ~ he'll be here by noon> **b :** to assure (a person) of the truth of what is said **2 a :** to guarantee to a person good title to and undisturbed possession of (as an estate) **b :** to provide a guarantee of the security of (as title to property sold) usu. by an express covenant in the deed of conveyance **c :** to guarantee to be as represented **d :** to guarantee (as goods sold) esp. in respect of the quality or quantity specified **3 :** to guarantee security or immunity to : SECURE <I'll ~ him from drowning —Shak.> **4 :** to give warrant or sanction to : AUTHORIZE <the law ~*s* this procedure> **5 a :** to give proof of the authenticity or truth of **b :** to give assurance of the nature of or for the undertaking of : GUARANTEE **6 :** to serve as or give adequate ground or reason for *syn* see JUSTIFY
war·rant·able \'wȯr-ənt-ə-bəl, 'wär-\ *adj* : capable of being warranted : JUSTIFIABLE — **war·rant·able·ness** *n* — **war·rant·ably** \-blē\ *adv*
war·ran·tee \,wȯr-ən-'tē, ,wär-\ *n* : the person to whom a warranty is made
warrant officer *n* **1 :** an officer in the armed forces holding rank by virtue of a warrant and ranking above a noncommissioned officer and below a commissioned officer **2 :** a commissioned officer in the navy or coast guard ranking below an ensign
war·ran·tor \,wȯr-ən-'tȯ(ə)r, ,wär-; 'wȯr-ənt-ər, 'wär-\ *also* **war·rant·er** \'wȯr-ənt-ər, 'wär-\ *n* : one that warrants or gives a warranty
war·ran·ty \'wȯr-ənt-ē, 'wär-\ *n, pl* **-ties** [ME *warantie*, fr. ONF, fr. *warantir* to warrant] **1 a :** a real covenant binding the grantor of an estate and his heirs to warrant and defend the title **b :** a collateral undertaking that a fact regarding the subject of a contract is or will be as it is expressly or by implication declared or promised to be **2 :** something that authorizes, sanctions, supports, or justifies : WARRANT **3 :** a usu. written guarantee of the integrity of a product and of the maker's responsibility for the repair or replacement of defective parts
warranty deed *n* : a deed warranting that the grantor has a good title free and clear of all liens and encumbrances and will defend the grantee against all claims
war·ren \'wȯr-ən, 'wär-\ *n* [ME *warenne*, fr. ONF] **1** *chiefly Brit* **a :** a place legally authorized for keeping small game (as hare or pheasant) **b :** the privilege of hunting game in such a warren **2 a (1) :** an area (as of uncultivated ground) where rabbits breed **(2) :** a structure where rabbits are kept or bred **b :** the rabbits of a warren **3 a :** a crowded tenement or district **b :** a maze of passageways or cubbies
war·ren·er \-ə-nər\ *n* **1 :** GAMEKEEPER **2 :** one that maintains a rabbit warren
war·rior \'wȯr-yər, 'wȯr-ē-ər, 'wär-ē- *also* 'wär-yər\ *n, often attrib* [ME *werriour*, fr. ONF *werreieur*, fr. *werreier* to make war, fr. *werre* war] : a man engaged or experienced in warfare
war risk insurance *n* **1 :** term insurance written by the government for members of the military and naval forces **2 :** insurance that protects against loss due to acts of war
war·saw \'wȯr-(,)sȯ\ *n* [modif. of AmerSp *guasa*] : a large grouper (esp. *Garrupa nigrita*)
war·ship \'wȯ(ə)r-,ship\ *n* : a military ship; *esp* : one armed for combat
war·sle *or* **wars·tle** \'wä(r)s-əl\ *vb* [ME *werstelen*, *warstelen*, alter. of *wrestlen*, *wrastlen*] *Scot* : WRESTLE, STRUGGLE — **warsle** *n*, *Scot*
wart \'wȯ(ə)rt\ *n* [ME, fr. OE *wearte*; akin to OHG *warza* wart, L *verruca*] **1 a :** a horny projection on the skin usu. of the extremities that is caused by a virus — called also *verruca vulgaris* **b :** any of numerous similar skin lesions **2 :** an excrescence or protuberance resembling a true wart; *esp* : a glandular excrescence or hardened protuberance on a plant **3 :** one that suggests a wart esp. in smallness, unpleasantness, or unattractiveness — **wart·ed** \'wȯrt-əd\ *adj* — **warty** \'wȯrt-ē\ *adj*
wart·hog \'wȯ(ə)rt-,hȯg, -,häg\ *n* : any of a genus (*Phacochoerus*) of African wild hogs with two pairs of rough warty excrescences on the face and large protruding tusks

warthog

war·time \'wȯ(ə)r-,tīm\ *n* : a period during which a war is in progress
Warw *abbr* Warwickshire
war whoop *n* : a war cry esp. of American Indians
wary \'wa(ə)r-ē, 'we(ə)r-\ *adj* **wari·er; -est** [[1]*ware*, fr. ME *war*, *ware*, fr. OE *wær* careful, aware, wary; akin to OHG gi*war* aware, attentive, L *vereri* to fear, Gk *horan* to see] : marked by keen caution, cunning, and watchful prudence in detecting and escaping danger *syn* see CAUTIOUS *ant* foolhardy, brash (*of persons*) — **wari·ly** \'war-ə-lē, 'wer-\ *adv* — **wari·ness** \'war-ē-nəs, 'wer-\ *n*
war zone *n* **1 :** a zone in which belligerents are waging war **2 :** a designated area esp. on the high seas within which rights of neutrals are not respected by a belligerent nation in time of war

was [ME, fr. OE, 1st & 3d sing. past indic. of *wesan* to be; akin to ON *vera* to be, *var* was, Skt *vasati* he lives, dwells] *past 1st & 3d sing of* BE

1wash \ˈwȯsh, ˈwäsh\ *vb* [ME *washen,* fr. OE *wascan;* akin to OHG *waskan* to wash, OE *wæter* water] *vt* **1 a :** to cleanse by or as if by the action of liquid (as water) **b :** to remove (as dirt) by rubbing or drenching with liquid **2 :** to cleanse (fur) by licking or by rubbing with a paw moistened with saliva **3 a :** to flush or moisten (a bodily part or injury) with a liquid **b** (1) **:** to wet thoroughly **:** DRENCH (2) **:** to overspread with light **:** SUFFUSE **c :** to pass water over or through esp. so as to carry off material from the surface or interior **4 :** to flow along or dash or overflow against **:** LAVE <waves *~ing* the shore> **5 :** to move, carry, or deposit by or as if by the force of water in motion <houses *~ed* away by the flood> **6 a :** to subject (as crushed ore) to the action of water to separate valuable material **b :** to separate (particles) from a substance (as ore) by agitation with or in water **c** (1) **:** to pass through a bath to carry off impurities or soluble components (2) **:** to pass (a gas or gaseous mixture) through or over a liquid to purify it esp. by removing soluble components **7 a :** to cover or daub lightly with or as if with an application of a thin liquid (as whitewash or varnish) **b :** to depict or paint by a broad sweep of thin color with a brush **8 :** to cause to swirl <*~ing* coffee around in his cup> ~ *vi* **1 :** to wash oneself or a part of one's body **2 :** to become worn away by the action of water **3 :** to clean something by rubbing or dipping in water **4 a :** to become carried along on water **:** DRIFT <cakes of ice *~ing* along> **b :** to pour, sweep, or flow in a stream or current <waves of pioneers *~ing* westward —Green Peyton> **5 :** to serve as a cleansing agent <this soap *~es* thoroughly> **6 a :** to undergo laundering <this dress doesn't ~ well> **b** (1) **:** to undergo testing successfully <an interesting theory, but it just won't ~> (2) **:** to gain acceptance **:** inspire belief <his story didn't ~ with me> — **wash one's hands of :** to disclaim interest in, responsibility for, or further connection with

2wash *n* **1 a :** the act or process or an instance of washing or being washed **b :** articles to be washed or being washed **2 :** the surging action of waves **3 a :** a piece of ground washed by the sea or river **b :** BOG, MARSH **c** (1) **:** a shallow body of water (2) **:** a shallow creek **d** *West* **:** the dry bed of a stream — called also *dry wash* **4 a :** worthless esp. liquid waste **:** REFUSE **b :** an insipid beverage **c :** vapid writing or speech **5 a :** a sweep or splash esp. of color made by or as if by a long stroke of a brush **b :** a thin coat of paint (as watercolor) **c :** a thin liquid used for coating a surface (as a wall) **6 :** LOTION **7 :** loose or eroded surface material of the earth (as rock debris) transported and deposited by running water **8 a :** BACKWASH 1 **b :** a disturbance in the air produced by the passage of an airfoil or propeller

3wash *adj* **1 :** involving essentially simultaneous purchase and sale of the same security <spurious market activity resulting from ~ trading> **2 :** WASHABLE <~ fabric>

Wash *abbr* Washington

wash·able \ˈwȯsh-ə-bəl, ˈwäsh-\ *adj* **:** capable of being washed without damage — **wash·abil·i·ty** \ˌwȯsh-ə-ˈbil-ət-ē, ˌwäsh-\ *n*

wash and wear *adj* **:** of, relating to, or constituting a fabric or garment that needs little or no ironing after washing

wash·ba·sin \ˈwȯsh-ˌbās-ᵊn, ˈwäsh-\ *n* **:** WASHBOWL

wash·board \ˈwȯsh-ˌbō(ə)rd, ˈwäsh-, -ˌbȯ(ə)rd\ *n* **1 :** a broad thin plank along a gunwale or on the sill of a lower deck port to keep out the sea **2 :** BASEBOARD **3 a :** a corrugated rectangular surface that is used for scrubbing clothes **b :** a road or pavement so worn by traffic as to be corrugated transversely

wash·bowl \-ˌbōl\ *n* **:** a large bowl for water that is used to wash one's hands and face

wash·cloth \-ˌklȯth\ *n* **:** a cloth that is used for washing one's face and body — called also *facecloth, washrag*

wash down *vt* **1 :** to move or carry downward by action of a liquid; *esp* **:** to facilitate the passage of (food) down the gullet with accompanying swallows of liquid **2 :** to wash the whole length or extent of <*washed down* and scrubbed the front porch>

wash drawing *n* **:** watercolor painting in or chiefly in washes esp. in black, white, and gray tones only

washed–out \ˈwȯsh-ˈtau̇t, ˈwäsh-\ *adj* **1 :** faded in color **2 :** depleted in vigor or animation **:** EXHAUSTED

wash·er \ˈwȯsh-ər, ˈwäsh-\ *n* **1 :** one that washes; *esp* **:** WASHING MACHINE **2 :** a flat thin ring or a perforated plate used in joints or assemblies to ensure tightness, prevent leakage, or relieve friction

wash·er·man \-mən\ *n* **:** LAUNDRYMAN; *esp* **:** one who takes in washing

wash·er·wom·an \-ˌwu̇m-ən\ *n* **:** LAUNDRYWOMAN; *esp* **:** one who takes in washing

wash·house \ˈwȯsh-ˌhau̇s, ˈwäsh-\ *n* **:** a building used or equipped for washing; *esp* **:** one for washing clothes

wash·ing \ˈwȯsh-iŋ, ˈwäsh-\ *n* **1 :** the act or action of one that cleanses with water **2 :** material obtained by washing **3 :** a thin covering or coat <a ~ of silver> **4 :** articles washed or to be washed **:** WASH

washing machine *n* **:** a machine for washing; *esp* **:** one for washing clothes and household linen

washing soda *n* **:** SAL SODA

Wash·ing·ton pie \ˌwȯsh-iŋ-tən-, ˌwäsh-\ *n* [George *Washington*] **:** cake layers put together with a jam or jelly filling

Washington's Birthday *n* [George *Washington*] **1 :** February 22 formerly observed as a legal holiday in most of the states of the U.S. **2 :** the third Monday in February observed as a legal holiday in most of the states of the U.S.

wash·out \ˈwȯsh-ˌau̇t, ˈwäsh-\ *n* **1 a :** the washing out or away of something and esp. of earth in a roadbed by a freshet **b :** a place where earth is washed away **2 :** one that fails to measure up **:** FAILURE; *specif* **:** one who fails in a course of training or study

wash out \(ˈ)wȯsh-ˈau̇t, (ˈ)wäsh-\ *vt* **1 :** to wash free of an extraneous substance (as dirt) **2 a :** to cause to fade by laundering **b :** to deplete the strength or vitality of **c :** to eliminate as useless or unsatisfactory **:** REJECT **3 a :** to destroy or make useless by the force or action of water <the storm *washed out* the bridge> **b :** to rain out <the game was *washed out*> ~ *vi* **1 :** to become depleted of color or vitality **:** FADE **2 :** to fail to meet requirements or measure up to a standard

wash·rag \ˈwȯsh-ˌrag, ˈwäsh-\ *n* **:** WASHCLOTH

wash·room \-ˌrüm, -ˌru̇m\ *n* **:** a room that is equipped with washing and toilet facilities **:** LAVATORY

wash·stand \-ˌ(s)tand\ *n* **1 :** a stand holding articles needed for washing one's face and hands **2 :** a washbowl permanently set in place and attached to water and drainpipes

wash·tub \-ˌtəb\ *n* **:** a tub in which clothes are washed or soaked

wash up *vi* **1 :** to wash one's face and hands **2** *Brit* **:** to wash the dishes after a meal ~ *vt* **1 :** to get rid of by washing <*wash up* the spilled milk> **2 :** EXHAUST, FINISH

wash·wom·an \ˈwȯsh-ˌwu̇m-ən, ˈwäsh-\ *n* **:** WASHERWOMAN

washy \ˈwȯsh-ē, ˈwäsh-\ *adj* **wash·i·er; -est 1 a :** WEAK, WATERY <~ tea> **b :** deficient in color **:** PALLID **c :** lacking in vigor, individuality, or definiteness **2 :** lacking in condition and in firmness of flesh

wasn't \ˈwəz-ᵊnt, ˈwäz-\ **:** was not

wasp \ˈwäsp, ˈwȯsp\ *n* [ME *waspe,* fr. OE *wæps, wæsp;* akin to OHG *wafsa* wasp, L *vespa* wasp, OE *wefan* to weave — more at WEAVE] **1 :** any of numerous social or solitary winged hymenopterous insects that usu. have a slender smooth body with the abdomen attached by a narrow stalk, well-developed wings, biting mouthparts, and in the females and workers an often formidable sting, and that are largely carnivorous and often provision their nests with caterpillars, insects, or spiders killed or paralyzed by stinging for their larvae to feed on — compare BEE **2 :** any of various hymenopterous insects with larvae that are parasitic on other arthropods — **wasp·like** \-ˌlīk\ *adj*

wasp 1

WASP *or* **Wasp** \ˈwäsp, ˈwȯsp\ *n* [*w*hite *A*nglo-*S*axon *P*rotestant] **:** an American of Northern European and esp. British stock and of Protestant background **:** one often considered to be a member of the dominating and the most privileged class of people in the U.S. — **Wasp·ish** \ˈwäs-pish, ˈwȯs-\ *adj* — **Waspy** \-pē\ *adj*

wasp·ish \ˈwäs-pish, ˈwȯs-\ *adj* **1 :** resembling a wasp in behavior; *esp* **:** SNAPPISH, PETULANT **2 :** resembling a wasp in form; *esp* **:** slightly built — **wasp·ish·ly** *adv* — **wasp·ish·ness** *n*

wasp waist *n* **:** a very slender waist — **wasp–waist·ed** \ˈwäsp-ˈwā-stəd, ˈwȯsp-\ *adj*

1was·sail \ˈwäs-əl *also* wä-ˈsā(ə)l\ *n* [ME *wæs hæil,* fr. ON *ves heill* be well, fr. *ves* (imper. sing. of *vera* to be) + *heill* healthy — more at WAS, WHOLE] **1 :** an early English toast to someone's health **2 :** a liquor that is made of ale or wine, spices, and often baked apples and that is served in a large bowl usu. at Christmastime **3 :** riotous drinking **:** REVELRY

2wassail *vi* **1 :** to hold a wassail **:** CAROUSE **2** *dial Eng* **:** to sing carols from house to house at Christmas ~ *vt* **:** to drink to the health or thriving of

was·sail bowl \ˈwäs-əl-\ *n* **1 :** a bowl that is used for the serving of wassail **2 :** WASSAIL 2

was·sail·er \ˈwäs-ə-lər *also* wä-ˈsā-lər\ *n* **1 :** one that carouses **:** REVELER **2** *archaic* **:** one who goes about singing carols

Was·ser·mann reaction \ˈwäs-ər-mən-, ˈväs-\ *n* [August von *Wassermann*] **:** a complement-fixing reaction occurring with the serum of syphilitic patients and used as a test for syphilis — called also *Wassermann*

Wassermann test *n* **:** a test for the detection of syphilitic infection using the Wassermann reaction

wast \wəst, (ˈ)wäst\ *archaic past 2d sing of* BE

wast·age \ˈwā-stij\ *n* **:** loss, decrease, or destruction of something (as by use, decay, erosion, or leakage); *esp* **:** wasteful or avoidable loss of something valuable

1waste \ˈwāst\ *n* [ME *waste, wast;* in sense 1, fr. ONF *wast,* fr. *wast,* adj., desolate, waste, fr. L *vastus;* akin to OHG *wuosti* desolate, waste, L *vanus* empty; in other senses, fr. ME *wasten* to waste — more at WANE] **1 a :** a sparsely settled or barren region **:** DESERT **b :** uncultivated land **c :** a broad and empty expanse (as of water) **2 :** the act or an instance of wasting **:** the state of being wasted **3 a :** loss through breaking down of bodily tissue **b :** gradual loss or decrease by use, wear, or decay **4 a :** damaged, defective, or superfluous material produced by a manufacturing process: as (1) **:** material rejected during a textile manufacturing process and used usu. for wiping away dirt and oil (2) **:** SCRAP (3) **:** fluid (as steam) allowed to escape without being utilized **b :** refuse from places of human or animal habitation: as (1) **:** GARBAGE, RUBBISH (2) *pl* **:** EXCREMENT (3) **:** SEWAGE **c :** material derived by mechanical and chemical weathering of the land and moved down sloping surfaces or carried by streams to the sea

2waste *vb* **wast·ed; wast·ing** [ME *wasten,* fr. ONF *waster,* fr. L *vastare,* fr. *vastus* desolate, waste] *vt* **1 :** to lay waste; *esp* **:** to damage or destroy gradually and progressively <reclaiming land *wasted* by strip-mining> **2 :** to cause to shrink in physical bulk or strength **:** EMACIATE, ENFEEBLE **3 :** to wear away or diminish gradually **:** CONSUME **4 a :** to spend or use carelessly **:** SQUANDER **b :** to allow to be used inefficiently or become dissipated ~ *vi* **1 :** to lose weight, strength, or vitality — often used with *away* **2 a :** to become diminished in bulk or substance **b :** to become

consumed **3 :** to spend money or consume property extravagantly or improvidently
***syn* 1** see RAVAGE
2 WASTE, SQUANDER, DISSIPATE, FRITTER, CONSUME *shared meaning element* : to spend or expend futilely or without gaining a proper or reasonable or normal return ***ant*** save, conserve
— **waste one's breath :** to accomplish nothing by speaking

[3]**waste** *adj* [ME *waste, wast,* fr. ONF *wast*] **1 a** (1) **:** being wild and uninhabited **:** DESOLATE (2) **:** ARID, EMPTY **b :** not cultivated **:** not productive **2 :** being in a ruined or devastated condition **3** [[1]*waste*] **:** discarded as worthless, defective, or of no use **:** REFUSE <~ material> **4** [[1]*waste*] **:** serving to conduct or hold refuse material; *specif* **:** carrying off superfluous water

waste·bas·ket \'wās(t)-ˌbas-kət\ *n* **:** a receptacle for refuse and esp. for wastepaper — called also *wastepaper basket*

wast·ed *adj* **1 :** laid waste **:** RAVAGED **2 :** impaired in strength or health **:** EMACIATED **3** *archaic* **:** gone by **:** ELAPSED <the chronicle of ~ time —Shak.> **4 :** unprofitably used, made, or expended <~ effort>

waste·ful \'wāst-fəl\ *adj* **:** given to or marked by waste **:** LAVISH, PRODIGAL — **waste·ful·ly** \-fə-lē\ *adv* — **waste·ful·ness** *n*

waste·land \'wāst-ˌland *also* -lənd\ *n* **1 :** barren or uncultivated land <a desert ~> **2 :** an ugly often devastated or barely inhabitable place or area **3 :** something (as a way of life) that is spiritually and emotionally arid and unsatisfying

waste·pa·per \'wās(t)-'pā-pər\ *n* **:** paper discarded as used, superfluous, or not fit for use

waste pipe *n* **:** a pipe for carrying off waste fluid

waste product *n* **1 :** debris resulting from a process (as of manufacture) that is of no further use to the system producing it **2 :** material discharged from or stored in an inert form in a living body as a by-product of its vital activities

wast·er \'wā-stər\ *n* **1 a** (1) **:** one that spends or consumes extravagantly and without thought for the future (2) **:** a dissolute person **b :** one that uses wastefully or causes or permits waste <a procedure that is a ~ of time> **c :** one that lays waste **:** DESTROYER **2 :** an imperfect or inferior manufactured article or object ***syn*** see SPENDTHRIFT

waste·wa·ter \'wāst-ˌwȯt-ər, -ˌwät-\ *n* **:** water that has been used (as in a manufacturing process) **:** SEWAGE

wast·ing \'wā-stiŋ\ *adj* **1 :** laying waste **:** DEVASTATING **2 :** undergoing or causing decay or loss of strength <~ diseases such as tuberculosis> — **wast·ing·ly** \-stiŋ-lē\ *adv*

wast·rel \'wā-strəl *also* 'wäs-trəl\ *n* [irreg. fr. *-waste*] **1 :** VAGABOND, WAIF **2 :** one who dissipates his resources foolishly and self-indulgently **:** PROFLIGATE ***syn*** see SPENDTHRIFT

Wat *abbr* Waterford

[1]**watch** \'wäch, 'wȯch\ *vb* [ME *wacchen,* fr. OE *wæccan* — more at WAKE] *vi* **1 a :** to keep vigil as a devotional exercise **b :** to be awake during the night **2 a :** to be attentive or vigilant **b :** to keep guard **3 a :** to keep someone or something under close observation **b :** to observe as a spectator <the country ~*ed* as stocks fell sharply> **4 :** to be expectant **:** WAIT <~ for the signal> ~ *vt* **1 :** to keep under guard **2 a :** to observe closely in order to check on action or change <he's being ~*ed* by the police> **b :** to look at **:** OBSERVE <sat and ~*ed* the crowd> **c :** to look on at <~ television> <~ a ball game> **3 a :** to take care of **:** TEND **b :** to be careful of <~*es* his diet> **4 :** to be on the alert for **:** BIDE <~*ed* his opportunity> ***syn*** see TEND, SEE — **watch it :** look out **:** be careful <*watch it* when you handle the glassware> — **watch one's step :** to proceed with extreme care **:** act or talk warily — **watch over :** to have charge of **:** SUPERINTEND

[2]**watch** *n* **1 a :** the act of keeping awake to guard, protect, or attend **b** *obs* **:** the state of being wakeful **c :** a wake over a dead body **d :** a state of alert and continuous attention **e :** close observation **:** SURVEILLANCE **2 a :** any of the definite divisions of the night made by ancient peoples **b :** one of the indeterminate wakeful intervals marking the passage of night — usu. used in pl. <the silent ~*es* of the night> **3 a :** one that watches **:** LOOKOUT, WATCHMAN **b** *archaic* **:** the office or function of a sentinel or guard **4 a :** a body of soldiers or sentinels making up a guard **b :** a watchman or body of watchmen formerly assigned to patrol the streets of a town at night, announce the hours, and act as police **5 a** (1) **:** a portion of time during which a part of a ship's company is on duty (2) **:** the part of a ship's company required to be on duty during a particular watch (3) **:** a sailor's assigned duty period **b :** a period of duty **:** SHIFT **6 a :** a portable timepiece that has a movement driven in any of several ways (as by a spring or a battery) and is designed to be worn (as on the wrist) or carried in the pocket — compare CLOCK **b :** a ship's chronometer

watch and ward *n* **1 :** continuous unbroken vigilance and guard **2 :** service as a watchman or sentinel required from a feudal tenant

watch·band \'wäch-ˌband, 'wȯch-\ *n* **:** the bracelet or strap of a wristwatch

watch cap *n* **:** a knitted close-fitting navy-blue cap worn esp by enlisted men in the U.S. navy in cold or stormy weather

watch·case \'wäch-ˌkās, 'wȯch-\ *n* **:** the outside metal covering of a watch

[1]**watch·dog** \-ˌdȯg\ *n* **1 :** a dog kept to guard property **2 :** one that guards against loss, waste, theft, or undesirable practices

[2]**watchdog** *vt* **:** to act as a watchdog for

watch·er \'wäch-ər, 'wȯch-\ *n* **:** one that watches: as **a :** one that sits up or continues awake at night **b :** WATCHMAN **c** (1) **:** one that keeps watch beside a dead person (2) **:** one that attends a sick person at night **d :** OBSERVER, VIEWER **e :** a representative of a party or candidate who is stationed at the polls on an election day to watch the conduct of officials and voters

watch·eye \-ˌī\ *n* **:** WALLEYE 1; *esp* **:** a walleye of a dog

watch fire *n* **:** a fire lighted as a signal or for the use of a guard

watch·ful \'wäch-fəl, 'wȯch-\ *adj* **1** *archaic* **a :** not able or accustomed to sleep or rest **:** WAKEFUL **b :** causing sleeplessness **c :** spent in wakefulness **:** SLEEPLESS **2 :** carefully observant or attentive **:** being on the watch — **watch·ful·ly** \-fə-lē\ *adv* — **watch·ful·ness** *n*

syn WATCHFUL, VIGILANT, WIDE-AWAKE, ALERT *shared meaning element* **:** being on the lookout, esp. for danger or opportunity

watch·mak·er \-ˌmā-kər\ *n* **:** one that makes or repairs watches or clocks

watch·mak·ing \-ˌmā-kiŋ\ *n* **:** the work or occupation of a watchmaker

watch·man \-mən\ *n* **:** one who keeps watch **:** GUARD

watch night *n* **:** a devotional service lasting until after midnight esp. on New Year's Eve

watch out *vi* **:** to be vigilant **:** look out — usu. used with *for*

watch pocket *n* **:** a small pocket just below the front waistband of men's trousers

watch·tow·er \'wäch-ˌtau̇(-ə)r, 'wȯch-\ *n* **:** a tower for a lookout

watch·word \-ˌwərd\ *n* **1 :** a word or phrase used as a sign of recognition among members of the same society, class, or group **2 :** a motto that embodies a principle or guide to action of an individual or group **:** SLOGAN

[1]**wa·ter** \'wȯt-ər, 'wät-\ *n, often attrib* [ME, fr. OE *wæter;* akin to OHG *wazzar* water, Gk *hydōr,* L *unda* wave] **1 a :** the liquid that descends from the clouds as rain, forms streams, lakes, and seas, and is a major constituent of all living matter and that is an odorless, tasteless, very slightly compressible liquid oxide of hydrogen H_2O which appears bluish in thick layers, freezes at 0° C and boils at 100° C, has a maximum density at 4° C and a high specific heat, is feebly ionized to hydrogen and hydroxyl ions, and is a poor conductor of electricity and a good solvent **b :** a natural mineral water — usu. used in pl. **2 a** (1) *pl* **:** the water occupying or flowing in a particular bed (2) *chiefly Brit* **:** LAKE, POND **b :** a quantity or depth of water adequate for some purpose (as navigation) **c** *pl* (1) **:** a band of seawater abutting on the land of a particular sovereignty and under the control of that sovereignty (2) **:** the sea of a particular part of the earth **d :** a water supply <threatened to turn off the ~> **3 :** travel or transportation on water <we went by ~> **4 :** the level of water at a particular state of the tide **:** TIDE **5 :** liquid containing or resembling water: as **a** (1) **:** a pharmaceutical or cosmetic preparation made with water (2) **:** a watery solution of a gaseous or readily volatile substance — compare AMMONIA WATER **b** *archaic* **:** a distilled fluid (as an essence); *esp* **:** a distilled alcoholic liquor **c :** a watery fluid (as tears, urine, or sap) formed or circulating in a living body **6 a :** the limpidity and luster of a precious stone and esp. a diamond **b :** degree of excellence <a scholar of the first ~> **c :** a wavy lustrous pattern (as of a textile) **7 :** WATERCOLOR **8 a :** capital stock not representing assets of the issuing company and not backed by earning power **b :** fictitious or exaggerated asset entries that give a stock an unrealistic book value — **above water :** out of difficulty

[2]**water** *vt* **1 :** to moisten, sprinkle, or soak with water **2 :** to supply with water for drink **3 :** to supply water to **4 :** to treat with or as if with water; *specif* **:** to impart a lustrous appearance and wavy pattern to (cloth) by calendering **5 a :** to dilute by the addition of water — often used with *down* <~ down the punch> **b :** to add to the aggregate par value of (securities) with a corresponding addition to the assets represented by the securities ~ *vi* **1 :** to form or secrete water or watery matter (as tears or saliva) **2 :** to get or take water: as **a :** to take on a supply of water **b :** to drink water

water back *n* **:** a water heater set in the firebox of a stove

water bag *n* **1 :** a bag for holding water; *esp* **:** one designed to keep water cool for drinking by evaporation through a slightly porous surface **2 :** the fetal membranes enclosing the amniotic fluid

water balance *n* **:** the ratio between the water assimilated into the body and that lost from the body; *also* **:** the condition of the body when this ratio approximates unity

water ballet *n* **:** a synchronized sequence of movements performed by a group of swimmers

water bear *n* **:** TARDIGRADE

Water Bearer *n* **:** AQUARIUS 1, 2a

water bed *n* **:** a bed whose mattress is a plastic bag filled with water

water beetle *n* **:** any of numerous oval flattened aquatic beetles (esp. family Dytiscidae) that swim by means of their fringed hind legs which act together as oars

water bird *n* **:** a swimming or wading bird — compare WATERFOWL

water biscuit *n* **:** a cracker of flour and water and sometimes fat

water blister *n* **:** a blister with a clear watery content that is not purulent or sanguineous

water bloom *n* **:** an accumulation of algae and esp. of blue-green algae at or near the surface of a body of water; *also* **:** an alga causing this

water boatman *n* **:** any of various aquatic bugs (family Corixidae) with one pair of legs modified into paddles

wa·ter·borne \'wȯt-ər-ˌbō(ə)rn, 'wät-, -ˌbȯ(ə)rn\ *adj* **:** supported or carried by water <~ commerce> <~ infection>

water boy *n* **:** one who keeps a group (as of football players) supplied with drinking water

wa·ter·buck \'wȯt-ər-ˌbək, 'wät-\ *n, pl* **waterbuck** *or* **water·bucks :** any of various Old World antelopes that commonly frequent streams or wet areas

water buffalo *n* **:** an often domesticated Asiatic buffalo (*Bubalus bubalis*)

water bug *n* **:** any of various small arthropods (as insects) that frequent water: as **a :** GERMAN COCKROACH **b :** WATER BOATMAN

water chestnut *n* **1 :** any of a genus (*Trapa* and esp. *T. natans* and *T. bicornis*) of aquatic herbs of the evening-primrose family; *also* **:** its edible nutlike spiny-angled fruit — called also *water caltrop* **2 :** a Chinese sedge (*Eleocharis tuberosa*); *also* **:** its edible tuber

water clock *n* **:** an instrument designed to measure time by the fall or flow of a quantity of water

water closet *n* **1 :** a compartment or room for defecation and excretion into a toilet bowl **:** BATHROOM **2 :** a toilet bowl and its accessories

wa·ter·col·or \'wȯt-ər-ˌkəl-ər, 'wät-\ *n* **1 :** a paint of which the liquid is a water dispersion of the binding material (as glue, casein, or gum) **2 :** the art or method of painting with watercolors **3 :** a picture or design executed in watercolors — **watercolor** *adj* — **wa·ter·col·or·ist** \-ˌkəl-ə-rəst\ *n*

wa·ter–cool \ˌwȯt-ər-'kül, ˌwät-\ *vt* **:** to cool by means of water and esp. circulating water (as in a water jacket)

wa·ter·course \'wȯt-ər-ˌkō(ə)rs, -ˌkȯ(ə)rs\ *n* **1 :** a natural or made channel through which water flows **2 :** a stream of water (as a river, brook, or underground stream)

wa·ter·craft \-ˌkraft\ *n* **1 :** skill in aquatic activities (as managing boats) **2 a :** SHIP, BOAT **b :** craft for water transport

wa·ter·cress \-ˌkres\ *n* **:** any of several water-loving cresses; *esp* **:** a perennial cress (*Nasturtium officinale*) found chiefly in springs or running water and used esp. in salads or as a potherb

water dog *n* **1 :** a dog accustomed to the water and usu. trained to retrieve waterfowl **2 :** any of several large American salamanders; *esp* **:** any of a genus (*Necturus* of the family Proteidae) with external gills **3 :** a person (as a skilled sailor or seaman) who is quite at ease in or on water

water down *vt* **:** to reduce or temper the force or effectiveness of <was urged to *water down* his inflammatory speeches> <a *watered down* report>

wa·ter·er \'wȯt-ər-ər, 'wät-\ *n* **:** one that waters: as **a :** a person who obtains or supplies drinking water **b :** a device used for supplying water to livestock and poultry

wa·ter·fall \-ˌfȯl\ *n* **1 a :** a perpendicular or very steep descent of the water of a stream **b :** an artificial waterfall (as in a hotel lobby or a nightclub) **2 :** something resembling a waterfall <deluged by a ~ of suggestions>

wa·ter–fast \-ˌfast\ *adj, chiefly Scot* **:** WATERTIGHT

water flea *n* **:** any of various small active dark or brightly colored aquatic entomostracan crustaceans (as of the genera *Cyclops* and *Daphnia*)

¹wa·ter·flood \-ˌfləd\ *vi* **:** to pump water into the ground around an oil well in order to loosen and force out oil

²waterflood *n* **:** the process of waterflooding an oil well

wa·ter·fowl \'wȯt-ər-ˌfau̇l, 'wät-\ *n* **1 :** a bird that frequents water; *esp* **:** a swimming bird **2 waterfowl** *pl* **:** swimming game birds as distinguished from upland game birds and shorebirds

wa·ter·fowl·er \-ˌfau̇-lər\ *n* **:** a hunter of waterfowl

wa·ter·front \-ˌfrənt\ *n* **:** land, land with buildings, or a section of a town fronting or abutting on a body of water

water gap *n* **:** a pass in a mountain ridge through which a stream runs

water gas *n* **:** a poisonous flammable gaseous mixture that consists chiefly of carbon monoxide and hydrogen with small amounts of methane, carbon dioxide, and nitrogen, is usu. made by blowing air and then steam over red-hot coke or coal, and is used as a fuel or after carbureting as an illuminant

water gate *n* **1 :** a gate (as of a building) giving access to a body of water **2 :** FLOODGATE

water gauge *n* **:** an instrument to measure or find the depth or quantity of water or to indicate the height of its surface esp. in a steam boiler

water glass *n* **1 :** WATER CLOCK **2 :** a glass vessel (as a drinking glass) for holding water **3 :** an instrument consisting of an open box or tube with a glass bottom used for examining objects in or under water **4 :** a substance that consists usu. of the silicate of sodium, is found in commerce as a glassy mass, a stony powder, or dissolved in water as a viscous syrupy liquid, and is used esp. as a cement, as a protective coating and fireproofing agent, and in preserving eggs **5 :** WATER GAUGE

water gum *n* **:** a gum tree (as a tupelo) that grows on wet land

water gun *n* **:** WATER PISTOL

water hammer *n* **:** a concussion or sound of concussion of moving water against the sides of a containing pipe or vessel (as a steam pipe)

water haul *n* [fr. the figure of a fishing net that catches nothing but water] **:** a fruitless effort

water heater *n* **:** an apparatus for heating and usu. storing hot water (as for domestic use)

water hemlock *n* **:** any of several poisonous plants (genus *Cicuta*) of the carrot family; *esp* **:** a tall Eurasian perennial herb (*C. virosa*)

water hen *n* **:** any of various birds (as a coot or gallinule) related to the rails

water hole *n* **1 :** a natural hole or hollow containing water **2 :** a hole in a surface of ice

water hyacinth *n* **:** a showy So. American floating aquatic plant (*Eichhornia crassipes* of the family Pontederiaceae) that often clogs waterways in warm regions (as of the southern U.S.)

water ice *n* **:** a frozen dessert of water, sugar, and flavoring

wa·ter–inch \ˌwȯt-ə-'rinch, ˌwät-\ *n* **:** a unit of hydraulic measure that equals the discharge from a circular orifice one inch in diameter which is commonly estimated at 14 pints per minute

watering hole *n* **:** a place where people gather socially; *esp* **:** WATERING PLACE 3

watering place *n* **1 :** a place where water may be obtained; *esp* **:** one where animals and esp. livestock come to drink **2 :** a health or recreational resort featuring mineral springs or bathing **3 :** a place (as a nightclub, bar, or lounge) where drink is available

watering pot *n* **:** a vessel usu. with a spout used to sprinkle or pour water esp. on plants — called also *watering can*

wa·ter·ish \'wȯt-ə-rish, 'wät-\ *adj* **:** somewhat watery — **wa·ter·ish·ness** *n*

water jacket *n* **:** an outer casing which holds water or through which water circulates to cool the interior; *specif* **:** the enclosed space surrounding the cylinder block of an internal-combustion engine and containing the cooling liquid

water jump *n* **:** an obstacle (as in a steeplechase) consisting of a pool, stream, or ditch of water

wa·ter·leaf \'wȯt-ər-ˌlēf, 'wät-\ *n, pl* **-leafs** \-ˌlēfs\ **:** any of a genus (*Hydrophyllum* of the family Hydrophyllaceae, the waterleaf family) of perennial woodland herbs with lobed or pinnate toothed leaves and cymes of bell-shaped flowers

wa·ter·less \-ləs\ *adj* **1 :** lacking or destitute of water **:** DRY **2 :** not requiring water (as for cooling or cooking) — **wa·ter·less·ly** *adv* — **wa·ter·less·ness** *n*

water level *n* **1 :** an instrument to show the level by means of the surface of water in a trough or in a U-shaped tube **2 :** the surface of still water: as **a :** the level assumed by the surface of a particular body or column of water **b :** the waterline of a vessel **c :** WATER TABLE 2

water lily *n* **:** any of a family (Nymphaeaceae, the water-lily family) of aquatic plants with floating leaves and usu. showy flowers; *broadly* **:** an aquatic plant (as a water hyacinth) with showy flowers

water lily

wa·ter·line \'wȯt-ər-ˌlīn, 'wät-\ *n* **:** any of several lines that are marked upon the outside of a ship and correspond with the surface of the water when it is afloat on an even keel

wa·ter·log \-ˌlȯg, -ˌläg\ *vt* [back-formation fr. *waterlogged*] **1 :** to make (as a boat) unmanageable by flooding **2 :** to saturate with water to the point of sogginess or loss of buoyancy

wa·ter·logged \-ˌlȯgd, -ˌlägd\ *adj* [¹*water* + *log* (to accumulate in the hold)] **:** so filled or soaked with water as to be heavy or hard to manage <~ boats>

wa·ter·loo \ˌwȯt-ər-'lü, ˌwät-\ *n, pl* **-loos** [*Waterloo*, Belgium, scene of Napoleon's defeat in 1815] **:** a decisive defeat

water main *n* **:** a pipe or conduit for conveying water

wa·ter·man \'wȯt-ər-mən, 'wät-\ *n* **:** a man who lives and works mostly in or near water; *esp* **:** a boatman who plies for hire

wa·ter·man·ship \-ˌship\ *n* **:** the business, skill, or art of a waterman: as **a :** technique or expertness in rowing **b :** technique or expertness in swimming

¹wa·ter·mark \'wȯt-ər-ˌmärk, 'wät-\ *n* **1 :** a mark indicating the height to which water has risen **2 :** a marking in paper resulting from differences in thickness usu. produced by pressure of a projecting design in the mold or on a processing roll and visible when the paper is held up to the light; *also* **:** the design or the metal pattern producing the marking

²watermark *vt* **1 :** to mark (paper) with a watermark **2 :** to impress (a given design) as a watermark

wa·ter·mel·on \-ˌmel-ən\ *n* **1 :** a large oblong or roundish fruit with a hard green or white rind often striped or variegated, a sweet watery pink, yellowish, or red pulp, and many seeds **2 :** a widely grown African vine (*Citrullus vulgaris*) of the gourd family whose fruits are watermelons

water meter *n* **:** an instrument for recording the quantity of water passing through a particular outlet

water milfoil *n* **:** any of a genus (*Myriophyllum* of the family Haloragaceae) of aquatic plants with finely pinnate submersed leaves

water mill *n* **:** a mill whose machinery is moved by water

water moccasin *n* **1 :** a venomous semiaquatic pit viper (*Agkistrodon piscivorus*) of the southern U.S. closely related to the copperhead **2 :** an American water snake (genus *Natrix*)

water mold *n* **:** an aquatic fungus (as of the genus *Saprolegnia*)

water nymph *n* **:** a nymph (as a naiad, Nereid, or Oceanid) associated with a body of water

water oak *n* **:** any of numerous American oaks that thrive in wet soils

water of constitution : water so combined into a molecule that it cannot be removed without disrupting the entire molecule — compare WATER OF HYDRATION

water of crystallization : water of hydration present in many crystallized substances that is usu. essential for maintenance of a particular crystal structure

water of hydration : water that is chemically combined with a substance to form a hydrate and can be expelled (as by heating) without essentially altering the composition of the substance — compare WATER OF CONSTITUTION

water ouzel *n* **:** any of several birds (genus *Cinclus* and esp. *C. cinclus* and *C. mexicanus*) that are related to the thrushes and are not web-footed but dive into swift mountain streams and walk on the bottom in search of food — called also *dipper*

water parting *n* **:** a summit or boundary line separating the drainage districts of two streams or coasts

water pepper *n* **:** an annual smartweed (*Polygonum hydropiper*) of moist soils with extremely acrid peppery juice

water pimpernel *n* **:** either of two small white-flowered herbs (*Samolus valerandi* of Europe and *S. floribundus* of the U.S.) of the primrose family that grow in wet places

water pipe *n* **1 :** a pipe for conveying water **2 :** a tobacco smoking device that consists of a bowl mounted on a vessel of water which is provided with a long tube and so arranged that the smoke is drawn through the water where it is cooled and up the tube to the mouth

water pistol *n* **:** a toy pistol designed to throw a jet of liquid — called also *water gun, squirt gun*

water plantain *n* **:** any of a genus (*Alisma* of the family Alismaceae, the water-plantain family) of marsh or aquatic herbs with acrid sap and scapose 3-petaled flowers

water polo *n* **:** a goal game similar to soccer that is played in water by teams of swimmers using a ball resembling a soccer ball

wa·ter·pow·er \ˈwȯt-ər-ˌpau̇(-ə)r, ˈwät-\ *n* **1 a :** the power of water employed to move machinery **b :** a fall of water suitable for such use **2 :** a water privilege for a mill

water privilege *n* **:** the right to use water esp. as a source of mechanical power

[1]**wa·ter·proof** \ˌwȯt-ər-ˈprüf, ˌwät-\ *adj* **:** impervious to water; *esp* **:** covered or treated with a material (as a solution of rubber) to prevent permeation by water — **wa·ter·proof·ness** *n*

[2]**waterproof** \ˈwȯt-ər-ˌ, ˈwät-\ *n* **1 :** a waterproof fabric **2** *chiefly Brit* **:** RAINCOAT

[3]**waterproof** \ˌwȯt-ər-ˈ, ˌwät-\ *vt* **:** to make waterproof

wa·ter·proof·er \ˈwȯt-ər-ˈprü-fər, ˌwät-\ *n* **:** one that waterproofs something (as roofs or fabrics)

wa·ter·proof·ing \-ˈprü-fiŋ\ *n* **1 a :** the act or process of making something waterproof **b :** the condition of being made waterproof **2 :** something (as a coating) capable of imparting waterproofness

water race *n* **:** [1]RACE 2c

water rat *n* **1 :** a rodent that frequents water **2 :** a waterfront loafer or petty thief

wa·ter–re·pel·lent \ˌwȯt-ə(r)-ri-ˈpel-ənt, ˌwät-\ *adj* **:** treated with a finish that is resistant but not impervious to penetration by water

wa·ter–re·sis·tant \-ri-ˈzis-tənt\ *adj* **:** WATER-REPELLENT

water right *n* **:** a right to the use of water (as for irrigation); *esp* **:** RIPARIAN RIGHT

water sapphire *n* **:** a deep blue cordierite sometimes used as a gem

wa·ter·scape \ˈwȯt-ər-ˌskāp, ˈwät-\ *n* **:** a water or sea view **:** SEASCAPE 1

water scorpion *n* **:** any of numerous aquatic bugs (family Nepidae) with the end of the abdomen prolonged by a long breathing tube

wa·ter·shed \ˈwȯt-ər-ˌshed, ˈwät-\ *n* **1 :** WATER PARTING **2 :** a region or area bounded peripherally by a water parting and draining ultimately to a particular watercourse or body of water **3 :** a crucial dividing point or line

water shield *n* **:** an aquatic plant (*Brasenia schreberi*) of the water-lily family having floating oval leaves with a gelatinous coating and small dull purple flowers; *also* **:** any of a related genus (*Cabomba*)

[1]**wa·ter·side** \ˈwȯt-ər-ˌsīd, ˈwät-\ *n* **:** the margin of a body of water **:** WATERFRONT

[2]**waterside** *adj* **1 :** of, relating to, or located on the waterside <a ~ café> **2 :** employed along the waterside <~ workers>; *also* **:** of or relating to the workers along the waterside <a ~ strike>

water ski *n* **:** a ski used in planing over water while being towed by a speedboat — **wa·ter–ski** *vi*

wa·ter–ski·er \ˈwȯt-ər-ˌskē-ər, ˈwät-\ *n* **:** one that water-skis

wa·ter·ski·ing \-ˌskē-iŋ\ *n* **:** the art or sport of planing and jumping on water skis

water snake *n* **:** any of numerous snakes (esp. genus *Natrix*) that frequent or inhabit fresh waters and feed largely on aquatic animals

wa·ter–soak \ˈwȯt-ər-ˌsōk, ˈwät-\ *vt* **:** to soak in water

water spaniel *n* **:** a rather large spaniel that has a heavy curly coat and is used esp. for retrieving waterfowl

water spot *n* **:** any of several diseases of fruits characterized by water-soaked lesions

wa·ter·spout \ˈwȯt-ər-ˌspau̇t, ˈwät-\ *n* **1 :** a pipe, duct, or orifice from which water is spouted or through which it is carried **2 :** a funnel-shaped or tubular column of rotating cloud-filled wind usu. extending from the underside of a cumulus or cumulonimbus cloud down to a cloud of spray torn up by the whirling winds from the surface of an ocean or lake

water sprite *n* **:** a sprite believed to inhabit or haunt water **:** WATER NYMPH

water sprout *n* **:** an extremely vigorous but usu. unproductive shoot from an adventitious or latent bud on a tree

water strider *n* **:** any of various long-legged bugs (family Gerridae) that move about on the surface of the water

water strider

water supply *n* **:** source, means, or process of supplying water (as for a community) usu. including reservoirs, tunnels, and pipelines

water system *n* **1 :** a river with its tributaries **2 :** WATER SUPPLY

water table *n* **1 :** a stringcourse or similar member when projecting so as to throw off water **2 :** the upper limit of the portion of the ground wholly saturated with water

water thrush *n* **1 :** any of several No. American warblers (genus *Seiurus*) usu. living in the vicinity of streams **2 :** a European water ouzel (*Cinclus cinclus*)

wa·ter·tight \ˌwȯt-ər-ˈtīt, ˌwät-\ *adj* **1 :** of such tight construction or fit as to be impermeable to water except when under sufficient pressure to produce structural discontinuity **2 :** leaving no possibility of misconstruction or evasion <a ~ lease> — **wa·ter·tight·ness** *n*

water tower *n* **:** a tower or standpipe serving as a reservoir to deliver water at a required head; *specif* **:** a fire apparatus having a vertical pipe that can be extended to various heights and supplied with water under high pressure

water turkey *n* **:** a New World snakebird (*Anhinga anhinga*) that occurs from the southern U.S. to northern Argentina

water vapor *n* **:** water in a vaporous form esp. when below boiling temperature and diffused (as in the atmosphere)

water–vascular system *n* **:** a system of vessels in echinoderms containing a circulating watery fluid that is used for the movement of tentacles and tube feet and may also function in excretion and respiration

water wagon *n* **:** a wagon or motortruck equipped with a tank or barrels for hauling water or for sprinkling — **on the water wagon** **:** abstaining from alcoholic beverages

water wave *n* **:** a method or style of setting hair by dampening with water and forming into waves — **wa·ter–waved** \ˈwȯt-ər-ˌwāvd, ˈwät-\ *adj*

wa·ter·way \ˈwȯt-ər-ˌwā, ˈwät-\ *n* **1 :** a way or channel for water **2 :** a groove at the edge of a ship's deck for draining the deck **3 :** a navigable body of water

wa·ter·weed \-ˌwēd\ *n* **:** any of various aquatic plants (as a pondweed) with inconspicuous flowers — compare WATER LILY

wa·ter·wheel \-ˌhwēl, -ˌwēl\ *n* **1 :** a wheel made to rotate by direct action of water **2 :** a wheel for raising water

waterwheel 1

water wings *n pl* **:** a pneumatic device to give support to the body of a person swimming or learning to swim

water witch *n* **:** one that dowses for water — **water witch·ing** \-ˌwich-iŋ\ *n*

water witch·er \-ˌwich-ər\ *n* **:** WATER WITCH

wa·ter·works \ˈwȯt-ər-ˌwərks, ˈwät-\ *n pl* **1 :** an ornamental fountain or cascade **2 :** the system of reservoirs, channels, mains, and pumping and purifying equipment by which a water supply is obtained and distributed (as to a city) **3 :** the shedding of tears **:** TEARS

wa·ter·worn \-ˌwō(ə)rn, -ˌwȯ(ə)rn\ *adj* **:** worn, smoothed, or polished by the action of water

wa·tery \ˈwȯt-ə-rē, ˈwät-\ *adj* **1 a :** consisting of or filled with water **b :** containing, sodden with, or yielding water or a thin liquid <a ~ solution> <~ vesicles> **2 a :** felt to resemble water or watery matter esp. in thin fluidity, soggy texture, paleness, or lack of savor <~ blood> <~ sunlight> <a ~ soup> **b :** exhibiting weakness and vapidity **:** WISHY-WASHY <a ~ writing style> — **wa·ter·i·ly** \-ə-rə-lē\ *adv* — **wa·ter·i·ness** \-ə-rē-nəs\ *n*

WATS *abbr* Wide Area Telephone Service

Wat·son–Crick model \ˌwät-sən-ˈkrik-\ *n* [J. D. *Watson* *b*1928 Am biologist and F. H. C. *Crick* *b*1916 E biologist] **:** a model deoxyribonucleic acid structure in which the molecule is visualized as a double-stranded helix cross-linked by hydrogen bonds

watt \ˈwät\ *n* [James *Watt* †1819 Sc engineer] **:** the absolute mks unit of power equal to the work done at the rate of one absolute joule per second or to the rate of work represented by a current of one ampere under a pressure of one volt and taken as the standard in the U.S. **:** $^1/_{746}$ horsepower

watt·age \ˈwät-ij\ *n* **:** amount of power expressed in watts

Wat·teau \(ˌ)wä-ˌtō\ *adj* [Antoine *Watteau*] **1** *of women's dress* **:** having back pleats falling loosely from neckline to hem **2** *of a hat* **:** shallow-crowned with wide brim turned up at the back to hold flower trimmings

-watt·er \ˈwät-ər\ *n comb form* **:** one having a specified wattage

watt–hour \ˈwät-ˈau̇(ə)r\ *n* **:** a unit of work or energy equivalent to the power of one watt operating for one hour

[1]**wat·tle** \ˈwät-ᵊl\ *n* [ME *wattel,* fr. OE *watel;* akin to OHG *wadal* bandage] **1 a :** a fabrication of poles interwoven with slender branches, withes, or reeds and used esp. formerly in building **b :** material for such construction **c** *pl* **:** poles laid on a roof to support thatch **2 a :** a fleshy dependent process usu. about the head or neck (as of a bird) — see COCK illustration **b :** [2]BARBEL **3** *Austral* **:** ACACIA 1 — **wat·tled** \-ᵊld\ *adj*

[2]**wattle** *vt* **wat·tled; wat·tling** \ˈwät-liŋ, -ᵊl-iŋ\ **1 :** to form or build of or with wattle **2 a :** to form into wattle **:** interlace to form wattle **b :** to unite or make solid by interweaving light flexible material

wattle and daub *n* **:** a framework of woven rods and twigs covered and plastered with clay and used in building construction

wat·tle·bird \ˈwät-ᵊl-ˌbərd\ *n* **:** any of several Australasian honey eaters (genus *Anthochaera*) having fleshy pendulous ear wattles

watt·me·ter \ˈwät-ˌmēt-ər\ *n* [ISV] **:** an instrument for measuring electric power in watts

waught \ˈwäkt\ *n, chiefly Scot* [Sc *waught* to drink deep, of unknown origin] **:** a copious draft (as of wine or ale)

W Aust *abbr* Western Australia

[1]**wave** \ˈwāv\ *vb* **waved; wav·ing** [ME *waven,* fr. OE *wafian* to wave with the hands; akin to OE *wǣfre* restless — more at WAVER] *vi* **1 :** to float, play, or shake in an air current **:** move loosely to and fro **:** FLUTTER **2 :** to motion with the hands or with something held in them in signal or salute **3** *of water* **:** to move in waves **:** HEAVE **4 :** to become moved or brandished to and fro <his sword *waved* and flashed> **5 :** to move before the wind with a wavelike motion <field of *waving* grain> **6 :** to follow a curving line or take a wavy form **:** UNDULATE ~ *vt* **1 :** to swing (something) back and forth or up and down **2 :** to impart a curving or undulating shape to <*waved* her hair> **3 a :** to motion to (someone) to go in an indicated direction or to stop **:** FLAG, SIGNAL <looked at his papers, then *waved* him on> **b :** to gesture with (the hand or an object) in greeting or farewell or in homage **c :** to dismiss or put out of mind **:** DISREGARD — usu. used with *aside* **d :** to convey by waving <*waved* farewell> **4 :** BRANDISH, FLOURISH <*waved* a pistol menacingly> ***syn*** see SWING

[2]**wave** *n* **1 a :** a moving ridge or swell on the surface of a liquid (as of the sea) **b :** open water **2 a :** a shape or outline having successive curves **b :** a waviness of the hair **c :** an undulating line or streak or a pattern formed by such lines **3 :** something that swells and dies away: as **a :** a surge of sensation or emotion <a ~ of anger swept over her> **b :** a movement sweeping large numbers in a common direction **:** CONTAGION <~*s* of protest> **c :** a peak or climax of activity <a ~ of buying> **4 :** a sweep of hand or arm or of some object held in the hand used as a signal or greeting **5 :** a rolling or undulatory movement or one of a series of such movements passing along a surface or through the air **6 :** a movement like that of an ocean wave: as **a :** a surging movement of a group <a big new ~ of incoming freshmen> **b :** one of a succession of influxes of people migrating into a region **c** (1) **:** a moving group of animals of one kind (2) **:** a sudden

rapid increase in a population **d :** a line of attacking or advancing troops or airplanes **7 a :** a disturbance or variation that transfers energy progressively from point to point in a medium and that may take the form of an elastic deformation or of a variation of pressure, electric or magnetic intensity, electric potential, or temperature **b :** one complete cycle of such a disturbance **8 :** a marked change in temperature : a period of hot or cold weather **9 :** an undulating or jagged line constituting a graphic representation of an action — **wave·like** \ˈwāv-ˌlīk\ *adj*

Wave \ˈwāv\ *n* [*W*omen *A*ccepted for *V*olunteer *E*mergency Service] : a woman serving in the navy

wave band *n* : a band of radio-wave frequencies

waved \ˈwāvd\ *adj* : having a wavelike form or outline: as **a :** marked by undulations : CURVING <the ~ cutting edge of a bread knife> **b :** having wavy lines of color : WATERED <~ cloth>

wave equation *n* : a partial differential equation of the second order whose solutions describe wave phenomena

wave·form \ˈwāv-ˌfȯrm\ *n* : a usu. graphic representation of the shape of a wave that indicates its characteristics (as frequency and amplitude) — called also *waveshape*

wave front *n* : a surface composed at any instant of all the points just reached by a vibrational disturbance in its propagation through a medium

wave·guide \ˈwāv-ˌgīd\ *n* : a metal pipe of usu. circular or rectangular cross section of a dielectric cylinder of such dimensions that it will propagate electromagnetic waves of a given frequency that is used for channeling ultrahigh-frequency waves

wave·length \-ˌleŋ(k)th\ *n* : the distance in the line of advance of a wave from any one point to the next point of corresponding phase

wave·less \-ləs\ *adj* : having no waves — **wave·less·ly** *adv*

wave·let \-lət\ *n* : a little wave : RIPPLE

wave mechanics *n pl but sing or pl in constr* : a theory of matter that is based on the concept of the possession of wave properties by elementary particles (as electrons, protons, or neutrons) and that affords a mathematical interpretation of the structure of matter on the basis of these properties

wave number *n* : the number of waves per unit distance of radiant energy of a given wavelength : the reciprocal of the wavelength

wave of the future : a movement that is viewed as representing forces or a trend that will inevitably prevail

wave packet *n* : a pulse of radiant energy that is the resultant of a number of wave trains of differing wavelengths

[1]**wa·ver** \ˈwā-vər\ *vi* **wa·vered; wa·ver·ing** \ˈwāv-(ə-)riŋ\ [ME *waveren;* akin to OE *wǣfre* restless, *wefan* to weave — more at WEAVE] **1 :** to vacillate irresolutely between choices : fluctuate in opinion, allegiance, or direction **2 a :** to weave or sway unsteadily to and fro : REEL, TOTTER **b :** QUIVER, FLICKER <~*ing* flames> **c :** to hesitate as if about to give way : FALTER **3 :** to give an unsteady sound : QUAVER ***syn*** see SWING, HESITATE — **wa·ver·er** \ˈwā-vər-ər\ *n* — **wa·ver·ing·ly** \ˈwāv-(ə-)riŋ-lē\ *adv*

[2]**waver** *n* : an act of wavering, quivering, or fluttering

[3]**wav·er** \ˈwā-vər\ *n* : one that waves

wa·very \ˈwāv-(ə-)rē\ *adj* : that waves : WAVERING

wave·shape \ˈwāv-ˌshāp\ *n* : WAVEFORM

wave theory *n* : UNDULATORY THEORY

wave train *n* : a succession of similar waves at equal intervals

wav·i·ness \ˈwā-vē-nəs\ *n* : the quality or state of being wavy

wavy \ˈwā-vē\ *adj* **wav·i·er; -est 1 :** rising or swelling in waves; *also* : abounding in waves <~ hair> **2 :** moving with an undulating motion : FLUCTUATING; *also* : marked by wavering **3 :** marked by undulation : ROLLING — **wav·i·ly** \ˈwā-və-lē\ *adv*

waw \ˈväv, ˈvȯv\ *n* [Heb *wāw*] : the 6th letter of the Hebrew alphabet — see ALPHABET table

wa–wa pedal \ˈwä-ˌwä-\ *n* [imit.] : an electronic device that is connected to an amplifier and operated by a foot pedal and that is used (as with an electric guitar) to produce a fluctuating muted effect

[1]**wax** \ˈwaks\ *n* [ME, fr. OE *weax;* akin to OHG *wahs* wax, Lith *vaškas*] **1 :** a substance secreted by bees and used by them for constructing the honeycomb that is dull yellow solid plastic when warm and composed of a mixture of esters, cerotic acid, and hydrocarbons — called also *beeswax* **2 :** any of various substances resembling beeswax: as **a :** any of numerous substances of plant or animal origin that differ from fats in being less greasy, harder, and more brittle and in containing principally esters of higher fatty acids and higher alcohols, free higher acids and alcohols, and saturated hydrocarbons **b :** a solid substance (as ozokerite or paraffin wax) of mineral origin consisting usu. of higher hydrocarbons **c :** a pliable or liquid composition used esp. in uniting surfaces, excluding air, making patterns or impressions, or producing a polished surface **d :** a resinous preparation used by shoemakers for rubbing thread **3 :** something likened to wax as soft, impressionable, or readily molded **4 :** a waxy secretion; *esp* : CERUMEN **5 :** a phonograph recording — **wax·like** \ˈwak-ˌslīk\ *adj*

[2]**wax** *vt* **1 :** to treat or rub with wax usu. for polishing or stiffening **2 :** to record on phonograph records

[3]**wax** *vi* [ME *waxen,* fr. OE *weaxan;* akin to OHG *wahsan* to increase, Gk *auxanein,* L *augēre* — more at EKE] **1 a :** to increase in size, numbers, strength, prosperity, or intensity **b :** to grow in volume or duration **c :** to grow toward full development **2 :** to increase in phase or intensity — used chiefly of the moon, other satellites, and inferior planets **3 :** to assume a (specified) characteristic, quality, or state : BECOME <~ indignant>

[4]**wax** *n* [ME, fr. *waxen* to increase, grow] : INCREASE, GROWTH — usu. used in the phrase *on the wax*

[5]**wax** *n* [perh. fr. [3]*wax*] : a fit of temper : RAGE

wax bean *n* : a kidney bean with pods that turn creamy yellow to bright yellow when mature enough for use as snap beans

wax·ber·ry \ˈwaks-ˌber-ē\ *n* **1 :** the wax-covered fruit of the wax myrtle; *also* : WAX MYRTLE **2 :** SNOWBERRY

wax·bill \-ˌbil\ *n* : any of numerous Old World birds (family Ploceidae and esp. genus *Estrilda*) having white, pink, or reddish bills of a waxy appearance

waxed paper *n* : paper coated or otherwise treated with wax to make it resistant to water and grease and used esp. as a wrapping

wax·en \ˈwak-sən\ *adj* **1 :** made of or covered with wax **2 :** resembling wax: as **a :** easily molded : PLIABLE **b :** seeming to lack vitality or animation : PALLID **c :** lustrously smooth

wax·er \-sər\ *n* : one whose work is applying or polishing with wax

wax·ing *n* : the act of applying wax (as in polishing)

wax insect *n* : a scale insect (family Coccidae) that secretes a wax from its body; *esp* : a Chinese insect (*Ericerus pe-la*) that yields a hard, friable, and commercially important wax

wax light *n* : a wax candle : TAPER

wax moth *n* : a dull brownish or ashen moth (*Galleria mellonella*) with a larva that feeds on the wax of the combs of the honeybee

wax museum *n* : an exhibition of wax effigies (as of famous historical persons)

wax myrtle *n* : any of a genus (*Myrica* of the family Myricaceae, the wax-myrtle family) of trees or shrubs with aromatic foliage; *esp* : an American shrub (*M. cerifera*) having small hard berries with a thick coating of white wax used for candles

wax palm *n* : any of several palms that yield wax: as **a :** an Andean pinnate-leaved palm (*Ceroxylon andicolum*) whose stem yields a resinous wax used in candles **b :** CARNAUBA

wax paper *n* : WAXED PAPER

wax·wing \ˈwak-ˌswiŋ\ *n* : any of several American and Eurasian passerine birds (genus *Bombycilla*) that are chiefly brown with a showy crest and velvety plumage

wax·work \ˈwak-ˌswərk\ *n* **1 :** an effigy in wax usu. of a person **2** *pl but sing or pl in constr* : an exhibition of wax effigies

waxy \ˈwak-sē\ *adj* **wax·i·er; -est 1 :** made of, abounding in, or covered with wax : WAXEN <a ~ surface> <~ berries> **2 :** resembling wax: as **a :** readily shaped or molded **b :** marked by smooth or lustrous whiteness <a ~ complexion> — **wax·i·ness** *n*

[1]**way** \ˈwā\ *n* [ME, fr. OE *weg;* akin to OHG *weg* way, OE *wegan* to move, L *vehere* to carry] **1 a :** a thoroughfare for travel or transportation from place to place **b :** an opening for passage <this door is the only ~ out of the room> **2 :** the course traveled from one place to another : ROUTE **3 a :** a course (as a series of actions or sequence of events) leading in a direction or toward an objective <led the ~ to eventual open heart operations —*Current Biog.*> **b (1) :** a course of action <took the easy ~ out> **(2) :** opportunity, capability, or fact of doing as one pleases <always manages to get her own ~> **c :** a possible decision, action, or outcome : POSSIBILITY <he was rude — there were no two ~*s* about it> **4 a :** manner or method of doing or happening; *also* : method of accomplishing : MEANS **b :** FEATURE, RESPECT <in no ~ resembles her mother> **c :** a usu. specified degree of participation in an activity or enterprise <active in real estate in a small ~> **5 :** characteristic, regular, or habitual manner or mode of being, behaving, or happening <knows nothing of the ~*s* of women> **6 :** the length of a course : DISTANCE <has come a long ~ in her studies> **7 :** movement or progress along a course <working his ~ through college> **8 a :** DIRECTION <is coming this ~> **b :** PARTICIPANT — usu. used in combination <three-*way* discussion> **9 :** state of affairs : CONDITION, STATE <that's the ~ things are> **10 a** *pl but sometimes sing in constr* : an inclined structure upon which a ship is built or supported in launching **b** *pl* : the guiding surfaces on the bed of a machine along which a table or carriage moves **11 :** CATEGORY, KIND — usu. used in the phrase *in the way of* <doesn't require much in the ~ of expensive equipment —*Forbes*> **12 :** motion or speed of a ship or boat through the water ***syn*** see METHOD — **by way of 1 :** for the purpose of **2 :** by the route through : VIA — **in a way 1 :** within limits : with reservations **2 :** from one point of view — **in one's way** *also* **in the way 1 :** in a position to be encountered by one : in or along one's course <an opportunity had been put *in my way* —Ellen Glasgow> **2 :** in a position to hinder or obstruct — **on the way** *or* **on one's way :** moving along in one's course : in progress — **out of the way 1 :** WRONG, IMPROPER <didn't know he'd said anything *out of the way*> **2 a :** in or to a secluded place **b :** UNUSUAL, REMARKABLE <the house wasn't anything *out of the way*> **3 :** DONE, COMPLETED <got his homework *out of the way*>

[2]**way** *adj* : of, connected with, or constituting an intermediate point on a route <visited five major countries plus ~ points>

[3]**way** *adv* **1 :** AWAY 7 <is ~ ahead of the class> **2 :** all the way <pull the switch ~ back> — **from way back :** of long standing <friends *from way back*>

way·bill \ˈwā-ˌbil\ *n* : a document prepared by the carrier of a shipment of goods that contains details of the shipment, route, and charges

way car *n* **1 :** CABOOSE 2 **2 :** a freight car for less-than-carload shipments to way stations

way·far·er \ˈwā-ˌfar-ər, -ˌfer-\ *n* [ME *weyfarere,* fr. *wey, way* way + *-farere* traveler, fr. *faren* to go — more at FARE] : a traveler esp. on foot — **way·far·ing** \-ˌfar-iŋ, -ˌfer-\ *adj*

way·go·ing \ˈwā-ˌgō-ən, -iŋ\ *n, chiefly Scot* : the act of leaving : DEPARTURE

Way·land \ˈwā-lən(d)\ *n* [OE *Wēland*] : a smith of Germanic legend

way·lay \ˈwā-ˌlā\ *vt* **-laid** \-ˌlād\; **-lay·ing :** to lie in wait for or attack from ambush ***syn*** see SURPRISE

way·less \-ləs\ *adj* : having no road or path

Way of the Cross : STATIONS OF THE CROSS

way–out \'wā-'au̇t\ *adj* [*way out* (adverbial phrase), fr. [3]*way* + *out*] **:** FAR-OUT

ways \'wāz\ *n pl but sing in constr* [ME *wayes,* fr. gen. of [1]*way*] **:** WAY 6 <a long ~ from home>

-ways \ˌwāz\ *adv suffix* [ME, fr. *ways,* gen. of *way*] **:** in (such) a way, course, direction, or manner <side*ways*> <flat*ways*>

ways and means *n pl* **1 :** methods and resources for accomplishing something and esp. for defraying expenses **2** *often cap W&M* **a :** methods and resources for raising the necessary revenues for the expenses of a nation or state **b :** a legislative committee concerned with this function

way·side \'wā-ˌsīd\ *n* **:** the side of or land adjacent to a road or path — **wayside** *adj*

way station *n* **1 :** an intermediate station between principal stations on a line of travel (as a railroad) **2 :** an intermediate stopping place

way·ward \'wā-wərd\ *adj* [ME, short for *awayward* turned away, fr. *away,* adv. + *-ward*] **1 :** following one's own capricious, wanton, or depraved inclinations **:** UNGOVERNABLE **2 :** following no clear principle or law **:** UNPREDICTABLE **3 :** opposite to what is desired or expected **:** UNTOWARD <~ fate> ***syn*** see CONTRARY — **way·ward·ly** *adv* — **way·ward·ness** *n*

way·worn \-ˌwō(ə)rn, -ˌwȯ(ə)rn\ *adj* **:** wearied by traveling

WB *abbr* **1** water ballast **2** waybill **3** weather bureau **4** westbound

WBC *abbr* white blood cells

WC *abbr* **1** water closet **2** without charge

WCTU *abbr* Women's Christian Temperance Union

wd *abbr* **1** wood **2** word **3** would

WD *abbr* War Department

we \(')wē\ *pron, pl in constr* [ME, fr. OE *wē;* akin to OHG *wir* we, Skt *vayam*] **1 :** I and the rest of a group that includes me **:** you and I **:** you and I and another or others **:** I and another or others not including you — used as pronoun of the first person plural; compare I, OUR, OURS, US **2 :** [1]I — used by sovereigns; used by writers to keep an impersonal character

weak \'wēk\ *adj* [ME *weike,* fr. ON *veikr;* akin to OE *wīcan* to yield, L *vicis* change — more at WEEK] **1 :** lacking strength: as **a :** deficient in physical vigor **:** FEEBLE, DEBILITATED **b :** not able to sustain or exert much weight, pressure, or strain **c :** not able to resist external force or withstand attack **2 a :** mentally or intellectually deficient **b :** not firmly decided **:** VACILLATING **c :** resulting from or indicating lack of judgment or discernment **d :** not able to withstand temptation or persuasion **3 :** not factually grounded or logically presented <a ~ argument> **4 a :** not able to function properly **b (1) :** lacking skill or proficiency <tutoring for ~*er* students> **(2) :** indicative of a lack of skill or aptitude <math was his ~*est* subject> **c :** wanting in vigor of expression or effect **5 a :** deficient in the usual or required ingredients **:** DILUTE <~ coffee> **b :** lacking normal intensity or potency <~ strain of virus> **6 a :** not having or exerting authority or political power <~ government> **b :** INEFFECTIVE, IMPOTENT **7 :** of, relating to, or constituting a verb or verb conjugation that in English forms the past tense and past participle by adding the suffix *-ed* or *-d* or *-t* **8 a :** bearing the minimal degree of stress occurring in the language <~ syllable> **b :** having little or no stress and obscured vowel sound <*d* is the ~ form of *would*> **9 :** tending toward a lower price <a ~ market> **10 :** ionizing only slightly in solution <~ acids and bases> — **weak·ly** *adv*

syn WEAK, FEEBLE, FRAIL, FRAGILE, INFIRM, DECREPIT *shared meaning element* **:** not strong enough to endure strain, stress, or strenuous effort ***ant*** strong

weak·en \'wē-kən\ *vb* **weak·ened; weak·en·ing** \'wēk-(ə-)niŋ\ *vt* **1 :** to make weak **:** lessen the strength of **2 :** to reduce in intensity or effectiveness ~ *vi* **:** to become weak — **weak·en·er** \-(ə-)nər\ *n*

syn WEAKEN, ENFEEBLE, DEBILITATE, UNDERMINE, SAP, CRIPPLE, DISABLE *shared meaning element* **:** to lose or cause to lose strength, vigor, or energy ***ant*** strengthen

weak·fish \'wēk-ˌfish\ *n* [obs. D *weekvis,* fr. D *week* soft + *vis* fish; fr. its tender flesh] **1 :** a common marine percoid sport and market fish (*Cynoscion regalis*) of the eastern coast of the U.S. — called also *gray trout, sea trout* **2 :** any of several food fishes congeneric with the weakfish

weak·heart·ed \-'härt-əd\ *adj* **:** lacking courage **:** FAINTHEARTED

weak interaction *n* **:** a fundamental interaction experienced by elementary particles that is responsible for some particle decay processes, for nuclear beta decay, and for emission and absorption of neutrinos

weak·ish \'wē-kish\ *adj* **:** somewhat weak <~ tea>

weak–kneed \'wēk-'nēd\ *adj* **:** lacking willpower or resolution

weak·ling \'wē-kliŋ\ *n* **:** one that is weak in body, character, or mind — **weakling** *adj*

weak·ly \'wē-klē\ *adj* **:** FEEBLE, WEAK — **weak·li·ness** *n*

weak–mind·ed \'wēk-'mīn-dəd\ *adj* **:** having or indicating a weak mind: **a :** lacking in judgment or good sense **:** FOOLISH **b :** FEEBLEMINDED — **weak–mind·ed·ness** *n*

weak·ness \-nəs\ *n* **1 :** the quality or state of being weak; *also* **:** an instance or period of being weak <agreed in a moment of ~ to go along> **2 :** FAULT, DEFECT **3 :** an object of special desire or fondness <she's my ~ now>

weak side *n* **:** the side of a football formation having the smaller number of players; *specif* **:** the side of a formation away from the tight end

weak sister *n* **:** a member of a group who needs aid; *also* **:** something that is weak and ineffective as compared with others in the group

[1]weal \'wē(ə)l\ *n* [ME *wele,* fr. OE *wela;* akin to OE *wel* well] **1 :** a sound, healthy, or prosperous state **:** WELL-BEING **2** *obs* **:** BODY POLITIC, COMMONWEAL

[2]weal *n* [alter. of *wale*] **:** WELT

weald \'wē(ə)ld\ *n* [the *Weald,* England] **1 :** a heavily wooded area **:** FOREST <*Weald* of Kent> **2 :** a wild or uncultivated usu. upland region

wealth \'welth\ *n* [ME *welthe,* fr. *wele* weal] **1** *obs* **:** WEAL, WELFARE **2 :** abundance of valuable material possessions or resources **3 :** abundant supply **:** PROFUSION **4 a :** all property that has a money value or an exchangeable value **b :** all material objects that have economic utility; *esp* **:** the stock of useful goods having economic value in existence at any one time <national ~>

wealthy \'wel-thē\ *adj* **wealth·i·er; -est 1 :** having wealth **:** extremely affluent **2 :** characterized by abundance **:** AMPLE ***syn*** see RICH ***ant*** indigent — **wealth·i·ly** \-thə-lē\ *adv* — **wealth·i·ness** \-thē-nəs\ *n*

wean \'wēn\ *vt* [ME *wenen,* fr. OE *wenian* to accustom, wean; akin to OE *wunian* to be used to — more at WONT] **1 :** to accustom (as a child) to take food otherwise than by nursing **2 :** to detach from a cause of dependence or preoccupation **:** free from a usu. unwholesome interest <to ~ your minds from hankering after false . . . standards —A. T. Quiller-Couch> ***syn*** see ESTRANGE ***ant*** addict

wean·er \'wē-nər\ *n* **1 :** one that weans **2 :** a young animal recently weaned from its mother

wean·ling \'wēn-liŋ\ *n* **:** a child or animal newly weaned — **weanling** *adj*

[1]weap·on \'wep-ən\ *n* [ME *wepen,* fr. OE *wǣpen;* akin to ON *vāpn* weapon] **1 :** an instrument of offensive or defensive combat **:** something to fight with **2 :** a means of contending against another

[2]weapon *vt* **:** ARM

weap·on·less \'wep-ən-ləs\ *adj* **:** lacking weapons **:** UNARMED

weap·on·ry \-rē\ *n* **1 :** the science of designing and making weapons **2 :** WEAPONS

[1]wear \'wa(ə)r, 'we(ə)r\ *vb* **wore** \'wō(ə)r, 'wȯ(ə)r\; **worn** \'wō(ə)rn, 'wȯ(ə)rn\; **wear·ing** [ME *weren,* fr. OE *werian;* akin to ON *verja* to clothe, invest, spend, L *vestis* clothing, garment, Gk *hennynai* to clothe] *vt* **1 :** to bear or have on the person <*wore* a coat> **2 a :** to use habitually for clothing or adornment <~*s* a toupee> **b :** to carry on the person <~ a sword> **3 a :** to hold the rank or dignity or position signified by (an ornament) <~ the royal crown> **b :** to have or show an appearance of <*wore* a happy smile> **c :** to show or fly (a flag or colors) on a ship **4 a :** to cause to deteriorate by use **b :** to impair or diminish by use or attrition **:** consume or waste gradually <letters on the stone *worn* away by weathering> **5 :** to produce gradually by friction or attrition <~ a hole in the rug> **6 :** to exhaust or lessen the strength of **:** WEARY, FATIGUE **7 :** to cause (a ship) to go about with the stern presented to the wind ~ *vi* **1 a :** to endure use **:** last under use or the passage of time <material that will ~ for years> **b :** to retain quality or vitality **2 a :** to diminish or decay through use <the heels of his shoes began to ~> **b :** to diminish or fail with the passage of time <the effect of the drug *wore* off> <the day *wore* on> **c :** to grow or become by attrition or use **3** *of a ship* **:** to change to an opposite tack by turning the stern to the wind — compare TACK — **wear·able** \'war-ə-bəl, 'wer-\ *adj* — **wear·er** *n* — **wear on :** IRRITATE, FRAY — **wear stripes :** to serve in prison — **wear the trousers** or **wear the pants :** to have the controlling authority in a household — **wear thin 1 :** to become weak or ready to give way <his patience was *wearing thin*> **2 :** to become trite, unconvincing, or out-of-date <an argument that quickly *wore thin*>

[2]wear *n* **1 :** the act of wearing **:** the state of being worn **:** USE <clothes for everyday ~> **2 a :** clothing or an article of clothing usu. of a particular kind; *esp* **:** clothing worn for a special occasion or popular during a specific period **b :** FASHION, VOGUE **3 :** wearing quality **:** durability under use **4 :** the result of wearing or use **:** diminution or impairment due to use <*wear*-resistant surface>

[1]wear·able \'war-ə-bəl, 'wer-\ *adj* **:** capable of being worn **:** suitable to be worn — **wear·abil·i·ty** \ˌwar-ə-'bil-ət-ē, ˌwer-\ *n*

[2]wearable *n* **:** GARMENT — usu. used in pl.

wear and tear *n* **:** the loss or injury to which something is subjected by or in the course of use; *esp* **:** normal depreciation

wear down *vt* **:** to weary and overcome by persistent resistance or pressure

wea·ri·ful \'wir-ē-fəl\ *adj* **1 :** causing weariness; *esp* **:** TEDIOUS **2 :** full of weariness **:** WEARIED — **wea·ri·ful·ly** \-fə-lē\ *adv* — **wea·ri·ful·ness** *n*

wea·ri·less \'wir-ē-ləs\ *adj* **:** TIRELESS — **wea·ri·less·ly** *adv*

wea·ri·ly \'wir-ə-lē\ *adv* **:** in a weary manner

wea·ri·ness \'wir-ē-nəs\ *n* **:** the quality or state of being weary

[1]wear·ing \'wa(ə)r-iŋ, 'we(ə)r-\ *adj* **:** intended for wear <~ apparel>

[2]wearing *adj* **:** subjecting to or inflicting wear; *esp* **:** causing fatigue <a ~ journey> — **wear·ing·ly** \-iŋ-lē\ *adv*

wea·ri·some \'wir-ē-səm\ *adj* **:** causing weariness **:** TIRESOME — **wea·ri·some·ly** *adv* — **wea·ri·some·ness** *n*

wear out *vt* **1 :** to make useless esp. by long or hard usage **2 :** TIRE, EXHAUST **3 :** ERASE, EFFACE **4 :** to endure through **:** OUTLAST <*wear out* a storm> **5 :** to consume (as time) tediously <*wear out* idle days> ~ *vi* **:** to become useless from long or excessive wear or use

[1]wea·ry \'wi(ə)r-ē\ *adj* **wea·ri·er; -est** [ME *wery,* fr. OE *wērig;* akin to OHG *wuorag* intoxicated, Gk *hōrakian* to faint] **1 :** exhausted in strength, endurance, vigor, or freshness **2 :** expressing or characteristic of weariness **3 :** having one's patience, tolerance, or pleasure exhausted — used with *of* **4 :** WEARISOME

[2]weary *vb* **wea·ried; wea·ry·ing** *vi* **:** to become weary ~ *vt* **:** to make weary ***syn*** see TIRE

wea·sand \'wēz-ᵊnd, 'wiz-ᵊn(d)\ *n* [ME *wesand,* fr. (assumed) OE *wǣsend* gullet; akin to OE *wāsend* gullet, OHG *weisunt* windpipe] **:** THROAT, GULLET; *also* **:** WINDPIPE

[1]wea·sel \'wē-zəl\ *n, pl* **weasels** [ME *wesele,* fr. OE *weosule;* akin to OHG *wisula* weasel, L *virus* slimy liquid, stench — more at

VIRUS] **1** *or pl* **weasel :** any of various small slender active carnivorous mammals (genus *Mustela* of the family **Mustelidae**, the weasel family) that consume small birds and mammals and esp. great numbers of vermin (as mice or rats) and are mostly reddish brown with white or yellowish underparts and in northern forms turn white in winter **2 :** a light self-propelled tracked vehicle built either for traveling over snow, ice, or sand or as an amphibious vehicle

weasel 1

[2]**weasel** *vi* **wea·seled; wea·sel·ing** \ˈwēz-(ə-)liŋ\ [*weasel word*] **1 :** to use weasel words : EQUIVOCATE **2 :** to escape from or evade a situation or obligation — often used with *out*

weasel word *n* [fr. the weasel's reputed habit of sucking the contents out of an egg while leaving the shell superficially intact] **:** a word used in order to evade or retreat from a direct or forthright statement or position

[1]**weath·er** \ˈweth-ər\ *n* [ME *weder*, fr. OE; akin to OHG *wetar* weather, OSlav *vetrŭ* wind] **1 :** state of the atmosphere with respect to heat or cold, wetness or dryness, calm or storm, clearness or cloudiness **2 :** state of life or fortune **3 :** disagreeable atmospheric conditions: as **a :** RAIN, STORM **b :** cold air with dampness **4 :** WEATHERING — **under the weather 1 :** ILL **2 :** DRUNK

[2]**weather** *adj* **:** WINDWARD — compare LEE

[3]**weather** *vb* **weath·ered; weath·er·ing** \ˈweth-(ə-)riŋ\ *vt* **1 :** to expose to the open air : subject to the action of the elements **2 :** to sail or pass to the windward of **3 :** to bear up against and come safely through <~ a storm> ~ *vi* **:** to undergo or endure the action of the elements

weath·er·abil·i·ty \ˌweth-(ə-)rə-ˈbil-ət-ē\ *n* **:** capability of withstanding the weathering process <~ of a plastic>

weath·er–beat·en \ˈweth-ər-ˌbēt-ᵊn\ *adj* **1 :** worn or damaged by exposure to weather **2 :** toughened, tanned, or bronzed by the weather <~ face>

weath·er·board \-ˌbō(ə)rd, -ˌbȯ(ə)rd\ *n* **1 :** CLAPBOARD, SIDING **2 :** the weather side of a ship

weath·er·board·ing \-ˌbōrd-iŋ, -ˌbȯrd-\ *n* **:** CLAPBOARDS, SIDING

weath·er–bound \-ˌbau̇nd\ *adj* **:** kept in port or at anchor or from travel or sport by bad weather

weather bureau *n* **:** a bureau engaged in the collection of weather reports as a basis for weather predictions, storm warnings, and the compiling of statistical records

weath·er–burned \ˈweth-ər-ˌbərnd\ *adj* **:** browned by sun and wind

weath·er·cock \-ˌkäk\ *n* **1 :** a vane often in the figure of a cock mounted so as to turn freely with the wind and show its direction **2 :** a person or thing that changes readily or often

weather deck *n* **:** a deck having no overhead protection from the weather

weath·ered \ˈweth-ərd\ *adj* **1 a :** seasoned by exposure to the weather **b :** altered in color, texture, composition, or form by such exposure or by artificial means producing a similar effect <~ oak> **2 :** made sloping so as to throw off water <~ windowsill>

weather eye *n* **1 :** an eye quick to observe coming changes in the weather **2 :** constant and shrewd watchfulness and alertness

weath·er·glass \ˈweth-ər-ˌglas\ *n* **:** a simple instrument for showing changes in atmospheric pressure by the changing level of liquid in a spout connected with a closed reservoir; *broadly* **:** BAROMETER

weath·er·ing *n* **:** the action of the elements in altering the color, texture, composition, or form of exposed objects; *specif* **:** the physical disintegration and chemical decomposition of earth materials at or near the earth's surface

weath·er·ly \ˈweth-ər-lē\ *adj* **:** able to sail close to the wind with little leeway

weath·er·man \-ˌman\ *n* **:** one who reports and forecasts the weather : METEOROLOGIST

weather map *n* **:** a map or chart showing the principal meteorological elements at a given hour and over an extended region

weath·er·proof \ˌweth-ər-ˈprüf\ *adj* **:** able to withstand exposure to weather without damage or loss of function — **weatherproof** *vt* — **weath·er·proof·ness** *n*

weather ship *n* **:** a ship that makes observations for use by meteorologists

weather station *n* **:** a station for taking, recording, and reporting meteorological observations

weather strip *n* **:** a strip of material to cover the joint of a door or window and the sill, casing, or threshold so as to exclude rain, snow, and cold air — called also *weather stripping* — **weath·er–strip** *vt*

weather vane *n* **:** VANE 1a

weath·er–wise \ˈweth-ər-ˌwīz\ *adj* **1 :** skillful in forecasting changes in the weather **2 :** skillful in forecasting changes in opinion or feeling <a ~ politician>

weath·er·worn \-ˌwō(ə)rn, -ˌwȯ(ə)rn\ *adj* **:** worn by exposure to the weather

[1]**weave** \ˈwēv\ *vb* **wove** \ˈwōv\ *or* **weaved; wo·ven** \ˈwō-vən\ *or* **weaved; weav·ing** [ME *weven*, fr. OE *wefan*; akin to OHG *weban* to weave, Gk *hyphos* web] *vt* **1 a :** to form (cloth) by interlacing strands (as of yarn); *specif* **:** to make (cloth) on a loom by interlacing warp and filling threads **b :** to interlace (as threads) into cloth **c :** to make (as a basket) by intertwining **2 :** SPIN — used of spiders and insects **3 :** to interlace esp. to form a texture, fabric, or design **4 a :** to produce by elaborately combining elements : CONTRIVE **b :** to unite in a coherent whole **c :** to introduce as an appropriate element : work in — usu. used with *in* or *into* **5 :** to direct (as the body) in a winding or zigzag course esp. to avoid obstacles ~ *vi* **1 :** to work at weaving : make cloth **2 :** to move in a devious, winding, or zigzag course esp. to avoid obstacles

[2]**weave** *n* **1 :** something woven; *esp* **:** woven cloth **2 :** any of the patterns or methods for interlacing the threads of woven fabrics

[3]**weave** *vi* **weaved; weav·ing** [ME *weven* to move to and fro, wave; akin to ON *veifa* to wave, Skt *vepate* he trembles] **:** to move waveringly from side to side : SWAY

weav·er \ˈwē-vər\ *n* **1 :** one that weaves esp. as an occupation **2 :** WEAVERBIRD

weav·er·bird \-ˌbərd\ *n* **:** any of numerous Old World passerine birds (family Ploceidae) that resemble finches and mostly construct elaborate nests of interlaced vegetation — called also *weaver*

weaver's knot *n* **:** SHEET BEND — called also *weaver's hitch*

[1]**web** \ˈweb\ *n* [ME, fr. OE; akin to ON *vefr* web, OE *wefan* to weave] **1 :** a fabric on a loom or in process of being removed from a loom **2 a :** COBWEB 1, 2 **b :** SNARE, ENTANGLEMENT **3 :** a tissue or membrane of an animal or plant; *esp* **:** that uniting fingers or toes either at their bases (as in man) or for a greater part of their length (as in many water birds) **4 a :** a thin metal sheet, plate, or strip **b :** the plate connecting the upper and lower flanges of a girder or rail **c :** the arm of a crank **5 :** an intricate structure suggestive of something woven : NETWORK **6 :** the series of barbs implanted on each side of the shaft of a feather : VANE **7 a :** a continuous sheet of paper manufactured or undergoing manufacture on a paper machine **b :** a roll of such paper for use in a rotary printing press **8 :** the part of a ribbed vault between the ribs — **webbed** \ˈwebd\ *adj* — **web·like** \ˈweb-ˌlīk\ *adj*

[2]**web** *vb* **webbed; web·bing** *vt* **1 :** to cover with a web or network **2 :** ENTANGLE, ENSNARE **3 :** to provide with a web ~ *vi* **:** to construct or form a web

web·bing \ˈweb-iŋ\ *n* **1 :** a strong narrow closely woven tape designed for bearing weight and used esp. for straps, harness, or upholstery **2 :** TRAP 3c

web·by \ˈweb-ē\ *adj* **:** of, relating to, or consisting of a web

we·ber \ˈweb-ər, ˈvā-bər\ *n* [Wilhelm E. *Weber* †1891 G physicist] **:** the practical mks unit of magnetic flux equal to that flux which in linking a circuit of one turn produces in it an electromotive force of one volt as the flux is reduced to zero at a uniform rate of one ampere per second : 10^8 maxwells

web·fed \ˈweb-ˌfed\ *adj* **:** of, relating to, or printed by a web press

web·foot *n* **1** \ˈweb-ˈfu̇t\ **:** a foot having webbed toes **2** \-ˌfu̇t\ **:** an animal having web feet — **web–foot·ed** \-ˈfu̇t-əd\ *adj*

web member *n* **:** one of the several members joining the top and bottom chords of a truss or lattice girder

web offset *n* **:** offset printing by web press

web press *n* **:** a press that prints a continuous roll of paper

web spinner *n* **:** an insect that spins a web; *esp* **:** any of an order (Embiodea) of small slender insects with biting mouthparts that live in silken tunnels which they spin

web·ster \ˈweb-stər\ *n* [ME, fr. OE *webbestre* female weaver, fr. *webbian* to weave; akin to OE *wefan* to weave] *archaic* **:** WEAVER

Web·ste·ri·an \web-ˈstir-ē-ən\ *adj* **1 :** of, relating to, or characteristic of the statesman Daniel Webster **2 :** of, relating to, or characteristic of the lexicographer Noah Webster or his dictionary

web·worm \ˈweb-ˌwərm\ *n* **:** any of various caterpillars that are more or less gregarious and spin large webs

wed \ˈwed\ *vb* **wed·ded** *also* **wed; wed·ding** [ME *wedden*, fr. OE *weddian*; akin to MHG *wetten* to pledge, OE *wedd* pledge, OHG *wetti*, Goth *wadi*, L *vad-*, *vas* bail, security] *vt* **1 :** to take for wife or husband by a formal ceremony : MARRY **2 :** to join in marriage **3 :** to unite as if by the bond of marriage ~ *vi* **:** to enter into matrimony — **wed·der** *n*

Wed *abbr* Wednesday

we'd \(ˌ)wēd\ **:** we had : we would : we should

wed·ding \ˈwed-iŋ\ *n, often attrib* **1 :** a marriage ceremony usu. with its accompanying festivities : NUPTIALS **2 :** an act, process, or instance of joining in close association **3 :** a wedding anniversary or its celebration — usu. used in combination

wedding march *n* **:** a march of slow tempo and stately character composed or played to accompany the bridal procession

wedding ring *n* **:** a ring often of plain gold or platinum given by the groom to the bride during the wedding service; *also* **:** a similar ring given by the bride to the groom in a double-ring service

we·del \ˈvād-ᵊl\ *vi* [back-formation fr. *wedeln*] **:** to ski downhill by means of wedeln

we·deln \ˈvād-ᵊln\ *n* [G, fr. *wedeln* to fan, wag the tail, fr. *vedel* fan, tail, fr. OHG *wadal*; akin to ON *vēl* bird's tail] **:** a style of skiing in which a skier moves the rear of the skis quickly from side to side while following the fall line

[1]**wedge** \ˈwej\ *n* [ME *wegge*, fr. OE *wecg*; akin to OHG *wecki* wedge, Lith *vagis*] **1 :** a piece of a substance (as wood or iron) that tapers to a thin edge and is used for splitting wood and rocks, raising heavy bodies, or for tightening by being driven into something **2 a :** something (as a policy) causing a breach or separation **b :** something used to initiate an action or development <a possible ~ for opening up a stalemate on negotiations —*Springfield (Mass.) Republican*> **3 :** something wedge-shaped: as **a :** an array of troops or tanks in the form of a wedge **b :** the wedge-shaped stroke in cuneiform characters **c :** a shoe having a heel extending from the back of the shoe to the front of the shank and a tread formed by an extension of the sole **d :** an iron golf club with a broad low-angled face for maximum loft

[2]**wedge** *vb* **wedged; wedg·ing** *vt* **1 :** to fasten or tighten by driving in a wedge **2 a :** to force or press (something) into a narrow space : CRAM **b :** to force (one's way) into or through

<~*ed* his way into the crowd> **3 :** to separate or force apart with or as if with a wedge ~ *vi* **:** to become wedged
wedged \'wejd, 'wej-əd\ *adj* **:** shaped like a wedge
Wedg·ies \'wej-ēz\ *trademark* — used for shoes having a wedge-shaped piece serving as the heel and joining the half sole to form a continuous flat undersurface
Wedg·wood \'wej-,wu̇d\ *trademark* — used for ceramic wares (as bone china or jasper)
wedgy \'wej-ē\ *adj* **:** resembling a wedge in shape
wed·lock \'wed-,läk\ *n* [ME *wedlok,* fr. OE *wedlāc* marriage bond, fr. *wedd* pledge + *-lāc,* suffix denoting activity] **:** the state of being married **:** MARRIAGE, MATRIMONY — **out of wedlock :** with the natural parents not legally married to each other
Wednes·day \'wenz-dē\ *n* [ME, fr. OE *wōdnesdæg;* akin to ON *ōthinsdagr* Wednesday; both fr. a prehistoric WGmc-NGmc compound whose components are represented by OE *Wōden* Odin, the chief god in Germanic mythology, and by OE *dæg* day] **:** the fourth day of the week — **Wednes·days** \-dēz\ *adv*
wee \'wē\ *adj* [ME *we,* fr. *we,* n., little bit, fr. OE *wǣge* weight; akin to OE *wegan* to move, weigh — more at WAY] **1 :** very small **:** DIMINUTIVE **2 :** very early <~ hours of the morning> ***syn*** see SMALL
[1]**weed** \'wēd\ *n* [ME, fr. OE *wēod;* akin to OS *wiod* weed] **1 a** (1) **:** a plant of no value and usu. of rank growth; *esp* **:** one that tends to overgrow or choke out more desirable plants (2) **:** a weedy growth of plants **b :** an aquatic plant; *esp* **:** SEAWEED **c** (1) **:** TOBACCO (2) **:** MARIJUANA **2 a :** an obnoxious growth, thing, or person <militarism is a tough ~ to kill —F. S. Oliver> **b :** something like a weed in detrimental quality; *esp* **:** an animal unfit to breed from
[2]**weed** *vi* **:** to remove weeds or something harmful ~ *vt* **1 a :** to clear of weeds <~ a garden> **b** (1) **:** to free from something hurtful or offensive (2) **:** to remove the less desirable portions of **:** CULL **2 :** to get rid of (something harmful or superfluous) — often used with *out*
[3]**weed** *n* [ME *wede,* fr. OE *wǣd, gewǣde;* akin to ON *vāth* cloth, clothing, Lith *austi* to weave] **1 :** GARMENT — often used in pl. **2 a :** dress worn as a sign of mourning (as by a widow) — usu. used in pl. **b :** a band of crape worn on a man's hat as a sign of mourning — usu. used in pl.
weed·er \'wēd-ər\ *n* **:** one that weeds; *specif* **:** any of various devices for freeing an area from weeds
weed·less \'wēd-ləs\ *adj* **:** free from weeds <a ~ garden>
weedy \'wēd-ē\ *adj* **1 :** abounding with or consisting of weeds <~ pastures> **2 :** resembling a weed esp. in rank growth or ready propagation **3 :** noticeably lean and scrawny **:** LANKY <light carriage with its pair of ~ young horses —Joseph Hergesheimer> — **weed·i·ness** *n*
week \'wēk\ *n* [ME *weke,* fr. OE *wicu, wucu;* akin to OHG *wehha* week, L *vicis* change, alternation, OE *wīr* wire — more at WIRE] **1 a :** one of a series of seven-day cycles used in various calendars **b** (1) **:** a week beginning with a specified day or containing a specified holiday <the ~ of the 18th> <Easter ~> (2) **:** a week appointed for public recognition of some cause <Fire Prevention *Week*> **2 a :** any seven consecutive days **b :** a series of regular working, business, or school days during each seven-day period **3 :** a time seven days before or after a specified day
week·day \'wēk-,dā\ *n* **:** a day of the week except Sunday or sometimes except Saturday and Sunday
week·days \-,dāz\ *adv* **:** on weekdays repeatedly **:** on any weekday <takes a bus ~>
[1]**week·end** \'wē-,kend\ *n* **:** the end of the week; *specif* **:** the period between the close of one working or business or school week and the beginning of the next
[2]**weekend** *vi* **:** to spend the weekend
weekend bag *n* **:** a traveling bag of a size to carry clothing and personal articles for a weekend trip — called also *weekend case*
week·end·er \'wē-'ken-dər\ *n* **1 :** one that vacations or visits for a weekend **2 :** WEEKEND BAG
week·ends \'wē-,ken(d)z\ *adv* **:** on weekends repeatedly **:** on any weekend <travels ~>
[1]**week·ly** \'wē-klē\ *adv* **:** every week **:** once a week **:** by the week
[2]**weekly** *adj* **1 :** occurring, appearing, or done weekly **2 :** reckoned by the week
[3]**weekly** *n, pl* **weeklies :** a weekly newspaper or periodical
week·night \'wēk-,nīt\ *n* **:** a weekday night
week·nights \-,nīts\ *adv* **:** on weeknights repeatedly **:** on any weeknight
ween \'wēn\ *vt* [ME *wenen,* fr. OE *wēnan;* akin to ON *væna* to hope, L *venus* love, charm — more at WIN] *archaic* **:** IMAGINE
wee·nie *var of* WIENIE
wee·ny \'wē-nē\ *also* **ween·sy** \'wēn(t)-sē\ *adj* [*wee* + *tiny*] **:** exceptionally small **:** TINY
weep \'wēp\ *vb* **wept** \'wept\; **weep·ing** [ME *wepen,* fr. OE *wēpan;* akin to OHG *wuoffan* to weep, OSlav *vabiti* to call to] *vt* **1 :** to express deep sorrow for usu. by shedding tears **:** BEWAIL **2 :** to pour forth (tears) from the eyes **3 :** to exude (a fluid) slowly **:** OOZE ~ *vi* **1 :** to express passion (as grief) by shedding tears **2 a :** to give off or leak fluid slowly **:** OOZE **b** *of a fluid* **:** to flow sluggishly or in drops **3 :** to droop over **:** BEND
weep·er \'wē-pər\ *n* **1 a :** one that weeps **b :** a professional mourner **2 :** a small statue of a figure in mourning on a funeral monument **3 :** a badge of mourning worn esp. in the 18th and 19th centuries **4** *pl* **:** long and flowing side-whiskers
weep·ing \'wē-piŋ\ *adj* **1 :** TEARFUL **2 :** RAINY **3 :** having slender pendent branches
weeping willow *n* **:** an Asiatic willow (*Salix babylonica*) with weeping branches
weepy \'wē-pē\ *adj* **:** inclined to weep **:** TEARFUL
weet \'wēt\ *vb* [ME *weten,* alter. of *witen* — more at WIT] *archaic* **:** KNOW
wee·ver \'wē-vər\ *n* [ONF *wivre* viper — more at WYVERN] **:** any of several edible marine percoid fishes (family Trachinidae) with a broad spinose head and venomous spines on the dorsal fin
wee·vil \'wē-vəl\ *n* [ME *wevel,* fr. OE *wifel;* akin to OHG *wibil* beetle, OE *wefan* to weave] **:** any of numerous mostly small beetles (group Rhynchophora) having the head elongated and usu. curved downward to form a snout bearing the jaws at the tip and including many very injurious esp. as larvae to nuts, fruit, and grain or to living plants — **wee·viled** *or* **wee·villed** \-vəld\ *adj* — **wee·vily** *or* **wee·vil·ly** \'wēv-(ə-)lē\ *adj*

weevil

weft \'weft\ *n* [ME, fr. OE; akin to ON *veptr* weft, OE *wefan* to weave — more at WEAVE] **1 a :** [1]WOOF 1a **b :** yarn used for the woof **2 :** WEB, FABRIC; *also* **:** an article of woven fabric
weft–knit·ted \-,nit-əd\ *adj* **:** produced in machine knitting with the yarns running crosswise or in a circle
wei·ge·la \wī-'jē-lə\ *n* [NL, genus name, fr. Christian E. *Weigel* †1831 G physician] **:** any of a genus (*Weigela*) of showy shrubs of the honeysuckle family; *esp* **:** one (*W. florida*) of China widely grown for its pink or red flowers
[1]**weigh** \'wā\ *vb* [ME *weyen,* fr. OE *wegan* to move, carry, weigh — more at WAY] *vt* **1 :** to ascertain the heaviness of by or as if by a balance **2 a :** OUTWEIGH **b :** COUNTERBALANCE **c :** to make heavy **:** WEIGHT **3 :** to consider carefully esp. by balancing opposing factors or aspects in order to reach a choice or conclusion **:** EVALUATE **4 :** to heave up (an anchor) preparatory to sailing **5 :** to measure or apportion (a definite quantity) on or as if on a scales ~ *vi* **1 a :** to have weight or a specified weight **b :** to register a weight (as on a scales) — used with *in* or *out* — compare WEIGH IN **2 :** to merit consideration as important **:** COUNT <evidence will ~ heavily against him> **3 a :** to press down with or as if with a heavy weight **b :** to have a saddening or disheartening effect **4 :** to weigh anchor ***syn*** see CONSIDER — **weigh·able** \'wā-ə-bəl\ *adj* — **weigh·er** *n*
[2]**weigh** *n* [alter. of *way*] **:** WAY — used in the phrase *under weigh*
weigh down *vt* **1 :** to cause to bend down **:** OVERBURDEN **2 :** OPPRESS, DEPRESS
weigh–in \'wā-,in\ *n* **:** an act or instance of weighing in as a contestant esp. in sport
weigh in \(')wā-'in\ *vi* **1 :** to have oneself or one's possessions (as baggage) weighed; *esp* **:** to have oneself weighed in connection with an athletic contest **2 :** to enter as a participant
[1]**weight** \'wāt\ *n* [ME *wight, weght,* fr. OE *wiht;* akin to ON *vætt* weight, OE *wegan* to weigh] **1 a :** the amount that a thing weighs **b** (1) **:** the standard or established amount that a thing should weigh (2) **:** one of the classes into which contestants in a sports event are divided according to body weight (3) **:** poundage required to be carried by a horse in a handicap race **2 a :** a quantity or thing weighing a fixed and usu. specified amount **b :** a heavy object (as a metal ball) thrown, put, or lifted as an athletic exercise or contest **3 a :** a unit of weight or mass — see METRIC SYSTEM table **b :** a piece of material (as metal) of known specified weight for use in weighing articles **c :** a system of related units of weight **4 a :** something heavy **:** LOAD **b :** a heavy object to hold or press something down or to counterbalance **5 a :** BURDEN, PRESSURE **b :** the quality or state of being ponderous **c :** CORPULENCE **6 a :** relative heaviness **b :** the force with which a body is attracted toward the earth or a celestial body by gravitation and which is equal to the product of the mass by the local gravitational acceleration **7 a :** the relative importance or authority accorded something **b :** measurable influence esp. upon others **8 :** overpowering force **9 :** the quality (as lightness) that makes a fabric or garment suitable for a particular use or season — often used in combination <summer-*weight*> **10 :** a numerical coefficient assigned to an item to express its relative importance in a frequency distribution ***syn*** see IMPORTANCE, INFLUENCE
[2]**weight** *vt* **1 a :** to load or make heavy with or as if with a weight **b :** to increase in heaviness by adding an ingredient **2 :** to oppress with a burden <~*ed* down with cares> **3 a :** WEIGH 1 **b :** to feel the weight of **:** HEFT **4 :** to assign a statistical weight to **5 :** to cause to incline in a particular direction by manipulation <the tax structure . . . which was ~*ed* so heavily in favor of the upper classes —A. S. Link> **6 :** to shift the burden of weight upon
weight·ed *adj* **1 :** made heavy **:** LOADED <~ silk> **2 a :** having a statistical weight attached **b :** compiled from weighted data <~ arithmetic mean>
weight·less \'wāt-ləs\ *adj* **:** having little weight **:** lacking apparent gravitational pull — **weight·less·ly** *adv* — **weight·less·ness** *n*
weight lifter *n* **:** one that lifts barbells in competition or as an exercise — **weight lifting** *n*
weight man *n* **:** an athlete who competes in any of the field events in which a weight is thrown or put
weighty \'wāt-ē\ *adj* **weight·i·er; -est 1 a :** of much importance or consequence **:** MOMENTOUS **b :** SOLEMN **2 a :** weighing a considerable amount **b :** heavy in proportion to its bulk <~ metal> **3 :** POWERFUL, TELLING <~ arguments> ***syn*** see HEAVY — **weight·i·ly** \'wāt-ᵊl-ē\ *adv* — **weight·i·ness** \'wāt-ē-nəs\ *n*
wei·ma·ra·ner \,vī-mə-'rän-ər, ,wī-; 'vī-mə-,, 'wī-\ *n* [G, fr. *Weimar,* Germany] **:** any of a German breed of large gray short-haired sporting dogs
wei·ner \'wē-nər, 'wē-nē, 'win-ē\ *var of* WIENER
weir \'wa(ə)r, 'we(ə)r, 'wi(ə)r\ *n* [ME *were,* fr. OE *wer;* akin to ON *ver* fishing place, OHG *werien, werren* to defend, L *aperire* to open, *operire* to close, cover] **1 :** a fence or enclosure set in a waterway for taking fish **2 :** a dam in a stream to raise the water level or divert its flow
[1]**weird** \'wi(ə)rd\ *n* [ME *wird, werd,* fr. OE *wyrd;* akin to ON *urthr* fate, OE *weorthan* to become — more at WORTH] **1 :** FATE, DESTINY; *esp* **:** ill fortune **2 :** SOOTHSAYER
[2]**weird** *adj* [[1]*weird*] **1 :** of, relating to, or caused by witchcraft or the supernatural **:** MAGICAL **2 :** of strange or extraordinary character **:** ODD, FANTASTIC — **weird·ly** *adv* — **weird·ness** *n*
syn WEIRD, EERIE, UNCANNY *shared meaning element* **:** mysteriously strange or fantastic

WEIGHTS AND MEASURES[1]

UNIT	ABBR. OR SYMBOL	EQUIVALENTS IN OTHER UNITS OF SAME SYSTEM	METRIC EQUIVALENT
		WEIGHT *avoirdupois*	
ton			
short ton		20 short hundredweight, 2000 pounds	0.907 metric tons
long ton		20 long hundredweight, 2240 pounds	1.016 metric tons
hundredweight	cwt		
short hundredweight		100 pounds, 0.05 short tons	45.359 kilograms
long hundredweight		112 pounds, 0.05 long tons	50.802 kilograms
pound	lb *or* lb av *also* #	16 ounces, 7000 grains	0.453 kilograms
ounce	oz *or* oz av	16 drams, 437.5 grains	28.349 grams
dram	dr *or* dr av	27.343 grains, 0.0625 ounces	1.771 grams
grain	gr	0.036 drams, 0.002285 ounces	0.0648 grams
		troy	
pound	lb t	12 ounces, 240 pennyweight, 5760 grains	0.373 kilograms
ounce	oz t	20 pennyweight, 480 grains	31.103 grams
pennyweight	dwt *also* pwt	24 grains, 0.05 ounces	1.555 grams
grain	gr	0.042 pennyweight, 0.002083 ounces	0.0648 grams
		apothecaries'	
pound	lb ap	12 ounces, 5760 grains	0.373 kilograms
ounce	oz ap *or* ℥	8 drams, 480 grains	31.103 grams
dram	dr ap *or* ʒ	3 scruples, 60 grains	3.887 grams
scruple	s ap *or* ℈	20 grains, 0.333 drams	1.295 grams
grain	gr	0.05 scruples, 0.002083 ounces, 0.0166 drams	0.0648 grams
		CAPACITY *U.S. liquid measure*	
gallon	gal	4 quarts (231 cubic inches)	3.785 liters
quart	qt	2 pints (57.75 cubic inches)	0.946 liters
pint	pt	4 gills (28.875 cubic inches)	0.473 liters
gill	gi	4 fluidounces (7.218 cubic inches)	118.291 milliliters
fluidounce	fl oz *or* *f* ℥	8 fluidrams (1.804 cubic inches)	29.573 milliliters
fluidram	fl dr *or* *f* ʒ	60 minims (0.225 cubic inches)	3.696 milliliters
minim	min *or* ♏	1/60 fluidram (0.003759 cubic inches)	0.061610 milliliters
		U.S. dry measure	
bushel	bu	4 pecks (2150.42 cubic inches)	35.238 liters
peck	pk	8 quarts (537.605 cubic inches)	8.809 liters
quart	qt	2 pints (67.200 cubic inches)	1.101 liters
pint	pt	1/2 quart (33.600 cubic inches)	0.550 liters
		British imperial liquid and dry measure	
bushel	bu	4 pecks (2219.36 cubic inches)	0.036 cubic meters
peck	pk	2 gallons (554.84 cubic inches)	0.009 cubic meters
gallon	gal	4 quarts (277.420 cubic inches)	4.545 liters
quart	qt	2 pints (69.355 cubic inches)	1.136 liters
pint	pt	4 gills (34.678 cubic inches)	568.26 cubic centimeters
gill	gi	5 fluidounces (8.669 cubic inches)	142.066 cubic centimeters
fluidounce	fl oz *or* *f* ℥	8 fluidrams (1.7339 cubic inches)	28.416 cubic centimeters
fluidram	fl dr *or* *f* ʒ	60 minims (0.216734 cubic inches)	3.5516 cubic centimeters
minim	min *or* ♏	1/60 fluidram (0.003612 cubic inches)	0.059194 cubic centimeters
		LENGTH	
mile	mi	5280 feet, 320 rods, 1760 yards	1.609 kilometers
rod	rd	5.50 yards, 16.5 feet	5.029 meters
yard	yd	3 feet, 36 inches	0.9144 meters
foot	ft *or* ′	12 inches, 0.333 yards	30.480 centimeters
inch	in *or* ″	0.083 feet, 0.027 yards	2.540 centimeters
		AREA	
square mile	sq mi *or* m^2	640 acres, 102,400 square rods	2.590 square kilometers
acre		4840 square yards, 43,560 square feet	0.405 hectares, 4047 square meters
square rod	sq rd *or* rd^2	30.25 square yards, 0.006 acres	25.293 square meters
square yard	sq yd *or* yd^2	1296 square inches, 9 square feet	0.836 square meters
square foot	sq ft *or* ft^2	144 square inches, 0.111 square yards	0.093 square meters
square inch	sq in *or* in^2	0.007 square feet, 0.00077 square yards	6.451 square centimeters
		VOLUME	
cubic yard	cu yd *or* yd^3	27 cubic feet, 46,656 cubic inches	0.765 cubic meters
cubic foot	cu ft *or* ft^3	1728 cubic inches, 0.0370 cubic yards	0.028 cubic meters
cubic inch	cu in *or* in^3	0.00058 cubic feet, 0.000021 cubic yards	16.387 cubic centimeters

[1] For U.S. equivalents of metric units see Metric System table

weird·ie \ˈwi(ə)rd-ē\ *or* **weirdy** *n, pl* **weird·ies** : one that is extraordinarily strange, eccentric, or queer

weirdo \ˈwi(ə)rd-(ˌ)ō\ *n, pl* **weird·os** : WEIRDIE

Weird Sisters *n pl* : FATES

wei·sen·hei·mer *var of* WISENHEIMER

Weis·mann·ism \ˈwī-smə-ˌniz-əm, ˈvī-\ *n* : the theories of heredity proposed by August Weismann stressing particularly the continuity of the germ plasm and the separateness of the germ cells and soma

weka \ˈwek-ə\ *n* [Maori] : any of several flightless New Zealand rails (genus *Gallirallus*)

welch \ˈwelch\, **welcher** *var of* WELSH, WELSHER

Welch \ˈwelch\ *var of* WELSH

¹wel·come \ˈwel-kəm\ *interj* [ME, alter. of *wilcume,* fr. OE, fr. *wilcuma* desirable guest; akin to OHG *willicomo* desirable guest; prob. both fr. a prehistoric WGmc compound whose constituents are represented by OE *willa, will* desire and by OE *cuma* guest; akin to OE *cuman* to come — more at WILL, COME] — used to express a greeting to a guest or newcomer upon his arrival

²welcome *vt* **wel·comed; wel·com·ing 1 :** to greet hospitably and with courtesy or cordiality **2 :** to accept with pleasure the occurrence of <~*s* danger> — **wel·com·er** *n*

³welcome *adj* **1 :** received gladly into one's presence or companionship <was always ~ in their home> **2 :** giving pleasure : received with gladness or delight esp. in response to a need <a ~ relief> **3 :** willingly permitted or admitted <he was ~ to come and go —W. M. Thackeray> *syn* see PLEASANT *ant* unwelcome — **wel·come·ly** *adv* — **wel·come·ness** *n*

⁴welcome *n* : a greeting or reception upon arrival

¹weld \ˈweld\ *vb* [alter. of obs. E *well* to weld, fr. ME *wellen* to boil, well, weld] *vi* : to become or be capable of being welded ~ *vt* **1 a :** to unite (metallic parts) by heating and allowing the metals to flow together or by hammering or compressing with or without previous heating **b :** to unite (plastics) in a similar manner by heating **c :** to repair (as an article) by this method **d :** to produce or create as if by such a process **2 :** to unite or reunite closely or intimately — **weld·able** \ˈwel-də-bəl\ *adj*

²weld *n* **1 :** a welded joint **2 :** union by welding : the state or condition of being welded

weld·er \ˈwel-dər\ *n* : one that welds: as **a** *or* **weldor :** one whose work is welding **b :** a machine used in welding

ə abut ᵊ kitten ər further a back ā bake ä cot, cart
aü out ch chin e less ē easy g gift i trip ī life
j joke ŋ sing ō flow ȯ flaw ȯi coin th thin t͟h this
ü loot u̇ foot y yet yü few yu̇ furious zh vision

weld·ment \ˈwel(d)-mənt\ *n* **:** a unit formed by welding together an assembly of pieces

[1]**wel·fare** \ˈwel-ˌfa(ə)r, -ˌfe(ə)r\ *n* [ME, fr. the phrase *wel faren* to fare well] **1 :** the state of doing well esp. in respect to good fortune, happiness, well-being, or prosperity **2 :** WELFARE WORK **3 :** RELIEF 2b

[2]**welfare** *adj* **1 :** of, relating to, or concerned with welfare and esp. with improvement of the welfare of disadvantaged social groups <~ legislation> **2 :** receiving public welfare benefits <~ mothers>

welfare state *n* **1 :** a social system based upon the assumption by a political state of primary responsibility for the individual and social welfare of its citizens **2 :** a nation or state characterized by the operation of the welfare state system

welfare work *n* **:** organized efforts by a community or organization for the social betterment of a group in society — **welfare worker** *n*

wel·far·ism \ˈwel-ˌfa(ə)r-ˌiz-əm, -ˌfe(ə)r-\ *n* **:** the complex of policies, attitudes, and beliefs associated with the welfare state — **wel·far·ist** \-əst\ *n or adj*

wel·kin \ˈwel-kən\ *n* [ME, lit., cloud, fr. OE *wolcen;* akin to OHG *wolkan* cloud, OSlav *vlaga* moisture] **1 a :** the vault of the sky **:** FIRMAMENT **b :** the celestial abode of God or the gods **:** HEAVEN **2 :** the upper atmosphere

[1]**well** \ˈwel\ *n* [ME *welle,* fr. OE (northern & Midland dial.) *welle;* akin to OHG *wella* wave, OE *weallan* to bubble, boil] **1 a :** an issue of water from the earth **:** a pool fed by a spring **b :** FOUNTAIN, WELLSPRING **2 :** a pit or hole sunk into the earth to reach a supply of water **3 a :** an enclosure in the middle of a ship's hold to protect from damage and facilitate the inspection of the pumps **b :** a compartment in the hold of a fishing boat in which fish are kept alive **4 :** a shaft or hole sunk to obtain oil, brine, or gas **5 :** an open space extending vertically through floors of a structure **6 :** a space having a construction or shape suggesting a well for water **7 a :** something resembling a well in being damp, cool, deep, or dark **b :** a deep vertical hole **c :** a source from which something may be drawn as needed **8 :** a pronounced minimum of a variable in physics <a potential ~>

[2]**well** *vb* [ME *wellen,* fr. OE (northern & Midland dial.) *wellan* to cause to well; akin to MHG *wellen* to cause to well, OE *weallan* to bubble, boil, L *volvere* to roll — more at VOLUBLE] *vi* **1 :** to rise to the surface and usu. flow forth <tears ~*ed* from her eyes> **2 :** to rise to the surface like a flood of liquid <longing ~*ed* up in his breast> ~ *vt* **:** to emit in a copious free flow

[3]**well** *adv* **bet·ter** \ˈbet-ər\; **best** \ˈbest\ [ME *wel,* fr. OE; akin to OHG *wela* well, OE *wyllan* to wish — more at WILL] **1 a :** in a good or proper manner **:** JUSTLY, RIGHTLY **b :** satisfactorily with respect to conduct or action <did ~ in math> **2 :** in a kindly or friendly manner <spoke ~ of your idea> **3 a :** with skill or aptitude **:** EXPERTLY <paints ~> **b :** SATISFACTORILY **c :** with good appearance or effect **:** ELEGANTLY <carried himself ~> **4 :** with careful or close attention **:** ATTENTIVELY **5 :** to a high degree <~ deserved the honor> <*well*-equipped kitchen> **6 :** FULLY, QUITE <~ worth the price> **7 a :** in a way appropriate to the facts or circumstances **:** FITTINGLY, RIGHTLY **b :** in a prudent manner **:** SENSIBLY — used with *do* **8 :** in accordance with the occasion or circumstances **:** NATURALLY <cannot ~ refuse> **9 a :** as one could wish **:** FAVORABLY **b :** with material success **:** ADVANTAGEOUSLY <married ~> **10 a :** EASILY, READILY <could ~ afford a new car> **b :** in all likelihood **:** INDEED <it may ~ be true> **11 :** in a prosperous or affluent manner <he lives ~> **12 :** to an extent approaching completeness **:** THOROUGHLY <after being ~ dried with a sponge> **13 :** without doubt or question **:** CLEARLY <~ knew the penalty> **14 :** in a familiar manner <knew her ~> **15 :** to a large extent or degree **:** CONSIDERABLY, FAR <~ over a million> — **as well 1 :** in addition **:** ALSO <there were other features *as well*> **2 :** to the same extent or degree **:** as much <open *as well* to the poor as to the rich> **3 :** with equivalent or comparable effect <might just *as well* have stayed home> — **as well as :** and in addition **:** AND <skillful *as well as* strong>

[4]**well** *interj* **1** — used to express surprise or expostulation **2** — used to indicate resumption of a thread of discourse or to introduce a remark

[5]**well** *adj* **1 :** being in good standing or favor **2 :** SATISFACTORY, PLEASING <all's ~ that ends well> **3 a :** PROSPEROUS, WELL-OFF **b :** being in satisfactory condition or circumstances **4 :** ADVISABLE, DESIRABLE <it might be ~ for you to leave> **5 a :** free or recovered from infirmity or disease **:** HEALTHY <a ~ man> **b :** completely cured or healed <the wound is nearly ~> **6 :** pleasing or satisfactory in appearance **7 :** being a cause for thankfulness **:** FORTUNATE <it is ~ that this has happened> ***syn*** see HEALTHY ***ant*** unwell, ill — **well·ness** *n*

we'll \(ˌ)wē(ə)l, wil\ **:** we will **:** we shall

well–ad·vised \ˌwel-əd-ˈvīzd\ *adj* **1 :** acting with wisdom, wise counsel, or proper deliberation **:** PRUDENT **2 :** resulting from, based on, or showing careful deliberation or wise counsel <~ plans>

well–ap·point·ed \ˌwel-ə-ˈpȯint-əd\ *adj* **:** having good and complete equipment **:** properly fitted out <a ~ house>

wel·la·way \ˌwel-ə-ˈwā, ˈwel-ə-ˌ\ *interj* [ME *welaway,* fr. OE *weilāwei,* lit., woe! lo! woe!, alter. of *wālāwā,* fr. *wā* woe + *lā* lo + *wā* woe — more at WOE] — used to express sorrow or lamentation

well–be·ing \ˈwel-ˈbē-iŋ\ *n* **:** the state of being happy, healthy, or prosperous **:** WELFARE

well–be·loved \ˌwel-bi-ˈləvd\ *adj* **1 :** sincerely and deeply loved <my ~ wife> **2 :** sincerely respected — used in various ceremonial forms of address

well·born \ˈwel-ˈbȯ(ə)rn\ *adj* **:** born of good stock either socially or genetically

well–bred \-ˈbred\ *adj* **1 :** having or displaying good breeding **:** REFINED **2 :** having a good pedigree <~ swine>

well–con·di·tioned \ˌwel-kən-ˈdish-ənd\ *adj* **1 :** characterized by proper disposition, morals, or behavior **2 :** having a good physical condition **:** SOUND <a ~ animal>

well–de·fined \ˌwel-di-ˈfīnd\ *adj* **1 :** having clearly distinguishable limits, boundaries, or features <a ~ scar> **2 :** clearly stated or described <~ policies>

well–dis·posed \-dis-ˈpōzd\ *adj* **:** having a good disposition; *esp* **:** disposed to be friendly, favorable, or sympathetic

well–done \ˈwel-ˈdən\ *adj* **1 :** rightly or properly performed **2 :** cooked thoroughly

Wel·ler·ism \ˈwel-ə-ˌriz-əm\ *n* [Sam *Weller,* witty servant of Mr. Pickwick in the story *Pickwick Papers* (1836-37) by Charles Dickens] **:** an expression of comparison comprising a usu. well-known quotation followed by a facetious sequel (as "'every one to his own taste,' said the old woman as she kissed the cow")

well–fa·vored \ˈwel-ˈfā-vərd\ *adj* **:** good-looking **:** HANDSOME — **well–fa·vored·ness** *n*

well–fixed \-ˈfikst\ *adj* **:** having plenty of money or property

well–found \-ˈfau̇nd\ *adj* **:** fully furnished **:** properly equipped <a ~ ship>

well–found·ed \-ˈfau̇n-dəd\ *adj* **:** based on excellent reasoning, information, judgment, or grounds

well–groomed \-ˈgrümd, -ˈgru̇md\ *adj* **1 :** well dressed and scrupulously neat <~ men> **2 :** made neat, tidy, and attractive down to the smallest details <a ~ lawn>

well–ground·ed \-ˈgrau̇n-dəd\ *adj* **:** having a firm foundation <~ in Latin and Greek>

well–han·dled \-ˈhan-dᵊld\ *adj* **1 :** managed or administered efficiently **2 :** having been handled a great deal <~ goods on a store counter>

well·head \ˈwel-ˌhed\ *n* **1 :** the source of a spring or a stream **2 :** principal source **:** FOUNTAINHEAD **3 :** the top of or a structure built over a well

well–heeled \-ˈhē(ə)ld\ *adj* **:** having plenty of money **:** WELL-FIXED

Wel·ling·ton \ˈwel-iŋ-tən\ *n* [Arthur Wellesley, 1st Duke of *Wellington*] **:** a leather boot having a loose top with the front usu. coming above the knee

well–in·ten·tioned \ˌwel-in-ˈten-chənd\ *adj* **:** WELL-MEANING

well–knit \ˈwel-ˈnit\ *adj* **:** firmly knit <a ~ group>; *esp* **:** firmly and strongly constructed, compacted, or framed <a ~ drama>

well–known \-ˈnōn\ *adj* **:** fully or widely known

well–mean·ing \-ˈmē-niŋ\ *adj* **:** having or based on good intentions <~ but misguided idealists>

well–nigh \-ˈnī\ *adv* **:** ALMOST, NEARLY

well–off \-ˈȯf\ *adj* **1 :** being in easy or affluent circumstances **:** WELL-TO-DO **2 :** suggesting prosperity <the house had a sleek ~ look> ***syn*** see RICH

well–or·dered \-ˈȯrd-ərd\ *adj* **1 :** having an orderly procedure or arrangement <a ~ household> **2 :** partially ordered with every subset containing a first element and exactly one of the relationships greater than, equal to, or less than holding for any given pair of elements

well–or·der·ing \-ˈȯrd-(ə-)riŋ\ *n* **:** an instance of being well-ordered

well–read \-ˈred\ *adj* **:** well informed or deeply versed through reading <~ in history>

well–round·ed \-ˈrau̇n-dəd\ *adj* **:** fully or broadly developed: as **a :** having a broad educational background <a ~ gentleman> **b :** COMPREHENSIVE <a ~ program of activities>

well–set \-ˈset\ *adj* **1 :** well or firmly established <~ in his own values —William Johnson> **2 :** strongly built <a ~ young man>

well–spo·ken \ˈwel-ˈspō-kən\ *adj* **1 :** speaking well, fitly, or courteously **2 :** spoken with propriety <~ words>

well·spring \-ˌspriŋ\ *n* **1 :** a source of continual supply **2 :** FOUNTAINHEAD 1

well–tak·en \-ˈtā-kən\ *adj* **:** WELL-GROUNDED, JUSTIFIABLE <his chief and ~ point>

well–thought–of \wel-ˈthȯt-ˌəv, -ˌäv\ *adj* **:** being of good repute

well–timed \ˈwel-ˈtīmd\ *adj* **:** happening at an opportune moment **:** TIMELY <a ~ announcement>

well–to–do \ˌwel-tə-ˈdü\ *adj* **:** having more than adequate financial resources **:** PROSPEROUS <a ~ family> ***syn*** see RICH

well–turned \ˈwel-ˈtərnd\ *adj* **1 :** symmetrically shaped or rounded **:** SHAPELY **2 :** concisely and appropriately expressed <a ~ phrase> **3 :** expertly rounded or turned <a ~ column>

well–wish·er \ˈwel-ˌwish-ər, -ˈwish-\ *n* **:** one that wishes well to another — **well–wish·ing** \-iŋ\ *adj or n*

well–worn \-ˈwō(ə)rn, -ˈwȯ(ə)rn\ *adj* **1 a :** having been much used or worn <~ shoes> **b :** made trite by overuse **:** HACKNEYED <a ~ quotation> **2 :** worn well or properly <~ honors>

Wels·bach \ˈwelz-ˌbak, -ˌbäk\ *trademark* — used for a burner for producing gaslight by the combustion of a mixture of air and gas or vapor to heat to incandescence a gas mantle or for the mantle used with such a burner

welsh \ˈwelsh, ˈwelch\ *vi* [prob. fr. *Welsh,* adj.] **1 :** to avoid payment — used with *on* <~*ed* on his debts> **2 :** to break one's word **:** go back on <~*ed* on his promises> — **welsh·er** *n*

Welsh \ˈwelsh *also* ˈwelch\ *n* [ME *Walsche, Welsse,* fr. *walisch, welisch,* adj., Welsh, fr. OE (northern & Midland dial.) *wælisc, welisc* Celtic, Welsh, foreign, fr. OE *Wealh* Celt, Welshman, foreigner, of Celtic origin; akin to the source of L *Volcae,* a Celtic people of southeastern Gaul] **1** *pl in constr* **:** the natives or inhabitants of Wales **2 :** the Celtic language of the Welsh people **3 :** a breed of cattle or of swine developed in Wales — **Welsh** *adj*

Welsh cor·gi \-ˈkȯr-gē\ *n* [W *corgi,* fr. *cor* dwarf + *ci* dog] **:** a short-legged long-backed dog with foxy head that is known in two varieties of Welsh origin

Welsh·man \-mən\ *n* **:** a native or inhabitant of Wales

Welsh rabbit *n* **:** melted often seasoned cheese poured over toast or crackers

Welsh rare·bit \-ˈra(ə)r-bət, -ˈre(ə)r-\ *n* [by alter.] **:** WELSH RABBIT

Welsh springer spaniel *n* **:** any of a Welsh breed of red and white or orange and white small-eared springer spaniels

Welsh terrier *n* : any of a breed of wiry-coated terriers resembling airedales but smaller and developed in Wales for hunting

Welsh corgi

Welsh·wom·an \ˈwelsh-ˌwu̇m-ən *also* ˈwelch-\ *n* : a female native or inhabitant of Wales
¹welt \ˈwelt\ *n* [ME *welte*] **1** : a strip between a shoe sole and upper through which they are stitched or stapled together **2** : a doubled edge, strip, insert, or seam (as on a garment) for ornament or reinforcement **3 a** : a ridge or lump raised on the body usu. by a blow **b** : a heavy blow
²welt *vt* **1** : to furnish with a welt **2 a** : to raise a welt on the body of **b** : to hit hard
welt·an·schau·ung \ˈvel-ˌtän-ˌshau̇-əŋ, -tən-\ *n, pl* **weltanschauungs** \-əŋz\ *or* **welt·an·schau·ung·en** \-əŋ-ən\ *often cap* [G, fr. *welt* world + *anschauung* view] : a comprehensive conception or apprehension of the world esp. from a specific standpoint
¹wel·ter \ˈwel-tər\ *vi* **wel·tered; wel·ter·ing** \-t(ə-)riŋ\ [ME *welteren;* akin to MD *welteren* to roll, OHG *walzan,* L *volvere* — more at VOLUBLE] **1 a** : WRITHE, TOSS; *also* : WALLOW **b** : to rise and fall or toss about in or with waves **2** : to become deeply sunk, soaked, or involved **3** : to be in turmoil
²welter *n* **1** : a state of wild disorder : TURMOIL **2** : a chaotic mass or jumble <a bewildering ~ of data>
³welter *n* [prob. fr. ¹*welt*] : WELTERWEIGHT
wel·ter·weight \ˈwel-tər-ˌwāt\ *n* [³*welter*] : a boxer who weighs more than 135 but not more than 147 pounds
welt·schmerz \ˈvelt-ˌshme(ə)rts\ *n, often cap* [G, fr. *welt* world + *schmerz* pain] **1** : mental depression or apathy caused by comparison of the actual state of the world with an ideal state **2** : a mood of sentimental sadness
¹wen \ˈwen\ *n* [ME *wenn,* fr. OE; akin to MLG *wene* wen] : a cyst formed by obstruction of a sebaceous gland and filled with sebaceous material
²wen *n* [OE] : a rune adopted into the Old English alphabet with the value of Modern English *w*
¹wench \ˈwench\ *n* [ME *wenche,* short for *wenchel* child, fr. OE *wencel;* akin to OHG *winchan* to stagger — more at WINK] **1 a** : a young woman : GIRL **b** : a female servant **2** : a lewd woman : PROSTITUTE
²wench *vi* : to consort with lewd women; *esp* : to practice fornication — **wench·er** *n*
wend \ˈwend\ *vb* [ME *wenden,* fr. OE *wendan;* akin to OHG *wenten* to turn, OE *windan* to twist — more at WIND] *vi* : to direct one's course : TRAVEL ~ *vt* : to proceed on (one's way) : DIRECT
Wend \ˈwend\ *n* [G *Wende,* fr. OHG *Winida;* akin to OE *Winedas,* pl., Wends] : a member of a Slavic people of eastern Germany
¹Wend·ish \ˈwen-dish\ *adj* : of or relating to the Wends or their language
²Wendish *n* : the West Slavic language of the Wends
went [ME, past & pp. of *wenden*] *past of* GO
wen·tle·trap \ˈwent-ᵊl-ˌtrap\ *n* [D *wenteltrap* winding stair, fr. MD *wendeltrappe,* fr. *wendel* turning + *trappe* stairs] : any of a family (Epitoniidae) of marine snails with usu. white shells; *also* : one of the shells
wept *past of* WEEP
were [ME *were* (suppletive sing. past subj. & 2d sing. past indic. of *been* to be), *weren* (suppletive past pl. of *been*), fr. OE *wǣre* (sing. past subj. & 2d sing. past indic. of *wesan* to be), *wǣron* (past pl. indic. of *wesan*), *wǣren* (past pl. subj. of *wesan*) — more at WAS] *past 2d sing, past pl, or past subjunctive of* BE
we're \(ˌ)wi(ə)r, (ˌ)wər, ˌwē-ər\ : we are
weren't \(ˈ)wərnt, ˈwər-ənt\ : were not
were·wolf \ˈwi(ə)r-ˌwu̇lf, ˈwe(ə)r-, ˈwər-\ *n, pl* **were·wolves** \-ˌwu̇lvz\ [ME, fr. OE *werwulf;* akin to OHG *werwolf* werewolf; both fr. a prehistoric WGmc compound whose constituents are represented by OE *wer* man and by OE *wulf* wolf — more at VIRILE, WOLF] : a person transformed into a wolf or capable of assuming a wolf's form : LYCANTHROPE
wer·gild \ˈwər-ˌgild\ *or* **wer·geld** \-ˌgeld\ *n* [ME *wergeld,* fr. OE; akin to OHG *wergelt* wergild; both fr. a prehistoric WGmc compound whose constituents are represented by OE *wer* man and by OE *gield, geld* payment, tribute — more at GELD] : the value set in Anglo-Saxon and Germanic law upon the life of a man in accordance with his rank and paid as compensation to the kindred or lord of a slain person
wert \(ˈ)wərt\ *archaic past 2d sing of* BE
wes·kit \ˈwes-kət\ *n* [alter. of *waistcoat*] : VEST 2a
Wes·ley·an·ism \ˈwes-lē-ə-ˌniz-əm *also* ˈwez-\ *n* : METHODISM 1; *specif* : the system of Arminian Methodism taught by John Wesley — **Wes·ley·an** \-lē-ən\ *adj or n*
¹west \ˈwest\ *adv* [ME, fr. OE; akin to OHG *westar* to the west and prob. to L *vesper* evening, Gk *hesperos*] : to, toward, or in the west
²west *adj* **1** : situated toward or at the west <the ~ exit> **2** : coming from the west <a ~ wind>
³west *n* **1 a** : the general direction of sunset : the direction to the left of one facing north **b** : the place on the horizon where the sun sets when it is near one of the equinoxes **c** : the compass point directly opposite to east **2** *cap* **a** : regions or countries lying to the west of a specified or implied point of orientation **b** : the noncommunist countries of Europe and America **3** : the end of a church opposite the chancel **4** *often cap* **a** : the one of four positions at 90-degree intervals that lies to the west or to the left of South **b** : a person (as a bridge player) occupying this position in the course of a specified activity
west·bound \ˈwes(t)-ˌbau̇nd\ *adj* : traveling or headed west
west by north : a compass point one point north of due west : N78°45′W
west by south : a compass point one point south of due west : S78°45′W
¹west·er \ˈwes-tər\ *vi* **west·ered; west·er·ing** \-t(ə-)riŋ\ [ME *westren,* fr. ¹*west*] : to turn or move westward <the half moon ~*s* low —A. E. Housman>
²wester *n* [²*west*] : a westerly wind; *esp* : a storm from the west
¹west·er·ly \ˈwes-tər-lē\ *adj or adv* [obs. *wester* (western)] **1** : situated toward or belonging to the west <the ~ end of the farm> **2** : coming from the west <a ~ breeze>
²westerly *n, pl* **-lies** : a wind from the west
¹west·ern \ˈwes-tərn\ *adj* [ME *westerne,* fr. OE; akin to OHG *westrōni* western, OE *west*] **1** *cap* : of, relating to, or characteristic of a region conventionally designated West: as **a** : steeped in or stemming from the Greco-Roman traditions **b** : European rather than Slavic in character **c** : of or relating to the noncommunist countries of Europe and America **2 a** : lying toward the west **b** : coming from the west <~ wind> **3** *cap* : of or relating to the Roman Catholic or Protestant segment of Christianity <*Western* liturgies> — **west·ern·most** \-ˌmōst\ *adj*
²western *n* **1** : one that is produced in or characteristic of a western region and esp. the western U.S. **2** *often cap* : a novel, story, motion picture, or broadcast dealing with life in the western U.S. esp. during the latter half of the 19th century
West·ern·er \ˈwes-tə(r)-nər\ *n* **1** : a native or inhabitant of the West; *esp* : a native or resident of the western part of the U.S. **2** : one advocating the adoption of western European culture esp. in 19th century Russia
western hemisphere *n* : the half of the earth comprising No. and So. America and surrounding waters
west·ern·iza·tion \ˌwes-tər-nə-ˈzā-shən\ *n, often cap* : conversion to or adoption of western traditions or techniques
west·ern·ize \ˈwes-tər-ˌnīz\ *vb* **-ized; -iz·ing** *vt* : to imbue with qualities native to or associated with a western region and esp. the noncommunist countries of Europe and America ~ *vi* : to become westernized
western saddle *n, often cap W* : STOCK SADDLE
West Germanic *n* : a subdivision of the Germanic languages including English, Frisian, Dutch, and German — see INDO-EUROPEAN LANGUAGES table
West Highland *n* [fr. *West Highlands,* western part of the Highlands of Scotland] : any of a breed of small very hardy beef cattle from the Highlands of Scotland
West Highland white terrier *n* : a small white long-coated dog of a breed developed in Scotland
west·ing \ˈwes-tiŋ\ *n* : westerly progress : a going westward
Westm *abbr* **1** Westmeath **2** Westmorland
west–northwest *n* : a compass point that is two points north of due west : N67°30′W
West·pha·lian ham \wes(t)-ˌfāl-yən-, -ˌfā-lē-ən-\ *n* [*Westphalia,* Germany] : a ham of distinctive flavor produced by smoking with juniper brush
West Saxon *n* **1** : a native or inhabitant of the West Saxon kingdom **2** : a dialect of Old English used as the chief literary dialect in pre-Conquest England
west–southwest *n* : a compass point that is two points south of due west : S67°30′W
¹west·ward \ˈwes-twərd\ *adv or adj* : toward the west — **west·wards** \-twərdz\ *adv*
²westward *n* : westward direction or part <sail to the ~>
¹wet \ˈwet\ *adj* **wet·ter; wet·test** [ME, partly fr. pp. of *weten* to wet & partly fr. OE *wǣt* wet; akin to ON *vātr* wet, OE *wæter* water] **1 a** : consisting of, containing, covered with, or soaked with liquid (as water) **b** *of natural gas* : containing appreciable quantities of readily condensable hydrocarbons **2** : RAINY **3** : still moist enough to smudge or smear <~ paint> **4 a** : DRUNK <a ~ driver> **b** (1) : permitting the manufacture and sale of alcoholic liquor <a ~ county> (2) : advocating a policy of permitting such traffic <a ~ candidate> **5** : preserved in liquid **6** : employing or done by means of or in the presence of water or other liquid <~ extraction of copper> — **wet·ly** *adv* — **wet·ness** *n*
syn WET, DAMP, DANK, MOIST, HUMID *shared meaning element* : more or less covered with or permeated by liquid *ant* dry
— **all wet** : completely wrong : in error — **wet behind the ears** : IMMATURE, INEXPERIENCED
²wet *n* **1** : WATER; *also* : MOISTURE, WETNESS **2** : rainy weather : RAIN **3** : an advocate of a policy of permitting the sale of intoxicating liquors
³wet *vb* **wet** *or* **wet·ted; wet·ting** [ME *weten,* fr. OE *wǣtan,* fr. *wǣt,* adj.] *vt* **1** : to make wet **2** : to urinate in or on ~ *vi* : to become wet — **wet one's whistle** : to take a drink esp. of liquor
wet·back \ˈwet-ˌbak\ *n* : a Mexican who enters the U.S. illegally (as by wading the Rio Grande)
wet–blan·ket *vt* : to quench or dampen with or as if with a wet blanket : DEPRESS
wet blanket *n* : one who quenches or dampens enthusiasm or pleasure
wet down *vt* : to dampen by sprinkling with water
wet dream *n* : an erotic dream culminating in orgasm and in the male accompanied by seminal emission
weth·er \ˈwet͟h-ər\ *n* [ME, ram, fr. OE; akin to OHG *widar* ram, L *vitulus* calf, *vetus* old, Gk *etos* year] : a male sheep castrated before sexual maturity
wet·land \ˈwet-ˌland, -lənd\ *n* : land or areas (as tidal flats or swamps) containing much soil moisture — usu. used in pl.
wet mop *n* : a long-handled mop for cleaning floors with water

wet–nurse *vt* **1 :** to act as wet nurse to **2 :** to give constant and often excessive care to

wet nurse *n* **:** one that cares for and suckles young not her own

wet suit *n* **:** a close-fitting suit made of material (as sponge rubber) that water will go through but that retains body heat and worn (as by a skin diver) esp. in cold water

wet·ta·bil·i·ty \\ˌwet-ə-ˈbil-ət-ē\\ *n* **:** the quality or state of being wettable **:** the degree to which something can be wet

wet·ta·ble \\ˈwet-ə-bəl\\ *adj* **:** capable of being wetted

wet·ter \\ˈwet-ər\\ *n* **:** one that wets; *also* **:** WETTING AGENT

wetting agent *n* **:** a substance that by becoming adsorbed prevents a surface from being repellent to a wetting liquid and is used esp in mixing solids with liquids or spreading liquids on surfaces

wet·tish \\ˈwet-ish\\ *adj* **:** somewhat wet **:** MOIST

wet wash *n* **:** laundry returned damp and not ironed

we've \\(ˌ)wēv\\ **:** we have

Wex *abbr* Wexford

WFTU *abbr* World Federation of Trade Unions

WGA *abbr* Writers Guild of America

wh *abbr* **1** which **2** white

WH *abbr* watt-hour

¹whack \\ˈhwak, ˈwak\\ *vb* [prob. imit.] *vt* **1 a :** to strike with a smart or resounding blow **b :** to cut with or as if with a whack **:** CHOP **2** *chiefly Brit* **:** to get the better of **:** DEFEAT ~ *vi* **:** to strike a smart or resounding blow — **whack·er** *n*

²whack *n* **1 :** a smart or resounding blow; *also* **:** the sound of or as if of such a blow **2 :** PORTION, SHARE **3 :** CONDITION; *esp* **:** proper working order **4 a :** an opportunity or attempt to do something **b :** a single action or occasion <borrowed $50 all at one ~>

whack·ing \\ˈhwak-iŋ, ˈwak-\\ *adj* **:** very large **:** WHOPPING

whack up *vt* **:** to divide into shares

whacky \\ˈhwak-ē, ˈwak-\\ *var of* WACKY

¹whale \\ˈhwā(ə)l, ˈwā(ə)l\\ *n, pl* **whales** *often attrib* [ME, fr. OE *hwæl;* akin to OHG *hwal* whale] **1** *or pl* **whale :** an aquatic mammal (order Cetacea) that superficially resembles a large fish and is valued commercially for its oil, flesh, and sometimes whalebone; *esp* **:** one of the larger members of this group **2 :** one that is impressive esp. in size <a ~ of a difference>

whale 1

²whale *vi* **whaled; whal·ing :** to engage in whale fishing

³whale *vt* **whaled; whal·ing** [origin unknown] **1 :** LASH, THRASH **2 :** to strike or hit vigorously **3 :** to defeat soundly

whale·back \\ˈhwā(ə)l-ˌbak, ˈwā(ə)l-\\ *n* **:** something shaped like the back of a whale; *specif* **:** a freight steamer with a convex upper deck

whale·boat \\-ˌbōt\\ *n* **1 :** a long narrow rowboat made with both ends sharp and raking, often steered with an oar, and formerly used by whalers for hunting whales **2 :** a long narrow rowboat or motorboat that is sharp and rounded at both ends in the manner of the original whaleboats and is often carried by warships and merchant ships

whale·bone \\-ˌbōn\\ *n* **1 :** a horny substance found in two rows of plates from 2 to 12 feet long attached along the upper jaw of whalebone whales and used esp. to stiffen stays or fans **2 :** an article made of whalebone

whalebone whale *n* **:** any of various usu. large whales (suborder Mysticeti) having whalebone instead of teeth — compare TOOTHED WHALE

whal·er \\ˈhwā-lər, ˈwā-\\ *n* **1 :** a person or ship engaged in whale fishing **2 :** WHALEBOAT 2

whal·ing \\-liŋ\\ *n* **:** the occupation of catching and extracting commercial products from whales

¹wham \\ˈhwam, ˈwam\\ *n* [imit.] **1 :** the loud sound of a hard impact **2 :** a solid blow

²wham *vb* **whammed; wham·ming** *vt* **:** to propel, strike, or beat so as to produce a loud impact ~ *vi* **:** to hit or explode with a loud impact

wham·my \\ˈhwam-ē, ˈwam-\\ *n, pl* **whammies** [prob. fr. ¹*wham*] **1 a :** a supernatural power bringing bad luck **b :** a magic curse or spell **2 :** a potent force or attack; *specif* **:** a paralyzing or lethal blow

¹whang \\ˈhwaŋ, ˈwaŋ\\ *n* [alter. of ME *thong, thwang*] **1** *dial* **a :** THONG **b :** RAWHIDE **2** *Brit* **:** a large piece **:** CHUNK

²whang *vt* **1** *dial* **:** BEAT, THRASH **2 :** to propel or strike with force ~ *vi* **:** to beat or work with force or violence

³whang *n* [imit.] **:** a loud sharp vibrant or resonant sound

⁴whang *vi* **:** to make a whang ~ *vt* **:** to strike with a whang

whan·gee \\hwaŋ-ˈ(g)ē, waŋ-\\ *n* [prob. fr. Chin (Pek) *huang² li²*, fr. *huang²* yellow + *li²* bamboo cane] **1 :** any of several Chinese bamboos (genus *Phyllostachys*) **2 :** a walking stick or riding crop of whangee

whap \\ˈhwäp, ˈwäp\\ *var of* WHOP

wharf \\ˈhwȯrf, ˈwȯrf\\ *n, pl* **wharves** \\ˈhwȯrvz, ˈwȯrvz\\ *also* **wharfs** [ME, fr. OE *hwearf* embankment, wharf; akin to OE *hweorfan* to turn, OHG *hwerban,* Gk *karpos* wrist] **1 :** a structure built along or at an angle from the shore of navigable waters so that ships may lie alongside to receive and discharge cargo and passengers **2** *obs* **:** the bank of a river or the shore of the sea

wharf·age \\ˈhwȯr-fij, ˈwȯr-\\ *n* **1 a :** the provision or the use of a wharf **b :** the handling or stowing of goods on a wharf **2 :** the charge for the use of a wharf **3 :** the wharf accommodations of a place **:** WHARVES

wharf·in·ger \\-fən-jər\\ *n* [irreg. fr. *wharfage*] **:** the operator or manager of a commercial wharf

wharf·mas·ter \\ˈhwȯrf-ˌmas-tər, ˈwȯrf-\\ *n* **:** the manager of a wharf

¹what \\(ˈ)hwät, (ˈ)hwət, (ˈ)wät, (ˈ)wət\\ *pron* [ME, fr. OE *hwæt,* neut. of *hwā* who — more at WHO] **1 a** (1) — used as an interrogative expressing inquiry about the identity, nature, or value of an object or matter <~ is this> <~ is wealth without friends> <~ does he earn> <~ hath God wrought> (2) — often used to ask for repetition of an utterance or part of an utterance not properly heard or understood <you said ~> **b** (1) *archaic* **:** WHO 1 — used as an interrogative expressing inquiry about the identity of a person (2) — used as an interrogative expressing inquiry about the character, nature, occupation, position, or role of a person <~ do you think I am, a fool> <~ is she, that all our swains commend her —Shak.> **c** — used as an exclamation expressing surprise or excitement and frequently introducing a question <~, no breakfast> **d** — used in expressions directing attention to a statement that the speaker is about to make <you know ~> **e** — used at the end of a question to express inquiry about additional possibilities <is it raining, or snowing, or ~> **f** *chiefly Brit* — used at the end of an utterance as a form of tag question <a clever play, ~> **2** *chiefly substand* **:** ⁴THAT 1, WHICH 3, WHO 3 **3 :** that which **:** the one or ones that <no income but ~ he gets from his writings> — sometimes used in reference to a clause or phrase that is yet to come or is not yet complete <gave also, ~ is more valuable, understanding> **4 a :** WHATEVER 1a <say ~ you will> **b** *obs* **:** WHOEVER — **what for 1 :** for what purpose or reason **:** WHY — usu. used with the other words of a question between *what* and *for* <*what* did you do that *for*> except when used alone **2 :** punishment esp. by blows or by a sharp reprimand <gave him *what for* in violent Spanish —*New Yorker*> — **what have you :** what not <novels, plays, short stories, travelogues, and *what have you* —Haldeen Braddy> — **what if 1 :** what will or would be the result if **2 :** what does it matter if — **what it takes :** the qualities or resources needed for success or for attainment of a goal — **what not :** any of various other things that might also be mentioned <paper clips, pins, and *what not*> — **what of 1 :** what is the situation with respect to **2 :** what importance can be assigned to — **what's what :** the true state of things <knows *what's what* when it comes to fashion> — **what though :** what does it matter if <*what though* the rose have prickles, yet 'tis plucked —Shak.>

²what *adv* [ME, fr. OE *hwæt,* fr. *hwæt,* pron.] **1** *obs* **:** WHY **2 :** in what respect **:** HOW <~ does he care> **3** — used to introduce prepositional phrases in parallel construction or a prepositional phrase that expresses cause and usu. has more than one object; used principally before phrases beginning with *with* <~ with unemployment and high prices> <~ with the war, ~ with the sweat, ~ with the gallows, and ~ with poverty, I am custom-shrunk —Shak.>

³what *adj* [¹*what*] **1 a** — used as an interrogative expressing inquiry about the identity, nature, or value of a person, object, or matter <~ minerals do we export> **b :** how remarkable or striking for good or bad qualities — used esp. in exclamatory utterances and dependent clauses <~ mountains> <remember ~ fun we had> <~ a suggestion> <~ a charming girl> **2 a** (1) **:** WHATEVER 1a (2) **:** ANY <ornament of ~ description soever> **b :** the . . . that **:** as much or as many . . . as <rescued ~ survivors they found>

¹what·ev·er \\hwät-ˈev-ər, wät-, (ˌ)(h)wət-\\ *pron* **1 a :** anything or everything that <take ~ you want> **b :** no matter what **c :** what not <buffalo or rhinoceros or ~ —Alan Moorehead> **2 :** WHAT 1a(1) — used to express astonishment or perplexity <~ do you mean by that>

²whatever *adj* **1 a :** any . . . that **:** all . . . that <buy peace . . . on ~ terms could be obtained —C. S. Forester> **b :** no matter what <money, in ~ hands, will confer power —Samuel Johnson> **2 :** of any kind at all — used after the substantive it modifies with *any* or with an expressed or implied negative <in any order ~ —W. G. Moulton> <no food ~>

what·not \\ˈhwät-ˌnät, ˈhwət-, ˈwät-, ˈwət-\\ *n* [*what not?*] **1 :** a nondescript person or thing **2 :** a light open set of shelves for bric-a-brac

what·so·ev·er \\ˌhwät-sə-ˈwev-ər, ˌhwət-, ˌwät-, ˌwət-\\ *pron or adj* **:** WHATEVER

whaup \\ˈhwȯp, ˈwȯp\\ *n, pl* **whaup** *also* **whaups** [imit.] *chiefly Scot* **:** a European curlew (*Numenius arquata*)

wheal \\ˈhwē(ə)l, ˈwē(ə)l\\ *n* [alter. of *wale*] **:** a suddenly formed elevation of the skin surface: as **a :** WELT **b :** a flat burning or itching eminence on the skin

wheat \\ˈhwēt, ˈwēt\\ *n, often attrib* [ME *whete,* fr. OE *hwǣte;* akin to OHG *weizzi* wheat, *hwīz, wīz* white — more at WHITE] **1 :** a cereal grain that yields a fine white flour, is the chief breadstuff of temperate climates, is used also in pastas (as macaroni or spaghetti), and is important in animal feeds **2 :** any of various grasses (genus *Triticum*) of wide climatic adaptability that are cultivated in most temperate areas for the wheat they yield; *esp* **:** an annual cereal grass (*T. aestivum*) known only as a cultigen

wheat bread *n* **:** a bread made of a combination of white and whole wheat flours as distinguished from bread made entirely of white or whole wheat flour

wheat cake *n* **:** a pancake made of wheat flour

wheat·ear \\ˈhwēt-ˌi(ə)r, ˈwēt-\\ *n* [back-formation fr. earlier *wheatears* wheatear, prob. by folk etymology or euphemism fr. *white* + *arse*] **:** a small white-rumped northern bird (*Oenanthe oenanthe*) related to the stonechat and whinchat

wheat·en \\ˈhwēt-ᵊn, ˈwēt-\\ *adj* **:** of, relating to, or made of wheat

wheat germ *n* **:** the embryo of the wheat kernel separated in milling and used esp. as a source of vitamins

wheat rust *n* **:** a destructive disease of wheat caused by rust fungi; *also* **:** a fungus (as *Puccinia graminis*) causing a wheat rust

Wheat·stone bridge \\ˌhwēt-ˌstōn-, ˌwēt-, *chiefly Brit* -stən-\\ *n* [Sir Charles *Wheatstone*] **:** a bridge for measuring electrical resistances that consists of a conductor joining two branches of a circuit

whee \\ˈhwē, ˈwē\\ *interj* — used to express delight or exuberance

whee·dle \ˈhwēd-ᵊl, ˈwēd-\ *vb* **whee·dled; whee·dling** \ˈ(h)wēd-liŋ, -ᵊl-iŋ\ [origin unknown] *vt* **1 :** to influence or entice by soft words or flattery **2 :** to gain or get by wheedling <~ his way into favor> ~ *vi* **:** to use soft words or flattery

[1]**wheel** \ˈhwē(ə)l, ˈwē(ə)l\ *n, often attrib* [ME, fr. OE *hweogol, hwēol;* akin to ON *hvēl* wheel, Gk *kyklos* circle, wheel, Skt *cakra,* L *colere* to cultivate, inhabit, Gk *telos* end] **1 :** a circular frame of hard material that may be solid, partly solid, or spoked and that is capable of turning on an axle **2 :** a contrivance or apparatus having as its principal part a wheel: as **a :** a chiefly medieval instrument of torture designed for mutilating a victim (as by stretching or disjointing) **b :** BICYCLE **c :** any of many revolving disks or drums used as gambling paraphernalia **3 :** an imaginary turning wheel symbolizing the inconstancy of fortune **4 :** something resembling a wheel in shape or motion; *specif* **:** a firework that rotates while burning **5 a :** a curving or circular movement **b :** a rotation or turn usu. about an axis or center; *specif* **:** a turning movement of troops or ships in line in which the units preserve alignment and relative positions as they change direction **6 a :** a moving or essential part of something compared to a machine <the ~*s* of government> **b :** a directing or controlling force **c :** a person of importance esp. in an organization <a big ~> **7 :** the refrain or burden of a song **8 a :** a circuit of theaters or places of entertainment **b :** a sports league **9** *pl, slang* **:** a motor vehicle; *esp* **:** CAR <those who cannot afford ~*s* must . . . hitch a ride —Denis Hayes> — **wheel·less** \ˈhwē(ə)l-ləs, ˈwē(ə)l-\ *adj*

[2]**wheel** *vi* **1 :** to turn on or as if on an axis **:** REVOLVE **2 :** to change direction as if revolving on a pivot <the battalion would have ~*ed* to the flank —Walter Bernstein> <~*ed* about and walked briskly aft —L. C. Douglas> <her mind will ~ around to the other extreme —Liam O'Flaherty> **3 :** to move or extend in a circle or curve <birds in ~*ing* flight> <valleys where young cotton ~*ed* slowly in fanlike rows —William Faulkner> **4 :** to drive or go on or as if on wheels or in a wheeled vehicle ~ *vt* **1 :** to cause to turn on or as if on an axis **:** ROTATE **2 :** to convey or move on or as if on wheels or in a wheeled vehicle; *esp* **:** to drive (a vehicle) at high speed **3 :** to cause to change direction as if revolving on a pivot **4 :** to make or perform in a circle or curve — **wheel and deal :** to pursue one's interest esp. in a shrewd or unscrupulous manner

wheel and axle *n* **:** a mechanical device consisting of a grooved wheel turned by a cord or chain with a rigidly attached axle (as for winding up a weight) together with the supporting standards

wheel animal *n* **:** ROTIFER — called also *wheel animalcule*

[1]**wheel·bar·row** \ˈhwē(ə)l-ˌbar-(ˌ)ō, ˈwē(ə)l-, -ˌbar-ə(-w)\ *n* **:** a small usu. single-wheeled vehicle that is used for carrying small loads and is fitted with handles at the rear by which it can be pushed and guided

[2]**wheelbarrow** *vt* **:** to convey in a wheelbarrow

wheel·base \ˈhwē(ə)l-ˌbās, ˈwē(ə)l-\ *n* **:** the distance in inches between the front and rear axles of an automotive vehicle

wheel bug *n* **:** a large No. American bug (*Arilus cristatus*) that has a high serrated crest on its prothorax and that sucks the blood of other insects

wheel·chair \ˈhwē(ə)l-ˌche(ə)r, ˈwē(ə)l-, -ˌcha(ə)r\ *n* **:** a chair mounted on wheels esp. for the use of invalids

wheeled \ˈhwē(ə)ld, ˈwē(ə)ld\ *adj* **1 :** equipped with wheels <~ vehicles> **2 :** moving or functioning by means of wheels <~ traffic>

wheel·er \ˈhwē-lər, ˈwē-\ *n* **1 :** one that wheels **2 :** a draft animal (as a horse) pulling in the position nearest the front wheels of a wagon **3 :** something (as a vehicle or ship) that has wheels — used esp. in combination <side-*wheeler*>

wheel·er–deal·er \ˌhwē-lər-ˈdē-lər, ˌwē-\ *n* [fr. the vb. phrase *wheel and deal*] **:** a shrewd operator esp. in business or politics

wheel·horse \ˈhwē(ə)l-ˌhȯ(ə)rs, ˈwē(ə)l-\ *n* **1 a :** a horse (as in a tandem) in a position nearest the wheels **b** *chiefly dial* **:** the left-hand one of a pair of horses **2 :** a steady and effective worker esp. in a political body

wheel·house \-ˌhau̇s\ *n* **:** PILOTHOUSE

wheel·ie \ˈhwē-lē, ˈwē-\ *n* **:** a maneuver in which a wheeled vehicle (as a bicycle) is momentarily balanced on its rear wheel or wheels

wheel·ing \ˈhwē-liŋ, ˈwē-\ *n* **1 :** the act or process of one that wheels **2 :** the condition of a road relative to passage on wheels

wheel lock *n* **:** an obsolete gunlock in which sparks are struck from a flint or a piece of iron pyrites by a revolving wheel

wheel·man \ˈhwē(ə)l-mən, ˈwē(ə)l-\ *n* **1 a :** HELMSMAN **b :** the driver of an automobile **2 :** CYCLIST

wheels·man \ˈhwē(ə)lz-mən, ˈwē(ə)lz-\ *n* **:** one who steers with a wheel; *esp* **:** HELMSMAN

wheel·work \ˈhwē(ə)l-ˌwərk, ˈwē(ə)l-\ *n* **:** wheels in gear and their connections in a machine or mechanism

wheel·wright \-ˌrīt\ *n* **:** a man whose occupation is the making or repairing of wheels and wheeled vehicles

[1]**wheen** \ˈhwēn, ˈwēn\ *adj* [ME (Sc) *quheyne,* fr. OE *hwǣne, hwēne,* adv., somewhat, fr. instr. of *hwōn* little, few] *dial Brit* **:** FEW 2

[2]**wheen** *n, dial Brit* **:** a considerable number or amount

[1]**wheeze** \ˈhwēz, ˈwēz\ *vi* **wheezed; wheez·ing** [ME *whesen,* prob. of Scand origin; akin to ON *hvæsa* to hiss; akin to OE *hwǣst* action of blowing, L *queri* to complain] **1 :** to breathe with difficulty usu. with a whistling sound **2 :** to make a sound resembling that of wheezing

[2]**wheeze** *n* **1 :** a sound of wheezing **2 a :** an often repeated and widely known joke used esp. by entertainers **b :** a trite saying or proverb

wheezy \ˈhwē-zē, ˈwē-\ *adj* **wheez·i·er; -est 1 :** inclined to wheeze **2 :** having a wheezing sound — **wheez·i·ly** \-zə-lē\ *adv* — **wheez·i·ness** \-zē-nəs\ *n*

[1]**whelk** \ˈhwelk, ˈwelk, ˈwilk\ *n* [ME *welke,* fr. OE *weoloc;* akin to L *volvere* to turn — more at VOLUBLE] **:** any of numerous large marine snails (as of the genus *Buccinum*); *esp* **:** one (*B. undatum*) much used as food in Europe

[2]**whelk** \ˈhwelk, ˈwelk\ *n* [ME *whelke,* fr. OE *hwylca,* fr. *hwelian* to suppurate] **1 :** PAPULE, PUSTULE **2 :** WELT, WHEAL

whelm \ˈhwelm, ˈwelm\ *vb* [ME *whelmen*] *vt* **1 :** to turn (as a dish or vessel) upside down usu. to cover something **:** cover or engulf completely with usu. disastrous effect **2 :** to overcome in thought or feeling **:** OVERWHELM ~ *vi* **:** to pass or go over something so as to bury or submerge it

[1]**whelp** \ˈhwelp, ˈwelp\ *n* [ME, fr. OE *hwelp;* akin to OHG *hwelf* whelp] **1 a :** one of the young of various carnivorous mammals and esp. of the dog **b :** a young boy or girl **2 :** an ill-considered or despised person or his offspring

[2]**whelp** *vt* **:** to give birth to — used of various carnivores and esp. the dog ~ *vi* **:** to bring forth young

[1]**when** \(ˈ)hwen, (ˈ)wen, (h)wən\ *adv* [ME, fr. OE *hwanne, hwenne;* akin to OHG *hwanne* when, OE *hwā* who — more at WHO] **1 :** at what time <~ will he return> **2 a :** at or during which time **b :** and then **3 :** at a former and usu. less prosperous time <brag fondly of having known him ~ —Vance Packard>

[2]**when** *conj* [ME, fr. OE *hwanne, hwenne,* fr. *hwanne, hwenne,* adv.] **1 a :** at or during the time that **:** WHILE <went fishing ~ he was a boy> **b :** just at the moment that <stop writing ~ the bell rings> **c :** at any or every time that <~ he listens to music, he falls asleep> **2 :** in the event that **:** IF <a contestant is disqualified ~ he disobeys the rules> **3 a :** considering that <why use water at all ~ you can drown in it —Stuart Chase> **b :** in spite of the fact that **:** ALTHOUGH <gave up politics ~ he might have made a great career in it>

[3]**when** \ˌhwen, ˌwen\ *pron* **:** what or which time <in 1934, since ~ he has been working at landscapes and portraits —*Horizon*>

[4]**when** \ˈhwen, ˈwen\ *n* **:** the time in which something is done or comes about <troubled his head very little about the hows and ~*s* of life —Laurence Sterne>

when·as \hwe-ˈnaz, we-, (h)wə-\ *conj* [ME (Sc) *when as,* fr. ME *when* + *as*] *archaic* **:** WHEN

[1]**whence** \(ˈ)hwen(t)s, (ˈ)wen(t)s\ *adv* [ME *whennes,* fr. *whenne* whence (fr. OE *hwanon*) + *-s,* adv. suffix, fr. *-s,* gen. sing. ending; akin to OHG *hwanān* whence, OE *hwā* who] **:** from what place, source, or cause <~ do these questionings well up —S. C. Pepper>

[2]**whence** *conj* **1 :** from what place, source, or cause <inquired ~ the water came —Maria Edgeworth> **2 a :** from or out of which place, source, or cause <the lawless society ~ the ballads sprang —DeLancey Ferguson> **b :** by reason of which fact **:** WHEREFORE <nothing broke — ~ I infer that my bones are not yet chalky —O. W. Holmes †1935>

whence·so·ev·er \ˈhwen(t)(s)-sə-ˌwev-ər, ˈwen(t)(s)-\ *conj* **:** from whatever place or source

[1]**when·ev·er** \hwe-ˈnev-ər, we-, (h)wə-\ *conj* **:** at any or every time that

[2]**whenever** *adv* **:** at whatever time

[1]**when·so·ev·er** \ˈhwen(t)-sə-ˌwev-ər, ˈwen(t)-\ *conj* **:** WHENEVER

[2]**whensoever** *adv, obs* **:** at any time whatever

[1]**where** \(ˈ)hwe(ə)r, (ˈ)hwa(ə)r, (ˈ)we(ə)r, (ˈ)wa(ə)r, (ˌ)(h)wər\ *adv* [ME, fr. OE *hwǣr;* akin to OHG *hwār* where, OE *hwā* who — more at WHO] **1 a :** at, in, or to what place <~ is the house> <~ are we going> **b :** at, in, or to what situation, position, direction, circumstances, or respect <~ does this plan lead> <~ is he wrong> **2** *archaic* **:** HERE, THERE <lo, ~ it comes again —Shak.>

[2]**where** *conj* **1 a :** at, in, or to what place <knows ~ the house is> **b :** at, in, or to what situation, position, direction, circumstances, or respect <shows ~ the plan leads> **2 :** WHEREVER <goes ~ he likes> **3 a :** at, in, or to which place <the town ~ she lives> **b :** at or in which <has reached the size ~ traffic is a problem> **4 a :** at, in, or to the place at, in, or to which <stay ~ you are> <send him away ~ he'll forget> **b :** in a case, situation, or respect in which <outstanding ~ endurance is called for>

[3]**where** \ˈhwe(ə)r, ˈhwa(ə)r, ˈwe(ə)r, ˈwa(ə)r\ *n* **1 :** PLACE, LOCATION <the ~ and the how of the accident> **2 :** what place, source, or cause <~ is he from>

[1]**where·abouts** \-ə-ˌbau̇ts\ *also* **where·about** \-ˌbau̇t\ *adv* [ME *wherabouts* (fr. *wher aboute* + *-s,* adv. suffix) & *wher aboute,* fr. *where, wher* where + *about, aboute* about — more at WHENCE] **:** about where **:** near what place <~ is the house>

[2]**whereabouts** *also* **whereabout** *conj* **1** *obs* **:** on what business or errand **2 :** near what place **:** WHERE <know ~ he lives>

[3]**whereabouts** *n pl but sing or pl in constr, also* **whereabout :** the place or general locality where a person or thing is <his present ~ are a secret>

[1]**where·as** \hwer-ˈaz, hwar-, wer-, war-, (ˌ)(h)wər-\ *conj* [ME *where as,* fr. *where* + *as*] **1 :** in view of the fact that **:** SINCE — used esp. to introduce a preamble **2 a :** while on the contrary **b :** ALTHOUGH

[2]**whereas** *n* **1 :** an introductory statement of a formal document **:** PREAMBLE **2 :** a conditional or qualifying statement

where·at \-ˈat\ *conj* **1 :** at or toward which **2 :** in consequence of which **:** WHEREUPON

[1]**where·by** \hwe(ə)r-ˈbī, hwa(ə)r-, we(ə)r-, wa(ə)r-, (ˌ)(h)wər-\ *conj* **:** by, through, or in accordance with which

[2]**whereby** *adv, obs* **:** by what **:** HOW

[1]**where·fore** \ˈhwe(ə)r-ˌfō(ə)r, ˈhwa(ə)r-, ˈwe(ə)r-, ˈwa(ə)r-, -ˌfȯ(ə)r\ *adv* [ME *wherfor, wherfore,* fr. *where, wher* + *for, fore* for] **1 :** for what reason or purpose **:** WHY **2 :** THEREFORE

[2]**wherefore** *n* **:** an answer or statement giving an explanation **:** REASON <wants to know the whys and ~*s*>

where·from \-ˌfrəm, -ˌfräm\ *conj* **:** from which

1**where·in** \hwer-ˈin, hwar-, wer-, war-, (ˌ)(h)wər-\ *adv* : in what : in what particular or respect <~ was he wrong>
2**wherein** *conj* **1 a** : in which : WHERE <the city ~ he lives> **b** : during which **2** : in what way : HOW <showed him ~ he was wrong>
where·in·to \-ˈin-(ˌ)tü, -tə(-w)\ *conj* : into which
1**where·of** \-ˈəv, -ˈäv\ *conj* **1** : of what <knows ~ she speaks> **2 a** : of which <books ~ the best are lost> **b** : of whom **3** *archaic* : with or by which
2**whereof** *adv, archaic* : of what <~ are you made —Shak.>
1**where·on** \-ˈȯn, -ˈän\ *conj* **1** *archaic* : on what <tell me ~ the likelihood depends —Shak.> **2** : on which <the base ~ it rests>
2**whereon** *adv, archaic* : on what <~ do you look —Shak.>
where·so·ev·er \ˈhwer-sə-ˌwev-ər, ˈhwar-, ˈwer-, ˈwar-\ *conj, archaic* : WHEREVER
where·through \ˈhwe(ə)r-ˌthrü, ˈhwa(ə)r-, ˈwe(ə)r-, ˈwa(ə)r-\ *conj* : through which
1**where·to** \-ˌtü\ *adv* : to what place, purpose, or end <~ tends all this —Shak.>
2**whereto** *conj* : to which
where·un·to \hwer-ˈən-(ˌ)tü, hwar-, wer-, war-, (ˌ)(h)wər-, -ˈən-tə(-w)\ *adv or conj* : WHERETO
where·up·on \ˈhwer-ə-ˌpȯn, ˈhwar-, ˈwer-, ˈwar-, -ˌpän\ *conj* **1** : on which **2** : closely following and in consequence of which
1**wher·ev·er** \hwer-ˈev-ər, hwar-, wer-, war-, (ˌ)(h)wər-\ *adv* **1** : where in the world <~ did she get that hat> **2** : anywhere at all <explore northward or ~ —Bernard De Voto>
2**wherever** *conj* **1** : at, in, or to any or all places that <thrives ~ he goes> **2** : in any circumstance in which <~ it is possible, he tries to help>
1**where·with** \ˈhwe(ə)r-ˌwith, ˈhwa(ə)r-, ˈwe(ə)r-, ˈwa(ə)r-, -ˌwith\ *conj* : with or by means of which <metal tools ~ to break ground —Russell Lord>
2**wherewith** *pron* : that with or by which — used with an infinitive <had not ~ to feed himself>
3**wherewith** *adv, obs* : with what <~ shall it be salted —Mt 5:13 (AV)>
1**where·with·al** \ˈhwe(ə)r-with-ˌȯl, ˈhwa(ə)r-, ˈwe(ə)r-, ˈwa(ə)r-, -with-\ *conj* [*where* + *withal*] : WHEREWITH
2**wherewithal** *pron* : WHEREWITH
3**wherewithal** *n* : MEANS, RESOURCES; *specif* : MONEY <didn't have the ~ for an expensive dinner>
wher·ry \ˈhwer-ē, ˈwer-\ *n, pl* **wherries** [ME *whery*] **1** : any of various light boats: as **a** : a long light rowboat made sharp at both ends and used to transport passengers on rivers and about harbors **b** : a racing scull for one person **2** : a large light barge, lighter, or fishing boat varying in type in different parts of Great Britain
1**whet** \ˈhwet, ˈwet\ *vt* **whet·ted; whet·ting** [ME *whetten*, fr. OE *hwettan*; akin to OHG *wezzen* to whet, *waz* sharp] **1** : to sharpen by rubbing on or with something (as a stone) <~ a knife> **2** : to make keen or more acute : EXCITE, STIMULATE <~ the appetite> — **whet·ter** *n*
2**whet** *n* **1** *dial* **a** : a spell of work between two whettings of the scythe **b** : TIME, WHILE **2** : something that sharpens or makes keen: **a** : GOAD, INCITEMENT **b** : APPETIZER; *also* : a drink of liquor
1**wheth·er** \ˈhweth-ər, ˈweth-, (ˌ)(h)wəth-\ *n* [ME, fr. OE *hwæther, hwether*; akin to OHG *hwedar* which of two, L *uter*, Gk *poteros*, OE *hwā* who — more at WHO] **1** *archaic* : which one of the two **2** *archaic* : whichever one of the two
2**whether** *conj* [ME, fr. OE *hwæther, hwether*, fr. *hwæther, hwether*, pron.] — used as a function word usu. with correlative *or* or with *or whether* to indicate (1) until the early 19th century a direct question involving alternatives; (2) an indirect question involving alternatives <decide ~ he should agree or raise objections>; (3) alternative conditions or possibilities <see me no more, ~ he be dead or no —Shak.> <seated him next to her ~ by accident or design> — **whether or no** *or* **whether or not** : in any case
whet·stone \ˈhwet-ˌstōn, ˈwet-\ *n* : a stone for whetting edge tools
whew *often read as* ˈhwü, ˈwü, ˈhyü; *the interj is a whistle concluded with a voiceless* ü\ *n* [imit.] **1** : a whistling sound **2** : a sound like a half-formed whistle uttered as an exclamation <gave a long ~ when he realized the size of the job> — used interjectionally chiefly to express amazement, discomfort, or relief
whey \ˈhwā, ˈwā\ *n* [ME, fr. OE *hwæg*; akin to MD *wey* whey] : the serum or watery part of milk that is separated from the coagulable part or curd esp. in the process of making cheese and that is rich in lactose, minerals, and vitamins and contains lactalbumin and traces of fat — **whey·ey** \ˈhwā-ē, ˈwā-\ *adj*
whey–face \ˈhwā-ˌfās, ˈwā-\ *n* : a person having a pale face (as from fear) — **whey–faced** \-ˌfāst\ *adj*
whf *abbr* wharf
1**which** \(ˈ)hwich, (ˈ)wich\ *adj* [ME, of what kind, which, fr. OE *hwilc*; akin to OHG *wilīh* of what kind, which; both fr. a prehistoric Gmc compound whose first constituent is akin to OE *hwā* who & whose second constituent is represented by OE *-līc* -ly — more at WHO, -LY] **1** : being what one or ones out of a group — used as an interrogative <~ tie should I wear> <kept a record of ~ employees took their vacations in July> **2** : 2WHICHEVER <it will not fit, turn it ~ way you like> **3** — used as a function word to introduce a nonrestrictive relative clause and to modify a noun in that clause and to refer together with that noun to a word or word group in a preceding clause or to an entire preceding clause or sentence or longer unit of discourse <in German, ~ language might . . . have been the medium of transmission —Thomas Pyles> <that this city is a rebellious city . . . : for ~ cause was this city destroyed —Ezra 4:15 (AV)>
2**which** *pron* **1** : what one or ones out of a group — used as an interrogative <~ of those houses do you live in> <~ of you want tea and ~ want lemonade> <he is swimming or canoeing, I don't know ~> **2** : WHICHEVER <take ~ you like> **3** — used as a function word to introduce a relative clause; used in any grammatical relation except that of a possessive; used esp. in reference to animals, inanimate objects, groups, or ideas <the bonds ~ represent the debt —G. B. Robinson> <the Samnite tribes, ~ settled south and southeast of Rome —Ernst Pulgram>; used freely in reference to persons as recently as the 17th century <our Father ~ art in heaven —Mt 6:9 (AV)>, and still occas. so used but usu. with some implication of emphasis on the function or role of the person rather than on the person himself <chiefly they wanted husbands, ~ they got easily —Lynn White>; used by speakers on all educational levels and by many reputable writers, though disapproved by some grammarians, in reference to an idea expressed by a word or group of words that is not necessarily a noun or noun phrase <in August of that year he resigned that post, after ~ he engaged in ranching —*Current Biog.*>
1**which·ev·er** \hwich-ˈev-ər, wich-\ *pron* : whatever one or ones out of a group <take two of the four elective subjects, ~ you prefer>
2**whichever** *adj* : being whatever one or ones out of a group : no matter which <walk . . . back to ~ chair he happened to be using at the time —Grace Metalious> <its soothing . . . effect will be the same ~ way you take it —*Punch*>
which·so·ev·er \ˌhwich-sə-ˈwev-ər, ˌwich-\ *pron or adj* : WHICHEVER
whick·er \ˈhwik-ər, ˈwik-\ *vi* **whick·ered; whick·er·ing** \-(ə-)riŋ\ [imit.] : NEIGH, WHINNY — **whicker** *n*
whid \ˈhwid, ˈwid\ *vi* **whid·ded; whid·ding** [Sc *whid* silent rapid motion] *Scot* : to move nimbly and silently
whidah *var of* WHYDAH
1**whiff** \ˈhwif, ˈwif\ *n* [imit.] **1 a** : a quick puff or slight gust esp. of air, odor, gas, smoke, or spray **b** : an inhalation of odor, gas, or smoke **c** : a slight puffing or whistling sound **2** : a slight trace
2**whiff** *vi* **1** : to move with or as if with a puff of air **2** : to emit whiffs : PUFF **3** : to inhale an odor **4** : FAN 3 ~ *vt* **1 a** : to carry or convey by or as if by a whiff : BLOW **b** : to expel or puff out in a whiff : EXHALE **c** : SMOKE 3 **2** : FAN 8
whif·fet \ˈhwif-ət, ˈwif-\ *n* [prob. alter. of *whippet*] : a small, young, or unimportant person
whif·fle \ˈhwif-əl, ˈwif-\ *vb* **whif·fled; whif·fling** \-(ə-)liŋ\ [prob. freq. of *whiff*] *vi* **1 a** *of the wind* : to blow unsteadily or in gusts **b** : VACILLATE **2** : to emit or produce a light whistling or puffing sound ~ *vt* : to blow, disperse, emit, or expel with or as if with a whiff
1**whif·fler** \ˈhwif-lər, ˈwif-\ *n* [alter. of earlier *wifler*, fr. obs. *wifle* (battle-ax)] *Brit* : one that clears the way for a procession
2**whif·fler** \ˈhwif-(ə-)lər, ˈwif-\ *n* [*whiffle*] **1** : one that frequently changes his opinion or course **2** : one that uses shifts and evasions in argument
whif·fle·tree \ˈhwif-əl-(ˌ)trē, ˈwif-\ *n* [alter. of *whippletree*] : the pivoted swinging bar to which the traces of a harness are fastened and by which a vehicle or implement is drawn

1 whiffletree

Whig \ˈhwig, ˈwig\ *n* [short for *Whiggamore* (member of a Scottish group that marched to Edinburgh in 1648 to oppose the court party)] **1** : a member or supporter of a major British political group of the 18th and early 19th centuries seeking to limit the royal authority and increase parliamentary power — compare TORY **2** : an American favoring independence from Great Britain during the American Revolution **3** : a member or supporter of an American political party formed about 1834 in opposition to the Jacksonian Democrats, associated chiefly with manufacturing, commercial, and financial interests, and succeeded about 1854 by the Republican party — **Whig** *adj* — **Whig·gish** \ˈhwig-ish, ˈwig-\ *adj* — **Whig·gism** \-ˌiz-əm\ *n*
Whig·gery \ˈhwig-ə-rē, ˈwig-\ *n* : the principles or practices of Whigs
whig·ma·lee·rie \ˌhwig-mə-ˈli(ə)r-ē, ˌwig-\ *n* [origin unknown] **1** : WHIM **2** : an odd or fanciful contrivance : GIMCRACK
1**while** \ˈhwī(ə)l, ˈwī(ə)l\ *n* [ME, fr. OE *hwīl*; akin to OHG *hwīla* time, L *quies* rest, quiet] **1** : a period of time esp. when short and marked by the occurrence of an action or a condition : TIME <stay here for a ~> **2** : the time and effort used (as in the performance of an action) : TROUBLE <worth your ~>
2**while** *conj* **1 a** : during the time that <take a nap ~ I'm out> **b** : as long as <~ there's life there's hope> **2 a** : when on the other hand : WHEREAS <easy for an expert, ~ it is dangerous for a novice> **b** : in spite of the fact that : ALTHOUGH <~ respected, he is not liked> **3** : similarly and at the same time that <~ the book will be welcomed by scholars, it will make an immediate appeal to the general reader —*Brit. Book News*>
3**while** *prep, archaic* : UNTIL
4**while** *vt* **whiled; whil·ing** : to cause to pass esp. without boredom or in a pleasant manner — usu. used with *away* <~ away the time>
syn WHILE, WILE, BEGUILE, FLEET *shared meaning element* : to pass idle or leisure time without being bored
1**whiles** \ˈhwī(ə)lz, ˈwī(ə)lz\ *conj* [ME, fr. *while* + *-s*, adv. suffix — more at WHENCE] *archaic* : WHILE
2**whiles** *adv, chiefly Scot* : SOMETIMES
1**whi·lom** \ˈhwī-ləm, ˈwī-\ *adv* [ME, lit., at times, fr. OE *hwīlum*, dat. pl. of *hwīl* time, while] *archaic* : FORMERLY
2**whilom** *adj* : FORMER
whilst \ˈhwī(ə)lst, ˈwī(ə)lst\ *conj* [ME *whilest*, alter. of *whiles*] *chiefly Brit* : WHILE
whim \ˈhwim, ˈwim\ *n* [short for *whim-wham*] **1** : a capricious or eccentric and often sudden idea or turn of the mind : FANCY **2** : a large capstan that is made with one or more radiating arms to which a horse may be yoked and that is used in mines for raising ore or water ***syn*** see CAPRICE
whim·brel \ˈhwim-brəl, ˈwim-\ *n* [perh. imit.] : a small European curlew (*Phaeopus phaeopus*); *broadly* : a small curlew

[1]**whim·per** \'hwim-pər, 'wim-\ *vi* **whim·pered; whim·per·ing** \-p(ə-)riŋ\ [imit.] **1 :** to make a low whining plaintive or broken sound **2 :** to complain or protest with or as if with a whimper

[2]**whimper** *n* **1 :** a whimpering cry or sound **2 :** a petulant complaint or protest

whim·si·cal \'hwim-zi-kəl, 'wim-\ *adj* [*whimsy*] **1 :** full of, actuated by, or exhibiting whims **2 a :** resulting from or characterized by whim or caprice **b :** subject to erratic behavior or unpredictable change — **whim·si·cal·i·ty** \ˌhwim-zə-'kal-ət-ē, ˌwim-\ *n* — **whim·si·cal·ly** \'hwim-zi-k(ə-)lē, 'wim-\ *adv* — **whim·si·cal·ness** \-kəl-nəs\ *n*

whim·sied \'hwim-zēd, 'wim-\ *adj* : WHIMSICAL

whim·sy *or* **whim·sey** \'hwim-zē, 'wim-\ *n, pl* **whimsies** *or* **whimseys** [irreg. fr. *whim-wham*] **1 :** WHIM, CAPRICE **2 :** a fanciful or fantastic device, object, or creation esp. in writing or art

whim–wham \'hwim-ˌhwam, 'wim-ˌwam\ *n* [origin unknown] **1 :** a whimsical object or device esp. of ornament or dress **2 :** FANCY, WHIM **3** *pl* **:** JITTERS

whin \'hwin, 'win\ *n* [ME *whynne,* of Scand origin; akin to Norw *kvein* bent grass] **:** FURZE

whin·chat \'hwin-ˌchat, 'win-\ *n* [[2]*whin*] **:** a small brown and buff European singing bird (*Saxicola rubetra*) of grassy meadows

[1]**whine** \'hwīn, 'wīn\ *vb* **whined; whin·ing** [ME *whinen,* fr. OE *hwīnan* to whiz; akin to ON *hvīna* to whiz] *vi* **1 a :** to utter a high-pitched plaintive or distressed cry **b :** to make a sound similar to such a cry <the wind *whined* in the chimney> **2 :** to utter a complaint with or as if with a whine **3 :** to move or proceed with the sound of a whine <the bullet *whined* . . . across the ice —Berton Roueché> ~ *vt* **:** to utter or express with or as if with a whine — **whin·er** *n* — **whin·ing·ly** \'hwī-niŋ-lē, 'wī-\ *adv*

[2]**whine** *n* **1 a :** a prolonged high-pitched cry usu. expressive of distress or pain **b :** a sound resembling such a cry **2 :** a complaint uttered with or as if with a whine — **whiny** *or* **whin·ey** \'hwī-nē, 'wī-\ *adj*

whing–ding \'wiŋ-ˌdiŋ, 'hwiŋ-\ *n* [by alter.] **:** WINGDING

[1]**whin·ny** \'hwin-ē, 'win-\ *vb* **whin·nied; whin·ny·ing** [prob. imit.] *vi* **:** to neigh esp. in a low or gentle way ~ *vt* **:** to utter with or as if with a whinny

[2]**whinny** *n, pl* **whinnies** **1 :** NEIGH **2 :** a sound resembling a neigh

whin·stone \'hwin-ˌstōn, 'win-\ *n* **:** basaltic rock **:** TRAP; *also* **:** any of various other dark resistant rocks (as chert)

[1]**whip** \'hwip, 'wip\ *vb* **whipped; whip·ping** [ME *wippen, whippen;* akin to MD *wippen* to move up and down, sway, OE *wipian* to wipe] *vt* **1 :** to take, pull, snatch, jerk, or otherwise move very quickly and forcefully <*whipped* out his gun —Green Peyton> **2 a (1) :** to strike with a slender lithe implement (as a lash or rod) esp. as a punishment **(2) :** SPANK **b :** to drive or urge on by or as if by using a whip **c :** to strike as a lash does <rain *whipped* the pavement> **3 a :** to bind or wrap (as a rope or fishing rod) with cord for protection and strength **b :** to wind or wrap around something **4 :** to belabor with stinging words **:** ABUSE **5 :** to seam or hem with shallow overcasting stitches **6 :** to overcome decisively **:** DEFEAT **7 :** to stir up **:** INCITE — usu. used with *up* <trying to ~ up a new emotion —Ellen Glasgow> **8 :** to produce in a hurry — usu. used with *up* <a sketch . . . an artist might ~ up —*N.Y. Times*> **9 :** to fish (water) with rod, line, and artificial lure **10 :** to beat (as eggs or cream) into a froth with a utensil (as a whisk or fork) **11 :** to gather together or hold together for united action in the manner of a party whip ~ *vi* **1 :** to move nimbly or quickly **:** WHISK <*whipping* through the supper dishes —C. B. Davis> **2 :** to thrash about flexibly in the manner of a whiplash <a flag . . . *whipping* out from its staff —H. A. Calahan> — **whip·per** *n* — **whip into shape :** to bring forcefully to a desired state or condition

[2]**whip** *n* **1 :** an instrument consisting usu. of a handle and lash forming a flexible rod that is used for whipping **2 :** a stroke or cut with or as if with a whip **3 a :** a dessert made by whipping a portion of the ingredients <prune ~> **b :** a kitchen utensil made of braided or coiled wire or perforated metal with a handle and used in whipping **4 :** one of the arms of a windmill **5 :** a hoisting apparatus; *esp* **:** a purchase consisting of a single block and a small rope for lifting light articles **6 :** one that handles a whip: as **a :** a driver of horses **:** COACHMAN **b :** WHIPPER-IN 1 **7 a :** a member of a legislative body appointed by his political party to enforce party discipline and to secure the attendance of party members at important sessions **b** *often cap* **:** a notice of forthcoming business sent weekly to each member of a political party in the British House of Commons **8 :** a whipping or thrashing motion **9 :** the quality of resembling a whip esp. in being flexible **10 :** any of various pieces of machinery that operate with a quick vibratory motion (as a spring in an electrical device for making a circuit) **11 :** a flexible radio antenna — called also *whip antenna* — **whip·like** \'hwip-ˌlīk, 'wip-\ *adj*

whip·cord \'hwip-ˌkȯ(ə)rd, 'wip-\ *n* [fr. its use in making whips] **1 a :** a thin tough cord made of braided or twisted hemp or catgut **b :** a cloth that is made of hard-twisted yarns and has fine diagonal cords or ribs **2 :** either of two marine brown algae (*Chorda filum* and *Chordaria flagelliformis*) having very long slender flexible fronds

whip hand *n* **1 :** the hand holding the whip in driving **2 :** positive control **:** ADVANTAGE

whip in *vt* **1 :** to keep (hounds in a pack) from scattering by use of a whip **2 :** to collect or keep together (members of a political party) for legislative action

whip·lash \'hwip-ˌlash, 'wip-\ *n* **1 :** the lash of a whip **2 :** something resembling a blow from a whip <the ~ of fear —R. S. Banay> **3 :** WHIPLASH INJURY

whiplash injury *n* **:** injury resulting from a sudden sharp whipping movement of the neck and head (as of a person in a vehicle that is struck head-on or from the rear by another vehicle)

whip·per–in \ˌhwip-ə-'rin, ˌwip-\ *n, pl* **whip·pers–in** \-ər-'zin\ **1 :** a huntsman's assistant who whips in the hounds **2 :** WHIP 7a

whip·per·snap·per \'hwip-ər-ˌsnap-ər, 'wip-\ *n* [alter. of *snippersnapper*] **:** a diminutive, insignificant, or presumptuous person

whip·pet \'hwip-ət, 'wip-\ *n* [prob. fr. [1]*whip*] **1 :** a small swift slender dog of greyhound type developed from a cross between the Italian greyhound and a terrier **2 :** a small tank used in World War I by the Allied armies

whip·ping *n* **1 :** the act of one that whips: as **a :** a severe beating or chastisement **b :** a stitching with small overcasting stitches **2 :** material used to whip or bind

whipping boy *n* **1 :** a boy formerly educated with a prince and punished in his stead **2 :** SCAPEGOAT

whipping post *n* **:** a post to which offenders are tied to be legally whipped

whip·ple·tree \'hwip-əl-(ˌ)trē, 'wip-\ *n* [perh. irreg. fr. *whip* + *tree*] **:** WHIFFLETREE

whip·poor·will \'hwip-ər-ˌwil, ˌhwip-ər-', 'wip-, ˌwip-\ *n* [imit.] **:** a nocturnal goatsucker (*Caprimulgus vociferus*) of the eastern U.S. and Canada related to the European nightjar

whippoorwill

whip·py \'hwip-ē, 'wip-\ *adj* **whip·pi·er; -est** **1 :** of, relating to, or resembling a whip **2 :** unusually resilient **:** SPRINGY <a ~ fishing rod>

whip–round \'hwip-ˌrau̇nd, 'wip-\ *n, chiefly Brit* **:** a collection of money made usu. for a benevolent purpose <had a ~ to help the couple pay for a Paris honeymoon —*The People*>

[1]**whip·saw** \'hwip-ˌsȯ, 'wip-\ *n* [[2]*whip*] **1 :** a narrow pit saw tapering from butt to point, having hook teeth, and averaging from 5 to 7½ feet in length **2 :** a two-man crosscut saw

[2]**whipsaw** *vt* **1 :** to saw with a whipsaw **2 :** to worst or victimize in two opposite ways at once, by a two-phase operation, or by the collusive action of two opponents

whip·sawed \-ˌsȯd\ *adj* **:** subjected to a double market loss through trying inopportunely to recoup a loss by a subsequent short sale of the same security

whip scorpion *n* **:** any of an order (Pedipalpida) of arachnids somewhat resembling true scorpions but having a long slender caudal process and no sting

whip stall *n* **:** a stall during a vertical climb in which the nose of the airplane whips violently forward and then downward

[1]**whip·stitch** \'hwip-ˌstich, 'wip-\ *vt* **:** WHIP 5

[2]**whipstitch** *n* **1 :** a shallow overcasting stitch **2 :** a small interval of time

whip·stock \-ˌstäk\ *n* **:** the handle of a whip

whip·worm \-ˌwərm\ *n* **:** a parasitic nematode worm (family Trichuridae) with a body that is thickened posteriorly and that is very long and slender anteriorly; *esp* **:** one (*Trichuris trichiura*) of the human intestine

[1]**whir** *also* **whirr** \'hwər, 'wər\ *vb* **whirred; whir·ring** [ME (Sc) *quirren,* prob. of Scand origin; akin to Dan *hvirre* to whirl, whir; akin to OE *hweorfan* to turn — more at WHARF] *vi* **:** to fly, revolve, or move rapidly with a whir ~ *vt* **:** to move or carry rapidly with a whir

[2]**whir** *also* **whirr** *n* **:** a continuous fluttering or vibratory sound made by something in rapid motion

[1]**whirl** \'hwər(-ə)l, 'wər(-ə)l\ *vb* [ME *whirlen,* prob. of Scand origin; akin to ON *hvirfla* to whirl; akin to OHG *wirbil* whirlwind, OE *hweorfan* to turn — more at WHARF] *vi* **1 :** to move in a circle or similar curve esp. with force or speed **2 a :** to turn on or around an axis like a wheel **:** ROTATE **b :** to turn abruptly around or aside **:** WHEEL **3 :** to pass, move, or go quickly <she ~*ed* down the hallway> **4 :** to become giddy or dizzy **:** REEL <my head is ~*ing*> ~ *vt* **1 :** to drive, impel, or convey with or as if with a rotary motion **2 a :** to cause to turn usu. rapidly on or around an axis **:** ROTATE **b :** to cause to turn abruptly around or aside **3** *obs* **:** to throw or hurl violently with a revolving motion — **whirl·er** \'hwər-lər, 'wər-\ *n*

[2]**whirl** *n* **1 a :** a rapid rotating or circling movement **b :** something undergoing such a movement **2 a :** a confused tumult **:** BUSTLE <plunged into a ~ of work —Will Irwin> **b :** a confused or disturbed mental state **:** TURMOIL <a ~ of febrile excitement —Emily Skeel> **3 :** an experimental or brief attempt **:** TRY <gave it a ~>

whirl·i·gig \'hwər-li-ˌgig, 'wər-\ *n* [ME *whirlegigg,* fr. *whirlen* to whirl + *gigg* top — more at GIG] **1 :** a child's toy having a whirling motion **2 :** MERRY-GO-ROUND **3 a :** one that continuously whirls, moves, or changes **b :** a whirling or circling course (as of events)

whirligig beetle *n* **:** any of numerous beetles (family Gyrinidae) that live mostly on the surface of water where they move swiftly about in curves

whirl·pool \'hwər(-ə)l-ˌpül, 'wər(-ə)l-\ *n* **1 :** water moving rapidly in a circle so as to produce a depression in the center into which floating objects may be drawn **:** EDDY, VORTEX **2 a :** a confused tumult and bustle **:** WHIRL **b :** a magnetic or impelling force by which something may be engulfed <a seething ~ of competition and intrigue —David Cecil>

whirl·wind \-ˌwind\ *n* **1 :** a small rotating windstorm of limited extent marked by an inward and upward spiral motion of the lower air that is followed by an outward and upward spiral motion and usu. a progressive motion at all levels **2 a :** a confused rush **:** WHIRL **b :** a destructive force or agency

[1]**whirly** \'hwər-lē, 'wər-\ *adj* : marked by or exhibiting a whirling motion

[2]**whirly** *n, pl* **whirl·ies** : a small whirlwind

whirly·bird \-ˌbərd\ *n* : HELICOPTER

whir·ry \'hwər-ē, 'wər-, '(h)wə-rē\ *vb* **whir·ried; whir·ry·ing** [perh. blend of *whir* and *hurry*] *vt, Scot* : to convey quickly ~ *vi, Scot* : HURRY

[1]**whish** \'hwish, 'wish\ *vb* [imit.] *vt* : to urge on or cause to move with a whish ~ *vi* **1** : to make a sibilant sound **2** : to move with a whish esp. at high speed <an elevator . . . ~*es* down to the lower level —Natalie Cooper>

[2]**whish** *n* : a rushing sound : SWISH

whisht \'hwisht, 'wisht\ *vi* [imit.] *chiefly Irish* : HUSH — often used interjectionally to enjoin silence

[1]**whisk** \'hwisk, 'wisk\ *n* [ME *wisk,* prob. of Scand origin; akin to ON *visk* wisp; akin to OE *wiscian* to plait, L *virga* branch, rod] **1** : a quick light brushing or whipping motion **2 a** : a small usu. wire kitchen utensil used for beating food by hand **b** : a flexible bunch (as of twigs, feathers, or straw) attached to a handle for use as a brush

[2]**whisk** *vi* : to move nimbly and quickly ~ *vt* **1** : to move or convey briskly <~*ed* the children off to bed> **2** : to mix or fluff up by or as if by beating with a whisk <~ egg whites> **3** : to brush or wipe off lightly

whisk broom *n* : a small broom with a short handle used esp. as a clothes brush

whis·ker \'hwis-kər, 'wis-\ *n* [back-formation fr. *whiskers* (mustache), fr. [2]*whisk*] **1 a** : a hair of the beard **b** *pl* (1) *archaic* : MUSTACHE (2) : the part of the beard growing on the sides of the face or on the chin **c** : HAIRBREADTH <lost the race by a ~> **2** : one of the long projecting hairs or bristles growing near the mouth of an animal (as a cat or bird) **3** : an outrigger extending on each side of the bowsprit to spread the jib and flying jib guys — usu. used in pl. **4 a** : a shred or filament resembling a whisker **b** : a thin hairlike crystal (as of sapphire or a metal) of exceptional mechanical strength — **whis·kered** \-kərd\ *adj* — **whis·kery** \-k(ə-)rē\ *adj*

whis·key *or* **whis·ky** \'hwis-kē, 'wis-\ *n, pl* **whiskeys** *or* **whis·kies** [IrGael *uisce beathadh* & ScGael *uisge beatha,* lit., water of life] **1** : a distilled alcoholic liquor made from fermented mash of grain (as rye, corn, barley, or wheat) **2** : a drink of whiskey

Whiskey — a communications code word for the letter *w*

whiskey sour *n* : a cocktail usu. made of whiskey, sugar, and lemon juice shaken with ice and served with a fruit garnish (as orange or maraschino cherry)

[1]**whis·per** \'hwis-pər, 'wis-\ *vb* **whis·pered; whis·per·ing** \-p(ə-)riŋ\ [ME *whisperen,* fr. OE *hwisperian;* akin to OHG *hwispalōn* to whisper, ON *hvísla* — more at WHISTLE] *vi* **1** : to speak softly with little or no vibration of the vocal cords esp. to avoid being overheard **2** : to make a sibilant sound that resembles whispering ~ *vt* **1** : to address in a whisper **2** : to utter or communicate in or as if in a whisper

[2]**whisper** *n* **1 a** : an act or instance of whispering; *esp* : speech without vibration of the vocal cords **b** : a sibilant sound that resembles whispered speech **2** : something communicated by or as if by whispering: as **a** : RUMOR <~*s* of scandal> **b** : HINT, TRACE

whis·per·er \-pər-ər\ *n* : one that whispers; *specif* : RUMORMONGER

[1]**whis·per·ing** *n* **1 a** : whispered speech **b** : GOSSIP, RUMOR **2** : a sibilant sound : WHISPER

[2]**whispering** *adj* **1** : making a sibilant sound **2** : spreading confidential and esp. derogatory reports <~ tongues can poison truth —S. T. Coleridge> — **whis·per·ing·ly** \-p(ə-)riŋ-lē\ *adv*

whispering campaign *n* : the systematic dissemination by word of mouth of derogatory rumors or charges esp. against a candidate for public office

whis·pery \'hwis-p(ə-)rē, 'wis-\ *adj* **1** : resembling a whisper **2** : full of whispers

[1]**whist** \'hwist, 'wist\ *vi* [imit.] *dial Brit* : to be silent : HUSH — often used interjectionally to enjoin silence

[2]**whist** *adj* : QUIET, SILENT

[3]**whist** *n* [alter. of earlier *whisk,* prob. fr. [2]*whisk;* fr. whisking up the tricks] : a card game for four players in two partnerships that is played with a pack of 52 cards and that scores one point for each trick in excess of six

[1]**whis·tle** \'hwis-əl, 'wis-\ *n, often attrib* [ME, fr. OE *hwistle;* akin to ON *hvísla* to whisper, *hvína* to whiz — more at WHINE] **1 a** : a small wind instrument in which sound is produced by the forcible passage of breath through a slit in a short tube <police ~> **b** : a device through which air or steam is forced into a cavity or against a thin edge to produce a loud sound <a factory ~> **2 a** : a shrill clear sound produced by forcing breath out or air in through the puckered lips **b** : the sound produced by a whistle **c** : a signal given by or as if by whistling **3** : a sound that resembles a whistle; *esp* : a shrill clear note of or as if of a bird

[2]**whistle** *vb* **whis·tled; whis·tling** \-(ə-)liŋ\ *vi* **1 a** : to utter a shrill clear sound by blowing or drawing air through the puckered lips **b** : to utter a shrill note or call resembling a whistle **c** : to make a shrill clear sound esp. by rapid movement **d** : to blow or sound a whistle **2 a** : to give a signal or issue an order or summons by or as if by whistling <~ to a dog> **b** : to make a demand without result <did a sloppy job so he can ~ for his money> ~ *vt* **1** : to send, bring, signal, or call by or as if by whistling **2** : to produce, utter, or express by whistling <~ a tune> — **whis·tle·able** \-ə-lə-bəl\ *adj* — **whistle in the dark** : to keep up one's courage by or as if by whistling

whis·tler \'hwis-(ə-)lər, 'wis-\ *n* : one that whistles: as **a** : any of various birds; *esp* : GOLDENEYE 1 **b** : a large mountain marmot (*Marmota caligata*) of northwestern No. America **c** : a broken-winded horse **d** : an electromagnetic signal of audio or radio frequency that is generated by lightning discharge and that travels along the earth's magnetic lines of force

[1]**whis·tle–stop** \'hwis-əl-ˌstäp, 'wis-\ *n* **1 a** : a small station at which trains stop only on signal : FLAG STOP **b** : a small community **2** : a brief personal appearance esp. by a political candidate usu. on the rear platform of a train during the course of a tour

[2]**whistle–stop** *vi* : to make a tour esp. in a political campaign with many brief personal appearances in small communities

whis·tling *n* : the act or sound of one that whistles : WHISTLE

whit \'hwit, 'wit\ *n* [alter. of ME *wiht, wight* creature, thing, bit — more at WIGHT] : the smallest part or particle imaginable : BIT <have not contributed one ~ to our knowledge of man — Nehemiah Jordan>

[1]**white** \'hwīt, 'wīt\ *adj* **whit·er; whit·est** [ME, fr. OE *hwīt;* akin to OHG *hwīz* white, Skt *śveta*] **1 a** : free from color **b** : of the color of new snow or milk; *specif* : of the color white **c** : light or pallid in color <~ hair> <lips ~ with fear> **d** : lustrous pale gray : SILVERY; *also* : made of silver **2 a** : being a member of a group or race characterized by reduced pigmentation and usu. specif. distinguished from persons belonging to groups marked by black, brown, yellow, or red skin coloration **b** : of, relating to, or consisting of white people <~ schools> **c** *slang* : marked by upright fairness <a ~ man if ever there was one> **3** : free from spot or blemish: as **a** (1) : free from moral impurity : INNOCENT (2) : marked by the wearing of white by the woman as a symbol of purity <a ~ wedding> **b** : unmarked by writing or printing **c** : not intended to cause harm <a ~ lie> <~ magic> **d** : FAVORABLE, FORTUNATE <one of the ~ days of his life —Sir Walter Scott> **4 a** : wearing or habited in white **b** : marked by the presence of snow : SNOWY <a ~ Christmas> **5 a** : heated to the point of whiteness **b** : notably ardent : PASSIONATE <~ fury> **6 a** : ultraconservative or reactionary in political outlook and action **b** : instigated or carried out by reactionary forces as a counterrevolutionary measure <a ~ terror> **7** : not featuring open warfare but involving oblique methods <a ~ war of propaganda and bribery> **8** : of, relating to, or constituting a musical tone quality characterized by a controlled pure sound, a lack of warmth and color, and a lack of resonance **9** : consisting of a wide range of frequencies — used of light, sound, and electromagnetic radiation

[2]**white** *n* **1** : the achromatic object color of greatest lightness characteristically perceived to belong to objects that reflect diffusely nearly all incident energy throughout the visible spectrum **2 a** : a white or light-colored part of something: as (1) : a mass of albuminous material surrounding the yolk of an egg (2) : the white part of the ball of the eye (3) : the light-colored pieces in a two-handed board game; *also* : the player by whom these are played **b** (1) *archaic* : a white target (2) : the fifth or outermost circle of an archery target; *also* : a shot that hits it **3** : one that is or approaches the color white: as **a** : white clothing — often used in pl. **b** : WHITE WINE **c** : a white mammal (as a horse or a hog) **d** : a white-colored product (as flour, pins, or sugar) — usu. used in pl. **4** *pl* : LEUKORRHEA **5** : a person belonging to a light-skinned race **6** : a member of an ultraconservative or reactionary political group

[3]**white** *vt* **whit·ed; whit·ing** [ME *whiten,* fr. *white,* adj.] *archaic* : WHITEN

white ant *n* : TERMITE

white·bait \'hwīt-ˌbāt, 'wīt-\ *n* **1** : the young of any of several European herrings and esp. of the common herring (*Clupea harengus*) or of the sprat (*C. sprattus*) **2** : any of various small fishes likened to the European whitebait and used as food

white bass *n* : a No. American freshwater food fish (*Lepibema chrysops*)

white·beard \'hwīt-ˌbi(ə)rd, 'wīt-\ *n* : an old man : GRAYBEARD

white blood cell *n* : a blood cell that does not contain hemoglobin : LEUKOCYTE — called also *white blood corpuscle*

white book *n* : an official report of government affairs bound in white

white·cap \'hwīt-ˌkap, 'wīt-\ *n* : a wave crest breaking into white foam

white cedar *n* : any of various No. American timber trees including true cedars, junipers, and cypress

white cell *n* : WHITE BLOOD CELL

white chip *n* **1** : a white-colored poker chip usu. of minimum value **2** : a thing or quantity of little worth — compare BLUE CHIP

white–col·lar \'hwīt-'käl-ər, 'wīt-\ *adj* : of, relating to, or constituting the class of salaried employees whose duties do not call for the wearing of work clothes or protective clothing — compare BLUE-COLLAR

white corpuscle *n* : WHITE BLOOD CELL

white crappie *n* : a silvery No. American sunfish (*Pomoxis annularis*) with 5 or 6 protruding spines on the dorsal fins that is highly esteemed as a panfish and often used for stocking small ponds

whit·ed \'hwīt-əd, 'wīt-\ *adj* **1** : covered with white or whiting and esp. with whitewash **2** : made white : WHITENED

whited sepulcher *n* [fr. the simile in Mt 23:27 (AV)] : a person inwardly corrupt or wicked but outwardly or professedly virtuous or holy : HYPOCRITE

white Dutch clover *n* : a Eurasian clover (*Trifolium repens*) with round heads of white flowers that is widely used in lawn and pasture grass-seed mixtures and is an important source of nectar for bees

white dwarf *n* : a whitish star of high surface temperature and low intrinsic brightness usu. with a mass approximately equal to that of the sun but with a density many times larger

white elephant *n* **1** : an Indian elephant of a pale color that is sometimes venerated in India, Ceylon, Thailand, and Burma **2 a** : a property requiring much care and expense and yielding little profit **b** : an object no longer of value to its owner but of value to others **c** : something of little or no value

white·face \'hwīt-ˌfās, 'wīt-\ *n* **1** : a white-faced animal; *specif* : HEREFORD **2** : dead-white facial makeup <a clown in ~>

white–faced \-'fāst\ *adj* **1 :** having a wan pale face **2 :** having the face white in whole or in part — used esp. of an animal otherwise dark in color

white feather *n* [fr. the superstition that a white feather in the plumage of a gamecock is a mark of a poor fighter] **:** a mark or symbol of cowardice — used chiefly in the phrase *show the white feather*

white·fish \'hwīt-ˌfish, 'wīt-\ *n* **1 a :** any of various freshwater food fishes (family Salmonidae and esp. genus *Coregonus*) related to the salmons and trouts **b :** any of various fishes in some respect resembling the true whitefishes **c** *Brit* **:** any of various market fishes with white flesh that is not oily **2 :** the flesh of a whitefish esp. as an article of food

white flag *n* **1 :** a flag of plain white used as a flag of truce or as a token of surrender **2 :** a token of weakness or yielding

white·fly \'hwīt-ˌflī, 'wīt-\ *n* **:** any of numerous small homopterous insects (family Aleyrodidae) that are injurious plant pests related to the scale insects

white–foot·ed mouse \ˌhwīt-ˌfu̇t-əd-, ˌwīt-\ *n* **:** a common woodland mouse (*Peromyscus leucopus*) of the eastern U.S.; *also* **:** any of several related mice

white friar *n, often cap W&F* [fr. his white habit] **:** CARMELITE

white–fringed beetle \ˌhwīt-ˌfrinj(d)-, ˌwīt-\ *n* **:** any of a genus (*Graphognathus*) of So. American flightless beetles of which one (*G. leucoloma*) has been accidentally introduced into the southeastern U.S. where it is a pest on cultivated plants

white gasoline *n* **:** gasoline containing no tetraethyl lead — called also *white gas*

white gold *n* **:** a pale alloy of gold esp. with nickel or palladium that resembles platinum in appearance

white goods *n pl* **1 a :** white fabrics esp. of cotton or linen **b :** articles (as sheets, towels, or curtains) orig. or typically made of white cloth **2 :** major household appliances (as stoves and refrigerators) that are typically finished in white enamel

white grub *n* **:** a grub that is the larva of a june beetle and a destructive pest of grass roots

White·hall \'hwīt-ˌhȯl, 'wīt-\ *n* [*Whitehall,* thoroughfare of London in which are located the chief offices of British government] **:** the British government

white·head \-ˌhed\ *n* **:** MILIUM

white–head·ed \-'hed-əd\ *adj* **1 :** having the hair, fur, or plumage of the head white or very light **2 :** specially favored **:** FORTUNATE — used esp. in the phrase *white-headed boy*

white heat *n* **1 :** a temperature (as for copper and iron from 1500° to 1600° C.) which is higher than red heat and at which a body becomes brightly incandescent **2 :** a state of intense mental or physical strain, emotion, or activity

white hope *n* **1** *slang* **:** a white contender for a boxing championship held by a Negro; *also* **:** one who is felt to represent whites **2 :** one from whom much is expected; *esp* **:** a person undertaking a difficult task

White Horde *n* **:** a Mongolian people powerful in Russia in the 14th century

white–hot \'hwīt-'hät, 'wīt-\ *adj* **1 :** being at or radiating white heat **2 :** ardently zealous **:** FERVID

White House \-ˌhau̇s\ *n* [the *White House,* mansion in Washington, D.C. assigned to the use of the president of the U.S.] **1 :** the executive department of the U.S. government **2 :** a residence of the president of the U.S.

white hunter *n* **:** a white man serving as guide and professional hunter to an African safari

white lead *n* **:** any of several white lead-containing pigments; *esp* **:** a heavy poisonous basic carbonate of lead of variable composition that is marketed as a powder or as a paste in linseed oil, has good hiding power, and is used chiefly in exterior paints

white leather *n* **:** leather prepared with alum and salt

white line *n* **:** a band or edge of something white; *esp* **:** a stripe painted on a road and used to guide traffic

white list \-ˌlist\ *n* **:** a list of approved or favored items — compare BLACKLIST — **white–list·ed** \-ˌlis-təd\ *adj*

white–liv·ered \-'liv-ərd\ *adj* [fr. the former belief that the choleric temperament depends on the body's producing large quantities of yellow bile] **:** PUSILLANIMOUS, LILY-LIVERED

white·ly \'hwīt-lē, 'wīt-\ *adv* **:** with an effect of whiteness **:** so as to show or appear white

white man's burden *n* ["The White Man's Burden" (1899), poem by Rudyard Kipling] **:** the alleged duty of the white peoples to manage the affairs of the less developed nonwhite peoples

white matter *n* **:** neural tissue that consists largely of medullated nerve fibers, has a whitish color, and underlies the gray matter of the brain and spinal cord or is gathered into nerves

white metal *n* **1 :** any of several lead-base or tin-base alloys (as babbitt metal) used esp. for bearings, fusible plugs, and type metal **2 :** any of several light-colored alloys used esp. as a base for plated silverware and ornaments and novelties

white mustard *n* **:** a Eurasian mustard (*Brassica hirta*) grown for its seeds which yield mustard and mustard oil

whit·en \'hwīt-ᵊn, 'wīt-\ *vb* **whit·ened; whit·en·ing** \'hwīt-niŋ, 'wīt-, -ᵊn-iŋ\ *vt* **:** to make white or whiter esp. by application of a covering coat <snow ~*ed* the hills> ~ *vi* **:** to become white or whiter

syn WHITEN, BLANCH, BLEACH *shared meaning element* **:** to change from a color to or nearly to white ***ant*** blacken

whit·en·er \'hwīt-nər, -ᵊn-ər, 'wīt-\ *n* **:** one that whitens; *specif* **:** an agent (as a bleach) used to impart whiteness to something

white·ness \'hwīt-nəs, 'wīt-\ *n* **1 :** the quality or state of being white: as **a :** white color **b :** PALLOR, PALENESS **c :** freedom from stain **:** CLEANNESS **2 :** white substance

whit·en·ing *n* **1 :** the act or process of making or becoming white **2 :** something that is used to make white **:** WHITING

white oak *n* **:** any of various oaks (esp. *Quercus sessiliflora* of Europe and *Q. alba* of No. America) with acorns that mature in one year and leaf veins that never extend beyond the margin of the leaf; *also* **:** the hard, strong, durable, and moisture-resistant wood of a white oak

white of egg *n, pl* **whites of egg** *or* **whites of eggs :** WHITE 2a(1)

white oil *n* **:** any of various colorless odorless tasteless mineral oils used esp. in medicine and in pharmaceutical and cosmetic preparations

white·out \'hwīt-ˌau̇t, 'wīt-\ *n* [*white* + *-out* (as in *blackout*)] **:** a surface weather condition in an arctic area in which no object casts a shadow, the horizon cannot be seen, and only dark objects are discernible

white paper *n* **:** a government report on any subject; *esp* **:** a British publication that is usu. less extensive than a blue book

white perch *n* **1 :** a small silvery anadromous sea bass (*Morone americana*) of the coast and coastal streams of the eastern U.S. **2 :** a croaker (*Aplodinotus grunniens*) of the Great Lakes and Mississippi valley that sometimes attains a weight of 50 pounds or more **3 :** WHITE CRAPPIE

white pine *n* **1 a :** a tall-growing pine (*Pinus strobus*) of eastern No. America with leaves in clusters of five — called also *eastern white pine* **b :** any of several trees felt to resemble the white pine esp. in having leaves in bundles of five **2 :** the wood of a white pine and esp. of the eastern white pine which is much used in building construction

white–pine blister rust *n* **:** a destructive disease of white pine caused by a rust fungus (*Cronartium ribicola*) that passes part of its complex life cycle on currant or gooseberry bushes; *also* **:** this fungus

white plague *n* **1 :** tuberculosis of the lungs **2 :** heroin addiction

white potato *n* **:** POTATO 2b

white primary *n* **:** a party primary in a southern state open to white voters only

white room *n* **:** CLEAN ROOM

White Russian *n* **:** BELORUSSIAN

white rust *n* **:** any of various plant diseases caused by lower fungi (order Peronosporales) and characterized by the presence of masses of white spores that escape through ruptures of the host tissue; *also* **:** a fungus causing a white rust

white sale *n* **:** a sale of white goods

white sauce *n* **:** a sauce consisting essentially of a roux with milk, cream, or stock and seasoning

white sea bass *n* **:** a large croaker (*Cynoscion nobilis*) of the Pacific coast that is closely related to the Atlantic weakfishes and is an important sport and food fish

white shark *n* **:** a large mackerel shark of warm seas that is bluish when young but becomes whitish with age and is a man-eater

white slave *n* **:** a woman or girl held unwillingly for purposes of commercial prostitution

white slav·er \-'slā-vər\ *n* **:** one engaged in white-slave traffic

white slavery *n* **:** enforced prostitution

white·smith \'hwīt-ˌsmith, 'wīt-\ *n* **1 :** TINSMITH **2 :** a worker in iron who finishes or polishes the work

white space *n* **:** the areas of a page (as in a book) not covered by print or pictures

white spruce *n* **1 :** any of several spruces; *esp* **:** a widely distributed spruce (*Picea glauca*) of cooler parts of No. America that has short blue-green leaves and slender cones **2 :** the wood of a white spruce; *esp* **:** the light pale tough straight-grained wood of the common white spruce (*Picea glauca*) used esp. for construction and as a source of paper pulp

white supremacist *n* **:** an advocate of or believer in white supremacy

white supremacy *n* **:** a doctrine based on a belief in the inherent superiority of the white race over the Negro race and the correlative necessity for the subordination of Negroes to whites in all relationships

white·tail \'hwīt-ˌtāl, 'wīt-\ *n* **:** a No. American deer (*Odocoileus virginianus*) with a rather long tail white on the undersurface and forward-arching antlers — see DEER illustration

white–tailed deer \ˌhwīt-ˌtāl-'di(ə)r\ *n* **:** WHITETAIL

white–tailed sea eagle \-ˌtāl(d)-\ *n* **:** a bulky long-winged sea eagle (*Haliäetus albicilla*) with a short white wedge-shaped tail

white·throat \'hwīt-ˌthrōt, 'wīt-\ *n* **:** any of several birds with white on the throat: as **a :** an Old World warbler (*Sylvia communis*) with rusty upper surfaces and largely pale buff underparts **b :** WHITE-THROATED SPARROW

white–throated sparrow \ˌhwīt-ˌthrōt-əd-, ˌwīt-\ *n* **:** a common brown sparrow (*Zonotrichia albicollis*) of eastern No. America with a striped crown and a large white patch on the throat

white–tie *adj* **:** characterized by or requiring the wearing of formal evening dress by men <a ~ dinner> — compare BLACK-TIE

white trash *n sing but pl in constr* **:** POOR WHITE — usu. used disparagingly

white·wall \'hwīt-ˌwȯl, 'wīt-\ *n* **:** an automobile tire having a white band on the sidewall

white walnut *n* **1 a :** a butternut tree **b :** WALNUT 1b **2 :** the light-colored wood of a white walnut

[1]**white·wash** \'hwīt-ˌwȯsh, 'wīt, -ˌwäsh\ *vt* **1 :** to whiten with whitewash **2 a :** to gloss over or cover up (as vices or crimes) **b :** to exonerate by means of a perfunctory investigation or through biased presentation of data **3 :** to hold (an opponent) scoreless in a game or contest

[2]**whitewash** *n* **1 :** a liquid composition for whitening a surface: as **a :** a preparation for whitening the skin **b :** a composition (as of lime and water or whiting, size, and water) for whitening

ə abut ᵊ kitten ər further a back ā bake ä cot, cart
au̇ out ch chin e less ē easy g gift i trip ī life
j joke ŋ sing ō flow ȯ flaw ȯi coin th thin t͟h this
ü loot u̇ foot y yet yü few yu̇ furious zh vision

structural surfaces **2** : an act or instance of glossing over or of exonerating **3** : a defeat in a contest in which the loser fails to score

white·wash·er \-ər\ *n* : one that whitewashes; *esp* : one who puts on whitewash

white·wash·ing \-iŋ\ *n* : an act or instance of applying whitewash; *also* : WHITEWASH 3

white water *n* : frothy water (as in breakers, rapids, or waterfalls)

white way *n* [the *Great White Way,* nickname for the theatrical section of Broadway, New York City] : a brilliantly lighted street or avenue esp. in a city's business or theater district

white wine *n* : a wine ranging in color from faintly yellow to amber that is produced from light-colored grapes

white·wing \'hwīt-,wiŋ, 'wīt-\ *n* : a person and esp. a street sweeper wearing a white uniform

white·wood \-,wu̇d\ *n* **1** : any of various trees with pale or white wood: as **a** : LINDEN 1b **b** : COTTONWOOD **c** : TULIP TREE 1 **2** : the wood of a whitewood; *esp* : the pale soft wood of the tulip tree

whit·ey \'hwīt-ē, 'wīt-\ *n, often cap* : the white man : white society — usu. used disparagingly

[1]**whith·er** \'hwith-ər, 'with-\ *adv* [ME, fr. OE *hwider;* akin to L *quis* who and to OE hi*der* hither — more at WHO, HITHER] **1** : to what place <~ will they go> **2** : to what situation, position, degree, or end <~ will this abuse drive him>

[2]**whither** *conj* **1 a** : to what place <knew ~ to go —Daniel Defoe> **b** : to what situation, position, degree, or end **2 a** : to the place at, in, or to which **b** : to which place **3** : to whatever place

whith·er·so·ev·er \,hwith-ər-sə-'wev-ər, ,with-\ *conj* : to whatever place <will go ~ you lead>

whith·er·ward \'hwith-ər-wərd, 'with-\ *adv* : toward what or which place

[1]**whit·ing** \'hwīt-iŋ, 'wīt-\ *n* [ME, fr. MD *witinc,* fr. *wit* white; akin to OE *hwīt* white] : any of various marine food fishes: as **a** (1) : a common European fish (*Merlangus merlangus*) related to the cod (2) : SILVER HAKE **b** : any of several No. American sciaenid fishes (genus *Menticirrhus*)

[2]**whiting** *n* [ME, fr. gerund of *whiten* to white]: calcium carbonate prepared as fine powder by grinding and washing and used esp. as a pigment and extender, in putty, and in rubber compounding and paper coating

whit·ish \'hwīt-ish, 'wīt-\ *adj* : somewhat white

whit·low \'hwit-(,)lō, 'wit-\ *n* [ME *whitflawe, whitflowe, whitlowe*] : FELON 3

Whit·mon·day \'hwit-,mən-dē, 'wit-, -'mən-\ *n* [*Whit-* (as in *Whitsunday*) + *Monday*] : the day after Whitsunday observed as a legal holiday in England, Wales, and Ireland

Whit·sun \'hwit-sən, 'wit-\ *adj* [ME *Whitson,* fr. *Whitsonday*] : of, relating to, or observed on Whitsunday or at Whitsuntide

Whit·sun·day \-'sən-dē, -sən-,dā\ *n* [ME *Whitsonday,* fr. OE *hwīta sunnandæg,* lit., white Sunday; prob. fr. the custom of wearing white robes by the newly baptized, who were numerous at this season] : PENTECOST 2

Whit·sun·tide \-sən-,tīd\ *n* : the week beginning with Whitsunday and esp. the first three days of this week

[1]**whit·tle** \'hwit-ᵊl, 'wit-\ *n* [ME *whittel,* alter. of *thwitel,* fr. *thwiten* to whittle, fr. OE *thwītan;* akin to ON *thveita* to hew] *archaic* : a large knife

[2]**whittle** *vb* **whit·tled; whit·tling** \'hwit-liŋ, -ᵊl-iŋ, 'wit-\ *vt* **1 a** : to pare or cut off chips from the surface of (wood) with a knife **b** : to shape or form by so paring or cutting **2** : to reduce, remove, or destroy gradually as if by cutting off bits with a knife : PARE — usu. used with an adverb <~ down expenses> ~ *vi* **1** : to cut or shape something (as wood) by or as if by paring it with a knife **2** : to wear oneself or another out with fretting — **whit·tler** \-lər, -ᵊl-ər\ *n*

whit·tling *n* : a piece cut away in whittling

whit·tret \'hwi-trət, 'wi-\ *n* [ME *whitrat,* fr. *white, whit* white + *rat*] *chiefly Scot* : WEASEL

whity *or* **whit·ey** \'hwīt-ē, 'wīt-\ *adj* : WHITISH — usu. used in combination

[1]**whiz** *or* **whizz** \'hwiz, 'wiz\ *vb* **whizzed; whiz·zing** [imit.] *vi* **1** : to hum, whir, or hiss like a speeding object (as an arrow or ball) passing through air **2** : to fly or move swiftly with a whiz ~ *vt* : to cause to whiz; *esp* : to rotate very rapidly

[2]**whiz** *or* **whizz** *n, pl* **whiz·zes** **1** : a hissing, buzzing, or whirring sound **2** : a movement or passage of something accompanied by a whizzing sound

[3]**whiz** *n, pl* **whiz·zes** [prob. by shortening & alter.] : WIZARD 3 <a ~ at math>

whiz·bang *or* **whizz·bang** \'hwiz-,baŋ, 'wiz-, -'baŋ\ *n* : one that is conspicuous for noise, speed, or startling effect

whiz–bang *adj* : EXCELLENT, EXPERT

whiz kid *n* [alter. (influenced by [3]*whiz*) of *Quiz Kid,* member of a panel of children on a former popular quiz show] : a person who is unusually intelligent, clever, or successful esp. at an early age

whiz·zer \'hwiz-ər, 'wiz-\ *n* : one that whizzes; *esp* : a centrifugal machine for drying something (as grain, sugar, or nitrated cotton)

who \(')hü, ü\ *pron* [ME, fr. OE *hwā;* akin to OHG *hwer,* interrog. pron., who, L *quis,* Gk *tis,* L *qui,* rel. pron., who] **1** : what or which person or persons — used as an interrogative <~ was elected president> <find out ~ they are>; used by speakers on all educational levels and by many reputable writers, though disapproved by some grammarians, as the object of a verb or a following preposition <~ did I see but a Spanish lady —Padraic Colum> <do not know ~ the message is from —G. K. Chesterton> **2** : the person or persons that : WHOEVER **3** — used as a function word to introduce a relative clause; used esp. in reference to persons <my father, ~ was a lawyer> but also in reference to groups <a generation ~ had known nothing but war —R. B. West> or to animals <dogs ~ . . . fawn all over tramps —Nigel Balchin> or to inanimate objects esp. with the implication that the reference is really to a person <earlier sources ~ maintain a Davidic ancestry —F. M. Cross>; used by speakers on all educational levels and by many reputable writers, though disapproved by some grammarians, as the object of a verb or a following preposition <a character ~ we are meant to pity —*Times Lit. Supp.*> — **as who** *archaic* : as one that : as if someone — **as who should say** *archaic* : so to speak — **who is who** *or* **who's who** *or* **who was who** : the identity of or the noteworthy facts about each of a number of persons

WHO *abbr* World Health Organization

whoa \'wō, 'hō, 'hwō\ *vb imper* [ME *whoo, who*] — a command (as to a draft animal) to stand still

who·dun·it *also* **who·dun·nit** \hü-'dən-ət\ *n* [substandard *who done it?*] : a detective story or mystery story presented as a novel, play, or motion picture

who·ev·er \hü-'ev-ər\ *pron* : whatever person : no matter who — used in any grammatical relation except that of a possessive

[1]**whole** \'hōl\ *adj* [ME *hool* healthy, unhurt, entire, fr. OE *hāl;* akin to OHG *heil* healthy, unhurt, ON *heill,* OSlav *cělŭ*] **1 a** (1) : free of wound or injury : UNHURT (2) : recovered from a wound or injury : RESTORED (3) : being healed <~ of an ancient evil, I sleep sound —A. E. Housman> **b** : free of defect or impairment : INTACT **c** : physically sound and healthy : free of disease or deformity **2** : having all its proper parts or components : COMPLETE, UNMODIFIED <~ milk> <a ~ egg> **3 a** : constituting the total sum or undiminished entirety of : ENTIRE <made the ~ class stay after school> **b** : each or all of the <took part in the ~ series of athletic events> **4 a** : constituting an undivided unit : UNBROKEN, UNCUT <a ~ roast suckling pig> **b** : directed to one end : CONCENTRATED <promised to give it his ~ attention> **5 a** : seemingly complete or total <the ~ idea is to help, not hinder> **b** : very great <feels a ~ lot better now> **6** : constituting a person in his full nature or development <the university is supposed to educate the ~ man —J. W. Scott> **7** : having the same father and mother <~ brother> — **whole·ness** *n*

[2]**whole** *n* **1** : a complete amount or sum : a number, aggregate, or totality lacking no part, member, or element **2** : something constituting a complex unity : a coherent system or organization of parts fitting or working together as one — **in whole** : to the full or entire extent : WHOLLY — usu. used in the phrase *in whole or in part* — **on the whole** **1** : in view of all the circumstances or conditions : all things considered **2** : in general : in most instances : TYPICALLY — **out of whole cloth** : out of pure fabrication : without basis

[3]**whole** *adv* : WHOLLY, ENTIRELY <a ~ new age group —Henry Chauncey>

whole gale *n* : wind having a speed of 55 to 63 miles per hour — see BEAUFORT SCALE table

whole·heart·ed \'hōl-'härt-əd\ *adj* **1** : completely and sincerely devoted, determined, or enthusiastic <a ~ student of social problems> **2** : marked by complete earnest commitment : free from all reserve or hesitation <gave the movement his ~ support>

whole–hog *adj* : committed without reservation : THOROUGHGOING <a ~ patriot>

[1]**whole hog** *n* : the whole way or farthest limit : ALL — usu. used adverbially in the phrase *go the whole hog*

[2]**whole hog** *adv* : to the fullest extent : without reservation : COMPLETELY <accepting *whole hog* the standards . . . of the majority —R. B. Kaplan>

whole note *n* : a musical note equal in time value to four quarter notes or two half notes — see NOTE illustration

whole number *n* : INTEGER

whole rest *n* : a musical rest corresponding in time value to a whole note

[1]**whole·sale** \'hōl-,sāl\ *n* : the sale of commodities in quantity usu. for resale (as by a retail merchant)

[2]**wholesale** *adj* **1** : of, relating to, or engaged in the sale of commodities in quantity for resale <a ~ grocer> **2** : performed on a large scale esp. without discrimination <~ slaughter> *syn* see INDISCRIMINATE

[3]**wholesale** *adv* : in a wholesale manner

[4]**wholesale** *vb* **wholesaled; whole·sal·ing** *vi* : to sell in quantity usu. for resale ~ *vt* : to sell (something) in quantity usu. for resale

whole·sal·er \'hōl-,sā-lər\ *n* : a merchant middleman who sells chiefly to retailers, other merchants, or industrial, institutional, and commercial users mainly for resale or business use

whole·some \'hōl-səm\ *adj* **1** : promoting health or well-being of mind or spirit **2** : promoting health of body **3 a** : sound in body, mind, or morals **b** : having the simple health or vigor of normal domesticity **4 a** : based on well-grounded fear : PRUDENT <a ~ respect for the law> **b** : SAFE <it wouldn't be ~ for you to go down there —Mark Twain> *syn* see HEALTHY — **whole·some·ly** *adv* — **whole·some·ness** *n*

whole–souled \'hōl-'sōld\ *adj* : moved by ardent enthusiasm or single-minded devotion : WHOLEHEARTED

whole step *n* : a musical interval (as C–D or G–A) comprising two half steps — called also *whole tone*

whole wheat *adj* : made of ground entire wheat kernels

whol·ly \'hōl-(l)ē\ *adv* [ME *hoolly,* fr. *hool* whole] **1** : to the full or entire extent : COMPLETELY <~ incompetent> **2** : to the exclusion of other things : SOLELY <a book dealing ~ with herbs>

whom \(')hüm, üm\ *pron, objective case of* WHO [ME, fr. OE *hwām,* dat. of *hwā* who] — used as an interrogative or relative; used as object of a verb or a preceding preposition <to know for ~ the bell tolls —John Donne> or less frequently as the object of a following preposition <the man ~ you wrote to> though now often considered stilted esp. as an interrogative and esp. in oral use; occas. used as predicate nominative with a copulative verb or as subject of a verb esp. in the vicinity of a preposition or a verb of which it might mistakenly be considered the object <~ say ye that I am — Mt 16:15 (AV)> <people . . . ~ you never thought would sympathize —Shea Murphy>

whom·ev·er \hü-'mev-ər\ *pron, objective case of* WHOEVER

[1]**whomp** \'hwämp, 'hwȯmp, 'wämp, 'wȯmp\ *n* [imit.] : a loud slap, crash, or crunch

2whomp *vi* : to strike with a sharp noise or thump ~ *vt* **1** : to hit or slap sharply **2** : to defeat decisively : TROUNCE
whomp up *vt* **1** : to stir up : AROUSE **2** : to put together esp. hastily
whom·so \ˈhüm-(ˌ)sō\ *objective case of* WHOSO
whom·so·ev·er \ˌhüm-sə-ˈwev-ər\ *objective case of* WHOSOEVER
1whoop \ˈhüp, ˈhu̇p, *least frequently for vi 3* ˈhwüp *or* ˈhwu̇p\ *vb* [ME *whopen*, fr. MF *houpper*, of imit. origin] *vi* **1** : to utter a whoop in expression of eagerness, enthusiasm, or enjoyment : SHOUT **2** : to utter the cry of an owl : HOOT **3** : to make the characteristic whoop of whooping cough **4 a** : to go or pass with a loud noise **b** : to be rushed through by acclamation or with noisy support <the bill ~*ed* through both houses> ~ *vt* **1 a** : to utter or express with a whoop **b** : to urge, drive, or cheer on with a whoop **2** : to agitate in behalf of **3** : BOOST, RAISE <~ up the price> — **whoop it up** **1** : to celebrate riotously : CAROUSE **2** : to stir up enthusiasm
2whoop *n* **1 a** : a loud yell expressive of eagerness, exuberance, or jubilation — often used interjectionally **b** : a shout of hunters or of men in battle or pursuit **2** : the cry of an owl : HOOT **3** : the crowing intake of breath following a paroxysm in whooping cough **4** : a minimum amount or degree (as of care or consideration) : the least bit <not worth a ~>
whoop–de–do *or* **whoop–de–doo** \ˌh(w)üp-dē-ˈdü, ˌh(w)u̇p-, -tē-\ *n* [prob. irreg. fr. 2*whoop*] **1** : noisy and exuberant or attention-getting activity (as at a social affair or in a political campaign) **2** : a lively social affair **3** : agitated public discussion or debate
1whoop·ee \ˈ(h)wu̇p-(ˌ)ē, ˈ(h)wü-(ˌ)pē; (h)wu̇-ˈpē, (h)wü-\ *interj* [irreg. fr. 2*whoop*] — used to express exuberance
2whoop·ee \ˈ(h)wu̇p-(ˌ)ē, ˈ(h)wü-(ˌ)pē\ *n* : boisterous convivial fun
whoop·er *n* : one that whoops; *specif* : WHOOPING CRANE
whooping cough *n* : an infectious disease esp. of children caused by a bacterium (*Bordetella pertussis*) and marked by a convulsive spasmodic cough sometimes followed by a crowing intake of breath — called also *pertussis*
whooping crane *n* : a large white nearly extinct No. American crane (*Grus americana*) noted for its loud whooping note
whoop·la \ˈh(w)üp-ˌlä, ˈh(w)u̇p-\ *n* [alter. of *hoopla*] **1** : a noisy commotion **2** : boisterous merrymaking
whoops \ˈ(w)u̇(ə)ps\ *interj* : OOPS
1whoosh \ˈhwüsh, ˈwüsh, ˈ(h)wu̇sh\ *vb* [imit.] *vi* : to rush past or move explosively <cars ~*ing* along the expressway> ~ *vt* : to move (a person or thing) with an explosive or sibilant rush
2whoosh *n* : a swift or explosive rush
1whop \ˈhwäp, ˈwäp\ *vt* **whopped; whop·ping** [ME *whappen*, alter. of *wappen* to throw violently] **1** : to pull or whip out **2 a** : BEAT, STRIKE **b** : to defeat totally

whooping crane

2whop *n* : a heavy blow : THUMP
whop·per \ˈhwäp-ər, ˈwäp-\ *n* [1*whop*] **1** : something unusually large or otherwise extreme of its kind **2** : an extravagant or monstrous lie
whop·ping \ˈhwäp-iŋ, ˈwäp-\ *adj* : extremely large; *also* : EXTRAORDINARY, EXTRAVAGANT
1whore \ˈhō(ə)r, ˈhȯ(ə)r, ˈhu̇(ə)r\ *n* [ME *hore*, fr. OE *hōre*; akin to ON *hōra* whore, *hōrr* adulterer, L *carus* dear — more at CHARITY] : a woman who practices promiscuous sexual intercourse esp. for hire : PROSTITUTE
2whore *vb* **whored; whor·ing** *vi* **1** : to have unlawful sexual intercourse as or with a whore **2** : to pursue a faithless, unworthy, or idolatrous desire ~ *vt, obs* : DEBAUCH
whore·dom \ˈhōrd-əm, ˈhȯrd-, ˈhu̇rd-\ *n* [ME *hordom* sexual immorality, idolatrous practices, fr. ON *hōrdōmr* adultery, fr. *hōrr*] **1** : the practice of whoring : PROSTITUTION **2** : faithless, unworthy, or idolatrous practices or pursuits
whore·house \ˈhō(ə)r-ˌhau̇s, ˈhȯ(ə)r-, ˈhu̇(ə)r-\ *n* : a building in which prostitutes are available
whore·mas·ter \-ˌmas-tər\ *n* : a man consorting with whores or given to lechery
whore·mon·ger \-ˌməŋ-gər, -ˌmäŋ-\ *n, archaic* : WHOREMASTER
whore·son \ˈhōrs-ᵊn, ˈhȯrs-, ˈhu̇rs-\ *n, often attrib* **1** : BASTARD **2** : a coarse fellow — used as a generalized term of abuse
whor·ish \ˈhōr-ish, ˈhȯr-, ˈhu̇r-\ *adj* : of or resembling a whore : LEWD
whorl \ˈhwȯr(ə)l, ˈwȯr(ə)l, ˈ(h)wər(-ə)l\ *n* [ME *wharle, whorle*, prob. alter. of *whirle*, fr. *whirlen* to whirl] **1** : a drum-shaped section on the lower part of a spindle in spinning or weaving machinery serving as a pulley for the tape drive that rotates the spindle **2** : an arrangement of similar anatomical parts (as leaves) in a circle around a point on an axis **3** : something that whirls, coils, or spirals or whose form suggests such movement : SWIRL <~*s* of snow> **4** : one of the turns of a univalve shell **5** : a fingerprint in which the central papillary ridges turn through at least one complete circle — see FINGERPRINT illustration
whorled \ˈhwȯr(ə)ld, ˈwȯr(ə)ld, ˈ(h)wər(-ə)ld\ *adj* : having or arranged in whorls; *esp* : VERTICILLATE <~ leaves>
whort \ˈhwərt, ˈwərt\ *or* **whor·tle** \ˈhwərt-ᵊl, ˈwərt-\ *n* : WHORTLEBERRY 1
whor·tle·ber·ry \ˈhwərt-ᵊl-ˌber-ē, ˈwərt-\ *n* [alter. of earlier *hurtleberry*, fr. ME *hurtilberye*, irreg. fr. OE *horte* whortleberry + ME *berye* berry] **1** : a European blueberry (*Vaccinium myrtillus*); *also* : its glaucous blackish edible berry **2** : BLUEBERRY
1whose \(ˈ)hüz, üz\ *adj* [ME *whos*, gen. of *who, what*] : of or relating to whom or which esp. as possessor or possessors <~ gorgeous vesture heaps the ground —Robert Browning>, agent or agents <the law courts, ~ decisions were important —F. L. Mott>, or object or objects of an action <the first poem ~ publication he ever sanctioned —J. W. Krutch>
2whose *pron, sing or pl in constr* : that which belongs to whom — used without a following noun as a pronoun equivalent in meaning to the adjective *whose* <tell me ~ it was —Shak.>
whose·so·ev·er \ˌhüz-sə-ˈwev-ər\ *adj* : of or relating to whomsoever <~ sins ye remit —Jn 20:23 (AV)>
who·so \ˈhü-(ˌ)sō\ *pron* : WHOEVER
who·so·ev·er \ˌhü-sə-ˈwev-ər\ *pron* : WHOEVER
who's who *n, often cap both Ws* : a compilation of brief biographical sketches of prominent persons in a particular field <a *who's who* of sports figures>
WHP *abbr* water horsepower
whr *abbr* watt-hour
whs *or* **whse** *abbr* warehouse
whsle *abbr* wholesale
whump \ˈhwəmp, ˈwəmp\ *vi* [imit.] : BANG, THUMP — **whump** *n*
1why \(ˈ)hwī, (ˈ)wī\ *adv* [ME, fr. OE *hwȳ*, instr. case of *hwæt* what — more at WHAT] : for what cause, reason, or purpose <~ did you do it>
2why *conj* **1** : the cause, reason, or purpose for which <know ~ you did it> <that is ~ you did it> **2** : for which : on account of which <know the reason ~ you did it>
3why \ˈhwī, ˈwī\ *n, pl* **whys** **1** : REASON, CAUSE <wants to know the ~*s* and wherefores> **2** : a baffling problem : ENIGMA
4why \(ˌ)wī, (ˌ)hwī\ *interj* [1*why*] — used to express mild surprise, hesitation, approval, disapproval, or impatience <~, here's what I was looking for>
whyd·ah \ˈhwid-ə, ˈwid-\ *n* [alter. of *widow (bird)*] : any of various mostly black and white African weaverbirds often kept as cage birds and distinguished in the male by long drooping tail feathers during the breeding season
wi *abbr* when issued
WI *abbr* **1** West Indies **2** Wisconsin **3** wrought iron
WIA *abbr* wounded in action
wick \ˈwik\ *n* [ME *weke, wicke*, fr. OE *wēoce*; akin to OHG *wiohha* wick, OIr *figim* I weave] : a bundle of fibers or a loosely twisted, braided, or woven cord, tape, or tube usu. of soft spun cotton threads that by capillary attraction draws up to be burned a steady supply of the oil in lamps or the melted tallow or wax in candles
Wick *abbr* Wicklow
wick·ed \ˈwik-əd\ *adj* [ME, alter. of *wicke* wicked] **1** : morally very bad : EVIL **2 a** : FIERCE, VICIOUS <a ~ dog> **b** : disposed to mischief : ROGUISH **3 a** : disgustingly unpleasant : VILE <a ~ odor> **b** : causing or likely to cause harm, distress, or trouble <a ~ storm> **4** : going beyond reasonable or predictable limits <a ~ loss of life> <~ skill at cards> ***syn*** see BAD — **wick·ed·ly** *adv*
wick·ed·ness *n* **1** : the quality or state of being wicked **2** : something wicked
wick·er \ˈwik-ər\ *n* [ME *wiker*, of Scand origin; akin to Sw dial. *vikker* willow, ON *veikr* weak — more at WEAK] **1** : a small pliant twig or branch : OSIER, WITHE **2 a** : WICKERWORK **b** : something made of wicker — **wicker** *adj*
wick·er·work \-ˌwərk\ *n* : work consisting of interlaced osiers, twigs, or rods <a cage of ~>
wick·et \ˈwik-ət\ *n* [ME *wiket*, fr. ONF, of Gmc origin; akin to MD *wiket* wicket, OE *wīcan* to yield — more at WEAK] **1** : a small gate or door; *esp* : one forming part of or placed near a larger gate or door **2** : an opening like a window; *esp* : a grilled or grated window through which business is transacted **3** : a small gate for emptying the chamber of a canal lock or regulating the amount of water passing through a channel **4 a** : either of the 2 sets of 3 stumps topped by 2 crosspieces and set 22 yards apart at which the ball is bowled in cricket **b** : an area 10 feet wide bounded by these wickets **c** : one innings of a batsman; *specif* : one that is not completed or never begun <win by 3 ~*s*> **5** : an arch or hoop in croquet
wick·ing \ˈwik-iŋ\ *n* : material for wicks
wick·i·up \ˈwik-ē-ˌəp\ *n* [Saç, Fox, & Kickapoo *wikiyap* dwelling] : a hut used by the nomadic Indians of the arid regions of the western and southwestern U.S. with a usu. oval base and a rough frame covered with reed mats, grass, or brushwood; *also* : a rude temporary shelter or hut

wickiup

wic·o·py *or* **wick·a·pe** \ˈwik-ə-pē\ *n* [Cree *wikupiy* inner bark of basswood] **1** : LEATHERWOOD **2** : a basswood (*Tilia glabra*) **3** : WILLOW HERB 1
wid *abbr* widow; widower
wid·der·shins \ˈwid-ər-shənz\ *adv* [MLG *weddersinnes*] : in a left-handed, wrong, or contrary direction : COUNTERCLOCKWISE — compare DEASIL
wid·dy \ˈwid-ē\ *n, pl* **widdies** [ME (Sc), fr. ME *withy*] **1** *Scot & dial Eng* : a rope of osiers : WITHY **2** *Scot & dial Eng* : a hangman's noose
1wide \ˈwīd\ *adj* **wid·er; wid·est** [ME, fr. OE *wīd*; akin to OHG *wīt* wide] **1 a** : having great extent : VAST <a ~ area> **b** : extending over a vast area : EXTENSIVE <a ~ reputation> **c** : extending throughout a specified area or scope <nation*wide*> **d** : COMPREHENSIVE 1, INCLUSIVE 1 <reaches a ~ public> **2 a** : having a specified extension from side to side <3 feet ~> **b** : having much extent between the sides : BROAD <a ~ doorway> **c** : fully opened <*wide*-eyed> **d** : LAX 4 **3 a** : extending or fluctuating considerably between limits <a ~ variation> **b** : straying or deviating from something specified <his remark was ~ of the truth> **4** *of an animal ration* : relatively rich in

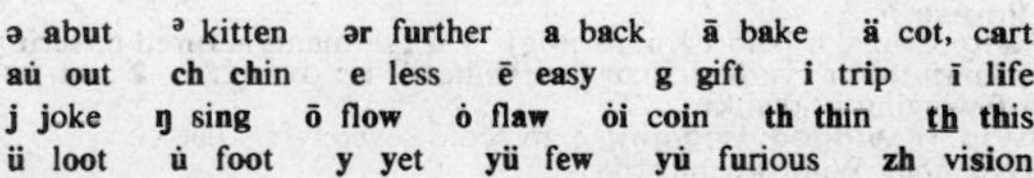

ə abut   ᵊ kitten   ər further   a back   ā bake   ä cot, cart
au̇ out   ch chin   e less   ē easy   g gift   i trip   ī life
j joke   ŋ sing   ō flow   ȯ flaw   ȯi coin   th thin   t͟h this
ü loot   u̇ foot   y yet   yü few   yu̇ furious   zh vision

carbohydrate as compared with protein *syn* see BROAD *ant* strait — **wide·ness** *n*

[2]wide *adv* **wid·er; wid·est** **1 a :** over a great distance or extent **:** WIDELY <searched far and ~> **b :** over a specified distance, area, or extent <expanded the business country-*wide*> **2 a :** so as to leave much space or distance between **b :** so as to pass at or clear by a considerable distance <ran ~ around left end> **3 :** to the fullest extent **:** COMPLETELY, FULLY <~ open>

wide–an·gle \'wī-'daŋ-gəl\ *adj* **1 :** having or covering an angle of view wider than the ordinary — used esp. of lenses of shorter than normal focal length **2 :** having, involving the use of, or relating to a wide-angle lens <a ~ camera>

wide–awake \ˌwīd-ə-'wāk\ *adj* **1 :** fully awake **2 :** alertly watchful esp. for advantages or opportunities *syn* see WATCHFUL — **wide–awake·ness** *n*

wide–eyed \'wīd-'īd\ *adj* **1 :** having the eyes wide open esp. with wonder or astonishment **2 :** marked by unsophisticated or uncritical acceptance or admiration **:** NAIVE <~ innocence>

wide·ly *adv* **1 :** over a broad range <persons with ~ fluctuating incomes —*Current Biog.*> **2 :** to a great extent <departed ~ from the previous edition> **3 :** by or among a large well= dispersed group of people <a ~ known political figure> **4 :** over or through a wide area <has traveled ~>

wide·mouthed \'wīd-'mau̇thd, -'mau̇tht\ *adj* **1 :** having a wide mouth <~ jars> **2 :** having one's mouth opened wide (as in awe)

wid·en \'wīd-ᵊn\ *vb* **wid·ened; wid·en·ing** \'wīd-niŋ, -ᵊn-iŋ\ *vt* **:** to increase the width, scope, or extent of ~ *vi* **:** to become wide or wider — **wid·en·er** \-nər, -ᵊn-ər\ *n*

wide receiver *n* **:** a football receiver who normally lines up several yards to the side of the offensive formation

wide–screen *adj* **:** of or relating to a projected picture whose aspect ratio is substantially greater than 1.33:1

wide·spread \'wīd-'spred\ *adj* **1 :** widely extended or spread out <low, ~ hood and fenders —*Time*> <a ~ erosion surface —C. B. Hitchcock> **2 :** widely diffused or prevalent <~ public interest>

wide–spread·ing \-iŋ\ *adj* **1 :** stretching or extending over a wide space or area <~ thatch roofs —*Nat'l Geographic*> **2** *archaic* **:** spreading over or affecting a wide area

wid·geon *also* **wi·geon** \'wij-ən\ *n, pl* **widgeon** *or* **widgeons** [origin unknown] **:** any of several freshwater ducks (genus *Mareca*) between the teal and the mallard in size

wid·get \'wij-ət\ *n* [alter. of *gadget*] **1 :** GADGET **2 :** an unnamed article considered for purposes of hypothetical example

wid·ish \'wīd-ish\ *adj* **:** somewhat wide

[1]wid·ow \'wid-(ˌ)ō, 'wid-ə(-w)\ *n* [ME *widewe,* fr. OE *wuduwe;* akin to OHG *wituwa* widow, L *vidua* widow, *-videre* to separate, Gk *ēitheos* unmarried youth] **1 a :** a woman who has lost her husband by death; *esp* **:** one who has not remarried **b :** GRASS WIDOW 2 **2 :** an extra hand or part of a hand of cards dealt face down and usu. placed at the disposal of the highest bidder **3 :** a single usu. short last line (as of a paragraph) separated from its related text and appearing at the top of a printed page or column

[2]widow *vt* **1 :** to bereave of a spouse; *esp* **:** to cause to become a widow **2** *obs* **:** to survive as the widow of **3 :** to deprive of something greatly valued or needed

wid·ow·er \'wid-ə-wər\ *n* [ME *widewer,* alter. of *wedow* widow, widower, fr. OE *wuduwa* widower; akin to OE *wuduwe* widow] **:** a man who has lost his wife by death and has not married again

wid·ow·er·hood \-ˌhu̇d\ *n* **1 :** the quality or state of being a widower **2 :** the period during which a man remains a widower

wid·ow·hood \'wid-ō-ˌhu̇d, 'wid-ə-ˌhu̇d\ *n* **1 :** the quality or state of being a widow **2 :** the period during which a woman remains a widow

widow's peak *n* **:** PEAK 7

widow's walk *n* [fr. its use by the wives of seamen during their absence on a voyage] **:** a railed observation platform atop a usu. coastal house

width \'width, 'witth\ *n* [[1]*wide*] **1 :** the measurement taken at right angles to the length **:** BREADTH **2 :** largeness of extent or scope **3 :** a measured and cut piece of material <a ~ of calico> <a ~ of lumber>

width·ways \-ˌwāz\ *adv* **:** WIDTHWISE

width·wise \-ˌwīz\ *adv* **:** in the direction of the width **:** CROSSWISE

wield \'wē(ə)ld\ *vt* [ME *welden* to control, fr. OE *wieldan;* akin to OHG *waltan* to rule, L *valēre* to be strong, be worth] **1** *chiefly dial* **:** to deal successfully with **:** MANAGE **2 :** to handle (as a tool) effectively <~ a broom> **3 a :** to exert one's authority by means of <~ influence> **b :** have at one's command or disposal <did not ~ appropriate credentials —G. W. Bonham> *syn* see HANDLE — **wield·er** *n*

wieldy \'wē(ə)l-dē\ *adj* **:** capable of wielding or of being wielded easily

wie·ner \'wē-nər, 'wē-nē, 'win-ē\ *n* [short for *wienerwurst*] **:** FRANKFURTER

Wie·ner schnit·zel \'vē-nər-ˌs(h)nit-səl, 'wē-nər-ˌsnit-\ *n* [G, lit., Vienna cutlet] **:** a thin breaded veal cutlet served with a garnish

wie·ner·wurst \'wē-nə(r)-ˌwərst, -ˌwu̇(ə)rst; 'wē-nər-ˌwu̇s(h)t\ *n* [G, fr. *Wiener* of Vienna + *wurst* sausage] **1 :** VIENNA SAUSAGE **2 :** FRANKFURTER

wie·nie \'wē-nē, 'win-ē\ *n* **:** FRANKFURTER

wife \'wīf\ *n, pl* **wives** \'wīvz\ [ME *wif,* fr. OE *wīf;* akin to OHG *wīb* wife] **1 a** *dial* **:** WOMAN **b :** a woman acting in a specified capacity — used in combination <fish*wife*> **2 :** a married woman — **wife·hood** \'wīf-ˌhu̇d, 'wī-ˌfu̇d\ *n* — **wife·less** \'wī-fləs\ *adj*

[1]wife·like \'wī-ˌflīk\ *adv* **:** in a wifely manner

[2]wifelike *adj* **:** WIFELY

wife·ly \'wī-flē\ *adj* **:** of, relating to, or befitting a wife — **wife·li·ness** *n*

[1]wig \'wig\ *n* [short for *periwig*] **1 a :** a manufactured covering of natural or synthetic hair for the head **b :** TOUPEE 2 **2 :** an act of wigging **:** REBUKE

[2]wig *vt* **wigged; wig·ging :** to scold severely **:** REBUKE

Wig *abbr* Wigtownshire

wig·an \'wig-ən\ *n* [*Wigan,* England] **:** a stiff plain-weave cotton fabric used for interlining

wigged \'wigd\ *adj* **:** wearing a wig <the mute, blond-*wigged* . . . member of the team —*Current Biog.*>

[1]wig·gle \'wig-əl\ *vb* **wig·gled; wig·gling** \-(ə-)liŋ\ [ME *wiglen,* fr. or akin to MD or MLG *wiggelen* to totter; akin to OE *wegan* to move — more at WAY] *vi* **1 :** to move to and fro with quick jerky or shaking motions **:** JIGGLE **2 :** to proceed with or as if with twisting and turning movements **:** WRIGGLE ~ *vt* **:** to cause to wiggle

[2]wiggle *n* **1 :** the act of wiggling **2 :** shellfish or fish in cream sauce with peas — **wig·gly** \'wig-(ə-)lē\ *adj*

wig·gler \'wig-(ə-)lər\ *n* **1 :** one that wiggles **2 :** a larva or pupa of the mosquito — called also *wriggler*

[1]wight \'wīt\ *n* [ME, creature, thing, fr. OE *wiht;* akin to OHG *wiht* creature, thing, OSlav *vĕstĭ* thing] **:** a living being **:** CREATURE; *esp* **:** a human being

[2]wight *adj* [ME, of Scand origin; akin to ON *vīgr* skilled in fighting (neut. *vīgt*); akin to OE *wīgan* to fight — more at VICTOR] *archaic* **:** VALIANT, STALWART

wig·let \'wig-lət\ *n* **:** a small wig used esp. to enhance a hairstyle

wig·mak·er \'wig-ˌmā-kər\ *n* **:** one that makes or deals in wigs

[1]wig·wag \'wig-ˌwag\ *vb* [E dial. *wig* to move + E *wag*] *vi* **1 :** to send a signal by or as if by a flag or light waved according to a code **2 :** to make a signal (as with the hand or arm) ~ *vt* **1 :** to signal by wigwagging **2 :** to cause to wigwag

[2]wigwag *n* **1 :** the art or practice of wigwagging **2 :** the act of wigwagging

wig·wam \'wig-ˌwäm\ *n* [Abnaki & Massachuset *wīkwām*] **:** a hut of the Indians of the Great Lakes region and eastward having typically an arched framework of poles overlaid with bark, rush mats, or hides; *also* **:** a rough hut

wigwam

wil·co \'wil-(ˌ)kō\ *interj* [*will* comply] — used esp. in radio and signaling to indicate that a message received will be complied with

[1]wild \'wī(ə)ld\ *adj* [ME *wilde,* fr. OE; akin to OHG *wildi* wild, W *gwyllt*] **1 a :** living in a state of nature and not ordinarily tame or domesticated <~ duck> **b (1) :** growing or produced without the aid and care of man <~ honey> **(2) :** related to or resembling a corresponding cultivated or domesticated organism **c :** of or relating to wild organisms <the ~ state> **2 a :** not inhabited or cultivated <~ land> **b :** not amenable to human habitation or cultivation **:** WASTE **3 a (1) :** loose from restraint or regulation **:** UNCONTROLLED <~ mobs> **(2) :** emotionally overcome <~ with grief>; *also* **:** passionately eager or enthusiastic <was ~ to own a toy train —J. C. Furnas> **(3) :** not amenable to control or restraint **:** UNRULY <the zebra is too ~ to be used as a draft animal> **b :** marked by turbulent agitation **:** STORMY <a ~ night> **c :** going beyond normal or conventional bounds **:** FANTASTIC **d :** indicative of strong passion, desire, or emotion <a ~ gleam of delight in his eyes —*Irish Digest*> **4 :** UNCIVILIZED, BARBARIC **5 :** characteristic of, appropriate to, or expressive of wilderness, wildlife, or a simple or uncivilized society **6 a :** deviating from the intended or expected course <~ spelling —C. W. Cunnington> <the throw was ~> **b :** having no basis in known or surmised fact <a ~ guess> **7** *of a playing card* **:** able to represent any card designated by the holder — **wild·ly** \'wī(ə)l-(d)lē\ *adv* — **wild·ness** \'wī(ə)l(d)-nəs\ *n*

[2]wild *n* **1 :** a sparsely inhabited or uncultivated region or tract **:** WILDERNESS **2 :** a wild, free, or natural state or existence <living in the ~>

[3]wild *adv* **:** in a wild manner: as **a :** without regulation or control **b :** off an intended or expected course

wild and woolly *adj* **:** marked by a boisterous and untamed lack of polish and refinement <a *wild and woolly* town>

wild bergamot *n* **:** a fragrant No. American herb (*Monarda fistulosa*) having a terminal capitate cluster of rather large pink or purple flowers

wild boar *n* **:** an Old World wild hog (*Sus scrofa*) from which most domestic swine have been derived

wild carrot *n* **:** a widely naturalized Eurasian weed (*Daucus carota*) that is prob. the original of the cultivated carrot and has an acrid ill-flavored root — called also *Queen Anne's lace*

[1]wild·cat \'wī(ə)l(d)-ˌkat\ *n, pl* **wildcats** **1 a :** either of two cats (*Felis sylvestris* of Europe and *F. ocreata* of Africa) that resemble but are heavier in build than the domestic tabby cat and are usu. held to be among the ancestors of the domestic cat **b** *or pl* **wildcat :** any of various small or medium-sized cats (as the lynx or ocelot) **c :** a feral domestic cat **2 :** a savage quick-tempered person **3 a :** wildcat money **b :** a wildcat oil or gas well **c :** a wildcat strike

[2]wildcat *adj* **1 a (1) :** financially irresponsible or unreliable <~ banks> **(2) :** issued by a financially irresponsible banking establishment <~ currency> **b :** operating, produced, or carried on outside the bounds of standard or legitimate business practices <~ insurance schemes —H. H. Reichard> **c :** of, relating to, or being an oil or gas well drilled in territory not known to be productive **d :** initiated by a group of workers without formal union approval or in violation of a contract <a ~ strike> <~ work stoppages> **2 a** *of a cartridge* **:** having a bullet of standard caliber but using an expanded case or a case designed for a bullet of greater caliber necked down for the smaller bullet **b** *of a rifle* **:** using wildcat cartridges

[3]wildcat *vt* **wild·cat·ted; wild·cat·ting :** to prospect and drill an experimental oil or gas well or sink a mine shaft in territory not known to be productive

wild·cat·ter \-ˌkat-ər\ *n* **1 :** one that drills wells in the hope of finding oil in territory not known to be an oil field **2 :** one that promotes unsafe and unreliable enterprises; *esp* **:** one that sells stocks in enterprises of this kind **3 :** one that designs, builds, or fires wildcat cartridges and rifles as a hobby **4 :** a worker who goes out on an unauthorized strike

wild celery *n* **:** TAPE GRASS

wil·de·beest \'wil-də-ˌbēst\ *n, pl* **wildebeests** *also* **wildebeest** [Afrik *wildebees,* fr. *wilde* wild + *bees* ox] **:** GNU

wil·der \'wil-dər\ *vb* [prob. irreg. fr. *wilderness*] *vt* **1** *archaic* **:** to lead astray **2** *archaic* **:** BEWILDER, PERPLEX ~ *vi, archaic* **:** to move at random **:** WANDER — **wil·der·ment** \-dər-mənt\ *n, archaic*

wil·der·ness \'wil-dər-nəs\ *n* [ME, fr. *wildern* wild, fr. OE *wilddēoren* of wild beasts] **1 a** (1) **:** a tract or region uncultivated and uninhabited by human beings (2) **:** an area essentially undisturbed by human activity together with its naturally developed life community **b :** an empty or pathless area or region <in remote ~*es* of space groups of nebulae are found —G. W. Gray †1960> **c :** a part of a garden devoted to wild growth **2** *obs* **:** WILDNESS **3 a :** a confusing multitude or mass **:** an indefinitely great number or quantity <I would not have given it for a ~ of monkeys —Shak.> **b :** a bewildering situation <those moral ~*es* of civilized life —Norman Mailer>

wilderness area *n, often cap W&A* **:** an often large tract of public land maintained essentially in its natural state and protected against introduction of intrusive artifacts (as roads and buildings)

wild–eyed \'wī(ə)l-'dīd\ *adj* **1 :** having a wild expression in the eyes **2 :** consisting of or favoring extreme political or social measures <~ schemes>

wild·fire \'wī(ə)l(d)-ˌfī(ə)r\ *n* **1 :** a sweeping and destructive conflagration **2 a :** GREEK FIRE **b :** something that acts intensely and usu. very rapidly — usu. used in the phrase *like wildfire* **3 :** a phosphorescent glow (as ignis fatuus or fox fire) **4 :** a destructive bacterial disease of tobacco

wild flax *n* **1 :** GOLD OF PLEASURE **2 :** BUTTER-AND-EGGS

wild flower *n* **:** the flower of a wild or uncultivated plant or the plant bearing it

wild·fowl \'wī(ə)l(d)-ˌfau̇l\ *n* **:** a game bird; *esp* **:** a game waterfowl (as a wild duck or goose) — **wild·fowl·er** \-ˌfau̇-lər\ *n* — **wild·fowl·ing** \-liŋ\ *n*

wild geranium *n* **1 :** a common geranium (*Geranium maculatum*) of eastern No. America with deeply parted leaves and flowers of rosy purple **2 :** any of several geraniums related to the wild geranium

wild ginger *n* **:** a No. American perennial herb (*Asarum canadense*) of the birthwort family with a pungent creeping rhizome

wild–goose chase *n* **:** a fruitless pursuit or search

wild hyacinth *n* **:** any of several plants with flowers suggestive of hyacinths: as **a :** a camas (*Camassia scilloides*) with white racemose flowers **b :** WOOD HYACINTH

wild indigo *n* **:** any of a genus (*Baptisia*) of American leguminous plants; *esp* **:** a tumbleweed (*B. tinctoria*) with bright yellow flowers and trifoliolate leaves

¹wild·ing \'wīl-diŋ\ *n* [¹*wild* + ²*-ing*] **1 a :** a plant growing uncultivated in the wild either as a native or an escape; *esp* **:** a wild apple or crab apple **b :** the fruit of a wilding **2 :** a wild animal

²wilding *adj* **:** not domesticated or cultivated **:** WILD

wild·ish \'wīl-dish\ *adj* **:** somewhat wild

wild land *n* **:** land that is uncultivated or unfit for cultivation

wild·life \'wī(ə)l-ˌ(d)līf\ *n, often attrib* **:** living things that are neither human nor domesticated; *esp* **:** mammals, birds, and fishes hunted by man

wild·ling \'wī(ə)l-(d)liŋ\ *n* **:** WILDING

wild madder *n* **1 :** MADDER 1, 2a **2 :** either of two bedstraws (*Gallium mollugo* and *G. tinctorium*)

wild marjoram *n* **:** OREGANO 1

wild mustard *n* **:** CHARLOCK

wild oat *n* **1 a :** any of several wild grasses (genus *Avena*); *esp* **:** a European annual weed (*A. fatua*) common in meadows and pastures **b :** any of a genus (*Uvularia*) of small herbs of the lily family with drooping bell-shaped yellowish flowers **2** *pl* **:** offenses and indiscretions ascribed to youthful exuberance — usu. used in the phrase *sow one's wild oats*

wild olive *n* **:** any of various trees that resemble the olive or have fruits resembling its fruit

wild pansy *n* **:** a common and long-cultivated European viola (*Viola tricolor*) which has short-spurred flowers usu. blue or purple mixed with white and yellow and from which most of the garden pansies are derived — called also *heartsease, Johnny-jump-up*

wild parsley *n* **:** any of numerous wild plants of the carrot family with finely divided foliage

wild pink *n* **:** an American catchfly (genus *Silene*); *esp* **:** one (*S. caroliniana*) of the eastern U.S. with pink or whitish flowers

wild pitch *n* **:** a pitched baseball not hit by the batter that cannot be caught or controlled by the catcher with ordinary effort and that enables a base runner to advance — compare PASSED BALL

wild rice *n* **:** a tall aquatic No. American perennial grass (*Zizania aquatica*) that yields an edible grain

wild rye *n* **:** any of several grasses (genus *Elymus*)

wild sarsaparilla *n* **:** a common No. American perennial herb (*Aralia nudicaulis*) with long-stalked basal compound leaves, umbels of greenish flowers, and an aromatic root used as a substitute of true sarsaparilla

wild type *n* **:** the typical form of an organism as ordinarily encountered in nature in contrast to atypical mutant individuals — **wild–type** *adj*

wild vanilla *n* **:** a perennial composite herb (*Trilisa odoratissima*) of the southeastern U.S. with vanilla-scented leaves

wild West *n* **:** the western U.S. in its frontier period

wild·wood \'wī(ə)l-ˌ(d)wu̇d\ *n* **:** a wood unaltered or unfrequented by man

¹wile \'wī(ə)l\ *n* [ME *wil,* fr. (assumed) ONF, prob. of Gmc origin; akin to OE *wigle* divination — more at WITCH] **1 :** a trick or stratagem intended to ensnare or deceive; *also* **:** a beguiling or playful trick **2 :** skill in outwitting **:** TRICKERY, GUILE ***syn*** see TRICK

²wile *vt* **wiled; wil·ing** **1 :** to lure by or as if by a magic spell **:** ENTICE **2** [perh. alter. of *while*] **:** to pass or spend pleasurably ***syn*** see WHILE

¹will \wəl, (ə)l, (ˈ)wil\ *vb, past* **would** \wəd, (ə)d, (ˈ)wu̇d\; *pres sing & pl* **will** [ME (1st & 3d sing. pres. indic.), fr. OE *wille* (infin. *wyllan*); akin to OHG *wili* (3d sing. pres. indic.) wills, L *velle* to wish, will] *vt* **:** DESIRE, WISH <call it what you ~> ~ *verbal auxiliary* **1** — used to express desire, choice, willingness, consent, or in negative constructions refusal <could find no one who *would* take the job> <if we ~ all do our best> <~ you please stop that racket> **2** — used to express frequent, customary, or habitual action or natural tendency or disposition <~ get angry over nothing> <~ work one day and loaf the next> **3** — used to express futurity <tomorrow morning I ~ wake up in this first-class hotel suite —Tennessee Williams> **4** — used to express capability or sufficiency <back seat ~ hold three passengers> **5** — used to express probability and often equivalent to the simple verb <that ~ be the milkman> **6 a** — used to express determination, insistence, persistence, or willfulness <I have made up my mind to go and go I ~> **b** — used to express inevitability <accidents ~ happen> **7** — used to express a command, exhortation, or injunction <you ~ do as I say, at once> ~ *vi* **:** to have a wish or desire <whether we ~ or no>

²will \'wil\ *n* [ME, fr. OE *willa* will, desire; akin to OE *wille*] **1 :** DESIRE, WISH: as **a :** DISPOSITION, INCLINATION <where there's a ~ there's a way> **b :** APPETITE, PASSION **c :** CHOICE, DETERMINATION **2 a :** something desired; *esp* **:** a choice or determination of one having authority or power **b** (1) *archaic* **:** REQUEST, COMMAND (2) [fr. the phrase *our will is* which introduces it] **:** the part of a summons expressing a royal command **3 :** the act, process, or experience of willing **:** VOLITION **4 a :** mental powers manifested as wishing, choosing, desiring, or intending **b :** a disposition to act according to principles or ends **c :** the collective desire of a group <the ~ of the people> **5 :** the power of control over one's own actions or emotions <a man of iron ~> **6 :** a legal declaration of a person's mind as to the manner in which he would have his property or estate disposed of after his death; *esp* **:** a written instrument legally executed by which a man makes disposition of his estate to take effect after his death — **at will** **:** as one wishes **:** as or when it pleases or suits oneself

³will \'wil\ *vt* **1 a :** to order or direct by a will **b :** to dispose of by or as if by a will **:** BEQUEATH **2 a :** to determine by an act of choice **b :** DECREE, ORDAIN <Providence ~*s* it> **c :** INTEND, PURPOSE ~ *vi* **1 :** to exercise the will **2 :** CHOOSE

will·able \'wil-ə-bəl\ *adj* **:** capable of being willed, wished, or determined by will

willed \'wild\ *adj* **:** having a will esp. of a specified kind — usu. used in combination <strong-*willed*>

wil·lem·ite \'wil-ə-ˌmīt\ *n* [G *willemit,* fr. *Willem* (William) I †1843 king of the Netherlands] **:** a mineral Zn_2SiO_4 consisting of zinc silicate, occurring in hexagonal prisms and in massive or granular forms, and varying in color

wil·let \'wil-ət\ *n, pl* **willet** [imit.] **:** a large shorebird (*Catoptrophorus semipalmatus*) of the eastern and Gulf coasts and the central parts of No. America

will·ful *or* **wil·ful** \'wil-fəl\ *adj* **1 :** obstinately and often perversely self-willed **2 :** done deliberately **:** INTENTIONAL ***syn*** **1** see VOLUNTARY **2** see UNRULY ***ant*** biddable — **will·ful·ly** \-fə-lē\ *adv* — **will·ful·ness** *n*

Wil·liam Tell \ˌwil-yəm-'tel\ *n* **:** a marksman of Swiss legend who complied with an order to shoot an apple off his son's head with an arrow

wil·lies \'wil-ēz\ *n pl* [origin unknown] **:** a fit of nervousness **:** JITTERS — used with *the*

wil·lie–waught \'wil-ē-ˌwäkt\ *n* [*guid willie-waught,* by incorrect division fr. Sc *guidwillie waught* cheering drink] **:** a deep draft (as of ale)

will·ing \'wil-iŋ\ *adj* **1 :** inclined or favorably disposed in mind **:** READY **2 :** prompt to act or respond **3 :** done, borne, or accepted by choice or without reluctance **4 :** of or relating to the will or power of choosing **:** VOLITIONAL — **will·ing·ly** \-iŋ-lē\ *adv* — **will·ing·ness** *n*

wil·li·waw \'wil-i-ˌwȯ\ *n* [origin unknown] **1 a :** a sudden violent gust of cold land air common along mountainous coasts of high latitudes **b :** a sudden violent wind **2 :** a violent commotion or agitation

will–less \'wil-ləs\ *adj* **1 :** involving no exercise of the will **:** INVOLUNTARY <~ obedience> **2 :** not exercising the will <~ human beings>

will–o'–the–wisp \ˌwil-ə-t͟hə-'wisp\ *n* [*Will* (nickname for *William*) + *of* + *the* + *wisp*] **1 :** IGNIS FATUUS **2 :** a delusive goal — **will–o'–the–wisp·ish** \-'wis-pish\ *adj*

¹wil·low \'wil-(ˌ)ō, 'wil-ə(-w)\ *n* [ME *wilghe, wilowe,* fr. OE *welig;* akin to MHG *wilge* willow, Gk *helikē*] **1 :** any of a genus (*Salix* of the family Salicaceae, the willow family) of trees and shrubs bearing aments of apetalous flowers and including forms of value for wood, osiers, or tanbark and a few ornamentals **2 :** an object made of willow wood; *esp* **:** a cricket bat **3** [alter. of ¹*willy*] **:** a textile machine in which cotton or wool is opened and cleaned by a spiked drum revolving in a box studded internally with spikes — called also *willower, willy* — **wil·low·like** \-ō-ˌlīk, -ə-ˌlīk\ *adj*

²willow *vt* **:** to open and clean (textile fibers) with a willow

wil·low·er \'wil-ə-wər\ *n* **1 :** a textile worker who operates a willow **2 :** WILLOW 3

willow herb *n* **1 :** any of a genus (*Epilobium*) of herbs of the evening-primrose family; *esp* **:** FIREWEED b **2 :** LOOSESTRIFE; *esp* **:** a purplish-flowered form (*Lythrum salicaria*) common in marshes

wil·low·ware \ˈwil-ə-ˌwa(ə)r, ˈwil-ō-, -ˌwe(ə)r\ *n* **:** dinnerware that is usu. blue-and-white and that is decorated with a story-telling design featuring a large willow tree by a little bridge

wil·lowy \ˈwil-ə-wē\ *adj* **1 :** abounding with willows **2 a :** resembling a willow **:** PLIANT **b :** gracefully tall and slender

will·pow·er \ˈwil-ˌpau̇(-ə)r\ *n* **:** energetic determination **:** RESOLUTENESS

will to power **1 :** the drive of the superman in the philosophy of Nietzsche to perfect and transcend the self through the possession and exercise of creative power **2 :** a conscious or unconscious desire to exercise authority over others

¹wil·ly \ˈwil-ē\ *n, pl* **willies** [(assumed) ME, basket, fr. OE *wiliga;* akin to OE *welig* willow] **:** WILLOW 3

²willy *vt* **wil·lied; wil·ly·ing :** WILLOW

wil·ly-nil·ly \ˌwil-ē-ˈnil-ē\ *adv or adj* [alter. of *will I nill I* or *will ye nill ye* or *will he nill he*] **:** by compulsion **:** without choice

Wil·son's disease \ˈwil-sənz-\ *n* [Samuel A. K. *Wilson* †1937 E neurologist] **:** a congenital disease that is characterized by inability to metabolize copper and is marked esp. by cirrhotic changes in the liver and severe mental disorder

¹wilt \wəlt, (ˈ)wilt\ *archaic pres 2d sing of* WILL

²wilt \ˈwilt\ *vb* [alter. of earlier *welk,* fr. ME *welken,* prob. fr. MD; akin to OHG *erwelkēn* to wilt] *vi* **1 :** to lose freshness and become flaccid (as a plant on a dry day) **:** DROOP **2 :** to grow weak or faint **:** LANGUISH ~ *vt* **:** to cause to wilt

³wilt \ˈwilt\ *n* **1 :** an act or instance of wilting **:** the state of being wilted **2 a :** a disorder (as a fungus disease) of plants marked by loss of turgidity in soft tissues with subsequent drooping and often shriveling — called also *wilt disease* **b :** a destructive virus disease of various caterpillars marked by visceral liquefaction and shriveling of the body

Wil·ton \ˈwilt-ᵊn\ *n* [*Wilton,* borough in England] **:** a carpet woven with loops like the Brussels carpet but having a velvet cut pile and being generally of better materials

Wilts *abbr* Wiltshire

wily \ˈwī-lē\ *adj* **wil·i·er; -est :** full of wiles **:** CRAFTY — **wil·i·ly** \-lə-lē\ *adv* — **wil·i·ness** \-lē-nəs\ *n*

¹wim·ble \ˈwim-bəl\ *n* [ME, fr. AF, fr. MD *wimmel* auger; akin to MLG *wimmel* auger] **:** any of various instruments for boring holes

²wimble *vt* **wim·bled; wim·bling** \-b(ə-)liŋ\ *archaic* **:** to bore with or as if with a wimble

¹wim·ple \ˈwim-pəl\ *n* [ME *wimpel,* fr. OE; akin to OE *wīpian* to wipe] **1 :** a cloth covering worn outdoors over the head and around the neck and chin esp. by women in the late medieval period and by some nuns **2** *Scot* **a :** a crafty turn **:** TWIST **b :** CURVE, BEND

wimple 1

²wimple *vb* **wim·pled; wim·pling** \-p(ə-)liŋ\ *vt* **1 :** to cover with or as if with a wimple **:** VEIL **2 :** to cause to ripple ~ *vi* **1 :** to fall or lie in folds **2** *chiefly Scot* **:** to follow a winding course **:** MEANDER **3 :** RIPPLE

¹win \ˈwin\ *vb* **won** \ˈwən\; **win·ning** [ME *winnen,* fr. OE *winnan* to struggle; akin to OHG *winnan* to struggle, L *venus* love, charm] *vi* **1 :** to gain the victory in a contest **:** SUCCEED **2 :** to succeed in arriving at a place or a state ~ *vt* **1 a :** to get possession of by effort or fortune **b :** to obtain by work **:** EARN <striving to ~ a living from the sterile soil> **2 a :** to gain in or as if in battle or contest **b :** to be the victor in <*won* the war> **3 :** to solicit and gain the favor of; *esp* **:** to induce to accept oneself in marriage **4 a :** to obtain (as ore, coal, or clay) by mining **b :** to prepare (as a vein or bed) for regular mining **c :** to recover (as metal) from ore **5 :** to reach by expenditure of effort ***syn*** see GET ***ant*** lose — **win·na·ble** \ˈwin-ə-bəl\ *adj*

²win *n* **:** VICTORY; *specif* **:** first place at the finish of a horse race

wince \ˈwin(t)s\ *vi* **winced; winc·ing** [ME *wenchen* to be impatient, dart about, fr. (assumed) ONF *wenchier,* of Gmc origin; akin to OHG *wankōn* to totter, OE *wincian* to wink] **:** to shrink back involuntarily (as from pain) **:** FLINCH ***syn*** see RECOIL — **wince** *n*

¹winch \ˈwinch\ *n* [ME *winche* roller, reel, fr. OE *wince;* akin to OE *wincian* to wink] **1 :** any of various machines or instruments for hauling or pulling; *esp* **:** a powerful machine with one or more drums on which to coil a rope, cable, or chain for hauling or hoisting **:** WINDLASS **2 :** a crank with a handle for giving motion to a machine (as a grindstone)

winch 1

²winch *vt* **:** to hoist or haul with or as if with a winch — **winch·er** *n*

¹wind \ˈwind, *archaic or poetic* ˈwīnd\ *n, often attrib* [ME, fr. OE; akin to OHG *wint* wind, L *ventus,* Gk *aēnai* to blow, Skt *vāti* it blows] **1 a :** a natural movement of air of any velocity; *esp* **:** air in natural motion horizontally **b :** an artificially produced movement of air **2 a :** a destructive force or influence **b :** a force or agency that carries along or influences **:** TENDENCY, TREND <withstood the ~*s* of popular opinion —Felix Frankfurter> **3 a :** BREATH 4a **b :** BREATH 2a **c :** the pit of the stomach **:** SOLAR PLEXUS **4 :** gas generated in the stomach or the intestines **5 a :** compressed air or gas **b** *archaic* **:** AIR **6 :** something that is insubstantial: as **a :** mere talk **:** idle words **b :** NOTHING, NOTHINGNESS **c :** vain self-satisfaction **7 a :** air carrying a scent (as of a hunter or game) **b :** slight information esp. about something secret **:** INTIMATION <got ~ of the rumors about him> **8 a :** musical wind instruments esp. as distinguished from strings and percussion **b** *pl* **:** players of wind instruments **9 a :** a direction from which the wind may blow **:** a point of the compass; *esp* **:** one of the cardinal points **b :** the direction from which the wind is blowing — **wind·less** \-ləs\ *adj* — **wind·less·ly** *adv* — **wind·less·ness** *n* — **before the wind :** in the same direction as the main force of the wind — **close to the wind :** as nearly as possible against the main force of the wind — **have the wind of 1 :** to be to windward of **2 :** to be on the scent of **3 :** to have a superior position to — **in the wind :** about to happen **:** ASTIR, AFOOT <other projects than a new building were *in the wind* —Ben Riker> — **near the wind 1 :** close to the wind **2 :** close to a point of danger **:** near the permissible limit — **off the wind :** away from the direction from which the wind is blowing — **on the wind :** toward the direction from which the wind is blowing — **under the wind 1 :** to leeward **2 :** in a place protected from the wind **:** under the lee

²wind \ˈwind\ *vt* **1 :** to detect or follow by scent **2 :** to expose to the air or wind **:** dry by exposing to air **3 :** to make short of breath **4 :** to regulate the wind supply of (an organ pipe) **5 :** to rest (as a horse) in order to allow the breath to be recovered ~ *vi* **1 :** to scent game **2** *dial* **:** to pause for breath

³wind \ˈwīnd, ˈwind\ *vb* **wind·ed** \ˈwīn-dəd, ˈwin-\ *or* **wound** \ˈwau̇nd\; **wind·ing** *vt* [¹*wind*] **1 :** to cause (as a horn) to sound by blowing **:** BLOW **2 :** to sound (as a call or note) on a horn <*wound* a rousing call —R. L. Stevenson> ~ *vi* **:** to produce a sound on a horn

⁴wind \ˈwīnd\ *vb* **wound** \ˈwau̇nd\ *also* **wind·ed; wind·ing** [ME *winden,* fr. OE *windan* to twist, move with speed or force, brandish; akin to OHG *wintan* to wind, Umbrian ohavendu let him turn aside] *vi* **1 :** BEND, WARP **2 :** to have a curving course or shape **:** extend in curves **3 :** to move so as to encircle **4 :** to turn when lying at anchor ~ *vt* **1 a** *obs* **:** WEAVE **b :** ENTANGLE, INVOLVE **c :** to introduce sinuously or stealthily **:** INSINUATE **2 a :** to encircle or cover with something pliable **:** bind with loops or layers **b :** to turn completely or repeatedly about an object **:** COIL, TWINE **c (1) :** to hoist or haul by means of a rope or chain and a windlass **(2) :** to move (a ship) by hauling on a capstan **d (1) :** to tighten the spring of <~ a clock> **(2)** *obs* **:** to make tighter **:** TIGHTEN, TUNE **(3) :** CRANK **e :** to raise to a high level (as of excitement or tension) **3 a :** to cause to move in a curving line or path **b** *archaic* **:** to turn the course of; *esp* **:** to lead (a person) as one wishes **c (1) :** to cause (as a ship) to change direction **:** TURN **(2) :** to turn (a ship) end for end **d :** to traverse on a curving course <the river ~*s* the valley> **e :** to effect by or as if by curving — **wind·er** *n*

⁵wind \ˈwīnd\ *n* **1 :** a mechanism (as a winch) for winding **2 :** an act of winding **:** the state of being wound **3 :** COIL, TURN **4 :** a particular method of winding

wind·age \ˈwin-dij\ *n* [¹*wind*] **1 a :** the space between the projectile of a smoothbore gun and the surface of the bore **b :** the difference between the diameter of the bore of a muzzle-loading rifled cannon and that of the projectile cylinder **2 a :** the amount of sight deflection necessary to compensate for wind displacement in aiming a gun **b (1) :** the influence of the wind in deflecting the course of a projectile **(2) :** the amount of deflection due to the wind **3 :** the disturbance of the air caused by a passing object (as a projectile) **4 :** the surface exposed (as by a ship) to the wind

wind·bag \ˈwin(d)-ˌbag\ *n* **:** an exhaustively talkative person

wind–bell \-ˌbel\ *n* **1 :** a cluster of small pieces of glass or metal tied loosely together in such a way that they tinkle when blown by the wind — usu. used in pl. **2 :** a bell that is light enough to be moved and sounded by the wind

wind·blast \-ˌblast\ *n* **:** the destructive effect of air friction on a pilot ejected from a high-speed airplane

wind·blown \-ˌblōn\ *adj* **1 :** blown by the wind; *esp* **:** having a permanent set or character of growth determined by the prevailing winds <~ trees> **2** *of hair* **:** cut so that the ends turn outward and to the front as if blown by a wind from behind

wind·break \-ˌbrāk\ *n* **:** a growth of trees or shrubs serving to break the force of wind; *broadly* **:** a shelter (as a fence) from the wind

Wind·break·er \-ˌbrā-kər\ *trademark* — used for an outer jacket made of wind-resistant material

wind–bro·ken \-ˌbrō-kən\ *adj, of a horse* **:** affected with pulmonary emphysema or with heaves

wind·burn \-ˌbərn\ *n* **:** irritation caused by wind — **wind·burned** \-ˌbərnd\ *adj*

wind·chill \ˈwin(d)-ˌchil\ *n* **:** a still-air temperature that would have the same cooling effect on exposed human flesh as a given combination of temperature and wind speed — called also *chill factor, windchill index*

wind chime *n* **:** WIND-BELL 1 — usu. used in pl.

wind cone *n* **:** WIND SOCK

wind·er \ˈwīn-dər\ *n* **:** one that winds: as **a :** a worker who winds yarn or thread **b :** any of various textile machines for winding thread and yarn **c :** a key for winding a mechanism (as a clock) **d :** a step that is wider at one end than at the other (as in a spiral staircase)

wind·fall \ˈwin(d)-ˌfȯl\ *n* **1 :** something (as a tree or fruit) blown down by the wind **2 :** an unexpected or sudden gain or advantage

wind·flaw \-ˌflȯ\ *n* **:** a gust of wind **:** FLAW

wind·flow·er \-ˌflau̇(-ə)r\ *n* **1 :** ANEMONE 1 **2 :** RUE ANEMONE

wind·gall \-ˌgȯl\ *n* **:** a soft tumor or synovial swelling on a horse's leg in the region of the fetlock joint — **wind·galled** \-ˌgȯld\ *adj*

wind gap *n* **:** a notch in the crest of a mountain ridge **:** a pass not occupied by a stream

wind harp *n* **:** AEOLIAN HARP

wind·hov·er \ˈwind-ˌhəv-ər, -ˌhäv-\ *n, Brit* **:** KESTREL

¹wind·ing \ˈwīn-diŋ\ *n* **1 :** material (as wire) wound or coiled about an object (as an armature); *also* **:** a single turn of the wound material **2 a :** the act of one that winds **b :** the manner of winding something **3 :** a curved or sinuous course, line, or progress

2**winding** *adj* **:** marked by winding: as **a :** having a pronounced curve; *esp* **:** SPIRAL <a ~ stairway> **b :** having a course that winds <a ~ road>

wind·ing–sheet \'wīn-diŋ-ˌshēt\ *n* **:** a sheet in which a corpse is wrapped

wind instrument *n* **:** a musical instrument (as a trumpet, clarinet, or organ) sounded by wind; *esp* **:** a musical instrument sounded by the player's breath

wind·jam·mer \'win(d)-ˌjam-ər\ *n* **:** a sailing ship; *also* **:** one of its crew

1**wind·lass** \'win-(d)ləs\ *n* [ME *wyndlas,* alter. of *wyndas,* fr. ON *vindāss,* fr. *vinda* to wind + *āss* pole; akin to OHG *wintan* to wind] **:** any of various machines for hoisting or hauling; as **a :** a horizontal barrel supported on vertical posts and turned by a crank so that the hoisting rope is wound around the barrel **b :** a steam or electric winch with horizontal or vertical shaft and two drums used to raise a ship's anchor

2**windlass** *vt* **:** to hoist or haul with a windlass

win·dle·straw \'win-(d)ᵊl-ˌstrȯ\ *n* [(assumed) ME, fr. OE *windelstrēaw,* fr. *windel* basket (fr. *windan* to wind) + *strēaw* straw] *Brit* **:** a dry thin stalk of grass

1**wind·mill** \'win(d)-ˌmil\ *n* **1 a :** a mill operated by the wind usu. acting on oblique vanes or sails which radiate from a horizontal shaft; *esp* **:** a wind-driven water pump **b :** the wind-driven wheel of a windmill **2 :** something that resembles or suggests a windmill: as **a :** PINWHEEL 1 **b :** HELICOPTER **3** [fr. the episode in *Don Quixote* by Cervantes in which the hero attacks windmills under the illusion that they are giants] **:** an imaginary wrong, evil, or opponent — used in the phrase *to tilt at windmills*

windmill 1

2**windmill** *vt* **:** to cause to move like a windmill ~ *vi* **:** to move like a windmill

win·dow \'win-(ˌ)dō, -də(-w)\ *n, often attrib* [ME *windowe,* fr. ON *vindauga,* fr. *vindr* wind + *auga* eye; akin to OE *wind* and to OE *ēage* eye — more at EYE] **1 :** an opening esp. in the wall of a building for admission of light and air that is usu. closed by casements or sashes containing transparent material (as glass) and capable of being opened and shut **2 :** WINDOWPANE **3 :** an opening (as a shutter, slot, or valve) that resembles or suggests a window **4 :** the transparent panel of a window envelope **5 :** the framework (as a shutter or sash with its fittings) that closes a window opening **6 :** CHAFF 4 **7 :** a range of wavelengths in the electromagnetic spectrum to which a planet's atmosphere is transparent **8 :** an interval of time within which a rocket or spacecraft must be launched to accomplish a particular mission **9 :** an area at the limits of the earth's sensible atmosphere through which a spacecraft must pass for successful reentry — **win·dow·less** \-dō-ləs, -də-\ *adj*

window box *n* **1 :** one of the hollows in the sides of a window frame for the weights that counterbalance a lifting sash **2 :** a box designed to hold soil for growing plants on a windowsill

win·dow–dress \'win-dō-ˌdres, -də-ˌdres\ *vt* [back-formation fr. *window dresser*] **:** to make appear more attractive or favorable

window dresser *n* **1 :** one that arranges merchandise and decorations in a show window **2 :** one that distorts facts or puts up a front in order to make a favorable impression

window dressing *n* **1 :** the display of merchandise in a retail store window **2 :** the act or an instance of making something appear more attractive or favorable often by means of false or misleading statements of facts

window envelope *n* **:** an envelope having a transparent panel through which the address on the enclosure is visible

win·dow·pane \'win-dō-ˌpān, -də-\ *n* **:** a pane in a window

window seat *n* **:** a seat built into a window recess

window shade *n* **:** a shade or curtain for a window

win·dow–shop \'win-dō-ˌshäp, -də-\ *vi* **:** to look at the displays in retail store windows without going inside the stores to make purchases — **win·dow–shop·per** *n*

win·dow·sill \-ˌsil\ *n* **:** the horizontal member at the bottom of a window opening

wind·pipe \'win(d)-ˌpīp\ *n* **:** the passage for the breath from the larynx to the lungs **:** TRACHEA

wind–pol·li·nat·ed \-'päl-ə-ˌnāt-əd\ *adj* **:** pollinated by wind-borne pollen

wind·proof \-'prüf\ *adj* **:** proof against the wind <a ~ jacket>

wind rose \'win-ˌdrōz\ *n* [G *windrose* compass card] **:** a diagram showing for a given place the relative frequency or frequency and strength of winds from different directions

1**wind·row** \'win-ˌ(d)rō\ *n* **1 a :** a row of hay raked up to dry before being baled or stored **b :** a similar row of cut vegetation (as grain) for drying **2 :** a row heaped up by or as if by the wind **3 a :** a long low ridge of road-making material scraped to the side of a road **b :** BANK, RIDGE, HEAP

2**windrow** *vt* **:** to form (as hay) into a windrow

wind scale *n* **:** a series of numbers or words corresponding to various ranges of wind speeds for indicating the force of the wind

wind·screen \'win(d)-ˌskrēn\ *n* **1 :** a screen that protects against the wind **2** *Brit* **:** an automobile windshield

wind shake *n* **:** shake in timber attributed to high winds — **wind–shak·en** \'win(d)-ˌshā-kən\ *adj*

wind·shield \'win(d)-ˌshēld\ *n* **:** a transparent screen (as of glass) in front of the occupants of a vehicle

wind sock *n* **:** a truncated cloth cone open at both ends and mounted in an elevated position to indicate the direction of the wind — called also *wind sleeve*

Wind·sor chair \ˌwin-zər-\ *n* [*Windsor,* England] **:** a wooden chair with spindle back, raking legs, and usu. a saddle seat

Windsor knot *n* **:** a knot used for tying four-in-hand ties that is wider than the usual four-in-hand knot

Windsor tie *n* **:** a broad necktie usu. tied in a loose bow

wind sprint *n* **:** a sprint performed as a training exercise to develop breathing capacity esp. during exertion

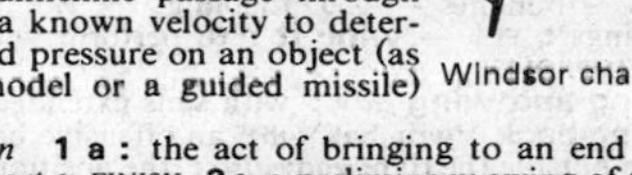

Windsor chair

wind·storm \'win(d)-ˌstȯ(ə)rm\ *n* **:** a storm marked by high wind with little or no precipitation

wind·swept \'win(d)-ˌswept\ *adj* **:** swept by or as if by wind

wind tee *n* **:** a large weather vane shaped like a horizontal letter T on or near a landing field

wind tunnel *n* **:** a tunnellike passage through which air is blown at a known velocity to determine the effects of wind pressure on an object (as an airplane part or model or a guided missile) placed in the passage

1**wind·up** \'wīn-ˌdəp\ *n* **1 a :** the act of bringing to an end **b :** a concluding act or part **:** FINISH **2 :** a preliminary swing of the arms before pitching a baseball

2**windup** *adj* **:** having a spring wound up by hand for operation

wind up \(')wīn-'dəp\ *vt* **1 :** to bring to a conclusion **:** END **2 :** to put in order **:** SETTLE ~ *vi* **1 a :** to come to a conclusion **b :** to arrive in a place, situation, or condition at the end or as a result of a course of action <*wound up* as millionaires> **2 :** to give a preliminary swing to the arms (as before pitching a baseball)

1**wind·ward** \'win-(d)wərd\ *adj* **:** being in or facing the direction from which the wind is blowing — compare LEEWARD

2**windward** *n* **:** the side or direction from which the wind is blowing — **to windward :** into or in an advantageous position

wind·way \'win-ˌ(d)wā\ *n* **:** a passage for air (as in an organ pipe)

wind–wing \-ˌ(d)wiŋ\ *n* **:** a small panel in an automobile window that can be turned outward for ventilation

windy \'win-dē\ *adj* **wind·i·er; -est 1 a (1) :** WINDSWEPT **(2) :** marked by strong wind or by more wind than usual **b :** VIOLENT, STORMY **2 :** FLATULENT 1 **3 a :** VERBOSE, BOMBASTIC **b :** lacking substance **:** EMPTY — **wind·i·ly** \-də-lē\ *adv* — **wind·i·ness** \-dē-nəs\ *n*

1**wine** \'wīn\ *n, often attrib* [ME *win,* fr. OE *wīn;* akin to OHG *wīn* wine; both fr. a prehistoric Gmc word borrowed fr. L *vinum* wine, of non-IE origin; akin to the source of Gk *oinos* wine] **1 a :** fermented grape juice containing varying percentages of alcohol together with ethers and esters that give it bouquet and flavor **b :** wine or a substitute used in Christian communion services **2 :** the usu. fermented juice of a plant product (as a fruit) used as a beverage **3 :** something that invigorates or intoxicates **4 :** a variable color averaging a dark red

2**wine** *vb* **wined; win·ing** *vt* **:** to give wine to <*wined* and dined his friends> ~ *vi* **:** to drink wine

wine cellar *n* **:** a room for storing wines; *also* **:** a stock of wines

wine cooler *n* **:** a vessel or container in which wine is cooled; *specif* **:** an often lidded metal-lined wooden container on legs with casters used esp. in the 18th and early 19th centuries for cooling wine

wine·glass \'wīn-ˌglas\ *n* **1 :** a stemware drinking glass for wine **2 :** a four-ounce unit of measure used in mixing drinks

wine·grow·er \-ˌgrō(-ə)r\ *n* **:** one that cultivates a vineyard and makes wine

wine·press \'wīn-ˌpres\ *n* **:** a vat in which juice is expressed from grapes by treading or by means of a plunger

win·ery \'wīn-(ə-)rē\ *n, pl* **-er·ies :** a wine-making establishment

wine·shop \'wīn-ˌshäp\ *n* **:** a tavern that specializes in serving wine

wine·skin \-ˌskin\ *n* **:** a bag that is made from the skin of an animal (as a goat) and that is used for holding wine

wine taster *n* **1 :** one that tests wine by tasting **2 :** a small flat bowl used to hold a sample of wine being tested

win·ey *var of* WINY

1**wing** \'wiŋ\ *n, often attrib* [ME *winge,* of Scand origin; akin to Dan & Sw *vinge* wing; akin to Skt *vāti* it blows — more at WIND] **1 a :** one of the movable feathered or membranous paired appendages by means of which a bird, bat, or insect is able to fly; *also* **:** such an appendage even though rudimentary if possessed by an animal belonging to a group characterized by the power of flight **b :** any of various organic structures esp. of a flying fish or flying lemur providing means of limited flight **2 :** an appendage or part resembling a wing in shape, appearance, or position: as **a :** a device worn under the arms to aid a person in swimming or staying afloat **b :** ALA **c :** a turned-back or extended edge on an article of clothing **d :** a sidepiece at the top of an armchair **e (1) :** a foliaceous, membranous, or woody expansion of a plant esp. along a stem or on a samara or capsule **(2) :** either of the two lateral petals of a papilionaceous flower **f :** a vane of a windmill or arrow **g :** SAIL **h :** one of the airfoils that develop a major part of the lift which supports a heavier-than-air aircraft **3 :** a means of flight or rapid progress **4 :** the act or manner of flying **:** FLIGHT **5 :** a side or outlying region or district **6 :** a part or feature usu. projecting from and subordinate to the main or central part **7 a :** one of the pieces of scenery at the side of a stage **b** *pl* **:** the area at the side of the stage out of sight **8 a :** a left or right section of an army or fleet **:** FLANK **b :** one of the offensive positions or players on either side of a center position in certain team sports; *also* **:** FLANKER **9 a :** either of two opposing groups within an organization or society **:** FACTION **b :** a section of an organized body (as a legislative chamber) representing a group or faction holding distinct opinions or policies — compare LEFT WING, RIGHT WING **10 a :** a unit of the U.S. Air Force higher than a group and lower than a division **b :** two or more squadrons of naval airplanes not carrier based **11 :** a dance step marked by a quick outward and inward rolling glide of one foot — **in the wings 1 :** out of sight in the stage wings **2 :** in the background **:** close at hand <when

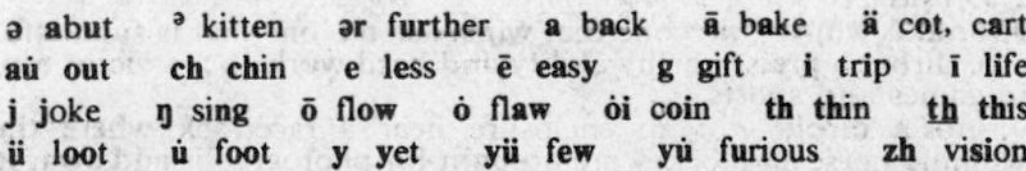

ə abut ᵊ kitten ər further a back ā bake ä cot, cart
aù out ch chin e less ē easy g gift i trip ī life
j joke ŋ sing ō flow ȯ flaw ȯi coin th thin t͟h this
ü loot ù foot y yet yü few yù furious zh vision

the president . . . of a . . . corporation dies . . . a dozen men are waiting *in the wings* to take his place —D. R. Cressey> — **on the wing :** in flight : FLYING — **under one's wing :** under one's protection : in one's care

2**wing** *vt* **1 a :** to fit with wings **b :** to enable to fly or move swiftly **2 a :** to wound in the wing : disable the wing of <~*ed* the duck> **b :** to wound (as with a bullet) without killing <~*ed* by a sniper> **3 a :** to traverse with or as if with wings **b :** to effect or achieve by flying **4 :** to let fly : DISPATCH <would start to ~ punches —A. J. Liebling> ~ *vi* : to go with or as if with wings : FLY — **wing it :** to perform without following a script : IMPROVISE

wing and wing *adv* **:** with sails extended on both sides

wing·back \ˈwiŋ-ˌbak\ *n* **:** an offensive back in football who lines up outside the tight end; *also* **:** the position of a player so stationed

wing bar *n* **:** a line of contrasting color across the middle of a bird's wing made by markings on the wing coverts — see COCK illustration

wing bow *n* **:** the lesser coverts of the upper part of a bird's wing when distinctively colored — see COCK illustration

wing case *n* **:** ELYTRON

wing chair *n* **:** an upholstered armchair with high solid back and sides that provide a rest for the head and protection from drafts

wing chair

wing commander *n* **:** a commissioned officer in the British air force who ranks with a lieutenant colonel in the army

wing covert *n* **:** one of the coverts of the wing quills

wing·ding \ˈwiŋ-ˌdiŋ\ *n* [origin unknown] **1 :** a wild, lively, or lavish party **2 :** a pretended fit or illness

winged \ˈwiŋd *also except for 1a(2)* ˈwiŋ-əd\ *adj* **1 a (1) :** having wings <~ seeds> **(2) :** having wings of a specified kind — used in combination <strong-*winged*> **b :** using wings in flight **2 a :** soaring with or as if with wings : ELEVATED **b :** SWIFT, RAPID

winged elm *n* **:** a No. American elm (*Ulmus alata*) having twigs and young branches with prominent corky projections

wing·er \ˈwiŋ-ər\ *n, chiefly Brit* **:** a player (as in soccer) in a wing position

wing–foot·ed \ˈwiŋ-ˈfu̇t-əd\ *adj* **:** having winged feet : SWIFT <a ~ messenger>

wing·less \ˈwiŋ-ləs\ *adj* **:** having no wings or very rudimentary wings — **wing·less·ness** *n*

wing·let \ˈwiŋ-lət\ *n* **1 :** a very small or rudimentary wing **2 :** BASTARD WING

wing·like \-ˌlīk\ *adj* **:** resembling a wing in form or lateral position

wing·man \-mən\ *n* **:** a pilot who flies behind and outside the leader of a flying formation

wing nut *n* **:** a nut with wings that provide a grip for the thumb and finger

wing·over \ˈwiŋ-ˌō-vər\ *n* **:** a flight maneuver in which a plane is put into a climbing turn until nearly stalled after which the nose is allowed to fall while the turn is continued until normal flight is attained in a direction opposite to that in which the maneuver was entered

wings \ˈwiŋz\ *n pl* **:** insignia consisting of an outspread pair of stylized bird's wings which are awarded on completion of prescribed training to a qualified pilot, aircrew member, or military balloon pilot

wing shooting *n* **:** the act or practice of shooting at game birds in flight or at flying targets

wing·span \ˈwiŋ-ˌspan\ *n* **:** the distance from the tip of one of a pair of wings to that of the other; *also* **:** SPAN 2c

wing·spread \-ˌspred\ *n* **:** the spread of the wings : WINGSPAN; *specif* **:** the extreme measurement between the tips or outer margins of the wings (as of a bird or insect)

wing tip *n* **1 :** a toe cap having a point that extends back toward the throat of the shoe and curving sides that extend toward the shank **2 :** a shoe having a wing tip

wingy \ˈwiŋ-ē\ *adj* **1 :** having wings **2 :** soaring with or as if with wings : LOFTY **3 :** resembling or suggesting a wing in shape or position <~ sleeves>

1**wink** \ˈwiŋk\ *vb* [ME *winken,* fr. OE *wincian;* akin to OHG *winchan* to stagger, wink, L *vacillare* to sway — more at PREVARICATE] *vi* **1 :** to shut one eye briefly as a signal or in teasing **2 :** to close and open the eyelids quickly **3 :** to avoid seeing or noting something — usu. used with *at* **4 :** to gleam or flash intermittently : TWINKLE **5 a :** to come to an end — usu. used with *out* **b :** to stop shining — usu. used with *out* **6 :** to signal a message with a light ~ *vt* **1 :** to cause to open and shut **2 :** to affect or influence by or as if by blinking the eyes
syn WINK, BLINK *shared meaning element* **:** to move one's eyelids

2**wink** *n* **1 :** a brief period of sleep : NAP **2 a :** a hint or sign given by winking **b :** an act of winking **3 :** the time of a wink : INSTANT <quick as a ~> **4 :** a flicker of the eyelids : BLINK

wink·er \ˈwiŋ-kər\ *n* **1 :** one that winks **2 a :** a horse's blinder : BLINKER **b (1) :** EYE **(2) :** EYELASH

1**win·kle** \ˈwiŋ-kəl\ *n* [short for *periwinkle*] **1 :** 2PERIWINKLE **2 :** any of various whelks (esp. genus *Busycon*) that destroy oysters and clams by drilling their shells and rasping away their flesh

2**winkle** *vt* **win·kled; win·kling** \-k(ə-)liŋ\ [1*winkle;* fr. the process of extracting a winkle from its shell] *chiefly Brit* **:** to displace, extract, or evict from a position — usu. used with *out*

3**winkle** *vi* **win·kled; win·kling** \-k(ə-)liŋ\ [freq. of *wink*] **:** TWINKLE

win·ner \ˈwin-ər\ *n* **:** one that wins: as **a :** one that is successful esp. through praiseworthy ability and hard work **b :** a victor esp. in games and sports

winner's circle *n* **:** an enclosure near a racetrack where the winning horse and jockey are brought for photographs and awards

Win·nie \ˈwin-ē\ *n* [*winner* + *-ie*] **:** an award presented annually by a professional organization for notable achievement in fashion design

1**win·ning** \ˈwin-iŋ\ *n* **1 :** the act of one that wins : VICTORY **2 :** something won: as **a :** a captured territory : CONQUEST **b :** money won by success in a game or competition — usu. used in pl. **3 a :** a shaft or pit opening made to win coal **b :** a more or less isolated section of a mine

2**winning** *adj* **1 a :** of, relating to, or used for or in the act of winning <the ~ ticket> **b :** successful in competition <a ~ team> **2 :** tending to please or delight <a ~ smile> ***syn*** see SWEET — **win·ning·ly** \-iŋ-lē\ *adv*

win·nock \ˈwin-ək\ *n* [ME (Sc) *windok, windowe*] *Scot* **:** WINDOW

1**win·now** \ˈwin-(ˌ)ō, ˈwin-ə(-w)\ *vb* [ME *winewen,* fr. OE *windwian* to fan, winnow; akin to OHG *wintōn* to fan, L *vannus* winnowing fan, *ventus* wind — more at WIND] *vt* **1 a (1) :** to remove (as chaff) by a current of air **(2) :** to get rid of (something undesirable or unwanted) : REMOVE — often used with *out* <~ out certain inaccuracies —Stanley Walker> **b :** SEPARATE, SIFT <an old hand at ~*ing* what is true and significant —Oscar Lewis> **2 :** to treat (as grain) by exposure to a current of air so that waste matter is eliminated **3 :** to blow on : FAN <the wind ~*ing* his thin white hair —*Time*> ~ *vi* **1 :** to separate chaff from grain by fanning **2 :** to separate desirable and undesirable elements

2**winnow** *n* **1 :** a device for winnowing **2 a :** the action of winnowing **b :** a motion resembling that of winnowing

win·now·er \ˈwin-ə-wər\ *n* **:** one (as a machine) that winnows something

wino \ˈwī-(ˌ)nō\ *n, pl* **win·os :** one who is chronically addicted to drinking wine

win·some \ˈwin(t)-səm\ *adj* [ME *winsum,* fr. OE *wynsum,* fr. *wynn* joy; akin to OHG *wunna* joy, L *venus* love — more at WIN] **1 :** generally pleasing and engaging often because of a childlike charm and innocence **2 :** CHEERFUL, GAY ***syn*** see SWEET — **win·some·ly** *adv* — **win·some·ness** *n*

1**win·ter** \ˈwint-ər\ *n* [ME, fr. OE; akin to OHG *wintar* winter] **1 :** the season between autumn and spring comprising in the northern hemisphere usu. the months December, January, and February or as reckoned astronomically extending from the December solstice to the March equinox **2 :** the colder half of the year **3 :** YEAR <happened many ~*s* ago> **4 :** a period of inactivity or decay

2**winter** *adj* **1 :** of, relating to, or suitable for winter <a ~ vacation> <~ clothes> **2 :** sown in the autumn and harvested in the following spring or summer <~ wheat> <~ rye> — compare SUMMER

3**winter** *vb* **win·tered; win·ter·ing** \ˈwint-ə-riŋ, ˈwin-triŋ\ *vi* **1 :** to pass the winter **2 :** to feed or find food during the winter — used with *on* ~ *vt* **:** to keep, feed, or manage during the winter

winter aconite *n* **:** a small Old World perennial herb (*Eranthis hyemalis*) of the crowfoot family grown for its bright yellow flowers which often bloom through the snow

win·ter·ber·ry \ˈwint-ər-ˌber-ē\ *n* **:** any of various American hollies with bright red berries persistent through the winter

win·ter·bourne \-ˌbō(ə)rn, -ˌbȯ(ə)rn, -ˌbu̇(ə)rn\ *n* **:** a stream that flows only or chiefly in winter

winter crookneck *n* **:** any of several crooknecks that are winter squashes of the pumpkin group noted for their keeping qualities

win·ter·er \ˈwint-ər-ər\ *n* **:** one that winters; *specif* **:** a winter resident or visitor

winter flounder *n* **:** a rusty brown flounder (*Pseudopleuronectes americanus*) of the northwestern Atlantic important as a market fish esp. in winter

win·ter·green \ˈwint-ər-ˌgrēn\ *n* **1 :** any of a genus (*Pyrola* of the family Pyrolaceae, the wintergreen family) of evergreen perennial herbs related to the heaths; *esp* **:** one (*P. minor*) with small round basal leaves **2 a :** any of a genus (*Gaultheria*) of the heath family; *esp* **:** a low evergreen plant (*G. procumbens*) with white flowers and spicy red berries — called also *checkerberry* **b (1) :** an essential oil from this plant **(2) :** the flavor of this oil <~ lozenges>

wintergreen 2a

win·ter·ize \ˈwint-ə-ˌrīz\ *vt* **-ized; -iz·ing :** to make ready for winter or winter use and esp. resistant or proof against winter weather <~ a car> — **win·ter·iza·tion** \ˌwint-ə-rə-ˈzā-shən\ *n*

win·ter–kill \ˈwint-ər-ˌkil\ *vt* **:** to kill (as a plant) by exposure to winter conditions ~ *vi* **:** to die as a result of exposure to winter conditions — **winterkill** *n*

win·ter·ly \ˈwint-ər-lē\ *adj* **:** of, relating to, or occurring in winter : WINTRY

winter melon *n* **:** a muskmelon (*Cucumis melo inodorus*) with smooth rind and sweet white or greenish flesh that keeps well

winter quarters *n pl but sing or pl in constr* **:** a winter residence or station (as of a military unit or a circus)

winter squash *n* **:** any of various squashes derived from a natural species (*Cucurbita maxima*) or pumpkins from a species (*C. moschata*) that can be stored for several months

win·ter·tide \ˈwint-ər-ˌtīd\ *n* **:** WINTERTIME

win·ter·time \-ˌtīm\ *n* **:** the season of winter

win through *vi* **:** to survive difficulties and reach a desired or satisfactory end

win·tle \ˈwin(t)-ᵊl\ *vi* **win·tled; win·tling** \ˈwin(t)-liŋ, -ᵊl-iŋ\ [perh. fr. Flem *windtelen* to reel] *Scot* **1 :** STAGGER, REEL **2 :** WRIGGLE

win·try \ˈwin-trē\ *or* **win·tery** \ˈwint-ə-rē, ˈwin-trē\ *adj* **win·tri·er; -est 1** *archaic* **:** of or relating to winter **2 :** characteristic of winter : COLD, STORMY **3 a :** weathered by or as if by winter : AGED, HOARY **b :** CHILLING, CHEERLESS <a bitter ~ smile> — **win·tri·ly** \ˈwin-trə-lē\ *adv* — **win·tri·ness** \ˈwin-trē-nəs\ *n*

winy \ˈwī-nē\ *adj* **win·i·er; -est 1 :** having the taste or qualities of wine : VINOUS **2** *of the air* **:** crisply fresh : EXHILARATING

[1]**winze** \ˈwinz\ *n* [alter. of earlier *winds,* prob. fr. pl. of [5]*wind*] **:** a steeply inclined passageway connecting a mine working place with a lower one

[2]**winze** *n* [Flem or D *wensch* wish] *Scot* **:** CURSE

[1]**wipe** \ˈwīp\ *vb* **wiped; wip·ing** [ME *wipen,* fr. OE *wīpian;* akin to OHG *wīfan* to wind around, L *vibrare* to vibrate] *vt* **1 a :** to rub with or as if with something soft for cleaning **b :** to clean or dry by rubbing **c :** to draw, pass, or move for or as if for rubbing or cleaning **2 a :** to remove by or as if by rubbing **b :** to expunge completely <~ from memory the gruesome scenes —*Amer. Guide Series: Del.*> **3 a :** to spread by or as if by wiping **b :** to form (a joint between lead pipes) by applying solder in repeated increments individually spread and shaped with greased cloth pads ~ *vi* **:** to make a motion of or as if of wiping something — **wipe one's boots on :** to treat with indignity — **wipe the floor with** *or* **wipe the ground with :** to defeat decisively

[2]**wipe** *n* **1 a :** BLOW, STRIKE **b :** GIBE, JEER **2 :** an act or instance of wiping **3 :** something (as a towel) used for wiping

wiped out \ˈwīp-ˈtau̇t\ *adj, slang* **:** INTOXICATED, HIGH

wipe·out \ˈwī-ˌpau̇t\ *n* **1 :** the act or an instance of wiping out **:** complete or utter destruction **2 :** a fall from a surfboard caused usu. by losing control, colliding with another surfer, or being knocked off by a wave

wipe out \(ˈ)wī-ˈpau̇t\ *vt* **:** to destroy completely **:** ANNIHILATE

wip·er \ˈwī-pər\ *n* **1 :** one that wipes **2 a :** something (as a towel or sponge) used for wiping **b :** a projecting tooth, tumbler, eccentric, tappet, or cam on a rotating or oscillating piece used esp. for raising a stamper, the helve of a power hammer, or other part intended to fall by its own weight **c :** a moving contact for making connections with the terminals of an electrical device (as a rheostat)

wipe up *vt* **1 :** to make clean by or as if by wiping **2 :** to mop up **:** DESTROY

[1]**wire** \ˈwī(ə)r\ *n, often attrib* [ME, fr. OE *wīr;* akin to OHG *wiara* fine gold, L *viēre* to plait, Gk *iris* rainbow] **1 a :** metal in the form of a usu. very flexible thread or slender rod **b :** a thread or rod of such material **2 a :** WIREWORK **b :** the meshwork of parallel or woven wire on which the wet web of paper forms **3 :** something (as a thin plant stem) that is wirelike **4** *pl* **a :** a system of wires used to operate the puppets in a puppet show **b :** hidden influences controlling the action of a person or organization **5 a :** a line of wire for conducting electrical current — compare CORD 3b **b :** a telephone or telegraph wire or system **c :** TELEGRAM, CABLEGRAM **6 :** fencing or a fence of usu. barbed wire **7 :** the finish line of a race — **wire·like** \-ˌlīk\ *adj* — **under the wire 1 :** at the finish line **2 :** at the last moment

[2]**wire** *vb* **wired; wir·ing** *vt* **1 :** to provide with wire **:** use wire on for a specific purpose **2 :** to send or send word to by telegraph ~ *vi* **:** to send a telegraphic message — **wir·able** \ˈwī-rə-bəl\ *adj* — **wir·er** \ˈwīr-ər\ *n*

wire cloth *n* **:** a fabric of woven metallic wire (as for strainers)

wire coat *n* **:** a coat (as of a dog) of harsh and dense outer hair

wired \ˈwī(ə)rd\ *adj* **1 :** reinforced by wire (as for strength) **2 :** furnished with wires (as for electric connections) **3 :** bound with wire <a ~ container> **4 :** having a wirework netting or fence

wire·draw \ˈwī(ə)r-ˌdrȯ\ *vt* **1 a :** to draw or stretch forcibly **:** ELONGATE **b :** to draw or spin out to great length, tenuity, or overrefinement **:** ATTENUATE **2 :** to draw (metal) into wire — **wire·draw·er** \-ˌdrȯ(-ə)r\ *n*

wire·drawn \-ˌdrȯn\ *adj* **:** excessively minute and subtle <curious speculations, ~ comparisons, obsolete erudition —Virginia Woolf>

wire gauge *n* **1 :** a gauge esp. for measuring the diameter of wire or the thickness of sheet metal **2 :** any of various systems consisting of a series of standard sizes used in describing the diameter of wire or the thickness of sheet metal

wire gauze *n* **:** a gauzelike texture of fine wires

wire glass *n* **:** a glass with wire netting embedded in it

wire grass *n* **:** any of various grasses having wiry culms or leaves; *esp* **:** a European slender-stemmed meadow grass (*Poa compressa*) widely naturalized in the U.S. and Canada

wire·hair \ˈwī(ə)r-ˌha(ə)r, -ˌhe(ə)r\ *n* **:** a wirehaired fox terrier

wire·haired \-ˈha(ə)rd, -ˈhe(ə)rd\ *adj* **:** having a stiff wiry outer coat of hair — used esp. of a dog

wirehaired pointing griffon *n* **:** any of a breed of sporting dogs that originated in Holland and have a long head and a harsh wiry gray or grayish outer coat often with chestnut markings

wirehaired terrier *n* **:** a wirehaired fox terrier

[1]**wire·less** \ˈwī(ə)r-ləs\ *adj* **1 :** having no wire or wires **2** *chiefly Brit* **:** of or relating to radiotelegraphy, radiotelephony, or radio

[2]**wireless** *n* **1 :** WIRELESS TELEGRAPHY **2 :** RADIOTELEPHONY **3** *chiefly Brit* **:** RADIO

[3]**wireless** *vt* **:** to send by wireless **:** RADIO <the lightship ~*ed* a warning to vessels in the vicinity —*Amer. Guide Series: N.C.*> ~ *vi* **:** to send a message by wireless

wireless telegraphy *n* **:** telegraphy carried on by radio waves and without connecting wires — called also *wireless telegraph*

wireless telephone *n* **:** RADIOTELEPHONE

wire·man \ˈwī(ə)r-mən\ *n* **:** a maker of or worker with wire; *esp* **:** LINEMAN 1

wire netting *n* **:** a texture of woven wire coarser than wire gauze

Wire·pho·to \ˈwī(ə)r-ˈfōt-(ˌ)ō\ *trademark* — used for a photograph transmitted by electrical signals over telephone wires

wire–pull·er \-ˌpu̇l-ər\ *n* **:** one who uses secret or underhand means to influence the acts of a person or organization — **wire–pull·ing** \-ˌpu̇l-iŋ\ *n*

wire–re·cord \ˌwī(ə)(r)-ri-ˈkȯ(ə)rd\ *vt* **:** to make a wire recording of

wire recorder *n* **:** a magnetic recorder using magnetic wire

wire recording *n* **:** magnetic recording on magnetic wire; *also* **:** the recording made by this process

wire rope *n* **:** a rope formed wholly or chiefly of wires

wire service *n* **:** a news agency that sends out syndicated news copy by wire to subscribers

[1]**wire·tap** \ˈwī(ə)r-ˌtap\ *vi* **:** to tap a telephone or telegraph wire in order to get information

[2]**wiretap** *n* **1 :** the act or an instance of wiretapping **2 :** an electrical connection for wiretapping

wire·tap·per \-ˌtap-ər\ *n* **:** one that taps telephone or telegraph wires

wire·way \ˈwī(ə)r-ˌwā\ *n* **:** a conduit for wires

wire·work \-ˌwərk\ *n* **1 :** a work of wires; *esp* **:** meshwork, netting, or grillwork of wire <plan the ~ for new circuitry> **2 :** walking on wires esp. by acrobats

wire·worm \-ˌwərm\ *n* **:** a worm that is the slender hard-coated larva of various click beetles and is esp. destructive to plant roots

wir·ing \ˈwī(ə)r-iŋ\ *n* **1 :** the act of providing or using wire **2 :** a system of wires; *esp* **:** an arrangement of wires used for electric distribution

wir·ra \ˈwir-ə\ *interj* [*oh wirra,* fr. IrGael *a Muire,* lit., O Mary] *Irish* — usu. used to express lament, grief, or concern

wiry \ˈwī(ə)r-ē\ *adj* **wir·i·er** \ˈwī-rē-ər\; **-est 1 a :** made of wire **b :** resembling wire esp. in form and flexibility **c** *of sound* **:** produced by or suggestive of the vibration of wire <the violinist . . . often let his tone go nasal and ~ —D. J. Henahan> **2 :** being lean, supple, and vigorous **:** SINEWY <a ~ slip of a girl —Ned Hoopes> — **wir·i·ly** \ˈwī-rə-lē\ *adv* — **wir·i·ness** \-rē-nəs\ *n*

wis \ˈwis\ *vb* [by incorrect division fr. *iwis* (understood as *I wis,* with *wis* taken to be an archaic pres. indic. of [1]*wit*)] *archaic* **:** KNOW

Wis *or* **Wisc** *abbr* Wisconsin

Wisd *abbr* Wisdom

wis·dom \ˈwiz-dəm\ *n* [ME, fr. OE *wīsdōm,* fr. *wīs* wise] **1 a :** accumulated philosophic or scientific learning **:** KNOWLEDGE **b :** ability to discern inner qualities and relationships **:** INSIGHT **c :** good sense **:** JUDGMENT **2 :** a wise attitude or course of action **3 :** the teachings of the ancient wise men ***syn*** see SENSE ***ant*** folly, injudiciousness

Wisdom *n* **:** a didactic book included in the Roman Catholic canon of the Old Testament and corresponding to the Wisdom of Solomon in the Protestant Apocrypha — see BIBLE table

Wisdom of Sol·o·mon \-ˈsäl-ə-mən\ **:** a didactic book included in the Protestant Apocrypha — see BIBLE table

wisdom tooth *n* [fr. being cut usu. in the late teens] **:** the last tooth of the full set on each half of each jaw in man

[1]**wise** \ˈwīz\ *n* [ME, fr. OE *wīse;* akin to OHG *wīsa* manner, Gk *eidos* form, *idein* to see — more at WIT] **:** MANNER, WAY <in any ~>

[2]**wise** *adj* **wis·er; wis·est** [ME *wis,* fr. OE *wīs;* akin to OHG *wīs* wise, OE *witan* to know — more at WIT] **1 a :** characterized by wisdom **:** marked by deep understanding, keen discernment, and a capacity for sound judgment **b :** exercising sound judgment **:** PRUDENT **2 :** evidencing or hinting at the possession of inside information **:** KNOWING, *also* **:** CRAFTY, SHREWD **3** *archaic* **:** skilled in magic or devination — **wise·ly** *adv* — **wise·ness** *n* ***syn*** WISE, SAGE, SAPIENT, JUDICIOUS, PRUDENT, SENSIBLE, SANE *shared meaning element* **:** having or showing ability to choose sound ends and appropriate means ***ant*** simple

[3]**wise** *vb* **wised; wis·ing** *vt* **:** to give instruction or information to **:** TEACH — usu. used with *up* ~ *vi* **:** to become informed or knowledgeable **:** LEARN — used with *up*

[4]**wise** *vt* **wised; wis·ing** [ME *wisen,* fr. OE *wīsian;* akin to ON *vīsa* to show the way, OE *wīs* wise] **1** *chiefly Scot* **a :** DIRECT, GUIDE **b :** ADVISE, PERSUADE **2** *chiefly Scot* **:** to divert or impel in a given direction **:** SEND

-wise \ˌwīz\ *adv comb form* [ME, fr. OE *-wīsan,* fr. *wīse* manner] **1 a :** in the manner of <crab*wise*> <fan*wise*> **b :** in the position or direction of <slant*wise*> <clock*wise*> **2 :** with regard to **:** in respect of <dollar*wise*>

wise·acre \ˈwī-ˌzā-kər\ *n* [MD *wijssegger* soothsayer, modif. of OHG *wīzzago;* akin to OE *wītega* soothsayer, *witan* to know] **:** one who pretends to knowledge or cleverness **:** SMART ALECK

[1]**wise·crack** \ˈwīz-ˌkrak\ *n* **:** a sophisticated or knowing witticism ***syn*** see JEST

[2]**wisecrack** *vi* **:** to make a wisecrack — **wise·crack·er** *n*

wise guy \ˈwīz-ˌgī\ *n* **:** a cocky conceited fellow **:** KNOW-IT-ALL

wise man *n* **1 :** a man of unusual learning, judgment, or insight **:** SAGE **2 :** a man versed in esoteric lore (as of magic or astrology); *specif* **:** MAGUS 2

wi·sen·hei·mer \ˈwīz-ᵊn-ˌhī-mər\ *n* [[2]*wise* + G *-enheimer* (as in G family names such as *Guggenheimer, Oppenheimer*)] **:** one who has the air of knowing all about something **:** WISEACRE

wi·sent \ˈvē-ˌzent\ *n* [G, fr. OHG *wisunt* — more at BISON] **:** a European bison (*Bison bonasus*) — called also *aurochs*

wise·wom·an \ˈwīz-ˌwu̇m-ən\ *n* **1 :** a woman versed in charms, conjuring, or fortune-telling **2 :** MIDWIFE

[1]**wish** \ˈwish\ *vb* [ME *wisshen,* fr. OE *wȳscan;* akin to OHG *wunsken* to wish, L *venus* love, charm — more at WIN] *vt* **1 :** to have a desire for (as something unattainable) **:** WANT <~*ed* he could live his life over> **2 :** to give expression to as a wish **:** BID <~ him good night> **3 a :** to give form to (a wish) **b :** to express a wish for **c :** to request in the form of a wish **:** ORDER **4 :** to confer (something unwanted) upon someone **:** FOIST ~ *vi* **1 :** to have a desire **:** WANT **2 :** to make a wish ***syn*** see DESIRE — **wish·er** *n*

[2]**wish** *n* **1 a :** an act or instance of wishing or desire **:** WANT **b :** an object of desire **:** GOAL **2 a :** an expressed will or desire **:** MANDATE **b :** a request or command couched as a wish **3 :** an invocation of good or evil fortune on someone

wisha \'wish-ə\ *interj* [IrGael *ō* oh + *muise* indeed] *chiefly Irish* — used as an intensive or to express surprise

wish·bone \'wish-,bōn\ *n* [fr. the superstition that when two persons pull it apart the one getting the longer fragment will have his wish granted] **1 :** a furcula in front of the breastbone in a bird consisting chiefly of the two clavicles fused at their median or lower end **2 :** a variation of the T formation in which the halfbacks line up farther from the line of scrimmage than the fullback does

wish·ful \'wish-fəl\ *adj* **1 a :** expressive of a wish : HOPEFUL **b :** having a wish : DESIROUS **2 :** according with wishes rather than reality — **wish·ful·ly** \-fə-lē\ *adv* — **wish·ful·ness** *n*

wish fulfillment *n* **:** the gratification of a desire esp. as gained symbolically (as in dreams, daydreams, or neurotic symptoms)

wishful thinking *n* **1 :** the attribution of reality to what one wishes to be true and the tenuous justification of what one wants to believe **2 :** AUTISM

wish·ing *adj* **1** *archaic* **:** WISHFUL **2 :** regarded as having the power to grant wishes <threw a coin in the ~ well>

wish–wash \'wish-,wŏsh, -,wäsh\ *n* [redupl. of [2]*wash*] **1 :** a weak drink **2 :** insipid talk or writing

wishy–washy \'wish-ē-,wŏsh-ē, -,wäsh-\ *adj* [redupl. of *washy*] **1 :** lacking in strength or flavor : WEAK **2 :** lacking in character or determination : INEFFECTUAL

[1]**wisp** \'wisp\ *n* [ME] **1 :** a small handful (as of hay or straw) **2 a :** a thin strip or fragment **b :** a thready streak <a ~ of smoke> **c :** something frail, slight, or fleeting <a ~ of a girl> <a ~ of a smile> **3 :** WILL-O'-THE-WISP — **wispy** \'wis-pē\ *adj*

[2]**wisp** *vt* **1 :** to roll into a wisp **2 a :** to make wisps of <a cigarette ~*ing* smoke at the corner of his mouth —Raymond Chandler> **b :** to cover with wisps <the sky all ~*ed* with mist —W. F. Wray> ~ *vi* **:** to emerge or drift in wisps <her hair began to ~ into her eyes —Mary Manning>

wisp·ish \'wis-pish\ *adj* **:** resembling a wisp : INSUBSTANTIAL

wist \'wist\ *vt* [alter. of *wis*] *archaic* **:** KNOW

wis·tar·ia \wis-'tir-ē-ə *also* -'ter-\ *n* [NL, alter. of *Wisteria*] **:** WISTERIA

wis·te·ria \-'tir-ē-ə\ *n* [NL, genus name, fr. Caspar *Wistar* †1818 Am physician] **:** any of a genus (*Wisteria*) of chiefly Asiatic mostly woody leguminous vines having pinnately-compound leaves and showy blue, white, purple, or rose pealike flowers in long racemes and including several grown as ornamentals

wist·ful \'wist-fəl\ *adj* [blend of *wishful* and obs. E *wistly* (intently)] **1 :** full of unfulfilled longing or desire : YEARNING **2 :** musingly sad : PENSIVE — **wist·ful·ly** \-fə-lē\ *adv* — **wist·ful·ness** *n*

[1]**wit** \'wit\ *vb* **wist** \'wist\; **wit·ting**; *pres 1st & 3d sing* **wot** \'wät\ [ME *witen* (1st & 3d sing. pres. *wot*, past *wiste*), fr. OE *witan* (1st & 3d sing. pres. *wāt*, past *wisse*, *wiste*); akin to OHG *wizzan* to know, L *vidēre* to see, Gk *eidenai* to know, *idein* to see] **1** *archaic* **:** KNOW **2** *archaic* **:** to come to know : LEARN

[2]**wit** *n* [ME, fr. OE; akin to OHG *wizzi* knowledge, OE *witan* to know] **1 a :** MIND, MEMORY **b :** reasoning power : INTELLIGENCE **2 a :** SENSE 2a — usu. used in pl. <alone and warming his five ~*s*, the white owl in the belfry sits —Alfred Tennyson> **b (1) :** mental soundness : SANITY — usu. used in pl. **(2) :** mental capability and resourcefulness : INGENUITY **3 a :** astuteness of perception or judgment : ACUMEN **b :** the ability to relate seemingly disparate things so as to illuminate or amuse **c (1) :** a talent for banter or persiflage **(2) :** a witty utterance or exchange **4 a :** a person of superior intellect : THINKER **b :** an imaginatively perceptive and articulate individual esp. skilled in banter or persiflage

syn WIT, HUMOR, IRONY, SARCASM, SATIRE, REPARTEE *shared meaning element* **:** a mode of expression intended to arouse amused interest or evoke attention and laughter or a quality of mind that predisposes to such expression. WIT suggests the power to evoke laughing attention by remarks showing verbal felicity or ingenuity and swift perception, especially of the incongruous <true *wit* is nature to advantage dressed, what oft was thought, but ne'er so well expressed —Alexander Pope> HUMOR implies an ability to perceive and effectively express the ludicrous, the comical, or the absurd, especially in human life <the modern sense of *humor* is the quiet enjoyment and implicit expression of the fun of things —Louis Cazamian> IRONY applies to a manner of presentation in which an intended meaning is subtly emphasized by appropriate expression of its opposite <*irony* properly suggests the opposite of what is explicitly stated, by means of peripheral clues — tone of voice, accompanying gestures, stylistic exaggeration . . . thus, for "Brutus is an honorable man" we understand "Brutus is a traitor" —Jacob Brackman> SARCASM applies to savagely humorous expression, frequently in the form of irony, intended to cut and wound <the arrows of *sarcasm* are barbed with contempt —Washington Gladden> SATIRE applies primarily to writing that holds up vices or follies to ridicule and reprobation often by use of irony or caricature <his dry wit and his easy, good-natured *satire* on the follies of the day —Eleanor M. Sickels> REPARTEE applies to the power or art of responding quickly, smoothly, pointedly, and wittily or to an interchange of such response <as for *repartee* . . . , as it is the very soul of conversation, so it is the greatest grace of comedy —John Dryden>

— **at one's wit's end** *or* **at one's wits' end :** at a loss for a means of solving a problem

wi·tan \'wi-,tän\ *n pl* [OE, pl. of *wita* sage, adviser; akin to OHG *wizzo* sage, OE *witan* to know] **:** members of the witenagemot

[1]**witch** \'wich\ *n* [ME *wicche*, fr. OE *wicca*, masc., wizard & *wicce*, fem., witch; akin to MHG *wicken* to bewitch, OE *wigle* divination, OHG *wīh* holy — more at VICTIM] **1 :** one that is credited with usu. malignant supernatural powers; *esp* **:** a woman practicing usu. black witchcraft often with the aid of a devil or familiar : SORCERESS — compare WARLOCK **2 :** an ugly old woman : HAG **3 :** a charming or alluring girl or woman — **witchy** \'wich-ē\ *adj*

[2]**witch** *vt* **1 :** to affect injuriously with witchcraft **2** *archaic* **:** to influence or beguile with allure or charm ~ *vi* **:** DOWSE

witch·craft \'wich-,kraft\ *n* **1 a :** the use of sorcery or magic **b :** communication with the devil or with a familiar **2 :** an irresistible influence or fascination : ENCHANTMENT

witch doctor *n* **:** a professional worker of magic usu. in a primitive society who often works to cure sickness

witch·ery \'wich-(ə-)rē\ *n, pl* **-er·ies 1 a :** the practice of witchcraft : SORCERY **b :** an act of witchcraft **2 :** an irresistible fascination : CHARM

witches' brew *n* **:** a potent or fearsome mixture <a *witches' brew* of untamed sex and brutality —Harrison Smith>

witch·es'–broom \'wich-əz-,brüm, -,brụm\ *n* **:** an abnormal tufted growth of small branches on a tree or shrub caused esp. by fungi or viruses — called also *hexenbesen*

witches' Sabbath *n* **:** a midnight assembly of witches, devils, and sorcerers for the celebration of rites and orgies

witch·grass \'wich-,gras\ *n* [prob. alter. of *quitch* (*grass*)] **1 :** QUACK GRASS **2** [[1]*witch*] **:** a No. American grass (*Panicum capillare*) with slender brushy panicles that is often a weed on cultivated land

witch ha·zel \'wich-,hā-zəl\ *n* [*witch* (a tree with pliant branches)] **1 :** any of a genus (*Hamamelis* of the family Hamamelidaceae, the witch-hazel family) of shrubs with slender-petaled yellow flowers borne in late fall or early spring; *esp* **:** one (*H. virginiana*) of eastern No. America that blooms in the fall **2 :** an alcoholic solution of a distillate of the bark of a witch hazel (*H. virginiana*) used as a soothing and mildly astringent lotion

witch hazel 1

witch–hunt \'wich-,hənt\ *n* **1 :** the searching out and deliberate harassment of those (as political opponents) with unpopular views **2 :** a searching out for persecution of persons accused of witchcraft — **witch–hunt·er** *n* — **witch–hunt·ing** *n or adj*

[1]**witch·ing** \'wich-iŋ\ *n* **:** the practice of witchcraft : SORCERY

[2]**witching** *adj* **:** of, relating to, or suitable for sorcery or supernatural occurrences <the very ~ time of night —Shak.>

witch·like \'wich-,līk\ *adj* **:** resembling or befitting a witch

witch moth *n* **:** any of various noctuid moths (as of the genus *Erebus*)

witch of Agne·si \-än-'yā-zē\ [Maria Gaetana *Agnesi* †1799 It mathematician; probably from its resemblance to the outline of a witch's hat] **:** a plane cubic curve that is symmetric about the y-axis, approaches the x-axis as an asymptote, and has the equation $x^2y = 4a^2(2a - y)$ — called also *witch*

witch·weed \'wich-,wēd\ *n* **:** any of a genus (*Striga* of the figwort family) of yellow-flowered Old World plants that are damaging root parasites of grasses (as sorghum and maize) and that include one (*S. asiatica*) which is an introduced pest in parts of the southeastern U.S.

[1]**wite** \'wīt\ *n* [ME, fr. OE *wīte* punishment; akin to OHG *wīzi* punishment, OE *witan* to know] *chiefly Scot* **:** BLAME, RESPONSIBILITY

[2]**wite** *vt* **wit·ed; wit·ing** *chiefly Scot* **:** BLAME

wi·te·na·ge·mot *or* **wi·te·na·ge·mote** \'wit-ᵊn-ə-gə-,mōt\ *n* [OE *witena gemōt*, fr. *witena* (gen. pl. of *wita* sage, adviser) + *gemōt* gemot] **:** an Anglo-Saxon council made up of a varying number of nobles, prelates, and influential officials and convened from time to time to advise the king on administrative and judicial matters — compare WITAN

with \(')with, (')with, wəth, wəth\ *prep* [ME, against, from, with, fr. OE; akin to OE *wither* against, OHG *widar* against, back, Skt *vi* apart] **1 a :** in opposition to : AGAINST <had a fight ~ his brother> **b :** so as to be separated or detached from <broke ~ his family> **2** — used as a function word to indicate one to whom a usu. reciprocal communication is made <talking ~ a friend> **3 a** — used as a function word to indicate one that shares in an action, transaction, or arrangement <works ~ his father> **b** — used as a function word to indicate the object of attention, behavior, or feeling <get tough ~ him> <angry ~ her> **c :** in respect to : so far as concerns <on friendly terms ~ all nations> **d** — used to indicate the object of an adverbial expression of imperative force <off ~ his head> **e :** OVER, ON <no longer has any influence ~ him> **f :** in the performance, operation, or use of <the trouble ~ this machine> **4 a** — used as a function word to indicate the object of a statement of comparison or equality <a dress identical ~ her hostess's> **b** — used as a function word to express agreement or sympathy <must conclude, ~ him, that the painting is a forgery> **c :** on the side of : FOR <if he's for lower taxes, I'm ~ him> **d :** as well as <can pitch ~ the best of them> **5 a** — used as a function word to indicate combination, accompaniment, presence, or addition <heat milk ~ honey> <went there ~ her> <his money, ~ his wife's, comes to a million> **b :** inclusive of <costs five dollars ~ the tax> **6 a :** in the judgment or estimation of <stood well ~ his classmates> **b :** in or according to the experience or practice of <~ many of us, our ideas seem to fall by the wayside —W. J. Reilly> **7 a** — used as a function word to indicate the means, cause, agent, or instrumentality <hit him ~ a rock> <pale ~ anger> <threatened ~ tuberculosis> <he amused the crowd ~ his antics> **b** *archaic* **:** by the direct act of **8 a** — used as a function word to indicate manner of action <ran ~ effort> <acknowledge your contribution ~ thanks> **b** — used as a function word to indicate an attendant fact or circumstance <stood there ~ his hat on> **c** — used as a function word to indicate a result attendant on a specified action <got off ~ a light sentence> **9 a (1) :** in possession of : HAVING <came ~ good news> **(2) :** in the possession or care of <left the money ~ his mother> **b :** characterized or distinguished by <a man ~ a sharp nose> **10 a** — used as a function word to indicate a close association in time <~ the outbreak of war they went home> <mellows ~ time> **b :** in proportion to <the pressure varies ~

the depth> **11 a :** in spite of : NOTWITHSTANDING <a really tip-top man, ~ all his wrongheadedness —H. J. Laski> **b :** except for <finds that, ~ one group of omissions and one important addition, they reflect that curriculum —Gilbert Highet> **12 :** in the direction of <~ the wind> <~ the grain> ***syn*** see BY

1with·al \with-'ȯl, with-\ *adv* [ME, fr. *with* + *all, al* all] **1 :** together with this : BESIDES <a supporter of all constructive work and ~ an excellent businessman —A. W. Long> **2** *archaic* : THEREWITH **3 :** on the other hand : NEVERTHELESS

2withal *prep, archaic* : WITH — used postpositively with a relative or interrogative pronoun as object

with·draw \with-'drȯ, with-\ *vb* **-drew** \-'drü\; **-drawn** \-'drȯn\; **-draw·ing** \-'drȯ(-)iŋ\ [ME, fr. *with* from + *drawen* to draw] *vt* **1 a :** to take back or away : REMOVE <pressure upon educational administrators to ~ academic credit —J. W. Scott> **b :** to remove from use or cultivation **c :** to remove (money) from a place of deposit **d :** to turn away (as the eyes) from an object of attention <*withdrew* his gaze> **e :** to draw (as a curtain) back or aside **2 a :** to remove from consideration or set outside a group <*withdrew* his name from the list of nominees> <*withdrew* his son from the school> **b (1) :** to take back : RETRACT **(2) :** to recall or remove (a motion) under parliamentary procedure ~ *vi* **1 a :** to move back or away : RETIRE **b :** to draw back from a battlefield : RETREAT **2 a :** to remove oneself from participation **b :** to become socially or emotionally detached <had *withdrawn* farther and farther into herself —Ethel Wilson> **3 :** to recall a motion under parliamentary procedure ***syn*** see GO — **with·draw·able** \-'drȯ-ə-bəl\ *adj*

with·draw·al \-'drȯ(-ə)l\ *n* **1 a :** retreat or retirement esp. into a more secluded or less exposed place or position **b :** an operation by which a military force disengages from the enemy **c (1) :** social or emotional detachment **(2) :** a pathological retreat from objective reality (as in some schizophrenic states) **2 :** RETRACTION, REVOCATION <threatened us with ~ of his consent> **3 :** the act of drawing someone or something back from or out of a place or position **4 a :** the act of taking back or away something that has been granted or possessed **b :** removal from a place of deposit or investment **c :** the discontinuance of administration or use of a drug

withdrawing room *n* : a room to retire to (as from a dining room); *esp* : DRAWING ROOM

with·drawn \with-'drȯn\ *adj* **1 :** removed from immediate contact or easy approach : ISOLATED **2 :** socially detached and unresponsive : INTROVERTED — **with·drawn·ness** \-'drȯn-nəs\ *n*

withe \'with, 'with, 'wīth\ *n* [ME, fr. OE *withthe;* akin to OE *wīthig* withy] : a slender flexible branch or twig; *esp* : one used as a band or line

with·er \'with-ər\ *vb* **with·ered; with·er·ing** \-(ə-)riŋ\ [ME *widren;* prob. akin to ME *weder* weather] *vi* **1 :** to become dry and sapless; *esp* : to shrivel from or as if from loss of bodily moisture **2 :** to lose vitality, force, or freshness ~ *vt* **1 :** to cause to wither **2 :** to make speechless or incapable of action : STUN <~*ed* him with a look —Dorothy Sayers>

with·er·ing *adj* : acting or serving to cut down or destroy : DEVASTATING <a ~ fire from the enemy> — **with·er·ing·ly** \-(ə-)riŋ-lē\ *adv*

with·er·ite \'with-ə-,rīt\ *n* [G *witherit,* irreg. fr. William *Withering* †1799 E physician] : a mineral $BaCO_3$ consisting of barium carbonate in the form of white or gray twin crystals or columnar or granular masses

withe rod *n* : either of two No. American viburnums (*Viburnum cassinoides* and *V. nudum*) with tough slender shoots

with·ers \'with-ərz\ *n pl* [prob. fr. obs. E *wither-* (against), fr. ME, fr. OE, fr. *wither* against; fr. the withers being the parts which resist the pull in drawing a load — more at WITH] **1 :** the ridge between the shoulder bones of a horse — see HORSE illustration **2 :** a part corresponding to the withers in a quadruped other than a horse

with·er·shins \'with-ər-shənz\ *var of* WIDDERSHINS

with·hold \with-'hōld, with-\ *vb* **-held** \-'held\; **-hold·ing** [ME *withholden,* fr. *with* from + *holden* to hold — more at WITH] *vt* **1 :** to hold back from action : CHECK **2** *archaic* : to keep in custody **3 :** to refrain from granting, giving, or allowing <~ permission> **4 :** to deduct (withholding tax) from income ~ *vi* : FORBEAR, REFRAIN ***syn*** see KEEP — **with·hold·er** *n*

withholding tax *n* : a deduction (as from wages, fees, or dividends) levied at a source of income as advance payment on income tax

1with·in \with-'in, with-\ *adv* [ME *withinne,* fr. OE *withinnan,* fr. *with* + *innan* inwardly, within, fr. *in*] **1 :** in or into the interior : INSIDE **2 :** in one's inner thought, disposition, or character : INWARDLY <search ~ for a creative impulse —Kingman Brewster, Jr.>

2within *prep* **1** — used as a function word to indicate enclosure or containment **2** — used as a function word to indicate situation or circumstance in the limits or compass of: as **a :** before the end of <gone ~ a week> **b (1) :** not beyond the quantity, degree, or limitations of <lives ~ his income> **(2) :** in or into the scope or sphere of <~ the jurisdiction of the state> **(3) :** in or into the range of <~ reach> <~ sight> **(4)** — used as a function word to indicate a specified difference or margin <came ~ two points of a perfect mark> <~ a mile of the town> **3 :** to the inside of : INTO

3within *n* : an inner place or area <revolt from ~>

4within *adj* : being inside : ENCLOSED <the ~ indictment>

with·in·doors \with-,in-'dō(ə)rz, with-, -'dȯ(ə)rz\ *adv* : INDOORS

with–it \'with-ət\ *adj* : attuned to a social or cultural vanguard : socially or culturally up-to-date <the intelligent, disaffected, ~ young —Eliot Fremont-Smith>

1with·out \with-'au̇t, with-\ *prep* [ME *withoute,* fr. OE *withūtan,* fr. *with* + *ūtan* outside, fr. *ūt* out] **1 :** OUTSIDE **2** — used as a function word to indicate the absence or lack of something or someone <fight ~ fear> <left ~ him> <looks ~ seeing>

2without *adv* **1 :** on the outside : EXTERNALLY **2 :** with something lacking or absent <has learned to do ~>

3without *conj, chiefly dial* : UNLESS <you don't know about me ~ you have read a book —Mark Twain>

4without *n* : an outer place or area <came from ~>

with·out·doors \with-,au̇t-'dō(ə)rz, with-\ *adv* : OUTDOORS

with·stand \with-'stand, with-\ *vt* **-stood** \-'stu̇d\; **-stand·ing** [ME *withstanden,* fr. OE *withstandan,* fr. *with* against + *standan* to stand — more at WITH] **1 a :** to stand up against : oppose with firm determination; *esp* : to resist successfully **b :** to be proof against : resist the effect of <~ the impact of a landing —*Current Biog.*> **2** *archaic* : to stop or obstruct the course of ***syn*** see OPPOSE

1withy \'with-ē\ *n, pl* **with·ies** [ME, fr. OE *wīthig;* akin to OHG *wīda* willow, L *vitis* vine, *viēre* to plait — more at WIRE] **1 :** WILLOW; *esp* : OSIER 1 **2 :** a flexible slender twig or branch (as of osier) : WITHE

2withy \'with-ē, 'with-ē, 'wī-thē\ *adj* [*withe*] : flexibly tough

wit·less \'wit-ləs\ *adj* **1 :** destitute of wit or understanding : FOOLISH **2 :** mentally deranged : CRAZY <drive one ~ with anxiety —William Styron>

wit·ling \-liŋ\ *n* : a person of little wit

wit·loof \'wit-,lōf, -,lüf\ *n* [D dial. *witloof* chicory, fr. D *wit* white + *loof* foliage] : CHICORY 1; *also* : ENDIVE 2

1wit·ness \'wit-nəs\ *n* [ME *witnesse,* fr. OE *witnes* knowledge, testimony, witness, fr. 1*wit*] **1 :** attestation of a fact or event : TESTIMONY **2 :** one that gives evidence; *specif* : one who testifies in a cause or before a judicial tribunal **3 :** one asked to be present at a transaction so as to be able to testify to its having taken place **4 :** one who has personal knowledge of something **5 a :** something serving as evidence or proof : SIGN **b :** public affirmation by word or example of usu. religious faith or conviction <the heroic ~ to divine life —*Pilot*> **6** *cap* : a member of the Jehovah's Witnesses

2witness *vt* **1 :** to testify to : ATTEST **2 :** to act as legal witness of **3 :** to furnish proof of : BETOKEN **4 a :** to have personal or direct cognizance of : see for oneself <~*ed* the historic event> **b :** to take note of <our grammar — ~ our verb system — is a marvel of flexibility, variety, and exactitude —Charlton Laird> **5 :** to constitute the scene or time of <structures . . . which this striking Dorset hilltop once ~*ed* —*Times Lit. Supp.*> ~ *vi* **1 :** to bear witness : TESTIFY **2 :** to bear witness to one's religious convictions <opportunity to ~ for Christ —W. F. Graham>

wit·ness–box \-,bäks\ *n, chiefly Brit* : an enclosure in which a witness sits or stands while testifying in court

witness stand *n* : a stand or an enclosure from which a witness gives evidence in a court

wit·ted \'wit-əd\ *adj* : having wit or understanding — usu. used in combination <dull-*witted*>

wit·ti·cism \'wit-ə-,siz-əm\ *n* [*witty* + *-cism* (as in *criticism*)] : a cleverly witty and often biting or ironic remark ***syn*** see JEST

1wit·ting \'wit-ᵊn, -iŋ\ *n* **1** *chiefly dial* : knowledge or awareness of something : COGNIZANCE **2** *chiefly dial* : information obtained or communicated : NEWS

2wit·ting \-iŋ\ *adj* **1 :** cognizant or aware of something : CONSCIOUS **2 :** done deliberately : INTENTIONAL — **wit·ting·ly** \-iŋ-lē\ *adv*

wit·tol \'wit-ᵊl\ *n* [ME *wetewold,* fr. *weten, witen* to know + *-wold* (as in *cokewold* cuckold) — more at WIT] **1** *archaic* : a man who knows of his wife's infidelity and puts up with it **2** *archaic* : a witless person

wit·ty \'wit-ē\ *adj* **wit·ti·er; -est** **1** *archaic* : having good intellectual capacity : INTELLIGENT **2 :** amusingly or ingeniously clever in conception or execution <the costumes are sumptuous and ~ —Virgil Thomson> <the musical background is . . . often ~ —Wolcott Gibbs> **3 :** marked by or full of wit : smartly facetious or jocular **4 :** quick or ready to see or express illuminating or amusing relationships or insights — **wit·ti·ly** \'wit-ᵊl-ē\ *adv* — **wit·ti·ness** \'wit-ē-nəs\ *n*

syn WITTY, HUMOROUS, FACETIOUS, JOCULAR, JOCOSE *shared meaning element* : provoking or tending to provoke amusement or laughter

wive \'wīv\ *vb* **wived; wiv·ing** [ME *wiven,* fr. OE *wīfian,* fr. *wīf* woman, wife] *vi* : to marry a woman ~ *vt* **1 :** to marry to a wife **2 :** to take for a wife

wives *pl of* WIFE

wiz \'wiz\ *n* : WIZARD 3

1wiz·ard \'wiz-ərd\ *n* [ME *wysard,* fr. *wis, wys* wise] **1** *archaic* : a wise man : SAGE **2 :** one skilled in magic : SORCERER **3 :** a very clever or skillful person

2wizard *adj* **1** *archaic* : having magical influence or power **2** *archaic* : of or relating to wizardry : ENCHANTED **3** *chiefly Brit* : worthy of the highest praise : EXCELLENT

wiz·ard·ly \'wiz-ərd-lē\ *adj* **1 :** having characteristics of a wizard **2 :** marvelous in construction or operation <uses ~ circuitry to distort images —*Time*>

wiz·ard·ry \'wiz-ə(r)-drē\ *n, pl* **-ries** **1 :** the art or practices of a wizard : SORCERY **2 :** a seemingly magical transforming power or influence

1wiz·en \'wiz-ᵊn\ *vb* [ME *wisenen,* fr. OE *wisnian;* akin to OHG *wesanēn* to wither, L *viēre* to twist together, plait — more at WIRE] *vi* : to become dry, shrunken, and wrinkled often as a result of aging or of failing vitality ~ *vt* : to cause to wizen ***syn*** see WITHER

2wizen *adj* [alter. of *wizened*] : that is wizened

wk *abbr* **1** week **2** work

WL *abbr* **1** waterline **2** wavelength

wm *abbr* wattmeter

wmk *abbr* watermark

WMO *abbr* World Meteorological Organization
WNW *abbr* west-northwest
WO *abbr* **1** warrant officer **2** water-in-oil
w/o *abbr* without
woad \'wōd\ *n* [ME *wod,* fr. OE *wād;* akin to OHG *weit* woad, L *vitrum* woad, glass] **:** a European herb (*Isatis tinctoria*) of the mustard family formerly grown for the blue dyestuff yielded by its leaves; *also* **:** this dyestuff
[1]**wob·ble** \'wäb-əl\ *vb* **wob·bled; wob·bling** \-(ə-)liŋ\ [prob. fr. LG *wabbeln;* akin to OE *wǣfre* restless — more at WAVER] *vi* **1 a :** to move or proceed with an irregular rocking or staggering motion or unsteadily and clumsily from side to side **b :** TREMBLE, QUAVER **2 :** WAVER, VACILLATE ~ *vt* **:** to cause to wobble — **wob·bler** \-(ə-)lər\ *n* — **wob·bli·ness** \'wäb-lē-nəs\ *n* — **wob·bly** \'wäb-(ə-)lē\ *adj*
[2]**wobble** *n* **1 a :** a hobbling or rocking unequal motion (as of a wheel unevenly hung) **b :** an uncertainly directed movement **2 :** an intermittent variation (as in volume of sound)
wobble pump *n* **:** an auxiliary hand pump used on an airplane to supply fuel to the carburetor of an engine when the power-driven pump fails or to force fuel from an extra tank
Wob·bly \'wäb-lē\ *n, pl* **Wobblies** [origin unknown] **:** a member of the Industrial Workers of the World
WOC *abbr* without compensation
Wo·den \'wōd-ᵊn\ *n* [OE *Wōden*] **:** ODIN
[1]**woe** \'wō\ *interj* [ME *wa, wo,* fr. OE *wā;* akin to ON *vei,* interj., woe, L *vae*] — used to express grief, regret, or distress
[2]**woe** *n* [ME *wo,* fr. *wo,* interj.] **1 :** a condition of deep suffering from misfortune, affliction, or grief **2 :** ruinous trouble **:** CALAMITY, AFFLICTION <economic ~*s*> *syn* see SORROW
woe·be·gone \'wō-bi-ˌgȯn *also* -ˌgän\ *adj* [ME *wo begon,* fr. *wo,* n. + *begon,* pp. of *begon* to go about, beset, fr. OE *begān,* fr. *be-* + *gān* to go — more at GO] **1 :** strongly affected with woe **:** WOEFUL **2 a :** exhibiting great woe, sorrow, or misery <a ~ expression> **b :** being in a sorry state <this ~ grass, where timothy had once grown head-high —S. H. Holbrook> — **woe·be·gone·ness** *n*
woe·ful *also* **wo·ful** \'wō-fəl\ *adj* **1 :** full of woe **:** GRIEVOUS <~ prophecies> **2 :** involving or bringing woe <it was ~ to see him spoiling it —Henry James> **3 :** lamentably bad or serious **:** DEPLORABLE <~ ignorance> — **woe·ful·ly** \-f(ə-)lē\ *adv* — **woe·ful·ness** \-fəl-nəs\ *n*
wok \'wäk\ *n* [Chin (Cant) *wôk*] **:** a bowl-shaped cooking utensil used esp. in the preparation of Chinese food
woke *past of* WAKE
woken *past part of* WAKE
wold \'wōld\ *n* [ME *wald, wold,* fr. OE *weald, wald* forest; akin to OHG *wald* forest] **1 :** a usu. upland area of open country **2** *cap* **:** a hilly or rolling region — used in names of various English geographical areas <Yorkshire ~*s*>
[1]**wolf** \'wu̇lf\ *n, pl* **wolves** \'wu̇lvz\ *often attrib* [ME, fr. OE *wulf;* akin to OHG *wolf,* L *lupus,* Gk *lykos*] **1** *pl also* **wolf a :** any of various large predatory mammals (genus *Canis* and esp. *C. lupus*) that resemble the related dogs, are destructive to game and livestock, and may rarely attack man esp. when in a pack — compare COYOTE, JACKAL **b :** the fur of a wolf **2 a (1) :** a fierce, rapacious, or destructive person **(2) :** a man forward, direct, and zealous in amatory attentions to women **b :** dire poverty **:** STARVATION <keep the ~ from the door> **c (1) :** a beetle grub or moth grub that infests granaries **(2) :** the maggot of a warble fly **3** [G; fr. the howling sound] **a (1) :** dissonance in some chords on organs, pianos, or other instruments with fixed tones tuned by unequal temperament **(2) :** an instance of such dissonance **b :** a harshness due to faulty vibration in various tones in a bowed instrument — **wolf·like** \'wu̇l-ˌflīk\ *adj* — **wolf in sheep's clothing :** one who cloaks a hostile intention with a friendly manner
[2]**wolf** *vt* **:** to eat greedily **:** DEVOUR
wolf·ber·ry \'wu̇lf-ˌber-ē\ *n* **:** a white-berried western American shrub (*Symphoricarpos occidentalis*) of the honeysuckle family
wolf dog *n* **1 :** any of various large dogs formerly kept for hunting wolves **2 :** the offspring of a wolf and a domestic dog **3 :** a wolfish dog
wolf·er \'wu̇l-fər\ *n* **:** a hunter of wolves
wolff·ian body \ˌwu̇l-fē-ən-\ *n, often cap W* [Kaspar Friedrich *Wolff*] **:** MESONEPHROS
Wolffian duct *n* **:** the duct of the mesonephros persisting in the female as the ureter and in the male as the common urogenital duct
wolf·fish \'wu̇lf-ˌfish\ *n* **:** any of several large marine blennies notable for their strong teeth and ferocity
wolf·hound \'wu̇lf-ˌhau̇nd\ *n* **:** any of several large dogs used esp. formerly in hunting large animals (as wolves)
wolf·ish \'wu̇l-fish\ *adj* **1 :** of or relating to wolves **2 a :** suggestive of a wolf <~ mongrel dogs —Hoffman Birney> <a ~ and withdrawn youth —Marshall Frady> **b :** befitting or characteristic of a wolf (as in fierceness or rapacity) <a ~ appetite> — **wolf·ish·ly** *adv* — **wolf·ish·ness** *n*
wolf pack *n* **:** a group of submarines that make a coordinated attack on shipping; *also* **:** a group of two or more fighter planes making a coordinated attack
wol·fram \'wu̇l-frəm\ *n* [G] **1 :** TUNGSTEN **2 :** WOLFRAMITE
wol·fram·ic \wu̇l-'fram-ik\ *adj* **:** TUNGSTIC
wol·fram·ite \'wu̇l-frə-ˌmīt\ *n* [G *wolframit,* fr. *wolfram*] **:** a mineral $(Fe,Mn)WO_4$ that consists of a tungstate of iron and manganese usu. of a brownish or grayish black color and slightly metallic luster, occurs in monoclinic crystals and in granular or columnar masses, and is used as a source of tungsten
wolfs·bane \'wu̇lfs-ˌbān\ *n* **:** ACONITUM 1; *esp* **:** a highly variable yellow-flowered Eurasian herb (*Aconitum lycoctonum*)
wolf spider *n* **:** any of various active wandering ground spiders (family Lycosidae)
wolf whistle *n* **:** a distinctive whistle sounded by a male to express sexual admiration for a girl or woman in his vicinity
wol·las·ton·ite \'wu̇l-ə-stə-ˌnīt, 'wäl-\ *n* [William H. *Wollaston* †1828 E chemist] **:** a triclinic mineral $CaSiO_3$ of a white to gray, red, yellow, or brown color consisting of a native calcium silicate occurring usu. in cleavable masses
Wo·lof \'wō-ˌlȯf\ *n* **:** a Niger-Congo language of Senegambia
wol·ver·ine \ˌwu̇l-və-'rēn\ *n, pl* **wolverines** [prob. irreg. fr. *wolv-* (as in *wolves*)] **1** *pl also* **wolverine a :** a carnivorous usu. solitary mammal (*Gulo gulo* of the weasel family) of northern forests and associated tundra that is blackish with a light brown band on each side of the body and is noted esp. for its strength — called also *carcajou* **b :** the fur of the wolverine **2** *cap* **:** a native or resident of Michigan — used as a nickname

wolverine 1a

wom·an \'wu̇m-ən\ *n, pl* **wom·en** \'wim-ən\ [ME, fr. OE *wīfman,* fr. *wīf* woman, wife + *man* human being, man] **1 a :** an adult female person **b :** a woman belonging to a particular category (as by birth, residence, membership, or occupation) — usu. used in combination <council*woman*> **2 :** WOMANKIND **3 :** distinctively feminine nature **:** WOMANLINESS **4 :** a female servant or personal attendant **5 a** *chiefly dial* **:** WIFE **b :** MISTRESS **c :** GIRL FRIEND 2 — **wom·an·less** \'wu̇m-ən-ləs\ *adj*
wom·an·hood \'wu̇m-ən-ˌhu̇d\ *n* **1 a :** the state of being a woman **b :** the distinguishing character or qualities of a woman or of womankind **2 :** WOMEN, WOMANKIND
wom·an·ish \'wu̇m-ə-nish\ *adj* **1 :** characteristic of or suitable for a woman **2 :** unsuitable to a man or to a strong character of either sex **:** EFFEMINATE <~ fears> — **wom·an·ish·ly** *adv* — **wom·an·ish·ness** *n*
wom·an·ize \'wu̇m-ə-ˌnīz\ *vb* **-ized; -iz·ing** *vt* **:** to make effeminate ~ *vi* **:** to pursue freewheeling relationships with women — **wom·an·iz·er** *n*
wom·an·kind \'wu̇m-ən-ˌkīnd\ *n sing but sing or pl in constr* **:** WOMENKIND
[1]**wom·an·like** \-ˌlīk\ *adj* **:** WOMANLY
[2]**womanlike** *adv* **:** in the manner of a woman
wom·an·ly \-lē\ *adj* **:** marked by qualities characteristic of a woman — **wom·an·li·ness** *n*
woman of the street : PROSTITUTE — called also *woman of the streets*
wom·an·pow·er \'wu̇m-ən-ˌpau̇(-ə)r\ *n* **:** women available and fitted for service (as in industry or a particular line of endeavor)
woman's rights *n pl* **1 :** legal, political, and social rights for women equal to those of men **2 :** FEMINISM 2
woman suffrage *n* **:** possession and exercise of suffrage by women
womb \'wüm\ *n* [ME *wamb, womb,* fr. OE; akin to OHG *wamba* belly] **1 :** UTERUS **2 a :** a cavity or space that resembles a womb in containing and enveloping **b :** a place where something is generated — **wombed** \'wümd\ *adj*
wom·bat \'wäm-ˌbat\ *n* [native name in New So. Wales] **:** any of several stocky Australian marsupials (family Vombatidae) resembling small bears
wom·en·folk \'wim-ən-ˌfōk\ *also* **wom·en·folks** \-ˌfōks\ *n pl* **:** WOMEN
wom·en·kind \-ˌkīnd\ *n* **:** female human beings **:** women esp. as distinguished from men
women's room *n* **:** LADIES' ROOM
wom·mera \'wäm-ə-rə\ *n* **:** WOOMERA
[1]**won** \'wən, 'wōn\ *vi* **wonned; won·ning** [ME *wonen,* fr. OE *wunian* — more at WONT] *archaic* **:** DWELL 2a, ABIDE 2
[2]**won** \'wən\ *past of* WIN
[3]**won** \'wȯn\ *n* [Korean *wŏn*] — see MONEY table
[1]**won·der** \'wən-dər\ *n* [ME, fr. OE *wundor;* akin to OHG *wuntar* wonder] **1 a :** a cause of astonishment or admiration **:** MARVEL <it's a ~ he wasn't killed> **b :** MIRACLE **2 :** the quality of exciting amazed admiration **3 a :** rapt attention or astonishment at something awesomely mysterious or new to one's experience <looked at each other in silent ~ —G. D. Brown> **b :** a feeling of doubt or uncertainty
[2]**wonder** *adj* **:** WONDROUS, WONDERFUL: as **a :** exciting amazement or admiration **b :** effective or efficient far beyond anything previously known or anticipated <~ drugs>
[3]**wonder** *vb* **won·dered; won·der·ing** \-d(ə-)riŋ\ *vi* **1 a :** to be in a state of wonder **:** MARVEL **b :** to feel surprise **2 :** to feel curiosity or doubt ~ *vt* **:** to be curious or in doubt about — **won·der·er** \-dər-ər\ *n*
won·der·ful \'wən-dər-fəl\ *adj* **1 :** exciting wonder **:** MARVELOUS, ASTONISHING <a sight ~ to behold> **2 :** unusually good **:** ADMIRABLE — **won·der·ful·ly** \-f(ə-)lē\ *adv* — **won·der·ful·ness** \-fəl-nəs\ *n*
won·der·land \'wən-dər-ˌland, -lənd\ *n* **1 :** a fairylike imaginary realm **2 :** a place that excites admiration or wonder
won·der·ment \-mənt\ *n* **1 :** ASTONISHMENT, SURPRISE **2 :** a cause of or occasion for wonder **3 :** curiosity about something
won·der·work \-də(r)-ˌwərk\ *n* **:** a marvelous act, work, or accomplishment
won·der–work·er \-ˌwər-kər\ *n* **:** one that performs wonders
won·der–work·ing \-kiŋ\ *adj* **:** producing wonders
won·drous \'wən-drəs\ *adj* [alter. of ME *wonders,* fr. gen. of [1]*wonder*] **:** that is to be marveled at **:** EXTRAORDINARY — **wondrous** *adv, archaic* — **won·drous·ly** *adv* — **won·drous·ness** *n*
won·ky \'wäŋ-kē\ *adj* [alter. of E dial. *wankle,* fr. ME *wankel,* fr. OE *wancol*] **1** *Brit* **:** UNSTEADY, SHAKY **2** *Brit* **:** AWRY, WRONG
[1]**wont** \'wȯnt, 'wōnt *also* 'wənt, 'wänt\ *adj* [ME *woned, wont,* fr. pp. of *wonen* to dwell, be used to, fr. OE *wunian;* akin to OHG *wonēn* to dwell, be used to, L *venus* love, charm — more at WIN] **1 :** ACCUSTOMED, USED <got up early as he is ~ to do> **2 :** INCLINED, APT <revealing as letters are ~ to be —Gladys M. Wrigley>
[2]**wont** *n* **:** habitual way of doing **:** USE *syn* see HABIT
[3]**wont** *vb* **wont; wont** *or* **wont·ed; wont·ing** *vt* **:** ACCUSTOM, HABITUATE ~ *vi* **:** to have the habit of doing something

won't \(ˈ)wōnt; *NewEng, upstate NY, nPa* ˌwənt, ˈwənt; *greater NYC* (ˈ)wünt; *eSC* (ˈ)wünt, (ˈ)wu̇nt\ : will not

wont·ed \ˈwȯnt-əd, ˈwōnt- *also* ˈwənt- *or* ˈwänt-\ *adj* : usual or ordinary esp. by reason of established habit <spoke with his ~ slowness> ***syn*** see USUAL — **wont·ed·ly** *adv* — **wont·ed·ness** *n*

won·ton \ˈwän-ˌtän\ *n* [Chin (Cant) *wan t'an*] : filled pockets of noodle dough boiled in and eaten with soup

woo \ˈwü\ *vb* [ME *wowen*, fr. OE *wōgian*] *vt* **1** : to sue for the affection of and usu. marriage with : COURT **2** : to solicit or entreat esp. with importunity **3** : to seek to gain or bring about ~ *vi* : to court a woman — **woo·er** *n*

1wood \ˈwüd, ˈwōd, ˈwu̇d\ *adj* [ME, fr. OE *wōd* insane; akin to OHG *wuot* madness — more at VATIC] *archaic* : violently mad : CRAZY

2wood \ˈwu̇d\ *n* [ME *wode*, fr. OE *widu, wudu;* akin to OHG *witu* wood, OIr *fid* tree] **1 a** : a dense growth of trees usu. greater in extent than a grove and smaller than a forest — often used in pl. but sing. or pl. in constr. **b** : WOODLAND **2 a** : the hard fibrous substance basically xylem that makes up the greater part of the stems and branches of trees or shrubs beneath the bark and is found to a limited extent in herbaceous plants **b** : wood suitable or prepared for some use (as burning or building) **3** : something made of wood; *esp* : a golf club having a wooden head — **out of the woods** : escaped from peril or difficulty

3wood \ˈwu̇d\ *adj* **1** : WOODEN **2** : suitable for cutting or working with wood <a ~ saw> **3** *or* **woods** \ˈwu̇dz\ : living, growing, or existing in woods <*woods* trails>

4wood \ˈwu̇d\ *vt* : to cover with a growth of trees or plant with trees ~ *vi* : to gather or take on wood

wood alcohol *n* : METHANOL

wood anemone *n* : any of several anemones; esp : a common anemone (*Anemone quinquefolia*) of the eastern U.S. with solitary often pink-tinged flowers

wood betony *n* : a lousewort (*Pedicularis canadensis*) of eastern No. America with pinnately parted leaves and red or yellowish flowers in bracted spikes

wood·bin \ˈwu̇d-ˌbin\ *n* : a bin for holding firewood

wood·bine \-ˌbīn\ *n* [ME *wodebinde*, fr. OE *wudubinde*, fr. *wudu* wood + *bindan* to tie, bind; fr. its winding around trees] **1** : any of several honeysuckles; *esp* : a European twining shrub (*Lonicera periclymenum*) **2** : VIRGINIA CREEPER

wood·block \-ˌbläk\ *n* : WOODCUT — **wood–block** *adj*

wood–bor·ing \-ˌbōr-iŋ, -ˌbȯr-\ *adj* : excavating galleries in wood in feeding or in constructing a nest — used chiefly of an insect

wood·box \-ˌbäks\ *n* : WOODBIN

wood–carv·er \-ˌkär-vər\ *n* : a person whose occupation is wood carving

wood carving *n* : the art of fashioning or ornamenting objects of wood by cutting with a sharp implement held in the hand; *also* : an object of wood so fashioned or ornamented

wood·chat \ˈwu̇d-ˌchat\ *n* **1** : any of several Asiatic thrushes (genus *Erithacus*) having brightly colored males **2** : a European shrike (*Lanius senator*)

wood·chop·per \-ˌchäp-ər\ *n* : one engaged esp. in chopping down trees

wood·chuck \-ˌchək\ *n* [by folk etymology fr. Ojibwa *otchig* fisher, marten, or Cree *otcheck*] **1** : a grizzled thickset marmot (*Marmota monax*) of the northeastern U.S. and Canada — called also *groundhog* **2** : any of several marmots of mountainous western No. America

woodchuck 1

wood coal *n* **1** : CHARCOAL **2** : LIGNITE

wood·cock \ˈwu̇d-ˌkäk\ *n, pl* **wood·cocks 1** *or pl* **woodcock** : a widespread Old World limicoline bird (*Scolopax rusticola*); *also* : a smaller related American bird (*Philohela minor*) prized as a game bird **2** [fr. the ease with which the woodcock is snared] *archaic* : SIMPLETON

wood·craft \-ˌkraft\ *n* **1** : skill and practice in anything relating to the woods and esp. in maintaining oneself and making one's way in the woods **2** : skill in shaping or constructing articles from wood

wood·cut \-ˌkət\ *n* **1** : a relief printing surface consisting of a wooden block with a usu. pictorial design cut with the grain **2** : a print from a woodcut

wood·cut·ter \-ˌkət-ər\ *n* : one that cuts wood

wood·cut·ting \-ˌkət-iŋ\ *n* **1** : the producing of woodcuts **2** : the action or occupation of cutting wood or timber

wood duck *n* : a showy American duck (*Aix sponsa*) that nests in trees and in the male has a large crest and plumage varied with green, purple, black, white, and chestnut

wood·ed \ˈwu̇d-əd\ *adj* : covered with growing trees

wood·en \ˈwu̇d-ᵊn\ *adj* **1** : made or consisting of wood **2** : lacking ease or flexibility : awkwardly stiff — **wood·en·ly** *adv* — **wood·en·ness** \-ᵊn-(n)əs\ *n*

wood engraving *n* **1** : a relief printing surface consisting of a wooden block with a usu. pictorial design cut in the end grain **2** : a print from a wood engraving

wood·en·head \ˈwu̇d-ᵊn-ˌhed\ *n* : BLOCKHEAD

wood·en·head·ed \ˌwu̇d-ᵊn-ˈhed-əd\ *adj* : DENSE, STUPID

wooden Indian *n* : a standing wooden image of an American Indian brave used esp. formerly as a sign for a cigar store

wood·en·ware \ˈwu̇d-ᵊn-ˌwa(ə)r, -ˌwe(ə)r\ *n* : articles made of wood for domestic use

wood fiber *n* : any of various fibers located in or associated with xylem

wood hyacinth *n* : a European squill (*Scilla nonscripta*) having scapose racemes of bell-shaped flowers

wood ibis *n* : a large wading bird (*Mycteria americana* of the family Ciconiidae) that frequents wooded swamps of So. and Central America and the southern U.S.

1wood·land \ˈwu̇d-lənd, -ˌland\ *n* : land covered with woody vegetation : TIMBERLAND, FOREST — **wood·land·er** \-ər\ *n*

2woodland *adj* **1** : of, relating to, or being woodland **2** : growing, living, or existing in woodland

wood·lore \-ˌlōr, -ˌlȯr\ *n* : knowledge of the woods

wood·lot \ˈwu̇d-ˌlät\ *n* : a restricted area of woodland usu. privately maintained as a source of fuel, posts, and lumber

wood louse *n* **1** : a terrestrial isopod crustacean (suborder Oniscoidea) with a flattened elliptical body often capable of being rolled into a ball — called also *pill bug, sowbug* **2** : any of several small wingless insects (order Corrodentia) that live under bark, in the crevices of walls, and among old books and papers

wood·man \ˈwu̇d-mən\ *n* **1** : WOODSMAN **2** *cap* [Modern *Woodmen* of America & *Woodmen* of the World] : a member of either of two independent benevolent and fraternal societies

wood·note \-ˌnōt\ *n* [fr. its likeness to the call of a bird in the woods] : verbal expression that is natural and artless

wood nymph *n* : a nymph living in woods — called also *dryad*

wood·peck·er \ˈwu̇d-ˌpek-ər\ *n* : any of numerous birds (family Picidae) with zygodactyl feet, stiff spiny tail feathers used in climbing or resting on tree trunks, a usu. extensile tongue, a very hard bill used to drill the bark or wood of trees for insect food or to excavate nesting cavities, and generally showy parti-colored plumage

wood·pile \-ˌpīl\ *n* : a pile of wood (as firewood) — **in the woodpile** : doing or responsible for covert mischief <the No. 1 villain *in the woodpile* — Howard Whitman>

wood pulp *n* : pulp from wood used in making cellulose derivatives (as paper or rayon)

wood pussy *n* : SKUNK

wood rat *n* : any of numerous native voles (family Cricetidae and esp. genus *Neotoma*) of the southern U.S. and western No. America with soft fur that is light gray to ocherous above and white below, well-furred tails, and large ears

wood ray *n* : XYLEM RAY

wood·ruff \ˈwu̇d-(ˌ)rəf\ *n* [ME *woderove*, fr. OE *wudurofe*, fr. *wudu* wood + *-rofe* (perh. akin to OHG *rāba* turnip) — more at RAPE] : any of a genus (*Asperula*) of herbs of the madder family; *esp* : a small European sweet-scented herb (*A. odorata*) used in perfumery and for flavoring wine

1wood·shed \-ˌshed\ *n* : a shed for storing wood and esp. firewood

2woodshed *vi* **-shed·ded; -shed·ding** [prob. fr. the former use of woodsheds for private practicing] : to practice on a musical instrument

wood shot *n* **1** : a golf shot played with a wood **2** : a stroke in a racket game in which the ball or shuttlecock is hit with the wooden part of the racket rather than the strings

woods·man \ˈwu̇dz-mən\ *n* : one who frequents or works in the woods; *esp* : one skilled in woodcraft

wood sorrel *n* **1** : any of a genus (*Oxalis* of the family Oxalidaceae, the wood-sorrel family) of herbs with acid sap, compound leaves, and regular flowers; *esp* : a stemless herb (*O. montana* or *O. acetosella*) with trifoliolate leaves sometimes held to be the original shamrock **2** : SHEEP SORREL

wood spirit *n* : METHANOL

wood sugar *n* **1** : XYLOSE **2** : a mixture of pentose and hexose sugars obtained by hydrolysis of pentosans and cellulose of wood

woodsy \ˈwu̇d-zē\ *adj* : characteristic or suggestive of woods

wood tar *n* : tar obtained by the destructive distillation of wood either as a deposit from pyroligneous acid or as a residue from the distillation of the acid or of wood turpentine

wood tick *n* : any of various ixodid ticks whose young cling to bushes whence they readily drop on and attach themselves to passing animals where they may produce troublesome sores or serve as vectors for disease-producing microorganisms — compare ROCKY MOUNTAIN SPOTTED FEVER

wood·turn·er \ˈwu̇d-ˌtər-nər\ *n* : one whose occupation is wood turning

wood turning *n* : the art or process of fashioning wooden pieces or blocks into various forms and shapes by means of a lathe

wood turpentine *n* : TURPENTINE 2b

wood warbler *n* : WARBLER 2b

wood·wax·en \ˈwu̇d-ˌwak-sən\ *n* [ME *wodewexen*, alter. of OE *wuduweaxe*, fr. *wudu* wood + *-weaxe* (prob. fr. *weaxan* to grow) — more at WAX] : a low bushy yellow-flowered Eurasian leguminous shrub (*Genista tinctoria*) grown for ornament or formerly as the source of a yellow dye

wood·wind \-ˌwind\ *n* **1** : one of a group of wind instruments (as a clarinet, flute, oboe, or saxophone) that is characterized by a cylindrical or conical tube of wood or metal usu. ending in a slightly flared bell, that produces tones by the vibration of one or two reeds in the mouthpiece or by the passing of air over a mouth hole, and that usu. has finger holes or keys by which the player may produce all the tones within the instrument's range **2** *pl* : the woodwind section of a band or orchestra

wood·work \-ˌwərk\ *n* : work made of wood; *esp* : interior fittings (as moldings or stairways) of wood

1wood·work·ing \-ˌwər-kiŋ\ *n* : the act, process, or occupation of working with wood — **wood·work·er** \-kər\ *n*

2woodworking *adj* : used for woodworking <~ tools>

woody \ˈwu̇d-ē\ *adj* **wood·i·er; -est 1** : abounding or overgrown with woods **2 a** : of or containing wood or wood fibers : LIGNEOUS <~ tissues> **b** : having woody parts : rich in xylem and associated structures <~ plants> **3** : characteristic of or suggestive of wood <wine with a ~ flavor> — **wood·i·ness** *n*

ə abut	ᵊ kitten	ər further	a back	ā bake	ä cot, cart	
au̇ out	ch chin	e less	ē easy	g gift	i trip	ī life
j joke	ŋ sing	ō flow	ȯ flaw	ȯi coin	th thin	t͟h this
ü loot	u̇ foot	y yet	yü few	yu̇ furious	zh vision	

[1]**woof** \'wu̇f, 'wüf\ *n* [alter. of ME *oof*, fr. OE *ōwef*, fr. *ō-* (fr. *on*) + *wefan* to weave — more at WEAVE] **1 a :** a filling thread or yarn in weaving **b :** woven fabric; *also* **:** the texture of such a fabric **2 :** a basic or essential element or material
[2]**woof** \'wu̇f\ *n* [imit.] **1 :** a low gruff sound typically produced by a dog **2 :** a low note emitted by sound reproducing equipment
[3]**woof** *vi* **:** to make the sound of a woof
woof·er \'wu̇f-ər\ *n* **:** a loudspeaker usu. larger than a tweeter, responsive only to the lower acoustic frequencies, and used for reproducing sounds of low pitch
wool \'wu̇l\ *n, often attrib* [ME *wolle*, fr. OE *wull;* akin to OHG *wolla* wool, L *vellus* fleece, *lana* wool, *lanugo* down] **1 :** the soft wavy or curly hypertrophied undercoat of various hairy mammals and esp. the sheep made up of fibers of keratin molecules within a matrix and covered with minute scales **2 :** a product of wool; *esp* **:** a woven fabric or garment of such fabric **3 a :** a dense felted pubescence esp. on a plant **:** TOMENTUM **b :** a filamentous mass — usu. used in combination; compare MINERAL WOOL, STEEL WOOL — **wooled** \'wu̇ld\ *adj*
-wooled \'wu̇ld\ *adj comb form* **:** having wool of (such) quality <coarse-*wooled*>
[1]**wool·en** *or* **wool·len** \'wu̇l-ən\ *adj* **1 :** made of wool — compare WORSTED **2 :** of or relating to the manufacture or sale of woolen products <~ mills> <the ~ industry>
[2]**woolen** *or* **woollen** *n* **1 :** a fabric made of wool **2 :** garments of woolen fabric — usu. used in pl.
wool fat *n* **:** wool grease esp. after refining **:** LANOLIN
wool·fell \'wu̇l-ˌfel\ *n, Brit* **:** WOOLSKIN
wool–gath·er \'wu̇l-ˌgat͟h-ər, -ˌget͟h-\ *vi* **:** to indulge in woolgathering — **wool·gath·er·er** \-ər-ər\ *n*
wool·gath·er·ing \-ˌgat͟h-(ə-)riŋ, -ˌget͟h-\ *n* **:** the act of indulging in idle daydreaming
wool grease *n* **:** a fatty slightly sticky wax coating the surface of the fibers of sheep's wool — compare WOOL FAT
[1]**wool·ly** *also* **wooly** \'wu̇l-ē\ *adj* **wool·li·er; -est** **1 a :** of, relating to, or bearing wool **b :** resembling wool **2 a :** lacking in clearness or sharpness of outline <a ~ TV picture> **b :** marked by mental confusion <~ thinking> **3 :** marked by boisterous roughness or lack of order or restraint <where the West is still ~ —Paul Schubert> — **wool·li·ness** *n*
[2]**wool·ly** *also* **wool·ie** *or* **wooly** \'wu̇l-ē\ *n, pl* **wool·lies** **1 :** a garment made from wool; *esp* **:** underclothing of knitted wool — usu. used in pl. **2** *West & Austral* **:** SHEEP
woolly aphid *n* **:** a plant louse (genus *Eriosoma*) covered with a dense coat of white filaments
woolly bear *n* **:** any of various rather large very hairy caterpillars; *esp* **:** one that is the larva of a tiger moth
wool·ly–head·ed \ˌwu̇l-ē-'hed-əd\ *adj* **1 :** having hair suggesting wool **2 :** marked by vague or confused perception or thinking
wool·pack \'wu̇l-ˌpak\ *n* **1 a :** a wrapper of strong fabric into which fleeces are packed for shipment **b :** the complete package of wool and wrapper **2 :** a rounded cumulus cloud springing from a horizontal base
wool·sack \-ˌsak\ *n* **1** *archaic* **:** WOOLPACK 1b **2 :** the official seat of the Lord Chancellor or his deputy in the House of Lords
wool·shed \-ˌshed\ *n* **:** a building or range of buildings (as on an Australian sheep station) in which sheep are sheared and wool is prepared for market
wool·skin \-ˌskin\ *n* **:** a sheepskin having the wool still on it
wool·sort·er's disease \'wu̇l-ˌsȯrt-ərz-\ *n* **:** pulmonary anthrax resulting esp. from inhalation of bacterial spores (*Bacillus anthracis*) from contaminated wool or hair
wool sponge *n* **:** a soft-fibered durable commercial sponge; *esp* **:** one (*Hippiospongia lachne*) found in the Gulf of Mexico, the Caribbean sea, and off the southern coast of Florida
wool stapler *n* **:** a dealer in wool
woom·era \'wu̇m-ə-rə\ *n* [native name in Australia] **:** a wooden rod with a hooked end used by Australian aborigines for throwing a spear
woops *interj* **:** OOPS
woo·zy \'wü-zē, 'wu̇z-ē\ *adj* **woo·zi·er; -est** [prob. alter. of *oozy*] **1 :** mentally unclear or hazy <seems a little ~, not quite knowing what to say —J. A. Lukacs> **2 :** affected with dizziness, mild nausea, or weakness **:** SICK — **woo·zi·ly** *adv* — **woo·zi·ness** *n*
wop \'wäp\ *n, often cap* [It dial. *guappo* blusterer, swaggerer, bully, tough] **:** ITALIAN — usu. used disparagingly
Worces·ter \'wu̇s-tər\ *n* **:** low-fired porcelain containing a frit and steatite produced at Worcester, England from about 1751 — called also *Worcester china, Worcester porcelain*
Worces·ter·shire sauce \ˌwu̇s-tə(r)-ˌshi(ə)r-, -shər- *also* -ˌshi(ə)r-\ *n* **:** a pungent sauce orig. made in Worcester, England whose ingredients include soy, vinegar, and garlic
Worcs *abbr* Worcestershire
[1]**word** \'wərd\ *n* [ME, fr. OE; akin to OHG *wort* word, L *verbum*, Gk *eirein* to say, speak] **1 a :** something that is said **b** *pl* (1) **:** TALK, DISCOURSE <putting one's feelings into ~*s*> (2) **:** the text of a vocal musical composition **c :** a brief remark or conversation <would like to have a ~ with you> **2 a** (1) **:** a speech sound or series of speech sounds that symbolizes and communicates a meaning without being divisible into smaller units capable of independent use (2) **:** the entire set of linguistic forms produced by combining a single base with various inflectional elements without change in the part of speech elements **b :** a written or printed character or combination of characters representing a spoken word <the number of ~*s* to a line> **c :** a combination of electrical or magnetic impulses conveying a quantum of information in communication and computer work **3 :** ORDER, COMMAND <don't move till I give the ~> **4** *often cap* **a :** LOGOS **b :** GOSPEL 1a **c :** the expressed or manifested mind and will of God **5 a :** NEWS, INFORMATION <sent ~ that he would be late> **b :** RUMOR **6 :** the act of speaking or of making verbal communication **7 :** SAYING, PROVERB **8 :** PROMISE, DECLARATION <kept her ~> **9 :** a quarrelsome utterance or conversation — usu. used in pl. **10 :** a verbal signal **:** PASSWORD — **good word** **1 :** a favorable statement <put in a *good word* for me> **2 :** good news <what's the *good word*> — **in a word :** in short — **in so many words** **1 :** in exactly those terms <implied that such actions were criminal but did not say so *in so many words*> **2 :** in plain forthright language <*in so many words*, she wasn't fit to be seen —Jean Stafford> — **of few words :** not inclined to say more than is necessary **:** LACONIC <a man *of few words*> — **of one's word :** that can be relied on to keep a promise — used only after *man* or *woman* <a man *of his word*> — **upon my word :** with my assurance **:** INDEED, ASSUREDLY <*upon my word*, I've never heard of such a thing>
[2]**word** *vi, archaic* **:** SPEAK ~ *vt* **:** to express in words **:** PHRASE
word·age \'wərd-ij\ *n* **1 a :** WORDS **b :** VERBIAGE 1 **2 :** the number or quantity of words **3 :** WORDING
word–association test *n* **:** a test of personality and mental function in which the subject is required to respond to each of a series of words with one that it evokes in his mind or with one of a specified class of words
word·book \'wərd-ˌbu̇k\ *n* **:** VOCABULARY, DICTIONARY
word class *n* **:** a linguistic form class whose members are words; *esp* **:** PART OF SPEECH
word–for–word *adj* **:** being in or following the exact words **:** VERBATIM
word for word *adv* **:** in the exact words **:** VERBATIM
word–hoard \'wərd-ˌhō(ə)rd, -ˌhȯ(ə)rd\ *n* **:** a supply of words **:** VOCABULARY
word·ing \'wərd-iŋ\ *n* **:** the act or manner of expressing in words
word·less \'wərd-ləs\ *adj* **1 :** not expressed in or accompanied by words **2 :** SILENT, INARTICULATE — **word·less·ly** *adv* — **word·less·ness** *n*
word·mon·ger \-ˌməŋ-gər, -ˌmäŋ-\ *n* **:** a writer who uses words for show or without particular regard for meaning
word–mon·ger·ing \-g(ə-)riŋ\ *n* **:** the use of empty or bombastic words
word–of–mouth \ˌwərd-ə(v)-'mau̇th\ *adj* **:** orally communicated
word of mouth : oral communication
word order *n* **:** the order of arrangement of words in a phrase, clause, or sentence
word·play \'wərd-ˌplā\ *n* **:** verbal wit
word square *n* **:** ACROSTIC 3
word stress *n* **:** the manner in which stresses are distributed on the syllables of a word — called also *word accent*
wordy \'wərd-ē\ *adj* **word·i·er; -est** **1 :** using or containing many and usu. too many words **2 :** of or relating to words **:** VERBAL — **word·i·ly** \'wərd-ᵊl-ē\ *adv* — **word·i·ness** \'wərd-ē-nəs\ *n*
syn WORDY, VERBOSE, DIFFUSE, PROLIX, REDUNDANT *shared meaning element* **:** using more words than effective expression requires
wore *past of* WEAR
[1]**work** \'wərk\ *n* [ME *werk, work*, fr. OE *werc, weorc;* akin to OHG *werc*, Gk *ergon*] **1 :** activity in which one exerts strength or faculties to do or perform something: **a :** sustained physical or mental effort to overcome obstacles and achieve an objective or result **b :** the labor, task, or duty that affords one his accustomed means of livelihood **c :** a specific task, duty, function, or assignment often being a part or phase of some larger activity **2 a :** energy expended by natural phenomena **b :** the result of such energy <sand dunes are the ~ of sea and wind> **c :** the transference of energy that is produced by the motion of the point of application of a force and is measured by multiplying the force and the displacement of its point of application in the line of action **3 a :** something that results from a particular manner or method of working, operating, or devising <careful police ~> <clever camera ~> **b :** something that results from the use or fashioning of a particular material <porcelain ~> **4 a :** a fortified structure (as a fort, earthen barricade, or trench) **b** *pl* **:** structures in engineering (as docks, bridges, or embankments) or mining (as shafts or tunnels) **5** *pl but sing or pl in constr* **:** a place where industrial labor is carried on **:** PLANT, FACTORY **6** *pl* **:** the working or moving parts of a mechanism <~*s* of a clock> **7 a :** something produced or accomplished by effort, exertion, or exercise of skill <this book is the ~ of many hands> **b :** something produced by the exercise of creative talent or expenditure of creative effort **:** artistic production **8** *pl* **:** performance of moral or religious acts <salvation by ~*s*> **9 a :** effective operation **:** EFFECT, RESULT <wait for time to do its healing ~> **b :** manner of working **:** WORKMANSHIP, EXECUTION **10 :** the material or piece of material that is operated upon at any stage in the process of manufacture **11** *pl* **a :** everything possessed, available, or belonging <the whole ~*s*, rod, reel, tackle box, went overboard> **b :** subjection to drastic treatment **:** all possible abuse — usu. used with <get the ~*s*> or *give* <gave him the ~*s*>
syn WORK, LABOR, TRAVAIL, TOIL, DRUDGERY, GRIND *shared meaning element* **:** activity involving effort or exertion ***ant*** play
— **at work** **1 :** engaged in working **:** BUSY; *esp* **:** engaged in one's regular occupation **2 :** having effect **:** OPERATING, FUNCTIONING — **in the works :** in process of preparation, development, or completion — **in work** **1 :** in process of being done **2** *of a horse* **:** in training — **out of work :** without regular employment **:** JOBLESS
[2]**work** *adj* **1 :** suitable or styled for wear while working <~ clothes> **2 :** used for work <~ elephant>
[3]**work** *vb* **worked** \'wərkt\ *or* **wrought** \'rȯt\; **work·ing** [ME *werken, worken*, fr. OE *wyrcan;* akin to OE *weorc*] *vt* **1 :** to bring to pass **:** EFFECT <~ miracles> **2 a :** to fashion or create by expending labor or exertion upon **:** FORGE, SHAPE <~ flint into tools> **b :** to make or decorate with needlework; *esp* **:** EMBROIDER **3 a :** to prepare for use by stirring or kneading **b :** to bring into a desired form by a gradual process of cutting, hammering, scraping, pressing, or stretching <~ cold steel> **4 :** to set or keep in motion, operation, or activity **:** cause to operate or produce <a pump ~*ed* by hand> <~ farmland> **5 :** to solve (a problem) by reasoning or calculation **6 a :** to cause to toil or labor **:** get work out of <~*ed* his horses nearly to death> **b :** to make use of **:** EXPLOIT **c :** to control or guide the operation

of <switches are ~*ed* from a central tower> **7 :** to carry on an operation through or in or along <the salesman ~*ed* both sides of the street> <fisherman ~*ed* the stream from the bridge down to the pool> **8 :** to pay for with labor or service <~*ed* his way through college> **9 a :** to get (oneself or an object) into or out of a condition or position by gradual stages **b :** CONTRIVE, ARRANGE <we can ~ it so that you can take your vacation> **10 a :** to practice trickery or cajolery on for some end <~*ed* the management for a free ticket> **b :** EXCITE, PROVOKE <~*ed* himself into a rage> ~ *vi* **1 a :** to exert oneself physically or mentally esp. in sustained effort for a purpose or under compulsion or necessity **b :** to perform or carry through a task requiring sustained effort or continuous repeated operations <~*ed* all day over a hot stove> **c :** to perform work or fulfill duties regularly for wages or salary **2 :** to function or operate according to plan or design <hinges ~ better with oil> **3 :** to exert an influence or tendency **4 :** to produce a desired effect or result : SUCCEED **5 a :** to make way slowly and with difficulty : move or progress laboriously <~*ed* his way up to the presidency> **b :** to sail to windward **6 :** to permit of being worked : react in a specified way to being worked <this wood ~*s* easily> **7 a :** to be in agitation or restless motion **b :** FERMENT 1 **c :** to move slightly in relation to another part **d :** to get into a specified condition by slow or imperceptible movements <the knot ~*ed* loose> — **work on 1 :** AFFECT <*worked on* his sympathies> **2 :** to strive to influence or persuade — **work upon :** to have effect upon : operate on : INFLUENCE

work·able \ˈwər-kə-bəl\ *adj* **1 :** capable of being worked **2 :** PRACTICABLE, FEASIBLE — **work·abil·i·ty** \ˌwər-kə-ˈbil-ət-ē\ *n* — **work·able·ness** \ˈwər-kə-bəl-nəs\ *n*

work·a·day \ˈwər-kə-ˌdā\ *adj* [alter. of earlier *workyday,* fr. obs. *workyday,* n., (workday)] **1 :** of, relating to, or suited for working days **2 :** PROSAIC, ORDINARY

work·bag \ˈwərk-ˌbag\ *n* **:** a bag for implements or materials for work; *esp* **:** a bag for needlework

work·bas·ket \-ˌbas-kət\ *n* **:** a basket for needlework

work·bench \-ˌbench\ *n* **:** a bench on which work esp. of mechanics, machinists, and carpenters is performed

work·boat \-ˌbōt\ *n* **:** a boat used for work purposes (as commercial fishing and ferrying supplies) rather than for sport or for passenger or naval service

work·book \-ˌbu̇k\ *n* **1 :** a booklet outlining a course of study **2 :** a workman's handbook or manual **3 :** a record book of work done **4 :** a student's individual exercise book of problems to be solved directly on the pages

work·box \-ˌbäks\ *n* **:** a box for work instruments and materials

work camp *n* **:** a camp for workers: as **a :** PRISON CAMP 1 **b :** a short-term group project in which individuals from one or more religious organizations volunteer their labor

work·day \ˈwərk-ˌdā\ *n* **1 :** a day on which work is performed as distinguished from Sunday or a holiday **2 :** the period of time in a day during which work is performed — **workday** *adj*

worked \ˈwərkt\ *adj* **:** that has been subjected to some process of development, treatment, or manufacture <a newly ~ field>

worked up *adj* **:** emotionally aroused : EXCITED

work·er \ˈwər-kər\ *n* **1 a :** one that works esp. at manual or industrial labor or with a particular material — often used in combination **b :** a member of the working class **2 :** one of the sexually underdeveloped and usu. sterile members of a colony of social ants, bees, wasps, or termites that perform most of the labor and protective duties of the colony — see HONEYBEE illustration **3 :** a usu. electrotype plate from which printing is done

worker–priest *n* **:** a French Roman Catholic priest who for missionary purposes spends part of each weekday as a worker in a secular job

work farm *n* **:** a farm on which persons guilty of minor law violations are confined

work·folk \ˈwərk-ˌfōk\ *or* **work·folks** \-ˌfōks\ *n pl* **:** working people; *esp* **:** farm workers

work force *n* **1 :** the workers engaged in a specific activity <the factory's *work force*> **2 :** the number of workers potentially assignable for any purpose <the nation's *work force*>

work·horse \ˈwərk-ˌhȯ(ə)rs\ *n* **1 :** a horse used chiefly for labor as distinguished from driving, riding, or racing **2 a :** a person who performs most of the work of a group task **b :** a markedly useful or durable vehicle, craft, or machine

work·house \-ˌhau̇s\ *n* **1** *Brit* **:** POORHOUSE **2 :** a house of correction for persons guilty of minor law violations

work in *vt* **1 :** to insert or cause to penetrate by repeated or continued effort **2 :** to interpose or insinuate gradually or unobtrusively <*worked in* a few topical jokes>

[1]**work·ing** *adj* **1 :** adequate to permit work to be done <a ~ majority> **2 :** assumed or adopted to permit or facilitate further work or activity <~ draft>

[2]**working** *n* **1 :** an excavation or group of excavations made in mining, quarrying, or tunneling — usu. used in pl. **2 :** the manner of functioning or operating : OPERATION — usu. used in pl.

working asset *n* **:** an asset other than a capital asset

working capital *n* **:** capital actively turned over in or available for use in the course of business activity: **a :** the excess of current assets over current liabilities **b :** all capital of a business except that invested in capital assets

work·ing–class *adj* **:** relating to, deriving from, or suitable to the class of wage earners <~ virtues>

working class *n* **:** the class of people who work for wages usu. at manual labor

working day *n* **:** WORKDAY

working dog *n* **:** a dog fitted by size, breeding, or training for useful work (as draft or herding) esp. as distinguished for one fitted primarily for pet, show, or sporting use

working fluid *n* **:** a fluid working substance

work·ing·man \ˈwər-kiŋ-ˌman\ *n* **:** one who works for wages usu. at manual labor

working papers *n pl* **:** official documents legalizing the employment of a minor

working substance *n* **:** a usu. fluid substance that through changes of temperature, volume, and pressure is the means of carrying out thermodynamic processes or cycles (as in a heat engine)

work·less \ˈwərk-ləs\ *adj* **:** being without work : UNEMPLOYED — **work·less·ness** *n*

work load *n* **1 :** the amount of work or of working time expected from or assigned to an employee **2 :** the amount of work performed or capable of being performed (as by a mechanical device) usu. within a specific period

work·man \ˈwərk-mən\ *n* **1 :** WORKINGMAN **2 :** ARTISAN, CRAFTSMAN

work·man·like \-ˌlīk\ *adj* **:** worthy of a good workman : SKILLFUL

work·man·ly \-lē\ *adj* **:** WORKMANLIKE

work·man·ship \-ˌship\ *n* **1 :** the art or skill of a workman : CRAFTSMANSHIP; *also* **:** the quality imparted to a thing in the process of making <a vase of exquisite ~> **2 :** something effected, made, or produced : WORK

workmen's compensation insurance *n* **:** insurance that reimburses an employer for damages that he is required to pay to an employee for injury occurring in the scope and course of his employment

work of art 1 : a product of one of the fine arts; *esp* **:** a painting or sculpture of high artistic quality **2 :** something giving high aesthetic satisfaction to the beholder or auditor <the wedding cake was a *work of art*>

work off *vt* **:** to dispose of or get rid of by work or activity <*worked off* his anger>

work·out \ˈwər-ˌkau̇t\ *n* **:** a practice or exercise to test or improve one's fitness esp. for athletic competition, ability, or performance

work out \ˌwər-ˈkau̇t, ˈwər-\ *vt* **1 :** to effect by labor and exertion **2 a :** SOLVE **b :** to devise, arrange, or achieve esp. by resolving difficulties <*worked out* a compromise> **c :** DEVELOP, ELABORATE **3 :** to discharge (as a debt) by labor **4 :** to exhaust (as a mine) by working ~ *vi* **1 a :** to prove effective, practicable, or suitable <hoped his plan *worked out*> **b :** to amount to a total or calculated figure — used with *at* **2 :** to go through a training or practice session esp. in an athletic specialty

work over *vt* **1 :** to subject to thorough examination, study, or treatment <shelf stock would get thoroughly *worked over* by shoppers> **2 :** to do over : REWORK <saved the play by *working* the first act *over*> **3 :** to beat up or manhandle with thoroughness <the gang *worked* him *over*>

work·peo·ple \ˈwərk-ˌpē-pəl\ *n pl, chiefly Brit* **:** WORKERS, EMPLOYEES

work·piece \-ˌpēs\ *n* **:** a piece of work in process of manufacture

work·room \ˈwər-ˌkrüm, -ˌkru̇m\ *n* **:** a room used esp. for manual work

work·shop \ˈwərk-ˌshäp\ *n* **1 :** a small establishment where manufacturing or handicrafts are carried on **2 :** WORKROOM **3 :** a usu. brief intensive educational program for a relatively small group of people in a given field that emphasizes participation in problem-solving efforts

work stoppage *n* **:** concerted cessation of work by a group of employees usu. more spontaneous and less serious than a strike

work·ta·ble \ˈwərk-ˌtā-bəl\ *n* **:** a table for holding working materials and implements; *esp* **:** a small table with drawers and other conveniences for needlework

work·up \ˈwər-ˌkəp\ *n* **:** an intensive diagnostic study <do an X ray ~ on the chest>

work–up \ˈwər-ˌkəp\ *n* **:** an unintended mark on a printed sheet caused by the rising of spacing material

work up \ˌwər-ˈkəp, ˈwər-\ *vt* **1 :** to stir up : ROUSE **2 :** to produce by mental or physical work <*worked up* a comedy act> <*worked up* a sweat in the gymnasium> ~ *vi* **:** to rise gradually in intensity or emotional tone

work·week \ˈwər-ˌkwēk\ *n* **:** the hours or days of work in a calendar week <40-hour ~> <a 5-day ~>

work·wom·an \ˈwər-ˌkwu̇m-ən\ *n* **:** a woman who works

[1]**world** \ˈwər(-ə)ld\ *n* [ME, fr. OE *woruld* human existence, this world, age; akin to OHG *weralt* age, world; both fr. a prehistoric WGmc-NGmc compound whose first constituent is represented by OE *wer* man and whose second constituent is akin to OE *eald* old — more at VIRILE, OLD] **1 a :** the earthly state of human existence **b :** life after death — used with a qualifier <the next ~> **2 :** the earth with its inhabitants and all things upon it **3 :** individual course of life : CAREER **4 :** the inhabitants of the earth : the human race **5 a :** the concerns of the earth and its affairs as distinguished from heaven and the life to come **b :** secular affairs **6 :** the system of created things : UNIVERSE **7 a :** a division, section, or generation of the inhabitants of the earth distinguished by living together at the same place or at the same time <the medieval ~> **b :** a distinctive class of persons or their sphere of interest <the academic ~> <the sports ~> **8 :** human society <withdraw from the ~> **9 :** a part or section of the earth that is a separate independent unit **10 :** the sphere or scene of one's life and action **11 :** an indefinite multitude or a great quantity or amount <makes a ~ of difference> **12 :** the whole body of living persons : PUBLIC <announced his discovery to the ~> **13 :** KINGDOM 5 <the animal ~> **14 a :** a celestial body (as a planet) **b :** one that is inhabited *syn* see EARTH — **for all the world :** in every way : EXACTLY <copies which look *for all the world* like the original> — **in the world :** among innumerable possibilities : EVER — used as an intensive <what *in the world* is

ə abut ə kitten ər further a back ā bake ä cot, cart
au̇ out ch chin e less ē easy g gift i trip ī life
j joke ŋ sing ō flow ȯ flaw ȯi coin th thin t͟h this
ü loot u̇ foot y yet yü few yu̇ furious zh vision

it> — **out of this world** : of extraordinary excellence : SUPERB

[2]world *adj* **1** : of or relating to the world <a ~ championship> **2 a** : extending or found throughout the world : WORLDWIDE <brought about ~ peace> **b** : involving or applying to the whole world <a ~ state>

world–beat·er \ˈwərl(d)-ˌbēt-ər\ *n* : one that excels all others of its kind : CHAMPION

world–class *adj* : being of the highest caliber in the world <a ~ polo player>

World Communion Sunday *n* : the first Sunday in October observed with a Communion service in many churches as an expression of Christian unity

World Day of Prayer : the first Friday in Lent observed by many churches esp. as a day of prayer for missions

world federalism *n* **1** : federalism on a worldwide basis **2** *cap W&F* **a** : the principles and policies of the World Federalists **b** : the body or movement composed of World Federalists

world federalist *n* **1** : an adherent or advocate of world federalism **2** *cap W&F* : a member of a movement arising after World War II advocating the formation of a federal union of the nations of the world with limited but positive governmental powers

World Island *n* : the landmass consisting of Europe, Asia, and Africa held by geopoliticians to have strategic advantages for mastery of the world

world·ling \ˈwər(-ə)l-dliŋ, ˈwərl-liŋ\ *n* : a person engrossed in the concerns of this present world

world·ly \ˈwər(-ə)l-dlē, ˈwərl-lē\ *adj* **1** : of, relating to, or devoted to this world and its pursuits rather than to religion or spiritual affairs **2** : WORLDLY-WISE ***syn*** see EARTHLY — **world·li·ness** *n*

world·ly–mind·ed \ˌwərl-(d)lē-ˈmīn-dəd\ *adj* : devoted to or engrossed in worldly interests — **world·ly–mind·ed·ness** *n*

world·ly–wise \ˈwərl-(d)lē-ˌwīz\ *adj* : possessing a practical and often shrewd and materialistic understanding of human affairs : SOPHISTICATED

world power *n* : a political unit (as a nation or state) powerful enough to affect the entire world by its influence or actions

world premiere *n* : the first regular performance (as of a theatrical production) anywhere in the world

world series *n* : a series of baseball games played each fall between the pennant winners of the major leagues to decide the professional championship of the U.S.

world's fair *n* : an international exposition featuring exhibits and participants from all over the world

world–shak·ing \ˈwərl(d)-ˌshā-kiŋ\ *adj* : EARTHSHAKING

world soul *n* : an animating spirit or creative principle related to the world as the soul is to the individual being

world view *n* : WELTANSCHAUUNG

world war *n* : a war engaged in by all or most of the principal nations of the world; *esp, cap both Ws* : either of two such wars of the first half of the 20th century

world–wea·ry \ˈwərl-ˌdwi(ə)r-ē\ *adj* : fatigued from or bored with the life of the world and esp. material pleasures — **world–wea·ri·ness** *n*

[1]world·wide \ˈwər(-ə)l-ˈdwīd\ *adj* : extended throughout or involving the entire world

[2]worldwide *adv* : throughout the world

[1]worm \ˈwərm\ *n, often attrib* [ME, fr. OE *wyrm* serpent, worm; akin to OHG *wurm* serpent, worm, L *vermis* worm] **1 a** : EARTHWORM; *broadly* : an annelid worm **b** : any of numerous relatively small elongated usu. naked and soft-bodied animals: as (1) : an insect larva; *esp* : one that is a destructive grub, caterpillar, or maggot (2) : SHIPWORM (3) : BLINDWORM **2 a** : a human being who is an object of contempt, loathing, or pity : WRETCH **b** : something that torments or devours from within **3** *archaic* : SNAKE, SERPENT **4** : HELMINTHIASIS — usu. used in pl. **5** : something (as a mechanical device) spiral or vermiculate in form or appearance: as **a** : the thread of a screw **b** : a short revolving screw whose threads gear with the teeth of a worm wheel or a rack **c** : a spiral condensing tube used in distilling **d** : ARCHIMEDES SCREW; *also* : a conveyor working on the principle of such a screw — **worm·like** \-ˌlīk\ *adj*

[2]worm *vi* : to move or proceed sinuously or insidiously ~ *vt* **1** : to free (as a dog) from worms **2 a** : to cause to move or proceed in or as if in the manner of a worm **b** : to insinuate or introduce (oneself) by devious or subtle means **c** : to proceed or make (one's way) insidiously or deviously <tried to ~ her way out of the situation> **3** : to wind rope or yarn spirally round and between the strands of (a cable or rope) before serving **4** : to obtain or extract by artful or insidious questioning or by pleading, asking, or persuading — usu. used with *out of* — **worm·er** *n*

worm–eat·en \ˈwər-ˌmēt-ᵊn\ *adj* **1 a** : eaten or burrowed by worms <~ timber> **b** : PITTED **2** : WORN-OUT, ANTIQUATED

worm fence *n* : a zigzag fence consisting of interlocking rails supported by crossed poles — called also *snake fence, Virginia fence*

worm gear *n* **1** : WORM WHEEL **2** : a gear of a worm and a worm wheel working together

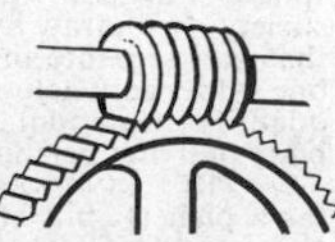

worm gear 2

worm·hole \ˈwərm-ˌhōl\ *n* : a hole or passage burrowed by a worm

worm·seed \-ˌsēd\ *n* **1** : any of various plants whose seeds possess anthelmintic properties: as **a** : any of several artemisias (as the santonica) **b** : a goosefoot (*Chenopodium ambrosioides*) **2** : SANTONICA 2

worm's–eye view \ˌwərm-ˌzī-\ *n* : a view from ground level or from the lowest levels of a hierarchy <the bird's-eye view of the executive and the *worm's-eye view* of the employee —*Current Biog.*>

worm snake *n* : any of various small harmless burrowing snakes suggesting earthworms

worm wheel *n* : a toothed wheel gearing with the thread of a worm

worm·wood \ˈwərm-ˌwu̇d\ *n* [ME *wormwode*, alter. of *wermode*, fr. OE *wermod*; akin to OHG *wermuota* wormwood] **1** : ARTEMISIA; *esp* : a European plant (*A. absinthium*) yielding a bitter slightly aromatic dark green oil used in absinthe **2** : something bitter or grievous : BITTERNESS

wormy \ˈwər-mē\ *adj* **worm·i·er; -est** **1** : containing, abounding in, or infested with worms <~ flour> <a ~ dog>; *also* : damaged by worms : WORM-EATEN <~ timbers> **2** : resembling or suggestive of a worm

worn *past part of* WEAR

worn–out \ˈwō(ə)r-ˈnau̇t, ˈwȯ(ə)r-\ *adj* : exhausted or used up by or as if by wear

wor·ri·ment \ˈwər-ē-mənt, ˈwə-rē-\ *n* : an act or instance of worrying; *also* : TROUBLE, WORRY

wor·ri·some \-səm\ *adj* **1** : causing distress or worry **2** : inclined to worry or fret — **wor·ri·some·ly** *adv* — **wor·ri·some·ness** *n*

[1]wor·ry \ˈwər-ē, ˈwə-rē\ *vb* **wor·ried; wor·ry·ing** [ME *worien*, fr. OE *wyrgan*; akin to OHG *wurgen* to strangle, Lith *veržti* to constrict] *vt* **1** *dial Brit* : CHOKE, STRANGLE **2 a** : to harass by tearing, biting, or snapping esp. at the throat **b** : to shake or pull at with the teeth <a terrier ~*ing* a rat> **c** : to touch or disturb something repeatedly **d** : to change the position of or adjust by repeated pushing or hauling **3 a** : to assail with rough or aggressive attack or treatment : TORMENT **b** : to subject to persistent or nagging attention or effort **4** : to afflict with mental distress or agitation : make anxious ~ *vi* **1** *dial Brit* : STRANGLE, CHOKE **2** : to move, proceed, or progress by unceasing or difficult effort : STRUGGLE **3** : to feel or experience concern or anxiety : FRET — **wor·ried·ly** \-(r)ēd-lē, -(r)əd-\ *adv* — **wor·ri·er** \-(r)ē-ər\ *n*

syn WORRY, ANNOY, HARASS, HARRY, PLAGUE, PESTER, TEASE, TANTALIZE *shared meaning element* : to torment to the point of destroying peace of mind or annoying acutely

[2]worry *n, pl* **worries** **1 a** : mental distress or agitation resulting from concern usu. for something impending or anticipated : ANXIETY **b** : an instance or occurrence of such distress or agitation **2** : a cause of worry : TROUBLE, DIFFICULTY ***syn*** see CARE

worry beads *n pl* : a string of beads fingered so as to keep one's hands occupied

wor·ry·wart \ˈwər-ē-ˌwȯ(ə)rt, ˈwə-rē-\ *n* : one who is inclined to worry unduly

[1]worse \ˈwərs\ *adj, comparative of* BAD *or of* ILL [ME *werse, worse*, fr. OE *wiersa, wyrsa*; akin to OHG *wirsiro* worse] **1** : of more inferior quality, value, or condition **2 a** : more unfavorable, unpleasant, or painful **b** : more faulty, unsuitable, or incorrect **c** : less skillful or efficient **3** : bad, evil, or corrupt in a greater degree : more reprehensible **4** : being in poorer health : SICKER

[2]worse *n* : one that is worse <thought he was an atheist and ~ —Van Wyck Brooks>

[3]worse *adv, comparative of* BAD *or of* ILL : in a worse manner : to a worse extent or degree

wors·en \ˈwərs-ᵊn\ *vb* **wors·ened; wors·en·ing** \ˈwərs-niŋ, -ᵊn-iŋ\ *vt* : to make worse ~ *vi* : to become worse

wors·er \ˈwər-sər\ *adj or adv* [*worse* + *-er*] *archaic* : WORSE <had chosen the ~ part — Robert Southey> <I cannot hate thee ~ than I do —Shak.>

[1]wor·ship \ˈwər-shəp\ *n* [ME *worshipe* worthiness, repute, respect, reverence paid to a divine being, fr. OE *weorthscipe* worthiness, repute, respect, fr. *weorth* worthy, worth + *-scipe* -ship] **1** *chiefly Brit* : a person of importance — used as a title for various officials (as magistrates and some mayors) <sent a petition to his *Worship*> **2** : reverence offered a divine being or supernatural power; *also* : an act of expressing such reverence **3** : a form of religious practice with its creed and ritual **4** : extravagant respect or admiration for or devotion to an object of esteem <~ of the dollar>

[2]worship *vb* **-shiped** *or* **-shipped; -ship·ing** *or* **-ship·ping** *vt* **1** : to honor or reverence as a divine being or supernatural power **2** : to regard with great, even extravagant respect, honor, or devotion ~ *vi* : to perform or take part in worship or an act of worship ***syn*** see REVERE — **wor·ship·er** *n*

wor·ship·ful \ˈwər-shəp-fəl\ *adj* **1 a** *archaic* : NOTABLE, DISTINGUISHED **b** *chiefly Brit* — used as a title for various persons or groups of rank or distinction **2** : giving worship or veneration — **wor·ship·ful·ly** \-fə-lē\ *adv* — **wor·ship·ful·ness** *n*

wor·ship·less \-shə-pləs\ *adj* : lacking worship or worshipers

[1]worst \ˈwərst\ *adj, superlative of* BAD *or of* ILL [ME *werste, worste*, fr. OE *wierresta, wyrsta*, superl. of the root of OE *wiersa* worse] **1** : most corrupt, bad, evil, or ill **2 a** : most unfavorable, unpleasant, or painful **b** : most unsuitable, faulty, unattractive, or ill-conceived **c** : least skillful or efficient **3** : most wanting in quality, value, or condition — **the worst way** : very much <such men . . . need indoctrination *the worst way* —J. G. Cozzens> — often used with *in* <wanted a new bicycle in *the worst way*>

[2]worst *n* : one that is worst — **at worst** : under the worst circumstances

[3]worst *adv, superlative of* ILL *or* ILLY *or of* BAD *or* BADLY **1** : to the extreme degree of badness or inferiority **2** : to the greatest or highest degree <groups who need the subsidies ~ lose out —T. W. Arnold>

[4]worst *vt* : to get the better of : DEFEAT

wor·sted \ˈwu̇s-təd, ˈwər-stəd\ *n* [ME, fr. *Worsted* (now *Worstead*), England] **1** : a smooth compact yarn from long wool fibers used esp. for firm napless fabrics, carpeting, or knitting **2** : a fabric made from worsted yarns — **worsted** *adj*

[1]wort \ˈwərt, ˈwȯ(ə)rt\ *n* [ME, fr. OE *wyrt* root, herb, plant — more at ROOT] **1** : PLANT; *esp* : an herbaceous plant — usu. used in combination <louse*wort*> **2** *archaic* : POTHERB

[2]wort *n* [ME, fr. OE *wyrt*; akin to MHG *würze* brewer's wort, OE *wyrt* root, herb] : a dilute solution of sugars obtained from malt by infusion and fermented to form beer

[1]worth \ˈwərth\ *vi* [ME *worthen*, fr. OE *weorthan*; akin to OHG *werdan* to become, L *vertere* to turn] *archaic* : BECOME — usu. used in the phrase *woe worth*

[2]worth *adj* [ME, fr. OE *weorth* worthy, of (a specified) value; akin to OHG *werd* worthy, worth] **1** *archaic* **:** having monetary or material value **2** *archaic* **:** ESTIMABLE

[3]worth *prep* **1 a :** equal in value to **b :** having possessions or income equal to **2 :** deserving of <well ~ the effort>

[4]worth *n* **1 a :** monetary value <farmhouse and lands of little ~> **b :** the equivalent of a specified amount or figure <a dollar's ~ of gas> **2 :** the value of something measured by its qualities or by the esteem in which it is held <a literary heritage of great ~> **3 a :** moral or personal value <trying to teach human ~> **b :** MERIT, EXCELLENCE <a field in which he has proved his ~> **4 :** WEALTH, RICHES <his personal ~ is several million>

worth·ful \'wərth-fəl\ *adj* **1 :** full of merit **:** HONORABLE <a good and ~ man> **2 :** having value **:** ESTEEMED <the ~ aspects of their culture>

worth·less \'wərth-ləs\ *adj* **1 a :** lacking worth **:** VALUELESS <~ currency> **b :** USELESS <~ to continue searching> **2 :** CONTEMPTIBLE, DESPICABLE — **worth·less·ly** *adv* — **worth·less·ness** *n*

worth·while \-'hwī(ə)l, -'wī(ə)l\ *adj* **:** being worth the time or effort spent — **worth·while·ness** *n*

[1]wor·thy \'wər-thē\ *adj* **wor·thi·er; -est** **1 a :** having worth or value **:** ESTIMABLE <a ~ cause> **b :** HONORABLE, MERITORIOUS <~ men> **2 :** having sufficient worth **:** important enough **:** DESERVING <a deed ~ to be remembered> <a ~ opponent> — **wor·thi·ly** \'wər-thə-lē\ *adv* — **wor·thi·ness** \-thē-nəs\ *n*

[2]worthy *n, pl* **worthies :** a worthy or prominent person

-wor·thy \,wər-thē\ *adj comb form* **1 :** fit or safe for <a sea*worthy* vessel> **2 :** of sufficient worth for <a news*worthy* event>

[1]wot *prest 1st & 3d sing of* WIT

[2]wot \'wät\ *vb* **wot·ted; wot·ting** [ME *woten,* alter. of *witen* — more at WIT] *chiefly Brit* **:** KNOW — often used with *of*

would \wəd, əd, d, (')wu̇d\ *past of* WILL [ME *wolde,* fr. OE; akin to OHG *wolta* wished, desired] **1 a** *archaic* **:** WISHED, DESIRED **b** *archaic* **:** wish for **:** WANT **c** (1) **:** strongly desire **:** WISH <I ~ I were young again> (2) — used in auxiliary function with *rather* or *sooner* to express preference <he ~ sooner die than face them> **2 a** — used in auxiliary function to express wish, desire, or intent <those who ~ forbid gambling> **b** — used in auxiliary function to express willingness or preference <as ye ~ that men should do to you —Lk 6:31 (AV)> **c** — used in auxiliary function to express plan or intention <said he ~ come> **3** — used in auxiliary function to express custom or habitual action <we ~ meet often for lunch> **4** — used in auxiliary function to express consent or choice <~ put it off if he could> **5 a** — used in auxiliary function in the conclusion of a conditional sentence to express a contingency or possibility <if he were coming, he ~ be here now> **b** — used in auxiliary function in a noun clause (as one completing a statement of desire, request, or advice) <we wish that he ~ go> **6** — used in auxiliary function to express probability or presumption in past or present time <~ have won if he had not tripped> **7 :** COULD <the barrel ~ hold 20 gallons> **8** — used in auxiliary function to express a request with which voluntary compliance is expected <~ you please help us> **9** — used in auxiliary function to express doubt or uncertainty <the explanation . . . ~ seem satisfactory> **10 :** SHOULD <knew I ~ enjoy the trip> <~ be glad to know the answer>

would–be \,wu̇d-,bē\ *adj* **:** desiring or professing to be

wouldn't \'wu̇d-ᵊnt\ **:** would not

wouldst \wədst, (')wu̇dst, wətst\ *or* **would·est** \'wu̇d-əst\ *archaic past 2d sing of* WILL

[1]wound \'wünd, *archaic or dial* 'wau̇nd\ *n* [ME, fr. OE *wund;* akin to OHG *wunta* wound] **1 a :** an injury to the body (as from violence, accident, or surgery) that involves laceration or breaking of a membrane (as the skin) and usu. damage to underlying tissues **b :** a cut or breach in a plant due to external violence **2 :** a mental or emotional hurt or blow

[2]wound *vt* **:** to cause a wound to or in ~ *vi* **:** to inflict a wound

[3]wound \'wau̇nd\ *past of* WIND

[1]wound·ed \'wün-dəd\ *adj* **:** injured, hurt by, or suffering from a wound <a ~ soldier> <~ pride>

[2]wounded *n pl* **:** wounded persons

wound·less \'wün-(d)ləs\ *adj* **1** *obs* **:** INVULNERABLE <the ~ air —Shak.> **2 :** free from wounds **:** UNWOUNDED

wound·wort \'wün-,dwərt, -,dwȯ(ə)rt\ *n* **:** any of various plants whose soft downy leaves have been used in the dressing of wounds; *esp* **:** any of several mints (genus *Stachys*)

wove *past of* WEAVE

woven *past part of* WEAVE

wove paper \'wōv-\ *n* [*wove* (archaic pp. of *weave*)] **:** paper made with a revolving roller covered with wires so woven as to produce no fine lines running across the grain — compare LAID PAPER

[1]wow \'wau̇\ *interj* — used to express strong feeling (as pleasure or surprise)

[2]wow *n* [[1]*wow*] **:** a striking success **:** HIT

[3]wow *vt* **:** to excite to enthusiastic admiration or approval

[4]wow *n* [imit.] **:** a distortion in reproduced sound consisting of a slow rise and fall of pitch caused by speed variation in the reproducing system

wow·ser \'wau̇-zər\ *n* [origin unknown] *chiefly Austral* **:** an obtrusively puritanical person

WP *abbr* **1** weather permitting **2** wettable powder **3** white phosphorus **4** without prejudice

WPA *abbr* **1** with particular average **2** Works Progress Administration

W particle *n* [*W,* abbr. for *weak*] **:** a hypothetical massive elementary particle held to be responsible for the weak interaction

WPC *abbr* watts per candle

WPM *abbr* words per minute

wpn *abbr* weapon

WR *abbr* **1** warehouse receipt **2** Wassermann reaction **3** with rights

WRAC *abbr* Women's Royal Army Corps

[1]wrack \'rak\ *n* [ME, fr. OE *wræc* misery, punishment, something driven by the sea; akin to OE *wrecan* to drive, punish — more at WREAK] **1 :** RUIN, DESTRUCTION **2 :** a remnant of something destroyed

[2]wrack *n* [ME *wrak,* fr. MD or MLG; akin to OE *wræc* something driven by the sea] **1 a :** a wrecked ship **b :** WRECKAGE **c :** WRECK **d** *dial* **:** the violent destruction of a structure, machine, or vehicle **2 a :** marine vegetation; *esp* **:** KELP **b :** dried seaweeds

[3]wrack *vt* **:** to utterly ruin **:** WRECK

[4]wrack *vb* [by alter.] **:** [4]RACK

[5]wrack *n* **:** [3]RACK 2

[6]wrack *n* **:** [1]RACK

wrack·ful \'rak-fəl\ *adj* **:** DESTRUCTIVE

WRAF *abbr* Women's Royal Air Force

wraith \'rāth\ *n, pl* **wraiths** \'rāths *also* 'rāthz\ [origin unknown] **1 a :** an apparition of a living person in his exact likeness seen usu. just before his death **b :** GHOST, SPECTER **2 :** an insubstantial appearance **:** SHADOW **3 :** a barely visible gaseous or vaporous column

[1]wran·gle \'raŋ-gəl\ *vb* **wran·gled; wran·gling** \-g(ə-)liŋ\ [ME *wranglen;* akin to OHG *ringan* to struggle — more at WRING] *vi* **1 :** to dispute angrily or peevishly **:** BICKER **2 :** to engage in argument or controversy ~ *vt* **1 :** to obtain by persistent arguing **:** WANGLE **2 :** to herd and care for (livestock and esp. horses) on the range

[2]wrangle *n* **1 :** an angry, noisy, or prolonged dispute or quarrel **2 :** the action or process of wrangling ***syn*** see QUARREL

wran·gler \-g(ə-)lər\ *n* **1 :** a bickering disputant **2 :** a ranch hand who takes care of the saddle horses; *broadly* **:** COWBOY

[1]wrap \'rap\ *vb* **wrapped; wrap·ping** [ME *wrappen*] *vt* **1 a :** to cover esp. by winding or folding **b :** to envelop and secure for transportation or storage **:** BUNDLE **c :** ENFOLD, EMBRACE **d :** to coil, fold, draw, or twine about something **2 a :** SURROUND, ENVELOP **b :** to suffuse or surround with an aura or state <the affair was *wrapped* in scandal> **c :** to involve completely **:** ENGROSS **3 :** to conceal or obscure as if by enveloping or enfolding **4 :** to enclose as if with a protective covering ~ *vi* **1 :** to wind, coil, or twine so as to encircle or cover something **2 :** to put on clothing **:** DRESS — usu. used with *up* **3 :** to be subject to covering, enclosing, or packaging — usu. used with *up*

[2]wrap *n* **1 a :** WRAPPER, WRAPPING **b :** an article of clothing that may be wrapped round a person; *esp* **:** an outer garment (as a coat or shawl) **c :** BLANKET **2 :** a single turn or convolution of something wound round an object **3** *pl* **a :** RESTRAINT **b :** SECRECY <a plan kept under ~*s*>

[1]wrap·around \'rap-ə-,rau̇nd\ *adj* **1 a :** made to be wrapped around the body <a ~ skirt> **b :** of or relating to a flexible printing surface wrapped around a plate cylinder **2 :** shaped to follow a contour; *esp* **:** made to curve from the front around to the side <~ sunglasses>

[2]wraparound *n* **1 :** a garment (as a dress or coat) made with a full-length opening and adjusted to the figure by wrapping around **2 :** an object that encircles or esp. curves and laps over another

wrap·per \'rap-ər\ *n* **1 :** that in which something is wrapped: as **a :** a tobacco leaf used for the outside covering esp. of cigars **b** (1) **:** JACKET 3c(1) (2) **:** the paper cover of a book not bound in boards **c :** a paper wrapped around a newspaper or magazine in the mail **2 :** one that wraps **3 :** an article of clothing worn wrapped around the body

wrap·ping \'rap-iŋ\ *n* **:** something used to wrap an object **:** WRAPPER

wrap–up \'rap-,əp\ *n* **:** a summarizing report

wrap up \(')rap-'əp\ *vt* **1 :** to bring to a usu. successful conclusion **:** END **2 :** to make a single comprehensive report of

wrasse \'ras\ *n* [Corn *gwragh, wragh*] **:** any of numerous elongate compressed usu. brilliantly colored marine spiny-finned fishes (family Labridae) that include important food fishes esp. of warm seas as well as some believed to be poisonous

[1]wrath \'rath, *chiefly Brit* 'rȯth\ *n* [ME, fr. OE *wrǣththo,* fr. *wrāth* wroth — more at WROTH] **1 :** strong vengeful anger or indignation **2 :** retributory punishment for an offense or a crime **:** divine chastisement ***syn*** see ANGER

[2]wrath *adj* [alter. of *wroth*] *archaic* **:** WRATHFUL

wrath·ful \-fəl\ *adj* **1 :** filled with wrath **:** IRATE **2 :** arising from, marked by, or indicative of wrath — **wrath·ful·ly** \-fə-lē\ *adv* — **wrath·ful·ness** *n*

wrathy \-ē\ *adj* **:** WRATHFUL

wreak \'rēk *also* 'rek\ *vt* [ME *wreken,* fr. OE *wrecan* to drive, punish, avenge; akin to OHG *rehhan* to avenge, L *urgēre* to drive on, urge] **1 a** *archaic* **:** AVENGE **b :** to cause the infliction of (vengeance or punishment) **:** EXACT **2 :** to give free play or course to (malevolent feeling) <~ one's wrath> **3 :** to bring about **:** CAUSE <~ havoc>

wreath \'rēth\ *n, pl* **wreaths** \'rēthz, 'rēths\ [ME *wrethe,* fr. OE *writha;* akin to OE *writhan* to twist — more at WRITHE] **:** something intertwined into a circular shape; *esp* **:** GARLAND, CHAPLET

wreathe \'rēth\ *vb* **wreathed; wreath·ing** [*wreath*] *vt* **1 :** to twist or contort so as to show folds or creases **2 a :** to shape into a wreath **b :** INTERWEAVE **c :** to cause to coil about something **3 :** to encircle or adorn with or as if with a wreath ~ *vi* **1 :** to twist in coils **:** WRITHE **2 a :** to take on the shape of a wreath **b :** to move or extend in circles or spirals

wreathy \'rē-thē, -thē\ *adj* **1 :** having the form of a wreath **2 :** constituting a wreath

[1]**wreck** \ˈrek\ *n* [ME *wrek,* fr. AF, of Scand origin; akin to ON *rek* wreck; akin to OE *wrecan* to drive] **1 :** something cast up on the land by the sea esp. after a shipwreck **2 a :** SHIPWRECK **b :** the action of wrecking or fact or state of being wrecked : DESTRUCTION **3 a :** a hulk or the ruins of a wrecked ship **b :** the broken remains of something wrecked or otherwise ruined **c :** something disabled or in a state of ruin or dilapidation; *also* **:** a person or animal of broken constitution, health, or spirits

[2]**wreck** *vt* **1 :** to cast ashore **2 a :** to reduce to a ruinous state by or as if by violence **b :** SHIPWRECK **c :** to ruin, damage, or imperil by a wreck **d :** to involve in disaster or ruin **3 :** WREAK 3 ~ *vi* **1 :** to become wrecked **2 :** to rob, salvage, or repair wreckage or a wreck ***syn*** see RUIN

wreck·age \ˈrek-ij\ *n* **1 :** the act of wrecking : the state of being wrecked **2 a :** something that has been wrecked **b :** broken, disrupted, and disordered parts or material from a wrecked structure

wreck·er \ˈrek-ər\ *n* **1 :** one that wrecks; *esp* **:** one whose work is the demolition of buildings **2 a :** one that searches for or works on the wrecks of ships (as for rescue or for plunder) **b :** an automotive vehicle with hoisting apparatus and equipment for towing wrecked or disabled automobiles or freeing automobiles stalled in snow or mud **c :** one that salvages junked automobile parts and material

wrecker's ball *n* **:** a heavy iron or steel ball swung or dropped by a derrick to demolish old buildings — called also *wrecking ball*

wrecking bar *n* **:** a small crowbar with a claw for pulling nails at one end and a slight bend for prying at the other end

wren \ˈren\ *n* [ME *wrenne,* fr. OE *wrenna;* akin to OHG *rentilo* wren] **1 :** any of numerous small more or less brown singing birds (family Troglodytidae); *esp* **:** a very small European bird (*Troglodytes troglodytes*) that has a short erect tail and is noted for its song **2 :** any of numerous small singing birds resembling the true wrens in size and habits

[1]**wrench** \ˈrench\ *vb* [ME *wrenchen,* fr. OE *wrencan;* akin to OHG *renken,* L *vergere* to bend, incline] *vi* **1 :** to move with a violent twist; *also* **:** to undergo twisting **2 :** to pull or strain at something with violent twisting ~ *vt* **1 :** to twist violently **2 :** to injure or disable by a violent twisting or straining **3 :** CHANGE; *esp* **:** DISTORT, PERVERT **4 a :** to pull or tighten by violent twisting or with violence **b :** to snatch forcibly : WREST **5 :** to cause to suffer mental anguish : RACK — **wrench·ing·ly** \ˈren-chiŋ-lē\ *adv*

[2]**wrench** *n* **1 a :** a violent twisting or a pull with or as if with twisting **b :** a sharp twist or sudden jerk straining muscles or ligaments; *also* **:** the resultant injury (as of a joint) **c :** a distorting or perverting alteration **d :** acute emotional distress **:** sudden violent mental change **2 :** a hand or power tool for holding, twisting, or turning an object (as a bolt or nut) **3 :** MONKEY WRENCH 2

[1]**wrest** \ˈrest\ *vt* [ME *wrasten, wresten,* fr. OE *wrǣstan;* akin to OE *writhan* to twist — more at WRITHE] **1 :** to pull, force, or move by violent wringing or twisting movements **2 :** to gain with difficulty by or as if by force, violence, or determined labor **3 a :** to divert to an unnatural or improper use **b :** to deflect or change from a true or normal bearing, significance, or interpretation : DISTORT — **wrest·er** *n*

[2]**wrest** *n* **1 :** the action of wresting : WRENCH **2 :** a key or wrench formerly used for turning wrest pins

[1]**wres·tle** \ˈres-əl, ˈras-\ *vb* **wres·tled; wres·tling** \-(ə-)liŋ\ [ME *wrastlen, wrestlen,* fr. OE *wrǣstlian,* freq. of *wrǣstan*] *vi* **1 :** to contend by grappling with and striving to trip or throw an opponent down or off balance **2 :** to combat an opposing tendency or force <*wrestling* with his conscience> **3 :** to engage in deep thought, consideration, or debate **4 :** to engage in or as if in a violent or determined struggle <*wrestling* with cumbersome luggage> ~ *vt* **1 a :** to engage in (a match, bout, or fall) in wrestling **b :** to wrestle with <~ an alligator> **2 :** to move by or as if by force — **wres·tler** \ˈres-lər, ˈras-\ *n*

[2]**wrestle** *n* **:** the action or an instance of wrestling : STRUGGLE; *esp* **:** a wrestling bout

wres·tling \ˈres-liŋ\ *n* **:** a sport or contest in which two unarmed individuals struggle hand to hand with each attempting to subdue or unbalance his opponent

wretch \ˈrech\ *n* [ME *wrecche,* fr. OE *wrecca* outcast, exile; akin to OE *wrecan* to drive, drive out — more at WREAK] **1 :** a miserable person : one who is profoundly unhappy or in great misfortune **2 :** a base, despicable, or vile person

wretch·ed \ˈrech-əd\ *adj* [irreg. fr. *wretch*] **1 :** deeply afflicted, dejected, or distressed in body or mind **2 :** extremely or deplorably bad or distressing <was in ~ health> <a ~ accident> **3 a** being or appearing mean, miserable, or contemptible <a ~ half-starved horse> <dressed in ~ old clothes> **b :** very poor in quality or ability : INFERIOR <~ workmanship> ***syn*** see MISERABLE — **wretch·ed·ly** *adv* — **wretch·ed·ness** *n*

[1]**wrig·gle** \ˈrig-əl\ *vb* **wrig·gled; wrig·gling** \-(ə-)liŋ\ [ME *wrigglen,* fr. or akin to MLG *wriggeln* to wriggle; akin to OE *wrigian* to turn — more at WRY] *vi* **1 :** to move the body or a bodily part to and fro with short writhing motions like a worm **:** SQUIRM **2 :** to move or advance by twisting and turning **3 :** to extricate or insinuate oneself or reach a goal by maneuvering, equivocation, or ingratiation ~ *vt* **1 :** to cause to move in short quick contortions **2 :** to introduce, insinuate, or bring into a state or place by or as if by wriggling — **wrig·gly** \-(ə-)lē\ *adj*

[2]**wriggle** *n* **1 :** a short or quick writhing motion or contortion **2 :** a formation or marking of sinuous design

wrig·gler \ˈrig-(ə-)lər\ *n* **:** one that wriggles; *esp* **:** WIGGLER 2

wright \ˈrīt\ *n* [ME, fr. OE *wyrhta, wryhta* worker, maker; akin to OE *weorc* work] **:** a workman in wood : CARPENTER — usu. used in combination <ship*wright*> <wheel*wright*>

wring \ˈriŋ\ *vb* **wrung** \ˈrəŋ\; **wring·ing** \ˈriŋ-iŋ\ [ME *wringen,* fr. OE *wringan;* akin to OHG *ringan* to struggle, OE *wyrgan* to strangle — more at WORRY] *vt* **1 :** to squeeze or twist esp. so as to make dry or to extract moisture or liquid <~ the towel dry> **2 a :** to extract or obtain by or as if by twisting and compressing <~ the water from the towel> **b :** to exact or acquire by coercion or with difficulty <~ a confession from the suspect> **3 a :** to twist so as to strain or sprain into a distorted shape : CONTORT **b :** to twist together (clasped hands) as a sign of anguish **4 :** to place or insert by a twisting movement **5 :** to affect painfully as if by wringing : TORMENT <a tragedy that ~*s* the heart> **6 :** to shake (a hand) vigorously in greeting ~ *vi* **:** SQUIRM, WRITHE — **wring** *n*

wring·er \ˈriŋ-ər\ *n* **:** one that wrings; *esp* **:** a machine or device for pressing out liquid or moisture <a clothes ~>

[1]**wrin·kle** \ˈriŋ-kəl\ *n* [ME, back-formation fr. *wrinkled* twisted, winding, prob. fr. OE *gewrinclod,* pp. of *gewrinclian* to wind, fr. *ge-,* perfective prefix + *-wrinclian* (akin to *wrencan* to wrench) — more at CO-] **1 :** a small ridge or furrow esp. when formed on a surface by the shrinking or contraction of a smooth substance : CREASE; *specif* **:** one in the skin esp. when due to age, care, or fatigue **2 a :** METHOD, TECHNIQUE; *also* **:** information about a method : HINT **b :** an innovation in method, technique, or equipment — **wrin·kly** \-k(ə-)lē\ *adj*

[2]**wrinkle** *vb* **wrin·kled; wrin·kling** \-k(ə-)liŋ\ *vi* **:** to become marked with or contracted into wrinkles ~ *vt* **:** to contract into wrinkles : PUCKER

wrist \ˈrist\ *n* [ME, fr. OE; akin to OE *wrǣstan* to twist, wrest — more at WREST] **1 :** the joint or the region of the joint between the human hand and the arm or a corresponding part on a lower animal **2 :** the part of a garment or glove covering the wrist

wrist·band \ˈris(t)-ˌband\ *n* **1 :** the part of a sleeve covering the wrist **2 :** a band encircling the wrist

wrist·let \ˈris(t)-lət\ *n* **:** a band encircling the wrist; *esp* **:** a close-fitting knitted band attached to the top of a glove or the end of a sleeve

wrist·lock \ˈrist-ˌläk\ *n* **:** a wrestling hold in which one contestant is thrown or made helpless by a twisting grip on the wrist

wrist pin *n* **:** a stud or pin that forms a journal (as in a crosshead) for a connecting rod

wrist shot *n* **:** a stroke (as in golf or hockey) in which a quick flip of the wrists provides all or most of the power

wrist·watch \ˈris-ˌtwäch\ *n* **:** a small watch that is attached to a bracelet or strap and is worn around the wrist

wrist wrestling *n* **:** a form of arm wrestling in which opponents interlock thumbs instead of gripping hands

wristy \ˈris-tē\ *adj* **:** characterized by or tending to use a lot of wrist movement (as in stroking a ball)

writ \ˈrit\ *n* [ME, fr. OE; akin to OE *wrītan* to write] **1 :** something written : WRITING <Sacred *Writ*> **2 a :** a formal written document; *specif* **:** a legal instrument in epistolary form issued under seal in the name of the English monarch **b :** an order or mandatory process in writing issued under seal in the name of the sovereign or of a court or judicial officer commanding the person to whom it is directed to perform or refrain from performing an act specified therein <~ of detinue> <~ of entry> <~ of execution> **c :** such a written order constituting a symbol of the power and authority of the issuer — usu. used with *run* <outside the United States where . . . our ~ does not run —Dean Acheson>

writ·able \ˈrīt-ə-bəl\ *adj* **:** capable of being put in writing

write \ˈrīt\ *vb* **wrote** \ˈrōt\; **writ·ten** \ˈrit-ᵊn\ *also* **writ** \ˈrit\; **writ·ing** \ˈrīt-iŋ\ [ME *writen,* fr. OE *wrītan* to scratch, draw, inscribe; akin to OHG *rīzan* to tear, Gk *rhinē* file, rasp] *vt* **1 a :** to form (as characters or symbols) on a surface with an instrument (as a pen) **b :** to form (as words) by inscribing the characters or symbols of on a surface **c :** to spell in writing <words *written* alike but pronounced differently> **d :** to cover, fill, or fill in by writing <*wrote* ten pages> <~ a check> **2 :** to set down in writing: as **a :** to draw up : DRAFT <~ a will> **b** (1) **:** to be the author of : COMPOSE <~*s* poems and essays> (2) **:** to compose in musical form <~ a string quartet> **c :** to express in literary form <if I could ~ the beauty of your eyes —Shak.> **d :** to communicate by letter <~*s* that he is coming> **e :** to use or exhibit (a specific script, language, or literary form or style) in writing <~ Braille> <~*s* French with ease> **f :** to write contracts or orders for; *esp* **:** UNDERWRITE <~ life insurance> **3 :** to make a permanent impression of **4 :** to communicate with in writing <*wrote* them on his arrival> **5 :** ORDAIN, FATE <so be it, it is *written* —D. C. Peattie> **6 :** to make evident or obvious <guilt *written* on his face> **7 :** to force, effect, introduce, or remove by writing <~ oneself into fame and fortune —Charles Lee> **8 :** to take part in or bring about (something worth recording) **9 a :** to introduce (information) into the storage device or medium of a computer **b :** to transfer (information) from the memory store of a computer to its output storage device or medium ~ *vi* **1 a :** to make significant characters or inscriptions; *also* **:** to permit or be adapted to writing **b :** to form or produce written letters, words, or sentences **2 :** to compose, communicate by, or send a letter **3 a :** to produce a written work **b :** to compose music — **write one's own ticket :** to select a course of action or position entirely according to one's wishes — **writ large :** written or manifested on an expanded scale or in a clearer manner <the problems of modern totalitarianism are only our own problems *writ large* —*Times Lit. Supp.*>

write–down \ˈrīt-ˌdau̇n\ *n* **:** a deliberate reduction in the book value of an asset (as to reflect the effect of obsolescence or deflation)

write down \(ˈ)rīt-ˈdau̇n\ *vt* **1 :** to record in written form **2 :** to record, regard, or reveal (as oneself) as being **3 a :** to depreciate, disparage, or injure by writing **b :** to reduce in status, rank, or value; *esp* **:** to reduce the book value of **c :** to play down in writing ~ *vi* **:** to write so as to appeal to a lower level of taste, comprehension, or intelligence

write–in \ˈrīt-ˌin\ *n* **1 :** a vote cast by writing in the name of a candidate **2 :** a candidate whose name is written in

write in \(ˈ)rīt-ˈin\ *vt* **1 :** to insert in a document or text **2 a :** to insert (a name not listed on a ballot or voting machine) in an appropriate space **b :** to cast (a vote) in this manner

write–in campaign \ˈrīt-ˌin-\ *n* **:** a political campaign carried on to encourage writing in a candidate's name

write–off \'rīt-,ȯf\ *n* **1 :** an elimination of an item from the books of account **2 :** a reduction in book value of an item (as by way of depreciation)

write off \(')rīt-'ȯf\ *vt* **1 :** to reduce the estimated or book value of : DEPRECIATE **2 :** to take off the books : CANCEL <*write off* a bad debt>

write out *vt* **1 :** to put in writing; *esp* **:** to put into a full and complete written form **2 :** to exhaust the ideas or resources of (oneself) by writing all one has to say <*wrote* himself *out* on the subject>

writ·er \'rīt-ər\ *n* **:** one who writes esp. as an occupation; *esp* **:** AUTHOR

writer's cramp *n* **:** a painful spasmodic cramp of muscles of the hand or fingers brought on by excessive writing

write–up \'rīt-,əp\ *n* **1 :** a written account; *esp* **:** a flattering article **2 :** a deliberate increase in the book value of an asset (as to reflect the effect of inflation)

write up \(')rīt-'əp\ *vt* **1 a :** to write an account of : DESCRIBE **b :** to put into finished written form **2 :** to bring up to date the writing of **3 :** to increase the book value of **4 :** to write a summons for

writhe \'rīth\ *vb* **writhed; writh·ing** [ME *writhen*, fr. OE *wrīthan;* akin to ON *rītha* to twist, OE *wrigian* to turn — more at WRY] *vt* **1 a :** to twist into coils or folds **b :** to twist so as to distort **:** WRENCH **c :** to twist (the body or a bodily part) in pain **2 :** INTERTWINE ~ *vi* **1 :** to move or proceed with twists and turns **2 :** to twist from or as if from pain or struggling **3 :** to suffer keenly — **writhe** *n*

writh·en \'rith-ən\ *adj* [ME, fr. OE, fr. pp. of *wrīthan*] **:** being twisted or contorted <~ trees> <a ~ smile>

writ·ing \'rīt-iŋ\ *n* **1 :** the act or process of one who writes: as **a :** the act or art of forming visible letters or characters; *specif* **:** HANDWRITING 1 **b :** the act or practice of literary or musical composition **2 :** something written: as **a :** letters or characters that serve as visible signs of ideas, words, or symbols **b :** a letter, note, or notice used to communicate or record **c :** a written composition **d :** INSCRIPTION **e (1) :** a written or printed paper or document **(2) :** an impression of characters on a material (as paper) **3 :** a style or form of composition **4 :** the occupation of a writer; *esp* **:** the profession of authorship — **writing on the wall :** HANDWRITING ON THE WALL

writing desk *n* **:** a desk that often has a sloping top for writing on; *also* **:** a portable case that contains writing materials and has a surface for writing

writing paper *n* **:** paper that is usu. finished with a smooth surface and sized and that can be written on with ink

Writ·ings \'rīt-iŋz\ *n pl* [trans. of LHeb *kĕthūbhīm*] **:** HAGIOGRAPHA

writ of assistance **1 :** a writ issued to a law officer (as a sheriff or marshal) for the enforcement of a court order or decree **2 :** a writ issued to a law officer to aid in the search for smuggled or illegal goods

writ of certiorari : CERTIORARI

writ of election : a writ used to order the holding of an election; *specif* **:** one used to call a special election for filling a vacancy in an elective office

writ of error : a writ used to direct a court usu. to remit the record of a legal action to an appellate court in order that some alleged error in the proceedings or in the judgment may be corrected if it exists

writ of extent : a writ formerly used to recover debts of record to the British crown and under which the lands, goods, and person of the debtor might all be seized to secure payment

writ of privilege : a writ used to deliver a privileged person from custody when arrested in a civil suit

writ of prohibition : a writ issued by a superior tribunal to direct an inferior court to cease from the prosecution of a suit depending before it

writ of protection : a judicial writ issued to a person required to attend court as party or juror and intended to secure him from arrest in coming, staying, and returning

writ of summons : a writ issued on behalf of the British monarch summoning a lord spiritual or a lord temporal to attend parliament

WRNS *abbr* Women's Royal Naval Service

wrnt *abbr* warrant

¹wrong \'rȯŋ\ *n* [ME, fr. OE *wrang*, fr. (assumed) *wrang*, adj., wrong] **1 a :** an injurious, unfair, or unjust act **:** action or conduct inflicting harm without due provocation or just cause **b :** a violation or invasion of the legal rights of another; *esp* **:** TORT **2 :** something wrong, immoral, or unethical; *esp* **:** principles, practices, or conduct contrary to justice, goodness, equity, or law **3 :** the state, position, or fact of being or doing wrong: as **a :** the state of being mistaken or incorrect **b :** the state of being guilty ***syn*** see INJUSTICE

²wrong *adj* **wrong·er** \'rȯŋ-ər\; **wrong·est** \'rȯŋ-əst\ [ME, fr. (assumed) OE *wrang*, of Scand origin; akin to ON *rangr* awry, wrong; akin to OE *wringan* to wring] **1 :** not according to the moral standard **:** SINFUL, IMMORAL <thought that war was ~> **2 :** not right or proper according to a code, standard, or convention **:** IMPROPER <it was ~ not to thank your host> **3 :** not according to truth or facts **:** INCORRECT <gave a ~ date> **4 :** not satisfactory (as in condition, results, health, or temper) **5 :** not in accordance with one's needs, intent, or expectations <took the ~ bus> **6 :** of, relating to, or constituting the side of something that is usu. held to be opposite to the principal one, that is the one naturally or by design turned down, inward, or away, or that is the least finished or polished ***syn*** see FALSE ***ant*** right — **wrong·ly** \'rȯŋ-lē\ *adv* — **wrong·ness** *n*

³wrong *adv* **1 :** without accuracy **:** INCORRECTLY <guessed ~> **2 :** without regard for what is proper or just **3 :** in a wrong direction **4 a :** in an unsuccessful or unfortunate way **b :** out of working order or condition **5 :** in a false light <don't get me ~>

⁴wrong *vt* **wronged; wrong·ing** \'rȯŋ-iŋ\ **1 a :** to do wrong to **:** INJURE, HARM **b :** to treat disrespectfully or dishonorably **:** VIOLATE **2 :** DEFRAUD — usu. used with *of* **3 :** DISCREDIT, MALIGN — **wrong·er** \'rȯŋ-ər\ *n*

wrong·do·er \'rȯŋ-'dü-ər\ *n* **:** one that does wrong; *esp* **:** one who transgresses moral laws

wrong·do·ing \-'dü-iŋ\ *n* **1 :** evil behavior or action **2 :** an instance of doing wrong

wronged *adj* **:** being injured unjustly **:** suffering a wrong

wrong·ful \'rȯŋ-fəl\ *adj* **1 :** WRONG, UNJUST **2 a :** having no legal sanction **:** UNLAWFUL **b :** ILLEGITIMATE — **wrong·ful·ly** \-fə-lē\ *adv* — **wrong·ful·ness** *n*

wrong·head·ed \'rȯŋ-'hed-əd\ *adj* **:** stubborn in adherence to wrong opinion or principles **:** PERVERSE — **wrong·head·ed·ly** *adv* — **wrong·head·ed·ness** *n*

wrote *past of* WRITE

wroth \'rȯth *also* 'rōth\ *adj* [ME, fr. OE *wrāth;* akin to OHG *reid* twisted, OE *wrīthan* to writhe] **:** highly incensed **:** WRATHFUL

wrought \'rȯt\ *adj* [ME, fr. pp. of *worken* to work] **1 :** worked into shape by artistry or effort **:** FASHIONED, FORMED <carefully ~ essays> **2 :** elaborately embellished **:** ORNAMENTED **3 :** processed for use **:** MANUFACTURED <~ silk> **4 :** beaten into shape by tools **:** HAMMERED — used of metals **5 :** deeply stirred **:** EXCITED — often used with *up* <gets easily ~ up over nothing>

wrought iron *n* **:** a commerical form of iron that is tough, malleable, and relatively soft, contains less than 0.3 percent and usu. less than 0.1 percent carbon, and carries 1 or 2 percent of slag mechanically mixed with it

wrung *past of* WRING

¹wry \'rī\ *vb* **wried; wry·ing** [ME *wrien*, fr. OE *wrigian* to turn; akin to MHG *rigel* kerchief wound around the head, Gk *rhoikos* crooked] *vi* **:** TWIST, WRITHE ~ *vt* **:** to pull out of or as if out of proper shape **:** make awry

²wry *adj* **wri·er** \'rī(-ə)r\; **wri·est** \'rī-əst\ **1 :** having a bent or twisted shape or condition <a ~ smile>; *esp* **:** turned abnormally to one side <a ~ neck> **2 :** marked by perversity **:** WRONGHEADED **3 :** cleverly and often ironically or grimly humorous — **wry·ly** \'rī-lē\ *adv* — **wry·ness** *n*

wry·neck \'rī-,nek\ *n* **1 :** any of various woodpeckers (genus *Jynx*) that differ from the typical woodpeckers in having soft tail feathers and a peculiar manner of writhing the neck **2 :** TORTICOLLIS

WSW *abbr* west-southwest

wt *abbr* weight

WT *abbr* **1** watertight **2** wireless telegraphy

Wu \'wü\ *n* [Chin (Pek) *wu²*] **:** a group of Chinese dialects spoken in the lower Yangtze valley

wud \'wüd\ *adj* [alter. of ¹*wood*] *chiefly Scot* **:** INSANE, MAD

wul·fen·ite \'wu̇l-fə-,nīt\ *n* [G *wulfenit*, fr. F. X. von *Wulfen* †1805 Austrian mineralogist] **:** a tetragonal mineral $PbMoO_4$ that is a complex oxide of lead and molybdenum and that occurs usu. in bright orange-yellow to red, gray, green, or brown tabular crystals

wun·der·kind \'vu̇n-dər-,kint\ *n, pl* **wun·der·kin·der** \-,kin-dər\ [G, fr. *wunder* wonder + *kind* child] **:** a child prodigy; *also* **:** one who succeeds in a competitive or highly difficult field or profession at an early age

wurst \'wərst, 'wu̇(ə)rst, 'wu̇s(h)t\ *n* [G; akin to OHG *werran* to confuse — more at WAR] **:** SAUSAGE 1

wurzel *n* **:** MANGEL-WURZEL

W Va *or* **WV** *abbr* West Virginia

WVS *abbr* Women's Voluntary Services

WW *abbr* **1** warehouse warrant **2** with warrants **3** world war

Wy·an·dot \'wī-ən-,dät *also* 'wīn-\ *n* **:** a member of a subgroup of the Hurons

wy·an·dotte \-,dät\ *n* [prob. fr. *Wyandotte* (Wyandot)] **:** any of an American breed of medium-sized domestic fowls derived largely from dark brahmas and spangled Hamburgs

Wyc·liff·ite \'wik-lə-,fīt\ *n* [John *Wycliffe*] **:** LOLLARD — **Wycliffite** *adj*

wye \'wī\ *n* **1 :** the letter *y* **2 :** a Y-shaped part or object

wy·lie·coat \'wī-lē-,kōt, 'wil-ē-\ *n* [ME (Sc) *wyle cot*] **1** *chiefly Scot* **:** a warm undergarment **2** *chiefly Scot* **:** PETTICOAT

wynd \'wīnd\ *n, chiefly Scot* [ME (Sc) *wynde*, prob. fr. *wynden* to wind, proceed, go, fr. OE *windan* to twist — more at WIND] **:** a very narrow street

Wyo *or* **WY** *abbr* Wyoming

wy·vern \'wī-vərn\ *n* [alter. of ME *wyvere* viper, fr. ONF *wivre*, modif. of L *vipera*] **:** a fabulous animal usu. represented as a 2-legged winged creature resembling a dragon

[1]**x** \'eks\ *n, pl* **x's** *or* **xs** \'ek-səz\ *often cap, often attrib* **1 a :** the 24th letter of the English alphabet **b :** a graphic representation of this letter **c :** a speech counterpart of orthographic *x* **2 :** TEN — see NUMBER table **3 :** a graphic device for reproducing the letter *x* **4 :** one designated *x* esp. as the 24th in order or class, or the first in an order or class that includes x, y, and sometimes z **5 :** an unknown quantity **6 :** something shaped like or marked with the letter X

[2]**x** *vt* **x-ed** *also* **x'd** *or* **xed** \'ekst\; **x-ing** *or* **x'ing** \'ek-siŋ\ **1 :** to mark with an *x* **2 :** to cancel or obliterate with a series of *x*'s — usu. used with *out*

[3]**x** *abbr, often cap* **1** ex **2** experimental **3** extra

[4]**x** *symbol* **1 a** times <3 *x* 2 is 6> **b** by <a 3 *x* 5 index card> **2** *often cap* power of magnification **3** halogen atom **4** crossed with

[1]**X** \'eks\ *adj, of a motion picture* **:** of such a nature that admission is denied to persons under a specified age (as 17) — compare G, PG, R

[2]**X** *symbol* reactance

Xan·a·du \'zan-ə-,d(y)ü\ *n* [*Xanadu,* locality in Coleridge's poem *Kubla Khan* (1798)]**:** a place (as a town or village) of idyllic beauty

xanth- *or* **xantho-** *comb form* [NL, fr. Gk, fr. *xanthos*] **1 :** yellow <*xanth*ene> **2 :** xanthic acid <*xanth*ate>

xan·thate \'zan-,thāt\ *n* **:** a salt or ester of a xanthic acid

xan·thene \-,thēn\ *n* **1 :** a white crystalline heterocyclic compound $C_{13}H_{10}O$; *also* **:** an isomer of this that is the parent of the colored forms of the xanthene dyes **2 :** any of various derivatives of xanthene

xanthene dye *n* **:** any of various brilliant fluorescent yellow to pink to bluish red dyes characterized by the presence of the xanthene nucleus

xan·thic \'zan(t)-thik\ *adj* [F *xanthique,* fr. Gk *xanthos*] **1 :** of, relating to, or tending toward a yellow color **2 a :** of or relating to xanthin or xanthine **b :** of, relating to, or being any of various unstable thio acids and esp. a colorless oily acid $C_3H_6OS_2$

xan·thin \-thən\ *n* [ISV]**:** a carotenoid pigment soluble in alcohol

xan·thine \'zan-,thēn\ *n* [ISV] **:** a feebly basic compound $C_5H_4N_4O_2$ that occurs esp. in animal or plant tissue, is formed by hydrolysis of guanine, and yields uric acid on oxidation; *also* **:** any of various derivatives of this

Xan·thip·pe \zan-'t(h)ip-ē\ *or* **Xan·tip·pe** \-'tip-ē\ *n* [Gk *Xanthippē,* shrewish wife of Socrates]**:** an ill-tempered woman

xan·thoch·roi \zan-'thäk-rə-,wī, -'thäk-,rȯi\ *n pl* [NL, fr. *xanth-* + Gk *ōchroi,* nom. pl. masc. of *ōchros* pale]**:** white persons having light hair and fair skin — **xan·tho·chro·ic** \,zan(t)-thə-'krō-ik\ *adj* — **xan·tho·chroid** \'zan(t)-thə-,krȯid, zan-'thäk-rȯid\ *adj or n*

xan·thone \'zan-,thōn\ *n* [ISV] **:** a ketone $C_{13}H_8O_2$ that is the parent of several natural yellow pigments

xan·tho·phyll \'zan(t)-thə-,fil\ *n* [F *xanthophylle,* fr. *xanth-* + *-phylle* -phyll]**:** any of several neutral yellow to orange carotenoid pigments that are oxygen derivatives of carotenes; *esp* **:** LUTEIN — **xan·tho·phyl·lic** \,zan(t)-thə-'fil-ik\ *adj* — **xan·tho·phyl·lous** \-'fil-əs\ *adj*

Xa·ve·ri·an Brother \zā-,vir-ē-ən-, za-\ *n* [*Xaverian* (of St. Francis Xavier)] **:** a member of a Roman Catholic congregation of lay brothers founded by Theodore J. Ryken in Bruges, Belgium in 1839 and dedicated to education

x–ax·is \'ek-,sak-səs\ *n* **1 :** the axis in a plane Cartesian coordinate system parallel to which abscissas are measured **2 :** one of the three axes in a three-dimensional rectangular coordinate system

XC *or* **xcp** *abbr* ex coupon

X chromosome *n* **:** a sex chromosome that usu. occurs paired in each female zygote and cell and single in each male zygote and cell in species in which the male typically has two unlike sex chromosomes — compare Y CHROMOSOME

x–co·or·di·nate \,ek-skō-'ȯrd-nət, -ᵊn-ət, -ᵊn-,āt\ *n* **:** a coordinate whose value is determined by measuring parallel to an x-axis; *specif* **:** ABSCISSA

XD *or* **x div** *abbr* ex dividend

X–dis·ease \'eks-diz-,ēz\ *n* **:** any of various usu. virus diseases of obscure etiology and relationships

Xe *symbol* xenon

xe·bec \'zē-,bek, zi-'\ *n* [prob. modif. of F *chebec,* fr. Ar *shabbāk*] **:** a usu. 3-masted Mediterranean sailing ship with long overhanging bow and stern

xebec

xen- *or* **xeno-** *comb form* [LL, fr. Gk, fr. *xenos* stranger, guest, host] **1 :** guest **:** foreigner <*xeno*phobia> **2 :** strange **:** foreign <*xeno*lith>

xe·nia \'zē-nē-ə, -nyə\ *n* [NL, fr. Gk, hospitality, fr. *xenos* host]**:** the effect of genes introduced by a male nucleus on structures (as endosperm or the fruit of a seed plant) other than the embryo

xe·nic \'zen-ik, 'zēn-\ *adj* [*xen-* + *-ic*] **:** of, relating to, or employing a culture medium containing one or more unidentified organisms <~ cultivation of insect larvae> — **xe·ni·cal·ly** \-i-k(ə-)lē\ *adv*

xe·no·di·ag·no·sis \,zen-ō-,dī-ig-'nō-səs, ,zēn-\ *n* [NL]**:** the detection of a parasite (as of man) by feeding a suitable intermediate host (as an insect) on supposedly infected material (as blood) and later examining it for the parasite — **xe·no·di·ag·nos·tic** \-'näs-tik\ *adj*

xe·no·ge·ne·ic \-jə-'nē-ik\ *adj* [*xen-* + *-geneic* (alter. of *-genic*] **:** derived from or originating in a member of another species <a ~ antibody>

xe·no·graft \'zen-ə-,graft, 'zēn-\ *n* **:** a tissue graft carried out between members of different species

xe·no·lith \'zen-ᵊl-,ith, 'zēn-\ *n* **:** a fragment of a rock included in another rock — **xe·no·lith·ic** \,zen-ᵊl-'ith-ik, ,zēn-\ *adj*

xe·non \'zē-,nän, 'zen-,än\ *n* [Gk, neut. of *xenos* strange]**:** a heavy, colorless, and relatively inert gaseous element that occurs in air as about one part in 20 million by volume and is used in thyratrons and specialized flashtubes — see ELEMENT table

xe·no·phile \'zen-ə-,fīl, 'zēn-\ *n* [ISV] **:** one attracted to foreign things (as manners, styles, or people) — **xe·noph·i·lous** \ze-'näf-ə-ləs, zi-\ *adj*

xe·no·phobe \'zen-ə-,fōb, 'zēn-\ *n* [ISV] **:** one unduly fearful of what is foreign and esp. of people of foreign origin — **xe·no·pho·bic** \,zen-ə-'fō-bik, ,zēn-\ *adj*

xe·no·pho·bia \,zen-ə-'fō-bē-ə, ,zēn-\ *n* [NL]**:** fear and hatred of strangers or foreigners or of anything that is strange or foreign

xer- *or* **xero-** *comb form* [LL, fr. Gk *xēr-, xēro-,* fr. *xēros* — more at SERENE] **:** dry <*xer*ic> <*xero*phyte>

xe·rarch \'zi(ə)r-,ärk\ *adj* **:** developing or originating in a dry place — used of an ecological succession

xe·ric \'zir-ik, 'zer-\ *adj* **:** characterized by, relating to, or requiring only a small amount of moisture <a ~ habitat> <a ~ plant> — compare HYDRIC, MESIC — **xe·ri·cal·ly** \-i-k(ə-)lē\ *adv*

xe·rog·ra·phy \zə-'räg-rə-fē, zir-'äg-\ *n* [ISV] **:** a process for copying graphic matter by the action of light on an electrically charged photoconductive insulating surface in which the latent image is developed with a resinous powder — **xe·ro·graph·ic** \,zir-ə-'graf-ik\ *adj* — **xe·ro·graph·i·cal·ly** \-i-k(ə-)lē\ *adv*

xe·roph·i·lous \zə-'räf-ə-ləs, zir-'äf-\ *or* **xe·ro·phile** \'zir-ə-,fīl\ *adj* **:** thriving in or tolerant or characteristic of xeric environment — **xe·roph·i·ly** \zə-'räf-ə-lē, zir-'äf-\ *n*

xe·roph·thal·mia \,zir-,äf-'thal-mē-ə, -,äp-'thal-\ *n* [LL, fr. Gk *xērophthalmia,* fr. *xēr-* xer- + *ophthalmia*] **:** a dry thickened lusterless condition of the eyeball resulting from a severe systemic deficiency of vitamin A — **xe·roph·thal·mic** \-mik\ *adj*

xe·ro·phyte \'zir-ə-,fīt\ *n* **:** a plant structurally adapted for life and growth with a limited water supply esp. by means of mechanisms that limit transpiration or that provide for the storage of water — **xe·ro·phyt·ic** \,zir-ə-'fit-ik\ *adj* — **xe·ro·phyt·i·cal·ly** \-i-k(ə-)lē\ *adv* — **xe·ro·phyt·ism** \'zir-ə-,fīt-,iz-əm\ *n*

xe·ro·ther·mic \,zir-ə-'thər-mik\ *adj* **1 :** characterized by heat and dryness **2 :** adapted to or thriving in a hot dry environment

xe·rox \'zi(ə)r-,äks, 'zē-,räks\ *vt, often cap* [*Xerox*] **:** to copy on a Xerox machine

Xerox *trademark* — used for a xerographic copier

x height *n* **:** the height of a lowercase x used to represent the height of the main body of a lowercase letter

xi \'zī, 'ksī\ *n* [Gk *xei*] **1 :** the 14th letter of the Greek alphabet — see ALPHABET table **2 :** an unstable elementary particle of the baryon family existing in negative and neutral charge states with masses respectively 2585 and 2572 times the mass of an electron

XI *or* **x in** *or* **x int** *abbr* ex interest

x–in·ter·cept \'ek-'sint-ər-,sept\ *n* **:** the x-coordinate of a point where a line, curve, or surface intersects the x-axis

xi·phi·ster·num \,zī-fə-'stər-nəm, ,zif-ə-\ *n, pl* **-na** \-nə\ [NL, fr. Gk *xiphos* sword + NL *sternum*]**:** the posterior segment of the sternum — called also *xiphoid process*

[1]**xi·phoid** \'zī-,fȯid, 'zif-,ȯid\ *adj* [NL *xiphoides,* fr. Gk *xiphoeidēs,* fr. *xiphos*] **1 :** shaped like a sword **:** ENSIFORM **2 :** of, relating to, or being the xiphisternum

[2]**xiphoid** *n* **:** XIPHISTERNUM

xi·phos·uran \,zī-fə-'sur-ən, ,zif-ə-\ *n* [deriv. of Gk *xiphos* + *oura* tail — more at SQUIRREL] **:** any of an order (Xiphosura) of arthropods comprising the horseshoe crabs and extinct related forms — **xiphosuran** *adj* — **xi·phos·ure** \'zī-fə-,su̇(ə)r, 'zif-ə-\ *n* — **xi·phos·urous** \,zī-fə-'su̇r-əs, ,zif-ə-\ *adj*

x–ir·ra·di·ate \,ek-sir-'ād-ē-,āt\ *vt, often cap* **:** to irradiate with X rays — **x–ir·ra·di·a·tion** \-,ād-ē-'ā-shən\ *n*

XL *abbr* extra large

Xmas \'kris-məs *also* 'ek-sməs\ *n* [*X* (symbol for *Christ,* fr. the Gk letter chi (X), initial of *Christos* Christ) + *-mas* (in *Christmas*)] **:** CHRISTMAS

Xn *abbr* Christian

Xnty *abbr* Christianity

XR *abbr* ex rights

x–ra·di·a·tion \,eks-,rād-ē-'ā-shən\ *n, often cap* **1 :** exposure to X rays **2 :** radiation composed of X rays

Xray \'eks-,rā\ — a communications code word for the letter x

x–ray \'eks-,rā\ *vt, often cap* **:** to examine, treat, or photograph with X rays

X ray \'eks-,rā\ *n* **1 :** any of the electromagnetic radiations of the same nature as visible radiation but of an extremely short wavelength less than 100 angstroms that is produced by bombarding a metallic target with fast electrons in vacuum or by transition of atoms to lower energy states and that has the properties of ionizing a gas upon passage through it, of penetrating various thicknesses of all solids, of producing secondary radiations by impinging on material bodies, of acting on photographic films and plates as light does, and of causing fluorescent screens to emit light **2 :** a photograph obtained by use of X rays

X–ray astronomy *n* **:** astronomy dealing with investigations of celestial bodies by means of the X rays they emit

X–ray diffraction *n* **:** a scattering of X rays by the atoms of a crystal that produces an interference effect so that the diffraction pattern gives information on the structure of the crystal or the identity of a crystalline substance

X–ray photograph *n* **:** a shadow picture made with X rays

X–ray star *n* **:** a luminous starlike celestial object emitting a major portion of its radiation in the form of X rays

X–ray therapy *n* **:** medical treatment (as of cancer) by controlled application of X rays

X–ray tube *n* **:** a vacuum tube in which a concentrated stream of electrons strikes a metal target and produces X rays

x–sec·tion \'krȯs-'sek-shən, -,sek-\ *n* [*x,* rebus for *cross*] **:** CROSS SECTION — **x–sec·tion·al** \-shnəl, -shən-ᵊl\ *adj*

xu \'sü\ *n, pl* **xu** [Vietnamese, fr. F *sou* sou] **1** — see DONG at MONEY table **2 :** a coin of South Vietnam equivalent to the cent

XW *abbr* ex warrants

xyl- *or* **xylo-** *comb form* [L, fr. Gk, fr. *xylon*] **1 :** wood <*xylo*phone> **2 :** xylene <*xyl*ic>

xy·lan \'zī-ˌlan\ *n* [ISV] **:** a yellow gummy pentosan that yields xylose on hydrolysis and is abundantly present in plant cell walls and woody tissue

xy·la·ry ray \ˌzī-lə-rē-\ *n* [*xyl*em + *-ary*] **:** XYLEM RAY

xy·lem \'zī-ləm, -ˌlem\ *n* [G, fr. Gk *xylon*] **:** a complex tissue in the vascular system of higher plants that consists of vessels, tracheids, or both usu. together with wood fibers and parenchyma cells, functions chiefly in conduction but also in support and storage, and typically constitutes the woody element (as of a plant stem) — compare PHLOEM

xylem ray *n* **:** a vascular ray or portion of a vascular ray located in xylem — called also *wood ray;* compare PHLOEM RAY

xy·lene \'zī-ˌlēn\ *n* [ISV] **:** any of three toxic flammable oily isomeric aromatic hydrocarbons C_8H_{10} that are di-methyl homologues of benzene and are obtained from wood tar, coal tar, or petroleum distillates; *also* **:** a mixture of xylenes and ethyl-benzene used chiefly as a solvent

xy·li·dine \'zī-lə-ˌdēn\ *n* [ISV] **:** any or a mixture of six toxic liquid or low-melting crystalline isomeric amino derivatives $C_8H_{11}N$ of the xylenes used chiefly as intermediates for azo dyes and in organic synthesis

xy·log·ra·phy \zī-'läg-rə-fē\ *n* [F *xylographie,* fr. *xyl-* + *-graphie* -graphy] **:** the art of making engravings on wood — **xy·lo·graph** \'zī-lə-ˌgraf\ *n* — **xy·log·ra·pher** \zī-'läg-rə-fər\ *n* — **xy·lo·graph·ic** \ˌzī-lə-'graf-ik\ *adj* — **xy·lo·graph·i·cal** \-i-kəl\ *adj*

xy·lol \'zī-ˌlȯl, -ˌlōl\ *n* [ISV] **:** XYLENE

xy·loph·a·gous \zī-'läf-ə-gəs\ *adj* [Gk *xylophagos,* fr. *xyl-* + *-phagos* -phagous] **:** feeding on or in wood

xy·loph·i·lous \-'läf-ə-ləs\ *adj* **:** growing or living in or on wood

xy·lo·phone \'zī-lə-ˌfōn *also* 'zil-ə-\ *n* **:** a percussion instrument consisting of a series of wooden bars graduated in length to produce the musical scale, supported on belts of straw or felt, and sounded by striking with two small wooden hammers — **xy·lo·phon·ist** \-ˌfō-nəst\ *n*

xylophone

xy·lose \'zī-ˌlōs, -ˌlōz\ *n* [ISV] **:** a crystalline aldose sugar $C_5H_{10}O_5$ that is not fermentable with ordinary yeasts and occurs esp. as a constituent of xylans from which it is obtained by hydrolysis

xy·lot·o·mous \zī-'lät-ə-məs\ *adj* **:** capable of boring or cutting wood — used of an insect

xy·lot·o·my \-mē\ *n* **:** the art of preparing sections of wood for microscopic examination — **xy·lo·tom·ic** \ˌzī-lə-'täm-ik\ *or* **xy·lo·tom·i·cal** \-i-kəl\ *adj*

¹y \'wī\ *n, pl* **y's** *or* **ys** \'wīz\ *often cap, often attrib* **1 a :** the 25th letter of the English alphabet **b :** a graphic representation of this letter **c :** a speech counterpart of orthographic *y* **2 :** a graphic device for reproducing the letter *y* **3 :** one designated *y* esp. as the 25th in order or class or the second in order or class when x is made the first **4 :** something shaped like the letter Y

²y *abbr* **1** yard **2** year **3** yen **4** yeoman

¹Y \'wī\ *n* **:** YMCA

²Y *symbol* **1** admittance — used of a circuit **2** yttrium

¹-y *also* **-ey** \ē\ *adj suffix* [ME, fr. OE *-ig;* akin to OHG *-ig, -y,* L *-icus,* Gk *-ikos,* Skt *-ika*] **1 a :** characterized by **:** full of <bloss*y*> <dirt*y*> <mudd*y*> <clay*ey*> **b :** having the character of **:** composed of <ic*y*> <wax*y*> **c :** like **:** like that of <hom*ey*> <wintr*y*> — often with a disparaging connotation <stag*y*> **d :** devoted to **:** addicted to **:** enthusiastic over <hors*y*> **2 a :** tending or inclined to <sleep*y*> <chatt*y*> **b :** giving occasion for (specified) action <tear*y*> **c :** performing (specified) action <curl*y*> **3 a :** somewhat **:** rather **:** -ISH <chill*y*> **b :** having (such) characteristics to a marked degree or in an affected or superficial way <French*y*>

²-y \ē\ *n suffix, pl* **-ies** [ME *-ie,* fr. OF, fr. L *-ia,* fr. Gk *-ia, -eia*] **1 :** state **:** condition **:** quality <beggar*y*> **2 :** activity, place of business, or goods dealt with <chandler*y*> <laundr*y*> **3 :** whole body or group <soldier*y*>

³-y *n suffix, pl* **-ies** [ME *-ie,* fr. AF, fr. L *-ium*] **:** instance of a (specified) action <entreat*y*> <inquir*y*>

⁴-y — see -IE

yab·ber \'yab-ər\ *n, Austral* [prob. modif. (influenced by E *jabber*) of *yabba,* native name in Australia] **:** TALK, JABBER <all ~ and chatter ceased around the campfires —Francis Birtles> — **yabber** *vi*

¹yacht \'yät\ *n* [obs. D *jaght,* fr. MLG *jacht,* short for *jachtschiff,* lit., hunting ship] **:** any of various relatively small sailing or mechanically driven ships that characteristically have a sharp prow and graceful lines and are ordinarily used for pleasure cruising or racing

²yacht *vi* **:** to race or cruise in a yacht

yacht club *n* **:** a club organized to promote and regulate yachting and boating

yacht·ing *n* **:** the action, fact, or pastime of racing or cruising in a yacht

yachts·man \'yät-smən\ *n* **:** a person who owns or sails a yacht

YAF *abbr* Young Americans for Freedom

YAG \'yag\ *n* [*y*ttrium *a*luminum *g*arnet] **:** a synthetic yttrium aluminium garnet of marked hardness and high refractive index that is used esp. as a gemstone and in laser technology

ya·gi \'yäg-ē, 'yag-\ *n* [Hidetsugu *Yagi b* 1886 Jap engineer] **:** a highly directional and selective shortwave antenna consisting of a horizontal conductor of one or two dipoles connected with the receiver or transmitter and of a set of nearly equal insulated dipoles parallel to and on a level with the horizontal conductor

ya·hoo \'yā-(ˌ)hü, 'yä-\ *n, pl* **yahoos** **1** *cap* **:** a member of a race of brutes in Swift's *Gulliver's Travels* who have the form and all the vices of man **2 :** an uncouth or rowdy person

Yah·weh \'yä-(ˌ)wā, -(ˌ)vā\ *also* **Yah·veh** \-(ˌ)vā\ *n* [Heb *Yahweh*] **:** the God of the Hebrews — compare TETRAGRAMMATON

Yah·wism \-ˌwiz-əm, -ˌviz-\ *n* **:** the worship of Yahweh among the ancient Hebrews

Yah·wis·tic \yä-'wis-tik, -'vis-\ *adj* **1 :** characterized by the use of *Yahweh* as the name of God **2 :** of or relating to Yahwism

¹yak \'yak\ *n, pl* **yaks** *also* **yak** [Tibetan *gyak*] **:** a large long-haired wild or domesticated ox (*Bos grunniens*) of Tibet and adjacent elevated parts of central Asia

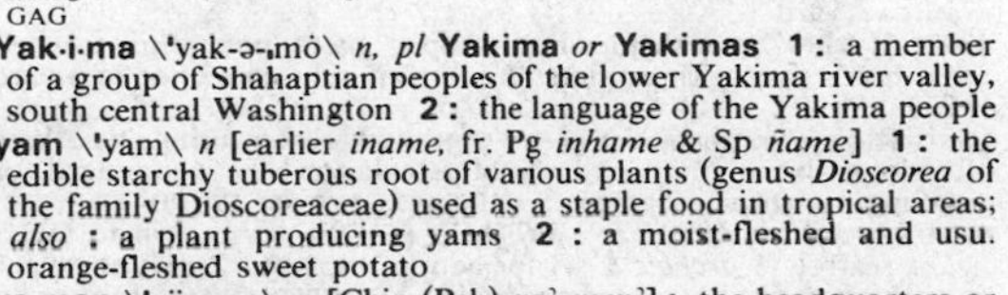

yak

²yak *also* **yack** \'yak\ *n* [prob. imit.] **:** persistent or voluble talk

³yak *also* **yack** *vi* **yakked** *also* **yacked; yak·king** *also* **yack·ing** **:** to talk persistently **:** CHATTER

⁴yak \'yäk, 'yak\ *n* [imit.] **1** *slang* **:** LAUGH **2** *slang* **:** JOKE, GAG

Yak·i·ma \'yak-ə-ˌmȯ\ *n, pl* **Yakima** *or* **Yakimas** **1 :** a member of a group of Shahaptian peoples of the lower Yakima river valley, south central Washington **2 :** the language of the Yakima people

yam \'yam\ *n* [earlier *iname,* fr. Pg *inhame* & Sp *ñame*] **1 :** the edible starchy tuberous root of various plants (genus *Dioscorea* of the family Dioscoreaceae) used as a staple food in tropical areas; *also* **:** a plant producing yams **2 :** a moist-fleshed and usu. orange-fleshed sweet potato

ya·men \'yäm-ən\ *n* [Chin (Pek) *ya²-men²*] **:** the headquarters or residence of a Chinese government official or department

yam·mer \'yam-ər\ *vi* **yam·mered; yam·mer·ing** \-(ə-)riŋ\ [alter. of ME *yomeren* to murmur, be sad, fr. OE *gēomrian;* akin to OHG *jāmaron* to be sad] **1 a :** to utter repeated cries of distress or sorrow **b :** WHIMPER **2 :** to utter persistent complaints **:** WHINE **3 :** to talk persistently or volubly and often loudly <caused the purists to ~ for censorship —D. W. Maurer> — **yammer** *n*

yang \'yäŋ, 'yaŋ\ *n* [Chin (Pek) *yang²*] **:** the masculine active principle in nature that in Chinese cosmology is exhibited in light, heat, or dryness and that combines with yin to produce all that comes to be

¹yank \'yaŋk\ *n* [origin unknown] **:** a strong sudden pull **:** JERK

²yank *vt* **:** to pull or extract with a quick vigorous movement ~ *vi* **:** to pull on something with a quick vigorous movement *syn* see JERK

Yank \'yaŋk\ *n* **:** YANKEE

¹Yan·kee \'yaŋ-kē\ *n* [origin unknown] **1 a :** a native or inhabitant of New England **b :** a native or inhabitant of the northern U.S. **2 :** a native or inhabitant of the U.S. — **Yan·kee·dom** \-kēd-əm\ *n* — **Yan·kee·ism** \-kē-ˌiz-əm\ *n*

²Yankee — a communications code word for the letter *y*

Yan·kee–Doo·dle \ˌyaŋ-kē-'düd-ᵊl\ *n* [*Yankee Doodle,* popular song during the American Revolution] **:** YANKEE

yan·qui \'yäŋ-kē\ *n, often cap* [Sp, fr. E [1]*Yankee*] **:** a citizen of the U.S. as distinguished from a Latin American

1yap \'yap\ *vi* **yapped; yap·ping** [imit.] **1 :** to bark snappishly **:** YELP **2 :** to talk in a shrill insistent way **:** CHATTER, SCOLD — **yap·per** *n*

2yap *n* **1 a :** a quick sharp bark **:** YELP **b :** shrill insistent talk **:** CHATTER **2 :** an unsophisticated, ignorant, or uncouth person **:** BUMPKIN **3** *slang* **:** MOUTH

ya·pock *or* **ya·pok** \yə-'päk\ *n* [*Oyapock, Oyapok,* river in So. America] **:** a gray and white So. American aquatic opossum (*Chironectes minimus*) with webbed hind feet

Yar·bor·ough \'yär-,bər-ə, -,bə-rə, -b(ə-)rə\ *n* [2d Earl of *Yarborough* †1897 E nobleman said to have bet a thousand to one against the dealing of such a hand] **:** a hand in bridge or whist containing no card higher than a nine

1yard \'yärd\ *n* [ME *yarde,* fr. OE *gierd* twig, measure, yard; akin to OHG *gart* stick, L *hasta* spear] **1 :** any of various units of measure: as **a :** a unit of length equal in the U.S. to 0.9144 meter — see WEIGHT table **b :** a unit of volume equal to a cubic yard **2 a :** a great length or quantity <remembered ~*s* of facts and figures> **b** *slang* **:** one hundred dollars **3 :** a long spar tapered toward the ends to support and spread the head of a square sail, lateen, or lugsail

2yard *n* [ME, fr. OE *geard* enclosure, yard; akin to OHG *gart* enclosure, L *hortus* garden] **1 a :** a small usu. walled and often paved area open to the sky and adjacent to a building **:** COURT **b :** the grounds of a building or group of buildings **2 a :** an enclosure for livestock (as poultry) **b (1) :** an area with its buildings and facilities set aside for a particular business or activity **(2) :** an assembly or storage area **c :** a system of tracks for storage and maintenance of cars and making up trains **3 :** a locality in a forest where deer herd in winter

3yard *adj* **1 :** of, relating to, or employed in the yard surrounding a building <~ light> **2 :** of, relating to, or employed in a railroad yard <~ engine>

4yard *vt* **1 :** to drive into or confine in a restricted area **:** HERD, PEN **2 :** to deliver to or store in a yard ~ *vi* **:** to congregate in or as if in a yard

1yard·age \'yärd-ij\ *n* [[2]*yard*] **1 :** the use of a livestock enclosure for animals in transit provided by a railroad at a station **2 :** a charge made by a railroad for the use of a livestock enclosure

2yardage *n* [[1]*yard*] **1 a :** an aggregate number of yards **b :** the length, extent, or volume of something as measured in yards **2 :** YARD GOODS

yard·arm \'yärd-,ärm\ *n* **:** either end of the yard of a square-rigged ship

yard·bird \-,bərd\ *n* [[2]*yard*] **1 :** a soldier assigned to a menial task or restricted to a limited area as a disciplinary measure **2 :** an untrained or inept enlisted man

yard goods *n pl* **:** fabrics sold by the yard **:** PIECE GOODS

yard grass *n* [[2]*yard*] **:** a coarse annual grass (*Eleusine indica*) with digitate spikes that is widely distributed as a weed

yard line *n* **:** any of a series of marked or imaginary lines one yard apart on a football field that are parallel to the goal lines and that indicate the distance to the nearest goal line

yard·man \'yärd-mən, -,man\ *n* **1 :** a man employed to do outdoor work (as mowing lawns) **2 :** one who works in the yard of a commercial establishment; *esp* **:** one who supervises the handling of building materials in a lumberyard **3 :** a railroad man employed in yard service

yard·mas·ter \-,mas-tər\ *n* **:** the man in charge of operations in a railroad yard

yard of ale 1 : a slender horn-shaped glass about three feet tall that holds two or three pints **2 :** the amount contained in a yard of ale

yard·stick \'yärd-,stik\ *n* **1 a :** a graduated measuring stick three feet long **b :** a standard basis of calculation **2 :** a standard for making a critical judgment **:** CRITERION ***syn*** see STANDARD

yare \'ya(ə)r, 'ye(ə)r, 'yär\ *adj* [ME, fr. OE *gearu;* akin to OHG *garo* ready] **1** *archaic* **:** set for action **:** READY **2** *or* **yar** \'yär\ **a :** characterized by speed and agility **:** NIMBLE, LIVELY **b** *of a ship* **:** easily handled **:** MANEUVERABLE — **yare** *adv, archaic* — **yare·ly** *adv, archaic*

yar·mul·ke *or* **yar·mel·ke** \'yär-məl-kə\ *n* [Yiddish, fr. Ukrainian & Pol *jarmutka* skullcap] **:** a skullcap worn esp. by Orthodox and Conservative Jewish males in the synagogue and the home

1yarn \'yärn\ *n* [ME, fr. OE *gearn;* akin to OHG *garn* yarn, Gk *chordē* string, L *hernia* rupture] **1 a :** a continuous often plied strand composed of fibers or filaments and used in weaving and knitting to form cloth **b :** a similar strand of metal, glass, asbestos, paper, or plastic **c :** THREAD **2 :** a narrative of adventures; *esp* **:** a tall tale

2yarn *vi* **:** to tell a yarn

yarn–dye \'yärn-,dī\ *vt* **:** to dye before weaving or knitting

yar·row \'yar-(,)ō, -ə(-w)\ *n* [ME *yarowe,* fr. OE *gearwe;* akin to OHG *garwa* yarrow] **:** a widely naturalized strong-scented Eurasian composite herb (*Achillea millefolium*) with finely dissected leaves and small usu. white corymbose flowers; *also* **:** any of several congeneric plants

yash·mak *also* **yas·mak** \'yas(h)-,mak\ *n* [Turk *yaşmak*] **:** a veil worn by Muslim women that is wrapped around the upper and lower parts of the face so that only the eyes remain exposed to public view

yat·a·ghan \'yat-ə-,gan, 'yat-i-gən\ *n* [Turk *yatağan*] **:** a long knife or short saber common among Muslims that is made without a cross guard and usu. with a double curve to the edge and a nearly straight back

yauld \'yòl(d)\ *adj* [origin unknown] *chiefly Scot* **:** VIGOROUS, ENERGETIC

yau·pon \'yü-,pän *also* 'yō-, 'yò-\ *n* [Catawba *yopún,* dim. of *yop* tree] **:** a holly (*Ilex vomitoria*) of the southern U.S. with smooth elliptical leaves and emetic and purgative properties

1yaw \'yò\ *n* [origin unknown] **1 :** the action of yawing; *esp* **:** a side to side movement **2 :** the extent of the movement in yawing

2yaw *vi* **1 a** *of a ship* **:** to deviate erratically from a course (as when struck by a heavy sea) **b** *of an airplane, spacecraft, or projectile* **:** to turn by angular motion about the vertical axis **2 :** to become deflected **:** SWERVE

yawl \'yòl\ *n* [LG *jolle*] **1 :** a ship's small boat **:** JOLLY BOAT **2 :** a fore-and-aft rigged sailboat carrying a mainsail and one or more jibs with a mizzenmast far aft

yawl 2

1yawn \'yòn, 'yän\ *vb* [ME *yenen, yanen,* fr. OE *ginian;* akin to OHG *ginēn* to yawn, L *hiare,* Gk *chainein*] *vi* **1 :** to open wide **:** GAPE **2 :** to open the mouth wide usu. as an involuntary reaction to fatigue or boredom ~ *vt* **:** to utter with a yawn — **yawn·er** *n*

2yawn *n* **1 :** GAP, CAVITY **2 :** a deep usu. involuntary intake of breath through the wide open mouth

yawn·ing *adj* **1 :** wide open **:** CAVERNOUS <a ~ hole> **2 :** showing fatigue or boredom by yawns <a ~ audience> — **yawn·ing·ly** \'yò-niŋ-lē\ *adv*

1yawp *or* **yaup** \'yòp\ *vi* [ME *yolpen*] **1 :** to make a raucous noise **:** SQUAWK **2 :** CLAMOR, COMPLAIN — **yawp·er** *n*

2yawp *also* **yaup** *n* **1 :** a raucous noise **:** SQUAWK **2 :** something suggestive of a raucous noise; *specif* **:** rough vigorous language

yawp·ing *n* **:** a strident utterance

yaws \'yòz\ *n pl but sing or pl in constr* [of Cariban origin; akin to Calinago *yáya* yaws] **:** an infectious contagious tropical disease caused by a spirochete (*Treponema pertenue*) and marked by ulcerating lesions with later bone involvement — called also *frambesia*

y–ax·is \'wī-,ak-səs\ *n* **1 :** the axis of ordinates in a plane Cartesian coordinate system **2 :** one of the three axes in a three-dimensional rectangular coordinate system

Yb *symbol* ytterbium

YB *abbr* yearbook

Y chromosome *n* **:** a sex chromosome that is characteristic of male zygotes in species in which the male typically has two unlike sex chromosomes — compare X CHROMOSOME

yclept *or* **ycleped** [ME, fr. OE *geclipod,* pp. of *clipian* to cry out, name] *past part of* CLEPE

y–co·or·di·nate \,wī-kō-'ȯrd-nət, -ᵊn-ət; -ᵊn-,āt\ *n* **:** a coordinate whose value is determined by measuring parallel to a y-axis; *specif* **:** ORDINATE

yd *abbr* yard

1ye \(')yē\ *pron* [ME, fr. OE *gē;* akin to OHG *ir* you — more at YOU] **:** YOU 1 — used orig. only as a plural pronoun of the second person in the subjective case and now used esp. in ecclesiastical or literary language and in various English dialects

2ye \yē, yə, *or like* 'THE\ *definite article* [alter. of OE *þē* the; fr. the use by early printers of the letter *y* to represent *þ* (*th*) of manuscripts] *archaic* **:** THE <*Ye* Olde Gifte Shoppe>

1yea \'yā\ *adv* [ME *ye, ya,* fr. OE *gēa;* akin to OHG *jā* yes] **1 :** YES — used in oral voting **2 :** more than this **:** not only so but — used as a function word to introduce a more explicit or emphatic phrase <men achieved the right to economic necessity, ~, even abundance —L. H. Harshbarger>

2yea *n* **1 :** AFFIRMATION, ASSENT **2 a :** an affirmative vote **b :** a person casting a yea vote

yeah \'ye-ə, 'yeü, 'ya-ə\ *adv* [by alter.] **:** YES

yean \'(y)ēn\ *vi* [ME *yenen,* fr. (assumed) OE *geēanian,* fr. OE *ge-,* perfective prefix + *ēanian* to yean; akin to L *agnus* lamb, Gk *amnos*] **:** to bring forth young — used of a sheep or goat

yean·ling \-liŋ, -lən\ *n* **:** LAMB, KID 1a

year \'yi(ə)r\ *n* [ME *yere,* fr. OE *gēar;* akin to OHG *jār* year, Gk *hōros* year, *hōra* season, hour, L *ire* to go — more at ISSUE] **1 a :** the period of about 365¼ solar days required for one revolution of the earth around the sun **b :** the time required for the apparent sun to return to an arbitrary fixed or moving reference point in the sky **2 a :** a cycle in the Gregorian calendar of 365 or 366 days divided into 12 months beginning with January and ending with December **b :** a period of time equal to one year of the Gregorian calendar but beginning at a different time **3 :** a calendar year specified usu. by a number **4** *pl* **:** a time or era having a special significance **5** *pl* **:** AGE <a man in ~*s* but a child in understanding>; *also* **:** the final stage of the normal life span **6 :** a period of time (as the usu. nine-month period in which a school is in session) other than a calendar year

year·book \-,bůk\ *n* **1 :** a book published yearly as a report or summary of statistics or facts **:** ANNUAL **2 :** a school publication that is compiled usu. by a graduating class and that serves as a record of the year's activities

1year–end \-'end\ *n* **:** the end of usu. the fiscal year

2year–end \,yi(ə)r-,end\ *adj* **:** made at the year-end <a ~ report> **:** occurring or existing at the year-end <a ~ upsurge of prices>

year·ling \'yi(ə)r-liŋ, 'yər-lən\ *n* **:** one that is a year old: as **a :** an animal one year old or in the second year of its age **b :** a racehorse between January 1st of the year after the year in which it was foaled and the next January 1st — **yearling** *adj*

year·long \'yi(ə)r-'lòŋ\ *adj* **:** lasting through a year

1year·ly \'yi(ə)r-lē\ *adj* **1 :** reckoned by the year **2 :** occurring, appearing, made, done, or acted upon every year or once a year **:** ANNUAL

2yearly *adv* **:** every year **:** ANNUALLY

Yearly Meeting *n* **:** an organization uniting several Quarterly Meetings of the Society of Friends

yearn \'yərn\ *vi* [ME *yernen,* fr. OE *giernan;* akin to OHG *gerōn* to desire, L *hortari* to urge, encourage, Gk *chairein* to rejoice] **1** : to long persistently, wistfully, or sadly **2** : to feel tenderness or compassion *syn* see LONG — **yearn·er** *n*

yearn·ing *n* : a tender or urgent longing

year of grace : a year of the Christian era <the *year of grace* 1962>

year–round \'yi(ə)r-'raủnd, 'yiə-'raủnd\ *adj* : effective, employed, or operating for the full year : not seasonal <a ~ resort>

yea–say·er \'yā-ˌsā-ər, -ˌse(-ə)r\ *n* **1** : one whose attitude is that of confident affirmation **2** : YES-MAN

¹yeast \'yēst, 'ēst (*the latter frequent or prevalent from mid Pa southward*)\ *n* [ME *yest,* fr. OE *gist;* akin to MHG *jest* foam, Gk *zein* to boil] **1 a** : a yellowish surface froth or sediment that occurs esp. in saccharine liquids (as fruit juices) in which it promotes alcoholic fermentation, consists largely of cells of a fungus (family Saccharomycetaceae), and is used esp. in the making of alcoholic liquors and as a leaven in baking **b** : a commercial product containing yeast plants in a moist or dry medium **c** (1) : a minute fungus (esp. *Saccharomyces cerevisiae*) that is present and functionally active in yeast, usu. has little or no mycelium, and reproduces by budding (2) : any of various similar fungi (esp. orders Endomycetales and Moniliales) **2** : the foam or spume of waves **3** : something that causes ferment or activity <were all seething with the ~ of revolt —J. F. Dobie>

²yeast *vi* : FERMENT, FROTH

yeasty \'yē-stē, 'ē-stē\ *adj* **yeast·i·er; -est** **1** : of, relating to, or resembling yeast **2 a** : IMMATURE, UNSETTLED **b** : marked by change **c** : EXUBERANT **d** : FRIVOLOUS — **yeast·i·ly** \-stə-lē\ *adv* — **yeast·i·ness** \-stē-nəs\ *n*

yegg \'yeg, 'yāg\ *n* [origin unknown] : SAFECRACKER, BOMBER

¹yell \'yel\ *vb* [ME *yellen,* fr. OE *giellan;* akin to OHG *gellan* to yell, OE *galan* to sing] *vi* **1** : to utter a loud cry, scream, or shout **2** : to give a cheer usu. in unison ~ *vt* : to utter or declare with or as if with a yell : SHOUT — **yell·er** *n*

²yell *n* **1** : SCREAM, SHOUT **2** : a usu. rhythmic cheer used esp. in schools or colleges to encourage athletic teams

¹yel·low \'yel-(ˌ)ō, -ə(-w)\ *adj* [ME *yelwe, yelow,* fr. OE *geolu;* akin to OHG *gelo* yellow, L *helvus* light bay, Gk *chlōros* greenish yellow, Skt *hari* yellowish] **1 a** : of the color yellow **b** : become yellowish through age, disease, or discoloration : SALLOW **c** : having a yellow or light brown complexion or skin **2 a** : featuring sensational or scandalous items or ordinary news sensationally distorted <~ journalism> **b** : MEAN, COWARDLY — **yel·low·ish** \'yel-ə-wish\ *adj*

²yellow *vt* : to make yellow : give a yellow tinge or color to <~*ed* by time> ~ *vi* : to become or turn yellow

³yellow *n* **1 a** : a color whose hue resembles that of ripe lemons or sunflowers or is that of the portion of the spectrum lying between green and orange **b** : a pigment or dye that colors yellow **2** : something yellow or marked by a yellow color: as **a** : a person having yellow or light brown skin **b** : the yolk of an egg **3** *pl* : JAUNDICE **4** *pl* : any of several plant diseases caused esp. by viruses and marked by yellowing of the foliage and stunting

yellow bile *n* : a humor believed in medieval physiology to be secreted by the liver and to cause irascibility

yellow birch *n* : a No. American birch (*Betula lutea*) with thin lustrous gray or yellow bark; *also* : its strong hard pale wood

yel·low·bird \'yel-ō-ˌbərd, -ə-bərd\ *n* **1** : any of various American goldfinches **2** : a small mostly yellow American warbler (*Dendroica petechia*)

yel·low–dog \ˌyel-ō-'dȯg, -ə-'dȯg\ *adj* **1** : MEAN, CONTEMPTIBLE **2** : of or relating to opposition to trade unionism or a labor union

yellow–dog contract *n* : an employment contract in which a worker disavows membership in and agrees not to join a labor union during the period of his employment

yellow dwarf *n* : any of several virus diseases of plants and esp. cereal grasses characterized by yellowing and stunting

yellow enzyme *n* : a yellow flavoprotein respiratory enzyme

yellow fever *n* : an acute destructive infectious disease of warm regions marked by sudden onset, prostration, fever, albuminuria, jaundice, and often hemorrhage and caused by a virus transmitted by a mosquito — called also *yellow jack*

yellow–fever mosquito *n* : a small dark-colored mosquito (*Aëdes aegypti*) that is the usual vector of yellow fever

yel·low·fin tuna \ˌyel-ō-ˌfin-, ˌyel-ə-\ *n* : a rather small and nearly cosmopolitan tuna (*Thunnus albacares*) with yellow-tipped fins and delicate light flesh — called also *yellowfin*

yellow–green alga *n* : any of a division (Chrysophyta) of algae with the chlorophyll masked by brown or yellow pigment

yel·low·ham·mer \'yel-ō-ˌham-ər, 'yel-ə-\ *n* [alter. of earlier *yelambre,* fr. (assumed) ME *yelwambre,* fr. ME *yelwe* yellow + (assumed) ME *ambre* yellowhammer, fr. OE *amore;* akin to OHG *amaro* yellowhammer, *amari* emmer] **1** : a common European finch (*Emberiza citrinella*) having the male largely bright yellow — called also *yellow bunting* **2** : YELLOW-SHAFTED FLICKER

yellow jack *n* **1** : YELLOW FEVER **2** : a flag raised on ships in quarantine **3** : a silvery and golden food fish (*Caranx bartholomaei*) of Florida and the West Indies

yellow jacket *n* **1** : any of various small yellow-marked social wasps (family Vespidae) that commonly nest in the ground **2** *slang* : a sedative or hypnotic drug; *esp* : THIOPENTAL

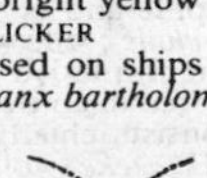
yellow jacket 1

yellow jessamine *n* : a twining evergreen shrub (*Gelsemium sempervirens*) of the family Loganiaceae with fragrant yellow flowers — called also *yellow jasmine*

yel·low·legs \'yel-ō-ˌlegz, 'yel-ə-, -ˌlāgz\ *n pl but sing or pl in constr* : either of two American shorebirds: **a** : GREATER YELLOWLEGS **b** : LESSER YELLOWLEGS

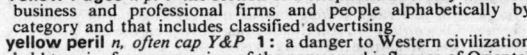

yellow ocher *n* **1** : a mixture of limonite usu. with clay and silica used as a pigment **2** : a moderate orange yellow

Yellow Pages *n pl* : the section of a telephone directory that lists business and professional firms and people alphabetically by category and that includes classified advertising

yellow peril *n, often cap Y&P* **1** : a danger to Western civilization held to arise from expansion of the power and influence of Oriental peoples **2** : a threat to Western living standards from the incursion into Western countries of Oriental laborers willing to work for very low wages

yellow pine *n* : the yellowish wood of any of several No. American pines; *also* : a tree yielding this

yellow poplar *n* **1 a** : the American tulip tree **b** : TULIPWOOD 1 **2** : the soft and light but durable wood of the common cucumber tree (*Magnolia acuminata*) of the southeastern U.S.

yel·low–shaft·ed flicker \ˌyel-ō-ˌshaf-təd-, ˌyel-ə-\ *n* : a common large woodpecker (*Colaptes auratus*) of eastern No. America with bright symmetrical markings among which are a black crescent on the breast, red nape, white rump, and yellow shafts to the tail and wing feathers — called also *yellowhammer*

yellow spot *n* : MACULA LUTEA

yel·low·tail \'yel-ō-ˌtāl, 'yel-ə-\ *n, pl* **yellowtail** *or* **yellowtails** : any of various fishes having a yellow or yellowish tail: as **a** : any of several carangid fishes (genus *Seriola*) **b** : SILVER PERCH a **c** : RAINBOW RUNNER **d** : PINFISH **e** : a common snapper (*Ocyurus chrysurus*) of the tropical western Atlantic and West Indies that is olive above and broadly striped with yellow along the sides and on the tail and highly esteemed for sport and food **f** : SPOT 6

yel·low·throat \-ˌthrōt\ *n* : any of several largely olive American warblers (genus *Geothlypis*); *esp* : one with yellow breast and throat

yel·low·wood \-ˌwủd\ *n* **1** : any of various trees having yellowish wood or yielding a yellow extract: as **a** : a leguminous tree (*Cladrastis lutea*) of the southern U.S. having showy white fragrant flowers and yielding a yellow dye **b** : OSAGE ORANGE **c** : BUCKTHORN **d** : SMOKE TREE **2** : the wood of a yellowwood tree

¹yelp \'yelp\ *vb* [ME *yelpen* to boast, cry out, fr. OE *gielpan* to boast, exult; akin to OHG *gelph* outcry, Lith *gulbinti* to praise] *vi* : to utter a sharp quick shrill cry <dogs ~> ~ *vt* : to utter with a yelp

²yelp *n* : a sharp shrill bark or cry (as of a dog)

yelp·er \'yel-pər\ *n* **1** : one that yelps; *esp* : a yelping dog **2** : an instrument used by hunters to produce a call or whistle imitating the yelp of the wild turkey hen

¹yen \'yen\ *n, pl* **yen** [Jap *en*] — see MONEY table

²yen *n* [obs. E slang *yen-yen* craving for opium, fr. Chin (Cant) *in-yǎn,* fr. *in* opium + *yǎn* craving] : a strong desire or propensity : LONGING; *also* : URGE

³yen *vi* **yenned; yen·ning** : to desire intensely : LONG, YEARN

yen–shee \'yen-'shē\ *n* [Chin (Cant) *in shí,* fr. *in* opium + *shí* excrement, filth] : the residue formed in the bowl of an opium pipe by smoking

yeo *or* **yeom** *abbr* yeomanry

yeo·man \'yō-mən\ *n* [ME *yoman*] **1 a** : an attendant or officer in a royal or noble household **b** : a person attending or assisting another : RETAINER **c** : YEOMAN OF THE GUARD **d** : a naval petty officer who performs clerical duties **2 a** : a small farmer who cultivates his own land; *specif* : one belonging to a class of English freeholders below the gentry **b** : a person of the social rank of yeoman **3** : one that performs great and laborious services

¹yeo·man·ly \-lē\ *adj* **1** : of, relating to, or having the rank of a yeoman **2** : becoming or suitable to a yeoman : STURDY, LOYAL

²yeomanly *adv* : in a manner befitting a yeoman : BRAVELY

yeoman of the guard : a member of a military corps attached to the British royal household that serves as ceremonial attendants of the sovereign and as warders of the Tower of London

yeo·man·ry \'yō-mən-rē\ *n* **1** : the body of yeomen; *specif* : the body of small landed proprietors of the middle class **2** : a British volunteer cavalry force created from yeomen in 1761 as a home defense force and reorganized in 1907 as part of the territorial force

yeoman's service *or* **yeoman service** *n* : great and loyal service, assistance, or support

yep \'yep, *or with glottal stop instead of* p\ *adv* [by alter.] : YES

-yer — see -ER

yer·ba ma·té \ˌyer-bə-'mä-ˌtā, ˌyər-\ *n* [AmerSp *yerba mate,* fr. *yerba* herb + *mate* maté] : MATÉ

¹yerk \'yərk\ *vt* [ME *yerken* to bind tightly] **1** *dial* : to beat vigorously : THRASH **2** *dial* : to attack or excite vigorously : GOAD

²yerk *n* **1** *Scot* : a lashing out : KICK **2** *dial* : JERK 1

¹yes \'yes, 'yeủ, 'e-(y)ə *are three of many variants*\ *adv* [ME, fr. OE *gēse*] **1** — used as a function word to express assent or agreement <are you ready? *Yes,* I am> **2** — used as a function word usu. to introduce correction or contradiction of a negative assertion or direction <don't say that! *Yes,* I will> **3** — used as a function word to introduce a more emphatic or explicit phrase **4** — used as a function word to indicate uncertainty or polite interest or attentiveness

²yes \'yes\ *n* : an affirmative reply : YEA

ye·shi·va *or* **ye·shi·vah** \yə-'shē-və\ *n, pl* **yeshivas** *or* **ye·shi·voth** \-ˌshē-'vōt(h)\ [LHeb *yĕshībhāh*] **1** : a school for Talmudic study **2** : an orthodox Jewish rabbinical seminary **3** : a Jewish day school providing secular and religious instruction

yes–man \'yes-ˌman\ *n* : a person who agrees with everything that is said to him; *esp* : one who endorses or supports without criticism every opinion or proposal of an associate or superior

yes·ter \'yes-tər\ *adj, archaic* : of or relating to yesterday

ə abut	ᵊ kitten	ər further	a back	ā bake	ä cot, cart
aủ out	ch chin	e less	ē easy	g gift	i trip	ī life
j joke	ŋ sing	ō flow	ȯ flaw	ȯi coin	th thin	t͟h this
ü loot	ủ foot	y yet	yü few	yủ furious	zh vision

1**yes·ter·day** \ˈyes-tərd-ē\ *adv* [ME *yisterday,* fr. OE *giestran dæg,* fr. *giestran* yesterday + *dæg* day; akin to OHG *gestaron* yesterday, L *heri,* Gk *chthes*] **1 :** on the day last past : on the day preceding today **2 :** at a time not long past : only a short time ago <I wasn't born ~> — **yesterday** *adj*

2**yesterday** *n* **1 :** the day last past : the day next before the present **2 :** recent time : time not long past **3 :** past time — usu. used in pl.

yes·ter·year \ˈyes-tər-ˌyi(ə)r\ *n* [*yester*day + *year*] **1 :** last year **2 :** the recent past — **yesteryear** *adv*

yes·treen \ye-ˈstrēn\ *n, chiefly Scot* : last evening or night — **yestreen** *adv*

1**yet** \(ˈ)yet\ *adv* [ME, fr. OE *giet;* akin to OFris *ieta* yet] **1 a :** in addition : BESIDES <gives ~ another reason> **b :** EVEN 2c <a ~ higher speed> **2 a (1) :** up to now : so far <hasn't done much ~> **(2) :** at this or that time : so soon as now <not time to go ~> **b :** continuously up to the present or a specified time : STILL <is ~ a new country> **c :** at a future time : EVENTUALLY <may ~ see the light> **3 :** NEVERTHELESS, HOWEVER — **as yet :** up to the present time

2**yet** *conj* : but nevertheless : BUT

ye·ti \ˈyet-ē, ˈyāt-\ *n* [Tibetan] : ABOMINABLE SNOWMAN

yeuk \ˈyük\ *vi* [ME (northern) *yukyn,* fr. OE *giccan*] *chiefly Scot* : ITCH — **yeuk** *n, chiefly Scot* — **yeuky** \ˈyü-kē\ *adj, chiefly Scot*

yew \ˈyü\ *n* [ME *ew,* fr. OE *īw;* akin to OHG *iwa* yew, OIr *ēo*] **1 a :** any of a genus (*Taxus* of the family Taxaceae, the yew family) of evergreen trees and shrubs with stiff linear leaves and fruits with a fleshy aril; *esp* : a long-lived Eurasian tree (*T. baccata*) — called also *English yew* **b :** the wood of a yew; *esp* : the heavy fine-grained wood of English yew **2** *archaic* : an archery bow made of yew

yew 1a

Ygerne \ē-ˈge(ə)rn\ *n* : IGRAINE

Ygg·dra·sil \ˈig-drə-ˌsil\ *n* [ON] : a huge ash tree in Norse mythology that overspreads the world and binds earth, hell, and heaven together

YHWH \ˈyä-(ˌ)wä, -(ˌ)vä\ *n* : YAHWEH — compare TETRAGRAMMATON

Yid *abbr* Yiddish

Yid·dish \ˈyid-ish\ *n* [Yiddish *yidish,* short for *yidish daytsh,* lit., Jewish German] : a High German language usu. written in Hebrew characters that is spoken by Jews chiefly in eastern Europe and areas to which eastern European Jews have migrated — **Yiddish** *adj*

1**yield** \ˈyē(ə)ld\ *vb* [ME *yielden,* fr. OE *gieldan;* akin to OHG *geltan* to pay] *vt* **1** *archaic* : RECOMPENSE, REWARD **2 :** to give or render as fitting, rightfully owed, or required **3 :** to give up possession of on claim or demand: as **a :** to give up (as one's breath) and so die **b :** to surrender or relinquish to the physical control of another : hand over possession of **c :** to surrender or submit (oneself) to another **d :** to give (oneself) up to an inclination, temptation, or habit **e :** to relinquish one's possession of (as a position of advantage or point of superiority) <~ precedence> **4 a :** to bear or bring forth as a natural product esp. as a result of cultivation <the tree always ~*s* good fruit> **b :** to furnish as return or result of expended effort <properly handled this soil should ~ good crops> **c (1) :** to produce as return from an expenditure or investment : furnish as profit or interest <a bond that ~*s* 12 percent> **(2) :** to produce as revenue : bring in <the tax is expected to ~ millions> **5 :** to give up (as a hit or run) in baseball <~*ed* two runs in the third inning> ~ *vi* **1 :** to be fruitful or productive : BEAR, PRODUCE **2 :** to give up and cease resistance or contention : SUBMIT, SUCCUMB **3 :** to give way to pressure or influence : submit to urging, persuasion, or entreaty **4 :** to give way under physical force (as bending, stretching, or breaking) **5 a :** to give place or precedence : acknowledge the superiority of someone else **b :** to be inferior <our beer ~*s* to none> **c :** to give way to or become succeeded by someone or something else **6 :** to relinquish the floor of a legislative assembly

syn **1** see RELINQUISH

2 YIELD, SUBMIT, CAPITULATE, SUCCUMB, RELENT, DEFER *shared meaning element* : to give way to someone or something that one can no longer resist. YIELD in reference to a person implies being overcome (as by force or entreaty) <after some further argument I *yielded* the point —W. H. Hudson †1922> but with reference to a thing it implies qualities (as elasticity or weakness) that facilitate giving way <the door suddenly *yielded* to her hand —Jane Austen> SUBMIT implies prior conflict or resistance and suggests submissiveness (as to the will or control of another) <not only has faith in divine Providence but *submits* to it humbly —Herbert Agar> CAPITULATE stresses the fact of ending all resistance and may imply either a coming to terms (as with an adversary) or hopelessness in the face of an irresistible opposing force or power <the universities would *capitulate* to a young, vigorous and revolutionary creed —Walter Moberly> SUCCUMB attributes weakness and helplessness to the one that gives way or overwhelming power to the opposing force <the best of constitutions will not prevent ambitious politicians from *succumbing* . . . to the temptations of power —Aldous Huxley> The word frequently implies a disastrous outcome (as death or destruction) <true passion must be crushed before it will *succumb* —George Meredith> RELENT implies a yielding through pity or mercy by one who holds the upper hand <can you hear a good man groan, and not *relent*? —Shak.> DEFER implies a voluntary yielding or submitting out of respect or reverence for or deference and affection toward another <she *deferred* in all things to her uncle —Upton Sinclair>

2**yield** *n* **1 :** something yielded : PRODUCT; *esp* : the amount or quantity produced or returned <~ of wheat per acre> **2 :** the capacity of yielding produce

yield·er \ˈyēl-dər\ *n* : one that yields: as **a :** a person who surrenders, concedes, or gives in **b :** something that yields produce or products

yield·ing \-diŋ\ *adj* **1 :** PRODUCTIVE <a high-*yielding* wheat> **2 :** lacking rigidity or stiffness : FLEXIBLE **3 :** disposed to submit or comply

yin \ˈyin\ *n* [Chin (Pek) *yin*[1]] : the feminine passive principle in nature that in Chinese cosmology is exhibited in darkness, cold, or wetness and that combines with yang to produce all that comes to be

y–in·ter·cept \ˈwī-ˈint-ər-ˌsept\ *n* : the y-coordinate of a point where a line, curve, or surface intersects the y-axis

yip \ˈyip\ *vi* **yipped; yip·ping** [imit.] **1 :** to bark sharply, quickly, and often continuously **2 :** to utter a short sharp cry — **yip** *n*

yip·pee \ˈyip-ē\ *interj* — used to express exuberant delight or triumph

-yl \əl, ᵊl, (ˌ)il, ˌēl, *chiefly Brit* ˌīl\ *n comb form* [Gk *hylē* matter, material, lit., wood] : chemical and usu. univalent radical <eth*yl*>

ylang–ylang *var of* ILANG-ILANG

YMCA \ˌwī-ˌem-(ˌ)sē-ˈā\ *n* [*Y*oung *M*en's *C*hristian *A*ssociation] : an international organization that promotes the spiritual, intellectual, social and physical welfare of young men

YMHA \ˌwī-ˌem-ˌā-ˈchā\ *n* [*Y*oung *M*en's *H*ebrew *A*ssociation] : an organization that promotes the religious, intellectual, social, and physical welfare of Jewish young men

Ymir \ˈē-ˌmi(ə)r\ *n* [ON] : a giant from whose body according to Norse mythology the gods created the world

YOB *abbr* year of birth

yod \ˈyȯd, ˈyu̇d\ *n* [Heb *yōdh*] : the 10th letter of the Hebrew alphabet — see ALPHABET table

1**yo·del** \ˈyōd-ᵊl\ *vb* **yo·deled** *or* **yo·delled; yo·del·ing** *or* **yo·del·ling** \ˈyōd-liŋ, -ᵊl-iŋ\ [G *jodeln*] *vi* : to sing by suddenly changing from a natural voice to a falsetto and back; *also* : to shout or call in a similar manner ~ *vt* : to sing (a tune) by yodeling — **yo·del·er** \ˈyōd-lər, -ᵊl-ər\ *n*

2**yodel** *n* : a song or refrain sung by yodeling; *also* : a yodeled shout or cry

yo·ga \ˈyō-gə\ *n* [Skt, lit., yoking, fr. *yunakti* he yokes; akin to L *jungere* to join — more at YOKE] **1** *cap* : a Hindu theistic philosophy teaching the suppression of all activity of body, mind, and will in order that the self may realize its distinction from them and attain liberation **2 :** a system of exercises for attaining bodily or mental control and well-being — **yo·gic** \-gik\ *adj, often cap*

yogh \ˈyȯk, ˈyōg\ *n* [ME *yogh,* ȝ*ogh*] : a letter ȝ used in Middle English to represent a velar or palatal fricative or \w\ between two vowels the second of which is unstressed

yo·gi \ˈyō-gē\ *or* **yo·gin** \-gən, -ˌgin\ *n* [Skt *yogin,* fr. *yoga*] **1 :** a person who practices yoga **2** *cap* : an adherent of Yoga philosophy **3 :** a markedly reflective or mystical person

yo·gurt *or* **yo·ghurt** \ˈyō-gərt\ *n* [Turk *yoğurt*] : a fermented slightly acid semisolid food made of whole and skimmed cow's milk and milk solids to which cultures of two bacteria (*Lactobacillus bulgaricus* and *Streptococcus thermophilus*) have been added

yo·him·bine \yō-ˈhim-ˌbēn, -bən\ *n* [ISV, fr. *yohimbē* (an African tree)] : an alkaloid $C_{21}H_{26}N_2O_3$ with sympathomimetic and hypotensive effects that has been used as an aphrodisiac

yoicks \ˈyȯiks\ *interj, archaic* — used as a cry of encouragement to foxhounds

1**yoke** \ˈyōk\ *n, pl* **yokes** [ME *yok,* fr. OE *geoc;* akin to OHG *joh* yoke, L *jugum,* Gk *zygon,* L *jungere* to join] **1 a :** a wooden bar or frame by which two draft animals (as oxen) are joined at the heads or necks for working together **b :** an arched device formerly laid upon the neck of a defeated person **c :** a frame fitted to a person's shoulders to carry a load in two equal portions **d :** a bar by which the end of the tongue of a wagon or carriage is suspended from the collars of the harness **e (1) :** a crosspiece on the head of a boat's rudder **(2) :** an airplane lever operating the elevators and the ailerons **f :** a frame from which a bell is hung **g :** a clamp or similar piece that embraces two parts to hold or unite them in position **2** *pl usu* **yoke :** two animals yoked or worked together **3 a (1) :** an oppressive agency **(2) :** SERVITUDE, BONDAGE **b :** TIE, LINK; *esp* : MARRIAGE **4 :** a fitted or shaped piece at the top of a skirt or at the shoulder of various garments

2**yoke** *vb* **yoked; yok·ing** *vt* **1 a (1) :** to put a yoke on **(2) :** to join in or with a yoke **b :** to attach a draft animal to; *also* : to attach (a draft animal) to something **2 :** to join as if by a yoke **3 :** to put to work ~ *vi* : to become joined or linked

yoke·fel·low \ˈyōk-ˌfel-(ˌ)ō, -ə(-w)\ *n* : a close companion : MATE

yo·kel \ˈyō-kəl\ *n* [perh. fr. E dial. *yokel* green woodpecker, of imit. origin] : a naive or gullible inhabitant of a rural area or small town

yolk \ˈyōk, ˈyelk (*as a cultivated pron, esp S*) *also* ˈyōlk, ˈyȯlk, ˈyälk, ˈyəlk\ *also* **yoke** \ˈyōk\ *n* [ME *yolke,* fr. OE *geoloca,* fr. *geolu* yellow — more at YELLOW] **1 a :** the yellow spheroidal mass of stored food that forms the inner portion of the egg of a bird or reptile and is surrounded by the white — see EGG illustration **b** *archaic* : the whole contents of an ovum consisting of a protoplasmic formative portion and an inert nutritive portion **c :** material stored in an ovum that supplies food to the developing embryo and consists chiefly of proteins, lecithin, and cholesterol **2** [akin to MD *ieke* yolk (of wool), OE *ēowu* ewe] : oily material in unprocessed sheep wool consisting of wool fat, suint, and debris — **yolked** *adj* — **yolky** *adj*

yolk sac *n* : a membranous sac that is attached to an embryo and encloses food yolk, that is continuous in most forms through the vitelline duct with the intestinal cavity of the embryo, that being abundantly supplied with blood vessels is throughout embryonic life and in some forms later the chief organ of nutrition, and that in placental mammals is nearly vestigial and functions chiefly prior to the elaboration of the placenta

yolk stalk *n* : the narrow tubular stalk connecting the yolk sac with the embryo

Yom Kip·pur \ˌyȯm-ˈkip-ər, ˌyəm-, ˌyōm-, ˌyäm-, -ki-ˈpu̇(ə)r\ *n* [Heb *yōm kippūr,* fr. *yōm* day + *kippūr* atonement] : a Jewish holiday observed with fasting and prayer on the 10th day of Tishri in accordance with the rites described in Leviticus 16 — called also *Day of Atonement*

[1]**yon** \'yän\ *adj* [ME, fr. OE *geon;* akin to OHG *ienēr,* adj., that, Gk *enē* day after tomorrow] : YONDER

[2]**yon** *pron, dial* : that or those yonder

[3]**yon** *adv* 1 : YONDER 2 : THITHER <ran hither and ~>

[1]**yond** \'yänd\ *adv* [ME, fr. OE *geond;* akin to OE *geon*] *archaic* : YONDER

[2]**yond** *adj, dial* : YONDER

[1]**yon·der** \'yän-dər\ *adv* [ME, fr. *yond* + *-er* (as in *hither*)] : at or in that indicated more or less distant place usu. within sight

[2]**yonder** *adj* 1 : farther removed : more distant 2 : being at a distance within view or at a place or in a direction known or indicated

[3]**yonder** *pron* : something that is or is in an indicated more or less distant place

yo·ni \'yō-nē\ *n* [Skt, vulva] : a stylized representation of the female genitalia symbolizing the feminine principle in Hindu cosmology — compare LINGAM

yoo-hoo \'yü-(,)hü\ *interj* — used to attract attention or as a call to persons

yore \'yō(ə)r, 'yȯ(ə)r\ *n* [ME, fr. *yore,* adv., long ago, fr. OE *geāra,* fr. *gēar* year] : time past and esp. long past — usu. used in the phrase *of yore*

York·ist \'yȯr-kəst\ *adj* [Edward, Duke of *York* (Edward IV of England)] : of or relating to the English royal house that ruled from 1461 to 1485 — **Yorkist** *n*

York rite \'yȯ(ə)rk-\ *n* [*York,* England] 1 : a ceremonial observed by one of the Masonic systems 2 : a system or organization that observes the York rite and confers in the U.S. 13 degrees of which the last three are in commanderies of Knights Templar — compare SCOTTISH RITE

Yorks *abbr* Yorkshire

York·shire \'yȯ(ə)rk-,shi(ə)r, -shər\ *n* : a white swine of any of several breeds or strains originated in Yorkshire, England

Yorkshire pudding *n* [*Yorkshire,* England] : a batter of eggs, flour, and milk baked in meat drippings

Yorkshire terrier *n* : a compact toy terrier with long straight silky hair mostly bluish gray but tan on the head and chest

Yor·u·ba \'yȯr-ə-bə\ *n, pl* **Yoruba** *or* **Yorubas** 1 : a member of a Negro people of the eastern Guinea coast mainly between Dahomey and the lower Niger 2 : the language of the Yorubas

you \(')yü, yə, yē\ *pron* [ME, fr. OE *ēow,* dat. & accus. of *gē* you; akin to OHG *iu,* dat. of *ir* you, Skt *yūyam* you] 1 : the one or ones being addressed — used as the pronoun of the second person singular or plural in any grammatical relation except that of a possessive <~ may sit in that chair> <~ are my friends> <can I pour ~ a cup of tea>; used formerly only as a plural pronoun of the second person in the dative or accusative case as direct or indirect object of a verb or as object of a preposition; compare THEE, THOU, YE, YOUR, YOURS 2 : [2]ONE 2

you-all \(')yü-'ȯl, 'yü-,; 'yȯl\ *pron, chiefly South* : YOU — usu. used in addressing two or more persons or sometimes one person as representing also another or others

you'd \(,)yüd, (,)yu̇d, yəd\ : you had : you would

you'll \(,)yü(ə)l, (,)yu̇l, yəl\ : you will : you shall

[1]**young** \'yəŋ\ *adj* **youn·ger** \'yəŋ-gər\; **youn·gest** \'yəŋ-gəst\ [ME *yong,* fr. OE *geong;* akin to OHG *jung* young, L *juvenis*] 1 a : being in the first or an early stage of life, growth, or development b : JUNIOR 1a c : of an early, tender, or desirable age for use as food <fresh ~ lamb> 2 : having little experience 3 a : recently come into being : NEW b : YOUTHFUL 5 4 : of, relating to, or having the characteristics of youth or a young person 5 *cap* : representing a new or rejuvenated esp. political group or movement — **young·ness** \'yəŋ-nəs\ *n*

[2]**young** *n, pl* **young** 1 *pl* a : young persons : YOUTH b : immature offspring esp. of lower animals 2 : a single recently born or hatched animal — **with young** : PREGNANT — used of a female animal

young·ber·ry \'yəŋ-,ber-ē\ *n* [B. M. *Young fl* 1900 Am fruit grower] : the large sweet reddish black fruit of a hybrid between a trailing blackberry and a southern dewberry grown in western and southern U.S.; *also* : the trailing hybrid bramble

youn·ger \'yəŋ-gər\ *n* : an inferior in age : JUNIOR — usu. used with a possessive pronoun <is several years his ~>

youn·gest \'yəŋ-gəst\ *n, pl* **youngest** : one that is the least old; *esp* : the youngest child or member of a family

young·ish \'yəŋ-ish\ *adj* : somewhat young

young·ling \'yəŋ-liŋ\ *n* : one that is young; *esp* : a young person or animal — **youngling** *adj*

young·ster \'yəŋ(k)-stər\ *n* 1 a : a young person : YOUTH b : CHILD c : a person in the relatively early years of manhood or of a career 2 : a young mammal, bird, or plant esp. of a domesticated or cultivated breed or type

Young Turk *n* [*Young Turks,* a 20th cent. revolutionary party in Turkey] : an insurgent or a member of an insurgent group esp. in a political party : RADICAL

youn·ker \'yəŋ-kər\ *n* [D *jonker* young nobleman] 1 : a young man 2 : CHILD, YOUNGSTER

your \yər, (')yu̇(ə)r, (')yō(ə)r, (')yȯ(ə)r\ *adj* [ME, fr. OE *ēower;* akin to OE *ēow* you — more at YOU] 1 : of or relating to you or yourself or yourselves esp. as possessor or possessors <~ bodies>, agent or agents <~ contributions>, or object or objects of an action <~ discharge> 2 : of or relating to one or oneself <when you face the north, east is at ~ right>

you're \yər, (,)yu̇(ə)r, (,)yō(ə)r, (,)yȯ(ə)r, ,yü-ər\ : you are

yours \'yu̇(ə)rz, 'yō(ə)rz, 'yȯ(ə)rz\ *pron, sing or pl in constr* [ME fr. *your* + *-s* -'s] : that which belongs to you — used without a following noun as a pronoun equivalent in meaning to the adjective *your;* often used esp. with an adverbial modifier in the complimentary close of a letter <~ truly> — **yours truly** : I, ME, MYSELF <I can take care of *yours truly*>

your·self \yər-'self\ *pron* 1 a : that identical one that is you — used reflexively <you might hurt ~>, for emphasis <carry them ~>, or in absolute constructions b : your normal, healthy, or sane condition 2 : ONESELF

your·selves \-'selvz\ *pron pl* 1 : those identical ones that are you — used reflexively <get ~ a treat>, for emphasis, or in absolute constructions 2 : your normal, healthy, or sane condition

youth \'yüth\ *n, pl* **youths** \'yüt͟hz, 'yüths\ [ME *youthe,* fr. OE *geoguth;* akin to OE *geong* young — more at YOUNG] 1 a : the time of life when one is young; *esp* : the period between childhood and maturity b : the early period of existence, growth, or development 2 a : a young person; *esp* : a young male between adolescence and maturity b : young persons or creatures — usu. pl. in constr. 3 : the quality or state of being youthful : YOUTHFULNESS

youth·ful \'yüth-fəl\ *adj* 1 : of, relating to, or characteristic of youth 2 : being young and not yet mature 3 : marked by or possessing youth 4 : having the vitality or freshness of youth : VIGOROUS 5 : having accomplished or undergone little erosion — **youth·ful·ly** \-fə-lē\ *adv* — **youth·ful·ness** *n*

youth hostel *n* : HOSTEL 2

you've \(,)yüv, yəv\ : you have

[1]**yowl** \'yau̇(ə)l\ *vb* [ME *yowlen*] *vi* 1 : to utter a loud long cry of grief, pain, or distress : WAIL 2 : to complain or protest with or as if with yowls ~ *vt* : to express with yowling

[2]**yowl** *n* : a loud long mournful wail or howl (as of a cat)

yo-yo \'yō-(,)yō\ *n, pl* **yo-yos** [native name in Philippines] : a thick grooved double disk with a string attached to its center which is made to fall and rise to the hand by unwinding and rewinding on the string

yr *abbr* 1 year 2 younger 3 your

yrbk *abbr* yearbook

YT *abbr* Yukon Territory

yt·ter·bic \i-'tər-bik, ə-\ *adj* : of, relating to, or containing ytterbium esp. when trivalent

yt·ter·bi·um \-bē-əm\ *n* [NL, fr. *Ytterby,* Sweden] : a bivalent or trivalent metallic element of the rare-earth group that resembles yttrium and occurs with it and related elements in several minerals (as gadolinite) — see ELEMENT table

yt·ter·bous \-bəs\ *adj* : of, relating to, or containing ytterbium when bivalent

yt·tri·um \'i-trē-əm\ *n* [NL, fr. *yttria*] : a trivalent metallic element usu. included among the rare-earth metals which it resembles chemically and with which it occurs in minerals — see ELEMENT table

yu·an \'yü-ən, yü-'än\ *n, pl* **yuan** [Chin (Pek) *yüan*²] — see MONEY table

Yu·ca·tec \'yü-kə-,tek\ *n* [Sp *yucateco,* fr. *Yucatán* peninsula, Mexico] 1 : a member of an American Indian people of the Yucatán peninsula, Mexico 2 : a Mayan language of the Yucatecs — **Yu·ca·tec·an** \,yü-kə-'tek-ən\ *adj or n*

yuc·ca \'yək-ə\ *n* [NL, genus name, fr. Sp *yuca,* of unknown origin] : any of a genus (*Yucca*) of sometimes arborescent plants of the lily family having long often rigid fibrous-margined leaves on a woody base and bearing a large panicle of white blossoms

Yug *abbr* Yugoslavia

yu·ga \'yu̇g-ə, 'yüg-\ *n* [Skt, yoke, age; akin to L *jugum* yoke — more at YOKE] : one of the four ages of a Hindu world cycle

Yu·kon time \'yü-,kän-\ *n* : the time of the 9th time zone west of Greenwich that includes the Yukon Territory and part of southern Alaska — called also *Yukon standard time*

yule \'yü(ə)l\ *n, often cap* [ME *yol,* fr. OE *geōl;* akin to ON *jōl* yule] : the feast of the nativity of Jesus Christ : CHRISTMAS

Yule log *n* : a large log formerly put on the hearth on Christmas Eve as the foundation of the fire

yule·tide \'yü(ə)l-,tīd\ *n, often cap* : CHRISTMASTIDE

Yu·man \'yü-mən\ *n* : an Amerindian language family of southwestern U.S. and northern Mexico — **Yuman** *adj*

yum·my \'yəm-ē\ *adj* **yum·mi·er; -est** [*yum-yum*] : highly attractive or pleasing : DELECTABLE, DELICIOUS

yum-yum \'yəm-'yəm\ *interj* [imit. of the sound of smacking the lips] — used to express pleasurable satisfaction esp. in the taste of food

yup \'yəp\ *var of* YEP

Yu·rak \yu̇-'rak, 'yu(ə)r-,ak\ *n* : a Uralic language of northern Russia & Siberia

yurt \'yu̇(ə)rt\ *n* [Russ *yurta,* of Turkic origin; akin to Turk *yurt* dwelling] : a circular domed tent of skins or felt stretched over a collapsible lattice framework and used by the Kirghiz and other Mongol nomads of Siberia

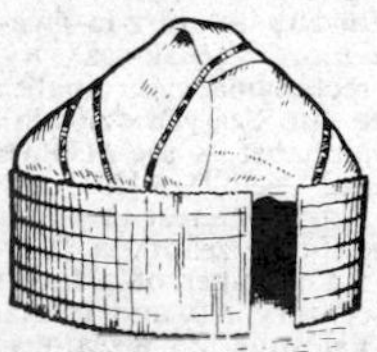
yurt

YWCA \,wī-,dəb-əl-yü-(,)sē-'ā, -,dəb-ə-yü-\ *n* [*Y*oung *W*omen's *C*hristian *A*ssociation] : an international organization that promotes the spiritual, intellectual, social, and physical welfare of young women

YWHA \-ā-'chā\ *n* [*Y*oung *W*omen's *H*ebrew *A*ssociation] : an organization that promotes the religious, intellectual, social, and physical welfare of Jewish young women

ə abut ᵊ kitten ər further a back ā bake ä cot, cart
au̇ out ch chin e less ē easy g gift i trip ī life
j joke ŋ sing ō flow ȯ flaw ȯi coin th thin t͟h this
ü loot u̇ foot y yet yü few yu̇ furious zh vision

1z \ˈzē, *Canad, Brit, & Austral* ˈzed, *chiefly dial* ˈiz-ərd\ *n, pl* **z's** *or* **zs** *often cap, often attrib* **1 a :** the 26th and last letter of the English alphabet **b :** a graphic representation of this letter **c :** a speech counterpart of orthographic *z* **2 :** a graphic device for reproducing the letter *z* **3 :** one designated *z* esp. as the 26th in order or class or the third in order or class when x is made the first **4 :** something shaped like the letter Z

2z *abbr* **1** zero **2** zone

Z *symbol* **1** atomic number **2** impedance **3** zenith distance

za·ba·glio·ne \ˌzäb-əl-ˈyō-nē\ *n* [It] **:** a mixture of eggs, sugar, and wine or fruit juice beaten over hot water until thick and light and served warm or cold

Zach *abbr* Zacharias

Zach·a·ri·as \ˌzak-ə-ˈrī-əs\ *n* [LL, fr. Gk, fr. Heb *Zĕkharyāh*] **:** ZECHARIAH

zad·dik \ˈtsäd-ik\ *n, pl* **zad·dik·im** \tsä-ˈdik-əm\ [Heb *ṣaddīq* just, righteous] **1 :** a righteous and saintly person by Jewish religious standards **2 :** the spiritual leader of a modern Hasidic community

zaf·fer *or* **zaf·fre** \ˈzaf-ər\ *n* [It *zaffera*] **:** an impure oxide of cobalt used in the manufacture of smalt and as a blue ceramic coloring

1zag \ˈzag\ *n* [zig*zag*] **1 a :** one of the sharp turns, angles, or alterations in a zigzag course **b :** one of the short straight lines or sections of a zigzag course at an angle to a zig **2 :** ZIG 2

2zag *vi* **zagged; zag·ging :** to execute a zag

zaire \ˈzī(ə)r, zä-ˈi(ə)r\ *n, pl* **zaire** [F *zaïre,* fr. *Zaïre,* former name of Congo river] — see MONEY table

za·mia \ˈzā-mē-ə\ *n* [NL, genus name, fr. L *zamiae nuces* false MS reading for *azaniae nuces* pine nuts] **:** any of a genus (*Zamia*) of American cycads with a short thick woody base, a crown of palmlike leaves, and oblong cones

za·min·dar *or* **ze·min·dar** \ˈzam-ən-ˌdär, ˈzem-; zə-ˌmēn-ˈdär\ *n* [Hindi *zamīndār,* fr. Per, fr. *zamīn* land + *-dār* holder] **1 :** a collector of the land revenue of a district for the government during the period of Muslim rule in India **2 :** a feudal landlord in British India paying the government a fixed revenue

za·min·dari *or* **ze·min·dary** \ˌzam-ən-ˈdär-ē, ˌzem-; zə-ˌmēn-\ *n, pl* **-dar·is** *or* **-dar·ies** [Hindi *zamīndārī,* fr. Per, fr. *zamīndār*] **1 :** the system of landholding and revenue collection by zamindars **2 :** the land held or administered by a zamindar

zan·der \ˈzan-dər, ˈtsän-\ *n, pl* **zander** *or* **zanders** [G] **:** a pike perch (*Lucioperca sandra*) of central Europe related to the walleyed pike

1za·ny \ˈzā-nē\ *n, pl* **zanies** [It *zanni,* a traditional masked clown, fr. It (dial.) *Zanni,* nickname for *Giovanni* John] **1 :** a subordinate clown or acrobat in old comedies who mimics ludicrously the tricks of his principal **:** MERRY-ANDREW **2 :** a slavish follower **:** TOADY **3 :** one who acts the buffoon to amuse others **4 :** SIMPLETON

2zany *adj* **za·ni·er; -est 1 :** being or having the characteristics of a zany **2 :** fantastically or absurdly ludicrous — **za·ni·ly** \ˈzā-nə-lē, ˈzān-ᵊl-ē\ *adv* — **za·ni·ness** \ˈzā-nē-nəs\ *n*

zan·za \ˈzan-zə\ *n* [Ar *ṣanj* castanets, cymbals, fr. Per *sanj*] **:** an African musical instrument that consists of a wooden box set with a graduated series of wooden or metal tongues which are plucked with the fingers or thumbs

1zap \ˈzap\ *interj* [imit.] — used to indicate a sudden or instantaneous occurrence

2zap *n* **:** ZIP 2

3zap *vb* **zapped; zap·ping** *vt* **1 a :** DESTROY, KILL **b :** OVERWHELM, OVERCOME **2 :** to impart speed or force to **:** ZIP ~ *vi* **:** to move with speed or force

za·pa·te·ado \ˌzäp-ə-tā-ˈäd-(ˌ)ō, ˌsäp-ə-tā-ˈaù\ *n* [Sp, fr. *zapatear* to strike or tap with the shoe, fr. *zapato* shoe] **:** a Latin American dance marked by rhythmic stamping or tapping of the feet

za·pa·teo \ˌzäp-ə-ˈtā-(ˌ)ō, ˌsäp-\ *n* [Sp, fr. *zapatear*] **:** ZAPATEADO

Za·po·tec \ˌzäp-ə-ˈtek, ˌsäp-\ *n* **:** a member of an Indian people of Mexico

za·re·ba *or* **za·ri·ba** \zə-ˈrē-bə\ *n* [Ar *zarībah* enclosure] **:** an improvised stockade constructed esp. of thorny bushes in parts of Africa

zar·zue·la \ˌzärz-(ə-)ˈwā-lə\ *n* [Sp] **:** a usu. comic Spanish operetta

z–ax·is \ˈzē-ˌak-səs\ *n* **:** one of the axes in a three-dimensional rectangular coordinate system

za·yin \ˈzä-yən, ˈzī(-ə)n\ *n* [Heb] **:** the 7th letter of the Hebrew alphabet — see ALPHABET table

zeal \ˈzē(ə)l\ *n* [ME *zele,* fr. LL *zelus,* fr. Gk *zēlos*] **:** eagerness and ardent interest in pursuit of something **:** FERVOR *syn* see PASSION

zeal·ot \ˈzel-ət\ *n* [LL *zelotes,* fr. Gk *zēlōtēs,* fr. *zēlos*] **1** *cap* **:** a member of a fanatical sect arising in Judea during the first century A.D. and militantly opposing the Roman domination of Palestine **2 :** a zealous person; *esp* **:** a fanatical partisan — **zealot** *adj*

zeal·ot·ry \ˈzel-ə-trē\ *n, pl* **-ries :** excess of zeal **:** fanatical devotion

zeal·ous \ˈzel-əs\ *adj* **:** filled with or characterized by zeal <~ missionaries> — **zeal·ous·ly** *adv* — **zeal·ous·ness** *n*

ze·atin \ˈzē-ə-tən\ *n* [NL *Zea,* genus of grasses including Indian corn + *-tin* (as in *kinetin*) — more at ZEIN] **:** a cytokinin first isolated from the endosperm of Indian corn

ze·bra \ˈzē-brə, *Canad & Brit also* ˈzeb-\ *n, pl* **zebras** *also* **zebra** [It, fr. Sp *cebra*] **:** any of several fleet African mammals (genus *Equus*) related to the horse but distinctively and conspicuously patterned in stripes of black or dark brown and white or buff — **ze·brine** \-ˌrīn\ *adj* — **ze·broid** \-ˌròid\ *adj*

zebra crossing *n, Brit* **:** a crosswalk marked by a series of broad white stripes to indicate a crossing-point at which pedestrians have the right of way

zebra finch *n* **:** a small largely gray-and-white Australian weaverbird (*Poephila castanotis*) that has black bars on the tail coverts and is often kept as a cage bird

zebra fish *n* **:** any of various barred fishes; *esp* **:** a very small blue-and-silver-striped Indian danio (*Brachydanio rerio*) often kept in the tropical aquarium — called also *zebra danio*

ze·bra·wood \ˈzē-brə-ˌwùd, ˈzeb-\ *n* **1 :** any of several trees or shrubs having mottled or striped wood; *esp* **:** a tropical tree (*Connarus guianensis* of the family Connaraceae) with strikingly marked hard wood used in cabinetwork **2 :** the wood of a zebrawood

ze·bu \ˈzē-(ˌ)b(y)ü\ *n* [F *zébu*] **:** an Asiatic ox (*Bos indicus*) domesticated and differentiated into many breeds, used chiefly for draft or for milk or flesh, and distinguished from European cattle with which it crosses freely by the presence of a large fleshy hump over the shoulders, a loose skin prolonged into dewlap and folds under the belly, large pendulous ears, and marked resistance to the injurious effects of heat and insect attack

zebu

Zeb·u·lun \ˈzeb-yə-lən\ *n* [Heb *Zĕbhūlūn*] **:** a son of Jacob and the traditional eponymous ancestor of one of the tribes of Israel

zec·chi·no \ze-ˈkē-(ˌ)nō, tse-\ *n, pl* **-ni** \-(ˌ)nē\ *or* **-nos** [It] **:** SEQUIN 1

Zech *abbr* Zechariah

Zech·a·ri·ah \ˌzek-ə-ˈrī-ə\ *n* [Heb *Zĕkharyāh*] **1 :** a Hebrew prophet of the 6th century B.C. **2 :** a prophetic book of canonical Jewish and Christian Scripture — see BIBLE table

ze·chin \ˈzek-ən, ze-ˈkēn\ *n* [It *zecchino*] **:** SEQUIN 1

zed \ˈzed\ *n* [ME, fr. MF *zede,* fr. LL *zeta* zeta, fr. Gk *zēta*] *chiefly Brit* **:** the letter *z*

zee \ˈzē\ *n* **:** the letter *z*

ze·in \ˈzē-ən\ *n* [NL *Zea,* genus of grasses including Indian corn, fr. Gk, wheat; akin to Skt *yava* barley] **:** a protein from Indian corn that lacks lysine and tryptophan and is used esp. in making textile fibers, plastics, printing inks, coatings (as varnish), and adhesives and sizes

zeit·geist \ˈtsīt-ˌgīst, ˈzīt-\ *n* [G, fr. *zeit* time + *geist* spirit] **:** the general intellectual, moral, and cultural climate of an era

zel·ko·va \ˈzel-kə-və, zel-ˈkō-və\ *n* [NL, genus name, fr. Georgian *tselkva*] **:** a tall widely spreading Japanese tree (*Zelkova serrata*) resembling the American elm and often replacing the latter as an ornamental and shade tree because of its resistance to Dutch elm disease

zemst·vo \ˈzem(p)st-(ˌ)vō, -və\ *n, pl* **zemstvos** [Russ; akin to Russ *zemlya* earth, land, L *humus* — more at HUMBLE] **:** one of the district and provincial assemblies established in Russia in 1864

Zen \ˈzen\ *n* [Jap, religious meditation, fr. Chin (Pek) *ch'an*2, fr. Pali *jhāna,* fr. Skt *dhyāna,* fr. *dhyāti* he thinks — more at SEMANTIC] **:** a Japanese sect of Mahayana Buddhism that aims at enlightenment by direct intuition through meditation

ze·na·na \zə-ˈnän-ə\ *n* [Hindi *zanāna*] **:** HAREM, SERAGLIO

Zend–Aves·ta \ˌzen-də-ˈves-tə\ *n* [F, fr. MPer *Avastāk va Zand* Avesta and commentary] **:** AVESTA

ze·ner diode \ˌzē-nər-, ˌzen-ər-\ *n, often cap Z* [origin unknown] **:** a silicon semiconductor device used esp. as a voltage regulator

ze·nith \ˈzē-nəth, *Canad also & Brit usu* ˈzen-əth, -ith\ *n* [ME *senith,* fr. MF *cenith,* fr. ML, fr. OSp *zenit,* modif. of Ar *samt* (*ar-ra's*) way (of the head)] **1 :** the point of the celestial sphere that is directly opposite the nadir and vertically above the observer **2 :** the highest point reached in the heavens by a celestial body **3 :** culminating point **:** ACME <at the ~ of his powers —John Buchan>

ze·nith·al \-əl\ *adj* **1 :** of, relating to, or located at or near the zenith **2 :** showing correct directions from the center <a ~ map>

ze·o·lite \ˈzē-ə-ˌlīt\ *n* [Sw *zeolit,* fr. Gk *zein* to boil + *-o-* + Sw *-lit* -lite, fr. F *-lite* — more at YEAST] **:** any of various hydrous silicates that are analogous in composition to the feldspars, occur as secondary minerals in cavities of lavas, and can act as ion-exchangers; *also* **:** any of various natural or synthesized silicates of similar structure used in water softening and as adsorbents — **ze·o·lit·ic** \ˌzē-ə-ˈlit-ik\ *adj*

Zeph *abbr* Zephaniah

Zeph·a·ni·ah \ˌzef-ə-ˈnī-ə\ *n* [Heb *Ṣĕphanyāh*] **1 :** a Hebrew prophet of the 7th century B.C. **2 :** an apocalyptic book of canonical Jewish and Christian Scripture — see BIBLE table

zeph·yr \ˈzef-ər\ *n* [ME *Zephirus,* west wind (personified), fr. L *Zephyrus,* god of the west wind, & *zephyrus* west wind, zephyr, fr. Gk *Zephyros,* god of the west wind, & *zephyros* west wind, zephyr] **1 a :** a breeze from the west **b :** a gentle breeze **2 :** any of various lightweight fabrics and articles of clothing

Zeph·y·rus \ˈzef-ə-rəs\ *n* [L] **:** the west wind personified

zep·pe·lin \ˈzep-(ə-)lən\ *n* [Count Ferdinand von *Zeppelin*] **:** a rigid airship consisting of a cylindrical trussed and covered frame supported by internal gas cells; *broadly* **:** AIRSHIP

1ze·ro \ˈzē-(ˌ)rō, ˈzi(ə)r-(ˌ)ō\ *n, pl* **zeros** *also* **zeroes** [F or It; F *zéro,* fr. It *zero,* fr. ML *zephirum,* fr. Ar *ṣifr*] **1 a :** the arithmetical symbol 0 or Ø denoting the absence of all magnitude or quantity **b :** ADDITIVE IDENTITY; *specif* **:** the number between the set of all negative numbers and the set of all positive numbers **c :** a value of the independent variable of a function that makes it equal to zero **2** — see NUMBER table **3 a (1) :** the point of departure in reckoning; *specif* **:** the point from which the graduation of a scale (as of a thermometer) begins **(2) :** the temperature represented by the zero mark on a thermometer **b :** the setting or adjustment of the rear sight of a firearm that causes it to shoot accurately **4 :** an insignificant person or thing **:** NONENTITY **5 a :** a state of total absence or neutrality **b :** the lowest point **:** NADIR **6 :** something arbitrarily or conveniently designated zero

[2]**zero** *adj* **1 a :** of, relating to, or being a zero **b :** having no magnitude or quantity <~ growth> **c (1) :** ABSENT, LACKING <the ~ modification in the past of *cut*> **(2) :** having no modified inflectional form <a ~ plural> **2 a** *of a cloud ceiling* **:** limiting vision to 50 feet or less **b** *of horizontal visibility* **:** limited to 165 feet or less

[3]**zero** *vt* **1 :** to determine or adjust the zero of (as a rifle) **2 a :** to concentrate firepower on the exact range of — usu. used with *in* **b :** to bring to bear on the exact range of a target — usu. used with *in* ~ *vi* **1 :** to adjust fire (as of artillery) on a specific target — usu. used with *in* **2 :** to move near to or focus attention as if on a target **:** CLOSE — usu. used with *in*

zero hour *n* [fr. its being marked by the count of zero in a countdown] **1 a :** the hour at which a planned military operation is scheduled to start **b :** the time at which a usu. significant or notable event is scheduled to take place **2 :** a time when a vital decision or decisive change must be made

zero–sum *adj* **:** of, relating to, or being a situation (as a game or relationship) in which a gain for one side entails a corresponding loss for the other side

zero–zero *adj* **1 :** characterized by or being atmospheric conditions that reduce ceiling and visibility to zero **2 :** limited to zero by atmospheric conditions

zest \'zest\ *n* [obs. F (now *zeste*), orange or lemon peel (used as flavoring)] **1 :** a quality of enhancing enjoyment **:** PIQUANCY **2 :** keen enjoyment **:** RELISH ***syn*** see TASTE — **zest·ful** \-fəl\ *adj* — **zest·ful·ly** \-fə-lē\ *adv* — **zest·ful·ness** *n*

zesty \'zes-tē\ *adj* **zest·i·er; -est :** having or characterized by zest **:** PIQUANT

ze·ta \'zāt-ə, 'zēt-\ *n* [Gk *zēta*] **:** the 6th letter of the Greek alphabet — see ALPHABET table

zeug·ma \'züg-mə\ *n* [L, fr. Gk, lit., joining, fr. *zeugnynai* to join; akin to L *jungere* to join — more at YOKE] **:** the use of a word to modify or govern two or more words usu. in such a manner that it applies to each in a different sense or makes sense with only one <"opened the door and her heart to the homeless boy" is an example of ~>

Zeus \'züs\ *n* [Gk] **:** the Greek god who is king of gods and men and husband of Hera — compare JUPITER

ZI *abbr* zone of interior

zib·e·line *or* **zib·el·line** \'zib-ə-,lēn, -,līn\ *n* [MF, sable, fr. OIt *zibellino*, of Slav origin; akin to Russ *sobol'* sable] **:** a soft lustrous wool fabric with mohair, alpaca, or camel's hair

[1]**zig** \'zig\ *n* [*zigzag*] **1 a :** one of the sharp turns, angles, or alterations in a zigzag course **b :** one of the short straight lines or sections of a zigzag course at an angle to a zag **2 :** a sharp alteration or change of direction (as in a process or policy) <the quick ~*s* and zags of his international maneuverings —*N.Y. Times*>

[2]**zig** *vi* **zigged; zig·ging :** to execute a zig

zig·gu·rat \'zig-ə-,rat\ *n* [Akkadian *ziqqurratu* pinnacle] **:** an ancient Mesopotamian temple tower consisting of a lofty pyramidal structure built in successive stages with outside staircases and a shrine at the top

[1]**zig·zag** \'zig-,zag\ *n* [F] **:** one of a series of short sharp turns, angles, or alterations in a course; *also* **:** something having the form or character of such a series <a blue necktie with cherry red ~*s* —Lawrence Williams>

[2]**zigzag** *adv* **:** in or by a zigzag path or course

[3]**zigzag** *adj* **:** having short sharp turns or angles <a ~ trail>

[4]**zigzag** *vb* **zig·zagged; zig·zag·ging** *vt* **:** to form into a zigzag ~ *vi* **:** to lie in, proceed along, or consist of a zigzag course

zilch \'zilch\ *adj or n* [by alter.] **:** ZERO

zil·lion \'zil-yən\ *n* [*z* + *-illion* (as in *million*)] **:** an indeterminately large number <~*s* of mosquitoes>

[1]**zinc** \'ziŋk\ *n, often attrib* [G *zink*] **:** a bluish white crystalline bivalent metallic element of low to intermediate hardness that is ductile when pure but in the commercial form is brittle at ordinary temperatures and becomes ductile on slight heating, occurs abundantly in minerals, is an essential micronutrient for both plants and animals, and is used esp. as a protective coating for iron and steel — see ELEMENT table — **zinc·ic** \'ziŋ-kik\ *adj* — **zin·cous** \-kəs\ *adj*

[2]**zinc** *vt* **zinced** *or* **zincked** \'ziŋ(k)t\; **zinc·ing** *or* **zinck·ing** \'ziŋ-kiŋ\ **:** to treat or coat with zinc **:** GALVANIZE

zinc·ate \'ziŋ-,kāt\ *n* **:** a compound formed by reaction of zinc oxide or zinc with solutions of alkalies

zinc blende *n* **:** SPHALERITE

zinc chloride *n* **:** a poisonous caustic deliquescent salt $ZnCl_2$ used esp. as a wood preservative, drying agent, and catalyst

zinc·ite \'ziŋ-,kīt\ *n* [G *zinkit*, fr. *zink*] **:** a brittle deep-red to orange-yellow hexagonal mineral that consists essentially of zinc oxide and occurs massive or in granular form

zincky *or* **zinky** *or* **zincy** \'ziŋ-kē\ *adj* **:** containing or having the appearance of zinc

zinc ointment *n* **:** an ointment that contains about 20 percent of zinc oxide and is used in treating skin disorders

zinc oxide *n* **:** an infusible white solid ZnO used esp. as a pigment, in compounding rubber, and in pharmaceutical and cosmetic preparations

zinc sulfide *n* **:** a fluorescent white to yellowish compound ZnS used esp. as a white pigment and a phosphor

zinc white *n* **:** a white pigment that consists of zinc oxide

zin·fan·del \'zin-fən-,del\ *n* [origin unknown] **:** a red table wine of the claret type made from a small black grape that is grown chiefly in California

[1]**zing** \'ziŋ\ *n* [imit.] **1 :** a shrill humming noise **2 :** ENERGY, VIM

[2]**zing** *vi* **:** to make or move with a humming sound <bees ~*ed* by>

zingy \'ziŋ-ē\ *adj* **zing·i·er; -est** [[1]*zing*] **1 :** enjoyably exciting <a ~ musical> **2 :** strikingly attractive or appealing <wore a ~ new outfit>

zinj·an·thro·pus \zin-'jan(t)-thrə-pəs, ,zin-,jan-'thrō-\ *n, pl* **-pi** \-,pī, -,pē\ *or* **-pus·es** [NL, genus name, fr. Ar *Zinj* eastern Africa + Gk *anthrōpos* human being] **:** a fossil hominid (*Australopithecus*, syn. *Zinjanthropus, boisei*) based on skeletal remains from the Late Pliocene or Early Pleistocene of eastern Africa and characterized by very low brow and large molars — **zin·jan·thro·pine** \zin-'jan(t)-thrə-,pīn\ *adj or n*

zin·ken·ite \'ziŋ-kə-,nīt\ *n* [G *zinkenit*, fr. J. K. L. *Zinken* †1862 G mineralogist] **:** a steel-gray mineral $Pb_6Sb_{14}S_{27}$ of metallic luster consisting of a lead antimony sulfide

zin·nia \'zin-ē-ə, 'zin-yə, 'zēn-\ *n* [NL, genus name, fr. Johann G. *Zinn* †1759 G botanist] **:** any of a small genus (*Zinnia*) of tropical American composite herbs and low shrubs with showy flower heads and long-lasting ray flowers

Zi·on \'zī-ən\ *n* [*Zion*, citadel in Palestine which was the nucleus of Jerusalem, fr. ME *Sion*, fr. OE, fr. LL, fr. Heb *Ṣiyōn*] **1 a :** the Jewish people **:** ISRAEL **b :** the Jewish homeland that is symbolic of Judaism or of Jewish national aspiration **c :** the ideal nation or society envisaged by Judaism **2 :** HEAVEN **3 :** UTOPIA

Zi·on·ism \'zī-ə-,niz-əm\ *n* **:** a theory, plan, or movement for setting up a Jewish national or religious community in Palestine — **Zi·on·ist** \-nəst\ *adj or n* — **Zi·on·is·tic** \,zī-ə-'nis-tik\ *adj*

[1]**zip** \'zip\ *vb* **zipped; zip·ping** [imit. of the sound of a speeding object] *vi* **1 :** to move or act with speed and vigor **2 :** to travel with a sharp hissing or humming sound ~ *vt* **1 :** to impart speed or force to **2 :** to add zest, interest, or life to — often used with *up* **3 :** to transport with speed

[2]**zip** *n* **1 :** a sudden sharp hissing or sibilant sound **2 :** ENERGY, VIM

[3]**zip** *n, chiefly Brit* **:** ZIPPER

[4]**zip** *vb* **zipped; zip·ping** [back-formation fr. *zipper*] *vt* **1 :** to close or open with or as if with a zipper **2 :** to cause (a zipper) to open or shut ~ *vi* **:** to become open, closed, or attached by means of a zipper

[5]**zip** *n, often cap Z&I&P* **:** ZIP CODE

zip–code *vt* **:** to furnish with a zip code

zip code *n, often cap Z&I&P* [*z*one *i*mprovement *p*lan] **:** a 5-digit number that identifies each postal delivery area in the U.S.

zip fastener *n, chiefly Brit* **:** ZIPPER

zip gun *n* **:** a gun that is made from a toy pistol or length of pipe, has a firing pin usu. powered by a rubber band, and fires a .22 caliber bullet

zip·per \'zip-ər\ *n* [fr. *Zipper*, a trademark] **:** a fastener consisting of two rows of metal or plastic teeth or spirals on strips of tape and a sliding piece that closes an opening by drawing the teeth or spirals together

zip·pered \-ərd\ *adj* **:** equipped with a zipper

zip·py \'zip-ē\ *adj* **zip·pi·er; -est :** full of zip **:** BRISK, SNAPPY

zi·ram \'zī-,ram\ *n* [*zinc* + *-ram* (as in *thiram*)] **:** an organic zinc salt $C_6H_{12}N_2S_4Zn$ used as a rubber accelerator and agricultural fungicide

zir·con \'zər-,kän, -kən\ *n* [G, modif. of F *jargon* jargoon, zircon, fr. It *giargone*] **:** a tetragonal mineral $ZrSiO_4$ consisting of a zirconium silicate and occurring usu. in brown or grayish square prisms of adamantine luster or sometimes in transparent forms which are used as gems

zir·co·nia \,zər-'kō-nē-ə\ *n* [NL, fr. ISV *zircon*] **:** ZIRCONIUM OXIDE

zir·con·ic \,zər-'kän-ik\ *adj* **:** of, relating to, or containing zirconium

zir·co·ni·um \,zər-'kō-nē-əm\ *n* [NL, fr. ISV *zircon*] **:** a steel-gray strong ductile chiefly tetravalent metallic element with a high melting point that occurs widely in combined form (as in zircon), is highly resistant to corrosion, and is used esp. in alloys and in refractories and ceramics — see ELEMENT table

zirconium oxide *n* **:** a white crystalline compound ZrO_2 used esp. in refractories, in thermal and electric insulation, in abrasives, and in enamels and glazes — called also *zirconia*

zith·er \'zit͟h-ər, 'zith-\ *n* [G, fr. L *cithara* lyre, fr. Gk *kithara*] **:** a stringed instrument having usu. 30 to 40 strings over a shallow horizontal soundboard and played with pick and fingers — **zith·er·ist** \-ə-rəst\ *n*

zi·zith \'tsit-səs, tsēt-'sēt\ *n pl* [Heb *ṣīṣith*] **:** the fringes or tassels worn on traditional or ceremonial garments by Jewish males as reminders of the commandments of Deut 22:12 and Num 15:37–41

zither

Zl *abbr* zloty

zlo·ty \'zlȯt-ē, zə-'lȯt-\ *n, pl* **zlo·tys** \-ēz\ *also* **zloty** [Pol *złoty*] — see MONEY table

Zn *symbol* **1** [*a*zimuth + *n*orth] azimuth **2** zinc

zo- *or* **zoo-** *comb form* [Gk *zōi-, zōio-*, fr. *zōion*; akin to Gk *zōē* life — more at QUICK] **1 :** animal **:** animal kingdom or kind <zooid> <zoology> **2** [Gk *zō-* alive, fr. *zōos*; akin to Gk *zōē*] **:** motile <zoospore>

-zoa \'zō-ə\ *n pl comb form* [NL, fr. Gk *zōia*, pl. of *zōion*] **:** animals — in taxa <Meta*zoa*>

zo·an·thar·i·an \,zō-ən-'ther-ē-ən, -'thar-\ *n* [deriv. of *zo-* + Gk *anthos* flower — more at ANTHOLOGY] **:** any of a subclass (Zoantharia) of anthozoans having a hexamerous arrangement of tentacles or septa or both and including most of the recent corals and sea anemones — **zoantharian** *adj*

zo·ar·i·um \zō-'ar-ē-əm, -'er-\ *n, pl* **-ia** \-ē-ə\ [NL] **:** a colony of colonial bryozoans — **zo·ar·i·al** \-ē-əl\ *adj*

zo·di·ac \'zōd-ē-,ak\ *n* [ME, fr. MF *zodiaque*, fr. L *zodiacus*, fr. Gk *zōidiakos*, fr. *zōidiakos*, adj., of carved figures, of the zodiac, fr. *zōidion* carved figure, sign of the zodiac, fr. dim. of *zōion* living being, figure; akin to Gk *zōē* life — more at QUICK] **1 a :** an imaginary belt in the heavens usu. 18 degrees wide that encompasses the apparent paths of all the principal planets except Pluto, has the ecliptic as its central line, and is divided into 12 constellations or signs each taken for astrological purposes to extend 30 degrees of longitude **b :** a figure representing the signs of the zodiac and their symbols **2 :** a cyclic course <a ~ of feasts and fasts —R. W. Emerson> — **zo·di·a·cal** \zō-ˈdī-ə-kəl, zə-\ *adj*

SIGNS OF THE ZODIAC

NUMBER	NAME	SYMBOL	SUN ENTERS
1	Aries the Ram	♈	March 21
2	Taurus the Bull	♉	April 20
3	Gemini the Twins	♊	May 21
4	Cancer the Crab	♋	June 22
5	Leo the Lion	♌	July 23
6	Virgo the Virgin	♍	August 23
7	Libra the Balance	♎	September 23
8	Scorpio the Scorpion	♏	October 24
9	Sagittarius the Archer	♐	November 22
10	Capricorn the Goat	♑	December 22
11	Aquarius the Water Bearer	♒	January 20
12	Pisces the Fishes	♓	February 19

zodiacal light *n* **:** a diffuse glow seen in the west after twilight and in the east before dawn

zo·ea \zō-ˈē-ə\ *n, pl* **zo·eae** \-ˈē-ˌē\ *or* **zo·eas** \-ˈē-əz\ [NL, fr. Gk *zōē* life] **:** an early larval form of many decapod crustaceans and esp. crabs with a relatively large cephalothorax, conspicuous eyes, and large fringed antennae and mouthparts used for swimming — **zo·e·al** \zō-ˈē-əl\ *adj*

¹-zo·ic \ˈzō-ik\ *adj comb form* [Gk *zōikos* of animals, fr. *zōion* animal — more at ZO-] **:** having a (specified) animal mode of existence <holo*zoic*> <endo*zoic*> <sapro*zoic*>

²-zoic *adj comb form* [Gk *zōē* life] **:** of, relating to, or being a (specified) geological era <Archeo*zoic*> <Meso*zoic*>

zois·ite \ˈzȯi-ˌsīt\ *n* [G *zoisit*, fr. Baron Sigismund *Zois* von Edelstein †1819 Slovenian nobleman] **:** an orthorhombic mineral $Ca_2Al_3Si_3O_{12}OH$ that consists of a basic calcium aluminum silicate and is related to epidote

zom·bie *also* **zom·bi** \ˈzäm-bē\ *n* [of Niger-Congo origin; akin to Kongo *nzambi* god] **1** *usu zombi* **a :** the voodoo snake deity **b :** the supernatural power that according to voodoo belief may enter into and reanimate a dead body **c :** a will-less and speechless human in the West Indies capable only of automatic movement who is held to have died and been reanimated but often believed to have been drugged into a catalepsy for the hours of interment **2 a :** a person held to resemble the so-called walking dead; *esp* **:** AUTOMATON **b :** a person markedly strange in appearance or behavior **3 :** a mixed drink made of several kinds of rum, liqueur, and fruit juice — **zom·bie·like** \-bē-ˌlīk\ *adj*

zom·bi·ism \-bē-ˌiz-əm\ *n* **:** the beliefs and practices of the cult of the zombi

zon·al \ˈzōn-ᵊl\ *adj* **1 :** of, relating to, affecting, or having the form of a zone <a ~ boundary> **2 :** of, relating to, or being a soil or a major soil group marked by well-developed characteristics that are determined primarily by the action of climate and organisms esp. vegetation — compare AZONAL, INTRAZONAL — **zon·al·ly** \-ᵊl-ē\ *adv*

zon·ate \ˈzō-ˌnāt\ *also* **zon·at·ed** \-ˌnāt-əd\ *adj* **:** marked with or arranged in zones

zo·na·tion \zō-ˈnā-shən\ *n* **1 :** zonate structure or arrangement **2 :** distribution of kinds of organisms in biogeographic zones

¹zone \ˈzōn\ *n* [L *zona* belt, zone, fr. Gk *zōnē*; akin to Lith *juosti* to gird] **1 a :** any of five great divisions of the earth's surface with respect to latitude and temperature — compare FRIGID ZONE, TEMPERATE ZONE, TORRID ZONE **b :** a portion of the surface of a sphere included between two parallel planes **2** *archaic* **:** GIRDLE, BELT **3 a :** an encircling anatomical structure **b** (1) **:** a subdivision of a biogeographic region that supports a similar fauna and flora throughout its extent (2) **:** such a zone dominated by a particular life form **c :** a distinctive belt, layer, or series of layers of earth materials (as rock) **4 :** a region or area set off as distinct from surrounding or adjoining parts **5 :** one of the sections of an area or territory created for a particular purpose: as **a :** a zoned section of a city **b :** any of the eight concentric bands of territory centered on a given postal shipment point designated as a distance bracket for U.S. parcel post to which mail is charged at a single rate — called also *parcel post zone* **c :** a distance within which the same fare is charged by a common carrier **d :** an area on a field of play **e :** a stretch of roadway or a space in which certain traffic regulations are in force

²zone *vt* **zoned; zon·ing 1 :** to surround with a zone **:** ENCIRCLE **2 :** to arrange in or mark off into zones; *specif* **:** to partition (a city, borough, or township) by ordinance into sections reserved for different purposes (as residence, business, or manufacturing) — **zon·er** *n*

³zone *adj* **1 :** ZONAL 1 **2 :** of, relating to, or being a system of defense (as in basketball or football) in which each player guards an assigned area rather than a specified opponent

zone melting *n* **:** a technique for the purification of a crystalline material and esp. a metal in which a molten region travels through the material to be refined, picks up impurities at its advancing edge, and then allows the purified part to recrystallize at its opposite edge

zone refine *vt* **:** to produce or refine by zone melting

zonked \ˈzäŋ(k)t\ *adj* [origin unknown]**:** being under the influence of alcohol or a drug (as LSD) **:** HIGH

Zon·ti·an \ˈzänt-ē-ən\ *n* [*Zonta International*] **:** a member of a service club made up of executive women each of whom is a sole representative of one business or profession in a community

zoo \ˈzü\ *n, pl* **zoos** [short for *zoological garden*] **:** a zoological garden or collection of living animals usu. for public display

zoo- — see ZO-

zoo·gen·ic \ˌzō-ə-ˈjen-ik\ *adj* [ISV] **:** caused by or associated with animals or their activities <~ humus>

zo·og·e·nous \zō-ˈäj-ə-nəs, zə-ˈwäj-\ *adj* **:** ZOOGENIC

zoogeog *abbr* zoogeography

zoo·ge·og·ra·phy \ˌzō-ə-jē-ˈäg-rə-fē\ *n* [ISV] **:** a branch of biogeography concerned with the geographical distribution of animals and esp. with the determination of the areas characterized by special groups of animals and the study of the causes and significance of such groups — **zoo·ge·og·ra·pher** \-fər\ *n* — **zoo·geo·graph·ic** \-ˌjē-ə-ˈgraf-ik\ *also* **zoo·geo·graph·i·cal** \-i-kəl\ *adj* — **zoo·geo·graph·i·cal·ly** \-i-k(ə-)lē\ *adv*

zoo·glea \zō-ˈäg-lē-ə, ˌzō-ə-ˈglē-ə\ *n, pl* **-gleas** *or* **-gle·ae** \-lē-ˌē, -ˈglē-ˌē, -ˌī\ [NL, fr. *zo-* + MGk *glia*, *gloea* glue — more at CLAY] **:** a gelatinous or mucilaginous mass formed by bacteria growing in fluid media rich in organic material and made up of bacterial bodies embedded in a matrix of swollen confluent capsule substance — **zoo·gle·al** \-lē-əl, -ˈglē-əl\ *adj*

zo·oid \ˈzō-ˌȯid\ *n* **:** an entity that resembles but is not wholly the same as a separate individual organism: as **a :** an organized body (as a phagocyte or a sperm cell) having locomotion **b :** a more or less independent animal produced (as by fission, proliferation, or strobilation) by other than direct sexual methods and so having an equivocal individuality — **zo·oi·dal** \zō-ˈȯid-ᵊl\ *adj*

zooks \ˈzu̇ks\ *interj, archaic* — used as a mild oath

zool *abbr* zoological; zoology

zo·ol·a·try \zō-ˈäl-ə-trē, zə-ˈwäl-\ *n* [NL *zoolatria*, fr. *zo-* + LL *-latria* -latry] **:** animal worship

zoo·log·i·cal \ˌzō-ə-ˈläj-i-kəl\ *also* **zoo·log·ic** \-ik\ *adj* **1 :** of, relating to, or occupied with zoology **2 :** of, relating to, or affecting lower animals often as distinguished from man — **zoo·log·i·cal·ly** \-i-k(ə-)lē\ *adv*

zoological garden *n* **:** a garden or park where wild animals are kept for exhibition

zo·ol·o·gy \zō-ˈäl-ə-jē, zə-ˈwäl-\ *n* [NL *zoologia*, fr. *zo-* + *-logia* -logy] **1 :** a science that deals with animals and is the branch of biology concerned with the animal kingdom and its members as individuals and classes and with animal life **2 :** a treatise on zoology **3 a :** animal life (as of a region) **:** FAUNA **b :** the properties and vital phenomena exhibited by an animal, animal type, or group — **zo·ol·o·gist** \-jəst\ *n*

¹zoom \ˈzüm\ *vb* [imit.] *vi* **1 :** to move with a loud low hum or buzz **2** *of an airplane* **:** to climb for a short time at an angle greater than that which can be maintained in steady flight so that the machine is carried upward at the expense of stored kinetic energy **3 :** to focus a camera or microscope using a special lens that permits the apparent distance of the object to be varied **4 :** to increase sharply <retail sales ~*ed*> ~ *vt* **:** to cause to zoom

²zoom *n* **1 :** an act or process of zooming; *specif* **:** a sharp upward movement **2 :** a zooming sound **3 :** ZOOM LENS

zoom lens *n* **:** a camera or projector lens in which the image size can be varied continuously so that the image remains in focus at all times

zoo·mor·phic \ˌzō-ə-ˈmȯr-fik\ *adj* [ISV] **1 :** having the form of an animal <a ~ orchid> **2 :** of, relating to, or being a deity conceived of in animal form or with the attributes of an animal

-zo·on \ˈzō-ˌän *also* -ən\ *n comb form, pl* **-zoa** \ˈzō-ə\ [NL, fr. Gk *zōion*] **:** animal **:** zooid <hemato*zoon*> <spermato*zoon*>

zoo·no·sis \zō-ˈän-ə-səs, ˌzō-ə-ˈnō-səs\ *n, pl* **-no·ses** \-ˌsēz\ [NL, fr. *zo-* + Gk *nosos* disease] **:** a disease communicable from lower animals to man under natural conditions — **zoo·not·ic** \ˌzō-ə-ˈnät-ik\ *adj*

zoo·par·a·site \ˌzō-ə-ˈpar-ə-ˌsīt\ *n* **:** a parasitic animal — **zoo·par·a·sit·ic** \-ˌpar-ə-ˈsit-ik\ *adj*

zo·oph·a·gous \zō-ˈäf-ə-gəs, zə-ˈwäf-\ *adj* [ISV] **:** feeding on animals **:** CARNIVOROUS

zoo·phil·ic \ˌzō-ə-ˈfil-ik\ *adj* **:** ZOOPHILOUS

zo·oph·i·lous \zō-ˈäf-ə-ləs, zə-ˈwäf-\ *adj* **:** having an attraction to or preference for animals: as **a :** adapted to pollination by animals other than insects — compare ENTOMOPHILOUS **b** *of an insect* **:** preferring lower animals to man as a source of food

zoo·phyte \ˈzō-ə-ˌfīt\ *n* [Gk *zōophyton*, fr. *zōi-*, *zō-* zo- + *phyton* plant — more at PHYT-] **:** an invertebrate animal (as a coral or sponge) more or less resembling a plant in appearance or mode of growth; *esp* **:** one that forms a branching arborescent colony attached to a substrate — **zoo·phyt·ic** \ˌzō-ə-ˈfit-ik\ *adj*

zoo·plank·ter \ˈzō-ə-ˌplaŋ(k)-tər\ *n* [*zo-* + *plankter*] **:** a planktonic animal

zoo·plank·ton \ˌzō-ə-ˈplaŋ(k)-tən, -ˌtän\ *n* **:** animal life of the plankton — **zoo·plank·ton·ic** \-ˌplaŋ(k)-ˈtän-ik\ *adj*

zoo·spo·ran·gi·um \ˌzō-ə-spə-ˈran-jē-əm\ *n* [NL] **:** a spore case or sporangium bearing zoospores

zoo·spore \ˈzō-ə-ˌspō(ə)r, -ˌspȯ(ə)r\ *n* [ISV] **:** an independently motile spore: as **a :** a motile usu. naked and flagellated asexual spore esp. of an alga or lower fungus **b :** a minute amoeboid or flagellated product of protozoan sporocyst division whether sexual or asexual — **zoo·spor·al** \ˌzō-ə-ˈspōr-əl, -ˈspȯr-\ *adj*

zo·os·ter·ol \zō-ˈäs-tə-ˌrōl, -ˌrȯl\ *n* **:** a sterol (as cholesterol) of animal origin — compare PHYTOSTEROL

zoo·tech·nics \ˌzō-ə-ˈtek-niks\ *n pl but sing or pl in constr* **:** the care and improving of animals under domestication **:** the technology of animal husbandry — **zoo·tech·ni·cal** \-ni-kəl\ *adj*

zoot suit \ˈzüt-\ *n* [origin unknown] **:** a flashy suit of extreme cut typically consisting of a thigh-length jacket with wide padded shoulders and peg-top trousers tapering to narrow cuffs — **zoot–suit·er** \-ˌsüt-ər\ *n*

zo·ri \ˈzōr-ē, ˈzȯr-\ *n, pl* **zori** [Jap *zōri*] **:** a flat thonged sandal usu. made of straw, leather, or rubber

Zorn's lemma \ˈzȯ(ə)rnz-\ *n* [Max August *Zorn* *b*1906 G mathematician] **:** a lemma in set theory: if a set is partially ordered and if each subset for which every pair of elements is related by exactly one of the relationships "less than", "equal to", or "greater than" has an upper bound in the set, the set contains at least one element for which there is no greater element in the set

Zo·ro·as·tri·an·ism \ˌzōr-ə-ˈwas-trē-ə-ˌniz-əm\ *n* **:** a Persian religion founded in the 6th century B.C. by the prophet Zoroaster, promulgated in the Avesta, and characterized by worship of a supreme god Ahura Mazda who requires men's good deeds for help in his cosmic struggle against the evil spirit Ahriman — **Zo·ro·as·tri·an** \-trē-ən\ *adj or n*

zoster *n* [L, fr. Gk *zōstēr* girdle; akin to Gk *zōnē* zone] **:** HERPES ZOSTER

Zou·ave \zü-ˈäv\ *n* [F, fr. Berber *Zwāwa,* Algerian tribe] **1 :** a member of a French infantry unit orig. composed of Algerians wearing a brilliant uniform and conducting a quick spirited drill **2 :** a member of a military unit adopting the dress and drill of the Zouaves

zounds \ˈz(w)au̇n(d)z, ˈz(w)ün(d)z\ *interj* [euphemism for *God's wounds*] — used as a mild oath

zoy·sia \ˈzȯi-shə, -zhə, -sē-ə, -zē-ə\ *n* [NL, alter. of *Zoisia,* genus name, fr. Karl von *Zois* †1800 G botanist] **:** any of a genus (*Zoisia*) of creeping perennial grasses having fine wiry leaves and including some suitable for lawn grasses esp. in warm regions

ZPG *abbr* zero population growth

Zr *symbol* zirconium

zuc·chet·to \zü-ˈket-(ˌ)ō, tsü-\ *n, pl* **-tos** [It, fr. *zucca* gourd, head, fr. LL *cucutia* gourd] **:** a small round skullcap worn by Roman Catholic ecclesiastics in colors that vary according to the rank of the wearer

zuc·chi·ni \zu̇-ˈkē-nē\ *n, pl* **-ni** *or* **-nis** [It, pl. of *zucchino,* dim. of *zucca* gourd] **:** a summer squash of bushy growth with smooth cylindrical dark green fruits; *also* **:** its fruit

[1]Zu·lu \ˈzü-(ˌ)lü\ *n* **1 :** a member of a Bantu-speaking people of Natal **2 :** a Bantu language of the Zulus — **Zulu** *adj*

[2]Zulu — a communications code word for the letter *z*

Zu·ni \ˈzü-nē\ *or* **Zu·ñi** \-nyē\ *n, pl* **Zuni** *or* **Zunis** *or* **Zuñi** *or* **Zuñis** [AmerSp] **1 a :** an Amerindian people of western New Mexico **b :** a member of this people **2 :** the language of the Zuni people — **Zu·ni·an** \-nē-ən\ *or* **Zu·ñi·an** \-nyē-\ *adj*

Zunian *or* **Zuñian** *n* **:** a language family consisting of Zuni only

zwie·back \ˈswē-ˌbak, ˈswī-, ˈzwē-, ˈzwī-, -ˌbäk\ *n* [G, lit., twice baked, fr. *zwie-* twice (fr. OHG *zwi-*) + *backen* to bake, fr. OHG *bahhan* — more at TWI-, BAKE] **:** a usu. sweetened bread enriched with eggs that is baked and then sliced and toasted until dry and crisp

Zwing·li·an \ˈzwiŋ-(g)lē-ən, ˈswiŋ-; ˈtsfiŋ-lē-\ *adj* **:** of or relating to Ulrich Zwingli or his teachings and esp. his doctrine that Christ's presence in the Eucharist is not corporeal but symbolic — **Zwinglian** *n* — **Zwing·li·an·ism** \-ə-ˌniz-əm\ *n*

zwit·ter·ion \ˈzwit-ə-ˌrī-ən, ˈswit-, -ˌrī-ˌän\ *n* [G, fr. *zwitter* hybrid + *ion*] **:** a dipolar ion — **zwit·ter·ion·ic** \ˌzwit-ə-rī-ˈän-ik, ˌswit-\ *adj*

zyg- *or* **zygo-** *comb form* [NL, fr. Gk, fr. *zygon* — more at YOKE] **1 :** yoke <*zygo*morphic> **2 :** pair <*zygo*dactyl> **3 :** union **:** zygosis <*zygo*spore>

zyg·apoph·y·sis \ˌzī-gə-ˈpäf-ə-səs\ *n, pl* **-y·ses** \-ˌsēz\ [NL] **:** one of the articular processes of the neural arch of a vertebra of which there are usu. two anterior and two posterior

zy·go·dac·tyl \ˌzī-gə-ˈdak-tᵊl\ *adj* [ISV *zyg-* + Gk *daktylos* toe] **:** having the toes arranged two in front and two behind — used of a bird — **zy·go·dac·tyl** \ˈzī-gə-ˌdak-tᵊl\ *n*

zy·go·dac·ty·lous \-tə-ləs\ *adj* **:** ZYGODACTYL

zy·go·ma \zī-ˈgō-mə\ *n, pl* **-ma·ta** \-mət-ə\ *also* **-mas** [NL *zygomat-, zygoma,* fr. Gk *zygōma,* fr. *zygoun* to join, fr. *zygon* yoke] **1 a :** ZYGOMATIC ARCH **b :** a slender bony process of the zygomatic arch **2 :** ZYGOMATIC BONE

zy·go·mat·ic \ˌzī-gə-ˈmat-ik\ *adj* **:** of, relating to, constituting, or situated in the region of the zygoma and esp. the zygomatic arch

zygomatic arch *n* **:** the arch of bone that extends along the front or side of the skull beneath the orbit

zygomatic bone *n* **:** a bone of the side of the face below the eye that in mammals forms part of the zygomatic arch and part of the orbit — called also *cheekbone*

zygomatic process *n* **:** any of several bony processes that enter into or strengthen the zygomatic arch

zy·go·mor·phic \ˌzī-gə-ˈmȯr-fik\ *adj* **:** bilaterally symmetrical and capable of division into essentially symmetrical halves by only one longitudinal plane passing through the axis — **zy·go·mor·phism** \-ˌfiz-əm\ *or* **zy·go·mor·phy** \ˈzī-gə-ˌmȯr-fē\ *n*

zy·gos·i·ty \zī-ˈgäs-ət-ē\ *n* **:** the makeup or characteristics of a particular zygote

zy·go·spore \ˈzī-gə-ˌspō(ə)r, -ˌspȯ(ə)r\ *n* [ISV] **:** a plant spore that is formed by union of two similar sexual cells, usu. serves as a resting spore, and produces the sporophytic phase of the plant — compare OOSPORE — **zy·go·spor·ic** \ˌzī-gə-ˈspōr-ik, -ˈspȯr-\ *adj*

zy·gote \ˈzī-ˌgōt\ *n* [Gk *zygōtos* yoked, fr. *zygoun* to join together — more at ZYGOMA] **:** a cell formed by the union of two gametes; *broadly* **:** the developing individual produced from such a cell — **zy·got·ic** \zī-ˈgät-ik\ *adj* — **zy·got·i·cal·ly** \-i-k(ə-)lē\ *adv*

zy·go·tene \ˈzī-gə-ˌtēn\ *n* [ISV] **:** the synaptic stage in meiosis in which homologous chromosomes pair intimately

-zy·gous \ˈzī-gəs\ *adj comb form* [Gk *-zygos* yoked, fr. *zygon* yoke — more at YOKE] **:** having (such) a zygotic constitution <hetero*zygous*>

zym- *or* **zymo-** *comb form* [NL, fr. Gk, leaven, fr. *zymē*] **1 :** fermentation <*zym*urgy> **2 :** enzyme <*zymo*gen>

zy·mase \ˈzī-ˌmās, -ˌmāz\ *n* [ISV] **:** an enzyme or enzyme complex that promotes glycolysis

-zyme \ˌzīm\ *n comb form* [Gk *zymē* leaven] **:** enzyme <lyso*zyme*>

zy·mo·gen \ˈzī-mə-jən\ *n* [ISV] **:** an inactive protein precursor of an enzyme secreted by living cells and activated by catalysis (as by a kinase or an acid) — called also *proenzyme*

zy·mo·gen·ic \ˌzī-mə-ˈjen-ik\ *adj* **1 :** producing fermentation **2 :** of or relating to a zymogen

zy·mol·o·gy \zī-ˈmäl-ə-jē\ *n* [NL *zymologia,* fr. *zym-* + *-logia* -logy] **:** a science that deals with fermentation

zy·mot·ic \zī-ˈmät-ik\ *adj* **1 :** of, relating to, causing, or caused by fermentation **2 :** relating to, constituting, or causing an infectious or contagious disease — **zy·mot·i·cal·ly** \-i-k(ə-)lē\ *adv*

zy·mur·gy \ˈzī-(ˌ)mər-jē\ *n* **:** a branch of applied chemistry that deals with fermentation processes

Foreign Words and Phrases

ab·eunt stu·dia in mo·res \ˈäb-ə-ˌu̇nt-ˈstüd-ē-ˌä-in-ˈmō-ˌrās\ [L] : practices zealously pursued pass into habits
à bien·tôt \à-bya^{n}-tō\ [F] : so long
ab in·cu·na·bu·lis \ˌäb-ˌiŋ-kə-ˈnäb-ə-ˌlēs\ [L] : from the cradle : from infancy
à bon chat, bon rat \à-bō^{n}-ˈshà bō^{n}-ˈrà\ [F] : to a good cat, a good rat : retaliation in kind
à bouche ou·verte \à-bü-shü-vert\ [F] : with open mouth : eagerly : uncritically
ab ovo us·que ad ma·la \äb-ˈō-vō-ˌu̇s-kwe-ˌäd-ˈmäl-ä\ [L] : from egg to apples : from soup to nuts : from beginning to end
à bras ou·verts \à-brà-zü-ver\ [F] : with open arms : cordially
ab·sit in·vi·dia \ˈäb-ˌsit-in-ˈwid-ē-ˌä\ [L] : let there be no envy or ill will
ab uno dis·ce om·nes \äb-ˈü-nō-ˌdis-ke-ˈȯm-ˌnās\ [L] : from one learn to know all
ab ur·be con·di·ta \äb-ˈu̇r-be-ˈkȯn-də-ˌtä\ [L] : from the founding of the city (Rome, founded 753 B.C.) — used by the Romans in reckoning dates
ab·usus non tol·lit usum \ˈäb-ˌü-səs-ˌnōn-ˌtȯ-lət-ˈü-səm\ [L] : abuse does not take away use, i.e., is not an argument against proper use
à compte \à-ˈkō^{n}t\ [F] : on account
à coup sûr \à-kü-sūēr\ [F] : with sure stroke : surely
ad ar·bi·tri·um \ˌad-är-ˈbit-rē-əm\ [L] : at will : arbitrarily
ad as·tra per as·pera \ad-ˈas-trə-ˌpər-ˈas-pə-rə\ [L] : to the stars by hard ways — motto of Kansas
ad ex·tre·mum \ˌad-ik-ˈstrē-məm\ [L] : to the extreme : at last
ad ka·len·das Grae·cas \ˌäd-kə-ˈlen-dəs-ˈgrī-ˌkäs\ [L] : at the Greek calends : never (since the Greeks had no calends)
ad ma·jo·rem Dei glo·ri·am \äd-mä-ˈyōr-ˌem-ˈde-ˌē-ˈglōr-ē-ˌäm, -ˈyȯr-, -ˈglȯr-\ [L] : to the greater glory of God — motto of the Society of Jesus
ad pa·tres \äd-ˈpä-ˌtrās\ [L] : (gathered) to his fathers : deceased
à droite \à-drwät\ [F] : to or on the right hand
ad un·guem \äd-ˈu̇ŋ-ˌgwem\ [L] : to the fingernail : to a nicety : exactly (from the use of the fingernail to test the smoothness of marble)
ad utrum·que pa·ra·tus \ˌäd-u̇-ˈtru̇m-kwe-pə-ˈrät-əs\ [L] : prepared for either (event)
ad vi·vum \äd-ˈwē-ˌwu̇m\ [L] : to the life
ae·gri som·nia \ˌī-grē-ˈsȯm-nē-ˌä\ [L] : a sick man's dreams
ae·quam ser·va·re men·tem \ˈī-ˌkwäm-sər-ˌwä-rē-ˈmen-ˌtem\ [L] : to preserve a calm mind
ae·quo ani·mo \ˌī-ˌkwō-ˈän-ə-ˌmō\ [L] : with even mind : calmly
ae·re per·en·ni·us \ˈī-rā-pə-ˈren-ē-ˌu̇s\ [L] : more lasting than bronze
à gauche \à-gōsh\ [F] : to or on the left hand
age quod agis \ˈäg-e-ˌkwȯd-ˈäg-ˌis\ [L] : do what you are doing : to the business at hand
à grands frais \à-grä^{n}-fre\ [F] : at great expense
à huis clos \à-w^{y}ē-klō\ [F] : with closed doors
aide–toi, le ciel t'aidera \ed-twà lə-ˈsyel-te-drà\ [F] : help yourself (and) heaven will help you
ai·né \e-nā\ [F] : elder : senior (masc.)
ai·née \e-nā\ [F] : elder : senior (fem.)
à l'aban·don \à-là-bä^{n}-dō^{n}\ [F] : carelessly : in disorder
à la belle étoile \à-là-bel-ā-twàl\ [F] : under the beautiful star : in the open air at night
à la bonne heure \à-là-bȯ-nœr\ [F] : at a good time : well and good : all right
à la fran·çaise \à-là-frä^{n}-sez\ [F] : in the French style
à l'an·glaise \à-lä^{n}-glez\ [F] : in the English style
alea jac·ta est \ˈäl-ē-ˌä-ˌyäk-tə-ˈest\ [L] : the die is cast
à l'im·pro·viste \à-la^{n}-prō-vēst\ [F] : unexpectedly
ali·quan·do bo·nus dor·mi·tat Ho·me·rus \ˌäl-ə-ˌkwän-dō-ˈbȯ-nəs-ˌdȯr-mə-ˌtät-hō-ˈmer-əs\ [L] : sometimes (even) good Homer nods
alis vo·lat pro·pri·is \ˈäl-ˌēs-ˈwȯ-ˌlät-ˈprō-prē-ˌēs\ [L] : she flies with her own wings — motto of Oregon
al-ki \ˈal-ˌkī, -kē\ [Chinook Jargon] : by and by — motto of Washington
alo·ha oe \ä-ˌlō-hä-ˈȯi, -ˈō-ē\ [Hawaiian] : love to you : greetings : farewell
al·ter idem \ˌȯl-tər-ˈī-ˌdem, ˌäl-tər-ˈē-\ [L] : second self
a max·i·mis ad mi·ni·ma \ä-ˈmäk-sə-ˌmēs-ˌäd-ˈmin-ə-ˌmä\ [L] : from the greatest to the least
ami·cus hu·ma·ni ge·ner·is \ä-ˈmē-kəs-hü-ˌmän-ē-ˈgen-ə-rəs\ [L] : friend of the human race
amicus us·que ad aras \-ˌu̇s-kwe-ˌäd-ˈär-ˌäs\ [L] : a friend as far as to the altars, i.e., except in what is contrary to one's religion; *also* : a friend to the last extremity
ami de cour \à-ˌmēd-ə-ˈku̇r\ [F] : court friend : insincere friend
amor pa·tri·ae \ˌäm-ˌȯr-ˈpä-trē-ˌī\ [L] : love of one's country
amor vin·cit om·nia \ˈä-ˌmȯr-ˌwiŋ-kət-ˈȯm-nē-ə\ [L] : love conquers all things
an·cienne no·blesse \ä^{n}-syen-nȯ-bles\ [F] : old-time nobility : the French nobility before the Revolution of 1789
an·guis in her·ba \ˌäŋ-gwəs-in-ˈher-ˌbä\ [L] : snake in the grass
ani·mal bi·pes im·plu·me \ˈän-i-ˌmäl-ˌbip-ˌās-im-ˈplü-me\ [L] : two-legged animal without feathers (i.e., man)
ani·mis opi·bus·que pa·ra·ti \ˈän-ə-ˌmēs-ˌō-pə-ˈbu̇s-kwe-pə-ˈrät-ē\ [L] : prepared in spirits and resources — one of the mottoes of South Carolina
an·no ae·ta·tis su·ae \ˈän-ō-ī-ˌtät-əs-ˈsü-ˌī\ [L] : in the (specified) year of his (or her) age
an·no mun·di \ˌän-ō-ˈmu̇n-dē\ [L] : in the year of the world — used in reckoning dates from the supposed period of the creation of the world, esp. as fixed by James Ussher at 4004 B.C. or by the Jews at 3761 B.C.
an·no ur·bis con·di·tae \ˌän-ō-ˌu̇r-bəs-ˈkȯn-də-ˌtī\ [L] : in the year of the founded city (Rome, founded 753 B.C.)
an·nu·it coep·tis \ˌän-ə-ˌwit-ˈkȯip-ˌtēs\ [L] : He (God) has smiled on our undertakings — motto on the reverse of the Great Seal of the United States
à peu près \à-pœ-pre\ [F] : nearly : approximately
à pied \à-pyā\ [F] : on foot
après moi le dé·luge \à-pre-mwà-lə-dā-lūēzh\ [F] : after me the deluge (attributed to Louis XV)
à pro·pos de bottes \à-prə-pōd-ə-bȯt\ [F] : apropos of boots — used to change the subject
à propos de rien \-rya^{n}\ [F] : apropos of nothing
aqua et ig·ni in·ter·dic·tus \ˌäk-wä-et-ˈig-nē-ˌint-ər-ˈdik-təs\ [L] : forbidden to be furnished with water and fire : outlawed
Ar·ca·des am·bo \ˌär-kə-ˌdes-ˈäm-bō\ [L] : both Arcadians : two persons of like occupations or tastes; *also* : two rascals
a ri·ve·der·ci \ˌär-ē-vā-ˈder-chē\ [It] : till we meet again — used as a formula of farewell
ar·rec·tis au·ri·bus \ä-ˈrek-ˌtēs-ˈau̇-ri-ˌbu̇s\ [L] : with ears pricked up : attentively
ars est ce·la·re ar·tem \ˌärs-ˌest-kā-ˌlär-ē-ˈär-ˌtem\ [L] : it is (true) art to conceal art
ars lon·ga, vi·ta bre·vis \ärs-ˈlȯŋ-ˌgä ˌwē-ˌtä-ˈbre-wəs\ [L] : art is long, life is short
à tort et à tra·vers \à-tȯr-tā-à-trà-ver\ [F] : wrong and crosswise : at random : without rhyme or reason
au bout de son la·tin \ō-büd-(ə-)sō^{n}-là-ta^{n}\ [F] : at the end of one's Latin : at the end of one's mental resources
au con·traire \ō-kō^{n}-trer\ [F] : on the contrary
au·de·mus ju·ra no·stra de·fen·dere \au̇-ˈdā-məs-ˌyu̇r-ə-ˈnȯ-strə-dā-ˈfen-də-rē\ [L] : we dare defend our rights — motto of Alabama
au·den·tes for·tu·na ju·vat \au̇-ˈden-ˌtās-fȯr-ˌtü-nə-ˈyü-ˌwät\ [L] : fortune favors the bold
au·di al·teram partem \ˈau̇-ˌdē-ˌäl-tə-ˌräm-ˈpär-ˌtem\ [L] : hear the other side
au grand sé·rieux \ō-grä^{n}-sā-ryœ\ [F] : in all seriousness
au pays des aveugles les borgnes sont rois \ō-pā-ē-dā-zà-vœgl^{ə}-lā-bȯrn^{y}-ə-sō^{n}-rwä\ [F] : in the country of the blind the one-eyed men are kings
au·rea me·di·o·cri·tas \ˈau̇-rē-ə-ˌmed-ē-ˈō-krə-ˌtäs\ [L] : the golden mean
au reste \ō-rest\ [F] : for the rest : besides
au·spi·ci·um me·li·o·ris ae·vi \au̇-ˈspik-ē-ˌu̇m-ˌmel-ē-ˌȯr-əs-ˈī-ˌwē\ [L] : an omen of a better age — motto of the Order of St. Michael and St. George
aus·si·tôt dit, aus·si·tôt fait \ō-sē-tō-dē ō-sē-tō-fe\ [F] : no sooner said than done
aut Cae·sar aut ni·hil \au̇t-ˈkī-sär-ˌau̇t-ˈni-ˌhil\ [L] : either a Caesar or nothing
aut Caesar aut nul·lus \-ˈnu̇l-əs\ [L] : either a Caesar or a nobody
au·tres temps, au·tres mœurs \ō-trə-tä^{n} ō-trə-mœrs\ [F] : other times, other customs
aut vin·ce·re aut mo·ri \au̇t-ˈwiŋ-kə-rē-ˌau̇t-ˈmȯ-ˌrē\ [L] : either to conquer or to die
aux armes \ō-zärm\ [F] : to arms
ave at·que va·le \ˈä-ˌwä-ˌät-kwe-ˈwä-ˌlā\ [L] : hail and farewell

à vo·tre san·té \ȧ-vȯt-sä^{n}-tā, -vȯ-trə-\ [F] : to your health — used as a toast
bal·lon d'es·sai \bȧ-lō^{n}-dā-se\ [F] : trial balloon
beaux yeux \bō-zyœ̄\ [F] : beautiful eyes : beauty of face
bien en·ten·du \bya^{n}-nä^{n}-tä^{n}-due̅\ [F] : well understood : of course
bien·sé·ance \bya^{n}-sā-ä^{n}s\ [F] : propriety
bis dat qui ci·to dat \ˌbis-ˌdät-kwē-ˈki-tō-ˌdät\ [L] : he gives twice who gives promptly
bon gré, mal gré \ˈbō^{n}-ˌgrā-ˈmȧl-ˌgrā\ [F] : whether with good grace or bad : willy-nilly
bo·nis avi·bus \ˌbō-ˌnēs-ˈä-wi-ˌbu̇s\ [L] : under good auspices
bon jour \bō^{n}-zhür\ [F] : good day : good morning
bonne foi \bȯn-fwä\ [F] : good faith
bon soir \bō^{n}-swȧr\ [F] : good evening
bru·tum ful·men \ˌbrüt-əm-ˈfu̇l-mən\ [L] : insensible thunderbolt : a futile threat or display of force
ca·dit quae·stio \ˌkäd-ət-ˈkwī-stē-ˌō\ [L] : the question drops : the argument collapses
cau·sa si·ne qua non \ˈkau̇-ˌsä-ˌsin-ē-kwä-ˈnōn\ [L] : an indispensable cause or condition
ca·ve ca·nem \ˌkä-wā-ˈkän-ˌem\ [L] : beware the dog
ce·dant ar·ma to·gae \ˈkā-ˌdänt-ˌär-mə-ˈtō-ˌgī\ [L] : let arms yield to the toga : let military power give way to civil power — motto of Wyoming
ce n'est que le pre·mier pas qui coûte \snek-lə-prə-myā-pä-kē-küt\ [F] : it is only the first step that costs
c'est a dire \se-tȧ-dēr\ [F] : that is to say : namely
c'est au·tre chose \se-tōt-shōz, -tō-trə-\ [F] : that's a different thing
c'est plus qu'un crime, c'est une faute \se-plue̅-kœ^{n}-krēm se-tue̅n-fōt\ [F] : it is worse than a crime, it is a blunder
ce·tera de·sunt \ˌkāt-ə-ˌrä-ˈdā-ˌsu̇nt\ [L] : the rest is missing
cha·cun à son gout \shȧ-kœ^{n}-nȧ-sō^{n}-gü\ [F] : everyone to his taste
châ·teau en Es·pagne \shä-tō-ä^{n}-nes-pȧn^{y}\ [F] : castle in Spain : a visionary project
cher·chez la femme \sher-shā-lȧ-fȧm\ [F] : look for the woman
che sa·rà, sa·rà \ˌkā-sä-ˌrä-sä-ˈrä\ [It] : what will be, will be
che·val de ba·taille \shə-vȧl-də-bȧ-tȧ^{y}\ [F] : war-horse : argument constantly relied on : favorite subject
co·gi·to, er·go sum \ˈkō-gə-ˌtō-ˌer-gō-ˈsu̇m\ [L] : I think, therefore I exist
com·pa·gnon de voy·age \kō^{n}-pȧ-n^{y}ō^{n}-də-vwȧ-yȧzh\ [F] : traveling companion
compte rendu \kō^{n}t-rä^{n}-due̅\ [F] : report (as of proceedings in an investigation)
cor·rup·tio op·ti·mi pes·si·ma \kə-ˈru̇p-tē-ˌō-ˈäp-tə-ˌmē-ˈpes-ə-ˌmä\ [L] : the corruption of the best is the worst of all
coup de mai·tre \küd-(ə-)metr^{ə}\ [F] : masterstroke
coup d'es·sai \kü-dā-se\ [F] : experiment : trial
coûte que coûte \küt-kə-küt\ [F] : cost what it may
cre·do quia ab·sur·dum est \ˌkrād-ō-ˈkwē-ä-äp-ˌsu̇rd-əm-ˈest\ [L] : I believe it because it is absurd
cres·cit eun·do \ˌkres-kət-ˈeu̇n-dō\ [L] : it grows as it goes — motto of New Mexico
crux cri·ti·co·rum \ˈkru̇ks-ˌkrit-ə-ˈkōr-əm\ [L] : crux of critics
cum gra·no sa·lis \ku̇m-ˌgrän-ō-ˈsäl-əs\ [L] : with a grain of salt
cus·tos mo·rum \ˌku̇s-tōs-ˈmōr-əm\ [L] : guardian of manners or morals : censor
d'ac·cord \dȧ-kȯr\ [F] : in accord : agreed
dame d'hon·neur \dȧm-dō-nœr\ [F] : lady-in-waiting
dam·nant quod non in·tel·li·gunt \ˈdäm-ˌnänt-ˌkwȯd-ˌnōn-in-ˈtel-ə-ˌgu̇nt\ [L] : they condemn what they do not understand
de bonne grâce \də-bȯn-gräs\ [F] : with good grace : willingly
de gus·ti·bus non est dis·pu·tan·dum \dā-ˈgu̇s-tə-ˌbu̇s-ˌnōn-ˌest-ˌdis-pu̇-ˈtän-ˌdu̇m\ [L] : there is no disputing about tastes
Dei gra·tia \ˌde-ē-ˈgrät-ē-ˌä\ [L] : by the grace of God
de in·te·gro \dā-ˈint-ə-ˌgrō\ [L] : anew : afresh
de l'au·dace, en·core de l'au·dace, et tou·jours de l'au·dace \də-lō-ˈdȧs ä^{n}-ˈkȯr-də-lō-dȧs ā-tü-ˈzhür-də-lō-dȧs\ [F] : audacity, more audacity, and ever more audacity
de·len·da est Car·tha·go \dā-ˈlen-dä-ˌest-kär-ˈtäg-ō\ [L] : Carthage must be destroyed
de·li·ne·a·vit \dā-ˌlē-nā-ˈä-wit\ [L] : he (or she) drew it
de mal en pis \də-mȧ-lä^{n}-pē\ [F] : from bad to worse
de mi·ni·mis non cu·rat lex \dā-ˈmin-ə-ˌmēs-ˌnōn-ˌkü-ˌrät-ˈleks\ [L] : the law takes no account of trifles
de mor·tu·is nil ni·si bo·num \dā-ˈmȯrt-ə-ˌwēs-ˌnēl-ˌnis-ē-ˈbō-ˌnu̇m\ [L] : of the dead (say) nothing but good
Deo fa·ven·te \ˌdā-ō-fə-ˈvent-ē\ [L] : with God's favor
Deo gra·ti·as \ˌdā-ō-ˈgrät-ē-ˌäs\ [L] : thanks (be) to God
de pro·fun·dis \ˌdā-prō-ˈfu̇n-dēs, -ˈfən-\ [L] : out of the depths
der Geist der stets ver·neint \dər-ˈgīst-dər-ˌshtāts-fer-ˈnīnt\ [G] : the spirit that ever denies — applied originally to Mephistopheles
de·si·pere in lo·co \dā-ˈsip-ə-rē-in-ˈlō-kō\ [L] : to indulge in trifling at the proper time
Deus vult \ˌdā-əs-ˈwu̇lt\ [L] : God wills it — rallying cry of the First Crusade
di·es fau·stus \ˌdē-ˌās-ˈfau̇-stəs\ [L] : lucky day
dies in·fau·stus \-ˈin-ˌfau̇-stəs\ [L] : unlucky day
dies irae \-ˈē-ˌrī, -ˌrā\ [L] : day of wrath — used of the Judgment Day
Dieu et mon droit \dyœ̄-ā-mō^{n}-drwä\ [F] : God and my right — motto on the British royal arms
Dieu vous garde \dyœ̄-vü-gȧrd\ [F] : God keep you
di·ri·go \ˈdē-ri-ˌgō\ [L] : I direct — motto of Maine
dis ali·ter vi·sum \ˌdēs-ˌal-ə-ˌter-ˈwē-ˌsu̇m\ [L] : the Gods decreed otherwise
di·tat De·us \ˌdē-ˌtät-ˈdā-ˌu̇s\ [L] : God enriches — motto of Arizona
di·vi·de et im·pe·ra \ˈdē-wi-ˌde-ˌet-ˈim-pə-ˌrä\ [L] : divide and rule
do·cen·do dis·ci·mus \dō-ˌken-dō-ˈdis-ki-ˌmu̇s\ [L] : we learn by teaching
Domine, dirige nos \ˈdō-mi-ˌne-ˌdē-ri-ˌge-ˈnōs\ [L] : Lord, direct us — motto of the City of London
Do·mi·nus vo·bis·cum \ˌdō-mi-ˌnu̇s-wō-ˈbēs-ˌku̇m\ [L] : the Lord be with you
dul·ce et de·co·rum est pro pa·tria mo·ri \ˌdu̇l-ˌket-de-ˈkōr-ˌəst-prō-ˌpä-trē-ˌä-ˈmō-ˌrē\ [L] : it is sweet and seemly to die for one's country
dum spi·ro, spe·ro \du̇m-ˈspē-rō-ˈspā-rō\ [L] : while I breathe I hope — one of the mottoes of South Carolina
dum vi·vi·mus vi·va·mus \ˌdu̇m-ˈwē-wē-ˌmu̇s-wē-ˈwäm-u̇s\ [L] : while we live, let us live
dux fe·mi·na fac·ti \ˌdu̇ks-ˌfā-mi-nä-ˈfäk-ˌtē\ [L] : a woman was leader of the exploit
ec·ce sig·num \ˌek-e-ˈsig-ˌnu̇m\ [L] : behold the sign : look at the proof
e con·tra·rio \ˌā-kōn-ˈträr-ē-ˌō\ [L] : on the contrary
écra·sez l'in·fâme \ā-krä-zā-la^{n}-fȧm\ [F] : crush the infamous thing
eheu fu·ga·ces la·bun·tur an·ni \ˌā-ˌheu̇-fu̇-ˈgä-ˌkās-lä-ˌbu̇n-ˌtu̇r-ˈän-ˌē\ [L] : alas! the fleeting years glide on
ein fes·te Burg ist un·ser Gott \īn-ˌfes-tə-ˈbu̇rk-ist-ˌu̇n-zər-ˈgȯt\ [G] : a mighty fortress is our God
em·bar·ras de ri·chesses \ä^{n}-bȧ-räd-(ə-)rē-shes\ [F] : embarrassing surplus of riches : confusing abundance
em·bar·ras du choix \ä^{n}-bȧ-rä-due̅-shwȧ\ [F] : embarrasing variety of choice
en ami \ä^{n}-nȧ-mē\ [F] : as a friend
en ef·fet \ä^{n}-nā-fe\ [F] : in fact : indeed
en fa·mille \ä^{n}-fȧ-mē^{y}\ [F] : in one's family : at home : informally
en·fant gâ·té \ä^{n}-fä^{n}-gä-tā\ [F] : spoiled child
en·fants per·dus \ä^{n}-fä^{n}-per-due̅\ [F] : lost children : soldiers sent to a dangerous post
en·fin \ä^{n}-fa^{n}\ [F] : in conclusion : in a word
en gar·çon \ä^{n}-gȧr-sō^{n}\ [F] : as or like a bachelor
en pan·tou·fles \ä^{n}-pä^{n}-tüfl^{ə}\ [F] : in slippers : at ease : informally
en plein air \ä^{n}-plen-er\ [F] : in the open air
en plein jour \ä^{n}-pla^{n}-zhür\ [F] : in broad day
en règle \ä^{n}-regl^{ə}\ [F] : in order : in due form
en re·tard \ä^{n}r-(ə-)tȧr\ [F] : behind time : late
en re·traite \ä^{n}-rə-tret\ [F] : in retreat : in retirement
en re·vanche \ä^{n}r-(ə-)vä^{n}sh\ [F] : in return : in compensation
en se·condes noces \ä^{n}s-(ə-)gō^{n}d-nȯs\ [F] : in a second marriage
en·se pe·tit pla·ci·dam sub li·ber·ta·te qui·e·tem \ˌen-se-ˌpet-ət-ˈpläk-i-ˌdäm-su̇b-ˌlē-ber-ˌtä-te-kwē-ˈā-ˌtem\ [L] : with the sword she seeks calm repose under liberty — motto of Massachusetts
épa·ter les bour·geois \ā-pȧ-tā-lā-bür-zhwȧ\ [F] : to shock the middle classes
e plu·ri·bus unum \ˌē-ˌplu̇r-ə-bəs-ˈ(y)ü-nəm, ˌā-ˌplu̇r-\ [L] : one out of many — motto of the United States
e pur si muo·ve \ā-ˌpür-sē-ˈmwō-vā\ [It] : and yet it does move — attributed to Galileo after recanting his assertion of the earth's motion
er·ra·re hu·ma·num est \e-ˈrär-e-hü-ˌmän-əm-ˈest\ [L] : to err is human
es·prit de l'es·ca·lier \es-prēd-les-kȧ-lyā\ *or* **es·prit d'es·ca·lier** \-prē-des-\ [F] : spirit of the staircase : repartee thought of only too late, on the way home
es·se quam vi·de·ri \ˈes-e-ˌkwäm-wi-ˈdā-rē\ [L] : to be rather than to seem — motto of North Carolina
est mo·dus in re·bus \est-ˈmō-ˌdu̇s-in-ˈrā-ˌbu̇s\ [L] : there is a proper measure in things, i.e., the golden mean should always be observed
es·to per·pe·tua \ˈes-ˌtō-pər-ˈpet-ə-ˌwä\ [L] : may she endure forever — motto of Idaho
et hoc ge·nus om·ne \et-ˌhōk-ˌgen-əs-ˈȯm-ne\ *or* **et id genus om·ne** \et-ˌid-\ [L] : and everything of this kind
et in Ar·ca·dia ego \ˌet-in-är-ˌkäd-ē-ə-ˈeg-ō\ [L] : I too (lived) in Arcadia
et sic de si·mi·li·bus \et-ˌsēk-dā-sə-ˈmil-ə-ˌbu̇s\ [L] : and so of like things
et tu Bru·te \et-ˈtü-ˈbrü-te\ [L] : thou too, Brutus — exclamation attributed to Julius Caesar on seeing his friend Brutus among his assassins
eu·re·ka \yu̇-ˈrē-kə\ [Gk] : I have found it — motto of California
Ewig–Weib·li·che \ˌā-vik̲-ˈvīp-li-k̲ə\ [G] : eternal feminine
ex ani·mo \ek-ˈsän-ə-ˌmō\ [L] : from the heart : sincerely
ex·cel·si·or \ik-ˈsel-sē-ər, eks-ˈkel-sē-ˌȯr\ [L] : still higher — motto of New York
ex·cep·tio pro·bat re·gu·lam de re·bus non ex·cep·tis \eks-ˈkep-tē-ˌō-ˌprō-bät-ˈrā-gə-ˌläm-dā-ˈrā-ˌbu̇s-ˌnōn-eks-ˈkep-ˌtēs\ [L] : an exception establishes the rule as to things not excepted
ex·cep·tis ex·ci·pi·en·dis \eks-ˈkep-ˌtēs-eks-ˌkip-ē-ˈen-ˌdēs\ [L] : with the proper or necessary exceptions
ex·i·tus ac·ta pro·bat \ˈek-sə-ˌtu̇s-ˌäk-tə-ˈprō-ˌbät\ [L] : the event justifies the deed
ex li·bris \eks-ˈlē-brəs\ [L] : from the books of — used on bookplates
ex me·ro mo·tu \ˌeks-ˌmer-ō-ˈmō-tü\ [L] : out of mere impulse : of one's own accord
ex ne·ces·si·ta·te rei \ˌeks-nə-ˌkes-ə-ˈtä-te-ˈrā-(ˌē)\ [L] : from the necessity of the case
ex ni·hi·lo ni·hil fit \eks-ˈni-hi-ˌlō-ˌni-ˌhil-ˈfit\ [L] : from nothing nothing is produced

ex pe·de Her·cu·lem \eks-ˌped-e-ˈher-kə-ˌlem\ [L] : from the foot (we may judge of the size of) Hercules : from a part we may judge of the whole
ex·per·to cre·di·te \eks-ˌpert-ō-ˈkrād-ə-ˌte\ [L] : believe one who has had experience
ex un·gue le·o·nem \eks-ˈu̇ŋ-gwe-le-ˈō-ˌnem\ [L] : from the claw (we may judge of) the lion : from a part we may judge of the whole
ex vi ter·mi·ni \eks-ˌwē-ˈter-mə-ˌnē\ [L] : from the force of the term
fa·ci·le prin·ceps \ˌfäk-i-le-ˈpriŋ-ˌkeps\ [L] : easily first
fa·ci·lis de·scen·sus Aver·no \ˈfäk-i-ˌlis-dā-ˌskän-ˌsu̇s-ä-ˈwer-nō\ *or* **facilis descensus Aver·ni** \-(ˌ)nē\ [L] : the descent to Avernus is easy : the road to evil is easy
faire suivre \fer-swʸēvrᵊ\ [F] : have forwarded : please forward
fas est et ab ho·ste do·ce·ri \ˌfäs-ˈest-et-äb-ˈhō-ste-dō-ˈkā-(ˌ)rē\ [L] : it is right to learn even from an enemy
Fa·ta vi·am in·ve·ni·ent \ˌfä-tä-ˈwē-ˌäm-in-ˈwen-ē-ˌent\ [L] : the Fates will find a way
fat·ti mas·chii, pa·ro·le fe·mi·ne \ˌfät-tē-ˈmäs-ˌkē pä-ˌrō-lä-ˈfā-mē-ˌnā\ [It] : deeds are males, words are females : deeds are more effective than words — motto of Maryland, where it is generally interpreted as meaning "manly deeds, womanly words"
faux bon·homme [F] : pretended good fellow
faux–naif \fō-nä-ēf\ [F] : pretending to be childlike
femme de cham·bre \fäm-də-shäⁿbrᵊ\ [F] : chambermaid : lady's maid
fe·sti·na len·te \fe-ˌstē-nə-ˈlen-ˌtā\ [L] : make haste slowly
feux d'ar·ti·fice \fœ-där-tē-fēs\ [F] : fireworks : display of wit
fi·at ex·pe·ri·men·tum in cor·po·re vi·li \ˈfē-ˌät-ek-ˌsper-ē-ˈmen-ˌtu̇m-in-ˌkȯr-pə-re-ˈwē-lē\ [L] : let experiment be made on a worthless body
fi·at ju·sti·tia, ru·at cae·lum \ˌfē-ˌät-yu̇s-ˈtit-ē-ä ˌrü-ˌät-ˈkī-ˌlu̇m\ [L] : let justice be done though the heavens fall
fi·at lux \ˌfē-ˌät-ˈlu̇ks\ [L] : let there be light
Fi·dei De·fen·sor \ˌfid-e-ˌē-dā-ˈfān-ˌsȯr\ [L] : Defender of the Faith — a title of the sovereigns of England
fi·dus Acha·tes \ˌfēd-əs-ä-ˈkä-ˌtās\ [L] : faithful Achates : trusty friend
fille de cham·bre \fēy-də-shäⁿbrᵊ\ [F] : lady's maid
fille d'hon·neur \fēy-dȯ-nœr\ [F] : maid of honor
fils \fēs\ [F] : son — used after French proper names to distinguish a son from his father
fi·nem re·spi·ce \ˌfē-ˌnem-ˈrā-spi-ˌke\ [L] : consider the end
fi·nis co·ro·nat opus \ˌfē-nəs-kə-ˌrō-ˌnät-ˈō-ˌpu̇s\ [L] : the end crowns the work
fluc·tu·at nec mer·gi·tur \ˈflu̇k-tə-ˌwät-ˌnek-ˈmer-gə-ˌtu̇r\ [L] : it is tossed by the waves but does not sink — motto of Paris
fors·an et haec olim me·mi·nis·se ju·va·bit \ˌfȯr-ˌsän-ˌet-ˈhīk-ˌō-lim-ˌmem-ə-ˈnis-e-yu̇-ˈwä-bit\ [L] : perhaps this too will be a pleasure to look back on one day
for·tes for·tu·na ju·vat \ˈfȯr-ˌtās-fȯr-ˌtü-nə-ˈyü-ˌwät\ [L] : fortune favors the brave
fron·ti nul·la fi·des \ˈfrȯn-ˌtē-ˌnu̇l-ə-ˈfid-ˌās\ [L] : no reliance can be placed on appearance
fu·it Ili·um \ˈfu̇-ət-ˈil-ē-əm\ [L] : Troy has been (i.e., is no more)
fu·ror lo·quen·di \ˌfu̇r-ˌȯr-lō-ˈkwen-(ˌ)dē\ [L] : rage for speaking
furor po·e·ti·cus \-pō-ˈāt-i-ku̇s\ [L] : poetic frenzy
furor scri·ben·di \-skrē-ˈben-(ˌ)dē\ [L] : rage for writing
Gal·li·ce \ˈgäl-ə-ˌke\ [L] : in French : after the French manner
gar·çon d'hon·neur \gär-sōⁿ-dȯ-nœr\ [F] : bridegroom's attendant
garde du corps \gärd-dᵫ-kȯr\ [F] : bodyguard
gar·dez la foi \gär-dā-lä-fwä\ [F] : keep faith
gau·de·a·mus igi·tur \ˌgau̇d-ē-ˈäm-əs-ˈig-ə-ˌtu̇r\ [L] : let us then be merry
gens d'é·glise \zhäⁿ-dā-glēz\ [F] : church people : clergy
gens de guerre \zhäⁿ-də-ger\ [F] : military people : soldiery
gens du monde \zhäⁿ-dᵫ-mōⁿd\ [F] : people of the world : fashionable people
gno·thi se·au·ton \gə-ˈnō-thē-ˌse-au̇-ˈtȯn\ [Gk] : know thyself
grand monde \gräⁿ-mōⁿd\ [F] : great world : high society
guerre à ou·trance \ger-ä-ü-träⁿs\ [F] : war to the uttermost
gu·ten Tag \ˌgüt-ᵊn-ˈtäk\ [G] : good day
has·ta la vis·ta \ˌäs-tə-lä-ˈvēs-tə\ [Sp] : good-bye
haut goût \ō-gü\ [F] : high flavor : slight taint of decay
hic et ubi·que \ˌhēk-et-ü-ˈbē-kwe\ [L] : here and everywhere
hic ja·cet \hik-ˈjā-sət, hēk-ˈyäk-ət\ [L] : here lies — used preceding a name on a tombstone
hinc il·lae la·cri·mae \ˌhiŋk-ˌil-ˌī-ˈläk-ri-ˌmī\ [L] : hence those tears
hoc age \hōk-ˈäg-e\ [L] : do this : apply yourself to what you are about
hoc opus, hic labor est \hōk-ˈō-ˌpu̇s-ˌhēk-ˌlä-ˌbȯr-ˈest\ [L] : this is the hard work, this is the toil
homme d'af·faires \ȯm-dä-fer\ [F] : man of business : business agent
homme d'es·prit \-des-prē\ [F] : man of wit
homme moyen sen·suel \ȯm-mwä-yaⁿ-säⁿ-swʸel\ [F] : the average nonintellectual man
ho·mo sum: hu·ma·ni nil a me ali·e·num pu·to \ˈhō-mō-ˌsu̇m hü-ˌmän-ē-ˈnēl-ä-ˌmā-ˌäl-ē-ˈā-nəm-ˈpu̇-tō\ [L] : I am a man; I regard nothing that concerns man as foreign to my interests
ho·ni soit qui mal y pense \ō-nē-swä-kē-mäl-ē-päⁿs\ [F] : shamed be he who thinks evil of it — motto of the Order of the Garter
hors com·merce \ȯr-kȯ-mers\ [F] : outside the trade : not offered through regular commercial channels
hô·tel–Dieu \ō-tel-dyœ\ [F] : hospital
hu·ma·num est er·ra·re \hü-ˌmän-əm-ˌest-e-ˈrär-e\ [L] : to err is human
ich dien \ik-ˈdēn\ [G] : I serve — motto of the Prince of Wales
ici on parle fran·çais \ē-sē-ōⁿ-pärl(-ə)-fräⁿ-se\ [F] : French is spoken here
id est \id-ˈest\ [L] : that is
ig·no·ran·tia ju·ris ne·mi·nem ex·cu·sat \ˌig-nə-ˌränt-ē-ä-ˈyu̇r-əs-ˈnā-mə-ˌnem-eks-ˈkü-ˌsät\ [L] : ignorance of the law excuses no one
ig·no·tum per ig·no·ti·us \ig-ˈnōt-əm-ˌper-ig-ˈnōt-ē-ˌu̇s\ [L] : (explaining) the unknown by means of the more unknown
il faut cul·ti·ver no·tre jar·din \ēl-fō-kᵫl-tē-vä-nȯt-zhär-daⁿ, -nō-trə-zhär-\ [F] : we must cultivate our garden : we must tend to our own affairs
in ae·ter·num \ˌin-ī-ˈter-ˌnu̇m\ [L] : forever
in du·bio \in-ˈdu̇b-ē-ˌō\ [L] : in doubt : undetermined
in fu·tu·ro \in-fə-ˈtu̇r-ō\ [L] : in the future
in hoc sig·no vin·ces \in-hōk-ˈsig-nō-ˈviŋ-ˌkās\ [L] : by this sign (the Cross) you will conquer
in li·mi·ne \in-ˈlē-mə-ˌne\ [L] : on the threshold : at the beginning
in om·nia pa·ra·tus \in-ˈōm-nē-ə-pə-ˈrä-ˌtu̇s\ [L] : ready for all things
in par·ti·bus in·fi·de·li·um \in-ˈpärt-ə-ˌbu̇s-ˌin-fə-ˈdā-lē-ˌu̇m\ [L] : in the regions of the infidels — used of a titular bishop having no diocesan jurisdiction, usu. in non-Christian countries
in prae·sen·ti \ˌin-prī-ˈsen-ˌtē\ [L] : at the present time
in sae·cu·la sae·cu·lo·rum \in-ˈsī-ku̇-ˌlä-ˌsī-kə-ˈlōr-əm, -ˈsä-ku̇-ˌlä-ˌsä-\ [L] : for ages of ages : forever and ever
in sta·tu quo an·te bel·lum \in-ˈstä-ˌtü-kwō-ˌänt-ē-ˈbel-əm\ [L] : in the same state as before the war
in·te·ger vi·tae sce·le·ris·que pu·rus \ˌin-tə-ˌger-ˈwē-ˌtī-ˌskel-ə-ˈris-kwe-ˈpü-rəs\ [L] : upright of life and free from wickedness
in·ter nos \ˌint-ər-ˈnōs\ [L] : between ourselves
in·tra mu·ros \ˌin-trä-ˈmü-ˌrōs\ [L] : within the walls
in usum Del·phi·ni \in-ˈü-səm-del-ˈfē-nē\ [L] : for the use of the Dauphin : expurgated
in utrum·que pa·ra·tus \ˌin-ü-ˈtru̇m-kwe-pə-ˈrä-ˌtu̇s\ [L] : prepared for either (event)
in·ve·nit \in-ˈwā-nit\ [L] : he (or she) devised it
in vi·no ve·ri·tas \in-wē-nō-ˈwā-rə-ˌtäs\ [L] : there is truth in wine
in·vi·ta Mi·ner·va \in-ˈwē-ˌtä-mi-ˈner-ˌwä\ [L] : Minerva being unwilling : without natural talent or inspiration
ip·sis·si·ma ver·ba \ip-ˌsis-ə-ˌmä-ˈwer-ˌbä\ [L] : the very words
ira fu·ror bre·vis est \ˌē-rä-ˈfu̇r-ˌȯr-ˈbre-wəs-ˌest\ [L] : anger is a brief madness
jacta alea est \ˈyäk-ˌtä-ˌä-lē-ˌä-ˈest\ [L] : the die is cast
j'adoube \zhä-düb\ [F] : I adjust — used in chess when touching a piece without intending to move it
ja·nu·is clau·sis \ˌyän-ə-ˌwēs-ˈklau̇-ˌsēs\ [L] : with closed doors
je main·tien·drai \zhə-maⁿ-tyaⁿ-drā\ [F] : I will maintain — motto of the Netherlands
jeu de mots \zhœ̄d-(ə-)mō\ [F] : play on words : pun
Jo·an·nes est no·men eius \yō-ˈän-ās-est-ˌnō-men-ˈā-yu̇s\ [L] : John is his name — motto of Puerto Rico
jour·nal in·time \zhür-näl-aⁿ-tēm\ [F] : intimate journal : private diary
jus di·vi·num \ˌyüs-di-ˈwē-ˌnu̇m\ [L] : divine law
jus·ti·tia om·ni·bus \yu̇s-ˌtit-ē-ä-ˈōm-ni-ˌbu̇s\ [L] : justice for all — motto of the District of Columbia
j'y suis, j'y reste \zhē-swʸē-zhē-rest\ [F] : here I am, here I remain
kte·ma es aei \(kə-)ˈtā-ˌmä-ˌes-ä-ˈā\ [Gk] : a possession for ever — applied to a work of art or literature of enduring significance
la belle dame sans mer·ci \lä-bel-däm-säⁿ-mer-sē\ [F] : the beautiful lady without mercy
la·bo·ra·re est ora·re \ˈläb-ō-ˌrär-e-ˌest-ˈō-ˌrär-e\ [L] : to work is to pray
la·bor om·nia vin·cit \ˈlä-ˌbȯr-ˌōm-nē-ä-ˈwiŋ-kit\ [L] : labor conquers all things — motto of Oklahoma
la·cri·mae re·rum \ˌläk-ri-ˌmī-ˈrā-ˌru̇m\ [L] : tears for things : pity for misfortune; *also* : tears in things : tragedy of life
lais·ser–al·ler \le-sā-ä-lā\ [F] : letting go : lack of restraint
lap·sus ca·la·mi \ˌläp-su̇s-ˈkäl-ə-ˌmē, ˌlap-səs-ˈkaˈ-ə-ˌmī\ [L] : slip of the pen
lap·sus lin·guae \ˌlap-səs-ˈliŋ-ˌgwī, ˌläp-ˌsu̇s-\ [L] : slip of the tongue
la reine le veut \lä-ren-lə-vœ\ [F] : the queen wills it
la·scia·te ogni spe·ran·za, voi ch'en·tra·te \ˌläsh-ˈshä-tä ˌō-nʸē-spā-ˈrän-tsä-ˌvō-ē-kān-ˈträ-tā\ [It] : abandon all hope, ye who enter
lau·da·tor tem·po·ris ac·ti \lau̇-ˈdä-ˌtȯr-ˌtem-pə-ris-ˈäk-ˌtē\ [L] : one who praises past times
laus Deo \ˌlau̇s-ˈdā-ō\ [L] : praise (be) to God
le cœur a ses rai·sons que la rai·son ne con·nait point \lə-kœr-ä-sā-re-zōⁿk-la-re-zōⁿn-(ə-)kō-ne-pwaⁿ\ [F] : the heart has its reasons that reason knows nothing of
le roi est mort, vive le roi \lə-rwä-e-mȯr vēv-lə-rwä\ [F] : the king is dead, long live the king
le roi le veut \-lə-vœ\ [F] : the king wills it
le roi s'avi·se·ra \-sä-vēz-rä\ [F] : the king will consider
le style, c'est l'homme \lə-stēl-se-lȯm\ [F] : the style is the man
l'état, c'est moi \lā-tä-se-mwä\ [F] : the state, it is I
l'étoile du nord \lā-twäl-dᵫ-nȯr\ [F] : the star of the north — motto of Minnesota
Lie·der·kranz \ˈlēd-ər-ˌkräns\ [G] : wreath of songs : German singing society
lit·tera scrip·ta ma·net \ˌlit-ə-ˌrä-ˌskrip-tə-ˈmän-et\ [L] : the written letter abides
lo·cus in quo \ˌlō-kəs-in-ˈkwō\ [L] : place in which
l'union fait la force \lᵫ-nyōⁿ-fe-lä-fȯrs\ [F] : union makes strength — motto of Belgium
lu·sus na·tu·rae \ˌlü-səs-nə-ˈtu̇r-ē, -ˈtu̇r-ˌī\ [L] : freak of nature
ma foi \mä-fwä\ [F] : my faith! : indeed
mag·na est ve·ri·tas et prae·va·le·bit \ˌmäg-nä-ˌest-ˈwā-ri-ˌtäs-et-ˌprī-wä-ˈlā-bit\ [L] : truth is mighty and will prevail
mag·ni no·mi·nis um·bra \ˌmäg-nē-ˌnō-mə-nis-ˈu̇m-brä\ [L] : the shadow of a great name
mai·son de san·té \mā-zōⁿd-(ə-)säⁿ-tā\ [F] : private hospital : asylum
ma·lade ima·gi·naire \mä-läd-ē-mä-zhē-ner\ [F] : imaginary invalid : hypochondriac
ma·lis avi·bus \ˌmäl-ˌēs-ˈä-wi-ˌbu̇s\ [L] : under evil auspices
man spricht Deutsch \män-shprikt-ˈdȯich\ [G] : German spoken

ma·riage de con·ve·nance \má-ryȧzh-də-kō^{n}v-nä^{n}s\ [F] : marriage of convenience
mau·vaise honte \mō-vez-ō^{n}t\ [F] : bad shame : bashfulness
mau·vais quart d'heure \mō-ve-kȧr-dœr\ [F] : bad quarter hour : an uncomfortable though brief experience
me·den agan \(,)mā-,den-'äg-,än\ [Gk] : nothing in excess
me·dio tu·tis·si·mus ibis \'med-ē-,ō-tü-,tis-ə-mu̇s-'ē-bəs\ [L] : you will go most safely by the middle course
me ju·di·ce \mā-'yüd-ə-ke\ [L] : I being judge : in my judgment
mens sa·na in cor·po·re sa·no \māns-'sän-ə-in-,kȯr-pə-re-'sän-ō\ [L] : a sound mind in a sound body
me·um et tu·um \,mē-əm-,et-'tü-əm, ,me-əm-\ [L] : mine and thine : distinction of private property
mi·ra·bi·le vi·su \mə-,räb-ə-lē-'wē-sü\ [L] : wonderful to behold
mi·ra·bi·lia \,mir-ə-'bil-ē-ə\ [L] : wonders : miracles
mo·le ru·it sua \'mō-le-,ru̇-it-,su̇-ä\ [L] : it collapses from its own bigness
monde \mō^{n}d\ [F] : world : fashionable world : society
mon·ta·ni sem·per li·be·ri \mȯn-'tän-ē-,sem-pər-'lē-bə-,rē\ [L] : mountaineers are always free men — motto of West Virginia
mo·nu·men·tum ae·re per·en·ni·us \,mȯ-nə-'men-tu̇m-,ī-re-pə-'ren-ē-u̇s\ [L] : a monument more lasting than bronze — used of an immortal work of art or literature
mo·ri·tu·ri te sa·lu·ta·mus \,mȯr-ə-'tu̇r-ē-,tā-,säl-ə-'täm-u̇s\ [L] : we who are about to die salute thee
mul·tum in par·vo \,mu̇l-təm-in-'pär-vō\ [L] : much in little
mu·ta·to no·mi·ne de te fa·bu·la nar·ra·tur \mü-,tät-ō-'nō-mə-ne-dā-'tā-,fäb-ə-lä-nä-'rä-,tu̇r\ [L] : with the name changed the story applies to you
na·tu·ram ex·pel·las fur·ca, ta·men us·que re·cur·ret \nä-'tü-,räm-ek-,spel-äs-'fu̇r-,kä ,tä-mən-'u̇s-kwe-re-'ku̇r-et\ [L] : you may drive nature out with a pitchfork, but she will keep coming back
na·tu·ra non fa·cit sal·tum \nä-'tü-rä-,nōn-,fäk-ət-'säl-,tu̇m\ [L] : nature makes no leap
ne ce·de ma·lis \nā-,kā-de-'mäl-,ēs\ [L] : yield not to misfortunes
ne·mo me im·pu·ne la·ces·sit \'nā-mō-'mā-im-,pü-nā-lä-'kes-ət\ [L] : no one attacks me with impunity — motto of Scotland and of the Order of the Thistle
ne quid ni·mis \nā-,kwid-'nim-əs\ [L] : not anything in excess
n'est-ce pas? \nes-pä\ [F] : isn't it so?
nil ad·mi·ra·ri \'nēl-,äd-mə-'rär-ē\ [L] : to be excited by nothing : equanimity
nil de·spe·ran·dum \'nēl-,dā-spā-'rän-du̇m\ [L] : never despair
nil si·ne nu·mi·ne \'nēl-,sin-e-'nü-mə-ne\ [L] : nothing without the divine will — motto of Colorado
n'im·porte \na^{n}-pȯrt\ [F] : it's no matter
no·lens vo·lens \,nō-,lenz-'vō-,lenz\ [L] : unwilling (or) willing : willy-nilly
non om·nia pos·su·mus om·nes \nōn-'ȯm-nē-ä-,pō-sə-mu̇s-'ȯm-,nās\ [L] : we can't all (do) all things
non om·nis mo·ri·ar \nōn-'ȯm-nəs-,mȯr-ē-,är\ [L] : I shall not wholly die
non sans droict \nō^{n}-sä^{n}-drwä\ [OF] : not without right — motto on Shakespeare's coat of arms
non sum qua·lis eram \nōn-,su̇m-,kwäl-əs-'er-,äm\ [L] : I am not what I used to be
nos·ce te ip·sum \nōs-ke-,tā-'ip-,su̇m\ [L] : know thyself
nos·tal·gie de la boue \nȯs-täl-zhē-d(ə-)lä-bü\ [F] : nostalgia for the mud : homesickness for the gutter
nous avons chan·gé tout ce·la \nü-zȧ-vō^{n}-shä^{n}-zhā-tü-s(ə)lȧ\ [F] : we have changed all that
nous ver·rons ce que nous ver·rons \nü-ve-rō^{n}s-(ə-)kə-nü-ve-rō^{n}\ [F] : we shall see what we shall see
no·vus ho·mo \,nȯ-wəs-'hȯ-mō\ [L] : new man : man newly ennobled : upstart
no·vus or·do se·clo·rum \-'ȯr-,dō-sā-'klōr-əm\ [L] : a new cycle of the ages — motto on the reverse of the Great Seal of the United States
nu·gae \'nü-,gī\ [L] : trifles
nuit blanche \nw^{y}ē-blä^{n}sh\ [F] : white night : a sleepless night
nyet \'nyet\ [Russ] : no
ob·iit \'ō-bē-,it\ [L] : he (or she) died
ob·scu·rum per ob·scu·ri·us \əb-'skyu̇r-əm-,per-əb-'skyu̇r-ē-əs\ [L] : (explaining) the obscure by means of the more obscure
ode·rint dum me·tu·ant \'ōd-ə-,rint-,du̇m-met-ə-,wänt\ [L] : let them hate, so long as they fear
odi et amo \'ō-,dē-et-'äm-(,)ō\ [L] : I hate and I love
om·ne ig·no·tum pro mag·ni·fi·co \,ȯm-ne-ig-'nō-,tu̇m-prō-mäg-'nif-i-,kō\ [L] : everything unknown (is taken) as grand : the unknown tends to be exaggerated in importance or difficulty
om·nia mu·tan·tur, nos et mu·ta·mur in il·lis \,ȯm-nē-ä-mü-'tän-,tu̇r ,nōs-,et-mü-,täm-ər-in-'il-,ēs\ [L] : all things are changing, and we are changing with them
om·nia vin·cit amor \'ȯm-nē-ä-'wiŋ-kət-'äm-,ȯr\ [L] : love conquers all
onus pro·ban·di \,ō-nəs-prō-'ban-,dī, -dē\ [L] : burden of proof
ora pro no·bis \,ō-rä-prō-'nō-,bēs\ [L] : pray for us
ore ro·tun·do \,ōr-ē-rō-'tən-dō\ [L] : with round mouth : eloquently
oro y pla·ta \,ōr-ō-ē-'plät-ə\ [Sp] : gold and silver — motto of Montana
o tem·po·ra! o mo·res! \ō-'tem-pə-rä-ō-'mō-,rās\ [L] : oh the times! oh the manners!
oti·um cum dig·ni·ta·te \'ōt-ē-,u̇m-ku̇m-,dig-nə-'tä-te\ [L] : leisure with dignity
où sont les neiges d'an·tan? \ü-sō^{n}-lā-nezh-dä^{n}-tä^{n}\ [F] : where are the snows of yesteryear?
pal·li·da Mors \,pal-əd-ə-'mȯrz\ [L] : pale Death
pa·nem et cir·cen·ses \'pän-,em-et-kir-'kān-,sēs\ [L] : bread and circuses : provision of the means of life and recreation by government to appease discontent
pan·ta rhei \,pän-,tä-'(h)rā, ,pant-ə-'rā\ [Gk] : all things are in flux
par avance \pȧr-ȧ-vä^{n}s\ [F] : in advance : by anticipation
par avion \pȧr-ȧ-vyō^{n}\ [F] : by airplane — used on airmail
par ex·em·ple \pȧr-äg-zä^{n}pl^{ə}\ [F] : for example
par·tu·ri·unt mon·tes, nas·ce·tur ri·di·cu·lus mus \pär-,tu̇r-ē-,u̇nt-'mōn-,tās näs-'kā-,tu̇r-ri-,dik-ə-lu̇s-'müs\ [L] : the mountains are in labor, and a ridiculous mouse will be brought forth
pa·ter pa·tri·ae \'pä-,ter-'pä-trē-,ī\ [L] : father of his country
pau·cis ver·bis \,pau̇-,kēs-'wer-,bēs\ [L] : in a few words
pax vo·bis·cum \,päks-vō-'bēs-,ku̇m\ [L] : peace (be) with you
peine forte et dure \pen-fȯr-tā-dūer\ [F] : strong and hard punishment : torture
per an·gus·ta ad au·gus·ta \per-'än-,gu̇s-tə-äd-'au̇-,gu̇s-tə, per-'äŋ-\ [L] : through difficulties to honors
pere \per\ [F] : father — used after French proper names to distinguish a father from his son
per·eant qui an·te nos nos·tra dix·e·runt \'per-e-,änt-kwē-,än-te-'nōs-'nōs-trä-dēk-'sā-,ru̇nt\ [L] : may they perish who have expressed our bright ideas before us
per·eunt et im·pu·tan·tur \'per-e-,u̇nt-et-,im-pə-'tän-,tu̇r\ [L] : they (the hours) pass away and are reckoned on (our) account
per·fide Al·bion \per-fēd-ȧl-byō^{n}\ [F] : perfidious Albion (England)
peu à peu \pœ̄-ȧ-pœ̄\ [F] : little by little
peu de chose \pœ̄d-(ə-)shōz\ [F] : a trifle
pièce d'oc·ca·sion \pyes-dȯ-kä-zyō^{n}\ [F] : piece for a special occasion
pinx·it \'piŋk-sət\ [L] : he (or she) painted it
place aux dames \plȧs-ō-dȧm\ [F] : (make) room for the ladies
ple·no ju·re \,plā-nō-'yu̇r-e\ [L] : with full right
plus ça change, plus c'est la même chose \plue̅-sȧ-shä^{n}zh plue̅-se-lȧ-mem-shōz\ [F] : the more that changes, the more it's the same thing
plus roy·a·liste que le roi \plue̅-rwȧ-yȧ-lēst-kəl-rwȧ\ [F] : more royalist than the king
po·cas pa·la·bras \,pō-käs-pä-'läv-räs\ [Sp] : few words
po·eta nas·ci·tur, non fit \pō-,ā-tä-'näs-kə-,tu̇r nōn-'fit\ [L] : a poet is born, not made
pol·li·ce ver·so \,pō-li-ke-'ver-sō\ [L] : with thumb turned : with a gesture or expression of condemnation
post hoc, er·go prop·ter hoc \'pōst-,hōk ,er-gō-'prōp-ter-,hōk\ [L] : after this, therefore on account of it (a fallacy of argument)
post ob·itum \pōst-'ō-bə-,tu̇m\ [L] : after death
pour ac·quit \pür-ȧ-kē\ [F] : received payment
pour le mé·rite \pür-lə-mā-rēt\ [F] : for merit
pro aris et fo·cis \prō-,ä-,rēs-et-'fō-,kēs\ [L] : for altars and firesides
pro bo·no pu·bli·co \prō-,bō-nō-'pü-bli-,kō\ [L] : for the public good
pro hac vi·ce \prō-,häk-'wik-e\ [L] : for this occasion
pro pa·tria \prō-'pä-trē-,ä\ [L] : for one's country
pro re·ge, le·ge, et gre·ge \prō-'rā-,ge-'lā-,ge-et-'greg-,e\ [L] : for the king, the law, and the people
pro re na·ta \,prō-,rā-'nät-ə\ [L] : for an occasion that has arisen : as needed — used in medical prescriptions
quand même \kä^{n}-mem\ [F] : even though : whatever may happen
quan·tum mu·ta·tus ab il·lo \,kwänt-əm-mü-'tät-əs-äb-'il-ō\ [L] : how changed from what he once was
quan·tum suf·fi·cit \,kwänt-əm-'səf-ə-,kit\ [L] : as much as suffices : a sufficient quantity — used in medical prescriptions
¿quién sa·be? \kyān-'sä-vā\ [Sp] : who knows?
qui fa·cit per ali·um fa·cit per se \kwē-,fäk-it-,per-'äl-ē-,u̇m-,fäk-it-,per-'sā\ [L] : he who does (anything) through another does it through himself
quis cus·to·di·et ip·sos cus·to·des? \,kwis-ku̇s-'tōd-ē-,et-ip-,sōs-ku̇s-'tō-,dās\ [L] : who will keep the keepers themselves?
qui s'ex·cuse s'ac·cuse \kē-'sek-,skue̅z-'sȧ-,kue̅z\ [F] : he who excuses himself accuses himself
quis se·pa·ra·bit? \,kwis-,sā-pə-'räb-it\ [L] : who shall separate (us)? — motto of the Order of St. Patrick
qui trans·tu·lit sus·ti·net \kwē-'träns-tə-,lit-'su̇s-tə-,net\ [L] : He who transplanted sustains (us) — motto of Connecticut
qui va là? \kē-vȧ-lȧ\ [F] : who goes there?
quo·ad hoc \kwō-,äd-'hōk\ [L] : as far as this : to this extent
quod erat de·mon·stran·dum \,kwōd-'er-,ät-,dem-ən-'stran-dəm, -,dā-,mōn-'strän-,du̇m\ [L] : which was to be proved
quod erat fa·ci·en·dum \-,fäk-ē-'en-,du̇m\ [L] : which was to be done
quod sem·per, quod ubi·que, quod ab om·ni·bus \kwōd-'sem-,per kwōd-'u̇b-i-,kwā ,kwōd-äb-'ōm-ni-,bu̇s, -,kwōd-u̇-'bē-(,)kwā-\ [L] : what (has been held) always, everywhere, by everybody
quod vi·de \kwōd-'wid-,e\ [L] : which see
quo·rum pars mag·na fui \'kwōr-əm-,pärs-,mäg-nə-'fu̇-ē\ [L] : in which I played a great part
quos de·us vult per·de·re pri·us de·men·tat \kwōs-'de-u̇s-,wu̇lt-'perd-ə-,re-,pri-u̇s-dā-'men-,tät\ [L] : those whom a god wishes to destroy he first drives mad
quot ho·mi·nes, tot sen·ten·ti·ae \kwōt-'hō-mə-,nās-,tōt-sen-'ten-tē-,ī\ [L] : there are as many opinions as there are men
quo va·dis? \kwō-'wäd-əs\ [L] : whither are you going?
rai·son d'état \re-zō^{n}-dā-tä\ [F] : reason of state
re·cu·ler pour mieux sau·ter \rə-kue̅-lā-pür-myœ̄-sō-tā\ [F] : to draw back in order to make a better jump
reg·nat po·pu·lus \,reg-,nät-'pō-pə-,lu̇s\ [L] : the people rule — motto of Arkansas
re in·fec·ta \,rā-in-'fek-,tä\ [L] : the business being unfinished

ə abut ᵊ kitten, F table ər further a back ā bake ä cot, cart ȧ F bac au̇ out ch chin e less ē easy g gift i trip ī life j joke k̲ G ich ^{n} F vin ŋ sing ō flow ȯ flaw œ F bœuf œ̄ F feu ȯi coin th thing t̲h̲ this ü loot u̇ foot ue G Füllen ue̅ F rue y yet ^{y} F digne \dēn^{y}\, nuit \nw^{y}ē\ yü few yu̇ furious zh vision

Alem·bert, d' \ˌdal-əm-ˈba(ə)r, -ˈbe(ə)r\ Jean Le Rond 1717?–1783 Fr. math. & philos.
Al·ex·an·der \ˌal-ig-ˈzan-dər, ˌel-\ name of 8 popes: esp. **VI** (*Rodrigo Lanzol y Borja*) 1431?–1503 (pope 1492–1503)
Alexander III of Macedon 356–323 B.C. *the Great* king (336-323)
Alexander *Russ.* **Alek·sandr** name of 3 emps. of Russia: **I** 1777–1825 (reigned 1801–25); **II** 1818–1881 (reigned 1855–81); **III** 1845–1894 (reigned 1881–94)
Alexander I Obre·no·vich \-ō-ˈbren-ə-ˌvich\ 1876–1903 king of Serbia (1889–1903)
Alexander I 1888–1934 king of Yugoslavia (1921–34)
Alexander of Hillsborough 1st Earl 1885–1965 *Albert Victor Alexander* Brit. polit.
Alexander Nev·ski \-ˈnev-skē, -ˈnef-\ 1220?–1263 Russ. saint & mil. hero
Alexander Se·ve·rus \-sə-ˈvir-əs\ 208?–235 Rom. emp. (222–235)
Alexander of Tunis 1st Earl 1891–1969 *Harold Rupert Leofric George Alexander* Brit. field marshal; gov. gen. of Canada (1946–52)
Alex·is I Mi·khai·lo·vich \ə-ˌlek-sə-smə-ˈkī-lə-ˌvich\ 1629–1676 *father of Peter the Great* czar of Russia (1645–76)
Alexis Pe·tro·vich \pə-ˈtrō-vich\ 1690–1718 *son of Peter the Great* czarevitch of Russia
Alex·i·us I Com·ne·nus \ə-ˈlek-sē-ə-ˌskäm-ˈnē-nəs\ 1048–1118 Eastern Rom. emp. (1081–1118)
Al·fie·ri \ˌal-fē-ˈe(ə)r-ē\ Count Vittorio 1749–1803 Ital. dram.
Al·fon·so \al-ˈfän(t)-(ˌ)sō, -ˈfän-(ˌ)zō\ *Port.* **Afon·so** *older* **Af·fon·so** \ə-ˈfōⁿ-(ˌ)sü\ name of 6 kings of Portugal: esp. **I** 1112–1185 (1st king; 1139–85); **V** 1432–1481 (reigned 1438–81)
Alfonso *or* **Al·phon·so XIII** 1886–1941 king of Spain (1886–1931)
Al·fred \ˈal-frəd, -fərd\ 849–899 *the Great* king of the West Saxons (871–899)
Al·ger \ˈal-jər\ Horatio 1832–1899 Am. author
Al·gren \ˈȯl-grən\ Nelson 1909– Am. author
Ali \ä-ˈlē, ˈal-ē, ˈäl-ē\ *Ar.* **Ali ibn-abi-Tālib** 600?–661 *cousin & son-in-law of Muhammad* 4th orthodox caliph (656–661)
Ali *or* **Ali Pa·sha** \-ˈpäsh-ə, -ˈpash-; -pə-ˈshä\ 1741–1822 *the Lion of Janina* Turk. pasha
Al·len \ˈal-ən\ Ethan 1738–1789 Am. Revolutionary soldier
Allen Frederick Lewis 1890–1954 Am. editor & hist.
Allen William 1532–1594 Eng. cardinal
Al·len·by \ˈal-ən-bē\ 1st Viscount 1861–1936 *Edmund Henry Hynman Allenby* Brit. field marshal
Allen·de Gos·sens \ä-ˌyen-dā-ˈgō-ˌsen(t)s\ Salvador 1908–1973 Chilean physician; pres. of Chile (1970–73)
Al·leyn \ˈal-ən, -ˌēn, -ˌān\ Edward 1566–1626 Eng. actor
All·ston \ˈȯl-stən\ Washington 1779–1843 Am. painter
Al·ma–Tad·e·ma \ˌal-mə-ˈtad-ə-mə\ Sir Lawrence 1836–1912 Eng. (Du.-born) painter
Al·va \ˈal-və\ *or* **Al·ba** \ˈal-bə\ Duke of 1508–1582 *Fernando Álvarez de Toledo* Span. gen.
Al·va·ra·do, de \-dä-ˌal-və-ˈräd-(ˌ)ō\ Alonso 1490?–1554 Span. soldier in Mexico (under Cortes) & Peru
Alvarado, de Pedro 1495?–1541 Span. soldier; companion of Cortes in Mexico
Al·ve·ar, de \ˌäl-vā-ˈär\ Carlos María 1789–1853 Argentine revolutionist
A·ma·ti \ä-ˈmät-ē, ə-\ family of Ital. violin makers of Cremona: esp. Nicolò or Nicola 1596–1684
Am·brose \ˈam-ˌbrōz\ Saint 340?–397 bishop of Milan — **Am·bro·sian** \am-ˈbrō-zhən, -zē-ən\ *adj*
Amen·ho·tep \ˌäm-ən-ˈhō-ˌtep, ˌam-\ *or* **Am·e·no·phis** \ˌam-ə-ˈnō-fəs\ name of 4 kings of Egypt: esp. **III** (reigned *ab* 1411–1375 B.C.); **IV** — see IKHNATON
Amerigo Vespucci — see VESPUCCI
Am·herst \ˈam-(ˌ)ərst\ Baron 1717–1797 *Jeffrey (or Jeffery) Amherst* Brit. gen.; gov.-gen. of Brit. No. Am. (1760–63)
Amis \ˈā-məs\ Kingsley 1922– Eng. author
Am·père \äⁿ-ˈpe(ə)r\ André Marie 1775–1836 Fr. physicist
Amund·sen \ˈäm-ən-sən\ Roald 1872–1928 Norw. polar explorer; disc. South Pole (1911)
Anac·re·on \ə-ˈnak-rē-ən\ 572?–?488 B.C. Greek poet
An·ax·ag·o·ras \ˌan-ˌak-ˈsag-ə-rəs\ 500?–428 B.C. Greek philos. — **An·ax·ag·o·re·an** \-ˌsag-ə-ˈrē-ən\ *adj*
Anax·i·man·der \ə-ˈnak-sə-ˌman-dər\ 611–547 B.C. Greek philos. & astron. — **Anax·i·man·dri·an** \-ˌnak-sə-ˈman-drē-ən\ *adj*
An·ders \ˈän-dərs, -dərz\ Wladyslaw 1892–1970 Pol. gen.
An·der·sen \ˈan-dər-sən\ Hans Christian 1805–1875 Danish writer of fairy tales
An·der·son \ˈan-dər-sən\ Carl David 1905– Am. physicist
Anderson John 1882–1958 1st Viscount *Wa·ver·ley* \ˈwā-vər-lē\ Brit. polit.
Anderson Dame Judith 1898– orig. *Frances Margaret Anderson* Australian actress
Anderson Marian 1902– Am. contralto
Anderson Maxwell 1888–1959 Am. dram.
Anderson Sherwood 1876–1941 Am. writer
An·drás·sy \ˈän-ˌdräsh-ē\ Count Gyula, father 1823–1890 & son 1860–1929 Hung. statesmen
An·dré \ˈan-drē, ˈän-(ˌ)drā\ John 1751–1780 Brit. major; spy in Am. Rev.
An·drea del Sar·to \än-ˌdrā-ə-ˌdel-ˈsärt-(ˌ)ō\ 1486–1531 *Andrea Domenico d'Agnolo di Francesco* Florentine painter
An·dre·ev \än-ˈdrā-(y)əf\ Andrei Andreevich 1895–1971 Russ. polit.
Andreev *or* **An·dre·yev** \än-ˈdrā-(y)əf\ Leonid Nikolaevich 1871–1919 Russ. nov., storywriter, & dram.
An·drews \ˈan-ˌdrüz\ Roy Chapman 1884–1960 Am. naturalist
An·dric \ˈän-drich\ Ivo 1890– Yugoslav author
An·dros \ˈan-ˌdräs, -drəs\ Sir Edmund 1637–1714 Brit. colonial gov. in Am.
An·ge·la Me·ri·ci \ˌan-jə-lə-mə-ˈrē-chē\ Saint 1474?–1540 Ital. religious; founder of Ursuline order (1535)
Angelico Fra — see FIESOLE
An·gell \ˈān-jəl\ Sir Norman 1872–1967 *Ralph Norman Angell Lane* Eng. author & lecturer
Ång·ström \ˈaŋ-strəm, ˈȯŋ-\ Anders Jonas 1814–1874 Swed. physicist
An·na Iva·nov·na \ˈan-ə-ē-ˈvän-əv-nə\ 1693–1740 empress of Russia (1730–40)
Anne \ˈan\ 1665–1714 *dau. of James II* queen of Gr. Brit. (1702–14)
Anne of Austria 1601–1666 *consort of Louis XIII of France* regent (1643–61) for her son Louis XIV
Anne of Cleves \ˈklēvz\ 1515–1557 *4th wife of Henry VIII of Eng.*
Annunzio, D' Gabriele — see D'ANNUNZIO
Anouilh \a-ˈnü-ē\ Jean 1910– Fr. dram.
An·selm \ˈan-ˌselm\ Saint 1033–1109 archbishop of Canterbury (1093–1109)
An·tho·ny \ˈan(t)-thə-nē, *chiefly Brit* ˈan-tə-\ Saint *ab* 250–350 Egyptian monk; regarded as founder of Christian monachism
Anthony Mark — see Marcus ANTONIUS
Anthony Susan Brownell 1820–1906 Am. suffragist
Anthony of Padua Saint 1195–1231 Franciscan monk
An·tig·o·nus I \an-ˈtig-ə-nəs\ 382–301 B.C. *Cyclops* gen. of Alexander the Great & king of Macedonia (306–301)
An·ti·o·chus \an-ˈtī-ə-kəs\ name of 13 Seleucid kings of Syria: esp. **III** *the Great* 242–187 B.C. (reigned 223–187); **IV** (*Epiph·a·nes* \-i-ˈpif-ə-ˌnēz\) *d* 163 B.C. (reigned 175–163)
An·tip·a·ter \an-ˈtip-ət-ər\ 398?–319 B.C. Macedonian gen. & statesman
An·tis·the·nes \an-ˈtis-thə-ˌnēz\ 444?–after 371 B.C. Athenian philos.; founder of Cynic school
An·toine Père \pe(ə)r-ˈan-ˌtwän\ 1748–1829 *Antonio de Se·di·lla* \sə-ˈdē-(y)ə\ Span. Capuchin priest in New Orleans
An·to·ne·scu \ˌan-tə-ˈnes-(ˌ)kü\ Ion \ˈyȯn\ 1882–1946 Rumanian gen.; dictator (1940–44)
An·to·ni·nus \ˌan-tə-ˈnī-nəs\ Marcus Au·re·lius \ȯ-ˈrēl-yəs, -ˈrē-lē-əs\ 121–180 *nephew, son-in-law, and adopted son of Antoninus Pius* Rom. emp. (161–180) & Stoic philos.
Antoninus Pi·us \ˈpī-əs\ 86–161 Rom. emp. (138–161)
An·to·ni·us \an-ˈtō-nē-əs\ Marcus *Eng.* Mark *or* Marc An·to·ny *or* An·tho·ny \ˈan(t)-thə-nē, *chiefly Brit* ˈan-tə-\ 83?–30 B.C. Rom. orator, triumvir, & gen.
Ao·ki \ˈä-ō-kē\ Viscount 1844–1914 *Shuzo Aoki* Jap. diplomat; 1st Jap. ambassador to U.S. (1905–09)
Apel·les \ə-ˈpel-ēz\ 4th cent. B.C. Greek painter
Apol·li·naire \ə-ˌpäl-ə-ˈna(ə)r, -ˈne(ə)r\ Guillaume 1880–1918 *Guillaume Apollinaire de Kostrowitsky* Fr. poet
Ap·ol·lo·ni·us \ˌap-ə-ˈlō-nē-əs\ **of Rhodes** 3d–2d cent. B.C. Greek poet — **Ap·ol·lo·nian** \-nē-ən, -nyən\ *adj*
Appius Claudius — see CLAUDIUS
Appleseed Johnny — see John CHAPMAN
Ap·ple·ton \ˈap-əl-tən, -əlt-ᵊn\ Sir Edward (Victor) 1892–1965 Eng. physicist
Aprak·sin *or* **Aprax·in** \ə-ˈprak-sən\ Fëdor Matveevich 1671–1728 Russ. admiral
Ap·u·le·ius \ˌap-yə-ˈlē-(y)əs\ Lucius 2d cent. A.D. Rom. philos. & satirist
Aqui·nas \ə-ˈkwī-nəs\ Saint Thomas 1225–1274 Ital. theol.
Ar·am \ˈar-əm, ˈer-\ Eugene 1704–1759 Eng. philologist & murderer
Ara·nha \ə-ˈran-yə\ Oswaldo 1894–1960 Brazil. lawyer & polit.
Ar·ber \ˈär-bər\ Edward 1836–1912 Eng. editor
Arblay, d' Madame — see Fanny BURNEY
Ar·buth·not \är-ˈbəth-nət, ˈär-bəth-ˌnät\ John 1667–1735 Scot. physician & author
Ar·cher \ˈär-chər\ William 1856–1924 Scot. critic & dram.
Ar·chi·me·des \ˌär-kə-ˈmēd-ēz\ 287?–212 B.C. Greek math. & inventor — **Ar·chi·me·de·an** \-ˈmēd-ē-ən, -mi-ˈdē-\ *adj*
Ar·chi·pen·ko \ˌär-kə-ˈpeŋ-(ˌ)kō\ Alexander 1887–1964 Am. (Russ.-born) sculptor
Are·ti·no \ˌar-ə-ˈtē-(ˌ)nō\ Pietro 1492–1556 Ital. satirist
Ar·gall \ˈär-ˌgȯl, -gəl\ Sir Samuel *fl* 1609–1625 Eng. mariner
Ar·gyll \är-ˈgī(ə)l, ˈär-ˌgīl\ 9th Duke of 1845–1914 *John Douglas Sutherland Campbell* gov. gen. of Canada (1878–83)
Ari·o·sto \ˌär-ē-ˈō-(ˌ)stō\ Lodovico 1474–1533 Ital. poet
Ar·is·tar·chus \ˌar-ə-ˈstär-kəs\ 220?–150 B.C. Greek grammarian
Aristarchus of Samos 3d cent. B.C. Greek astron.
Ar·is·ti·des *or* **Ar·is·tei·des** \ˌar-ə-ˈstīd-ēz\ 530?–?468 B.C. *the Just* Athenian statesman
Ar·is·tip·pus \ˌar-ə-ˈstip-əs\ 435?–?356 B.C. Greek philos.
Ar·is·toph·a·nes \ˌar-ə-ˈstäf-ə-ˌnēz\ 448?–?380 B.C. Athenian dram.
Aristophanes of Byzantium 257?–?180 B.C. Greek scholar
Ar·is·tot·le \ˈar-ə-ˌstät-ᵊl\ 384–322 B.C. Greek philos.
Ar·i·us \ə-ˈrī-əs; ˈar-ē-əs, ˈer-\ *d* 336 A.D. Greek theol.
Ark·wright \ˈär-ˌkrīt\ Sir Richard 1732–1792 Eng. inventor
Ar·len \ˈär-lən\ Michael 1895–1956 *Di·kran* \dik-ˈrän\ *Kou·youmdjian* \kü-ˈyüm-jē-ən\ Brit. (Bulg.-born) nov.
Ar·min·i·us \är-ˈmin-ē-əs\ *or* **Ar·min** \är-ˈmēn\ 17 B.C.?–A.D. 21 sometimes *Her·mann* \ˈhe(ə)r-ˌmän\ Ger. hero
Arminius Jacobus 1560–1609 *Jacob Har·men·sen* \ˈhär-mən-sən\ or *Her·mansz* \ˈhe(ə)r-ˌmän(t)s\ Du. theol.
Ar·mour \ˈär-mər\ Philip Danforth 1832–1901 Am. meat packer
Arm·strong \ˈärm-ˌstrȯŋ\ Hamilton Fish 1893–1973 Am. editor
Armstrong Louis 1900–1971 *Satch·mo* \ˈsach-ˌmō\ Am. jazz musician
Armstrong Neil Alden 1930– Am. astronaut; 1st man on the moon
Armstrong William George 1810–1900 Baron *Armstrong of Cragside* Eng. inventor & industrialist
Armstrong–Jones \-ˈjōnz\ Antony Charles Robert 1930– Earl of *Snowdon; husband of Princess Margaret Rose of Gr. Brit.*
Arne \ˈärn\ Thomas Augustine 1710–1778 Eng. composer
Ar·nim, von \ˈär-nəm\ Jürgen 1889– Ger. gen.
Ar·nold \ˈärn-ᵊld\ Benedict 1741–1801 Am. Revolutionary gen. & traitor
Arnold Henry Harley 1886–1950 Am. gen.

Arnold Matthew 1822–1888 *son of Thomas* Eng. poet & critic
Arnold Thomas 1795–1842 Eng. educ.
Ar·nold·son \'ärn-ᵊl-sən\ Klas Pontus 1844–1916 Swed. pacifist
Arouet François Marie — see VOLTAIRE
Arp \'ärp\ Jean (or Hans) 1887–1966 Fr. artist & poet
Ar·pád \'är-ˌpäd\ *d* 907 Hung. national hero
Ar·rhe·ni·us \ə-'rē-nē-əs, -'rā-\ Svante August 1859–1927 Swed. physicist & chem.
Ar·son·val, d' \ˌdärs-ᵊn-ˌväl, -ˌval\ Jacques Arsène 1851–1940 Fr. physicist
Ar·ta·xer·xes \ˌärt-ə(g)-'zərk-ˌsēz\ name of 3 Pers. kings: **I** *d* 424 B.C. (reigned 464–24); **II** *d* 359 B.C. (reigned 404–359); **III** *d* 338 B.C. (reigned 359–338)
Ar·te·vel·de, van \'ärt-ə-ˌvel-də\ Jacob 1290?–1345 & his son Philip 1340?–1382 Flem. leaders
Ar·thur \'är-thər\ Chester Alan 1829–1886 21st pres. of the U.S. (1881–85)
Ar·tzy·ba·sheff \ˌärt-si-'bäsh-əf\ Boris 1899–1965 Am. (Russ.-born) illustrator
As·bury \'az-ˌber-ē, -b(ə-)rē\ Francis 1745–1816 1st Methodist bishop in Am.
Asch \'ash\ Sho·lem \'shō-ləm\ *or* Sha·lom \shə-'lōm\ *or* Sho·lom \'shō-ləm\ 1880–1957 Am. (Pol.-born) Yiddish writer
As·cham \'as-kəm\ Roger 1515–1568 Eng. scholar & author
Ashburton Baron — see Alexander BARING
Ashton Winifred — see Clemence DANE
Ashur·ba·ni·pal *also* **A(s·)sur·ba·ni·pal** \ˌäs(h)-ər-'bän-ə-ˌpäl\ king of Assyria (669–626 B.C.)
Aso·ka *or* **Aço·ka** \ə-'s(h)ō-kə\ *d* 232 B.C. king of Magadha, India (273–232)
As·pa·sia \as-'pā-zh(ē-)ə\ 470?–410 B.C. *consort of Pericles*
As·quith \'as-ˌkwith, -kwəth\ Herbert Henry 1852–1928 *1st Earl of Oxford and Asquith* Brit. statesman
As·ser \'äs-ər\ Tobias Michael Carel 1838–1913 Du. jurist
Astaire \ə-'sta(ə)r, -'ste(ə)r\ Fred 1899– Am. dancer & actor
As·ton \'as-tən\ Francis William 1877–1945 Eng. physicist
As·tor \'as-tər\ John Jacob 1763–1848 Am. (Ger.-born) fur trader & capitalist
Astor Viscountess 1879–1964 *Nancy Langhorne Astor* 1st woman member of Brit. Parliament (1919–45)
As·tu·ri·as \ə-'st(y)u̇r-ē-əs, a-\ Miguel Angel 1899– Guatemalan author
Ata·hual·pa \ˌät-ə-'wäl-pə\ 1500?–1533 last Inca king of Peru
Ath·a·na·sius \ˌath-ə-'nā-zh(ē-)əs, -'nā-sh(ē-)əs\ Saint 293?–373 Greek church father
Ath·el·stan \'ath-əl-ˌstan\ 895–940 king of Eng. (*ab* 924–940)
Ath·er·ton \'ath-ərt-ᵊn\ Gertrude Franklin 1857–1948 née *Horn* Am. nov.
At·tar \'at-ər, 'a-ˌtär\ 1119–?1299 Pers. poet
At·ti·la \'at-ᵊl-ə\ 406?–453 *the Scourge of God* king of the Huns
Att·lee \'at-lē\ 1st Earl 1883–1967 *Clement Richard Attlee* Brit. polit.
At·tucks \'at-əks\ Crispus 1723?–1770 Am. Negro; one of 3 men killed in Boston Massacre
Au·ber \ō-'be(ə)r\ Daniel François Esprit 1782–1871 Fr. composer
Au·brey \'ȯ-brē\ John 1626–1697 Eng. antiquarian
Au·chin·closs \'ȯ-kən-ˌkläs\ Louis Stanton 1917– Am. writer
Au·den \'ȯd-ᵊn\ Wystan Hugh 1907–1973 Am. (Eng.-born) poet — **Au·den·esque** \ˌȯd-ᵊn-'esk\ *adj*
Au·du·bon \'ȯd-ə-bən, -ˌbän\ John James 1785–1851 Am. (Haitian-born) artist & naturalist
Au·er·bach \'au̇(-ə)r-ˌbäk, -ˌbäk\ Berthold 1812–1882 Ger. nov.
Au·gier \ō-'zh(y)ā, ˌō-zhē-'ā\ Émile 1820–1889 Fr. poet & dram.
Au·gus·tine \'ȯ-gə-ˌstēn; ȯ-'gəs-tən, ə-\ Saint 354–430 church father; bishop of Hippo (396–430)
Augustine *also* **Austin** Saint *d* 604 *Apostle of the English* 1st archbishop of Canterbury (601–04)
Au·gus·tus \ȯ-'gəs-təs, ə-\ 63 B.C.–A.D. 14) *Gaius Julius Caesar Octavianus* 1st Rom. emp. (27 B.C.–A.D. 14)
Au·rang·zeb *or* **Au·rung·zeb** *or* **Au·rung·zebe** \'ȯr-əŋ-ˌzeb, 'au̇-rəŋ-\ 1618–1707 emp. of Hindustan (1658–1707)
Au·re·lian \ȯ-'rēl-yən\ 212?–275 *Lucius Domitius Aurelianus* Rom. emp. (270-275)
Au·ri·ol \ˌȯr-ē-ˌōl, -'ōl\ Vincent 1884–1966 Fr. lawyer; 1st pres. of 4th Republic (1947–54)
Aus·ten \'ȯs-tən, 'äs-\ Jane 1775–1817 Eng. nov.
Aus·tin \'ȯs-tən, 'äs-\ Alfred 1835–1913 Eng. poet; poet laureate (1896–1913)
Austin John 1790–1859 Eng. jurist
Austin Mary 1868–1934 née *Hunter* Am. nov.
Austin Stephen Fuller 1793–1836 Am. colonizer in Texas
Avebury 1st Baron — see LUBBOCK
Av·en·zo·ar \ˌav-ən-'zō-ər, -zō-'är\ 1091?–1162 Arab physician in Spain
Aver·ro·ës *or* **Aver·rho·ës** \ə-'ver-ə-ˌwēz, ˌav-ə-'rō-(ˌ)ēz\ 1126–1198 also *ibn-Rushd* Span.-Arab philos. & physician
Avery \'āv-(ə-)rē\ Milton Clark 1893–1965 Am. artist
Av·i·cen·na \ˌav-ə-'sen-ə\ 980–1037 also *ibn-Sina* Arab (Persian-born) philos. & physician
Ávila Camacho Manuel — see CAMACHO
Avo·ga·dro \ˌav-ə-'gäd-(ˌ)rō, ˌäv-\ Count Amedeo 1776–1856 Ital. chemist & physicist
Avon Earl of — see Anthony EDEN
Ay·de·lotte \'ād-ᵊl-ˌät\ Frank 1880–1956 Amer. educ.
Aza·ña \ə-'zän-yə\ Manuel 1880–1940 Span. lawyer; pres. of Spain (1936–39)
Azu·ma \ə-'zü-mə, 'äz-ə-ˌmä\ Tokuho 1909– Jap. dancer
Bab·bitt \'bab-ət\ Irving 1865–1933 Am. scholar
Ba·ber *or* **Ba·bur** *or* **Ba·bar** \'bäb-ər\ 1483–1530 *Zahir ud-Din Muhammad* founder of Mogul dynasty of India; emp. (1526–30)
Ba·beuf *or* **Ba·boeuf** \bä-'bəf, bȧ-bœf\ François Émile 1760–1797 Fr. agitator
Bab·ing·ton \'bab-iŋ-tən\ Anthony 1561–1586 Eng. R.C. conspirator against Queen Elizabeth I
Bab·son \'bab-sən\ Roger Ward 1875–1967 Am. statistician
Bach \'bäk, 'bäk\ Carl Philipp Emanuel 1714–1788 *son of J.S.* Ger. composer
Bach Johann Sebastian 1685–1750 Ger. organist & composer
Bach Wilhelm Friedmann 1710–1784 *son of J.S.* Ger. organist & composer
Ba·con \'bā-kən\ Francis 1561–1626 1st Baron *Ver·u·lam* \'ver-(y)ə-ləm\ Viscount *St. Al·bans* \sānt-'ȯl-bənz, sənt-\ Eng. philos.
Bacon Nathaniel 1647–1676 Am. colonial leader
Bacon Roger, Friar 1214?–1294 Eng. philos.
Ba·den–Pow·ell \ˌbād-ᵊn-'pō-əl\ Robert Stephenson Smyth 1857–1941 1st Baron of *Gilwell* Brit. gen.; founder of Boy Scout movement
Ba·do·glio \bə-'dōl-(ˌ)yō\ Pietro 1871–1956 Ital. gen.; premier (1943–44)
Bae·yer, von \'bā-(y)ər\ Adolf 1835–1917 Ger. chem.
Baez \'bä-ˌez, 'bīz\ Joan 1941– Am. folk singer
Baf·fin \'baf-ən\ William 1584–1622 Eng. navigator
Bage·hot \'baj-ət\ Walter 1826–1877 Eng. econ. & journalist
Ba·gra·tion \bə-ˌgrät-ē-'ōn, ˌbäg-rə-'tyōn\ Prince Pëtr Ivanovich 1765–1812 Russ. gen.
Ba·ha·ul·lah \bä-ˌhä-ü-'lä\ Mirza Husayn Ali 1817–1892 Pers. founder of Bahaism
Bai·ley \'bā-lē\ Liberty Hyde 1858–1954 Am. botanist
Bailey Nathan *or* Nathaniel *d* 1742 Eng. lexicographer
Bailey Pearl Mae 1918– Am. singer
Bail·lie \'bā-lē\ Joanna 1762–1851 Scot. dram. & poet
Bain \'bān\ Alexander 1818–1903 Scot. psychol.
Baird \'ba(ə)rd, 'be(ə)rd\ John Logie 1888–1946 *father of television* Scot. inventor
Bairns·fa·ther \'ba(ə)rnz-ˌfät͟h-ər, 'be(ə)rnz-\ Bruce 1888–1959 Eng. cartoonist
Ba·jer \'bī(-ə)r\ Fredrik 1837–1922 Dan. statesman & writer
Ba·ker \'bā-kər\ Newton Diehl 1871–1937 Am. statesman
Baker Ray Stannard 1870–1946 pseud. *David Gray·son* \'grās-ᵊn\ Am. author
Baker Sir Samuel White 1821–1893 Eng. explorer in Africa
Bakst \'bäkst\ Léon Nikolaevich 1866?–1924 Russ. painter
Ba·ku·nin \bə-'kün-(y)ən, bä-\ Mikhail Aleksandrovich 1814–1876 Russ. anarchist
Bal·an·chine \ˌbal-ən-'chin, -'chēn\ George 1904– *George Meletonovitch Balanchinvadze* Am. (Russ.-born) choreographer
Bal·bo \'bäl-(ˌ)bō\ Italo 1896–1940 Ital. aviator & polit.
Bal·boa, de \bal-'bō-ə\ Vasco Núñez 1475–1519 Span. explorer; disc. Pacific Ocean
Balch \'bȯlch\ Emily Greene 1867–1961 Am. econ. & sociol.
Bal·dwin I \'bȯl-dwən\ 1058–1118 *bro. of Godfrey of Bouillon* king of Jerusalem (1100–18)
Baldwin James 1924– Am. writer
Baldwin James Mark 1861–1934 Am. psychol.
Baldwin Stanley 1867–1947 1st Earl *Baldwin of Bewd·ley* \'byüd-lē\ Brit. statesman
Balfe \'balf\ Michael William 1808–1870 Irish composer & singer
Bal·four \'bal-fər, -ˌfōr, -ˌfȯr\ 1st Earl of 1848–1930 *Arthur James Balfour* Brit. philos. & statesman
Ba·liol, de \'bāl-yəl\ John 1249–1315 king of Scotland (1292–96)
Ball \'bȯl\ John *d* 1381 Eng. priest & social agitator
Bal·lan·tyne \'bal-ən-ˌtīn\ James 1772–1833 Scot. printer
Baltimore Lord — see George CALVERT
Bal·zac, de \'bȯl-ˌzak, 'bal-, *Fr.* bȧl-zȧk\ Honoré 1799–1850 Fr. nov. — **Bal·za·cian** \bȯl-'zā-shən, bal-, -'zak-ē-ən\ *adj*
Ban·croft \'ban-ˌkrȯft, 'baŋ-\ George 1800–1891 Am. hist.
Bancroft Richard 1544–1610 Eng. prelate; archbishop of Canterbury (1604–10)
Ban·del·lo \ban-'del-(ˌ)ō, bän-\ Matteo 1480?–1562 Ital. writer
Bangs \'baŋz\ John Kendrick 1862–1922 Am. humorist
Bank·head \'baŋk-ˌhed\ Tallulah Brockman 1903–1968 Am. actress
Banks \'baŋ(k)s\ Sir Joseph 1743–1820 Eng. naturalist
Ban·ting \'bant-iŋ\ Sir Frederick Grant 1891–1941 Canad. physician; discovered (with others) insulin treatment of diabetes
Ba·ra·nov \bə-'rän-əf\ Aleksandr Andreevich 1747–1819 Russ. fur trader; 1st gov. of Russ. America
Bá·rány \'bär-ˌän-yə\ Robert 1876–1936 Austrian physician
Bar·ba·ros·sa \ˌbär-bə-'räs-ə, -'rȯs-\ — see FREDERICK I
Barbarossa name of 2 Algerian corsairs, brothers: **I** 1473?–1518; **II** 1466?–1546
Bar·ber \'bär-bər\ Samuel 1910– Am. composer
Bar·busse \bär-bu̅e̅s, bär-'b(y)üs\ Henri 1873–1935 Fr. author
Bar·clay \'bär-klē\ Robert 1648–1690 Scot. Quaker author
Bar·clay de Tol·ly \ˌbär-ˌklī-də-'tō-lē, -ˌklā-\ Prince Mikhail 1761–1818 Russ. field marshal
Bar·deen \bär-'dēn\ John 1908– Am. physicist
Ba·rents \'bar-ən(t)s, 'bär-\ Willem *d* 1597 Du. navigator
Bar·ing \'ba(ə)r-iŋ, 'be(ə)r-\ Alexander 1774–1848 1st Baron *Ash·bur·ton* \'ash-ˌbərt-ᵊn\ Brit. financier & diplomat
Baring Evelyn 1841–1917 1st Earl of *Cro·mer* \'krō-mər\ Brit. diplomat
Bark·la \'bär-klə\ Charles Glover 1877–1944 Eng. physicist
Bark·ley \'bär-klē\ Al·ben \'al-bən\ William 1877–1956 Am. lawyer & polit.; vice-pres. of U.S. (1949–53)
Bar·low \'bär-ˌlō\ Joel 1754–1812 Am. poet & diplomat
Bar·nard \'bär-nərd, -ˌnärd\ Christiaan Neethling 1922– So. African surgeon
Bar·nard \'bär-nərd\ George Grey 1863–1938 Am. sculptor
Barnes \'bärnz\ Harry Elmer 1889–1968 Am. sociol.

Bar·ne·veldt *or* **Bar·ne·veld** \'bär-nə-ˌvelt\ Jan van Olden 1547–1619 Du. statesman
Bar·num \'bär-nəm\ Phineas Taylor 1810–1891 Am. showman
Barocchio *or* **Barozzi** Giacomo — see VIGNOLA
Ba·ro·ja \bä-'rō-(ˌ)hä\ Pío 1872–1956 Span. writer
Bar·rès \ba-'res\ Auguste Maurice 1862–1923 Fr. nov. & polit.
Bar·rie \'bar-ē\ Sir James Matthew 1860–1937 Scot. nov. & dram.
Bar·ros, de \'bär-ˌüsh\ João 1496–1570 Port. hist.
Bar·row \'bar-(ˌ)ō, 'bar-ə(-w)\ Isaac 1630–1677 Eng. math. & theol.
Bar·ry \'bar-ē\ Philip 1896–1949 Am. dram.
Bar·ry·more \'bar-i-ˌmō(ə)r, -ˌmȯ(ə)r\ family of Am. actors: Maurice 1847–1905 real name *Herbert Blythe;* his wife Georgiana Emma 1856–1893 *dau. of John Drew;* their children Lionel 1878–1954, Ethel 1879–1959, & John Blythe 1882–1942
Bart \'bär\ *or* **Barth** \'bärt\ Jean 1651?–1702 Fr. naval hero
Barth \'bärth\ John Simmons 1930– Am. author
Barth \'bärt, 'barth\ Karl 1886–1968 Swiss theol. — **Barth·ian** \-ē-ən\ *adj*
Bar·thol·di \bär-'t(h)äl-dē, -'t(h)ȯl-\ Frédéric Auguste 1834–1904 Fr. sculptor
Bart·lett \'bärt-lət\ John 1820–1905 Am. publisher & editor
Bartlett Vernon 1894– Eng. author
Bar·tók \'bär-ˌtäk, -ˌtȯk\ **Bé·la** \'bā-lə\ 1881–1945 Hung. composer
Bar·to·lom·meo \ˌbär-ˌtōl-ə-'mā-(ˌ)ō\ Fra 1475–1517 *Baccio della Porta* Florentine painter
Bar·ton \'bärt-ᵊn\ Clara *in full* Clarissa Harlowe 1821–1912 founder of Am. Red Cross Society
Bar·tram \'bär-trəm\ John 1699–1777 Am. botanist
Ba·ruch \bə-'rük\ Bernard Man·nes \'man-əs\ 1870–1965 Am. businessman & statesman
Ba·sil \'baz-əl, 'bās-, 'bas-, 'bāz-\ *or* **Ba·sil·i·us** \bə-'sil-ē-əs, -'zil-\ Saint 330?–?379 *the Great* church father; bishop of Caesarea
Bas·ker·ville \'bas-kər-ˌvil\ John 1706–1775 Eng. typographer
Bates \'bāts\ Katharine Lee 1859–1929 Am. poet & educ.
Ba·tis·ta y Zal·dí·var \bə-'tēs-tə-ˌē-zäl-'dē-ˌvär\ Fulgencio 1901–1973 Cuban soldier; pres. of Cuba (1940–44; 1952–59)
Bat·ta·ni, al- \ˌal-bə-'tän-ē\ *ab* 850–929 *Al·ba·teg·ni·us* \ˌal-bə-'teg-nē-əs\ or *Al·ba·te·ni·us* \-'tē-nē-\ Arab astron.
Bau·de·laire \bōd-'la(ə)r, -'le(ə)r\ Charles Pierre 1821–1867 Fr. poet
Bau·douin \bō-'dwa^n\ 1930– king of Belgium (1951–)
Baum \'bäm\ Lyman Frank 1856–1919 Am. journalist & writer
Baum \'bau̇m\ Vicki 1888–1960 Am. (Austrian-born) nov.
Bau·mé \bō-'mā\ Antoine 1728–1804 Fr. chem.
Bax·ter \'bak-stər\ Richard 1615–1691 Eng. Puritan scholar & writer
Ba·yard, de \'bī-ərd, 'bā-ərd, *F.* bá-yár\ Seigneur Pierre Terrail 1473?–1524 Fr. mil. hero
Bayle \'bā(ə)l, 'bel\ Pierre 1647–1706 Fr. philos. & critic
Bay·lor \'bā-lər\ Robert Emmet Bledsoe 1793?–1873 Am. jurist
Beaconsfield Earl of — see Benjamin DISRAELI
Bea·dle \'bēd-ᵊl\ George Wells 1903– Am. biologist
Beard \'bi(ə)rd\ Charles Austin 1874–1948 & his wife Mary *née Ritter* 1876–1958 Am. historians
Beard Daniel Carter 1850–1941 Am. painter & illustrator; organizer of Boy Scouts in U.S. (1910)
Beards·ley \'bi(ə)rdz-lē\ Aubrey Vincent 1872–1898 Eng. illustrator
Beat·tie \'bēt-ē\ James 1735–1803 Scot. poet
Beau·fort \'bō-fərt\ Sir Francis 1774–1857 Brit. admiral
Beaufort Henry 1377?–1447 Eng. cardinal & statesman
Beau·har·nais, de \ˌbō-ˌär-'nā\ Fr. family including: Vicomte Alexandre 1760–1794 gen.; his wife Joséphine 1763–1814 later the 1st wife of Napoleon I; their son Eugene 1781–1824 prince of Eich·stätt \'īk-ˌshtet\; their daughter Hortense 1783–1837 wife of Louis Bonaparte & mother of Napoleon III
Beau·mar·chais, de \ˌbō-ˌmär-'shā\ Pierre Augustin Caron 1732–1799 Fr. dram. & man of affairs
Beau·mont \'bō-ˌmänt, -mənt\ Francis 1584–1616 Eng. dram.
Beau·mont \-ˌmänt\ William 1785–1853 Am. surgeon
Beau·re·gard, de \'bōr-ə-ˌgärd, 'bȯr-\ Pierre Gustave Toutant 1818–1893 Am. Confed. gen.
Beau·voir, de \bōv-'wär\ Simone 1908– Fr. author
Bea·ver·brook \'bē-vər-ˌbru̇k\ 1st Baron 1879–1964 *William Maxwell Aitken* Brit. (Canad.-born) newspaper publisher
Be·bel \'bā-bəl\ August 1840–1913 Ger. Social Democrat leader & writer
Beck·et, à \ə-'bek-ət, ä-\ Saint Thomas 1118?–1170 archbishop of Canterbury (1162–70)
Beck·ett \'bek-ət\ Samuel 1906– Irish author in France
Beck·ford \'bek-fərd\ William 1760–1844 Eng. author
Bec·que·rel \be-'krel, ˌbek-ə-'rel\ family of Fr. physicists including: Antoine César 1788–1878; his son Alexandre Edmond 1820–1891; the latter's son Antoine Henri 1852–1908
Bed·does \'bed-(ˌ)ōz\ Thomas Lovell 1803–1849 Eng. writer
Bede \'bēd\ *or* **Bae·da** *or* **Be·da** \'bēd-ə\ Saint 673–735 *the Venerable Bede* Eng. scholar, hist., & theol.
Bed·ford \'bed-fərd\ Duke of 1389–1435 *John of Lancaster; son of Henry IV of England* regent for Henry V
Bee·be \'bē-bē\ (Charles) William 1877–1962 Am. naturalist & explorer
Bee·cham \'bē-chəm\ Sir Thomas 1879–1961 Eng. conductor
Bee·cher \'bē-chər\ Henry Ward 1813–1887 Am. clergyman
Beecher Lyman 1775–1863 *father of H.W. & of Harriet Beecher Stowe* Am. Presbyterian clergyman
Beer·bohm \'bi(ə)r-ˌbōm, -bəm\ Sir Max 1872–1956 Eng. critic & caricaturist
Beer·naert \'be(ə)r-ˌnärt\ Auguste Marie François 1829–1912 Belg. statesman
Bee·tho·ven, van \'bā-ˌtō-vən\ Ludwig 1770–1827 Ger. composer — **Bee·tho·vi·an** \bā-'tō-vē-ən\ *also* **Bee·tho·ve·nian** \ˌbā-ˌtō-'vē-nyən\ *adj*
Be·han \'bē-ən\ Brendan Francis 1923–1964 Irish dram.
Beh·ring, von \'be(ə)r-iŋ\ Emil 1854–1917 Ger. bacteriol.
Behr·man \'be(ə)r-mən\ Samuel Nathaniel 1893–1973 Am. dram.
Bel·a·fon·te \ˌbel-ə-'fänt-ē\ Harry 1927– Am. singer
Be·las·co \bə-'las-(ˌ)kō\ David 1853–1931 Am. dram. & producer
Bel·i·sar·i·us \ˌbel-ə-'sar-ē-əs, -'ser-\ 505?–565 gen. of the Eastern Rom. Empire
Bell \'bel\ Alexander Graham 1847–1922 Am. (Scot.-born) inventor of the telephone
Bel·la·my \'bel-ə-mē\ Edward 1850–1898 Am. author
Bel·lay, du \ˌd(y)ü-bə-'lā\ Joachim 1522–1560 Fr. poet
Bel·li·ni \bə-'lē-nē\ family of Venetian painters including: Iacopo *ab* 1400–*ab* 1470 and his sons Gentile 1429?–1507 and Giovanni 1430?–1516
Bellini Vincenzo 1801–1835 Ital. composer
Bel·loc \'bel-äk, -ək\ Hil·a·ry \'hil-ə-rē\ pen name *Hi·laire* \hil-'a(ə)r, -'e(ə)r\ 1870–1953 Eng. author
Bel·low \'bel-(ˌ)ō, -ə(-w)\ Saul 1915– Am. (Canad.-born) writer
Bel·lows \'bel-(ˌ)ōz, -əz\ Albert Fitch 1829–1883 Am. painter
Bellows George Wesley 1882–1925 Am. painter & lithographer
Be·na·ven·te y Mar·ti·nez \ˌben-ə-ˌvent-ē-ˌē-mär-'tē-nəs\ Jacinto 1866–1954 Span. dram.
Bench·ley \'bench-lē\ Robert Charles 1889–1945 Am. humorist
Ben·e·dict \'ben-ə-ˌdikt\ name of 15 popes: esp. **XIV** (*Prospero Lambertini*) 1675–1758 (pope 1740–58); **XV** (*Giacomo della Chiesa*) 1854–1922 (pope 1914–22)
Benedict of Nur·sia \'nər-sh(ē-)ə\ Saint 480?–?543 Ital. founder of Benedictine order
Benedict Ruth 1887–1948 née *Fulton* Am. anthropologist
Be·neš \'ben-ˌesh\ Eduard 1884–1948 Czech statesman; pres. (1935–38; 1939–48)
Be·nét \bə-'nā\ Stephen Vincent 1898–1943 *bro. of W.R.* Am. poet & storywriter
Benét William Rose 1886–1950 Am. poet, nov., & editor
Ben–Gu·rion \ˌben-gu̇r-'yȯn, ben-'gu̇r-ē-ən\ David 1886–1973 Israeli (Pol.-born) statesman; prime min. of Israel (1949–53; 1955–63)
Ben·ja·min \'benj-(ə-)mən\ Judah Philip 1811–1884 Am. Confed. statesman & lawyer
Ben·nett \'ben-ət\ (Enoch) Arnold 1867–1931 Eng. nov.
Bennett James Gordon 1795–1872 Am. (Scot.-born) journalist
Bennett Viscount 1870–1947 *Richard Bedford Bennett* Canad. prime min. (1930–35)
Be·noît de Sainte–Maure \ben-'wäd-ə-(ˌ)sa^n(n)t-'mȯ(ə)r\ 12th cent. Fr. trouvère
Ben·son \'ben(t)-sən\ Arthur Christopher 1862–1925 Eng. educ. & author
Benson Edward White 1829–1896 Brit. prelate; archbishop of Canterbury (1882–96)
Benson Ezra Taft 1899– U.S. secy. of agric. (1953–61)
Ben·tham \'ben(t)-thəm\ Jeremy 1748–1832 Eng. jurist & philos.
Ben·tinck \'bent-i(ŋ)k\ Lord William Cavendish 1774–1839 *son of W.H.C.* 1st gov. gen. of India (1833)
Bentinck William Henry Cavendish 1738–1809 3d Duke of *Portland* Brit. prime min. (1783; 1807–09)
Bent·ley \'bent-lē\ Richard 1662–1742 Eng. clergyman, scholar, & critic
Ben·ton \'bent-ᵊn\ Thomas Hart 1782–1858 *Old Bullion* Am. polit.
Benton Thomas Hart 1889– Am. painter
Bé·ran·ger, de \bā-rä^n-zhā\ Pierre Jean 1780–1857 Fr. poet
Ber·dya·ev \bərd-'yä-yəf, bər-'jä-\ Nikolai Aleksandrovich 1874–1948 Russ. philos.
Ber·en·son \'ber-ən-sən\ Bernard 1865–1959 Am. art critic
Berg \'be(ə)rg\ Alban 1885–1935 Austrian composer
Bergerac, de Cyrano — see CYRANO DE BERGERAC
Ber·gi·us \'ber-gē-əs\ Friedrich 1884–1949 Ger. chem.
Berg·son \'be(ə)rg-sən, berk-sō^n\ Henri 1859–1941 Fr. philos.
Be·ria *or* **Be·ri·ya** \'ber-ē-ə\ Lavrenti Pavlovich 1899–1953 Russ. polit.
Be·ring \'bi(ə)r-iŋ, 'be(ə)r-\ Vitus 1680–1741 Dan. navigator; disc. Bering Strait and Bering Sea
Berke·ley \'bär-klē, 'bər-\ George 1685–1753 Irish bishop & philos.
Berke·ley \'bər-klē\ Sir William 1606–1677 colonial gov. of Virginia
Ber·le \'bər-lē\ Adolf Augustus 1895–1971 Am. diplomat
Ber·lich·ing·en, von \'ber-lik-ˌiŋ-ən\ Götz *or* Gottfried 1480–1562 Ger. knight
Ber·lin \(ˌ)bər-'lin\ Irving 1888– Am. (Russ.-born) composer
Ber·li·ner \'bər-lə-nər\ Emile 1851–1929 Am. (Ger.-born) inventor
Ber·li·oz \'ber-lē-ˌōz\ (Louis) Hector 1803–1869 Fr. composer
Ber·na·dette of Lourdes \ˌbər-nə-'det\ 1844–1879 *Bernadette Sou·bi·rous* \ˌsü-bē-'rü\ Fr. religious
Ber·na·dotte \'bər-nə-ˌdät\ Jean Baptiste Jules 1763?–1844 Fr. gen.; king (1818–44) of Sweden as *Charles XIV John* founding present Swed. dynasty
Ber·nard \ber-'när\ Claude 1813–1878 Fr. physiol.
Ber·nard of Clair·vaux \bər-'närd-əv-ˌkla(ə)r-'vō, ber-'när-, -ˌkle(ə)r-\ Saint 1091–1153 Fr. ecclesiastic — **Ber·nar·dine** \'bər-nə(r)-ˌdēn\ *adj*
Ber·nar·din de Saint–Pierre \ˌber-nər-'da^n-də-ˌsänt-pē-'e(ə)r\ Jacques Henri 1737–1814 Fr. author
Berners Baron — see TYRWHITT-WILSON
Bern·hardt \'bərn-ˌhärt, ber-'när\ Sarah 1844–1923 orig. *Rosine Ber·nard* \ber-nár\ Fr. actress
Ber·ni·ni \bər-'nē-nē\ Giovanni Lorenzo 1598–1680 Ital. sculptor, architect, & painter
Bern·stein \'bərn-ˌstīn, -ˌstēn\ Leonard 1918– Am. conductor & composer
Bern·storff \'be(ə)rn-ˌshtȯrf\ Count Johann-Heinrich 1862–1939 Ger. diplomat
Ber·ry·man \'ber-ē-mən\ John 1914–1972 Am. poet
Ber·thier \ber-'tyā\ Louis Alexandre 1753–1815 Prince *de Neuchatel;* Duc *de Valangin;* Prince *de Wagram* Fr. soldier; marshal of France
Ber·til·lon \ˌbert-ē-'(y)ō^n, 'bərt-ᵊl-ˌän\ Alphonse 1853–1914 Fr. anthropol. & criminol.

Ber·ze·li·us \(ˌ)bər-ˈzē-lē-əs, -ˈzā-\ Baron Jöns Jakob 1779–1848 Swed. chem.
Bes·ant \ˈbes-ᵊnt, ˈbez-\ Annie née *Wood* 1847–1933 Eng. theosophist
Bes·se·mer \ˈbes-ə-mər\ Sir Henry 1813–1898 Eng. engineer
Be·tan·court \ˌbe-ˌtän-ˈkü(ə)r(t), -täŋ-\ Rómulo 1908– Venezuelan pres. (1959–63)
Beth·mann-Holl·weg, von \ˌbet-mən-ˈhōl-ˌväg, -ˌmän-\ Theobald 1856–1921 Ger. statesman; chancellor (1909–17)
Be·thune \bə-ˈth(y)ün\ Mary McLeod 1875–1955 Am. educ.
Bet·je·man \ˈbech-ə-mən\ John 1906– Eng. poet
Bet·ter·ton \ˈbet-ərt-ᵊn\ Thomas 1635?–1710 Eng. actor
Bev·an \ˈbev-ən\ Aneu·rin \ə-ˈnī-rən\ 1897–1960 Brit. socialist leader
Bev·er·idge \ˈbev-(ə-)rij\ Albert Jeremiah 1862–1927 Am. polit. & hist.
Beveridge 1st Baron 1879–1963 *William Henry Beveridge* Eng. econ.
Bev·in \ˈbev-ən\ Ernest 1881–1951 Brit. labor leader & polit.
Beyle Marie Henri — see STENDHAL
Bhumibol Adulyadej — see PHUMIPHON ADULDET
Bi·dault \bē-ˈdō\ Georges 1899– Fr. statesman
Bid·dle \ˈbid-ᵊl\ John 1615–1662 founder of Eng. Unitarianism
Biddle Nicholas 1786–1844 Am. financier
Bien·ville, de \bē-ˈen-ˌvil, -vəl; bya^{n}-ˈvē(ə)l\ Sieur Jean Baptiste Lemoyne 1680–1768 Fr. colonial gov. of Louisiana
Bierce \ˈbi(ə)rs\ Ambrose (Gwinnett) 1842–?1914 Am. author
Bier·stadt \ˈbi(ə)r-ˌstat\ Albert 1830–1902 Am. (Ger.-born) painter
Bing·ham \ˈbiŋ-əm\ George Caleb 1811–1879 Am. painter
Bi·on \ˈbī-ˌän, -ən\ 2d cent. B.C. Greek poet
Birk·beck \ˈbər(k)-ˌbek\ George 1776–1841 Eng. physician; founder of mechanics' institutions
Bir·ken·head \ˈbər-kən-ˌhed\ 1st Earl of 1872–1930 *Frederick Edwin Smith* Eng. jurist & statesman
Bi·ron \bē-ˌrōn\ Ernst Johann 1691–1772 orig. *Büh·ren* \ˈbue-rən\ Duke of *Kurland* Russ. statesman
Bir·rell \ˈbir-əl\ Augustine 1850–1933 Eng. author
Bish·op \ˈbish-əp\ Elizabeth 1911– Am. poet
Bis·marck, von \ˈbiz-ˌmärk\ Prince Otto Eduard Leopold 1815–1898 in full *Bismarck-Schön·hau·sen* \-shœn-ˈhaúz-ᵊn\ 1st chancellor of Ger. Empire (1871–90) — **Bis·marck·ian** \biz-ˈmärk-ē-ən\ *adj*
Bi·zet \bē-ˈzā\ Alexandre César Léopold 1838–1875 Fr. composer
Björn·son \ˈbyərn-sən\ Björnstjerne 1832–1910 Norw. poet, dram., & nov.
Black \ˈblak\ Hugo LaFayette 1886–1971 Am. jurist & polit.
Black·ett \ˈblak-ət\ Patrick Maynard Stuart 1897– Brit. physicist
Black Hawk \ˈblak-ˌhók\ 1767–1838 *Ma-ka-tae-mish-kia-kiak* Am. Indian chief
Black·more \ˈblak-ˌmō(ə)r, -ˌmó(ə)r\ Richard Doddridge 1825–1900 Eng. nov.
Black·mun \ˈblak-mən\ Harry Andrew 1908– Am. jurist
Black·stone \ˈblak-ˌstōn, *chiefly Brit* -stən\ Sir William 1723–1780 Eng. jurist
Black·wood \ˈblak-ˌwúd\ William 1776–1834 Scot. publisher
Blaine \ˈblān\ James Gillespie 1830–1893 Am. statesman
Blake \ˈblāk\ Eugene Carson 1906– Am. clergyman
Blake Robert 1599–1657 Eng. admiral
Blake William 1757–1827 Eng. artist, poet, & mystic — **Blak·ean** \ˈblā-kē-ən\ *adj*
Blas·co-Ibá·ñez \ˈbläs-(ˌ)kō-ē-ˈbän-(ˌ)yās\ Vicente 1867–1928 Span. nov.
Bla·vat·sky \blə-ˈvat-skē, -ˈvät-\ Elena Petrovna 1831–1891 née (*Helena*) *Hahn* Russ. traveler & theosophist
Blé·ri·ot \ˈbler-ē-ˌō\ Louis 1872–1936 Fr. engineer & pioneer aviator
Bligh \ˈblī\ William 1754–1817 Eng. naval officer
Bloc \ˈblók, ˈbläk\ André 1896–1966 Fr. sculptor
Bloch \ˈbläk, ˈblók, ˈblók\ Ernest 1880–1959 Am. (Swiss-born) composer
Bloch \ˈbläk\ Felix 1905– Am. physicist
Block \ˈbläk\ Herbert Lawrence 1909– *Her·block* \ˈhər-ˌbläk\ Am. editorial cartoonist
Bloom·field \ˈblüm-ˌfēld\ Leonard 1887–1949 Am. linguist
Blount \ˈblənt\ Winton Malcolm 1921– U.S. postmaster gen. (1969–71)
Blü·cher, von \ˈblü-kər, ˈbluek-ər\ Gebhard Leberecht 1742–1819 Pruss. field marshal
Blum \ˈblüm\ Léon 1872–1950 Fr. polit.; provisional pres. (1946)
Bluntsch·li \ˈblúnch-lē\ Johann Kaspar 1808–1881 Swiss legal scholar
Bo·ab·dil \ˌbō-əb-ˈdē(ə)l\ *d* 1533 *or* 1534 last Moorish king of Granada
Bo·ad·i·cea \(ˌ)bō-ˌad-ə-ˈsē-ə\ *d* 62 queen of the Iceni
Bo·as \ˈbō-ˌaz\ Franz 1858–1942 Am. (Ger.-born) anthropol. & ethnol.
Bo·ba·di·lla, de \ˌbō-bə-ˈdē-(y)ə\ Francisco *d* 1502 Span. viceroy of Indies
Boc·cac·cio \bō-ˈkäch-(ē-ˌ)ō\ Giovanni 1313–1375 Ital. author
Boc·che·ri·ni \ˌbäk-ə-ˈrē-nē\ Luigi 1743–1805 Ital. composer
Bod·ley \ˈbäd-lē\ Sir Thomas 1545–1613 Eng. diplomat & founder of Bodleian library
Bo·do·ni \bə-ˈdō-nē\ Giambattista 1740–1813 Ital. printer & type designer
Bo·ethi·us \bō-ˈē-thē-əs\ Anicius Manlius Severinus 480?–?524 Rom. philos.
Boh·len \ˈbō-lən\ Charles Eustis 1904– Am. diplomat
Böh·me \ˈbə(r)m-ə, ˈbœ-mə\ *or* **Böhm** \ˈbə(r)m, ˈbœm\ Ja·kob \ˈyä-ˌkóp\ 1575–1624 Ger. mystic & theosophist
Bohr \ˈbō(ə)r, ˈbó(ə)r\ Niels 1885–1962 Dan. physicist
Bo·iar·do \bói-ˈärd-(ˌ)ō, bō-ˈyärd-\ Matteo Maria 1434–1494 Ital. poet
Boi·leau-Des·pré·aux \ˈbwäl-ō-ˌdā-prē-ˈō\ Nicolas 1636–1711 Fr. critic & poet
Bo·jer \ˈbói-ər\ Johan \yō-ˈhän\ 1872–1959 Norw. writer
Bok \ˈbäk\ Edward William 1863–1930 Am. (Du.-born) editor
Bo·leyn \bú-ˈlin, ˈbúl-ən\ Anne 1507–1536 *2d wife of Henry VIII of England & mother of Queen Elizabeth I*
Bo·ling·broke \ˈbäl-iŋ-ˌbrúk, ˈbúl-(*usu Brit pronuncs*), ˈbō-liŋ-, -ˌbrōk\ 1st Viscount 1678–1751 *Henry St. John* \ˈsin-jən (*usu Brit pronunc*); (ˌ)sānt-ˈjän, sənt-\ Eng. statesman
Bo·lí·var Si·món \sē-ˌmōn-bə-ˈlē-ˌvär, ˌsī-mən-ˈbäl-ə-vər\ 1783–1830 So. Am. liberator
Böll \ˈbəl, ˈbər(-ə)l, ˈbœl\ Heinrich Theodor 1917– Ger. writer
Bo·na·parte \ˈbō-nə-ˌpärt\ *Ital.* **Buo·na·par·te** \ˌbwón-ə-ˈpärt-ē\ Corsican family including Na·po·leon I \nə-ˈpōl-yən, -ˈpō-lē-ən\ (*q.v.*) & his bros.: Joseph 1768–1844 king of Naples & Spain; Lucien 1775–1840 prince of Ca·ni·no \kə-ˈnē-(ˌ)nō\; Louis 1778–1846 king of Holland & father of Napoleon III; Jérôme 1784–1860 king of Westphalia
Bonar Law — see LAW
Bon·a·ven·tu·ra \ˌbän-ə-ˌven-ˈt(y)úr-ə\ *or* **Bon·a·ven·ture** \ˌbän-ə-ˈven-chər, ˈbän-ə-ˌ\ Saint 1221–1274 *the Seraphic Doctor* Ital. philos.
Bone \ˈbōn\ Sir Muirhead 1876–1953 Scot. etcher & painter
Bon·heur \bä-ˈnər\ Rosa 1822–1899 *Marie Rosalie* Fr. painter
Bon·i·face \ˈbän-ə-fəs, -ˌfās\ Saint 680?–755 *Winfrid* or *Wynfrith* Eng. missionary in Germany
Boniface name of 9 popes: esp. **VIII** (*Benedetto Caetani*) 1235?–1303 (pope 1294–1303)
Bon·nard \bó-ˈnär\ Pierre 1867–1947 Fr. painter
Bon·ner *or* **Bon·er** \ˈbän-ər\ Edmund 1500?–1569 Eng. prelate
Bon·net \bó-ˈnā\ Georges 1889–1973 Fr. polit. & diplomat
Bonnet Henri 1888– Fr. hist. & diplomat
Boone \ˈbün\ Daniel 1734–1820 Am. pioneer
Booth \ˈbüth, *chiefly Brit* ˈbüth\ family of Am. actors: Junius Brutus 1796–1852 *b* in England & his sons Edwin Thomas 1833–1893 & John Wilkes 1838–1865 assassin of Lincoln
Booth William 1829–1912 Eng. founder of Salvation Army & father of: William Bramwell 1856–1929 Salvation Army gen.; Ballington 1859–1940 founder of Volunteers of America; Evangeline Cory 1865–1950 Salvation Army gen.
Boothe Clare — see Clare Boothe LUCE
Bo·rah \ˈbōr-ə, ˈbór-\ William Edgar 1865–1940 Am. polit.
Bor·den \ˌbórd-ᵊn\ Sir Robert (Laird) 1854–1937 Canad. lawyer & statesman; prime min. (1911–20)
Bor·det \bór-ˈdā\ Jules 1870–1961 Belg. bacteriol.
Bor·ges \ˈbór-ˌhās\ Jorge Luis 1899– Argentinean author
Bor·gia \ˈbór-(ˌ)jä, -jə, -zhə\ Cesare 1475(or 1476)–1507 *son of Rodrigo* Ital. cardinal & mil. leader
Borgia Lucrezia 1480–1519 *dau. of Rodrigo* duchess of Ferrara
Borgia Rodrigo 1431?–1503 — see Pope ALEXANDER VI
Bor·glum \ˈbór-gləm\ (John) Gut·zon \ˈgət-sən\ (de la Mothe) 1871–1941 Am. sculptor
Bo·ri \ˈbōr-ē, ˈbór-\ Lucrezia 1887–1960 Span. soprano in U.S.
Bo·ris III \ˈbōr-əs, ˈbór-, ˈbär-\ 1894–1943 czar of Bulgaria (1918–43)
Bor·laug \ˈbór-ˌlóg\ Norman Ernest 1914– Am. agronomist
Born \ˈbó(ə)rn\ Max 1882–1970 Ger. physicist
Bo·ro·din \ˌbór-ə-ˈdēn, ˌbär-\ Aleksandr Porfirevich 1834–1887 Russ. composer & chem.
Bor·row \ˈbär-(ˌ)ō, -ə(-w)\ George 1803–1881 Eng. author
Bosch \ˈbäsh, ˈbósh, *Du* ˈbäs, ˈbós\ Hieronymus *ab* 1450–1516 Du. painter
Bosch \ˈbäsh, ˈbósh\ Karl 1874–1940 Ger. industrial chem.
Bose \ˈbōs, ˈbōs(h)\ Sir Ja·ga·dis \ˌjəg-ə-ˈdēs\ Chan·dra \ˈchən-drə\ 1858–1937 Indian physicist & plant physiol.
Bos·suet \bó-ˈswā\ Jacques Bénigne 1627–1704 Fr. bishop
Bos·well \ˈbäz-ˌwel, -wəl\ James 1740–1795 *Boz·zy* \ˈbäz-ē\ Scot. lawyer & author; biographer of Samuel Johnson
Bo·tha \ˈbō-ˌtä, ˈbōt-ə\ Louis 1862–1919 Boer gen.; 1st prime min. of Transvaal (1907) & of Union of So. Africa (1910–19)
Bo·the \ˈbōt-ə\ Walter 1891–1957 Ger. physicist
Bot·ti·cel·li \ˌbät-ə-ˈchel-ē\ Sandro 1444?–1510 *Alessandro di Mariano dei Filipepi* Ital. painter
Bou·cher \bü-ˈshā\ François 1703–1770 Fr. painter
Bou·ci·cault \ˈbü-si-ˌkō\ *or* **Bour·ci·cault** \ˈbúr-\ Dion 1820?–1890 *Dionysius Lardner Boursiquot* Irish actor & dram.
Bou·gain·ville, de \ˈbü-gən-ˌvil, bü-ga^{n}-vēl\ Louis Antoine 1729–1811 Fr. navigator
Bou·lan·ger \bü-lä^{n}-zhā\ Georges Ernest Jean Marie 1837–1891 Fr. gen.
Bou·lez \bü-ˈlez\ Pierre 1925– Fr. composer
Bour·bon, de \ˈbú(ə)r-bən, búr-ˈbō^{n}\ Duc Charles 1490–1527 Fr. gen.; constable of France
Bour·geois \búrzh-ˈwä, ˈbú(ə)rzh-ˌ\ Léon Victor Auguste 1851–1925 Fr. statesman
Bour·get \búr-ˈzhā\ (Charles Joseph) Paul 1852–1935 Fr. poet, critic, & nov.
Bour·gui·ba \búr-ˈgē-bə\ Habib Ben Ali 1903– Tunisian pres. (1957–)
Bo·vet \bō-ˈvā\ Daniel 1907– Ital. (Swiss-born) physiol.
Bow·ditch \ˈbaúd-ich\ Nathaniel 1773–1838 Am. math. & astron.
Bow·ell \ˈbō-əl\ Mackenzie 1823–1917 prime min. of Canada (1894–96)
Bow·en \ˈbō-ən\ Elizabeth 1899–1973 Brit. (Irish-born) author
Bow·ers \ˈbaú-ərz\ Claude Ger·nade \zhər-ˈnäd\ 1878–1958 Am. hist. & diplomat

---

ə abut ᵊ kitten, F table ər further a back ā bake
ä cot, cart á F bac aú out ch chin e less ē easy
g gift i trip ī life j joke k G ich ^{n} F vin ŋ sing
ō flow ó flaw œ F bœuf œ̄ F feu ói coin th thing
th this ü loot ú foot ue G Füllen ue F rue y yet
^{y} F digne \dēn^{y}\, nuit \nw^{y}ē\ yü few yú furious zh vision

Bowles \ˈbōlz\ Chester 1901– Am. econ. & diplomat

Boyd \ˈbȯid\ Alan Stephenson 1922– U.S. secy. of transportation (1967–69)

Boy·den \ˈbȯid-^{ə}n\ Seth 1788–1870 Am. inventor

Boyd Orr \ˈbȯid-ˈō(ə)r, -ˈȯ(ə)r\ 1st Baron 1880–1971 *John Boyd Orr* Scot. agriculturist

Boyle \ˈbȯi(ə)l\ Kay 1903– Am. author

Boyle Robert 1627–1691 Brit. physicist & chem.

Brabazon of Tara Baron — see MOORE-BRABAZON

Brad·bury \ˈbrad-ˌber-ē, -b(ə-)rē\ Ray Douglas 1920– Am. writer

Brad·dock \ˈbrad-ək\ Edward 1695–1755 Brit. gen. in Am.

Brad·ford \ˈbrad-fərd\ Gamaliel 1863–1932 Am. biographer

Bradford Roark 1896–1948 Am. writer

Bradford William 1590–1657 Pilgrim father; 2d gov. of Plymouth colony

Bradford William 1663–1752 Am. printer

Brad·ley \ˈbrad-lē\ Francis Herbert 1846–1924 Eng. philos. — **Brad·le·ian** *also* **Brad·ley·an** \ˈbrad-lē-ən, brad-ˈ\ *adj*

Bradley Henry 1845–1923 Eng. philologist & lexicographer

Bradley Omar Nelson 1893– Am. gen.

Brad·street \ˈbrad-ˌstrēt\ Anne 1612?–1672 née *Dudley; wife of Simon* Am. poet

Bradstreet Simon 1603–1697 colonial gov. of Mass.

Bra·dy \ˈbrād-ē\ Mathew B. 1823?–1896 Am. photographer

Bragg \ˈbrag\ Braxton 1817–1876 Am. Confed. gen.

Bragg Sir William (Henry) 1862–1942 Eng. physicist

Bragg Sir (William) Lawrence 1890–1971 *son of prec.* Eng. physicist

Brahe \ˈbrä; ˈbrä-hē, -hə\ Ty·cho \ˈtē-(ˌ)kō\ 1546–1601 Dan. astron.

Brahms \ˈbrämz\ Johannes 1833–1897 Ger. composer & pianist — **Brahms·ian** \ˈbräm-zē-ən\ *adj*

Braille \ˈbrā(ə)l, ˈbrī\ Louis 1809–1852 Fr. blind teacher of the blind

Bra·man·te \brə-ˈmänt-ē, -ˈmän-(ˌ)tā\ 1444–1514 *Donato d'Agnolo* or *d'Angelo* Ital. architect

Bran·cu·si \bran-ˈkü-sē\ Constantin 1876–1957 Fr. (Rumanian-born) sculptor

Bran·deis \ˈbran-ˌdīs, -ˌdīz\ Louis Dembitz 1856–1941 Am. jurist

Bran·des \ˈbrän-dəs\ Georg Morris 1842–1927 Dan. lit. critic

Brandt \ˈbränt, ˈbrant\ Wil·ly \ˈvil-ē, ˈwil-ē\ 1913– W. Ger. polit.; chancellor West Germany (1969–)

Bran·ting \ˈbrant-iŋ\ Karl Hjal·mar \ˈyäl-ˌmär\ 1860–1925 Swed. statesman & socialist leader

Braque \ˈbrak, ˈbräk\ Georges 1882–1963 Fr. painter

Brat·tain \ˈbrat-^{ə}n\ Walter Houser 1902– Am. physicist

Brau·chitsch, von \ˈbrau̇k-ich, ˈbrau̇k-\ Heinrich Alfred Hermann Walther 1881–1948 Ger. gen.

Braun \ˈbrau̇n\ Karl Ferdinand 1850–1918 Ger. physicist

Breas·ted \ˈbres-təd\ James Henry 1865–1935 Am. orientalist

Brecht \ˈbrekt, ˈbrekt\ Bertolt 1898–1956 Ger. dram. — **Brecht·ian** \-ē-ən\ *adj*

Breck·in·ridge \ˈbrek-ən-(ˌ)rij\ John Cabell 1821–1875 Am. lawyer; vice-pres. of the U.S. (1857–61)

Bren·nan \ˈbren-ən\ Francis 1894–1968 Am. cardinal

Brennan Peter J. 1918– U.S. secy. of labor (1973–)

Brennan William Joseph, Jr. 1906– Am. jurist

Bresh·kov·sky \bresh-ˈkȯf-skē, -ˈkȯv-\ Catherine 1844–1934 Russ. revolutionist

Bre·ton \brə-tō^{n}\ André 1896–1966 Fr. surrealist poet

Brew·ster \ˈbrü-stər\ William 1567–1644 Pilgrim father

Brezh·nev \ˈbrezh-ˌnef\ Leonid I. 1906– Russ. polit.; pres. U.S.S.R. (1960–64); 1st secy. of Communist party (1964–)

Bri·an Bo·ru \ˌbrī-ən-bə-ˈrü\ *Irish* **Brian Bo·ram·ha** *or* **Bo·raim·he** \ˌbrēn-bə-ˈrō, -ˈrü\ 926–1014 king of Ireland (1002–14)

Bri·and \brē-ä^{n}\ Aristide 1862–1932 Fr. statesman

Brid·ger \ˈbrij-ər\ James 1804–1881 Am. pioneer & scout

Brid·ges \ˈbrij-əz\ Robert Seymour 1844–1930 Eng. poet; poet laureate (1913–30)

Bridg·man \ˈbrij-mən\ Percy Williams 1882–1961 Am. physicist

Briggs \ˈbrigz\ Lyman James 1874–1963 Am. physicist

Bright \ˈbrīt\ John 1811–1889 Eng. orator & statesman

Brig·id \ˈbrij-əd, ˈbrē-əd\ *also* **Brid·get** \ˈbrij-ət\ *or* **Brig·it** \ˈbrij-ət, ˈbrē-ət\ *or* **Brighid** \ˈbrēd\ *or* **Bride** \ˈbrīd\ **of Kildare** Saint 453–523 a patron saint of Ireland

Bril·lat-Sa·va·rin \brē-ˈ(y)ä-ˌsav-ə-ˈra^{n}, -ˈsav-ə-rən\ Anthelme 1755–1826 Fr. gastronome

Brin·e·gar \ˈbrin-e-gər\ Claude S. 1926– U.S. secy. of transportation (1973–)

Brit·ten \ˈbrit-^{ə}n\ (Edward) Benjamin 1913– Eng. composer

Bro·gan \ˈbrō-gən\ Sir Denis William 1900– Brit. hist.

Broglie, de \brȯi\ Louis Victor 1892– Fr. physicist

Brom·field \ˈbräm-ˌfēld\ Louis 1896–1956 Am. nov.

Bron·të \ˈbränt-ē\ a family of Eng. writers: Charlotte 1816–1855 & her sisters Emily 1818–1848 & Anne 1820–1849

Brooke \ˈbru̇k\ Alan Francis 1883–1963 1st Viscount *Al·an·brooke* \ˈal-ən-ˌbru̇k\ Brit. field marshal

Brooke Edward William 1919– Am. polit.

Brooke Rupert 1887–1915 Eng. poet

Brooks \ˈbru̇ks\ Phillips 1835–1893 Am. bishop

Brooks Van Wyck \van-ˈwīk, vən-\ 1886–1963 Am. essayist & critic

Bro·sio \ˈbrō-zē-ˌō, ˈbrō-\ Manlio 1897– Ital. lawyer & diplomat; secy.-gen. of N.A.T.O. (1964–)

Brow·der \ˈbrau̇d-ər\ Earl 1891–1973 Am. Communist polit.

Brown \ˈbrau̇n\ Charles Brockden 1771–1810 Am. nov.

Brown Ford Mad·ox \ˈmad-əks\ 1821–1893 Eng. painter

Brown John Mason 1900–1969 Am. literary critic

Brown John *of Osa·wat·o·mie* \ˌō-sə-ˈwät-ə-mē\ 1800–1859 Am. abolitionist

Browne \ˈbrau̇n\ Charles Farrar 1834–1867 pseud. *Ar·te·mus* \ˈärt-ə-məs\ *Ward* Am. humorist

Browne Sir Thomas 1605–1682 Eng. physician & author

Brow·ning \ˈbrau̇-niŋ\ Elizabeth Barrett 1806–1861 *wife of Robert* Eng. poet

Browning Robert 1812–1889 Eng. poet

Broz \ˈbrōz, ˈbrȯz\ *or* **Bro·zo·vitch** \ˈbrō-zə-ˌvich, ˈbrȯ-\ Josip 1892– *Ti·to* \ˈtēt-(ˌ)ō\ Yugoslav marshal; prime min. (1945–53); pres. (1953–)

Bruce \ˈbrüs\ Sir David 1855–1931 Brit. physician & bacteriol.

Bruce David Kirkpatrick Este 1898– Am. diplomat

Bruce Robert 1274–1329 liberator & king (1306–29) of Scotland

Bruce Viscount 1883–1967 *Stanley Melbourne Bruce* Austral. statesman; prime min. (1923–29)

Bruck·ner \ˈbru̇k-nər\ Anton 1824–1896 Austrian composer

Brue·ghel *or* **Breu·ghel** \ˈbrü-gəl, ˈbrȯi-, ˈbrə(r)-\ family of Flem. painters including: Pieter 1520?–1569 & his sons Pieter 1564?–?1638 & Jan 1568–1625

Brum·mell \ˈbrəm-əl\ George Bryan 1778–1840 *Beau Brummell* Eng. dandy

Bru·nel·le·schi \ˌbrün-^{ə}l-ˈes-kē\ *or* **Bru·nel·le·sco** \-(ˌ)kō\ Filippo 1377?–1446 Ital. architect

Bru·ne·tière \ˌbrü-nə-ˈtye(ə)r, ˌbrᵫ-\ Vincent de Paul Marie Ferdinand 1849–1906 Fr. critic

Brü·ning *or* **Brue·ning** \ˈbrü-niŋ, ˈbrᵫ-\ Heinrich 1885–1970 chancellor of Germany (1930–32)

Bru·no \ˈbrü-(ˌ)nō\ Giordano 1548?–1600 Ital. philos.

Bru·tus \ˈbrüt-əs\ Marcus Junius 85?–42 B.C. Rom. polit.; one of Caesar's assassins

Bry·an \ˈbrī-ən\ William Jennings 1860–1925 Am. lawyer & polit.

Bry·ant \ˈbrī-ənt\ William Cul·len \ˈkəl-ən\ 1794–1878 Am. poet & editor

Bryce \ˈbrīs\ Viscount 1838–1922 *James Bryce* Brit. jurist, hist., & diplomat

Bu·ber \ˈbü-bər\ Martin 1878–1965 Israeli (Austrian-born) philos.

Buch·an \ˈbək-ən, ˈbək-\ John 1875–1940 1st Baron *Tweeds·muir* \ˈtwēdz-ˌmyu̇(ə)r\ Scot. author; gov. gen. of Canada (1935–40)

Bu·chan·an \byü-ˈkan-ən, bə-\ James 1791–1868 Am. polit. & diplomat; 15th pres. of the U.S. (1857–61)

Buch·man \ˈbu̇k-mən, ˈbək-\ Frank Nathan Daniel 1878–1961 Am. evangelist

Buch·ner \ˈbu̇k-nər, ˈbük-\ Eduard 1860–1917 Ger. chem.

Buck \ˈbək\ Pearl 1892–1973 née *Sy·den·strick·er* \ˈsīd-^{ə}n-ˌstrik-ər\ Am. nov.

Buckingham 1st & 2d Dukes of — see GEORGE VILLIERS

Buck·ley \ˈbək-lē\ William Frank 1925– Am. editor & writer

Buck·ner \ˈbək-nər\ Simon Bolivar 1823–1914 Am. Confed. gen. & polit.

Buckner Simon Bolivar 1886–1945 *son of S.B.* Am. gen.

Buddha — see GAUTAMA BUDDHA

Bu·dën·ny \bü-ˈdyȯn-ē, bü-ˈden-\ Semën Mikhailovich 1883–1973 Russ. gen.

Buffalo Bill — see William Frederick CODY

Buf·fon, de \ˌbə-ˈfō^{n}, byü-, bᵫ-\ Comte Georges Louis Leclerc 1707–1788 Fr. naturalist

Buis·son \bwē-ˈsō^{n}\ Ferdinand 1841–1932 Fr. educ.

Bu·kha·rin \bü-ˈkär-ən\ Nikolai Ivanovich 1888–1938 Russ. Communist leader & editor

Bul·finch \ˈbu̇l-ˌfinch\ Charles 1763–1844 Am. architect

Bul·ga·nin \bu̇l-ˈgan-ən\ Nikolai Aleksandrovich 1895– Russ. polit. & marshal

Bull \ˈbu̇l\ Ole \ˈō-lə\ Bornemann 1810–1880 Norw. violinist

Bul·litt \ˈbu̇l-ət\ William Christian 1891–1967 Am. diplomat

Bü·low, von \ˈbyü-(ˌ)lō, ˈbᵫ-\ Prince Bernhard 1849–1929 Ger. diplomat & statesman; chancellor of Germany (1900–09)

Bul·wer \ˈbu̇l-wər\ William Henry Lytton Earle 1801–1872 *bro. of 1st Baron Lytton* Brit. diplomat

Bulwer-Lytton — see LYTTON

Bunche \ˈbənch\ Ralph Johnson 1904–1971 Am. diplomat

Bu·nin \ˈbün-(y)ən, -ˌ(y)ēn\ Ivan Alekseevich 1870–1953 Russ. poet & nov.

Bun·ker \ˈbəŋ-kər\ Ellsworth 1894– Am. diplomat

Bun·sen \ˈbu̇n-zən, ˈbən(t)-sən\ Robert Wilhelm 1811–1899 Ger. chem.

Bun·yan \ˈbən-yən\ John 1628–1688 Eng. preacher & author

Buonaparte Ital. spelling of BONAPARTE

Bur·bage \ˈbər-bij\ Richard 1567?–1619 Eng. actor

Bur·bank \ˈbər-ˌbaŋk\ Luther 1849–1926 Am. horticulturist

Burch·field \ˈbərch-ˌfēld\ Charles Ephraim 1893–1967 Am. painter

Bur·ger \ˈbər-gər\ Warren Earl 1907– Am. jurist; chief justice U.S. Supreme Court (1969–)

Bür·ger \ˈbu̇r-gər, ˈbir-, ˈbᵫr-\ Gottfried August 1747–1794 Ger. poet

Bur·gess \ˈbər-jəs\ Anthony 1917– Brit. writer

Burgess (Frank) Gelett 1866–1951 Am. humorist & illustrator

Burgess Thornton Waldo 1874–1965 Am. writer

Burghley *or* **Burleigh** 1st Baron — see CECIL

Bur·goyne \ˈbər-ˌgȯin, (ˌ)bər-ˈ\ John 1722–1792 Brit. gen. in Am. & dram.

Burke \ˈbərk\ Edmund 1729–1797 Brit. statesman & orator — **Burk·ean** *or* **Burk·ian** \ˈbər-kē-ən\ *adj*

Burke Martha Jane 1852?–1903 *Calamity Jane* née *Canary* Am. frontier markswoman

Bur·lin·game \ˈbər-lən-ˌgām\ **An·son** \ˈan(t)-sən\ 1820–1870 Am. lawyer & diplomat

Burne-Jones \ˈbərn-ˈjōnz\ Sir Edward Co·ley \ˈkō-lē\ 1833–1898 orig. *Jones* Eng. painter & designer

Bur·net \(ˌ)bər-ˈnet, ˈbər-nət\ Sir (Frank) Macfarlane 1899– Austral. physician

Bur·nett \(ˌ)bər-ˈnet, ˈbər-nət\ Frances Eliza 1849–1924 née *Hodgson* \ˈhäj-sən\ Am. (Eng.-born) writer

Bur·ney \ˈbər-nē\ Fanny 1752–1840 orig. *Frances; Madame d'Arblay* \där-ˌblā\ Eng. nov. & diarist

Burns \ˈbərnz\ Robert 1759–1796 Scot. poet — **Burns·ian** \ˈbərn-zē-ən\ *adj*

Burn·side \ˈbərn-ˌsīd\ Ambrose Everett 1824–1881 Am. gen.

Burr \ˈbər\ Aaron 1756–1836 3d vice-pres. of the U.S. (1801–05)

Bur·roughs \'bər-(,)ōz, 'bə-(,)rōz\ Edgar Rice 1875–1950 Am. writer
Burroughs John 1837–1921 Am. naturalist
Burroughs William Seward 1914– Am. writer
Bur·ton \'bərt-ᵊn\ Harold Hitz 1888–1964 Am. jurist
Burton Sir Richard Francis 1821–1890 Brit. explorer & orientalist
Burton Robert 1577–1640 Eng. clergyman & author
Bush \'bu̇sh\ **Van·ne·var** \və-'nē-vər, va-\ 1890– Am. electrical engineer
Bu·so·ni \b(y)ü-'zō-nē\ Ferruccio Benvenuto 1866–1924 Ital. composer & pianist
Bu·te·nandt \'büt-ᵊn-,änt\ Adolph 1903– Ger. chem.
But·ler \'bət-lər\ Benjamin Franklin 1818–1893 Am. gen. & polit.
Butler Joseph 1692–1752 Eng. theol.
Butler Nicholas Murray 1862–1947 Am. educ.
Butler Samuel 1612–1680 Eng. satirical poet
Butler Samuel 1835–1902 Eng. nov. & satirist
Butz \'bəts\ Earl Lauer 1909– U.S. secy. of agric. (1971–)
Bux·te·hu·de \,bu̇k-stə-'hüd-ə\ Dietrich 1637?–1707 Dan. organist & composer
Buys Bal·lot \,bīs-bə-'lät, ,bȯis-\ Christoph Hendrik Didericus 1817–1890 Du. meteorologist
Byng \'biŋ\ George 1663–1733 Brit. admiral
Byng Julian Hed·worth George 1862–1935 1st Baron *Byng of Vimy* Brit. gen.; gov. gen. of Canada (1921–26)
Byrd \'bərd\ Richard Evelyn 1888–1957 Am. admiral & polar explorer
Byrnes \'bərnz\ James Francis 1879–1972 Am. polit. & jurist
By·ron \'bī-rən\ 6th Baron 1788–1824 *George Gordon Byron* Eng. poet
Caballero Francisco Largo — see LARGO CABALLERO
Cab·ell \'kab-əl\ James Branch 1879–1958 Am. nov. & essayist
Ca·be·za de Va·ca \kə-,bā-zə-də-'väk-ə\ Álvar Núñez 1490?–?1577 Span. explorer
Ca·ble \'kā-bəl\ George Washington 1844–1925 Am. nov.
Cab·ot \'kab-ət\ John 1450–1498 *Giovanni Ca·bo·to* \kä-'bō-(,)tō\ Venetian navigator; disc. continent of No. America for England
Cabot Sebastian 1476?–1557 *son of John* Eng. navigator
Ca·bral \kə-'bräl\ Pedro Álvares 1460?–?1526 Port. navigator; claimed Brazil for Portugal
Ca·bril·lo \kə-'brē-(,)(y)ō, -'bril-(,)ō\ Juan Rodríguez *d* 1543 Span. (Port.-born) explorer in Mex. & Calif.
Ca·bri·ni \kə-'brē-nē\ Saint Frances Xavier 1850–1917 *Mother Cabrini* 1st Am. citizen canonized (1946)
Cade \'kād\ Jack *d* 1450 Eng. rebel
Cad·il·lac \'kad-ᵊl-,ak, *F* kȧ-dē-yȧk\ Sieur Antoine de la Mothe 1658–1730 Fr. founder of Detroit
Caed·mon \'kad-mən\ *fl* 670 Anglo-Saxon poet
Cae·sar \'sē-zər\ Gaius Julius 100–44 B.C. Rom. gen., statesman, & writer
Cage \'kāj\ John Milton 1912– Am. composer
Ca·glio·stro, di \kal-'yō-(,)strō, käl-\ Count Alessandro 1743–1795 real name *Giuseppe Bal·sa·mo* \'bäl-sə-,mō\ Ital. imposter
Caine \'kān\ Sir (Thomas Henry) Hall 1853–1931 Eng. nov.
Calamity Jane — see Martha Jane BURKE
Cal·der \'kȯl-dər\ Alexander 1898– Am. sculptor
Cal·de·rón de la Bar·ca \,käl-də-'rōn-,dä-lə-'bär-kə, -'rȯn-\ Pedro 1600–1681 Span. dram. & poet
Cald·well \'kȯl-,dwel, -dwəl, 'käl-\ Erskine 1903– Am. nov.
Caldwell (Janet) Taylor 1900– Am. author
Cal·houn \kal-'hün\ John Caldwell 1782–1850 Am. lawyer; vice-pres. of the U.S. (1825–32)
Ca·lig·u·la \kə-'lig-yə-lə\ 12–41 *Gaius Caesar* Rom. emp. (37–41)
Cal·las \'kal-əs, 'käl-\ Maria 1923– Am. soprano
Cal·les \'kī-,äs, 'kä-,yäs\ Plutarco Elías 1877–1945 Mex. gen.; pres. of Mexico (1924–28)
Cal·lim·a·chus \kə-'lim-ə-kəs\ 5th cent. B.C. Greek sculptor
Callimachus *b ab* 310 B.C. Greek scholar & Alexandrian librarian
Cal·lis·the·nes \kə-'lis-thə-,nēz\ 360?–?328 B.C. Greek philos. & hist.
Cal·lis·tra·tus \kə-'lis-trət-əs\ *d* 355 B.C. Athenian orator & gen.
Cal·vert \'kal-vərt\ George 1580?–1632 1st Baron *Baltimore* Eng. proprietor in Am.
Calvert Leonard 1606–1647 *son of George* gov. of Maryland province (1634–47)
Cal·vin \'kal-vən\ John 1509–1564 orig. *Jean Chau·vin* \shō-vaⁿ\ or *Caul·vin* \kōl-vaⁿ\ Fr. theol. & reformer
Ca·ma·cho \kə-'mäch-(,)ō\ Manuel Ávila 1897–1955 Mex. gen.; pres. of Mex. (1940–46)
Cam·ba·cé·rès, de \,käⁿ-,bas-ə-'res, -,bäs-\ Duc 1753–1824 *Jean Jacques Ré·gis* \rā-'zhēs\ Fr. jurist; counsellor of Napoleon I
Cambridge 1st Baron of — see Edgar Douglas ADRIAN
Cam·by·ses \kam-'bī-(,)sēz\ *d* 522 B.C. *son of Cyrus the Great* king of Persia (529–22)
Cam·den \'kam-dən\ William 1551–1623 Eng. antiquarian & hist.
Cam·er·on of Loch·iel \'kam-(ə-)rə-nəv-lä-'kē(ə)l, -'k̲ē(ə)l\ 1629–1719 Sir *Ewen Cameron* Scot. chieftain
Cameron of Lochiel 1695?–1748 *Donald Cameron; the gentle Lochiel* Scot. chieftain
Ca·mões, Vaz de \,väzh-də-kə-'mōiⁿsh\ *Eng.* **Ca·mo·ëns** \kə-'mō-ənz, 'kam-ə-wənz\ Luiz 1524–1580 Port. poet
Camp \'kamp\ Walter Chauncey 1859–1925 Am. football coach
Camp·bell \'kam-(b)əl\ Alexander 1788–1866 Am. (Irish-born) founder of Disciples of Christ
Campbell Colin 1792–1863 orig. *Mac·li·ver* \mə-'klē-vər\; Baron *Clyde* Brit. field marshal
Campbell John 1705–1782 4th Earl of *Lou·doun* \'lau̇d-ᵊn\ Brit. gen. in Am.
Campbell John D.S. — see Duke of ARGYLL
Campbell Thomas 1777–1844 Brit. poet
Campbell–Ban·ner·man \-'ban-ər-mən\ Sir Henry 1836–1908 Brit. statesman; prime min. (1905–08)

Cam·pi \'käm-(,)pē\ Ital. family of painters in Cremona including: Galeazzo 1477–1536 & his three sons Giulio *ab* 1502–1572, Antonio *d* 1591?, & Vincenzo 1536–1591
Cam·pi·on \'kam-pē-ən\ Thomas 1567–1620 Eng. poet & musician
Ca·mus \kȧ-mᵫ\ Albert 1913–1960 Fr. nov., essayist, & dram.
Ca·na·let·to \,kan-ᵊl-'et-(,)ō\ Antonio 1697–1768 orig. *Antonio Canale* or *Canal* Ital. painter
Can·by \'kan-bē\ Henry Sei·del \'sīd-ᵊl\ 1878–1961 Am. editor & educ.
Can·dolle, de \käⁿ-dȯl\ Augustin Pyrame 1778–1841 Swiss botanist
Canfield Dorothy — see Dorothy Canfield FISHER
Can·ning \'kan-iŋ\ Earl Charles John 1812–1862 Brit. gov. gen. of India (1856–62)
Canning George 1770–1827 *father of C.J.* Brit. statesman; prime min. (1827)
Canning Stratford 1786–1880 1st Viscount *Stratford de Red·cliffe* \'red-,klif\ Brit. diplomat
Can·non \'kan-ən\ Joseph Gurney 1836–1926 *Uncle Joe* Am. lawyer & polit.
Ca·no·va \kə-'nō-və, -'nȯ-\ Antonio 1757–1822 Ital. sculptor
Can·til·lon \,käⁿ-tē-'(y)ōⁿ, 'kant-ᵊl-,än\ Richard 1680?–1734 Irish econ.
Ca·nute \kə-'n(y)üt\ 994?–1035 *the Great* king of England (1016–35); of Denmark (1018–35); of Norway (1028–35)
Ča·pek \'chäp-,ek\ Ka·rel \'kär-əl\ 1890–1938 Czech nov. & dram.
Capet Hugh — see HUGH CAPET
Ca·po·te \kə-'pōt-ē\ Truman 1924– Am. author
Car·a·cal·la \,kar-ə-'kal-ə\ 188–217 *Marcus Aurelius Antoninus* orig. *Bas·si·a·nus* \,bas-ē-'ān-əs\ Rom. emp. (211–217)
Ca·rac·ta·cus \kə-'rak-ti-kəs\ *or* **Ca·rat·a·cus** \kə-'rat-i-\ *Eng.* **Ca·rad·oc** \kə-'rad-ək\ *fl* 43–50 Brit. chieftain
Ca·ra·vag·gio, da \,kar-ə-'väj-(ē-,)ō, -'väzh-ō\ Michelangelo 1569?–?1609 *Michelangelo Merisi* Ital. painter
Car·ber·ry \'kär-,ber-ē, -bə-rē\ John Joseph 1904– Am. cardinal
Cár·de·nas \'kärd-ᵊn-,äs, 'kär-t͟hə-,näs\ Lázaro 1895–1970 Mex. gen. & polit.; pres. of Mex. (1934–40)
Car·do·zo \kär-'dō-(,)zō\ Benjamin Nathan 1870–1938 Am. jurist
Car·duc·ci \kär-'dü-(,)chē\ Giosuè 1835–1907 Ital. poet
Ca·rew \kə-'rü; 'ka(ə)r-ē, 'ke(ə)r-\ Thomas 1595?–?1645 Eng. poet
Carl XVI Gus·taf \'kärl-'gəs-,täv, -'gús-, -,täf\ 1946– king of Sweden (1973–)
Carle·ton \'kär(-ə)l-tən, 'kärlt-ᵊn\ Guy 1724–1808 1st Baron *Dorchester* Brit. gen. & administrator in Am.
Car·los \'kär-ləs, -,lōs\ Don 1788–1855 infante & pretender to Span. throne
Carlos de Austria 1545–1568 prince of Asturias & heir to Span. throne
Car·lo·ta \kär-'lōt-ə, -'lät-\ *Eng.* **Charlotte** 1840–1927 empress of Mexico (1864–67)
Car·lyle \kär-'lī(ə)l, 'kär-,\ Thomas 1795–1881 Scot. essayist & hist. — **Car·lyl·ian** \kär-'lī-lē-ən\ *adj*
Car·man \'kär-mən\ (William) Bliss 1861–1929 Canad. poet
Car·mo·na \kär-'mō-nə\ Antonio Oscar de Fragoso 1869–1951 Port. gen.; pres. of Portugal (1926–51)
Car·ne·gie \'kär-nə-gē, kär-'neg-ē\ Andrew 1835–1919 Am. (Scot-born) industrialist & philanthropist
Car·not \kär-'nō\ Lazare Nicolas Marguerite 1753–1823 Fr. statesman & gen.
Carnot Marie François Sadi 1837–1894 pres. of France (1887–94)
Car·ol II \'kar-əl\ 1893–1953 king of Rumania (1930–40)
Car·pac·cio \kär-'päch-(ē-,)ō\ Vittore 1460?–?1525 Ital. painter
Car·ran·za \kə-'ran-zə, -'rän-\ Venustiano 1859–1920 pres. of Mexico (1915–20)
Car·rel \kə-'rel, 'kar-əl\ Alexis 1873–1944 Fr. surgeon & biologist
Car·rère \kə-'re(ə)r\ John Merven 1858–1911 Am. architect
Car·roll \'kar-əl\ Charles 1737–1832 *Carroll of Carrollton* Am. patriot
Carroll Lewis — see Charles Lutwidge DODGSON — **Car·roll·ian** \ka-'rō-lē-ən\ *adj*
Car·son \'kärs-ᵊn\ Christopher 1809–1868 *Kit* \'kit\ Am. trapper & frontiersman
Carson Rachel Louise 1907–1964 Am. scientist & writer
Carte, D'Oy·ly \,dȯi-lē-'kärt\ Richard 1844–1901 Eng. opera impresario
Car·ter \'kärt-ər\ Howard 1873–1939 Eng. archaeologist
Car·ter·et \,kärt-ə-'ret, 'kärt-ə-,\ John 1690–1763 Earl *Gran·ville* \'gran-,vil\ Eng. statesman
Car·tier \kär-'tyā, 'kärt-ē-,ā\ George Étienne 1814–1873 Canad. statesman
Cartier Jacques 1491–1557 Fr. navigator & explorer; disc. St. Lawrence river
Cart·wright \'kärt-,rīt\ Edmund 1743–1823 Eng. inventor
Ca·ru·so \kə-'rü-(,)sō, -(,)zō\ En·ri·co \en-'rē-(,)kō\ 1873–1921 orig. *Errico* Ital. tenor
Car·ver \'kär-vər\ George Washington 1864–1943 Am. botanist
Carver John 1576?–1621 Eng. *Mayflower* pilgrim; 1st gov. of Plymouth colony
Cary \'ka(ə)r-ē, 'ke(ə)r-ē\ (Arthur) Joyce (Lunel) 1888–1957 Brit. nov.
Cary Henry Francis 1772–1844 Eng. clergyman; translator of Dante
Ca·sa·bian·ca, de \,käz-ə-'byäŋ-kə, ,käs-\ Louis 1755?–1798 Fr. naval officer
Ca·sals \kə-'sälz, -'zälz\ Pablo 1876–1973 Span.-born cellist, conductor, & composer

ə abut	ᵊ kitten, F table	ər further	a back	ā bake	
ä cot, cart	ȧ F bac	au̇ out	ch chin	e less	ē easy
g gift	i trip	ī life	j joke	k̲ G ich	ⁿ F vin	ŋ sing
ō flow	ȯ flaw	œ F bœuf	œ̄ F feu	ȯi coin	th thing
t͟h this	ü loot	u̇ foot	ue G Füllen	ue̅ F rue	y yet
ʸ F digne \dēnʸ\, nuit \nwʸē\	yü few	yu̇ furious	zh vision		

Ca·sa·no·va \ˌkaz-ə-ˈnō-və, ˌkas-\ *or* **Casanova de Sein·galt** \sa^{n}-gält Giacomo Girolamo 1725–1798 also *Giovanni Jacopo* Ital. adventurer

Ca·sau·bon \kə-ˈsȯ-bən, ˌkaz-ō-ˈbō^{n}\ Isaac 1559–1614 Fr. theol. & scholar

Case·ment \ˈkā-smənt\ Sir Roger David 1864–1916 Irish rebel

Ca·si·mir–Pé·rier \ˈkaz-ə-ˌmi(ə)r-ˈper-ē-ˌā\ Jean Paul Pierre 1847–1907 Fr. statesman; pres. of France (1894–95)

Cas·lon \ˈkaz-lən\ William 1692–1766 Eng. typefounder

Cass \ˈkas\ Lewis 1782–1866 Am. statesman

Cas·satt \kə-ˈsat\ Mary 1845–1926 Am. painter in Fr.

Cas·sin \ka-ˈsa^{n}, kä-\ René 1887– Fr. statesman

Cas·si·o·do·rus \ˌkas-ē-ə-ˈdōr-əs, -ˈdȯr-\ Flavius Magnus Aurelius *d* A.D. 575 Rom. statesman & author

Cas·sius Lon·gi·nus \ˈkash-(ē)-ə-ˌslän-ˈjī-nəs, ˈkas-ē-ə-\ Gaius *d* 42 B.C. Rom. gen. & conspirator

Cas·te·lar y Ri·poll \ˌkas-tə-ˈlär-ē-rē-ˈpȯl^{y}\ Emilio 1832–1899 Span. statesman & writer

Ca·stel·ve·tro \kä-ˌstel-ˈve-(ˌ)trō\ Lodovico 1505–1571 Ital. critic & philologist

Ca·sti·glio·ne \ˌkäs-tēl-ˈyō-(ˌ)nā\ Con·te \ˌkōn-tā-\ Baldassare 1478–1529 Ital. statesman & author

Cas·ti·lho, de \kas(h)-ˈtēl-(ˌ)yü\ Vis·con·de \vēs(h)-ˈkō^{n}-dē\ Antônio Feliciano 1800–1875 Port. poet

Castlereagh Viscount — see Robert STEWART

Castriota George — see SCANDERBEG

Cas·tro \ˈkas-(ˌ)trō, ˈkäs-\ Cipriano 1858?–1924 Venezuelan gen.; pres. of Venezuela (1902–08)

Castro, de Inés *Eng.* Agnes 1320?–1355 Span. noblewoman

Castro (Ruz) \ˈrüs\ Fi·del \fē-ˈdel\ 1927– Cuban premier (1959–)

Cates·by \ˈkāts-bē\ Mark 1679?–1749 Eng. naturalist

Catesby Robert 1573–1605 Eng. rebel

Cath·er \ˈkath-ər\ Willa Sibert 1873–1947 Am. nov.

Cath·er·ine \ˈkath-(ə-)rən\ name of 1st, 5th, & 6th wives of Henry VIII of England: Catherine of Aragon 1485–1536; Catherine Howard 1520?–1542; Catherine Parr \-ˈpär\ 1512–1548

Catherine I 1684?–1727 *wife of Peter the Great* empress of Russia (1725–27)

Catherine II 1729–1796 *the Great* empress of Russia (1762–96)

Catherine of Braganza 1638–1705 *queen of Charles II of England*

Cath·er·ine de Mé·di·cis \ˈkath-(ə-)rən-də-ˈmed-ə-(ˌ)chē, -ˌmād-ə-ˈsē(s)\ *Ital* **Caterina de' Me·di·ci** \ˈmed-ə-(ˌ)chē\ 1519–1589 *queen of Henry II of France*

Cat·i·line \ˈkat-^{ə}l-ˌīn\ 108?–62 B.C. *Lucius Sergius Cat·i·li·na* \ˌkat-^{ə}l-ˈī-nə, -ˈē-nə\ Rom. polit. & conspirator

Cat·lin \ˈkat-lən\ George 1796–1872 Am. artist

Ca·to \ˈkāt-(ˌ)ō\ Marcus Porcius 234–149 B.C. *the Elder; the Censor* Rom. statesman

Cato Marcus Porcius 95–46 B.C. *the Younger; great-grandson of prec.* Rom. Stoic philos.

Catt \ˈkat\ Carrie Chapman 1859–1947 née *Lane* Am. suffragist

Cat·tell \kə-ˈtel\ James McKeen 1860–1944 Am. psychol. & editor

Cat·ton \ˈkat-^{ə}n\ (Charles) Bruce 1899– Am. journalist & hist.

Ca·tul·lus \kə-ˈtəl-əs\ Gaius Valerius 84?–54 B.C. Rom. poet

Cau·lain·court, de \ˌkō-ˌla^{n}-ˈku̇(ə)r\ Marquis Armand Augustin Louis 1772–1827 Fr. gen. & diplomat

Ca·vell \ˈkav-əl, kə-ˈvel\ Edith Louisa 1865–1915 Eng. nurse

Cav·en·dish \ˈkav-ən-(ˌ)dish\ Henry 1731–1810 Eng. scientist

Cavendish Spencer Compton 1833–1908 8th Duke of *Devonshire* Eng. statesman

Cavendish Sir William 1505?–1557 Eng. statesman

Cavendish William 1640–1707 1st Duke of *Devonshire* Eng. statesman

Ca·vour, di \kə-ˈvu̇(ə)r, kä-\ Con·te \ˈkōn-(ˌ)tā-\ Camillo Benso 1810–1861 Ital. statesman

Ca·xi·as, de \kə-ˈshē-əs\ Du·que \ˈdü-kə\ 1803–1880 *Luiz Alves de Lima e Silva* Brazil. gen. & statesman

Cax·ton \ˈkak-stən\ William 1422?–1491 first Eng. printer

Cay·ce \ˈkā-sē\ Edgar 1877–1945 Am. photographer & psychic

Cec·il \ˈses-əl, ˈsis-\ (Edgar Algernon) Robert 1864–1958 1st Viscount *Cecil of Chel·wood* \ˈchel-ˌwu̇d\ Eng. statesman

Cecil Lord (Edward Christian) David 1902– Eng. biographer

Cecil Robert 1563?–1612 1st Earl of *Salisbury* & 1st Viscount *Cran·borne* \ˈkran-ˌbȯ(ə)rn\ Eng. statesman

Cecil Gas·coyne· \ˈgas-ˌkȯin-\ Robert Arthur Talbot 1830–1903 3d Marquis of *Salisbury* Eng. statesman

Cecil William 1520–1598 1st Baron *Burgh·ley* or *Bur·leigh* \ˈbər-lē\ Eng. statesman

Cel·e·brez·ze \ˌsel-ə-ˈbrē-zē\ Anthony Joseph 1910– U.S. secy. of health, ed. & welfare (1962–65)

Cel·li·ni \chə-ˈlē-nē\ Ben·ve·nu·to \ˌben-və-ˈnü-(ˌ)tō\ 1500–1571 Ital. goldsmith & sculptor

Cel·sius \ˈsel-sē-əs, -shəs\ Anders 1701–1744 Swed. astron.

Cen·ci \ˈchen-(ˌ)chē\ Be·a·tri·ce \ˌbā-ä-ˈtrē-(ˌ)chā\ 1577–1599 Ital. woman executed for parricide

Cer·van·tes Saa·ve·dra, de \sər-ˈvan-ˌtēz-ˌsä-(ə-)ˈvā-drə\ Miguel 1547–1616 Span. writer

Cé·zanne \sā-ˈzan\ Paul 1839–1906 Fr. painter — **Cé·zann·esque** \(ˌ)sā-ˌzan-ˈesk\ *adj*

Cha·bri·er \ˌshäb-rē-ˈā, ˌshab-\ 1841–1894 Fr. composer

Chad·wick \ˈchad-(ˌ)wik\ Sir James 1891– Eng. physicist

Cha·gall \shə-ˈgäl-, -ˈgal\ Marc 1887– Russ. painter in France

Chain \ˈchān\ Ernst Boris 1906– Brit. (Ger. born) biochem.

Cha·lia·pin \shəl-ˈyäp-(ˌ)ēn, -ən\ Feodor Ivanovitch 1873–1938 Russ. basso

Chal·mers \ˈchal-mərz, ˈchäm-ərz\ Alexander 1759–1834 Scot. biographer & editor

Cham·ber·lain \ˈchām-bər-lən\ Joseph 1836–1914 & his sons Sir (Joseph) Austen 1863–1937 & (Arthur) Neville 1869–1940 Brit. statesmen

Chamberlain Owen 1920– Am. physicist

Cham·ber·lin \ˈchām-bər-lən\ Thomas Chrow·der \ˈkrau̇d-ər\ 1843–1928 Am. geologist

Cham·bers \ˈchām-bərz\ Robert 1802–1871 Scot. publisher & editor

Cham·bord, de \shä^{n}-ˈbȯ(ə)r\ Comte 1820–1883 Duc *de Bordeaux* Bourbon claimant to Fr. throne

Cham·plain, de \(ˈ)sham-ˈplān, shä^{n}-pla^{n}\ Samuel 1567?–1635 Fr. explorer in Am.; founder of Quebec

Cham·pol·lion \shä^{n}-pȯl-yō^{n}\ Jean François 1790–1832 Fr. Egyptologist

Champollion–Fi·geac \-fē-zhäk\ Jean Jacques 1778–1867 *bro. of prec.* Fr. archaeologist

Chan·dra·gup·ta \ˌchən-drə-ˈgu̇p-tə\ 4th cent. B.C. also *San·dro·cot·tus* or *San·dra·cot·tus* \ˌsan-drə-ˈkät-əs\ Indian ruler of Maurya dynasty

Chandragupta II Indian ruler of Gupta dynasty (383?–413)

Cha·nel \shə-ˈnel, sha-\ Gabrielle 1883–1971 *Co·co* \ˈkō-(ˌ)kō\ Fr. fashion designer & perfumer

Chang Hsüeh-liang \ˈjäŋ-shu̇-ˈä-lē-ˈäŋ\ *son of Chang Tso-lin* 1898– Chin. gen.

Chang Tso-lin \-ˈ(t)sō-ˈlin\ 1873–1928 Chin. gen.

Chan·ning \ˈchan-iŋ\ William Ellery 1780–1842 Am. clergyman

Chao K'uang-yin \ˈjau̇-ˈkwäŋ-ˈyin\ *d* 976 *T'ai-tsu* \ˈtīd-ˈzü\ Chin. emp. (960–976); founder of Sung dynasty

Chap·lin \ˈchap-lən\ Charles Spencer 1889– Brit. actor & producer

Chap·man \ˈchap-mən\ Frank Mich·ler \ˈmik-lər\ 1864–1945 Am. ornithologist

Chapman George 1559?–1634 Eng. dram. & translator

Chapman John 1774–1845 *Johnny Ap·ple·seed* \ˈap-əl-ˌsēd\ Am. pioneer

Char·cot \shär-ˈkō, ˈshär-ˌ\ Jean Mar·tin \mär-ˈta^{n}\ 1825–1893 Fr. neurologist

Char·le·magne \ˈshär-lə-ˌmān\ 742–814 *Charles the Great* or *Charles I* Frankish king (768–814) & emp. of the West (800–814)

Charles I \ˈchär(-ə)lz\ 1600–1649 *Charles Stuart* king of Gr. Brit. (1625–49)

Charles II 1630–1685 *son of Charles I* king of Gr. Brit. (1660–85)

Charles 1948– *son of Elizabeth II* prince of Wales

Charles I 1887–1922 *Charles Francis Joseph; nephew of Francis Ferdinand* emp. of Austria & (as *Charles IV*) king of Hungary (1916–18)

Charles I *or* **II** 823–877 *the Bald* king of France as *Charles I* (840–877); emp. as *Charles II* (875–877)

Charles IV 1294–1328 *the Fair* king of France (1322–28)

Charles V 1337–1380 *the Wise* king of France (1364–80)

Charles VI 1368–1422 *the Mad* or *the Beloved* king of France (1380–1422)

Charles VII 1403–1461 *the Victorious* king of France (1422–61)

Charles IX 1550–1574 king of France (1560–74)

Charles X 1757–1836 king of France (1824–30)

Charles V 1500–1558 Holy Rom. emp. (1519–56); king of Spain as *Charles I* (1516–56)

Charles XII 1682–1718 king of Sweden (1697–1718)

Charles Prince 1903– *bro. of King Leopold* regent of Belgium (1944–50)

Charles XIV John — see BERNADOTTE

Charles Edward Stuart 1720–1788 *the Young Pretender; (Bonnie) Prince Charlie* Brit. prince

Charles *or* **Karl Ludwig** 1771–1847 archduke of Austria

Charles Mar·tel \mär-ˈtel\ 689?–741 *grandfather of Charlemagne* Frankish ruler (715–741)

Charlotte Empress of Mexico — see CARLOTA

Chase \ˈchās\ Mary Ellen 1887–1973 Am. educ. & author

Chase Sal·mon \ˈsam-ən, ˈsal-mən\ Portland 1808–1873 Am. statesman, chief justice U.S. Supreme Court (1864–73)

Cha·teau·bri·and, de \(ˌ)sha-ˌtō-brē-ˈä^{n}\ Vi·comte \vē-kō^{n}t\ François René 1768–1848 Fr. author

Chatham 1st Earl of — see William PITT

Chatrian Alexandre — see ERCKMANN-CHATRIAN

Chat·ter·ji \ˈchät-ər-jē\ Ban·kim \ˈbȯŋ-kim\ Chan·dra \ˈchȯn-(ˌ)drō\ 1838–1894 Indian nov.

Chat·ter·ton \ˈchat-ərt-^{ə}n\ Thomas 1752–1770 Eng. poet

Chau·cer \ˈchȯ-sər\ Geoffrey 1340?–1400 Eng. poet — **Chau·ce·ri·an** \chȯ-ˈsir-ē-ən\ *adj*

Chau·temps \shō-tä^{n}\ Camille 1885–1963 Fr. lawyer & polit.; premier (1930; 1933–34; 1937–38)

Chavannes, de — see PUVIS DE CHAVANNES

Chá·vez \ˈchäv-əs, -ˌez\ Carlos 1899– Mex. conductor & composer

Chee·ver \ˈchē-vər\ John 1912– Am. writer

Che·khov *also* **Che·kov** \ˈchek-ˌȯf, -ˌȯv\ Anton Pavlovich 1860–1904 Russ. dram. & storywriter — **Che·kho·vi·an** \che-ˈkō-vē-ən\ *adj*

Ché·nier, de \shān-ˈyā\ André Marie 1762–1794 Fr. poet

Chen·nault \shə-ˈnȯlt\ Claire Lee 1890–1958 Am. gen.

Cheops — see KHUFU

Che·ren·kov \chə-ˈreŋ-kəf\ Pavel Alekseevich 1904– Russ. physicist

Cher·ny·shev·ski \ˌcher-ni-ˈshef-skē, -ˈshev-\ Nikolai Gavrilovich 1829–1889 Russ. revolutionist & author

Che·ru·bi·ni \ˌker-ə-ˈbē-nē, ˌkā-ru̇-\ Lu·i·gi \lü-ˈē-(ˌ)jē\ Carlo Zenobio Salvatore 1760–1842 Ital. composer

Ches·ter·field \ˈches-tər-ˌfēld\ 4th Earl of 1694–1773 *Philip Dormer Stan·hope* \ˈstan-əp\ Eng. statesman & author

Ches·ter·ton \ˈches-tərt-^{ə}n\ Gilbert Keith 1874–1936 Eng. journalist & author

Che·va·lier \shə-ˈval-(ˌ)yā\ Mau·rice \mȯ-ˈrēs\ 1888–1972 Fr. entertainer

Chiang Kai-shek \jē-ˈäŋ-ˈkī-ˈshek, ˈchaŋ-\ 1887– Chin. gen. & statesman; pres. of China (1948–49, 1950–54; 1954–)

Ch'ien-lung \ˈchē-ˈen-ˈlu̇ŋ\ 1711–1799 Chin. emp. (1736–96)

Chif·ley \ˈchif-lē\ Joseph Benedict 1885–1951 prime min. of Austral. (1945–49)

Chi·ka·ma·tsu Mon·za·e·mon \ˌchē-kə-ˈmät-(ˌ)sü-mən-ˈzī-ˌmȯn\ 1653–?1724 *the Shakespeare of Japan* Jap. dram.
Child \ˈchī(ə)ld\ Francis James 1825–1896 Am. philologist & ballad editor
Childe \ˈchī(ə)ld\ Vere Gordon 1892–1957 Brit. anthropol. & archaeol.
Chil·ders \ˈchil-dərz\ Erskine Hamilton 1905– Irish (Eng.-born) polit.; pres. of Ireland (1973–)
Chip·pen·dale \ˈchip-ən-ˌdāl\ Thomas 1718?–1779 Eng. cabinetmaker
Chi·ri·co, de \ˈkir-i-ˌkō, ˈkē-ri-\ Gior·gio \ˈjȯr-(ˌ)jō\ 1888– Ital. painter
Chit·ty \ˈchit-ē\ Joseph 1776–1841 Eng. lawyer & legal writer
Choate \ˈchōt\ Joseph Hod·ges \ˈhäj-əz\ 1832–1917 Am. lawyer & diplomat
Choate Rufus 1799–1859 Am. jurist
Choi·seul, de \shwä-ˈzəl, -ˈzər(-ə)l, -ˈzœ̄l\ Duc Étienne 1719–1785 Fr. statesman
Cho·pin \ˈshō-ˌpan, -ˌpa^{n}\ Fréderic François 1810–1849 Pol. pianist & composer
Chou En-lai \ˈjō-ˈen-ˈlī\ 1898– Chin. Communist polit.
Chré·tien de Troyes \krā-tya^{n}-də-trwä\ also *Chres·tien* \krā-tya^{n}\ 12th cent. Fr. trouvère
Christ Jesus — see JESUS
Chris·tian X \ˈkris(h)-chən\ 1870–1947 king of Denmark (1912–47)
Chris·tie \ˈkris-tē\ Agatha 1891– née *Miller* Eng. writer
Chris·ti·na \kris-ˈtē-nə\ 1626–1689 *dau. of Gustavus Adolphus* queen of Sweden (1632–54)
Chris·tophe \krē-stȯf\ Henri 1767–1820 king of Haiti (1811–20)
Chris·ty \ˈkris-tē\ Howard Chandler 1873–1952 Am. painter & illustrator
Chry·sos·tom \ˈkris-əs-təm, kris-ˈäs-təm\ Saint John 345?–407 church father & patriarch of Constantinople
Chu Hsi \ˈjü-ˈshē\ 1130–1200 Chin. philos.
Chu Teh \-ˈdə\ 1886– Chin. Communist gen.
Chur·chill \ˈchər-ˌchil, ˈchərch-ˌhil\ John 1650–1722 1st Duke of *Marl·bor·ough* \ˈmärl-ˌbər-ə, ˈmȯl-, -ˌbə-rə, -b(ə-)rə\ Eng. gen.
Churchill Randolph Henry Spencer 1849–1895 Lord *Randolph Churchill* Brit. statesman
Churchill Winston 1871–1947 Amer. nov.
Churchill Sir Winston Leonard Spencer 1874–1965 *son of Lord Randolph* Brit. statesman; prime min. (1940–45; 1951–55) — **Chur·chill·ian** \ˌchər-ˈchil-ē-ən, ˈchərch-ˈhil-\ *adj*
Cia·no \ˈchän-(ˌ)ō\ Con·te \ˌkōn-(ˌ)tā\ Galeazzo 1903–1944 *son-in-law of Mussolini* Ital. statesman
Ciar·di \ˈchärd-ē\ John 1916– Am. poet
Cib·ber \ˈsib-ər\ Col·ley \ˈkäl-ē\ 1671–1757 Eng. dram. & actor; poet laureate (1730–57)
Cic·ero \ˈsis-ə-ˌrō\ Marcus Tullius 106–43 B.C. Rom. statesman, orator, & author — **Cic·ero·nian** \ˌsis-ə-ˈrō-nyən, -nē-ən\ *adj*
Cid, the \ˈsid\ 1040?–1099 *Rodrigo* (or *Ruy*) *Díaz de Bi·var* \bē-ˈvär\ Span. soldier & hero
Ci·ma·bue \ˌchē-mə-ˈbü-(ˌ)ā\ Giovanni *ab* 1240–*ab* 1302 properly *Cenni de Pepo* Florentine painter
Ci·mon \ˈsī-mən, -ˌmän\ 507?–449 B.C. Athenian gen. & statesman
Cin·cin·na·tus \ˌsin(t)-sə-ˈnat-əs, -ˈnāt-\ Lucius Quinctius 5th cent. B.C. Rom. gen. & statesman
Clare \ˈkla(ə)r, ˈkle(ə)r\ Saint 1194–1253 Ital. nun
Clarendon Earl of — see Edward HYDE
Clark \ˈklärk\ Champ \ˈchamp\ 1850–1921 *James Beau·champ* \ˈbē-chəm\ *Clark* Am. polit.
Clark George Rogers 1752–1818 Am. soldier & frontiersman
Clark Kenneth Bancroft 1914– Am. psychologist
Clark Mark Wayne 1896– Am. gen.
Clark Thomas Campbell 1899– Am. jurist
Clark William 1770–1838 Am. explorer (with Meriwether Lewis)
Clark (William) Ramsey 1927– Am. lawyer; U.S. attorney general (1967–69)
Clarke \ˈklärk\ Charles Cow·den \ˈkau̇d-ᵊn\ 1787–1877 & his wife Mary Victoria Cowden-Clarke 1809–1898 Eng. Shakespearean scholars
Clau·di·us \ˈklȯd-ē-əs\ Rom. gens including: **Ap·pi·us** \ˈap-ē-əs\ **Claudius Cras·sus** \ˈkras-əs\ consul (471 & 451 B.C.) & decemvir (451–450 B.C.); **Appius Claudius Cae·cus** \ˈsē-kəs\ censor (312–307 B.C.), consul (307 & 296 B.C.), & dictator who began building of the Appian Way (312 B.C.)
Claudius I 10 B.C.–A.D. 54 *Tiberius Claudius Drusus Ne·ro* \ˈnē-(ˌ)rō, ˈni(ə)r-(ˌ)ō\ *Germanicus* Rom. emp. (41–54)
Claudius II 214–270 *Marcus Aurelius Claudius Gothicus* Rom. emp. (268–270)
Clau·se·witz, von \ˈklau̇-zə-ˌvits\ Karl 1780–1831 Pruss. gen. & military strategist
Clay \ˈklā\ Henry 1777–1852 Am. statesman & orator
Clay Lucius Du Bi·gnon \du̇-ˈbin-yən\ 1897– Am. gen.
Cle·an·thes \klē-ˈan-ˌthēz\ 3d cent. B.C. Greek Stoic philos.
Cle·ar·chus \klē-ˈär-kəs\ *fl* 408–401 B.C. Greek soldier; gov. of Byzantium
Clea·ver \ˈklē-vər\ (Leroy) Eldridge 1935– Am. writer & Negro leader
Cleis·the·nes \ˈklīs-thə-ˌnēz\ *or* **Clis·the·nes** \ˈklis-\ *fl ab* 507 B.C. Athenian statesman
Cle·men·ceau \ˌklem-ən-ˈsō, klā-mä^{n}-sō\ Georges 1841–1929 *the Tiger* Fr. statesman
Clem·ens \ˈklem-ənz\ Samuel Langhorne 1835–1910 pseud. *Mark Twain* \ˈtwān\ Am. writer
Clem·ent \ˈklem-ənt\ name of 14 popes: esp. **VII** (*Giulio de' Me·di·ci* \ˈmed-ə-(ˌ)chē\) 1478–1534 (pope 1523–34)
Cle·men·ti \klə-ˈment-ē\ Muzio 1752–1832 Ital. pianist & composer in Eng.
Clement of Alexandria 150?–?220 *Titus Flavius Cle·mens* \ˈklem-ˌenz\ Greek Christian theologian & church father

Cle·om·e·nes \klē-ˈäm-ə-ˌnēz\ name of 3 kings of Sparta: esp. **III** (reigned 235–219 B.C.)
Cle·o·pa·tra \ˌklē-ə-ˈpa-trə, -ˈpā-, -ˈpä-\ 69–30 B.C. queen of Egypt (51–49; 48–30)
Clerk–Maxwell James — see James Clerk MAXWELL
Cleve·land \ˈklēv-lənd\ (Stephen) Grover 1837–1908 22d & 24th pres. of the U.S. (1885–89; 1893–97)
Cli·burn \ˈklī-bərn\ Van \ˈvan\ 1934– *Harvey Lavan Cliburn* Am. pianist
Clif·ford \ˈklif-ərd\ Clark McAdams 1906– Am. lawyer; U.S. secy. of defense (1968–69)
Clin·ton \ˈklint-ᵊn\ De Witt \di-ˈwit\ 1769–1828 Am. statesman
Clinton George 1739–1812 vice-pres. of the U.S. (1805–12)
Clinton Sir Henry 1738?–1795 Eng. gen. in Am.
Clive \ˈklīv\ Robert 1725–1774 Baron *Clive of Plassey* Brit. gen.; founder of the empire of Brit. India
Cloots, de \ˈklōts\ Baron 1755–1794 *Jean Baptiste du Val-de-Grâce; An·a·char·sis* \ˌan-ə-ˈkär-səs\ *Cloots* Prussian-Fr. revolutionist
Clough \ˈkləf\ Arthur Hugh 1819–1861 Eng. poet
Clo·vis I \ˈklō-vəs\ *Ger.* **Chlod·wig** \ˈklōt-(ˌ)vik\ 466?–511 Frankish king of Merovingian dynasty (481–511)
Clyde Baron — see Colin CAMPBELL
Cnut \kə-ˈn(y)üt\ *var of* CANUTE
Coates \ˈkōts\ Joseph Gordon 1878–1943 N. Z. statesman
Cobb \ˈkäb\ Irvin Shrewsbury 1876–1944 Am. journalist & humorist
Cob·bett \ˈkäb-ət\ William 1763–1835 *Peter Porcupine* Eng. polit. writer
Cob·den \ˈkäb-dən\ Richard 1804–1865 Eng. statesman & econ.
Cobham Lord — see Sir John OLDCASTLE
Co·chise \kō-ˈchēs\ *d* 1874 Apache Indian chief
Cock·croft \ˈkäk-ˌ(k)rȯft\ Sir John Douglas 1897–1967 Brit. physicist
Coc·teau \käk-ˈtō, kȯk-\ Jean 1889–1963 Fr. author
Co·dy \ˈkōd-ē\ John Patrick 1907– Am. cardinal
Cody William Frederick 1846–1917 *Buffalo Bill* Am. scout, Indian fighter, & showman
Coen \ˈkün\ Jan Pie·ters·zoon \ˈpēt-ər-sən\ 1587–1629 Du. colonial gov.; founder of Du. East Indian empire
Coeur de Lion — see RICHARD I of England
Cof·fin \ˈkȯf-ən, ˈkäf-\ Robert Peter Tristram 1892–1955 Am. author
Co·han \ˈkō-ˌhan\ George Michael 1878–1942 Am. actor, dram., & producer
Co·hen \ˈkō-ən\ Octavus Roy 1891–1959 Am. author
Cohen Wilbur Joseph 1913– U.S. secy. of health, ed. & welfare (1968–69)
Cohn \ˈkōn\ Ferdinand Julius 1828–1898 Ger. botanist; called founder of bacteriology
Coke \ˈku̇k, ˈkōk\ Sir Edward 1552–1634 *Lord Coke* Eng. jurist
Col·bert \kȯl-ˈbe(ə)r, ˈkōl-ˌ\ Jean Baptiste 1619–1683 Fr. statesman & financier
Cole \ˈkōl\ Thomas 1801–1848 Am. (Eng.-born) painter
Cole·pep·er \ˈkəl-ˌpep-ər\ Thomas 1635–1689 2d Baron *Colepeper of Thores·way* \ˈthō(ə)rz-ˌwā, ˈthȯ(ə)rz-\ Eng. colonial administrator; gov. of Virginia
Cole·ridge \ˈkōl-rij, ˈkō-lə-rij\ Samuel Taylor 1772–1834 Eng. poet — **Cole·ridg·ean** *also* **Cole·ridg·ian** \ˌkōl-(ə-)ˈrij-ē-ən\ *adj*
Col·et \ˈkäl-ət\ John 1466?–1519 Eng. theol. & scholar
Co·lette \kȯ-ˈlet\ Sidonie Gabrielle Claudine 1873–1954 Fr. author
Col·fax \ˈkōl-ˌfaks\ Schuy·ler \ˈskī-lər\ 1823–1885 vice-pres. of the U.S. (1869–73)
Co·li·gny *or* **Co·li·gni, de** \ˌkȯ-lēn-ˈyē, kə-ˈlēn-yē\ Gaspard (II) 1519–1572 Fr. admiral & Huguenot leader
Col·lier \ˈkäl-yər, ˈkäl-ē-ər\ Jeremy 1650–1726 Eng. clergyman
Collier John Payne 1789–1883 Eng. editor
Collier Peter Fen·e·lon \ˈfen-ᵊl-ən\ 1849–1909 Am. publisher
Col·lins \ˈkäl-ənz\ Michael 1890–1922 Irish revolutionist
Collins Michael 1930– Am. astronaut
Collins William 1721–1759 Eng. poet
Collins (William) Wilkie 1824–1889 Eng. nov.
Col·man \ˈkōl-mən\ George 1732–1794 Eng. dram.
Col·um \ˈkäl-əm\ Mary Gun·ning \ˈgən-iŋ\ 1887?–1957 née *Maguire* \mə-ˈgwī(ə)r\ *wife of Padraic* Am. (Irish-born) writer
Colum Pad·raic \ˈpȯth-rig\ 1881–1972 Am. (Irish-born) poet & dram.
Co·lum·ba \kə-ˈləm-bə\ *Irish* **Col·um** \ˈkəl-əm\ *or* **Col·um·cille** \ˈkəl-əm-ˌkil\ Saint 521–597 *apostle of Caledonia* Irish missionary in Scot.
Co·lum·bus \kə-ˈləm-bəs\ Christopher *Ital.* Cristoforo **Co·lom·bo** \kə-ˈləm-(ˌ)bō\ *Span.* Cristóbal **Co·lón** \kə-ˈlōn\ 1451–1506 Ital. navigator; disc. Am.
Co·me·ni·us \kə-ˈmē-nē-əs\ *Czech* **Ko·men·ský** \ˈkȯ-mən-skē\ John Amos 1592–1670 Czech theol. & educ.
Co·mines *or* **Com·mines** *or* **Com·mynes** *or* **Co·mynes, de** \kȯ-ˈmēn\ Philippe 1447?–?1511 Sire *d'Ar·gen·ton* \ˌsiər-ˌdär-ˌzhä^{n}-ˈtō^{n}\ Fr. chronicler
Com·ma·ger \ˈkäm-i-jər\ Henry Steele 1902– Am. hist.
Com·mo·dus \ˈkäm-ə-dəs\ Lucius Aelius Aurelius 161–192 Rom. emp. (180–192)
Com·mo·ner \ˈkäm-ə-nər\ Barry 1917– Am. biologist & educ.
Comp·ton \ˈkäm(p)-tən\ Arthur Holly 1892–1962 Am. physicist
Compton Karl Taylor 1887–1954 *bro. of A.H.* Am. physicist
Com·stock \ˈkäm-ˌstäk *also* ˈkəm-\ Anthony 1844–1915 Am. reformer

---

ə abut   ᵊ kitten, F table   ər further   a back   ā bake
ä cot, cart   å F bac   au̇ out   ch chin   e less   ē easy
g gift   i trip   ī life   j joke   k G ich ^{n} F vin   ŋ sing
ō flow   ȯ flaw   œ F bœuf   œ̄ F feu   ȯi coin   th thing
th this   ü loot   u̇ foot   ue G Füllen   ue̅ F rue   y yet
^{y} F digne \dēn^{y}\, nuit \nw^{y}ē\   yü few   yu̇ furious   zh vision

Comte \'kō^{n}(n)t\ Auguste 1798–1857 *Isidore Auguste Marie François Comte* Fr. math. & philos.
Conan Doyle — see DOYLE
Co·nant \'kō-nənt\ James Bryant 1893– Am. chem. & educ.
Con·dé, de \kō^{n}-dā\ Prince 1621–1687 *Louis II de Bour·bon* \'bu̇(ə)r-bən, bu̇r-'bō^{n}\; Duc *d'En·ghien* \dä^{n}-ga^{n}\ Fr. gen.
Con·don \'kän-dən\ Edward Uhler 1902– Am. physicist
Con·dor·cet, de \kō^{n}-dȯr-sā\ Marquis 1743–1794 *Marie Jean Antoine Nicholas de Ca·ri·tat* \ˌkar-ə-'tä\ Fr. philos. & polit.
Con·fu·cius \kən-'fyü-shəs\ *Chin.* **K'ung Fu-tzu** *or* **Kung Fu-tse** *ab* 551–479 B.C. Chin. philos.
Con·greve \'kän-ˌgrēv, 'käŋ-\ William 1670–1729 Eng. dram.
Con·ing·ham \'kən-iŋ-ˌham, *chiefly Brit* -iŋ-əm\ Sir Arthur 1895–1948 Brit. air marshal
Con·nal·ly \'kän-^{ə}l-ē, 'kän-lē\ John Bowden 1917– U.S. secy. of the treasury (1971–72)
Con·nor \'kän-ər\ John Thomas 1914– Am. lawyer; U.S. secy. of commerce (1965–67)
Con·rad \'kän-ˌrad\ Joseph 1857–1924 orig. *Teodor Józef Konrad Kor·ze·niow·ski* \ˌkȯr-zən-'yȯf-skē, -'yȯv-\Brit. (Ukrainian-born of Pol. parents) nov.
Con·sta·ble \'kən(t)-stə-bəl, 'kän(t)-\ John 1776–1837 Eng. painter
Cons·tant \kō^{n}-stä^{n}\ Benjamin 1845–1902 Fr. painter
Constant de Re·becque \rə-'bek\ Benjamin 1767–1830 Fr. writer & polit.
Con·stan·tine \'kän(t)-stən-ˌtēn, -ˌtīn\ 1940– king of Greece (1964–73; deposed)
Constantine I 280?–337 *the Great* Rom. emp. (306–337) — **Con·stan·tin·ian** \ˌkän(t)s-tən-'tin-ē-ən\ *adj*
Constantine I 1868–1923 king of Greece (1913–17; 1920–22)
Con·ta·ri·ni \ˌkänt-ə-'rē-nē\ Venetian family including esp. Gasparo 1483–1542 cardinal & diplomat
Con·ti, de' \'kōnt-ē, 'känt-\ Niccolò 15th cent. Venetian traveler
Cook \'ku̇k\ Capt. James 1728–1779 Eng. navigator & explorer
Cooke \'ku̇k\ (Alfred) **Al·is·tair** \'al-ə-stər\ 1908– Am. (Brit.-born) essayist & journalist
Cooke Terence James 1921– Am. cardinal
Coo·lidge \'kü-lij\ (John) Calvin 1872–1933 30th pres. of the U.S. (1923–29)
Coolidge Julian Lowell 1873–1954 Am. math.
Coo·per \'kü-pər, 'ku̇p-ər\ Anthony Ashley — see SHAFTESBURY
Cooper James **Fen·i·more** \'fen-ə-ˌmō(ə)r, -ˌmȯ(ə)r\ 1789–1851 Am. nov.
Cooper Peter 1791–1883 Am. manufacturer & philanthropist
Co·per·ni·cus \kō-'pər-ni-kəs\ Nicolaus *Pol.* Mikolaj **Ko·per·nik** \kȯ-'per-nēk\ *or* Niklas **Kop·per·nigk** \'käp-ər-ˌnik\ 1473–1543 Pol. (or Prussian) astron.; founder of modern astronomy
Cop·land \'kō-plənd\ Aaron 1900– Am. composer
Cop·ley \'käp-lē\ John **Sin·gle·ton** \'siŋ-gəl-tən\ 1738–1815 Am. portrait painter
Co·que·lin \ˌkȯk-(ə-)'la^{n}\ Benoît Constant 1841–1909 Fr. actor
Cor·co·ran \'kȯr-k(ə-)rən\ Thomas Gardiner 1900– Am. lawyer & polit.
Cor·day \kȯr-'dā, 'kȯr-ˌ\ Charlotte 1768–1793 *Marie Anne Charlotte Corday d'Ar·mont* \där-'mō^{n}\ Fr. patriot; assassinated Marat
Co·rel·li \kə-'rel-ē\ Arcangelo 1653–1713 Ital. violinist & composer
Co·ri \'kōr-ē, 'kȯr-\ Carl Ferdinand 1896– & his wife **Ger·ty** \'gert-ē\ Theresa 1896–1957 née *Rad·nitz* \'räd-ˌnits\ Am.(Czech.-born) biochemists
Corneille \kȯr-'nā\ Pierre 1606–1684 Fr. dram.
Cor·ne·lia \kȯr-'nēl-yə, -'nē-lē-ə\ 2d cent. B.C. *Mother of the Gracchi* Rom. matron
Cornelia *d* ?67 B.C. *wife of Julius Caesar*
Cor·ne·lius, von \kȯr-'nāl-yəs, -'nā-lē-əs\ **Pe·ter** \'pāt-ər\ 1783–1867 Ger. painter
Cor·nell \kȯr-'nel\ Ezra 1807–1874 Am. financier & philanthropist
Cornell Katharine 1898– Am. actress
Corn·wal·lis \kȯrn-'wäl-əs\ 1st Marquis 1738–1805 *Charles Cornwallis* Brit. gen. & statesman
Co·ro·na·do \ˌkȯr-ə-'näd-(ˌ)ō, ˌkär-\ Francisco Vásquez de 1510–1554 Span. explorer of southwestern U.S.
Co·rot \kə-'rō, kȯ-\ Jean Baptiste Camille 1796–1875 Fr. painter
Cor·reg·gio \kə-'rej-(ē-ˌ)ō\ 1494–1534 *Antonio Allegri da Correggio* Ital. painter
Cor·tes *or* **Cor·tez** \kȯr-'tez, 'kȯr-ˌ\ Hernando 1485–1547 Span. conqueror of Mexico
Cos·grave \'käz-ˌgrāv\ Liam 1920– prime min. of Ireland (1973–)
Cosgrave William Thomas 1880–1965 Irish statesman
Cos·ta Ca·bral, da \ˌkäs(h)-tə-kə-'bräl\ Antonio Bernardo 1803–1889 *Conde de Thomar* Port. statesman
Cos·tel·lo \'käs-tə-ˌlō\ John Aloysius 1891– prime min. of Ireland (1948–51; 1954–57)
Cot·ton \'kät-^{ə}n\ Charles 1630–1687 Eng. author & translator
Cotton John 1584–1652 Eng. Puritan clergyman in Am.
Co·ty \kȯ-'tē, kō-\ René 1882–1962 Fr. lawyer; 2d pres. of 4th Republic (1954–59)
Cou·lomb, de \kü-lō^{n}; 'kü-ˌläm, -ˌlōm, kü-'\ Charles Augustin 1736–1806 Fr. physicist
Cou·pe·rin \ˌküp-(ə-)'ra^{n}\ François 1668–1733 Fr. composer
Cou·pe·rus \kü-'pā-rəs, -'per-əs\ 1863–1923 Du. nov.
Cour·bet \ku̇r-'bā\ Gustave 1819–1877 Fr. painter
Cour·nand \ku̇r-'nä^{n}\ André Frédéric 1895– Am. (Fr.-born) physiologist
Cou·sin \kü-za^{n}\ Victor 1792–1867 Fr. philos.
Cous·ins \'kəz-^{ə}nz\ Norman 1912– Am. editor & essayist
Cous·teau \kü-'stō\ Jacques Yves 1910– Fr. marine explorer
Co·var·ru·bias \ˌkō-və-'rü-bē-əs\ Miguel 1904–1957 Mex. illustrator
Cov·er·dale \'kəv-ər-ˌdāl\ Miles 1488–1568 Eng. Bible translator
Cow·ard \'kau̇(-ə)rd\ Sir Noel Pierce 1899–1973 Eng. actor & dram.
Cow·ell \'kau̇(-ə)l\ Henry Dixon 1897–1965 Am. composer
Cowl \'kau̇(ə)l\ Jane 1884–1950 orig. *Cowles* Am. actress
Cow·ley \'kau̇-lē\ Abraham 1618–1667 Eng. poet
Cowley Malcolm 1898– Am. literary critic
Cow·per \'kü-pər, 'ku̇p-ər, 'kau̇-pər\ William 1731–1800 Eng. poet
Cox·ey \'käk-sē\ Jacob Sechler 1854–1951 Am. polit. reformer
Coz·zens \'kəz-^{ə}nz\ James Gould 1903– Am. author
Crabbe \'krab\ George 1754–1832 Eng. poet
Craig·av·on \krā-'gav-ən\ 1st Viscount 1871–1940 *James Craig Craigavon* Brit. statesman; 1st prime min. of Northern Ireland (1921–40)
Crai·gie \'krā-gē\ Sir William Alexander 1867–1957 Brit. philologist & lexicographer
Cram \'kram\ Ralph Adams 1863–1942 Am. architect & author
Cra·nach \'krän-ˌäk\ Lucas 1472–1553 Ger. painter & engraver
Cranborne Viscount — see Robert CECIL
Crane \'krān\ (Harold) Hart 1899–1932 Am. poet
Crane Stephen 1871–1900 Am. writer
Cran·mer \'kran-mər\ Thomas 1489–1556 Eng. reformer; archbishop of Canterbury (1533–56)
Cras·sus \'kras-əs\ Marcus Licinius 115?–53 B.C. *Di·ves* \'dī-(ˌ)vēz\ Rom. polit.
Crazy Horse \'krā-zē-ˌhȯrs\ 1849?–1877 *Tashunca-Uitco* Sioux Indian chief
Cré·bil·lon \ˌkrā-bē-'(y)ō^{n}\ 1674–1762 pseud. of *Prosper Jolyot* Fr. dram.
Cre·mer \'krē-mər\ Sir William Randal 1838–1908 Eng. pacifist
Cres·ton \'kres-tən\ Paul 1906– real name *Joseph Guttoveggio* Am. composer
Crève·coeur, de \krev-'kər, krēv-, -'ku̇(ə)r\ Michel Guillaume St. Jean 1735–1813 Am. (Fr.-born) essayist
Crich·ton \'krīt-^{ə}n\ James 1560?–1582 *the Admirable Crichton* Scot. prodigy
Crile \'krī(ə)l\ George Washington 1864–1943 Am. surgeon
Cripps \'krips\ Sir (Richard) Stafford 1889–1952 Brit. lawyer & socialist statesman
Cri·spi \'kris-pē, 'krēs-\ Francesco 1819–1901 Ital. statesman; premier (1887–91; 1893–96)
Cro·ce \'krō-(ˌ)chā\ Benedetto 1866–1952 Ital. philos. & statesman
Crock·ett \'kräk-ət\ David 1786–1836 *Davy* Am. frontiersman & polit.
Croe·sus \'krē-səs\ *d* 546 B.C. king of Lydia (560–546)
Cro·ker \'krō-kər\ John Wilson 1780–1857 Brit. essayist & editor
Cromer 1st Earl of — see Evelyn BARING
Cromp·ton \'kräm(p)-tən\ Samuel 1753–1827 Eng. inventor of the spinning mule
Crom·well \'kräm-ˌwel, 'krəm-, -wəl\ Oliver 1599–1658 Eng. gen. & statesman; lord protector of England (1653–58)
Cromwell Richard 1626–1712 *son of Oliver* lord protector (1658–59)
Cromwell Thomas 1485?–1540 Earl of *Essex* Eng. statesman
Cro·nin \'krō-nən\ Archibald Joseph 1896– Eng. physician & nov.
Cron·jé \krȯn-'yā\ Piet Arnoldus 1840?–1911 Boer leader & gen.
Crookes \'kru̇ks\ Sir William 1832–1919 Eng. physicist & chem.
Cross \'krȯs\ Wilbur Lucius 1862–1948 Am. educ. & polit.
Crouse \'krau̇s\ Russel 1893–1966 Am. journalist & dram.
Cru·den \'krüd-^{ə}n\ Alexander 1701–1770 Scot. compiler of a biblical concordance
Cruik·shank \'kru̇k-ˌshaŋk\ George 1792–1878 Eng. caricaturist & illustrator
Cud·worth \'kəd-(ˌ)wərth\ Ralph 1617–1688 Eng. philos.
Cul·pep·er \'kəl-ˌpep-ər\ *var of* COLEPEPER
Cum·mings \'kəm-iŋz\ Edward Estlin 1894–1962 Am. poet
Cu·nha, da Tris·tão \ˌtris-tən-də-'kü-nə, trēs(h)-ˌtau̇^{n}-də-'kün-yə\ 1460?–?1540 Port. navigator & explorer
Cun·ning·ham \'kən-iŋ-ˌham, *chiefly Brit* -iŋ-əm\ Allan 1784–1842 Scot. author
Cunningham Merce 1922?– Am. choreographer
Cu·rie \kyu̇-'rē, 'kyu̇(ə)r-(ˌ)ē\ Eve 1904– *dau. of Marie & Pierre* Fr. author
Curie Marie 1867–1934 née *Marja Sklo·dow·ska* \sklə-'dȯf-skə, -'dȯv-\ Fr. (Pol.-born) chem.
Curie Pierre 1859–1906 *husband of Marie* Fr. chem.
Curie Joliot — see JOLIOT-CURIE
Cur·ley \'kər-lē\ James Michael 1874–1958 Am. polit.
Cur·ri·er \'kər-ē-ər, 'kə-rē-\ Nathaniel 1813–1888 Am. lithographer
Cur·ry \'kər-ē, 'kə-rē\ John Steuart 1897–1946 Am. painter
Cur·tin \'kərt-^{ə}n\ John 1885–1945 Austral. polit.; prime min. (1941–45)
Cur·tis \'kərt-əs\ Charles 1860–1936 vice-pres. of the U.S. (1929–33)
Curtis Cyrus Hermann Kotzschmar 1850–1933 Am. publisher
Curtis George Ticknor 1812–1894 Am. lawyer & writer
Curtis George William 1824–1892 Am. author & editor
Cur·tiss \'kərt-əs\ Glenn Hammond 1878–1930 Am. aviator & inventor
Cur·ti·us \'ku̇rt-sē-əs\ Ernst 1814–1896 Ger. philologist & archaeologist
Cur·wen \'kər-wən\ John 1816–1880 Eng. music teacher
Cur·zon \'kərz-^{ə}n\ George Nathaniel 1859–1925 1st Baron & 1st Marquis *Curzon of Ked·le·ston* \'ked-^{ə}l-stən\ Eng. statesman; viceroy of India (1899–1905)
Cush·ing \'ku̇sh-iŋ\ Caleb 1800–1879 Am. lawyer & diplomat
Cushing Harvey 1869–1939 Am. surgeon
Cushing Richard James 1895–1970 Am. cardinal
Cush·man \'ku̇sh-mən\ Charlotte Saunders 1816–1876 Am. actress
Cus·ter \'kəs-tər\ George Armstrong 1839–1876 Am. gen.
Cuth·bert \'kəth-bərt\ Saint 635?–687 Eng. monk
Cu·vier \'k(y)ü-vē-ˌā, kɶ-vyā\ Baron Georges Léopold Chrétien Frédéric Dagobert 1769–1832 Fr. naturalist
Cyn·e·wulf \'kin-ə-ˌwu̇lf\ *or* **Cyn·wulf** \'kin-ˌwu̇lf\ *fl* 750 Anglo-Saxon poet

Cyp·ri·an \ˈsip-rē-ən\ Saint *d* 258 *Thascius Caecilius Cyprianus* Christian martyr; bishop of Carthage (248–258)

Cy·ran·kie·wicz \ˌ(t)sir-ən-ˈkyā-vich\ Jozef 1911– Pol. polit.; prime min. (1947; 1954; 1961)

Cy·ra·no de Ber·ge·rac, de \ˌsir-ə-ˌnō-də-ˈber-zhə-ˌrak\ Savinien 1619–1655 Fr. poet & soldier

Cyr·il \ˈsir-əl\ Saint 827–869 *Constantine* Slavic apostle

Cy·rus \ˈsī-rəs\ 600?–529 B.C. *the Great* or *the Elder* king of Persia (550–529)

Cyrus 429?–401 B.C. *the Younger* Persian prince & satrap

Czer·ny \ˈcher-nē, ˈchər-\ Carl 1791–1857 Austrian pianist & composer

D', De, Du, etc. for many names beginning with these elements see the specific family names

Da·guerre \də-ˈge(ə)r\ Louis Jacques Mandé 1789–1851 Fr. painter; inventor of the daguerrotype

Daim·ler \ˈdīm-lər\ Gottlieb 1834–1900 Ger. automotive manufacturer

Da·kin \ˈdā-kən\ Henry Drys·dale \ˈdrīz-ˌdāl\ 1880–1952 Eng. chem.

Da·la·dier \də-ˈläd-ē-ˌā, ˌdal-əd-ˈyā\ Édouard 1884–1970 Fr. statesman

D' Al·bert \ˈdal-bərt\ Eugen Francis Charles 1864–1932 Scot. pianist & composer

Dalcroze Émile Jaques — see Émile JAQUES-DALCROZE

Dale \ˈdā(ə)l\ Sir Henry Hallett 1875–1968 Eng. physiol.

Dale Sir Thomas *d* 1619 Eng. colonial administrator in Virginia (1611–16)

Da·lén \də-ˈlān\ Nils Gustaf 1869–1937 Swed. inventor

Da·ley \ˈdā-lē\ Richard Joseph 1902– Am. polit.

Dalhousie Earl & Marquis of — see RAMSAY

Da·li \ˈdäl-ē, *by himself* dä-ˈlē\ Salvador 1904– Span. surrealistic painter — **Da·li·esque** \ˌdäl-ē-ˈesk\ *adj*

Dal·las \ˈdal-ə, -is\ George Mifflin 1792–1864 vice-pres. of the U.S. (1845–49)

Dal·rym·ple \dal-ˈrim-pəl, ˈdal-ˌ\ Sir James 1619–1695 1st Viscount *Stair* Scot. jurist

Dalrymple Sir John 1673–1747 2d Earl of *Stair* Brit. gen. & diplomat

Dal·ton \ˈdȯlt-ᵊn\ Baron 1887–1962 *Hugh Dalton* Brit. polit.

Dalton John 1766–1844 Eng. chem. & physicist

Da·ly \ˈdā-lē\ (John) Augustin 1838–1899 Am. dram. & theater manager

Dam \ˈdam, ˈdäm\ (Carl Peter) Henrik 1895– Dan. biochem.

Da·mien de Veus·ter \ˌdā-mē-ən-də-ˈvyüs-tər, ˌdam-ē-ˌa^{n}-də-ˌvə(r)s-ˈte(ə)r\ Joseph 1840–1889 *Father Damien* Belg. R.C. missionary to lepers on Molokai

Dam·pi·er \ˈdam-pē-ər\ William 1652–1715 Eng. buccaneer & navigator

Dam·rosch \ˈdam-ˌräsh\ Walter Johannes 1862–1950 Am. (Ger.-born) musician & conductor

Da·na \ˈdā-nə\ Charles Anderson 1819–1897 Am. newspaper editor

Dana Edward Salisbury 1849–1935 Am. mineralogist

Dana James Dwight 1813–1895 Am. geologist

Dana Richard Henry 1815–1882 Am. lawyer & author

Dane \ˈdān\ Clemence 1888–1965 pseud. of *Winifred Ash·ton* \ˈash-tən\ Eng. nov.

Dan·iel \ˈdan-yəl\ Samuel 1562?–1619 Eng. poet

Dan·iels \ˈdan-yəlz\ Josephus 1862–1948 Am. journalist & statesman

Da·nil·o·va \də-ˈnē-lə-və\ **Alexandra** 1906– Russ. ballet dancer in U.S.

D'An·nun·zio \dä-ˈnün(t)-sē-ˌō\ Gabriele 1863–1938 Ital. author & soldier

Dan·te \ˈdant-ē, ˈdän-(ˌ)tā\ 1265–1321 *Dante Ali·ghie·ri* \ˌal-əg-ˈye(ə)r-ē\ Ital. poet — **Dan·te·an** \ˈdant-ē-ən, ˈdänt-\ *or* **Dan·tes·can** \dan-ˈtes-kən, dän-\ *or* **Dan·tesque** \-ˈtesk\ *adj*

Dan·ton \dä^{n}-tō^{n}\ Georges Jacques 1759–1794 Fr. revolutionist

Dare \ˈda(ə)r, ˈde(ə)r\ Virginia 1587–? 1st child born in Am. of Eng. parents

Da·ri·us \də-ˈrī-əs\ name of 3 kings of Persia: esp. **I** 558?–486 B.C. (reigned 521–486) *Darius Hys·tas·pis* \his-ˈtas-pəs\; *the Great*

Dar·lan \där-ˈlä^{n}\ Jean Louis Xavier 1881–1942 Fr. admiral

Darn·ley \ˈdärn-lē\ Lord 1545–1567 *Henry Stewart* or *Stuart; husband of Mary, Queen of Scots*

Dar·row \ˈdar-(ˌ)ō\ Clarence Seward 1857–1938 Am. lawyer & author

Dar·win \ˈdär-wən\ Charles Robert 1809–1882 Eng. naturalist

Darwin Erasmus 1731–1802 *grandfather of C. R.* Eng. physiol. & poet

Dau·bi·gny \ˌdō-bēn-ˈyē, dō-ˈbē-nyē\ Charles François 1817–1878 Fr. painter

Dau·det \dō-ˈdā\ Alphonse 1840–1897 Fr. nov.

Daudet Léon 1867–1942 *son of Alphonse* Fr. journalist & writer

Dau·mier \dō-myā, ˈdō-mē-ˌā\ Honoré 1808–1879 Fr. caricaturist & painter

Dav·e·nant *or* **D'Av·e·nant** \ˈdav-(ə-)nənt\ Sir William 1606–1668 Eng. poet & dram.; poet laureate (1638–68)

Dav·en·port \ˈdav-ən-ˌpō(ə)rt, ˈdav-ᵊm-, -ˌpȯ(ə)rt\ John 1597–1670 Eng. clergyman; founder of New Haven colony

Da·vid \ˈdā-vəd\ **I** 1084–1153 king of Scotland (1124–53)

David \ˈdäv-ət\ Gerard 1450? or 1460?–1523 Du. painter

Da·vid \dä-ˈvēd\ Jacques Louis 1748–1825 Fr. painter

Da·vid d'An·gers \dä^{n}-ˌzhā\ Pierre Jean 1788–1856 Fr. sculptor

Da·vid·son \ˈdā-vəd-sən\ Jo 1883–1952 Am. sculptor

Davidson Randall Thomas 1848–1930 archbishop of Canterbury (1903–28)

Da·vies \ˈdā-vēz\ Arthur Bowen 1862–1928 Am. painter

Dá·vi·la y Pa·di·lla \ˈdäv-i-lə-ˌē-pä-ˈdē-(y)ə\ Agustín 1562–1604 Mex. monk & hist.

Da·vis \ˈdā-vəs\ Dwight Filley 1879–1945 Am. statesman

Da·vis Elmer Holmes 1890–1958 Am. radio broadcaster & news commentator

Davis Harold Le·noir \lə-ˈnō(ə)r, -ˈnȯ(ə)r\ 1896–1960 Am. writer

Davis Jefferson 1808–1889 Am. statesman; pres. of Confed. states (1861–65)

Davis Richard Harding 1864–1916 Am. author

Da·vis·son \ˈdā-və-sən\ Clinton Joseph 1881–1958 Am. physicist

Da·vout \da-ˈvü\ Louis Nicolas 1770–1823 Duc *d'Au·er·staedt* \ˈdaů(ə)r-ˌstet\ & Prince *d'Eck·mühl* \ˈdek-ˌmyül\ marshal of France

Da·vy \ˈdā-vē\ Sir Humphry 1778–1829 Eng. chem.

Dawes \ˈdȯz\ Charles Gates 1865–1951 Am. lawyer & financier; vice-pres. of U.S. (1925–29)

Daw·son \ˈdȯs-ᵊn\ Sir John William 1820–1899 Canad. geologist

Day \ˈdā\ Clarence Shepard 1874–1935 Am. author

Day Thomas 1748–1789 Eng. author

Day William Rufus 1849–1923 Am. statesman & jurist

Da·yan \dī-ˈän, dä-ˈyän\ Moshe 1915– Israeli soldier and statesman

Day–Le·wis \ˈdā-ˈlü-əs\ Cecil 1904–1972 pseud. *Nicholas Blake* Brit. writer; poet laureate (1968–72)

De·ák \ˈdā-ˌäk\ Fe·rencz \ˈfer-ˌen(t)s\ 1803–1876 Hung. statesman

Dean \ˈdēn\ Sir Patrick 1909– Brit. diplomat

Deane \ˈdēn\ Silas 1737–1789 Am. lawyer & diplomat

Dear·den \ˈdi(ə)rd-ᵊn\ John Francis 1907– Am. cardinal

De·bierne \də-ˈbye(ə)rn\ André Louis 1874–1949 Fr. chem.

Debs \ˈdebz\ Eugene Victor 1855–1926 Am. socialist

De·bus·sy \ˌdeb-yù-ˈsē, ˌdāb-; də-ˈbyü-sē\ Claude Achille 1862–1918 Fr. composer

De·bye \də-ˈbī\ Peter Joseph Wilhelm 1884–1966 Du.-born physicist in Am.

De·ca·tur \di-ˈkāt-ər\ Stephen 1779–1820 Am. naval officer

De·cazes \də-käz\ Duc Élie 1780–1860 Fr. jurist & statesman

De·cius \ˈdē-sh(ē-)əs\ 201–251 *Gaius Messius Quintus Trajanus Decius* Rom. emp. (249–51)

Dee·ping \ˈdē-piŋ\ (George) Warwick 1877–1950 Eng. nov.

Deere \ˈdi(ə)r\ John 1804–1886 Am. inventor

Def·fand, du \dā-fä^{n}\ Marquise 1697–1780 née *Marie de Vichy-Cham·rond* \-shä^{n}-rō^{n}\ Fr. noblewoman

De·foe \di-ˈfō\ Daniel *ab* 1660–1731 Eng. journalist & nov.

De For·est \di-ˈfȯr-əst, -ˈfär-\ Lee 1873–1961 Am. inventor

De·gas \də-gä\ (Hilaire Germain) Edgar 1834–1917 Fr. artist

de Gaulle \di-ˈgōl, -ˈgȯl\ Charles André Joseph Mario 1890–1970 Fr. gen.; interim pres. of France (1945–46); pres. of Fifth Republic (1959–69)

Dek·ker *or* **Deck·er** \ˈdek-ər\ Thomas 1572?–?1632 Eng. dram.

de Koo·ning \də-ˈkō-niŋ\ Willem 1904– Am. (Du.-born) painter

De Kruif \də-ˈkrīf\ Paul 1890–1971 Am. bacteriol. & author

De·la·croix \ˌdel-ə-ˈk(r)wä\ (Ferdinand Victor) Eugène 1798–1863 Fr. painter

de la Mare \ˌdel-ə-ˈma(ə)r, -ˈme(ə)r\ Walter John 1873–1956 Eng. poet & nov.

De·land \də-ˈland\ Margaret 1857–1945 née (*Margaretta Wade*) *Campbell* Am. nov.

De La Rey \ˌdel-ə-ˈrī, -ˈrā\ Jacobus Hercules 1847–1914 Boer gen. & statesman

De·la·roche \ˌdel-ə-ˈrōsh, -ˈrȯsh\ Hippolyte Paul 1797–1856 Fr. painter

De·la·vigne \ˌdel-ə-ˈvēn^{y}, -ˈvēn-yə\ Casimir 1793–1843 Fr. poet & dram.

De La Warr \ˈdel-ə-ˌwa(ə)r, -ˌwe(ə)r\ Baron 1577–1618 *Thomas West; Lord Delaware* Eng. colonial administrator in Am.

De·led·da \dā-ˈled-ə, də-\ Grazia 1875–1936 Ital. author

De·libes \də-ˈlēb\ Leo 1836–1891 Fr. composer

De·lius \ˈdē-lē-əs, ˈdēl-yəs\ Frederick 1862–1934 Eng. composer

Del·lin·ger \ˈdel-ən-jər\ John Howard 1886–1962 Am. radio engineer

De Long \də-ˈlȯŋ\ George Washington 1844–1881 Am. naval officer & explorer

De·lorme *or* **de l'Orme** \de-ˈlȯ(ə)rm\ Philibert 1515?–1570 Fr. architect

De Mille \də-ˈmil\ Agnes George 1906?– Am. dancer & choreographer

De Mille Cec·il \ˈses-əl\ Blount \ˈblənt\ 1881–1959 Am. motion-picture producer

De·moc·ri·tus \di-ˈmäk-rət-əs\ *b ab* 460 B.C. *the Laughing Philosopher* Greek philos.

De Mor·gan \di-ˈmȯr-gən\ William Frend 1839–1917 Eng. artist & nov.

De·mos·the·nes \di-ˈmäs-thə-ˌnēz\ 385?–322 B.C. Athenian orator & statesman — **De·mos·then·ic** \di-ˌmäs-ˈthen-ik, ˌdē-\ *adj*

De·ni·ker \ˌdā-nē-ˈke(ə)r\ Joseph 1852–1918 Fr. anthropol.

De·nis *or* **De·nys** \ˈden-əs, də-nē\ Saint 3d cent. A.D. 1st bishop of Paris; patron saint of France

Dent \ˈdent\ Frederick B. 1922– U.S. secy. of commerce (1973–)

Dent Joseph Mal·a·by \ˈmal-ə-bē\ 1849–1926 Eng. publisher

De·pew \di-ˈpyü\ Chauncey Mitchell 1834–1928 Am. lawyer & polit.

De Quin·cey \di-ˈkwin(t)-sē, -ˈkwin-zē\ Thomas 1785–1859 Eng. author

De·rain \də-ra^{n}\ André 1880–1954 Fr. painter

Der·vish Pa·sha \ˌdər-vish-ˈpäsh-ə, -ˈpash-ə, -pə-ˈshä\ Ibrahim 1817–1896 Turk. gen.

Der·zha·vin \der-ˈzhäv-ən\ Gavriil Romanovich 1743–1816 Russ. poet

De·saix de Vey·goux \də-ˌsād-ə-(ˌ)vā-ˈgü\ Louis Charles Antoine 1768–1800 Fr. gen.

ə abut ᵊ kitten, F table ər further a back ā bake
ä cot, cart á F bac aů out ch chin e less ē easy
g gift i trip ī life j joke k̲ G ich ^{n} F vin ŋ sing
ō flow ȯ flaw œ F bœuf œ̄ F feu ȯi coin th thing
t̲h̲ this ü loot ù foot ue G Füllen ue̅ F rue y yet
^{y} F digne \dēn^{y}\, nuit \nw^{y}ē\ yü few yù furious zh vision

De·sargues \dā-ˈzärg\ Gérard 1593–1662 Fr. math.
Des·cartes \dā-ˈkärt\ René 1596–1650 Lat. *Renatus Cartesius* Fr. math. & philos.
Des·cha·nel \ˌdā-shə-ˈnel\ Paul Eugène Louis 1856–1922 Fr. statesman; pres. of France (1920)
de Se·ver·sky \də-sə-ˈver-skē\ Alexander Procofieff 1894– Am. (Russ.-born) aeronautical engineer
Des·mou·lins \dā-mü-laⁿ\ Camille 1760–1794 *Lucie Simplice Camille Benoît Desmoulins* Fr. revolutionist
de So·to \di-ˈsōt-(ˌ)ō\ Hernando *or* Fernando 1500?–1542 Span. explorer in Am.
Des Prez \dā-prā\ Jos·quin \zhȯs-kaⁿ\ 1450?–1521 Du. composer
Des·saix \də-ˈsā\ Comte Joseph Marie 1764–1834 Fr. gen. under Napoleon
Des·sa·lines \ˌdās-ə-ˈlēn, ˌdes-\ Jean Jacques 1758–1806 emp. as *Jacques I* of Haiti (1804–06)
De·taille \də-ˈtī\ (Jean Baptiste) Édouard 1848–1912 Fr. painter
De·us Ra·mos, de \ˌdā-əsh-ˈram-(ˌ)üsh\ João \zhwauⁿ\ 1830–1896 Port. poet
De Va·le·ra \ˌdev-ə-ˈler-ə, -ˈlir-ə\ Ea·mon \ˈā-mən\ 1882– Irish polit.; prime min. of Ireland (1937–48; 1951–54; 1957–59); pres. of Ireland (1959–73)
de Vere \də-ˈvi(ə)r\ Aubrey Thomas 1814–1902 Irish poet
Dev·er·eux \ˈdev-ə-ˌrü(ks)\ Robert 1566–1601 2d Earl of *Essex* Eng. soldier & courtier
Devonshire dukes of — see CAVENDISH
De Vo·to \di-ˈvōt-(ˌ)ō\ Bernard Augustine 1897–1955 Am. author
De Vries \də-ˈvrēs\ Hugo 1848–1935 Du. botanist
Dew·ar \ˈd(y)ü-ər\ Sir James 1842–1923 Scot. chem. & physicist
De Wet \də-ˈvet\ Christiaan Rudolph 1854–1922 Boer soldier & polit.
Dew·ey \ˈd(y)ü-ē\ George 1837–1917 Am. admiral
Dewey John 1859–1952 Am. philos. & educ. — **Dew·ey·an** \-ən\ *adj*
Dewey Melvil 1851–1931 Am. librarian
Dewey Thomas Edmund 1902–1971 Am. lawyer & polit.
De Witt \də-ˈvit\ Jan 1625–1672 Du. statesman
Dia·ghi·lev \dē-ˈäg-ə-ˌlef\ Sergei Pavlovich 1872–1929 Russ. ballet producer & art critic
Di·as *or* **Di·az** \ˈdē-ˌäsh\ Bartholomeu 1450?–1500 Port. navigator; disc. Cape of Good Hope
Dí·az \ˈdē-ˌäts\ Armando 1861–1928 *Duca della Vittoria* Ital. gen.; marshal of Italy
Dí·az \ˈdē-ˌäs, -ˌäz\ Porfirio 1830–1915 *José de la Cruz Porfirio* Mex. gen.; pres. of Mexico (1877–80; 1884–1911)
Díaz de Bivar — see CID
Dí·az Or·daz \ˌdē-ə-sȯr-ˈdäz\ Gustavo 1911– pres. of Mex. (1964–70)
Dick \ˈdik\ George Frederick 1881–1967 Am. physician
Dick·ens \ˈdik-ənz\ Charles John Huffam 1812–1870 *Boz* \ˈbäz, ˈbōz\ Eng. nov. — **Dick·en·si·an** \dik-ˈen-zē-ən, -sē-\ *adj*
Dick·in·son \ˈdik-ən-sən\ Emily Elizabeth 1830–1886 Am. poet
Dickinson John 1732–1808 Am. statesman
Di·de·rot \dē-ˈdrō, ˈdēd-ə-ˌrō\ Denis 1713–1784 Fr. encyclopedist
Die·fen·ba·ker \ˈdē-fən-ˌbā-kər\ John George 1895– prime min. of Canada (1957–63)
Diels \ˈdē(ə)lz, ˈdē(ə)ls\ Otto 1876–1954 Ger. chem.
Die·sel \ˈdē-zəl, -səl\ Rudolf 1858–1913 Ger. mechanical engineer
Diez \ˈdēts\ Friedrich Christian 1794–1876 Ger. philologist
Dig·by \ˈdig-bē\ Sir Ken·elm \ˈken-ˌelm\ 1603–1665 Eng. naval commander, diplomat, & author
Dill \ˈdil\ Sir John Greer 1881–1944 Brit. gen.
Dil·lon \ˈdil-ən\ (Clarence) Douglas 1909– U.S. secy. of the treasury (1961–65)
Dillon John 1851–1927 Irish nationalist polit.
Dim·net \dim-ˈnā\ Ernest 1866–1954 Fr. abbé & writer
Di·ne·sen \ˈdē-nə-sən, ˈdin-ə-\ Isak \ˈē-ˌsäk\ 1885–1962 pen name of *Baroness Karen Blix·en* \ˈblik-sən\ née *Dinesen* Dan. author
Din·wid·die \din-ˈwid-ē\ Robert 1693–1770 Eng. colonial administrator in Am.
Di·o·cle·tian \ˌdī-ə-ˈklē-shən\ 245–313 *Gaius Aurelius Valerius Diocletianus* Rom. emp. (284–305)
Di·og·e·nes \dī-ˈäj-ə-ˌnēz\ 412?–323 B.C. Greek Cynic philos.
Di·o·ny·sius \ˌdī-ə-ˈnis(h)-ē-əs, -ˈnish-əs, -ˈnī-sē-əs\ 430?–?367 B.C. *the Elder* Greek tyrant of Syracuse (405–367)
Dionysius *the Younger* tyrant of Syracuse (367–356; 347–344 B.C.)
Dionysius Ex·ig·u·us \eg-ˈzig-yə-wəs\ 6th cent. Christian monk; introduced method of reckoning the Christian era
Dionysius of Alexandria Saint 3d cent. theol. & bishop of Alexandria (247)
Dionysius of Halicarnassus *d ab* 7 B.C. Greek scholar
Di·rac \di-ˈrak\ Paul Adrien Maurice 1902– Eng. physicist
Dirk·sen \ˈdərk-sən\ Everett McKinley 1896–1969 Am. polit.
Dis·ney \ˈdiz-nē\ Walter Elias 1901–1966 Am. producer of animated motion-picture cartoons
Dis·rae·li \diz-ˈrā-lē\ Benjamin 1804–1881 1st Earl of *Bea·cons·field* \ˈbē-kənz-ˌfēld\; *Diz·zy* \ˈdiz-ē\ Brit. polit. & author; prime min. (1868; 1874–80)
Dit·mars \ˈdit-ˌmärz\ Raymond Lee 1876–1942 Am. naturalist
Dix \ˈdiks\ Dorothea Lynde 1802–1887 Am. social reformer
Dix Dorothy — see Elizabeth Meriwether GILMER
Dix·on \ˈdik-sən\ Jeremiah *fl* 1763–1767 Eng. surveyor in Am.
Dmow·ski \də-ˈmȯf-skē, -ˈmȯv-\ Roman 1864–1939 Pol. statesman
Dö·be·rei·ner \ˈdə(r)b-ə-ˌrī-nər, ˈdœb-\ Johann Wolfgang 1780–1849 Ger. chem.
Do·bie \ˈdō-bē\ James Frank 1888–1964 Am. folklorist
Do·brée \ˈdō-ˌbrā\ Bon·a·my \ˈbän-ə-mē\ 1891– Eng. scholar
Dob·son \ˈdäb-sən\ (Henry) Austin 1840–1921 Eng. poet & essayist
Dodge \ˈdäj\ Mary Elizabeth 1831–1905 née *Mapes* \ˈmāps\ Am. author
Dodg·son \ˈdäj-sən, ˈdäd-\ Charles Lut·widge \ˈlət-wij\ 1832–1898 pseud. *Lewis Car·roll* \ˈkar-əl\ Eng. math. & storywriter
Dods·ley \ˈdädz-lē\ Robert 1703–1764 Eng. author & bookseller
Doi·sy \ˈdȯi-zē\ Edward Adelbert 1893– Am. biochem.
Dole \ˈdōl\ Sanford Ballard 1844–1926 Am. jurist; pres. (1894–98) & gov. (1900–03) of Hawaii
Doll·fuss \ˈdȯl-ˌfüs\ Engelbert 1892–1934 Austrian statesman
Do·magk \ˈdō-ˌmäk\ Gerhard 1895–1964 Ger. chem.
Do·me·ni·chi·no, Il \(ˌ)dō-ˌmā-nə-ˈkē-(ˌ)nō\ 1581–1641 *Domenico Zam·pie·ri* \ˌtsäm-pē-ˈe(ə)r-ē, ˌzäm-\ Ital. painter
Dom·i·nic \ˈdäm-ə-(ˌ)nik\ Saint 1170–1221 *Domingo de Guz·mán* \güz-ˈmän, güs-\ Span.-born founder of the Dominican order of friars
Do·mi·tian \də-ˈmish-ən\ 51–96 *Titus Flavius Domitianus Augustus* Rom. emp. (81–96)
Don·a·tel·lo \ˌdän-ə-ˈtel-(ˌ)ō\ 1386?–1466 *Donato di Niccolò di Betto Bardi* Ital. sculptor
Dö·nitz \ˈdə(r)n-əts, ˈdœn-\ Karl 1891– Ger. admiral
Don·i·zet·ti \ˌdän-ə(d)-ˈzet-ē, ˌdōn-\ Gaetano 1797–1848 Ital. composer
Donne \ˈdən *also* ˈdän\ John *ab* 1572–1631 Eng. poet & clergyman — **Donn·ean** *or* **Donn·ian** \ˈdən-ē-ən, ˈdän-\ *adj*
Don·o·van \ˈdän-ə-vən, ˈdən-\ William Joseph 1883–1959 *Wild Bill* Am. lawyer & gen.
Doo·lit·tle \ˈdü-ˌlit-ᵊl\ James Harold 1896– Am. aviator & gen.
Dopp·ler \ˈdäp-lər\ Christian Johann 1803–1853 Austrian physicist & math.
Do·ra·ti \də-ˈrät-ē\ An·tal \ˈän-ˌtäl\ 1906– Am. (Hung.-born) conductor
Do·ré \dȯ-ˈrā, də-\ Paul Gustave 1833–1883 Fr. illustrator & painter
Dor·ge·les \ˌdȯr-zhə-ˈles\ Roland 1886–1973 Fr. nov.
Dor·nier \ˈdȯrn-ˌyā\ Claude 1884–1969 Ger. airplane builder
Dorr \ˈdȯ(ə)r\ Thomas Wilson 1805–1854 Am. lawyer & polit.
Dorset 1st Earl of — see Thomas SACKVILLE
Dos Pas·sos \də-ˈspas-əs\ John Roderigo 1896–1970 Am. writer
Dos·to·ev·ski \ˌdäs-tə-ˈyef-skē, -ˈyev-\ Fëdor Mikhailovich 1821–1881 Russ. nov. — **Dos·to·ev·ski·an** \-skē-ən\ *adj*
Dou *or* **Douw** \ˈdau̇\ Gerard 1613–1675 Du. painter
Dou·gher·ty \ˈdȯ-(h)ərt-ē\ Denis Joseph 1865–1951 Am. cardinal
Dough·ty \ˈdau̇t-ē\ Charles Montagu 1843–1926 Eng. poet & traveler
Doug·las \ˈdəg-ləs\ John Shol·to \ˈshōl-(ˌ)tō\ 1844–1900 8th Marquis & Earl of *Queens·ber·ry* \ˈkwēnz-ˌber-ē, -b(ə-)rē\ Scot. boxing patron
Douglas Norman 1868–1952 Eng. author
Douglas Stephen Arnold 1813–1861 Am. polit.
Douglas William Orville 1898– Am. jurist
Douglas–Home — see HOME
Douglas of Kir·tle·side \ˈkərt-ᵊl-ˌsīd\ 1st Baron 1893–1969 *William Sholto Douglas* Brit. air marshal
Doug·lass \ˈdəg-ləs\ Frederick 1817?–1895 orig. *Frederick Augustus Washington Bailey* Am. abolitionist
Dou·mer \dü-ˈme(ə)r\ Paul 1857–1932 pres. of France (1931–32)
Dou·mergue \dü-ˈme(ə)rg\ Gaston 1863–1937 Fr. statesman; pres. of France (1924–31)
Dow·den \ˈdau̇d-ᵊn\ Edward 1843–1913 Irish literary critic
Dow·ie \ˈdau̇-ē\ John Alexander 1847–1907 Scot.-born religious leader in Am.
Downes \ˈdau̇nz\ (Edwin) Olin \ˈō-lən\ 1886–1955 Am. music critic
Dow·son \ˈdau̇s-ᵊn\ Ernest Christopher 1867–1900 Eng. lyric poet
Dox·ia·dis \ˌdȯk-sē-ˈä-t͟hēs\ Constantinos Apostolos 1913– Gk. architect
Doyle \ˈdȯi(ə)l\ Sir Arthur Co·nan \ˈkō-nən\ 1859–1930 Brit. physician, nov., & detective-story writer
D'Oyly Carte — see CARTE
Drach·mann \ˈdräk-mən\ Holger Henrik Herholdt 1846–1908 Dan. author
Dra·co \ˈdrā-(ˌ)kō\ late 7th cent. B.C. Athenian lawgiver
Drake \ˈdrāk\ Sir Francis 1540?–1596 Eng. navigator & admiral
Dra·per \ˈdrā-pər\ Henry 1837–1882 Am. astron.
Draper John William 1811–1882 Am. (Eng.-born) scientist & writer
Dray·ton \ˈdrāt-ᵊn\ Michael 1563–1631 Eng. poet
Drayton William Henry 1742–1779 Am. Revolutionary polit.
Drei·ser \ˈdrī-sər, -zər\ Theodore Herman Albert 1871–1945 Am. editor & nov.
Drew \ˈdrü\ John 1826–1862 Am. (Irish-born) actor
Drew John 1853–1927 *son of prec.* Am. actor
Drey·fus \ˈdrī-fəs, ˈdrā-; drē-fᵫs\ Alfred 1859–1935 Fr. army officer
Driesch \ˈdrēsh\ Hans Adolf Eduard 1867–1941 Ger. biologist & philos.
Drink·wa·ter \ˈdriŋ-ˌkwȯt-ər, -ˌkwät-\ John 1882–1937 Eng. poet & dram.
Drou·et d'Er·lon \drü-ˌā-der-ˈlōⁿ\ Comte Jean Baptiste 1765–1844 Fr. gen.; marshal of France
Drum·mond \ˈdrəm-ənd\ Henry 1851–1897 Scot. clergyman & writer
Drummond William 1585–1649 1st Laird of *Haw·thorn·den* \ˈhȯ-ˌthȯrn-dən\ Scot. poet
Drummond William Henry 1854–1907 Canad. (Irish-born) poet
Dru·sus \ˈdrü-səs\ 38–9 B.C. *Ne·ro* \ˈnē-(ˌ)rō, ˈni(ə)r-(ˌ)ō\ *Claudius Drusus Ger·man·i·cus* \(ˌ)jer-ˈman-i-kəs\ Rom. gen.
Dry·den \ˈdrīd-ᵊn\ John 1631–1700 Eng. poet & dram.; poet laureate (1670–88) — **Dry·de·ni·an** *adj*
Du Bar·ry \d(y)ü-ˈbar-ē\ Comtesse 1746 (or 1743?)–1793 *Marie Jeanne Bécu; mistress of Louis XV of France*
Du·bois \d(y)üb-ˈwä, dᵫ-bwä\ Paul 1829–1905 Fr. sculptor
Dubois Théodore 1837–1924 Fr. composer
Du Bois \d(y)ü-ˈbȯis\ William Edward Burghardt 1868–1963 Am. educ. & writer
Du·buf·fet \ˌd(y)ü-bə-ˈfā, dᵫ-bᵫ-fe\ Jean 1901– Fr. artist
Du Cange \d(y)ü-ˈkäⁿzh\ Sieur Charles du Fresne 1610–1688 Fr. scholar & glossarist
Du Chail·lu \də-ˈshal-(ˌ)yü, -ˈshī-(ˌ)ü\ Paul Belloni 1831–1903 Am. (Fr.-born) explorer in Africa

Du·champ \d(y)ü-'shäⁿ\ Marcel 1887–1968 Fr. painter
Du·com·mun \ˌd(y)ü-kə-'mœⁿ\ Élie 1833–1906 Swiss journalist
Dudevant Aurore — see George SAND
Dud·ley \'dəd-lē\ Robert 1532?–1588 1st Earl of *Leicester* Eng. courtier
Dudley Thomas 1576–1653 colonial administrator in Massachusetts Bay Colony
Duf·fer·in and Ava \ˌdəf-(ə-)rə-nə-'näv-ə\ 1st Marquis of 1826–1902 *Frederick Temple Hamilton-Temple-Blackwood* Brit. diplomat & administrator
Duff–Gor·don \'dəf-'gȯrd-ᵊn\ Lady Lucie *or* Lucy 1821–1869 Eng. author
Duf·fy \'dəf-ē\ Sir Charles Gavan 1816–1903 Irish nationalist & Austral. polit.
Du·fy \d(y)ü-'fē\ Raoul 1877–1953 Fr. painter
Du Gard Roger Martin — see MARTIN DU GARD
Du Gues·clin \ˌd(y)ü-ˌgā-'klaⁿ, d(y)u-'gā-ˌ\ Bertrand 1320?–1380 constable of France
Du·ha·mel \ˌd(y)ü-ä-'mel, dᵫ-á-mel\ Georges 1884–1966 pseud. *Denis Thévenin* Fr. writer
Duke \d(y)ük\ Benjamin Newton 1855–1929 & his bro. James Buchanan 1856–1925 Am. tobacco industrialists
Dul·les \'dəl-əs\ John Foster 1888–1959 Am. lawyer; secy. of state (1953–59)
Du·mas \d(y)ü-'mä, 'd(y)ü-ˌ\ Alexandre 1802–1870 *Dumas père* \'pe(ə)r\ Fr. nov. & dram.
Dumas Alexandre 1824–1895 *Dumas fils* \'fēs\ Fr. nov. & dram.
du Mau·rier \d(y)ü-'mȯr-ē-ˌā\ Daphne 1907– Brit. writer
du Maurier George Louis Palmella Busson 1834–1896 Brit. artist & nov.
Du·mou·riez \d(y)ü-'mu̇r-ē-ˌā\ Charles François 1739–1823 Fr. gen.
Du·nant \d(y)ü-'näⁿ\ Jean Henri 1828–1910 Swiss philanthropist; founder of the Red Cross
Dun·bar \'dən-ˌbär\ Paul Laurence 1872–1906 Am. poet
Dunbar \'dən-ˌbär, ˌdən-'\ William 1460?–?1520 Scot. poet
Dun·can \'dəŋ-kən\ Isadora 1878–1927 Am. dancer
Dun·das \ˌdən-'das\ Henry 1742–1811 1st Viscount *Mel·ville* & Baron *Dun·ira* \ˌdə-'nir-ə\ Brit. statesman
Dun·lop \ˌdən-'läp, 'dən-ˌ\ John Boyd 1840–1921 Scot. inventor
Dun·more \ˌdən-'mō(ə)r, -'mȯ(ə)r\ 4th Earl of 1732–1809 *John Murray* Scot. colonial administrator in Am.
Dunne \'dən\ Finley Peter 1867–1936 Am. humorist
Du·nois, de \d(y)ün-'wä\ Comte Jean 1403?–1468 *the bastard of Orléans* Fr. gen.
Dun·sa·ny \ˌdən-'sā-nē\ 18th Baron 1878–1957 *Edward John Moreton Drax Plunkett; Lord Dunsany* Irish poet & dram.
Duns Sco·tus \ˌdən(z)-'skōt-əs\ John 1265?–?1308 Scot. scholastic theol.
Dun·stan \'dən(t)-stən\ Saint 925?–988 archbishop of Canterbury (961–988)
Du·pleix \d(y)ü-'pleks\ Marquis Joseph François 1697–1763 Fr. colonial administrator in India
Duplessis-Mornay — see Philippe de MORNAY
Du Pont \d(y)ü-'pänt, 'd(y)ü-ˌ\ Éleuthère Irénée 1771–1834 *son of P.S. Du Pont de Nemours* Am. (Fr.-born) industralist
Du Pont de Ne·mours \-də-nə-'mu̇(ə)r\ Pierre Samuel 1739–1817 Fr. econ. & statesman
Du·quesne \d(y)ü-'kān\ Marquis Abraham 1610–1688 Fr. naval officer
Du·rant \d(y)u̇-'rant\ William James 1885– Am. educ. & writer
Dü·rer \'d(y)u̇r-ər, 'dᵫr-\ Albrecht 1471–1528 Ger. painter & engraver — **Dü·rer·esque** \ˌd(y)u̇r-ər-'esk, ˌdᵫr-\ *adj*
D'Ur·fey \'dər-fē\ Thomas 1653–1723 Eng. songwriter & dram.
Dur·kheim \du̇r-'kem\ Émile 1858–1917 Fr. sociol.
Du·roc \d(y)u̇-'räk\ Géraud Christophe Michel 1772–1813 Duc *de Friuli* Fr. gen. under Napoleon
Dur·rell \'dər-əl, 'də-rəl\ Lawrence 1912– Eng. author & poet
Dur·ren·matt \'dᵫr-ən-ˌmät, 'du̇r-\ Friedrich 1921– Swiss author
Du·ruy \ˌdu̇r-(ə-)'wē, dᵫ-rwʸē\ Victor 1811–1894 Fr. hist.
Du·se \'dü-(ˌ)zā\ Eleanora 1859–1924 Ital. actress
Du·tra \'dü-trə\ Eurico Gaspar 1885– Brazilian gen.; pres. of Brazil (1946–51)
Du·va·lier \d(y)u̇-'val-(ˌ)yā\ François 1907–1971 pres. of Haiti (1957–71)
du Vi·gneaud \d(y)u̇-'vēn-(ˌ)yō\ Vincent 1901– Am. biochem.
Dvo·rak \(də-)'vȯr-ˌzhäk\ Anton 1841–1904 Czech composer
Dwig·gins \'dwig-ənz\ William Addison 1880–1956 Am. type designer
Dwight \'dwīt\ Timothy 1752–1817 Am. clergyman; pres. Yale U. (1795–1817)
Dwight Timothy 1828–1916 *grandson of prec.* Am. clergyman; pres. Yale U. (1886–98)
Dwyfor Earl of — see LLOYD GEORGE
Dyce \'dīs\ Alexander 1798–1869 Scot. editor
Dy·er \'dī(-ə)r\ John 1700?–1758 Brit. poet
Eads \'ēdz\ James Buchanan 1820–1887 Am. engineer & inventor
Ea·ker \'ā-kər\ Ira Clarence 1896– Am. aviator & gen.
Ea·kins \'ā-kənz\ Thomas 1844–1916 Am. artist
Ear·hart \'e(ə)r-ˌhärt, 'i(ə)r-\ Amelia 1898–1937 Am. aviator
Ear·ly \'ər-lē\ Ju·bal \'jü-bəl\ Anderson 1816–1894 Am. Confed. gen.
Earp \'ərp\ Wyatt 1848–1929 Am. lawman
East·man \'ēst-mən\ Charles Alexander 1858–1939 Indian name *Ohiyesa* Am. (Sioux Indian) physician & author
Eastman George 1854–1932 Am. inventor & industrialist
Eastman Max Forrester 1883–1969 Am. editor & writer
Ea·ton \'ēt-ᵊn\ Theophilus 1590–1658 Eng. colonial administrator in Am.; gov. of New Haven colony (1638–58)
Ebert \'ā-bərt\ Friedrich 1871–1925 Ger. polit.; pres. of Germany (1919–25)
Ec·cles \'ek-əlz\ Marriner Stoddard 1890– Am. banker & econ.
Eche·ga·ray y Ei·za·guir·re \ˌā-chə-gə-'rī-ˌē-ˌā-sə-'gwi(ə)r-(ˌ)ā, -ˌē-ˌā-sə-\ José 1832–1916 Span. dram.
Eche·ver·ría Al·va·rez \ˌā-chə-və-'rē-ə-'al-və-ˌrez, ˌech-ə-\ Luis 1922– pres. of Mex. (1970–)
Eck \'ek\ Johann 1486–1543 orig. *Mayer* Ger. R.C. theol.
Eck·er·mann \'ek-ər-ˌmän, -mən\ Johann Peter 1792–1854 Ger. writer
Eck·hart *or* **Eck·art** *or* **Eck·ardt** \'ek-ˌ(h)ärt\ Johannes 1260?–?1327 Ger. Dominican theol.; founder of Ger. mysticism
Ed·ding·ton \'ed-iŋ-tən\ Sir Arthur Stanley 1882–1944 Eng. astron.
Ed·dy \'ed-ē\ Mary Morse 1821–1910 née *Baker* Am. founder of the Christian Science Church
Eden \'ēd-ᵊn\ (Robert) Anthony 1897– Earl of *Avon* \'ā-vən\ Eng. statesman; prime min. (1955–57)
Edge·worth \'ej-(ˌ)wərth\ Maria 1767–1849 Brit. nov.
Edinburgh Duke of — see PHILIP
Ed·i·son \'ed-ə-sən\ Thomas Alva 1847–1931 Am. inventor
Ed·mund *or* **Ead·mund II** \'ed-mənd\ 980?–1016 *Ironside* king of the English (1016)
Ed·ward \'ed-wərd\ name of 8 post-Norman Eng. (Brit.) kings: **I** 1239–1307 (reigned 1272–1307) *Longshanks*
Edward II 1284–1327 (reigned 1307–27)
Edward III 1312–1377 (reigned 1327–77)
Edward IV 1442–1483 (reigned 1461–70; 1471–83)
Edward V 1470–1483 (reigned 1483)
Edward VI 1537–1553 (reigned 1547–53) *son of Henry VIII & Jane Seymour*
Edward VII 1841–1910 (reigned 1901–10) *Albert Edward, son of Victoria*
Edward VIII 1894–1972 (reigned 1936; abdicated) Duke of *Windsor, son of George V*
Edward 1330–1376 *the Black Prince; son of Edward III* prince of Wales
Edward *or* **Ead·ward** \'ed-\ 1002?–1066 *the Confessor* king of the English (1042–66)
Ed·wards \'ed-wərdz\ Jonathan 1703–1758 Am. theol. — **Ed·ward·ean** \ed-'wärd-ē-ən, -'wȯrd-\ *adj*
Ed·win *or* **Ead·wine** \'ed-wən\ 585?–633 king of Northumbria (617–633)
Eg·bert \'eg-bərt\ 775?–839 king of the West Saxons (802–839) & 1st king of the English (828–839)
Eg·gle·ston \'eg-əl-stən\ Edward 1837–1902 Am. writer
Eggleston George Cary 1839–1911 *bro. of Edward* Am. writer
Eg·mont, d' \'deg-ˌmänt\ Comte Lamoral 1522–1568 Flem. gen. & statesman
Eh·ren·burg \'er-ən-ˌbu̇(ə)rg, -ˌbu̇(ə)rk\ Ilya Grigorievich 1891–1967 Russ. writer
Ehr·lich \'e(ə)r-lik\ Paul 1854–1915 Ger. bacteriol.
Ehr·lich \'ər-lik\ Paul Ralph 1932– Am. biologist
Eich·mann \'īk-ˌmän, 'īsh-\ Adolf 1906–1962 Ger. Nazi leader
Eif·fel \'ī-fəl, e-fel\ Alexandre Gustave 1832–1923 Fr. engineer
Eijk·man \'īk-ˌmän, 'āk-\ Christiaan 1858–1930 Du. hygienist
Ein·stein \'īn-ˌstīn\ Albert 1879–1955 Am. (Ger.-born) physicist
Eint·ho·ven \'īnt-ˌhō-vən, 'ānt-\ Willem 1860–1927 Du. physiol.
Ei·sen·how·er \'īz-ᵊn-ˌhau̇(-ə)r\ Dwight David 1890–1969 Am. gen.; 34th pres. of the U.S. (1953–61)
El·a·gab·a·lus \ˌel-ə-'gab-ə-ləs\ *var of* HELIOGABALUS
El·don \'el-dən\ 1st Earl of 1751–1838 *John Scott* Eng. jurist
El·ea·nor \'el-ə-nər, -ˌnȯ(ə)r\ **of Aquitaine** 1122?–1204 *queen of Louis VII of France (divorced 1152) & of Henry II of England*
Eleanor of Castile *d* 1290 *queen of Edward I of England*
Eleanor of Provence *d* 1291 *queen of Henry III of England*
El·gar \'el-ˌgär, -gər\ Sir Edward 1857–1934 Eng. composer
El·iot \'el-ē-ət, 'el-yət\ Charles William 1834–1926 Am. educ.; pres. Harvard U. (1869–1909)
Eliot George 1819–1880 pseud. of *Mary Ann (or Marian) Evans* Eng. nov.
Eliot Sir John 1592–1632 Eng. statesman
Eliot John 1604–1690 *apostle to the Indians* Am. clergyman
Eliot Thomas Stearns 1888–1965 Brit. (Am.-born) poet & critic — **El·i·ot·ic** \ˌel-ē-'ät-ik\ *adj*
Eliz·a·beth \i-'liz-ə-bəth\ name of 2 Eng. (Brit.) queens: **I** 1533–1603 *dau. of Henry VIII & Anne Boleyn* (reigned 1558–1603); **II** 1926– *Elizabeth Alexandra Mary; dau. of George VI, wife of Prince Philip; mother of Prince Charles* (reigned 1952–)
Elizabeth 1596–1662 *Queen of Hearts; queen of Frederick V of Bohemia*
Elizabeth 1900– *Elizabeth Angela Marguerite Bowes-Ly·on* \'-bōz-'lī-ən\; *queen of George VI of Gr. Brit.*
Elizabeth 1843–1916 pseud. *Carmen Syl·va* \ˌkär-mən-'sil-və\ queen of Rumania & writer
Elizabeth psued. of Countress RUSSELL
Elizabeth Pe·trov·na \pə-'trȯv-nə\ 1709–1762 empress of Russia (1741–62)
Ellenborough 1st Baron — see LAW
El·ling·ton \'el-iŋ-tən\ Edward Kennedy 1899– *Duke Ellington* Am. band leader & composer
El·liott \'el-ē-ət, 'el-yət\ Maxine 1871–1940 pseud. of *Jessie Dermot* Am. actress
El·lis \'el-əs\ Alexander John 1814–1890 orig. surname *Sharpe* Eng. philologist
Ellis (Henry) Have·lock \'hav-ˌläk, -lək\ 1859–1939 Eng. psychol. & writer
El·li·son \'el-ə-sən\ Ralph Waldo 1914– Am. writer
Ells·worth \'elz-(ˌ)wərth\ Lincoln 1880–1951 Am. explorer

ə abut	ᵊ kitten, F table	ər further	a back	ā bake	
ä cot, cart	á F bac	au̇ out	ch chin	e less	ē easy
g gift	i trip	ī life	j joke	k G ich	ⁿ F vin	ŋ sing
ō flow	ȯ flaw	œ F bœuf	ᵫ F feu	ȯi coin	th thing
th this	ü loot	u̇ foot	ue G Füllen	ᵫ F rue	y yet
ʸ F digne \dēnʸ\, nuit \nwʸē\	yü few	yu̇ furious	zh vision		

Ellsworth Oliver 1745–1807 Am. jurist; chief justice U.S. Supreme Court (1796–99)

El·man \'el-mən\ Mi·scha \'mē-shə\ 1891–1967 Am. (Russ.-born) violinist

El·phin·stone \'el-fən-stōn, *chiefly Brit* -stən\ Mount·stu·art \maůnt-'st(y)ü-ərt\ 1779–1859 Brit. statesman in India

Elphinstone William 1431–1514 Scot. bishop & statesman

El·yot \'el-ē-ət, 'el-yət\ Sir Thomas 1490?–1546 Eng. scholar & diplomat

El·ze·vir *or* **El·ze·vier** \'el-zə-ˌvi(ə)r\ family of Du. printers including esp. Louis 1540?–1617, his son Bonaventure 1583–1652, & his grandson Abraham 1592?–1652

Em·er·son \'em-ər-sən\ Ralph Waldo 1803–1882 Am. essayist & poet — **Em·er·so·nian** \ˌem-ər-'sō-nē-ən, -nyən\ *adj*

Em·met \'em-ət\ Robert 1778–1803 Irish nationalist & rebel

Em·ped·o·cles \em-'ped-ə-ˌklēz\ 5th cent. B.C. Greek philos. & statesman

En·de·cott *or* **En·di·cott** \'en-di-kət, -də-ˌkät\ John 1589?–1665 colonial gov. of Massachusetts

En·ders \'en-dərz\ John Franklin 1897– Am. bacteriol.

Enes·co \ə-'nes-(ˌ)kō\ Georges 1881–1955 Rumanian composer

Eng·els \'eŋ-(g)əlz, *Ger* 'eŋ-əls\ Friedrich 1820–1895 Ger. socialist; collaborator with Karl Marx

En·ver Pa·sha \'en-ˌve(ə)r-'päsh-ə, 'pash-ə, -pə-'shä\ 1881?–1922 *Enver Bey* Turk. soldier & polit.

Epam·i·non·das \i-ˌpam-ə-'nän-dəs\ 418?–362 B.C. Theban gen. & statesman

Ep·ic·te·tus \ˌep-ik-'tēt-əs\ 1st–2d cent. A.D. Greek Stoic philos. in Rome — **Ep·ic·te·tian** \-'tē-shən\ *adj*

Ep·i·cu·rus \ˌep-i-'kyůr-əs\ 342?–270 B.C. Greek philos.

Ep·stein \'ep-ˌstīn\ Sir Jacob 1880–1959 Brit. (Am.-born) sculptor

Eras·mus \i-'raz-məs\ Desiderius 1466?–1536 *Gerhard Gerhards* or *Geert Geerts* Du. scholar — **Eras·mi·an** \-mē-ən\ *adj*

Er·a·tos·the·nes \ˌer-ə-'täs-thə-ˌnēz\ 3d cent. B.C. Greek astron.

Erck·mann–Cha·tri·an \'erk-ˌmän-ˌshä-trē-'äⁿ, -ˌsha-\ joint pseud. of *Émile Erckmann* 1822–1899 & *Alexandre Chatrian* 1826–1890 Fr. authors

Er·hard \'e(ə)r-härt\ Ludwig 1897– chancellor of West Germany (1963–66)

Er·ic \'er-ik\ 10th cent. *the Red* Norw. navigator; explored Greenland coast

Er·ic·son \'er-ik-sən\ Leif \'lāv, 'lēf\ *Old Norse* Leifr **Eiriksson** *fl* 1000 *son of Eric the Red* Norw. mariner; disc. "Vinland"

Er·ics·son \'er-ik-sən\ John 1803–1889 Am. (Swed.-born) engineer & inventor

Erig·e·na \i-'rij-ə-nə\ Johannes Scotus 815?–?877 Scot.-Irish (?) philos. & theol.

Er·lan·der \er-'län-dər\ Tage Frithiof 1901– Swed. polit.

Er·lang·er \'ər-ˌlaŋ-ər\ Joseph 1874–1965 Am. physiol.

Er·len·mey·er \'ər-lən-ˌmī(-ə)r, 'er-\ Emil 1825–1909 Ger. chem.

Ernst \'e(ə)rn(t)st, 'ərn(t)st\ Max 1891– Ger. painter

Er·skine \'ər-skən\ John 1695–1768 Scot. jurist

Erskine John 1879–1951 Am. educ. & writer

Er·vine \'ər-vən\ St. John \sānt-'jän, sənt-; 'sin-jən\ Greer 1883–1971 Irish dram. & nov.

Erz·ber·ger \'erts-ˌber-gər\ Matthias 1875–1921 Ger. statesman

Ese·nin \(y)is-'ān-yən\ Sergei Aleksandrovich 1895–1925 Russ. poet

Esh·kol \esh-'kōl\ Levi 1895–1969 premier of Israel (1963–69)

Es·par·te·ro \ˌes-pər-'te(ə)r-(ˌ)ō\ Baldomero 1792–1879 Conde *de Luchana* Span. gen. & statesman

Esquemeling — see EXQUEMELIN

Es·sen, von \'es-ᵊn\ Count Hans Henrik 1755–1824 Swed. field marshal & statesman

Essex 2d Earl of — see DEVEREUX

Es·taing, d' \des-taⁿ\ Comte Jean Baptiste Charles Henri Hector 1729–1794 Fr. admiral

Este \'es-(ˌ)tā\ Ital. princely family beginning with *Alberto Az·zo II* \'äd-(ˌ)zō\ 996–1097 & ending with *Er·co·le III* \'er-kə-ˌlā\ *Rinaldo* 1727–1803

Es·ter·ha·zy \'es-tər-ˌhäz-ē\ Marie Charles Ferdinand Walsin 1847–1923 Fr. army officer

Es·tienne \ā-'tyen\ *or* **Étienne** Fr. family of printers & booksellers including esp.: Henri I *d* 1520; his son Robert 1503–1559; & Robert's son Henri II 1528?–1598

Es·tour·nelles de Cons·tant, d' \ˌdes-ˌtůr-'nel-də-kōⁿ-'stäⁿ\ Baron Constant de Rebecque 1852–1924 *Paul Henri Benjamin Bal·luat* \bá-lwȧ\ Fr. diplomat & polit.

Eth·el·bert \'eth-əl-(ˌ)bərt\ 552?–616 king of Kent

Eth·el·red II \'eth-əl-ˌred\ 968?–1016 *the Unready* king of England (978–1016)

Eth·er·ege \'eth-(ə-)rij\ Sir George 1635?–1691 Eng. dram.

Euck·en \'ȯi-kən\ Rudolf Christoph 1846–1926 Ger. philos.

Eu·clid \'yü-kləd\ *fl ab* 300 B.C. Greek geometer

Eu·gene *or* **Eu·gène** \yü-'jēn, 'yü-ˌ, *F* œ-zhen\ 1663–1736 *François Eugène de Savoie-Carignan* prince of Savoy & Austrian gen.

Eu·gé·nie \'yü-jə-ˌnē; yü-'jā-nē, -'jē-; *F* œ-zhā-nē\ 1826–1920 *Eugénie Marie de Montijo de Guzmán; wife of Napoleon III* empress of the French (1853–71)

Eu·ler \'ȯi-lər\ Leonhard 1707–1783 Swiss math. & physicist

Eu·ler–Chel·pin, von \ȯi-lər-'kel-pən\ Hans August Simon 1873–1964 Swed. (Ger.-born) chem.

Eu·rip·i·des \yů-'rip-ə-ˌdēz\ 480?–?406 B.C. Greek dram. — **Eu·rip·i·de·an** \-ˌrip-ə-'dē-ən\ *adj*

Eus·den \'yüz-dən\ Laurence 1688–1730 Eng. poet; poet laureate (1718–30)

Eu·se·bi·us of Caesarea \yü-'sē-bē-əs\ 260?–?340 theol. & church hist.

Eu·sta·chio \eů-'stäk-ē-ˌō\ Bartolommeo 1524?–1574 Lat. *Eu·sta·chius* \yů-'stā-kē-əs, -'stā-sh(ē-)əs\ Ital. anatomist

Ev·ans \'ev-ənz\ Sir Arthur John 1851–1941 Eng. archaeologist

Evans Herbert McLean 1882–1971 Am. anatomist & embryologist

Evans Maurice 1901– Eng. actor

Evans Walker 1903– Am. photographer

Ev·arts \'ev-ərts\ William Maxwell 1818–1901 Am. lawyer & statesman

Ev·att \'ev-ət\ Herbert Vere 1894–1965 Austral. lawyer & statesman

Eve·lyn \'ēv-lən, 'ev-\ John 1620–1706 Eng. diarist

Ev·er·ett \'ev-(ə-)rət\ Edward 1794–1865 Am. clergyman, orator, & statesman

Ewald *or* **Evald** \'iv-ˌäl\ Johannes 1743–1781 Dan. poet & dram.

Ew·ell \'yü-əl\ Richard Stoddert 1817–1872 Am. Confed. gen.

Ex·que·me·lin \ik-'skā-mə-lən\ Alexandre Olivier 1645?–1707 Fr. pirate, surgeon, & author

Eyck, van \'īk\ Hubert *or* Huybrecht 1366?–1426 & his bro. Jan 1370?–1440 Flem. painters

Eze·kiel \i-'zēk-yəl\ Moses Jacob 1844–1917 Am. sculptor

Fa·bio·la \ˌfab-ē-'ō-lə, fəb-'yō-\ 1928– *queen of King Baudouin I of Belgium*

Fa·bi·us \'fā-bē-əs\ *d* 203 B.C. *Quintus Fabius Maximus Verrucosus Cunc·ta·tor* \ˌkəŋk-'tāt-ər\ Rom. gen. against Hannibal

Fa·bre \fäbrᵊ\ Jean Henri 1823–1915 Fr. entomologist

Fad·den \'fad-ᵊn\ Arthur William 1895–1973 Austral. statesman

Fad·i·man \'fad-ə-mən\ Clifton 1904– Am. writer & editor

Fah·ren·heit \'far-ən-ˌhīt, 'fär-\ Gabriel Daniel 1686–1736 Ger. physicist

Fair·banks \'fa(ə)r-ˌbaŋ(k)s, 'fe(ə)r-\ Charles Warren 1852–1918 Am. lawyer & polit.; vice-pres. of U.S. (1905–09)

Fairbanks Douglas Elton 1883–1939 Am. actor

Fair·child \'fa(ə)r-ˌchīld\ David Grandison 1869–1954 Am. botanist

Fair·fax \'fa(ə)r-ˌfaks, 'fe(ə)r-\ Baron Thomas 1612–1671 Eng. gen.

Fairfax Baron Thomas 1692–1782 proprietor in Va.

Fai·sal \'fī-səl, 'fā-\ 1904– king of Saudi Arabia (1964–)

Fai·sal *or* **Fei·sal** *or* **Fei·sul I** \'fī-səl, 'fā-\ 1885–1933 king of Syria (1920), of Iraq (1921–1933)

Faisal *or* **Feisal** *or* **Feisul II** 1935–1958 king of Iraq (1939–58)

Fa·lie·ri \fəl-'ye(ə)r-ē\ *or* **Fa·lie·ro** \-(ˌ)ō\ Marino 1278?–1355 doge of Venice (1354–55)

Fal·ken·hau·sen, von \'fäl-kən-ˌhaůz-ᵊn, 'fal-\ Baron Ludwig 1844–1936 Ger. gen.

Fal·ken·hayn, von \'fäl-kən-ˌhīn, 'fal-\ Erich 1861–1922 Ger. gen.

Falkner William — see FAULKNER

Fal·la, de \'fä-yə, 'fī-ə\ Manuel 1876–1946 Span. composer

Fal·lières \fal-'ye(ə)r\ Clément Armand 1841–1931 Fr. statesman; pres. of France (1906–13)

Fan·euil \'fan-yəl, 'fan-ᵊl, 'fan-yə-wəl\ Peter 1700–1743 Am. merchant

Far·a·day \'far-ə-ˌdā, -əd-ē\ Michael 1791–1867 Eng. chem. & physicist

Fa·ri·na \fə-'rē-nə\ Salvatore 1846–1918 Ital. nov.

Far·ley \'fär-lē\ James Aloysius 1888– Am. polit.

Far·man \fär-'mäⁿ, 'fär-mən\ Henri 1874–1958 & his brother Maurice 1877–1964 Fr. pioneer aviators and airplane manufacturers

Far·mer \'fär-mər\ Fannie Merritt 1857–1915 Am. cookery expert

Farmer James Leonard 1920– Am. civil rights leader

Far·ne·se \fär-'nā-zē, -sē\ Alessandro 1545–1592 Duke of *Parma* Ital. gen. in Span. service

Far·quhar \'fär-k(w)ər\ George 1678–1707 Brit. dram.

Far·ra·gut \'far-ə-gət\ David Glasgow 1801–1870 Am. admiral

Far·rar \'far-ər\ Frederic William 1831–1903 Eng. clergyman & writer

Far·rar \fə-'rär\ Geraldine 1882–1967 Am. soprano

Far·rell \'far-əl\ James Thomas 1904– Am. nov.

Fa·ruk *or* **Fa·rouk** \fə-'rük\ **I** 1920–1965 king of Egypt (1936–52; abdicated); citizen of Monaco (1959–65)

Fat·i·ma \'fat-ə-mə\ 606–632 *dau. of Muhammad*

Faulk·ner \'fȯk-nər\ William Cuthbert 1897–1962 sometimes *Falkner* Am. nov.

Faure \'fȯ(ə)r, fō(ə)r\ François Félix 1841–1899 Fr. statesman; pres. of France (1895–99)

Fau·ré \fȯ-'rā\ Gabriel Urbain 1845–1924 Fr. composer

Faus·ta \'fȯ-stə, 'faů-\ 289–326 *Flavia Maximiana Fausta; wife of Constantine the Great* Rom. empress

Fawkes \'fȯks\ Guy 1570–1606 Eng. R. C. conspirator

Faÿ \'fī, fä-'ē\ Bernard 1893– Fr. hist.

Fech·ner \'fek-nər, 'fek-\ Gustav Theodor 1801–1887 Ger. physicist & psychol.

Fei·ning·er \'fī-niŋ-ər\ Lyonel Charles Adrian 1871–1956 Am. painter

Feke \'fēk\ Robert 1705?–?1750 Am. painter

Fell·tham *or* **Fel·tham** \'fel-thəm\ Owen 1602?–1668 Eng. writer

Fé·ne·lon \ˌfān-ᵊl-'ōⁿ, fen-'lōⁿ\ François de Salignac de La Mothe 1651–1715 Fr. prelate & writer

Feng Yü-hsiang \'fəŋ-'yü-shē-'äŋ\ 1880–1948 Chin. gen.

Fer·ber \'fər-bər\ Edna 1887–1968 Am. writer

Fer·di·nand I \'fərd-ᵊn-ˌand\ 1503–1564 Holy Rom. emp. (1556–64)

Ferdinand II 1578–1637 king of Bohemia (1617–19; 1620–37) & of Hungary (1621–37); Holy Rom. emp. (1619–37)

Ferdinand III 1608–1657 king of Hungary (1625–57); Holy Rom. emp. (1637–57)

Ferdinand I 1861–1948 *Maximilian Karl Leopold Maria* king of Bulgaria (1908–18)

Ferdinand I *d* 1065 *the Great* king of Castile (1033–65); of Navarre and León (1037–65); emp. of Spain (1056–65)

Ferdinand V of Castile *or* **II** of Aragon 1452–1516 *the Catholic* king of Castile (1474–1504); of Aragon (1479–1516); of Naples (1504–16); founder of the Span. monarchy

Ferdinand VII 1784–1833 king of Spain (1808; 1814–33)

Fe·rish·tah \ˌfer-ish-'tä\ Mohammed Kasim 1550?–?1626 Pers. hist.

Fer·mat, de \fer-'mä\ Pierre 1601–1665 Fr. math.

Fer·mi \'fe(ə)r-(ˌ)mē\ Enrico 1901–1954 Ital. physicist

Fer·nán·dez \fər-'nan-ˌdez\ Juan 1536–?1602 Span. navigator

Fer·re·ro \fə-'re(ə)r-(ˌ)ō\ Guglielmo 1871–1942 Ital. hist. & author

Fes·sen·den \'fes-^{ə}n-dən\ William Pitt 1806–1869 Am. polit.; secy. of the treas. (1864–65)

Fes·tus \'fes-təs\ Porcius *d ab* A.D. 62 Rom. procurator of Judea (58 or 60-62)

Feucht·wang·er \'fȯikt-ˌväŋ-ər, 'fȯik̲t-\ Li·on \'lē-ˌȯn\ 1884–1958 Ger. nov. & dram.

Feuil·let \fə-'yā\ Octave 1821–1890 Fr. nov. & dram.

Fey \'fī\ Emil 1888–1938 Austrian soldier & polit.

Fi·bi·ger \'fē-bē-gər\ Johannes 1867–1928 Dan. pathologist

Fich·te \'fik-tə, 'fik̲-\ Johann Gottlieb 1762–1814 Ger. philos. — **Fich·te·an** \-tē-ən\ *adj*

Fied·ler \'fēd-lər\ Arthur 1894– Am. conductor

Field \'fē(ə)ld\ Cyrus West 1819–1892 Am. financier

Field Eugene 1850–1895 Am. poet & journalist

Field Marshall 1834–1906 Am. merchant

Fiel·ding \'fē(ə)l-diŋ\ Henry 1707–1754 Eng. nov.

Fie·so·le, da \fē-'ā-zə-ˌlā, -lē\ Giovanni 1387–1455 *Fra An·ge·li·co* \an-'jel-i-ˌkō\ orig. *Guido di Pietro* Ital. painter

Figl \'fē-gəl\ Leopold 1902–1965 Austrian agrarian & polit.

Fi·gue·roa, de \fē-gə-'rō-ə\ Francisco 1536?–1620 Span. poet

Fill·more \'fil-ˌmō(ə)r, -ˌmȯ(ə)r\ Millard 1800–1874 13th pres. of the U.S. (1850–53)

Finch \'finch\ Robert Hutchison 1925– U.S. secy. of health, ed. & welfare (1969–70)

Fin·lay \fin-'lī\ Carlos Juan 1833–1915 Cuban physician & biologist

Fin·sen \'fin(t)-sən\ Niels Ryberg 1860–1904 Dan. physician

Fir·bank \'fər-ˌbaŋk\ Ronald 1886–1926 Eng. author

Fir·dau·si \fər-'dau̇-sē, -'dō-\ *or* **Fir·du·si** \-'dü-\ 940?–?1020 *Abul Qasim Mansur* or *Hasan* Pers. epic poet

Fire·stone \'fī(ə)r-ˌstōn\ Harvey Samuel 1868–1938 Am. industrialist

Fi·scher \'fish-ər\ Emil 1852–1919 Ger. chem.

Fischer Hans 1881–1945 Ger. chem.

Fish \'fish\ Hamilton 1808–1893 Am. statesman

Fish·bein \'fish-ˌbīn\ Morris 1889– Am. physician & editor

Fish·er \'fish-ər\ Dorothy 1879–1958 *Dorothea Frances* née *Canfield* \'kan-ˌfēld\ Am. nov.

Fisher Geoffrey Francis 1887–1972 archbishop of Canterbury (1945–61)

Fisher Herbert Albert Laurens 1865–1940 Eng. hist. & educ.

Fisher Irving 1867–1947 Am. econ.

Fisher John Arbuthnot 1841–1920 1st Baron *Fisher of Kil·ver·stone* \'kil-vər-stən\ Brit. admiral

Fiske \'fisk\ John 1842–1901 orig. *Edmund Fisk Green* Am. philos. & hist.

Fitch \'fich\ John 1743–1798 Am. inventor

Fitch (William) Clyde 1865–1909 Am. dram.

Fitz·ger·ald \fits-'jer-əld\ Ella 1918– Am. singer

Fitzgerald Francis Scott Key 1896–1940 Am. writer

FitzGerald Edward 1809–1883 Eng. poet & translator

Fitz·her·bert \fits-'hər-bərt\ Maria Anne 1756–1837 née *Smythe; wife of George IV of England*

Flagg \'flag\ James Montgomery 1877–1960 Am. painter, illustrator, & writer

Flag·stad \'fläg-ˌstä, 'flag-ˌstad\ Kir·sten \'kish-tən, 'ki(ə)r-stən\ 1895 –1962 Norw. soprano

Fla·min·i·us \flə-'min-ē-əs\ Gaius *d* 217 B.C. Rom. gen. & statesman

Flam·ma·rion \flə-ˌmar-ē-'ō^{n}\ (Nicolas) Camille 1842–1925 Fr. astron. & writer

Flan·a·gan \'flan-i-gən\ Edward Joseph 1886–1948 Am. (Irish-born) R. C. priest & founder of Boys Town

Flan·din \flä^{n}-da^{n}\ Pierre Étienne 1889–1958 Fr. lawyer; premier (1934–35)

Flau·bert \flō-'be(ə)r\ Gustave 1821–1880 Fr. nov. — **Flau·ber·tian** \-'bər-shən, -'bert-ē-ən\ *adj*

Flax·man \'flak-smən\ John 1755–1826 Eng. sculptor

Fleet·wood \'flēt-ˌwu̇d\ Charles *d* 1692 Eng. gen.

Flem·ing \'flem-iŋ\ Sir Alexander 1881–1955 Brit. bacteriol.

Fleming Ian Lancaster 1908–1964 Brit. writer

Fleming Sir John Ambrose 1849–1945 Eng. electrical engineer

Fletch·er \'flech-ər\ John 1579–1625 Eng. dram.

Fleu·ry, de \ˌflər-'ē\ André Hercule 1653–1743 Fr. cardinal & statesman

Fleury Claude 1640–1723 Fr. ecclesiastical hist.

Flint \'flint\ Austin: father 1812–1886 & son 1836–1915 Am. physicians

Flo·res \'flōr-ˌās, 'flȯr-\ Juan José 1800–1864 Ecuadorian soldier; pres. of Ecuador (1830–35; 1839–45)

Flo·rey \'flōr-ē, 'flȯr-\ Sir Howard Walter 1898–1968 Brit. pathologist

Flo·rio \'flōr-ē-ˌō, 'flȯr-\ John 1553?–1625 Eng. lexicographer & translator

Flo·tow, von \'flō-(ˌ)tō\ Baron Friedrich 1812–1883 Ger. composer

Foch \'fȯsh, 'fäsh\ Ferdinand 1851–1929 Fr. gen.; marshal of France

Fo·kine \'fō-ˌkēn, fō-'\ Michel 1880–1942 Am. (Russ.-born) choreographer

Fok·ker \'fäk-ər, 'fȯk-\ Anthony Herman Gerard 1890–1939 Am. (Du.-born) aircraft designer & builder

Fo·ley \'fō-lē\ John Henry 1818–1874 Irish sculptor

Fol·ger \'fōl-jər\ Henry Clay 1857–1930 Am. bibliophile

Fon·tanne \fän-'tan, 'fän-ˌ\ Lynn 1887?– *wife of Alfred Lunt* Am. (Eng.-born) actress

Fon·teyn \fän-'tān, 'fän-ˌ\ Dame Margot 1919– *Margot Hookham* \'hu̇k-əm\ Eng. dancer

Foote \'fu̇t\ Andrew Hull 1806–1863 Am. admiral

Foote Samuel 1720–1777 Eng. actor & playwright

Forbes–Rob·ert·son \'fȯrbz-'räb-ərt-sən\ Sir Johnston 1853–1937 Eng. actor

Ford \'fō(ə)rd, 'fȯ(ə)rd\ Ford Mad·ox \'mad-əks\ 1873–1939 orig. *Huef·fer* \'(h)wef-ər\ Eng. author

Ford Gerald Rudolph 1913– Am. polit.; vice-pres. of the U.S. (1973–)

Ford Henry 1863–1947 Am. automobile manuf.

Ford John 1586?–1639 Eng. dram.

For·es·ter \'fȯr-əs-tər, 'fär-\ Cecil Scott 1899–1966 Brit. writer in Am.

For·rest \'fȯr-əst, 'fär-\ Edwin 1806–1872 Am. actor

Forrest Nathan Bedford 1821–1877 Am. Confed. gen.

For·res·tal \'fȯr-əs-t^{ə}l, 'fär-, -ˌtȯl\ James Vincent 1892–1949 Am. banker; 1st U.S. secy. of defense (1947–49)

Forss·mann \'fȯr-ˌsmän\ Werner Theodor Otto 1904– Ger. surgeon

For·ster \'fȯr-stər\ Edward Morgan 1879–1970 Brit. nov. — **For·ste·ri·an** \fȯr-'stir-ē-ən\ *adj*

For·syth \fȯr-'sīth, fər-\ John 1780–1841 Am. statesman

For·tas \'fȯrt-əs\ Abe 1910– Am. jurist

Fos·dick \'fäz-(ˌ)dik\ Harry Emerson 1878–1969 Am. clergyman

Fos·ter \'fȯs-tər, 'fäs-\ Stephen Collins 1826–1864 Am. songwriter

Foster William Zebulon 1881–1961 Am. Communist

Fou·cault \fü-'kō\ Jean Bernard Léon 1819–1868 Fr. physicist

Fouqué — see LA MOTTE-FOUQUÉ

Fou·quet *or* **Fouc·quet** \fü-'kā\ Nicolas 1615–1680 Fr. superintendent of finance

Fou·quier–Tin·ville \fü-kyā-ta^{n}-vēl\ Antoine Quentin 1746–1795 Fr. polit.

Four·dri·nier \ˌfōr-drə-'ni(ə)r, ˌfȯr-; fu̇r-'drin-ē-ər, fōr-, fȯr-\ Henry 1766–1854 & his bro. Sealy *d* 1847 Eng. papermakers & inventors

Fou·ri·er \'fu̇r-ē-ˌā\ François Marie Charles 1772–1837 Fr. sociol. & reformer

Fow·ler \'fau̇-lər\ Henry Hamill 1908– U.S. secy. of the treas. (1965–68)

Fowler Henry Watson 1858–1933 Eng. lexicographer

Fox \'fäks\ Charles James 1749–1806 Eng. statesman & orator

Fox Dixon Ryan 1887–1945 Am. educ. & hist.

Fox George 1624–1691 Eng. preacher; founder of Society of Friends (Quakers)

Fox Henry 1705–1774 1st Baron *Hol·land* \'häl-ənd\ Brit. statesman

Fox John William 1863–1919 *John Fox, Jr.* Am. nov.

Foxe \'fäks\ John 1517–1587 Eng. martyrologist

Foxe *or* **Fox** Richard 1448?–1528 Eng. prelate & statesman

Fra·go·nard \ˌfrag-ə-'när\ Jean Honoré 1732–1806 Fr. painter & engraver

France \'fran(t)s, frä^{n}s\ Anatole 1844–1924 pseud. of *Jacques Anatole François Thibault* Fr. nov. & satirist

Fran·ces·ca, della \fran-'ches-kə, frän-\ Piero 1420?–1492 *Piero dei Fran·ce·schi* \-'ches-kē\ Ital. painter

Fran·ces·ca da Ri·mi·ni \fran-ˌches-kəd-ə-'rim-ə-(ˌ)nē, frän-, -'rē-mə-\ *d* 1285? Ital. lady celebrated in Dante's *Inferno*

Fran·cis I \'fran(t)-səs\ 1494–1547 king of France (1515–47)

Francis II 1768–1835 last Holy Rom. emp. (1792–1806); emp. of Austria (as *Francis I*) 1804–35

Francis Ferdinand 1863–1914 archduke of Austria; assassinated

Francis Joseph I 1830–1916 emp. of Austria (1848–1916)

Francis of Assisi Saint 1182–1226 *Giovanni Francesco Bernardone* Ital. friar; founder of Franciscan order

Francis of Sales \'sā(ə)lz\ Saint 1567–1622 Fr. R. C. bishop of Geneva

Franck \'fräŋk\ César Auguste 1822–1890 Belg.-Fr. organist & composer

Franck James 1882–1964 Am. (Ger.-born) physicist

Francke \'fräŋ-kə\ Kuno 1855–1930 Am. (Ger.-born) hist. & educ.

Fran·co \'fräŋ-(ˌ)kō, 'fraŋ-\ Francisco 1892– *Francisco Paulino Hermenegildo Teódulo Franco-Bahamonde* Span. gen. & head of Span. state

Frank \'fraŋk, 'fräŋk\ Ilya Mikhailovich 1908– Russ. physicist

Frank·furt·er \'fraŋk-fə(r)t-ər, -ˌfərt-\ Felix 1882–1965 Am. (Austrian-born) jurist

Frank·lin \'fraŋ-klən\ Benjamin 1706–1790 Am. statesman & philos.

Franklin Sir John 1786–1847 Eng. arctic explorer

Franks \'fraŋ(k)s\ Baron 1905– *Oliver Shewell Franks* Eng. philos. & diplomat

Fra·ser \'frā-zər, -zhər\ James Earle 1876–1953 Am. sculptor

Fraser Peter 1884–1950 N.Z. statesman; prime min. (1940–49)

Fraser Simon 1667?–1747 12th Baron *Lov·at* \'ləv-ət\ Scot. Jacobite

Fraun·ho·fer, von \'frau̇n-ˌhō-fər\ Joseph 1787–1826 Bavarian optician & physicist

Fra·zer \'frā-zər, -zhər\ Sir James (George) 1854–1941 Scot. anthropologist

Fré·chette \frā-'shet\ Louis Honoré 1839–1908 Canad. journalist & poet

Fred·er·ick I \'fred-(ə-)rik\ 1123?–1190 *Frederick Bar·ba·ros·sa* \ˌbär-bə-'räs-ə, -'rōs-\ Holy Rom. emp. (1152–90)

Frederick II 1194–1250 Holy Rom. emp. (1215–50); king of Sicily (1198–1250)

Frederick I 1657–1713 king of Prussia (1701–13)

Frederick II 1712–1786 *Frederick the Great* king of Prussia (1740–86)

Frederick IX 1899–1972 king of Denmark (1947–72)

Frederick William 1620–1688 *the great Elector* elector of Brandenburg (1640–88)

Frederick William name of 4 kings of Prussia: **I** 1688–1740 (reigned 1713–40); **II** 1744–1797 (reigned 1786–97); **III** 1770–1840 (reigned 1797–1840); **IV** 1795–1861 (reigned 1840–61)

Free·man \'frē-mən\ Douglas Sou·thall \'sau̇-ˌthȯl, -ˌthȯl\ 1886–1953 Am. editor & hist.

ə abut	^{ə} kitten, F table	ər further	a back	ā bake
ä cot, cart	ȧ F bac	au̇ out	ch chin	e less	ē easy
g gift	i trip	ī life	j joke	k̲ G ich	^{n} F vin	ŋ sing
ō flow	ȯ flaw	œ F bœuf	œ̄ F feu	ȯi coin	th thing
t͟h this	ü loot	u̇ foot	ue G Füllen	ue̅ F rue	y yet
^{y} F digne \dēn^{y}\, nuit \nw^{y}ē\	yü few	yu̇ furious	zh vision	

Freeman Mary Eleanor 1852–1930 née *Wilkins* Am. writer
Freeman Orville Lothrop 1918– U.S. secy. of agric. (1961–69)
Fre·ling·huy·sen \ˈfrē-liŋ-ˌhīz-ᵊn\ Frederick Theodore 1817–1885 Am. statesman
Fré·mont \ˈfrē-ˌmänt\ John Charles 1813–1890 Am. gen. & explorer
French \ˈfrench\ Daniel Chester 1850–1931 Am. sculptor
Fre·neau \fri-ˈnō\ Philip Morin 1752–1832 Am. poet
Fres·co·bal·di \ˌfres-kə-ˈbäl-dē, -ˈbȯl\ Girolamo 1583–1643 Ital. composer
Fres·nel \frā-ˈnel\ Augustin Jean 1788–1827 Fr. physicist
Freud \ˈfrȯid\ Sigmund 1856–1939 Austrian neurologist; founder of psychoanalysis
Frey·berg \ˈfrī-ˌbərg\ 1st Baron 1889–1963 *Bernard Cyril Freyberg* N.Z. gen.
Frey·tag \ˈfrī-ˌtäk, -ˌtäg\ Gustav 1816–1895 Ger. author
Frick \ˈfrik\ Henry Clay 1849–1919 Am. industrialist
Fried \ˈfrēt, ˈfrēd\ Alfred Hermann 1864–1921 Austrian pacifist
Fro·bi·sher \ˈfrō-bi-shər\ Sir Martin 1535?–1594 Eng. navigator
Froe·bel or **Frö·bel** \ˈfrā-bəl, ˈfrē-, ˈfrœ-\ Friedrich 1782–1852 Ger. educ.
Froh·man \ˈfrō-mən\ Charles 1860–1915 Am. theater manager
Frois·sart \ˈfrȯi-ˌsärt, f(r)wä-ˈsär\ Jean 1333?–?1400 Fr. chronicler
Fromm \ˈfrōm, ˈfräm\ Erich 1900– Am. (Ger.-born) psychoanalyst
Fron·di·zi \frän-ˈdē-zē, -sē\ Arturo 1908– Argentinian pres. (1958–62)
Fron·te·nac, de \ˈfränt-ᵊn-ˌak\ Comte *de Pal·lu·au* \pá-lwʸō\ *et* 1620–1698 *Louis de Buade* \ˈbwʸád\ Fr. gen. & colonial administrator
Frost \ˈfrȯst\ Robert Lee 1874–1963 Am. poet — **Frost·ian** \-ē-ən\ *adj*
Froude \ˈfrüd\ James Anthony 1818–1894 Eng. hist.
Fry \ˈfrī\ Christopher 1907– Eng. dram.
Fu·ad I \fü-ˈäd\ 1868–1936 orig. *Ahmed Fuad Pasha* sultan (1917–22) & king (1922–36) of Egypt
Fu·en·tes \fü-ˈen-ˌtās\ Carlos 1928– Mex. author
Fuer·tes \ˈfyü(ə)rt-ēz\ Louis Agassiz 1874–1927 Am. illustrator
Ful·bright \ˈfu̇l-ˌbrīt\ James William 1905– Am. polit.
Ful·da \ˈfu̇l-də\ Ludwig 1862–1939 Ger. writer
Ful·ler \ˈfu̇l-ər\ Melville Weston 1833–1910 Am. jurist; chief justice U.S. Supreme Court (1888–1910)
Fuller Richard Buckminster 1895– Am. engineer
Fuller (Sarah) Margaret 1810–1850 Marchioness *Os·so·li* \ˈó-sə-(ˌ)lē\ Am. critic & reformer
Fuller Thomas 1608–1661 Eng. divine & author
Ful·ton \ˈfu̇lt-ᵊn\ Robert 1765–1815 Am. engineer & inventor
Funk \ˈfu̇ŋk, ˈfəŋk\ Casimir 1884–1967 Am. (Pol.-born) biochem.
Funk \ˈfəŋk\ Isaac Kauffman 1839–1912 Am. editor & publisher
Funk \ˈfu̇ŋk\ Walther 1890–1960 Ger. journalist & econ.
Fun·ston \ˈfən(t)-stən\ Frederick 1865–1917 Am. gen.
Fur·ness \ˈfər-nəs, -ˌnes\ Horace Howard: father 1833–1912 & son 1865–1930 Am. Shakespeare scholars
Fur·ni·vall \ˈfər-nə-vəl\ Frederick James 1825–1910 Eng. philologist
Furt·wäng·ler \ˈfu̇(ə)rt-ˌveŋ-lər\ Wilhelm 1886–1954 Ger. conductor
Ga·bo \ˈgäb-(ˌ)ō\ Naum 1890– orig. *Naum Pevs·ner* \ˈpevz-nər\ Am. (Russ.-born) sculptor
Ga·bo·riau \gə-ˈbȯr-ē-ˌō\ Emile 1835–1873 Fr. writer
Ga·bri·eli \ˌgäb-rē-ˈel-ē\ Giovanni 1557–1612 Ital. composer
Gads·den \ˈgadz-dən\ James 1788–1858 Am. army officer & diplomat
Gad·ski \ˈgät-skē\ Johanna 1872–1932 Ger. soprano
Ga·ga·rin \gə-ˈgär-ən\ Yu·ri \ˈyu̇(ə)r-ē\ Alekseyevich 1934–1968 Russ. astronaut; first man in space (1961)
Gage \ˈgāj\ Thomas 1721–1787 Brit. gen. & colonial gov. in Am.
Gail·lard \gil-ˈyärd\ David DuBose \-d(y)ü-ˈbōz\ 1859–1913 Am. army officer & engineer
Gaines \ˈgānz\ Edmund Pendelton 1777–1849 Am. gen.
Gains·bor·ough \ˈgānz-ˌbər-ə, -ˌbə-rə, -b(ə-)rə\ Thomas 1727–1788 Eng. painter
Gait·skell \ˈgāt-skəl\ Hugh Todd Naylor 1906–1963 Brit. socialist leader
Ga·ius \ˈgā-(y)əs, ˈgī-əs\ *or* **Ca·ius** \ˈkā-, ˈkī-\ 2d cent. A.D. Rom. jurist
Gal·ba \ˈgal-bə, ˈgȯl-\ Servius Sulpicius 5 B.C.?–A.D. 69 Rom. emp. (68–69)
Gal·braith \ˈgal-ˌbrāth\ John Kenneth 1908– Am. (Canad.-born) econ.
Gale \ˈgā(ə)l\ Zona 1874–1938 Am. nov.
Ga·len \ˈgā-lən\ *ab* 130– *ab* 200 Greek physician & writer
Ga·le·ri·us \gə-ˈlir-ē-əs\ *d* 311 *Gaius Galerius Valerius Maximianus* Rom. emp. (305–311)
Ga·li·lei \ˌgal-ə-ˈlā-ˌē\ Ga·li·leo \ˌgal-ə-ˈlē-(ˌ)ō, -ˈlā-\ 1564–1642 *Galileo* Ital. astron. & physicist
Gal·land \ga-ˈlä^n\ Antoine 1646–1715 Fr. orientalist & translator
Gal·la·tin \ˈgal-ət-ᵊn\ (Abraham Alfonse) Albert 1761–1849 Am. (Swiss-born) financier & statesman
Gal·lau·det \ˌgal-ə-ˈdet\ Thomas Hopkins 1787–1851 Am. teacher of the deaf & dumb
Ga·lle·gos Fre·ire \gä-ˈyā-(ˌ)gōs-ˈfrā-(ˌ)rā\ Rómulo 1884–1969 Venezuelan nov.; pres. of Venezuela (1948)
Gal·li–Cur·ci \ˌgal-i-ˈkür-chē, ˌgäl-, -ˈkər-\ Amelita 1889–1963 née *Galli* Am. (Ital.-born) soprano
Gal·lie·ni \ˌgal-yā-ˈnē, gal-ˈyā-nē\ Joseph Simon 1849–1916 Fr. gen. & colonial administrator
Gal·li·e·nus \ˌgal-ē-ˈē-nəs, -ˈā-nəs\ Publius Licinius Valerianus Egnatius *d* 268 Rom. emp. (253–268)
Gal·lup \ˈgal-əp\ George Horace 1901– Am. statistician
Ga·lois \gal-ˈwä\ Évariste 1811–1832 Fr. math.
Gals·wor·thy \ˈgȯlz-ˌwər-thē\ John 1867–1933 Eng. nov. & dram.
Galt \ˈgȯlt\ John 1779–1839 Scot. nov.
Gal·ton \ˈgȯlt-ᵊn\ Sir Francis 1822–1911 Eng. scientist — **Gal·to·nian** \gȯl-ˈtō-nē-ən, -nyən\ *adj*
Gal·va·ni \gal-ˈvän-ē, gäl-\ Luigi *or* Aloisio 1737–1798 Ital. physician & physicist
Gál·vez \ˈgäl-ˌves\ José 1729–1787 Marqués *de la Sonora* Span. jurist & colonial administrator
Ga·ma, da \ˈgam-ə, ˈgäm-\ Vasco 1469?–1524 Port. navigator
Ga·mar·ra \gə-ˈmär-ə\ Agustín 1785–1841 Peruvian gen.; pres. of Peru (1829–33; 1839–41)
Gam·bet·ta \gam-ˈbet-ə, ˌgä^n-bə-ˈtä\ Léon 1838–1882 Fr. lawyer & statesman
Ga·me·lin \ˌgam-(ə-)ˈla^n\ Maurice Gustave 1872–1958 Fr. gen.
Gan·dhi \ˈgän-dē, ˈgan-\ In·dira \ˈin-də-rə, in-ˈdir-ə\ Nehru 1917– *dau. of Jawaharlal Nehru* prime minister of India (1966–)
Gandhi Mohandas Karamchand 1869–1948 *Ma·hat·ma* \mə-ˈhät-mə, -ˈhat-\ *Gandhi* Hindu nationalist leader
Gar·a·mond \ˈgar-ə-ˌmänd, ˌgar-ə-ˈmō^n\ Claude *d* 1561 Fr. typefounder
Ga·rand \gə-ˈrand, ˈgar-ənd\ John Cantius 1888– Am. (Canad.-born) inventor
Gar·cía Gu·tiér·rez \gär-ˈsē-ə-gü-ˈtyer-əs\ Antonio 1813–1884 Span. dram.
García Iñi·guez \-ˈēn-yi-ˌgās\ Calixto 1836?–1898 Cuban lawyer & revolutionist
García Lor·ca \-ˈlȯr-kə\ Federico 1899–1936 Span. poet & dram.
García Mo·re·no \-mə-ˈrā-(ˌ)nō\ Gabriel 1821–1875 Ecuadorian journalist; pres. of Ecuador (1861–65; 1869–75)
Gar·ci·la·so de la Ve·ga \ˌgär-sə-ˈläs-ō-ˌdä-lə-ˈvā-gə\ 1539?–1616 *El Inca* Peruvian hist.
Gar·den \ˈgärd-ᵊn\ Mary 1874–1967 Am. (Scot.-born) soprano
Gar·di·ner \ˈgärd-nər, -ᵊn-ər\ Samuel Rawson 1829–1902 Eng. hist.
Gardiner Stephen 1483?–1555 Eng. prelate & statesman
Gard·ner \ˈgärd-nər\ Erle Stanley 1889–1970 Am. writer
Gardner John William 1912– U.S. secy. health, ed. & welfare (1965–68)
Gar·field \ˈgär-ˌfēld\ James Abram 1831–1881 20th pres. of the U.S. (1881)
Gar·i·bal·di \ˌgar-ə-ˈbȯl-dē\ Giuseppe 1807–1882 Ital. patriot — **Gar·i·bal·di·an** \-dē-ən\ *adj*
Gar·land \ˈgär-lənd\ (Hannibal) Hamlin 1860–1940 Am. nov.
Gar·ner \ˈgär-nər\ John Nance 1868–1967 Am. polit.; vice-pres. of the U.S. (1933–41)
Gar·nett \ˈgär-nət\ Constance 1862–1946 née *Black* Eng. translator
Gar·rick \ˈgar-ik\ David 1717–1779 Eng. actor
Gar·ri·son \ˈgar-ə-sən\ Mabel 1886–1963 Am. soprano
Garrison William Lloyd 1805–1879 Am. abolitionist
Gar·shin \ˈgär-shən\ Vsevolod Mikhailovich 1855–1888 Russ. writer
Gar·vey \ˈgär-vē\ Marcus 1887–1940 Jamaican Black Nationalist
Gary \ˈga(ə)r-ē, ˈge(ə)r-\ Elbert Henry 1846–1927 Am. lawyer & industrialist
Gas·coigne \ˈgas-ˌkȯin\ George 1535?–1577 Eng. poet
Gas·kell \ˈgas-kəl\ Elizabeth Cleghorn 1810–1865 née *Stevenson* Eng. nov.
Gas·ser \ˈgas-ər\ Herbert Spencer 1888–1963 Am. physiol.
Gasset — see José ORTEGA Y GASSET
Gates \ˈgāts\ Horatio 1728?–1806 Am. gen. in Revolution
Gau·guin \gō-ga^n\ (Eugène Henri) Paul 1848–1903 Fr. painter — **Gau·guin·esque** \(ˌ)gō-ˌga(^{n})n-ˈesk\ *adj*
Gauss \ˈgau̇s\ Karl Frie·drich 1777–1855 Ger. math. & astron.
Gau·ta·ma Bud·dha \ˌgau̇t-ə-mə-ˈbüd-ə, -ˈbu̇d-\ 563?–?483 B.C. orig. Prince *Siddhartha* Indian philos.; founder of Buddhism
Gau·tier \gō-tyā\ Théophile 1811–1872 Fr. author
Gay \ˈgā\ John 1685–1732 Eng. poet & dram.
Gay–Lus·sac \ˌgā-lə-ˈsak\ Joseph Louis 1778–1850 Fr. chem. & physicist
Ge·ber \ˈjē-bər\ *fl* 721–766 Arab scholar
Ged·des \ˈged-əs\ Sir Eric (Campbell) 1875–1937 & his bro. 1st Baron 1879–1954 *Auckland Campbell Geddes* Eng. statesmen
Geddes \ˈged-ēz\ Norman Bel \ˈbel\ 1893–1958 Am. designer
Gei·kie \ˈgē-kē\ Sir Archibald 1835–1924 Scot. geologist
Gei·sel \ˈgī-zəl\ Theodor Seuss 1904– pseud. *Dr. Seuss* \ˈsüs\ Am. writer & illustrator
Gellée Claude — see Claude LORRAIN
Ge·net \zhə-ˈnā\ Jean 1910– Fr. dram.
Ge·nêt \zhə-ˈnā\ Edmond Charles Edouard 1763–1834 Fr. diplomat in U.S.
Gen·ghis Khan \ˌjeŋ-gə-ˈskän, ˌgeŋ-\ 1162–1227 Mongol conqueror
Gen·ser·ic \ˈgen(t)-sə-rik, ˈjen(t)-\ *d* 477 king of the Vandals (428–477)
Gen·ti·le da Fa·bri·a·no \jen-ˈtē-lē-də-ˌfäb-rē-ˈän-(ˌ)ō\ 1370?–?1427 *Gentile Massi* Ital. painter
Geof·frey of Monmouth \ˈjef-rē\ 1100?–1154 Brit. ecclesiastic & chronicler
George \ˈjȯ(ə)rj\ Saint *d ab* 303 Christian martyr & patron saint of Eng.
George name of 6 kings of Gr. Brit.: **I** 1660–1727 (reigned 1714–27); **II** 1683–1760 (reigned 1727–60); **III** 1738–1820 (reigned 1760–1820); **IV** 1762–1830 (reigned 1820–30); **V** 1865–1936 (reigned 1910–36); **VI** 1895–1952 (reigned 1936–52)
George I 1845–1913 king of Greece (1863–1913)
George II 1890–1947 king of Greece (1922–23; 1935–47)
George David Lloyd — see David LLOYD GEORGE
George Henry 1839–1897 Am. econ.
Ge·rard \jə-ˈrärd, ˈjer-ˌärd\ Charles 1618?–1694 1st Baron *Gerard of Bran·don* \ˈbran-dən\; Viscount *Brandon* Eng. royalist commander
Ge·rard \jə-ˈrärd\ James Watson 1867–1951 Am. lawyer & diplomat
Gé·rard \zhā-ˈrär\ Comte Étienne Maurice 1773–1852 Fr. Napoleonic gen.; marshal of France
Ger·hard·sen \ˈge(ə)r-ˌhärs-ᵊn\ Einar 1897– Norw. polit.

Gé·ri·cault \ˌzhā-ri-ˈkō\ (Jean Louis André) Théodore 1791–1824 Fr. painter
Ger·man·i·cus Cae·sar \jər-ˌman-i-kə(s)-ˈsē-zər\ 15 B.C.–A.D. 19 Rom. gen.
Gé·rôme \zhā-ˈrōm\ Jean Léon 1824–1904 Fr. painter
Ge·ron·i·mo \jə-ˈrän-ə-ˌmō\ 1829–1909 Apache chieftain
Ger·ry \ˈger-ē\ Elbridge 1744–1814 Am. statesman; vice-pres. of the U.S. (1813–14)
Gersh·win \ˈgərsh-wən\ George 1898–1937 Am. composer
Ge·sell \gə-ˈzel\ Arnold Lucius 1880–1961 Am. psychol. & pediatrician
Ges·ner, von \ˈges-nər\ Konrad 1516–1565 Swiss naturalist
Get·ty \ˈget-ē\ George Washington 1819–1901 Am. gen.
Getty Jean Paul 1892– Am. business executive
Ghaz·za·li *or* **Gha·za·li, al-** \ˌal-gə-ˈzäl-ē\ 1058–1111 Arab (Persian-born) philos.
Ghi·ber·ti \gē-bert-ē\ Lorenzo 1378–1455 Florentine goldsmith, painter, & sculptor
Ghir·lan·da·jo \ˌgir-lən-ˈdä-(ˌ)yō, -ˈdī-(ˌ)ō\ Domenico 1449–1494 Florentine painter & mosaicist
Ghose \ˈgōs\ Sri Aurobindo 1872–1950 Indian philos. & nationalist statesman
Gia·co·met·ti \ˌjäk-ə-ˈmet-ē\ Albert 1901–1966 Swiss artist
Gi·auque \jē-ˈōk\ William Francis 1895– Am. chem.
Gib·bon \ˈgib-ən\ Edward 1737–1794 Eng. hist.
Gib·bons \ˈgib-ənz\ James 1834–1921 Am. cardinal
Gibbons Orlando 1538–1625 Eng. organist & composer
Gibbs \ˈgibz\ Josiah Willard 1839–1903 Am. math. & physicist
Gibbs Sir Philip 1877–1962 Eng. journalist & nov.
Gib·ran \jə-ˈbrän\ Gibran Khalil 1883–1931 Lebanese nov., poet, & artist in U.S.
Gib·son \ˈgib-sən\ Charles Dana 1867–1944 Am. illustrator
Gibson William 1914– Am. dram.
Gide \ˈzhēd\ André 1869–1951 Fr. nov., critic, & essayist
Giel·gud \ˈgil-ˌgu̇d, ˈgēl-\ Sir (Arthur) John 1904– Eng. actor
Gie·se·king \ˈgē-zə-kiŋ\ Walter Wilhelm 1895–1956 Ger. (Fr.-born) pianist
Gil·bert \ˈgil-bərt\ Cass 1859–1934 Am. architect
Gilbert Sir Humphrey 1539?–1583 Eng. navigator
Gilbert William 1540–1603 Eng. physician & physicist
Gilbert Sir William Schwenck 1836–1911 Eng. librettist & poet; collaborator with Sir Arthur Sullivan
Gil·der \ˈgil-dər\ Richard Watson 1844–1909 Am. poet & editor
Gil·lette \jə-ˈlet\ King Camp 1855–1932 Am. inventor & manuf.
Gillette William 1855–1937 Am. actor
Gil·man \ˈgil-mən\ Arthur 1837–1909 Am. educ.; developed Radcliffe College
Gilman Daniel Coit \ˈkȯit\ 1831–1908 Am. educ.; pres. Johns Hopkins U. (1875–1901)
Gil·mer \ˈgil-mər\ Elizabeth 1870–1951 née *Mer·i·weth·er* \ˈmer-ə-ˌweth-ər\ pseud. *Dorothy Dix* \ˈdiks\ Am. journalist
Gil·pin \ˈgil-pən\ Charles Sidney 1878–1930 Am. actor
Gilwell 1st Baron of — see BADEN-POWELL
Gi·na·ste·ra \ˌhē-nə-ˈster-ə\ Alberto 1916– Argentine composer
Gins·berg \ˈginz-ˌbərg\ Allen 1926– Am. poet
Gior·gio·ne, Il \ˌel-(ˌ)jȯr-ˈjō-nē\ *ab* 1478–1511 *Giorgione da Castelfranco*, orig. *Giorgio Barbarelli* Venetian painter
Giot·to \ˈjȯt(ˌ)-(ˌ)tō, jē-ˈät-(ˌ)ō\ 1266?–1337 *Giotto di Bondone* Florentine painter, architect, & sculptor
Gi·rard \zhē-ˈrär\ Jean Baptiste 1765–1850 Swiss Franciscan & educ.
Gi·rard \jə-ˈrärd\ Stephen 1750–1831 Am. (Fr.-born) financier & philanthropist
Gi·raud \zhē-ˈrō\ Henri Honoré 1879–1949 Fr. gen.
Gi·rau·doux \ˌzhē-rō-ˈdü\ Jean 1882–1944 Fr. writer
Gir·tin \ˈgərt-^{ə}n\ Thomas 1775–1802 Eng. founder of art of modern watercolor painting
Gis·sing \ˈgis-iŋ\ George Robert 1857–1903 Eng. nov.
Gjel·le·rup \ˈgel-ə-ˌru̇p\ Karl 1857–1919 Dan. writer
Glad·stone \ˈglad-ˌstōn, *chiefly Brit.* -stən\ William Ewart 1809–1898 Brit. statesman; prime min. (1868–74; 1880–85; 1886; 1892–94)
Gla·ser \ˈglā-zər\ Donald Arthur 1926– Am. physicist
Glas·gow \ˈglas-(ˌ)kō, -(ˌ)gō, ˈglaz-(ˌ)gō\ Ellen Anderson Gholson 1874–1945 Am. nov.
Glas·pell \ˈglas-ˌpel\ Susan 1882–1948 Am. nov. & dram.
Glass \ˈglas\ Carter 1858–1946 Am. statesman
Gla·zu·nov \ˈglaz-ə-ˌnȯf, -ˌnȯv, ˌgläz-ü-ˈ\ Aleksandr 1865–1936 Russ. composer
Glen·dow·er \glen-ˈdau̇(-ə)r\ Owen 1359?–?1416 Welsh chieftain & rebel against Henry IV of Eng.
Glenn \ˈglen\ John Herschel 1921– Am. astronaut; first Am. to orbit the earth (1962)
Glen·nan \ˈglen-ən\ Thomas Keith 1905– Am. engineer
Glin·ka \ˈgliŋ-kə\ Mikhail Ivanovich 1803–1857 Russ. composer
Gloucester Duke of — see HUMPHREY
Glov·er \ˈgləv-ər\ John 1732–1797 Am. Revolutionary gen.
Glover Sarah Ann 1785–1867 Eng. music teacher; invented tonic sol-fa system of notation
Gluck \ˈglu̇k\ Alma 1884–1938 née *(Reba) Fiersohn* Am. (Rumanian-born) soprano
Gluck Christoph Willibald 1714–1787 Ger. composer
Glyn \ˈglin\ Elinor 1864–1943 née *Sutherland* Brit. nov.
Go·bat \gō-ˈbä\ Charles Albert 1843–1914 Swiss statesman
God·dard \ˈgäd-ərd\ Robert Hutchings 1882–1945 Am. physicist
God·frey of Bouil·lon \ˌgäd-frē-əv-(ˌ)bü-ˈyōⁿ\ *Fr.* **Godefroy de Bouillon** 1061?–1100 Fr. crusader
Go·dol·phin \gə-ˈdäl-fən\ Sidney 1645–1712 1st Earl of *Godolphin* Eng. statesman
Go·doy, de \gō-ˈdȯi\ Manuel 1767–1851 Span. statesman
Go·du·nov \ˈgōd-^{ə}n-ˌȯf, ˈgȯd-, ˈgäd-\ Boris Fëdorovich 1551?–1605 czar of Russia (1598–1605)
God·win \ˈgäd-wən\ *d* 1053 earl of the West Saxons
Godwin William 1756–1836 Eng. philos. & nov. — **God·win·ian** \gäd-ˈwin-ē-ən\ *adj*
Godwin–Aus·ten \-ˈȯs-tən, -ˈäs-\ Henry Haversham 1834–1923 Eng. explorer & geologist
Goeb·bels \ˈgə(r)b-əlz, ˈgœb-əls\ Joseph Paul 1897–1945 Ger. Nazi propagandist
Goering — see GÖRING
Goes \ˈgüs\ Hugo van der 1440?–1482 Du. painter
Goe·thals \ˈgō-thəlz\ George Washington 1858–1928 Am. gen. & engineer
Goe·the, von \ˈgə(r)-tə, ˈgœ̄-tə *also* ˈgə(r)-tē\ Johann Wolfgang 1749–1832 Ger. poet & dram. — **Goe·the·an** \-tē-ən\ *adj*
Gogh, van \van-ˈgō, -ˈgäk, -ˈkȯk\ Vincent 1853–1890 Du. painter
Go·gol \ˈgȯ-gəl, ˈgō-ˌgȯl\ Nikolai Vasilievich 1809–1852 Russ. writer — **Go·gol·ian** \gȯ-ˈgōl-yən, gō-ˈgȯl-\ *adj*
Gold·berg \ˈgōl(d)-ˌbərg\ Arthur Joseph 1908– Am. lawyer; U.S. ambassador to U.N. (1965–68)
Gol·den \ˈgōl-dən\ Harry Lewis 1902– Am. journalist
Gol·den·wei·ser \ˈgōl-dən-ˌwī-zər\ Alexander A. 1880–1940 Am. (Russ.-born) anthropologist & sociologist
Gol·ding \ˈgōl-diŋ\ William Gerald 1911– Eng. author
Gol·do·ni \gäl-ˈdō-nē, gȯl-\ Carlo 1707–1793 Ital. dram.
Gold·smith \ˈgōl(d)-ˌsmith\ Oliver 1728–1774 Brit. author
Gold·wa·ter \ˈgōl-ˌdwȯt-ər, -ˌdwät-\ Barry Morris 1909– Am. polit.
Gol·gi \ˈgȯl-(ˌ)jē\ Camillo \kä-ˈmēl-(ˌ)lō\ 1844–1926 Ital. physician
Gol·lancz \gə-ˈlan(t)s\ Sir Hermann 1852–1930 Eng. Semitic scholar
Gó·mez \ˈgō-ˌmez\ Juan Vicente 1857?–1935 Venezuelan gen. & polit.; dictator (1908–35)
Gom·pers \ˈgäm-pərz\ Samuel 1850–1924 Am. (Brit.-born) labor leader
Go·mul·ka \gō-ˈmu̇l-kə, -ˈməl-\ Wladyslaw 1905– Pol. polit.
Gon·çal·ves Di·as \gən-ˌsäl-vəs-ˈdē-əs\ Antônio 1823–1864 Brazilian poet
Gon·cha·ro·va \gən-ˈchär-ə-və\ Nathalie 1883–1962 Russ. artist
Gon·court, de \gōⁿ-ˈkü(ə)r\ Edmond Louis Antoine 1822–1896 & his bro. Jules Alfred Huot 1830–1870 Fr. nov. & collaborators
Gon·do·mar \ˌgän-də-ˈmär\ Count of 1567–1626 *Diego Sarmiento de Acuña* Span. diplomat
Gon·za·ga \gən-ˈzäg-ə, gän-, -ˈzag-\ Saint Aloysius 1568–1591 Ital. Jesuit cleric
Gon·zá·lez \gən-ˈzäl-əs\ Manuel 1833–1893 Mex. gen.; pres. of Mexico (1880–84)
Gon·za·lo de Cór·do·ba \gən-ˌzäl-ō-də-ˈkȯrd-ə-bə, -ˈkȯrd-ə-və\ Hernández 1453–1515 *el Gran Capitán* Span. soldier
Good·hue \ˈgu̇d-(ˌ)(h)yü\ Bertram Grosvenor 1869–1924 Am. architect
Good·man \ˈgu̇d-mən\ Paul 1911–1972 Am. educ.
Good·rich \ˈgu̇d-(ˌ)rich\ Samuel Griswold 1793–1860 pseud. *Peter Par·ley* \ˈpär-lē\ Am. writer
Good·year \ˈgu̇d-ˌyi(ə)r, ˈgu̇j-ˌi(ə)r\ Charles 1800–1860 Am. inventor
Gor·cha·kov \ˌgȯr-chə-ˈkȯf, -ˈkȯv\ Prince Aleksandr Ivanovich 1764–1825 Russ. gen. & statesman
Gorchakov Prince Aleksandr Mikhailovich 1798–1883 Russ. statesman & diplomat
Gor·din \ˈgȯrd-^{ə}n\ Jacob 1853–1909 Am. (Russ.-born) Yiddish dram.
Gor·don \ˈgȯrd-^{ə}n\ Charles George 1833–1885 *Chinese Gordon, Gordon Pasha* Brit. soldier
Gordon Charles William 1860–1937 pseud. *Ralph Connor* Canad. clergyman & nov.
Gordon Lord George 1751–1793 Eng. polit. agitator
Go·re·my·kin \ˌgȯr-ə-ˈmē-kən\ Ivan Longinovich 1839–1917 Russ. statesman; prime min. (1906; 1914–16)
Gor·gas \ˈgȯr-gəs\ William Crawford 1854–1920 Am. army surgeon & sanitation expert
Gö·ring \ˈgər-iŋ, ˈger-, ˈgœr-\ Hermann Wilhelm 1893–1946 Ger. Nazi polit.
Gor·ki \ˈgȯr-kē\ Maksim *also* Maxim **Gorky** 1868–1936 pseud. of *Aleksei Maksimovich Pesh·kov* \ˈpesh-ˌkȯf, -ˌkȯv\ Russ. writer
Gor·ky \ˈgȯr-kē\ Arshile 1904–1948 Am. (Turk.-born) artist
Gort \ˈgȯ(ə)rt\ 6th Viscount 1886–1946 *John Standish Surtees Prendergast Ver·e·ker* \ˈver-i-kər\ Brit. field marshal
Gor·ton \ˈgȯrt-^{ə}n\ John Grey 1911– Austral. polit.; prime minister (1968–71)
Gosse \ˈgäs\ Sir Edmund William 1849–1928 Eng. poet & critic
Go·ta·ma Buddah \ˈgōt-ə-mə-\ *var of* GAUTAMA BUDDHA
Gott·schalk \ˈgäch-ˌȯk, ˈgät-ˌshȯk\ Louis Moreau 1829–1869 Am. composer
Gou·dy \ˈgau̇d-ē\ Frederic William 1865–1947 Am. type designer
Gough \ˈgäf\ Sir Hugh 1st Viscount 1779–1869 Eng. field marshal
Gouin \gü-ˈaⁿ, ˈgwaⁿ\ Felix 1884– pres. of Fr. (1946)
Gould \ˈgüld\ Jay *orig.* Jason 1836–1892 Am. financier
Gou·nod \ˈgü-ˌnō\ Charles François 1818–1893 Fr. composer
Gou·raud \gu̇-ˈrō\ Henri Joseph Eugène 1867–1946 Fr. gen.
Gour·mont, de \gu̇r-ˈmōⁿ\ Remy 1858–1915 Fr. writer
Gow·er \ˈgau̇(-ə)r, ˈgō(-ə)r, ˈgȯ(-ə)r\ John 1325?–1408 Eng. poet
Go·ya y Lu·cien·tes, de \ˈgȯi-(y)ə-ˌē-ˌlü-sē-ˈen-ˌtās\ Francisco José 1746–1828 Span. painter — **Go·ya·esque** \ˌgȯi-(y)ə-ˈesk\ *or* **Go·yesque** \gȯi-ˈ(y)esk\ *adj*
Grac·chus \ˈgrak-əs\ Gaius Sempronius 153–121 B.C. & his bro. Tiberius Sempronius 163–133 B.C. *the Grac·chi* \ˈgrak-ˌī\ Rom. statesmen

ə abut	^{ə} kitten, F table	ər further	a back	ā bake
ä cot, cart	ȧ F bac	au̇ out	ch chin	e less	ē easy
g gift	i trip	ī life	j joke	k G ich	ⁿ F vin	ŋ sing
ō flow	ȯ flaw	œ F bœuf	œ̄ F feu	ȯi coin	th thing
th this	ü loot	u̇ foot	ue G Füllen	ue̅ F rue	y yet
ʸ F digne \dēnʸ\, nuit \nwʸē\	yü few	yu̇ furious	zh vision		

Gra·ham \'grā-əm, 'gra(-ə)m\ John 1649?–1689 *Graham of Claver·house* \'klā-vər-ˌhau̇s\; *Bonny Dundee;* 1st Viscount of *Dundee* Scot. Jacobite
Graham Martha 1894?– Am. dancer
Graham Thomas 1805–1869 Scot. chem.
Graham William Franklin 1918– *Billy* Am. evangelist
Gra·hame \'grā-əm, 'gra(-ə)m\ Kenneth 1859–1932 Brit. writer
Gramme \'gram\ Zénobe Théophile 1826–1901 Belg. electrician
Gra·mont, de \gra-'mōⁿ\ Comte Philibert 1621?–1707 Fr. soldier & courtier
Gra·na·dos \'grə-'näd-(ˌ)ōs\ Enrique 1867–1916 Span. composer
Gran·di \'grän-(ˌ)dē\ Count (di Mordano) Dino 1895– Ital. Fascist polit.
Grant \'grant\ Heber Jedediah 1856–1945 Am. Mormon; pres. of the church (1918–45)
Grant Ulysses Simpson 1822–1855 *Ulysses Hiram* (baptized *Hiram Ulysses*) *Grant* Am. gen.; 18th pres. of the U.S. (1869–77)
Gran·ville–Bar·ker \ˌgran-ˌvil-'bär-kər\ Harley Granville 1877–1946 Eng. actor-manager & dram.
Grass \'gräs\ Günter Wilhelm 1927– Ger. writer
Grasse, de \'gras, 'gräs\ Comte François Joseph Paul 1722–1788 Marquis *de Grasse-Tilly* \-tē-'yē\ Fr. naval officer
Gra·tian \'grā-sh(ē-)ən\ *Lat.* **Flavius Gratianus** 359–383 Rom. emp. (375–383)
Grat·tan \'grat-ᵊn\ Henry 1746–1820 Irish orator & statesman
Grau San Mar·tín \'grau̇-ˌsan-(ˌ)mär-'tēn, -ˌsän-\ Ramón 1887–1969 Cuban physician & polit.; pres. of Cuba (1944–48)
Graves \'grāvz\ Robert Ranke 1895– Brit. author
Gray \'grā\ Asa 1810–1888 Am. botanist
Gray Thomas 1716–1771 Eng. poet
Grayson David — see Ray Stannard BAKER
Gra·zia·ni \ˌgrät-sē-'ä-nē\ Rodolfo 1882–1955 Marchese *di Neghelli* Ital. marshal & colonial administrator
Gre·co, El \'grek-(ˌ)ō, 'grāk-, 'grēk-\ 1548?–?1614 or ?1625 *Domenico Teotocopulo* Span. (Cretan-born) painter
Gree·ley \'grē-lē\ Horace 1811–1872 Am. journalist & polit.
Gree·ly \'grē-lē\ Adolphus Washington 1844–1935 Am. gen. & arctic explorer
Green \'grēn\ John Richard 1837–1883 Eng. hist.
Green Julian 1900– Am. (Fr.-born) nov.
Green William 1873–1952 Am. labor leader
Gree·na·way \'grē-nə-ˌwā\ Catherine 1846–1901 *Kate* Eng. painter & illustrator
Greene \'grēn\ Graham 1904– Brit. nov.
Greene Nathanael 1742–1786 Am. Revolutionary gen.
Greene Robert 1558–1592 Eng. poet & dram.
Gree·nough \'grē-ˌnō\ Horatio 1805–1852 Am. sculptor
Greg·o·ry \'greg-(ə-)rē\ name of 16 popes: esp. **I** Saint 540?–604 *the Great* (pope 590–604); **VII** Saint (*Hil·de·brand* \'hil-də-ˌbrand\) 1020?–1085 (pope 1073–85); **XIII** (*Ugo Buoncompagni*) 1502–1585 (pope 1572–85)
Gregory Lady Augusta 1859?–1932 née *Persse* Irish dram.
Gregory of Nys·sa \-'nis-ə\ Saint 331?–?396 Eastern church father
Gregory of Tours Saint 538?–593 Frankish ecclesiastic & hist.
Gren·fell \'gren-ˌfel, -fəl\ Sir Wilfred Thomason 1865–1940 Eng. medical missionary to Labrador
Gren·ville \'gren-ˌvil, -vəl\ George 1712–1770 Eng. statesman
Grenville *or* **Greyn·ville** \'grān-\ Sir Richard 1541?–1591 Brit. admiral
Gresh·am \'gresh-əm\ Sir Thomas 1519?–1579 Eng. financier
Greuze \'grə(r)z, 'grœz\ Jean Baptiste 1725–1805 Fr. painter
Gré·vy \grā-'vē\ François Paul Jules 1807–1891 Fr. lawyer; 3d pres. of the Republic (1879–87)
Grey \'grā\ 2d Earl 1764–1845 *Charles Grey* Eng. statesman; prime min. (1830–34)
Grey Edward 1862–1933 Viscount *Grey of Fal·lo·don* \'fal-əd-ᵊn\ Eng. statesman
Grey Lady Jane 1537–1554 Eng. noblewoman beheaded as a possible rival for the throne
Grey (Pearl) Zane 1875–1939 Am. nov.
Grieg \'grēg, 'grig\ Edvard Hagerup 1843–1907 Norw. composer
Grier·son \'gri(ə)rs-ᵊn\ Sir Herbert John Clifford 1866–1960 Brit. scholar
Grieve Christopher Murray — see Hugh MACDIARMID
Grif·fin \'grif-ən\ Walter Burley 1876–1937 Am. architect
Grif·fith \'grif-əth\ Arthur 1872–1922 Irish poet
Griffith David Lewelyn Wark 1875–1948 Am. motion-picture producer
Gri·gnard \grēn-ˌyär\ Victor 1871–1934 Fr. chem.
Grill·par·zer \'gril-ˌpärt-sər\ Franz 1791–1872 Austrian dram. & poet
Grimm \'grim\ Jacob 1785–1863 & his bro. Wilhelm 1786–1859 Ger. philologists & fairy tale collaborators
Gris \'grēs\ Juan 1887–1927 Span. painter in France
Gro·fé \'grō-ˌfā\ Fer·de \'fərd-ē\ 1892–1972 Am. conductor & composer
Gro·lier de Ser·vières \'grōl-ˌyā-də-ˌser-vē-'e(ə)r, 'grōl-yər-\ Jean 1479–1565 Fr. bibliophile
Gro·my·ko \grə-'mē-(ˌ)kō, grō-\ Andrei Andreevich 1909– Russ. econ. & diplomat
Gro·nou·ski \grə-'nau̇-skē\ John Austin 1919– U.S. postmaster general (1963–65)
Groo·te \'grōt-ə\ Gerhard 1340–1384 *Ge·rar·dus Mag·nus* \jə-ˌrärd-ə-'smag-nəs\ Du. religious reformer
Gro·pi·us \'grō-pē-əs\ Walter 1883–1969 Ger.-born architect in Am.
Grop·per \'gräp-ər\ William 1897– Am. artist
Gros·ve·nor \'grōv-(ə-)nər\ Gilbert Hovey 1875–1966 Am. geographer
Grosz \'grōs\ George 1893–1959 Ger. painter
Grote \'grōt\ George 1794–1871 Eng. hist.
Gro·tius \'grō-sh(ē-)əs\ Hugo 1583–1645 *Huig de Groot* \'grōt\ Du. jurist & statesman
Grou·chy, de \grü-'shē\ Marquis Emmanuel 1766–1847 Fr. gen.
Grove \'grōv\ Sir George 1820–1900 Eng. writer on music
Groves \'grōvz\ Leslie Richard 1896–1970 Am. gen.
Grü·ne·wald \'grü-nə-ˌwȯld, 'grüe-nə-ˌvält\ Matthias *fl* 1500–1530 Ger. painter
Gryph·i·us \'grif-ē-əs\ Andreas 1616–1664 *Ger.* **Greif** \'grīf\ Ger. poet & dram.
Guar·ne·ri \gwär-'ne(ə)r-ē\ *Lat.* **Guar·ne·ri·us** \gwär-'nir-ē-əs, -'ner-\ family of Italian violin makers: esp. Giuseppe Antonio 1683–1745
Gu·de·ri·an \gü-'der-ē-ən\ Heinz 1886–1954 Ger. gen.
Gue·dal·la \gwi-'dal-ə\ Philip 1889–1944 Eng. writer
Gué·rard \gā-'rär(d)\ Albert Léon 1880–1959 Am. (Fr.-born) educ. & writer
Gue·rin \'ger-ən\ Jules 1866–1946 Am. painter
Guesde \ged\ Jules 1845–1922 *Mathieu Basile* Fr. socialist
Guest \'gest\ Edgar Albert 1881–1959 Am. journalist & poet
Gue·va·ra \gā-'vär-ə\ Ernesto 1928–1967 *Ché* Latin Am. revolutionary leader
Gui·do d' Arez·zo \'gwēd-(ˌ)ō-də-'ret-(ˌ)sō\ *or* **Guido Are·ti·no** \ˌar-ə-'tē-(ˌ)nō\ 995?–?1050 Benedictine monk & music reformer
Guil·laume \gē-'yōm\ Charles Édouard 1861–1938 Fr. physicist
Guis·card \gē-'skär\ Robert 1015?–1085 Norman conqueror in Italy
Guise, de \'gēz *also* 'gwēz\ 2d Duc 1519–1563 *François de Lorraine; le Balafré* Fr. soldier & polit.
Guise, de 3d Duc 1550–1588 *Henri I de Lorraine;* also *le Balafré* Fr. soldier & polit.
Gui·te·ras \gē-'ter-əs\ Juan 1852–1925 Cuban physician
Gui·zot \gē-'zō\ François Pierre Guillaume 1787–1874 Fr. hist. & statesman
Gull·strand \'gəl-ˌstran(d)\ Allvar 1862–1930 Swed. ophthalmologist
Gun·nars·son \'gən-ər-sən\ Gunnar 1889– Icelandic writer
Gun·ter \'gənt-ər\ Edmund 1581–1626 Eng. math.
Gun·ther \'gən(t)-thər\ John 1901–1970 Am. writer
Gus·ta·vus \(ˌ)gə-'stā-vəs, -'stäv-əs\ name of 6 kings of Sweden: **I** (*Gustavus Va·sa* \-'väs-ə\) 1496–1560 (reigned 1523–60); **II** (*Gustavus Adolphus*) 1594–1632 (reigned 1611–32); **III** 1746–1792 (reigned 1771–92); **IV** (*Gustavus Adolphus*) 1778–1837 (reigned 1792–1809); **V** (*Gus·taf* \'gəs-ˌtäv, 'gu̇s-, -ˌtäf\) 1858–1950 (reigned 1907–50); **VI** (*Gustavus Adolphus*) 1882–1973 (reigned 1950–73)
Gu·ten·berg \'güt-ᵊn-ˌbərg\ Johann 1400?–?1468 *Johann Gensfleisch* Ger. inventor of printing from movable type
Guth·rie \'gəth-rē\ Woodrow Wilson 1912–1967 *Woody* Am. folk singer
Gutz·kow \'gu̇ts-(ˌ)kō\ Karl 1811–1878 Ger. journalist, nov., & dram.
Guz·mán Blan·co \gü-ˌsmän-'bläŋ-(ˌ)kō\ Antonio 1829–1899 Venezuelan soldier & statesman; pres. of Venezuela (alternate terms of two years 1870–89)
Gwin·nett \gwin-'et\ Button 1735–1777 Am. Revolutionary leader
Gwyn *or* **Gwynne** \'gwin\ Eleanor 1650–1687 *Nell* Eng. actress; *mistress of Charles II*
Haa·kon VII \'hȯ-kən, -ˌkän\ 1872–1957 king of Norway (1905–57)
Ha·ber \'häb-ər\ Fritz 1868–1934 Ger. chem.
Há·cha \'hä-(ˌ)kä\ Emil 1872–1945 Czech jurist & statesman
Had·field \'had-ˌfēld\ Sir Robert Abbott 1858–1940 Eng. metallurgist
Had·ley \'had-lē\ Henry Kimball 1871–1937 Am. composer
Had·ow \'had-(ˌ)ō\ Sir (William) Henry 1859–1937 Eng. educ. & writer on music
Ha·dri·an \'hā-drē-ən\ *var of* ADRIAN
Hadrian 76–138 Rom. emp. (117–138)
Haeck·el \'hek-əl\ Ernst Heinrich 1834–1919 Ger. biologist & philos.
Ha·fiz \hä-'fiz\ 14th cent. *Shams ud-din Mohammed* Pers. poet
Hag·e·dorn \'hag-ə-ˌdȯ(ə)rn\ Hermann 1882–1964 Am. poet, nov., & critic
Hag·gard \'hag-ərd\ Sir (Henry) Ri·der \-'rīd-ər\ 1856–1925 Eng. nov.
Hahn \'hän\ Otto 1879–1968 Ger. physical chem.
Hah·ne·mann \'hän-ə-mən\ (Christian Friedrich) Samuel 1755–1843 Ger. physician; founder of homeopathy
Hai·dar (*or* **Hy·der**) **Ali** \ˌhīd-ə-rä-'lē\ 1722–1782 Muslim ruler of Mysore, India
Haig \'hāg\ 1st Earl 1861–1928 *Douglas Haig* Brit. field marshal
Hai·le Se·las·sie \ˌhī-lē-sə-'las-ē, -'läs-\ 1892– Ras *Taffari* or *Tafari* emp. of Ethiopia (1930–36; 1941–)
Hak·luyt \'hak-ˌlüt\ Richard 1552–1616 Eng. geographer & hist.
Hal·dane \'hȯl-ˌdān, -dən\ John Burdon Sanderson 1892–1964 Brit. scientist
Haldane John Scott 1860–1936 Brit. physiologist
Haldane Richard Burdon 1856–1928 Viscount *Haldane of Cloan* \'klōn\; *bro. of J.S.* Brit. lawyer, philos., & statesman
Hal·der \\'häl-dər\ Franz 1884–1972 Ger. gen.
Hale \'hā(ə)l\ Edward Everett 1822–1909 Am. Unitarian clergyman & writer
Hale George Ellery 1868–1938 Am. astron.
Hale Sir Matthew 1609–1676 Eng. jurist
Hale Nathan 1755–1776 Am. Revolutionary officer; executed as a spy by the British
Ha·lé·vy \ˌ(h)al-ā-'vē, ˌ(h)äl-\ 1799–1862 pseud. of *Jacques Fromental Élie Lé·vy* \lā-'vē\ Fr. composer
Halévy Ludovic 1834–1908 *nephew of prec.* Fr. dram. & nov.
Hal·i·fax \'hal-ə-ˌfaks\ Earl of 1881–1959 *Edward Frederick Lindley Wood* Eng. statesman & diplomat
Hall \'hȯl\ Charles Francis 1821–1871 Am. arctic explorer
Hall Charles Martin 1863–1914 Am. chem. & manuf.
Hall Granville Stanley 1846–1924 Am. psychol. & educ.
Hall James Norman 1887–1951 Am. nov.
Hal·lam \'hal-əm\ Henry 1777–1859 Eng. hist.
Hal·leck \'hal-ək, -ik\ Fitz-Greene 1790–1867 Am. poet
Halleck Henry Wager 1815–1872 Am. gen.

Hal·ler \ˈhäl-ər\ Józef 1873–1960 Pol. soldier
Hal·ley \ˈhal-ē, ˈhā-lē\ Edmund 1656–1742 Eng. astron.
Hals \ˈhälz, ˈhäls\ Frans 1580?–1666 Du. painter
Hal·sey \ˈhȯl-sē, -zē\ William Frederick 1882–1959 Am. admiral
Hal·sted \ˈhȯl-stəd, -ˌsted\ William Stewart 1852–1922 Am. surgeon
Ham·bro \ˈhäm-ˌbrō\ Carl Joachim 1885–1964 Norw. statesman
Ha·mil·car Bar·ca \hə-ˈmil-ˌkär-ˈbär-kə, ˈham-əl-\ 270?–228 B.C. *father of Hannibal* Carthaginian gen.
Ham·il·ton \ˈham-əl-tən, -əlt-ᵊn\ Alexander 1757–1804 Am. statesman
Hamilton Edith 1867–1963 Am. classicist
Hamilton Lady Emma 1761?–1815 née *Lyon, mistress of Lord Nelson*
Ham·lin \ˈham-lən\ Hannibal 1809–1891 Am. polit.; vice-pres. of the U.S. (1861–65)
Ham·mar·skjöld \ˈham-ər-ˌshəld, ˈhäm-, -ˌshu̇ld, -ˌshēld\ Dag \ˈdäg\ Hjalmar Agné Carl 1905–1961 Swed. U.N. official; secy.-gen. (1953–61)
Ham·mer·stein \ˈham-ər-ˌstīn, -ˌstēn\ Oscar 1847?–1919 Ger.-born theater manager in Am.
Hammerstein Oscar 1895–1960 *grandson of prec.* Am. dram.
Ham·mond \ˈham-ənd\ John Hays 1855–1936 Am. mining engineer
Hammond John Hays 1888–1965 *son of prec.* Am. electrical engineer & inventor
Hammond Laurens 1895– Am. inventor
Ham·mu·ra·bi \ˌham-ə-ˈräb-ē\ king of Babylon (*ab* 1955–1913 B.C. or earlier)
Hamp·den \ˈham(p)-dən\ John 1594–1643 Eng. statesman
Hampden Walter 1879–1955 stage name of *W. H. Dougherty* Am. actor
Hamp·ton \ˈham(p)-tən\ Wade 1752?–1835 Am. gen.
Hampton Wade 1818–1902 *grandson of prec.* Am. polit. & Confed. gen.
Ham·sun \ˈhäm-sən\ Knut 1859–1952 pseud. of *Knut Pedersen* Norw. writer
Han·cock \ˈhan-ˌkäk\ John 1737–1793 Am. Revolutionary statesman
Hancock Winfield Scott 1824–1886 Am. gen. & polit.
Hand \ˈhand\ Learned 1872–1961 Am. jurist
Han·del \ˈhan-dᵊl\ George Frederick 1685–1759 Brit. (Ger.-born) composer — **Han·de·li·an** \han-ˈdē-lē-ən\ *adj*
Han·dy \ˈhan-dē\ William Christopher 1873–1958 *W. C.* Am. blues musician
Han·na \ˈhan-ə\ Marcus Alonzo 1837–1904 *Mark* Am. businessman & polit.
Han·nay \ˈhan-ˌā, ˈhan-ē\ James Owen 1865–1950 Irish clergyman & nov.
Han·ni·bal \ˈhan-ə-bəl\ 247–183 B.C. *son of Hamilcar Barca* Carthaginian gen.
Han·no \ˈhan-(ˌ)ō\ 3d cent. B.C. Carthaginian statesman
Ha·no·taux \ˌan-ə-ˈtō, ˌän-\ (Albert Auguste) Gabriel 1853–1944 Fr. hist. & statesman
Han·sard \ˈhan-ˌsärd, ˈhan(t)-sərd\ Luke 1752–1828 Eng. printer
Han·son \ˈhan(t)-sən\ Howard 1896– Am. composer
Hans·son \ˈhan(t)-sən\ Per Albin 1885–1946 Swed. statesman
Han Yü \ˈhän-ˈyü\ 768–824 *Han Wen-kung* Chin. poet, essayist, & philos.
Har·bach \ˈhär-ˌbäk\ Otto Abels 1873–1963 Am. dram. & musical-comedy librettist
Har·de·ca·nute \ˌhärd-i-kə-ˈn(y)üt\ 1019?–1042 king of Denmark (1035–42) and of Eng. (1040–42)
Har·den \ˈhärd-ᵊn\ Sir Arthur 1865–1940 Eng. chem.
Harden Maximilian 1861–1927 orig. *Witkowski* Ger. journalist & writer
Har·den·berg, von \ˈhärd-ᵊn-ˌbərg, -ˌbe(ə)rg\ Prince Karl August 1750–1822 Pruss. statesman
Har·din \ˈhärd-ᵊn\ Clifford Morris 1915– U.S. secy. of agric. (1969–71)
Har·ding \ˈhärd-iŋ\ Warren Gamaliel 1865–1923 29th pres. of the U.S. (1921–23)
Hard·wicke \ˈhär-ˌdwik\ Sir Ce·dric \ˈsē-drik\ Webster 1893–1964 Eng. actor
Har·dy \ˈhärd-ē\ Thomas 1840–1928 Eng. nov. & poet
Har·greaves \ˈhär-ˌgrēvz\ James *d* 1778 Eng. inventor of the spinning jenny
Har·ing·ton *or* **Har·ring·ton** \ˈhar-iŋ-tən\ Sir John 1561–1612 Eng. writer & translator
Ha·ri·ri, al– \ˌal-hə-ˈri(ə)r-ē\ 1054–1122 Arab scholar & poet
Har·lan \ˈhär-lən\ John Marshall 1833–1911 & his grandson 1899–1971 Am. jurists
Har·ley \ˈhär-lē\ Robert 1661–1724 1st Earl of *Oxford* Eng. statesman
Harms·worth \ˈhärmz-(ˌ)wərth\ Alfred Charles William 1865–1922 Viscount *North·cliffe* \ˈnȯrth-ˌklif\ Eng. publisher & polit.
Harmsworth Harold Sidney 1868–1940 1st Viscount *Roth·er·mere* \ˈräth-ər-mi(ə)r\ *bro. of A.C.W.* Eng. publisher & polit.
Har·old I \ˈhar-əld\ *d* 1040 *Harold Hare·foot* \ˈha(ə)r-ˌfu̇t, ˈhe(ə)r-\ king of Eng. (1035–40)
Harold II 1022?–1066 king of Eng. (1066)
Harold name of 3 kings of Norway; esp. **III** *Haard·raa·de* \ˈhȯr-ˌrȯd-ə\ 1015–1066 (reigned 1047–66)
Har·ri·man \ˈhar-ə-mən\ (William) Aver·ell \ˈāv-(ə-)rəl\ 1891– Am. businessman, diplomat, & polit.
Har·ring·ton \ˈhar-iŋ-tən\ (Edward) Michael 1928– Am. writer
Har·ris \ˈhar-əs\ Frank 1854–1931 Am. (Irish-born) writer
Harris Joel Chandler 1848–1908 Am. writer
Harris Roy 1898– Am. composer
Harris William Torrey 1835–1909 Am. philos. & educ.
Har·ri·son \ˈhar-ə-sən\ Benjamin 1833–1901 *grandson of W. H. Harrison* 23d pres. of the U.S. (1889–93)
Harrison Frederic 1831–1923 Eng. writer & philos.
Harrison William Henry 1773–1841 9th pres. of the U.S. (1841)
Hart \ˈhärt\ Albert Bushnell 1854–1943 Am. hist. & editor
Hart Basil Henry Liddell — see LIDDELL HART
Hart Lorenz 1895–1943 Am. lyricist
Hart Moss 1904–1961 Am. librettist & dram.
Hart Sir Robert 1835–1911 Brit. diplomat
Hart William Surrey 1872–1946 Am. actor
Harte \ˈhärt\ Francis Brett 1836–1902 *Bret* Am. writer
Ha·run al–Ra·shid \hə-ˌrü-ˌnal-rə-ˈshēd, -ˌnär-rə-\ 764?–809 caliph of Baghdad (786–809)
Har·vard \ˈhär-vərd\ John 1607–1638 Eng. clergyman in Am.
Har·vey \ˈhär-vē\ George Brinton McClellan 1864–1928 Am. journalist & diplomat
Harvey Sir John Martin 1863–1944 Eng. actor & producer
Harvey William 1578–1657 Eng. physician & anatomist
Has·dru·bal \ˈhaz-ˌdrü-bəl, haz-ˈ\ *d* 207 B.C. *bro. of Hannibal* Carthaginian gen.
Has·sam \ˈhas-əm\ (Frederick) Childe 1859–1935 Am. artist
Hass·ler \ˈhäs-lər\ Hans Leo 1564–1612 Ger. composer
Has·tings \ˈhā-stiŋz\ 1st Marquis of 1754–1826 *Francis Raw·don-Hastings* \ˌrȯd-ᵊn-\ Brit. gen. & colonial administrator
Hastings Thomas 1860–1929 Am. architect
Hastings Warren 1732–1818 Eng. statesman & administrator in India
Haupt·mann \ˈhau̇p(t)-ˌmän\ Gerhart 1862–1946 Ger. writer
Haus·ho·fer \ˈhau̇s-ˌhō-fər\ Karl 1869–1946 Ger. gen. & geographer
Hauss·mann \ō-ˈsmän, ˈhau̇s-mən\ Baron Georges Eugène 1809–1891 Fr. administrator; improver of Paris
Have·lock \ˈhav-ˌläk, -lək\ Sir Henry 1795–1857 Brit. gen.
Hawke \ˈhȯk\ 1st Baron 1705–1781 *Edward Hawke* Eng. admiral
Haw·kins \ˈhȯ-kənz\ Sir Anthony Hope 1863–1933 pseud. *Anthony Hope* Eng. nov. & dram.
Hawkins *or* **Hawkyns** Sir John 1532–1595 Eng. admiral
Haw·orth \ˈhau̇-ərth\ Sir (Walter) Norman 1883–1950 Eng. chem.
Haw·thorne \ˈhȯ-ˌthȯ(ə)rn\ Nathaniel 1804–1864 Am. author
Hay \ˈhā\ John Milton 1838–1905 Am. statesman
Hay·den \ˈhād-ᵊn\ Carl Trumbull 1877–1972 Am. polit.
Haydn \ˈhīd-ᵊn\ (Franz) Joseph 1732–1809 Austrian composer
Hayes \ˈhāz\ Carlton Joseph Huntley 1882–1964 Am. hist. & diplomat
Hayes Helen 1900– *Helen Hayes Brown, wife of Charles MacArthur* Am. actress
Hayes Isaac Israel 1832–1881 Am. arctic explorer
Hayes Patrick Joseph 1867–1938 Am. cardinal
Hayes Roland 1887– Am. tenor
Hayes Rutherford Birchard 1822–1893 19th pres. of the U.S. (1877–81)
Haynes \ˈhānz\ Elwood 1857–1925 Am. inventor
Hays \ˈhāz\ Will Harrison 1879–1954 Am. lawyer & polit.
Haz·ard \ˈhaz-ərd\ Caroline 1856–1945 Am. educ.; pres. Wellesley College (1899–1910)
Ha·zard \ä-ˈzär\ Paul Gustave Marie Camille 1878–1944 Fr. literary hist.
Haz·litt \ˈhaz-lət, ˈhāz-\ William 1778–1830 Eng. essayist
Hea·ly \ˈhē-lē\ Timothy Michael 1855–1931 Irish statesman
Hearn \ˈhərn\ Laf·ca·dio \laf-ˈkäd-ē-ˌō\ 1850–1904 *Yakumo Koizumi* Jap. (Greek-born) writer of Irish-Greek descent
Hearst \ˈhərst\ William Randolph 1863–1951 Am. newspaper publisher
Heath \ˈhēth\ Edward 1916– Brit. prime min. (1970–)
Heav·i·side \ˈhev-ē-ˌsīd\ Oliver 1850–1925 Eng. physicist & electrician
Heb·bel \ˈheb-əl\ Friedrich 1813–1863 Ger. dram.
He·ber \ˈhē-bər\ Reginald 1783–1826 Eng. prelate & hymn writer
Hé·bert \ā-ˈbe(ə)r\ Jacques René 1755–1794 Fr. revolutionary journalist
He·din \hā-ˈdēn\ Sven Anders 1865–1952 Swed. explorer
He·gel \ˈhā-gəl\ Georg Wilhelm Friedrich 1770–1831 Ger. philos.
Hei·deg·ger \ˈhī-ˌdeg-ər, ˈhīd-i-gər\ Martin 1889– Ger. philos.
Hei·den·stam, von \ˈhād-ᵊn-ˌstam, -ˌstäm\ Verner 1859–1940 Swed. writer
Hei·fetz \ˈhī-fəts\ Ja·scha \ˈyäsh-ə\ 1901– Am. (Russ.-born) violinist
Hei·ne \ˈhī-nə *also* -nē\ Heinrich 1797–1856 Ger. poet & critic
Hei·sen·berg \ˈhīz-ᵊn-ˌbərg, -ˌbe(ə)rg\ Werner 1901– Ger. physicist
Hei·ser \ˈhī-zər\ Victor George 1873–1972 Am. public-health physician & writer
He·li·o·gab·a·lus \ˌhē-lē-ō-ˈgab-ə-ləs\ 204–222 *Varius Avitus Bassianus* Rom. emp. (218–222)
Hell·man \ˈhel-mən\ Lillian 1905– Am. dram.
Helm·holtz, von \ˈhelm-ˌhōlts\ Hermann Ludwig Ferdinand 1821–1894 Ger. physicist, anatomist, & physiol.
Hé·lo·ïse \ˈā-lə-ˌwēz, ˈel-ə-\ 1101?–1164 *wife of Abelard* Fr. abbess
Hel·vé·tius \hel-ˈvā-sh(ē-)əs, -ˈvē-; ˌ(h)el-ˌvās-ˈyüs, -ˈyᵫs\ Claude Adrien 1715–1771 Fr. philos.
He·mans \ˈhem-ənz, ˈhē-mənz\ Felicia Dorothea 1793–1835 née *Browne* Eng. poet
Hem·ing *or* **Hem·minge** \ˈhem-iŋ\ John 1556?–1630 Eng. actor
Hem·ing·way \ˈhem-iŋ-ˌwā\ Ernest Miller 1899–1961 Am. story-writer & journalist
Hench \ˈhench\ Philip Showalter 1896–1965 Am. physician
Hen·der·son \ˈhen-dər-sən\ Arthur 1863–1935 Brit. labor leader & statesman
Henderson Leon 1895– Am. econ. & administrator

ə abut ᵊ kitten, F table ər further a back ā bake ä cot, cart á F bac au̇ out ch chin e less ē easy g gift i trip ī life j joke k̲ G ich ⁿ F vin ŋ sing ō flow ȯ flaw œ F bœuf ᵫ F feu ȯi coin th thing t̲h̲ this ü loot u̇ foot ue G Füllen ᵫ F rue y yet ʸ F digne \dēnʸ\, nuit \nwʸē\ yü few yu̇ furious zh vision

Henderson Sir Nev·ile \'nev-əl\ Meyrick 1882–1942 Brit. diplomat
Hen·dricks \'hen-driks\ Thomas Andrews 1819–1885 Am. polit.; vice-pres. of the U.S. (1885)
Hen·gist \'heŋ-gəst, -ˌgist\ *and* **Hor·sa** \'hȯr-sə\ *d* 488 and 455 A.D. resp. *bros.* Jute invaders of Britain (*ab* 449)
Hen·ley \'hen-lē\ William Ernest 1849–1903 Eng. editor & author
Hen·ne·pin \'hen-ə-pən, ˌen-ə-'paⁿ\ Louis 1640?–1701 Belg. friar & explorer in Am.
Hen·ri \'hen-rē\ Robert 1865–1929 *Robert Henry Cozad* Am. painter
Hen·ry \'hen-rē\ name of 8 kings of Eng.: **I** 1068–1135 (reigned 1100–35); **II** 1133–1189 (reigned 1154–89); **III** 1207–1272 (reigned 1216–72); **IV** 1367–1413 (reigned 1399–1413); **V** 1387–1422 (reigned 1413–22); **VI** 1421–1471 (reigned 1422–61 & 1470–71); **VII** 1457–1509 (reigned 1485–1509); **VIII** 1491–1547 (reigned 1509–47)
Henry name of 4 kings of France: **I** 1008–1060 (reigned 1031–60); **II** 1519–1559 (reigned 1547–59); **III** 1551–1589 (reigned 1574–89); **IV of Navarre** 1553–1610 (reigned 1589–1610)
Henry 1394–1460 *the Navigator* Port. prince; promoter of navigation
Henry Joseph 1797–1878 Am. physicist
Henry O. — see William Sydney PORTER
Henry Patrick 1736–1799 Am. statesman & orator
Hens·lowe \'henz-(ˌ)lō\ Philip *d* 1616 Eng. theater manager & diarist
Hep·burn \'hep-(ˌ)bərn\ Katharine 1909– Am. actress
Hep·ple·white \'hep-əl-ˌ(h)wīt\ George *d* 1786 Eng. cabinetmaker
Hep·worth \'hep-(ˌ)wərth\ Dame Barbara 1903– Brit. sculptor
Her·a·cli·tus \ˌher-ə-'klīt-əs\ 6th–5th cent. B.C. Greek philos. — **Her·a·cli·te·an** \-'klīt-ē-ən, -klī-'tē-\ *adj*
He·ra·cli·us \ˌher-ə-'klī-əs, hi-'rak-lē-\ 575?–641 Byzantine emp. (610–641)
Her·bart \'he(ə)r-ˌbärt\ Johann Friedrich 1776–1841 Ger. philos. & educ.
Her·bert \'hər-bərt\ George 1593–1633 Eng. divine & poet
Herbert Victor 1859–1924 Am. (Irish-born) composer & conductor
Herbert William 1580–1630 3d Earl of *Pembroke* Eng. statesman & poet
Herblock — see Herbert Lawrence BLOCK
Her·der, von \'herd-ər\ Johann Gottfried 1744–1803 Ger. philos. & writer
He·re·dia, de \ā-rā-'dyä, (h)ā-'rād-ē-ə\ José María 1842–1905 Fr. (Cuban-born) poet
Her·ford \'hər-fərd\ Oliver 1863–1935 Eng. writer & illustrator
Her·ges·hei·mer \'hər-gəs-ˌhī-mər, -gə-ˌshī-\ Joseph 1880–1954 Am. nov.
He·ring \'her-iŋ, 'hā-riŋ\ Ewald 1834–1918 Ger. physiol. & psychol.
Her·ki·mer \'hər-kə-mər\ Nicholas 1728–1777 Am. Revolutionary gen.
Hern·don \'hərn-dən\ William Henry 1818–1891 Am. lawyer
He·ro \'hē-(ˌ)rō, 'hi(ə)r-(ˌ)ō\ *or* **He·ron** \'hē-ˌrän\ 3d cent. A.D. Greek scientist
Her·od \'her-əd\ 73?–4 B.C. *the Great* Rom. king of Judea (37–4)
Herod An·ti·pas \'ant-ə-ˌpas, -pəs\ *d* after A.D. 40 *son of prec.* Rom. tetrarch of Galilee (4 B.C.–A.D. 40)
He·rod·o·tus \hi-'räd-ə-təs\ 5th cent. B.C. Greek hist. — **He·rod·o·te·an** \-ˌräd-ə-'tē-ən\ *adj*
Her·re·ra, de \(h)ə-'rer-ə\ Francisco 1576–1656 *el Viejo* Span. painter
Her·rick \'her-ik\ Myron Timothy 1854–1929 Am. diplomat
Herrick Robert 1591–1674 Eng. poet
Her·riot \ˌer-ē-'ō\ Édouard 1872–1957 Fr. statesman
Her·schel \'hər-shəl\ Sir John Frederick William 1792–1871 & his father Sir William 1738–1822 Eng. astronomers
Her·sey \'hər-sē\ John Richard 1914– Am. nov.
Her·ter \'hərt-ər\ Christian Archibald 1895–1966 Am. diplomat; secy. of state (1959–61)
Her·ty \'hərt-ē\ Charles Holmes 1867–1938 Am. chem.
Hertz \'he(ə)rts, 'hərts\ Gustav 1887– Ger. physicist
Hertz Heinrich Rudolf 1857–1894 Ger. physicist
Her·tzog \'hərt-ˌsȯg, 'hert-, -ˌsäg; 'er-ˌsȯg\ Enrique 1897?– pres. of Bolivia (1947–49)
Hert·zog James Barry Munnik 1866–1942 So. African gen. & statesman
Herzl \'hert-səl\ Theodor 1860–1904 Austrian (Hung.-born) Zionist
He·si·od \'hē-sē-əd, 'hes-ē-\ 8th cent. B.C. Greek poet
Hess \'hes\ Dame Myra 1890–1965 Eng. pianist
Hess Victor Franz 1883–1964 Austrian physicist
Hess (Walther Richard) Rudolf 1894– Ger. Nazi polit.
Hess Walter Rudolf 1881–1973 Swiss physiol.
Hes·se \'hes-ə\ Hermann 1877–1962 Ger. author
He·ve·sy, de \'hev-ə-shē, -ˌesh-ē\ George 1885–1966 Hung. chem.
Hey·drich \'hī-drik, -drik\ Reinhard 1904–1942 *the Hangman* Ger. Nazi administrator
Hey·er·dahl \'hā-ər-ˌdäl\ Thor 1914– Norw. explorer & writer
Hey·mans \ā-'män(t)s, -'man(t)s\ Corneille 1892–1968 Belg. physiol.
Hey·rov·sky \'hā-ˌrȯf-skē, -ˌrȯv-\ Jaroslav 1890–1967 Czech chem.
Hey·se, von \'hī-zə\ Paul 1830–1914 Ger. nov., dram., & poet
Hey·ward \'hā-wərd\ Du·Bose \d(y)ü-'bōz\ 1885–1940 Am. author
Hey·wood \'hā-ˌwu̇d\ John 1497?–?1580 Eng. author
Heywood Thomas 1574?–1641 Eng. dram.
Hich·ens \'hich-ənz\ Robert Smythe 1864–1950 Eng. nov.
Hick·el \'hik-əl\ Walter Joseph 1919– U.S. secy. of the interior (1969–71)
Hick·ok \'hik-ˌäk\ James Butler 1837–1876 *Wild Bill* Am. scout & U.S. marshal
Hicks \'hiks\ Edward 1780–1849 Am. painter
Hi·ero I \'hī-ə-ˌrō\ *or* **Hi·er·on** \-ˌrän\ *d* 466 B.C. tyrant of Syracuse (478–466)
Hieronymus Saint Eusebius — see JEROME
Hig·gin·son \'hig-ən-sən\ Thomas Wentworth Storrow 1823–1911 Am. clergyman & writer
High·et \'hī-ət\ Gilbert 1906– Am. (Scot.-born) writer
Hildebrand — see Pope GREGORY VII
Hill \'hil\ Ambrose Powell 1825–1865 Am. Confed. gen.
Hill Archibald Vivian 1886– Eng. physiol.
Hill James Jerome 1838–1916 Am. financier & railway promoter
Hill Sir Rowland 1795–1879 Eng. postal reformer
Hil·la·ry \'hil-ə-rē\ Sir Edmund Percival 1919– N.Z. mountaineer & explorer
Hil·lel \'hil-əl, -ˌel\ *fl* 30 B.C.–A.D. 9 Jewish teacher; first to formulate definite hermeneutic principles
Hill·man \'hil-mən\ Sidney 1887–1946 Am. labor leader
Hil·precht \'hil-ˌprekt\ Hermann Volrath 1859–1925 Am. (Ger.-born) Assyriologist
Hil·ton \'hilt-ᵊn\ Conrad Nicholson 1887– Am. businessman
Hilton James 1900–1954 Eng. nov.
Himm·ler \'him-lər\ Heinrich 1900–1945 Ger. Nazi polit.
Hin·de·mith \'hin-də-ˌmit(h), -mət(h)\ Paul 1895–1963 Am. (Ger.-born) violist & composer
Hin·den·burg, von \'hin-dən-ˌbərg, -ˌbu̇(ə)rg\ Paul 1847–1934 *Paul Ludwig Hans Anton von Beneckendorff und von Hindenburg* Ger. field marshal; pres. of Germany (1925–34)
Hin·shel·wood \'hin-chəl-ˌwu̇d\ Sir Cyril Norman 1897–1967 Brit. chem.
Hip·par·chus \hip-'är-kəs\ 6th cent. B.C. tyrant of Athens (527–514 B.C.)
Hipparchus *fl* 130 B.C. Greek astron.
Hip·pi·as \'hip-ē-əs\ 6th cent. B.C. *bro. of Hipparchus* ruled Athens with his brother
Hip·poc·ra·tes \hip-'äk-rə-ˌtēz\ 460?–?377 B.C. *father of medicine* Greek physician
Hi·ra·nu·ma \hi-'rän-ə-ˌmä\ Baron Kiichiro 1867–1952 Jap. statesman
Hi·ro·hi·to \ˌhir-ō-'hē-(ˌ)tō\ 1901– emp. of Japan (1926–)
Hi·ro·shi·ge \ˌhir-ə-'shē-ˌgā\ Ando 1797–1858 Jap. painter
Hitch·cock \'hich-ˌkäk\ Edward 1793–1864 Am. geologist
Hitchcock Ethan Allen 1835–1909 Am. diplomat & administrator
Hit·ler \'hit-lər\ Adolf 1889–1945 Ger. chancellor & führer
Hit·ti \'hit-ē\ Philip Khuri 1886– Am. (Lebanese-born) orientalist
Hit·torf \'hi-ˌtȯrf\ Johann Wilhelm 1824–1914 Ger. physicist
Hoare \'hō(ə)r, 'hȯ(ə)r\ Samuel John Gurney 1880–1959 Viscount *Templewood* Eng. statesman
Ho·bart \'hō-ˌbärt, -bərt\ Garret Augustus 1844–1899 Am. lawyer; vice-pres. of the U.S. (1897–99)
Hob·be·ma \'häb-ə-mə\ Meindert 1638–1709 Du. painter
Hobbes \'häbz\ Thomas 1588–1679 Eng. philos.
Hob·son \'häb-sən\ Richmond Pearson 1870–1937 Am. naval officer
Hoc·cleve \'häk-ˌlēv\ Thomas 1370?–?1450 Eng. poet
Ho Chi Minh \ˌhō-ˌchē-'min, ˌhō-ˌshē-\ 1890–1969 pres. of North Vietnam (1954–69)
Hock·ing \'häk-iŋ\ William Ernest 1873–1966 Am. philos.
Hodg·es \'häj-əz\ Luther Hartwell 1898– U.S. secy. of commerce (1961–65)
Hodg·son \'häj-sən\ James Day 1915– U.S. secy. of labor (1970–72)
Hoe \'hō\ Richard March 1812–1886 *son of Robert* Am. inventor
Hoe Robert 1784–1833 Am. (Eng.-born) printing-press manuf.
Ho·fer \'hō-fər\ Andreas 1767–1810 Tyrolese patriot
Hof·fa \'häf-ə\ James Riddle 1913– Am. labor leader
Hoff·man \'häf-mən, 'hȯf-\ **Mal·vi·na** \mal-'vē-nə\ 1887–1966 Am. sculptor
Hoff·mann \'häf-mən, 'hȯf-, -ˌmän\ August Heinrich 1798–1874 Ger. poet, philologist, & hist.
Hoffman Ernst Theodor Wilhelm 1776–1822 *Ernst Theodor Amadeus* Ger. composer, writer, & illustrator
Hof·mann \'häf-mən, 'hȯf-, -ˌmän\ Hans 1880–1966 Am. (Ger.-born) painter
Hofmann Josef Casimir 1876–1957 Pol. pianist
Hof·mann, von \'häf-mən, 'hȯf-, -ˌmän\ August Wilhelm 1818–1892 Ger. chem.
Hof·manns·thal, von \'häf-mənz-ˌtäl, 'hȯf-\ Hugo 1874–1929 Austrian poet & dram.
Ho·garth \'hō-ˌgärth\ William 1697–1764 Eng. painter & engraver
Hog·ben \'hȯg-bən, 'häg-\ Lancelot Thomas 1895– Eng. scientist & writer
Hogg \'hȯg, 'häg\ James 1770–1835 Scot. poet
Hohenzollern Michael — see MICHAEL
Ho·ku·sai \'hō-kü-ˌsī, ˌhō-kü-'\ Katsushika 1760–1849 Jap. artist
Hol·bein \'hōl-ˌbīn, 'hȯl-\ Hans father 1465?–1524 & son 1497?–1543 Ger. painters
Hol·comb \'häl-kəm\ Thomas 1879–1965 Am. marine-corps gen.
Hol·in·shed \'häl-ən-ˌshed\ *or* **Hol·lings·head** \-iŋz-ˌhed\ Raphael *d ab* 1580 Eng. chronicler
Hol·land \'häl-ənd\ John Philip 1840–1914 Irish-born inventor in Am.
Holland Sidney George 1893–1961 prime min. of N.Z. (1945–57)
Holman-Hunt William — see Holman HUNT
Holmes \'hōmz, 'hōlmz\ John Haynes 1879–1964 Am. clergyman
Holmes Oliver Wendell 1809–1894 Am. physician & author
Holmes Oliver Wendell 1841–1935 *son of prec.* Am. jurist
Holst \'hōlst\ Gustav Theodore 1874–1934 Eng. composer
Holt \'hōlt\ Harold Edward 1908–1967 Austral. polit.; prime min. (1966–67)
Holt Luther Emmett 1855–1924 Am. pediatrician
Hol·yoake \'hōl-ˌyōk, 'hō-lē-ˌōk\ Keith Jacka 1904– prime min. of N.Z. (1960–72)
Home \'hyüm\ Sir Alec Douglas- 1903– Brit. prime min. (1963–64)
Home William Douglas- 1912– Brit. dram.
Ho·mer \'hō-mər\ *fl* 850? B.C.; traditional Greek epic poet
Homer Winslow 1836–1910 Am. artist

Ho·neg·ger \ˌō-nä-ˈge(ə)r, ˈ(h)än-i-gər\ Arthur 1892–1955 Fr. composer
Ho·no·ri·us \hə-ˈnōr-ē-əs, -ˈnȯr-\ Flavius 384–423 Rom. emp. of the West (395–423)
Hood \ˈhu̇d\ John Bell 1831–1879 Am. Confed. gen.
Hood Samuel 1st Viscount 1724–1816 Brit. admiral
Hood Thomas 1799–1845 Eng. poet
Hooke \ˈhu̇k\ Robert 1635–1703 Eng. experimental philos.
Hook·er \ˈhu̇k-ər\ Joseph 1814–1879 Am. army officer
Hooker Sir Joseph Dalton 1817–1911 Eng. botanist
Hooker Richard 1554–1600 Eng. theol.
Hooker Thomas 1586?–1647 Eng. Puritan clergyman; a founder of Connecticut
Hoo·ton \ˈhüt-ᵊn\ Earnest Albert 1887–1954 Am. anthropol.
Hoo·ver \ˈhü-vər\ Herbert Clark 1874–1964 31st pres. of the U.S. (1929–33)
Hoover John Edgar 1895–1972 Am. criminologist; F.B.I. director (1924–72)
Hope \ˈhōp\ Anthony — see Sir Anthony Hope HAWKINS
Hope Victor Alexander John 1887–1951 *son of prec.* 8th Earl of *Hope·toun* \ˈhōp-tən\ & 2d Marquis of *Lin·lith·gow* \lin-ˈlith-(ˌ)gō\ Brit. soldier; viceroy of India (1936–43)
Hop·kins \ˈhäp-kənz\ Sir Frederick Gow·land \ˈgau̇-lənd\ 1861–1947 Eng. biochem.
Hopkins Gerard Manley 1844–1889 Eng. poet
Hopkins Harry Lloyd 1890–1946 Am. polit. & administrator
Hopkins Johns \ˈjänz\ 1795–1873 Am. financier
Hopkins Mark 1802–1887 Am. educ.
Hop·kin·son \ˈhäp-kən-sən\ Francis 1737–1791 Am. lawyer & satirist
Hop·pe \ˈhäp-ē\ William Frederick 1887–1959 Am. billiard player
Hop·per \ˈhäp-ər\ Edward 1882–1967 Am. artist
Hopper (William) DeWolf 1858–1935 Am. actor
Hop·wood \ˈhäp-ˌwu̇d\ (James) Avery 1882–1928 Am. dram.
Hor·ace \ˈhȯr-əs, ˈhär-\ 65–8 B.C. *Quintus Horatius Flaccus* Rom. poet & satirist
Hore–Be·li·sha \ˌhō(ə)r-bə-ˈlē-shə, ˌhȯ(ə)r-\ Leslie 1893–1957 Eng. polit.
Hor·na·day \ˈhȯr-nə-ˌdā\ William Temple 1854–1937 Am. zool.
Hor·ney \ˈhȯr-ˌnī\ Karen 1885–1952 née *Danielson* Am. (Ger.-born) psychoanalyst & author
Ho·ro·witz \ˈhȯr-ə-ˌwits, ˈhär-\ Vladimir 1904– Am. (Russ.-born) pianist
Horsa — see HENGIST
Hortense de Beauharnais — see BEAUHARNAIS
Hor·thy \ˈhȯrt-ē\ Miklós von Nagybánya 1868–1957 Hung. admiral; regent of Hungary (1920–44)
Hos·kins \ˈhäs-kənz\ Roy Graham 1880–1964 Am. physiol.
Hou·di·ni \hü-ˈdē-nē\ Harry 1874–1926 *Ehrich Weiss* Am. magician
Hou·don \ˈhü-ˌdän, ü-dō^{n}\ Jean Antoine 1741–1828 Fr. sculptor
Hou·dry \ˈhü-drē\ Eugene Jules 1892–1962 Am. (Fr.-born) engineer
House \ˈhau̇s\ Edward Mandell 1858–1938 *Colonel House* Am. diplomat
Hous·man \ˈhau̇-smən\ Alfred Edward 1859–1936 Eng. classical scholar & poet
Housman Laurence 1865–1959 *bro. of prec.* Eng. writer & illustrator
Hous·say \ü-ˈsī\ Bernardo Alberto 1887–1971 Argentine physiol.
Hous·ton \ˈ(h)yü-stən\ Samuel 1793–1863 *Sam* Am. gen.; pres. of the Republic of Texas (1836–38; 1841–44)
Hov·ey \ˈhəv-ē\ Richard 1864–1900 Am. poet
How·ard \ˈhau̇(-ə)rd\ Catherine — see CATHERINE
Howard Henry 1517?–1547 Earl of *Surrey* Eng. soldier & poet
Howard Oliver Otis 1830–1909 Am. gen. & educ.
Howard Sidney Coe 1891–1939 Am. dram.
Howe \ˈhau̇\ Ed 1853–1937 *Edgar Watson* Am. journalist
Howe Elias 1819–1867 Am. inventor
Howe Julia 1819–1910 née *Ward* Am. suffragist & reformer
Howe Mark Antony De Wolfe 1864–1960 Am. writer
Howe Earl 1726–1799 *Richard Howe* Eng. admiral
Howe 5th Viscount 1729–1814 *William Howe* Eng. gen. in Am.
How·ells \ˈhau̇-əlz\ William Dean 1837–1920 Am. author
Hoyt \ˈhȯit\ Charles Hale 1860–1900 Am. dram.
Hr·dlič·ka \ˈhərd-lich-ˌkä\ Aleš \ˈäl-ˌesh\ 1869–1943 Am. (Bohemian-born) anthropol.
Hsü Shih-ch'ang \ˈshü-ˈshi(ə)r-ˈchäŋ, -ˈshē-\ 1858–1939 Chin. gen.; pres. of China (1918–22)
Hsüan–t'ung \ˈshü-ˈän-ˈtu̇ŋ\ 1906–1967 *Henry P'u-yi* \ˈpü-ˈ(y)ē\ Chin. emp. (1908–12); last of Manchu dynasty; puppet emp. of Manchukuo (1934–45)
Hu Shih \ˈhü-ˈshi(ə)r, -ˈshē\ 1891–1962 Chin. philos. & diplomat
Huás·car \ˈwäs-ˌkär\ 1495?–1533 Inca prince
Hub·bard \ˈhəb-ərd\ Elbert Green 1856–1915 Am. writer
Hud·son \ˈhəd-sən\ Henry *d* 1611 erroneously *Hen·drick* \ˈhen-drik\ Eng. navigator & explorer
Hudson Manley Ottmer 1886–1960 Am. jurist
Hudson William Henry 1841–1922 Eng. naturalist & writer
Huer·ta \ˈwert-ə, ü-ˈert-\ Victoriano 1854–1916 Mex. gen.; provisional pres. of Mexico (1913–14)
Hug·gins \ˈhəg-ənz\ Sir William 1824–1910 Eng. astron.
Hugh Ca·pet \ˈkā-pət, ˈkap-ət, ka-ˈpā\ *Fr.* **Hugues Ca·pet** \ᵫg-kä-pe\ 940?–996 king of France (987–996)
Hughes \ˈhyüz *also* ˈyüz\ Charles Evans 1862–1948 Am. jurist; chief justice of the U.S. Supreme Court (1930–41)
Hughes Howard Robard 1905– Am. businessman
Hughes (James) Langston 1902–1967 Am. writer
Hughes Rupert 1872–1956 Am. writer
Hughes Ted 1930– Brit. poet
Hughes Thomas 1822–1896 Eng. jurist, reformer, & writer
Hughes William Morris 1864–1952 Austral. statesman
Hu·go \ˈ(h)yü-(ˌ)gō\ Victor Marie 1802–1885 Fr. poet, nov., & dram. — **Hu·go·esque** \ˌ(h)yü-(ˌ)gō-ˈesk\ *adj*
Hui·zinga \ˈhī-ziŋ-ə\ Johan 1872–1945 Du. historian
Hu·la·gu \hü-ˈlä-(ˌ)gü\ 1217–1265 *grandson of Genghis Khan* Mongol ruler
Hull \ˈhəl\ Cordell 1871–1955 Am. statesman; U.S. secy. of state (1933–44)
Hull Isaac 1773–1843 Am. naval officer
Hull William 1753–1825 Am. gen.
Hu·ma·yun \hü-ˈmä-ˌyün\ 1508–1556 emp. of Hindustan (1530–56)
Hum·bert I \ˈhəm-bərt\ *Ital.* **Um·ber·to** \üm-ˈbe(ə)r-(ˌ)tō\ 1844–1900 king of Italy (1878–1900)
Humbert II 1904– Prince of *Piedmont;* Count of *Sarre;* king of Italy (1946)
Hum·boldt, von \ˈhəm-ˌbōlt, ˈhu̇m-\ Baron (Friedrich Heinrich) Alexander 1769–1859 Ger. naturalist, traveler, & statesman
Humboldt, von Baron Wilhelm 1767–1835 *bro. of prec.* Ger. philologist & diplomat
Hume \ˈhyüm *also* ˈyüm\ David 1711–1776 Scot. philos. & hist. — **Hum·ean** *or* **Hum·ian** \ˈ(h)yü-mē-ən\ *adj*
Hum·per·dinck \ˈhu̇m-pər-ˌdiŋk, ˈhəm-\ Engelbert 1854–1921 Ger. composer
Hum·phrey \ˈhəm(p)-frē\ 1391–1447 *son of Henry IV* Duke of *Gloucester* (*the Good Duke*) & Earl of *Pembroke* Eng. statesman & book collector
Humphrey Hubert Horatio 1911– Am. polit.; vice-pres. of the U.S. (1965–69)
Hun·e·ker \ˈhən-i-kər\ James Gibbons 1860–1921 Am. critic
Hung–wu \ˈhu̇ŋ-ˈwü\ 1328–1398 *Chu Yüan-chang* \ˈjü-yü-ˈän-ˈjäŋ\ Chin. emp. (1368–98); founder of Ming dynasty
Hunt \ˈhənt\ (James Henry) Leigh 1784–1859 Eng. writer
Hunt (William) Hol·man \ˈhōl-mən\ 1827–1910 Eng. painter
Hun·ter \ˈhənt-ər\ John 1728–1793 Brit. anatomist & surgeon
Hun·ting·ton \ˈhənt-iŋ-tən\ Collis Potter 1821–1900 Am. pioneer railroad builder
Huntington Ellsworth 1876–1947 Am. geographer & explorer
Huntington Henry E. 1850–1927 Am. bibliophile
Huntington Samuel 1731–1796 Am. Revolutionary polit.
Hun·tzi·ger \ˌ(h)ənt-sē-ˈzhe(ə)r\ Charles Léon Clément 1880–1941 Fr. gen.
Hu·nya·di *or* **Hu·nya·dy** \ˈhu̇n-ˌyäd-ē, -ˌyȯd-\ Já·nos \ˈyän-(ˌ)ōsh\ 1387?–1456 Hung. soldier & hero
Hur·ley \ˈhər-lē\ Patrick Jay 1883–1963 Am. lawyer & diplomat
Hurst \ˈhərst\ Sir Cecil James Barrington 1870–1963 Eng. jurist
Hurst Fannie 1889–1968 Am. writer
Hu·sein ibn–Ali \hü-ˈsā-ˌnib-ən-ä-ˈlē\ 1856–1931 first king of the Hejaz (1916–24)
Huss *or* **Hus** \ˈhəs, ˈhu̇s\ John *or* Jan *ab* 1374–1415 *Johannes Hus von Husinetz* Bohemian religious reformer
Hus·sein I \hü-ˈsān\ 1935– king of Jordan (1953–)
Hus·serl \ˈhu̇s-ə-rəl\ Edmund 1859–1938 Ger. philos.
Hu·szár \ˈhu̇s-ˌär\ Károly 1882– Hung. journalist & polit.
Hutch·ins \ˈhəch-ənz\ Robert Maynard 1899– Am. educ.
Hutch·in·son \ˈhəch-ə(n)-sən\ Anne 1591–1643 née *Marbury* religious liberal in Am.
Hutchinson Thomas 1711–1780 Am. colonial administrator
Hut·ten, von \ˈhu̇t-ᵊn\ Ulrich 1488–1523 Ger. humanist & supporter of Luther
Hux·ley \ˈhək-slē\ Al·dous \ˈȯl-dəs\ Leonard 1894–1963 *bro. of J.S.* Eng. nov. & critic — **Hux·lei·an** \ˌhək-ˈslē-ən, ˈhək-slē-\ *or* **Hux·ley·an** \ˈhək-slē-ən\ *adj*
Huxley Andrew Fielding 1917– Brit. physiol. & educ.
Huxley Sir Julian Sorell 1887– *grandson of T.H.* Eng. biologist
Huxley Thomas Henry 1825–1895 Eng. biologist
Huy·gens *or* **Huy·ghens** \ˈhī-gənz, ˈhȯi-\ Christian 1629–1695 Du. math., physicist, & astron.
Huys·mans \wē-ˈsmä^{n}s\ Camille 1871–1968 Belg. polit.
Huysmans Joris Karl 1848–1907 orig. *Charles Marie Georges* Fr. nov.
Hy·att \ˈhī-ət\ Alpheus 1838–1902 Am. naturalist
Hyde \ˈhīd\ Douglas 1860–1949 Irish author; pres. of Republic of Ireland (1938–45)
Hyde Edward 1609–1674 1st Earl of *Clarendon* Eng. statesman & hist.
Hyder Ali — see HAIDAR ALI
Hy·mans \ˈhī-ˌmän(t)s, ē-mä^{n}s\ Paul 1865–1941 Belg. statesman
Hy·pse·lan·tes \ˌēp-sə-ˈlän-dēs\ *var of* YPSILANTI
Ibáñez Vicente Blasco- — see BLASCO-IBÁÑEZ
Iber·ville, d' \ˈdē-bər-ˌvil, -ˌvēl; ˈdī-bər-ˌvil\ Sieur 1661–1706 *Pierre Lemoyne* Fr.-Canad. explorer; founder of Louisiana
ibn–Khal·dun \ˌib-ən-ˌkal-ˈdün\ 1332–1406 Arab hist.
ibn–Rushd — see AVERROËS
ibn–Saud \ˌib-ən-sä-ˈüd, -ˈsau̇d\ Abdul-Aziz 1880–1953 king of Saudi Arabia (1932–53)
ibn–Zuhr \ˌib-ən-ˈzü(ə)r\ *or* **ibn–Zohr** \-ˈzō(ə)r, -ˈzȯ(ə)r\ *var of* AVENZOAR
Ibra·him Pa·sha \i-ˌbrä-ˈhim-ˈpäsh-ə, -ˈpash-ə, -pə-ˈshä\ 1789–1848 Egyptian gen. & viceroy
Ib·sen \ˈib-sən, ˈip-\ Henrik 1828–1906 Norw. poet & dram. — **Ib·se·ni·an** \ib-ˈsē-nē-ən, ip-, -ˈsen-ē-\ *adj*
Ick·es \ˈik-əs\ Harold LeClair 1874–1952 Am. lawyer
Ic·ti·nus \ik-ˈtī-nəs\ 5th cent. B.C. Greek architect
Ig·na·tius \ig-ˈnā-sh(ē-)əs\ Saint 1st–2d cent. A.D. *Theophorus* bishop of Antioch & church father
Ignatius of Loyola Saint — see LOYOLA — **Ig·na·tian** \-sh(ē-)ən\ *adj*
Ike·da \ē-ˈkād-ə, -ˈked-\ Hayato 1899–1965 Jap. polit.; premier (1960–64)

ə abut ᵊ kitten, F table ər further a back ā bake
ä cot, cart ȧ F bac au̇ out ch chin e less ē easy
g gift i trip ī life j joke k G ich ⁿ F vin ŋ sing
ō flow ȯ flaw œ F bœuf ᵫ F feu ȯi coin th thing
th this ü loot u̇ foot ue G Füllen ᵫ F rue y yet
ʸ F digne \dēnʸ\, nuit \nwʸē\ yü few yu̇ furious zh vision

Ikh·na·ton \ik-ˈnät-ᵊn\ *Amen·ho·tep IV* \ˌäm-ən-ˈhō-ˌtep, ˌam-\ king of Egypt (*ab* 1375–1358 B.C.); religious reformer
Im·mel·mann \ˈim-əl-ˌmän, -mən\ Max 1890–1916 Ger. aviator
In·dy, d' \ˈdan-dē; dan-ˈdē, daⁿ-\ Vincent 1851–1931 Fr. composer
Inés de Castro — see CASTRO
Inge \ˈinj\ William 1913–1973 Am. playwright
Inge \ˈiŋ\ William Ralph 1860–1954 Eng. prelate & author
In·ger·soll \ˈiŋ-gər-ˌsȯl, -səl\ Robert Green 1833–1899 Am. lawyer & agnostic
In·gram \ˈiŋ-grəm\ Arthur Foley Winnington 1858–1946 Eng. prelate; bishop of London (1901–39)
In·gres \ˈaⁿ(ŋ)grᵊ\ Jean Auguste Dominique 1780–1867 Fr. painter
In·ness \ˈin-əs\ George, father 1825–1894 & son 1854–1926 Am. painters
In·no·cent \ˈin-ə-sənt\ name of 13 popes: esp **II** *d* 1143 (pope 1130–43); **III** 1161–1216 (pope 1198–1216); **IV** *d* 1254 (pope 1243–54); **XI** 1611–1689 (pope 1676–89)
İnö·nü \ˌin-ə-ˈn(y)ü\ Is·met \is-ˈmet\ 1884– Turk. statesman; pres. of Turkey (1938–50); premier (1961–65)
In·sull \ˈin(t)-səl\ Samuel 1859–1938 Am. (Eng.-born) utilities executive
Io·nes·co \ˌē-ə-ˈnes-(ˌ)kō\ Eugene 1912– Fr. (Rumanian-born) dram.
Ipa·tieff *or* **Ipa·tiev** \i-ˈpät-ē-ˌef, -ˈpäch-əf\ Vladimir Nikolaevich 1867–1952 Russ.-born chem. in Am.
Ire·dell \ˈī(ə)r-ˌdel\ James 1751–1799 Am. jurist
Ire·ton \ˈī(ə)rt-ᵊn\ Henry 1611–1651 Eng. Parliamentary commander & regicide
Iri·go·yen \ˌir-i-ˈgō-ˌyen\ Hi·pó·li·to \ē-ˈpȯ-lē-ˌtō\ 1850–1933 pres. of Argentina (1916–22; 1928–30)
Iron·side \ˈī(-ə)rn-ˌsīd\ William Edmund 1880–1959 1st Baron of *Archangel and Ironside* Brit. field marshal
Ir·ving \ˈər-viŋ\ Sir Henry 1838–1905 orig. *John Henry Brodribb* Eng. actor
Irving Washington 1783–1859 Am. essayist, nov., & hist.
Ir·win \ˈər-wən\ Wallace 1875–1959 Am. journalist & humorist
Irwin William Henry 1873–1948 *Will* Am. journalist & writer
Isaacs \ˈī-ziks, -zəks\ Sir Isaac Alfred 1855–1948 Austral. jurist & statesman; gov.-gen. of Australia (1931–36)
Isaacs Rufus Daniel — see Marquis of READING
Is·a·bel·la I \ˌiz-ə-ˈbel-ə\ 1451–1504 *wife of Ferdinand II of Aragon* queen of Castile (1474–1504); aided Columbus
Ish·er·wood \ˈish-ər-ˌwu̇d\ Christopher William Bradshaw 1904– Am. (Brit.-born) writer
Ishii \ˈē-shē-ˌē, ˈish-ē-ˌē\ Viscount Kikujiro 1866–1945 Jap. diplomat
Is·i·dore of Seville \ˈiz-ə-ˌdō(ə)r, -ˌdȯ(ə)r\ Saint *ab* 570–636 *Isidorus Hispalensis* Span. prelate & scholar
Iskender Bey — see SCANDERBEG
Is·ma·il Pa·sha \is-ˈmä-ˌēl-ˈpäsh-ə, ˈpash-ə, pə-ˈshä\ 1830–1895 *Ismail I* khedive of Egypt (1863–79)
Isoc·ra·tes \ī-ˈsäk-rə-ˌtēz\ 436–338 B.C. Athenian orator
Ito \ˈē-(ˌ)tō\ Prince Hirobumi 1841–1909 Jap. statesman
Ito Yuko *or* Sukenori 1843–1914 Jap. admiral
Itur·bi \i-ˈtu̇r-bē\ José 1895– Span.-born pianist & conductor
Itur·bi·de, de \ˌē-ˌtu̇r-ˈbē-(ˌ)thā\ Agustín 1783–1824 Mex. soldier; emp. of Mex. (1822–23)
Ivan III \ē-ˈvän, ˈī-vən\ **Va·si·lie·vich** \və-ˈsil-yə-ˌvich\ 1440–1505 *Ivan the Great* grand duke of Russia (1462–1505)
Ivan IV Vasilievich \və-ˈsil-yə-ˌvich\ 1530–1584 *Ivan the Terrible* ruler of Russia (1533–84)
Ives \ˈīvz\ Charles Edward 1874–1954 Am. composer — **Ives·ian** \ˈīv-zē-ən\ *adj*
Ives James Merritt 1824–1895 Am. lithographer
Iye·ya·su *or* **Ie·ya·su** \ˌē-ə-ˈyäs-(ˌ)ü, ˌē-yā-ˈyäs-\ 1542–1616 Jap. gen.; founder (1603) of Tokugawa shogunate
Izard \ˈī-ˌzärd, ˈiz-ərd\ Ralph 1742–1804 Am. Revolutionary leader
Jabir *var of* GEBER
Jack·son \ˈjak-sən\ Andrew 1767–1845 Am. gen.; 7th pres. of the U.S. (1829–37)
Jackson Helen Maria Hunt 1830–1885 née *Fiske* Am. nov.
Jackson Robert Hough·wout \ˈhau̇-ət\ 1892–1954 Am. jurist
Jackson Thomas Jonathan 1824–1863 *Stone·wall* \ˈstōn-ˌwȯl\ *Jackson* Am. Confed. gen.
Jac·quard \zha-ˈkär, ˈjak-ˌärd\ Joseph Marie 1752–1834 Fr. inventor
Jacques I — see Jean Jacques DESSALINES
Jag·a·tai \ˈjag-ə-ˌtī\ *d* 1242 *2d son of Genghis Khan* Mongol ruler
Ja·han·gir \jə-ˈhän-ˌgi(ə)r\ 1569–1627 emp. of Hindustan (1605–27)
Ja·lal–ud–din Ru·mi \jə-ˈläl-ə-ˌdēn-ˈrü-mē\ 1207–1273 Pers. poet
James \ˈjāmz\ name of 6 kings of Scot. & 2 kings of Gr. Brit.: **VI** 1566–1625 of Scot. (reigned 1567–1603) *or* **I** of Gr. Brit. (reigned 1603–25); **II** 1633–1701 (reigned 1685–88)
James Henry 1811–1882 Am. philos.
James Henry 1843–1916 *son of prec.* Brit. (Am.-born) writer
James Jesse Woodson 1847–1882 Am. outlaw
James William 1842–1910 *bro. of Henry.* Am. psychol. & philos.
James Edward Stuart 1688–1766 *the Old Pretender* Eng. prince
Jame·son \ˈjām-sən, ˈjem-ə-sən\ Sir Leander Starr 1853–1917 *Doctor Jameson* Scot. physician & administrator in So. Africa
Ja·mi \ˈjäm-ē\ 1414–1492 Pers. poet & mystic
Ja·na·ček \ˈyän-ə-ˌchek\ Leoš 1854–1928 Czech composer
Jan·sen \ˈjan(t)-sən, ˈyän(t)-\ Cor·ne·lis \kȯr-ˈnā-ləs\ 1585–1638 *Cornelius Jansenius* Du. R.C. theol.
Jaques–Dal·croze \ˈzhäk-ˌdal-ˈkrōz, ˈzhak-\ Emile 1865–1950 Swiss composer & creator of eurythmics
Ja·rir \jə-ˈri(ə)r\ *d* 729? Arab poet
Jar·rell \jə-ˈrel, ja-\ Randall 1914–1965 Am. writer
Jas·pers \ˈyäs-pərs\ Karl 1883–1969 Ger. philos.
Jauregg Julius Wagner von — see WAGNER VON JAUREGG
Jau·rès \zhō-res\ Jean Léon 1859–1914 Fr. socialist
Jay \ˈjā\ John 1745–1829 Am. jurist & statesman; 1st chief justice of the U.S. Supreme Court (1789–95)
Jeanne d'Arc — see JOAN OF ARC
Jeans \ˈjēnz\ Sir James Hopwood 1877–1946 Eng. physicist, astron., & author
Jebb \ˈjeb\ Sir Richard Claverhouse 1841–1905 Scot. scholar
Jef·fers \ˈjef-ərz\ (John) Robinson 1887–1962 Am. poet
Jef·fer·son \ˈjef-ər-sən\ Joseph 1829–1905 Am. actor
Jefferson Thomas 1743–1826 3d pres. of the U.S. (1801–09)
Jef·frey \ˈjef-rē\ Lord Francis 1773–1850 Scot. critic & jurist
Jef·freys \ˈjef-rēz\ George 1648–1689 1st Baron *Jeffreys of Wem* Eng. jurist
Jel·li·coe \ˈjel-i-ˌkō\ 1st Earl 1859–1935 *John Rushworth Jellicoe* Brit. admiral
Jenghiz Khan *var of* GENGHIS KHAN
Jen·ner \ˈjen-ər\ Edward 1749–1823 Eng. physician — **Jen·ne·ri·an** \je-ˈnir-ē-ən\ *adj*
Jenner Sir William 1815–1898 Eng. physician
Jen·sen \ˈyen(t)-sən, ˈjen(t)-\ Johannes Vilhelm 1873–1950 Dan. poet & nov.
Jen·son \ˈjen-sən, zhäⁿ-ˈsōⁿ\ Nicolas 1420–*ab* 1481 Fr. printer & engraver in Venice
Je·ri·tza \ˈyer-ət-sə\ Maria 1887– Am. (Austrian-born) soprano
Je·rome \jə-ˈrōm\ Saint 340?–420 *Eusebius Hieronymus* Latin church father
Jer·vis \ˈjər-vəs\ John 1735–1823 Earl of *St. Vincent* Brit. admiral
Jes·per·sen \ˈyes-pər-sən\ (Jens) Otto (Harry) 1860–1943 Dan. philologist
Je·sus \ˈjē-zəs, -zəz\ *or* **Jesus Christ** \ˈkrīst\ *or* **Christ Jesus** 4–8? B.C.–A.D.? 29 *Jesus of Nazareth; the Son of Mary* source of the Christian religion & Savior in the Christian faith
Jev·ons \ˈjev-ənz\ William Stanley 1835–1882 Eng. econ.
Jew·ett \ˈjü-ət\ Sarah Orne 1849–1909 Am. writer
Ji·mé·nez \hē-ˈmā-nəs\ Juan Ramón 1881–1958 Span. poet
Jiménez de Cis·ne·ros \ˌdā-sis-ˈner-əs\ Francisco 1436–1517 Span. prelate & statesman
Jin·nah \ˈjin-(ˌ)ä, ˈjin-ə\ Mohammed Ali 1876–1948 Muslim lawyer; 1st gov.-gen. of dominion of Pakistan (1947–48)
Jo·achim \yō-ˈäk-im, -ˈäk-; ˈyō-ə-ˌkim, -ˌkim\ Joseph 1831–1907 Hung. violinist
Joan of Arc \ˌjō-nə-ˈvärk *also* ˌjō-ə-nə-, jō-ˌan-ə-\ *Fr.* **Jeanne d'Arc** \zhän-dark\ Saint 1412–1431 *the Maid of Orleans* Fr. national heroine
Jodl \ˈyōd-ᵊl\ Alfred 1892?–1946 Ger. gen.
Jof·fre \zhȯfrᵊ\ Joseph Jacques Césaire 1852–1931 Fr. field marshal; marshal of France
John \ˈjän\ name of 21 popes: esp. **XXIII** (*Angelo Giuseppe Roncalli*) 1881–1963 (pope 1958–63)
John 1167?–1216 *John Lack·land* \ˈlak-ˌland\ king of England (1199–1216)
John I 1357–1433 *the Great* king of Portugal (1385–1433)
John Augustus Edwin 1878–1961 Brit. painter & etcher
John of Austria 1547–1578 Don *John* Span. gen.
John of Gaunt \ˈgȯnt, ˈgänt\ 1340–1399 Duke of *Lancaster; son of Edward III of Eng.*
John of Lancaster — see Duke of BEDFORD
John of Leiden 1509–1536 Du. Anabaptist fanatic
John of Salisbury *d* 1180 Eng. ecclesiastic
John III So·bies·ki \sō-ˈbyes-kē, ˌsō-bē-ˈes-\ 1624–1697 king of Poland (1674–96)
John·son \ˈjän(t)-sən\ Andrew 1808–1875 17th pres. of the U.S. (1865–69) — **John·so·nian** \jän-ˈsō-nē-ən, -nyən\ *adj*
Johnson (Jonathan) Eastman 1824–1906 Am. painter
Johnson Gerald White 1890– Am. author
Johnson James Weldon 1871–1938 Am. author
Johnson Lyndon Baines 1908–1973 Am. polit.; 36th pres. of the U.S. (1963–69) — **John·so·nian** \jän-ˈsō-nē-ən, -nyən\ *adj*
Johnson Richard Mentor 1780–1850 vice-pres. of the U.S. (1837–41)
Johnson Samuel 1709–1784 *Dr. Johnson* Eng. lexicographer & author — **John·so·nian** \jän-ˈsō-nē-ən, -nyən\ *adj*
Johnson Sir William 1715–1774 Brit. administrator in Am.
John·ston \ˈjän(t)-stən, -sən\ Albert Sidney 1803–1862 Am. Confed. gen.
Johnston Joseph Eggleston 1807–1891 Am. Confed. gen.
Johnston Mary 1870–1936 Am. nov.
Join·ville, de \zhwaⁿ-ˈvē(ə)l\ Jean 1224?–1317 Fr. chronicler
Jó·kai \ˈyō-ˌkȯi\ Mau·rus \ˈmȯr-əs\ *or* Mó·ricz \ˈmōr-əts, ˈmȯr-\ 1825–1904 Hung. nov. & dram.
Jo·liet *or* **Jol·liet** \zhȯl-ˈyā\ Louis 1645–1700 Fr.-Canadian explorer
Jo·liot–Cu·rie \ˈzhȯl-ˌyō-kyu̇-ˈrē, -ˈkyu̇(ə)r-(ˌ)ē\ Frédéric 1900–1958 orig. *Joliot* Fr. physicist
Joliot–Curie Irène 1897–1956 formerly *Irène Curie-Joliot, dau. of Marie & Pierre Curie & wife of prec.* Fr. physicist
Jo·mi·ni \ˌzhō-mə-ˈnē\ Baron Henri 1779–1869 Swiss-born soldier & military strategist
Jones \ˈjōnz\ Anson 1798–1858 pres. of the Republic of Texas (1844–46)
Jones Daniel 1881–1967 Eng. phonetician
Jones Henry Arthur 1851–1929 Eng. dram.
Jones Howard Mumford 1892– Am. educ. & critic
Jones In·i·go \ˈin-i-ˌgō\ 1573–1652 Eng. architect
Jones Jesse Holman 1874–1956 Am. financier & administrator
Jones John Paul 1747–1792 orig. in full *John Paul* Am. (Scot.-born) naval officer
Jones Thomas Hudson 1892–1969 Am. sculptor
Jon·son \ˈjän(t)-sən\ Ben 1573?–1637 orig. *Benjamin* Eng. dram.; poet laureate (1619–37) — **Jon·so·nian** \jän-ˈsō-nē-ən, -nyən\ *adj*
Jop·lin \ˈjäp-lən\ Scott 1868–1917 Am. pianist & composer
Jor·dan \ˈjȯrd-ᵊn\ David Starr 1851–1931 Am. biologist & educ.
Jo·seph \ˈjō-zəf *also* -səf\ 1840?–1904 Nez Percé Indian chief

Jo·seph II \ˈjō-zəf *also* -səf\ 1741–1790 king of Germany (1764–90); Holy Rom. emp. (1765–90)
Josephine Empress — see BEAUHARNAIS
Jo·se·phus \jō-ˈsē-fəs\ Flavius 37–?100 Jewish hist.
Jou·bert \zhü-ˈbe(ə)r\ Joseph 1754–1824 Fr. essayist & moralist
Joubert \yü-ˈbe(ə)r, yō-\ Petrus Jacobus 1834–1900 *Piet* Boer gen. & statesman
Jou·haux \zhü-ō\ Léon 1879–1954 Fr. trade-union leader
Joule \ˈjül, ˈjau̇(ə)l, ˈjōl\ James Prescott 1818–1889 Eng. physicist
Jour·dan \zhu̇r-ˈdä^{n}\ Comte Jean Baptiste 1762–1833 Fr. soldier; marshal of France
Jo·vi·an \ˈjō-vē-ən\ 331?–364 *Flavius Claudius Jovianus* Rom. emp. (363–364)
Jow·ett \ˈjau̇-ət, ˈjō-\ Benjamin 1817–1893 Eng. Greek scholar
Joyce \ˈjȯis\ James 1882–1941 Irish writer — **Joyc·ean** \ˈjȯi-sē-ən\ *adj*
Juan Car·los \ˈ(h)wän-ˈkär-ləs, -ˌlōs\ 1938– Span. king-designate
Juan Ma·nuel \ˈ(h)wän-män-ˈwel\ Don 1282–1349 Span. writer
Juá·rez \ˈ(h)wär-əs\ Benito Pablo 1806–1872 Mex. lawyer; pres. of Mexico (1857–72)
Ju·das Mac·ca·bae·us \ˈjüd-ə-ˌsmak-ə-ˈbē-əs\ *d* 160 B.C. Jewish patriot; with 4 bros. (the Mac·ca·bees \ˈmak-ə-(ˌ)bēz\) revolted against Antiochus Epiphanes
Ju·gur·tha \ju̇-ˈgər-thə\ *d* 104 B.C. king of Numidia (113–104 B.C.)
Ju·lian \ˈjül-yən\ 331–363 *Flavius Claudius Julianus, the Apostate* Rom. emp. (361–363)
Ju·li·ana \ˌjü-lē-ˈan-ə\ 1909– *dau. of Wilhelmina* queen of the Netherlands (1948–)
Jung \ˈyu̇ŋ\ Carl Gustav 1875–1961 Swiss psychol.
Ju·nius \ˈjü-nyəs, -nē-əs\ Franciscus 1589–1677 Eng. (Ger.-born) philologist
Jun·kers \ˈyu̇ŋ-kərz, -kərs\ Hugo 1859–1935 Ger. airplane designer & builder
Ju·not \zhü-ˈnō\ Andoche 1771–1813 Duc *d'Abran·tès* \ˌdab-ˌrä^{n}-ˈtes\ Fr. gen. under Napoleon
Jus·se·rand \zhūēs-(ə-)rä^{n}\ Jean Jules 1855–1932 *Jean Adrien Antoine Jules Jusserand* Fr. scholar & diplomat
Jus·tin \ˈjəs-tən\ Saint 100?–?165 *Justin (the) Martyr* church father
Jus·tin·i·an I \ˌjə-ˈstin-ē-ən\ 483–565 *the Great* Byzantine emp. (527–565)
Ju·ve·nal \ˈjü-vən-^{ə}l\ 60?–?140 *Decimus Junius Juvenalis* Rom. poet & satirist — **Ju·ve·na·lian** \ˌjü-və-ˈnāl-yən\ *adj*
Kaf·ka \ˈkäf-kə, ˈkaf-\ Franz 1883–1924 Austrian writer — **Kaf·ka·esque** \ˌkäf-kə-ˈesk, ˌkaf-\ *adj*
Ka·ga·wa \kä-ˈgä-wə\ Toyohiko 1888–1960 Jap. social reformer
Kai·ser \ˈkī-zər\ Henry John 1882–1967 Am. industrialist
Kalb \ˈkälp, ˈkalb\ Johann 1721–1780 Baron *de Kalb* \di-ˈkalb\ Ger. gen. in Am.
Ka·li·da·sa \ˌkäl-i-ˈdäs-ə\ 5th cent. A.D. Hindu dram. & poet
Ka·li·nin \kə-ˈlē-n(y)ən\ Mikhail Ivanovich 1875–1946 Russ. polit.; pres. U.S.S.R. (1923–46)
Ka·me·ha·me·ha I \kə-ˌmā-ə-ˈmā-(ˌ)hä\ 1758?–1819 *the Great* king of Hawaii (1795–1819)
Ka·me·nev \ˈkäm-ə-ˌnef, ˈkam-\ Lev Borisovich 1883–1936 Russ. Communist leader
Ka·mer·lingh On·nes \ˌkäm-ər-liŋ-ˈȯn-əs\ Heike 1853–1926 Du. physicist
Kan·din·ski \kan-ˈdin(t)-skē\ Vasili 1866–1944 Russ. painter
Kane \ˈkān\ Elisha Kent 1820–1857 Am. arctic explorer
K'ang–hsi \ˈkäŋ-ˈshē\ 1654–1722 Chin. emp. (1662–1722)
Kant \ˈkant, ˈkänt\ Immanuel 1724–1804 Ger. philos.
Kar·a·george \ˌkar-ə-ˈjȯ(ə)rj\ 1766?–1817 orig. *George Petrović* Serbian nationalist; founder of Kar·a·geor·ge·vich \-ˈjȯr-jə-ˌvich\ dynasty
Ka·ra·jan \ˈkär-ə-ˌyän\ Herbert von 1908– Austrian conductor
Karl·feldt \ˈkär(ə)l-ˌfelt\ Erik Axel 1864–1931 Swed. poet
Ka·ro·lyi \ˈkar-əl-yē, ˈkär-\ Count Mihály 1875–1955 Hung. polit.
Kar·rer \ˈkär-ər\ Paul 1889–1971 Swiss chemist
Kar·sa·vi·na \kär-ˈsäv-ə-nə, -ˈsav-\ Tamara 1885– Russ. dancer
Kat·zen·bach \ˈkat-sən-ˌbak\ Nicholas deBelleville 1922– U.S. atty. gen. (1965–66)
Kauf·man \ˈkȯf-mən\ George Simon 1889–1961 Am. dram.
Kau·nitz, von \ˈkau̇-nəts\ Count Wenzel Anton 1711–1794 Prince *von Kaunitz-Rietberg* Austrian statesman
Kaut·sky \ˈkau̇t-skē\ Karl Johann 1854–1938 Ger. socialist writer
Ka·wa·ba·ta \ˌkä-wə-ˈbät-e, kə-ˈwäb-ə-ˌtä\ Yasunari 1899– Jap. writer
Kaye–Smith \ˈkā-ˈsmith\ Sheila 1887–1956 Eng. nov.
Ka·zan·tza·kis \ˌkäz-^{ə}n-ˈtsäk-ēs\ Nikos 1885–1957 Greek poet, nov., & translator
Kean \ˈkēn\ Edmund 1787–1833 Eng. actor
Kear·ny \ˈkär-nē\ Philip 1814–1862 Am. gen.
Keats \ˈkēts\ John 1795–1821 Eng. poet — **Keats·ian** \ˈkēt-sē-ən\ *adj*
Ke·ble \ˈkē-bəl\ John 1792–1866 Eng. clergyman & poet
Kee·ley \ˈkē-lē\ Leslie Enraught 1834–1900 Am. physician
Ke·fau·ver \ˈkē-ˌfȯ-vər\ Estes 1903–1963 Am. polit.
Kei·tel \ˈkīt-^{ə}l\ Wilhelm 1882–1946 Ger. field marshal
Kek·ko·nen \ˈkek-ə-nən, -ˌnen\ Urho Kaleva 1900– pres. of Finland (1956–)
Kel·land \ˈkel-ənd\ Clarence Budington 1881–1964 Am. nov.
Kel·ler \ˈkel-ər\ Helen Adams 1880–1968 Am. deaf & blind lecturer
Kel·logg \ˈkel-ˌȯg, -ˌäg\ Frank Billings 1856–1937 Am. statesman
Kel·vin \ˈkel-vən\ 1st Baron 1824–1907 *William Thomson* Brit. math. & physicist
Ke·mal Ata·türk \kə-ˌmal-ˈat-ə-ˌtərk, -ˈät-\ 1881–1938 *Mustafa* or *Mustapha Kemal* Turk. gen.; pres. of Turkey (1923–38)
Kem·ble \ˈkem-bəl\ Frances Anne 1809–1893 *Fanny* Eng. actress
Kemble John Philip 1757–1823 Eng. actor
Kempis Thomas a — see THOMAS A KEMPIS
Ken *or* **Kenn** \ˈken\ Thomas 1637–1711 Eng. prelate & hymn writer
Ken·dall \ˈken-d^{ə}l\ Edward Calvin 1886–1972 Am. biochem.
Kendall (William) Sergeant 1869–1938 Am. painter & sculptor
Ken·nan \ˈken-ən\ George Frost 1904– Am. hist. & diplomat
Ken·ne·dy \ˈken-əd-ē\ David Matthew 1905– Am. banker; U.S. secy. of the treasury (1969–71)
Kennedy John Fitzgerald 1917–1963 Am. polit.; 35th pres. of the U.S. (1961–63)
Kennedy Joseph Patrick 1888–1969 *father of J. F. & R. F.* Am. businessman & diplomat
Kennedy Robert Francis 1925–1968 Am. polit. & lawyer; atty. gen. of the U.S. (1961–64)
Ken·nel·ly \ˈken-^{ə}l-ē\ Arthur Edwin 1861–1939 Am. electrical engineer
Ken·ny \ˈken-ē\ Elizabeth 1886–1952 Austral. nurse & physiotherapist
Kent \ˈkent\ James 1763–1847 Am. jurist
Kent Rockwell 1882–1971 Am. painter
Ken·wor·thy \ˈken-ˌwər-t͟hē\ Joseph Montague 1886–1953 10th Baron *Stra·bol·gi* \strə-ˈbō-gē\ Brit. naval officer
Ken·yon \ˈken-yən\ John Samuel 1874–1959 Am. phonetician
Kep·ler \ˈkep-lər\ Johannes 1571–1630 Ger. astronomer
Kep·pel \ˈkep-əl\ 1st Viscount 1725–1786 *Augustus Keppel* Brit. admiral
Ker \ˈke(ə)r, ˈkər, ˈkär\ William Paton 1855–1923 Brit. scholar
Ke·ren·ski \ˈker-ən-skē\ Aleksandr Feodorovich 1881–1970 Russ. revolutionist
Kern \ˈkərn\ Jerome David 1885–1945 Am. composer
Ker·ou·ac \ˈker-ə-ˌwak\ Jack 1922–1969 Am. writer
Kes·sel·ring \ˈkes-əl-riŋ\ Albert 1887–1960 Ger. field marshal
Ket·ter·ing \ˈket-ə-riŋ\ Charles Franklin 1876–1958 Am. electrical engineer & inventor
Key \ˈkē\ Francis Scott 1779–1843 Am. lawyer; author of "The Star-Spangled Banner"
Keynes \ˈkānz\ 1st Baron 1883–1946 *John Maynard Keynes* Eng. econ.
Key·ser·ling \ˈkī-zər-liŋ\ Count Hermann Alexander 1880–1946 Ger. philos. & writer
Kha·cha·tu·ri·an \ˌkäch-ə-ˈtu̇r-ē-ən, ˌkach-\ Aram 1903– Russ.-Armenian composer
Khe·ra·skov \kə-ˈräs-kəf\ Mikhail Matveevich 1733–1807 Russ. poet
Khru·shchev \kru̇sh-ˈ(ch)ȯf, -ˈ(ch)ȯv, -ˈ(ch)ev, ˈkru̇sh-ˌ\ Ni·ki·ta \nə-ˈkēt-ə\ Sergeevich 1894–1971 Russ. polit.; premier of Soviet Union (1958–64) — **Khru·shchev·ian** \kru̇sh-ˈ(ch)ȯv-ē-ən, -ˈ(ch)ȯv-, -ˈ(ch)ev-\ *adj* — **Khru·shchev·ite** *adj*
Khu·fu \ˈkü-(ˌ)fü\ *Greek* **Che·ops** \ˈkē-ˌäps\ king of Egypt (*ab* 2900–2877 B.C.) & pyramid builder
Khwa·riz·mi, al– \al-ˈkwär-əz-mē\ 780–?850 Arab math.
Kidd \ˈkid\ William 1645?–1701 *Captain Kidd* Scot. pirate
Kie·ran \ˈkir-ən\ John Francis 1892– Am. journalist
Kier·ke·gaard \ˈkir-kə-ˌgär(d), -ˌgȯ(ə)r\ Sören Aabye 1813–1855 Dan. philos. & theol. — **Kier·ke·gaard·ian** \ˌkir-kə-ˈgärd-ē-ən, -ˈgȯrd-\ *adj*
Kie·sing·er \ˈkē-ziŋ-ər\ Kurt Georg 1904– chancellor of West Germany (1966–69)
Kil·learn \kil-ˈərn\ 1st Baron 1880–1964 *Miles Wedderburn Lampson* Brit. diplomat
Kil·lian \ˈkil-ē-ən, ˈkil-yən\ James Rhyne 1904– Am. educator
Kil·mer \ˈkil-mər\ (Alfred) Joyce 1886–1918 Am. poet
Kil·pat·rick \kil-ˈpa-trik\ Hugh Judson 1836–1881 Am. gen.
Kim·mel \ˈkim-əl\ Husband Edward 1882–1968 Am. admiral
Kin·di, al– \al-ˈkin-dē\ 9th cent. A.D. Arab philos.
King \ˈkiŋ\ Ernest Joseph 1878–1956 Am. admiral
King Martin Luther 1929–1968 Am. clergyman
King Rufus 1755–1827 Am. polit. & diplomat
King William Lyon Mackenzie 1874–1950 Canad. statesman; prime min. (1921–26; 1926–30; 1935–48)
King William Rufus DeVane 1786–1853 Am. polit.; vice-pres. of the U.S. (1853)
King·lake \ˈkiŋ-ˌlāk\ Alexander William 1809–1891 Eng. hist.
Kings·ley \ˈkiŋz-lē\ Charles 1819–1875 Eng. clergyman & nov.
Kingsley Sidney 1906– Am. dram.
Kinkaid \kin-ˈkād\ Thomas Cassin 1888–1972 Am. admiral
Kin·sey \ˈkin-zē\ Alfred Charles 1894–1956 Am. zoologist
Kip·ling \ˈkip-liŋ\ Rud·yard \ˈrəd-yərd, ˈrəj-ərd\ 1865–1936 Eng. author — **Kip·ling·esque** \ˌkip-liŋ-ˈesk\ *adj*
Kir·by–Smith \ˌkər-bē-ˈsmith\ Edmund 1824–1893 Am. Confed. gen.
Kirch·hoff \ˈki(ə)r-ˌkȯf\ Gustav Robert 1824–1887 Ger. physicist
Kirch·ner \ˈki(ə)rk-nər, ˈki(ə)r$\underline{k}$-\ Ernst Ludwig 1880–1938 Ger. painter
Kirk \ˈkərk\ Norman 1923– prime min. of N.Z. (1972–)
Ki·rov \ˈkē-ˌrȯf, -ˌrȯv\ Sergei Mironovich 1888–1934 Russ. revolutionist
Kir·sten \ˈki(ə)r-stən\ Dorothy 1917– Am. soprano
Kir·wan \ˈkər-wən\ Richard 1733–1812 Irish chem.
Kis·sin·ger \ˈkis-^{ə}n-jər\ Henry Alfred 1923– Am. (Ger.-born) scholar & govt. official; U.S. secy. of state (1973–)
Kitch·e·ner \ˈkich-(ə-)nər\ Horatio Herbert 1850–1916 1st Earl *Kitchener of Khartoum and of Broome* Brit. field marshal
Kit·tredge \ˈki-trij\ George Lyman 1860–1941 Am. educ.
Klee \ˈklā\ Paul 1879–1940 Swiss painter
Klein·dienst \ˈklīn-ˌdēnst\ Richard Gordon 1923– U.S. attorney general (1972–73)
Kleist, von \ˈklīst\ Heinrich 1777–1811 Ger. dram.

ə abut	^{ə} kitten, F table	ər further	a back	ā bake
ä cot, cart	ȧ F bac	au̇ out	ch chin	e less	ē easy
g gift	i trip	ī life	j joke	$\underline{k}$ G ich	^{n} F vin	ŋ sing
ō flow	ȯ flaw	œ F bœuf	ǣ F feu	ȯi coin	th thing
t͟h this	ü loot	u̇ foot	ue G Füllen	ūē F rue	y yet
^{y} F digne \dēn^{y}\, nuit \nw^{y}ē\	yü few	yu̇ furious	zh vision	

Kleist, von Paul Ludwig Ewald 1881–1954 Ger. gen.
Klem·per·er \'klem-pər-ər\ Otto 1885–1973 Ger. conductor
Klop·stock \'kläp-ˌstäk, 'klȯp-ˌshtȯk\ Friedrich Gottlieb 1724–1803 Ger. poet
Knel·ler \'nel-ər\ Sir Godfrey 1646–1723 orig. *Gottfried Kniller* Ger.-born portrait painter in Eng.
Knox \'näks\ Frank 1874–1944 *William Franklin* Am. publisher
Knox Henry 1750–1806 Am. Revolutionary gen.
Knox John 1505–1572 Scot. reformer & statesman
Knox Philander Chase 1853–1921 Am. statesman
Knud·sen \(kə-)'nüd-sən\ William Signius 1879–1948 Am. (Dan.-born) industrialist & administrator
Knut \kə-'n(y)üt\ *var of* CANUTE
Koch \'kȯk, 'kȯk, *or* ō, ä\ Robert 1843–1910 Ger. bacteriologist
Ko·cher \'kȯk-ər, 'kȯk-\ Emil Theodor 1841–1917 Swiss surgeon
Kock, de \'kȯk\ Paul 1794–1871 Fr. nov. & dram.
Ko·dály \'kō-ˌdī\ Zol·tán \'zōl-ˌtän\ 1882–1967 Hung. composer
Koest·ler \'kes(t)-lər\ Arthur 1905– Brit. (Hung.-born) writer
Koh·ler \'kō-lər\ Foy David 1908– Am. diplomat
Koi·so \'kȯi-(ˌ)sō, 'kō-ē-(ˌ)sō\ Kuniaki 1880–1950 Jap. gen.
Ko·kosch·ka \kə-'kȯsh-kə\ Oskar 1886– Brit. (Austrian-born) painter
Kol·chak \kȯl-'chäk\ Aleksandr Vasilievich 1874–1920 Russ. admiral & counterrevolutionist
Kol·lon·tai \ˌkäl-ən-'tī\ Aleksandra Mikhailovna 1872–1952 Russ. diplomat
Koll·witz \'kōl-ˌwits, 'kȯl-ˌvits\ Käthe 1867–1945 née *Schmidt* Ger. artist
Kol·tsov \kōlt-'sȯf, -'sȯv\ Aleksei Vasilievich 1808–1842 Russ. poet
Ko·mu·ra \kō-'mu̇r-ä, 'kō-mə-ˌrä\ Marquis Jutaro 1855–1911 Jap. diplomat
Kon·dy·les \kȯn-'dē-ləs, -lēs\ Georgios 1879–1936 Greek gen. & statesman
Ko·nev \'kȯn-ˌyef, -ˌyev, -yəf\ Ivan Stepanovich 1897–1973 Russ. gen. & marshal of Soviet Union
Ko·no·ye \kə-'nȯi-(ˌ)ā\ Prince Fumimaro 1891–1945 Jap. statesman
Koo \'kü\ Vi Kyuin Wel·ling·ton \'wel-iŋ-tən\ 1887– orig. *Ku Wei-chün* Chin. statesman & diplomat
Kopernik *or* **Koppernigk** — see COPERNICUS
Korn·berg \'kȯ(ə)rn-ˌbərg\ Arthur 1918– Am. biochemist
Korn·gold \'kȯ(ə)rn-ˌgōld, -ˌgȯlt\ Erich Wolfgang 1897–1957 Am. (Austrian-born) composer, conductor, & pianist
Kor·ni·lov \kȯr-'nē-ləf\ Lavr Georgievich 1870–1918 Russ. gen. & counterrevolutionist
Ko·ro·len·ko \ˌkȯr-ə-'leŋ-(ˌ)kō, ˌkär-\ Vladimir Galaktionovich 1853–1921 Russ. nov.
Kor·zyb·ski \kȯr-'zip-skē, -'zib-\ Alfred Habdank Skarbek 1879–1950 Am. (Pol.-born) scientist & writer
Kos·cius·ko \ˌkäs-ē-'əs-ˌkō, kȯsh-'chu̇sh-(ˌ)kō\ Thaddeus 1746–1817 Pol. patriot
Kos·sel \'kȯs-əl\ Albrecht 1853–1927 Ger. physiological chem.
Kos·suth \'kä-ˌsüth, kä-'; 'kȯ-ˌshu̇t\ Fe·renc \'fer-ˌen(t)s\ 1841–1914 *son of La·jos* Hung. polit.
Kossuth La·jos \'lȯi-ˌōsh\ 1802–1894 Hung. patriot & statesman
Ko·sy·gin \kə-'sē-gən\ Aleksei Nikolaevich 1904– Russ. polit.; premier of Soviet Union (1964–)
Kot·ze·bue, von \'kät-sə-ˌbü, 'kȯt-\ August Friedrich Ferdinand 1761–1819 Ger. dram.
Koun·dou·rio·tes \(ˌ)kün-ˌdu̇r-ē-'ōt-ēs\ Pavlos 1855–1935 Greek admiral & statesman
Kous·se·vitz·ky \ˌkü-sə-'vit-skē\ Serge \'sərj, 'se(ə)rzh\ 1874–1951 *Sergei Alexandrovitch* Russ.-born conductor
Krafft–Ebing, von \'kräf-'tā-biŋ, 'kraf-\ Baron Richard 1840–1902 Ger. neurologist
Krebs \'krebz\ Sir Hans (Adolf) 1900– Brit. (Ger.-born) biochemist
Kreis·ler \'krī-slər\ Fritz 1875–1962 Am. (Austrian-born) violinist
Kreym·borg \'krām-ˌbȯ(ə)rg\ Alfred 1883–1966 Am. poet
Krock \'kräk\ Arthur 1886– Am. journalist
Krogh \'krȯg\ August 1874–1949 Dan. physiol.
Krol \'krōl\ John Joseph 1910– Am. cardinal
Kroll \'krōl\ Leon 1884– Am. painter
Kro·pot·kin \krə-'pät-kən\ Prince Pëtr Alekseevich 1842–1921 Russ. geographer & revolutionist
Kru·ger \'krü-gər *Afrik* 'krue-ər\ Stephanus Johannes Paulus 1825–1904 *Oom Paul* \'ōm-'pōül\ So. African statesman
Krupp \'kru̇p, 'krəp\ family of Ger. munition makers including: Friedrich 1787–1826; his son Alfred 1812–1887; Alfred's son Friedrich Alfred 1854–1902; Friedrich Alfred's daughter Bertha 1886–1957; & Bertha's son Alfred-Felix 1907–1967
Krup·ska·ya \'kru̇p-skə-yə\ Nadezhda Konstantinovna 1869–1939 *wife of Nikolai Lenin* Russ. social worker
Krutch \'krüch\ Joseph Wood 1893–1970 Am. author & critic
Ku·bi·tschek \'kü-bə-ˌchek\ Juscelino 1901– pres. of Brazil (1956–61)
Ku·blai Khan \ˌkü-ˌblī-'kän, -blə-\ 1216–1294 founder of Mongol dynasty in China
Kuhn \'kün\ Richard 1900–1967 Austrian chem.
Kui·by·shev \'kwē-bə-ˌshef, 'kü-ē-bə-, -ˌshev\ Valerian Vladimirovich 1888–1935 Russ. Bolshevik
Kun \'kün\ Bé·la \'bā-lə\ 1885–1937 Hung. Communist
Kung \'gu̇ŋ\ Prince 1833–1898 Manchu statesman
Kung \'ku̇ŋ\ H. H. 1881–1967 orig. *K'ung Hsiang-hsi* Chin. statesman
Ku·ro·pat·kin \ˌku̇r-ə-'pat-kən, -'pät-\ Aleksei Nikolaevich 1848–1925 Russ. gen.
Ku·ru·su \ku̇-'rü-(ˌ)sü, ˌku̇r-ə-'sü\ Saburo 1888–1954 Jap. diplomat
Kusch \'ku̇sh\ Polykarp 1911– Am. (Ger.-born) physicist
Ku·tu·zov \kə-'tü-ˌzȯf, -ˌzȯv\ Mikhail Ilarionovich 1745–1813 *Prince of Smolensk* Russ. field marshal
Kyd *or* **Kid** \'kid\ Thomas 1558–1594 Eng. dram.
Kynewulf *var of* CYNEWULF
La Bru·yère, de \ˌlä-brü-'ye(ə)r, -brē-'e(ə)r\ Jean 1645–1696 Fr. moralist
La·chaise \lə-'shāz\ Gaston 1882–1935 Am. (Fr.-born) sculptor
La Chaise, de \lə-'shāz\ François d'Aix 1624–1709 Fr. Jesuit
La Farge \lə-'färzh, -'färj\ John 1835–1910 Am. artist
La Farge Oliver Hazard Perry 1901–1963 Am. writer & anthropol.
La·fa·yette, de \ˌläf-ē-'et, ˌlaf-\ Marquis 1757–1834 *Marie Joseph Paul Yves Roch Gilbert du Motier* Fr. gen. & statesman
Laf·fite *or* **La·fitte** \lə-'fēt, la-\ Jean *ab* 1780–*ab* 1826 Fr. pirate
La Fol·lette \lə-'fäl-ət\ Robert Marion 1855–1925 Am. polit.
La·fon·taine \lə-ˌfän-'tān, -'fän-ˌ; -ˌfōⁿ-'ten\ Henri 1854–1943 Belg. lawyer & statesman
La Fon·taine, de \lə-ˌfän-'tān, -'fän-ˌ; -ˌfōⁿ-'ten\ Jean 1621–1695 Fr. fabulist
La·ger·kvist \'läg-ər-ˌkfist, -ˌkwist\ Pär Fabian 1891– Swed. dram., poet, & nov.
La·ger·löf \'läg-ər-ˌlə(r)v\ Selma Ottiliana Lovisa 1858–1940 Swed. nov. & poet
La·grange \lə-'gränj, -'gräⁿzh\ Comte Joseph Louis 1736–1813 Fr. geometer & astron.
La Guar·dia \lə-'g(w)ärd-ē-ə\ Fi·o·rel·lo \ˌfē-ə-'rel-(ˌ)ō\ Henry 1882–1947 Am. lawyer & polit.
Laird \'la(ə)rd, 'le(ə)rd\ Melvin Robert 1922– U.S. polit.; U.S. secy. of defense (1969–72)
Lake \'lāk\ Simon 1866–1945 Am. naval architect
La·marck, de \lə-'märk\ Chevalier 1744–1829 *Jean Baptiste Pierre Antoine de Monet* Fr. naturalist
La·mar·tine, de \ˌläm-är-'tēn, -ˌlam-ər-\ Alphonse Marie Louis de Prat 1790–1869 Fr. poet
Lamas Carlos Saavedra — see Carlos SAAVEDRA LAMAS
Lamb \'lam\ Charles 1775–1834 Eng. essayist & critic
Lamb William 1779–1848 2d Viscount *Melbourne* Eng. statesman
Lamb Willis Eugene 1913– Am. physicist
Lam·bert \'lam-bərt\ John 1619–1683 Eng. parliamentary gen.
Lam·masch \'läm-ˌäsh\ Heinrich 1853–1920 Austrian jurist
La Motte–Fou·qué \lə-ˌmät-fü-'kā\ Baron Friedrich Heinrich Karl 1777–1843 Ger. nov.
Land \'land\ Edwin Herbert 1909– Am. inventor & industrialist
Lan·dis \'lan-dəs\ Ken·e·saw \'ken-ə-ˌsȯ\ Mountain 1866–1944 Am. jurist & baseball commissioner
Lan·don \'lan-dən\ Alfred Mossman 1887– Am. polit.
Lan·dor \'lan-ˌdȯ(ə)r, -dər\ Walter Savage 1775–1864 Eng. author
Lan·dow·ska \lan-'dȯf-skə, -'dȯv-\ Wanda 1877–1959 Pol. pianist
Land·seer \'lan(d)-ˌsi(ə)r\ Sir Edwin Henry 1802–1873 Eng. painter
Land·stei·ner \'lan(d)-ˌstī-nər, 'länt-ˌshtī-\ Karl 1868–1943 Austrian-born pathologist in Am.
Lane \'lān\ Edward William 1801–1876 Eng. orientalist
Lan·franc \'lan-ˌfraŋk\ 1005?–1089 Ital.-born prelate in Eng.
Lang \'laŋ\ Andrew 1844–1912 Scot. scholar & author
Lang Cosmo Gordon 1864–1945 Brit. prelate; archbishop of Canterbury (1928–42)
Lange \'läŋ-ə\ Christian Louis 1869–1938 Norw. pacifist & hist.
Lang·er \'laŋ-ər\ Susanne Knauth 1895– Am. philos. & educ.
Lang·land \'laŋ-lənd\ *or* **Lang·ley** \'laŋ-lē\ William 1332?–?1400 Eng. poet
Lang·ley \'laŋ-lē\ Samuel Pierpont 1834–1906 Am. astron. & airplane pioneer
Lang·muir \'laŋ-ˌmyu̇(ə)r\ Irving 1881–1957 Am. chem.
Lang·ton \'laŋ(k)-tən\ Stephen *d* 1228 Eng. theol., hist., & poet
Lang·try \'laŋ(k)-trē\ Lillie 1853–1929 née (*Emilie Charlotte*) *Le Breton;* the *Jersey Lily* Brit. actress
La·nier \lə-'ni(ə)r\ Sidney 1842–1881 Am. poet
Lan·kes·ter \'laŋ-kəs-tər; 'lan-ˌkes-, 'laŋ-\ Sir Edwin Ray 1847–1929 Eng. zool.
Lannes \'län, 'lan\ Jean 1769–1809 Duc *de Montebello* Fr. soldier under Napoleon; marshal of France
Lan·sing \'lan(t)-siŋ\ Robert 1864–1928 Am. lawyer & statesman
Lao–tzu *or* **Lao–tse** *or* **Lao–tze** \'lau̇d-'zə\ 604?–?531 B.C. Chin. philos.
La Pé·rouse, de \-ˌlä-pā-'rüz, -pə-\ Comte 1741–1788 *Jean François de Galoup* Fr. navigator & explorer
La·place, de \lə-'pläs\ Marquis Pierre Simon 1749–1827 Fr. astron. & math.
Lard·ner \'lärd-nər\ Ring 1885–1933 *Ringgold Wilmer* Am. writer
La·re·do Brú \lə-ˌrād-ō-'brü\ Federico 1875–1946 Cuban soldier; pres. of Cuba (1936–40)
Lar·go Ca·ba·lle·ro \'lär-(ˌ)gō-ˌkab-ə(l)-'ye(ə)r-(ˌ)ō, -ˌkäb-, -ə-'le(ə)r-\ Francisco 1869–1946 Span. labor leader; prime min. (1936–37)
La Roche·fou·cauld, de \lä-ˌrōsh-ˌfü-'kō, -ˌrōsh-\ Duc François 1613–1680 Fr. writer & moralist
La·rousse \lə-'rüs\ Pierre Athanase 1817–1875 Fr. grammarian & lexicographer
Lar·tet \lär-tā\ Édouard Armand Isidore Hippolyte 1801–1871 Fr. archaeologist
La Salle, de \lə-'sal\ Sieur 1643–1687 *René Robert Cavelier* Fr. explorer in Am.
Las Ca·sas, de \lä-'skäs-əs\ Bartolomé 1474–1566 Span. Dominican missionary & hist.
Las·ki \'las-kē\ Harold Joseph 1893–1950 Eng. polit. scientist
Las·salle \lə-'sal, -'säl\ Ferdinand 1825–1864 Ger. socialist
Lat·i·mer \'lat-ə-mər\ Hugh 1485?–1555 Eng. Protestant martyr
La·tou·rette \ˌlät-ə-'ret\ Kenneth Scott 1884–1968 Am. religious hist. & sinologue
La·trobe \lə-'trōb\ Benjamin Henry 1764–1820 Am. (Eng.-born) architect & engineer
Lat·ti·more \'lat-ə-ˌmō(ə)r, -ˌmȯ(ə)r\ Owen 1900– Am. orientalist
Laud \'lȯd\ William 1573–1645 Eng. prelate; archbishop of Canterbury (1633–45)
Lau·der \'lȯd-ər\ Sir Harry 1870–1950 orig. *MacLennan* Scot. singer

Laue, von \'lau̇-ə\ Max 1879–1960 Ger. physicist
Laugh·ton \'lȯt-^{ə}n\ Charles 1899–1962 Am. (Eng.-born) actor
Lau·ren·cin \lȯ-rä^{n}-sa^{n}\ Marie 1885–1956 Fr. painter
Lau·rens \lȯ-rä^{n}s\ Henri 1885–1954 Fr. sculptor
Lau·ri·er \'lȯr-ē-ˌā, 'lär-\ Sir Wilfrid 1841–1919 Canad. statesman
Lautrec — see TOULOUSE-LAUTREC
La·val \lə-'val, -'väl\ Pierre 1883–1945 Fr. lawyer & polit.
La Val·lière, de \ˌlä-vəl-'ye(ə)r\ Duchesse 1644–1710 *mistress of Louis XIV of France*
La·ve·ran \ˌlav-ə-'rä^{n}\ Charles Louis Alphonse 1845–1922 Fr. physiol. & bacteriol.
La Vé·ren·drye, de \lä-ˌver-ən-'drē, -'ver-ən-ˌdrī\ Sieur 1685–1749 *Pierre Gaultier de Varennes* Canad. explorer in Am.
La·very \'lāv-(ə-)rē, 'lav-\ Sir John 1856–1941 Brit. painter
La·voi·sier \ləv-'wäz-ē-ˌā\ Antoine Laurent 1743–1794 Fr. chem.
Law \'lȯ\ (Andrew) Bon·ar \'bän-ər\ 1858–1923 Brit. (Canad.-born) statesman
Law Edward 1750–1818 1st Baron *Ellenborough* Eng. jurist
Law John 1671–1729 Scot. financier & speculator
Law William 1686–1761 Eng. devotional writer
Lawes \'lȯz\ Henry 1596–1662 Eng. composer
Lawes Lewis Edward 1883–1947 Am. penologist
Law·rence \'lȯr-ən(t)s, 'lär-\ David 1888–1973 Am. journalist
Lawrence David Herbert 1885–1930 Eng. nov.
Lawrence Ernest Orlando 1901–1958 Am. physicist
Lawrence Gertrude 1901–1952 orig. *Gertrud Alexandra Dagmar Lawrence Klasen* Eng. actress
Lawrence James 1781–1813 Am. naval officer
Lawrence Sir Thomas 1769–1830 Eng. painter
Lawrence Thomas Edward 1888–1935 *Lawrence of Arabia* later surname *Shaw* Brit. archaeologist, soldier, & writer
Law·rie \'lȯr-ē, 'lär-ē\ Lee 1877–1963 Am. sculptor
Lax·ness \'läk-ˌsnes\ Hall·dór \'häl-ˌdō(ə)r, -ˌdȯ(ə)r\ Kiljan 1902– Icelandic writer
Lay·a·mon \'lī-ə-mən, 'lā-ə-\ *fl* 1200 Eng. poet
Lay·ard \'lā-ˌärd, -ərd\ Sir Austen Henry 1817–1894 Eng. archaelogist & diplomat
Lea·cock \'lē-ˌkäk\ Stephen Butler 1869–1944 Canad. econ. & humorist
Leadbelly — see Huddie LEDBETTER
Leaf \'lēf\ Walter 1852–1927 Eng. banker & scholar
Lea·hy \'lā-(ˌ)hē\ William Daniel 1875–1959 Am. admiral
Lea·key \'lē-kē\ Louis Seymour Bazett 1903–1972 Brit. paleontologist
Lear \'li(ə)r\ Edward 1812–1888 Eng. painter & nonsense poet
Le·brun \lə-'brə^{n}n, -'brœ^{n}\ Albert 1871–1950 Fr. statesman; pres. of France (1932–40)
Lebrun Mme. Vigée- — see VIGÉE-LEBRUN
Le Brun *or* **Le·brun** Charles 1619–1690 Fr. painter
Lecky \'lek-ē\ William Edward Hartpole 1838–1903 Irish hist. & essayist
Le·conte de Lisle \lə-ˌkō^{n}(n)t-də-'lē(ə)l\ Charles Marie 1818–1894 orig. *Leconte* Fr. poet
Le Cor·bu·sier \lə-ˌkȯr-'b(y)ü-zē-ˌā\ 1887–1965 pseud. of *Charles Édouard Jeanneret-Gris* Fr. (Swiss-born) architect, painter, & writer
Led·bet·ter \'led-ˌbet-ər\ Huddie 1888–1949 *Lead·bel·ly* \'led-ˌbel-ē\ Am. folk singer
Le·der·berg \'lād-ər-ˌbərg\ Joshua 1925– Am. geneticist
Lee \'lē\ Ann 1736–1784 Eng. mystic; founder of Shaker society in U.S.
Lee Charles 1731–1782 Am. (Eng.-born) gen.
Lee Fitzhugh 1835–1905 *nephew of R. E. Lee* Am. gen.
Lee Francis Lightfoot 1734–1797 Am. Revolutionary statesman
Lee Henry 1756–1818 *Light-Horse Harry* Am. gen.
Lee Richard Henry 1732–1794 Am. Revolutionary statesman
Lee Robert Edward 1807–1870 Am. Confed. gen.
Lee Sir Sidney 1859–1926 Eng. editor & scholar
Lee Tsung-Dao \'lē-'dzüŋ-'dau̇\ 1926– Chin. physicist
Leeu·wen·hoek *or* **Leu·wen·hoek, van** \'lā-vən-ˌhu̇k\ Anton 1632–1723 Du. naturalist
Le·feb·vre \lə-'fevr^{ə}\ François Joseph 1755–1820 Duc *de Dantzig* Fr. gen.; marshal of France
Le Gal·lienne \lə-'gal-yən, -ˌyen\ Eva 1899– *dau. of Richard* Eng. actress in Am.
Le Gallienne Richard 1866–1947 Eng. writer
Le·gen·dre \lə-'zhä^{n}(n)dr^{ə}\ Adrien Marie 1752–?1833 Fr. math.
Lé·ger \lā-'zhā\ Alexis Saint-Léger 1887– pseud. *St. John Perse* \sa^{n}-ˌjȯn-'pe(ə)rs\ Fr. diplomat & poet
Léger Fernand 1881–1955 Fr. painter
Le·guía y Sal·ce·do \lə-'gē-ə-ˌē-säl-'säd-(ˌ)ō, -'sā-(ˌ)t͟hō\ Augusto Bernardino 1863–1932 Peruvian banker; pres. of Peru (1908–12; 1919–30)
Le·hár \'lā-ˌhär\ Franz 1870–1948 Hung. composer
Leh·man \'lē-mən\ Herbert Henry 1878–1963 Am. banker & polit.
Leh·mann \'lā-ˌmän\ Lot·te \'lȯt-ə\ 1888– Ger. soprano
Leib·niz *or* **Leib·nitz, von** \'līb-nəts, *Ger* 'līp-nits\ Baron Gottfried Wilhelm 1646–1716 Ger. philos. & math.
Leicester 1st Earl of — see Robert DUDLEY; see also de MONTFORT
Leif Ericson — see ERICSON
Leigh–Mal·lo·ry \'lē-'mal-(ə-)rē\ Sir Trafford Leigh 1892–1944 Brit. air marshal
Leigh·ton \'lāt-^{ə}n\ Frederick 1830–1896 Baron *Leighton of Stretton* Eng. painter
Leins·dorf \'līnz-ˌdȯrf, 'līn(t)s-\ Erich 1912– Am. (Austrian-born) conductor
Leith–Ross \'lē-'thrȯs\ Sir Frederick (William) 1887–1968 Brit. econ. & financier
Le·jeune \lə-'jün\ John Archer 1867–1942 Am. gen.
Le·land \'lē-lənd\ *or* **Ley·land** \'lā-\ John 1506?–1552 Eng. antiquarian
Le·ly \'lē-lē\ Sir Peter 1618–1680 orig. *Pieter Van der Faes* Du. painter in Eng.
Le·maî·tre \lə-'metr^{ə}\ (François Élie) Jules 1853–1914 Fr. writer
Lemaître Abbé Georges Henri 1894–1966 Belg. astrophysicist
Lem·ass \'lem-əs\ Seán \'shȯn\ Francis 1899–1971 prime min. of Ireland (1959–66)
Lemoyne Pierre — see IBERVILLE
Le·nard \'lā-ˌnärt\ Philipp 1862–1947 Ger. physicist
Len·clos \lä^{n}-klō\ Anne 1620–1705 *Ninon de Lenclos* Fr. wit & lady of fashion
L'En·fant \'län-ˌfänt, lä^{n}-fä^{n}\ Pierre Charles 1754–1825 Fr. engineer in Am.
Le·nin \'len-ən\ Nikolai 1870–1924 *Vladimir Ilich Ul·ya·nov* \ül-'yän-əf, -ˌȯf, -ˌȯv\ Russ. Communist leader
Leo \'lē-(ˌ)ō\ name of 13 popes: esp. **I** Saint 390?–461 (pope 440–61); **III** Saint 750?–816 (pope 795–816); **XIII** 1810–1903 (pope 1878–1903)
Leon·ard \'len-ərd\ William Ellery 1876–1944 Am. educ. & poet
Leonardo da Vinci — see Leonardo da VINCI
Le·on·ca·val·lo \ˌlā-ˌōn-kə'väl-(ˌ)ō\ Ruggiero 1858–1919 Ital. composer & librettist
Le·on·i·das \lē-'än-əd-əs\ 5th cent. B.C. Greek hero; king of Sparta (490?–480)
Le·o·par·di \ˌlā-ə-'pärd-ē\ Conte Giacomo 1798–1837 Ital. poet
Le·o·pold I \'lē-ə-ˌpōld\ 1640–1705 king of Hungary (1655–1705) & Holy Rom. emp. (1658–1705)
Leopold II 1747–1792 Holy Rom. emp. (1790–92)
Leopold I 1790–1865 king of Belgium (1831–65)
Leopold II 1835–1909 king of Belgium (1865–1909)
Leopold III 1901– king of Belgium (1934–51)
Lep·i·dus \'lep-əd-əs\ Marcus Aemilius *d* 13 B.C. Rom. triumvir
Ler·mon·tov \'ler-mən-ˌtȯf, -ˌtȯv\ Mikhail Yurievich 1814–1841 Russ. poet & nov.
Ler·ner \'lər-nər\ Alan Jay 1918– Am. dram.
Le·sage \lə-'säzh\ Alain René 1668–1747 Fr. nov. & dram.
Le·sche·tiz·ky \ˌlesh-ə-'tit-skē\ Theodor 1830–1915 Pol. pianist & composer
Les·seps, de \lā-'seps, 'les-əps\ Vicomte Ferdinand Marie 1805–1894 Fr. diplomat; promoter of Suez Canal
Les·sing \'les-iŋ\ Gotthold Ephraim 1729–1781 Ger. critic & dram.
Les·ter \'les-tər\ Seán \'shȯn\ 1889–1959 Irish journalist & diplomat; last secy.-gen. of League of Nations (1940–46)
L'Es·trange \lə-'strānj\ Sir Roger 1616–1704 Eng. journalist & translator
Leu·tze \'lȯit-sə\ Emanuel 1816–1868 Am. (Ger.-born) painter
Le·vas·seur \lə-ˌväs-'ər\ Pierre Émile 1828–1911 Fr. econ.
Le·ver \'lē-vər\ Charles James 1806–1872 Brit. nov.
Lew·es \'lü-əs\ George Henry 1817–1878 Eng. philos. & critic
Lew·is \'lü-əs\ Cecil Day — see DAY-LEWIS
Lewis Clive Staples 1898–1963 Eng. nov. & essayist
Lewis (Harry) Sinclair 1885–1951 Am. nov.
Lewis Isaac Newton 1858–1931 Am. army officer & inventor
Lewis John Llewellyn 1880–1969 Am. labor leader
Lewis Matthew Gregory 1775–1818 *Monk Lewis* Eng. author
Lewis Meriwether 1774–1809 Am. explorer
Lewis (Percy) Wyndham 1884–1957 Brit. painter & author
Lew·i·sohn \'lü-ə-zən, -sən\ Ludwig 1883–1955 Am. (Ger.-born) nov. & critic
Ley \'lī\ Robert 1890–1945 Ger. Nazi leader
Li Hung-chang \'lē-'hu̇ŋ-'jäŋ\ 1823–1901 Chin. statesman
Li Po \-'bō, -'pō\ *or* Tai-po \-'tī-\ *d* 762 A.D. Chin. poet
Li Shih-min \-'shē-'min\ 597–649 *T'ai-tsung* \-'tīd-'zu̇ŋ\ Chin. emp. (627–649)
Lib·by \'lib-ē\ Willard Frank 1908– Am. chem.
Lich·ten·stein \'lik-tən-ˌstīn, -ˌstēn\ Roy 1923– Am. artist
Li·cin·i·us \lə-'sin-ē-əs\ 270?–325 *Valerius Licinianus Licinius* Rom. emp. (308–324)
Lid·dell Hart \ˌlid-^{ə}l-'härt\ Basil Henry 1895–1970 Eng. military scientist
Lie \'lē\ Jonas 1833–1909 Norw. nov. & dram.
Lie Jonas 1880–1940 *nephew of prec.* Norw.-born painter in Am.
Lie Trygve 1896–1968 Norw. lawyer & statesman; secy.-gen. of U.N. (1946–53)
Lie·big, von \'lē-big\ Baron Justus 1803–1873 Ger. chem.
Lieb·knecht \'lēp-(kə-)ˌnekt\ Karl 1871–1919 Ger. socialist leader
Li·far \'lē-ˌfär, lē-'\ Serge 1905– Russ. dancer
Lil·ien·thal \'lil-yən-ˌthȯl\ David Eli 1899– Am. lawyer & administrator
Lil·ien·thal \'lil-yən-ˌtäl, -ˌthȯl\ Otto 1848–1896 Ger. aeronautical engineer
Li·li·u·o·ka·la·ni \li-ˌlē-ə-(ˌ)wō-kə-'län-ē\ Lydia Kamekeha 1838–1917 queen of the Hawaiian Islands (1891–93)
Lil·lo \'lil-(ˌ)ō\ George 1693?–1739 Eng. dram.
Li·món \li-'mōn\ José 1908–1972 Mex. dancer & choreographer in the U.S.
Lin Sen \'lin-'sen\ *or* Shen \-'shen\ 1876?–1943 Chin. statesman; pres. of the National government (1932–43)
Lin Yu-tang \-'yü-'täŋ, -'taŋ\ 1895– Chin. author & philologist
Lin·a·cre \'lin-i-kər\ Thomas 1460?–1524 Eng. humanist & physician
Lin·coln \'liŋ-kən\ Abraham 1809–1865 16th pres. of the U.S. (1861–65)
Lincoln Benjamin 1733–1810 Am. Revolutionary gen.
Lincoln Joseph Crosby 1870–1944 Am. nov.
Lind \'lind\ Jenny 1820–1887 *Johanna Maria; the Swedish Nightingale* Swed. soprano
Lind·bergh \'lin(d)-ˌbərg\ Anne Spencer 1906– née *Morrow; wife of C. A.* Am. author
Lindbergh Charles Augustus 1902– Am. aviator

ə abut	^{ə} kitten, F table	ər further	a back	ā bake
ä cot, cart	ȧ F bac	au̇ out	ch chin	e less	ē easy
g gift	i trip	ī life	j joke	k̲ G ich	^{n} F vin	ŋ sing
ō flow	ȯ flaw	œ F bœu f	œ̄ F feu	ȯi coin	th thing
t͟h this	ü loot	u̇ foot	ue G Füllen	ue̅ F rue	y yet
^{y} F digne \dēn^{y}\, nuit \nw^{y}ē\	yü few	yu̇ furious	zh vision		

Lind·ley \'lin-(d)lē\ John 1799–1865 Eng. botanist — **Lind·ley·an** \-ən\ *adj*
Lind·say \'lin-zē\ Howard 1889–1968 Am. dram. & actor
Lindsay John Vliet 1921– Am. polit.
Lindsay (Nicholas) Va·chel \'vā-chəl\ 1879–1931 Am. poet
Link·la·ter \'liŋ-ˌklāt-ər, -klət-\ Eric 1899– Brit. writer
Linlithgow Marquis of — see HOPE
Lin·nae·us \lə-'nē-əs, -'nā-\ Carolus 1707–1778 Carl *von Lin·né* \lə-'nā\ Swed. botanist — **Lin·nae·an** *or* **Lin·ne·an** \lə-'nē-ən, -'nā-; 'lin-ē-\ *adj*
Lip·chitz \'lip-shəts\ Jacques 1891–1973 Am. (Lithuanian-born) sculptor
Lip·mann \'lip-mən\ Fritz Albert 1899– Am. (Ger.-born) biochem.
Lip·pi \'lip-ē\ Fra Filippo *or* Lippo 1406?–1469 Florentine painter
Lippi Filippo *or* Filippino 1457?–1504 *son of prec.* Florentine painter
Lipp·mann \lep-'män, -'man\ Gabriel 1845–1921 Fr. physicist
Lipp·mann \'lip-mən\ Walter 1889– Am. journalist & author
Lip·ton \'lip-tən\ Sir Thomas Johnstone 1850–1931 Eng. merchant & yachtsman
Lisle, de — see LECONTE DE LISLE, ROUGET DE LISLE
Lis·ter \'lis-tər\ Joseph 1827–1912 1st Baron *Lister of Lyme Regis* Eng. surgeon
Liszt \'list\ Franz 1811–1886 Hung. pianist & composer — **Liszt·ian** \-ē-ən\ *adj*
Lit·tle·ton \'lit-^{ə}l-tən\ Sir Thomas 1407?–1481 Eng. jurist
Lit·tré \li-'trā\ Maximilien Paul Émile 1801–1881 Fr. lexicographer
Lit·vi·nov \lit-'vē-ˌnȯf, -ˌnȯv, -nəf\ Maksim Maksimovich 1876–1951 Russ. Communist
Liu Shao-ch'i \lē-'ü-'shau̇-'chē\ 1898– Chin. Communist
Liv·ing·ston \'liv-iŋ-stən\ Robert R. 1746–1813 Am. statesman
Liv·ing·stone \'liv-iŋ-stən\ David 1813–1873 Scot. explorer in Africa
Livy \'liv-ē\ 59 B.C.–A.D. 17 *Titus Livius* Rom. hist.
Lloyd George \'lȯid-'jȯ(ə)rj\ David 1863–1945 1st Earl of *Dwy·for* \'dü-ē-ˌvȯ(ə)r\ Brit. statesman; prime min. (1916–22)
Lo·ba·chev·ski \ˌlō-bə-'chef-skē, ˌläb-ə-, -'chev-\ Nikolai Ivanovich 1793–1856 Russ. math.
Lo·ben·gu·la \ˌlō-bən-'g(y)ü-lə\ 1833–1894 Zulu king of the Matabele
Locke \'läk\ John 1632–1704 Eng. philos.
Lock·er–Lamp·son \ˌläk-ər-'lam(p)-sən\ Frederick 1821–1895 Eng. poet
Lock·hart \'läk-ərt, 'läk-ˌ(h)ärt\ John Gibson 1794–1854 Scot. nov. & biographer
Lock·yer \'läk-yər\ Sir Joseph Norman 1836–1920 Eng. astron.
Lodge \'läj\ Henry Cabot 1850–1924 Am. statesman & author
Lodge Henry Cabot 1902– *grandson of prec.* Am. polit. & diplomat
Lodge Sir Oliver Joseph 1851–1940 Eng. physicist
Lodge Thomas 1558–1625 Eng. poet & dram.
Loeb \'lōb\ Jacques 1859–1924 Ger.-born physiol. in Am.
Loewe \'lō(-ē)\ Frederick 1904– Am. (Austrian-born) composer
Loewi \'lō-ē\ Otto 1873–1961 Am. (Ger.-born) pharmacologist
Löff·ler \'lef-lər\ Friedrich August Johannes 1852–1915 Ger. bacteriol.
Lo·max \'lō-ˌmaks\ John Avery 1872–1948 Am. folklorist
Lom·bard \'läm-ˌbärd, -bərd\ Peter 1100?–1160 or 1164 *Petrus Lombardus* Ital. theol.
Lom·bro·so \lȯm-'brō-(ˌ)sō\ Ce·sa·re \'chā-zä-ˌrā\ 1836–1909 Ital. physician & psychiatrist
Lon·don \'lən-dən\ John Griffith 1876–1916 *Jack* Am. writer
Long \'lȯŋ\ Crawford Williamson 1815–1878 Am. surgeon
Long Hu·ey \'hyü-e\ Pierce 1893–1935 Am. lawyer & polit.
Long Stephen Harriman 1784–1864 Am. army officer & explorer
Long·fel·low \'lȯŋ-ˌfel-(ˌ)ō, -ˌfel-ə(-w)\ Henry Wads·worth \'wädz-(ˌ)wərth\ 1807–1882 Am. poet
Lon·gi·nus \län-'jī-nəs\ Dionysius Cassius *d* A.D. 273 Greek philos.
Long·ley \'lȯŋ-lē\ Charles Thomas 1794–1868 archbishop of Canterbury (1862–68)
Long·street \'lȯŋ-ˌstrēt\ James 1821–1904 Am. Confed. gen.
Lönn·rot \'len-ˌrüt, 'lə(r)n-, -ˌrüt\ Elias 1802–1884 Finnish scholar
Lons·dale \'länz-ˌdāl\ Frederick 1881–1954 Brit. dram.
Ló·pez \'lō-ˌpez\ Carlos Antonio 1790–1862 pres. of Paraguay (1844–62)
López Francisco Solano 1827–1870 *son of prec.* pres. of Paraguay (1862–70)
López Ma·te·os \-mə-'tā-əs, -(ˌ)ōs\ Adolfo 1910–1969 pres. of Mex. (1958–64)
Lorca Federico García — see Federico GARCÍA-LORCA
Lo·rentz \'lōr-ˌen(t)s, 'lȯr-\ Hendrik Antoon 1853–1928 Du. physicist
Lo·renz \'lōr-ˌen(t)s, 'lȯr-\ Adolf 1854–1946 Austrian orthopedic surgeon
Lor·rain \lə-'rān, lȯ-, -'ran\ Claude 1600–1682 pseud. of *Claude Gellée* Fr. painter
Lo·thair I \lō-'t(h)a(ə)r, -'t(h)e(ə)r, 'lō-ˌ\ 795?–855 king of Germany (840–43) & Holy Rom. emp. (840–855)
Lothair II (*or* **III**) 1070?–1137 *the Saxon* king of Germany & Holy Rom. emp. (1125–37)
Lo·ti \lō-'tē, lō-\ Pierre 1850–1923 pseud. of *Louis Marie Julien Viaud* Fr. naval officer & nov.
Lou·bet \lü-'bā\ Émile 1838–1929 Fr. statesman; pres. of France (1899–1906)
Loudoun 4th Earl of — see John CAMPBELL
Lou·is \'lü-ē, 'lü-əs\ name of 18 kings of France: esp. **I** (*le Débonnaire*) 778–840 (reigned 814–840); **V** (*le Fainéant*) 966?–987 (reigned — last Carolingian — 986–987); **IX** (*Saint*) 1214–1270 (reigned 1226–70); **XI** 1423–1483 (reigned 1461–83); **XII** 1462–1515 (reigned 1498–1515); **XIII** 1601–1643 (reigned 1610–43); **XIV** 1638–1715 (reigned 1643–1715); **XV** 1710–1774 (reigned 1715–74); **XVI** 1754–1793 (reigned 1774–92; guillotined); **XVII** 1785–1795 (nominally reigned 1793–95); **XVIII** 1755–1824 (reigned 1814–15; 1815–24)
Louis IV 1287?–1347 *Duke of Bavaria* king of Germany & Holy Rom. emp. (1314–47)
Louis II de Bourbon — see CONDÉ
Louis Napoleon — see NAPOLEON III
Louis Phi·lippe \fi-'lēp\ 1773–1850 *the Citizen King* king of the French (1830–48)
Louns·bury \'lau̇nz-ˌber-ē, -b(ə-)rē\ Thomas Raynesford 1838–1915 Am. scholar & educ.
L'Ouverture — see Pierre Dominique TOUSSAINT L'OUVERTURE
Louÿs \lü-'ē\ Pierre 1870–1925 Fr. writer
Lovat 12th Baron — see Simon FRASER
Love·lace \'ləv-ˌlās\ Richard 1618–1658 Eng. Cavalier poet
Lov·ell \'ləv-əl\ Sir (Alfred Charles) Bernard 1913– Brit. radio astron.
Lov·er \'ləv-ər\ Samuel 1797–1868 Irish nov.
Low \'lō\ Sir David Alexander Cecil 1891–1963 Brit. cartoonist
Low·ell \'lō-əl\ Amy 1874–1925 Am. poet & critic
Lowell James Russell 1819–1891 Am. poet, essayist, & dram.
Lowell Percival 1855–1916 *bro. of Amy* Am. astron.
Lowell Robert Traill Spence 1917– Am. poet
Lowes \'lōz\ John Livingston 1867–1945 Am. educ.
Lowndes \'lau̇n(d)z\ William Thomas 1798–1843 Eng. bibliographer
Low·ry \'lau̇(ə)r-ē\ Malcolm 1909–1957 Brit. writer
Loy·o·la \lȯi-'ō-lə\ Saint Ignatius of 1491–1556 *Íñigo de Oñez y Loyola* Span. soldier & ecclesiastic; founder of the Society of Jesus
Lu Hsun \'lü-'shün\ 1881–1936 Chin. writer
Lub·bock \'ləb-ək\ Sir John 1834–1913 1st Baron *Avebury; son of Sir J. W.* Eng. financier & author
Lubbock Sir John William 1803–1865 Eng. astron. & math.
Luc·an \'lü-kən\ 39–65 *Marcus Annaeus Lucanus* Rom. poet
Luce \'lüs\ Clare 1903– née *Boothe* \'büth\ *wife of H. R.* Am. dram., polit., & diplomat
Luce Henry Robinson 1898–1967 Am. editor & publisher
Lu·cre·tius \lü-'krē-sh(ē-)əs\ 96?–55 B.C. *Titus Lucretius Carus* Rom. poet & philos. — **Lu·cre·tian** \-shən\ *adj*
Lu·cul·lus \lü-'kəl-əs\ Lucius Licinius *fl* 79?–?57 B.C. Rom. gen. & epicure
Lu·den·dorff \'lüd-^{ə}n-ˌdȯrf\ Erich Friedrich Wilhelm 1865–1937 Ger. gen.
Lul·ly \lü-'lē\ Jean Baptiste 1632–1687 Fr. (Ital.-born) composer
Lul·ly \'ləl-ē\ Raymond 1235?–1315 Span. ecclesiastic & philos.
Lunt \'lənt\ Alfred 1893– Am. actor
Lu·ther \'lü-thər\ Martin 1483–1546 Ger. Reformation leader
Lu·thu·li \lü-'t(h)ü-lē\ Albert John 1898–1967 So. African reformer
Lux·em·burg \'lək-səm-ˌbərg, 'lük-səm-ˌbu̇(ə)rg\ Rosa 1870–1919 Ger. socialist leader
Lyau·tey \lē-ˌō-'tā\ Louis Hubert Gonzalve 1854–1934 Fr. soldier; marshal of France
Ly·cur·gus \lī-'kər-gəs\ 9th cent. B.C. Spartan lawgiver
Lyd·gate \'lid-ˌgāt, -gət\ John 1370?–?1451 Eng. poet
Ly·ell \'lī-əl\ Sir Charles 1797–1875 Brit. geologist
Lyly \'lil-ē\ John 1554?–1606 Eng. author
Lynch \'linch\ John Mary 1917– prime min. of Ireland (1966–73)
Lynd \'lind\ Robert Staugh·ton \'stȯt-^{ə}n\ 1892–1970 & his wife Helen née *Merrell* 1897– Am. sociologists
Ly·on \'lī-ən\ Mary 1797–1849 Am. educ.
Ly·ons \'lī-ənz\ Joseph Aloysius 1879–1939 Austral. statesman; prime min. (1932–39)
Ly·san·der \lī-'san-dər\ *d* 395 B.C. Spartan commander
Ly·sen·ko \lə-'seŋ-(ˌ)kō\ Trofim Denisovich 1898– Russ. scientist
Lys·i·as \'lis-ē-əs\ 450?–?380 B.C. Athenian orator
Ly·sim·a·chus \lī-'sim-ə-kəs\ 361?–281 B.C. Macedonian gen. under Alexander the Great; king of Thrace (306)
Ly·sip·pus \lī-'sip-əs\ 4th cent. B.C. Greek sculptor
Lyt·ton \'lit-^{ə}n\ 1st Baron 1803–1873 *Edward George Earle Lytton Bul·wer-Lytton* \ˌbu̇l-wər-\; *bro. of Sir Henry Bulwer* Eng. nov. & dram.
Lytton 1st Earl of 1831–1891 *Edward Robert Bulwer-Lytton;* pseud. *Owen Meredith; son of prec.* Brit. statesman & poet
Lytton 2d Earl of 1876–1947 *Victor Alexander George Robert Lytton; son of 1st Earl* Brit. administrator & author
M'–, Mc– names beginning with these prefixes are alphabetized as if spelled MAC-
Mc·Adoo \'mak-ə-ˌdü\ William Gibbs 1863–1941 Am. lawyer & administrator
Mac·Ar·thur \mə-'kär-thər\ Arthur 1845–1912 Am. gen.
MacArthur Charles 1895–1956 Am. dram.
MacArthur Douglas 1880–1964 *son of Arthur* Am. gen.
Ma·cau·lay \mə-'kȯ-lē\ Dame Rose 1881–1958 Eng. nov.
Macaulay 1st Baron 1800–1859 *Thomas Babington Macaulay* Eng. hist., author, & statesman
Mac·beth \mək-'beth\ *d* 1057 king of Scotland (1040–57)
Mc·Bur·ney \mək-'bər-nē\ Charles 1845–1913 Am. surgeon
Mc·Car·thy \mə-'kär-thē *also* -'kärt-ē\ Eugene Joseph 1916– Am. polit.
McCarthy Joseph Raymond 1908–1957 Am. polit.
McCarthy Mary 1912– Am. writer
M'·Car·thy \mə-'kär-thē *also* -'kärt-ē\ Justin 1830–1912 Irish writer & polit.
M'Carthy Justin Huntly 1861–1936 *son of Justin* Irish dram., nov., & hist.
Mc·Clel·lan \mə-'klel-ən\ George Brinton 1826–1885 Am. gen. & polit.
Mc·Clos·key \mə-'kläs-kē\ John 1810–1885 1st Am. cardinal
Mc·Cloy \mə-'klȯi\ John Jay 1895– Am. banker & govt. official
Mc·Clure \mə-'klu̇(ə)r\ Samuel Sidney 1857–1949 Am. (Irish-born) editor & publisher
Mc·Cor·mack \mə-'kȯr-mək, -mik\ John 1884–1945 Am. (Irish-born) tenor

McCormack John William 1891– Am. polit.
Mc·Cor·mick \mə-ˈkȯr-mik\ Cyrus Hall 1809–1884 Am. inventor
McCormick Joseph Me·dill \mə-ˈdil\ 1877–1925 & his bro. Robert Rutherford 1880–1955 Am. newspaper publishers
Mac·Crack·en \mə-ˈkrak-ən\ Henry Noble 1880–1970 Am. educ.
Mc·Crae \mə-ˈkrā\ John 1872–1918 Canad. physician & poet
Mc·Cul·lers \mə-ˈkəl-ərz\ Carson Smith 1917–1967 Am. writer
MacDiar·mid \mək-ˈdər-məd, -mət\ Hugh 1892– pseud. of *Christopher Murray Grieve* Scot. poet
Mac·don·ald \mək-ˈdän-^{ə}ld\ George 1824–1905 Scot. nov. & poet
Macdonald Sir John Alexander 1815–1891 Canad. statesman; 1st prime min. of Dominion of Canada (1867–73) and again (1878–91)
MacDon·ald \mək-ˈdän-^{ə}ld\ James Ramsay 1866–1937 Brit. statesman
Mac·don·ough \mək-ˈdän-ə, -ˈdən-\ Thomas 1783–1825 Am. naval officer
Mac·Dow·ell \mək-ˈdau̇(-ə)l\ Edward Alexander 1861–1908 Am. composer
Mc·Dow·ell \mək-ˈdau̇(-ə)l\ Ephraim 1771–1830 Am. surgeon
McDowell Irvin 1818–1885 Am. gen.
Mc·Fee \mək-ˈfē\ William 1881–1966 Eng. writer
Mc·Gill \mə-ˈgil\ James 1744–1813 Canad. (Scot.-born) businessman & philanthropist
McGill Ralph Emerson 1898–1969 Am. journalist
Mc·Gov·ern \mə-ˈgəv-ərn\ George Stanley 1922– Am. polit.
Mc·Guf·fey \mə-ˈgəf-ē\ William Holmes 1800–1873 Am. educ.
Mach \ˈmäk, ˈmäk\ Ernst 1838–1916 Austrian physicist & philos.
Ma·cha·do y Mo·ra·les \mä-ˈchäd-ō-ˌē-mə-ˈräl-əs\ Gerardo 1871–1939 pres. of Cuba (1925–33)
Ma·chi·a·vel·li \ˌmak-ē-ə-ˈvel-ē\ Niccolò 1469–1527 Ital. statesman & polit. philos.
Mc·In·tyre \ˈmak-ən-ˌtī(ə)r\ James Francis Aloysius 1886– Am. cardinal
Mac·Kaye \mə-ˈkī\ Percy 1875–1956 Am. poet & dram.
Mc·Ken·na \mə-ˈken-ə\ Sio·bhan \shə-ˈvȯn\ 1923– Irish actress
Mack·en·sen, von \ˈmäk-ən-zən\ August 1849–1945 Ger. field marshal
Mac·ken·zie \mə-ˈken-zē\ Alexander 1822–1892 Canad. (Scot.-born) statesman; prime min. (1873–78)
Mackenzie Sir Alexander Campbell 1847–1935 Brit. composer & conductor
Mackenzie Sir Compton 1883–1972 Eng. nov.
Mackenzie William Lyon 1795–1861 Canad. (Scot.-born) insurgent leader
Mc·Kim \mə-ˈkim\ Charles Follen 1847–1909 Am. architect
Mac·kin·der \mə-ˈkin-dər\ Sir Halford John 1861–1947 Eng. geographer
Mc·Kin·ley \mə-ˈkin-lē\ William 1843–1901 25th pres. of the U.S. (1897–1901)
Mack·in·tosh \ˈmak-ən-ˌtäsh\ Sir James 1765–1832 Scot. philos. & hist.
Maclaren Ian — see John WATSON
Mac·Leish \mə-ˈklēsh\ Archibald 1892– Am. poet & administrator
Mac·Len·nan \mə-ˈklen-ən\ Hugh 1907– Canad. nov.
Mac·leod \mə-ˈklau̇d\ John James Rickard 1876–1935 Scot. physiol.
Mc·Lu·han \mə-ˈklü-ən\ (Herbert) Marshall 1911– Canad. educ.
Mac·Ma·hon, or Mac·ma·hon, de \ˌmäk-ˌmä-ō^{n}; mək-ˈma(-ə)n, -ˈmän\ Comte Marie Edme Patrice Maurice 1808–1893 marshal (1859) & pres. (1873–79) of France
McMa·hon \mək-ˈmä(-ə)n\ William 1908– prime min. of Austral. (1971–72)
Mac·mil·lan \mək-ˈmil-ən\ Harold 1894– Brit. prime min. (1957–63)
Mac·Mil·lan \mək-ˈmil-ən\ Donald Baxter 1874–1970 Am. arctic explorer
Mc·Mil·lan \mək-ˈmil-ən\ Edwin Mattison 1907– Am. chem.
Mac·Mon·nies \mək-ˈmän-ēz\ Frederick William 1863–1937 Am. sculptor
Mc·Na·mara \ˌmak-nə-ˈmar-ə, ˈmak-nə-ˌmar-ə\ Robert Strange 1916– U.S. secy. of defense (1961–68)
Mc·Naugh·ton \mək-ˈnȯt-^{ə}n\ Andrew George Latta 1887–1966 Canad. gen. & diplomat
Mac·Neice \mək-ˈnēs\ Louis 1907–1963 Brit. (Irish-born) poet
Mac·Neil \mək-ˈnē(ə)l\ Hermon Atkins 1866–1947 Am. sculptor
Mc·Nutt \mək-ˈnət\ Paul Vories 1891–1955 Am. lawyer & administrator
Mac·pher·son \mək-ˈfərs-^{ə}n\ James 1736–1796 Scot. writer
Mac·rea·dy \mə-ˈkrēd-ē\ William Charles 1793–1873 Eng. actor
Ma·da·ria·ga y Ro·jo, de \ˌmäd-ə-rē-ˈäg-ə-(ˌ)ē-ˈrō-(ˌ)hō\ Salvador 1886– Span. writer & diplomat
Ma·de·ro \mə-ˈde(ə)r-(ˌ)ō\ Francisco Indalecio 1873–1913 pres. of Mexico (1911–13)
Mad·i·son \ˈmad-ə-sən\ Dolley 1768–1849 née (*Dorothea*) *Payne; wife of James* Am. hostess
Madison James 1751–1836 4th pres. of the U.S. (1809–17) — **Mad·i·so·nian** \ˌmad-ə-ˈsō-nē-ən, -nyən\ *adj*
Mae·ce·nas \mi-ˈsē-nəs\ Gaius 70?–8 B.C. Rom. statesman & patron of literature
Maes *or* **Maas** \ˈmäs\ Nicolaes 1632–1693 Du. painter
Mae·ter·linck \ˈmāt-ər-ˌliŋk *also* ˈmet-, ˈmat-\ Count Maurice 1862–1949 Belg. poet, dram., & essayist — **Mae·ter·linck·ian** \ˌmāt-ər-ˈliŋ-kē-ən, ˌmet-, ˌmat-\ *adj*
Ma·gel·lan \mə-ˈjel-ən, *chiefly Brit* -ˈgel-\ Ferdinand 1480?–1521 *Fernão de Magalhães* Port. navigator
Ma·gi·not \ˌmazh-ə-ˈnō, ˌmaj-\ André 1877–1932 Fr. polit.
Ma·gritte \mə-ˈgrēt\ René 1898–1967 Belgian painter
Mah·ler \ˈmäl-ər\ Gustav 1860–1911 Austrian composer
Mah·mud II \mä-ˈmüd\ 1785–1839 sultan of Turkey (1803–39)
Ma·ho·met \mə-ˈhäm-ət, ˈmā-ə-mət\ *or* **Ma·hom·ed** \-əd\ *var of* MUHAMMAD
Mai·ler \ˈmā-lər\ Norman 1923– Am. author
Mail·lol \mä-ˈyȯl, -ˈyōl\ Aristide 1861–1944 Fr. sculptor
Mai·mon·i·des \mī-ˈmän-ə-ˌdēz\ 1135–1204 Rabbi *Moses ben Maimon* Span.-born philos.
Maine \ˈmān\ Sir Henry James Sumner 1822–1888 Eng. jurist
Main·te·non, de \ˌma^{n}(n)t-^{ə}n-ˈō^{n}, ma^{n}(n)t-ˈnō^{n}\ Marquise 1635–1719 *Françoise d'Aubigné; consort of Louis XIV*
Mait·land \ˈmāt-lənd\ Frederic William 1850–1906 Eng. hist.
Ma·ki·no \mä-ˈkē-(ˌ)nō\ Count Nobuaki 1861–1949 Jap. statesman
Mal·a·mud \ˈmal-ə-(ˌ)məd\ Bernard 1914– Am. writer
Ma·lan \mə-ˈlan, -ˈlän\ Daniel François 1874–1959 So. African editor; prime min. (1948–54)
Mal·colm X \ˌmal-kə-ˈmeks\ 1925–1965 *Malcolm Little* Am. civil rights leader
Male·branche, de \ˌmal-(ə-)ˈbrä^{n}sh, ˌmäl-\ Nicolas 1638–1715 Fr. philos.
Ma·len·kov \mə-ˈlen-ˌkȯf, -ˌkȯv, -ˈleŋ-kəf; ˌmal-ən-ˈkȯf, -ˈkȯv\ Georgi Maximilianovich 1901– Russ. polit.
Mal·herbe, de \ma-ˈle(ə)rb, mä-\ François 1555–1628 Fr. poet
Ma·li·nov·sky \ˌmal-ə-ˈnȯf-skē, ˌmäl-, -ˈnȯv-\ Rodion Yakovlevich 1899–1967 Russ. gen.
Ma·li·now·ski \ˌmal-ə-ˈnȯf-skē, ˌmäl-, -ˈnȯv-\ Bronislaw Kasper 1884–1942 Pol.-born anthropologist
Mal·lar·mé \ˌmal-ˌär-ˈmā\ Stéphane 1842–1898 Fr. poet
Ma·lone \mə-ˈlōn\ Edmund *or* Edmond 1741–1812 Irish Shakespearean scholar
Mal·o·ry \ˈmal-(ə-)rē\ Sir Thomas *fl* 1470 Eng. author
Mal·pi·ghi \mal-ˈpē-gē, -ˈpig-ē\ Marcello 1628–1694 Ital. anatomist
Mal·raux \mal-ˈrō\ André 1901– Fr. writer & polit.
Mal·thus \ˈmal-thəs\ Thomas Robert 1766–1834 Eng. econ.
Man·del \mä^{n}(n)-ˈdel\ Georges 1885–1943 orig. *Jéroboam Rothschild* Fr. polit.
Man·de·ville \ˈman-də-ˌvil\ Bernard 1670?–1733 Du.-born physician & satirist in Eng.
Mandeville Sir John *d* 1372 pseud. of an unidentified author of travel books
Ma·net \ma-ˈnā, mä-\ Édouard 1832–1883 Fr. painter
Ma·nil·i·us \mə-ˈnil-ē-əs\ Gaius 1st cent. B.C. Rom. polit.
Mann \ˈman\ Horace 1796–1859 Am. educ.
Mann \ˈmän, ˈman\ Thomas 1875–1955 Am. (Ger.-born) author
Man·ner·heim, von \ˈmän-ər-ˌhām, ˈman-, -ˌhīm\ Baron Carl Gustaf Emil 1867–1951 Finn. gen. & statesman
Man·ning \ˈman-iŋ\ Henry Edward 1808–1892 Eng. cardinal
Manning Timothy 1909– Am. cardinal
Mans·field \ˈmans-ˌfēld, ˈmanz-\ Katherine 1888–1923 pseud. of *Kathleen née Beau·champ* \ˈbē-chəm\ *Murry* Brit. (N.Z.-born) writer
Mansfield Richard 1854–1907 Eng. actor in Am.
Man·son \ˈman(t)-sən\ Sir Patrick 1844–1922 Brit. parasitologist
Man·sur, al- \ˌal-ˌman-ˈsu̇(ə)r\ 712?–775 Arab caliph (754–775); founder of Baghdad
Man·te·gna \män-ˈtān-yə\ Andrea 1431–1506 Ital. painter & engraver
Man·tle \ˈmant-^{ə}l\ (Robert) Burns 1873–1948 Am. journalist
Manuel Don Juan — see JUAN MANUEL
Ma·nu·tius \mə-ˈn(y)ü-sh(ē-)əs\ Al·dus \ˈȯl-dəs, ˈal-\ 1450–1515 *Teobaldo Mannucci or Manuzio* Ital. printer & classical scholar
Man·zo·ni \män(d)-ˈzō-nē\ Alessandro Francesco Tommaso Antonio 1785–1873 Ital. nov. & poet
Mao Tse-tung \ˌmau̇(d)-zə-ˈdu̇ŋ, ˌmau̇t-sə-\ 1893– Chin. Communist
Map \ˈmap\ Walter 1140?–?1209 Welsh writer
Ma·rat \mə-ˈrä\ Jean Paul 1743–1793 Fr. (Swiss-born) revolutionist
Mar·cel·lus \mär-ˈsel-əs\ Marcus Claudius 268?–208 B.C. Rom. gen.
March 1st Earl of — see Roger de MORTIMER
Mar·co·ni \mär-ˈkō-nē\ Marchese Guglielmo 1874–1937 Ital. electrical engineer & inventor
Marco Polo — see POLO
Mar·cos \ˈmär-kəs, -ˌkōs\ Ferdinand Edralin 1917– pres. of the Philippine Republic (1965–)
Marcus Aurelius — see Marcus Aurelius ANTONINUS
Mar·cu·se \mär-ˈkü-zə\ Herbert 1898– Am. (Ger.-born) philos.
Mar·ga·ret \ˈmär-g(ə-)rət\ **of Anjou** 1430–1482 *queen of Henry VI of England*
Margaret of Navarre 1492–1549 queen of Navarre (1544–49) & writer
Margaret of Valois 1553–1615 queen of Navarre
Margaret Rose 1930– *wife of Earl of Snowdon* princess of Gr. Brit.
Mar·gre·the II \mär-ˈgrāt-ə\ 1940– queen of Denmark (1972–)
Ma·ria The·re·sa \mə-ˌrē-ə-tə-ˈrā-sə, -ˈrā-zə\ 1717–1780 *wife of Emp. Francis I* queen of Hungary & Bohemia
Ma·rie \mə-ˈrē\ 1875–1938 queen of Rumania (1914–27); queen dowager (1927–38)
Marie An·toi·nette \ˌan-t(w)ə-ˈnet\ 1755–1793 *dau. of Maria Theresa & wife of Louis XVI of France*
Marie Louise 1791–1847 *dau. of Francis I of Austria & 2d wife of Napoleon I*
Marie de Mé·di·cis \-də-ˈmed-ə-(ˌ)chē, -ˌmäd-ə-ˈsē(s)\ 1573–1642 *2d wife of Henry IV of France*

ə abut	^{ə} kitten, F table	ər further	a back	ā bake	
ä cot, cart	à F bac	au̇ out	ch chin	e less	ē easy
g gift	i trip	ī life	j joke	k̲ G ich	^{n} F vin	ŋ sing
ō flow	ȯ flaw	œ F bœuf	œ̄ F feu	ȯi coin	th thing
th̲ this	ü loot	u̇ foot	ue G Füllen	ue̅ F rue	y yet
^{y} F digne \dēn^{y}\, nuit \nw^{y}ē\	yü few	yu̇ furious	zh vision		

Mar·in \ˈmar-ən\ John Cheri 1870–1953 Am. painter

Ma·ri·net·ti \ˌmar-ə-ˈnet-ē, ˌmär-\ Emilio Filippo Tommaso 1876–1944 Ital. poet

Ma·ri·ni \mə-ˈrē-nē\ *or* **Ma·ri·no** \-(ˌ)nō\ Giambattista 1569–1625 Ital. poet

Mar·i·on \ˈmer-ē-ən, ˈmar-ē-\ Francis 1732?–1795 *the Swamp Fox* Am. Revolutionary commander

Ma·ri·tain \ˌmar-ə-ˈta^{n}\ Jacques 1882–1973 Fr. philos. & diplomat

Mar·i·us \ˈmer-ē-əs, ˈmar-\ Gaius 155?–86 B.C. Rom. gen.

Ma·ri·vaux, de \ˌmar-ə-ˈvō\ Pierre Carlet de Chamblain 1688–1763 Fr. dram. & nov.

Mark Antony *or* **Anthony** — see Marcus ANTONIUS

Mark·ham \ˈmär-kəm\ (Charles) Edwin 1852–1940 Am. poet

Mar·ko·va \mär-ˈkō-və\ Ali·cia \ə-ˈlē-sē-ə\ 1910– *Alice Marks* Eng. dancer

Marlborough 1st Duke of — see John CHURCHILL

Mar·lowe \ˈmär-ˌlō\ Christopher 1564–1593 Eng. dram. — **Mar·lo·vi·an** \mär-ˈlō-vē-ən, -vyən\ *adj*

Marlowe Julia 1866–1950 pseud. of *Sarah Frances Frost* Am. (Eng.-born) actress

Mar·mont, de \mär-ˈmō^{n}\ Auguste Frédéric Louis Viesse 1774–1852 Duc *de Raguse* Fr. gen.; marshal of France

Mar·mon·tel \ˌmär-(ˌ)mō^{n}-ˈtel\ Jean François 1723–1799 Fr. author

Ma·rot \ma-ˈrō\ Clément 1495?–1544 Fr. poet

Mar·quand \mär-ˈkwänd\ John Phillips 1893–1960 Am. writer

Mar·quette \mär-ˈket\ Jacques 1637–1675 *Père* \ˌpi(ə)r, ˌpe(ə)r\ *Marquette* Jesuit missionary & explorer in Am.

Mar·quis \ˈmär-kwəs\ Donald Robert Perry 1878–1937 *Don* Am. humorist

Marquis Frederick James — see WOOLTON

Mar·ry·at \ˈmar-ē-ət\ Frederick 1792–1848 Eng. naval commander & nov.

Marsh \ˈmärsh\ Dame Ngaio \ˈnī-(ˌ)ō\ 1899– N.Z. writer

Mar·shall \ˈmär-shəl\ George Catlett 1880–1959 Am. gen. & diplomat

Marshall John 1755–1835 Am. jurist; chief justice U.S. Supreme Court (1801–35)

Marshall John Ross 1912– prime min. of N.Z. (1972)

Marshall Thomas Riley 1854–1925 vice-pres. of the U.S. (1913–21)

Marshall Thurgood 1908– Am. jurist

Mar·sil·i·us of Padua \mär-ˈsil-ē-əs\ 1290?–?1343 Ital. scholar

Mar·ston \ˈmär-stən\ John 1575?–1634 Eng. dram.

Martel Charles — see CHARLES MARTEL

Mar·tens \ˈmärt-ᵊnz\ Fëdor Fëdorovich 1845–1909 Russ. jurist

Mar·tial \ˈmär-shəl\ *ab* 40–*ab* 102 *Marcus Valerius Martialis* Rom. epigrammatist

Mar·tin \ˈmärt-ᵊn, mär-ta^{n}\ Saint 315?–?399 *Martin of Tours* \-ˈtu̇(ə)r\ patron saint of France

Mar·tin \ˈmärt-ᵊn\ Archer John Porter 1910– Brit. chem.

Martin Glenn Luther 1886–1955 Am. airplane manuf.

Martin Homer Dodge 1836–1897 Am. painter

Martin Joseph William 1884–1968 Am. publisher & polit.

Mar·tin du Gard \mär-ta^{n}-dü̅-gär\ Roger 1881–1958 Fr. nov.

Mar·ti·neau \ˈmärt-ᵊn-ˌō\ Harriet 1802–1876 Eng. nov. & econ.

Martineau James 1805–1900 *bro. of Harriet* Eng. theol. & philos.

Mar·ti·ni \mär-ˈtē-nē\ Simone 1283?–1344 Ital. painter

Mar·vell \ˈmär-vəl\ Andrew 1621–1678 Eng. poet & satirist

Marx \ˈmärks\ Karl 1818–1883 Ger. polit. philos. & socialist

Mary \ˈme(ə)r-ē, ˈma(ə)r-ē, ˈmā-rē\ 1867–1953 Princess *Victoria Mary of Teck; queen of George V of Eng.*

Mary I 1516–1558 *Mary Tudor; Bloody Mary* queen of Eng. (1553–58)

Mary II 1662–1694 joint Brit. sovereign with William III

Mary Stuart 1542–1587 *Mary, Queen of Scots* queen of Scot. (1542–67)

Ma·sac·cio \mə-ˈzäch-(ē-ˌ)ō\ 1401–1428 orig. *Tommaso Guidi* Ital. painter

Ma·sa·ryk \ˈmäs-ə-(ˌ)rik, ˈmas-\ Jan \ˈyän, ˈyan\ Gar·rigue \gə-ˈrēg\ 1886–1948 *son of T. G.* Czech diplomat & polit.

Ma·sa·ryk To·máš \ˈtō-ˌmäsh, ˈtäm-əs\ Garrigue 1850–1937 Czech philos; 1st pres. of Czechoslovakia (1918–35)

Ma·sca·gni \mä-ˈskän-yē, ma-\ Pietro 1863–1945 Ital. composer

Mase·field \ˈmās-ˌfēld\ John 1878–1967 Eng. author; poet laureate (1930–67)

Mas·i·nis·sa *or* **Mas·si·nis·sa** \ˌmas-ə-ˈnis-ə\ 238?–149 B.C. king of Numidia

Ma·son \ˈmās-ᵊn\ Charles 1730–1787 Eng. astron. & surveyor

Mason George 1725–1792 Am. revolutionary statesman

Mas·sa·soit \ˌmas-ə-ˈsȯit\ *d* 1661 sachem of Wampanoag Indians in eastern Massachusetts

Mas·sé·na \ˌmas-ā-ˈnä, mə-ˈsā-nə\ André 1758–1817 Duc *de Rivoli;* Prince *d'Ess·ling* \des-lēŋ\ Fr. soldier under Napoleon; marshal of France

Mas·se·net \ˌmas-ᵊn-ˈā, ma-ˈsnā\ Jules Émile Frédéric 1842–1912 Fr. composer

Mas·sey \ˈmas-ē\ Raymond 1896– Am. (Canad.-born) actor & producer

Massey William Ferguson 1856–1925 N.Z. statesman

Mas·sine \ma-ˈsēn\ Léonide 1894– Am. (Russ.-born) dancer & choreographer

Mas·sin·ger \ˈmas-ᵊn-jər\ Philip 1583–1640 Eng. dram.

Mas·son \ˈmas-ᵊn\ David 1822–1907 Scot. editor & author

Mas·ters \ˈmas-tərz\ Edgar Lee 1869–1950 Am. author

Math·er \ˈma$\underline{th}$-ər, ˈmath-\ Cotton 1663–1728 Am. clergyman & author

Mather Increase 1639–1723 *father of Cotton* Am. clergyman & author; pres. Harvard College (1685–1701)

Ma·tisse \ma-ˈtēs, mə-\ Henri 1869–1954 Fr. painter

Ma·tsu·o·ka \ˌmat-sə-ˈwō-kə, ˌmät-, -(ˌ)kä\ Yosuke 1880–1946 Jap. statesman

Mat·te·ot·ti \ˌmat-ē-ˈōt-ē, ˌmät-, -ˈȯt-\ Giacomo 1885–1924 Ital. socialist

Mat·thews \ˈmath-(ˌ)yüz\ (James) Brander 1852–1929 Am. educ. & author

Mat·ting·ly \ˈmat-iŋ-lē\ Garrett 1900–1962 Am. hist.

Maugham \ˈmȯm\ William Somerset 1874–1965 Eng. nov. & dram.

Mau·nou·ry \ˌmō-nə-ˈrē\ Michel-Joseph 1847–1923 Fr. gen.

Mau·pas·sant, de \ˌmō-pə-ˈsä^{n}\ (Henri René Albert) Guy 1850–1893 Fr. short-story writer

Mau·riac \ˌmȯr-ˈyäk, ˌmȯr-ē-ˈäk\ François 1885–1970 Fr. author

Mau·rice \ˈmȯr-əs, ˈmär-; mȯ-ˈrēs\ *Ger.* **Mo·ritz** \ˈmōr-əts, ˈmȯr-\ 1521–1553 elector of Saxony (1547–53) & gen.

Maurice of Nassau 1567–1625 Prince of *Orange* Du. gen. & statesman

Mau·rois \mȯr-ˈwä\ André 1885–1967 pseud. of *Émile Salomon Wilhelm Her·zog* \er-zȯg\ Fr. writer

Mau·ry \ˈmȯr-ē, ˈmär-\ Matthew Fontaine 1806–1873 Am. naval officer & oceanographer

Mau·ser \ˈmau̇-zər\ Peter Paul 1838–1914 & his bro. Wilhelm 1834–1882 Ger. inventors

Maw·son \ˈmȯs-ᵊn\ Sir Douglas 1882–1958 Brit. antarctic explorer & geologist

Max·im \ˈmak-səm\ Sir Hiram Stevens 1840–1916 Brit. (Am.-born) inventor

Maxim Hudson 1853–1927 *bro. of Sir Hiram* Am. inventor & explosives expert

Max·i·mil·ian \ˌmak-sə-ˈmil-yən\ 1832–1867 *bro. of Francis Joseph I of Austria* emp. of Mexico (1864–67)

Maximilian I 1459–1519 Holy Rom. emp. (1493–1519)

Maximilian II 1527–1576 Holy Rom. emp. (1564–76)

Max·well \ˈmak-ˌswel, -swəl\ James Clerk \ˈklärk\ 1831–1879 Scot. physicist

May \ˈmā\ Sir Thomas Erskine 1815–1886 1st Baron *Farn·bor·ough* \ˈfärn-ˌbər-ə, -ˌbə-rə, -b(ə-)rə\ Eng. constitutional jurist

Ma·ya·kov·ski \ˌmä-yə-ˈkȯf-skē, ˌmī-ə-, -ˈkȯv-\ Vladimir Vladimirovich 1893–1930 Russ. poet

Mayo \ˈmā-(ˌ)ō\ Charles Horace 1865–1939 & his bro. William James 1861–1939 Am. surgeons

Mayo Henry Thomas 1856–1937 Am. admiral

Ma·za·rin \ˌmaz-ə-ˈra^{n}\ Jules 1602–1661 Fr. cardinal & statesman

Maz·zi·ni \mät-ˈsē-nē, mäd-\ Giuseppe 1805–1872 Ital. patriot

Mc- — see MAC-

Mead \ˈmēd\ Margaret 1901– Am. anthropol.

Meade \ˈmēd\ George Gordon 1815–1872 Am. gen.

Mea·ny \ˈmē-nē\ George 1894– Am. labor leader

Med·a·war \ˈmed-ə-wər\ Peter Brian 1915– Eng. anatomist

Me·dei·ros \mə-ˈder-əs, -(ˌ)ōs\ Humberto 1915– Am. (Port.-born) cardinal

Me·di·ci, de \ˈmed-ə-(ˌ)chē\ Catherine — see CATHERINE DE MEDICIS

Medici, de' Cosimo *or* Cosmo 1389–1464 Florentine financier & polit.

Medici, de' Cosimo I 1519–1574 *Cosimo the Great;* Duke of *Florence;* Grand Duke of *Tuscany*

Medici, de' Giulio — see CLEMENT VII

Medici, de' Lorenzo 1449–1492 *Lorenzo the Magnificent* Florentine statesman, ruler, & patron

Me·di·na–Si·do·nia \mə-ˈdē-nə-sə-ˈdōn-yə\ 7th Duke of 1550–1615 *Alonso Pérez de Guzmán* Span. admiral

Meer van Delft, van der — see Jan VERMEER

Me·he·met Ali \mā-ˌmet-ä-ˈlē\ *or* **Mohammed Ali** 1769–1849 viceroy of Egypt (1805–48)

Meigh·en \ˈmē-ən\ Arthur 1874–1960 Canad. statesman; prime min. (1920–21; 1926)

Me·ir \me-ˈi(ə)r\ Golda 1898– *G. Mabovitz* or *Mabovich* prime min. of Israel (1969–)

Meis·so·nier \ˌmās-ᵊn-ˈyā, mā-ˈsən-(ˌ)yā\ (Jean Louis) Ernest 1815–1891 Fr. painter

Meit·ner \ˈmīt-nər\ Li·se \ˈlē-zə\ 1878–1968 Ger. physicist

Me·lanch·thon \mə-ˈlaŋ(k)-t(h)ən\ 1497–1560 *Philipp Schwarzert* Ger. scholar & religious reformer

Mel·ba \ˈmel-bə\ Dame Nellie 1861–1931 orig. *Helen Porter Mitchell* Austral. soprano

Mel·chers \ˈmel-chərz\ Gari 1860–1932 Am. painter

Mel·chi·or \ˈmel-kē-ˌȯ(ə)r\ Lau·ritz \ˈlau̇-rəts\ Lebrecht Hommel 1890–1973 Am. (Dan.-born) tenor

Mel·lon \ˈmel-ən\ Andrew William 1855–1937 Am. financier

Mel·ville \ˈmel-ˌvil\ Herman 1819–1891 Am. nov.

Mem·ling \ˈmem-liŋ\ *or* **Mem·linc** \-liŋk\ Hans 1430?–1495 Flem. painter

Me·nan·der \mə-ˈnan-dər\ 343?–?291 B.C. Greek dram.

Men·cius \ˈmen-ch(ē-)əs\ 372?–?289 B.C. *Mêng-tzŭ* or *Meng-tse* Chin. philos.

Menck·en \ˈmeŋ-kən, ˈmen-\ Henry Louis 1880–1956 Am. editor — **Menck·e·nian** \meŋ-ˈkē-nē-ən, men-\ *adj*

Men·del \ˈmen-dᵊl\ Gregor Johann 1822–1884 Austrian botanist

Men·de·le·ev \ˌmen-də-ˈlā-əf\ Dmitri Ivanovich 1834–1907 Russ. chem.

Men·dels·sohn \ˈmen-dᵊl-sən\ Moses 1729–1786 Ger. philos.

Mendelssohn–Bar·thol·dy \-bär-ˈt(h)ȯl-dē\ Jakob Ludwig Felix 1809–1847 *grandson of Moses Mendelssohn* Ger. composer, pianist, & conductor

Mendès-France \ma^{n}-des-fräns\ Pierre 1907– Fr. statesman

Men·do·za, de \men-ˈdō-zə\ Antonio 1485?–1552 Span. colonial administrator

Men·e·lik II \ˈmen-ᵊl-(ˌ)ik\ 1844–1913 emp. of Ethiopia (1889–1913)

Me·nén·dez de Av·i·lés \mə-ˈnen-dəs-dā-ˌäv-ə-ˈlās\ Pedro 1519–1574 Span. admiral; colonizer of Florida

Me·nes \ˈmē-(ˌ)nēz\ *fl* 3400 (3500?) B.C. Egyptian king; uniter of north & south kingdoms

Men·ning·er \ˈmen-iŋ-ər\ Karl Augustus 1893– Am. psychiatrist

Me·not·ti \mə-'nät-ē, -'nȯt-\ Gian-Carlo 1911– Am. (Ital.-born) composer
Me·nu·hin \'men-yə-wən\ Ye·hu·di \yə-'hüd-ē\ 1916– Am. violinist
Men·zies \'men-(,)zēz\ Sir Robert Gordon 1894– Austral. statesman; prime min. (1939–41; 1949–66)
Mer·ca·tor \(,)mər-'kāt-ər\ Gerhardus 1512–1594 *Gerhard Kremer* Flem. geographer
Mer·cier \mer-'syā, 'mer-sē-,ā\ Désiré Joseph 1851–1926 Belg. cardinal; primate of Belgium
Mer·e·dith \'mer-əd-əth\ George 1828–1909 Eng. nov. & poet
Meredith Owen — see E. R. Bulwer LYTTON
Mer·gen·tha·ler \'mər-gən-,thäl-ər, 'mer-gən-,täl-\ Ottmar 1854–1899 Am. (Ger.-born) inventor
Mé·ri·mée \'mer-ə-,mā, ,mā-rə-'\ Prosper 1803–1870 Fr. writer
Mer·ton \'mərt-^{ə}n\ Thomas 1915–1968 Am. clergyman & author
Mes·mer \'mez-mər, 'mes-\ Franz *or* Friedrich Anton 1734–1815 Austrian physician
Mes·sa·la Cor·vi·nus \mə-'säl-ə-,kȯr-'vī-nəs\ Marcus Valerius 1st cent. B.C. Rom. gen. & statesman
Mes·sa·li·na \,mes-ə-'lī-nə, -'lē-\ Valeria *d* A.D. 48 *3d wife of Emp. Claudius*
Mes·ser·schmitt \'mes-ər-,shmit\ Willy 1898– Ger. aircraft designer & manuf.
Mes·sier \mās-yā, 'mes-ē-,ā\ Charles 1730–1817 Fr. astron.
Mes·tro·vic \'mes(h)-trə-,vich\ Ivan 1883–1962 Am. (Yugoslavian-born) sculptor
Me·tax·as \me-,täk-'säs\ Joannes 1871–1941 Greek gen. & dictator
Metch·ni·koff \'mech-nə-,kȯf\ Élie 1845–1916 Russ. zool. & bacteriol.
Met·ter·nich, von \'met-ər-(,)nik, -(,)ni<u>k</u>\ Prince Klemens Wenzel Nepomuk Lothar 1773–1859 Austrian statesman
Mey·er \'mī(-ə)r\ Albert Gregory 1903–1965 Am. cardinal
Meyer Annie 1867–1951 née *Nathan* Am. educ. & writer
Mey·er·beer \'mī-ər-,bi(ə)r, -,be(ə)r\ Giacomo 1791–1864 *Jakob Liebmann Beer* Ger. composer
Mey·er·hof \'mī-ər-,hōf\ Otto 1884–1951 Ger. physiol.
Mi·chael \'mī-kəl\ *Rumanian* **Mi·hai** \mē-'hī\ 1921– *Michael Hohenzollern* king of Rumania (1927–30; 1940–47); abdicated
Mi·chel·an·ge·lo Buo·nar·ro·ti \,mī-kə-'lan-jə-,lō-,bwȯn-ə-'rȯt-ē, ,mik-ə-'lan-, ,mē-kə-'län-\ 1475–1564 Ital. sculptor, painter, architect, & poet — **Mi·chel·an·ge·lesque** \-,lan-jə-'lesk, -,län-\ *adj*
Mi·che·let \,mēsh-(ə-)'lā\ Jules 1798–1874 Fr. hist.
Mi·chel·son \'mī-kəl-sən\ Albert Abraham 1852–1931 Am. (Ger.-born) physicist
Mich·e·ner \'mich-(ə-)nər\ James Albert 1907– Am. author
Mich·ener \'mish-nər\ Roland 1900– Canad. polit.; gov.-gen. of Canada (1967–)
Mic·kie·wicz \mits-'kyā-vich\ Adam 1798–1855 Pol. poet
Mid·dle·ton \'mid-^{ə}l-tən\ Thomas 1570?–1627 Eng. dram.
Mies van der Ro·he \,mēs-,vän-də-'rō(-ə), ,mēz-\ Ludwig 1886–1969 Am. (Ger.-born) architect
Miff·lin \'mif-lən\ Thomas 1744–1800 Am. Revolutionary gen.
Mi·haj·lo·vić *or* **Mi·khai·lo·vitch** \mi-'hī-lə-,vich\ Draža *or* Dra·ja \'dräzh-ə\ 1893?–1946 Yugoslav gen.
Mi·ko·yan \,mē-kō-'yän\ Anas·tas \,än-ə-'stäs\ Ivanovich 1895– Russ. polit.; pres. U.S.S.R. (1964–65)
Miles \'mī(ə)lz\ Nelson Appleton 1839–1925 Am. gen.
Mi·lhaud \mē-'(y)ō\ Darius 1892– Fr. composer
Mill \'mil\ James 1773–1836 Scot. philos., hist., & econ.
Mill John Stuart 1806–1873 *son of James* Eng. philos. & econ.
Mil·lais \'mil-,ā, mil-'ā\ Sir John Everett 1829–1896 Eng. painter
Mil·lay \mil-'ā\ Edna St. Vincent 1892–1950 Am. poet
Mil·ler \'mil-ər\ Arthur 1915– Am. dram. & nov.
Miller Cincinnatus Hiner 1839–1913 pseud. *Joa·quin* \wä-'kēn, wȯ-\ *Miller* Am. poet
Miller Henry 1891– Am. writer
Miller Perry Gilbert Eddy 1905–1963 Am. literary critic & scholar
Miller William 1782–1849 Am. Adventist
Mil·le·rand \mēl-(ə-)rä^{n}\ Alexandre 1859–1943 Fr. statesman; pres. of France (1920–24)
Mil·let \mē-'yā, mi-'lā\ Jean François 1814–1875 Fr. painter
Mil·li·kan \'mil-i-kən\ Robert Andrew 1868–1953 Am. physicist
Mil·man \'mil-mən\ Henry Hart 1791–1868 Eng. poet & hist.
Milne \'mil(n)\ Alan Alexander 1882–1956 Eng. poet & dram.
Mil·ti·a·des \mil-'tī-ə-,dēz\ 540?–?489 B.C. Athenian gen.
Mil·ton \'milt-^{ə}n\ John 1608–1674 Eng. poet — **Mil·to·nian** \mil-'tō-nē-ən, -nyən\ *or* **Mil·ton·ic** \-'tän-ik\ *adj*
Mil·yu·kov \,mil-yə-'kȯf, -'kȯv\ Pavel Nikolaevich 1859–1943 Russ. polit. & hist.
Mi·not \'mī-nət\ George Richards 1885–1950 Am. physician
Min·ton \'mint-^{ə}n\ Sherman 1890–1965 Am. jurist
Min·u·it \'min-yə-wət\ *or* **Min·ne·wit** \'min-ə-,wit\ Peter 1580–1638 Du. colonial administrator in Am.
Mi·ra·beau, de \'mir-ə-,bō\ Comte 1749–1791 *Honoré Gabriel Victor Riqueti* Fr. orator & revolutionist
Mi·ró \mē-'rō\ Joan \zhü-'än\ 1893– Span. painter
Mi·shi·ma \'mē-shi-,mä, mə-'shē-mə\ Yukio 1925– Jap. writer
Mis·tral \mi-'sträl, -'stral\ Frédéric 1830–1914 Provençal poet
Mis·tral \mi-'sträl, -'stral\ Gabriela 1889–1957 *Lucila Godoy de Alcayaga* Chilean poet & educ.
Mitch·ell \'mich-əl\ John 1870–1919 Am. labor leader
Mitchell John Newton 1913– Am. lawyer; U.S. attorney general (1969–72)
Mitchell Maria 1818–1889 Am. astron.
Mitchell William 1879–1936 *Billy Mitchell* Am. gen.
Mit·ford \'mit-fərd\ Mary Russell 1787–1855 Eng. nov. & dram.
Mitford William 1744–1827 Eng. hist.
Mith·ri·da·tes VI \,mith-rə-'dāt-ēz\ *ab* 132–63 B.C. *the Great* king of Pontus (120–63)
Mi·tro·pou·los \mə-'träp-ə-ləs\ Di·mi·tri \də-'mē-trē\ 1896–1960 Am. (Greek-born) conductor
Mo·di·glia·ni \,mō-dēl-'yän-ē, ,mōd-^{ə}l-\ Amedeo 1884–1920 Ital. painter in France
Mo·djes·ka \mə-'jes-kə\ Helena 1840–1909 orig. *Modrzejewska* née *Opid* Pol.-born actress in Am.
Mohammed *var of* MUHAMMAD
Mo·ham·med Ri·za Pah·la·vi *or* **Pah·le·vi** \mō-'ham-əd-ri-'zä-'pal-ə-(,)vē, -'häm-\ 1919– shah of Iran (1941–)
Mois·san \mwä-'sä^{n}\ Henri 1852–1907 Fr. chem.
Mo·ley \'mō-lē\ Raymond 1886– Am. journalist
Mo·lière \mōl-'ye(ə)r, 'mōl-,\ 1622–1673 pseud. of *Jean Baptiste Poquelin* Fr. actor & dram.
Molina, de Tirso — see TIRSO DE MOLINA
Mol·nár \'mōl-,när, 'mȯl-\ Fe·renc \'fer-ən(t)s\ 1878–1952 Hung. author
Mo·lo·tov \'mäl-ə-,tȯf, 'mȯl-, 'mōl-, -,tȯv\ Vyacheslav Mikhailovich 1890– orig. *Skryabin* Russ. statesman
Molt·ke, von \'mōlt-kə\ Count Helmuth 1800–1891 Pruss. field marshal
Momm·sen \'mōm-zən\ Theodor \'tā-ō-,dōr\ 1817–1903 Ger. classical scholar & hist.
Monck *or* **Monk** \'məŋk\ George 1608–1670 1st Duke of *Albemarle* Eng. gen.
Mon·dri·an \'mȯn-drē-,än\ Piet 1872–1944 *Pieter Cornelis Mondriaan* Du. painter
Mo·net \mō-'nā\ Claude 1840–1926 Fr. painter
Mo·ne·ta \mō-'nāt-ə\ Ernesto Teodoro 1833–1918 Ital. journalist & pacifist
Mon·i·er–Wil·liams \,mən-ē-ər-'wil-yəmz, ,män-\ Sir Monier 1819–1899 Eng. Sanskrit scholar
Mo·niz \mü-'nēsh\ Antonio Caetano de Abrere Freire Egas 1874–1955 Port. medical scientist
Mon·mouth \'mən-məth, 'män-\ Duke of 1649–1685 *James Scott, son of Charles II of Eng.* Eng. rebel & claimant to the throne
Mon·roe \mən-'rō\ James 1758–1831 5th pres. of U.S. (1817–25)
Mon·ta·gna \mən-'tän-yə\ Bartolommeo 1450?–1523 Ital. painter
Mon·ta·gu \'mänt-ə-,gyü, 'mənt-\ Lady Mary Wortley 1689–1762 Eng. letter writer
Mon·taigne, de \män-'tān, mō^{n}-ten^{y}\ Michel Eyquem 1533–1592 Fr. essayist
Mont·calm de Saint–Vé·ran, de \mänt-'kä(l)m-də-,sa^{n}-vā-'rä^{n}\ Marquis Louis Joseph 1712–1759 Fr. field marshal in Canada
Mon·tes·pan, de \'män-tes-pä^{n}, 'mänt-ə-,span\ Marquise 1641–1707 née (*Françoise Athénaïs*) *Rochechouart; mistress of Louis XIV*
Mon·tes·quieu, de \,mänt-əs-'kyü, -'kyə(r), -'kyœ\ Baron *de La Brède et* 1689–1755 *Charles de Secondat* Fr. lawyer & polit. philos.
Mon·tes·so·ri \,mänt-ə-'sōr-ē, -'sȯr-\ Maria 1870–1952 Ital. physician & educator
Mon·teux \mō^{n}-'tə(r), -'tœ\ Pierre 1875–1964 Am. (Fr.-born) conductor
Mon·te·ver·di \,mänt-ə-'ve(ə)rd-ē, -'vərd-\ Claudio Giovanni Antonio 1567–1643 Ital. composer
Mon·te·zu·ma II \,mänt-ə-'zü-mə\ 1480?–1520 last Aztec emp. of Mexico (1502–20)
Mont·fort, de \'mänt-fərt\ Simon 1208?–1265 Earl of *Leicester* Eng. soldier & statesman
Mont·fort l'Amau·ry, de \,mänt-fərt-'lā-mə-rē, mō^{n}-'fō(ə)r-,lā-,mō-'rē\ Simon IV 1160?–1218 Earl of *Leicester* & Comte de *Toulouse; father of prec.* Fr. crusader
Mont·gol·fier \mänt-'gäl-fē-ər, ,fē-,ā\ Joseph Michel 1740–1810 & his bro. Jacques Étienne 1745–1799 Fr. inventors & acronauts
Mont·gom·ery \(,)mən(t)-'gəm-(ə-)rē, män(t)-, -'gäm-\ Bernard Law 1887– 1st Viscount Brit. field marshal
Mont·mo·ren·cy, de \,mänt-mə-'ren(t)-sē\ Duc Anne 1493–1567 Fr. soldier; constable (1537)
Mon·trose \män-'trōz\ James Graham 1st Marquis of 1612–1650 Scot. Royalist
Moo·dy \'müd-ē\ Dwight Lyman 1837–1899 Am. evangelist
Moody William Vaughn 1869–1910 Am. poet & dram.
Moo·ney \'mü-nē\ Edward 1882–1958 Am. cardinal
Moore \'mō(ə)r, 'mȯ(ə)r, 'mu(ə)r\ George 1852–1933 Irish author
Moore George Edward 1873–1958 Eng. philos.
Moore Henry 1898– Brit. sculptor
Moore John Bassett 1860–1947 Am. jurist
Moore Marianne Craig 1887–1972 Am. poet
Moore Thomas 1779–1852 Irish poet
Moore–Brab·a·zon \-'brab-ə-zən\ John Theodore Cuthbert 1884–1964 1st Baron *Brabazon of Ta·ra* \'tär-ə\ Brit. aviator & administrator
Mo·ra·via \mō-'räv-ē-ə\ Alberto 1907– real name *Pincherle* Ital. writer
More \'mō(ə)r, 'mȯ(ə)r\ Hannah 1745–1833 Eng. religious writer
More Henry 1614–1687 Eng. philos.
More Paul Elmer 1864–1937 Am. essayist & critic
More Sir Thomas 1478–1535 *Saint* Eng. statesman & author
Mo·reau \mȯ-rō\ Jean Victor 1763–1813 Fr. gen.
Mor·gan \'mȯr-gən\ Conway Lloyd 1852–1936 Eng. zool. & psychol.
Morgan Daniel 1736–1802 Am. Revolutionary gen.
Morgan Sir Henry 1635?–1688 Eng. buccaneer
Morgan John Hunt 1825–1864 Am. Confed. cavalry officer
Morgan John Pier·pont \'pi(ə)r-,pänt\ 1837–1913 Am. financier
Morgan John Pierpont 1867–1943 *son of J. P.* Am. financier
Morgan Thomas Hunt 1866–1945 Am. zool.
Mor·gen·thau \'mȯr-gən-,thȯ\ Henry 1891–1967 U.S. secy. of the treas. (1934–45)
Mor·i·son \'mȯr-ə-sən, 'mär-\ Samuel Eliot 1887– Am. hist.

ə abut · ^{ə} kitten, F table · ər further · a back · ā bake · ä cot, cart · å F bac · au̇ out · ch chin · e less · ē easy · g gift · i trip · ī life · j joke · <u>k</u> G ich · ^{n} F vin · ŋ sing · ō flow · ȯ flaw · œ F bœu f · $\bar{\text{œ}}$ F feu · ȯi coin · th thing · <u>th</u> this · ü loot · u̇ foot · ue G Füllen · $\bar{\text{ue}}$ F rue · y yet · ^{y} F digne \dēn^{y}\, nuit \nw^{y}ē\ · yü few · yu̇ furious · zh vision

Morison Stanley 1889–1968 Eng. type designer
Mo·ri·sot \mȯ-rē-zō\ Berthe 1841–1895 Fr. painter
Mor·ley \'mȯr-lē\ Christopher Darlington 1890–1957 Am. writer
Morley John 1838–1923 Viscount *Morley of Blackburn* Eng. statesman & writer
Mor·nay, de \mȯr-nā\ Philippe 1549–1623 Seigneur du *Plessis-Marly; Duplessis-Mornay* Fr. Huguenot
Mor·ris \'mȯr-əs, 'mär-\ Gou·ver·neur \ˌgəv-ə(r)-'ni(ə)r\ 1752–1816 Am. statesman & diplomat
Morris Robert 1734–1806 Am. financier & statesman
Morris William 1834–1896 Eng. poet, artist, & socialist
Mor·ri·son \'mȯr-ə-sən, 'mär-\ Robert 1782–1834 Scot. missionary in China
Morrison of Lambeth Baron 1888–1965 *Herbert Stanley Morrison* Eng. labor leader & polit.
Morse \'mȯ(ə)rs\ Samuel Finley Breese 1791–1872 Am. artist & inventor
Mor·ti·mer, de \'mȯrt-ə-mər\ Roger (IV) 1287–1330 1st Earl of *March* Welsh rebel & paramour of Isabella, Queen of Edward II of Eng.
Mor·ton \'mȯrt-ᵊn\ Levi Parsons 1824–1920 Am. banker; vice-pres. of the U.S. (1889–93)
Morton Rogers Clark Ballard 1914– U.S. secy. of the interior (1971–)
Morton William Thomas Green 1819–1868 Am. dentist
Mos·by \'mōz-bē\ John Singleton 1833–1916 Am. lawyer & Confed. cavalry officer
Mos·cic·ki \mȯsh-'chēt-skē, -'chit-\ Ignacy 1867–1946 Pol. chem.; pres. of Poland (1926–39)
Mo·ses \'mō-zəz *also* -zəs\ Anna Mary née *Robertson* 1860–1961 *Grandma Moses* Am. painter
Mos·ley \'mōz-lē\ Sir Oswald Er·nald \'ərn-ᵊld\ 1896– Eng. polit.
Moth·er·well \'məth-ər-ˌwel, -wəl\ Robert 1915– Am. artist
Mo Ti \'mō-'dē\ *or* **Mo–tzu** \'mōd-'zə\ 5th-4th cent. B.C. Chin. philos.
Mot·ley \'mät-lē\ John Lothrop 1814–1877 Am. hist.
Mo·ton \'mōt-ᵊn\ Robert Russa 1867–1940 Am. educ.
Mott \'mät\ John Raleigh 1865–1955 Am. Y.M.C.A. leader
Mott Lucretia 1798–1880 née *Coffin* Am. social reformer
Mot·teux \mä-'tə(r), 'mä-ˌ\ Peter Anthony 1660 or 1663–1718 Eng. (Fr.-born) dram. & translator
Moul·ton \'mōlt-ᵊn\ Forest Ray 1872–1952 Am. astron.
Moul·trie \'mül-trē, 'mōl-\ William 1730–1805 Am. Revolutionary gen.
Mount·bat·ten \maůnt-'bat-ᵊn\ Louis, Earl 1900– Prince *Louis of Bat·ten·berg* \'bat-ᵊn-ˌbərg\ Brit. admiral; 1st gov.-gen. of India (1947–48); chief of defense staff (1959–65)
Mountbatten Philip, Duke of Edinburgh — see PHILIP
Mo·zart \'mōt-ˌsärt\ Wolfgang Amadeus 1756–1791 Austrian composer — **Mo·zart·ean** *also* **Mo·zart·ian** \mōt-'särt-ē-ən\ *adj*
Muench \'minch\ Aloisius Joseph 1889–1962 Am. cardinal
Mu·ham·mad \mō-'ham-əd, -'häm- *also* mü-\ 570–632 Arab prophet & founder of Islam
Mu·ham·mad \mō-'ham-əd, mü-\ Elijah 1897– *E. Poole* Am. religious leader
Müh·len·berg \'myü-lən-ˌbərg\ Henry Melchior 1711–1787 Ger.-born Lutheran clergyman in Am.
Muir \'myů(ə)r\ John 1838–1914 Am. (Scot.-born) naturalist
Mul·ler \'məl-ər\ Hermann Joseph 1890–1967 Am. geneticist
Mül·ler \'myül-ər, 'mil-, 'məl-\ Friedrich Max 1823–1900 Brit. (Ger.-born) philologist
Müller Johann 1436–1476 *Regiomontanus* Ger. astron.
Müller Paul 1899–1965 Swiss chem.
Mum·ford \'məm(p)-fərd\ Lewis 1895– Am. writer
Munch \'můnch, 'mᵫnch\ Charles 1891–1968 Fr.-born conductor
Munch \'můŋk\ Edvard 1863–1944 Norw. artist
Münch·hau·sen, von \'mᵫnk-ˌhaůz-ᵊn\ Baron Karl Friedrich Hieronymus 1720–1797 Baron *Mun·chau·sen* \'mən-ˌchaůz-ᵊn, 'mün-, -ˌchȯz-\ Ger. hunter, soldier, & supposed teller of absurdly exaggerated stories
Mun·de·lein \'mən-də-ˌlīn\ George William 1872–1939 Am. cardinal
Mu·ñoz Ma·rín \(ˌ)mün-ˌyōs-mə-'rēn, -ˌyōz-\ Luis 1898– Puerto Rican polit.
Munro H. H. — see SAKI
Mun·sey \'mən(t)-sē, 'mən-zē\ Frank Andrew 1854–1925 Am. publisher
Mün·ster·berg \'mün(t)-stər-ˌbərg, 'myün(t), 'mən(t)-\ Hugo 1863–1916 Ger.-born psychol. in Am.
Mu·ra·sa·ki \ˌm(y)ůr-ə-'säk-ē\ Baroness 11th cent. *Murasaki Shikibu* Jap. novelist
Mu·rat \myů-'rä, mᵫ-\ Joachim 1767?–1815 Fr. gen.; marshal of France; king of Naples (1808–15)
Mur·doch \'mər-dək, -ˌdäk\ (Jean) Iris 1919– Brit. (Irish-born) writer
Mu·ril·lo \myů-'ril-(ˌ)ō, m(y)ů-'rē-(ˌ)ō\ Bartolomé Esteban 1617–1682 Span. painter
Mur·phy \'mər-fē\ Frank 1890–1949 Am. jurist
Murphy Robert Daniel 1894– Am. diplomat
Murphy William Parry 1892– Am. physician
Mur·ray \'mər-ē, 'mə-rē\ (George) Gilbert (Aimé) 1866–1957 Brit. classical scholar
Murray Sir James Augustus Henry 1837–1915 Brit. lexicographer
Murray Lindley 1745–1826 Am. grammarian
Murray Philip 1886–1952 Am. labor leader
Mur·row \'mər-(ˌ)ō, 'mə-(ˌ)rō\ Edward Roscoe 1908–1965 Am. news commentator
Mus·kie \'məs-kē\ Edmund Sixtus 1914– Am. polit.
Mu·sorg·ski *or* **Mous·sorg·sky** \mů-'sȯrg-skē, -'zȯrg-\ Mo·dest \mō-'dest\ Petrovich 1835–1881 Russ. composer
Mus·set, de \myü-'sā\ (Louis Charles) Alfred 1810–1857 Fr. poet
Mus·so·li·ni \ˌmü-sə-'lē-nē, ˌmůs-ə-\ Be·ni·to \bə-'nēt-(ˌ)ō\ 1883–1945 *Il Du·ce* \ēl-'dü-(ˌ)chā\ Ital. Fascist premier (1922–45)

Mustafa (*or* **Mustapha**) **Kemal Pasha** — see KEMAL ATATÜRK
Mu·tsu·hi·to \ˌmüt-sə-'hē-(ˌ)tō\ 1852–1912 *Mei·ji* \'mā-(ˌ)jē\ emp. of Japan (1867–1912)
Muz·zey \'məz-ē\ David Saville 1870–1965 Am. hist.
My·ron \'mī-rən\ 5th cent. B.C. Greek sculptor
Na·bo·kov \nə-'bȯ-kəf\ Vladimir Vladimirovich 1899– Am. (Russ.-born) nov. & poet
Na·der \'nād-ər\ Ralph 1934– Am. lawyer & writer
Nai·du \'nīd-(ˌ)ü\ Sarojini 1879–1949 Hindu poet & reformer
Namby–Pamby — see Ambrose PHILIPS
Na·mier \'na-ˌmi(ə)r\ Sir Lewis Bernstein 1888–1960 Brit. hist.
Na·nak \'nän-ək\ 1469–1538 founder of the Sikh faith in India
Nan·sen \'nän(t)-sən, 'nan(t)-\ Frid·tjof \'frich-ˌȯf\ 1861–1930 Norw. arctic explorer, zool., & statesman
Na·pier \'nā-pē-ər, -ˌpi(ə)r; nə-'pi(ə)r\ Sir Charles James 1782–1853 Brit. gen.
Napier John 1550–1617 Laird of *Mer·chis·ton* \'mər-kə-stən\ Scot. math.
Napier Robert Cornelis 1810–1880 1st Baron *Napier of Mag·da·la* \'mag-də-lə\ Brit. field marshal
Na·po·leon I \nə-'pōl-yən, -'pō-lē-ən\ *or* **Napoleon Bo·na·parte** \'bō-nə-ˌpärt\ 1769–1821 emp. of the French (1804–15)
Napoleon II 1811–1832 *L'Ai·glon* \lā-'glō^{n}\; Duc *de Reichstadt; son of Napoleon I & Marie Louise*
Napoleon III 1808–1873 *Louis Napoleon; son of Louis Bonaparte & Hortense de Beauharnais* emp. of the French (1852–70)
Nar·vá·ez, de \när-'vä-ˌäs\ Pánfilo 1480?–1528 Span. soldier in Am.
Nash \'nash\ Ogden 1902–1971 Am. poet
Nash *or* **Nashe** \'nash\ Thomas 1567–1601 Eng. satirist & dram.
Nash Walter 1882–1968 prime min. of N.Z. (1957–60)
Na·smyth \'nā-ˌsmith, 'näz-məth\ Alexander 1758–1840 Scot. painter
Nas·ser \'näs-ər, 'nas-\ Ga·mal \gə-'mäl\ Ab·del \'äb-dᵊl\ 1918–1970 Egyptian polit.; pres. of Egypt (1956–70)
Nast \'nast\ Thomas 1840–1902 Am. (Ger.-born) cartoonist
Na·than \'nā-thən\ George Jean 1882–1958 Am. editor & dramatic critic
Nathan Robert 1894– Am. nov.
Na·tion \'nā-shən\ Car·ry \'kar-ē\ Amelia 1846–1911 née *Moore* Am. temperance agitator
Neb·u·chad·nez·zar \ˌneb-(y)ə-kəd-'nez-ər\ *or* **Neb·u·cha·drez·zar** \-kə-'drez-\ *d* 562 B.C. Chaldean king of Babylon (605–562)
Nec·ker \nā-'ke(ə)r, 'nek-ər\ Jacques 1732–1804 *father of Mme. de Staël* Fr. (Swiss-born) financier & statesman
Neh·ru \'ne(ə)r-(ˌ)ü, 'nā-(ˌ)rü\ Ja·wa·har·lal \jə-'wä-hər-ˌläl\ 1889–1964 *son of Motilal* Indian nationalist; prime min. (1947–64)
Nehru Pun·dit \'pən-dət\ Mo·ti·lal \'mōt-ᵊl-ˌäl\ 1861–1931 Indian nationalist
Neill \'nē(ə)l\ Alexander Sutherland 1883–1973 Brit. educ.
Neil·son \'nē(ə)l-sən\ William Allan 1869–1946 Am. (Scot.-born) educ.; pres. Smith Coll. (1917–39)
Nel·son \'nel-sən\ Viscount 1758–1805 *Horatio Nelson* Brit. admiral
Ne·pos \'nē-ˌpäs, 'nep-ˌäs\ Cornelius 1st cent. B.C. Rom. hist.
Ne·ri, de' \'ne(ə)r-ē, 'nā-rē\ San Filippo 1515–1595 Saint *Philip Neri* Ital. founder (1564) of "Fathers of the Oratory"
Nernst \'ne(ə)rn(t)st\ Walther Hermann 1864–1941 Ger. physicist & chem.
Ne·ro \'nē-(ˌ)rō, 'ni(ə)r-(ˌ)ō\ 37–68 *Nero Claudius Caesar Drusus Germanicus* orig. *Lucius Domitius Ahenobarbus* Rom. emp. 54–68 — **Ne·ro·ni·an** \ni-'rō-nē-ən\ *or* **Ne·ron·ic** \-'rän-ik\ *adj*
Ne·ru·da \nā-'rüd-ə, -'rü-(ˌ)thä\ Pablo 1904–1973 Chilean poet & diplomat
Ner·va \'nər-və\ Marcus Cocceius 35?–98 Rom. emp. (96–98)
Ner·vi \'ne(ə)r-vē\ Pier Luigi 1891– Ital. structural engineer
Nes·to·ri·us \ne-'stōr-ē-əs, -'stȯr-\ *d ab* 451 patriarch of Constantinople (428–431)
Neu·rath, von \'nȯi-ˌrät\ Baron Konstantin 1873–1956 Ger. diplomat
Nev·el·son \'nev-əl-sən\ Louise 1900– Am. (Russ.-born) sculptor
Neville Richard — see Earl of WARWICK
Nev·in \'nev-ən\ Ethelbert Woodbridge 1862–1901 Am. composer
Nev·ins \'nev-ənz\ Allan 1890–1971 Am. hist.
New·bolt \'n(y)ü-ˌbōlt\ Sir Henry John 1862–1938 Eng. author
New·comb \'n(y)ü-kəm\ Simon 1835–1909 Am. (Canad.-born) astron.
New·man \'n(y)ü-mən\ John Henry 1801–1890 Eng. cardinal & writer
New·ton \'n(y)üt-ᵊn\ Sir Isaac 1642–1727 Eng. math. & natural philos.
Ney \'nā\ Michel 1769–1815 Duc *d'Elchingen;* Prince *de la Moskova* Fr. soldier; marshal of France
Nich·o·las \'nik-(ə-)ləs\ Saint 4th cent. Christian prelate; patron saint of children
Nicholas I 1796–1855 czar of Russia (1825–55)
Nicholas II 1868–1918 czar of Russia (1894–1917)
Nicholas Grand Duke 1856–1929 Russ. gen. & monarchist
Nicholas of Cu·sa \-'kyü-sə, -zə\ 1401–1464 R.C. prelate, math., & philos.
Nich·ols \'nik-əlz\ Anne 1891–1966 Am. dram.
Nich·ol·son \'nik-əl-sən\ Ben 1894– Brit. artist
Nicholson Sir Francis 1655–1728 Brit. administrator in Am.
Nicholson Francis 1753–1844 Eng. watercolorist
Ni·ci·as \'nis(h)-ē-əs\ *d* 413 B.C. Athenian gen. & statesman
Nic·o·lay \'nik-ə-ˌlā\ John George 1832–1901 Am. biographer
Ni·co·let \ˌnik-ə-'lā, -'let\ Jean 1598–1642 Fr. explorer in North America
Ni·colle \nē-kȯl\ Charles Jean Henri 1866–1936 Fr. physician & bacteriol.
Nic·ol·son \'nik-əl-sən\ Sir Harold George 1886–1968 Eng. biographer & diplomat

Nie·buhr \ˈnē-ˌbu̇(ə)r, -bər\ Barthold Georg 1776–1831 Ger. hist., statesman, & philologist
Niebuhr Rein·hold \ˈrīn-ˌhōld\ 1892–1971 Am. theol. — **Nie·buhr·ian** \nē-ˈbu̇r-ē-ən\ *adj*
Niel·sen \ˈnē(ə)l-sən\ Carl August 1865–1931 Dan. composer
Niem·ce·wicz \n(e-)em-ˈsā-vich\ Julian Ursyn 1758–1841 Pol. patriot & writer
Nie·mey·er \ˈnē-ˌmī(-ə)r\ Oscar 1907– Brazilian architect
Nie·möl·ler \ˈnē-ˌmə(r)l-ər, -ˌmœl-\ Martin 1892– Ger. anti-Nazi Protestant theol.
Nietz·sche \ˈnē-chə, -chē\ Friedrich Wilhelm 1844–1900 Ger. philos. — **Nietz·sche·an** \-chē-ən\ *adj*
Night·in·gale \ˈnīt-ᵊn-ˌgāl, -iŋ-\ Florence 1820–1910 Eng. nurse & philanthropist
Ni·jin·ska \nə-ˈzhin-skə, -ˈjin-\ Bro·ni·sla·va \ˌbrän-ə-ˈsläv-ə\ 1891–1972 *sister of following* Russ. dancer & choreographer
Ni·jin·sky \-skē\ Was·law \ˈvät-släf\ 1890–1950 Russ. ballet dancer
Nils·son \ˈnil-sən\ Birgit 1918– Swed. soprano
Nim·itz \ˈnim-əts\ Chester William 1885–1966 Am. admiral
Nin \ˈnēn\ Anaïs 1903– Am. (Fr.-born) author
Nit·ti \ˈnit-ē, ˈnēt-\ Francesco Saverio 1868–1953 Ital. econ. & statesman
Nix·on \ˈnik-sən\ Richard Mil·hous \ˈmil-ˌhau̇s\ 1913– Am. lawyer; 37th pres. of the U.S. (1969–)
Nkru·mah \en-ˈkrü-mə, eŋ-\ Kwa·me \ˈkwäm-ē\ 1909–1972 Ghanaian prime min. (1957–60); 1st president (1960–66)
No·bel \nō-ˈbel\ Alfred Bernhard 1833–1896 Swed. manuf., inventor, & philanthropist
No·bi·le \ˈnō-bə-ˌlā\ Umberto 1885– Ital. arctic explorer & aeronautical engineer
No·el–Ba·ker \ˌnō-əl-ˈbā-kər\ Philip John 1889– Brit. polit.
No·gu·chi \nō-ˈgü-chē\ Hideyo 1876–1928 Am. (Jap.-born) bacteriol.
No·gu·chi Isamu 1904– Am. sculptor
No·guès \nō-ˈges\ Auguste 1876–1971 Fr. gen.
No·mu·ra \nō-ˈmu̇r-ə\ Kichisaburo 1877–1964 Jap. admiral & diplomat
Nor·dau \ˈnȯ(ə)r-ˌdau̇\ Max Simon 1849–1923 orig. *Süd·feld* \ˈzu̇et-ˌfelt\ Ger. physician, author, & Zionist
Nor·den·skjöld \ˈnu̇rd-ᵊn-ˌshəld, -ˌshu̇ld, -ˌshēld\ Baron Nils Adolf Erik 1832–1901 Swed. arctic explorer
Nor·di·ca \ˈnȯrd-i-kə\ Lillian 1857–1914 pseud. *of Lillian Norton* Am. soprano
Nor·ris \ˈnȯr-əs, ˈnär-\ Charles Gilman 1881–1945 Am. nov.
Norris Frank 1870–1902 *Benjamin Franklin; bro. of C. G.* Am. nov.
Norris George William 1861–1944 Am. statesman
Norris Kathleen 1880–1966 *wife of C. G.* Am. nov.
North \ˈnȯ(ə)rth\ Christopher — see WILSON
North Frederick 1732–1792 *Lord North* Eng. statesman; prime min. (1770–82)
North Sir Thomas 1535–?1601 Eng. translator
Northcliffe Viscount — see HARMSWORTH
Nor·throp \ˈnȯr-thrəp\ John Howard 1891– Am. scientist
Nor·ton \ˈnȯrt-ᵊn\ Charles Eliot 1827–1908 Am. author & educ.
Norton Thomas 1532–1584 Eng. lawyer & poet
Nos·tra·da·mus \ˌnäs-trə-ˈdā-məs, ˌnōs-trə-ˈdäm-əs\ 1503–1566 Fr. physician & astrologer
No·vi·kov \ˈnō-və-ˌkȯf, -ˌkȯv\ Nikolai Vasilievich 1903– Russ. diplomat
Noyes \ˈnȯiz\ Alfred 1880–1958 Eng. poet
Nu·re·yev \nu̇-ˈrā-yəf\ Rudolph 1939– Brit. (Russ.-born) ballet dancer
Nut·ting \ˈnət-iŋ\ Wallace 1861–1941 Am. antiquarian
Nye \ˈnī\ Edgar Wilson 1850–1896 *Bill* Am. humorist
Oates \ˈōts\ Joyce Carol 1938– Am. writer
Oates Titus 1649–1705 Brit. fabricator of the Popish Plot
O'·Boyle \ō-ˈbȯi(ə)l\ Patrick Aloysius 1896– Am. cardinal
Obrenović Alexander I — see ALEXANDER
O'·Bri·en \ō-ˈbrī-ən\ Lawrence Francis 1917– U.S. postmaster general (1965–68)
O'·Ca·sey \ō-ˈkā-sē\ Sean \ˈshȯn\ 1880–1964 Irish dram.
Oc·cam *or* **Ock·ham** \ˈäk-əm\ William of 1300?–?1349 Eng. philos. — **Oc·cam·is·tic** *or* **Ock·ham·is·tic** \ˌäk-ə-ˈmis-tik\ *adj*
Oc·cleve \ˈäk-ˌlēv\ *var of* HOCCLEVE
Ochoa \ō-ˈchō-ə\ Severo 1905– Am. (Span.-born) biochem.
Ochs \ˈäks\ Adolph Simon 1858–1935 Am. newspaper publisher
O'·Con·nell \ō-ˈkän-ᵊl\ Daniel 1775–1847 Irish polit. agitator
O'Connell William Henry 1859–1944 Am. cardinal
O'·Con·nor \ō-ˈkän-ər\ Frank 1903–1966 pseud. of *Michael John O'Donovan* Irish author
O'Connor Thomas Power 1848–1929 *Tay Pay* \ˈtā-ˈpā\ Irish journalist
Octavian *or* **Octavianus** — see AUGUSTUS
Odets \ō-ˈdets\ Clifford 1906–1963 Am. playwright
Odo·a·cer \ˈōd-ə-ˌwā-sər, ˈäd-\ 434?–493 1st barbarian ruler of Italy (476–493)
Oeh·len·schlä·ger \ˈə(r)l-ən-ˌshlā-gər, ˈœl-\ Adam Gottlob 1779–1850 Dan. poet & dram.
O'·Fao·láin \ˌō-fə-ˈlȯn\ Seán \ˈshȯn\ 1900– Irish author
Of·fen·bach \ˈȯf-ən-ˌbäk, -ˌbäk\ Jacques 1819–1880 Fr. composer
O'·Fla·her·ty \ō-ˈfla-(h)ər-tē\ Li·am \ˈlē-əm\ 1896– Irish nov.
Og·a·dai \ˈäg-ə-ˌdī\ 1185–1241 Mongol khan (1229–41)
Og·den \ˈȯg-dən, ˈäg-\ Charles Kay 1889–1957 Brit. psychol.
Ogle·thorpe \ˈō-gəl-ˌthȯrp\ James Edward 1696–1785 Eng. philanthropist & gen.; founder of Georgia
O'·Hara \ō-ˈhar-ə\ John Henry 1905–1970 Am. author
O'·Hig·gins \ō-ˈhig-ənz, ō-ˈē-gən(t)s\ Bernardo 1778–1842 *Liberator of Chile* Chilean soldier & stateman
Ohm \ˈōm\ Georg Simon 1787–1854 Ger. physicist
Ois·trakh \ˈȯis-trək\ David Fyodorovich 1908– Russ. violinist
O'·Keeffe \ō-ˈkēf\ Georgia 1887– Am. painter
O'·Kel·ly \ō-ˈkel-ē\ Seán \ˈshȯn\ Thomas 1883–1966 Irish journalist; pres. of Republic of Ireland (1945–59)
O'Kelly Seu·mas \ˈshā-məs\ 1881–1918 Irish writer
Olaf I \ˈō-ləf, -ləv\ 969–1000 *Olaf Trygg·ves·son* \ˈtrig-və-sən\ king of Norway (995–1000)
Olaf II 995?–1030 Saint *Olaf* king of Norway (1016–28)
Olav V \ˈō-ləf, -ləv\ 1903– king of Norway (1957–)
Old·cas·tle \ˈōl(d)-ˌkas-əl\ Sir John 1377?–1417 Baron *Cob·ham* \-ˈkäb-əm\ Eng. Lollard leader
Oliv·i·er \ō-ˈliv-ē-ˌā\ Laurence Kerr 1907– Baron *Olivier of Brighton* Eng. actor
Olm·sted \ˈōm-ˌsted, ˈäm-, -stəd\ Frederick Law 1822–1903 Am. landscape architect
Omar Khay·yám \ˌō-ˌmär-ˌkī-ˈ(y)äm, ˌō-mər-, -ˈ(y)am\ *d ab* 1123 Pers. poet & astron.
O'·Neill \ō-ˈnē(ə)l\ Eugene Gladstone 1888–1953 Am. dram.
On·ions \ˈən-yənz\ Charles Talbut 1873–1965 Eng. lexicographer
Op·pen·heim \ˈäp-ən-ˌhīm\ Edward Phillips 1866–1946 Eng. nov.
Op·pen·hei·mer \-ˌhī-mər\ Julius Robert 1904–1967 Am. physicist
Or·ca·gna \ȯr-ˈkän-yə\ 1308?–?1368 *Andrea di Cione* Florentine painter, sculptor, & architect
Or·czy \ˈȯrt-sē\ Baroness Em·mus·ka \ˈem-əsh-kə\ 1865–1947 Eng. (Hung.-born) nov. & dram.
Orff \ˈȯ(ə)rf\ Carl 1895– Ger. composer
Or·i·gen \ˈȯr-ə-jən, ˈär-\ 185?–?254 Greek writer, teacher, & church father
Or·lan·do \ȯr-ˈlan-(ˌ)dō, -ˈlän-\ Vittorio Emanuele 1860–1952 Ital. statesman
Or·man·dy \ˈȯr-mən-dē\ Eugene 1899– Am. (Hung.-born) conductor
Orms·by–Gore \ˌȯrmz-bē-ˈgō(ə)r, -ˈgȯ(ə)r\ (William) David 1918– 5th Baron *Harlech* Brit. diplomat
Oroz·co \ō-ˈrō-(ˌ)skō\ José Clemente 1883–1949 Mex. painter
Orozco Romero \rō-ˈme(ə)r-(ˌ)ō\ Carlos 1898– Mex. caricaturist & painter
Or·te·ga y Gas·set \ȯr-ˈtā-gə-ˌē-gä-ˈset\ José 1883–1955 Span. philos., writer, & statesman
Or·tiz Ru·bio \ˌȯr-ˌtēz-ˈrü-bē-ˌō\ Pascual 1877–1963 pres. of Mexico (1930–32)
Or·well \ˈȯr-ˌwel, -wəl\ George 1903–1950 pseud. of *Eric Blair* Eng. author — **Or·well·ian** \ȯr-ˈwel-ē-ən\ *adj*
Os·born \ˈäz-bərn, -ˌbȯrn\ Henry Fairfield 1857–1935 Am. paleontologist
Os·borne \ˈäz-bərn, -ˌbȯ(ə)rn, -ˌbō(ə)rn\ John James 1929– Brit. dram.
Osborne Thomas Mott 1859–1926 Am. penologist
Os·car II \ˈäs-kər\ 1829–1907 king of Sweden (1872–1907) & of Norway (1872–1905)
Osce·o·la \ˌäs-ē-ˈō-lə, ˌō-sē-\ 1800?–1838 Seminole Indian chief
Os·ler \ˈō-slər, ˈōz-lər\ Sir William 1849–1919 Canad. physician
Os·man \ōs-ˈmän\ *or* **Oth·man** \ōth-\ 1259–1326 founder of the Ottoman Empire
Os·me·ña \ōz-ˈmān-yə, ōs-\ Sergio 1878–1961 pres. of Philippine Commonwealth (1944–46)
Os·si·etz·ky, von \ˌäs-ē-ˈet-skē\ Carl 1889–1938 Ger. writer & pacifist
Ossoli Marchioness — see Margaret FULLER
Os·ten·so \ˈäs-tən-ˌsō\ Martha 1900–1963 Norw.-born nov. in U.S.
Ost·wald \ˈōs-ˌtwȯld\ Wilhelm 1853–1932 Ger. physical chem. & philos.
Otis \ˈōt-əs\ Elwell Stephen 1838–1909 Am. gen.
Otis Harrison Gray 1837–1917 Am. gen. & journalist
Otis James 1725–1783 Am. Revolutionary statesman
Ot·ter·bein \ˈät-ər-ˌbīn\ Philip William 1726–1813 Ger.-born clergyman in Am.
Ot·to I \ˈät-(ˌ)ō\ 912–973 *the Great* Holy Rom. emp. (936–973)
Ot·way \ˈät-ˌwā\ Thomas 1652–1685 Eng. dram.
Ouida — see Marie Louise de la RAMÉE
Ov·id \ˈäv-əd\ 43 B.C.–?A.D. 17 *Publius Ovidius Naso* Rom. poet — **Ovid·ian** \ä-ˈvid-ē-ən\ *adj*
Ow·en \ˈō-ən\ Robert 1771–1858 Welsh social reformer
Owen Wilfred 1893–1918 Brit. poet
Ox·en·stier·na *or* **Ox·en·stjer·na** \ˈu̇k-sən-ˌsher-nə, ˈäk-\ *or* **Ox·en·stiern** \ˈäk-sən-ˌsti(ə)rn\ Count Axel Gustafsson 1583–1654 Swed. statesman
Oxford Earl of — see Robert HARLEY
Paa·si·ki·vi \ˈpäs-ə-ˌkē-vē\ Ju·ho \ˈyü-(ˌ)hō\ K. 1870–1956 Finnish businessman; pres. of Finland (1946–56)
Pa·de·rew·ski \ˌpad-ə-ˈref-skē, -ˈrev-\ Ignace \ēn-ˈyäs\ Jan \ˈyän\ 1860–1941 Pol. pianist & statesman
Pa·ga·ni·ni \ˌpag-ə-ˈnē-nē, ˌpäg-\ Niccolò 1782–1840 Ital. violinist
Page \ˈpāj\ Thomas Nelson 1853–1922 Am. nov. & diplomat
Page Walter Hines 1855–1918 Am. journalist & diplomat
Pag·et \ˈpaj-ət\ Sir James 1814–1899 Eng. surgeon & pathologist
Paine \ˈpān\ Albert Bigelow 1861–1937 Am. author
Paine Thomas 1737–1809 Am. (Eng.-born) polit. philos. & author
Pain·le·vé \paⁿ-lə-vā\ Paul 1863–1933 Fr. math. & statesman
Pa·le·stri·na, da \ˌpal-ə-ˈstrē-nə\ Giovanni Pierluigi 1526?–1594 Ital. composer
Pa·ley \ˈpā-lē\ William 1743–1805 Eng. theol. & philos.
Pal·grave \ˈpal-ˌgrāv, ˈpȯl-\ Francis Turner 1824–1897 Eng. poet & anthologist
Pal·la·dio \pə-ˈläd-ē-ˌō\ Andrea 1518–1580 Ital. architect
Pal·ma \ˈpäl-mə\ Tomás Estrada 1835–1908 1st pres. of Cuba (1902–06)

ə abut	ᵊ kitten, F table	ər further	a back	ā bake
ä cot, cart	å F bac	au̇ out	ch chin	e less	ē easy
g gift	i trip	ī life	j joke	k G ich	ⁿ F vin	ŋ sing
ō flow	ȯ flaw	œ F bœuf	œ̄ F feu	ȯi coin	th thing
t͟h this	ü loot	u̇ foot	u̇e G Füllen	ue̅ F rue	y yet
ʸ F digne \dēnʸ\, nuit \nwʸē\	yü few	yu̇ furious	zh vision		

Palm·er \ˈpäm-ər, ˈpäl-mər\ Alice Elvira 1855–1902 née *Freeman; wife of G. H.* Am. educ.
Palmer Daniel David 1845–1913 Canad.-born father of chiropractic
Palmer George Herbert 1842–1933 Am. scholar & educ.
Palm·er·ston \ˈpäm-ər-stən, ˈpäl-mər-\ 3d Viscount 1784–1865 *Henry John Temple* Eng. statesman; prime min. (1855–58; 1859–65) — **Palm·er·sto·nian** \ˌpäm-ər-ˈstō-nē-ən, ˌpäl-mər-, -nyən\ *adj*
Palm·gren \ˈpäm-grən, ˈpälm-\ Selim 1878–1951 Finnish pianist & composer
Pa·ni·ni \ˈpän-(y)ə-(ˌ)nē\ *fl* 350 B.C. Indian grammarian of Sanskrit
Pank·hurst \ˈpaŋk-ˌhərst\ Emmeline 1858–1928 née *Goulden* Eng. suffragist
Pa·o·li, di \ˈpau̇-lē, ˈpä-ō-(ˌ)lē\ Pasquale 1725–1807 Corsican patriot
Pa·pen, von \ˈpäp-ən\ Franz 1879–1969 Ger. diplomat
Pap·pen·heim, zu \ˈpäp-ən-ˌhīm, ˈpap-\ Count Gottfried Heinrich 1594–1632 Ger. gen.
Par·a·cel·sus \ˌpar-ə-ˈsel-səs\ Philippus Aureolus 1493–1541 *Theophrastus Bombastus von Hohenheim* Swiss-born alchemist & physician
Pares \ˈpa(ə)rz, ˈpe(ə)rz\ Sir Bernard 1876–1949 Eng. hist.
Pa·re·to \pə-ˈrāt-(ˌ)ō\ Vilfredo 1848–1923 Ital. econ. & sociol.
Pa·ris \pä-ˈrēs, pə-\ Gaston 1839–1903 Fr. philologist
Par·is \ˈpar-əs\ Matthew 1200?–1259 Eng. monk & hist.
Park \ˈpärk\ Mungo 1771–1806 Scot. explorer in Africa
Par·ker \ˈpär-kər\ Dorothy 1893–1967 née *Rothschild* Am. writer
Parker Sir Gilbert 1862–1932 Canad. author
Parker Matthew 1504–1575 Eng. theol.
Parker Theodore 1810–1860 Am. Unitarian clergyman
Parkes \ˈpärks\ Sir Henry 1815–1896 Austral. statesman
Park·man \ˈpärk-mən\ Francis 1823–1893 Am. hist.
Parley Peter — see Samuel Griswold GOODRICH
Par·men·i·des \pär-ˈmen-ə-ˌdēz\ 5th cent. B.C. Greek philos.
Par·mi·gia·ni·no \ˌpär-mi-jä-ˈnē-(ˌ)nō\ *or* **Par·mi·gia·no** \-mə-ˈjän-(ˌ)ō\ Il 1503–1540 *Girolamo Francesco Maria Mazzuoli* or *Mazzola* Ital. painter
Par·nell \pär-ˈnel *also* ˈpärn-ᵊl\ Charles Stewart 1846–1891 Irish nationalist
Parr Catherine — see CATHERINE
Par·ring·ton \ˈpar-iŋ-tən\ Vernon Louis 1871–1929 Am. literary hist.
Par·rish \ˈpar-ish\ Maxfield 1870–1966 Am. painter
Par·ry \ˈpar-ē\ Sir William Edward 1790–1855 Eng. arctic explorer
Par·sons \ˈpärs-ᵊnz\ William 1800–1867 3d Earl of *Rosse* Eng. astron.
Pas·cal \pas-ˈkal, pȧs-kȧl\ Blaise 1623–1662 Fr. math. & philos.
Pa·šić \ˈpäsh-(ˌ)ich\ Nikola \ˈnē-kō-lä\ 1845?–1926 Serbian & Yugoslav statesman
Passfield 1st Baron — see WEBB
Pas·sy \pa-ˈsē, pä-\ Frédéric 1822–1912 Fr. econ. & statesman
Passy Paul Édouard 1859–1940 *son of prec.* Fr. phonetician
Pas·ter·nak \ˈpas-tər-ˌnak\ Boris Leonidovich 1890–1960 Russ. poet, nov., & translator
Pas·teur \pas-ˈtər\ Louis 1822–1895 Fr. chem. — **Pas·teur·ian** \-ē-ən\ *adj*
Pa·ter \ˈpāt-ər\ Walter Horatio 1839–1894 Eng. essayist & critic
Pat·more \ˈpat-ˌmō(ə)r, -ˌmȯ(ə)r\ Coventry Kersey Dighton 1823–1896 Eng. poet
Pa·ton \ˈpāt-ᵊn\ Alan Stewart 1903– So. African writer
Pa·tri \ˈpa-trē\ Angelo 1877–1965 Am. (Ital.-born) educ. & author
Pat·rick \ˈpa-trik\ Saint 389?–?461 apostle & patron saint of Ireland
Pat·ti \ˈpat-ē, ˈpät-ē\ Adelina 1843–1919 Ital. (Span.-born) operatic soprano
Pat·ti·son \ˈpat-ə-sən\ Mark 1813–1884 Eng. scholar & author
Pat·ton \ˈpat-ᵊn\ George Smith 1885–1945 Am. gen.
Pau·ker \ˈpau̇-kər\ Ana 1889?–1960 née *Ra·bin·sohn* Rumanian Communist
Paul \ˈpȯl\ name of 6 popes: esp. **III** 1468–1549 (pope 1534–49); **V** 1552–1621 (pope 1605–21); **VI** (*Giovanni Battista Montini*) 1897– (pope 1963–)
Paul I 1754–1801 emp. of Russia (1796–1801)
Paul I 1901–1964 king of Greece (1947–64)
Paul Jean — see RICHTER
Paul–Bon·cour \ˈpȯl-(ˌ)bō^{n}-ˈkü(ə)r\ Joseph 1873–1972 Fr. lawyer & statesman
Paul·ding \ˈpȯl-diŋ\ James Kirke 1778–1860 Am. author
Pau·li \ˈpau̇-lē\ Wolfgang 1900–1958 Austrian-born physicist in Am.
Pau·ling \ˈpȯ-liŋ\ Li·nus \ˈlī-nəs\ Carl 1901– Am. chem.
Pau·lus \ˈpau̇-ləs\ Friedrich 1890–1957 Ger. field marshal
Paulus \ˈpȯ-ləs\ Julius 2d–3d cent. A.D. Rom. jurist
Pau·sa·ni·as \pȯ-ˈsā-nē-əs\ 2d cent. A.D. Greek traveler & geographer
Pav·lov \ˈpäv-ˌlȯf, ˈpav-, -ˌlȯv\ Ivan Petrovich 1849–1936 Russ. physiol.
Pa·vlo·va \ˈpav-lə-və, pav-ˈlō-\ Anna 1885–1931 Russ. ballerina
Payne \ˈpān\ John Howard 1791–1852 Am. actor & dram.
Paz \ˈpäs, ˈpäz\ Octavio 1914– Mex. author
Pea·body \ˈpē-ˌbäd-ē, -bəd-ē\ Endicott 1857–1944 Am. educ.
Peabody George 1795–1869 Am. merchant & philanthropist
Pea·cock \ˈpē-ˌkäk\ Thomas Love 1785–1866 Eng. nov. & poet
Peale \ˈpē(ə)l\ Charles Willson 1741–1827 & his bro. James 1749–1831 & Charles's son Rembrandt 1778–1860 Am. painters
Pear·son \ˈpi(ə)rs-ᵊn\ Karl 1857–1936 Eng. scientist
Pearson Lester Bowles 1897–1972 prime min. of Canada (1963–68)
Pea·ry \ˈpi(ə)r-ē\ Robert Edwin 1856–1920 Am. arctic explorer
Pe·co·ra \pi-ˈkōr-ə, -ˈkȯr-\ Ferdinand 1882–1971 Am. jurist
Peel \ˈpē(ə)l\ Sir Robert 1788–1850 Eng. statesman
Peele \ˈpē(ə)l\ George 1556–1596 Eng. dram. & poet
Pe·gram \ˈpē-grəm\ George Braxton 1876–1958 Am. physicist
Pei \ˈpā\ Ieoh Ming 1917– Am. (Chin.-born) architect
Peirce \ˈpərs, ˈpi(ə)rs\ Charles Sanders 1839–1914 Am. physicist, math., & logician
Pei·xot·to \pā-ˈshōt-(ˌ)ō\ Ernest Clifford 1869–1940 Am. painter & illustrator
Pe·la·gius \pə-ˈlā-j(ē-)əs\ 360?–?420 Brit. monk & theol.
Pe·lop·i·das \pə-ˈläp-əd-əs\ *d* 364 B.C. Theban gen.
Pen·de·rec·ki \ˌpen-də-ˈret-skē\ Krzysztof 1933– Pol. composer
Penn \ˈpen\ Sir William 1621–1670 Eng. admiral
Penn William 1644–1718 *son of prec.* Eng. Quaker; founder of Pennsylvania
Pen·nell \ˈpen-ᵊl, pə-ˈnel\ Joseph 1857–1926 Am. etcher
Pep·in the Short \ˌpep-ən-\ 714?–768 king of the Franks (751–768)
Pepys \ˈpēps\ Samuel 1633–1703 Eng. diarist — **Pepys·ian** \-ē-ən\ *adj*
Per·cy \ˈpər-sē\ Sir Henry 1364–1403 *Hotspur* Eng. soldier
Percy Thomas 1729–1811 Eng. antiquarian & poet
Per·el·man \ˈper-əl-mən (*his own pron.*), ˈpər(-ə)l-\ Sidney Joseph 1904– Am. writer
Pé·rez Gal·dós \ˌper-əs-(ˌ)gäl-ˈdōs\ Benito 1843–1920 Span. nov. & dram.
Per·go·le·si \ˌpər-gə-ˈlā-zē, ˌper-gə-ˈlā-sē\ Giovanni Battista 1710–1736 Ital. composer
Per·i·cles \ˈper-ə-ˌklēz\ *d* 429 B.C. Athenian statesman — **Per·i·cle·an** \ˌper-ə-ˈklē-ən\ *adj*
Per·kins \ˈpər-kənz\ Frances 1882–1965 Am. social worker & administrator
Pe·rón \pā-ˈrōn, pə-\ Juan Domingo 1895– Argentine polit.; pres. of Argentina (1946–55; 1973–)
Per·rault \pə-ˈrō, pe-\ Charles 1628–1703 Fr. fairy tale writer
Per·rin \pə-ra^{n}(n), pe-\ Jean Baptiste 1870-1942, Fr. physicist
Per·ry \ˈper-ē\ Bliss 1860–1954 Am. educ. & critic
Perry Matthew Calbraith 1794–1858 Am. commodore
Perry Oliver Hazard 1785–1819 *bro. of prec.* Am. naval officer
Perry Ralph Barton 1876–1957 Am. philos. & educ.
Perse St. John — see Alexis Saint-Léger LÉGER
Per·shing \ˈpər-shiŋ, -zhiŋ\ John Joseph 1860–1948 Am. gen.
Per·sius \ˈpər-shəs, -shē-əs\ 34–62 *Aulus Persius Flaccus* Rom. satirist
Pe·ru·gi·no, Il \ˌper-ə-ˈjē-(ˌ)nō\ 1446–1523 *Pietro Vannucci* Ital. painter
Pe·ruz·zi \pə-ˈrüt-sē, pā-\ Baldassare 1481–1536 Ital. architect & painter
Pes·ta·loz·zi \ˌpes-tə-ˈlät-sē\ Johann Heinrich 1746–1827 Swiss educ.
Pé·tain \pā-ta^{n}\ Henri Philippe 1856–1951 Fr. gen.; marshal of France; premier of Vichy France (1940–44)
Pe·ter \ˈpēt-ər\ Saint *d* A.D. ?67 disciple of Jesus; regarded, esp. by Roman Catholics, as vicar of Christ on earth [Mt. 16:16–19]
Peter I 1672–1725 *the Great* czar of Russia (1682–1725)
Peter I Ka·ra·geor·ge·vich \ˌkar-ə-ˈjȯr-jə-ˌvich\ 1844–1921 king of Serbia (1903–21)
Peter II 1923–1970 king of Yugoslavia (1934–45)
Peter the Hermit 1050?–?1115 Fr. preacher of the 1st Crusade
Pe·ters \ˈpāt-ərz, -ərs\ Carl 1856–1918 Ger. explorer in Africa
Pe·ter·son \ˈpēt-ər-sən\ Peter George 1926– U.S. secy. of commerce (1972)
Pe·tö·fi \ˈpet-ə-fē\ Sán·dor \ˈshän-ˌdȯ(ə)r\ 1823–1849 Hung. poet
Pe·trarch \ˈpē-ˌträrk, ˈpe-\ *or* **Pe·trar·ca** \pä-ˈträr-kə\ Francesco 1304–1374 Ital. poet — **Pe·trarch·an** \pē-ˈträr-kən, pe-\ *adj*
Pe·trie \ˈpē-trē\ Sir (William Matthew) Flin·ders \ˈflin-dərz\ 1853–1942 Eng. Egyptologist
Pe·tro·ni·us \pə-ˈtrō-nē-əs\ Gaius 1st cent. A.D. *Ar·bi·ter Ele·gan·ti·ae* \ˈär-bət-ər-ˌel-ə-ˈgan-chē-ˌē\ Rom. satirist — **Pe·tro·ni·an** \-nē-ən\ *adj*
Pet·ty \ˈpet-ē\ Sir William 1623–1687 Eng. polit. econ.
Pevs·ner \ˈpevz-nər\ Antoine 1886–1962 *bro. of Naum Gabo* Fr. (Russ.-born) sculptor & painter
Pevsner Sir Nikolaus 1902– Brit. (Ger.-born) art hist.
Phae·drus \ˈfē-drəs\ 5th cent. B.C. Greek philos.
Phaedrus 1st cent. A.D. Rom. fabulist
Phid·i·as \ˈfid-ē-əs\ 5th cent. B.C. Greek sculptor
Phil·ip \ˈfil-əp\ 1639?–1676 *Met·a·com·et* \ˌmet-ə-ˈkäm-ət\ sachem of the Wampanoag Indians
Philip name of 6 kings of France: esp. **II** *or* **Philip Augustus** 1165–1223 (reigned 1180–1223); **IV** (*the Fair*) 1268–1314 (reigned 1285–1314); **VI** 1293–1350 (reigned 1328–50)
Philip name of 5 kings of Spain: esp. **II** 1527–1598 (reigned 1556–98); **V** 1683–1746 (reigned 1700–46)
Philip II 382–336 B.C. king of Macedon (359–336)
Philip Prince 1921– *consort of Queen Elizabeth II of Gr. Brit.* 3d Duke of Edinburgh
Philip the Good 1396–1467 Duke of Burgundy (1419–67)
Phil·ips \ˈfil-əps\ Ambrose 1675?–1749 *Nam·by-Pam·by* \ˌnam-bē-ˈpam-bē\ Eng. poet & dram.
Phil·lipps \ˈfil-əps\ Sir Thomas 1792–1872 Eng. antiquarian
Phil·lips \ˈfil-əps\ Wendell 1811–1884 Am. orator & reformer
Phill·potts \ˈfil-ˌpäts\ Eden 1862–1960 Eng. nov. & dram.
Phi·lo Ju·dae·us \ˈfī-(ˌ)lō-jü-ˈdē-əs, -ˈdā-\ 1st cent. B.C.–1st cent. A.D. Hellenistic Jewish philos. of Alexandria
Pho·ci·on \ˈfō-sē-ˌän\ 402?–317 B.C. Athenian gen. & statesman
Phu·mi·phon Adul·det \ˈpü-mē-ˌpōn-ä-ˈdün-lə-ˌdāt— *sic*\ 1927– *Ra·ma IX* \ˈräm-ə\ king of Thailand (1946–)
Phyfe \ˈfīf\ Duncan 1768–1854 Am. (Scot.-born) cabinetmaker
Pia·get \pyä-ˈzhä\ Jean 1896– Swiss psychol.
Pi·card \pē-ˈkär, pik-ˈärd\ Jean 1620–1682 Fr. astron.
Pi·cas·so \pi-ˈkäs-(ˌ)ō, -ˈkas-\ Pablo 1881–1973 Span. painter & sculptor in Fr.
Pic·card \pi-ˈkär, pik-ˈärd\ Auguste 1884–1962 Swiss physicist & aeronaut
Piccard Jacques Ernst *son of Auguste* 1922– Swiss (Belg.-born) oceanographer; developer of bathyscaphe
Pick·er·ing \ˈpik-(ə-)riŋ\ Edward Charles 1846–1919 & his bro. William Henry 1858–1938 Am. astronomers
Pick·ett \ˈpik-ət\ George Edward 1825–1875 Am. Confed. gen.

Pi·co del·la Mi·ran·do·la \ˈpē-(ˌ)kō-ˌdel-ə-mə-ˈran-də-lə, -ˈrän-\ Count Giovanni 1463–1494 Ital. humanist
Pieck \ˈpēk\ Wilhelm 1876–1960 Ger. Communist
Pierce \ˈpi(ə)rs\ Franklin 1804–1869 14th pres. of the U.S. (1853–57)
Piero della Francesca — see FRANCESCA
Pike \ˈpīk\ Zebulon Montgomery 1779–1813 Am. gen. & explorer
Pi·late \ˈpī-lət\ **Pon·tius** \ˈpän-chəs, ˈpən-chəs\ 1st cent. A.D. Rom. procurator of Judea; tried & condemned Jesus Christ
Pil·sud·ski \pil-ˈsüt-skē, -ˈzüt-\ Józef 1867–1935 Pol. gen. & statesman
Pin·chot \ˈpin-ˌshō\ Gifford 1865–1946 Am. forester & polit.
Pinck·ney \ˈpiŋk-nē\ Charles Cotesworth 1746–1825 Am. statesman
Pin·dar \ˈpin-dər, -ˌdär\ 522?–443 B.C. Greek poet
Pi·ne·ro \pə-ˈni(ə)r-(ˌ)ō, -ˈne(ə)r-\ Sir Arthur Wing 1855–1934 Eng. dram.
Pin·ker·ton \ˈpiŋ-kərt-ᵊn\ Allan 1819–1884 Scot.-born detective in Am.
Pin·ter \ˈpint-ər\ Harold 1930– Eng. dram.
Pin·tu·ric·chio \ˌpint-ə-ˈrē-kē-ˌō\ 1454–1513 *Bernardino Betti* Ital. painter
Pin·zón \pin-ˈzōn\ Martín Alonso 1440?–1493 & his bro. Vicente Yáñez 1460?–?1524 Span. navigators with Columbus
Pioz·zi \pē-ˈót-sē\ Hester Lynch 1741–1821 *Mrs. Thrale* \ˈthrā(ə)l\ Eng. writer
Pi·ran·del·lo \ˌpir-ən-ˈdel-(ˌ)ō\ Luigi 1867–1936 Ital. author — **Pi·ran·del·li·an** \-ˈdel-ē-ən\ *adj*
Pire \ˈpi(ə)r\ Dominique-Georges 1910–1969 Belg. priest; founder of charitable organizations
Pi·sa·no \pi-ˈsän-(ˌ)ō, -ˈzän-\ Giovanni 1245–1314 & his father Nicola 1220–1284 Ital. sculptors
Pi·sis·tra·tus *or* **Pei·sis·tra·tus** \pī-ˈsis-trət-əs, pə-\ *d* 527 B.C. tyrant of Athens
Pis·sar·ro \pə-ˈsär-(ˌ)ō\ Camille 1830–1903 Fr. painter
Pis·ton \ˈpis-tən\ Walter 1894– Am. composer
Pit·man \ˈpit-mən\ Sir Isaac 1813–1897 Eng. phonographer
Pitt \ˈpit\ William 1708–1778 Earl of *Chatham; the Elder Pitt* Eng. statesman
Pitt William 1759–1806 *the Younger Pitt; son of prec.* Eng. statesman
Pitt–Riv·ers \ˈpit-ˈriv-ərz\ Augustus Henry 1827–1900 Eng. archaeologist
Pi·us \ˈpī-əs\ name of 12 popes: esp. **II** (*Enea Silvio de Piccolomini* or *Aeneas Silvius* or *Sylvius*) 1405–1464 (pope 1458–64); **VII** 1742–1823 (pope 1800–23); **IX** 1792–1878 (pope 1846–78); **X** 1835–1914 (pope 1903–14); **XI** (*Achille Ratti*) 1857–1939 (pope 1922–39); **XII** (*Eugenio Pacelli*) 1876–1958 (pope 1939–58)
Pi·zar·ro \pə-ˈzär-(ˌ)ō\ Francisco 1470?–1541 Span. conqueror of Peru
Planck \ˈpläŋk\ Max Karl Ernst Ludwig 1858–1947 Ger. physicist
Plan·tin \plänⁿ-taⁿ\ Christophe 1514–1589 Fr. printer
Plath \ˈplath\ Sylvia 1932–1963 *S. P. Hughes* Am. poet
Pla·to \ˈplāt-(ˌ)ō\ 427?–347 B.C. Greek philos.
Plau·tus \ˈplót-əs\ Titus Maccius 254?–184 B.C. Rom. dram. — **Plau·tine** \ˈplò-ˌtīn\ *adj*
Ple·kha·nov \plə-ˈkän-ˌóf, -ˌóv\ Georgi Valentinovich 1857–1918 Russ. Marxist philos.
Ple·ven \plā-ˈven\ René 1901– Fr. polit.
Plim·soll \ˈplim(p)-səl, ˈplim-ˌsòl\ Samuel 1824–1898 *the Sailor's Friend* Eng. shipping reformer
Pliny \ˈplin-ē\ 23–79 *Gaius Plinius Secundus; the Elder* Rom. scholar
Pliny 62–113 *Gaius Plinius Caecilius Secundus; the Younger; nephew of prec.* Rom. author
Plo·ti·nus \plō-ˈtī-nəs\ 205?–270 Rom. (Egyptian-born) philos. — **Plo·tin·i·an** \-ˈtin-ē-ən\ *adj*
Plu·tarch \ˈplü-ˌtärk\ 46?–?120 Greek biographer & moralist — **Plu·tarch·an** \plü-ˈtär-kən\ *or* **Plu·tarch·ian** \-kē-ən\ *adj*
Po·ca·hon·tas \ˌpō-kə-ˈhänt-əs\ 1595?–1617 *dau. of Powhatan* Am. Indian
Pod·gor·ny \päd-ˈgòr-nē\ Nikolai Viktorovich 1903– Soviet polit.; pres. U.S.S.R. (1965–)
Poe \ˈpō\ Edgar Allan 1809–1849 Am. poet & storywriter
Poin·ca·ré \ˌpwaⁿ(ŋ)-ˌkä-ˈrā\ Jules Henri 1854–1912 Fr. math.
Poincaré Raymond 1860–1934 *cousin of J. H.* Fr. statesman; pres. of France (1913–20)
Poi·tier \ˈpwä-ˌtyā\ Sidney 1924– Am. actor
Pole \ˈpōl, ˈpül\ Reginald 1500–1558 Eng. cardinal; archbishop of Canterbury (1556–58)
Po·li·tian \pə-ˈlish-ən\ 1454–1494 *Angelo Poliziano* Ital. classical scholar & poet
Polk \ˈpōk\ James Knox 1795–1849 11th pres. of the U.S. (1845–49)
Pol·lio \ˈpäl-ē-ˌō\ Gaius Asinius 75 B.C.–A.D. 5 Rom. soldier, orator, & polit.
Pol·lock \ˈpäl-ək\ Channing 1880–1946 Am. nov. & dram.
Pollock Sir Frederick 1845–1937 Eng. jurist
Pollock Jackson 1912–1956 Am. painter
Po·lo \ˈpō-(ˌ)lō\ **Mar·co** \ˈmär-(ˌ)kō\ 1254?–?1324 Ital. traveler
Po·lyb·i·us \pə-ˈlib-ē-əs\ 205?–?125 B.C. Greek hist.
Pol·y·carp \ˈpäl-i-ˌkärp\ Saint 69?–?155 Christian martyr & Apostolic Father; bishop of Smyrna
Pol·y·cli·tus *or* **Pol·y·clei·tus** \ˌpäl-i-ˈklīt-əs\ 5th cent. B.C. Greek sculptor & architect
Po·lyc·ra·tes \pə-ˈlik-rə-ˌtēz\ *d ab* 522 B.C. tyrant of Samos
Pol·y·do·rus \ˌpäl-i-ˈdōr-əs, -ˈdòr-\ 1st cent. B.C. Rhodian sculptor
Pol·yg·no·tus \ˌpäl-ig-ˈnōt-əs\ 5th cent. B.C. Greek painter
Pom·pa·dour, de \ˈpäm-pə-ˌdō(ə)r, -ˌdò(ə)r, -ˌdü(ə)r\ Marquise 1721–1764 *Jeanne Antoinette Poisson; mistress of Louis XV*
Pom·pey \ˈpäm-pē\ 106–48 B.C. *Gnaeus Pompeius Magnus; the Great* Rom. gen. & statesman
Pom·pi·dou \ˈpäm-pi-ˌdü\ Georges Jean Raymond 1911– Fr. polit.; premier of France (1962–68); pres. of France (1969–)
Ponce de Le·ón \ˌpän(t)s-də-ˈlē-ən, ˌpän(t)-sə-ˌdā-lē-ˈōn\ Juan 1460?–1521 Span. explorer; disc. Florida
Pon·chi·el·li \ˌpóŋ-kē-ˈel-ē\ Amilcare 1834–1886 Ital. composer
Pons \ˈpōⁿs\ Lily 1904– Am. (Fr.-born) soprano
Pon·selle \pän-ˈsel\ Rosa Melba 1897– Am. soprano
Pon·ti·ac \ˈpänt-ē-ˌak\ 1720?–1769 Ottawa Indian chief
Pon·top·pi·dan \pän-ˈtäp-ə-ˌdan\ Henrik 1857–1943 Dan. nov.
Pon·tor·mo, da \pōn-ˈtȯr-(ˌ)mō\ Jacopo 1494–1557 orig. *J. Carrucci* Ital. painter
Pope \ˈpōp\ Alexander 1688–1744 Eng. poet — **Pop·ian** *also* **Pop·ean** \ˈpō-pē-ən\ *adj*
Pope John 1822–1892 Am. gen.
Por·son \ˈpòrs-ᵊn\ Richard 1759–1808 Eng. scholar
Por·tal \ˈpōrt-ᵊl, ˈpòrt-\ Charles Frederick Algernon 1893–1971 1st Viscount *Portal of Hungerford* Brit. air marshal
Por·ter \ˈpōrt-ər, ˈpòrt-\ Cole Albert 1891–1964 Am. composer & songwriter
Porter David 1780–1843 & his son David Dixon 1813–1891 Am. naval officers
Porter Gene 1868–1924 née *Stratton* Am. nov.
Porter Katherine Anne 1890– Am. writer
Porter Noah 1811–1892 Am. philos. & lexicographer; pres. Yale U. (1871–86)
Porter William Sydney 1862–1910 pseud. ***O. Hen·ry*** \(ˈ)ō-ˈhen-rē\ Am. short-story writer
Portland Duke of — see BENTINCK
Post \ˈpōst\ Emily 1873?–1960 née *Price* Am. columnist & writer; authority on etiquette
Po·tëm·kin \pə-ˈtyòm(p)-kən, pō-ˈtem(p)-\ Grigori Aleksandrovich 1739–1791 Russ. field marshal & statesman
Pot·ter \ˈpät-ər\ Beatrix 1866–1943 Brit. writer & illustrator
Potter Paul 1625–1654 Du. painter
Pou·lenc \ˈpü-ˌlaŋk\ **Fran·cis** \fräⁿ-sēs\ 1899–1963 Fr. composer
Pound \ˈpau̇nd\ Ezra Loomis 1885–1972 Am. poet
Pound Roscoe 1870–1964 Am. jurist
Pous·sin \pü-saⁿ\ Nicolas 1594–1665 Fr. painter
Pow·ell \ˈpau̇(-ə)l\ Adam Clayton 1908–1972 Am. clergyman & polit.
Powell Anthony 1905– Eng. writer
Powell Cecil Frank 1903–1969 Brit. physicist
Powell John Wesley 1834–1902 Am. geologist & explorer
Powell Lewis Franklin 1907– Am. jurist
Powell Maud 1868–1920 Am. violinist
Pow·ers \ˈpau̇(-ə)rz\ Hiram 1805–1873 Am. sculptor
Pow·ha·tan \ˌpau̇-ə-ˈtan, pau̇-ˈhat-ᵊn\ 1550?–1618 *father of Pocahontas* Am. Indian chief
Pow·ys \ˈpō-əs\ **John Cow·per** \ˈkü-pər\ 1872–1963 & his bros. Theodore Francis 1875–1953 & Llewelyn 1884–1939 Eng. authors
Pra·do Ugar·te·che \ˈpräd-(ˌ)ō-ˌü-gär-ˈtā-chē\ Manuel 1889–1967 Peruvian banker; pres. of Peru (1939–45; 1956–62)
Pra·ja·dhi·pok \prə-ˈchät-i-ˌpäk\ 1893–1941 king of Siam (1925–35)
Pratt \ˈprat\ Bela Lyon 1867–1917 Am. sculptor
Pratt Edwin John 1883–1964 Canad. poet
Prax·it·e·les \prak-ˈsit-ᵊl-ˌēz\ 4th cent. B.C. Athenian sculptor — **Prax·it·e·le·an** \(ˌ)prak-ˌsit-ᵊl-ˈē-ən\ *adj*
Pre·ble \ˈpreb-əl\ Edward 1761–1807 Am. naval officer
Pregl \ˈprā-gəl\ Fritz 1869–1930 Austrian chem.
Pres·cott \ˈpres-kət *also* -ˌkät\ William Hickling 1796–1859 Am. hist.
Pre·to·ri·us \pri-ˈtōr-ē-əs, -ˈtòr-\ Andries Wilhelmus Jacobus 1799–1853 & his son Marthinus Wessels 1819–1901 So. African Du. colonizers & soldiers
Pré·vost d'Ex·iles \prā-ˈvō-ˌdeg-ˈzē(ə)l\ Antoine François 1697–1763 Fr. abbé & writer
Price \ˈprīs\ Byron 1891– Am. journalist
Price (Mary) **Le·on·tyne** \lē-ˈän-ˌtēn\ 1927– Am. singer
Pride \ˈprīd\ Thomas *d* 1658 Eng. Parliamentary commander
Priest·ley \ˈprēst-lē\ John Boynton 1894– Eng. author
Priestley Joseph 1733–1804 Eng. clergyman & chem.
Primo de Rivera y Orbaneja — see RIVERA Y ORBANEJA
Primrose Archibald Philip — see ROSEBERY
Prior \ˈprī(-ə)r\ Matthew 1664–1721 Eng. poet
Pri·scian \ˈprish-ən, ˈprish-ē-ən\ *fl* 500 *Priscianus Caesariensis* Latin grammarian at Constantinople
Pro·clus \ˈprō-kləs, ˈpräk-ləs\ 410?–485 Greek philos.
Pro·co·pi·us \prə-ˈkō-pē-əs\ 6th cent. A.D. Byzantine hist.
Pro·kof·iev \prə-ˈkòf-yəf, -ˌyef, -ˌyev\ Sergei Sergeevich 1891–1953 Russ. composer — **Pro·kof·iev·ian** \-ˌkòf-ˈyev-ē-ən\ *adj*
Pro·per·tius \prō-ˈpər-sh(ē-)əs\ Sextus 50?–?15 B.C. Rom. poet
Pro·tag·o·ras \prō-ˈtag-ə-rəs\ 5th cent. B.C. Greek philos. — **Pro·tag·o·re·an** \-ˌtag-ə-ˈrē-ən\ *adj*
Prou·dhon \prü-dōⁿ\ Pierre Joseph 1809–1865 Fr. journalist
Proust \prüst\ Marcel 1871–1922 Fr. nov. — **Proust·ian** \ˈprü-stē-ən\ *adj*
Prynne \ˈprin\ William 1600–1669 Eng. Puritan pamphleteer
Przhe·val·ski \ˌpər-zhə-ˈväl-skē, ˌ(p)shə-ˈväl-\ Nikolai Mikhailovich 1839–1888 Russ. explorer
Ptol·e·my \ˈtäl-ə-mē\ name of 14 kings of Egypt
Ptolemy 2d cent. A.D. *Claudius Ptolemaeus* Alexandrian astron.
Puc·ci·ni \pü-ˈchē-nē\ Giacomo 1858–1924 Ital. composer
Pu·las·ki \pə-ˈlas-kē, pyü-\ Casimir 1748?–1779 Pol. soldier in Am. Rev.
Pu·lit·zer \ˈpu̇l-ət-sər (*family's pronunciation*), ˈpyü-lət-\ Joseph 1847–1911 Am. (Hung.-born) journalist
Pull·man \ˈpu̇l-mən\ George Mortimer 1831–1897 Am. inventor

ə abut ᵊ kitten, F table ər further a back ā bake
ä cot, cart á F bac au̇ out ch chin e less ē easy
g gift i trip ī life j joke k G ich ⁿ F vin ŋ sing
ō flow ȯ flaw œ F bœuf œ̄ F feu ȯi coin th thing
th this ü loot u̇ foot ue G Füllen ue̅ F rue y yet
ʸ F digne \dēnʸ\, nuit \nwʸē\ yü few yu̇ furious zh vision

Pu·pin \p(y)ü-ˈpēn\ Michael Idvorsky 1858–1935 Am. (Yugoslavian-born) physicist & inventor
Pur·cell \(ˌ)pər-ˈsel\ Edward Mills 1912– Am. physicist
Pur·cell \ˈpər-səl, (ˌ)pər-ˈsel\ Henry 1658?–1695 Eng. composer
Pur·chas \ˈpər-chəs\ Samuel 1575?–1626 Eng. compiler
Pur·kin·je \ˈpu̇r-kən-ˌyä, (ˌ)pər-ˈkin-jē\ Johannes Evangelista 1787–1869 Czech physiol.
Pu·sey \ˈpyü-zē\ Edward Bouverie 1800–1882 Eng. theol.
Push·kin \ˈpu̇sh-kən\ Aleksander Sergeevich 1799–1837 Russ. poet — **Push·kin·ian** \pu̇sh-ˈkin-ē-ən\ *adj*
Put·nam \ˈpət-nəm\ Israel 1718–1790 Am. Revolutionary gen.
Putnam Rufus 1738–1824 *cousin of Israel* Am. Revolutionary gen. & pioneer in Ohio region
Pu·vis de Cha·vannes \pu̅e-vē-də-shȧ-vȧn, -vēs-; pyü-ˌvē(s)-də-shä-ˈvän\ Pierre 1824–1898 Fr. painter & muralist
P'u-yi Henry — see HSÜAN-T'UNG
Pye \ˈpī\ Henry James 1745–1813 Eng. poet laureate (1790–1813)
Pyle \ˈpī(ə)l\ Ernest Taylor 1900–1945 *Ernie* Am. journalist
Pym \ˈpim\ John 1584–1643 Eng. parliamentary statesman
Pyr·rhus \ˈpir-əs\ 318?–272 B.C. king of Epirus (306–272 B.C.)
Py·thag·o·ras \pə-ˈthag-ə-rəs, pī-\ *d ab* 497 B.C. Greek philos. & math.
Qua·dros \ˈkwäd-ˌrōs\ Jânio da Silva 1917– Brazilian pres. (1961)
Quarles \ˈkwȯr(ə)lz, ˈkwär(ə)lz\ Francis 1592–1644 Eng. poet
Qua·si·mo·do \kwä-ˈzē-mə-ˌdō\ Salvatore \ˌsäl-vä-ˈtō-(ˌ)rā\ 1901–1968 Ital. poet & critic
Queensberry Marquis of — see DOUGLAS
Quer·cia, del·la \ˈkwer-chə\ Jacopo 1378?–1438 Sienese sculptor
Ques·nay \kā-ˈnā\ François 1694–1774 Fr. physician & econ.
Que·zon y Mo·li·na \ˈkā-ˌsō-ˌnē-mə-ˈlē-nə\ Manuel Luis 1878–1944 *Manuel Quezon* pres. of the Philippine Commonwealth (1935–44)
Quid·de \ˈkfid-ə, ˈkwid-\ Ludwig 1858–1941 Ger. hist. & pacifist
Quil·ler–Couch \ˈkwil-ər-ˌküch\ Sir Arthur Thomas 1863–1944 Eng. author
Quin·cy \ˈkwin-zē, ˈkwin(t)-sē\ Josiah 1744–1775 Am. lawyer
Quin·te·ro, Ál·va·rez \ˈäl-və-ˌrās-kēn-ˈte(ə)r-(ˌ)ō\ Serafín 1871–1938 & his bro. Joaquín 1873–1944 Span. dramatists
Quin·til·ian \kwin-ˈtil-yən\ 1st cent. A.D. *Marcus Fabius Quintilianus* Rom. rhetorician
Qui·ri·no \ki-ˈrē-(ˌ)nō\ Elpidio 1891?–1956 pres. of the Philippine Republic (1948–53)
Quo Tai-chi \ˈgwō-ˈtī-ˈchē\ 1889–1952 Chin. diplomat
Quoirez Françoise — see Françoise SAGAN
Ra·be·lais \ˈrab-ə-ˌlā, ˌrab-ə-ˈlā\ François 1494?–1553 Fr. humorist & satirist
Ra·bi \ˈräb-ē\ Isidor Isaac 1898– Am. (Austrian-born) physicist
Rabinowitz Solomon — see Shalom ALEICHEM
Ra·chel \ra-ˈshel\ Mlle. 1820–1858 pseud. of *Élisa Félix* Fr. actress
Rach·ma·ni·noff \rak-ˈman-ə-ˌnȯf, räk-ˈmän-, -ˌnȯv\ Sergei Wassilievitch 1873–1943 Russ. composer, pianist, & conductor
Ra·cine \ra-ˈsēn, rə-\ Jean Baptiste 1639–1699 Fr. dram.
Rack·ham \ˈrak-əm\ Arthur 1867–1939 Brit. illustrator
Rad·cliffe \ˈrad-ˌklif\ Ann 1764–1823 née *Ward* Eng. nov.
Ra·detz·ky \rə-ˈdet-skē\ Joseph Wenzel 1766–1858 Count *Radetzky von Radetz* Austrian field marshal
Rae \ˈrā\ John 1813–1893 Scot. arctic explorer
Rae·burn \ˈrā-(ˌ)bərn\ Sir Henry 1756–1823 Scot. painter
Rae·der \ˈräd-ər\ Erich 1876–1960 Ger. admiral
Rae·mae·kers \ˈräm-ˌäk-ərz, -ərs\ Louis 1869–1956 Du. cartoonist
Rag·lan \ˈrag-lən\ 1st Baron 1788–1855 *Fitzroy James Henry Somerset* Brit. field marshal
Rai·mon·di \rī-ˈmän-dē, -ˈmōn-\ Marcantonio 1475?–?1534 Ital. engraver
Ra·ja·go·pa·la·cha·ri \ˈräj-ə-(ˌ)gō-ˌpäl-ə-ˈchär-yə\ Chakravarti 1879–1972 Indian lawyer; gov. gen. of India (1948–50)
Ra·leigh *or* **Ra·legh** \ˈrȯl-ē, ˈräl- *also* ˈral-\ Sir Walter 1552?–1618 Eng. courtier, navigator, & hist.
Ra·ma·krish·na \ˌräm-ə-ˈkrish-nə\ 1836–1886 Hindu saint
Ra·man \ˈräm-ən\ Sir Chan·dra·se·kha·ra \ˌchən-drə-ˈshā-kə-rə\ Venkata 1888–1970 Indian physicist
Ra·meau \ra-ˈmō\ Jean Philippe 1683–1764 Fr. composer
Ra·mée, de la \ˌdel-ə-rə-ˈmā\ Marie Louise 1839–1908 pseud. *Oui·da* \ˈwēd-ə\ Eng. nov.
Ra·món y Ca·jal \rə-ˌmōn-(ˌ)ē-kə-ˈhäl\ Santiago 1852–1934 Span. histologist
Ram·say \ˈram-zē\ Allan 1686–1758 Scot. poet
Ramsay James Andrew Broun 1812–1860 10th Earl & 1st Marquis of *Dal·hou·sie* \dal-ˈhau̇-zē\ Brit. colonial administrator
Ramsay Sir William 1852–1916 Brit. chem.
Ram·ses \ˈram-ˌsēz\ *or* **Ram·e·ses** \ˈram-ə-ˌsēz\ name of 12 kings of Egypt: esp. **II** (reigned 1292–1225 B.C.); **III** (reigned 1198–1167 B.C.)
Ram·sey \ˈram-zē\ Arthur Michael 1904– archbishop of Canterbury (1961–)
Rand \ˈrand\ Ayn \ˈīn\ 1905– Am. (Russ.-born) writer
Ran·dolph \ˈran-ˌdälf\ Asa Philip 1889– Am. labor leader
Randolph Edmund Jennings 1753–1813 Am. statesman
Randolph John 1773–1833 Am. statesman
Ran·jit Singh \ˌrən-jət-ˈsiŋ\ Maharaja 1780–1839 founder of Sikh kingdom
Ran·ke, von \ˈräŋ-kə\ Leopold 1795–1886 Ger. hist.
Ran·som \ˈran(t)-səm\ John Crowe 1888– Am. educator & poet
Ra·pha·el \ˈraf-ē-əl, ˈrā-fē-, ˈräf-ē-\ 1483–1520 *Raffaello Santi* or *Sanzio* Ital. painter — **Ra·pha·el·esque** \ˌraf-ē-ə-ˈlesk, ˌrā-fē-, ˌräf-ē-\ *adj*
Rask \ˈräsk, ˈrask\ Rasmus Christian 1787–1832 Dan. philologist & orientalist
Ras·mus·sen \ˈras-mə-sən, ˈräs-ˌmu̇s-ᵊn\ Knud Johan Victor 1879–1933 Dan. arctic explorer & ethnologist
Ras·pu·tin \ra-ˈsp(y)üt-ᵊn, -ˈpu̇t-\ Grigori Efimovich 1871?–1916 Russ. monk
Ra·the·nau \ˈrät-ᵊn-ˌau̇, ˈrath-ən-\ Emil 1838–1915 Ger. industrialist
Rausch·en·berg \ˈrau̇-shən-ˌbərg\ Robert 1925– Am. artist
Rausch·ning \ˈrau̇-shniŋ\ Hermann 1887– Am. (Ger.-born) polit. & writer
Ra·vel \rə-ˈvel, ra-\ Mau·rice \mȯ-ˈrēs\ Joseph 1875–1937 Fr. composer
Raw·lin·son \ˈrȯ-lən-sən\ George 1812–1902 Eng. hist.
Rawlinson Sir Henry Cres·wicke \ˈkrez-ik\ 1810–1895 *bro. of prec.* Eng. Assyriologist
Ray \ˈrā\ John 1627?–1705 Eng. naturalist
Ray·burn \ˈrā-(ˌ)bərn\ Samuel Tal·ia·ferro \ˈtäl-ə-vər\ 1882–1961 *Sam* Am. lawyer & polit.
Ray·leigh \ˈrā-lē\ 3d Baron 1842–1919 *John William Strutt* Eng. math. & physicist
Read \ˈrēd\ George 1733–1798 Am. lawyer & revolutionist
Read Sir Herbert 1893–1968 Eng. writer
Read Thomas Buchanan 1822–1872 Am. poet & painter
Reade \ˈrēd\ Charles 1814–1884 Eng. nov. & dram.
Read·ing \ˈred-iŋ\ 1st Marquis of 1860–1935 *Rufus Daniel Isaacs* Brit. statesman; viceroy of India (1921–26)
Ré·au·mur, de \ˌrā-ō-ˈmyu̇(ə)r; rā-ˈō-mər, -ˌmyu̇(ə)r\ René Antoine Ferchault 1683–1757 Fr. naturalist & physicist
Ré·ca·mi·er \rā-ˈkam-ē-ˌā, rā-kȧ-myā\ Jeanne Françoise Julie Adélaïde 1777–1849 Fr. society wit
Red Cloud \ˈred-ˌklau̇d\ 1822–1909 Oglala Sioux Indian chief
Red·mond \ˈred-mənd\ John Edward 1856–1918 Irish polit.
Re·don \rə-ˈdōⁿ\ Odilon 1840–1916 Fr. artist
Reed \ˈrēd\ John 1887–1920 Am. journalist, poet, & Communist
Reed Stanley Forman 1884– Am. jurist
Reed Thomas Brackett 1839–1902 Am. polit.
Reed Walter 1851–1902 Am. army surgeon
Reg·u·lus \ˈreg-yə-ləs\ Marcus Atilius *d ab* 250 B.C. Rom. gen.
Rehn·quist \ˈren-ˌkwist\ William Hubbs 1924– Am. jurist
Reich·stein \ˈrīk-ˌs(h)tīn\ Tadeus 1897– Swiss (Pol.-born) chem.
Reid \ˈrēd\ Thomas 1710–1796 Scot. philos.
Reid Whitelaw 1837–1912 Am. journalist & diplomat
Rei·nach \rā-ˈnäk, re-nȧk\ Salomon 1858–1932 Fr. archaeologist
Rei·ner \ˈrī-nər\ Fritz 1888–1963 Am. (Hung.-born) conductor
Rein·hardt \ˈrīn-ˌhärt\ Max 1873–1943 orig. *Goldmann* Austrian theater director
Re·marque \rə-ˈmärk\ Erich Maria 1898–1970 Am. (Ger.-born) nov.
Rem·brandt van Rijn *or* **Ryn** \ˈrem-ˌbrant-vän-ˈrīn *also* -ˌbränt-\ 1606–1669 Du. painter — **Rem·brandt·esque** \ˌrem-ˌbrant-ˈesk, -ˌbränt-\ *adj*
Rem·ing·ton \ˈrem-iŋ-tən\ Frederic 1861–1909 Am. artist
Rem·sen \ˈrem(p)-sən, ˈrem-zən\ Ira 1846–1927 Am. chem.
Re·nan \rə-ˈnäⁿ(n)\ Joseph Ernest 1823–1892 Fr. philologist & hist.
Re·nault \rə-ˈnō\ Louis 1843–1918 Fr. jurist & pacifist
Re·ni \ˈrā-nē\ Guido 1575–1642 Ital. painter
Ren·ner \ˈren-ər\ Karl 1870–1950 Austrian statesman; pres. of Austria (1945–50)
Re·noir \ˈren-ˌwär, rən-ˈ\ Jean 1894– *son of P. A.* Fr. film producer & writer
Renoir Pierre Auguste 1841–1919 Fr. painter
Ren·wick \ˈren-(ˌ)wik\ James 1818–1895 Am. architect
Rep·plier \ˈrep-ˌli(ə)r, -lē-ər\ Agnes 1855–1950 Am. essayist
Re·spi·ghi \rə-ˈspē-gē, re-\ Ottorino 1879–1936 Ital. composer
Res·ton \ˈres-tən\ James Barrett 1909– Am. journalist
Resz·ke, de \ˈresh-kē\ Jean \ˈzhäⁿ\ 1850–1925 *Jan Mieczislaw* Pol. tenor
Retz, de \ˈrets, *Fr* re(s)\ Cardinal 1614–1679 *Jean François Paul de Gondi* Fr. ecclesiastic & polit.
Reuch·lin \ˈrȯik-lən; ˈrȯi-ˌklēn, rȯi-ˈ\ Johann 1455–1522 *Cap·nio* \ˈkap-nē-ˌō\ Ger. humanist
Reu·ter, von \ˈrȯit-ər\ Baron Paul Julius 1816–1899 orig. *Israel Beer Josaphat* Brit. (Ger.-born) newsagent
Reu·ter·dahl \ˈrȯit-ər-ˌdäl\ Henry 1871–1925 Swed.-born painter in U.S.
Reu·ther \ˈrü-thər\ Walter Philip 1907–1970 Am. labor leader
Re·vere \ri-ˈvi(ə)r\ Paul 1735–1818 Am. patriot & silversmith
Rex·roth \ˈreks-ˌrȯth\ Kenneth 1905– Am. writer
Rey·mont \ˈrā-ˌmänt\ Wła·dy·sław \vlä-ˈdis-ˌläf\ Sta·ni·sław \stä-ˈnē-ˌsläf\ 1867–1925 Pol. nov.
Rey·naud \rā-ˈnō\ Paul 1878–1966 premier of France (1940)
Reyn·olds \ˈren-ᵊl(d)z\ Sir Joshua 1723–1792 Eng. painter
Rhee \ˈrē\ Syng·man \ˈsiŋ-mən, ˈsig-\ 1875–1965 So. Korean polit.
Rhodes \ˈrōdz\ Cecil John 1853–1902 Brit. administrator & financier in So. Africa
Rhond·da \ˈrän-də, -thə\ Viscount 1856–1918 *David Alfred Thomas* Brit. industrialist & administrator
Rib·ben·trop, von \ˈrib-ən-ˌträp, -ˌtrōp\ Joachim 1893–1946 Ger. diplomat
Ri·be·ra, de \rē-ˈber-ə\ Jusepe 1588–1652 *Lo Spa·gno·let·to* \ˌlō-ˌspän-yə-ˈlet-(ˌ)ō\ Span. painter & etcher
Rib·i·coff \ˈrib-ə-ˌkȯf\ Abraham A. 1910– U.S. secy. of health, ed. & welfare (1961–62)
Ri·car·do \rik-ˈärd-(ˌ)ō\ David 1772–1823 Eng. econ.
Rice \ˈrīs\ Elmer L. 1892–1967 orig. *Elmer Reizenstein* Am. dram.
Rich·ard \ˈrich-ərd\ name of 3 kings of England: **I** (*Coeur de Li·on* \ˌkərd-ᵊl-ˈī-ən, -ˈē-ən, -ē-ˈōⁿ\) 1157–1199 (reigned 1189–99); **II** 1367–1400 (reigned 1377–99); **III** 1452–1485 (reigned 1483–85)
Rich·ards \ˈrich-ərdz\ Dickinson Woodruff 1895–1973 Am. physician
Richards Theodore William 1868–1928 Am. chem.
Rich·ard·son \ˈrich-ərd-sən\ Elliot Lee 1920– U.S. secy. of health, ed. & welfare (1970–73); atty. gen. (1973)
Richardson Henry Handel 1870–1946 pseud. of *Ethel Florence Lindesay Richardson* Austral. nov.
Richardson Henry Hobson 1838–1886 Am. architect
Richardson Sir Owen Willans 1879–1959 Eng. physicist

Richardson Sir Ralph David 1902– Brit. actor
Richardson Samuel 1689–1761 Eng. nov.
Ri·che·lieu, de \'rish-əl-ˌ(y)ü, rē-shə-lyœ̄\ Duc 1585–1642 *Armand Jean du Plessis* Fr. cardinal & statesman
Ri·chet \rē-'shā\ Charles Robert 1850–1935 Fr. physiol.
Rich·ter \'rik-tər, 'ri<u>k</u>-\ Jean Paul Friedrich 1763–1825 pseud. *Jean Paul* \'zhä^{n}-'paů(ə)l, 'jēn-'pȯl\ Ger. writer
Ri·ci·mer \'ris-ə-mər\ *d* 472 Rom. gen.
Rick·en·back·er \'rik-ən-ˌbak-ər\ Edward Vernon 1890–1973 Am. aviator
Rick·o·ver \'rik-ˌō-vər\ **Hy·man** \'hī-mən\ George 1900– Am. admiral
Rid·ley \'rid-lē\ Nicholas 1500?–1555 Eng. reformer & martyr
Rid·path \'rid-ˌpath, -ˌpȧth\ John Clark 1840–1900 Am. hist.
Ri·el \rē-'el\ Louis 1844–1885 Canad. insurgent
Rie·mann \'rē-ˌmän\ Georg Friedrich Bernhard 1826–1866 Ger. math. — **Rie·mann·ian** \rē-'män-ē-ən\ *adj*
Ri·en·zi \rē-'en-zē\ *or* **Ri·en·zo** \-(ˌ)zō\, **di** Cola 1313–1354 *Niccolo Gabrini; Last of the Romans* Ital. patriot; tribune of Rome
Ries·man \'rēs-mən\ David 1909– Am. social scientist
Riis \'rēs\ Jacob August 1849–1914 Am. (Dan.-born) social worker & writer
Ri·ley \'rī-lē\ James **Whit·comb** \'hwit-kəm, 'wit-\ 1849–1916 Am. poet
Ril·ke \'ril-kə, -kē\ **Rai·ner** \'rī-nər\ Maria 1875–1926 Ger. poet
Rim·baud \ra^{n}(m)-'bō, 'ram-ˌ\ (Jean Nicholas) Arthur 1854–1891 Fr. poet
Rimini Francesca da — see FRANCESCA DA RIMINI
Rim·ski–Kor·sa·kov \ˌrim(p)-skē-'kȯr-sə-ˌkȯf, -ˌkȯv, -ˌkȯr-sə-'\ Nikolai Andreevich 1844–1908 Russ. composer
Rin·cón, del \riŋ-'kōn\ Antonio 1446–1500 Span. painter
Rine·hart \'rīn-ˌhärt\ Mary 1876–1958 née *Roberts* Am. writer
Rí·os \'rē-ˌōs\ Juan Antonio 1888–1946 Chilean lawyer; pres. of Chile (1942–46)
Rip·ley \'rip-lē\ George 1802–1880 Am. literary critic & socialist
Ri·sto·ri \ri-'stōr-ē, -'stȯr-\ Adelaide 1822–1906 Ital. actress
Rit·ter \'rit-ər\ Joseph Elmer 1891–1967 Am. cardinal
Ri·ve·ra \ri-'ver-ə\ Diego 1886–1957 Mex. painter
Ri·ve·ra y Or·ba·ne·ja, de \-ˌē-ˌȯr-bə-'nā-(ˌ)hä\ Miguel Primo 1870–1930 Marqués *de Estella* Span. gen.; dictator (1925–30)
Riv·ers \'riv-ərz\ Larry 1923– Am. artist
Ri·zal \ri-'zäl, -'säl\ José 1861–1896 Filipino patriot
Ri·za Shah Pah·la·vi *or* **Pah·le·vi** \ri-'zä-ˌshä-'päl-ə-(ˌ)vē, -ˌshȯ-\ 1877–1944 shah of Iran (1925–41)
Riz·zio \'rit-sē-ˌō\ *or* **Ric·cio** \'rich-ē-ˌō\ David 1533?–1566 Ital. musician & favorite of Mary, Queen of Scots
Robbe–Gril·let \ˌrō-bə-grē-'yā\ Alain 1922– Fr. writer
Rob·bia, del·la \ˌdel-ə-'räb-ē-ə, -'rōb-\ Luca 1400?–1482 Florentine sculptor
Rob·bins \'räb-ənz\ Frederick C. 1916– Am. physician
Robbins Jerome 1918– Am. dancer & choreographer
Rob·ert \'räb-ərt\ — see Robert BRUCE
Robert I *d* 1035 *Robert the Devil* Duke of Normandy (1028–35) *father of William the Conqueror*
Rob·erts \'räb-ərts\ Sir Charles George Douglas 1860–1943 Canad. poet
Roberts Frederick Sleigh 1832–1914 1st Earl *Roberts of Kandahar, Pretoria, and Waterford* Brit. field marshal
Roberts Kenneth 1885–1957 Am. nov.
Roberts Owen Josephus 1875–1955 Am. jurist
Rob·ert·son \'räb-ərt-sən\ William 1721–1793 Scot. hist.
Robe·son \'rōb-sən\ Paul Bustill 1898– Am. actor & singer
Robes·pierre, de \'rōbz-ˌpi(ə)r, -ˌpyc(ə)r; ˌrō-ˌbes-'pye(ə)r\ Maximilien François Marie Isidore 1758–1794 Fr. revolutionist
Rob·in·son \'räb-ən-sən\ Edwin Arlington 1869–1935 Am. poet
Robinson George Frederick Samuel 1827–1909 1st Marquis of *Ripon* Brit. statesman
Robinson James Harvey 1863–1936 Am. hist.
Robinson Sir Robert 1886– Eng. chem.
Ro·cham·beau, de \ˌrō-ˌsham-'bō\ Comte 1725–1807 *Jean Baptiste Donatien de Vimeur* Fr. gen.
Rocke·fel·ler \'räk-i-ˌfel-ər, 'räk-ˌfel-\ John Davison father 1839–1937 & son 1874–1960 Am. oil magnates & philanthropists
Rockefeller Nelson Aldrich 1908– *grandson & son of prec.* Am. polit.
Rock·ing·ham \'räk-iŋ-əm, *US also* -iŋ-ˌham\ 2d Marquis of 1730–1782 *Charles Watson-Wentworth* Eng. statesman
Rock·ne \'räk-nē\ Knute \'nüt\ Kenneth 1888–1931 Norw.-born football coach in U.S.
Rock·well \'räk-ˌwel, -wəl\ Norman 1894– Am. illustrator
Ro·de \'rō-<u>th</u>ə\ **Hel·ge** \'hel-gə\ 1870–1937 Dan. poet
Rod·gers \'räj-ərz\ Richard 1902– Am. composer
Ro·din \'rō-da^{n}(n)\ (François) Auguste (René) 1840–1917 Fr. sculptor
Rod·ney \'räd-nē\ George **Bryd·ges** \'brij-əz\ 1719–1792 1st Baron *Rodney* Eng. admiral
Ro·dzin·ski \rō-'jin(t)-skē\ **Ar·tur** \'är-ˌtů(ə)r\ 1894–1958 Am. conductor
Roeb·ling \'rō-bliŋ\ John Augustus 1806–1869 Am. (Ger.-born) civil engineer
Roent·gen *or* **Rönt·gen** \'rent-gən, 'rənt-, -jən; 'ren-chən, 'rən-\ Wilhelm Conrad 1845–1923 Ger. physicist
Roe·rich \'rer-ik, 're(ə)r-\ Nicholas Konstantin 1874–1947 Russ. painter
Roeth·ke \'ret(h)-kē\ Theodore 1908–1963 Am. poet
Rog·ers \'räj-ərz\ Bruce 1870–1957 Am. printer & book designer
Rogers Henry **Hut·tle·ston** \'hət-^{ə}l-stən\ *or* **Hud·dle·ston** \'həd-^{ə}l-\ 1840–1909 Am. financier
Rogers James Gamble 1867–1947 Am. architect
Rogers Samuel 1763–1855 Eng. poet
Rogers William Penn Adair 1879–1935 *Will* Am. actor & humorist
Rogers William Pierce 1913– U.S. secy. of state (1969–73)
Ro·get \rō-'zhā, 'rō-ˌ\ Peter Mark 1779–1869 Eng. physician & scholar

Ro·kos·sov·ski \ˌräk-ə-'sȯf-skē, -'sȯv-\ Konstantin 1896–1968 Russ. marshal
Rolfe \'rälf\ John 1585–1622 *husband of Pocahontas* Eng. colonist
Rol·land \rō-'lä^{n}, rȯ-\ Romain 1866–1944 Fr. author
Rol·lo \'räl-(ˌ)ō\ *or* **Hrolf** \'(h)rälf\ 860?–?931 Norse chieftain
Röl·vaag \'rōl-ˌväg\ Ole \'ō-lə\ **Ed·vart** \'ed-ˌvärt\ 1876–1931 Norw.-born educ. & nov. in Am.
Ro·mains \rō-'ma^{n}\ Jules 1885–1972 pseud. of *Louis Farigoule* Fr. author
Ro·ma·no \rō-'män-(ˌ)ō\ Giulio 1499–1546 *Giulio Pippi de' Gianuzzi* Ital. painter & architect
Ro·ma·nov *or* **Ro·ma·noff** \rō-'män-əf, 'rō-mə-ˌnäf\ Mikhail Feodorovich 1596–1645 1st czar (1613–45) of Russ. Romanov dynasty (1613–1917)
Rom·berg \'räm-ˌbərg\ Sigmund 1887–1951 Hung.-born composer in Am.
Rom·mel \'räm-əl\ Erwin 1891–1944 Ger. field marshal
Rom·ney \'räm-nē, 'rəm-\ George 1734–1802 Eng. painter
Rom·ney \'räm-nē\ George Wilcken 1907– U.S. secy. of housing & urban development (1969–72)
Ron·sard, de \rō^{n}-'sär\ Pierre 1524–1585 Fr. poet
Roo·se·velt \'rō-zə-vəlt (*Roosevelts' usual pronunciation*), -ˌvelt *also* 'rü-\ (Anna) Eleanor 1884–1962 née *Roosevelt, wife of F.D.* Am. lecturer & writer
Roosevelt Franklin **Del·a·no** \'del-ə-ˌnō\ 1882–1945 32d pres. of the U.S. (1933–45)
Roosevelt Theodore 1858–1919 26th pres. of the U.S. (1901–09)
Roosevelt Theodore 1887–1944 *son of prec.* Am. gen. & polit.
Root \'rüt, 'růt\ Elihu 1845–1937 Am. lawyer & statesman
Ro·rem \'rōr-əm, 'rȯr-\ Ned 1923– Am. composer
Ro·sa \'rō-zə\ Salvator 1615–1673 Ital. painter & poet
Rose·bery \'rōz-ˌber-ē, -b(ə-)rē\ 5th Earl of 1847–1929 *Archibald Philip Primrose* Eng. statesman
Rose·crans \'rō-zə-ˌkranz, 'rōz-ˌkran(t)s\ William Starke 1819–1898 Am. gen.
Ro·sen·berg \'rōz-^{ə}n-ˌbərg, -ˌbe(ə)rg\ Alfred 1893–1946 Ger. Nazi & writer
Ro·sen·wald \'rōz-^{ə}n-ˌwȯld\ Julius 1862–1932 Am. merchant & philanthropist
Ross \'rȯs\ Betsy 1752–1836 née *Griscom* maker of first Am. flag
Ross Sir James Clark 1800–1862 Scot. polar explorer
Ross Sir John 1777–1856 *uncle of prec.* Scot. arctic explorer
Ross Sir Ronald 1857–1932 Brit. physician
Rosse Earl of — see William PARSONS
Ros·set·ti \rō-'zet-ē, -'set-\ Christina Georgina 1830–1894 *sister of D.G.* Eng. poet
Rossetti Dante Gabriel 1828–1882 Eng. painter & poet
Ros·si \'rȯs-ē\ Bruno 1905– Ital.-born physicist in Am.
Ros·si·ni \rō-'sē-nē, rə-\ **Gio·ac·chi·no** \ˌjō-ə-'kē-(ˌ)nō\ Antonio 1792–1868 Ital. composer
Ros·tand \rō-'stä^{n}, 'räs-ˌtand\ Edmond 1868–1918 Fr. poet & dram.
Roth \'rȯth\ Philip 1933– Am. writer
Roth·ko \'räth-(ˌ)kō\ Mark 1903–1970 Am. (Russ.-born) painter
Roth·schild \'rȯth(s)-ˌchīld, 'rȯs-, *Ger* 'rōt-ˌshilt\ Meyer Amschel 1743–1812 Ger. financier
Rothschild Nathan Meyer 1777–1836 *son of prec.* financier in London
Rou·ault \rü-'ō\ Georges 1871–1958 Fr. painter
Rou·get de Lisle \(ˌ)rü-ˌzhā-də-'lē(ə)l\ Claude Joseph 1760–1836 Fr. army officer & composer
Rous·seau \rü-'sō, 'rü-ˌ\ Henri 1844–1910 *the Douanier* Fr. painter
Rousseau Jean Jacques 1712–1778 Fr. (Swiss-born) philos. & writer
Rousseau Théodore 1812–1867 Fr. painter
Rowe \'rō\ Nicholas 1674–1718 Eng. poet & dram.; poet laureate (1715–18)
Row·ley \'rō-lē, 'raů-\ William 1585?–?1642 Eng. actor & dram.
Ro·xas y Acu·ña \'rō-ˌhäs-ˌē-ə-'kün-yə\ Manuel 1892–1948 Philippine statesman; pres. of the Philippine Republic (1946–48)
Roy·all \'rȯi(-ə)l\ Kenneth Claiborne 1894–1971 Am. lawyer & statesman
Royce \'rȯis\ Josiah 1855–1916 Am. philos.
Rozh·dest·ven·ski \rȯzh-'dest-vən-skē\ Zinovi Petrovich 1848–1909 Russ. admiral
Ru·bens \'rü-bənz\ Peter Paul 1577–1640 Flem. painter — **Ru·ben·esque** \ˌrü-bə-'nesk\ *adj* — **Ru·ben·si·an** \rü-'ben-zē-ən\ *adj*
Ru·bin·stein \'rü-bən-ˌstīn\ **An·ton** \än-'tōn\ 1829–1894 Russ. pianist & composer
Rubinstein Arthur 1889– Pol.-born pianist in Am.
Ru·dolf I of Hapsburg \'rü-ˌdälf\ 1218–1291 Holy Rom. emp. (1273–91); 1st of the Hapsburgs
Rudolf *or* **Rudolph of Hapsburg** 1858–1889 archduke & crown prince of Austria
Ruis·dael *or* **Ruys·dael, van** \'rīz-ˌdäl, 'rīs-\ Jacob 1628?–1682 & his uncle Salomon 1600?–1670 Du. painters
Ruiz Cor·ti·nes \rü-ˌēs-kȯr-'tē-nəs\ Adolfo 1891– pres. of Mex. (1952–58)
Rumford Count — see Benjamin THOMPSON
Rund·stedt, von \'rün(t)-ˌs(h)tet\ Karl Rudolf Gerd 1875–1953 Ger. field marshal
Ru·ne·berg \'rü-nə-ˌbərg, -ˌber-ē\ Johan Ludvig 1804–1877 Finnish poet
Runjit Singh — see RANJIT SINGH
Run·yon \'rən-yən\ (Alfred) **Da·mon** \'dā-mən\ 1880–1946 Am. author

Ru·pert \'rü-pərt\ Prince 1619–1682 *nephew of Charles I of Eng.* Ger.-Eng. gen. & admiral
Rupert *or* **Rup·precht** \'rüp-ˌrekt, -ˌrekt\ 1869–1955 crown prince of Bavaria & Ger. field marshal
Rush \'rəsh\ Benjamin 1745?–1813 Am. physician & Revolutionary patriot
Rush Richard 1780–1859 *son of prec.* Am. lawyer & statesman
Rusk \'rəsk\ (David) Dean 1909– U.S. secy. of state (1961–69)
Rus·kin \'rəs-kən\ John 1819–1900 Eng. essayist, critic, & reformer — **Rus·kin·ian** \ˌrəs-'kin-ē-ən\ *adj*
Rus·sell \'rəs-əl\ 3d Earl 1872–1970 *Bertrand Arthur Russell* Eng. math. & philos.
Russell Charles Marion 1864–1926 Am. artist
Russell Charles Taze 1852–1916 Am. pastor
Russell Countess 1866–1941 *Elizabeth Mary Beauchamp Russell* pseud. *Elizabeth* Austral.-born nov.
Russell George William 1867–1935 pseud. *Æ* Irish author
Russell Lord John 1792–1878 1st Earl *Russell of Kingston Russell* Brit. statesman
Russell Lillian 1861–1922 *Helen Louise Leonard* Am. singer & actress
Rus·tin \'rəs-tən\ Bayard 1910– Am. civil rights leader
Ruth·er·ford \'rəth-ə(r)-fərd, 'rəth-\ Ernest 1871–1937 1st Baron *Rutherford of Nelson* Brit. physicist
Rutherford Joseph Franklin 1869–1942 *Judge* Am. leader of Jehovah's Witnesses
Rut·ledge \'rət-lij\ Ann 1816–1835 fiancée of Abraham Lincoln
Rutledge John 1739–1800 Am. statesman & jurist; chief justice U.S. Supreme Court (1795)
Rutledge Wiley Blount \'blənt\ 1894–1949 Am. jurist
Ruy·ter *or* **Rui·ter, de** \'rīt-ər\ Michel Adriaanszoon 1607–1676 Du. admiral
Ru·zic·ka \'rü-ˌz(h)ich-kə, -ˌzhits-\ Leopold 1887– Yugoslav chem.
Ry·der \'rīd-ər\ Albert Pinkham 1847–1917 Am. painter
Rys·kind \'ris-kənd\ Morris 1895– Am. dram.
Saa·ri·nen \'sär-ə-nən\ Ee·ro \'e(ə)r-(ˌ)ō\ 1910–1961 Am. architect
Saarinen (Gottlieb) Eliel 1873–1950 *father of prec.* Finnish architect
Saa·ve·dra La·mas \sä-ˌväd-rə-'läm-əs, -ˌväth-\ Carlos 1880–1959 Argentine lawyer & diplomat
Sa·ba·tier \ˌsab-ə-'tyā\ Paul 1854–1941 Fr. chem.
Sa·ba·ti·ni \ˌsab-ə-'tē-nē, ˌsäb-\ Rafael 1875–1950 Ital. author
Sac·co \'sak-(ˌ)ō\ Nicola 1891–1927 & **Van·zet·ti** \van-'zet-ē\ Bartolomeo 1888–1927 Am. (Ital.-born) anarchists
Sachs \'zäks, 'saks\ Hans 1494–1576 Ger. cobbler & Meistersinger
Sachs \'saks, 'zäks\ Nelly 1891–1970 Swed. dram. & poet
Sack·ville \'sak-ˌvil\ Thomas 1536–1608 1st Earl of *Dorset* Eng. poet & diplomat
Sackville–West \-'west\ Victoria Mary 1892–1962 Eng. writer
Sa·dat, el- \ˌel-sə-'dat, -'dät\ Anwar 1918– pres. of Egypt (1970–)
Sade, de \'säd, 'sād, 'sad\ Comte Donatien Alphonse François 1740–1814 Marquis *de Sade* Fr. soldier & pervert
Sa·gan \sà-'gäⁿ, sä-\ Françoise 1935– pseud. of *Françoise Quoirez* Fr. writer
Sage \'sāj\ Russell 1816–1906 Am. financier
Saint–Cyr \saⁿ-'si(ə)r\ Marquis Laurent de Gouvion 1764–1830 Fr. gen. under Napoleon; marshal of France
St. Den·is \sānt-'den-əs, sənt-\ Ruth 1878–1968 Am. dancer
Sainte–Beuve \saⁿt-bœv; sānt-'bə(r)v, sənt-\ Charles Augustin 1804–1869 Fr. critic & author
Saint–Gau·dens \sānt-'gȯd-ᵊnz, sənt-\ Augustus 1848–1907 Irish-born sculptor in Am.
St. John Henry — see BOLINGBROKE
Saint–Just, de \saⁿ-zhüest; sānt-'jəst, sənt-\ Louis Antoine Léon 1767–1794 Fr. Revolutionist
St. Lau·rent \saⁿ-lȯ-räⁿ\ Louis Stephen 1882–1973 Canad. lawyer; prime min. (1948–57)
Saint–Pierre — see BERNARDIN DE SAINT-PIERRE
Saint–Saëns \saⁿ-säⁿs\ (Charles) Camille 1835–1921 Fr. composer
Saints·bury \'sānts-ˌber-ē, -b(ə-)rē\ George Edward Bateman 1845–1933 Eng. critic
Saint–Si·mon, de \saⁿ-sē-mōⁿ\ Comte 1760–1825 *Claude Henri de Rouvroy* Fr. philos. & social scientist
Saint–Simon, de Duc 1675–1755 *Louis de Rouvroy* Fr. soldier, statesman, & writer
Sai·on·ji \sī-'än-jē, -'ȯn-\ Marquis Kimmochi 1849–1940 Jap. statesman
Sa·kha·rov \'säk-ə-ˌrȯf, 'säk-, -ˌrȯv\ Andrei Dimitrievich 1921– Russ. physicist
Sa·ki \'säk-ē\ 1870–1916 pseud. of *Hector Hugh Mun·ro* \(ˌ)mən-'rō\ Brit. writer
Sal·a·din \'sal-əd-ən\ 1138–1193 sultan of Egypt & Syria
Sa·la·zar \ˌsal-ə-'zär, ˌsäl-\ Antonio de Oliveira 1889–1970 Port. chief of state
Sal·in·ger \'sal-ən-jər\ Jerome David 1919– Am. nov.
Salisbury 1st Earl of & 3d Marquis of — see CECIL
Salk \'sȯ(l)k\ Jonas 1914– Am. physician
Sal·lust \'sal-əst\ 86–34 B.C. *Gaius Sallustius Crispus* Rom. hist. & polit. — **Sal·lus·ti·an** \sə-'ləs-tē-ən, sa-\ *adj*
Sal·ve·mi·ni \sal-'vā-mə-nē, säl-\ Gaetano 1873–1957 Ital. hist.
Sal·vi·ni \sal-'vē-nē, säl-\ Tommaso 1829–1916 Ital. actor
Sán·chez de Bus·ta·man·te y Sir·vén \'sän-chəz-də-ˌbüs-tə-'mänt-ē-ē-si(ə)r-'ven\ Antonio 1865–1951 Cuban jurist
Sand \'sand, 'säⁿ(n)d, säⁿ\ George 1804–1876 pseud. of *Amandine Aurore Lucie* née *Dupin;* Baronne *Dudevant* Fr. writer
Sand·burg \'san(d)-ˌbərg\ Carl 1878–1967 orig. *Charles August Sandburg* Am. author
Sandracottus *or* **Sandrocottus** — see CHANDRAGUPTA
San·gal·lo, da \sän-'gäl-(ˌ)ō, säŋ-\ Giuliano 1445–1516 Florentine architect & sculptor
Sang·er \'saŋ-ər\ Frederick 1918– Brit. chem.
Sanger Margaret 1883–1966 née *Higgins* Am. birth-control leader
San Mar·tín, de \ˌsan-(ˌ)mär-'tēn, ˌsän-\ José 1778–1850 So. Am. soldier & statesman
San·ta An·na *or* **San·ta Ana, de** \ˌsant-ə-'an-ə, ˌsänt-ə-'än-ə\ Antonio López 1795?–1876 Mex. gen. & pres.
San·tan·der \ˌsän-ˌtän-'de(ə)r, ˌsan-ˌtan-\ Francisco de Paula 1792–1840 gen. & polit. of New Granada
San·ta·ya·na \ˌsant-ə-'yän-ə, ˌsant-ē-'än-, ˌsänt-\ George 1863–1952 Am. (Span.-born) poet & philos.
San·tos–Du·mont \ˌsant-əs-d(y)ü-'mänt, säⁿ-tōs-dūē-'mōⁿ\ Alberto 1873–1932 Brazilian aeronaut in France
Sa·pir \sə-'pi(ə)r\ Edward 1884–1939 Am. (Pomerania-born) anthropol. & linguist
Sap·pho \'saf-(ˌ)ō\ *fl ab* 600 B.C. Greek poet
Sa·ra·gat \ˌsär-ə-'gät\ Giuseppe 1898– pres. of Italy (1964–71)
Sar·da·na·pa·lus \ˌsäˌd-ᵊn-'ap-(ə-)ləs, -ᵊn-ə-'pā-ləs\ king of Assyria (*ab* 822 B.C.); sometimes identified with Ashurbanipal
Sar·dou \sär-'dü\ Victorien 1831–1908 Fr. dram.
Sar·gent \'sär-jənt\ John Sing·er \'siŋ-ər\ 1856–1925 Am. painter
Sar·gon II \'sär-ˌgän, -gən\ *d* 705 B.C. king of Assyria (722–705)
Sa·roy·an \sə-'rȯi-ən\ William 1908– Am. writer
Sar·tre \'särtrᵊ\ Jean-Paul 1905– Fr. philos., dram., & nov. — **Sar·tri·an** \'sär-trē-ən\ *adj*
Sas·soon \sa-'sün, sə-\ Siegfried Lorraine 1886–1967 Eng. writer
Sa·tie \sa-'tē, sä-\ Erik 1866–1925 *Alfred Erik Leslie-Satie* Fr. composer
Sa·to \'sä-(ˌ)tō\ Eisaku 1901– Jap. premier (1964–72)
Sato Naotake 1882–1971 Jap. diplomat
Sa'ud Ibn Abd·ul \sä-'üd-ˌib-ə-nəb-'dül, 'saůd-\ 1902–1969 king of Saudi Arabia (1953–64)
Sav·age \'sav-ij\ Michael Joseph 1872–1940 prime min. of N.Z. (1935–40)
Savage Richard 1697?–1743 Eng. poet
Sa·vo·na·ro·la \ˌsav-ə-nə-'rō-lə, sə-ˌvän-ə-'rō-\ Gi·ro·la·mo \ji-'rōl-ə-ˌmō\ 1452–1498 Ital. reformer
Saw·yer \'sȯ-yər, 'sȯi-ər\ Charles 1887– Am. lawyer & administrator
Saxe, de \'saks\ Comte Hermann Maurice 1696–1750 Fr. soldier; marshal of France
Saxo Gram·mat·i·cus \ˌsak-(ˌ)sō-grə-'mat-i-kəs\ 1150?–?1220 Dan. hist.
Say·ers \'sa(ə)rz, 'se(ə)rz, 'sā-ərz\ Dorothy Leigh 1893–1957 Eng. writer
Scal·i·ger \'skal-ə-jər\ Joseph Justus 1540–1609 Ital.-born physician & scholar
Scaliger Julius Caesar 1484–1558 *father of prec.* Ital. physician
Scan·der·beg \'skan-dər-ˌbeg\ *Turk.* **Iskender Bey** 1403?–1468 *George Castriota* Albanian chieftain
Scar·lat·ti \skär-'lät-ē\ Alessandro 1659–1725 & his son Domenico 1685–1757 Ital. composers
Scar·ron \ska-'rōⁿ\ Paul 1610–1660 Fr. author
Schacht \'shäkt, 'shäkt\ (Horace Greeley) Hjal·mar \'yäl-ˌmär\ 1877–1970 Ger. financier
Scharn·horst, von \'shärn-ˌhȯrst\ Gerhard Johann David 1755–1813 Prussian gen.
Schar·wen·ka \shär-'veŋ-kə\ Philipp 1847–1917 & his bro. Xaver 1850–1924 Ger. pianists & composers
Schei·de·mann \'shīd-ə-ˌmän\ Philipp 1865–1939 Ger. polit.
Schel·ling, von \'shel-iŋ\ Friedrich Wilhelm Joseph 1775–1854 Ger. philos. — **Schel·ling·ian** \she-'liŋ-ē-ən\ *adj*
Schia·pa·rel·li \skē-ˌäp-ə-'rel-ē, ˌskap-\ Giovanni Virginio 1835–1910 Ital. astron.
Schick \'shik\ Bé·la \'bā-lə\ 1877–1967 Am. (Hung.-born) pediatrician
Schil·ler, von \'shil-ər\ Johann Christoph Friedrich 1759–1805 Ger. poet & dram.
Schi·rach, von \'shē-ˌräk, -ˌräk\ Baldur 1907– Ger. Nazi polit.
Schle·gel, von \'shlā-gəl\ August Wilhelm 1767–1845 Ger. author
Schlegel, von Friedrich 1772–1829 *bro. of prec.* Ger. philos. & writer
Schlei·cher, von \'shlī-kər, -kər\ Kurt 1882–1934 Ger. soldier & statesman
Schlei·er·ma·cher \'shlī-ər-ˌmäk-ər, -ˌmäk-\ Friedrich Ernst Daniel 1768–1834 Ger. theol. & philos.
Schle·sing·er \'shlā-ziŋ-ər\ Arthur Meier father 1888–1965 & son 1917– Am. historians
Schlesinger James R. 1929– U.S. secy. of defense (1973–)
Schley \'s(h)lī\ Winfield Scott 1839–1911 Am. admiral
Schlie·mann \'shlē-ˌmän\ Heinrich 1822–1890 Ger. archaeologist
Schna·bel \'shnäb-əl\ Ar·tur \'är-ˌtů(ə)r\ 1882–1951 Am. (Austrian-born) pianist & composer
Schnitz·ler \'shnit-slər\ Arthur 1862–1931 Austrian physician, dram., & nov.
Scho·field \'skō-ˌfēld\ John McAllister 1831–1906 Am. gen.
Schön·berg \'shə(r)n-ˌbərg, 'shœn-ˌberk\ Arnold 1874–1951 Am. (Austrian-born) composer
Scho·pen·hau·er \'shō-pən-ˌhaů(-ə)r\ Arthur 1788–1860 Ger. pessimist philos.
Schrö·ding·er \'shrād-iŋ-ər, 'shrœd-\ Erwin 1887–1961 Austrian physicist
Schu·bert \'shü-bərt, -ˌbert\ Franz Peter 1797–1828 Austrian composer
Schulz \'shůlts\ Charles Monroe 1922– Am. cartoonist
Schu·man \'shü-ˌmän, -mən\ Robert 1886–1963 Fr. statesman
Schu·man \'shü-mən\ William Howard 1910– Am. composer
Schu·mann \'shü-ˌmän, -mən\ Robert 1810–1856 Ger. composer
Schu·mann–Heink \ˌshü-mən-'hīŋk\ Ernestine 1861–1936 née *Roessler* Austrian-born contralto
Schur·man \'shů(ə)r-mən, 'shər-\ Jacob Gould 1854–1942 Am. philos. & diplomat
Schurz \'shů(ə)rts, 'shərts\ Carl 1829–1906 Am. (Ger.-born) lawyer, gen., & polit.
Schusch·nigg, von \'shůsh-(ˌ)nik, -(ˌ)nig\ Kurt 1897– Austrian statesman
Schuy·ler \'skī-lər\ Philip John 1733–1804 Am. gen. & statesman

Schweit·zer \'s(h)wīt-sər, 'shvīt-\ Albert 1875–1965 Fr. Protestant clergyman, philos., physician, & music scholar
Scip·io \'sip-ē-ˌō, 'skip-\ **Aemilianus Af·ri·ca·nus** \ˌaf-rə-'kan-əs, -'kän-, -'kān-\ **Numantinus** Publius Cornelius 185–129 B.C. *Scipio the Younger* Rom. gen.
Scipio Africanus Publius Cornelius 237–183 B.C. *Scipio the Elder* Rom. gen.
Scopes \'skōps\ John Thomas 1900–1970 Am. teacher
Scott \'skät\ Dred \'dred\ 1795?–1858 Am. Negro slave; central figure in U.S. lawsuit
Scott Sir George Gilbert 1811–1878 Eng. architect
Scott Robert Falcon 1868–1912 Eng. antarctic explorer
Scott Sir Walter 1771–1832 Scot. poet & nov.
Scott Winfield 1786–1866 Am. gen.
Scotus Duns — see DUNS SCOTUS
Scotus Johannes — see ERIGENA
Scria·bin *or* **Scria·bine** \skrē-'äb-ən\ Alexander 1872–1915 Russ. composer
Scribe \skrēb\ Augustin Eugène 1791–1861 Fr. dram.
Scud·der \'skəd-ər\ Horace Elisha 1838–1902 Am. author
Scu·dé·ry, de \ˌsküd-ə-'rē, skue̅-dā-rē\ Magdeleine 1607–1701 *Sa·pho* \sȧ-fō\ Fr. poet, nov., & lady of fashion
Sea·borg \'sē-ˌbȯ(ə)rg\ Glenn Theodore 1912– Am. chem.
Sears \'si(ə)rz\ Richard Warren 1863–1914 Am. merchant
See \'sē\ Thomas Jefferson Jackson 1866–1962 Am. astronomer & math.
Seeckt, von \'zākt\ Hans 1866–1936 Ger. army officer
See·ger \'sē-gər\ Alan 1888–1916 Am. poet
Seeger Peter 1919– *Pete* Am. folk singer
Se·fe·ri·a·des \ˌsef-ˌer-'yäth-ēs\ Giorgos Stylianou 1900–1971 pseud. *George Se·fe·ris* \se-'fer-ēs\ Greek diplomat & poet
Se·go·via \sā-'gō-vyə, -vē-ə\ Andrés 1894– Span. guitarist & composer
Se·grè \sə-'grā, sā-\ Emilio 1905– Am. (Ital.-born) physicist
Se·ja·nus \si-'jā-nəs\ Lucius Aelius *d* A.D. 31 Rom. conspirator
Sel·den \'sel-dən\ George Baldwin 1846–1922 Am. lawyer & inventor
Selden John 1584–1654 Eng. jurist & antiquarian
Se·leu·cus I \sə-'lü-kəs\ 358?–280 B.C. ruler (306–280) of a Greek dynasty in Syria
Sel·in·court, de \'sel-ən-ˌkō(ə)rt, -ˌkȯ(ə)rt\ Hugh 1878–1951 Eng. nov. & dram.
Sel·kirk \'sel-ˌkərk\ Alexander 1676–1721 Scot. sailor marooned on one of Juan Fernández islets; original of Defoe's Robinson Crusoe
Sem·brich \'sem-brik\ Marcella 1858–1935 *Praxede Marcelline Kochanska* Austrian-born soprano
Se·më·nov \sə-'myȯn-əf\ Nikolai Nikolaevitch 1896– Russ. chem.
Semmes \'semz\ Raphael 1809–1877 Am. Confed. admiral
Sen·e·ca \'sen-i-kə\ Lucius Annaeus 4 B.C.?–A.D. 65 Rom. statesman & philos. — **Sen·e·can** \-kən\ *adj*
Sen·ghor \seŋ-'gȯ(ə)r, sä^{n}-'gȯ(ə)r\ Leopold Sedar 1906– pres. of Senegal (1960–)
Sen·nach·er·ib \sə-'nak-ə-rəb\ *d* 681 B.C. king of Assyria (705–681)
Se·quoya \si-'kwȯi-ə\ 1770?–1843 Cherokee Indian scholar
Ser·kin \'sər-kən\ Rudolf 1903– Am. (Bohemian-born) pianist
Ser·ra \'ser-ə\ **Ju·ní·pe·ro** \hü-'nē-pə-ˌrō\ 1713–1784 orig. *Miguel José* Span. missionary in Mexico & California
Ser·ra·no Su·ñer \sə-ˌrän-ō-sün-'ye(ə)r\ Ramón 1901– *bro.-in-law of Franco* Span. lawyer & polit.
Ser·to·ri·us \(ˌ)sər-'tōr-ē-əs, -'tȯr-\ Quintus *d* 72 B.C. Rom. gen. & statesman
Ser·ve·tus \(ˌ)sər-'vēt-əs\ Michael 1511–1553 Span. theol. & martyr
Ser·vice \'sər-vəs\ Robert William 1874–1958 Canad. writer
Ses·sions \'sesh-ənz\ Roger 1896– Am. composer
Se·ton \'sēt-ᵊn\ Elizabeth Ann née *Bayley* 1774–1821 *Mother Seton* Am. religious leader
Seton Ernest Thompson 1860–1946 orig. surname *Thompson* Eng.-born writer & illustrator in Am.
Seu·rat \sə-'rä\ Georges 1859–1891 Fr. painter
Seuss — see Theodor Seuss GEISEL
Se·ve·rus \sə-'vir-əs\ Lucius Septimius 146–211 Rom. emp. (193–211)
Sé·vi·gné, de \ˌsā-(ˌ)vēn-'yā, sā-'vēn-(ˌ)yā\ Marquise 1626–1696 née *Marie de Rabutin-Chantal* Fr. writer & lady of fashion
Sew·ard \'sü-ərd, 'sü(-ə)rd\ William Henry 1801–1872 Am. statesman; secy. of state (1861–69)
Sew·ell \'sü-əl\ Anna 1820–1878 Brit. writer
Sey·mour \'sē-ˌmō(ə)r, -ˌmȯ(ə)r\ Jane 1509?–1537 *3d wife of Henry VIII of Eng. & mother of Edward VI*
Seyss–In·quart, von \'zī-'siŋ(k)-ˌfärt\ **Ar·tur** \'är-ˌtü(ə)r\ 1892–1946 Ger. Nazi polit.
Sfor·za \'sfȯrt-(ˌ)sä, -sə\ Count Carlo 1873–1952 Ital. anti-Fascist statesman
Shack·le·ton \'shak-əl-tən, -əlt-ᵊn\ Sir Ernest Henry 1874–1922 Brit. antarctic explorer
Shad·well \'shad-ˌwel, -wəl\ Thomas 1642?–1692 Eng. dram.; poet laureate (1688–92)
Shaf·ter \'shaf-tər\ William Rufus 1835–1906 Am. gen.
Shaftes·bury \'shaf(t)s-ˌber-ē, -b(ə-)rē\ 1st Earl of 1621–1683 *Anthony Ashley Cooper* Eng. statesman
Shah Ja·han \ˌshäj-ə-'hän\ 1592–1666 Mogul emp. of Hindustan (1628–58)
Shahn \'shän\ Ben 1898–1969 Am. (Lithuanian-born) painter
Shake·speare *or* **Shak·spere** \'shāk-ˌspi(ə)r\ William 1564–1616 Eng. dram. & poet
Sha·piro \shə-'pi(ə)r-(ˌ)ō\ Karl Jay 1913– Am. poet & critic
Shas·tri \'shäs-trē\ Shri Lal \'läl\ Bahadur 1904–1966 Indian polit.; prime min. of India (1964–66)
Shaw \'shȯ\ George Bernard 1856–1950 Brit. (Irish-born) author & socialist
Shaw Thomas Edward — see T. E. LAWRENCE

Shawn \'shȯn\ Ted 1891–1972 Am. dancer & choreographer
Shays \'shāz\ Daniel 1747?–1825 Am. Revolutionist & rebel
Shee·ler \'shē-lər\ Charles 1883–1965 Am. painter & photographer
She·han \'shē-ən\ Lawrence Joseph 1898– Am. cardinal
Shel·ley \'shel-ē\ Mary Woll·stone·craft \'wu̇l-stən-ˌkraft\ 1797–1851 née *Godwin; wife of P. B.* Eng. nov.
Shelley Percy Bysshe \'bish\ 1792–1822 Eng. poet — **Shel·ley·an** \'shel-ē-ən\ *or* **Shel·ley·esque** \ˌshel-ē-'esk\ *adj*
Shen·stone \'shen-ˌstōn, 'shen(t)-stən\ William 1714–1763 Eng. poet
Shep·ard \'shep-ərd\ Alan Bartlett 1923– Am. astronaut; 1st Am. in space (1961)
Sher·a·ton \'sher-ət-ᵊn\ Thomas 1751–1806 Eng. furniture maker
Sher·i·dan \'sher-əd-ᵊn\ Philip Henry 1831–1888 Am. gen.
Sheridan Richard Brins·ley \'brinz-lē\ 1751–1816 Irish dram. & orator
Sher·man \'shər-mən\ James Schoolcraft 1855–1912 vice-pres. of the U.S. (1909–12)
Sherman John 1823–1900 *bro. of W. T.* Am. statesman
Sherman Roger 1721–1793 Am. jurist & statesman
Sherman Stuart Pratt 1881–1926 Am. critic
Sherman William Tecumseh 1820–1891 Am. gen.
Sher·riff \'sher-əf\ Robert Cedric 1896– Eng. writer
Sher·ring·ton \'sher-iŋ-tən\ Sir Charles Scott 1861–1952 Eng. physiol.
Sher·wood \'shər-ˌwu̇d *also* 'she(ə)r-\ Robert Emmet 1896–1955 Am. dram.
Shi·de·ha·ra \ˌshēd-ə-'här-ə\ Baron Kijuro 1872–1951 Jap. diplomat & statesman
Shi·ge·mit·su \ˌshē-gə-'mit-(ˌ)sü, ˌshig-ə-\ Mamoru 1887–1957 Jap. diplomat
Shih Huang–ti \'shi(ə)r-'hwäŋ-'tē, 'shē-\ 259–210 B.C. Chin. emp. Ch'in dynasty
Shin·well \'shin-ˌwel, -wəl\ Emanuel 1884– Brit. polit.
Shi·rer \'shīr-ər\ William Lawrence 1904– Am. journalist
Shir·ley \'shər-lē\ James 1596–1666 Eng. dram.
Shock·ley \'shäk-lē\ William Bradford 1910– Am. physicist
Sho·lo·khov \'shȯl-ə-ˌkȯf, -ˌkȯv\ Mikhail Aleksandrovich 1905– Russ. nov.
Sho·sta·ko·vich \ˌshäs-tə-'kō-vich, ˌshȯs-, -'kȯ-\ **Di·mi·tri** \də-'mē-trē\ Dimitrievich 1906– Russ. composer
Shri·ver \'shrī-vər, *esp South* 'srī-\ Robert Sargent 1915 – Am. lawyer
Shultz \'shu̇lts\ George Pratt 1920– U.S. secy. of labor (1969–70), of the treasury (1972–)
Shute \'shüt\ Nev·il \'nev-əl\ 1899–1960 *Nevil Shute Norway* Eng. aeronautical engineer & writer
Shver·nik \'shfer-nik\ Nikolai M. 1888–1970 Russ. polit.; pres. U.S.S.R. (1946–53)
Si·be·lius \sə-'bāl-yəs, -'bā-lē-əs\ Jean \'zhän, 'yän\ 1865–1957 Finnish composer
Sick·les \'sik-əlz\ Daniel Edgar 1825–1914 Am. gen. & polit.
Sid·dons \'sid-ᵊnz\ Sarah 1755–1831 née *Kemble* Eng. actress
Sid·ney \'sid-nē\ Sir Philip 1554–1586 Eng. poet, statesman, & soldier
Sieg·bahn \'sēg-ˌbän\ Karl Manne Georg 1886– Swed. physicist
Sie·mens \'sē-mənz\ Sir William 1823–1883 Brit. (Ger.-born) inventor
Sien·kie·wicz \shen-'kyā-vich\ Henryk 1846–1916 Pol. nov.
Sie·vers \'sē-vərz; 'zē-fərs, -vərs\ Eduard 1850–1932 Ger. philologist
Sie·yès \sē-ā-'yes\ Emmanuel Joseph 1748–1836 *Abbé Sieyès* Fr. Revolutionist
Sig·is·mund \'sig-ə-smənd\ 1368–1437 Holy Rom. emp. (1411–37)
Sigs·bee \'sigz-bē\ Charles Dwight 1845–1923 Am. admiral
Si·gurds·son \'sig-ərd-sən, -ərth-\ Jón \'yōn\ 1811–1879 Icelandic statesman & author
Si·kor·ski \sə-'kȯr-skē\ Władysław 1881–1943 Pol. gen. & statesman
Si·kor·sky \sə-'kȯr-skē\ Igor Ivan 1889–1972 Am. (Russ.-born) aeronautical engineer
Sil·lan·pää \'sil-ən-ˌpa\ Frans Eemil 1888–1964 Finnish nov.
Si·lo·ne \si-'lō-nē\ Ignazio 1900– real name *Secondo Tranquilli* Ital. author
Si·me·non \ˌsē-mə-'nō^{n}\ Georges Joseph Christian 1903– Fr. (Belg.-born) writer
Sim·e·on Sty·li·tes \ˌsim-ē-ən-stə-'līt-ēz, -ˌstī-\ Saint 390?–459 Syrian ascetic & stylite
Si·mon \'sī-mən\ 1st Viscount 1873–1954 *John Allsebrook Simon* Brit. jurist & statesman
Simon Neil 1927– Am. playwright
Si·mon·i·des \sī-'män-ə-ˌdēz\ **of Ceos** 6th–5th cent. B.C. Greek poet
Simp·son \'sim(p)-sən\ William Hood 1888– Am. gen.
Sims \'simz\ William Sow·den \'sau̇d-ᵊn\ 1858–1936 Am. admiral
Sin·clair \'sin-ˌkla(ə)r, 'siŋ-, -ˌkle(ə)r, sin-', siŋ-'\ May 1865?–1946 Eng. nov.
Sinclair Upton Beall \'bel\ 1878–1968 Am. writer & polit.
Sing·er \'siŋ-ər\ Isaac Bashevis 1904– Am. (Pol.-born) author
Singer Isaac Merrit 1811–1875 Am. inventor
Si·quei·ros \si-'kā-(ˌ)rōs\ David **Al·fa·ro** \äl-'fär-(ˌ)ō\ 1898– Mex. muralist
Si·raj–ud–dau·la \sə-ˌräj-ə-'dau̇-lə\ 1728?–1757 nawab of Bengal (1756–57)
Sis·ley \'siz-lē, sēs-le\ Alfred 1839–1899 Eng.-born painter in France

---

ə abut ᵊ kitten, F table ər further a back ā bake
ä cot, cart ȧ F bac au̇ out ch chin e less ē easy
g gift i trip ī life j joke k̲ G ich ^{n} F vin ŋ sing
ō flow ȯ flaw œ F bœuf œ̄ F feu ȯi coin th thing
th̲ this ü loot u̇ foot ue G Füllenue̅ F rue y yet
^{y} F digne \dēn^{y}\, nuit \nw^{y}ē\ yü few yu̇ furious zh vision

Sis·mon·di, de \sis-ˈmän-dē, sēs-mō^{n}-dē\ Jean Charles Léonard Simonde 1773–1842 Swiss hist. & econ.
Sit·ter, de \ˈsit-ər\ Willem 1872–1934 Du. astron.
Sit·ting Bull \ˌsit-iŋ-ˈbu̇l\ 1834–1890 Sioux leader & medicine man
Sit·well \ˈsit-ˌwel, -wəl\ Sir George Reres·by \ˈri(ə)rz-bē\ 1860–1943 & his 3 children: Dame Edith 1887–1964; Sir Osbert 1892–1969; & Sa·chev·er·ell \sə-ˈshev-(ə-)rəl\ 1897– Eng. authors
Skeat \ˈskēt\ Walter William 1835–1912 Eng. philologist
Skel·ton \ˈskelt-ᵊn\ John 1460?–1529 Eng. poet — **Skel·ton·ic** \skel-ˈtän-ik\ *adj*
Skin·ner \ˈskin-ər\ Burrhus Frederick 1904– Am. psychol.
Skinner Cornelia Otis 1901– *dau. of Otis* Am. actress
Skinner Otis 1858–1942 Am. actor
Sko·da, von \ˈskōd-ə, ˈshkōd-(ˌ)ä\ Emil 1839–1900 Czech engineer & industrialist
Sla·ter \ˈslāt-ər\ Samuel 1768–1835 Eng.-born industrialist in Am.
Slich·ter \ˈslik-tər\ Sumner Huber 1892–1959 Am. economist
Sli·dell \slī-ˈdel, *by collateral descendants* ˈslīd-ᵊl\ John 1793–1871 Am. Confed. diplomat
Sloan \ˈslōn\ John French 1871–1951 Am. painter
Slo·cum \ˈslō-kəm\ Henry Warner 1827–1894 Am. gen.
Slo·nim·sky \slō-ˈnim(p)-skē\ Nicolas 1894– Russ.-born composer & musicologist in U.S.
Sme·ta·na \ˈsmet-ᵊn-ə\ Be·dřich \ˈbed-ər-ˌzhik\ 1824–1884 Czech pianist, composer, & conductor
Śmig·ly–Rydz \ˌs(h)mig-lē-ˈrits, -ˈridz\ Edward 1886– Pol. gen.
Smith \ˈsmith\ Adam 1723–1790 Scot. econ.
Smith Alfred Emanuel 1873–1944 Am. polit.
Smith Bessie 1894–1937 Am. blues singer
Smith Cyrus Rowlett 1899– U.S. secy. of commerce (1968–69)
Smith David 1906–1965 Am. sculptor
Smith Edmund Kirby — see KIRBY-SMITH
Smith John 1580–1631 Eng. colonist in Am.
Smith Joseph 1805–1844 Am. founder of Mormon Church
Smith Sydney 1771–1845 Eng. essayist
Smith Walter Be·dell \bə-ˈdel\ 1895–1961 Am. gen. & diplomat
Smith William 1769–1839 Eng. geologist
Smith–Dor·ri·en \ˈsmith-ˈdȯr-ē-ən, -ˈdär-\ Sir Horace Lockwood 1858–1930 Brit. gen.
Smith·son \ˈsmith-sən\ James 1765–1829 Brit. chem. & mineralogist & founder of Smithsonian Inst.
Smol·lett \ˈsmäl-ət\ Tobias George 1721–1771 Brit. author
Smuts \ˈsməts, ˈsmœts\ Jan \ˈyän\ Christiaan 1870–1950 So. African field marshal; prime min. (1919–24; 1939–48)
Smyth \ˈsmith\ Henry DeWolf 1898– Am. physicist
Snor·ri Stur·lu·son \ˌsnȯr-ē-ˈstər-lə-sən, ˌsnär-\ 1178–1241 Icelandic statesman & hist.
Snow \ˈsnō\ Baron 1905– *Charles Percy Snow* Eng. nov. & physicist
Snow·den \ˈsnōd-ᵊn\ Philip 1864–1937 1st Viscount *Snowden of Ick·orn·shaw* \ˈik-ˌȯrn-ˌshȯ\ Eng. econ. & polit.
Snow·don \ˈsnōd-ᵊn\ Earl of — see ARMSTRONG-JONES
Sny·der \ˈsnīd-ər\ John Wesley 1895– Am. banker & administrator
Sobieski John — see JOHN III SOBIESKI
So·ci·nus \sō-ˈsī-nəs\ Faustus 1539–1604 *Fausto Soz·zi·ni* \-sōt-ˈsē-nē\ Ital. religious reformer
Soc·ra·tes \ˈsäk-rə-ˌtēz\ 470?–399 B.C. Greek philos.
Sod·dy \ˈsäd-ē\ Frederick 1877–1956 Eng. chem.
Sö·der·blom \ˈsə(r)d-ər-ˌblüm, ˈsœd-\ Nathan 1866–1931 Swed. theol.
So·do·ma, Il \ˈsȯd-ə-mə\ 1477?–1549 *Giovanni Antonio de' Bazzi* Ital. painter
So·kol·ni·kov \sə-ˈkȯl-ni-ˌkȯf, -ˌkȯv\ Grigori Yakovlevich 1888– Russ. polit.
So·lon \ˈsō-lən, -ˌlän\ 638?–?559 B.C. Athenian lawgiver
Sol·y·man \ˈsäl-i-mən\ *var of* SULEIMAN
Sol·zhe·ni·tsyn \ˌsōl-zhə-ˈnēt-sən, ˌsȯl-\ Aleksandr Isayevich 1918– Russ. nov.
Som·er·ville \ˈsəm-ər-ˌvil\ Sir James Fownes \ˈfōnz\ 1882–1949 Brit. admiral
Soong \ˈsu̇ŋ\ Ai-ling \ˈī-ˈliŋ\ 1888– *wife of H. H. Kung*
Soong Ch'ing-ling \ˈchiŋ-ˈliŋ\ 1890– *wife of Sun Yat-Sen*
Soong Mei-ling \ˈmā-ˈliŋ\ 1898– *wife of Chiang Kai-shek*
Soong Tse-ven *or* Tsŭ-wên \ˈtsu̇-ˈwən\ 1891–1971 *T. V. Soong, bro. of the 3 prec.* Chin. financier & statesman
Soph·o·cles \ˈsäf-ə-ˌklēz\ 496?–406 B.C. Greek dram. — **Soph·o·cle·an** \ˌsäf-ə-ˈklē-ən\ *adj*
Sor·del·lo \sȯr-ˈdel-(ˌ)ō\ 13th cent. Ital. troubadour
So·rol·la y Bas·ti·da \sə-ˈrōl-yə-ē-bä-ˈstē-də, -ˈrōi-ə-, -ˈstē-t͟hə\ Joaquín 1863–1923 Span. painter
Soult \ˈsült\ Nicolas Jean de Dieu 1769–1851 *Duc de Dal·ma·tie* \dál-má-sē\ Fr. soldier; marshal of France
Sou·sa \ˈsü-zə, ˈsü-sə\ John Philip 1854–1932 *the March King* Am. bandmaster & composer
South \ˈsau̇th\ Robert 1634–1716 Eng. clergyman
Sou·they \ˈsau̇-t͟hē, ˈsət͟h-ə\ Robert 1774–1843 Eng. author; poet laureate (1813–43)
Sou·tine \sü-ˈtēn\ Chaim 1894–1943 Lith.-born painter in France
Spaak \ˈspäk\ Paul-Henri Charles 1899–1972 Belg. lawyer & polit.; premier (1938–39; 1947–49); secy.-gen. of N.A.T.O. (1957–61)
Spaatz \ˈspäts\ Carl 1891– orig. *Spatz* Am. gen.
Spal·ding \ˈspȯl-diŋ\ Albert 1888–1953 Am. violinist & composer
Spark \ˈspärk\ Muriel Sarah 1918– Brit. writer
Sparks \ˈspärks\ Jar·ed \ˈjar-əd, ˈjer-\ 1789–1866 Am. hist.
Spar·ta·cus \ˈspärt-ə-kəs\ *d* 71 B.C. Rom. slave & insurrectionist
Spell·man \ˈspel-mən\ Francis Joseph 1889–1967 Am. cardinal
Spe·mann \ˈshpā-ˌmän\ Hans 1869–1941 Ger. zool.
Spen·cer \ˈspen(t)-sər\ Herbert 1820–1903 Eng. philos.
Spen·der \ˈspen-dər\ Stephen Harold 1909– Eng. poet & critic
Speng·ler \ˈs(h)peŋ-lər\ Oswald 1880–1936 Ger. philos.
Spen·ser \ˈspen(t)-sər\ Edmund 1552–1599 Eng. poet — **Spen·se·ri·an** \spen-ˈsir-ē-ən\ *adj*
Sper·ry \ˈsper-ē\ Elmer Ambrose 1860–1930 Am. inventor
Spin·garn \ˈspin-ˌgärn\ Joel Elias 1875–1939 Am. author
Spi·no·za \spin-ˈō-zə\ Baruch *or* Benedict 1632–1677 Du. philos. — **Spi·no·zis·tic** \spə-ˌnō-ˈzis-tik, ˌspin-ə-\ *adj*
Spit·te·ler \ˈs(h)pit-ᵊl-ər, ˈs(h)pit-lər\ Carl 1845–1924 pseud. *Felix Tan·dem* \ˈtän-ˌdem\ Swiss writer
Spock \ˈspäk\ Benjamin McLane 1903– Am. physician
Spode \ˈspōd\ Josiah 1754–1827 Eng. potter
Spru·ance \ˈsprü-ən(t)s\ Raymond Ames 1886–1969 Am. admiral
Spy·ri \ˈs(h)pi(ə)r-ē\ Johanna 1827–1901 née *Heusser* Swiss author
Staël, de \ˈstäl, stål\ Mme. Anne Louise Germaine 1766–1817 Baronne *de Staël Holstein* née *Necker* Fr. writer
Ståhl·berg \ˈstȯl-ˌbərg, -ˌber-ē\ Kaarlo Ju·ho \ˈyü-(ˌ)hō\ 1865–1952 Finnish statesman
Stair Viscount & Earl of — see DALRYMPLE
Sta·lin \ˈstäl-ən, ˈstal-, -ˌēn\ Joseph 1879–1953 *Iosif Vissarionovich Dzhu·gash·vi·li* \ˌjü-gəsh-ˈvē-lē\ Russ. Communist leader
Stan·dish \ˈstan-dish\ Myles *or* Miles 1584?–1656 Eng. colonist in Am.
Stan·is·las \ˈstan-ə-ˌslȯs, -ˌsläs\ **I Lesz·czyń·ski** \lesh-ˈchin-skē\ 1677–1766 king of Poland (1704–09; 1733–35)
Stan·i·slav·ski \ˌstan-ə-ˈslaf-skē, -ˈslav-\ Konstantin 1863–1938 Russ. actor
Stan·ley \ˈstan-lē\ Edward George Geoffrey Smith 1799–1869 *Earl of Derby* Brit. statesman
Stanley Sir Henry Morton 1841–1904 orig. *John Rowlands* Brit. explorer in Africa
Stanley Wendell Meredith 1904–1971 Am. biochem.
Stans \ˈstanz\ Maurice Hubert 1908– U.S. secy. of commerce (1969–72)
Stan·ton \ˈstant-ᵊn\ Edwin McMasters 1814–1869 Am. lawyer & secy. of war (1862–68)
Stanton Elizabeth 1815–1902 née *Cady* Am. suffragist
Star·hem·berg, von \ˈstär-əm-ˌbərg, ˈshtär-əm-ˌberk\ Prince Ernst Rüdiger 1899–1956 Austrian anti-Nazi statesman
Stark \ˈstärk\ Harold Raynsford 1880–1972 Am. admiral
Stark \ˈs(h)tärk\ Johannes 1874–1957 Ger. physicist
Stark \ˈstärk\ John 1728–1822 Am. Revolutionary gen.
Star·zyń·ski \stär-ˈzin(t)-skē\ Stefan 1893–?1940 Pol. polit. & hero
Stas·sen \ˈstas-ᵊn\ Harold Edward 1907– Am. lawyer & polit.
Sta·tius \ˈstā-sh(ē-)əs\ Publius Papinius 45?–?96 Rom. poet
Stau·ding·er \ˈs(h)tau̇d-iŋ-ər\ Hermann 1881–1965 Ger. chem.
Steed \ˈstēd\ Henry Wick·ham \ˈwik-əm\ 1871–1956 Eng. journalist
Steele \ˈstē(ə)l\ Sir Richard 1672–1729 Brit. essayist & dram.
Steen \ˈstān\ Jan 1626–1679 Du. painter
Ste·fans·son \ˈstef-ən-sən\ Vil·hjal·mur \ˈvil-ˌyau̇l-mər\ 1879–1962 Canad. arctic explorer
Stef·fens \ˈstef-ənz\ (Joseph) Lincoln 1866–1936 Am. journalist & editor
Stei·chen \ˈstī-kən\ Edward 1879–1973 Am. photographer
Stein \ˈstīn\ Gertrude 1874–1946 Am. writer
Stein, vom und zum \ˌfōm-ənt-ˌsu̇m-ˈs(h)tīn, -ˌsüm-\ Baron Heinrich Friedrich Karl 1757–1831 Prussian statesman
Stein·beck \ˈstīn-ˌbek\ John Ernst 1902–1968 Am. nov.
Stein·metz \ˈs(h)tīn-ˌmets\ Charles Proteus 1865–1923 Am. (Ger.-born) electrical engineer
Sten·dhal \sten-ˈdäl, stan-, *F* sta^{n}-dál\ 1783–1842 pseud. of *Marie Henri Beyle* Fr. writer — **Sten·dhal·ian** \-ˈdäl-ē-ən\ *adj*
Ste·phen \ˈstē-vən\ 1097?–1154 king of England (1135–54)
Stephen Sir Leslie 1832–1904 Eng. philos., critic, & biographer
Ste·phens \ˈstē-vənz\ Alexander Hamilton 1812–1883 Am. polit.; vice-pres. of the Confed. states
Stephens James 1882–1950 Irish poet & nov.
Ste·phen·son \ˈstē-vən-sən\ George 1781–1848 Eng. inventor & founder of railroads
Stephenson Robert 1803–1859 *son of George* Eng. engineer
Stern \ˈstərn\ Gladys Bertha 1890–1973 Eng. nov.
Stern Isaac 1920– Russ.-born violinist in Am.
Stern Otto 1888–1969 Am. physicist
Stern·berg \ˈstərn-ˌbərg\ George Miller 1838–1915 Am. physician & bacteriol.
Sterne \ˈstərn\ Laurence 1713–1768 Brit. nov.
Stet·tin·i·us \stə-ˈtin-ē-əs, ste-\ Edward Riel·ley \ˈrī-lē\ 1900–1949 Am. financier & statesman
Steu·ben, von \ˈst(y)ü-bən, ˈshtȯi-; st(y)ü-ˈben\ Baron Friedrich Wilhelm Ludolf Gerhard Augustin 1730–1794 Prussian-born gen. in Am.
Ste·vens \ˈstē-vənz\ John 1749–1838 Am. inventor
Stevens Thaddeus 1792–1868 Am. lawyer & polit.
Stevens Wallace 1879–1955 Am. poet
Ste·ven·son \ˈstē-vən-sən\ Ad·lai \ˈad-lē\ Ewing 1835–1914 Am. polit.; vice-pres. of U.S. (1893–97)
Stevenson Adlai Ewing 1900–1965 *grandson of prec.* Am. lawyer & diplomat
Stevenson Robert Louis Balfour 1850–1894 *R. L. S.* Scot. author
Stew·art \ˈst(y)ü-ərt, ˈst(y)u̇(-ə)rt\ Du·gald \ˈdü-gəld\ 1753–1828 Scot. philos.
Stewart Potter 1915– Am. jurist
Stewart Robert 1769–1822 Viscount *Cas·tle·reagh* \ˈkas-əl-ˌrā\ Eng. statesman
Steyn \ˈstīn\ Martinus Theunis 1857–1916 So. African lawyer & statesman
Stieg·litz \ˈstēg-ləts, -ˌlits\ Alfred 1864–1946 Am. photographer & editor
Stik·ker \ˈstik-ər\ Dirk 1897– Dutch diplomat & statesman; secy.-gen. of N.A.T.O. (1961–64)
Stil·i·cho \ˈstil-i-ˌkō\ Flavius 359?–408 Rom. gen. & statesman
Still \ˈstil\ Andrew Taylor 1828–1917 Am. physician; founder of osteopathy
Stil·well \ˈstil-ˌwel, -wəl\ Joseph Warren 1883–1946 Am. gen.
Stim·son \ˈstim(p)-sən\ Henry Lewis 1867–1950 Am. statesman
Stin·nes \ˈs(h)tin-əs\ Hugo 1870–1924 Ger. industrialist

Stock·mar, von \'stäk-ˌmär\ Baron Christian Friedrich 1787–1863 Anglo-Belg. statesman
Stock·ton \'stäk-tən\ Francis Richard 1834–1902 *Frank R.* Am. writer
Stod·dard \'städ-ərd\ Richard Henry 1825–1903 Am. poet & critic
Sto·ker \'stō-kər\ Bram 1847–1912 Brit. writer
Stokes \'stōks\ Sir Frederick Wilfrid Scott 1860–1927 Eng. engineer & inventor
Sto·kow·ski \stə-'kȯf-skē, 'kȯv-\ Leopold Antoni Stanislaw 1882– Eng.-born conductor in Am.
Stone \'stōn\ Edward Durell 1902– Am. architect
Stone Harlan Fiske 1872–1946 Am. jurist; chief justice U.S. Supreme Court (1941–46)
Stone Irving 1903– *I. Tannenbaum* Am. writer
Stone Lucy 1818–1893 Mrs. *Henry Brown Blackwell* Am. suffragist
Sto·ry \'stōr-ē, 'stȯr-ē\ Joseph 1779–1845 Am. jurist
Story William Wetmore 1819–1895 *son of Joseph* Am. sculptor
Stow \'stō\ John 1525?–1605 Eng. hist. & antiquarian
Stowe \'stō\ Harriet Elizabeth 1811–1896 née *Beecher* Am. author
Stra·bo \'strā-(ˌ)bō\ 63 B.C.?–?A.D. 24 Greek geographer
Stra·chey \'strā-chē\ Evelyn John St. Loe 1901–1963 Eng. socialist
Strachey (Giles) Lytton 1880–1932 Eng. biographer
Strachey John St. Loe 1860–1927 *father of Evelyn* Eng. journalist
Stra·di·va·ri \ˌstrad-ə-'vär-ē, -'var-, -'ver-\ Antonio 1644–1737 *Antonius Strad·i·var·i·us* \ˌstrad-ə-'var-ē-əs, -'ver-\ Ital. violin maker
Straf·ford \'straf-ərd\ 1st Earl of 1593–1641 *Thomas Wentworth* Eng. statesman
Stratford de Redcliffe Viscount — see CANNING
Strath·co·na \strath-'kō-nə\ **and Mount Royal** 1st Baron 1820–1914 *Donald Alexander Smith* Canad. (Scot.-born) railroad builder & administrator
Straus \'s(h)trau̇s\ Oskar 1870–1954 Fr. (Austrian-born) composer
Strauss \'s(h)trau̇s\ David Friedrich 1808–1874 Ger. theol. & philos.
Strauss Johann father 1804–1849 & his sons Johann 1825–1899 & Josef 1827–1870 Austrian composers
Strauss Richard \'rik-ˌärt, 'rik-\ 1864–1949 Ger. composer
Stra·vin·sky \strə-'vin(t)-skē\ Igor \'ē-ˌgȯ(ə)r\ Fëdorovich 1882–1971 Am. (Russ.-born) composer — **Stra·vin·sky·an** *or* **Stra·vin·ski·an** \-skē-ən\ *adj*
Strei·cher \'s(h)trī-kər, -k̲ər\ Julius 1885–1946 Ger. Nazi administrator
Stre·se·mann \'s(h)trā-zə-ˌmän\ Gustav 1878–1929 Ger. statesman
Strij·dom \'strīd-əm, 'strād-\ Johannes Gerhardus 1893–1958 prime min. of So. Africa (1954–58)
Strind·berg \'strin(d)-ˌbərg, 'strin-ˌber-ē\ August 1849–1912 Swed. dram. & nov. — **Strind·berg·ian** \strin(d)-'bər-gē-ən\ *adj*
Stritch \'strich\ Samuel Alphonsus 1887–1958 Am. cardinal
Stroess·ner \'stres-nər\ Alfredo 1912– pres. of Paraguay (1954–)
Stru·en·see, von \'s(h)trü-ən-ˌzā\ Count Johann Friedrich 1737–1772 Ger.-Dan. statesman & philos.
Struth·er \'strət̲h̲-ər\ Jan \'jan\ 1901–1953 pseud. of *Joyce Maxtone Graham* née *Anstruther* Eng. writer
Strutt \'strət\ Joseph 1749–1802 Eng. antiquarian
Stu·art \'st(y)ü-ərt, 'st(y)u̇(-ə)rt\ — see CHARLES I & MARY STUART
Stuart Charles *the Young Pretender* — see CHARLES
Stuart Gilbert Charles 1755–1828 Am. painter
Stuart James Ewell Brown 1833–1864 *Jeb* Am. Confed. gen.
Stuart James Francis Edward *the Old Pretender* — see JAMES
Stubbs \'stəbz\ William 1825–1901 Eng. hist. & prelate
Stülp·na·gel, von \'s(h)tu̇lp-ˌnäg-əl, 's(h)tuelp-\ Otto 1880–1948 Ger. gen.
Stur·gis \'stər-jəs\ Russell 1836–1909 Am. architect & writer
Sturluson — see SNORRI STURLUSON
Stur·sa \'shtu̇(ə)r-sə\ Jan \'yän\ 1880–1925 Czech sculptor
Stuy·ve·sant \'stī-və-sənt\ Peter 1592–1672 Du. administrator in Am.
Sty·ron \'stī-rən\ William 1925– Am. writer
Suck·ling \'sək-liŋ\ Sir John 1609–1642 Eng. Cavalier poet
Su·cre, de \'sü-(ˌ)krā\ Antonio José 1795–1830 So. Am. liberator
Sue \'sü, sue\ Eugène 1804–1857 *Marie Joseph* Fr. nov.
Sue·to·ni·us \swē-'tō-nē-əs, ˌsü-ə-'tō-\ 2d cent. A.D. *Gaius Suetonius Tranquillus* Rom. biographer & hist.
Su·gi·ya·ma \ˌsü-gē-'yäm-ə\ Hajime 1880–1945 Jap. field marshal
Su·kar·no \sü-'kär-(ˌ)nō\ 1901–1970 pres. of Indonesian Republic (1945–1967)
Su·lei·man I \'sü-lā-ˌmän, -li-\ 1496?–1566 *the Magnificent* Ottoman sultan (1520–66)
Sul·la \'səl-ə\ 138–78 B.C. *Lucius Cornelius Sulla Felix* Rom. gen. & polit.
Sul·li·van \'səl-ə-vən\ Sir Arthur Seymour 1842–1900 Eng. composer
Sullivan John 1740–1795 Am. Revolutionary gen.
Sullivan John Lawrence 1858–1918 Am. boxer
Sullivan John Lawrence 1899– Am. lawyer & administrator
Sullivan Louis Henri 1856–1924 Am. architect
Sul·ly \'səl-ē\ Thomas 1783–1872 Eng.-born painter in Am.
Sul·ly, de \'səl-ē, (ˌ)sə-'le, sue-lē\ Duc 1560–1641 *Maximilien de Béthune* Baron *de Ros·ny* \-rō-'nē\ Fr. statesman
Sully Pru·dhomme \-prü-dəm, prue-, -'dȯm\ René François Armand 1839–1907 Fr. poet & critic
Sum·ner \'səm-nər\ Charles 1811–1874 Am. statesman & orator
Sumner James Batcheller 1887–1955 Am. biochem.
Sumner John Bird 1780–1862 archbishop of Canterbury (1848–62)
Sumner William Graham 1840–1910 Am. sociol. & educ.
Sun Yat-sen \'sün-'yät-'sen\ 1866–1925 Chin. statesman
Sun·day \'sən-dē\ William Ashley 1862–1935 *Billy* Am. evangelist
Sur·raj·ah Dow·lah *var of* SIRAJ-UD-DAULA
Surrey Earl of — see Henry HOWARD
Sur·tees \'sərt-(ˌ)ēz\ Robert Smith 1803–1864 Eng. nov. & editor
Suth·er·land \'sət̲h̲-ər-lənd\ Joan 1926– Austral. operatic soprano
Sut·ter \'sət-ər, 'süt-\ John Augustus 1803–1880 Ger.-born pioneer in California
Sutt·ner, von \'zu̇t-nər, 'su̇t-\ Bertha 1843–1914 née Countess *Kinsky* Austrian writer & pacifist
Su·vo·rov \su̇-'vȯr-əf, -'vär-\ Count Aleksandr Vasilievich 1730–1800 Russ. field marshal
Sved·berg \'sfed-ˌbərg, -ˌber-ē\ The *or* Theodor 1884–1971 Swed. chem.
Sver·drup \'sve(ə)r-drəp\ Otto Neumann 1855–1930 Norw. arctic explorer
Sver·re \'sver-ə\ 1152?–1202 *Sverre Si·gurds·son* \'sig-ərd-sən\ king of Norway (1184–1202)
Swe·den·borg \'swēd-ᵊn-ˌbȯrg\ Emanuel 1688–1772 orig. *Svedberg* Swed. philos. & religious writer
Swee·linck \'swā-liŋk\ Jan Pieterszoon 1562–1621 Du. organist & composer
Sweet \'swēt\ Henry 1845–1912 Eng. phonetician & philologist
Swift \'swift\ Gustavus Franklin 1839–1903 Am. meat packer
Swift Jonathan 1667–1745 Eng. (Irish-born) satirist — **Swift·ian** \'swif-tē-ən\ *adj*
Swin·burne \'swin-(ˌ)bərn\ Algernon Charles 1837–1909 Eng. poet — **Swin·burn·ian** \swin-'bər-nē-ən\ *adj*
Swin·ner·ton \'swin-ərt-ᵊn\ Frank Arthur 1884– Eng. nov. & critic
Swin·ton \'swint-ᵊn\ 1st Earl of 1884–1972 *Philip Cunliffe-Lister* Eng. statesman
Sylva Carmen — see ELIZABETH Queen of Rumania
Sy·ming·ton \'sī-miŋ-tən\ (William) Stuart 1901– Am. industrialist & polit.
Sy·monds \'sim-ən(d)z, 'sīm-\ John Addington 1840–1893 Eng. scholar
Sy·mons \'sīm-ənz, 'sīm-\ Arthur 1865–1945 Brit. poet & critic
Synge \'siŋ\ John Millington 1871–1909 Irish poet & dram.
Synge Richard Laurence Millington 1914– Brit. biochem.
Szell \'sel, 'zel\ George 1897–1970 Am. (Hung.-born) conductor
Szent–Györ·gyi \sānt-'jȯrj(-ē)\ **von Nagy·ra·polt** \'näj-'räp-ˌōlt\ Albert 1893– Hung. chem.
Szi·ge·ti \'sig-ət-ē, sə-'get-\ Joseph 1892–1973 Am. (Hung.-born) violinist
Szi·lard \'zil-ˌärd, zə-'lärd\ Leo 1898–1964 Am. (Hung.-born) physicist
Szold \'zōld\ Henrietta 1860–1945 Am. Zionist; founder of Hadassah
Tabb \'tab\ John Banister 1845–1909 Am. clergyman & poet
Tac·i·tus \'tas-ət-əs\ Cornelius 55?–after 117 Rom. hist. — **Tac·i·te·an** \ˌtas-ə-'tē-ən\ *adj*
Taft \'taft\ Lo·ra·do \lə-'räd-(ˌ)ō\ 1860–1936 Am. sculptor
Taft Robert Alphonso 1889–1953 *son of W.H.* Am. polit.
Taft William Howard 1857–1930 27th pres. of the U.S. (1909–13); chief justice U.S. Supreme Court (1921–30)
Ta·gore \tə-'gō(ə)r, -'gȯ(ə)r\ Sir Ra·bin·dra·nath \rə-'bin-drə-ˌnät\ 1861–1941 Hindu poet
Taine \'tān, 'ten\ Hippolyte Adolphe 1828–1893 Fr. philos. & critic
Tait \'tāt\ Archibald Campbell 1811–1882 archbishop of Canterbury (1869–82)
T'ai–tsu — see CHAO K'ung-yin
Tall·chief \'tȯl-ˌchēf\ Maria 1925– Am. dancer
Tal·ley·rand–Pé·ri·gord, de \'tal-ē-ˌran(d)-ˌper-ə-'gȯ(ə)r, *F* tal-(e-)räⁿ\ Charles Maurice 1754–1838 Prince *de Bénévent* Fr. statesman
Ta·ma·yo \tə-'mī-(ˌ)ō\ Rufino 1899– Mex. painter
Tam·er·lane \'tam-ər-ˌlān\ *or* **Tam·bur·laine** \'tam-bər-ˌlān\ 1336?–1405 *Timur Lenk* also *Timour* Eastern conqueror
Tamm \'täm, 'tam\ Igor Yevgenievich 1895–1971 Russ. physicist
Ta·na·ka \tə-'näk-ə\ Kakuei 1918– Jap. premier (1972–)
Tan·cred \'taŋ-krəd\ 1078?–1112 Norman leader in 1st crusade
Ta·ney \'tȯ-nē\ Roger Brooke 1777–1864 Am. jurist; chief justice U.S. Supreme Court (1836–64)
Tan·guy \täⁿ-'gē\ Yves 1900–1955 Am. (Fr.-born) artist
Tar·bell \'tär-ˌbel\ Ida Minerva 1857–1944 Am. author
Tar·dieu \tär-'dyə(r), -'dyœ\ André Pierre Gabriel Amédée 1876–1945 Fr. statesman
Tar·king·ton \'tär-kiŋ-tən\ (Newton) Booth 1869–1946 Am. nov.
Tas·man \'taz-mən\ Abel Janszoon 1603–1659 Du. mariner
Tas·so \'tas-(ˌ)ō, 'täs-\ Tor·qua·to \tȯr-'kwät-(ˌ)ō\ 1544–1595 Ital. poet
Tate \'tāt\ Allen 1899– Am. poet & critic
Tate Nahum 1652–1715 Brit. dram.; poet laureate (1692–1715)
Ta·tum \'tāt-əm\ Edward Lawrie 1909– Am. biochem.
Taus·sig \'tau̇-sig\ Frank William 1859–1940 Am. econ.
Taw·ney \'tȯ-nē\ Richard Henry 1880–1962 Eng. economic hist.
Tay·lor \'tā-lər\ (James) Bay·ard \'bī-ərd, 'bā-\ 1825–1878 Am. writer
Taylor (Joseph) Deems 1885–1966 Am. composer & music critic
Taylor Edward 1645?–1729 Am. clergyman & poet
Taylor Jeremy 1613–1667 Eng. prelate & author
Taylor Maxwell Davenport 1901– Am. gen.
Taylor Myron Charles 1874–1959 Am. businessman & diplomat
Taylor Tom 1817–1880 Eng. dram.
Taylor Zachary 1784–1850 12th pres. of the U.S. (1849–50)
Tchai·kov·sky \chī-'kȯf-skē, chə-, -'kȯv-\ Pëtr Ilich 1840–1893 Russ. composer — **Tchai·kov·sky·an** *or* **Tchai·kov·ski·an** \-skē-ən\ *adj*
Tchekhov *var of* CHEKHOV

ə abut ᵊ kitten, F table ər further a back ā bake
ä cot, cart á F bac au̇ out ch chin e less ē easy
g gift i trip ī life j joke k̲ G ich ⁿ F vin ŋ sing
ō flow ȯ flaw œ F bœuf œ̄ F feu ȯi coin th thing
t̲h̲ this ü loot u̇ foot ue G füllen ue̅ F rue y yet
ʸ F digne \dēnʸ\, nuit \nwʸē\ yü few yu̇ furious zh vision

Teas·dale \'tēz-ˌdāl\ Sara 1884–1933 Am. poet
Te·cum·seh \tə-'kəm(p)-sə, -sē\ *or* **Te·cum·tha** \-'kəm(p)-thə\ 1768?–1813 Shawnee Indian chief
Ted·der \'ted-ər\ 1st Baron 1890–1967 *Arthur William Tedder* Brit. air marshal
Teil·hard de Char·din \tā-yär-də-shär-da^{n}\ Pierre 1881–1955 Fr. priest & author
Tek·a·kwitha \ˌtek-ə-'kwith-ə\ Ka·teri \'kät-ə-rē\ 1656–1680 *Lily of the Mohawks* Am. Indian ascetic
Te·le·mann \'tā-lə-ˌmän\ Georg Philipp 1681–1767 Ger. composer
Tel·ler \'tel-ər\ Edward 1908– Am. (Hung.-born) physicist
Téllez Gabriel — see TIRSO DE MOLINA
Tem·ple \'tem-pəl\ Frederick 1821–1902 archbishop of Canterbury (1896–1902)
Temple Sir William 1628–1699 Brit. statesman
Temple William 1881–1944 *son of Frederick* archbishop of Canterbury (1942–44)
Templewood Viscount — see HOARE
Te·niers \tə-'ni(ə)rs, tä-'nyā\ David father 1582–1649 & son 1610–1690 Flemish painters
Ten·niel \'ten-yəl\ Sir John 1820–1914 Eng. cartoonist & illustrator
Ten·ny·son \'ten-ə-sən\ 1st Baron 1809–1892 *Alfred Tennyson* Eng. poet; poet laureate (1850–92) — **Ten·ny·so·nian** \ˌten-ə-'sō-nē-ən, -nyən\ *adj*
Ter·borch *or* **Ter Borch** \tər-'bȯrk, -'bȯrk\ Gerard 1617–1681 Du. painter
Ter·ence \'ter-ən(t)s\ 190?–159 B.C. *Publius Terentius Afer* Rom. dram.
Te·resh·ko·va \ˌter-əsh-'kȯ-və, -'kō-\ Valentina Vladimirovna 1937– Russ. astronaut; first woman in space (1963)
Ter·hune \(ˌ)tər-'hyün\ Albert Payson 1872–1942 Am. author
Ter·ry \'ter-ē\ Ellen Alicia *or* Alice 1847–1928 Eng. actress
Ter·tul·lian \(ˌ)tər-'təl-yən\ 160?–?230 *Quintus Septimius Florens Tertullianus* Latin church father
Tes·la \'tes-lə\ Nikola 1856–1943 Am. (Austrian-born) electrician & inventor
Tet·zel *or* **Te·zel** \'tet-səl\ Johann 1465?–1519 Ger. Dominican monk
Thack·er·ay \'thak-(ə-)rē\ William Makepeace 1811–1863 Eng. author — **Thack·er·ay·an** \-rē-ən\ *adj*
Tha·les \'thā-(ˌ)lēz\ 640?–546 B.C. Greek philos. — **Tha·le·sian** \thā-'lē-zhən\ *adj*
Thant \'thant, 'thänt\ U \'ü\ 1909– Burmese U.N. official; secy.-gen. (1961–71)
Thayer \'tha(ə)r, 'the(ə)r\ Sylvanus 1785–1872 *father of West Point* Am. army officer & educ.
Thayer William Roscoe 1859–1923 Am. hist. & biographer
Thei·ler \'tī-lər\ Max 1899–1972 So. African-born specialist in tropical medicine in U.S.
The·mis·to·cles \thə-'mis-tə-ˌklēz\ 527?–?460 B.C. Athenian gen. & statesman
The·oc·ri·tus \thē-'äk-rət-əs\ 3d cent. B.C. Greek poet
The·od·o·ric \thē-'äd-ə-rik\ 454?–526 *the Great* king of the Ostrogoths (474–526)
The·o·do·sius I \ˌthē-ə-'dō-sh(ē-)əs\ 346?–395 *the Great* Rom. gen. & emp. (379–395)
The·o·phras·tus \ˌthē-ə-'fras-təs\ *ab* 371–287 B.C. Greek philos. & naturalist
The·o·rell \ˌtā-ə-'rel\ Axel Hugo Theodor 1903– Swed. biochem.
The·re·sa *or* **Te·re·sa** \tə-'rē-sə, -'rā-sə, -'rā-zə\ Saint 1515–1582 Span. Carmelite nun
Thes·pis \'thes-pəs\ 6th cent. B.C. Greek poet
Thiers \tē-'e(ə)r\ Louis Adolphe 1797–1877 Fr. statesman & hist.
Tho·mas \tȯ-'mä\ Ambroise 1811–1896 Fr. composer
Thom·as \'täm-əs\ Augustus 1857–1934 Am. dram.
Thomas Dyl·an \'dil-ən\ 1914–1953 Brit. poet
Thomas Norman Mat·toon \ma-'tün, mə-\ 1884–1969 Am. socialist polit.
Thomas Seth 1785–1859 Am. clock manufacturer
Thomas Theodore 1835–1905 Ger.-born conductor in Am.
Thomas à Becket — see BECKET
Thomas a Kem·pis \ə-'kem-pəs, (ˌ)ä-'kem-\ 1380–1471 Ger. ecclesiastic & writer
Thomas of Er·cel·doune \'ər-səl-ˌdün\ *fl* 1220–1297 *Thomas the Rhymer* Scot. seer & poet
Thomp·son \'täm(p)-sən\ Benjamin 1753–1814 Count *Rum·ford* \'rəm(p)-fərd\ Brit. (Am.-born) physicist & statesman
Thompson Dorothy 1894–1961 Am. journalist
Thompson Francis 1859–1907 Eng. poet
Thompson Sir John Sparrow David 1844–1894 Canad. statesman; prime min. (1892–94)
Thompson Llewellyn E. 1904–1972 Am. diplomat
Thom·son \'täm(p)-sən\ George Pag·et \'paj-ət\ 1892– *son of Sir Joseph John* Eng. physicist
Thomson James 1700–1748 Scot. poet
Thomson James 1834–1882 *B. V.* Scot. poet
Thomson John Arthur 1861–1933 Scot. biologist
Thomson Sir Joseph John 1856–1940 Eng. physicist
Thomson Virgil Garnett 1896– Am. composer & critic
Thomson William — see Baron KELVIN
Tho·reau \thə-'rō, thȯ-; 'thȯr-(ˌ)ō\ Henry David 1817–1862 orig. *David Henry Thoreau* Am. writer — **Tho·reau·vi·an** \thə-'rō-vē-ən, thȯ-\ *adj*
Tho·rez \tȯ-'rez\ Maurice 1900–1964 Fr. Communist
Thorn·dike \'thȯrn-ˌdīk\ Ashley Horace 1871–1933 & his brother Lynn 1882–1965 Am. educators
Thorndike Dame Sybil 1882– Brit. actress
Thorn·ton \'thȯrnt-^{ə}n\ William 1759–1828 Am. architect
Thor·vald·sen *or* **Thor·wald·sen** \'t(h)ȯr-ˌwȯl-sən, 'tür-ˌväl-sən\ Ber·tel \'bert-^{ə}l\ 1768–1844 Dan. sculptor
Thras·y·bu·lus \ˌthras-ə-'byü-ləs\ *d* 389 B.C. Athenian gen.
Thu·cyd·i·des \th(y)ü-'sid-ə-ˌdēz\ 471?–?400 B.C. Greek hist. — **Thu·cyd·i·de·an** \(ˌ)th(y)ü-ˌsid-ə-'dē-ən\ *adj*

Thur·ber \'thər-bər\ James Grover 1894–1961 Am. writer
Thys·sen \'tis-^{ə}n\ Fritz 1873–1951 Ger. industrialist
Tib·bett \'tib-ət\ Lawrence Mervil 1896–1960 Am. baritone
Ti·be·ri·us \tī-'bir-ē-əs\ 42 B.C.–A.D. 37 *Tiberius Claudius Nero Caesar* Rom. emp. (14–37)
Ti·bul·lus \tə-'bəl-əs\ Albius 54?–?18 B.C. Rom. poet
Tieck \'tēk\ Ludwig 1773–1853 Ger. author
Tie·po·lo \tē-'ā-pə-ˌlō, -'ep-ə-\ Giovanni Battista 1696–1770 Ital. painter
Tif·fa·ny \'tif-ə-nē\ Charles Lewis 1812–1902 Am. jeweler
Tiffany Louis Comfort 1848–1933 *son of C.L.* Am. artist & glass manuf.
Tig·lath–pi·le·ser III \'tig-ˌlath-(ˌ)pī-'lē-zər-, -pə-\ *d* 727 B.C. king of Assyria (745–727)
Til·den \'til-dən\ Samuel Jones 1814–1886 Am. lawyer & polit.
Til·dy \'til-dē\ Zol·tán \'zōl-ˌtän\ 1889–1961 Hung. polit.
Til·lich \'til-ik\ Paul Johannes 1886–1965 Am. (Ger.-born) theol.
Til·lot·son \'til-ət-sən\ John 1630–1694 Eng. divine
Til·ly \'til-ē\ Count of 1559–1632 *Johan Tser·claes* \tsər-'kläs\ Flem. field marshal
Ti·mo·shen·ko \ˌtim-ə-'sheŋ-(ˌ)kō\ Se·mën \səm-'yȯn\ Konstantinovich 1895–1970 Russ. marshal
Timour, Timur, Timur Lenk — see TAMERLANE
Ting·ley \'tiŋ-lē\ Katherine Augusta 1847–1929 née *Westcott* Am. theosophist
Tin·to·ret·to, Il \ˌtin-tə-'ret-(ˌ)ō\ 1518–1594 *Jacopo Robusti* Ital. painter
Ti·pu Sa·hib *or* **Tip·poo Sa·hib** \ˌtip-(ˌ)ü-'sä-ˌ(h)ib\ 1751–1799 sultan of Mysore (1782–99)
Tir·pitz, von \'ti(ə)r-pəts, 'tər-\ Alfred 1849–1930 Ger. admiral
Tir·so de Mo·li·na \'ti(ə)r-(ˌ)sō-ˌdā-mə-'lē-nə\ 1571?–1648 pseud. of *Gabriel Téllez* Span. dram.
Ti·se·li·us \tə-'sā-lē-əs, -'zā-\ Arne Wilhelm Kaurin 1902–1971 Swed. biochem.
Ti·so \'tē-(ˌ)sō\ Josef 1887–1947 Slovakian pres.
Titch·e·ner \'tich-ə-nər\ Edward Bradford 1867–1927 Eng. psychol.
Ti·tian \'tish-ən\ 1477–1576 *Tiziano Vecellio* Ital. painter — **Ti·tian·esque** \ˌtish-ə-'nesk\ *adj*
Tito — see BROZ
Ti·tus \'tīt-əs\ 40?–81 *Titus Flavius Sabinus Vespasianus* Rom. emp. (79–81)
Tocque·ville, de \'tōk-ˌvil, 'tȯk-, 'täk-, -ˌvēl, -vəl\ Alexis Charles Henri Maurice Clérel 1805–1859 Fr. statesman & author
Todd \'täd\ Sir Alexander Robertus 1907– Brit. chem.
Todd David 1855–1939 Am. astron.
Todt \'tōt\ Fritz 1891–1942 Ger. military engineer
To·gliat·ti \tōl-'yät-ē\ Pal·mi·ro \päl-'mē-(ˌ)rō\ 1893?–1964 Ital. Communist
To·go \'tō-(ˌ)gō\ Marquis Heihachiro 1847–1934 Jap. admiral
Togo Shigenori 1882–1950 Jap. diplomat & polit.
To·jo \'tō-(ˌ)jō\ Hideki 1885–1948 Jap. gen. & polit.
Tol·bert \'tōl-bərt\ William Richard 1913– pres. of Liberia (1971–)
Tol·kien \'täl-ˌkēn\ John Ronald Reuel 1892–1973 Eng. author
Tol·ler \'tȯl-ər, 'täl-\ Ernst 1893–1939 Ger. dram. & polit.
Tol·stoy *or* **Tol·stoi** \tōl-'stȯi, tōl-', täl-', 'tōl-ˌ, 'tōl-ˌ, 'täl-ˌ\ Count Lev Nikolaevich 1828–1910 Russ. nov., philos., & mystic — **Tol·stoy·an** *or* **Tol·stoi·an** \-ən\ *adj*
Tom·baugh \'täm-ˌbȯ\ Clyde William 1906– Am. astron.; disc. Pluto
Tom·ma·si·ni \ˌtäm-ə-'zē-nē\ Vicenzo 1880–1950 Ital. composer
Tomp·kins \'täm(p)-kənz\ Daniel D. 1774–1825 Am. polit.; vice-pres. of the U.S. (1817–25)
Tone \'tōn\ (Theobald) Wolfe 1763–1798 Irish revolutionist
Tooke \'tük\ (John) Horne 1736–1812 Eng. polit. radical & philologist
Toombs \'tümz\ Robert Augustus 1810–1885 Am. lawyer & Confed. statesman
Tor·que·ma·da, de \ˌtȯr-kə-'mäd-ə, -'mäth-ə\ Tomás 1420?–1498 Span. grand inquisitor
Tor·ri·cel·li \ˌtȯr-ə-'chel-ē, ˌtär-\ Evangelista 1608–1647 Ital. math. & physicist
Tos·ca·ni·ni \ˌtäs-kə-'nē-nē, ˌtȯs-\ Ar·tu·ro \är-'tù(ə)r-(ˌ)ō\ 1867–1957 Ital. conductor
Tot·le·ben *or* **Tod·le·ben** \'tōt-lə-bən\ Count Frants Eduard Ivanovich 1818–1884 Russ. gen.
Tou·louse–Lau·trec, de \tü-ˌlüz-lō-'trek\ Henri 1864–1901 Fr. painter
Tour·neur \'tər-nər\ Cyril 1575?–1626 Eng. dram.
Tous·saint L'Ou·ver·ture \'tü-ˌsa^{n}-'lü-vər-ˌt(y)ù(ə)r\ Pierre Dominique 1743–1803 Haitian gen. & liberator
Toyn·bee \'tȯin-bē\ Arnold Joseph 1889– Eng. hist.
Tra·jan \'trā-jən\ 52 *or* 53–117 *Marcus Ulpius Trajanus* Rom. emp. (98–117)
Trau·bel \'traù-bəl\ Helen 1903–1972 Am. opera singer
Tree \'trē\ Sir Herbert Beerbohm 1853–1917 Eng. actor-manager
Treitsch·ke, von \'trīch-kə\ Heinrich 1834–1896 Ger. hist.
Trench \'trench\ Richard Chen·e·vix \'shen-ə-ˌvē\ 1807–1886 Eng. poet & prelate
Tre·vel·yan \tri-'vel-yən, -'vil-\ George Macaulay 1876–1962 Eng. hist.
Trevelyan Sir George Otto 1838–1928 *father of prec.* Eng. polit., biographer, & hist.
Trol·lope \'träl-əp\ Anthony 1815–1882 Eng. nov. — **Trol·lo·pi·an** \trä-'lō-pē-ən\ *adj*
Tromp \'trȯmp, 'trämp\ Maarten Harpertszoon 1597–1653 Du. admiral
Trots·ky *or* **Trots·ki** \'trät-skē, 'trȯt-\ Leon 1879–1940 *Leib* or *Lev Davydovich Bronstein* Russ. Communist
Trow·bridge \'trō-(ˌ)brij\ Alexander Buel 1929– U.S. secy. of commerce (1967–68)
Troy·on \t(r)wä-'yō^{n}\ Constant 1813–1865 Fr. painter

Tru·deau \'trü-(,)dō, trü-'\ Pierre Elliott 1919– Canad. polit.; prime min. (1968–)

Tru·ji·llo Mo·li·na \trü-'hē-(,)(y)ō-mə-'lē-nə\ Rafael Leonidas 1891–1961 Dominican gen. & polit.; pres. of Dominican Republic (1930–38; 1942–52)

Tru·man \'trü-mən\ Harry S 1884–1972 33d pres. of the U.S. (1945–53)

Trum·bull \'trəm-bəl\ John 1756–1843 Am. painter

Trumbull Jonathan 1710–1785 *father of prec.* Am. patriot & statesman

Tsai Ting-kai \'(t)sī-'tiŋ-'gī\ 1892–1968 Chin. gen.

Tsal·da·res *or* **Tsal·da·ris** \(t)säl-'där-əs, -ēs\ **Pa·na·ges** *or* **Pa·na·gis** \,pän-ə-'yēs\ 1868–1936 Greek statesman

Tsao Hsueh-chin \'tsaü-'shüe-'chin\ *d.* 1764 Chin. author

Tschaikovsky *var of* TCHAIKOVSKY

Tu Fu \'tü-'fü\ 712–770 Chin. poet

Tub·man \'təb-mən\ William Vacanarat Shadrach 1895–1971 Liberian lawyer; pres. of Liberia (1944–71)

Tul·si Das \,tül-sē-'däs\ 1532–1623 Hindu poet

Tup·per \'təp-ər\ Sir Charles 1821–1915 prime min. of Canada (1896)

Tu·renne, de \tü-'ren\ Vicomte 1611–1675 *Henri de la Tour d'Auvergne* Fr. marshal

Tur·ge·nev \tür-'gān-yəf, -'gen-\ Ivan Sergeevich 1818–1883 Russ. nov.

Tur·got \tür-'gō\ Anne Robert Jacques 1727–1781 Baron *de l'Aulne* \'lōn\ Fr. statesman & econ.

Tur·ner \'tər-nər\ Frederick Jackson 1861–1932 Am. hist.

Turner Joseph Mallord William 1775–1851 Eng. painter

Turner Nat 1800–1831 Am. insurrectionist

Tut·ankh·a·men \,tü-,taŋ-'käm-ən, -,täŋ-\ *or* **Tut·enkh·a·mon** \-,teŋ-'käm-ən\ *fl ab* 1358 B.C. king of Egypt

Twacht·man \'twäk(t)-mən\ John Henry 1853–1902 Am. painter

Twain Mark — see CLEMENS

Tweed \'twēd\ William Marcy 1823–1878 *Boss Tweed* Am. polit.

Tweedsmuir — see BUCHAN

Ty·ler \'tī-lər\ John 1790–1862 10th pres. of the U.S. (1841–45)

Tyler Wat \'wät\ *or* Walter *d* 1381 Eng. leader of Peasants' Revolt (1381)

Tyn·dale \'tin-dᵊl\ William 1492?–1536 Eng. reformer & martyr

Tyn·dall \'tin-dᵊl\ John 1820–1893 Brit. physicist

Tyr·whitt–Wil·son \,tir-ət-'wil-sən\ Gerald Hugh 1883–1950 14th Baron *Ber·ners* \'bər-nərz\ Eng. composer & painter

Tz'u–hsi \'tsü-'shē\ 1835–1908 Chin. empress dowager

Uc·cel·lo \ü-'chel-(,)ō\ Paolo 1397–1475 *Paolo di Dono* Florentine painter

Udall \'yü-,döl, 'yüd-ᵊl\ *or* **Uve·dale** \'yüv-,dāl\ Nicholas 1505–1556 Eng. schoolmaster & dram.

Udall \'yü-,döl\ Stewart Lee 1920– U.S. secy. of interior (1961–69)

Ugar·te \ü-'gärt-ē\ Manuel 1874–1951 Argentine writer

Uh·land \'ü-,länt\ Johann Ludwig 1787–1862 Ger. poet & hist.

Ul·bricht \'ül-(,)brikt, -(,)brikt\ Walter 1893–1973 East German statesman

Ul·fi·las \'ül-fə-,läs, 'əl-, -ləs, -,las\ *or* **Ul·fi·la** \-lə\ *or* **Wul·fi·la** \'wül-fə-lə\ 311?–381 bishop of the Goths

Ul·pi·an \'əl-pē-ən\ 170?–228 *Domitius Ulpianus* Rom. jurist

Una·mu·no y Ju·go, de \,ü-nə-'mü-(,)nō-(,)ē-'hü-(,)gō\ Miguel 1864–1936 Span. philos. & writer

Un·cas \'əŋ-kəs\ 1588?–?1683 Pequot Indian chief

Und·set \'ün-,set\ Si·grid \'sig-rē, -rəd\ 1882–1949 Norw. nov.

Un·ter·mey·er \'ənt-ər-,mī(-ə)r\ Louis 1885– Am. poet

Up·dike \'əp-,dīk\ John 1932– Am. writer

Up·john \'əp-,jän\ Richard 1802–1878 Am. (Eng.-born) architect

Up·ton \'əp-tən\ Emory 1839–1881 Am. gen. & author

Ur·ban \'ər-bən\ name of 8 popes: esp. **II** (*Odo* \'ōd-(,)ō\ or *Udo* \'üd-\) 1042?–1099 (pope 1088–99)

Urey \'yü(ə)r-ē\ Harold Clayton 1893– Am. chem.

Ur·quhart \'ər-kərt, -,kärt\ Sir Thomas 1611–1660 Scot. author & translator

Ussh·er \'əsh-ər\ James 1581–1656 Irish archbishop

Utril·lo \yü-'tril-(,)ō; ,yü-trē-'ō, ,ue-\ Maurice 1883–1955 Fr. painter

Vail·lant \vä-'yä^{n}, vī-'ä^{n}\ Jean Baptiste Philibert 1790–1872 Fr. army officer; marshal of France

Valdemar — see WALDEMAR

Val·di·via, de \val-'dē-vē-ə\ Pedro 1500?–1553 Span. conqueror of Chile

Va·lens \'vā-lənz, -,lenz\ 328?–378 Rom. emp. of the East (364–378)

Val·en·tin·ian \,val-ən-'tin-ē-ən, -'tin-yən\ *Lat.* **Valentinianus** name of 3 Rom. emperors: **I** 321–375 (reigned 364–375); **II** 372–392 (reigned 375–392); **III** 419–455 (reigned 425–455)

Valera Eamon de — see DE VALERA

Va·le·ra y Al·ca·lá Ga·lia·no \və-'ler-ə-,ē-,al-kə-'lä-,gal-ē-'än-(,)ō, -äl-kə-, -,gäl-\ Juan 1824–1905 Span. writer & statesman

Va·le·ri·an \və-'lir-ē-ən\ *d* ?269 *Publius Licinius Valerianus* Rom. emp. (253–260)

Va·le·ry \,val-ə-'rē, 'val-ə-rē\ Paul Ambroise 1871–1945 Fr. poet & philos.

Va·llar·ta \vä-'yärt-ə, vī-'ärt-\ Manuel Sandoval 1899– Mex. physicist

Val·le·jo \və-'lā-(,)ō, -'yā-(,)(h)ō\ Mariano Guadalupe 1808–1890 soldier & pioneer in Calif.

Van Al·len \va-'nal-ən, və-\ James Alfred 1914– Am. physicist

Van·brugh \'van-brə, van-'brü\ Sir John 1664–1726 Eng. dram. & architect

Van Bu·ren \van-'byür-ən, vən-\ Martin 1782–1862 8th pres. of the U.S. (1837–41)

Van·cou·ver \van-'kü-vər\ George 1757–1798 Eng. navigator & explorer

Van·de·grift \'van-də-,grift\ Alexander Archer 1887– Am. marine-corps gen.

Van·den·berg \'van-dən-,bərg\ Arthur Hendrick 1884–1951 Am. journalist & polit.

Van·der·bilt \'van-dər-,bilt\ Cornelius 1794–1877 Am. capitalist

Van Dine — see Willard Huntington WRIGHT

van Dong·en \van-'däŋ-ən, vän-, vən-, 'döŋ-\ Cornelius 1877–1968 *Kees van Dongen* Fr. (Dutch-born) painter

Van Do·ren \van-'dōr-ən, vən-, -'dȯr-\ Carl Clinton 1885–1950 & his bro. Mark 1894–1972 Am. writers & editors

Van·dyke *or* **Van Dyck** \van-'dīk, vən-\ Sir Anthony 1599–1641 Flem.-born painter in Eng.

Vane \'vān\ Sir Henry *or* Harry 1613–1662 Eng. statesman

Van Rens·se·laer \,van-,ren(t)-sə-'li(ə)r, -,ren-'sli(ə)r, van-; -'ren(t)-s(ə-)lər\ Stephen 1764–1839 Am. gen. & polit.

Van·sit·tart \van-'sit-ərt, vən-\ Robert Gilbert 1881–1957 1st Baron *Vansittart of Den·ham* \'den-əm\ Brit. diplomat

van't Hoff \vänt-'hȯf, vant-\ Jacobus **Hen·dri·cus** \hen-'drē-kəs\ 1852–1911 Du. physical chem.

Vanzetti Bartolomeo — see Nicola SACCO

Van Zyl \van-'zī(ə)l, fän-'sail\ Gideon Brand 1873–1956 So. African lawyer

Va·rese \və-'räz, -'rez\ Edgard 1883–1965 Am. (Fr.-born) composer

Var·gas \'vär-gəs\ Getulio Dornelles 1883–1954 Braz. lawyer; pres. of Brazil (1930–45; 1951–54)

Var·ro \'var(,)ō\ Marcus Terentius 116–27 B.C. Rom. author

Va·sa·ri \və-'zär-ē\ Giorgio 1511–1574 Ital. painter

Vasco da Gama — see GAMA

Va·tu·tin \və-'tü-tin\ Nikolai 1900?–1944 Russ. gen.

Vau·ban, de \vō-'bä^{n}\ Marquis 1633–1707 *Sébastien Le Pres·tre* \lə-'pretrᵊ\ Fr. mil. engineer; marshal of France

Vaughan \'vȯn, 'vän\ Henry 1622–1695 *the Sil·u·rist* \'sil-yə-rəst\ Brit. poet

Vaughan Wil·liams \-'wil-yəmz\ Ralph 1872–1958 Eng. composer

Veb·len \'veb-lən\ Thor·stein \'thȯ(ə)r-,stīn\ Bunde 1857–1929 Am. sociol. & econ. — **Veb·le·ni·an** \veb-'lē-nē-ən\ *adj*

Ve·ga, de \'vā-gə\ Lo·pe \'lō-(,)pā\ 1562–1635 *Lope Félix de Vega Carpio* Span. dram.

Ve·láz·quez *or* **Ve·lás·quez** \və-'las-kəs\ Diego Rodríguez de Silva y 1599–1660 Span. painter

Ven·dôme, de \vä^{n}(n)-'dōm\ Duc Louis Joseph 1654–1712 Fr. soldier; marshal of France

Ve·ni·ze·los \,ven-ə-'zā-ləs, -'zel-əs\ Eleutherios 1864–1936 Greek statesman

Ver·di \'ve(ə)rd-ē\ Giuseppe 1813–1901 Ital. composer — **Ver·di·an** \-ən\ *adj*

Vereker — see GORT

Ve·re·shcha·gin \,ver-əsh-'chäg-ən, ,ver-ə-'shäg-\ Vasili Vasilievich 1842–1904 Russ. painter

Ver·gil *or* **Vir·gil** \'vər-jəl\ 70–19 B.C. *Publius Vergilius Maro* Rom. poet — **Ver·gil·ian** *or* **Vir·gil·ian** \(,)vər-'jil-ē-ən\ *adj*

Ver·laine \ve(ə)r-'lān, -'len\ Paul 1844–1896 Fr. poet

Ver·meer \vər-'me(ə)r, -'mi(ə)r\ Jan 1632–1675 *Jan van der Meer van Delft* Du. painter

Verne Jules \'jülz-'vərn, 'zhüel-'ve(ə)rn\ 1828–1905 Fr. writer

Ver·ner \'ve(ə)r-nər\ Karl Adolph 1846–1896 Dan. philologist

Ver·nier \ve(ə)rn-'yā, 'vər-nē-ər\ Pierre 1580–1637 Fr. math.

Ver·non \'vər-nən\ Edward 1684–1757 Eng. admiral

Ve·ro·ne·se \,ver-ə-'nā-sē, -'nā-zē\ Paolo 1528–1588 *Paolo Cagliari* Ital. painter

Ver·ra·za·no, da *or* **Ver·raz·za·no** \,ver-ə-'zän-(,)ō, -ət-'sän-\ Giovanni 1485?–?1528 Florentine navigator

Ver·roc·chio, del \və-'rōk-ē-,ō\ Andrea 1435–1488 *Andrea di Michele Cione* Florentine sculptor & painter

Verulam — see Francis BACON

Ve·rus \'vir-əs\ Lucius Aurelius 130–169 *Lucius Ceionius Commodus* Rom. emp. (161–169)

Ver·woerd \fər-'vü(ə)rt, fer-\ Hendrik Frensch 1901–1966 So. African polit.; prime min. (1958–66)

Ve·sey \'vē-zē\ Denmark 1762–1822 Am. insurrectionist

Ves·pa·sian \ve-'spā-zh(ē-)ən\ 9–79 *Titus Flavius Sabinus Vespasianus* Rom. emp. (69–79)

Ves·puc·ci \ve-'spü-chē\ **Ame·ri·go** \,äm-ə-'rē-(,)gō\ 1454–1512 *Amer·i·cus Ves·pu·cius* \ə-'mer-ə-kəs-,ves-'pyü-sh(ē-)əs\ Ital. navigator; eponym of *America*

Victor Emmanuel I 1759–1824 king of Sardinia (1802–21)

Victor Emmanuel II 1820–1878 king of Sardinia (1849–61) & 1st king of Italy (1861–78)

Victor Emmanuel III 1869–1947 king of Italy (1900–46)

Vic·to·ria \vik-'tōr-ē-ə, -'tȯr-\ Alexandrina 1819–1901 queen of Gr. Brit. (1837–1901)

Vic·to·ria \vik-'tōr-ē-ə, -'tȯr-\ Tomás Luis de 1540?–1611 Span. composer

Vi·da \'vēd-ə\ Marco Girolamo 1480?–1566 Ital. poet

Vi·ë·tor \'fē-ə-,tō(ə)r\ Wilhelm 1850–1918 Ger. philologist

Vi·gée–Le·brun \vē-'zhā-lə-'brə^{n}(n), -'brœ^{n}\ Marie Ann Élisabeth 1755–1842 Fr. painter

Vi·gno·la, da \vēn-'yō-lə\ Giacomo 1507–1573 *Giacomo Barocchio* or *Barozzi* Ital. architect

Vi·gny, de \vēn-'yē\ Comte Alfred Victor 1797–1863 Fr. author

Vil·la \'vē-(y)ə\ Francisco *or* **Pan·cho** \'pän-(,)chō, 'pan-\ 1877–1923 orig. *Doroteo Arango* Mex. bandit & revolutionist

Vil·la–Lo·bos \,vil-ə-'lō-bəs, ,vē-lə-'lō-,büs\ Heitor 1881–1959 Braz. composer

Vil·lard \və-'lär(d)\ Oswald Garrison 1872–1949 Am. journalist

ə abut	ᵊ kitten, F table	ər further	a back	ā bake	
ä cot, cart	å F bac	aù out	ch chin	e less	ē easy
g gift	i trip	ī life	j joke	k̲ G ich	^{n} F vin	ŋ sing
ō flow	ȯ flaw	œ F bœuf	œ̄ F feu	ȯi coin	th thing
th̲ this	ü loot	u̇ foot	ue G Füllen	ue̅ F rue	y yet
^{y} F digne \dēn^{y}\, nuit \nw^{y}ē\	yü few	yu̇ furious	zh vision		

Vil·lars, de \vi-ˈlär\ Duc Claude Louis Hector 1653–1734 Fr. soldier; marshal of France

Ville·neuve, de \ˌvēl(-ə)-ˈnə(r)v, -ˈnœv\ Pierre Charles Jean Baptiste Silvestre 1763–1806 Fr. admiral

Vil·liers \ˈvil-(y)ərz\ George 1592–1628 1st Duke of *Buck·ing·ham* \ˈbək-iŋ-əm, *US also* -iŋ-ˌham\ Eng. statesman & admiral

Villiers George 1628–1687 2d Duke of *Buckingham, son of prec.* Eng. courtier & dram.

Vil·lon \vē-ˈ(y)ōⁿ *also* -ˈlāⁿ\ François 1431–after 1462 *François de Montcorbier* Fr. poet

Vil·lon \vē-ˈlōⁿ\ Jacques 1875–1963 real name *Gaston Duchamp* Fr. painter

Vin·cent de Paul \ˌvin(t)-sənt-də-ˈpȯl\ Saint 1581?–1660 Fr. priest

Vin·ci, da \ˈvin-chē, ˈvēn-\ Le·o·nar·do \ˌlē-ə-ˈnärd-(ˌ)ō, ˌlā-\ 1452–1519 Florentine painter, sculptor, architect, & engineer

Vi·no·gra·doff \ˌvin-ə-ˈgrad-ˌȯf\ Sir Paul Gavrilovich 1854–1925 Russ. jurist & hist. in Eng.

Vin·son \ˈvin(t)-sən\ Carl 1883– Am. lawyer & polit.

Vinson Frederick Moore 1890–1953 Am. chief justice U.S. Supreme Court (1946–53)

Viol·let–le–Duc \ˌvē-ə-ˈlā-lə-ˈd(y)ük, vyȯ-ˌle-lə-dūēk\ Eugène Emmanuel 1814–1879 Fr. architect

Vir·chow \ˈfi(ə)r-(ˌ)kō, ˈvi(ə)r-\ Rudolf 1821–1902 Ger. pathologist

Vir·ta·nen \ˈvi(ə)r-tə-ˌnen\ Art·tu·ri \ˈärt-ə-rē\ Ilmari 1895–1973 Finnish biochem.

Vi·tru·vi·us Pol·lio \və-ˈtrü-vē-ə-ˈspäl-ē-ˌō\ Marcus 1st cent. B.C. Rom. architect & engineer

Vi·val·di \vi-ˈväl-dē, -ˈvȯl-\ Antonio 1675?–1741 Ital. composer

Vla·di·mir \ˈvlad-ə-ˌmi(ə)r, vlə-ˈdē-ˌmi(ə)r\ 956?–1015 *the Great* ruler of Russia (980–1015)

Vla·minck, de \vlə-ˈmaŋk\ Maurice 1876–1958 Fr. painter

Vo·gler \ˈfō-glər\ Georg Joseph 1749–1814 Abt \äpt, apt\ *or* Abbé *Vogler* Ger. musician

Vol·pe \ˈvōl-pē\ John Anthony 1908– U.S. secy. of transportation (1969–72)

Vol·stead \ˈväl-ˌsted, ˈvȯl-, ˈvōl-, -stəd\ Andrew John 1860–1947 Am. legislator

Vol·ta \ˈvōl-tə, ˈväl-, ˈvȯl-\ Count Alessandro 1745–1827 Ital. physicist

Vol·taire \vōl-ˈta(ə)r, väl-, vȯl-, -ˈte(ə)r\ 1694–1778 *François Marie Arouet* Fr. writer — **Vol·tair·ean** *or* **Vol·tair·ian** \-ˈtar-ē-ən, -ˈter-\ *adj*

Von Braun \vän-ˈbraùn, fən-, vən-\ Wern·her \ˈve(ə)r-nər\ 1912– Am. (Ger.-born) engineer

Von·ne·gut \ˈvän-i-gət\ Kurt 1922– Am. writer

Vo·ro·shi·lov \ˌvȯr-ə-ˈshē-ˌlȯf, ˌvär-, -ˌlȯv\ Kliment Efremovich 1881–1969 Russ. marshal; pres. U.S.S.R. (1953–60)

Vor·ster \ˈfȯr-stər\ Balthazar Johannes 1915– prime min. of Rep. of South Africa (1966–)

Voz·ne·sen·sky \ˌväz-nə-ˈsen(t)-skē\ Andrei 1933– Russ. poet

Vuil·lard \vwē-ˈyär\ Jean Édouard 1868–1940 Fr. painter

Vy·shin·sky \və-ˈshin(t)-skē\ Andrei Yanuarievich 1883–1954 Russ. lawyer & statesman

Waals, van der \ˈvan-dər-ˌwȯlz\ Johannes Diderik 1837–1923 Du. physicist

Wace \ˈwās, ˈwäs\ 12th cent. Anglo-Norman poet

Wag·ner \ˈväg-nər\ (Wilhelm) Ri·chard \ˈrik-ˌärt, ˈrik-\ 1813–1883 Ger. composer

Wagner von Jau·regg \ˈyaù-ˌrek\ Julius 1857–1940 Austrian neurologist & psychiatrist

Wag·ner \ˈwag-nər\ Robert Ferdinand 1910– Am. polit.

Wain·wright \ˈwān-ˌrīt\ Jonathan Mayhew 1883–1953 Am. gen.

Wainwright Richard father 1817–1862 & his son 1849–1926 Am. naval officers

Waite \ˈwāt\ Morrison Remick 1816–1888 Am. jurist; chief justice U.S. Supreme Court (1874–88)

Waks·man \ˈwäk-smən, ˈwak-\ Sel·man \ˈsel-mən\ Abraham 1888–1973 Am. (Ukrainian-born) microbiologist

Wald \ˈwȯld\ Lillian D. 1867–1940 Am. social worker

Wal·de·mar \ˈwȯl-də-ˌmär\ *Dan.* **Val·de·mar** \ˈväl-, ˈval-\ name of 4 kings of Denmark: esp. **I** (*the Great*) 1131–1182 (reigned 1157–82)

Wal·der·see, von \ˈväl-dər-ˌzā, ˈwȯl-\ Count Alfred 1832–1904 Ger. field marshal

Wald·heim \ˈvält-ˌhīm\ Kurt 1918– Austrian U.N. official; secy.-gen. (1972–)

Wal·do \ˈwȯl-(ˌ)dō, ˈwäl-\ *or* **Val·do** \ˈval-(ˌ)dō, ˈväl-\ Peter *fl* 1173–1179 Fr. heretic

Walk·er \ˈwȯ-kər\ Francis Am·a·sa \ˈam-ə-sə\ 1840–1897 Am. econ.

Walker William 1824–1860 Am. adventurer in Mex. & Nicaragua

Wal·lace \ˈwäl-əs\ Alfred Russel 1823–1913 Eng. naturalist

Wallace George Corley 1919– Am. polit.

Wallace Henry Agard \ˈā-ˌgärd\ 1888–1965 Am. agriculturist, editor, & polit.; vice-pres. of U.S. (1941–45)

Wallace Lewis 1827–1905 *Lew* Am. lawyer, gen., & nov.

Wallace Sir William 1272?–1305 Scot. patriot

Wal·lach \ˈwäl-ək, ˈväl-\ Otto 1847–1931 Ger. chem.

Wal·len·stein, von \ˈwäl-ən-ˌstīn\ Albrecht Eusebius Wenzel 1583–1634 Duke of *Friedland and Mecklenburg;* Prince of *Sagan* Austrian gen.

Wal·ler \ˈwäl-ər\ Edmund 1606–1687 Eng. poet

Wal·pole \ˈwȯl-ˌpōl, ˈwäl-\ Horace *or* Horatio 1717–1797 4th Earl of *Orford* Eng. author

Walpole Sir Hugh Seymour 1884–1941 Eng. nov.

Walpole Sir Robert 1676–1745 1st Earl of *Orford; father of Horace* Eng. statesman — **Wal·pol·ian** \wȯl-ˈpō-lē-ən, wäl-\ *adj*

Wal·ter \ˈväl-tər, ˈwȯl-\ Bruno 1876–1962 orig. *Bruno Schle·sing·er* \ˈs(h)lā-ziŋ-ər\ Am. (Ger.-born) conductor

Wal·ter \ˈwȯl-tər\ John 1739–1812 Eng. journalist

Wal·ther von der Vo·gel·wei·de \ˈväl-tər-ˌfȯn-dər-ˈfō-gəl-ˌvīd-ə\ 1170?–?1230 Ger. minnesinger

Wal·ton \ˈwȯlt-ᵊn\ Ernest Thomas Sinton 1903– Irish physicist

Walton Izaak \ˈī-zik, -zək\ 1593–1683 Eng. writer

Walton Sir William Turner 1902– Eng. composer

Wan·a·ma·ker \ˈwän-ə-ˌmā-kər\ John 1838–1922 Am. merchant

Wang Ching-wei \ˈwäŋ-ˈjiŋ-ˈwā\ 1884–1944 Chin. polit.

War·beck \ˈwȯr-ˌbek\ Perkin 1474–1499 Walloon imposter; pretender to the Eng. throne

War·burg \ˈwȯr-ˌbərg, ˈvär-ˌbù(ə)rk\ Otto Heinrich 1883–1970 Ger. physiol.

Ward \ˈwȯ(ə)rd\ Aaron Montgomery 1843–1913 Am. merchant

Ward Sir Adolphus William 1837–1924 Eng. hist.

Ward Ar·te·mas \ˈärt-ə-məs\ 1727–1800 Am. Revolutionary gen.

Ward Artemus — see Charles Farrar BROWNE

Ward Barbara 1914– *Lady Jackson* Eng. econ.

Ward Sir Joseph George 1856–1930 N.Z. statesman

Ward Mary Augusta 1851–1920 *Mrs. Humphry Ward,* née *Arnold* Eng. nov.

War·field \ˈwȯr-fēld\ William Caesar 1920– Am. baritone

War·hol \ˈwȯr-ˌhȯl, -ˌhōl\ Andy 1930?– Am. artist & filmmaker

War·ner \ˈwȯr-nər\ Charles Dudley 1829–1900 Am. editor & essayist

War·ren \ˈwȯr-ən, ˈwär-\ Earl 1891– Am. lawyer & polit.; chief justice U.S. Supreme Court (1953–69)

Warren Gou·ver·neur \ˌgəv-ə(r)-ˈni(ə)r\ Kemble 1830–1882 Am. gen.

Warren Joseph 1741–1775 Am. physician & gen.

Warren Robert Penn 1905– Am. author & educ.

Warren Whitney 1864–1943 Am. architect

War·ton \ˈwȯrt-ᵊn\ Thomas 1728–1790 Eng. literary hist. & critic; poet laureate (1785–90)

War·wick \ˈwär-ik, *US also* ˈwȯr-ik, ˈwȯr-(ˌ)wik\ Earl of 1428–1471 *Richard Nev·ille* \ˈnev-əl\; *the Kingmaker* Eng. soldier & statesman

Wash·ing·ton \ˈwȯsh-iŋ-tən, ˈwäsh-\ Book·er \ˈbùk-ər\ Tal·ia·ferro \ˈtäl-ə-vər\ 1856–1915 Am. educ.

Washington George 1732–1799 Am. gen.; 1st pres. of the U.S. (1789–97) — **Wash·ing·to·nian** \ˌwȯsh-iŋ-ˈtō-nē-ən, ˌwäsh-, -nyən\ *adj*

Was·ser·mann, von \ˈwäs-ər-mən, ˈväs-\ August 1866–1925 Ger. bacteriol.

Wa·ters \ˈwȯt-ərz, ˈwät-\ Ethel 1900– Am. actress & singer

Wat·son \ˈwät-sən\ John 1850–1907 pseud. *Ian Mac·lar·en* \mə-ˈklar-ən\ Scot. clergyman & author

Watson John Broadus 1878–1958 Am. psychol.

Watson Thomas John 1874–1956 Am. businessman

Watson Sir William 1858–1935 Eng. poet

Watt \ˈwät\ James 1736–1819 Scot. inventor

Watt Sir Robert Alexander Watson 1892– Scot. physicist

Wat·teau \wä-ˈtō, vä-\ Jean Antoine 1684–1721 Fr. painter

Wat·ter·son \ˈwät-ər-sən, ˈwȯt-\ Henry 1840–1921 Am. journalist & polit.

Watts \ˈwäts\ George Frederic 1817–1904 Eng. painter & sculptor

Watts Isaac 1674–1748 Eng. theol. & hymn writer

Watts–Dun·ton \-ˈdənt-ᵊn\ Walter Theodore 1832–1914 Eng. critic & poet

Waugh \ˈwȯ\ Evelyn Arthur St. John 1903–1966 Eng. writer

Wa·vell \ˈwā-vəl\ 1st Earl 1883–1950 *Archibald Percival Wavell* Brit. field marshal; viceroy of India (1943–47)

Wayne \ˈwān\ Anthony 1745–1796 *Mad Anthony* Am. Revolutionary gen.

Wea·ver \ˈwē-vər\ Robert Clifton 1907– Am. econ.; U.S. secy. of housing and urban development (1966–69)

Webb \ˈweb\ Beatrice 1858–1943 née *Potter; wife of S.J.* Eng. socialist

Webb Sidney James 1859–1947 1st Baron *Passfield* Eng. socialist

We·ber \ˈvā-bər\ Ernst Heinrich 1795–1878 Ger. physiol.

Weber, von Baron Karl Maria Friedrich Ernst 1786–1826 Ger. composer & conductor

Weber Max 1864–1930 Ger. sociol. & econ. — **We·be·ri·an** \vā-ˈbir-ē-ən\ *adj*

Weber Max 1881–1961 Am. (Russ.-born) painter

We·bern \ˈvā-bərn\ Anton von 1883–1945 Austrian composer

Web·ster \ˈweb-stər\ Daniel 1782–1852 Am. statesman & orator

Webster John 1580?–?1625 Eng. dram.

Webster Noah 1758–1843 Am. lexicographer & author

Wedg·wood \ˈwej-ˌwùd\ Josiah 1730–1795 Eng. potter

Weems \ˈwēmz\ Mason Locke 1759–1825 *Parson Weems* Am. clergyman & biographer

Weill \ˈwī(ə)l, ˈvī(ə)l\ Kurt \ˈkù(ə)rt\ 1900–1950 Ger.-born composer in the U.S.

Wein·ber·ger \ˈwīn-ˌbər-gər\ Caspar W. 1917– U.S. secy. of health, ed., & welfare (1973–)

Weir \ˈwi(ə)r\ Robert Walter 1803–1889 & his 2 sons John Ferguson 1841–1926 & Julian Alden 1852–1919 Am. painters

Weis·mann \ˈvī-ˌsmän, ˈwī-smən\ August 1834–1914 Ger. biologist

Weiz·mann \ˈvīt-smən, ˈwīt-\ Chaim \ˈḵīm, ˈhīm\ 1874–1952 Israeli (Russ.-born) chem.; 1st pres. of Israel (1948–52)

Welch \ˈwelch, ˈwelsh\ William Henry 1850–1934 Am. pathologist

Wel·ler \ˈwel-ər\ Thomas Huckle 1915– Am. public health specialist

Welles \ˈwelz\ (George) Or·son \ˈȯrs-ᵊn\ 1915– Am. actor & producer

Welles Gideon 1802–1878 Am. polit. & writer

Welles Sumner 1892–1961 Am. diplomat

Welles·ley \ˈwelz-lē\ 1st Marquis 1760–1842 *Richard Colley Wellesley* Brit. statesman; gov. gen. of India (1797–1805)

Wel·ling·ton \ˈwel-iŋ-tən\ 1st Duke of 1769–1852 *Arthur Wellesley; the Iron Duke* Brit. gen. & statesman

Wells \ˈwelz\ Herbert George 1866–1946 Eng. nov. & hist. — **Wells·ian** \ˈwel-zē-ən\ *adj*

Wel·ty \ˈwel-tē\ Eudora 1909– Am. writer

Wemyss \ˈwēmz\ Sir Henry Colville Barclay 1891–1959 Brit. gen.

Wen·ces·laus \ˈwen(t)-sə-ˌslȯs, -sləs\ *Ger.* **Wen·zel** \ˈven(t)-səl\ 1361–1419 king of Germany & Holy Rom. Emp. (1378–1400) & (as Wenceslaus IV) king of Bohemia (1378–1419)

Wen·dell \ˈwen-dᵊl\ Barrett 1855–1921 Am. scholar

Geographical Names

Aa·chen \'äk-ən\ *or* F **Aix–la–Cha·pelle** \äk-ˌslä-shə-'pel, ˌek-\ city W Germany near Belgian & Dutch borders *pop* 176,800
Aaland — see AHVENANMAA
Aal·borg *or* **Al·borg** \'ȯl-bȯ(ə)rg\ city & port Denmark in NE Jutland *pop* 154,737
Aalst \'älst\ *or* **Alost** \ä-'lȯst\ commune *cen* Belgium WNW of Brussels *pop* 46,619
Aa·rau \'är-ˌau̇\ commune N Switzerland * of Aargau canton *pop* 16,881
Aa·re \'är-ə\ *or* **Aar** \'är\ river 175 *m, cen* & N Switzerland flowing E & NE into the Rhine
Aar·gau \'är-ˌgau̇\ *or* F **Ar·go·vie** \är-gə-'vē\ canton N Switzerland * Aarau *area* 542, *pop* 433,284
Aar·hus *or* **År·hus** \'ȯ(ə)r-ˌhüs\ city & port Denmark in E Jutland on the Kattegat *pop* 111,266
Ab·a·co \'ab-ə-ˌkō\ two islands of the Bahamas (**Great Abaco & Little Abaco**) N of New Providence I. *area* 776
Aba·dan \ˌäb-ə-'dän, ˌab-ə-'dan\ **1** island W Iran in Shatt-al-Arab delta **2** city & port on Abadan I. *pop* 272,962
Ab·bai \ä-'bī\ the upper course of the Blue Nile
Ab·be·ville \ab-'vēl, 'ab-i-ˌvil\ commune N France on the Somme NW of Amiens *pop* 23,999
Ab·er·dare \ˌab-ər-'da(ə)r, -'de(ə)r\ urban district S Wales in Glamorganshire *pop* 37,760
Ab·er·deen, 1 \'ab-ər-ˌdēn\ city NE S.Dak. *pop* 26,476 **2** city & port W Wash. on Grays Harbor *pop* 18,489 **3** \ˌab-ər-'dēn\ *or* **Ab·er·deen·shire** \-ˌshi(ə)r, -shər\ county NE Scotland *area* 1971, *pop* 319,887 **4** burgh & port * of Aberdeenshire *pop* 182,006 — **Ab·er·do·ni·an** \ˌab-ər-'dō-nē-ən\ *adj or n*
Ab·er·yst·wyth \ˌab-ə-'ris-ˌtwith\ municipal borough W Wales on Cardigan Bay * of Cardiganshire
Ab–i–Diz — see DIZ
Ab·i·djan \ˌab-i-'jän\ city & port * of Ivory Coast *pop* 285,000
Abila — see MUSA (Jebel)
Ab·i·lene \'ab-ə-ˌlēn\ city NW *cen* Tex. *pop* 89,653
Ab·i·tibi \ˌab-ə-'tib-ē\ **1** lake Canada on E boundary of Ont. *area* 356 **2** river 230 *m* Canada flowing N into Moose river
Ab·kha·sia *or* **Ab·kha·zia** \ab-'kā-zh(ē)-ə, -'käz-ē-ə\ *or* **Ab·kha·sian Republic** \-'kā-zhən, -'käz-ē-ən\ autonomous republic U.S.S.R. in NW Georgia on Black sea * Sukhumi *area* 3358, *pop* 487,000 — **Ab·khas** \-'käs\ *n* — **Ab·kha·sian** *or* **Ab·kha·zian** \-'kā-zhən, -'käz-ē-ən\ *adj or n*
Åbo — see TURKU
Abo·mey \ˌab-ə-'mā, ə-'bō-mē\ city S Dahomey *pop* 34,000
Abruz·zi \ä-'brüt-sē, ə-\ area *cen* Italy bordering on the Adriatic & including highest of the Apennines; with Molise (to S), forms **Abruzzi e Mo·li·se** \-ˌā-'mȯ-lə-ˌzā\ region (* Aquila)
Ab·sa·ro·ka \ab-'sär-ə-kə, -'sȯ(ə)r-kē\ mountain range S Mont. & NW Wyo. E of Yellowstone National Park — see FRANKS PEAK
Ab·se·con inlet \ab-'sē-kən\ strait SE N.J. through barrier reef N of Atlantic City
Ab·u·kir \ˌab-(ˌ)ü-'ki(ə)r, ˌäb-\ **1** bay N Egypt between Alexandria & Rosetta mouth of the Nile **2** village on the bay — see CANOPUS
Abu Sim·bel \ˌäb-ˌü-'sim-bəl\ *or* **Ip·sam·bul** \ˌip-səm-'bül\ locality S Egypt on left bank of the Nile 140 *m* SW of Aswân; site of two rock temples
Aby·dos \ə-'bīd-əs\ **1** ancient town Asia Minor on the Hellespont **2** ancient town S Egypt on left bank of the Nile S of Thebes
Abyla — see MUSA (Jebel)
Ab·ys·sin·ia \ˌab-ə-'sin-ē-ə, -'sin-yə\ — see ETHIOPIA — **Ab·ys·sin·ian** \-ē-ən, -yən\ *adj or n*
Aca·dia \ə-'kād-ē-ə\ *or* F **Aca·die** \á-ká-dē\ NOVA SCOTIA — an early name — **Aca·di·an** \ə-'kād-ē-ən\ *adj or n*
Acadia National Park section of coast of Me. including chiefly mountainous areas on Mount Desert I. & Isle au Haut *area* 42
Aca·pul·co \ˌäk-ə-'pül-(ˌ)kō, ˌak-\ *or* **Acapulco de Juá·rez** \-də-'wär-əs\ city & port S Mexico in Guerrero on the Pacific SSW of Mexico City *pop* 234,866
Ac·ar·na·nia \ˌak-ər-'nā-nē-ə, -'nā-nyə\ *or* NGk **Akar·na·nía** \ˌäk-ˌär-nə-'nē-ə\ region W Greece on Ionian sea — **Ac·ar·na·nian** \ˌak-ər-'nā-nē-ən, -'nā-nyən\ *adj or n*
Ac·cad \'ak-ˌad, 'äk-ˌäd\ — see AKKAD — **Ac·ca·di·an** \ə-'kād-ē-ən, -'käd-\ *adj or n*
Ac·cra *or* **Ak·kra** \ə-'krä\ city & port * of Ghana on Gulf of Guinea *pop* 615,800
Ac·cring·ton \'ak-riŋ-tən\ municipal borough NW England in SE Lancashire N of Manchester *pop* 36,838

Achaea \ə-'kē-ə\ *or* **Acha·ia** \ə-'kī-ə, -'kā-(y)ə\ region S Greece in N Peloponnesus bordering on gulfs of Corinth & Patras — **Achae·an** \ə-'kē-ən\ *or* **Acha·ian** \ə-'kī-ən, -'kā-(y)ən\ *adj or n*
Ach·e·lo·us *or* NGk **Akhe·ló·os** *or* **Ach·e·lo·os** \ˌak-ə-'lō-əs\ river 100 *m* W Greece flowing S to Ionian sea
Ach·ill \'ak-əl\ island 15 *m* long NW Ireland in County Mayo
Achray, Loch \ə-'krā\ lake *cen* Scotland in SW Perthshire
Acon·ca·gua \ˌak-ən-'käg-wə, ˌäk-\ mountain 22,831 *ft* W Argentina WNW of Mendoza near Chilean border; highest in Andes & western hemisphere
Açores — see AZORES
Acragas — see AGRIGENTO
Acre \'äk-rə, 'ā-(ˌ)krā\ state W Brazil bordering on Peru & Bolivia * Rio Branco *area* 57,153, *pop* 203,900
Acre \'äk-ər, 'ā-kər, 'äk-rə\ *or* Heb **Ak·ko** *or* **Ac·cho** \ä-'kō\ *or anc* **Ptol·e·ma·is** \ˌtäl-ə-'mā-əs\ city & port NW Israel at N end of Bay of Acre N of Mt. Carmel *pop* 33,900
Acroceraunia — see LINGUETTA (Cape)
Ac·te *or* **Ak·te** \'ak-(ˌ)tē\ peninsula NE Greece, the most easterly of the three peninsulas of Chalcidice — see ATHOS
Ac·ti·um \'ak-shē-əm, 'ak-tē-\ promontory & ancient town W Greece in NW Acarnania
Ac·ton \'ak-tən\ former municipal borough SE England in Middlesex, W suburb of London, now part of Ealing
Adak \'ā-ˌdak\ island SW Alaska in Andreanof group of the Aleutians
Adalia — see ANTALYA
Ad·ams, Mount \'ad-əmz\ **1** mountain 5798 *ft* N N.H. in White mountains N of Mt. Washington **2** mountain 12,307 *ft* SW Wash. in Cascade range SSE of Mt. Rainier
Ad·am's Bridge \ˌad-əmz-\ chain of shoals 30 *m* long between Ceylon & SE India
Adam's Peak mountain 7365 *ft* S *cen* Ceylon
Ada·na \'äd-ə-nə, -ˌnä, ə-'dän-ə\ *or* **Sey·han** \sā-'hän\ city S Turkey on Seyhan river *pop* 289,919
Ada·pa·za·ri \ˌäd-ə-ˌpäz-ə-'rē\ city NW Turkey in Asia E of Istanbul *pop* 152,171
Ad·dis Aba·ba \ˌad-ə-'sab-ə-bə\ city * of Ethiopia *pop* 795,900
Ad·di·son \'ad-ə-sən\ village NE Ill. W of Chicago *pop* 24,482
Ad·e·laide \'ad-ᵊl-ˌād\ city Australia * of So. Australia *pop* (with suburbs) 742,300
Aden \'äd-ᵊn, 'ād-, 'ad-\ **1** former Brit. protectorate S Arabia comprising coast area between Yemen on W & Oman on E; since 1967 part of Southern Yemen *area* 112,000 **2** former Brit. colony on coast of & surrounded by Aden protectorate comprising Aden & Little Aden peninsulas, a small area of hinterland, & Perim I.; since 1967 part of Southern Yemen *area* 75 **3** city & port * of People's Democratic Republic of Yemen (Southern Yemen) & former * of Aden colony & protectorate *pop* 225,000
Aden, Gulf of arm of Indian ocean between Aden & Somalia
Adi·ge \'äd-ə-ˌjā\ river 220 *m* N Italy flowing SE into the Adriatic
Ad·i·ron·dack \ˌad-ə-'rän-ˌdak\ mountains NE N.Y. — see MARCY (Mount)
Ad·mi·ral·ty \'ad-m(ə-)rəl-tē\ **1** island 100 *m* long SE Alaska in N Alexander archipelago **2** islands W Pacific N of New Guinea in Bismarck archipelago *area* 800, *pop* 21,588
Adour \ə-'dù(ə)r\ river 200 *m* SW France flowing from the Pyrenees NW & W into Bay of Biscay
Adri·an \'ā-drē-ən\ city SE Mich. *pop* 20,382
Adrianople — see EDIRNE
Adri·at·ic \ˌā-drē-'at-ik, ˌad-rē-\ sea arm of the Mediterranean between Italy & Balkan peninsula
Adu·wa *or* **Ado·wa** \'äd-ə-wə, 'ad-\ *or* **Ad·wa** \'äd-(ˌ)wä\ city N Ethiopia *pop* 15,712
Ad·vent Bay \ˌad-ˌvent-, -vənt-\ inlet of Arctic ocean West Spitsbergen on W coast
Ady·gei *or* **Adi·gey** \ˌäd-ə-'gā\ autonomous region U.S.S.R. in S Soviet Russia, Europe * Maikop *area* 1505, *pop* 386,000
Adzha·ria \ə-'jär-ē-ə\ *or* **Adzhar Republic** \ˌaj-ˌär-\ autonomous republic U.S.S.R. in SW Georgia on Black sea * Batum *area* 1080,

* capital or seat of administration
NESW indicate direction and are not part of a place-name

ə abut ᵊ kitten, F table ər further a back ā bake ä cot, cart á F bac au̇ out ch chin e less ē easy g gift i trip ī life j joke k̲ G ich ⁿ F vin ŋ sing ō flow ȯ flaw œ F bœuf œ̄ F feu oi coin th thing t̲h̲ this ü loot u̇ foot ue G Füllen ue̅ F rue y yet ʸ F digne \dēnʸ\, nuit \nwʸē\ yü few yu̇ furious zh vision

pop 310,000 — **Adzhar** \ˈäj-ˌär\ *n* — **Adzhar·i·an** \ə-ˈjär-ē-ən\ *adj or n*
Aegadian, Aegates — see EGADI
Ae·ge·an \i-ˈjē-ən\ **1** sea arm of the Mediterranean between Asia Minor & Greece **2** islands Aegean sea including the Cyclades & the Northern & Southern Sporades
Ae·gi·na \i-ˈjī-nə\ or NGk **Ai·gi·na** \ˈā-yē-ˌnä\ island & ancient state SE Greece in Saronic gulf — **Ae·gi·ne·tan** \ˌē-jə-ˈnēt-ᵊn\ *adj or n*
Ae·gos·pot·a·mi \ˌē-gə-ˈspät-ə-ˌmī\ *or* **Ae·gos·pot·a·mos** \-məs\ river & town of ancient Thrace in the Chersonese
Aemilia — see EMILIA-ROMAGNA
Aeolian islands — see LIPARI
Ae·o·lis \ˈē-ə-ləs\ *or* **Ae·o·lia** \ē-ˈō-lē-ə, -ˈōl-yə\ ancient country of NW Asia Minor
Aetna — see ETNA
Ae·to·lia \ē-ˈtō-lē-ə, -ˈtōl-yə\ region W *cen* Greece N of Gulf of Patras & E of Acarnania — **Ae·to·lian** \-lē-ən, -yən\ *adj or n*
Afars and the Issas, French Territory of the — see FRENCH TERRITORY OF THE AFARS AND THE ISSAS
Af·ghan·i·stan \af-ˈgan-ə-ˌstan\ country W Asia E of Iran; a republic since 1973 ✱ Kabul *area* 250,000 *pop* 17,480,000
Afog·nak \ə-ˈfög-ˌnak, -ˈfäg-\ island S Alaska N of Kodiak I.
Af·ri·ca \ˈaf-ri-kə\ continent of the eastern hemisphere S of the Mediterranean & adjoining Asia on NE *area* 11,596,000
Afyon *or* **Afyon Ka·ra·hi·sar** \ä-ˈfyōn-ˌkär-ə-his-ˈär\ city W *cen* Turkey *pop* 44,026
Aga·dir \ˌäg-ə-ˈdi(ə)r, ˌag-\ city & port SW Morocco *pop* 34,000
Aga·na \ə-ˈgän-yə\ town ✱ of Guam on W coast *pop* 2119
Agar·ta·la \ˌəg-ər-tə-ˈlä\ city E India ✱ of Tripura *pop* 54,878
Ag·as·siz, Lake \ˈag-ə-(ˌ)sē\ prehistoric lake 700 *m* long in S Man., E Sask., E N.Dak., & NW Minn.
Ag·a·wam \ˈag-ə-ˌwäm\ town SW Mass. SW of Springfield *pop* 21,717
Age·nais \ˌäzh-ə-ˈnā\ *or* **Age·nois** \ˌäzh-ən-ˈwä\ ancient region SW France S of Périgord ✱ Agen
Aghrim — see AUGHRIM
Agincourt — see AZINCOURT
Ag·no \ˈäg-(ˌ)nō\ river 128 *m* Philippines in NW Luzon
Agra \ˈäg-rə\ **1** region N India roughly equivalent to present Uttar Pradesh excluding Oudh region **2** city N India in W Uttar Pradesh SSE of Delhi *pop* 628,070
Agram — see ZAGREB
Agri Dagi — see ARARAT
Agri·gen·to \ˌäg-ri-ˈjen-(ˌ)tō, ˌag-\ *or formerly* **Gir·gen·ti** \jər-ˈjent-ē\ *or anc* **Ag·ri·gen·tum** \ˌag-rə-ˈjent-əm\ *or* **Ac·ra·gas** \ˈak-rə-gəs\ commune Italy in SW Sicily near coast *pop* 51,682
Agua·di·lla \ˌäg-wə-ˈthē-(y)ə\ city & port NW Puerto Rico *pop* 21,031
Aguas·ca·lien·tes \ˌäg-wə-ˌskäl-ˈyen-ˌtās\ **1** state *cen* Mexico *area* 2499, *pop* 334,936 **2** city, its ✱ *pop* 222,105
Agul·has, Cape \ə-ˈgəl-əs\ headland Republic of So. Africa in S Cape Province; southernmost point of Africa, at 34°50′S, 20°E
Ahag·gar \ə-ˈhäg-ər, ˌä-hə-ˈgär\ *or* **Hog·gar** \ˈhäg-ər, hə-ˈgär\ mountains S Algeria in W *cen* Sahara; highest Tahat 9573 *ft*
Ah·mad·abad *or* **Ah·med·abad** \ˈäm-əd-ə-ˌbäd\ city W India N of Bombay ✱ of Gujarat *pop* 1,550,779
Ah·ven·an·maa \ˈä(k)-və-ˌnän-ˌmä\ *or* Sw **Åland** *or* **Aa·land** \ˈō-ˌländ\ **1** archipelago SW Finland in Baltic sea ✱ Maarianhamina (Sw Mariehamn) **2** island, chief of the group
Ah·waz \ä-ˈwäz\ city SW Iran on Karun river *pop* 206,375
Ail·sa Craig \ˈāl-zə-ˌkrāg\ small rocky island Scotland S of Arran at mouth of Firth of Clyde
Ain \a^{n}\ river 118 *m* E France rising in Jura mountains & flowing SSW into the Rhone
Aintab — see GAZIANTEP
Air·drie \ˈa(ə)r-drē, ˈe(ə)r-\ burgh S *cen* Scotland in Lanark E of Glasgow *pop* 37,908
Aire \ˈa(ə)r, ˈe(ə)r\ river 70 *m* N England in W Yorkshire flowing to the Ouse; its valley is **Aire·dale** \-ˌdāl\
Aisne \ˈān\ river *ab* 175 *m* N France flowing NW & W from Argonne Forest into the Oise near Compiègne
Aix \ˈāks, ˈeks\ *or* **Aix–en–Pro·vence** \ˌāk-ˌsä^{n}-prō-ˈvä^{n}s, ˌek-\ city SE France N of Marseilles *pop* 89,556
Aix–la–Chapelle — see AACHEN
Aix–les–Bains \ˌāk-slā-ˈba^{n}, ˌek-\ commune E France N of Chambéry *pop* 20,627
Ajac·cio \ä-ˈyäch-(ˌ)ō\ city & port France ✱ of Corsica *pop* 40,834
Ajan·ta \ə-ˈjənt-ə\ village W *cen* India in N *cen* Maharashtra in Ajanta range NNE of Aurangabad; caves
Aj·mer \ˌəj-ˈmi(ə)r, -ˈme(ə)r\ **1** *or* **Ajmer–Mer·wa·ra** \-ˌme(ə)r-ˈwär-ə\ former state NW India, now part of Rajasthan *area* 2425 **2** city, its ✱, SW of Delhi *pop* 269,233
Ajodh·ya *or* **Ayodh·ya** \ə-ˈyōd-yə\ former city N India, now part of city of Faizabad
Akaba — see ʻAQABA
Akarnanía — see ACARNANIA
Aka·shi \ä-ˈkäsh-ē\ city Japan in SW Honshu on Akashi strait W of Kobe *pop* 196,000
Akhelóos — see ACHELOUS
Ak·hi·sar \ˌäk-(h)is-ˈär\ *or anc* **Thy·a·ti·ra** \ˌthī-ə-ˈtī-rə\ city W Turkey in Asia NE of Izmir *pop* 46,167
Aki·ta \ä-ˈkēt-ə, ˈäk-i-ˌtä\ city & port Japan in N Honshu on Sea of Japan *pop* 237,000
Ak·kad *or* **Ac·cad** \ˈak-ˌad, ˈäk-ˌäd\ **1** the N division of ancient Babylonia **2** *or* **Aga·de** \ə-ˈgäd-ə\ ancient city, its ✱
Akkerman — see BELGOROD-DNESTROVSKI
Akko — see ACRE
Akkra — see ACCRA
Ak·ron \ˈak-rən\ city NE Ohio *pop* 275,425
Ak·sum *or* **Ax·um** \ˈäk-ˌsüm\ town N Ethiopia ✱ of an ancient kingdom (the Axumite Empire)
Akte — see ACTE
Akyab — see SITTWE
Al·a·bama \ˌal-ə-ˈbam-ə\ **1** river 315 *m* S Ala. flowing SW into Tensaw & Mobile rivers **2** state SE U.S. ✱ Montgomery *area* 51,609, *pop* 3,444,165 — **Al·a·bam·i·an** \-ˈbam-ē-ən\ *or* **Al·a·bam·an** \-ˈbam-ən\ *adj or n*
Ala·go·as \ˌal-ə-ˈgō-əs\ state NE Brazil ✱ Maceió *area* 11,031, *pop* 1,606,165
Alai \ˈä-ˌlī\ mountain range U.S.S.R. in Soviet Central Asia in SW Kirgiz Republic; highest peak 19,554 *ft*
Al·a·me·da \ˌal-ə-ˈmēd-ə\ city & port W Calif. on island in San Francisco Bay near Oakland *pop* 70,968
Ala·mein *or* **El Alamein** \ˌel-ˌal-ə-ˈmān\ village NW Egypt on the Mediterranean N of NE corner of Qattara Depression
Al·a·mo·gor·do \ˌal-ə-mə-ˈgȯrd-(ˌ)ō\ city S N.Mex. *pop* 23,035
Ala·se·hir \ˌal-ə-shə-ˈhi(ə)r, ˌäl-\ *or anc* **Philadelphia** city W Turkey 75 *m* E of Izmir *pop* 16,012
Alas·ka \ə-ˈlas-kə\ **1** state (territory 1912–59) of the U.S. NW No. America ✱ Juneau *area* 586,412, *pop* 302,173 **2** peninsula SW Alaska SW of Cook inlet **3** mountain range S Alaska extending from Alaska peninsula to Yukon boundary — see MCKINLEY (Mount) — **Alas·kan** \-kən\ *adj or n*
Alaska, Gulf of inlet of the Pacific off S Alaska between Alaska peninsula on W & Alexander archipelago on E
Ala Tau \ˌal-ə-ˈtau̇, ˌäl-\ several ranges of the Tien Shan mountain system Soviet Central Asia in E Kazakh & Kirgiz republics around & NE of Issyk Kul; 10,000 to 18,000 *ft* high
Ála·va \ˈäl-ə-və\ province N Spain S of Vizcaya; one of the Basque Provinces ✱ Vitoria *area* 1175, *pop* 204,323
Al·a·va, Cape \ˈal-ə-və\ cape NW Wash. 17 *m* S of Cape Flattery; westernmost point of conterminous U.S., at 124°44′W
Al·ba·ce·te \ˌal-bə-ˈsāt-ē\ **1** province SE Spain N of Murcia province *area* 5737, *pop* 335,026 **2** commune, its ✱ *pop* 93,233
Al·ba Lon·ga \ˌal-bə-ˈlȯŋ-gə\ ancient city *cen* Italy SE of Rome
Al·ban hills \ˌȯl-bən-, ˌal-\ *or anc* **Al·ba·nus Mons** \äl-ˌbän-ə-ˈsmōn(t)s\ mountain group Italy SE of Rome
Al·ba·nia \al-ˈbā-nē-ə, -nyə *also* ȯl-\ **1** ancient country Europe in E Caucasus region on W side of Caspian sea **2** country S Europe in Balkan peninsula on the Adriatic; a republic ✱ Tirane *area* 10,630, *pop* 2,230,000
Al·ba·no, Lake \al-ˈbän-(ˌ)ō, äl-\ *or anc* **La·cus Al·ba·nus** \ˌläk-ə-säl-ˈbän-əs\ lake Italy SE of Rome
Al·ba·ny \ˈȯl-bə-nē\ **1** city SW Ga. *pop* 72,623 **2** city ✱ of N.Y. *pop* 114,873 **3** city NW Oreg. S of Salem *pop* 18,181 **4** river 610 *m* Canada in N Ont. flowing E into James Bay — **Al·ba·ni·an** \ȯl-ˈbā-nē-ən\ *adj or n*
Al·be·marle \ˈal-bə-ˌmärl\ **1** sound inlet of Atlantic ocean NE N.C. **2** — see ISABELA
Al·bert, Lake \ˈal-bərt\ lake 100 *m* long E Africa between Uganda & Zaire in course of the Victoria Nile
Al·ber·ta \al-ˈbərt-ə\ province W Canada ✱ Edmonton *area* 248,-800, *pop* 1,634,000 — **Al·ber·tan** \-ˈbərt-ᵊn\ *adj or n*
Al·bert Lea \ˌal-bərt-ˈlē\ city S Minn. *pop* 19,418
Albert Nile — see NILE
Albertville — see KALIMA
Al·bi \al-ˈbē\ commune S France NE of Toulouse *pop* 42,930
Ål·borg — see AALBORG
Al·bu·quer·que \ˈal-b(y)ə-ˌkər-kē\ city *cen* N.Mex. *pop* 243,751
Al·ca·mo \ˈäl-kə-ˌmō\ commune NW Sicily *pop* 42,758
Al·ca·traz \ˈal-kə-ˌtraz\ island Calif. in San Francisco Bay
Al·coy \äl-ˈkȯi\ commune E Spain N of Alicante *pop* 61,371
Al·da·bra \ˈal-də-brə\ island (atoll) NW Indian ocean N of Madagascar, chief of Aldabra group; in Brit. Indian Ocean Territory
Al·dan \äl-ˈdän\ river 1500 *m* U.S.S.R. in E Soviet Russia, Asia, in SE Yakutsk Republic flowing into the Lena
Al·der·ney \ˈȯl-dər-nē\ island in English channel, northernmost of the Channel islands ✱ St. Anne *area* 3, *pop* 1686
Al·der·shot \ˈȯl-dər-ˌshät\ municipal borough S England in Hampshire *pop* 33,311
Aleksandrovsk — see ZAPOROZHE
Aleksandrovsk Grushevski — see SHAKHTY
Alen·çon \ˌal-ˌä^{n}-ˈsō^{n}\ city NW France N of Le Mans *pop* 31,656
Alep·po \ə-ˈlep-(ˌ)ō\ *or* **Alep** \ä-ˈlep\ *or* Ar **Ha·leb** \hə-ˈleb\ *or* **Ha·lab** \-ˈlab\ *or anc* **Be·roea** *or* **Be·rea** \bə-ˈrē-ə\ city N Syria *pop* 639,000 — **Alep·pine** \ə-ˈlep-ən, -ˌīn, -ˌēn\ *adj or n*
Ales·san·dria \ˌal-ə-ˈsan-drē-ə\ commune NW Italy *pop* 99,023
Aleu·tian \ə-ˈlü-shən\ **1** islands SW Alaska extending in an arc 1200 *m* SW & W from Alaska peninsula — see ANDREANOF, FOX, NEAR, RAT **2** mountain range SW Alaska, the SW extension of Alaska range, running along NW shore of Cook inlet to SW tip of Alaska peninsula with mountains of the Aleutian chain forming its SW extension — see SHISHALDIN
Al·ex·an·der \ˌal-ig-ˈzan-dər, ˌel-\ archipelago of *ab* 1100 islands SE Alaska — see ADMIRALTY, BARANOF, CHICHAGOF, KUPREANOF, PRINCE OF WALES, REVILLAGIGEDO
Alexander I island Antarctica W of base of Antarctic peninsula
Alexandretta — see ISKENDERUN
Al·ex·an·dria \ˌal-ig-ˈzan-drē-ə, ˌel-\ **1** city *cen* La. *pop* 41,557 **2** city N Va. on the Potomac S of Washington, D.C. *pop* 110,938 **3** city & port N Egypt between Lake Mareotis & the Mediterranean *pop* 2,032,000 — **Al·ex·an·dri·an** \-drē-ən\ *adj or n*
Al·föld \ˈȯl-ˌfə(r)ld\ the central plain of Hungary
Al·gar·ve \äl-ˈgär-və, al-\ medieval Moorish kingdom now a province of Portugal on S coast
Al·ge·ci·ras \ˌal-jə-ˈsir-əs\ city & port SW Spain W of Gibraltar on Bay of Algeciras *pop* 81,662
Al·ge·ria \al-ˈjir-ē-ə\ country NW Africa bordering on the Mediterranean ✱ Algiers *area* 919,352, *pop* 14,770,000 — **Al·ge·ri·an** \-ē-ən\ *adj or n*
Al·giers \al-ˈji(ə)rz\ **1** former Barbary state N Africa now Algeria **2** *or* F **Al·ger** \äl-zhā\ *or* Ar **Al-je·zair** \ˌal-jə-ˌza(ə)r\ city & port ✱ of Algeria on Bay of Algiers *pop* 903,530 — **Al·ge·rine** \ˌal-jə-ˈrēn\ *adj or n*
Al·goa Bay \al-ˌgō-ə-\ inlet of Indian ocean S Republic of So. Africa on SE coast of Cape Province

Al·ham·bra \al-ˈham-brə\ **1** city SW Calif. E of Los Angeles *pop* 62,125 **2** hill in Granada, Spain; site of remains of Moorish palace & fortifications
Ali·can·te \ˌal-ə-ˈkant-ē, ˌäl-ə-ˈkänt-ē\ **1** province E Spain on the Mediterranean S of Valencia province *area* 2185, *pop* 920,105 **2** city & port, its ✱ *pop* 137,504
Al·ice \ˈal-əs\ city S Tex. W of Corpus Christi *pop* 20,121
Ali·garh \ˌal-i-ˈgär\ city N India in NW Uttar Pradesh N of Agra *pop* (including old town of **Ko·il** \ˈkō-əl\) 237,954
Al·i·quip·pa \ˌal-ə-ˈkwip-ə\ borough W Pa. *pop* 22,277
Al Ittihad — see MEDINA AS-SHAAB
Alk·maar \ˈalk-ˌmär\ commune NW Netherlands *pop* 52,091
Al–Kut — see KUT-AL-IMARA
Al Kuwait — see KUWAIT
Al·lah·abad \ˈal-ə-hə-ˌbad, -ˌbäd\ city N India in S Uttar Pradesh on the Ganges W of Banaras *pop* 534,676
Al·le·ghe·ny \ˌal-ə-ˈgā-nē *also* -ˈgen-ē\ **1** river 325 *m* W Pa. uniting with the Monongahela at Pittsburgh to form the Ohio **2** mountains of Appalachian system E U.S. in Pa., Md., Va., & W.Va.; 2000 to over 4800 *ft* high — **Al·le·ghe·ni·an** \-ˈgā-nē-ən, -ˈgen-ē-\ *adj*
Al·len Park \ˌal-ən-\ city SE Mich. WSW of Detroit *pop* 40,747
Allenstein — see OLSZTYN
Al·len·town \ˈal-ən-ˌtau̇n\ city E Pa. on the Lehigh *pop* 109,527
Al·lep·pey \ə-ˈlep-ē\ city & port S India in Kerala NW of Trivandrum *pop* 163,977
Al·li·ance \ə-ˈlī-ən(t)s\ city NE Ohio NE of Canton *pop* 26,547
Al·lier \al-ˈyā\ river *ab* 250 *m* S *cen* France flowing to the Loire
Al·ma \ˈal-mə\ **1** river 50 *m* U.S.S.R. in S Soviet Russia, Europe, in SW Crimea **2** city Canada in E Que. on the Saguenay *pop* 22,622
Al·ma–Ata \ˌal-mə-ə-ˈtä\ *or formerly* **Ver·nyi** \ˈve(ə)rn-yē\ city U.S.S.R. in Soviet Central Asia ✱ of Kazakh Republic *pop* 730,000
Al·ma·dén \ˌal-mə-ˈdān, ˌäl-\ town S *cen* Spain in the Sierra Morena
Al·me·lo \ˈäl-mə-ˌlō\ commune E Netherlands *pop* 58,941
Al·me·ría \ˌal-mə-ˈrē-ə\ **1** province S Spain SE of Granada province *area* 3360, *pop* 375,004 **2** city & port, its ✱ *pop* 114,510
Alor \ˈal-ˌȯ(ə)r, ˈäl-\ *or* **Om·bai** \ˈōm-ˌbī\ island Indonesia in Lesser Sundas N of Timor; with **Pan·tar** \ˈpan-ˌtär\, forms **Alor islands** group
Alor Se·tar \sə-ˈtär\ city NW Malaya ✱ of Kedah *pop* 66,179
Alost — see AALST
Al·phe·us \al-ˈfē-əs\ *or* NGk **Al·fiós** \äl-ˈfyȯs\ river *ab* 75 *m* S Greece in W Peloponnesus flowing NW into Ionian sea
Alps \ˈalps\ mountain system S *cen* Europe extending from Mediterranean coast at border between France & Italy into NW & W Yugoslavia — see MONT BLANC
Al·sace \al-ˈsas, -ˈsās, ˈal-ˌ\ *or* G **El·sass** \ˈel-ˌzäs\ *or anc* **Al·sa·tia** \al-ˈsā-sh(ē-)ə\ region & former province NE France between Rhine river & Vosges mountains — **Al·sa·tian** \al-ˈsā-shən\ *adj or n*
Alsace–Lor·raine \-lə-ˈrān, -lȯ-\ *or* G **El·sass–Lo·thring·en** \ˌel-ˌzäs-ˈlō-triŋ-ən\ region NE France including Alsace & part of Lorraine
Al·sek \ˈal-ˌsek\ river 260 *m* NW Canada & SE Alaska flowing S into the Pacific
Al·ta California \ˈal-tə-\ former Spanish & Mexican province (1772–1848) comprising the present state of Calif. — a name used to differentiate it from Baja California
Al·tai \ˈal-ˌtī\ **1** mountain system *cen* Asia between Outer Mongolia & Sinkiang region of W China & between Kazakh & Russian republics — see TABUN BOGDO **2** territory U.S.S.R. in SW Soviet Russia, Asia ✱ Barnaul *area* 71,885, *pop* 2,670,000
Al·ta·ma·ha \ˈȯl-tə-mə-ˌhȯ\ river 137 *m* SE Ga. formed by junction of Ocmulgee & Oconee rivers & flowing SE into **Altamaha Sound** (estuary)
Al·ta·mi·ra \ˌal-tə-ˈmir-ə\ caverns N Spain WSW of Santander
Alt·dorf \ˈalt-ˌdȯrf, ˈält-\ *or* **Al·torf** \ˈal-ˌtȯrf, ˈäl-\ town *cen* Switzerland ✱ of Uri canton
Al·ten·burg \ˈält-^{ə}n-ˌbu̇(ə)rg\ city E Germany E of Weimar *pop* 46,737
Altin Tagh *or* **Altyn Tagh** — see ASTIN TAGH
Al·to Adi·ge \ˌäl-(ˌ)tō-ˈäd-i-ˌjā\ *or* **Upper Adige** *or* **South Tirol** district N Italy in S Tirol in N Trentino-Alto Adige region
Al·ton \ˈȯlt-^{ə}n\ city SW Ill. on the Mississippi *pop* 39,700
Al·too·na \al-ˈtü-nə\ city S *cen* Pa. *pop* 62,900
Alto Paraná — see PARANÁ
Al·trin·cham \ˈȯl-triŋ-əm\ municipal borough NW England in Cheshire SSW of Manchester *pop* 40,752
Al·tus \ˈal-təs\ city SW Okla. *pop* 23,302
Aluta — see OLT
Ama·ga·sa·ki \ˌam-ə-gə-ˈsäk-ē\ city Japan in W *cen* Honshu on Osaka Bay *pop* 539,000
Amal·fi \ə-ˈmäl-fē\ commune & port S Italy in Campania on Gulf of Salerno — **Amal·fi·an** \-fē-ən\ *adj or n*
Ama·mi \ə-ˈmäm-ē\ island group W Pacific in *cen* Ryukyus belonging to Japan *area* 498
Ama·pá \ˌam-ə-ˈpä\ territory N Brazil NW of Amazon delta ✱ Macapá *area* 55,489, *pop* 116,481
ˈAma·ra \ə-ˈmär-ə\ city SE Iraq on the Tigris *pop* 64,847
Am·a·ril·lo \ˌam-ə-ˈril-(ˌ)ō, -ˈril-ə\ city NW Tex. *pop* 127,010
Am·a·zon \ˈam-ə-ˌzän, -zən\ river *ab* 3900 *m* N So. America flowing from Peruvian Andes into the Atlantic in N Brazil — see UCAYALI, SOLIMÕES
Ama·zo·nas \ˌam-ə-ˈzō-nəs\ state NW Brazil ✱ Manaus *area* 595,474, *pop* 714,803
Am·ba·to \äm-ˈbät-(ˌ)ō\ city *cen* Ecuador S of Quito *pop* 75,300
Am·bon \ˈam-ˌbän\ *or* **Am·boi·na** \am-ˈbȯi-nə\ **1** island E Indonesia in the Moluccas S of Ceram *area* 314, *pop* 72,679 **2** city & port on Ambon I. ✱ of Maluku province *pop* 56,000 — **Am·bo·nese** \ˌam-bə-ˈnēz, -ˈnēs\ *or* **Am·boi·nese** \ˌam-ˌbȯi-ˈnēz, am-ˈbȯi-ˌ\ *adj or n*
Am·bra·cian Gulf \am-ˌbrā-shən-\ *or* **Gulf of Ar·ta** \ˈärt-ə\ *or* NGk **Am·vra·ki·kós Kól·pos** \ˌam-ˈvräk-i-ˌkȯ-ˈskȯl-ˌpȯs\ inlet of Ionian sea 25 *m* long W Greece in S Epirus
Am·brose channel \ˌam-ˌbrōz\ dredged channel SE N.Y. at entrance to N.Y. harbor N of Sandy Hook; 40 *ft* deep, 2000 *ft* wide
Am·chit·ka \am-ˈchit-kə\ island SW Alaska in the Aleutians at E end of Rat group
Amer·i·ca \ə-ˈmer-ə-kə\ **1** either continent (No. America or So. America) of the western hemisphere **2** *or* **the Amer·i·cas** \-kəz\ the lands of the western hemisphere including No., Central, & So. America & the West Indies **3** UNITED STATES OF AMERICA
American Samoa *or* **Eastern Samoa** island group of E Samoa SW *cen* Pacific ✱ Pago Pago (on Tutuila I.) *area* 76, *pop* 27,159
Amer·i·cus \ə-ˈmer-ə-kəs\ city SW *cen* Ga. *pop* 16,091
Amers·foort \ˈäm-ərz-ˌfō(ə)rt, -ərs-, -ˌfȯ(ə)rt\ commune *cen* Netherlands NE of Utrecht *pop* 78,189
Ames \ˈāmz\ city *cen* Iowa N of Des Moines *pop* 39,505
Am·ga \äm-ˈgä\ river 800 *m* U.S.S.R. in E Soviet Russia, Asia, flowing NE to the Aldan
Am·hara \am-ˈhar-ə,-ˈhär-ə\ former kingdom now province of NW Ethiopia ✱ Gondar
Am·herst \ˈam-(ˌ)ərst\ town W *cen* Mass. N of Springfield *pop* 26,331
Amiens \am-ˈya^n\ city N France on the Somme *pop* 117,888
Amin·di·vi \ˌəm-ən-ˈdē-vē\ island group India in the N Laccadives
Am·i·rante \ˈam-ə-ˌrant\ islands W Indian ocean SW of Seychelles; a dependency of Seychelles
Am·man \a-ˈmän, -ˈman\ *or anc* **Philadelphia** *or Bib* **Rab·bah** \ˈrab-ə\ *or* **Rab·bath** \ˈrab-əth\ city ✱ of Jordan *pop* 500,000
Am·mon \ˈam-ən\ ancient country NW Arabia E of Gilead ✱ Rabbah
Ammonium — see SIWA
Am·ne Ma·chin \ˌam-nē-mə-ˈjin\ **1** range of the Kunlun mountains W China in E *cen* Tsinghai **2** its highest peak *ab* 25,000 *ft*
Amnok — see YALU
Amor·gos \ə-ˈmȯr-gəs\ *or* NGk **Amor·gós** \ˌäm-(ˌ)ȯr-ˈgȯs\ island Greece in the Aegean in SE Cyclades SE of Naxos *area* 52
Amoy \ä-ˈmȯi, a-, ə-\ *or* **Sze·ming** \ˈsü-ˈmiŋ\ city & port SE China in S Fukien on Amoy & Kulangsu islands *pop* 400,000
Am·ra·va·ti \ˌəm-ˈräv-ət-ē, äm-\ *or* **Am·rao·ti** \-ˈrau̇t-ē\ city *cen* India in NE Maharashtra WSW of Nagpur; chief city of Berar region *pop* 181,774
Am·rit·sar \ˌəm-ˈrit-sər\ city N India in NW Punjab *pop* 430,783
Am·ster·dam \ˈam(p)-stər-ˌdam\ **1** city E N.Y. on the Mohawk *pop* 25,524 **2** city & port, official ✱ of Netherlands *pop* 838,642
Amu Dar·ya \ˌäm-ü-ˈdär-yə\ *or* **Ox·us** \ˈäk-səs\ river over 1400 *m*, *cen* & W Asia flowing from Pamir plateau into Lake Aral
Amund·sen \ˈäm-ən-sən, ˈam-\ **1** sea arm of the S Pacific W Antarctica off Marie Byrd Land **2** gulf arm of Beaufort sea N Canada
Amur \ä-ˈmu̇(ə)r\ *or* **Hei·lung·kiang** \ˈhā-ˈlu̇ŋ-jē-ˈäŋ\ river 1780 *m* E Asia formed by junction of Shilka & Argun rivers, flowing into the Pacific at N end of Tatar strait, & forming part of boundary between Manchuria & Soviet Russia, Asia
Ana·dyr *or* **Ana·dir** \ˌän-ə-ˈdi(ə)r, ˌan-\ river 450 *m* U.S.S.R. in Soviet Russia, Asia, flowing S & E to Gulf of Anadyr
Anadyr, Gulf of inlet of N Bering sea U.S.S.R. in Soviet Russia, Asia, S of Chukotski peninsula
An·a·heim \ˈan-ə-ˌhīm\ city SW Calif. *pop* 166,701
Aná·huac \ə-ˈnä-ˌwäk\ the central plateau of Mexico
Anarajapura — see ANURADHAPURA
An·a·to·lia \ˌan-ə-ˈtō-lē-ə, -ˈtōl-yə\ the part of Turkey comprising the peninsula of Asia Minor
An·chor·age \ˈaŋ-k(ə-)rij\ city S *cen* Alaska at head of Cook inlet *pop* 48,029
An·co·hu·ma \ˌaŋ-kə-ˈh(y)ü-mə\ mountain peak 20,873 *ft* W Bolivia; highest in the Illampu massif
An·co·na \aŋ-ˈkō-nə, an-\ city & port *cen* Italy ✱ of the Marches on the Adriatic *pop* 64,501
An·da·lu·sia \ˌan-də-ˈlü-zh(ē-)ə\ *or* Sp **An·da·lu·cía** \ˌän-də-(ˌ)lü-ˈsē-ə\ region S Spain including Sierra Nevada & valley of the Guadalquivir — **An·da·lu·sian** \ˌan-də-ˈlü-zhən\ *adj or n*
An·da·man \ˈan-də-mən, -ˌman\ **1** islands India in Bay of Bengal S of Burma & N of Nicobar islands *area* 2508 **2** sea SE Asia, the E section of Bay of Bengal — **An·da·man·ese** \ˌan-də-mə-ˈnēz, -ˈnēs\ *adj or n*
Andaman and Nic·o·bar \ˈnik-ə-ˌbär\ territory India comprising Andaman & Nicobar groups ✱ Port Blair *area* 3143, *pop* 115,090
An·der·lecht \ˈän-dər-ˌlekt\ commune *cen* Belgium, WSW suburb of Brussels *pop* 104,157
An·der·matt \ˈän-dər-ˌmät\ commune *cen* Switzerland S of Altdorf
An·der·son \ˈan-dər-sən\ **1** city *cen* Ind. *pop* 70,787 **2** city NW S.C. *pop* 27,556 **3** river 430 *m* Canada in NW Mackenzie District flowing W & N into Beaufort sea
An·des \ˈan-(ˌ)dēz\ mountain system of So. America extending along W coast from Panama to Tierra del Fuego — see ACONCAGUA — **An·de·an** \ˈan-(ˌ)dē-ən, an-ˈ\ *adj*
An·dhra Pra·desh \ˌän-drə-prə-ˈdāsh, -ˈdesh\ state SE India N of Madras state bordering on Bay of Bengal ✱ Hyderabad *area* 105,677, *pop* 43,394,951
An·di·zhan \ˌan-di-ˈzhan, ˌän-di-ˈzhän\ city U.S.S.R. in Uzbekistan ESE of Tashkent *pop* 188,000
An·dor·ra \an-ˈdȯr-ə, -ˈdär-ə\ country SW Europe in E Pyrenees between France & Spain; a republic ✱ Andorra la Vella *area* 179, *pop* 20,550 — **An·dor·ran** \-ən\ *adj or n*
An·do·ver \ˈan-ˌdō-vər, -də-\ town NE Mass. S of Lawrence *pop* 23,695
An·dre·a·nof \ˌan-drē-ˈan-əf, -ˌȯf\ islands SW Alaska in *cen* Aleutian chain — see ADAK, ATKA
An·dria \ˈän-drē-ə\ commune SE Italy in Apulia *pop* 67,900

ə abut	**^{ə}** kitten, F table	**ər** further	**a** back	**ā** bake	
ä cot, cart	**ȧ** F bac	**au̇** out	**ch** chin	**e** less	**ē** easy
g gift	**i** trip	**ī** life	**j** joke	**k̲** G ich	**^{n}** F vin	**ŋ** sing
ō flow	**ȯ** flaw	**œ** F bœuf	**œ̄** F feu	**oi** coin	**th** thing
th̲ this	**ü** loot	**u̇** foot	**ue** G Füllen	**ue̅** F rue	**y** yet
^{y} F digne \dēn^y\, nuit \nw^{y}ē\	**yü** few	**yu̇** furious	**zh** vision		

An·dros, 1 \'an-drəs\ island, largest of the Bahamas *area* 1600 **2** \'an-drəs, -ˌdräs\ island 25 *m* long Greece in N Cyclades
An·dros·cog·gin \ˌan-drə-'skäg-ən\ river 157 *m* NE N.H. & SW Me. flowing into the Kennebec
Ane·to, Pi·co de \'pē-(ˌ)kō-ˌdā-ə-'nāt-(ˌ)ō\ *or* F **Pic de Né·thou** \ˌpēk-də-(ˌ)nā-'tü\ mountain 11,174 *ft* NE Spain; highest in the Pyrenees
An·ga·ra \ˌäŋ-gə-'rä\ river 1100 *m* U.S.S.R. in Soviet Russia, Asia, flowing from Lake Baikal into the Yenisei — see TUNGUSKA
An·garsk \an-'gärsk\ city U.S.S.R. in E *cen* Soviet Russia, Asia, on the Angara NW of Irkutsk *pop* 204,000
An·gel Falls \ˌän-jəl-\ waterfall 3212 *ft* SE Venezuela on Auyán-tepuí Mountain in a headstream of the Caroní
An·gers \ä^{n}-zhā\ city W France ENE of Nantes *pop* 128,533
Ang·kor \'aŋ-ˌkō(ə)r\ ruins of ancient city NW Cambodia N of Tonle Sap; ✱ of the Khmers
An·gle·sey *or* **An·gle·sea** \'aŋ-gəl-sē\ **1** *or anc* **Mo·na** \'mō-nə\ island NW Wales **2** county comprising Anglesey I. & Holyhead I. ✱ Llangefni *area* 276, *pop* 59,705
Anglia, 1 — see ENGLAND **2** — see EAST ANGLIA — **An·gli·an** \'aŋ-glē-ən\ *adj or n*
Anglo–Egyptian Sudan — see SUDAN
An·go·la \aŋ-'gō-lə, an-\ *or* **Portuguese West Africa** country SW Africa S of mouth of the Congo river; a dependency of Portugal ✱ Luanda *area* 481,351, *pop* 5,430,000 — **An·go·lan** \-lən\ *adj or n*
An·gou·lême \ˌä^{n}-gü-'läm, -'lem\ city W France NE of Bordeaux *pop* 47,822
An·gou·mois \ˌä^{n}-güm-'wä\ region & former duchy & province W France S of Poitou ✱ Angoulême
An·guil·la \aŋ-'gwil-ə, an-\ island Brit. West Indies NW of St. Kitts *area* 34
An·gus \'aŋ-gəs\ *or formerly* **For·far** \'fōr-fər\ *or* **For·far·shire** \-ˌshi(ə)r, -shər\ county E Scotland ✱ Forfar *area* 874, *pop* 279,396
An·halt \'än-ˌhält\ former state *cen* Germany ✱ Dessau
An·hwei *or* **An·hui** \'än-'(h)wā\ province E China W of Kiangsu ✱ Hofei *area* 54,015, *pop* 35,000,000
An·i·ak·chak Crater \ˌan-ē-'ak-ˌchak\ active volcano 4420 *ft* SW Alaska on Alaska peninsula; crater 6 *m* in diameter
An·jou \'an-ˌjü, ä^{n}-zhü\ **1** region & former province NW France in Loire valley SE of Brittany ✱ Angers **2** town Canada in S Que. N of Montreal *pop* 33,886
An·ka·ra \'aŋ-kə-rə, 'äŋ-\ *or formerly* **An·go·ra** \aŋ-'gōr-ə, an-, -'gȯr-\ *or anc* **An·cy·ra** \an-'sī-rə\ city ✱ of Turkey in N *cen* Anatolia *pop* 905,660
An·king \'än-'kiŋ\ *or* **Hwai·ning** \'(h)wī-'niŋ\ city E China in Anhwei on the Yangtze *pop* 105,300
Ann, Cape \'an\ peninsula NE Mass.
An·na·ba \ə-'näb-ə\ *or formerly* **Bône** \'bōn\ commune & port NE Algeria *pop* 152,006
An Najaf — see NAJAF
An·nam \ə-'nam, a-; 'an-ˌam\ region & former kingdom E Indochina in *cen* Vietnam ✱ Hue *area* 57,000
An·nap·o·lis \ə-'nap-(ə-)ləs\ city & port ✱ of Md. *pop* 29,592
Annapolis Basin inlet of Bay of Fundy Canada in W N.S.
An·na·pur·na *or* **An·a·pur·na** \ˌan-ə-'pu̇r-nə, -'pər-\ massif N Nepal in the Himalayas; highest peak Annapurna I 26,503 *ft*
Ann Ar·bor \a-'när-bər\ city SE Mich. *pop* 99,797
An·ne·cy \ˌan-ə-'sē\ city E France ENE of Lyons *pop* 54,484
An Nhon \'än-'nōn\ *or formerly* **Binh Dinh** \'bin-'din\ city South Vietnam in S Annam *pop* 112,050
An·nis·ton \'an-ə-stən\ city NE Ala. *pop* 31,533
An·shan \'än-'shän\ city NE China in E *cen* Liaoning SSW of Mukden *pop* 805,000
An·so·nia \an-'sō-nē-ə, -'sōn-yə\ city SW Conn. *pop* 21,160
An·ta·kya \ˌant-ə-'kyä\ *or* **An·ta·ki·yah** \-'kē-(y)ə\ *or anc* **An·ti·och** \'ant-ē-ˌäk\ city S Turkey on Orontes river *pop* 57,855
An·tal·ya \ˌant-ᵊl-'yä\ *or formerly* **Ada·lia** \ˌäd-ᵊl-'ē-(y)ä\ city & port SW Turkey on Gulf of Antalya *pop* 71,833
Antananarivo — see TANANARIVE
Ant·arc·tic \(')ant-'ärk-tik, -'ärt-ik\ **1** ocean surrounding Antarctica including the southern regions of the So. Atlantic, So. Pacific, & Indian oceans esp. S of *ab* 60° S **2** the Antarctic regions **3** *or formerly* **Palm·er peninsula** \ˌpäm-ər-, ˌpäl-mər-\ *or* **Gra·ham Land** \'grā-əm, 'gra(-ə)m\ peninsula 1200 *m* long W Antarctica S of S end of So. America **4** *or* **Palmer archipelago** islands W of N end of Antarctic peninsula in Falkland Islands Dependencies
Ant·arc·ti·ca \-'ärk-ti-kə, -'ärt-i-\ *or* **Antarctic continent** body of land around the So. Pole; a plateau 6000 to 10,000 *ft* covered by a great ice cap & having mountain peaks 10,000 to 15,000 *ft* high *area ab* 6,000,000
An·tibes \ä^{n}-'tēb\ city & port SE France SW of Nice *pop* 47,547
Antibes, Cap d' — see CAP D'ANTIBES
An·ti·cos·ti \ˌant-ə-'kō-stē\ island E Canada in E Que. at mouth of the St. Lawrence *area* 3043
An·tie·tam \an-'tēt-əm\ creek S Pa. & N Md. flowing S into the Potomac N of Harpers Ferry, W.Va.
An·ti·gua \an-'tē-gə\ **1** island Brit. West Indies in the Leewards ✱ St. Johns *area* 108, *pop* (with Barbuda & Redonda) 60,000 — see WEST INDIES ASSOCIATED STATES **2** *or* **Antigua Guatemala** city S *cen* Guatemala WSW of Guatemala City; former ✱ of Guatemala *pop* 21,984 — **An·ti·guan** \an-'tē-g(w)ən\ *adj or n*
An·ti–Leb·a·non \'ant-i-'leb-ə-nən, -ˌnän\ mountains SW Asia E of Bika valley on Syria-Lebanon border — see HERMON (Mount)
Antilles the West Indies excluding the Bahamas — see GREATER ANTILLES, LESSER ANTILLES — **An·til·le·an** \an-'til-ē-ən\ *adj*
An·ti·och \'ant-ē-ˌäk\ **1** city W Calif. NE of Oakland *pop* 28,060 **2** — see ANTAKYA **3** ancient city Asia Minor in Pisidia, at certain periods within boundaries of Phrygia; its ruins are near Yalvac in W *cen* Turkey
An·ti·sa·na \ˌant-i-'sän-ə\ volcano 18,714 *ft* N *cen* Ecuador
An·to·fa·gas·ta \ˌant-ə-fə-'gäs-tə\ city & port N Chile *pop* 125,081
An·trim \'an-trəm\ county E Northern Ireland ✱ Belfast *area* 1098, *pop* 353,417 (with Belfast, 712,408)
Antung — see TAN-TUNG

Ant·werp \'ant-(ˌ)wərp\ *or* F **An·vers** \ä^{n}-'ve(ə)r(s)\ *or* Flem **Ant·wer·pen** \'änt-ˌver-pə(n)\ **1** province N Belgium *area* 1104, *pop* 1,535,680 **2** city & port, its ✱, on the Scheldt *pop* 230,184
Anu·ra·dha·pu·ra \ˌən-ə-ˌräd-ə-'pu̇r-ə\ *or* **Ana·ra·ja·pu·ra** \-ˌräj-ə-\ town N *cen* Ceylon; an ancient ✱ of Ceylon
An·yang \'än-'yäŋ\ city E China in N Honan N of Kaifeng *pop* 124,900
An·zio \'an-zē-ˌō, 'än-\ city & port Italy SSE of Rome *pop* 22,108
Ao·mo·ri \'au̇-mə-(ˌ)rē\ city & port N Japan in NE Honshu on Mutsu Bay *pop* 255,000
Aorangi — see COOK (Mount)
Aos·ta \ä-'ō-stə\ **1** commune NW Italy in Piedmont at junction of Great & Little St. Bernard passes *pop* 35,257 **2** — see VAL D'AOSTA
Ap·a·lach·i·co·la \ˌap-ə-ˌlach-i-'kō-lə\ river 90 *m* NW Fla. flowing from Lake Seminole S into **Apalachicola Bay** (inlet of Gulf of Mexico)
Apa·po·ris \ˌäp-ə-'pōr-(ˌ)ēs, -'pȯr-\ river *ab* 500 *m* S Colombia flowing SE into the Japurá on Colombia-Brazil boundary
Apel·doorn \'ap-əl-ˌdō(ə)rn, -ˌdȯ(ə)rn\ commune E *cen* Netherlands N of Arnhem *pop* 122,287
Ap·en·nines \'ap-ə-ˌnīnz\ mountain chain Italy extending the length of the peninsula — see CORNO (Monte) — **Ap·en·nine** \-ˌnīn\ *adj*
Apia \ə-'pē-ə\ town & port Samoa ✱ of Western Samoa on Upolu I.
Apo, Mount \'äp-(ˌ)ō\ volcano 9689 *ft* S Philippines in SE Mindanao; highest peak in the Philippines
Ap·pa·la·chia \ˌap-ə-'lā-chə, -'lach-ə\ region SE U.S. comprising Appalachian mountains from S *cen* N.Y. southward
Ap·pa·la·chian \ˌap-ə-'lā-chən, -'lach-ən\ mountain system E No. America extending from S Que. to N Ala.; highest peak Mt. Mitchell (N.C.; in Blue Ridge) 6684 *ft*
Ap·pen·zell \'ap-ən-ˌzel, 'äp-ən(t)-ˌsel\ canton NE Switzerland; subdivided into half cantons: **Appenzell In·ner Rhodes** \-'in-ə(r)-ˌrōdz\ *or* G **Appenzell Inner Rho·den** \-ˌrōd-ᵊn\ (✱ Appenzell, *area* 61, *pop* 13,124) & **Appenzell Out·er Rhodes** \-'au̇t-ə(r)-\ *or* G **Appenzell Aus·ser Rhoden** \-'au̇-sə(r)-\ (✱ Herisau, *area* 101, *pop* 49,023)
Ap·ple·ton \'ap-əl-tən\ city E Wis. *pop* 57,143
Ap·po·mat·tox Court House National Historical Park \ˌap-ə-'mat-əks\ reservation *cen* Va. E of Lynchburg & ENE of town of Appomattox
Apra Harbor \'äp-rə\ seaport Guam on W coast
Ap·she·ron \ˌäp-shə-'rōn\ peninsula U.S.S.R. projecting into the Caspian sea on coast of E Azerbaidzhan Republic
Apu·lia \ə-'pyül-yə, -'pyü-lē-ə\ *or It* **Pu·glia** \'pül-(ˌ)yä\ *or* **Le Pu·glie** \lā-'pül-(ˌ)yā\ region SE Italy bordering on the Adriatic & Gulf of Taranto ✱ Bari — **Apu·lian** \ə-'pyül-yən, -'pyü-lē-ən\ *adj or n*
Apu·re \ə-'pu̇(ə)r-(ˌ)ā\ river 420 *m* W Venezuela flowing E into the Orinoco
Apu·ri·mac \ˌäp-ə-'rē-ˌmäk\ river 550 *m* S & *cen* Peru flowing N to unite with the Urubamba forming the Ucayali
'Aqa·ba *or* **Aka·ba** \'äk-ə-bə, 'ak-\ *or anc* **Elath** \'ē-ˌlath\ town & port SW Jordan on border of Israel at head of NE arm (**Gulf of 'Aqaba**) of Red sea
Aquid·neck \ə-'kwid-ˌnek\ *or* **Rhode** island SE R.I. in Narragansett Bay; site of city of Newport
Aqui·la \'äk-wi-lə, 'ak-\ *or* **L'A·qui·la** \'läk-, 'lak-\ *or* **Aquila de·gli Abruz·zi** \ˌdāl-yē-ä-'brüt-sē, -yē-ə-\ commune *cen* Italy NE of Rome ✱ of Abruzzi e Molise *pop* 58,631
Aq·ui·taine \'ak-wə-ˌtān\ old region of SW France comprising area later known as Guienne ✱ Toulouse
Aq·ui·ta·nia \ˌak-wə-'tā-nyə, -nē-ə\ a Roman division of SW Gaul under Caesar consisting of country between Pyrenees mountains & Garonne river & under Augustus expanded to Loire & Allier rivers — **Aq·ui·ta·nian** \-nyən, -nē-ən\ *adj or n*
Ara·ba, Wa·di el \ˌwäd-ē-ˌel-'ar-ə-bə\ *or* **Ar·a·bah** \'ar-ə-bə\ valley extending S from Dead sea to Gulf of 'Aqaba
Arab Emirates UNITED ARAB EMIRATES
Ara·bia \ə-'rā-bē-ə\ peninsula of SW Asia *ab* 1400 *m* long & 1250 *m* wide including Saudi Arabia, Yemen Arab Republic, Southern Yemen, & Persian Gulf States; in earlier times divided into **Arabia Pe·traea** \-pə-'trē-ə\, "Rocky Arabia", the NW part; **Arabia De·ser·ta** \-di-'zərt-ə\, "Desert Arabia", the N part; & **Arabia Fe·lix** \-'fē-liks\, "Fertile Arabia", the main part of the peninsula but by some geographers restricted to Yemen — **Ara·bi·an** \-bē-ən\ *adj or n*
Arabian, 1 desert E Egypt between the Nile & the Red sea **2** sea, NW section of the Indian ocean between India & Arabia
Arab Republics, Federation of confederation formed 1971 comprising Egypt, Libya, & Syria
Ara·ca·ju \ˌar-ə-kə-'zhü\ city & port NE Brazil ✱ of Sergipe *pop* 183,333
Arad \ä-'räd\ city W Rumania on Mures river *pop* 135,181
Ara·fu·ra \ˌar-ə-'fu̇r-ə\ sea between N Australia & West New Guinea
Ar·a·gon \'ar-ə-ˌgän, -gən\ region NE Spain bordering on France; once an independent kingdom ✱ Zaragoza — **Ar·a·go·nese** \ˌar-ə-gə-'nēz, -'nēs\ *adj or n*
Ara·gua·ia *or* **Ara·gua·ya** \ˌar-ə-'gwī-ə\ river *ab* 1100 *m*, *cen* Brazil flowing N into the Tocantins
Arak \ä-'räk, ə-'rak\ *or* **Iraq** \i-'räk, i-'rak\ *or* **Sul·tan·abad** \ˌsu̇l-'tän-ə-ˌbäd\ city W Iran SW of Tehran *pop* 72,930
Ara·kan \ˌar-ə-'kän, -'kan\ coast region SW Burma on Bay of Bengal; chief town Sittwe
Araks \ə-'räks\ *or* **Aras** \ə-'räs\ *or anc* **Arax·es** \ə-'rak-(ˌ)sēz\ river 635 *m* W Asia rising in mountains of Turkish Armenia & flowing E to join the Kura in E Azerbaidzhan, U.S.S.R.
Ar·al sea \'ar-əl\ *or* **Lake Aral** brackish lake U.S.S.R. in SW Soviet Central Asia between Kazakhstan & Uzbekistan *area* 26,000
Ar·am \'ar-əm, 'er-\ ancient Syria — its Hebrew name
Ar·an \'ar-ən\ islands W Ireland off coast of Galway; largest island Inishmore

Aran·sas Bay \ə-ˈran(t)-səs\ inlet of Gulf of Mexico S Tex. NE of Corpus Christi Bay between mainland & St. Joseph I.

Aransas Pass channel S Tex. between Mustang & St. Joseph islands leading to Corpus Christi & Aransas bays

Ar·a·rat \ˈar-ə-ˌrat\ *or* **Ag·ri Da·gi** \ˌä(g)-rē-dä(g)-ˈē\ mountain 16,946 *ft* E Turkey near border of Iran

Arau·ca·nia \ə-ˌrau̇-ˈkän-ē-ə, ˌär-ˌau̇-\ region *cen* Chile S of Bío-Bío river

Ara·val·li \ə-ˈräv-ə-(ˌ)lē\ mountain range NW India E of Thar desert 300 *m* long; highest peak Mt. Abu 5650 *ft*

Arbela, Arbil — see ERBIL

Ar·bon \är-ˈbō^{n}\ commune NE Switzerland in Thurgau canton on Lake Constance

Ar·buck·le mountains \ˈär-ˌbək-əl\ hilly region S *cen* Okla.

Ar·ca·dia \är-ˈkād-ē-ə\ **1** city SW Calif. ENE of Los Angeles *pop* 42,868 **2** mountainous region S Greece in *cen* Peloponnesus

Archangel — see ARKHANGELSK

Archangel, Gulf of — see DVINA GULF

Arch·es National Park \ˈär-chəz\ reservation E Utah including wind-eroded natural arch formations *area* 114

Ar·cos de la Fron·te·ra \ˈär-ˌkōz-ˌdel-ə-ˌfrən-ˈter-ə\ commune SW Spain NE of Cádiz *pop* 29,966

Ar·cot \är-ˈkät\ city SE India in N Tamil Nadu WSW of Madras; once ✱ of the nawabs of Carnatic *pop* 25,029

Arc·tic \ˈärk-tik, ˈärt-ik\ **1** ocean N of the Arctic circle **2** the Arctic regions **3** archipelago N Canada in Arctic ocean constituting larger part of Franklin District, Northwest Territories

Arctic Red river 310 *m* Canada in NW Mackenzie District, Northwest Territories, flowing N into the Mackenzie

Ar·cueil \är-ˈkəi, -ˈkə(r)\ commune N France S of Paris *pop* 21,877

Ar·de·bil *or* **Ar·da·bil** \ˌärd-ə-ˈbē(ə)l\ city NW Iran in E Azerbaijan province *pop* 88,000

Ar·den \ˈärd-ᵊn\ district *cen* England in N Warwickshire W of Stratford-upon-Avon; site of former **Forest of Arden**

Ar·dennes \är-ˈden\ wooded plateau region in NE France, W Luxembourg, & SE Belgium E of the Meuse

Ard·more \ˈärd-ˌmō(ə)r, -ˌmȯ(ə)r\ city S Okla. *pop* 20,881

Are·ci·bo \ˌar-ə-ˈsē-(ˌ)bō\ city & port N Puerto Rico *pop* 35,484

Are·na, Point \ə-ˈrē-nə\ promontory N Calif. in the Pacific *ab* midway between Cape Mendocino & San Francisco Bay

Are·qui·pa \ˌar-ə-ˈkē-pə\ city S Peru *pop* 187,400

Arez·zo \ə-ˈret-(ˌ)sō, ä-\ commune *cen* Italy in Tuscany SE of Florence *pop* 84,839

Ar·gen·tan \ˌär-zhän-ˈtä^{n}\ commune NW France in Normandy NNW of Alençon

Ar·gen·teuil \ˌär-zhän-ˈtəi, -ˈtə(r)\ commune N France on the Seine NNW of Paris *pop* 90,480

Ar·gen·ti·na \ˌär-jən-ˈtē-nə\ *or* **Ar·gen·tine Republic** \ˌär-jən-ˌtēn-\ *or* **the Ar·gen·tine** \ˈär-jən-ˌtēn\ country S So. America between the Andes & the Atlantic S of Pilcomayo river; a federal republic ✱ Buenos Aires *area* 1,079,965, *pop* 23,550,000 — **Argentine** *adj or n* — **Ar·gen·tin·ean** *or* **Ar·gen·tin·i·an** \ˌär-jən-ˈtin-ē-ən\ *adj or n*

Ar·gi·nu·sae \ˌär-jə-ˈn(y)ü-(ˌ)sē\ group of small islands in the Aegean SE of Lesbos

Ar·go·lis \ˈär-gə-ləs\ district & ancient country S Greece in E Peloponnesus comprising a plain around Argos & area between Gulf of Argolis & Saronic gulf — **Ar·gol·ic** \är-ˈgäl-ik\ *adj*

Argolis, Gulf of *or* **Gulf of Nau·plia** \ˈnȯ-plē-ə\ inlet of the Aegean S Greece on E coast of Peloponnesus

Ar·gonne \är-ˈgän, ˈär-ˌ\ wooded plateau NE France S of the Ardennes near Belgian border between Meuse & Aisne rivers

Ar·gos \ˈär-ˌgäs, -gəs\ town Greece in E Peloponnesus on Argive plain at head of Gulf of Argolis; once a Greek city-state

Argovie — see AARGAU

Ar·guel·lo, Point \är-ˈgwel-(ˌ)ō\ cape SW Calif. WNW of Santa Barbara

Ar·gun \är-ˈgün\ river 450 *m* NE Asia forming boundary between Inner Mongolia (China) & U.S.S.R. & uniting with the Shilka to form the Amur

Ar·gyll \är-ˈgī(ə)l, ˈär-ˌgīl\ *or* **Ar·gyll·shire** \-ˌshi(ə)r, -shər\ county W Scotland ✱ Lochgilphead *area* 3110, *pop* 59,909

Arhus — see AARHUS

Aria \ˈar-ē-ə, ˈer-; ə-ˈrī-ə\ **1** an E province of ancient Persian Empire; district now in NW Afghanistan & E Iran **2** — see HERAT

Ari·ca \ə-ˈrē-kə\ city & port N Chile near Peruvian border *pop* 63,160 — see TACNA

Ar·i·ma·thea *or* **Ar·i·ma·thaea** \ˌar-ə-mə-ˈthē-ə\ town in ancient Palestine; location not certainly identified

Ariminum — see RIMINI

Ari·pua·nã \ˌar-əp-wə-ˈna^{n}\ river 600 *m* W *cen* Brazil rising in Mato Grosso state & flowing N into the Madeira

Arius — see HARI RUD

Ar·i·zo·na \ˌar-ə-ˈzō-nə\ state SW U.S. ✱ Phoenix *area* 113,909, *pop* 1,772,482 — **Ar·i·zo·nan** \-nən\ *or* **Ar·i·zo·nian** \-nē-ən, -nyən\ *adj or n*

Ar·kan·sas \ˈär-kən-ˌsȯ; *1 is also* är-ˈkan-zəs\ **1** river 1450 *m* SW *cen* U.S. rising in *cen* Colo. & flowing E & SE through S Kans., NE Okla., & Ark. into the Mississippi **2** state S *cen* U.S. ✱ Little Rock *area* 53,104, *pop* 1,923,295 — **Ar·kan·san** \är-ˈkan-zən\ *adj or n*

Ar·khan·gelsk \är-ˈkan-ˌgelsk\ *or* **Arch·an·gel** \ˈär-ˌkān-jəl\ city & port U.S.S.R. in N Soviet Russia, Europe, on the Northern Dvina *pop* 343,000

Arl·berg \ˈär(ə)l-ˌbərg, -ˌbe(ə)rg\ Alpine valley, pass, & tunnel W Austria in the Tirol

Arles \ˈär(ə)l\ **1** medieval kingdom E & SE France; also called Kingdom of Burgundy **2** *or anc* **Ar·e·las** \ˈar-ə-ˌlas\ *or* **Ar·e·la·te** \ˌar-ə-ˈlāt-ē\ city SE France on the Rhone *pop* 45,774 — **Ar·le·sian** \är-ˈlē-zhən\ *n*

Ar·ling·ton \ˈär-liŋ-tən\ **1** town E Mass. NW of Boston *pop* 53,524 **2** city N Tex. E of Fort Worth *pop* 90,643

Arlington Heights village NE Ill. NW of Chicago *pop* 64,884

Ar·lon \är-ˈlō^{n}\ commune SE Belgium ✱ of Luxembourg province *pop* 14,343

Ar·magh \är-ˈmä, ˈär-ˌ\ **1** county S Northern Ireland *area* 489, *pop* 131,441 **2** urban district, its ✱, *pop* 11,724

Ar·ma·gnac \ˌär-mən-ˈyak\ district SW France in old province of Gascony; chief town Auch

Ar·me·nia \är-ˈmē-nē-ə, -nyə\ **1** *or bib* **Min·ni** \ˈmin-ˌī\ former kingdom W Asia in mountainous region SE of Black sea & SW of Caspian sea; area now divided between U.S.S.R., Turkey, & Iran **2** *or* **Armenian Republic** constituent republic of U.S.S.R. in S Transcaucasia ✱ Yerevan *area* 11,580, *pop* 2,493,000 — see LESSER ARMENIA

Ar·men·tières \ˌär-mən-ˈtye(ə)r, -ˈti(ə)rz\ commune N France W of Lille *pop* 26,916

Ar·mor·i·ca \är-ˈmȯr-ə-kə, -ˈmär-\ **1** *or* **Ar·e·mor·i·ca** \ˌar-ə-\ ancient region NW France between Seine & Loire rivers **2** BRITTANY

Arn·hem \ˈärn-ˌhem, ˈär-nəm\ commune E Netherlands ✱ of Gelderland *pop* 133,391

Arn·hem Land \ˈär-nəm\ region N Australia on N coast of Northern Territory

Ar·no \ˈär-(ˌ)nō\ *or anc* **Ar·nus** \-nəs\ river 140 *m, cen* Italy flowing W from the Apennines through Florence into Ligurian sea

Aroos·took \ə-ˈrüs-tək, -ˈrüs-\ river 140 *m* N Me. flowing NE across N.B. border & into St. John river

Ar·ran \ˈar-ən\ island SW Scotland in Firth of Clyde *area* 165

Ar·ras \ə-ˈräs, ˈar-əs\ city N France SSW of Lille *pop* 49,144

Ar Rimal — see RUB' AL KHALI

Arsanias — see MURAT

Arta, Gulf of — see AMBRACIAN GULF

Ar·te·movsk \är-ˈtem-əfsk\ *or formerly* **Bakh·mut** \ˈbäk-ˌmüt\ city U.S.S.R. in E Ukraine in the Donets basin N of Donetsk *pop* 81,000

Ar·tois \är-ˈtwä\ former province N France between Flanders & Picardy ✱ Arras

Aru *or* **Aroe** *or* **Ar·roe** \ˈär-(ˌ)ü\ islands E Indonesia S of W New Guinea *area* 3305, *pop* 29,604

Aru·ba \ə-ˈrü-bə\ island Netherlands Antilles off coast of NW Venezuela; chief town Oranjestad *area* 69, *pop* 59,813

Aru·wi·mi \ˌär-ə-ˈwē-mē, ˌar-\ river 800 *m* N Zaire flowing SW & W into Congo river

Ar·vada \är-ˈvad-ə\ city N *cen* Colo. NW of Denver *pop* 46,814

Ar·vi·da \är-ˈvīd-ə\ city Canada in S Que. on the Saguenay *pop* 18,448

Ar·wad \är-ˈwad, -ˈwäd\ *or* **Ru·ad** \rü-ˈad\ *or bib* **Ar·vad** \ˈär-ˌvad\ island Syria off coast of S Latakia

Asa·hi·ka·wa \ˌäs-ə-hē-ˈkä-wə\ *or* **Asa·hi·ga·wa** \-ˈgä-wə\ city Japan in *cen* Hokkaido *pop* 297,000

Asa·ma \ə-ˈsäm-ə\ *or* **Asa·ma·ya·ma** \ə-ˌsäm-ə-ˈyäm-ə\ volcano 8340 *ft* Japan in *cen* Honshu

Asan·sol \ˈäs-ᵊn-ˌsōl\ city NE India in West Bengal *pop* 137,725

As·bury Park \ˈaz-ˌber-ē, -b(ə-)rē\ city E N.J. on the Atlantic *pop* 16,533

As·cen·sion \ə-ˈsen-chən\ island in S Atlantic at 7°55′S, 14°25′W belonging to Brit. colony of St. Helena *area* 34, *pop* 1363

As·co·li Pi·ce·no \ˌäs-kə-(ˌ)lē-pi-ˈchā-(ˌ)nō\ *or anc* **As·cu·lum Pi·ce·num** \ˌas-kyə-ləm-(ˌ)pī-ˈsē-nəm\ commune *cen* Italy in the Marches 87 *m* NE of Rome *pop* 54,536

Ascoli Sa·tria·no \-ˌsä-trē-ˈän-(ˌ)ō\ *or anc* **As·cu·lum Ap·u·lum** \ˌas-kyə-lə-ˈmap-yə-ləm\ *or* **Aus·cu·lum Apulum** \ˌȯs-\ commune SE Italy in Apulia S of Foggia

As·cot \ˈas-kət\ village S England in Berkshire SW of London

As·cut·ney, Mount \ə-ˈskət-nē\ mountain 3320 *ft* SE Vermont

Ashan·ti \ə-ˈshant-ē, -ˈshänt-\ region *cen* Ghana; formerly a native kingdom & later a Brit. colony ✱ Kumasi *area* 24,379, *pop* 1,477,397

Ash·bur·ton \ˈash-ˌbərt-ᵊn\ river 500 *m* Australia in NW Western Australia flowing NW into Indian ocean

Ash·dod \ˈash-ˌdäd\ city & port Israel W of Jerusalem *pop* 37,600

Ashe·ville \ˈash-ˌvil, -vəl\ city W N.C. *pop* 57,681

Ashi·ka·ga \ˌäsh-i-ˈkäg-ə\ city Japan in *cen* Honshu *pop* 155,000

Ash·ke·lon \ˈash-kə-ˌlän\ *or* **As·ca·lon** \ˈas-kə-\ ancient city & port SW Palestine, site in Israel WSW of Jerusalem

Ashkh·a·bad \ˈash-kə-ˌbad, -ˌbäd\ *or formerly* **Pol·to·ratsk** \ˌpäl-tə-ˈrätsk\ city U.S.S.R. in Soviet Central Asia ✱ of Turkmen Republic *pop* 253,000

Ash·land \ˈash-lənd\ **1** city NE Ky. on the Ohio *pop* 29,245 **2** city N *cen* Ohio *pop* 19,872

Ash·ley \ˈash-lē\ river 40 *m* S S.C. flowing SE into Charleston harbor

Ash·ta·bu·la \ˌash-tə-ˈbyü-lə\ city NE Ohio on Lake Erie *pop* 24,313

Asia \ˈā-zhə, -shə\ continent of the eastern hemisphere N of equator forming a single landmass with Europe (the conventional dividing line between Asia & Europe being the Ural mountains & main range of the Caucasus mountains); has numerous large offshore islands including Cyprus, Ceylon, Malay archipelago, Formosa, the Japanese chain, & Sakhalin *area* 16,988,000

Asia Mi·nor \-ˈmī-nər\ peninsula forming W extremity of Asia between Black sea on N, Mediterranean sea on S, & Aegean sea on W — see ANATOLIA

Asir \a-ˈsi(ə)r\ principality SW Arabia on Red sea; dependency of the Nejd, Saudi Arabia ✱ As Sabya *area* 13,857

As·ma·ra \az-ˈmär-ə, -ˈmar-ə\ city N Ethiopia ✱ of Eritrea *pop* 190,500

ə abut ᵊ kitten, F table ər further a back ā bake
ä cot, cart á F bac au̇ out ch chin e less ē easy
g gift i trip ī life j joke k̲ G ich ^{n} F vin ŋ sing
ō flow ȯ flaw œ F bœuf œ̄ F feu ȯi coin th thing
t̲h̲ this ü loot u̇ foot ue G Füllen ue̅ F rue y yet
^{y} F digne \dēn^{y}\, nuit \nw^{y}ē\ yü few yu̇ furious zh vision

As·nières \an-'ye(ə)r, än-\ commune N France NW of Paris *pop* 80,530
Aso \'äs-(ˌ)ō\ *or* **Aso·san** \ˌäs-ō-'sän\ volcanic mountain Japan in *cen* Kyushu; has five volcanic cones (highest 5225 *ft*) grouped around crater 15 *m* long with walls 2000 *ft* high
Aso·lo \'äz-ə-ˌlō\ commune NE Italy NW of Treviso
As·pern \'äs-pərn\ former village Austria ENE of Vienna; since 1905 part of Vienna
Asphaltites, Lacus — see DEAD SEA
Aspinwall — see COLÓN
As·sam \ə-'sam, a-; 'as-ˌam\ state NE India on edge of Himalayas ✱ Shillong *area* 85,012, *pop* 14,857,314
As·sin·i·boine \ə-'sin-ə-ˌbȯin\ river 450 *m* Canada rising in SE Sask. & flowing S & E across S Man. into Red river
Assiniboine, Mount mountain 11,870 *ft* Canada in SW Alta. on B.C. border
As·si·si \ə-'sis-ē, -'sē-zē, -'sē-sē, -'siz-ē\ commune *cen* Italy ESE of Perugia *pop* 24,755
As·syr·ia \ə-'sir-ē-ə\ *or bib* **As·sur** \ä-'sü(ə)r, 'ä-ˌ\ *or* **Ash·ur** \'ash-ər\ ancient empire W Asia extending along middle Tigris & over foothills to the E; early ✱ Calah, later ✱ Nineveh
Astacus — see IZMIT
Asterabad — see GURGAN
Asti \'äs-tē\ commune NW Italy W of Alessandria *pop* 73,211
As·tin Tagh \ˌas-tən-'tä(g)\ *or* **Al·tin Tagh** *or* **Al·tyn Tagh** \ˌal-tən-\ mountain range W China in S Sinkiang; highest peak 20,213 *ft*
As·tra·khan \'as-trə-ˌkan, -kən\ city U.S.S.R. in Soviet Russia, Europe, on the Volga at head of its delta; 50 *ft* below sea level *pop* 411,000
As·tu·ri·as \ə-'st(y)ür-ē-əs, a-\ **1** region & old kingdom NW Spain on Bay of Biscay **2** OVIEDO (province)
Asun·ción \ə-ˌsün(t)-sē-'ōn, (ˌ)ä-\ city ✱ of Paraguay on Paraguay river at confluence with the Pilcomayo *pop* 288,882
As·wân *or* **As·souan** *or* **As·suan** \a-'swän, ä-\ *or anc* **Sy·e·ne** \sī-'ē-nē\ city S Egypt on right bank of the Nile near site of dam built 1898–1902 & of **Aswân High Dam** (completed 1970 to form **Lake Nas·ser** \'näs-ər, 'nas-\) *pop* 201,500
As·yût *or* **As·siout** *or* **As·siut** \ˌas-ē-'üt, ˌäs-\ city *cen* Egypt on left bank of the Nile *pop* 175,700
Ata·ca·ma \ˌat-ə-'käm-ə\ **1** desert N Chile between Copiapó & Peru border **2** — see PUNA DE ATACAMA
At·ba·ra \'at-bə-rə\ river *ab* 500 *m* NE Africa rising in N Ethiopia & flowing through E Sudan into the Nile
Atchaf·a·laya \(ə-)ˌchaf-ə-'lī-ə\ river 225 *m* S La. flowing S into **Atchafalaya Bay** (inlet of Gulf of Mexico)
Ath·a·bas·ca *or* **Ath·a·bas·ka** \ˌath-ə-'bas-kə\ **1** river 765 *m* Canada in Alta. flowing NE & N into Lake Athabasca **2** lake Canada on Alta.-Sask. boundary *area* 3058
Ath·ens \'ath-ənz\ **1** city NE Ga. *pop* 44,342 **2** city SE Ohio on Hocking river *pop* 23,310 **3** *or* NGk **Athí·nai** \ä-'thē-(ˌ)nā\ *or anc* **Athe·nae** \ə-'thē-(ˌ)nē\ city ✱ of Greece near Saronic Gulf *pop* 627,564 — **Athe·nian** \ə-'thē-nē-ən, -nyən\ *adj or n*
Athos \'ath-ˌäs, 'ä-ˌthäs\ mountain NE Greece at E end of Acte peninsula; site of a number of monasteries comprising **Mount Athos** (autonomous area)
Ati·tlán \ˌät-ē-'tlän\ lake 24 *m* long SW Guatemala at 4700 *ft* altitude occupying a crater 1000 *ft* deep N of Atitlán Volcano
At·ka \'at-kə, 'ät-\ island SW Alaska in Andreanof group of the Aleutians
At·lan·ta \ət-'lant-ə, at-\ city ✱ of Ga. *pop* 496,973 — **At·lan·tan** \-'lant-ᵊn\ *adj or n*
At·lan·tic \ət-'lant-ik, at-\ ocean separating No. & So. America from Europe & Africa *area* 41,105,000
Atlantic City city SE N.J. on Atlantic coast *pop* 47,859
At·las \'at-ləs\ mountains NW Africa extending from SW Morocco to NE Tunisia; its highest peaks (over 13,000 *ft*) are in the **Grand,** or **High, Atlas** in SW *cen* Morocco — see TOUBKAL (Jebel)
Atrek \ə-'trek\ *or* **Atrak** \-'trak\ river 300 *m* NE Iran flowing into the Caspian on U.S.S.R. border
Atropatene — see AZERBAIJAN
At·ta·wa·pis·kat \ˌat-ə-wə-'pis-kət\ river 465 *m* Canada in N Ont. flowing E into James Bay
At·ti·ca \'at-i-kə\ region E Greece, chief city Athens; a state of ancient Greece
At·tle·boro \'at-ᵊl-ˌbər-ə, -ˌbə-rə\ city SE Mass. *pop* 32,907
At·tu \'a-(ˌ)tü\ island SW Alaska, most westerly of the Aleutians, in Near group
Aube \'ōb\ river 125 *m* N *cen* France flowing into the Seine
Au·ber·vil·liers \ˌō-bər-ˌvēl-'yā\ commune N France NNE of Paris *pop* 73,695
Au·burn \'ȯ-bərn\ **1** city E Ala. *pop* 22,767 **2** town E *cen* Mass. SW of Worcester *pop* 15,347 **3** city SW Me. *pop* 24,151 **4** city *cen* N.Y. *pop* 34,599 **5** city W Wash. NE of Tacoma *pop* 21,817
Auck·land \'ȯ-klənd\ city & port N New Zealand on North I. *pop* 152,300
Audenarde — see OUDENAARDE
Au·ghra·bies Falls \ȯ-'gräb-ēz\ *or* **King George's Falls** waterfall 480 *ft* Republic of So. Africa in Orange river in NW Cape Province
Au·ghrim *or* **Aghrim** \'ȯ-grəm, -krəm\ town W Ireland in E Galway
Augs·burg \'ȯgz-ˌbərg, 'aùgz-ˌbü(ə)rg\ city W Germany in Bavaria on Lech river *pop* 213,000
Au·gus·ta \ȯ-'gəs-tə, ə-\ **1** city E Ga. on Savannah river *pop* 59,864 **2** city ✱ of Me. on the Kennebec *pop* 21,945
Au·lis \'ȯ-ləs\ harbor E Greece in Boeotia on Evripos strait
Au·nis \ō-'nēs\ former province W France on Gironde estuary & Bay of Biscay ✱ La Rochelle
Au·rang·a·bad \aù-'rəŋ-(g)ə-ˌbäd\ city W India in *cen* Maharashtra ENE of Bombay *pop* 87,579
Au·rès \ō-'res\ massif *ab* 7600 *ft* NE Algeria in Saharan Atlas
Au·ri·gnac \ˌō-rēn-'yak\ village SW France SW of Toulouse
Au·ril·lac \ˌō-rē-'(y)ak\ city S *cen* France NW of Cahors *pop* 28,226
Au·ro·ra \ə-'rōr-ə, ȯ-, -'rȯr-\ **1** city N *cen* Colo. E of Denver *pop* 74,974 **2** city NE Ill. *pop* 74,182
Au·sa·ble \ȯ-'sā-bəl\ river 20 *m* NE N.Y. flowing E into Lake Champlain through **Ausable Chasm** (gorge 2 *m* long)
Auschwitz — see OSWIECIM
Aus·ter·litz \'ȯ-stər-ˌlits, 'aù-\ *or* Czech **Slav·kov** \'släf-ˌkȯf, 'släv-ˌkȯv\ town Czechoslovakia ESE of Brno
Aus·tin \'ȯs-tən, 'äs-\ **1** city S Minn. *pop* 25,074 **2** city ✱ of Tex. on the Colorado *pop* 251,808
Austral — see TUBUAI
Aus·tral·asia \ˌȯs-trə-'lā-zhə, ˌäs-, -'lā-shə\ **1** Australia, Tasmania, New Zealand, & Melanesia **2** the Brit. Commonwealth nations of the SW Pacific: Australia, New Zealand, Fiji, & Western Samoa — **Aus·tral·asian** \-zhən, -shən\ *adj or n*
Aus·tra·lia \ȯ-'strāl-yə, ä-\ **1** continent of the eastern hemisphere SE of Asia & S of the equator *area* 2,948,366 **2** *or* **Commonwealth of Australia** dominion of the British Commonwealth of Nations including the continent of Australia & the island of Tasmania ✱ Canberra *area* 2,967,909, *pop* 12,730,000
Australian Alps mountain range SE Australia in E Victoria & SE New So. Wales forming S end of Great Dividing range
Australian Capital Territory *or formerly* **Federal Capital Territory** district SE Australia including two areas, one around Canberra & the other on Jervis Bay, surrounded by New So. Wales *area* 939, *pop* 133,100
Aus·tra·sia *or* **Os·tra·sia** \ȯ-'strā-zhə, ä-, -shə\ the E dominions of the Merovingian Franks extending from Meuse river to Bohemian Forest — **Aus·tra·sian** \-zhən, -shən\ *adj or n*
Aus·tria \'ȯs-trē-ə, 'äs-\ *or* G **Ös·ter·reich** \'œ-stə(r)-ˌrīk\ country *cen* Europe in & N of E Alps with the Danube crossing it in N; a republic *area* 32,375, *pop* 7,460,000 — **Aus·tri·an** \-ən\ *adj or n*
Austria–Hun·ga·ry \-'həŋ-gə-rē\ dual monarchy 1867–1918 *cen* Europe including Austria, Hungary, Czechoslovakia, Bukovina & Transylvania in Rumania, NW half of Yugoslavia, Galicia in Poland, & NE Italy — **Aus·tro–Hun·gar·i·an** *adj or n* \'ȯs-(ˌ)trō-ˌhəŋ-'gar-ē-ən, 'äs-, -'ger-\
Aus·tro·ne·sia \ˌȯs-trə-'nē-zhə, ˌäs-, -'nē-shə\ **1** the islands of the S Pacific **2** area extending from Madagascar through the Malay peninsula & archipelago to Hawaii & Easter I.
Au·teuil \ō-'təi, -'tə(r)\ district in W Paris, France
Au·vergne \ō-'ve(ə)rn(-yə), -'vərn\ **1** region & former province S *cen* France ✱ Clermont (now Clermont-Ferrand) **2** mountains S *cen* France; highest in the Massif Central — see SANCY (Puy de)
Aux Cayes — see CAYES
Aux Sources, Mont \ˌmōⁿ-ˌtō-'sü(ə)rs\ mountain 10,822 *ft* N Lesotho in Drakensberg mountains on Natal border
Au·yán–te·puí \aù-ˌyän-təp-'wē\ *or* **Devil Mountain** plateau *ab* 20 *m* long SE Venezuela E of Caroní river — see ANGEL FALLS
Av·a·lon \'av-ə-ˌlän\ **1** peninsula Canada in SE Nfld. **2** *or* **Isle of Avalon** district, orig. an island, SW England in Somerset including Glastonbury; considered by some to be the Avalon of Arthurian legend
Ave·bury \'āv-b(ə-)rē, *US also* -ˌber-ē\ village S England in Wiltshire E of Bristol
Ave·lla·ne·da \ˌav-ə-zhə-'nā-də\ city E Argentina, E suburb of Buenos Aires, on Rio de la Plata *pop* 329,626
Avenches \a-'väⁿsh\ *or anc* **Aven·ti·cum** \ə-'vent-i-kəm\ town W Switzerland in Vaud canton ✱ of ancient Helvetia
Av·en·tine \'av-ən-ˌtīn, -ˌtēn\ hill in Rome, Italy, one of seven (including also the Caelian, Capitoline, Esquiline, Palatine, Quirinal, & Viminal) on which the ancient city was built
Aver·nus \ə-'vər-nəs\ *or* It **Aver·no** \ä-'ve(ə)r-(ˌ)nō\ lake S Italy in crater of extinct volcano W of Naples
Avi·gnon \ˌa-(ˌ)vēn-'yōⁿ\ city SE France near confluence of Rhone & Durance rivers *pop* 86,096
Ávi·la \'äv-i-lə\ **1** province *cen* Spain *area* 3042, *pop* 203,798 **2** city, its ✱, WNW of Madrid *pop* 30,938
Avlona — see VLONE
Avon \'ā-vən, 'av-ən, *US also* 'ā-ˌvän\ **1** river 96 *m*, *cen* England rising in Northamptonshire & flowing WSW past Stratford-upon-Avon into the Severn at Tewkesbury **2** river 65 *m* S England rising near Devizes in Wiltshire & flowing S into English channel **3** river 62 *m* SW England rising in Gloucestershire & flowing S & W through city of Bristol into Bristol channel at Avonmouth **4** \'av-ən\ — see SWAN
Avranches \av-'räⁿsh\ town NW France in SW Normandy
Awa·ji \ə-'wäj-ē\ island Japan S of Honshu & NE of Shikoku I.
Awash — see HAWASH
Ax·el Hei·berg \ˌak-səl-'hī-ˌbərg\ island N Canada in the Sverdrup islands W of Ellesmere I. *area* 15,779
Axum — see AKSUM — **Ax·um·ite** \'ak-sə-mit\ *adj or n*
Aya·cu·cho \ˌī-ə-'kü-(ˌ)chō\ town S Peru SE of Lima
Ay·din \ī-'din\ city SW Turkey SE of Izmir *pop* 43,483
Ayers Rock \'a(ə)rz-, 'e(ə)rz-\ monolith *cen* Australia in SW Northern Territory; 1½ *m* long, 1143 *ft* high
Ayles·bury \'ā(ə)lz-b(ə-)rē, *US also* -ˌber-ē\ municipal borough SE *cen* England ✱ of Buckinghamshire *pop* 41,288
Ayodhya — see AJODHYA
Ayr \'a(ə)r, 'e(ə)r\ **1** *or* **Ayr·shire** \-ˌshi(ə)r, -shər\ county SW Scotland *area* 1132, *pop* 361,074 **2** burgh & port, its ✱ *pop* 47,884
Ayut·tha·ya *or* **Ayu·dhya** \ä-'yùt-ə-yə\ city S Thailand N of Bangkok on an island in the lower Chao Phraya *pop* 40,352
Azer·bai·dzhan *or* **Azer·bai·jan** *or* **Azerbaidzhan Republic** \ˌaz-ər-ˌbī-'jän, ˌäz-\ constituent republic of the U.S.S.R. in E Transcaucasia bordering on Caspian sea ✱ Baku *area* 33,200, *pop* 5,111,000
Azerbaijan *or anc* **At·ro·pa·te·ne** *or* **Me·dia Atropatene** \'mēd-ē-ə-ˌa-trō-pə-'tē-nē\ region NW Iran; chief city Tabriz
Azin·court \ä-zaⁿ-'kür\ *or earlier* **Agin·court** \'aj-ən-ˌkō(ə)rt, -ˌkȯ(ə)rt; 'àzh-ən-ˌkù(ə)r\ village N France WNW of Arras
Azores \'ā-ˌzō(ə)rz, -ˌzȯ(ə)rz, ə-'\ *or* Port **Aço·res** \ə-'sōr-ēsh\ islands N Atlantic belonging to Portugal & lying *ab* 800 *m* off coast of Portugal; chief town Ponta Delgada *area* 888, *pop* 336,100 — **Azor·e·an** *or* **Azor·i·an** \ā-'zōr-ē-ən, -'zȯr-, ə-\ *adj or n*

Azov, Sea of \'az-,òf, 'äz-, -,äv\ gulf of the Black sea E of Crimea connected with the Black sea by the Kerch strait *area* 14,520

Az·tec Ruins National Monument \,az-,tek-\ reservation NW N. Mex. NE of Farmington; site of a prehistoric pueblo

Azu·sa \ə-'zü-sə\ city SW Calif. ENE of Los Angeles *pop* 25,217

Baal·bek \'bā-əl-,bek, 'bäl-,bek\ town E Lebanon N of Damascus on site of ancient city of **He·li·op·o·lis** \,hē-lē-'äp-(ə-)ləs\

Ba·bar \'bäb-,är\ islands Indonesia ENE of Timor

Bab el Man·deb \,bab-əl-'man-dəb\ strait between SW Arabia & Africa connecting Red sea & Gulf of Aden

Ba·bel·thu·ap \,bäb-əl-'tü-,äp\ *or* **Pa·lau** \pə-'lau̇\ *or* **Pe·lew** \pə-'lü\ island W Pacific, chief island in the Palau district *area* 143

Ba·bu·yan \,bäb-ü-'yän\ **1** islands N Philippines N of Luzon *area* 225 **2** chief island of the group

Bab·y·lon \'bab-ə-lən, -,län\ ancient city ✱ of Babylonia; its site *ab* 50 *m* S of Baghdad near the Euphrates

Bab·y·lo·nia \,bab-ə-'lō-nyə, -nē-ə\ ancient country in valley of lower Euphrates & Tigris rivers ✱ Babylon

Back \'bak\ river 605 *m* Canada in NE Mackenzie District & NW Keewatin District flowing ENE into Arctic ocean

Ba·co·lod \bä-'kō-,lòd\ city Philippines on Negros I. *pop* 156,900

Bactra — see BALKH

Bac·tria \'bak-trē-ə\ *or* **Bac·tri·a·na** \,bak-trē-'an-ə, -'än-ə, -'ā-nə\ ancient country SW Asia between Hindu Kush & Oxus river ✱ Bactra — see BALKH — **Bac·tri·an** \'bak-trē-ən\ *adj or n*

Ba·da·joz \,bäth-ə-'hōs, ,bäd-ə-'hōz\ **1** province SW Spain in valley of Guadiana river *area* 8451, *pop* 687,599 **2** city, its ✱ *pop* 112,836

Ba·da·lo·na \,bäd-ᵊl-'ō-nə\ city & port NE Spain on the Mediterranean NE of Barcelona *pop* 139,223

Bad Ems — see EMS

Ba·den \'bäd-ᵊn\ **1** region SW Germany bordering on Switzerland & France; formerly a grand duchy (1805–1918), a state of the Weimar republic (1918–33), an administrative division of the Third Reich (1933–49), & a state of the Bonn Republic (1949–51) ✱ Karlsruhe — see BADEN-WÜRTTEMBERG **2** BADEN-BADEN

Ba·den–Ba·den \,bäd-ᵊn-'bäd-ᵊn\ city & spa SW Germany in Baden-Württemberg SSW of Karlsruhe *pop* 34,074

Ba·den–Würt·tem·berg \,bäd-ᵊn-'wərt-əm-,bərg, -'wu̇rt-; -'vuert-əm-,berk\ state W Germany W of Bavaria; formed 1951 from former Baden, Württemberg-Baden, & Württemberg-Hohenzollern states ✱ Stuttgart *area* 13,800, *pop* 8,959,700

Badgastein — see GASTEIN

Bad Godesberg — see GODESBERG

Badlands National Monument reservation SW S.Dak. E of Black hills comprising an area of badlands topography *area* 156

Bad Mergentheim — see MERGENTHEIM

Baf·fin \'baf-ən\ island NE Canada N of Hudson strait; largest in Arctic archipelago *area* 183,810

Baffin Bay inlet of the Atlantic between W Greenland & E Baffin I.

Ba·fing \bə-'faŋ\ river 350 *m* W Africa in W Mali & Guinea; the upper course of the Senegal

Bagh·dad *or* **Bag·dad** \'bag-,dad\ city ✱ of Iraq on the middle Tigris *pop* 1,490,759 — **Bagh·dadi** \bag-'dad-ē\ *n*

Ba·guio \,bäg-ē-'ō\ city, summer ✱ of the Philippines, in NW *cen* Luzon *pop* 71,400

Ba·ha·ma \bə-'häm-ə, *by outsiders also* -'hā-mə\ islands in the Atlantic SE of Florida; an independent member of Brit. Commonwealth since 1973 (officially **Commonwealth of the Bahamas**) ✱ Nassau *area* 4404, *pop* 190,000 — see TURKS AND CAICOS — **Ba·ha·mi·an** \bə-'hā-mē-ən, -'häm-ē-\ *adj or n*

Ba·ha·wal·pur \bə-'hä-wəl-,pu̇(ə)r\ region Pakistan in SW Punjab in Thar desert; until 1947 a princely state of India

Ba·hia \bə-'hē-ə, bä-'ē-ə\ state E Brazil ✱ Salvador *area* 215,329, *pop* 7,420,906

Ba·hía Blan·ca \bə-,hē-ə-'blaŋ-kə, bä-,ē-ə-'bläŋ-\ city & port E Argentina 350 *m* SW of Buenos Aires *pop* 120,580

Bahnasa, El — see OXYRHYNCHUS

Bah·rain *or* **Bah·rein** \bä-'rān\ **1** islands in Persian gulf off coast of Arabia; an independent sultanate ✱ Manama (on Bahrain I.) *area* 213, *pop* 220,000 **2** island, largest of the group, 27 *m* long — **Bah·raini** *or* **Bah·reini** \-'rā-nē\ *adj or n*

Bahr el Ghazal \,ba(ə)r-,el-gə-'zal, ,bär-\ river *ab* 500 *m* SW Sudan flowing E to unite at Lake No with the Bahr el Jebel forming the White Nile

Bahr el Je·bel \'jeb-əl\ section of the Albert Nile in Sudd region above Lake No

Bai·kal *or* **Bay·kal** \bi-'kòl, -'kal\ lake U.S.S.R. in S Soviet Russia, Asia, in mountains N of Mongolia; 5712 *ft* deep, *ab* 375 *m* long *area* 13,200

Baile Atha Cliath — see DUBLIN

Ba·ja \'bä-(,)hä\ BAJA CALIFORNIA

Ba·ja California \,bä-(,)hä-\ *or* **Lower California** peninsula 760 *m* long NW Mexico between the Pacific & Gulf of California; divided into the state of **Baja California** (to the N ✱ Mexicali *area* 27,653, *pop* 856,773) & the territory of **Baja California Sur** \'su̇(ə)r\ (to the S ✱ La Paz *area* 27,976, *pop* 123,786)

Bakan — see SHIMONOSEKI

Ba·ker \'bā-kər\ island (atoll) *cen* Pacific near the equator at 176°31′W; belongs to U.S.

Baker, Mount mountain 10,750 *ft* NW Wash. in Cascade range

Baker Lake — see DUBAWNT

Ba·kers·field \'bā-kərz-,fēld\ city S *cen* Calif. at SE end of San Joaquin valley *pop* 69,515

Bakhmut — see ARTEMOVSK

Ba·ku \bä-'kü\ city U.S.S.R. ✱ of Azerbaidzhan Republic on W shore of Caspian sea *pop* 847,000

Bakwanga — see MBUJI-MAYI

Ba·la·kla·va *or* **Ba·la·cla·va** \,bal-ə-'klav-ə, ,bäl-ə-'kläv-ə\ village U.S.S.R. in S Soviet Russia, Europe, in Crimea on Black sea SE of Sevastopol

Bal·a·ton \'bal-ə-,tän, 'bòl-ə-,tōn\ *or* G **Plat·ten·see** \'plät-ᵊn-,zā\ lake W Hungary; largest in *cen* Europe *area* 266

Bal·boa Heights \(,)bal-,bō-ə-\ town Panama Canal Zone, suburb of Balboa, at Pacific entrance to the canal adjacent to Panama City; administrative center of Canal Zone

Bal·dwin \'bòl-dwən\ borough SW Pa. S of Pittsburgh *pop* 26,729

Baldwin Park city SW Calif. E of Los Angeles *pop* 47,285

Bâle — see BASEL

Bal·e·ar·es \,bal-ē-'ar-ēz\ **1** the Balearic islands **2** province E Spain comprising the Balearic islands ✱ Palma *area* 1936, *pop* 558,287

Bal·e·ar·ic \,bal-ē-'ar-ik\ islands E Spain in the W Mediterranean — see BALEARES, IVIZA, MAJORCA, MINORCA

Ba·li \'bäl-ē\ island Indonesia off E end of Java; chief town Singaradja *area* 2147, *pop* 2,247,000 — **Ba·li·nese** \,bäl-i-'nēz, ,bal-, -'nēs\ *adj or n*

Ba·li·ke·sir \,bäl-ē-ke-'si(ə)r\ city NW Turkey in Asia SW of Bursa *pop* 69,341

Ba·lik·pa·pan \,bäl-ik-'päp-,än\ city & port Indonesia on SE Borneo on inlet of Makassar strait *pop* 91,706

Bal·kan \'bòl-kən\ **1** mountain range *cen* Bulgaria extending from Yugoslavia border to Black sea; highest point Botev Peak 7795 *ft* **2** peninsula SE Europe between Adriatic & Ionian seas on W & Aegean & Black seas on E

Balkan States *or* **Bal·kans** \'bòl-kənz\ the countries occupying the Balkan peninsula: Yugoslavia, Rumania, Bulgaria, Albania, Greece, & Turkey in Europe

Bal·kar·ia \bòl-'kar-ē-ə, bal-, -'ker-\ mountain region U.S.S.R. in S Soviet Russia, Europe, in S Kabardinian Republic

Balkh \'bälk\ **1** district N Afghanistan corresponding closely to ancient Bactria **2** *or anc* **Bac·tra** \'bak-trə\ town N Afghanistan ✱ of ancient Bactria

Bal·khash *or* **Bal·kash** \bal-'kash, bäl-'käsh\ lake 440 *m* long U.S.S.R. in Soviet Central Asia in SE Kazakh Republic *area* 6700

Bal·la·rat \'bal-ə-,rat\ city SE Australia in *cen* Victoria WNW of Melbourne *pop* 41,910

Bal·sas \'bòl-səs, 'bäl-\ river 426 *m, cen* Mexico flowing from Tlaxcala to the Pacific on border between Michoacán & Guerrero

Bal·tic \'bòl-tik\ sea arm of the Atlantic N Europe enclosed by Denmark & the Scandinavian peninsula *area ab* 160,000

Bal·ti·more \'bòl-tə-,mō(ə)r, -,mò(ə)r, -mər\ city & port N *cen* Md. on Patapsco river estuary near Chesapeake Bay *pop* 905,759 — **Bal·ti·mor·ean** \,bòl-tə-'mōr-ē-ən, -'mòr-\ *n*

Bal·ti·stan \,bòl-tə-'stan\ region N Kashmir; the W section of Ladakh district

Ba·lu·chi·stan \bə-,lü-chə-'stan\ arid region S Asia bordering on Arabian sea in SW Pakistan & SE Iran S & SW of Afghanistan

Ba·ma·ko \,bäm-ə-'kō\ city ✱ of Mali on the Niger *pop* 182,000

Bam·berg \'bam-,bərg, 'bäm-,be(ə)rg\ city W Germany in N Bavaria NNW of Nuremberg *pop* 69,303

Ba·na·hao \bə-'nä-,hau̇\ extinct volcano 7141 *ft* Philippines on S Luzon *ab* 50 *m* SE of Manila

Ba·nana river \bə-,nan-ə-\ lagoon E Fla. between Canaveral peninsula & Merritt I.

Ba·na·ras *or* **Be·na·res** \bə-'när-əs, -ēz\ *or* **Va·ra·na·si** \və-'rän-ə-(,)sē\ city N India in SE Uttar Pradesh *pop* 637,612

Ba·nat \bə-'nät, 'bän-,ät\ region SE *cen* Europe in Danube basin between Tisza & Mures rivers & the Transylvanian Alps; once entirely in Hungary, divided 1919 between Yugoslavia & Rumania

Ban·da \'ban-də, 'bän-\ **1** islands Indonesia in Moluccas S of Ceram *area* 16 **2** sea E Malay archipelago SE of Celebes, S of the Moluccas, W of Aru islands, & NE of Timor

Ban·da Ori·en·tal \'bän-də-,ōr-ē-,en-'täl, -,òr-\ URUGUAY — a former name, used with reference to its position on E shore of Río de la Plata

Bandar — see MASULIPATNAM

Ban·dare Shah·pur \,bən-dər-,ē-shə-'pu̇(ə)r, ,ban-\ town & port SW Iran at head of Persian gulf ENE of Abadan

Ban·de·lier National Monument \,ban-də-'li(ə)r\ reservation N *cen* N.Mex. W of Santa Fe containing cliff-dweller ruins *area* 42

Ban·djar·ma·sin *or* **Ban·jer·ma·sin** \,ban-jər-'mäs-ᵊn, ,bän-\ city Indonesia in S Borneo on Martapura river *pop* 214,096

Ban·dol \bäⁿ-dòl\ town SE France W of Toulon

Ban·dung *or* D **Ban·doeng** \'bän-,du̇ŋ\ city Indonesia in W Java SE of Djakarta *pop* 972,566

Banff \'bam(p)f\ **1** *or* **Banff·shire** \-,shi(ə)r, -shər\ county NE Scotland *area* 630, *pop* 43,501 **2** burgh, its ✱

Banff National Park reservation W Canada in SW Alta. on E slopes of Rocky mountains *area* 2585

Ban·ga·lore \'baŋ-gə-,lō(ə)r, -,lò(ə)r\ city S India W of Madras ✱ of Mysore *pop* 1,041,900

Bang·ka *or* **Ban·ka** \'baŋ-kə\ island, Indonesia off SE Sumatra; chief town Pangkalpinang *area* 4609, *pop* 251,639

Bang·kok \'baŋ-,käk, baŋ-'\ city & port ✱ of Thailand on the Chao Phraya *ab* 20 *m* above its mouth *pop* 2,132,000

Ban·gla·desh \,bäŋ-glə-'desh, -'däsh\ country S Asia E of India on Bay of Bengal; a republic in Brit. Commonwealth since 1971 ✱ Dacca *area* 55,126, *pop* 75,000,000 — see EAST PAKISTAN

Ban·gor \'baŋ-,gò(ə)r & 'ban-,gò(ə)r (*these usual for 1*), 'baŋ-gər\ **1** city E *cen* Me. on Penobscot river *pop* 33,168 **2** municipal borough SE Northern Ireland in County Down *pop* 35,105 **3** municipal borough & city NW Wales in Caernarvonshire

Ban·gui \bäⁿ-gē\ city ✱ of Central African Republic *pop* 150,000

Bang·we·u·lu \,baŋ-wē-'ü-(,)lü\ lake *ab* 50 *m* long N Zambia in swamp region; its area fluctuates seasonally; drains into the Luapula, a headstream of the Congo

Banks \'baŋ(k)s\ **1** island N Canada at W end of Canadian Arctic archipelago *area* 23,230 **2** islands SW Pacific N of New Hebrides

Ban·nock·burn \'ban-ək-,bərn, ,ban-ək-'\ town *cen* Scotland in Stirlingshire SSE of Stirling
Ban·tam \'bant-əm\ village Indonesia in NW corner of Java; once ✱ of Sultanate of Bantam
Ban·try Bay \,ban-trē-\ bay SW Ireland in SW County Cork
Ba·paume \bä-'pōm, ba-\ town N France S of Arras
Ba·ra·cal·do \,bar-ə-'käl-(,)dō, ,bär-\ commune N Spain W of Bilbao *pop* 110,516
Ba·ra·coa \,bar-ə-'kō-ə, ,bär-\ city & port E Cuba on N coast near E tip of island *pop* (municipality) 105,070
Ba·ra·na·gar \bə-'rän-ə-gər\ city E India in West Bengal N of Calcutta *pop* 147,920
Ba·ra·nof \'bar-ə-,nȯf, bə-'rän-əf\ island SE Alaska in Alexander archipelago S of Chichagof I. *area ab* 1600
Bar·a·tar·ia Bay \,bar-ə-'tar-ē-ə, -'ter-\ lagoon SE La. on coast NW of delta of the Mississippi
Bar·ba·dos *or* **Bar·ba·does** \bär-'bād-(,)äs, -əs\ island Brit. West Indies in Lesser Antilles E of the Windward group; a dominion of the Brit. Commonwealth since 1966 ✱ Bridgetown *area* 166, *pop* 240,000 — **Bar·ba·di·an** \-'bād-ē-ən\ *adj or n*
Bar·ba·ry \'bär-b(ə-)rē\ region N Africa on **Barbary Coast** extending from Egyptian border to the Atlantic & including the former **Barbary States** (Morocco, Algiers, Tunis, & Tripoli) — a former name
Bar·bers Point \,bär-bərz-\ *or* **Ka·la·eloa Point** \kə-,lä-(,)ä-,lō-ə-\ cape Hawaii at SW corner of Oahu W of Pearl Harbor
Bar·ber·ton \'bär-bərt-ᵊn\ city NE Ohio SW of Akron *pop* 33,052
Bar·bi·zon \,bär-bə-'zōⁿ\ village N France SSE of Paris near Forest of Fontainebleau
Bar·bu·da \bär-'büd-ə\ island Brit. West Indies in the Leewards N of Antigua, of which it is a dependency *area* 62
Bar·ca *or* **Bar·ka** \'bär-kə\ town Libya in NW Cyrenaica
Bar·ce·lo·na \,bär-sə-'lō-nə\ **1** province NE Spain in Catalonia on the Mediterranean *area* 2968, *pop* 3,929,194 **2** city & port, its ✱ *pop* 1,837,838 **3** city NE Venezuela near coast *pop* 54,916 — **Bar·ce·lo·nese** \-lō-'nēz, -'nēs, -'lō-,\ *adj or n*
Bar·dia \'bärd-ē-ə\ town & port Libya in NE Cyrenaica
Ba·reil·ly *or* **Ba·re·li** \bə-'rā-lē\ **1** city N India in NW *cen* Uttar Pradesh ESE of Delhi *pop* 334,064 **2** — see ROHILKHAND
Ba·rents \'bar-ən(t)s, 'bär-\ sea comprising the part of the Arctic ocean between Spitsbergen & Novaya Zemlya
Ba·ri \'bär-ē\ *or anc* **Bar·i·um** \'bar-ē-əm, 'ber-\ commune & port SE Italy ✱ of Apulia on the Adriatic *pop* 350,670
Ba·ri·lo·che *or* **San Car·los de Bariloche** \san-'kär-ləs-də-,bar-ə-'lō-chē\ city SW Argentina on Lake Nahuel Huapí *pop* 15,995
Bar·i·sal \'bar-ə-,sȯl\ city S Bangladesh in Ganges delta *pop* 79,300
Bar·king \'bär-kiŋ\ *or* **Barking Town** borough of E Greater London, England *pop* 160,499
Bar·let·ta \bär-'let-ə\ commune & port SE Italy in Apulia on the Adriatic *pop* 75,097
Bar·na·ul \,bär-nə-'ül\ city U.S.S.R. in Soviet Russia, Asia, on the Ob ✱ of Altai Territory *pop* 439,000
Bar·ne·gat Bay \'bär-ni-,gat, -gət-\ inlet of the Atlantic E N.J.
Barnes \'bärnz\ former municipal borough SE England, now part of Richmond upon Thames
Bar·net \'bär-nət\ borough of N Greater London, England *pop* 303,578
Barns·ley \'bärnz-lē\ county borough N England in West Riding, Yorkshire *pop* 75,330
Barn·sta·ble \'bärn-stə-bəl\ town SE Mass. on Cape Cod *pop* 19,842
Ba·ro·da \bə-'rōd-ə\ **1** former state W India near head of Gulf of Cambay ✱ Baroda *area* 8176 **2** city W India in SE Gujarat SE of Ahmadabad *pop* 404,229
Ba·rot·se·land \bə-'rät-sē-,land\ province W Zambia ✱ Mongu Lealui; a protectorate
Bar·qui·si·me·to \,bär-kə-sə-'māt-(,)ō\ city NW Venezuela *pop* 280,086
Bar·ran·qui·lla \,bär-ən-'kē-(y)ə\ city & port N Colombia on the Magdalena *pop* 816,706
Barren Grounds treeless plains N Canada W of Hudson Bay
Bar·rie \'bar-ē\ city Canada in SE Ont. *pop* 27,676
Bar·ring·ton \'bar-iŋ-tən\ town E R.I. SE of Providence *pop* 17,554
Bar·row \'bar-(,)ō\ *or* **Barrow-in-Fur·ness** \,bar-ə-wən-'fər-nəs\ county borough NW England in NW Lancashire *pop* 63,998
Barrow, Point most northerly point of Alaska & of the U.S., at *ab* 71°25'N, 156°30'W
Bar·stow \'bär-,stō\ city S Calif. NNE of San Bernardino *pop* 17,442
Bar·tles·ville \'bärt-ᵊlz-vil\ city NE Okla. *pop* 29,683
Ba·sel \'bäz-əl\ *or* F **Bâle** *or older* **Basle** \'bäl\ **1** canton NW Switzerland *area* 179, *pop* 439,834 **2** city, its ✱ & ✱ of **Basel-Stadt** \'bäz-əl-,shtät\ (half canton) *pop* 213,200
Ba·shan \'bā-shən\ region in ancient Palestine E & NE of Sea of Galilee
Ba·shi channel \'bäsh-ē\ strait between Philippines & Formosa
Bash·kir·ia \bash-'kir-ē-ə\ *or* **Bash·kir Republic** \,bash-,ki(ə)r-\ autonomous republic U.S.S.R. in E Soviet Russia, Europe, in S Ural mountains ✱ Ufa *area* 54,233, *pop* 3,819,000
Ba·si·lan \bä-'sē-,län\ **1** island Philippines SW of Mindanao *area* 495 **2** city comprising Basilan Island and several small nearby islands *pop* 209,100
Bas·il·don \'baz-əl-dən\ urban district SE England in Essex *pop* 129,073
Ba·si·li·ca·ta \bə-,zil-ə-'kät-ə, -,sil-\ *or formerly* **Lu·ca·nia** \lü-'kān-yə, 'kän-\ region S Italy on Gulf of Taranto ✱ Potenza
Basin ranges — see GREAT BASIN
Basque Provinces \'bask\ region N Spain on Bay of Biscay including provinces of Álava, Guipúzcoa, & Vizcaya
Bas·ra \'bäs-rə, 'bəs-, 'bas-, 'bäz-, 'bəz-, 'baz-\ *or* **Bus·ra** \'bäs-rə, 'bəs-\ city & port S Iraq on Shatt-al-Arab *pop* 310,950
Bass \'bas\ strait separating Tasmania & continent of Australia
Bas·sein \bə-'sān\ city S Burma W of Rangoon *pop* 175,000
Basse·terre \bas-'te(ə)r, bäs-\ town & port Brit. West Indies ✱ of St. Kitts I. & of St. Kitts-Nevis state
Basse-Terre \bas-'te(ə)r, bäs-\ **1** island French West Indies constituting the W part of Guadeloupe *area* 364 **2** town & port ✱ of Guadeloupe
Bas·tia \'bas-tē-ə, 'bäs-\ city & port France on NE coast of Corsica *pop* 49,375
Bas·togne \ba-'stōn\ town SE Belgium in the Ardennes
Basutoland — see LESOTHO
Ba·taan \bə-'tan, -'tän\ peninsula Philippines in W Luzon on W side of Manila Bay
Ba·ta·via \bə-'tā-vē-ə\ **1** city NW N.Y. *pop* 17,338 **2** — see DJAKARTA — **Ba·ta·vi·an** \-vē-ən\ *adj & n*
Batavian Republic the Netherlands under the French (1795-1806)
Bath \'bath, 'bäth\ city & county borough SW England in Somerset ESE of Bristol *pop* 84,545
Bath·urst \'bath-(,)ərst\ **1** city Canada in NE N.B. *pop* 16,674 **2** city & port ✱ of Gambia on Island of St. Mary in Gambia river *pop* 36,570 **3** island N Canada in Parry group *area* 6041
Bat·on Rouge \,bat-ᵊn-'rüzh\ city ✱ of La. on the Mississippi *pop* 165,963
Bat·ter·sea \'bat-ər-sē\ former metropolitan borough SW London, England, on S bank of the Thames, now part of Wandsworth
Bat·tle Creek \'bat-ᵊl-,krēk\ city S Mich. *pop* 38,931
Ba·tu·mi \bə-'tü-mē\ *or* **Ba·tum** \-'tüm\ city & port U.S.S.R. in SW Georgia on Black sea ✱ of Adzhar Republic *pop* 82,000
Baut·zen \'bau̇t-sən\ city E Germany on Spree river ENE of Dresden *pop* 43,670
Ba·var·ia \bə-'ver-ē-ə, -'var-\ *or* G **Bay·ern** \'bī-ərn\ state S Germany bordering on Austria & Czechoslovakia ✱ Munich *area* 27,232, *pop* 10,603,200
Ba·ya·mon \,bī-ə-'mōn\ city NE *cen* Puerto Rico *pop* 147,552
Bay City city E Mich. near head of Saginaw Bay *pop* 49,449
Ba·yeux \bī-'(y)ü, bā-; bä-'yə(r); bȧ-yœ\ town NW France WNW of Caen
Baykal — see BAIKAL
Bay·onne \bā-'ōn\ city & port NE N.J. *pop* 72,743
Ba·yonne \bā-'ōn, bä-'yȯn\ city SW France on the Adour near Bay of Biscay *pop* 42,743
Bay·reuth \bī-'rȯit, 'bī-,\ city W Germany in Bavaria NE of Nuremberg *pop* 63,530
Bay·town \'bā-,tau̇n\ city SE Tex. on Galveston Bay *pop* 43,980
Bay Village city NE Ohio W of Cleveland *pop* 18,163
Beachy Head \,bē-chē-\ headland SE England on coast of East Sussex
Bea·cons·field \'bē-kənz-,fēld\ city Canada in S Que. on Montreal I. SSW of Montreal *pop* 19,389
Bear \'ba(ə)r, 'be(ə)r\ **1** river 75 *m* N Calif. flowing SW to Feather river **2** river 350 *m* N Utah, SW Wyo., & SE Idaho flowing to Great Salt Lake
Beard·more \'bi(ə)rd-,mō(ə)r, -,mȯ(ə)r\ glacier Antarctica descending to Ross Ice Shelf at *ab* 170°E
Bear Mountain mountain 1305 *ft* SE N.Y. on the Hudson
Bé·arn \bā-'ärn\ region & former province SW France in Pyrenees SW of Gascony ✱ Pau
Be·as *or* **Bi·as** \'bē-,äs\ river 300 *m* N India in the Punjab flowing to the Sutlej
Beau·fort \'bō-fərt\ sea comprising the part of the Arctic ocean NE of Alaska & NW of Canada
Beau·mar·is \bō-'mar-əs\ municipal borough NW Wales in Anglesey on E Anglesey I. on Beaumaris Bay
Beau·mont \'bō-,mänt, bō-'\ city & port SE Tex. on Neches river *pop* 115,919
Beaune \'bōn\ commune E France SSW of Dijon *pop* 16,874
Beau·so·leil \,bō-sə-'lā\ commune SE France N of Monaco
Beau·vais \bō-'vā\ commune N France NNW of Paris *pop* 46,777
Bea·ver \'bē-vər\ **1** river 280 *m* NW Okla. forming upper course of the North Canadian **2** river 305 *m* Canada in Alta. & Sask. flowing E into the Churchill
Bea·ver·head \'bē-vər-,hed\ mountains on Idaho-Mont. boundary; SE part of Bitterroot range of the Rockies — see GARFIELD
Bea·ver·ton \'bē-vərt-ᵊn\ city NW Oreg. W of Portland *pop* 18,577
Bech·u·a·na·land \,bech-(ə-)'wän-ə-,land\ **1** region S Africa N of Orange river & W of Transvaal & including Kalahari desert & Okovanggo Basin **2** — see BOTSWANA **3** *or* **British Bechuanaland** former Brit. colony in the region S of Molopo river; became part of Union of So. Africa 1895 — **Bech·u·a·na** \,bech-(ə-)'wän-ə\ *adj or n*
Beck·en·ham \'bek-(ə-)nəm\ former urban district SE England in Kent, now part of Bromley
Beck·ley \'bek-lē\ city S W.Va. *pop* 19,884
Bed·ford \'bed-fərd\ **1** city NE Ohio SE of Cleveland *pop* 17,552 **2** *or* **Bed·ford·shire** \-,shi(ə)r, -shər\ county SE *cen* England *area* 473, *pop* 463,493 **3** municipal borough, its ✱ *pop* 73,064
Bed·loe's \'bed-,lōz\ — see LIBERTY
Be·dzin \'ben-,jēn\ *or* **Ben·din** \'ben-,dēn\ commune S Poland in Silesia *pop* 42,800
Beer·she·ba \bi(ə)r-'shē-bə, be(ə)r-, bər-\ city S Israel in N Negeb, in Bible times marking extreme S limit of Palestine *pop* 77,400
Behar — see BIHAR
Be·his·tun \,bā-his-'tün\ *or* **Bi·su·tun** \,bē-sə-'tün\ village W Iran 22 *m* E of Kermanshah
Bei·da \'bād-ə\ town NE Libya in Cyrenaica NE of Benghazi
Bei·ra \'bā-rə\ town & port SE Mozambique *pop* 58,970
Bei·rut *or* **Bay·rut** *or* **Bey·routh** \bā-'rüt\ *or anc* **Be·ry·tus** \bə-'rīt-əs\ city & port ✱ of Lebanon *pop* 700,000
Bekaa — see BIKA
Bé·kés·csa·ba \'bā-,kāsh-,chȯ-,bȯ\ city SE Hungary *pop* 55,408
Be·la·ya \'bel-ə-yə\ river 700 *m* U.S.S.R. in Soviet Russia, Europe, rising in the S Urals & flowing S, W, & NW to the Kama
Be·lém \bə-'lem\ *or* **Pa·rá** \pə-'rä\ city N Brazil ✱ of Pará state on Pará river *pop* 563,996

Bel·fast \ˈbel-ˌfast, bel-ˈ\ county borough & port ✱ of Northern Ireland & of County Antrim at head of **Belfast Lough** (inlet) *pop* 358,991

Bel·fort \bel-ˈfȯ(ə)r, bā-ˈfȯ(ə)r\ commune E France commanding **Belfort Gap** (wide pass between Vosges & Jura mountains) *pop* 53,214

Belgian Congo *or earlier* **Congo Free State** former Belgian colony W *cen* Africa — see ZAIRE

Belgian East Africa — see RUANDA-URUNDI

Bel·gium \ˈbel-jəm\ *or F* **Bel·gique** \bel-zhēk\ *or Flem* **Bel·gië** \ˈbel-gē-ə\ country W Europe bordering on North sea; a constitutional monarchy ✱ Brussels *area* 11,774, *pop* 9,730,000

Bel·go·rod–Dnes·trov·ski *or* **Byel·go·rod–Dnes·trov·ski** \ˈbel-gə-ˌräd-(ˌ)ne-ˈstrȯf-skē, -ˈstrȯv-, ˈbyel-gə-rət-\ *or Rum* **Ce·ta·tea Al·ba** \chə-ˌtät-ē-ə-ˈäl-bə\ *or formerly Turk & Russ* **Ak·ker·man** \ˌäk-ər-ˈmän\ city U.S.S.R. in SW Ukraine on the Dniester estuary *pop* 29,000

Bel·grade \ˈbel-ˌgrād, -ˌgräd, -ˌgrad, bel-ˈ\ *or* **Beo·grad** \ˈbeȯ-ˌgräd\ city ✱ of Yugoslavia & of Serbia *pop* 772,000

Bel·gra·via \bel-ˈgrā-vē-ə\ district of W *cen* London, England

Be·li·tung \bə-ˈlēt-əŋ\ *or* **Bil·li·ton** \-ˈlē-ˌtän\ island Indonesia between Bangka & Borneo *area* 1866, *pop* 102,375

Be·lize \bə-ˈlēz\ **1** city & port, former ✱ of Brit. Honduras *pop* 39,257 **2** BRITISH HONDURAS — **Be·liz·ean** \-ˈlē-zē-ən\ *adj or n*

Bell \ˈbel\ city SW Calif. SE of Los Angeles *pop* 21,836

Bel·la Coo·la \ˌbel-ə-ˈkü-lə\ river *ab* 60 *m* Canada in B.C. flowing W to Burke channel E of Queen Charlotte Sound

Bel·laire \be-ˈla(ə)r, bə-, -ˈle(ə)r\ city SE Tex. within city of Houston *pop* 19,009

Bel·leau \be-ˈlō, ˈbe-ˌ\ village N France NW of Château-Thierry & N of **Bel·leau Wood** (*F* **Bois de Bel·leau** \ˌbwäd-ə-be-ˈlō\)

Belle Fourche \(ˈ)bel-ˈfüsh\ river *ab* 290 *m* NE Wyo. & W S.Dak. flowing NE & E into the Cheyenne

Belle Glade \ˈbel-ˌglād, bel-ˈ\ city SE Fla. W of West Palm Beach *pop* 15,949

Belle Isle, Strait of \be-ˈlī(ə)l\ channel between N tip of Newfoundland I. & SE Labrador

Belle·ville \ˈbel-ˌvil\ **1** city SW Ill. *pop* 41,699 **2** town NE N.J. N of Newark *pop* 34,643 **3** city Canada in SE Ont. *pop* 35,128

Belle·vue \ˈbel-ˌvyü\ **1** city E Nebr. S of Omaha *pop* 19,449 **2** city W Wash. E of Seattle *pop* 61,102

Bell·flow·er \ˈbel-ˌflau̇(-ə)r\ city SW Calif. E of Los Angeles *pop* 51,454

Bell Gardens city SW Calif. E of Los Angeles *pop* 29,308

Bel·ling·ham \ˈbel-iŋ-ˌham\ city & port NW Wash. on **Bellingham Bay** (inlet at N end of Puget Sound) *pop* 39,375

Bel·lings·hau·sen \ˈbel-iŋz-ˌhau̇z-ᵊn\ sea comprising a large bay of the S Pacific W of base of Antarctic peninsula

Bel·lin·zo·na \ˌbel-ən-ˈzō-nə\ commune S Switzerland E of Locarno ✱ of Ticino *pop* 16,979

Bell·mawr \ˈbel-ˌmär, -ˌmȯ(ə)r\ borough SW N.J. S of Camden *pop* 15,618

Bel·lu·no \bə-ˈlü-(ˌ)nō\ commune N Italy on Piave river *pop* 33,721

Bell·wood \ˈbel-ˌwu̇d\ village NE Ill. W of Chicago *pop* 22,096

Bel·mont \ˈbel-ˌmänt\ **1** city W Calif. SE of San Francisco *pop* 23,667 **2** town E Mass. W of Boston *pop* 28,285

Bel·mo·pan \ˌbel-mō-ˈpan\ city *cen* Brit. Honduras ✱ (since 1970) of Brit. Honduras

Beloe More — see WHITE

Be·lo Ho·ri·zon·te \ˈbā-lō-ˌhȯr-ə-ˈzänt-ē, ˈbel-ō-, -ˌhär-\ city E Brazil ✱ of Minas Gerais *pop* 1,106,722

Be·loit \bə-ˈlȯit\ city S Wis. on Ill. border *pop* 35,729

Be·lo·rus·sia \ˌbel-ō-ˈrəsh-ə\ *or* **Bye·lo·rus·sia** \bē-ˌel-ō-\ *or* **White Russia, 1** former region E Europe N of & including the Pripet Marshes inhabited by the White Russians **2** *or* **Be·lo·rus·sian Republic** \-ˌrəsh-ən-\ constituent republic of the U.S.S.R. bordering on Poland, Lithuania, & Latvia ✱ Minsk *area* 88,044, *pop* 9,003,000

Belostok — see BIALYSTOK

Bel·sen *or* **Ber·gen–Belsen** \ˌber-gən-ˈbel-zən, ˌbər-\ locality NW Germany on Lüneburg Heath NW of Celle

Be·lu·kha \bə-ˈlü-kə\ mountain 15,157 *ft* U.S.S.R. in S Soviet Russia, Asia; highest in Altai mountain region

Benares — see BANARAS

Ben·di·go \ˈben-di-ˌgō\ city SE Australia in N Victoria NNW of Melbourne *pop* (with suburbs) 31,350

Be·ne·lux \ˈben-ᵊl-ˌəks\ economic union comprising Belgium, the Netherlands, & Luxembourg; formed 1947

Be·ne·ven·to \ˌben-ə-ˈven-(ˌ)tō\ commune S Italy in Campania NE of Naples *pop* 59,578

Ben·gal \ben-ˈgȯl, beŋ-\ region E India (subcontinent) including delta of Ganges & Brahmaputra rivers; formerly a presidency & (1937–47) a province of Brit. India; divided 1947 between Pakistan & Republic of India — see EAST BENGAL, EAST PAKISTAN, WEST BENGAL — **Ben·gal·ese** \ˌbeŋ-gə-ˈlēz, ˌben-, -ˈlēs\ *adj or n*

Bengal, Bay of arm of the Indian ocean between India & Ceylon on the W & Burma & Malay peninsula on the E

Ben·gha·zi *or* **Ben·ga·zi** *or* **Ben·gha·si** *or* **Ben·ga·si** \ben-ˈgäz-ē, beŋ-ˈgaz-\ *or anc* **Ber·e·ni·ce** \ˌber-ə-ˈnī-sē\ city & port NE Libya, a ✱ of Libya *pop* 137,295

Ben·guela \ben-ˈg(w)el-ə\ city & port W Angola *pop* 35,162

Be·ni \ˈbā-nē\ river 1000 *m, cen* & N Bolivia flowing N to unite with Mamoré river forming the Madeira

Be·nin \bə-ˈnin, -ˈnēn; ˈben-ən\ **1** river *ab* 100 *m* S Nigeria W of the Niger flowing into Bight of Benin **2** *or* **Benin City** city SW Nigeria in W delta of the Niger *pop* 119,692

Benin, Bight of the N section of Gulf of Guinea W Africa off coast of SW Nigeria & Dahomey

Be·ni Su·ef \ˌben-ē-sü-ˈāf\ city N *cen* Egypt SSW of Cairo *pop* 99,400

Ben Lomond — see LOMOND (Ben)

Ben Nevis — see NEVIS (Ben)

Be·no·ni \bə-ˈnō-nē\ city NE Republic of So. Africa in S Transvaal on the Witwatersrand E of Johannesburg *pop* 122,502

Ben·ton \ˈbent-ᵊn\ city *cen* Ark. SW of Little Rock *pop* 16,499

Benton Harbor city SW Mich. *pop* 16,481

Be·nue \ˈbān-(ˌ)wā\ *or* **Bin·ue** \ˈbin-(ˌ)wā\ river 870 *m* W Africa flowing W into the Niger

Bep·pu \ˈbep-(ˌ)ü\ city Japan in NE Kyushu on **Beppu Bay** (arm of Inland sea) *pop* 146,000

Be·rar \bā-ˈrär, bə-\ region W *cen* India; in Central Provinces & Berar 1903–47, in Madhya Pradesh 1947–56, in Bombay 1956–60, in Maharashtra since 1960; chief city Amravati

Ber·be·ra \ˈbər-b(ə-)rə\ town & port N Somalia

Berch·tes·ga·den \ˈberk-təs-ˌgäd-ᵊn\ town W Germany in E Bavarian Alps S of Salzburg, Austria

Be·rea \bə-ˈrē-ə\ **1** city NE Ohio SW of Cleveland *pop* 22,396 **2** — see ALEPPO **3** — see VÉROIA

Be·re·zi·na \bə-ˈrāz-ᵊn-ə, -ˈrez-\ river 350 *m* U.S.S.R. in Belorussia flowing SE into the Dnieper

Bergama — see PERGAMUM

Ber·ga·mo \ˈbe(ə)r-gə-ˌmō, ˈbər-\ commune N Italy in Lombardy NE of Milan *pop* 124,968

Ber·gen, 1 \ˈbər-gən, ˈbe(ə)r-\ city & port SW Norway *pop* 115,964 **2** — see MONS

Ber·gen·field \ˈbər-gən-ˌfēld\ borough NE N.J. *pop* 33,131

Be·ring \ˈbi(ə)r-iŋ, ˈbe(ə)r-\ **1** sea arm of the N Pacific between Alaska & NE Siberia & between the Aleutians & Bering strait *area* 878,000 **2** strait *ab* 56 *m* wide separating Asia (U.S.S.R.) from No. America (Alaska)

Berke·ley \ˈbər-klē\ **1** city & port W Calif. on San Francisco Bay N of Oakland *pop* 116,716 **2** city E Mo. NW of St. Louis *pop* 19,743

Berk·ley \ˈbər-klē\ city SE Mich. NW of Detroit *pop* 22,618

Berk·shire \ˈbərk-ˌshi(ə)r, -shər\ **1** hills W Mass. W of the Connecticut — see GREYLOCK (Mount) **2** *Brit usu* ˈbärk-\ county S England in Thames river basin ✱ Reading *area* 725, *pop* 633,457

Ber·lin, 1 \ˈbər-lən\ city N N.H. *pop* 15,256 **2** \(ˌ)bər-ˈlin, *Ger* ber-ˈlēn\ city E *cen* Germany on Spree river, before 1945 ✱ of Germany & of Prussia, divided under postwar occupation between East & West Germany, East Berlin being made ✱ of East Germany (1949) & West Berlin a state (not formally incorporated) of West Germany *pop* 3,218,273 — **Ber·lin·er** \(ˌ)bər-ˈlin-ər\ *n*

Ber·me·jo \bər-ˈmā-(ˌ)hō, ber-\ river 1000 *m* N Argentina rising on Bolivian frontier & flowing SE into Paraguay river

Ber·mond·sey \ˈbər-mən(d)-zē\ former metropolitan borough E *cen* London, England, now part of Southwark

Ber·mu·da \(ˌ)bər-ˈmyüd-ə\ islands W Atlantic ESE of Cape Hatteras; a British colony ✱ Hamilton *area* 21, *pop* 50,000 — **Ber·mu·di·an** \-ˈmyüd-ē-ən\ *or* **Ber·mu·dan** \-ˈmyüd-ᵊn\ *adj or n*

Bern *or* **Berne** \ˈbərn, ˈbe(ə)rn\ **1** canton NW & W *cen* Switzerland *area* 2658, *pop* 983,296 **2** city, its ✱ & ✱ of Switzerland on the Aare *pop* 166,800 — **Bern·ese** \(ˌ)bər-ˈnēz, -ˈnēs\ *adj or n*

Bern·burg \ˈbərn-ˌbərg, ˈbe(ə)rn-ˌbu̇(ə)rg\ city E Germany W of Dessau *pop* 45,322

Bernese Alps *or* **Bernese Oberland** — see OBERLAND

Ber·ni·cia \(ˌ)bər-ˈnish-(ē-)ə\ Anglian kingdom of 6th century A.D. located between Tyne & Forth rivers ✱ Bamborough

Ber·ni·na \(ˌ)bər-ˈnē-nə\ the S extension of Rhaetian Alps on border between Italy & Switzerland; highest peak **Piz Bernina** \ˌpēts-\ (highest in the Rhaetian Alps) 13,295 *ft*

Beroea, 1 — see ALEPPO **2** — see VÉROIA

Ber·ry *or* **Ber·ri** \be-ˈrē\ former province *cen* France S of Orléanais ✱ Bourges

Ber·thoud \ˈbər-thəd\ mountain pass 11,315 *ft* N Colo. in Front range WNW of Denver

Ber·wick \ˈber-ik\ *or* **Ber·wick·shire** \-ˌshi(ə)r, -shər\ county SE Scotland ✱ Duns *area* 457, *pop* 22,523

Ber·wyn \ˈbər-wən\ city NE Ill. W of Chicago *pop* 52,502

Berytus — see BEIRUT

Be·san·çon \bə-ˈzan(t)-sən, bə-zäⁿ-sōⁿ\ city E France *pop* 113,220

Bes·kids \ˈbes-ˌkidz, be-ˈskēdz\ mountain ranges *cen* Europe in W Carpathians; include **West Beskids** (in Poland & Czechoslovakia W of Tatra mountains) & **East Beskids** (in NE Czechoslovakia)

Bes·sa·ra·bia \ˌbes-ə-ˈrā-bē-ə\ region SE Europe between Dniester & Prut rivers; now mostly in Moldavian Republic of the U.S.S.R. — **Bes·sa·ra·bi·an** \-bē-ən\ *adj or n*

Bes·se·mer \ˈbes-ə-mər\ city N *cen* Ala. *pop* 33,428

Beth·a·ny \ˈbeth-ə-nē\ village Palestine E of Jerusalem on Mount of Olives; now in W Jordan

Be·thel \ˈbeth-əl, be-ˈthel\ ruined town Palestine in W Jordan *ab* 11 *m* N of Jerusalem

Beth·el Park \ˌbeth-əl-\ borough SW Pa. S of Pittsburgh *pop* 34,791

Beth·le·hem \ˈbeth-li-ˌhem, -lē-(h)əm\ **1** city E Pa. on the Lehigh *pop* 72,686 **2** city Palestine in Judea SW of Jerusalem; now in W Jordan *pop* 16,313

Beth·nal Green \ˌbeth-nəl-\ former metropolitan borough E London, England, now part of Tower Hamlets

Beth·sa·i·da \beth-ˈsā-əd-ə\ ruined town Palestine on NE side of Sea of Galilee E of the Jordan; its site in SE Syria

Be·tio \ˈbā-chē-ˌō, -shē-; ˈbāt-sē-\ islet & village W Pacific in N Gilbert islands at S end of Tarawa

Bet·ten·dorf \ˈbet-ᵊn-ˌdȯrf\ city E Iowa E of Davenport *pop* 22,126

Beuthen — see BYTOM

Bev·er·ley \ˈbev-ər-lē\ municipal borough N England ✱ of East Riding, Yorkshire *pop* 17,124

Bev·er·ly \ˈbev-ər-lē\ city NE Mass. *pop* 38,348

Beverly Hills city SW Calif. W of Los Angeles *pop* 33,416

Bex·ley \'bek-slē\ borough of E Greater London, England *pop* 216,172

Bey·o·glu \,bā-ə-'(g)lü\ *or formerly* **Pera** \'per-ə\ section of Istanbul, Turkey, comprising area N of the Golden Horn

Beyrouth — see BEIRUT

Bé·ziers \bāz-'yā\ city S France SW of Montpellier *pop* 80,492

Bezwada — see VIJAYAWADA

Bha·gal·pur \'bäg-əl-,pu̇(ə)r\ city E India in E Bihar on the Ganges *pop* 178,216

Bhak·ra Dam \,bäk-rə-\ hydroelectric & irrigation dam 680 *ft* high N India in Punjab NW of Bilaspur in gorge of the Sutlej

Bha·mo \bə-'mō, -'mō\ city N Burma on the upper Irrawaddy *pop* 16,000

Bharat — see INDIA

Bhat·pa·ra \bät-'pär-ə\ city E India in West Bengal N of Calcutta *pop* 160,607

Bhav·na·gar *or* **Bhau·na·gar** \bau̇-'nəg-ər\ city & port W India in S Gujarat on Gulf of Cambay *pop* 222,462

Bho·pal \bō-'päl\ **1** former state N *cen* India in & N of Vindhya mountains ✻ Bhopal; now part of Madhya Pradesh **2** city N *cen* India NW of Nagpur ✻ of Madhya Pradesh *pop* 325,721

Bhu·ba·nes·war *or* **Bhu·va·nesh·war** \,bu̇v-ə-'näsh-wər\ city E India S of Cuttack ✻ of Orissa *pop* 38,211

Bhu·tan \bü-'tan, -'tän\ country Asia in Himalayas on NE border of India; a protectorate of India ✻ Thimbu *area* 18,000, *pop* 800,000 — **Bhu·ta·nese** \,büt-ᵊn-'ēz, -'ēs\ *adj or n*

Bi·a·fra, Bight of \bē-'af-rə, bi-, -'äf-\ the E section of Gulf of Guinea, W Africa

Bi·ak \bē-'(y)äk\ island off West New Guinea; largest of the Schouten islands

Bia·ly·stok \bē-'äl-i-,stȯk\ *or* Russ **Be·lo·stok** \,bel-ə-'stȯk\ city NE Poland *pop* 162,700

Biar·ritz \,bē-ə-'rits, 'bē-ə-,\ commune SW France on Bay of Biscay *pop* 26,750

Bias — see BEAS

Bid·de·ford \'bid-ə-fərd\ city SW Me. SW of Portland *pop* 19,983

Biel \'bē(ə)l\ *or* F **Bienne** \bē-'en\ commune NW Switzerland in Bern canton NE of NE end of **Lake of Biel** (10 *m* long) *pop* 64,333

Bie·le·feld \'bē-lə-,felt\ city W Germany E of Münster *pop* 168,700

Big Bend, 1 area W Tex. in large bend of the Rio Grande; partly included in **Big Bend National Park** (reservation *area* 1094) **2** section of Columbia river E *cen* Wash.

Big Black river 330 *m* W *cen* Miss. flowing to the Mississippi

Big Diomede — see DIOMEDE

Big Hole National Battlefield reservation SW Mont. in mountain valley SW of Anaconda near Idaho border

Big·horn \'big-,hȯ(ə)rn\ *or* **Big Horn, 1** river 336 *m* N Wyo. & SE Mont. flowing N into Yellowstone river — see WIND **2** mountains N Wyo. extending S from Mont. border E of Bighorn river — see CLOUD PEAK

Big Sandy river 22 *m* between W.Va. & Ky. formed by confluence of Levisa Fork & Tug Fork & flowing N into the Ohio

Big Sioux \'sü\ river 300 *m* S.Dak. & Iowa flowing S to the Missouri & forming Iowa-S.Dak. boundary

Big Spring city W Tex. NE of Odessa *pop* 28,735

Big Stone lake *ab* 30 *m* long between W Minn. & NE S.Dak. — see MINNESOTA (river)

Big Sur \'sər\ region W Calif. centering on Big Sur river & extending *ab* 80 *m* along coast SE of Point Sur

Bi·har *or* **Be·har** \bi-'här\ **1** state NE India bordering on Nepal; winter ✻ Patna, summer ✻ Ranchi *area* 67,164, *pop* 56,387,296 **2** city *cen* Bihar state SE of Patna *pop* 78,581

Bijanagar — see VIJAYANAGAR

Bi·ka *or* **Be·kaa** \bi-'kä\ *or* **El Bika** *or* **El Bekaa** \,el-\ *or anc* **Coe·le–Syria** \,sē-lē-\valley Lebanon & Syria between Lebanon & Anti-Lebanon mountain ranges

Bi·ka·ner \,bik-ə-'ne(ə)r, ,bē-kə-, -'ni(ə)r\ city NW India in N Rajasthan in Thar desert *pop* 190,868

Bi·ki·ni \bə-'kē-nē\ island (atoll) W Pacific in Marshall islands at NW end of Ratak chain

Bi·las·pur \bə-'läs-,pu̇(ə)r\ city E *cen* India in SE Madhya Pradesh SE of Jabalpur *pop* 86,706

Bil·bao \bil-'bä-,ō, -'bau̇, -'bä-(,)ō\ city N Spain ✻ of Vizcaya *pop* 369,559

Bil·ler·i·ca \(')bil-'rik-ə, ,bel-ə-'rik-ə\ town NE Mass. S of Lowell *pop* 31,648

Bil·lings \'bil-iŋz\ city S *cen* Mont. *pop* 61,581

Billiton — see BELITUNG

Bi·loxi \bə-'lək-sē, -'läk-\ city & port SE Miss. *pop* 48,486

Bim·i·ni \'bim-ə-nē\ two islands of the Bahamas NW of Andros

Bing·en \'biŋ-ən\ city W Germany at confluence of the Rhine & the Nahe *pop* 24,350

Bing·ham·ton \'biŋ-əm-tən\ city S *cen* N.Y. *pop* 64,123

Binh Dinh — see AN NHON

Binue — see BENUE

Bío–Bío \,bē-ō-'bē-(,)ō\ river 238 *m* S *cen* Chile flowing into the Pacific at Concepción

Bir·ken·head \'bər-kən-,hed, ,bər-kən-'\ county borough NW England in Cheshire on the Mersey estuary opposite Liverpool *pop* 137,738

Bir·ming·ham \'bər-miŋ-,ham, *Brit usu* -miŋ-əm\ **1** city N *cen* Ala. *pop* 300,910 **2** city SE Mich. N of Detroit *pop* 26,170 **3** city & county borough W *cen* England in Warwickshire, Staffordshire, & Worcestershire *pop* 1,013,366

Bi·ro·bi·dzhan \,bir-ō-bi-'jän, -'jan\ **1** — see JEWISH AUTONOMOUS REGION **2** city U.S.S.R. ✻ of Jewish Autonomous Region *pop* 56,000

Bisayas — see VISAYAN

Biscay *or* **Biscaya** — see VIZCAYA

Bis·cay, Bay of \'bis-,kā, -kē\ inlet of the Atlantic between W coast of France & N coast of Spain

Bis·cayne Bay \bis-'kān, 'bis-,\ inlet of the Atlantic SE Fla.

Bisk \'bisk, 'bēsk\ *or* **Biysk** *or* **Biisk** \'bē(-ə)sk\ city U.S.S.R. in Soviet Russia, Asia, in E Altai Territory *pop* 186,000

Bis·kra \'bis-krə, -(,)krä\ city NE Algeria at an oasis on S edge of Atlas mountains *pop* 53,177

Bis·marck \'biz-,märk\ **1** sea comprising the part of the W Pacific enclosed by the islands of the Bismarck archipelago **2** archipelago W Pacific N of E end of New Guinea *area* 22,290, *pop* 176,471 **3** mountain range North-East New Guinea NW of Owen Stanley range; highest point Mt. Wilhelm 15,400 *ft* **4** city ✻ of N.Dak. on the Missouri *pop* 34,703

Bis·sau *or* **Bis·são** \bis-'au̇(ⁿ)\ city & port ✻ of Portuguese Guinea *pop* 62,101

Bisutun — see BEHISTUN

Bi·thyn·ia \bə-'thin-ē-ə\ ancient country NW Asia Minor bordering on the Propontis & Euxine — **Bi·thyn·i·an** \-ē-ən\ *adj or n*

Bitola *or* **Bitolj** — see MONASTIR

Bitter Lakes two lakes (Great Bitter Lake & Little Bitter Lake) in NE Egypt N of Suez; connected & traversed by the Suez canal

Bit·ter·root \'bit-ə(r)-,rüt, -,ru̇t\ range of the Rocky mountains on Idaho-Mont. boundary — see BEAVERHEAD, GARFIELD

Bi·wa \'bē-(,)wä\ lake 40 *m* long Japan on Honshu NE of Kyoto

Bi·zerte \bə-'zərt-ē, bi-'ze(ə)rt\ *or* **Bi·zer·ta** \bə-'zərt-ə\ city & port N Tunisia on **Lake Bizerte** (a deep lagoon) *pop* 51,708

Björneborg — see PORI

Black, 1 mountains W N.C.; a range of the Blue Ridge mountains — see MITCHELL (Mount) **2** hills W S.Dak. & NE Wyo. — see HARNEY PEAK **3** canyon of the Colorado between Ariz. & Nev. S of Hoover Dam **4** canyon of the Gunnison SW *cen* Colo. partly in **Black Canyon of the Gunnison National Monument** (*area* 21) **5** — see BO

Black·burn \'blak-(,)bərn\ county borough NW England in Lancashire *pop* 101,672

Blackburn, Mount mountain 16,523 *ft* S Alaska; highest in the Wrangell mountains

Black Forest *or* G **Schwarz·wald** \'shfärts-,vält, 'shwȯrt-,swȯld\ forested mountain region SW Germany along the upper Rhine between the Neckar & Swiss border

Black·pool \'blak-,pül\ county borough NW England in Lancashire on Irish sea *pop* 151,311

Black Sea *or* **Eux·ine Sea** \'yük-sən, -,sīn\ *or anc* **Pon·tus Eux·i·nus** \'pänt-əs-,yük-'sī-nəs\ *or* **Pontus** sea between Europe & Asia connected with Aegean sea through the Bosporus, Sea of Marmara, & Dardanelles *area* 168,500

Black Volta — see VOLTA

Black Warrior river 178 *m*, *cen* Ala. flowing into the Tombigbee

Bla·go·vesh·chensk \,bläg-ə-'vesh-(ch)ən(t)sk\ city U.S.S.R. in E Soviet Russia, Asia, on the Amur *pop* 128,000

Blaine \'blān\ city E Minn. N of St. Paul *pop* 20,640

Blanc, Cape \'blaŋk, 'bläⁿ\ **1** cape N Tunisia; northernmost point of Africa, at 37°14'N **2** promontory NW Africa on the Atlantic at tip of peninsula divided by Mauritania–Spanish Sahara boundary

Blanc, Mont — see MONT BLANC

Blan·ca Peak \'blaŋ-kə\ mountain 14,317 *ft* S Colo.; highest in Sangre de Cristo mountains

Blan·co, Cape \'blaŋ-(,)kō\ cape SW Oreg.

Blan·tyre–Lim·be \'blan-,tī(ə)r-'lim-bā\ city S Malawi *pop* 109,461

Blar·ney \'blär-nē\ town SW Ireland in *cen* County Cork

Blas·ket \'blas-kət\ islands SW Ireland N of Dingle Bay

Bled \'bled\ resort village NW Yugoslavia in Slovenia NW of Ljubljana

Blen·heim \'blen-əm\ *or* G **Blind·heim** \'blint-,hīm\ village W Germany in Bavaria NNW of Augsburg

Bli·da \'blēd-ə\ city N Algeria SW of Algiers *pop* 85,683

Block \'bläk\ island R.I. SSW of Point Judith

Bloem·fon·tein \'blüm-fən-,tān, -,fän-\ city Republic of So. Africa ✻ of Orange Free State & judicial ✻ of the Republic *pop* 112,606

Blois \blə-'wä\ city N *cen* France SW of Orléans *pop* 44,264

Bloom·field \blüm-,fēld\ **1** town N *cen* Conn. NW of Hartford *pop* 18,301 **2** town NE N.J. *pop* 52,029

Bloo·ming·ton \'blü-miŋ-tən\ **1** city *cen* Ill. *pop* 39,992 **2** city SW *cen* Ind. *pop* 42,890 **3** village SE Minn. SW of Minneapolis *pop* 81,970

Blooms·bury \'blümz-b(ə-)rē, *US also* -,ber-ē\ district of *cen* London, England

Blue, 1 mountains NE Oreg. & SE Wash. W of Wallowa mountains; highest Rock Creek Butte 9097 *ft* **2** mountains SE Australia in Great Dividing range in E New So. Wales; highest 4460 *ft* **3** mountains E Jamaica; highest Blue Mountain Peak 7402 *ft*

Blue·field \'blü-,fēld\ city S W.Va. *pop* 15,921

Blue Grotto sea cave Italy on N shore of Capri

Blue Island city NE Ill. S of Chicago *pop* 22,958

Blue Nile river 850 *m* Ethiopia & Sudan flowing from Lake Tana NNW into the Nile at Khartoum — see ABBAI

Blue Ridge *or* **Blue Ridge Mountains** the E range of the Appalachian mountains E U.S. extending from South Mountain, S Pa. into N Ga. — see MITCHELL (Mount)

Bluff \'bləf\ town S New Zealand; port for Invercargill

Blythe·ville \'blī-vəl, 'blīth-,vil\ city NE Ark. *pop* 24,752

Bo \'bō\ *or* **Black** \'blak\ river 500 *m* SE Asia rising in *cen* Yunnan, China, & flowing SE to Red river

Bo·bruisk \bō-'brü-isk\ city U.S.S.R. in White Russia on the Berezina *pop* 138,000

Bo·ca Ra·ton \,bō-kə-rə-'tōn\ city SE Fla. N of Fort Lauderdale *pop* 28,506

Bo·chum \'bō-kəm\ city W Germany in Ruhr valley *pop* 346,000

Bodensee — see CONSTANCE (Lake)

Boe·o·tia \bē-'ō-sh(ē-)ə\ *or* NGk **Voi·o·tía** \vyō-'tē-ə\ district E *cen* Greece NW of Attica — **Boe·o·tian** \bē-'ō-shən\ *adj or n*

Boetoeng — see BUTUNG

Bo·ga·lu·sa \,bō-gə-'lü-sə\ city E La. *pop* 18,412

Bo·gor \'bō-,gȯ(ə)r\ *or formerly* **Bul·ten·zorg** \'bīt-ᵊn-,zȯ(ə)rg\ city Indonesia in W Java S of Djakarta *pop* 154,092

Bo·go·tá \,bō-gə-'tō, -'tä\ city ✻ of Colombia on plateau of the Andes at altitude of 8563 *ft*, *pop* 2,293,919

Bo·he·mia \bō-'hē-mē-ə\ region W Czechoslovakia; once a kingdom, later a province ✻ Prague

Bohemian Forest *or* G **Böh·mer·wald** \ˈbə(r)m-ər-ˌvält, ˈbœm-\ forested mountain region Czechoslovakia & Germany along boundary between E Bavaria & SW Bohemia
Bo·hol \bō-ˈhȯl\ island S *cen* Philippines, one of the Visayan islands, N of Mindanao *area* 1492
Bois de Belleau — see BELLEAU
Bois de Bou·logne \ˌbwäd-ə-bü-ˈlōn, -ˈlȯin\ park France W of Paris *area* 2155 acres
Boi·se \ˈbȯi-sē, -zē\ city ✻ of Idaho on Boise river (60 *m* long) *pop* 74,990
Bo·ja·dor, Cape \ˈbäj-ə-ˌdȯ(ə)r\ headland NW Africa in the Atlantic on W coast of Spanish Sahara
Bokhara — see BUKHARA
Boks·burg \ˈbäks-ˌbərg\ city NE Republic of So. Africa in S Transvaal E of Johannesburg *pop* 108,850
Bo·lan \bō-ˈlän\ mountain pass 5900 *ft* Pakistan in N Baluchistan SE of Quetta
Bolbitine — see ROSETTA
Bo·li·var, Cer·ro \ˌser-(ˌ)ō-bə-ˈlē-ˌvär\ *or* **La Pa·ri·da** \ˌläp-ə-ˈrē-də\ iron mountain 2018 *ft* E Venezuela S of Ciudad Bolívar
Bo·li·var, Pi·co \ˌpē-(ˌ)kō-bə-ˈlē-ˌvär\ *or* **La Co·lum·na** \ˌläk-ə-ˈlüm-nə\ mountain 16,411 *ft* W Venezuela in Cordillera Mérida: highest in Venezuela
Bo·liv·ia \bə-ˈliv-ē-ə\ country W *cen* So. America; a republic; administrative ✻ La Paz, constitutional ✻ Sucre *area* 424,200, *pop* 5,060,000 — **Bo·liv·i·an** \-ē-ən\ *adj or n*
Bo·lo·gna \bə-ˈlōn-(y)ə\ *or anc* **Bo·no·nia** \bə-ˈnō-nē-ə\ commune N Italy ✻ of Emilia-Romagna at foot of the Apennines *pop* 489,593 — **Bo·lo·gnan** \bə-ˈlōn-yən\ *or* **Bo·lo·gnese** \ˌbō-lən-ˈ(y)ēz, -ˈ(y)ēs\ *adj or n*
Bol·se·na, Lake \bōl-ˈsā-nə\ lake *cen* Italy in NW Latium NW of Viterbo
Bol·ton *or* **Bolton–le–Moors** \ˌbōlt-ᵊn-lə-ˈmu̇(ə)rz\ county borough NW England in Lancashire NW of Manchester *pop* 153,977
Bol·za·no \bōlt-ˈsän-(ˌ)ō, bōl-ˈzän-\ **1** former province N Italy in S Tirol, now part of Trentino-Alto Adige region **2** commune in Trentino-Alto Adige region *pop* 104,089
Bo·ma \ˈbō-mə\ city & port W Congo on Congo river *pop* 79,230
Bom·bay \bäm-ˈbā\ **1** former state W India ✻ Bombay; divided 1960 into Gujarat & Maharashtra states; once a presidency & (1937–47) a province of Brit. India **2** island W India on which city of Bombay is situated *area* 24 **3** city & port W India ✻ of Maharashtra & of former Bombay state *pop* 5,700,358
Bo·mu \ˈbō-(ˌ)mü\ *or* **Mbo·mu** \-əm-ˈbō-\ river 500 *m* W *cen* Africa forming boundary between Zaire & Central African Republic & uniting with Uele river to form the Ubangi
Bon, Cape \ˈbō^{n}\ *or* **Ras el Tib** \ˌräs-ˌel-ˈtib\ *or* **Ras Ad·dar** \ˌräs-ə-ˈdär\ headland NE Tunisia on **Cape Bon Peninsula**
Bo·na, Mount \ˈbō-nə\ mountain 16,421 *ft* S Alaska at W end of Wrangell mountains
Bon·aire \bə-ˈna(ə)r, -ˈne(ə)r\ island Netherlands Antilles E of Curaçao *area* 95, *pop* 8099
Bon·di \ˈbän-ˈdī\ town SE Australia, SE suburb of Sydney, S of entrance to Port Jackson on **Bondi Beach**
Bône — see ANNABA
Bo·nin \ˈbō-nən\ *or* **Oga·sa·wa·ra** \(ˌ)ō-ˌgäs-ə-ˈwär-ə\ islands W Pacific *ab* 600 *m* SSE of Tokyo; belong to Japan; administered by U.S. 1945–68 *area* 40, *pop* 205
Bonn \ˈbän, ˈbȯn\ city W Germany on the Rhine SSE of Cologne ✻ of West German Federal Republic (often called **Bonn Republic**) *pop* 300,400
Bon·ne·ville, Lake \ˈbän-ə-ˌvil\ prehistoric lake 350 *m* long in Utah, E Nev., & S Idaho; its remnant is Great Salt Lake
Bonneville Dam dam in Columbia river *ab* 35 *m* above Vancouver, Wash.
Bonneville Salt Flats *or* **Bonneville Flats** broad level area of Great Salt Lake desert E of Wendover, Utah
Boo·thia \ˈbü-thē-ə\ peninsula N Canada W of Baffin I.; its N tip (at *ab* 72°N, 94°W) is the northernmost point on No. American mainland
Boothia, Gulf of gulf N Canada between Baffin I. & Melville peninsula on E & Boothia peninsula on W
Boo·tle \ˈbüt-ᵊl\ county borough NW England in Lancashire, N suburb of Liverpool *pop* 74,208
Bo·ra Bo·ra \ˌbōr-ə-ˈbōr-ə, ˌbȯr-ə-ˈbȯr-ə\ island S Pacific in Leeward group of the Society islands NW of Tahiti *area* 14.6
Bo·rah Peak \ˌbōr-ə-, ˌbȯr-\ mountain 12,662 *ft* E *cen* Idaho in Lost River range; highest point in state
Bo·rås \bü-ˈrōs\ city SW Sweden E of Göteborg *pop* 71,227
Bor·deaux \bȯr-ˈdō\ city & port SW France on the Garonne *pop* 266,662
Bor·di·ghe·ra \ˌbȯrd-i-ˈger-ə\ commune & port NW Italy in Liguria SW of San Remo
Bor·ger·hout \ˈbȯr-gər-ˌhau̇t\ commune N Belgium, E suburb of Antwerp *pop* 48,766
Borgne, Lake \ˈbȯ(ə)rn\ inlet of the Mississippi Sound E of New Orleans, La.
Bo·ri·sov \bə-ˈrē-səf\ city U.S.S.R. in N *cen* Belorussia on the Berezina *pop* 77,000
Bor·neo \ˈbȯr-nē-ˌō\ island Malay archipelago SW of Philippines *area* 290,012 — see BRUNEI, KALIMANTAN, SABAH, SARAWAK — **Bor·ne·an** \-nē-ən\ *adj or n*
Born·holm \ˈbȯrn-ˌhō(l)m\ island Denmark in Baltic sea ✻ Rönne *area* 228, *pop* 47,241
Bos·nia \ˈbäz-nē-ə\ region W *cen* Yugoslavia; formerly a kingdom, now part of **Bosnia and Her·ze·go·vi·na** \ˌhert-sə-gō-ˈvē-nə, ˌhərt-\ federated republic (✻ Sarajevo *area* 19,904, *pop* 3,742,852) — **Bos·ni·an** \-nē-ən\ *adj or n*
Bos·po·rus \ˈbäs-p(ə-)rəs\ *or* **Bos·pho·rus** \-f(ə-)rəs\ strait *ab* 18 *m* long between Turkey in Europe & Turkey in Asia connecting Sea of Marmara & Black sea — **Bos·po·ran** \-pə-rən\ *adj*
Bos·sier City \ˌbō-zhər-\ city NW La. *pop* 41,595
Bos·ton \ˈbȯ-stən\ **1** mountains NW Ark. & E Okla. in Ozark plateau; highest over 2000 *ft* **2** city & port ✻ of Mass. on Massachusetts Bay *pop* 641,071 **3** municipal borough & port E England in Lincolnshire ✻ of Parts of Holland *pop* 25,995 — **Bos·ton·ese** \ˌbȯ-stə-ˈnēz, -ˈnēs\ *adj* — **Bos·to·nian** \bȯ-ˈstō-nē-ən, -nyən\ *adj or n*
Bo·ta·fo·go Bay \ˌbōt-ə-ˈfō-(ˌ)gō\ inlet of Guanabara Bay in Rio de Janeiro, Brazil
Bot·a·ny Bay \ˈbät-ᵊn-ē, ˈbät-nē\ inlet of the S Pacific SE Australia in New So. Wales on S border of city of Sydney
Both·nia, Gulf of \ˈbäth-nē-ə\ arm of Baltic sea between Sweden & Finland
Bo·tswa·na \bät-ˈswän-ə\ country S Africa N of Molopo river; an independent republic since 1966, formerly Brit. protectorate of **Bechuanaland** ✻ Gaberones *area ab* 222,000, *pop* 670,000
Bot·trop \ˈbä-ˌträp\ city W Germany NNW of Essen *pop* 108,200
Bou·cher·ville \ˈbü-shər-ˌvil, ˌbü-ˌshā-\ town Canada in S Que. NE of Montreal *pop* 19,997
Bou·gain·ville \ˈbüg-ən-ˌvil, ˈbōg-, ˈbu̇g-\ island S Pacific, largest of the Solomons; chief town Kieta *area* 3880
Bou·gie \bü-ˈzhē\ city & port NE Algeria *pop* 49,930
Bouil·lon \bü-ˈyō^{n}\ town SE Belgium in the Ardennes
Boul·der \ˈbōl-dər\ **1** canyon of the Colorado between Ariz. & Nev. now covered by Lake Mead **2** city N *cen* Colo. *pop* 66,870
Boulder Dam — see HOOVER DAM
Bou·logne \bü-ˈlōn, -ˈlȯin\ *or* **Bou·logne–sur–Mer** \-ˌsu̇(ə)r-ˈme(ə)r\ city & port N France on English channel *pop* 49,276
Boulogne–Bil·lan·court \-ˌbē-ˌ(y)ä^{n}-ˈku̇(ə)r\ commune N France SW of Paris on the Seine *pop* 109,008
Boundary Peak mountain 13,145 *ft* SW Nev. in White mountains; highest in state
Bountiful city N Utah *pop* 27,853
Bour·bon·nais \ˌbu̇r-bə-ˈnā\ former province *cen* France W of Burgundy ✻ Moulins
Bourges \ˈbu̇(ə)rzh\ commune *cen* France SSE of Orléans *pop* 70,814
Bourgogne — see BURGUNDY
Bourne·mouth \ˈbō(ə)rn-məth, ˈbȯ(ə)rn-, ˈbu̇(ə)rn-\ county borough S England in Hampshire on English channel SW of Southampton *pop* 153,425
Bou·vet \ˈbü-(ˌ)vā\ island S Atlantic SSW of Cape of Good Hope at *ab* 54°S, 5°E; belongs to Norway
Bow \ˈbō\ river 315 *m* Canada in SW Alta. rising in Banff National Park & joining the Oldman to form the So. Saskatchewan
Bow·ie \ˈbü-ē\ town NE Md. NE of Washington, D.C. *pop* 35,028
Bowling Green **1** city S Ky. *pop* 36,253 **2** city NW Ohio S of Toledo *pop* 21,760
Boyne \ˈbȯin\ river 70 *m* E Ireland in Leinster flowing to Irish sea S of Drogheda
Boyn·ton Beach \ˌbȯint-ᵊn-\ city SE Fla. S of Palm Beach *pop* 18,115
Boz·caa·da \ˌbōz-jä-ˈdä\ *or anc* **Ten·e·dos** \ˈten-ə-ˌdäs\ island Turkey in NE Aegean sea S of the Dardanelles
Boze·man \ˈbōz-mən\ city SW Mont. *pop* 18,670
Bra·bant \brə-ˈbant, -ˈbänt\ **1** old duchy of W Europe including region now forming No. Brabant province of the Netherlands & Brabant & Antwerp provinces of Belgium **2** *or* **South Brabant** province *cen* Belgium ✻ Brussels *pop* 2,177,975
Bra·den·ton \ˈbrād-ᵊn-tən\ city & port W Fla. *pop* 21,040
Brad·ford \ˈbrad-fərd\ city & county borough N England in West Riding, Yorkshire *pop* 293,756
Bra·ga \ˈbräg-ə\ commune NW Portugal *pop* 101,877
Bra·gan·ça \brə-ˈgan(t)-sə\ *or* **Bra·gan·za** \-ˈgan-zə\ commune NE Portugal near Spanish border *pop* 33,928
Brah·ma·pu·tra \ˌbräm-ə-ˈp(y)ü-trə\ river 1680 *m* S Asia flowing from the Himalayas in Tibet to the Ganges delta in E India (subcontinent) — see JAMUNA, TSANGPO
Bra·ila \brə-ˈē-lə\ city E Rumania on the Danube *pop* 149,686
Brain·tree \ˈbrān-(ˌ)trē\ town E Mass. S of Boston *pop* 35,050
Brak·pan \ˈbrak-ˌpan\ city NE Republic of So. Africa in S Transvaal on the Witwatersrand S of Johannesburg *pop* 63,997
Bramp·ton \ˈbram(p)-tən\ town Canada in SE Ont. W of Toronto *pop* 41,211
Bran·co \ˈbraŋ-(ˌ)kō, -(ˌ)kü\ river 350 *m* N Brazil flowing S into the Negro
Bran·den·burg \ˈbran-dən-ˌbərg, ˈbrän-dən-ˌbu̇(ə)rg\ **1** region & former province NE *cen* Germany **2** city E Germany on the Havel WSW of Berlin *pop* 93,660
Bran·don \ˈbran-dən\ city Canada in SW Man. *pop* 31,150
Bran·dy·wine \ˈbran-dē-ˌwīn\ creek *ab* 20 *m* SE Pa. & N Del. flowing SE to join Christina river at Wilmington, Del.
Bran·ford \ˈbran-fərd\ town S Conn. E of New Haven *pop* 20,444
Brant·ford \ˈbrant-fərd\ city Canada in SE Ont. *pop* 64,421
Bras d'Or Lake \ˌbrad-ˈō(ə)r\ tidal lake *ab* 50 *m* long Canada in N.S. on Cape Breton I.
Bra·si·lia \brə-ˈzil-yə\ city ✻ (since 1960) of Brazil in Federal District in E Goiás *pop* 379,699
Bra·sov \brä-ˈshȯv\ *or formerly* **Sta·lin** \ˈstäl-ən, ˈstal-, -ˌēn\ *or* **Ora·sul Stalin** \ˌȯr-ə-ˌshül-, ˌȯr-\ city *cen* Rumania *pop* 179,316
Bra·ti·sla·va \ˌbrat-ə-ˈsläv-ə, ˌbrät-\ *or* G **Press·burg** \ˈpres-ˌbərg, -ˌbu̇(ə)rg\ *or* Hung **Po·zsony** \ˈpō-ˌzhōn-yə\ city Czechoslovakia, chief city of Slovakia, on the Danube *pop* 283,234
Bratsk \ˈbrätsk\ city U.S.S.R. in E *cen* Soviet Russia, Asia, NNE of Irkutsk near site of **Bratsk Dam** (in Angara river) *pop* 155,000
Braunschweig — see BRUNSWICK
Bravo, Rio — see RIO GRANDE
Bra·zil \brə-ˈzil\ *or* Port **Bra·sil** *or* **Es·ta·dos Uni·dos do Bra·sil** \ish-ˈtät͟h-ə-zü-ˈnē-t͟həz-ˌdü-brə-ˈzil\ country E & *cen* So. America; a federal republic ✻ Brasília *area* 3,286,169, *pop* 95,410,000 — **Bra·zil·ian** \brə-ˈzil-yən\ *adj or n*
Braz·os \ˈbraz-əs\ river *ab* 950 *m*, *cen* Tex. flowing SE into Gulf of Mexico
Braz·za·ville \ˈbraz-ə-ˌvil, ˈbräz-ə-ˌvēl\ city & port ✻ of Congo Republic on W bank of Stanley Pool in Congo river *pop* 175,000

Brea \'brā-ə\ city SW Calif. SE of Los Angeles *pop* 18,447

Breck·nock \'brek-ˌnäk, -nək\ *or* **Brec·on** \'brek-ən\ **1** *or* **Breck·nock·shire** \-ˌshi(ə)r, -shər\ *or* **Brec·on·shire** county SE Wales *area* 733, *pop* 53,234 **2** municipal borough, its ✱

Brecknock Beacons *or* **Brecon Beacons** two mountain peaks SE Wales in Brecknockshire; highest Pen y Fan 2907 *ft*

Bre·da \brā-'dä\ commune S Netherlands *pop* 120,582

Bre·genz \'brā-ˌgen(t)s\ commune W Austria on Lake Constance ✱ of Vorarlberg *pop* 24,078

Brei·ten·feld \'brīt-ᵊn-ˌfelt\ village E Germany NNW of Leipzig

Bre·men \'brem-ən, 'brä-mən\ **1** former duchy N Germany between the lower Weser & the lower Elbe **2** state NW Germany including cities of Bremen & Bremerhaven *area* 156, *pop* 754,400 **3** city & port, its ✱ *pop* 606,100

Bre·mer·ha·ven \'brem-ər-ˌhäv-ən, ˌbrā-mər-'häf-ən\ city & port NW Germany in Bremen state at mouth of the Weser; includes former city of **We·ser·mün·de** \ˌvā-zər-'m(y)ün-də, -'mœn-\ *pop* 149,300

Brem·er·ton \'brem-ər-tən, -ərt-ᵊn\ city & port W Wash. *pop* 35,307

Bren·ner \'bren-ər\ mountain pass 4494 *ft* in the Alps between Austria & Italy

Brent \'brent\ *or formerly* **Brent·ford and Chis·wick** \ˌbrent-fərd-ᵊn-'chiz-ik\ borough of W Greater London, England *pop* 278,541

Bren·ta \'brent-ə\ river 100 *m* N Italy flowing SE into the Adriatic S of Chioggia

Bre·scia \'bresh-ə, 'brā-shə\ *or anc* **Brix·ia** \'brik-sē-ə\ commune N Italy in E Lombardy ENE of Milan *pop* 204,369

Breslau — see WROCLAW

Brest \'brest\ **1** commune & port NW France in Brittany *pop* 154,023 **2** *or* **Brest Li·tovsk** \ˌbrest-lə-'tȯfsk, -'tȯvsk\ city U.S.S.R. in SW Belorussia on the Bug *pop* 122,000

Bre·ton, Cape \kāp-'bret-ᵊn, kə-'bret-, -'brit-\ headland Canada, easternmost point of Cape Breton I. & of N.S., at 59°48′ W

Bri·an·çon \brē-äⁿ-sōⁿ\ town SE France SE of Grenoble

Bridge·port \'brij-ˌpō(ə)rt, -ˌpȯ(ə)rt\ city SW Conn. on Long Island Sound *pop* 156,542

Bridge·ton \'brij-tən\ **1** city E Mo. NW of St. Louis *pop* 19,992 **2** city SW N.J. *pop* 20,435

Bridge·town \'brij-ˌtaůn\ city & port Brit. West Indies ✱ of Barbados *pop* 12,300

Brie \brē\ district & medieval county NE France E of Paris; chief town Meaux

Bri·enne \brē-en\ **1** former county NE France in the Champagne NNE of Troyes **2** town, its ✱

Bri·enz \brē-'en(t)s\ town Switzerland in SE Bern canton at NE end of **Lake of Brienz** (9 *m* long, in course of the Aare)

Brigh·ton \'brīt-ᵊn\ county borough S England in East Sussex on English channel *pop* 166,081

Brin·di·si \'brin-də-(ˌ)zē, 'brēn-\ *or anc.* **Brun·di·si·um** \ˌbrən-'diz(h)-ē-əm\ city & port SE Italy in Apulia *pop* 80,357

Bris·bane \'briz-bən, -ˌbān\ city & port E Australia ✱ of Queensland on Brisbane river near its mouth *pop* (with suburbs) 680,000

Bris·tol \'bris-tᵊl\ **1** city W *cen* Conn. WSW of Hartford *pop* 55,487 **2** town E R.I. SE of Providence *pop* 17,860 **3** city NE Tenn. *pop* 20,064 **4** channel between S Wales & SW England **5** city & county borough & port SW England in Gloucestershire on Avon river near Severn estuary *pop* 425,203 — **Bris·to·li·an** \bris-'tō-lē-ən, -'tōl-yən\ *n*

Bristol Bay arm of Bering Sea SW Alaska W of Alaska peninsula

Brit·ain \'brit-ᵊn\ **1** *or* L **Bri·tan·nia** \brə-'tan-yə, -'tan-ē-ə\ the island of Great Britain **2** UNITED KINGDOM **3** BRITISH COMMONWEALTH OF NATIONS

British America, 1 *or* **British North America** CANADA **2** all Brit. possessions in & adjacent to No. & So. America

British Bechuanaland — see BECHUANALAND

British Cameroons former Brit. trust territory W equatorial Africa comprising two areas in the Cameroons between Nigeria & Republic of Cameroon ✱ Buea *area* 34,081; divided 1961 between Nigeria (N section) & Cameroon (S section)

British Columbia province W Canada on Pacific coast ✱ Victoria *area* 359,279, *pop* 2,196,000

British Commonwealth of Nations *or* **British Commonwealth** Great Britain & Northern Ireland, the Brit. dominions & republics, & the Brit. dependencies

British East Africa, 1 KENYA — a former name **2** the former Brit. dependencies in E Africa: Kenya, Uganda, Zanzibar, & Tanganyika

British Empire Great Britain & the Brit. dominions & dependencies — a former usage

British Guiana — see GUYANA

British Honduras country Central America bordering on the Caribbean; a Brit. colony ✱ Belmopan *area* 8866, *pop* 120,000

British India the part of India formerly under direct Brit. administration — see INDIAN STATES

British Indian Ocean Territory Brit. colony in Indian ocean comprising Chagos archipelago & Aldabra, Farquhar, & Desroches islands *area* 30, *pop* 560

British Isles island group W Europe comprising Great Britain, Ireland, & adjacent islands

British Malaya former dependencies of Great Britain on Malay peninsula & in Malay archipelago including Federation of Malaya, Singapore, No. Borneo, Sarawak, & Brunei

British Solomon Islands Brit. protectorate comprising the Solomons (except Bougainville, Buka, & adjacent small islands) & the Santa Cruz islands ✱ Honiara *area* 11,500, *pop* 166,280

British Somaliland former Brit. protectorate E Africa bordering on Gulf of Aden ✱ Hargeisa; since 1960 part of Somalia

British Virgin Islands the E islands of the Virgin islands group; a Brit. possession ✱ Road Town (on Tortola I.) *area* 58, *pop* 8650

British West Indies islands of the West Indies including Jamaica, the Bahamas, Caymans, Brit. Virgin islands, Brit. Leeward & Windward islands, Trinidad, & Tobago

Brit·ta·ny \'brit-ᵊn-ē\ *or* F **Bre·tagne** \brə-tän'\ region & former province NW France SW of Normandy

Br·no \'bər-(ˌ)nō\ *or* G **Brünn** \'brüen, 'brůn\ city *cen* Czechoslovakia, chief city of Moravia *pop* 335,935

Broads \'brȯdz\ low-lying district E England in Norfolk (the **Norfolk Broads**) & Suffolk (the **Suffolk Broads**)

Brock·en \'bräk-ən\ mountain 3747 *ft* E Germany; highest in Harz mountains

Brock·ton \'bräk-tən\ city SE Mass. *pop* 89,040

Brock·ville \'bräk-ˌvil\ city Canada in SE Ont. on the St. Lawrence *pop* 19,765

Bro·ken Hill \ˌbrō-kən-\ **1** city SE Australia in W New So. Wales *pop* 30,320 **2** — see KABWE

Bromberg — see BYDGOSZCZ

Brom·ley \'bräm-lē\ borough of SE Greater London, England *pop* 304,357

Bronx \'bräŋ(k)s\ *or* **The Bronx** borough of New York City on the mainland NE of Manhattan I. *pop* 1,472,216

Brook·field \'brůk-ˌfēld\ **1** village NE Ill. W of Chicago *pop* 20,284 **2** city SE Wis. W of Milwaukee *pop* 32,140

Brook·line \'brůk-ˌlīn\ town E Mass. W of Boston *pop* 58,886

Brook·lyn \'brůk-lən\ borough of New York City at SW end of Long I. *pop* 2,601,852 — **Brook·lyn·ite** \-lə-ˌnīt\ *n*

Brooklyn Center village SE Minn. NW of Minneapolis *pop* 35,173

Brooklyn Park village E Minn. NW of Minneapolis *pop* 26,230

Brooks \'brůks\ mountain range N Alaska extending from Kotzebue Sound to Canada border; highest peak Mt. Michelson 9239 *ft*

Bros·sard \brō-'sär(d)\ town Canada in S Que. SE of Montreal *pop* 23,452

Browns·ville \'braůnz-ˌvil, -vəl\ city & port S Tex. on Rio Grande *pop* 52,522

Brown·wood \'braůn-ˌwůd\ city *cen* Tex. *pop* 17,368

Bruges \'brüzh, brüezh\ *or* Flem **Brug·ge** \'brœg-ə\ commune NW Belgium ✱ of West Flanders *pop* 51,303

Bru·nei \'brü-ˌnī, -(ˌ)nā\ **1** sultanate & Brit. protectorate NW Borneo *area* 2226, *pop* 140,000 **2** city & port, its ✱ *pop* 36,574

Bruns·wick \'brənz-(ˌ)wik\ **1** city & port SE Ga. on Atlantic coast *pop* 19,585 **2** town SW Me. *pop* 16,195 **3** city NE Ohio SSW of Cleveland *pop* 15,852 **4** *or* G **Braun·schweig** \'braůn-ˌshwīg, -ˌshfīk\ former state *cen* Germany ✱ Brunswick **5** *or* G **Braunschweig** city W *cen* Germany W of Berlin *pop* 225,600

Brus·sels \'brəs-əlz\ *or* F **Bru·xelles** \brüe(k)-sel\ *or* Flem **Brus·sel** \'brœs-əl\city ✱ of Belgium & of Brabant *pop* 164,013

Bruttium — see CALABRIA

Bry·an \'brī-ən\ city E *cen* Tex. *pop* 33,719

Bryansk *or* **Briansk** \brē-'än(t)sk\ city U.S.S.R. in SW Soviet Russia, Europe, SW of Moscow *pop* 318,000

Bryce Canyon National Park \'brīs\ reservation S Utah NE of Zion National Park *area* 56

Bu·bas·tis \byü-'bas-təs\ ancient city N Egypt; ruins near modern city of Zagazig

Bu·ca·ra·man·ga \ˌbü-kə-rə-'mäŋ-gə\ city N Colombia NNE of Bogotá *pop* 279,703

Bu·cha·rest \'b(y)ü-kə-ˌrest\ *or* Rum **Bu·cu·res·ti** \ˌbü-kə-'resht(-ē)\ city ✱ of Rumania *pop* 1,457,802

Bu·chen·wald \'bü-kən-ˌwȯld, -ˌvält\ village E Germany NW of Weimar

Buck·ing·ham \'bək-iŋ-əm, *US also* -iŋ-ˌham\ *or* **Buck·ing·ham·shire** \-ˌshi(ə)r, -shər\ *or* **Bucks** \'bəks\ county SE *cen* England ✱ Aylesbury *area* 749, *pop* 586,211

Bu·da·pest \'büd-ə-ˌpest *also* 'byüd-, 'bůd-, -ˌpesht\ city ✱ of Hungary on the Danube *pop* 1,934,000

Buddh Ga·ya \ˌbůd-gə-'yä\ village NE India in *cen* Bihar

Budweis — see CESKE BUDEJOVICE

Bue·na Park \ˌbyü-nə-\ city Calif. near Los Angeles *pop* 63,646

Bue·na·ven·tu·ra \ˌbwen-ə-ˌven-'t(y)ůr-ə, ˌbwā-nə-\ city & port W Colombia on the Pacific *pop* 279,703

Bue·nos Ai·res \ˌbwā-nə-'sa(ə)r-ēz, ˌbō-nə-, -'se(ə)r-, -'sī(ə)r-\ city & port ✱ of Argentina on Río de la Plata *pop* 3,600,000

Buenos Aires, Lake lake 80 *m* long S Argentina & S Chile in the Andes; drains to the Pacific

Buf·fa·lo \'bəf-ə-ˌlō\ city & port W N.Y. on Lake Erie & Niagara river *pop* 462,768

Bug \'büg\ **1** river 450 *m, cen* Poland rising in W Ukraine, U.S.S.R., & flowing into the Vistula **2** river 500 *m* U.S.S.R. in SW Ukraine flowing SE to the Dnieper estuary

Bu·gan·da \b(y)ü-'gan-də\ province & former native kingdom E Africa in SE Uganda ✱ Kampala

Buitenzorg — see BOGOR

Bu·jum·bu·ra \ˌbü-jəm-'bůr-ə\ *or formerly* **Usum·bu·ra** \ˌü-səm-\ city ✱ of Burundi on Lake Tanganyika *pop* 70,000

Bu·ka \'bü-kə\ island W Pacific in the Solomons N of Bougainville

Bu·ka·vu \bü-'käv-(ˌ)ü\ *or formerly* **Cos·ter·mans·ville** \'käs-tər-mənz-ˌvil\ city E Zaire at S end of Lake Kivu *pop* 134,861

Bu·kha·ra \bü-'kär-ə, -'kar-, -'här-, -'har-\ *or* **Bo·kha·ra** \bō-\ **1** former emirate W Asia occupying region around city of Bukhara **2** city U.S.S.R. in Soviet Central Asia in W Uzbek Republic E of the Amu Darya *pop* 112,000 — **Bu·kha·ran** *or* **Bo·kha·ran** \-ən\ *adj or n*

Bu·kit·ting·gi \ˌbü-kə-'tiŋ-gē\ *or formerly* **Fort de Kock** \-də-'kȯk, -'käk\ city Indonesia in W *cen* Sumatra *pop* 51,456

Bu·ko·vi·na *or* **Bu·co·vi·na** \ˌbü-kə-'vē-nə\ region E *cen* Europe in foothills of E Carpathians; now in NE Rumania & W Ukraine

Bu·la·wayo *or* **Bu·lu·wayo** \ˌbůl-ə-'wā-(ˌ)ō, -'wī-\ city SW Southern Rhodesia, chief town of Matabeleland *pop* 210,000

Bul·gar·ia \ˌbəl-'gar-ē-ə, bůl-, -'ger-\ country SE Europe on Black sea; a republic ✱ Sofia *area* 42,858, *pop* 8,540,000

Bull Run \'bůl-'rən\ stream 20 *m* N Va. W of Washington, D.C., flowing into Occoquan creek (small tributary of the Potomac)

Bun·del·khand \'bůn-dᵊl-ˌkənd\ region N *cen* India containing headwaters of the Jumna; now chiefly in N Madhya Pradesh

Bun·ker Hill \ˌbəŋ-kər-\ height in Charlestown section of Boston, Mass.

Bur·bank \'bər-ˌbaŋk\ city SW Calif. *pop* 88,871

Bur·gas \bu̇r-ˈgäs\ city & port SE Bulgaria *pop* 129,128
Bur·gen·land \ˈbər-gən-ˌland, ˈbu̇r-gən-ˌlänt\ province E Austria SE of Vienna on Hungarian border ✽ Eisenstadt
Bur·gos \ˈbu̇(ə)r-ˌgōs\ **1** province N Spain *area* 5480, *pop* 358,075 **2** city, its ✽ & once ✽ of Old Castile *pop* 119,915
Bur·gun·dy \ˈbər-gən-dē\ *or* F **Bour·gogne** \bür-gȯn^{y}\ **1** region & former kingdom, duchy, & province E France S of Champagne **2** county France E of Burgundy province; later called **Franche-Com·té** \frä^{n}sh-(ə-)kō^{n}-tā\ — **Bur·gun·di·an** \(ˌ)bər-ˈgən-dē-ən\ *adj or n*
Bur·lin·game \ˈbər-lən-ˌgām\ city W Calif. SSE of San Francisco on San Francisco Bay *pop* 27,320
Bur·ling·ton \ˈbər-liŋ-tən\ **1** city SE Iowa *pop* 32,366 **2** town NE Mass. N of Boston *pop* 21,980 **3** city N *cen* N.C. *pop* 35,930 **4** city NW Vt. *pop* 38,633 **5** town Canada in SE Ont. N of Hamilton *pop* 87,023
Bur·ma \ˈbər-mə\ *or* **Union of Burma** country SE Asia on Bay of Bengal; a federal republic ✽ Rangoon *area* 261,789, *pop* 26,980,000 — **Bur·man** \ˈbər-mən\ *adj or n*
Burn·ley \ˈbərn-lē\ county borough NW England in Lancashire N of Manchester *pop* 76,483
Burns·ville \ˈbərnz-ˌvil\ village SE Minn. S of Minneapolis *pop* 19,940
Bur·rard \bə-ˈrärd\ inlet of Strait of Georgia, W Canada, in B.C.; city of Vancouver is situated on it
Bur·sa \bu̇r-ˈsä, ˈbər-sə\ *or formerly* **Bru·sa** \brü-ˈsä, ˈbrü-sə\ city NW Turkey in Asia near Sea of Marmara *pop* 211,644
Bu·run·di \bu̇-ˈrün-dē\ *or formerly* **Urun·di** \u̇-ˈrün-\ country E *cen* Africa; a kingdom ✽ Usumbura *area* 10,744, *pop* 3,620,000 — see RUANDA-URUNDI — **Bu·run·di·an** \-dē-ən\ *adj or n*
Bury \ˈber-ē\ county borough NW England in Lancashire NNW of Manchester *pop* 67,776
Bur·yat, *or* **Bur·iat, Republic** \bu̇r-ˌyät-, ˌbu̇-ē-ˌät-\ autonomous republic U.S.S.R. in S Soviet Russia, Asia, adjacent to Outer Mongolia & E of Lake Baikal ✽ Ulan-Ude *area* 127,020, *pop* 812,000 — **Buryat** *or* **Buriat** *n*
Bury Saint Ed·munds \ˌber-ē-sānt-ˈed-mən(d)z, -sənt-\ municipal borough SE England ✽ of West Suffolk *pop* 25,629
Bu·shire \bü-ˈshi(ə)r\ city & port SW Iran *pop* 40,000
Busra — see BASRA
Butaritari — see MAKIN
Bute \ˈbyüt\ **1** island SW Scotland W of Firth of Clyde **2** *or* **Bute·shire** \-ˌshi(ə)r, -shər\ county SW Scotland comprising Bute, Arran, the Cumbraes, & several smaller islands in the Firth of Clyde ✽ Rothesay (on Bute) *area* 218, *pop* 14,357
But·ler \ˈbət-lər\ city W Pa. N of Pittsburgh *pop* 18,691
Butte \ˈbyüt\ city SW Mont. *pop* 23,368
Bu·tung \ˈbü-ˌtüŋ\ *or* **Bu·ton** \ˈbü-ˌtȯn\ *or* D **Boe·toeng** \ˈbü-ˌtüŋ\ island Indonesia off SE Celebes *area ab* 2000
Bu·zau \bə-ˈzō, -ˈzau̇\ city E Rumania *pop* 55,382
Buzzards Bay \ˌbəz-ərdz-\ inlet of the Atlantic SE Mass. W of Cape Cod
Byd·goszcz \ˈbid-ˌgȯsh(ch)\ *or* G **Brom·berg** \ˈbräm-ˌbərg, ˈbrȯm-ˌberk\ city NW *cen* Poland NE of Poznan *pop* 279,000
Byelgorod–Dnestrovski — see BELGOROD-DNESTROVSKI
Byelorussia — see BELORUSSIA — **Byelorussian** *adj or n*
Byrd Land — see MARIE BYRD LAND
By·tom \ˈbē-ˌtȯm, ˈbi-\ *or* G **Beu·then** \ˈbȯit-ᵊn\ city SW Poland in Silesia *pop* 186,700
Byzantium — see ISTANBUL
Ca·ba·na·tuan \ˌkäb-ə-nə-ˈtwän\ city Philippines in S *cen* Luzon *pop* 97,000
Ca·bin·da \kə-ˈbin-də\ territory W equatorial Africa on the Atlantic between Congo Republic & Zaire; belongs to Angola ✽ Cabinda *area* 3000, *pop* 58,547
Cab·ot \ˈkab-ət\ strait *ab* 70 *m* wide E Canada between SW Nfld. & Cape Breton I. connecting Gulf of St. Lawrence with the Atlantic
Ca·ca·hua·mil·pa \ˌkäk-ə-wə-ˈmil-pə\ caverns S Mexico in Guerrero NNE of Taxco
Cá·ce·res \ˈkäs-ə-ˌräs\ **1** province W Spain in N Estremadura *area* 7667, *pop* 457,777 **2** city, its ✽ *pop* 56,064
Cache la Pou·dre \ˌkash-lə-ˈpüd-ər\ river 125 *m* N Colo. flowing into the So. Platte
Cad·do \ˈkad-(ˌ)ō\ lake 20 *m* long NW La. & NE Tex. draining to Red river
Cá·diz \kə-ˈdiz; ˈkād-əz, ˈkäd-, ˈkad-; *Sp* ˈkä-(ˌ)thēs\ **1** province SW Spain in Andalusia *area* 2834, *pop* 885,433 **2** *or anc* **Ga·dir** \ˈgād-ər\ *or* **Ga·des** \ˈgād-(ˌ)ēz\ city & port, its ✽, on Bay of Cádiz NW of Gibraltar *pop* 134,315
Cae·li·an \ˈsē-lē-ən\ hill in Rome, Italy, one of seven on which the ancient city was built — see AVENTINE
Caen \kä^{n}\ city NW France in Normandy *pop* 110,262
Caer·nar·von *or* **Car·nar·von** \kär-ˈnär-vən, kər-\ **1** *or* **Caer·nar·von·shire** *or* **Car·nar·von·shire** \-ˌshi(ə)r, -shər\ county NW Wales *area* 569, *pop* 122,852 **2** municipal borough, its ✽
Cae·sa·rea \ˌsē-zə-ˈrē-ə; ˌses-ə-, ˌsez-\ **1** ancient seaport Palestine 22 *m* S of Haifa **2** *or* **Caesarea Mazaca** — see KAYSERI
Caesarea Phi·lip·pi \-ˈfil-ə-ˌpī, -fə-ˈlip-ˌī\ ancient city N Palestine SW of Mt. Hermon; site at modern village of Baniyas \ˌban-ē-ˈyas\ in SW Syria
Caesena — see CESENA
Ca·ga·yan \ˌkäg-ə-ˈyän\ *or* **Rio Gran·de de Cagayan** \ˌrē-ō-ˈgrän-dē-ˌdā-\ river 220 *m* Philippines in NE Luzon flowing N
Ca·glia·ri \ˈkäl-yə-(ˌ)rē\ commune & port Italy ✽ of Sardinia *pop* 221,427
Ca·guas \ˈkä(g)-ˌwäs\ city E *cen* Puerto Rico *pop* 63,215
Ca·ho·kia \kə-ˈhō-kē-ə\ village SW Ill. S of East St. Louis *pop* 20,649
Cahokia Mounds group of prehistoric Indian mounds Ill. ENE of East St. Louis
Ca·hors \kä-ˈ(h)ȯ(ə)r\ city S *cen* France on the Lot N of Toulouse *pop* 19,203
Caicos — see TURKS AND CAICOS
Cairn·gorm \ˈka(ə)rn-ˌgȯ(ə)rm, ˈke(ə)rn-\ **1** mountain range of the Grampians NE *cen* Scotland; highest point Ben Macdhui 4296 *ft* **2** mountain 4084 *ft* in Cairngorm mountains in W Banffshire
Cai·ro \ˈkī-(ˌ)rō\ city N Egypt ✽ of Egypt *pop* 4,961,000 — **Cai·rene** \kī-ˈrēn\ *adj or n*
Caith·ness \ˈkāth-nəs\ *or* **Caith·ness–shire** \-nəs(h)-ˌshi(ə)r, -shər\ county N Scotland ✽ Wick *area* 684, *pop* 27,481
Ca·ja·mar·ca \ˌkä-hə-ˈmär-kə\ city NW Peru *pop* 27,600
Ca·jon \kə-ˈhōn\ pass 4301 *ft* S Calif. NW of San Bernardino between San Bernardino & San Gabriel mountains
Cal·a·bar \ˈkal-ə-ˌbär\ city & port SE Nigeria *pop* 88,621
Ca·la·bria \kə-ˈlā-brē-ə, -ˈläb-rē-\ **1** district of ancient Italy comprising area forming heel of the Italian peninsula; now the S part of Apulia **2** *or* It **Le Ca·la·brie** \ˌlā-kə-ˈläb-rē-ˌā\ *or anc* **Brut·ti·um** \ˈbru̇t-ē-əm, ˈbrət-\ region S Italy occupying toe of the Italian peninsula ✽ Catanzaro *area* 5823, *pop* 2,067,154 — **Ca·la·bri·an** \kə-ˈlā-brē-ən, -ˈläb-rē-\ *adj or n*
Ca·lah \ˈkā-lə\ *or* **Kal·hu** \ˈkal-(ˌ)hü\ ancient city ✽ of Assyria on the Tigris 20 *m* SW of modern Mosul; its site now called **Nim·rud** \nim-ˈrüd\
Ca·lais \ka-ˈlā, ˈkal-(ˌ)ā\ city & port N France on Strait of Dover *pop* 74,624
Calais, Pas de — see DOVER (Strait of)
Ca·la·mian \ˌkäl-ə-mē-ˈän\ islands W Philippines NE of Palawan I.
Cal·ca·sieu \ˈkal-kə-ˌshü\ river 200 *m* SW La. flowing through **Calcasieu Lake** (*ab* 15 *m* long) & **Calcasieu Pass** (channel 5 *m* long) into Gulf of Mexico
Cal·cut·ta \kal-ˈkət-ə\ city & port E India on Hooghly river ✽ of West Bengal *pop* 3,158,838 — **Cal·cut·tan** \-ˈkət-ᵊn\ *n*
Cal·e·do·nia \ˌkal-ə-ˈdō-nyə, -nē-ə\ — see SCOTLAND — **Cal·e·do·nian** \-nyən, -nē-ən\ *adj or n*
Caledonian Canal ship canal N Scotland in the Great Glen connecting Loch Linnhe & Moray firth & uniting lochs Ness, Oich, Lochy, & Eil
Cal·ga·ry \ˈkal-gə-rē\ city Canada in SW Alta. *pop* 403,319
Ca·li \ˈkäl-ē\ city W Colombia on the Cauca *pop* 820,809
Calicut — KOZHIKODE
Cal·i·for·nia \ˌkal-ə-ˈfȯr-nyə\ state SW U.S. ✽ Sacramento *area* 158,693, *pop* 19,953,134 — **Cal·i·for·nian** \-nyən\ *adj or n*
California, Gulf of arm of the Pacific NW Mexico between Baja California & states of Sonora & Sinaloa
Ca·llao \kə-ˈyä-(ˌ)ō, -ˈyau̇\ city & port W Peru on Callao Bay W of Lima *pop* 321,700
Ca·loo·sa·hatch·ee \kə-ˌlü-sə-ˈhach-ē\ river 75 *m* S Fla. flowing W into Gulf of Mexico
Calpe — see GIBRALTAR (Rock of)
Cal·ta·nis·set·ta \ˌkäl-tə-ni-ˈset-ə, ˌkal-\ commune Italy in *cen* Sicily *pop* 64,402
Cal·u·met \ˈkal-yə-ˌmet, -mət\ industrial region NW Ind. & NE Ill. SE of & adjacent to Chicago; includes chiefly cities of East Chicago, Gary, & Hammond, Ind., & Calumet City & Lansing, Ill.
Calumet City city NE Ill. S of Chicago *pop* 32,956
Calumet Harbor harbor district SE Chicago, Ill., on Lake Michigan at mouth of Calumet river draining Lake Calumet in S Chicago
Cal·va·dos reef \ˌkal-və-ˈdōs\ *or* F **Ro·chers du Calvados** \rō-ˌshād-ə-\ long reef of rocks NW France in English channel at mouth of Orne river
Cal·va·ry \ˈkalv-(ə-)rē\ *or* Heb **Gol·go·tha** \ˈgäl-gə-thə, gäl-ˈgäth-ə\ place outside ancient Jerusalem where Christ was crucified
Cal·y·don \ˈkal-ə-ˌdän, -əd-ᵊn\ ancient city *cen* Greece in S Aetolia near Gulf of Patras — **Cal·y·do·nian** \ˌkal-ə-ˈdō-nyən, -nē-ən\ *adj*
Calydon, Gulf of — see PATRAS (Gulf of)
Cam \ˈkam\ river 40 *m* E *cen* England in Cambridgeshire flowing into the Ouse
Ca·ma·güey \ˌkam-ə-ˈgwā\ city E *cen* Cuba *pop* (municipality) 178,600
Ca·margue \kə-ˈmärg\ *or* **La Camargue** \ˌläk-ə-\ marshy island S France in delta of the Rhone
Cam·a·ril·lo \ˌkam-ə-ˈrē-(ˌ)ō\ city SW Calif. W of Los Angeles *pop* 19,219
Cam·ba·luc \ˈkam-bə-ˌlək\ KHANBALIK
Cam·bay \kam-ˈbā\ city & former port W India in Gujarat W of Baroda *pop* 51,291
Cambay, Gulf of inlet of Arabian sea in India N of Bombay
Cam·ber·well \ˈkam-bər-ˌwel, -wəl\ **1** city SE Australia in S Victoria E of Melbourne *pop* 99,908 **2** former metropolitan borough S London, England, now part of Southwark
Cambodia — see KHMER REPUBLIC
Cam·brai *or formerly* **Cam·bray** \kam-ˈbrā, kä^{n}-\ city N France on the Scheldt *pop* 37,532
Cam·bria \ˈkam-brē-ə\ — see WALES
Cam·bri·an \ˈkam-brē-ən\ mountains *cen* Wales
Cam·bridge \ˈkām-brij\ **1** city E Mass. W of Boston *pop* 100,361 **2** *or* **Cam·bridge·shire and Isle of Ely** \-ˌshi(ə)r[-shər], -ˈē-lē\ county E England enlarged 1965 by amalgamation with Isle of Ely ✽ Cambridge *area* 831, *pop* 302,507 **3** *or* ML **Can·ta·brig·ia** \ˌkant-ə-ˈbrij-(ē-)ə\ municipal borough E England on the Cam ✽ of Cambridgeshire *pop* 98,519
Cam·den \ˈkam-dən\ **1** city S Ark. *pop* 15,147 **2** city & port SW N.J. on the Delaware opposite Philadelphia, Pa. *pop* 102,551 **3** borough of N Greater London, England *pop* 200,784
Cam·er·oon \ˌkam-ə-ˈrün\ **1** *or* **Fa·ko** \ˈfäk-(ˌ)ō\ massif 13,353 *ft* Republic of Cameroon NW of Buea near coast **2** *or* **Cam·er·oun** \-ˈrün\ country W equatorial Africa in Cameroons region; a republic, formerly a trust territory under France ✽ Yaoundé *area*

ə abut ᵊ kitten, F table ər further a back ā bake
ä cot, cart ȧ F bac au̇ out ch chin e less ē easy
g gift i trip ī life j joke k̲ G ich ^{n} F vin ŋ sing
ō flow ȯ flaw œ F bœuf œ̄ F feu ȯi coin th thing
th̲ this ü loot u̇ foot ue G Füllen ue̅ F rue y yet
^{y} F digne \dēn^{y}\, nuit \nw^{y}ē\ yü few yu̇ furious zh vision

183,080, *pop* 5,840,000 — **Cam·er·oo·nian** \-'rü-nē-ən, -nyən\ *adj or n*

Cam·er·oons \,kam-ə-'rünz\ region W Africa bordering on NE Gulf of Guinea formerly comprising Brit. & French Cameroons but now divided between Nigeria & Republic of Cameroon — **Cam·er·oo·nian** \-'rü-nē-ən, -nyən\ *adj or n*

Ca·mi·guin \,kam-ə-'gēn\ **1** island N Philippines N of Luzon; site of Camiguin Volcano 2750 *ft* **2** island S Philippines off N coast of Mindanao — see HIBOKHIBOK

Ca·mo·ni·ca \kə-'mò-ni-kə\ valley N Italy in the Alps N of Brescia

Ca·mo·tes \,kä-'mō-,tās\ sea S *cen* Philippines W of Leyte

Cam·pa·gna di Ro·ma \kam-,pän-yə-dē-'rō-mə, -'pan-\ *or* **Roman Campagna** region *cen* Italy around Rome *area ab* 800

Cam·pa·nia\kam-'pā-nyə, -nē-ə\ region S Italy bordering on Tyrrhenian sea ✱ Naples *area* 5214, *pop* 5,132,860 — **Cam·pa·nian** \-nyən, -nē-ən\ *adj or n*

Camp·bell \'kam-(b)əl\ city W Calif. SW of San José *pop* 24,770

Cam·pe·che \kam-'pē-chē, käm-'pā-chā\ **1** state SE Mexico in W Yucatán peninsula *area* 19,670, *pop* 250,391 **2** city & port, its ✱, on Bay of Campeche *pop* 59,627

Campeche, Bay of the SW section of Gulf of Mexico

Cam·pi·na Gran·de \kam-,pē-nə-'gran-də, -dē\ city E Brazil in E Paraíba *pop* 157,149

Cam·pi·nas \kam-'pē-nəs\ city SE Brazil in E São Paulo state *pop* 252,145

Cam·po·bel·lo \,kam-pə-'bel-(,)ō\ island Canada in SW N.B.

Cam·po·for·mi·do \,kam-(,)pō-'fòr-mə-,dō\ *or formerly* **Cam·po For·mio** \-mē-,ō\ village NE Italy SW of Udine

Cam·pos \'kam-pəs\ city SE Brazil in Rio de Janeiro state on the Paraíba *pop* 389,045

Cam Ranh Bay \,kam-,ran-\ inlet of So. China sea SE Vietnam *ab* 180 *m* NE of Saigon

Ca·na \'kā-nə\ village N Palestine in Galilee 4 *m* NE of Nazareth; now in Israel

Ca·naan \'kā-nən\ ancient region corresponding vaguely to later Palestine

Can·a·da \'kan-əd-ə\ country N No. America including Nfld. & Arctic islands N of mainland; a dominion of the British Commonwealth ✱ Ottawa *area* 3,560,238, *pop* 21,681,000

Ca·na·di·an \kə-'nād-ē-ən\ *or, above its junction with the No. Canadian,* **South Canadian** river 906 *m* S *cen* U.S. flowing E from NE N. Mex. to Arkansas river in E Okla.

Canadian Shield — see LAURENTIAN HIGHLANDS

Canal Zone *or* **Panama Canal Zone** strip of territory Panama under perpetual lease to the U.S. for Panama canal; administrative center Balboa Heights; *area* 553, *pop* 44,198

Can·an·dai·gua \,kan-ən-'dā-gwə\ lake 15 *m* long W *cen* N.Y.; one of the Finger Lakes

Ca·nary \kə-'ne(ə)r-ē\ islands in the Atlantic off NW coast of Africa S of Madeira belonging to Spain *area* 2807, *pop* 1,170,224 — see LAS PALMAS, SANTA CRUZ DE TENERIFE — **Ca·nar·i·an** \kə-'ner-ē-ən\ *adj or n*

Ca·nav·er·al \kə-'nav-(ə-)rəl\ **1** peninsula E Fla. enclosing Mosquito lagoon & Indian river (lagoon) **2** — see KENNEDY (Cape)

Can·ber·ra \'kan-,ber-ə, -b(ə-)rə\ city ✱ of Australia in Australian Capital Territory SW of Sydney *pop* 119,235

Can·dia \'kan-dē-ə\ **1** CRETE **2** *or* **He·rak·li·on** \hi-'rak-lē-ən\ *or* NGk **Irá·kli·on** \i-'rak-\ city & port Greece on N coast of Crete *pop* 77,783

Candia, Sea of — see CRETE (Sea of)

Ca·nea \kə-'nē-ə\ *or* NGk **Kha·niá** \kän-'yä\ *or anc.* **Cy·do·nia** \sī-'dō-nē-ə, -nyə\ city & port Greece ✱ of Crete *pop* 40,452

Ca·ney *or* **El Caney** \,el-kə-'nā\ town E Cuba NE of Santiago de Cuba

Can·nae \'kan-(,)ē\ ancient town SE Italy in Apulia WSW of modern Barletta

Can·na·nore \'kan-ə-,nō(ə)r, -,nò(ə)r\ *or* **Ka·na·nur** \,kən-ə-'nù(ə)r\ city SW India in Kerala on Malabar coast NNW of Calicut *pop* 48,960

Cannes \'kan\ commune & port SE France *pop* 67,152

Ca·no·pus \kə-'nō-pəs\ ancient city N Egypt E of Alexandria at modern Abukir — **Ca·no·pic** \kə-'nō-pik, -'näp-ik\ *adj*

Can·so, Cape \'kan(t)-(,)sō\ cape Canada at NE end of N.S. mainland

Canso, Strait of narrow channel Canada separating Cape Breton I. from mainland of Nova Scotia

Can·ta·bri·an \kan-'tā-brē-ən\ mountains N & NW Spain running E–W near coast of Bay of Biscay — see CERREDO

Cantabrigia — see CAMBRIDGE

Can·ter·bury \'kant-ə(r)-,ber-ē\ **1** city SE Australia in E New So. Wales, SW suburb of Sydney *pop* 115,802 **2** city & county borough SE England in Kent *pop* 33,157 — **Can·ter·bu·ri·an** \,kant-ə(r)-'byùr-ē-ən\ *adj*

Can·ti·gny \,kä^n-,tēn-'yē\ village N France S of Amiens

Can·ton \'kant-ᵊn\ **1** town E Mass. S of Boston *pop* 17,100 **2** city NE Ohio *pop* 110,053 **3** island (atoll) *cen* Pacific in Phoenix islands; controlled jointly by U.S. & Great Britain

Can·ton \'kan-,tän, kan-'\ **1** — see PEARL **2** *or* **Kwang·chow** *or* **Kuang–chou** \'gwäŋ-'jō\ city & port SE China ✱ of Kwangtung on Pearl river *pop* 1,840,000

Cantyre — see KINTYRE

Canyon de Chelly National Monument \də-'shā\ reservation NE Ariz. containing cliff-dweller ruins *area* 131

Can·yon·lands National Park \'kan-yən-,lan(d)z\ reservation SE Utah surrounding junction of Colorado & Green rivers *area* 403

Cap d'An·tibes \,kap-dä^n-'tēb\ cape SE France SW of Antibes

Cap–de–la–Ma·de·leine \,kap-də-,lä-,mad-ᵊl-'än\ city Canada in S Que. on the St. Lawrence ENE of Trois-Rivières *pop* 31,463

Cape Bret·on \käp-'bret-ᵊn, kə-'bret-, -'brit-\ **1** island Canada in NE N.S. *area* 3970 **2** — see BRETON (Cape)

Cape Breton Highlands National Park reservation Canada in NE N.S. near N end of Cape Breton I. *area* 390

Cape Cod Bay the S end of Massachusetts Bay W of Cape Cod

Cape Cod National Seashore — see COD (Cape)

Cape Fear \'fi(ə)r\ **1** river 202 *m, cen* & SE N.C. flowing SE into the Atlantic **2** — see FEAR (Cape)

Cape Gi·rar·deau \jə-'rä(r)d-(,)ō\ city SE Mo. *pop* 31,282

Cape Hatteras National Seashore Recreational Area — see HATTERAS

Cape of Good Hope, 1 — see GOOD HOPE (Cape of) **2** *or* **Cape Province** *or* **Kaap·land** \'käp-,länt\ *or formerly* **Cape Colony** province S Republic of So. Africa ✱ Cape Town *area* 278,465, *pop* 6,199,634

Ca·per·na·um \kə-'pər-nē-əm\ city of ancient Palestine on NW shore of Sea of Galilee

Cape Sa·ble \'sā-bəl\ **1** island 7 *m* long Canada off S coast of N.S. **2** — see SABLE (Cape)

Cape Town *or* **Cape·town** \'käp-,taùn\ *or* Afrikaans **Kaap·stad** \'käp-,stät\ city & port, legislative ✱ of Republic of So. Africa & ✱ of Cape of Good Hope, on Table Bay *pop* 508,341 — **Cape·to·ni·an** \käp-'tō-nē-ən\ *n*

Cape Verde \'vərd\ **1** islands in the Atlantic off W Africa belonging to Portugal ✱ Praia (on São Tiago) *area* 1557, *pop* 246,000 **2** — see VERT (Cape) — **Cape Verd·ian** \'vərd-ē-ən\ *n*

Cape York peninsula \'yó(ə)rk\ peninsula NE Australia in N Queensland having at its N tip **Cape York** (on Torres strait)

Cap Fer·rat \,kap-fə-'rä\ cape SE France E of Nice

Cap Hai·tien \kap-'hā-shən\ *or* F **Cap–Ha·i·tien** \kà-pà-ē-syaⁿ, -ē-tyaⁿ\ city & port N Haiti *pop* 44,123

Cap·i·to·line \'kap-ət-ᵊl-,īn, *Brit often* kə-'pit-ᵊl-\ hill in Rome, Italy, one of seven on which the ancient city was built — see AVENTINE

Capitol Reef National Park reservation S *cen* Utah containing archaeological remains, petrified forests, & unusual erosion forms *area* 378

Capodistria — see KOPER

Caporetto — see KOBARID

Cap·pa·do·cia \kap-ə-'dō-sh(ē-)ə\ ancient district E Asia Minor chiefly in valley of the upper Kizil Irmak in modern Turkey ✱ Caesarea Mazaca — **Cap·pa·do·cian** \-sh(ē-)ən\ *adj or n*

Ca·pri \kə-'prē, kə-; 'käp-(,)rē, 'kap-\ *or anc* **Cap·re·ae** \'kap-rē-,ē\ island Italy S Bay of Naples *area* 5 — **Ca·pri·ote** \'kap-rē-,ōt, 'käp-, -rē-ət\ *n*

Capsa — see GAFSA

Cap·ua \'kap-yə-wə\ commune S Italy on the Volturno N of Naples NW of site of ancient city of Capua *pop* 19,176 — **Cap·u·an** \-wən\ *adj or n*

Cap·u·lin, Mount \'kap-(y)ə-lən\ **1** cinder cone 8215 *ft* NE N.Mex. ESE of Raton; main feature of **Capulin Mountain National Monument** (*area* 1) **2** *or* **Capulin Peak** mountain 9198 *ft* N N.Mex. NW of Los Alamos

Ca·ra·cas \kə-'rak-əs, -'räk-\ city ✱ of Venezuela near Caribbean coast *pop* 786,863

Car·bon·dale \'kär-bən-,dāl\ city SW Ill. *pop* 22,816

Car·cas·sonne \,kär-kə-'sòn, -'sōn\ city S France on the Aude SE of Toulouse *pop* 43,616

Car·che·mish \'kär-kə-,mish, kär-'kē-mish\ ruined city S Turkey on Euphrates river at Syrian border N of modern Jerablus, Syria

Cár·de·nas \'kärd-ᵊn-,äs\ city & port N Cuba E of Matanzas *pop* 73,460

Car·diff \'kärd-əf\ county borough & port ✱ of Wales & of Glamorganshire on Bristol channel *pop* 278,221

Car·di·gan \'kärd-i-gən\ *or* **Car·di·gan·shire** \-,shi(ə)r, -shər\ county W Wales ✱ Aberystwyth *area* 692, *pop* 54,844

Cardigan Bay inlet of St. George's channel on W coast of Wales

Carelia — see KARELIA

Ca·ren·tan \,kar-ən-'täⁿ\ town NW France at base of Cotentin peninsula

Car·ia \'kar-ē-ə, 'ker-\ ancient region SW Asia Minor bordering on Aegean sea ✱ Halicarnassus — **Car·i·an** \-ē-ən\ *adj or n*

Ca·rib·be·an \,kar-ə-'bē-ən, kə-'rib-ē-\ sea arm of Atlantic ocean bounded on N & E by West Indies, on S by So. America, & on W by Central America

Car·ib·bees \'kar-ə-,bēz\ LESSER ANTILLES

Car·i·boo \'kar-ə-,bü\ mountains W Canada in E *cen* B.C. W of the Rocky mountains; highest point *ab* 11,750 *ft*

Ca·rin·thia \kə-'rin(t)-thē-ə\ region *cen* Europe in E Alps; once a duchy, Austrian crown land 1849–1918, divided between Austria & Yugoslavia 1918 — **Ca·rin·thi·an** \-thē-ən\ *adj or n*

Car·lisle \kär-'lī(ə)l, kər-, 'kär-,\ **1** borough S *cen* Pa. *pop* 18,079 **2** city & county borough NW England ✱ of Cumberland *pop* 71,497

Car·low \'kär-,lō\ **1** county SE Ireland in Leinster *area* 346, *pop* 34,025 **2** urban district, its ✱

Carls·bad \'kär(ə)lz-,bad\ **1** caverns SE N.Mex. in **Carlsbad Caverns National Park** (*area* 72) **2** city SE N.Mex. on the Pecos *pop* 21,297 **3** — see KARLOVY VARY

Carmana, Carmania — KERMAN

Car·mar·then \kär-'mär-t͟hən, kər-\ **1** *or* **Car·mar·then·shire** \-,shi(ə)r, -shər\ county S Wales *area* 919, *pop* 162,313 **2** municipal borough & port, its ✱, on Towy river

Car·mel, Mount \'kär-məl\ mountain ridge NW Palestine; highest point 1791 *ft*

Carnarvon, Carnarvonshire — see CAERNARVON

Car·nat·ic \kär-'nat-ik\ region SE India between Eastern Ghats & Coromandel coast

Car·nic Alps \,kär-nik-\ mountain range E Alps between Austria & Italy — see KELLERWAND

Car·nio·la \,kär-nē-'ō-lə, kärn-'yō-\ region NW Yugoslavia NE of Istrian peninsula — **Car·nio·lan** \-lən\ *adj*

Car·o·li·na \,kar-ə-'lī-nə\ English colony 1663–1729 on E coast of No. America divided 1729 into No. Carolina & So. Carolina (the **Car·o·li·nas** \-nəz\)

Ca·ro·li·na \,kär-ə-'lē-nə\ city NE *cen* Puerto Rico *pop* 94,271

Car·o·line \'kar-ə-,līn, -lən\ islands W Pacific E of S Philippines; part of Trust Territory of the Pacific Islands *area* 463 — see PALAU, PONAPE, TRUK, YAP

Ca·ro·ní \ˌkär-ə-ˈnē\ river 373 *m* E Venezuela flowing N into the Orinoco
Car·pa·thi·an \kär-ˈpā-thē-ən\ mountain system E *cen* Europe along boundary between Czechoslovakia & Poland & in N & *cen* Rumania — see GERLACHOVKA, TATRA, TRANSYLVANIAN ALPS
Carpathian Ruthenia — see RUTHENIA
Carpathos — see KARPATHOS
Car·pen·tar·ia, Gulf of \ˌkär-pən-ˈter-ē-ə, -ˈtar-\ inlet of Arafura sea on N coast of Australia
Car·pen·ters·ville \ˈkär-pən-tərz-ˌvil, ˈkärp-ᵊm-\ village NE Ill. NW of Chicago *pop* 24,059
Car·qui·nez \kär-ˈkē-nəs\ strait 8 *m* long Calif. joining San Pablo & Suisun bays
Car·ran·tuo·hill \ˌkar-ən-ˈtü-əl\ mountain 3414 *ft* SW Ireland in County Kerry; highest in Macgillicuddy's Reeks & in Ireland
Car·ra·ra \kə-ˈrär-ə\ commune N Italy ESE of La Spezia *pop* 66,821
Car·rhae \ˈkar-(ˌ)ē\ ancient city N Mesopotamia
Car·rick on Shan·non \ˌkar-i-ˌkȯn-ˈshan-ən, -ˌkän-\ town N *cen* Ireland ✻ of County Leitrim
Car·shal·ton \kär-ˈshȯlt-ᵊn, kər-\ former urban district S England in Surrey, now part of Sutton
Carso — see KRAS
Car·son \ˈkärs-ᵊn\ **1** river 125 *m* W Nev. flowing NE into **Carson Lake** **2** city SW Calif. SE of Los Angeles *pop* 71,150
Carson City city ✻ of Nev. E of Lake Tahoe *pop* 15,468
Carson Sink intermittent lake W Nev. S of Humboldt Lake
Car·stensz, Mount \ˈkär-stənz\ mountain 16,404 *ft* W New Guinea in Nassau range of Snow mountains; highest in New Guinea
Car·ta·ge·na \ˌkärt-ə-ˈgā-nə, -ˈhā-\ **1** city & port NW Colombia *pop* 299,040 **2** city & port SE Spain *pop* 144,316
Car·ta·go \kär-ˈtäg-(ˌ)ō\ city *cen* Costa Rica *pop* 21,596
Car·ter·et \ˌkärt-ə-ˈret\ borough NE N.J. S of Elizabeth *pop* 23,137
Car·thage \ˈkär-thij\ *or anc* **Car·tha·go** \kär-ˈtäg-(ˌ)ō\ ancient city & state N Africa on coast NE of modern Tunis — **Car·tha·gin·ian** \ˌkär-thə-ˈjin-yən, -ˈjin-ē-ən\ *adj or n*
Ca·sa·blan·ca \ˌkas-ə-ˈblaŋ-kə, ˌkaz-\ *or* Ar **Dar el Bei·da** \ˌdär-ˌel-bā-ˈdä\ city & port W Morocco on the Atlantic *pop* 1,395,000
Casa Gran·de National Monument \ˌkas-ə-ˈgran-dē\ reservation S Ariz. SE of Phoenix *area* 473 acres; prehistoric ruins
Cas·cade \(ˈ)kas-ˈkād\ mountain range W U.S., N continuation of the Sierra Nevada extending N from Lassen Peak, N Calif., across Oreg. & Wash. — see RAINIER (Mount), COAST
Cas·co Bay \ˈkas-(ˌ)kō\ inlet of the Atlantic S Me. on which Portland is situated
Ca·ser·ta \kə-ˈzert-ə, -ˈzərt-\ commune S Italy NNE of Naples *pop* 59,223
Cash·el \ˈkash-əl\ urban district S Ireland in *cen* Tipperary at base of **Rock of Cashel** (hill with ruins of cathedral & castle)
Cashmere — see KASHMIR
Ca·si·quia·re \ˌkäs-i-ˈkyär-ē\ river 125 *m* S Venezuela connecting the upper course of the Negro with the Orinoco
Cas·per \ˈkas-pər\ city *cen* Wyo. on No. Platte river *pop* 39,361
Cas·pi·an \ˈkas-pē-ən\ sea (salt lake) between Europe & Asia; *ab* 85 *ft* below sea level *area* 169,381
Caspian Gates pass on W shore of Caspian sea near Derbent
Cassel — see KASSEL
Cas·si·no \kə-ˈsē-(ˌ)nō\ commune *cen* Italy ESE of Frosinone; site of Monte Cassino monastery *pop* 25,088
Cas·tel Gan·dol·fo \(ˌ)käs-ˌtel-gän-ˈdȯl-(ˌ)fō\ commune *cen* Italy on Lake Albano SE of Rome
Cas·tel·lón *or* **Castellón de la Pla·na** \ˌkas-tə(l)-ˈyōn-ˌdel-ə-ˈplän-ə\ **1** province E Spain *area* 2495, *pop* 385,823 **2** city & port, its ✻, on the Mediterranean NE of Valencia *pop* 93,968
Castellorizo *or* **Castelrosso** — see KASTELLORIZON
Cas·tile \kas-ˈtē(ə)l\ *or* Sp **Cas·ti·lla** \kä-ˈstē-lʸä, -ˈstē-yä\ region & ancient kingdom *cen* & N Spain divided by the Sierra de Guadarrama into regions & old provinces of **Old Castile** (to the N, ✻ Burgos) & **New Castile** (to the S, ✻ Toledo)
Castilla la Nue·va \-lä-ˈnwā-vä\ NEW CASTILE
Castilla la Vie·ja \-lä-ˈvye-k̲ä\ OLD CASTILE
Cas·tle·bar \ˌkas-əl-ˈbär\ urban district NW Ireland ✻ of Mayo
Castres \ˈkästrᵊ\ city S France E of Toulouse *pop* 40,457
Cas·tries \ˈkas-ˌtrēz, -ˌtrēs\ *or* **Port Castries** city & port Brit. West Indies in the Windward islands ✻ of St. Lucia
Ca·strop–Raux·el *or* **Ka·strop–Rauxel** \ˌkäs-ˌtrȯp-ˈrau̇k-səl\ city W Germany SSW of Münster *pop* 83,892
Ca·tal·ca *or* **Cha·tal·ja** \ˌchät-ᵊl-ˈjä\ city Turkey in Europe W of Istanbul *pop* 22,000
Cat·a·li·na *or* **San·ta Catalina** \ˌsant-ə-ˌkat-ᵊl-ˈē-nə\ island SW Calif. in Santa Barbara islands *area* 70
Cat·a·lo·nia \ˌkat-ᵊl-ˈō-nyə, -nē-ə\ *or* Sp **Ca·ta·lu·ña** \ˌkät-ᵊl-ˈü-nyə\ region NE Spain bordering on France & the Mediterranean; chief city Barcelona *area* 12,431 — **Cat·a·lo·nian** \-ˈō-nyən, -nē-ən\ *adj or n*
Ca·ta·mar·ca \ˌkät-ə-ˈmär-kə\ city NW Argentina SSW of Tucumán *pop* 45,929
Ca·ta·nia \kə-ˈtān-yə, -ˈtän-\ *or anc* **Cat·a·na** \ˈkat-ə-nə\ commune Italy in E Sicily on E coast on Gulf of Catania at foot of Mt. Etna *pop* 410,905
Ca·ta·ño \kə-ˈtän-(ˌ)yō\ town NE *cen* Puerto Rico *pop* 26,459
Ca·tan·za·ro \ˌkä-ˌtän-ˈ(d)zär-(ˌ)ō\ city S Italy ✻ of Calabria *pop* 81,548
Ca·taw·ba \kə-ˈtȯ-bə\ river 250 *m* flowing S from W N.C. into S.C. — see WATEREE
Ca·thay \ka-ˈthā, ka-\ CHINA — an old name
Catherine, Mount — see KATHERINA (Gebel)
Ca·toc·tin Mountain \kə-ˈtäk-tən\ mountain ridge NW Md. & N Va. in Blue Ridge mountains
Cats·kill \ˈkat-ˌskil\ mountains SE N.Y. in the Appalachian system W of the Hudson — see SLIDE MOUNTAIN
Cattaro — see KOTOR
Cau·ca \ˈkau̇-kə\ river 600 *m* W Colombia flowing N into the Magdalena
Cau·ca·sia \kȯ-ˈkā-zhə, -shə\ *or* **Cau·ca·sus** \ˈkȯ-kə-səs\ region U.S.S.R. between the Black & Caspian seas; divided by Caucasus mountains into **Cis·cau·ca·sia** \ˌsis-\ (to the N) & **Trans·cau·ca·sia** \ˌtran(t)s-\ (to the S)
Caucasus mountain system U.S.S.R. in Caucasia — see ELBORUS
Caucasus Indicus — see HINDU KUSH
Cau·dine Forks \ˌkȯ-ˌdīn-, -ˌdēn-\ two mountain passes S Italy in the Apennines between Benevento & Capua
Caul·field \ˈkȯl-ˌfēld\ city SE Australia in S Victoria SE of Melbourne; part of Greater Melbourne *pop* 76,119
Causses \kōs\ limestone region S *cen* France on S border of Massif Central
Cau·ve·ry \ˈkȯ-və-rē\ *or* **Ka·ve·ri** \ˈkäv-ə-rē\ river 475 *m* S India flowing E & entering Bay of Bengal in a wide delta
Cauvery Falls waterfall 300 *ft* India in Cauvery river on Mysore-Tamil Nadu boundary
Cav·an \ˈkav-ən\ **1** county NE Republic of Ireland in Ulster *area* 730, *pop* 52,674 **2** urban district, its ✻
Ca·vi·te \kə-ˈvēt-ē\ city Philippines in Luzon on Cavite peninsula in Manila Bay SW of Manila *pop* 77,100
Cawnpore — see KANPUR
Ca·xi·as \kə-ˈshē-əs\ **1** town NE Brazil in Maranhão WNW of Teresina *pop* 124,403 **2** — see DUQUE DE CAXIAS **3** *or* **Caxias do Sul** \-də-ˈsül\ city S Brazil in Rio Grande do Sul N of Pôrto Alegre *pop* 110,241
Ca·yam·be \kä-ˈyäm-(ˌ)bā\ mountain 18,996 *ft* N Ecuador
Cay·enne \kī-ˈen, kā-\ city & port ✻ of French Guiana on island in Cayenne river near the coast *pop* 24,518
Cayes *or* **Aux Cayes** \(ō-)ˈkī\ city & port SW Haiti on Tiburon peninsula *pop* 15,213
Ca·yey \kä-ˈyā\ city SE *cen* Puerto Rico *pop* 21,562
Cay·man \(ˈ)kā-ˈman, *attributively* ˈkā-mən\ islands West Indies NW of Jamaica; a Brit. colony ✻ Georgetown (on **Grand Cayman,** chief island) *area* 93, *pop* 10,652
Ca·yu·ga \kē-ˈü-gə, ˈkyü-, kä-ˈ(y)ü-\ lake 40 *m* long W *cen* N.Y.; one of the Finger Lakes
Ce·a·rá \ˌsā-ə-ˈrä\ **1** state NE Brazil bordering on the Atlantic ✻ Fortaleza *area* 57,371, *pop* 4,440,286 **2** — see FORTALEZA
Ce·bu \sā-ˈbü\ **1** island E *cen* Philippines, one of the Visayan islands *area* 1707 **2** city on E coast of Cebu I. *pop* 332,100
Ce·dar \ˈsēd-ər\ river 329 *m* SE Minn. & E Iowa flowing SE into the Iowa
Cedar Breaks National Monument reservation SW Utah NE of Zion National Park containing unusual erosion forms *area* 8
Cedar Falls city NE Iowa NW of Waterloo *pop* 29,597
Cedar Rapids city E Iowa on Cedar river *pop* 110,642
Ce·le·bes \ˈsel-ə-ˌbēz, sə-ˈlē-bēz\ **1** *or* **Su·la·we·si** \ˌsü-lə-ˈwā-sē\ island Indonesia E of Borneo ✻ Makassar *area* 69,255, *pop* 8,925,000 **2** sea arm of SW Pacific enclosed on N by Mindanao & Sulu archipelago, on S by Celebes, & on W by Borneo — **Cel·e·be·sian** \ˌsel-ə-ˈbē-zhən\ *adj*
Celestial Empire the former Chinese Empire
Cel·le \ˈ(t)sel-ə\ city W Germany NE of Hannover *pop* 156,505
Ce·nis, Mont \ˌmōⁿ-sə-ˈnē\ *or* It **Mon·te Ce·ni·sio** \ˌmōnt-ē-chə-ˈnē-zē-ˌō\ **1** mountain pass 6831 *ft* between France & Italy over Mont Cenis massif (11,792 *ft*) in Graian Alps **2** tunnel piercing the Fréjus massif SW of Mont Cenis
Central African Republic country N *cen* Africa, formerly Ubangi-Shari; a republic ✻ Bangui *area* 238,224, *pop* 1,640,000
Central America, 1 the narrow S portion of No. America connecting that continent with So. America & extending from the Isthmus of Tehuantepec to the Isthmus of Panama **2** the republics of Guatemala, El Salvador, Honduras, Nicaragua, & Costa Rica & often also Panama & Brit. Honduras
Central Falls city N R.I. N of Providence *pop* 18,716
Cen·tra·lia \sen-ˈtrāl-yə\ city S *cen* Ill. *pop* 15,217
Central India former group of 89 Indian states N *cen* India ✻ Indore; area now chiefly in W & N Madhya Pradesh
Central Karroo — see KARROO
Central Provinces and Be·rar \bā-ˈrär, bə-\ former province of India reorganized 1950 & renamed Madhya Pradesh
Central Valley valley *cen* Calif. comprising the valleys of the Sacramento & San Joaquin rivers
Ceos — see KEOS
Ceph·a·lo·nia \ˌsef-ə-ˈlō-nyə, -nē-ə\ *or* NGk **Ke·fal·li·nía** \ˌkef-ə-lə-ˈnē-ə\ island W Greece in the Ionian islands *area* 277
Ce·phi·sus \sə-ˈfī-səs\ *or* **Ce·phis·sus** \-ˈfis-əs\ any of three small rivers *cen* Greece in Attica & Boeotia
Ce·ram *or* **Se·ram** \ˈsā-ˌräm\ island E Indonesia in *cen* Moluccas *area* 6621
Cerigo — see KÍTHIRA
Cernauti — see CHERNOVTSY
Cer·re·do *or* **Tor·re de Cerredo** \(ˈtȯr-ē-)də-sə-ˈrād-(ˌ)ō\ mountain 8687 *ft* N Spain SW of Santander; highest in the Cantabrians
Cer·ri·tos \sə-ˈrēt-əs\ city SW Calif. NE of Long Beach *pop* 15,856
Cerro Bolívar — see BOLÍVAR (Cerro)
Cer·ro de Pas·co \ˌser-ō-də-ˈpas-(ˌ)kō\ **1** mountain 15,100 *ft*, *cen* Peru NE of Lima **2** city near the mountain *pop* 21,363
Cerro de Pun·ta \ˈpünt-ə\ mountain 4389 *ft*, *cen* Puerto Rico in Cordillera Central; highest on the island
Cer·ro Gor·do \ˌser-ə-ˈgȯrd-(ˌ)ō\ mountain pass E Mexico between Veracruz & Jalapa
Cervin, Mont — see MATTERHORN
Ce·se·na \chə-ˈzā-nə\ *or anc* **Cae·se·na** \sə-ˈzē-nə\ commune N Italy in Emilia-Romagna SE of Forlì *pop* 85,140

Čes·ké Bu·dě·jo·vi·ce \'ches-kə-'bùd-ə-ˌyò-vət-sə\ *or* G **Bud·weis** \'bùt-ˌvīs\ city W Czechoslovakia in S Bohemia on the Vltava *pop* 75,684
Cetatea Alba — see BELGOROD-DNESTROVSKI
Ce·ti·nje \'(t)set-ᵊn-ˌyā\ town S Yugoslavia SE of Kotor near coast; formerly ✱ of Montenegro
Cette — see SÈTE
Ceu·ta \'sā-ˌüt-ə, 'seù-(ˌ)tä\ city & port N Morocco opposite Gibraltar; a Spanish presidio *pop* 67,187
Cé·vennes \sā-'ven\ mountain range S France W of the Rhone at E edge of Massif Central — see MÉZENC
Cey·lon \si-'län, sā-\ *or* **Lan·ka** \'laŋ-kə\ **1** *or* Ar **Ser·en·dib** \'ser-ən-ˌdib, -ˌdip\ *or* L & Gk **Ta·prob·a·ne** \tə-'präb-ə-(ˌ)nē\ island 270 *m* long & 140 *m* wide in Indian ocean off S India **2** — see SRI LANKA — **Cey·lon·ese** \ˌsā-lə-'nēz, ˌsē-lə-, ˌsel-ə-, -'nēs\ *adj or n*
Cha·co *or* **Gran Chaco** \((ˈ)grän-)'chäk-(ˌ)ō\ region S *cen* So. America drained by the Paraguay & its chief W tributaries the Pilcomayo & Bermejo; divided between Argentina, Bolivia, & Paraguay
Cha·co Canyon National Monument \ˌchäk-(ˌ)ō-\ reservation NW N.Mex. containing cliff-dweller ruins *area* 28
Chad *or* F **Tchad** \'chad\ **1** shallow lake N *cen* Africa at junction of boundaries of Chad, Niger, & Nigeria *maximum area ab* 8000 **2** country N *cen* Africa ✱ Fort-Lamy; a republic within French Community; before 1959 a territory of French Equatorial Africa *area* 495,752, *pop* 3,800,000 — **Chad·ian** \'chad-ē-ən\ *adj or n*
Chae·ro·nea \ˌker-ə-'nē-ə, ˌkir-\ *or* **Chae·ro·neia** \-'nī-ə\ ancient city E *cen* Greece in W Boeotia SE of Mt. Parnassus
Cha·gres \'chäg-rəs, 'chag-\ river Panama flowing through Gatun Lake to the Caribbean
Cha·gua·ra·mas \ˌchäg-wə-'räm-əs\ district NW Trinidad W of Port of Spain on **Chaguaramas Bay** (inlet of Gulf of Paria)
Cha·har \'chä-'här\ former province NE China in E Inner Mongolia ✱ Kalgan
Chalcedon — see KADIKOY
Chal·cid·i·ce \kal-'sid-ə-(ˌ)sē\ *or* NGk **Khal·ki·di·kí** \ˌkäl-kə-thi-'kē\ peninsula NE Greece in E Macedonia projecting SE into N Aegean sea; terminates in three peninsulas: Kassandra (*anc* Pallene), Sithonia, & Acte — see ACTE
Chal·cis \'kal-səs\ *or* **Chal·kis** \-kəs\ *or* NGk **Khal·kis** \käl-'kēs\ city *cen* Greece ✱ of Euboea on Evripos strait *pop* 36,381 — **Chal·cid·i·an** \kal-'sid-ē-ən\ *adj or n*
Chal·dea *or* **Chal·daea** \kal-'dē-ə\ ancient region SW Asia on Euphrates river & Persian gulf
Cha·leur Bay \shə-'lù(ə)r, -'lər\ inlet of Gulf of St. Lawrence SE Canada between N N.B. & Gaspé peninsula, Que.
Cha·lon *or* **Chalon-sur-Saône** \sha-'lō^n(-ˌsù(ə)r-'sōn)\ city E *cen* France N of Mâcon *pop* 50,589
Châ·lons *or* **Châlons-sur-Marne** \shä-'lō^n(-ˌsù(ə)r-'märn)\ commune NE France on the Marne *pop* 50,764
Cham·bal \'chəm-bəl\ river 650 *m, cen* India flowing from Vindhya mountains E into the Jumna
Cham·bers·burg \'chām-bərz-ˌbərg\ borough S Pa. *pop* 17,315
Cham·bé·ry \shä^n-bā-rē\ city E France E of Lyons *pop* 51,066
Cham·bord \shä^n-'bò(ə)r\ village N *cen* France NE of Blois
Cham·do \'chäm-'dō\ **1** region E Tibet; chief town Changtu **2** — see CHANGTU
Cha·mi·zal \ˌsham-ə-'zäl, ˌchäm-i-'säl\ tract of land 630 acres on N bank of the Rio Grande formerly in El Paso, Tex.; ceded to Mexico 1963
Cha·mo·nix \ˌsham-ə-'nē\ town & valley SE France NW of Mont Blanc
Cham·pagne \sham-'pān\ region & former province NE France W of Lorraine & N of Burgundy ✱ Troyes
Cham·paign \sham-'pān\ city E *cen* Ill. *pop* 56,532
Cham·pi·gny-sur-Marne \ˌshä^n-(ˌ)pēn-'yē-ˌsù(ə)r-'märn\ commune N France, SSE suburb of Paris *pop* 70,419
Cham·plain, Lake \sham-'plān\ lake 125 *m* long between N.Y. & Vt. extending N into Quebec *area* 600
Chan·der·na·gore \ˌchən-dər-nə-'gō(ə)r, -'gò(ə)r\ *or* **Chan·dan·na·gar** \ˌchən-də-'nəg-ər\ city E India in West Bengal N of Calcutta; before 1950 part of French India *pop* 67,105
Chan·di·garh \'chən-dē-gər\ city N India N of Delhi; a union territory administered by the national government; joint ✱ of Punjabi Suba & Haryana; founded 1953, *pop* 256,979
Changan — see SIAN
Chang·chow \'jäŋ-'jō, 'chaŋ-'chaù\ **1** *or* **Lung·ki** \'lùŋ-'kē\ city SE China in S Fukien W of Amoy *pop* 81,200 **2** *or formerly* **Wu·tsin** \'wü-'jin\ city E China in S Kiangsu *pop* 296,500
Chang·chun \'chäŋ-'chùn\ city NE China ✱ of Kirin *pop* 975,000
Chang·hua \'chäŋ-'(h)wä\ city China in W Formosa *pop* 133,514
Chang·jin \'chäŋ-'jin\ **1** river 160 *m* N Korea flowing NE into the Yalu **2** reservoir in Changjin river
Changkiakow — see KALGAN
Chang·sha \'chäŋ-'shä\ city SE *cen* China ✱ of Hunan on Siang river *pop* 975,000
Chang·shu \'chäŋ-'shü\ city E China in S Kiangsu *pop* 101,400
Chang·teh \'chäŋ-'də\ city SE *cen* China in N Hunan on Yuan river *pop* 225,000
Chang·tu \'chäŋ-'tü\ *or* **Cham·do** \'chäm-'dō\ town E Tibet on the Mekong
Chan·kiang \'chän-jē-'äŋ\ *or* **Tsam·kong** \'jäm-'goŋ\ *or formerly* **Fort Bay·ard** \'bā-ərd, 'bī-\ city SE China in SE Kwangtung on Luichow peninsula *pop* 220,000
Channel, 1 — see SANTA BARBARA (islands) **2** islands in English channel; a possession of Brit. Crown *area* 75, *pop* 125,240 — see ALDERNEY, GUERNSEY, JERSEY, SARK
Channel Islands National Monument reserve SW Calif. in Santa Barbara islands including areas on Anacapa islands (E of Santa Cruz I.) & Santa Barbara I. (W of Santa Catalina I.)
Chan·til·ly \shä^n-tē-yē, shan-'til-ē\ town N France NNE of Paris
Chao·chow \'chaù-'jō\ *or* **Chao·an** \'chaù-'än\ city E China in NE Kwangtung on Han river above Swatow *pop* 101,300
Chao Phra·ya \chaù-'prī-ə\ *or* **Me Nam** \mā-'näm\ river 160 *m* W *cen* Thailand formed by confluence of Nan & Ping rivers & flowing S into Gulf of Siam
Cha·pa·la \chə-'päl-ə\ lake 50 *m* long W *cen* Mexico in Jalisco & Michoacán SE of Guadalajara
Chapel Hill town N N.C. SW of Durham *pop* 25,537
Cha·pul·te·pec \chə-'pül-tə-ˌpek\ fortress *cen* Mexico on a hill 3 *m* SW of Mexico City
Cha·rente \shə-'ränt\ river 225 *m* W France flowing W into Bay of Biscay
Chari — see SHARI
Char·i·ton \'shar-ət-ᵊn\ river 280 *m* S Iowa & N Mo. flowing S into the Missouri
Charle·roi \'shär-lə-ˌròi, -lər-ˌwä\ city SW Belgium in Hainaut *pop* 23,911
Charles \'chär(ə)lz\ river 47 *m* Mass. flowing into Boston harbor
Charles, Cape cape E Va. N of entrance to Chesapeake Bay
Charles·bourg \shärl-'bù(ə)r, 'chärlz-ˌbərg\ city Canada in SE Que. NE of Quebec city *pop* 33,443
Charles·ton \'chärl-stən\ **1** city E *cen* Ill. *pop* 16,421 **2** city & port SE S.C. *pop* 66,945 **3** city ✱ of W.Va. on the Kanawha *pop* 71,505 — **Charles·to·nian** \chärl-'stō-nē-ən, -nyən\ *n*
Charleston Peak mountain 10,874 *ft* SE Nev. WNW of Las Vegas
Charles·town \'chärl-ˌstaùn\ section of Boston, Mass., on Boston harbor between mouths of Charles & Mystic rivers
Char·lotte \'shär-lət\ city S N.C. *pop* 241,178
Charlotte Ama·lie \ə-'mäl-yə\ *or formerly* **Saint Thomas** city & port ✱ of Virgin Islands of the U.S., on St. Thomas I.
Charlotte Harbor inlet of Gulf of Mexico SW Fla.
Char·lot·ten·burg \shär-'lät-ᵊn-ˌbərg, -ˌbù(ə)rg\ a W section of Berlin, Germany
Char·lottes·ville \'shär-ləts-ˌvil, -vəl\ city *cen* Va. *pop* 38,880
Char·lotte·town \'shär-lət-ˌtaùn\ city & port Canada ✱ of P.E.I. on Northumberland Strait *pop* 19,133
Chartres \'shärt, 'shärtrᵊ\ city N *cen* France SW of Paris *pop* 34,469
Chatalja — see CATALCA
Châ·teau·guay \'shat-ə-ˌgā\ town Canada in S Que. SW of Montreal *pop* 15,797
Châteauguay-Cen·tre \-'sent-ər\ town Canada in S Que. *pop* 17,942
Châ·teau·roux \shä-tō-rü\ commune *cen* France S of Orléans *pop* 49,138
Châ·teau-Thier·ry \ˌsha-ˌtō-ˌtye-'rē, ˌshä-\ town N France on the Marne SW of Reims
Chat·ham \'chat-əm\ **1** — see SAN CRISTÓBAL **2** islands S Pacific belonging to New Zealand & comprising two islands (Chatham & Pitt) *area* 372 **3** strait SE Alaska between Admiralty I. & Kuiu I. on E & Baranof I. & Chichagof I. on W **4** city Canada in SE Ont. E of Lake St. Clair *pop* 35,317 **5** municipal borough SE England in Kent *pop* 56,921
Chat·ta·hoo·chee \ˌchat-ə-'hü-chē\ river 410 *m* SE U.S. rising in N Ga., flowing SW & S along Ala.-Ga. boundary into Lake Seminole
Chat·ta·noo·ga \ˌchat-ə-'nü-gə, ˌchat-ᵊn-'ü-\ city SE Tenn. on the Tennessee *pop* 119,082
Chau·tau·qua \shə-'tò-kwə\ lake 18 *m* long SW N.Y.
Che·bok·sa·ry \ˌcheb-ˌäk-'sär-ē\ city U.S.S.R. in Soviet Russia, Europe ✱ of Chuvash Republic WNW of Kazan *pop* 216,000
Che·cheno-In·gush Republic \chə-ˌchen-ō-in-'güsh\ autonomous republic of the U.S.S.R. in SE Soviet Russia, Europe, on N slopes of Caucasus mountains *area* 6064, *pop* 1,065,000
Che·du·ba \chə-'dü-bə\ island W Bengal *area* 220
Che·foo \'jə-'fü\ *or* **Yen·tai** \'yen-'tī\ city & port E China in NE Shantung on Shantung peninsula on Po Hai *pop* 116,000
Che·ju \'chē-ˌjü\ *or* **Quel·part** \'kwel-ˌpärt\ *or* Jap **Sai·shu** \'sī-(ˌ)shü\ **1** island S Korea in N East China sea *area* 710 **2** city & port on N coast of the island *pop* 106,456
Che·kiang \'jəj-ē-'äŋ\ province E China bordering on East China sea ✱ Hangchow *area* 39,305, *pop* 31,000,000
Che·lan \shə-'lan\ lake *ab* 55 *m* long N *cen* Wash.
Chelms·ford **1** \'chem-sfərd *also* 'chelm-\ town NE Mass. S of Lowell *pop* 31,432 **2** \'chelm-, 'chem-\ municipal borough SE England ✱ of Essex *pop* 58,125
Chel·sea \'chel-sē\ **1** city E Mass. NE of Boston *pop* 30,625 **2** former metropolitan borough SW London, England, on N bank of the Thames, now part of Kensington and Chelsea
Chel·ten·ham \'chelt-ᵊn-ˌham, *Brit usu* 'chelt-nəm *or* -ᵊn-əm\ municipal borough SW *cen* England in Gloucestershire *pop* 69,734
Che·lya·binsk \chel-'yä-bən(t)sk\ city U.S.S.R. in W Soviet Russia, Asia, S of Sverdlovsk *pop* 874,000
Che·lyu·skin, Cape \chel-'yü-skən\ headland U.S.S.R. in NW Soviet Russia, Asia, on Taimyr peninsula; northernmost point of Asian mainland, at 77°35'N, 105°E
Chem·nitz \'kem-ˌnits, -nəts\ *or* **Karl-Marx-Stadt** \(ˈ)kärl-'märk-ˌs(h)tät\ city E Germany SE of Leipzig *pop* 297,133
Chemulpo — see INCHON
Che·nab \chə-'näb\ river 590 *m* NW India (subcontinent) in Kashmir & the Punjab flowing SW to unite with the Sutlej forming the Panjnad
Cheng·chow \'jəŋ-'jō\ city NE *cen* China ✱ of Honan on Yellow river *pop* 766,000
Cheng·teh \'chəŋ-'də\ *or formerly* **Je·hol** \jə-'hōl, 'rō-'hō\ city NE China in NE Hopei NE of Peking *pop* 200,000
Cheng·tu \'chəŋ-'dü\ city SW *cen* China ✱ of Szechwan on Min river *pop* 1,107,000
Chenstokhov — see CZESTOCHOWA
Cher \'she(ə)r\ river 220 *m, cen* France flowing into the Loire
Cher·bourg \'she(ə)r-ˌbù(ə)r(g), sher-'bù(ə)r\ city & port NW France on Cotentin peninsula on English channel *pop* 38,243
Che·rem·kho·vo \chə-'rem-kə-və, ˌcher-əm-'kò-və\ city U.S.S.R. in E *cen* Soviet Russia, Asia, NW of Irkutsk *pop* 104,000
Cheribon — see TJIREBON

Cher·kessk \chər-ˈkesk\ city U.S.S.R. in SE Soviet Russia, Europe, in N Caucasia SE of Stavropol ✱ of Karachayevo-Cherkess Autonomous Region *pop* 67,000
Cher·ni·gov \cher-ˈnē-gəf\ city U.S.S.R. in Ukraine *pop* 159,000
Cher·nov·tsy \cher-ˈnȯft-sē\ *or* Rum **Cer·na·u·ti** \ˌcher-nə-ˈüts(-ē)\ city U.S.S.R. in W Ukraine on the Prut *pop* 187,000
Cher·o·kee Outlet *or* **Cherokee Strip** \ˌcher-ə-(ˌ)kē-\ strip of land N Okla. along S border of Kans. E of 100°W opened to settlement 1893; 50 *m* wide, *ab* 220 *m* long
Cher·so·nese \ˈkər-sə-ˌnēz, -ˌnēs\ *or anc* **Cher·so·ne·sus** \ˌkər-sə-ˈnē-səs\ any of several peninsulas: as (1) Jutland (the **Cim·bri·an** \ˈsim-brē-ən\, *or* **Cim·bric** \-brik\, **Chersonese**); (2) the Malay peninsula (the **Golden Chersonese**); (3) the Crimea (the **Tau·ric Chersonese** \ˈtȯr-ik\); (4) the Gallipoli peninsula (the **Thra·cian Chersonese** \ˈthrā-shən\)
Cher·well \ˈchär-wəl\ river 30 *m, cen* England in Northamptonshire & Oxfordshire flowing S into the Thames at Oxford
Ches·a·peake \ˈches-(ə-)ˌpēk\ city SE Va. *pop* 89,580
Chesapeake Bay inlet of the Atlantic 200 *m* long in Va. & Md.
Chesh·ire \ˈchesh-ər, ˈchesh-ˌi(ə)r\ **1** town S Conn. SW of Meriden *pop* 19,051 **2** *or* **Ches·ter** \ˈches-tər\ county NW England ✱ Chester *area* 973, *pop* 1,542,624
Ches·ter \ˈches-tər\ **1** city SE Pa. *pop* 56,331 **2** city & county borough NW England ✱ of Cheshire on the Dee *pop* 62,696
Ches·ter·field \ˈches-tər-ˌfēld\ **1** inlet *ab* 250 *m* long N Canada on NW coast of Hudson Bay in Keewatin District **2** municipal borough N *cen* England in Derbyshire S of Sheffield *pop* 70,153
Chev·i·ot \ˈchev-ē-ət, ˈchē-vē-ət\ **1** hills extending NE to SW along English-Scottish border **2** peak 2676 *ft*, highest in the Cheviots
Chey·enne \shī-ˈan, -ˈen\ **1** river 290 *m* S.Dak. flowing NE into the Missouri **2** city ✱ of Wyo. *pop* 40,914
Chi·ai \jē-ˈī\ city China in W *cen* Formosa *pop* 234,359
Chiang Mai \jē-ˈäŋ-ˈmī\ *or* **Chieng·mai** \jē-ˈeŋ-ˈmī\ city NW Thailand on Ping river *pop* 89,272
Chi·a·pas \chē-ˈäp-əs\ state SE Mexico bordering on the Pacific ✱ Tuxtla Gutiérrez *area* 28,729, *pop* 1,578,180
Chi·ba \ˈchē-bə\ city E Japan in Honshu on Tokyo Bay E of Tokyo *pop* 456,000
Chi·ca·go \shə-ˈkäg-(ˌ)ō, -ˈkȯg-\ **1** river Chicago, Ill., having two branches (No. Branch & So. Branch) & orig. flowing E into Lake Michigan but now flowing S through So. Branch & Chicago Sanitary & Ship canal into Des Plaines river **2** city & port NE Ill. on Lake Michigan *pop* 3,366,957 — **Chi·ca·go·an** \-ˈkäg-ə-wən, -ˈkȯg-\ *n*
Chicago Heights city NE Ill. S of Chicago *pop* 40,900
Chich·a·gof \ˈchich-ə-ˌgȯf, -ˌgäf\ island SE Alaska in Alexander archipelago N of Baranof I. *area* 2100
Chi·chén Itzá \chə-ˌchen-ət-ˈsä\ village SE Mexico in Yucatán 75 *m* ESE of Mérida at site of ruins of important Mayan city
Chich·es·ter \ˈchich-ə-stər\ municipal borough S England ENE of Portsmouth ✱ of West Sussex *pop* 20,547
Chick·a·hom·i·ny \ˌchik-ə-ˈhäm-ə-nē\ river 90 *m* E Va. flowing SE into the James
Chi·cla·yo \chə-ˈklī-(ˌ)ō\ city NW Peru near coast *pop* 134,100
Chi·co \ˈchē-(ˌ)kō\ city W Calif. N of Sacramento *pop* 19,580
Chic·o·pee \ˈchik-ə-(ˌ)pē\ city SW Mass. *pop* 66,676
Chi·cou·timi \shə-ˈküt-ə-mē\ **1** river 100 *m* Canada in S Que. flowing N into the Saguenay **2** city Canada in S *cen* Que. on the Saguenay *pop* 33,893
Chihli — see HOPEI
Chihli, Gulf of — see PO HAI
Chi·hua·hua \chə-ˈwä-(ˌ)wä, shə-, -wə\ **1** state N Mexico bordering on the U.S. *area* 94,822, *pop* 1,730,012 **2** city, its ✱ *pop* 363,850
Chilachap — see TJILATJAP
Chile \ˈchil-ē\ country S So. America between the Andes & Pacific ocean; a republic ✱ Santiago *area* 286,396, *pop* 8,990,000 — **Chil·ean** \ˈchil-ē-ən, chə-ˈlā-ən\ *adj or n*
Chil·koot \ˈchil-ˌküt\ pass 3502 *ft* between SE Alaska & SW Yukon Territory, Canada, in N Coast mountains
Chi·llán \chē-ˈ(y)än\ city *cen* Chile NE of Concepción *pop* 77,654
Chil·li·cothe \ˌchil-ə-ˈkäth-ē, -ˈkȯ-thē\ city S Ohio *pop* 24,842
Chi·loé \ˌchil-ə-ˈwā\ island S *cen* Chile *area* 4700
Chil·pan·cin·go \ˌchil-pən-ˈsiŋ-(ˌ)gō\ city S Mexico ✱ of Guerrero *pop* 56,904
Chil·tern \ˈchil-tərn\ hills S *cen* England in Oxfordshire, Buckinghamshire, Hertfordshire, & Bedfordshire
Chim·bo·ra·zo \ˌchim-bə-ˈräz-(ˌ)ō, ˌshim-\ mountain 20,702 *ft* W *cen* Ecuador
Chim·kent \chim-ˈkent\ city U.S.S.R. in S Kazakh Republic N of Tashkent *pop* 247,000
Chin \ˈchin\ hills W Burma; highest Mt. Victoria 10,018 *ft*
Chi·na \ˈchī-nə\ country E Asia; a republic, until 1912 an empire ✱ Peking; *area* 3,691,502, *pop* 787,180,000 — see FORMOSA
China sea the East & So. China seas
Chin·chow \ˈjin-ˈjō\ city NE China in SW Liaoning on Gulf of Liaotung *pop* 352,200
Chin·co·teague \ˌshiŋ-kə-ˈtēg\ bay Md. & Va. on Atlantic coast
Chin·dwin \ˈchin-ˈdwin\ river 550 *m* NW Burma flowing S into the Irrawaddy
Chinese Turkestan *or* **Kash·gar·ia** \kash-ˈgar-ē-ə, -ˈger-\ region W China in W & *cen* Sinkiang
Chinghai — see TSINGHAI
Chin·ju \ˈjin-ˈjü\ city S Korea W of Pusan *pop* 121,622
Chin·kiang \ˈjin-jē-ˈäŋ\ city & port E China in NW *cen* Kiangsu on the Yangtze at its junction with the Grand canal *pop* 201,400
Chinmen — see QUEMOY
Chinnampo — see NAMPO
Chinnereth, Sea of — see GALILEE (Sea of)
Chi·no \ˈchē-(ˌ)nō\ city SW Calif. E of Los Angeles *pop* 20,411
Chin·wang·tao \ˈchin-ˈ(h)wäŋ-ˈdau̇\ city & port NE China in NE Hopei on Po Hai *pop* 186,800
Chiog·gia \kē-ˈō-jə\ commune & port NE Italy on island in Lagoon of Venice *pop* 48,347
Chi·os \ˈkī-ˌäs\ *or* NGk **Khí·os** \ˈkē-ˌȯs\ **1** island E Greece in the Aegean off W coast of Turkey *area* 355 **2** *or* NGk **Ká·stron** \ˈkäs-trȯn\ city & port Greece on E coast of Chios *pop* 24,074 — **Chi·an** \ˈkī-ən\ *adj or n*
Chip·pe·wa \ˈchip-ə-ˌwä, -wə\ river 183 *m* NW Wis. flowing S into the Mississippi
Chire — see SHIRE
Chir·i·ca·hua National Monument \ˌchir-i-ˈkä-wə, *locally also* ˈchir-i-ˌkau̇\ reservation SE Ariz. containing curious natural rock formations *area* 16.5
Chi·ri·quí \ˌchir-i-ˈkē\ volcano 11,070 *ft* Panama near Costa Rican border
Chis·holm Trail \ˌchiz-əm-\ pioneer cattle trail between San Antonio, Tex., & Abilene, Kans., used esp. 1866–85
Chisinau — see KISHINEV
Chis·le·hurst and Sid·cup \ˈchiz-əl-ˌhərst-ən-ˈsid-kəp\ former urban district SE England in Kent, now partly in Bexley, partly in Bromley
Chi·ta \chi-ˈtä\ city U.S.S.R. in SE Soviet Russia, Asia, E of Lake Baikal *pop* 242,000
Chi·tral \chi-ˈträl\ **1** river 300 *m* N Pakistan & Afghanistan flowing SW into the Kabul **2** district N Pakistan ✱ Chitral
Chit·ta·gong \ˈchit-ə-ˌgäŋ, -ˌgȯŋ\ city & port SE Bangladesh on Bay of Bengal *pop* 437,000
Chiu·si \kē-ˈü-sē\ *or anc* **Clu·si·um** \ˈklü-z(h)ē-əm\ town *cen* Italy in Tuscany SE of Siena
Chkalov — see ORENBURG
Choaspes — see KARKHEH
Choi·seul \shwä-ˈzə(r)l\ island W Pacific in the Solomons SE of Bougainville I. *area* 1500
Choi·sy *or* **Choisy–le–Roi** \shwä-ˌzē-lər-ˈwä\ commune N France on Seine river SSE of Paris *pop* 41,440
Cho·lon \shə-ˈlōn, chə-ˈlən\ former city S Vietnam, now part of Saigon
Cho·lu·la \chə-ˈlü-lə\ town SE *cen* Mexico in Puebla state
Cho·mo Lha·ri \ˌchō-mō-ˈlär-ē\ mountain 23,997 *ft* in the Himalayas between Tibet & NW Bhutan; sacred to Buddhists
Chomolungma — see EVEREST
Chong·jin \ˈchȯŋ-ˌjin\ city & port NE Korea on Sea of Japan *pop* 184,301
Chong·ju \ˈchȯŋ-ˌjü\ city S *cen* Korea N of Taejon *pop* 123,736
Chon·ju \ˈjən-ˌjü\ city SW Korea SW of Taejon *pop* 220,654
Cho Oyu \ˌchō-ō-ˈyü\ mountain 26,967 *ft* Nepal & Tibet in the Himalayas; 6th highest in the world
Cho·ras·mia \kə-ˈraz-mē-ə\ province of ancient Persia on the Oxus extending W to Caspian sea; equiv. to Khwarazm — see KHIVA
Cho·rzow \ˈkō-ˌzhüf, -ˌzhüv\ city SW Poland in Silesia *pop* 151,300
Chosen — see KOREA
Cho·ta Nag·pur \ˌchōt-ə-ˈnäg-ˌpu̇(ə)r\ plateau region E India N of Mahanadi basin in N Orissa & S Bihar
Cho·wan \chə-ˈwän\ river 50 *m* NE N.C. formed by confluence of Blackwater & Nottoway rivers & flowing into Albemarle sound
Christ·church \ˈkrīs(t)-ˌchərch\ city New Zealand on E coast of South I. *pop* 166,100
Christiania — see OSLO
Chris·tians·haab \ˈkris(h)-chənz-ˌhȯb\ town W Greenland on Disko Bay SE of Godhavn
Chris·tian·sted \ˈkris(h)-chən-ˌsted\ town Virgin Islands of the U.S. on N coast of St. Croix I.
Christ·mas \ˈkris-məs\ **1** island E Indian ocean 225 *m* S of W end of Java; administered by Australia *area* 64, *pop* 3361 **2** island (atoll) in the Line islands belonging to Great Britain; largest atoll in the Pacific *area* (including lagoon) 234
Chu \ˈchü\ **1** — see PEARL **2** river 600 *m* U.S.S.R. in Soviet Central Asia in SE Kazakh Republic flowing E into Issyk Kul
Chü·an·chow \chə-ˈwän-ˈjō\ city & port SE China in SE Fukien on Formosa strait *pop* 107,700
Chubb Crater — see NEW QUEBEC CRATER
Chu·but \chə-ˈbüt, -ˈvüt\ river 500 *m* S Argentina flowing E across Patagonia into the Atlantic
Chu·chow \ˈchü-ˈjō\ city SE China in E Hunan *pop* 127,300
Chudskoe — see PEIPUS (Lake)
Chu·gach \ˈchü-ˌgach *also* -ˌgash\ mountains S Alaska extending along coast from Cook inlet to St. Elias range; highest Mt. Marcus Baker 13,250 *ft*
Chuk·chi *or* **Chuck·chee** \ˈchək-chē, ˈchu̇k-\ sea of the Arctic ocean N of Bering Strait
Chu·kot·ski \chə-ˈkät-skē\ *or* **Chu·kot** \-ˈkät\ peninsula U.S.S.R. in NE Soviet Russia, Asia, between Bering & Chukchee seas — see EAST CAPE
Chu·la Vis·ta \ˌchü-lə-ˈvis-tə\ city SW Calif. S of San Diego *pop* 67,901
Chu·lym *or* **Chu·lim** \chə-ˈlim\ river 700 *m* U.S.S.R. in E *cen* Soviet Russia, Asia, flowing W into the Ob
Chun·chon \ˈchu̇n-ˌchȯn\ city S *cen* Korea NE of Seoul *pop* 122,672
Chung·king \ˈchu̇ŋ-ˈkiŋ\ *or* **Pa·hsien** \ˈbä-shē-ˈen\ city ✱ of China 1937–46 in SE Szechwan on the Yangtze *pop* 3,500,000
Chur \ˈku̇(ə)r\ *or* F **Coire** \ˈkwär\ commune E Switzerland ✱ of Graubünden canton *pop* 30,200
Chur·chill \ˈchər-ˌchil\ **1** river *ab* 1000 *m* Canada flowing E across N Sask. & N Man. into Hudson Bay **2** *or formerly* **Hamilton** river 208 *m* Canada in Nfld. in S *cen* Labrador flowing E to Lake Melville
Churchill Falls *or formerly* **Grand Falls** waterfall 245 *ft* high Canada in W Labrador in Churchill river

---

ə abut ᵊ kitten, F table ər further a back ā bake
ä cot, cart à F bac au̇ out ch chin e less ē easy
g gift i trip ī life j joke k̲ G ich ⁿ F vin ŋ sing
ō flow ȯ flaw œ F bœuf œ̄ F feu ȯi coin th thing
t͟h this ü loot u̇ foot ue G Füllen ue̅ F rue y yet
ʸ F digne \dēnʸ\, nuit \nwʸē\ yü few yu̇ furious zh vision

Chu Shan \'chü-'shän\ archipelago E China in East China sea at entrance to Hangchow Bay

Chu·vash Republic \chu̇-ˌväsh-\ *or* **Chu·vash·ia** \-'väsh-ē-ə\ autonomous republic U.S.S.R. in E *cen* Soviet Russia, Europe, S of the Volga ✱ Cheboksary *area* 6909, *pop* 1,224,000

Chu·zen·ji \chü-'zen-jē\ lake Japan in *cen* Honshu W of Nikko

Ci·bo·la \'sē-bə-lə, 'sib-ə-\ historical region in present N N.Mex. including seven pueblos (the **Seven Cities of Cibola**) believed by early Spanish explorers to contain vast treasures

Cic·ero \'sis-ə-ˌrō\ town NE Ill. W of Chicago *pop* 67,058

Cien·fue·gos \sē-ˌen-'fwā-(ˌ)gōs\ city & port W *cen* Cuba on S coast on Cienfuegos Bay *pop* 91,800

Cieszyn — see TESCHEN

Ci·li·cia \sə-'lish-(ē-)ə\ ancient country SE Asia Minor extending along Mediterranean coast S of Taurus mountains — see LESSER ARMENIA — **Ci·li·cian** \-'lish-ən\ *adj or n*

Cilician Gates mountain pass S Turkey in Taurus mountains

Cim·ar·ron \'sim-ə-ˌrän, -ˌrōn, -rən\ river 600 *m* flowing E from NE N.Mex. through SW Kans. into the Arkansas in NE Okla.

Cimbrian, *or* **Cimbric, Chersonese** — see CHERSONESE

Cim·me·ri·an Bosporus \sə-ˌmir-ē-ən-\ the Kerch strait

Cin·cin·nati \ˌsin(t)-sə-'nat-ē, -'nat-ə\ city SW Ohio *pop* 452,524 — **Cin·cin·nati·an** \-'nat-ē-ən\ *n*

Cinque Ports \'siŋk\ group of seaport towns SE England on coast of Kent & Sussex, orig. five (Dover, Sandwich, Romney, Hastings, & Hythe) to which were later added Winchelsea, Rye, & other minor places, granted special privileges (abolished in 19th century) in return for services in coast defense

Cintra — see SINTRA

Circars — see NORTHERN CIRCARS

Cir·cas·sia \(ˌ)sər-'kash-(ē-)ə\ region U.S.S.R. in S Soviet Russia, Europe, on Black sea N of W end of Caucasus mountains

Cirenaica — see CYRENAICA

Cis·al·pine Gaul \sis-ˌal-ˌpīn-\ the part of Gaul lying S & E of the Alps

Ciscaucasia — see CAUCASIA

Ci·thae·ron \sə-'thē-ˌrän\ *or* NGk **Ki·thai·rón** \ˌkē-the-'rȯn\ *or formerly* **El·a·tea** \ˌel-ə-'tē-ə\ mountain 4629 *ft* Greece on NW border of ancient Attica

Ci·tlal·te·petl \sē-ˌtläl-'tā-ˌpet-ᵊl\ *or* **Ori·za·ba** \ˌȯr-ə-'zäb-ə, ˌȯr-\ inactive volcano 18,700 *ft* SE Mexico on Puebla-Veracruz boundary; highest point in Mexico

Città del Vaticano — see VATICAN CITY

Ci·u·dad Bo·li·var \ˌsē-ü-ˌdä-bə-'lē-ˌvär, -ü-ˌdad-\ city & port E *cen* Venezuela on the Orinoco *pop* 103,663

Ciudad Guayana — see SANTO TOMÉ DE GUAYANA

Ciudad Juá·rez \'(h)wär-əs\ *or* **Juárez** city Mexico in Chihuahua on Rio Grande opposite El Paso, Tex. *pop* 436,054

Ciudad Re·al \-rā-'äl\ **1** province S *cen* Spain *area* 7620, *pop* 507,650 **2** commune, its ✱, S of Toledo *pop* 41,708

Ciudad Trujillo — see SANTO DOMINGO

Ciudad Vic·to·ria \ˌvik-'tōr-ē-ə, -'tȯr-\ city E *cen* Mexico ✱ of Tamaulipas *pop* 94,304

Ci·vi·ta·vec·chia \ˌchē-vē-tä-'vek-(ˌ)yä\ commune & port *cen* Italy in Latium on Tyrrhenian sea WNW of Rome *pop* 42,570

Clack·man·nan \klak-'man-ən\ *or* **Clack·man·nan·shire** \-ˌshi(ə)r, -shər\ **1** county *cen* Scotland bordering on Forth river *area* 55, *pop* 45,553 **2** town, its ✱

Clac·ton \'klak-tən\ *or* **Clacton-on-Sea** urban district SE England in Essex on North sea *pop* 37,942

Clair·ton \'kla(ə)rt-ᵊn, 'kle(ə)rt-\ city SW Pa. SE of Pittsburgh *pop* 15,051

Clare \'kla(ə)r, 'kle(ə)r\ county W Ireland in Munster ✱ Ennis *area* 1231, *pop* 74,844

Clare·mont \-ˌmänt\ city SW Calif. E of Los Angeles *pop* 23,464

Clark Fork \'klärk\ river 300 *m* W Mont. & N Idaho flowing NW into Pend Oreille Lake

Clarks·burg \'klärks-ˌbərg\ city N W.Va. *pop* 24,864

Clarks·dale \'klärks-ˌdāl\ city NW Miss. *pop* 21,673

Clarks·ville \'klärks-ˌvil, -vəl\ city N Tenn. NW of Nashville *pop* 31,719

Claw·son \'klȯs-ᵊn\ city SE Mich. N of Detroit *pop* 17,617

Clay·ton \'klāt-ᵊn\ city E Mo. W of St. Louis *pop* 16,222

Clear, Cape \'kli(ə)r\ cape SW Ireland at S end of Clear I.

Clear·wa·ter \'kli(ə)r-ˌwȯt-ər, -ˌwät-\ **1** mountains N *cen* Idaho; highest *ab* 8000 *ft* **2** city W Fla. NW of St. Petersburg on Gulf of Mexico *pop* 52,074

Cle·burne \'klē-bərn\ city NE *cen* Tex. *pop* 16,015

Clee \'klē\ hills W England in S Shropshire; highest 1790 *ft*

Cler·mont-Fer·rand \ˌkler-ˌmōⁿ-fə-'räⁿ\ city S *cen* France in Allier valley on edge of Auvergne mountains *pop* 148,896

Cleve·land \'klēv-lənd\ **1** city & port NE Ohio on Lake Erie *pop* 750,903 **2** city SE Tenn. ENE of Chattanooga *pop* 20,651 **3** district N England in N Yorkshire between Tees estuary & the **Cleveland hills** — **Cleve·land·er** \-lən-dər\ *n*

Cleveland, Mount mountain 10,438 *ft* N Mont., highest in Glacier National Park

Cleveland Heights city NE Ohio E of Cleveland *pop* 60,767

Cleves \'klēvz\ *or* G **Kle·ve** *or* **Cle·ve** \'klā-və\ city NW Germany WSW of Münster near the Rhine *pop* 22,423

Cli·chy *or* **Clichy-la-Ga·renne** \kli-ˌshē-ˌläg-ə-'ren\ commune N France NW of Paris *pop* 52,477

Clif·ton \'klif-tən\ city NE N.J. N of Newark *pop* 82,437

Clinch \'klinch\ river 200 *m* SW Va. & E Tenn. flowing SW into the Tennessee

Cling·mans Dome \ˌkliŋ-mənz-\ mountain 6642 *ft* on N.C.-Tenn. boundary; highest in Great Smoky mountains

Clin·ton \'klint-ᵊn\ city E Iowa on the Mississippi *pop* 34,719

Clip·per·ton \'klip-ərt-ᵊn\ island E Pacific at 10°N, 109°W belonging to France

Clon·mel \klän-'mel\ municipal borough S Ireland ✱ of County Tipperary

Cloud Peak mountain 13,165 *ft* N Wyo.; highest in Bighorn mountains

Clo·vel·ly \klō-'vel-ē\ village SW England in NW Devon

Clo·vis \'klō-vəs\ city E N.Mex. *pop* 28,495

Cluj \'klüzh\ city NW *cen* Rumania in Transylvania *pop* 197,902

Clu·ny \'klü-nē, klü-'\ town E *cen* France NNW of Lyons

Clusium — see CHIUSI

Clu·tha \'klü-thə\ river 210 *m* New Zealand in SE South I. flowing SE into the Pacific

Clyde \'klīd\ river 106 *m* SW Scotland flowing NW into **Firth of Clyde** (estuary)

Clyde·bank \'klīd-ˌbaŋk\ burgh W *cen* Scotland in Dunbartonshire on the Clyde *pop* 48,296

Clydes·dale \'klīdz-ˌdāl\ valley of the upper Clyde, Scotland

Cni·dus \'nīd-əs\ ancient town SW Asia Minor in Caria at end of a long promontory

Cnossus — see KNOSSOS

Coa·chel·la \kō-'chel-ə\ valley SE Calif. between Salton sea & San Bernardino mountains

Coa·hui·la \ˌkō-ə-'wē-lə, kwä-'wē-\ state N Mexico bordering on the U.S. ✱ Saltillo *area* 58,062, *pop* 1,140,989

Coast, 1 mountains Canada in W B.C.; N continuation of Cascade range **2** mountain ranges W No. America extending along Pacific coast W of Sierra Nevada & Cascade range & N through Vancouver I., B.C., to Kenai peninsula & Kodiak I., Alaska — see LOGAN (Mount)

Coat·bridge \'kōt-(ˌ)brij\ burgh S *cen* Scotland in Lanark E of Glasgow *pop* 52,131

Coats Land \'kōts\ section of Antarctica SE of Weddell sea

Cobh \'kōv\ *or formerly* **Queens·town** \'kwēnz-ˌtau̇n\ urban district & port SW Ireland on island in Cork Harbor

Coblenz — see KOBLENZ

Co·burg, 1 \'kō-ˌbərg\ city SE Australia in S Victoria, N suburb of Melbourne *pop* 68,568 **2** \-ˌbərg, -ˌbu̇(ə)rg\ city W Germany in N Bavaria NW of Bayreuth *pop* 41,456

Cocanada — see KAKINADA

Co·cha·bam·ba \ˌkō-chə-'bäm-bə\ city W *cen* Bolivia *pop* 157,000

Co·chin \'kō-chən\ region SW India in Kerala on Malabar coast — see TRAVANCORE AND COCHIN

Co·chin China \ˌkō-chən-\ region S Vietnam bordering on So. China sea & Gulf of Siam *area* 29,974

Cochinos Bay — see PIGS (Bay of)

Co·co \'kō-(ˌ)kō\ *or* **Se·go·via** \sā-'gō-vyə, -vē-ə\ river 450 *m* N Nicaragua flowing NE into the Caribbean & forming part of Honduras-Nicaragua boundary

Cocoa city E Fla. SE of Orlando *pop* 16,110

Co·co·ni·no \ˌkō-kə-'nē-(ˌ)nō, -'nē-nə\ plateau NW Ariz. S of Grand Canyon

Co·cos \'kō-kəs\ *or* **Kee·ling** \'kē-liŋ\ islands E Indian ocean belonging to Australia *area* 1

Cod, Cape \'käd\ peninsula 65 *m* long SE Mass.; part of area is included in **Cape Cod National Seashore** (created 1961; *area* 42)

Coele-Syria — see BIKA

Coeur d'Alene \ˌkȯrd-ᵊl-'ān\ **1** lake *ab* 25 *m* long N Idaho E of Spokane, Wash.; drained by Spokane river **2** city N Idaho *pop* 16,228

Cof·fey·ville \'kȯf-ē-ˌvil\ city SE Kans. *pop* 15,116

Coglians, Monte — see KELLERWAND

Co·hoes \kə-'hōz\ city E N.Y. NW of Troy *pop* 18,613

Coi — see RED

Coim·ba·tore \ˌkȯim-bə-'tō(ə)r, -'tȯ(ə)r\ city S India in W Tamil Nadu on S slope of Nilgiri hills *pop* 405,952

Co·im·bra \kō-'im-brə, kü-\ city W *cen* Portugal *pop* 108,046

Coire — see CHUR

Col·ches·ter \'kōl-ˌches-tər, -chəs-\ municipal borough SE England in Essex *pop* 76,145

Col·chis \'käl-kəs\ ancient country bordering on Black sea S of Caucasus mountains; area now constitutes W part of Georgian Republic, U.S.S.R. — **Col·chi·an** \'käl-kē-ən\ *adj or n*

Co·li·ma \kə-'lē-mə\ **1** volcano 12,792 *ft* SW Mexico in S Jalisco **2** state SW Mexico bordering on the Pacific *area* 2009, *pop* 240,235 **3** city, its ✱, SSW of Guadalajara *pop* 72,074

College Park, 1 city NW Ga. S of Atlanta *pop* 18,203 **2** city SW Md. NE of Washington, D.C. *pop* 26,156

College Station city E *cen* Tex. SE of Bryan *pop* 17,676

Col·lings·wood \'käl-iŋz-ˌwu̇d\ borough SW N.J. E of Camden *pop* 17,422

Col·lins·ville \'käl-ənz-ˌvil\ city SW Ill. NE of East St. Louis *pop* 17,773

Col·mar *or* **Kol·mar** \'kōl-ˌmär, kōl-'\ commune NE France at E edge of Vosges mountains *pop* 59,550

Co·logne \kə-'lōn\ *or* G **Köln** \'kœln\ city W Germany in No. Rhine-Westphalia on the Rhine *pop* 860,800

Co·lomb-Bé·char \kə-ˌlōⁿ(m)-bā-'shär\ commune NW Algeria SSE of Oran *pop* 42,090

Co·lombes \kə-'lōⁿ(m)b\ commune N France, NW suburb of Paris *pop* 80,357

Co·lom·bia \kə-'ləm-bē-ə *also* -'lōm-\ country NW So. America bordering on Caribbean sea & Pacific ocean ✱ Bogotá *area* 439,825, *pop* 21,770,000 — **Co·lom·bi·an** \-bē-ən\ *adj or n*

Co·lom·bo \kə-'ləm-(ˌ)bō\ city & port ✱ of Sri Lanka *pop* 510,947

Co·lón \kə-'lōn\ *or formerly* **As·pin·wall** \'as-pən-ˌwȯl\ city & port N Panama on the Caribbean at entrance to Panama canal *pop* 95,308

Colón archipelago — see GALÁPAGOS ISLANDS

Colonial Heights city SE Va. N of Petersburg *pop* 15,097

Col·o·phon \'käl-ə-fən, -ˌfän\ ancient city W Asia Minor in Lydia

Col·o·ra·do \ˌkäl-ə-'rad-(ˌ)ō, -'räd-\ **1** river 1450 *m* SW U.S. & NW Mexico rising in N Colo. & flowing SW into Gulf of California **2** river 840 *m* S Tex. flowing SE into Gulf of Mexico **3** desert SE Calif. W of Colorado river **4** plateau SW U.S. W of Rocky mountains in Colorado river basin in N Ariz., S & E Utah, W Colo., & NW N.Mex. **5** state W U.S. ✱ Denver *area* 104,247, *pop* 2,207,259 **6** river 530 *m*, *cen* Argentina flowing SE to the Atlantic — **Col·o·ra·dan** \-'rad-ᵊn, -'räd-\ *adj or n* — **Col·o·ra·do·an** \-'rad-ə-wən, -'räd-\ *adj or n*

Colorado National Monument reservation W Colo. W of Grand Junction containing many unusual erosion formations *area* 28
Colorado Springs city *cen* Colo. E of Pikes Peak *pop* 135,060
Co·los·sae \kə-'läs-(,)ē\ ancient city SW *cen* Asia Minor in SW Phrygia — **Co·los·sian** \kə-'läsh-ən\ *adj or n*
Col·ton \'kōlt-^{ə}n\ city SW Calif. S of San Bernardino *pop* 19,974
Co·lum·bia \kə-'ləm-bē-ə\ **1** river 1270 *m* SW Canada & NW U.S. rising in SE B.C. & flowing S & W into the Pacific **2** plateau E Wash., E Oreg., & SW Idaho in Columbia river basin **3** city *cen* Mo. *pop* 58,804 **4** city ✱ of S.C. *pop* 113,542 **5** city *cen* Tenn. *pop* 21,471 — **Co·lum·bi·an** \-bē-ən\ *adj or n*
Columbia, Cape cape N Canada on Ellesmere I.; northernmost point of Canada, at 83°07′N
Columbia, District of — see DISTRICT OF COLUMBIA
Columbia Heights city SE Minn. N of Minneapolis *pop* 17,533
Co·lum·bus \kə-'ləm-bəs\ **1** city W Ga. on the Chattahoochee *pop* 154,168 **2** city S *cen* Ind. *pop* 27,141 **3** city E Miss. *pop* 25,795 **4** city E Nebr. *pop* 15,471 **5** city ✱ of Ohio on the Scioto *pop* 539,677
Col·ville \'kōl-,vil, 'käl-\ river 320 *m* N Alaska flowing NE into Beaufort sea
Col·wyn Bay \,käl-wən-\ urban district N Wales in Denbighshire *pop* 25,535
Co·mil·la \kə-'mil-ə\ city Bangladesh *pop* 54,504
Commander — see KOMANDORSKIE
Commerce City \,käm-(,)ərs-\ city N *cen* Colo. N of Denver *pop* 17,407
Communism Peak — see GARMO PEAK
Co·mo \'kō-(,)mō\ commune N Italy in Lombardy at SW end of **Lake Como** (37 *m* long) *pop* 93,199
Comodoro Rivadavia — see RIVADAVIA
Com·o·rin, Cape \'käm-ə-rən; kə-'mōr-ən, -'mȯr-, -'mär-\ cape S India in Tamil Nadu; southernmost point of India, at 8°5′N
Com·o·ro \'käm-ə-,rō\ islands off SE Africa between Mozambique & Madagascar belonging to France *area* 790, *pop* 267,000
Com·piègne \kōmp-'yän\ town N France E of Beauvais on the Oise *pop* 29,700
Compostela SANTIAGO DE COMPOSTELA
Comp·ton \'käm(p)-tən\ city SW Calif. SSE of Los Angeles *pop* 78,611
Com·stock lode \,käm-,stäk-\ gold & silver lode at Virginia City, Nev., discovered 1859
Con·a·kry *or* **Kon·a·kry** \'kän-ə-krē\ city & port ✱ of Guinea on the Atlantic *pop* 197,267
Co·nan·i·cut \kə-'nan-i-kət\ island R.I. in Narragansett Bay W of Aquidneck I.
Con·cep·ción \kən-,sep-sē-'ōn, -'sep-shən\ city S *cen* Chile *pop* 191,746
Con·chos \'kän-chəs\ river 300 *m* N Mexico flowing NE into Rio Grande
Concord, 1 \'kän-,kȯ(ə)rd, 'käŋ-\ city W Calif. NE of Oakland *pop* 85,164 **2** \'käŋ-kərd\ town E Mass. NW of Boston *pop* 16,148 **3** \'käŋ-kərd\ city ✱ of N.H. on the Merrimack *pop* 30,022 **4** \'kän-,kȯ(ə)rd, 'käŋ-\ city S *cen* N.C. *pop* 18,464
Co·ney Island \,kō-nē-\ resort section of New York City in S Brooklyn; formerly an island
Con·ga·ree \'käŋ-gə-(,)rē\ river 60 *m*, *cen* S.C. flowing SE to unite with the Wateree forming the Santee
Con·go \'käŋ-(,)gō\ **1** *or* **Zaire** river *ab* 3000 *m*, *cen* Africa flowing N, W, & SW into the Atlantic — see LUALABA **2** — see ZAIRE **3** *or* **Congo Republic** *or formerly* **Middle Congo** country W *cen* Africa W of the lower Congo ✱ Brazzaville *area* 132,046, *pop* 960,000 — see FRENCH EQUATORIAL AFRICA — **Con·go·lese** \,käŋ-gə-'lēz, -'lēs\ *adj or n*
Congo Free State — see BELGIAN CONGO
Conjeeveram — see KANCHIPURAM
Con·nacht \'kän-,ȯt\ *or formerly* **Con·naught** province W Ireland *area* 6611, *pop* 389,763
Con·nect·i·cut \kə-'net-i-kət\ **1** river 407 *m* NE U.S. rising in N N.H. & flowing S into Long Island Sound **2** state NE U.S. ✱ Hartford *area* 5009, *pop* 3,032,217
Con·ne·ma·ra \,kän-ə-'mär-ə\ district W Ireland in W Galway on Atlantic coast
Con·ners·ville \'kän-ərz-,vil\ city E Ind. *pop* 17,604
Con·stance \'kän(t)-stən(t)s\ *or* G **Kon·stanz** \'kȯn-,stän(t)s\ commune W Germany on Lake Constance *pop* 60,821
Constance, Lake *or* G **Bo·den·see** \'bōd-^{ə}n-,zā\ lake 46 *m* long W Europe on border between Germany, Austria, & Switzerland
Con·stan·tine \'kän(t)-stən-,tēn\ city NE Algeria *pop* 243,558
Constantinople — see ISTANBUL
Con·stan·tsa \kən-'stän(t)-sə\ city & port SE Rumania on Black sea *pop* 170,026
Con·way \'kän-,wā\ city *cen* Ark. N of Little Rock *pop* 15,510
Cooch Be·har \,küch-bə-'här\ former state NE India W of Assam, since 1947 attached to West Bengal *area* 1321
Cook \'ku̇k\ **1** islands S Pacific SW of Society islands; belong to New Zealand ✱ Avarua (on Rarotonga I.) *area* 89, *pop* 22,000 **2** strait New Zealand between North I. & South I. **3** inlet of the Pacific S Alaska W of Kenai peninsula
Cook, Mount *or* **Ao·rangi** \au̇-'räŋ-ē\ mountain 12,349 *ft* New Zealand in W *cen* South I.; highest peak in Southern Alps & New Zealand
Coomassie — see KUMASI
Coon Rapids \'kün\ city E Minn. N of St. Paul *pop* 30,505
Coorg *or* **Kurg** \ku̇(ə)rg\ former state S India ✱ Mercara; merged with Mysore state 1956
Coo·sa \'kü-sə\ river 286 *m* NW Ga. & N Ala. flowing SW to join the Tallapoosa forming the Alabama
Coos Bay \'küs\ inlet of the Pacific SW Oreg.
Co·pán \kō-'pän\ ruined Mayan city W Honduras
Co·pen·ha·gen \,kō-pən-'hā-gən, -'häg-ən\ *or* Dan **Kø·ben·havn** \,kœ̄-bən-'hau̇n\ city & port ✱ of Denmark on E Sjælland I. & N Amager I. *pop* 643,262 — **Co·pen·ha·gen·er** \,kō-pən-'hā-gə-nər, -'häg-ə-\ *n*
Co·pia·pó \,kō-pē-ə-'pō\ **1** volcano 19,947 *ft* N *cen* Chile **2** city W of the volcano *pop* 36,767
Cop·per·mine \'käp-ər-,mīn\ river 525 *m* N Canada in Northwest Territories flowing NW into Arctic ocean
Coquilhatville — see MBANDAKA
Co·quim·bo \kō-'kim-(,)bō, -'kēm-\ city & port N *cen* Chile *pop* 39,610
Coral sea arm of the SW Pacific bounded on W by Queensland, Australia, on N by the Solomons, & on E by New Hebrides & New Caledonia
Coral Gables city SE Fla. SW of Miami *pop* 42,494
Cor·co·va·do \,kȯr-kə-'väd-(,)ō\ mountain 2310 *ft* SE Brazil on S side of city of Rio de Janeiro
Cor·dil·le·ra Cen·tral \,kȯrd-^{ə}l-'(y)er-ə-,sen-'träl, ,kȯrd-ē-'er-\ **1** range of the Andes in Colombia **2** range of the Andes in Peru E of the Marañón **3** chief range of the Dominican Republic **4** range Philippines in N Luzon — see PULOG **5** range S *cen* Puerto Rico — see CERRO DE PUNTA
Cordillera Mé·ri·da \-'mer-əd-ə\ *or* **Sier·ra Ne·va·da de Mérida** \sē-,er-ə-nə-'väd-ə-də-, -'vad-\ mountain range W Venezuela — see BOLÍVAR (Pico)
Cór·do·ba \'kȯrd-ə-bə, -ə-və\ **1** province S Spain *area* 5299, *pop* 724,116 **2** *or* **Cor·do·va** \'kȯrd-ə-və\ city, its ✱, on the Guadalquivir *pop* 229,407 **3** city N *cen* Argentina *pop* 586,015 — **Cor·do·ban** \-bən\ *adj or n*
Cor·do·va Island \,kȯrd-ə-və\ tract on the Rio Grande 382 acres adjoining Chemizal, formerly belonging to Mexico; 191 acres ceded to U.S. in 1963
Cor·fu \kȯr-'fü, 'kȯr-(,)f(y)ü\ *or* NGk **Kér·ky·ra** *or* **Kér·ki·ra** \'ker-ki-rə\ *or anc* **Cor·cy·ra** \kȯr-'sī-rə\ **1** island NW Greece, one of the Ionian islands *area* 227 **2** city & port on E Corfu *pop* 29,374 — **Cor·fi·ote** \'kȯr-fē-,ōt, -ət\ *n*
Cor·inth \'kȯr-ən(t)th, 'kär-\ *or* NGk **Kó·rin·thos** \'kȯr-ən-,thȯs\ **1** *or* **Co·rin·thia** \kə-'rin(t)-thē-ə\ region of ancient Greece occupying most of Isthmus of Corinth & part of NE Peloponnesus **2** city & port Greece on Isthmus of Corinth at head of Gulf of Corinth NE of site of ancient city of Corinth *pop* 15,892
Corinth, Gulf of *or* **Gulf of Le·pan·to** \'lep-ən-,tō, li-'pan-(,)tō\ inlet of Ionian sea *cen* Greece W of **Isthmus of Corinth** (neck of land 20 *m* long connecting Peloponnesus with rest of Greece)
Cork \'kȯ(ə)rk\ **1** county SW Ireland in Munster *area* 2881, *pop* 351,735 **2** city & county borough & port, its ✱, at head of Cork Harbor *pop* 122,146
Corn \'kȯ(ə)rn\ two small islands in the Caribbean 40 *m* off E coast of Nicaragua leased by Nicaragua to U.S.
Cor·ner Brook \'kȯ(r)-nər-,bru̇k\ city Canada in W Nfld. on Gulf of St. Lawrence *pop* 26,309
Corneto — see TARQUINIA
Cor·ning \'kȯr-niŋ\ city S N.Y. W of Elmira *pop* 15,792
Cor·no, Mon·te \,mänt-ē-'kȯr-(,)nō\ mountain 9585 *ft*, *cen* Italy NE of Rome; highest in the Apennines
Corn·wall \'kȯrn-,wȯl, -wəl\ **1** city Canada in SE Ont. on the St. Lawrence *pop* 47,116 **2** county SW England on peninsula projecting into the Atlantic ✱ Truro *area* 1375, *pop* 379,842
Co·ro \'kōr-(,)ō, 'kȯr-\ city NW Venezuela near coast at base of Paraguaná peninsula *pop* 55,955
Cor·o·man·del \,kȯr-ə-'man-d^{ə}l, ,kär-\ coast region SE India on Bay of Bengal S of the Kistna
Co·ro·na \kə-'rō-nə\ city SW Calif. E of Los Angeles *pop* 27,519
Cor·o·na·do \,kȯr-ə-'näd-(,)ō, ,kär-\ city SW Calif. on San Diego Bay opposite San Diego *pop* 20,910
Cor·pus Chris·ti \,kȯr-pə-'skris-tē\ city & port S Tex. on Corpus Christi Bay at mouth of Nueces river *pop* 204,525
Cor·reg·i·dor \kə-'reg-ə-,dȯ(ə)r\ island N Philippines at entrance to Manila Bay *area ab* 2
Cor·rien·tes \,kȯr-ē-'en-,tās, ,kär-\ city NE Argentina on the Paraná *pop* 97,507
Cor·si·ca \'kȯr-si-kə\ *or* F **Corse** \kȯrs\ island France in the Mediterranean N of Sardinia ✱ Ajaccio *area* 3367, *pop* 269,831 — **Cor·si·can** \'kȯr-si-kən\ *adj or n*
Cor·si·cana \,kȯr-sə-'kan-ə\ city NE *cen* Tex. *pop* 19,972
Cor·ti·na *or* **Cortina d'Am·pez·zo** \kȯr-'tē-nə-,däm-'pet-(,)sō\ resort village N Italy in the Dolomites N of Belluno
Cort·land \'kȯrt-lənd\ city S *cen* N.Y. *pop* 19,621
Cor·to·na \kȯr-'tō-nə\ commune *cen* Italy NW of Perugia *pop* 23,564
Coruña, La; Corunna — see LA CORUÑA
Cor·val·lis \kȯr-'val-əs\ city W Oreg. SW of Salem *pop* 35,153
Cos — see KOS
Co·sen·za \kō-'zen(t)-sə\ commune S Italy in Calabria *pop* 94,800
Cos·ta Bra·va \,käs-tə-'bräv-ə, ,kōs-, ,kȯs-\ coast region NE Spain in Catalonia on the Mediterranean extending NE from Barcelona
Costa del Sol \-del-'sȯl, -'sōl\ coast region S Spain on the Mediterranean extending E from Gibraltar
Cos·ta Me·sa \,kōs-tə-'mā-sə\ city SW Calif. SE of Long Beach on Pacific coast *pop* 72,660
Cos·ta Ri·ca \,käs-tə-'rē-kə, ,kȯs-, ,kōs-\ country Central America between Nicaragua & Panama; a republic ✱ San José *area* 19,238, *pop* 1,790,000 — **Cos·ta Ri·can** \-kən\ *adj or n*
Costermansville — see BUKAVU
Côte d'A·zur \,kōt-də-'zu̇(ə)r\ coast region SE France on the Mediterranean; part of the Riviera
Côte d'Ivoire — see IVORY COAST
Côte d'Or \kōt-'dȯ(ə)r\ range of hills E France SW of Dijon
Co·ten·tin \kō-tä^{n}-'ta^{n}\ peninsula NW France projecting into English channel W of mouth of the Seine
Côte–Saint–Luc \kōt-sänt-'lük, -sənt-\ city Canada in S Que. W of Montreal *pop* 24,375
Co·to·nou \,kōt-ə-'nü\ city & port S Dahomey *pop* 208,000
Co·to·paxi \,kōt-ə-'pak-sē, -'päk-\ volcano 19,347 *ft* N *cen* Ecuador
Cots·wold \'kät-,swōld\ hills SW *cen* England in Gloucestershire; highest point Cleeve Cloud 1031 *ft*
Cott·bus *or* **Kott·bus** \'kät-bəs, -,bu̇s\ city E Germany on Spree river SE of Berlin *pop* 82,897

Cot·ti·an Alps \ˌkät-ē-ən-\ range of W Alps France & Italy — see VISO

Couls·don and Pur·ley \'kōlz-də-nən-'pər-lē\ former urban district S England in Surrey, now part of Croydon

Coun·cil Bluffs \ˌkau̇n(t)-səl-'bləfs\ city SW Iowa *pop* 60,348

Cou·ran·tyne *or* **Co·ren·tyne** \'kōr-ən-ˌtīn, 'kȯr-\ *or* D **Co·ran·tijn** \-ˌtīn\ river 300 *m* N So. America flowing N into the Atlantic & forming boundary between Guyana & Surinam

Cour·be·voie \ˌku̇r-bəv-'wä\ commune N France on the Seine NW of Paris *pop* 58,118

Courland — see KURLAND

Cour·ma·yeur \ˌku̇r-mə-'yər\ resort village NW Italy in Val d'Aosta SE of Mont Blanc

Courtrai — see KORTRIJK

Cov·en·try 1 \'kəv-ən-trē\ town W R.I. SW of Providence *pop* 22,947 2 \'käv-, 'kəv-\ city & county borough *cen* England in Warwickshire *pop* 334,839

Co·vi·na \kō-'vē-nə\ city SW Calif. E of Los Angeles *pop* 30,380

Cov·ing·ton \'kəv-iŋ-tən\ city N Ky. *pop* 52,535

Cowes \'kau̇z\ urban district S England in N Isle of Wight *pop* 18,895

Cow·litz \'kau̇-ləts\ river 150 *m* SW Wash. flowing into the Columbia

Co·zu·mel \ˌkō-zə-'mel\ island SE Mexico off NE coast of Quintana Roo

Crab — see VIEQUES

Cracow — see KRAKOW

Cra·io·va \krə-'yō-və\ city S Rumania *pop* 171,676

Cran·ston \'kran(t)-stən\ city E R.I. S of Providence *pop* 73,037

Cra·ter \'krāt-ər\ lake 1932 *ft* deep SW Oreg. in Cascade range at altitude of 6164 *ft;* main feature of **Crater Lake National Park** (*area* 250) — see MAZAMA (Mount)

Craters of the Moon National Monument reservation SE *cen* Idaho including lava flows & other volcanic formations *area* 74

Cré·cy \krā-'sē, 'kres-ē\ *or* **Cres·sy** \'kres-ē\ *or* **Cré·cy–en–Pon·thieu** \krā-'sē-ä^{n}-pō^{n}-'tyə(r), -'tyœ\ commune N France NW of Amiens

Cre·mo·na \kri-'mō-nə\ commune N Italy in Lombardy on the Po ESE of Milan *pop* 80,798

Crest·wood \'krest-ˌwu̇d\ city E Mo. SW of St. Louis *pop* 15,398

Crete \'krēt\ *or* NGk **Kríti** \'krēt-ē\ island Greece in the E Mediterranean ✱ Canea *area* 3199, *pop* 483,075 — **Cre·tan** \'krēt-^{ə}n\ *adj or n*

Crete, Sea of *or* **Sea of Can·dia** \'kan-dē-ə\ the S section of Aegean sea between Crete & the Cyclades

Crewe \'krü\ municipal borough NW England in Cheshire *pop* 51,302

Cri·mea \krī-'mē-ə, krə-\ *or* Russ **Krim** \'krim\ peninsula U.S.S.R. in S Soviet Russia, Europe, extending into Black sea SW of Sea of Azov — **Cri·me·an** \krī-'mē-ən, krə-\ *adj*

Cris·to·bal \kris-'tō-bəl\ *or* Sp **Cris·tó·bal** town NW Panama Canal Zone adjoining Colón, Panama

Cro·atan \ˌkrō-ə-'tan\ *or* **Cro·ato·an** \-'tō-ən\ island of uncertain identity, probably Okracoke I., off coast of N.C. between Pamlico Sound & the Atlantic thought to be place to which Raleigh's Roanoke I. colony moved 1587

Cro·atia \krō-'ā-sh(ē-)ə\ 1 region SE Europe in NW Yugoslavia SE of Slovenia 2 constituent republic of Yugoslavia comprising Croatia, Slavonia, & most of Istria & the Dalmatian coast ✱ Zagreb *area* 21,726, *pop* 4,442,564

Crocodile — see LIMPOPO

Cros·by \'krȯz-bē\ *or* **Great Crosby** municipal borough NW England in Lancashire on Irish sea NNW of Liverpool *pop* 57,405

Cross \'krȯs\ river 300 *m* W Africa in W Cameroon & SE Nigeria flowing W & S into Gulf of Guinea

Cro·to·ne \krə-'tō-nē\ *or anc* **Cro·to·na** \-nə\ *or* **Cro·ton** \'krōˌtän, 'krōt-^{ə}n\ commune S Italy in Calabria on Gulf of Taranto *pop* 49,732

Croy·don \'krȯid-^{ə}n\ borough of S Greater London, England *pop* 331,851

Cro·zet \krō-'zā\ islands S Indian ocean WNW of Kerguelen

Crys·tal \'krist-t^{ə}l\ city SE Minn. N of Minneapolis *pop* 30,925

Cte·si·phon \'tes-əˌfän, 'tē-sə-\ ancient city *cen* Iraq on the Tigris opposite Seleucia ✱ of Parthia & of later Sassanid empire

Cuan·za \'kwän-zə\ river 500 *m* SW Africa in *cen* Angola flowing NW into the Atlantic

Cu·ba \'kyü-bə\ 1 island in the West Indies N of Caribbean sea *area* 41,634 2 country largely coextensive with island; a republic ✱ Havana *area* 46,736, *pop* 8,660,000 — **Cu·ban** \-bən\ *adj or n*

Cubango — see OKOVANGGO

Cú·cu·ta \'kü-kət-ə\ city N Colombia *pop* 207,091

Cud·a·hy \'kəd-ə-(ˌ)hē\ 1 city SW Calif. NW of Downey *pop* 16,998 2 city SE Wis. *pop* 22,078

Cuen·ca \'kweŋ-kə\ 1 city S Ecuador *pop* 77,300 2 province E *cen* Spain *area* 6636, *pop* 247,158 3 commune, its ✱, ESE of Madrid *pop* 34,485

Cuer·na·va·ca \ˌkwer-nə-'väk-ə, -'vak-\ city S *cen* Mexico S of Mexico City ✱ of Morelos *pop* 44,278

Cufra — see KUFRA

Cu·lia·cán \ˌkül-yə-'kän\ 1 river 175 *m* NW Mexico flowing SW into the Pacific at mouth of Gulf of California 2 city NW Mexico on the Culiacán ✱ of Sinaloa *pop* 358,812

Cul·lo·den Moor \kə-ˌläd-^{ə}n-, -ˌlōd-\ moorland N Scotland in N Inverness-shire E of Inverness

Cul·ver City \ˌkəl-vər\ city SW Calif. *pop* 31,035

Cu·mae \'kyü-(ˌ)mē\ ancient town S Italy on Tyrrhenian coast W of modern Naples — **Cu·mae·an** \kyü-'mē-ən\ *adj*

Cu·ma·ná \ˌkü-mə-'nä\ city & port NE Venezuela on the Caribbean NE of Barcelona *pop* 100,498

Cum·ber·land \'kəm-bər-lənd\ 1 river 687 *m* S Ky. & N Tenn. flowing W into the Ohio 2 falls SE Ky. in upper course of the Cumberland 3 caverns *cen* Tenn. SE of McMinnville 4 city NW Md. on the Potomac *pop* 29,724 5 town NE R.I. *pop* 26,605 6 county NW England ✱ Carlisle *area* 1511, *pop* 292,009 — **Cum·bri·an** \'kəm-brē-ən\ *adj or n*

Cumberland Gap mountain pass 1304 *ft* NE Tenn. through a ridge of the Cumberlands SE of Middlesboro, Ky.

Cumberland plateau *or* **Cumberland mountains** mountain region E U.S., part of the S Appalachian mountains W of Tennessee river extending from S W.Va. to NE Ala.

Cumbre, La — see USPALLATA

Cumbria — see STRATHCLYDE

Cum·bri·an \'kəm-brē-ən\ mountains NW England in Cumberland, Westmorland, & Lancashire — see SCAFELL PIKE

Cu·naxa \kyü-'nak-sə\ town in ancient Babylonia E of the Euphrates 87 *m* NW of Babylon

Cu·ne·ne *or* **Ku·ne·ne** \kü-'nā-nə\ river 700 *m* SW Africa in SW Angola flowing S & W into the Atlantic

Cu·par \'kü-pər\ burgh E Scotland ✱ of Fifeshire

Cu·per·ti·no \ˌkyü-pər-'tē-(ˌ)nō\ city W Calif. W of San José *pop* 18,216

Cuquenán — see KUKENAAM

Cu·ra·çao \'k(y)u̇r-ə-ˌsō, -ˌsau̇, ˌk(y)u̇r-ə-'\ island Netherlands Antilles in the S Caribbean; chief town Willemstad *area* 210, *pop* 143,778

Cu·ri·ti·ba \ˌku̇r-ə-'tē-bə\ city S Brazil SW of São Paulo ✱ of Paraná *pop* 616,548

Cush or **Kush** \'kəsh, 'ku̇sh\ ancient country NE Africa in Nile valley S of Egypt — **Cush·ite** \-ˌīt\ *adj or n* — **Cush·it·ic** \ˌkəsh-'it-ik, ku̇sh-\ *adj*

Cus·ter Battlefield National Monument \'kəs-tər\ site SE Mont. on Little Bighorn river of battle 1876

Cutch — see KUTCH

Cut·tack \'kət-ək\ city E India in Orissa *pop* 204,656

Cux·ha·ven \ku̇ks-'häf-ən\ city & port W Germany on North sea at mouth of the Elbe *pop* 45,383

Cuy·a·hoga \ˌkī-(ə-)'hō-gə, kə-'hȯ-, -'hä-, -'hō-\ river 100 *m* NE Ohio flowing into Lake Erie at Cleveland

Cuyahoga Falls city NE Ohio N of Akron *pop* 49,678

Cu·yu·ni \ku̇-'yü-nē\ river 300 *m* N So. America rising in E Venezuela & flowing E into the Essequibo in N Guyana

Cuz·co *or* **Cus·co** \'kü-(ˌ)skō\ city S Peru *pop* 105,400

Cyc·la·des \'sik-lə-ˌdēz\ *or* NGk **Ki·klá·dhes** \kē-'klät͟h-əs\ islands Greece in the S Aegean *area* 996 — **Cy·clad·ic** \sik-'lad-ik, sī-'klad-\ *adj*

Cydonia — see CANEA — **Cy·do·nian** \sī-'dō-nē-ən, -'dō-nyən\ *adj or n*

Cymru see WALES

Cy·press \'sī-prəs\ city SW Calif. SE of Los Angeles *pop* 31,026

Cy·prus \'sī-prəs\ 1 island E Mediterranean S of Turkey 2 country coextensive with the island; a republic of the Brit. Commonwealth ✱ Nicosia *area* 3572, *pop* 640,000 — **Cyp·ri·ot** \'sip-rē-ət, -rē-ˌät\ *or* **Cyp·ri·ote** \-ˌōt, -ət\ *adj or n*

Cy·re·na·ica \ˌsir-ə-'nā-ə-kə, ˌsī-rə-\ *or* It **Ci·re·na·ica** \ˌchē-rā-'nä-ē-kä\ 1 *or* **Cy·re·ne** \sī-'rē-(ˌ)nē\ ancient coastal region N Africa dominated by city of Cyrene 2 region E Libya, formerly a province — **Cy·re·na·ican** \ˌsir-ə-'nā-ə-kən, ˌsī-rə-\ *adj or n* — **Cy·re·ni·an** \sī-'rē-nē-ən\ *n*

Cy·re·ne \sī-'rē-(ˌ)nē\ ancient city N Africa on the Mediterranean in NE Libya; site at modern village of Shahat — **Cy·re·ni·an** \-nē-ən\ *adj or n*

Cythera — see KÍTHIRA

Cyz·i·cus \'siz-i-kəs\ 1 — see KAPIDAGI 2 ancient city in Mysia on isthmus leading to Kapidagi peninsula

Czecho·slo·va·kia \ˌchek-ə-slō-'väk-ē-ə, -'vak-\ country *cen* Europe; a republic ✱ Prague *area* 49,373, *pop* 14,500,000 — **Czecho·slo·vak** \-'slō-ˌväk, -ˌvak\ *adj or n* — **Czecho·slo·va·ki·an** \-slō-'väk-ē-ən, -'vak-\ *adj or n*

Cze·sto·cho·wa \ˌchen(t)-stə-'kō-və\ *or* Russ **Chen·sto·khov** \'chen(t)-stə-'kȯf, -'kȯv\ city S Poland on the Warta *pop* 186,200

Dac·ca \'dak-ə, 'däk-ə\ city ✱ of Bangladesh *pop* 829,000

Da·chau \'däk-ˌau̇\ city W Germany in S Bavaria *pop* 32,713

Da·cia \'dā-sh(ē-)ə\ ancient country & Roman province SE Europe roughly equivalent to Rumania & Bessarabia — **Da·cian** \-shən\ *adj or n*

Dag·en·ham \'dag-(ə-)nəm\ former municipal borough SE England in Essex, now part of Barking

Da·ge·stan *or* **Da·ghe·stan** \ˌdag-ə-'stan, ˌdäg-ə-'stän\ autonomous republic U.S.S.R. in SE Soviet Russia, Europe, on W shore of the Caspian ✱ Makhachkala *area* 13,124, *pop* 1,429,000

Da·ho·mey \də-'hō-mē\ country W Africa on Gulf of Guinea; a republic within the French Community; formerly a territory of French West Africa ✱ Porto-Novo *area* 44,749, *pop* 2,760,000 — **Da·ho·man** \-mən\ *adj or n* — **Da·ho·me·an** \-mē-ən\ *adj or n* — **Da·ho·mey·an** \-mē-ən\ *adj or n*

Dai·ren \'dī-'ren\ city & port NE China in S Liaoning on Liaotung peninsula — see LÜTA

Da·kar \'dakˌ-är, də-'kär\ city & port ✱ of Senegal *pop* 581,000

Da·ko·ta \də-'kōt-ə\ 1 — see JAMES 2 territory (1861–89) NW U.S. divided 1889 into states of N.Dak. & S.Dak. (the **Da·ko·tas** \-əz\) — **Da·ko·tan** \-'kōt-^{ə}n\ *adj or n*

Dal·e·car·lia \ˌdal-ə-'kär-lē-ə\ region W *cen* Sweden — **Dal·e·car·li·an** \-lē-ən\ *adj*

Dal·las \'dal-əs, 'da-lis\ city NE Tex. E of Fort Worth *pop* 844,401

Dal·ma·tia \dal-'mā-sh(ē-)ə\ region W Yugoslavia on the Adriatic — **Dal·ma·tian** \-shən\ *adj or n*

Dal·ton \'dȯlt-^{ə}n\ city NW Ga. *pop* 18,872

Da·ly City \ˌdā-lē-\ city W Calif. S of San Francisco *pop* 66,922

Da·man \də-'man\ *or* **Da·mão** \də-'mau̇^{n}\ 1 district W India, formerly part of Portuguese India, on Gulf of Cambay *area* 148 2 its chief town & port — see GOA

Da·man·hûr \ˌdam-ən-'hu̇(ə)r\ city N Egypt E of Alexandria *pop* 161,400

Da·mas·cus \də-'mas-kəs\ *or* Ar **Esh Sham** \esh-'sham\ city ✱ of Syria *pop* 835,000

Damavand — see DEMAVEND

Dam·i·et·ta \ˌdam-ē-'et-ə\ city & port N Egypt *pop* 98,000

Dam·mam \də-'mam\ town & port Saudi Arabia on Persian gulf
Da·mo·dar \'däm-ə-ˌdär\ river 350 *m* NE India in *cen* Bihar & West Bengal flowing ESE into the Hooghly
Dan \'dan\ **1** river 180 *m* S Va. & N N.C. flowing E into the Roanoke **2** ancient village at N extremity of Palestine N of Waters of Merom
Da Nang \(ʹ)dä-'näŋ\ *or* **Tou·rane** \tü-'rän\ city & port S Vietnam in Annam SE of Hue *pop* 334,229
Dan·bury \'dan-ˌber-ē, -b(ə-)rē\ city SW Conn. *pop* 50,781
Danger islands — see PUKAPUKA
Dangerous archipelago — see TUAMOTU
Danish West Indies the W islands of the Virgin islands group that were until 1917 a Danish possession & now constitute the Virgin Islands of the U.S.
Danmark — see DENMARK
Dan·ube \'dan-(ˌ)yüb\ *or* G **Do·nau** \'dō-ˌnau̇\ *or anc* **Da·nu·bi·us** \də-'n(y)ü-bē-əs, da-\ *or* **Is·ter** \'is-tər\river 1725 *m, cen* & SE Europe flowing SE from S Germany into Black sea — **Da·nu·bi·an** \da-'nyü-bē-ən\ *adj*
Dan·vers \'dan-vərz\ town NE Mass. N of Lynn *pop* 26,151
Dan·ville, **1** \'dan-ˌvil\ city E Ill. *pop* 42,570 **2** \-ˌvil, -vəl\ city S Va. on the Dan *pop* 46,391
Dan·zig \'dan(t)-sig, 'dän(t)-\ **1** — see GDANSK **2** territory surrounding & including Danzig that (1920–39) constituted a free city under the League of Nations *area* 754
Danzig, Gulf of inlet of S Baltic sea in N Poland & W U.S.S.R.
Dapsang — see GODWIN AUSTEN
Dar·da·nelles \ˌdärd-ᵊn-'elz\ *or* **Hel·les·pont** \'hel-ə-ˌspänt\ *or anc* **Hel·les·pon·tus** \ˌhel-ə-'spänt-əs\ strait NW Turkey connecting Sea of Marmara with the Aegean
Dar el Beida — see CASABLANCA
Dar es Sa·laam \ˌdär-ˌes-sə-'läm\ city & port ✱ of Tanzania & of Tanganyika on Indian ocean *pop* 343,911
Dar·fur \där-'fu̇(ə)r\ region W Sudan; chief city El Fasher
Dar·i·en \ˌdar-ē-'en, ˌder-\ **1** town SW Conn. on Long Island Sound *pop* 20,411 **2** Spanish colonial settlement Central America W of Gulf of Darien
Darien, Gulf of inlet of the Caribbean between E Panama & NW Colombia
Darien, Isthmus of — see PANAMA (Isthmus of)
Dar·jee·ling *or* **Dar·ji·ling** \där-'jē-liŋ\ city NE India in West Bengal on Sikkim border *pop* 40,651
Dar·ling \'där-liŋ\ **1** river 1160 *m* SE Australia in Queensland & New So. Wales flowing SW into the Murray **2** mountain range SW Western Australia extending *ab* 250 *m* N–S along coast; highest point Mt. Cooke 1910 *ft*
Dar·ling·ton \'där-liŋ-tən\ county borough N England in Co. Durham *pop* 85,889
Darm·stadt \'därm-ˌstat, -ˌs(h)tät\ city W Germany in Hesse SSW of Frankfurt *pop* 140,200
Dart·moor \'därt-ˌmu̇(ə)r, -ˌmō(ə)r, -ˌmȯ(ə)r\ tableland SW England in S Devonshire *area* 215
Dart·mouth \'därt-məth\ **1** town SE Mass. W of New Bedford *pop* 18,800 **2** city Canada in S N.S. on Halifax harbor opposite Halifax *pop* 64,770 **3** municipal borough & port SW England in S Devon on Dart river
Dar·win \'där-wən\ *or formerly* **Port Darwin** city & port N Australia ✱ of Northern Territory on Port Darwin (inlet of Timor sea) *pop* 21,617
Dar·yal Gorge *or* **Dar·lal Gorge** \där-ˌyal-\ mountain pass U.S.S.R. in S Soviet Russia, Europe, through Caucasus mountains; a gorge cut by Terek river
Dau·gav·pils \'dau̇-gəf-ˌpilz\ *or* Russ **Dvinsk** \də-'vin(t)sk\ city U.S.S.R. in E Latvia on the Dvina *pop* 101,000
Dau·phi·né \ˌdō-fi-'nā\ region & former province SE France N of Provence ✱ Grenoble
Da·vao \'däv-ˌau̇, dä-'vau̇\ **1** gulf of the Pacific Philippines in SE Mindanao **2** city Philippines on Davao gulf *pop* 337,000
Dav·en·port \'dav-ən-ˌpō(ə)rt, 'dav-ᵊm-, -ˌpȯ(ə)rt\ city E Iowa *pop* 98,469
Da·vis \'dā-vəs\ **1** mountains W Texas N of the Big Bend of the Rio Grande **2** strait between SW Greenland & E Baffin I. connecting Baffin Bay with the Atlantic **3** city W Calif. W of Sacramento *pop* 23,488
Da·vos \dä-'vōs\ commune E Switzerland in Graubünden
Dax \'daks\ commune SW France in the Landes on the Adour NE of Biarritz *pop* 19,348
Day·ton \'dāt-ᵊn\ city SW Ohio on the Miami *pop* 243,601
Day·to·na Beach \dā-ˌtō-nə, də-\ city NE Fla. *pop* 45,327
Dead sea \'ded\ *or bib* **Salt sea** \'sȯlt\ *or* L **La·cus As·phal·ti·tes** \'lā-kə-ˌsas-ˌfȯl-'tīt-ēz\salt lake *ab* 50 *m* long on boundary between Israel & Jordan *area* 370, surface 1286 *ft* below sea level
Dean, Forest of \'dēn\ forested district SW England in W Gloucestershire between Severn & Wye rivers; an ancient royal forest
Dear·born \'di(ə)r-ˌbȯ(ə)rn, -bərn\ city SE Mich. *pop* 104,199
Dearborn Heights city SE Mich. W of Detroit *pop* 80,069
Death Valley arid valley E Calif. & S Nev. containing lowest point in the U.S. (280 *ft* below sea level); most of area included in **Death Valley National Monument** (*area* 2891)
Deau·ville \'dō-ˌvil, dō-'vē(ə)l\ town NW France on Bay of the Seine SSW of Le Havre
De·bre·cen \'deb-rət-ˌsen\ city E Hungary *pop* 154,000
De·cap·o·lis \di-'kap-ə-ləs\ confederation of 10 ancient cities N Palestine in region chiefly SE of Sea of Galilee
De·ca·tur \di-'kāt-ər\ **1** city N Ala. *pop* 38,044 **2** city NW *cen* Ga. E of Atlanta *pop* 21,943 **3** city *cen* Ill. *pop* 90,397
Dec·can \'dek-ən, -ˌan\ plateau region S *cen* India lying between Eastern & Western Ghats
Ded·ham \'ded-əm\ town E Mass. SW of Boston *pop* 26,938
Dee \'dē\ **1** river 90 *m* NE Scotland flowing E into North sea **2** river 50 *m* S Scotland flowing S into Solway firth **3** river 70 *m* N Wales & W England flowing E & N into Irish sea
Deer·field \'di(ə)r-ˌfēld\ village NE Ill. NW of Chicago *pop* 18,949
Deerfield Beach city SE Fla. N of Fort Lauderdale *pop* 17,130
Defiance \di-'fī-ən(t)s\ city NW Ohio *pop* 16,281
Deh·ra Dun \ˌder-ə-'dün\ city N India in NW Uttar Pradesh *pop* 137,604
De Kalb \di-'kalb\ city N Ill. *pop* 32,949
Del·a·goa Bay \ˌdel-ə-ˌgō-ə-\ inlet of Indian ocean S Mozambique
Del·a·ware \'del-ə-ˌwa(ə)r, -ˌwe(ə)r, -wər\ **1** river 296 *m* E U.S. flowing S from S N.Y. into Delaware Bay **2** state E U.S. ✱ Dover *area* 2057, *pop* 548,104 **3** city *cen* Ohio NNW of Columbus *pop* 15,008 — **Del·a·war·ean** *or* **Del·a·war·ian** \ˌdel-ə-'war-ē-ən, -'wer-\ *adj or n*
Delaware Bay inlet of the Atlantic between SW N.J. & E Del.
Del City \'del\ city *cen* Okla. E of Oklahoma City *pop* 27,133
Delft \'delft\ commune SW Netherlands *pop* 83,698
Del·ga·do, Cape \del-'gäd-(ˌ)ō\ cape NE Mozambique
Del·hi \'del-ē\ **1** territory N India W of Uttar Pradesh ✱ Delhi *area* 578, *pop* 4,044,338 **2** city, its ✱ *pop* 3,772,457 — see NEW DELHI
Dells of the Wisconsin *or* **Wisconsin Dells** \'delz\ gorge of Wisconsin river in S *cen* Wis. N of Baraboo
Del·mar·va \del-'mär-və\ *or* **Del·mar·via** \-vē-ə\ peninsula E U.S. between Chesapeake & Delaware bays comprising Del. & parts of Md. & Va. — see EASTERN SHORE
Del·men·horst \'del-mən-ˌhȯrst\ city NW Germany in Lower Saxony WSW of Bremen *pop* 63,068
De·los \'dē-ˌläs\ *or* NGk **Dhí·los** \'thē-\ island Greece in *cen* Cyclades *area* 2 — **De·lian** \'dē-lē-ən, 'dēl-yən\ *adj or n*
Del·phi \'del-ˌfī\ ancient town *cen* Greece in Phocis on S slope of Mt. Parnassus near present village of **Dhel·foí** \thel-'fē\
Del·ray Beach \(ˌ)del-ˌrā\ city SE Fla. S of Palm Beach *pop* 19,366
Del Rio \del-'rē-(ˌ)ō, -'rē-ə\ city S Tex. on Rio Grande *pop* 21,330
Del·ta, The \'del-tə\ region NW Miss. between Mississippi & Yazoo rivers
Dem·a·vend \'dem-ə-ˌvend\ *or* **Dam·a·vand** \'dam-ə-ˌvand\ mountain 18,934 *ft* N Iran NE of Tehran; highest in Elburz mountains
Dem·e·ra·ra \ˌdem-ə-'rär-ə, -'rar-, -'rer-\ river 200 *m* Guyana flowing N into the Atlantic
Denali — see MCKINLEY (Mount)
Den·bigh \'den-bē\ *or* **Den·bigh·shire** \-ˌshi(ə)r, -shər\ county N Wales ✱ Ruthin *area* 669, *pop* 184,824
Den·der·mon·de \ˌden-dər-'män-də\ *or* **Ter·monde** \te(ə)r-'mōⁿ(n)d\ commune NW *cen* Belgium
Den Hel·der \də(n)-'hel-dər\ commune W Netherlands in No. Holland on an outlet from Wadden Zee to North sea *pop* 60,612
Den·i·son \'den-ə-sən\ city NE Tex. on Red river *pop* 24,923
De·niz·li \ˌden-əz-'lē\ city SW Turkey SE of Izmir *pop* 64,331
Den·mark \'den-ˌmärk\ *or* Dan **Dan·mark** \'dän-ˌmärk\ **1** country N Europe occupying most of Jutland peninsula & adjacent islands in Baltic & North seas; a kingdom ✱ Copenhagen *area* 16,576, *pop* 4,970,000 **2** strait 130 *m* wide between SE Greenland & Iceland connecting Arctic ocean with the Atlantic
Dent Blanche \däⁿ-bläⁿsh\ mountain 14,304 *ft* S Switzerland in Pennine Alps
Dent du Mi·di \ˌdäⁿ-də-mi-'dē\ mountain 10,686 *ft* SW Switzerland in W Alps
Den·ton \'dent-ᵊn\ city N Tex. NW of Dallas *pop* 39,874
D'En·tre·cas·teaux \ˌdän-trə-'kas-(ˌ)tō\ islands SW Pacific N of E tip of New Guinea belonging to Territory of Papua *area* 1200, *pop* 32,336
Den·ver \'den-vər\ city ✱ of Colo. *pop* 514,678 — **Den·ver·ite** \-və-ˌrīt\ *n*
De·pew \di-'pyü\ village NW N.Y. E of Buffalo *pop* 22,158
Dept·ford \'det-fərd\ former metropolitan borough SE London, England, now part of Lewisham
Der·be \'dər-(ˌ)bē\ ancient town S Asia Minor in S Lycaonia on border of Cilicia; exact site unknown
Der·bent *or* **Der·bend** \dər-'bent\ city U.S.S.R. in SE Soviet Russia, Europe, in Dagestan on Caspian sea *pop* 61,000
Der·by \'där-bē, *U.S. also* 'dər-\ **1** *or* **Der·by·shire** \-ˌshi(ə)r, -shər\ county N *cen* England *area* 1012, *pop* 884,339 **2** county borough, its ✱ *pop* 219,348
Der·na \'de(ə)r-nə\ city & port NE Libya *pop* 26,000
Derry — see LONDONDERRY
Der·went \'dər-wənt\ river 130 *m* Australia in Tasmania flowing SE into Tasman sea
Derwent Water lake NW England in Lake District in Cumberland
Desaguadero — see SALADO
Des·chutes \dā-'shüt\ river 250 *m, cen* & N Oreg. E of Cascade range flowing N into the Columbia
Des·er·et \ˌdez-ə-'ret\ provisional state of the U.S. S of 42d parallel & W of the Rockies organized 1849 by Mormons; part of it became Utah territory 1850
Des Moines \di-'mȯin\ **1** river 327 *m* Iowa flowing SE into the Mississippi **2** city ✱ of Iowa on Des Moines river *pop* 200,587
Des·na \də-'snä\ river 550 *m* U.S.S.R. in SW Soviet Russia, Europe, & N Ukraine flowing S into the Dnieper
Des Plaines \des-'plānz\ **1** river 150 *m* NE Ill. flowing S to unite with the Kankakee forming the Illinois **2** city NE Ill. NW of Chicago *pop* 57,239
Des·sau \'des-ˌau̇\ city E Germany N of Halle *pop* 98,261
Destêrro — see FLORIANÓPOLIS
De·troit \di-'trȯit\ **1** river 31 *m* Ont. & SE Mich. connecting Lakes Erie & St. Clair **2** city SE Mich. *pop* 1,511,482 — **De·troit·er** \-ər\ *n*
Detskoe Selo — see PUSHKIN
Deur·ne \'dərn(-ə)\ commune N Belgium, E suburb of Antwerp *pop* 79,106

Deutschland — see GERMANY
De·ven·ter \'dā-vən-tər\ commune E Netherlands *pop* 65,319
Devil Mountain — see AUYÁN-TEPUÍ
Devil's Island *or* F **Île du Dia·ble** \ēl-dūe-dyäblᵊ\ island French Guiana in the Safety islands group; former penal colony
Devils Post·pile \'pōst-ˌpīl\ lava formation E *cen* Calif. SE of Yosemite National Park; feature of **Devils Postpile National Monument** (*area* 1.3)
Devils Tower *or* **Ma·to Tepee** \ˌmät-(ˌ)ō-\ columnar rock formation NE Wyo. rising 865 *ft* above base, in **Devils Tower National Monument** (*area* 2)
Dev·on \'dev-ən\ **1** island N Canada in Franklin District in E Parry islands N of Baffin I. *area* 20,861 **2** *or* **Dev·on·shire** \-ˌshi(ə)r, -shər\ county SW England between Bristol & English channels ✱ Exeter *area* 2612, *pop* 896,245
Dews·bury \'d(y)üz-ˌber-ē, -b(ə-)rē\ county borough N England in West Riding, Yorkshire S of Leeds *pop* 51,310
Dezhnev, Cape — see EAST CAPE
Dhah·ran \dä-'rän, ˌdä-hə-'rän\ town SE Saudi Arabia on Persian gulf near Bahrein islands
Dhau·la·gi·ri \ˌdau̇-lə-'gi(ə)r-ē\ mountain 26,810 *ft* W *cen* Nepal in the Himalayas
Di·a·blo, Mount \dē-'äb-(ˌ)lō, dī-'ab-\ mountain 3849 *ft*, *cen* Calif. E of Oakland
Di·a·man·ti·na, **1** \ˌdī-ə-ˌman-'tē-nə\ river 470 *m* E *cen* Australia in SW Queensland flowing SW into the Warburton **2** \ˌdē-ə-\ town E Brazil in *cen* Minas Gerais *pop* 34,267
Diamond — see KUMGANG
Diamond Head promontory Hawaii on Oahu I. in SE Honolulu
Dié·go–Sua·rez \dē-ˌā-gō-'swär-əs\ city & port Malagasy Republic near N tip of Madagascar *pop* 40,237
Dien Bien Phu \ˌdyen-ˌbyen-'fü\ village NW Vietnam
Di·eppe \dē-'ep\ city & port N France N of Rouen *pop* 29,970
Di·jon \dē-zhōⁿ\ city E France *pop* 145,357
Diks·mui·de *or* **Dix·mui·de** \dik-'smīd-ə\ *or* **Dix·mude** \dēk-smu̅ed\ town W Belgium in West Flanders N of Ieper
Di·li \'dē-lē\ city & port N Timor ✱ of Portuguese Timor *pop* 29,312
Di·mi·trov·grad \də-'mē-trəf-ˌgrad\ city S Bulgaria on Maritsa river ESE of Plovdiv *pop* 44,302
Di·mi·tro·vo — see PERNIK
Di·nar·ic Alps \də-ˌnar-ik-\ range of E Alps W Yugoslavia; highest point Djeravica (SW of Pec) 8714 *ft*
Din·gle Bay \ˌdiŋ-gəl-\ inlet of the Atlantic SW Ireland
Ding·wall \'diŋ-ˌwȯl\ burgh N Scotland ✱ of Ross and Cromarty
Dinosaur National Monument reservation NW Colo. & NE Utah at junction of Green & Yampa rivers; rich fossil deposits *area* 328
Di·o·mede \'dī-ə-ˌmēd\ islands in Bering strait comprising **Big Diomede** (U.S.S.R.) & **Little Diomede** (U.S.)
Diospolis — see THEBES
Di·re·dawa \ˌdir-ə-'dau̇-ə\ city E Ethiopia *pop* 60,925
Dis·ko \'dis-(ˌ)kō\ island W Greenland in Davis strait
Dismal swamp SE Va. & NE N.C. between Chesapeake Bay & Albemarle Sound *ab* 40 *m* long, 10 *m* wide
District of Co·lum·bia \kə-'ləm-bē-ə\ federal district E U.S. coextensive with city of Washington *area* 67, *pop* 756,510
Distrito Federal — see FEDERAL DISTRICT
Diu \'dē-(ˌ)ü\ district W India, formerly part of Portuguese India, at S end of Kathiawar peninsula *area* 20 — see GOA
Dix·on \'dik-sən\ city NW Ill. on Rock river *pop* 18,147
Dixon Entrance strait between N Queen Charlotte islands, B.C., & Prince of Wales I., Alaska
Di·yar·ba·kir \di-ˌ(y)är-bä-'ki(ə)r\ *or* **Di·ar·bekr** \-'bek-ər\ city SE Turkey on the Tigris *pop* 102,653
Diz *or* **Ab–i–Diz** \ˌäb-ə-'dēz, ˌab-ə-'diz\ river 250 *m* W Iran flowing S to the Karun
Diz·ful \diz-'fül\ city SW Iran on the Karun *pop* 88,000
Djailolo — see HALMAHERA
Dja·ja·pu·ra \ˌjä-yə-'pu̇r-ə\ *or formerly* **Hol·lan·dia** \hä-'lan-dē-ə\ *or* **Ko·ta·ba·ru** \ˌkōt-ə-'bär-(ˌ)ü\ *or* **Su·kar·na·pu·ra** \sü-ˌkär-nə-'pu̇r-ə\ city & port Indonesia ✱ of West Irian
Dja·kar·ta *or* **Ja·kar·ta** \jə-'kärt-ə\ *or formerly* **Ba·ta·via** \bə-'tā-vē-ə\ city & port ✱ of Indonesia on NW coast of Java *pop* 2,906,533
Djam·bi *or* **Jam·bi** \'jäm-bē\ city & port Indonesia in SE *cen* Sumatra on Hari river *pop* 113,080
Djawa — see JAVA
Djer·ba *or* **Jer·ba** \'jər-bə, 'je(ə)r-\ island SE Tunisia in the Mediterranean at entrance to Gulf of Gabes *area* 16, *pop* 62,446
Dji·bou·ti *or* **Ji·bu·ti** \jə-'büt-ē\ city ✱ of French Territory of the Afars and the Issas on Gulf of Tadjoura *pop* 41,536
Djokjakarta — see JOGJAKARTA
Dne·pro·dzer·zhinsk \'nep-(ˌ)rō-dər-'zhin(t)sk\ city U.S.S.R. in E *cen* Ukraine on the Dnieper W of Dnepropetrovsk *pop* 227,000
Dne·pro·pe·trovsk \-pə-'trōfsk\ *or formerly* **Eka·te·ri·no·slav** \i-ˌkat-ə-'rē-nə-ˌsläf, -ˌsläv\ city U.S.S.R. in E *cen* Ukraine on the Dnieper *pop* 863,000
Dnie·per \'nē-pər\ river 1400 *m* U.S.S.R. rising in S Valdai hills & flowing S through Ukraine into Black sea
Dnies·ter \'nēs-tər\ river 850 *m* U.S.S.R. rising on N slope of Carpathian mountains & flowing SE into Black sea
Do·bru·ja *or* **Do·bru·dja** \'dō-brə-ˌjä\ region S Europe in Rumania & Bulgaria on Black sea S of the Danube
Do·de·ca·nese \dō-'dek-ə-ˌnēz, ˌdō-di-kə-, -ˌnēs\ islands Greece in the SE Aegean comprising the Southern Sporades S of Icaria & Samos; belonged to Italy 1923–47 *area* 486 — see RHODES — **Do·de·ca·ne·sian** \(ˌ)dō-ˌdek-ə-'nē-zhən, ˌdō-di-kə-, -shən\ *adj or n*
Do·do·na \də-'dō-nə\ ancient city NW Greece in Epirus on Mt. Tomarus
Dog·ger Bank \ˌdȯg-ər-, ˌdäg-\ submerged sandbank *ab* 150 *m* long in North sea *ab* 60 *m* E of N England
Do·ha \'dō-(ˌ)hä\ city & port ✱ of Qatar on Persian Gulf *pop* 95,000
Dol·gel·lau \däl-'gel-ˌī\ *or* **Dol·gel·ley** *or* **Dol·gel·ly** \-'gel-ē\ urban district W Wales ✱ of Merionethshire
Dol·lard–des–Or·meaux \dȯ-'lär-ˌdā-ˌzȯr-'mō\ town Canada in S Que. NW of Montreal *pop* 25,217
Do·lo·mites \'dō-lə-ˌmīts, 'däl-ə-\ *or* **Dolomite Alps** range of E Alps NE Italy between Adige & Piave rivers — see MARMOLADA
Dol·ton \'dōlt-ᵊn\ village NE Ill. S of Chicago *pop* 25,937
Dôme, Puy de \ˌpwēd-ə-'dōm\ mountain 4805 *ft* S *cen* France in Auvergne mountains
Dom·i·ni·ca \ˌdäm-ə-'nē-kə\ island Brit. West Indies in the Leeward islands ✱ Roseau *area* 305, *pop* 70,302 — see WEST INDIES ASSOCIATED STATES
Do·min·i·can Republic \də-ˌmin-i-kən-\ *or formerly* **San·to Do·min·go** \ˌsant-əd-ə-'miŋ-(ˌ)gō\ *or* **San Domingo** \ˌsan-də-\ country West Indies on E Hispaniola; a republic ✱ Santo Domingo *area* 18,700, *pop* 4,190,000 — **Do·min·i·can** \-'min-\ *adj or n*
Dom·ré·my–la–Pu·celle \ˌdōⁿr-ə-ˌmē-(ˌ)läp-(y)ü-'sel\ village NE France on the Meuse SW of Nancy
Don \'dän\ river 1200 *m* U.S.S.R. in SW Soviet Russia, Europe, flowing SE & then SW into Sea of Azov
Donau — see DANUBE
Don·cas·ter \'däŋ-kə-stər\ county borough N England in West Riding, Yorkshire *pop* 82,505
Don·e·gal \ˌdän-i-'gȯl, ˌdən-\ county NW Republic of Ireland in Ulster ✱ Lifford *area* 1865, *pop* 108,000
Donegal Bay inlet of the Atlantic NW Ireland
Do·nets \də-'nets\ river 670 *m* U.S.S.R. in SE Ukraine & SW Soviet Russia, Europe, flowing SE into the Don
Donets Basin *or* **Don·bass** *or* **Don·bas** \ˌdən-'bas\ region U.S.S.R. in E Ukraine SW of Donets river
Do·netsk \də-'netsk\ *or formerly* **Sta·li·no** \'stäl-i-ˌnō, 'stal-\ *or* **Sta·lin** \'stäl-ən, 'stal-, -ˌēn\ *or* **Yu·zov·ka** \'yü-zəf-kə\ city U.S.S.R. in E Ukraine in Donets basin *pop* 879,000
Don·ner \'dän-ər\ mountain pass 7135 *ft* E Calif. in Sierra Nevada NW of Lake Tahoe
Don·ny·brook \'dän-ē-ˌbru̇k\ city E Ireland in Leinster, SE suburb of Dublin *pop* 37,228
Door \'dōr\ peninsula E Wis. between Green Bay & Lake Michigan
Doornik — see TOURNAI
Dor·ches·ter \'dȯr-chə-stər, -ˌches-tər\ municipal borough S England ✱ of Dorset *pop* 19,424
Dor·dogne \dȯr-'dōn(-yə)\ river 300 *m* SW France flowing SW & W to unite with the Garonne forming the Gironde estuary
Dor·drecht \'dȯr-ˌdrekt\ *or* **Dordt** *or* **Dort** \'dȯ(ə)rt\ commune SW Netherlands in So. Holland on the Maas *pop* 88,699
Dore, Monts \mōⁿ-'dō(ə)r, -'dȯ(ə)r\ mountain group S *cen* France in Auvergne mountains — see SANCY (Puy de)
Do·ris \'dōr-əs, 'dȯr-, 'där-\ **1** ancient country *cen* Greece between Mounts Oeta & Parnassus **2** ancient district SW Asia Minor on coast of Caria
Dor·noch \'dȯr-nək\ burgh N Scotland ✱ of Sutherland
Dorpat — see TARTU
Dor·set \'dȯr-sət\ *or* **Dor·set·shire** \-ˌshi(ə)r, -shər\ county S England ✱ Dorchester *area* 973, *pop* 361,213
Dorset, Cape cape Canada in SW Baffin I. at S tip of Foxe peninsula
Dort·mund \'dȯ(ə)rt-ˌmu̇nt, -mənd\ city W Germany in the Ruhr *pop* 647,000
Dor·val \dȯr-'val, -'väl\ city Canada in S Que. SW of Montreal *pop* 20,469
Do·than \'dō-thən\ city SE Ala. *pop* 36,733
Dou·ai *or formerly* **Dou·ay** \dü-'ā\ city N France S of Lille *pop* 49,187
Dou·a·la *or* **Du·a·la** \du̇-'äl-ə\ city & port SW Cameroon on Bight of Biafra *pop* 250,000
Doug·las \'dəg-ləs\ city & port ✱ of Isle of Man *pop* 20,385
Dou·ro \'dōr-(ˌ)ü, 'dȯr-\ *or* Sp **Due·ro** \'dwe(ə)r-(ˌ)ō\ river 485 *m* N Spain & N Portugal flowing W into the Atlantic
Do·ver \'dō-vər\ **1** city ✱ of Del. *pop* 17,488 **2** city SE N.H. *pop* 20,850 **3** town N N.J. NW of Morristown *pop* 15,039 **4** municipal borough SE England in Kent on Strait of Dover *pop* 34,322
Dover, Strait of *or* F **Pas de Ca·lais** \päd-(ə-)kȧ-le\ channel between SE England & N France, easternmost section of English channel; 20 *m* wide at narrowest point
Down \'dau̇n\ county SE Northern Ireland ✱ Downpatrick *area* 952, *pop* 311,266
Dow·ners Grove \ˌdau̇-nərz-\ village NE Ill. W of Chicago *pop* 32,751
Dow·ney \'dau̇-nē\ city SW Calif. SE of Los Angeles *pop* 88,445
Down·pat·rick \dau̇n-'pa-trik\ urban district SE Northern Ireland ✱ of County Down
Downs \'dau̇nz\ **1** two ranges of hills SE England — see NORTH DOWNS, SOUTH DOWNS **2** roadstead in English channel along E coast of Kent protected by the Goodwin Sands
Dra·chen·fels \'dräk-ən-ˌfelz\ hill 1053 *ft* W Germany in the Siebengebirge on the Rhine S of Bonn
Dra·cut \'drā-kət\ town NE Mass. N of Lowell *pop* 18,214
Dra·kens·berg \'dräk-ənz-ˌbərg\ *or* **Quath·lam·ba** \kwät-'läm-bə\ mountains E Republic of So. Africa & in Lesotho; highest Thabana Ntlenyana 11,425 *ft*
Drake Passage *or* **Drake Strait** \'drāk\ strait S of So. America between Cape Horn & So. Shetlands
Dram·men \'dräm-ən\ city & port SE Norway on a branch of Oslo Fjord *pop* 49,271
Dran·cy \dräⁿ-'sē\ commune N France, NE suburb of Paris *pop* 69,444
Dra·va *or* **Dra·ve** \'dräv-ə\ river 450 *m* S Austria & N Yugoslavia flowing SE into the Danube
Dren·the *or* **Dren·te** \'dren-tə\ province NE Netherlands ✱ Assen *area* 1030, *pop* 366,590
Dres·den \'drez-dən\ city E Germany in Saxony *pop* 500,726
Dri·na \'drē-nə\ river 160 *m*, *cen* Yugoslavia flowing N along the border between Bosnia & Serbia into the Sava
Dro·ghe·da \'drȯ(i)-əd-ə, 'drȯid-ə\ municipal borough E Ireland in County Louth on the Boyne *pop* 19,744
Drug \'drüg\ — see DURG
Drum·mond·ville \'drəm-ən-ˌ(d)vil\ city Canada in S Que. NE of Montreal *pop* 31,813

Druz, Jebel (ed) — see JEBEL ED DRUZ
Dry Tor·tu·gas \(,)tȯr-'tü-gəz\ small island group S Fla. WNW of Key West; site of **Fort Jef·fer·son National Monument** \'jef-ər-sən\
Du·bawnt \dü-'bȯnt\ **1** lake N Canada in SE Northwest Territories E of Great Slave Lake *area* 1654 **2** river 580 *m* N Canada flowing NE through Dubawnt Lake to **Ba·ker Lake** \'bā-kər-\ (W expansion of Chesterfield inlet)
Dub·lin \'dəb-lən\ **1** city *cen* Ga. *pop* 15,143 **2** *or* Gael **Bai·le Atha Cli·ath** \blä-'klē-ə\ county E Ireland in Leinster *area* 356, *pop* 849,542 **3** *or* Gael **Baile Atha Cliath** city & county borough & port ✱ of Republic of Ireland & of County Dublin at mouth of the Liffey on **Dublin Bay** (inlet of Irish sea) *pop* 568,772 — **Dub·lin·er** \'dəb-lə-nər\ *n*
Du·brov·nik \'dü-,brȯv-nik\ *or* It **Ra·gu·sa** \rə-'gü-zə\ city & port SW Yugoslavia in Croatia *pop* 26,000
Du·buque \də-'byük\ city E Iowa on the Mississippi *pop* 62,309
Dud·ley \'dəd-lē\ county borough W *cen* England in Worcestershire & Staffordshire WNW of Birmingham *pop* 185,535
Dui·no \dü-'ē-(,)nō, 'dwē-\ village NE Italy on the Adriatic NW of Trieste
Duis·burg \'dü-əs-,bərg, 'd(y)üz-, *Ger* 'düs-,bu̇rk\ *or formerly* **Duisburg–Ham·born** \-häm-'bȯ(ə)rn\ city W Germany at junction of Rhine & Ruhr rivers *pop* 460,500
Du·luth \də-'lüth\ city & port NE Minn. at W end of Lake Superior *pop* 100,578 — **Du·luth·ian** \-'lü-thē-ən\ *adj or n*
Dul·wich \'dəl-ij, -ich\ a SE district of London, England, in Southwark borough
Dum·bar·ton \,dəm-'bärt-ᵊn\ **1** burgh W *cen* Scotland ✱ of Dunbartonshire *pop* 25,640 **2** *or* **Dum·bar·ton·shire** \-,shi(ə)r, -shər\ DUNBARTON
Dum·fries \,dəm-'frēs\ **1** *or* **Dum·fries·shire** \-'frēs(h)-,shi(ə)r, -shər\ county S Scotland *area* 1073, *pop* 88,215 **2** burgh, its ✱ *pop* 29,384
Du·mont \'d(y)ü-,mänt\ borough NE N.J. E of Paterson *pop* 17,534
Dun·barton \,dən-'bärt-ᵊn\ *or* **Dun·bar·ton·shire** \-,shi(ə)r, -shər\ county W *cen* Scotland ✱ Dumbarton *area* 244, *pop* 237,518
Dun·can \'dəŋ-kən\ city S Okla. *pop* 19,718
Dun·dalk \,dən-'dȯ(l)k\ urban district & port NE Republic of Ireland on Dundalk Bay ✱ of County Louth *pop* 21,718
Dun·das \'dən-dəs\ town Canada in SE Ont. NW of Hamilton *pop* 17,208
Dun·dee \,dən-'dē\ burgh & port E Scotland in Angus on Firth of Tay *pop* 182,084
Dun·edin \,də-'nēd-ᵊn\ **1** city W Fla. N of Clearwater *pop* 17,639 **2** — see EDINBURGH **3** city New Zealand on SE coast of South I. at head of Otago Harbor *pop* 59,400
Dun·ferm·line \,dən-'fərm-lən\ burgh E Scotland in Fife *pop* 49,-882
Dun·kerque *or* **Dun·kirk** \'dən-,kərk, ,dən-'\ city & port N France on Strait of Dover *pop* 27,504
Dun·kirk \'dən-,kərk\ city W N.Y. on Lake Erie *pop* 16,855
Dun Laoghai·re \,dən-'le(ə)r-ə\ *or* **Dun·lea·ry** \-'li(ə)r-ē\ *or formerly* **Kings·town** \'kiŋ-,stau̇n\ city borough & port E Ireland in Leinster on Dublin Bay *pop* 52,990
Dun·more \'dən-,mō(ə)r, -,mȯ(ə)r\ borough NE Pa. E of Scranton *pop* 17,300
Dun·net Head \,dən-ət-\ headland N Scotland on N coast in Caithness W of John o' Groat's; northernmost point of mainland of Scotland, at 58°50'N
Duns \'dənz\ burgh SE Scotland ✱ of Berwick
Duque de Caxias \,dü-kə-də-kə-'shē-əs\ city SE Brazil in Rio de Janeiro state N of city of Rio de Janeiro *pop* 324,261
Du·rance \d(y)u̇-'räⁿs\ river 160 *m* SE France flowing SW into the Rhone
Du·ran·go \d(y)u̇-'raŋ-(,)gō\ **1** state NW *cen* Mexico *area* 42,272, *pop* 919,381 **2** city, its ✱ *pop* 192,934
Dur·ban \'dər-bən\ city & port E Republic of So. Africa in E Natal on Natal Bay *pop* (with suburbs) 560,100
Durg \'du̇(ə)rg\ *or formerly* **Drug** \'drüg\ city E *cen* India in SE Madhya Pradesh E of Nagpur *pop* 64,132
Dur·ham \'dər-əm, 'də-rəm, 'du̇r-əm\ **1** city NE *cen* N.C. NW of Raleigh *pop* 95,438 **2** county N England bordering on North sea *area* 1015, *pop* 1,408,103 **3** municipal borough, its ✱, S of Newcastle *pop* 24,744
Dur·res \'du̇r-əs\ *or* It **Du·raz·zo** \du̇-'rät-(,)sō\ *or anc* **Ep·i·dam·nus** \'ep-ə-'dam-nəs\ *or* **Dyr·ra·chi·um** \də-'rā-kē-əm\ city & port Albania on Adriatic sea W of Tirane *pop* 53,160
Du·shan·be \d(y)ü-'sham-bə, -'shäm-\ *or formerly* **Sta·lin·abad** \,stäl-i-nə-'bäd, ,stal-i-nə-'bad\ city U.S.S.R. in Soviet Central Asia ✱ of Tadzhik Republic *pop* 374,000
Düs·sel·dorf \'d(y)üs-əl-,dȯrf, 'dues-\ city W Germany on the Rhine N of Cologne ✱ of No. Rhine-Westphalia *pop* 683,000
Dutch Borneo — see KALIMANTAN
Dutch East Indies NETHERLANDS EAST INDIES
Dutch Guiana — see SURINAM
Dutch New Guinea NETHERLANDS NEW GUINEA
Dutch West Indies — see NETHERLANDS ANTILLES
Dvi·na \də-,vē-'nä\ **1** river 630 *m* U.S.S.R. rising in Valdai hills & flowing W into Gulf of Riga **2** — see NORTHERN DVINA
Dvina Gulf *or* **Dvina Bay** *or formerly* **Gulf of Arch·an·gel** \'är-,kān-jəl\ arm of White sea U.S.S.R. in N Soviet Russia, Europe
Dvinsk — see DAUGAVPILS
Dzaudzhikau — see ORDZHONIKIDZE
Dzer·zhinsk \dər-'zhin(t)sk\ city U.S.S.R. in *cen* Soviet Russia, Europe, on Oka river W of Gorki *pop* 221,000
Dzun·gar·ia *or* **Zun·gar·ia** \,(d)zən-'gar-ē-ə, (d)zu̇ŋ-, -'ger-\ region W China in N Sinkiang N of the Tien Shan
E¹ — see LHOTSE
Ea·gle \'ē-gəl\ lake 13 *m* long N Calif. ENE of Lassen Peak
Eagle Pass city SW Tex. on Rio Grande *pop* 15,364
Ea·ling \'ē-liŋ\ borough of W Greater London, England *pop* 299,-450
East An·glia \'aŋ-glē-ə\ region E England including Norfolk & Suffolk; one of kingdoms in Anglo-Saxon heptarchy — **East An·gli·an** \-ən\ *adj or n*
East Bengal the part of Bengal now in Bangladesh
East Beskids — see BESKIDS
East·bourne \'ēs(t)-,bō(ə)rn, -,bȯ(ə)rn\ county borough S England in East Sussex on English channel *pop* 70,495
East Cape *or* **Cape Dezh·nev** \-,dezh-nē-'ȯf, -,desh-, -'ȯv\ cape U.S.S.R. in NE Soviet Russia, Asia, at E end of Chukotski peninsula
East Chicago city NW Ind. SE of Chicago, Ill. *pop* 46,982
East China sea W Pacific between China (on W), Korea (on N), Japan & Ryukyu islands (on E), & Formosa (on S)
East Cleveland city NE Ohio NE of Cleveland *pop* 39,600
East Detroit city SE Mich. NE of Detroit *pop* 45,920
Eas·ter \'ē-stər\ *or* **Ra·pa Nui** \,räp-ə-'nü-ē\ *or* Sp **Is·la de Pas·cua** \,ēz-lä-də-'päs-kwə\ island SE Pacific 2000 *m* W of Chilean coast belonging to Chile *area* 50
Eastern Ghats chain of mountains SE India extending SW & S from near delta of Mahanadi river in Orissa to W Madras & S Kerala; highest point Mt. Dodabetta (in Nilgiri hills) 8647 *ft* — see WESTERN GHATS
Eastern Rumelia *or* **Eastern Roumelia** region S Bulgaria including Rhodope mountains & Maritsa river valley *area* 12,585
Eastern Samoa — see AMERICAN SAMOA
Eastern Shore region E Md. & E Va E of Chesapeake Bay; sometimes considered as including Del. — see DELMARVA
Eastern Thrace — see THRACE
East Flanders province NW *cen* Belgium ✱ Ghent *area* 1147, *pop* 1,314,031
East Frisian — see FRISIAN
East Germany the German Democratic Republic — see GERMANY
East Ham \'ēst-'ham\ former county borough SE England in Essex, now part of Newham
East Hartford town *cen* Conn. *pop* 57,583
East Haven \'ēst-,hā-vən\ town S Conn. SE of New Haven *pop* 25,120
East Indies, 1 *or* **East India** southeastern Asia including India, Indochina, Malaya, & Malay archipelago — a chiefly former name **2** the Malay archipelago — **East Indian** *adj or n*
East Kil·do·nan \kil-'dō-nən\ city Canada in SE Man. NE of Winnipeg *pop* 30,152
East·lake \'ēst-,lāk\ city NE Ohio NE of Cleveland *pop* 19,690
East Lansing city S Mich. *pop* 47,540
East Liverpool city E Ohio on the Ohio *pop* 20,020
East London city & port S Republic of So. Africa in SE Cape of Good Hope on Indian ocean *pop* 113,746
East Lo·thi·an \'lō-th̲ē-ən\ *or* **Had·ding·ton** \'had-iŋ-t ən\ *or* **Had·ding·ton·shire** \-,shi(ə)r, -shər\ county SE Scotland ✱ Haddington *area* 267, *pop* 55,891
East·main \'ēst-,mān\ river 375 *m* Canada in W Que. flowing W into James Bay
East Malaysia the parts of Malaysia on the island of Borneo, comprising Sabah and Sarawak
East Moline city NW Ill. on the Mississippi *pop* 20,832
Eas·ton \'ē-stən\ city E Pa. NE of Bethlehem at junction of Lehigh & Delaware rivers *pop* 30,256
East Orange city NE N.J. NW of Newark *pop* 75,471
East Pakistan the former E division of Pakistan comprising the E portion of Bengal; now independent — see BANGLADESH
East Paterson borough NE N.J. *pop* 22,749
East Peoria city N *cen* Ill. *pop* 18,455
East Point \'ēst-,pȯint\ city NW *cen* Ga. SW of Atlanta *pop* 39,315
East Providence city E R.I. *pop* 48,151
East Prussia region N Europe bordering on the Baltic E of Pomerania; formerly a province of Prussia, for a time (1919–39) forming an exclave separated from rest of Prussia by Polish Corridor; since 1945 in Poland & U.S.S.R.
East Punjab — see PUNJAB
East Ridge \'ēst-,rij\ town SE Tenn. SE of Chattanooga *pop* 21,799
East Riding — see YORK
East river strait SE N.Y. connecting Upper New York Bay with Long Island Sound & separating Manhattan I. from Long I.
East Saint Louis city SW Ill. *pop* 69,996
East Siberian sea arm of Arctic ocean N of Yakutsk Republic, U.S.S.R., extending from New Siberian islands to Wrangel I.
East Suffolk — see SUFFOLK
East Sussex — see SUSSEX
Eastview — see VANIER
Eau Claire \ō-'kla(ə)r, -'kle(ə)r\ city W Wis. *pop* 44,619
Eb·bw Vale \'eb-ü-,vāl\ urban district SE Wales in Monmouthshire N of Cardiff *pop* 26,049
Eboracum — see YORK
Ebro \'ā-(,)brō\ river 480 *m* NE Spain flowing from Cantabrian mountains ESE into the Mediterranean
Ecbatana — see HAMADAN
Ecorse \'ē-,kȯrs\ city SE Mich. SSW of Detroit *pop* 17,515
Ec·ua·dor \'ek-wə-,dȯ(ə)r\ country W So. America bordering on the Pacific; a republic ✱ Quito *area* 104,510, *pop* 6,300,000 — **Ec·ua·dor·an** \,ek-wə-'dȯr-ən, -'dōr-\ *adj or n* — **Ec·ua·dor·ian** \-ē-ən\ *adj or n*
Edam \'ēd-əm, 'ē-,dam, *Du* ā-'däm\ commune NW Netherlands on the IJsselmeer NNE of Amsterdam *pop* 18,184
Ede, 1 \'ād-ə\ commune E Netherlands NW of Arnhem *pop* 71,952 **2** \'ā-,dā\ city SW Nigeria NE of Ibadan *pop* 156,036
Eden \'ēd-ᵊn\ town N N.C. *pop* 15,871

ə abut	ᵊ kitten, F table	ər further	a back	ā bake	
ä cot, cart	ȧ F bac	au̇ out	ch chin	e less	ē easy
g gift	i trip	ī life	j joke	k̲ G ich	ⁿ F vin	ŋ sing
ō flow	ȯ flaw	œ F bœuf	œ̄ F feu	ȯi coin	th thing
th̲ this	ü loot	u̇ foot	ue G Füllen	ue̅ F rue	y yet
ʸ F digne \dēnʸ\, nuit \nwʸē\	yü few	yu̇ furious	zh vision		

Edes·sa \i-ˈdes-ə\ **1** *or* **Vo·de·na** \ˌvō-t͟he-ˈnä\ town N Greece in W Macedonia; ancient ✱ of Macedonian kings *pop* 16,521 **2** — see URFA
Edfu — see IDFU
Edi·na \i-ˈdī-nə\ village SE Minn. SW of Minneapolis *pop* 44,046
Edin·burg \ˈed-ᵊn-ˌbərg\ city S Tex. NW of Brownsville *pop* 17,163
Ed·in·burgh \ˈed-ᵊn-ˌbər-ə, -ˌbə-rə, -b(ə-)rə\ **1** *or* Gael **Dun·edin** \ˌdə-ˈnēd-ᵊn\ city & burgh ✱ of Scotland & of Midlothian on Firth of Forth *pop* 453,422 **2** *or* **Edinburghshire** — see MIDLOTHIAN
Edir·ne \ā-ˈdir-nə\ *or formerly* **Adri·a·no·ple** \ˌā-drē-ə-ˈnō-pəl\ city Turkey in Europe on Maritsa river *pop* 46,091
Ed·is·to \ˈed-ə-ˌstō\ river 150 *m* S S.C. flowing SE into the Atlantic
Edith Ca·vell, Mount \-ˈkav-əl, -kə-ˈvel\ mountain 11,033 *ft* Canada in SW Alta. in Jasper National Park
Ed·mond \ˈed-mənd\ city *cen* Okla. N of Oklahoma City *pop* 16,-633
Ed·monds \ˈed-mən(d)z\ city W Wash. N of Seattle *pop* 23,998
Ed·mon·ton \ˈed-mən-tən\ **1** city Canada ✱ of Alta. on the No. Saskatchewan *pop* 438,152 **2** former municipal borough SE England in Middlesex, now part of Enfield
Edo — see TOKYO
Edom \ˈēd-əm\ *or* **Id·u·maea** *or* **Id·u·mea** \ˌij-ə-ˈmē-ə\ ancient country SW Asia S of Judea & the Dead sea
Ed·ward, Lake \ˈed-wərd\ lake E Africa SW of Lake Albert on boundary between NE Zaire & SW Uganda *area* 830
Ed·wards \ˈed-wərdz\ plateau 2000–5000 *ft* SW Tex.
Efa·te \ā-ˈfä-ˌtā\ *or* **Va·té** *Fr* vá-tā\ island SW Pacific in *cen* New Hebrides; chief town Vila (✱ of New Hebrides) *area* 200
Effigy Mounds National Monument site NE Iowa on the Mississippi including prehistoric mounds *area* 2
Ega·di \ˈeg-əd-ē\ *or* **Ae·ga·di·an** \ē-ˈgād-ē-ən\ *or anc* **Ae·ga·tes** \ē-ˈgāt-ēz\ islands Italy off W coast of Sicily *area* 15
Eger \ˈā-gər\ *or* Czech **Ohre** \ˈȯr-zhə\ river 193 *m* S Germany & W Czechoslovakia flowing NE into the Elbe
Eg·mont, Mount \ˈeg-ˌmänt\ *or* **Ta·ra·na·ki** \ˌtar-ə-ˈnak-ē, ˌtär-\ mountain 8260 *ft* New Zealand in W *cen* North I.
Egorevsk — see YEGOREVSK
Egypt \ˈē-jəpt\ *or* Ar **Misr** \ˈmisrᵊ\ country NE Africa & Sinai peninsula bordering on Mediterranean & Red seas ✱ Cairo *area* 386,198, *pop* 34,130,000 — see UNITED ARAB REPUBLIC
Ei·fel \ˈī-fəl\ plateau region W Germany NW of the Moselle & NE of Luxembourg
Ei·ger \ˈī-gər\ mountain 13,036 *ft* W *cen* Switzerland NE of the Jungfrau
Eind·ho·ven \ˈīnt-ˌhō-vən, ˈānt-\ commune S Netherlands in No. Brabant *pop* 187,930
Eire — see IRELAND
Ei·se·nach \ˈīz-ᵊn-ˌäk, -ˌäḵ\ city E Germany in Thuringia W of Erfurt *pop* 50,777
Ekaterinburg — see SVERDLOVSK
Ekaterinodar — see KRASNODAR
Ekaterinoslav — see DNEPROPETROVSK
El Alamein — see ALAMEIN
Elam \ˈē-ləm\ *or* **Su·si·ana** \ˌsü-zē-ˈan-ə, -ˈän-ə, -ˈā-nə\ ancient kingdom SW Asia at head of Persian gulf E of Babylonia ✱ Susa — **Elam·ite** \ˈē-lə-ˌmīt\ *adj or n*
Elatea — see CITHAERON
Elath \ˈē-ˌläth\ **1** — see ʻAQABA **2** *or* **Ei·lat** \ā-ˈlät\ town & port S Israel at head of Gulf of ʻAqaba
Ela·zig \ˌel-ə-ˈzig\ city E *cen* Turkey in valley of the upper Murat *pop* 78,605
El·ba \ˈel-bə\ island Italy in the Mediterranean between Corsica & mainland; chief town Portoferraio *area* 86, *pop* 27,602
El Bahnasa — see OXYRHYNCHUS
El·be \ˈel-bə, ˈelb\ *or* Czech **La·be** \ˈlä-be\ river 720 *m* NW Czechoslovakia & N Germany flowing NW into North sea
El·bert, Mount \ˈel-bərt\ mountain 14,431 *ft*, *cen* Colo. in Sawatch mountains; highest in Colo. & Rocky mountains
El Bika *or* **El Bekaa** — see BIKA
El·blag \ˈel-ˌblȯŋ\ *or* G **El·bing** \ˈel-biŋ\ city & port N Poland near the Frisches Haff *pop* 89,800
El·brus \el-ˈbrüz\ *or* **El·bo·rus** \ˌel-bə-ˈrüz\ mountain 18,481 *ft* U.S.S.R. in Kabardino-Balkar Republic; highest in the Caucasus & in Europe
El·burz \el-ˈbu̇(ə)rz\ mountains N Iran parallel with S shore of Caspian sea — see DEMAVEND
El Ca·jon \ˌel-kə-ˈhōn\ city SW Calif. E of San Diego *pop* 52,273
El Caney — see CANEY
El Cen·tro \el-ˈsen-(ˌ)trō\ city S Calif. in Imperial valley *pop* 19,272
El Cer·ri·to \ˌel-sə-ˈrēt-(ˌ)ō\ city W Calif. on San Francisco Bay N of Berkeley *pop* 25,190
El·che \ˈel-(ˌ)chā\ city SE Spain SW of Alicante *pop* 101,028
El Do·ra·do \ˌel-də-ˈräd-(ˌ)ō, -ˈrād-ə\ city S Ark. *pop* 25,283
Electric Peak mountain 11,155 *ft* S Mont. in Yellowstone National Park; highest in Gallatin range
El·e·phan·ta \ˌel-ə-ˈfant-ə\ *or* **Gha·ra·pu·ri** \ˌgär-ə-ˈpu̇(ə)r-ē\ island W India in Bombay harbor
El·e·phan·ti·ne \ˌel-ə-ˌfan-ˈtī-nē, -fən-, -ˈtē-\ island S Egypt in the Nile opposite Aswân
Eleu·sis \i-ˈlü-səs\ ancient deme E Greece in Attica NW of Athens; ruins at modern town of **Elev·sis** \ˌel-əf-ˈsēs\— **El·eu·sin·i·an** \ˌel-yu̇-ˈsin-ē-ən\ *adj or n*
Eleu·thera \i-ˈlü-thə-rə\ island Bahamas E of New Providence I. *area* 164
El Faiyûm *or* **El Fayum** — see FAIYÛM
El Fa·sher \el-ˈfash-ər\ city W Sudan in Darfur *pop* 46,380
El Fer·rol \ˌel-fə-ˈrōl\ *or* **El Ferrol del Cau·di·llo** \-ˌdel-kau̇-ˈt͟hē-(ˌ)(y)ō, -ˈt͟hēl-(ˌ)yō\ city & port NW Spain on the Atlantic NE of La Coruña *pop* 87,736
El·gin, 1 \ˈel-jən\ city NE Ill. *pop* 55,691 **2** \ˈel-gən\ *or* **El·gin·shire** \-ˌshi(ə)r, -shər\ — see MORAY **3** \ˈel-gən\ borough NE Scotland ✱ of Moray
El Giza *or* **El Gizeh** — see GIZA
El·gon, Mount \ˈel-ˌgän\ extinct volcano 14,178 *ft* E Africa on boundary between Uganda & Kenya NE of Lake Victoria
El Hamad — see HAMAD
El Hasa — see HASA
Elis \ˈē-ləs\ *or* NGk **Ilía** \ē-ˈlē-ə\ region S Greece in NW Peloponnesus S of Achaea bordering on Ionian sea
Elisabethville — see LUBUMBASHI
Elisavetgrad — see KIROVOGRAD
Elisavetpol — see KIROVABAD
Eliz·a·beth \i-ˈliz-ə-bəth\ **1** short river SE Va. flowing between cities of Norfolk & Portsmouth into Hampton Roads **2** islands SE Mass. between Buzzards Bay & Vineyard Sound **3** city & port NE N.J. SW of Newark on Newark Bay *pop* 112,654
El Jezira — see GEZIRA
Elk Grove Village village NE Ill. NW of Chicago *pop* 24,516
Elk·hart \ˈel-ˌkärt\ city N Ind. E of So. Bend *pop* 43,152
Elk Island National Park reservation Canada in E *cen* Alta. *area* 51
Ellás — see GREECE
Elles·mere \ˈelz-ˌmi(ə)r\ island Canada in Franklin District of Northwest Territories W of NW Greenland — see COLUMBIA (Cape)
El·lice \ˈel-əs\ islands W Pacific N of Fiji & SSE of Gilbert islands *area* 10, *pop* 5782 — see GILBERT
El·lis \ˈel-əs\ island SE N.Y. in Upper New York Bay
El·lo·ra \e-ˈlōr-ə, -ˈlȯr-\ *or* **Elu·ra** \-ˈlu̇r-ə\ village W India in *cen* Maharashtra NW of Aurangabad; caves
El·lore \e-ˈlō(ə)r, -ˈlȯ(ə)r\ *or* **Elu·ru** \e-ˈlu̇(ə)r-(ˌ)ü\ city SE India in E Andhra Pradesh N of Masulipatnam *pop* 132,791
Ells·worth Land \ˈelz-(ˌ)wərth\ region W Antarctica on Bellingshausen sea
El Maghreb al Aqsa — see MAGHREB
El Mansûra — see MANSÛRA
Elm·hurst \ˈelm-ˌhərst\ city NE Ill. W of Chicago *pop* 50,547
El Minya — see MINYA
El·mi·ra \el-ˈmī-rə\ city S N.Y. *pop* 39,945
El Misti — see MISTI
El Mon·te \el-ˈmänt-ē\ city SW Calif. E of Los Angeles *pop* 69,837
El Mor·ro National Monument \el-ˈmär-(ˌ)ō, -ˈmȯr-\ reservation W N.Mex. SE of Gallup; rock carvings, pueblo *area* 1.4
Elm·wood Park \ˌelm-ˌwu̇d-\ village NE Ill. NW of Chicago *pop* 26,160
El Obeid \ˌel-ō-ˈbād\ city *cen* Sudan in Kordofan *pop* 66,270
El Paso \el-ˈpas-(ˌ)ō\ city Tex. at W tip on Rio Grande *pop* 322,261 — **El Paso·an** \-ˈpas-ə-wən\ *n*
El Sal·va·dor \el-ˈsal-və-ˌdȯ(ə)r, ˌsal-və-ˈ\ country Central America bordering on the Pacific; a republic ✱ San Salvador *area* 8236 *pop* 3,533,628
El Se·gun·do \ˌel-sə-ˈgən-(ˌ)dō, -ˈgün-\ city SW Calif. SW of Los Angeles *pop* 15,620
Elsass, Elsass–Lothringen — see ALSACE, ALSACE-LORRAINE
Elsene — see IXELLES
Elsinore — see HELSINGÖR
El Uqsor — see LUXOR
Ely \ˈē-lē\ urban district E England in Isle of Ely on the Ouse
Ely, Isle of former administrative county E England; now part of Cambridgeshire
Elyr·ia \i-ˈlir-ē-ə\ city NE Ohio SW of Cleveland *pop* 53,427
Em·bar·ras *or* **Em·bar·rass** \ˈam-ˌbrō\ river 150 *m* E Ill. flowing SE into the Wabash
Em·den \ˈem-dən\ city & port W Germany at the mouth of the Ems *pop* 48,098
Emesa — see HOMS
Emi·lia \ā-ˈmēl-yə\ **1** district N Italy comprising the W part of Emilia-Romagna region **2** — see EMILIA-ROMAGNA
Emi·lia–Ro·ma·gna \ā-ˌmēl-yə-rō-ˈmän-yə\ *or formerly* **Emilia** *or anc* **Ae·mil·ia** \ē-ˈmil-yə\ region N Italy bounded by the Po, the Adriatic, & the Apennines ✱ Bologna *area* 8546, *pop* 3,815,254
Em·men \ˈem-ən\ commune NE Netherlands *pop* 79,707
Em·men·thal *or* **Em·men·tal** \ˈem-ən-ˌtäl\ valley of the upper **Em·me** \ˈem-ə\ *or* **Em·men** \ ˈem-ən\(river 45 *m*) *cen* Switzerland in E Bern canton
Em·po·ria \em-ˈpōr-ē-ə, -ˈpȯr-\ city E *cen* Kans. *pop* 23,327
Empty Quarter RUBʻ AL KHALI
Ems \ˈemz, ˈem(p)s\ **1** river 200 *m* W Germany flowing N into North sea **2** *or* **Bad Ems** \bät-\ town W Germany SE of Koblenz
Enchanted Mesa sandstone butte W N.Mex. NE of Acoma
En·der·bury \ˈen-dər-ˌber-ē\ island (atoll) *cen* Pacific in the Phoenix islands controlled jointly by U.S. & Great Britain
En·di·cott \ˈen-di-kət, -də-ˌkät\ mountains N Alaska, the central range of Brooks range
En·field \ˈen-ˌfēld\ **1** town N Conn. *pop* 46,189 **2** borough of N Greater London, England *pop* 266,788
En·ga·dine \ˌeŋ-gə-ˈdēn\ valley of upper Inn river 60 *m* long E Switzerland in Graubünden
En·gland \ˈiŋ-glənd *also* ˈiŋ-lənd\ **1** *or* LL **An·glia** \ˈaŋ-glē-ə\ country S Great Britain; a division of the United Kingdom of Great Britain & Northern Ireland ✱ London *area* 50,331, *pop* 45,870,062 **2** England & Wales **3** UNITED KINGDOM
En·gle·wood \ˈen-gəl-ˌwu̇d\ **1** city N *cen* Colo. S of Denver *pop* 33,695 **2** city NE N.J. on the Hudson *pop* 24,985
English channel *or* F **La Manche** \lá-mäⁿsh\ channel between S England & N France connecting North sea & Atlantic ocean
Enid \ˈē-nəd\ city N Okla. *pop* 44,008
Enisei — see YENISEI
Eni·we·tok \ˌen-i-ˈwē-ˌtäk\ island (atoll) W Pacific in the NW Marshalls
En·na \ˈen-ə\ commune Italy in *cen* Sicily *pop* 28,653
En·nis \ˈen-əs\ urban district W Ireland ✱ of County Clare
En·nis·kil·len \ˌen-ə-ˈskil-ən\ *or* **In·nis·kil·ling** \ˌin-ə-ˈskil-iŋ\ municipal borough SW Northern Ireland ✱ of County Fermanagh
Enns \ˈenz, ˈen(t)s\ river 160 *m*, *cen* Austria flowing E & N from Styria into the Danube
En·sche·de \ˈen(t)-skə-ˌdā\ commune E Netherlands in Overijssel near German frontier *pop* 138,064

En·se·na·da \ˌen(t)-sə-ˈnäd-ə\ city & port NW Mexico in Baja California state on the Pacific SE of Tijuana *pop* 113,320

En·teb·be \en-ˈteb-ə\ town S Uganda on N shore of Lake Victoria; former ✱ of Uganda

En·ter·prise \ˈent-ər-ˌprīz\ city SE Ala. *pop* 15,591

Eolie, Isole — see LIPARI

E¹ — see LHOTSE

Eph·e·sus \ˈef-ə-səs\ ancient city W Asia Minor in Ionia near Aegean coast; its site SSE of Izmir — **Ephe·sian** \i-ˈfē-zhən\ *adj or n*

Ephra·im \ˈē-frē-əm\ **1** *or* **Mount Ephraim** hilly region *cen* Palestine N of Judaea **2** — see ISRAEL

Epidamnus — see DURRES

Ep·i·dau·rus \ˌep-ə-ˈdȯr-əs\ ancient town S Greece in Argolis on Saronic gulf

Épi·nal \ˌā-pi-ˈnäl\ commune NE France on the Moselle SW of Strasbourg *pop* 36,856

Epi·rus *or* **Epei·rus** \i-ˈpī-rəs\ *or* NGk **Ípi·ros** \ˈē-pē-ˌrȯs\ region NW Greece bordering on Ionian sea — **Epi·rote** \i-ˈpī-ˌrōt, -rət\ *n*

Ep·ping Forest \ˈep-iŋ\ forested region SE England in Essex NE of London & S of **Epping** urban district

Ep·som and Ew·ell \ˌep-sə-mən-ˈ(d)yü-əl\ municipal borough SE England in Surrey SW of London *pop* 72,054

Equatorial Guinea country W Africa on Bight of Biafra comprising former Spanish Guinea; an independent republic since 1968 ✱ Santa Isabel *area* 10,831, *pop* 290,000 — see SPANISH GUINEA

Er·bil \ˈe(ə)r-ˌbil\ *or* **Ar·bil** \ˈär-\ *or anc* **Ar·be·la** \är-ˈbē-lə\ city N Iraq E of Mosul *pop* 90,320

Er·ci·yas Da·gi \ˌer-jē-ˌ(y)äs-dä-ˈ(g)ē\ mountain 12,848 *ft, cen* Turkey; highest in Asia Minor

Er·e·bus, Mount \ˈer-ə-bəs\ volcano 12,450 *ft* E Antarctica on Ross I. in SW Ross sea

Ere·gli \ˌer-ā-ˈ(g)lē\ **1** city S Turkey SSE of Ankara *pop* 38,362 **2** town & port NW Turkey in Asia on Black Sea NW of Ankara *pop* 18,978

Erevan — see YEREVAN

Er·furt \ˈe(ə)r-fərt, -ˌfü(ə)rt\ city E Germany WSW of Leipzig *pop* 193,997

Erie \ˈi(ə)r-ē\ **1** city & port NW Pa. on Lake Erie *pop* 129,231 **2** canal 363 *m* long N N.Y. from Hudson river at Albany to Lake Erie at Buffalo; built 1817–25; superseded by **New York State Barge Canal** (*ab* 525 *m* long)

Erie, Lake lake E *cen* No. America on boundary between the U.S. & Canada; one of the Great Lakes *area* 9940

Eriha — see JERICHO

Er·i·trea \ˌer-ə-ˈtrē-ə, -ˈtrā-\ former country NE Africa bordering on Red sea ✱ Asmara; incorporated (1962) into Ethiopia *area* 46,000 — **Er·i·tre·an** \-ən\ *adj*

Erivan — see YEREVAN

Er·lang·en \ˈe(ə)r-ˌläŋ-ən\ city W Germany in Bavaria NNW of Nuremberg *pop* 84,619

Er·moú·po·lis *or* **Her·moú·po·lis** \er-ˈmü-pə-ləs\ *or* **Her·mop·o·lis** \(ˌ)hər-ˈmäp-ə-ləs\ *or* **Sy·ros** \ˈsī-ˌräs\ town & port Greece on Syros; chief town of the Cyclades

Er Rif *or* **Er Riff** — see RIF

Erz·ge·bir·ge \ˈerts-gə-ˌbir-gə\ *or* **Ore mountains** mountain range E *cen* Germany & NW Czechoslovakia on boundary between Saxony & Bohemia; highest Klinovec (in Czechoslovakia) 4000 *ft*

Er·zin·can \ˌer-zin-ˈjän\ city E *cen* Turkey on the Euphrates W of Erzurum *pop* 45,197

Er·zu·rum \ˌerz-(ə-)ˈrüm, ˌərz-\ city NE Turkey in mountains of W Turkish Armenia *pop* 105,317

Es·bjerg \ˈes-bē-ˌe(ə)r(g)\ city & port SW Denmark in SW Jutland peninsula on North sea *pop* 76,056

Es·ca·na·ba \ˌes-kə-ˈnäb-ə\ city NW Mich. on Green Bay *pop* 15,368

Escaut — see SCHELDT

Es·con·di·do \ˌes-kən-ˈdēd-(ˌ)ō\ city SW Calif. N of San Diego *pop* 36,792

Es·dra·e·lon, Plain of \ˌez-drə-ˈē-lən\ *or* **Plain of Jez·re·el** \ˈjez-rē-ˌel, -ˌrē(ə)l\ plain N Palestine NE of Mt. Carmel in valley of the upper Qishon

Esfahan — see ISFAHAN

Esher \ˈē-shər\ urban district S England in Surrey SW of London *pop* 64,186

Esh Sham — see DAMASCUS

Es·kils·tu·na \ˈes-kəl-ˌstü-nə\ city SE Sweden S of Malar Lake *pop* 67,536

Es·ki·se·hir \ˌes-ki-shə-ˈhi(ə)r\ *or* **Es·ki·shehr** \-ˈshe(ə)r\ city W *cen* Turkey on tributary of the Sakarya *pop* 173,882

España — see SPAIN

Española — see HISPANIOLA

Es·pí·ri·to San·to \ə-ˌspir-ə-ˌtü-ˈsan-(ˌ)tü\ state E Brazil bordering on the Atlantic ✱ Vitória *area* 16,543, *pop* 1,597,389

Es·pí·ri·tu San·to \ə-ˌspir-ə-ˌtü-ˈsan-(ˌ)tü\ island SW Pacific in the NW New Hebrides; largest in the group *area* 1875

Es·qui·line \ˈes-kwə-ˌlīn, -lən\ hill in Rome, Italy, one of seven on which the ancient city was built — see AVENTINE

Es·sa·oui·ra \ˌes-ə-ˈwir-ə\ *or* **Mog·a·dor** \ˈmäg-ə-ˌdȯ(ə)r\ city & port W Morocco on the Atlantic W of Marrakesh *pop* 26,392

Es·sen \ˈes-ᵊn\ city W Germany in the Ruhr *pop* 705,700

Es·se·qui·bo \ˌes-ə-ˈkē-(ˌ)bō\ river 600 *m* Guyana flowing N into the Atlantic through a wide estuary

Es·sex \ˈes-iks\ county SE England bordering on North sea & N shore of the Thames; one of kingdoms in Anglo-Saxon heptarchy ✱ Chelmsford *area* 1528, *pop* 1,353,564

Ess·ling·en \ˈes-liŋ-ən\ city W Germany on the Neckar ESE of Stuttgart *pop* 85,350

Es Sur — see TYRE

Es·te·rel \ˌes-tə-ˈrel\ forested mountain region SE France on coast between Fréjus & Cannes; highest point 2020 *ft*

Es·tes Park \ˌes-tēz-\ valley N Colo. in Front range of the Rocky mountains at E border of Rocky Mountain National Park

Es·to·nia \e-ˈstō-nē-ə, -nyə\ *or* **Es·tho·nia** \e-ˈstō-, es-ˈthō-\ country N Europe bordering on Baltic sea; one of the Baltic Provinces of Russia 1721–1917, an independent republic 1918–40, since 1940 a constituent republic (**Estonian Republic**) of the U.S.S.R. ✱ Tallin *area* 18,361 *pop* 1,357,000

Es·to·ril \ˌesh-tə-ˈril\ resort town Portugal on coast W of Lisbon *pop* 15,740

Es·tre·ma·du·ra \ˌes-trə-mə-ˈdu̇r-ə\ **1** region & old province W *cen* Portugal ✱ Lisbon; SW part included in present Estremadura province **2** *or* **Ex·tre·ma·du·ra** \ˌek-strə-\ region & old province W Spain bordering on Portugal; area included in present Cáceres & Badajoz provinces

Ethi·o·pia \ˌē-thē-ˈō-pē-ə\ **1** ancient country NE Africa S of Egypt bordering on Red sea **2** *or* **Ab·ys·sin·ia** \ˌab-ə-ˈsin-yə, -ˈsin-ē-ə\ country E Africa; an empire ✱ Addis Ababa *area* 400,000, *pop* 25,250,000

Et·na *or* **Aet·na** \ˈet-nə\ volcano 10,902 *ft* Italy in NE Sicily

Eton \ˈēt-ᵊn\ urban district SE *cen* England in Buckinghamshire on the Thames

Etru·ria \i-ˈtru̇r-ē-ə\ ancient country *cen* Italy coextensive with modern Tuscany & part of Umbria

Et·trick Forest \ˌe-trik-\ region, formerly a forest & hunting ground, in SE Scotland in Selkirkshire

Eu·boea \yu̇-ˈbē-ə\ *or* **Neg·ro·pont** \ˈneg-rə-ˌpänt\ *or* NGk **Év·voia** \ˈev-(ˌ)yä\ island 90 *m* long E Greece in the Aegean NE of Attica & Boeotia ✱ Chalcis *area* 1457 — **Eu·boe·an** \yu̇-ˈbē-ən\ *adj or n*

Eu·clid \ˈyü-kləd\ city NE Ohio NE of Cleveland *pop* 71,552

Eu·ga·ne·an \yü-ˈgā-nē-ən, ˌyü-gə-ˈnē-\ hills NE Italy in SW Veneto between Padua & the Adige

Eu·gene \yü-ˈjēn\ city W Oreg. on the Willamette *pop* 76,346

Eu·less \ˈyü-ləs\ village NE Tex. NE of Fort Worth *pop* 19,316

Eu·pen \ˈȯi-pən; ˌə(r)-ˈpen, œ̄-\ commune E Belgium E of Liège; formerly in Germany, transferred (with Malmédy) to Belgium 1919

Eu·phra·tes \yu̇-ˈfrāt-(ˌ)ēz\ river 1700 *m* SW Asia flowing from E Turkey SW & SE to unite with the Tigris forming the Shatt-al-Arab — see KARA SU

Eur·asia \yu̇-ˈrā-zhə, -shə\ continental landmass comprising Asia & Europe

Eure \ˈər\ river 140 *m* NW France flowing N into the Seine above Rouen

Eu·re·ka \yu̇-ˈrē-kə\ city & port NW Calif. *pop* 24,337

Eu·ri·pus \yu̇-ˈrī-pəs\ *or* NGk **Evri·pou Porth·mós** \ev-ˈrē-ˌpü-pȯrth-ˈmȯs\ narrow strait E Greece between Euboea & mainland

Eu·rope \ˈyu̇r-əp\ **1** continent of the eastern hemisphere between Asia & the Atlantic *area ab* 3,800,000 **2** the European continent as distinguished from the British Isles

Euxine Sea — see BLACK SEA

Ev·ans, Mount \ˈev-ənz\ mountain 14,260 *ft* N *cen* Colo. in Front range WSW of Denver

Ev·ans·ton \ˈev-ən(t)-stən\ city NE Ill. N of Chicago *pop* 79,808

Ev·ans·ville \ˈev-ənz-ˌvil\ city SW Ind. on the Ohio *pop* 138,764

Ev·er·est, Mount \ˈev-(ə-)rəst\ *or* Tibetan **Cho·mo·lung·ma** \ˌchō-mə-ˈlu̇ŋ-mə\ mountain 29,028 *ft* S Asia on border between Nepal & Tibet in the Himalayas; highest in the world

Ev·er·ett \ˈev-(ə-)rət\ **1** city E Mass. N of Boston *pop* 42,485 **2** city NW *cen* Wash. on Puget Sound N of Seattle *pop* 53,622

Ev·er·glades \ˈev-ər-ˌglādz\ swamp region S Fla. S of Lake Okeechobee; now partly drained; S part forms **Everglades National Park** (*area* 2188)

Evergreen Park village NE Ill. S of Chicago *pop* 25,487

Eve·sham \ˈēv-shəm\ municipal borough W *cen* England in Worcestershire S of Birmingham in **Vale of Evesham**

Évian *or* **Évian-les-Bains** \ā-vyäⁿ-le-baⁿ\ commune E France on Lake Geneva; health resort

Évo·ra \ˈev-ə-rə\ city S *cen* Portugal *pop* 47,806

Évreux \āv-ˈrə(r)\ commune N France WNW of Paris *pop* 42,550

Évros — see MARITSA

Ex·e·ter \ˈek-sət-ər\ city & county borough SW England ✱ of Devonshire *pop* 95,598

Ex·moor \ˈek-ˌsmu̇(ə)r, -ˌsmō(ə)r, -ˌsmȯ(ə)r\ moorland SW England in Somerset *area* 32

Ex·u·ma \ik-ˈsü-mə, ig-ˈzü-\ islands in *cen* Bahamas S of **Exuma Sound** (SE of New Providence I.); chief island **Great Exuma**

Eyre \ˈa(ə)r, ˈe(ə)r\ peninsula Australia in S So. Australia W of Spencer gulf

Eyre, Lake intermittent lake *cen* Australia in NE So. Australia

Eyzies, Les — see LES EYZIES

Fa·en·za \fä-ˈen-zə, -ˈen(t)-sə\ commune N Italy SW of Ravenna *pop* 54,065

Faer·oe *or* **Far·oe** \ˈfa(ə)r-(ˌ)ō, ˈfe(ə)r-\ islands Denmark in the NE Atlantic NW of the Shetlands ✱ Thorshavn *area* 540, *pop* 38,681

Fa·ial *or* **Fa·yal** \fə-ˈyäl, fī-ˈäl\ island *cen* Azores *area* 64

Fair·born \ˈfa(ə)r-ˌbō(ə)rn, ˈfe(ə)r-\ city SW *cen* Ohio NE of Dayton *pop* 32,267

Fair·fax \ˈfa(ə)r-ˌfaks, ˈfe(ə)r-\ city NE Va. W of Alexandria *pop* 21,970

Fair·field \ˈfa(ə)r-ˌfēld, ˈfe(ə)r-\ **1** city W Calif. NE of Berkeley *pop* 44,146 **2** town SW Conn. SW of Bridgeport *pop* 56,487

Fair·ha·ven \fa(ə)r-ˈhā-vən, fe(ə)r-\ town SE Mass. E of New Bedford *pop* 16,332

Fair Lawn borough NE N.J. NE of Paterson *pop* 37,975

Fair·mont \ˈfa(ə)r-ˌmänt, ˈfe(ə)r-\ city N W.Va. *pop* 26,093

Fair·view Park \ˌfa(ə)r-ˌvyü, ˌfe(ə)r-\ city NE Ohio SW of Cleveland *pop* 21,681

ə abut ᵊ kitten, F table ər further a back ā bake
ä cot, cart ȧ F bac au̇ out ch chin e less ē easy
g gift i trip ī life j joke k̲ G ich ⁿ F vin ŋ sing
ō flow ȯ flaw œ F bœu f œ̄ F feu ȯi coin th thing
t̲h̲ this ü loot u̇ foot ue G Füllen ue̅ F rue y yet
ʸ F digne \dēnʸ\, nuit \nwʸē\ yü few yu̇ furious zh vision

Fair·weath·er, Mount \'fa(ə)r-ˌweth-ər, 'fe(ə)r-\ mountain 15,300 *ft* on boundary between Alaska & B.C.; highest in **Fairweather range** of the Coast ranges
Fai·yûm *or* **Fa·yum** *or* **El Faiyûm** *or* **El Fayum** \(ˌel-)fā-'(y)üm, -(ˌ)fī-\ city N Egypt SSW of Cairo *pop* 150,900
Faiz·abad \'fī-zə-ˌbad\ **1** city NE Afghanistan *pop* 62,853 **2** *or* **Fyz·abad** \'fī-\ city N India in Uttar Pradesh *pop* 83,700
Fa·jar·do \fə-'härd-(ˌ)ō\ town NE Puerto Rico *pop* 18,249
Fa·ka·ra·va \ˌfäk-ə-'räv-ə\ island (atoll) S Pacific, principal island of the Tuamotu archipelago
Fako — see CAMEROON
Fa·laise \fa-'lāz\ town NW France SSE of Caen
Fal·kirk \'fȯl-(ˌ)kərk\ burgh *cen* Scotland in Stirlingshire ENE of Glasgow *pop* 37,587
Falk·land \'fō(l)-klənd\ *or* Sp **Is·las Mal·vi·nas** \ˌēz-läz-mäl-'vē-näs\ islands SW Atlantic E of S end of Argentina; a British crown colony ✱ Stanley *area* 4618, *pop* 2045
Falkland Islands Dependencies islands & territories in the S Atlantic & in Antarctica administered by the British from Falkland islands, including So. Orkney, So. Sandwich, & So. Shetland islands, So. Georgia I., Antarctic (Palmer) peninsula, & Antarctic (Palmer) archipelago
Fall River \'fȯl\ city & port SE Mass. *pop* 96,898
Fal·mouth \'fal-məth\ town SE Mass. on Cape Cod *pop* 15,942
False Bay \'fȯls\ inlet Republic of So. Africa in SW Cape Province E of Cape of Good Hope
Fal·ster \'fäl-stər, 'fȯl-\ island Denmark in Baltic sea S of Sjælland *area* 198
Fa·ma·gus·ta \ˌfäm-ə-'güs-tə, ˌfam-\ city & port E Cyprus on **Famagusta Bay** (inlet of the Mediterranean) *pop* 42,500
Fan·ning \'fan-iŋ\ island *cen* Pacific in the Line islands belonging to Great Britain *area* 15
Far·al·lon \'far-ə-ˌlän\ islands Calif. 27 *m* W of San Francisco
Far East the countries of E Asia & the Malay archipelago — usu. considered as comprising the Asian countries bordering on the Pacific but sometimes as including also India, Ceylon, Bangladesh, Tibet, & Burma — **Far Eastern** *adj*
Fare·well, Cape \'fa(ə)r-ˌwel, 'fe(ə)r-\ cape Greenland at S tip
Far·go \'fär-(ˌ)gō\ city E N.Dak. on Red river *pop* 53,365
Far·i·bault \'far-ə-ˌbō\ city SE Minn. *pop* 16,595
Farm·ers Branch \'fär-mərz\ city NE Tex. NW of Dallas *pop* 27,-492
Far·ming·ton \'fär-miŋ-tən\ city NW N.Mex. *pop* 21,979
Far·rukh·abad \fə-'rü-kə-ˌbad, -ˌbäd\ city N India in Uttar Pradesh on the Ganges WNW of Lucknow *pop* 94,951
Fars \'färz, 'färs\ *or* **Far·si·stan** \ˌfär-si-'stan, -'stän\ region SW Iran, chief city Shiraz, corresponding closely with ancient region of **Per·sis** \'pər-səs\
Fársala — see PHARSALUS
Farther India — see INDOCHINA
Fashoda — see KODOK
Fá·ti·ma \'fat-ə-mə\ village *cen* Portugal NNE of Lisbon
Fat·shan \'fät-'shän\ *or* **Nam·hoi** \'näm-'hȯi\ city SE China in *cen* Kwangtung SW of Canton *pop* 122,500
Fayal — see FAIAL
Fay·ette·ville \'fā-ət-ˌvil, -vəl; *2 is also* 'fed-vəl\ **1** city NW Ark. *pop* 30,729 **2** city SE *cen* N.C. on Cape Fear river *pop* 53,510
Fear, Cape \'fi(ə)r\ cape SE N.C. at mouth of Cape Fear river
Feath·er \'feth-ər\ river 100 *m* N *cen* Calif. flowing S into the Sacramento
Federal Capital Territory — see AUSTRALIAN CAPITAL TERRITORY
Federal District *or* Sp & Port **Dis·tri·to Fe·de·ral** \di-'strē-tō-ˌfeth-ə-'räl, dish-'trē-tü-\ **1** *or* **Federal Capital** *or* Sp **Ca·pi·tal Fe·de·ral** \ˌkäp-ə-'täl-\ district E Argentina largely comprising ✱ city of Buenos Aires *area* 74, *pop* 2,972,453 **2** district E *cen* Brazil including ✱ city of Brasília *area* 2260, *pop* 544,862 **3** — see GUANABARA **4** district *cen* Mexico including ✱, Mexico City *area* 573, *pop* 7,005,855 **5** district N Venezuela including ✱ city of Caracas *area* 745, *pop* 2,009,561
Federated Malay States former Brit. protectorate (1895–1945) comprising the Malay states of Negri Sembilan, Pahang, Perak, & Selangor ✱ Kuala Lumpur
Federated Shan States — see SHAN STATE
Fen \'fen, 'fən\ river 300 *m* N China in *cen* Shansi flowing SSE into Yellow river
Fengtien, 1 — see LIAONING **2** — see MUKDEN
Fer·ga·na *or* **Fer·gha·na** \fər-'gän-ə\ valley U.S.S.R. in the Tien Shan in Kirgiz, Tadzhik, & Uzbek republics SE of Tashkent
Fer·gu·son \'fər-gə-sən\ city E Mo. N of St. Louis *pop* 28,915
Fer·man·agh \fər-'man-ə\ county SW Northern Ireland ✱ Enniskillen *area* 653, *pop* 49,902
Fer·nan·do de No·ro·nha \fər-'nan-(ˌ)dō-də-nə-'rōn-yə\ island Brazil in the Atlantic 300 *m* NE of city of Natal *area* 7
Fer·nan·do Po *or* **Fer·nan·do Poo** \fər-ˌnan-(ˌ)dō-'pō\ island Equatorial Guinea in Bight of Biafra *area* 778, *pop* 61,197
Fern·dale \'fərn-ˌdāl\ city SE Mich. N of Detroit *pop* 30,850
Fer·ra·ra \fə-'rär-ə\ commune N Italy in Emilia-Romagna NE of Bologna near the Po *pop* 156,426
Ferro — see HIERRO
Ferrol, El — see EL FERROL
Ferryville — see MENZEL-BOURGUIBA
Fez \'fez\ *or* **Fès** \'fes\ city N *cen* Morocco *pop* 290,000
Fez·zan \fe-'zan\ region SW Libya, chiefly desert *area ab* 150,000
Fich·tel·ge·bir·ge \'fik-tᵊl-gə-ˌbir-gə\ mountains S *cen* Germany in NE Bavaria; highest Schneeberg 3447 *ft*
Fie·so·le \fē-'ā-zə-lē, -ˌlā\ *or anc* **Fae·su·lae** \'fē-zə-ˌlē\ commune *cen* Italy in Tuscany NE of Florence
Fife \'fīf\ *or* **Fife·shire** \-ˌshi(ə)r, -shər\ county E Scotland between firths of Tay & Forth ✱ Cupar *area* 505, *pop* 326,989
Fi·ji \'fē-(ˌ)jē\ islands SW Pacific E of New Hebrides constituting (with Rotuma I.) an independent dominion of Brit. Commonwealth ✱ Suva (on Viti Levu) *area* 7083, *pop* 530,000
Filch·ner Ice Shelf \'filk-nər\ area of shelf ice Antarctica in Weddell sea
Filipinas, República de — see PHILIPPINES
Finch·ley \'finch-lē\ former municipal borough SE England in Middlesex, now part of Barnet
Find·lay \'fin-(d)lē\ city NW Ohio *pop* 35,800
Fin·gal's Cave \ˌfiŋ-gəlz-\ sea cave W Scotland on Staffa I.
Fin·ger Lakes \'fiŋ-gər\ group of long narrow lakes W *cen* N.Y. comprised of Cayuga, Seneca, Keuka, Canandaigua, Skaneateles, Owasco, & several smaller lakes
Fin·is·terre, Cape \ˌfin-ə-'ste(ə)r, -'ster-ē\ cape NW Spain on coast of La Coruña province; westernmost point of Spanish mainland, at 9°18′W
Fin·land \'fin-lənd\ *or* Finn **Suo·mi** \'swȯ-mē\ country N Europe bordering on Gulf of Bothnia & Gulf of Finland; a republic ✱ Helsinki *area* 130,165 *pop* 4,680,000 — **Fin·land·er** *n*
Finland, Gulf of arm of Baltic sea between Finland & Estonia
Fin·lay \'fin-lē\ river 250 *m* Canada in N *cen* B.C. flowing SE to unite with **Pars·nip** \ˌpär-snəp-\ river (145 *m*) forming the Peace
Fins·bury \'finz-ˌber-ē, -b(ə-)rē\ former metropolitan borough E *cen* London, England, now part of Islington
Fin·ster·aar·horn \ˌfin(t)-stər-'är-ˌhȯ(ə)rn\ mountain 14,022 *ft* S Switzerland; highest of the Bernese Alps
Fiord·land \fē-'ȯ(ə)rd-ˌland\ mountain region S New Zealand in SW South I.
Fitch·burg \'fich-ˌbərg\ city N *cen* Mass. *pop* 43,343
Fiume — see RIJEKA
Fiu·mi·ci·no \ˌfyü-mə-'chē-(ˌ)nō\ town *cen* Italy on Tyrrhenian sea SW of Rome & WNW of Ostia
Flag·staff \'flag-ˌstaf\ city N *cen* Ariz. *pop* 26,117
Flam·bor·ough Head \ˌflam-ˌbər-ə-, -ˌbə-rə-, -b(ə-)rə-\ promontory NE England on Yorkshire coast
Flan·ders \'flan-dərz\ *or* F **Flan·dre** \fläⁿdrᵊ\ *or* Flem **Vlaan·de·ren** \'vlän-də-rə(n)\ region W Belgium & N France bordering on North sea; a medieval county ✱ Lille — see EAST FLANDERS, WEST FLANDERS
Flat·head \'flat-ˌhed\ river 250 *m* SE B.C. & NW Mont. flowing S through **Flathead Lake** (30 *m* long, in Mont.) into Clark Fork
Flat·tery, Cape \'flat-ə-rē\ cape NW Wash. at entrance to Juan de Fuca strait
Flens·burg \'flenz-ˌbərg, 'flen(t)s-ˌbu̇rk\ city & port W Germany on inlet of the Baltic near Danish border *pop* 95,488
Fletsch·horn \'flech-ˌhȯ(ə)rn\ *or* **Ross·bo·den·horn** \'rȯs-'bōd-ᵊn-ˌhȯ(ə)rn\ mountain 13,127 *ft* S Switzerland in Pennine Alps S of Simplon Pass
Flin·ders \'flin-dərz\ **1** river 500 *m* Australia in *cen* Queensland flowing NW into Gulf of Carpentaria **2** mountain ranges Australia in E So. Australia E of Lake Torrens
Flint \'flint\ **1** river 265 *m* W Ga. flowing S & SW into Lake Seminole **2** city SE *cen* Mich. *pop* 193,317 **3** *or* **Flint·shire** \-ˌshi(ə)r, -shər\ county NE Wales ✱ Mold *area* 256, *pop* 175,396
Flod·den \'fläd-ᵊn\ hill N England in N Northumberland near Scottish border
Floral Park village SE N.Y. on E Long I. *pop* 18,422
Flor·ence \'flȯr-ən(t)s, 'flär-\ **1** city NW Ala. on the Tennessee *pop* 34,031 **2** city E S.C. *pop* 25,997 **3** *or* It **Fi·ren·ze** \fē-'rent-sā\ commune *cen* Italy on the Arno ✱ of Tuscany *pop* 458,359 — **Flor·en·tine** \'flȯr-ən-ˌtēn, 'flär-, -ˌtīn\ *adj or n*
Flo·res \'flōr-əs, 'flȯr-\ **1** island NW Azores *area* 57 **2** island Indonesia in Lesser Sunda islands *area* 5509
Flo·ri·a·nó·po·lis \ˌflōr-ē-ə-'näp-ə-ləs, ˌflȯr-\ *or formerly* **Des·têr·ro** \dēsh-'ter-ü\ city S Brazil ✱ of Santa Catarina state on island off coast *pop* 130,012
Flor·i·da \'flȯr-əd-ə, 'flär-\ **1** state SE U.S. ✱ Tallahassee *area* 58,560, *pop* 6,789,443 **2** \'flȯr-əd-ə, 'flär-; flə-'rēd-ə\ *or* **N'Ge·la** \en-'gā-lə\ *or* **Ge·la** \'gā-lə\ island W Pacific in SE Solomons N of Guadalcanal — **Flo·rid·i·an** \flə-'rid-ē-ən\ *adj or n* — **Flor·i·dan** \'flȯr-əd-ᵊn, 'flär-\ *adj or n*
Florida, Straits of *or* **Florida Strait** channel between Florida Keys (on NW) & Cuba & Bahamas (on S & E) connecting Gulf of Mexico with the Atlantic
Florida Keys chain of islands off the S tip of Florida peninsula
Flo·ris·sant \'flōr-ə-sənt, 'flȯr-\ city E Mo. NNW of St. Louis *pop* 65,908
Flush·ing \'fləsh-iŋ\ **1** section of New York City on Long I. in Queens **2** — see VLISSINGEN
Fly \'flī\ river 650 *m* S New Guinea flowing SE into Gulf of Papua
Foc·sa·ni \fȯk-'shän(-ē)\ city E Rumania in S Moldavia *pop* 39,629
Fog·gia \'fȯ-jə, -(ˌ)jä\ commune SE Italy in Apulia *pop* 139,117
Foggy Bottom section of Washington, D.C., along the Potomac
Foix \'fwä\ region & former province S France in the Pyrenees SE of Gascony
Folke·stone \'fōk-stən, *US also* -ˌstōn\ municipal borough SE England in Kent on Strait of Dover *pop* 43,760
Fond du Lac \'fän-dᵊl-ˌak, 'fän-jə-ˌlak\ city E Wis. on Lake Winnebago *pop* 35,515
Fon·se·ca, Gulf of \fän-'sā-kə\ *or* **Fonseca Bay** inlet of the Pacific in Central America in El Salvador, Honduras, & Nicaragua
Fon·taine·bleau \'fänt-ᵊn-ˌblō\ commune N France SSE of Paris *pop* 18,094
Fon·tana \fän-'tan-ə\ city SW Calif. E of Los Angeles *pop* 20,673
Foo·chow \'fü-'jō, -'chau̇\ *or* **Min·how** \'min-'hō\ city & port SE China ✱ of Fukien on Min river *pop* 616,000
For·a·ker, Mount \'fȯr-i-kər, 'fär-\ mountain 17,395 *ft* S Alaska in Alaska range SW of Mt. McKinley
Forest Hill village Canada in SE Ont. near Toronto *pop* 23,135
Forest Park **1** city N Ga. SE of Atlanta *pop* 19,994 **2** village NE Ill. W of Chicago *pop* 15,472 **3** city SW Ohio N of Cincinnati *pop* 15,139
For·far \'fȯr-fər\ **1** *or* **For·far·shire** \-ˌshi(ə)r, -shər\ — see ANGUS **2** burgh E Scotland ✱ of Angus
For·lì \fȯr-'lē\ commune N Italy in Emilia-Romagna *pop* 103,666
For·mo·sa \fȯr-'mō-sə, fər-, -zə\ *or* **Tai·wan** \'tī-'wän\ **1** island China off SE coast E of Fukien; belonged to Japan 1895–1945; since 1949 seat of (Nationalist) Republic of China (✱ Taipei); provincial ✱ Taichung *area* 13,900, *pop* 14,810,929 **2** strait between For-

mosa & China mainland connecting East China & So. China seas — **For·mo·san** \-'mōs-ᵊn, -'mōz-\ *adj or n*
For·ta·le·za \ˌfȯrt-ᵊl-'ā-zə\ *or* **Ce·a·rá** \ˌsā-ə-'rä\ city & port NE Brazil on the Atlantic ✱ of Ceará *pop* 846,069
Fort Bayard — see CHANKIANG
Fort Col·lins \'käl-ənz\ city N Colo. *pop* 43,337
Fort–de–France \ˌfȯrd-ə-'fräⁿs\ city French West Indies ✱ of Martinique on W coast *pop* 96,943
Fort de Kock — see BUKITTINGGI
Fort Dodge \'däj\ city NW *cen* Iowa *pop* 31,263
Fort Erie \'i(ə)r-ē\ town Canada in SE Ont. on Niagara river *pop* 23,113
Fort Fred·e·ri·ca National Monument \ˌfred-ə-'rē-kə, fre-'drē-\ reservation SE Ga. on W shore of St. Simon I. containing site of fort built by Oglethorpe 1736
Fort George \'jȯ(ə)rj\ river 480 *m* Canada in *cen* Que. flowing W into James Bay
Forth \'fō(ə)rth, 'fȯ(ə)rth\ river 114 *m* S *cen* Scotland flowing E into **Firth of Forth** (estuary 48 *m* long, inlet of North sea)
Fort Jefferson National Monument — see DRY TORTUGAS
Fort Knox \'näks\ military reservation N *cen* Ky. SSW of Louisville; location of U.S. Gold Bullion Depository
Fort–La·my \ˌfȯr-lə-'mē\ city ✱ of Chad *pop* 99,000
Fort Lar·a·mie National Monument \'lar-ə-mē\ site SE Wyo. on the No. Platte of a trading post & fort (1834–90) on Oregon Trail
Fort Lau·der·dale \'lȯd-ər-ˌdāl\ city SE Fla. *pop* 139,590
Fort Lee \'lē\ borough NE N.J. on the Hudson *pop* 30,631
Fort Mc·Hen·ry National Monument \mə-'ken-rē\ site in Baltimore, Md., of a fort bombarded 1814 by the British
Fort Ma·tan·zas National Monument \mə-'tan-zəs\ reservation *ab* 15 *m* SSE of St. Augustine, Fla., containing Fort Matanzas, built *ab* 1736 by the Spanish
Fort My·ers \'mī(-ə)rz\ city SW Fla. on estuary of the Caloosahatchee *pop* 27,351
Fort Nel·son \'nel-sən\ river 260 *m* Canada in NE B.C. flowing NW into Liard river
Fort Peck Reservoir \'pek\ reservoir *ab* 130 *m* long NE Mont. formed in Missouri river by **Fort Peck Dam**
Fort Pierce \'pi(ə)rs\ city E Fla. on the Atlantic *pop* 29,721
Fort Pu·las·ki National Monument \pə-'las-kē, pyü-\ reservation E Ga. comprising island in mouth of Savannah river, site of a fort built 1829–47 to replace Revolutionary Fort Greene
Fort Randall Dam — see FRANCIS CASE (Lake)
Fort Smith \'smith\ city NW Ark. on Arkansas river *pop* 62,802
Fort Sum·ter National Monument \'səm(p)-tər\ reservation S.C. at entrance to Charleston harbor containing site of Fort Sumter
Fort Thom·as \'täm-əs\ city N Ky. SE of Covington *pop* 16,338
Fort Union National Monument reservation NE N.Mex. 50 *m* ENE of Santa Fe containing site of military post 1851–91
Fort Vancouver National Monument site SW Wash. in city of Vancouver of a trading & military post (founded 1825) that was W terminus of the Oregon Trail
Fort Wal·ton Beach \'wȯlt-ᵊn\ city NW Fla. E of Pensacola *pop* 19,994
Fort Wayne \'wān\ city NE Ind. *pop* 177,671
Fort William — see THUNDER BAY
Fort Worth \'wərth\ city N Tex. W of Dallas *pop* 393,476
Fos·to·ria \fō-'stōr-ē-ə, fä-, -'stȯr-\ city NW Ohio *pop* 16,037
Fountain Valley city SW Calif. SE of Los Angeles *pop* 31,826
Four Forest Cantons the cantons of Uri, Schwyz, Unterwalden, & Lucerne in *cen* Switzerland surrounding the Lake of Lucerne
Four Forest Cantons, Lake of the — see LUCERNE (Lake of)
Fou·ta Djal·lon *or* **Fu·ta Jal·lon** \ˌfüt-ə-jə-'lōn\ mountain region W Guinea; highest point *ab* 4200 *ft*
Fox \'fäks\ **1** islands SW Alaska in the E Aleutians — see UMNAK, UNALASKA, UNIMAK **2** river 220 *m* SE Wis. & NE Ill. flowing S into the Illinois **3** river 175 *m* E Wis. flowing NE & N through Lake Winnebago into Green Bay
Foxe Basin \'fäks\ inlet of the Atlantic N Canada in E Franklin District W of Baffin I.; connected with Hudson Bay by **Foxe Channel**
Foyle \'fȯi(ə)l\ river *ab* 20 *m* N Ireland flowing NE past city of Londonderry to **Lough Foyle** (inlet of the Atlantic 18 *m* long)
Fra·ming·ham \'frā-miŋ-ˌham\ town E Mass. *pop* 64,048
France \'fran(t)s\ country W Europe between English channel & the Mediterranean; a republic ✱ Paris *area* 212,659, *pop* 51,260,000
Franche–Com·té \'fräⁿsh-kōⁿ-tā\ region & former county & province E France E of the Saône ✱ Besançon — see BURGUNDY
Fran·cis Case, Lake \-ˌfran(t)-səs-'kās\ reservoir *ab* 100 *m* long S S.Dak. formed in the Missouri by **Fort Ran·dall Dam** \'ran-dᵊl\
Fran·co·nia \fraŋ-'kō-nē-ə, -nyə\ **1** former duchy in Austrasia **2** region W Germany in N & NW Bavaria — **Fran·co·ni·an** \-nē-ən, -nyən\ *adj or n*
Frank·fort \'fraŋk-fərt\ city ✱ of Ky. *pop* 21,356
Frank·furt \'fraŋk-fərt, 'fräŋk-ˌfu̇(ə)rt\ *or* **Frank·fort** \'fraŋk-fərt\ **1** *or* **Frankfurt am Main** \-(ˌ)äm-'mīn\ *or* **Frankfort on the Main** city W Germany on Main river *pop* 661,800 **2** *or* **Frankfurt an der Oder** \-än-də-'rōd-ər\ *or* **Frankfort on the Oder** city E Germany on Oder river *pop* 62,011
Frank·lin \'fraŋ-klən\ **1** town E *cen* Mass. SW of Boston *pop* 17,830 **2** district Canada in N Northwest Territories including Arctic islands & Boothia & Melville peninsulas *area* 541,753
Franklin D. Roosevelt Lake reservoir 151 *m* long NE Wash. formed in Columbia river by Grand Coulee Dam
Franklin Park village NE Ill. W of Chicago *pop* 20,497
Franks Peak *or* **Francs Peak** \'fraŋ(k)s\ mountain 13,140 *ft* NW Wyo; highest in Absaroka range
Franz Jo·sef Land \'fran(t)s-'jō-zəf-ˌland *also* -səf-; frän(t)s-'yō-zəf-ˌlänt\ archipelago U.S.S.R. in Soviet Russia, Europe, in Arctic ocean N of Novaya Zemlya
Fras·ca·ti \fra-'skät-ē, frä-\ commune *cen* Italy in Latium 11 *m* SE of Rome *pop* 18,023
Fra·ser \'frā-zər, -zhər\ river 850 *m* Canada in S *cen* B.C. flowing into Strait of Georgia
Frau·en·feld \'frau̇(-ə)n-ˌfelt\ commune NE Switzerland ✱ of Thurgau canton *pop* 17,576
Fred·er·ick \'fred-(ə-)rik\ city N Md. *pop* 23,641
Fred·er·ic·ton \'fred-(ə-)rik-tən\ city Canada ✱ of N.B. on St. John river *pop* 24,254
Fred·er·iks·berg \'fred-(ə-)riks-ˌbərg\ city Denmark on Sjælland I., W suburb of Copenhagen *pop* 103,621
Free·port \'frē-ˌpō(ə)rt, -ˌpȯ(ə)rt\ **1** city N Ill. W of Rockford *pop* 27,736 **2** village SE N.Y. on Long I. *pop* 40,374 **3** city NW Bahamas on *cen* Grand Bahama I. *pop* 25,859
Free·town \'frē-ˌtau̇n\ city & port ✱ of Sierra Leone on the Atlantic *pop* 178,600
Frei·burg \'frī-ˌbu̇(ə)rg, -ˌbərg\ *or* **Freiburg im Breisgau** \-im-'brīs-ˌgau̇\ **1** city W Germany at W foot of Black Forest *pop* 163,-500 **2** — see FRIBOURG
Fré·jus, Mas·sif du \ma-ˌsēf-də-frā-'zhüs, -'zhuͤs\ mountain on border between France & Italy at SW end of Graian Alps
Fre·man·tle \frē-'mant-ᵊl\ city Australia in SW Western Australia at mouth of Swan river; port for Perth *pop* 25,284
Fre·mont \'frē-ˌmänt\ **1** city W Calif. SE of Oakland *pop* 100,869 **2** city E Nebr. *pop* 22,962 **3** city N Ohio *pop* 18,490
French Community *or* F **Com·mu·nau·té fran·çaise** \kō-muͤ-nō-tā-fräⁿ-sez\ federation (formed 1958) comprising metropolitan France, its overseas departments & territories, & the former French territories in Africa that on becoming republics chose to maintain their ties with France
French Equatorial Africa *or* **French Congo** former country W *cen* Africa N of Congo river comprising a federation of Chad, Gabon, Middle Congo, & Ubangi-Shari territories ✱ Brazzaville
French Guiana country N So. America; an overseas department of France ✱ Cayenne *area* 34,740, *pop* 50,000
French Guinea — see GUINEA
French India former French possessions in India including Chandernagore (ceded to India 1950) & Pondicherry, Karikal, Yanaon, & Mahé (ceded to India 1954) ✱ Pondicherry
French Indochina — see INDOCHINA
French Morocco — see MOROCCO
French Polynesia *or formerly* **French Oceania** islands in S Pacific belonging to France & including Society, Marquesas, Tuamotu, Gambier, & Tubuaï groups ✱ Papeete (on Tahiti) *pop* 120,000
French Sudan — see MALI
French Territory of the Afars and the Is·sas \'äf-ˌär(z) . . . ē-'sä(z)\ *or formerly* **French Somaliland** country E Africa on Gulf of Aden belonging to France ✱ Djibouti *area* 8492, *pop* 95,000
French Togo — see TOGO
French Union former federation (1946–58) comprising metropolitan France & its overseas departments, territories, & associated states — see FRENCH COMMUNITY
French West Africa area W Africa comprising the former French territories of Dahomey, French Guinea, French Sudan, Ivory Coast, Mauritania, Niger, Senegal, & Upper Volta
French West Indies islands of the West Indies belonging to France and including Guadeloupe, Martinique, Désirade, Les Saintes, Marie Galante, St. Barthélemy, & part of St. Martin
Fres·no \'frez-(ˌ)nō\ city S *cen* Calif. *pop* 165,972
Fria, Cape \'frē-ə\ cape NW South-West Africa on the Atlantic
Fri·bourg \frē-'bu̇(ə)r\ *or* G **Frei·burg** \'frī-ˌbu̇(ə)rg, -bərg\ **1** canton W *cen* Switzerland *area* 647, *pop* 180,309 **2** commune, its ✱, SW of Bern *pop* 39,659
Frid·ley \'frid-lē\ city SE Minn. N of St. Paul *pop* 29,233
Friendly — see TONGA
Fries·land \'frēz-lənd, 'frēs-, -ˌland\ **1** old region N Europe bordering on North sea **2** province N Netherlands ✱ Leeuwarden *area* 1431, *pop* 521,751
Frio, Cape \'frē-(ˌ)ō\ cape SE Brazil E of Rio de Janeiro
Fri·sches Haff \'frish-əs-ˌhäf\ lagoon N Poland & E Soviet Russia, Europe; inlet of Gulf of Danzig
Fri·sian \'frizh-ən, 'frē-zhən\ islands NW Europe in North sea including **West Frisian** islands (off N coast of Netherlands), **East Frisian** islands (off NW coast of Germany), & **North Frisian** islands (off coast of Germany & Denmark, including Helgoland & Sylt)
Fri·u·li \'frē-ə-(ˌ)lē, frē-'ü-lē\ district N Italy in Friuli-Venezia Giulia on Yugoslav border — **Fri·u·li·an** \frē-'ü-lē-ən\ *adj or n*
Friuli–Ve·ne·zia Giu·lia \-və-ˌnet-sē-ə-'jül-yə\ region N Italy E of Veneto ✱ Udine *area* 6223, *pop* 1,225,894
Fro·bi·sher Bay \ˌfrō-bi-shər-\ inlet of the Atlantic N Canada in Franklin District on SE coast of Baffin I.
Front \'frənt\ range of the Rockies extending from *cen* Colo. N into SE Wyo. — see GRAYS PEAK
Fro·ward, Cape \'frō-(w)ərd\ headland S Chile on N side of Strait of Magellan; southernmost point of mainland of So. America, at *ab* 53°54′S lat.
Frun·ze \'frün-zə\ *or formerly* **Pish·pek** \pish-'pek\ city U.S.S.R. on Chu river ✱ of Kirgiz Republic *pop* 431,000
Fu·ji \'f(y)ü-(ˌ)jē\ *or* **Fu·ji·ya·ma** \ˌf(y)ü-jē-'(y)äm-ə\ *or* **Fu·ji–no–ya·ma** \-(ˌ)nō-'yäm-ə\ *or* **Fu·ji–san** \-'sän\ mountain 12,388 *ft* Japan in S *cen* Honshu; highest in Japan
Fu·kien \'fü-'kyen, -kē-'en\ province SE China bordering on Formosa strait ✱ Foochow *area* 47,529, *pop* 17,000,000
Fu·ku·o·ka \ˌfü-kə-'wō-kə\ city & port Japan on N Kyushu on inlet of Tsushima strait *pop* 825,000
Ful·da \'fu̇l-də\ city W Germany NE of Frankfurt *pop* 44,365
Ful·ham \'fu̇l-əm\ former metropolitan borough SW London, England, now part of Hammersmith
Ful·ler·ton \'fu̇l-ərt-ᵊn\ city SW Calif. *pop* 85,826

Fu·na·fu·ti \ˌf(y)ü-nə-ˈf(y)üt-ē\ island (atoll) S Pacific in *cen* Ellice islands
Fun·chal \fün-ˈshäl, ˌfən-\ city & port Portugal ✱ of Madeira I. *pop* 105,791
Fun·dy, Bay of \ˈfən-dē\ inlet of the Atlantic SE Canada between N.B. & N.S.
Fundy National Park reservation SE Canada in N.B. on upper Bay of Fundy *area* 80
Fur·neaux \ˈfər-(ˌ)nō\ islands Australia off NE Tasmania
Fur·ness \ˈfər-nəs\ district N England comprising peninsula in Irish sea in NW Lancashire
Fürth \ˈfü(ə)rt, ˈfuert\ city W Germany NW of Nuremberg *pop* 94,-252
Fu·se \ˈfü-(ˌ)sā\ city Japan in S Honshu E of Osaka *pop* 253,000
Fu·shun \ˈfü-ˈshün\ city NE China in NE Liaoning E of Mukden *pop* 985,000
Fu·sin \ˈfü-ˈshin\ city NE China in NE Liaoning WNW of Mukden *pop* 188,600
Futa Jallon — see FOUTA DJALLON
Fu·tu·na \fə-ˈtü-nə\ **1** *or* **Hoorn** \ˈhō(ə)rn, ˈhȯ(ə)rn\ islands SW Pacific NE of Fiji; formerly a French protectorate, since 1959 part of Wallis & Futuna islands territory **2** island SW Pacific in Futuna group **3** island SW Pacific in SE New Hebrides
Fyn \ˈfin\ *or* G **Fü·nen** \ˈf(y)ü-nən, ˈfue-\ island Denmark in the Baltic between Sjælland & Jutland; chief city Odense *area* 1149
Fyzabad — see FAIZABAD
Ga·be·ro·nes \ˌgäb-ə-ˈrō-nəs\ town ✱ of Botswana on SE border
Ga·bes \ˈgäb-əs, -ˌes\ city & port SE Tunisia on **Gulf of Gabes** (*anc* **Syr·tis Mi·nor** \ˌsərt-ə-ˈsmī-nər\, arm of the Mediterranean) *pop* 32,300
Ga·bon \ga-ˈbōⁿ\ **1** *or* **Ga·boon** *or* **Ga·bun** \gə-ˈbün, ga-\ river NW Gabon flowing into the Atlantic through long wide estuary **2** country W Africa bordering on the Atlantic; formerly a territory of French Equatorial Africa, since 1958 a republic within the French Community ✱ Libreville *area* 103,089, *pop* 500,000 — **Gab·o·nese** \ˌgab-ə-ˈnēz, -ˈnēs\ *adj or n*
Gad·a·ra \ˈgad-ə-rə\ ancient town Palestine SE of Sea of Galilee — **Gad·a·rene** \ˈgad-ə-ˌrēn, ˌgad-ə-ˈ\ *adj or n*
Gades *or* **Gadir** — see CÁDIZ — **Gad·i·tan** \ˈgad-ə-tən\ *adj or n*
Gads·den \ˈgadz-dən\ city NE Ala. on Coosa river *pop* 53,928
Gadsden Purchase tract of land S of Gila river in present Ariz. & N.Mex. purchased 1853 by the U.S. from Mexico *area* 29,640
Ga·e·ta \gä-ˈāt-ə\ city & port *cen* Italy in Latium on **Gulf of Gaeta** (inlet of Tyrrhenian sea N of Bay of Naples) *pop* 22,799
Gaf·sa \ˈgaf-sə\ *or anc* **Cap·sa** \ˈkap-sə\ oasis W *cen* Tunisia
Gaines·ville \ˈgānz-ˌvil, -vəl\ **1** city N *cen* Fla. *pop* 64,510 **2** city N Ga. *pop* 15,459
Gaird·ner, Lake \ˈga(ə)rd-nər, ˈge(ə)rd-\ salt lake Australia in So. Australia W of Lake Torrens *area* 1840
Ga·lá·pa·gos islands \gə-ˈläp-ə-gəs, -ˈlap-\ *or* **Co·lón archipelago** \kə-ˈlōn-\ island group Ecuador in the Pacific 600 *m* W of mainland ✱ San Cristóbal *area* 3029 — see ISABELA
Gal·a·ta \ˈgal-ət-ə\ port & commercial section of Istanbul, Turkey
Ga·la·ti \gə-ˈläts(-ē)\ *or* **Ga·latz** \ˈgäl-ˌäts\ city E Rumania on the Danube *pop* 172,687
Ga·la·tia \gə-ˈlā-sh(ē-)ə\ ancient country & Roman province *cen* Asia Minor in region centering around modern Ankara, Turkey — **Ga·la·tian** \-shən\ *adj or n*
Gald·hö·pig·gen \ˈgäl-ˌhə(r)-ˌpig-ən\ mountain 8100 *ft* S *cen* Norway in Jotunheim mountains
Gales·burg \ˈgā(ə)lz-ˌbərg\ city NW Ill. *pop* 36,290
Ga·li·cia \gə-ˈlish-(ē-)ə\ **1** region E *cen* Europe including N slopes of the Carpathians & valleys of the upper Vistula, Dniester, Bug, & Seret; former Austrian crown land; belonged to Poland between the two world wars; now divided between Poland & Ukraine **2** region & ancient kingdom NW Spain bordering on the Atlantic — **Ga·li·cian** \-ˈlish-ən\ *adj or n*
Gal·i·lee \ˈgal-ə-ˌlē\ hill region N Palestine N of Esdraelon plain — **Gal·i·le·an** \ˌgal-ə-ˈlē-ən\ *adj or n*
Galilee, Sea of *or bib* **Lake of Gen·nes·a·ret** \gə-ˈnes-ə-ˌret, -rət\ *or* **Sea of Ti·be·ri·as** \tī-ˈbir-ē-əs\ *or* **Sea of Chin·ne·reth** \ˈkin-ə-ˌreth\ *or* Heb **Yam Kin·ne·ret** \ˈyäm-ˈkin-ə-ˌret\ lake 14 *m* long & 8 *m* wide N Israel on Syrian border traversed by the Jordan; 686 *ft* below sea level
Gal·la·tin \ˈgal-ət-ᵊn\ **1** mountain range S Mont. — see ELECTRIC PEAK **2** river 125 *m* SW Mont. — see THREE FORKS
Ga·lli·nas, Point \gə-ˈyē-nəs\ cape N Colombia; northernmost point of So. America, at 12°15′ N
Gal·lip·o·li \gə-ˈlip-ə-lē\ *or* **Ge·li·bo·lu** \ˌgel-ə-bə-ˈlü\ peninsula Turkey in Europe between the Dardanelles & Saros gulf — see CHERSONESE
Gal·lo·way \ˈgal-ə-ˌwā\ district SW Scotland comprising Wigtown & Kirkcudbright — **Gal·we·gian** \gal-ˈwē-j(ē-)ən\ *adj or n*
Galt \ˈgȯlt\ city Canada in SE Ont. NW of Hamilton *pop* 38,897
Gal·ves·ton \ˈgal-və-stən\ city SE Tex. on **Galveston Island** (30 *m* long) at entrance to **Galveston Bay** (inlet of Gulf of Mexico) *pop* 61,809
Gal·way \ˈgȯl-ˌwā\ **1** county W Ireland in Connacht bordering on the Atlantic *area* 2293, *pop* 148,220 **2** municipal borough & port, its ✱, on **Galway Bay** (inlet) *pop* 26,896
Gam·bia \ˈgam-bē-ə\ **1** river 460 *m* W Africa flowing from Fouta Djallon in W Guinea W through Senegal into the Atlantic in Gambia **2** *or* **The Gambia** country W Africa; a republic in the Brit. Commonwealth ✱ Bathurst *area* 3977, *pop* 370,000 — **Gam·bi·an** \-bē-ən\ *adj or n*
Gam·bier \ˈgam-ˌbi(ə)r\ islands S Pacific SE of Tuamotu archipelago belonging to France — see MANGAREVA
Gana — see GHANA
Gand — see GHENT
Gan·dak \ˈgən-(ˌ)dək\ river 400 *m* Nepal & N India flowing SW & SE into the Ganges
Gandzha — see KIROVABAD
Gan·ges \ˈgan-ˌjēz\ river 1550 *m* N India flowing from the Himalayas SE & E to unite with the Brahmaputra & empty into Bay of Bengal through the vast **Ganges delta** — see HOOGHLY — **Gan·get·ic** \gan-ˈjet-ik\ *adj*
Gang·tok \ˈgaŋ-ˈtäk, ˈgan-\ town ✱ of Sikkim
Gan·nett Peak \ˌgan-ət-\ mountain 13,785 *ft*, *cen* Wyo.; highest in Wind River range & in the state
Gar·da, Lake \ˈgärd-ə\ lake 35 *m* long N Italy between Lombardy & Veneto draining through the Mincio into the Po
Gar·de·na \gär-ˈdē-nə\ city SW Calif. S of Los Angeles *pop* 41,021
Garden City, 1 city SE Mich. SW of Detroit *pop* 41,864 **2** village SE N.Y. on Long I. *pop* 25,373
Garden Grove city SW Calif. SW of Los Angeles *pop* 122,524
Gard·ner \ˈgärd-nər\ city N *cen* Mass. *pop* 19,748
Gar·field \ˈgär-ˌfēld\ **1** mountain 10,961 *ft* SW Mont. near Idaho border; highest in Beaverhead & Bitterroot ranges **2** city NE N.J. N of Newark *pop* 30,722
Garfield Heights city NE Ohio SSE of Cleveland *pop* 41,417
Ga·ri·glia·no \ˌgär-ēl-ˈyän-(ˌ)ō\ river 100 *m*, *cen* Italy in Latium flowing SE & SW into Gulf of Gaeta
Gar·land \ˈgär-lənd\ city NE Tex. NNE of Dallas *pop* 81,437
Gar·misch–Par·ten·kir·chen \ˈgär-mish-ˈpärt-ᵊn-ˌki(ə)r-kən\ city W Germany in Bavaria SW of Munich in foothills of the Alps *pop* 27,367
Gar·mo Peak \ˈgär-(ˌ)mō\ *or* **Sta·lin Peak** \ˈstäl-ən, ˈstal-, -ˌēn\ *or since 1961* **Communism Peak** mountain 24,590 *ft* Soviet Central Asia in SE Tadzhik Republic in the Pamirs; highest in the U.S.S.R.
Ga·ronne \gə-ˈrän, -ˈrōn\ river 355 *m* SW France flowing NW to unite with the Dordogne forming Gironde estuary
Gar·ri·son Reservoir \ˈgar-ə-sən\ reservoir 140 *m* long W N.Dak. formed in the Missouri by the **Garrison Dam**
Gar·tok \ˈgär-ˌtäk\ town SW Tibet on the upper Indus
Gary \ˈga(ə)r-ē, ˈge(ə)r-\ city NW Ind. *pop* 175,415
Gas·co·nade \ˌgas-kə-ˈnād\ river 250 *m* S *cen* Mo. flowing NE into the Missouri
Gas·co·ny \ˈgas-kə-nē\ *or* F **Gas·cogne** \gȧ-skȯnʸ\ region & former province SW France ✱ Auch
Ga·sher·brum \ˈgəsh-ər-ˌbrüm, -ˌbrum\ mountain 26,470 *ft* N Kashmir in Karakoram range SE of Mt. Godwin Austen
Gas·pé \gas-ˈpā, ˈgas-ˌ\ **1** peninsula Canada in SE Que. between mouth of St. Lawrence river & Chaleur Bay **2** city Canada in E Que. *pop* 17,211 — **Gas·pe·sian** \-ˈspē-zhən\ *adj*
Ga·stein *or* **Badga·stein** \(ˌ)bät-)gä-ˈstīn\ town W *cen* Austria S of Salzburg
Gas·ti·neau \ˈgas-tə-ˌnō\ channel SE Alaska between Douglas I. & mainland; Juneau is situated on it
Gas·to·nia \ga-ˈstō-nē-ə, -nyə\ city S N.C. *pop* 47,142
Gates·head \ˈgāts-ˌhed\ county borough N England in Co. Durham on the Tyne opposite Newcastle *pop* 94,457
Gath \ˈgath\ city of ancient Philistia ENE of Gaza
Gat·i·neau \ˌgat-ᵊn-ˈō\ **1** river 240 *m* Canada in SW Que. flowing S into the Ottawa at Hull **2** town Canada in SW Que. NW of Hull *pop* 22,321
Ga·tun \gə-ˈtün\ lake Panama Canal Zone formed by the **Gatun Dam** in Chagres river
Gaul \ˈgȯl\ *or* L **Gal·lia** \ˈgal-ē-ə\ ancient country W Europe comprising chiefly the region occupied by modern France & Belgium & at one time including also the Po valley in N Italy — see CISALPINE GAUL, TRANSALPINE GAUL
Ga·var·nie \ˌgav-ər-ˈnē\ waterfall 1385 *ft* SW France S of Lourdes in the **Cirque de Gavarnie** \ˌsi(ə)rk-də-\ (natural amphitheater at head of Gave de Pau) — see PAU (Gave de)
Gave de Pau — see PAU
Gav·ins Point Dam \ˌgav-ənz-\ dam SE S.Dak. & NE Nebr. in the Missouri — see LEWIS AND CLARK
Gäv·le \ˈyev-lə\ city & port E Sweden on Gulf of Bothnia NNW of Stockholm *pop* 72,987
Ga·ya \gə-ˈyä\ city NE India in *cen* Bihar *pop* 169,464
Ga·za \ˈgäz-ə, ˈgaz-, ˈgāz-\ *or* Ar **Ghaz·ze** \ˈgaz-ē\ city S Palestine near the Mediterranean; with surrounding coastal district (**Gaza Strip,** adjoining Sinai peninsula), administered since 1949 by Egypt *pop* 118,300
Ga·zi·an·tep \ˌgäz-ē-(ˌ)än-ˈtep\ *or formerly* **Ain·tab** \īn-ˈtab\ city S Turkey N of Alep, Syria *pop* 160,152
Gdansk \gə-ˈdän(t)sk, -ˈdan(t)sk\ *or* G **Dan·zig** \ˈdan(t)-sig, ˈdän(t)-\ city & port N Poland on Gulf of Danzig *pop* 369,900
Gdyn·ia \gə-ˈdin-ē-ə\ city & port N Poland on Gulf of Danzig NNW of Gdansk *pop* 182,400
Gebel Katherina — see KATHERINA (Gebel)
Gebel Musa — see MUSA (Gebel)
Ge·diz \gə-ˈdēz\ *or* **Sa·ra·bat** \ˌsär-ə-ˈbät\ river 200 *m* W Turkey in Asia flowing W into Gulf of Izmir
Gee·long \jə-ˈlȯŋ\ city & port SE Australia in S Victoria on Port Phillip Bay SW of Melbourne *pop* (with suburbs) 104,974
Geel·vink Bay \ˌgā(ə)l-(ˌ)viŋk-\ inlet of W Pacific N West New Guinea
Gela — see FLORIDA
Gel·der·land \ˈgel-dər-ˌland\ province E Netherlands bordering on IJsselmeer ✱ Arnhem *area* 1965, *pop* 1,505,760
Gelibolu — see GALLIPOLI
Gel·sen·kir·chen \ˌgel-zən-ˈki(ə)r-kən\ city W Germany in the Ruhr W of Dortmund *pop* 351,000
General San Martín — see SAN MARTÍN
Gen·e·see \ˌjen-ə-ˈsē\ river 144 *m* W N.Y. flowing N into Lake Ontario
Ge·ne·va \jə-ˈnē-və\ **1** city *cen* N.Y. on Seneca Lake *pop* 16,793 **2** *or* F **Ge·nève** \zhə-ˈnev\ *or* G **Genf** \ˈgenf\ canton SW Switzerland *area* 107, *pop* 331,599 **3** *or* F **Genève** *or* G **Genf** city, its ✱, at SW tip of Lake Geneva on the Rhone *pop* 169,500 — **Gen·e·vese** \ˌjen-ə-ˈvēz, -ˈvēs\ *adj or n*
Geneva, Lake *or* **Lake Le·man** \ˈlē-mən, ˈlem-ən, lə-ˈman\ lake 45 *m* long on border between SW Switzerland & E France; traversed by the Rhone
Gennesaret, Lake of — see GALILEE (Sea of)
Gen·oa \ˈjen-ə-wə\ *or* It **Ge·no·va** \ˈje-nō-vä\ *or anc* **Gen·ua** \ˈjen-yə-wə\ commune & port NW Italy ✱ of Liguria at foot of the

Apennines & at head of **Gulf of Genoa** (arm of Ligurian sea) *pop* 842,303 — **Gen·o·ese** \ˌjen-ə-ˈwēz, -ˈwēs\ *adj or n* — **Gen·o·vese** \-ə-ˈvēz, -ˈvēs\ *adj or n*

Gen·tof·te \ˈgen-ˌtəf-tə\ city Denmark on Sjælland I., N suburb of Copenhagen *pop* 77,970

George \ˈjȯ(ə)rj\ river 345 *m* Canada in NE Que. flowing N into Ungava Bay

George, Lake, 1 lake 14 *m* long NE Fla. in course of St. Johns river WNW of Daytona Beach 2 lake 33 *m* long E N.Y. S of Lake Champlain

George·town \ˈjȯ(ə)rj-ˌtau̇n\ 1 section of Washington, D.C., in W part of the city 2 town Canada in SE Ont. W of Toronto *pop* 17,053 3 city & port ✱ of Guyana on the Atlantic at mouth of the Demerara *pop* 162,000

George Town \ˈjȯ(ə)rj-ˌtau̇n\ *or* **Pe·nang** \pə-ˈnaŋ\ city & port Federation of Malaysia ✱ of Penang on Penang I. *pop* 234,930

Geor·gia \ˈjȯr-jə\ 1 state SE U.S. ✱ Atlanta *area* 58,876, *pop* 4,589,575 2 *or* **Geor·gian Republic** \ˌjȯr-jən-\ constituent republic of the U.S.S.R. S of Caucasus mountains bordering on Black sea; an ancient & medieval kingdom ✱ Tiflis *area* 26,875, *pop* 4,688,000

Georgia, Strait of channel 150 *m* long NW Wash. & SW B.C. between S Vancouver I. & mainland

Georgian Bay inlet of Lake Huron, Canada, in SE Ont.

Georgian Bay Islands National Park reservation SE Canada including Flowerpot I. SE of Manitoulin I. & a group of small islands N of Midland, Ont. *area* 5.4

Ge·ra \ˈger-ə\ city E Germany ESE of Erfurt *pop* 111,188

Ger·la·chov·ka \ˈge(ə)r-lə-ˌkȯf-kə, -ˌkȯv-\ mountain 8737 *ft* E Czechoslovakia in N Slovakia in Tatra mountains; highest in Carpathian mountains

German East Africa former country E Africa comprising Tanganyika & Ruanda-Urundi (now Rwanda & Burundi); a German protectorate 1885–1920

Ger·ma·nia \(ˌ)jər-ˈmā-nē-ə, -nyə\ 1 region of ancient Europe E of the Rhine & N of the Danube including modern Germany 2 region of Roman Empire just W of the Rhine in what is now NE France & part of Belgium & the Netherlands

German ocean — see NORTH SEA

German Southwest Africa — see SOUTH-WEST AFRICA

Ger·man·town \ˈjər-mən-ˌtau̇n\ a NW section of Philadelphia, Pa.

Ger·ma·ny \ˈjərm-(ə-)nē\ *or* G **Deutsch·land** \ˈdȯich-ˌlänt\ country *cen* Europe bordering on North & Baltic seas, since 1949 constituting two republics: the West German Federal Republic (✱ Bonn, *area* 94,634, *pop* 59,180,000) & the East German Democratic Republic (✱ East Berlin, *area* 41,700, *pop* 15,950,000)

Ger·mis·ton \ˈjər-mə-stən\ city NE Republic of So. Africa in S Transvaal E of Johannesburg *pop* 214,393

Ge·ro·na \hā-ˈrō-nə, jə-\ 1 province NE Spain in Catalonia bordering on the Mediterranean *area* 2264, *pop* 414,397 2 commune, its ✱ *pop* 50,338

Get·tys·burg National Military Park \ˈget-ēz-ˌbərg\ reservation S Pa. near borough of Gettysburg including site of battle 1863

Ge·zi·ra *or* **Je·zi·ra** *or* **El Jezira** \(ˌel-)jə-ˈzir-ə\ district E *cen* Sudan between the Blue Nile & White Nile

Gha·da·mes \gə-ˈdam-əs, -ˈdäm-\ oasis & town NW Libya in Tripolitania near Algerian border

Gha·gha·ra \ˈgäg-ə-ˌrä\ *or* **Gog·ra** \ˈgäg-rə, -ˌrä\ river 570 *m* S *cen* Asia flowing S from SW Tibet through Nepal into the Ganges in N India

Gha·na \ˈgän-ə, ˈgan-ə\ 1 *or* **Ga·na** ancient empire W Africa in what is now W Mali; flourished 4th–13th centuries 2 *or formerly* **Gold Coast** country W Africa bordering on Gulf of Guinea; a republic within Brit. Commonwealth; formerly (as Gold Coast) a Brit. territory comprising Gold Coast colony, Ashanti, Northern Territories, & Togoland trust territory ✱ Accra *area* 91,843, *pop* 8,860,000 — **Gha·na·ian** \gä-ˈnā-(y)ən, ga-, -ˈnī-ən\ *adj or n* — **Gha·nian** \ˈgän-ē-ən, ˈgän-yən, ˈgan-\ *adj or n* — **Gha·nese** \gä-ˈnēz, ga-, -ˈnēs\ *adj*

Gharapuri — see ELEPHANTA

Ghar·da·ia \gär-ˈdī-ə\ commune N *cen* Algeria 300 *m* S of Algiers *pop* 30,167

Ghats — see EASTERN GHATS, WESTERN GHATS

Ghazal, Bahr el — see BAHR EL GHAZAL

Ghaz·ni \ˈgäz-nē\ city E *cen* Afghanistan; once ✱ of a Muslim kingdom extending from the Tigris to the Ganges *pop* 43,423

Ghazze — see GAZA

Ghent \ˈgent\ *or* Flem **Gent** \ˈgent\ *or* F **Gand** \gä^{n}\ city NW *cen* Belgium ✱ of East Flanders at confluence of Scheldt & Lys rivers *pop* 151,614

Giant's Causeway formation of prismatic basaltic columns Northern Ireland on N coast of Antrim

Gib·e·on \ˈgib-ē-ən\ city of ancient Palestine NW of Jerusalem — **Gib·e·on·ite** \-ə-ˌnīt\ *n*

Gi·bral·tar \jə-ˈbrȯl-tər\ town & port on Rock of Gibraltar; a Brit. colony *area* 2.5, *pop* 26,833 — **Gi·bral·tar·i·an** \jə-ˌbrȯl-ˈter-ē-ən, ˌjib-ˌrȯl-, -ˈtar-\ *n*

Gibraltar, Rock of *or anc* **Cal·pe** \ˈkal-(ˌ)pē\ headland on S coast of Spain at E end of Strait of Gibraltar; highest point 1396 *ft* — see PILLARS OF HERCULES

Gibraltar, Strait of passage between Spain & Africa connecting the Atlantic & Mediterranean *ab* 8 *m* wide at narrowest point

Gies·sen \ˈgēs-^{ə}n\ city W Germany N of Frankfort *pop* 74,380

Gi·fu \ˈgē-(ˌ)fü\ city Japan in *cen* Honshu *pop* 393,000

Gi·jón \hē-ˈhōn\ city & port NW Spain in Oviedo province on Bay of Biscay *pop* 148,784

Gi·la \ˈhē-lə\ river 630 *m* N.Mex. & Ariz. flowing W into the Colorado

Gila Cliff Dwellings National Monument reservation SW N.Mex. including cliff-dweller ruins

Gil·bert \ˈgil-bərt\ islands (*area* 166) W Pacific SSE of the Marshalls forming with other islands the Brit. colony of **Gilbert and El·lice Islands** \ˈel-əs\ (✱ Tarawa *area* 342, *pop* 56,400) — **Gil·bert·ese** \ˌgil-bər-ˈtēz, -ˈtēs\ *n*

Gil·boa, Mount \gil-ˈbō-ə\ mountain 1696 *ft* N Palestine W of the Jordan & S of Valley of Jezreel

Gil·e·ad \ˈgil-ē-əd\ mountainous region of Palestine E of Jordan river; now in Jordan — **Gil·e·ad·ite** \-ē-ə-ˌdīt\ *n*

Gil·git \ˈgil-gət\ 1 district NW Kashmir 2 town NW Kashmir on Gilgit river

Gil·ling·ham \ˈjil-iŋ-əm\ municipal borough SE England in Kent *pop* 86,714

Gin·za \ˈgin-zə, -ˌzä\ shopping street & entertainment district in downtown Tokyo, Japan

Gi·re·sun \ˌgir-ə-ˈsün\ *or* **Ke·ra·sun** \ˌker-ə-\ city & port NE Turkey on Black sea 70 *m* W of Trabzon *pop* 25,331

Girgenti — see AGRIGENTO

Gi·ronde \jə-ˈränd, zhə-; zhē-rō^{n}d\ estuary 45 *m* W France formed by junction of the Garonne & the Dordogne & flowing NW into Bay of Biscay

Gis·borne \ˈgiz-bərn, -ˌbȯ(ə)rn\ borough & port New Zealand on E North I. *pop* 26,500

Gi·za *or* **Gi·zeh** \ˈgē-zə\ *or* **El Giza** *or* **El Gizeh** \el-\ city N Egypt on W bank of the Nile near Cairo *pop* 711,900

Glace Bay \ˈgläs\ town Canada in NE N.S. on Cape Breton I. *pop* 22,440

Gla·cier Bay \ˌglā-shər-\ inlet SE Alaska at S end of St. Elias range in **Glacier Bay National Monument** (*area* 4381)

Glacier National Park, 1 reservation NW Mont. (*area* 1602) adjoining Waterton Lakes National Park, Canada (*area* 203), and with it forming **Wa·ter·ton–Glacier International Peace Park** \ˌwȯt-ərt-^{ə}n-, ˌwät-\ 2 reservation W Canada in SE B.C. in Selkirk mountains W of Yoho National Park *area* 521

Glad·beck \ˈglät-ˌbek, ˈglad-\ city W Germany in the Ruhr *pop* 82,810

Glad·stone \ˈglad-ˌstōn\ city W Mo. N of Kansas City *pop* 23,128

Gla·mor·gan \glə-ˈmȯr-gən\ *or* **Gla·mor·gan·shire** \-ˌshi(ə)r, -shər\ county SE Wales ✱ Cardiff *area* 813, *pop* 1,255,374

Gla·rus \ˈglär-əs\ *or* F **Gla·ris** \gla-ˈrēs\ 1 canton E *cen* Switzerland *area* 267, *pop* 38,155 2 commune, its ✱

Glas·gow \ˈglas-(ˌ)kō, ˈglas-(ˌ)gō, ˈglaz-(ˌ)gō\ burgh & port S *cen* Scotland on the Clyde *pop* 896,958 — **Glas·we·gian** \glas-ˈwē-jən\ *n*

Glas·ton·bury \ˈglas-tən-ˌber-ē\ 1 town *cen* Conn. SE of Hartford *pop* 20,651 2 municipal borough SW England in Somerset SSW of Bristol

Glatzer Neisse — see NEISSE

Glen Canyon Dam \ˈglen\ dam N Ariz. in Glen Canyon of Colorado river forming **Lake Pow·ell** \ˈpau̇(-ə)l\ (chiefly in SE Utah)

Glen·coe \glen-ˈkō\ valley W Scotland in Argyll

Glen Cove \ˈglen-ˈkōv\ city SE N.Y. on NW Long I. *pop* 25,770

Glen·dale \ˈglen-ˌdāl\ 1 city *cen* Ariz. NW of Phoenix *pop* 36,228 2 city SW Calif. NE of Los Angeles *pop* 132,752

Glen·do·ra \glen-ˈdōr-ə, -ˈdȯr-\ city SW Calif. ENE of Los Angeles *pop* 31,349

Glen El·lyn \gle-ˈnel-ən\ village NE Ill. W of Chicago *pop* 21,909

Glen More — see GREAT GLEN

Glens Falls \ˈglenz\ city E N.Y. S of Lake George *pop* 17,222

Glen·view \ˈglen-ˌvyü\ village NE Ill. *pop* 24,880

Glit·ter·tind \ˈglit-ər-ˌtin\ mountain 8110 *ft* S *cen* Norway in Jotunheim mountains; highest in Scandinavia

Gli·wi·ce \gli-ˈvēt-sə\ *or* G **Glei·witz** \ˈglī-(ˌ)vits\ city SW Poland in Silesia W of Katowice *pop* 167,800

Glom·ma \ˈglȯ-ˌmä, ˈgläm-ə\ river 185 *m* E Norway flowing S into the Skagerrak

Glossa, Cape — see LINGUETTA (Cape)

Glouces·ter \ˈgläs-tər, ˈglȯs-\ 1 city NE Mass. on Cape Ann *pop* 27,941 2 *or* **Glouces·ter·shire** \-ˌshi(ə)r, -shər\ county SW *cen* England *area* 1257, *pop* 1,069,454 3 city & county borough, its ✱, on the Severn *pop* 90,134

Glov·ers·ville \ˈgləv-ərz-ˌvil\ city E N.Y. *pop* 19,677

Gnossus — see KNOSSOS

Goa \ˈgō-ə\ *or* Port **Gôa** district W India on Malabar Coast, with Daman & Diu forming a Union Territory; before 1962 belonged to Portugal ✱ Pangim *area* 1301, *pop* 626,978 — see PORTUGUESE INDIA — **Go·an** \ˈgō-ən\ *adj or n* — **Goa·nese** \ˌgō-ə-ˈnēz, -ˈnēs\ *adj*

Go·bi \ˈgō-(ˌ)bē\ desert E *cen* Asia in Mongolia *area ab* 500,000

Go·da·va·ri \gə-ˈdäv-ə-rē\ river 900 *m*, *cen* India flowing SE across the Deccan into Bay of Bengal

Go·des·berg \ˈgōd-əs-ˌbərg, -ˌbe(ə)rg\ *or* **Bad Godesberg** \ˈbät-\ commune W Germany on the Rhine S of Bonn *pop* 73,512

Godt·haab \ˈgȯt-ˌhȯb, ˈgät-\ town ✱ of Greenland on SW coast

God·win Aus·ten \ˌgäd-wə-ˈnȯ-stən, -ˈnäs-tən\ *or* K^2 \ˈkā-ˈtü\ *or* **Dap·sang** \ˈdap-ˌsaŋ, ˈdəp-ˌsəŋ\ mountain 28,250 *ft* N Kashmir in Karakoram range; 2d highest mountain in the world

Go·ge·bic \gō-ˈgē-bik\ iron range N Wis. & W upper peninsula of Mich.

Gogra — see GHAGHARA

Goi·â·nia *or formerly* **Goy·a·nia** \gȯi-ˈan-ē-ə\ city SE *cen* Brazil ✱ of Goiás *pop* 345,085

Goi·ás *or* **Goi·az** *or* **Goy·az** \gȯi-ˈäs\ state SE *cen* Brazil ✱ Goiânia *area* 244,330, *pop* 2,989,414

Gokcha — see SEVAN

Gol·con·da \gäl-ˈkän-də\ ruined city *cen* India in W Andhra Pradesh W of Hyderabad ✱ (1512–1687) of Golconda kingdom

Gold Coast, 1 region W Africa on N shore of Gulf of Guinea between the Ivory Coast (on W) & the Slave Coast (on E) 2 — see GHANA 3 former Brit. colony in S Gold Coast region ✱ Accra; now part of Ghana

Golden Chersonese — see CHERSONESE
Golden Gate strait 2 *m* wide W Calif. connecting San Francisco Bay with Pacific ocean
Golden Horn inlet of the Bosporus, Turkey in Europe; harbor of Istanbul
Golden Valley village E Minn. W of Minneapolis *pop* 24,246
Golds·boro \'gōl(d)z-ˌbər-ə, -ˌbə-rə\ city E *cen* N.C. *pop* 26,810
Golgotha — see CALVARY
Go·mel \'gō-məl, 'gȯ-\ city U.S.S.R. in SE Belorussia *pop* 272,000
Go·mor·rah \gə-'mär-ə, -'mȯr-\ city of ancient Palestine in the plain of the Jordan
Go·nâve, Gulf of \gō-'näv\ arm of Caribbean sea on W coast of Haiti
Gon·dar \'gän-dər, -ˌdär\ city NW Ethiopia N of Lake Tana ✱ of Amhara & former ✱ of Ethiopia *pop* 35,331
Good Hope, Cape of \ˌgu̇d-'hōp\ cape S Republic of So. Africa in SW Cape Province W of False Bay, at 34°21′S — see CAPE OF GOOD HOPE
Good·win Sands \ˌgu̇d-wən-\ shoals SE England in Strait of Dover off E coast of Kent — see DOWNS
Go·rakh·pur \'gōr-ək-ˌpu̇(ə)r, 'gȯr-\ city NE India in E Uttar Pradesh N of Banaras *pop* 241,000
Go·ri·zia \gə-'rēt-sē-ə\ commune NE Italy in Venetia on Isonzo river *pop* 43,663
Gor·ki *or* **Gor·ky** *or* **Gor·kiy** \'gȯr-kē\ *or formerly* **Nizh·ni Nov·go·rod** \ˌnizh-nē-'näv-gə-ˌräd\ city U.S.S.R. in *cen* Soviet Russia, Europe, at confluence of Oka & Volga rivers *pop* 1,170,000
Gör·litz \'gər-ˌlits, -ləts\ city E Germany on the Neisse *pop* 87,308
Gor·lov·ka \gȯr-'lȯf-kə, -'lȯv-\ city U.S.S.R. in E Ukraine in the Donets basin N of Donetsk *pop* 335,000
Gor·no–Al·tai \ˌgȯr-(ˌ)nō-ˌal-'tī\ *or formerly* **Oi·rot** \'ȯi-rət\ autonomous region U.S.S.R. in S Soviet Russia, Asia, in SE Altai Territory in Altai mountains ✱ Gorno-Altaisk (formerly Oirot-Tura) *area* 35,800, *pop* 168,000
Gor·no–Ba·dakh·shan \'gȯr-(ˌ)nō-ˌbäd-ˌäk-'shän\ autonomous region U.S.S.R. in Soviet Central Asia in SE Tadzhik Republic in the Pamirs ✱ Khorog *area* 25,784, *pop* 98,000
Go·shen \'gō-shən\ **1** city N Ind. *pop* 17,171 **2** district of ancient Egypt E of Nile delta
Gos·port \'gäs-ˌpō(ə)rt, -ˌpȯ(ə)rt\ municipal borough S England in Hampshire on Portsmouth harbor *pop* 75,947
Gö·te·borg \ˌyə(r)t-ə-'bȯr-ē\ *or* **Goth·en·burg** \'gäth-ən-ˌbərg\ city & port SW Sweden *pop* 446,875
Go·tha \'gōt-ə, 'gō-thə\ city W Germany W of Erfurt *pop* 57,328
Got·land *or* **Gott·land** \'gät-ˌland, -lənd\ island Sweden in the Baltic off SE coast; chief town Visby *area* 1167, *pop* 54,093
Göt·ting·en \'gə(r)t-iŋ-ən, 'get-\ city W Germany SSW of Brunswick *pop* 114,000
Gott·wal·dov \'gät-vəl-ˌdȯf, -ˌdȯv\ *or formerly* **Zlin** \zə-'lēn\ city *cen* Czechoslovakia in SE Moravia *pop* 64,499
Gou·da \'gau̇d-ə, 'güd-\ commune SW Netherlands in So. Holland *pop* 45,990
Gra·ham Land \'grā-əm, 'gra(-ə)m\ **1** — see ANTARCTIC **2** the N section of the Antarctic peninsula
Gra·hams·town \'grā-əmz-ˌtau̇n, 'gra(-ə)mz-\ city S Republic of So. Africa in SE Cape Province ENE of Port Elizabeth *pop* 37,600
Gra·ian Alps \ˌgrā-(y)ən-, ˌgrī-ən-\ section of W Alps S of Mont Blanc on border between France & Italy — see GRAN PARADISO
Grain coast \'grān\ region W Africa in Liberia bordering on Gulf of Guinea
Gram·pi·an \'gram-pē-ən\ hills *cen* Scotland between the Lowlands & the Great Glen — see NEVIS (Ben)
Gra·na·da \grə-'näd-ə\ **1** city SW Nicaragua on NW shore of Lake Nicaragua *pop* 51,363 **2** medieval Moorish kingdom S Spain **3** province S Spain in Andalusia bordering on the Mediterranean *area* 4928, *pop* 733,375 **4** city, its ✱, in the Sierra Nevada *pop* 158,477
Gran·by \'gran-bē\ city Canada in S Que. *pop* 34,385
Gran Chaco — see CHACO
Grand, 1 river 260 *m* SW Mich. flowing N & W into Lake Michigan **2** river 300 *m* NW Mo. flowing SE into the Missouri **3** river 140 *m* W Mo. flowing SE into Lake of the Ozarks **4** river 200 *m* N S.Dak. flowing E into the Missouri **5** the Colorado river from its source to junction with Green river in SE Utah — a former name **6** — see NEOSHO **7** canal *ab* 1000 *m* long E China from Hangchow to Tientsin
Grand Atlas — see ATLAS
Grand Bahama island Bahamas, NW island of group *area* 430
Grand Bank *or* **Grand Banks** shoals in W Atlantic SE of Nfld.
Grand Canary *or* Sp **Gran Ca·na·ria** \ˌgräŋ-kə-'när-yä\ island Spain in the Canaries; chief city Las Palmas *area* 523
Grand Canyon gorge of the Colorado NW Ariz. extending from mouth of the Little Colorado W to the Grand Wash Cliffs; over 1 *m* deep; area largely comprised in **Grand Canyon National Park** (at E end *area* 1008) & **Grand Canyon National Monument** (to the W *area* 306) — see MARBLE CANYON
Grand Canyon of the Snake — see HELLS CANYON
Grand Cayman — see CAYMAN
Grand Cou·lee \'kü-lē\ valley E Wash. extending SSW from S wall of canyon of the Columbia where it turns W in forming the Big Bend
Grand Coulee Dam dam NE *cen* Wash. in the Columbia — see FRANKLIN D. ROOSEVELT LAKE
Grande, Rio, 1 \ˌrē-ō-'grand(-ē) *also* ˌrī-ō-'grand\ river U.S. & Mexico — see RIO GRANDE **2** \ˌrē-ō-'gran-də, -dē\ river 680 *m* E Brazil in Minas Gerais flowing W to unite with the Paranaíba forming the Paraná
Grande Soufrière — see SOUFRIÈRE
Grande–Terre \gran-'te(ə)r\ island French West Indies constituting the E portion of Guadeloupe *area* 220
Grand Falls — see CHURCHILL FALLS
Grand Forks city E N.Dak. on Red river *pop* 39,008
Grand Island city SE *cen* Nebr. on the Platte *pop* 31,269
Grand Junction city W Colo. on the Colorado *pop* 20,170
Grand Lac — see TONLE SAP
Grand Ma·nan \mə-'nan\ island 20 *m* long Canada in N.B. at entrance to Bay of Fundy
Grand'Mère \grän-'me(ə)r\ city Canada in S Que. NNW of Trois-Rivières *pop* 17,137
Grand Mesa mountain *ab* 10,000 *ft* W Colo. near junction of Colorado & Gunnison rivers; summit area *ab* 53
Grand Prairie city NE *cen* Tex. W of Dallas *pop* 50,904
Grand Rapids city SW Mich. *pop* 197,649
Grand Te·ton \'tē-ˌtän\ mountain 13,766 *ft* W Wyo.; highest in Teton range
Grand Teton National Park reservation NW Wyo. including Jackson Lake & main part of Teton range
Grand Trav·erse Bay \-ˌtrav-ərs-\ inlet of Lake Michigan in Mich. on NW coast of lower peninsula
Grand Turk — see TURKS AND CAICOS
Grand·view \'gran(d)-ˌvyü\ city W Mo. S of Kansas City *pop* 17,456
Grange·mouth \'grānj-məth, -ˌmau̇th\ burgh & port *cen* Scotland in Stirling county on Firth of Forth *pop* 24,572
Granicus — see KOCABAS
Granite City city SW Ill. on the Mississippi *pop* 40,440
Granite Peak mountain 12,799 *ft* S Mont. NE of Yellowstone National Park in Beartooth range (spur of Absaroka range); highest point in state
Gran Pa·ra·di·so \ˌgran-ˌpar-ə-'dē-(ˌ)zō\ mountain 13,324 *ft* NW Italy in NW Piedmont; highest in Graian Alps
Gran Qui·vi·ra National Monument \ˌgran-kə-'vir-ə\ reservation *cen* N.Mex. containing ruins of a pueblo & Spanish mission
Gras·mere \'gras-ˌmi(ə)r\ lake 1 *m* long NW England in Westmorland in Lake District
Grasse \'gras, 'gräs\ commune SE France W of Nice *pop* 30,907
Grau·bün·den \grau̇-'bin-dən, -'bün-, -'bɶn-\ *or* F **Gri·sons** \grē-zōⁿ\ canton E Switzerland ✱ Chur *area* 2744, *pop* 162,086
Graudenz — see GRUDZIADZ
Gravenhage, 's — see HAGUE (The)
Graves·end \'grāv-'zend\ municipal borough SE England in Kent on Thames estuary *pop* 54,044
Grays Harbor \'grāz\ inlet of the Pacific W Wash.
Grays Peak mountain 14,274 *ft, cen* Colo.; highest in Front range
Graz \'gräts\ city S Austria ✱ of Styria on the Mur *pop* 253,800
Great Abaco — see ABACO
Great Australian Bight wide bay on S coast of Australia
Great Barrier Reef coral reef 1250 *m* long Australia off NE coast of Queensland
Great Basin region W U.S. between Sierra Nevada & Wasatch mountains including most of Nev. & parts of Calif., Idaho, Utah, Wyo. & Oreg. & having no drainage to ocean; contains many isolated mountain ranges (the **Basin ranges**)
Great Bear lake Canada in N Mackenzie District, Northwest Territories *area* 12,000
Great Bend city W *cen* Kans. *pop* 16,133
Great Brit·ain \'brit-ᵊn\ *or* **Britain, 1** island W Europe comprising England, Scotland, & Wales *area* 88,745, *pop* 53,821,364 **2** UNITED KINGDOM
Great Crosby — see CROSBY
Great Dividing mountain range E Australia extending from Cape York peninsula to S Victoria &, interrupted by Bass strait, into Tasmania — see KOSCIUSKO (Mount)
Greater An·til·les \an-'til-ēz\ group of islands in the West Indies including Cuba, Hispaniola, Jamaica, & Puerto Rico
Greater Khingan — see KHINGAN
Greater London county SE England comprising City of London and 32 surrounding boroughs *area* 620, *pop* 7,379,014
Greater Sunda — see SUNDA
Greater Walachia — see MUNTENIA
Great Exuma — see EXUMA
Great Falls, 1 *or* **Great Falls of the Potomac** waterfall 35 *ft* in the Potomac *ab* 15 *m* above Washington **2** city W *cen* Mont. on Missouri river WSW of the **Great Falls of the Missouri** (92 *ft*) *pop* 60,091
Great Glen \'glen\ *or* **Glen More** \glen-'mō(ə)r, -'mȯ(ə)r\ valley *ab* 50 *m* long N Scotland cutting through the Highlands from SW to NE & connecting Loch Linnhe & Moray firth — see CALEDONIAN CANAL
Great Inagua — see INAGUA
Great Kabylia — see KABYLIA
Great Karroo — see KARROO
Great Lakes, 1 chain of five lakes (Superior, Michigan, Huron, Erie, & Ontario) *cen* No. America in the U.S. & Canada **2** group of lakes E *cen* Africa including Lakes Rudolf, Albert, Victoria, Tanganyika, & Nyasa
Great Namaqualand — see NAMAQUALAND
Great Ouse — see OUSE
Great Plains elevated plains region W *cen* U.S. & W Canada E of Rocky mountains & chiefly W of 100th meridian extending from NE B.C. & NW Alta. SE & S to include the Llano Estacado of N.Mex. & Tex.
Great Rift valley \'rift\ depression SW Asia & E Africa extending with several breaks from valley of the Jordan S to *cen* Mozambique
Great Saint Ber·nard \ˌsānt-bər-'närd\ mountain pass 8111 *ft* through Pennine Alps between Switzerland & Italy
Great Salt lake *ab* 70 *m* long N Utah having strongly saline waters & no outlet
Great Salt Lake desert flat barren region NW Utah
Great Sand Dunes National Monument reservation S Colo. on W slope of Sangre de Cristo mountains *area* 56
Great Slave, 1 lake NW Canada in S Mackenzie District receiving Slave river on S & draining into the Mackenzie on W *area* 11,170 **2** — see SLAVE
Great Smoky mountains of N.C.-Tenn. boundary partly in **Great Smoky Mountains National Park** (*area* 720) — see CLINGMANS DOME
Great Yarmouth — see YARMOUTH

Greece \ˈgrēs\ *or* Gk **Hel·las** \ˈhel-əs\ *or* NGk **El·lás** \e-ˈläs\ country S Europe at S end of Balkan peninsula; a kingdom ✱ Athens *area* 50,147, *pop* 8,850,000

Gree·ley \ˈgrē-lē\ city N Colo. *pop* 38,902

Green \ˈgrēn\ **1** river 730 *m* W U.S. flowing from Wind River range in W Wyo. S into the Colorado in SE Utah **2** mountains E No. America in the Appalachian system extending from S Que. S through Vt. into W Mass. — see MANSFIELD (Mount)

Green Bay, **1** inlet of NW Lake Michigan 120 *m* long in NW Mich. & NE Wis. **2** city NE Wis. on Green Bay *pop* 87,809

Green·belt \ˈgrēn-ˌbelt\ city *cen* Md. NE of Washington, D.C. *pop* 18,199

Green·dale \ˈgrēn-ˌdāl\ village SE Wis. SW of Milwaukee *pop* 15,089

Green·field \ˈgrēn-ˌfēld\ **1** town NW Mass. on the Connecticut *pop* 18,116 **2** city SE Wis. near Milwaukee *pop* 24,424

Greenfield Park town Canada in S Que. E of Montreal *pop* 15,348

Green·land \ˈgrēn-lənd, -ˌland\ **1** island in N Atlantic off NE No. America belonging to Denmark ✱ Godthaab *area* 839,800, *pop* 46,331 **2** sea arm of Arctic ocean between Greenland and Spitsbergen — **Green·land·er** \-lən-dər, -ˌlan-\ *n*

Gree·nock \ˈgrēn-ək\ burgh & port SW Scotland in Renfrewshire on Firth of Clyde *pop* 69,004

Greens·boro \ˈgrēnz-ˌbər-ə, -ˌbə-rə\ city N *cen* N.C. *pop* 144,076

Greens·burg \ˈgrēnz-ˌbərg\ city SW Pa. *pop* 15,870

Green·ville \ˈgrēn-ˌvil, -vəl\ **1** city W Miss. on the Mississippi *pop* 39,648 **2** city E N.C. *pop* 29,063 **3** city NW S.C. *pop* 61,208 **4** city NE Tex. NE of Dallas on the Sabine *pop* 22,043

Green·wich, **1** \ˈgren-ich, ˈgrēn-ˌwich, ˈgrin-ˌwich\ town SW Conn. on Long Island Sound *pop* 59,755 **2** \ˈgrin-ij, ˈgren-, -ich\ SE borough of Greater London, England *pop* 216,441

Green·wich Village \ˌgren-ich-, ˌgrin-, -ij-\ section of New York City in Manhattan on lower W side

Green·wood \ˈgrēn-ˌwu̇d\ **1** city W Miss. *pop* 22,400 **2** city W S.C. *pop* 21,069

Gre·na·da \grə-ˈnād-ə\ island Brit. West Indies in S Windward islands; with S Grenadines, constitutes an Associated State of Brit. Commonwealth ✱ St. George's *area* 133, *pop* 87,300

Gren·a·dines \ˌgren-ə-ˈdēnz\ islands Brit. West Indies in *cen* Windwards between Grenada & St. Vincent; divided administratively between Grenada & St. Vincent

Gre·no·ble \grə-ˈnō-bəl, -ˈnōblᵊ\ city SE France *pop* 161,616

Gret·na \ˈgret-nə\ city SE La. S of New Orleans *pop* 24,875

Grey·lock, Mount \ˈgrā-ˌläk\ mountain 3505 *ft* NW Mass.; highest in Berkshire hills & in state

Grif·fin \ˈgrif-ən\ city W *cen* Ga. *pop* 22,734

Grif·fith \ˈgrif-əth\ town NW Ind. S of Hammond *pop* 18,168

Grims·by \ˈgrimz-bē\ **1** town Canada in SE Ont. E of Hamilton *pop* 15,770 **2** county borough E England in Lincolnshire in Parts of Lindsey near mouth of the Humber *pop* 95,685

Grin·del·wald \ˈgrin-dᵊl-ˌwȯld, -ˌvält\ valley & village *cen* Switzerland in Bern canton in the Bernese Alps E of Interlaken

Gri·qua·land West \ˈgrik-wə-ˌland\ district NW Republic of So. Africa in N Cape of Good Hope N of Orange river; chief town Kimberley

Gris–Nez, Cape \grē-nā\ headland N France projecting into Strait of Dover

Grisons — see GRAUBÜNDEN

Grod·no \ˈgräd-(ˌ)nō, ˈgrȯd-\ city U.S.S.R. in W Belorussia on Neman river *pop* 132,000

Gro·ning·en \ˈgrō-niŋ-ən\ **1** province NE Netherlands *area* 866, *pop* 517,305 **2** city, its ✱ *pop* 168,256

Grosse Pointe Park \ˌgrōs-ˌpȯint-\ city SE Mich. NE of Detroit *pop* 15,585

Grosse Pointe Woods \ˌgrōs-ˌpȯint-\ city SE Mich. NE of Detroit *pop* 21,878

Gross·glock·ner \ˈgrōs-ˈgläk-nər\ mountain 12,457 *ft* SW Austria, highest in the Hohe Tauern & in Austria

Gros Ventre \ˈgrō-ˌvänt\ river 100 *m* W Wyo. flowing W into the Snake

Grot·on \ˈgrät-ᵊn\ town SE Conn. E of New London *pop* 38,523

Groves \ˈgrōvz\ city SE Tex. NE of Port Arthur *pop* 18,067

Groz·ny *or* **Groz·nyy** \ˈgrȯz-nē, ˈgräz-\ city U.S.S.R. in S Soviet Russia, Europe, N of Caucasus mountains *pop* 341,000

Gru·dziadz \ˈgrü-ˌjōⁿ(n)ts\ *or* G **Grau·denz** \ˈgrau̇-ˌden(t)s\ city N Poland on the Vistula NE of Bydgoszcz *pop* 75,500

Gua·da·la·ja·ra \ˌgwäd-ə-lə-ˈhär-ə\ **1** city W *cen* Mexico ✱ of Jalisco *pop* 1,196,218 **2** province E *cen* Spain in NE New Castile *area* 4676, *pop* 147,732 **3** commune, its ✱ *pop* 31,917

Gua·dal·ca·nal \ˌgwäd-ᵊl-kə-ˈnal, ˌgwäd-ə-kə-\ island W Pacific in the SE Solomons *area* 2500, *pop* 23,922

Gua·dal·qui·vir \ˌgwäd-ᵊl-ˈkwiv-ər, -ki-ˈvi(ə)r\ river 374 *m* S Spain flowing W & SW into Gulf of Cádiz

Gua·da·lupe \ˈgwäd-ᵊl-ˌüp\ **1** mountains S N.Mex. & W Tex., the S extension of Sacramento mountains; highest point **Guadalupe Peak** 8751 *ft* (highest in Tex.) in **Guadalupe Mountains National Park** (in Tex. *area* 127) **2** river 300 *m* SE Tex. flowing SE into San Antonio river

Gua·da·lupe Hi·dal·go \ˈgwäd-ᵊl-ˌüp(-ē)-hi-ˈdal-(ˌ)gō\ former city *cen* Mexico N of Mexico City now part of city of Gustavo A. Madero **2** GUSTAVO A. MADERO

Gua·de·loupe \ˈgwäd-ᵊl-ˌüp\ two islands, Basse-Terre (or Guadeloupe proper) & Grande-Terre, in French West Indies in *cen* Leeward islands; an overseas department of France ✱ Basse-Terre (on Basse-Terre I.) *area* 583, *pop* 327,000

Gua·di·a·na \ˌgwäd-ē-ˈän-ə, -ˈan-\ river 515 *m* Spain & Portugal flowing W & S into Gulf of Cádiz

Guai·rá Falls \gwī-ˌrä-\ *or* **Se·te Que·das** \ˌsāt-ə-ˈkā-t͟həsh\ cataract in gorge of the Alto Paraná on Brazil-Paraguay boundary; total descent 374 *ft*

Guam \ˈgwäm\ island W Pacific in S Marianas belonging to U.S. ✱ Agana *area* 212, *pop* 84,996 — **Gua·ma·ni·an** \gwä-ˈmā-nē-ən\ *adj or n*

Gua·na·ba·coa \ˌgwän-ə-bə-ˈkō-ə\ city W Cuba E of Havana *pop* (municipality) 203,010

Gua·na·ba·ra \ˌgwän-ə-ˈbar-ə, -ˈbär-ə\ state SE Brazil bordering on the Atlantic; created 1960 from former Federal District ✱ Rio de Janeiro *area* 451, *pop* 4,296,782

Guanabara Bay *or* **Rio de Janeiro Bay** inlet of Atlantic ocean SE Brazil

Gua·na·jua·to \ˌgwän-ə-ˈ(h)wät-(ˌ)ō\ **1** state *cen* Mexico *area* 11,804, *pop* 2,285,249 **2** city, its ✱ *pop* 65,258

Guan·tá·na·mo \gwän-ˈtän-ə-ˌmō\ city SE Cuba NW of **Guantánamo Bay** (inlet of the Caribbean; site of U.S. naval station) *pop* (municipality) 238,700

Gua·po·ré \ˌgwäp-ə-ˈrā\ **1** *or* **Ité·nez** \ē-ˈtā-nəs\ river 950 *m* W Brazil & NE Bolivia flowing NW to the Mamoré **2** — see RONDÔNIA

Guar·da·fui, Cape \ˌg(w)ärd-əf-ˈwē, -ə-ˈfü-ē\ cape NE Somalia at entrance to Gulf of Aden

Guá·ri·co \ˈgwär-i-ˌkō\ river 225 *m* W Venezuela flowing SW & S into the Apure

Gua·te·ma·la \ˌgwät-ə-ˈmäl-ə\ **1** country Central America S of Mexico bordering on the Pacific & the Caribbean; a republic *area* 42,042, *pop* 5,350,000 **2** *or* **Guatemala City** city, its ✱ *pop* 730,991 — **Gua·te·ma·lan** \-ˈmäl-ən\ *adj or n*

Gua·via·re \gwäv-ˈyär-ē\ river 650 *m* Colombia flowing E into the Orinoco

Gua·ya·ma \gwə-ˈyäm-ə\ town SE Puerto Rico *pop* 20,318

Gua·ya·quil \ˌgwī-ə-ˈkē(ə)l, -ˈkil\ city & port W Ecuador on Guayas river 40 *m* from **Gulf of Guayaquil** (inlet of the Pacific) *pop* 738,591

Gua·yas \ˈgwī-əs\ river *ab* 100 *m* W Ecuador forming delta in Gulf of Guayaquil

Guay·mas \ˈgwī-məs\ city & port NW Mexico in Sonora on Gulf of California *pop* 60,981

Guay·na·bo \gwī-ˈnäb-(ˌ)ō\ city NE *cen* Puerto Rico *pop* 55,310

Gub·bio \ˈgü-bē-ˌō\ commune *cen* Italy NE of Perugia *pop* 31,085

Guelph \ˈgwelf\ city Canada in SE Ont. *pop* 60,087

Guer·ni·ca \ger-ˈnē-kə\ town N Spain ENE of Bilbao

Guern·sey \ˈgərn-zē\ island English channel in the Channel islands ✱ St. Peter Port *area* 25, *pop* 46,182

Guer·re·ro \gə-ˈre(ə)r-(ˌ)ō\ state S Mexico bordering on the Pacific ✱ Chilpancingo *area* 24,885, *pop* 1,573,098

Gui·a·na \gē-ˈan-ə, -ˈän-ə; gī-ˈan-ə\ region N So. America bordering on the Atlantic & bounded on W & S by the Orinoco, the Negro, & the Amazon; includes Guyana, French Guiana, Surinam, & adjoining parts of Brazil & Venezuela — **Gui·a·nan** \-ən\ *adj or n* — **Gui·a·nese** \ˌgi-ə-ˈnēz, ˌgē-ə-, -ˈnēs\ *adj or n*

Gui·enne *or* **Guy·enne** \gwē-ˈ(y)en\ region & former province SW France bordering on Bay of Biscay ✱ Bordeaux — see AQUITAINE

Guin·ea \ˈgin-ē\ *or* F **Gui·née** \gē-nā\ **1** region W Africa bordering on the Atlantic from Gambia (on N) to Angola (on S) **2** *or formerly* **French Guinea** country W Africa bordering on the Atlantic; a republic, formerly a territory of French West Africa ✱ Conakry *area* 108,455, *pop* 4,010,000 — **Guin·ean** \ˈgin-ē-ən\ *adj or n*

Guinea, Gulf of arm of the Atlantic W *cen* Africa; includes bights of Benin & Biafra

Gui·púz·coa \gē-ˈpüs-kə-wə\ province N Spain; one of the Basque provinces ✱ San Sebastian *area* 728, *pop* 631,003

Gu·ja·rat *or* **Gu·je·rat** \ˌgüj-ə-ˈrät, ˌgu̇j-ə-\ **1** region W India where Gujarati is spoken **2** state W India N & E of Gulf of Cambay; formed 1960 from NW portion of former Bombay state ✱ Ahmadabad *area* 72,226, *pop* 26,660,929

Guj·ran·wala \ˌgüj-rən-ˈwäl-ə, ˌgu̇j-\ city NE Pakistan N of Lahore *pop* 289,000

Gulf·port \ˈgəlf-ˌpō(ə)rt, -ˌpȯ(ə)rt\ city & port SE Miss. *pop* 40,791

Gulf Stream warm ocean current in N Atlantic flowing from Gulf of Mexico NE along coast of U.S. to Nantucket I. & thence to Brit. Isles

Gum·ti \ˈgu̇m(p)-tē\ river 500 *m* N India flowing SE into the Ganges

Gun·ni·son \ˈgən-ə-sən\ river 150 *m* W *cen* Colo. flowing W & NW into the Colorado

Gun·tur \gu̇n-ˈtu̇(ə)r\ city E India in *cen* Andhra Pradesh W of Masulipatnam *pop* 273,385

Gur·gan \gu̇r-ˈgän\ *or* **As·ter·abad** \ˈas-t(ə-)rə-ˌbad, -ˌbäd\ city N Iran near SE coast of Caspian sea *pop* 55,000

Gus·ta·vo A. Ma·de·ro \gə-ˈstäv-(ˌ)ō-ˈä-mə-ˈde(ə)r-(ˌ)ō\ city *cen* Mexico in Federal District N of Mexico City *pop* 1,182,895

Guy·ana \gī-ˈan-ə\ *or formerly* **British Guiana** country N So. America on Atlantic coast; a republic within Brit. Commonwealth since 1970 ✱ Georgetown *area* 83,000 *pop* 740,000 — **Guy·a·nese** \ˌgī-ə-ˈnēz, -ˈnēs\ *adj or n*

Gwa·dar *or* **Gwa·dur** \ˈgwäd-ər\ town & port SW Pakistan on Arabian sea; until 1958 belonged to Sultan of Oman

Gwa·li·or \ˈgwäl-ē-ˌȯ(ə)r\ **1** former state N *cen* India ✱ Lashkar; part of Madhya Pradesh since 1956 **2** city N *cen* India in NW Madhya Pradesh SSE of Agra *pop* (including adjacent city of **Lash·kar** \ˈläsh-kər\) 369,121

Gyor \ˈjər\ *or* G **Raab** \ˈräp\ city NW Hungary *pop* 100,065

Haar·lem \ˈhär-ləm\ city W Netherlands ✱ of No. Holland *pop* 172,588

Haar·lem·mer·meer \ˌhär-lə-mər-ˈme(ə)r\ commune W Netherlands *pop* 58,966

Habana — see HAVANA

Hab·ba·ni·ya \hə-ˈban-ē-(y)ə\ lake *cen* Iraq along S bank of the Euphrates W of Baghdad

Hack·en·sack \ˈhak-ən-ˌsak\ city NE N.J. *pop* 35,911

ə abut	ᵊ kitten, F table	ər further	a back	ā bake
ä cot, cart	à F bac	au̇ out	ch chin	e less
ē easy	g gift	i trip	ī life	j joke
k̲ G ich	ⁿ F vin	ŋ sing	ō flow	ȯ flaw
œ F bœuf	œ̄ F feu	ȯi coin	th thing	t͟h this
ü loot	u̇ foot	ue G Füllen	ue̅ F rue	y yet
ʸ F digne \dēnʸ\, nuit \nwʸē\	yü few	yu̇ furious	zh vision	

Hack·ney \ˈhak-nē\ borough of N Greater London, England *pop* 216,659

Had·ding·ton \ˈhad-iŋ-tən\ **1** *or* **Had·ding·ton·shire** \-ˌshi(ə)r, -shər\ — see EAST LOTHIAN **2** burgh Scotland ✻ of East Lothian

Ha·dhra·maut *or* **Ha·dra·maut** \ˌhäd-rə-ˈmau̇t\ region S Arabia bordering on Arabian sea E of Aden in South Yemen; chief city Mukalla *area* 58,500

Hadrumetum — see SOUSSE

Hae·ju \ˈhī-(ˌ)jü\ city N Korea on inlet of Yellow sea S of Pyongyang *pop* 70,000

Ha·gen \ˈhäg-ən\ *or* **Hagen in West·fa·len** \-in-ˌvest-ˈfäl-ən\ city W Germany ENE of Düsseldorf *pop* 201,500

Ha·gers·town \ˈhā-gərz-ˌtau̇n\ city N Md. *pop* 35,862

Hague, The \thə-ˈhāg\ *or* **D 's Gra·ven·ha·ge** \ˌs(k)räv-ən-ˈhäg-ə\ city SW Netherlands in So. Holland near coast of North sea; de facto ✻ of the Netherlands *pop* 557,114

Haichow — see SINHAILIEN

Haidarabad — see HYDERABAD

Hai·fa \ˈhī-fə\ city & port NW Israel *pop* 214,500

Haikow — see HOIHOW

Hai·nan \ˈhī-ˈnän\ **1** island SE China in Kwangtung in So. China sea *area* 13,000 **2** strait between Hainan I. & Luichow peninsula connecting Gulf of Tonkin with So. China sea

Hai·naut \(h)ā-ˈnō\ **1** medieval county in Low Countries SE of Flanders in modern SW Belgium & N France **2** province SW Belgium ✻ Mons *area* 1436, *pop* 1,330,789

Hai·phong \ˈhī-ˈfȯŋ\ city & port N Vietnam in Tonkin in delta of Red river *pop* 182,490

Hai·ti *or formerly* **Hay·ti** \ˈhāt-ē\ **1** — see HISPANIOLA **2** country West Indies on W Hispaniola; a republic ✻ Port-au-Prince *area* 10,714, *pop ab* 4,970,000

Ha·ko·da·te \ˌhäk-ə-ˈdät-ē\ city & port Japan in SW Hokkaido on Tsugaru strait *pop* 247,000

Halab *or* **Haleb** — see ALEPPO

Ha·le·a·ka·la \ˌhäl-ē-ˌäk-ə-ˈlä\ dormant volcano 10,023 *ft* Hawaii in E Maui I.; crater 2720 *ft* deep, 20 *m* in circumference; in **Haleakala National Park** (*area* 33)

Hal·fa·ya Pass \hal-ˌfī-ə-\ pass NW Egypt through hills near Mediterranean coast

Hal·i·car·nas·sus \ˌhal-ə-kär-ˈnas-əs\ ancient city SW Asia Minor in SW Caria on Aegean sea

Hal·i·fax \ˈhal-ə-ˌfaks\ **1** city & port Canada ✻ of N.S. *pop* 122,035 **2** county borough N England in West Riding, Yorkshire *pop* 91,171

Hal·lan·dale \ˈhal-ən-ˌdāl\ city SE Fla. S of Fort Lauderdale *pop* 23,849

Hal·le \ˈhäl-ə\ city E Germany on Saale river *pop* 261,190

Hall·statt \ˈhȯl-ˌstat, ˈhäl-ˌs(h)tät\ village W *cen* Austria on shore of **Hall·stät·ter Lake** \ˌhȯl-ˌstet-ər, ˌhäl-ˌs(h)tet-\

Hal·ma·hera \ˌhal-mə-ˈher-ə, ˌhäl-\ *or* **Djai·lo·lo** \jī-ˈlō-(ˌ)lō\ island E Indonesia in Moluccas; largest in group *area* 6928

Halm·stad \ˈhälm-ˌstä(d)\ city & port SW Sweden *pop* 46,723

Häl·sing·borg \ˈhel-siŋ-ˌbȯ(ə)rg, ˌhel-siŋ-ˈbȯr-ē\ city & port SW Sweden on Öresund opposite Helsingör, Denmark *pop* 82,137

Hal·tom City \ˌhȯl-təm-\ village N Tex. NE of Fort Worth *pop* 28,127

Halys — see KIZIL IRMAK

Ha·ma \ˈham-ˌä\ *or bib* **Ha·math** \ˈhā-ˌmath\ city W Syria on the Orontes *pop* 137,000

Ha·mad *or* **El Hamad** \(ˌel-)-hə-ˈmad\ the SW portion of Syrian desert

Ha·ma·dan \ˌham-ə-ˈdan, -ˈdän\ *or anc* **Ec·bat·a·na** \ek-ˈbat-ᵊn-ə\ city W Iran WSW of Tehran *pop* 124,167

Ha·ma·ma·tsu \ˌhäm-ə-ˈmät-(ˌ)sü\ city Japan is S Honshu SE of Nagoya near Pacific coast *pop* 425,000

Ham·burg \ˈham-ˌbərg; ˈhäm-ˌbu̇(ə)rg\ city & port W Germany on the Elbe 90 *m* from its mouth; since 1948 a state of the Bonn Republic *area* 288, *pop* 1,818,600 — **Ham·burg·er** \-ˌbər-gər, -ˌbu̇r-\ *n*

Ham·den \ˈham-dən\ town S Conn. N of New Haven *pop* 49,357

Ha·meln \ˈhäm-əln\ city W Germany in Lower Saxony SW of Hannover *pop* 46,986

Ham·hung \ˈhäm-ˌhu̇ŋ\ city N Korea NW of Hungnam near coast *pop* 125,000

Ha·mi \ˈhä-ˈmē\ *or* **Qo·mul** \ˈkō-ˈmül\ oasis W China in E Sinkiang NE of Takla Makan desert

Ham·il·ton \ˈham-əl-tən, -əlt-ᵊn\ **1** city SW Ohio N of Cincinnati *pop* 67,865 **2** town & port ✻ of Bermuda *pop* 2,127 **3** — see CHURCHILL **4** city & port Canada in SE Ont. on Lake Ontario *pop* 309,173 **5** borough New Zealand on *cen* North I. *pop* 71,600

Hamilton, Mount mountain 4209 *ft* W Calif. E of San Jose

Hamilton Inlet inlet of the Atlantic 150 *m* long (with Lake Melville) Canada in SE Labrador

Hamm \ˈhäm, ˈham\ city W Germany on the Lippe SSE of Münster *pop* 84,266

Ham·mer·fest \ˈham-ər-ˌfest, ˈhäm-\ town & port N Norway on island in Arctic ocean; northernmost town in Europe, at 70°38′N

Ham·mer·smith \ˈham-ər-ˌsmith\ borough SW Greater London, England *pop* 184,935

Ham·mond \ˈham-ənd\ city NW Ind. SE of Chicago *pop* 107,790

Hamp·shire \ˈham(p)-ˌshi(ə)r, -shər\ **1** *or* **Hants** \ˈhan(t)s\ formerly, and still as a postal and geographical name, a county of S England comprising the modern administrative counties of Hampshire & Isle of Wight **2** *or officially* **South·amp·ton** \sau̇th-ˈ(h)am(p)-tən\ administrative county S England on English channel ✻ Winchester *area* 1503, *pop* 1,561,605

Hamp·stead \ˈham(p)-stəd, -ˌsted\ former metropolitan borough NW London, England, now part of Camden

Hamp·ton \ˈham(p)-tən\ city & port SE Va. E of Newport News on Hampton Roads *pop* 120,779

Hampton Roads channel SE Va. through which the James & Elizabeth rivers flow into Chesapeake Bay

Ham·tramck \ham-ˈtram-ik\ city SE Mich. within city of Detroit *pop* 27,245

Han \ˈhän\ **1** river 900 *m* E *cen* China in Shensi & Hupei flowing SE into the Yangtze **2** river 220 *m* S Korea flowing W & NW into Yellow sea

Han Cities WUHAN

Han·ford \ˈhan-fərd\ city S *cen* Calif. SE of Fresno *pop* 15,179

Hang·chow \ˈhaŋ-ˈchau̇, ˈhäŋ-ˈjō\ city E China ✻ of Chekiang at head of **Hangchow Bay** (inlet of East China sea) *pop* 784,000

Hanka — see KHANKA

Han·ko \ˈhaŋ-ˌkȯ\ *or* Sw **Hangö** \ˈhäŋ-ˌə(r)\ town & port SW Finland on Hanko (Hangö) peninsula in the Baltic SE of Turku

Han·kow \ˈhaŋ-ˈkau̇, -ˈkō; ˈhän-ˈkō\ former city E *cen* China — see WUHAN

Han·ni·bal \ˈhan-ə-bəl\ city NE Mo. on the Mississippi *pop* 18,609

Han·no·ver *or* **Han·o·ver** \ˈhan-ˌō-vər, ˈhan-ə-vər, *G* hä-ˈnō-vər, -ˈnō-fər\ city W Germany WNW of Brunswick *pop* 519,700

Ha·noi \ha-ˈnȯi, hə-, hä-\ city ✻ of No. Vietnam in Tonkin on Red river; formerly ✻ of French Indochina *pop* 414,600

Han·o·ver \ˈhan-ˌō-vər, ˈhan-ə-vər\ borough S Pa. SW of York *pop* 15,623

Han·yang \ˈhän-ˈyäŋ\ former city E *cen* China — see WUHAN

Ha·rap·pa \hə-ˈrap-ə\ locality W Pakistan in Indus valley NE of Multan; center of a prehistoric civilization

Ha·rar \ˈhär-ər\ city E Ethiopia E of Addis Ababa *pop* 45,033

Har·bin \ˈhär-bən, här-ˈbin\ *or* **Pin·kiang** \ˈbin-jē-ˈäŋ\ city NE China ✻ of Heilungkiang on Sungari river *pop* 1,552,000

Har·in·gey \ˈhar-iŋ-ˌgā\ borough of N Greater London, England *pop* 236,956

Ha·ri Rud \ˌhar-ē-ˈrüd\ *or* **He·ri Rud** \ˌher-\ *or anc* **Ari·us** \ˈar-ē-əs, ˈer-; ə-ˈrī-əs\ river 700 *m* NW Afghanistan, NE Iran, & S Turkmen Republic flowing W & N into Kara Kum desert

Har·lech \ˈhär-lək, -lək\ village NW Wales on Cardigan Bay

Har·lem \ˈhär-ləm\ **1** river channel SE N.Y. NE of Manhattan I.; with Spuyten Duyvil Creek, connects Hudson & East rivers **2** section of New York City in NE Manhattan bordering on Harlem & East rivers **3** HAARLEM — **Har·lem·ite** \-lə-ˌmīt\ *n*

Har·lin·gen **1** \ˈhär-lən-jən\ city S Tex. NNW of Brownsville *pop* 33,503 **2** \-liŋ-ən\ town & port N Netherlands in Friesland

Har·ney Lake \ˈhär-nē\ salt lake SE Oreg. in **Harney basin** (depression, *area* 2500)

Harney Peak mountain 7242 *ft* SW S.Dak.; highest in Black hills & in state

Har·pers Fer·ry National Monument \ˌhär-pərz-ˈfer-ē\ historical site Md.-W.Va. at town of Harpers Ferry, W.Va., near junction of Shenandoah & Potomac rivers

Har·per Woods \ˌhär-pər-\ city SE Mich. NE of Detroit *pop* 20,186

Harris — see LEWIS WITH HARRIS

Har·ris·burg \ˈhar-əs-ˌbərg\ city ✻ of Pa. *pop* 68,061

Har·ro·gate \ˈhar-ə-gət, -ˌgāt\ municipal borough N England in West Riding, Yorkshire N of Leeds *pop* 62,290

Har·row \ˈhar-(ˌ)ō\ borough of NW Greater London, England *pop* 202,718

Hart·ford \ˈhärt-fərd\ city ✻ of Conn. *pop* 158,017

Hart·le·pool \ˈhärt-lē-ˌpül\ county borough N England in Co. Durham on North sea *pop* 96,898

Har·vard, Mount \ˈhär-vərd\ mountain 14,420 *ft, cen* Colo. in Collegiate range of Sawatch mountains SE of Mt. Elbert

Har·vey \ˈhär-vē\ city NE Ill. S of Chicago *pop* 34,636

Har·wich \ˈhar-ij, -ich, *US also* ˈhär-(ˌ)wich\ municipal borough SE England in Essex on North sea

Ha·ry·a·na *or* **Ha·ri·a·na** \ˌhə-rē-ˈän-ə\ state NW India in E Punjab formed 1966 from southern part of former state of Punjab ✻ Chandigarh *area* 17,010, *pop* 9,971,165

Harz \ˈhärts\ mountains *cen* Germany between Elbe & Leine rivers — see BROCKEN

Ha·sa *or* **El Hasa** \(el-)ˈhas-ə\ region NE Saudi Arabia in E Nejd bordering on Persian gulf

Has·selt \ˈhäs-əlt\ commune NE Belgium ✻ of Limburg *pop* 39,673

Has·tings \ˈhā-stiŋz\ **1** city S Nebr. *pop* 23,580 **2** county borough SE England in East Sussex on Strait of Dover *pop* 72,169

Ha·tay \hä-ˈtī\ district S Turkey E of Gulf of Iskenderun; chief city Iskenderun

Hat·ter·as \ˈhat-ə-rəs, ˈha-trəs\ island N.C. between Pamlico sound & Atlantic ocean; a long barrier island, mostly in **Cape Hatteras National Seashore Recreational Area** (*area* 39)

Hatteras, Cape cape N.C. on SE Hatteras I.

Hat·ties·burg \ˈhat-ēz-ˌbərg\ city SE Miss. *pop* 38,277

Hau·ra·ki Gulf \hau̇-ˌrak-ē-, -ˌräk-\ inlet of the Pacific N New Zealand on N coast of North I.

Haute–Volta — see UPPER VOLTA

Ha·vana *or* **Ha·bana** \hə-ˈvan-ə\ *or* Sp **La Ha·ba·na** \ˌlä-(ä-)ˈvän-ə\ city & port ✻ of Cuba on Gulf of Mexico *pop* 990,000 — **Ha·van·an** \hə-ˈvan-ən\ *adj or n*

Hav·ant and Wa·ter·loo \ˈhav-ənt-ᵊn-ˌwȯt-ər-ˈlü-, -ˌwät-\ urban district S England in Hampshire NE of Portsmouth *pop* 108,999

Ha·vel \ˈhäf-əl\ river 225 *m* E Germany flowing SW through Berlin into the Elbe

Hav·er·ford·west \ˌhav-ər-fərd-ˈwest, ˌhär-fərd-\ municipal borough & port SW Wales ✻ of Pembrokeshire

Ha·ver·hill \ˈhāv-(ə-)rəl\ city NE Mass. *pop* 46,120

Ha·ver·ing \ˈhāv-(ə-)riŋ\ borough of NE Greater London, England *pop* 246,778

Havre — see LE HAVRE

Hawaii \hə-ˈwä-(ˌ)(y)ē, -ˈwī-(ˌ)(y)ē, -ˈwȯ-(ˌ)(y)ē, -ˈwä-yə, -ˈwȯ-yə, -ˈwī-(y)ə\ **1** *or* **Ha·wai·ian islands** \hə-ˌwä-yən-, -ˌwī-(y)ən-, -ˌwȯ-yən-\ *or formerly* **Sand·wich islands** \ˌsan-ˌ(d)wich-\ group of islands *cen* Pacific belonging to U.S. **2** island SE Hawaii, largest of the group; chief city Hilo *area* 4021 **3** state of the U.S. comprising Hawaiian islands except Midway islands; annexed 1898, a territory 1900–59 ✻ Honolulu *area* 6450, *pop* 768,561

Hawaii Volcanoes National Park reservation Hawaii including Mauna Loa & Kilauea volcanoes on Hawaii I. *area* 344

Ha·wash \ˈhä-ˌwäsh\ *or* **Awash** \ˈä-\ river 500 *m* E Ethiopia flowing NE into the desert

Hawke Bay \'hȯk\ inlet of the S Pacific N New Zealand on SE coast of North I.

Haw·thorne \'hȯ-ˌthȯ(ə)rn\ **1** city SW Calif. SW of Los Angeles *pop* 53,304 **2** borough NE N.J. N of Paterson *pop* 19,173

Hay \'hā\ river 530 *m* Canada in N Alta. & SW Mackenzie District flowing NE into Great Slave Lake

Hayes \'hāz\ **1** river 300 *m* Canada in E Man. flowing NE into Hudson Bay **2** *or* **Hayes and Har·ling·ton** \'här-liŋ-tən\ former urban district SE England in Middlesex, now part of Hillingdon

Hays \'hāz\ city NW *cen* Kans. *pop* 15,396

Hayti — see HAITI

Hay·ward \'hā-wərd\ city W Calif. SE of Oakland *pop* 93,058

Ha·zel Park \ˌhā-zəl-\ city SE Mich. N of Detroit *pop* 23,784

Ha·zle·ton \'hā-zəl-tən\ city E Pa. S of Wilkes-Barre *pop* 30,426

Heard \'hərd\ island S Indian ocean SE of Kerguelen, at 53°10'S, 74°10'E; claimed by Australia

Heb·ri·des \'heb-rə-ˌdēz\ *or* **Western** islands W Scotland in the Atlantic divided by Little Minch into **Inner Hebrides** (near the mainland) & **Outer Hebrides** (to NW) *area* 2900, *pop* 60,000 — see LEWIS WITH HARRIS — **Heb·ri·de·an** \ˌheb-rə-'dē-ən\ *adj or n*

He·bron \'hē-brən\ *or anc* **Kir·jath·ar·ba** \ˌkər-ˌjath-'är-bə, ˌki(ə)r-\ city *cen* Palestine SSW of Jerusalem in modern Jordan *pop* 38,300

Hec·ate \'hek-ət\ strait Canada in W B.C., inlet of the Pacific between Queen Charlotte islands & the coast

Heer·len \'he(ə)r-lən\ commune SE Netherlands in Limburg NE of Maastricht *pop* 75,147

Hei·del·berg \'hīd-ᵊl-ˌbərg, -ˌbe(ə)rg\ city W Germany on the Neckar SE of Mannheim *pop* 122,000

Heil·bronn \'hī(ə)l-ˌbrän, hīl-'brȯn\ city W Germany on the Neckar N of Stuttgart *pop* 98,481

Hei·lung·kiang \'hā-'lu̇ŋ-jē-'äŋ\ **1** — see AMUR **2** province NE China in N Manchuria bordering on the Amur ✻ Harbin *area* 178,996, *pop* 21,000,000

He·jaz *or* **He·djaz** \hej-'az, hij-\ region W Saudi Arabia on Red sea; a viceroyalty ✻ Mecca *area* 150,000, *pop* 2,000,000 — **He·jazi** \-ē\ *adj or n*

Hek·la *or* **Hec·la** \'hek-lə\ volcano 4747 *ft* SW Iceland

Hel·e·na \'hel-ə-nə\ city ✻ of Mont. *pop* 22,730

Hel·go·land \'hel-gō-ˌland\ *or* **Hel·i·go·land** \'hel-ə-gō-ˌland, -ˌlänt\ island NW Germany in North sea, in No. Frisian islands

Hel·i·con \'hel-ə-ˌkän, -i-kən\ mountain 5735 *ft* E *cen* Greece in SW Boeotia near Gulf of Corinth

He·li·op·o·lis \ˌhē-lē-'äp-ə-ləs\ **1** — see BAALBEK **2** ancient ruined city N Egypt S of modern Cairo **3** ancient ruined city 6 *m* N of modern Cairo

Hellas — see GREECE

Hel·les, Cape \'hel-(ˌ)ēz\ headland Turkey in Europe at S tip of Gallipoli peninsula

Hellespont, Hellespontus — see DARDANELLES

Hell Gate a narrow part of East river in New York City between Long I. & Manhattan I.

Hells Canyon \'helz\ *or* **Grand Canyon of the Snake** canyon of Snake river on Idaho-Oreg. border 40 *m* long; deepest point over 7000 *ft*

Hel·mand *or* **Hel·mund** \'hel-mənd\ river 650 *m* SW Afghanistan flowing SW & W into a morass on Iranian border

Hel·mond \'hel-ˌmȯnt\ commune S Netherlands *pop* 57,889

Helm·stedt \'helm-ˌs(h)tet\ city *cen* Germany E of Brunswick on border between East and West Germany *pop* 27,267

Hel·sing·ör \ˌhel-siŋ-'ər\ *or* **El·si·nore** \'el-sə-ˌnō(ə)r, -ˌnȯ(ə)r\ city & port Denmark on N Sjælland I. *pop* 30,211

Hel·sin·ki \'hel-ˌsiŋ-kē, hel-'\ *or* Sw **Hel·sing·fors** \'hel-siŋ-ˌfȯ(ə)rz\ city & port ✻ of Finland on Gulf of Finland *pop* 529,091

Hel·vel·lyn \hel-'vel-ən\ mountain 3118 *ft* NW England on Cumberland-Westmorland border in Lake District

Helvetia — see SWITZERLAND

Hemp·stead \'hem(p)-ˌsted, -stəd\ village SE N.Y. on Long I. *pop* 39,411

Hen·der·son \'hen-dər-sən\ **1** city NW Ky. *pop* 22,976 **2** city S Nev. *pop* 16,395

Hen·don \'hen-dən\ former urban district SE England in Middlesex, now part of Barnet

Heng·e·lo \'heŋ-ə-ˌlō\ commune E Netherlands in Overijssel *pop* 69,618

Heng·yang \'həŋ-'yäŋ\ city SE *cen* China in SE Hunan on the Siang *pop* 235,000

Hen·ley \'hen-lē\ *or* **Henley on Thames** municipal borough SE *cen* England in Oxfordshire W of London *pop* 31,744

Hen·lo·pen, Cape \hen-'lō-pən\ headland SE Del. at entrance to Delaware Bay

Hen·ry, Cape \'hen-rē\ headland SE Va. S of entrance to Chesapeake Bay

Her·a·clea \ˌher-ə-'klē-ə\ ancient city S Italy in Lucania near Gulf of Taranto

Heraklion — see CANDIA

He·rat \he-'rät, hə-\ *or anc* **Ar·ia** \'ar-ē-ə, 'er-; ə-'rī-ə\ city NW Afghanistan on the Hari Rud *pop* 101,579

Her·cu·la·ne·um \ˌhər-kyə-'lā-nē-əm\ ancient city S Italy in Campania on Tyrrhenian sea; destroyed A.D. 79 by eruption of Mt. Vesuvius

Her·e·ford \'her-ə-fərd, *U.S. also* 'hər-fərd\ **1** *or* **Her·e·ford·shire** \-ˌshi(ə)r, -shər\ county W England on Welsh border *area* 842, *pop* 138,425 **2** municipal borough, its ✻, on the Wye *pop* 46,503

Her·ford \'he(ə)r-fō(ə)rt\ city W Germany in North Rhine-Westphalia NE of Bielefeld *pop* 67,377

Heri Rud — see HARI RUD

He·ri·sau \'her-ə-ˌzau̇\ commune NE Switzerland ✻ of Appenzell Outer Rhodes half canton

Her·mon, Mount \'hər-mən\ mountain 9232 *ft* on border between Syria & Lebanon; highest in Anti-Lebanon mountains

Hermopolis *or* **Hermoúpolis** — see ERMOÚPOLIS

Her·mo·sa Beach \(ˌ)hər-ˌmō-sə-\ city SW Calif. SW of Los Angeles *pop* 17,412

Her·mo·si·llo \ˌer-mə-'sē-(ˌ)(y)ō\ city NW Mexico ✻ of Sonora on Sonora river *pop* 206,663

Her·ne \'he(ə)r-nə\ city W Germany in the Ruhr *pop* 101,500

Herst·mon·ceux *or* **Hurst·mon·ceux** \ˌhərs(t)-mən-'sü\ village S England in East Sussex NE of Eastbourne

Her·ten \'he(ə)rt-ᵊn\ city W Germany in North Rhine-Westphalia N of Essen *pop* 52,258

Hert·ford \'här-fərd *also* 'härt-, *US also* 'hərt-\ **1** *or* **Hert·ford·shire** \-ˌshi(ə)r, -shər\ county SE England *area* 632, *pop* 922,188 **2** municipal borough, its ✻, N of London *pop* 20,379

Hertogenbosch, 's — see 'S HERTOGENBOSCH

Her·ze·go·vi·na \ˌhert-sə-gō-'vē-nə, ˌhərt-\ *or* Serb **Her·ce·go·vi·na** \ˈkert-sə-gō-vē-nə\ region W *cen* Yugoslavia S of Bosnia & NW of Montenegro; now part of Bosnia & Herzegovina federated republic — see BOSNIA — **Her·ze·go·vi·nian** \ˌhert-sə-gō-'vē-nē-ən, ˌhərt-, -nyən\ *n*

Hesse \'hes, 'hes-ē\ *or* G **Hes·sen** \'hes-ᵊn\ **1** region SW Germany N of Baden-Württemberg divided into **Hesse–Darmstadt** (in the S) & **Hes·se–Cas·sel** \'kas-əl, 'käs-\ (in the N), the latter being united with Prussia in 1866 as part of the province of **Hesse–Nassau** along with the duchy of Nassau & the city of Frankfurt **2** state of the Weimar Republic, equivalent to Hesse-Darmstadt **3** state of the Bonn Republic, including larger part of Hesse-Darmstadt & part of Hesse-Nassau ✻ Wiesbaden *area* 8148, *pop* 5,441,300

Hes·ton and Isle·worth \ˌhes-tə-nə-'nī-zəl-(ˌ)wərth, ˌhes-ᵊn-ə-'nī-\ former municipal borough SE England in Middlesex, now part of Hounslow

Hi·a·le·ah \ˌhī-ə-'lē-ə\ city SE Fla. N of Miami *pop* 102,297

Hib·bing \'hib-iŋ\ village NE Minn. *pop* 16,104

Hibernia — see IRELAND

Hi·bok·hi·bok \ˌhē-ˌbȯk-'hē-ˌbȯk\ volcano 5620 *ft* S Philippines on Camiguin I.

Hick·o·ry \'hik-(ə-)rē\ city W *cen* N.C. *pop* 20,569

Hi·dal·go \hid-'al-(ˌ)gō\ state *cen* Mexico ✻ Pachuca *area* 8057, *pop* 1,156,177

Hierosolyma — see JERUSALEM

Hier·ro \'ye(ə)r-(ˌ)ō\ *or formerly* **Fer·ro** \'fe(ə)r-(ˌ)ō\ island Spain, westernmost of the Canary islands *area* 107

High Atlas — see ATLAS

High·land \'hī-lənd\ town NW Ind. S of Hammond *pop* 24,947

Highland Park, 1 city NE Ill. N of Chicago *pop* 32,263 **2** city SE Mich. within city of Detroit *pop* 35,444

High·lands \'hī-lən(d)z\ the chiefly mountainous N part of Scotland N of a line connecting Firth of Clyde & Firth of Tay

Highlands of Navesink — see NAVESINK HIGHLANDS

Highlands of the Hudson hilly region SE N.Y. on both sides of the Hudson; includes Storm King 1340 *ft*

High Plains the Great Plains esp. from Nebr. southward

High Point \'hī-ˌpȯint\ city N *cen* N.C. SW of Greensboro *pop* 63,204

High Sierra the Sierra Nevada (in Calif.)

High Tatra — see TATRA

High Wyc·ombe \'wik-əm\ municipal borough SE *cen* England in Buckinghamshire WNW of London *pop* 59,298

Hiiumaa — see KHIUMA

Hil·des·heim \'hil-dəs-ˌhīm\ city W Germany SSE of Hannover *pop* 96,018

Hil·ling·don \'hil-iŋ-dən\ borough of W Greater London, England *pop* 234,718

Hi·lo \'hē-(ˌ)lō\ city & port Hawaii in E Hawaii I. *pop* 26,353

Hil·ver·sum \'hil-vər-səm\ city *cen* Netherlands in No. Holland SE of Amsterdam *pop* 100,098

Hi·ma·chal Pra·desh \hi-ˌmäch-əl-prə-'desh, -'dāsh\ territory NW India NW of Uttar Pradesh ✻ Simla *area* 21,629, *pop* 3,424,332

Hi·ma·la·ya \ˌhim-ə-'lā-ə, hə-'mäl-(ə-)yə\ mountains S Asia on border between India & Tibet & in Kashmir, Nepal, Sikkim, & Bhutan — see EVEREST — **Hi·ma·la·yan** \ˌhim-ə-'lā-ən, hə-'mäl-(ə-)yən\ *adj*

Hi·me·ji \hi-'mej-ē\ city Japan in W Honshu *pop* 405,000

Hindenburg — see ZABRZE

Hin·du Kush \ˌhin-(ˌ)dü-'ku̇sh, -'kəsh\ *or anc* **Cau·ca·sus In·di·cus** \ˌkȯ-kə-sə-'sin-di-kəs\ mountain range *cen* Asia SW of the Pamirs on border of Kashmir & in Afghanistan — see TIRICH MIR

Hin·du·stan *or* **Hin·do·stan** \ˌhin-(ˌ)dü-'stan, -də-, -'stän\ **1** region N India N of the Deccan including the plain drained by the Indus, the Ganges, & the Brahmaputra **2** the subcontinent of India **3** the Republic of India

Hing·ham \'hiŋ-əm\ town E Mass. SE of Boston *pop* 18,845

Hins·dale \'hinz-ˌdāl\ village NE Ill. W of Chicago *pop* 15,918

Hip·po \'hip-(ˌ)ō\ *or* **Hippo Re·gi·us** \-'rē-j(ē-)əs\ ancient city N Africa S of modern Bône, Algeria; chief town of Numidia

Hi·ro·sa·ki \hi-'rō-sə-kē, ˌhir-ə-'säk-ē\ city Japan in N Honshu SW of Aomori *pop* 160,000

Hi·ro·shi·ma \ˌhir-ə-'shē-mə, hə-'rō-shə-mə\ city & port Japan in SW Honshu on Inland sea *pop* 549,000

His·pa·nia \his-'pān-ē-ə, -'pän-yə, -'pan-\ the Iberian peninsula

His·pan·io·la \ˌhis-pən-'yō-lə\ *or* Sp **Es·pa·ño·la** \ˌes-ˌpän-'yō-lə\ *or formerly* **Hai·ti** \'hāt-ē\ *or* **San·to Do·min·go** \ˌsant-əd-ə-'miŋ-(ˌ)gō\ *or* **San Domingo** \ˌsan-də-\ island West Indies in the Greater Antilles; divided between Haiti (on W) & Dominican Republic (on E) *area* 29,979

His·sar·lik \ˌhis-ər-'lik\ site of ancient Troy NW Turkey in Asia 4 *m* SE of mouth of the Dardanelles

Hi·va Oa \ˌhē-və-'ō-ə\ island S Pacific in SE Marquesas *area* 154

Hi·was·see \hī-'wäs-ē\ river 150 *m* E U.S. flowing from NE Ga. WNW through W N.C. into the Tennessee in Tenn.
Ho·bart, 1 \'hō-bərt\ city NW Ind. *pop* 21,485 **2** \-,bärt\ city & port Australia ✻ of Tasmania *pop* (with suburbs) 123,500
Hobbs \'häbz\ city SE N.Mex. *pop* 26,025
Ho·bo·ken \'hō-,bō-kən\ **1** city NE N.J. N of Jersey City *pop* 45,380 **2** commune N Belgium, suburb of Antwerp *pop* 33,278
Höch·städt \'hə(r)k-,s(h)tet, 'hœ̄k-,shtet\ town W Germany in Bavaria on the Danube NE of Ulm
Ho·dei·da \hō-'dād-ə\ city & port W Yemen *pop* 40,000
Hod·me·zo·va·sar·hely \'hōd-mə-,zə(r)-'väsh-ər-,hā\ city SE Hungary NE of Szeged near Tisza river *pop* 52,797
Hof \'hōf, 'hȯf\ city W Germany in Bavaria on the Saale NE of Bayreuth *pop* 54,964
Ho·fei \'hə-'fā\ *or* **Lu·chow** \'lü-'jō\ city E China ✻ of Anhwei W of Nanking *pop* 304,000
Hoff·man Estates \'häf-mən, 'hȯf-\ village NE Ill. NW of Chicago *pop* 22,238
Ho·fuf \hü-'füf, hō-\ city NE Saudi Arabia in E Nejd; chief town of Hasa region *pop* 100,000
Hoggar — see AHAGGAR
Ho·hen·lin·den \'hō-ən-,lin-dən, ,hō-ən-'\ village SE Germany in Bavaria E of Munich
Ho·hen·zol·lern \'hō-ən-,zäl-ərn\ region SW Germany, formerly a province of Prussia — see WÜRTTEMBERG
Ho·he Tau·ern \,hō-ə-'taủ(-ə)rn\ range of the E Alps W Austria between Carinthia & Tirol — see GROSSGLOCKNER
Hoi·how \'hȯi-'haủ, 'hī-'hō\ *or* **Hai·kow** \'hī-'kaủ, -'kō\ city & port SE China in Kwangtung on NE Hainan I. *pop* 135,300
Hok·kai·do \hä-'kīd-(,)ō\ *or* **Ye·zo** \'yez-(,)ō\ island N Japan N of Honshu *area* 30,077
Hol·born \'hō(l)-bərn\ former metropolitan borough W *cen* London, England, now part of Camden
Hol·guín \(h)ȯl-'gēn\ city E Cuba NW of Santiago de Cuba *pop* (municipality) 350,250
Hol·land \'häl-ənd\ **1** city W Mich. on Lake Michigan *pop* 26,337 **2** medieval county of Holy Roman Empire bordering on North sea, now forming No. & So. Holland provinces of the Netherlands **3** — see NETHERLANDS — **Hol·land·er** \-ən-dər\ *n*
Holland, Parts of administrative county E England in SE Lincolnshire ✻ Boston *area* 420, *pop* 105,643
Hollandia — see DJAJAPURA
Hol·ly·wood \'häl-ē-,wủd\ **1** section of Los Angeles, Calif. NW of the downtown district **2** city SE Fla. N of Miami *pop* 106,873
Hol·stein \'hōl-,stīn, -,stēn\ region NW Germany S of Jutland peninsula adjoining Schleswig; once a duchy of Denmark, became a part of Prussia 1866 — see SCHLESWIG-HOLSTEIN
Hol·ston \'hōl-stən\ river 140 *m* E Tenn. flowing SW to unite with the French Broad forming the Tennessee
Ho·ly \'hō-lē\ **1** *or* **Lin·dis·farne** \'lin-dəs-,färn\ island N England off NE coast of Northumberland **2** *or* **Holy·head** \'häl-ē-,hed\ island NW Wales in St. George's channel off W coast of Anglesey
Holy Cross, Mount of the mountain 14,005 *ft* NW *cen* Colo. in Sawatch range
Holy·head \'häl-ē-,hed\ urban district & port NW Wales in Anglesey on Holy I.
Holy Land PALESTINE
Holy Loch inlet of Firth of Clyde W Scotland on NW shore of the firth opposite mouth of Clyde river
Hol·yoke \'hōl-,yōk\ city SW Mass. *pop* 50,112
Hom·burg \'häm-,bərg, -,bủ(ə)rg\ *or* **Bad Homburg** \(')bät-\ city W Germany N of Frankfurt *pop* 40,485
Homestead National Monument site SE Nebr. W of Beatrice of first homestead entered under General Homestead Act of 1862
Home·wood \'hōm-,wủd\ **1** city *cen* Ala. *pop* 21,245 **2** village NE Ill. S of Chicago *pop* 18,871
Homs \'hōmz, 'hōm(p)s\ **1** *or formerly* **Leb·da** \'leb-də\ *or anc* **Lep·tis Mag·na** \,lep-tə-'smag-nə\ town & port Libya ESE of Tripoli **2** *or anc* **Em·e·sa** \'em-ə-sə\ city W Syria *pop* 136,474
Ho·nan \'hō-'nan\ province E *cen* China ✻ Chengchow *area* 64,479, *pop* 50,000,000
Hon·du·ras \hän-'d(y)ủr-əs\ country Central America bordering on the Caribbean & the Pacific; a republic ✻ Tegucigalpa *area* 59,160, *pop* 2,580,000 — **Hon·du·ran** \-ən\ *adj or n* — **Hon·du·ra·ne·an** *or* **Hon·du·ra·ni·an** \,hän-d(y)ủ-'rā-nē-ən\ *adj or n*
Honduras, Gulf of inlet of the Caribbean between S Brit. Honduras, E Guatemala, & N Honduras
Hon·fleur \ōⁿ-'flər\ town & port N France on Seine estuary
Hong Kong *or* **Hong·kong** \'häŋ-,käŋ, -'käŋ; 'hȯŋ-,kȯŋ, -'kȯŋ\ **1** Brit. crown colony on SE coast of China E of mouth of Pearl river including Hong Kong I., Kowloon peninsula & adjacent area (New Territories) on mainland, & nearby islands ✻ Victoria *area* 391, *pop* 3,950,000 **2** — see VICTORIA
Ho·ni·a·ra \,hō-nē-'är-ə\ town W Pacific ✻ of the Brit. Solomons on Guadalcanal I.
Ho·no·lu·lu \,hän-ᵊl-'ü-(,)lü, ,hōn-ᵊl-\ city & port ✻ of Hawaii on Oahu I. *pop* 324,871 — **Ho·no·lu·lan** \-'ü-lən\ *n*
Hon·shu \'hän-(,)shü\ *or* **Hon·do** \-(,)dō\ island Japan, chief island of the group *area* 88,000
Hood, Mount \'hủd\ mountain 11,245 *ft* NW Oreg. in Cascade range; highest point in state
Hood Canal inlet of Puget Sound 80 *m* long W Wash. along E shore of Olympic peninsula
Hoo·ghly *or* **Hu·gli** \'hü-glē\ river 120 *m* E India flowing S into Bay of Bengal; most westerly channel of the Ganges in its delta
Hook of Holland \,hủk-\ headland SW Netherlands in So. Holland on coast SW of the Hague
Hoorn — see FUTUNA
Hoo·sac \'hü-sək, -sik\ mountain range NW Mass. & SW Vt., a southern extension of Green mountains; highest peak Spruce Hill 2588 *ft*
Hoo·ver Dam \,hü-vər-\ *or* **Boul·der Dam** \,bōl-dər-\ dam 726 *ft* high in Colorado river between Nev. & Ariz. — see MEAD (Lake)
Ho·pat·cong, Lake \hə-'pat-,kän, -,käŋ\ lake 8 *m* long N N.J.
Ho·pei *or* **Ho·peh** \'hō-'pā\ *or formerly* **Chih·li** \'chē-'lē\ province NE China bordering on Po Hai ✻ Tientsin *area* 84,865, *pop* 47,000,000
Hope·well \'hōp-,wel, -wəl\ city SE Va. *pop* 23,471
Hop·kins·ville \'häp-kənz-,vil\ city SW Ky. *pop* 21,250
Hor \'hȯ(ə)r\ mountain 4430 *ft* SW Jordan
Ho·reb \'hōr-,eb, 'hȯr-\ *or* **Si·nai** \'sī-,nī *also* -nē-,ī\ mountain where according to the Bible the Law was given to Moses; thought to be in the Gebel Musa on Sinai peninsula
Hor·muz *or* **Or·muz** \'(h)ȯr-,məz, (h)ȯr-'müz\ **1** ancient town S Iran on **Strait of Hormuz** (strait between Iran & Arabian peninsula connecting Persian gulf & Gulf of Oman) **2** island SE Iran in Strait of Hormuz
Horn \'hȯ(ə)rn\ *or* **North Cape** cape NW Iceland
Horn, Cape headland S Chile on Horn I. in Tierra del Fuego; southernmost point of So. America, at 55°59′S
Horn·church \'hȯ(ə)rn-,chərch\ former urban district SE England in Essex, now part of Havering
Horn of Africa the easternmost projection of Africa S of Gulf of Aden including Somalia & SE Ethiopia; its E tip is Cape Guardafui
Horn·sey \'hȯrn-zē\ former municipal borough SE England in Middlesex, now part of Haringey
Hor·sens \'hȯrs-ᵊnz, -ᵊn(t)s\ city & port Denmark in E Jutland *pop* 35,621
Hos·pi·ta·let \,(h)äs-,pit-ᵊl-'et\ city NE Spain in Barcelona province, SW suburb of Barcelona *pop* 206,512
Hot Springs city W *cen* Ark. adjoining **Hot Springs National Park** (reservation containing numerous hot mineral springs *area* 5.5) *pop* 35,631
Hou·ma \'hō-mə, 'hü-\ city SE La. *pop* 30,922
Houns·low \'haủnz-(,)lō\ borough of SW Greater London, England *pop* 206,182
Hou·sa·ton·ic \,hü-sə-'tän-ik, ,hü-zə-\ river 148 *m* W Mass. & W Conn. flowing from Berkshire hills S into Long Island Sound
Hous·ton \'(h)yü-stən\ city & port SE Tex. NW of Galveston; connected with Galveston Bay by ship canal *pop* 1,232,802
Hove \'hōv\ municipal borough S England in East Sussex on English channel, W suburb of Brighton *pop* 72,659
Ho·ven·weep National Monument \'hō-vən-,wēp\ site SE Utah & SW Colo. of prehistoric pueblos & cliff dwellings
How·rah \'haủ-rə\ city E India in West Bengal on the Hooghly opposite Calcutta *pop* 599,740
Hra·dec Kra·lo·ve \,(h)räd-,ets-'kräl-ə-,vā\ *or* G **Kö·nig·grätz** \'kā-nig-,gräts, 'kə(r)n-ig-\ city W Czechoslovakia *pop* 66,744
Hsiang — see SIANG
Hsin·chu \'shin-'chü\ city & port China in NW Formosa on coast SW of Taipei *pop* 201,678
Hua·lla·ga \wä-'yäg-ə\ river 700 *m* N *cen* Peru flowing N into the Marañón
Huambo — see NOVA LISBOA
Huang — see YELLOW
Huas·ca·rán \,wäs-kə-'rän\ *or* **Huas·cán** \wä-'skän\ mountain 22,205 *ft* W Peru; highest in the country
Hu·bli \'hủb-lē\ city SW India in W Mysore *pop* 222,775
Hud·ders·field \'həd-ərz-,fēld\ county borough N England in West Riding, Yorkshire, NE of Manchester *pop* 130,964
Hud·son \'həd-sən\ **1** river 306 *m* E N.Y. flowing from Adirondack mountains S into New York Bay **2** town E *cen* Mass. *pop* 16,084 **3** bay inlet of the Atlantic in N Canada; an inland sea 850 *m* long **4** strait 450 *m* long NE Canada between S Baffin I. & N Que. connecting Hudson Bay with the Atlantic — **Hud·so·ni·an** \,həd-'sō-nē-ən\ *adj*
Hue *or* F **Hué** \'(h)wā, h(y)ü-'ā\ city & port S *cen* Vietnam in Annam; formerly ✻ of Annam *pop* 156,537
Huel·va \'(h)wel-və\ **1** province SW Spain in Andalusia on Gulf of Cádiz *area* 3913, *pop* 397,683 **2** city, its ✻ *pop* 96,689
Hues·ca \'(h)wes-kə\ **1** province NE Spain in Aragon *area* 5848, *pop* 222,238 **2** commune, its ✻ *pop* 33,185
Hu·he·hot \'hü-(,)hā-'hōt\ *or* **Kwei·sui** \'gwā-'swā\ *or* **Ku·ku-Kho·to** \,kü-(,)kü-'kōt-(,)ō, -'hōt-\ city N China ✻ of Inner Mongolia E of Paotow *pop* 314,000
Hui·la \'(h)wē-(,)lä\ volcano 18,700 *ft* SW *cen* Colombia
Hull \'həl\ **1** city Canada in SW Que. on Ottawa river opposite Ottawa, Ont. *pop* 63,580 **2** *or* **Kings·ton upon Hull** \'kiŋ(k)-stən\ county borough & port N England in East Riding, Yorkshire, on the Humber *pop* 285,472
Hum·ber \'həm-bər\ estuary 40 *m* E England formed by the Ouse & the Trent & flowing E & SE into North sea
Hum·boldt \'həm-,bōlt\ **1** river 290 *m* N Nev. flowing W & SW into Rye Patch reservoir & formerly into Humboldt Lake **2** glacier NW Greenland; largest known glacier **3** bay NW Calif. on which Eureka is situated
Humboldt Lake *or* **Humboldt Sink** intermittent lake 20 *m* long W Nev. formerly receiving Humboldt river; has no outlet
Hum·phreys, Mount \'həm(p)-frēz\ mountain peak 12,633 *ft* N *cen* Ariz. — see SAN FRANCISCO PEAKS
Hu·nan \'hü-'nän\ province SE *cen* China ✻ Changsha *area* 81,274, *pop* 38,000,000
Hun·ga·ry \'həŋ-g(ə-)rē\ *or* Hung **Ma·gyar·or·szag** \,mäj-,är-'ȯr-,säg\ country *cen* Europe; formerly a kingdom, since 1946 a republic ✻ Budapest *area* 35,912, *pop* 10,360,000
Hung·nam \'hủŋ-,näm\ city & port N Korea on Sea of Japan *pop* 143,600
Hung·shui \'hủŋ-'shwā\ river 800 *m* S China flowing from E Yunnan E to unite with the Yü in E Kwangsi forming West river
Hung·tze \'hủŋ-'(d)zə\ lake 65 *m* long E China in W Kiangsu; traversed by Yellow river
Hun·ter \'hənt-ər\ river 287 *m* SE Australia in E New So. Wales flowing E into the Pacific
Hun·ting·don \'hənt-iŋ-dən\ **1** *or* **Hun·ting·don·shire** \-,shi(ə)r, -shər\ *or* **Huntingdon and Pe·ter·bor·ough** \'pēt-ər-,bər-ə, -,bə-rə, -b(ə-)rə\ *or* **Hunts** \'hən(t)s\ county E *cen* England enlarged 1965 by amalgamation with the Soke of Peterborough *area* 486, *pop* 202,337 **2** *or* **Huntingdon and God·man·ches·ter** \'gäd-mən-

ˌches-tər\ municipal borough ✱ of Huntingdon and Peterborough, on the Great Ouse *pop* 16,540
Hun·ting·ton \ˈhənt-iŋ-tən\ **1** city NE Ind. *pop* 16,217 **2** city W W.Va. on the Ohio *pop* 74,315
Huntington Beach city SW Calif. SE of Los Angeles *pop* 115,960
Huntington Park city SW Calif. S of Los Angeles *pop* 33,744
Hunts·ville \ˈhən(t)s-ˌvil, -vəl\ **1** city N Ala. *pop* 137,802 **2** city E Tex. N of Houston *pop* 17,610
Hun·za \ˈhu̇n-zə\ district NW Jammu & Kashmir N of Hunza river ✱ Baltit *area* 8000
Hu·on Gulf \ˈhyü-ˌän\ inlet of Solomon sea on SE coast of North-East New Guinea S of Huon peninsula
Hu·pei *or* **Hu·peh** \ˈhü-ˈpā\ province E *cen* China ✱ Wuhan *area* 72,394, *pop* 32,000,000
Hu·ron, Lake \ˈhyu̇r-ən, ˈhyu̇(ə)r-ˌän, *or without* h\ lake E *cen* No. America between the U.S. & Canada; one of the Great Lakes *area* 23,010
Hurst \ˈhərst\ city NE Tex. NE of Fort Worth *pop* 27,215
Hurstmonceux — see HERSTMONCEUX
Hutch·in·son \ˈhəch-ə(n)-sən\ city *cen* Kans. *pop* 36,885
Hutt \ˈhət\ city New Zealand on S North I. *pop* 59,400
Huy \ˈ(h)wē\ commune E Belgium SW of Liège
Huy·ton with Ro·by \ˌhīt-ᵊn-with-ˈrō-bē, -with-\ urban district NW England in Lancashire E of Liverpool *pop* 66,629
Hwai \ˈ(h)wī\ river 600 *m* E China flowing from S Honan E into Hungtze Lake
Hwai·nan \ˈ(h)wī-ˈnän\ *or formerly* **Show·hsien** \ˈshō-shē-ˈen\ city E China in N *cen* Anhwei SW of Pengpu *pop* 286,900
Hwaining — see ANKING
Hwang Ho — see YELLOW
Hwang Pu *or* **Whang·poo** \ˈ(h)wäŋ-ˈpü\ river 70 *m* E China flowing E & N past Shanghai into the Yangtze
Hwang·shih \ˈ(h)wäŋ-ˈshē\ city E China in E Hupei on the Yangtze SE of Wuhan *pop* 110,500
Hy·bla \ˈhī-blə\ ancient town in Sicily on S slope of Mt. Etna
Hydaspes — see JHELUM
Hy·der·abad \ˈhīd-(ə-)rə-ˌbad, -ˌbäd\ **1** former state S *cen* India in the Deccan ✱ Hyderabad **2** *or* **Hai·dar·abad** city S *cen* India ✱ of Andhra Pradesh *pop* 1,316,802 **3** city S Pakistan in Sind on the Indus *pop* 698,000
Hy·dra \ˈhī-drə\ *or* NGk **Ídhra** \ˈēth-rə\ island Greece in S Aegean sea off E coast of Peloponnesus *area* 20 — **Hy·dri·ot** \ˈhī-drē-ət, -drē-ˌät\ *or* **Hy·dri·ote** \-ˌōt, -ət\ *n*
Hydraotes — see RAVI
Hy·ères \ē-ˈe(ə)r, ˈye(ə)r\ **1** islands (F **Îles d'Hyères** \ˌēl-dē-ˈe(ə)r, ēl-ˈdye(ə)r\) in the Mediterranean off SE coast of France **2** commune SE France on Côte d'Azur E of Toulon *pop* 34,875
Hy·met·tus \hī-ˈmet-əs\ mountain ridge 3370 *ft*, *cen* Greece E & SE of Athens — **Hy·met·ti·an** \-ˈmet-ē-ən\ *adj*
Hyr·ca·nia \(ˌ)hər-ˈkā-nē-ə\ province of ancient Persia on SE coast of Caspian sea NE of Media & NW of Parthia — **Hyr·ca·ni·an** \-nē-ən\ *adj*
Ia·si \ˈyäsh(-ē)\ *or* **Jas·sy** \ˈyäs-ē\ city NE Rumania *pop* 179,405
Iba·dan \i-ˈbäd-ᵊn, -ˈbad-\ city SW Nigeria *pop* 745,756
Ibe·ria \ī-ˈbir-ē-ə\ **1** ancient Spain **2** the Iberian peninsula **3** ancient region S of the Caucasus W of Colchis in modern Georgia
Ibe·ri·an \-ē-ən\ peninsula SW Europe between the Mediterranean & the Atlantic occupied by Spain & Portugal
Ibi·cui \ˌē-bi-ˈkwē\ river 400 *m* S Brazil in Rio Grande do Sul flowing W into the Uruguay
Ibiza — see IVIZA
Içá — see PUTUMAYO
Icar·ia \ī-ˈker-ē-ə, -ˈkar-; ik-ˈer-, -ˈar-\ *or* NGk **Ika·ria** \ˌē-kə-ˈrē-ə\ island Greece in Southern Sporades WSW of Samos *area* 99
Icel — see MERSIN
Ice·land \ˈī-slənd, ˈī-ˌsland\ *or* Dan **Is·land** \ˈē-ˌslän\ *or* Icelandic **Is·land** \ˈē-ˌslänt\ island between the Arctic & the Atlantic SE of Greenland; a republic formerly (1380–1944) belonging to Denmark, later (1918–44) an independent kingdom in personal union with Denmark ✱ Reykjavik *area* 39,709, *pop* 210,000 — **Ice·land·er** \ˈī-ˌslan-dər, ˈī-slən-\ *n*
Ichang \ˈē-ˈchäŋ\ city *cen* China in W Hupei *pop* 160,000
Iconium — see KONYA
Ida \ˈīd-ə\ **1** *or* NGk **Ídhi** \ˈē-thē\ mountain 8195 *ft* Greece in *cen* Crete; highest on island **2** *or* Turk **Kaz Da·gi** \ˌkäz-dä-ˈ(g)ē\ mountain 5810 *ft* NW Turkey in Asia SE of ancient Troy
Ida·ho \ˈīd-ə-ˌhō\ state NW U.S. ✱ Boise *area* 83,557, *pop* 712,567 — **Ida·ho·an** \ˌīd-ə-ˈhō-ən\ *adj or n*
Idaho Falls city SE Idaho on the Snake *pop* 35,776
Id·fu \ˈid-(ˌ)fü\ *or* **Ed·fu** \ˈed-\ city S Egypt on Nile *pop* 27,300
Idumaea *or* **Idumea** — see EDOM — **Id·u·mae·an** *or* **Id·u·me·an** \ˌij-ə-ˈmē-ən\ *adj or n*
Ie·per \ˈyā-pər\ *or* F **Ypres** \ˈēprᵊ\ commune NW Belgium in West Flanders *pop* 18,696
Ife \ˈē-(ˌ)fā\ city SW Nigeria NE of Ibadan *pop* 154,589
If·ni \ˈif-nē\ territory SW Morocco; administered by Spain 1934–69 ✱ Sidi Ifni *area* 741
Igua·çu *or* **Iguas·su** *or* Sp **Igua·zú** \ˌē-gwə-ˈsü\ river 380 *m* S Brazil in Paraná state flowing W into the Alto Paraná; contains **Iguaçu Falls** (waterfall over 2 *m* wide composed of numerous cataracts averaging 200 *ft* in height)
IJs·sel *or* **Ijs·sel** *or* **Ys·sel** \ˈī-səl\ river 70 *m* E Netherlands flowing out of Rhine river N into IJsselmeer
IJs·sel·meer \ˌī-səl-ˈme(ə)r\ *or* **Lake IJs·sel** \ˈī-səl\ *or formerly* **Zui·der,** *or* **Zuy·der, Zee** \ˌzīd-ər-ˈzā, -ˈzē\ lake N Netherlands separated from North sea by a dike & bordered by reclaimed lands
Île-de-France \ˌēl-də-ˈfräⁿs\ region & former province N *cen* France bounded on N by Picardy, on E by Champagne, on S by Orléanais, & on W by Normandy ✱ Paris
Île du Diable — see DEVIL'S ISLAND
Îles de la Société — see SOCIETY
Îles du Vent — see WINDWARD
Îles sous le Vent — see LEEWARD
Il·ford \ˈil-fərd\ former municipal borough SE England in Essex, now part of Redbridge
Il·fra·combe \ˈil-frə-ˌküm\ urban district SW England in Devon on Bristol channel
Ili \ˈē-ˈlē\ river 800 *m*, *cen* Asia flowing from W Sinkiang, China, W & NW into Lake Balkhash in Kazakhstan
Ilia — see ELIS
Il·i·am·na \ˌil-ē-ˈam-nə\ **1** lake 80 *m* long SW Alaska NE of Bristol Bay **2** volcano 10,085 *ft* NE of Iliamna Lake
Ilion *or* **Ilium** — see TROY — **Il·i·an** \ˈil-ē-ən\ *adj or n*
Illam·pu \ē-ˈ(y)äm-(ˌ)pü\ **1** *or* **So·ra·ta** \sə-ˈrät-ə\ massif in the Andes W Bolivia E of Lake Titicaca — see ANCOHUMA **2** peak 20,867 *ft* in the Illampu massif
Illi·ma·ni \ˌē-(y)ə-ˈmän-ē\ mountain 21,201 *ft* Bolivia E of La Paz
Il·li·nois \ˌil-ə-ˈnoi *also* -ˈnȯiz\ **1** river 273 *m* Ill. flowing SW into the Mississippi **2** state *cen* U.S. ✱ Springfield *area* 56,400, *pop* 11,113,976 — **Il·li·nois·an** \ˌil-ə-ˈnȯi-ən, -ˈnȯiz-ᵊn\ *adj or n*
Il·lyr·ia \il-ˈir-ē-ə\ ancient region S Europe in Balkan peninsula bordering on the Adriatic — **Il·lyr·ic** \-ˈlir-ik\ *adj*
Il·lyr·i·cum \il-ˈir-i-kəm\ province of Roman Empire in Illyria
Il·men \ˈil-mən\ lake U.S.S.R. in NW Soviet Russia, Europe, S of Lake Ladoga
Ilo·ilo \ˌē-lə-ˈwē-(ˌ)lō\ city Philippines on S coast of Panay I. *pop* 201,000
Im·pe·ria \im-ˈpir-ē-ə, -ˈper-\ commune & port NW Italy in Liguria SW of Genoa *pop* 39,307
Im·pe·ri·al \im-ˈpir-ē-əl\ valley U.S. & Mexico in SE Calif. & NE Baja California in Colorado desert; most of area below sea level
Imperial Beach city SW Calif. S of San Diego *pop* 20,244
Imp·hal \ˈimp-ˌhəl\ city NE India ✱ of Manipur *pop* 67,717
Im·roz \im-ˈrȯz\ *or* Gk **Im·bros** \ˈim-brəs, ˈēm-ˌvrȯs\ island Turkey in the NE Aegean W of Gallipoli peninsula *area* 110
Ina·gua \in-ˈäg-wə\ two islands in the SE Bahamas: **Great Inagua** (50 *m* long) & **Little Inagua** (8 *m* long)
In·chon \ˈin-ˌchän\ *or* **Che·mul·po** \jə-ˈmu̇l-(ˌ)pō\ city & port S Korea W of Seoul *pop* 525,072
In·de·pen·dence \ˌin-də-ˈpen-dən(t)s\ city W Mo. *pop* 111,662
In·dia \ˈin-dē-ə\ **1** peninsula region (often called a subcontinent) S Asia S of the Himalayas between Bay of Bengal & Arabian sea occupied by India, Pakistan & Bangladesh & formerly often considered as also including Burma (but not Ceylon) **2** those parts of India until 1947 under Brit. rule or protection together with Baluchistan & the Andaman & Nicobar islands &, prior to 1937, Burma **3** *or* **Indian Union** *or* **Bha·rat** \ˈbər-ət, ˈbə-rət\ country comprising major portion of peninsula; a republic within the Brit. Commonwealth; until 1947 a part of the Brit. Empire ✱ New Delhi *area* 1,262,275, *pop* 550,370,000
In·di·an \ˈin-dē-ən\ **1** ocean E of Africa, S of Asia, W of Australia & Tasmania, & N of Antarctica *area* 28,925,000 **2** — see THAR
In·di·ana \ˌin-dē-ˈan-ə\ **1** state E *cen* U.S. ✱ Indianapolis *area* 36,291, *pop* 5,193,669 **2** borough W *cen* Pa. *pop* 16,199 — **In·di·an·an** \-ˈan-ən\ *adj or n* — **In·di·an·i·an** \-ˈan-ē-ən\ *adj or n*
Indiana Harbor harbor district in East Chicago, Ind., on Lake Michigan
In·di·a·nap·o·lis \ˌin-dē-ə-ˈnap-(ə-)ləs\ city ✱ of Ind. *pop* 744,624
Indian river lagoon 165 *m* long E Fla. between mainland & coastal islands
Indian States *or* **Native States** former semi-independent states of the Indian Empire ruled by native princes subject to varying degrees of Brit. authority — see BRITISH INDIA
Indian Territory former territory S U.S. in present state of Okla.
In·dies \ˈin-(ˌ)dēz\ **1** EAST INDIES **2** WEST INDIES
In·di·gir·ka \ˌin-də-ˈgi(ə)r-kə\ river 850 *m* U.S.S.R. in NE Yakutsk Republic flowing N into East Siberian sea
In·do·chi·na \ˈin-(ˌ)dō-ˈchī-nə\ **1** *or* **Farther India** peninsula SE Asia; includes Burma, Cambodia, Laos, Malay peninsula, Thailand, & Vietnam **2** *or* **French Indochina** former country SE Asia bordering on So. China sea & Gulf of Siam & comprising Annam, Cambodia, Cochin China, Laos, & Tonkin ✱ Hanoi
In·do·ne·sia \ˌin-də-ˈnē-zhə, -shə\ **1** country SE Asia in Malay archipelago comprising Sumatra, Java, S & E Borneo, Celebes, W Timor, W New Guinea, the Moluccas, & many adjacent smaller islands; a republic since 1949; formerly (as **Netherlands East Indies**) an overseas territory of the Netherlands ✱ Djakarta *area* 575,450, *pop* 124,890,000 **2** the Malay archipelago
In·dore \in-ˈdō(ə)r, -ˈdȯ(ə)r\ **1** former state *cen* India in Narbada valley ✱ Indore; area now in Madhya Pradesh **2** city NW *cen* India in W Madhya Pradesh *pop* 494,664
In·dus \ˈin-dəs\ river 1800 *m* S Asia flowing from Tibet NW & SSW through Pakistan into Arabian sea
In·gle·wood \ˈiŋ-gəl-ˌwu̇d\ city SW Calif. SW of Los Angeles *pop* 89,985
In·gol·stadt \ˈiŋ-gəl-ˌs(h)tät\ city W Germany in Bavaria N of Munich *pop* 70,841
Ink·ster \ˈiŋ(k)-stər\ village SE Mich. W of Detroit *pop* 38,595
In·land \ˈin-ˌland, -lənd\ sea inlet of the Pacific 240 *m* long SW Japan between Honshu on E & N, Kyushu on W, & Shikoku on S
Inland Empire region NW U.S. between Cascade range & Rocky mountains in E Wash., N Idaho, NW Mont., & NE Oreg.
Inn \ˈin\ river 320 *m* flowing from SE Switzerland NE through Austria into the Danube in Germany — see ENGADINE
Inner Hebrides — see HEBRIDES
Inner Mongolia region N China in SE Mongolia & W Manchuria ✱ Huhehot *area* 454,633, *pop* 13,000,000
Inniskilling — see ENNISKILLEN
Inns·bruck \ˈinz-ˌbru̇k, ˈin(t)s-\ city W Austria *pop* 112,824

Inside Passage *or* **Inland Passage** protected shipping route from Puget Sound, Wash., to Skagway, Alaska, following channels between mainland & coastal islands
In·ter·la·ken \ˈint-ər-ˌläk-ən\ commune W *cen* Switzerland in Bern canton on the Aare between Lake of Thun & Lake of Brienz
International Zone — see MOROCCO
Inu·vik \in-ˈü-vik\ town NW Canada in NW Mackenzie District in Mackenzie delta
In·ver·car·gill \ˌin-vər-ˈkär-gəl\ borough & port New Zealand on S coast of South I. *pop* 46,700
In·ver·ness \ˌin-vər-ˈnes\ **1** *or* **In·ver·ness–shire** \-ˈnes(h)-ˌshi(ə)r, -shər\ county NW Scotland *area* 4211, *pop* 89,545 **2** burgh, its ✱ *pop* 34,870
Io·an·ni·na \yō-ˈän-ē-(ˌ)nä\ *or* **Yan·ni·na** \ˈyän-ē-(ˌ)nä\ city NW Greece in N Epirus *pop* 39,814
Io·na \ī-ˈō-nə\ island Scotland in S Inner Hebrides off SW tip of Mull I. *area* 6
Io·nia \ī-ˈō-nē-ə\ ancient region W Asia Minor bordering on the Aegean W of Lydia & Caria — **Io·ni·an** \-nē-ən\ *adj or n*
Ionian, 1 sea arm of the Mediterranean between SE Italy & W Greece **2** islands W Greece in Ionian sea
Io·wa \ˈī-ə-wə\ **1** river 291 *m* Iowa flowing SE into the Mississippi **2** state *cen* U.S. ✱ Des Moines *area* 56,290, *pop* 2,825,041 — **Io·wan** \-wən\ *adj or n*
Iowa City city E Iowa *pop* 46,850
Ipin \ˈē-ˈpin, -ˈpēn\ *or formerly* **Sü·chow** \ˈs(h)ü-ˈjō, ˈsü-ˈchau̇\ *or* **Sui·fu** \ˈswā-ˈfü\ city *cen* China in S Szechwan *pop* 177,500
Ipiros — see EPIRUS
Ipoh \ˈē-(ˌ)pō\ city Federation of Malaysia in Perak *pop* 125,766
Ipsambul — see ABU SIMBEL
Ip·sus \ˈip-səs\ ancient village W *cen* Asia Minor in S Phrygia
Ips·wich \ˈip-(ˌ)swich\ **1** city E Australia in SE Queensland SW of Brisbane *pop* 54,500 **2** county borough SE England ✱ of East Suffolk *pop* 122,814
Iqui·que \i-ˈkē-kē\ city & port N Chile on the Pacific *pop* 65,288
Iqui·tos \i-ˈkēt-(ˌ)ōs\ city NE Peru on the Amazon *pop* 74,000
Iráklion — see CANDIA
Iran \i-ˈran, -ˈrän; ī-ˈran\ *or esp formerly* **Per·sia** \ˈpər-zhə, *esp Brit* -shə\ country SW Asia bordering in N on Caspian sea & in S on Persian gulf & Gulf of Oman; a kingdom ✱ Tehran *area* 628,000, *pop* 29,780,000 — **Irani** \-ˈran-ē, -ˈrän-\ *adj or n*
Iraq \i-ˈräk, -ˈrak\ **1** *or* **Irak** country SW Asia in Mesopotamia; a republic since 1958, formerly a kingdom ✱ Baghdad *area* 171,555, *pop* 9,750,000 **2** — see ARAK — **Iraqi** \-ˈräk-ē, -ˈrak-\ *adj or n*
Ire·land \ˈī(ə)r-lənd\ **1** *or* L **Hi·ber·nia** \hī-ˈbər-nē-ə\ island W Europe in the Atlantic, one of the Brit. Isles *area* 32,375; divided between Republic of Ireland & Northern Ireland **2** *or* **Republic of Ireland** *or* **Irish Republic** *or* **Ei·re** \ˈar-ə, ˈar-ē, ˈer-, ˈär-, ˈīr-\ country occupying major portion of island; a republic since 1949; a division of the United Kingdom of Great Britain & Ireland 1801–1921 & (as **Irish Free State**) a dominion of the Brit. Commonwealth 1922–37 ✱ Dublin *area* 26,602, *pop* 2,970,000 **3** — see NORTHERN IRELAND
Irian — see NEW GUINEA
Irian Barat — see WEST IRIAN
Irish sea arm of the Atlantic between Great Britain & Ireland
Ir·kutsk \i(ə)r-ˈkütsk, ˌər-\ city U.S.S.R. in E *cen* Soviet Russia, Asia, on the Angara near Lake Baikal *pop* 451,000
Iron Gate \ˈī(-ə)rn-\ gorge 2 *m* long of the Danube at place where it cuts around end of Transylvanian Alps on border between Rumania & Yugoslavia
Iron·ton \ˈī-rən-tən, ˈīrnt-ᵊn\ city SE Ohio on the Ohio *pop* 15,030
Ir·ra·wad·dy \ˌir-ə-ˈwäd-ē\ river 1350 *m* Burma flowing S into Bay of Bengal through several mouths
Ir·tysh *or* **Ir·tish** \i(ə)r-ˈtish, ˌər-\ river 2200 *m, cen* Asia flowing from Altai mountains in Sinkiang, China, NW & N into the Ob in U.S.S.R.
Irún \ē-ˈrün\ commune N Spain in Guipúzcoa E of San Sebastián near French border *pop* 45,060
Ir·ving \ˈər-viŋ\ city NE Tex. W of Dallas *pop* 97,260
Ir·ving·ton \-tən\ town NE N.J. WSW of Newark *pop* 59,743
Is·a·bela \ˌiz-ə-ˈbel-ə\ *or* **Al·be·marle** \ˈal-bə-ˌmärl\ island Ecuador; largest of the Galápagos *area* 1650
Isar \ˈē-ˌzär\ river 219 *m* W Europe flowing from Tirol, Austria, NW through Bavaria, Germany, into the Danube
Isau·ria \i-ˈsȯr-ē-ə\ ancient district in E Pisidia S Asia Minor on N slope of W Taurus mountains — **Isau·ri·an** \-ē-ən\ *adj or n*
Is·chia \ˈis-kē-ə\ island Italy WSW of Naples *area* 18
Ise Bay \ˌē-ˌsā-\ inlet of the Pacific S Japan on S coast of Honshu
Iseo, Lake \ē-ˈzā-(ˌ)ō\ lake 14 *m* long N Italy in Lombardy NW of Bergamo
Isère \ē-ˈze(ə)r\ river 150 *m* SE France flowing from Graian Alps WSW into the Rhone
Iser·lohn \ˌē-zər-ˈlōn, ˈē-zər-ˌ\ city W Germany in Ruhr valley SE of Dortmund *pop* 57,615
Is·fa·han \ˌis-fə-ˈhän, -ˈhan\ *or* **Es·fa·han** \ˌes-\ *or* **Is·pa·han** \ˌis-pə-\ city W *cen* Iran; former ✱ of Persia *pop* 424,045
Ishim \i-ˈshim\ river 1330 *m* U.S.S.R. flowing from N Kazakh Republic N into the Irtysh
Isis \ˈī-səs\ the Thames river, England, at & above Oxford
Is·ken·de·run \(ˌ)is-ˌken-də-ˈrün\ *or* **Is·ken·de·ron** \-ˈrän\ *or formerly* **Al·ex·an·dret·ta** \ˌal-ig-(ˌ)zan-ˈdret-ə, ˌel-\ city & port S Turkey on **Gulf of Iskenderun** (inlet of the Mediterranean) *pop* 69,382
Is·lam·abad \is-ˈläm-ə-ˌbäd, iz-ˈlam-ə-ˌbad\ city ✱ of Pakistan in NE Pakistan in Murree hills NE of Rawalpindi *pop* 50,000
Island *or* **Island** — see ICELAND
Is·lay \ˈī-(ˌ)lā, -lə\ island Scotland in S Inner Hebrides *area* 234
Isle au Haut \ˌī-lə-ˈhō(t), ˌē-lə-ˈhō\ island Me. at entrance to Penobscot Bay — see ACADIA NATIONAL PARK
Isle of Ely — see ELY (Isle of)
Isle of Man — see MAN (Isle of)
Isle of Pines, 1 *or* Sp **Is·la de Pi·nos** \ˌēz-lä-də-ˈpē-nōs\ island W Cuba in the Caribbean *area* 1180 **2** — see KUNIE
Isle of Wight — see WIGHT (Isle of)
Isle Roy·ale \(ˈ)ī(ə)l-ˈrȯi(-ə)l\ island Mich. in NW Lake Superior in **Isle Royale National Park** (*area* 209)
Is·ling·ton \ˈiz-liŋ-tən\ borough of N Greater London, England *pop* 199,129
Is·ma·ilia \ˌiz-mā-ə-ˈlē-ə\ city NE Egypt on the Suez canal *pop* 167,500
Ison·zo \ē-ˈzȯn(t)-(ˌ)sō\ river 75 *m* NW Yugoslavia & NE Italy flowing S into Gulf of Trieste
Is·par·ta \ˌis-(ˌ)pär-ˈtä\ city SW Turkey N of Antalya *pop* 42,901
Is·ra·el \ˈiz-rē-əl\ **1** ancient kingdom Palestine comprising the lands occupied by the Hebrew people; established *ab* 1025 B.C.; divided *ab* 933 B.C. into a S kingdom (Judah) & a N kingdom (Israel) **2** *or* **Northern Kingdom** *or* **Ephra·im** \ˈē-frē-əm\ the N portion of the Hebrew kingdom after the division ✱ Samaria **3** country Palestine bordering on the Mediterranean; a republic established 1948 ✱ Jerusalem *area* 7993, *pop* 3,010,000 — see PALESTINE
Is·sus \ˈis-əs\ ancient town S Asia Minor N of modern Iskenderun, Turkey
Is·syk Kul \ˌis-ik-ˈkəl\ lake 115 *m* long U.S.S.R. in Soviet Central Asia in NE Kirgiz Republic *area* 2250
Is·tan·bul \ˌis-təm-ˈbül, -ˌtäm-, -ˌtam-, -ˌtän-\ *or formerly* **Con·stan·ti·no·ple** \ˌkän-ˌstant-ᵊn-ˈō-pəl\ *or anc* **By·zan·ti·um** \bə-ˈzan-sh(ē-)əm, -ˈzant-ē-əm\ city NW Turkey on the Bosporus & Sea of Marmara; former ✱ of Turkey & of Ottoman Empire *pop* 1,742,978
Ister — see DANUBE
Is·tok·po·ga \ˌis-ˌtäk-ˈpō-gə\ lake S Fla. NW of Lake Okeechobee
Is·tria \ˈis-trē-ə\ peninsula NW Yugoslavia in Croatia & Slovenia projecting into the N Adriatic — **Is·tri·an** \-trē-ən\ *adj or n*
Italian East Africa former territory E Africa comprising Eritrea, Ethiopia, & Italian Somaliland
Italian Somaliland former Italian colony E Africa bordering on Indian ocean ✱ Mogadiscio (Mogadishu) *area* 194,000; since 1960 part of Somalia
It·a·ly \ˈit-ᵊl-ē\ *or* It **Ita·lia** \ē-ˈtäl-yə\ *or* L **Ita·lia** \ə-ˈtal-yə, i-\ **1** peninsula 760 *m* long S Europe projecting into the Mediterranean between Adriatic & Tyrrhenian seas **2** country comprising the peninsula of Italy, Sicily, Sardinia, & numerous other islands; a republic since 1946, formerly a kingdom ✱ Rome *area* 119,764, *pop* 54,080,000
Itas·ca, Lake \ī-ˈtas-kə\ lake NW *cen* Minn.; source of the Mississippi
Iténez — see GUAPORÉ
Ith·a·ca \ˈith-i-kə\ **1** city S *cen* N.Y. on Cayuga Lake *pop* 26,226 **2** *or* NGk **Ithá·ki** \ē-ˈthäk-ē\ island W Greece in the Ionian islands NE of Cephalonia *area* 36 — **Ith·a·can** \ˈith-i-kən\ *adj or n*
Itsukushima — see MIYAJIMA
It·u·raea *or* **It·u·rea** \ˌich-ə-ˈrē-ə\ ancient country NE Palestine S of Damascus — **It·u·rae·an** *or* **It·u·re·an** \-ˈrē-ən\ *adj or n*
Iva·no–fran·kovsk \i-ˌvän-ə-frän-ˈkȯfsk\ *or formerly* **Sta·ni·slav** \ˌstan-ə-ˈslaf, -ˈslav\ city U.S.S.R. in SW Ukraine *pop* 105,000
Iva·no·vo \i-ˈvän-ə-və\ *or formerly* **Ivanovo Voz·ne·sensk** \-ˌväz-nə-ˈsen(t)sk\ city U.S.S.R. in *cen* Soviet Russia, Europe, WNW of Gorki *pop* 419,000
Ivi·za *or* Sp **Ibi·za** \ē-ˈvē-zə, -ˈbē-\ island Spain in the Balearics SW of Majorca *area* 230
Ivory Coast *or* **Côte d'Ivoire** \ˌkōt-dēv-ˈwär\ **1** region W Africa bordering on the Atlantic W of the Gold Coast **2** country W Africa including the Ivory Coast & its hinterland; a republic of the French Community since 1959, formerly a territory of French West Africa ✱ Abidjan *area* 127,520, *pop* 4,420,000 — **Ivo·ry Coast·er** \ˌīv-(ə-)rē-ˈkō-stər\ *n*
Iwo \ˈē-(ˌ)wō\ city SW Nigeria NE of Ibadan *pop* 188,506
Iwo Ji·ma \ˌē-(ˌ)wō-ˈjē-mə\ island W Pacific in the Volcano islands 660 nautical *m* S of Tokyo *area* 8
Ix·elles \ēk-ˈsel\ *or* Flem **El·se·ne** \ˈel-sə-nə\ commune *cen* Belgium in Brabant; suburb of Brussels *pop* 88,970
Iza·bal \ˌē-zə-ˈbäl, -sə-\ lake 25 *m* long E Guatemala
Izal·co \i-ˈzal-(ˌ)kō, ē-ˈsäl-\ volcano 7828 *ft* W El Salvador
Izhevsk \ˈē-ˌzhefsk\ city U.S.S.R. in E Soviet Russia, Europe ✱ of Udmurt Republic *pop* 422,000
Iz·ma·il *or* Rum **Is·ma·il** \ˌiz-mä-ˈē(ə)l\ city U.S.S.R. in SW Ukraine on the Danube delta *pop* 63,000
Iz·mir \iz-ˈmi(ə)r\ *or* **Smyr·na** \ˈsmər-nə\ city & port W Turkey in Asia on an inlet of the Aegean *pop* 411,626
Iz·mit *or* **Iz·mid** \iz-ˈmit\ *or anc* **As·ta·cus** \ˈas-tə-kəs\ *or* **Nic·o·me·dia** \ˌnik-ə-ˈmēd-ē-ə\ city & port NW Turkey in Asia on **Gulf of Izmit** (E arm of Sea of Marmara) *pop* 89,547
Iz·nik \iz-ˈnik\ lake 14 *m* long NW Turkey in Asia S of E arm of Sea of Marmara
Iz·tac·ci·huatl *or* **Ix·ta·ci·huatl** \ˌēs-(ˌ)tä(k)-ˈsē-ˌwät-ᵊl\ extinct volcano 17,343 *ft* S Mexico N of Popocatepetl
Ja·bal·pur \ˈjəb-əl-ˌpu̇(ə)r\ *or* **Jub·bul·pore** \ˈjəb-əl-ˌpō(ə)r, -ˌpȯ(ə)r\ city *cen* India in *cen* Madhya Pradesh *pop* 419,462
Jack·son \ˈjak-sən\ **1** city S Mich. *pop* 45,484 **2** city ✱ of Miss. on Pearl river *pop* 153,968 **3** city W Tenn. *pop* 39,996
Jackson Hole valley NW Wyo. E of Teton range & partly in Grand Teton National Park; contains **Jackson Lake** (reservoir)
Jack·son·ville \ˈjak-sən-ˌvil\ **1** city *cen* Ark. NE of Little Rock *pop* 19,832 **2** city NE Fla. near mouth of the St. Johns *pop* 528,865 **3** city W *cen* Ill. *pop* 20,553 **4** city E N.C. *pop* 16,021
Jadotville — see LIKASI
Ja·én \hä-ˈän\ **1** province S Spain in N Andalusia *area* 5203, *pop* 661,146 **2** commune, its ✱ *pop* 78,156
Jaf·fa \ˈjaf-ə, ˈyaf-ə\ *or* **Jop·pa** \ˈjäp-ə\ *or* **Ya·fo** \yä-ˈfō\ former city & port W Israel, since 1950 a S section of Tel Aviv
Jaff·na \ˈjäf-nə\ city N Ceylon on Palk strait *pop* 101,700
Jagannath — see PURI
Jain·tia \ˈjīnt-ē-ə\ hills E India in N *cen* Assam E of Khasi hills
Jai·pur \ˈjī-ˌpu̇(ə)r\ **1** former state NW India; now part of Rajasthan **2** city, its ✱, now ✱ of Rajasthan *pop* 548,684
Jakarta — see DJAKARTA

Ja·la·pa \hə-'läp-ə\ city E Mexico ✱ of Veracruz *pop* 127,081
Ja·lis·co \hə-'lis-(,)kō\ state W *cen* Mexico ✱ Guadalajara *area* 31,149, *pop* 3,322,750
Jal·u·it \'jal-(y)ə-wət\ island (atoll) 38 *m* long & 21 *m* wide W Pacific, in Ralik chain of the Marshalls
Ja·mai·ca \jə-'mā-kə\ island West Indies in the Greater Antilles; a dominion of Brit. Commonwealth since 1962; formerly a Brit. colony ✱ Kingston *area* 4411, *pop* 1,900,000 — **Ja·mai·can** \-kən\ *adj or n*
Jamaica Bay inlet SE N.Y. in SW Long I.
Jambi — see DJAMBI
James \'jāmz\ **1** *or* **Da·ko·ta** \də-'kōt-ə\ river 710 *m* N. & S.Dak. flowing S to the Missouri **2** river 340 *m* Va. flowing E into Chesapeake Bay at Hampton Roads
James Bay the S extension of Hudson Bay 280 *m* long & 150 *m* wide Canada between NE Ont. & W Que.
James·town \'jām-,staun\ **1** city SW N.Y. *pop* 39,795 **2** city E *cen* N.D. *pop* 15,385
Jam·mu \'jəm-(,)ü\ **1** district N India (subcontinent) S of Kashmir in valley of the upper Chenab **2** city S of Srinagar, winter ✱ of Jammu & Kashmir *pop* 135,522
Jammu and Kashmir — see KASHMIR
Jam·na·gar \jäm-'nəg-ər\ *or* **Na·va·na·gar** \,näv-ə-'nəg-ər\ city W India in W Gujarat on Gulf of Kutch *pop* 207,199
Jam·shed·pur \'jäm-,shed-,pu̇(ə)r\ city E India in S Bihar SE of Ranchi *pop* 414,330
Ja·mu·na \'jəm-ə-nə\ the lower Brahmaputra
Janes·ville \'jānz-,vil\ city S Wis. SE of Madison *pop* 46,426
Ja·nic·u·lum \jə-'nik-yə-ləm\ hill in Rome, Italy, on right bank of the Tiber opposite the Seven Hills — see AVENTINE
Jan Ma·yen \yän-'mī-ən\ island in Arctic ocean E of Greenland & NNE of Iceland belonging to Norway *area* 147
Ja·pan \jə-'pan, ji-, ja-\ *or* Jap **Nip·pon** \nip-'än\ *or* **Ni·hon** \'nē-'hōn\ country E Asia comprising Honshu, Hokkaido, Kyushu, Shikoku, & other islands in the W Pacific; an empire ✱ Tokyo *area* 146,690, *pop* 104,660,000
Japan, Sea of arm of the N Pacific W of Japan
Ja·pu·rá \,zhäp-ə-'rä\ river 1750 *m* S Colombia & NW Brazil flowing SE into the Amazon
Jar·vis \'jär-vəs\ island *cen* Pacific in the Line islands; claimed by the U.S.
Jas·per National Park \'jas-pər\ reservation W Canada in W Alta. on E slopes of the Rockies NE of & adjoining Banff National Park *area* 4200
Jassy — see IASI
Ja·va \'jäv-ə, 'jav-ə\ *or* Indonesian **Dja·wa, 1** island Indonesia SE of Sumatra; chief city Djakarta *area* 51,007, *pop* 78,201,001 **2** sea arm of the Pacific bounded on S by Java, on W by Sumatra, on N by Borneo, & on E by Celebes
Java Head cape Indonesia at W end of Java on Sunda strait
Ja·va·ri \,zhäv-ə-'rē\ *or* Sp **Ya·va·ri** \,yäv-ə-'rē\ *or formerly* **Ya·ca·ra·na** \,yäk-ə-'rän-ə\river 650 *m* Peru & Brazil flowing NE on the boundary & into the Amazon
Jaxartes — see SYR DARYA
Jean·nette \jə-'net\ city SW Pa. *pop* 15,209
Jebel, Bahr el — see BAHR EL GHAZAL
Je·bel ed Druz \,jeb-ə-,led-'drüz\ *or* **Jebel Druz** region S Syria E of Sea of Galilee on border of Jordan; formerly (1921–42) an autonomous state of Syria
Jebel Musa — see MUSA (Jebel)
Jebel Toubkal — see TOUBKAL (Jebel)
Jed·burgh \'jed-b(ə-)rə\ burgh SE Scotland ✱ of Roxburgh
Jef·fer·son \'jef-ər-sən\ river 250 *m* SW Mont. — see THREE FORKS
Jefferson, Mount mountain 10,495 *ft* NW Oreg. in Cascades
Jefferson City city ✱ of Mo. on the Missouri *pop* 32,407
Jef·fer·son·ville \'jef-ər-sən-,vil\ city S Ind. *pop* 20,008
Je·hol \jə-'hōl, 'rō-'hō\ **1** former province NE China ✱ Chengteh; divided 1955 among Hopei, Liaoning, & Inner Mongolia **2** — see CHENGTEH
Je·mappes \zhə-'map\ commune SW Belgium W of Mons
Je·na \'yā-nə, -(,)nä\ city E Germany on the Saale E of Erfurt *pop* 88,346
Jen·nings \'jen-iŋz\ city E Mo., N suburb of St. Louis *pop* 19,379
Je·qui·ti·nho·nha \zhə-,kēt-ə-'n(y)ōn-yə\ river 500 *m* E Brazil flowing NE into the Atlantic
Jerba — see DJERBA
Je·rez \hə-'rās\ *or* **Je·rez de la Fron·te·ra** \hə-'rez-də-lə-,frən-'ter-ə\ *or formerly* **Xe·res** \'sher-ēz\ city SW Spain NE of Cádiz *pop* 147,633
Jer·i·cho \'jer-i-,kō\ **1** *or* Ar **Eri·ha** \ə-'rē-ə\ town W Jordan 5 *m* NW of Dead sea **2** ancient Palestinian city near site of modern Jericho
Jer·sey \'jər-zē\ **1** island English channel in the Channel islands ✱ St. Helier *area* 45 **2** NEW JERSEY — **Jer·sey·an** \-ən\ *n* — **Jer·sey·ite** \-,īt\ *n*
Jersey City city & port NE N.J. *pop* 260,545
Je·ru·sa·lem \jə-'rü-s(ə-)ləm, -'rüz-(ə-)ləm\ *or anc* **Hi·ero·sol·y·ma** \,hī-(ə-)rō-'säl-ə-mə\ city *cen* Palestine NW of Dead sea; divided since 1948 between Jordan (old city) & Israel (new city) ✱ of Israel since 1950 & formerly ✱ of ancient kingdoms of Israel & Judah *pop* 283,100
Jer·vis Bay \,jär-vəs-\ inlet of the Pacific SE Australia on SE coast of New So. Wales on which is situated district (*area* 28) that is part of Australian Capital Territory
Jesselton — see KOTA KINABALU
Jewel Cave National Monument limestone cave SW S.Dak.
Jewish Autonomous Region *or* **Bi·ro·bi·dzhan** \,bir-ō-bi-'jän\ autonomous region U.S.S.R. in E Soviet Russia, Asia, bordering on the Amur ✱ Birobidzhan *area* 14,085, *pop* 173,000
Jezira — see GEZIRA
Jez·re·el \'jez-rē-,el, -,rē(ə)l\ ancient town *cen* Palestine in Samaria NW of Mt. Gilboa in Valley of Jezreel
Jezreel, Plain of the Plain of Esdraelon
Jezreel, Valley of the E end of the Plain of Esdraelon
Jhan·si \'jän(t)-sē\ city N India in S Uttar Pradesh SW of Kanpur *pop* 181,904
Jhe·lum \'jā-ləm\ *or anc* **Hy·das·pes** \hī-'das-(,)pēz\ river 450 *m* NW India (subcontinent) flowing from Kashmir S & SW into the Chenab
Jibuti — see DJIBOUTI
Jid·da \'jid-ə\ *or* **Jed·da** \'jed-ə\ city W Saudi Arabia in Hejaz on Red sea; port for Mecca *pop* 194,000
Jin·ja \'jin-jə\ city & port SE Uganda on Lake Victoria *pop* 47,298
João Pes·soa \,zhwaü^{n}(m)-pə-'sō-ə\ *or formerly* **Pa·ra·í·ba** \,par-ə-'ē-bə\ city NE Brazil ✱ of Paraíba *pop* 189,096
Jodh·pur \'jäd-pər, -,pu̇(ə)r\ **1** *or* **Mar·war** \'mär-,wär\ former state NW India bordering on Thar desert & Rann of Kutch; since 1949 part of Rajasthan state **2** city, its ✱ *pop* 275,893
Jod·rell Bank \,jäd-rəl-\ locality W England in NE Cheshire near Macclesfield
Jog·ja·kar·ta \,jäg-yə-'kärt-ə\ *or* **Djok·ja·kar·ta** \,jäk-\ city Indonesia in S Java *pop* 312,698
Jo·han·nes·burg \jō-'han-əs-,bərg, -'hän-\ city NE Republic of So. Africa in S Transvaal in *cen* Witwatersrand *pop* 595,083
John Day \'jän-'dā\ river 281 *m* N Oreg. flowing W & N into the Columbia
John o' Groat's \,jän-ə-'grōts\ *or* **John o' Groat's House** locality N Scotland on N coast in Caithness; popularly considered the northernmost point of mainland of Scotland & Great Britain — see DUNNET HEAD
John·son City \,jän(t)-sən-\ **1** village S N.Y. NW of Binghamton *pop* 18,025 **2** city NE Tenn. *pop* 33,770
John·ston \'jän(t)-stən, -sən\ **1** island (atoll) *cen* Pacific 700 *m* SW of Honolulu, Hawaii; belongs to the U.S. **2** town S R.I. NW of Providence *pop* 22,037
Johns·town \'jänz-,staun\ city SW *cen* Pa. *pop* 42,476
Jo·hore \jə-'hō(ə)r, -'hȯ(ə)r\ state S Federation of Malaysia at S end of Malay peninsula ✱ Johore Bahru *area* 7321, *pop* 1,273,990
Johore Bah·ru \-'bär-(,)ü\ city S Federation of Malaysia ✱ of Johore on an inlet opposite Singapore I. *pop* 135,936
Join·vi·le *or formerly* **Join·vil·le** \zhȯin-'vē-lē\ city S Brazil NNW of Florianópolis *pop* 88,647
Jo·li·et \,jō-lē-'et, *chiefly by outsiders* ,jäl-ē-\ city NE Ill. SW of Chicago *pop* 80,378
Jo·liette \,zhō-lē-'et\ city Canada in S Que. N of Montreal *pop* 20,127
Jo·lo \hō-'lō\ *or* **Su·lu** \'sü-(,)lü\ island S Philippines, chief island of Sulu archipelago *area* 345
Jones·boro \'jōnz-,bər-ə, -,bə-rə\ city NE Ark. *pop* 27,050
Jön·kö·ping \'yə(r)n-,chə(r)p-iŋ\ city S Sweden at S end of Lake Vatter *pop* 55,372
Jon·quière \,zhō^{n}-kē-'e(ə)r\ city Canada in S *cen* Que. *pop* 28,430
Jop·lin \'jäp-lən\ city SW Mo. *pop* 39,256
Joppa — see JAFFA
Jor·dan \'jȯrd-^{ə}n\ **1** river 45 *m*, *cen* Utah flowing from Utah Lake N into Great Salt Lake **2** river 200 *m* NE Palestine flowing from Anti-Lebanon mountains S through Sea of Galilee into Dead sea **3** *or* **Trans·jor·dan** \(')tran(t)s-, (')tranz-\ *or officially* **Hash·im·ite Kingdom of Jordan** \'hash-ə-,mīt\ country SW Asia in NW Arabia ✱ Amman *area* 37,737, *pop* 2,380,000 — **Jor·da·ni·an** \jȯr-'dā-nē-ən\ *adj or n*
Josh·ua Tree National Monument \'jäsh-(ə-)wə\ reservation S Calif. N of Salton sea containing unusual desert flora *area* 1025
Jo·tun·heim \'yōt-^{ə}n-,hām\ *or* Norw **Jo·tun·hei·men** \-,hā-mən\ mountains S *cen* Norway — see GLITTERTIND
Juan de Fu·ca \,(h)wän-də-'fyü-kə\ strait 100 *m* long between Vancouver I., B.C., & Olympic peninsula, Wash.
Juan Fer·nán·dez \,(h)wän-fər-'nan-dəs\ group of three islands SE Pacific 400 *m* W of Chile; belongs to Chile *area* 70
Juan–les–Pins \,zhwä^{n}-lā-'pa^{n}\ town SE France on Cap d'Antibes
Juárez — see CIUDAD JUÁREZ
Ju·ba \'jü-bə\ river 1000 *m* E Africa flowing from S Ethiopia S through Somalia into Indian ocean
Jubbulpore — see JABALPUR
Juby, Cape — see YUBI (Cape)
Jú·car \'hü-,kär\ river 300 *m* E Spain flowing S & E into the Mediterranean S of Valencia
Ju·dah \'jüd-ə\ ancient kingdom S Palestine ✱ Jerusalem — see ISRAEL
Ju·dea *or* **Ju·daea** \jü-'dē-ə, -'dā-\ ancient region Palestine constituting the S division (Judah) of the country under Persian, Greek, & Roman rule — **Ju·de·an** *or* **Ju·dae·an** \-ən\ *adj or n*
Juggernaut — see PURI
Jugoslavia — see YUGOSLAVIA — **Jugoslav** *or* **Jugoslavian** *adj or n*
Juiz de Fo·ra \,zhwēzh-də-'fōr-ə, -'fȯr-\ city E Brazil in S Minas Gerais *pop* 194,135
Ju·juy \hü-'hwē\ city NW Argentina N of Tucumán *pop* 44,188
Ju·lian Alps \,jül-yən-\ section of E Alps NW Yugoslavia N of Istrian peninsula; highest peak Triglav 9393 *ft*
Julian Venetia — see VENEZIA GIULIA
Jul·lun·dur \'jəl-ən-dər\ city NW India in Punjab *pop* 288,694
Jum·na \'jəm-nə\ river 860 *m* N India in Uttar Pradesh flowing from the Himalayas S & SE into the Ganges
Junction City city NE *cen* Kans. *pop* 19,018
Ju·neau \'jü-(,)nō, jü-'\ city & port ✱ of Alaska in SE coastal strip *pop* 6050
Jung·frau \'yu̇ŋ-,frau̇\ mountain 13,642 *ft* SW *cen* Switzerland in Bernese Alps between Bern & Valais cantons

ə abut ^{ə} kitten, F table ər further a back ā bake
ä cot, cart a̓ F bac au̇ out ch chin e less ē easy
g gift i trip ī life j joke k̲ G ich ^{n} F vin ŋ sing
ō flow ȯ flaw œ F bœuf œ̄ F feu ȯi coin th thing
t̲h̲ this ü loot u̇ foot ue G Füllen ue̅ F rue y yet
^{y} F digne \dēn^{y}\, nuit \nw^{y}ē\ yü few yu̇ furious zh vision

Ju·ni·ata \ˌjü-nē-ˈat-ə\ river 150 *m* S *cen* Pa. flowing E into the Susquehanna
Ju·nín \hü-ˈnēn\ **1** city E Argentina 150 *m* W of Buenos Aires *pop* 53,489 **2** town *cen* Peru at S end of **Lake Junín** (25 *m* long)
Ju·ra \ˈju̇r-ə\ **1** mountains France & Switzerland extending 200 *m* along the boundary; highest Crêt de la Neige 5652 *ft* **2** island 24 *m* long W Scotland in the Inner Hebrides S of Mull
Juramento — see SALADO
Ju·ruá \ˌzhu̇r-(ə-)ˈwä\ river 1200 *m* NW *cen* So. America flowing from E *cen* Peru NE into the Solimões in NW Brazil
Ju·rue·na \ˌzhu̇r-(ə-)ˈwā-nə\ river 600 *m* W *cen* Brazil flowing N to unite with the São Manuel forming the Tapajoz
Jut·land \ˈjət-lənd\ *or* Dan **Jyl·land** \ˈyuel-ˌän, ˈyœl-\ **1** peninsula N Europe projecting into North sea & comprising mainland of Denmark & N portion of Schleswig-Holstein, Germany **2** the mainland of Denmark
K² — see GODWIN AUSTEN
Kaapland — see CAPE OF GOOD HOPE
Kaapstad — see CAPE TOWN
Kab·ar·din·i·an Republic \ˌkab-ər-ˌdin-ē-ən-\ *or* **Kab·ar·di·no–Bal·kar·i·an Republic** \ˌkab-ər-ˈdē-(ˌ)nō-bȯl-ˈkar-ē-ən-, -bal-, -ˈker-\ *or* **Kabardino–Bal·kar Republic** \-ˈbȯl-ˌkär, -ˈbal-\ autonomous republic U.S.S.R. in S Soviet Russia, Europe, on N slopes of the Caucasus ✱ Nalchik *area* 4600, *pop* 539,000 — **Kabardinian** *adj or n*
Ka·bul \ˈkäb-əl, kə-ˈbül\ **1** river 360 *m* Afghanistan & N Pakistan flowing E into the Indus **2** city ✱ of Afghanistan on Kabul river *pop* 307,338 — **Ka·buli** \ˈkäb-ə-(ˌ)lē, kə-ˈbü-lē\ *adj or n*
Kab·we \ˈkäb-(ˌ)wā\ *or formerly* **Bro·ken Hill** \ˌbrō-kən-\ city *cen* Zambia *pop* 49,000
Ka·by·lia \kə-ˈbī-lē-ə, -ˈbil-ē-\ mountainous region N Algeria on coast E of Algiers; comprises two areas: **Great Kabylia** (to W) & **Little Kabylia** (to E)
Ka·chin \kə-ˈchin\ state N Burma between China & India
Ka·desh–bar·nea \ˌkā-ˌdesh-ˈbär-nē-ə\ ancient town S Palestine SW of Dead sea; exact location uncertain
Kadiak — see KODIAK
Ka·di·koy \ˌkäd-i-ˈkȯi\ *or anc* **Chal·ce·don** \ˈkal-sə-ˌdän, kal-ˈsēd-ᵊn\ former city NW Turkey in Asia on the Bosporus; now a district of Istanbul
Ka·di·yev·ka *or* **Ka·di·ev·ka** \kə-ˈdē-(y)əf-kə\ city U.S.S.R. in E Ukraine in Donets basin *pop* 137,000
Kae·song \ˈkā-ˌsȯŋ\ city N Korea SE of Pyongyang *pop* 265,000
Kaf·fe·klub·ben \ˈkäf-ə-ˌklu̇b-ən, -ˌkləb-\ island in Arctic ocean off N coast of Greenland; northernmost point of land in the world, at 83°40′N
Kaf·frar·ia \kə-ˈfrar-ē-ə, ka-, -ˈfrer-\ region Republic of So. Africa in E Cape Province S of Natal & bordering on Indian ocean
Kafiristan — see NURISTAN
Ka·fue \kə-ˈfü-ē\ river 500 *m* Zambia flowing into the Zambezi
Ka·ge·ra \kə-ˈger-ə\ river 430 *m* Burundi, Rwanda, & NW Tanganyika flowing N & E into Lake Victoria on Uganda border
Ka·go·shi·ma \ˌkäg-ə-ˈshē-mə, kä-ˈgō-shə-\ city & port S Japan in S Kyushu on **Kagoshima Bay** (inlet of the Pacific) *pop* 407,000
Ka·hoo·la·we \ˌkä-hō-ˈlä-vē, -wē\ island Hawaii SW of Maui *area* 45
Kai·bab \ˈkī-ˌbab\ plateau N Ariz. N of Grand Canyon
Kai·e·teur Falls \ˌkī-ə-ˌtu̇(ə)r-, ˌkī-ˌchu̇(ə)r-\ waterfall 741 *ft* high & 350 *ft* wide *cen* Guyana in Potaro river
Kai·feng \ˈkī-ˈfəŋ\ city E *cen* China in NE Honan *pop* 299,100
Kai·lua \kī-ˈlü-ə\ city Hawaii in NE Oahu *pop* 33,783
Kair·ouan \ker-ˈwän\ *or* **Kair·wan** \kī(ə)r-ˈwän\ city NE Tunisia *pop* 46,199
Kai·sers·lau·tern \kī-zərz-ˈlau̇t-ərn\ city W Germany W of Ludwigshafen *pop* 99,917
Ka·ki·na·da *or* **Coc·a·na·da** \ˌkäk-ə-ˈnäd-ə\ city & port E India in NE Andhra Pradesh on Bay of Bengal *pop* 149,146
Ka Lae \kä-ˈlä-ā\ *or* **South Cape** *or* **South Point** headland Hawaii, southernmost point of Hawaii I.
Kalaeloa Point — see BARBERS POINT
Kal·a·ha·ri \ˌkal-ə-ˈhär-ē\ desert region S Africa N of Orange river & S of Lake Ngami in Botswana & NW Republic of So. Africa
Ka·la·ma·ta \ˌkal-ə-ˈmät-ə\ *or* NGk **Ka·lá·mai** \kə-ˈläm-ē\ city & port S Greece in SW Peloponnesus *pop* 39,346
Kal·a·ma·zoo \ˌkal-ə-mə-ˈzü\ city SW Mich. *pop* 85,555
Ka·lat *or* **Khe·lat** \kə-ˈlät\ region NW Pakistan including S & *cen* Baluchistan; a former princely state ✱ Kalat
Kal·gan \ˈkal-ˈgan\ *or* **Chang·kia·kow** \ˈjäŋ-jē-ˈä-ˈkō\ city NE China in NW Hopei NW of Peking *pop* 229,300
Kal·goor·lie \kal-ˈgu̇(ə)r-lē\ town Australia in S *cen* Western Australia
Kalhu — see CALAH
Ka·li·ma \kə-ˈlē-mə\ *or formerly* **Al·bert·ville** \ˌal-ˌber-ˈvē(ə)l, ˈal-bərt-ˌvil\ city & port E Zaire on Lake Tanganyika *pop* 86,687
Ka·li·man·tan \ˌkal-ə-ˈman-ˌtan, ˌkäl-ə-ˈmän-ˌtän\ **1** BORNEO — its Indonesian name **2** the S & E part of Borneo belonging to Indonesia; formerly (as **Dutch Borneo**) part of Netherlands India
Ka·li·nin \kə-ˈlē-nən, -ˈlēn-ˌyēn\ *or formerly* **Tver** \tə-ˈve(ə)r\ city U.S.S.R. in W *cen* Soviet Russia, Europe, on the Volga *pop* 345,000
Ka·li·nin·grad \kə-ˈlē-n(y)ən-ˌgrad\ *or* G **Kö·nigs·berg** \ˈkā-nigz-ˌbərg, ˈkə(r)n-igz-, -ˌbe(ə)rg\ city & port U.S.S.R. in W Soviet Russia, Europe, near the Frisches Haff; formerly ✱ of East Prussia *pop* 297,000
Ka·lisz \ˈkäl-ish\ commune *cen* Poland W of Lodz *pop* 81,200
Kal·mar \ˈkäl-ˌmär, ˈkal-\ city & port SE Sweden *pop* 38,912
Kal·myk Republic \(ˌ)kal-ˌmik-\ autonomous republic of the U.S.S.R. in S Soviet Russia, Europe, on NW shore of Caspian sea W of the Volga ✱ Elista *area* 29,417 *pop* 268,000
Ka·lu·ga \kə-ˈlü-gə\ city U.S.S.R. in W *cen* Soviet Russia, Europe, on the Oka WNW of Tula *pop* 211,000
Ka·ma \ˈkäm-ə\ river 1200 *m* U.S.S.R. in E Soviet Russia, Europe, flowing SW into the Volga S of Kazan
Ka·ma·ku·ra \kä-ˈmäk-ə-ˌrä, ˌkäm-ə-ˈku̇r-ə\ city Japan in SE Honshu on Sagami sea S of Yokohama *pop* 135,000
Kam·chat·ka \kam-ˈchat-kə\ peninsula 750 *m* long U.S.S.R. in NE Soviet Russia, Asia, between Sea of Okhotsk & Bering sea
Ka·met \ˈkəm-āt\ mountain 25,447 *ft* N India in Uttar Pradesh in the NW Himalayas
Kam·loops \ˈkam-ˌlüps\ city Canada in S B.C. *pop* 26,168
Kam·pa·la \käm-ˈpäl-ə\ city ✱ of Uganda in Buganda N of Entebbe *pop* 331,889
Kan \ˈgän\ river 350 *m* SE China in Kiangsi flowing N through Poyang Lake into the Yangtze
Kananur — see CANNANORE
Ka·na·wha \kə-ˈnȯ-(w)ə\ river 97 *m* W W.Va. flowing NW into the Ohio
Ka·na·za·wa \kə-ˈnäz-ə-wə, ˌkan-ə-ˈzä-wə\ city & port Japan in W *cen* Honshu near Sea of Japan *pop* 342,000
Kan·chen·jun·ga \ˌkan-chən-ˈjəŋ-gə, -ˈju̇ŋ-\ *or* **Kang·chen·jun·ga** \ˌkaŋ-ˌchen-\ *or* **Kin·chin·jun·ga** \ˌkin-chən-\ mountain 28,146 *ft* Nepal & Sikkim in the Himalayas; 3d highest in world
Kan·chi·pu·ram \kän-ˈchē-pə-rəm\ *or* **Con·jee·ve·ram** \kən-ˈjē-və-rəm\ city SE India in N Tamil Nadu SW of Madras *pop* 92,714
Kan·da·har \ˈkan-də-ˌhär\ city SE Afghanistan *pop* 130,212
Kand·la \ˈkən-dlə\ town & port W India in Gujarat near E end of Gulf of Kutch
Kan·dy \ˈkan-dē\ city W *cen* Ceylon ENE of Colombo *pop* 78,000
Kane Basin \ˈkān\ section of the passage between NW Greenland & Ellesmere I. N of Baffin Bay
Ka·ne·o·he \ˌkän-ē-ˈō-ē, -ˈō-(ˌ)hā\ city Hawaii in E Oahu on **Kaneohe Bay** (inlet) *pop* 29,903
Kan·i·a·pis·kau \ˌkan-ē-ə-ˈpis-(ˌ)kō\ river *m* Canada in N Que. flowing N to unite with the Larch forming the **Kok·so·ak** \ˈkäk-sə-ˌwak\ river (85 *m* flowing into Ungava Bay)
Kan·ka·kee \ˌkaŋ-kə-ˈkē\ **1** river 225 *m* Ind. & Ill. flowing SW & W to unite with the Des Plaines forming the Illinois **2** city NE Ill. on the Kankakee *pop* 30,944
Ka·no \ˈkän-(ˌ)ō\ city N *cen* Nigeria *pop* 351,175
Ka·noya \kə-ˈnȯi-ə\ city Japan in S Kyushu *pop* 66,995
Kan·pur \ˈkän-ˌpu̇(ə)r\ *or* **Cawn·pore** \ˈkȯn-ˌpō(ə)r, -ˌpȯ(ə)r\ city N India in S Uttar Pradesh on the Ganges *pop* 1,197,255
Kan·sas \ˈkan-zəs\ **1** *or* **Kaw** \ˈkȯ\ river 169 *m* E Kans. flowing E into the Missouri — see SMOKY HILL **2** state *cen* U.S. ✱ Topeka *area* 82,264, *pop* 2,249,071 — **Kan·san** \ˈkan-zən\ *adj or n*
Kansas City, **1** city NE Kans. adjacent to Kansas City, Mo. *pop* 168,213 **2** city W Mo. *pop* 507,087
Kan·su \ˈkan-ˈsü, ˈgän-\ province N *cen* China ✱ Lanchow *area* 137,104, *pop* 13,000,000
Kanto Plain — see KWANTO PLAIN
Kaoh·siung \ˈkau̇-shē-ˈu̇ŋ, ˈgau̇-\ city & port China in SW Formosa *pop* 784,502
Kaolan — see LANCHOW
Ka·pi·da·gi \ˌkäp-ē-dä-ˈ(g)ē\ *or anc* **Cyz·i·cus** \ˈsiz-i-kəs\ peninsula NW Turkey in Asia projecting into Sea of Marmara
Ka·ra, **1** \ˈkär-ə\ sea arm of Arctic ocean off coast of N U.S.S.R. E of Novaya Zemlya **2** — see MESTA
Ka·ra·cha·ye·vo–Cher·kess \ˌkär-ə-ˈchī-ə-ˌvō-cher-ˈkes\ autonomous region U.S.S.R. in SE Soviet Russia, Europe, in N Caucasus *area* 5442, *pop* 345,000 ✱ Cherkessk
Ka·ra·chi \kə-ˈräch-ē\ city & port S Pakistan on an arm of Arabian sea NW of mouths of the Indus *pop* 3,060,000
Karafuto — see SAKHALIN
Ka·ra·gan·da \ˌkar-ə-gən-ˈdä\ city U.S.S.R. in *cen* Kazakhstan *pop* 522,000
Ka·ra–Kal·pak Republic \ˌkar-ə-ˌkal-ˈpak\ autonomous republic U.S.S.R. in NW Uzbek Republic SE of Lake Aral ✱ Nukus *area* 61,600, *pop* 702,000
Kar·a·ko·ram *or* **Kar·a·ko·rum** \ˌkar-ə-ˈkōr-əm, -ˈkȯr-\ mountain system S *cen* Asia in N Kashmir & NW Tibet on Sinkiang border; westernmost system of the Himalaya complex, connecting the Himalayas with the Pamirs — see GODWIN AUSTEN
Karakoram Pass *or* **Karakorum Pass** mountain pass 18,290 *ft* NE Kashmir through Karakoram range
Kar·a·ko·rum \-əm\ ruined city Outer Mongolia on the upper Orkhon ✱ of Mongol Empire
Ka·ra Kum \ˌkar-ə-ˈküm\ desert U.S.S.R. in Turkmen Republic S of Lake Aral between the Caspian sea & the Amu Darya *area* 110,000
Karashahr — see YENCH'I
Ka·ra Su \ˌkar-ə-ˈsü\ the Euphrates above its junction with the Murat in E *cen* Turkey
Kar·ba·la \ˈkär-bə-lə\ *or* **Ker·be·la** \ˈkər-bə-lə\ city *cen* Iraq SSW of Baghdad *pop* 83,301
Ka·re·lia *or* **Ca·re·lia** \kə-ˈrē-lē-ə, -ˈrēl-yə\ **1** region NE Europe between Gulf of Finland & White sea in the U.S.S.R. & Finland **2** *or* **Ka·re·lian Republic** \-ˌrē-lē-ən-, -ˌrēl-yən-\ autonomous republic U.S.S.R. in NW Soviet Russia, Europe, in Karelia region; formerly (1940–56), as the **Ka·re·lo–Finnish Republic** \kə-ˌrē-(ˌ)lō-\, constituent republic of the U.S.S.R. ✱ Petrozavodsk *area* 68,900, *pop* 714,000
Ka·re·lian \-ˌrē-lē-ən-, -ˌrēl-yən-\ isthmus U.S.S.R. in Karelia between Gulf of Finland & Lake Ladoga
Ka·ren \kə-ˈren\ state S Burma bordering on Andaman sea
Ka·ri·ba \kə-ˈrē-bə\ lake 165 *m* long SE Zambia & N Rhodesia formed in the Zambezi by **Kariba Dam**
Ka·ri·kal \ˌkar-ə-ˈkäl\ **1** territory of former French India S of Pondicherry; incorporated 1954 in India *area* 52 **2** city & port, its ✱, on Bay of Bengal *pop* 22,252
Kar·kheh *or* **Ker·kheh** \kər-ˈkā\ *or anc* **Cho·as·pes** \kō-ˈas-(ˌ)pēz\ river 340 *m* flowing from W Iran S & W into marshlands E of the Tigris in SE Iraq
Karl–Marx–Stadt — see CHEMNITZ
Kar·lo·vy Va·ry \ˌkär-lə-vē-ˈvär-ē\ *or* **Carls·bad** *or* G **Karls·bad** \ˈkär(ə)lz-ˌbad, -ˌbät\ city NW Czechoslovakia in NW Bohemia NNW of Plzen *pop* 45,310
Karls·kro·na \kärl-ˈskrü-nə\ city & port SE Sweden on Baltic sea *pop* 36,236

Karls·ru·he \ˈkärlz-ˌrü-ə\ city W Germany in Baden-Württemberg on the Rhine *pop* 256,200 — **Karls·ru·her** \-ˌrü-ər\ *n*
Karl·stad \ˈkär(ə)l-ˌstä(d)\ city SW Sweden *pop* 54,072
Kar·nak \ˈkär-ˌnak\ town S Egypt on the Nile N of Luxor on N part of site of ancient Thebes
Kár·pa·thos *or* **Car·pa·thos** \ˈkär-pə-ˌthäs\ *or* It **Scar·pan·to** \ˈskär-pən-ˌtō\ island Greece in the S Dodecanese *area* 118
Kar·roo *or* **Ka·roo** \kə-ˈrü\ plateau region W Republic of So. Africa W of Drakensberg mountains divided into **Little**, or **Southern**, **Karroo** (in S Cape Province); **Great**, or **Central**, **Karroo** (in S *cen* Cape Province); and **Northern**, or **Upper**, **Karroo** (in N Cape Province, Orange Free State, & W Transvaal)
Kars \ˈkärz, ˈkärs\ city NE Turkey *pop* 41,376
Karst — see KRAS
Ka·run \kə-ˈrün\ river 450 *m* W Iran flowing into Shatt-al-Arab
Ka·sai \kə-ˈsī\ **1** river 1200 *m* N Angola & W Zaire flowing N & W into the Congo **2** region S *cen* Zaire
Ka·shan \kə-ˈshän\ city *cen* Iran N of Isfahan *pop* 62,000
Kash·gar \ˈkash-ˌgär\ city W China in SW Sinkiang at oasis on Kashgar river *pop* 175,000
Kashgaria — see CHINESE TURKESTAN
Kash·mir \ˈkash-ˌmi(ə)r, ˈkazh-, kash-ˈ, kazh-ˈ\ *or formerly* **Cash·mere, 1** mountainous region N India (subcontinent) W of Tibet & SW of Sinkiang; includes valley (**Vale of Kashmir**) watered by Jhelum & Kishenganga rivers **2** *or* **Jam·mu and Kashmir** \ˈjəm-(ˌ)ü\ state N India including Kashmir region & Jammu (to the S); claimed also by Pakistan; summer ✱ Srinagar, winter ✱ Jammu *area* 92,780, *pop* 4,615,176 — **Kash·mir·i·an** \kash-ˈmir-ē-ən, kazh-\ *adj or n*
Kas·kas·kia \ka-ˈskas-kē-ə\ river 300 *m* SW Ill. flowing SW into the Mississippi
Kas·sa·la \ˈkas-ə-lə\ city NE Sudan *pop* 81,230
Kas·sel *or* **Cas·sel** \ˈkas-əl, ˈkäs-\ city W Germany WNW of Erfurt *pop* 213,100
Kas·ser·ine Pass \ˌkas-ə-ˌrēn-\ mountain pass *cen* Tunisia
Ka·stel·lór·i·zon \ˌkäs-tə-ˈlór-ə-ˌzän\ *or* It **Ca·stel·lo·ri·zo** \käs-tə-ˈlór-ə-ˌzō\ *or* **Cas·tel·ros·so** \ˌkäs-ˌtel-ˈrós-(ˌ)ō\ island Greece in the E Dodecanese off SW coast of Turkey *area* 4
Kastro — see MYTILENE
Ká·stron \ˈkäs-ˌtrón\ **1** town Greece on Lemnos **2** — see CHIOS
Kastrop–Rauxel — see CASTROP-RAUXEL
Ka·tah·din, Mount \kə-ˈtäd-^{ə}n\ mountain 5268 *ft* N *cen* Me.; highest point in state
Katanga — see SHABA
Katar — see QATAR
Kath·er·i·na, Ge·bel \ˌjeb-əl-ˌkath-ə-ˈrē-nə\ *or* **Mount Kath·er·ine** \ˈkath-(ə-)rən\ mountain 8652 *ft* NE Egypt on Sinai peninsula; highest in the Gebel Musa
Ka·thi·a·war \ˌkät-ē-ə-ˈwär\ peninsula W India in Gujarat between Gulf of Kutch & Gulf of Cambay
Kat·mai, Mount \ˈkat-ˌmī\ volcano 6715 *ft* S Alaska in Aleutian range at NE end of Alaska peninsula
Katmai National Monument reservation S Alaska including Mt. Katmai & Valley of Ten Thousand Smokes *area* 4363
Kat·man·du *or* **Kath·man·du** *or* **Khat·man·du** \ˌkat-ˌman-ˈdü, -mən-\ city ✱ of Nepal *pop* 121,019
Ka·to·wi·ce \ˌkät-ə-ˈvēt-sə\ city S Poland in Silesia WNW of Krakow *pop* 295,600
Kat·rine, Loch \ˈka-trən\ lake 9 *m* long *cen* Scotland in SW Perthshire E of Loch Lomond
Kat·te·gat \ˈkat-i-ˌgat\ arm of North sea between Sweden & Jutland peninsula of Denmark
Kau·ai \ˈkaù-ˌī\ island Hawaii WNW of Oahu *area* 551
Kau·nas \ˈkaù-nəs, -ˌnäs\ *or* Russ **Kov·no** \ˈkȯv-(ˌ)nō\ city U.S.S.R. in *cen* Lithuania on Neman river; a former (1918–40) ✱ of Lithuania *pop* 306,000
Ka·vál·la \kə-ˈval-ə, -ˈväl-\ city & port NE Greece in Macedonia on coast *pop* 46,679
Kaveri — see CAUVERY
Kaw — see KANSAS
Ka·wa·gu·chi \ˌkä-wə-ˈgü-chē, kä-ˈwäg-ü-(ˌ)chē\ city Japan in E Honshu N of Tokyo *pop* 294,000
Ka·war·tha Lakes \kə-ˌwȯr-thə-\ group of lakes Canada in SE Ont. E of Lake Simcoe; traversed by Trent canal system
Ka·wa·sa·ki \ˌkä-wə-ˈsäk-ē\ city Japan in E Honshu on Tokyo Bay, S suburb of Tokyo *pop* 932,000
Ka·yah \ˈkī-ə\ *or formerly* **Ka·ren·ni** \kə-ˈren-ē\ state S Burma
Kay·se·ri \ˌkī-zə-ˈrē\ *or anc* **Cae·sa·rea** \ˌsē-zə-ˈrē-ə, ˌsez-ə-, ˌses-ə-\ *or* **Ma·za·ca** \ˈmaz-ə-kə\ *or* **Caesarea Mazaca** city *cen* Turkey in Asia at foot of Erciyas Dagi; chief city of ancient Cappadocia *pop* 126,653
Ka·zakh·stan *or* **Ka·zak·stan** \kə-ˌzak-ˈstan; kə-ˌzäk-ˈstän, ˌkä-\ *or* **Ka·zakh Republic** \kə-ˌzak-, -ˌzäk-\ constituent republic of the U.S.S.R. in Soviet Central Asia extending from Caspian sea to Altai mountains ✱ Alma-Ata *area* 1,047,930, *pop* 12,850,000
Ka·zan, 1 \kə-ˈzan\ river 455 *m* Canada flowing through a series of lakes into Baker Lake **2** \kə-ˈzan, -ˈzän(-yə)\ city U.S.S.R. in E Soviet Russia, Europe ✱ of Tatar Republic *pop* 869,000
Kazan Retto — see VOLCANO ISLANDS
Kaz·bek *or* **Kas·bek** \käz-ˈbek\ mountain 16,541 *ft* U.S.S.R. in S Soviet Russia, Europe, in *cen* Caucasus mountains
Kaz Dagi — see IDA
Kaz·vin *or* **Qaz·vin** \kaz-ˈvēn\ city NW Iran S of Elburz mountains & NW of Tehran *pop* 92,000
Ke·a·la·ke·kua Bay \kä-ˌäl-ə-kə-ˌkü-ə-\ inlet of the Pacific Hawaii in W Hawaii I. on Kona coast W of Mauna Loa
Kear·ney \ˈkär-nē\ city S *cen* Nebr. on the Platte *pop* 19,181
Kear·ny \ˈkär-nē\ town NE N.J. N of Newark *pop* 37,585
Kecs·ke·met \ˈkech-kə-ˌmāt\ city *cen* Hungary *pop* 77,484
Ked·ah \ˈked-ə\ state Federation of Malaysia in N Malaya bordering on Strait of Malacca ✱ Alor Star *area* 3660, *pop* 955,374
Kedron — see KIDRON
Keeling — see COCOS
Kee·lung \ˈkē-ˈlùŋ\ city & port China in N Formosa *pop* 317,780
Keene \ˈkēn\ city SW N.H. *pop* 20,467
Kee·wa·tin \kē-ˈwāt-^{ə}n\ district Canada in E Northwest Territories N of Manitoba & Ontario & including the islands in Hudson Bay *area* 218,460
Kefallinia — see CEPHALONIA
Kef·la·vik \ˈkyeb-lə-ˌvēk, ˈkef-\ town SW Iceland WSW of Reykjavík
Keigh·ley \ˈkēth-lē—*sic*\ municipal borough N England in West Riding, Yorkshire, NW of Leeds *pop* 55,263
Ke·lan·tan \kə-ˈlan-ˌtan\ state Federation of Malaysia in N Malaya on So. China sea ✱ Kota Bharu *area* 5746, *pop* 680,626
Kel·ler·wand \ˈkel-ər-ˌvänt\ *or* **Mon·te Co·glians** \ˌmōnt-ē-kōl-ˈyän(t)s\ mountain 9217 *ft* on Austria-Italy border; highest in the Carnic Alps
Ke·low·na \kə-ˈlō-nə\ city Canada in S B.C. *pop* 19,412
Keltsy — see KIELCE
Ke·me·ro·vo \ˈkem-ə-rə-və, -ˌrō-və, -rə-ˌvō\ city U.S.S.R. in S Soviet Russia, Asia, in Kuznetsk basin on the Tom *pop* 385,000
Ke·nai \ˈkē-ˌnī\ peninsula S Alaska E of Cook inlet
Ken·dal \ˈken-d^{ə}l\ municipal borough NW England ✱ of Westmorland *pop* 21,572
Ken·il·worth \ˈken-^{ə}l-ˌwərth\ urban district *cen* England in Warwickshire *pop* 20,121
Ke·ni·tra \kə-ˈnē-trə\ *or formerly* **Port Lyau·tey** \ˌpōr-lē-ˌō-ˈtā, -ˈō-ˌ\ city N Morocco NE of Rabat *pop* 130,000
Ken·more \ˈken-ˌmō(ə)r, -ˌmȯ(ə)r\ village W N.Y. N of Buffalo *pop* 20,980
Ken·ne·bec \ˈken-i-ˌbek, ˌken-i-ˈ\ river 164 *m* S Me. flowing S from Moosehead Lake into the Atlantic
Ken·ne·dy, Cape \ˈken-əd-ē\ cape E Fla. in the Atlantic on E shore of Canaveral peninsula; site of Air Force Missile Test Center; formerly called **Cape Ca·nav·er·al** \kə-ˈnav-(ə-)rəl\
Kennedy, Mount mountain 13,095 *ft* NW Canada in Yukon Territory in St. Elias range SE of Mt. Logan near Alaska border
Ken·ner \ˈken-ər\ city SE La. W of New Orleans *pop* 29,858
Ken·ne·saw Mountain \ˌken-ə-ˌsȯ-\ mountain 1809 *ft* NW Ga. NW of Atlanta
Ken·ne·wick \ˈken-ə-ˌwik\ city SE Wash. *pop* 15,212
Ke·no·sha \kə-ˈnō-shə\ city SE Wis. S of Racine *pop* 78,805
Ken·sing·ton and Chel·sea \ˈken-ziŋ-tən-ən-ˈchel-sē, ˈken(t)-siŋ-\ royal borough of W Greater London, England *pop* 184,392; includes former boroughs of Kensington & Chelsea
Kent \ˈkent\ **1** city NE Ohio SE of Cleveland *pop* 28,183 **2** city W Wash. S of Seattle *pop* 21,510 **3** county SE England bordering on Strait of Dover; one of kingdoms in Anglo-Saxon heptarchy ✱ Maidstone *area* 1525, *pop* 1,396,032 — **Kent·ish** \ˈkent-ish\ *adj*
Ken·tucky \kən-ˈtək-ē\ **1** river 259 *m* N *cen* Ky. flowing NW into the Ohio **2** state E *cen* U.S. ✱ Frankfort *area* 40,395, *pop* 3,219,311 — **Ken·tucki·an** \-ē-ən\ *adj or n*
Kent·wood \ˈkent-ˌwu̇d\ city SW Mich. SE of Grand Rapids *pop* 20,310
Ke·nya \ˈken-yə, ˈkēn-\ **1** extinct volcano 17,040 *ft*, *cen* Kenya near equator **2** republic E Africa S of Ethiopia bordering on Indian ocean; former Brit. crown colony & protectorate ✱ Nairobi *area* 224,960, *pop* 11,690,000 — **Ke·nyan** \-yən\ *adj or n*
Ke·os \ˈkē-ˌäs\ *or* **Kea** \ˈkē-ə\ *or anc* **Ce·os** \ˈsē-ˌäs\ island Greece in NW Cyclades; chief town Kea *area* 67
Ker·a·la \ˈker-ə-lə\ state SW India bordering on Arabian sea; formed 1956 from former Travancore and Cochin state & part of Madras state ✱ Trivandrum *area* 15,035, *pop* 21,280,397
Kerasun — see GIRESUN
Kerbela — see KARBALA
Kerch \ˈke(ə)rch\ **1** peninsula U.S.S.R. in S Soviet Russia, Europe, projecting E from the Crimea **2** strait between Kerch peninsula & Taman peninsula connecting Sea of Azov & Black Sea **3** city & port in the Crimea on Kerch strait *pop* 128,000
Ker·gue·len \ˈkər-gə-lən, ˌkər-gə-ˈlen\ **1** archipelago S Indian ocean belonging to France *area* 7000 **2** island in the archipelago
Ke·rin·tji \kə-ˈrin-chē\ volcano 12,484 *ft* Indonesia in W *cen* Sumatra; highest on the island
Kerkheh — see KARKHEH
Kérkira *or* **Kérkyra** — see CORFU
Kerk·ra·de \ˈke-(ə)r-ˌkräd-ə\ commune SE Netherlands *pop* 48,150
Ker·mad·ec \(ˌ)kər-ˈmad-ək\ islands SW Pacific *ab* 500 *m* NE of New Zealand; belong to New Zealand *area* 13
Ker·man \kər-ˈmän, ke(ə)r-\ **1** *or anc* **Car·ma·nia** \kär-ˈmā-nē-ə, -nyə\ region SE Iran bordering on Gulf of Oman & Persian gulf S of ancient Parthia **2** *or anc* **Car·ma·na** \kär-ˈmān-ə, -ˈman-, -ˈmän-\ city SE *cen* Iran in NW Kerman region *pop* 88,000
Ker·man·shah \ˈker-ˌmän-ˈshä, -ˈshȯ\ city W Iran *pop* 187,930
Kern \ˈkərn\ river 150 *m* S *cen* Calif. flowing SW into Buena Vista reservoir
Ker·ry \ˈker-ē\ county SW Ireland in Munster ✱ Tralee *area* 1815, *pop* 112,941
Ker·u·len \ˈker-ə-ˌlen\ river 650 *m* E Mongolia flowing S & E into the Argun in Manchuria
Kes·te·ven, Parts of \ke-ˈstē-vən\ administrative county E England in SW Lincolnshire ✱ Sleaford *area* 724, *pop* 232,215
Kes·wick \ˈkez-ik\ urban district NW England in Cumberland
Ket·ter·ing \ˈket-ə-riŋ\ city SW Ohio S of Dayton *pop* 69,599
Keu·ka \ˈkyü-kə, kā-ˈyü-\ lake 18 *m* long W *cen* N.Y.; one of the Finger Lakes
Kew \ˈkyü\ **1** city SE Australia in S Victoria, NE suburb of Melbourne *pop* 32,816 **2** parish S England in Surrey, now in the Greater London borough of Richmond upon Thames
Ke·wa·nee \ki-ˈwän-ē\ city NW Ill. *pop* 15,762

ə abut ^{ə} kitten, F table   ər further   a back   ā bake
ä cot, cart   ȧ F bac   aù out   ch chin   e less   ē easy
g gift   i trip   ī life   j joke   k̲ G ich ^{n} F vin   ŋ sing
ō flow   ȯ flaw   œ F bœuf   œ̄ F feu   ȯi coin   th thing
th̲ this   ü loot   u̇ foot   ue G Füllen   ue̅ F rue   y yet
^{y} F digne \dēn^{y}\, nuit \nw^{y}ē\   yü few   yu̇ furious   zh vision

Ke·wee·naw \'kē-wə-ˌnȯ\ peninsula NW Mich. projecting from upper Mich. peninsula into Lake Superior W of **Keweenaw Bay**
Key Lar·go \'lär-(ˌ)gō\ island S Fla. in the Florida Keys
Key West \'west\ city SW Fla. on Key West I. at W end of Florida Keys *pop* 27,563
Kha·ba·rovsk \kə-'bär-əfsk\ **1** territory U.S.S.R. in E Soviet Russia, Asia, bordering on Sea of Okhotsk & Bering sea *area* 965,400, *pop* 1,346,000 **2** city, its ✻, on the Amur *pop* 437,000
Kha·kass \kə-'kas\ autonomous region U.S.S.R. in S Soviet Russia, Asia, in SW Krasnoyarsk Territory N of the Sayan mountains ✻ Abakan *area* 24,000, *pop* 446,000
Khalkidiki — see CHALCIDICE
Khalkis — see CHALCIS
Khan·ba·lik \ˌkän-bə-'lēk\ ancient city ✻ of China under the Mongols, corresponding to modern Peking
Khania — see CANEA
Khan·ka \'kaŋ-kə\ *or* **Han·ka** \'haŋ-kə\ lake E Asia between Maritime Territory, U.S.S.R., & Heilungkiang, China *area* 1700
Khan Tengri — see TENGRI KHAN
Kha·rag·pur \'kär-əg-ˌpu̇(ə)r, 'kər-\ city E India in SW West Bengal WSW of Calcutta *pop* 165,925
Khar·kov \'kär-ˌkȯf, -ˌkȯv, -kəf\ city U.S.S.R. in NE Ukraine on edge of Donets Basin *pop* 1,223,000
Khar·toum *or* **Khar·tum** \kär-'tüm\ city ✻ of Sudan at junction of the White Nile & Blue Nile *pop* 194,000
Khartoum North city *cen* Sudan *pop* 39,082
Kha·si \'käs-ē\ hills E India in NW *cen* Assam
Kha·tan·ga \kə-'täŋ-gə, -'taŋ-\ river 800 *m* U.S.S.R. in N Soviet Russia, Asia, in NE Krasnoyarsk Territory flowing N into Laptev sea
Khatmandu — see KATMANDU
Khelat — see KALAT
Kher·son \ke(ə)r-'sȯn\ city & port U.S.S.R. in S Ukraine on the Dnieper near its mouth *pop* 261,000
Khing·an \'shiŋ-'än\ mountains NE China divided into the **Greater Khingan** (running N–S in NE Inner Mongolia) & the **Lesser Khingan** (extending NW–SE in Heilungkiang
Khios — see CHIOS
Khirbat Qumran — see QUMRAN
Khi·u·ma \'kē-ə-ˌmä\ *or* Estonian **Hii·u·maa** \'hē-ə-ˌmä\ island U.S.S.R. in Estonia in Baltic sea N of Sarema I. *area* 371
Khi·va \'kē-və\ **1** *or* **Kho·rezm** \kə-'rez-əm\ oasis U.S.S.R. in Uzbekistan on the lower Amu Darya **2** *or* **Khwa·razm** \kwə-'raz-əm, kwä-\ former khanate *cen* Asia including Khiva oasis **3** city in the oasis, ✻ of the khanate *pop* 22,000
Khmer Republic \kə-'me(ə)r-\ *or* **Cam·bo·dia** \kam-'bōd-ē-ə\ country SE Asia bordering on Gulf of Siam ✻ Phnom Penh *area* 69,866, *pop* 6,818,200
Khor·ram·shahr \ˌkȯr-əm-'shär, ˌkär-\ city & port W Iran on Shatt-al-Arab NNW of Abadan *pop* 90,000
Kho·tan \'kō-'tän\ town & oasis W China in SW Sinkiang on S edge of the Takla Makan at foot of Kunlun mountains *pop* 50,000
Khu·ra·san \ˌku̇r-ə-'sän\ *or* **Khor·a·san** \ˌkȯr-ə-'sän, ˌkär-\ region NE Iran; chief city Meshed
Khu·zi·stan \ˌkü-zi-'stän, -'stan\ region SW Iran bordering on Persian gulf; chief city Khorramshahr
Khy·ber \'kī-bər\ mountain pass 33 *m* long on border between Afghanistan & Pakistan in Safed Koh range WNW of Peshawar
Kia·mu·sze \jē-'ä-'mü-'sü\ city NE China in NE Heilungkiang on the Sungari *pop* 146,000
Kiang·si \jē-'äŋ-'sē\ province SE China ✻ Nanchang *area* 63,629, *pop* 22,000,000
Kiang·su \jē-'äŋ-'sü\ province E China bordering on Yellow sea ✻ Nanking *area* 41,699, *pop* 47,000,000
Kiangtu — see YANGCHOW
Kiao·chow Bay \jē-'au̇-'jō\ inlet of Yellow sea E China in E Shantung *area* 200
Ki·bo \'kē-(ˌ)bō\ mountain peak 19,317 *ft* Tanzania in NE Tanganyika; highest peak of Kilimanjaro & highest point in Africa
Kid·der·min·ster \'kid-ər-ˌmin(t)-stər\ municipal borough W *cen* England in Worcestershire SW of Birmingham *pop* 47,255
Kid·ron \'kid-rən, 'kī-drən\ *or* **Ked·ron** \'ked-rən, 'kē-drən\ valley *cen* Palestine between Jerusalem & Mount of Olives; source of stream (Kidron) flowing E to Dead sea
Kiel \'kē(ə)l\ **1** city & port N Germany ✻ of Schleswig-Holstein on SE coast of Jutland peninsula *pop* 269,200 **2** ship canal 61 *m* N Germany across base of Jutland peninsula connecting Baltic sea & North sea
Kiel·ce \kē-'elt-(ˌ)sä\ *or* Russ **Kelt·sy** \'kelt-sē\ city S Poland S of Warsaw *pop* 121,200
Ki·ev *or* **Ki·yev** \'kē-ˌ(y)ef, -ˌ(y)ev, -(y)əf\ city U.S.S.R. ✻ of Ukraine on the Dnieper *pop* 1,632,000
Ki·ga·li \ki-'gäl-ē\ city E *cen* Africa ✻ of Rwanda *pop* 60,000
Kikládhes — see CYCLADES
Ki·lau·ea \ˌkē-ˌlau̇-'ā-ə\ volcanic crater 2 *m* wide Hawaii on Hawaii I. on E slope of Mauna Loa
Kil·dare \kil-'da(ə)r, -'de(ə)r\ county E Ireland in Leinster ✻ Naas *area* 654, *pop* 71,522
Kil·i·man·ja·ro \ˌkil-ə-mən-'jär-(ˌ)ō, -'jar-\ mountain Tanzania in NE Tanganyika near Kenya border — see KIBO
Kil·ken·ny \kil-'ken-ē\ **1** county SE Ireland in Leinster *area* 796, *pop* 61,811 **2** municipal borough, its ✻
Kil·lar·ney, Lakes of \kil-'är-nē\ three lakes SW Ireland in County Kerry
Kill Dev·il \'kil-ˌdev-əl\ hill E N.C. near village of **Kit·ty Hawk** \'kit-ē-ˌhȯk\ on sand barrier opposite Albemarle Sound; included in Wright Brothers National Memorial
Kil·leen \kil-'ēn\ city *cen* Tex. N of Austin *pop* 35,507
Kil·lie·cran·kie \ˌkil-ē-'kraŋ-kē\ mountain pass *cen* Scotland in Perthshire in the SE Grampians
Kill Van Kull \ˌkil-(ˌ)van-'kəl, -vən-\ channel between N.J. & Staten I., N.Y., connecting Newark Bay & Upper New York Bay
Kil·mar·nock \kil-'mär-nək\ burgh SW Scotland in Ayrshire *pop* 48,785
Kim·ber·ley \'kim-bər-lē\ city Republic of So. Africa in N Cape of Good Hope WNW of Bloemfontein *pop* 96,200
Kim·ber·leys \-lēz\ plateau region N Western Australia N of 19°30'S lat.
Kin·a·ba·lu *or* **Kin·a·bu·lu** \ˌkin-ə-bə-'lü\ mountain 13,455 *ft* N *cen* No. Borneo in Crocker range; highest in Borneo I.
Kin·car·dine \kin-'kärd-ᵊn\ *or* **Kin·car·dine·shire** \-ˌshi(ə)r, -shər\ *or formerly* **The Mearns** \'mərnz, 'me(ə)rnz\ county E Scotland bordering on North sea ✻ Stonehaven *area* 382, *pop* 25,050
Kinchinjunga — see KANCHENJUNGA
Ki·nesh·ma \'kē-nish-mə\ city U.S.S.R. in *cen* Soviet Russia, Europe, NE of Moscow *pop* 94,000
King George's Falls — see AUGHRABIES FALLS
King·man \'kiŋ-mən\ reef *cen* Pacific at N end of Line islands enclosing deep lagoon
King's — see OFFALY
Kings Canyon National Park \'kiŋz-\ reservation SE *cen* Calif. in the Sierra Nevada N of Sequoia National Park *area* 719
King's Lynn \'kiŋz-'lin\ *or* **Lynn** *or* **Lynn Re·gis** \-'rē-jəs\ municipal borough E England in Norfolk near the Wash *pop* 30,102
Kings Mountain ridge N.C. & S.C. SW of Gastonia, N.C.
Kings Peak mountain 13,528 *ft* NE Utah in Uinta mountains; highest point in state
Kings·port \'kiŋz-ˌpō(ə)rt, -ˌpȯ(ə)rt\ city NE Tenn. *pop* 31,938
Kings·ton \'kiŋ-stən\ **1** city SE N.Y. on the Hudson *pop* 25,544 **2** borough E Pa. SW of Scranton *pop* 18,325 **3** city Canada in SE Ont. on Lake Ontario *pop* 59,047 **4** *or* **Kingston on** (*or* **upon**) **Thames** royal borough of SW Greater London, England ✻ of Surrey *pop* 140,210 **5** city & port ✻ of Jamaica on **Kingston Harbor** (inlet of the Caribbean) *pop* 117,400
Kingston upon Hull — see HULL
Kings·town \'kiŋ-ˌstau̇n\ **1** town & port Brit. West Indies on St. Vincent I. ✻ of St. Vincent territory **2** — see DUN LAOGHAIRE
Kings·ville \'kiŋz-ˌvil, -vəl\ city S Tex. *pop* 28,711
Kinmen — see QUEMOY
Kinneret, Yam — see GALILEE (Sea of)
Kin·ross \kin-'rȯs\ **1** *or* **Kin·ross–shire** \-'rȯs(h)-ˌshi(ə)r, -shər\ county E *cen* Scotland *area* 82, *pop* 6422 **2** burgh, its ✻
Kin·sha·sa \kin-'shäs-ə\ *or formerly* **Lé·o·pold·ville** \'lē-ə-ˌpōld-ˌvil, 'lā-\ city ✻ of Zaire on Congo river at outlet of Stanley Pool *pop* 1,288,122
Kin·ston \'kin(t)-stən\ city E N.C. *pop* 22,309
Kin·tyre \kin-'tī(ə)r\ *or* **Can·tyre** \kan-\ peninsula 40 *m* long SW Scotland between the Atlantic & Firth of Clyde; terminates in **Mull of Kintyre** \ˌməl-\ (cape in No. channel)
Kioga — see KYOGA
Kir·giz Republic *or* **Kir·ghiz Republic** \(ˌ)ki(ə)r-ˌgēz-\ *or* **Kir·gi·zia** *or* **Kir·ghi·zia** \ki(ə)r-'gē-z(h)ē-ə, -zhə\ constituent republic of the U.S.S.R. in Soviet Central Asia on China border NE of Tadzhikistan ✻ Frunze *area* 76,100, *pop* 2,933,000
Ki·rik·ka·le \kə-'rik-ə-ˌlā\ city *cen* Turkey E of Ankara *pop* 57,668
Ki·rin \'kē-'rin\ **1** province NE China in E Manchuria ✻ Changchun *area* 72,201, *pop* 17,000,000 **2** *or formerly* **Yung·ki** \'yuŋ-'jē\ city NE China in Kirin E of Changchun *pop* 568,000
Kirjath–arba — see HEBRON
Kirk·caldy \(ˌ)kər-'kȯ(l)d-ē, -'käd-\ burgh & port E Scotland in Fife on Firth of Forth N of Edinburgh *pop* 52,097
Kirk·cud·bright \(ˌ)kər-'kü-brē\ **1** *or* **Kirk·cud·bright·shire** \-ˌshi(ə)r, -shər\ county S Scotland on Solway firth *area* 899, *pop* 30,472 **2** burgh, its ✻, SW of Dumfries
Kirk·land \'kər-klənd\ city W Wash. NE of Seattle *pop* 15,249
Kirk·pat·rick, Mount \ˌkərk-'pa-trik\ mountain 14,800 *ft* E Antarctica in Queen Alexandra Range S of Ross sea
Kirks·ville \'kərks-ˌvil\ city NE Mo. *pop* 15,560
Kir·kuk \ki(ə)r-'kük\ city NE Iraq SE of Mosul *pop* 175,303
Kirk·wall \'kər-ˌkwȯl\ burgh & port N Scotland ✻ of Orkney, on Mainland I.
Kirk·wood \'kər-ˌkwu̇d\ city E Mo. W of St. Louis *pop* 31,890
Ki·rov \'kē-ˌrȯf, -ˌrȯv, -rəf\ *or formerly* **Vyat·ka** \vē-'at-kə, -'ät-\ city U.S.S.R. in E Soviet Russia, Europe, on Vyatka river *pop* 332,000
Ki·ro·va·bad \ki-'rō-və-ˌbad\ *or formerly* **Gan·dzha** \'gän-jə\ *or* **Eli·sa·vet·pol** \i-ˌliz-ə-'vet-ˌpȯl\ city U.S.S.R. in W Azerbaidzhan *pop* 190,000
Ki·ro·vo·grad \ki-'rō-və-ˌgrad\ *or formerly* **Zi·nov·ievsk** \zə-'nȯv-ˌyefsk\ *or* **Eli·sa·vet·grad** \i-ˌliz-ə-'vet-ˌgrad\ city U.S.S.R. in S *cen* Ukraine *pop* 189,000
Ki·ru·na \'kē-rə-ˌnä\ city N Sweden in Lapland *pop* 28,942
Ki·san·ga·ni \ˌkē-sən-'gän-ē\ *or formerly* **Stan·ley·ville** \'stan-lē-ˌvil\ city NE Zaire on Congo river *pop* 229,596
Kish \'kish\ ancient city of Sumer & Akkad E of site of Babylon
Ki·shi·nev \'kish-ə-ˌnef, -ˌnev\ *or* Rum **Chi·si·nau** \ˌkē-shi-'nau̇\ city U.S.S.R. ✻ of Moldavia *pop* 357,000
Kishm — see QISHM
Kishon — see QISHON
Kis·ka \'kis-kə\ island SW Alaska in Rat group of the Aleutians
Kis·ma·yu \kis-'mī-(ˌ)ü\ city & port S Somalia on Indian ocean *pop* 17,872
Kis·sim·mee \kis-'im-ē\ river 150 *m* S *cen* Fla. flowing SSE from Lake Tohopekaliga through **Lake Kissimmee** (12 *m* long) into Lake Okeechobee
Kistna — see KRISHNA
Ki·su·mu \ki-'sü-(ˌ)mü\ city E Kenya on Lake Victoria *pop* 30,700
Ki·ta·kyu·shu \kē-'tä-kē-'ü-(ˌ)shü\ city & port Japan in N Kyushu formed 1963 by amalgamation of former cities of Kokura, Moji, Tobata, Wakamatsu, & Yahata *pop* 1,050,000
Kitch·e·ner \'kich-(ə-)nər\ city Canada in SE Ont. *pop* 111,804
Kithairón — see CITHAERON
Kí·thi·ra *or* **Ky·the·ra** \'kē-thə-(ˌ)rä\ *or* **Cy·the·ra** \sə-'thir-ə, sī-\ *or* It **Ce·ri·go** \'cher-i-ˌgō\ island W Greece, southernmost of the Ionian islands ✻ Kíthira *area* 110
Kit·i·mat \'kit-ə-ˌmat\ river *ab* 50 *m* W Canada in NW B.C. flowing to Douglas channel (inlet of the Pacific)

Kit·ta·tin·ny Mountain \ˌkit-ə-ˌtin-ē-\ ridge E U.S. in the Appalachians extending from SE N.Y. through NW N.J. into E Pa.
Kit·tery Point \ˌkit-ə-rē-\ cape Me. at S tip
Kitt Peak \ˈkit\ mountain 6875 *ft* S Ariz. in Baboquivari mountains SW of Tucson
Kitty Hawk — see KILL DEVIL
Kitz·bü·hel \ˈkits-ˌbyü(-ə)l, -ˌbue(-ə)l\ resort town W Austria in the Tirol
Ki·vu, Lake \ˈkē-(ˌ)vü\ lake 60 *m* long & 30 *m* wide E Zaire in Great Rift valley N of Lake Tanganyika *area* 1025
Ki·zil Ir·mak \kə-ˌzil-i(ə)r-ˈmäk\ *or anc* **Ha·lys** \ˈhā-ləs\ river 600 *m* N *cen* Turkey flowing W & NE into Black sea
Kjö·len \ˈchə(r)l-ən\ mountains on border between NE Norway & NW Sweden; highest Kebnekaise (in Sweden) 6963 *ft*
Kla·gen·furt \ˈkläg-ən-ˌfu̇(ə)rt\ city S Austria ✻ of Carinthia WSW of Graz *pop* 73,156
Klaipeda — see MEMEL
Klam·ath \ˈklam-əth\ **1** river 250 *m* S Oreg. & NW Calif. flowing from Upper Klamath Lake SW into the Pacific **2** mountains S Oreg. & NW Calif. in the Coast ranges; highest Mt. Eddy (in Calif.) 9038 *ft*
Klamath Falls city SW Oreg. *pop* 15,775
Kleve — see CLEVES
Klon·dike \ˈklän-ˌdīk\ **1** river 90 *m* Canada in *cen* Yukon Territory flowing W into the Yukon **2** the Klondike river valley
Kly·az·ma \klē-ˈaz-mə\ river 425 *m* U.S.S.R. in W *cen* Soviet Russia, Europe, flowing E to join the Oka W of Gorki
Knok·ke \kə-ˈnäk-ə\ town NW Belgium NNE of Bruges
Knos·sos *or* **Cnos·sus** \(kə-)ˈnäs-əs\ *or* **Gnos·sus** \(gə-)ˈnäs-əs\ ruined city ✻ of ancient Crete near N coast SE of modern Candia
Knox·ville \ˈnäks-ˌvil, -vəl\ city E Tenn. *pop* 174,587
Knud Ras·mus·sen Land \ˈnüd-ˈräs-ˌmu̇s-ᵊn, ˈras-mə-sən\ region N & NW Greenland NE of Baffin Bay
Ko·ba·rid \ˈkō-bə-ˌrēd\ *or* It **Ca·po·ret·to** \ˌkap-ə-ˈret-(ˌ)ō, ˌkäp-\ village NW Yugoslavia on the Isonzo NE of Udine, Italy
Ko·be \ˈkō-bē, -ˌbā\ city & port Japan in S Honshu on Osaka Bay *pop* 1,267,000
København — see COPENHAGEN
Ko·blenz *or* **Co·blenz** \ˈkō-ˌblen(t)s\ city W Germany SSE of Cologne at confluence of the Rhine & the Moselle *pop* 105,700
Koca — see XANTHUS
Ko·ca·bas \ˌkō-jə-ˈbäsh\ *or anc* **Gra·ni·cus** \grə-ˈnī-kəs\ river *ab* 30 *m* NW Turkey in Asia flowing NE to Sea of Marmara
Ko·chi \ˈkō-chē\ city & port Japan in S Shikoku *pop* 249,000
Ko·di·ak \ˈkōd-ē-ˌak\ *or* **Ka·diak** \kəd-ˈyak, -ˈyäk\ island S Alaska in Gulf of Alaska E of Alaska peninsula *area* 3465
Ko·dok \ˈkōd-ˌäk\ *or formerly* **Fa·sho·da** \fə-ˈshōd-ə\ town SE Sudan on the White Nile
Koedoes — see KUDUS
Ko·fu \ˈkō-(ˌ)fü\ city Japan in S *cen* Honshu *pop* 184,000
Ko·ha·la \kō-ˈhäl-ə\ mountains Hawaii in N Hawaii I.; highest *ab* 5500 *ft*
Ko·hi·ma \kō-ˈhē-mə\ town NE India ✻ of Nagaland
Kol — see RED
Koil — see ALIGARH
Ko·kand \kō-ˈkand\ **1** region & former khanate U.S.S.R. in Soviet Central Asia in E Uzbekistan **2** city in Kokand region SE of Tashkent *pop* 133,000
Ko·kiu *or* **Ko·chiu** \ˈgō-jē-ˈō\ city S China in SE Yunnan S of Kunming *pop* 159,700
Ko·ko·mo \ˈkō-kə-ˌmō\ city N *cen* Ind. *pop* 44,042
Koko Nor — see TSINGHAI
Koksoak — see KANIAPISKAU
Ko·ku·ra \ˈkō-kə-ˌrä, kō-ˈku̇r-ə\ former city Japan in N Kyushu — see KITAKYUSHU
Ko·la \ˈkō-lə\ peninsula 250 *m* long & 150 *m* wide U.S.S.R. in NW Soviet Russia, Europe, between Barents & White seas
Ko·lar Gold Fields \kō-ˈlär\ city S India in SE Mysore *pop* 167,610
Kol·ha·pur \ˈkō-lə-ˌpu̇(ə)r\ city W India in SW Maharashtra SSE of Bombay *pop* 252,109
Kolmar — see COLMAR
Köln — see COLOGNE
Ko·ly·ma *or* **Ko·li·ma** \kə-ˈlē-mə\ **1** river 1110 *m* U.S.S.R. in NE Soviet Russia, Asia, flowing from Kolyma range NE into East Siberian sea **2** mountain range Soviet Russia, Asia, in NE Khabarovsk Territory parallel to coast of Penzhinskaya Bay
Ko·man·dor·skie \ˌkäm-ən-ˈdȯr-skē\ *or* **Com·mand·er** \kə-ˈmandər\ islands U.S.S.R. in E Soviet Russia, Asia, in Bering sea E of Kamchatka peninsula *area* 850
Ko·ma·ti \kə-ˈmät-ē\ river 500 *m* S Africa flowing from N Drakensberg mountains in NE Republic of So. Africa E & N into Delagoa Bay in S Mozambique
Ko·mi Republic \ˈkō-mē\ autonomous republic U.S.S.R. in NE Soviet Russia, Europe, W of N Ural mountains ✻ Syktyvkar *area* 145,221, *pop* 965,000
Ko·mo·do \kə-ˈmōd-(ˌ)ō\ island Indonesia in the Lesser Sundas E of Sumbawa I. & W of Flores I. *area* 185
Kom·so·molsk \ˌkäm(p)-sə-ˈmȯlsk\ city U.S.S.R. in E Soviet Russia, Asia, in S Khabarovsk Territory on the Amur *pop* 218,000
Ko·na \ˈkō-nə\ coast region Hawaii in W Hawaii I.
Konakry — see CONAKRY
Königgrätz — see HRADEC KRALOVE
Königsberg — see KALININGRAD
Kon·kan \ˈkäŋ-kən\ region W India in W Maharashtra bordering on Arabian sea & extending from Bombay S to Goa
Konstanz — see CONSTANCE
Kon·ya *or* **Kon·ia** \kȯn-ˈyä\ *or anc* **Ico·ni·um** \ī-ˈkō-nē-əm\ city SW *cen* Turkey *pop* 157,934
Ko·o·lau \ˌkō-ə-ˈlä-(ˌ)ü\ mountains Hawaii in E Oahu; highest peak Konahuanui 3105 *ft*
Koo·te·nai *or (in Canada)* **Koo·te·nay** \ˈküt-ᵊn-ˌā, -ᵊn-ē\ river 407 *m* SW Canada & NW U.S. in B.C., Mont., & Idaho flowing through **Kootenay Lake** (65 *m* long, in B.C.) into the Columbia
Kootenay National Park reservation Canada in SE B.C. including section of the upper Kootenay *area* 587
Ko·per \ˈkō-ˌpe(ə)r\ *or* **Ko·par** \-ˌpär\ *or* It **Ca·po·dis·tria** \ˌkap-ə-ˈdis-trē-ə, ˌkäp-ə-ˈdēs-\ town & port Yugoslavia at N end of Istrian peninsula SSW of Trieste
Ko·peysk *or* **Ko·peisk** \kō-ˈpāsk\ city U.S.S.R. in W Soviet Russia, Asia, SE of Chelyabinsk *pop* 156,000
Kor·do·fan \ˌkȯrd-ə-ˈfan\ region *cen* Sudan W & N of the White Nile; chief city El Obeid
Ko·rea \kə-ˈrē-ə, *esp South* (ˈ)kō-\ **1** peninsula 600 *m* long & 135 *m* wide E Asia between Yellow sea & Sea of Japan **2** strait 120 *m* wide between S Korea & SW Japan connecting Sea of Japan & Yellow sea **3** *or* **Cho·sen** \ˈchō-ˈsen\ country coextensive with Korea peninsula; once a kingdom & (1910–1945) a Japanese dependency ✻ Seoul; divided 1948 at 38th parallel into republics of No. Korea (✻ Pyongyang *area* 47,839, *pop* 14,280,000) & So. Korea (✻ Seoul *area* 37,427, *pop* 31,920,000)
Korea Bay arm of Yellow sea between Liaotung peninsula & NW Korea
Kórinthos — see CORINTH
Kort·rijk \ˈkȯrt-ˌrīk\ *or* **Cour·trai** \ku̇r-ˈtrā\ commune NW Belgium in West Flanders on the Lys NNE of Lille *pop* 45,138
Kos *or* **Cos** \ˈkäs, ˈkȯs\ **1** island Greece in the Dodecanese *area* 111, *pop* 19,987 **2** chief town on the island
Kos·ci·us·ko, Mount \ˌkäz-ē-ˈəs-(ˌ)kō\ mountain 7316 *ft* SE Australia in SE New So. Wales; highest in Great Dividing range & Australia
Ko·si·ce \ˈkȯ-shət-ˌsā\ city E Czechoslovakia *pop* 119,757
Ko·stro·ma \ˌkäs-trə-ˈmä\ city U.S.S.R. in N *cen* Soviet Russia, Europe, on the Volga *pop* 223,000
Kotabaru — see DJAJAPURA
Ko·ta Bha·ru \ˌkōt-ə-ˈbär-(ˌ)ü\ city Federation of Malaysia in Malaya ✻ of Kelantan *pop* 55,052
Ko·ta Kin·a·ba·lu \ˈkōt-ə-ˌkin-ə-bə-ˈlü\ *or formerly* **Jes·sel·ton** \ˈjes-əl-tən\ city & port Malaysia ✻ of Sabah *pop* 41,830
Ko·tor \ˈkō-ˌtȯ(ə)r\ *or* It **Cat·ta·ro** \ˈkät-ə-ˌrō\ town & port SE Yugoslavia in Montenegro on an inlet of the Adriatic
Kottbus — see COTTBUS
Kot·ze·bue Sound \ˌkät-si-ˌbyü-\ arm of Chuckchee sea NW Alaska NE of Bering strait
Kovno — see KAUNAS
Kowait — see KUWAIT
Kow·loon \ˈkau̇-ˈlün\ **1** peninsula SE China in Hong Kong colony opposite Hong Kong I. **2** city on Kowloon peninsula *pop* 715,440
Koy·u·kuk \ˈkī-ə-ˌkək\ river 425 *m* N *cen* Alaska flowing from Brooks range SW into the Yukon
Ko·zhi·kode \ˈkō-zhə-ˌkōd\ *or* **Cal·i·cut** \ˈkal-i-kət\ city & port SW India on Malabar coast in Kerala *pop* 330,225
Kozlov — see MICHURINSK
Kra, Isthmus of \ˈkrä\ isthmus S Thailand in N *cen* Malay peninsula; 40 *m* wide at narrowest part
Krak·a·toa \ˌkrak-ə-ˈtō-ə\ *or* **Krak·a·tau** *or* **Krak·a·tao** \-ˈtau̇\ island & volcano Indonesia between Sumatra & Java
Kra·kow *or* **Cra·cow** \ˈkräk-ˌau̇, ˈkrak-, ˈkräk-, -(ˌ)ō, *Pol* ˈkräk-ˌüf\ city S Poland on the Vistula *pop* 570,700
Kras \ˈkräs\ *or* G **Karst** \ˈkärst\ *or* It **Car·so** \ˈkär-(ˌ)sō\ limestone plateau NW Yugoslavia NE of Istrian peninsula
Kras·no·dar \ˈkras-nə-ˌdär\ **1** territory U.S.S.R. in S Soviet Russia, Europe, in N Caucasus region *area* 32,800, *pop* 4,511,000 **2** *or formerly* **Eka·te·ri·no·dar** \i-ˌkat-ə-ˈrē-nə-ˌdär\ city, its ✻, on Kuban river *pop* 465,000
Kras·no·yarsk \ˌkras-nə-ˈyärsk\ **1** territory U.S.S.R. in W *cen* Soviet Russia, Asia, extending along valley of the Yenisei from Arctic ocean to Sayan mountains *area* 928,000, *pop* 2,962,000 **2** city, its ✻, on the upper Yenisei *pop* 648,000
Kre·feld \ˈkrā-ˌfelt\ *or formerly* **Krefeld–Uer·ding·en** \-ˈu̇rd-iŋ-ən, -ˈuer-\ city W Germany on the Rhine WSW of Essen *pop* 226,800
Krim — see CRIMEA
Krish·na \ˈkrish-nə\ *or formerly* **Kist·na** \ˈkist-nə\ river 800 *m* S India flowing from Western Ghats E into Bay of Bengal
Kristiania — see OSLO
Kris·tian·sand \ˈkris(h)-chən-ˌsan(d)\ city & port SW Norway on the Skagerrak SW of Oslo *pop* 56,152
Kris·tian·sund \-ˌsu̇n(d)\ city & port W Norway WSW of Trondheim *pop* 18,621
Kríti — see CRETE
Kri·voy Rog *or* **Kri·voi Rog** \ˌkriv-ˌȯi-ˈrōg, -ˈrȯk\ city U.S.S.R. in SE *cen* Ukraine NE of Odessa *pop* 573,000
Kron·shtadt *or* **Kron·stadt** \ˈkrōn-ˌstat, krän-ˈs(h)tät\ city U.S.S.R. in Soviet Russia, Europe, on island in E Gulf of Finland W of Leningrad *pop* 45,000
Kru·ger National Park \ˈkrü-gər\ game reserve NE Republic of So. Africa in E Transvaal on Mozambique border *area* 8652
Kru·gers·dorp \ˈkrü-gərz-ˌdȯrp, ˈkrue-ərz-\ city NE Republic of So. Africa in S Transvaal W of Johannesburg *pop* 100,500
K² — see GODWIN AUSTEN
Kua·la Lum·pur \ˌkwäl-ə-ˈlu̇m-ˌpu̇(ə)r, -ˈləm-\ city ✻ of Federation of Malaysia & of Selangor in W Malaya *pop* 451,728
Kuang-chou — see CANTON
Ku·ban \kü-ˈban, -ˈbän\ river 512 *m* U.S.S.R. flowing from the Caucasus N & W into Sea of Azov
Ku·ching \ˈkü-chiŋ\ city & port Malaysia ✻ of Sarawak *pop* 63,491
Ku·dus *or* D **Koe·does** \küd-ˌüs\ city Indonesia in *cen* Java NE of Semarang *pop* 74,911
Ku·fra *or* **Cu·fra** \ˈkü-frə\ group of five oases SE Libya

Kui·by·shev *or* **Kuy·by·shev** \'kwē-bə-,shef, 'kü-ē-bə-, -,shev\ *or formerly* **Sa·ma·ra** \sə-'mär-ə\ city U.S.S.R. in SE Soviet Russia, Europe, in valley of the Volga *pop* 1,047,000

Ku·ke·naam \,kü-kə-'näm\ *or* **Cu·que·nán** \,kü-kə-'nän\ **1** mountain 8620 on border between Guyana & Venezuela near Roraima **2** waterfall 2000 *ft* on this mountain

Kuku–Khoto — see HUHEHOT

Ku·la Gulf \,kü-lə-\ body of water 17 *m* long in the Solomons between New Georgia & adjacent islands

Kul·dja \'kül-(,)jä\ city W China in NW Sinkiang *pop* 160,000

Kum \'küm\ river 247 *m* S Korea flowing into Yellow sea

Ku·ma·mo·to \,küm-ə-'mōt-(,)ō\ city Japan in W Kyushu *pop* 435,-000

Ku·ma·si *or* **Coo·mas·sie** \kü-'mäs-ē, -'mas-\ city S *cen* Ghana in Ashanti *pop* 281,600

Kum·chon \'küm-,chän\ city S Korea NW of Taegu *pop* 51,300

Kum·gang \'küm-,gäŋ\ *or* **Di·a·mond** \'dī-(ə-)mənd\ mountains NE *cen* Korea; highest 5374 *ft*

Kunene — see CUNENE

Ku·nie \'kün-(,)yā\ *or* **Isle of Pines** island SW Pacific in New Caledonia territory SE of New Caledonia I. *area* 58

Kun·lun *or* **Kuen·lun** \'kün-'lün\ mountains W China extending from the Pamirs & Karakoram range E along N edge of Tibetan plateau to SE Tsinghai — see ULUGH MUZTAGH

Kun·ming \'kün-'miŋ\ *or formerly* **Yun·nan** \yü-'nän\ *or* **Yun·nan·fu** \-'fü\ city S China ✻ of Yunnan *pop* 1,700,000

Kun·san \'gün-,sän\ city & port S Korea on Yellow sea at mouth of Kum river *pop* 112,453

Kun·tse·vo \'kün(t)-sə-,vō\ city U.S.S.R. in Soviet Russia, Europe, SW suburb of Moscow *pop* 129,000

Ku·pre·a·nof \,kü-prē-'an-,ȯf\ island SE Alaska in E Alexander archipelago

Ku·ra \kə-'rä, 'kür-ə\ river 825 *m* W Asia in Transcaucasia flowing from NE Turkey ESE through Georgia & Azerbaidzhan, U.S.S.R., into Caspian sea

Kur·di·stan \,kürd-ə-'stan, ,kərd-\ region SW Asia chiefly in E Turkey, NW Iran, & N Iraq

Ku·re \'k(y)ü(ə)r-ē, 'kü-(,)rā\ **1** *or* **Ocean** island *cen* Pacific in Hawaii, westernmost of the Leewards **2** city & port Japan in SW Honshu on Inland sea SSE of Hiroshima *pop* 237,000

Kurg — see COORG

Kur·gan \kü(ə)r-'gan, -'gän\ city U.S.S.R. in W Soviet Russia, Asia, E of Chelyabinsk *pop* 240,000

Ku·ria Mu·ria \,k(y)ür-ē-ə-'m(y)ür-ē-ə\ islands in Arabian sea off SW coast of Oman belonging to Oman *area* 28

Ku·ril *or* **Ku·rile** \'kyü(ə)r-,ēl, kyü-'rē(ə)l\ islands U.S.S.R. in the Pacific between S Kamchatka & NE Hokkaido, Japan; belonged 1875–1945 to Japan *area* 3960

Kur·land *or* **Cour·land** \'kü(ə)r-lənd\ region U.S.S.R. in W Latvia bordering on the Baltic & Gulf of Riga

Kurland Gulf inlet of the Baltic W U.S.S.R. on border between Lithuania & Soviet Russia *area* 625

Kur·nool \kər-'nül\ city S India in W Andhra Pradesh SSW of Hyderabad *pop* 164,248

Kursk \'kü(ə)rsk\ city U.S.S.R. in SW Soviet Russia, Europe, on Seim river *pop* 284,000

Kush — see CUSH

Kus·ko·kwim \'kəs-kə-,kwim\ river 550 *m* SW Alaska flowing SW into **Kuskokwim Bay** (inlet of Bering sea)

Ku·tah·ya \kü-'tä-yə\ city W *cen* Turkey *pop* 49,301

Kut–al–Ima·ra \,küt-,al-ə-'mär-ə\ *or* **Al–Kut** \al-'küt\ city SE *cen* Iraq on the Tigris SE of Baghdad *pop* 42,116

Kutch *or* **Cutch** \'kəch\ former principality & state W India N of Gulf of Kutch ✻ Bhuj; now part of Gujarat

Kutch, Gulf of inlet of Arabian sea W India N of Kathiawar

Kutch, Rann of \,rən-\ salt marsh in S Pakistan & W India stretching in an arc from the mouths of the Indus to the head of Gulf of Kutch

Ku·wait *or* **Ku·weit** *or* **Ko·wait** \kə-'wāt\ *or* **Al Kuwait** \,al-\ **1** country SW Asia in Arabia at head of Persian gulf; a sheikhdom, before 1961 under Brit. protection *area* 6178, *pop* 830,000 **2** city & port, its ✻ *pop* 80,008 — **Ku·waiti** \-'wāt-ē\ *adj or n*

Kuz·netsk \küz-'netsk\ city U.S.S.R. in SE *cen* Soviet Russia, Europe, E of Penza *pop* 79,000

Kuznetsk Basin *or* **Kuz·bass** *or* **Kuz·bas** \'küz-,bas\ basin of Tom river U.S.S.R. in W *cen* Soviet Russia, Asia, extending from Novokuznetsk to Tomsk

Kwa·ja·lein \'kwäj-ə-lən, -,lān\ island (atoll) 78 *m* long W Pacific in Ralik chain of the Marshalls; encloses lagoon (*area* 650)

Kwan·do \'kwän-(,)dō\ river 600 *m* S Africa flowing from *cen* Angola SE & E into the Zambezi just above Victoria Falls

Kwangchow — see CANTON

Kwang·cho·wan \'gwäŋ-'jō-'wän, 'kwäŋ-\ former territory SE China in Kwangtung on Luichow peninsula; leased 1898–1946 to France ✻ Fort Bayard *area* 325

Kwang·ju \'gwäŋ-(,)jü, 'kwäŋ-\ city SW Korea NE of Mokpo *pop* 502,753

Kwang·si \'gwäŋ-'sē, 'kwäŋ\ *or* **Kwangsi–Chu·ang Region** \-chü-'äŋ\ region & former province S China W of Kwangtung ✻ Nanning *area* 85,096, *pop* 24,000,000

Kwang·tung \'gwäŋ-'düŋ, 'kwäŋ-, -'tüŋ\ province SE China bordering on So. China sea & Gulf of Tonkin ✻ Canton *area* 89,344, *pop* 40,000,000

Kwan·to Plain \,kwän-(,)tō-\ *or* **Kan·to Plain** \,kän-\ *or* **Tokyo Plain** region Japan in E *cen* Honshu; Tokyo is situated on it

Kwan·tung \'gwän-'düŋ, 'kwän-, -'tüŋ\ former territory NE China in S Manchuria at tip of Liaotung peninsula; leased to Russia 1898–1905, to Japan 1905–45, & to Russia again 1945–55; included cities of Port Arthur & Dairen *area* 1444

Kwei \'gwā, 'kwā\ river 200 *m* SE China in E Kwangsi flowing S into West river

Kwei·chow \'gwā-'jō, 'kwā-\ province S China S of Szechwan ✻ Kweiyang *area* 67,181, *pop* 17,000,000

Kwei·lin \'gwā-'lin, 'kwā-\ city S China in NE Kwangsi on the Kwei *pop* 235,000

Kweisui — see HUHEHOT

Kwei·yang \'gwā-'yäŋ, 'kwā-\ *or* **Kwei·chu** \-'jü\ city S China ✻ of Kweichow *pop* 1,500,000

Kyo·ga *or* **Kio·ga** \kē-'ō-gə\ lake *cen* Uganda N of Lake Victoria traversed by the Victoria Nile *area* 1000

Kyongsong — see SEOUL

Kyo·to \kē-'ōt-(,)ō\ city Japan in W *cen* Honshu NNE of Osaka; formerly (794–1869) ✻ of Japan *pop* 1,422,000

Kythera — see KÍTHIRA

Kyu·shu \kē-'ü-(,)shü\ island S Japan S of W end of Honshu *area* 16,240

Laaland — see LOLLAND

Labe — see ELBE

Lab·ra·dor \'lab-rə-,dȯ(ə)r\ **1** peninsula E Canada between Hudson Bay & the Atlantic; divided between Que. & Nfld. **2** the section of the peninsula belonging to Nfld. *area* 101,881 **3** sea arm of the Atlantic between Labrador & Greenland — **Lab·ra·dor·ean** *or* **Lab·ra·dor·ian** \,lab-rə-'dȯr-ē-ən, -'dōr-\ *adj or n*

La·bu·an \lə'bü-ən\ island Sabah off W coast *pop* 14,904

Lac·ca·dive \'lak-ə-,dēv, -,dīv\ islands India in Arabian sea N of Maldive islands

Laccadive, Min·i·coy, and Amin·di·vi Islands \'min-i-,kȯi; ,əm-ən-'dē-vē\ territory India comprising the Laccadive group ✻ Kavaratti *area* 11, *pop* 31,798

Lacedaemon — see SPARTA — **Lac·e·dae·mo·nian** \,las-əd-i-'mō-nē-ən, -nyən\ *adj or n*

La Chaux–de–Fonds \lä-,shōd-ə-'fōⁿ\ commune W Switzerland in Neuchâtel canton in Jura mountains WNW of Bern *pop* 42,347

La·chine \lə-'shēn\ city Canada in S Que. above the **Lachine rapids** on the St. Lawrence SW of Montreal *pop* 44,423

La·chish \'lā-kish\ ancient city S Palestine W of Hebron

Lach·lan \'läk-lən\ river 800 *m* SE Australia in *cen* New So. Wales flowing W into the Murrumbidgee

Lack·a·wan·na \,lak-ə-'wän-ə\ city W N.Y. on Lake Erie S of Buffalo *pop* 28,657

La·co·nia \lə-'kō-nē-ə, -nyə\ ancient country S Greece in SE Peloponnesus bordering on the Aegean & the Mediterranean ✻ Sparta — **La·co·nian** \-nē-ən, -nyən\ *adj or n*

Laconia, Gulf of inlet of the Mediterranean on S coast of Greece in Peloponnesus between capes Matapan & Malea

La Co·ru·ña \,läk-ə-'rün-yə\ **1** province NW Spain in Galicia bordering on the Atlantic *area* 3051, *pop* 1,004,188 **2** *or* **Co·run·na** \kə-'rən-ə\ commune & port, its ✻ *pop* 224,055

La Crosse \lə-'krȯs\ city W Wis. *pop* 51,153

La·dakh \lə-'däk\ district N India in E Kashmir on border of Tibet ✻ Leh *area* 45,762 — **La·dakhi** \-'däk-ē\ *adj or n*

Lad·o·ga \'lad-ə-gə, 'läd-\ lake 130 *m* long & 75 *m* wide U.S.S.R. in NW Soviet Russia, Europe, NE of Gulf of Finland *area* 7000; largest in Europe

Ladrone — see MARIANA

La·dy·smith \'lād-ē-,smith\ city E Republic of So. Africa in W Natal *pop* 27,900

Lae \'lā-,ā\ city Papua New Guinea on SE coast on Huon Gulf *pop* 24,339

La·fay·ette \,laf-ē-'et, ,läf-, ,lāf-\ **1** city W Calif. E of Berkeley *pop* 20,484 **2** city W *cen* Ind. *pop* 44,955 **3** city S La. WSW of Baton Rouge *pop* 68,908

La·fleche \lə-'flesh\ city Canada in S Que. E of Montreal *pop* 15,113

La·gash \'lā-,gash\ ancient city of Sumer between the Euphrates & the Tigris at modern village of Telloh \te-'lō\ in S Iraq

Lagoa dos Patos — see PATOS (Lagoa dos)

La·gos \'lā-,gäs\ city & port ✻ of Nigeria on an offshore island in Bight of Benin & on mainland opposite *pop* 875,417

La Gou·lette \,lä-gü-'let\ city N Tunisia on Bay of Tunis; port for Tunis *pop* 31,830

La Grange \lə-'grānj\ **1** city W Ga. *pop* 23,301 **2** village NE Ill. W of Chicago *pop* 16,773

La Grange Park village NE Ill. W of Chicago *pop* 15,626

La Granja — see SAN ILDEFONSO

La Guai·ra \lə-'gwī-rə\ city N Venezuela on the Caribbean; port for Caracas *pop* 20,497

Laguna Madre — see MADRE (Laguna)

La Habana — see HAVANA

La Ha·bra \lə-'häb-rə\ city SW Calif. SE of Los Angeles *pop* 41,350

La Hague, Cape \lə-'hāg, -'häg\ *or* F **Cap de la Hague** \käp-də-lä-äg\ headland NW France at tip of Cotentin peninsula projecting into English channel

La Hogue \lə-'hōg\ roadstead NW France in English channel off E coast of Cotentin peninsula

La·hon·tan, Lake \lə-'hänt-ᵊn\ prehistoric lake NW Nev. & NE Calif.

La·hore \lə-'hō(ə)r, -'hȯ(ə)r\ city Pakistan in E Punjab province near the Ravi *pop* 1,823,000

Lah·ti \'lät-ē\ city S Finland NNE of Helsinki *pop* 89,360

La Jol·la \lə-'hȯi-ə\ a NW section of San Diego, Calif.

Lake Charles \'chär(ə)lz\ city SW La. *pop* 77,998

Lake District region NW England in S Cumberland, W Westmorland, & N Lancashire containing many lakes & peaks

Lake Forest city NE Ill. N of Chicago *pop* 15,642

Lake·land \'lā-klənd\ city *cen* Fla. E of Tampa *pop* 41,550

Lake·wood \'lā-,kwüd\ **1** city SW Calif. NE of Long Beach *pop* 82,973 **2** city N *cen* Colo. W of Denver *pop* 92,787 **3** city NE Ohio on Lake Erie W of Cleveland *pop* 70,173

Lake Worth \'wərth\ city SE Fla. on Lake Worth (lagoon) S of West Palm Beach *pop* 23,714

La Lí·nea \lä-'lē-nē-ə\ commune SW Spain on Bay of Algeciras N of Gibraltar *pop* 57,127

La Man·cha \lə-'män-chə, -'man-\ region S *cen* Spain in S New Castile

La Marque \lə-'märk\ city SE Tex. SE of Houston *pop* 16,131

Lam·ba·ré·né \ˌläm-bə-'rā-nē, -rə-'nā\ city W Gabon, Africa *pop* 17,770

Lam·beth \'lam-bəth, -ˌbeth\ borough of S Greater London, England *pop* 302,616

La Me·sa \lə-'mā-sə\ city SW Calif. NE of San Diego *pop* 39,178

La·mia \lə-'mē-ə\ city E *cen* Greece NW of Thermopylae *pop* 38,495

La Mi·ra·da \ˌläm-ə-'räd-ə\ city SW Calif. SE of Los Angeles *pop* 30,808

Lam·mer·muir \'lam-ər-ˌmyu̇(ə)r\ *or* **Lam·mer·moor** \-ˌmu̇(ə)r\ hills SE Scotland in East Lothian & Berwick — see SAYS LAW

Lam·pe·du·sa \ˌlam-pə-'dü-sə, -zə\ island Italy in the Pelagian islands

La·nai \lə-'nī\ island Hawaii W of Maui *area* 141

Lan·ark \'lan-ərk\ **1** *or* **Lan·ark·shire** \-ˌshi(ə)r, -shər\ county S *cen* Scotland; chief city Glasgow *area* 892, *pop* 1,524,848 **2** burgh, its ✻, on the Clyde SE of Glasgow

Lan·ca·shire \'laŋ-kə-ˌshi(ə)r, -shər\ *or* **Lan·cas·ter** \'laŋ-kə-stər\ county NW England bordering on Irish sea ✻ Preston *area* 1875, *pop* 5,106,123

Lan·cas·ter \'laŋ-kə-stər; 'lan-ˌkas-tər, 'laŋ-\ **1** city S *cen* Ohio SE of Columbus *pop* 32,911 **2** city SE Pa. *pop* 57,690 **3** municipal borough NW England in Lancashire *pop* 49,525 — **Lan·cas·tri·an** \laŋ-'kas-trē-ən, lan-\ *adj or n*

Lan·chow \'län-'jō\ *or* **Kao·lan** \'kau̇-'län\ city N *cen* China ✻ of Kansu *pop* 1,500,000

Landes \'lä^{n}(n)d\ coastal region SW France on Bay of Biscay between Gironde estuary & the Adour

Lands End *or* **Land's End** \'lan(d)-'zend\ cape SW England at SW tip of Cornwall; extreme W point of England, at 5°41'W

Lang·dale Pikes \ˌlaŋ-ˌdāl-\ two mountain peaks NW England in Westmorland in Lake District

Lan·gue·doc \ˌlaŋ-gə-'däk, ˌlä^{n}(ŋ)-gə-'dȯk\ region & former province S France extending from Auvergne to the Mediterranean ✻✻ Toulouse & Montpellier

Lanka — see CEYLON

Lans·dale \'lanz-ˌdāl\ borough SE Pa. NW of Philadelphia *pop* 18,451

Lan·sing \'lan(t)-siŋ\ **1** village NE Ill. SSE of Chicago *pop* 25,805 **2** city ✻ of Mich *pop* 131,546

Lan·tao \'län-'dau̇\ island Hong Kong colony W of Hong Kong I. *area* 58

La·nús \lə-'nüs\ city E Argentina, S suburb of Buenos Aires *pop* 375,428

La·od·i·cea \(ˌ)lā-ˌäd-ə-'sē-ə\ **1** ancient city W *cen* Asia Minor in Phrygia **2** — see LATAKIA — **La·od·i·ce·an** \-'sē-ən\ *adj or n*

Laoighis \'lāsh, 'lēsh\ *or* **Leix** \'lāsh, 'lēsh\ *or formerly* **Queen's** county *cen* Ireland in Leinster ✻ Maryborough *area* 664, *pop* 45,349

Laon \'lä^{n}\ commune N France NE of Paris *pop* 26,316

Laos \'lau̇s, 'läōs\ country SE Asia bordering on the Mekong; a kingdom, formerly a state of French Indochina; administrative ✻ Vientiane, royal ✻ Luang Prabang *area* 91,482, *pop ab* 3,030,000

La Pal·ma \lə-'päl-mə\ island Spain in Canary islands; chief town Santa Cruz de la Palma *area* 280

La Paz \lə-'paz, -'päz, -'päs\ **1** city, administrative ✻ of Bolivia E of Lake Titicaca at altitude of 11,910 *ft*, *pop* 525,000 **2** town W Mexico ✻ of Baja California Sur on La Paz Bay (inlet of Gulf of California)

Lap·land \'lap-ˌland, -lənd\ region N Europe above the arctic circle in N Norway, N Sweden, N Finland, & Kola peninsula of the U.S.S.R. — **Lap·land·er** \-ˌlan-dər, -lən-\ *n*

La Pla·ta \lə-'plät-ə\ city E Argentina SE of Buenos Aires *pop* 337,060

La Plata Peak \lə-ˌplat-ə\ mountain 14,340 *ft*, *cen* Colo. in Sawatch mountains

La Porte \lə-'pō(ə)rt, -'pȯ(ə)rt\ city N Ind. *pop* 22,140

Lap·tev \'lap-ˌtef, -ˌtev\ *or formerly* **Nor·den·skjöld** \'nȯrd-^{ə}n-ˌshəld, -ˌshüld, -ˌshēld\ sea arm of Arctic ocean U.S.S.R. between Taimyr peninsula & New Siberian islands

La Pu·en·te \ˌläp-ü-'ent-ē\ city SW Calif. ESE of Los Angeles *pop* 31,092

L'Aquila — see AQUILA

Lar·a·mie \'lar-ə-mē\ **1** river 200 *m* N Colo. & SE Wyo. flowing N & NE into the No. Platte **2** city SE Wyo. *pop* 23,143

Larch \'lärch\ river 270 *m* Canada in W Que. flowing NE to unite with the Kaniapiskau forming the Koksoak

La·re·do \lə-'rād-(ˌ)ō\ city S Tex. on Rio Grande *pop* 69,024

Lar·go \'lär-(ˌ)gō\ town W Fla. S of Clearwater *pop* 22,031

La·ris·sa \lə-'ris-ə\ city N *cen* Greece in E Thessaly *pop* 72,762

Lar·i·stan \ˌlar-ə-'stan\ region S Iran bordering on Persian gulf

La Ro·chelle \ˌlär-ə-'shel\ city & port W France *pop* 73,347

Lar·vik \'lär-vik\ town & port SE Norway

La·Salle \lə-'sal\ city Canada in S Que. on the St. Lawrence SSW of Montreal *pop* 72,912

Las·caux \la-'skō\ cave SW *cen* France SE of Périgueux near town of Montignac

Las Cru·ces \lä-'skrü-səs\ city S N.Mex. *pop* 37,857

La·shio \lə-'shō\ town E *cen* Burma

Lashkar — see GWALIOR

Las Pal·mas \lä-'späl-məs\ **1** province Spain compising the E Canary islands *area* 1279, *pop* 579,710 **2** city & port, its ✻, in NE Grand Canary I. *pop* 235,061

La Se·re·na \ˌläs-ə-'rā-nə\ city N *cen* Chile *pop* 48,647

La Spe·zia *or* **Spezia** \(lä-)'spet-sē-ə\ city & port NW Italy in Liguria *pop* 112,245

Lassa — see LHASA

Las·sen Peak *or* **Mount Lassen** \'las-^{ə}n\ volcano 10,453 *ft* N Calif. at S end of Cascade range; central feature of **Lassen Volcanic National Park** (area 161)

Las Ve·gas \läs-'vā-gəs\ city SE Nev. *pop* 125,787

Lat·a·kia \ˌlat-ə-'kē-ə\ **1** region NW Syria bordering on the Mediterranean **2** *or anc* **La·od·i·cea** \(ˌ)lā-ˌäd-ə-'sē-ə\ city & port, its chief town, on the Mediterranean *pop* 126,000

Latin America, 1 Spanish America & Brazil **2** all of the Americas S of the U.S. — **Latin–American** *adj* — **Latin American** *n*

La·tium \'lā-sh(ē-)əm\ *or* It **La·zio** \'lät-sē-ˌō\ region *cen* Italy bordering on Tyrrhenian sea & traversed by the Tiber ✻ Rome

Lat·via \'lat-vē-ə\ country N *cen* Europe bordering on the Baltic; an independent republic 1918–40, since 1940 a constituent republic (**Lat·vi·an Republic** \ˌlat-vē-ən-\) of the U.S.S.R. ✻ Riga *area* 25,200, *pop* 2,365,000

Laun·ces·ton \'lȯn(t)-sə-stən, 'län(t)-\ city & port Australia in N Tasmania *pop* (with suburbs) 36,620

Lau·rel \'lȯr-əl, 'lär-\ city SE Miss. *pop* 24,145

Lau·ren·tian \lȯ-'ren-chən\ *or* **Lau·ren·tide** \'lȯr-ən-ˌtīd, 'lär-\ hills Canada in S Que. N of the St. Lawrence on S edge of Laurentian Highlands

Laurentian Highlands *or* **Laurentian Upland** *or* **Canadian Shield** plateau region E Canada & NE U.S. extending from Mackenzie basin E to Davis strait & S to S Que., S Ont., NE Minn., N Wis., NW Mich., & NE N.Y. including the Adirondacks

Lau·ri·um \'lȯr-ē-əm, 'lär-\ mountain SE Greece at SE tip of Attica

Lau·sanne \lō-'zän, -'zan\ commune W Switzerland ✻ of Vaud canton on Lake Geneva *pop* 138,300

Lausitz — see LUSATIA

Lausitzer Neisse — see NEISSE

Lava Beds National Monument reservation N Calif. SE of Lower Klamath Lake *area* 72

La·val \lə-'val\ city Canada in S Que. NW of Montreal *pop* 220,010

La Vendée — see VENDÉE

Lawn·dale \'lȯn-ˌdāl, 'län-\ city SW Calif. SSW of Los Angeles *pop* 24,825

Law·rence \'lȯr-ən(t)s, 'lär-\ **1** town *cen* Ind. NE of Indianapolis *pop* 16,646 **2** city NE Kans. WSW of Kansas City *pop* 45,698 **3** city NE Mass. *pop* 66,915

Law·ton \'lȯt-^{ə}n\ city SW Okla. *pop* 74,470

Lay·san \'lī-ˌsän\ island Hawaii in the Leewards *ab* 750 *m* NW of Niihau I.

Leam·ing·ton \'lem-iŋ-tən\ *or* **Royal Leamington Spa** municipal borough S *cen* England in Warwickshire *pop* 44,989

Leav·en·worth \'lev-ən-ˌwərth\ city NE Kans. on the Missouri NW of Kansas City *pop* 25,147

Leb·a·non, 1 \'leb-ə-nən\ city SE *cen* Pa. E of Harrisburg *pop* 28,572 **2** \-nən, -ˌnän\ *or anc* **Lib·a·nus** \'lib-ə-nəs\ mountains Lebanon running parallel to coast W of Bika valley; highest point Dahr el Qadib 10,131 *ft* **3** country SW Asia bordering on the Mediterranean; a republic since 1944, formerly (1920–44) a French mandate ✻ Beirut *area* 4105, *pop* 2,870,000 — **Leb·a·nese** \ˌleb-ə-'nēz, -'nēs\ *adj or n*

Lebda — see HOMS

Le Bour·get \lə-ˌbu̇r-'zhā\ commune N France, NE suburb of Paris

Lec·ce \'lā-chē, 'lech-ē\ commune SE Italy in Apulia SE of Brindisi *pop* 81,048

Lec·co \'lā-(ˌ)kō, 'lek-(ˌ)ō\ commune N Italy in Lombardy on SE arm (**Lake Lecco**) of Lake Como *pop* 51,991

Lech \'lek, 'lek\ river 177 *m* Austria & Germany flowing from the Vorarlberg N into the Danube

Le·do \'lēd-(ˌ)ō, 'lād-\ town NE India in NE Assam

Leeds \'lēdz\ city & county borough N England in West Riding, Yorkshire, on the Aire *pop* 494,971

Lee's Summit \'lēz-\ city W Mo. SE of Kansas City *pop* 16,230

Leeu·war·den \'lā-ˌvärd-^{ə}n\ commune N Netherlands ✻ of Friesland *pop* 88,668

Lee·ward \'lē-wərd\ **1** island chain *cen* Pacific extending 1250 *m* WNW from main islands of the Hawaiian group; includes Nihoa, Necker, Laysan, Midway, & Kure islands **2** *or* F **Iles sous le Vent** \ēl-sü-lə-vä^{n}\ islands S Pacific, W group of the Society islands **3** islands West Indies in the N Lesser Antilles extending from Virgin islands (on N) to Dominica (on S) **4** former colony Brit. West Indies in the Leewards including territories of Antigua, St. Kitts-Nevis, & Montserrat

Leg·horn \'leg-ˌ(h)ō(ə)rn\ *or* It **Li·vor·no** \lē-'vȯr-(ˌ)nō\ commune & port *cen* Italy in Tuscany on Tyrrhenian sea *pop* 173,317

Leh \'lā\ town E Kashmir on the Indus ✻ of Ladakh

Le Ha·vre \lə-'hävr^{ə}\ *or* **Havre** *or formerly* **Le Ha·vre–de–Grâce** \lə-ˌhäv-rəd-ə-'gräs, -ˌhäv-də-\ city & port N France on English channel on N side of Seine estuary *pop* 199,509

Le·high \'lē-ˌhī\ river 100 *m* E Pa. flowing SW & SE into the Delaware

Leh·man Caves \ˌlē-mən-\ limestone caverns E Nev. on E slope of Wheeler Peak in **Lehman Caves National Monument** *area* 1

Leices·ter \'les-tər\ **1** *or* **Leices·ter·shire** \-ˌshi(ə)r, -shər\ county *cen* England *area* 832, *pop* 771,213 **2** city & county borough, its ✻, ENE of Birmingham *pop* 283,549

Lei·den *or* **Ley·den** \'līd-^{ə}n, *Du usu* 'lā-yə\ city W Netherlands in So. Holland on a branch of the lower Rhine *pop* 101,878

Leie — see LYS

Lein·ster \'len(t)-stər\ province E Ireland *area* 7580, *pop* 1,494,544

Leip·zig \'līp-sig, -sik\ *or* **Leip·sic** \-sik\ city E Germany in Saxony SSW of Berlin *pop* 587,761

Lei·ria \lā-'rē-ə\ town W *cen* Portugal SSW of Coimbra

Leith \'lēth\ port section of Edinburgh, Scotland, on Firth of Forth; formerly a burgh

Lei·tha \'lī-(ˌ)tä\ river 112 *m* E Austria & NW Hungary flowing SE into the Raba

Lei·trim \'lē-trəm\ county NW Ireland in Connacht ✻ Carrick on Shannon *area* 589, *pop* 28,313

Leix — see LAOIGHIS

ə abut ^{ə} kitten, F table   ər further   a back   ā bake
ä cot, cart   ȧ F bac   au̇ out   ch chin   e less   ē easy
g gift   i trip   ī life   j joke   k̲ G ich ^{n} F vin   ŋ sing
ō flow   ȯ flaw   œ F bœuf   œ̄ F feu   ȯi coin   th thing
t̲h̲ this   ü loot   u̇ foot   ue G Füllen   ūē F rue   y yet
^{y} F digne \dēn^{y}\, nuit \nw^{y}ē\   yü few   yu̇ furious   zh vision

Lei·xões \lā-'shōiⁿsh\ town NW Portugal on the Atlantic; port for Oporto
Lek \'lek\ river 40 *m* Netherlands flowing W into the Atlantic; the N branch of the lower Rhine
Le Maine — see MAINE
Leman, Lake — see GENEVA (Lake)
Le Mans \lə-'mäⁿ\ city NW France *pop* 143,246
Le Marche — see MARCHES
Lemberg — see LVOV
Lem·nos \'lem-,näs, -nəs\ *or* NGk **Lím·nos** \'lēm-,nȯs\ island Greece in the Aegean ESE of Chalcidice peninsula; chief town Kástron *area* 175
Le·na \'lē-nə, 'lā-\ river 3000 *m* U.S.S.R. in W Soviet Russia, Asia, flowing from mountains W of Lake Baikal NE & N into Laptev sea through wide delta
Len·in·grad \'len-ən-,grad\ *or formerly* (1703–1914) **Saint Pe·ters·burg** \sānt-'pēt-ərz-,bərg, sənt-\ *or* (1914–24) **Pet·ro·grad** \'pe-trə-,grad\ city U.S.S.R. in NW Soviet Russia, Europe, at E end of Gulf of Finland ✱ of Russian Empire 1712–1917, *pop* 3,513,000 — **Len·in·grad·er** \'len-ən-,grad-ər\ *n*
Le·nin Peak \,len-ən-, ,län-, -,ēn-\ mountain 23,386 *ft* on border between Kirgiz & Tadzhik republics; highest in Trans Alai range
Leom·in·ster \'lem-ən-stər\ city *cen* Mass. N of Worcester *pop* 32,939
Le·ón \lā-'ōn\ **1** *or* **León de los Al·da·mas** \-də-,lō-,sal-'däm-əs\ city *cen* Mexico in Guanajuato *pop* 453,976 **2** city W Nicaragua *pop* 90,897 **3** region & ancient kingdom NW Spain W of Old Castile **4** province NW Spain in N León region *area* 5936, *pop* 648,721 **5** city, its ✱ *pop* 105,235
Le·o·ne, Mon·te \,mōn-tē-lā-'ō-nē\ mountain 11,684 *ft* on border between Switzerland & Italy SW of Simplon Pass; highest in Lepontine Alps
Le·o·pold II, Lake \'lē-ə-,pōld, 'lā-\ lake 90 *m* long W Zaire
Léopoldville — see KINSHASA
Lepanto — see NÁVPAKTOS
Lepanto, Gulf of —see CORINTH (Gulf of)
Le·pon·tine Alps \li-,pän-,tīn-, ,lep-ən-\ range of *cen* Alps on border between Switzerland & Italy — see LEONE (Monte)
Leptis Magna — see HOMS
Lé·ri·da \'lā-rəd-ə, 'ler-əd-\ **1** province NE Spain in NW Catalonia *area* 4690, *pop* 347,015 **2** commune, its ✱ *pop* 90,884
Ler·wick \'lər-(,)wik, 'le(ə)r-\ burgh & port N Scotland ✱ of Shetland on Mainland I.
Les·bos \'lez-,bäs, -bəs\ *or* **Myt·i·le·ne** \,mit-ᵊl-'ē-nē\ *or* NGk **Lés·vos** \'lez-,vȯs\ *or* **Mi·ti·lí·ni** \,mit-ᵊl-'ē-nē\ island Greece in the Aegean off NW coast of Turkey *area* 623
Les Ey·zies \,lā-zā-'zē\ commune SW *cen* France SE of Périgueux
Le·so·tho \lə-'sō-(,)tō\ *or formerly* **Ba·su·to·land** \bə-'süt-ə-,land\ country S Africa surrounded by Republic of So. Africa; a constitutional monarchy in Brit. Commonwealth ✱ Maseru *area* 11,716, *pop* 930,000
Lesser An·til·les \an-'til-ēz\ islands in the West Indies including Virgin, Leeward, & Windward islands, Trinidad, Barbados, Tobago, & islands in the S Caribbean N of Venezuela
Lesser Armenia region S Turkey corresponding to ancient Cilicia
Lesser Khingan — see KHINGAN
Lesser Slave \'slāv\ lake Canada in *cen* Alta. draining through the Lesser Slave river to the Athabasca *area* 461
Lesser Sunda — see SUNDA
Leth·bridge \'leth-(,)brij\ city Canada in S Alta. *pop* 41,217
Le·ti·cia \lə-'tē-sē-ə\ town SE Colombia on the Amazon on Colombia-Peru border
Letzeburg — see LUXEMBOURG
Leu·cas \'lü-kəs\ *or* **Leu·ca·dia** \lü-'kād-ē-ə\ *or* NGk **Lev·kás** \lef-'käs\ island Greece in Ionian islands at entrance to Ambracian Gulf *area* 111
Leuc·tra \'lük-trə\ ancient village Greece in Boeotia SW of Thebes
Leuven — see LOUVAIN
Le·val·lois-Per·ret \lə-'val-,wä-pə-'rā\ commune N France on the Seine, NW suburb of Paris *pop* 59,941
Le·vant \lə-'vant\ the countries bordering on the E Mediterranean — **Le·van·tine** \'lev-ən-,tīn, -,tēn, lə-'van-\ *adj or n*
Levant States — see SYRIA
Le·ven, Loch \'lē-vən\ **1** inlet of Loch Linnhe W Scotland between Argyll & Inverness counties **2** lake 4 *m* long E Scotland in Kinross SSE of Perth
Le·ver·ku·sen \lā-vər-'küz-ᵊn\ city W Germany on the Rhine SE of Düsseldorf *pop* 110,800
Lé·vis \'lē-vəs\ city Canada in S Que. *pop* 16,597
Lew·es \'lü-əs\ **1** the upper Yukon river S of its junction with the Pelly **2** municipal borough S England ✱ of East Sussex on the Ouse S of London
Lew·is and Clark \,lü-ə-sən-'klärk\ **1** lake 30 *m* long SE S.Dak. & NE Nebr. formed by Gavins Point Dam **2** *or* **Mor·ri·son Cave** \'mȯr-ə-sən-, 'mär-\ cavern *cen* Mont. WNW of Bozeman
Lew·i·sham \'lü-ə-shəm\ borough of SE Greater London, England *pop* 264,800
Lew·is·ton \'lü-ə-stən\ **1** city NW Idaho on Wash. border *pop* 26,068 **2** city SW Me. on the Androscoggin opposite Auburn *pop* 41,779
Lew·is with Har·ris \,lü-ə-swəth-'har-əs, -swəth-\ island NW Scotland in the Outer Hebrides divided administratively into **Lewis** (in the N, in Ross and Cromarty county, chief town & port Stornoway) & **Harris** (in the S, in Inverness county); largest of the Hebrides *area* 770
Lex·ing·ton \'lek-siŋ-tən\ **1** city N *cen* Ky. *pop* 108,137 **2** town NE Mass. NW of Boston *pop* 31,886 **3** city N *cen* N.C. *pop* 17,205
Leyden — see LEIDEN
Ley·te \'lāt-ē\ island Philippines in the Visayans S of Samar; chief town Tacloban *area* 2785
Leyte Gulf inlet of the Pacific in Philippines E of Leyte & S of Samar
Ley·ton \'lāt-ᵊn\ former municipal borough SE England in Essex, now part of Waltham Forest

Lha·sa *or* **Las·sa** \'läs-ə, 'las-\ city SE Tibet ✱ of Tibet *pop* 175,000
Lho·tse \'(h)lōt-'sā\ *or* **E¹** \'ē-'wən\ mountain 27,923 *ft* in Mt. Everest massif S of Mt. Everest; 4th highest in the world
Liao \lē-'aů\ river 700 *m* NE China flowing into Gulf of Liaotung
Liao·ning \lē-'aů-'niŋ\ *or formerly* **Feng·tien** \'fəŋ-tē-'en\ province NE China in S Manchuria ✱ Mukden *area* 58,301, *pop* 28,000,000
Liao·si \lē-'aů-'shē\ former province (1948–54) NE China in S Manchuria bordering on Gulf of Liaotung ✱ Chinchow *area* 2500
Liao·tung \lē-'aů-'důŋ\ peninsula NE China in S Liaoning between Korea Bay & **Gulf of Liaotung** (arm of Po Hai)
Liao·yang \lē-'aů-'yäŋ\ city NE China in *cen* Liaoning NE of Anshan *pop* 250,000
Liao·yüan \lē-'aů-yů-'än\ city NE China in W Kirin S of Changchun on the Liao *pop* 123,100
Li·ard \'lē-ərd\ river 755 *m* W Canada flowing from Stikine mountains in Yukon Territory E & N into the Mackenzie
Libanus — see LEBANON
Li·be·rec \'lib-ə-,rets\ city W Czechoslovakia in N Bohemia *pop* 72,640
Li·be·ria \lī-'bir-ē-ə\ country W Africa; a republic ✱ Monrovia *area* 43,000, *pop* 1,570,000 — **Li·be·ri·an** \-ē-ən\ *adj or n*
Lib·er·ty \'lib-ərt-ē\ *or* **Bed·loe's** \'bed-,lōz\ island SE N.Y. in Upper New York Bay; comprises **Statue of Liberty National Monument**
Li·bre·ville \'lē-brə-,vil, -,vē(ə)l\ city & port ✱ of Gabon at mouth of Gabon river *pop* 57,000
Lib·ya \'lib-ē-ə\ **1** the part of Africa N of the Sahara between Egypt & Syrtis Major (Gulf of Sidra) — an ancient name **2** northern Africa W of Egypt — an ancient name **3** *or* **Lib·y·an Arab Republic** \'lib-ē-ən\ country N Africa bordering on the Mediterranean; a colony of Italy 1912–43, an independent kingdom 1951–69, a republic since 1969 ✱ ✱ Tripoli & Benghazi *area* 679,358, *pop* 2,010,000
Lib·y·an \'lib-ē-ən\ desert N Africa W of the Nile in Libya, Egypt, & Sudan
Lich·field \'lich-,fēld\ municipal borough W *cen* England in Staffordshire *pop* 22,672
Lick·ing \'lik-iŋ\ river 350 *m* NE Ky. flowing NW into the Ohio
Li·di·ce \'lid-ə(t)-sē, -,sā\ village W Czechoslovakia in W *cen* Bohemia WNW of Prague
Li·do \'lēd-(,)ō\ island Italy in the Adriatic separating Lagoon of Venice & Gulf of Venice
Liech·ten·stein \'lik-tən-,s(h)tīn\ country W Europe between Switzerland & Austria bordering on the Rhine; a principality ✱ Vaduz *area* 62, *pop* 20,000 — **Liech·ten·stein·er** \-,s(h)tī-nər\ *n*
Li·ège \lē-'ezh, -'āzh\ *or* Flem **Luik** \'līk\ **1** province E Belgium *area* 1525, *pop* 1,019,309 **2** city, its ✱ *pop* 148,599
Lie·pa·ja \lē-'ep-ə-yə, -'ep-,ä-yə\ *or* G **Li·bau** \'lē-,baů\ city & port U.S.S.R. in W Latvia on the Baltic *pop* 88,000
Lif·fey \'lif-ē\ river 50 *m* E Ireland flowing into Dublin Bay
Lif·ford \'lif-ərd\ town NW Republic of Ireland in Ulster ✱ of County Donegal
Li·gu·ria \lə-'gyůr-ē-ə\ region NW Italy bordering on Ligurian sea ✱ Genoa — **Li·gu·ri·an** \-ē-ən\ *adj or n*
Ligurian sea arm of the Mediterranean N of Corsica
Li·ka·si \li-'käs-ē\ *or formerly* **Ja·dot·ville** \,zhad-ō-'vē(ə)l, zha-'dō-,vil\ city SE Zaire in SE Shaba *pop* 146,394
Lille \'lē(ə)l\ *or formerly* **Lisle** \'lē(ə)l, 'lī(ə)l city N France; medieval ✱ of Flanders *pop* 190,546
Li·ma, 1 \'lī-mə\ city NW Ohio *pop* 53,734 **2** \'lē-mə\ city ✱ of Peru E of Callao *pop* 2,541,300
Li·may \lē-'mī\ river 250 *m* W Argentina flowing out of Lake Nahuel Huapí & joining the Neuquén forming the Negro
Lim·burg \'lim-,bərg\ **1** region W Europe E of the Meuse including parts of present Limburg province, Netherlands, & Limburg province, Belgium **2** province NE Belgium ✱ Hasselt *area* 929, *pop* 656,477 **3** province SE Netherlands ✱ Maastricht *area* 851, *pop* 998,570
Lime·house \'līm-,haůs\ district E London, England, in Tower Hamlets on N bank of the Thames
Lim·er·ick \'lim-(ə-)rik\ **1** county SW Ireland in Munster *area* 1037, *pop* 140,370 **2** city & county borough & port, its ✱, on the Shannon *pop* 57,137
Límnos — see LEMNOS
Li·moges \lē-'mōzh, -'mȯzh\ city SW *cen* France *pop* 132,935
Li·món *or* **Puer·to Limón** \(,pwert-ō-)li-'mōn\ city & port E Costa Rica on the Caribbean *pop* 22,555
Li·mou·sin \,lē-mü-'zaⁿ\ region & former province S *cen* France W of Auvergne ✱ Limoges
Lim·po·po \lim-'pō-(,)pō\ *or* **Croc·o·dile** \'kräk-ə-,dīl\ river 1000 *m* S Africa flowing from Transvaal, Republic of So. Africa, into Indian ocean in Mozambique
Li·na·res \li-'när-əs\ commune S Spain N of Jaén *pop* 31,878
Lin·coln \'liŋ-kən\ **1** city *cen* Ill. *pop* 17,582 **2** city ✱ of Nebr. *pop* 149,518 **3** town N R.I. *pop* 16,182 **4** *or* **Lin·coln·shire** \-,shi(ə)r, -shər\ county E England bordering on North sea between Humber river & the Wash — see HOLLAND (Parts of), KESTEVEN (Parts of), LINDSEY (Parts of) **5** city & county borough E England in Lincolnshire ✱ of Parts of Lindsey *pop* 74,207
Lincoln Park city SE Mich. SW of Detroit *pop* 52,984
Lin·den \'lin-dən\ city NE N.J. SSW of Elizabeth *pop* 41,409
Lin·den·hurst \'lin-dən-,hərst\ village SE N.Y. in *cen* Long I. *pop* 28,338
Lin·des·nes \'lin-də-,snās\ *or* **the Naze** \'nāz\ cape Norway at S tip projecting into North sea
Lindisfarne — see HOLY
Lind·sey, Parts of \'lin-zē\ administrative county E England in N Lincolnshire ✱ Lincoln *area* 1520, *pop* 470,526
Line \'līn\ islands *cen* Pacific S of Hawaii divided between the U.S. (Kingman Reef & Palmyra) & Great Britain (Washington, Fanning, & Christmas) with some in dispute
Lin·ga·yen Gulf \,liŋ-gə-,yen-\ inlet of So. China sea Philippines in NW Luzon

Lin·guet·ta, Cape \liŋ-'gwet-ə\ *or* **Cape Glos·sa** \'gläs-ə\ *or anc* **Ac·ro·ce·rau·nia** \ˌak-rō-sə-'rò-nē-ə\ cape SW Albania projecting into Strait of Otranto

Lin·kö·ping \'lin-ˌchə(r)p-iŋ\ city SE Sweden *pop* 80,760

Lin·lith·gow \lin-'lith-(ˌ)gō\ **1** *or* **Lin·lith·gow·shire** \-ˌshi(ə)r, -shər\ — see WEST LOTHIAN **2** burgh SE Scotland ✻ of West Lothian

Linn·he, Loch \'lin-ē\ inlet of the Atlantic on W coast of Scotland in Argyll extending NE from head of Firth of Lorne

Linz \'lin(t)s, 'linz\ city N Austria on the Danube *pop* 205,808

Li·ons, Gulf of \'lī-ənz\ *or* F **Golfe du Lion** \gȯlf-dü̅e-lyō^{n}\ arm of the Mediterranean on S coast of France

Lip·a·ri \'lip-ə-rē\ **1** *or* **Ae·o·lian islands** \ē-'ō-lē-ən, -'ōl-yən\ *or* It **Iso·le Eo·lie** \'ē-zə-ˌlā-ā-'ō-lē-ˌā\ islands Italy in SE Tyrrhenian sea off NE Sicily *area* 45 — see STROMBOLI **2** *or anc* **Lip·a·ra** \'lip-ə-rə\ island, chief of the Lipari group

Li·petsk \'lē-ˌpetsk\ city U.S.S.R. in S *cen* Soviet Russia, Europe, N of Voronezh *pop* 290,000

Lip·pe \'lip-ə\ **1** river 150 *m* W Germany flowing from Teutoberger Wald W into the Rhine **2** former principality & state Germany between Teutoberger Wald & the Weser ✻ Detmold

Li·ri \'lir-ē\ river 100 *m, cen* Italy flowing into Gulf of Gaeta

Lis·bon \'liz-bən\ *or* Port **Lis·boa** \lēzh-'vō-ə\ city & port ✻ of Portugal on estuary of the Tagus *pop* 830,600 — **Lis·bo·an** \liz-'bō-ən\ *n*

Lis·burne, Cape \'liz-bərn\ cape NW Alaska projecting into Arctic ocean near W end of Brooks range

Li·sieux \lēz-'yə(r), -'yœ̅\ city NW France E of Caen *pop* 23,830

Lith·u·a·nia \ˌlith-(y)ə-'wā-nē-ə, -nyə\ *or* Lith **Lie·tu·va** \lē-ˌe-tü-'vä\ country N *cen* Europe bordering on the Baltic; remnant of a medieval principality extending from Baltic sea to Black sea; a republic 1918–40, since 1940 a constituent republic **(Lithuanian Republic)** of the U.S.S.R. ✻ Vilnius *area* 31,200, *pop* 3,129,000

Little Abaco — see ABACO

Little Bighorn river 80 *m* N Wyo. & S Mont. flowing N into the Bighorn

Little Colorado river 300 *m* NE Ariz. flowing NW into the Colorado

Little Diomede — see DIOMEDE

Little Inagua — see INAGUA

Little Kabylia — see KABYLIA

Little Karroo — see KARROO

Little Minch — see MINCH

Little Missouri river 560 *m* W U.S. flowing from NE Wyo. N into the Missouri in W N.Dak.

Little Namaqualand — see NAMAQUALAND

Lit·tle Rock \'lit-ᵊl-ˌräk\ city ✻ of Ark. on Arkansas river *pop* 132,483

Little Saint Bernard mountain pass 7177 *ft* over Savoy Alps between France & Italy S of Mont Blanc

Lit·tle·ton \'lit-əl-tən\ town N *cen* Colo. S of Denver *pop* 26,466

Little Walachia — see OLTENIA

Liuchiu — see RYUKYU

Liu·chow \lē-'ü-'jō\ city S China in *cen* Kwangsi *pop* 158,800

Liv·er·more \'liv-ər-ˌmō(ə)r, -ˌmȯ(ə)r\ city W Calif. SE of Oakland *pop* 37,703

Liv·er·pool \'liv-ər-ˌpül\ city & county borough & port NW England in Lancashire on Mersey estuary *pop* 606,834 — **Liv·er·pud·li·an** \ˌliv-ər-'pəd-lē-ən\ *adj or n*

Liv·ing·stone \'liv-iŋ-stən\ city S Zambia on the Zambezi near Victoria Falls *pop* 41,000

Livingstone Falls rapids in lower Congo river W equatorial Africa below Stanley Pool; a series of cascades dropping *ab* 900 *ft* in 220 *m*

Li·vo·nia \lə-'vō-nē-ə, -nyə\ **1** region *cen* Europe bordering on the Baltic in Latvia & Estonia **2** city SE Mich. W of Detroit *pop* 110,109 — **Li·vo·nian** \-nē-ən, -nyən\ *adj or n*

Livorno — see LEGHORN

Lizard Head *or* **Lizard Point** headland SW England in S Cornwall at S tip of the **Lizard** (peninsula projecting into English channel); extreme S point of Great Britain, at 49°57′30″N, 5°12′W

Lju·blja·na \lē-ˌü-blē-'än-ə\ city NW Yugoslavia ✻ of Slovenia on the Sava *pop* 172,000

Llan·ber·is \(h)lan-'ber-əs\ village NW Wales in Caernarvonshire near Mt. Snowdon at entrance to **Pass of Llanberis** (1169 *ft*)

Llan·drin·dod Wells \(h)lan-'drin-ˌdäd\ urban district E Wales ✻ of Radnorshire

Llan·dud·no \(h)lan-'did-(ˌ)nō, -'dəd-\ urban district NW Wales on coast of Caernarvonshire *pop* 19,009

Lla·nel·li \(h)la-'nel-ē\ municipal borough & port S Wales in Carmarthenshire *pop* 26,320

Llan·gef·ni \(h)lan-'gev-nē\ urban district NW Wales ✻ of Anglesey, on Anglesey I.

Lla·no Es·ta·ca·do \'lan-(ˌ)ō-ˌes-tə-'käd-(ˌ)ō, 'län-\ *or* **Staked Plain** \'stāk(t)-\ plateau region SE N.Mex. & NW Tex.

Llu·llai·lla·co \ˌyü-ˌyī-'yäk-(ˌ)ō\ volcano 22,057 *ft* N Chile in Andes mountains on Argentina border SE of Antofagasta

Loanda — see LUANDA

Lo·an·ge \lō-'aŋ-gə\ *or* Port **Lu·an·gue** \lü-'aŋ-gə\ river 425 *m* NE Angola & SW Congo flowing N into the Kasai

Lo·bi·to \lō-'bēt-(ˌ)ō\ city & port W Angola *pop* 97,758

Lo·bos, Point \'lō-bəs\ **1** promontory Calif. in San Francisco on S side of entrance to the Golden Gate **2** promontory Calif. on the Pacific SW of Monterey

Lo·car·no \lō-'kär-(ˌ)nō\ commune SE *cen* Switzerland in Ticino canton on N shore of Lake Maggiore

Loch·gilp·head \läk-'gilp-ˌhed\ burgh W Scotland ✻ of Argyll

Lock·port \'läk-ˌpō(ə)rt, -ˌpȯ(ə)rt\ city W N.Y. NE of Buffalo *pop* 25,399

Lo·cris \'lō-krəs, 'läk-rəs\ region of ancient Greece N of Gulf of Corinth — **Lo·cri·an** \'lō-krē-ən, 'läk-rē-\ *adj or n*

Lod — see LYDDA

Lo·di, **1** \'lōd-ˌī\ city *cen* Calif. SSE of Sacramento *pop* 28,691 **2** \'lōd-ˌī\ borough NE N.J. SE of Paterson *pop* 25,213 **3** \'lȯd-(ˌ)ē\ commune N Italy in Lombardy SE of Milan *pop* 42,577

Lodz \'lüj, 'lädz\ city *cen* Poland WSW of Warsaw *pop* 751,300

Lo·fo·ten \'lō-ˌfōt-ᵊn\ island group Norway off NW coast SW of Vesterålen *area* 475

Lo·gan \'lō-gən\ city N Utah *pop* 22,333

Logan, Mount mountain 19,850 *ft* Canada in SW Yukon Territory; highest in St. Elias & Coast ranges & in Canada

Lo·gans·port \'lō-gən-ˌspō(ə)rt, -ˌspȯ(ə)rt\ city N *cen* Ind. NNW of Kokomo *pop* 19,255

Lo·gro·ño \lə-'grōn-(ˌ)yō\ **1** province N Spain in NE Old Castile *area* 1946, *pop* 235,713 **2** commune, its ✻, on the Ebro *pop* 84,456

Loire \lə-'wär\ river 625 *m, cen* France flowing from the Massif Central NW & W into Bay of Biscay

Lol·land \'läl-ənd\ *or* **Laa·land** \'lō-ˌlän\ island Denmark in the Baltic S of Sjælland *area* 477

Lo·ma·mi \lō-'mäm-ē\ river 900 *m, cen* Zaire flowing N into Congo river

Lo·mas \'lō-ˌmäs\ *or* **Lo·mas de Za·mo·ra** \-ˌmäz-də-zə-'mōr-ə, -'mȯr-\ city E Argentina SW of Buenos Aires *pop* 275,219

Lom·bard \'läm-ˌbärd\ village NE Ill. W of Chicago *pop* 35,977

Lom·bar·dy \-ˌbärd-ē, -bərd-\ *or* It **Lom·bar·dia** \ˌläm-bər-'dē-ə\ region N Italy chiefly N of Po river ✻ Milan

Lom·blen \läm-'blen\ island Indonesia in the Lesser Sundas E of Flores *area* 468

Lom·bok \'läm-ˌbäk\ island Indonesia in the Lesser Sundas E of Bali; chief town Mataram *area* 1825

Lo·mé \lō-'mā\ city & port ✻ of Togo *pop* 94,800

Lo·mi·ta \lō-'mēt-ə\ city SW Calif. S of Los Angeles *pop* 19,784

Lo·mond, Ben \ben-'lō-mənd\ mountain 3192 *ft* S *cen* Scotland on E side of Loch Lomond

Lomond, Loch lake 24 *m* long S *cen* Scotland *area* 27

Lom·poc \'läm-ˌpōk\ city SW Calif. W of Santa Barbara *pop* 25,284

Lon·don \'lən-dən\ **1** city Canada in SE Ont. on the Thames *pop* 223,222 **2** city & port SE England formerly constituting an administrative county ✻ of United Kingdom; comprises City of London & 12 inner boroughs of Greater London *area* 117, *pop* 2,723,483 **3** *or* **City of London** *or anc* **Lon·din·i·um** \län-'din-ē-əm, ˌlən-\ city within Greater London, England, on the Thames *area* 675 acres, *pop* 4234 **4** GREATER LONDON — **Lon·don·er** \-də-nər\ *n*

Lon·don·der·ry \ˌlən-dən-'der-ē, 'lən-dən-ˌ\ *or* **Der·ry** \'der-ē\ **1** county NW Northern Ireland *area* 804, *pop* 182,173 **2** county borough & port, its ✻, on the Foyle *pop* 51,617

Long Beach, **1** city & port SW Calif. S of Los Angeles on San Pedro Bay *pop* 358,633 **2** city SE N.Y. on island S of Long I. *pop* 33,127

Long Branch city E *cen* N.J. on the Atlantic *pop* 31,774

Long·fel·low mountains \'lȯŋ-ˌfel-ō, -ˌfel-ə\ the Appalachian mountains in Me.; so named 1959

Long·ford \'lȯŋ-fərd\ **1** county E *cen* Ireland in Leinster *area* 403, *pop* 28,227 **2** urban district, its ✻

Long Island island 118 *m* long SE N.Y. S of Conn. *area* 1401

Long Island City section of New York City in NW Queens

Long Island Sound inlet of the Atlantic between Conn. & Long I.

Long·mead·ow \'lȯŋ-'med-(ˌ)ō, -ə(-w)\ town SW Mass. S of Springfield *pop* 15,630

Long·mont \'lȯŋ-ˌmänt\ city N Colo. N of Denver *pop* 23,209

Longs Peak \'lȯŋz-\ mountain 14,255 *ft* N *cen* Colo. in Front range in Rocky Mountain National Park

Lon·gueuil \lȯŋ-'gā(ə)l\ city Canada in S Que. E of Montreal *pop* 97,590

Long·view \'lȯŋ-ˌvyü\ **1** city NE Tex. *pop* 45,547 **2** city SW Wash. on the Columbia *pop* 28,373

Long·xuyên \laùŋ-'swē-ən\ city S Vietnam in SW Cochin China on S side of Mekong delta *pop* 47,401

Lookout, Cape cape E N.C. on the Atlantic SW of Cape Hatteras

Lookout Mountain ridge 2126 *ft* SE Tenn., NW Ga., & NE Ala. near Chattanooga, Tenn.

Lo·rain \lə-'rān, lō-\ city N Ohio on Lake Erie *pop* 78,185

Lor·ca \'lȯr-kə\ commune SE Spain SW of Murcia *pop* 60,609

Lord Howe \lȯ(ə)rd-'haù\ island Australia in Tasman sea 436 *m* ENE of Sydney belonging to New So. Wales *area* 5

Lo·re·to \lə-'rāt-(ˌ)ō, -'ret-\ commune *cen* Italy in the Marches S of Ancona

Lo·ri·ent \ˌlȯr-ē-'ä^{n}\ commune & port NW France in Brittany on Bay of Biscay *pop* 66,444

Lorne, Firth of \'lȯ(ə)rn\ strait W Scotland between E Mull I. & mainland

Lor·raine \lə-'rān, lō-\ *or* G **Lo·thring·en** \'lō-triŋ-ən\ region & former duchy NE France around upper Moselle & Meuse rivers; remnant (Upper Lorraine) of medieval kingdom of **Lo·tha·rin·gia** \ˌlō-thə-'rin-j(ē)ə\ including also territory to N (Lower Lorraine) between the Rhine & the Scheldt — see ALSACE-LORRAINE

Los Al·tos \lō-'sal-təs\ city W Calif. SSE of Palo Alto *pop* 24,956

Los An·ge·les, **1** \lō-'san-jə-ləs *also* -'saŋ-g(ə-)ləs\ city & port SW Calif. on the Pacific *pop* 2,816,061 **2** \lō-'säŋ-hā-ˌlās\ city S *cen* Chile *pop* 41,719

Los Gat·os \lōs-'gat-əs\ city W Calif. S of San José *pop* 23,735

Lot \'lät, 'lōt\ river 300 *m* S France flowing W into the Garonne

Lo·thi·an \'lō-th̲ē-ən\ region S Scotland bordering on Firth of Forth; now divided into three counties (the **Lothians**): East Lothian, Midlothian, & West Lothian

Lough·bor·ough \'ləf-ˌbər-ə, -ˌbə-rə, -b(ə-)rə\ municipal borough *cen* England in Leicestershire S of Nottingham *pop* 45,863

Lou·ise, Lake \lu̇-ˈēz\ lake W Canada in SW Alta. in Banff National Park
Lou·i·si·ade \lu̇-ˌē-zē-ˈäd, -ˈad\ archipelago in Solomon sea SE of New Guinea; belongs to Papua
Lou·i·si·ana \lu̇-ˌē-zē-ˈan-ə, ˌlü-ə-zē-, ˌlü-zē-\ state S U.S. ✱ Baton Rouge *area* 48,523, *pop* 3,643,180 — **Lou·i·si·an·an** \-ˈan-ən\ *adj or n* — **Lou·i·si·an·ian** \-ˈan-ē-ən, -ˈan-yən\ *adj or n*
Louisiana Purchase region W *cen* U.S. between the Mississippi & the Rockies purchased (1803) from France *area* 885,000
Lou·is·ville \ˈlü-i-ˌvil, -vəl\ city N Ky. on the Ohio *pop* 361,472
Loup \ˈlüp\ river 70 *m* (290 *m* with longest headstream, the Middle Loup) E *cen* Nebr. flowing E into the Platte
Lourdes \ˈlu̇(ə)rd(z)\ commune SW France on the Gave de Pau SSW of Tarbes *pop* 17,939
Lou·ren·ço Mar·ques \lə-ˌren(t)-(ˌ)sō-ˌmär-ˈkes, -ˈmärk(s)\ city & port ✱ of Mozambique on Delagoa Bay *pop* (with suburbs) 383,775
Louth \ˈlau̇t͟h\ county E Ireland in Leinster bordering on Irish sea ✱ Dundalk *area* 317, *pop* 74,899
Lou·vain \lü-ˈva^{n}\ *or* Flem **Leu·ven** \ˈlə(r)v-ə(n)\ city *cen* Belgium in Brabant E of Brussels *pop* 32,419
Love·land \ˈləv-lənd\ city N Colo. N of Denver *pop* 16,220
Low see TUAMOTU
Low Countries region W Europe bordering on North sea & comprising modern Belgium, Luxembourg, & the Netherlands
Low·ell \ˈlō-əl\ city NE Mass. NW of Boston *pop* 94,239
Lower California — see BAJA CALIFORNIA
Lower Canada the chiefly French province of Canada 1791–1841 corresponding to modern Quebec — see UPPER CANADA
Lower Klamath lake N Calif. on Oreg. border SSE of Upper Klamath Lake (in Oreg.); now usu. dry
Lower Saxony *or* G **Nie·der·sach·sen** \ˌnēd-ər-ˈzäk-sən\ state of the Bonn Republic W Germany bordering on North sea ✱ Hannover *area* 18,289, *pop* 7,067,200 — see SAXONY
Lowes·toft \ˈlō-stəf(t), -ˌstȯft\ municipal borough & port E England in East Suffolk on North sea *pop* 52,182
Low·lands \ˈlō-lən(d)z, -ˌlan(d)z\ the *cen* & E part of Scotland lying between the Highlands & the Southern Uplands
Loyalty islands SW Pacific E of New Caledonia; a dependency of New Caledonia *area* 800, *pop* 11,409
Lo·yang \ˈlō-ˈyäŋ\ city E China in N Honan in Yellow river basin *pop* 171,200
Lu·a·la·ba \ˌlü-ə-ˈläb-ə\ river 400 *m* SE Zaire flowing N to join the **Lu·a·pu·la** \-ˈpü-lə\ (350 *m*, outlet of Lake Bangweulu) forming the Congo
Lu·an·da \lu̇-ˈan-də\ *or* **Lo·an·da** \lō-\ city & port ✱ of Angola *pop* 475,328
Luang Pra·bang \lu̇-ˌäŋ-prə-ˈbäŋ\ city, royal ✱ of Laos, on the Mekong NNW of Vientiane *pop* 25,000
Luangue — see LOANGE
Lub·bock \ˈləb-ək\ city NW Tex. *pop* 149,101
Lü·beck \ˈlü-ˌbek, ˈlue-\ city & port N Germany NE of Hamburg *pop* 242,900
Lu·blin \ˈlü-blən, -ˌblēn\ city E Poland SE of Warsaw *pop* 238,600
Lu·bum·ba·shi \ˌlü-ˌbüm-ˈbäsh-ē\ *or formerly* **Elis·a·beth·ville** \i-ˈliz-ə-bəth-ˌvil\ city SE Zaire in SE Shaba *pop* 318,000
Lucania — see BASILICATA
Lu·ca·nia, Mount \lü-ˈkā-nē-ə, -nyə\ mountain 17,150 *ft* Canada in SW Yukon Territory in St. Elias range N of Mt. Logan
Luc·ca \ˈlü-kə\ commune *cen* Italy in Tuscany NW of Florence *pop* 91,401
Lu·cerne \lü-ˈsərn\ *or* G **Lu·zern** \lüt-ˈse(ə)rn\ **1** canton *cen* Switzerland *area* 579, *pop* 289,641 **2** commune, its ✱, on Lake of Lucerne *pop* 73,000
Lucerne, Lake of *or* **Lake of the Four Forest Cantons** lake 24 *m* long *cen* Switzerland *area* 44
Lu·chow \ˈlü-ˈjō\ **1** city S *cen* China in SE Szechwan on the Yangtze SW of Chungking *pop* 225,000 **2** — see HOFEI
Luck·now \ˈlək-ˌnau̇\ city N India ✱ of Uttar Pradesh *pop* 783,718
Lü·de·ritz \ˈlüd-ə-rəts\ town & port SW South-West Africa
Lu·dhi·a·na \ˌlu̇d-ē-ˈän-ə\ city NW India in Punjab SE of Amritsar *pop* 337,664
Lud·low \ˈləd-(ˌ)lō\ town SW Mass. NE of Springfield *pop* 17,580
Lud·wigs·burg \ˈlüt-vigz-ˌbu̇(ə)rg, ˈlüd-\ city SW Germany in Baden-Württemberg N of Stuttgart *pop* 78,812
Lud·wigs·ha·fen \ˌlüt-vigz-ˈhäf-ən, ˌlüd-\ city W Germany on the Rhine opposite Mannheim *pop* 174,000
Luf·kin \ˈləf-kən\ city E Tex. NNE of Houston *pop* 23,049
Lu·ga·no \lü-ˈgän-(ˌ)ō\ commune S Switzerland in Ticino canton on Lake Lugano *pop* 22,280
Lugano, Lake lake on border between Switzerland & Italy E of Lake Maggiore *area* 19
Lugansk — see VOROSHILOVGRAD
Lu·go \ˈlü-(ˌ)gō\ **1** province NW Spain in NE Galicia on Bay of Biscay *area* 3814, *pop* 415,052 **2** commune, its ✱ *pop* 63,830
Lui·chow \ˈlā-ˈjō\ peninsula SE China in Kwangtung between So. China sea & Gulf of Tonkin
Luik — see LIÈGE
Lu·lea \ˈlü-lə-ˌō, -lē-ˌō\ city & port N Sweden near head of Gulf of Bothnia *pop* 57,838
Lu·le·bur·gaz \ˌlü-lə-bu̇r-ˈgäz\ city *cen* Turkey in Europe *pop* 25,667
Lu·lua·bourg \lü-ˈlü-ə-ˌbu̇(ə)r(g)\ city S *cen* Zaire *pop* 428,960
Lum·ber·ton \ˈləm-bərt-^{ə}n\ city S N.C. *pop* 16,961
Lund \ˈlənd, ˈlu̇nd\ city SW Sweden NE of Malmö *pop* 54,410
Lun·dy \ˈlən-dē\ island SW England at mouth of Bristol channel off coast of Devonshire *area* 2
Lü·ne·burg \ˈlü-nə-ˌbu̇(ə)rg, ˈlue-\ city W Germany SE of Hamburg & NE of **Lüneburg Heath** *or* G **Lü·ne·bur·ger Hei·de** \-ˌbu̇r-gər-ˌhīd-ə\ (tract of moorland 50 *m* long) *pop* 59,728
Lü·nen \ˈlü-nən, ˈlue-\ city W Germany S of Münster *pop* 72,207
Lu·né·ville \ˈlü-nə-ˌvil\ city NE France on the Meurthe SE of Nancy *pop* 23,177
Lungki — see CHANGCHOW
Lungkiang — see TSITSIHAR
Lu·ray \ˈlü-ˌrā, lü-ˈ\ caverns N Va. in Blue Ridge mountains
Lu·ri·stan \ˈlu̇r-ə-ˌstan, -ˌstän\ region W Iran; chief town Burujird
Lu·sa·ka \lü-ˈsäk-ə\ city ✱ of Zambia *pop* 238,200
Lu·sa·tia \lü-ˈsā-sh(ē-)ə\ *or* G **Lau·sitz** \ˈlau̇-(ˌ)zits\ region E Germany NW of Silesia between Elbe & Oder rivers
Lüshun — see PORT ARTHUR
Lusitania — see PORTUGAL — **Lu·si·ta·ni·an** \ˌlü-sə-ˈtā-nē-ən, -nyən\ *adj or n*
Lü·ta *or* **Lü·da** \ˈlü-ˈdä\ *or* **Port Arthur–Dairen** municipality NE China in Liaoning including cities of Dairen & Port Arthur & adjacent area *pop* 4,000,000
Lutetia — see PARIS
Lu·ton \ˈlüt-^{ə}n\ municipal borough SE *cen* England in Bedfordshire *pop* 161,178
Lüt·zen \ˈlüt-sən, ˈlue̅t-\ town E Germany in Saxony SW of Leipzig
Lux·em·bourg *or* **Lux·em·burg** \ˈlək-səm-ˌbərg, ˈlu̇k-səm-ˌbu̇(ə)rg\ *or* **Let·ze·burg** \ˈlet-sə-ˌbu̇(ə)rg\ **1** province SE Belgium ✱ Arlon *area* 1705, *pop* 219,186 **2** country W Europe between Belgium, France, & Germany; a grand duchy *area* 999, *pop* 339,484 **3** city, its ✱ *pop* 77,463 — **Lux·em·bourg·er** *or* **Lux·em·burg·er** \-ˌbər-gər, -ˌbu̇r-\ *n* — **Lux·em·bourg·ian** *or* **Lux·em·burg·ian** \ˌlək-səm-ˈbər-gē-ən, ˌlu̇k-səm-ˈbu̇r-\ *adj*
Lux·or \ˈlək-ˌsȯ(ə)r, ˈlu̇k-\ *or* Ar **El Uq·sor** \e-ˈlu̇k-ˌsu̇(ə)r\ city S Egypt on the Nile on S part of site of ancient Thebes *pop* 84,600
Lu·zon \lü-ˈzän\ island N Philippines, chief island of the group *area* 40,420, *pop* 16,669,724
Lvov \lə-ˈvȯf, -ˈvȯv\ *or* Pol **Lwów** \lə-ˈvüf, -ˈvüv\ *or* G **Lem·berg** \ˈlem-ˌbərg, -ˌbe(ə)rg\ city U.S.S.R. in W Ukraine *pop* 238,600
Ly·all·pur \ˈlī-əl-ˌpu̇(ə)r\ city NE Pakistan W of Lahore *pop* 854,000
Ly·ca·bet·tus *or* Gk **Ly·ka·bet·tos** \ˌlik-ə-ˈbet-əs, ˌlī-kə-\ mountain 909 *ft* in NE part of Athens, Greece
Ly·ca·o·nia \ˌlik-ā-ˈō-nē-ə, ˌlī-kā-, -nyə\ ancient region & Roman province SE *cen* Asia Minor N of Cilicia
Ly·cia \ˈlish-(ē-)ə\ ancient region & Roman province SW Asia Minor on coast SE of Caria — **Ly·cian** \-(ē-)ən\ *adj or n*
Lyd·da \ˈlid-ə\ *or* **Lod** \ˈlōd\ city *cen* Israel *pop* 29,300
Lyd·ia \ˈlid-ē-ə\ ancient country W Asia Minor bordering on the Aegean ✱ Sardis — **Lyd·i·an** \-ən\ *adj or n*
Lyn·brook \ˈlin-ˌbru̇k\ village SE N.Y. on Long I. *pop* 23,776
Lynch·burg \ˈlinch-ˌbərg\ city S *cen* Va. on the James *pop* 54,083
Lynd·hurst \ˈlind-ˌhərst\ city NE Ohio E of Cleveland *pop* 19,749
Lynn \ˈlin\ **1** city NE Mass. NE of Boston *pop* 90,294 **2** *or* **Lynn Regis** — see KING'S LYNN
Lynn Canal narrow inlet of the Pacific 80 *m* long SE Alaska extending N from Juneau
Lynn·wood \ˈlin-ˌwu̇d\ city W Wash. N of Seattle *pop* 16,919
Lyn·wood \ˈlin-ˌwu̇d\ city SW Calif. S of Los Angeles *pop* 43,353
Ly·on·nais *or* **Ly·o·nais** \ˌlē-ə-ˈnā\ former province SE *cen* France NE of Auvergne & W of the Saône & the Rhone ✱ Lyons
Ly·ons \lē-ˈō^{n}, ˈlī-ənz\ *or* F **Lyon** \lyō^{n}\ *or anc* **Lug·du·num** \ˌlu̇g-ˈdü-nəm, ˌləg-\ city SE *cen* France *pop* 527,800
Lys \lēs\ *or* **Leie** \ˈlā-ə, ˈlī-ə\ river 120 *m* France & Belgium flowing NE into the Scheldt
Lyt·tel·ton \ˈlit-^{ə}l-tən\ borough New Zealand on South I.; port for Christchurch, on Port Lyttelton (inlet)
Maas — see MEUSE
Maas·tricht *or* **Maes·tricht** \ˈmäs-ˌtrikt\ commune SE Netherlands on the Meuse ✱ of Limburg *pop* 98,927
Mc·Al·es·ter \mə-ˈkal-ə-stər\ city E *cen* Okla. *pop* 18,802
Mc·Al·len \mə-ˈkal-ən\ city S Tex. WNW of Brownsville *pop* 37,636
Ma·cao *or* **Ma·cau** \mə-ˈkau̇\ **1** island SE China in Kwangtung in Si delta W of Hong Kong **2** Portuguese colony comprising peninsula on SE Macao I. & adjacent islands *area* 6, *pop* 314,000 **3** city & port, its ✱ — **Mac·a·nese** \ˌmak-ə-ˈnēz, -ˈnēs\ *n*
Ma·ca·pá \ˌmak-ə-ˈpä\ city & port N Brazil ✱ of Amapá *pop* 87,755
Macassar — see MAKASSAR
Mac·cles·field \ˈmak-əlz-ˌfēld\ municipal borough W England in E Cheshire SSE of Manchester *pop* 44,240
Mac·don·nell ranges \mək-ˈdän-^{ə}l\ series of mountain ridges *cen* Australia in S Northern Territory; highest point Mt. Ziel 4955 *ft*
Mac·e·do·nia \ˌmas-ə-ˈdō-nyə, -nē-ə\ **1** region S Europe in Balkan peninsula in NE Greece, SE Yugoslavia, & SW Bulgaria including territory of ancient kingdom of Macedonia (*or* **Mac·e·don** \ˈmas-əd-ən, -ə-ˌdän\ ✱ Pella) **2** the Yugoslav section of Macedonia; a federated republic ✱ Skoplje *area* 10,229, *pop* 1,647,104
Ma·ceió \ˌmas-ā-ˈō\ city NE Brazil ✱ of Alagoas *pop* 221,250
Mac·gil·li·cud·dy's Reeks \mə-ˌgil-ə-ˌkəd-ēz-\ mountain range SW Ireland in County Kerry — see CARRANTUOHILL
Ma·chu Pic·chu \ˌmäch-(ˌ)ü-ˈpēk-(ˌ)chü\ site SE Peru of ancient Inca city on a mountain NW of Cuzco
Mc·Kees·port \mə-ˈkēz-ˌpō(ə)rt, -ˌpȯ(ə)rt\ city SW Pa. S of Pittsburgh *pop* 37,977
Mac·ken·zie \mə-ˈken-zē\ **1** river 1120 *m* NW Canada flowing from Great Slave Lake NW into Beaufort sea; sometimes considered to include the Finlay, Peace, & Slave rivers (total length 2635 *m*) **2** mountain range NW Canada in the Rockies in Yukon Territory & Mackenzie District **3** district Canada in W Northwest Territories in basin of Mackenzie river *area* 493,225
Mack·i·nac \ˈmak-ə-ˌnak, -ˌnȯ\ *or formerly* **Mich·i·li·mack·i·nac** \ˌmish-ə-lē-\ island N Mich. in Straits of Mackinac
Mack·i·nac, Straits of \ˈmak-ə-ˌnȯ\ channel N Mich. connecting Lakes Huron & Michigan; 4 *m* wide at narrowest point; site of Mackinac bridge connecting upper & lower peninsulas of Mich.
Mc·Kin·ley, Mount \mə-ˈkin-lē\ *or native* **De·na·li** \də-ˈnäl-ē\ mountain 20,320 *ft*, *cen* Alaska in Alaska range; highest in U.S. & No. America; in **Mount McKinley National Park** (*area* 3030)
Mc·Kin·ney \mə-ˈkin-ē\ city NE Tex. N of Dallas *pop* 15,193
Mc·Mur·do Sound \mək-ˌmərd-ō-\ inlet of W Ross sea Antarctica between Ross I. & coast of Victoria Land
Ma·comb \mə-ˈkōm\ city W Ill. SW of Peoria *pop* 19,643
Ma·con \ˈmā-kən\ city *cen* Ga. *pop* 122,423
Mâ·con \mä-kō^{n}\ city E *cen* France *pop* 33,445
Mac·quar·ie \mə-ˈkwär-ē\ river 750 *m* SE Australia in E *cen* New So. Wales flowing NNW to Darling river

Mac·tan \mäk-'tän\ island S *cen* Philippines off E coast of Cebu
Mad·a·gas·car \,mad-ə-'gas-kər\ island W Indian ocean off SE coast of Africa; formerly a French territory; became (1958), as the **Mal·a·gasy Republic** \,mal-ə-,gas-ē-\ *or* F **Ré·pu·blique Mal·gache** \rā-pue-blēk-mal-gash\, a republic of the French Community ✻ Tananarive *area* 227,678, *pop* 6,750,000 — **Mad·a·gas·can** \,mad-ə-'gas-kən\ *adj or n*
Ma·dei·ra \mə-'dir-ə, -'der-ə\ **1** river 2100 *m* W Brazil formed at Bolivian border by confluence of Mamoré & Beni rivers & flowing NE to the Amazon **2** islands in N Atlantic N of the Canaries belonging to Portugal ✻ Funchal *area* 302, *pop* 268,700 **3** island, chief of group *area* 285 — **Ma·dei·ran** \-'dir-ən, -'der-\ *adj or n*
Ma·de·ra \mə-'der-ə\ city S *cen* Calif. NW of Fresno *pop* 16,044
Ma·dhya Bha·rat \,mäd-yə-'bär-ət\ former state *cen* India; a union of 20 states icluding Gwalior, Indore, & Malwa formed 1948; became part of Madhya Pradesh 1956
Madhya Pra·desh \-prə-'desh, -'dāsh\ state *cen* India ✻ Bhopal *area* 171,201, *pop* 41,449,729 — see CENTRAL PROVINCES AND BERAR, MADHYA BHARAT
Mad·i·son \'mad-ə-sən\ **1** river 180 *m* SW Mont. — see THREE FORKS **2** borough N N.J. SE of Morristown *pop* 16,710 **3** city ✻ of Wis. *pop* 173,258
Madison Heights city SE Mich. N of Detroit *pop* 38,599
Mad·i·son·ville \'mad-ə-sən-,vil\ city W Ky. *pop* 15,332
Ma·dras \mə-'dras, -'dräs\ **1** — see TAMIL NADU **2** city & port ✻ of Tamil Nadu *pop* 2,086,036
Ma·dre, La·gu·na \lə-,gü-nə-'mäd-rē\ inlet of Gulf of Mexico S Tex. between Padre I. & mainland
Ma·dre de Dios \,mäd-rē-,dād-ē-'ōs\ river 900 *m* rising in SE Peru & flowing E into the Beni in Brazil
Ma·drid \mə-'drid\ **1** province *cen* Spain in NW New Castile *area* 3084, *pop* 3,792,561 **2** city, its ✻ & ✻ of Spain *pop* 2,939,175 — **Mad·ri·le·nian** \,mad-rə-'lē-nē-ən, -nyən\ *adj or n*
Ma·du·ra *or* D **Ma·doe·ra** \mə-'dur-ə\ island Indonesia off coast of NE Java *area* (with adjacent islands) 2113 — **Mad·u·rese** \,mad-ə-'rēz, ,maj-, -'rēs\ *adj or n*
Ma·du·rai \,mäd-ə-'rī\ *or* **Mad·u·ra** \'maj-ə-rə\ city S India in S Tamil Nadu *pop* 493,842
Maeander — see MENDERES
Maf·e·king \'maf-ə-kiŋ\ town S Republic of So. Africa in N Cape Province near W Transvaal border
Ma·fia \'mäf-ē-ə, 'maf-\ island Tanzania in Indian ocean S of Zanzibar *area* 170
Ma·ga·dan \,mäg-ə-'dan, -'dän\ city & port U.S.S.R. in E Soviet Russia, Asia, on N shore of Sea of Okhotsk *pop* 92,000
Magallanes — see PUNTA ARENAS
Mag·da·la \'mag-də-lə\ **1** ancient city N Palestine on W shore of Sea of Galilee N of Tiberias **2** town N *cen* Ethiopia
Mag·da·len \'mag-də-lən\ *or* F **Iles de la Ma·de·leine** \ēl-də-lä-mäd-(ə-)len\ islands Canada in Que. in Gulf of St. Lawrence between Nfld. & P.E.I. *area* 102, *pop* 13,151
Mag·da·le·na \,mag-də-'lā-nə, -'lē-\ river 1000 *m* Colombia flowing N into the Caribbean
Mag·de·burg \'mäg-də-,bu(ə)rg, 'mag-də-,bərg\ city E Germany on the Elbe WSW of Berlin *pop* 269,031
Ma·ge·lang \,mäg-ə-'läŋ\ city Indonesia in *cen* Java *pop* 94,089
Ma·gel·lan, Strait of \mə-'jel-ən, *chiefly Brit* -'gel-\ strait 370 *m* long at S end of So. America between mainland & Tierra del Fuego archipelago
Mageröy — see NORTH CAPE
Mag·gio·re, Lake \mə-'jōr-ē, -'jor-\ lake 40 *m* long N Italy & S Switzerland traversed by the Ticino
Ma·ghreb *or* **Ma·ghrib** \'məg-rəb\ **1** northwestern Africa &, at time of the Moorish occupation, Spain; now considered as including Morocco, Algeria, Tunisia, & sometimes Libya **2** *or* **El Ma·ghreb al Aq·sa** \el-,məg-rə-ba-'lək-sə\ MOROCCO — **Ma·ghre·bi** *or* **Ma·ghri·bi** \'məg-rə-bē\ *adj or n* — **Ma·ghreb·i·an** \mə-'greb-ē-ən\ *or* **Ma·ghrib·i·an** \-'grib-\ *adj or n*
Mag·na Grae·cia \,mag-nə-'grē-shə\ the ancient Greek colonies in S Italian peninsula including Tarentum, Sybaris, Crotona, Heraclea, & Neapolis
Magnesia — see MANISA
Mag·ni·to·gorsk \mag-'nēt-ə-,gorsk\ city U.S.S.R. in W Soviet Russia, Asia, on Ural river *pop* 364,000
Magyarorszag — see HUNGARY
Ma·hal·la el Ku·bra \mə-,hal-ə-el-'kü-brə\ city N Egypt in Nile delta NE of Tanta *pop* 255,800
Ma·ha·na·di \mə-'hän-əd-ē\ river 512 *m* E India flowing into Bay of Bengal in Orissa through several mouths
Ma·ha·rash·tra \,mä-hə-'räsh-trə\ **1** region W *cen* India S of the Narbada; the original home of the Marathas **2** state W India bordering on Arabian sea formed 1960 from SE part of former Bombay state ✻ Bombay *area* 118,717 *pop* 50,295,081
Ma·hé \ma-'hā\ **1** island in Indian ocean, chief of the Seychelles group **2** *or formerly* **May·ya·li** \mī-'yäl-ē\ city SW India in N Kerala NW of Kozhikode; a settlement of French India until 1954 *pop* 18,298
Ma·hón \mə-'hōn\ *or* **Port Ma·hon** \mə-'hōn\ city & port Spain on Minorca I. *pop* 19,279
Ma·hone Bay \mə-,hōn-\ inlet of the Atlantic E Canada in S N.S. SW of Halifax
Maid·en·head \'mād-ᵊn-,hed\ municipal borough S England in Berkshire on the Thames W of London *pop* 45,306
Maid·stone \'mād-stən, -,stōn\ municipal borough SE England ✻ of Kent on the Medway ESE of London *pop* 70,918
Mai·kop \mī-'kop\ city U.S.S.R. in S Soviet Russia, Europe ✻ of Adygei Autonomous Region *pop* 111,000
Main \'mīn, 'mān\ river 305 *m* W Germany rising in N Bavaria in the Fichtel gebirge & flowing W into the Rhine
Maine \'mān\ **1** state NE U.S. ✻ Augusta *area* 33,215, *pop* 992,-048 **2** *or* **Le Maine** \lə-\ region & former province NW France S of Normandy ✻ Le Mans **3** — see MAYENNE
Main·land \'mān-,land, -lənd\ **1** Honshu, the chief island of Japan **2** *or* **Po·mo·na** \pə-'mō-nə\ island N Scotland, largest of the Orkneys **3** island N Scotland, largest of the Shetlands
Mainz \'mīn(t)s\ *or* F **Ma·yence** \mä-yäⁿs\ city W Germany on the Rhine ✻ of Rhineland-Palatinate *pop* 174,100
Ma·jor·ca \mə-'jor-kə, -'yor-\ *or* Sp **Ma·llor·ca** \mə-'yor-kə\ island Spain, largest of the Balearic Islands; chief city Palma *area* 1405 — **Ma·jor·can** \-'jor-kən, -'yor-\ *adj or n*
Ma·jun·ga \mə-'jəŋ-gə\ city & port NW Madagascar *pop* 53,993
Ma·ka·lu \'mək-ə-,lü\ mountain 27,824 *ft* in the Himalayas in NE Nepal SE of Mt. Everest; 5th highest in world
Ma·ka·ri·ka·ri \mə-,kär-i-'kär-ē\ large salt basin S Africa in NE Botswana
Ma·kas·sar *or* **Ma·kas·ar** *or* **Ma·cas·sar** \mə-'kas-ər\ **1** city & port Indonesia ✻ of Celebes on SW coast of the island *pop* 384,159 **2** strait Indonesia between E Borneo & W Celebes — **Ma·kas·sa·rese** *or* **Ma·cas·sa·rese** \mə-,kas-ə-'rēz, -'rēs\ *n*
Ma·ka·téa \,mäk-ə-'tā-ə\ island S Pacific in NW Tuamotu archipelago *area* 8
Ma·ke·ev·ka *or* **Ma·ke·yev·ka** \mə-'kā-(y)əf-kə\ city U.S.S.R. in E Ukraine in Donets basin NE of Donetsk *pop* 393,000
Ma·khach·ka·la \mə-,käch-kə-'lä\ *or formerly* **Pe·trovsk** \pə-'trofsk\ city U.S.S.R. in SE Soviet Russia, Europe, on the Caspian ✻ of Dagestan *pop* 186,000
Ma·kin \'mäk-ən, 'mā-kən\ *or* **Bu·ta·ri·ta·ri** \bu-,tär-ē-'tär-ē\ island (atoll) W Pacific at N end of the Gilberts *area* 4
Makira — see SAN CRISTOBAL
Makka — see MECCA
Mal·a·bar \'mal-ə-,bär\ coast region SW India on Arabian sea in Mysore & Kerala states
Ma·lac·ca *or* **Ma·lak·ka** \mə-'lak-ə, -'läk-\ **1** state Federation of Malaysia on W coast of Malaya; formerly in Straits Settlements *area* 633, *pop* 403,722 **2** city & port, its ✻, on Strait of Malacca *pop* 86,357 — **Ma·lac·can** \-ən\ *adj*
Malacca, Strait of channel 500 *m* long between S Malay peninsula & island of Sumatra
Má·la·ga \'mal-ə-gə\ **1** province S Spain in Andalusia *area* 2812, *pop* 867,330 **2** city & port, its ✻ *pop* 321,622
Malagasy Republic — see MADAGASCAR
Ma·lai·ta \mə-'lāt-ə\ island SW Pacific in the SE Solomons NE of Guadalcanal *area* 2500, *pop* 50,661
Ma·la·moc·co \,mal-ə-'mäk-(,)ō\ village N Italy on Lido I.
Ma·lang \mə-'läŋ\ city Indonesia in E Java *pop* 341,452
Ma·lar \'mā-,lär\ *or* **Mä·lar·en** \'mā-,lär-ən\ lake SE Sweden extending from Baltic sea 70 *m* inland
Mal·a·spi·na \,mal-ə-'spē-nə\ glacier S Alaska SE of Mt. St. Elias
Ma·la·tya \,mäl-ə-'tyä\ *or anc* **Mel·i·te·ne** \,mel-ə-'tē-nē\ city E Turkey NE of Gaziantep *pop* 104,428
Ma·la·wi \mə-'lä-wē, -'lau-ē\ *or formerly* **Ny·asa·land** \nī-'as-ə-,land, nē-\ country SE Africa bordering on Lake Malawi; formerly a Brit. protectorate; independent within Brit. Commonwealth since 1964; a republic since 1966 ✻ Zomba *area* 37,374, *pop* 4,550,000 — **Ma·la·wi·an** \-ən\ *adj or n*
Malawi, Lake *or formerly* **Lake Ny·asa** \nī-'as-ə, nē-\ lake SE Africa in Great Rift valley in Malawi, Mozambique, & Tanganyika
Ma·lay \mə-'lā, 'mā-(,)lā\ **1** archipelago SE Asia including Sumatra, Java, Borneo, Celebes, Moluccas, & Timor; usu. considered as including also the Philippines & sometimes New Guinea **2** peninsula 700 *m* long SE Asia divided between Thailand & Federation of Malaysia **3** sea SE Asia surrounding the Malay archipelago
Ma·laya \mə-'lā-ə, mā-\ **1** the Malay peninsula **2** BRITISH MALAYA **3** *or* **Federation of Malaya** former country SE Asia; a Brit. dominion 1957–63, since 1963 a territory (**West Malaysia**) of Federation of Malaysia ✻ Kuala Lumpur *area* 50,690, *pop* 8,980,000
Ma·lay·sia \mə-'lā-zh(ē-)ə, -sh(ē-)ə\ **1** the Malay archipelago **2** *or* **Federation of Malaysia** country SE Asia, a union of Malaya, Sabah (No. Borneo), Sarawak, & (until 1965) Singapore; a limited constitutional monarchy in Brit. Commonwealth ✻ Kuala Lumpur *area* 128,703 *pop* 10,650,000 — **Ma·lay·sian**\mə-'lā-zhən, -shən\ *adj or n*
Mal·den \'mol-dən\ **1** city E Mass. N of Boston *pop* 56,127 **2** island *cen* Pacific, one of the Line islands; claimed by U.S. & Great Britain
Mal·dive \'mol-,dēv, -,dīv- *also* 'mal-, -div\ islands in Indian ocean S of the Laccadives; a sultanate under Brit. protection until 1965; now **Republic of Maldives** ✻ Male *area* 115, *pop* 114,469 — **Mal·div·i·an** \mol-'div-ē-ən, mal-\ *adj or n*
Ma·le \'mäl-ē\ island (atoll), chief of the Maldives
Ma·lea, Cape \mə-'lē-ə\ cape S Greece at extremity of E peninsula of the Peloponnesus
Malgache, République — see MADAGASCAR
Mal·heur \mal-'hu(ə)r\ lake SE Oreg. in Harney basin
Ma·li \'mäl-ē, 'mal-ē\ **1** federation 1959–60 of Senegal and Sudanese Republic **2** *or formerly* **Sudanese Republic** country W Africa in W Sahara & Sudan regions; a republic; before 1958 constituted **French Sudan** (a territory of France) ✻ Bamako *area* 461,389, *pop* 5,140,000 — **Ma·li·an** \-ē-ən\ *adj or n*
Malines — see MECHLIN
Mal·in Head \,mal-ən-\ cape Republic of Ireland in County Donegal; northernmost tip of Ireland
Mal·mé·dy \,mal-mə-'dē\ commune E Belgium SE of Liège; formerly in Germany, transferred (with Eupen) to Belgium 1919
Malmö \'mal-,mə(r)\ city & port SW Sweden on Öresund opposite Copenhagen, Denmark *pop* 258,311

ə abut ᵊ kitten, F table ər further a back ā bake
ä cot, cart ȧ F bac au out ch chin e less ē easy
g gift i trip ī life j joke k̲ G ich ⁿ F vin ŋ sing
ō flow o flaw œ F bœuf œ̄ F feu oi coin th thing
t̲h̲ this ü loot u foot ue G Füllen ue̅ F rue y yet
ʸ F digne \dēnʸ\, nuit \nwʸē\ yü few yu furious zh vision

Mal·ta \'mȯl-tə\ *or anc* **Mel·i·ta** \'mel-ət-ə\ **1** *or* **Mal·tese islands** \ˌmȯl-ˌtēz, -ˌtēs-\ group of islands in the Mediterranean S of Sicily; a dominion of Brit. Commonwealth since 1964 ✱ Valletta *area* 122, *pop* 330,000 **2** island, chief of the group *area* 95
Maluku — see MOLUCCAS
Mal·vern \'mȯ(l)-vərn\ hills W England between Worcestershire & Herefordshire; highest point 1395 *ft*
Malvinas, Islas — see FALKLAND
Ma·mar·o·neck \mə-'mar-ə-ˌnek, -nik\ village SE N.Y. NE of New Rochelle *pop* 18,909
Mam·be·ra·mo \ˌmam-bə-'räm-(ˌ)ō\ river 500 *m* West New Guinea flowing NW into the Pacific
Mam·moth Cave \ˌmam-əth-\ limestone caverns SW *cen* Ky. in **Mammoth Cave National Park** (*area* 79)
Ma·mo·ré \ˌmäm-ə-'rā\ river 1200 *m* Bolivia flowing N to unite with the Beni on Brazilian border forming the Madeira
Man, Isle of \'man\ *or anc* **Mo·na·pia** \mə-'nā-pē-ə\ *or* **Mo·na** \'mō-nə\ island Brit. Isles in Irish sea; a possession of the Brit. Crown; has own legislature & laws ✱ Douglas *area* 221, *pop* 49,743 — **Manx·man** \'maŋ(k)-smən\ *n*
Ma·na·do *or* **Me·na·do** \mə-'näd-(ˌ)ō\ city & port Indonesia in NE Celebes I. on Celebes sea *pop* 129,912
Ma·na·gua \mə-'näg-wə\ **1** lake 38 *m* long W Nicaragua draining S through Tipitipa river to Lake Nicaragua **2** city ✱ of Nicaragua on Lake Managua *pop* 262,047
Ma·na·ma \mə-'nam-ə\ city ✱ of Bahrain *pop* 89,728
Ma·naus \mə-'naủs\ *or* **Ma·ná·os** \-'naủs\ city W Brazil ✱ of Amazonas on the Negro 12 *m* from its junction with the Amazon *pop* 303,155
Mancha, La — see LA MANCHA
Manche, La — see ENGLISH CHANNEL
Man·ches·ter \'man-ˌches-tər, -chə-stər\ **1** town *cen* Conn. E of Hartford *pop* 47,994 **2** city S N.H. on the Merrimack *pop* 87,754 **3** city & county borough NW England in Lancashire *pop* 541,468 — **Man·cu·nian** \man-'kyü-nē-ən, -nyən\ *adj or n*
Man·chu·kuo \'man-'chü-'kwō, man-'chü-ˌ\ former country (1931–45) E Asia in Manchuria & E Inner Mongolia ✱ Changchun
Man·chu·ria \man-'chủr-ē-ə\ region NE China E of the Great Khingan mountains & S of the Amur including Heilungkiang, Kirin, & Liaoning provinces & part of Inner Mongolia — **Man·chu·ri·an** \-ē-ən\ *adj or n*
Man·da·lay \ˌman-də-'lā\ city *cen* Burma *pop* 195,348
Man·ga·ia \mäŋ-'(g)ī-ə\ island S Pacific in SE Cook islands; completely encircled by reef *area* 25
Man·ga·lore \'maŋ-gə-ˌlō(ə)r, -ˌlȯ(ə)r\ city S India in Mysore on Malabar coast W of Bangalore *pop* 171,759
Man·ga·re·va \ˌmäŋ-(g)ə-'rā-və\ island S Pacific, chief of the Gambier islands *area* 7
Man·hat·tan \man-'hat-^{ə}n, mən-\ **1** city NE *cen* Kans. on Kansas river *pop* 27,575 **2** island 13 *m* long SE N.Y. on New York Bay **3** borough of New York City comprising Manhattan I., several small adjacent islands, & a small area (Marble Hill) on mainland *pop* 1,524,541 — **Man·hat·tan·ite** \-ˌīt\ *n*
Manhattan Beach city SW Calif. SW of Los Angeles *pop* 35,352
Ma·ni·hi·ki \ˌmän-ə-'hē-kē\ **1** *or* **Northern Cook** \'kủk\ islands S *cen* Pacific N of Cook islands; belong to New Zealand *pop* 3000 **2** island, chief of the group; an atoll
Ma·nila \mə-'nil-ə\ city & port Philippines on W coast of Luzon on **Manila Bay** (inlet of So. China sea) ✱ of the Philippines until 1948 & present seat of government *pop* 1,499,000 — see QUEZON CITY
Man·i·pur \ˌman-ə-'pủ(ə)r, ˌmən-\ **1** river 210 *m* NE India & W Burma flowing into the Chindwin **2** territory NE India between Assam & Burma ✱ Imphal *area* 8628, *pop* 1,069,555
Ma·ni·sa *or* **Ma·nis·sa** \ˌmän-ə-'sä\ *or anc* **Mag·ne·sia** \mag-'nē-shə, -zhə\ city W Turkey NE of Izmir *pop* 69,711
Man·i·to·ba \ˌman-ə-'tō-bə\ province S *cen* Canada ✱ Winnipeg *area* 251,000, *pop* 988,000 — **Man·i·to·ban** \-bən\ *adj or n*
Manitoba, Lake lake 120 *m* long Canada in S Man. *area* 1817
Man·i·tou·lin \ˌman-ə-'tü-lən\ island 80 *m* long Canada in Ont. in Lake Huron NW of Georgian Bay; largest freshwater island in the world *area* 1068
Man·i·to·woc \'man-ət-ə-ˌwäk\ city E Wis. *pop* 33,430
Ma·ni·za·les \ˌman-ə-'zäl-əs, -'zal-\ city W *cen* Colombia in Cauca valley *pop* 267,543
Man·ka·to \man-'kät-(ˌ)ō\ city S Minn. on Minnesota river SW of Minneapolis *pop* 30,895
Man·nar, Gulf of \mə-'när\ inlet of Indian ocean between Ceylon & S tip of India S of Palk strait
Mann·heim \'man-ˌhīm, 'män-\ city W Germany at confluence of the Rhine & the Neckar *pop* 328,000
Mans·field \'man(t)s-ˌfēld, 'manz-\ **1** town *cen* Conn. *pop* 19,994 **2** city N *cen* Ohio *pop* 55,047 **3** municipal borough N *cen* England in Nottinghamshire N of Nottingham *pop* 57,598
Mansfield, Mount mountain 4393 *ft* N Vt.; highest in Green mountains & in state
Man·sû·ra *or* **El Mansûra** \(ˌel-)man-'sủr-ə\ city N Egypt in Nile delta *pop* 212,300
Man·tua \'manch-(ə-)wə, 'mant-ə-wə\ *or* **Man·to·va** \'män-tə-və\ commune N Italy in Lombardy WSW of Venice *pop* 66,089 — **Man·tu·an** \'manch-(ə-)wən, 'mant-ə-wən\ *adj or n*
Ma·nua \mə-'nü-ə\ islands SW Pacific in American Samoa E of Tutuila *area* 22
Ma·nus \'män-əs\ island SW Pacific in Admiralty islands; largest of group *area* 600
Man·za·la, Lake \man-'zäl-ə\ *or anc* **Ta·nis** \'tā-nəs\ lagoon N Egypt in Nile delta W of N entrance of Suez canal
Man·za·ni·llo \ˌman-zə-'nē-(ˌ)(y)ō\ **1** city & port E Cuba on the Caribbean *pop* (municipality) 183,900 **2** town & port SW Mexico in Colima *pop* 29,347
Maple Heights city NE Ohio SE of Cleveland *pop* 34,093
Ma·ple·wood \'mā-pəl-ˌwủd\ village SE Minn. E of St. Paul *pop* 25,222
Ma·quo·ke·ta \mə-'kō-kət-ə\ river 150 *m* E Iowa flowing SE into the Mississippi
Mar·a·cai·bo \ˌmar-ə-'kī-(ˌ)bō\ city NW Venezuela on channel between Lake Maracaibo & Gulf of Venezuela *pop* 625,101
Maracaibo, Gulf of — see VENEZUELA (Gulf of)
Maracaibo, Lake the S extension of Gulf of Venezuela in NW Venezuela *area* 6300
Maracanda — see SAMARKAND
Ma·ra·cay \ˌmär-ə-'kī\ city N Venezuela WSW of Caracas *pop* 185,655
Marais des Cygnes \'merd-ə-ˌzēn\ river 150 *m* E Kans. & W Mo. flowing into the Osage
Ma·ra·nhão \ˌmar-ən-'yaủ^{n}\ state NE Brazil bordering on the Atlantic ✱ São Luis *area* 133,674, *pop* 2,883,211
Ma·ra·ñón \ˌmär-ən-'yōn\ river 800 *m* N Peru flowing from the Andes NNW & E to join the Ucayali forming the Amazon
Ma·ras *or* **Ma·rash** \mə-'räsh\ city S *cen* Turkey *pop* 63,284
Mar·a·thon \'mar-ə-ˌthän, -thən\ **1** plain E Greece in Attica NE of Athens on the Aegean **2** ancient town on the plain
Marble Canyon canyon of Colorado river N Ariz. just above the Grand Canyon, sometimes considered its upper portion; in **Marble Canyon National Monument** (*area* 42)
Mar·ble·head \'mär-bəl-ˌhed, ˌmär-bəl-'\ town E Mass. NE of Lynn on Massachusetts Bay *pop* 21,295
Mar·burg \'mär-ˌbủ(ə)rg, -ˌbərg\ city W Germany in Hesse N of Frankfurt *pop* 51,070
March \'märch\ **1** *or* **Mo·ra·va** \'mȯr-ə-və\ river 180 *m, cen* Czechoslovakia in Moravia flowing S into the Danube **2** urban district E England ✱ of Isle of Ely E of Leicester
Marche \'märsh\ region & former province *cen* France NW of Auvergne ✱ Guéret
March·es \'mär-chəz\ *or* **Le Mar·che** \lā-'mär-(ˌ)kā\ region *cen* Italy on the Adriatic NW of Abruzzi e Molise ✱ Ancona
Mar·cus \'mär-kəs\ island W Pacific E of the Bonins; occupied by the U.S. *area* 1
Mar·cy, Mount \'mär-sē\ mountain 5344 *ft* NE N.Y.; highest in Adirondack mountains & in state
Mar del Pla·ta \ˌmär-ˌdel-'plät-ə\ city & port E Argentina SSE of Buenos Aires *pop* 211,365
Mare \'ma(ə)r, 'me(ə)r\ island W Calif. in San Pablo Bay
Ma·rem·ma \mə-'rem-ə\ low-lying district W Italy on Tyrrhenian coast in SW Tuscany
Ma·ren·go \mə-'reŋ-(ˌ)gō\ village NW Italy in SE Piedmont SE of Alessandria
Mar·eo·tis, Lake \ˌmar-ē-'ōt-əs\ *or* Ar **Mar·yût** \mər-'yüt\ lake N Egypt in Nile delta; Alexandria is situated between it & the Mediterranean
Ma·reth \'mär-əth, 'mar-\ town SE Tunisia SSE of Gabes
Mar·ga·ri·ta \ˌmär-gə-'rēt-ə\ island N Venezuela in the Caribbean, chief of the **Neu·va Es·par·ta** \nủ-ˌā-və-es-'pärt-ə\ group; chief town & port Porlamar *area* 444
Mar·gate \'mär-ˌgāt, -gət\ municipal borough SE England in Kent on coast of Isle of Thanet *pop* 50,145
Mar·i·ana \ˌmar-ē-'an-ə, ˌmer-\ *or formerly* **La·drone** \lə-'drōn\ islands W Pacific S of Bonin islands; except Guam, a Japanese mandate 1919–45 & since 1947 in Trust Territory of the Pacific Islands administered by the U.S. *area* (*excluding Guam*) 184, *pop* 9640
Ma·ri·a·nao \ˌmär-ē-ə-'naủ\ city W Cuba, W suburb of Havana *pop* (municipality) 350,260
Ma·ri·an·ske Laz·ne \ˌmär-ē-ˌän(t)-skə-'läz-nə\ *or* G **Ma·ri·en·bad** \mə-'rē-ən-ˌbad, -ˌbät\ town W Czechoslovakia in NW Bohemia NE of Plzen
Ma·ri·as \mə-'rī-əs, -əz\ **1** river 250 *m* NW Mont. flowing SE to the Missouri **2** mountain pass 5213 *ft* NW Mont. in Lewis range at SE corner of Glacier National Park
Ma·ri·bor \'mär-i-ˌbȯ(ə)r\ city NW Yugoslavia *pop* 97,167
Ma·rie Byrd Land \mə-ˌrē-'bərd-\ *or* **Byrd Land** region W Antarctica E of Ross Ice Shelf & Ross sea
Ma·rie Ga·lante \mə-ˌrē-gə-'länt\ island E West Indies in the Leewards; a dependency of Guadeloupe *area* 60, *pop* 16,341
Mar·i·et·ta \ˌmar-ē-'et-ə, ˌmer-\ **1** city NW Ga. NW of Atlanta *pop* 27,216 **2** city SE Ohio *pop* 16,861
Ma·rin·du·que \ˌmar-ən-'dü-(ˌ)kā, ˌmär-\ island Philippines in Sibuyan sea S of Luzon; chief town Boac *area* 355
Mar·i·on \'mer-ē-ən, 'mar-\ **1** city N *cen* Ind. *pop* 39,607 **2** city E Iowa NE of Cedar Rapids *pop* 18,028 **3** city *cen* Ohio *pop* 38,646
Ma·ri Republic \'mär-ē\ autonomous republic U.S.S.R. in E *cen* Soviet Russia, Europe ✱ Ioshkar Ola *area* 8900, *pop* 685,000
Maritime Alps section of the W Alps SE France & NW Italy extending to the Mediterranean; highest point Punta Argentera 10,814 *ft*
Maritime Provinces *or* **Maritimes** the Canadian provinces of N.B., N.S., & P.E.I.
Maritime Territory *or* Russ **Pri·mor·ye** \prē-'mȯr-yə\ territory U.S.S.R. in E Soviet Russia, Asia, bordering on Sea of Japan ✱ Vladivostok *area* 64,900, *pop* 1,722,000
Ma·ri·tsa \mə-'rēt-sə\ *or* NGk **Ev·ros** \'ev-ˌrȯs\ *or* Turk **Me·ric** \mə-'rēch\ river 320 *m* S Europe flowing from W Rhodope mountains in S Bulgaria E & S through Thrace into the Aegean
Mariupol — see ZHDANOV
Mar·ken \'mär-kən\ island W Netherlands in SW Lake IJssel
Mark·ham \'mär-kəm\ **1** village NE Ill. SW of Chicago *pop* 15,987 **2** town Canada in SE Ont. NE of Toronto *pop* 36,684 **3** river 200 *m* E New Guinea flowing S & SE into Solomon sea
Markham, Mount mountain 14,275 *ft* Antarctica in Queen Elizabeth Range W of Ross Ice Shelf
Marl \'mär(ə)l\ city W Germany in the Ruhr *pop* 75,905
Marl·bor·ough *or* **Marl·boro** \'märl-ˌbər-ə, 'mȯl-, -ˌbə-rə, -brə\ city E Mass. E of Worcester *pop* 27,936
Mar·ly–le–Roi \ˌmär-'lē-lə-rə-'wä, -lər-'wä\ town N France, NW suburb of Versailles, on edge of Marly Forest
Mar·ma·ra, Sea of *or* **Sea of Mar·mo·ra** \'mär-mə-rə\ *or anc* **Pro·pon·tis** \prə-'pänt-əs\ sea NW Turkey connected with Black Sea by the Bosporus & with Aegean sea by the Dardanelles *area* 4250

Mar·mo·la·da \ˌmär-mə-ˈläd-ə\ mountain 10,965 *ft* NE Italy; highest in the Dolomites
Marne \ˈmärn\ river 325 *m* NE France flowing W into the Seine
Ma·ro·ni \mə-ˈrō-nē\ *or* D **Ma·ro·wij·ne** \ˌmär-ə-ˈvī-nə\ river 420 *m* on border between Surinam & French Guiana flowing N into the Atlantic
Maros — see MURES
Mar·que·sas \mär-ˈkā-zəz, -zəs, -səz, -səs\ *or* **Mar·que·zas** \-zəz, -zəs\ *or* F **Iles Mar·quises** \ˌē(ə)l-mär-ˈkēz\islands S Pacific N of Tuamotu archipelago in French Polynesia *area* 480, *pop* 5147
Mar·quette \mär-ˈket\ city NW Mich. in upper peninsula on Lake Superior *pop* 21,967
Mar·ra·kesh *or* **Mar·ra·kech** \mə-ˈräk-ish, ˌmar-ə-ˈkesh\ *or formerly* **Mo·roc·co** \mə-ˈräk-(ˌ)ō\city *cen* Morocco in foothills of the Grand Atlas *pop* 305,000
Mar·sa·la \mär-ˈsäl-ə\ city & port Italy on W coast of Sicily S of Trapani *pop* 82,724
Mar·seilles \mär-ˈsā, -ˈsā(ə)lz\ *or* F **Mar·seille** \mär-ˈsā\ *or anc* **Mas·sil·ia** \mə-ˈsil-ē-ə\ city & port SE France on Gulf of Lions *pop* 889,029
Mar·shall \ˈmär-shəl\ **1** city NE Tex. *pop* 22,937 **2** islands W Pacific E of the Carolines comprising the Ratak & Ralik chains; a Japanese mandate 1920–45; now part of Trust Territory of the Pacific Islands administered by the U.S. *area* 70, *pop* 22,888 — **Mar·shall·ese** \ˌmär-shə-ˈlēz, -ˈlēs\ *adj or n*
Mar·shall·town \ˈmär-shəl-ˌtau̇n\ city *cen* Iowa *pop* 26,219
Marsh·field \ˈmärsh-ˌfēld\ **1** town E Mass. N of Plymouth *pop* 15,223 **2** city N *cen* Wis. *pop* 15,619
Mar·ston Moor \ˌmär-stən-\ locality N England in West Riding, Yorkshire, W of York
Mar·ta·ban, Gulf of \ˌmärt-ə-ˈban\ arm of Andaman sea S Burma
Mar·tha's Vineyard \ˌmär-thəz-\ island 20 *m* long SE Mass. in the Atlantic off SW coast of Cape Cod WNW of Nantucket
Mar·ti·nez \mär-ˈtē-nəs\ city W Calif. NE of Oakland *pop* 16,506
Mar·ti·nique \ˌmärt-ᵊn-ˈēk\ island West Indies in the Windwards; an overseas department of France ✱ Fort-de-France *area* 385, *pop* 292,062
Mar·tins·ville \ˈmärt-ᵊnz-ˌvil, -vəl\ city S Va. *pop* 19,653
Marwar — see JODHPUR
Mary·bor·ough \ˈmer-ē-ˌbər-ə, ˈmar-, -ˌbə-rə, -b(ə-)rə\ *or* **Port Laoigh·i·se** \ˈlā-ə-shə\ town *cen* Ireland ✱ of County Laoighis
Mary·land \ˈmer-ə-lənd\ state E U.S. ✱ Annapolis *area* 10,577, *pop* 3,922,399 — **Mary·land·er** \-lən-dər, -ˌlan-\ *n*
Mary·le·bone \ˈmar-(ə-)lə-bən, ˈmar-i-bən\ *or* **Saint Marylebone** former metropolitan borough W *cen* London, England, now part of Westminster
Ma·sa·da \mə-ˈsäd-ə\ fortress town of ancient Palestine, site in SE Israel W of Dead sea
Ma·san \ˈmäs-ˌän\ *or formerly* **Ma·sam·po** \ˈmäs-ˌäm-ˌpō\ city & port S Korea on an inlet of Korea strait E of Pusan *pop* 154,856
Mas·ba·te \mäz-ˈbät-ē\ island *cen* Philippines in the Visayans NE of Panay *area* 1571
Mas·ca·rene \ˌmas-kə-ˈrēn\ islands W Indian ocean E of Madagascar including Mauritius, Réunion, and Rodrigues
Mashhad — see MESHED
Mas·e·ru \ˈmaz-ə-ˌrü\ city ✱ of Lesotho on NW border on Caledon river *pop* 16,000
Maskat, Masqat — see MUSCAT
Ma·son City \ˌmās-ᵊn-\ city N Iowa *pop* 30,491
Mas·sa·chu·setts \ˌmas-(ə-)ˈchü-səts, -zəts\ state NE U.S. ✱ Boston *area* 8257, *pop* 5,689,170
Massachusetts Bay inlet of the Atlantic E Mass.
Mas·sa·nut·ten Mountain \ˌmas-ə-ˈnət-ᵊn\ ridge N Va. in Blue Ridge mountains
Mas·sa·pe·qua Park \ˌmas-ə-ˈpē-kwə\ village SE N.Y. on Long I. *pop* 22,112
Mas·sa·wa *or* **Mas·saua** \mə-ˈsä-wə, -ˈsau̇-ə\ city & port N Ethiopia in Eritrea on an inlet of Red sea *pop* 18,490
Mas·sif Cen·tral \ma-ˌsēf-ˌsen-ˈträl, -ˌsäⁿ-\ plateau *cen* France rising sharply just W of the Rhone-Saône valley & sloping N to the Paris basin & W to the basin of Aquitaine
Mas·sil·lon \ˈmas-ə-lən, -ˌlän\ city NE Ohio *pop* 32,539
Mas·sive, Mount \ˈmas-iv\ mountain 14,418 *ft, cen* Colo. in Sawatch mountains N of Mt. Elbert
Ma·su·li·pat·nam \ˌməs-ə-li-ˈpət-nəm\ *or* **Ma·su·li·pa·tam** \-ˈpət-əm\ *or* **Ban·dar** \ˈbən-dər\ city & port SE India in E Andhra Pradesh SW of Kakinada *pop* 129,905
Ma·su·ria \mə-ˈzu̇r-ē-ə, -ˈsu̇r-\ *or* G **Ma·su·ren** \mə-ˈzu̇r-ən\ region NE Poland SE of Gulf of Danzig; formerly in East Prussia, Germany — **Ma·su·ri·an** \mə-ˈzu̇r-ē-ən, -ˈsu̇r-\ *adj*
Mat·a·be·le·land \ˌmat-ə-ˈbē-lē-ˌland\ region SW Rhodesia between the Limpopo & the Zambezi; chief town Bulawayo
Ma·ta·di \mə-ˈtäd-ē\ town & port W Zaire on Congo river *pop* 110,436
Mat·a·gor·da Bay \ˌmat-ə-ˈgȯrd-ə\ inlet of Gulf of Mexico 30 *m* long SE Tex.
Mat·a·mo·ros \ˌmat-ə-ˈmōr-əs, -ˈmȯr-\ city NE Mexico in Tamaulipas on Rio Grande opposite Brownsville, Tex. *pop* 182,887
Mat·a·nus·ka \ˌmat-ə-ˈnü-skə\ river 90 *m* S Alaska flowing SW to head of Cook inlet
Ma·tan·zas \mə-ˈtan-zəs\ city & port W Cuba on Straits of Florida E of Havana *pop* (municipality) 84,100
Mat·a·pan \ˌmat-ə-ˈpan\ *or* **Ma·ta·pás** \ˌmät-ə-ˈpäs\ *or* **Tai·na·ron** \ˈtā-nə-ˌrȯn\ cape S Greece at S tip of Peloponnesus between gulfs of Laconia & Messenia
Ma·thu·ra \ˈmət-ə-rə\ *or* **Mut·tra** \ˈmə-trə\ city N India in W Uttar Pradesh NW of Agra *pop* 137,345
Ma·to Gros·so *or formerly* **Mat·to Gros·so** \ˌmat-ə-ˈgrō-(ˌ)sō\ **1** state SW Brazil ✱ Cuiabá *area* 485,405, *pop* 1,475,117 **2** plateau region in E *cen* Mato Grosso state
Mato Tepee — see DEVILS TOWER
Ma·trûh *or* **Mer·sa Matrûh** \(ˌ)mər-ˌsä-)mə-ˈtrü\ town NW Egypt
Mat·su \ˈmät-ˈsü, ˈmat-, -(ˌ)sü\ island SE China in Formosa strait E of Foochow
Ma·tsue \ˈmät-sə-ˌwā, -sü-ˌyā\ city of Japan in W Honshu NW of Hiroshima *pop* 116,000
Ma·tsu·mo·to \ˌmät-sə-ˈmōt-(ˌ)ō\ city Japan in *cen* Honshu NE of Nagoya *pop* 161,000
Ma·tsu·shi·ma \ˌmät-sü-ˈshē-mə, mät-ˈsü-shi-mə\ group of over 800 islets Japan off N Honshu in Ishinomaki Bay NE of Sendai
Mat·su·ya·ma \ˌmät-sə-ˈyäm-ə\ city & port Japan in W Shikoku *pop* 323,000
Mat·tag·a·mi \mə-ˈtag-ə-mē\ river 275 *m* Canada in E Ont. flowing into Moose river
Mat·ta·po·ni \ˌmat-ə-pə-ˈnī\ river 125 *m* E Va. uniting with the Pamunkey to form York river
Mat·ter·horn \ˈmat-ər-ˌhȯ(ə)rn, ˈmät-\ *or* F **Mont Cer·vin** \mōⁿ-ser-ˈvaⁿ\ mountain 14,690 *ft* in Pennine Alps on border between Switzerland & Italy
Mat·toon \mə-ˈtün, ma-\ city SE *cen* Ill. *pop* 19,681
Ma·tu·rín \ˌmät-ə-ˈrēn\ city NE Venezuela *pop* 97,257
Maui \ˈmau̇-ē\ island Hawaii NW of Hawaii I. *area* 728
Mau·mee \(ˈ)mȯ-ˈmē\ **1** river 175 *m* NE Ind. & NW Ohio flowing NE into Lake Erie at Toledo **2** city NW Ohio SW of Toledo *pop* 15,937
Mau·na Kea \ˌmau̇-nə-ˈkā-ə\ extinct volcano 13,796 *ft* Hawaii in N *cen* Hawaii I.
Mauna Loa \-ˈlō-ə\ volcano 13,680 *ft* Hawaii in S *cen* Hawaii I. in Hawaii National Park — see KILAUEA
Maures, Monts des \ˌmōⁿ-dā-ˈmō(ə)r, -ˈmȯ(ə)r\ mountains SE France along the Riviera SW of Fréjus
Mau·re·ta·nia *or* **Mau·ri·ta·nia** \ˌmȯr-ə-ˈtā-nē-ə, ˌmär-, -nyə\ ancient country N Africa W of Numidia in modern Morocco & W Algeria — **Mau·re·ta·nian** *or* **Mau·ri·ta·nian** \-nē-ən, -nyən\ *adj or n*
Mauritania *or* F **Mau·ri·ta·nie** \mȯ-rē-tȧ-nē\ country NW Africa bordering on the Atlantic N of Senegal river; a republic (**Islamic Republic of Mauritania**) within the French Community, formerly a territory ✱ Nouakchott *area* 419,229, *pop* 1,200,000 — **Mau·ri·ta·ni·an** \ˌmȯr-ə-ˈtā-nē-ən, ˌmär-, -nyən\ *adj or n*
Mau·ri·ti·us \mȯ-ˈrish-(ē-)əs\ island in Indian ocean in *cen* Mascarenes; constitutes with Rodrigues & other dependencies a dominion of the Brit. Commonwealth ✱ Port Louis *area* 720, *pop* 820,000 — **Mau·ri·tian** \-ˈrish-ən\ *adj or n*
May, Cape \ˈmā\ cape S N.J. at entrance to Delaware Bay
May·a·gua·na \ˌmā-ə-ˈgwän-ə\ island in the SE Bahamas NNE of Great Inagua I. *area* 96
Ma·ya·güez \ˌmī-ə-ˈgwez, -ˈgwes\ city & port W Puerto Rico *pop* 68,872
Ma·ya·pán \ˌmī-ə-ˈpän\ ruined city ✱ of the Mayas SE Mexico in Yucatán SSE of Mérida
Mayence — see MAINZ
Ma·yenne \mä-ˈyen, mī-ˈen\ river 125 *m* NW France uniting with the Sarthe to form the **Maine** \ˈmān\ (8 *m* long, flowing into the Loire)
May·fair \ˈmā-ˌfa(ə)r, -ˌfe(ə)r\ district of W London, England, in Westminster borough
May·field Heights \ˌmā-ˌfēld-\ city NE Ohio E of Cleveland *pop* 22,139
May·nooth \mā-ˈnüth\ town E Ireland in County Kildare
Mayo, 1 \ˈmī-(ˌ)ō\ river 250 *m* NW Mexico in Sonora flowing SW into Gulf of California **2** \ˈmā-(ˌ)ō\ county NW Ireland in Connacht ✱ Castlebar *area* 2084, *pop* 109,497
Ma·yon \mä-ˈyōn\ volcano 7943 *ft* Philippines in SE Luzon
May·wood \ˈmā-ˌwu̇d\ **1** city SW Calif. W of Whittier *pop* 16,996 **2** village NE Ill. W of Chicago *pop* 30,036
Mayyali — see MAHÉ
Mazaca — see KAYSERI
Ma·za·ma, Mount \mə-ˈzäm-ə\ prehistoric volcano SW Oreg. the collapse of whose summit formed Crater Lake
Ma·za·tlán \ˌmäz-ə-ˈtlän, ˌmäs-\ city & port W Mexico in Sinaloa on the Pacific *pop* 171,835
Mba·bane \ˌem-bə-ˈbän\ town ✱ of Swaziland *pop* 14,000
Mban·da·ka \ˌem-ˌbän-ˈdäk-ə\ *or formerly* **Co·qui·lhat·ville** \ˌkō-kē-ˈat-ˌvil\ city W Zaire on Congo river *pop* 107,910
Mbomu — see BOMU
Mbu·ji–Ma·yi \em-ˌbü-jē-ˈmī-ˌē\ *or formerly* **Ba·kwan·ga** \bə-ˈkwäŋ-gə\ city S Zaire *pop* 305,818
M'·Clure Strait \mə-ˌklu̇(ə)r-\ channel N Canada between Banks I. & Melville I. opening on the W into Arctic ocean
Mead, Lake \ˈmēd\ reservoir NW Ariz. & SE Nev. formed by Hoover Dam in Colorado river — see BOULDER
Mead·ville \ˈmēd-ˌvil\ city NW Ohio *pop* 16,573
Mearns, The — see KINCARDINE
Meath \ˈmēth, ˈmēth\ county E Ireland in NE Leinster ✱ Trim *area* 903, *pop* 71,616
Meaux \ˈmō\ commune N France ENE of Paris *pop* 30,167
Mec·ca \ˈmek-ə\ *or* **Mak·ka** \ˈmak-ə\ city Saudi Arabia ✱ of Hejaz *pop* 185,000 — **Mec·can** \ˈmek-ən\ *adj or n*
Mech·lin \ˈmek-lən\ *or* Flem **Me·che·len** \ˈmek-ə-lə(n)\ *or* F **Ma·lines** \mə-ˈlēn\ commune N Belgium *pop* 65,823
Meck·len·burg \ˈmek-lən-ˌbərg\ region E Germany SE of Jutland peninsula & E of the Elbe; in 18th & 19th centuries divided into duchies of **Mecklenburg–Schwe·rin** \-shfā-ˈrēn\ & **Mecklenburg–Stre·litz** \-ˈs(h)trā-ləts\ which became grand duchies 1815 & states of Weimar Republic 1919
Me·dan \mā-ˈdän\ city Indonesia in NE Sumatra *pop* 479,098
Me·del·lín \ˌmed-ᵊl-ˈēn, ˌmā-thə-ˈyēn\ city NW Colombia NW of Bogotá *pop* 967,825

ə abut ᵊ kitten, F table ər further a back ā bake
ä cot, cart ȧ F bac au̇ out ch chin e less ē easy
g gift i trip ī life j joke k G ich ⁿ F vin ŋ sing
ō flow ȯ flaw œ F bœuf œ̄ F feu ȯi coin th thing
th this ü loot u̇ foot ue G Füllen ue̅ F rue y yet
ʸ F digne \dēnʸ\, nuit \nwʸē\ yü few yu̇ furious zh vision

Med·ford \'med-fərd\ **1** city E Mass. N of Boston *pop* 64,397 **2** city SW Oreg. *pop* 28,454
Me·dia \'mēd-ē-ə\ ancient country & province of Persian Empire SW Asia in NW modern Iran — **Me·di·an** \-ē-ən\ *adj or n*
Media Atropatene — see AZERBAIJAN
Medicine Bow \-,bō\ **1** river 120 *m* S Wyo. flowing into the No. Platte **2** mountains N Colo. & S Wyo. in the Rockies; highest **Medicine Bow Peak** (in Wyo.) 12,005 *ft*
Medicine Hat city Canada in SE Alta. *pop* 26,518
Me·di·na \mə-'dē-nə\ city W Saudi Arabia *pop* 100,000
Medina as-Shaab \-,ash-'shäb\ city; administrative ✻ of People's Democratic Republic of Yemen & formerly (as **Al It·ti·had** \,al-,it-i-'had, -'häd\) ✻ of Federation of So. Arabia *pop* 20,000
Mediolanum — see MILAN
Med·i·ter·ra·nean \,med-ə-tə-'rā-nē-ən, -nyən\ sea 2330 *m* long between Europe & Africa connecting with the Atlantic through Strait of Gibraltar & with Red sea through Suez canal
Mé·doc \mā-'däk\ district SW France N of Bordeaux
Med·way \'med-,wā\ river 60 *m* SE England in Kent flowing NE into the Thames
Mee·rut \'mā-rət, 'mir-ət\ city N India in NW Uttar Pradesh NE of Delhi *pop* 250,126
Meg·a·ra *or* NGk **Mé·ga·ra** \'meg-ə-rə\ city & port Greece on Saronic gulf W of Athens *pop* 15,450; chief town of ancient **Meg·a·ris** \'meg-ə-rəs\ (district between Saronic gulf & Gulf of Corinth) — **Me·gar·i·an** \mə-'gar-ē-ən, me-, -'ger-\ *adj or n*
Megh·na \'meg-nə\ the lower course of the Surma river, India
Me·gid·do \mi-'gid-(,)ō\ ancient city N Palestine N of Samaria
Meis·sen \'mīs-ᵊn\ city E Germany NW of Dresden *pop* 45,571
Méjico — see MEXICO
Mek·nes \mek-'nes\ city N Morocco WSW of Fez; former ✻ of Morocco *pop* 245,000
Me·kong \'mā-'kȯŋ, -'käŋ\ river 2600 *m* SE Asia flowing from S Tsinghai, China, S & SE into So. China sea in S Vietnam
Mel·a·ne·sia \,mel-ə-'nē-zhə, -shə\ the islands in the Pacific NE of Australia & S of Micronesia including Bismarck archipelago, the Solomons, New Hebrides, New Caledonia, & the Fijis
Mel·bourne \'mel-bərn\ **1** city E Fla. SSW of Cape Kennedy *pop* 40,236 **2** city & port SE Australia ✻ of Victoria on Port Phillip Bay *pop* (with suburbs) 2,425,300 — **Mel·bur·ni·an** \mel-'bər-nē-ən\ *n*
Me·li·lla \mə-'lē-(y)ə\ city & port NE Morocco on coast NE of Fez; a Spanish presidio *pop* 60,843
Melita — see MALTA
Melitene — see MALATYA
Me·li·to·pol \,mel-ə-'tō-pəl\ city U.S.S.R. in S Ukraine near Sea of Azov *pop* 137,000
Me·los *or* NGk **Mi·los** \mē-,läs\ *or* It **Mi·lo** \'mē-(,)lō\ island Greece in SW Cyclades *area* 57 — **Me·li·an** \'mē-lē-ən\ *adj or n*
Mel·rose \'mel-,rōz\ city E Mass. N of Boston *pop* 33,180
Melrose Park village NE Ill. W of Chicago *pop* 22,706
Mel·ville \'mel-,vil\ **1** island Canada in NW Franklin District in Parry islands *area* 16,141 **2** peninsula Canada in SE Franklin District between Foxe Basin & an arm of Gulf of Boothia
Melville, Lake lake Canada in Nfld. in Labrador; the inner basin of Hamilton inlet *area* 1133
Me·mel \'mā-məl\ **1** — see NEMAN **2** *or* **Klai·pe·da** \'klī-pəd-ə\ city & port U.S.S.R. in W Lithuania on the Baltic *pop* 140,000
Mem·phis \'mem(p)-fəs\ **1** city SW Tenn. *pop* 623,530 **2** ancient city N Egypt on the Nile S of modern Cairo; once ✻ of Egypt — **Mem·phi·an** \-fē-ən\ *adj or n* — **Mem·phite** \'mem-,fīt\ *adj or n*
Mem·phre·ma·gog, Lake \,mem(p)-fri-'mā-,gäg\ lake 30 *m* long on border between Canada & the U.S. in Que. & Vt.
Menado — see MANADO
Men·ai \'men-,ī\ strait 14 *m* long N Wales between Anglesey I. & mainland
Me Nam — see CHAO PHRAYA
Men·den·hall \'men-dən-,hȯl\ glacier SE Alaska N of Juneau
Men·de·res \,men-də-'res\ **1** *or anc* **Mae·an·der** \mē-'an-dər\ river 240 *m* W Turkey in Asia flowing SW & W into the Aegean **2** *or anc* **Sca·man·der** \skə-'man-dər\ river 60 *m* NW Turkey in Asia flowing from Mt. Ida W & NW across the plain of ancient Troy into the Dardanelles
Men·dip \'men-,dip, -dəp\ hills SW England in NE Somerset; highest Blackdown 1068 *ft*
Men·do·ci·no, Cape \,men-də-'sē-(,)nō\ headland NW Calif. SSW of Eureka; extreme W point of Calif., at 124°8′W
Men·do·ta \men-'dōt-ə\ lake 6 *m* long S Wis. NW of Madison
Men·do·za \men-'dō-zə\ city W Argentina *pop* 109,122
Men·lo Park \,men-(,)lō-\ city W Calif. SE of San Francisco *pop* 22,734
Me·nom·i·nee \mə-'näm-ə-nē\ **1** river 125 *m* NE Wis. flowing SE on Mich.–Wis. border into Green Bay **2** iron range NE Wis. & NW Mich. in upper peninsula
Me·nom·o·nee Falls \mə-,näm-ə-nē-\ village SE Wis. NW of Milwaukee *pop* 31,697
Menorca — see MINORCA
Men·ton \mäⁿ-tōⁿ\ *or* It **Men·to·ne** \men-'tō-nē\ city SE France on the Mediterranean ENE of Nice *pop* 25,040
Men·tor \'ment-ər\ city NE Ohio NE of Cleveland *pop* 36,912
Men·zel–Bour·gui·ba \men-,zel-bu̇r-'gē-bə\ *or formerly* **Fer·ry·ville** \'fer-ē-,vil\ city N Tunisia on Lake Bizerte *pop* 33,800
Me·ra·no \mə-'rän-(,)ō\ commune N Italy in Trentino-Alto Adige NW of Bolzano *pop* 33,594
Mer·ced \(,)mər-'sed\ **1** river 150 *m*, *cen* Calif. flowing W through Yosemite valley into San Joaquin river **2** city *cen* Calif. in San Joaquin valley *pop* 22,670
Mer·ce·da·rio \,mer-sə-'där-ē-,ō\ mountain 22,210 *ft* W Argentina in the Andes N of Aconcagua
Mer·cer Island \,mər-sər-\ city W Wash. E of Seattle *pop* 19,047
Mer·cia \'mər-sh(ē-)ə\ ancient Anglian kingdom *cen* England; one of kingdoms in the Anglo-Saxon heptarchy
Mer·gent·heim \'mer-gənt-,hīm\ *or* **Bad Mergentheim** \(')bät-\ town W Germany in Baden-Württemberg NNE of Stuttgart
Meric — see MARITSA
Mé·ri·da \'mer-əd-ə\ **1** city SE Mexico ✻ of Yucatán *pop* 253,856 **2** city W Venezuela S of Lake Maracaibo *pop* 75,634
Mer·i·den \'mer-əd-ᵊn\ city S *cen* Conn. S of Hartford *pop* 55,959
Me·rid·i·an \mə-'rid-ē-ən\ city E *cen* Miss. *pop* 45,083
Merín — see MIRIM
Mer·i·on·eth \,mer-ē-'än-əth\ *or* **Mer·i·on·eth·shire** \-,shi(ə)r, -shər\ county NW Wales ✻ Dolgellau *area* 660, *pop* 35,277
Mer·o·ë \'mer-ə-,wē\ ancient city, site in N *cen* Sudan on the Nile — **Mero·ite** \'mer-ə-,wīt\ *n* — **Mero·it·ic** \,mer-ə-'wit-ik\ *adj*
Meroë, Isle of ancient region E Sudan between the Nile & Blue Nile & the Atbara
Mer·ri·mack \'mer-ə-,mak\ river 110 *m* S N.H. & NE Mass. flowing S & NE into the Atlantic
Mer·ritt \'mer-ət\ island 40 *m* long E Fla. W of Canaveral peninsula between Indian & Banana rivers
Mersa Matrûh — see MATRÛH
Mers–el–Ke·bir \,me(ə)r-,sel-kə-'bi(ə)r\ town NW Algeria on the Mediterranean W of Oran
Mer·sey \'mər-zē\ river 70 *m* NW England flowing NW & W into Irish sea through a large estuary
Mer·sin \me(ə)r-'sēn\ *or* **Icel** \ē-'chel\ city & port S Turkey on the Mediterranean WSW of Adana *pop* 86,692
Mer·thyr Tyd·fil \,mər-thər-'tid-,vil\ county borough SE Wales in Glamorganshire *pop* 55,215
Mer·ton \'mərt-ᵊn\ borough of SW Greater London, England *pop* 176,524
Me·ru \'mā-(,)rü\ mountain 14,954 *ft* Tanzania in Tanganyika W of Kilimanjaro
Me·sa \'mā-sə\ city SW *cen* Ariz. E of Phoenix *pop* 62,853
Me·sa·bi \mə-'säb-ē\ iron range NE Minn. NW of Duluth
Me·sa Verde National Park \,mā-sə-'vərd(-ē)\ reservation SW Colo. containing prehistoric cliff dwellings *area* 80
Me·se·ta \mə-'sāt-ə\ the central plateau of Spain
Me·shed \mə-'shed\ *or* **Mash·had** \mə-'shad\ city NE Iran *pop* 425,000
Me·so·lón·gi·on \,mes-ə-'lȯŋ-gē(-,ȯn)\ *or* **Mis·so·lon·ghi** \,mis-ə-'lȯŋ-gē\ town SW *cen* Greece on Gulf of Patras
Mes·o·po·ta·mia \,mes-(ə-)pə-'tā-mē-ə, -myə\ **1** region SW Asia between Tigris & Euphrates rivers extending from the mountains of E Asia Minor to the Persian gulf **2** the entire Tigris-Euphrates valley — **Mes·o·po·ta·mian** \-mē-ən, -myən\ *adj or n*
Mes·quite \mə-'skēt, me-\ city NE Tex. E of Dallas *pop* 55,131
Mes·se·ne *or* NGk **Mes·sí·ni** \mə-'sē-nē\ town S Greece in SW Peloponnesus, ancient ✻ of Messenia
Mes·se·nia \mə-'sē-nē-ə, -nyə\ region S Greece in SW Peloponnesus bordering on Ionian sea
Messenia, Gulf of inlet of the Mediterranean S Greece on S coast of Peloponnesus
Mes·si·na \mə-'sē-nə\ *or anc* **Mes·sa·na** \mə-'sän-ə\ *or* **Zan·cle** \'zaŋ-(,)klē\ city & port Italy in NE Sicily *pop* 271,279
Messina, Strait of channel between S Italy & NE Sicily
Mes·ta \me-'stä\ *or* Turk **Ka·ra** \'kär-ə\ *or* Gk **Nes·tos** \'nes-,tȯs\ river 130 *m* SW Bulgaria & NE Greece flowing from W end of Rhodope mountains SE into the Aegean
Me·ta \'māt-ə\ river 685 *m* NE Colombia flowing into the Orinoco on Venezuela-Colombia boundary
Me·tau·ro \mə-'tau̇(ə)r-(,)ō\ *or anc* **Me·tau·rus** \-'tȯr-əs\ river 70 *m* E *cen* Italy flowing E into the Adriatic
Me·thu·en \mə-'th(y)ü-ən\ town NE Mass. *pop* 35,456
Me·tuch·en \mə-'təch-ən\ borough N cen N.J. WNW of Perth Amboy *pop* 16,031
Metz \'mets, *F* mes\ city NE France on the Moselle *pop* 107,537
Meurthe \'mərt\ river 100 *m* NE France flowing NW from Vosges mountains to the Moselle
Meuse \'myüz, 'mə(r)z\ *or* D **Maas** \'mäs\ river 575 *m* W Europe flowing from NE France through S Belgium into North sea in the Netherlands
Mewar — see UDAIPUR
Mex·i·cali \,mek-si-'kal-ē\ city NW Mexico ✻ of Baja California state on Mexico–Calif. border *pop* 281,333
Mex·i·co \'mek-si-,kō\ *or* Sp **Mé·ji·co** \'me-hē-(,)kō\ *or* MexSp **Mé·xi·co** \'me-hē-(,)kō\ **1** *or* **Es·ta·dos Uni·dos Me·xi·ca·nos** \ä-,stäth-(,)ō-sü-,nē-(,)thōz-,me-hē-'kän-(,)ōs\ country S No. America S of the U.S.; a republic ✻ Mexico *area* 761,830, *pop* 50,830,000 **2** state S *cen* Mexico ✻ Toluca *area* 8267, *pop* 3,797,-861 **3** *or* **Mexico City** city ✻ of Republic of Mexico in Federal District (area surrounded on three sides by state of Mexico) *pop* 3,025,564 — see TENOCHTITLÁN
Mexico, Gulf of inlet of the Atlantic on SE coast of No. America
Mé·zenc \mā-'zaŋk\ mountain 5753 *ft* S France; highest in the Cévennes
Mez·zo·gior·no \,met-sō-'jȯr-(,)nō, ,med-zō-\ the Italian peninsula S of *ab* the latitude of Rome
Mfumbiro — see VIRUNGA
Mi·ami \mī-'am-ē, -'am-ə\ city & port SE Fla. on Biscayne Bay *pop* 334,859 — **Mi·ami·an** \-'am-ē-ən\ *n*
Miami Beach city SE Fla. *pop* 87,072
Mich·i·gan \'mish-i-gən\ state N U.S. in Great Lakes region including an upper(NW) & a lower (SE) peninsula ✻ Lansing *area* 58,216, *pop* 8,875,083 — **Mich·i·gan·der** \,mish-i-'gan-dər\ *n* — **Mich·i·gan·ite** \'mish-i-gə-,nīt\ *n*
Michigan, Lake lake N *cen* U.S.; one of the Great Lakes *area* 22,400
Michigan City city N Ind. on Lake Michigan *pop* 39,369
Michilimackinac — see MACKINAC
Mi·cho·a·cán \,mē-chə-wä-'kän\ state SW Mexico bordering on the Pacific ✻ Morelia *area* 23,200, *pop* 2,341,556
Mi·chu·rinsk \mi-'chu̇r-ən(t)sk\ *or formerly* **Kos·lov** \käz-'lȯf, -'lȯv\ city U.S.S.R. in S *cen* Soviet Russia, Europe *pop* 93,000
Mi·cro·ne·sia \,mī-krə-'nē-zhə, -shə\ the islands of the W Pacific E of the Philippines & N of Melanesia including the Caroline, Gilbert, Mariana, & Marshall groups

Mid·del·burg \ˈmid-əl-ˌbərg\ city SW Netherlands on Walcheren I. ✻ of Zeeland *pop* 30,211
Middle Congo former French territory W *cen* Africa — see CONGO, FRENCH EQUATORIAL AFRICA
Middle East *or* **Mid·east** \ˈmid-ˈēst\ the countries of SW Asia & N Africa — usu. considered as including the countries extending from Libya on the W to Afghanistan on the E — **Middle Eastern** *or* **Mid·east·ern** \ˈmid-ˈē-stərn\ *adj*
Mid·dles·brough \ˈmid-əlz-brə\ former county borough N England in No. Riding, Yorkshire, on the Tees; now part of Teesside
Mid·dle·sex \ˈmid-əl-ˌseks\ **1** borough N *cen* N.J. SW of Plainfield *pop* 15,038 **2** former county SE England, now absorbed in Greater London
Mid·dle·town \ˈmid-əl-ˌtau̇n\ **1** city *cen* Conn. S of Hartford *pop* 36,924 **2** city SE N.Y. *pop* 22,607 **3** city SW Ohio SW of Dayton *pop* 48,767 **4** town S R.I. N of Newport *pop* 29,621
Middle West *or* **Mid·west** \ˈmid-ˈwest\ region N *cen* U.S. including area around Great Lakes & in upper Mississippi valley from Ohio & sometimes Ky. on the E to N. & S.Dak., Nebr., & Kans. on the W — **Middle Western** *or* **Mid·west·ern** \ˈmid-ˈwes-tərn\ *adj* — **Middle Westerner** *or* **Mid·west·ern·er** \ˈmid-ˈwes-tə(r)-nər\ *n*
Mi·di \mē-ˈdē\ the south of France
Mid·i·an \ˈmid-ē-ən\ ancient region NW Arabia E of Gulf of ʻAqaba
Mid·land \ˈmid-lənd\ **1** city *cen* Mich. NW of Saginaw *pop* 35,176 **2** city W Tex. NE of Odessa *pop* 59,463
Mid·lands \ˈmid-lən(d)z\ the central counties of England usu. considered as comprising Derby, Nottingham, Lincoln, Stafford, Leicester, Rutland, Worcester, Warwick, Northampton, Huntingdon, Cambridge, Oxford, Buckingham, & Bedford
Mid·lo·thi·an, **1** \mid-ˈlō-thē-ən\ village NE Ill. SW of Chicago *pop* 15,939 **2** \-thē-ən\ *or formerly* **Ed·in·burgh** \ˈed-ən-ˌbər-ə, -ˌbə-rə, -b(ə-)rə\ *or* **Ed·in·burgh·shire** \-ˌshi(ə)r, -shər\ county SE Scotland ✻ Edinburgh *area* 366, *pop* 595,631
Mid·way \ˈmid-ˌwā\ islands (atoll) *cen* Pacific 1300 *m* WNW of Honolulu belonging to the U.S., in Hawaiian group but not incorporated in state of Hawaii *area* 2
Midwest City city *cen* Okla. E of Oklahoma City *pop* 48,114
Mie·res \mē-ˈer-əs\ commune NW Spain in Oviedo province SSE of Oviedo *pop* 64,552
Mikonos — see MYKONOS
Mi·lan \mə-ˈlan, -ˈlän\ *or* It **Mi·la·no** \mi-ˈlän-(ˌ)ō\ *or anc* **Me·dio·la·num** \ˌmed-ē-ō-ˈlä-nəm\ commune N Italy ✻ of Lombardy *pop* 1,696,230 — **Mil·a·nese** \ˌmil-ə-ˈnēz, -ˈnēs\ *adj or n*
Mi·laz·zo \mi-ˈlät-(ˌ)sō\ *or anc* **My·lae** \ˈmī-(ˌ)lē\ city & port Italy in NE Sicily W of Messina *pop* 25,651
Mi·le·tus \mī-ˈlēt-əs, mə-\ ancient city on W coast of Asia Minor in Caria near mouth of the Maeander
Mil·ford \ˌmil-fərd\ **1** city S Conn. on Long Island Sound *pop* 50,858 **2** town E Mass. SE of Worcester *pop* 19,352
Milford Haven urban district & port SW Wales in Pembrokeshire on Milford Haven (inlet of St. George's channel)
Milk \ˈmilk\ river 625 *m* Canada & U.S. in Alta. & Mont. flowing SE into the Missouri
Mill·brae \ˈmil-ˌbrā\ city W Calif. on San Francisco Bay S of San Francisco *pop* 20,781
Mille Lacs \mil-ˈak(s)\ lake 20 *m* long E *cen* Minn.
Mil·ling·ton \ˈmil-iŋ-tən\ town SW Tenn. N of Memphis *pop* 21,106
Mill·ville \ˈmil-ˌvil\ city S N.J. *pop* 21,366
Milo *or* **Mílos** — see MELOS
Mil·pi·tas \mil-ˈpēt-əs\ city W Calif. N of San José *pop* 27,149
Mil·ton \ˈmilt-ən\ town E Mass. S of Boston *pop* 27,190
Mil·wau·kee \mil-ˈwȯ-kē\ city & port SE Wis. *pop* 717,099
Mil·wau·kie \mil-ˈwȯ-kē\ city NW Oreg. S of Portland *pop* 16,379
Min \ˈmin\ **1** river 350 *m*, *cen* China in Szechwan flowing SE into the Yangtze **2** river 250 *m* SE China in Fukien flowing SE into East China sea
Mi·nas Basin \ˌmī-nəs-\ landlocked bay E Canada in *cen* N.S.; the NE extension of Bay of Fundy
Mi·nas de Ri·o·tin·to \ˈmē-nəs-(ˌ)dā-ˌrē-ə-ˈtin-(ˌ)tō\ commune SW Spain in Huelva province NE of Huelva
Mi·nas Ge·rais \ˌmē-nə-zhə-ˈrīs\ state E Brazil ✻ Belo Horizonte *area* 226,179, *pop* 11,279,872
Minch \ˈminch\ channel NW Scotland comprising **North Minch** & **Little Minch** between Outer Hebrides & NW coast of Scotland
Min·cio \ˈmēn-(ˌ)chō, ˈmin-chē-ˌō\ *or anc* **Min·cius** \ˈmin-sh(ē-)əs, ˈmin(t)-sē-əs\ river 115 *m* N Italy issuing from Lake Garda & emptying into the Po
Min·da·nao \ˌmin-də-ˈnä-ˌō, -ˈnau̇\ **1** island S Philippines *area* (including adjacent islands) 36,537, *pop* 7,292,691 **2** sea S Philippines N of Mindanao
Min·do·ro \min-ˈdōr-(ˌ)ō, -ˈdȯr-\ island *cen* Philippines SW of Luzon *area* 3759, *pop* 473,940
Min·e·o·la \ˌmin-ē-ˈō-lə\ village SE N.Y. on Long I. *pop* 21,845
Mineral Wells city N *cen* Texas W of Fort Worth *pop* 18,411
Minhow — see FOOCHOW
Mi·ni·coy \ˈmin-i-ˌkȯi\ island India, southernmost of the Laccadive group
Min·ne·ap·o·lis \ˌmin-ē-ˈap-(ə-)ləs\ city SE Minn. pop 434,400 — **Min·ne·apol·i·tan** \-ē-ə-ˈpäl-ət-ən\ *n*
Min·ne·so·ta \ˌmin-ə-ˈsōt-ə\ **1** river 332 *m* S Minn. flowing from Big Stone Lake to the Mississippi **2** state N U.S. ✻ St. Paul *area* 84,068, *pop* 3,805,069 — **Min·ne·so·tan** \-ˈsōt-ən\ *adj or n*
Min·ne·ton·ka \ˌmin-ə-ˈtäŋ-kə\ village SE Minn. E of **Lake Minnetonka** (12 *m* long) *pop* 35,776
Minni — see ARMENIA
Mi·nor·ca \mə-ˈnȯr-kə\ *or* Sp **Me·nor·ca** \mā-\ island Spain in the Balearic islands ENE of Majorca; chief city Mahón *area* 264 — **Mi·nor·can** \mə-ˈnȯr-kən\ *adj or n*
Mi·not \ˈmī-ˌnät, -nət\ city NW *cen* N.Dak. on Souris river *pop* 32,290
Minsk \ˈmin(t)sk\ city U.S.S.R. ✻ of Belorussia *pop* 907,000
Min·ya *or* **El Minya** \(el-)ˈmin-yə\ city *cen* Egypt *pop* 122,100
Min·ya Kon·ka \ˌmin-yə-ˈkäŋ-kə\ mountain 24,900 *ft* W China in SW *cen* Szechwan; highest in China
Mi·que·lon \ˌmik-ə-ˌlän, ˌmēk-\ island off S coast of Nfld., Canada, belonging to France — see SAINT PIERRE
Mir·a·mar \ˈmir-ə-ˌmär\ city SE Fla. S of Fort Lauderdale *pop* 23,973
Mi·rim \mə-ˈrim\ *or* Sp **Me·rín** \mā-ˈrēn\ lake 108 *m* long on boundary between Brazil & Uruguay near Atlantic coast
Mir·za·pur \ˈmi(ə)r-zə-ˌpu̇(ə)r\ city N India in SE Uttar Pradesh on the Ganges SW of Banaras *pop* 114,741
Mi·se·num \mī-ˈsē-nəm\ ancient port & naval station S Italy at NW corner of Bay of Naples
Mish·a·wa·ka \ˌmish-ə-ˈwȯ-kə, -ˈwäk-ə\ city N Ind. *pop* 35,517
Mis·kolc \ˈmish-ˌkōlts\ city NE Hungary *pop* 172,952
Misr — see EGYPT
Missionary Ridge mountain SE Tenn. & NW Ga. SE of Chattanooga & E of Lookout Mountain
Mis·sis·sau·ga \ˌmis-ə-ˈsȯ-gə\ town Canada in S Ont. SW of Toronto *pop* 156,070
Mis·sis·sip·pi \ˌmis-(ə-)ˈsip-ē\ **1** river 2470 *m*, *cen* U.S. flowing from N *cen* Minn. to Gulf of Mexico — see ITASCA (Lake) **2** river 105 *m* Canada in SE Ont. flowing NE & N into the Ottawa **3** sound inlet of Gulf of Mexico E of Lake Pontchartrain **4** state S U.S. ✻ Jackson *area* 47,716, *pop* 2,216,912
Missolonghi — see MESOLÓNGION
Mis·sou·la \mə-ˈzü-lə\ city W Mont. *pop* 29,497
Mis·sou·ri \mə-ˈzu̇(ə)r-ē, -ˈzu̇r-ə\ **1** river 2700 *m* W U.S. flowing from SW Mont. into the Mississippi in E Mo. — see THREE FORKS **2** state *cen* U.S. ✻ Jefferson City *area* 69,686, *pop* 4,677,399 — **Mis·sou·ri·an** \-ˈzu̇r-ē-ən\ *adj or n*
Mis·tas·si·ni \ˌmis-tə-ˈsē-nē\ **1** lake Canada in S *cen* Que. draining W to James Bay *area* 840 **2** river 185 *m* Canada in S Que. flowing S into Lake St. John
Mis·ti *or* **El Misti** \(el-)ˈmēs-tē, ˈmis-\ dormant volcano 19,098 *ft* S Peru NE of Arequipa
Mitch·am \ˈmich-əm\ former municipal borough S England in Surrey, now part of Merton
Mitch·ell, Mount \ˈmich-əl\ mountain 6684 *ft* W N.C. in Black mountains of the Blue Ridge mountains; highest point in U.S. E of Mississippi river
Mitilini — see MYTILENE
Mi·ya·ji·ma \mē-(y)ə-ˈjē-mə\ *or* **Itsu·ku·shi·ma** \it-ˌsü-kə-ˈshē-mə\ island *ab* 5 *m* long Japan in Inland sea SW of Hiroshima
Mi·ya·za·ki \mē-ˌ(y)äz-ˈäk-ē, mē-ˈ(y)äz-ə-(ˌ)kē\ city & port Japan in Kyushu on SE coast *pop* 214,000
Mo·ab \ˈmō-ˌab\ region Jordan E of Dead sea; in biblical times a kingdom between Edom & the country of the Amorites
Mo·bile \mō-ˈbē(ə)l, ˈmō-ˌbēl\ **1** river 38 *m* long SW Ala. formed by Alabama & Tombigbee rivers & flowing S into **Mobile Bay** (inlet of Gulf of Mexico) **2** city & port SW Ala. *pop* 190,026
Moçambique — see MOZAMBIQUE
Moçâmedes — see MOSSÂMEDES
Mo·cha \ˈmō-kə\ *or* Ar **Mu·kha** \mu̇-ˈkä\ town & port SW Arabia in SW Yemen on the Red sea
Mod·der \ˈmäd-ər\ river 180 *m* Republic of So. Africa in Orange Free State; a tributary of the Vaal
Mo·de·na \ˈmȯd-ən-ə, -ən-ˌä\ *or anc* **Mu·ti·na** \ˈmyüt-ən-ə\ commune N Italy in Emilia SW of Venice *pop* 166,061 — **Mod·e·nese** \ˌmȯd-ən-ˈēz, -ˈēs\ *n*
Mo·des·to \mə-ˈdes-(ˌ)tō\ city *cen* Calif. *pop* 61,712
Moe·sia \ˈmē-sh(ē-)ə\ ancient country & Roman province SE Europe in modern Serbia & Bulgaria S of the Danube from the Drina to Black sea
Mog·a·di·shu \ˌmäg-ə-ˈdish-(ˌ)ü, -ˈdēsh-\ *or* **Mog·a·di·scio** \-(ˌ)ō\ city & port ✻ of Somalia & formerly ✻ of Italian Somaliland on Indian ocean *pop* 172,677
Mogador — see ESSAOUIRA
Mo·gi·lev \ˌmäg-ə-ˌlef, -ˌlev\ city U.S.S.R. in E Belorussia on the Dnieper *pop* 202,000
Mo·gol·lon \ˌməg-ē-ˈōn, ˌmōg-\ **1** mountains SW N.Mex.; highest Whitewater Baldy 10,892 *ft* **2** plateau *ab* 8000 *ft*, *cen* Ariz.
Mo·hacs \ˈmō-ˌhach, -ˌhäch\ town S Hungary *pop* 19,583
Mo·hawk \ˈmō-ˌhȯk\ river 148 *m* E *cen* N.Y. flowing E into the Hudson
Mo·hen·jo–Da·ro \mō-ˌhen-(ˌ)jō-ˈdär-(ˌ)ō\ prehistoric city Pakistan in Indus valley 140 *m* NE of modern Karachi
Mo·ja·ve *or* **Mo·ha·ve** \mə-ˈhäv-ē\ desert S Calif. SE of S end of the Sierra Nevada
Mo·ji \ˈmō-(ˌ)jē\ former city Japan in N Kyushu on Shimonoseki strait — see KITAKYUSHU
Mok·po \ˈmäk-(ˌ)pō\ city & port SW Korea on Yellow sea SW of Kwangju *pop* 162,322
Mold \ˈmōld\ urban district NE Wales ✻ of Flintshire
Moldau — see VLTAVA
Mol·da·via \mäl-ˈdā-vē-ə, -vyə\ **1** region Europe in NE Rumania & SE U.S.S.R. between the Carpathians & Transylvanian Alps on the W & the Dniester on the E **2** *or* **Moldavian Republic** constituent republic of the U.S.S.R. in E Moldavia region ✻ Kishinev *area* 13,100, *pop* 3,572,000 — **Mol·da·vian** \-vē-ən, -vyən\ *adj or n*
Mo·len·beek \ˈmō-lən-ˌbāk\ *or* **Sint–Jans–Molenbeek** \sint-ˈyän(t)s-\ *or* **Molenbeek–Saint–Jean** \-san-ˈzhän\ commune *cen* Belgium in Brabant W of Brussels *pop* 68,515
Mo·line \mō-ˈlēn\ city NW Ill. on the Mississippi *pop* 46,237
Mo·li·se \ˈmȯ-li-ˌzā\ area *cen* Italy between the Apennines & the Adriatic S of Abruzzi — see ABRUZZI
Mo·lo·kai \ˌmäl-ə-ˈkī, ˌmō-lə-\ island *cen* Hawaii ESE of Oahu *area* 259
Mo·lo·po \mə-ˈlō-(ˌ)pō\ river 600 *m* S Africa flowing W along border between Botswana & Republic of So. Africa & thence S into the Orange; now usu. dry
Molotov — see PERM
Mo·luc·cas \mə-ˈlək-əz\ *or* **Spice** \ˈspīs\ *or* Indonesian **Ma·lu·ku** \mə-ˈlü-(ˌ)kü\ islands Indonesia in Malay archipelago between

Celebes & New Guinea *area* 32,300, *pop* 995,000 — see HALMAHERA — **Mo·luc·ca** \mə-ˈlək-ə\ *or* **Mo·luc·can** \-ən\ *adj*

Mom·ba·sa \mäm-ˈbäs-ə\ **1** island Kenya on coast N of Pemba **2** city & port on Mombasa I. & adjacent mainland *pop* 255,400

Mona, 1 — see ANGLESEY **2** *or* **Monapia** — see MAN (Isle of)

Mo·na·co \ˈmän-ə-ˌkō *also* mə-ˈnäk-(ˌ)ō\ **1** country S Europe on the Mediterranean coast of France; a principality *area* 368 acres, *pop* 20,000 **2** commune, its ✻ — **Mo·na·can** \ˈmän-ə-kən, mə-ˈnäk-ən\ *adj or n* — **Mon·e·gasque** \ˌmän-i-ˈgask\ *adj or n*

Mo·nad·nock, Mount \mə-ˈnad-ˌnäk\ mountain 3186 *ft* SW N.H.

Mon·a·ghan \ˈmän-ə-hən, -ˌhan\ **1** county NE Republic of Ireland in Ulster *area* 498, *pop* 46,231 **2** urban district, its ✻

Mo·na Passage \ˌmō-nə-\ strait West Indies between Hispaniola & Puerto Rico connecting the Caribbean & the Atlantic

Mon·a·stir \ˌmän-ə-ˈsti(ə)r\ *or* **Bi·tolj** \ˈbē-ˌtōl(-yə), -ˌtȯi\ *or* **Bi·to·la** \ˈbēt-^{ə}l-ˌyä\ city S Yugoslavia in S Macedonia *pop* 20,400

Mön·chen–Glad·bach \ˌmə(r)n-kən-ˈglät-ˌbäk, ˌmœn-kən-ˈglät-ˌbäk\ *or* **Mün·chen–Glad·bach** \ˌm(y)ün-, ˌmuen-\ city W Germany W of Düsseldorf *pop* 152,200

Monc·ton \ˈməŋ(k)-tən\ city Canada in E N.B. *pop* 47,891

Mo·nes·sen \mə-ˈnes-^{ə}n\ city SW Pa. *pop* 15,216

Mon·go·lia \män-ˈgōl-yə, mäŋ-, -ˈgō-lē-ə\ **1** region E Asia W of Khingan mountains & E of Altai mountains; includes Gobi desert **2** *or* **Mongolian Republic** *or* **Outer Mongolia** country E Asia comprising major portion of Mongolia region; a republic ✻ Ulan Bator *area* 580,158, *pop* 1,280,000 **3** INNER MONGOLIA

Mon·he·gan \män-ˈhē-gən\ island Me. ESE of Boothbay Harbor

Mon·mouth \ˈmän-məth, ˈmən-\ *or* **Mon·mouth·shire** \-ˌshi(ə)r, -shər\ county SE Wales; formerly regarded as part of England ✻ Newport *area* 546, *pop* 461,459

Mo·no \ˈmō-(ˌ)nō\ saline lake 14 *m* long E Calif.

Mo·noc·a·cy \mə-ˈnäk-ə-sē\ river 60 *m* S Pa. & N Md. flowing S into the Potomac

Mo·non·ga·he·la \mə-ˌnän-gə-ˈhē-lə, -ˌnäŋ-gə-, -ˈhā-lə\ river 128 *m* N W.Va. & SW Pa. flowing N to unite with the Allegheny at Pittsburgh forming the Ohio

Mon·roe \(ˌ)mən-ˈrō\ **1** city N La. *pop* 56,374 **2** city SE Mich. SSW of Detroit on Lake Erie *pop* 23,894

Mon·roe·ville \(ˌ)mən-ˈrō-ˌvil\ borough SW Pa. E of Pittsburgh *pop* 29,011

Mon·ro·via \(ˌ)mən-ˈrō-vē-ə\ **1** city SW Calif. E of Pasadena *pop* 30,015 **2** city & port ✻ of Liberia on the Atlantic *pop* 100,000

Mons \mō^{n}s\ *or* Flem **Ber·gen** \ˈber-kə(n)\ commune SW Belgium ✻ of Hainaut *pop* 28,727

Mon·tana \män-ˈtan-ə\ state NW U.S. ✻ Helena *area* 147,138, *pop* 694,409 — **Mon·tan·an** \-ən\ *adj or n*

Mont·au·ban \ˌmänt-ō-ˈbä^{n}, mō^{n}-tō-bä^{n}\ city SW France on the Tarn N of Toulouse *pop* 45,895

Mon·tauk Point \ˌmän-ˌtȯk-\ headland SE N.Y. at E tip of Long I.

Mont Blanc \mō^{n}-blä^{n}\ **1** mountain 15,771 *ft* SE France on Italian border in Savoy Alps; highest of the Alps **2** tunnel 7½ *m* long France & Italy under Mont Blanc

Mont·clair \mänt-ˈkla(ə)r, -ˈkle(ə)r\ **1** city SW Calif. E of Los Angeles *pop* 22,546 **2** town NE N.J. SSW of Paterson *pop* 44,043

Mon·te Al·bán \ˌmänt-ē-äl-ˈbän\ ruined city of the Zapotecs S Mexico in Oaxaca state SW of Oaxaca

Mon·te·bel·lo \ˌmänt-ə-ˈbel-(ˌ)ō\ city SW Calif. ESE of Los Angeles *pop* 42,807

Mon·te Car·lo \ˌmänt-i-ˈkär-(ˌ)lō\ commune Monaco

Mon·te·go Bay \män-ˌtē-(ˌ)gō-\ city & port NW Jamaica on Montego Bay (inlet of the Caribbean) *pop* 42,800

Mon·te·ne·gro \ˌmänt-ə-ˈnē-(ˌ)grō, -ˈnā-\ federated republic S Yugoslavia on the Adriatic; formerly a kingdom (✻ Cetinje) ✻ Titograd *area* 5343, *pop* 530,361 — **Mon·te·ne·grin** \-grən\ *adj or n*

Mon·te·rey \ˌmänt-ə-ˈrā\ city W Calif. on Monterey peninsula at S end of **Monterey Bay** (inlet of the Pacific) *pop* 26,302

Monterey Park city SW Calif. E of Los Angeles *pop* 49,166

Mon·ter·rey \ˌmänt-ə-ˈrā\ city NE Mexico ✻ of Nuevo León *pop* 830,336

Mon·te·vi·deo \ˌmänt-ə-və-ˈdā-(ˌ)ō, -ˈvid-ē-ˌō\ city & port ✻ of Uruguay on N shore of Río de la Plata *pop* 1,154,465

Mon·te·zu·ma Castle National Monument \ˌmänt-ə-ˈzü-mə\ reservation *cen* Ariz. containing prehistoric cliff dwellings

Mont·gom·ery \(ˌ)mən(t)-ˈgəm-(ə-)rē, män(t)-, -ˈgäm-\ **1** city ✻ of Ala. on the Alabama *pop* 133,386 **2** *or* **Mont·gom·ery·shire** \-ˌshi(ə)r, -shər\ county E Wales ✻ Welshpool *area* 797, *pop* 42,761

Mont·mar·tre \mō^{n}-ˈmärtr^{ə}\ section of Paris, France, on a hill in N *cen* part of the city

Mont·mo·ren·cy \ˌmänt-mə-ˈren(t)-sē, mō^{n}-mȯ-rä^{n}-sē\ commune N France, N suburb of Paris *pop* 18,691

Mont·mo·ren·cy Falls \ˌmänt-mə-ˌren(t)-sē-\ waterfall 270 *ft* Canada in S Que. NE of Quebec city in **Montmorency** river (60 *m* flowing S into the St. Lawrence)

Mont·par·nasse \ˌmō^{n}-(ˌ)pär-ˈnäs, -ˈnas\ section of Paris, France, in S *cen* part of the city — **Mont·par·nas·sian** \-ˈnash-ən, -ˈnas-ē-ən\ *adj*

Mont·pe·lier \mänt-ˈpēl-yər, -ˈpil-\ city ✻ of Vt. *pop* 8609

Mont·pel·lier \mō^{n}-pe-lyā\ city S France WNW of Marseilles *pop* 161,910

Mon·tre·al \ˌmän-trē-ˈȯl, ˌmən-\ *or* **Mont·ré·al** \mō^{n}-rā-ál\ city & port Canada in S Que. on **Montreal Island** (32 *m* long, in the St. Lawrence) *pop* 1,214,352 — **Mon·tre·al·er** \ˌmän-trē-ˈȯ-lər, ˌmən-\ *n*

Montreal North *or* **Montréal–Nord** \-nȯr\ town Canada in S Que. on Montreal I. *pop* 89,139

Mon·treuil \mō^{n}-ˈtrə(r), -ˈtrəi\ *or* **Montreuil–sous–Bois** \-(ˌ)süb-ˈwä\ commune N France, E suburb of Paris *pop* 95,714

Mon·treux \mō^{n}-ˈtrə(r), -ˈtrœ\ group of villages W Switzerland in Vaud canton at E end of Lake Geneva *pop* 20,421

Mont–Roy·al \mō^{n}-rwä-yál\ *or* **Mount Roy·al** \maùnt-ˈrȯi(-ə)l\ **1** town Canada in S Que. on Montreal I. *pop* 21,561 **2** height 769 *ft* in Montreal, Que.

Mont–Saint–Mi·chel \mō^{n}-sa^{n}-mē-shel\ small island NW France in Gulf of St-Malo

Mont·ser·rat \ˌmän(t)-sə-ˈrat\ island Brit. West Indies in the Leewards SW of Antigua; chief town Plymouth *area* 33, *pop* 12,302

Mont·ville \ˈmänt-ˌvil\ town SE Conn. N of New London *pop* 15,662

Monument Valley region NE Ariz. & SE Utah containing red sandstone buttes, mesas, & arches

Mon·za \ˈmōn(t)-sə, ˈmän-zə\ commune N Italy in Lombardy SE of Milan *pop* 106,590

Moore \ˈmō(ə)r, ˈmȯ(ə)r\ city *cen* Okla. S of Oklahoma City *pop* 18,761

Mo·oréa \ˌmō-ə-ˈrā-ə\ island S Pacific in Society islands NW of Tahiti *area* 51

Moor·head \ˈmō(ə)r-ˌhed, ˈmȯ(ə)r-, ˈmu̇(ə)r-\ city W Minn. on Red river opposite Fargo, N.Dak. *pop* 29,687

Moose \ˈmüs\ river 50 *m* Canada in NE Ont. flowing NE into James Bay; estuary of Abitibi, Mattagami, & other rivers

Moose·head \ˈmüs-ˌhed\ lake 35 *m* long NW *cen* Me.

Moose Jaw city Canada in S Sask. W of Regina *pop* 31,854

Mo·rad·abad \mə-ˈräd-ə-ˌbäd, -ˈrad-ə-ˌbad\ city N India in NW Uttar Pradesh ENE of Delhi *pop* 208,556

Mo·ra·tu·wa \mə-ˈrət-ə-wə\ city W Ceylon on Indian ocean S of Colombo *pop* 86,000

Mo·ra·va \ˈmȯr-ə-və\ **1** — see MARCH **2** river 134 *m* E Yugoslavia in Serbia flowing N into the Danube

Mo·ra·via \mə-ˈrā-vē-ə\ region *cen* Czechoslovakia S of Silesia traversed by Morava river; chief city Brno

Mo·ra·vi·an Gate *or* **Moravian Gap** \mə-ˌrā-vē-ən-\ mountain pass *cen* Europe between Sudeten & Carpathian mountains

Moravska Ostrava — see OSTRAVA

Mor·ay \ˈmər-ē, ˈmə-rē\ *or* **Mor·ay·shire** \-ˌshi(ə)r, -shər\ *or* **El·gin** \ˈel-gən\ *or* **El·gin·shire** \-ˌshi(ə)r, -shər\ county NE Scotland bordering on North sea ✻ Elgin *area* 476, *pop* 51,485

Moray firth inlet of North sea N Scotland

Mor·do·vi·an Republic \(ˌ)mȯr-ˌdō-vē-ən-\ *or* **Mord·vin·i·an Republic** \(ˌ)mȯrd-ˌvin-ē-ən-\ autonomous republic U.S.S.R. in *cen* Soviet Russia, Europe, S & W of middle Volga ✻ Saransk *area* 10,100, *pop* 1,030,000

Morea — see PELOPONNESUS

Mo·reau \ˈmōr-(ˌ)ō, ˈmȯr-\ river 250 *m* NW S.Dak. flowing E into the Missouri

More·cambe and Hey·sham \ˌmōr-kəm-ən(d)-ˈhē-shəm, ˌmȯr-\ municipal borough NW England in N Lancashire on **Morecambe Bay** (inlet of Irish sea) *pop* 41,863

Mo·re·lia \mə-ˈrāl-yə\ city SW Mexico ✻ of Michoacán *pop* 209,507

Mo·re·los \mə-ˈrā-ləs\ state S *cen* Mexico ✻ Cuernavaca *area* 1916, *pop* 620,392

More·ton Bay \ˌmōrt-^{ə}n-, ˌmȯrt-\ inlet of the Pacific Australia in SE Queensland at mouth of Brisbane river

Mor·gan City \ˌmȯr-gən-\ city SE La. *pop* 16,586

Mor·gan·town \ˈmȯr-gən-ˌtau̇n\ city N W.Va. *pop* 29,431

Mo·ri·ah \mə-ˈrī-ə\ hill *cen* Palestine in E part of Jerusalem

Mo·ri·o·ka \ˌmōr-ē-ˈō-kə, ˌmȯr-\ city Japan in N Honshu E of Akita *pop* 195,000

Mo·roc·co \mə-ˈräk-(ˌ)ō\ **1** country NW Africa bordering on the Atlantic & the Mediterranean; a kingdom ✻ Rabat, summer ✻ Tangier *area ab* 175,000, *pop* 15,230,000; formerly (1911–56) divided into **French Morocco** (protectorate ✻ Rabat *area* 153,870), **Spanish Morocco** (protectorate ✻ Tetuán *area* 18,009), **Southern Morocco** (Spanish protectorate, chief town Cabo Yubi *area* 10,039), & the **International Zone** of Tangier (*area* 225) **2** — see MARRAKESH — **Mo·roc·can** \-ˈräk-ən\ *adj or n*

Mo·ro Gulf \ˌmōr-(ˌ)ō-, ˌmȯr-\ arm of Celebes sea S Philippines off SW coast of Mindanao

Mor·ris Jes·up, Cape \ˌmȯr-əs-ˈjes-əp, ˌmär-\ headland N Greenland in Peary Land on Arctic ocean

Mor·ri·son, Mount \ˈmȯr-ə-sən, ˈmär-\ *or* **Yü Shan** \ˈyü-ˈshän\ mountain 13,599 *ft* China in *cen* Formosa; highest on island

Morrison Cave — see LEWIS AND CLARK

Mor·ris·town \ˈmȯr-ə-ˌstau̇n, ˈmär-\ **1** town NE *cen* N.J. *pop* 17,662 **2** city E Tenn. ENE of Knoxville *pop* 20,318

Mor·ton Grove \ˌmȯrt-^{ə}n-\ village NE Ill. W of Evanston *pop* 26,369

Mos·cow \ˈmäs-ˌkau̇, -(ˌ)kō\ *or* Russ **Mos·kva** \mäsk-ˈvä\ **1** river 315 *m* U.S.S.R. in W *cen* Soviet Russia, Europe, flowing E into the Oka **2** city ✻ of U.S.S.R. & of the Russian Republic on Moscow river *pop* 7,061,000 — see MUSCOVY

Mo·selle \mō-ˈzel\ *or* G **Mo·sel** \ˈmō-zəl\ river 320 *m* E France & W Germany flowing from the Vosges into the Rhine at Koblenz

Mosquito coast *or* **Mos·qui·tia** \mə-ˈskēt-ē-ə\ region Central America bordering on the Caribbean in E Honduras & E Nicaragua

Mos·sâ·me·des *or* **Mo·çâ·me·des** \mə-ˈsam-əd-ish\ town & port SW Angola

Mos·sel Bay \ˌmō-səl-\ city & port S Republic of So. Africa in S Cape of Good Hope on Mossel Bay (inlet of Indian ocean) *pop* 15,600

Moss Point city SE Miss. E of Gulfport *pop* 19,321

Mos·tag·a·nem \mə-ˈstag-ə-ˌnem\ city & port NW Algeria ENE of Oran *pop* 63,297

Mo·sul \mō-ˈsül, ˈmō-səl\ city N Iraq on the Tigris *pop* 264,146

Moth·er·well and Wish·aw \ˈməth-ər-ˌwel-ən-ˈwish-ˌȯ, -wə-lən-\ burgh S *cen* Scotland in Lanark SE of Glasgow *pop* 73,384

Moul·mein \mül-ˈmān, mōl-, -ˈmīn\ city S Burma on Gulf of Martaban at mouth of the Salween *pop* 108,020

Mound City Group National Monument reservation S Ohio N of Chillicothe containing prehistoric mounds

Mountain Brook city N *cen* Ala. E of Birmingham *pop* 19,474

Mountain View city W Calif. NW of San Jose *pop* 51,092

Mount Clem·ens \ˈklem-ənz\ city SE Mich. *pop* 20,476

Mount De·sert \də-ˈzərt, ˈdez-ərt\ island S Me. in the Atlantic E of Penobscot Bay *area* 100 — see ACADIA NATIONAL PARK

Mount·lake Terrace \ˌmau̇nt-ˌlāk-\ city W Wash. N of Seattle *pop* 16,600
Mount McKinley National Park — see MCKINLEY (Mount)
Mount Pleasant city *cen* Mich. NW of Saginaw *pop* 20,504
Mount Pros·pect \'präs-ˌpekt\ village NE Ill. *pop* 34,995
Mount Rainier National Park — see RAINIER (Mount)
Mount Rev·el·stoke National Park \'rev-əl-ˌstōk\ reservation Canada in SE B.C. on a plateau including Mt. Revelstoke (over 7000 *ft*) W of Selkirk mountains *area* 100
Mount Royal — see MONT-ROYAL
Mount Ver·non \'vər-nən\ **1** city S Ill. *pop* 15,980 **2** city SE N.Y. N of New York City *pop* 72,778
Mourne \'mō(ə)rn, 'mȯ(ə)rn\ mountains SE Northern Ireland
Mouse — see SOURIS
Mo·zam·bique \ˌmō-zəm-'bēk\ *or* Port **Mo·çam·bi·que** \ˌmü-səm-'bē-kə\ **1** channel 950 *m* long SE Africa between Madagascar & Mozambique **2** *or* **Portuguese East Africa** country SE Africa bordering on Mozambique channel; a dependency of Portugal ✱ Lourenço Marques *area* 297,654, *pop* 8,233,034 — **Mo·zam·bi·can** \ˌmō-zəm-'bē-kən\ *adj*
Mtwa·ra \em-'twär-ə\ city & port Tanzania in SE Tanganyika *pop* 20,413
Mu·gu, Point \mə-'gü\ cape SW Calif. W of Los Angeles
Muir Woods National Monument \'myu̇(ə)r\ reservation N Calif. NW of San Francisco containing a redwood grove
Mui·zen·berg \'mīz-ᵊn-ˌbərg\ town Republic of So. Africa on False Bay, SSE suburb of Cape Town
Mu·kal·la \mu̇-'kal-ə\ city & port South Yemen on Gulf of Aden; chief town of the Hadhramaut *pop* 65,000
Muk·den \'mu̇k-dən, 'mək-; mu̇k-'den\ *or* **Shen·yang** \'shən-'yäŋ\ *or formerly* **Feng·tien** \'fəŋ-tē-'en\ city NE China ✱ of Liaoning on Hun river; chief city of Manchuria *pop* 2,411,000
Mukha — see MOCHA
Mül·heim \'m(y)ül-ˌhīm, 'mu̅e̅l-\ *or* **Mülheim an der Ruhr** \-än-də(r)-'ru̇(ə)r\ city W Germany on Ruhr river *pop* 190,400
Mul·house \mə-'lüz\ commune NE France in Alsace *pop* 116,336
Mull \'məl\ island W Scotland in the Inner Hebrides *area* 351
Mul·lin·gar \ˌməl-ən-'gär\ town N *cen* Ireland ✱ of Westmeath
Mul·tan \mu̇l-'tän\ city NE Pakistan SW of Lahore *pop* 597,000
Mult·no·mah Falls \ˌməlt-'nō-mə\ waterfall 620 *ft* NW Oreg. E of Portland in a tributary of the Columbia
München-Gladbach — see MÖNCHEN-GLADBACH
Mun·cie \'mən(t)-sē\ city E Ind. *pop* 69,080
Mun·de·lein \'mən-də-ˌlīn\ village NE Ill. NW of Chicago *pop* 16,128
Mun·hall \'mən-ˌhȯl\ borough SW Pa. SE of Pittsburgh *pop* 16,674
Mu·nich \'myü-nik\ *or* G **Mün·chen** \'mu̅e̅n-kən\ city S Germany ✱ of Bavaria on the Isar *pop* 1,302,600
Mun·ster \'mən(t)-stər\ **1** town NW Ind. SW of Hammond *pop* 16,514 **2** province S Ireland *area* 9317, *pop* 880,000
Mün·ster \'mən(t)-stər, 'm(y)ün(t)-, 'mu̅e̅n-\ city W Germany; formerly ✱ of Westphalia *pop* 203,300
Mun·te·nia \ˌmən-'tē-nē-ə, mün-'ten-ē-ə\ *or* **Greater Walachia** region SE Rumania in E part of Walachia
Mur \'mu̇(ə)r\ *or* **Mu·ra** \'mu̇r-ə\ river 230 *m* Austria & N Yugoslavia flowing into the Drava
Mu·ra·no \mu̇-'rän-(ˌ)ō\ town NE Italy in Venetia on islands in Lagoon of Venice N of Venice
Mu·rat \mü-'rät\ *or anc* **Ar·sa·ni·as** \är-'sā-nē-əs\ river 380 *m* E Turkey flowing WSW into the Euphrates
Mur·chi·son \'mər-chə-sən\ river 400 *m* Australia in W Western Australia flowing W into Indian ocean
Murchison Falls waterfall 120 *ft* W Uganda in the Victoria Nile above Lake Albert
Mur·cia \'mər-sh(ē-)ə\ **1** region & ancient kingdom SE Spain bordering on the Mediterranean **2** province SE Spain bordering on the Mediterranean *area* 4453, *pop* 832,313 **3** commune, its ✱ & ✱ of ancient kingdom of Murcia, on Segura river *pop* 277,948
Mu·res *or* **Mu·resh** \'mü-ˌresh\ *or* **Ma·ros** \'mȯr-ˌōsh\ river 400 *m*, *cen* Rumania & E Hungary flowing W into the Tisza
Mur·frees·boro \'mər-f(r)ēz-ˌbər-ə, -ˌbə-rə\ city *cen* Tenn. SE of Nashville *pop* 26,360
Mur·mansk \mu̇r-'man(t)sk, -'män(t)sk\ city & port U.S.S.R. in NW Soviet Russia, Europe, on Kola peninsula on an inlet of Barents sea *pop* 309,000
Mu·ro·ran \ˌmu̇r-ə-'rän\ city & port Japan in SW Hokkaido on an inlet of the Pacific *pop* 183,000
Mur·ray \'mər-ē, 'mə-rē\ **1** city N Utah *pop* 21,206 **2** river 1200 *m* SE Australia flowing from near Mt. Kosciusko in E Victoria W into Indian ocean in SE So. Australia
Mur·ree \'mər-ē, 'mə-rē\ **1** hills NE Pakistan **2** town in the Murree hills NE of Rawalpindi
Mur·rum·bidg·ee \ˌmər-əm-'bij-ē, ˌmə-rəm-\ river 1000 *m* SE Australia in New So. Wales flowing W into the Murray
Murua — see WOODLARK
Murviedro — see SAGUNTO
Mu·sa, Ge·bel \ˌjeb-əl-'mü-sə\ mountain group NE Egypt in S Sinai peninsula — see HOREB, KATHERINA (Gebel)
Mu·sa, Je·bel \ˌjeb-əl-'mü-sə\ *or anc* **Ab·i·la** *or* **Ab·y·la** \'ab-ə-lə\ mountain 2775 *ft* N Morocco opposite Rock of Gibraltar — see PILLARS OF HERCULES
Mus·cat *or* **Mas·qat** *or* **Mas·kat** \'məs-ˌkat, -kət\ town & port ✱ of Oman on Gulf of Oman
Muscat and Oman — see OMAN
Mus·ca·tine \ˌməs-kə-'tēn\ city E Iowa *pop* 22,405
Mus·co·vy \(ˌ)mə-'skō-vē; 'məs-kə-, -ˌkō-\ **1** the principality of Moscow (founded 1295) which in 15th century came to dominate Russia **2** RUSSIA
Mus·ke·gon \mə-'skē-gən\ **1** river 200 *m* W *cen* Mich. flowing SW into Lake Michigan **2** city & port SW Mich. *pop* 44,631
Muskegon Heights city SW Mich. *pop* 17,304
Mus·kin·gum \mə-'skiŋ-(g)əm\ river 120 *m* E Ohio flowing SSE into the Ohio
Mus·ko·gee \mə-'skō-gē\ city E Okla. *pop* 37,331
Mus·ko·ka, Lake \mə-'skō-kə\ lake Canada in SE Ont. E of Georgian Bay & N of Lake Simcoe *area* 54
Mus·sel·shell \'məs-əl-ˌshel\ river 300 *m*, *cen* Mont. flowing E & N into the Missouri
Mu·tan·kiang \'mü-'dän-jē-'äŋ\ city NE China in S Heilungkiang on the **Mu·tan** \'mü-'dän\ river (310 *m* flowing NE into the Sungari) SE of Harbin *pop* 400,000
Mutina — see MODENA
Mu·tsu Bay \ˌmüt-(ˌ)sü-\ inlet N Japan on NE Honshu on Tsugaru strait
Muttra — see MATHURA
Mwe·ru \mə-'we(ə)r-(ˌ)ü\ lake 80 *m* long on border between Zaire & Zambia SW of Lake Tanganyika
Myc·a·le \'mik-ə-(ˌ)lē\ promontory W Turkey opposite Samos I.
My·ce·nae \mī-'sē-(ˌ)nē\ ancient city S Greece in NE Peloponnesus N of Argos
Myit·kyi·na \ˌmē-chi-'nȯ\ town N Burma ✱ of Kachin
Myk·o·nos \'mik-ə-ˌnäs, -nəs\ *or* NGk **Mí·ko·nos** \'mē-kə-ˌnȯs\ island Greece in the Aegean in NE Cyclades SE of Tenos *area* 35
Mylae — see MILAZZO
My·men·singh \ˌmī-mən-'siŋ\ city N Bangladesh *pop* 53,256
My·ra \'mī-rə\ ancient city S Asia Minor on coast of Lycia
My·sia \'mish-(ē-)ə\ ancient country NW Asia Minor bordering on the Propontis — **My·sian** \-(ē-)ən\ *adj or n*
My·sore \mī-'sō(ə)r, -'sȯ(ə)r\ **1** state SW India ✱ Bangalore *area* 74,326, *pop* 29,224,046 **2** city in S Mysore state *pop* 263,131
Mys·tic \'mis-tik\ river E Mass. flowing SE into Boston harbor
Myt·i·le·ne *or* NGk **Mi·ti·li·ni** \ˌmit-ᵊl-'ē-nē\ **1** — see LESBOS **2** *or formerly* **Ka·stro** \'käs-(ˌ)trō\ city & port Greece on E coast of Lesbos I. *pop* 24,157
Naas \'nās\ urban district E Ireland in Leinster ✱ of Kildare
Nab·a·taea *or* **Nab·a·tea** \ˌnab-ə-'tē-ə\ ancient Arab kingdom SE of Palestine — **Nab·a·tae·an** *or* **Nab·a·te·an** \-'tē-ən\ *adj or n*
Nab·lus \'nab-ləs, 'näb-\ *or anc* **She·chem** \'shē-kəm, -ˌkem\ *or* **Ne·ap·o·lis** \nē-'ap-ə-ləs\ city *cen* Palestine in Samaria; now in W Jordan *pop* 44,223
Nac·og·do·ches \ˌnak-ə-'dō-chəz, -chəs\ city E Tex. *pop* 22,544
Na·fud *or* **Ne·fud** \nə-'füd\ desert N Saudi Arabia in N Nejd
Na·ga \'näg-ə\ hills E India & N Burma SE of the Brahmaputra; highest Saramati 12,553 *ft*
Na·ga·land \'näg-ə-ˌland\ state E India N of Manipur in Naga hills ✱ Kohima *area* 6336, *pop* 515,561
Na·ga·o·ka \ˌnä-gə-'ō-kə, nä-'gä-ō-(ˌ)kä\ city Japan in N *cen* Honshu SSW of Niigata *pop* 160,000
Na·ga·sa·ki \ˌnäg-ə-'säk-ē, ˌnag-ə-'sak-ē\ city & port Japan in W Kyushu on East China sea *pop* 425,000
Na·gor·no-Ka·ra·bakh Region \nə-ˌgȯr-(ˌ)nō-'kär-ə-ˌbäk-\ autonomous region U.S.S.R. in SW Azerbaidzhan ✱ Stepanakert *area* 1700, *pop* 149,000
Na·goya \nə-'gȯi-ə, 'näg-ə-(ˌ)yä\ city Japan in S *cen* Honshu *pop* 2,014,000
Nag·pur \'näg-ˌpu̇(ə)r\ city E *cen* India in NE Maharashtra *pop* 903,826
Nagyvarad — see ORADEA
Na·ha \'nä-(ˌ)hä\ *or* **Na·wa** \'nä-(ˌ)wä\ city & port Ryukyu islands in SW Okinawa I. ✱ of Okinawa *pop* 276,380
Nairn \'na(ə)rn, 'ne(ə)rn\ **1** *or* **Nairn·shire** \-ˌshi(ə)r, -shər\ county NE Scotland bordering Moray firth *area* 163, *pop* 11,049 **2** burgh, its ✱, on Moray firth
Nai·ro·bi \nī-'rō-bē\ city ✱ of Kenya *pop* 535,200
Na·jaf *or* **An Najaf** \(an-)'naj-ˌaf\ city S *cen* Iraq *pop* 134,027
Najd — see NEJD — **Najdi** \'naj-dē\ *adj or n*
Na·khi·che·van \ˌnäk-i-chə-'vän\ **1** *or* **Nakhichevan Republic** autonomous republic U.S.S.R.; part of Azerbaidzhan *area* 2100, *pop* 202,000 **2** city, its ✱, on the Araks *pop* 33,000
Nak·tong \'näk-ˌtȯŋ\ river 260 *m* S Korea flowing S & E into Korea strait near Pusan
Na·ma·qua·land \nə-'mäk-wə-ˌland\ *or* **Na·ma·land** \'näm-ə-\ region SW Africa; divided by Orange river into **Great Namaqualand** (in South-West Africa) & **Little Namaqualand** (in Cape Province, Republic of So. Africa, chief town Springbok)
Namhoi — see FATSHAN
Namibia — see SOUTH-WEST AFRICA
Nam·pa \'nam-pə\ city SW Idaho W of Boise *pop* 20,768
Nam·po \'nam-(ˌ)pō\ *or* **Chin·nam·po** \'chē(n)-ˌnäm-(ˌ)pō\ city & port N Korea SW of Pyongyang *pop* 82,162
Na·mur \nə-'m(y)u̇(ə)r\ **1** province S Belgium *area* 1413, *pop* 384,689 **2** commune, its ✱ *pop* 32,507
Nan \'nän\ river 350 *m* N Thailand flowing S to join the Ping forming the Chao Phraya
Nan·chang \'nän-'chäŋ\ city SE China ✱ of Kiangsi on the Kan SW of Poyang Lake *pop* 508,000
Nan·chung \'nän-'chu̇ŋ\ city *cen* China in E *cen* Szechwan on Kialing river *pop* 164,700
Nan·cy \'nan(t)-sē, näⁿ-sē\ city NE France *pop* 123,428
Nan·da De·vi \ˌnən-də-'dā-vē\ mountain 25,645 *ft* N India in the Himalayas in Uttar Pradesh
Nan·di *or* **Na·di** \'nän-(ˌ)dē\ village Fiji on W Viti Levu I.
Nan·ga Par·bat \ˌnəŋ-gə-'pər-bət\ mountain 26,660 *ft* NW Kashmir in the W Himalayas
Nan·king \'nan-'kiŋ, 'nän-\ city E China on the Yangtze ✱ of Kiangsu & (1928–37 & 1946–49) ✱ of China *pop* 1,419,000
Nan Ling \'nän-'liŋ\ *or* **Nan Shan** \-'shän\ mountain system SE China roughly separating Kwangtung & Kwangsi from Hunan & Kweichow

Nan·ning \'nän-'niŋ\ *or formerly* **Yung·ning** \'yu̇ŋ-'niŋ\ city S China ✻ of Kwangsi on Yü river *pop* 264,000

Nansei — see RYUKYU

Nan Shan \'nän-'shän\ mountain range W China extending from Kunlun mountains along NE edge of Tibetan plateau to NE Tsinghai

Nan·terre \nä(n)-'te(ə)r\ commune N France W of Paris *pop* 90,332

Nantes \'nan(t)s\ city NW France on the Loire *pop* 259,208

Nan·tuck·et \nan-'tək-ət\ island Mass. in the Atlantic S of Cape Cod on **Nantucket Sound** (inlet of the Atlantic)

Nan·tung \'nän-'tu̇ŋ\ city & port E China in SE Kiangsu on Yangtze estuary NW of Shanghai *pop* 300,000

Napa \'nap-ə\ city W Calif. N of Vallejo *pop* 35,978

Na·per·ville \'nā-pər-ˌvil\ city NE Ill. W of Chicago *pop* 23,885

Na·pi·er \'nā-pē-ər\ borough & port New Zealand in E North I. on Hawke Bay *pop* 38,200

Na·ples \'nā-pəlz\ *or* It **Na·po·li** \'näp-ə-lē\ *or anc* **Ne·ap·o·lis** \nē-'ap-ə-ləs\ city & port S Italy on **Bay of Naples** (inlet of Tyrrhenian sea) ✻ of Campania *pop* 1,273,806

Na·po \'näp-(ˌ)ō\ river 550 *m* NW So. America rising near Mt. Cotopaxi in *cen* Ecuador & flowing E & SE into the Amazon

Na·ra \'när-ə\ city Japan in W *cen* Honshu E of Osaka; an early ✻ of Japan *pop* 200,000

Nar·ba·da \nər-'bəd-ə\ river 800 *m, cen* India flowing W between Vindhya mountains & Satpura range into Gulf of Cambay

Nar·bonne \när-'bän, -'bən\ city S France near the Mediterranean sea E of Carcassonne *pop* 38,441

Na·rew \'när-ˌef, -ˌev\ *or* Russ **Na·rev** \nər-'yȯf, -'yȯv\ river 285 *m* NE Poland flowing W & SW into the Bug

Nar·ra·gan·sett Bay \ˌnar-ə-'gan(t)-sət\ inlet of the Atlantic SE R.I.

Nar·vik \'när-vik\ town & port N Norway

Nash·ua \'nash-ə-wə, -ə-ˌwä\ city S N.H. *pop* 55,820

Nash·ville \'nash-ˌvil, -vəl\ city ✻ of Tenn. *pop* 447,877

Nas·sau \'nas-ˌȯ, *Ger* 'näs-ˌau̇\ **1** city & port ✻ of the Bahamas on New Providence I. *pop* 101,182 **2** region W Germany N & E of the Rhine; chief city Wiesbaden **3** — see SUDIRMAN

Nasser, Lake — see ASWÂN

Na·tal \nə-'tal, -'täl\ **1** city & port NE Brazil ✻ of Rio Grande do Norte *pop* 239,590 **2** province E Republic of So. Africa between Drakensberg mountains & Indian ocean ✻ Pietermaritzburg *area* 35,284, *pop* 3,418,942

Natch·ez \'nach-əz\ city SW Miss. on the Mississippi *pop* 19,704

Natchez Trace pioneer road between Natchez, Miss., & Nashville, Tenn., used in the early 19th century

Natch·i·toches \'nak-ə-ˌtäsh, 'nak-(ə-)təsh\ city NW *cen* La. *pop* 15,974

Na·tick \'nāt-ik\ town E Mass. W of Boston *pop* 31,057

National City city SW Calif. S of San Diego *pop* 43,184

Native States — see INDIAN STATES

Natural Bridges National Monument reservation SE Utah containing three large natural bridges

Nau·cra·tis \'nȯ-krət-əs\ ancient Greek city N Egypt in Nile delta W of Rosetta branch

Nau·ga·tuck \'nȯ-gə-ˌtək\ borough SW *cen* Conn. *pop* 23,034

Nau·plia \'nȯ-plē-ə\ *or* NGk **Náv·pli·on** \'näf-plē-ˌȯn\ town & port S Greece in E Peloponnesus near head of Gulf of Argolis

Nauplia, Gulf of — see ARGOLIS (Gulf of)

Na·u·ru \nä-'ü-(ˌ)rü\ *or formerly* **Pleas·ant** \'plez-ᵊnt\ island (atoll) W Pacific 26 *m* S of the equator; formerly a joint Brit., New Zealand, & Australian trust territory; since 1968 an independent republic *area* 8, *pop* 6603

Nav·a·jo National Monument \'nav-ə-ˌhō, 'näv-\ reservation N Ariz. SW of Monument Valley near Utah line

Navanagar — see JAMNAGAR

Navarino — see PYLOS

Na·varre \nə-'vär\ *or* Sp **Na·var·ra** \nə-'vär-ə\ **1** region & former kingdom N Spain & SW France in W Pyrenees **2** province N Spain ✻ Pamplona *area* 4055, *pop* 466,867

Nav·e·sink, Highlands of \'nav-ə-ˌsiŋk, 'nev-ə(r)-\ *or* **Navesink Highlands** *or* **Navesink Hills** range of hills E N.J. extending from near Sandy Hook to Raritan Bay

Navigators — see SAMOA

Náv·pak·tos \'näf-ˌpäk-təs\ *or* It **Le·pan·to** \'lep-ən-ˌtō, li-'pan-(ˌ)tō\ *or anc* **Nau·pac·tus** \nȯ-'pak-təs\ town & port Greece on N shore of strait connecting gulfs of Corinth & Patras

Nawa — see NAHA

Nax·os \'nak-səs, -ˌsäs\ **1** *or* NGk **Ná·xos** \'näk-ˌsȯs\ island Greece, largest of the Cyclades *area* 171 **2** oldest Greek colony in Sicily; ruins SW of Taormina

Na·ya·rit \ˌnī-ə-'rēt\ state W Mexico bordering on the Pacific ✻ Tepic *area* 10,444, *pop* 547,992

Naz·a·reth \'naz-(ə-)rəth\ city N Israel in Galilee SE of Haifa *pop* 34,000

Naze, The \'nāz\ **1** headland SE England on E coast of Essex **2** — see LINDESNES

Na·zil·li \ˌnäz-ə-'lē\ city SW Turkey SE of Izmir *pop* 41,330

Neagh, Lough \'nā\ lake *cen* Northern Ireland *area* 153; largest in British Isles

Neapolis, 1 — see NABLUS **2** — see NAPLES

Near \'ni(ə)r\ islands SW Alaska at W end of the Aleutians — see ATTU

Near East, 1 the region included in the Ottoman Empire at its greatest extent — a former usage **2** the countries of SW Asia & NE Africa — **Near Eastern** *adj*

Nebo — see PISGAH

Ne·bras·ka \nə-'bras-kə\ state *cen* U.S. ✻ Lincoln *area* 77,227, *pop* 1,483,791 — **Ne·bras·kan** \-kən\ *adj or n*

Ne·chako \ni-'chak-(ˌ)ō\ river 287 *m* Canada in *cen* B.C. flowing N & E into the Fraser

Ne·ches \'nā-chəz\ river 280 *m* E Tex. flowing S & SE into Sabine Lake

Neck·ar \'nek-ər, -ˌär\ river 246 *m* SW Germany rising in the Black Forest & flowing N & W into the Rhine

Neck·er \'nek-ər\ island Hawaii in Leewards 300 *m* NW of Niihau I.

Ne·der·land \'nēd-ər-lənd\ city SE Tex. SE of Beaumont *pop* 16,810

Need·ham \'nēd-əm\ town E Mass. WSW of Boston *pop* 29,748

Nee·nah \'nē-nə\ city E Wis. on Lake Winnebago *pop* 22,892

Nefud — see NAFUD

Neg·ev \'neg-ˌev\ *or* **Neg·eb** \-ˌeb\ region S Israel, a triangular wedge of desert touching Gulf of ʿAqaba in S

Ne·gri Sem·bi·lan \nə-ˌgrē-səm-'bē-lən\ state Federation of Malaysia on Strait of Malacca ✻ Seremban *area* 2550, *pop* 479,312

Ne·gro \'nā-(ˌ)grō\ **1** river 630 *m* S *cen* Argentina flowing E into the Atlantic **2** river 1400 *m* E Colombia & N Brazil flowing into the Amazon **3** river 290 *m, cen* Uruguay flowing SW into Uruguay river

Negropont — see EUBOEA

Ne·gros \'nā-(ˌ)grōs\ island Philippines, one of the Visayan islands *area* 4905

Nei·kiang \'nā-jē-'äŋ\ city *cen* China in S *cen* Szechwan SE of Chengtu *pop* 190,200

Neis·se \'nī-sə\ *or* Pol **Ny·sa** \'nis-ə\ **1** *or* **Lau·sitz·er Neisse** \'lau̇-zət-sər-ˌ\ river 140 *m* N Europe flowing from N Czechoslovakia N into the Oder **2** *or* **Glatz·er Neisse** \'glät-sər-ˌ\ river 120 *m* SW Poland rising on Czechoslovak border & flowing NE into the Oder

Nejd \'nejd, 'nezhd\ *or* **Najd** \'najd, 'nazhd\ region *cen* & E Saudi Arabia; a viceroyalty ✻ Riyadh *area* 447,000, *pop* 4,000,000 — **Nejdi** \'nej-dē, 'nezh-\ *adj or n*

Nel·son \'nel-sən\ **1** river 400 *m* Canada in Man. flowing from N end of Lake Winnipeg to Hudson Bay **2** city & port New Zealand on N coast of South I. *pop* 28,300

Ne·man \'nem-ən\ *or* **Nie·men** \nē-'em-ən, 'nē-mən\ *or* **Me·mel** \'mā-məl\ river 500 *m* W U.S.S.R. flowing from *cen* Belorussia N & W into Kurland Gulf

Ne·mea \'nē-mē-ə\ valley & town Greece in NE Peloponnesus W of Corinth — **Ne·me·an** \'nē-mē-ən, ni-'mē-\ *adj*

Ne·o·sho \nē-'ō-(ˌ)shō, -shə\ *or* **Grand** river 460 *m* SE Kans. & NE Okla. flowing SE & S into Arkansas river

Ne·pal \nə-'pȯl, -'päl, -'pal\ country Asia on NE border of India in the Himalayas; a kingdom ✻ Katmandu *area* 54,000, *pop* 11,290,000 — **Nep·a·lese** \ˌnep-ə-'lēz, -'lēs\ *adj or n*

Ness, Loch \'nes\ lake 23 *m* long NW Scotland in Inverness

Nestos — see MESTA

Neth·er·lands \'neth-ər-lən(d)z\ **1** LOW COUNTRIES — an historical usage **2** *or* **Hol·land** \'häl-ənd\ *or* D **Ne·der·land** \'nād-ər-ˌlänt\ country NW Europe on North sea; a kingdom, official ✻ Amsterdam, de facto ✻ The Hague *area* 15,785, *pop* 13,190,000 — **Neth·er·land** \'neth-ər-lənd\ *adj* — **Neth·er·land·er** \-ˌlan-dər, -lən-\ *n* — **Neth·er·land·ish** \-dish\ *adj*

Netherlands An·til·les \an-'til-ēz\ *or* **Dutch West Indies** the islands of the West Indies belonging to the Netherlands: Aruba, Bonaire, Curaçao, Saba, St. Eustatius, & S part of St. Martin; an overseas territory ✻ Willemstad (on Curaçao) *area* 403, *pop* 220,084

Netherlands Guiana — see SURINAM

Netherlands East Indies — see INDONESIA

Netherlands India *or* **Netherlands Indies** NETHERLANDS EAST INDIES

Netherlands New Guinea — see WEST IRIAN

Netherlands Timor — see TIMOR

Néthou, Pic de — see ANETO (Pico de)

Net·tu·no \nā-'tü-(ˌ)nō\ commune Italy on Tyrrhenian sea SSE of Rome adjoining Anzio *pop* 22,698

Neu·châ·tel \ˌn(y)ü-shə-'tel, ˌnə(r)sh-ə-, nœ-shä-tel\ *or* G **Neu·en·burg** \'nȯi-ən-ˌbərg\ **1** canton W Switzerland in Jura mountains *area* 312, *pop* 169,173 **2** commune, its ✻, on **Lake of Neuchâtel** (*area* 84) *pop* 38,784

Neuil·ly–sur–Seine \ˌnə(r)-ˌyē-ˌsu̇(ə)r-'sān\ commune N France NW of Paris near the Bois de Boulogne *pop* 70,995

Neu·mün·ster \nȯi-'mu̇en-stər\ city W Germany SSW of Kiel *pop* 73,175

Neu·quén \nyü-'kān, neu̇-\ river 375 *m* W Argentina flowing from the Andes E to join the Limay forming the Negro

Neuse \'n(y)üs\ river 260 *m* E *cen* N.C. flowing SE into Pamlico Sound

Neuss \'nȯis\ city W Germany W of Düsseldorf *pop* 116,500

Neus·tria \'n(y)ü-strē-ə\ **1** the western part of the dominions of the Franks after the conquest by Clovis in 511, comprising the NW part of modern France between the Meuse, the Loire, & the Atlantic **2** NORMANDY — **Neus·tri·an** \-ən\ *adj or n*

Ne·va \'nē-və, 'nā-\ river 40 *m* U.S.S.R. in NW Soviet Russia, Europe, flowing from Lake Ladoga to Gulf of Finland at Leningrad

Ne·va·da \nə-'vad-ə, -'väd-ə\ state W U.S. ✻ Carson City *area* 110,540, *pop* 488,738 — **Ne·va·dan** \-'vad-ᵊn, -'väd-ᵊn\ *or* **Ne·va·di·an** \-'vad-ē-ən, -'väd-\ *adj or n*

Ne·vers \nə-'ve(ə)r\ city *cen* France on the Loire SE of Orléans *pop* 42,222

Ne·ves \'nā-vəs\ city SE Brazil on Guanabara Bay *pop* 53,052

Ne·vis \'nē-vəs\ island Brit. West Indies, part of St. Kitts-Nevis Associated State, in the Leewards; chief town Charlestown *area* 50

Nev·is, Ben \ben-'nev-əs\ mountain 4406 *ft* W Scotland in SW Inverness in the Grampians; highest peak in Great Britain

New Al·ba·ny \'ȯl-bə-nē\ city S Ind. *pop* 38,402

New Am·ster·dam \'am(p)-stər-ˌdam\ town founded 1625 on Manhattan I. by the Dutch; renamed New York 1664 by the British

New·ark \'n(y)ü-ərk, 'n(y)u̇(-ə)rk\ **1** city W Calif. SE of San Francisco *pop* 27,153 **2** city NE Del. W of Wilmington *pop* 20,757 **3** city & port NE N.J. on **Newark Bay** (W extension of Upper New York Bay) *pop* 382,417 **4** city *cen* Ohio *pop* 41,836

New Bed·ford \'bed-fərd\ city & port SE Mass. *pop* 101,777

New Ber·lin \'bər-lən\ city SE Wis. W of Milwaukee *pop* 26,937

New Braun·fels \'brau̇n-fəlz\ city SE *cen* Tex. *pop* 17,859

New Brigh·ton \'brīt-ᵊn\ village SE Minn. N of St. Paul *pop* 19,507

New Brit·ain \'brit-ᵊn\ **1** city *cen* Conn. *pop* 83,441 **2** island Bismarck archipelago; largest of group *area* 14,000, *pop* 138,689
New Bruns·wick \'brənz-(ˌ)wik\ **1** city N *cen* N.J. *pop* 41,885 **2** province SE Canada bordering on Gulf of St. Lawrence & Bay of Fundy ✻ Fredericton *area* 27,985, *pop* 632,000
New·burgh \'n(y)ü-ˌbərg\ city SE N.Y. on the Hudson S of Poughkeepsie *pop* 26,219
New·bury·port \'n(y)üb-ə-rē-ˌpō(ə)rt, -ˌpȯ(ə)rt *also* 'nu̇b-\ city NE Mass. *pop* 15,807
New Cal·e·do·nia \ˌkal-ə-'dō-nyə, -nē-ə\ island SW Pacific SW of the New Hebrides; with nearby islands, constitutes an overseas department of France ✻ Nouméa *area* 8548, *pop* 113,680
New Ca·naan \'kā-nən\ town SW Conn. NW of Norwalk *pop* 17,455
New Castile — see CASTILE
New·cas·tle \'n(y)ü-ˌkas-əl, *2 is locally* n(y)ü-'\ **1** city & port SE Australia in E New So. Wales NE of Sydney at mouth of Hunter river *pop* 144,450 **2** *or* **Newcastle upon Tyne** \'tīn\ city & county borough & port N England ✻ of Northumberland *pop* 222,-153 **3** *or* **Newcastle under Lyme** \'līm\ municipal borough W *cen* England in Staffordshire *pop* 76,970
New Cas·tle \'n(y)ü-ˌkas-əl\ **1** city E Ind. S of Muncie *pop* 21,215 **2** city W Pa. ESE of Youngstown, Ohio *pop* 38,559
Newchwang — see YINGKOW
New Delhi city ✻ of India in Delhi Territory S of city of (Old) Delhi *pop* 324,283
New England, 1 the NE section of the U.S. comprising the states of Me., N.H., Vt., Mass., R.I., & Conn. **2** mountain range & plateau SE Australia in NE New So. Wales; part of Great Dividing range — **New En·gland·er** \-'iŋ-glən-dər *also* -'iŋ-lən-\ *n*
New Forest forested area S England in Hampshire between the Avon & Southampton Water; once a royal hunting ground
New·found·land \'n(y)ü-fən-(d)lənd, -ˌ(d)land; ˌn(y)ü-fən-'(d)land\ **1** island Canada in the Atlantic E of Gulf of St. Lawrence *area* 42,734 **2** province E Canada comprising Newfoundland I. & Labrador ✻ St. John's *area* 154,734, *pop* 524,000 — **New·found·land·er** \-(d)lən-dər, -'(d)lan-dər\ *n*
New France the possessions of France in No. America before 1763
New Geor·gia \'jȯr-jə\ **1** island group W Pacific in *cen* Solomons **2** island 50 *m* long, chief island of the group
New Goa — see PANGIM
New Gra·na·da \grə-'näd-ə\ Spanish viceroyalty in NW So. America 1717–1819 comprising area included in modern Panama, Colombia, Venezuela, & Ecuador
New Guin·ea \'gin-ē\ **1** *or* **Pa·pua** \'pap-yə-wə, 'päp-ə-wə\ *or* Indonesian **Iri·an** \ˌir-ē-'än\ island in Malay archipelago N of E Australia divided between West Irian on W and Papua New Guinea on E *area* 306,600 **2** the NE portion of the island of New Guinea with the Bismarck archipelago, Bougainville, Buka, and adjacent small islands; part of territory of Papua New Guinea — **New Guin·e·an** \'gin-ē-ən\ *adj or n*
New·ham \'n(y)ü-əm\ borough of E Greater London, England *pop* 235,700
New Hamp·shire \'ham(p)-shər, -ˌshi(ə)r\ state NE U.S. ✻ Concord *area* 9304, *pop* 737,681 — **New Hamp·shire·man** \-mən\ *n* — **New Hamp·shir·ite** \-ˌīt\ *n*
New Ha·ven \'hā-vən\ city & port S Conn. *pop* 137,707
New Heb·ri·des \'heb-rə-ˌdēz\ islands SW Pacific NE of New Caledonia & W of Fiji; under joint Brit. & French administration ✻ Vila (on Efate) *area* 5700, *pop* 86,000
New Hope \'n(y)ü-ˌhōp\ village E Minn. N of Minneapolis *pop* 23,180
New Ibe·ria \ī-'bir-ē-ə\ city S La. SE of Lafayette *pop* 30,147
New·ing·ton \'nyü-iŋ-tən\ town *cen* Conn. SW of Hartford *pop* 26,037
New Ire·land \'ī(ə)r-lənd\ island W Pacific in Bismarck archipelago N of New Britain ✻ Kavieng *area* 3340, *pop* (with adjacent islands) 48,774
New Jer·sey \'jər-zē\ state E U.S. ✻ Trenton *area* 7836, *pop* 7,168,164 — **New Jer·sey·ite** \-ˌīt\ *n*
New Ken·sing·ton \'ken-ziŋ-tən\ city SW Pa. NE of Pittsburgh on the Allegheny *pop* 20,312
New Lon·don \'lən-dən\ city & port SE Conn. on Long Island Sound at mouth of Thames river *pop* 31,630
New·mar·ket \'n(y)ü-ˌmär-kət\ **1** town Canada in SE Ont. N of Toronto *pop* 18,941 **2** urban district E England in West Suffolk
New Mex·i·co \'mek-si-ˌkō\ state SW U.S. ✻ Santa Fe *area* 121,-666, *pop* 1,016,000 — **New Mex·i·can** \-si-kən\ *adj or n*
New Mil·ford \'mil-fərd\ borough NE N.J. *pop* 20,201
New Neth·er·land \'net͟h-ər-lənd\ Dutch colony in No. America 1613–64 occupying lands bordering on the Hudson & later also on the lower Delaware ✻ New Amsterdam
New Or·leans \'ȯr-lē-ənz, 'ȯrl-(y)ənz, (ˌ)ȯr-'lēnz\ city & port SE La. between Lake Pontchartrain & the Mississippi *pop* 593,471 — **New Or·lea·nian** \(ˌ)ȯr-'lē-nyən, -nē-ən\ *n*
New Philadelphia city E Ohio *pop* 15,184
New·port \'n(y)ü-ˌpō(ə)rt, -ˌpȯ(ə)rt\ **1** city N Ky. on the Ohio opposite Cincinnati, Ohio *pop* 25,998 **2** city & port SE R.I. on Narragansett Bay *pop* 34,562 **3** municipal borough S England ✻ of Isle of Wight *pop* 22,286 **4** county borough SE Wales ✻ of Monmouthshire WNW of Bristol *pop* 112,048
Newport Beach city SW Calif. SE of Long Beach *pop* 49,422
Newport News \ˌn(y)ü-ˌpōrt-'n(y)üz, -ˌpȯrt-, -pərt-\ city & port SE Va. on the James & Hampton Roads *pop* 138,177
New Prov·i·dence \'präv-əd-ən(t)s, -ə-ˌden(t)s\ island in NW *cen* Bahamas E of Andros; site of Nassau *area* 58
New Quebec region Canada in N Que. N of Eastmain river between Hudson Bay & Labrador — see UNGAVA
New Quebec Crater *or* **Chubb Crater** \'chəb\ lake-filled meteoric crater Canada in N Que., in N Ungava peninsula; 3 *m* in diameter
New Ro·chelle \ˌn(y)ü-rə-'shel\ city SE N.Y. on Long Island Sound E of Mount Vernon *pop* 75,385
New Sarum — see SALISBURY
New Siberian islands U.S.S.R. in N Soviet Russia, Asia, in Arctic ocean between Laptev & East Siberian seas *area* 11,000
New South Wales state SE Australia bordering on the Pacific ✻ Sydney *area* 309,432, *pop* 4,567,000
New Spain Spanish viceroyalty 1521–1821 including territory now in SW U.S., Mexico, Central America N of Panama, the West Indies, & the Philippines ✻ Mexico City
New Sweden Swedish colony in No. America 1638–55 bordering on W bank of the Delaware from modern Trenton, N.J., to its mouth
New·ton \'n(y)üt-ᵊn\ **1** city *cen* Iowa *pop* 15,619 **2** city *cen* Kans. *pop* 15,439 **3** city E Mass. W of Boston *pop* 91,066
New·town \'n(y)ü-ˌtau̇n\ town SW Conn. E of Danbury *pop* 16,942
New West·min·ster \wes(t)-'min(t)-stər\ city Canada in SW B.C. *pop* 42,835
New Windsor — see WINDSOR
New York \'yȯ(ə)rk\ **1** state NE U.S. ✻ Albany *area* 49,576, *pop* 18,190,740 **2** *or* **New York City** city & port SE N.Y. at mouth of the Hudson; includes boroughs of Bronx, Brooklyn, Manhattan, Queens, & Richmond *pop* 7,867,760 **3** the borough of Manhattan in New York City — **New York·er** \'yȯr-kər\ *n*
New York Bay inlet of the Atlantic SE N.Y. & NE N.J. at mouth of the Hudson forming harbor of metropolitan New York & consisting of **Upper New York Bay** & **Lower New York Bay** connected by the **Narrows** (strait separating Staten I. & Long I.)
New York State Barge Canal — see ERIE
New Zea·land \'zē-lənd\ country SW Pacific ESE of Australia comprising chiefly North I. & South I.; a dominion of the Brit. Commonwealth ✻ Wellington *area* 103,736, *pop* 2,850,000 — **New Zea·land·er** \-lən-dər\ *n*
Ngaliema, Mount — see STANLEY (Mount)
Nga·mi, Lake \eŋ-'gäm-ē\ marshy depression NW Botswana N of Kalahari desert; formerly a large lake
Ngau·ru·hoe \eŋ-ˌgau̇-rə-'hō-ē\ volcano 7515 *ft* New Zealand in *cen* North I. in Tongariro National Park
N'Gela — see FLORIDA
Ni·ag·a·ra Falls \(ˌ)nī-'ag-(ə-)rə\ **1** waterfalls on border between N.Y. & Ont. in the **Niagara** river (36 *m* flowing from Lake Erie N into Lake Ontario); divided by Goat I. into Horseshoe, or Canadian, Falls (158 *ft* high, 3010 *ft* wide at crest) & American Falls (167 *ft* high, 1060 *ft* wide) **2** city W N.Y. at the falls *pop* 85,615 **3** city Canada in SE Ont. *pop* 67,163
Nia·mey \nē-'äm-(ˌ)ā, nyä-'mā\ city ✻ of Niger on Niger river *pop* 78,991
Ni·as \'nē-ˌäs\ island Indonesia in Indian ocean off W coast of Sumatra *area* 1569 — **Ni·as·san** \'nē-ə-sən\ *n*
Ni·caea \nī-'sē-ə\ *or* **Nice** \'nīs\ ancient city of Byzantine Empire, site at modern village of Iznik in NW Turkey in Asia at E end of Iznik Lake — **Ni·cae·an** \nī-'sē-ən\ *adj*
Nic·a·ra·gua \ˌnik-ə-'räg-wə\ **1** lake 100 *m* long S Nicaragua *area* 3000 **2** country Central America bordering on the Pacific & the Caribbean; a republic ✻ Managua *area* 57,143, *pop* 1,980,000 — **Nic·a·ra·guan** \-'räg-wən\ *adj or n*
Nice \'nēs\ *or anc* **Ni·caea** \nī-'sē-ə\ city & port SE France on the Mediterranean *pop* 392,635
Nic·o·bar \'nik-ə-ˌbär\ islands India in Indian ocean S of Andaman islands *area* 635 — see ANDAMAN AND NICOBAR
Nicomedia — see IZMIT
Ni·cop·o·lis \nə-'käp-ə-ləs, nī-\ ancient city NW Greece in Epirus near entrance to Ambracian gulf
Nic·o·sia \ˌnik-ə-'sē-ə\ city ✻ of Cyprus *pop* 114,000
Nidwald, Nidwalden — see UNTERWALDEN
Niedersachsen — see LOWER SAXONY
Niemen — see NEMAN
Nieuw·poort *or* **Nieu·port** \'n(y)ü-ˌpō(ə)rt, -ˌpȯ(ə)rt, *Fr* nyœ-pȯr\ commune NW Belgium in West Flanders on the Yser SW of Ostend
Ni·ger \'nī-jər\ **1** river 2600 *m* W Africa flowing from Fouta Djallon NE, SE, & S into Gulf of Guinea **2** country W Africa; a republic of the French Community since 1958, formerly a territory of French West Africa ✻ Niamey *area* 458,874, *pop* 4,130,000
Ni·ge·ria \nī-'jir-ē-ə\ country W Africa bordering on Gulf of Guinea; a republic within the Brit. Commonwealth, formerly a colony & protectorate ✻ Lagos *area* 356,669, *pop* 56,510,000 — **Ni·ge·ri·an** \-ē-ən\ *adj or n*
Nihon — see JAPAN
Nii·ga·ta \nē-'gät-ə, 'nē-gə-ˌtä\ city & port Japan in N Honshu on Sea of Japan *pop* 382,000
Nii·hau \'nē-ˌhau̇\ island Hawaii WSW of Kauai *area* 72
Nij·me·gen \'nī-ˌmā-gən\ *or* **Nim·we·gen** \'nim-ˌvā-gən\ *or* **Ni·me·guen** \'nī-ˌmā-gən\ commune E Netherlands in Gelderland on the Waal S of Arnhem *pop* 147,996
Nik·ko \'nik-(ˌ)ō\ city Japan in E *cen* Honshu *pop* 28,502
Ni·ko·la·ev *or* **Ni·ko·la·yev** \ˌnik-ə-'lī-əf\ *or* **Ver·no·len·insk** \ˌver-nə-'len-ən(t)sk\ city & port U.S.S.R. in S Ukraine at confluence of Bug & Ingul rivers *pop* 331,000
Ni·ko·pol \ni-'kō-pəl\ city U.S.S.R. in E *cen* Ukraine on the Dnieper *pop* 125,000
Nile \'nī-(ə)l\ river 4037 *m* E Africa flowing from Lake Victoria in Uganda N into the Mediterranean in Egypt; in various sections called specifically: **Vic·to·ria** \vik-'tōr-ē-ə, -'tȯr-\, *or* **Som·er·set** \'səm-ər-sət, -ˌset\, **Nile,** between Lake Victoria & Lake Albert; **Al·bert** \'al-bərt\ **Nile,** between Lake Albert & Lake No; & **White Nile,** from Lake No to Khartoum — see BLUE NILE
Niles \'nī(ə)lz\ **1** village NE Ill. NW of Chicago *pop* 31,432 **2** city NE Ohio SE of Warren *pop* 21,581

ə abut ᵊ kitten, F table ər further a back ā bake ä cot, cart ȧ F bac au̇ out ch chin e less ē easy g gift i trip ī life j joke k̲ G ich ⁿ F vin ŋ sing ō flow ȯ flaw œ F bœuf œ̄ F feu ȯi coin th thing t͟h this ü loot u̇ foot ue G Füllen ue̅ F rue y yet ʸ F digne \dēnʸ\, nuit \nwʸē\ yü few yu̇ furious zh vision

Nil·gi·ri \'nil-gə-rē\ hills S India in W Tamil Nadu; highest point Mt. Dodabetta 8647 *ft*
Nimes \'nēm\ city S France NE of Montpellier *pop* 123,292
Nimrud — see CALAH
Nin·e·veh \'nin-ə-və\ *or* L **Ni·nus** \'nī-nəs\ ancient city ✻ of Assyria; ruins in Iraq on the Tigris opposite Mosul
Ning·po \'niŋ-'pō\ *or formerly* **Ning·hsien** \'niŋ-shē-'en\ city E China in N Chekiang ESE of Hangchow *pop* 237,500
Ning·sia *or* **Ning·hsia** \'niŋ-shē-'ä\ **1** region N China; formerly a province ✻ Yinchwan *area* 30,039 **2** — see YINCHWAN
Ni·o·brara \,nī-ə-'brar-ə, -'brer-\ river 431 *m* E Wyo. & N Nebr. flowing E into the Missouri
Niort \nē-'ó(ə)r\ city W France ENE of La Rochelle *pop* 48,469
Nip·i·gon, Lake \'nip-ə-,gän\ lake Canada in W Ont. N of Lake Superior *area* 1870
Nip·is·sing, Lake \'nip-ə-siŋ\ lake Canada in SE Ont. NE of Georgian Bay *area* 330
Nippon — see JAPAN
Nip·pur \nip-'ù(ə)r\ ancient city of Sumer 100 *m* SSE of Babylon
Nis *or* **Nish** \'nish\ city E Yugoslavia in E Serbia *pop* 127,178
Ni·shi·no·mi·ya \,nish-ə-'nō-mē-,(y)ä\ city Japan in *cen* Honshu on Osaka Bay E of Kobe *pop* 366,000
Ni·te·rói *or formerly* **Nic·the·roy** \,nēt-ə-'ròi\ city SE Brazil ✻ of Rio de Janeiro state on Guanabara Bay opposite Rio de Janeiro *pop* 303,575
Ni·u·a·foo \nē-'ü-ə-,fō\ island SW *cen* Pacific in the N Tongas
Ni·ue \nē-'ü-(,)(w)ā\ *or* **Sav·age** \'sav-ij\ island S *cen* Pacific W of Cook islands; a dependency of New Zealand *area* 100
Ni·velles \nē-'vel\ commune *cen* Belgium *pop* 15,903
Ni·ver·nais \,nē-vər-'nā\ region & former province *cen* France E of the upper Loire ✻ Nevers
Nizhni Novgorod — see GORKI
Nizh·ni Ta·gil \,nizh-nē-tə-'gil\ city U.S.S.R. in W Soviet Russia, Asia, on E slope of the Urals *pop* 378,000
No \'nō\ lake S *cen* Sudan where Bahr el Jebel & Bahr el Ghazal join to form the White Nile *area* 40
Noem·foor *or* **Num·for** \'nüm-,fō(ə)r, -,fò(ə)r\ island West New Guinea in W Schouten islands *area* 28
No·gal·es \nō-'gal-əs, -'gäl-\ city NW Mexico in Sonora adjacent to Nogales, Ariz. *pop* 52,865
No·ga·ta \nō-'gät-ə\ city Japan in N Kyushu *pop* 55,615
Nome, Cape \'nōm\ cape W Alaska on S side of Seward peninsula
Non·ni \'nən-'nē\ river 660 *m* NE China in N Manchuria flowing from the Great Khingan mountains S into the Sungari
Noot·ka Sound \,nùt-kə-, ,nüt-\ inlet of the Pacific Canada in SW B.C. on W coast of Vancouver I.
Nordenskjöld — see LAPTEV
Nord·kyn, Cape \'nō(ə)r-kən, 'nó(ə)r-\ cape NE Norway on Barents sea E of North Cape; northernmost point of European mainland, at 71°8′N
Nor·folk \'nòr-fək, *US also* -,fòk\ **1** city NE Nebr. *pop* 16,607 **2** city & port SE Va. on Elizabeth river S of Hampton Roads *pop* 307,951 **3** island S Pacific between New Caledonia & New Zealand; administered by Australia *area* 13 **4** county E England bordering on North sea ✻ Norwich *area* 2055, *pop* 616,427
Norfolk Broads — see BROADS
Norge — see NORWAY
Nor·i·cum \'nòr-i-kəm, 'när-\ ancient country & Roman province S *cen* Europe S of the Danube in modern Austria & S Germany
No·rilsk \nə-'rēlsk\ city U.S.S.R. in NW Soviet Russia, Asia, N of Arctic circle near mouth of the Yenisei *pop* 136,000
Nor·mal \'nòr-məl\ town *cen* Ill. N of Bloomington *pop* 26,396
Nor·man \'nòr-mən\ city *cen* Okla. on Canadian river *pop* 52,117
Nor·man·dy \'nòr-mən-dē\ *or* F **Nor·man·die** \nòr-mäⁿ-dē\ region & former province NW France NE of Brittany ✻ Rouen
Nor·ridge \'nòr-ij, 'när-\ village NE Ill. NW of Chicago *pop* 16,880
Nor·ris·town \'nòr-ə-,staùn, 'när-\ borough SE Pa. NW of Philadelphia on the Schuylkill *pop* 38,169
Norr·kö·ping \'nó(ə)r-,chə(r)p-iŋ\ city & port SE Sweden SW of Stockholm at head of an inlet of the Baltic *pop* 95,851
North island N New Zealand *area* 44,280, *pop* 1,956,411
North Ad·ams \'ad-əmz\ city NW Mass. *pop* 19,195
North·al·ler·ton \nòr-'thal-ərt-ᵊn\ urban district N England ✻ of No. Riding, Yorkshire
North America continent of the western hemisphere NW of So. America bounded by Atlantic, Arctic, & Pacific oceans *area* 9,385,000 — **North American** *adj or n*
North·amp·ton \nòrth-'(h)am(p)-tən\ **1** city W *cen* Mass. on the Connecticut N of Holyoke *pop* 29,664 **2** *or* **North·amp·ton·shire** \-,shi(ə)r, -shər\ county *cen* England *area* 914, *pop* 467,843 **3** county borough, its ✻ *pop* 126,608
North Andover town NE Mass. E of Lawrence *pop* 16,284
North Arlington borough NE N.J. NE of Newark *pop* 18,096
North At·tle·boro \'at-ᵊl-,bər-ə, -,bə-rə\ town SE Mass. NE of Providence, R.I. *pop* 18,665
North Bay \'nó(ə)rth-,bā\ city Canada in SE Ont. on Lake Nipissing *pop* 49,187
North Borneo — see SABAH
North Brabant *or* D **Noord·bra·bant** \,nōrt-brä-'bänt\ province S Netherlands ✻ 's Hertogenbosch *area* 1965, *pop* 1,787,783
North·brook \'nòrth-,brùk\ village NE Ill. NW of Chicago *pop* 27,-297
North Canadian river 760 *m* S *cen* U.S. flowing ESE from NE N.Mex. into the Canadian in E Okla. — see BEAVER
North Canton city NE Ohio *pop* 15,228
North Cape, 1 cape New Zealand at N tip of North I. **2** cape NE Norway on **Ma·ger·öy** \,mäg-ə-'rəi\ island (*area* 111) at 71°10′20″N **3** — see HORN
North Car·o·li·na \,kar-ə-'lī-nə\ state E U.S. ✻ Raleigh *area* 52,-586, *pop* 5,082,059 — **North Car·o·lin·ian** \-'lin-ē-ən, -'lin-yən\ *adj or n*
North Cas·cades National Park \kas-'kādz, 'kas-,\ reservation N *cen* Wash. on Canadian border *area* 789
North channel strait between NE Ireland & SW Scotland connecting Irish sea & the Atlantic
North Chicago city NE Ill. S of Waukegan *pop* 47,275
North Da·ko·ta \də-'kōt-ə\ state NW *cen* U.S. ✻ Bismarck *area* 70,665, *pop* 617,761 — **North Da·ko·tan** \-'kōt-ᵊn\ *adj or n*
North Downs hills S England chiefly in Kent & Surrey
North–East Frontier Agency autonomous district NE India in N Assam bordering on China
North–East New Guinea the NE section of Papua New Guinea on the island of New Guinea
Northern Cir·cars \(,)sər-'kärz\ coast region E India now in E Andhra Pradesh but historically constituting the four N districts of Madras province
Northern Cook — see MANIHIKI
Northern Dvi·na \də-,vē-'nä\ *or* Russ **Se·ver·na·ya Dvina** \'sā-vər-nə-yə\ river 1100 *m* U.S.S.R. in N Soviet Russia, Europe, flowing NW into White sea
Northern Ireland region NE Ireland; a division of the United Kingdom of Great Britain & Northern Ireland ✻ Belfast *area* 5461, *pop* 1,525,187
Northern Karroo — see KARROO
Northern Kingdom — see ISRAEL
Northern Region region N Ghana ✻ Tamale *area* 37,600, *pop* 728,572
Northern Rhodesia — see ZAMBIA
Northern Sporades — see SPORADES
Northern Territory territory *cen* & N Australia bordering on Arafura sea ✻ Darwin *area* 523,620, *pop* 71,400
North Frisian — see FRISIAN
North Glenn \'glen\ city N *cen* Colo. NE of Denver *pop* 27,937
North Ha·ven \'nó(ə)rth-,hā-vən\ town S Conn. N of New Haven *pop* 22,194
North Holland *or* D **Noord·hol·land** \'nōrt-'hò-,länt\ province NW Netherlands ✻ Haarlem *area* 1163, *pop* 2,244,456
North Kings·town \'kiŋ-stən\ town S R.I. S of Providence *pop* 27,673
North Las Vegas city SE Nev. *pop* 36,216
North Little Rock city *cen* Ark. *pop* 60,040
North Miami city SE Fla. *pop* 34,767
North Miami Beach city SE Fla. *pop* 30,723
North Minch — see MINCH
North Olm·sted \'ōm-,sted\ city NE Ohio *pop* 34,861
North Ossetia *or* **North Ossetian Republic** autonomous republic U.S.S.R. in SE Soviet Russia, Europe, on the N slopes of Caucasus mountains ✻ Dzaudzhikau *area* 3500, *pop* 553,000
North Plainfield borough NE N.J. SW of Elizabeth *pop* 21,796
North Platte, 1 river 618 *m* W U.S. flowing from N Colo. N & E through Wyo. into Nebr. to unite with the So. Platte forming the Platte **2** city SW *cen* Nebr. *pop* 19,447
North Providence town NE R.I. *pop* 24,337
North Rhine–Westphalia *or* G **Nord·rhein–West·fa·len** \'nòrt-,rīn-,vest-'fä-lən\ state W Germany formed 1946 by union of former Westphalia province, Lippe state, & N Rhine Province ✻ Düsseldorf *area* 13,107, *pop* 17,167,500
North Rich·land Hills \-,rich-lən(d)-\ town N Tex. N of Fort Worth *pop* 16,514
North Riding — see YORK
North river estuary of the Hudson between SE N.Y. & NE N.J.
North Saskatchewan — see SASKATCHEWAN
North sea *or* **German ocean** arm of the Atlantic 600 *m* long & 350 *m* wide E of Great Britain
North Tonawanda city W N.Y. N of Buffalo *pop* 36,012
North Truchas Peak — see TRUCHAS PEAK
North·um·ber·land \nòr-'thəm-bər-lənd\ **1** strait 180 *m* long Canada in Gulf of St. Lawrence between P.E.I. & the mainland **2** county N England ✻ Newcastle upon Tyne *area* 2019, *pop* 794,975
North·um·bria \nòr-'thəm-brē-ə\ ancient country Great Britain between the Humber & Firth of Forth; one of kingdoms in Anglo-Saxon heptarchy
North Vancouver city Canada in SW B.C. *pop* 31,847
North–West Frontier Province province of Pakistan & formerly of British India on Afghanistan border ✻ Peshawar
Northwest Territories territory N Canada comprising the arctic islands, the mainland N of 60° between Yukon Territory & Hudson Bay, & the islands in Hudson Bay; divided into Mackenzie, Keewatin, & Franklin districts ✻ Yellowknife *area* 1,253,438, *pop* 36,000
Nor·ton Shores \,nòrt-ᵊn-\ city W Mich. SW of Muskegon *pop* 22,271
Norton Sound arm of Bering sea W Alaska between Seward peninsula & the mouths of the Yukon
Nor·walk \'nó(ə)r-,wòk\ **1** city SW Calif. SE of Los Angeles *pop* 91,827 **2** city SW Conn. on Long Island Sound *pop* 79,113
Nor·way \'nó(ə)r-,wā\ *or* Norw **Nor·ge** \'nòr-gə\ country N Europe in Scandinavia bordering on Atlantic & Arctic oceans; a kingdom ✻ Oslo *area* 119,085, *pop* 3,910,000
Nor·we·gian \nòr-'wē-jən\ sea arm of the N Atlantic W of Norway
Nor·wich \'nó(ə)r-(,)wich; 'nòr-ich, 'när-\ **1** city SE Conn. N of New London *pop* 41,433 **2** \'när-ij, -ich\ city & county borough E England ✻ of Norfolk *pop* 121,688
Nor·wood \'nó(ə)r-,wùd\ **1** town E Mass. SW of Boston *pop* 30,-815 **2** city SW Ohio within city of Cincinnati *pop* 30,420
Not·ta·way \'nät-ə-,wā\ river 400 *m* Canada in SW Que. flowing NW into James Bay
Not·ting·ham \'nät-iŋ-əm, *US also* -,ham\ **1** *or* **Not·ting·ham·shire** \-,shi(ə)r, -shər\ *or* **Notts** \'näts\ county N *cen* England *area* 844, *pop* 974,640 **2** city & county borough, its ✻, on the Trent *pop* 299,758
Nouak·chott \nù-'äk-,shät\ town ✻ of Mauritania, in SW part on the Atlantic *pop* 35,000
Nou·méa \nü-'mā-ə\ city & port ✻ of New Caledonia *pop* 57,839
No·va Igua·çu \,nò-və-,ē-gwə-'sü\ city SE Brazil in Rio de Janeiro state NW of Rio de Janeiro *pop* 100,545

No·va Lis·boa \'nó-və-lēzh-'bō-ə\ *or formerly* **Huam·bo** \'(h)wäm-(,)bō\ city Angola in W *cen* highlands *pop* 49,823
No·va·ra \nō-'vär-ə\ commune NW Italy in Piedmont *pop* 98,941
No·va Sco·tia \,nō-və-'skō-shə\ province SE Canada comprising a peninsula (375 *m* long) & Cape Breton I. ✱ Halifax *area* 21,103, *pop* 770,000 — see ACADIA — **No·va Sco·tian** \-shən\ *adj or n*
No·va·to \nō-'vät-(,)ō\ city W Calif. N of San Francisco *pop* 31,006
No·va·ya Zem·lya \,nō-və-yə-,zem-lē-'ä\ two islands U.S.S.R. in NE Soviet Russia, Europe, in Arctic ocean between Barents sea & Kara sea *area* 36,000
Nov·go·rod \'näv-gə-,räd\ 1 medieval principality E Europe extending from Lake Peipus & Lithuania to the Urals 2 city U.S.S.R. in NW Soviet Russia, Europe, N of Lake Ilmen *pop* 128,-000
No·vi Sad \,nō-vē-'säd\ city NE Yugoslavia on the Danube; chief city of Voivodina *pop* 162,000
No·vo·kuz·netsk \,nō-(,)vō-kůz-'netsk\ *or formerly* **Sta·linsk** \'stäl-(y)ən(t)sk, 'stal-\ city U.S.S.R. in SW Soviet Russia, Asia, at S end of Kuznetsk Basin *pop* 499,000
No·vo·si·birsk \,nō-(,)vō-sə-'bi(ə)rsk\ *or formerly* **No·vo·ni·ko·la·evsk** \-,nik-ə-'lī-əfsk\ city U.S.S.R. in SW Soviet Russia, Asia, on the Ob *pop* 1,161,000
Nu·bia \'n(y)ü-bē-ə\ region & ancient kingdom NE Africa along the Nile in S Egypt & N Sudan
Nu·bi·an \'n(y)ü-bē-ən\ desert NE Sudan E of the Nile
Nu·e·ces \n(y)ü-'ā-səs\ river 338 *m* S Tex. flowing S & SE into Nueces Bay at head of Corpus Christi Bay
Nueva Esparta — see MARGARITA
Nue·vo La·re·do \nü-,ā-(,)vō-lə-'rād-(,)ō\ city N Mexico in Tamaulipas on Rio Grande opposite Laredo, Tex. *pop* 150,922
Nue·vo Le·ón \lā-'ōn\ state N Mexico in the Sierra Madre Oriental ✱ Monterrey *area* 25,134, *pop* 1,653,808
Nu·ku·a·lo·fa \,nü-kə-wə-'lō-fə\ town ✱ of Tonga on Tongatapu I. *pop* 15,545
Nu·ku Hi·va *or* **Nu·ku·hi·va** \,nü-kə-'hē-və\ island S Pacific in the Marquesas; largest in group *area* 186
Null·ar·bor Plain \,nəl-ə-,bó(ə)r-\ treeless plain SW Australia in Western Australia & So. Australia bordering on Great Australian Bight
Numfor — see NOEMFOOR
Nu·mid·ia \n(y)ü-'mid-ē-ə\ ancient country N Africa E of Mauretania in modern Algeria; chief city Hippo — **Nu·mid·i·an** \-ē-ən\ *adj or n*
Nun·ea·ton \nə-'nēt-ᵊn\ municipal borough *cen* England in Warwickshire E of Birmingham *pop* 66,979
Nu·ni·vak \'nü-nə-,vak\ island 50 *m* long W Alaska in Bering sea
Nu·rem·berg \'n(y)ůr-əm-,bərg\ *or G* **Nürn·berg** \'nœrn-,berk\ city W Germany in N *cen* Bavaria on Pegnitz river *pop* 474,200
Nu·ri·stan \,nůr-i-'stan\ *or formerly* **Kaf·i·ri·stan** \,kaf-ə-ri-'stan\ district E Afghanistan S of the Hindu Kush ✱ Puchal
Nut·ley \'nət-lē\ town NE N.J. N of Newark *pop* 32,099
Nyasa, Lake — see MALAWI (Lake)
Nyasaland — see MALAWI
Nyir·a·gon·go \nē-,ir-ə-'gȯŋ-(,)gō, -'gäŋ-\ volcano *ab* 11,400 *ft* E Zaire in Virunga mountains NE of Lake Kivu
Nysa — see NEISSE
Oa·he Reservoir \ə-'wä-(,)hē\ reservoir *ab* 225 *m* long N S.Dak. & S N.Dak. formed in Missouri river by **Oahe Dam**
Oa·hu \ə-'wä-(,)hü\ island Hawaii, site of Honolulu *area* 589
Oak Forest village NE Ill. S of Chicago *pop* 17,870
Oak·ham \'ō-kəm\ urban district E *cen* England ✱ of Rutland
Oak·land \'ō-klənd\ city & port W Calif. on San Francisco Bay opposite San Francisco *pop* 361,561
Oakland Park city SE Fla. N of Fort Lauderdale *pop* 16,261
Oak Lawn village NE Ill. SW of Chicago *pop* 60,305
Oak Park, 1 village NE Ill. W of Chicago *pop* 62,511 2 city SE Mich. N of Detroit *pop* 36,762
Oak Ridge city E Tenn. W of Knoxville *pop* 28,319
Oak·ville \'ōk-,vil\ town Canada in SE Ont. SW of Toronto *pop* 61,483
Oa·xa·ca \wə-'häk-ə\ 1 state SE Mexico bordering on the Pacific *area* 36,371, *pop* 2,011,946 2 city, its ✱ *pop* 116,826
Ob \'äb, 'ób\ river 2500 *m* U.S.S.R. in W Soviet Russia, Asia, flowing NW & N into **Gulf of Ob** (inlet of Arctic ocean 500 *m* long); with the Irtysh, 3200 *m* long
Ober·am·mer·gau \,ō-bə-'räm-ər-,gaů\ town SW Germany in Bavaria SSW of Munich
Ober·hau·sen \'ō-bər-,haůz-ᵊn\ city W Germany in the Ruhr WNW of Essen *pop* 249,900
Ober·land \'ō-bər-,land, -,länt\ *or* **Bernese Oberland** *or* **Bernese Alps** section of the Alps S Switzerland in Bern & Valais cantons between the Lakes of Thun & Brienz on the N & the valley of the upper Rhone on the S — see FINSTERAARHORN
Oberpfalz — see PALATINATE
Obwald *or* **Obwalden** — see UNTERWALDEN
Ocala \ō-'kal-ə\ city N *cen* Fla. S of Gainesville *pop* 22,583
Ocean, 1 island W Pacific between Nauru I. & Gilbert islands; belongs to Gilbert & Ellice Islands colony *area* 2 2 — see KURE
Oce·a·nia \,ō-shē-'an-ē-ə, -'ā-nē-ə\ *or* **Oce·an·i·ca** \-'an-i-kə\ the lands of the *cen* & S Pacific including Micronesia, Melanesia, Polynesia (including New Zealand), often Australia, & sometimes the Malay archipelago — **Oce·a·ni·an** \-'an-ē-ən, -'ā-nē-\ *adj or n*
Ocean·side \'ō-shən-,sīd\ city SW Calif. NNW of San Diego *pop* 40,494
Oc·mul·gee \ōk-'məl-gē\ river 255 *m, cen* Ga. flowing SE to join the **Oco·nee** \ō-'kō-nē\ (250 *m*) forming the Altamaha
Ocmulgee National Monument reservation *cen* Ga. at Macon containing Indian mounds & other remains
Ocra·coke \'ō-krə-,kōk\ island off *cen* N.C. coast between Pamlico Sound & the Atlantic — see CROATAN
Oden·se \'ōd-ᵊn-sə, 'ü-ən-zə\ city Denmark in N Fyn I. *pop* 103,850
Oder \'ōd-ər\ *or* **Odra** \'ō-drə\ river 563 *m, cen* Europe rising in the mountains of Silesia, Czechoslovakia, & flowing N to join the Neisse & thence N into the Baltic sea
Odes·sa \ō-'des-ə\ 1 city W Tex. *pop* 78,380 2 city & port U.S.S.R. in S Ukraine on Black Sea *pop* 892,000
Oea — see TRIPOLI
Oe·ta \'ēt-ə\ mountains *cen* Greece, E spur of Pindus mountains
Of·fa·ly \'óf-ə-lē, 'äf-\ *or formerly* **King's** county *cen* Ireland in Leinster ✱ Tullamore *area* 771, *pop* 51,834
Of·fen·bach \'óf-ən-,bäk, -,bäk̲\ city W Germany on the Main E of Frankfurt *pop* 117,500
Oga·den \ō-'gäd-,än\ plateau region SE Ethiopia
Ogasawara — see BONIN
Og·bo·mo·sho \,äg-bə-'mō-(,)shō\ city W Nigeria *pop* 380,239
Og·den \'óg-dən, 'äg-\ city N Utah *pop* 69,478
Ogee·chee \ō-'gē-chē\ river 250 *m* E Ga. flowing SE into the Atlantic
Ohio \ō-'hī-(,)ō\ 1 river 981 *m* E U.S. flowing from junction of Allegheny & Monongahela rivers in W Pa. into the Mississippi 2 state E *cen* U.S. ✱ Columbus *area* 41,222, *pop* 10,652,017 — **Ohio·an** \-'hī-ə-wən\ *n*
Ohre — see EGER
Oil City city NW Pa. *pop* 15,033
Oirot — see GORNO-ALTAI
Oise \'wäz\ river 186 *m* N France flowing SW into the Seine
Oi·ta \'ói-,tä\ city & port Japan in NE Kyushu *pop* 247,000
Oji·na·ga \,ō-hē-'näg-ə\ town N Mexico on Rio Grande opposite Presidio, Tex.
Ojos del Sa·la·do \'ō-(,)hōz-,del-sə-'läd-(,)ō\ mountain 22,539 *ft* NW Argentina in the Andes W of Tucumán
Oka \ō-'kä\ 1 river 530 *m* U.S.S.R. in S *cen* Soviet Russia, Asia, flowing N from the Sayan mountains into the Angara 2 river 950 *m* U.S.S.R. in *cen* Soviet Russia, Europe, flowing into the Volga
Oka·nog·an *or (in Canada)* **Oka·na·gan** \,ō-kə-'näg-ən\ river 300 *m* U.S. & Canada flowing from **Okanagan Lake** (70 *m* long, in SE B.C.) into the Columbia in NE Wash.
Oka·ya·ma \,ō-kə-'yäm-ə\ city & port Japan in W Honshu on Inland sea *pop* 375,000
Oka·za·ki \,ō-kə-'zäk-ē, ō-'käz-ə-kē\ city Japan in S *cen* Honshu SE of Nagoya *pop* 204,000
Okee·cho·bee, Lake \,ō-kə-'chō-bē\ lake 37 *m* long S *cen* Fla.
Oke·fe·no·kee \,ō-kə-fə-'nō-kē\ swamp 40 *m* long SE Ga. & NE Fla.
Okhotsk, Sea of \ō-'kätsk\ inlet of the Pacific U.S.S.R. in E Soviet Russia, Asia, W of Kamchatka peninsula & Kuril islands
Oki \'ō-(,)kē\ archipelago Japan in Sea of Japan off SW Honshu
Oki·na·wa \,ō-kə-'nä-wə, -'naů-ə\ 1 island group Japan in *cen* Ryukyu islands ✱ Naha; occupied by the U.S. 1945–1972 2 island in the group; largest in the Ryukyus *area* 579, *pop* 812,339 — **Oki·na·wan** \-'nä-wən, -'naů-ən\ *adj or n*
Okla·ho·ma \,ō-klə-'hō-mə\ state S *cen* U.S. ✱ Oklahoma City *area* 69,919, *pop* 2,559,253 — **Okla·ho·man** \-mən\ *adj or n*
Oklahoma City city ✱ of Okla. on the No. Canadian *pop* 366,481
Ok·mul·gee \ōk-'məl-gē\ city E Okla. *pop* 15,180
Oko·vang·go *or* **Oka·van·go** \,ō-kə-'vaŋ-(,)gō\ *or* Port **Cu·ban·go** \kü-'vaⁿ(ŋ)-(,)gü\ river 1000 *m* SW *cen* Africa rising in *cen* Angola & flowing S & E to empty into **Okovanggo basin** (great marsh N of Lake Ngami in NW Botswana)
Öland \'ə(r)l-,änd\ island Sweden in Baltic sea off SE coast; chief town Borgholm *area* 519
Ola·the \ō-'lā-thə\ city NE Kans. SW of Kansas City *pop* 17,917
Old Castile — see CASTILE
Ol·den·burg \'ōl-dən-,bərg\ 1 former state NW Germany bordering on North sea 2 city NW Germany W of Bremen *pop* 131,200
Old·ham \'ōl-dəm\ county borough NW England in Lancashire NE of Manchester *pop* 105,705
Old Point Comfort cape SE Va. on N shore of Hampton Roads
Old Sar·um \'sar-əm, 'ser-\ *or anc* **Sor·bi·o·du·num** \,sór-bē-ə-'d(y)ü-nəm\ ancient city S England in Wiltshire N of Salisbury
Ol·du·vai Gorge \'ōl-də-,vī\ canyon Tanzania in N Tanganyika SE of Serengeti Plain; fossil beds
Ole·an \'ō-lē-,an, ,ō-lē-'\ city SW N.Y. *pop* 19,169
Olek·ma \ō-'lek-mə\ river 700 *m* U.S.S.R. in E Soviet Russia, Asia, rising in Yablonoi mountains & flowing N into the Lena
Ole·nek \,äl-ən-'yök\ river 1325 *m* U.S.S.R. in N *cen* Soviet Russia, Asia, flowing NE into Laptev sea W of the Lena
Ol·i·fants \'äl-ə-fən(t)s\ river 350 *m* S Africa in Republic of So. Africa & Mozambique flowing from Transvaal into the Limpopo
Olives, Mount of *or* **Ol·i·vet** \'äl-ə-,vet, ,äl-ə-'\ mountain ridge 2680 *ft* W Jordan running N & S on E side of Jerusalem
Olo·mouc \'ō-lə-,mōts\ *or G* **Ol·mütz** \'ōl-,m(y)üts\ city Czechoslovakia in *cen* Moravia on March river *pop* 79,545
Olsz·tyn \'ólsh-tən\ *or G* **Al·len·stein** \'al-ən-,s(t)īn, 'äl-\ city N Poland NNW of Warsaw *pop* 94,100
Olt \'ólt\ *or* **Alu·ta** \ə-'lüt-ə\ river 308 *m* S Rumania flowing S through the Transylvanian Alps into the Danube
Ol·te·nia \äl-'tē-nē-ə\ *or* **Little Walachia** region S Rumania W of the Olt; the W division of Walachia
Olym·pia \ə-'lim-pē-ə, ō-\ 1 city ✱ of Wash. on Puget Sound *pop* 23,111 2 plain S Greece in NW Peloponnesus along Alpheus river — **Olym·pi·an** \-pē-ən\ *adj or n* — **Olym·pic** \-pik\ *adj*
Olympic, 1 mountains NW Wash. in *cen* Olympic peninsula — see OLYMPUS (Mount) 2 peninsula NW Wash. W of Puget Sound
Olympic National Park scenic area NW Wash. including part of Olympic mountains & strip of land along coast to W *area* 1388
Olym·pus \ə-'lim-pəs, ō-\ 1 mountains NE Greece in Thessaly near coast of Gulf of Salonika; highest peak 9550 *ft* 2 — see ULU DAG

ə abut ᵊ kitten, F table ər further a back ā bake
ä cot, cart á F bac aů out ch chin e less ē easy
g gift i trip ī life j joke k̲ G ich ⁿ F vin ŋ sing
ō flow ó flaw œ F bœu f œ̄ F feu ói coin th thing
t̲h̲ this ü loot ů foot ue G Füllen ue̅ F rue y yet
ʸ F digne \dēnʸ\, nuit \nwʸē\ yü few yů furious zh vision

Olympus, Mount mountain 7954 *ft* NW Wash.; highest in Olympic mountains
Olyn·thus \ō-'lin(t)-thəs\ ancient city NE Greece in Macedonia on Chalcidice peninsula
Om \'ōm\ river 450 *m* U.S.S.R. in SW Soviet Russia, Asia, flowing into the Irtysh
Omagh \'ō-mə\ town W Northern Ireland ✱ of Tyrone
Oma·ha \'ō-mə-,hò, -,hä\ city E Nebr. *pop* 347,328
Oman \ō-'män, -'man\ *or formerly* **Muscat and Oman** country SW Asia in SE Arabia bordering on Arabian sea; a sultanate ✱ Muscat *area* 82,000, *pop* 680,000 — **Omani** \ō-'män-ē, -'man-\ *adj or n*
Oman, Gulf of arm of Arabian sea between Oman & SE Iran
Ombai — see ALOR
Om·dur·man \,äm-dər-'man, -'män\ city *cen* Sudan on the Nile opposite Khartoum & Khartoum North *pop* 206,000
Omo·lon \,äm-ə-'lòn\ river 600 *m* U.S.S.R. in NE Soviet Russia, Asia, flowing from the Kolyma range N into Kolyma river
Omsk \'òm(p)sk, 'äm(p)sk\ city U.S.S.R. in SW Soviet Russia, Asia, at confluence of Irtysh & Om rivers *pop* 821,000
Omu·ra \'ō-mə-,rä\ city & port Japan in NW Kyushu on Omura Bay NNE of Nagasaki *pop* 56,538
Omu·ta \'ō-mə-,tä\ city & port Japan in NW Kyushu *pop* 188,000
One·ga \ō-'neg-ə\ lake U.S.S.R. in NW Soviet Russia, Europe, in S Karelo-Finnish Republic *area* 3764
Onei·da \ō-'nīd-ə\ lake *ab* 22 *m* long *cen* N.Y. NE of Syracuse
One·on·ta \,ō-nē-'änt-ə\ city *cen* N.Y. *pop* 16,030
On·tar·io \än-'ter-ē-,ō, -'tar-\ **1** city SW Calif. NW of Riverside *pop* 64,118 **2** province E Canada between Great Lakes & Hudson Bay ✱ Toronto *area* 363,282, *pop* 7,815,000 — **On·tar·i·an** \-ē-ən\ *adj or n*
Ontario, Lake lake U.S. & Canada in N.Y. & Ont.; easternmost of the Great Lakes *area* 7540
Ope·li·ka \,ō-pə-'lī-kə\ city E Ala. *pop* 19,027
Op·e·lou·sas \,äp-ə-'lü-səs\ city S La. N of Lafayette *pop* 20,121
Opo·le \ō-'pò-lə\ *or* G **Op·peln** \'ò-pəln\ city SW Poland on the Odra *pop* 86,500
Opor·to \ō-'pōrt-(,)ō, -'pòrt-\ *or* **Pôr·to** \'pōr-tü\ city & port NW Portugal on the Douro *pop* 325,400 — see LEIXÕES
Oquirrh \'ō-kər\ mountain range N *cen* Utah S of Great Salt Lake; highest point *ab* 11,000 *ft*
Ora·dea *or* **Oradea Ma·re** \ò-,räd-ē-ə-'mär-(,)ā\ *or* Hung **Nagy·va·rad** \'näj-'vär-,òd\ city NW Rumania in Transylvania near Hungarian border *pop* 135,361
Oran \ò-'rän\ city & port NW Algeria *pop* 327,493
Or·ange \'òr-inj, 'är-, -ənj\ **1** city SW Calif. N of Santa Ana *pop* 77,374 **2** city NE N.J. NW of Newark *pop* 32,566 **3** city E Tex. E of Beaumont on the Sabine *pop* 24,457 **4** river 1300 *m* S Africa flowing from the Drakensbergs in Lesotho W into the Atlantic
Orange \ò-rä^{n}zh\ city SE France N of Avignon *pop* 24,562
Orange Free State \'òr-inj, 'är-, -ənj\ *or* **Oran·je Vry·staat** \ō-,rä^{n}-yə-'frai-,stät\ province E *cen* Republic of So. Africa between Orange & Vaal rivers ✱ Bloemfontein *area* 49,647, *pop* 1,661,756
Orasul Stalin — see BRASOV
Or·dos \'òrd-əs\ desert N China in SW Inner Mongolia N of Great Wall in N bend of Yellow river
Or·dzho·ni·kid·ze \,òr-,jän-ə-'kid-zə\ *or* **Dzau·dzhi·kau** \(d)zaù-'jē-,kaù\ city U.S.S.R. in SE Soviet Russia, Europe, on Terek river ✱ of No. Ossetia *pop* 236,000
Öre·bro \,ər-ə-'brü\ city S *cen* Sweden *pop* 90,930
Or·e·gon \'òr-i-gən, 'är-, *chiefly by outsiders* -,gän\ **1** the Columbia river — an old name used esp. prior to discovery of mouth & renaming of river (1791) by Capt. Robert Gray **2** state NW U.S. ✱ Salem *area* 96,981, *pop* 2,091,385 **3** city NW Ohio E of Toledo *pop* 16,563 — **Or·e·go·nian** \,òr-i-'gō-nē-ən, ,är-, -nyən\ *adj or n*
Oregon Caves limestone caverns SW Oreg. SW of Medford in **Oregon Caves National Monument**
Oregon Country region W No. America between Pacific coast & the Rockies extending from N border of Calif. to Alaska — often so called *ab* 1818–46
Oregon Trail pioneer route to the Pacific Northwest *ab* 2000 *m* long from vicinity of Independence, Mo., to Fort Vancouver, Wash.; used esp. 1842–60
Orel \ò-'rel, òr-'yòl\ city U.S.S.R. in S Soviet Russia, Europe, on the Oka S of Moscow *pop* 232,000
Orem \'ōr-əm, 'òr-\ city N *cen* Utah N of Provo *pop* 25,729
Ore mountains — see ERZGEBIRGE
Oren·burg \'ōr-ən-,bərg, 'òr-, -,bù(ə)rg\ *or formerly* **Chka·lov** \chə-'käl-əf\ city U.S.S.R. in E Soviet Russia, Europe, on Ural river *pop* 345,000
Oren·se \ò-'ren(t)-(,)sā\ **1** province NW Spain *area* 2694, *pop* 413,733 **2** city, its ✱ *pop* 73,379
Öre·sund \'ər-ə-,sən\ *or* **The Sound** strait between Sjælland I., Denmark, & S Sweden connecting Kattegat with Baltic sea
Orfani, Gulf of — see STRYMONIC GULF
Organ Pipe Cactus National Monument reservation S Ariz. on Mexican border S of Ajo *area* 513
Oril·lia \ò-'ril-yə\ city Canada in SE Ont. on Lake Simcoe *pop* 24,040
Ori·no·co \,ōr-ə-'nō-(,)kō, ,òr-\ river 1600 *m* Venezuela flowing from Brazilian border to Colombia border & thence into the Atlantic through wide delta
Oris·sa \ò-'ris-ə\ state E India bordering on Bay of Bengal ✱ Bhubaneswar *area* 60,136, *pop* 21,934,827
Ori·za·ba \,ōr-ə-'zäb-ə, ,òr-\ **1** — see CITLALTEPETL **2** city E Mexico in Veracruz state *pop* 92,728
Or·khon \'òr-,kän\ river 450 *m* N Outer Mongolia flowing NE from N edge of the Gobi into the Selenga
Ork·ney \'òrk-nē\ islands N Scotland constituting a county ✱ Kirkwall (on Mainland I.) *area* 376, *pop* 17,075 — **Ork·ney·an** \'òrk-nē-ən, òrk-'\ *adj or n*
Or·lan·do \òr-'lan-(,)dō\ city E cen Fla. *pop* 99,006
Or·lé·a·nais \,òr-lē-ə-'nā\ region & former province N *cen* France ✱ Orléans
Or·lé·ans \òr-lā-ä^{n}\ commune N *cen* France *pop* 95,828
Or·ly \òr-'lē, 'òr-lē\ commune France, SSE suburb of Paris *pop* 30,202
Or·moc Bay \òr-'mäk\ inlet of Camotes sea Philippines in NW Leyte I.
Ormuz — see HORMUZ
Orne \'ò(ə)rn\ river 95 *m* NW France flowing N into Bay of the Seine
Oron·tes \ò-'ränt-ēz, -'rän-,tēz\ river 246 *m* Syria & Turkey rising in Lebanon in the Bika & flowing into the Mediterranean
Or·ping·ton \'òr-piŋ-tən\ former urban district SE England in Kent, now part of Bromley
Or·re·fors \,òr-ə-'fòrz, -'fòsh\ town SE Sweden NW of Kalmar
Orsk \'ò(ə)rsk\ city U.S.S.R. in SE Soviet Russia, Europe, on Ural river S of Magnitogorsk *pop* 225,000
Or·te·gal, Cape \,òrt-i-'gäl\ cape NW Spain
Ort·les \'òrt-,lās\ *or* G **Ort·ler** \-lər\ mountain range of E Alps N Italy between Venezia Tridentina & Lombardy; highest peak Ortles (*or* **Ort·ler·spit·ze** \-lər-,s(h)pit-sə\) 12,793 *ft*
Oru·ro \ò-'rù(ə)r-(,)ō\ city W Bolivia *pop* 86,985
Or·vie·to \,òr-vē-'ät-(,)ō\ *or anc* **Vel·su·na** \vel-'sü-nə\ *or* **Vol·sin·ii** \väl-'sin-ē-,ī\ commune *cen* Italy WNW of Terni *pop* 24,246
Osage \ō-'sāj, 'ō-,\ river 360 *m* E Kans. & Mo. flowing E into the Missouri
Osa·ka \ō-'säk-ə\ city & port Japan in S Honshu *pop* 3,018,000
Osh·a·wa \'äsh-ə-,wä\ city Canada in SE Ont. on Lake Ontario ENE of Toronto *pop* 91,587
Osh·kosh \'äsh-,käsh\ city E Wis. on Lake Winnebago *pop* 53,221
Osi·jek \'ō-sē-,(y)ek\ city N Yugoslavia in Slavonia *pop* 93,912
Os·lo \'äz-(,)lō, 'äs-\ *or formerly* **Chris·ti·a·nia** *or* **Kris·ti·a·nia** \,kris(h)-chē-'an-ē-ə, ,kris-tē-, -'än-\ city ✱ of Norway at N end of **Oslo Fjord** (inlet of the Skagerrak) *pop* 487,846
Os·na·brück \'äz-nə-,brùk\ city NW Germany *pop* 140,400
Osor·no \ō-'sòr-(,)nō\ **1** volcano 8727 *ft* S *cen* Chile in lake district **2** city S *cen* Chile S of Valdivia *pop* 69,220
Os·sa \'äs-ə\ mountain 6490 *ft* NE Greece in E Thessaly
Os·se·tia \ä-'sē-sh(ē-)ə\ region U.S.S.R. in SE Soviet Russia, Europe, in *cen* Caucasus — see NORTH OSSETIA, SOUTH OSSETIA
Os·si·ning \'äs-^{ə}n-iŋ, 'äs-niŋ\ village SE N.Y. *pop* 21,659
Ost·end \äs-'tend, 'äs-,\ *or* Flem **Oost·en·de** \ō-'sten-də\ *or* F **Os·tende** \ò-stä^{n}d\ city & port NW Belgium *pop* 56,954
Österreich — see AUSTRIA
Os·tia \'äs-tē-ə\ town *cen* Italy at mouth of the Tiber E of site of ancient town of the same name which was the port for Rome
Ostrasia — see AUSTRASIA
Ostra·va \'ò-strə-və\ *or* **Mo·rav·ska Ostrava** \,mòr-əf-skə-\ city *cen* Czechoslovakia in Moravia *pop* 273,280
Osu·mi \'ō-sə-(,)mē, ō-'sü-mē\ island group Japan in N Ryukyus
Os·we·go \ä-'swē-(,)gō\ city N N.Y. on Lake Ontario *pop* 23,844
Os·wie·cim \,òsh-vē-'en(t)-səm\ *or* **Ausch·witz** \'aùsh-,vits\ commune S Poland W of Krakow *pop* 39,600
Ota·go Harbor \ō-'täg-ō\ inlet of the Pacific S New Zealand on E coast of South I.; Dunedin is situated on it
Ota·ru \ō-'tär-(,)ü\ city & port Japan on Otaru Bay on W coast of Hokkaido I. *pop* 202,000
Otran·to \ō-'tran-(,)tō, 'ò-trən-,tō\ commune & port S Italy on coast at SE tip of Apulia
Otranto, Strait of strait between SE Italy & W Albania
Otsu \'ōt-(,)sü\ city Japan in W *cen* Honshu NE of Kyoto *pop* 165,000
Ot·ta·wa \'ät-ə-,wä, -wə, -,wò\ **1** city N *cen* Ill. *pop* 18,716 **2** river 696 *m* E Canada in SE Ont. & S Que. flowing E into the St. Lawrence **3** city ✱ of Canada in SE Ont. *pop* 302,341
Ot·to·man Empire \,ät-ə-mən-\ former Turkish sultanate (✱ Constantinople) in SE Europe, W Asia, & N Africa including at greatest extent Turkey, Syria, Mesopotamia, Palestine, Egypt, Barbary States, Balkan States, & parts of Russia & Hungary
Ot·tum·wa \ə-'təm-wə, ō-'təm-\ city SE Iowa *pop* 29,610
Oua·chi·ta \'wäsh-ə-,tò\ **1** mountains W Ark. & SE Okla. S of the Arkansas **2** *or* **Wash·i·ta** \'wäsh-ə-,tò\ river 605 *m* SW Ark. & E La. flowing into Black river
Oua·ga·dou·gou \,wäg-ə-'dü-(,)gü\ city ✱ of Upper Volta *pop* 115,500
Ouar·gla *or* **War·gla** \'wòr-glə, 'wär-, -,glä\ town & oasis Algeria in the Sahara SW of Touggourt *pop* 18,206
Oubangui — see UBANGI
Oubangui–Chari — see UBANGI-SHARI
Ou·den·aar·de \,aùd-^{ə}n-'ärd-ə, ,ōd-\ *or* F **Au·de·narde** \,ōd-^{ə}n-'ärd\ commune Belgium in E Flanders on the Scheldt *pop* 22,084
Oudh \'aùd\ region N India in E *cen* Uttar Pradesh ✱ Lucknow
Oudts·hoorn \'ōts-,hò(ə)rn\ city S Republic of So. Africa in S Cape Province 220 *m* E of Cape Town *pop* 25,800
Ouessant, Ile d' — see USHANT
Ouj·da \üzh-'dä\ city NE Morocco *pop* 128,645
Ou·lu \'aù-(,)lü, 'ō-\ *or* Sw **Uleå·borg** \'ü-lē-ō-,bòr-ē\ city N *cen* Finland on Gulf of Bothnia *pop* 87,224
Ou·ro Prê·to \,ō-,rü-'prāt-(,)ü\ city E Brazil in Minas Gerais *pop* 38,372
Ouse \'üz\ **1** *or* **Great Ouse** river 160 *m*, *cen* & E England flowing into the Wash **2** river 57 *m* NE England flowing SE to unite with the Trent forming the Humber
Outer Banks chain of sand islands & peninsulas along N.C. coast
Outer Hebrides — see HEBRIDES
Outer Mongolia — see MONGOLIA — **Outer Mongolian** *adj or n*
Out islands islands of the Bahamas group excepting New Providence
Ou·tre·mont \'ü-trə-,mänt, *F* ü-trə-mō^{n}\ city Canada in S Que. on Montreal I. *pop* 28,552
Ova·lle \ō-'vī-,ā, -'vä-,yā\ city N *cen* Chile *pop* 29,377
Over·ijs·sel \,ō-və-'rī-səl\ province E Netherlands ✱ Zwolle *area* 1318, *pop* 920,882
Over·land \'ō-vər-lənd\ city E Mo. NW of St. Louis *pop* 24,949
Overland Park city NE Kans. S of Kansas City *pop* 76,623

Ovie·do \ˌō-vē-ˈā-(ˌ)thō\ **1** province NW Spain on Bay of Biscay *area* 4025, *pop* 1,045,635 — see ASTURIAS **2** city ✱ of Oviedo province *pop* 147,172
Owas·co \ō-ˈwäs-(ˌ)kō\ lake 11 *m* long *cen* N.Y.; one of the Finger lakes
Owa·ton·na \ˌō-wə-ˈtän-ə\ city SE Minn. *pop* 15,341
Ow·en Falls \ˌō-ən-\ former waterfall 65 *ft* E Africa in Uganda in the Nile N of Lake Victoria; now submerged by **Owen Falls Dam**
Ow·ens \ˈō-ənz\ river E Calif. formerly flowing into **Owens Lake** (now dry), now supplying water to city of Los Angeles by way of Los Angeles Aqueduct
Ow·ens·boro \ˈō-ənz-ˌbər-ə, -ˌbə-rə\ city NW Ky. *pop* 50,329
Owen Sound city Canada in SE Ont. on Georgian Bay *pop* 18,469
Owen Stan·ley \ˈstan-lē\ mountain range E New Guinea; highest peak Mt. Victoria 13,240 *ft*
Owos·so \ə-ˈwäs-(ˌ)ō, ō-ˈwäs-\ city S *cen* Mich. W of Flint *pop* 17,179
Owy·hee \ō-ˈwī-(ˌ)(h)ē\ river 250 *m* SW Idaho & SE Oreg. flowing N into Snake river
Ox·ford \ˈäks-fərd\ **1** village SW Ohio *pop* 15,868 **2** *or* **Ox·ford·shire** \-ˌshi(ə)r, -shər\ county S *cen* England *area* 749, *pop* 380,-814 **3** *or* ML **Ox·o·nia** \äk-ˈsō-nē-ə\ city & county borough, its ✱, on the Thames WNW of London *pop* 108,564 — **Ox·ford·ian** \äks-ˈfōrd-ē-ən, -ˈfȯrd-\ *adj or n*
Ox·nard \ˈäk-ˌsnärd\ city S Calif. SE of Santa Barbara *pop* 71,225
Oxus — see AMU DARYA
Oxy·rhyn·chus \ˌäk-si-ˈriŋ-kəs\ *or* Ar **Eli Bah·na·sa** \el-ˈban-ə-sə\ archaeological site Egypt N of Minya & S of Faiyûm
Ozark plateau \ˈō-ˌzärk\ *or* **Ozark mountains** eroded tableland 1500–2500 *ft* high *cen* U.S. N of Arkansas river in N Ark., S Mo., & NE Okla. with E extension in S Ill. — **Ozark·er** \ˈō-ˌzär-kər\ *n* — **Ozark·ian** \ō-ˈzär-kē-ən\ *adj or n*
Ozarks, Lake of the reservoir 130 *m* long *cen* Mo. formed in Osage river by Bagnell Dam
Pa·bia·ni·ce \ˌpäb-yə-ˈnēt-sə\ commune *cen* Poland SSW of Lodz *pop* 62,300
Pa·chu·ca \pə-ˈchü-kə\ city *cen* Mexico NE of Mexico City ✱ of Hidalgo *pop* 84,543
Pa·cif·ic \pə-ˈsif-ik\ ocean extending from the arctic circle to the antarctic regions & from W No. America & W So. America to E Asia & Australia *area* 69,375,000
Pa·cif·i·ca \pə-ˈsif-i-kə\ city W Calif. S of San Francisco on the Pacific *pop* 36,020
Pacific Islands, Trust Territory of the islands in W Pacific under U.S. administration: the Marianas (except Guam), the Carolines (including the Palaus), & the Marshalls ✱ on Saipan I.; a Japanese mandate 1919–45, *land area* 717, *pop* 90,940
Pac·to·lus \pak-ˈtō-ləs\ river Asia Minor in ancient Lydia flowing into the Hermus (modern Gediz) near Sardis
Pa·dang \ˈpäd-ˌäŋ\ city & port Indonesia in W Sumatra *pop* 143,699
Pad·ding·ton \ˈpad-iŋ-tən\ former metropolitan borough NW London, England, now part of Westminster
Pa·dre \ˈpäd-rē, ˈpad-\ island 100 *m* long S Tex. between Laguna Madre & Gulf of Mexico
Pad·ua \ˈpaj-ə-wə, ˈpad-ə-wə\ *or* It **Pa·do·va** \ˈpäd-ə-ˌvä\ commune NE Italy W of Venice *pop* 225,231 — **Pad·u·an** \ˈpaj-ə-wən, ˈpad-ə-\ *adj or n*
Pa·du·cah \pə-ˈd(y)ü-kə\ city W Ky. on the Ohio *pop* 31,627
Padus — see PO
Paes·tum \ˈpēs-təm, ˈpes-\ *or earlier* **Po·sei·do·nia** \ˌpäs-ˌī-ˈdō-nē-ə, ˌpō-ˌsī-\ ancient city S Italy in W Lucania on Gulf of Salerno (ancient **Bay of Paestum**)
Pa·go Pa·go \ˌpäŋ-(ˌ)(g)ō-ˈpäŋ-(ˌ)(g)ō, ˌpäg-(ˌ)ō-ˈpäg-(ˌ)ō\ *or* **Pan·go Pan·go** \ˌpäŋ-(ˌ)(g)ō-ˈpäŋ-(ˌ)(g)ō\ town & port ✱ of American Samoa on Tutuila I. *pop* 2451
Pa·hang \pə-ˈhaŋ\ state E Federation of Malaysia bordering on So. China sea ✱ Kuala Lipis *area* 13,873, *pop* 503,131
Pahsien — see CHUNGKING
Paines·ville \ˈpānz-ˌvil\ city NE Ohio on Lake Erie *pop* 16,536
Painted desert region NE Ariz. E of the Little Colorado
Pais·ley \ˈpāz-lē\ burgh SW Scotland ✱ of Renfrewshire WSW of Glasgow *pop* 95,344
Pa·ki·stan \ˌpak-i-ˈstan, ˌpäk-i-ˈstän\ country S Asia orig. comprising an eastern division & a western division; a dominion 1947–56 & a republic 1956–72 of the Brit. Commonwealth, formed from parts of former Brit. India; ✱ Islamabad *area* 310,236, *pop* 53,990,173 — see EAST PAKISTAN, WEST PAKISTAN — **Pa·ki·stani** \-ˈstan-ē, -ˈstän-ē\ *adj or n*
Pa·lat·i·nate \pə-ˈlat-^{ə}n-ət\ *or* G **Pfalz** \ˈ(p)fälts\ either of two districts SW Germany once ruled by counts palatine of the Holy Roman Empire: **Rhenish,** *or* **Rhine, Palatinate** *or* G **Rheinpfalz** \ˈrīn-ˌ(p)fälts\ (on the Rhine E of Saarland) & **Upper Palatinate** *or* G **Ober·pfalz** \ˈō-bər-ˌ(p)fälts\ (on the Danube around Regensburg) — see RHINELAND-PALATINATE
Pal·a·tine \ˈpal-ə-ˌtīn\ **1** hill in Rome, Italy, one of seven on which the ancient city was built — see AVENTINE **2** village NE Ill. NW of Chicago *pop* 25,904
Pa·lau \pə-ˈlau̇\ *or* **Pe·lew** \pə-ˈlü\ **1** district SW Trust Territory of the Pacific Islands; usu. considered part of the Carolines *land area* 192, *pop* 11,210 **2** — see BABELTHUAP
Pa·la·wan \pə-ˈlä-wən, -ˌwän\ island 278 *m* long W Philippines W of the Visayans *area* 4550, *pop* (with adjacent islands) 232,322
Pa·lem·bang \ˌpäl-əm-ˈbäŋ\ city & port Indonesia in SE Sumatra on Musi river *pop* 474,971
Pa·len·cia \pə-ˈlen-ch(ē-)ə\ **1** province N Spain *area* 3256, *pop* 198,763 **2** city, its ✱, NNE of Valladolid *pop* 58,320
Pa·len·que \pə-ˈleŋ-(ˌ)kā\ ruined Mayan city S Mexico in N Chiapas SW of present town of Palenque
Pa·ler·mo \pə-ˈlər-(ˌ)mō, -ˈle(ə)r-\ *or anc* **Pan·or·mus** \pa-ˈnȯr-məs\ *or* **Pan·hor·mus** \pan-ˈhȯr-\ city & port Italy ✱ of Sicily *pop* 656,355 — **Pa·ler·mi·tan** \pə-ˈlər-mət-^{ə}n, -ˈler-\ *adj or n*
Pal·es·tine \ˈpal-ə-ˌstīn, -ˌstēn\ *or* L **Pal·aes·ti·na** \ˌpal-ə-ˈstē-nə, -ˈstī-\ **1** ancient region SW Asia bordering on E coast of the Mediterranean & extending E of the Jordan **2** former country bordering on the Mediterranean on W & Dead sea on E; a part of the Ottoman Empire 1516–1917, a Brit. mandate 1923–48; now divided between Israel & Jordan, with Gaza Strip administered by Egypt — **Pal·es·tin·ian** \ˌpal-ə-ˈstin-ē-ən, -ˈstin-yən\ *adj or n*
Pal·i·sades \ˌpal-ə-ˈsādz\ line of cliffs 15 *m* long SE N.Y. & NE N.J. on W bank of the Hudson
Palk \ˈpȯ(l)k\ strait 40 *m* wide between N Ceylon & SE India connecting Gulf of Mannar & Bay of Bengal
Pal·ma \ˈpäl-mə\ *or* **Palma de Ma·llor·ca** \-ˌdā-mə(l)-ˈyȯr-kə\ commune & port Spain ✱ of Baleares province on Majorca *pop* 179,572
Pal·mas, Cape \ˈpäl-məs\ cape Liberia on extreme SE coast
Palmer archipelago, Palmer peninsula — see ANTARCTIC
Palm·er Land \ˈpäm-ər, ˈpäl-mər\ the S section of Antarctic peninsula
Palm·er·ston \ˈpäm-ər-stən, ˈpäl-mər-\ island (atoll) *cen* Pacific NW of Rarotonga I.; belongs to New Zealand *area* 1
Palmerston North city New Zealand on S North I. NE of Wellington *pop* 51,000
Palm Springs city SW Calif. E of Los Angeles *pop* 20,936
Pal·my·ra \pal-ˈmī-rə\ **1** island *cen* Pacific in Line islands *area* 1 **2** *or bib* **Tad·mor** \ˈtad-ˌmȯ(ə)r\ *or* **Ta·mar** \ˈtā-ˌmär, -mər\ ancient city Syria on N edge of Syrian desert NE of Damascus — **Pal·my·rene** \ˌpal-mə-ˈrēn, -mī-\ *adj or n*
Palo Al·to \ˌpal-ə-ˈwal-(ˌ)tō\ city W Calif. SE of San Francisco on San Francisco Bay *pop* 55,966
Pal·o·mar, Mount \ˈpal-ə-ˌmär\ mountain 6126 *ft* S Calif. NNE of San Diego
Pa·los \ˈpä-ˌlōs\ *or* **Palos de la Fron·te·ra** \-ˌlōz-ˌdā-lə-ˌfrən-ˈter-ə\ town & former port SW Spain on Tinto river SE of Huelva
Pa·louse \pə-ˈlüs\ **1** river 150 *m* NW Idaho & SE Wash. flowing W & S into the Snake **2** fertile hilly region E Wash. & NW Idaho N of Snake & Clearwater rivers
Pa·mirs \pə-ˈmi(ə)rz\ *or* **Pa·mir** \-ˈmi(ə)r\ mountain region *cen* Asia in Tadzhik Republic & on borders of Sinkiang, Kashmir, & Afghanistan from which radiate Tien Shan to N, Kunlun & Karakoram to E, & Hindu Kush to W; has many peaks ove 20,000 *ft,* highest Kungur 25,146 *ft*
Pam·li·co \ˈpam-li-ˌkō\ river E N.C., estuary of Tar river, flowing E into **Pamlico Sound** (inlet of the Atlantic between the mainland & offshore islands)
Pam·pa \ˈpam-pə\ city NW Tex. ENE of Amarillo *pop* 21,726
Pam·phyl·ia \pam-ˈfil-ē-ə\ ancient district & Roman province S Asia Minor on coast S of Pisidia — **Pam·phyl·i·an** \-ē-ən\ *adj or n*
Pam·plo·na \pam-ˈplō-nə\ *or formerly* **Pam·pe·lu·na** \ˌpam-pə-ˈlü-nə\ city N Spain ✱ of Navarra province & once ✱ of Navarre kingdom *pop* 125,595
Pan·a·ma *or* Sp **Pa·na·má** \ˈpan-ə-ˌmä, -ˌmȯ, ˌpan-ə-ˈ\ **1** country S Central America; a republic; before 1903 part of Colombia *area* (including Canal Zone) 29,129, *pop* 1,480,000 **2** *or* **Panama City** city & port, its ✱, on Gulf of Panama *pop* 418,013 **3** ship canal 51 *m,* cen Panama in the Canal Zone connecting the Atlantic (Caribbean sea) & the Pacific (Gulf of Panama) — **Pan·a·ma·ni·an** \ˌpan-ə-ˈmā-nē-ən\ *adj or n*
Panama, Gulf of inlet of the Pacific on S coast of Panama
Panama, Isthmus of *or formerly* **Isthmus of Dar·i·en** \-ˌdar-ē-ˈen, -ˌder-\ isthmus Central America connecting No. America & So. America & comprised in Republic of Panama
Panama Canal Zone — see CANAL ZONE
Panama City, 1 city & port NW Fla. on Gulf of Mexico *pop* 32,096 **2** — see PANAMA
Pan·a·mint \ˈpan-ə-ˌmint, -mənt\ mountains E Calif. W of Death valley — see TELESCOPE PEAK
Pa·nay \pə-ˈnī\ island Philippines in the Visayans; chief town Iloilo *area* 4446
Pan·gim *or* **Pan·jim** \pan-ˈjim\ *or* **New Goa** \ˈgō-ə\ town & port W India in Goa; former ✱ of Portuguese India
Pa·ni·pat \ˈpän-ˌi-ˌpət\ city NW India in SE Haryana state NNW of Delhi *pop* 67,026
Panjab — see PUNJAB
Panj·nad \ˌpənj-ˈnäd\ river 50 *m* Pakistan, the combined stream of the Chenab & the Sutlej, flowing SW into the Indus
Pan·kow \ˈpäŋ-(ˌ)kō\ NE suburb of Berlin, Germany; seat of East German government
Pan·mun·jom \ˌpän-ˌmün-ˈjəm\ village S Korea SE of Kaesong
Pan·no·nia \pə-ˈnō-nē-ə\ Roman province SE Europe including territory W of the Danube now in Hungary & N Yugoslavia
Pantar — see ALOR
Pan·tel·le·ria \ˌpan-ˌtel-ə-ˈrē-ə\ island Italy in the Mediterranean between Sicily & Tunisia
Pá·nu·co \ˈpän-ə-ˌkō\ river 240 *m,* cen Mexico flowing from Hidalgo state NE into Gulf of Mexico
Pão de Açú·car \ˌpau̇ⁿ(n)-dē-ə-ˈsü-kər\ *or* **Sugarloaf Mountain** peak 1280 *ft* SE Brazil in city of Rio de Janeiro on W side of entrance to Guanabara Bay
Pao·ki \ˈpau̇-ˈkē\ city N *cen* China in SW Shensi on Wei river W of Sian *pop* 130,100
Paoking — see SHAOYANG
Pao·ting \ˈbau̇-ˈdiŋ\ *or formerly* **Tsing·yuan** \ˈchiŋ-yü-ˈän\ city NE China SW of Peking *pop* 265,000
Pao·tow \ˈbau̇-ˈdō\ city N China in SW Inner Mongolia on Yellow river W of Huhehot *pop* 800,000
Papal States — see STATES OF THE CHURCH
Pa·pee·te \ˌpäp-ē-ˈāt-ē; pə-ˈpāt-ē, -ˈpēt-\ commune & port Society islands on Tahiti ✱ of French Polynesia *pop* 24,000

ə abut ^{ə} kitten, F table   ər further   a back   ā bake
ä cot, cart   ȧ F bac   au̇ out   ch chin   e less   ē easy
g gift   i trip   ī life   j joke   k̲ G ich   ⁿ F vin   ŋ sing
ō flow   ȯ flaw   œ F bœuf   œ̄ F feu   ȯi coin   th thing
t̲h̲ this   ü loot   u̇ foot   u̇e G Füllen   ue̅ F rue   y yet
^{y} F digne \dēnʸ\, nuit \nwʸē\   yü few   yu̇ furious   zh vision

Paph·la·go·nia \ˌpaf-lə-ˈgō-nē-ə, -nyə\ ancient country & Roman province N Asia Minor bordering on Black Sea — **Paph·la·go·nian** \-nē-ən, -nyən\ *adj or n*

Pa·phos \ˈpā-ˌfäs\ town SW Cyprus on coast 10 *m* WNW of site of ancient city of Paphos

Pa·pua \ˈpap-yə-wə, ˈpäp-ə-wə\ **1** — see NEW GUINEA **2** the SE portion of the island of New Guinea; part of territory of Papua New Guinea

Papua, Gulf of arm of Coral sea SE New Guinea

Papua New Guinea territory comprising Papua & New Guinea; a U.N. trust territory administered by Australia ✱ Port Moresby *area* 182,700, *pop* 2,276,632

Pa·rá \pə-ˈrä\ **1** river 200 *m* N Brazil, the E mouth of the Amazon **2** state N Brazil S of the Amazon ✱ Belém *area* 470,752, *pop* 1,984,785 **3** — see BELÉM

Par·a·guay \ˈpar-ə-ˌgwī, -ˌgwā\ **1** river 1500 *m, cen* So. America flowing from Mato Grosso plateau in Brazil S into the Paraná in Paraguay **2** country *cen* So. America traversed by Paraguay river; a republic ✱ Asunción *area* 157,006, *pop* 2,390,000 — **Par·a·guay·an** \ˌpar-ə-ˈgwī-ən, -ˈgwā-\ *adj or n*

Par·a·í·ba \ˌpar-ə-ˈē-bə\ **1** *or* **Paraíba do Nor·te** \-də-ˈnȯrt-ē\ river 240 *m* NE Brazil flowing E into the Atlantic **2** *or* **Paraíba do Sul** \-ˈsül\ river 660 *m* SE Brazil flowing NE into the Atlantic **3** state NE Brazil bordering on the Atlantic ✱ João Pessoa *area* 21,591, *pop* 2,383,518

Par·a·mar·i·bo \ˌpar-ə-ˈmar-ə-ˌbō\ city & port ✱ of Surinam on Suriname river *pop* 110,867

Par·a·mount \ˈpar-ə-ˌmau̇nt\ city SW Calif. N of Long Beach *pop* 34,734

Pa·ram·us \pə-ˈram-əs\ borough NE N.J. *pop* 29,495

Pa·ra·ná \ˌpar-ə-ˈnä\ **1** *or in upper course* **Al·to Paraná** \ˌal-(ˌ)tō-\ river 2040 *m, cen* So. America flowing from junction of Rio Grande & the Paraíba in Brazil SSW into the Río de la Plata in Argentina **2** state S Brazil E of the Paraná ✱ Curitiba *area* 82,741, *pop* 6,741,-520 **3** city NE Argentina *pop* 107,551

Pa·ra·na·í·ba *or formerly* **Pa·ra·na·hi·ba** \ˌpar-ə-nə-ˈē-bə\ river 530 *m* S Brazil flowing SW to unite with the Rio Grande forming the Paraná

Par·du·bi·ce \ˈpärd-ə-ˌbit-sə\ city Czechoslovakia in Bohemia on the Elbe E of Prague *pop* 69,508

Pa·ria \ˈpär-ē-ə\ peninsula NE Venezuela

Paria, Gulf of inlet of the Atlantic between Trinidad & Venezuela

Pa·ri·cu·tin \pə-ˈrē-kə-ˌtēn\ volcano 7451 *ft* SW Mexico in NW Michoacán; first eruption 1943

Parida, La — see BOLÍVAR (Cerro)

Par·is \ˈpar-əs\ **1** city NE Tex. *pop* 23,441 **2** *or anc* **Lu·te·tia** \lü-ˈtē-sh(ē-)ə\ city ✱ of France on the Seine *pop* 2,590,771 — **Pa·ri·sian** \pə-ˈrizh-ən, -ˈrēzh-\ *adj or n*

Par·kers·burg \ˈpär-kərz-ˌbərg\ city NW W.Va. *pop* 44,208

Park Forest village NE Ill. S of Chicago *pop* 30,638

Park Ridge city NE Ill. NW of Chicago *pop* 42,466

Par·ma \ˈpär-mə\ **1** city NE Ohio S of Cleveland *pop* 100,216 **2** commune N Italy in Emilia-Romagna *pop* 171,304

Parma Heights city NE Ohio S of Cleveland *pop* 27,192

Par·na·í·ba *or formerly* **Par·na·hy·ba** \ˌpär-nə-ˈē-bə\ river 900 *m* NE Brazil flowing NE into the Atlantic

Par·nas·sus \pär-ˈnas-əs\ *or* NGk **Par·nas·sós** \ˌpär-nə-ˈsȯs\ mountain 8060 *ft, cen* Greece N of Gulf of Corinth

Par·os \ˈpar-ˌäs, ˈper-\ *or* NGk **Pá·ros** \ˈpär-ˌȯs\ island Greece in *cen* Cyclades W of Naxos *area* 81

Par·ra·mat·ta \ˌpar-ə-ˈmat-ə\ town SE Australia, W suburb of Sydney, on Parramatta river (estuary, W arm of Port Jackson) *pop* 106,996

Par·ris \ˈpar-əs\ island S S.C. in Port Royal sound

Par·ry \ˈpar-ē\ islands Canada in N Northwest Territories in Arctic ocean N of Victoria I.

Parsnip — see FINLAY

Par·thia \ˈpär-thē-ə\ ancient country SW Asia in NE modern Iran

Pas·a·de·na \ˌpas-ə-ˈdē-nə\ **1** city SW Calif. E of Glendale *pop* 113,327 **2** city SE Tex. E of Houston *pop* 89,277

Pa·sar·ga·dae \pə-ˈsär-gə-ˌdē\ city of ancient Persia built by Cyrus the Great; ruins NE of site of later Persepolis

Pa·say \ˈpäs-ˌī\ *or* **Ri·zal** \ri-ˈzäl, -ˈsäl\ municipality Philippines in Luzon on Manila Bay S of Manila *pop* 174,100

Pas·ca·gou·la \ˌpas-kə-ˈgü-lə\ city & port SE Miss. *pop* 27,264

Pasco, Cerro de — see CERRO DE PASCO

Pascua, Isla de — see EASTER

Pas de Calais — see DOVER (Strait of)

Pa·sig \ˈpäs-ig\ river 12 *m* Philippines in Luzon flowing from the Laguna de Bay through Manila into Manila Bay

Pas·sa·ic \pə-ˈsā-ik\ **1** river 100 *m* NE N.J. flowing into Newark Bay **2** city NE N.J. SSE of Paterson *pop* 55,124

Pas·sa·ma·quod·dy Bay \ˌpas-ə-mə-ˈkwäd-ē\ inlet of Bay of Fundy between E Me. & SW N.B. at mouth of St. Croix river

Pas·se·ro, Cape \ˈpäs-ə-ˌrō, ˈpas-\ headland Italy at SE tip of Sicily

Pas·sy \pa-ˈsē\ section of Paris, France, on right bank of the Seine near the Bois de Boulogne

Pas·ta·za \pə-ˈstäz-ə, -ˈstäs-\ river 400 *m* Ecuador & Peru flowing S into the Marañón

Pat·a·go·nia \ˌpat-ə-ˌgō-nyə, -nē-ə\ region So. America in S Argentina & S Chile between the Andes & the Atlantic S of *ab* 40° S lat.; sometimes considered as including Tierra del Fuego — **Pat·a·go·nian** \-nyən, -nē-ən\ *adj or n*

Pa·tan \ˈpä-ˌtən\ city E *cen* Nepal adjoining Katmandu *pop* 53,930

Pa·tap·sco \pə-ˈtap-(ˌ)skō, -si-ˌkō\ river 80 *m* N *cen* Md. flowing SE into Chesapeake Bay

Pat·er·son \ˈpat-ər-sən\ city NE N.J. N of Newark *pop* 144,824

Pa·ti·a·la \ˌpət-ē-ˈäl-ə\ **1** former state NW India, now part of Punjab state **2** city, its ✱, 70 *m* SW of Simla *pop* 157,920

Pat·mos \ˈpat-məs\ island Greece in the NW Dodecanese

Pat·na \ˈpət-nə\ city NE India on the Ganges, winter ✱ of Bihar *pop* 459,717

Pa·tos, La·goa dos \lə-ˌgō-əd-ə-ˈspat-əs\ lagoon 124 *m* long S Brazil in Rio Grande do Sul

Pa·tras \pə-ˈtras, ˈpa-trəs\ *or* NGk **Pa·trai** \ˈpä-trā\ *or anc* **Pa·trae** \ˈpā-(ˌ)trē\ city & port W Greece in N Peloponnesus on Gulf of Patras *pop* 111,238

Patras, Gulf of *or* **Gulf of Cal·y·don** \ˈkal-ə-ˌdän, -əd-ᵊn inlet of Ionian sea W Greece W of Gulf of Corinth

Patrimony of St. Peter — see ROME (Duchy of)

Pa·tux·ent \pə-ˈtək-sənt\ river 100 *m, cen* Md. flowing S & SE into Chesapeake Bay

Pau \ˈpō\ **1** *or* F **Gave de Pau** \gȧv-də-pō\ river 100 *m* SW France rising in the Pyrenees SW of Pau & flowing to the Adour — see GAVARNIE **2** commune SW France on the Pau *pop* 74,005

Paumotu — see TAUMOTU

Pa·via \pə-ˈvē-ə\ commune N Italy S of Milan *pop* 85,160

Pav·lof, Mount \ˈpav-ˌlȯf\ volcano 8215 *ft* SW Alaska on SW Alaska peninsula in Aleutian range

Paw·tuck·et \pə-ˈtək-ət, pȯ-\ city NE R.I. *pop* 76,984

Pay·san·dú \ˌpī-ˌsän-ˈdü\ city & port W Uruguay on Uruguay river NW of Montevideo *pop* 52,472

Pea·body \ˈpē-ˌbäd-ē, -bəd-ē\ city NE Mass. N of Lynn *pop* 48,080

Peace \ˈpēs\ river 945 *m* W Canada flowing E & NE in N B.C. & N Alta. into the Slave — see FINLAY

Pearl \ˈpər(-ə)l\ **1** river 490 *m* S Miss. flowing S into Gulf of Mexico **2** *or* **Chu** \ˈjü\ *or* **Canton** river SE China SE of Canton at E side of West river delta

Pearl City city Hawaii in S Oahu *pop* 19,552

Pearl Harbor inlet Hawaii on S coast of Oahu W of Honolulu

Pea·ry Land \ˈpi(ə)r-ē\ region N Greenland — see MORRIS JESUP

Pe·chen·ga \ˈpech-ən-gə\ *or* Finn **Pet·sa·mo** \ˈpet-sə-ˌmō\ town & port U.S.S.R. in NW Soviet Russia, Europe, on inlet of Barents sea in district that belonged to Finland 1920–44

Pe·cho·ra \pə-ˈchōr-ə, -ˈchȯr-\ river 1125 *m* U.S.S.R. in NE Soviet Russia, Europe, flowing N into Barents sea

Pe·cos \ˈpā-kəs\ river 735 *m* E N.Mex. & W Tex. flowing SE into the Rio Grande

Pecs \ˈpāch\ city S Hungary W of the Danube *pop* 144,000

Ped·er·nal·es \ˌpərd-ᵊn-ˈal-əs\ river 150 *m, cen* Tex. flowing E into the Colorado

Pee·bles \ˈpē-bəlz\ **1** *or* **Pee·bles·shire** \ˈpē-bəl-ˌshi(ə)r, -shər\ *or* **Tweed·dale** \ˈtwēd-ˌdāl\ county SE Scotland including upper course of the Tweed *area* 347, *pop* 13,675 **2** burgh, its ✱

Pee Dee \ˈpē-ˌdē\ river 233 *m* N.C. & S.C. flowing SE into Winyah Bay — see YADKIN

Peeks·kill \ˈpēk-ˌskil\ city SE N.Y. N of Yonkers *pop* 18,881

Peel \ˈpē(ə)l\ river 425 *m* NW Canada rising in W Yukon Territory & flowing E & N into the Mackenzie

Pee·ne \ˈpā-nə\ river 70 *m* N Germany flowing E through Pomerania into Stettiner Haff

Pee·ne·mün·de \ˌpā-nə-ˈm(y)ün-də, -ˈmu̇en-\ village NE Germany on island at mouth of Peene river

Pei·pus \ˈpī-pəs\ *or* Estonian **Peip·si** \ˈpāp-sē\ *or* Russ **Chudskoe** \ˈchüt-skə-yə\ lake U.S.S.R. in E Estonia & NW Soviet Russia, Europe *area* 1357

Peiraeus — see PIRAEUS

Pe·ka·long·an \ˌpek-ə-ˈlȯŋ-ˌän\ city Indonesia in *cen* Java on N coast *pop* 102,380

Pe·kin \ˈpē-kən, -ˌkin\ city N *cen* Ill. SSW of Peoria *pop* 31,375

Pe·king \ˈpē-ˈkiŋ\ *or* **Pei·ping** \ˈpā-ˈpiŋ, ˈbā-\ municipality N China; before 1928 ✱ of China; since 1949 ✱ of Communist China *pop* 8,000,000

Pe·la·gian \pə-ˈlā-j(ē-)ən\ islands Italy in the Mediterranean S of Sicily between Malta & Tunisia

Pe·lee \ˈpē-lē\ island SE Canada in W Lake Erie SW of Point Pelee, Ont. *area* 18

Pe·lée, Mount \pə-ˈlā\ volcano French West Indies in N Martinique

Pelee, Point — see POINT PELEE NATIONAL PARK

Pel·e·liu \ˌpel-ə-ˈlē-(ˌ)ü\ island W Pacific at S end of Palau islands

Pelew — see PALAU

Pe·li·on \ˈpē-lē-ən\ *or* NGk **Pí·lion** \ˈpēl-ˌyȯn\ mountain 5417 *ft* NE Greece in E Thessaly SE of Mt. Ossa

Pel·la \ˈpel-ə\ ancient city NE Greece, ancient ✱ of Macedonia

Pel·ly \ˈpel-ē\ river 330 *m* NW Canada in Yukon Territory flowing W into the Yukon

Pel·o·pon·ne·sus \ˌpel-ə-pə-ˈnē-səs\ *or* **Pel·o·pon·ne·sos** \-səs\ *or* **Pel·o·pon·nese** \ˈpel-ə-pə-ˌnēz, -ˌnēs\ *or* **Mo·rea** \mə-ˈrē-ə\ peninsula forming S part of mainland of Greece — **Pel·o·pon·ne·sian** \ˌpəl-ə-pə-ˈnē-zhən, -shən\ *adj or n*

Pe·lo·tas \pə-ˈlōt-əs\ city S Brazil in SE Rio Grande do Sul at S end of Lagoa dos Patos *pop* 208,672

Pem·ba \ˈpem-bə\ island Tanzania in Indian ocean N of island of Zanzibar

Pem·broke \ˈpem-ˌbru̇k, *U.S. also* -ˌbrōk\ **1** city Canada in SE Ont. WNW of Ottawa *pop* 16,544 **2** *or* **Pem·broke·shire** \-ˌshi(ə)r, -shər\ county SW Wales ✱ Haverfordwest *area* 614, *pop* 92,295

Pem·broke Pines \ˈpem-ˌbrōk\ city SE Fla. S of Fort Lauderdale *pop* 15,520

Pe·nang \pə-ˈnaŋ\ island SE Asia at N end of Strait of Malacca *area* 108 **2** state Federation of Malaysia comprising Penang I. & mainland opposite: until 1948 one of the Straits Settlements ✱ George Town *area* 400, *pop* 776,770 **3** — see GEORGE TOWN

Pend Oreille \ˌpän-də-ˈrā\ river 100 *m* N Idaho & NE Wash. flowing from **Pend Oreille Lake** (35 *m* long, in Idaho) W & N into the Columbia in B.C.

Pe·ne·us \pə-ˈnē-əs\ *or* NGk **Pi·niós** \pēn-ˈyȯs\ *or formerly* **Sa·lam·bria** \sə-ˈlam-brē-ə\ river 125 *m* N Greece in Thessaly flowing E into Gulf of Salonika

Peng·pu \ˈpəŋ-ˈpü\ city E China in N Anhwei *pop* 253,000

Pen·ki \ˈbən-ˈchē\ city NE China in E *cen* Liaoning *pop* 750,000

Pen·nine Alps \ˈpen-ˌīn\ section of Alps on border between Switzerland & Italy NE of Graian Alps — see ROSA (Monte)

Pennine Chain mountains N England extending S from Scottish border to Derbyshire & Staffordshire; highest Cross Fell 2930 *ft*

Penn·syl·va·nia \ˌpen(t)-səl-ˈvā-nyə, -nē-ə\ state NE U.S. ✱ Harrisburg *area* 45,333, *pop* 11,793,909

Pe·nob·scot \pə-ˈnäb-ˌskät, -skət\ river 101 *m*, *cen* Me. flowing S into **Penobscot Bay** (inlet of the Atlantic)

Penrhyn — see TONGAREVA

Pen·sa·co·la \ˌpen(t)-sə-ˈkō-lə\ city & port NW Fla. on **Pensacola Bay** (inlet of Gulf of Mexico) *pop* 59,507

Pen·tap·o·lis \pen-ˈtap-ə-ləs\ any one of several groups of five ancient cities in Italy, Asia Minor, & Cyrenaica

Pen·tel·i·cus \pen-ˈtel-i-kəs\ *or* **Pen·tel·i·kon** \-kən, -ˌkän\ *or* NGk **Pen·de·li·kón** \ˌpen-ˌdel-ē-ˈkȯn\ mountain 3639 *ft* E Greece in Attica NE of Athens

Pen·tic·ton \pen-ˈtik-tən\ city Canada in S B.C. *pop* 18,146

Pent·land \ˈpent-lənd\ **1** firth channel between Orkneys & mainland of Scotland **2** hills S Scotland in Midlothian, Lanark, & Peebles; highest peak Scald Law 1898 *ft*

Pen·za \ˈpen-zə\ city U.S.S.R. in S Soviet Russia, Europe, on Sura river 225 *m* W of Kuibyshev *pop* 374,000

Pen·zance \pen-ˈzan(t)s, pən-\ municipal borough & port SW England in Cornwall on English channel *pop* 19,352

Pen·zhin·ska·ya Bay \ˌpen-ˈzhin(t)-skə-yə\ *or* **Pen·zhi·na Bay** \ˈpen-zhə-nə\ arm of Sea of Okhotsk, U.S.S.R., between Kamchatka peninsula & mainland

People's Democratic Republic of Yemen — see YEMEN

Pe·o·ria \pē-ˈōr-ē-ə, -ˈȯr-\ city N *cen* Ill. *pop* 126,963

Pep·in, Lake \ˈpip-ən, ˈpep-\ expansion of the upper Mississippi 34 *m* long between SE Minn. & W Wis.

Pera — see BEYOGLU

Pe·raea *or* **Pe·rea** \pə-ˈrē-ə\ ancient region of Palestine E of the Jordan

Pe·rak \ˈper-ə, ˈpir-ə, ˈper-ˌak\ state W Federation of Malaysia on Strait of Malacca ✱ Kuala Kangsar *area* 7980, *pop* 1,562,566

Per·di·do \pər-ˈdēd-(ˌ)ō\ river 60 *m* rising in SE Ala. & flowing S into Gulf of Mexico forming part of Ala.-Fla. boundary

Per·ga \ˈpər-gə\ ancient city S Asia Minor in Pamphylia

Per·ga·mum \ˈpər-gə-məm\ *or* **Per·ga·mus** \-məs\ *or* **Per·ga·mos** \-məs, ˌmäs\ **1** ancient Greek kingdom covering most of Asia Minor; at its height 263–133 B.C. **2** *or modern* **Ber·ga·ma** \bər-ˈgäm-ə\ city W Turkey NNE of Izmir ✱ of ancient Pergamum *pop* 24,121

Pé·ri·gord \ˌper-ə-ˈgō(ə)r\ old division of N Guienne in SW France ✱ Périgueux

Pé·ri·gueux \-ˈgə(r), -ˈgœ̄\ commune SW France NE of Bordeaux *pop* 37,450

Pe·rim \pə-ˈrim, -ˈrēm\ island in Bab el Mandeb strait at entrance to Red sea; belongs to (Southern) Yemen

Per·lis \ˈper-ləs\ state N Federation of Malaysia bordering on Thailand & Andaman sea ✱ Kangar *area* 310, *pop* 121,062

Perm \ˈpərm, ˈpe(ə)rm\ *or formerly* **Mo·lo·tov** \ˈmäl-ə-ˌtȯf, ˈmōl-, ˈmōl-, -ˌtȯv\ city U.S.S.R. in E Soviet Russia, Europe, on the Kama *pop* 850,000

Per·nam·bu·co \ˌpər-nəm-ˈb(y)ü-(ˌ)kō, ˌper-nəm-ˈbü-\ **1** state NE Brazil ✱ Recife *area* 38,315, *pop* 5,208,011 **2** — see RECIFE

Per·nik \ˈpe(ə)r-nik\ *or* **Dimitrovo** \də-ˈmē-trə-ˌvō\ city W Bulgaria S of Sofia *pop* 79,335

Per·pi·gnan \per-pē-nyäⁿ\ city S France SE of Toulouse near Mediterranean coast *pop* 102,191

Per·sep·o·lis \pər-ˈsep-ə-ləs\ city of ancient Persia, site in SW Iran NE of Shiraz

Persia — see IRAN

Persian Gulf arm of Arabian sea between SW Iran & Arabia

Persian Gulf States Kuwait, Bahrein, Qatar, & United Arab Emirates

Persis — see FARS

Perth \ˈpərth\ **1** city ✱ of Western Australia on Swan river *pop* (with suburbs) 499,969 — see FREMANTLE **2** *or* **Perth·shire** \-ˌshi(ə)r, -shər\ county *cen* Scotland *area* 249, *pop* 127,138 **3** burgh, its ✱ *pop* 48,051

Perth Am·boy \ˌpər-ˈtham-ˌbȯi\ city & port NE N.J. on Raritan Bay at mouth of Raritan river *pop* 38,798

Pe·ru \pə-ˈrü\ country W So. America; a republic ✱ Lima *area* 482,257, *pop* 14,010,000 — **Pe·ru·vi·an** \-ˈrü-vē-ən\ *adj or n*

Pe·ru·gia \pə-ˈrü-j(ē-)ə, pā-\ commune *cen* Italy between Lake Trasimeno & the Tiber ✱ of Umbria *pop* 125,926

Perugia, Lake of — see TRASIMENO (Lake)

Pe·sa·ro \ˈpā-zə-ˌrō\ commune & port *cen* Italy on the Adriatic NW of Ancona *pop* 79,943

Pes·ca·do·res \ˌpes-kə-ˈdōr-ēz, -ˈdȯr-, -əs\ *or* **Peng·hu** \ˈpəŋ-ˈhü\ islands E China in Formosa strait, attached to Formosa; chief town Makung (on Penghu, chief island) *area* 49

Pe·sca·ra \pe-ˈskär-ə\ commune & port *cen* Italy on the Adriatic *pop* 115,122

Pe·sha·war \pə-ˈshä-wər, -ˈshau̇(-ə)r\ city N Pakistan ESE of Khyber pass *pop* 296,000

Pe·tah Tiq·va *or* **Pe·tah Tik·vah** \ˌpet-ə-ˈtik-(ˌ)vä, ˌpāt- city W Israel E of Tel Aviv *pop* 83,200

Pet·a·lu·ma \ˌpet-ᵊl-ˈü-mə\ city W Calif. N of San Francisco *pop* 24,870

Pe·ter·bor·ough \ˈpēt-ər-ˌbər-ə, -ˌbə-rə, -b(ə-)rə\ **1** city Canada in SE Ont. NE of Oshawa *pop* 58,111 **2** municipal borough E *cen* England *pop* 70,021

Peterborough, Soke of \ˌsōk\ former administrative county E *cen* England in Northamptonshire; now part of Huntingdonshire

Pe·ters·burg \ˈpēt-ərz-ˌbərg\ **1** city SE Va. *pop* 36,103 **2** SAINT PETERSBURG — see LENINGRAD

Pet·it·co·di·ac \ˌpet-ē-ˈkōd-ē-ˌak\ river 60 *m* SE Canada in SE N.B. flowing to head of Bay of Fundy

Pe·ti·tot \ˈpet-i-ˌtō\ river 295 *m* W *cen* Canada flowing W into Liard river

Pe·tra \ˈpē-trə, ˈpe-trə\ ancient city of NW Arabia on slope of Mt. Hor, site now in SW Jordan; ✱ of the Edomites & Nabataeans

Petrified Forest National Park reservation E Ariz. in Painted desert containing natural exhibit of petrified wood *area* 147

Pe·tro·dvo·rets \ˌpe-trəd-və-ˈrets\ *or formerly* **Pe·ter·hof** \ˈpēt-ər-ˌhȯf, -ˌhäf\ town U.S.S.R. in NW Soviet Russia, Europe, W of Leningrad

Petrograd — see LENINGRAD

Pet·ro·pav·lovsk \ˌpe-trə-ˈpav-ˌlȯfsk\ city U.S.S.R. in Soviet Central Asia in N Kazakhstan *pop* 173,000

Petropavlovsk–Kam·chat·ski \-kam-ˈchat-skē\ city & port U.S.S.R. in E Soviet Russia, Asia on Kamchatka peninsula *pop* 154,000

Pe·tró·po·lis \pə-ˈträp-ə-ləs\ city SE Brazil in Rio de Janeiro state *pop* 200,052

Petrovsk — see MAKHACHKALA

Pet·ro·za·vodsk \ˌpe-trə-zə-ˈvätsk\ city U.S.S.R. in NW Soviet Russia, Europe ✱ of Karelian Republic on Lake Onega *pop* 185,000

Petsamo — see PECHENGA

Pfalz — see PALATINATE

Pforz·heim \ˈ(p)fōrts-ˌhīm\ city W Germany SE of Karlsruhe *pop* 90,022

Pha·ros \ˈfa(ə)r-ˌäs, ˈfe(ə)r-\ peninsula N Egypt in city of Alexandria; formerly an island

Pharr \ˈfär\ city S Tex. E of McAllen *pop* 15,829

Phar·sa·lus \fär-ˈsā-ləs\ *or modern* **Phar·sa·la** \ˈfär-sə-lə\ *or* NGk **Fár·sa·la** \ˈfär-\ town NE Greece in E Thessaly in ancient district of **Phar·sa·lia** \fär-ˈsāl-yə, -ˈsā-lē-ə\

Phe·nix City \ˌfē-niks-\ city E Ala. *pop* 25,281

Phil·a·del·phia \ˌfil-ə-ˈdel-fyə, -fē-ə\ **1** city & port SE Pa. on the Delaware *pop* 1,948,609 **2** — see ALASEHIR **3** — see AMMAN — **Phil·a·del·phian** \-fyən, -fē-ən\ *adj or n*

Phi·lae \ˈfī-(ˌ)lē\ island S Egypt in the Nile above Aswân; now submerged

Philippeville — see SKIKDA

Phi·lip·pi \ˈfil-ə-ˌpī *also* fə-ˈlip-ˌī\ ancient town NE Greece in N *cen* Macedonia 10 *m* from the coast — **Phi·lip·pi·an** \fə-ˈlip-ē-ən\ *adj or n*

Phil·ip·pine \ˌfil-ə-ˈpēn, ˈfil-ə-ˌ\ **1** islands of the Malay archipelago NE of Borneo — see PHILIPPINES **2** sea comprising the waters of the W Pacific E of & adjacent to the Philippines

Phil·ip·pines \-ˈpēnz, -ˌpēnz\ *or* **Republic of the Philippines** *or* Sp **Re·pú·bli·ca de Fi·li·pi·nas** \re-ˈpüv-lē-kä-thä-ˌfē-lē-ˈpē-(ˌ)näs\ country E Asia comprising the Philippine islands; a republic, once a Spanish possession & (1898–1945) a U.S. possession ✱ Manila, official ✱ Quezon City *land area* 114,830, *pop* 37,960,000 — **Philippine** *adj*

Philippopolis — see PLOVDIV

Phi·lis·tia \fə-ˈlis-tē-ə\ ancient country SW Palestine on the coast; the land of the Philistines

Phil·lips·burg \ˈfil-əps-ˌbərg\ town W N.J. *pop* 17,849

Phnom Penh *or* **Pnom·penh** \(pə-)ˈnȯm-ˈpen, (pə-)ˈnäm-\ city ✱ of Khmer Republic on the Mekong *pop* 393,995

Pho·caea \fō-ˈsē-ə\ ancient city of Asia Minor on Aegean sea in N Ionia — **Pho·cae·an** \-ən\ *adj or n*

Pho·cis \ˈfō-səs\ region *cen* Greece N of Gulf of Corinth

Phoe·ni·cia *or* **Phe·ni·cia** \fi-ˈnish-(ē-)ə, -ˈnēsh-\ *or* **Phe·ni·ce** \-ˈnī-sē\ ancient country SW Asia at E end of the Mediterranean in modern Syria & Lebanon

Phoe·nix \ˈfē-niks\ **1** city ✱ of Ariz. on Salt river *pop* 581,562 **2** islands *cen* Pacific ESE of the Gilberts belonging (except for Canton & Enderbury) to Gilbert & Ellice Islands colony

Phryg·ia \ˈfrij-(ē-)ə\ ancient country W *cen* Asia Minor divided *ab* 400 B.C. into **Greater Phrygia** (the inland region) & **Lesser Phrygia** (region along the Hellespont)

Pia·cen·za \pyä-ˈchen(t)sə, ˌpē-ə-ˈ\ *or anc* **Pla·cen·tia** \plə-ˈsen-ch(ē-)ə\ commune N Italy on the Po SE of Milan *pop* 103,439

Pi·auí *or formerly* **Pi·au·hy** \pyau̇-ˈē, pē-ˌau̇-\ state NE Brazil bordering on the Atlantic E of Parnaíba river ✱ Teresina *area* 94,819, *pop* 1,735,568

Pia·ve \ˈpyäv-(ˌ)ā, pē-ˈäv-\ river 137 *m* NE Italy flowing S & SE into the Adriatic

Pic·ar·dy \ˈpik-ərd-ē\ *or* F **Pi·car·die** \pē-kȧr-dē\ region & former province N France bordering on English channel N of Normandy ✱ Amiens — **Pi·card** \ˈpik-ˌärd, -ərd; pik-ˈärd\ *adj or n*

Pi·ce·num \pī-ˈsē-nəm\ district of ancient Italy on the Adriatic SE of Umbria

Pi·co Ri·ve·ra \ˌpē-(ˌ)kō-rə-ˈvir-ə\ city SW Calif. SE of Los Angeles *pop* 54,170

Pied·mont \ˈpēd-ˌmänt\ **1** plateau E U.S. lying E of the Appalachian mountains between SE N.Y. & *cen* Ala. **2** *or* It **Pie·mon·te** \pyā-ˈmōn-(ˌ)tā\ region NW Italy bordering on France & Switzerland W of Lombardy ✱ Turin — **Pied·mon·tese** \ˌpēd-mən-ˈtēz, -(ˌ)män-, -ˈtēs\ *adj or n*

Pie·dras Ne·gras \pē-ˌā-drə-ˈsnā-grəs, -ˌed-rə-ˈsneg-rəs\ city N Mexico in Coahuila on Rio Grande opposite Eagle Pass, Tex. *pop* 65,883

Pi·e·ria \pī-ˈir-ē-ə, -ˈer-\ ancient region NE Greece in Macedonia N of Thessaly

Pierre \ˈpi(ə)r\ city ✱ of S.Dak. on the Missouri *pop* 9699

Pierre·fonds \pē-ˌe(ə)r-ˈfōⁿ\ city Canada in S Que. W of Montreal *pop* 33,010

Pie·ter·mar·itz·burg \ˌpēt-ər-ˈmar-əts-ˌbərg\ city E Republic of So. Africa ✱ of Natal *pop* 128,598

Pigs, Bay of \ˈpigz\ *or* **Co·chi·nos Bay** \kō-ˌchē-nəs-\ bay W Cuba on S coast

Pikes Peak \ˈpīks\ mountain 14,110 *ft* E *cen* Colo. at S end of Front range

Pik Pobedy — see POBEDA (Peak)

ə abut	ᵊ kitten, F table	ər further	a back	ā bake	
ä cot, cart	ȧ F bac	au̇ out	ch chin	e less	ē easy
g gift	i trip	ī life	j joke	k̲ G ich	ⁿ F vin	ŋ sing
ō flow	ȯ flaw	œ F bœuf	œ̄ F feu	ȯi coin	th thing
th̲ this	ü loot	u̇ foot	u̇e G Füllen	ue̅ F rue	y yet
ʸ F digne \dēnʸ\, nuit \nwʸē\	yü few	yu̇ furious	zh vision		

Pi·la·tus \pi-'lät-əs\ mountain 6995 *ft, cen* Switzerland in Unterwalden SW of Lucerne
Pil·co·ma·yo \ˌpil-kə-'mī-(ˌ)ō\ river 1000 *m* S *cen* So. America rising in Bolivia & flowing SE on Argentina-Paraguay boundary into Paraguay river
Pilion — see PELION
Pillars of Her·cu·les \'hər-kyə-ˌlēz\ the two promontories at E end of Strait of Gibraltar: Rock of Gibraltar (in Europe) & Jebel Musa (in Africa)
Pílos — see PYLOS
Pim·li·co \'pim-li-ˌkō\ district of W London, England in SW Westminster
Pi·nar del Río \pi-ˌnär-ˌdel-'rē-(ˌ)ō\ city & port W Cuba SW of Havana *pop* 67,600
Pin·dus \'pin-dəs\ mountains N Greece between Epirus & Thessaly; highest point over 7500 *ft*
Pine Bluff \'pīn-'bləf, -ˌbləf\ city SE *cen* Ark. *pop* 57,389
Pi·nel·las \pī-'nel-əs\ peninsula W Fla. between Tampa Bay & Gulf of Mexico
Pinellas Park city W Fla. NW of St. Petersburg *pop* 22,287
Pines, Isle of, 1 — see ISLE OF PINES **2** — see KUNIE
Ping \'piŋ\ river 360 *m* W Thailand flowing SSE to join the Nan forming the Chao Phraya
Piniós — see PENEUS
Pinkiang — see HARBIN
Pinnacles National Monument reservation W *cen* Calif. in Coast range SSE of Hollister *area* 20
Pi·nole \pē-'nōl\ city W Calif. N of Berkeley *pop* 15,850
Pinsk \'pin(t)sk\ city U.S.S.R. in SW Belorussia *pop* 62,000
Pinsk Marshes — see PRIPET
Piotr·kow \'pyȯt-ər-ˌküf, pē-'ȯt-, -ˌküv\ *or* Russ **Pe·tro·kov** \'petrə-ˌkȯf, -ˌkȯv\ commune *cen* Poland SSE of Lodz *pop* 59,700
Pipe Spring National Monument reservation NW Ariz. containing old stone fort
Pipe·stone National Monument \'pīp-ˌstōn\ reservation SW Minn. containing quarry once used by Indians
Piq·ua \'pik-(ˌ)wä, -wə\ city W Ohio N of Dayton *pop* 20,741
Pi·rae·us *or* **Pei·rae·us** \pī-'rē-əs\ *or* NGk **Pi·rai·évs** \ˌpē-re-'efs\ city E Greece on Saronic gulf; port for Athens *pop* 183,957
Pirineos — see PYRENEES
Pir·ma·sens \ˌpi(ə)r-mə-'zen(t)s\ city W Germany near French border E of Saarbrücken *pop* 56,420
Pir·na \'pi(ə)r-nə\ city E Germany SE of Dresden *pop* 47,468
Pi·sa \'pē-zə, *It* -sä\ commune W *cen* Italy in Tuscany on the Arno *pop* 102,864 — **Pi·san** \'pēz-ᵊn\ *adj or n*
Pis·cat·a·qua \pis-'kat-ə-ˌkwȯ\ river 12 *m* Me. & N.H. formed by junction of Cocheco & Salmon Falls rivers & flowing SE on Me.-N.H. boundary into the Atlantic
Pis·gah \'piz-gə\ *or* **Ne·bo** \'nē-(ˌ)bō\ mountain 2644 *ft* Palestine in Jordan E of N end of Dead sea
Pishpek — see FRUNZE
Pi·sid·ia \pə-'sid-ē-ə, pī-\ ancient country S Asia Minor N of Pamphylia — **Pi·sid·i·an** \-ē-ən\ *adj*
Pi·sto·ia \pi-'stȯi-ə, -'stō-yə\ commune *cen* Italy NW of Florence *pop* 90,463
Pit \'pit\ river 280 *m* N Calif. flowing SW into the Sacramento
Pit·cairn \'pit-ˌka(ə)rn, -ˌke(ə)rn\ island S Pacific SE of Tuamotu archipelago; a Brit. colony, with several smaller islands
Pitts·burg \'pits-ˌbərg\ **1** city W Calif. NE of Oakland on San Joaquin river *pop* 20,651 **2** city SE Kans. *pop* 20,171
Pitts·burgh \'pits-ˌbərg\ city SW Pa. *pop* 520,117
Pitts·field \'pits-ˌfēld\ city W Mass. *pop* 57,020
Piz Bernina — see BERNINA
Pla·cen·tia \plə-'sen-chə\ city SW Calif. SE of Los Angeles *pop* 21,948
Placentia Bay inlet of the Atlantic E Canada in SE Nfld.
Plac·id, Lake \'plas-əd\ lake 5 *m* long NE N. Y. in the Adirondacks
Plain·field \'plān-ˌfēld\ city NE N. J. *pop* 46,862
Plains of Abra·ham \'ā-brə-ˌham\ plateau Canada in W part of city of Quebec
Plain·view \'plān-vyü\ city NW Tex. N of Lubbock *pop* 19,096
Plain·ville \'plān-ˌvil\ town *cen* Conn. SW of Hartford *pop* 16,733
Pla·no \'plā-(ˌ)nō\ city NE Tex. N of Dallas *pop* 17,872
Plantation city SE Fla. W of Fort Lauderdale *pop* 23,523
Plant City \'plant-\ city W *cen* Fla. E of Tampa *pop* 15,451
Plas·sey \'plas-ē\ village NE India in West Bengal N of Calcutta
Pla·ta, Río de la \ˌrē-(ˌ)ō-ˌdel-ə-'plät-ə\ *or* **River Plate** \'plāt\ estuary of Paraná & Uruguay rivers So. America between Uruguay & Argentina; 225 *m* long
Pla·taea \plə-'tē-ə\ *or* **Pla·tae·ae** \-'tē-ˌē\ ancient city Greece in SE Boeotia S of Thebes — **Pla·tae·an** \-'tē-ən\ *adj or n*
Platte \'plat\ **1** river 310 *m* (with No. Platte, 900 *m*) *cen* Nebr. formed by junction of the No. Platte & So. Platte & flowing E into the Missouri **2** river 300 *m* SW Iowa & NW Mo. flowing into the Missouri
Plattensee — see BALATON
Platt National Park \'plat\ reservation S Okla. containing numerous sulfur & other mineral springs *area* 912 acres
Platts·burgh *or* **Platts·burg** \'plats-ˌbərg\ city NE N.Y. on Lake Champlain *pop* 18,715
Plau·en \'plaů-ən\ *or* **Plauen im Vogt·land** \ˌplaů-ə-ˌnim-'fōk-ˌtlänt\ city E Germany on the Weisse Elster SW of Zwickau *pop* 81,907
Pleasant — see NAURU
Pleasant Hill city W Calif. ENE of Oakland *pop* 24,610
Pleas·an·ton \'plez-ᵊn-tən\ city W Calif. SE of Oakland *pop* 18,328
Plenty, Bay of inlet of the So. Pacific N New Zealand on NE coast of North I.
Ple·ven \'plev-ən\ *or* **Plev·na** \'plev-nə\ city NW Bulgaria *pop* 89,814
Plo·eș·ti \plȯ-'(y)esht(-ē)\ city SE *cen* Rumania *pop* 160,011
Plov·div \'plȯv-ˌdif, -ˌdiv\ *or* Gk **Phil·ip·pop·o·lis** \ˌfil-ə-'päp-ə-ləs\ city S Bulgaria on the Maritsa N of the Rhodope mountains *pop* 242,050
Plym·outh \'plim-əth\ **1** town SE Mass. *pop* 18,606 **2** village SE Minn. NW of Minneapolis *pop* 17,593 **3** city & county borough & port SW England in Devonshire *pop* 239,314
Plzen \'pəl-ˌzen(-yə)\ *or* G **Pil·sen** \'pil-zən, -sən\ city Czechoslovakia in Bohemia WSW of Prague *pop* 145,299
Pnompenh — see PHNOM PENH
Po \'pō\ *or anc* **Pa·dus** \'päd-əs\ river 418 *m* N Italy flowing from slopes of Mt. Viso E into the Adriatic through several mouths
Po·be·da, Peak \pō-'bed-ə, pə-\ *or* Russ **Pik Po·be·dy** \ˌpēk-pə-'bed-ē\ mountain 24,406 *ft* U.S.S.R. in S Soviet Russia, Asia; highest in Tien Shan
Po·ca·tel·lo \ˌpō-kə-'tel-(ˌ)ō, -'tel-ə\ city SE Idaho *pop* 40,036
Po·co·no \'pō-kə-ˌnō\ mountains E Pa. NW of Kittatinny Mountain; highest point *ab* 1600 *ft*
Podgorica *or* **Podgoritsa** — see TITOGRAD
Po·do·lia \pə-'dō-lē-ə, -'dōl-yə\ *or* Russ **Po·dolsk** \pə-'dȯlsk\ region U.S.S.R. in W Ukraine N of middle Dniester river
Po·dolsk \pə-'dȯlsk\ city U.S.S.R. in S *cen* Soviet Russia, Europe, S of Moscow *pop* 169,000
Po Hai \'bō-'hī\ *or* **Gulf of Chih·li** \'chē-'lē, 'ji(ə)r-\ arm of Yellow sea NE China bounded on NE by Liaotung peninsula & on SE by Shantung peninsula
Po·hang \'pō-ˌhäŋ\ *or* **Pohang–dong** \-'dȯŋ\ city & port S Korea on Sea of Japan *pop* 79,451
Pointe–à–Pi·tre \ˌpwant-ə-'pētrᵊ\ city & port French West Indies in Guadeloupe on Grande-Terre *pop* 29,757
Pointe–aux–Trem·bles \ˌpȯint-ō-'trem-bəlz\ city Canada in S Que. N of Montreal *pop* 35,567
Pointe–Claire \pȯint-'kla(ə)r, -'kle(ə)r\ city Canada in S Que. on St. Lawrence river SW of Montreal *pop* 27,303
Pointe–Ga·ti·neau \ˌpȯint-ˌgat-ᵊn-'ō\ town Canada in SW Que. NE of Hull *pop* 15,640
Pointe–Noire \ˌpwant-nə-'wär\ city & port SW Congo Republic on the Atlantic; formerly ✻ of Middle Congo *pop* 135,000
Point Pe·lee National Park \pȯint-'pē-lē\ reservation Canada in SE Ont. on **Point Pelee** (cape projecting into Lake Erie)
Point Pleasant borough E N.J. SSW of Asbury Park *pop* 15,968
Poi·tiers *or formerly* **Poic·tiers** \pwä-'tyā, 'pwät-ē-ˌā\ city W *cen* France SW of Tours *pop* 70,681
Poi·tou \pwä-'tü\ region & former province W France SE of Brittany ✻ Poitiers
Pola — see PULA
Po·land \'pō-lənd\ *or* Pol **Pol·ska** \'pȯl-skä\ country E *cen* Europe bordering on Baltic sea; in medieval period a kingdom, at one time extending to the lower Dnieper; partitioned 1772, 1793, 1795 among Russia, Prussia, & Austria; again a kingdom 1815–30; lost autonomy 1830–1918; since 1918 a republic ✻ Warsaw *area* 120,355, *pop* 32,750,000
Polish Corridor strip of land N Europe in Poland that between World War I & World War II separated East Prussia from main part of Germany; area was before 1919 part of Germany
Pol·ta·va \pəl-'täv-ə\ city U.S.S.R. in *cen* Ukraine on Vorskla river WSW of Kharkov *pop* 220,000
Poltoratsk — see ASHKHABAD
Pol·y·ne·sia \ˌpäl-ə-'nē-zhə, -shə\ the islands of the *cen* & S Pacific including Hawaii, the Line, Ellice, Phoenix, Tonga, Cook, & Samoa islands, Easter I., French Polynesia, & often New Zealand
Pom·er·a·nia \ˌpäm-ə-'rā-nē-ə, -nyə\ *or* G **Pom·mern** \'pȯ-mərn\ *or* Pol **Po·mo·rze** \pȯ-'mȯ-zhe\ **1** region N Europe on Baltic sea; formerly in Germany, now mostly in Poland **2** former province of Prussia
Pom·er·e·lia \ˌpäm-ə-'rē-lē-ə, -'rēl-yə\ *or* G **Pom·me·rel·len** \ˌpȯmə-'rel-ən\ region E Europe on the Baltic W of the Vistula & E of Pomerania; orig. part of Pomerania
Po·mo·na \pə-'mō-nə\ **1** city SW Calif. E of Los Angeles *pop* 87,384 **2** — see MAINLAND
Pom·pa·no Beach \'päm-pə-ˌnō, 'pəm-\ city SE Fla. on the Atlantic N of Fort Lauderdale *pop* 37,724
Pom·pe·ii \päm-'pā, -'pā-ˌē\ ancient city S Italy SE of Naples destroyed A.D. 79 by eruption of Mt. Vesuvius — **Pom·pe·ian** *or* **Pom·pei·ian** \-'pā-ən\ *adj or n*
Po·na·pe \'pō-nə-ˌpā\ **1** district Trust Territory of the Pacific Islands in the E Carolines *land area* 176, *pop* 18,536 **2** island, chief in district
Pon·ca City \ˌpäŋ-kə-\ city N Okla. on Arkansas river *pop* 25,940
Pon·ce \'pȯn(t)-(ˌ)sā\ city & port S Puerto Rico *pop* 128,233
Pon·di·cher·ry \ˌpän-də-'cher-ē, -'sher-\ *or* F **Pon·di·ché·ry** \pōⁿ-dē-shā-rē\ **1** territory SE India SSW of Madras surrounded by Tamil Nadu; a settlement of French India before 1954, *area* 112, *pop* 471,347 **2** city & port, its ✻ *pop* 40,421
Pon·ta Del·ga·da \ˌpänt-ə-del-'gäd-ə, -'gad-\ city & port Portugal in the Azores on São Miguel I. *pop* 69,930
Pont·char·train, Lake \'pän-chər-ˌtrān, ˌpän-chər-'\ lake SE La. E of the Mississippi & N of New Orleans *area* 600
Pon·te·fract \'pänt-i-ˌfrakt\ municipal borough N England in West Riding, Yorkshire, SE of Leeds *pop* 31,335
Pon·te·ve·dra \ˌpänt-ə-'vā-drə\ **1** province NW Spain in SW Galicia on the Atlantic *area* 1695, *pop* 750,701 **2** commune & port, its ✻, NW of Vigo *pop* 52,452
Pon·ti·ac \'pänt-ē-ˌak\ city SE Mich. NW of Detroit *pop* 85,279
Pon·ti·a·nak \ˌpänt-ē-'än-ˌäk\ city Indonesia on SW coast of Borneo ✻ of West Kalimantan *pop* 150,220
Pon·tine \'pän-ˌtīn, -ˌtēn\ islands Italy in Tyrrhenian sea W of Naples; chief islands **Pon·za** \'pōn(t)-sə\ & **Pon·ti·ne** \pōn-'tē-nē\
Pontine marshes district *cen* Italy in SW Latium, separated from sea by low sand hills that prevent natural drainage; now reclaimed
Pon·tus \'pänt-əs\ **1** ancient country NE Asia Minor; a kingdom 4th century B.C. to 66 B.C. later a Roman province **2** *or* **Pontus Euxinus** — see BLACK SEA
Pon·ty·pool \ˌpänt-i-'pül\ urban district SE Wales in Monmouthshire *pop* 37,014

Pon·ty·pridd \ˌpänt-i-ˈprēth\ urban district SE Wales in Glamorganshire *pop* 34,465
Poole \ˈpül\ municipal borough S England in Dorset on English channel *pop* 106,697
Poo·na \ˈpü-nə\ city W India in Maharashtra ESE of Bombay *pop* 732,731
Po·o·pó \ˌpō-ə-ˈpō, (ˌ)pō-ˈpō\ lake 60 *m* long W *cen* Bolivia S of Lake Titicaca at altitude of 12,000 *ft*
Pop·lar \ˈpäp-lər\ former metropolitan borough E London, England, on N bank of the Thames, now part of Tower Hamlets
Poplar Bluff city SE Mo. *pop* 16,653
Po·po·ca·te·petl \ˌpō-pə-ˌkat-ə-ˈpet-^{ə}l\ volcano 17,887 *ft* SE *cen* Mexico in Puebla
Porcupine river 590 *m* in N Yukon Territory & NE Alaska flowing N & W into the Yukon
Po·ri \ˈpȯr-ē\ *or* Sw **Björ·ne·borg** \ˈbyər-nə-ˌbȯr-ē\ city & port SW Finland *pop* 72,938
Pork·ka·la \ˈpȯr-kə-lə, -ˌlä\ peninsula S Finland projecting into Gulf of Finland W of Helsinki
Por·la·mar \ˌpȯr-lə-ˈmär\ city & port NE Venezuela on Margarita I. *pop* 36,184
Port Ad·e·laide \ˈad-^{ə}l-ˌād\ city SE So. Australia on Gulf of St. Vincent at mouth of Torrens river; port for Adelaide *pop* 39,823
Por·tage \ˈpōrt-ij, ˈpȯrt-\ **1** city NW Ind. E of Gary *pop* 19,127 **2** city SW Mich. S of Kalamazoo *pop* 33,590
Port Al·ber·ni \al-ˈbər-nē\ city Canada in SW B.C. on Vancouver I. *pop* 20,063
Port An·ge·les \ˈan-jə-ləs\ city NW Wash. *pop* 16,367
Port Ar·thur \ˈär-thər\ **1** city & port SE Tex. on Sabine Lake SE of Beaumont *pop* 57,371 **2** — see THUNDER BAY **3** *or* **Lü·shun** \ˈlü-ˈshün\ city & port NE China in S Liaoning at tip of Liaotung peninsula SW of Dairen — see LÜTA
Port–au–Prince \ˌpōrt-ō-ˈprin(t)s, ˌpȯrt-; ˌpōr(t)-ō-ˈpran(t)s, ˌpȯr(t)-, -ˈpra^{n}s\ city & port ✻ of Republic of Haiti *pop* 340,175
Port Blair \ˈbla(ə)r, ˈble(ə)r\ town & port India on So. Andaman I. ✻ of Andaman & Nicobar Islands Territory
Port Castries — see CASTRIES
Port Ches·ter \ˈpōrt-ˌches-tər, ˈpȯrt-\ village SE N.Y. NE of New Rochelle on Long Island Sound *pop* 25,803
Port Col·borne \ˈkōl-bərn\ city Canada in SE Ont. W of Buffalo, N.Y. *pop* 21,420
Port Co·quit·lam \kō-ˈkwit-ləm\ city Canada in SW B.C. E of Vancouver *pop* 19,560
Port Darwin — see DARWIN
Port Eliz·a·beth \-^{ə}l-ˈiz-ə-bəth, -i-ˈliz-\ city & port S Republic of So. Africa in SE Cape Province on Algoa Bay *pop* 249,211
Port Ev·er·glades \ˈev-ər-ˌgladz\ seaport SE Fla. on the Atlantic S of Fort Lauderdale
Port Hu·ron \ˈ(h)yür-ən\ city E Mich. on Lake Huron & St. Clair river *pop* 35,794
Port Jack·son \ˈjak-sən\ inlet of S Pacific SE Australia in New So. Wales; the harbor of Sydney
Port·land \ˈpōrt-lənd, ˈpȯrt-\ **1** city & port SW Me. on Casco Bay *pop* 65,116 **2** city & port NW Oreg. at confluence of Columbia & Willamette rivers *pop* 382,619
Portland Canal inlet of the Pacific *ab* 80 *m* long Canada & U.S. between B.C. & SE tip of Alaska
Port Laoighise — see MARYBOROUGH
Port Lou·is \ˈlü-əs, ˈlü-ē, lü-ˈē\ city & port ✻ of Mauritius *pop* (with suburbs) 138,140
Port Lyautey see — KENITRA
Port Mahon — see MAHÓN
Port Mores·by \ˈmō(ə)rz-bē, ˈmȯ(ə)rz-\ city & port SE New Guinea in Papua ✻ of Papua New Guinea *pop* 56,206
Pôrto — see OPORTO
Pôr·to Ale·gre \ˌpōrt-(ˌ)ō-ə-ˈleg-rə, ˌpȯrt-\ city & port S Brazil ✻ of Rio Grande do Sul state at N end of Lagoa dos Patos *pop* 932,801
Por·to·be·lo *or* **Por·to Bel·lo** \ˌpōrt-ə-ˈbel-(ˌ)ō, ˌpȯrt-\ *or* **Puer·to Bello** *same, or* ˌpwert-\ town & port Panama on Caribbean coast; the great emporium of So. American trade in 16th & 17th centuries
Por·to·fi·no \ˌpōrt-ə-ˈfē-(ˌ)nō, ˌpȯrt-\ village N Italy in Liguria on the coast SE of Genoa
Port of Spain city & port ✻ of Trinidad & Tobago, on NW Trinidad I. *pop* 93,954
Por·to–No·vo \ˌpōrt-ə-ˈnō-(ˌ)vō, ˌpȯrt-\ city & port ✻ of Dahomey *pop* 74,500
Porto Rico — see PUERTO RICO
Port Phil·lip Bay \ˈfil-əp\ inlet of Bass strait SE Australia in Victoria; the harbor of Melbourne
Port Roy·al \ˈroi(-ə)l\ town Jamaica at entrance to Kingston Harbor; early ✻ of Jamaica, destroyed by earthquakes 1692 & 1907 & partly engulfed by the sea
Port Royal sound inlet of the Atlantic S S.C.
Port Said \sä-ˈēd, ˈsīd\ city & port NE Egypt on the Mediterranean at N end of Suez canal *pop* 313,000
Ports·mouth \ˈpōrt-sməth, ˈpȯrt-\ **1** city & port SE N.H. on the Atlantic *pop* 25,717 **2** city S Ohio at junction of Ohio & Scioto rivers *pop* 27,633 **3** city & port SE Va. on Elizabeth river opposite Norfolk *pop* 110,963 **4** city & county borough S England in Hampshire on **Port·sea** \ˈpōrt-sē, ˈpȯrt-\ (island in English channel) *pop* 196,973
Port Stanley — see STANLEY
Port Sudan city & port NE Sudan on Red sea *pop* 100,700
Por·tu·gal \ˈpōr-chi-gəl, ˈpȯr-\ *or anc* **Lu·si·ta·nia** \ˌlü-sə-ˈtā-nē-ə, -nyə\ country SW Europe in W Iberian peninsula bordering on the Atlantic; a republic, before 1910 a kingdom ✻ Lisbon *area* (not including Azores & Madeira) 34,240, *pop* 8,950,000
Portuguese East Africa — see MOZAMBIQUE
Por·tu·guese Guinea \ˌpōr-chə-ˌgēz-, ˌpȯr-, -ˌgēs-\ country W Africa S of Senegal; a Portuguese colony ✻ Bissau *area* 13,948, *pop* 530,000
Portuguese India former Portuguese possessions on W coast of India peninsula, annexed 1962 by India; comprised territory of Goa & districts of Damão & Diu
Portuguese Timor — see TIMOR
Portuguese West Africa — see ANGOLA
Porz am Rhein \ˌpȯrt-säm-ˈrīn\ city W Germany E of Cologne *pop* 76,762
Poseidonia — see PAESTUM
Po·si·ta·no \ˌpō-zə-ˈtän-(ˌ)ō\ commune S Italy on Gulf of Salerno
Potch·ef·stroom \ˈpäch-əf-ˌstrōm\ city NE Republic of So. Africa in S Transvaal SW of Johannesburg *pop* 51,800
Po·to·mac \pə-ˈtō-mək, -mik\ river 287 *m* E U.S. flowing from W.Va. into Chesapeake Bay & forming S boundary of Md.
Po·to·sí \ˌpōt-ə-ˈsē\ city S Bolivia *pop* 63,590
Pots·dam \ˈpäts-ˌdam\ city E Germany SW of Berlin *pop* 110,949
Potts·town \ˈpät-ˌstaün\ borough SE Pa. *pop* 25,355
Potts·ville \ˈpäts-ˌvil\ city E *cen* Pa. NNW of Reading *pop* 19,715
Pough·keep·sie \pə-ˈkip-sē, pō-\ city SE N.Y. *pop* 32,029
Pow·der \ˈpaüd-ər\ **1** river 150 *m* E Oreg. flowing into the Snake **2** river 375 *m* N Wyo. & SE Mont. flowing N into the Yellowstone
Powell, Lake — see GLEN CANYON DAM
Po·yang \ˈpō-ˈyäŋ\ lake 90 *m* long E China in N Kiangsi
Poz·nan \ˈpōz-ˌnan(-yə), ˈpȯz-, -ˌnän(-yə)\ *or* G **Po·sen** \ˈpōz-^{ə}n\ city W *cen* Poland on the Warta *pop* 459,700
Poz·zuo·li \pȯt-ˈswō-lē\ *or anc* **Pu·te·o·li** \p(y)ü-ˈtē-ə-ˌlī\ commune & port S Italy in Campania W of Naples *pop* 61,912
Prades \ˈpräd\ village S France in the Pyrenees 25 *m* SW of Perpignan
Prague \ˈpräg\ *or* Czech **Pra·ha** \ˈprä-(ˌ)hä\ city ✻ of Czechoslovakia in Bohemia on Vltava river *pop* 1,102,060
Prairie Provinces the Canadian provinces of Man., Sask., & Alta.
Prairie Village city NE Kans. S of Kansas City *pop* 28,138
Pra·to \ˈprät-ō\ commune *cen* Italy in Tuscany *pop* 138,717
Presque Isle \pre-ˈskī(ə)l\ peninsula NW Pa. in Lake Erie forming **Presque Isle Bay** (harbor of Erie, Pa.)
Pressburg — see BRATISLAVA
Pres·ton \ˈpres-tən\ **1** town Canada in SE Ont. SE of Kitchener *pop* 16,723 **2** county borough NW England ✻ of Lancashire *pop* 97,365
Prest·wich \ˈpres-(ˌ)twich\ municipal borough NW England in Lancashire NNW of Manchester *pop* 32,838
Prest·wick \ˈpres-(ˌ)twik\ burgh SW Scotland in Ayrshire
Pre·to·ria \pri-ˈtōr-ē-ə, -ˈtȯr-\ city, administrative ✻ of Republic of So. Africa & ✻ of Transvaal *pop* 303,684
Prib·i·lof \ˈprib-ə-ˌlȯf\ islands Alaska in Bering sea
Prich·ard \ˈprich-ərd\ city SW Ala. N of Mobile *pop* 41,578
Primorye — see MARITIME TERRITORY
Prince Al·bert \ˈal-bərt\ city Canada in *cen* Sask. *pop* 28,464
Prince Albert National Park reservation Canada in *cen* Sask. on No. Saskatchewan river *area* 1496
Prince Ed·ward Island \ˌed-wərd-\ island SE Canada in Gulf of St. Lawrence off E N.B. & N N.S.; a province ✻ Charlottetown *area* 2184, *pop* 111,000
Prince Edward Island National Park reservation Canada in P.E.I. *area* 7
Prince George \ˈjȯ(ə)rj\ city Canada in E *cen* B.C. on Fraser river *pop* 33,101
Prince of Wales \ˈwā(ə)lz\ **1** island SE Alaska, largest in Alexander archipelago *area* 1500 **2** island N Canada between Victoria I. & Somerset I. *area* 12,830
Prince of Wales, Cape cape Alaska at W tip of Seward peninsula; most westerly point of mainland of No. America, at 168°W
Prince Ru·pert \ˈrü-pərt\ city & port Canada in NW B.C. at head of Dixon Entrance *pop* 15,747
Prince Ru·pert's Land \ˈrü-pərts\ historical region N & W Canada comprising drainage basin of Hudson Bay granted 1670 by King Charles II to Hudson's Bay company
Prince Wil·liam Sound \ˌwil-yəm-\ inlet of Gulf of Alaska S Alaska E of Kenai peninsula
Prin·ci·pe \ˈprin(t)-sə-pə\ *or* **Prince** \ˈprin(t)s\ island W Africa in Gulf of Guinea N of São Tomé; belongs to Portugal *area* 58 — see SÃO TOMÉ
Prip·et \ˈprip-ˌet, -ət\ *or* Russ **Pri·pyat** \ˈprip-yət\ river 500 *m* E *cen* Europe in the U.S.S.R. in NW Ukraine & S White Russia flowing E through the **Pripet,** *or* **Pinsk, marshes** (marshlands *ab* 300 *m* long & 140 *m* wide) to the Dnieper
Pro·gre·so \prə-ˈgres-(ˌ)ō\ city SE Mexico on Yucatán peninsula; port for Mérida *pop* 22,100
Pro·ko·pevsk *or* **Pro·ko·pyevsk** \prə-ˈkȯp-yəfsk\ city U.S.S.R. in SW Soviet Russia, Asia, at S end of Kuznetsk basin NW of Novokuznetsk *pop* 275,000
Propontis — see MARMARA (Sea of)
Pro·vence \prə-ˈvä^{n}s\ region & former province SE France bordering on the Mediterranean ✻ Aix
Prov·i·dence \ˈpräv-əd-ən(t)s, -ə-ˌden(t)s\ city & port ✻ of R.I. *pop* 179,213
Pro·vo \ˈprō-(ˌ)vō\ city N *cen* Utah on Utah Lake *pop* 53,131
Prud·hoe Bay \ˈprüd-ˌ(h)ō, ˈprəd-\ inlet of Beaufort sea N Alaska
Prus·sia \ˈprəsh-ə\ *or* G **Preus·sen** \ˈprois-^{ə}n\ **1** historical region N Germany bordering on Baltic sea **2** former kingdom & state of Germany ✻ Berlin — see EAST PRUSSIA, WEST PRUSSIA — **Prus·sian** \ˈprəsh-ən\ *adj or n*
Prut \ˈprüt\ river 500 *m* E Europe flowing from the Carpathians SSE into the Danube & since World War II forming the boundary between Rumania & the U.S.S.R.
Pskov \pə-ˈskȯf, -ˈskȯv\ city U.S.S.R. in Soviet Russia, Europe, near **Lake Pskov** (S arm of Lake Peipus) *pop* 127,000

Ptol·e·ma·is \ˌtäl-ə-ˈmā-əs\ 1 ancient town in upper Egypt on left bank of the Nile NW of Thebes 2 ancient town in Cyrenaica NW of Barca; site at modern village of Tolmeta 3 — see ACRE
Pueb·la \pü-ˈeb-lə, ˈpweb-, pyü-ˈeb-\ 1 state SE *cen* Mexico *area* 13,124, *pop* 2,483,770 2 *or* **Puebla de Za·ra·go·za** \də-ˌzar-ə-ˈgō-zə\ city, its ✱ *pop* 521,885
Pueb·lo \pü-ˈeb-(ˌ)lō, ˈpweb-, pyü-ˈeb-\ city SE *cen* Colo. *pop* 97,453
Puer·to Bar·rios \ˌpwert-ō-ˈbär-ē-ˌōs\ city & port E Guatemala on Gulf of Honduras *pop* 29,425
Puerto Bello — see PORTOBELO
Puerto Ca·be·llo \-kə-ˈbā-(ˌ)(y)ō\ city & port N Venezuela 70 *m* W of Caracas *pop* 70,598
Puerto La Cruz \lə-ˈkrüz, -ˈkrüs\ city NE Venezuela NE of Barcelona *pop* 82,059
Puerto Limón — see LIMÓN
Puerto Montt \ˈmȯnt\ city & port S *cen* Chile *pop* 49,473
Puer·to Ri·co \ˌpōrt-ə-ˈrē-(ˌ)kō, ˌpȯrt-, ˌpwert-\ *or formerly* **Por·to Rico** island West Indies E of Hispaniola; a self-governing commonwealth in union with the U.S. ✱ San Juan *area* 3435, *pop* 2,712,033 — **Puerto Ri·can** \-ˈrē-kən\ *adj or n*
Pu·get Sound \ˌpyü-jət-\ arm of the Pacific extending 80 *m* S into W Wash. from E end of Juan de Fuca strait
Puglia *or* **Le Puglie** — see APULIA
Pu·ka·pu·ka \ˌpü-kə-ˈpü-kə\ *or* **Dan·ger islands** \ˈdān-jər\ atoll *cen* Pacific N of Cook islands; chief island Pukapuka; administered with Cook islands by New Zealand
Pu·la \ˈpü-lə\ *or* **Pulj** \ˈpül-yə\ *or* It **Po·la** \ˈpō-lə\ city & port NW Yugoslavia at tip of Istrian peninsula *pop* 45,000
Pul·ko·vo \ˈpül-kə-və, -ˌvō\ village U.S.S.R. in Soviet Russia, Europe, 10 *m* S of Leningrad
Pull·man \ˈpu̇l-mən\ city SE Wash. *pop* 20,509
Pu·log \ˈpü-ˌlȯg\ mountain 9606 *ft* Philippines in N Luzon at S end of Cordillera Central; highest in Luzon
Pu·na de Ata·ca·ma \ˈpü-nə-ˌdā-ˌat-ə-ˈkäm-ə, -ˌät-\ high plateau region NW Argentina NW of Tucumán
Pun·jab *or* **Pan·jab** \ˌpən-ˈjäb, -ˈjab, ˈpən-ˌ\ 1 region NW Indian subcontinent in Pakistan & NW India occupying valleys of the Indus & its five tributaries; formerly a province of Brit. India ✱ Lahore 2 *or* **East Punjab** former state NW India in E Punjab divided 1966 into two states of Punjabi Suba & Haryana 3 *or* **West Punjab** province NE Pakistan 4 *or* **Pun·jabi Su·ba** \ˌpən-ˌjäb-ē-ˈsü-bə, -ˌjab-\ state NW India formed from northern part of former state of Punjab ✱ Chandigarh *area* 19,495, *pop* 13,472,972
Punt \ˈpu̇nt\ — ancient Egyptian name for a part of Africa not certainly identified, probably Somaliland
Pun·ta Are·nas \ˌpün-tə-ə-ˈrā-nəs\ *or* **Ma·ga·lla·nes** \ˌmäg-ə-ˈyän-əs\ city & port S Chile on Strait of Magellan *pop* 67,514
Punta del Es·te \-ˌdel-ˈes-tē\ town S Uruguay E of Montevideo
Pu·ra·cé \ˌpu̇r-ə-ˈsā\ volcano 15,420 *ft* SW *cen* Colombia
Pur·beck, Isle of \ˈpər-ˌbek\ peninsula region S England in Dorset extending E into English channel
Pur·ga·toire \ˈpər-gə-ˌtwär, ˈpik-ət-ˌwī(ə)r\ river 190 *m* SE Colo. flowing into the Arkansas
Pu·ri \ˈpu̇r-ē\ *or* **Ja·gan·nath** \ˈjəg-ə-ˌnät\ *or* **Jug·ger·naut** \ˈjəg-ər-ˌnȯt, -ˌnät\ city & port E India in SE Orissa on Bay of Bengal *pop* 60,815
Pu·rus \pə-ˈrüs\ river 2000 *m* NW *cen* So. America rising in the Andes in SE Peru & flowing NE into the Amazon in Brazil
Pu·san \ˈpü-ˌsän\ city & port SE Korea on Korea strait *pop* 1,425,-703
Push·kin \ˈpu̇sh-kən\ *or formerly* **Tsar·skoe Se·lo** \ˌ(t)sär-skə-yə-sə-ˈlō\ *or* **Det·skoe Selo** \ˌdet-skə-yə-\ city U.S.S.R. in NW Soviet Russia, Europe, S of Leningrad *pop* 73,000
Puteoli — see POZZUOLI
Put–in–Bay \ˌpu̇t-ˌin-\ inlet of Lake Erie in Ohio on So. Bass I. N of Sandusky Bay; site of Perry's Victory and International Peace Memorial National Monument
Pu·tu·ma·yo \ˌpüt-ə-ˈmī-(ˌ)ō\ *or* (*in Brazil*) **Içá** \ē-ˈsä\ river 980 *m* NW So. America flowing from SW Colombia into the Amazon in NW Brazil
Puy de Dôme — see DÔME (Puy de)
Puy de Sancy — see SANCY (Puy de)
Pya·ti·gorsk \pē-ˌat-i-ˈgȯ(ə)rsk\ city U.S.S.R. in S Soviet Russia, Europe, in N Caucasus SE of Stavropol *pop* 84,000
Pyd·na \ˈpid-nə\ ancient town Macedonia on W shore of Gulf of Salonika
Py·los \ˈpī-ˌläs\ *or* **Na·va·ri·no** \ˌnav-ə-ˈrē-(ˌ)nō\ *or* NGk **Pí·los** \ˈpē-ˌlȯs\ town and port SW Greece in SW Peloponnesus
Pyong·yang \pē-ˈȯŋ-ˌyäŋ, pē-ˈəŋ-, -ˌyaŋ\ city ✱ of No. Korea on the Taedong *pop* 653,100
Pyramid lake 30 *m* long NW Nev. NE of Reno
Pyr·e·nees \ˈpir-ə-ˌnēz\ *or* F **Py·ré·nées** \pē-rā-nā\ *or* Sp **Pi·ri·ne·os** \ˌpē-rē-ˈnā-(ˌ)ōs\ mountains along French-Spanish border from Bay of Biscay to Gulf of Lions — see ANETO (Pico de) — **Pyr·e·ne·an** \ˌpir-ə-ˈnē-ən\ *adj or n*
Qa·tar *or* **Ka·tar** \ˈkät-ər, ˈgät-, ˈgət-\ country E Arabia on peninsula projecting into Persian gulf; an independent emirate ✱ Doha *area* 6000, *pop* 80,000
Qat·ta·ra Depression \kə-ˈtär-ə\ region NW Egypt, a low area 40 *m* from coast; lowest point 440 *ft* below sea level
Qazvin — see KAZVIN
Qe·na \ˈken-ə, ˈkā-nə\ city S Egypt N of Luxor *pop* 77,600
Qeshm \ˈkesh-əm\ *or* **Qishm** \ˈkish-\ island S Iran in Strait of Hormuz
Qi·shon *or* **Ki·shon** \ˈkē-ˌshōn, kē-ˈ\ river 50 *m* N Palestine flowing NW through Plain of Esdraelon to the Mediterranean
Qomul — see HAMI
Qu'Ap·pelle \kwə-ˈpel\ river 270 *m* Canada in S Sask. flowing E into the Assiniboine
Quathlamba — see DRAKENSBERG
Que·bec \kwi-ˈbek *also* ki-\ *or* **Qué·bec** \kā-bek\ 1 province E Canada extending from Hudson Bay to Gaspé peninsula *area* 523,860, *pop* 6,030,000 2 city & port, its ✱, on the St. Lawrence *pop* 186,088 — **Que·bec·er** *or* **Que·beck·er** \kwi-ˈbek-ər *also* ki-\ *n*
Queen·bor·ough–in–Shep·pey \ˈkwēn-ˌbər-ə-in-ˈshep-ē, -ˌbə-rə-, -b(ə-)rə-\ municipal borough SE England in Kent at mouth of the Thames *pop* 31,541
Queen Char·lotte \ˈshär-lət\ 1 islands Canada in W B.C. in Pacific ocean *area* 3970 2 sound S of Queen Charlotte islands
Queen Eliz·a·beth \-ᵊl-ˈiz-ə-bəth, -i-ˈliz-\ islands N Canada N of water passage extending from M'Clure strait to Lancaster Sound; include Parry, Sverdrup, Devon, & Ellesmere islands
Queen Maud Land \ˈmȯd\ section of Antarctica on the Atlantic
Queens \ˈkwēnz\ borough of New York City on Long I. E of Brooklyn *pop* 1,973,708
Queen's — see LAOIGHIS
Queens·land \ˈkwēnz-ˌland, -lənd\ state NE Australia ✱ Brisbane *area* 670,500, *pop* 1,799,200 — **Queens·land·er** \-ər\ *n*
Queenstown — see COBH
Quelpart — see CHEJU
Que·moy \k(w)i-ˈmȯi, ˈkwē-ˌ\ *or* **Kin·men** *or* **Chin·men** \ˈjin-ˈmən\ island SE China in Formosa strait 15 *m* E of Amoy
Que·ré·ta·ro \kə-ˈret-ə-ˌrō\ 1 state *cen* Mexico *area* 4432, *pop* 464,226 2 city, its ✱ *pop* 140,379
Quet·ta \ˈkwet-ə\ city Pakistan in N Baluchistan *pop* 130,000
Que·zal·te·nan·go *or* **Quet·zal·te·nan·go** \ke(t)-ˌsäl-tə-ˈnäŋ-(ˌ)gō\ city SW Guatemala *pop* 54,478
Que·zon City \ˈkā-ˌsȯn\ city Philippines in Luzon NE of Manila; official ✱ of the Philippines *pop* 545,500
Quil·mes \ˈkē(ə)l-ˌmās, -ˌmes\ city E Argentina SE of Buenos Aires *pop* 318,144
Quim·per \kaⁿ(m)-ˈpe(ə)r\ commune NW France W of Rennes near Bay of Biscay *pop* 52,496
Qui·nault \kwin-ˈȯlt\ river 65 *m* W Wash. flowing to the Pacific
Quin·cy, 1 ˈkwin(t)-sē\ city W Ill. on the Mississippi *pop* 45,288 2 \ˈkwin-zē\ city E Mass. SE of Boston *pop* 87,966
Quin·ta·na Roo \kēn-ˌtän-ə-ˈrō\ territory SE Mexico in E Yucatán ✱ Chetumal *area* 19,438, *pop* 91,044
Quin·te, Bay of \ˈkwint-ē\ inlet of Lake Ontario in Canada in SE Ont.; connected with Georgian Bay by Trent canal
Quir·i·nal \ˈkwir-ən-ᵊl\ hill in Rome, Italy, one of seven on which the ancient city was built — see AVENTINE
Qui·to \ˈkē-(ˌ)tō\ city ✱ of Ecuador *pop* 496,410
Quoddy Bay PASSAMAQUODDY BAY
Qum \ˈku̇m\ city NW *cen* Iran *pop* 110,000
Qum·ran *or* **Khir·bat Qumran** \kir-ˌbät-ku̇m-ˈrän\ site Palestine in NW Jordan on Wadi Qumran near NW shore of Dead sea of an Essene community (*ab* 100 B.C.–A.D. 68) near a series of caves in which the Dead Sea Scrolls were found
Raab — see GYOR
Ra·ba \ˈräb-ə\ river 160 *m* SE Austria & W Hungary flowing E & NE into the Danube
Ra·bat \rə-ˈbät\ city ✱ of Morocco on Atlantic coast *pop* 325,000
Ra·baul \rə-ˈbau̇(ə)l\ city Bismarck archipelago at E end of New Britain; formerly ✱ of Territory of New Guinea *pop* 21,453
Rabbah, Rabbath — see AMMAN
Race, Cape \ˈrās\ headland, SE point of Nfld., Canada
Ra·ci·bórz \rät-ˈsē-ˌbu̇sh\ *or* G **Ra·ti·bor** \ˈrät-ə-ˌbȯ(ə)r\ city SW Poland in Silesia on the Odra *pop* 40,400
Ra·cine \rə-ˈsēn, rā-\ city SE Wis. S of Milwaukee *pop* 95,162
Rad·nor \ˈrad-nər, -ˌnȯ(ə)r\ *or* **Rad·nor·shire** \-ˌshi(ə)r, -shər\ county E Wales ✱ Llandrindod Wells *area* 471, *pop* 18,262
Ra·dom \ˈräd-ˌȯm\ commune Poland NE of Kielce *pop* 154,500
Raetia — see RHAETIA — **Rae·tian** \ˈrē-shən\ *adj or n*
Rages — see RHAGES
Ra·gu·sa \rə-ˈgü-zə\ 1 commune Italy in SE Sicily *pop* 59,787 2 — see DUBROVNIK
Rah·way \ˈrȯ-ˌwā\ city NE N.J. SW of Elizabeth *pop* 29,114
Ra·ia·téa \ˌrī-ə-ˈtā-ə\ island S Pacific in Leeward group of the Society islands 130 *m* WNW of Tahiti *area* 75
Rainbow Bridge National Monument reservation S Utah near Ariz. line containing **Rainbow Bridge** (large natural bridge)
Rai·nier, Mount \rə-ˈni(ə)r, rā-\ *or formerly* **Mount Ta·co·ma** \tə-ˈkō-mə\ mountain 14,410 *ft* W *cen* Wash., highest in the Cascade range & in Wash.; in **Mount Rainier National Park** (*area* 377)
Rainy \ˈrā-nē\ 1 river 80 *m* on Canada-U.S. boundary between Ont. & Minn. flowing from Rainy Lake into Lake of the Woods 2 lake Canada & U.S. between Ont. & Minn. *area* 366
Rai·pur \ˈrī-ˌpu̇(ə)r\ city E India in SE Madhya Pradesh E of Nagpur *pop* 212,414
Rai·sin \ˈrāz-ᵊn\ river 150 *m* SE Mich. flowing into Lake Erie
Ra·jah·mun·dry \ˌräj-ə-ˈmu̇n-drē\ city E India in E Andhra Pradesh on Godavari river W of Kakinada *pop* 158,498
Ra·ja·sthan \ˈräj-ə-ˌstän\ 1 RAJPUTANA 2 state NW India bordering on Pakistan ✱ Jaipur *area* 132,077, *pop* 25,724,142
Raj·kot \ˈräj-ˌkōt\ 1 former state W India in N *cen* Kathiawar peninsula 2 city, its ✱, now in Gujarat *pop* 277,457
Raj·pu·ta·na \ˌräj-pə-ˈtän-ə\ region NW India bordering on Pakistan & including part of Thar desert
Ra·leigh \ˈrȯ-lē, ˈräl-ē\ city ✱ of N.C. *pop* 121,577
Ra·lik \ˈräl-ik\ the W chain of the Marshall islands
Ram·a·po \ˈram-ə-ˌpō\ mountains of the Appalachians N N.J. & S N.Y.; highest point 1164 ft.
Ra·mat Gan \rə-ˈmät-ˌgän\ city W Israel E of Tel Aviv *pop* 112,600
Ram·bouil·let \räⁿ-bü-yā\ town N France 28 *m* SW of Paris
Ram·gan·ga \räm-ˈgəŋ-gə\ river 370 *m* N India in Uttar Pradesh flowing S into the Ganges
Ram·pur \ˈräm-ˌpu̇(ə)r\ 1 former state N India NW of Bareilly, now in Uttar Pradesh 2 city, its ✱, ENE of Delhi *pop* 136,463
Rams·gate \ˈramz-ˌgāt, -gət\ municipal borough SE England in Kent on North sea N of Dover *pop* 39,482
Ran·chi \ˈrän-chē\ city E India, summer ✱ of Bihar, NW of Calcutta *pop* 139,052
Rand \ˈrand, ˈränd\ WITWATERSRAND
Ran·ders \ˈrän-ərs\ city & port NE Denmark *pop* 41,253

Ran·dolph \ˈran-ˌdälf\ town E Mass. S of Boston *pop* 27,035
Range·ley Lakes \ˌrānj-lē-\ chain of Lakes W Me. & N N.H. including Rangeley, Mooselookmeguntic, Upper Richardson, Lower Richardson, & Umbagog
Ran·goon \ran-ˈgün, ˌraŋ-\ **1** river 185 *m* S Burma, the E outlet of the Irrawaddy **2** city & port ✱ of Burma on Rangoon river 21 *m* from its mouth *pop* 1,717,649
Ran·noch, Loch \ˈran-ək, -ək\ lake 9 *m* long *cen* Scotland
Rann of Kutch — see KUTCH (Rann of)
Ran·toul \ran-ˈtül\ village E Ill. NNE of Champaign *pop* 25,562
Ra·pa \ˈräp-ə\ island S Pacific in SE Tubuaï group *area* 15
Ra·pal·lo \rə-ˈpäl-(ˌ)ō\ commune NW Italy in Liguria ESE of Genoa on Gulf of Rapallo (inlet of Ligurian sea) *pop* 25,311
Rapa Nui — see EASTER
Rap·i·dan \ˌrap-ə-ˈdan\ river 70 *m* N Va. rising in Blue Ridge mountains & flowing E into the Rappahannock
Rap·id City \ˌrap-əd-\ city W S.Dak. in Black hills *pop* 43,836
Rap·pa·han·nock \ˌrap-ə-ˈhan-ək\ river 185 *m* NE Va. flowing into Chesapeake Bay
Rap·ti \ˈräp-tē\ river 400 *m* Nepal & N India flowing SE into the Gogra
Rar·i·tan \ˈrar-ət-ᵊn\ river 75 *m* N *cen* N.J. flowing E into **Raritan Bay** (inlet of the Atlantic S of Staten I., N.Y.)
Rar·o·ton·ga \ˌrar-ə-ˈtäŋ-(g)ə\ island S Pacific in SW part of Cook islands; site of Avarua, ✱ of the group
Ras Addar — see BON (Cape)
Ras Da·shan \ˌräs-də-ˈshän\ mountain 15,158 *ft* N Ethiopia NE of Lake Tana; highest in Ethiopia
Ras el Tib — see BON (Cape)
Rashid — see ROSETTA
Rasht \ˈrasht\ *or* **Resht** \ˈresht\ city NW Iran *pop* 143,557
Rat \ˈrat\ islands SW Alaska in W Aleutians — see AMCHITKA, KISKA
Ra·tak \ˈrä-ˌtäk\ *or* **Ra·dak** \ˈräd-ˌäk\ the E chain of the Marshall islands
Rath·mines and Rath·gar \rath-ˈmīn-zən-(ˌ)rath-ˈgär\ town E Ireland, S suburb of Dublin *pop* 45,629
Ra·ton \ra-ˈtōn, rə-, -ˈtün; *usu* -ˈtōn *in N. Mex.*, -ˈtün *in Colo.*\ pass 7834 *ft* SE Colo. on Colo.-N. Mex. border in **Raton range** (E spur of Sangre de Cristo mountains)
Ra·ven·na \rə-ˈven-ə\ commune N Italy NE of Florence near Adriatic coast *pop* 130,708
Ra·vi \ˈräv-ē\ *or anc* **Hy·dra·o·tes** \ˌhī-drə-ˈōt-(ˌ)ēz\ river 450 *m* N India flowing SW to the Chenab & forming part of boundary between East Punjab (Republic of India) & West Punjab (Pakistan)
Ra·wal·pin·di \ˌrä-wəl-ˈpin-dē, raủl-ˈ, rȯl-ˈ\ city NE Pakistan NNW of Lahore *pop* 455,000
Ray·town \ˈrā-ˌtaủn\ city W Mo. SE of Kansas City *pop* 33,632
Read·ing \ˈred-iŋ\ **1** town E Mass. N of Boston *pop* 22,539 **2** city SE Pa. on the Schuylkill *pop* 87,643 **3** county borough S England ✱ of Berkshire *pop* 132,023
Re·bild \ˈrā-ˌbil\ village N Denmark in N Jutland S of Aalborg in **Rebild hills** (site of **Rebild National Park**)
Re·ci·fe \rə-ˈsē-fə\ *or formerly* **Per·nam·bu·co** \ˌpər-nəm-ˈb(y)ü-(ˌ)kō, ˌper-nəm-ˈbü-\ city & port NE Brazil ✱ of Pernambuco state *pop* 1,100,464
Reck·ling·hau·sen \ˌrek-liŋ-ˈhauz-ᵊn\ city W Germany SW of Münster *pop* 125,733
Red \ˈred\ **1** sea 1450 *m* long between Arabia & NE Africa **2** river 1018 *m* flowing E on Okla.-Tex. boundary & into the Atchafalaya & Mississippi in La. **3** river 310 *m* N *cen* U.S. & S *cen* Canada flowing N on Minn.-N.Dak. boundary & into Lake Winnipeg in Man. **4** — see ARCTIC RED **5** *or* **Col** *or* **Koi** \ˈkȯi\ river 500 *m* SE Asia rising in *cen* Yunnan, China, & flowing SE across N Vietnam into Gulf of Tonkin
Red·bridge \ˈred-(ˌ)brij\ borough of NE Greater London, England *pop* 238,614
Red Deer **1** river 385 *m* Canada in S Alta. flowing E & SE into the So. Saskatchewan **2** city Canada in S *cen* Alta. S of Edmonton *pop* 27,674
Red·ding \ˈred-iŋ\ city N Calif. *pop* 16,659
Red Lake lake 38 *m* long N Minn. divided into **Upper Red Lake** & **Lower Red Lake**; drained by **Red Lake river** (135 *m* flowing W into Red river)
Red·lands \ˈred-lən(d)z\ city S Calif. SE of San Bernardino *pop* 36,355
Re·don·do Beach \ri-ˈdän-dō\ city SW Calif. *pop* 56,075
Red Volta river 200 *m* S Upper Volta & N Ghana flowing into the White Volta
Red·wood City \ˈred-ˌwủd\ city W Calif. SE of San Francisco *pop* 55,686
Redwood National Park reservation NW Calif. *area* 89
Reel·foot \ˈrē(ə)l-ˌfủt\ lake NW Tenn. near the Mississippi
Re·gens·burg \ˈrā-gənz-ˌbərg, -ˌbủ(ə)rg\ *or* **Rat·is·bon** \ˈrat-əs-ˌbän, -əz-\ city W Germany in Bavaria on the Danube 65 *m* NNE of Munich *pop* 126,600
Reg·gan *or* **Reg·gane** \re-ˈgän, -ˈgan\ oasis *cen* Algeria in Tanezrouft SSE of Béchar
Reg·gio, 1 *or* **Reggio di Ca·la·bria** *or* **Reggio Calabria** \ˌrej-(ē-)(ˌ)ō-ˌdē-kə-ˈläb-rē-ə\ *or anc* **Rhe·gi·um** \ˈrē-jē-əm\ commune & port S Italy on Strait of Messina *pop* 165,421 **2** *or* **Reggio nel·l'Emi·lia** \-ˌnel-ə-ˈmēl-yə\ *or* **Reggio Emilia** commune N Italy in Emilia-Romagna NW of Bologna *pop* 127,086
Re·gi·na \ri-ˈjī-nə\ city Canada ✱ of Sask. *pop* 139,469
Reims *or* **Rheims** \ˈrēmz, *F* raⁿs\ city NE France ENE of Paris *pop* 152,967
Reindeer lake Canada on Man.-Sask. border *area* 2444
Re·ma·gen \ˈrā-ˌmäg-ən\ town W Germany on W bank of the Rhine NW of Koblenz
Rem·scheid \ˈrem-ˌshīt\ city W Germany in No. Rhine-Westphalia ESE of Düsseldorf *pop* 136,400
Ren·do·va \ren-ˈdō-və\ island W Pacific in *cen* Solomons off SW *cen* coast of New Georgia I.
Ren·frew \ˈren-ˌfrü\ *or* **Ren·frew·shire** \-ˌshi(ə)r, -shər\ county SW Scotland ✱ Paisley *area* 227, *pop* 362,144
Rennes \ˈren\ city NW France N of Nantes *pop* 180,943
Re·no \ˈrē-(ˌ)nō\ city W Nev. NNE of Lake Tahoe *pop* 72,863
Ren·ton \ˈrent-ᵊn\ city W Wash. SE of Seattle *pop* 25,258
Re·pen·ti·gny \rə-ˌpäⁿ-tēn-ˈyē\ town Canada in S Que. N of Montreal *pop* 19,520
Republican river 445 *m* Nebr. & Kans. rising in E Colo. & flowing E to unite with the Smoky Hill forming Kansas river
Re·si·ta \ˈresh-ət-ˌsä\ *or* **Re·ci·ta** \ˈrech-\ commune SW Rumania 65 *m* SE of Arad *pop* 67,980
Re·thondes \rə-tōⁿd\ village N France E of Compiègne
Ré·union \rē-ˈyün-yən\ island W Indian ocean in the W Mascarenes ✱ St-Denis; an overseas department of France *area* 970, *pop* 455,200
Reut·ling·en \ˈrȯit-liŋ-ən\ city W Germany in Baden-Württemberg S of Stuttgart *pop* 77,034
Reval *or* **Revel** — see TALLIN
Re·vere \ri-ˈvi(ə)r\ city E Mass. NE of Boston *pop* 43,159
Re·vil·la·gi·ge·do \ri-ˌvil-ə-gə-ˈgēd-(ˌ)ō\ island SE Alaska in SE Alexander archipelago E of Prince of Wales I.
Re·vi·lla Gi·ge·do \ri-ˌvē-(y)ə-hi-ˈhād-(ˌ)ō\ islands Mexico in the Pacific *ab* 300 *m* SW of S end of Baja California
Reyes, Point \ˈrāz\ cape W Calif. at S extremity of peninsula extending into the Pacific 30 *m* NW of Golden Gate, in **Point Reyes National Seashore** (*area* 101)
Reyk·ja·vik \ˈräk-(y)ə-ˌvik, -ˌvēk\ city & port ✱ of Iceland *pop* 81,288
Rey·no·sa \rā-ˈnō-sə\ city NE Mexico in Tamaulipas on Rio Grande *pop* 143,514
Rezaieh *or* **Rezayeh** — see RIZAIYEH
Rhae·tia *or* **Rae·tia** \ˈrē-sh(ē-)ə\ ancient Roman province *cen* Europe S of the Danube including most of modern Tirol & Vorarlberg region of Austria & Graubünden canton of E Switzerland — **Rhae·tian** \-shən\ *adj or n*
Rhaetian Alps section of Alps E Switzerland in E Graubünden — see BERNINA
Rha·ges \ˈrā-jəz\ *or* **Rha·gae** \-(ˌ)jē\ *or bib* **Ra·ges** \ˈrā-jəz\ city of ancient Media; ruins at modern village of Rai \ˈrī\ S of Tehran, Iran
Rheinfall — see SCHAFFHAUSEN
Rheinpfalz — see PALATINATE
Rhenish Palatinate *or* **Rhine Palatinate** — see PALATINATE
Rheydt \ˈrīt\ city W Germany S of München-Gladbach *pop* 100,300
Rhine \ˈrīn\ *or G* **Rhein** \ˈrīn\ *or F* **Rhin** \raⁿ\ *or D* **Rijn** \ˈrīn\ river 820 *m* W Europe flowing from SE Switzerland to North sea in the Netherlands — **Rhe·nish** \ˈren-ish, ˈrē-nish\ *adj*
Rhine, Falls of the — see SCHAFFHAUSEN
Rhine·land \ˈrīn-ˌland, -lənd\ *or G* **Rhein·land** \ˈrīn-ˌlänt\ **1** the part of W Germany W of the Rhine **2** RHINE PROVINCE — **Rhine·land·er** \ˈrīn-ˌlan-dər, -lən-\ *n*
Rhineland-Palatinate *or G* **Rheinland-Pfalz** \-ˈ(p)fälts\ state of Federal Republic of Germany chiefly W of the Rhine ✱ Mainz *area* 7654, *pop* 3,677,000
Rhine Province *or* **Rhenish Prussia** former province of Prussia, Germany, bordering on Belgium ✱ Koblenz
Rhode Is·land \rō-ˈdī-lənd\ **1** *or officially* **Rhode Island and Providence Plantations** state NE U.S. ✱ Providence *area* 1214, *pop* 949,723 **2** — see AQUIDNECK — **Rhode Is·land·er** \-lən-dər\ *n*
Rhodes \ˈrōdz\ *or NGk* **Ró·dhos** \ˈrō-ˌthȯs\ **1** island Greece in the SE Aegean, chief island of the Dodecanese *area* 545 **2** city, its ✱ *pop* 32,019 — **Rho·di·an** \ˈrōd-ē-ən\ *adj or n*
Rho·de·sia \rō-ˈdē-zh(ē-)ə\ **1** region *cen* S Africa S of Zaire comprising Southern Rhodesia & Zambia **2** *or formerly* **Southern Rhodesia** country S Africa S of the Zambezi; a self-governing Brit. colony ✱ Salisbury *area* 150,333, *pop* 5,500,000 — **Rho·de·sian** \-zh(ē-)ən\ *adj or n*
Rhodesia and Nyasaland, Federation of former country S Africa comprising Southern Rhodesia, Northern Rhodesia, & Nyasaland; a federal state within the Brit. Commonwealth; dissolved 1963
Rhod·o·pe \ˈräd-ə-(ˌ)pē\ mountains S Bulgaria & NE Greece; highest point Slav Peak 7576 *ft*
Rhon·dda \ˈrän-də, ˈ(h)rän-thə\ urban district SE Wales in Glamorganshire *pop* 88,924
Rhone *or F* **Rhône** \ˈrōn\ river 500 *m* Switzerland & France flowing through Lake of Geneva into the Mediterranean
Rhyl \ˈril\ urban district & port NE Wales in Flintshire at mouth of the Clwyd *pop* 21,715
Ri·al·to \rē-ˈal-(ˌ)tō\ **1** city SW Calif. W of San Bernardino *pop* 28,370 **2** island & district of Venice, Italy
Ri·au *or formerly* **Ri·ouw** \ˈrē-ˌaủ\ archipelago Indonesia S of Singapore; chief island Bintan *area* 2279, *pop* 278,966
Riazan — see RYAZAN
Ri·bei·rão Prê·to \ˌrē-və-ˈraủⁿ-ˈprā-(ˌ)tü\ city SE Brazil in N *cen* São Paulo state *pop* 169,845
Rich·ard·son \ˈrich-ərd-sən\ city NE Tex. N of Dallas *pop* 48,582
Rich·e·lieu \ˈrish-ə-ˌlü\ river 210 *m* Canada in S Que. flowing N from Lake Champlain to head of Lake St. Peter in the St. Lawrence
Rich·field \ˈrich-ˌfēld\ village SE Minn. *pop* 47,231
Rich·land \ˈrich-lənd\ city SE Wash. at confluence of Yakima & Columbia rivers *pop* 26,290
Rich·mond \ˈrich-mənd\ **1** city W Calif. NNW of Oakland on San Francisco Bay *pop* 79,043 **2** city E Ind. *pop* 43,999 **3** city *cen* Ky. *pop* 16,861 **4** borough of New York City coextensive with Staten

I. *pop* 295,443 **5** city ✻ of Va. on James river *pop* 249,621 **6** *or* **Richmond upon Thames** royal borough of SW Greater London, England *pop* 173,592 — **Rich·mond·er** \-mən-dər\ *n*
Richmond Hill town Canada in SE Ont. N of Toronto *pop* 32,384
Ri·deau \ri-'dō\ canal system Canada 126 *m* long in SE Ont. connecting Lake Ontario & Ottawa river & including **Rideau Lake** (20 *m* long) & **Rideau river** (flowing into the Ottawa)
Ridge·field \'rij-ˌfēld\ town SW Conn. NW of Norwalk *pop* 18,188
Ridge·wood \'rij-ˌwu̇d\ village NE N.J. NNE of Paterson *pop* 27,547
Rid·ing Mountain National Park \ˌrīd-iŋ-\ reservation Canada in SW Man. *area* 1148
Rif *or* **Riff** *or* **Er Rif** *or* **Er Riff** \er-'rif\ mountain range N Morocco on the Mediterranean; highest Tidiguin 8058 *ft*
Rift valley GREAT RIFT VALLEY
Ri·ga \'rē-gə\ city & port U.S.S.R. ✻ of Latvia *pop* 733,000
Riga, Gulf of inlet of Baltic sea bordering on Estonia & Latvia
Ri·je·ka *or* **Ri·e·ka** \rē-'(y)ek-ə\ *or* It **Fiu·me** \'fyü-(ˌ)mā, fē-'ü-\ city & port NW Yugoslavia in Croatia *pop* 136,000
Rijs·wijk \'ris-ˌvīk\ *or* **Rys·wick** \'riz-(ˌ)wik\ commune SW Netherlands near The Hague *pop* 50,172
Ri·mac \'rē-ˌmäk\ river 80 *m* W Peru flowing SW through Lima into the Pacific
Ri·mi·ni \'rim-ə-(ˌ)nē, 'rē-mə-\ *or anc* **Arim·i·num** \ə-'rim-ə-nəm\ commune & port N Italy on the Adriatic ESE of Ravenna *pop* 115,573
Ri·mou·ski \rim-'ü-skē\ city Canada in E Que. on Gaspé peninsula *pop* 26,887
Rio RIO DE JANEIRO
Rio Bran·co \ˌrē-(ˌ)ō-'braŋ-(ˌ)kō\ **1** — see BRANCO **2** territory NW Brazil bordering on Venezuela & Guyana ✻ Boa Vista *area* 97,438, *pop* 72,835
Rio de Ja·nei·ro \'rē-(ˌ)ō-ˌdā-zhə-'ne(ə)r-(ˌ)ō, -ˌdē-, -də-, -jə-'ne(ə)r-, -'ni(ə)r-\ **1** city & port SE Brazil ✻ of Guanabara state on Guanabara Bay; former ✻ of Brazil *pop* 4,207,322 **2** state SE Brazil ✻ Niterói *area* 16,372, *pop* 4,694,089
Rio de Janeiro Bay — see GUANABARA BAY
Río de la Plata — see PLATA (Río de la)
Río de Oro \ˌrē-(ˌ)ōd-ē-'ōr-(ˌ)ō, -'ȯr-\ **1** territory NW Africa comprising the S zone of Spanish Sahara **2** SPANISH SAHARA
Rio Grande \ˌrē-(ˌ)ō-'grand(-ē) *also* ˌrī-ō-'grand\ **1** *or* Mex **Río Bra·vo** \ˌrē-(ˌ)ō-'bräv-(ˌ)ō\ river 1885 *m* SW U.S. forming part of Mexico-U.S. boundary & flowing from San Juan mountains in SW Colo. to Gulf of Mexico **2** *or* **Rio Gran·de do Sul** \ˌrē-ō-ˌgrand-ē-də-'sül\ city S Brazil in Rio Grande do Sul state W of entrance to Lagoa dos Patos *pop* 117,500 **3** — see GRANDE (Rio)
Rio Grande de Cagayan — see CAGAYAN
Rio Gran·de do Nor·te \ˌrē-ō-ˌgrand-ē-də-'nȯrt-ə\ state NE Brazil ✻ Natal *area* 20,236, *pop* 1,603,094
Rio Grande do Sul \-'sül\ state SE Brazil bordering on Uruguay ✻ Pôrto Alegre *area* 100,150, *pop* 6,652,618
Río Mu·ni \ˌrē-(ˌ)ō-'mü-nē\ mainland portion of Equatorial Guinea bordering on Gulf of Guinea ✻ Bata *area* 10,040, *pop* 203,000
Río Pie·dras \ˌrē-(ˌ)ō-pē-'ā-drəs\ former city, since 1951 part of San Juan, Puerto Rico
Riouw — see RIAU
Rip·on Falls \ˌrip-ən-, -ˌän-\ former waterfall in the Victoria Nile N of Lake Victoria; submerged by Owen Falls Dam
Ri·va·da·via \ˌrē-və-'däv-ē-ə\ *or* **Co·mo·do·ro Rivadavia** \ˌkäm-ə-'dōr-(ˌ)ō-, -'dȯr-\ city & port S Argentina *pop* 35,966
Riv·er·dale \'riv-ər-ˌdāl\ village NE Ill. S of Chicago *pop* 15,806
River Rouge \'rüzh\ city SE Mich. S of Detroit *pop* 15,947
Riv·er·side \'riv-ər-ˌsīd\ city S Calif. *pop* 140,089
Riv·i·era \ˌriv-ē-'er-ə\ coast region SE France & NW Italy bordering on the Mediterranean — see CÔTE D'AZUR
Riviera Beach city SE Fla. N of West Palm Beach *pop* 21,401
Ri·yadh \rē-'(y)äd\ city ✻ of the Nejd & of Saudi Arabia *pop* 225,000
Ri·za·iyeh *or* **Re·za·ieh** *or* **Re·za·yeh** \ri-ˌzä-'ē-(y)ə\ *or* **Ur·mia** \'u̇r-mē-ə\ **1** shallow saline lake NW Iran **2** city NW Iran W of Lake Rizaiyeh *pop* 120,000
Rizal — see PASAY
Rju·kan \rē-'ü-ˌkän\ town S Norway 75 *m* W of Oslo near **Rjukan Falls** (waterfall 780 *ft*)
Ro·a·noke \'rō-(ə-)ˌnōk\ **1** river 380 *m* S Va. & NE N.C. flowing E & SE into Albemarle Sound **2** island N.C. S of entrance to Albemarle Sound **3** city W *cen* Va. *pop* 92,115
Rob·bins·dale \'räb-ənz-ˌdāl\ city SE Minn. NW of Minneapolis *pop* 16,845
Rob·erts, Point \'räb-ərts\ cape NW Wash., tip of a peninsula extending S into Strait of Georgia from B.C. & separated from U.S. mainland by Boundary Bay
Rob·son, Mount \'räb-sən\ mountain 12,972 *ft* W Canada in E B.C.; highest in Canadian Rockies
Ro·ca, Cape \'rō-kə\ *or* Port **Ca·bo da Ro·ca** \ˌkä-vü-t͟hə-'rō-kə\ cape Portugal; westernmost point of continental Europe, at 9°30′W
Roch·dale \'räch-ˌdāl\ county borough NW England in Lancashire NNE of Manchester *pop* 91,344
Roche·fort \rōsh-'fō(ə)r, 'rōsh-fərt\ *or* **Rochefort–sur–Mer** \-ˌsu̇r-'me(ə)r\ city W France SSE of La Rochelle *pop* 29,225
Roch·es·ter \'räch-ə-stər, -ˌes-tər\ **1** city SE Minn. *pop* 53,766 **2** city SE N.H. *pop* 17,938 **3** city W N.Y. on Genesee river *pop* 296,233 **4** municipal borough SE England in Kent *pop* 55,460
Rock \'räk\ river 300 *m* S Wis. & N Ill. flowing S & SW into the Mississippi at Rock Island
Rock·all \'räk-ˌȯl\ islet N Atlantic NW of Ireland, at 57°36′ N, 13°41′ W
Rock·ford \'räk-fərd\ city N Ill. *pop* 147,370
Rock·hamp·ton \räk-'(h)am(p)-tən\ city & port E Australia in E Queensland on Fitzroy river *pop* 47,000
Rock Hill city N S.C. SSW of Charlotte, N.C. *pop* 33,846
Rock Island city NW Ill. on the Mississippi *pop* 50,166
Rock·land \'räk-lənd\ town E Mass. NE of Brockton *pop* 15,674
Rock·ville \'räk-ˌvil, -vəl\ city SW Md. *pop* 41,564
Rockville Centre village SE N.Y. in W *cen* Long I. *pop* 27,444
Rocky \'räk-ē\ mountains W No. America extending from N Alaska SE to *cen* N.Mex. — see ELBERT (Mount), ROBSON (Mount)
Rocky Mount city NE *cen* N.C. *pop* 34,284
Rocky Mountain National Park reservation N Colo. NW of Denver *area* 400
Rocky River city NE Ohio on Lake Erie W of Cleveland *pop* 22,958
Ródhos — see RHODES
Ro·dri·gues *or* **Ro·dri·guez** \rō-'drē-gəs\ island Indian ocean in the Mascarenes; a dependency of Mauritius; chief town Port Mathurin *area* 40, *pop* 18,335
Rogue \'rōg\ river 220 *m* SW Oreg. rising in Crater Lake National Park & flowing W & SW into the Pacific
Ro·hil·khand \'rō-ˌhil-ˌkənd\ *or* **Ba·reil·ly** \bə-'rā-lē\ region N India in Uttar Pradesh; chief city Bareilly
Rolling Meadows city NE Ill. NW of Chicago *pop* 19,178
Ro·ma·gna \rō-'män-yə\ district N Italy on the Adriatic comprising the E part of Emilia-Romagna region
Roman Campagna — see CAMPAGNA DI ROMA
Romania — see RUMANIA
Rom·blon \räm-'blōn\ **1** islands Philippines in N Visayan islands in Sibuyan sea *area* 512 **2** island, largest of the group
Rome \'rōm\ **1** city NW Ga. NW of Atlanta *pop* 30,759 **2** city E *cen* N.Y. NW of Utica *pop* 50,148 **3** *or* It **Ro·ma** \'rō-mä\ *or anc* **Ro·ma** \'rō-mə\ city ✻ of Italy on the Tiber *pop* 2,706,535 **4** the Roman Empire
Rome, Duchy of division of Byzantine Empire 6th to 8th century *cen* Italy comprising most of modern Latium; later a province of the States of the Church called **Patrimony of Saint Pe·ter** \'pēt-ər\
Rom·ford \'räm(p)-fərd, 'rəm(p)-\ former municipal borough SE England in Essex, now part of Havering
Ron·ces·va·lles \ˌrȯn(t)-səs-'vī-əs\ *or* F **Ron·ce·vaux** \rōⁿs-(ə-)vō\ commune N Spain 5 *m* from French boundary in the Pyrenees near **Pass of Roncesvalles** (3648 *ft*)
Ron·dô·nia \rōⁿ(n)-'dōn-yə\ *or formerly* **Gua·po·ré** \ˌgwäp-ə-'rā\ territory W Brazil ✻ Porto Velho *area* 96,986, *pop* 95,311
Rong·er·ik \'räŋ-ə-ˌrik, 'rȯŋ-\ island W *cen* Pacific in the Marshalls in Ratak chain E of Bikini
Ron·ne Ice Shelf \'rō-nə, 'rən-ə\ area of shelf ice Antarctica in Weddell sea
Roo·de·poort–Ma·rais·burg \'rōd-ə-ˌpō(ə)rt-mə-'rā-ˌbərg, 'rō-i-ˌpō(ə)rt, -ˌpȯ(ə)rt\ city Republic of So. Africa in Transvaal W of Johannesburg *pop* 115,600
Roo·se·velt \'rō-zə-ˌvelt, -vəlt *also* 'rü-\ river 200 *m* W *cen* Brazil flowing from W Mato Grosso state N into the Aripuanã
Ro·rai·ma \rō-'rī-mə\ mountain 8620 *ft* N So. America in Serra Pacaraima on boundary between Venezuela, Guyana, & Brazil; has flat top 9 *m* long & 3 *m* wide
Ror·schach \'rō(ə)r-ˌshäk, 'rȯ(ə)r-, -ˌshäk\ commune NE Switzerland on S shore of Lake Constance
Ro·sa, Mon·te \ˌmōnt-ē-'rō-zə\ mountain 15,217 *ft* on Swiss-Italian border; highest in Pennine Alps
Ro·sa·rio \rō-'zär-ē-ˌō, -'sär-\ city E *cen* Argentina on the Paraná *pop* 591,428
Ros·com·mon \rä-'skäm-ən\ **1** county *cen* Ireland in Connacht *area* 951, *pop* 53,497 **2** town, its ✻
Rose, Mount \'rōz\ mountain 10,800 *ft* W Nev. in Carson range SW of Reno
Ro·selle \rō-'zel\ borough NE N.J. W of Elizabeth *pop* 22,585
Rose·mead \'rōz-ˌmēd\ city SW Calif. E of Los Angeles *pop* 40,972
Ro·set·ta \rō-'zet-ə\ *or* **Ra·shid** \rä-'shēd\ *or anc* **Bol·bi·ti·ne** \ˌbäl-bə-'tī-nē\ **1** river 146 *m* N Egypt forming W branch of the Nile in its delta **2** city N Egypt on the Rosetta *pop* 36,700
Rose·ville \'rōz-ˌvil\ **1** city W Calif. NE of Sacramento *pop* 17,895 **2** city SE Mich. NE of Detroit *pop* 60,529 **3** village SE Minn. N of St. Paul *pop* 34,518
Ross \'rȯs\ sea arm of S Pacific extending into Antarctica E of Victoria Land
Ross and Crom·ar·ty \'kräm-ərt-ē\ county N Scotland ✻ Dingwall *area* 3089, *pop* 58,267
Rossbodenhorn — see FLETSCHHORN
Ross Ice Shelf area of shelf ice Antarctica in S Ross sea
Ros·tock \'räs-ˌtäk, 'rō-ˌstōk\ city & port E Germany on Warnow river near the Baltic coast *pop* 193,699
Ros·tov \rə-'stȯf, -'stȯv\ *or* **Rostov–on–Don** \-ˌȯn-'dän, -ˌän-\ city U.S.S.R. in SE Soviet Russia, Europe, on the Don *pop* 789,000
Ros·well \'räz-ˌwel, -wəl\ city SE N.Mex. *pop* 33,908
Ro·ta \'rōt-ə\ **1** island W Pacific at S end of the Marianas *area* 35 **2** town & port SW Spain on the Atlantic NW of Cádiz
Roth·er·ham \'rät͟h-ə-rəm\ county borough N England in West Riding, Yorkshire, NE of Sheffield *pop* 84,646
Rothe·say \'räth-sē\ burgh SW Scotland on island of Bute ✻ of Buteshire
Ro·to·rua \ˌrōt-ə-'rü-ə\ city New Zealand in N *cen* North I. *pop* 29,300
Rot·ter·dam \'rät-ər-ˌdam\ city & port SW Netherlands on the Nieuwe Maas *pop* 692,915
Ro·tu·ma \rō-'tü-mə\ island SW Pacific N of Fiji Islands *area* 14; belongs to Fiji
Rou·baix \rü-'bā\ city N France NE of Lille *pop* 114,547
Rou·en \rü-'äⁿ(n)\ city & port N France on the Seine *pop* 120,471
Roumania — see RUMANIA
Rous·sil·lon \ˌrü-sē-'(y)ōⁿ\ region & former province S France bordering on the Pyrenees & the Mediterranean ✻ Perpignan
Rou·yn \'rü-ən, ru̇-'aⁿ\ city Canada in SW Que. *pop* 17,821
Rox·burgh \'räks-ˌbər-ə, -ˌbə-rə, -b(ə-)rə\ *or* **Rox·burgh·shire** \-ˌshi(ə)r, -shər\ county SE Scotland ✻ Jedburgh *area* 666, *pop* 41,942
Royal Gorge section of the canyon of Arkansas river S *cen* Colo. W of Canon City
Royal Leamington Spa — see LEAMINGTON
Royal Oak city SE Mich. N of Detroit *pop* 85,499

Royal Tun·bridge Wells \-ˌtən-brij-\ municipal borough SE England in Kent *pop* 44,506

Ruad — see ARWAD

Ru·an·da–Urun·di \rü-ˌän-də-ü-ˈrün-dē\ *or* **Belgian East Africa** former country E *cen* Africa bordering on Lake Tanganyika & comprising two districts, **Ruanda** (✱ Kigali) & **Urundi** (✱ Usumbura), administered by Belgium under League of Nations mandate 1919–45 & under UN trusteeship 1946–62 ✱ Usumbura — see BURUNDI, RWANDA

Ru·a·pe·hu \ˌrü-ə-ˈpā-(ˌ)hü\ volcano 9175 *ft* New Zealand, highest peak in North I., in Tongariro National Park

Rub' al Kha·li \ˌrüb-ˌal-ˈkäl-ē\ *or* **Ar Ri·mal** \ˌar-rə-ˈmal\ desert region S Arabia extending from Nejd S to Hadhramaut *area* 300,000

Ru·bi·con \ˈrü-bi-ˌkän\ river 15 *m* N *cen* Italy flowing E into the Adriatic

Ru·dolf, Lake \ˈrü-ˌdälf\ lake N Kenya in Great Rift valley *area* 3500

Ru·fisque \rü-ˈfēsk\ city & port W Senegal *pop* 60,000

Rug·by \ˈrəg-bē\ municipal borough *cen* England in Warwickshire on the Avon *pop* 59,372

Rü·gen \ˈrü-gən, ˈrue-\ island E Germany in Baltic sea off coast of Pomerania *area* 374; chief town Bergen

Ruhr \ˈrü(ə)r\ **1** river 144 *m* W Germany flowing NW & W to the Rhine **2** industrial district in valley of the Ruhr

Ruis·lip North·wood \ˌrī-sləp-ˈnȯrth-ˌwu̇d\ former urban district S England in Middlesex, now part of Hillingdon

Ru·ma·nia \ru̇-ˈmā-nē-ə, -nyə\ *or* **Ro·ma·nia** \rō-\ *or* **Rou·ma·nia** \ru̇-\ country SE Europe bordering on Black Sea ✱ Bucharest *area* 91,934, *pop* 20,470,000

Ru·me·lia *or* **Rou·me·lia** \rü-ˈmēl-yə, -ˈmē-lē-ə\ a division of the old Ottoman Empire including Albania, Macedonia, & Thrace

Run·ny·mede \ˈrən-ē-ˌmēd\ meadow S England in Surrey on S bank of the Thames in Egham urban district

Ru·pert \ˈrü-pərt\ river 380 *m* Canada in W Que. flowing W into James Bay

Rupert's Land PRINCE RUPERT'S LAND

Ru·se \ˈrü-(ˌ)sā\ *or* Turk **Rus·chuk** \ru̇s-ˈchük\ city NE Bulgaria on the Danube S of Bucharest *pop* 147,448

Rush·more, Mount \ˈrəsh-ˌmō(ə)r, -ˌmȯ(ə)r\ mountain 6200 *ft* W S.Dak. in Black hills on which are carved gigantic faces of Washington, Jefferson, Lincoln, Theodore Roosevelt; a national memorial

Rus·sell Cave National Monument \ˌrəs-əl-\ reservation NE Ala. including cavern where remains of early pre-Columbian man have been found

Rus·sia \ˈrəsh-ə\ *or* Russ **Ros·si·ya** \rä-ˈsē-(y)ə\ **1** former empire E Europe & N Asia coextensive (except for Finland & Kars region) with the present U.S.S.R. ✱ Petrograd **2** RUSSIAN REPUBLIC **3** the U.S.S.R.

Russian Republic *or* **Soviet Russia** constituent republic of the U.S.S.R. in E Europe (**Soviet Russia, Europe**) & N Asia (**Soviet Russia, Asia**) bordering on Arctic & Pacific oceans & on Baltic & Black seas ✱ Moscow *area* 6,501,500, *pop* 130,090,000

Russian Turkestan region comprising the republics of Soviet Central Asia

Rus·ton \ˈrəs-tən\ city N La. *pop* 17,365

Ru·the·nia \rü-ˈthē-nyə, -nē-ə\ *or* **Carpathian Ruthenia** *or* **Za·kar·pat·ska·ya** \ˌzäk-ər-ˈpät-skə-yə\ region U.S.S.R. in W Ukraine S of the Carpathian mountains; part of Hungary before 1918 & 1939–45; a province of Czechoslovakia 1918–38 ✱ Uzhgorod — **Ru·thene** \-ˈthēn\ *n* — **Ru·the·nian** \-ˈthē-nyən, -nē-ən\ *adj or n*

Ruth·er·ford \ˈrəth-ə(r)-fərd, ˈrəth-\ borough NE N.J. SSE of Paterson on Passaic river *pop* 20,802

Ruth·in \ˈrith-ən\ municipal borough N Wales ✱ of Denbighshire

Rut·land \ˈrət-lənd\ **1** city W *cen* Vt. *pop* 19,293 **2** *or* **Rut·land·shire** \-lən(d)-ˌshi(ə)r, -shər\ county E *cen* England ✱ Oakham *area* 152, *pop* 27,463

Ru·vu·ma *or* Port **Ro·vu·ma** \ru̇-ˈvü-mə\ river 400 *m* SE Africa rising in S Tanganyika & flowing E into Indian ocean

Ru·wen·zo·ri \ˌrü-(w)ən-ˈzōr-ē, -ˈzȯr-\ mountain group E *cen* Africa between Uganda & Zaire — see STANLEY (Mount)

Rwan·da \ru̇-ˈän-də\ *or formerly* **Ru·an·da** country E *cen* Africa; a republic ✱ Kigali *area* 10,166, *pop* 3,830,000 — see RUANDA-URUNDI — **Rwan·dan** \-dən\ *adj or n*

Rya·zan *or* **Ria·zan** \ˌrē-ə-ˈzan(-yə)\ city U.S.S.R. in *cen* Soviet Russia, Europe, on Oka river SE of Moscow *pop* 351,000

Ry·binsk \ˈrib-ən(t)sk\ *or* **Shcher·ba·kov** \ˌsh(ch)er-bə-ˈkȯf, -ˈkȯv\ city U.S.S.R. in N *cen* Soviet Russia, Europe, NNE of Moscow on the Volga at SE end of Rybinsk reservoir *pop* 218,000

Rye \ˈrī\ municipal borough SE England in East Sussex

Ryswick — see RIJSWIJK

Ryu·kyu \rē-ˈ(y)ü-(ˌ)k(y)ü\ *or* **Liu·chiu** \ˈlü-ˈchü\ *or* **Nan·sei** \ˈnän-ˈsā\ islands W Pacific extending between Kyushu, Japan, & Formosa, China; belonged to Japan 1895–1945; occupied by U.S. 1945; returned to Japan in 1953 (N islands) and 1972 (S islands) *area* 1803 — see AMAMI, OKINAWA, OSUMI, SAKISHIMA, TOKARA — **Ryu·kyu·an** \-ˌ(y)ü-ˈk(y)ü-ən\ *adj or n*

Saa·le \ˈzäl-ə, ˈsäl-\ river 226 *m* Germany rising in NE Bavaria in the Fichtelgebirge & flowing N into the Elbe

Saar \ˈsär, ˈzär\ **1** *or* F **Sarre** \ˈsȧr\ river 84 *m* Europe flowing from Vosges mountains in France N to the Moselle in Germany **2** *or* **Saar·land** \ˈsär-ˌland, ˈzär-\ region W Europe in basin of Saar river between France & Germany; once part of Lorraine, became part of Germany in 19th century; administered by League of Nations 1919–35; became a state of Germany 1935; came under control of France after World War II; to West Germany by a plebiscite Jan. 1, 1957, as a state (**Saarland**) ✱ Saarbrücken *area* 898, *pop* 1,127,000

Saar·brück·en \zär-ˈbru̇k-ən, sär-, -ˈbruek-\ city W Germany ✱ of Saarland *pop* 131,500

Saaremaa — see SAREMA

Sa·ba, **1** \ˈsäb-ə\ island SE West Indies in Netherlands Antilles ✱ The Bottom *area* 5, *pop* 972 **2** — see SHEBA

Sa·ba·dell \ˌsab-ə-ˈdel\ commune NE Spain N of Barcelona *pop* 145,979

Sa·bah \ˈsäb-ə\ *or formerly* **North Borneo** state Federation of Malaysia in NE Borneo, formerly a Brit. colony ✱ Kota Kinabalu *area* 29,388, *pop* 655,622

Sa·bar·ma·ti \ˌsäb-ər-ˈmət-ē\ river 200 *m* W India flowing S into head of Gulf of Cambay

Sa·bi \ˈsäb-ē\ *or* **Sa·ve** \ˈsäv-ə\ river 400 *m* SE Africa rising in *cen* Rhodesia & flowing E across S Mozambique to Mozambique channel

Sa·bine \sə-ˈbēn\ river 380 *m* E Tex. & W La. flowing SE through **Sabine Lake** (15 *m* long) & **Sabine Pass** (channel) into Gulf of Mexico

Sa·ble, Cape \ˈsā-bəl\ **1** cape at SW tip of Fla., southernmost point of U.S. mainland, at *ab* 25°7′N **2** headland E Canada on an islet S of **Cape Sable Island** (20 *m* long, at S end of N.S.)

Sab·ra·tha \ˈsab-rə-thə\ *or anc* **Sab·ra·ta** \-rət-ə\ town Libya on the coast WNW of Tripoli

Sachsen — see SAXONY

Sa·co \ˈsȯ-(ˌ)kō\ river 104 *m* E N.H. & SW Me. flowing SE into the Atlantic

Sac·ra·men·to \ˌsak-rə-ˈment-(ˌ)ō\ **1** mountains S N.Mex. — see GUADALUPE, SIERRA BLANCA **2** river 382 *m* N Calif. flowing S into Suisun Bay **3** city ✱ of Calif. on Sacramento river *pop* 254,413

Sa·do·wa \zä-ˈdō-və, ˈsäd-ə-ˌvä\ village Czechoslovakia in NE Bohemia

Sa·fed Koh \sə-ˌfed-ˈkō\ mountain range E Afghanistan on Pakistan border; a S extension of the Hindu Kush

Sa·fi \ˈsaf-ē\ city & port W Morocco *pop* 130,000

Sa·ga·mi \sə-ˈgäm-ē\ sea inlet of the Pacific Japan in *cen* Honshu SW of Tokyo Bay

Saghalien — see SAKHALIN

Sag·i·naw \ˈsag-ə-ˌnȯ\ city E *cen* Mich. *pop* 91,849

Saginaw Bay inlet of Lake Huron in E Mich.

Sa·gres \ˈsag-rēsh\ village SW Portugal E of Cape St. Vincent

Saguache — see SAWATCH

Sa·gua·ro National Monument \sə-ˈwär-ə, -ˈ(g)wär-(ˌ)ō\ reservation SE Ariz. E of Tucson *area* 84

Sag·ue·nay \ˈsag-ə-ˌnā, ˌsag-ə-ˈ\ river 125 *m* Canada in S Que. flowing from Lake St. John E into the St. Lawrence

Sa·guia el Ham·ra \sə-ˌgē-ə-ˌel-ˈham-rə\ *or* **Se·kia el Hamra** \-ˌkē-ə-\ territory NW Africa, the N zone of Spanish Sahara

Sa·gun·to \sə-ˈgün-(ˌ)tō\ *or formerly* **Mur·vie·dro** \ˌmu̇r-vē-ˈā-(ˌ)drō\ commune E Spain NNE of Valencia *pop* 47,026

Sahama — see SAJAMA

Sa·ha·ra \sə-ˈhar-ə, -ˈher-, -ˈhär-\ desert region N Africa N of the Sudan region extending from the Atlantic coast to Red sea or, as sometimes considered, to the Nile — **Sa·ha·ran** \-ən\ *adj*

Sa·ha·ran·pur \sə-ˈhär-ən-ˌpu̇(ə)r\ city N India in NW Uttar Pradesh NNE of Delhi *pop* 228,053

Saida — see SIDON

Sai·gon \sī-ˈgän, ˈsī-ˌ\ city & port ✱ of So. Vietnam in Cochin China on Saigon river *pop* 1,681,893 — **Sai·gon·ese** \ˌsī-gə-ˈnēz, -ˈnēs\ *adj or n*

Sai·maa \ˈsī-ˌmä\ lake SE Finland, largest of the **Saimaa Lakes**

Saint Al·bans \ˈȯl-bənz\ city & municipal borough SE England in Hertfordshire *pop* 52,057

Saint Ann \ˈan\ city E Mo. NW of St. Louis *pop* 18,215

Saint Bar·thol·o·mew \ˌsānt-bär-ˈthäl-ə-ˌmyü, -bər-\ *or* **Saint Bar·thé·le·my** \saⁿ-bȧr-tā-lə-mē\ *or* **Saint Barts** \sānt-ˈbärts, sənt-\ island French West Indies in department of Guadeloupe; chief town Gustavia

Saint Ber·nard \ˌsant-bə(r)-ˈnärd\ two Alpine passes — see GREAT SAINT BERNARD, LITTLE SAINT BERNARD

Saint Bon·i·face \ˈbän-ə-fəs, -ˌfās\ city Canada in SE Man. on Red river opposite Winnipeg *pop* 46,714

Saint–Bru·no–de–Mon·tar·ville \sānt-ˈbrü-ˌnō-də-ˈmänt-ər-ˌvil, sənt-\ town Canada in S Que. E of Montreal *pop* 15,780

Saint Cath·a·rines \ˈkath-(ə-)rənz\ city Canada in SE Ont. NW of Niagara Falls on Welland ship canal *pop* 109,722

Saint Charles \ˈchär(ə)lz\ city E Mo. on the Missouri *pop* 31,834

Saint Clair, Lake \ˈkla(ə)r, ˈkle(ə)r\ lake SE Mich. & SE Ont. *area* 460, connected by **Saint Clair river** (40 *m*) with Lake Huron & draining through Detroit river into Lake Erie

Saint Clair Shores city SE Mich. NE of Detroit *pop* 88,093

Saint Cloud \ˈklau̇d\ city *cen* Minn. on the Mississippi *pop* 39,691

Saint–Cloud \sānt-ˈklau̇d, sənt-; saⁿ-klü\ commune France, WSW suburb of Paris *pop* 28,162

Saint Croix \sānt-ˈkrȯi, sənt-\ **1** river 75 *m* Canada & U.S. between N.B. & Me. **2** river 164 *m* NW Wis. & E Minn. flowing into the Mississippi **3** *or* **San·ta Cruz** \ˌsant-ə-ˈkrüz\ island, West Indies, largest of the Virgin Islands of the U.S. *area* 80; chief town Christiansted

Saint–Cyr–l'École \saⁿ-si(ə)r-lā-ˈkəl\ commune N France W of Versailles *pop* 16,000

Saint–De·nis \saⁿ(t)-də-ˈnē\ **1** commune N France NNE of Paris *pop* 99,268 **2** commune ✱ of Réunion I. *pop* 94,104

Sainte–Foy \sānt-ˈfȯi, sənt-; saⁿt-(ə-)fwä\ city Canada in SE Que. SW of Quebec city *pop* 68,385

Saint Eli·as \ˌsānt-əl-ˈī-əs\ mountain range of the Coast ranges SW Yukon Territory & E Alaska — see LOGAN (Mount)

Saint Elias, Mount mountain 18,008 *ft* on Alaska-Canada boundary in St. Elias range

Sainte–Thé·rèse \ˌsānt-tə-ˈrāz\ city Canada in S Que. NW of Montreal *pop* 17,175

Saint–Étienne \saⁿ-tā-tyen\ city SE *cen* France *pop* 213,468

ə abut ᵊ kitten, F table ər further a back ā bake
ä cot, cart ȧ F bac au̇ out ch chin e less ē easy
g gift i trip ī life j joke k G ich ⁿ F vin ŋ sing
ō flow ȯ flaw œ F bœuf œ̄ F feu ȯi coin th thing
t͟h this ü loot u̇ foot ue G Füllen ue̅ F rue y yet
ʸ F digne \dēnʸ\, nuit \nwʸē\ yü few yu̇ furious zh vision

Saint Eu·sta·ti·us \ˌsānt-yu̇-ˈstā-sh(ē-)əs\ *or* **Sta·tia** \ˈstā-shə\ island West Indies in Netherlands Antilles NW of St. Kitts *area* 7

Saint Fran·cis \sānt-ˈfran(t)-səs, sənt-\ **1** river 425 *m* SE Mo. & E Ark. flowing S into the Mississippi **2** *or* **Saint Fran·çois** \sa^n-frä^n-swä\ river 165 *m* Canada in S Que. flowing NW into the St. Lawrence

Saint Fran·cis, Lake \ˈfran(t)-səs\ expansion of St. Lawrence river Canada above Valleyfield, Que.

Saint Gall \sānt-ˈgȯl, sənt-; sa^n-ˈgäl\ *or* G **Sankt Gal·len** \zäŋ(k)t-ˈgäl-ən\ **1** canton NE Switzerland *area* 800, *pop* 384,475 **2** commune, its ✱ *pop* 78,600

Saint George's channel \ˌjȯr-jəz-\ strait British Isles between SW Wales & Ireland

Saint–Ger·main \ˌsa^n-zhər-ˈma^n\ *or* **Saint–Ger·main–en–Laye** \-ˌma^n-ˌä^n-ˈlā\ commune N France WNW of Paris *pop* 38,808

Saint–Gilles \sa^n-ˈzhē(ə)l\ *or* Flem **Sint–Gil·lis** \sənt-ˈgil-əs\ commune *cen* Belgium near Brussels *pop* 54,272

Saint Gott·hard *or* **Saint Got·hard** \sānt-ˈgät(h)-ərd, sənt-; ˌsa^n-gə-ˈtär\ *or* G **Sankt Gott·hard** \zäŋ(k)t-ˈgȯt-ˌhärt\ **1** mountains Switzerland in Lepontine Alps between Uri & Ticino cantons **2** mountain pass 6935 *ft* in St. Gotthard range

Saint He·le·na \ˌsānt-^{ə}l-ˈē-nə, ˌsānt-hə-ˈlē-\ island S Atlantic; a Brit. colony ✱ Jamestown *area* 47, *pop* 4829

Saint Hel·ens \sānt-ˈhel-ənz, sənt-\ county borough NW England in Lancashire ENE of Liverpool *pop* 104,173

Saint Helens, Mount mountain 9671 *ft* SW Wash. in Cascades

Saint Hel·ier \ˈhel-yər\ town Channel islands ✱ of Jersey *pop* 28,135

Saint–Hu·bert \sānt-ˈhyü-bərt, sənt-\ town Canada in S Que. E of Montreal *pop* 21,741

Saint–Hy·a·cinthe \sānt-ˈhī-ə-(ˌ)sin(t)th, sənt-; ˌsant-yə-ˈsant\ city Canada in S Que. E of Montreal *pop* 24,562

Saint James–As·sin·i·boia \sānt-ˌjāmz-ə-ˌsin-ə-ˈbȯi-ə, sənt-\ city Canada in SE Man. W of Winnipeg *pop* 71,431

Saint–Jean \sa^n-zhä^n\ *or* **Saint Johns** \sānt-ˈjänz, sənt-\ city Canada in S Que. SE of Montreal *pop* 32,863

Saint–Jean–Cap–Fer·rat \sa^n-ˈzhä^n-ˌkap-fə-ˈrä\ commune SE France on coast E of Nice

Saint–Jean–de–Luz \sa^n-ˌzhä^n-də-ˈlüz, -ˈlu̵ez\ town SW France on Bay of Biscay SW of Biarritz

Saint–Jé·rôme \ˌsa^n-zhā-ˈrōm, ˌsānt-jə-ˈrōm\ city Canada in S Que. NW of Montreal *pop* 26,524

Saint John \sānt-ˈjän, sənt-\ **1** river 450 *m* NE U.S. & SE Canada flowing from N Me. into Bay of Fundy in N.B. **2** city & port Canada in S N.B. on Bay of Fundy at mouth of the St. John *pop* 89,039 **3** island West Indies, one of the Virgin Islands of the U.S. *area* 20

Saint John, Lake *or* **Lac Saint–Jean** \lȧk-sa^n-zhä^n\ lake Canada in S Que. draining through the Saguenay to the St. Lawrence *area* 350

Saint Johns \sānt-ˈjänz, sənt-\ **1** river 276 *m* NE Fla. flowing N & E into the Atlantic **2** town Brit. West Indies ✱ of Antigua on Antigua I. **3** — see SAINT-JEAN

Saint John's \sānt-ˈjänz, sənt-\ city & port Canada ✱ of Nfld. *pop* 88,102

Saint Jo·seph \ˈjō-zəf *also* -səf\ city NW Mo. *pop* 72,691

Saint Kitts \ˈkits\ *or* **Saint Chris·to·pher** \ˈkris-tə-fər\ island Brit. West Indies in the Leewards; chief town Basseterre *area* 68; with Nevis, forms **Saint Kitts–Nevis** Associated State (✱ Basseterre *area* 152, *pop* 52,020)

Saint–Lam·bert \sānt-ˈlam-bərt, sənt-\ city Canada in S Que. E of Montreal *pop* 18,616

Saint–Lau·rent \ˌsa^n-lȯ-ˈrä^n, ˌsant-lȯ-ˈrent\ city Canada in S Que. on Montreal I. *pop* 62,955

Saint Law·rence \sānt-ˈlȯr-ən(t)s, sənt-, -ˈlär-\ **1** island 95 *m* long W Alaska in N Bering sea **2** river 760 *m* E Canada in Ont. & Que. bordering on the U.S. in N.Y., flowing from Lake Ontario NE into the Atlantic, & forming at its mouth a wide bay (the **Gulf of Saint Lawrence**) **3** seaway Canada & U.S. in & along the St. Lawrence between Lake Ontario & Montreal

Saint Lawrence, Lake expansion of St. Lawrence river Canada & U.S. above Cornwall, Ont.

Saint Lawrence Islands National Park reservation E Canada in Ont. comprising a number of islands in the Thousand islands group & an area on shore of the St. Lawrence *area* 166 acres

Saint–Lé·o·nard \ˌsa^n-ˌlā-ə-ˈnär; sānt-ˈlen-ərd, sənt-\ city Canada in S Que. N of Montreal *pop* 52,040

Saint–Lô \sānt-ˈlō, sənt-; sa^n-lō\ commune NW France W of Caen *pop* 18,615

Saint Lou·is \sānt-ˈlü-əs, sənt-\ **1** river 220 *m* NE Minn. flowing to W tip of Lake Superior **2** city E Mo. *pop* 622,236

Saint–Lou·is \ˌsa^n-lü-ˈē\ **1** city & port Senegal on island at mouth of Senegal river; formerly ✱ of Senegal *pop* 75,000 **2** city & port Réunion I. *pop* 26,740

Saint Lou·is, Lake \sānt-ˈlü-ē, sənt-\ expansion of St. Lawrence river Canada above Lachine rapids

Saint Louis Park \ˈlü-əs\ city SE Minn. *pop* 48,883

Saint Lu·cia \sānt-ˈlü-shə, sənt-\ island Brit. West Indies in the Windwards S of Martinique; an Associated State ✱ Castries *area* 233, *pop* 101,100

Saint–Ma·lo \ˌsa^n-mə-ˈlō\ city & port NW France in Brittany on island in Gulf of St-Malo *pop* 42,297

Saint–Malo, Gulf of arm of English channel NW France between Cotentin peninsula & Brittany

Saint Mar·tin \sānt-ˈmärt-^{ə}n, sənt-\ island West Indies in the N Leewards; divided between France & Netherlands *area* 38

Saint Marylebone — see MARYLEBONE

Saint Mar·ys \ˈme(ə)r-ēz, ˈma(ə)r-ēz, ˈmā-rēz\ **1** river 175 *m* on Fla.-Ga. border flowing from Okefenokee swamp to the Atlantic **2** river 63 *m* between Canada & U.S. in Ont. & upper peninsula of Mich. flowing from Lake Superior into Lake Huron; descends 20 *ft* in a mile at **Saint Marys Falls** — see SAULT SAINTE MARIE CANALS

Saint–Maur–des–Fos·sés \sa^n-mȯr-dā-fō-sā\ commune N France SE of Paris on the Marne *pop* 77,251

Saint Mau·rice \sānt-ˈmȯr-əs, sənt-, -ˈmär-; ˌsa^n-mə-ˈris\ river 325 *m* Canada in S Que. flowing S into the St. Lawrence

Saint–Mi·hiel \sa^n-mē-yel\ town NE France on the Meuse NW of Nancy

Saint Mo·ritz \ˌsānt-mə-ˈrits, ˌsa^n-mə-\ *or* G **Sankt Mo·ritz** \ˌzäŋ(k)t-mə-ˈrits\ town E Switzerland in Graubünden canton SSE of Chur

Saint–Na·zaire \ˌsa^n-nə-ˈza(ə)r, -ˈze(ə)r\ commune & port NW France at mouth of the Loire *pop* 63,289

Sain·tonge \sa^n-tō^{n}zh\ region & former province of France on Bay of Biscay N of the Gironde ✱ Saintes

Saint–Ouen \sa^n-twa^n\ commune France, N suburb of Paris *pop* 48,886

Saint Pan·cras \sānt-ˈpaŋ-krəs, sənt-\ former metropolitan borough NW London, England, now part of Camden

Saint Paul \ˈpȯl\ city ✱ of Minn. *pop* 309,980 — **Saint Paul·ite** \ˈpȯ-ˌlīt\ *n*

Saint Paul Rocks *or* **Saint Paul's Rocks** *or* **Saint Peter and Saint Paul Rocks** *or* Port **Ro·che·dos Sao Pau·lo** \rə-ˌshā-thəs-ˌsau̇^{n}(m)-ˈpau̇-(ˌ)lü\ rocky islets in the Atlantic 600 *m* NE of Natal, Brazil, at 1°N, 29°15′W; belong to Brazil

Saint Pe·ter, Lake \sānt-ˈpēt-ər, sənt-\ expansion of St. Lawrence river Canada between Sorel & Trois-Rivières, Que.

Saint Pe·ters·burg \ˈpēt-ərz-ˌbərg\ **1** city W Fla. on Pinellas peninsula SW of Tampa *pop* 216,232 **2** — see LENINGRAD

Saint Pierre \sānt-ˈpi(ə)r, sənt-, -pē-ˈe(ə)r, *F* sa^n-pyer\ island in the Atlantic off S Nfld.; with nearby island of Miquelon and others, constitutes French territory of **Saint Pierre and Miq·ue·lon** \ˈmik-ə-ˌlän, *F* mēk-(ə-)lō^n\ (✱ St. Pierre, *area* 93, *pop* 5600)

Saint–Quen·tin \sānt-ˈkwent-^{ə}n, sənt-, *F* sa^n-kä^n-ta^n\ commune N France on the Somme NW of Laon *pop* 64,196

Saint Si·mon \sānt-ˈsī-mən, sənt-\ island SE Ga. in the Atlantic

Saint Thom·as \ˈtäm-əs\ **1** island West Indies, one of the Virgin Islands of the U.S. *area* 32 **2** — see CHARLOTTE AMALIE **3** city Canada in SE Ont. S of London *pop* 25,545

Saint–Tro·pez \sa^n-trō-pā\ commune SE France on the Mediterranean SW of Cannes

Saint Vin·cent \sānt-ˈvin(t)-sənt, sənt-\ island Brit. West Indies in *cen* Windwards; with N Grenadines, constitutes an Associated State ✱ Kingstown *area* 150, *pop* 89,129

Saint Vincent, Cape *or* Port **Ca·bo de São Vi·cen·te** \ˈkä-vü-thə-ˌsau̇^{n}-vē-ˈsā^n(n)-tə\ cape SW Portugal

Saint Vincent, Gulf of inlet of Indian ocean Australia in So. Australia E of Yorke peninsula

Saint–Vi·tal \ˌsānt-və-ˈtal\ city Canada in SE Man. SE of Winnipeg *pop* 32,963

Sai·pan \sī-ˈpan, -ˈpän, ˈsī-ˌ\ island W Pacific in S *cen* Marianas *area* 70, *pop* 7967 — **Sai·pa·nese** \ˌsī-pə-ˈnēz, -ˈnēs\ *adj or n*

Sa·is \ˈsā-əs\ ancient city Egypt in Nile delta on Canopic branch

Saishu — see CHEJU

Sa·ja·ma *or* **Sa·ha·ma** \sə-ˈhäm-ə\ mountain 21,391 *ft* W Bolivia near Chilean boundary

Sa·kai \(ˈ)sä-ˈkī\ city Japan in S Honshu on Osaka Bay *pop* 569,000

Sa·kar·ya \sə-ˈkär-yə\ river 300 *m* NW Turkey in Asia flowing into the Black Sea 80 *m* E of the Bosporus

Sa·kha·lin \ˈsak-ə-ˌlēn, -lən; ˌsak-ə-ˈlēn\ *or formerly* **Sa·gha·lien** \ˈsag-ə-ˌlēn, ˌsag-ə-ˈ\ *or* Jap **Ka·ra·fu·to** \kə-ˈräf-ə-ˌtō\ island U.S.S.R. in Sea of Okhotsk N of Hokkaido; formerly (1905–45) divided between Russia & Japan *area* 24,560

Sakhar — see SUKKUR

Sa·ki·shi·ma \ˌsäk-i-ˈshē-mə, sä-ˈkish-ə-mə\ island group Japan in S Ryukyus off E coast of N Formosa; occupied 1945–72 by the U.S. *area* 343

Sakkara — see SAQQARA

Sa·kon·net river \sə-ˈkän-ət\ inlet of the Atlantic SE R.I.

Salaberry–de–Valleyfield — see VALLEYFIELD

Sa·la·do \sə-ˈläd-(ˌ)ō\ **1** *or in upper course* **Ju·ra·men·to** \ˌhür-ə-ˈmen-(ˌ)tō\ river 1120 *m* N Argentina flowing from the Andes SE into the Paraná **2** *or* **Des·agua·de·ro** \ˌdā-ˌsäg-wə-ˈde(ə)r-(ˌ)ō\ river 850 *m* W *cen* Argentina flowing S into the Colorado

Sa·la·jar *or* **Sa·la·yar** \sə-ˈlä-ˌyär\ island Indonesia off SW Celebes I. *area* 256

Sal·a·man·ca \ˌsal-ə-ˈmaŋ-kə, ˌsäl-ə-ˈmäŋ-\ **1** province W Spain *area* 4829, *pop* 371,607 **2** commune, its ✱, WNW of Madrid *pop* 114,574

Sal·a·maua \ˌsal-ə-ˈmau̇-ə\ town & port E North-East New Guinea

Salambria — see PENEUS

Sal·a·mis \ˈsal-ə-məs\ **1** ancient city Cyprus on E coast **2** island Greece in Saronic gulf off Attica

Sa·lé \sa-ˈlā\ *or* **Sla** \ˈslä\ *or* **Sal·li** *or formerly* **Sal·lee** \ˈsal-ē\ city & port NW Morocco, N suburb of Rabat *pop* 75,799

Sa·lem \ˈsā-ləm\ **1** city & port NE Mass. NE of Lynn *pop* 40,556 **2** town SE N.H. E of Nashua *pop* 20,142 **3** city ✱ of Oreg. on Willamette river *pop* 68,296 **4** town W *cen* Va. WNW of Roanoke *pop* 21,982 **5** city S India in N Tamil Nadu SW of Madras *pop* 302,935 **6** JERUSALEM — an ancient name

Sa·ler·no \sə-ˈlər-(ˌ)nō, -ˈle(ə)r-\ commune & port S Italy on **Gulf of Salerno** (inlet of Tyrrhenian sea) ESE of Naples *pop* 149,392 — **Sa·ler·ni·tan** \-ˈlər-nə-tən\ *adj or n*

Sal·ford \ˈsȯl-fərd\ city & county borough NW England in Lancashire, W suburb of Manchester *pop* 130,641

Sa·li·na \sə-ˈlī-nə\ city *cen* Kans. on Smoky Hill river *pop* 37,714

Sa·li·nas \sə-ˈlē-nəs\ **1** river 150 *m* W Calif. flowing NW into Monterey Bay **2** city W Calif. near Monterey Bay *pop* 58,896

Salis·bury \ˈsȯlz-ˌber-ē, -b(ə)-rē\ **1** city SE Md. *pop* 15,252 **2** city W *cen* N.C. SSW of Winston-Salem *pop* 22,515 **3** city ✱ of Rhodesia *pop* 314,200 **4** *or* **New Sar·um** \ˈsar-əm, ˈser-\ municipal borough S England in Wiltshire on the Avon *pop* 35,271

Salisbury Plain plateau S England in Wiltshire NW of Salisbury

Salm·on \ˈsam-ən\ river 420 *m*, *cen* Idaho flowing into the Snake

Salmon River mountains *cen* Idaho; many peaks over 9000 *ft*

Sa·lo·ni·ka *or* **Sa·lo·ni·ca** \sə-ˈlän-i-kə, ˌsal-ə-ˈnē-kə\ *or* **Thes·sa·lo·ni·ca** \ˌthes-ə-lə-ˈnī-kə, -ˈlän-i-\ *or* NGk **Thes·sa·lo·ní·ki** \ˌthes-ə-lə-ˈnē-kē\ *or* **Sa·lo·ni·ki** \ˌsal-ə-ˈnē-kē\ city & port N Greece in Macedonia *pop* 250,920

Salonika, Gulf of *or* **Ther·ma·ic Gulf** \(ˌ)thər-ˌmā-ik-\ arm of Aegean sea N Greece W of Chalcidice

Salop, 1 — see SHROPSHIRE **2** — see SHREWSBURY — **Sa·lo·pi·an** \sə-ˈlō-pē-ən\ *adj or n*

Salt \ˈsȯlt\ **1** river 200 *m* Ariz. flowing W into the Gila **2** river 100 *m* N *cen* Ky. flowing into the Ohio **3** river 200 *m* NE Mo. flowing SE into the Mississippi

Sal·ta \ˈsäl-tə\ city NW Argentina N of San Miguel de Tucumán *pop* 117,400

Sal·ti·llo \säl-ˈtē-(ˌ)(y)ō, sal-\ city NE Mexico ✻ of Coahuila *pop* 191,879

Salt Lake City *or* **Salt Lake** city ✻ of Utah *pop* 175,885

Sal·to \ˈsäl-(ˌ)tō\ city & port NW Uruguay on Uruguay river *pop* 57,958

Sal·ton sea \ˌsȯlt-ᵊn-\ saline lake *ab* 235 *ft* below sea level SE Calif. at N end of Imperial valley formed by diversion of water from Colorado river into depression formerly called **Salton sink**

Salt sea — see DEAD SEA

Sa·lu·da \sə-ˈlüd-ə\ river 200 *m* W *cen* S.C. flowing SE to unite with the Broad forming the Congaree

Sal·va·dor \ˈsal-və-ˌdȯ(ə)r, ˌsal-və-ˈ\ **1** EL SALVADOR **2** *or formerly* **São Salvador** \saùⁿ-\ city & port NE Brazil ✻ of Bahia *pop* 892,392 — **Sal·va·dor·an** \ˌsal-və-ˈdȯr-ən, -ˈdōr-\ *adj or n* — **Sal·va·dor·ean** *or* **Sal·va·dor·ian** \-ē-ən\ *adj or n*

Sal·ween \ˈsal-ˌwēn\ river 1750 *m* SE Asia flowing from Tibet S into Gulf of Martaban in Burma

Salz·burg \ˈsȯlz-ˌbərg, ˈsälz-, ˈsalz-, ˈsȯlts-, -ˌbù(ə)rg, *G* ˈzälts-ˌbùrk\ city W Austria *pop* 121,306

Salz·git·ter \ˈzälts-ˌgit-ər\ *or formerly* **Wa·ten·stedt–Salzgitter** \ˈvät-ᵊn-ˌs(h)tet-\ city N *cen* Germany SW of Brunswick *pop* 117,300

Salz·kam·mer·gut \ˈzälts-ˌkäm-ər-ˌgüt\ district N Austria E of Salzburg; chief town Bad Ischl

Sa·mar \ˈsäm-ˌär\ island *cen* Philippines in the Visayans N of Leyte *area* 5050

Samara — see KUIBYSHEV

Samarang — see SEMARANG

Sa·mar·ia \sə-ˈmer-ē-ə, -ˈmar-\ **1** district of ancient Palestine W of the Jordan between Galilee & Judaea **2** city, its ✻ & ✻ of the Northern Kingdom (Israel); rebuilt by Herod the Great & renamed **Se·bas·te** \sə-ˈbas-tē\; site in Jordan at modern village of Sebastye

Sam·ar·kand \ˈsam-ər-ˌkand\ *or anc* **Mar·a·can·da** \ˌmar-ə-ˈkan-də\ city U.S.S.R. in E Uzbekistan *pop* 267,000

Sam·ni·um \ˈsam-nē-əm\ ancient country *cen* Italy E & SE of Latium — **Sam·nite** \-ˌnīt\ *adj or n*

Sa·moa \sə-ˈmō-ə\ *or formerly* **Navigators** islands SW *cen* Pacific N of Tonga islands; divided at long. 171°W into American, or Eastern, Samoa & Western Samoa *area* 1209

Sa·mos \ˈsā-ˌmäs\ island Greece in the Aegean off coast of Turkey N of the Dodecanese *area* 171 — **Sa·mi·an** \-mē-ən\ *adj or n*

Sam·o·thrace \ˈsam-ə-ˌthrās\ *or* NGk **Sa·mo·thrá·ke** \ˌsäm-ə-ˈthräk-ē\ island Greece in the NE Aegean — **Sam·o·thra·cian** \ˌsam-ə-ˈthrā-shən\ *adj or n*

Sam·sun \säm-ˈsün\ city & port N Turkey on Black Sea NW of Ankara *pop* 107,510

San·'a *or* **San·aa** \ˈsan-ˌä, san-ˈä\ city S Arabia ✻ of Yemen *pop* 125,093

San An·ge·lo \sa-ˈnan-jə-ˌlō\ city W *cen* Tex. *pop* 63,884

San An·to·nio \ˌsan-ən-ˈtō-nē-ˌō\ **1** river 200 *m* S Tex. flowing SE into Gulf of Mexico **2** city S Tex. *pop* 654,153 — **San An·to·ni·an** \-nē-ən\ *n*

San Be·ni·to \ˌsan-bə-ˈnēt-(ˌ)ō\ city S Tex. NW of Brownsville *pop* 15,176

San Ber·nar·di·no \ˌsan-ˌbər-nə(r)-ˈdē-(ˌ)nō\ **1** mountains S Calif. S of Mojave desert; highest Mt. San Gorgonio 11,485 *ft* **2** city SW Calif. E of Los Angeles *pop* 104,251

San Bru·no \san-ˈbrü-(ˌ)nō\ city W Calif. S of San Francisco *pop* 36,254

San Buenaventura — see VENTURA

San Car·los \san-ˈkär-ləs\ city W Calif. SE of San Francisco *pop* 25,924

San Carlos de Bariloche — see BARILOCHE

San Cle·men·te \ˌsan-klə-ˈment-ē\ **1** island S Calif., southernmost of the Santa Barbara islands **2** city SW Calif. NW of San Diego *pop* 17,063

San Cris·to·bal \ˌsan-kris-ˈtō-bəl\ *or* **San Cris·to·val** \-vəl\ *or* **Ma·ki·ra** \mə-ˈkir-ə\ island W Pacific in SE Solomons SE of Guadalcanal

San Cris·tó·bal \ˌsan-kris-ˈtō-bəl\ **1** *or* **Chat·ham** \ˈchat-əm\ island Ecuador in the Galápagos **2** city W Venezuela 100 *m* SSW of Lake Maracaibo *pop* 149,063

Sanc·ti Spí·ri·tus \ˌsäŋ(k)-tē-ˈspir-ə-ˌtüs\ city W *cen* Cuba *pop* (municipality) 146,450

San·cy, Puy de \ˌpwēd-ə-ˌsäⁿ-ˈsē\ mountain 6185 *ft* S *cen* France; highest in the Monts Dore & Auvergne mountains

San·da·kan \san-ˈdäk-ən\ city & port Sabah on Sulu sea; former ✻ of No. Borneo *pop* 28,806

Sandalwood — see SUMBA

Sand·hurst \ˈsand-ˌhərst\ town S England in E Berkshire SE of Reading

San·dia \san-ˈdē-ə\ mountains N *cen* N.Mex. E of Albuquerque; highest **Sandia Crest** 10,678 *ft*

San Di·ego \ˌsan-dē-ˈā-(ˌ)gō\ city & port SW Calif. on **San Diego Bay** (inlet of the Pacific) *pop* 696,769 — **San Di·egan** \-gən\ *adj or n*

San Di·mas \san-ˈdē-məs\ city SW Calif. NW of Pomona *pop* 15,692

San Domingo, 1 — see HISPANIOLA **2** — see DOMINICAN REPUBLIC **3** — see SANTO DOMINGO

San·dring·ham \ˈsan-driŋ-əm\ village E England in NW Norfolk

San·dus·ky \sən-ˈdəs-kē, san-\ **1** river 150 *m* N Ohio flowing N into Lake Erie **2** city N Ohio at entrance to **Sandusky Bay** (inlet of Lake Erie) *pop* 32,674

Sand·wich \ˈsan-(ˌ)(d)wich\ **1** islands — see HAWAII **2** municipal borough SE England in Kent on the Stour

Sandy Hook peninsula E N.J. extending N toward New York Bay

San Fer·nan·do \ˌsan-fər-ˈnan-(ˌ)dō\ **1** valley S Calif. NW of Los Angeles; partly within Los Angeles city limits **2** city SW Calif. in San Fernando valley *pop* 16,571

San·ford \ˈsan-fərd\ **1** city NE Fla. N of Orlando *pop* 17,393 **2** town SW Me. *pop* 15,812

Sanford, Mount mountain 16,208 *ft* S Alaska at W end of Wrangell mountains

San Fran·cis·co \ˌsan-frən-ˈsis-(ˌ)kō\ city & port W Calif. on **San Francisco Bay** & the Pacific *pop* 715,674 — **San Fran·cis·can** \-kən\ *adj or n*

San Francisco Peaks mountain N *cen* Ariz. N of Flagstaff; includes three peaks; Mt. Humphreys 12,633 *ft* (highest point in the state), Mt. Agassiz 12,340 *ft*, & Mt. Fremont 11,940 *ft*

San Ga·bri·el \san-ˈgā-brē-əl\ **1** mountains S Calif. SW of Mojave desert & NE of Los Angeles; highest San Antonio Peak 10,080 *ft* **2** city SW Calif. S of Pasadena *pop* 29,176

San·ga·mon \ˈsaŋ-gə-mən\ river 225 *m*, *cen* Ill. flowing SW & W into the Illinois

San·gay \säŋ-ˈgī\ volcano 17,159 *ft* SE *cen* Ecuador

San·gi·he \ˌsäŋ-gē-ˈā\ *or* **San·gi** \ˈsäŋ-gē\ **1** islands Indonesia NE of Celebes *area* 134 **2** island, chief of the group

San Gi·mi·gna·no \ˌsän-ˌjē-mēn-ˈyän-(ˌ)ō\ commune *cen* Italy NW of Siena

San·gre de Cris·to \ˌsaŋ-grēd-ə-ˈkris-(ˌ)tō\ mountains S Colo. & N N.Mex. in Rocky mountains — see BLANCA PEAK

San·i·bel \ˈsan-ə-bəl, -ˌbel\ island SW Fla. SW of Fort Myers

San Il·de·fon·so \ˌsan-ˌil-də-ˈfän(t)-(ˌ)sō\ *or* **La Gran·ja** \lə-ˈgräŋ-(ˌ)hä\ commune *cen* Spain SE of Segovia

San Isi·dro \ˌsan-ə-ˈsē-(ˌ)drō\ city E Argentina *pop* 196,188

San Ja·cin·to \ˌsan-jə-ˈsint-ə\ river 100 *m* SE Tex. flowing S into Galveston Bay

San Joa·quin \ˌsan-wä-ˈkēn, -wȯ-\ river 350 *m*, *cen* Calif. flowing from the Sierra Nevada SW & then NW into the Sacramento

San Jo·se \ˌsan-ə-ˈzā *also* ˌsan-(h)ō-ˈzā\ city W Calif. SSE of San Francisco *pop* 445,779

San Jo·sé \ˌsan-ə-ˈzā, ˌsan-(h)ō-ˈzā\ city ✻ of Costa Rica *pop* 203,148

San Juan \san-ˈ(h)wän\ **1** river 360 *m* SW Colo., NW N.Mex., & SE Utah flowing W into the Colorado **2** mountains SW Colo. in the Rocky mountains — see UNCOMPAHGRE PEAK **3** islands NW Wash. between Vancouver I. & the mainland **4** city & port ✻ of Puerto Rico *pop* 452,749 **5** city W Argentina N of Mendoza *pop* 106,564 **6** hill E Cuba near Santiago de Cuba — **San Jua·ne·ro** \ˌsan-(h)wä-ˈne(ə)r-(ˌ)ō\ *n*

Sankt An·ton am Arl·berg \zäŋ(k)-ˈtän-ˌtōn-ˌäm-ˈär(ə)l-ˌbərg, -ˌbe(ə)rg\ village W Austria in Tirol W of Innsbruck

Sankt Gallen — see SAINT GALL

Sankt Gotthard — see SAINT GOTTHARD

Sankt Moritz — see SAINT MORITZ

San Le·an·dro \ˌsan-lē-ˈan-(ˌ)drō\ city W Calif. SE of Oakland *pop* 68,698

San Lu·cas, Cape \san-ˈlü-kəs\ headland NW Mexico, the S extremity of Baja California

San Lu·is \san-ˈlü-əs\ valley S Colo. & N N.Mex. along the upper Rio Grande between San Juan & Sangre de Cristo mountains

San Luis Obis·po \san-ˌlü-ə-sə-ˈbis-(ˌ)pō\ city W Calif. NW of Santa Barbara *pop* 28,036

San Lu·is Po·to·sí \ˌsän-lü-ˌē-ˌspōt-ə-ˈsē\ **1** state *cen* Mexico *area* 24,415, *pop* 1,257,028 **2** city, its ✻ *pop* 274,320

San Mar·cos \san-ˈmär-kəs\ city S Tex. NE of San Antonio *pop* 18,860

San Ma·ri·no \ˌsan-mə-ˈrē-(ˌ)nō\ **1** country S Europe on Italian peninsula SSW of Rimini; a republic *area* 24, *pop* 18,320 **2** town, its ✻ — **San Mar·i·nese** \ˌsan-ˌmar-ə-ˈnēz, -ˈnēs\ *adj or n*

San Mar·tín \ˌsan-mär-ˈtēn\ *or* **Ge·ne·ral San Martín** \ˌhā-nā-ˌräl-\ city E Argentina, NW suburb of Buenos Aires *pop* 279,213

San Ma·teo \ˌsan-mə-ˈtā-(ˌ)ō\ city W Calif. SSE of San Francisco *pop* 78,991

San Mi·guel de Tu·cu·mán \ˌsan-mig-ˌel-də-ˌtü-kə-ˈmän\ *or* **Tucumán** city NW Argentina *pop* 271,546

San Pab·lo \san-ˈpab-(ˌ)lō\ city W Calif. N of Oakland on **San Pablo Bay** (N extension of San Francisco Bay) *pop* 21,461

San Pe·dro \san-ˈpē-(ˌ)drō, -ˈpā-\ channel SW Calif. between Santa Catalina I. & the mainland

San Ra·fael \ˌsan-rə-ˈfel\ city W Calif. N of San Francisco on San Pablo Bay *pop* 38,977

San Re·mo \sän-ˈrā-(ˌ)mō, san-ˈrē-\ city & port NW Italy in Liguria near French border *pop* 63,735

San Sal·va·dor \san-ˈsal-və-ˌdȯ(ə)r\ **1** *or* **Wat·ling** \ˈwät-liŋ\ *or* **Wat·lings** \-liŋz\ island *cen* Bahama islands *area* 60 — see GUANAHANI **2** city ✻ of El Salvador *pop* 349,333

San Se·bas·tián \ˌsan-si-ˈbas-chən, ˌsän-ˌseb-əs-ˈchän\ city & port N Spain ✻ of Guipúzcoa on Bay of Biscay *pop* 155,346

San Stefano — see YESILKOY

San·ta Ana \ˌsant-ə-ˈan-ə\ **1** city SW Calif. ESE of Long Beach *pop* 156,601 **2** city NW El Salvador *pop* 168,047

Santa Bar·ba·ra \-ˈbär-b(ə-)rə\ **1** channel SW Calif. between the N Santa Barbara islands & mainland **2** *or* **Channel** islands Calif. in the Pacific off SW coast — see CATALINA, SAN CLEMENTE, SANTA CRUZ, SANTA ROSA **3** city S Calif. *pop* 70,215

ə abut ᵊ kitten, F table ər further a back ā bake
ä cot, cart å F bac aù out ch chin e less ē easy
g gift i trip ī life j joke k̲ G ich ⁿ F vin ŋ sing
ō flow ȯ flaw œ F bœuf œ̄ F feu ȯi coin th thing
t̲h̲ this ü loot ù foot ue G Füllen ue̅ F rue y yet
ʸ F digne \dēnʸ\, nuit \nwʸē\ yü few yù furious zh vision

Santa Catalina — see CATALINA
San·ta Ca·ta·ri·na \ˌsant-ə-ˌkat-ə-ˈrē-nə\ state S Brazil bordering on the Atlantic ✱ Florianópolis *area* 31,118, *pop* 2,911,749
Santa Clara \-ˈklar-ə, -ˈkler-\ **1** city W Calif. NW of San Jose *pop* 87,717 **2** city W *cen* Cuba *pop* (municipality) 202,120
Santa Cruz \-ˈkrüz\ **1** island SW Calif. in NW Santa Barbara islands **2** city W Calif. S of San Jose on Monterey Bay *pop* 32,076 **3** — see SAINT CROIX **4** river 250 *m* S Argentina flowing E into the Atlantic **5** city E Bolivia *pop* 108,720 **6** islands SW Pacific N of the New Hebrides, chief island Ndeni; administratively attached to Brit. Solomon islands *area* 380
Santa Cruz de Te·ne·rife \-də-ˌten-ə-ˈrēf[-(ˌ)ā], -ˈrif\ **1** province Spain comprising W Canary islands *area* 1528, *pop* 590,514 **2** city & port, its ✱, on NE Tenerife I. *pop* 163,743
San·ta Fe \ˌsant-ə-ˈfā\ **1** city ✱ of N.Mex. *pop* 41,167 **2** city *cen* Argentina *pop* 208,900 — **San·ta Fe·an** \-ˈfā-ən\ *n*
Santa Fe Trail pioneer route to the Southwest used esp. 1821–80 from vicinity of Kansas City, Mo., to Santa Fe, N.Mex.
San·ta Is·a·bel \ˌsant-ə-ˈiz-ə-ˌbel\ **1** *or* **Santa Ys·a·bel** \-ˈiz-\ island W Pacific in the E *cen* Solomons NE of Guadalcanal *area* 1500 **2** city N Fernando Po, ✱ of Equatorial Guinea *pop* 37,152
Santa Ma·ria \-mə-ˈrē-ə\ city W Calif. NW of Santa Barbara *pop* 32,749
Santa Ma·ría \-mə-ˈrē-ə\ volcano 12,300 *ft* W Guatemala
Santa Mar·ta \-ˈmärt-ə\ city & port N Colombia on the Caribbean E of Barranquilla *pop* 137,474
Santa Mon·i·ca \-ˈmän-i-kə\ city SW Calif. adjacent to Los Angeles on **Santa Monica Bay** (inlet of the Pacific) *pop* 88,289
San·tan·der \ˌsän-ˌtän-ˈde(ə)r, ˌsan-ˌtan-\ **1** province N Spain in N Old Castile bordering on Bay of Biscay *area* 2108, *pop* 467,138 **2** city & port, its ✱, on Bay of Biscay *pop* 133,014
San·ta Pau·la \ˌsant-ə-ˈpȯ-lə\ city SW Calif. NW of Los Angeles *pop* 18,001
San·ta·rém \ˌsant-ə-ˈrem\ city N Brazil in W Pará at confluence of the Tapajoz & Amazon rivers *pop* 111,706
San·ta Ro·sa \ˌsant-ə-ˈrō-zə\ **1** island SW Calif. in NW Santa Barbara islands **2** city W Calif. N of San Francisco *pop* 50,006
San·tee \(ˈ)san-ˈtē, ˈsan-ˌ\ river 143 *m* S.C. flowing SE into the Atlantic — see CONGAREE
San·ti·a·go \ˌsant-ē-ˈäg-(ˌ)ō, ˌsänt-\ **1** city ✱ of Chile *pop* 2,516,421 **2** *or* **Santiago de los Ca·ba·lle·ros** \-də-ˌlōs-ˌkäb-ə-ˈye(ə)r-(ˌ)ōs\ city N *cen* Dominican Republic *pop* 103,861 **3** *or* **Santiago de Com·pos·te·la** \-də-ˌkäm-pə-ˈstel-ə\ commune NW Spain S of La Coruña *pop* 70,893 — **San·ti·a·gan** \ˌsant-ē-ˈäg-ən, ˌsänt-\ *n*
Santiago de Cu·ba \-də-ˈkyü-bə\ city & port SE Cuba *pop* (municipality) 264,200
Santiago del Es·te·ro \-ˌdel-ə-ˈste(ə)r-(ˌ)ō\ city N Argentina SE of San Miguel de Tucumán *pop* 80,395
San·to Do·min·go \ˌsant-əd-ə-ˈmiŋ-(ˌ)gō\ *or* **San Domingo** \ˌsan-də-\ **1** *or* **Santo Domingo de Guz·mán** \-də-gü-ˈsmän\ *or formerly* **Tru·ji·llo** \trü-ˈhē-(ˌ)(y)ō\ *or* **Ci·u·dad Trujillo** \ˌsē-ü-ˌthä-, ˌsē-ü-ˌdad-\ city & port ✱ of Dominican Republic on Caribbean sea *pop* 654,757 **2** — see HISPANIOLA **3** — see DOMINICAN REPUBLIC — **San·to Do·min·gan** \ˌsant-əd-ə-ˈmiŋ-gən\ *adj or n*
San·to·rin \ˌsant-ə-ˈrēn, -ˈrin\ *or* NGk **San·to·ri·ni** \-ˈrē-nē\ *or* **Thi·ra** \ˈthir-ə\ *or anc* **The·ra** \ˈthir-ə\ island Greece in S Cyclades *area* 30
San·tos \ˈsant-əs\ city & port SE Brazil in SE São Paulo state SSE of São Paulo on an island in a tidal inlet *pop* 313,771
San·to To·mé de Gua·ya·na \ˌsänt-ō-tə-ˈmād-ə-gwə-ˈyän-ə\ *or* **San To·mé de Guayana** \ˌsän-tō-ˈmād-\ *or* **Ci·u·dad Guayana** \ˌsē-ü-ˌthä-, -ü-ˌdad-\ city E Venezuela near junction of the Caroní & Orinoco *pop* 140,319
San·tur·ce \sän-ˈtü(ə)r-(ˌ)sā\ a NE section of San Juan, Puerto Rico
São Fran·cis·co \ˌsaùⁿ(m)-frən-ˈsis-(ˌ)kō\ river 1800 *m* E Brazil flowing from S *cen* Minas Gerais NE & E into the Atlantic
São Luís \ˌsaùⁿ-lù-ˈēs\ city & port NE Brazil ✱ of Maranhão state on Maranhão I. *pop* 218,783
São Ma·nuel \ˌsaùⁿ-mən-ˈwel\ river 600 *m, cen* Brazil flowing NW to join the Juruena forming the Tapajoz
São Mi·guel \ˌsaùⁿ-mi-ˈgel\ island Portugal in E Azores; chief town Ponta Delgada *area* 297
Saône \ˈsōn\ river 275 *m* E France flowing SSW into the Rhone
São Pau·lo \saùⁿ(m)-ˈpaù-(ˌ)lü, -(ˌ)lō\ **1** state SE Brazil *area* 95,-459, *pop* 17,716,186 **2** city, its ✱, on Tietê river *pop* 5,684,706
São Ro·que, Cape \saùⁿ-ˈrō-kə\ headland NE Brazil N of Natal
São Salvador — see SALVADOR
São Tia·go \ˌsaùⁿ(n)t-ē-ˈäg-(ˌ)ü, -(ˌ)ō\ *or* **San·ti·a·go** \ˌsant-ē-ˈäg-(ˌ)ō\ island Cape Verde islands, largest of the group; chief town Praia *area* 359
São To·mé *or* **Sao Tho·mé** \ˌsaùⁿ(n)t-ə-ˈmā\ island W Africa in Gulf of Guinea; with Príncipe I., forms Portuguese overseas territory of **São Tomé and Príncipe** (✱ São Tomé *area* 377, *pop* 70,000)
São Vicente, Cabo de — see SAINT VINCENT (Cape)
Sap·po·ro \ˈsäp-ə-ˌrō; sə-ˈpōr-(ˌ)ō, -ˈpȯr-\ city Japan on W Hokkaido *pop* 957,000
Sa·pul·pa \sə-ˈpəl-pə\ city NE Okla. SW of Tulsa *pop* 15,159
Saq·qa·ra *or* **Sak·ka·ra** \sə-ˈkär-ə\ village N Egypt SW of ruins of Memphis
Sarabat — see GEDIZ
Saragossa — see ZARAGOZA
Sa·ra·je·vo \ˈsär-ə-ye-ˌvō\ *or* **Se·ra·je·vo** \ˈser-\ city *cen* Yugoslavia ✱ of Bosnia & Herzegovina *pop* 223,000
Sar·a·nac \ˈsar-ə-ˌnak\ river 100 *m* NE N.Y. flowing NE from **Saranac Lakes** (three lakes in the Adirondacks: Upper Saranac, Middle Saranac, & Lower Saranac) into Lake Champlain
Sa·ransk \sə-ˈrän(t)sk, -ˈran(t)sk\ city U.S.S.R. in *cen* Soviet Russia, Europe ✱ of Mordvinian Republic *pop* 190,000
Sar·a·so·ta \ˌsar-ə-ˈsōt-ə\ city W Fla. S of Tampa *pop* 40,237
Sar·a·to·ga \ˌsar-ə-ˈtō-gə\ lake 7 *m* long E N.Y. S of Lake George **2** city W Calif. SW of San Jose *pop* 27,110
Saratoga Springs *or* **Saratoga** city NE N.Y. *pop* 18,845
Sa·ra·tov \sə-ˈrät-əf\ city U.S.S.R. in SE Soviet Russia, Europe, on a reservoir of Volga river *pop* 758,000
Sa·ra·wak \sə-ˈrä-(ˌ)wä(k), -ˌwak\ country N Borneo bordering on So. China sea; formerly a Brit. colony, since 1963 a territory of Federation of Malaysia ✱ Kuching *area* 47,000, *pop* 977,013
Sardica — see SOFIA
Sar·din·ia \sär-ˈdin-ē-ə, -ˈdin-yə\ *or* It **Sar·de·gna** \sär-ˈdän-yə\ island Italy S of Corsica; with surrounding smaller islands, constitutes a region of Italy ✱ Cagliari *area* 9283, *pop* 1,488,008
Sar·dis \ˈsärd-əs\ *or* **Sar·des** \ˈsärd-(ˌ)ēz\ ancient city W Asia Minor ✱ of ancient kingdom of Lydia; site *ab* 50 *m* E of Izmir — **Sar·di·an** \ˈsärd-ē-ən\ *adj or n*
Sa·re·ma *or* Estonian **Saa·re·maa** \ˈsär-ə-ˌmä\ island U.S.S.R. in Estonia at mouth of Gulf of Riga *area* 1010
Sar·gas·so sea \sär-ˌgas-(ˌ)ō-\ tract of comparatively still water N Atlantic lying chiefly between 25° & 35° N & 40° & 70° W
Sark \ˈsärk\ island in the English channel, one of the Channel islands; a dependency of Guernsey *area* 2
Sar·ma·tia \sär-ˈmā-sh(ē-)ə\ ancient region E Europe in modern Poland & Russia between the Vistula & the Volga — **Sar·ma·tian** \-shən\ *adj or n*
Sar·nia \ˈsär-nē-ə\ city Canada in SE Ont. on St. Clair river opposite Port Huron, Mich. *pop* 57,644
Sa·ron·ic Gulf \sə-ˌrän-ik\ inlet of the Aegean SE Greece between Attica & the Peloponnesus
Sa·ros, Gulf of \ˈsa(ə)r-ˌäs, ˈse(ə)r-\ inlet of the Aegean SW Turkey in Europe N of Gallipoli peninsula
Sarre — see SAAR
Sarthe \ˈsärt\ river 175 *m* NW France flowing S to unite with the Mayenne forming the Maine
Sarum, 1 New Sarum — see SALISBURY **2** OLD SARUM
Sa·se·bo \ˈsäs-ə-ˌbō\ city & port Japan in NW Kyushu on an inlet of East China sea *pop* 266,000
Sas·katch·e·wan \sə-ˈskach-ə-wən, sa-, -ˌwän\ **1** river 340 *m* S *cen* Canada formed by confluence in *cen* Sask. of two branches rising in the Rockies in Alta., the **North Saskatchewan** (760 *m*) & the **South Saskatchewan** (865 *m*), & flowing E into Lake Winnipeg **2** province SW Canada ✱ Regina *area* 237,975, *pop* 928,000 — **Sas·katch·e·wan·ian** \-ˌskach-ə-ˈwän-ē-ən\ *adj or n*
Sas·ka·toon \ˌsas-kə-ˈtün\ city Canada in *cen* Sask. *pop* 126,449
Sas·sa·ri \ˈsäs-ə-(ˌ)rē\ commune Italy in NW Sardinia *pop* 106,143
Sa·til·la \sə-ˈtil-ə\ river 220 *m* SE Ga. flowing E into the Atlantic
Sat·pu·ra \ˈsät-pə-rə\ range of hills W *cen* India between Narbada & Tapti rivers
Sa·tu–Ma·re \ˌsä-(ˌ)tü-ˈmär-(ˌ)ā\ city NW Rumania in Transylvania on the Somes *pop* 78,812
Sau·di Arabia \ˌsaùd-ē-, sä-ˌüd-ē-\ country SW Asia occupying most of Arabian peninsula; a kingdom, comprising former kingdoms of Nejd & Hejaz & principality of Asir ✱ Riyadh *area* 870,000, *pop* 7,200,000 — **Saudi** *adj or n* — **Saudi Arabian** *adj or n*
Sau·gus \ˈsȯ-gəs\ town NE Mass. W of Lynn *pop* 25,110
Sault Sainte Ma·rie \ˌsü-(ˌ)sānt-mə-ˈrē\ **1** city NE Mich. in upper peninsula *pop* 15,136 **2** city Canada in S Ont. *pop* 80,332
Sault Sainte Marie canals *or* **Soo canals** \ˌsü-\ *or* **Soo locks** three ship canals, two in the U.S. (four parallel locks) & one in Canada (one lock), at rapids in St. Marys river connecting Lakes Superior & Huron
Sau·mur \sō-ˈm(y)ù(ə)r, -ˈmœr\ commune NW France on the Loire SE of Angers *pop* 21,551
Sau·rash·tra \saù-ˈräsh-trə\ former state (1948–56) W India on Kathiawar peninsula; in Bombay state 1956–60 & since 1960 in Gujarat
Sa·va \ˈsäv-ə\ river 450 *m* N Yugoslavia flowing from Italian border E into the Danube at Belgrade
Savage — see NIUE
Sa·vaii \sə-ˈvī-ˌē\ island SW *cen* Pacific, largest in Samoa, in Western Samoa
Sa·van·nah \sə-ˈvan-ə\ **1** river 314 *m* E Ga. flowing SE to the Atlantic & forming Ga.-S.C. boundary **2** city & port E Ga. at mouth of Savannah river *pop* 118,349
Save — see SABI
Sa·vo \ˈsäv-(ˌ)ō\ island W Pacific in SE Solomon islands N of W end of Guadalcanal
Sa·vo·na \sə-ˈvō-nə\ commune & port NW Italy SW of Genoa *pop* 17,168
Sa·voy \sə-ˈvȯi\ *or* F **Sa·voie** \sá-vwá\ *or* It **Sa·vo·ia** \sä-ˈvȯ-yä\ region SE France in Savoy Alps SW of Switzerland & bordering on Italy; duchy 1416–1720, part of kingdom of Sardinia 1720–1860; became part of France 1860 — **Sa·voy·ard** \sə-ˈvȯi-ˌärd, ˌsav-ˌȯi-ˈärd, ˌsav-ˌwä-ˈyär(d)\ *adj or n*
Savoy Alps section of W Alps SE France — see MONT BLANC
Sa·watch *or* **Sa·guache** \sə-ˈwäch, ˈsə-wəsh\ mountain range *cen* Colo. in Rocky mountains — see ELBERT (Mount)
Saxe \ˈsaks\ SAXONY — its French form, used in English chiefly in names of former duchies in Thuringia: **Saxe–Al·ten·burg** \ˈält-ᵊn-ˌbù(ə)rg\, **Saxe–Co·burg** \ˈkō-ˌbərg\, **Saxe–Go·tha** \ˈgōt-ə, ˈgō-thə\, **Saxe–Mei·ning·en** \ˈmī-niŋ-ən\, & **Saxe–Wei·mar–Ei·se·nach** \-ˈvī-ˌmär-ˈīz-ᵊn-ˌäk, -ˌäk\
Sax·o·ny \ˈsak-s(ə-)nē\ *or* G **Sach·sen** \ˈzäk-sən\ **1** region & former duchy NW Germany S of Jutland peninsula between the Elbe & the Rhine **2** region & former state E Germany N of the Erzgebirge — see LOWER SAXONY, SAXE
Sa·yan \sə-ˈyän\ mountains U.S.S.R. in S Soviet Russia, Asia, on border of Tuva N of Altai mountains
Sayre·ville \ˈsa(ə)r-ˌvil, ˈse(ə)r-\ borough E *cen* N.J. *pop* 32,508
Says Law \ˈsäz-ˌlȯ\ mountain 1749 *ft* SE Scotland; highest in Lammermuir hills
Sa·zan \ˈsäz-ˌän\ *or* It **Sa·se·no** \sə-ˈzā-(ˌ)nō, sä-\ island Albania at entrance to Bay of Vlone
Sca·fell \ˈskȯ-ˈfel\ mountain 3162 *ft* NW England in Cumbrians SW of Keswick; second highest peak in England

Scafell Pike mountain 3210 *ft* NW England in Cumberland 1 *m* NE of Scafell; highest in the Cumbrians & in England
Scamander — see MENDERES
Scan·di·na·via \ˌskan-də-ˈnā-vē-ə, -vyə\ **1** peninsula N Europe occupied by Norway & Sweden **2** Denmark, Norway, Sweden, & sometimes also Iceland, the Faeroe islands, & Finland
Scapa Flow \ˌskap-ə-ˈflō\ sea basin N Scotland in the Orkneys
Scar·bor·ough \ˈskär-ˌbər-ə, -ˌbə-rə, -b(ə-)rə\ municipal borough & port NE England in North Riding, Yorkshire *pop* 44,370
Scarpanto — see KARPATHOS
Scars·dale \ˈskärz-ˌdāl\ village SE N.Y. NE of Yonkers *pop* 19,229
Schaer·beek *or* **Schaar·beek** \ˈskär-ˌbāk\ commune *cen* Belgium, NE suburb of Brussels *pop* 119,810
Schaff·hau·sen \shäf-ˈhau̇z-ᵊn\ *or* F **Schaff·house** \shȧ-füz\ **1** *or* **Falls of the Rhine** *or* G **Rhein·fall** \ˈrīn-ˌfäl\ waterfall in the Rhine N Switzerland 370 *ft* wide, with two principal falls 50 *ft* & 60 *ft* high **2** canton N Switzerland bordering on Germany *area* 114, *pop* 72,854 **3** commune, its ✻ *pop* 37,035
Schaum·burg \ˈshäm-(ˌ)bərg\ village NE Ill. NW of Chicago *pop* 18,730
Schaum·burg–Lip·pe \ˌshau̇m-ˌbu̇(ə)rg-ˈlip-ə\ state of Germany 1918–33 in NW between Westphalia & Hannover
Schei·degg \ˈshī-ˌdek\ village *cen* Switzerland in Bern canton on Little Scheidegg Pass
Scheldt \ˈskelt\ *or* **Schel·de** \ˈskel-də\ *or* F **Es·caut** \es-kō\ river 270 *m* W Europe flowing from N France through Belgium into North sea in Netherlands
Sche·nec·ta·dy \skə-ˈnek-təd-ē\ city E N.Y. *pop* 77,859
Sche·ve·ning·en \ˈskā-və-ˌniŋ-ən\ town SW Netherlands on North sea W of The Hague
Schie·dam \skē-ˈdäm\ commune SW Netherlands *pop* 83,049
Schles·wig \ˈs(h)les-(ˌ)wig, -(ˌ)wik\ **1** *or* Dan **Sles·vig** \ˈslis-vē\ region N Germany & S Denmark in S Jutland peninsula **2** city N Germany *pop ab* 33,265
Schleswig–Hol·stein \-ˈhōl-ˌstīn\ state N Germany consisting of Holstein & part of Schleswig ✻ Kiel *area* 6052, *pop* 2,561,200
Schou·ten \ˈskau̇t-ᵊn\ islands W New Guinea at mouth of Geelvink Bay *area* 1230
Schuyl·kill \ˈskül-ˌkil, ˈskü-kəl\ river 131 *m* SE Pa. flowing SE into the Delaware at Philadelphia
Schwaben — see SWABIA
Schwarzwald — see BLACK FOREST
Schwein·furt \ˈshfīn-ˌfu̇(ə)rt\ city W Germany on Main river *pop* 59,402
Schweiz — see SWITZERLAND
Schwe·rin \shfā-ˈrēn\ city E Germany in Mecklenburg E of Hamburg *pop* 96,949
Schwyz \ˈshfēts\ **1** canton E *cen* Switzerland *area* 351, *pop* 92,-072 **2** town, its ✻, E of Lucerne
Scil·ly \ˈsil-ē\ island group SW England off Lands End comprised of 140 islands ✻ Hugh Town (on St. Mary's, largest island) *area* 6, *pop* 2428 — **Scil·lo·ni·an** \sil-ˈō-nē-ən\ *adj or n*
Sci·o·to \sī-ˈōt-ə\ river 237 *m* Ohio flowing S into the Ohio
Scit·u·ate \ˈsich-ə-wət\ town E Mass. SE of Boston *pop* 16,973
Scone \ˈskün\ locality E Scotland NE of Perth
Sco·pus, Mount \ˈskō-pəs\ mountain Palestine in W Jordan in small area belonging to Israel
Scores·by Sound \ˈskō(ə)rz-bē, ˈskȯ(ə)rz-\ inlet of Norwegian sea E Greenland N of 70°N
Sco·tia \ˈskō-shə\ sea part of the S Atlantic SE of Falkland islands, W of So. Sandwich islands, & N of So. Orkney islands
Scot·land \ˈskät-lənd\ *or* L **Cal·e·do·nia** \ˌkal-ə-ˈdō-nyə, -nē-ə\ *or* ML **Sco·tia** \ˈskō-shə\ country N Great Britain; a division of United Kingdom of Great Britain & Northern Ireland ✻ Edinburgh *area* 29,794, *pop* 5,230,152
Scotts Bluff National Monument \ˈskäts\ reservation W Nebr. on the No. Platte including **Scotts Bluff** (high butte that was a landmark on the Oregon Trail)
Scotts·dale \ˈskäts-ˌdāl\ city SW *cen* Ariz. E of Phoenix *pop* 67,823
Scran·ton \ˈskrant-ᵊn\ city NE Pa. *pop* 103,564
Scun·thorpe \ˈskən-ˌthȯ(ə)rp\ municipal borough E England in Parts of Lindsey, Lincolnshire, WSW of Hull *pop* 70,880
Scu·ta·ri *or* **Sku·ta·ri** \ˈsküt-ə-rē\ **1** *or Albanian* **Shko·der** \ˈshkōd-ər\ city NW Albania *pop* 49,830 **2** lake NW Albania & S Yugoslavia *area* 130 **3** — see USKUDAR
Scyros — see SKYROS
Scyth·ia \ˈsith-ē-ə, ˈsit͟h-\ the country of the ancient Scythians comprising parts of Europe & Asia now in U.S.S.R. in regions N & NE of Black sea & E of Aral sea
Sea islands islands SE U.S. in the Atlantic off coast of S.C., Ga., & Fla. between mouths of Santee & St. Johns rivers
Seal Beach city SW Calif. SE of Los Angeles *pop* 24,441
Sea·side \ˈsē-ˌsīd\ city W Calif. on Monterey Bay *pop* 35,935
Se·at·tle \sē-ˈat-ᵊl\ city & port W Wash. between Puget Sound & Lake Washington *pop* 530,831 — **Se·at·tle·ite** \-ᵊl-ˌīt\ *n*
Se·ba·go \sə-ˈbā-(ˌ)gō\ lake 13 *m* long SW Me.
Sebaste, 1 *or* **Sebastia** — see SIVAS **2** — see SAMARIA
Sebha — see SABHA
Se·cun·der·abad *or* **Si·kan·dar·abad** \si-ˈkən-də-rə-ˌbad, -ˌbäd\ city S *cen* India in Andhra Pradesh, NE suburb of Hyderabad *pop* 187,471
Se·da·lia \sə-ˈdāl-yə\ city W *cen* Mo. *pop* 22,847
Se·dan \si-ˈdan, *F* sə-däⁿ\ city NE France on the Meuse NE of Reims *pop* 23,037
Sedge·moor \ˈsej-ˌmu̇(ə)r, -ˌmō(ə)r, -ˌmȯ(ə)r\ tract of moorland SW England in *cen* Somerset
Sedom — see SODOM
Se·go·via \sā-ˈgō-vyə, -vē-ə\ **1** — see COCO **2** province N *cen* Spain in Old Castile *area* 2635, *pop* 162,770 **3** commune, its ✻, NW of Madrid *pop* 41,880
Se·guin \sə-ˈgēn\ city SE *cen* Tex. *pop* 15,934
Seim *or* **Seym** \ˈsām\ river 435 *m* U.S.S.R. in SW *cen* Soviet Russia, Europe, flowing W into the Desna
Seine \ˈsān, ˈsen\ river 480 *m* N France flowing NW into **Bay of the Seine** (inlet of English channel)
Sekia el Hamra — see SAGUIA EL HAMRA
Sek·on·di \ˌsek-ən-ˈdē\ city & port SW Ghana NE of Takoradi *pop* (with Takoradi) 89,686
Se·lang·or \sə-ˈlaŋ-ər, -ˌō(ə)r\ state *cen* Federation of Malaysia on Strait of Malacca ✻ Kuala Lumpur *area* 3166, *pop* 1,629,386
Sel·en·ga \ˌsel-ən-ˈgä\ river 750 *m* N *cen* Asia rising in W Outer Mongolia & flowing to Lake Baikal
Se·leu·cia \sə-ˈlü-sh(ē-)ə\ **1** *or* **Seleucia Tra·che·o·tis** \ˌtrā-kē-ˈōt-əs\ ancient city SE Asia Minor in Cilicia SW of Tarsus **2** ancient city, chief city of the Seleucid Empire; ruins now in Iraq on the Tigris SSE of Baghdad **3** *or* **Seleucia Pi·eria** \pī-ˈir-ē-ə, -ˈer-\ ancient city Asia Minor N of mouth of the Orontes; port for Antioch
Sel·kirk \ˈsel-ˌkərk\ **1** mountains SW Canada in SE B.C. W of the Rockies; highest Mt. Sir Sandford 11,590 *ft* **2** *or* **Sel·kirk·shire** \-ˌshi(ə)r, -shər\ county SE Scotland *area* 267, *pop* 20,868 **3** burgh, its ✻, SE of Edinburgh
Sel·ma \ˈsel-mə\ city *cen* Ala. W of Montgomery *pop* 27,379
Se·ma·rang *or* **Sa·ma·rang** \sə-ˈmär-ˌäŋ\ city & port Indonesia in *cen* Java on N coast *pop* 503,153
Sem·i·nole, Lake \ˈsem-ə-ˌnōl\ reservoir SW Ga. & NW Fla. formed by confluence of Chattahoochee & Flint rivers & emptying by the Apalachicola
Sem·i·pa·la·tinsk \ˌsem-i-pə-ˈlä-ˌtin(t)sk\ city U.S.S.R. in Soviet Central Asia in NE Kazakhstan on Irtysh river *pop* 236,000
Sen·dai \(ˈ)sen-ˈdī\ city Japan in NE Honshu *pop* 520,000
Sen·e·ca \ˈsen-i-kə\ lake 35 *m* long W *cen* N.Y.; one of the Finger lakes
Sen·e·gal \ˌsen-i-ˈgȯl\ **1** river 1050 *m* W Africa flowing from Fouta Djallon NW & W into the Atlantic **2** country W Africa on the Atlantic; a republic of the French Community, formerly a territory of French West Africa ✻ Dakar *area* 81,081, *pop* 4,020,000 — **Sen·e·ga·lese** \ˌsen-i-gə-ˈlēz, -ˈlēs\ *adj or n*
Sen·e·gam·bia \ˌsen-ə-ˈgam-bē-ə\ region W Africa around Senegal & Gambia rivers — **Sen·e·gam·bi·an** \-ən\ *adj or n*
Sen·lac \ˈsen-ˌlak\ hill SE England in Sussex NW of Hastings
Sen·lis \säⁿ-lēs\ commune N France NNE of Paris
Sen·nar *or* **Sen·naar** \sə-ˈnär\ region E Sudan chiefly between the White Nile & the Blue Nile; an ancient kingdom
Sens \ˈsäⁿs\ city NE *cen* France WSW of Troyes *pop* 23,035
Seoul \ˈsōl\ *or* **Kyong·song** \kē-ˈōŋ-ˈsȯŋ\ city S Korea on Han river; formerly ✻ of Korea, since 1948 ✻ of So. Korea *pop* 3,794,959
Se·pik \ˈsā-pik\ river 600 *m* N New Guinea
Sept–Iles \se-ˈtē(ə)l\ *or* **Seven Islands** city Canada in E Que. at the mouth of the St. Lawrence *pop* 24,320
Se·quoia National Park \si-ˈkwȯi-ə\ reservation SE *cen* Calif. *area* 602; includes Mt. Whitney
Serajevo — see SARAJEVO
Seram — see CERAM
Ser·bia \ˈsər-bē-ə\ *or formerly* **Ser·via** \-vē-ə\ federated republic SE Yugoslavia traversed by the Morava; once a kingdom ✻ Belgrade *area* 34,080, *pop* 8,436,547
Serdica — see SOFIA
Serendib — see CEYLON
Ser·en·geti Plain \ˌser-ən-ˈget-ē\ area N Tanzania including **Serengeti National Park** (wild game reserve *area ab* 5000)
Ser·gi·pe \sər-ˈzhē-pə\ state NE Brazil ✻ Aracajú *area* 8321, *pop* 900,119
Se·rin·ga·pa·tam \sə-ˌriŋ-gə-pə-ˈtam\ *or* **Sri·ran·ga·pat·nam** \srē-ˌrəŋ-gə-ˈpət-nəm\ town S India N of city of Mysore
Se·rowe \sə-ˈrō-ē\ city S Africa in E Botswana *pop* 34,186
Ser·ra da Es·tre·la \ˌser-ə-ˌdä-e-ˈstrel-ə\ mountain range Portugal; highest point Malhão da Estrela (highest in Portugal) 6532 *ft*
Serra do Mar \-də-ˈmär\ mountain range S Brazil along coast; highest point 7323 *ft*
Serra Pa·ca·rai·ma \-ˌpak-ə-ˈrī-mə\ *or* **Si·er·ra Pacaraima** \sē-ˌer-ə-\ mountain range N So. America in SE Venezuela, N Brazil, & W Guyana — see RORAIMA
Ser·ra Pa·ri·ma \ˌser-ə-pə-ˈrē-mə\ *or* **Si·er·ra Parima** \sē-ˌer-ə-\ mountain range N So. America on Venezuela-Brazil border SW of Serra Pacaraima; source of the Orinoco; highest peak *ab* 8000 *ft*
Ses·tos \ˈses-təs\ ruined town Turkey in Europe on the Dardanelles (Hellespont) at narrowest point
Sète \ˈset\ *or formerly* **Cette** \ˈset\ commune & port S France SSW of Montpellier *pop* 40,576
Sete Quedas — see GUAIRÁ FALLS
Sé·tif \sā-ˈtēf\ commune NE Algeria *pop* 98,000
Se·tú·bal \sə-ˈtü-bəl, -ˌbäl\ city & port SW Portugal *pop* 64,531
Se·van \sə-ˈvän\ *or* **Se·vang** \-ˈväŋ\ *or* Turk **Gok·cha** \ˈgə(r)k-chə\ lake U.S.S.R. in N Armenian Republic *area* 540
Se·vas·to·pol \sə-ˈvas-tə-ˌpōl, -ˌpȯl, -pəl; ˌsev-ə-ˈstō-pəl, -ˈstō-\ *or formerly* **Se·bas·to·pol** \-ˈbas-; ˌseb-ə-\ city & port U.S.S.R. in Soviet Russia, Europe, in SW Crimea *pop* 229,000
Sev·ern \ˈsev-ərn\ **1** inlet (**Severn river**) of Chesapeake Bay, Md., on which Annapolis is situated **2** river 610 *m* Canada in NW Ont. flowing NE into Hudson Bay **3** river 210 *m* Great Britain flowing from E *cen* Wales into Bristol channel in England
Severnaya Dvina — see NORTHERN DVINA
Se·ver·na·ya Zem·lya \ˈsev-ər-nə-ˌyä-ˌzem-lē-ˈä\ islands U.S.S.R. in N Soviet Russia, Asia, N of Taimyr peninsula in Arctic ocean between Kara & Laptev seas *area* 14,300
Se·vier \sə-ˈvi(ə)r\ river 280 *m* SW *cen* Utah flowing into **Sevier Lake** (25 *m* long; saline)

ə abut ᵊ kitten, F table ər further a back ā bake
ä cot, cart ȧ F bac au̇ out ch chin e less ē easy
g gift i trip ī life j joke k̲ G ich ⁿ F vin ŋ sing
ō flow ȯ flaw œ F bœuf œ̄ F feu ȯi coin th thing
t͟h this ü loot u̇ foot u̯e G Füllen ue̅ F rue y yet
ʸ F digne \dēnʸ\, nuit \nwʸē\ yü few yu̇ furious zh vision

Se·ville \sə-'vil\ *or* Sp **Se·vi·lla** \sä-'vē-(,)(y)ä\ **1** province SW Spain *area* 5428, *pop* 1,327,190 **2** city, its ✱ *pop* 503,489
Sè·vres \'sevrᵊ\ commune N France SW of Paris *pop* 20,083
Sew·ard \'sü-ərd\ peninsula 180 *m* long & 130 *m* wide W Alaska projecting into Bering sea between Kotzebue & Norton sounds — see PRINCE OF WALES (Cape)
Sey·chelles \sä-'shel(z)\ island group W Indian ocean NE of Madagascar; a Brit. colony ✱ Victoria (on Mahé I.) *area* 100, *pop* 54,000
Sey·han \sā-'hän\ **1** *or* **Sei·hun** \-'hün\ river 300 *m* Turkey flowing SSW into the Mediterranean **2** — see ADANA
Seym — see SEIM
Sfax \'sfaks\ city & port Tunisia on Gulf of Gabes *pop* 79,585
's Gravenhage — see HAGUE (The)
Sha·ba \'shäb-ə\ *or formerly* **Ka·tan·ga** \kə-'täŋ-gə, -'taŋ-\ region SE Zaire; chief city Lubumbashi
Shah·ja·han·pur \,shäj-ə-'hän-,pu̇(ə)r\ city N India in *cen* Uttar Pradesh NNW of Kanpur *pop* 122,381
Shah·pur \shä-'pu̇(ə)r\ ancient city SW Iran W of Shiraz
Sha·ker Heights \,shā-kər-\ city NE Ohio E of Cleveland *pop* 36,306
Shakh·ty \'shäk-tē\ *or* **Ale·ksan·drovsk Gru·shev·ski** \,al-ik-'san-drəfsk-grü-'shef-skē, ,el-, -ig-'zan-, -'shev-\ city U.S.S.R. in SE Soviet Russia, Europe, NE of Rostov *pop* 205,000
Shang·hai \shaŋ-'hī\ municipality & port E China in SE Kiangsu on the Hwang Pu near the Yangtze estuary *pop* 11,000,000
Shang·kiu \'shäŋ-kē-'ü\ city E China in E Honan *pop* 250,000
Shan·non \'shan-ən\ river 240 *m* W Ireland flowing S & W into the Atlantic
Shan·si \'shän-'sē\ province N China bordering on Yellow river ✱ Taiyuan *area* 60,656, *pop* 18,000,000
Shan State \'shän, 'shan\ *or formerly* **Federated Shan States** province E Burma comprising a mountainous region (the **Shan hills**) ✱ Taunggyi *pop* 2,725,000
Shan·tung \'shan-'təŋ\ **1** peninsula E China projecting ENE between Yellow sea & Po Hai **2** province E China including Shantung peninsula ✱ Tsinan *area* 59,189, *pop* 57,000,000
Shao·hing *or* **Shao·hsing** \'shau̇-'shiŋ\ city E China in N Chekiang SE of Hangchow *pop* 225,000
Shao·yang \'shau̇-'yäŋ\ *or formerly* **Pao·king** \'bau̇-'chiŋ\ city SE China in *cen* Hunan W of Hengyang *pop* 275,000
Sha·ri *or* **Cha·ri** \'shär-ē\ river 1400 *m* N *cen* Africa in Chad flowing NW into Lake Chad
Shark Bay inlet of Indian ocean 150 *m* long W Western Australia, at *ab* 25°S
Shar·on \'shar-ən, 'sher-\ city NW Pa. *pop* 22,653
Sharon, Plain of region Israel on coast between Mt. Carmel & Jaffa
Sha·si \'shä-'sē\ city E *cen* China in S Hupei on the Yangtze *pop* 125,000
Shas·ta, Mount \'shas-tə\ mountain 14,162 *ft* N Calif. in Cascade range; an isolated volcanic cone
Shatt–al–Ar·ab \,shat-,al-'ar-əb\ river 120 *m* SE Iraq formed by Tigris & Euphrates rivers & flowing SE into Persian Gulf
Shaw·an·gunk Mountains \,shäŋ-gəm-, shə-,wän-(,)gəŋk-\ mountain ridge SE N.Y.; part of Kittatinny Mountain
Sha·win·i·gan \shə-'win-i-gən\ city Canada in S Que. on St. Maurice river NW of Trois-Rivières *pop* 27,792
Shaw·nee \shȯ-'nē, 'shȯ-,; shä-'nē, 'shä-,\ **1** city NE Kans. S of Kansas City *pop* 20,482 **2** city *cen* Okla. *pop* 25,075
Shcherbakov — see RYBINSK
She·ba \'shē-bə\ *or* **Sa·ba** \'sā-bə\ ancient country S Arabia
She·boy·gan \shi-'bȯi-gən\ city & port E Wis. *pop* 48,484
Shechem — see NABLUS
Sheer·ness \shi(ə)r-'nes\ former urban district & port SE England in Kent at mouth of the Thames; now part of Queenborough-in-Sheppey
Shef·field \'shef-,ēld\ city & county borough N England in West Riding, Yorkshire *pop* 519,703
Shel·by \'shel-bē\ city S N.C. *pop* 16,328
Shel·by·ville \'shel-bē-,vil\ city SE *cen* Ind. *pop* 15,094
Shel·i·kof \'shel-i-,kȯf\ strait S Alaska between Alaska peninsula & islands of Kodiak & Afognak
Shel·ton \'shelt-ᵊn\ city SW Conn. *pop* 27,165
Shen·an·do·ah \,shen-ən-'dō-ə, ,shan-ə-'dō-ə\ river 55 *m* N Va. flowing NE between Allegheny & Blue Ridge mountains across NE tip of W.Va. & into the Potomac
Shenandoah National Park reservation N Va. in Blue Ridge mountains *area* 302
Shen·si \'shen-'sē\ province N *cen* China bordering on Yellow river ✱ Sian *area* 75,598, *pop* 21,000,000
Shenyang — see MUKDEN
Sher·brooke \'shər-,bru̇k\ city E Canada in S Que. *pop* 80,711
Sher·man \'shər-mən\ city NE Tex. N of Dallas *pop* 29,061
's Her·to·gen·bosch \,ser-,tō-gən-'bȯs\ city S Netherlands ✱ of No. Brabant *pop* 81,574
Sher·wood Forest \,shər-,wu̇d- *also* ,she(ə)r-\ ancient royal forest *cen* England chiefly in Nottinghamshire
Shet·land \'shet-lənd\ **1** islands N Scotland NE of the Orkneys **2** *or* **Zet·land** \'zet-\ county comprising the Shetlands ✱ Lerwick (on Mainland I.) *area* 550, *pop* 17,298 — **Shet·land·er** \'shet-lən-dər\ *n*
Shey·enne \shī-'an, -'en\ river 325 *m* SE *cen* N.Dak. flowing SE into Red river
Shi·beli *or* **She·beli** *or* **Web·be Shibeli** \,web-ē-shə-'bel-ē\ river 700 *m* E Africa rising in *cen* Ethiopia & flowing SE to a swamp near Juba river in Somalia
Shi·bin el Kôm \shib-,ē-,nel-'kōm\ city N Egypt in Nile delta NNW of Cairo *pop* 75,600
Shi·ga·tse \shi-'gät-sə\ town W China in SE Tibet on Tsangpo river W of Lhasa
Shih·kia·chwang \'shi(ə)r-jē-'äj-'wäŋ, 'shē-jē-\ city NE China in SW Hopei SW of Paoting *pop* 1,500,000
Shi·kar·pur \shi-'kär-,pu̇(ə)r\ city S *cen* Pakistan in Sind *pop* 62,500
Shi·ko·ku \shi-'kō-(,)kü\ island S Japan E of Kyushu *area* 7246
Shil·ka \'shil-kə\ river 300 *m* U.S.S.R. in SE Soviet Russia, Asia, flowing NE to unite with the Argun forming the Amur
Shil·long \shil-'ȯŋ\ city NE India ✱ of Assam *pop* 84,269
Shi·loh \'shī-(,)lō\ ancient village Palestine W of the Jordan on slope of Mt. Ephraim; site in modern Jordan at village of Seilun
Shi·mi·zu \shi-'mē-(,)zü, 'shē-mi-,zü\ city & port Japan in *cen* Honshu on Suruga Bay; port for Shizuoka *pop* 232,000
Shi·mo·da \shi-'mōd-ə, -'mō-,dä\ city & port Japan in S Honshu SW of Yokohama on Sagami sea *pop* 30,318
Shi·mo·no·se·ki \,shim-ə-nō-'sek-ē\ **1** strait Japan between Honshu & Kyushu connecting Inland sea & Korea strait **2** *or formerly* **Ba·kan** \'bäk-,än\ city & port Japan in SW Honshu on Shimonoseki strait *pop* 267,000
Shi·nar \'shī-nər, -,när\ a country known to the early Hebrews as a plain in Babylonia; probably Sumer
Ship Rock isolated mountain 7178 *ft* N.Mex. in NW corner
Shi·raz \shi-'räz\ city SW Iran in Fars *pop* 269,865
Shi·re *or* **Chi·re** \'shē-(,)rā\ river 370 *m* S Malawi & *cen* Mozambique flowing from Lake Nyasa S into the Zambezi
Shi·shal·din \shish-'al-dən\ volcano 9387 *ft* SW Alaska on Unimak I.; highest in Aleutian range
Shive·ly \'shīv-lē\ city N Ky. SW of Louisville *pop* 19,223
Shi·zu·o·ka \,shiz-ə-'wō-kə, ,shē-zə-'ō-kə\ city Japan in *cen* Honshu near Suruga Bay SW of Shimizu *pop* 414,000
Shkoder — see SCUTARI
Sho·la·pur \'shō-lə-,pu̇(ə)r\ city W India in SE Maharashtra SE of Bombay *pop* 406,349
Shore·ditch \'shō(ə)r-,dich, 'shȯ(ə)r-\ former metropolitan borough N *cen* London, England, now part of Hackney
Shore·wood \-,wu̇d\ village SE Wis. N of Milwaukee *pop* 15,576
Short·land \'shȯrt-lənd\ islands W Pacific in the Solomons off S end of Bougainville; in Brit. Solomon Islands Protectorate
Sho·sho·ne \shə-'shō-nē\ river 120 *m* NW Wyo. flowing NE into the Bighorn
Shoshone Falls waterfall 210 *ft* S Idaho in Snake river near Twin Falls
Showhsien — see HWAINAN
Shreve·port \'shrēv-,pō(ə)rt, -,pȯ(ə)rt, *esp South* 'srēv-\ city NW La. *pop* 182,064
Shrews·bury **1** \'sh(r)üz-,ber-ē, -b(ə-)rē, *esp South* 'srüz-\ town E Mass. E of Worcester *pop* 19,196 **2** *Brit often* 'shrōz-\ *or* **Sal·op** \'sal-əp\ municipal borough W England ✱ of Shropshire on the Severn *pop* 56,140
Shrop·shire \'shräp-,shi(ə)r, -shər, *esp South* 'sräp-\ *or* **Sal·op** \'sal-əp\ county W England on border of Wales ✱ Shrewsbury *area* 1347, *pop* 336,934
Shu·ma·gin \'shü-mə-gən\ islands SW Alaska S of Alaska peninsula; largest Unga
Shushan — see SUSA
Si — see WEST
Si·al·kot \sē-'äl-,kōt\ city NE Pakistan NNE of Lahore *pop* 167,000
Siam — see THAILAND
Siam, Gulf of *or* **Gulf of Thailand** arm of So. China sea between Indochina & Malay peninsula
Si·an \'shē-'än\ *or formerly* **Chang·an** \'chäŋ-'än\ city E *cen* China ✱ of Shensi on Wei river *pop* 1,900,000
Siang *or* **Hsiang** \shē-'äŋ\ **1** river 350 *m* SE *cen* China flowing from N Kwangsi N into Tungting Lake in Hunan **2** — see YÜ
Siang·tan \shē-'äŋ-'tän\ city SE China in E Hunan on the Siang S of Changsha *pop* 300,000
Si·be·ria \sī-'bir-ē-ə\ region N Asia in U.S.S.R. extending from the Urals to the Pacific; roughly coextensive with Soviet Russia, Asia — **Si·be·ri·an** \-ən\ *adj or n*
Si·biu \sē-'byü\ city W *cen* Rumania in Transylvania *pop* 118,893
Si·bu·yan \,sē-bü-'yän\ sea *cen* Philippines bounded by Mindoro, S Luzon, & the Visayans
Sic·i·ly \'sis-(ə-)lē\ *or* It **Si·ci·lia** \sē-'chēl-yä\ *or anc* **Si·cil·ia** \sə-'sil-yə\ *or* **Tri·nac·ria** \trə-'nak-rē-ə, trī-\ island S Italy in the Mediterranean; a region ✱ Palermo *area* 9926, *pop* 4,867,650 — **Si·cil·ian** \sə-'sil-yən\ *adj or n*
Si·cy·on \'sis(h)-ē-,än\ *or* Gk **Sik·y·on** \'sik-ē-\ ancient city S Greece in NE Peloponnesus NW of Corinth
Si·di Bar·râ·ni \,sēd-ē-bə-'rän-ē\ village NW Egypt on coast
Si·di–bel–Ab·bès \-,bel-ə-'bes\ commune NW Algeria on S of Oran *pop* 86,581
Sid·ney \'sid-nē\ city W Ohio *pop* 16,332
Si·don \'sīd-ᵊn\ *or* Ar **Sai·da** \'sīd-ə\ city & port SW Lebanon; a chief city of ancient Phoenicia *pop* 17,739 — **Si·do·ni·an** \sī-'dō-nē-ən\ *adj or n*
Sid·ra, Gulf of \'sid-rə\ *or anc* **Syr·tis Ma·jor** \,sərt-ə-'smā-jər\ inlet of the Mediterranean on coast of Libya
Sie·ben·ge·bir·ge \'zē-bən-gə-,bi(ə)r-gə\ hills W Germany on right bank of the Rhine SSE of Bonn — see DRACHENFELS
Si·ena *or* **Si·en·na** \sē-'en-ə\ commune *cen* Italy in Tuscany *pop* 65,966 — **Si·enese** *or* **Si·en·nese** \,sē-ə-'nēz, -'nēs\ *adj or n*
Si·er·ra Blan·ca \sē-,er-ə-'blaŋ-kə\ *or* **Sierra Blanca Peak** mountain 12,003 *ft* S *cen* N.Mex. in Sierra Blanca range of the Sacramento mountains
Sierra de Cór·do·ba \-də-'kȯrd-ə-bə\ mountain range *cen* Argentina chiefly in Córdoba province; highest peak Cerro Champaquí 9462 *ft*
Sierra de Gre·dos \-də-'gräd-(,)ōs\ mountain range W *cen* Spain, SW extension of Sierra de Guadarrama; highest peak Plaza de Almanzor 8692 *ft*
Sierra de Gua·dar·ra·ma \-də-,gwäd-ə-'räm-ə\ mountain range *cen* Spain; highest peak Pico de Peñalara 7890 *ft*
Si·er·ra Le·one \sē-,er-ə-lē-'ōn, ,sir-ə-\ country W Africa on the Atlantic; a dominion of Brit. Commonwealth ✱ Freetown *area* 27,925, *pop* 2,600,000 — **Sier·ra Le·on·ean** \-'ō-nē-ən\ *adj or n*
Si·er·ra Ma·dre del Sur \sē-,er-ə-,mäd-rē-,del-'su̇(ə)r\ mountain range S Mexico along Pacific coast in Guerrero & Oaxaca
Sierra Madre Oc·ci·den·tal \-,äk-sə-,den-'täl\ mountain range NW Mexico parallel to the Pacific coast

Sierra Madre Ori·en·tal \-ˌōr-ē-ˌen-'täl, -ˌȯr-\ mountain range E Mexico parallel to coast of Gulf of Mexico

Sierra Mo·re·na \-mə-'rā-nə\ mountain range SW Spain between Guadiana & Guadalquivir rivers; highest peak Estrella 4274 *ft*

Sierra Ne·va·da \-nə-'vad-ə, -'väd-\ **1** mountain range E Calif. — see WHITNEY (Mount) **2** mountain range S Spain; highest peak Mulhacén 11,420 *ft*

Sierra Nevada de Mérida — see CORDILLERA MÉRIDA

Sierra Nevada de San·ta Mar·ta \-də-ˌsant-ə-'märt-ə\ mountain range N Colombia on Caribbean coast; highest peak 19,030 *ft*

Sierra Pacaraima — see SERRA PACARAIMA

Sierra Parima — see SERRA PARIMA

Sikandarabad — see SECUNDERABAD

Si·kang \'shē-'käŋ\ former province S China ✱ Yaan; divided 1955 between Szechwan & Chamdo

Si·kho·te Alin \ˌsē-kə-ˌtā-ə-'lēn\ mountain range U.S.S.R. in Soviet Russia, Asia, in Maritime Territory; highest point 6575 *ft*

Sik·kim \'sik-əm, -ˌim\ territory SE Asia on S slopes of the Himalayas between India & Tibet; a protectorate of Republic of India ✱ Gangtok *area* 2818, *pop* 200,000 — **Sik·kim·ese** \ˌsik-ə-'mēz, -'mēs\ *adj or n*

Si·le·sia \sī-'lē-zh(ē-)ə, sə-, -sh(ē-)ə\ region E *cen* Europe in valley of the upper Oder bordering on Sudeten mountains; formerly chiefly in Germany, now chiefly in N Czechoslovakia & SW Poland — **Si·le·sian** \-zh(ē-)ən, -sh(ē-)ən\ *adj or n*

Simbirsk — see ULYANOVSK

Sim·coe, Lake \'sim-(ˌ)kō\ lake E Canada in SE Ont. SE of Georgian Bay *area* 280

Sim·fe·ro·pol \ˌsim(p)-fə-'rō-pəl, -'rō-\ city U.S.S.R. in S Soviet Russia, Europe, in the Crimea *pop* 250,000

Si·mi Valley \si-'mē\ city SW Calif. W of Los Angeles *pop* 56,464

Sim·la \'sim-lə\ city N India N of Delhi ✱ of Himachal Pradesh & former summer ✱ of India *pop* 42,597

Si·mons·town \'sī-mənz-ˌtau̇n\ town & port SW Republic of So. Africa in Cape Province on False Bay S of Cape Town

Sim·plon \'sim-ˌplän\ **1** mountain pass 6589 *ft* in Lepontine Alps between Switzerland & Italy in Valais & Piedmont **2** tunnel 12.3 *m* long through Monte Leone near the pass

Sims·bury \'simz-ˌber-ē, -b(ə-)rē\ town N Conn. NW of Hartford *pop* 17,475

Si·nai \'sī-ˌnī *also* -nē-ˌī\ **1** peninsula extension of continent of Asia NE Egypt between Red sea & the Mediterranean **2** — see HOREB — **Si·na·it·ic** \ˌsī-nē-'it-ik\ *adj*

Si·na·loa \ˌsē-nə-'lō-ə, ˌsin-ə-\ state W Mexico bordering on Gulf of California ✱ Culiacán *area* 22,580, *pop* 1,273,228

Sind \'sind\ region S Pakistan in lower Indus river valley; chief city Karachi

Sin·ga·pore \'siŋ-(g)ə-ˌpō(ə)r, -ˌpȯ(ə)r\ **1** island Malay archipelago in So. China sea off S end of Malay peninsula; formerly a Brit. crown colony, from 1963 to 1965 a state of Federation of Malaysia, an independent republic in Brit. Commonwealth since 1965, *area* 225, *pop* 2,110,400 **2** city & port, its ✱, on Singapore Strait *pop* 206,500 — **Sin·ga·por·ean** \ˌsiŋ-(g)ə-'pōr-ē-ən, -'pȯr-\ *adj or n*

Singapore Strait channel SE Asia between Singapore I. & Riau archipelago connecting Strait of Malacca & So. China sea

Sin·hai·lien \'shin-'hī-lē-'en\ *or formerly* **Tung·hai** \'tu̇ŋ-'hī\ *or* **Hai·chow** \'hī-'jō\ city E China in N Kiangsu near coast *pop* 207,600

Si·ning \'shē-'niŋ\ city NW China WNW of Lanchow ✱ of Tsinghai *pop* 250,000

Sin·kiang \'shin-jē-'äŋ\ *or* **Sinkiang–Ui·ghur Region** \'wē-gər\ region W China between Kunlun & Altai mountains; formerly a province ✱ Urumchi *area* 635,829, *pop* 8,000,000

Si·nop \sə-'nȯp\ *or anc* **Si·no·pe** \-'nō-pē\ town & port N Turkey on peninsula in Black Sea NW of Ankara

Sin·siang \'shin-shē-'äŋ\ city E China in N Honan N of Chengchow *pop* 170,500

Sint–Gillis — see SAINT-GILLES

Sint–Jans–Molenbeek — see MOLENBEEK

Sin·tra *or* **Cin·tra** \'sēn-trə\ city W Portugal NW of Lisbon *pop* 20,321

Sin·ui·ju \'shin-ē-ˌjü\ city N Korea on the Yalu opposite Antung, China *pop* 118,414

Sion, 1 \sē-'ōⁿ\ *or* G **Sit·ten** \'zit-ᵊn, 'sit-\ commune SW *cen* Switzerland ✱ of Valais *pop* 21,925 **2** — see ZION

Sioux City \'sü\ city NW Iowa on Missouri river *pop* 85,925

Sioux Falls city SE S.Dak. on Big Sioux river *pop* 72,488

Sip·par \sip-'är\ ancient city of Babylonia on the Euphrates SSW of modern Baghdad; Sargon's capital

Sira *or* **Síros** — see SYROS

Siracusa — see SYRACUSE

Si·ret \si-'ret\ river 270 *m* E Rumania flowing from the Carpathians SE into the Danube

Sis·ki·you \'sis-ki-ˌ(y)ü\ mountains N Calif. & SW Oreg., a range of Klamath mountains; highest Mt. Ashland (in Oreg.) 7530 *ft*

Sit·ka National Monument \'sit-kə\ reservation SE Alaska on Baranof I. near town of Sitka; Indian & Russian relics

Sit·tang \'si-ˌtäŋ\ river 350 *m* E *cen* Burma flowing S into Gulf of Martaban

Sit·twe \'si-ˌtwā\ *or* **Akyab** \ak-'yab\ city & port W Burma; chief town of Arakan coast *pop* 86,451

Si·vas \si-'väs\ *or anc* **Se·bas·te** \sə-'bas-tē\ *or* **Se·bas·tia** \sə-'bas-ch(ē-)ə, -tē-ə\ city E *cen* Turkey *pop* 108,320

Si·wa \'sē-wə\ *or anc* **Am·mo·ni·um** \ə-'mō-nē-əm\ oasis & town NW Egypt W of Qattara Depression

Si·wa·lik \si-'wäl-ik\ range of foothills of the Himalayas N India extending SE from N Punjab into Uttar Pradesh

Sjæl·land \'shel-ˌän\ *or* **Zea·land** \'zē-lənd\ island, largest of islands of Denmark; site of Copenhagen *area* 2709

Skag·er·rak \'skag-ə-ˌrak\ arm of the North sea between Norway & Denmark

Skag·it \'skaj-ət\ river 200 *m* SW B.C. & NW Wash. flowing S & W into Puget sound

Skan·e·at·e·les \ˌskan-ē-'at-ləs, ˌskin-\ lake 16 *m* long *cen* N.Y. SW of Syracuse; one of the Finger Lakes

Skaw, The \'skȯ\ *or* **Cape Ska·gen** \'skäg-ən\ cape Denmark at N extremity of Jutland

Skee·na \'skē-nə\ river 360 *m* Canada in W B.C. flowing S & W into Hecate strait

Skid·daw \'skid-ˌȯ\ mountain 3054 *ft* NW England in *cen* Cumberland

Skik·da \'skik-(ˌ)dä\ *or formerly* **Phi·lippe·ville** \'fil-əp-ˌvil, fi-ˌlēp-'vē(ə)l\ city & port NE Algeria N of Constantine *pop* 60,535

Sko·kie \'skō-kē\ village NE Ill. N of Chicago *pop* 68,627

Skop·lje \'skȯp-ˌlā, -ˌyä\ *or* **Skop·je** \'skȯp-ˌyä\ *or* Turk **Us·kub** \u̇-'sküb\ city S Yugoslavia ✱ of Macedonia on Vardar river *pop* 290,000

Skunk river 264 *m* SE Iowa flowing SE into the Mississippi

Skutari — see SCUTARI, USKUDAR

Skye \'skī\ island Scotland, one of the Inner Hebrides *area* 670

Sky·ros \'skī-rəs, -ˌräs\ *or* **Scy·ros** \'sī-\ *or* NGk **Ský·ros** \'skē-ˌrȯs\ island Greece in the Northern Sporades E of Euboea

Sla — see SALÉ

Slave \'slāv\ *or* **Great Slave** river 258 *m* Canada flowing from W end of Lake Athabasca N into Great Slave Lake

Slave coast region W Africa bordering on Bight of Benin between Benin & Volta rivers

Slavkov — see AUSTERLITZ

Sla·vo·nia \slə-'vō-nē-ə, -nyə\ region N Yugoslavia in E Croatia between the Sava, the Drava, & the Danube

Slea·ford \'slē-fərd\ urban district E England ✱ of Parts of Kesteven, Lincolnshire

Slesvig — see SCHLESWIG

Sli·dell \slī-'del\ town SE La. NE of New Orleans *pop* 16,101

Slide Mountain \'slīd\ mountain 4204 *ft* SE N.Y. W of Kingston; highest in the Catskills

Sli·go \'slī-(ˌ)gō\ **1** county N Republic of Ireland in N Connacht *area* 694, *pop* 50,236 **2** municipal borough & port, its ✱, on Sligo Bay

Slough \'slau̇\ urban district SE *cen* England in Buckinghamshire W of London *pop* 66,757

Slo·va·kia \slō-'väk-ē-ə, -'vak-\ region E Czechoslovakia E of Moravia; chief city Bratislava

Slo·ve·nia \slō-'vē-nē-ə, -nyə\ federated republic NW Yugoslavia N & W of Croatia ✱ Ljubljana *area* 7708, *pop* 1,725,088

Smoky Hill river 540 *m*, *cen* Kans. flowing E to unite with Republican river forming the Kansas

Smo·lensk \smō-'len(t)sk\ city U.S.S.R. in W Soviet Russia, Europe, on upper Dnieper river WSW of Moscow *pop* 211,000

Smyr·na \'smər-nə\ **1** town NW Ga. NW of Atlanta *pop* 19,157 **2** — see IZMIR

Snake \'snāk\ river 1038 *m* NW U.S. flowing from NW Wyo. across S Idaho & into the Columbia in Wash.

Sno·qual·mie \snō-'kwäl-mē\ **1** mountain pass 3004 *ft* W *cen* Wash. in Cascade range SE of Seattle **2** waterfall 268 *ft* W *cen* Wash. in Snoqualmie river

Snow \'snō\ mountains West Irian; include Nassau & Orange ranges — see CARSTENSZ (Mount)

Snow·don \'snōd-ᵊn\ massif 3560 *ft* N Wales; highest point in Wales

Snow·do·nia \snō-'dō-nē-ə, -nyə\ mountain region NW Wales centering around Mt. Snowdon

Snowy, 1 mountains SE Australia in SE New So. Wales **2** river 240 *m* SE Australia flowing from Snowy mountains to the Pacific

So·bat \'sō-ˌbat\ river 460 *m* W Ethiopia & SE Sudan flowing W into the White Nile

Soche — see YARKAND

So·chi \'sō-chē\ city & port U.S.S.R. in S Soviet Russia, Europe, on NE coast of Black Sea *pop* 224,000

So·ci·e·ty Islands \sə-'sī-ət-ē\ *or* F **Îles de la So·cié·té** \ēl-də-lä-sȯ-syā-tā\ islands S Pacific belonging to France ✱ Papeete (on Tahiti) *area* 650, *pop* 81,424

So·co·tra *or* **So·ko·tra** \sə-'kō-trə\ island Indian ocean E of Gulf of Aden in So. Yemen ✱ Tamrida (Hadibu) *area* 1400

Sod·om \'säd-əm\ **1** city of ancient Palestine in plain of the Jordan **2** *or* **Se·dom** \sə-'dōm\ town Israel near S end of Dead sea

Soemba — see SUMBA

Soembawa — see SUMBAWA

Soenda — see SUNDA

Soerabaja — see SURABAJA

Soerakarta — see SURAKARTA

So·fia \'sō-fē-ə, 'sȯ-, sō-'\ *or* Bulg **So·fi·ya** \'sȯ-fē-(y)ə\ *or anc* **Ser·di·ca** \'sərd-i-kə\ *or* **Sar·di·ca** \'särd-\ city ✱ of Bulgaria *pop* 858,140

Sog·di·a·na \ˌsäg-dē-'an-ə, -'än-ə, -'ā-nə\ province of ancient Persian Empire between the Jaxartes (Syr Darya) & Oxus (Amu Darya) ✱ Maracanda (Samarkand)

Sog·ne Fjord \ˌsȯŋ-nə-\ inlet of Norwegian sea SW Norway

So·hâg \sō-'haj\ city *cen* Egypt on the Nile SE of Asyût *pop* 85,300

So·ho \'sō-ˌhō\ district of *cen* London, England, in Westminster

Sois·sons \swä-'sōⁿ\ commune N France NW of Paris *pop* 25,890

So·lent, The \'sō-lənt\ channel S England between Isle of Wight & the mainland

So·li·hull \ˌsō-li-'həl\ county borough *cen* England in Warwickshire SE of Birmingham *pop* 106,968

So·li·mões \ˌsü-lē-'mōiⁿsh\ the upper Amazon, Brazil, from Peruvian border to the mouth of the Negro

So·ling·en \'zō-liŋ-ən, 'sō-\ city W Germany in the Ruhr ESE of Düsseldorf *pop* 175,200

ə abut	ᵊ kitten, F table	ər further	a back	ā bake	
ä cot, cart	ȧ F bac	au̇ out	ch chin	e less	ē easy
g gift	i trip	ī life	j joke	k̲ G ich	ⁿ F vin	ŋ sing
ō flow	ȯ flaw	œ F bœuf	œ̄ F feu	ȯi coin	th thing
th̲ this	ü loot	u̇ foot	ue G Füllen	ue̅ F rue	y yet
ʸ F digne \dēnʸ\, nuit \nwʸē\	yü few	yu̇ furious	zh vision		

Sol·na \'sōl-ˌnä\ city E Sweden, N suburb of Stockholm *pop* 56,607
Solo — see SURAKARTA
Sol·o·mon \'säl-ə-mən\ **1** islands W Pacific E of New Guinea divided between the Australian trust territory of New Guinea & the Brit. Solomon islands *area* 16,120 **2** sea arm of Coral sea W of Solomon islands
So·lo·thurn \'zō-lə-ˌtu̇(ə)rn, 'sō-\ *or* F **So·leure** \sō-'lər\ **1** canton NW Switzerland *area* 306, *pop* 224,133 **2** commune, its ✱, on the Aare *pop* 17,708
Sol·way firth \ˌsäl-ˌwā-\ inlet of Irish sea in Great Britain on boundary between England & Scotland
So·ma·lia \sō-'mäl-ē-ə, sə-, -'mäl-yə\ *or* **So·ma·li Republic** \-ˌmäl-ē-\ country E Africa bordering on Gulf of Aden & Indian ocean; formed 1960 by union of Brit. Somaliland & Italian Somaliland ✱ Mogadishu *area* 262,000, *pop* 2,860,000 — **So·ma·lian** \-'mäl-ē-ən, -'mäl-yən\ *adj or n*
So·ma·li·land \sō-'mäl-ē-ˌland, sə-\ region E Africa comprising Somalia, French Territory of the Afars and the Issas, & Ogaden region of E Ethiopia
Som·er·set \'səm-ər-ˌset, -sət\ **1** town SE Mass. N of Fall River *pop* 18,088 **2** island N Canada in Franklin District N of Boothia peninsula *area* 9370 **3** *or* **Som·er·set·shire** \-ˌshi(ə)r, -shər\ county SW England ✱ Taunton *area* 1620, *pop* 681,974
Somerset Nile — see NILE
Som·er·ville \'səm-ər-ˌvil\ city E Mass. N of Cambridge *pop* 88,779
So·mes \sō-'mesh\ *or* Hung **Sza·mos** \'sȯm-ˌōsh\ river 200 *m* NE Hungary & NW Rumania flowing NW into the Tisza
Somme \'säm, 'səm\ river 147 *m* N France flowing NW into the English channel
So·no·ra \sə-'nōr-ə, -'nȯr-\ **1** river 300 *m* NW Mexico flowing SW into upper Gulf of California **2** state NW Mexico bordering on U.S. & Gulf of California ✱ Hermosillo *area* 70,477, *pop* 1,092,458 — **So·no·ran** \-ən\ *adj or n*
Sonoran *or* **Sonora** desert SW U.S. & NW Mexico in S Ariz. & SE Calif. & N Sonora
Soo canals *or* **Soo locks** — see SAULT SAINTE MARIE CANALS
Soo·chow *or* **Su·chou** \'sü-'jō, -'chau̇\ *or* **Wu·hsien** \'wü-shē-'en\ city E China in SE Kiangsu W of Shanghai *pop* 633,000
So·pot \'sȯ-ˌpȯt\ city N Poland NNW of Gdansk *pop* 47,600
Sop·ron \'shō-ˌprōn\ city W Hungary *pop* 47,100
Sorata — see ILLAMPU
Sorbiodunum — see OLD SARUM
So·rel \sə-'rel\ city Canada in S Que. on the St. Lawrence SW of Trois-Rivières *pop* 19,347
So·ria \'sōr-ē-ə, 'sȯr-\ **1** province N *cen* Spain *area* 3983, *pop* 114,956 **2** commune, its ✱, W of Zaragoza *pop* 25,030
So·ro·ca·ba \ˌsōr-ə-'kab-ə, ˌsȯr-\ city SE Brazil in SE São Paulo state *pop* 142,835
Sor·ren·to \sə-'ren-(ˌ)tō\ *or anc* **Sur·ren·tum** \sə-'rent-əm\ commune & port S Italy on S side of Bay of Naples
Sos·no·wiec \sä-'snōv-ˌyets\ *or* **Sos·no·wi·ce** \ˌsōs-nə-'vēt-sə\ city SW Poland NE of Katowice *pop* 144,000
Soudan — see SUDAN
Sou·fri·ère \ˌsü-frē-'e(ə)r\ **1** *or* **Grande Soufrière** \ˌgrän(n)d-\ volcano 4869 *ft* French West Indies in S Basse-Terre, Guadeloupe **2** volcano 4048 *ft* Brit. West Indies on St. Vincent I.
Sound, The — see ÖRESUND
Sou·ris \'su̇r-əs\ *or* **Mouse** \'mau̇s\ river 450 *m* Canada & U.S. flowing from SE Sask. SE into N N.Dak. & N into the Assiniboine in SW Man.
Sousse \'süs\ *or* **Su·sa** \'sü-zə\ *or anc* **Had·ru·me·tum** \ˌhad-rə-'mēt-əm\city & port NE Tunisia *pop* 58,161
South island S New Zealand *area* 58,092, *pop* 798,681
South Africa, Republic of country S Africa S of the Limpopo, Molopo, & Orange rivers bordering on Atlantic & Indian oceans; a republic, until 1961 (as **Union of South Africa**) a Brit. dominion; administrative ✱ Pretoria, legislative ✱ Cape Town, judicial ✱ Bloemfontein *area* 472,359, *pop* 22,090,000
Sou·thall \'sau̇-ˌthȯl\ former municipal borough S England in Middlesex, now part of Ealing
South America continent of the western hemisphere lying between the Atlantic & Pacific oceans SE of No. America & chiefly S of the equator *area* 7,035,357 — **South American** *adj or n*
South·amp·ton \sau̇th-'(h)am(p)-tən\ **1** island N Canada in Keewatin District, Northwest Territories, between Hudson Bay & Foxe channel *area* 15,700 **2** — see HAMPSHIRE **3** county borough & port S England in Hampshire on **Southampton Water** (estuary of Test river) *pop* 214,826
South Arabia, Federation of — see YEMEN
South Australia state S Australia ✱ Adelaide *area* 380,070, *pop* 1,164,700
South Bend \'bend\ city N Ind. *pop* 125,580
South Brabant — see BRABANT
South·bridge \'sau̇th-(ˌ)brij\ town S Mass. SW of Worcester *pop* 17,057
South Canadian — see CANADIAN
South Cape — see KA LAE
South Car·o·li·na \ˌkar-ə-'lī-nə\ state SE U.S. ✱ Columbia *area* 31,055, *pop* 2,590,516 — **South Car·o·lin·ian** \-'lin-ē-ən, -'lin-yən\ *adj or n*
South Charleston city SW W.Va. *pop* 16,333
South China sea W Pacific enclosed by SE China, Formosa, Philippines, Indochina, Malaya, & Borneo
South Da·ko·ta \də-'kōt-ə\ state NW *cen* U.S. ✱ Pierre *area* 77,047, *pop* 665,507 — **South Da·ko·tan** \-'kōt-ən\ *adj or n*
South Downs \'dau̇nz\ hills S England chiefly in Sussex
South·end on Sea \ˌsau̇-ˌthend-\ county borough SE England in Essex at mouth of Thames estuary *pop* 162,326
Southern Alps mountain range New Zealand in W South I. extending almost the length of the island — see COOK (Mount)
Southern Morocco *or* **Southern Protectorate of Morocco** former Spanish protectorate W Africa S of former French Morocco
Southern ocean the Antarctic ocean
Southern Rhodesia — see RHODESIA
Southern Uplands elevated moorland region S Scotland extending from English border to a line joining Girvan & Dunbar
Southern Yemen — see YEMEN
South Euclid city NE Ohio E of Cleveland *pop* 29,579
South·field \'sau̇th-ˌfēld\ city SE Mich. NW of Detroit *pop* 69,285
South·gate, 1 \'sau̇th-ˌgāt\ city SE Mich. S of Detroit *pop* 33,909 **2** \-ˌgāt, -gət\ former municipal borough SE England in Middlesex, now part of Enfield
South Gate \-ˌgāt\ city SW Calif. SE of Los Angeles *pop* 56,909
South Georgia island S Atlantic E of Tierra del Fuego in Falkland Islands Dependencies *area* 1450
South Had·ley \'had-lē\ town W Mass. NE of Holyoke *pop* 17,033
South Holland, 1 village NE Ill. S of Chicago *pop* 23,931 **2** *or* D **Zuid·hol·land** \zīt-'hȯ-ˌlänt\ province SW Netherlands ✱ Rotterdam *area* 1212, *pop* 2,968,700
South·ing·ton \'səth-iŋ-tən\ town W *cen* Conn. *pop* 30,946
South Kingstown town S R.I. *pop* 16,913
South Miami city SE Fla. *pop* 19,571
South Milwaukee city SE Wis. on Lake Michigan *pop* 23,297
South Mountain mountain ridge S Pa. & W Md. at N end of Blue Ridge mountains
South Na·han·ni \nə-'han-ē\ river 350 *m* Canada in SW Mackenzie District flowing SE into the Liard
South Orange village NE N.J. *pop* 16,971
South Orkney islands S Atlantic SE of the Falklands in Falkland Islands Dependencies *area* 400
South Ossetia *or* **South Ossetian Region** autonomous region U.S.S.R. in N Georgia on S slopes of the Caucasus ✱ Tskhinvali *area* 1500, *pop* 100,000
South Pasadena city SW Calif. *pop* 22,979
South Pass broad level valley SW *cen* Wyo. crossing continental divide near SE end of Wind River range
South Plainfield borough NE N.J. SW of Elizabeth *pop* 21,142
South Platte river 424 *m* Colo. & Nebr. flowing E to join the No. Platte forming the Platte
South Point — see KA LAE
South·port \'sau̇th-ˌpō(ə)rt, -ˌpȯ(ə)rt\ county borough NW England in Lancashire on coast N of Liverpool *pop* 84,349
South Portland city SW Me. *pop* 23,267
South River borough N *cen* N.J. SE of New Brunswick *pop* 15,428
South Saint Paul city SE Minn. on the Mississippi *pop* 25,016
South Sandwich islands S Atlantic SE of So. Georgia I. in Falkland Islands Dependencies *area* 120
South San Francisco city W Calif. *pop* 46,646
South Saskatchewan — see SASKATCHEWAN
South sea *or* **South seas** the areas of the Atlantic, Indian, & Pacific oceans in the southern hemisphere, esp. the S Pacific
South Shetland islands S Atlantic SE of Cape Horn off tip of Antarctic peninsula in Falkland Islands Dependencies
South Shields \'shē(ə)l(d)z\ county borough N England in Co. Durham at mouth of the Tyne E of Newcastle *pop* 100,513
South Tirol — see ALTO ADIGE
South·wark \'səth-ərk, 'sau̇th-wərk\ borough of S London, England *pop* 259,982
South–West Africa *or* **Suid·wes–Afri·ka** \ˌsīt-ˌves-'äf-rē-kə\ *or* **Na·mib·ia** \nə-'mib-ē-ə\ *or formerly* **German Southwest Africa** territory SW Africa on the Atlantic; belonged to Germany before 1919, assigned as mandate by League of Nations to Union of So. Africa 1919 ✱ Windhoek *area* 318,099, *pop* 650,000
South Windsor town N Conn. *pop* 15,553
South Yemen SOUTHERN YEMEN
So·vetsk \səv-'yetsk\ *or* G **Til·sit** \'til-sət, -zət\ city U.S.S.R. in W Soviet Russia, Europe, on Neman river *pop* 36,000
So·vet·ska·ya Ga·van \səv-ˌyet-skə-yə-'gäv-ən(-yə)\ city & port U.S.S.R. in SE Soviet Russia, Asia, in Khabarovsk Territory on Tatar strait *pop* 26,000
Soviet Central Asia the portion of *cen* Asia belonging to the U.S.S.R. & comprising the Kirgiz, Tadzhik, Turkmen, & Uzbek republics & sometimes the Kazakh Republic
Soviet Russia, 1 — see RUSSIAN REPUBLIC **2** the U.S.S.R.
Soviet Union — see UNION OF SOVIET SOCIALIST REPUBLICS
Spa \'spä\ town E Belgium SE of Liège
Spain \'spān\ *or* Sp **Es·pa·ña** \ā-'spän-yä\ country SW Europe in the Iberian peninsula; nominally a kingdom ✱ Madrid *area* 193,144, *pop* 34,130,000
Span·dau \'s(h)pän-ˌdau̇\ a W section of Berlin, Germany
Spanish America, 1 the Spanish-speaking countries of Central & So. America **2** the parts of America settled & formerly governed by the Spanish
Spanish Guinea former Spanish colony W Africa bordering on Gulf of Guinea including Rio Muni & Fernando Po & other islands — see EQUATORIAL GUINEA
Spanish Main, 1 the mainland of Spanish America esp. along N coast of So. America **2** the Caribbean sea & adjacent waters esp. at the time when region was infested with pirates
Spanish Morocco — see MOROCCO
Spanish Peaks two mountains (East Spanish Peak & West Spanish Peak) S Colo. E of Sangre de Cristo mountains; highest, W peak 13,623 *ft*
Spanish Sahara region NW Africa SW of Morocco comprising the Spanish possessions Río de Oro & Saguia el Hamra ✱ El Aaiún *area* 105,448, *pop* 76,425
Spanish Town town SE *cen* Jamaica; former ✱ of Jamaica
Sparks \'spärks\ city W Nev. E of Reno *pop* 24,187
Spar·ta \'spärt-ə\ *or* **Lac·e·dae·mon** \ˌlas-ə-'dē-mən\ ancient city S Greece in Peloponnesus ✱ of Laconia
Spar·tan·burg \'spärt-ən-ˌbərg\ city NW S.C. *pop* 44,546
Speed·way \'spēd-ˌwā\ town *cen* Ind. W of Indianapolis *pop* 15,056
Spen·cer Gulf \ˌspen(t)-sər-\ inlet of Indian ocean SE So. Australia
Spey \'spā\ river 110 *m* NE Scotland flowing into Moray firth
Spey·er \'s(h)pī(-ə)r\ *or* **Spires** \'spī(ə)rz\ city W Germany on W bank of the Rhine SW of Heidelberg *pop* 41,957

Spezia — see LA SPEZIA
Spice — see MOLUCCAS
Spits·ber·gen \'spits-,bər-gən\ group of islands in Arctic ocean N of Norway; belongs to Norway *area* 24,280 — see SVALBARD
Split \'split\ *or* **Spljet** \'spl^{y}et\ *or* It **Spa·la·to** \'späl-ə-,tō\ city & port W Yugoslavia in Croatia on Dalmatian coast *pop* 108,000
Spo·kane \spō-'kan\ **1** river 120 *m* N Idaho & E Wash. flowing from Coeur d'Alene Lake W into the Columbia **2** city E Wash. at Spokane Falls in Spokane river *pop* 170,516
Spo·le·to \spə-'lāt-(,)ō\ commune *cen* Italy SE of Perugia *pop* 37,-036
Spor·a·des \'spȯr-ə-,dēz, 'spär-\ two island groups Greece in the Aegean: the **Northern Sporades** (chief island Skyros, N of Euboea & E of Thessaly) & the **Southern Sporades** (chiefly Samos, Icaria, & the Dodecanese, off SW Turkey)
Spree \'s(h)prā\ river 220 *m* E Germany flowing N into the Havel
Spree·wald \-,vält\ marshy district E Germany in Spree valley
Spring·dale \'spriŋ-,dāl\ city NW Ark. *pop* 16,783
Spring·field \'spriŋ-,fēld\ **1** city ✱ of Ill. on the Sangamon *pop* 91,753 **2** city SW Mass. on the Connecticut *pop* 163,905 **3** city SW Mo. *pop* 120,096 **4** city W *cen* Ohio NE of Dayton *pop* 81,926 **5** city W Oreg. on the Willamette E of Eugene *pop* 27,047
Springs \'spriŋz\ city NE Republic of So. Africa in S Transvaal *pop* 137,253
Spuy·ten Duy·vil Creek \,spīt-^{ə}n-'dī-vəl\ channel New York City N of Manhattan I. connecting Hudson & Harlem rivers
Sri Lan·ka \(')srē-'läŋ-kə\ *or formerly* **Cey·lon** \si-'län, sā-\ country coextensive with island of Ceylon; an independent republic in Brit. Commonwealth ✱ Colombo *area* 25,332, *pop* 9,172,042
Sri·na·gar \sri-'nəg-ər\ city, summer ✱ of Jammu & Kashmir, in W Kashmir on Jhelum river NNE of Lahore *pop* 327,076
Srirangapatnam — see SERINGAPATAM
Staf·fa \'staf-ə\ islet W Scotland in the Inner Hebrides W of Mull — see FINGAL'S CAVE
Staf·ford \'staf-ərd\ **1** *or* **Staf·ford·shire** \-,shi(ə)r, -shər\ county W *cen* England *area* 1153, *pop* 1,856,890 **2** municipal borough, its ✱, NNW of Birmingham *pop* 54,890
Staked Plain — see LLANO ESTACADO
Stalin, 1 — see BRASOV **2** — see DONETSK **3** — see VARNA
Stalinabad — see DUSHANBE
Stalingrad — see VOLGOGRAD
Stalino — see DONETSK
Stalin Peak — see GARMO PEAK
Stalinsk — see NOVOKUZNETSK
Stam·boul *or* **Stam·bul** \stam-'bül\ **1** the older part of Istanbul S of the Golden Horn **2** ISTANBUL
Stam·ford \'stam(p)-fərd\ city SW Conn. *pop* 108,798
Stanislav — see IVANO-FRANKOVSK
Stan·ley \'stan-lē\ *or* **Port Stanley** town ✱ of the Falklands
Stanley, Mount *or* **Mount Nga·lle·ma** \,eŋ-gäl-'yā-mə\ mountain with two peaks (higher Margherita Peak 16,763 *ft*) E *cen* Africa; highest of Ruwenzori
Stanley Falls series of seven cataracts NE Zaire in Lualaba river near head of Congo river with total fall of *ab* 200 *ft* in 60 *m*
Stanley Pool expansion of Congo river *ab* 20 *m* long 300 *m* above its mouth between Congo Republic & Zaire; Brazzaville & Kinshasa are situated on its banks
Stanleyville — see KISANGANI
Stan·o·voi \,stan-ə-'vȯi\ mountain range U.S.S.R. in E Soviet Russia, Asia, N of Amur river; highest point 8143 *ft*
Stan·ton \'stant-^{ə}n\ city SW Calif. SE of Los Angeles *pop* 17,947
Sta·ra Za·go·ra \,stär-ə-zə-'gȯr-ə, -'gȯr-\ city *cen* Bulgaria *pop* 106,468
State College borough *cen* Pa. NE of Altoona *pop* 33,778
Stat·en \'stat-^{ə}n\ island SE N.Y. SW of mouth of the Hudson; part of New York City, constituting borough of Richmond
States of the Church *or* **Papal States** temporal domain of the popes in *cen* Italy 755–1870
States·ville \'stāts-,vil, -vəl\ city W *cen* N.C. *pop* 19,996
Statia — see SAINT EUSTATIUS
Statue of Liberty National Monument — see LIBERTY
Staun·ton \'stant-^{ə}n\ city NW *cen* Va. *pop* 24,504
Sta·vang·er \stə-'väŋ-ər, -'vaŋ-\ city & port SW Norway *pop* 82,-079
Stav·ro·pol \stav-'rō-pəl, -'rō-\ **1** territory U.S.S.R. in S Soviet Russia, Europe, N of the Caucasus *area* 29,600, *pop* 2,306,000 **2** city, its ✱ *pop* 198,000
Ste·bark \'ste(^{n})m-,bärk\ *or* G **Tan·nen·berg** \'tan-ən-,bərg, 'tän-ən-,berk\ village NE Poland SW of Olsztyn
Steens \'stēnz\ mountains SE Oreg.; highest **Steens Mountain** (massif) 9354 *ft*
Stel·len·bosch \'stel-ən-,bäs(h), *Afrik* ,stel-əm-'bȯs\ city SW Republic of So. Africa in SW Cape Province E of Cape Town *pop* 29,900
Step·ney \'step-nē\ former metropolitan borough E London, England, on N bank of the Thames, now part of Tower Hamlets
Ster·ling \'stər-liŋ\ city NW Ill. *pop* 16,113
Sterling Heights city SE Mich. N of Detroit *pop* 61,365
Stettin — see SZCZECIN
Stet·ti·ner Haff \s(h)te-'tē-nər-,häf\ lagoon on Baltic coast between NE Germany & NW Poland at mouth of the Oder
Steu·ben·ville \'st(y)ü-bən-,vil\ city E Ohio on the Ohio N of Wheeling, W.Va. *pop* 30,771
Ste·vens Point \,stē-vənz-\ city *cen* Wis. *pop* 23,479
Stew·art \'st(y)ü-ərt, 'st(y)u̇(-ə)rt\ **1** river 320 *m* Canada in *cen* Yukon Territory flowing W into the Yukon **2** island New Zealand S of South I. *area* 670
Sti·kine \stik-'ēn\ river 335 *m* Canada & Alaska flowing from **Stikine mountains** (in B.C. & Yukon Territory; highest 8670 ft) into the Pacific
Still·wa·ter \'stil-,wȯt-ər, -,wät-\ city N *cen* Okla. *pop* 31,126
Stir·ling \'stər-liŋ\ **1** *or* **Stir·ling·shire** \-,shi(ə)r, -shər\ county *cen* Scotland *area* 451, *pop* 208,956 **2** burgh, its ✱ *pop* 29,769
Stock·holm \'stäk-,hō(l)m\ city & port ✱ of Sweden on Lake Malar *pop* 747,490 — **Stock·holm·er** \-,hō(l)-mər\ *n*
Stock·port \'stäk-,pō(ə)rt, -,pȯ(ə)rt\ county borough NW England in Cheshire S of Manchester *pop* 139,633
Stock·ton \'stäk-tən\ **1** city *cen* Calif. on San Joaquin river E of Oakland *pop* 107,644 **2** *or* **Stockton on Tees** \'tēz\ former municipal borough N England in Durham, now part of Teesside
Stoke New·ing·ton \stōk-'n(y)ü-iŋ-tən\ former metropolitan borough N London, England, now part of Hackney
Stoke on Trent \,stō-,kȯn-'trent, -,kän-\ city & county borough W *cen* England in Staffordshire *pop* 265,153
Stone·ham \'stō-nəm, 'stōn-,(h)am\ town E Mass. N of Boston *pop* 20,725
Stone·ha·ven \stōn-'hā-vən, stān-'hī\ burgh & port E Scotland ✱ of Kincardine
Stone·henge \'stōn-,henj, (')stōn-'\ assemblage of megaliths S England in Wiltshire on Salisbury Plain erected by a prehistoric people
Stone Mountain mountain 1686 *ft* NW *cen* Georgia E of Atlanta
Stones \'stōnz\ river 60 *m*, *cen* Tenn. flowing NW into the Cumberland
Sto·ning·ton \'stō-niŋ-tən\ town SE Conn. *pop* 15,940
Stor·mont \'stȯr-mənt\ E suburb of Belfast, Ireland; site of Parliament House of Northern Ireland
Stough·ton \'stōt-^{ə}n\ town E Mass. NW of Brockton *pop* 23,459
Stour \'stau̇(ə)r, 'stu̇(ə)r, 'stō(ə)r\ **1** river 60 *m* SE England flowing E between Essex & Suffolk into the North sea **2** river 55 *m* S England in Dorset & Hampshire flowing SE into the Avon **3** river 40 *m* SE England in Kent flowing NE into the North sea **4** river 20 *m*, *cen* England in Oxfordshire & Warwickshire flowing NW into the Avon **5** river 20 *m* W *cen* England in Staffordshire & Worcestershire flowing S into the Severn
Stour·bridge \'stau̇(ə)r-(,)brij, 'stō(ə)r-\ municipal borough W *cen* England in Worcestershire W of Brimingham *pop* 54,331
Stow \'stō\ city NE Ohio NE of Akron *pop* 19,847
Straits Settlements former country SE Asia bordering on Strait of Malacca & comprising Singapore I., Penang, & Malacca; now divided between Republic of Singapore & Federation of Malaysia *area* 1242
Stral·sund \'s(h)träl-,zünt, -,sünt\ city & port E Germany on the Baltic opposite Rügen I. *pop* 71,551
Stras·bourg \'sträs-,bu̇(ə)rg, 'sträz-, -,bərg\ *or* G **Strass·burg** \'shträs-,bu̇rk\ city NE France on Ill river *pop* 249,396
Strat·ford \'strat-fərd\ **1** town SW Conn. *pop* 49,775 **2** city Canada in SE Ont. W of Kitchener *pop* 24,508
Stratford–upon–Avon \'ā-vən\ municipal borough *cen* England in Warwick *pop* 19,449
Strath·clyde \strath-'klīd\ Celtic kingdom of 6th to 11th centuries S Scotland & NW England ✱ Dumbarton; its S part called **Cumbria** \'kəm-brē-ə\
Strath·more \strath-'mō(ə)r, -'mȯ(ə)r\ great valley of E *cen* Scotland S of the Grampians
Stream·wood \'strēm-,wu̇d\ village NE Ill. E of Elgin *pop* 18,176
Strea·tor \'strēt-ər\ city NE *cen* Ill. *pop* 15,600
Stre·sa \'strā-zə\ town NW Italy in Piedmont on Lake Maggiore
Stret·ford \'stret-fərd\ municipal borough NW England in Lancashire SW of Manchester *pop* 54,011
Strom·bo·li \'sträm-bə-(,)lē\ *or anc* **Stron·gy·le** \'strän-jə-,lē\ **1** island Italy in Lipari islands **2** volcano 3040 *ft* on the island
Strom·lo, Mount \'sträm-(,)lō\ hill 2500 *ft* SE Australia in New So. Wales W of Canberra
Strongs·ville \'strȯŋz-,vil\ city NE Ohio SW of Cleveland *pop* 15,-182
Struth·ers \'strəth-ərz\ city NE Ohio SE of Youngstown *pop* 15,-343
Stry·mon \'strī-,män\ *or* NGk **Stri·món** \strē-'mȯn\ *or* Bulg **Stru·ma** \'strü-mə\ river 225 *m* W Bulgaria & NE Greece flowing SE into Strymonic gulf
Stry·mon·io Gulf \(,)strī-,män-ik-\ *or* **Gulf of Stri·món** \strē-'mȯn\ *or* **Gulf of Or·fa·ni** \ȯr-'fän-ē\ inlet of the Aegean NE Greece NE of Chalcidice peninsula
Stutt·gart \'s(h)tu̇t-,gärt, 'stət-\ city W Germany ✱ of Baden-Württemberg on the Neckar *pop* 621,000
Styr \'sti(ə)r\ river 300 *m* U.S.S.R. in NW Ukraine flowing N into Pripet river in the Pripet marshes
Styr·ia \'stir-ē-ə\ *or* G **Stei·er·mark** \'s(h)tī(-ə)r-,märk\ region *cen* & SE Austria; chief city Graz — **Styr·i·an** \'stir-ē-ən\ *adj or n*
Sua·kin \'swäk-ən\ town & port NE Sudan on Red sea
Süan·hwa \sü-'än-'(h)wä\ city NE China in NW Hopei near Kalgan *pop* 114,100
Su·bic \'sü-bik\ town Philippines in W Luzon at head of **Subic Bay** (inlet of So. China sea NW of Bataan peninsula)
Su·bo·ti·ca \'sü-bə-,tēt-sə\ city NE Yugoslavia in N Voivodina near Hungarian border *pop* 88,787
Suchon — see SOOCHOW
Sü·chow *or* **Hsü–chou** \'s(h)ü-'jō, 'sü-'chau̇\ **1** *or* **Tung·shan** \'tu̇ŋ-'shän\ city E China in NW Kiangsu N of Pengpu *pop* 1,500,-000 **2** — see IPIN
Su·cre \'sü-(,)krā\ city, constitutional ✱ of Bolivia, 265 *m* SE of La Paz *pop* 58,359
Su·da Bay \'süd-ə\ inlet of Aegean sea Greece on N coast of Crete E of Canea
Su·dan \sü-'dan, -'dän\ *or* F **Sou·dan** \sü-dä^{n}\ **1** region N Africa between the Atlantic & the upper Nile S of the Sahara including basins of Lake Chad & the Niger & upper Nile **2** country NE Africa S of Egypt; a republic, until 1956 a territory (**Anglo–Egyp-**

ə abut ^{ə} kitten, F table ər further a back ā bake
ä cot, cart á F bac au̇ out ch chin e less ē easy
g gift i trip ī life j joke k G ich ^{n} F vin ŋ sing
ō flow ȯ flaw œ F bœuf œ̄ F feu ȯi coin th thing
th this ü loot u̇ foot ue G Füllen ue̅ F rue y yet
^{y} F digne \dēn^{y}\, nuit \nw^{y}ē\ yü few yu̇ furious zh vision

tian Sudan) under joint Brit. & Egyptian rule ✱ Khartoum *area* 967,500, *pop* 16,090,000 — **Su·da·nese** \ˌsüd-ᵊn-ˈēz, -ˈēs\ *adj or n*
Sud·bury \ˈsəd-ˌber-ē, -b(ə-)rē\ city Canada in SE Ont. N of Georgian Bay *pop* 90,535
Sudd \ˈsəd\ swamp region S Sudan drained by the White Nile
Su·de·ten \sü-ˈdāt-ᵊn\ **1** *or* **Su·de·tes** \-ˈdēt-(ˌ)ēz\ *or* **Su·det·ic** \-ˈdet-ik\ mountains *cen* Europe W of the Carpathians between Czechoslovakia & Poland **2** *or* **Su·de·ten·land** \sü-ˈdāt-ᵊn-ˌland\ region N Czechoslovakia in Sudeten mountains — **Sudeten** *adj or n*
Su·dir·man \sü-ˈdi(ə)r-mən\ *or formerly* **Nas·sau** \ˈnas-ˌȯ\ mountain range *cen* West Irian
Su·ez \sü-ˈez, ˈsü-ˌez, *chiefly Brit* ˈsü-iz\ **1** city & port NE Egypt at S end of Suez canal on **Gulf of Suez** (arm of Red sea) *pop* 315,000 **2** canal 92 *m* long NE Egypt traversing Isthmus of Suez
Suez, Isthmus of isthmus NE Egypt between Mediterranean & Red seas connecting Africa & Asia
Suf·folk \ˈsəf-ək, *US also* -ˌȯk\ county E England bordering on North sea; divided into administrative counties of **East Suffolk** (✱ Ipswich *area* 871, *pop* 380,524) & **West Suffolk** (✱ Bury St. Edmunds *area* 611, *pop* 164,201)
Suffolk Broads — see BROADS
Sugarloaf Mountain — see PÃO DE AÇÚCAR
Suidwes–Afrika — see SOUTH-WEST AFRICA
Suifu — see IPIN
Suisse — see SWITZERLAND
Sui·sun Bay \sə-ˈsün\ the E extension of San Pablo Bay *cen* Calif.
Sukarnapura — see DJAJAPURA
Su·khu·mi \ˈsu̇k-ə-mē\ city & port U.S.S.R. in NW Georgia ✱ of Abkhazian Republic on Black Sea *pop* 102,000
Suk·kur *or* **Sa·khar** \ˈsək-ər\ city Pakistan in N Sind on the Indus *pop* 131,000
Sulawesi — see CELEBES
Sul·grave \ˈsəl-ˌgrāv\ village England in S Northamptonshire
Sultanabad — see ARAK
Su·lu \ˈsü-(ˌ)lü\ **1** archipelago SW Philippines SW of Mindanao **2** — see JOLO **3** sea W Philippines N of Celebes sea
Su·ma·tra \su̇-ˈmä-trə\ island W Indonesia S of Malay peninsula *area* 166,789 — **Su·ma·tran** \-trən\ *adj or n*
Sum·ba *or* D **Soem·ba** \ˈsüm-bə\ *or* **San·dal·wood** \ˈsan-dᵊl-ˌwu̇d\ island Indonesia in the Lesser Sundas *area* 4306
Sum·ba·wa *or* D **Soem·ba·wa** \süm-ˈbä-wə\ island Indonesia in the Lesser Sundas *area* 5693
Su·mer \ˈsü-mər\ the S division of ancient Babylonia — see AKKAD, SHINAR
Sum·ga·it \ˌsu̇m-gä-ˈēt\ city & port U.S.S.R. in Azerbaidzhan on the Caspian NW of Baku *pop* 124,000
Sum·mit \ˈsəm-ət\ city NE N.J. W of Newark *pop* 23,620
Sum·ter \ˈsəm(p)-tər\ city E *cen* S.C. E of Columbia *pop* 24,435
Sun·da \ˈsün-də\ *or* D **Soen·da** \ˈsün-\ **1** islands Malay archipelago comprising the **Greater Sunda** islands (Sumatra, Java, Borneo, Celebes, & adjacent islands) & the **Lesser Sunda** islands (extending E from Bali to Timor); with exception of N Borneo & Portuguese Timor, belong to Indonesia **2** strait between Java & Sumatra
Sun·der·land \ˈsən-dər-lənd\ county borough N England in Co. Durham on North sea at mouth of the Wear *pop* 216,892
Sunds·vall \ˈsən(t)s-ˌväl, ˈsün(t)s-\ city & port E Sweden on Gulf of Bothnia *pop* 63,939
Sun·ga·ri \ˈsu̇ŋ-gə-rē\ **1** river 800 *m* NE China in E Manchuria flowing from Chang Pai Shan on Korean border NW & NE into the Amur **2** reservoir formed by dam in the upper Sungari
Sun·ny·vale \ˈsən-ē-ˌvāl\ city W Calif. WNW of San Jose *pop* 95,408
Sunset Crater volcanic crater N *cen* Ariz. in **Sunset Crater National Monument** (*area* 5)
Suomi — see FINLAND
Su·pe·ri·or \su̇-ˈpir-ē-ər\ city & port NW Wis. *pop* 32,237
Superior, Lake lake U.S. & Canada; largest, northernmost, & westernmost of the Great Lakes *area* 31,820
Superstition mountain range S *cen* Ariz. E of Phoenix; highest point **Superstition Mountain** 5060 *ft*
Sur, Point \ˈsər\ promontory Calif. on the Pacific 20 *m* SSW of Monterey
Su·ra·ba·ja *or* **Su·ra·ba·ya** *or* D **Soe·ra·ba·ja** \ˌsu̇r-ə-ˈbī-ə\ city & port Indonesia in NE Java on **Surabaja strait** (between Java & W end of Madura) *pop* 1,007,945
Su·ra·kar·ta \ˌsu̇r-ə-ˈkärt-ə\ *or* **So·lo** \ˈsō-(ˌ)lō\ *or* D **Soe·ra·kar·ta** \ˌsu̇r-ə-ˈkärt-ə\ city Indonesia in *cen* Java *pop* 367,626
Su·rat \ˈsu̇r-ət, sə-ˈrat\ city W India in SE Gujarat *pop* 393,915
Sur·bi·ton \ˈsər-bət-ᵊn\ former municipal borough S England in Surrey WSW of London, now part of Kingston upon Thames
Su·ri·ba·chi, Mount \ˌsu̇r-ə-ˈbäch-ē\ volcano 548 *ft* in the Volcano islands at S end of Iwo Jima
Su·ri·nam \ˈsu̇r-ə-ˌnam, ˌsu̇r-ə-ˈnäm\ *or* **Su·ri·na·me** \ˌsu̇r-ə-ˈnäm-ə\ *or* **Dutch Guiana** *or* **Netherlands Guiana** country N So. America between Guyana & French Guiana; a territory of the Netherlands ✱ Paramaribo *area* 55,142, *pop* 410,000 — **Su·ri·nam·er** \ˈsu̇r-ə-ˌnam-ər, ˌsu̇r-ə-ˈnäm-\ *n* — **Su·ri·nam·ese** \ˌsu̇r-ə-ˌnə-ˈmēz, -ˈmēs\ *adj or n*
Suriname *or* **Surinam** river 400 *m* N Surinam flowing N into the Atlantic
Sur·ma \ˈsu̇(ə)r-mə\ river 560 *m* NE India (subcontinent) in Manipur & Bangladesh — see MEGHNA
Surrentum — see SORRENTO
Sur·rey \ˈsər-ē, ˈsə-rē\ county SE England S of London ✱ Kingston on Thames *area* 722, *pop* 999,588
Surts·ey \ˈsərt-ˌsā, ˈsu̇(ə)rt-\ island Iceland off S coast *area* 1; formed 1963 by volcanic eruption
Su·ru·ga Bay \ˈsu̇r-ə-gə\ inlet of the Pacific Japan on coast of SE Honshu W of Sagami sea
Su·sa \ˈsü-zə\ **1** *or bib* **Shu·shan** \ˈshü-shən, -ˌshan\ ancient city ✱ of Elam; ruins in SW Iran **2** — see SOUSSE
Su·sak \ˈsü-ˌshäk\ former city NW Yugoslavia, now an E section of Rijeka; seaport
Susiana — see ELAM
Sus·que·han·na \ˌsəs-kwə-ˈhan-ə\ river 444 *m* E U.S. flowing from *cen* N.Y. S through Pa. & into Chesapeake Bay in N Md.
Sus·sex \ˈsəs-iks, *US also* -ˌeks\ county SE England bordering on English channel; one of kingdoms in Anglo-Saxon heptarchy; divided into administrative counties of **East Sussex** (✱ Lewes *area* 829, *pop* 750,312) & **West Sussex** (✱ Chichester *area* 628, *pop* 491,020)
Suth·er·land \ˈsəth-ər-lənd\ *or* **Suth·er·land·shire** \-lən(d)-ˌshi(ə)r, -shər\ county N Scotland ✱ Dornoch *area* 2028, *pop* 13,053
Sutherland Falls waterfall 1904 *ft* New Zealand in SW South I.
Sut·lej \ˈsət-ˌlej\ river 900 *m* N India (subcontinent) flowing from Tibet W & SW through the Punjab to join the Chenab
Sut·ton \ˈsət-ᵊn\ borough of S Greater London, England *pop* 168,775
Sut·ton Cold·field \ˈkōl(d)-ˌfēld\ municipal borough *cen* England in Warwickshire NE of Birmingham *pop* 83,130
Sutton in Ash·field \ˈash-ˌfēld\ urban district N *cen* England in Nottinghamshire N of Nottingham *pop* 40,725
Su·va \ˈsü-və\ city & port ✱ of Fiji, on Viti Levu I. *pop* 63,200
Su·wal·ki *or* Russ **Su·val·ki** \su̇-ˈväl-kē\ *or* Lithuanian **Su·val·kai** \-ˌkī\ **1** district NE Poland E of Masurian Lakes **2** city in the district *pop* 25,400
Su·wan·nee \sə-ˈwän-ē\ river 240 *m* SE Ga. & N Fla. flowing SW into Gulf of Mexico
Su·won \ˈsü-ˌwän\ city S Korea S of Seoul *pop* 170,518
Sval·bard \ˈsfäl-ˌbär\ the Norwegian islands in the Arctic ocean including Spitsbergen, Bear I., & other small islands *area* 25,000
Sverd·lovsk \sferd-ˈlȯfsk\ *or formerly* **Eka·te·rin·burg** \i-ˈkat-ə-rən-ˌbərg\ city U.S.S.R. in W Soviet Russia, Asia, in *cen* Ural mountains *pop* 1,026,000
Sver·drup \ˈsfer-drəp\ islands N Canada W of Ellesmere I. including Axel Heiberg, Ellef Ringnes, & Amund Ringnes Islands
Swa·bia \ˈswā-bē-ə\ *or* G **Schwa·ben** \ˈshfäb-ən\ region and medieval county SW Germany chiefly in area comprising modern Baden-Wurttemberg & W Bavaria — **Swa·bi·an** \ˈswā-bē-ən\ *adj or n*
Swan \ˈswän\ **1** two islands in the Caribbean NE of Honduras **2** *or in its upper course* **Av·on** \ˈav-ən\ river 150 *m* SW Western Australia flowing W into Indian ocean
Swan·sea \ˈswän-zē (*usual Brit pron*), ˈswän(t)-sē\ county borough & port SE Wales in Glamorganshire *pop* 172,566
Swat \ˈswät\ river 400 *m* Pakistan flowing into the Kabul
Swa·tow \ˈswä-ˈtau̇\ city & port SE China in E Kwangtung on So. China sea *pop* 400,000
Swa·zi·land \ˈswäz-ē-ˌland\ country SE Africa N of Natal between Transvaal & Mozambique; a former Brit. protectorate, an independent kingdom since 1968 ✱ Mbabane *area* 6705, *pop* 420,000
Swe·den \ˈswēd-ᵊn\ *or* Swed **Sve·ri·ge** \ˈsfer-yə\ country N Europe on Scandinavian peninsula W of Baltic sea; a kingdom ✱ Stockholm *area* 173,349, *pop* 8,110,000
Swift Current \ˈswift\ city Canada in SW Sask. *pop* 15,415
Swin·don \ˈswin-dən\ municipal borough S England in Wiltshire *pop* 90,830
Świ·no·ujś·cie \ˌshfē-nō-ˈüish-(ˌ)chā\ *or* G **Swi·ne·mün·de** \ˌsfē-nə-ˈmu̇n-də, -ˈmuen-\ city & port NW Poland on N coast of Uznam (Usedom) I. at mouth of Swina river NNW of Szczecin *pop* 27,900
Swin·ton and Pen·dle·bury \ˌswint-ᵊn-ən-ˈpen-dᵊl-ˌber-ē, -b(ə-)rē\ municipal borough NW England in Lancashire NW of Manchester *pop* 40,124
Swit·zer·land \ˈswit-sər-lənd\ *or* F **Suisse** \swᵊēs\ *or* G **Schweiz** \ˈshfīts\ *or* It **Sviz·ze·ra** \ˈzvēt-tsā-rä\ *or* L **Hel·ve·tia** \hel-ˈvē-sh(ē-)ə\ country W Europe in the Alps; a federal republic ✱ Bern *area* 15,940, *pop* 6,310,000
Syb·a·ris \ˈsib-ə-rəs\ ancient Greek city S Italy on Gulf of Tarentum; destroyed 510 B.C.
Syd·ney \ˈsid-nē\ **1** city & port SE Australia on Port Jackson ✱ of New So. Wales *pop* (with suburbs) 2,780,310 **2** city Canada in NE N.S. on Cape Breton I. *pop* 33,230 — **Syd·ney·ite** \-ˌīt\ *n*
Syene — see ASWÂN
Sylt \ˈzilt, ˈsilt\ island N Germany, chief of the No. Frisian islands
Syr·a·cuse \ˈsir-ə-ˌkyüs, -ˌkyüz\ **1** city *cen* N.Y. *pop* 197,208 **2** *or* It **Si·ra·cu·sa** \ˌsē-rə-ˈkü-zə\ *or anc* **Syr·a·cu·sae** \ˌsir-ə-ˈkyü-(ˌ)sē, -(ˌ)zē\ city & port Italy in SE Sicily *pop* 103,202 — **Syr·a·cu·san** \ˌsir-ə-ˈkyüs-ᵊn, -ˈkyüz-\ *adj or n*
Syr Dar·ya \ˈsir-ˈdär-yə\ *or anc* **Jax·ar·tes** \jak-ˈsärt-(ˌ)ēz\ river 1500 *m* U.S.S.R. in Soviet Central Asia flowing from Tien Shan W & NW into Lake Aral
Syr·ia \ˈsir-ē-ə\ **1** ancient region SW Asia bordering on the Mediterranean & covering modern Syria, Lebanon, Israel, & Jordan **2** former French mandate (1920–44) comprising the **Le·vant States** \li-ˈvant \ (Syria, Lebanon, Latakia, & Jebel ed Druz), administrative ✱ Beirut, legislative ✱ Damascus *area* 76,030 **3** *or* **Syrian Arab Republic** country SW Asia bordering on the Mediterranean; a republic 1944–58 & since 1961; a province of United Arab Republic 1958–61 ✱ Damascus *area* 72,234, *pop* 6,450,000 — **Syr·i·an** \ˈsir-ē-ən\ *adj or n*
Syrian desert W Asia between Mediterranean coast & the Euphrates covering N Saudi Arabia, NE Jordan, SE Syria, & W Iraq
Sy·ros \ˈsī-ˌräs\ *or* **Sy·ra** \ˈsī-rə\ *or* NGk **Si·ros** \ˈsē-ˌrȯs\ *or* **Si·ra** \ˈsē-rə\ **1** island Greece in the Cyclades S of Andros **2** — see ERMOÚPOLIS
Syrtis Major — see SIDRA (Gulf of)
Syrtis Minor — see GABES (Gulf of)
Szamos — see SOMES
Szcze·cin \ˈshchet-ˌsēn\ *or* G **Stet·tin** \s(h)te-ˈtēn\ city & port NW Poland on the Oder near its mouth *pop* 335,400
Sze·chwan \ˈsech-ˈwän\ province SW China ✱ Chengtu *area* 219,691, *pop* 70,000,000
Sze·ged \ˈseg-ˌed\ city S Hungary on Yugoslav border *pop* 117,000
Szé·kes·fe·hér·var \ˈsā-ˌkesh-ˌfe-ər-ˌvär\ city W *cen* Hungary *pop* 72,940
Szeming — see AMOY

Sze·ping \'sü-'piŋ\ *or formerly* **Sze·ping·kai** \-'gī\ city NE China in W Kirin SW of Changchun *pop* 125,900
Szom·bat·hely \'sōm-ˌbot-ˌhā\ city W Hungary *pop* 64,745
Ta·bas·co \tə-'bas-(ˌ)kō\ state SE Mexico on the Caribbean SW of Yucatán peninsula ✱ Villahermosa *area* 9782, *pop* 766,346
Ta·blas \'täb-ləs\ island *cen* Philippines in Romblon group
Table Bay harbor of Cape Town, Republic of So. Africa
Table Mountain mountain 3550 *ft* Republic of So. Africa S of Cape Town
Ta·bor, Mount \'tā-bər, -ˌbȯ(ə)r\ mountain 1929 *ft* N Palestine E of Nazareth
Ta·bo·ra \tə-'bōr-ə, -'bȯr-\ city Tanzania in W *cen* Tanganyika *pop* 21,012
Ta·briz \tə-'brēz\ *or anc* **Tau·ris** \'tȯr-əs\ city NW Iran in Azerbaljan *pop* 403,413
Ta·bun Bog·do \ˌtäb-ˌün-'bȯg-(ˌ)dō\ mountain 15,266 *ft* W Outer Mongolia; highest in Altai mountains
Tac·na \'tak-nə\ city S Peru near Chilean border *pop* 30,500; in region (**Tacna–Ari·ca** \-ə-'rē-kə\) occupied 1884–1930 by Chile & now divided between Chile & Peru
Ta·co·ma \tə-'kō-mə\ **1** city & port W Wash. on Puget Sound S of Seattle *pop* 154,581 **2** — see RAINIER (Mount)
Ta·con·ic \tə-'kän-ik\ mountains along Mass.-N.Y. boundary & in SW Vt.; highest Mt. Equinox (in Vt.) 3816 *ft*
Ta·djou·ra, Gulf of *or* **Gulf of Ta·ju·ra** \tə-'ju̇r-ə\ inlet of Gulf of Aden in E French Territory of the Afars and the Issas
Tadmor — see PALMYRA
Ta·dzhik·i·stan *or* **Ta·jik·i·stan** \tä-ˌjik-i-'stan, tə-, -ˌjēk-, -'stän\ *or* **Ta·dzhik Republic** \tä-'jik, -jēk\ constituent republic of the U.S.S.R. in Soviet Central Asia bordering on China (Sinkiang) & Afghanistan ✱ Dushanbe *area* 54,900, *pop* 2,900,000
Tae·dong \ta-'du̇ŋ, tī-\ river 200 *m* N Korea flowing SW into Korea Bay
Tae·gu \ta-'gü, tī-\ city SE Korea NNW of Pusan *pop* 845,073
Tae·jon \ta-'jȯn, tī-\ city S Korea NW of Taegu *pop* 315,094
Ta·gan·rog \'tag-ən-ˌräg\ city U.S.S.R. in Soviet Russia, Europe, on **Gulf of Taganrog** (NE arm of Sea of Azov) *pop* 254,000
Ta·gus \'tā-gəs\ *or* Sp **Ta·jo** \'tä-(ˌ)hō\ *or* Port **Te·jo** \'tā-(ˌ)zhü\ river 566 *m* Spain & Portugal flowing W into the Atlantic
Ta·hi·ti \tə-'hēt-ē\ island S Pacific in Windward group of the Society Islands; chief town Papeete *area* 402, *pop* 61,519
Ta·hoe, Lake \'tä-ˌhō\ lake 22 *m* long on Calif.-Nev. boundary
Tai \'tī\ lake 40 *m* long & 35 *m* wide E China in Kiangsu
Tai·chow \'tī-'jō, -'chau̇\ city E China in *cen* Kiangsu NW of Shanghai *pop* 275,000
Tai·chung \'tī-'chu̇ŋ\ city China in W Formosa *pop* 428,426
Tai·myr *or* **Tai·mir** \tī-'mi(ə)r\ peninsula U.S.S.R. in NW Soviet Russia, Asia, between Yenisei & Khatanga rivers — see CHELYUSKIN
Tai·nan \'tī-'nän\ city China in SW Formosa *pop* 284,200
Tainaron — see MATAPAN
Tai·pei *or* **Tai·peh** \'tī-'pā, -'bā\ city ✱ of (Nationalist) China, on Formosa *pop* 1,712,108
Tai Shan \'tī-'shän\ mountain 5069 *ft* E China in W Shantung S of Tainan
Taiwan — see FORMOSA — **Tai·wan·ese** \ˌtī-wə-'nēz, -'nēs\ *adj or n*
Tai·yu·an \'tī-yü-'än\ *or formerly* **Yang·ku** \'yäŋ-'kü\ city N China ✱ of Shansi *pop* 2,725,000
Ta·ju·mul·co \ˌtä-hü-'mül-(ˌ)kō\ mountain 13,816 *ft* W Guatemala; highest in Central America
Ta·ka·mat·su \ˌtäk-ə-'mät-(ˌ)sü, tä-'käm-ət-ˌsü\ city & port Japan in NE Shikoku on Inland sea *pop* 270,000
Ta·ka·o·ka \tə-'kau̇-kə\ city Japan in *cen* Honshu *pop* 159,000
Tak·ka·kaw \'tak-ə-ˌkȯ\ waterfall 1650 *ft* Canada in SE B.C. in Yoho National Park; highest in Canada
Ta·kla Ma·kan \ˌtäk-lə-mə-'kän\ desert W China in *cen* Sinkiang between Tien Shan & Kunlun mountains
Ta·ko·ma Park \tə-'kō-mə\ city SW Md. *pop* 18,455
Ta·ko·ra·di \ˌtäk-ə-'räd-ē\ city & port SW Ghana SW of Sekondi *pop* (with Sekondi) 89,686
Ta·la·ud \'täl-ˌä-ˌüd\ *or* **Ta·laur** \-ˌä-ˌu̇(ə)r\ islands Indonesia NE of Celebes *area* 494
Tal·ca \'täl-kə\ city *cen* Chile 155 *m* S of Santiago *pop* 80,777
Tal·ca·hua·no \ˌtal-kə-'(h)wän-(ˌ)ō\ city & port S cen Chile NW of Concepción *pop* 112,087
Tal·la·de·ga \ˌtal-ə-'dē-gə, -'dig-ə\ city E *cen* Ala. *pop* 17,662
Tal·la·has·see \ˌtal-ə-'has-ē\ city ✱ of Fla. *pop* 71,897
Tal·la·hatch·ie \ˌtal-ə-'hach-ē\ river 301 *m* N Miss. flowing SW to unite with the Yalobusha forming the Yazoo
Tal·la·poo·sa \ˌtal-ə-'pü-sə\ river 268 *m* NW Ga. & E Ala. flowing SW to join Coosa river forming the Alabama
Tal·linn *or* **Tal·lin** \'tal-ən, 'täl-\ *or* **Re·vel** \'rā-vəl\ *or* **Re·val** \-ˌväl\ city & port U.S.S.R. ✱ of Estonia *pop* 363,000
Tall·madge \'tal-mij\ city NE Ohio NE of Akron *pop* 15,274
Tam·al·pais, Mount \ˌtam-əl-'pī-əs\ mountain 2606 *ft* W Calif. NW of San Francisco
Ta·man \tə-'män\ peninsula U.S.S.R. in S Soviet Russia, Europe, in Ciscaucasia between Sea of Azov & Black Sea
Tam·an·ras·set \ˌtam-ən-'ras-ət\ wadi & oasis SE Algeria
Ta·mar, 1 \'tā-mər\ river 40 *m* Australia in N Tasmania flowing N to Bass strait **2** \'tā-mər\ river 60 *m* SW England flowing SE from NW Devon into English channel **3** — see PALMYRA
Ta·ma·tave \ˌtam-ə-'täv, ˌtäm-\ city & port NE Malagasy Republic *pop* 56,910
Ta·mau·li·pas \ˌtäm-ˌau̇-'lē-pəs, təm-\ state NE Mexico bordering on Gulf of Mexico ✱ Ciudad Victoria *area* 30,731, *pop* 1,438,350
Tam·bo·ra \täm-'bōr-ə, -'bȯr-\ volcano 9354 *ft* Indonesia on Sumbawa I.
Tam·bov \täm-'bȯf, -'bȯv\ city U.S.S.R. in *cen* Soviet Russia, Europe, SE of Moscow *pop* 229,000
Tam·il Na·du \ˌtam-əl-'näd-(ˌ)ü\ *or formerly* **Madras** state SE India bordering on Bay of Bengal ✱ Madras *area* 50,110, *pop* 41,103,125
Tam·pa \'tam-pə\ city W Fla. on **Tampa Bay** (inlet of Gulf of Mexico) *pop* 277,767 — **Tam·pan** \-pən\ *adj or n*
Tam·pe·re \'tam-pə-ˌrā, 'täm-\ *or* Sw **Tam·mer·fors** \ˌtäm-ər-'fō(ə)rz, -'fȯsh\ city SW Finland *pop* 151,278
Tam·pi·co \tam-'pē-(ˌ)kō\ city & port E Mexico in S Tamaulipas on the Pánuco 7 *m* from its mouth *pop* 196,147
Ta·na \'tän-ə\ *or* **Tsa·na** \'(t)sän-ə\ **1** lake NW Ethiopia; source of the Blue Nile *area* 1418 **2** river 500 *m* E Africa in Kenya flowing into Indian ocean
Ta·na·gra \'tan-ə-grə, tə-'nag-rə\ village E *cen* Greece E of Thebes; an important town of ancient Boeotia
Tan·a·na \'tan-ə-ˌnȯ\ river 475 *m* E & *cen* Alaska flowing NW into the Yukon
Ta·nan·a·rive \tə-'nan-ə-ˌrēv\ *or formerly also* **An·ta·nan·a·ri·vo** \ˌan-tə-ˌnan-ə-'rē-(ˌ)vō\ city ✱ of Malagasy Republic *pop* 339,233
Tan·ez·rouft \ˌtan-əz-'rüft\ extremely arid region of W Sahara in SW Algeria & N Mali
Tan·ga \'taŋ-gə\ city & port Tanzania in NE Tanganyika *pop* 61,058
Tan·gan·yi·ka \ˌtan-gən-'yē-kə, ˌtaŋ-gən-, -gə-'nē-\ former country E Africa between Lake Tanganyika & Indian ocean; administered by Britain 1920–61; became an independent member of Brit. Commonwealth 1961 ✱ Dar es Salaam *area* 361,800; since 1964 united with Zanzibar as United Republic of Tanzania — see GERMAN EAST AFRICA — **Tan·gan·yi·kan** \-kən\ *adj or n*
Tanganyika, Lake lake E Africa in Great Rift Valley between Zaire & Tanzania *area* 12,700
Tan·gier \tan-'ji(ə)r\ *or* **Tan·giers** \-'ji(ə)rz\ *or* Sp **Tán·ger** \'täŋ-ˌher\ **1** city & port N Morocco on Strait of Gibraltar; summer ✱ of Morocco *pop* 170,000 **2** the International Zone of Tangier — see MOROCCO — **Tan·ger·ine** \ˌtan-jə-'rēn\ *adj or n*
Tang·shan \'täŋ-'shän\ city NE China in E Hopei *pop* 1,200,000
Ta·nim·bar \tə-'nim-ˌbär, tä-\ *or* **Ti·mor·laut** \ˌtē-ˌmȯr-'lau̇t\ islands Indonesia in SE Moluccas ENE of Timor
Ta·nis \'tā-nəs\ *or bib* **Zo·an** \'zō-ˌan\ancient city N Egypt in E Nile delta near Lake Tanis
Tanis, Lake — see MANZALA (Lake)
Tan·jung·pri·ok \ˌtän-ˌju̇ŋ-prē-'ȯk\ port of Djakarta, Indonesia
Tannenberg — see STEBARK
Tan·ta \'tänt-ə\ city N Egypt in *cen* Nile delta *pop* 253,600
Tan–tung \'dän-'du̇ŋ, 'tän-'tu̇ŋ\ *or* **An·tung** \'än-\ city & port NE China in SE Liaoning at mouth of the Yalu *pop* 450,000
Tan·za·nia \ˌtan-zə-'nē-ə\ republic E Africa formed 1964 by union of Tanganyika & Zanzibar ✱ Dar es Salaam *area* 362,844 *pop* 13,630,000 — **Tan·za·ni·an** \-nē-ən\ *adj or n*
Taor·mi·na \tau̇r-'mē-nə\ *or anc* **Tau·ro·me·ni·um** \ˌtȯr-ə-'mē-nē-əm\ commune Italy in NE Sicily
Ta·pa·joz \ˌtap-ə-'zhȯs\ river 500 *m* N Brazil flowing NE into the Amazon — see JURUENA
Tap·pan Zee \ˌtap-ən-'zē\ expansion of Hudson river SE N.Y.
Taprobane — see CEYLON
Tap·ti \'täp-tē\ river 436 *m* W India S of Satpura range flowing W into Gulf of Cambay
Ta·qua·ri \ˌtak-wə-'rē\ river 450 *m* S *cen* Brazil rising in S *cen* Mato Grosso & flowing WSW into the Paraguay
Tar \'tär\ river 215 *m* NE N.C. — see PAMLICO
Tara \'tar-ə\ village Ireland in County Meath NW of Dublin near **Hill of Tara** (seat of ancient Irish kings)
Tarabulus — see TRIPOLI
Taranaki — see EGMONT
Ta·ran·to \'tär-ən-ˌtō, tə-'rant-(ˌ)ō\ *or anc* **Ta·ren·tum** \tə-'rent-əm\ city & port SE Italy on **Gulf of Taranto** (inlet of Ionian sea) *pop* 218,025
Ta·ra·wa \tə-'rä-wə, 'tar-ə-ˌwä\ island *cen* Pacific in N Gilbert islands ✱ of Gilbert & Ellice Islands colony *area* 8
Tarbes \'tärb\ city SW France ESE of Pau *pop* 55,375
Ta·ri·fa, Cape \tä-'rē-fə\ cape S Spain; southernmost point of continental Europe, at 36°01′N
Ta·rim \'dä-'rēm, 'tä-\ river 1250 *m* W China in Sinkiang in the Takla Makan flowing E & SE into Lop Nor (marshy depression)
Tar·lac \'tär-ˌläk\ city Philippines in *cen* Luzon *pop* 121,400
Tarn \'tärn\ river 233 *m* S France flowing W into the Garonne
Tar·now \'tär-ˌnüf\ city S Poland E of Krakow *pop* 85,500
Tar·qui·nia \tär-'kwēn-yə, -'kwēn-ē-ə, -'kwin-\ *or formerly* **Cor·ne·to** \kȯr-'nāt-(ˌ)ō\ *or anc* **Tar·quin·ii** \tär-'kwin-ē-ˌī\ town *cen* Italy in N Latium NW of Viterbo
Tar·ra·go·na \ˌtar-ə-'gō-nə\ **1** province NE Spain on the Mediterranean *area* 2505, *pop* 431,961 **2** commune & port, its ✱, SW of Barcelona *pop* 78,238
Tar·ra·sa \tə-'räs-ə\ commune NE Spain NNW of Barcelona *pop* 127,814
Tar·shish \'tär-(ˌ)shish\ ancient maritime country referred to in the Bible, by some located in S Spain & identified with Tartessus
Tar·sus \'tär-səs\ city S Turkey near the Cilician Gates ✱ of ancient Cilicia *pop* 57,737
Tar·tes·sus *or* **Tar·tes·sos** \tär-'tes-əs\ ancient kingdom on SW coast of Spanish peninsula — see TARSHISH
Tar·tu \'tär-(ˌ)tü\ *or* G **Dor·pat** \'dȯ(ə)r-ˌpät\ city E Estonia W of Lake Peipus *pop* 87,000
Tash·kent \tash-'kent\ *or* **Tash·kend** \-'kent, -'kend\ city U.S.S.R. in Soviet Central Asia E of the Syr Darya ✱ of Uzbekistan *pop* 1,385,000
Tas·man \'taz-mən\ sea comprising the part of the S Pacific between SE Australia & W New Zealand
Tasman, Mount mountain 11,475 *ft* New Zealand in South I. in Southern Alps NE of Mt. Cook

ə abut ᵊ kitten, F table ər further a back ā bake
ä cot, cart ȧ F bac au̇ out ch chin e less ē easy
g gift i trip ī life j joke k G ich ⁿ F vin ŋ sing
ō flow ȯ flaw œ F bœuf œ̄ F feu ȯi coin th thing
t͟h this ü loot u̇ foot ue G Füllen ue̅ F rue y yet
ʸ F digne \dēnʸ\, nuit \nwʸē\ yü few yu̇ furious zh vision

Tas·ma·nia \taz-ˈmā-nē-ə, -nyə\ *or formerly* **Van Die·men's Land** \van-ˈdē-mənz\ island SE Australia S of Victoria; a state ✱ Hobart *area* 26,215, *pop* 392,200 — **Tas·ma·nian** \taz-ˈmā-nē-ən, -nyən\ *adj or n*

Ta·tar \ˈtät-ər\ strait between Sakhalin I. & mainland of Asia

Tatar Republic autonomous republic U.S.S.R. in E Soviet Russia, Europe, at bend of the middle Volga ✱ Kazan *area* 26,100, *pop* 3,131,000

Ta·ta·ry \ˈtät-ə-rē\ *or* **Tar·ta·ry** \ˈtärt-ə-\ an indefinite historical region in Asia & Europe extending from Sea of Japan to the Dnieper

Ta·tra \ˈtä-trə\ *or* **High Tatra** mountains E Czechoslovakia in *cen* Carpathian mountains — see GERLACHOVKA

Ta·tung \ˈdä-ˈtůŋ\ city NE China in N Shansi *pop* 300,000

Tau·ghan·nock Falls \tə-ˌgan-ək-\ waterfall 215 *ft* S *cen* N.Y. NW of Ithaca

Taung·gyi \ˈtaůn-ˈjē\ town E Burma ✱ of Shan State

Taun·ton \ˈtȯnt-^{ə}n, ˈtänt-, ˈtant-\ city SE Mass. *pop* 43,756

Tau·nus \ˈtaů-nəs\ mountain range W Germany E of the Rhine & N of the lower Main; highest peak Grosser Feldberg 2886 *ft*

Tauric Chersonese — see CHERSONESE

Tauris — see TABRIZ

Tau·rus \ˈtȯr-əs\ *or* Turk **To·ros** \tō-ˈrȯs\mountains S Turkey parallel to Mediterranean coast; highest Ala Dag 12,251 *ft*

Tax·co \ˈtäs-(ˌ)kō\ *or* **Taxco de Alar·cón** \-(ˌ)dā-ˌäl-ˌär-ˈkōn\ city S Mexico in Guerrero SSW of Mexico City *pop* 64,368

Tay \ˈtā\ river 120 *m* E *cen* Scotland flowing into North sea through **Firth of Tay** (estuary 25 *m* long)

Tay·lor \ˈtā-lər\ city SE Mich. SW of Detroit *pop* 70,020

Tbilisi — see TIFLIS

Tchad — see CHAD

Teche, Bayou \ˈtesh\ stream 175 *m* S La. flowing SE into the Atchafalaya

Tees \ˈtēz\ river 70 *m* N England flowing E along boundary between Yorkshire & Durham & into North sea

Tees·side \ˈtēz-ˌsīd\ county borough N England in North Riding, Yorkshire on the Tees *pop* 395,477

Te·gu·ci·gal·pa \tə-ˌgü-sə-ˈgal-pə\ city ✱ of Honduras *pop* 232,276

Te·hach·a·pi \ti-ˈhach-ə-pē\ **1** mountains SE Calif. N of Mojave desert running E–W between S end of Sierra Nevada & the Coast ranges; highest Double Mountain 7988 *ft* **2** pass 3793 *ft* at E end of the mountains

Teh·ran *or* **Te·he·ran** \ˌtā-ə-ˈran, -ˈrän\ city ✱ of Iran at foot of S slope of Elburz mountains *pop* 2,719,730

Teh·ri \ˈtā-rē\ *or* **Tehri Garh·wal** \-(ˌ)gər-ˈwäl\district N India in NW Uttar Pradesh on Tibet border; chief town Tehri

Te·huan·te·pec, Isthmus of \tə-ˈwänt-ə-ˌpek\ the narrowest section of Mexico, between **Gulf of Tehuantepec** (on Pacific side) & Bay of Campeche; 130 *m* wide

Tejo — see TAGUS

Te·jon \tē-ˈhōn\ pass 4183 *ft* SW Calif. in Tehachapi mountains NW of Los Angeles

Tel Aviv \ˌtel-ə-ˈvēv\ city W Israel *pop* 386,612 — see JAFFA

Tel·e·mark \ˈtel-ə-ˌmärk\ mountain region SW Norway

Telescope Peak mountain 11,045 *ft* E Calif., highest in Panamint mountains

Tell el ʻAmar·na *or* **Tel el ʻAmar·na** \ˌtel-ˌel-ə-ˈmär-nə\ *or* **Tell Amarna** locality *cen* Egypt on E bank of the Nile NW of Asyût; site of Egyptian ruins

Te·ma \ˈtē-mə\ city & port Ghana E of Accra *pop* 58,815

Temes — see TIMIS

Temesvar — see TIMISOARA

Tem·pe, 1 \tem-ˈpē\ city S *cen* Ariz. SE of Phoenix *pop* 62,907 **2** \ˈtem-pē\ *or* NGk **Tém·bi** \ˈtem-bē\ valley (**Vale of Tempe**) in NE Thessaly between Mounts Olympus & Ossa

Tem·pel·hof \ˈtem-pəl-ˌhōf\ residential district of S Berlin, Germany

Tem·ple \ˈtem-pəl\ city NE *cen* Tex. SSW of Waco *pop* 33,431

Temple City city SW Calif. SE of Pasadena *pop* 29,673

Te·mu·co \tā-ˈmü-(ˌ)kō\ city S *cen* Chile *pop* 100,973

Tenedos — see BOZCAADA

Te·ner·ife \ˌten-ə-ˈrēf-[(ˌ)ā], -ˈrif\ *or formerly* **Te·ner·iffe** \ˌten-ə-ˈrif, -ˈrēf\ island Spain, largest of the Canary islands; chief town Santa Cruz de Tenerife *area* 782

Ten·gri Khan \ˌteŋ-(g)rē-ˈkän\ *or* **Khan Tengri** mountain 23,620 *ft* on border between Kirgiz Republic (U.S.S.R.) & Sinkiang (China) in Tien Shan

Ten·nes·see \ˌten-ə-ˈsē, ˈten-ə-ˌ\ **1** river 652 *m* E U.S., in Tenn., Ala., & Ky. flowing into the Ohio **2** state SE *cen* U.S. ✱ Nashville *area* 42,244, *pop* 3,924,164 — **Ten·nes·se·an** *or* **Ten·nes·see·an** \ˌten-ə-ˈsē-ən\ *adj or n*

Te·noch·ti·tlán \tā-ˌnōch-tē-ˈtlän\ MEXICO CITY — its name when capital of the Aztec Empire

Te·nos \ˈtē-ˌnäs\ *or* NGk **Tí·nos** *or* **Té·nos** \ˈtē-ˌnȯs\ island Greece in N Cyclades SE of Andros

Ten·sas \ˈten-ˌsȯ\ river 250 *m* NE La. uniting with the Ouachita to form the Black

Ten·saw \ˈten-ˌsȯ\ river 40 *m* SW Ala. formed by Tombigbee & Alabama rivers & flowing S into Mobile Bay

Te·o·ti·hua·cán \ˌtā-ō-ˌtē-wə-ˈkän\ city S *cen* Mexico in Mexico state NE of Mexico City; once ✱ of the Toltecs *pop* 15,704

Te·pic \tā-ˈpēk\ city W Mexico ✱ of Nayarit *pop* 110,402

Te·quen·da·ma Falls \ˌtā-kən-ˈdäm-ə\ waterfall 475 *ft*, *cen* Colombia S of Bogotá

Ter·cei·ra \tər-ˈser-ə, -ˈsir-\ island *cen* Azores *area* 233

Ter·ek \ˈter-ək\ river 380 *m* U.S.S.R. in S Soviet Russia, Europe, N of Caucasus mountains flowing into the Caspian

Te·re·si·na \ˌter-ə-ˈzē-nə\ city NE Brazil ✱ of Piauí *pop* 184,836

Termonde — see DENDERMONDE

Ter·na·te \tər-ˈnä-(ˌ)tā\ **1** island Indonesia in N Moluccas off W Halmahera **2** city & port, chief city of Ternate I. *pop* 24,287

Ter·ni \ˈte(ə)r-nē\ commune *cen* Italy NNE of Rome *pop* 105,508

Ter·ra·ci·na \ˌter-ə-ˈchē-nə\ city & port *cen* Italy in Latium SE of Pontine marshes *pop* 32,729

Ter·ra No·va National Park \ˌter-ə-ˈnō-və\ reservation E Canada in E Newfoundland *area* 153

Ter·re Haute \ˌter-ə-ˈhōt *also* -ˈhət, *rapid* ter-ˈhōt, -ˈhət\ city W Ind. on Wabash river *pop* 70,286

Te·ruel \ˌter-ə-ˈwel\ **1** province E Spain in S Aragon *area* 5720, *pop* 170,284 **2** commune, its ✱, S of Zaragoza *pop* 21,638

Te·schen \ˈtesh-ən\ *or* Czech **Te·sin** \ˈtē-ˌesh-ˌēn\ *or* Pol **Cie·szyn** \ˈchesh-ən\region *cen* Europe in Silesia; once an Austrian duchy; divided 1920 between Poland & Czechoslovakia

Tessin — see TICINO

Te·ton \ˈtē-ˌtän\ mountain range NW Wyo. — see GRAND TETON

Té·touan \tā-twä^{n}\ *or* Sp **Te·tuán** \te-ˈtwän, ˌtet-ə-ˈwän\city & port N Morocco on the Mediterranean SE of Tangier; formerly ✱ of Spanish Morocco *pop* 101,352

Teu·to·burg Forest \ˈt(y)üt-ə-ˌbərg\ *or* G **Teu·to·bur·ger Wald** \ˈtȯit-ə-ˌbůr-gər-ˌvält\ range of forested hills W Germany in region between the Ems & the Weser; highest point 1530 *ft*

Tewkes·bury \ˈt(y)üks-ˌber-ē, ˈtüks-, -b(ə-)rē\ **1** town NE Mass. SE of Lowell *pop* 22,755 **2** municipal borough SW *cen* England in Gloucestershire on Avon & Severn rivers

Tex·ar·kana \ˌtek-sər-ˈkan-ə\ **1** city SW Ark. adjacent to Texarkana, Tex. *pop* 21,682 **2** city NE Tex. *pop* 30,497

Tex·as \ˈtek-səs, -siz\ state S U.S. ✱ Austin *area* 267,339, *pop* 11,196,730 — **Tex·an** \-sən\ *adj or n*

Texas City city & port SE Tex. on Galveston Bay *pop* 38,908

Tex·co·co \tes-ˈkō-(ˌ)kō\ *or* **Tez·cu·co** \tes-ˈkü-\ city *cen* Mexico in Mexico state E of Mexico City *pop* 67,220

Thai·land \ˈtī-ˌland, -lənd\ *or* **Si·am** \sī-ˈam\ country SE Asia bordering on Gulf of Siam; a kingdom ✱ Bangkok *area* 198,247, *pop* 35,340,000 — **Thai·land·er** \-ˌlan-dər, -lən-\ *n*

Thailand, Gulf of — see SIAM (Gulf of)

Thames, 1 \ˈtemz, ˈthāmz, ˈtāmz\ river 15 *m* SE Conn., an estuary flowing S into Long Island Sound **2** \ˈtemz\ river 135 *m* Canada in SE Ont. flowing S & SW into Lake St. Clair **3** \ˈtemz\ river 209 *m* S England flowing from the Cotswolds in Gloucestershire E into the North sea — see ISIS

Than·et, Isle of \ˈthan-ət\ tract of land SE England in NE Kent cut off from mainland by arms of Stour river *area* 42

Thar \ˈtär\ *or* **Indian** desert NW India (subcontinent) in Pakistan & Republic of India between Aravalli range & the Indus *area ab* 100,000

Tha·sos \ˈthā-ˌsäs\ *or* NGk **Thá·sos** \ˈthäs-ˌȯs\ island Greece in the N Aegean E of Chalcidice peninsula *area* 152

The·ba·id \thi-ˈbā-əd, ˈthē-bā-ˌid\ district about Thebes, Egypt

Thebes \ˈthēbz\ **1** *or anc* **The·bae** \ˈthē-(ˌ)bē\ *or* **Di·os·po·lis** \dī-ˈäs-pə-ləs\ ancient city S Egypt on the Nile S of modern Qena — see KARNAK, LUXOR **2** ancient city E Greece on site of modern village of Thívai 33 *m* NNW of Athens — **The·ban** \ˈthē-bən\ *adj or n*

The Hague — see HAGUE (The)

The·lon \ˈthē-ˌlän\ river *ab* 550 *m* N Canada in E Northwest Territories flowing NE to Baker Lake

Thera — see SANTORIN

Thermaic Gulf — see SALONIKA (Gulf of)

Ther·mop·y·lae \(ˌ)thər-ˈmäp-ə-(ˌ)lē\ locality E Greece between Mt. Oeta & Gulf of Lamia; once a narrow pass along the coast, now a rocky plain 6 *m* from the sea

Thessalonica *or* **Thessaloníki** — see SALONIKA

Thes·sa·ly \ˈthes-ə-lē\ *or* G **Thes·sa·lia** \the-ˈsā-lē-ə, -ˈsāl-yə\ region E Greece between Pindus mountains & the Aegean — **Thes·sa·lian** \the-ˈsā-lē-ən, -ˈsāl-yən\ *adj or n*

Thet·ford Mines \ˌthet-fərd-\ city Canada in S Que. *pop* 22,003

Thim·bu \ˈthim-(ˌ)bü\ town NW Bhutan ✱ of Bhutan *pop* (district) 60,027

Thira — see SANTORIN

Thom·as·ville \ˈtäm-əs-ˌvil, -vəl\ **1** city S Ga. *pop* 18,155 **2** city *cen* N.C. SE of Winston-Salem *pop* 15,230

Thomp·son \ˈtäm(p)-sən\ **1** river 304 *m* Canada in S B.C. flowing S (as the **North Thompson** 210 *m*) & thence W & SW into the Fraser; joined by a branch, the **South Thompson** (206 *m*) **2** city Canada in S Man. *pop* 19,001

Thorn — see TORUN

Thor·old \ˈthȯr-əld, ˈthär-\ town Canada in S Ont. W of Niagara Falls *pop* 15,065

Thors·havn \tȯrs-ˈhaůn\ town & port ✱ of the Faeroe islands, on Strömö I.

Thousand Islands island group Canada & U.S. in the St. Lawrence in Ont. & N.Y.

Thousand Oaks city SW Calif. W of Los Angeles *pop* 36,334

Thrace \ˈthrās\ region SE Europe in Balkan peninsula N of the Aegean; as ancient country (**Thra·ce** \ˈthrā-(ˌ)sē\ *or* **Thra·cia** \ˈthrā-sh(ē-)ə\), extended to the Danube; modern remnant divided between Greece (**Western Thrace**) & Turkey (**Eastern Thrace,** constituting Turkey in Europe) — **Thra·cian** \ˈthrā-shən\ *adj or n*

Thracian Chersonese — see CHERSONESE

Three Forks locality SW Mont. where Missouri river is formed by confluence of the Gallatin, Jefferson, & Madison

Three Rivers TROIS-RIVIÈRES

Thu·le \ˈtü-lē\ settlement & district NW Greenland N of Cape York

Thun, Lake of \ˈtün\ *or* G **Thu·ner·see** \ˈtü-nər-ˌzā\ lake 10 *m* long *cen* Switzerland; an expansion of Aare river

Thunder Bay city & port Canada in SW Ont. on Lake Superior, formed 1970 by consolidation of Fort William & Port Arthur *pop* 108,411

Thur·gau \ˈtů(ə)r-ˌgaů\ *or* F **Thur·go·vie** \tu̇ēr-gō-vē\ canton NE Switzerland ✱ Frauenfeld *area* 397, *pop* 182,835

Thu·rin·gia \th(y)ů-ˈrin-j(ē-)ə\ *or* G **Thü·ring·en** \ˈtu̇ē-riŋ-ən\region E Germany including the **Thu·rin·gian Forest** \th(y)ů-ˈrin-j(ē-)ən\ *or* G **Thü·ring·er Wald** \ˈtu̇ē-riŋ-ər-ˌvält\ (wooded mountain range between the upper Werra & Czech border)

Thur·rock \ˈthər-ək, ˈthə-rək\ urban district SE England in Essex *pop* 124,682

Thursday island NE Australia off N Queensland in Torres strait

Thyatira — see AKHISAR

Ti·a·hua·na·co \ˌtē-ə-wə-ˈnäk-(ˌ)ō\ locality W Bolivia near SE end of Lake Titicaca; site of prehistoric ruins

Ti·ber \ˈtī-bər\ *or* It **Te·ve·re** \ˈtā-vä-rā\ river 224 *m, cen* Italy flowing through Rome into Tyrrhenian sea

Ti·be·ri·as \tī-ˈbir-ē-əs\ city N Palestine in Galilee on W shore of Sea of Galilee; now in NE Israel *pop* 23,900

Tiberias, Sea of — see GALILEE (Sea of)

Ti·bes·ti \tə-ˈbes-tē\ mountains N *cen* Africa in the Sahara in NW Chad; highest Emi Koussi 11,204 *ft*

Ti·bet \tə-ˈbet\ region SW China on high plateau (average altitude 16,000 *ft*) N of the Himalayas ✻ Lhasa *area* 471,660, *pop* 1,400,000

Ti·bu·rón \ˌtē-bə-ˈrōn\ island 34 *m* long NW Mexico in Gulf of California off coast of Sonora

Ti·ci·no \ti-ˈchē-(ˌ)nō\ **1** river 154 *m* Switzerland & Italy flowing from slopes of St. Gotthard range SE & SW through Lake Maggiore into the Po **2** *or* F **Tes·sin** \tā-saⁿ\ canton S Switzerland bordering on Italy ✻ Bellinzona *area* 1085, *pop* 245,458

Tien Shan *or* **Tian Shan** \tē-ˈen-ˈshän, tē-ˈän-\ mountain system *cen* Asia extending from the Pamirs NE into Sinkiang — see POBEDA (Peak)

Tien·tsin \tē-ˈen(t)-ˈsin, ˈtin(t)-\ city & port NE China ✻ of Hopei SE of Peking *pop* 4,500,000

Tier·ra del Fue·go \tē-ˈer-ə-ˌdel-f(y)ü-ˈā-(ˌ)gō\ **1** archipelago off S So. America S of Strait of Magellan; in Argentina & Chile *area* 27,600 **2** chief island of the archipelago; divided between Chile and Argentina *area* 18,530

Tif·fin \ˈtif-ən\ city N Ohio on Sandusky river *pop* 21,596

Ti·flis \ˈtif-ləs, tə-ˈflēs\ *or* **Tbi·li·si** *or* **Tpl·li·si** \tə-ˈbil-ə-sē, -ˈpil-\ city U.S.S.R. ✻ of Georgia on Kura river *pop* 889,000

Ti·gre, 1 \ˈtē-(ˌ)grā\ city E Argentina, NW suburb of Buenos Aires, on islands in Paraná delta *pop* 91,725 **2** \ti-ˈgrā, ˈtig-(ˌ)rā\ region N Ethiopia bordering on Eritrea

Ti·gris \ˈtī-grəs\ river 1150 *m* Iraq & SE Turkey flowing SSE & uniting with the Euphrates to form the Shatt-al-Arab

Tihwa — see URUMCHI

Ti·jua·na \tē-(ə-)ˈwän-ə\ city NW Mexico on U.S. border in Baja California state *pop* 335,125

Ti·kal \ti-ˈkäl\ ancient Mayan city N Guatemala

Til·burg \ˈtil-ˌbərg\ commune S Netherlands *pop* 151,897

Til·bury \ˈtil-ˌber-ē, -b(ə-)rē\ town & port SE England in Essex on the Thames E of London in Thurrock urban district

Til·la·mook Bay \ˈtil-ə-ˌmu̇k\ inlet of the Pacific NW Oreg.

Tilsit — see SOVETSK

Ti·ma·ga·mi, Lake \tə-ˈmäg-ə-mē\ lake Canada in Ont. N of Lake Nipissing

Tim·buk·tu *or* **Tim·buc·too** \ˌtim-ˌbək-ˈtü, tim-ˈbək-(ˌ)tü\ *or* F **Tom·bouc·tou** \tōⁿ-bük-tü\ town W Africa in Mali (formerly French Sudan) near the Niger

Tim·gad \ˈtim-ˌgad\ ancient Roman city NE Algeria

Ti·mis \ˈtē-mish\ *or* **Te·mes** \ˈtem-ˌesh\ river 270 *m* Rumania & Yugoslavia flowing W & S into the Danube below Belgrade

Ti·mi·soa·ra \ˌtē-mish-(ə-)ˈwär-ə\ *or* Hung **Te·mes·var** \ˈtem-ˌesh-ˌvär\ city SW Rumania near Yugoslav border *pop* 189,264

Tim·mins \ˈtim-ənz\ town Canda in E Ont. N of Sudbury *pop* 28,542

Ti·mor \ˈtē-ˌmȯ(ə)r, tē-ˈ\ **1** island SE Malay archipelago; W half (formerly **Netherlands Timor**) belonged to the Dutch until 1946, now part of Indonesia ✻ Kupang *area* 18,485, *pop* 2,475,000; E half (**Portuguese Timor**) an overseas territory of Portugal ✻ Dili *area* 5762, *pop* 517,079 **2** sea between Timor I. & Australia — **Ti·mor·ese** \(ˌ)tē-ˌmō-ˈrēz, -ˈrēs\ *n*

Timorlaut — see TANIMBAR

Tim·pa·no·gos, Mount \ˌtim-pə-ˈnō-gəs\ mountain 12,008 *ft* N *cen* Utah N of Provo; highest in Wasatch mountains

Timpanogos Cave National Monument series of limestone caverns N *cen* Utah on N slope of Mt. Timpanogos

Ti·ni·an \ˌtin-ē-ˈan\ island W Pacific in the S Marianas

Tinos — see TENOS

Tin·tag·el Head \tin-ˌtaj-əl-\ headland SW England in NW Cornwall

Tip·pe·ca·noe \ˌtip-ē-kə-ˈnü\ river 200 *m* N Ind. flowing SW into the Wabash

Tip·per·ary \ˌtip-ə-ˈre(ə)r-ē\ **1** county S Ireland in Munster ✻ Clonmel *area* 1643, *pop* 123,196 **2** urban district in SW County Tipperary

Ti·ra·ne *or* **Ti·ra·na** \ti-ˈrän-ə\ city ✻ of Albania *pop* 169,300

Tir·gu–Mu·res \ˌti(ə)r-(ˌ)gü-ˈmü-ˌresh\ city NE *cen* Rumania ESE of Cluj *pop* 98,201

Ti·rich Mir \ˌtir-ich-ˈmi(ə)r\ mountain 25,263 *ft* Pakistan on Afghan border; highest in the Hindu Kush

Ti·rol *or* **Ty·rol** \tə-ˈrōl; ˈtī-ˌrōl, tī-ˈ; ˈtir-əl\ *or* It **Ti·ro·lo** \tē-ˈrō-(ˌ)lō\ region Europe in E Alps chiefly in Austria; the section S of Brenner pass has belonged since 1919 to Italy — **Ti·ro·le·an** \tə-ˈrō-lē-ən, ti-; ˌtir-ə-ˈ, ˌtī-rə-ˈ\ *adj or n* — **Ti·ro·lese** \ˌtir-ə-ˈlēz, ˌtī-rə-, -ˈlēs\ *adj or n*

Ti·ruch·chi·rap·pal·li \ˌtir-ə-chə-ˈräp-ə-lē\ *or* **Trich·i·nop·o·ly** \ˌtrich-ə-ˈnäp-ə-lē\ city S India in *cen* Tamil Nadu *pop* 282,819

Ti·ryns \ˈtir-ənz, ˈtī-rənz\ city of pre-Homeric Greece; ruins in E Peloponnesus SE of Argos

Ti·sza \ˈtis-ˌȯ\ *or* **Ti·sa** \ˈtē-sə\ river 800 *m* E Europe flowing from the Carpathians in W Ukraine W & SW into the Danube

Ti·ti·ca·ca \ˌtit-i-ˈkäk-ə\ lake on Peru-Bolivia boundary at altitude of 12,500 *ft, area* 3200

Ti·to·grad \ˈtēt-(ˌ)ō-ˌgrad\ *or* **Pod·go·ri·ca** *or* **Pod·go·ri·tsa** \ˈpäd-gə-ˌrēt-sə\ city S Yugoslavia ✻ of Montenegro *pop* 54,509

Ti·tus·ville \ˈtīt-əs-ˌvil, -vəl\ city E Fla. E of Orlando *pop* 30,515

Tiv·o·li \ˈtiv-ə-lē\ *or anc* **Ti·bur** \ˈtī-bər\ commune *cen* Italy in Latium ENE of Rome *pop* 40,501

Tji·la·tjap *or* **Chi·la·chap** \chi-ˈläch-ˌäp\ city & port Indonesia in S Java ESE of Bandung *pop* 55,333

Tjir·e·bon \ˌchir-ə-ˈbȯn\ *or* **Cher·i·bon** \ˌcher-ə-\ city Indonesia in W Java on N coast E of Djakarta *pop* 158,299

Tlax·ca·la \tlä-ˈskäl-ə\ **1** state *cen* Mexico *area* 1555, *pop* 418,334 **2** city, its ✻, E of Mexico City *pop* 21,421

Tlem·cen *or* **Tlem·sen** \tlem-ˈsen\ city NW Algeria SW of Oran *pop* 71,186

To·ba·go \tə-ˈbā-(ˌ)gō\ island SE West Indies, a territory of Trinidad & Tobago; chief town Scarborough *area* 116, *pop* 39,280

To·bol \tə-ˈbȯl\ river 800 *m* U.S.S.R. flowing from SE foothills of the Urals NNE into the Irtysh

To·bruk \ˈtō-ˌbru̇k\ city & port NE Libya *pop* 28,000

To·can·tins \ˌtō-kən-ˈtēnz, ˌtü-kən-ˈtēⁿs\ river 1700 *m* E *cen* & NE Brazil rising in S *cen* Goiás & flowing N into the Pará

To·go \ˈtō-(ˌ)gō\ *or* **To·go·land** \-ˌland\ **1** region W Africa on Gulf of Guinea between Dahomey & Ghana; until 1919 a German protectorate, then divided into two trust territories: **British Togoland** (in W, *area* 13,041; since 1957 part of Ghana) & **French Togo** (in E, since 1958 the Republic of Togo) **2** republic W Africa ✻ Lomé *area* 21,893, *pop* 1,440,000 — **To·go·lese** \ˌtō-(ˌ)gō-ˈlēz, -ˈlēs\ *adj or n* — **To·go·land·er** \ˈtō-(ˌ)gō-ˌlan-dər\ *n*

To·ho·pe·kal·i·ga \tə-ˌhō-pi-ˈkal-i-gə\ lake *cen* Fla. S of Orlando

To·ka·ra \tō-ˈkär-ə\ island group Japan in N Ryukyus

To·ke·lau \ˈtō-kə-ˌlau̇\ *or* **Union** islands *cen* Pacific N of Samoa belonging to New Zealand

To·ku·shi·ma \ˌtō-kə-ˈshē-mə\ city & port Japan on E coast of Shikoku I. *pop* 228,000

To·kyo \ˈtō-kē-ˌō\ *or formerly* **Edo** \ˈed-(ˌ)ō\ *or* **Ye·do** \ˈyed-(ˌ)ō\ city ✻ of Japan in SE Honshu on **Tokyo Bay** (inlet of the Pacific) *pop* 9,005,000 — **To·kyo·ite** \ˈtō-kē-(ˌ)ō-ˌīt\ *n*

Tokyo Plain — see KWANTO PLAIN

To·le·do \tə-ˈlēd-(ˌ)ō, -ˈlēd-ə\ **1** city & port NW Ohio *pop* 383,818 **2** province *cen* Spain in W New Castile *area* 5919, *pop* 468,925 **3** commune, its ✻ *pop* 44,382 — **To·le·dan** \-ˈlēd-ᵊn\ *adj or n* — **To·le·do·an** \-ˈlēd-ə-wən\ *adj or n*

Tol·i·ganj *or* **Tol·ly·ganj** *or* **Tol·ly·gunge** \ˈtäl-ē-ˌgənj\ city E India in S West Bengal, SSE suburb of Calcutta *pop* 357,000

To·li·ma \tə-ˈlē-mə\ dormant volcano W *cen* Colombia 17,717 *ft*

To·lu·ca \tə-ˈlü-kə\ *or* **Toluca de Ler·do** \-də-ˈle(ə)r-(ˌ)dō\ city *cen* Mexico ✻ of Mexico state *pop* 220,195

To·lu·ca, Ne·va·do de \nə-ˈväd-ō-ˌdāt-ᵊl-ˈü-kə\ extinct volcano 15,016 *ft* S *cen* Mexico in Mexico state

Tom \ˈtäm, ˈtȯm\ river 450 *m* U.S.S.R. in W Soviet Russia, Asia, rising in NW Altai mountains & flowing into the Ob

Tom·big·bee \täm-ˈbig-bē\ river 300 *m* NE Miss. & W Ala. flowing S to the Mobile & Tensaw

Tomsk \ˈtäm(p)sk, ˈtȯm(p)sk\ city U.S.S.R. in W *cen* Soviet Russia, Asia, on the Tom near its junction with the Ob *pop* 339,000

Ton·a·wan·da \ˌtän-ə-ˈwän-də\ city W N.Y. N of Buffalo *pop* 21,898

Ton·ga \ˈtäŋ-(g)ə\ *or* **Friendly** islands SW Pacific E of Fiji islands; a kingdom in Brit. Commonwealth ✻ Nukualofa *area* 270, *pop* 90,000

Ton·ga·re·va \ˌtäŋ-(g)ə-ˈrev-ə\ *or* **Pen·rhyn** \pen-ˈrin, ˈpen-ˌ\ island S Pacific in the Manihiki islands

Ton·ga·ri·ro \ˌtäŋ-(g)ə-ˈri(ə)r-(ˌ)ō\ volcano 6458 *ft* New Zealand in *cen* North I. in **Tongariro National Park**

Tongue \ˈtəŋ\ river 240 *m* N Wyo. & S Mont. flowing N into the Yellowstone

Ton·kin \ˈtäŋ-kən; ˈtän-ˈkin, ˈtäŋ-\ *or* **Tong·king** \ˈtäŋ-ˈkiŋ\ region N Indochina bordering on China, since 1946 forming N part of Vietnam; chief city Hanoi *area* 44,660 — **Ton·kin·ese** \ˌtäŋ-kə-ˈnēz, ˌtän-, -ˈnēs\ *or* **Tong·king·ese** \ˌtäŋ-kiŋ-ˈēz, -ˈēs\ *adj or n*

Tonkin, Gulf of arm of So. China sea between Indochina & Hainan I.

Ton·le Sap \ˌtän-ˌlā-ˈsap\ *or* F **Grand Lac** \gräⁿ-läk\ lake 87 *m* long SW Indochina in W Cambodia

Ton·to National Monument \ˈtän-(ˌ)tō\ reservation S *cen* Ariz. E of Phoenix containing cliff-dweller ruins

Too·woom·ba \tə-ˈwu̇m-bə\ city E Australia in SE Queensland W of Brisbane *pop* 58,000

To·pe·ka \tə-ˈpē-kə\ city ✻ of Kans. on Kansas river *pop* 125,011

To·po·lo·bam·po \tə-ˌpō-lə-ˈbäm-(ˌ)pō\ town & port NW Mexico in Sinaloa on Gulf of California

Tor·bay \(ˈ)tȯr-ˈbā\ county borough SW England in Devonshire on **Tor Bay** (inlet of English channel) *pop* 108,888

Tor·cel·lo \tȯr-ˈchel-(ˌ)ō\ island Italy in Lagoon of Venice

Tor·de·si·llas \ˌtȯrd-ə-ˈsē-(y)əs\ village NW Spain on the Duero SW of Valladolid

Torino — see TURIN

Tor·ne \ˈtȯr-nə\ *or* Finn **Tor·nio** \ˈtȯr-nē-ˌō\ river 250 *m* NE Sweden flowing S, forming part of Finnish-Swedish border, to head of Gulf of Bothnia

To·ron·to \tə-ˈränt-(ˌ)ō, -ˈränt-ə\ city & port Canada ✻ of Ont. on Lake Ontario *pop* 712,786 — **To·ron·to·ni·an** \tə-ˌrän-ˈtō-nē-ən; ˌtȯr-ən-, ˌtär-ən-\ *adj or n*

Toros — see TAURUS

Tor·quay \(ˈ)tȯr-ˈkē\ former municipal borough SW England, now part of Torbay

Tor·rance \ˈtȯr-ən(t)s, ˈtär-\ city SW Calif. *pop* 134,584

Tor·re An·nun·zi·a·ta \ˈtȯr-ē-ə-ˌnün(t)-sē-ˈät-ə\ commune S Italy on Bay of Naples SE of Naples *pop* 63,070

Torre de Cerredo — see CERREDO

Tor·re del Gre·co \ˈtȯr-ē-ˌdel-ˈgrek-(ˌ)ō, -ˈgrāk-\ commune S Italy on Bay of Naples *pop* 91,439

Tor·rens, Lake \ˈtȯr-ənz, ˈtär-\ salt lake Australia in E So. Australia N of Spencer Gulf; 25 *ft* below sea level

Tor·re·ón \ˌtȯr-ē-ˈōn\ city N Mexico in Coahuila *pop* 257,045

Tor·res \ˈtȯr-əs\ strait 80 *m* wide between island of New Guinea & N tip of Cape York peninsula, Australia

Tor·res Ve·dras \ˌtȯr-əs-ˈvā-drəs\ town W Portugal N of Lisbon

ə abut ᵊ kitten, F table ər further a back ā bake
ä cot, cart ȧ F bac au̇ out ch chin e less ē easy
g gift i trip ī life j joke k̲ G ich ⁿ F vin ŋ sing
ō flow ȯ flaw œ F bœuf œ̄ F feu ȯi coin th thing
th̲ this ü loot u̇ foot ue G Füllen ue̅ F rue y yet
ʸ F digne \dēnʸ\, nuit \nwʸē\ yü few yu̇ furious zh vision

Tor·ring·ton \'tȯr-iŋ-tən, 'tär-\ city NW Conn. *pop* 31,952

Tor·to·la \tȯr-'tō-lə\ island Brit. West Indies, chief of the British Virgin islands; site of Road Town *area* 24, *pop* 9730

Tor·tu·ga \tȯr-'tü-gə\ island Haiti off N coast *area* 70; a resort of pirates in 17th century

To·run \'tȯr-ˌün(-yə)\ *or* G **Thorn** \'tȯ(ə)rn\ city N Poland on the Vistula *pop* 126,200

Toscana — see TUSCANY

Tot·ten·ham \'tät-^{ə}n-əm, 'tät-nəm\ former municipal borough SE England in Middlesex, now part of Haringey

Toub·kal, Je·bel \ˌjeb-əl-tüb-'käl\ mountain 13,671 *ft* W *cen* Morocco; highest in Atlas mountains

Toug·gourt *or* **Tug·gurt** \tə-'gu̇(ə)rt\ town & oasis NE Algeria S of Biskra *pop* 50,000

Tou·lon \tü-lō^n\ commune & port SE France *pop* 174,746

Tou·louse \tu̇-'lüz\ city SW France on the Garonne *pop* 370,796

Tou·raine \tu̇-'rān, -'ren\ region & former province NW *cen* France ✻ Tours

Tourane — see DA NANG

Tour·coing \tu̇(ə)r-'kwa^n\ city N France NE of Lille *pop* 98,755

Tour·nai *or* **Tour·nay** \tu̇(ə)r-'nā\ *or* Flem **Door·nik** \'dōr-nik, 'dȯr-\ commune SW Belgium on the Scheldt *pop* 33,625

Tours \'tu̇(ə)r\ city NW *cen* France *pop* 128,120

Tower Hamlets borough of E Greater London, England *pop* 164,948

Towns·ville \'tau̇nz-ˌvil, -vəl\ city & port NE Australia in NE Queensland *pop* 63,300

To·ya·ma \tō-'yäm-ə\ city Japan in *cen* Honshu near **Toyama Bay** (inlet of Sea of Japan) *pop* 267,000

To·yo·ha·shi \ˌtȯi-ə-'häsh-ē\ city Japan in S Honshu SE of Nagoya *pop* 344,000

Tpilisi — see TIFLIS

Trab·zon \trab-'zän\ *or* **Treb·i·zond** \'treb-ə-ˌzänd\ *or anc* **Trap·e·zus** \'trap-i-zəs\ city & port NE Turkey on Black sea *pop* 65,516

Tra·fal·gar, Cape \trə-'fal-gər, *Sp* ˌträ-fäl-'gär\ cape SW Spain SE of Cádiz at W end of Strait of Gibraltar

Tra·lee \trə-'lē\ urban district & port SW Ireland ✻ of Kerry

Trans Alai \ˌtran(t)s-ə-'lī, ˌtranz-\ mountain range U.S.S.R. in NW Pamirs in Kirgiz & Tadzhik republics — see LENIN PEAK

Transalpine Gaul the part of Gaul included chiefly in modern France & Belgium

Transcaucasia — see CAUCASIA — **Trans·cau·ca·sian** \ˌtran(t)s-kō-'kā-zhən, -'kazh-ən\ *adj or n*

Trans·co·na \tran(t)s-'kō-nə\ city Canada in SE Man. W of Winnipeg *pop* 22,490

Transjordan — see JORDAN — **Transjordanian** *adj or n*

Trans·kei \(')tran(t)s-'kī\ territory E Republic of So. Africa in Cape Province S of Natal; a Bantustan ✻ Umtata *area* 16,675, *pop* 1,439,195

Trans·vaal \tran(t)s-'väl, tranz-\ province NE Republic of So. Africa between Vaal & Limpopo rivers; in 19th century a Boer republic (**South African Republic**) ✻ Pretoria *area* 110,450, *pop* 7,394,961

Tran·syl·va·nia *or* Rum **Tran·sil·va·nia** \ˌtran(t)s-əl-'vā-nyə, -nē-ə\ region W Rumania bounded on the N, E, & S by the Carpathians & the Transylvanian Alps; part of Hungary 1867–1918 — **Tran·syl·va·nian** \-nyən, -nē-ən\ *adj or n*

Transylvanian Alps a S extension of the Carpathian mountains in *cen* Rumania

Tra·pa·ni \'träp-ə-nē\ commune & port Italy at NW tip of Sicily *pop* 77,029

Tra·si·me·no, Lake \ˌtraz-ə-'men-(ˌ)ō\ *or* **Lake of Pe·ru·gia** \pə-'rü-j(ē-)ə, 'pā-\ lake 10 *m* wide *cen* Italy W of Perugia

Trav·an·core \'trav-ən-ˌkō(ə)r, -ˌkȯ(ə)r\ region & former state SW India on Malabar coast extending N from Cape Comorin; included (1949–56) in former **Travancore and Co·chin** \'kō-chən\ state (✻ Trivandrum) — see KERALA

Trav·erse, Lake \'trav-ərs\ lake NE S.Dak. & W Minn.; drained by the Bois de Sioux (headstream of Red river)

Trav·erse City \ˌtrav-ərs-\ city NW Mich. on Grand Traverse Bay *pop* 18,048

Treb·bia \'treb-ē-ə\ *or anc* **Tre·bia** \'trē-bē-ə\ river 71 *m* NW Italy flowing N into the Po

Treb·i·zond \'treb-ə-ˌzänd\ **1** — see TRABZON **2** Greek empire 1204–1461, an offshoot of Byzantine Empire; at greatest extent included Georgia, Crimea, & S coast of Black Sea E of Sakarya river

Trem·blant, Mont \mō^n-trä^n-blä^n\ mountain 3150 *ft* Canada in S Que. in Laurentian hills NW of Montreal

Treng·ga·nu \treŋ-'gän-(ˌ)ü\ state Federation of Malaysia bordering on So. China sea ✻ Kuala Trengganu *area* 5050

Trent \'trent\ **1** river 150 *m* Canada in SE Ont. flowing from Kawartha Lakes through Rice Lake into Lake Ontario (Bay of Quinte) **2** *or* **Trent–Sev·ern** \-'sev-ərn\ canal system Canada 224 *m* long in SE Ont. connecting Lake Huron (Georgian Bay) with Lake Ontario (Bay of Quinte) **3** river 170 *m*, *cen* England flowing NNE & uniting with the Ouse to form the Humber **4** *or* **Tren·to** \'tren-(ˌ)tō\ *or* G **Tri·ent** \trē-'ent\ *or anc* **Tri·den·tum** \trī-'dent-əm\ commune N Italy ✻ of Trentino-Alto Adige on Adige river *pop* 88,544

Tren·ti·no \tren-'tē-(ˌ)nō\ district N Italy in S Tirol; with Alto Adige, forms **Trentino–Alto Adige** region (✻ Trent *area* 6327, *pop* 834,675)

Tren·ton \'trent-^{ə}n\ **1** city SE Mich. on Detroit river *pop* 24,127 **2** city ✻ of N.J. on Delaware river *pop* 104,638

Tre·vi·so \trā-'vē-(ˌ)zō\ commune NE Italy NW of Venice *pop* 88,148

Trichinopoly — see TIRUCHCHIRAPPALLI

Trier \'tri(ə)r\ *or* **Treves** \'trēvz\ *or* F **Trèves** \'trev\ city W Germany on the Moselle near Luxembourg border *pop* 104,100

Tri·este \trē-'est, -'es-tē\ *or* G **Tri·est** \trē-'est\ *or* Serbo-Croatian **Trst** \'tərst\ city & port NE Italy on **Gulf of Trieste** (inlet at head of the Adriatic NW of the Istrian peninsula) *pop* 278,873; once belonged to Austria; part of Italy 1919–47; in 1947 made with surrounding territory the **Free Territory of Trieste** (*area* 293) under administration of the United Nations; city with N part of Free Territory returned to Italy 1953, S part of territory having previously been absorbed into Yugoslavia — **Tri·es·tine** \trē-'es-tən, -ˌtēn\ *adj*

Trim \'trim\ urban district E Ireland ✻ of County Meath

Trinacria — see SICILY — **Tri·nac·ri·an** \trə-'nak-rē-ən, trī-\ *adj*

Trin·co·ma·lee *or* **Trin·co·ma·li** \ˌtriŋ-kō-mə-'lē, triŋ-'kəm-ə-lē\ city & port NE Ceylon on inlet of Koddiyar Bay *pop* 39,000

Trin·i·dad \'trin-ə-ˌdad\ island SE West Indies off coast of NE Venezuela; with Tobago, a dominion (**Trinidad and Tobago**) of Brit. Commonwealth since 1962; formerly a Brit. colony ✻ Port of Spain *area* 1864, *pop* 938,600 — **Trin·i·da·di·an** \ˌtrin-ə-'dād-ē-ən, -'dad-\ *adj or n*

Trin·i·ty \'trin-ət-ē\ river 360 *m* E Tex. flowing SE into Galveston Bay

Trip·o·li \'trip-ə-lē\ **1** *or* Ar **Ta·ra·bu·lus** \tə-'räb-ə-ləs\ *or anc* **Oea** \'ē-ə\ city & port NW Libya a ✻ of Libya *pop* 247,365 **2** *or* Ar **Tarabulus** *or anc* **Trip·o·lis** \'trip-ə-ləs\ city & port NW Lebanon *pop* 127,611 **3** Tripolitania when it was one of the Barbary States — **Tri·pol·i·tan** \trip-'äl-ət-^{ə}n\ *adj or n*

Tri·po·li·ta·nia \ˌtrip-ˌäl-ə-'tān-yə, ˌtrip-ə-lə-\ *or anc* **Trip·o·lis** \'trip-ə-ləs\ region NW Libya bordering on the Mediterranean; formerly a province of Libya — **Tri·po·li·ta·nian** \trip-ˌäl-ə-'tān-yən, ˌtrip-ə-lə-\ *adj or n*

Tri·pu·ra \'trip-ə-rə\ territory E India between Bangladesh & Assam ✻ Agartala *area* 4032, *pop* 1,556,822

Tris·tan da Cu·nha \ˌtris-tən-də-'kü-nə\ island S Atlantic, chief of the Tristan da Cunha islands attached to Brit. colony of St. Helena *area* 42; volcanic eruptions 1961

Tri·van·drum \triv-'an-drəm\ city & port S India NW of Cape Comorin ✻ of Kerala *pop* 359,580

Tro·as \'trō-ˌas\ **1** *or* **Tro·ad** \-ˌad\ territory surrounding the ancient city of Troy in NW Mysia, Asia Minor **2** ancient city of Mysia S of site of Troy — **Tro·ad·ic** \trō-'ad-ik\ *adj*

Tro·bri·and \'trō-brē-ˌänd\ islands SW Pacific in Solomon sea; attached to Territory of Papua New Guinea *area* 170 — **Tro·bri·and·er** \ˌtrō-brē-'än-dər\ *n*

Trois–Ri·vières \ˌt(r)wä-rīv-'ye(ə)r\ city Canada in S Que. NE of Montreal on N bank of the St. Lawrence *pop* 55,869

Trom·sö \'träm-ˌsō, -ˌsə(r)\ city & port N Norway *pop* 38,064

Trond·heim \'trän-ˌhām\ city & port *cen* Norway on **Trondheim Fjord** (80 *m* long) *pop* 124,870

Tros·sachs \'träs-əks, -ˌaks\ valley *cen* Scotland in Perth between Lochs Katrine & Achray

Trou·ville \trü-'vē(ə)l\ *or* **Trouville–sur–Mer** \-(ˌ)su̇r-'me(ə)r\ town & port N France on English channel S of Le Havre

Trow·bridge \'trō-(ˌ)brij\ urban district S England ✻ of Wiltshire *pop* 19,245

Troy \'trȯi\ **1** city SE Mich. N of Detroit *pop* 39,419 **2** city E N.Y. on the Hudson NNE of Albany *pop* 62,918 **3** city W Ohio *pop* 17,186 **4** *or* **Il·i·um** \'il-ē-əm\ *or* **Il·i·on** \'il-ē-ˌän, -ē-ən\ *or* **Troia** \'trȯi-ə, 'trō-yə\ *or* **Tro·ja** \'trō-jə, -yə\ ancient city NW Asia Minor in Troas SW of the Dardanelles — see HISSARLIK

Troyes \trə-'wä\ city NE France SE of Paris *pop* 74,898

Tru·chas Peak \ˌtrü-chəs-\ *or* **North Truchas Peak** mountain 13,110 *ft* N N.Mex. in Sangre de Cristo mountains NE of Santa Fe; highest of three peaks forming **Truchas Peaks**

Trucial Oman, Trucial States — see UNITED ARAB EMIRATES

Truck·ee \'trək-ē\ river 120 *m* E Calif. & W Nev. flowing from Lake Tahoe into Pyramid Lake

Tru·ji·llo \trü-'hē-(ˌ)(y)ō\ **1** city NW Peru NW of Lima *pop* 149,000 **2** — see SANTO DOMINGO

Trujillo Al·to \-'äl-(ˌ)tō\ town NE *cen* Puerto Rico *pop* 18,477

Truk \'trək, 'tru̇k\ **1** district Trust Territory of the Pacific Islands in *cen* Carolines *land area* 49, *pop* 21,041 **2** islands, chief group in district

Trum·bull \'trəm-bəl\ town SW Conn. N of Bridgeport *pop* 31,394

Tru·ro \'tru̇(ə)r-(ˌ)ō\ municipal borough SW England ✻ of Cornwall

Tsamkong — see CHANKIANG

Tsana — see TANA

Tsang·po \'(t)säŋ-'pō\ the upper Brahmaputra in Tibet

Tsaritsyn — see VOLGOGRAD

Tsarskoe Selo — see PUSHKIN

Tsi·nan \'jē-'nän\ city E China ✻ of Shantung *pop* 1,500,000

Tsing·hai *or* **Ching·hai** \'chiŋ-'hī\ **1** *or* **Ko·ko Nor** \ˌkō-(ˌ)kō-'nȯ(ə)r\ shallow saline lake W *cen* China in NE Tsinghai province S of Nan Shan mountains at altitude of *ab* 10,000 *ft*, *area* 2300 **2** province W China ✻ Sining *area* 278,378, *pop* 2,000,000

Tsing·tao \'chiŋ-'dau̇, '(t)siŋ-'tau̇\ city & port E China in E Shantung on Kiaochow Bay *pop* 1,900,000

Tsingyuan — see PAOTING

Tsi·tsi·har \'(t)sēt-sē-ˌhär, 'chē-chē-\ *or formerly* **Lung·kiang** \'lu̇ŋ-jē-'äŋ\ city NE China in W Heilungkiang *pop* 1,500,000

Tskhin·va·li \'(t)skin-və-lē\ town N Georgia, U.S.S.R., NW of Tiflis ✻ of South Ossetia *pop* 30,000

Tsu·ga·ru \'(t)sü-gə-ˌrü\ strait Japan between Honshu & Hokkaido connecting Pacific ocean & Sea of Japan

Tsu·shi·ma \(t)sü-'shē-mə\ islands Japan in Korea strait separated from Kyushu and Honshu by **Tsushima strait** (the SE part of Korea strait) *area* 271

Tu·a·mo·tu \ˌtü-ə-'mō-(ˌ)tü\ *or* **Pau·mo·tu** \pau̇-'mō-\ *or* **Dan·ger·ous** \'dānj-(ə-)rəs\ *or* **Low** \'lō\ archipelago S Pacific E of Society islands; belongs to France *area* 330

Tü·bing·en \'t(y)ü-biŋ-ən, 'tue-\ city W Germany on the Neckar S of Stuttgart *pop* 55,795

Tu·buai \tüb-'wä-ˌē\ *or* **Aus·tral** \'ȯs-trəl, 'äs-\ islands S Pacific S of Tahiti belonging to France *area* 115, *pop* 5053

Tuc·son \tü-'sän, 'tü-ˌ\ city SE Ariz. *pop* 262,933

Tucumán — see SAN MIGUEL DE TUCUMÁN

Tu·ge·la \tü-'gā-lə\ river 300 *m* E Republic of So. Africa in *cen* Natal flowing E to Indian ocean; near its source on Mont Aux Sources are the **Tugela Falls** (3110 *ft*)

Tuggurt — see TOUGGOURT

Tu·la \'tü-lə\ **1** *or* **Tula de Allen·de** \-ˌdä-ä-'yen-dē\ city *cen* Mexico in SW Hidalgo N of Mexico City; ancient ✱ of the Toltecs *pop* 36,460 **2** city U.S.S.R. in *cen* Soviet Russia, Europe, S of Moscow on a tributary of the Oka *pop* 462,000

Tu·la·gi \tü-'läg-ē\ island S Pacific in S *cen* Solomons off S coast of Florida I. & N of Guadalcanal

Tu·lare \tü-'la(ə)r(-ē), -'le(ə)r(-ē)\ **1** former lake S *cen* Calif. S of Fresno; now drained for farmland **2** city S *cen* Calif. SE of Fresno *pop* 16,235

Tul·la·ho·ma \ˌtəl-ə-'hō-mə\ city S *cen* Tenn. *pop* 15,311

Tul·la·more \ˌtəl-ə-'mō(ə)r, -'mȯ(ə)r\ urban district *cen* Ireland ✱ of County Offaly

Tul·sa \'təl-sə\ city NE Okla. on Arkansas river *pop* 331,638

Tu·men \'tü-'mən\ river 220 *m* E Asia on border between Korea, China, & the U.S.S.R. flowing NE & SE into Sea of Japan

Tu·muc–Hu·mac *or* Pg **Tu·mu·cu·maque** \tə-ˌmü-kə-'mäk\ range of low mountains NE Brazil on Surinam-French Guiana boundary

Tunbridge Wells ROYAL TUNBRIDGE WELLS

Tunghai — see SINHAILIEN

Tung·hwa \'tu̇ŋ-'(h)wä\ city NE China in SW Kirin *pop* 275,000

Tungshan — see SÜCHOW

Tung·ting \'du̇ŋ-'tiŋ\ lake SE *cen* China in NE Hunan W of Poyang lake *area* 1450

Tun·gu·ska \tu̇ŋ-'gü-skə, tən-\ any of three rivers in Soviet Russia, Asia, tributaries of the Yenisei: **Lower Tunguska** (2000 *m*), **Stony Tunguska** (1000 *m*), & **Upper Tunguska** (lower course of the Angara)

Tu·nis \'t(y)ü-nəs\ **1** city ✱ of Tunisia near site of ancient Carthage *pop* 468,997 **2** TUNISIA — used esp. of the former Barbary state

Tu·ni·sia \t(y)ü-'nē-zh(ē-)ə, -'nizh-(ē-)ə\ country N Africa bordering on the Mediterranean; formerly one of the Barbary states; a French protectorate 1881–1956, a monarchy 1956–57, & a republic since 1957 ✱ Tunis *area* 48,300, *pop* 5,140,000 — **Tu·ni·sian** \-'nē-zh(ē-)ən, -'nizh-(ē-)ən\ *adj or n*

Tu·ol·um·ne \tu̇-'äl-ə-mē\ river 155 *m*, *cen* Calif. flowing W from Yosemite National Park into the San Joaquin

Tu·pe·lo \'t(y)ü-pə-ˌlō\ city NE Miss. *pop* 20,471

Tu·pun·ga·to \ˌtü-pən-'gät-(ˌ)ō\ mountain 22,310 *ft* in the Andes on Argentina-Chile boundary ENE of Santiago, Chile

Tur·fan \'tu̇(ə)r-'fän\ depression W China in E Sinkiang in NE part of Tarim basin; *ab* 425 *ft* below sea level at lowest point

Tu·rin \'t(y)u̇r-ən, t(y)u̇-'rin\ *or* It **To·ri·no** \tō-'rē-(ˌ)nō\ commune NW Italy on the Po ✱ of Piedmont *pop* 1,164,919 — **Tu·rin·ese** \ˌt(y)u̇r-ə-'nēz, -'nēs\ *adj or n*

Tur·ke·stan *or* **Tur·ki·stan** \ˌtər-kə-'stan, -'stän\ region *cen* Asia between Iran & Siberia; now divided between U.S.S.R., China, & Afghanistan — see CHINESE TURKESTAN, RUSSIAN TURKESTAN

Tur·key \'tər-kē\ country W Asia (**Turkey in Asia**) & SE Europe (**Turkey in Europe**) between Mediterranean & Black seas; formerly center of an empire (✱ Constantinople), since 1923 a republic ✱ Ankara *area* 301,302, *pop* 36,160,000 — see OTTOMAN EMPIRE

Turk·men Republic \ˌtərk-mən-\ *or* **Turk·me·nia** \ˌtərk-'mē-nē-ə\ *or* **Turk·men·i·stan** \ˌtərk-'men-ə-ˌstan\ constituent republic U.S.S.R. in *cen* Asia bordering on Afghanistan, Iran, & the Caspian ✱ Ashkhabad *area* 187,200, *pop* 2,158,000 — **Turk·man** \'tərk-mən\ *n* — **Turk·men** \-mən\ *adj* — **Turk·me·ni·an** \ˌtərk-'mē-nē-ən\ *adj*

Turks and Cai·cos \ˌtərk-sən-'kā-kəs\ two groups of islands (Turks Islands & Caicos islands) Brit. West Indies at SE end of the Bahamas; a Brit. colony; seat of government Grand Turk on **Grand Turk** island (7 *m* long) *area* 166, *pop* 5675

Tur·ku \'tu̇(ə)r-(ˌ)kü\ *or* Sw **Abo** \'ō-(ˌ)bü\ city & port SW Finland *pop* 150,568

Turn·hout \'tu̇(ə)rn-ˌhau̇t, tu̇r-'nüt\ commune N Belgium *pop* 37,927

Tur·tle Bay \ˌtərt-ᵊl-\ section of New York City in E *cen* Manhattan on East river; site of United Nations headquarters

Tus·ca·loo·sa \ˌtəs-kə-'lü-sə\ city W *cen* Ala. on Black Warrior river SW of Birmingham *pop* 65,773

Tus·ca·ny \'təs-kə-nē\ *or* It **To·sca·na** \tō-'skän-ə\ region NW *cen* Italy bordering on Ligurian & Tyrrhenian seas ✱ Florence *area* 8861, *pop* 3,434,618

Tus·cu·lum \'təs-k(y)ə-ləm\ ancient town Italy in Latium SE of Rome & N of Alban hills near modern Frascati

Tus·tin \'təs-tən\ city SW Calif. E of Santa Ana *pop* 21,178

Tu·tu·ila \ˌtüt-ə-'wē-lə\ island, chief of American Samoa group *area* 52, *pop* 24,548 — **Tu·tu·ilan** \-lən\ *adj or n*

Tu·va \'tü-və\ autonomous republic U.S.S.R. in S Soviet Russia, Asia, N of Outer Mongolia *area* 65,810, *pop* 231,000

Tux·tla \'tüst-lə\ *or* **Tuxtla Gu·tiér·rez** \-gü-'tyer-əs\ city SE Mexico ✱ of Chiapas *pop* 69,326

Tu·zi·goot National Monument \'tü-zi-ˌgüt\ reservation *cen* Ariz. SW of Flagstaff containing ruins of prehistoric pueblo

Tver — see KALININ

Tweed \'twēd\ river 96 *m* SE Scotland & NE England flowing E into North sea

Tweeddale — see PEEBLES

Twick·en·ham \'twik-(ə-)nəm\ former municipal borough SE England in Middlesex, now part of Richmond upon Thames

Twin Cities the cities of Minneapolis & St. Paul, Minn.

Twin Falls city S Idaho SW of Twin Falls (waterfall 125 *ft* in Snake River) *pop* 21,914

Ty·ler \'tī-lər\ city E Tex. ESE of Dallas *pop* 57,770

Tyn·dall, Mount \'tin-dᵊl\ **1** mountain 14,025 *ft* S *cen* Calif. in Sierra Nevada NW of Mt. Whitney **2** mountain 8280 *ft* New Zealand in *cen* South I. in Southern Alps

Tyne \'tīn\ river 35 *m* N England in Northumberland flowing E into North sea

Tyne·mouth \'tīn-ˌmau̇th\ county borough N England in Northumberland on North sea at mouth of the Tyne *pop* 68,861

Tyre \'tī(ə)r\ *or* Ar **Es Sur** \es-'su̇(ə)r\ *or* Heb **Zor** \'tsȯ(ə)r, 'zȯ(ə)r\ town S Lebanon on the coast; ancient ✱ of Phoenicia — **Tyr·i·an** \'tir-ē-ən\ *adj or n*

Ty·ree, Mount \tī-'rē\ mountain 16,290 *ft* W Antarctica in Sentinel Range of Ellsworth mountains NW of Vinson Massif

Tyrol — see TIROL — **Tyrolean** *adj or n* — **Tyrolese** *adj or n*

Ty·rone \tir-'ōn\ county W *cen* Northern Ireland ✱ Omagh *area* 1218, *pop* 137,997

Tyr·rhe·ni·an \tə-'rē-nē-ən\ sea, the part of the Mediterranean W of Italy, N of Sicily, & E of Sardinia & Corsica

Tyu·men \tyü-'men\ city U.S.S.R. in W Soviet Russia, Asia, on the Tura (a tributary of the Tobol) *pop* 269,000

Tze·kung \'dzə-'gu̇ŋ\ city S *cen* China in S Szechwan W of Chungking *pop* 350,000

Tze·po \'dzə-'pō\ city E China in *cen* Shantung E of Tsinan *pop* 806,000

Uap see YAP

Uau·pés \wau̇-'pes\ *or* Sp **Vau·pés** \vau̇-'\ river 700 *m* Colombia & Brazil flowing ESE into the Negro

Uban·gi \(y)ü-'baŋ-(g)ē\ *or* F **Ou·ban·gui** \ü-bäⁿ-gē\ river 700 *m* W *cen* Africa on NW border of Zaire flowing W & S into Congo river — see UELE

Ubangi–Sha·ri \-'shär-ē\ *or* F **Oubangui–Cha·ri** \-shä-rē\ former French territory N *cen* Africa — see CENTRAL AFRICAN REPUBLIC

Ube \'ü-(ˌ)bā\ city & port Japan in SW Honshu on Inland sea *pop* 150,000

Uca·ya·li \ˌü-kə-'yäl-ē\ river 1200 *m*, *cen* & N Peru flowing N to unite with the Marañón forming the Amazon

Uc·cle \'üklᵊ, 'ᵫklᵊ\ *or* Flem **Uk·kel** \'ək-əl\ commune *cen* Belgium *pop* 78,070

Udai·pur \ü-'dī-ˌpu̇(ə)r\ **1** *or* **Me·war** \mā-'wär\ former state NW India, now part of Rajasthan state **2** city, its ✱, NE of Ahmadabad *pop* 136,045

Udi·ne \'üd-i-ˌnā\ commune NE Italy NE of Venice ✱ of Friuli-Venezia Giulia region *pop* 95,675

Ud·murt Republic \'u̇d-ˌmu̇(ə)rt\ autonomous republic U.S.S.R. in E Soviet Russia, Europe, in W foothills of the Urals ✱ Izhevsk *area* 16,200, *pop* 1,417,000

Ue·le *or* **Wel·le** \'wel-ē\ river 700 *m*, *cen* Africa flowing W in N Zaire to unite with the Bomu forming the Ubangi

Ufa \ü-'fä\ **1** river 430 *m* U.S.S.R. in E Soviet Russia, Europe, in S Urals flowing NW & SW into the Belaya **2** city U.S.S.R. in E Soviet Russia, Europe ✱ of Bashkir Republic on the Belaya *pop* 773,000

Ugan·da \yü-'gan-də\ republic E Africa N of Lake Victoria; member of Brit. Commonwealth ✱ Kampala *area* 93,981, *pop* 10,130,000 — **Ugan·dan** \-dən\ *adj or n*

Uin·ta \yü-'int-ə\ mountain range NE Utah — see KINGS PEAK

Uj·jain \'ü-ˌjīn\ city NW *cen* India in W Madhya Pradesh NNW of Indore *pop* 159,024

Ukraine \yü-'krān, *also* -'krīn, 'yü-ˌ\ *or* **Ukrai·ni·an Republic** \yü-ˌkrā-nē-ən-\ *or* Russ **Ukrai·na** \ü-'krī-nə\ constituent republic of the U.S.S.R. in E Europe on N coast of Black Sea ✱ Kiev (✱ Kharkov 1921–34) *area* 222,600, *pop* 47,136,000

Ulan Ba·tor \ˌü-ˌlän-'bä-ˌtȯ(ə)r\ *or formerly* **Ur·ga** \'u̇(ə)r-gə\ city ✱ of Mongolian Republic *pop* 195,300

Ulan–Ude \ˌü-ˌlän-ü-'dā\ *or formerly* **Verkh·ne·udinsk** \ˌverk-nə-'ü-ˌdin(t)sk\ city U.S.S.R. in E Soviet Russia, Asia ✱ of Buryat Republic on Selenga river *pop* 254,000

Uleåborg — see OULU

Ulls·wa·ter \'əlz-ˌwȯt-ər, -ˌwät-\ lake 7 *m* long NW England in Cumberland & Westmorland

Ulm \'u̇lm\ city S Germany in E Baden-Wurttemburg on the Danube SE of Stuttgart *pop* 91,852

Ul·ster \'əl-stər\ **1** region N Ireland comprising Northern Ireland & N Republic of Ireland; ancient kingdom, later a province comprising nine counties three of which in 1921 joined Irish Free State (now Republic of Ireland) while the rest remained with United Kingdom **2** province N Republic of Ireland comprising counties Cavan, Donegal, & Monaghan *area* 3093, *pop* 208,283 **3** Northern Ireland comprising counties Antrim, Armagh, Down, Fermanagh, Londonderry, & Tyrone ✱ Belfast — **Ul·ster·ite** \-stə-ˌrīt\ *n* — **Ul·ster·man** \-stər-mən\ *n*

Ulu Dag \ˌü-lə-'dä(g)\ *or anc* **Olym·pus** \ə-'lim-pəs, ō-\ mountain 8343 *ft* NW Turkey in Asia SE of Bursa

Ulugh Muz·tagh \ˌü-lə-məz-'tä(g)\ mountain 25,340 *ft* W China in S Sinkiang; highest in Kunlun mountains

Ul·ya·novsk *or* **Ul·ia·novsk** \ül-'yän-əfsk\ *or formerly* **Sim·birsk** \sim-'bi(ə)rsk\ city U.S.S.R. in E *cen* Soviet Russia, Europe, on the Volga *pop* 351,000

Uma·til·la \ˌyü-mə-'til-ə\ river 80 *m* NE Oreg. flowing W & N into the Columbia

Um·bria \'əm-brē-ə\ region *cen* Italy in the Apennines; ✱ Perugia

Um·nak \'üm-ˌnak\ island SW Alaska in Fox group of the Aleutians

Ump·qua \'əm(p)-ˌkwȯ\ river 200 *m* SW Oreg. flowing into the Pacific

Un·alas·ka \ˌən-ə-'las-kə\ island SW Alaska in Fox group of the Aleutians

Unalaska Bay bay SW Alaska on N coast of Unalaska I.

Un·com·pah·gre Peak \ˌən-kəm-'päg-rē\ mountain 14,309 *ft* SW Colo.; highest in San Juan mountains

Uncompahgre Plateau tableland W Colo. SW of Gunnison river

Un·gava \ˌən-'gav-ə\ **1** peninsula Canada in N Que. between Hudson Bay & Ungava Bay **2** region Canada N of Eastmain river & W of Labrador including Ungava peninsula, divided 1927 between Que. & Nfld. — see NEW QUEBEC

Ungava Bay inlet of Hudson strait Canada in N Que.

Uni·mak \'yü-nə-ˌmak\ island SW Alaska in Fox group of the Aleutians

ə abut   ᵊ kitten, F table   ər further   a back   ā bake
ä cot, cart   a̍ F bac   au̇ out   ch chin   e less   ē easy
g gift   i trip   ī life   j joke   k̲ G ich   ⁿ F vin   ŋ sing
ō flow   ȯ flaw   œ F bœuf   œ̄ F feu   ȯi coin   th thing
th̲ this   ü loot   u̇ foot   ue G Füllen   ue̅ F rue   y yet
ʸ F digne \dēnʸ\, nuit \nwʸē\   yü few   yu̇ furious   zh vision

Union \'yün-yən\ — TOKELAU
Union City city NE N.J. N of Jersey City *pop* 58,537
Union of South Africa — see SOUTH AFRICA (Republic of)
Union of Soviet Socialist Republics *or* **Soviet Union** country E Europe & N Asia bordering on the Arctic & Pacific oceans & Baltic & Black seas; a union of 15 constituent republics ✱ Moscow *area* 8,662,400, *pop* 245,070,000 — see RUSSIA
Union·town \'yün-yən-ˌtau̇n\ city SW Pa. *pop* 16,282
United Arab Emirates *or formerly* **Trucial States** \'trü-shəl-\ *or* **Trucial Oman** country NE Arabia on Persian Gulf between Qatar & Oman; a republic composed of seven sheikhdoms (Abu Dhabi, Ajman, Dubai, Fujaira, Ras al Khaima, Sharja, & Umm al Qaiwan) formerly under Brit. protection ✱ Abu Dhabi *area* 32,000, *pop* 179,138
United Arab Republic former name (1961–71) of republic of Egypt & previously (1958–61) of union of Egypt & Syria
United Kingdom, 1 *or* **United Kingdom of Great Britain and Northern Ireland** country W Europe in British Isles comprising Great Britain & Northern Ireland ✱ London *area* 89,034, *pop* 55,346,551 **2** *or* **United Kingdom of Great Britain and Ireland** country 1801–1921 comprising Great Britain & all of Ireland
United Nations international territory, a small area in New York City in E *cen* Manhattan overlooking East river; seat since 1951 of permanent headquarters of the United Nations — see TURTLE BAY
United Provinces *or* **United Provinces of Agra and Oudh** former province N India formed 1902 ✱ Allahabad; as Uttar Pradesh, became a state of Republic of India 1950
United States of America *or* **United States** \yu̇-ˌnīt-əd-'stāts, *esp South* 'yü-\ **1** country No. America bordering on Atlantic, Pacific, & Arctic oceans; a federal republic ✱ Washington *area* 3,615,222, *pop* 203,184,772 **2** the United States of America with dependencies & possessions
University City city E Mo. WNW of St. Louis *pop* 46,309
University Heights city NE Ohio E of Cleveland *pop* 17,055
University Park city NE Tex. within city of Dallas *pop* 23,498
Un·ter·wal·den \'u̇nt-ər-ˌväl-dən\ *or* F **Un·ter·wald** \ün-tər-vald\ canton *cen* Switzerland subdivided into half cantons **Nid·wal·den** \'nēt-ˌväl-dən\ *or* F **Nid·wald** \nēd-vald\ (✱ Stans *area* 112, *pop* 25,634) & **Ob·wal·den** \'ōp-väl-dən\ *or* F **Ob·wald** \ōb-vald\ (✱ Sarnen *area* 183, *pop* 24,509)
Up·land \'əp-lənd\ city SW Calif. W of San Bernardino *pop* 32,551
Upo·lu \ü-'pō-(ˌ)lü\ island S Pacific in Western Samoa
Upper Adige — see ALTO ADIGE
Upper Arlington city *cen* Ohio W of Columbus *pop* 38,630
Upper Canada the Canadian province 1791–1841 corresponding to modern Ontario — see LOWER CANADA
Upper Karroo — see KARROO
Upper Klamath lake 30 *m* long S Oreg. SSE of Crater Lake National Park drained by Klamath river — see LOWER KLAMATH
Upper Palatinate — see PALATINATE
Upper Vol·ta \'väl-tə, 'vōl-, 'vȯl-\ *or* F **Haute–Vol·ta** \ōt-vȯl-tä\ country W Africa N of Ivory Coast, Ghana, & Togo; a republic; until 1958 a French territory ✱ Ouagadougou *area* 121,892, *pop* 5,490,000 — **Upper Vol·tan** \'vält-ᵊn, 'vōlt-, 'vȯlt-\ *adj or n*
Upp·sa·la *or* **Up·sa·la** \'əp-sə-ˌlä, -ˌsäl-ə; ˌəp-'säl-ə\ city E Sweden NW of Stockholm *pop* 101,696
Ur \'ər, 'u̇(ə)r\ city of ancient Sumer in S Babylonia; site in S Iraq near the Euphrates 105 *m* NW of Basra
Ural \'yu̇r-əl\ **1** river 1400 *m* U.S.S.R. rising at S end of Ural mountains & flowing S into the Caspian **2** mountain system U.S.S.R. extending from Kara sea to steppes N of Lake Aral; usu. considered the dividing line between Asia & Europe; highest Narodnaya 6214 *ft*
Uralsk \yu̇-'ralsk\ city U.S.S.R. in Soviet Central Asia in W Kazakh Republic on Ural river *pop* 134,000
Ura·ri·coe·ra \ü-ˌrär-i-'kwer-ə\ river 360 *m* N Brazil, a headstream of the Branco
Ura·wa \ü-'rä-wə\ city Japan in Honshu N of Tokyo *pop* 258,000
Ur·bana \ˌər-'ban-ə\ city E *cen* Ill. *pop* 32,800
Ur·bi·no \u̇(ə)r-'bē-(ˌ)nō\ commune *cen* Italy WNW of Ancona *pop* 16,720
Ur·fa \u̇r-'fä\ *or anc* **Edes·sa** \i-'des-ə\ city SE Turkey E of Gaziantep *pop* 73,498
Urga — see ULAN BATOR
Uri \'u̇(ə)r-ē\ canton *cen* Switzerland S of Lake of Lucerne ✱ Altdorf *area* 415, *pop* 34,091
Urmia — see RIZAIYEH
Uru·bam·ba \u̇r-ə-'bäm-bə\ river 450 *m*, *cen* Peru flowing NNW to unite with the Apurímac forming the Ucayali
Uru·guay \'(y)u̇r-ə-ˌgwī, 'yu̇r-ə-ˌgwā\ **1** river 980 *m* SE So. America rising in Brazil & flowing into the Río de la Plata **2** *or* **Re·pú·bli·ca Ori·en·tal del Uru·guay** \re-'pü-bli-(ˌ)kä-ˌōr-ē-ˌen-'täl-ˌdel-ˌu̇r-ə-'gwī, -ˌōr-\ country SE So. America between the Lower Uruguay & the Atlantic; a republic ✱ Montevideo *area* 72,172, *pop* 2,920,000 — see BANDA ORIENTAL — **Uru·guay·an** \ˌ(y)u̇r-ə-'gwī-ən, ˌyu̇r-ə-'gwā-\ *adj or n*
Urum·chi \ü-'rüm-chē, ˌu̇r-əm-'\ *or* **Ti·hwa** \'dē-'(h)wä\ city NW China ✱ of Sinkiang on N side of Tien Shan *pop* 500,000
Urundi — see BURUNDI
Ush·ant \'əsh-ənt\ *or* F **Île d'Oues·sant** \ēl-dwā-säⁿ\ island NW France off tip of Brittany
Us·hua·ia \ü-'swī-ə\ town S Argentina on S coast of Tierra del Fuego I., at 54°48'S; farthest S city in the world
Usk \'əsk\ river 60 *m* S Wales & W England flowing E & S into Severn estuary
Uskub — see SKOPLJE
Us·ku·dar \ˌu̇s-kə-'där\ *or* **Scu·ta·ri** *or* **Sku·ta·ri** \'sküt-ə-rē\ suburb of Istanbul, Turkey, on Asian side of the Bosporus
Us·pa·lla·ta \ˌü-spə-'yät-ə, -'zhät-\ *or* **La Cum·bre** \lə-'küm-(ˌ)brā\ mountain pass (12,572 *ft*) & tunnel S So. America in the Andes between Mendoza, Argentina, & Santiago, Chile
Us·su·ri \ü-'su̇(ə)r-ē\ river 450 *m* E Asia on border between U.S.S.R. & China flowing N into the Amur
Usti nad La·bem \'ü-stē-'näd-lä-ˌbem\ city W Czechoslovakia in N Bohemia on the Elbe *pop* 73,897
Usumbura — see BUJUMBURA
Utah \'yü-ˌtȯ, -ˌtä\ **1** lake 30 *m* long N *cen* Utah drained by Jordan river **2** state W U.S. ✱ Salt Lake City *area* 84,916, *pop* 1,059,273 — **Utah·an** \-ˌtȯ(-ə)n, -ˌtä(-ə)n\ *adj or n* — **Utahn** \-ˌtȯ(-ə)n, -ˌtä(-ə)n\ *n*
Uti·ca \'yüt-i-kə\ **1** city E *cen* N.Y. on the Mohawk *pop* 91,611 **2** ancient city N Africa on Mediterranean coast NW of Carthage
Utrecht \'yü-ˌtrekt\ **1** province *cen* Netherlands S of the IJsselmeer *area* 535, *pop* 801,285 **2** city, its ✱ *pop* 277,647
Utsu·no·mi·ya \ˌüt-sə-'nō-mē-ˌ(y)ä\ city Japan in *cen* Honshu N of Tokyo *pop* 292,000
Ut·tar Pra·desh \ˌu̇t-ər-prə-'desh, -'dāsh\ state N India bordering on Tibet & Nepal ✱ Lucknow *area* 113,409, *pop* 88,299,453 — see UNITED PROVINCES
Ux·bridge \'əks-(ˌ)brij\ former municipal borough SE England in Middlesex, now part of Hillingdon
Ux·mal \üsh-'mäl\ ancient city SE Mexico in Yucatán S of modern Mérida ✱ of the later Mayan Empire
Uz·bek Republic \'u̇z-ˌbek, 'əz-, u̇z-'\ *or* **Uz·bek·i·stan** \(ˌ)u̇z-ˌbek-i-'stan, ˌəz-, -'stän\ constituent republic U.S.S.R. in W *cen* Asia E of the Amu Darya ✱ Tashkent *area* 171,070, *pop* 11,963,000
Vaal \'väl\ river 700 *m* Republic of So. Africa rising in SE Transvaal & flowing W into the Orange in N Cape Province
Vaa·sa *or* Sw **Va·sa** \'väs-ə\ city & port W Finland *pop* 44,316
Vaca·ville \'vak-ə-ˌvil\ city W Calif. SW of Sacramento *pop* 21,690
Va·duz \vä-'düts\ commune ✱ of Liechtenstein on the upper Rhine
Vah \'vä(k)\ *or* Hung **Vag** \'väg\ river 210 *m* Czechoslovakia rising in Tatra mountains & flowing W & S into the Danube
Va·lais \va-'lā\ *or* G **Wal·lis** \'väl-əs\ canton SW *cen* Switzerland bordering on France & Italy ✱ Sion *area* 2026, *pop* 206,563
Val·dai \väl-'dī\ hills U.S.S.R. in W Soviet Russia, Europe, SE of Lake Ilmen; highest point 1053 *ft*
Val d'Ao·sta \ˌväl-dä-'ȯs-tə\ *or* **Val·le d'Ao·sta** \ˌväl-ā-\ autonomous region NW Italy bordering on France & Switzerland NW of Piedmont ✱ Aosta *area* 1260, *pop* 107,861
Val·di·via \val-'dēv-ē-ə\ city & port S *cen* Chile *pop* 80,035
Val d'Or \'val-ˌdȯ(ə)r\ town Canada in SW Que. *pop* 17,421
Val·dos·ta \val-'däs-tə\ city S Ga. *pop* 32,303
Va·lence \va-'läⁿs\ commune SE France S of Lyons *pop* 62,358
Va·len·cia \və-'len-ch(ē-)ə, -'len(t)-sē-ə\ **1** region & ancient kingdom E Spain between Andalusia & Catalonia **2** province E Spain *area* 4150, *pop* 1,767,327 **3** commune & port, its ✱ *pop* 498,159 **4** city N Venezuela WSW of Caracas *pop* 224,552
Va·len·ci·ennes \və-ˌlen(t)-sē-'en(z)\ city N France SE of Lille *pop* 46,626
Va·len·tia *or* **Va·len·cia** \və-'len-ch(ē-)ə\ island SW Ireland in County Kerry in the Atlantic S of entrance to Dingle Bay
Val·la·do·lid \ˌval-əd-ə-'lid, -'lē\ **1** province NW *cen* Spain *area* 2922, *pop* 412,572 **2** commune, its ✱ *pop* 177,797
Val·lau·ris \ˌval-ō-'rēs\ village SE France NE of Cannes
Va·lle·cas \vä-'yā-kəs, vī-'ā-\ commune *cen* Spain, SE suburb of Madrid
Val·le·jo \və-'lā-(ˌ)ō\ city W Calif. on San Pablo Bay *pop* 66,733
Val·let·ta *or* **Va·let·ta** \və-'let-ə\ city & port ✱ of Malta *pop* 15,547
Val·ley·field \'val-ē-ˌfēld\ *or* **Sal·a·ber·ry–de–Valleyfield** \'sal-ə-ˌber-ē-də-\ city Canada in S Que. on the St. Lawrence SW of Montreal *pop* 30,173
Valley of Ten Thousand Smokes volcanic region SW Alaska in Katmai National Monument
Valley Stream village SE N.Y. on Long I. *pop* 40,413
Va·lois \'val-ˌwä\ medieval county & duchy N France in NE Île-de-France ✱ Crépy-en-Valois
Valona — see VLONE
Val·pa·rai·so, 1 \ˌval-pə-'rā-(ˌ)zō\ city NW Ind. SE of Gary *pop* 20,020 **2** \-'rī-(ˌ)zō, -'rā-\ *or* Sp **Val·pa·ra·í·so** \ˌväl-pä-rä-'ē-sō\ city & port *cen* Chile 75 *m* WNW of Santiago *pop* 289,456
Van \'van\ lake E Turkey in mountains of Armenia *area* 1425
Van·cou·ver \van-'kü-vər\ **1** island W Canada in B.C. off SW coast; chief city Victoria *area* 12,408 **2** city SW Wash. on the Columbia opposite Portland, Oreg. *pop* 42,493 **3** city & port Canada in SW B.C. on Burrard Inlet *pop* 426,256
Vancouver, Mount mountain 15,700 *ft* on Alaska-Canada boundary in St. Elias range
Van Die·men \van-'dē-mən\ gulf inlet of Arafura sea N Australia in N Northern Territory
Van Diemen's Land — see TASMANIA
Va·ner *or* **Vä·ner** *or* **Ve·ner** \'vā-nər\ *or* **Vä·nern** \-nərn\ lake SW Sweden *area* 2141
Va·nier \'van-ˌyā\ *or formerly* **East·view** \'ēst-ˌvyü\ city Canada in SE Ont. NE of Ottawa on Ottawa river *pop* 22,477
Va·nua Le·vu \və-ˌnü-ə-'lev-(ˌ)ü\ island S Pacific in the Fijis NE of Viti Levu *area* 2128
Varanasi — see BANARAS
Var·dar \'vär-ˌdär\ *or* NGk **Var·dá·ris** \vär-'där-əs\ river 200 *m* SE Yugoslavia & N Greece flowing S into Gulf of Salonika
Va·re·se \və-'rā-sē\ commune N Italy NW of Milan *pop* 80,324
Var·na \'vär-nə\ *or formerly* **Sta·lin** \'stäl-ən, 'stal-, -ˌēn\ city & port E Bulgaria on Black sea *pop* 212,642
Väs·ter·ås \ˌves-tə-'rōs\ city E Sweden on Lake Malar NW of Stockholm *pop* 113,389
Vaté — see EFATE
Vat·i·can City *or* **Vatican City State** \ˌvat-i-kən-\ *or* It **Cit·tà del Va·ti·ca·no** \chēt-'tä-del-ˌvä-tē-'kä-nō\ independent papal state within commune of Rome, Italy; created Feb. 11, 1929 *area* 108.7 acres, *pop* 648
Vat·ter *or* **Vät·ter** *or* **Vet·ter** \'vet-ər\ *or* **Vät·tern** \-ərn\ lake S Sweden *area* 733
Vaud \'vō\ *or* G **Waadt** \'vät\ canton W Switzerland N of Lake of Geneva ✱ Lausanne *area* 1256, *pop* 511,851
Vaughan \'vȯn, 'vän\ town Canada in SE Ont. N of Toronto *pop* 15,873
Vaupés — see UAUPÉS

Ve·ga Ba·ja \ˌvä-gə-ˈbä-(ˌ)hä\ town N Puerto Rico *pop* 17,089
Vegas LAS VEGAS
Ve·ii \ˈvē-ˌ(y)ī\ ancient city of Etruria in *cen* Italy NNW of Rome
Vel·bert \ˈfel-bərt\ city W Germany in North Rhine-Westphalia in Ruhr valley NE of Düsseldorf *pop* 27,307
Vel·la La·vel·la \ˌvel-ə-lə-ˈvel-ə\ island SW Pacific in *cen* Solomons SW of Choiseul
Vel·lore \və-ˈlō(ə)r, ve-, -ˈlȯ(ə)r\ city SE India in N Tamil Nadu WSW of Madras *pop* 121,465
Vel·sen \ˈvel-zən, -sən\ commune W Netherlands; outer port for Amsterdam *pop* 67,580
Velsuna — see ORVIETO
Vence \väns\ commune SE France W of Nice
Ven·dée \vän(n)-ˈdā\ *or* **La Vendée** \lä-\ region W France bordering on Bay of Biscay S of Brittany
Ven·dôme \vän(n)-ˈdōm\ town N *cen* France WSW of Orléans
Ve·ne·tia \vi-ˈnē-sh(ē-)ə\ *or* It **Ve·ne·zia** \və-ˈnet-sē-ə\ **1** area NE Italy & NW Yugoslavia including territory between lower Po river & the Alps **2** VENEZIA EUGANEA
Ve·ne·to \ˈven-ə-ˌtō, ˈvā-nə-\ region NE Italy comprising most of Venezia Euganea ✱ Venice *area* 7092, *pop* 4,054,017
Ve·ne·zia Eu·ga·nea \və-ˌnet-sē-ə-ˌeü-ˈgän-ē-ə\ the S portion of Venetia
Venezia Giu·lia \-ˈjül-yə\ the E portion of Venetia including Julian Alps & Istria; now mainly in Yugoslavia
Venezia Tri·den·ti·na \ˌtrē-ˌden-ˈtē-nə\ the NW portion of Venetia N of Lake Garda; included in Trentino-Alto Adige region
Ven·e·zu·e·la \ˌven-əz(-ə)-ˈwā-lə, -ˈwē-\ country N So. America; a republic ✱ Caracas *area* 352,141, *pop* 10,400,000 — **Ven·e·zu·e·lan** \-lən\ *adj or n*
Venezuela, Gulf of *or* **Gulf of Maracaibo** inlet of the Caribbean NW Venezuela N of Lake Maracaibo
Ven·iam·i·nof Crater \ven-ˈyam-ə-ˌnȯf\ volcano 8225 *ft* SW Alaska on *cen* Alaska peninsula in Aleutian range
Ven·ice \ˈven-əs\ *or* It **Ve·ne·zia** \və-ˈnet-sē-ə\ *or* L **Ve·ne·tia** \vi-ˈnē-sh(ē-)ə\ city & port NE Italy ✱ of Veneto, on islands in **Lagoon of Venice** (inlet of Gulf of Venice) *pop* 367,732 — **Ve·ne·tian** \və-ˈnē-shən\ *adj or n*
Venice, Gulf of arm of the Adriatic between Po delta & Istria
Ven·lo *or formerly* **Ven·loo** \ˈven-(ˌ)lō\ commune SE Netherlands on the Maas near German border *pop* 62,694
Ven·ta \ˈvent-ə\ *or* G **Win·dau** \ˈvin-ˌdau̇\ river 200 *m* U.S.S.R. in Lithuania & Latvia flowing into the Baltic
Ven·ti·mi·glia \ˌvent-i-ˈmēl-yə\ commune NW Italy on Ligurian sea W of San Remo near Menton, France *pop* 25,564
Vents·pils \ˈven(t)-ˌspils, -ˌspilz\ *or* G **Win·dau** \ˈvin-ˌdau̇\ city & port Latvia at mouth of the Venta *pop* 37,000
Ven·tu·ra \ven-ˈt(y)u̇r-ə\ *or officially* **San Buen·a·ven·tu·ra** \(ˌ)san-ˌbwen-ə-ˌven-\ city & port SW Calif. on Santa Barbara channel ESE of Santa Barbara *pop* 55,797
Ve·nue, Ben \ˌben-və-ˈn(y)ü\ mountain 2393 *ft*, *cen* Scotland in SW Perth S of Loch Katrine
Ve·ra·cruz *or* **Ve·ra Cruz** \ˌver-ə-ˈkrüz, -ˈkrüs\ **1** state E Mexico ✱ Jalapa *area* 27,736, *pop* 3,813,613 **2** *or* **Vera Cruz Lla·ve** \-ˈyä-(ˌ)vā\ city & port E Mexico in Veracruz state on Gulf of Mexico *pop* 242,351
Ver·cel·li \ver-ˈchel-ē, (ˌ)vər-\ commune NW Italy *pop* 56,098
Ver·di·gris \ˈvərd-ə-grəs\ river 280 *m* SE Kans. & NE Okla. flowing into Arkansas river
Ver·dun \(ˌ)vər-ˈdən, ver-\ **1** city Canada in S Que. on Montreal I. *pop* 74,718 **2** *or* **Verdun–sur–Meuse** \-ˌsu̇(ə)r-\ city NE France on the Meuse ESE of Reims *pop* 22,013
Ver·ee·ni·ging \fə-ˈrā-nə-giŋ, -nək-əŋ\ city NE Republic of So. Africa in S Transvaal on the Vaal S of Johannesburg *pop* 94,500
Verkhneudinsk — see ULAN-UDE
Ver·mont \vər-ˈmänt\ state NE U.S. ✱ Montpelier *area* 9609, *pop* 444,330 — **Ver·mont·er** \-ər\ *n*
Vernoleninsk — see NIKOLAEV
Ver·non \ˈvər-nən\ town N *cen* Conn. NE of Hartford *pop* 27,237
Vernyi — see ALMA-ATA
Vé·roia \ˈve(ə)r-yə\ *or anc* **Be·rea** *or* **Be·roea** \bə-ˈrē-ə\ town NE Greece in Macedonia W of Salonika
Ve·ro·na \və-ˈrō-nə\ **1** borough NE N.J. SW of Paterson *pop* 15,067 **2** commune NE Italy on the Adige *pop* 256,711 — **Ver·o·nese** \ˌver-ə-ˈnēz, -ˈnēs\ *adj or n*
Ver·sailles \(ˌ)vər-ˈsī, ver-\ city N France, WSW suburb of Paris *pop* 90,829
Vert, Cape \ˈvərt\ *or* **Cape Verde** \ˈvərd\ promontory W Africa on Cape Vert peninsula in Senegal; westernmost point of Africa, at 17°30′W
Ver·viers \ver-ˈvyā\ commune E Belgium E of Liège *pop* 34,402
Ves·ter·ålen \ˈves-tə-ˌrō-lən\ island group Norway off NW coast NE of Lofoten islands
Ve·su·vi·us \və-ˈsü-vē-əs\ *or* It **Ve·su·vio** \vā-ˈzüv-yō\ volcano 4190 *ft* Italy on Bay of Naples — **Ve·su·vi·an** \və-ˈsü-vē-ən\ *adj*
Vet·lu·ga \vet-ˈlü-gə\ river 500 *m* U.S.S.R. in *cen* Soviet Russia, Europe, flowing S into the Volga
Ve·vey \və-ˈvā\ commune W Switzerland in Vaud on NE shore of Lake Geneva *pop* 17,957
Viatka — see VYATKA
Vi·cen·te Ló·pez \və-ˌsent-ə-ˈlō-ˌpez\ city E Argentina, N suburb of Buenos Aires, on Río de la Plata *pop* 250,853
Vi·cen·za \vi-ˈchen(t)-sə\ commune NE Italy W of Venice *pop* 111,973
Vichegda — see VYCHEGDA
Vi·chu·ga \vi-ˈchü-gə\ city U.S.S.R. in *cen* Soviet Russia, Europe, NE of Moscow *pop* 53,000
Vi·chy \ˈvish-ē, ˈvē-shē\ commune *cen* France on the Allier NE of Clermont-Ferrand *pop* 33,506
Vicks·burg \ˈviks-ˌbərg\ city W Miss. *pop* 25,478
Vic·to·ria \vik-ˈtōr-ē-ə, -ˈtȯr-\ **1** city SE Tex. on Guadalupe river *pop* 41,349 **2** city Canada ✱ of B.C. on SE Vancouver I. *pop* 61,761 **3** island N Canada SE of Banks I. *area* 81,930 **4** river 350 *m* Australia in NW Northern Territory flowing N & NW to Timor sea **5** state SE Australia ✱ Melbourne *area* 87,884, *pop* 3,443,800 **6** *or* **Hong Kong** \ˈhäŋ-ˌkäŋ, -ˈkäŋ; ˈhȯŋ-ˌkȯŋ, -ˈkȯŋ\ city & port ✱ of Hong Kong colony on NW Hong Kong I. *pop* 633,138 — **Vic·to·ri·an** \vik-ˈtōr-ē-ən, -ˈtȯr\ *adj or n*
Victoria, Lake lake E Africa in Tanzania, Kenya, and Uganda *area* 26,200
Victoria Falls waterfall 200 to 350 *ft* high & 5580 *ft* wide S Africa in the Zambezi on border between Zambia & Rhodesia
Victoria Land region E Antarctica S of New Zealand on W shore of Ross sea & Ross Ice Shelf
Victoria Nile — see NILE
Vic·to·ria·ville \vik-ˈtōr-ē-ə-ˌvil, -ˈtȯr-\ town Canada in S Que. NE of Drummondville *pop* 22,047
Vi·en·na \vē-ˈen-ə\ **1** town N Va. W of Washington, D.C. *pop* 17,152 **2** *or* G **Wien** \ˈvēn\ city ✱ of Austria on the Danube *pop* 1,644,976 — **Vi·en·nese** \ˌvē-ə-ˈnēz, -ˈnēs\ *adj or n*
Vi·enne \vē-ˈen\ **1** river 217 *m* SW *cen* France flowing NW into the Loire **2** city SE France on the Rhone *pop* 29,057
Vien·tiane \(ˈ)vyen-ˈtyän\ city, administrative ✱ of Laos, on the Mekong *pop* 132,253
Vie·ques \vē-ˈā-kəs\ *or* **Crab** \ˈkrab\ island West Indies off E Puerto Rico, belonging to Puerto Rico; chief town Isabela Secunda
Viet·nam *or* **Viet–Nam** *or* **Viet Nam** \vē-ˈet-ˈnäm, vyet-, ˌvē-ət-, vēt-, -ˈnam\ country SE Asia in Indochina; state, including Tonkin & N Annam, set up 1945–46; with S Annam & Cochin China, an associated state of French Union 1950–54; after civil war, divided 1954 at 17th parallel into republics of No. Vietnam (✱ Hanoi *area* 63,344, *pop* 21,600,000) & So. Vietnam (✱ Saigon *area* 66,262, *pop* 18,330,000)
Vi·go \ˈvē-(ˌ)gō\ city & port NW Spain *pop* 186,461
Viipuri — see VYBORG
Vi·ja·ya·na·gar \ˌvij-ə-yə-ˈnəg-ər\ *or* **Bi·ja·na·gar** \ˌbij-ə-ˈnəg-\ Hindu kingdom (1336–1565) S India S of the Krishna
Vi·ja·ya·wa·da \ˌvij-ə-yə-ˈwäd-ə\ *or* **Vi·ja·ya·va·da** \-ˈväd-ə\ *or formerly* **Bez·wa·da** \bez-ˈwäd-ə\ city SE India in E Andhra Pradesh on Krishna river, at head of its delta *pop* 322,717
Vi·la \ˈvē-lə\ town & port ✱ of New Hebrides in SW Efate I.
Vi·lla Cis·ne·ros \ˌvē-(y)ə-sis-ˈner-əs\ town & port NW Africa ✱ of Rio de Oro in Spanish Sahara
Vi·lla·her·mo·sa \ˌvē-(y)ə-ˌer-ˈmō-sə\ city SE Mexico ✱ of Tabasco state *pop* 78,034
Vil·la Park \ˌvil-ə-\ village NE Ill. W of Chicago *pop* 25,891
Ville·franche \ˌvēl-(ə-)ˈfränsh\ **1** *or* **Villefranche–sur–Mer** \-sur-ˈme(ə)r\ commune & port SE France E of Nice **2** *or* **Villefranche–sur–Saône** \-ˈsōn\ commune E *cen* France NNW of Lyons *pop* 26,338
Vil·leur·banne \(ˌ)vē-ˌyər-ˈban, -ˈbän\ commune E France, E suburb of Lyons *pop* 119,879
Vil·ni·us *or* **Vil·ny·us** \ˈvil-nē-əs\ *or* Pol **Wil·no** \ˈvil-(ˌ)nō\ *or* Russ **Vil·na** \ˈvil-nə\ *or* **Vil·no** \-(ˌ)nō\ city U.S.S.R. ✱ of Lithuania *pop* 372,000
Vi·lyui \vil-ˈyü-ē\ river 1500 *m* U.S.S.R. in *cen* Soviet Russia, Asia, flowing E into the Lena
Vim·i·nal \ˈvim-ən-ᵊl\ hill in Rome, Italy, one of seven upon which the ancient city was built — see AVENTINE
Vi·my Ridge \ˌvē-mē-, vi-ˌmē-\ ridge near Vimy commune N France N of Arras
Vi·ña del Mar \ˌvēn-yə-(ˌ)del-ˈmär\ city & port *cen* Chile E of Valparaiso *pop* 149,344
Vin·cennes \(ˈ)vin-ˈsenz; *for 2, F* van-sen\ **1** city SW Ind. *pop* 19,867 **2** commune N France, E suburb of Paris *pop* 49,143
Vin·dhya \ˈvin-dyə, -dē-ə\ mountain range N *cen* India N of & parallel to Narbada river
Vin·dhya Pra·desh \prə-ˈdesh, -ˈdāsh\ former state NE *cen* India ✱ Rewa; became (1956) part of Madhya Pradesh
Vine·land \ˈvīn-lənd\ city S N.J. *pop* 47,399
Vin·land \ˈvin-lənd\ a portion of the coast of No. America visited & so called by Norse voyagers *ab* A.D. 1000; perhaps N tip of Newfoundland
Vin·ni·tsa \ˈvin-ət-sə\ city U.S.S.R. in W *cen* Ukraine *pop* 211,000
Vin·son Massif \ˈvin(t)-sən\ mountain 16,860 *ft* W Antarctica S of Ellsworth Land in Sentinel range of Ellsworth mountains; highest in Antarctica
Vir·gin \ˈvər-jən\ **1** river 200 *m* SW Utah & SE Nev. flowing to Lake Mead **2** islands West Indies E of Puerto Rico — see BRITISH VIRGIN ISLANDS, VIRGIN ISLANDS OF THE UNITED STATES
Vir·gin·ia \vər-ˈjin-yə, -ˈjin-ē-ə\ state E U.S. ✱ Richmond *area* 40,817, *pop* 4,648,841 — **Vir·gin·ian** \-yən, -ē-ən\ *adj or n*
Virginia Beach city SE Va. *pop* 172,106
Virginia Capes Cape Charles & Cape Henry in Va. forming entrance to Chesapeake Bay
Virgin Islands National Park reservation West Indies in Virgin Islands of the U.S. on St. John I. *area* 8
Virgin Islands of the United States the W islands of the Virgin islands group including St. Croix, St. John, & St. Thomas; a territory ✱ Charlotte Amalie (on St. Thomas I.) *area* 132, *pop* 62,468 — see DANISH WEST INDIES
Vi·run·ga \və-ˈru̇ŋ-gə\ *or* **Mfum·bi·ro** \em-ˈfüm-bə-ˌrō\ volcanic mountain range E *cen* Africa in E Zaire & SW Uganda N of Lake Kivu; highest peak Karisimbi 14,786 *ft*
Vi·sa·kha·pat·nam \vi-ˌsäk-ə-ˈpət-nəm\ *or* **Vi·za·ga·pa·tam** \-ˌzag-ə-ˈpət-əm\ city & port E India in NE Andhra Pradesh *pop* 298,305
Vi·sa·lia \vī-ˈsāl-yə\ city S *cen* Calif. SE of Fresno *pop* 27,268

ə abut	ᵊ kitten, F table	ər further	a back	ā bake
ä cot, cart	a̐ F bac	au̇ out	ch chin	e less
ē easy	g gift	i trip	ī life	j joke
k̲ G ich	n F vin	ŋ sing	ō flow	ȯ flaw
œ F bœuf	œ̄ F feu	ȯi coin	th thing	t͟h this
ü loot	u̇ foot	ue G Füllen	ue̅ F rue	y yet
y F digne \dēny\, nuit \nwyē\	yü few	yu̇ furious	zh vision	

Vi·sa·yan \bə-'sī-ən\ *or* **Bi·sa·yas** \bə-'sī-əz\ islands *cen* Philippines between Luzon & Mindanao — see BOHOL, CEBU, LEYTE, MASBATE, NEGROS, PANAY, ROMBLON, SAMAR
Vis·by \'viz-bē\ city & port Sweden on Gotland I. in the Baltic *pop* 19,319
Vi·so \'vē-(,)zō\ mountain 12,605 ft NW Italy in Piedmont SW of Turin near French border; highest in Cottian Alps
Vis·ta \'vis-tə\ city SW Calif. N of San Diego *pop* 24,688
Vis·tu·la \'vis(h)-chə-lə, 'vis-tə-\ *or* Pol **Wis·la** \'vē-(,)slä\ *or* Russ **Vis·la** \'vē-slə\ *or* G **Weich·sel** \'vīk-səl\ river 630 *m* Poland flowing N from the Carpathians into Gulf of Danzig
Vistula Lagoon FRISCHES HAFF
Vi·tebsk \'vē-,tepsk, -,tebsk, və-'\ city U.S.S.R. in NE Belorussia on the Dvina *pop* 231,000
Vi·ter·bo \vi-'te(ə)r-(,)bō\ commune *cen* Italy in Latium NNW of Rome *pop* 52,522
Vi·ti Le·vu \,vēt-ē-'lev-(,)ü\ island SW Pacific, largest of the Fiji group *area* 4053
Vi·tim \və-'tēm\ river 1100 *m* U.S.S.R. in S Soviet Russia, Asia, flowing NE & N into the Lena
Vi·to·ria \vi-'tōr-ē-ə, -'tòr-\ city N Spain ✱ of Álava province SSE of Bilbao *pop* 126,098
Vi·tó·ria \vi-'tōr-ē-ə, -'tòr-\ city & port E Brazil ✱ of Espírito Santo state on Espírito Santo I. *pop* 121,843
Vi·try–sur–Seine \vi-,trē-,sù(ə)r-'sān, -'sen\ commune N France, SSE suburb of Paris *pop* 77,846
Viz·ca·ya \vis-'kī-ə\ *or* **Bis·ca·ya** \bis-\ *or* **Bis·cay** \'bis-(,)kā, -kē\ province N Spain on Bay of Biscay; one of the Basque provinces ✱ Bilbao *area* 836, *pop* 1,043,310
Vlaanderen — see FLANDERS
Vlaar·ding·en \'vlär-diŋ-ən\ commune & port SW Netherlands W of Rotterdam *pop* 79,085
Vla·di·mir \'vlad-ə-,mi(ə)r, vlə-'dē-,mi(ə)r\ city U.S.S.R. in *cen* Soviet Russia, Europe, on Klyazma river E of Moscow *pop* 234,000
Vlad·i·vos·tok \,vlad-ə-və-'stäk, -'väs-,täk\ city & port U.S.S.R. in SE Soviet Russia, Asia ✱ of Maritime Territory *pop* 442,000
Vlis·sing·en \'vlis-iŋ-ən\ *or* **Flush·ing** \'fləsh-iŋ\ city & port SW Netherlands on Walcheren I. *pop* 40,197
Vlo·ne *or* **Vlo·na** \'vlō-nə\ *or* **Vlo·re** *or* **Vlo·ra** \'vlōr-ə, 'vlòr-\ *or* **Va·lo·na** \və-'lō-nə\ *or formerly* **Avlo·na** \av-'lō-nə\city & port S Albania *pop* 50,351
Vlotslavsk — see WLOCLAWEK
Vlta·va \'vəl-tə-və\ *or* **Mol·dau** \'mōl-,daù, 'mòl-\ river 270 *m* W Czechoslovakia in Bohemia flowing N into the Elbe
Vodena — see EDESSA
Vo·gel·kop \'vō-gəl-,käp\ peninsula NW New Guinea
Voiotia — see BOEOTIA
Voi·vo·di·na *or* **Voj·vo·di·na** \'vòi-və-,dē-nə, -di-,nä\ autonomous region NE Yugoslavia N of the Danube; chief city Novi Sad *area* 8683, *pop* 1,950,268
Volcano *or* Jap **Ka·zan Ret·to** \,käz-,än-'ret-(,)ō\ islands W Pacific S of Bonin islands; belong to Japan; under U.S. control 1945–68 *area* 11 — see IWO JIMA
Vo·len·dam \'vō-lən-,dam, ,vō-lən-'däm\ village NW Netherlands on IJsselmeer SE of Edam
Vol·ga \'väl-gə, 'vòl-, 'vōl-\ river 2325 *m* U.S.S.R. in Soviet Russia, Europe, rising in Valdai hills & flowing into the Caspian
Vol·go·grad \'väl-gə-,grad, 'vòl-, 'vōl-\ *or formerly* **Sta·lin·grad** \'stäl-ən-,grad, 'stal-\ *or* **Tsa·ri·tsyn** \(t)sə-'rēt-sən\city U.S.S.R. in S Soviet Russia, Europe, on the Volga *pop* 818,000
Vo·log·da \'vò-ləg-də\ city U.S.S.R. in N *cen* Soviet Russia, Europe, NNE of Moscow *pop* 178,000
Vo·los \'vō-,läs\ *or* NGk **Vó·los** \'vò-,lòs\ city & port E Greece on **Gulf of Volos** (inlet of the Aegean) *pop* 51,340
Volsinii — see ORVIETO
Vol·ta \'väl-tə, 'vōl-, 'vòl-\ river *ab* 100 *m* W Africa flowing from **Lake Volta** (reservoir *area* 3275) receiving the **Black Volta** (540 *m*) & **White Volta** (450 *m*) in N *cen* Ghana & flowing S into Bight of Benin — see RED VOLTA
Vol·ta Re·don·da \,väl-tə-ri-'dän-də, ,vōl-, ,vòl-\ city E Brazil on the Paraíba NW of city of Rio de Janeiro *pop* 118,114
Vol·ter·ra \väl-'ter-ə, vōl-, vòl-\ *or anc* **Vo·la·ter·rae** \,vō-lə-'te(ə)r-,ī, -(,)ē\ commune *cen* Italy in Tuscany SE of Pisa *pop* 16,558
Vol·tur·no \väl-'tù(ə)r-(,)nō, vōl-, vòl-\ river 110 *m* S *cen* Italy flowing from the Apennines SE & SW into Gulf of Gaeta
Voor·burg \'vō(ə)r-,bərg, 'vò(ə)r-\ commune SW Netherlands, E suburb of The Hague *pop* 45,011
Vor·arl·berg \'fō(ə)r-,ärl-,bərg, 'fò(ə)r-\ province W Austria W of Tirol bordering on Switzerland ✱ Bregenz
Vo·ro·nezh \və-'rò-nish\ city U.S.S.R. in S *cen* Soviet Russia, Europe, near the Don *pop* 660,000
Vo·ro·shi·lov·grad \,vòr-ə-'shē-ləf-,grad, ,vär-, -ləv-\ *or formerly* **Lu·gansk** \lü-'gan(t)sk\ city U.S.S.R. in E Ukraine in Donets basin *pop* 382,000
Vosges \'vōzh\ mountains NE France on W side of Rhine valley; highest Ballon de Guebwiller 4672 *ft*
Voy·a·geurs National Park \,vòi-ə-'zhərz\ reservation N Minn. on Canadian border *area* 343
Vrangelya — see WRANGEL
Vyat·ka *or* **Viat·ka** \vē-'ät-kə\ **1** river 800 *m* U.S.S.R. in E Soviet Russia, Europe, flowing into the Kama **2** — see KIROV
Vy·borg \'vē-,bò(ə)rg, -,bòr-ē\ *or* Finn **Vii·pu·ri** \'vē-pə-rē\ city & port U.S.S.R. in NW Soviet Russia, Europe, on arm of Gulf of Finland; belonged to Finland 1917–40 *pop* 65,000
Vy·cheg·da *or* **Vi·cheg·da** \'vich-ig-də\ river 700 *m* U.S.S.R. in N Soviet Russia, Europe, flowing W to the Northern Dvina
Waadt — see VAUD
Waal \'väl\ river Netherlands, the S branch of the Lower Rhine
Wa·bash \'wò-,bash\ river 475 *m* Ind. & Ill. flowing into the Ohio
Wa·co \'wā-(,)kō\ city NE *cen* Tex. on Brazos river *pop* 95,326
Wad·den Zee \,väd-ᵊn-'zā\ inlet of North sea N Netherlands between West Frisian islands & IJsselmeer
Wad·ding·ton, Mount \'wäd-iŋ-tən\ mountain 13,260 *ft* W Canada in SW B.C. in Coast mountains; highest in province
Wa·gram \'väg-,räm\ village Austria NE of Vienna
Wa·hi·a·wa \,wä-hē-ə-'wä\ city Hawaii in *cen* Oahu *pop* 17,598
Wai·a·le·ale \wī-,äl-ē-'äl-ē\ mountain 5080 *ft* Hawaii in *cen* Kauai
Wai·ka·to \wī-'kät-(,)ō\ river 220 *m* New Zealand in NW North I. flowing NW into Tasman sea
Wai·ki·ki \,wī-kə-'kē\ resort section of Honolulu, Hawaii NW of Diamond Head on **Waikiki Beach**
Wai·mea Canyon \wī-,mā-ə-\ gorge Hawaii on SW coast of Kauai I.
Wai·pa·hu \wī-'pä-(,)hü\ city Hawaii in SW Oahu *pop* 22,798
Wai·ta·ki \wī-'täk-ē\ river 135 *m* New Zealand in SE *cen* South I. flowing ESE into the Pacific
Wa·ka·ya·ma \,wäk-ə-'yäm-ə\ city & port Japan in SW Honshu on Inland sea *pop* 362,000
Wake \'wāk\ island N Pacific N of Marshall islands belonging to the U.S.
Wake·field \'wāk-,fēld\ **1** town E Mass. N of Boston *pop* 25,402 **2** city & county borough N England ✱ of West Riding, Yorkshire *pop* 59,650
Wa·la·chia *or* **Wal·la·chia** \wä-'lā-kē-ə\ region S Rumania between the Transylvanian Alps & the Danube; includes Muntenia & Oltenia; chief city Bucharest — **Wa·la·chi·an** *or* **Wal·la·chi·an** \-ən\ *adj or n*
Wal·deck \'väl-,dek\ former county, principality, & state of Germany between Westphalia & Hesse-Nassau ✱ Arolsen
Wal·den Pond \,wòl-dən-\ pond NE Mass. S of Concord
Wales \'wā(ə)lz\ *or* Welsh **Cym·ru** \'kəm-,rē\ *or* ML **Cam·bria** \'kam-brē-ə\principality SW Great Britain; a division of the United Kingdom ✱ Cardiff *area* 7469, *pop* 2,723,596
Wal·la·sey \'wäl-ə-sē\ county borough NW England in Cheshire on coast W of Liverpool *pop* 97,061
Wal·la Wal·la \,wäl-ə-'wäl-ə, 'wäl-ə-,\ city SE Wash. *pop* 23,619
Wal·ling·ford \'wäl-iŋ-fərd\ town S Conn. NNE of New Haven *pop* 35,714
Wal·lis, **1** \'wäl-əs\ islands SW Pacific NE of Fiji islands; with Futuna Islands, constitute a French overseas territory (**Wallis and Futuna Islands** *pop* 8546) **2** — see VALAIS
Wal·lops \'wäl-əps\ island E Va. on the Atlantic SW of Chincoteague Bay
Wal·lowa \wä-'laù-ə\ mountains NE Oreg. E of Blue mountains; highest Sacajawea Peak 10,033 *ft*
Walnut Canyon National Monument reservation N *cen* Ariz. ESE of Flagstaff containing cliff dwellings
Walnut Creek city W Calif. E of Berkeley *pop* 39,844
Wal·pole \'wòl-,pōl, 'wäl-\ town E Mass. SW of Boston *pop* 18,149
Wal·sall \'wòl-,sòl, -səl\ county borough W *cen* England in Staffordshire NNW of Birmingham *pop* 184,606
Wal·tham \'wòl-,tham, *chiefly by outsiders* -thəm\ city E Mass. W of Boston *pop* 61,582
Wal·tham Forest \,wòl-thəm\ borough of NE Greater London, England *pop* 233,528
Wal·tham·stow \'wòl-thəm-,stō\ former municipal borough SE England in Essex, now part of Waltham Forest
Wal·vis Bay \,wòl-vəs-\ town, port, & district SW Africa on Walvis Bay (inlet) W of Windhoek; an exclave of Republic of So. Africa in South-West Africa *area* (of district) 374
Wands·worth \'wän(d)z-(,)wərth\ borough of SW Greater London, England *pop* 298,931
Wang·a·nui \,wäŋ-(g)ə-'nü-ē\ **1** river 150 *m* New Zealand in SW *cen* North I., flowing into Cook strait **2** city & port New Zealand in North I. on Cook strait *pop* 36,600
Wan·ne–Eick·el \,vän-ə-'ī-kəl\ city W Germany in the Ruhr N of Bochum *pop* 100,300
Wan·stead and Wood·ford \,wän-stəd-ᵊn-'wùd-fərd\ former municipal borough S England in Essex, now part of Redbridge
Wap·si·pin·i·con \,wäp-si-'pin-i-kən\ river 225 *m* SE Minn. & E Iowa flowing SE into the Mississippi
Wa·ran·gal \wə-'rəŋ-gəl\ city S *cen* India in N Andhra Pradesh NE of Hyderabad *pop* 181,255
War·bur·ton, The \'wòr-(,)bərt-ᵊn\ watercourse 275 *m* Australia in NE So. Australia flowing SW into Lake Eyre
Wargla — see OUARGLA
War·ley \'wòr-lē\ county borough W *cen* England in Worcestershire NW of Birmingham *pop* 163,388
War·ner Rob·ins \,wòr-nər-'räb-ənz\ city *cen* Ga. *pop* 33,491
War·ren \'wòr-ən, 'wär-\ **1** city SE Mich. N of Detroit *pop* 179,-260 **2** city NE Ohio NW of Youngstown *pop* 63,494
War·ren·ville Heights \-,vil\ city NE Ohio SE of Cleveland *pop* 18,925
War·ring·ton \'wòr-iŋ-tən, 'wär-\ county borough NW England in Lancashire on the Mersey E of Liverpool *pop* 68,262
War·saw \'wòr-,sò\ *or* Pol **War·sza·wa** \vär-'shäv-ə\ city ✱ of Poland on the Vistula *pop* 1,283,900
War·ta \'värt-ə\ *or* G **War·the** \'värt-ə\ river 445 *m* Poland flowing NW & W into the Oder
War·wick \'wär-ik, *US also* 'wòr-ik, 'wòr-(,)wik\ **1** city *cen* R.I. S of Providence on Narragansett Bay *pop* 83,694 **2** *or* **War·wick·shire** \-,shi(ə)r, -shər\ county *cen* England *area* 976, *pop* 2,079,-799 **3** municipal borough, its ✱ *pop* 18,289
Wa·satch \'wò-,sach\ mountain range SE Idaho & N & *cen* Utah — see TIMPANOGOS (Mount)
Wash, The \'wòsh, 'wäsh\ inlet of North sea E England between Norfolk & Lincoln
Wash·ing·ton \'wòsh-iŋ-tən, 'wäsh-\ **1** state NW U.S. ✱ Olympia *area* 68,192, *pop* 3,409,169 **2** city ✱ of the U.S., coextensive with District of Columbia *pop* 756,510 **3** city SW Pa. *pop* 19,827 — **Wash·ing·to·nian** \,wòsh-iŋ-'tō-nē-ən, ,wäsh-, -nyən\ *adj or n*
Washington, Lake lake 20 *m* long W Wash. E of Seattle
Washington, Mount mountain 6288 *ft* N N.H.; highest in White mountains
Wash·i·ta \'wäsh-ə-,tò\ **1** river 500 *m* NW Tex. & SW Okla. flowing SE into Red river **2** — see OUACHITA
Wa·tau·ga \wä-'tò-gə\ river 60 *m* NW N.C. & NE Tenn. flowing into S fork of the Holston

Watenstedt–Salzgitter — see SALZGITTER
Wa·ter·bury \'wȯt-ə(r)-ˌber-ē, 'wät-\ city W *cen* Conn. on Naugatuck river *pop* 108,033
Wa·ter·ee \'wȯt-ə-ˌrē, 'wät-\ river S.C., lower course of the Catawba — see CONGAREE
Wa·ter·ford \'wȯt-ər-fərd, 'wät-\ **1** town SE Conn. SW of New London *pop* 17,227 **2** county S Ireland in Munster *area* 710, *pop* 76,932 **3** city & port, its ✱, on Suir river *pop* 31,692
Wa·ter·loo \ˌwȯt-ər-'lü, ˌwät-\ **1** city NE *cen* Iowa *pop* 75,533 **2** city Canada in SE Ont. W of Kitchener *pop* 36,677 **3** town *cen* Belgium S of Brussels *pop* 16,924
Waterton–Glacier International Peace Park — see GLACIER NATIONAL PARK
Wa·ter·ton Lakes National Park \'wȯt-ərt-^{ə}n, 'wät-\ reservation Canada in Rocky mountains in S Alta. on Mont. border *area* 521
Wa·ter·town \'wȯt-ər-ˌtaůn, 'wät-\ **1** town SW Conn. NW of Waterbury *pop* 18,610 **2** town E Mass. W of Boston *pop* 39,307 **3** city N *cen* N.Y. SE of Kingston, Ont. *pop* 30,787 **4** city SE Wis. *pop* 15,683
Wa·ter·ville \'wȯt-ər-ˌvil, 'wät-\ city S *cen* Me. *pop* 18,192
Wat·ford \'wät-fərd\ municipal borough SE England in Hertfordshire NW of London *pop* 78,117
Watling *or* **Watlings** — see SAN SALVADOR
Wat·ten·scheid \'vät-^{ə}n-ˌshīt\ city W Germany E of Essen *pop* 80,527
Watts \'wäts\ section of Los Angeles, Calif. S of the downtown district
Wau·ke·gan \wȯ-'kē-gən\ city NE Ill. N of Chicago *pop* 65,269
Wau·ke·sha \'wȯ-kə-ˌshȯ\ city SE Wis. *pop* 40,258
Wau·sau \'wȯ-ˌsȯ, -sə\ city N *cen* Wis. on Wisconsin river *pop* 32,806
Wau·wa·to·sa \ˌwȯ-wə-'tō-sə\ city SE Wis. *pop* 58,676
Way·cross \'wā-ˌkrȯs\ city SE Ga. *pop* 18,996
Wayne \'wān\ village SE Mich. SW of Detroit *pop* 21,054
Wa·ziri·stan \wə-ˌzir-i-'stan, -'stän\ region W Pakistan on border of Afghanistan NE of Baluchistan
Weald \'wē(ə)ld\ region SE England in Kent, Surrey, & Sussex, between North Downs & South Downs; once heavily forested
Webbe Shibeli — see SHIBELI
Web·ster Groves \ˌweb-stər-\ city E Mo. *pop* 26,995
Wed·dell \wə-'del, 'wed-^{ə}l\ sea arm of the S Atlantic E of Antarctic peninsula
Wei \'wā\ river 400 *m* N *cen* China flowing E to join Yellow river
Weichsel — see VISTULA
Wei·fang \'wā-'fäŋ\ city E China in E *cen* Shantung NW of Tsingtao *pop* 260,000
Wei·hai \'wā-'hī\ *or formerly* **Wei·hai·wei** \ˌwā-ˌhī-'wā\ city & port E China in NE Shantung on Yellow sea *pop* 175,000
Wei·mar \'vī-ˌmär, 'wī-\ city E Germany E of Erfurt *pop* 63,689
Weimar Republic the German republic 1919–33
Weir·ton \'wi(ə)rt-^{ə}n\ city N W.Va. on the Ohio *pop* 27,131
Weiss·horn \'vīs-ˌhȯ(ə)rn\ mountain 14,804 *ft* SW *cen* Switzerland in Pennine Alps
Wel·land \'wel-ənd\ **1** city Canada in SE Ont. SW of Niagara Falls *pop* 44,397 **2** ship canal 28 *m* Canada in SE Ont. connecting Lake Erie & Lake Ontario
Welle — see UELE
Welles·ley \'welz-lē\ town E Mass. WSW of Boston *pop* 28,051
Wel·ling·ton \'wel-iŋ-tən\ city & port New Zealand in SW North I. on Port Nicholson (Wellington Harbor) on Cook strait ✱ of New Zealand *pop* 134,900
Wells \'welz\ municipal borough SW England in Somerset
Welsh·pool \'welsh-ˌpül\ municipal borough E Wales ✱ of Montgomeryshire
Wel·wyn Garden City \'wel-ən\ urban district SE England in Hertfordshire N of London *pop* 40,369
Wem·bley \'wem-blē\ former municipal borough SE England in Middlesex, now part of Brent
We·natch·ee \wə-'nach-ē\ city *cen* Wash. *pop* 16,912
Wen·chow \'wən-'jō\ *or formerly* **Yung·kia** \'yůŋ-jē-'ä\ city & port E China in S Chekiang on East China sea *pop* 250,000
Wer·ra \'ver-ə\ river 180 *m*, *cen* Germany flowing N to join the Fulda forming the Weser
We·ser \'vā-zər, 'wē-\ river 280 *m* W Germany formed by confluence of the Fulda & Werra & flowing into North sea
Wesermünde former city NW Germany — see BREMERHAVEN
Wes·la·co \'wes-li-ˌkō\ city S Tex. W of Harlingen *pop* 15,313
Wes·sex \'wes-iks\ ancient Anglian kingdom S England ✱ Winchester; one of kingdoms in Anglo-Saxon heptarchy
West \'west\ *or* **Si** \'shē\ river 300 *m* SE China in Kwangsi & Kwangtung formed by confluence of the Hungshui & the Yü & flowing E into So. China sea
West Al·lis \'al-əs\ city SE Wis. *pop* 71,723
West Bend \'bend\ city SE Wis. NNW of Milwaukee *pop* 16,555
West Bengal state E India comprising the W third of former Bengal province ✱ Calcutta *area* 33,945, *pop* 44,440,095
West Beskids — see BESKIDS
West Brom·wich \'brəm-ij, 'bräm-, -ich\ county borough W *cen* England in Staffordshire NW of Birmingham *pop* 166,626
West·ches·ter \'wes(t)-ˌches-tər\ village NE Ill. W of Chicago *pop* 20,033
West Ches·ter \'wes(t)-ˌches-tər\ borough SE Pa. *pop* 19,301
West Co·vi·na \kō-'vē-nə\ city SW Calif. *pop* 68,034
West Des Moines city S *cen* Iowa *pop* 16,441
Wes·ter·ly \'wes-tər-lē\ town SW R.I. *pop* 17,248
Western — see HEBRIDES
Western Australia state W Australia on Indian ocean ✱ Perth *area* 975,920, *pop* 980,000
Western Ghats \'gȯts\ chain of mountains SW India extending SSE parallel to coast from mouth of Tapti river to Cape Comorin; highest Anai Mudi 8841 *ft* — see EASTERN GHATS
Western Reserve tract of land NE Ohio on S shore of Lake Erie; part of western lands of Conn., ceded 1800 to Ohio *area ab* 5470
Western Samoa group of islands of Samoa W of 171°W; an independent state; until 1962 a territory administered by New Zealand ✱ Apia (on Upolu I.) *area* 1133, *pop* 140,000
Western Thrace — see THRACE
West·field \'wes(t)-ˌfēld\ **1** city SW Mass. WNW of Springfield *pop* 31,433 **2** town NE N.J. WSW of Elizabeth *pop* 33,720
West Flanders province NW Belgium bordering on North sea ✱ Bruges *area* 1248, *pop* 1,056,855
West Frisian — see FRISIAN
West Germany the Federal Republic of Germany — see GERMANY
West Ham \'ham\ former county borough SE England in Essex, now part of Newham
West Hartford town *cen* Conn. *pop* 68,031
West Ha·ven \'west-ˌhā-vən\ city S Conn. *pop* 52,851
West Indies, **1** the islands lying between SE No. America & N So. America bordering the Caribbean & comprising the Greater Antilles, Lesser Antilles, & Bahamas **2** *or* **West Indies Federation** former country including all of the Brit. West Indies except the Bahamas & the Brit. Virgin islands; established 1958, dissolved 1961 — **West Indian** *adj or n*
West Indies Associated States the self-governing states of Antigua, Dominica, Grenada, St. Kitts-Nevis, & St. Lucia, associated with Great Britain in foreign relations & defense
West Iri·an \ˌir-ē-'än\ *or* **West New Guinea** *or* Indonesian **Irian Ba·rat** \'bär-ˌät\ *or formerly* **Netherlands New Guinea** territory of Indonesia comprising the W half of New Guinea & adjacent islands; belonged to the Netherlands until 1963 ✱ Djajapura *area* 164,159 *pop* 957,000
West Kil·do·nan \kil-'dō-nən\ city Canada in SE Man. N of Winnipeg *pop* 23,959
West Lafayette city W *cen* Ind. *pop* 19,157
West·lake \'west-ˌlāk\ city N Ohio W of Cleveland *pop* 15,689
West·land \'wes-(t)lənd\ city SE Mich. W of Detroit *pop* 86,749
West Lo·thi·an \'lō-thē-ən\ *or* **Lin·lith·gow** \lin-'lith-(ˌ)gō\ *or* **Lin·lith·gow·shire** \-ˌshi(ə)r, -shər\ county SE Scotland bordering on Firth of Forth ✱ Linlithgow *area* 120, *pop* 108,474
West Malaysia — see MALAYA
West·meath \(ˈ)wes(t)-'mēth, -'mēth\ county E *cen* Ireland in Leinster ✱ Mullingar *area* 681, *pop* 53,557
West Memphis city E Ark. on the Mississippi *pop* 25,892
West Miff·lin \'mif-lən\ borough SW Pa. SE of Pittsburgh on the Monongahela *pop* 28,070
West·min·ster \'wes(t)-ˌmin(t)-stər\ **1** city SW Calif. E of Long Beach *pop* 59,865 **2** city N *cen* Colo. NW of Denver *pop* 19,432 **3** city constituting a borough of W *cen* Greater London, England *pop* 225,632
West·mor·land \'wes(t)-mər-lənd, *US also* wes(t)-'mō(ə)r- *or* -'mȯ(ə)r-\ county NW England ✱ Kendal *area* 789, *pop* 72,724
West·mount \'wes(t)-ˌmaůnt\ city Canada in S Que. within city of Montreal *pop* 23,606
West New York town NE N.J. on the Hudson *pop* 40,627
Wes·ton–su·per–Mare \'wes-tən-ˌsü-pər-'ma(ə)r, -'me(ə)r\ municipal borough SW England in Somerset on Bristol channel *pop* 50,794
West Orange town NE N.J. NW of Newark *pop* 43,715
West Pakistan the former W division of Pakistan, now coextensive with Pakistan
West Palm Beach city SE Fla. on Lake Worth inlet *pop* 57,375
West·pha·lia \wes(t)-'fāl-yə, -'fā-lē-ə\ *or* G **West·fa·len** \vest-'fäl-ən\ region W Germany bordering on the Netherlands E of the Rhine; includes Ruhr valley; a province of Prussia 1816–1945 ✱ Münster — see NORTH RHINE-WESTPHALIA — **West·pha·lian** \wes(t)-'fāl-yən, -'fā-lē-ən\ *adj or n*
West·port \'wes(t)-ˌpō(ə)rt, -ˌpȯ(ə)rt\ town SW Conn. on Long Island Sound *pop* 27,414
West Prussia *or* G **West·preus·sen** \'vest-ˌprȯis-^{ə}n\ region N Europe, now in Poland; the W part of original region of Prussia
West Punjab — see PUNJAB
West Quod·dy Head \ˌkwäd-ē\ cape NE Maine at entrance to Passamaquoddy Bay; easternmost point of the U.S., at 66°57'W
Wes·tra·lia \we-'strāl-yə, -'strā-lē-ə\ WESTERN AUSTRALIA
West Riding — see YORK
West Saint Paul city SE Minn. S of St. Paul *pop* 18,799
West Spitsbergen island in Arctic ocean, largest of the Spitsbergen group *area* 14,600
West Springfeld town SW Mass. on the Connecticut *pop* 28,461
West Suffolk — see SUFFOLK
West Sussex — see SUSSEX
West Virginia state E U.S. ✱ Charleston *area* 24,181, *pop* 1,744,-237 — **West Virginian** *adj or n*
West Warwick town *cen* R.I. *pop* 24,323
Weth·ers·field \'weth-ərz-ˌfēld\ town *cen* Conn. *pop* 26,662
Wet·ter·horn \'vet-ər-ˌhȯ(ə)rn\ mountain 12,153 *ft* Switzerland in Bernese Alps N of the Finsteraarhorn
Wex·ford \'weks-fərd\ **1** county SE Ireland in Leinster *area* 908, *pop* 85,892 **2** municipal borough & port, its ✱
Wey·mouth \'wā-məth\ town E Mass. SE of Boston *pop* 54,610
Whales, Bay of inlet of Ross sea Antarctica in Ross Ice Shelf
Wham·poa \'hwäm-'pō-'ä, 'wäm-\ town & port SE China in Kwangtung on Pearl river below Canton
Whangpoo — see HWANG PU
Whea·ton \'hwēt-^{ə}n, 'wēt-\ city NE Ill. W of Chicago *pop* 31,138
Wheat Ridge city N *cen* Colo. W of Denver *pop* 29,795
Whee·ler Peak \ˌhwē-lər-, ˌwē-\ **1** mountain 13,063 *ft* E Nev. in Snake range **2** mountain 13,160 *ft* N N.Mex in Sangre de Cristo mountains; highest in the state

Whee·ling \'hwē-liŋ, 'wē-\ city N W.Va. on the Ohio *pop* 48,188
Whid·bey \'hwid-bē, 'wid-\ island 40 *m* long NW Wash. at N end of Puget Sound E of Admiralty inlet
Whit·by \'hwit-bē, 'wit-\ town Canada in S Ont. NE of Toronto *pop* 25,324
White, 1 river 690 *m* N Ark. & SW Mo. flowing SE into the Mississippi **2** river 160*m* NW Colo. & E Utah flowing W into the Green **3** river 50 *m* SW Ind. formed by confluence of West Fork (300 *m*) & East Fork (250 *m*) & flowing W into the Wabash **4** river 325 *m* S S.Dak. flowing E into the Missouri **5** river 75 *m* NW Tex. flowing SE into the Salt Fork **6** mountains N N.H. in the Appalachians — see WASHINGTON (Mount) **7** mountain pass 2885 *ft* SE Alaska N of Skagway **8** *or* Russ **Be·loe Mo·re** \,bel-ə-yə-'mȯr-yə\ sea inlet of Barents sea U.S.S.R. on N coast of Soviet Russia, Europe, enclosed on the N by Kola peninsula
White Bear Lake city E Minn. NE of St. Paul *pop* 23,313
White·chap·el \'hwīt-,chap-əl, 'wīt-\ district of E London, England, N of the Thames in Tower Hamlets
White·fish Bay \'hwīt-,fish, 'wīt-\ village SE Wis. N of Milwaukee *pop* 17,394
White·friars \'hwīt-,frī(-ə)rz, 'wīt-\ district of *cen* London, England on the Thames
White·hall \-,hȯl\ **1** city *cen* Ohio, E suburb of Columbus *pop* 25,263 **2** borough SW Pa. S of Pittsburgh *pop* 16,551
White·horse \'hwīt-,hō(ə)rs, 'wīt-\ town NW Canada ✱ of Yukon Territory on the upper Yukon *pop* 11,084
White Nile — see NILE
White Plains city SE N.Y. NE of Yonkers *pop* 50,220
White Russia — see BELORUSSIA
White Sands National Monument reservation S N.Mex. SW of Alamogordo comprising an area of gypsum sand dunes *area* 219
White Volta — see VOLTA
Whit·man National Monument \'hwit-mən, 'wit-\ reservation SE Wash. NW of Walla Walla, site of Marcus Whitman mission
Whit·ney, Mount \'hwit-nē, 'wit-\ mountain 14,494 *ft* SE *cen* Calif. in Sierra Nevada in Sequoia National Park; highest in the U.S. outside of Alaska
Whit·ti·er \'hwit-ē-ər, 'wit-\ city SW Calif. SE of Los Angeles *pop* 72,863
Wich·i·ta \'wich-ə-,tȯ\ **1** city S *cen* Kans. on Arkansas river *pop* 276,554 **2** river 230 *m* N Tex. flowing ENE into Red river **3** mountains SW Okla.; highest Mt. Scott 2464 *ft*
Wichita Falls city N Tex. on Wichita river *pop* 97,564
Wick \'wik\ burgh N Scotland ✱ of Caithness
Wick·liffe \'wik-ləf, -(,)lif\ city NE Ohio NE of Cleveland *pop* 21,354
Wick·low \'wik-(,)lō\ **1** county E Ireland in Leinster *area* 782, *pop* 66,730 **2** urban district & port, its ✱, SSE of Dublin **3** mountains Ireland along E coast; highest Lugnaquilla 3039 *ft*
Wien — see VIENNA
Wies·ba·den \'vēs-,bäd-^{ə}n, 'vis-\ city W Germany on the Rhine W of Frankfurt ✱ of Hesse *pop* 259,900
Wig·an \'wig-ən\ county borough NW England in Lancashire W of Manchester *pop* 81,258
Wight, Isle of \'wīt\ island S England in English channel constituting **Isle of Wight** administrative county (✱ Newport *area* 147, *pop* 109,284) — see HAMPSHIRE
Wig·town \'wig-tən, -,taun\ **1** *or* **Wig·town·shire** \-,shi(ə)r, -shər\ county SW Scotland *area* 487, *pop* 27,335 **2** burgh, its ✱
Wilderness Road trail from SW Va. to *cen* Ky. through Cumberland Gap blazed to site of Boonesborough by Daniel Boone 1775 & later extended to Falls of the Ohio at Louisville
Wil·helms·ha·ven \,vil-,helmz-'häf-ən, 'vil-əmz-,\ city & port W Germany NW of Bremen *pop* 102,700
Wilkes–Barre \'wilks-,bar-ə, -,bar-ē, -,ba(ə)r\ city NE Pa. on the Susquehanna SW of Scranton *pop* 58,866
Wilkes Land \'wilks\ coast region E Antarctica extending along Indian ocean S of Australia
Wil·kins·burg \'wil-kənz-,bərg\ borough SW Pa. *pop* 26,780
Wil·lam·ette \wə-'lam-ət\ river 190 *m* NW Oreg. flowing N into the Columbia
Wil·la·pa Bay \'wil-ə-,pȯ, -,pä\ inlet of the Pacific SW Wash.
Wil·lem·stad \'vil-əm-,stät\ city ✱ of Netherlands Antilles on Curaçao I. *pop* 43,547
Willes·den \'wilz-dən\ former municipal borough SE England in Middlesex, now part of Brent
Wil·liam·son, Mount \'wil-yəm-sən\ mountain 14,384 *ft* SE *cen* Calif. in Sierra Nevada NNW of Mt. Whitney
Wil·liams·port \'wil-yəmz-,pō(ə)rt, -,pȯ(ə)rt\ city N *cen* Pa. on West Branch of the Susquehanna *pop* 37,918
Wil·lough·by \'wil-ə-bē\ city NE Ohio NE of Cleveland *pop* 18,634
Wil·lo·wick \'wil-ə-,wik\ city NE Ohio E of Cleveland *pop* 21,237
Wil·mette \wil-'met\ village NE Ill. N of Chicago *pop* 32,134
Wil·ming·ton \'wil-miŋ-tən\ **1** city & port N Del. *pop* 80,386 **2** town NE Mass. SE of Lowell *pop* 17,102 **3** city & port SE N.C. *pop* 46,169
Wilno — see VILNYUS
Wil·son \'wil-sən\ city E *cen* N.C. E of Raleigh *pop* 29,347
Wilson, Mount mountain 5704 *ft* SW Calif. NE of Pasadena
Wilt·shire \'wilt-,shi(ə)r; 'wil-chər, 'wilt-shər\ county S England ✱ Trowbridge *area* 1345, *pop* 486,048
Wim·ble·don \'wim-bəl-dən\ former municipal borough SE England in Surrey, now part of Merton
Win·ches·ter \'win-,ches-tər, -chə-stər\ **1** town E Mass. NW of Boston *pop* 22,269 **2** municipal borough S England ✱ of Hampshire *pop* 31,041
Wind \'wind\ river W *cen* Wyo., the upper course of the Bighorn
Windau — see VENTA, VENTSPILS
Wind Cave limestone cavern SW S.Dak. in Black hills in **Wind Cave National Park** (*area* 42)
Win·der·mere \'win-də(r)-,mi(ə)r\ lake 10 *m* long NW England on Westmorland-Lancashire border; largest in England
Wind·ham \'win-dəm\ town E *cen* Conn. *pop* 19,626
Wind·hoek \'vint-,hu̇k\ city ✱ of South-West Africa *pop* 36,051
Wind River mountain range W *cen* Wyo. — see GANNETT PEAK
Wind River Canyon gorge of the Bighorn river W *cen* Wyo.
Wind·sor \'win-zər\ **1** town N *cen* Conn. N of Hartford *pop* 22,502 **2** city Canada in SE Ont. opposite Detroit, Mich. *pop* 203,300 **3** *or* **New Windsor** municipal borough S England in Berkshire on the Thames W of London *pop* 30,065
Windsor Locks town N Conn. N of Hartford *pop* 15,080
Wind·ward \'win-dwərd\ **1** islands West Indies in the S Lesser Antilles extending S from Martinique but not including Barbados, Tobago, or Trinidad **2** former colony Brit. West Indies comprising territories of St. Lucia, St. Vincent, & Grenada in the Windward group & Dominica in the Leewards **3** *or* F **Îles du Vent** \ēl-dūe-vä^{n}\ islands S Pacific, E group of the Society islands, including Tahiti
Windward Passage channel between Cuba & Hispaniola
Win·ne·ba·go, Lake \,win-ə-'bā-(,)gō\ lake 30 *m* long E Wis.
Win·ni·peg \'win-ə-,peg\ **1** river 200 *m* Canada in W Ont. & SE Man. flowing from Lake of the Woods to Lake Winnipeg **2** city Canada ✱ of Man. *pop* 246,246 — **Win·ni·peg·ger** \-,peg-ər\ *n*
Winnipeg, Lake lake 275 *m* long Canada in S *cen* Man. drained by Nelson river *area* 9460
Win·ni·pe·go·sis, Lake \,win-ə-pə-'gō-səs\ lake Canada in W Man. W of Lake Winnipeg *area* 2086
Win·ni·pe·sau·kee, Lake \,win-ə-pə-'sȯ-kē\ lake *cen* N.H. *area* 71
Wi·no·na \wə-'nō-nə\ city SE Minn. *pop* 26,438
Wi·noo·ski \wə-'nü-skē\ river 100 *m* N *cen* Vt. flowing into Lake Champlain
Win·ston–Sa·lem \,win(t)-stən-'sā-ləm\ city N *cen* N.C. *pop* 132,913
Winter Haven city *cen* Fla. E of Lakeland *pop* 16,136
Winter Park city E Fla. N of Orlando *pop* 21,895
Win·ter·thur \'vint-ər-,tu̇(ə)r\ commune N Switzerland in Zurich canton NE of Zurich *pop* 92,500
Win·throp \'win(t)-thrəp\ town E Mass. ENE of Boston on Massachusetts Bay *pop* 20,335
Win·yah Bay \'win-,yȯ\ inlet of the Atlantic E S.C.
Wis·con·sin \wis-'kän(t)-sən\ **1** river 430 *m*, *cen* Wis. flowing S & W into the Mississippi **2** state N *cen* U.S. ✱ Madison *area* 56,164, *pop* 4,417,933 — **Wis·con·sin·ite** \-sə-,nīt\ *n*
Wisconsin Dells — see DELLS OF THE WISCONSIN
Wisconsin Rapids city *cen* Wis. *pop* 18,587
Wisla — see VISTULA
Wis·mar \'vis-,mär, 'wiz-,mär\ city & port NE Germany SW of Rostock *pop* 56,057
Wis·sa·hick·on \,wis-ə-'hik-ən\ creek SE Pa. flowing into the Schuylkill at Philadelphia
With·la·coo·chee \,with-lə-'kü-chē\ **1** river 110 *m* S Ga. & NW Fla. flowing SE into the Suwannee **2** river 120 *m* NW *cen* Fla. flowing NW into Gulf of Mexico
Wit·ten \'vit-^{ə}n\ city W Germany SW of Dortmund *pop* 97,472
Wit·ten·berg \'wit-^{ə}n-,bərg\ city E Germany E of Dessau *pop* 47,151
Wit·wa·ters·rand \'wit-,wȯt-ərz-,rand, -,wät-, -,ränd, -,ränt\ ridge of auriferous rock 62 *m* long & 23 *m* wide NE Republic of So. Africa in S Transvaal
Wlo·cla·wek \vlȯt-'släv-,ek\ *or* Russ **Vlo·tslavsk** \vlät-'släfsk\ commune N *cen* Poland on the Vistula *pop* 77,200
Wo·burn \'wü-bərn, 'wō-\ city E Mass. NW of Boston *pop* 37,406
Wolds, The \-'wōl(d)z\ chalk hills NE England in E Yorkshire & NE Lincolnshire on both sides of the Humber
Wolfs·burg \'wu̇lfs-,bərg, 'vȯlfs-,bu̇(ə)rg\ city W Germany NE of Brunswick *pop* 88,024
Wol·lon·gong \'wu̇l-ən-,gäŋ, -,gȯŋ\ city & port SE Australia in E New So. Wales S of Sydney *pop* (with suburbs) 155,160
Wol·ver·hamp·ton \'wu̇l-vər-,ham(p)-tən\ county borough W *cen* England in Staffordshire NW of Birmingham *pop* 268,847
Won·san \'wən-,sän\ city & port N Korea on E coast *pop* 300,000
Wood Buffalo National Park reservation W Canada in N Alta. & S Mackenzie District *area* 17,300
Wood Green former municipal borough SE England in Middlesex, now part of Haringey
Wood·land \'wu̇d-lənd\ city W Calif. NW of Sacramento *pop* 20,677
Wood·lark \'wu̇d-,lärk\ *or* **Mu·rua** \'mu̇r-ə-wə\ island W Pacific in Solomon sea off SE end of New Guinea; attached to Papua New Guinea *area* 400
Woods, Lake of the lake S Canada & N U.S. in Ont., Man., & Minn. SE of Lake Winnipeg *area* 1485
Wood·stock \'wu̇d-,stäk\ city Canada in SE Ont. ENE of London on Thames river *pop* 26,173
Wool·wich \'wu̇l-ij, -ich\ former metropolitan borough E London, England, now part of Greenwich
Woom·era \'wu̇m-ə-rə\ town So. Australia W of Lake Torrens
Woon·sock·et \wün-'säk-ət, 'wün-,\ city N R.I. *pop* 46,820
Woos·ter \'wu̇s-tər\ city N *cen* Ohio SW of Akron *pop* 18,703
Worces·ter \'wu̇s-tər\ **1** city E *cen* Mass. *pop* 176,572 **2** *or* **Worces·ter·shire** \-tə(r)-,shi(ə)r, -shər\ county W *cen* England *area* 699, *pop* 692,605 **3** city & county borough, its ✱ *pop* 73,445
Worms \'wərmz, 'vȯrm(p)s\ city W Germany on the Rhine NNW of Mannheim *pop* 77,642
Worth, Lake \'wərth\ inlet (lagoon) of the Atlantic SE Fla.
Wor·thing \'wər-thiŋ\ municipal borough S England in West Sussex on English channel *pop* 88,210
Wor·thing·ton \'wər-thiŋ-tən\ city *cen* Ohio N of Columbus *pop* 15,326
Wran·gel \'raŋ-gəl\ *or* Russ **Vran·ge·lya** \'vrän-gəl-yə\ island U.S.S.R. off NE Soviet Russia, Asia, in Arctic ocean
Wran·gell \'raŋ-gəl\ **1** island SE Alaska NE of Prince of Wales I. **2** mountain range S Alaska NW of St. Elias range — see BLACKBURN (Mount)
Wrangell, Cape cape on Attu I. in Aleutians, Alaska; westernmost point of U.S. at 172°27′E
Wrangell, Mount active volcano 14,006 *ft* S Alaska in Wrangell mountains NW of Mt. Blackburn

Wrath, Cape \'rath, *Scot* 'rȯth *or* 'räth\ extreme NW point of Scotland, at 58°35′N
Wrex·ham \'rek-səm\ municipal borough N Wales in Denbighshire *pop* 38,955
Wro·claw \'vrȯt-ˌsläf, -ˌsläv\ *or* G **Bres·lau** \'bres-ˌlau̇\ city SW Poland, chief city of Silesia *pop* 514,100
Wu \'wü\ river 500 *m, cen* China rising in W Kweichow & flowing through Szechwan into the Yangtze
Wu·chang \'wü-'chäŋ\ former city E *cen* China — see WUHAN
Wu·chow \'wü-'jō\ city S China in E Kwangsi at junction of Kwei & West rivers *pop* 150,000
Wu·han \'wü-'hän\ city E *cen* China ✱ of Hupei at junction of Han & Yangtze rivers; formed from the former separate cities of Hankow, Hanyang, & Wuchang *pop* 4,250,000
Wuhsien — see SOOCHOW
Wu·hu \'wü-'hü\ city E China in E Anhwei *pop* 300,000
Wu·pat·ki National Monument \wü-'pat-kē\ reservation N Ariz. NNE of Flagstaff containing prehistoric Indian dwellings
Wup·per·tal \'vu̇p-ər-ˌtäl\ city W Germany in Ruhr valley ENE of Düsseldorf *pop* 413,000
Würt·tem·berg \'wərt-əm-ˌbərg, 'wu̇rt-; 'vuert-əm-ˌberk\ region SW Germany between Baden & Bavaria; chief city Stuttgart; once a duchy, kingdom 1813–1918, state 1918–45; divided 1945–51, S part being joined to Hohenzollern forming **Württemberg–Hohenzollern** state & N part to N Baden forming **Württemberg–Baden** state; since 1951 part of Baden–Württemberg state
Würz·burg \'wərts-ˌbərg, 'wu̇rts-; 'vuerts-ˌbu̇rk\ city W Germany on the Main in N Bavaria NW of Nuremberg *pop* 120,100
Wu·sih \'wü-'shē\ city E China in S Kiangsu NW of Soochow *pop* 900,000
Wutsin — see CHANGCHOW
Wu·tung·kiao \ˌwü-ˌtu̇ŋ-chē-'au̇\ city SW *cen* China in S Szechwan S of Chengtu *pop* 199,100
Wy·an·dotte \'wī-ən-ˌdät *also* 'wīn-\ city SE Mich. *pop* 41,061
Wye \'wī\ river 130 *m* E Wales & W England flowing into the Severn
Wy·o·ming \wī-'ō-miŋ\ **1** state NW U.S. ✱ Cheyenne *area* 97,914, *pop* 332,416 **2** valley NE Pa. along the Susquehanna **3** city SW Mich. SW of Grand Rapids *pop* 56,560 — **Wy·o·ming·ite** \-miŋ-ˌīt\ *n*
Xan·thus \'zan(t)-thəs\ **1** *or* Turk **Ko·ca** \kō-'jä\ river 75 *m* S Turkey flowing SW & S into the Mediterranean **2** city of ancient Lycia near mouth of the Xanthus
Xe·nia \'zē-nyə, -nē-ə\ city SW *cen* Ohio *pop* 25,373
Xeres — see JEREZ
Xin·gu \shēŋ-'gü\ river 1300 *m, cen* & N Brazil rising on Mato Grosso plateau & flowing N into the Amazon near its mouth
Xo·chi·mil·co \ˌsō-chi-'mēl(ˌ)-kō, ˌsō-shi-, -'mil-\ city S *cen* Mexico, SE suburb of Mexico City *pop* 117,083
Ya·blo·noi \ˌyäb-lə-'nȯi\ *or* **Ya·blo·no·voi** \-lə-nə-'vȯi\ mountain range U.S.S.R. in S Soviet Russia, Asia, on E border of Buryat Republic; highest peak Sokhondo 8228 *ft*
Yacarana — see JAVARÍ
Yad·kin \'yad-kən\ river 202 *m, cen* N.C., the upper course of the Pee Dee
Yafo — see JAFFA
Ya·ha·ta \yə-'hät-ə\ *or* **Ya·wa·ta** \-'wät-\ former city Japan in N Kyushu — see KITAKYUSHU
Yak·i·ma \'yak-ə-ˌmȯ\ **1** river 200 *m* S Wash. flowing SE into the Columbia **2** city S *cen* Wash. *pop* 45,588
Yak·u·tat Bay \'yak-ə-ˌtat\ inlet of the Pacific SE Alaska
Ya·kutsk \yə-'kütsk\ city U.S.S.R. in E *cen* Soviet Russia, Asia ✱ of Yakutsk Republic *pop* 108,000
Yakutsk Republic *or* **Ya·kut Republic** \yə-'küt\ *or* **Ya·ku·tia** \-'k(y)ü-sh(ē-)ə\ autonomous republic U.S.S.R. in E *cen* Soviet Russia, Asia ✱ Yakutsk *area* 1,182,300, *pop* 664,000
Yal·ta \'yȯl-tə\ city & port U.S.S.R. in S Soviet Russia, Europe, on S coast of Crimea *pop* 57,000
Ya·lu \'yäl-(ˌ)ü\ *or* **Am·nok** \'am-ˌnäk\ river 300 *m* SE Manchuria & NW Korea flowing N, W, & SW into Korea Bay
Ya·lung \'yä-'lu̇ŋ\ river 725 *m* SW China in W Szechwan flowing S into the Yangtze
Ya·mal \yə-'mäl\ peninsula U.S.S.R. in NW Soviet Russia, Asia, at N end of Ural mountains between Gulf of Ob & Kara sea
Yam·pa \'yam-pə\ river 200 *m* NW Colo. flowing W into the Green
Ya·na \'yän-ə\ river 750 *m* U.S.S.R. in N Soviet Russia, Asia, flowing N into Laptev sea
Ya·naon \yə-'nau̇n\ *or* **Ya·nam** \yə-'näm\ town SE India in E Andhra Pradesh on N mouth of the Godavari; a territory of French India before 1954
Yang·chow \'yäŋ-'jō\ *or formerly* **Kiang·tu** \jē-'äŋ-'dü\ city E China in SW Kiangsu NW of Nanking *pop* 210,000
Yang·chuan \'yäŋ-chü-'än\ city N China in E Shansi E of Taiyuan *pop* 177,400
Yangku — see TAIYUAN
Yang·tze *or* **Yang·tse** \'yaŋ-'sē, 'yaŋ(k)t-'sē\ *or* **Yangtze Kiang** \kē-'aŋ\ river 3100 *m, cen* China flowing from Kunlun Shan in SW Tsinghai E into East China sea
Yannina — see IOANNINA
Yaoun·dé *or* **Yaun·de** \yau̇n-'dā\ city W Africa ✱ of Cameroon *pop* 178,000
Yap \'yap, 'yäp\ *or* **Uap** \'wäp\ **1** district Trust Territory of the Pacific Islands in W Carolines *land area* 46, *pop* 7625 **2** islands, chief group in district *pop* 2856
Ya·qui \yä-'kē\ river 420 *m* NW Mexico in Sonora flowing SW into Gulf of California
Yar·kand \yär-'kand\ **1** river 500 *m* Kashmir & China flowing from Karakoram range N & W to join the Khotan in Sinkiang forming the Tarim **2** *or* **So·che** \'swä-'chə\ city W China in SW Sinkiang at oasis on Yarkand river *pop* 80,000
Yar·mouth \'yär-məth\ *or* **Great Yarmouth** county borough & port E England in Norfolk on North sea *pop* 50,152
Ya·ro·slavl \ˌyär-ə-'släv-əl\ city U.S.S.R. in W *cen* Soviet Russia, Europe, on the Volga NE of Moscow *pop* 517,000
Yaz·oo \ya-'zü, 'yaz-(ˌ)ü\ river 188 *m* Miss. flowing SW into the Mississippi
Yedo — see TOKYO
Ye·gor·yevsk *or* **Ye·gor·evsk** \yə-'gȯr-(y)əfsk\ city W *cen* Soviet Russia, Europe, SE of Moscow *pop* 65,000
Yellow, 1 *or* **Hwang Ho** \'hwäŋ-'hō, 'wäŋ- \ *or* **Huang** river 3000 *m* N China flowing from Kunlun mountains in Tsinghai E into Po Hai **2** sea inlet of East China sea between N China & Korea
Yel·low·knife \'yel-ə-ˌnīf\ town Canada ✱ of Northwest Territories in Mackenzie District on Great Slave Lake *pop* 5867
Yel·low·stone \'yel-ə-ˌstōn\ river 671 *m* NW Wyo. & S & E Mont. flowing N through **Yellowstone Lake** (*area* 140) & **Grand Canyon of the Yellowstone** in Yellowstone National Park & NE into the Missouri in NW N.Dak. near Mont. border
Yellowstone Falls two waterfalls NW Wyo. in Yellowstone river at head of Grand Canyon of the Yellowstone; upper fall 109 *ft*, lower fall 308 *ft*
Yellowstone National Park reservation NW Wyo., E Idaho, & S Mont. including plateau region notable for numerous geysers & hot springs *area* 3458
Ye·men \'yem-ən\ **1** *or* **Yemen Arab Republic** country SW Arabia bordering on Red sea; republic since 1962 ✱ San'a *area* 75,000, *pop* 5,900,000 **2** *or* **People's Democratic Republic of Yemen** *or* **Southern Yemen** country S Arabian peninsula on Gulf of Aden formed 1967 from former **Federation of South Arabia** (Brit. protectorate comprising crown colony of Aden & numerous semi-independent Arab sultanates & emirates) ✱ Aden *area* 111,074, *pop* 1,470,000 — **Ye·me·ni** \'yem-ə-nē\ *adj or n* — **Ye·men·ite** \-ə-nīt\ *n*
Yen·an \'yen-'än\ city NE *cen* China in *cen* Shensi *pop* 45,000
Yen·ch'i \'yen-'chē\ *or* **Ka·ra·shahr** \ˌkär-ə-'shär\ city W China in *cen* Sinkiang on N edge of Takla Makan desert *pop* 130,000
Yen·i·sey *or* **Yen·i·sei** *or* **En·i·sei** \ˌyen-ə-'sā\ river *ab* 2300 *m* U.S.S.R. in Soviet Russia, Asia, flowing N into Arctic ocean
Yentai — see CHEFOO
Ye·re·van \ˌyer-ə-'vän\ *or* **Ere·van** *or* **Eri·van** \ˌ(y)er-ə-\ city U.S.S.R. ✱ of Armenian Republic *pop* 767,000
Ye·ru·pa·ja \ˌyer-ə-'pä-(ˌ)hä\ mountain 21,758 *ft* W *cen* Peru
Ye·sil Ir·mak \yə-'shē(ə)l-ir-'mäk\ river *ab* 250 *m* N Turkey in Asia flowing N into Black Sea
Ye·sil·koy \ˌyesh-(ˌ)ēl-'kȯi\ *or formerly* **San Ste·fa·no** \san-'stef-ə-ˌnō\ town Turkey in Europe on Sea of Marmara W of Istanbul
Yezd \'yezd\ *or* **Yazd** \'yazd\ city *cen* Iran *pop* 98,000
Yezo — see HOKKAIDO
Yin·chwan \'yin-chü-'än\ *or formerly* **Ning·sia** *or* **Ning·hsia** \'niŋ-shē-'ä\ city N China ✱ of Ningsia on Yellow river *pop* 84,000
Ying·kow \'yiŋ-'kau̇, -'kō\ *or* **New·chwang** \'n(y)ü-chü-'äŋ\ city & port NE China in *cen* Liaoning on Gulf of Liaotung at mouth of Liao river *pop* 215,000
Yo·ho National Park \'yō-(ˌ)hō\ reservation W Canada in SE B.C. on Alta. border *area* 507
Yok·kai·chi \yō-'kī-chē\ city & port Japan in S Honshu SW of Nagoya *pop* 218,981
Yo·ko·ha·ma \ˌyō-kə-'häm-ə\ city & port Japan in SE Honshu on Tokyo Bay S of Tokyo *pop* 2,144,000
Yo·ko·su·ka \yō-'kō-s(ə-)kə\ city & port Japan in Honshu W of entrance to Tokyo Bay *pop* 345,000
Yo·ne·za·wa \ˌyō-nə-'zä-wə\ city Japan in N Honshu E of Niigata *pop* 92,764
Yon·kers \'yäŋ-kərz\ city SE N.Y. N of New York City on the Hudson *pop* 204,370
Yonne \'yän\ river 120 *m* NE *cen* France flowing NNW into the Seine
York \'yȯ(ə)rk\ **1** city SE Pa. SE of Harrisburg *pop* 50,335 **2** *or* **York·shire** \-ˌshi(ə)r, -shər\ county N England bordering on North sea; comprises city of York & administrative counties of **East Riding** (✱ Beverley *area* 1172, *pop* 542,565), **North Riding** (✱ Northallerton *area* 2128, *pop* 724,463), & **West Riding** (✱ Wakefield *area* 2781, *pop* 3,780,539) **3** *or anc* **Ebo·ra·cum** \i-'bȯr-ə-kəm, -'bär-\ city & county borough in Yorkshire on the Ouse *pop* 104,513
York, Cape — see CAPE YORK PENINSULA
Yorke \'yȯ(ə)rk\ peninsula Australia in SE So. Australia between Spencer gulf and Gulf of St. Vincent
York river estuary 40 *m* E Va. formed by confluence of Pamunkey & Mattaponi rivers & flowing SE into Chesapeake Bay
Yo·sem·i·te \yō-'sem-ət-ē\ **1** waterfall E *cen* Calif. descending from rim of Yosemite valley in two falls (upper fall 1430 *ft*, lower fall 320 *ft* connected by a cascade 815 *ft* high) **2** glaciated valley of the Merced river E *cen* Calif. on W slope of Sierra Nevada in **Yosemite National Park** (*area* 1182)
Yo·su \'yō-(ˌ)sü\ city & port S Korea on Korea strait *pop* 113,651
Yough·io·ghe·ny \ˌyäk-ə-'gā-nē, ˌyō-hə-, -'gen-ē\ river 135 *m* NE W.Va., NW Md., & SW Pa. flowing N & NW into the Monongahela
Youngs·town \'yəŋ-ˌstau̇n\ city NE Ohio *pop* 139,788
Ypres — see IEPER
Yp·si·lan·ti \ˌip-sə-'lant-ē\ city SE Mich. *pop* 29,538
Yser \ē-'ze(ə)r\ river 55 *m* France & Belgium flowing into North sea
Yssel — see IJSSEL
Yü \'yü\ *or* **Siang** \shē-'äŋ\ river 400 *m* SE China in Yunnan & Kwangsi flowing E to unite with the Hungshui forming West river
Yu·an \yü-'än\ *or* **Yu·en** \-'än, -'en\ river 500 *m* SE *cen* China flowing from Kweichow NE to Tungting Lake
Yu·bi \'yü-bē\ *or* **Ju·by** \'jü-\, **Cape** cape NW Africa on NW coast of Spanish Sahara

---

ə abut ᵊ kitten, F table ər further a back ā bake
ä cot, cart ȧ F bac au̇ out ch chin e less ē easy
g gift i trip ī life j joke k̲ G ich ⁿ F vin ŋ sing
ō flow ȯ flaw œ F bœuf œ̄ F feu ȯi coin th thing
t͟h this ü loot u̇ foot ue G Füllen ue̅ F rue y yet
ʸ F digne \dēnʸ\, nuit \nwʸē\ yü few yu̇ furious zh vision

Yu·ca·tán \ˌyü-kə-ˈtan, -ˈtän\ **1** peninsula SE Mexico & N Central America including Brit. Honduras & part of Guatemala **2** channel between Yucatán & W end of Cuba **3** state SE Mexico at N end of Yucatan peninsula ✱ Mérida *area* 23,926, *pop* 774,011
Yu·go·sla·via *or* **Ju·go·sla·via** \ˌyü-gō-ˈsläv-ē-ə\ country S Europe bordering on the Adriatic; established 1918 as a kingdom (**Kingdom of the Serbs, Croats, and Slo·venes** \ˈsərbz-ˈkrōt-sən-ˈslō-ˌvēnz *also* -ˈkrō-ˌat-sən-\), became a federal republic 1945 ✱ Belgrade *area* 99,044, *pop* 20,550,000 — **Yu·go·slav** \ˌyü-gō-ˈsläv, -ˈslav\ *or* **Yu·go·sla·vi·an** \-ˈsläv-ē-ən\ *adj or n*
Yu·kon \ˈyü-ˌkän\ **1** river 1979 *m* Yukon Territory & Alaska flowing NW & SW into Bering sea — see LEWES **2** *or* **Yukon Territory** territory NW Canada between Alaska & B.C. bordering on Arctic ocean ✱ Whitehorse *area* 205,346, *pop* 17,000
Yu·ma \ˈyü-mə\ city SW Ariz. on Colorado river *pop* 29,007
Yungki — see KIRIN
Yungkia — see WENCHOW
Yungning — see NANNING
Yun·nan *or* **Yün·nan** \yü-ˈnän\ **1** province SW China bordering on Indochina & Burma ✱ Kunming *area* 168,417, *pop* 23,000,000 **2** *or* **Yunnanfu** — see KUNMING — **Yun·nan·ese** \ˌyü-nə-ˈnēz, -ˈnēs\ *adj or n*
Yun·que *or* **El Yunque** \el-ˈyüŋ-(ˌ)kā\ mountain 3496 *ft* E Puerto Rico
Yü Shan — see MORRISON (Mount)
Yuzovka — see DONETSK
Yver·don \ē-ver-dōⁿ\ commune W Switzerland N of Lausanne *pop* 20,538
Zaan·dam \zän-ˈdam, -ˈdäm\ commune W Netherlands NW of Amsterdam *pop* 63,535
Zab·rze \ˈzäb-(ˌ)zhā\ *or* G **Hin·den·burg** \ˈhin-dən-bərg, -ˌbu̇(ə)rg\ city SW Poland in Silesia *pop* 199,800
Za·ca·te·cas \ˌzak-ə-ˈtā-kəs, -ˈtek-əs\ **1** state N *cen* Mexico *area* 28,122, *pop* 949,663 **2** city, its ✱ *pop* 56,829
Za·dar \ˈzäd-ˌär\ *or* It **Za·ra** \ˈzär-ə\ city & port W Yugoslavia in Croatia; held by Italy 1920-47 *pop* 31,000
Zag·a·zig \ˈzag-ə-ˌzig\ *or* **Za·qa·ziq** \zə-ˌkä-ˈzēk\ city N Egypt NNE of Cairo *pop* 173,300
Za·greb \ˈzäg-ˌreb\ *or* G **Agram** \ˈäg-ˌräm\ city NW Yugoslavia ✱ of Croatia *pop* 565,000
Zag·ros \ˈzag-rəs, -ˌrōs\ mountains W & S Iran bordering on Turkey, Iraq, & Persian gulf; highest over 14,000 *ft*
Zaire \ˈzi(ə)r, zä-ˈi(ə)r\ **1** river in Africa — see CONGO **2** *or formerly* **Congo** *or* **Republic of the Congo** *or earlier* **Belgian Congo** country *cen* Africa comprising most of Congo river basin E of lower Congo river; a republic ✱ Kinshasa *area* 893,000, *pop* 22,480,000 — **Zair·ian** \ˈzī-rē-ən, zä-ˈir-ē-\ *adj or n*
Zakarpatskaya — see RUTHENIA
Zá·kin·thos *or* **Zá·kyn·thos** \ˈzäk-ən-ˌthōs\ *or* **Zan·te** \ˈzant-ē\ *or anc* **Za·cyn·thus** \zə-ˈsin(t)-thəs\ **1** island W Greece, one of the Ionian islands, SSE of Cephalonia *area* 156 **2** its chief town
Za·ko·pa·ne \ˌzäk-ə-ˈpän-(ˌ)ā\ city S Poland in Tatra mountains S of Krakow *pop* 27,000
Za·ma \ˈzā-mə, ˈzäm-ə\ ancient town N Africa SW of Carthage
Zam·be·zi *or* **Zam·be·si** \zam-ˈbē-zē\ river 1650 *m* SE Africa flowing from NW Zambia into Mozambique channel
Zam·bia \ˈzam-bē-ə\ *or formerly* **Northern Rhodesia** country S Africa; formerly a Brit. protectorate; independent republic within the Brit. Commonwealth since 1964 ✱ Lusaka *area* 290,410, *pop* 4,280,000 — **Zam·bi·an** \ˈzam-bē-ən\ *adj or n*
Zam·bo·an·ga \ˌzam-bə-ˈwäŋ-gə\ city & port Philippines on SW coast of Mindanao *pop* 176,800
Za·mo·ra \zə-ˈmōr-ə, -ˈmȯr-\ **1** province NW Spain in *cen* León *area* 4097, *pop* 251,934 **2** city, its ✱ *pop* 49,029
Zancle — see MESSINA
Zanes·ville \ˈzānz-ˌvil\ city E *cen* Ohio *pop* 33,045
Zan·zi·bar \ˈzan-zə-ˌbär\ **1** island E Africa off NE Tanganyika *area* 640, *pop* 190,494; formerly a sultanate, with Pemba & adjacent islands forming a Brit. protectorate; became independent 1963; united 1964 with Tanganyika in United Republic of Tanzania **2** city & port ✱ of the island & protectorate *pop* 68,490 — **Zan·zi·bari** \ˌzan-zə-ˈbär-ē\ *n*
Za·po·ro·zhe *or* **Za·po·ro·zhye** \ˌzäp-ə-ˈrō-zhə\ *or formerly* **Alek·san·drovsk** \ˌal-ik-ˈsan-drəfsk, ˌel-\ city U.S.S.R. in SE Ukraine *pop* 658,000
Za·ra·go·za \ˌzar-ə-ˈgō-zə\ *or* **Sar·a·gos·sa** \ˌsar-ə-ˈgäs-ə\ **1** province NE Spain in W Aragon *area* 6726, *pop* 760,186 **2** city, its ✱, on the Ebro *pop* 387,529
Zealand — see SJÆLLAND
Zee·brug·ge \ˈzā-ˌbrəg-ə\ town NW Belgium; port for Bruges
Zee·land \ˈzē-lənd, ˈzā-; ˈzā-ˌlänt\ province SW Netherlands ✱ Middelburg *area* 1040, *pop* 305,754
Zeist \ˈzīst\ commune *cen* Netherlands E of Utrecht *pop* 55,619
Zem·po·al·te·pec \ˌzem-pə-ˈwäl-tə-ˌpek\ *or* **Zem·po·al·te·petl** \-ˌwäl-ˈtā-ˌpet-ᵊl, -ˌwäl-tə-ˈ\ mountain 11,138 *ft* SE Mexico in Oaxaca
Zer·matt \(t)ser-ˈmät\ village SW *cen* Switzerland in Valais in Pennine Alps NE of the Matterhorn
Zetland — see SHETLAND
Zhda·nov \zhə-ˈdän-əf, ˈshtän-\ *or formerly* **Ma·ri·u·pol** \ˌmar-ē-ˈü-ˌpȯl\ city U.S.S.R. in E Ukraine on Sea of Azov *pop* 417,000
Zhi·to·mir \zhi-ˈtȯ-ˌmi(ə)r\ city U.S.S.R. in W Ukraine *pop* 161,000
Zim·ba·bwe \zim-ˈbäb-wē\ archaeological site NE Rhodesia
Zinovievsk — see KIROVOGRAD
Zi·on \ˈzī-ən\ city NE Ill. N of Waukegan *pop* 17,268
Zi·on \ˈzī-ən\ *or* **Si·on** \ˈsī-\ **1** the stronghold of Jerusalem conquered by David **2** a hill in Jerusalem occupied in ancient times by the Jewish Temple **3** JERUSALEM **4** ISRAEL
Zi·on National Park \ˈzī-ən\ reservation SW Utah (*area* 204) centering around **Zion Canyon** of Virgin river
Zi·pan·gu \zə-ˈpaŋ-(ˌ)gü\ JAPAN — the name used by Marco Polo
Zi·pa·qui·rá \ˌsē-pə-ki-ˈrä\ town *cen* Colombia N of Bogotá
Zla·to·ust \ˌzlät-ə-ˈüst\ city U.S.S.R. in W Soviet Russia, Asia, in the S Urals *pop* 181,000
Zlin — see GOTTWALDOV
Zoan — see TANIS
Zom·ba \ˈzäm-bə\ city ✱ of Malawi 70 *m* S of Lake Nyasa *pop* 20,000
Zon·gul·dak \ˌzȯŋ-gəl-ˈdäk\ city & port NW Turkey *pop* 55,404
Zor — see TYRE
Zug \ˈ(t)sük, ˈzüg\ *or* F **Zoug** \ˈzüg\ **1** canton N *cen* Switzerland *area* 92, *pop* 67,996 **2** commune, its ✱, on Lake of Zug *pop* 22,972
Zug, Lake of lake N *cen* Switzerland in Zug & Schwyz cantons N of Lake of Lucerne *area* 15
Zug·spit·ze \ˈ(t)sük-ˌs(h)pit-sə, ˈzüg-\ mountain 9721 *ft* S Germany; highest in Bavarian Alps & in Germany
Zuider Zee *or* **Zuyder Zee** — see IJSSELMEER
Zuidholland — see SOUTH HOLLAND
Zu·lu·land \ˈzü-(ˌ)lü-ˌland\ territory E Republic of So. Africa in NE Natal bordering on Indian ocean N of Tugela river *area* 10,427, *pop* 570,160
Zungaria — see DZUNGARIA
Zu·rich \ˈzu̇(ə)r-ik\ *or* G **Zü·rich** \ˈtsue-rik\ **1** canton N Switzerland *area* 665, *pop* 1,107,788 **2** city, its ✱, at NW end of Lake of Zurich *pop* 432,400
Zurich, Lake of lake 25 *m* long N *cen* Switzerland
Zut·phen \ˈzət-fən\ commune E Netherlands on IJssel river *pop* 27,610
Zwick·au \ˈtsfik-ˌau̇, ˈzwik-\ city E Germany S of Leipzig *pop* 127,477
Zwol·le \ˈzvȯl-ə, ˈzwȯl-\ city E Netherlands ✱ of Overijssel *pop* 76,167

Catonsville Comm. C. Catonsville, Md. 21228; junior, 1957
Cazenovia C. Cazenovia, N.Y. 13035; junior, 1824
Cecil Comm. C. North East, Md. 21901; junior, 1968
Cedar Crest C. Allentown, Pa. 18104; 1867
Centenary C. for Women Hackettstown, N.J. 07840; 1867
Centenary C. of Louisiana Shreveport, La. 71104; 1825
Central Arizona C. Coolidge, Ariz. 85228; junior, 1969
Central Baptist C. Conway, Ark. 72032; 1950
Central Bible C. Springfield, Mo. 65802; 1922
Central Carolina Technical Inst. Sanford, N.C. 27330; junior, 1961
Central C. McPherson, Kans. 67460; junior, 1914
Central Connecticut State C. New Britain, Conn. 06050; 1849
Central Florida Comm. C. Ocala, Fla. 32670; junior, 1958
Centralia C. Centralia, Wash. 98531; junior, 1925
Central Inst. of Tech. Kansas City, Mo. 64108; 1937
Central Methodist C. Fayette, Mo. 65248; 1854
Central Michigan U. Mount Pleasant, Mich. 48858; 1892
Central Missouri State U. Warrensburg, Mo. 64093; 1871
Central Oregon Comm. C. Bend, Oreg. 97701; junior, 1949
Central Piedmont Comm. C. Charlotte, N.C. 28204; junior, 1963
Central State U. Wilberforce, Ohio 45384; 1887
Central State U. Edmond, Okla. 73034; 1890
Central Texas C. Killeen, Tex. 76541; junior, 1967
Central U. of Iowa Pella, Iowa 50219; 1853
Central Virginia Comm. C. Lynchburg, Va. 24502; junior, 1966
Central Washington State C. Ellensburg, Wash. 98926; 1891
Central Wesleyan C. Central, S.C. 29630; 1906
Central Wyoming C. Riverton, Wyo. 82501; junior, 1966
Central YMCA Comm. C. Chicago, Ill. 60606; junior, 1960
Centre C. of Kentucky Danville, Ky. 40422; 1819
Cerritos C. Norwalk, Calif. 90650; junior, 1955
Chabot C. Hayward, Calif. 94545; junior, 1961
Chadron State C. Chadron, Nebr. 69337; 1911
Chaffey C. Alta Loma, Calif. 91701; junior, 1883
Chamberlayne Junior C. Boston, Mass. 02116; 1892
Chaminade C. of Honolulu Honolulu, Hawaii 96816; 1955
Champlain C. Burlington, Vt. 05401; junior, 1861
Chapman C. Orange, Calif. 92666; 1861
Charles County Comm. C. La Plata, Md. 20646; junior, 1958
Charleston, C. of Charleston, S.C. 29401; 1770
Chatham C. Pittsburgh, Pa. 15232; 1869
Chattanooga State Technical Inst. Chattanooga, Tenn. 37406; junior, 1963
Chemeketa Comm. C. Salem, Oreg. 97303; junior, 1954
Chesapeake C. Wye Mills, Md. 21679; junior, 1967
Chestnut Hill C. Philadelphia, Pa. 19118; 1871
Cheyney State C. Cheyney, Pa. 19319; 1837
Chicago, U. of Chicago, Ill. 60637; 1891
Chicago, City Colleges of Chicago, Ill. 60601; junior, 1931
Chicago C. of Osteopathic Medicine Chicago, Ill. 60615; 1913
Chicago State U. Chicago, Ill. 60621; 1869
Chicago Technical C. Chicago, Ill. 60616; 1904
Chipola Junior C. Marianna, Fla. 32446; 1947
Chowan C. Murfreesboro, N.C. 27855; junior, 1848
Christian Brothers C. Memphis, Tenn. 38104; 1871
Christ the Saviour Sem. of Johnstown, Pa. 15906; 1940
Church C. of Hawaii, The Laie, Oahu, Hawaii 96762; 1955
Cincinnati, U. of Cincinnati, Ohio 45221; 1819
Cincinnati Bible Sem., The Cincinnati, Ohio 45204; 1924
Cisco Junior C. Cisco, Tex. 76437; 1940
Citadel, The Charleston, S.C. 29409; 1842
Citrus C. Azusa, Calif. 91702; junior, 1915
City C. New York, N.Y. 10033; 1847
City C. of San Francisco San Francisco, Calif. 94112; junior, 1935
City U. of New York New York, N.Y. 10021; 1961
Clackamas Comm. C. Oregon City, Oreg. 97045; junior, 1966
Claflin C. Orangeburg, S.C. 29115; 1869
Claremont Men's C. Claremont, Calif. 91711; 1946
Claremore Junior C. Claremore, Okla. 74017; 1910
Clarendon C. Clarendon, Tex. 79226; junior, 1927
Clarion State C. Clarion, Pa. 16214; 1866
Clark C. Atlanta, Ga. 30314; 1869
Clark C. Vancouver, Wash. 98663; junior, 1933
Clarke C. Dubuque, Iowa 52001; 1843
Clarke C. Newton, Miss. 39345; junior, 1908
Clarkson C. of Tech. Potsdam, N.Y. 13676; 1896
Clark U. Worcester, Mass. 01610; 1887
Clatsop Comm. C. Astoria, Oreg. 97103; junior, 1958
Clayton Junior C. Morrow, Ga. 30260; 1965
Cleary C. Ypsilanti, Mich. 48197; 1883
Clemson U. Clemson, S.C. 29631; 1889
Cleveland Inst. of Art Cleveland, Ohio 44106; 1882
Cleveland Inst. of Music Cleveland, Ohio 44106; 1920
Cleveland State Comm. C. Cleveland, Tenn. 37311; junior, 1967
Cleveland State U. Cleveland, Ohio 44102; 1923
Clinton Comm. C. Plattsburgh, N.Y. 12901; junior, 1966
Cloud County Comm. Junior C. Concordia, Kans. 66901; 1965
Coahoma Junior C. Clarksdale, Miss. 38614; 1926
Cochise C. Douglas, Ariz. 85607; junior, 1962
Coe C. Cedar Rapids, Iowa 52402; 1851
Coffeyville Comm. Junior C. Coffeyville, Kans. 67337; 1923
Cogswell Polytechnical C. San Francisco, Calif. 94110; 1930
Coker C. Hartsville, S.C. 29550; 1894
Colby C. Waterville, Me. 04901; 1813
Colby Comm. Junior C. Colby, Kans. 67701; 1964
Colby Junior C. for Women New London, N.H. 03257; 1837
Colgate U. Hamilton, N.Y. 13346; 1819
Colorado, U. of Boulder, Colo. 80302; 1861
Colorado C. Colorado Springs, Colo. 80903; 1874
Colorado Mountain C. Glenwood Springs, Colo. 81601; junior, 1967
Colorado Sch. of Mines Golden, Colo. 80401; 1874
Colorado State U. Fort Collins, Colo. 80521; 1870
Columbia Basin C. Pasco, Wash. 99301; junior, 1955
Columbia Bible C. Columbia, S.C. 29203; 1923
Columbia Christian C. Portland, Oreg. 97220; 1956
Columbia C. Chicago, Ill. 60611; 1890
Columbia C. Columbia, Mo. 65201; junior, 1851
Columbia C. Columbia, S.C. 29203; 1854
Columbia-Greene Comm. C. Athens, N.Y. 12015; junior, 1967
Columbia Junior C. Columbia, Calif. 95310; 1968
Columbia State Comm. C. Columbia, Tenn. 38401; junior, 1966
Columbia Union C. Takoma Park, Md. 20012; 1904
Columbia U. New York, N.Y. 10027; 1754
Columbus C. Columbus, Ga. 31907; 1958
Columbus Technical Inst. Columbus, Ohio 43215; junior, 1963
Combs C. of Music Philadelphia, Pa. 19119; 1885
Compton Comm. C. Compton, Calif. 90221; junior, 1927
Concord C. Athens, W.Va. 24712; 1872
Concordia C. Moorhead, Minn. 56560; 1891
Concordia C. St. Paul, Minn. 55104; 1893
Concordia C. Bronxville, N.Y. 10708; 1881
Concordia C. Portland, Oreg. 97211; junior, 1905
Concordia C. Milwaukee, Wis. 53208; junior, 1881
Concordia Lutheran C. Austin, Tex. 78705; junior, 1926
Concordia Lutheran Junior C. Ann Arbor, Mich. 48105; 1963
Concordia Sem. St. Louis, Mo. 63105; 1839
Concordia Senior C. Fort Wayne, Ind. 46825; 1839
Concordia Teachers C. River Forest, Ill. 60305; 1864
Concordia Teachers C. Seward, Nebr. 68434; 1894
Connecticut, U. of Storrs, Conn. 06268; 1881
Connecticut C. New London, Conn. 06320; 1911
Connors State C. Warner, Okla. 74469; junior, 1908
Contra Costa C. San Pablo, Calif. 94806; junior, 1949
Converse C. Spartanburg, S.C. 29301; 1889
Cooke County Junior C. Gainesville, Tex. 76240; 1924
Cooper Union New York, N.Y. 10003; 1859
Copiah-Lincoln Junior C. Wesson, Miss. 39191; 1915
Coppin State C. Baltimore, Md. 21216; 1900
Cornell C. Mount Vernon, Iowa 52314; 1853
Cornell U. Ithaca, N.Y. 14850; 1865
Corning Comm. C. Corning, N.Y. 14830; junior, 1956
Corpus Christi, U. of Corpus Christi, Tex. 78411; 1947
Cosumnes River C. Sacramento, Calif. 95823; junior, 1969
Cottey C. Nevada, Mo. 64772; junior, 1884
County C. of Morris Dover, N.J. 07801; junior, 1968
Covenant C. Lookout Mountain, Tenn. 37350; 1955
Cowley County Comm. Junior C. Arkansas City, Kans. 67005; 1922
Cranbrook Acad. of Art Bloomfield Hills, Mich. 48013; 1927
Craven County Technical Inst. New Bern, N.C. 28560; junior, 1965
Creighton U. Omaha, Nebr. 68131; 1878
Crosier Sem. Onamia, Minn. 56359; junior, 1922
Crowder C. Neosho, Mo. 64850; junior, 1963
Crowley's Ridge C. Paragould, Ark. 72450; junior, 1964
Cuesta C. San Luis Obispo, Calif. 93401; junior, 1963
Cullman C. Cullman, Ala. 35055; junior, 1940
Culver-Stockton C. Canton, Mo. 63435; 1853
Cumberland C. Williamsburg, Ky. 40769; 1888
Cumberland C. of Tennessee Lebanon, Tenn. 37087; junior, 1842
Cumberland County C. Vineland, N.J. 08360; junior, 1964
Curry C. Milton, Mass. 02186; 1879
Curtis Inst. of Music Philadelphia, Pa. 19103; 1924
Cuyahoga Comm. C. Cleveland, Ohio 44115; junior, 1963
Cypress C. Cypress, Calif. 90630; junior, 1966
Dabney S. Lancaster Comm. C. Clifton Forge, Va. 24422; junior, 1964
Dakota State C. Madison, S.Dak. 57042; 1881
Dakota Wesleyan U. Mitchell, S.Dak. 57301; 1883
Dallas, U. of Irving, Tex. 75060; 1956
Dallas Baptist C. Dallas, Tex. 75211; 1891
Dallas Bible C. Dallas, Tex. 75228; 1940
Dalton Junior C. Dalton, Ga. 30720; 1966
Dana C. Blair, Nebr. 68008; 1884
Daniel Payne C. Birmingham, Ala. 35212; 1889
Danville Comm. C. Danville, Va. 24541; junior, 1936
Danville Junior C. Danville, Ill. 61832; 1946
Dartmouth C. Hanover, N.H. 03755; 1769
Davenport C. of Business Grand Rapids, Mich. 49502; junior, 1910
David Lipscomb C. Nashville, Tenn. 37203; 1891
Davidson C. Davidson, N.C. 28036; 1836
Davidson County Comm. C. Lexington, N.C. 27292; junior, 1961
Davis and Elkins C. Elkins, W.Va. 26241; 1903
Davis Junior C. Toledo, Ohio 43624; 1858
Dawson C. Glendive, Mont. 59330; junior, 1940
Dayton, U. of Dayton, Ohio 45409; 1850
Daytona Beach Comm. C. Daytona Beach, Fla. 32015; junior, 1958
Dean Junior C. Franklin, Mass. 02038; 1865
DeAnza C. Cupertino, Calif. 95014; junior, 1967
Deep Springs C. Deep Springs, Calif. 89010; junior, 1917
Defiance C. Defiance, Ohio 43512; 1850
DeKalb Comm. C. Clarkston, Ga. 30021; junior, 1963
Delaware, U. of Newark, Del. 19711; 1743
Delaware County, Comm. C. of Media, Pa. 19063; junior, 1967
Delaware State C. Dover, Del. 19901; 1891
Delaware Technical and Comm. C. Dover, Del. 19901; junior, 1967
Delaware Valley C. of Science and Agric. Doylestown, Pa. 18901; 1896
Delgado Vocational Technical Junior C. New Orleans, La. 70119; 1921
Del Mar C. Corpus Christi, Tex. 78404; junior, 1935
De Lourdes C. Des Plaines, Ill. 60016; 1951

Delta C. University Center, Mich. 48710; junior, 1961
Delta State C. Cleveland, Miss. 38732; 1924
Denison U. Granville, Ohio 43023; 1831
Denver, Comm. C. of Denver, Colo. 80204; junior, 1967
Denver, U. of Denver, Colo. 80210; 1864
De Paul U. Chicago, Ill. 60604; 1898
DePauw U. Greencastle, Ind. 46135; 1837
Desert, C. of the Palm Desert, Calif. 92260; junior, 1961
Des Moines Area Comm. C. Ankeny, Iowa 50021; junior, 1927
Detroit, U. of Detroit, Mich. 48221; 1877
Detroit Bible C. Detroit, Mich. 48235; 1945
Detroit C. of Business Dearborn, Mich. 48126; 1936
Detroit Inst. of Tech. Detroit, Mich. 48201; 1891
DeVry Inst. of Tech. Chicago, Ill. 60641; 1931
Diablo Valley C. Pleasant Hill, Calif. 94523; junior, 1949
Dickinson C. Carlisle, Pa. 17013; 1773
Dickinson State C. Dickinson, N.Dak. 58601; 1918
Dillard U. New Orleans, La. 70122; 1869
District of Columbia Teachers C. Washington, D.C. 20009; 1851
Divine Word C. Epworth, Iowa 52045; 1913
Dixie C. St. George, Utah 84770; junior, 1911
Doane C. Crete, Nebr. 68333; 1872
Dodge City Comm. Junior C. Dodge City, Kans. 67801; 1935
Dodge County Teachers C. Mayville, Wis. 53050; junior, 1925
Dominican C. Houston, Tex. 77021; 1946
Dominican C. Racine, Wis. 53402; 1935
Dominican C. of Blauvelt Blauvelt, N.Y. 10913; 1952
Dominican C. of San Rafael San Rafael, Calif. 94901; 1890
Don Bosco C. Newton, N.J. 07860; 1929
Don Bosco Technical Inst. Rosemead, Calif. 91790; junior, 1955
Donnelly C. Kansas City, Kans. 66102; junior, 1949
Dordt C. Sioux Center, Iowa 51250; 1955
Dowling C. Oakdale, N.Y. 11769; 1959
Drake U. Des Moines, Iowa 50311; 1881
Drew U. Madison, N.J. 07940; 1866
Drexel U. Philadelphia, Pa. 19104; 1891
Dr. Martin Luther C. New Ulm, Minn. 56073; 1884
Drury C. Springfield, Mo. 65802; 1873
Dubuque, U. of Dubuque, Iowa 52001; 1852
Duke U. Durham, N.C. 27706; 1838
Dunbarton C. of Holy Cross Washington, D.C. 20008; 1935
Duns Scotus C. Southfield, Mich. 48075; 1930
DuPage, C. of Glen Ellyn, Ill. 60137; junior, 1966
Duquesne U. Pittsburgh, Pa. 15219; 1878
Durham Technical Inst. Durham, N.C. 27703; junior, 1958
Dutchess Comm. C. Poughkeepsie, N.Y. 12601; junior, 1957
Dyersburg State Comm. C. Dyersburg, Tenn. 38024; junior, 1967
Dyke C. Cleveland, Ohio 44114; 1848
D'Youville C. Buffalo, N.Y. 14201; 1908
Earlham C. Richmond, Ind. 47374; 1847
East Carolina U. Greenville, N.C. 27834; 1907
East Central Junior C. Decatur, Miss. 39327; 1914
East Central Missouri District Junior C. Union, Mo. 63084; 1968
East Central State C. Ada, Okla. 74820; 1909
East Coast U. Brooksville, Fla. 33519; 1947
Eastern Arizona C. Thatcher, Ariz. 85552; junior, 1891
Eastern C. St. Davids, Pa. 19087; 1952
Eastern Connecticut State C. Willimantic, Conn. 06226; 1889
Eastern Illinois U. Charleston, Ill. 61920; 1895
Eastern Iowa Comm. C. Davenport, Iowa 52806; junior, 1929
Eastern Kentucky U. Richmond, Ky. 40475; 1906
Eastern Mennonite C. Harrisonburg, Va. 22801; 1917
Eastern Michigan U. Ypsilanti, Mich. 48197; 1849
Eastern Montana C. Billings, Mont. 59101; 1925
Eastern Nazarene C. Wollaston, Mass. 02170; 1900
Eastern New Mexico U. Portales, N.Mex. 88130; 1934
Eastern Oklahoma State C. Wilburton, Okla. 74578; junior, 1909
Eastern Oregon C. La Grande, Oreg. 97850; 1929
Eastern Utah, C. of Price, Utah 84501; junior, 1937
Eastern Washington State C. Cheney, Wash. 99004; 1890
Eastern Wyoming C. Torrington, Wyo. 82240; junior, 1948
Eastfield C. Mesquite, Tex. 75149; junior, 1970
East Los Angeles C. Los Angeles, Calif. 90022; junior, 1945
East Mississippi Junior C. Scooba, Miss. 39358; 1927
East Stroudsburg State C. East Stroudsburg, Pa. 18301; 1893
East Tennessee State U. Johnson City, Tenn. 37601; 1909
East Texas Baptist C. Marshall, Tex. 75670; 1914
East Texas State U. Commerce, Tex. 75428; 1889
Eckerd C. St. Petersburg, Fla. 33733; 1960
Edgecliff C. Cincinnati, Ohio 45206; 1935
Edgewood C. Madison, Wis. 53711; 1927
Edinboro State C. Edinboro, Pa. 16412; 1859
Edison Comm. C. Fort Myers, Fla. 33901; junior, 1962
Edmonds Comm. C. Lynnwood, Wash. 98036; junior, 1967
Edward Waters C. Jacksonville, Fla. 32209; 1866
Eisenhower C. Seneca Falls, N.Y. 13148; 1965
El Camino C. El Camino College, Calif. 90506; junior, 1946
El Centro C. Dallas, Tex. 75202; junior, 1965
Elgin Comm. C. Elgin, Ill. 60120; junior, 1949
Elizabeth City State U. Elizabeth City, N.C. 27909; 1891
Elizabeth Seton C. Yonkers, N.Y. 10701; junior, 1961
Elizabethtown C. Elizabethtown, Pa. 17022; 1899
Elko Comm. C. Elko, Nev. 89801; junior, 1967
Ellen Cushing Junior C. Bryn Mawr, Pa. 19010; 1892
Ellsworth Comm. C. Iowa Falls, Iowa 50126; junior, 1890
Elmhurst C. Elmhurst, Ill. 60126; 1871
Elmira C. Elmira, N.Y. 14901; 1853
Elon C. Elon College, N.C. 27244; 1889
El Paso Comm. C. Colorado Springs, Colo. 80903; junior, 1967
El Reno C. El Reno, Okla. 73036; junior, 1938
Embry–Riddle Aeronautical U. Daytona Beach, Fla. 32015; 1926
Emerson C. Boston, Mass. 02116; 1880
Emmanuel C. Boston, Mass. 02115; 1919
Emmaus Bible Sch. Oak Park, Ill. 60301; 1941
Emory and Henry C. Emory, Va. 24327; 1838
Emory U. Atlanta, Ga. 30322; 1836
Emporia, C. of Emporia, Kans. 66801; 1882
Endicott Junior C. Beverly, Mass. 01915; 1939
Englewood Cliffs C. Englewood Cliffs, N.J. 07632; junior, 1962
Enterprise State Junior C. Enterprise, Ala. 36330; 1965
Erie Comm. C. Amherst, N.Y. 14226; junior, 1946
Erskine C. Due West, S.C. 29639; 1839
Essex Comm. C. Baltimore, Md. 21237; junior, 1957
Essex County C. Newark, N.J. 07102; junior, 1968
Eureka C. Eureka, Ill. 61530; 1855
Evangel C. Springfield, Mo. 65802; 1955
Evansville, U. of Evansville, Ind. 47701; 1854
Everett Comm. C. Everett, Wash. 98201; junior, 1941
Fairbury Junior C. Fairbury, Nebr. 68352; 1941
Fairfield U. Fairfield, Conn. 06430; 1942
Fairleigh Dickinson U. Rutherford, N.J. 07070; 1942
Fairmont State C. Fairmont, W.Va. 26554; 1867
Faith Baptist Bible C. Ankeny, Iowa 50021; 1924
Fashion Inst. of Tech. New York, N.Y. 10001; junior, 1944
Faulkner State Junior C. Bay Minette, Ala. 36507; 1965
Fayetteville State U. Fayetteville, N.C. 28301; 1867
Fayetteville Technical Inst. Fayetteville, N.C. 28303; junior, 1961
Federal City C. Washington, D.C. 20001; 1966
Felician C. Lodi, N.J. 07644; 1923
Felician C., The Chicago, Ill. 60645; junior, 1926
Fergus Falls State Junior C. Fergus Falls, Minn. 56537; 1960
Ferris State C. Big Rapids, Mich. 49307; 1884
Ferrum C. Ferrum, Va. 24088; junior, 1914
Finch C. New York, N.Y. 10021; 1900
Findlay C. Findlay, Ohio 45840; 1882
Finger Lakes, Comm. C. of the Canandaigua, N.Y. 14424; junior, 1965
Fisher Junior C. Boston, Mass. 02116; 1903
Fisk U. Nashville, Tenn. 37203; 1866
Fitchburg State C. Fitchburg, Mass. 01420; 1894
Flagler C. St. Augustine, Fla. 32084; 1963
Flathead Valley Comm. C. Kalispell, Mont. 59901; junior, 1967
Florence–Darlington Technical Ed. Center Florence, S.C. 29501; junior, 1962
Florence State U. Florence, Ala. 35630; 1830
Florida, U. of Gainesville, Fla. 32601; 1853
Florida A. & M. U. Tallahassee, Fla. 32307; 1887
Florida Atlantic U. Boca Raton, Fla. 33432; 1964
Florida C. Temple Terrace, Fla. 33617; junior, 1944
Florida Inst. of Tech. Melbourne, Fla. 32901; 1958
Florida Junior C. at Jacksonville 32205; 1963
Florida Keys Comm. C. Key West, Fla. 33040; junior, 1965
Florida Memorial C. Miami, Fla. 33054; 1879
Florida Southern C. Lakeland, Fla. 33802; 1885
Florida State U. Tallahassee, Fla. 32306; 1857
Florida Technological U. Orlando, Fla. 32816; 1968
Florissant Valley Comm. C. St. Louis, Mo. 63135; junior, 1962
Floyd Junior C. Rome, Ga. 30161; 1968
Fontbonne C. St. Louis, Mo. 63105; 1923
Foothill C. Los Altos Hills, Calif. 94022; junior, 1957
Fordham U. Bronx, N.Y. 10458; 1841
Forest Park Comm. C. St. Louis, Mo. 63110; junior, 1962
Forsyth Technical Inst. Winston-Salem, N.C. 27103; junior, 1960
Fort Hays Kansas State C. Hays, Kans. 67601; 1901
Fort Lauderdale U. Fort Lauderdale, Fla. 33301; 1940
Fort Lewis C. Durango, Colo. 81301; 1911
Fort Scott Comm. Junior C. Fort Scott, Kans. 66701; 1919
Fort Steilacoom Comm. C. Tacoma, Wash. 98499; junior, 1965
Fort Valley State C. Fort Valley, Ga. 31030; 1895
Fort Wayne Bible C. Fort Wayne, Ind. 46807; 1904
Fort Wright C. of the Holy Names Spokane, Wash. 99204; 1907
Framingham State C. Framingham, Mass. 01701; 1839
Francis Marion C. Florence, S.C. 29501; 1970
Franconia C. Franconia, N.H. 03580; junior, 1962
Franklin and Marshall C. Lancaster, Pa. 17604; 1787
Franklin C. of Indiana Franklin, Ind. 46131; 1834
Franklin Inst. of Boston Boston, Mass. 02116; junior, 1908
Franklin Pierce C. Rindge, N.H. 03461; 1962
Franklin U. Columbus, Ohio 43215; 1902
Frank Phillips C. Borger, Tex. 79007; junior, 1946
Frederick Comm. C. Frederick, Md. 21701; junior, 1957
Freed–Hardeman C. Henderson, Tenn. 38340; junior, 1908
Freeman Junior C. Freeman, S.Dak. 57029; 1900
Free Will Baptist Bible C. Nashville, Tenn. 37205; 1942
Fresno City C. Fresno, Calif. 93704; junior, 1910
Friends Bible C. Haviland, Kans. 67059; 1917
Friendship Junior C. Rock Hill, S.C. 29730; 1891
Friends U. Wichita, Kans. 67213; 1898
Frostburg State C. Frostburg, Md. 21532; 1898
Fullerton Junior C. Fullerton, Calif. 92634; 1913
Fulton–Montgomery Comm. C. Johnstown, N.Y. 12095; junior, 1963
Furman U. Greenville, S.C. 29613; 1825
Gadsden State Junior C. Gadsden, Ala. 35903; 1965
Gainesville Junior C. Gainesville, Ga. 30501; 1965
Gallaudet C. Washington, D.C. 20002; 1864
Galveston C. Galveston, Tex. 77550; junior, 1967
Gannon C. Erie, Pa. 16501; 1933
Garden City Comm. Junior C. Garden City, Kans. 67846; 1919
Gardner–Webb C. Boiling Springs, N.C. 28017; 1905
Garland Junior C. Boston, Mass. 02215; 1872
Gaston C. Dallas, N.C. 28034; junior, 1963
Gateway Technical Inst., Kenosha Kenosha, Wis. 53140; junior, 1912
Gavilan C. Gilroy, Calif. 95020; junior, 1919
General Motors Inst. Flint, Mich. 48502; 1919

Genesee Comm. C. Flint, Mich. 48503; junior, 1923
Genesee Comm. C. Batavia, N.Y. 14020; junior, 1966
Geneva C. Beaver Falls, Pa. 15010; 1848
George C. Wallace State Technical Junior C. Dothan, Ala. 36301; 1963
George Fox C. Newberg, Oreg. 97132; 1891
George Mason U. Fairfax, Va. 22030; 1960
George Peabody C. for Teachers Nashville, Tenn. 37203; 1875
Georgetown C. Georgetown, Ky. 40324; 1787
Georgetown U. Washington, D.C. 20007; 1789
George Washington U. Washington, D.C. 20006; 1821
George Williams C. Downers Grove, Ill. 60515; 1884
Georgia, U. of Athens, Ga. 30601; 1785
Georgia C. at Milledgeville Milledgeville, Ga. 31061; 1889
Georgia Inst. of Tech. Atlanta, Ga. 30332; 1885
Georgia Military C. Milledgeville, Ga. 31061; junior, 1879
Georgian Court C. Lakewood, N.J. 08701; 1908
Georgia Southern C. Statesboro, Ga. 30458; 1908
Georgia Southwestern C. Americus, Ga. 31709; 1906
Georgia State U. Atlanta, Ga. 30303; 1913
Germanna Comm. C. Fredericksburg, Va. 22401; junior, 1969
Gettysburg C. Gettysburg, Pa. 17325; 1832
Glassboro State C. Glassboro, N.J. 08028; 1923
Glendale C. Glendale, Calif. 91208; junior, 1927
Glen Oaks Comm. C. Centreville, Mich. 49032; junior, 1965
Glenville State C. Glenville, W.Va. 26351; 1872
Gloucester County C. Sewell, N.J. 08080; junior, 1968
Goddard C. Plainfield, Vt. 05667; 1938
Gogebic Comm. C. Ironwood, Mich. 49938; junior, 1932
Golden Gate U. San Francisco, Calif. 94105; 1901
Golden West C. Huntington Beach, Calif. 92647; junior, 1966
Goldey Beacom C. Wilmington, Del. 19899; junior, 1886
Gonzaga U. Spokane, Wash. 99202; 1887
Gordon C. Wenham, Mass. 01984; 1889
Gordon Junior C. Barnesville, Ga. 30204; 1852
Goshen C. Goshen, Ind. 46526; 1894
Goucher C. Towson, Md. 21204; 1885
Grace Bible C. Grand Rapids, Mich. 49509; 1946
Grace Bible Inst. Omaha, Nebr. 68108; 1943
Grace C. Winona Lake, Ind. 46590; 1948
Graceland C. Lamoni, Iowa 50140; 1895
Grahm Junior C. Boston, Mass. 02215; 1950
Grambling C. Grambling, La. 71245; 1929
Grand Canyon C. Phoenix, Ariz. 85017; 1949
Grand Rapids Baptist Bible C. and Sem. Grand Rapids, Mich. 49505; 1941
Grand Rapids Junior C. Grand Rapids, Mich. 49502; 1914
Grand Valley State C. Allendale, Mich. 49401; 1963
Grand View C. Des Moines, Iowa 50316; junior, 1896
Gratz C. Philadelphia, Pa. 19141; 1895
Grays Harbor C. Aberdeen, Wash. 98520; junior, 1930
Grayson County C. Denison, Tex. 75020; junior, 1963
Greater Hartford Comm. C. Hartford, Conn. 06106; junior, 1967
Great Falls, C. of Great Falls, Mont. 59401; 1932
Greenbrier C. Lewisburg, W.Va. 24901; junior, 1808
Greenfield Comm. C. Greenfield, Mass. 01301; junior, 1962
Green Mountain C. Poultney, Vt. 05764; junior, 1834
Green River Comm. C. Auburn, Wash. 98002; junior, 1965
Greensboro C. Greensboro, N.C. 27402; 1838
Greenville C. Greenville, Ill. 62246; 1855
Greenville Technical Ed. Center Greenville, S.C. 29606; junior, 1962
Grinnell C. Grinnell, Iowa 50112; 1846
Grossmont C. El Cajon, Calif. 92020; junior, 1961
Grove City C. Grove City, Pa. 16127; 1876
Guam, U. of Agana, Guam 96910; 1952
Guilford C. Greensboro, N.C. 27410; 1834
Guilford Technical Inst. Jamestown, N.C. 27282; junior, 1958
Gulf-Coast Bible C. Houston, Tex. 77008; 1953
Gulf Coast Comm. C. Panama City, Fla. 32401; junior, 1957
Gustavus Adolphus C. St. Peter, Minn. 56082; 1862
Gwynedd-Mercy C. Gwynedd Valley, Pa. 19437; 1948
Hagerstown Junior C. Hagerstown, Md. 21740; 1946
Hamilton C. Clinton, N.Y. 13323; 1793
Hamline U. St. Paul, Minn. 55101; 1854
Hampden-Sydney C. Hampden-Sydney, Va. 23943; 1776
Hampshire C. Amherst, Mass. 01002; 1970
Hampton Inst. Hampton, Va. 23368; 1868
Hanover C. Hanover, Ind. 47243; 1827
Harcum Junior C. Bryn Mawr, Pa. 19010; 1915
Harding C. Searcy, Ark. 72143; 1924
Hardin-Simmons U. Abilene, Tex. 79601; 1891
Harford Comm. C. Bel Air, Md. 21014; junior, 1957
Harriman C. Harriman, N.Y. 10926; junior, 1956
Harrisburg Area Comm. C. Harrisburg, Pa. 17110; junior, 1964
Harris Teachers C. St. Louis, Mo. 63103; 1857
Hartford, U. of West Hartford, Conn. 06117; 1877
Hartford C. for Women Hartford, Conn. 06105; junior, 1933
Hartford State Technical C. Hartford, Conn. 06106; junior, 1946
Hartnell C. Salinas, Calif. 93901; junior, 1920
Hartwick C. Oneonta, N.Y. 13820; 1928
Harvard U. Cambridge, Mass. 02138; 1636
Harvey Mudd C. Claremont, Calif. 91711; 1955
Hastings C. Hastings, Nebr. 68901; 1882
Haverford C. Haverford, Pa. 19041; 1833
Hawaii, U. of Honolulu, Hawaii 96822; 1907
Hawaii, Hilo, U. of 96720; 1965
Hawaii Loa C. Kaneohe, Hawaii 96744; 1963
Hawaii Pacific C. Honolulu, Hawaii 96813; 1965
Haywood Technical Inst. Clyde, N.C. 28721; junior, 1965
Heald Engineering C. San Francisco, Calif. 94109; 1863
Hebrew C. Brookline, Mass. 02146; 1918
Hebrew Theol. C. Skokie, Ill. 60076; 1922
Hebrew Union C. Cincinnati, Ohio 45220; 1875
Heidelberg C. Tiffin, Ohio 44883; 1850
Hellenic C. Brookline, Mass. 02146; 1937
Henderson County Junior C. Athens, Tex. 75751; 1946
Henderson State C. Arkadelphia, Ark. 71923; 1929
Hendrix C. Conway, Ark. 72032; 1876
Henry Ford Comm. C. Dearborn, Mich. 48128; junior, 1938
Herbert H. Lehman C. Bronx, N.Y. 10468; 1931
Herkimer County Comm. C. Herkimer, N.Y. 13357; junior, 1966
Herron Sch. of Art Indianapolis, Ind. 46202; 1878
Hesston C. Hesston, Kans. 67062; junior, 1909
Hibbing State Junior C. Hibbing, Minn. 55746; 1916
Highland Comm. C. Freeport, Ill. 61032; junior, 1961
Highland Comm. Junior C. Highland, Kans. 66035; 1858
Highland Park Comm. C. Highland Park, Mich. 48203; junior, 1918
Highline Comm. C. Midway, Wash. 98031; junior, 1961
High Point C. High Point, N.C. 27262; 1924
Hilbert C. Hamburg, N.Y. 14075; junior, 1928
Hill Junior C. Hillsboro, Tex. 76645; 1962
Hillsborough Comm. C. Tampa, Fla. 33622; junior, 1968
Hillsdale C. Hillsdale, Mich. 49242; 1844
Hinds Junior C. Raymond, Miss. 39154; 1917
Hiram C. Hiram, Ohio 44234; 1850
Hiwassee C. Madisonville, Tenn. 37354; junior, 1849
Hobart and William Smith Colleges Geneva, N.Y. 14456; 1822
Hofstra U. Hempstead, N.Y. 11550; 1935
Hollins C. Hollins College, Va. 24020; 1842
Holmes Junior C. Goodman, Miss. 39079; 1911
Holy Apostles Sem. and C. Cromwell, Conn. 06416; 1956
Holy Cross, C. of the Worcester, Mass. 01610; 1843
Holy Cross Junior C. Notre Dame, Ind. 46556; 1966
Holy Family C. San Francisco, Calif. 94117; 1945
Holy Family C. Philadelphia, Pa. 19114; 1954
Holy Family C. Manitowoc, Wis. 54220; 1869
Holy Family Junior C. Fremont, Calif. 91738; 1952
Holy Names, C. of the Oakland, Calif. 94619; 1868
Holyoke Comm. C. Holyoke, Mass. 01040; junior, 1946
Holy Redeemer C. Waterford, Wis. 53185; 1965
Hood C. Frederick, Md. 21701; 1893
Hope C. Holland, Mich. 49423; 1851
Hostos Comm. C. Bronx, N.Y. 10451; junior, 1970
Houghton C. Houghton, N.Y. 14744; 1883
Housatonic Regional Comm. C. Bridgeport, Conn. 06608; junior, 1966
Houston, U. of Houston, Tex. 77004; 1934
Houston Baptist C. Houston, Tex. 77036; 1960
Howard Comm. C. Clarksville, Md. 21029; junior, 1970
Howard County Junior C. Big Spring, Tex. 79720; 1945
Howard Payne C. Brownwood, Tex. 76801; 1889
Howard U. Washington, D.C. 20001; 1867
Hudson Valley Comm. C. Troy, N.Y. 12180; junior, 1953
Humphreys C. Stockton, Calif. 95207; junior, 1896
Hunter C. New York, N.Y. 10021; 1870
Huntingdon C. Montgomery, Ala. 36106; 1854
Huntington C. Huntington, Ind. 46750; 1897
Huron C. Huron, S.Dak. 57350; 1883
Husson C. Bangor, Me. 04401; 1898
Huston-Tillotson C. Austin, Tex. 78702; 1877
Hutchinson Comm. Junior C. Hutchinson, Kans. 67501; 1928
Idaho, C. of Caldwell, Idaho 83605; 1891
Idaho, U. of Moscow, Idaho 83843; 1889
Idaho State U. Pocatello, Idaho 83201; 1901
Illinois, U. of Urbana, Ill. 61801; 1867
Illinois Benedictine C. Lisle, Ill. 60532; 1887
Illinois Central C. East Peoria, Ill. 61611; junior, 1966
Illinois C. Jacksonville, Ill. 62650; 1829
Illinois C. of Optometry Chicago, Ill. 60616; 1872
Illinois Inst. of Tech. Chicago, Ill. 60616; 1892
Illinois State U. Normal, Ill. 61761; 1857
Illinois Valley Comm. C. Oglesby, Ill. 61348; junior, 1924
Illinois Wesleyan U. Bloomington, Ill. 61701; 1850
Immaculata C. Immaculata, Pa. 19345; 1920
Immaculata C. of Washington Washington, D.C. 20016; junior, 1905
Immaculate Conception Sem. Conception, Mo. 64433; 1883
Immaculate Conception Sem. Mahwah, N.J. 07430; 1856
Immaculate Conception Sem. Troy, N.Y. 12180; 1959
Immaculate Heart C. Los Angeles, Calif. 90027; 1916
Imperial Valley C. Imperial, Calif. 92251; junior, 1922
Incarnate Word C. San Antonio, Tex. 78209; 1881
Independence Comm. Junior C. Independence, Kans. 67301; 1925
Indiana Central C. Indianapolis, Ind. 46227; 1902
Indiana Inst. of Tech. Fort Wayne, Ind. 46803; 1930
Indiana State U. Terre Haute, Ind. 47809; 1865
Indiana U. Bloomington, Ind. 47401; 1820
Indiana U. of Pennsylvania Indiana, Pa. 15701; 1875
Indian Hills Comm. C. Ottumwa, Iowa 52501; junior, 1930
Indian River Comm. C. Fort Pierce, Fla. 33450; junior, 1960
Insurance, C. of New York, N.Y. 10038; 1962
Inter American U. of Puerto Rico San Germán, Puerto Rico 00753; 1912
Inver Hills State Junior C. Inver Grove Heights, Minn. 55075; 1969
Iona C. New Rochelle, N.Y. 10801; 1940
Iowa, U. of Iowa City, Iowa 52240; 1847
Iowa Central Comm. C. Fort Dodge, Iowa 50501; junior, 1921
Iowa Lakes Comm. C. Estherville, Iowa 51334; junior, 1924
Iowa State U. of Science and Tech. Ames, Iowa 50010; 1858
Iowa Wesleyan C. Mount Pleasant, Iowa 52641; 1842
Iowa Western Comm. C. Council Bluffs, Iowa 51501; junior, 1923
Isothermal Comm. C. Spindale, N.C. 28160; junior, 1966
Itasca State Junior C. Grand Rapids, Minn. 55744; 1922
Itawamba Junior C. Fulton, Miss. 38843; 1948

Ithaca C. Ithaca, N.Y. 14850; 1892
Jackson C. Honolulu, Hawaii 96822; 1949
Jackson Comm. C. Jackson, Mich. 49201; junior, 1928
Jackson State C. Jackson, Miss. 39217; 1877
Jackson State Comm. C. Jackson, Tenn. 38301; junior, 1965
Jacksonville C. Jacksonville, Tex. 75766; junior, 1899
Jacksonville State U. Jacksonville, Ala. 36265; 1883
Jacksonville U. Jacksonville, Fla. 32211; 1934
Jamestown C. Jamestown, N.Dak. 58401; 1884
Jamestown Comm. C. Jamestown, N.Y. 14701; junior, 1934
Jarvis Christian C. Hawkins, Tex. 75765; 1912
Jefferson C. Hillsboro, Mo. 63050; junior, 1963
Jefferson Comm. C. Louisville, Ky. 40201; junior, 1967
Jefferson Comm. C. Watertown, N.Y. 13601; junior, 1963
Jefferson Davis State Junior C. Brewton, Ala. 36426; junior, 1963
Jefferson State Junior C. Birmingham, Ala. 35215; 1963
Jersey City State C. Jersey City, N.J. 07305; 1921
Jewish Theol. Sem. of America New York, N.Y. 10027; 1886
John A. Gupton C. Nashville, Tenn. 37203; junior, 1946
John A. Logan C. Carterville, Ill. 62918; junior, 1967
John Brown U. Siloam Springs, Ark. 72761; 1919
John Carroll U. Cleveland, Ohio 44118; 1886
John C. Calhoun State Technical Junior C. Decatur, Ala. 35601; 1965
John F. Kennedy C. Wahoo, Nebr. 68006; 1965
John F. Kennedy U. Martinez, Calif. 94553; 1964
John Jay C. of Criminal Justice New York, N.Y. 10003; 1965
Johns Hopkins U. Baltimore, Md. 21218; 1876
Johnson and Wales C. Providence, R.I. 02903; 1914
Johnson Bible C. Knoxville, Tenn. 37920; 1893
Johnson C. Smith U. Charlotte, N.C. 28208; 1867
Johnson County Comm. Junior C. Overland Park, Kans. 66210; 1967
Johnson State C. Johnson, Vt. 05656; 1867
Johnstown C. Johnstown, Pa. 15902; junior, 1927
John Tyler Comm. C. Chester, Va. 23831; junior, 1967
John Wesley C. Owosso, Mich. 48867; 1909
Joliet Junior C. Joliet, Ill. 60436; 1902
Jones C. Jacksonville, Fla. 33211; junior, 1918
Jones County Junior C. Ellisville, Miss. 39437; 1911
Judaism, U. of Los Angeles, Calif. 90028; 1947
Judson Baptist C. Portland, Oreg. 97220; 1956
Judson C. Marion, Ala. 36756; 1838
Judson C. Elgin, Ill. 60120; 1913
Juilliard Sch., The New York, N.Y. 10023; 1905
Juniata C. Huntingdon, Pa. 16652; 1876
Kalamazoo C. Kalamazoo, Mich. 49001; 1833
Kalamazoo Valley Comm. C. Kalamazoo, Mich, 49001; junior, 1966
Kankakee Comm. C. Kankakee, Ill. 60901; junior, 1966
Kansas, U. of Lawrence, Kans. 66044; 1863
Kansas City Art Inst. Kansas City, Mo. 64111; 1885
Kansas City Kansas Comm. Junior C. 66101; 1923
Kansas Newman C. Wichita, Kans. 67213; 1933
Kansas State C. of Pittsburg 66762; 1903
Kansas State Teachers C. of Emporia 66801; 1863
Kansas State U. of Agric. and Applied Science Manhattan, Kans. 66502; 1863
Kansas Wesleyan U. Salina, Kans. 67401; 1886
Kaskaskia C. Centralia, Ill. 62801; junior, 1940
Kearney State C. Kearney, Nebr. 68847; 1905
Keene State C. Keene, N.H. 03431; 1909
Kellogg Comm. C. Battle Creek, Mich. 49016; junior, 1956
Kemper Military Sch. and C. Boonville, Mo. 65233; junior, 1844
Kendall C. Evanston, Ill. 60204; junior, 1934
Kennesaw Junior C. Marietta, Ga. 30060; 1963
Kent State U. Kent, Ohio 44240; 1910
Kentucky, U. of Lexington, Ky. 40506; 1865
Kentucky Christian C. Grayson, Ky. 41143; 1919
Kentucky State U. Frankfort, Ky. 40601; 1886
Kentucky Wesleyan C. Owensboro, Ky. 42301; 1866
Kenyon C. Gambier, Ohio 43022; 1824
Kettering C. of Medical Arts Kettering, Ohio 45429; junior, 1967
Keuka C. Keuka Park, N.Y. 14478; 1890
Keystone Junior C. La Plume, Pa. 18440; 1868
Kilgore C. Kilgore, Tex. 75662; junior, 1935
King C. Bristol, Tenn. 37620; 1867
Kingsborough Comm. C. Brooklyn, N.Y. 11235; junior, 1963
King's C. Charlotte, N.C. 28201; junior, 1901
King's C. Wilkes-Barre, Pa. 18702; 1946
King's C., The Briarcliff Manor, N.Y. 10510; 1938
Kirkland C. Clinton, N.Y. 13323; 1965
Kirkland Hall C. Ocean City, Md. 21842; junior, 1967
Kirkwood Comm. C. Cedar Rapids, Iowa 52406; junior, 1965
Kirtland Comm. C. Roscommon, Mich. 48653; junior, 1966
Kishwaukee C. Malta, Ill. 60150; junior, 1967
Kittrell C. Kittrell, N.C. 27544; 1886
Knox C. Galesburg, Ill. 61401; 1837
Knoxville C. Knoxville, Tenn. 37921; 1863
Kutztown State C. Kutztown, Pa. 19530; 1860
Labette Comm. Junior C. Parsons, Kans. 67357; 1923
Lackawanna Junior C. Scranton, Pa. 18503; 1894
Ladycliff C. Highland Falls, N.Y. 10928; 1933
Lafayette C. Easton, Pa. 18042; 1826
LaGrange C. LaGrange, Ga. 30240; 1831
Lake City Comm. C. Lake City, Fla. 32055; junior, 1947
Lake County, C. of Grayslake, Ill. 60030; junior, 1967
Lake Erie C. Painesville, Ohio 44077; 1856
Lake Forest C. Lake Forest, Ill. 60045; 1857
Lake Land C. Mattoon, Ill. 61938; junior, 1966
Lakeland C. Sheboygan, Wis. 53081; 1862
Lakeland Comm. C. Mentor, Ohio 44060; junior, 1967
Lake Michigan C. Benton Harbor, Mich. 49022; junior, 1946
Lake Region Junior C. Devils Lake, N.Dak. 58301; 1941
Lake–Sumter Comm. C. Leesburg, Fla. 32748; junior, 1962
Lake Superior State C. Sault Ste. Marie, Mich. 49783; 1946
Lakewood State Junior C. White Bear Lake, Minn. 55110; 1967
Lamar Comm. C. Lamar, Colo. 81052; junior, 1937
Lamar U. Beaumont, Tex. 77705; 1923
Lambuth C. Jackson, Tenn. 38301; 1843
Lancaster Sch. of the Bible Lancaster, Pa. 17601; 1933
Lander C. Greenwood, S.C. 29646; 1872
Lane C. Jackson, Tenn. 38301; 1882
Lane Comm. C. Eugene, Oreg. 97405; junior, 1965
Laney C. Oakland, Calif. 94606; junior, 1927
Langston U. Langston, Okla. 73050; 1897
Lansing Comm. C. Lansing, Mich. 48914; junior, 1957
Laramie County Comm. C. Cheyenne, Wyo. 82001; junior, 1968
Laredo Junior C. Laredo, Tex. 78040; 1947
La Roche C. Allison Park, Pa. 15101; 1963
La Salette Sem. Altamont, N.Y. 12009; junior, 1924
La Salle C. Philadelphia, Pa. 19141; 1863
Lasell Junior C. Auburndale, Mass. 02166; 1851
Lassen C. Susanville, Calif. 96130; junior, 1925
Latter-day Saints Business C. Salt Lake City, Utah 84111; junior, 1886
La Verne C. La Verne, Calif. 91750; 1891
Lawrence Inst. of Tech. Southfield, Mich., 48075; 1932
Lawrence U. Appleton, Wis. 54911; 1847
Layton Sch. of Art and Design Milwaukee, Wis. 53202; 1920
Lebanon Valley C. Annville, Pa. 17003; 1866
Lee C. Cleveland, Tenn. 37311; 1918
Lee C. Baytown, Tex. 77520; junior, 1934
Lees Junior C. Jackson, Ky. 41339; 1883
Lees–McRae C. Banner Elk, N.C. 28604; junior, 1900
Lehigh County Comm. C. Schnecksville, Pa., 18078; junior, 1966
Lehigh U. Bethlehem, Pa. 18015; 1865
Leicester Junior C. Leicester, Mass. 01524; 1784
Le Moyne C. Syracuse, N.Y. 13214; 1946
LeMoyne–Owen C. Memphis, Tenn. 38126; 1870
Lenoir Comm. C. Kinston, N.C. 28501; junior, 1960
Lenoir Rhyne C. Hickory, N.C. 28601; 1891
Lesley C. Cambridge, Mass. 02138; 1909
LeTourneau C. Longview, Tex. 75601; 1946
Lewis and Clark C. Portland, Oreg. 97219; 1867
Lewis–Clark State C. Lewiston, Idaho 83501; 1955
Lewis C. Lockport, Ill. 60441; 1930
Limestone C. Gaffney, S.C. 29340; 1845
Lincoln Christian C. Lincoln, Ill. 62656; 1944
Lincoln C. Lincoln, Ill. 62656; junior, 1865
Lincoln Land Comm. C. Springfield, Ill. 62703; junior, 1967
Lincoln Memorial U. Harrogate, Tenn. 37752; 1897
Lincoln U. Jefferson City, Mo. 65101; 1866
Lincoln U. Lincoln University, Pa. 19352; 1854
Lindenwood C. St. Charles, Mo. 63301; 1827
Lindsey Wilson C. Columbia, Ky. 42728; junior, 1903
Linfield C. McMinnville, Oreg. 97128; 1849
Linn–Benton Comm. C. Albany, Oreg. 97321; junior, 1966
Livingstone C. Salisbury, N.C. 28144; 1879
Livingston U. Livingston, Ala. 35470; 1840
Lock Haven State C. Lock Haven, Pa. 17745; 1870
Loma Linda U. Loma Linda, Calif. 92354; 1905
Lone Mountain C. San Francisco, Calif. 94118; 1921
Long Beach City C. Long Beach, Calif. 90808; junior, 1913
Long Island U. Greenvale, N.Y. 11548; 1926
Longview C. Enfield, Conn. 06082; junior, 1945
Longview Comm. C. Lee's Summit, Mo. 64063; junior, 1969
Longwood C. Farmville, Va. 23901; 1884
Lon Morris C. Jacksonville, Tex. 75766; junior, 1873
Lorain County Comm. C. Elyria, Ohio 44035; junior, 1963
Loras C. Dubuque, Iowa 52001; 1839
Lord Fairfax Comm. C. Middletown, Va. 22645; junior, 1969
Loretto Heights C. Denver, Colo. 80236; 1891
Los Angeles Baptist C. Newhall, Calif. 91321; 1927
Los Angeles City C. Los Angeles, Calif. 90029; junior, 1929
Los Angeles C. of Optometry Los Angeles, Calif. 90007; 1904
Los Angeles Harbor C. Wilmington, Calif. 90744; junior, 1949
Los Angeles Pierce C. Woodland Hills, Calif. 91364; junior, 1947
Los Angeles Southwest C. Los Angeles, Calif. 90047; junior, 1967
Los Angeles Trade–Technical C. Los Angeles, Calif. 90015; junior, 1949
Los Angeles Valley C. Van Nuys, Calif. 91401; junior, 1949
Louisburg C. Louisburg, N.C. 27549; junior, 1787
Louisiana C. Pineville, La. 71360; 1906
Louisiana State U. and A. & M. C. Baton Rouge, La. 70803; 1860
Louisiana State U. at Alexandria 71301; junior, 1959
Louisiana State U. at Eunice 70535; junior, 1964
Louisiana State U. at New Orleans 70112; 1958
Louisiana State U. at Shreveport 71105; junior, 1965
Louisiana Tech U. Ruston, La. 71270; 1894
Louisville, U. of Louisville, Ky. 40208; 1798
Lourdes Junior C. Sylvania, Ohio 43560; 1957
Lowell State C. Lowell, Mass. 01850; 1894
Lowell Technological Inst. Lowell, Mass. 01854; 1895
Lower Columbia C. Longview, Wash. 98632; junior, 1934
Loyola C. Baltimore, Md. 21210; 1852
Loyola U. Chicago, Ill. 60611; 1869
Loyola U. New Orleans, La. 70118; 1849
Loyola U. of Los Angeles Los Angeles, Calif. 90045; 1865
Lubbock Christian C. Lubbock, Tex. 79407; 1957
Lurleen B. Wallace State Junior C. Andalusia, Ala. 36420; 1968
Luther C. Decorah, Iowa 52101; 1861
Luther C. of the Bible and Liberal Arts Teaneck, N.J. 07666; junior, 1948
Luther Rice C. Alexandria, Va. 22310; 1967
Luther Theol. Sem. St. Paul, Minn. 55108; 1876

Luzerne County Comm. C. Wilkes-Barre, Pa. 18700; junior, 1966
Lycoming C. Williamsport, Pa. 17701; 1812
Lynchburg C. Lynchburg, Va. 24504; 1903
Lyndon State C. Lyndonville, Vt. 05851; 1911
Macalester C. St. Paul, Minn. 55101; 1853
McCook C. McCook, Nebr. 69001; junior, 1926
MacCormac C. Chicago, Ill. 60604; junior, 1904
McHenry County Junior C. Crystal Lake, Ill. 60014; 1967
McKendree C. Lebanon, Ill. 62254; 1828
McLennan Comm. C. Waco, Tex. 76703; junior, 1966
MacMurray C. Jacksonville, Ill. 62650; 1846
McMurry C. Abilene, Tex. 79605; 1923
McNeese State U. Lake Charles, La. 70601; 1939
Macomb County Comm. C. Warren, Mich. 48093; junior, 1953
Macon Junior C. Macon, Ga. 31206; 1968
McPherson C. McPherson, Kans. 67460; 1887
Madison Area Technical C. Madison, Wis. 53703; junior, 1912
Madison Business C. Madison, Wis. 53703; 1856
Madison C. Harrisonburg, Va. 22802; 1908
Madonna C. Livonia, Mich. 48150; 1937
Maine at Augusta, U. of 04330; junior, 1965
Maine at Bangor, U. of 04401; junior, 1968
Maine at Farmington, U. of 04938; 1864
Maine at Fort Kent, U. of 04743; 1878
Maine at Machias, U. of 04654; 1909
Maine at Orono, U. of 04473; 1865
Maine at Portland–Gorham, U. of Gorham, 04038; 1878
Maine at Presque Isle, U. of 04769; 1903
Maine Maritime Acad. Castine, Me. 04421; 1941
Mainland, C. of the Texas City, Tex. 77590; junior, 1966
Mallinckrodt C. Wilmette, Ill. 60091; junior, 1918
Malone C. Canton, Ohio 44709; 1892
Manatee Junior C. Bradenton, Fla. 33505; 1958
Manchester C. North Manchester, Ind. 46962; 1889
Manchester Comm. C. Manchester, Conn. 06040; junior, 1963
Manhattan Christian C. Manhattan, Kans. 66502; 1927
Manhattan C. Bronx, N.Y. 10471; 1853
Manhattan Sch. of Music New York, N.Y. 10027; 1917
Manhattanville C. Purchase, N.Y. 10577; 1841
Mankato State C. Mankato, Minn. 56001; 1866
Mannes C. of Music New York, N.Y. 10021; 1916
Manor Junior C. Jenkintown, Pa. 19046; 1947
Mansfield State C. Mansfield, Pa. 16933; 1857
Maple Woods Comm. C. Kansas City, Mo. 64156; junior, 1969
Maria C. Albany, N.Y. 12208; junior, 1958
Marian C. Indianapolis, Ind. 46222; 1851
Marian C. of Fond du Lac Fond du Lac, Wis. 54935; 1936
Maria Regina C. Syracuse, N.Y. 13208; junior, 1934
Maricopa County Comm. C. Phoenix, Ariz. 85004; junior, 1962
Marietta C. Marietta, Ohio 45750; 1797
Marillac C. St. Louis, Mo. 63121; 1955
Marin, C. of Kentfield, Calif. 94904; junior, 1926
Marion C. Marion, Ind. 46952; 1920
Marion Inst. Marion, Ala. 36756; junior, 1842
Marist C. Poughkeepsie, N.Y. 12601; 1946
Marjorie Webster Junior C. Washington, D.C. 20012; 1920
Marlboro C. Marlboro, Vt. 05344; 1946
Marquette U. Milwaukee, Wis. 53233; 1857
Marshalltown Comm. C. Marshalltown, Iowa 50158; junior, 1927
Marshall U. Huntington, W.Va. 25701; 1837
Mars Hill C. Mars Hill, N.C. 28754; 1856
Martin C. Pulaski, Tenn. 38478; junior, 1870
Martin Technical Inst. Williamston, N.C. 27892; junior, 1967
Mary Baldwin C. Staunton, Va. 24401; 1842
Mary C. Bismarck, N.Dak. 58501; 1959
Marycrest C. Davenport, Iowa 52804; 1939
Maryglade C. Memphis, Mich. 48041; 1960
Marygrove C. Detroit, Mich. 48221; 1906
Mary Hardin-Baylor C. Belton, Tex. 76513; 1845
Mary Holmes C. West Point, Miss. 39773; junior, 1892
Mary Immaculate Sem. and C. Northampton, Pa. 18067; 1939
Maryland, College Park, U. of 20742; 1807
Maryland, Eastern Shore, U. of Princess Anne, Md. 21853; 1886
Maryland Inst., C. of Art, The Baltimore, Md. 21217; 1826
Marylhurst C. Marylhurst, Oreg. 97036; 1893
Mary Manse C. Toledo, Ohio 43620; 1922
Marymount C. Boca Raton, Fla. 33432; 1963
Marymount C. Salina, Kans. 67401; 1922
Marymount C. Tarrytown, N.Y. 10591; 1907
Marymount C. Arlington, Va. 22207; junior, 1950
Marymount C. at Loyola U. Los Angeles, Calif. 90045; 1933
Marymount C. of Palos Verdes Palos Verdes Peninsula, Calif. 90274; junior, 1932
Marymount Manhattan C. New York, N.Y. 10021; 1948
Maryville C. St. Louis, Mo. 63141; 1846
Maryville C. Maryville, Tenn. 37801; 1819
Mary Washington C. Fredericksburg, Va. 22401; 1908
Marywood C. Scranton, Pa. 18509; 1915
Massachusetts, Amherst, U. of 01002; 1863
Massachusetts, Boston, U. of 02116; 1964
Massachusetts Bay Comm. C. Watertown, Mass. 02172; junior, 1961
Massachusetts C. of Art Boston, Mass. 02215; 1873
Massachusetts C. of Optometry Boston, Mass. 02116; 1894
Massachusetts C. of Pharmacy Boston, Mass. 02115; 1823
Massachusetts Inst. of Tech. Cambridge, Mass. 02139; 1859
Massachusetts Maritime Acad. Buzzards Bay, Mass. 02532; 1891
Massasoit Comm. C. Brockton, Mass. 02379; junior, 1966
Mater Dei C. Ogdensburg, N.Y. 13369; junior, 1960
Mattatuck Comm. C. Waterbury, Conn. 06702; junior, 1967
Maysville Comm. C. Maysville, Ky. 41056; junior, 1968
Mayville State C. Mayville, N.Dak. 58257; 1889
Medaille C. Buffalo, N.Y. 14214; 1937
Medical C. of Pennsylvania Philadelphia, Pa. 19129; 1850
Medical U. of South Carolina Charleston, S.C. 29401; 1824
Meharry Medical C. Nashville, Tenn. 37208; 1876
Memphis, State Technical Inst. at Memphis, Tenn. 38128; junior, 1963
Memphis Acad. of Arts Memphis, Tenn. 38112; 1936
Memphis State U. Memphis, Tenn. 38111; 1909
Menlo C. Menlo Park, Calif. 94025; 1915
Meramec Comm. C. Kirkwood, Mo. 63137; junior, 1964
Merced C. Merced, Calif. 95340; junior, 1963
Mercer County Comm. C. Trenton, N.J. 08608; junior, 1947
Mercer U. Macon, Ga. 31207; 1833
Mercy C. Dobbs Ferry, N.Y. 10522; 1950
Mercy C. Cumberland, R.I. 02864; 1957
Mercy C. of Detroit Detroit, Mich. 48219; 1941
Mercyhurst C. Erie, Pa. 16501; 1871
Mercy Inst. Portland, Me. 04103; junior, 1956
Meredith C. Raleigh, N.C. 27602; 1891
Meridian Junior C. Meridian, Miss. 39301; 1937
Merrimack C. North Andover, Mass. 01845; 1947
Merritt C. Oakland, Calif. 94609; junior, 1953
Mesabi State Junior C. Virginia, Minn. 55792; 1918
Mesa C. Grand Junction, Colo. 81501; junior, 1925
Messiah C. Grantham, Pa. 17027; 1909
Methodist C. Fayetteville, N.C. 28301; 1956
Metropolitan State C. Denver, Colo. 80204; 1963
Metropolitan State Junior C. Minneapolis, Minn. 55403; 1965
Miami, U. of Coral Gables, Fla. 33124; 1925
Miami Christian U. Miami, Fla. 33167; 1946
Miami-Dade Junior C. Miami, Fla. 33156; 1960
Miami-Jacobs Junior C. of Business Dayton, Ohio 45402; 1860
Miami U. Oxford, Ohio 45056; 1809
Michigan, U. of Ann Arbor, Mich. 48104; 1817
Michigan Christian Junior C. Rochester, Mich. 48063; 1955
Michigan State U. East Lansing, Mich. 48823; 1855
Michigan Technological U. Houghton, Mich. 49931; 1885
Mid-America Nazarene C. Olathe, Kans. 66061; 1966
Middlebury C. Middlebury, Vt. 05753; 1800
Middle Georgia C. Cochran, Ga. 31014; junior, 1920
Middlesex Comm. C. Middletown, Conn. 06457; junior, 1966
Middlesex County C. Edison, N.J. 08817; junior, 1964
Middle Tennessee State U. Murfreesboro, Tenn. 37130; 1909
Midland Lutheran C. Fremont, Nebr. 68025; 1883
Midlands Technical Ed. Center Columbia, S.C. 29205; junior, 1962
Mid Michigan Comm. C. Harrison, Mich. 48625; junior, 1965
Mid-South Bible C. Memphis, Tenn. 38112; 1944
Midway C. Midway, Ky. 40347; junior, 1847
Midwestern U. Wichita Falls, Tex. 76308; 1922
Midwest Inst. of Business Administration Eureka, Kans. 67045; 1946
Miles C. Birmingham, Ala. 35208; 1907
Miles Comm. C. Miles City, Mont. 59301; junior, 1939
Millersville State C. Millersville, Pa. 17551; 1854
Milligan C. Milligan College, Tenn. 37682; 1882
Millikin U. Decatur, Ill. 62522; 1901
Millsaps C. Jackson, Miss. 39210; 1890
Mills C. Oakland, Calif. 94613; 1852
Mills C. of Ed. New York, N.Y. 10011; 1909
Milton C. Milton, Wis. 53563; 1844
Miltonvale Wesleyan C. Miltonvale, Kans. 67466; junior, 1909
Milwaukee Area Technical C. Milwaukee, Wis. 53203; junior, 1923
Milwaukee Sch. of Engineering Milwaukee, Wis. 53201; 1903
Mineral Area Comm. C. Flat River, Mo. 63601; junior, 1922
Minneapolis C. of Art and Design Minneapolis, Minn. 55404; 1886
Minnesota, U. of Minneapolis, Minn. 55455; 1851
Minnesota, Duluth, U. of 55812; 1895
Minnesota, Morris, U. of 56267; 1960
Minnesota Bible C. Rochester, Minn. 55901; 1913
Minnesota Technical Inst., U. of Crookston, Minn. 56716; junior, 1966
Minot State C. Minot, N.Dak. 58701; 1913
Mira Costa C. Oceanside, Calif. 92054; junior, 1934
Misericordia, C. Dallas, Pa. 18612; 1923
Mississippi, U. of University, Miss. 38677; 1844
Mississippi C. Clinton, Miss. 39056; 1826
Mississippi Delta Junior C. Moorhead, Miss. 38761; 1911
Mississippi Gulf Coast Junior C. Perkinston, Miss. 39573; 1911
Mississippi Industrial C. Holly Springs, Miss. 38635; 1905
Mississippi State C. for Women Columbus, Miss. 39701; 1884
Mississippi State U. State College, Miss. 39762; 1878
Mississippi Valley State C. Itta Bena, Miss. 38941; 1946
Missouri, U. of Columbia, Mo. 65201; 1839
Missouri at Kansas City, U. of 64110; 1929
Missouri at Rolla, U. of 65401; 1870
Missouri at St. Louis, U. of 63121; 1960
Missouri Baptist C.–Hannibal–Lagrange Hannibal, Mo. 63401; junior, 1858
Missouri Southern State C. Joplin, Mo. 64801; 1937
Missouri Valley C. Marshall, Mo. 65340; 1888
Missouri Western C. St. Joseph, Mo. 64507; 1915
Mitchell C. New London, Conn. 06320; junior, 1938
Mitchell C. Statesville, N.C. 28677; junior, 1852
Moberly Junior C. Moberly, Mo. 65270; 1927
Mobile C. Mobile, Ala. 36613; 1961
Modesto Junior C. Modesto, Calif. 95350; 1921
Mohawk Valley Comm. C. Utica, N.Y. 13501; junior, 1946
Molloy C. Rockville Centre, N.Y. 11570; 1955
Monmouth C. Monmouth, Ill. 61462; 1853
Monmouth C. West Long Branch, N.J. 07764; 1933
Monroe Comm. C. Rochester, N.Y. 14607; junior, 1961
Monroe County Comm. C. Monroe, Mich. 48161; junior, 1964

Montana, U. of Missoula, Mont. 59801; 1893
Montana C. of Mineral Science and Tech. Butte, Mont. 59701; 1893
Montana State U. Bozeman, Mont. 59715; 1893
Montcalm Comm. C. Sidney, Mich. 48885; junior, 1965
Montclair State C. Upper Montclair, N.J. 07043; 1908
Monterey Inst. of Foreign Studies Monterey, Calif. 93940; 1955
Monterey Peninsula C. Monterey, Calif. 93940; junior, 1947
Montevallo, U. of Montevallo, Ala. 35115; 1896
Montgomery C. Rockville, Md. 20850; junior, 1946
Montgomery County Comm. C. Blue Bell, Pa. 19422; junior, 1964
Montreat-Anderson C. Montreat, N.C. 28757; junior, 1916
Moody Bible Inst. Chicago, Ill. 60610; 1886
Moore C. of Art Philadelphia, Pa. 19103; 1844
Moorhead State C. Moorhead, Minn. 56560; 1885
Moorpark C. Moorpark, Calif. 93021; junior, 1963
Moraine Valley Comm. C. Palos Hills, Ill. 60465; junior, 1967
Moravian C. Bethlehem, Pa. 18018; 1807
Morehead State U. Morehead, Ky. 40351; 1922
Morehouse C. Atlanta, Ga. 30314; 1867
Morgan State C. Baltimore, Md. 21212; 1867
Morningside C. Sioux City, Iowa 51106; 1889
Morris Brown C. Atlanta, Ga. 30314; 1881
Morris C. Sumter, S.C. 29150; 1908
Morris Harvey C. Charleston, W.Va. 25304; 1888
Morristown C. Morristown, Tenn. 37814; junior, 1881
Morse C. Hartford, Conn. 06103; junior, 1860
Morton C. Cicero, Ill. 60650; junior, 1924
Motlow State Comm. C. Tullahoma, Tenn. 37388; junior, 1967
Mountain View C. Dallas, Tex. 75211; junior, 1970
Mount Aloysius Junior C. Cresson, Pa. 16630; 1848
Mount Alvernia C. Newton, Mass. 02158; 1959
Mount Angel C. Mount Angel, Oreg. 97362; 1887
Mount Angel Sem. St. Benedict, Oreg. 97373; 1887
Mount Carmel Junior C. New Orleans, La. 70124; 1924
Mount Holyoke C. South Hadley, Mass. 01075; 1837
Mount Hood Comm. C. Gresham, Oreg. 97030; junior, 1965
Mount Ida Junior C. Newton Centre, Mass. 02159; 1899
Mount Marty C. Yankton, S.Dak. 57078; 1922
Mount Mary C. Milwaukee, Wis. 53222; 1913
Mount Mercy C. Cedar Rapids, Iowa 52402; 1875
Mount Olive C. Mount Olive, N.C. 28365; junior, 1951
Mount Providence Junior C. Baltimore, Md. 21227; 1952
Mount Sacred Heart C. Hamden, Conn. 06514; junior, 1954
Mount St. Clare C. Clinton, Iowa 52732; junior, 1895
Mount Saint Joseph C. Wakefield, R.I. 02880; 1953
Mount St. Joseph-on-the-Ohio, C. of Mount St. Joseph, Ohio 45051; 1854
Mount St. Mary C. Hooksett, N.H. 03106; 1934
Mount St. Mary C. Newburgh, N.Y. 12550; 1930
Mount St. Mary's C. Los Angeles, Calif. 90049; 1925
Mount St. Mary's C. Emmitsburg, Md. 21727; 1808
Mount St. Vincent, C. of Bronx, N.Y. 10471; 1847
Mount San Antonio C. Walnut, Calif. 91789; junior, 1945
Mount San Jacinto C. Gilman Hot Springs, Calif. 92340; junior, 1963
Mount Senario C. Ladysmith, Wis. 54848; 1962
Mount Union C. Alliance, Ohio 44601; 1846
Mount Vernon C. Washington, D.C. 20007; junior, 1875
Mount Vernon Nazarene C. Mount Vernon, Ohio 43050; junior, 1966
Mount Wachusett Comm. C. Gardner, Mass. 01440; junior, 1963
Muhlenberg C. Allentown, Pa. 18104; 1848
Multnomah Sch. of the Bible Portland, Oreg. 97220; 1936
Mundelein C. Chicago, Ill. 60626; 1930
Murray State C. Tishomingo, Okla. 73460; junior, 1908
Murray State U. Murray, Ky. 42071; 1922
Muskegon Business C. Muskegon, Mich. 49442; junior, 1885
Muskegon Comm. C. Muskegon, Mich. 49443; junior, 1926
Muskingum Area Technical Inst. Zanesville, Ohio 43701; junior, 1969
Muskingum C. New Concord, Ohio 43762; 1837
Napa C. Napa, Calif. 94558; junior, 1941
Nassau Comm. C. Garden City, N.Y. 11533; junior, 1959
Nasson C. Springvale, Me. 04083; 1912
Natchez Junior C. Natchez, Miss. 39120; 1885
Nathaniel Hawthorne C. Antrim, N.H. 03440; 1962
National Business C. Roanoke, Va. 24009; junior, 1886
National C. of Ed. Evanston, Ill. 60201; 1886
Navajo Comm. C. Chinle, Ariz. 86503; junior, 1969
Navarro Junior C. Corsicana, Tex. 75110; 1946
Nazareth C. Kalamazoo, Mich. 49074; 1924
Nazareth C. of Rochester Rochester, N.Y. 14610; 1924
Nebraska at Lincoln, U. of 68508; 1869
Nebraska at Omaha, U. of 68132; 1908
Nebraska Wesleyan U. Lincoln, Nebr. 68504; 1887
Nebraska Western C. Scottsbluff, Nebr. 69361; junior, 1926
Neosho County Comm. Junior C. Chanute, Kans. 66720; 1936
Ner Israel Rabbinical C. Baltimore, Md. 21215; 1933
Nevada at Las Vegas, U. of 89109; 1957
Nevada at Reno, U. of 89507; 1874
Newark C. of Engineering Newark, N.J. 07102; 1881
Newark State C. Union, N.J. 07083; 1855
Newberry C. Newberry, S.C. 29108; 1856
New Church, Acad. of the Bryn Athyn, Pa. 19009; 1876
New C. Sarasota, Fla. 33578; 1960
Newcomb C. New Orleans, La. 70118; 1886
New England Aeronautical Inst. Nashua, N.H. 03060; junior, 1965
New England C. Henniker, N.H. 03242; 1946
New England Conservatory of Music Boston, Mass. 02115; 1867
New Hampshire, U. of Durham, N.H. 03824; 1866
New Hampshire C. Manchester, N.H. 03101; 1932
New Hampshire Technical Inst. Concord, N.H. 03301; junior, 1961
New Haven, U. of West Haven, Conn. 06516; 1920
New Mexico, U. of Albuquerque, N.Mex. 87106; 1889
New Mexico Highlands U. Las Vegas, N.Mex. 87701; 1893
New Mexico Inst. of Mining and Tech. Socorro, N.Mex. 87801; 1889
New Mexico Junior C. Hobbs, N.Mex. 88240; 1965
New Mexico Military Inst. Roswell, N.Mex. 88201; junior, 1891
New Mexico State U. Las Cruces, N.Mex. 88001; 1888
New River Comm. C. Dublin, Va. 24084; junior, 1966
New Rochelle, C. of New Rochelle, N.Y. 10801; 1904
New Sch. for Social Research New York, N.Y. 10011; 1919
Newton C. of the Sacred Heart Newton, Mass. 02159; 1946
Newton Junior C. Newtonville, Mass. 02160; 1946
New York Agricultural and Technical C., State U. of Alfred, N.Y. 14802; junior, 1908
New York Agricultural and Technical C., State U. of Canton, N.Y. 13617; junior, 1907
New York Agricultural and Technical C., State U. of Cobleskill, N.Y. 12043; junior, 1911
New York Agricultural and Technical C., State U. of Delhi, N.Y. 13753; junior, 1913
New York Agricultural and Technical C., State U. of Farmingdale, N.Y. 11735; junior, 1912
New York Agricultural and Technical C., State U. of Morrisville, N.Y. 13408; junior, 1908
New York at Albany, State U. of 12203; 1844
New York at Binghamton, State U. of 13901; 1946
New York at Buffalo, State U. of 14214; 1846
New York at Stony Brook, State U. of 11790; 1957
New York City Comm. C. of Applied Arts and Sciences Brooklyn, N.Y. 11201; junior, 1946
New York C. at Brockport, State U. of 14420; 1841
New York C. at Buffalo, State U. of 14222; 1867
New York C. at Cortland, State U. of 13045; 1863
New York C. at Fredonia, State U. of 14063; 1866
New York C. at Geneseo, State U. of 14454; 1867
New York C. at New Paltz, State U. of 12561; 1828
New York C. at Old Westbury, State U. of 11771; 1966
New York C. at Oneonta, State U. of 13820; 1889
New York C. at Oswego, State U. of 13126; 1861
New York C. at Plattsburgh, State U. of 12901; 1889
New York C. at Potsdam, State U. of 13676; 1816
New York C. at Purchase, State U. of 10577; 1967
New York C. of Podiatric Medicine New York, N.Y. 10035; 1911
New York Downstate Medical Center, State U. of Brooklyn, N.Y. 11203; 1930
New York Inst. of Tech. Old Westbury, N.Y. 11568; 1910
New York Maritime C., State U. of Bronx, N.Y. 10465; 1874
New York U. New York, N.Y. 10003; 1831
New York Upstate Medical Center, State U. of Syracuse, N.Y. 13210; 1834
Niagara County Comm. C. Niagara Falls, N.Y. 14303; junior, 1962
Niagara U. Niagara University, N.Y. 14109; 1856
Nicholls State U. Thibodaux, La. 70301; 1948
Nichols C. Dudley, Mass. 01570; 1815
Norfolk State C. Norfolk, Va. 23504; 1935
Normandale State Junior C. Bloomington, Minn. 55431; 1968
North Adams State C. North Adams, Mass. 01247; 1894
North American Baptist Sem. Sioux Falls, S.Dak. 57105; 1850
Northampton County Area Comm. C. Bethlehem, Pa. 18017; junior, 1966
North Carolina Agricultural and Technical State U. Greensboro, N.C. 27411; 1891
North Carolina at Asheville, U. of 28801; 1927
North Carolina Central U. Durham, N.C. 27707; 1909
North Carolina at Chapel Hill, U. of 27514; 1789
North Carolina at Charlotte, U. of 28213; 1946
North Carolina at Greensboro, U. of 27412; 1891
North Carolina at Wilmington, U. of 28401; 1947
North Carolina Sch. of the Arts Winston-Salem, N.C. 27107; 1965
North Carolina State U. at Raleigh 27607; 1887
North Carolina Wesleyan C. Rocky Mount, N.C. 27801; 1956
North Central Bible C. Minneapolis, Minn. 55404; 1930
North Central C. Naperville, Ill. 60540; 1861
North Central Michigan C. Petoskey, Mich. 49770; junior, 1958
North Central Technical Inst. Wausau, Wis. 54401; junior, 1912
North Country Comm. C. Saranac Lake, N.Y. 12983; junior, 1967
North Dakota, U. of Grand Forks, N.Dak. 58201; 1883
North Dakota, Williston, U. of 58801; junior, 1957
North Dakota State Sch. of Science Wahpeton, N.Dak. 58075; junior, 1889
North Dakota State U. Fargo, N.Dak. 58102; 1890
Northeast Alabama State Junior C. Rainsville, Ala. 35986; 1963
Northeast Bible Inst. Green Lane, Pa. 18054; 1938
Northeastern Christian Junior C. Villanova, Pa. 19085; 1956
Northeastern Collegiate Bible Inst. Essex Fells, N.J. 07021; 1950
Northeastern Illinois State U. Chicago, Ill. 60625; 1961
Northeastern Junior C. of Colorado Sterling, Colo. 80751; 1941
Northeastern Nebraska C. Norfolk, Nebr. 68701; junior, 1927
Northeastern Oklahoma A. & M. C. Miami, Okla. 74354; junior, 1919
Northeastern State C. Tahlequah, Okla. 74464; 1846
Northeastern U. Boston, Mass. 02115; 1898
Northeast Louisiana U. Monroe, La. 71201; 1931
Northeast Mississippi Junior C. Booneville, Miss. 38829; 1948
Northeast Missouri State C. Kirksville, Mo. 63501; 1867
Northern Arizona U. Flagstaff, Ariz. 86001; 1899
Northern Colorado, U. of Greeley, Colo. 80631; 1889
Northern Conservatory of Music Bangor, Me. 04401; 1929
Northern Essex Comm. C. Haverhill, Mass. 01830; junior, 1961

Northern Illinois U. De Kalb, Ill. 60115; 1895
Northern Iowa, U. of Cedar Falls, Iowa 50613; 1876
Northern Michigan U. Marquette, Mich. 49855; 1899
Northern Montana C. Havre, Mont. 59501; 1913
Northern Oklahoma C. Tonkawa, Okla. 74653; junior, 1901
Northern State C. Aberdeen, S.Dak. 57401; 1901
Northern Virginia Comm. C. Annandale, Va. 22003; junior, 1965
North Florida Junior C. Madison, Fla. 32340; 1958
North Georgia C. Dahlonega, Ga. 30533; 1873
North Greenville C. Tigerville, S.C. 29688; junior, 1892
North Hennepin State Junior C. Brooklyn Park, Minn. 55428; 1966
North Idaho C. Coeur d'Alene, Idaho 83814; junior, 1939
North Iowa Area Comm. C. Mason City, Iowa 50401; junior, 1918
Northland C. Ashland, Wis. 54806; 1892
Northland State Junior C. Thief River Falls, Minn. 56701; 1965
North Park C. Chicago, Ill. 60625; 1891
North Platte C. North Platte, Nebr. 69101; junior, 1964
Northrop Inst. of Tech. Inglewood, Calif. 90306; 1942
North Seattle Comm. C. Seattle, Wash. 98103; junior, 1969
North Shore Comm. C. Beverly, Mass. 01915; junior, 1965
North Texas State U. Denton, Tex. 76203; 1890
Northwest Alabama State Junior C. Phil Campbell, Ala. 35581; 1963
Northwest Bible C. Minot, N.Dak. 58701; 1934
Northwest Christian C. Eugene, Oreg. 97401; 1895
Northwest C. Kirkland, Wash. 98033; 1934
Northwest Comm. C. Powell, Wyo. 82435; junior, 1946
Northwestern C. Orange City, Iowa 51041; 1882
Northwestern C. Watertown, Wis. 53094; 1865
Northwestern Connecticut Comm. C. Winsted, Conn. 06098; junior, 1965
Northwestern Michigan C. Traverse City, Mich. 49684; junior, 1951
Northwestern State C. Alva, Okla. 73717; 1897
Northwestern State C. of Louisiana Natchitoches, La. 71457; 1884
Northwestern U. Evanston, Ill. 60201; 1851
Northwest Mississippi Junior C. Senatobia, Miss. 38668; 1915
Northwest Missouri State U. Maryville, Mo. 64468; 1905
Northwest Nazarene C. Nampa, Idaho 83651; 1913
Northwood Inst. Midland, Mich. 48640; 1959
Norwalk Comm. C. Norwalk, Conn. 06854; junior, 1961
Norwalk State Technical C. Norwalk, Conn. 06854; junior, 1961
Norwich U. Northfield, Vt. 05663; 1819
Notre Dame, C. of Belmont, Calif. 94002; 1851
Notre Dame, U. of Notre Dame, Ind. 46556; 1842
Notre Dame C. St. Louis, Mo. 63125; 1896
Notre Dame C. Manchester, N.H. 03104; 1950
Notre Dame C. Cleveland, Ohio 44121; 1922
Notre Dame of Maryland, C. of Baltimore, Md. 21210; 1848
Notre Dame Sem. New Orleans, La. 70118; 1923
Nyack C. Nyack, N.Y. 10960; 1882
Oakland City C. Oakland City, Ind. 47560; 1885
Oakland Comm. C. Bloomfield Hills, Mich. 48013; junior, 1964
Oakland U. Rochester, Mich. 48063; 1959
Oakwood C. Huntsville, Ala. 35806; 1896
Oberlin C. Oberlin, Ohio 44074; 1832
Oblate C. Washington, D.C. 20017; 1904
Occidental C. Los Angeles, Calif. 90041; 1887
Ocean County C. Toms River, N.J. 08753; junior, 1964
Odessa C. Odessa, Tex. 79760; junior, 1946
Oglethorpe C. Atlanta, Ga. 30319; 1835
Ohio C. of Podiatric Medicine Cleveland, Ohio 44106; 1916
Ohio Dominican C. Columbus, Ohio 43219; 1911
Ohio Inst. of Technology Columbus, Ohio 43219; 1952
Ohio Northern U. Ada, Ohio 45810; 1871
Ohio State U. Columbus, Ohio 43210; 1870
Ohio U. Athens, Ohio 45701; 1804
Ohio Valley C. Parkersburg, W.Va. 26101; junior, 1960
Ohio Wesleyan U. Delaware, Ohio 43015; 1841
Ohlone C. Fremont, Calif. 94537; junior, 1966
Okaloosa-Walton Junior C. Niceville, Fla. 32578; 1963
Oklahoma, U. of Norman, Okla. 73069; 1890
Oklahoma Baptist U. Shawnee, Okla. 74801; 1906
Oklahoma Christian C. Oklahoma City, Okla. 73111; 1950
Oklahoma City U. Oklahoma City, Okla. 73106; 1911
Oklahoma C. of Liberal Arts Chickasha, Okla. 73018; 1908
Oklahoma Panhandle State C. of Agriculture and Applied Sciences Goodwell, Okla. 73939; 1909
Oklahoma Sch. of Business, Accountancy, Law, and Finance Tulsa, Okla. 74119; junior, 1919
Oklahoma State U. of Agric. and Applied Science Stillwater, Okla. 74074; 1890
Old Dominion U. Norfolk, Va. 23508; 1930
Olivet C. Olivet, Mich. 49076; 1844
Olivet Nazarene C. Kankakee, Ill. 60901; 1907
Olney Central C. Olney, Ill. 62450; junior, 1963
Olympic C. Bremerton, Wash. 98310; junior, 1946
Onondaga Comm. C. Syracuse, N.Y. 13210; junior, 1961
Open Bible C. Des Moines, Iowa 50321; 1931
Oral Roberts U. Tulsa, Okla. 74105; 1963
Orangeburg-Calhoun Technical Center Orangeburg, S.C. 29115; junior, 1966
Orange Coast C. Costa Mesa, Calif. 92626; junior, 1947
Orange County Comm. C. Middletown, N.Y. 10940; junior, 1950
Oregon, U. of Eugene, Oreg. 97403; 1872
Oregon C. of Ed. Monmouth, Oreg. 97361; 1856
Oregon State U. Corvallis, Oreg. 97331; 1868
Oregon Technical Inst. Klamath Falls, Oreg. 97601; 1947
Otero Junior C. La Junta, Colo. 81050; 1941
Ottawa U. Ottawa, Kans. 66067; 1865
Otterbein C. Westerville, Ohio 43081; 1847
Ottumwa Heights C. Ottumwa, Iowa 52501; junior, 1925
Ouachita Baptist U. Arkadelphia, Ark. 71923; 1885
Our Lady of Holy Cross C. New Orleans, La. 70114; 1916
Our Lady of Providence, Sem. of Warwick, R.I. 02889; 1939
Our Lady of the Elms, C. of Chicopee, Mass. 01013; 1928
Our Lady of the Lake C. San Antonio, Tex. 78207; 1911
Ozark Bible C. Joplin, Mo. 64801; 1942
Ozarks, C. of the Clarksville, Ark. 72830; 1834
Ozarks, Sch. of the Point Lookout, Mo. 65726; 1906
Pace U. New York, N.Y. 10038; 1906
Pacific, U. of the Stockton, Calif. 95204; 1851
Pacific Christian C. Long Beach, Calif. 90804; 1928
Pacific C. Fresno, Calif. 93702; 1944
Pacific Lutheran U. Tacoma, Wash. 98447; 1890
Pacific Oaks C. Pasadena, Calif. 91105; 1945
Pacific Union C. Angwin, Calif. 94508; 1882
Pacific U. Forest Grove, Oreg. 97116; 1849
Pacific Western C. Renton, Wash. 98055; 1965
Packer C. Brooklyn, N.Y. 11201; junior, 1845
Paine C. Augusta, Ga. 30901; 1882
Palm Beach, U. of West Palm Beach, Fla. 33402; 1926
Palm Beach Atlantic C. West Palm Beach, Fla. 33401; 1968
Palm Beach Junior C. Lake Worth, Fla. 33460; 1933
Palmer C. Charleston, S.C. 29401; junior, 1903
Palmer Junior C. Davenport, Iowa 52803; 1965
Palomar C. San Marcos, Calif. 92069; junior, 1946
Palo Verde C. Blythe, Calif. 92225; junior, 1947
Pan American U. Edinburg, Tex. 78539; 1927
Panola Junior C. Carthage, Tex. 75633; 1947
Paris Junior C. Paris, Tex. 75460; 1924
Park C. Kansas City, Mo. 64152; 1875
Parkland C. Champaign, Ill. 61820; junior, 1965
Pasadena City C. Pasadena, Calif. 91106; junior, 1924
Pasadena C. Pasadena, Calif. 91104; 1902
Passionist Monastic Sem. Jamaica, N.Y. 11432; 1929
Patrick Henry State Junior C. Monroeville, Ala. 36460; 1965
Paul Quinn C. Waco, Tex. 76703; 1881
Paul Smith's C. Paul Smiths, N.Y. 12970; junior, 1937
Peabody Conservatory of Music Baltimore, Md. 21202; 1857
Peace C. Raleigh, N.C. 27602; junior, 1857
Pearl River Junior C. Poplarville, Miss. 39470; 1909
Peirce Junior C. Philadelphia, Pa. 19102; 1865
Pembroke C. Providence, R.I. 02912; 1891
Pembroke State U. Pembroke, N.C. 28372; 1887
Peninsula C. Port Angeles, Wash. 98362; junior, 1961
Penn Hall Junior C. Chambersburg, Pa. 17201; 1906
Pennsylvania, U. of Philadelphia, Pa. 19104; 1740
Pennsylvania C. of Optometry Philadelphia, Pa. 19141; 1919
Pennsylvania State U. University Park, Pa. 16802; 1855
Penn Valley Comm. C. Kansas City, Mo. 64111; junior, 1915
Pensacola Junior C. Pensacola, Fla. 32504; 1948
Pepperdine U. Los Angeles, Calif. 90044; 1937
Perry Normal Sch. Milton, Mass. 02186; 1898
Peru State C. Peru, Nebr. 68421; 1867
Pfeiffer C. Misenheimer, N.C. 28109; 1887
Philadelphia, Comm. C. of Philadelphia, Pa. 19107; junior, 1965
Philadelphia C. of Art Philadelphia, Pa. 19102; 1876
Philadelphia C. of Bible Philadelphia, Pa. 19103; 1913
Philadelphia C. of Pharmacy and Science Philadelphia, Pa. 19104; 1821
Philadelphia C. of Textiles and Science Philadelphia, Pa. 19144; 1884
Philadelphia Musical Acad. Philadelphia, Pa. 19103; 1870
Philander Smith C. Little Rock, Ark. 72203; 1868
Phillips County Comm. C. Helena, Ark. 72342; junior, 1965
Phillips U. Enid, Okla. 73701; 1906
Piedmont Bible C. Winston-Salem, N.C. 27101; 1945
Piedmont C. Demorest, Ga. 30535; 1897
Pikeville C. Pikeville, Ky. 41501; 1889
Pima Comm. C. Tucson, Ariz. 85709; junior, 1967
Pinebrook Junior C. East Stroudsburg, Pa. 18301; 1950
Pine Manor Junior C. Chestnut Hill, Mass. 02167; 1911
Pittsburgh, U. of Pittsburgh, Pa. 15213; 1787
Pitt Technical Inst. Greenville, N.C. 27834; junior, 1961
Pitzer C. Claremont, Calif. 91711; 1964
Plano, U. of Plano, Tex. 75074; 1964
Platte Junior C. Columbus, Nebr. 68601; 1967
Plymouth State C. Plymouth, N.H. 03264; 1871
Point Park C. Pittsburgh, Pa. 15222; 1933
Polk Comm. C. Winter Haven, Fla. 33880; junior, 1964
Polytechnic Inst. of Brooklyn Brooklyn, N.Y. 11201; 1854
Pomona C. Claremont, Calif. 91711; 1887
Pontifical C. Josephinum Worthington, Ohio 43085; 1888
Porterville C. Porterville, Calif. 93257; junior, 1927
Portland, U. of Portland, Oreg. 97203; 1901
Portland Comm. C. Portland, Oreg. 97201; junior, 1961
Portland State U. Portland, Oreg. 97207; 1946
Post Junior C. Waterbury, Conn. 06708; 1890
Potomac State C. of West Virginia U. Keyser, W.Va. 26726; junior, 1901
Prairie State C. Chicago Heights, Ill. 60411; junior, 1958
Prairie View A. & M. C. Prairie View, Tex. 77445; 1876
Pratt Comm. Junior C. Pratt, Kans. 67124; 1938
Pratt Inst. Brooklyn, N.Y. 11205; 1887
Prentiss Normal and Industrial Inst. Prentiss, Miss. 39474; junior, 1907
Presbyterian C. Clinton, S.C. 29325; 1880
Presbyterian Sch. of Christian Ed. Richmond, Va. 23227; 1914
Prescott C. Prescott, Ariz. 86301; 1966
Presentation C. Aberdeen, S.Dak. 57401; junior, 1922
Prince George's Comm. C. Largo, Md. 20870; junior, 1958
Princeton U. Princeton, N.J. 08540; 1746
Principia C., The Elsah, Ill. 62028; 1898

Providence C. Providence, R.I. 02918; 1917
Puerto Rico, U. of Río Piedras, Puerto Rico 00931; 1900
Puerto Rico Junior C. Río Piedras, Puerto Rico 00928; 1949
Puget Sound, U. of Tacoma, Wash. 98416; 1888
Purdue U. Lafayette, Ind. 47907; 1865
Queensborough Comm. C. Bayside, N.Y. 11364; junior, 1960
Queens C. Flushing, N.Y. 11367; 1937
Queens C. Charlotte, N.C. 28207; 1857
Quincy C. Quincy, Ill. 62301; 1860
Quincy Junior C. Quincy, Mass. 02169; 1958
Quinnipiac C. Hamden, Conn. 06518; 1929
Quinsigamond Comm. C. Worcester, Mass. 01605; junior, 1963
Rabbinical C. of Telshe Wickliffe, Ohio 44092; 1876
Radcliffe C. Cambridge, Mass. 02138; 1879
Radford C. Radford, Va. 24141; 1910
Rainy River State Junior C. International Falls, Minn. 56649; 1967
Ramapo C. of New Jersey Mahwah, N.J. 07430; 1971
Randolph-Macon C. Ashland, Va. 23005; 1830
Randolph-Macon Woman's C. Lynchburg, Va. 24504; 1891
Randolph Technical Inst. Asheboro, N.C. 27203; junior, 1962
Rangely C. Rangely, Colo. 81648; junior, 1962
Ranger Junior C. Ranger, Tex. 76470; 1926
Redlands, U. of Redlands, Calif. 92373; 1907
Redwoods, C. of the Eureka, Calif. 95501; junior, 1964
Reed C. Portland, Oreg. 97202; 1904
Reedley C. Reedley, Calif. 93654; junior, 1926
Reformed Bible C. Grand Rapids, Mich. 49506; 1940
Regis C. Denver, Colo. 80221; 1877
Regis C. Weston, Mass. 02193; 1927
Reinhardt C. Waleska, Ga. 30183; junior, 1883
Rend Lake C. Ina, Ill. 62846; junior, 1956
Rensselaer Polytechnic Inst. Troy, N.Y. 12181; 1824
Rhode Island, U. of Kingston, R.I. 02881; 1892
Rhode Island C. Providence, R.I. 02908; 1854
Rhode Island Junior C. Providence, R.I. 02908; 1964
Rhode Island Sch. of Design Providence, R.I. 02903; 1877
Richard Stockton State C. Pomona, N.J. 08240; 1971
Rice U. — see WILLIAM MARSH RICE U.
Richmond, U. of Richmond, Va. 23173; 1840
Richmond Technical Inst. Hamlet, N.C. 28345; junior, 1964
Ricker C. Houlton, Me. 04730; 1848
Ricks C. Rexburg, Idaho 83440; junior, 1888
Rider C. Trenton, N.J. 08602; 1865
Rio Grande C. Rio Grande, Ohio 45674; 1876
Rio Hondo C. Whittier, Calif. 90608; junior, 1963
Ripon C. Ripon, Wis. 54971; 1850
Riverside City C. Riverside, Calif. 92506; junior, 1916
Rivier C. Nashua, N.H. 03060; 1933
Roanoke C. Salem, Va. 24153; 1842
Robert Morris C. Carthage, Ill. 62321; junior, 1965
Robert Morris C. Coraopolis, Pa. 15108; 1921
Roberts Wesleyan C. Rochester, N.Y. 14624; 1866
Rochester, U. of Rochester, N.Y. 14627; 1850
Rochester Inst. of Tech. Rochester, N.Y. 14623; 1829
Rochester State Junior C. Rochester, Minn. 55901; 1915
Rockford C. Rockford, Ill. 61101; 1847
Rockhurst C. Kansas City, Mo. 64110; 1910
Rockingham Comm. C. Wentworth, N.C. 27375; junior, 1964
Rockland Comm. C. Suffern, N.Y. 10901; junior, 1959
Rockmont C. Denver, Colo. 80226; 1914
Rock Valley C. Rockford, Ill. 61101; junior, 1964
Rocky Mountain C. Billings, Mont. 59102; 1883
Rogers C. Maryknoll, N.Y. 10545; 1931
Roger Williams C. Bristol, R.I. 02809; 1919
Rollins C. Winter Park, Fla. 32789; 1885
Roosevelt U. Chicago, Ill. 60605; 1945
Rosary C. River Forest, Ill. 60305; 1848
Rosary Hill C. Buffalo, N.Y. 14226; 1948
Rose-Hulman Inst. of Tech. Terre Haute, Ind. 47803; 1874
Rosemont C. Rosemont, Pa. 19010; 1921
Rowan Technical Inst. Salisbury, N.C. 28144; junior, 1961
Royalton C. South Royalton, Vt. 05068; 1965
Russell C. Burlingame, Calif. 94010; 1928
Russell Sage C. Troy, N.Y. 12180; 1916
Rust C. Holly Springs, Miss. 38635; 1866
Rutgers-The State U. New Brunswick, N.J. 08903; 1766
Sacramento City C. Sacramento, Calif. 95822; junior, 1916
Sacred Heart, C. of the Santurce, Puerto Rico 00914; 1935
Sacred Heart C. Belmont, N.C. 28012; 1892
Sacred Heart Novitiate Monroe, Mich. 48161; 1949
Sacred Hearts, C. of the Fall River, Mass. 02720; 1934
Sacred Heart Sem. Detroit, Mich. 48206; 1919
Sacred Heart U. Bridgeport, Conn. 06604; 1963
Saddleback C. Mission Viejo, Calif. 92675; junior, 1967
Saginaw Valley C. University Center, Mich. 48710; 1963
Saint Alphonsus C. Suffield, Conn. 06078; 1963
Saint Ambrose C. Davenport, Iowa 52803; 1882
Saint Andrews Presbyterian C. Laurinburg, N.C. 28352; 1857
Saint Anselm's C. Manchester, N.H. 03102; 1889
Saint Anthony Sem. Hudson, N.H. 03051; 1956
Saint Augustine's C. Raleigh, N.C. 27602; 1867
Saint Basil's C. Stamford, Conn. 06902; 1939
Saint Benedict, C. of St. Joseph, Minn. 56374; 1913
Saint Bernard C. St. Bernard, Ala. 35138; 1892
Saint Bonaventure U. St. Bonaventure, N.Y. 14778; 1859
Saint Catharine C. St. Catharine, Ky. 40061; junior, 1932
Saint Catherine, C. of St. Paul, Minn. 55116; 1906
Saint Charles Borromeo Sem. Philadelphia, Pa, 19151; 1832
Saint Clair County Comm. C. Port Huron, Mich. 48060; junior, 1923
Saint Cloud State C. St. Cloud, Minn. 56301; 1866
Saint Edward's U. Austin, Tex. 78704; 1876
Saint Elizabeth, C. of Convent Station, N.J. 07961; 1899
Saint Fidelis C. Herman, Pa. 16039; 1877
Saint Francis, C. of Joliet, Ill. 60435; 1874
Saint Francis C. Fort Wayne, Ind. 46808; 1890
Saint Francis C. Biddeford, Me. 04005; 1953
Saint Francis C. Brooklyn, N.Y. 11201; 1858
Saint Francis C. Loretto, Pa. 15940; 1847
Saint Francis de Sales C. Milwaukee, Wis. 53207; 1856
Saint Gertrude, C. of Cottonwood, Idaho 83522; junior, 1956
Saint Gregory's C. Shawnee, Okla. 74801; junior, 1915
Saint Hyacinth C. and Sem. Granby, Mass. 01033; 1957
Saint John C. of Cleveland Cleveland, Ohio 44114; 1928
Saint John Fisher C. Rochester, N.Y. 14618; 1952
Saint John's C. Camarillo, Calif. 93010; 1939
Saint John's C. Winfield, Kans. 67156; junior, 1893
Saint John's C. Annapolis, Md. 21404; 1696
Saint Johns River Junior C. Palatka, Fla. 32077; 1958
Saint John's Sem. Brighton, Mass. 02135; 1884
Saint John's U. Collegeville, Minn. 56321; 1857
Saint John's U. Jamaica, N.Y. 11432; 1870
Saint John Vianney Minor Sem. Miami, Fla. 33165; junior, 1960
Saint John Vianney Sem. East Aurora, N.Y. 14052; 1961
Saint Joseph C. West Hartford, Conn. 06117; 1925
Saint Joseph C. Emmitsburg, Md. 21727; 1809
Saint Joseph C. Old Bennington, Vt. 05201; junior, 1926
Saint Joseph C. of Florida Jensen Beach, Fla. 33457; junior, 1957
Saint Joseph's C. Rensselaer, Ind. 47978; 1889
Saint Joseph's C. North Windham, Me. 04062; 1915
Saint Joseph's C. Brooklyn, N.Y. 11205; 1916
Saint Joseph's C. Philadelphia, Pa. 19131; 1851
Saint Joseph Sem. St. Benedict, La. 70457; 1891
Saint Joseph's Sem. and C. Yonkers, N.Y. 10704; 1839
Saint Joseph the Provider, C. of Rutland, Vt. 05701; 1957
Saint Lawrence U. Canton, N.Y. 13617; 1856
Saint Leo C. St. Leo, Fla. 33574; 1959
Saint Louis C. of Pharmacy St. Louis, Mo. 63110, 1864
Saint Louis Inst. of Music Saint Louis, Mo. 63105; 1924
Saint Louis U. St. Louis, Mo. 63103; 1818
Saint Martin's C. Olympia, Wash. 98501; 1895
Saint Mary, C. of Omaha, Nebr. 68124; 1923
Saint Mary C. Leavenworth, Kans. 66048; 1882
Saint Mary of the Plains C. Dodge City, Kans. 67801; 1952
Saint Mary-of-the-Woods C. Saint Mary-of-the-Woods, Ind. 47876; 1840
Saint Mary's C. Notre Dame, Ind. 46556; 1844
Saint Mary's C. St. Mary, Ky. 40063; 1821
Saint Mary's C. Orchard Lake, Mich. 48034; 1885
Saint Mary's C. Winona, Minn. 55987; 1912
Saint Mary's C. of California Moraga, Calif. 94575; 1863
Saint Mary's C. of Maryland St. Mary's City, Md. 20686; 1839
Saint Mary's C. of O'Fallon O'Fallon, Mo. 63366; junior, 1929
Saint Mary's Dominican C. New Orleans, La. 70118; 1910
Saint Mary's Junior C. Minneapolis, Minn. 55406; 1964
Saint Mary's Junior C. Raleigh, N.C. 27602; 1842
Saint Mary's Sem. Cleveland, Ohio 44108; 1848
Saint Mary's Sem. and C. Perryville, Mo. 63775; 1818
Saint Mary's Sem. and U. Baltimore, Md. 21210; 1791
Saint Mary's U. of San Antonio San Antonio, Tex. 78228; 1852
Saint Meinrad C. St. Meinrad, Ind. 47577; 1854
Saint Michael's C. Winooski, Vt. 05404; 1903
Saint Norbert C. West De Pere, Wis. 54178; 1898
Saint Olaf C. Northfield, Minn. 55057; 1874
Saint Patrick's C. Mountain View, Calif. 94040; 1898
Saint Paul Bible C. St. Bonifacius, Minn. 55375; 1916
Saint Paul's C. Washington, D.C. 20017; 1889
Saint Paul's C. Concordia, Mo. 64020; junior, 1883
Saint Paul's C. Lawrenceville, Va. 23868; 1888
Saint Paul Sem. St. Paul, Minn. 55101; 1895
Saint Petersburg Junior C. St. Petersburg, Fla. 33733; 1927
Saint Peter's C. Jersey City, N.J. 07306; 1872
Saint Philip's C. San Antonio, Tex. 78203; junior, 1898
Saint Pius X Sem. Garrison, N.Y. 10524; 1956
Saint Rose, C. of Albany, N.Y. 12203; 1920
Saint Scholastica, C. of Duluth, Minn. 55811; 1912
Saints C. Lexington, Miss. 39095; junior, 1918
Saint Teresa, C. of Winona, Minn. 55987; 1907
Saint Thomas, C. of St. Paul, Minn. 55101; 1885
Saint Thomas, U. of Houston, Tex. 77006; 1947
Saint Thomas Aquinas C. Sparkill, N.Y. 10976; 1952
Saint Thomas Sem. Denver, Colo. 80210; 1906
Saint Thomas Sem. Bloomfield, Conn. 06002; junior, 1897
Saint Vincent C. Latrobe, Pa. 15650; 1846
Saint Xavier C. Chicago, Ill. 60655; 1846
Salem C. Winston-Salem, N.C. 27108; 1772
Salem C. Salem, W.Va. 26426; 1888
Salem State C. Salem, Mass. 01970; 1854
Salesian C. North Haledon, N.J. 07508; junior, 1948
Salisbury State C. Salisbury, Md. 21801; 1925
Salve Regina C. Newport, R.I. 02840; 1934
Samford U. Birmingham, Ala. 35209; 1842
Sam Houston State U. Huntsville, Tex. 77340; 1879
San Antonio C. San Antonio, Tex. 78212; junior, 1925
San Bernardino Valley C. San Bernardino, Calif. 92403; junior, 1926
Sandhills Comm. C. Southern Pines, N.C. 28387; junior, 1963
San Diego City C. San Diego, Calif. 92101; junior, 1914
San Diego C. for Men, U. of San Diego, Calif. 92110; 1949
San Diego C. for Women San Diego, Calif. 92110; 1952
San Diego Evening C. San Diego, Calif. 92101; junior, 1962
San Diego Mesa C. San Diego, Calif. 92111; junior, 1964
San Francisco, U. of San Francisco, Calif. 94117; 1855
San Francisco Art Inst. C. San Francisco, Calif. 94133; 1874
San Francisco C. of Mortuary Science San Francisco, Calif. 94109; junior, 1930

San Francisco Conservatory of Music San Francisco, Calif. 94122; 1917
Sangamon State U. Springfield, Ill. 62703; 1969
San Jacinto C. Pasadena, Tex. 77505; junior, 1961
San Joaquin Delta C. Stockton, Calif. 95204; junior, 1935
San Jose Bible C. San Jose, Calif. 95108; 1939
San Jose City C. San Jose, Calif. 95114; junior, 1921
San Mateo, C. of San Mateo, Calif. 94402; junior, 1922
Santa Ana C. Santa Ana, Calif. 92706; junior, 1915
Santa Barbara City C. Santa Barbara, Calif. 93105; junior, 1946
Santa Clara, U. of Santa Clara, Calif. 95053; 1851
Santa Fe, C. of Santa Fe, N.Mex. 87501; 1947
Santa Fe Comm. C. Gainesville, Fla. 32601; junior, 1965
Santa Monica C. Santa Monica, Calif. 90406; junior, 1929
Santa Rosa Junior C. Santa Rosa, Calif. 95401; 1918
Sarah Lawrence C. Bronxville, N.Y. 10708; 1926
Sauk Valley C. Dixon, Ill. 61021; junior, 1965
Savannah State C. Savannah, Ga. 31404; 1890
Sayre Junior C. Sayre, Okla. 73662; 1938
Scarritt C. for Christian Workers Nashville, Tenn. 37203; 1924
Schenectady County Comm. C. Schenectady, N.Y. 12305; junior, 1967
Schoolcraft C. Livonia, Mich. 48151; junior, 1961
Schreiner Inst. Kerrville, Tex. 78028; junior, 1923
Scranton, U. of Scranton, Pa. 18510; 1888
Scripps C. Claremont, Calif. 91711; 1926
S. D. Bishop State Junior C. Mobile, Ala. 36603; 1965
Seat of Wisdom C. Litchfield, Conn. 06759; 1958
Seattle Central Comm. C. Seattle, Wash. 98122; junior, 1965
Seattle Pacific C. Seattle, Wash. 98119; 1891
Seattle U. Seattle, Wash. 98122; 1892
Selma U. Selma, Ala. 36701; 1878
Seminole Junior C. Sanford, Fla. 32771; 1965
Seminole Junior C. Seminole, Okla. 74868; 1931
Sequoias, C. of the Visalia, Calif. 93277; junior, 1926
Seton Hall U. South Orange, N.J. 07079; 1856
Seton Hill C. Greensburg, Pa. 15601; 1883
Seward County Comm. Junior C. Liberal, Kans. 67901; 1967
Shasta C. Redding, Calif. 96001; junior, 1949
Shaw C. at Detroit Detroit, Mich. 48202; 1962
Shaw U. Raleigh, N.C. 27602; 1865
Shawnee C. Ullin, Ill. 62956; junior, 1967
Sheboygan County Teachers C. Sheboygan Falls, Wis. 53085; junior, 1909
Sheldon Jackson C. Sitka, Alaska 99835; junior, 1878
Shenandoah C. and Shenandoah Conservatory of Music Winchester, Va. 22601; 1875
Shepherd C. Shepherdstown, W.Va. 25443; 1871
Sheridan C. Sheridan, Wyo. 82801; junior, 1948
Shimer C. Mount Carroll, Ill. 61053; 1853
Shippensburg State C. Shippensburg, Pa. 17257; 1871
Shoreline Comm. C. Seattle, Wash. 98133; junior, 1964
Shorter C. North Little Rock, Ark. 72114; 1884
Shorter C. Rome, Ga. 30161; 1873
Siena C. Loudonville, N.Y. 12211; 1937
Siena C. Memphis, Tenn. 38117; 1921
Siena Heights C. Adrian, Mich. 49221; 1919
Sierra C. Rocklin, Calif. 95677; junior, 1914
Simmons C. Boston, Mass. 02115; 1899
Simmons U. Louisville, Ky. 40210; 1879
Simpson C. San Francisco, Calif. 94134; 1921
Simpson C. Indianola, Iowa 50125; 1860
Sinclair Comm. C. Dayton, Ohio 45402; junior, 1887
Sioux Empire C. Hawarden, Iowa 51023; junior, 1967
Sioux Falls C. Sioux Falls, S.Dak. 57101; 1883
Siskiyous, C. of the Weed, Calif. 96094; junior, 1959
Skagit Valley C. Mount Vernon, Wash. 98273; junior, 1926
Skidmore C. Saratoga Springs, N.Y. 12866; 1911
Skyline C. San Bruno, Calif. 94066; junior, 1969
Slippery Rock State C. Slippery Rock, Pa. 16057; 1889
Smith C. Northampton, Mass. 01060; 1875
Snead State Junior C. Boaz, Ala. 35957; 1898
Snow C. Ephraim, Utah 84627; junior, 1888
Solano C. Suisun City, Calif. 94585; junior, 1945
Somerset County C. Somerville, N.J. 08876; junior, 1968
South, U. of the Sewanee, Tenn. 37375; 1857
South Alabama, U. of Mobile, Ala. 36608; 1963
South Carolina, U. of Columbia, S.C. 29208; 1801
South Carolina State C. Orangeburg, S.C. 29115; 1896
South Central Comm. C. New Haven, Conn. 06511; junior, 1967
South Dakota, U. of Vermillion, S.Dak. 57069; 1862
South Dakota at Springfield, U. of 57062; 1881
South Dakota Sch. of Mines and Tech. Rapid City, S.Dak. 57701; 1885
South Dakota State U. Brookings, S.Dak. 57006; 1881
Southeastern Baptist C. Laurel, Miss. 39440; junior, 1948
Southeastern Bible C. Birmingham, Ala. 35205; 1934
South-Eastern Bible C. Lakeland, Fla. 33801; 1935
Southeastern Christian C. Winchester, Ky. 40391; junior, 1949
Southeastern Comm C. Burlington, Iowa 52601; junior, 1920
Southeastern Comm. C. Whiteville, N.C. 28472; junior, 1964
Southeastern Illinois C. Harrisburg, Ill. 62946; junior, 1961
Southeastern Louisiana U. Hammond, La. 70401; 1925
Southeastern Massachusetts U. North Dartmouth, Mass. 02747; 1895
Southeastern State C. Durant, Okla. 74701; 1909
Southeastern U. Washington, D.C. 20006; 1879
Southeast Missouri State C. Cape Girardeau, Mo. 63701; 1873
Southern Baptist C. Walnut Ridge, Ark. 72476; junior, 1941
Southern Bible C. Houston, Tex. 77028; 1958
Southern California, U. of Los Angeles, Calif. 90007; 1879
Southern California C. Costa Mesa, Calif. 92626; 1920
Southern C. of Optometry Memphis, Tenn. 38104; 1932
Southern Colorado State C. Pueblo, Colo. 81005; 1933
Southern Connecticut State C. New Haven, Conn. 06515; 1893
Southern Idaho, C. of Twin Falls, Idaho 83301; junior, 1964
Southern Illinois U. Carbondale, Ill. 62901; 1874
Southern Maine Vocational Technical Inst. South Portland, Me. 04106; junior, 1946
Southern Methodist U. Dallas, Tex. 75222; 1910
Southern Missionary C. Collegedale, Tenn. 37315; 1893
Southern Mississippi, U. of Hattiesburg, Miss. 39401; 1910
Southern Oregon C. Ashland, Oreg. 97520; 1926
Southern Sem. Junior C. Buena Vista, Va. 24416; 1868
Southern State C. Magnolia, Ark. 71753; 1909
Southern Union State Junior C. Wadley, Ala. 36276; 1934
Southern U. and A. & M. C. Baton Rouge, La. 70813; 1880
Southern Utah State C. Cedar City, Utah 84720; 1897
Southern West Virginia Comm. C. Williamson, W.Va. 25661; junior, 1971
South Florida, U. of Tampa, Fla. 33620; 1956
South Florida Junior C. Avon Park, Fla. 33825; 1965
South Georgia C. Douglas, Ga. 31533; junior, 1906
South Plains C. Levelland, Tex. 79336; junior, 1958
Southside Virginia Comm. C. Alberta, Va. 23821; junior, 1969
South Texas Junior C. Houston, Tex. 77002; 1948
Southwest, C. of the Hobbs, N.Mex. 88240; 1957
Southwest Baptist C. Bolivar, Mo. 65613; 1878
Southwestern at Memphis Memphis, Tenn. 38112; 1848
Southwestern Christian C. Terrell, Tex. 75160; junior, 1950
Southwestern C. Chula Vista, Calif. 92010; junior, 1961
Southwestern C. Winfield, Kans. 67156; 1885
Southwestern C. Oklahoma City, Okla. 73127; junior, 1946
Southwestern Comm. C. Creston, Iowa 50801; junior, 1926
Southwestern Junior C. of the Assemblies of God Waxahachie, Tex. 75165; 1927
Southwestern Louisiana, The U. of Lafayette, La. 70501; 1900
Southwestern Michigan C. Dowagiac, Mich. 49047; junior, 1964
Southwestern Oregon Comm. C. Coos Bay, Oreg. 97420; junior, 1961
Southwestern State C. Weatherford, Okla. 73096; 1901
Southwestern Technical Inst. Sylva, N.C. 28779; junior, 1964
Southwestern Union C. Keene, Tex. 76059; 1893
Southwestern U. Los Angeles, Calif. 90015; 1911
Southwestern U. Georgetown, Tex. 78626; 1840
Southwest Minnesota State C. Marshall, Minn. 56258; 1963
Southwest Mississippi Junior C. Summit, Miss. 39666; 1918
Southwest Missouri State C. Springfield, Mo. 65802; 1905
Southwest Texas Junior C. Uvalde, Tex. 78801; 1946
Southwest Texas State U. San Marcos, Tex. 78666; 1899
Southwest Virginia Comm. C. Richlands, Va. 24641; junior, 1968
Southwood C. Salemburg, N.C. 28385; junior, 1875
Spalding C. Louisville, Ky. 40203; 1829
Spartanburg County Technical Ed. Center Spartanburg, S.C. 29303; junior, 1961
Spartanburg Junior C. Spartanburg, S.C. 29301; 1911
Spelman C. Atlanta, Ga. 30314; 1881
Spertus C. of Judaica Chicago, Ill. 60605; 1925
Spokane Comm. C. Spokane, Wash. 99202; junior, 1963
Spokane Falls Comm. C. Spokane Falls, Wash. 99204; junior, 1963
Spoon River C. Canton, Ill. 61520; junior, 1959
Spring Arbor C. Spring Arbor, Mich. 49283; 1873
Springfield C. Springfield, Mass. 01109; 1885
Springfield C. in Illinois Springfield, Ill. 62702; junior, 1929
Springfield Technical Comm. C. Springfield, Mass. 01105; junior, 1965
Spring Garden C. Philadelphia, Pa. 19118; 1850
Spring Hill C. Mobile, Ala. 36608; 1830
Stanford U. Stanford, Calif. 94305; 1885
State Fair Comm. C. Sedalia, Mo. 65301; junior, 1966
Staten Island Comm. C. Staten Island, N.Y. 10301; junior, 1956
Stephen F. Austin State U. Nacogdoches, Tex. 75961; 1917
Stephens C. Columbia, Mo. 65201; 1833
Sterling C. Sterling, Kans. 67579; 1887
Stetson U. De Land, Fla. 32720; 1883
Steubenville, C. of Steubenville, Ohio 43952; 1946
Stevens C. Hubbardston, Mass. 01452; junior, 1895
Stevens Henager C. Salt Lake City, Utah 84102; junior, 1907
Stevens Inst. of Tech. Hoboken, N.J. 07030; 1867
Stillman C. Tuscaloosa, Ala. 35401; 1876
Stonehill C. North Easton, Mass. 02356; 1948
Stratford C. Danville, Va. 24541; 1852
Strayer C. Washington, D.C. 20005; 1904
Sue Bennett C. London, Ky. 40741; junior, 1896
Suffolk County Comm. C. Lake Ronkonkoma, N.Y. 11779; junior, 1960
Suffolk U. Boston, Mass. 02114; 1906
Sullins C. Bristol, Va. 24201; junior, 1870
Sullivan County Comm. C. South Fallsburg, N.Y. 12779; junior, 1963
Sulpician Sem. of the Northwest Kenmore, Wash. 98028; 1930
Sul Ross State U. Alpine, Tex. 79830; 1920
Sumter Area Technical Ed. Center Sumter, S.C. 29105; junior, 1961
Suomi C. Hancock, Mich. 49930; junior, 1896
Surry Comm. C. Dobson, N.C. 27017; junior, 1965
Susquehanna U. Selinsgrove, Pa. 17870; 1858
Swarthmore C. Swarthmore, Pa. 19081; 1864
Sweet Briar C. Sweet Briar, Va. 24595; 1901
Syracuse U. Syracuse, N.Y. 13210; 1870
Syracuse U., Utica C. Utica, N.Y. 13502; 1946
Tabor C. Hillsboro, Kans. 67063; 1908
Tacoma Comm. C. Tacoma, Wash. 98465; junior, 1965
Taft C. Taft, Calif. 93268; junior, 1922
Tahoe C. Tahoe Paradise, Calif. 95705; 1967
Talladega C. Talladega, Ala. 35160; 1867
Tallahassee Comm. C. Tallahassee, Fla. 32304; junior, 1965

Tampa, U. of Tampa, Fla. 33606; 1931
Tarkio C. Tarkio, Mo. 64491; 1883
Tarleton State C. Stephenville, Tex. 76401; 1899
Tarrant County Junior C. Fort Worth, Tex. 76102; 1965
Taylor U. Upland, Ind. 46989; 1846
Teachers C. New York, N.Y. 10027; 1888
Temple Buell C. Denver, Colo. 80220; 1909
Temple Junior C. Temple, Tex. 76501; 1926
Temple U. Philadelphia, Pa. 19122; 1884
Tennessee at Chattanooga, U. of 37403; 1886
Tennessee at Knoxville, U. of 37916; 1794
Tennessee at Martin, U. of 38237; 1900
Tennessee State U. Nashville, Tenn. 37203; 1909
Tennessee Technological U. Cookeville, Tenn. 38501; 1915
Tennessee Temple C. Chattanooga, Tenn. 37404; 1946
Tennessee Wesleyan C. Athens, Tenn. 37303; 1857
Texarkana C. Texarkana, Tex. 75501; junior, 1927
Texas, U. of Austin, Tex. 78712; 1881
Texas A. & M. U. College Station, Tex. 77843; 1876
Texas Arts and Industries U. Kingsville, Tex. 78363; 1917
Texas at Arlington, U. of 76010; 1895
Texas at El Paso, U. of 79999; 1913
Texas Christian U. Fort Worth, Tex. 76129; 1873
Texas C. Tyler, Tex. 75701; 1894
Texas Lutheran C. Seguin, Tex. 78155; 1891
Texas Southern U. Houston, Tex. 77004; 1927
Texas Southmost C. Brownsville, Tex. 78520; junior, 1926
Texas State Technical Inst. Waco, Tex. 76705; junior, 1965
Texas Tech U. Lubbock, Tex. 79409; 1923
Texas Wesleyan C. Fort Worth, Tex. 76105; 1890
Texas Woman's U. Denton, Tex. 76204; 1901
Thames Valley State Technical C. Norwich, Conn. 06360; junior, 1963
Theodore A. Lawson State Junior C. Birmingham, Ala. 35228; 1963
Thiel C. Greenville, Pa. 16125; 1866
Thomas C. Waterville, Me. 04901; 1894
Thomas Jefferson U. Philadelphia, Pa. 19107; 1825
Thomas More C. Fort Mitchell, Ky. 41017; 1921
Thomas Nelson Comm. C. Hampton, Va. 23366; junior, 1967
Thornton Comm. C. South Holland, Ill. 60473; junior, 1927
Three Rivers Comm. C. Poplar Bluff, Mo. 63901; junior, 1966
Tidewater Comm. C. Portsmouth, Va. 23703; junior, 1958
Tiffin U. Tiffin, Ohio 44883; 1924
Tift C. Forsyth, Ga. 31029; 1847
Toccoa Falls Inst. Toccoa Falls, Ga. 30577; 1911
Toledo, U. of Toledo, Ohio 43606; 1872
Tolentine C. Olympia Fields, Ill. 60461; 1958
Tombrock C. West Paterson, N.J. 07424; junior, 1956
Tomlinson C. Cleveland, Tenn. 37311; junior, 1966
Tompkins-Cortland Comm. C. Groton, N.Y. 13073; junior, 1967
Tougaloo C. Tougaloo, Miss. 39174; 1869
Towson State C. Towson, Md. 21204; 1866
Transylvania U. Lexington, Ky. 40508; 1780
Treasure Valley Comm. C. Ontario, Oreg. 97914; junior, 1962
Trenton Junior C. Trenton, Mo. 64683; 1925
Trenton State C. Trenton, N.J. 08625; 1855
Trevecca Nazarene C. Nashville, Tenn. 37210; 1901
Trinidad State Junior C. Trinidad, Colo. 81082; 1925
Trinity Christian C. Palos Heights, Ill. 60463; 1959
Trinity C. Hartford, Conn. 06106; 1823
Trinity C. Washington, D.C. 20017; 1897
Trinity C. Deerfield, Ill. 60015; 1897
Trinity C. Burlington, Vt. 05401; 1925
Trinity U. San Antonio, Tex. 78212; 1869
Tri-State C. Angola, Ind. 46703; 1884
Triton C. River Grove, Ill. 60171; junior, 1964
Trocaire C. Buffalo, N.Y. 14220; junior, 1958
Troy State U. Troy, Ala. 36081; 1887
Truett McConnell C. Cleveland, Ga. 30528; junior, 1947
Tufts U. Medford, Mass. 02155; 1852
Tulane U. of Louisiana New Orleans, La. 70118; 1834
Tulsa, U. of Tulsa, Okla. 74104; 1894
Tunxis Comm. C. Farmington, Conn. 06032; junior, 1970
Tusculum C. Greeneville, Tenn. 37743; 1794
Tuskegee Inst. Tuskegee Institute, Ala. 36088; 1881
Tyler Junior C. Tyler, Tex. 75701; 1926
Ulster County Comm. C. Stone Ridge, N.Y. 12484; junior, 1963
Umpqua Comm. C. Roseburg, Oreg. 97470; junior, 1964
Union C. Barbourville, Ky. 40906; 1879
Union C. Lincoln, Nebr. 68506; 1891
Union C. Cranford, N.J. 07016; junior, 1933
Union C. and U. Schenectady, N.Y. 12308; 1795
Union U. Jackson, Tenn. 38301; 1834
United States Air Force Acad. Colorado Springs, Colo. 80840; 1954
United States Coast Guard Acad. New London, Conn. 06320; 1876
United States International U. San Diego, Calif. 92101; 1924
United States Merchant Marine Acad. Kings Point, N.Y. 11024; 1938
United States Military Acad. West Point, N.Y. 10996; 1802
United States Naval Acad. Annapolis, Md. 21402; 1845
United States Naval Postgraduate Sch. Monterey, Calif. 93940; 1909
United Wesleyan C. Allentown, Pa. 18103; 1921
Unity C. Unity, Me. 04988; 1966
Upper Iowa U. Fayette, Iowa 52142; 1857
Upsala C. East Orange, N.J. 07019; 1893
Urbana C. Urbana, Ohio 43078; 1850
Ursinus C. Collegeville, Pa. 19426; 1869
Ursuline C. Cleveland, Ohio 44124; 1871
Utah, U. of Salt Lake City, Utah 84112; 1850
Utah State U. Logan, Utah 84321; 1888
Utah Technical C. at Provo 84601; junior, 1941
Utah Technical C. at Salt Lake Salt Lake City, Utah 84107; junior, 1947
Utica Junior C. Utica, Miss. 39175; 1903
Valdosta State C. Valdosta, Ga. 31601; 1906
Valencia Comm. C. Orlando, Fla. 32802; junior, 1967
Valley City State C. Valley City, N.Dak. 58072; 1889
Valley Forge Military Junior C. Wayne, Pa. 19087; 1928
Valparaiso Technical Inst. Valparaiso, Ind. 46383; 1934
Valparaiso U. Valparaiso, Ind. 46383; 1859
Vanderbilt U. Nashville, Tenn. 37203; 1872
Vassar C. Poughkeepsie, N.Y. 12601; 1861
Vennard C. University Park, Iowa 52595; 1910
Ventura C. Ventura, Calif. 93003; junior, 1925
Vermilion State Junior C. Ely, Minn. 55731; 1922
Vermont, U. of Burlington, Vt. 05401; 1791
Vermont C. Montpelier, Vt. 05602; 1834
Vermont Technical C. Randolph Center, Vt. 05061; junior, 1957
Vernon Court Junior C. Newport, R.I. 02840; 1963
Victoria C. Victoria, Tex. 77901; junior, 1925
Victor Valley C. Victorville, Calif. 92392; junior, 1961
Villa Julie C. Stevenson, Md. 21153; junior, 1947
Villa Maria C. Erie, Pa. 16505; 1925
Villa Maria C. of Buffalo Buffalo, N.Y. 14225; junior, 1960
Villanova U. Villanova, Pa. 19085; 1842
Vincennes U. Vincennes, Ind. 47591; junior, 1804
Virginia, U. of Charlottesville, Va. 22903; 1819
Virginia Commonwealth U. Richmond, Va. 23220; 1838
Virginia Highlands Comm. C. Abingdon, Va. 24210; junior, 1967
Virginia Intermont C. Bristol, Va. 24201; 1884
Virginia Military Inst. Lexington, Va. 24450; 1839
Virginia Polytechnic Inst. and State U. Blacksburg, Va. 24061; 1872
Virginia C. Lynchburg, Va. 24501; junior, 1888
Virginia State C. Petersburg, Va. 23803; 1882
Virginia Union U. Richmond, Va. 23220; 1865
Virginia Wesleyan C. Norfolk, Va. 23502; 1961
Virginia Western Comm. C. Roanoke, Va. 24015; junior, 1966
Virgin Islands, C. of the St. Thomas, Virgin Islands 00802; 1963
Viterbo C. La Crosse, Wis. 54601; 1931
Voorhees C. Denmark, S.C. 29042; 1897
Wabash C. Crawfordsville, Ind. 47933; 1832
Wabash Valley C. Mt. Carmel, Ill. 62863; junior, 1961
Wadhams Hall Ogdensburg, N.Y. 13669; 1924
Wagner C. Staten Island, N.Y. 10301; 1883
Wake Forest U. Winston-Salem, N.C. 27109; 1834
Waldorf C. Forest City, Iowa 50436; junior, 1903
Walker C. Jasper, Ala. 35501; junior, 1938
Walla Walla C. College Place, Wash. 99324; 1892
Walla Walla Comm. C. Walla Walla, Wash. 99362; junior, 1967
Walsh C. Canton, Ohio 44720; 1960
Walters State Comm. C. Morristown, Tenn. 37814; junior, 1970
Warner Pacific C. Portland, Oreg. 97215; 1937
Warren Wilson C. Swannanoa, N.C. 28778; 1893
Wartburg C. Waverly, Iowa 50677; 1852
Washburn U. of Topeka Topeka, Kans. 66621; 1865
Washington, U. of Seattle, Wash. 98105; 1861
Washington and Jefferson C. Washington, Pa. 15301; 1780
Washington and Lee U. Lexington, Va. 24450; 1749
Washington Bible C. Lanham, Md. 20801; 1938
Washington C. Chestertown, Md. 21620; 1706
Washington State U. Pullman, Wash. 99163; 1890
Washington Technical Inst. Washington, D.C. 20008; junior, 1966
Washington U. St. Louis, Mo. 63130; 1853
Washtenaw Comm. C. Ann Arbor, Mich. 48107; junior, 1965
Waterbury State Technical C. Waterbury, Conn. 06708; junior, 1964
Waubonsee Comm. C. Sugar Grove, Ill. 60554; junior, 1966
Wayland Baptist C. Plainview, Tex. 79072; 1909
Wayne Comm. C. Goldsboro, N.C. 27530; junior, 1957
Wayne County Comm. C. Detroit, Mich. 48201; junior, 1968
Waynesburg C. Waynesburg, Pa. 15370; 1850
Wayne State C. Wayne, Nebr. 68787; 1891
Wayne State U. Detroit, Mich. 48202; 1868
Weatherford C. Weatherford, Tex. 76086; junior, 1869
Webber C. Babson Park, Fla. 33827; junior, 1927
Webb Inst. of Naval Architecture Glen Cove, N.Y. 11542; 1889
Weber State C. Ogden, Utah 84403; 1889
Webster C. St. Louis, Mo. 63119; 1915
Wellesley C. Wellesley, Mass. 02181; 1870
Wells C. Aurora, N.Y. 13026; 1868
Wenatchee Valley C. Wenatchee, Wash. 98801; junior, 1939
Wentworth Inst. Boston, Mass. 02115; junior, 1904
Wentworth Military Acad. Lexington, Mo. 64067; junior, 1880
Wesleyan C. Macon, Ga. 31201; 1836
Wesleyan U. Middletown, Conn. 06457; 1831
Wesley C. Dover, Del. 19901; junior, 1873
Westark Comm. C. Fort Smith, Ark. 72901; junior, 1928
Westbrook C. Portland, Me. 04103; junior, 1831
Westchester Comm. C. Valhalla, N.Y. 10595; junior, 1946
West Chester State C. West Chester, Pa. 19380; 1812
West Coast U. Los Angeles, Calif. 90005; 1909
Western Baptist Bible C. Salem, Oreg. 97302; 1946
Western Bible Inst. Morrison, Colo. 80465; 1948
Western Carolina U. Cullowhee, N.C. 28723; 1889
Western C. Oxford, Ohio 45056; 1853
Western Connecticut State C. Danbury, Conn. 06810; 1903
Western Illinois U. Macomb, Ill. 61455; 1899
Western Kentucky U. Bowling Green, Ky. 42101; 1906
Western Maryland C. Westminster, Md. 21157; 1867
Western Michigan U. Kalamazoo, Mich. 49001; 1903
Western Montana C. Dillon, Mont. 59725; 1893
Western New England C. Springfield, Mass. 01119; 1919

Western New Mexico U. Silver City, N.Mex. 88061; 1893
Western Piedmont Comm. C. Morganton, N.C. 28655; junior, 1964
Western State C. of Colorado Gunnison, Colo. 81230; 1901
Western States C. of Engineering Inglewood, Calif. 90301; 1946
Western Washington State C. Bellingham, Wash. 98225; 1893
Western Wisconsin Technical Inst. La Crosse, Wis. 54601; junior, 1912
Western Wyoming Comm. C. Rock Springs, Wyo. 82901; junior, 1959
Westfield State C. Westfield, Mass. 01085; 1839
West Florida, U. of Pensacola, Fla. 32504; 1967
West Georgia C. Carrollton, Ga. 30117; 1933
West Hills C. Coalinga, Calif. 93210; junior, 1932
West Liberty State C. West Liberty, W.Va. 26074; 1938
West Los Angeles C. Culver City, Calif. 90230; junior, 1968
Westmar C. Le Mars, Iowa 51031; 1900
Westminster Choir C. Princeton, N.J. 08540; 1926
Westminster C. Fulton, Mo. 65251; 1851
Westminster C. New Wilmington, Pa. 16142; 1852
Westminster C. Salt Lake City, Utah 84105; 1875
Westmont C. Santa Barbara, Calif. 93103; 1940
West Shore Comm. C. Scottville, Mich. 49454; junior, 1967
West Texas State U. Canyon, Tex. 79015; 1910
West Valley C. Campbell, Calif. 95008; junior, 1963
West Virginia Inst. of Tech. Montgomery, W.Va. 25136; 1895
West Virginia State C. Institute, W.Va. 25112; 1891
West Virginia U. Morgantown, W.Va. 26506; 1867
West Virginia Wesleyan C. Buckhannon, W.Va. 26201; 1890
Wharton County Junior C. Wharton, Tex. 77488; 1946
Wheaton C. Wheaton, Ill. 60187; 1853
Wheaton C. Norton, Mass. 02766; 1834
Wheeling C. Wheeling, W.Va. 26003; 1954
Wheelock C. Boston, Mass. 02215; 1889
White Pines C. Chester, N.H. 03036; junior, 1965
White Plains, C. of White Plains, N.Y. 10603; 1923
Whitman C. Walla Walla, Wash. 99362; 1859
Whittier C. Whittier, Calif. 90608; 1901
Whitworth C. Brookhaven, Miss. 39601; 1818
Whitworth C. Spokane, Wash. 99218; 1890
Wichita State U. Wichita, Kans. 67208; 1892
Widener C. Chester, Pa. 19013; 1821
Wilberforce U. Wilberforce, Ohio 45384; 1856
Wiley C. Marshall, Tex. 75670; 1873
Wilkes C. Wilkes-Barre, Pa. 18703; 1933
Wilkes Comm. C. Wilkesboro, N.C. 28697; junior, 1965
Willamette U. Salem, Oreg. 97301; 1842
William and Mary, C. of Williamsburg, Va. 23185; 1693
William Carey C. Hattiesburg, Miss. 39401; 1911
William Carter C. Goldsboro, N.C. 27530; 1952
William Jewell C. Liberty, Mo. 64068; 1849
William Marsh Rice U. Houston, Tex. 77001; 1891
William Paterson C. Wayne, N.J. 07470; 1855
William Penn C. Oskaloosa, Iowa 52577; 1873
William Rainey Harper C. Palatine, Ill. 60067; junior, 1965
Williams C. Williamstown, Mass. 01267; 1785
Williamsport Area Comm. C. Williamsport, Pa. 17701; junior, 1920
William Woods C. Fulton, Mo. 65251; 1870
Willmar State Junior C. Willmar, Minn. 56201; 1961
Wilmington C. New Castle, Del. 19720; 1967
Wilmington C. Wilmington, Ohio 45177; 1863
Wilson C. Chambersburg, Pa. 17201; 1869
Wilson County Technical Inst. Wilson, N.C. 27893; junior, 1958
Windham C. Putney, Vt. 05346; 1951
Wingate C. Wingate, N.C. 28174; junior, 1896
Winona State C. Winona, Minn. 55987; 1858
Winston-Salem State U. Winston-Salem, N.C. 27102; 1892
Winthrop C. Rock Hill, S.C. 29730; 1886
Wisconsin C. Conservatory Milwaukee, Wis. 53202; 1899
Wisconsin-Eau Claire, U. of 57401; 1916
Wisconsin-Green Bay, U. of 54305; 1969
Wisconsin-La Crosse, U. of 54601; 1909
Wisconsin-Madison, U. of 53706; 1836
Wisconsin-Milwaukee, U. of 53201; 1908
Wisconsin-Oshkosh, U. of 54901; 1871
Wisconsin-Parkside, U. of Kenosha, Wis. 53140; 1969
Wisconsin-Platteville, U. of 53818; 1866
Wisconsin-River Falls, U. of 54022; 1875
Wisconsin-Stevens Point, U. of 54481; 1894
Wisconsin-Stout, U. of Menomonie, Wis. 54751; 1893
Wisconsin-Superior, U. of 54880; 1896
Wisconsin-Whitewater, U. of 53190; 1868
Wittenberg U. Springfield, Ohio 45501; 1842
Wofford C. Spartanburg, S.C. 29301; 1854
Woodbury C. Los Angeles, Calif. 90017; 1884
Wood Junior C. Mathiston, Miss. 39752; 1886
Wooster, C. of Wooster, Ohio 44691; 1866
Worcester Junior C. Worcester, Mass. 01608; 1905
Worcester Polytechnic Inst. Worcester, Mass. 01609; 1865
Worcester State C. Worcester, Mass. 01620; 1871
Worthington State Junior C. Worthington, Minn. 56187; 1936
Wright State U. Fairborn, Ohio 45324; 1964
W.W. Holding Technical Inst. Raleigh, N.C. 27603; junior, 1958
Wyoming, U. of Laramie, Wyo. 82070; 1886
Wytheville Comm. C. Wytheville, Va. 24382; junior, 1963
Xavier U. Cincinnati, Ohio 45207; 1831
Xavier U. of Louisiana New Orleans, La. 70125; 1915
Yakima Valley C. Yakima, Wash. 98902; junior, 1928
Yale U. New Haven, Conn. 06520; 1701
Yankton C. Yankton, S.Dak. 57078; 1881
Yavapai C. Prescott, Ariz. 86301; 1966
Yeshiva U. New York, N.Y. 10033; 1886
York C. York, Nebr. 68467; junior, 1890
York C. Jamaica, N.Y. 11365; 1967
York C. of Pennsylvania York, Pa. 17405; 1941
York County Technical Ed. Center Rock Hill, S.C. 29730; junior, 1962
Young Harris C. Young Harris, Ga. 30582; junior, 1886
Youngstown State U. Youngstown, Ohio 44503; 1908
Yuba C. Marysville, Calif. 95901; junior, 1927

Canada

Acadia U. Wolfville, N.S., 1838
Alberta, U. of Edmonton, Alta., 1906
Aldersgate C. Moose Jaw, Sask., 1940
Algoma C. Sault Ste. Marie, Ont., 1965
Amos, Sém. d' Amos, P.Q., 1940
André-Grasset, C. Montreal, P.Q., 1927
Angèle Mérici, C. Quebec, P.Q., 1936
Anglican Theol. C. of British Columbia Vancouver, B.C., 1912
Assumption U. Windsor, Ont., 1857
Basile-Moreau, C. St. Laurent, P.Q., 1929
Bathurst, C. de Bathurst, N.B., 1899
Bishop's U. Lennoxville, P.Q., 1843
Bon Pasteur, C. du Chicoutimi, P.Q., 1947
Bourget, C. Rigaud, P.Q., 1850
Brandon U. Brandon, Man., 1899
Brescia C. London, Ont., 1919
British Columbia, U. of Vancouver, B.C., 1890
Brock U. St. Catharines, Ont., 1962
Bruyère, C. Ottawa, Ont., 1925
Calgary, U. of Calgary, Alta., 1945
Campion C. Regina, Sask., 1917
Camrose Junior C. Camrose, Alta., 1911
Canadian Bible C. Regina, Sask., 1941
Canadian Mennonite Bible C. Winnipeg, Man., 1944
Canterbury C. Windsor, Ont., 1957
Carey Hall Vancouver, B.C., 1960
Carleton U. Ottawa, Ont., 1942
Chicoutimi, Sém. de Chicoutimi, P.Q., 1873
Christian Training Inst. Edmonton, Alta., 1939
Christ the King, Sem. of Mission City, B.C., 1932
Concordia C. Edmonton, Alta., junior, 1921
Confederation C. Thunder Bay, Ont., 1967
Conrad Grebel C. Waterloo, Ont., 1961
Cornwall, C. Classique de Cornwall, Ont., 1949
Dalhousie U. Halifax, N.S., 1818
Emmanuel and Saint Chad, C. of Saskatoon, Sask., 1879
Gardes-Malades, École des Edmundston, N.B., 1946
Gaspé, Sém. de Gaspé, P.Q., 1926
Gravelbourg, C. Catholique de Gravelbourg, Sask., 1917
Guelph, U. of Guelph, Ont., 1964
Hautes Études Commerciales, École des Montreal, P.Q., 1907
Hearst, C. de Hearst, Ont., 1952
Holy Heart Sem. Halifax, N.S., 1895
Holy Names C. Windsor, Ont., 1934
Holy Redeemer C. Windsor, Ont., 1956
Huntington U. Sudbury, Ont., 1960
Huron C. London, Ont., 1863
Ignatius C. Guelph, Ont., 1913
Iona C. Windsor, Ont., 1964
Jean-de-Brébeuf, C. Montreal, P.Q., 1928
Jean-Jacques Olier, C. Verdun, P.Q., 1951
Jésuites, C. des Quebec, P.Q., 1635
Jésus-Marie, C. Shippegan, N.B., 1960
Jésus-Marie de Sillery, C. Quebec, P.Q., 1857
Jésus-Marie d'Outremont, C. Outremont, P.Q., 1933
Joliette, Sém. de Joliette, P.Q., 1846
Journalism, Sch. of Halifax, N.S., 1945
King's C. London, Ont., 1912
King's C., U. of Halifax, N.S., 1789
Knox C. Toronto, Ont., 1844
Lakehead U. Thunder Bay, Ont., 1946
L'Assomption, C. Moncton, N.B., 1943
L'Assomption, C. de L'Assomption, P.Q., 1832
Laurentian U. of Sudbury Sudbury, Ont., 1960
Laval, U. Quebec, P.Q., 1852
Lethbridge, U. of Lethbridge, Alta., 1967
Lethbridge Junior C. Lethbridge, Alta., 1957
Lévis, C. de Levis, P.Q., 1853
London C. of Bible and Missions London, Ont., 1935
Longueuil, Externat Classique de Ville Jacques-Cartier, P.Q., 1950
Loyola C. Montreal, P.Q., 1896
Lutheran Theol. Sem. Saskatoon, Sask., 1913
Luther C. Regina, Sask., junior, 1921
McGill U. Montreal, P.Q., 1821
McMaster Divinity C. Hamilton, Ont., 1957
McMaster U. Hamilton, Ont., 1887
Maillet, C. Saint-Basile, N.B., 1949
Manitoba, U. of Winnipeg, Man., 1877
Manitoba Law Sch. Winnipeg, Man., 1914
Marguerite-Bourgeoys, C. Montreal, P.Q., 1908
Marguerite d'Youville, C. Hull, P.Q., 1945
Marguerite d'Youville, Inst. Montreal, P.Q., 1934
Marianopolis C. Montreal, P.Q., 1943
Marie-Anne, C. Ahuntsic, Montreal, P.Q., 1932
Marie de France, C. Montreal, P.Q., 1939
Marie-de-la-Présentation, C. Drummondville, P.Q., 1955
Marie de l'Incarnation, C. Trois-Rivières, P.Q., 1697
Marie-Immaculée, Sém. Oblat de Chambly, P.Q., 1926
Marie-Médiatrice, C. Hull, P.Q., 1938
Maritime C. of Pharmacy Halifax, N.S., 1911

Maritime Sch. of Social Work Halifax, N.S., 1941
Médecine Vétérinaire, L'École St. Hyacinthe, P.Q., 1886
Medicine Hat Junior C. Medicine Hat, Alta., 1965
Memorial U. of Newfoundland St. John's, Nfld., 1925
Mennonite Brethren C. of Arts Winnipeg, Man., 1944
Moncton, U. de Moncton, N.B., 1864
Montréal, C. de Montreal, P.Q., 1767
Montréal, U. de Montreal, P.Q., 1876
Montreal Diocesan Theol. C. Montreal, P.Q., 1873
Mont-St.-Louis, C. Montreal, P.Q., 1888
Mount Allison U. Sackville, N.B., 1839
Mount Royal C. Calgary, Alta., junior, 1910
Mount St. Bernard C. Antigonish, N.S., 1883
Mount St. Vincent U. Halifax, N.S., 1873
Musique, École de Edmundston, N.B., 1950
New Brunswick, U. of Fredericton, N.B., 1785
Nicolet, Sém. de Nicolet, P.Q., 1801
Nipissing C. North Bay, Ont., 1967
Normale Secondaire, École Montreal, P.Q., 1941
North American Baptist C. South Edmonton, Alta., 1939
Notre-Dame, C. Prince Albert, Sask., 1958
Notre Dame C. Wilcox, Sask., 1933
Notre-Dame d'Acadie, C. Moncton, N.B., 1943
Notre-Dame de Bellevue, C. Quebec, P.Q., 1937
Notre-Dame de Grâce, Scolasticat Hull, P.Q., 1940
Notre-Dame de l'Assomption, C. Nicolet, P.Q., 1937
Notre-Dame du Perpétuel Secours, Sém. Moncton, N.B., 1956
Notre-Dame du St.-Rosaire, Scolasticat Rimouski, P.Q., 1957
Notre Dame U. of Nelson Nelson, B.C., 1950
Nova Scotia Agricultural C. Truro, N.S., junior, 1905
Nova Scotia C. of Art Halifax, N.S., 1887
Nova Scotia Technical C. Halifax, N.S., 1907
Oka, Inst. Agricole d' La Trappe, P.Q., 1893
Ontario Agricultural C. Guelph, Ont., 1874
Ontario Bible C. Toronto, Ont., 1935
Ontario Veterinary C. Guelph, Ont., 1862
Optométrie, École d' Montreal, P.Q., 1910
Osgoode Hall Law Sch. Toronto, Ont., 1872
Ottawa, Grand Sém. d' Ottawa, Ont., 1847
Ottawa, Petit Sém. d' Ottawa, Ont., 1925
Ottawa, U. d' Ottawa, Ont., 1848
Pédagogie Familiale, Inst. de Montreal, P.Q., 1943
Pédagogique, Inst. Montreal, P.Q., 1926
Pédagogique St.-Georges, Inst. Laval des Rapides, P.Q., 1929
Philosophie, Sém. de Montreal, P.Q., 1876
Pine Hill Divinity Hall Halifax, N.S., 1820
Polytechnique, École Montreal, P.Q., 1873
Pontifical Inst. of Mediaeval Studies Toronto, Ont., 1929
Presbyterian C. of Montreal Montreal, P.Q., 1865
Prince Edward Island, U. of Charlottetown, P.E.I., 1969
Provincial Inst. of Tech. and Art Calgary, Alta., junior, 1916
Québec, Acad. de Quebec, P.Q., 1862
Québec, Sém. de Quebec, P.Q. 1663
Queen's C. St. John's, Nfld., 1841
Queen's Theol. C. Kingston, Ont., 1912
Queen's U. at Kingston Kingston, Ont., 1841
Red Deer Junior C. Red Deer, Alta., 1964
Regis C. Toronto, Ont., 1930
Renison C. Waterloo, Ont., 1959
Rimouski, C. de Rimouski, P.Q., 1855
Rouyn, C. Classique de Rouyn, P.Q., 1948
Royal Military C. of Canada Kingston, Ont., 1876
Royal Roads Victoria, B.C., junior, 1942
Sacré-Coeur, C. du Sherbrooke, P.Q., 1945
Sacré-Coeur, Scolasticat du Lebret, Sask., 1926
Sacré-Coeur, Sém. du St. Victor, P.Q., 1910
Sacred Heart, Convent of the Halifax, N.S., junior, 1849
Saint-Alexandre, C. Limbour, P.Q., 1912
Saint-Alphonse, Sém. Aylmer, P.Q., 1896
Saint Andrew's C. Winnipeg, Man., 1946
Saint Andrew's C. Saskatoon, Sask., 1912
Saint Andrew's Hall Vancouver, B.C., 1957
Saint-Antoine, Sém. Quebec, P.Q., 1902
Saint-Augustin, Sém. Cap-Rouge, P.Q., 1965
Saint Augustine's C. Scarborough, Ont., 1913
Saint-Boniface, C. de St. Boniface, Man., 1818
Saint Bride's C. Littledale, Nfld., 1884
Saint-Denis, C. Montreal, P.Q., 1950
Sainte-Anne, C. Church Point, N.S., 1890
Sainte-Anne-de-la-Pocatière, C. Ste. Anne de la Pocatière, P.Q., 1827
Sainte-Croix, C. Montreal, P.Q., 1929
Sainte-Croix, Sém. St. Laurent, P.Q., 1899
Sainte-Marie, C. Montreal, P.Q., 1848
Sainte-Marie, Sém. Shawinigan, P.Q., 1947
Sainte-Thérèse, Sém. de Sainte-Thérèse-de-Blainville, P.Q., 1825
Saint Francis Xavier U. Antigonish, N.S., 1853
Saint-Georges, Sém. de Saint-Georges, P.Q., 1946
Saint-Hyacinthe, Sém. de St. Hyacinthe, P.Q., 1811
Saint-Jean, C. Edmonton, Alta., 1908
Saint-Jean, C. de Saint-Jean, P.Q., 1911
Saint-Jean, C. Militaire Royal de Saint Jean, P.Q., 1952
Saint-Jean, Scolasticat Ottawa, Ont., 1902
Saint-Jean-Eudes, Externat Classique Quebec, P.Q., 1937
Saint Jerome's C., U. of Waterloo, Ont., 1864
Saint John's C. Winnipeg, Man., 1829
Saint-Joseph, Sém. Mont Laurier, P.Q., 1915
Saint-Joseph, Sém. Trois-Rivières, P.Q., 1663
Saint-Joseph, C. Moncton, N.B., 1864
Saint Joseph's C. Edmonton, Alta., 1927
Saint Joseph's C. Yorkton, Sask., 1919
Saint-Laurent, C. de St. Laurent, P.Q., 1847
Saint-Louis, C. Edmundston, N.B., 1946
Saint Mark's C. Vancouver, B.C., 1956
Saint Martha's Sch. of Nursing Antigonish, N.S., 1933
Saint Mary's U. Halifax, N.S., 1802
Saint-Maurice, C. St. Hyacinthe, P.Q., 1935
Saint Michael's C., U. of Toronto, Ont., 1852
Saint Patrick's C. Ottawa, Ont., 1932
Saint-Paul, C. Montreal, P.Q., 1957
Saint Paul's C. Winnipeg, Man., 1926
Saint Paul's United C. Waterloo, Ont., 1961
Saint Paul U. Ottawa, Ont., 1848
Saint Peter's C. Muenster, Sask., junior, 1922
Saint-Sacrement, Sém. des Pères du Terrebonne, P.Q., 1902
Saints-Apôtres, Sém. des Côte Sainte-Catherine, Comté de Laprairie, P.Q., 1952
Saint Stephen's C. Edmonton, Alta., 1903
Saint Thomas C. North Battleford, Sask., 1932
Saint Thomas More C. Saskatoon, Sask., 1936
Saint Thomas U. Fredericton, N.B., 1876
Saint-Viateur, C. Montreal, P.Q., 1951
Saskatchewan, U. of Saskatoon, Sask., 1907
Sciences Domestiques, École des Sherbrooke, P.Q., 1956
Sherbrooke, Sém. de Sherbrooke, P.Q., 1875
Sherbrooke, U. de Sherbrooke, P.Q., 1954
Simon Fraser U. Burnaby, B.C., 1963
Sir George Williams U. Montreal, P.Q., 1873
Spiritain de Sainte-Foy, Sém. Ste.-Foy, P.Q., 1940
Stanislas, C. Montreal, P.Q., 1938
Sudbury, U. de Sudbury, Ont., 1913
Thomas More Inst. for Adult Ed. Montreal, P.Q., 1948
Thorneloe U. Sudbury, Ont., 1961
Toronto, U. of Toronto, Ont., 1827
Toronto Bible C. Toronto, Ont., 1894
Trent U. Peterborough, Ont., 1960
Trinity C., U. of Toronto, Ont., 1852
Trois-Rivières, Sém. de Trois-Rivières, P.Q., 1860
Union C. of British Columbia Vancouver, B.C., 1927
United C. Winnipeg, Man., 1871
United Theol. C. of Montreal Montreal, P.Q., 1926
Ursulines, C. des Rimouski, P.Q., 1906
Valleyfield, Sém. de Valleyfield, P.Q., 1893
Victoria, U. of Victoria, B.C., 1902
Victoria U. Toronto, Ont., 1836
Victoriaville, C. de Victoriaville, P.Q., 1872
Vocations Tardives, Sém. des Nicolet, P.Q., 1956
Waterloo, U. of Waterloo, Ont., 1959
Waterloo Lutheran U. Waterloo, Ont., 1910
Western Ontario, U. of London, Ont., 1878
Windsor, U. of Windsor, Ont., 1963
Winnipeg, U. of Winnipeg, Man., 1871
Winnipeg Bible C. Winnipeg, Man., 1925
Wycliffe C. Toronto, Ont., 1877
York U. Toronto, Ont., 1959

Signs and Symbols

Astronomy

SUN, GREATER PLANETS, ETC.

☉ the sun; Sunday
◐, ☾, *or* ☽ the moon; Monday
● new moon
☽, ◐, ◑, ☽ first quarter
○ *or* ☺ full moon
☾, ◑, ☾, ☾ last quarter
☿ Mercury; Wednesday
♀ Venus; Friday
⊕, ⊖, *or* ♁ the earth
♂ Mars; Tuesday
♃ Jupiter; Thursday
♄ *or* ♄ Saturn; Saturday
♅, ♅, *or* ♅ Uranus
♆, ♆, *or* ♆ Neptune
♇ Pluto

☄ comet
✳ *or* ✳ fixed Star

ASPECTS AND NODES

☌ conjunction—indicating that the bodies have the same longitude, or right ascension
□ quadrature—indicating a difference of 90° in longitude, or right ascension
△ trine—indicating a difference of 120° in longitude, or right ascension
☍ opposition—indicating a difference of 180° in longitude, or right ascension; as, ☍ ♆ ☉, opposition of Neptune to the sun
☊ ascending node
☋ descending node

Biology

○ an individual, specif., a female—used chiefly in inheritance charts
□ an individual, specif., a male—used chiefly in inheritance charts
♀ female
♂ *or* ♁ male

× crossed with; hybrid
+ wild type
F_1 offspring of the first generation
F_2 offspring of the second generation
F_3, F_4, F_5, etc. offspring of the third, fourth, fifth, etc., generation

Business

a/c account ⟨in a/c with⟩
@ at; each ⟨4 apples @ 5¢ = 20¢⟩
℘ per
c/o care of
number if it precedes a numeral ⟨track #3⟩; pounds if it follows ⟨a 5# sack of sugar⟩
℔ pound; pounds
% percent

‰ per thousand
$ dollars
¢ cents
£ pounds
/ shillings
(for other currency symbols see MONEY table)
© copyrighted
® registered trademark

Chemistry

\+ signifies "plus", "and", "together with", and is used between the symbols of substances brought together for, or produced by, a reaction; placed above a symbol or to its right above the line, it signifies a unit charge of positive electricity: Ca^{++} denotes the ion of calcium, which carries two positive charges; the plus sign is used also to indicate dextrorotation (as +143°); it is sometimes used to indicate a base or alkaloid when placed above the initial letter of the name of the substance; (as $\overset{+}{M}$, morphine or $\overset{+}{Q}$, quinine)

— signifies a single "bond", or unit of attractive force or affinity, and is used between the symbols of elements or groups which unite to form a compound: H—Cl for HCl, H—O—H for H_2O; placed above a symbol or to its right above the line, it signifies a unit charge of negative electricity: Cl^- denotes a chlorine ion carrying a negative charge; the dash indicates levorotation (as −92°); it also indicates an acid, when placed above the initial letter of the name of the acid (as $\overline{C}$, citric acid); it is used also to indicate the removal of a part from a compound

′ often indicates valence (as $Fe^{\prime\prime}$ denotes bivalent iron, $Fe^{\prime\prime\prime}$, trivalent iron); sometimes its use is restricted to negative ions so that it is equivalent to —

. is often used: (1) to indicate a bond (as H.Cl for H—Cl) or (2) to denote a unit positive charge of electricity (as Ca., denotes two positive charges) or (3) to separate parts of a compound regarded as loosely joined (as $CuSO_4.5H_2O$)

○ denotes the benzene ring

= indicates a double bond; placed above a symbol or to its right above the line, it signifies two unit charges of negative electricity (as SO_4 =, the negative ion of sulfuric acid, carrying two negative charges)

≡ signifies a triple bond or negative charge

: indicates a double bond

⋮ indicates a triple bond

() mark groups or radicals within a compound [as in $C_6H_4(CH_3)_2$, the formula for xylene which contains two methyl radicals (CH_3)]

⌐ *or* ⌙ join separated atoms or groups in structural formulas, as in that for glucose:

$$CH_2OH\overbrace{CH(CHOH)_3C}^{O}HOH$$

= give or form

→ give, pass over to, or lead to

⇄ forms and is formed from

↓ indicates precipitation of the substance

↑ indicates that the substance passes off as a gas

≡ *or* ⇌ is equivalent—used in statements to show how much of one substance will react with a given quantity of another so as to leave no excess of either

1-, 2-, etc. used initially in names, referring to the positions of substituting groups, attached to the first, etc., of the numbered atoms of the parent compound

H^2 *or* ^2H deuterium

H^3 *or* ^3H tritium

(for element symbols see ELEMENT table)

Flowchart symbols

⬭ TERMINAL. Marks the beginning and the end of the flowchart.

▭ PROCESSING. Indicates the performance of a given task.

⏢ MANUAL OPERATION.

◇ DECISION. Indicates a juncture at which a choice must be made.

[ANNOTATION. Connected to the flowchart proper by a dotted line.

○ CONNECTOR. Used to indicate common points in the flow when connecting lines cannot be drawn.

▱ INPUT/OUTPUT. This is the general symbol for input/output. It may be replaced by one of the more specific symbols below.

▭ PUNCHED CARD.

⌇ PUNCHED TAPE.

Q MAGNETIC TAPE.

⏢ MANUAL INPUT. Usually indicates a keyboard device.

⬯ DISPLAY OUTPUT. Indicates a video display.

▭ DOCUMENT. Indicates output from a printing device (as a line printer).

⊂ ON-LINE STORAGE. Indicates a mass storage unit (as a drum or disk).

▽ OFF-LINE STORAGE. Indicates data storage that cannot be accessed directly by a computer.

↑← DIRECTION OF FLOW. Arrowheads need not be used when direction of flow is from top to bottom or from left to right.

↯ COMMUNICATION LINK. Indicates a transfer of data from one location to another (as by a telephone connection).

Mathematics

$+$ plus; positive ⟨$a+b=c$⟩—used also to indicate omitted figures or an approximation

$-$ minus; negative

$\pm$ plus or minus ⟨the square root of $4a^2$ is $\pm 2a$⟩

$\times$ multiplied by; times ⟨$6\times 4=24$⟩—also indicated by placing a dot between the factors ⟨$6\cdot 4=24$⟩ or by writing factors other than numerals without signs

$\div$ *or* : divided by ⟨$24\div 6=4$⟩—also indicated by writing the divisor under the dividend with a line between ⟨$\frac{24}{6}=4$⟩ or by writing the divisor after the dividend with an oblique line between ⟨3/8⟩

$=$ equals ⟨$6+2=8$⟩

$\neq$ *or* $\ne$ is not equal to

$>$ is greater than ⟨$6>5$⟩

$\gg$ is much greater than

$<$ is less than ⟨$3<4$⟩

$\ll$ is much less than

$\geqq$ *or* $\geq$ is greater than or equal to

$\leqq$ *or* $\leq$ is less than or equal to

$\ngtr$ is not greater than

$\nless$ is not less than

$\approx$ is approximately equal to

$\equiv$ is identical to

$\sim$ equivalent; similar

$\cong$ is congruent to

$\propto$ varies directly as; is proportional to

$:$ is to; the ratio of

$\therefore$ therefore

∞ infinity

$\angle$ angle; the angle ⟨$\angle$ABC⟩

∟ right angle ⟨∟ABC⟩

$\perp$ the perpendicular; is perpendicular to ⟨AB $\perp$ CD⟩

$\parallel$ parallel; is parallel to ⟨AB $\parallel$ CD⟩

$\odot$ *or* ○ circle

⌒ arc of a circle

$\triangle$ triangle

□ square

▭ rectangle

$\vee$ *or* $\surd$ root—used without a figure to indicate a square root ⟨as in $\sqrt{4}=2$⟩ or with an index above the sign to indicate another degree ⟨as in $\sqrt[3]{3}$, $\sqrt[5]{7}$⟩; also denoted by a fractional index at the right of a number whose denominator expresses the degree of the root ⟨$3^{1/3}=\sqrt[3]{3}$⟩

( ) parentheses, [ ] brackets, { } braces — indicate that the quantities enclosed by them are to be taken together

— (above the quantities) vinculum

δ variation ⟨δx; the variation of x⟩

Δ increment

$\int$ integral; integral of ⟨$\int 2xdx=x^2$⟩

$\int_b^a$ the integral taken between the values a and b of the variable

σ standard deviation of a population

Σ sum; summation

$\bar{x}$ arithmetic mean of a sample of a variable x

μ arithmetic mean of a population

μ_2 *or* σ^2 variance

χ^2 chi-square

π pi; the number 3.14159265+; the ratio of the circumference of a circle to its diameter

Π product

! factorial

e *or* ϵ (1) the number 2.7182818+; the base of the natural system of logarithms (2) the eccentricity of a conic section

° degree ⟨60°⟩

′ minute; foot ⟨30′⟩—used also to distinguish between different values of the same variable or between different variables (as a', a'', a''', usu. read *a* prime, *a* double prime, *a* triple prime)

″ second, inch ⟨30″⟩

^{2}, ^{3}, etc. —used as exponents placed above and at the right of an expression to indicate that it is raised to a power whose degree is indicated by the figure ⟨a^2, the square of a⟩

$^{-2}$, $^{-3}$, —used as exponents placed above and at the right of an expression to indicate that the reciprocal of the expression is raised to the power whose degree is indicated by the figure ⟨a^{-2} equals $1/a^2$⟩

$\sin^{-1}x$ arc sine of x

$\cos^{-1}x$ arc cosine of x

$\tan^{-1}x$ arc tangent of x

$\cot^{-1}x$ arc cotangent of x

$\sec^{-1}x$ arc secant of x

$\operatorname{cosec}^{-1}x$ arc cosecant of x

f^{-1} the inverse of the function f

$|z|$ the absolute value of z

$\oplus$ an operation in a mathematical system (as a group or ring) indicating the sum of two elements

$\otimes$ an operation in a mathematical system (as a group or ring) indicating the product of two elements

$[x]$ the greatest integer not greater than x

(a,b) the open interval $a<x<b$

$[a,b]$ the closed interval $a\leqq x\leqq b$

$\aleph_0$ aleph-null

ω the ordinal number of the positive integers

$\cup$ union of two sets

$\cap$ intersection of two sets

$\subset$ is included in, is a subset of

$\supset$ contains as a subset

$\in$ *or* ϵ is an element of

$\notin$ is not an element of

Λ *or* 0 *or* ϕ *or* { } empty set, null set

Medicine

- $\overline{AA}$, $\overline{A}$, *or* $\bar{a}\bar{a}$ ana; of each
- ℞ take—used on prescriptions; prescription; treatment
- ☠ poison

APOTHECARIES' MEASURES

- ℥ ounce
- *f*℥ fluidounce
- *f*ʒ fluidram

- ♏, ♍, ♍, *or* min minim

APOTHECARIES' WEIGHTS

- ℔ pound
- ℥ ounce (as ℥ i or ℥ j, one ounce; ℥ ss, half an ounce; ℥ iss *or* ℥ jss, one ounce and a half; ℥ ij, two ounces)
- ʒ dram
- ℈ scruple

Miscellaneous

- & and
- &c et cetera; and so forth
- " *or* " ditto marks
- / diagonal *or* slant *or* solidus *or* virgule; used to mean "or" (as in *and/or*), "and/or" (as in *dead/wounded*), "per" (as in *feet/second*), indicates end of a line of verse; separates the figures of a date (4/4/73)
- ☞ index *or* fist
- < derived from — used in etymologies
- > whence derived — used in etymologies
- + and — used in etymologies
- * assumed — used in etymologies
- † died—used esp. in genealogies
- ✚ cross (for variations see CROSS illustration)
- ☧ monogram from Greek XP signifying Christ
- 卐 swastika
- ✡ Magen David
- ☥ ankh
- ℣ versicle
- ℟ response
- ✳ —used in Roman Catholic and Anglican service books to divide each verse of a psalm, indicating where the response begins
- ✠ *or* + —used in some service books to indicate where the sign of the cross is to be made; also used by certain Roman Catholic and Anglican prelates as a sign of the cross preceding their signatures
- LXX Septuagint
- *f*/ *or f*: relative aperture of a photographic lens
- ◉ civil defense
- ☮ peace

Physics

- α alpha particle
- β beta ray
- γ conductivity, gamma, photon, surface tension
- ϵ electric field intensity, electromotive force, permittivity
- η efficiency, viscosity
- κ kaon
- λ wavelength
- Λ lambda particle
- μ magnetic moment, micro-, micron, modulus, muon, permeability, viscosity
- $\mu\mu$ micromicron
- ν frequency, neutrino, reluctivity
- Ξ xi particle
- π pion
- ρ density, resistivity, rho particle
- σ conductivity, cross section, surface tension
- Σ sigma particle
- τ transmittance
- ϕ electric potential, luminous flux, magnetic flux
- Ω ohm, omega particle

Reference marks

- ⁂ asterisk *or* star
- † dagger
- ‡ double dagger
- § section *or* numbered clause
- ‖ parallels
- ¶ *or* ⁋ paragraph

Stamps and stamp collecting

- ★ unused
- ○ used
- ⊞ block of four or more
- ✉ entire cover or card
- △ on a piece of cover

Weather

- barometer, changes of
- ╱╲ Rising, then falling
- ╱‾ Rising, then steady; or rising, then rising more slowly
- ╱ Rising steadily, or unsteadily
- ✓ Falling or steady, then rising; or rising, then rising more quickly
- — Steady, same as 3 hours ago
- ╲╱ Falling, then rising, same or lower than 3 hours ago
- ╲_ Falling, then steady; or falling, then falling more slowly
- ╲ Falling steadily, or unsteadily
- ╱╲ Steady or rising, then falling; or falling, then falling more quickly
- ◎ calm
- ○ clear
- ◐ cloudy (partly)
- ● cloudy (completely overcast)
- ✛ drifting or blowing snow
- , drizzle
- ≡ fog
- ∾ freezing rain
- ▲▲▲ front, cold
- ●●● warm
- ▲●▲ occluded
- ▲●▼ stationary
-)(funnel clouds
- ∞ haze
- ● hurricane
- 6 tropical storm
- ↔ ice needles
- • rain
- ⁎ rain and snow
- ⩛ rime
- S sandstorm or dust storm
- ▽ shower(s)
- ▽ shower of rain
- ▽ shower of hail
- △ sleet
- * snow
- ⇂ thunderstorm
- ~ visibility reduced by smoke

Handbook of Style

Punctuation

The English writing system uses punctuation marks to separate groups of words for meaning and emphasis; to convey an idea of the variations of pitch, volume, pauses, and intonations of speech; and to help avoid contextual ambiguity. English punctuation marks, together with general rules and bracketed examples of their use, follow.

Apostrophe ’

1. indicates the possessive case of nouns and indefinite pronouns	⟨Senator Smith’s constituents⟩ ⟨the boy’s mother⟩ ⟨the boys’ mothers⟩ ⟨It is anyone’s guess how much it will cost.⟩ ⟨Rodgers and Hammerstein’s musicals⟩
2. marks omissions in contracted words	⟨didn’t⟩ ⟨o’clock⟩
3. often forms plurals of letters, figures, and words referred to as words	⟨You should dot your *i*’s and cross your *t*’s.⟩ ⟨His *1*’s and his *7*’s looked alike.⟩ ⟨She has trouble pronouncing her *the*’s.⟩

Brackets [ ]

1. set off extraneous data such as editorial interpolations especially within quoted material	⟨He wrote, “I recieved [sic] your letter.”⟩
2. function as parentheses within parentheses	⟨Bowman Act (22 Stat., ch. 4, § [or sec.] 4, p. 50)⟩

Colon :

1. introduces a clause or phrase that explains, illustrates, amplifies, or restates what has gone before	⟨The sentence was poorly constructed: it lacked both unity and coherence.⟩
2. directs attention to an appositive	⟨He had only one pleasure: eating.⟩
3. introduces a series	⟨Three countries were represented: England, France, and Belgium.⟩
4. introduces lengthy quoted material set off from the rest of a text by indentation but not by quotation marks	⟨I quote from the text of Chapter One:⟩
5. separates data in time-telling and data in bibliographic and biblical references	⟨8:30 a.m.⟩ ⟨New York: Smith Publishing Co.⟩ ⟨John 4:10⟩
6. separates titles and subtitles (as of books)	⟨*The Tragic Dynasty: A History of the Romanovs*⟩
7. follows the salutation in formal correspondence	⟨Dear Sir:⟩ ⟨Gentlemen:⟩

, Comma

1. separates main clauses joined by a coordinating conjunction (as *and, but, or, nor,* or *for*) and very short clauses not so joined
   ⟨She knew very little about him, and he volunteered nothing.⟩
   ⟨I came, I saw, I conquered.⟩
2. sets off an adverbial clause (or a long phrase) that precedes the main clause
   ⟨When she found that her friends had deserted her, she sat down and cried.⟩
3. sets off from the rest of the sentence transitional words and expressions (as *on the contrary, on the other hand*), conjunctive adverbs (as *consequently, furthermore, however*), and expressions that introduce an illustration or example (as *namely, for example*)
   ⟨Your second question, on the other hand, remains open.⟩
   ⟨The mystery, however, remains unsolved.⟩
   ⟨She expects to travel through two countries, namely, France and England.⟩
4. separates words, phrases, or clauses in series
   ⟨Men, women, and children crowded into the square.⟩
   ⟨He was young, eager, and restless.⟩
   ⟨It requires one to travel constantly, to have no private life, and to need no income other than living expenses on the road.—Sara Davidson⟩
5. sets off from the rest of the sentence parenthetic elements (as nonrestrictive modifiers and nonrestrictive appositives)
   ⟨Our guide, who wore a blue beret, was an experienced traveler.⟩
   ⟨We visited Gettysburg, the site of a famous battle.⟩
   ⟨The captain, John Jones, was an experienced mariner.⟩
6. introduces a direct quotation, terminates a direct quotation that is neither a question nor an exclamation, and encloses split quotations
   ⟨John said, "I am leaving."⟩
   ⟨"I am leaving," John said.⟩
   ⟨"I am leaving," John said with determination, "even if you want me to stay."⟩
7. sets off words in direct address, absolute phrases, and mild interjections
   ⟨You may go, Mary, if you wish.⟩
   ⟨I fear the encounter, his temper being what it is.⟩
   ⟨Ah, that's my idea of an excellent dinner.⟩
8. separates a tag question from the rest of the sentence
   ⟨It's a fine day, isn't it?⟩
9. indicates the omission of a word or words, and especially a word or words used earlier in the sentence
   ⟨Common stocks are preferred by some investors; bonds, by others.⟩
10. is used to avoid ambiguity and also to emphasize a particular phrase
    ⟨To Mary, Jane was someone special.⟩
    ⟨The more embroidery on a dress, the higher the price.⟩
11. is used to group numbers into units of three in separating thousands, millions, etc.; however, it is generally not used in numbers of four figures, in pagination, in dates, or in street numbers
    ⟨Smithville, pop. 100,000⟩
    but
    ⟨3600 rpm⟩ ⟨the year 1973⟩
    ⟨page 1411⟩ ⟨4507 Smith Street⟩
12. punctuates an inverted name
    ⟨Smith, John W., Jr.⟩
13. separates a proper name from a following academic, honorary, governmental, or military title
    ⟨John Smith, M.D.⟩
14. sets off geographical names (as state or country from city), items in dates, and addresses from the rest of a text
    ⟨Shreveport, Louisiana, is the site of a large air base.⟩
    ⟨On Sunday, June 23, 1940, he was wounded.⟩
    ⟨Number 10 Downing Street, London, is a famous address.⟩
15. follows the salutation in informal correspondence and follows the complimentary close of a formal or informal letter
    ⟨Dear Mary,⟩
    ⟨Affectionately,⟩
    ⟨Very truly yours,⟩

— Dash

1. usually marks an abrupt change or break in the continuity of a sentence
   ⟨When in 1960 the stockpile was sold off—indeed, dumped as surplus—natural-rubber sales were hard hit.—Barry Commoner⟩
2. introduces a summary statement that follows a series of words or phrases
   ⟨Oil, steel, and wheat—these are the sinews of industrialization.⟩
3. often precedes the attribution of a quotation
   ⟨My foot is on my native heath . . . . —Sir Walter Scott⟩

Ellipsis ... .

1. indicates the omission of one or more words within a quoted passage ⟨The head is not more native to the heart . . . than is the throne of Denmark to thy father.—Shak.⟩

2. indicates halting speech or an unfinished sentence in dialogue ⟨"I'd like to . . . that is . . . if you don't mind . . . ." He faltered and then stopped speaking.⟩

3. indicates the omission of one or more sentences within a quoted passage or the omission of words at the end of a sentence by using four spaced dots the last of which represents the period ⟨That recovering the manuscripts would be worth almost any effort is without question . . . . The monetary value of a body of Shakespeare's manuscripts would be almost incalculable—Charlton Ogburn⟩ ⟨It will take scholars years to determine conclusively the origins, the history, and, most importantly, the significance of the finds . . . .—Robert Morse⟩

4. usually indicates omission of one or more lines of poetry when ellipsis is extended the length of the line

⟨ Thus driven
By the bright shadow of that lovely dream,
. . . .
He fled.
—P. B. Shelley⟩

Exclamation Point !

1. terminates an emphatic phrase or sentence ⟨Get out of here!⟩

2. terminates an emphatic interjection ⟨Encore!⟩

Hyphen -

1. marks separation or division at the end of a line terminating with a syllable of a word that is to be carried over to the next line ⟨mill-
stone⟩ ⟨pas-
sion⟩

2. is used between some prefix and root combinations, as
   - prefix + proper name; ⟨pre-Renaissance⟩
   - prefix ending with a vowel + root word beginning often with the same vowel; ⟨co-opted⟩ ⟨re-ink⟩
   - stressed prefix + root word, especially when this combination is similar to a different word ⟨re-cover a sofa⟩ *but* ⟨recover from an illness⟩

3. is used in some compounds, especially those containing prepositions ⟨president-elect⟩ ⟨sister-in-law⟩ ⟨attorney-at-law⟩ ⟨good-for-nothing⟩

4. is often used between elements of a unit modifier in attributive position in order to avoid ambiguity ⟨He is a small-business man.⟩ ⟨She has gray-green eyes.⟩ ⟨He looked at her with a know-it-all expression.⟩

5. suspends the first part of a hyphened compound when used with another hyphened compound ⟨a six- or eight-cylinder engine⟩

6. is used in writing out compound numbers between 21 and 99 ⟨thirty-four⟩ ⟨one hundred twenty-eight⟩

7. is used between the numerator and the denominator in writing out fractions especially when they are used as modifiers; however, fractions used as nouns are usually styled as open compounds ⟨a two-thirds majority of the vote⟩ *but* ⟨ate two thirds of a box of candy⟩

8. serves as an arbitrary equivalent of the phrase "(up) to and including" when used between numbers and dates ⟨pages 40-98⟩ ⟨the decade 1960-69⟩

9. is used in the compounding of capitalized names ⟨the New York-Moscow flight⟩

⸗ Hyphen, Double

is used in the end-of-line division of a hyphened compound to indicate that the compound is hyphened and not closed

⟨self⸗[end of line]seeker⟩
but
⟨self-[end of line]same⟩

● The styling of compounds varies: they may be open, closed, or hyphened. When in doubt, one should consult the main vocabulary of this dictionary for the most commonly used styling.

( ) Parentheses

1. set off supplementary, parenthetic, or explanatory material when the interruption is more marked than that usually indicated by commas and when the inclusion of such material does not essentially alter the meaning of the sentence

   ⟨Three old destroyers (all now out of commission) will be scrapped.⟩
   ⟨He is hoping (as we all are) that this time he will succeed.⟩

2. enclose arabic numerals which confirm a written number in a text

   ⟨Delivery will be made in thirty (30) days.⟩

3. enclose numbers or letters in a series

   ⟨We must set forth (1) our long-term goals, (2) our immediate objectives, and (3) the means at our disposal.⟩

• Period

1. terminates sentences or sentence fragments that are neither interrogatory nor exclamatory

   ⟨Obey the law.⟩
   ⟨He obeyed the law.⟩
   ⟨He asked whether the law had been obeyed.⟩

2. follows some abbreviations and contractions

   ⟨Dr.⟩ ⟨A.D.⟩ ⟨Esq.⟩
   ⟨Jr.⟩ ⟨etc.⟩ ⟨cont.⟩

? Question Mark

1. terminates a direct question

   ⟨Who threw the bomb?⟩
   ⟨"Who threw the bomb?" he asked.⟩
   ⟨To ask the question Who threw the bomb? is unnecessary.⟩

2. indicates the writer's ignorance or uncertainty

   ⟨Omar Khayyám, Persian poet (?–?1123)⟩

" " Quotation Marks, Double

1. enclose direct quotations in conventional usage

   ⟨He said, "I am leaving."⟩

2. enclose words or phrases borrowed from others, words used in a special way, and often slang when it is introduced into formal writing

   ⟨As the leader of a gang of "droogs," he is altogether frightening, as is this film.—Liz Smith⟩
   ⟨He called himself "emperor," but he was really just a dictator.⟩
   ⟨He was arrested for smuggling "smack."⟩

3. enclose titles of short poems, short stories, articles, lectures, chapters of books, songs, short musical compositions, and radio and TV programs

   ⟨Robert Frost's "Dust of Snow"⟩
   ⟨Pushkin's "Queen of Spades"⟩
   ⟨The third chapter of *Treasure Island* is entitled "The Black Spot."⟩
   ⟨"America the Beautiful"⟩
   ⟨Ravel's "Bolero"⟩
   ⟨NBC's "Today Show"⟩

4. are used with other punctuation marks in the following ways:

   the period and the comma fall *within* the quotation marks
   〈"I am leaving," he said.〉
   〈His camera was described as "waterproof," but "moisture-resistant" would have been a better description.〉

   the semicolon falls *outside* the quotation marks
   〈He spoke of his "little cottage in the country"; he might have called it a mansion.〉

   the dash, question mark, and the exclamation point fall *within* the quotation marks when they refer to the quoted matter only; they fall *outside* when they refer to the whole sentence
   〈He asked, "When did you leave?"〉
   〈What is the meaning of "the open door"?〉
   〈The sergeant shouted, "Halt!"〉
   〈Save us from his "mercy"!〉

Quotation Marks, Single 

1. enclose a quotation within a quotation in conventional usage
   〈The witness said, "I distinctly heard him say, 'Don't be late,' and then I heard the door close."〉
2. are sometimes used in place of double quotation marks especially in British usage
   〈The witness said, 'I distinctly heard him say, "Don't be late," and then I heard the door close.'〉

Semicolon ;

1. links main clauses not joined by coordinating conjunctions
   〈Some people have the ability to write well; others do not.〉
2. links main clauses joined by conjunctive adverbs (as *consequently, furthermore, however*)
   〈Speeding is illegal; furthermore, it is very dangerous.〉
3. links clauses which themselves contain commas even when such clauses are joined by coordinating conjunctions
   〈Thus our search was for people who could think in very fundamental ways, who could buttress their views with careful analysis; people who were able to hang in during deliberations with their own ideas, but who could also comfortably and effectively work within the confines of a small group.—Frank Newman〉

Virgule /

1. separates alternatives
   〈. . . designs intended for high-heat and/or high-speed applications—F. S. Badger, Jr.〉
   〈. . . sit hour after hour . . . and finally year after year in a catatonic/frenzied trance rewriting the Bible—William Saroyan〉
2. separates successive divisions (as months or years) of an extended period of time
   〈the fiscal year 1972/73〉
3. serves as a dividing line between run-in lines of poetry
   〈Say, sages, what's the charm on earth/Can turn death's dart aside?—Robert Burns〉
4. often represents *per* in abbreviations
   〈9 ft/sec〉 〈20 km/hr〉
5. sets off phonemes and phonemic transcription
   〈/b/ as in *but*〉

Italicization

The following are usually italicized in print and underlined in manuscript and typescript:

1. titles of books, magazines, newspapers, plays, movies, works of art, and music
   〈Eliot's *The Waste Land*〉〈*Saturday Review*〉
   〈*Christian Science Monitor*〉〈Shakespeare's *Othello*〉
   〈the movie *Gone With the Wind*〉
   〈Gainsborough's *Blue Boy*〉〈Mozart's *Don Giovanni*〉

2. names of ships and aircraft, and often spacecraft

⟨M.V. *West Star*⟩
⟨Lindbergh's *Spirit of St. Louis*⟩
⟨*Apollo 13*⟩

3. words, letters, and figures when referred to as words, letters, and figures

⟨The word *receive* is often misspelled.⟩
⟨The *g* in *align* is silent.⟩
⟨You should dot your *i*'s and cross your *t*'s.⟩
⟨The first *2* and the last *0* in the address are barely legible.⟩

4. foreign words and phrases that have not been naturalized in English

⟨*aere perennius*⟩
⟨*che sarà, sarà*⟩
⟨*sans peur et sans reproche*⟩
⟨*ich dien*⟩

5. New Latin scientific names of genera, species, subspecies, and varieties (but not groups of higher rank, as phyla, classes, or orders) in botanical and zoological names

⟨a thick-shelled American clam (*Mercenaria mercenaria*)⟩
⟨a cardinal (*Richmondena cardinalis*)⟩

Capitalization

Capitals are used for two broad purposes in English: they mark a beginning (as of a sentence) and they signal a proper noun or adjective. The following principles, each with bracketed examples, describe the most common uses of capital letters.

1. The first word of a sentence or sentence fragment is capitalized.

⟨The play lasted nearly three hours.⟩
⟨How are you feeling?⟩
⟨Bravo!⟩
⟨"Have you hand grenades?"
"Plenty."
"How many rounds per rifle?"
"Plenty."
"How many?"
"One hundred fifty. More maybe."
—Ernest Hemingway⟩

2. The first word of a direct quotation is capitalized.

⟨And God said, Let there be light.—Gen 1:3 (AV)⟩
⟨He replied, "We can stay only a few minutes."⟩

3. The first word of a direct question within a sentence is capitalized.

⟨That question is this: Is man an ape or an angel?
—Benjamin Disraeli⟩

4. The first word of a line of poetry is conventionally capitalized.

⟨The best lack all conviction, while the worst
Are full of passionate intensity.—W. B. Yeats⟩

5. Words in titles are capitalized with the exception of internal conjunctions, prepositions, and articles.

⟨*The Way of the World*⟩
⟨*Of Mice and Men*⟩
⟨*Quo Vadis*⟩
⟨Deuteronomy⟩

6. The first word of the salutation of a letter and the first word of the complimentary close are capitalized.

⟨Dear Mary⟩
⟨My dear Mrs. Smith⟩
⟨Sincerely yours⟩ ⟨Yours sincerely⟩

7. The names of persons and places, of organizations and their members, of congresses and councils, and of historical periods and events are capitalized.

⟨Noah Webster⟩ ⟨Rome⟩ ⟨Texas⟩
⟨England⟩ ⟨Rotary International⟩
⟨Kiwanians⟩ ⟨Baptists⟩ ⟨the United Methodist Church⟩
⟨the Atomic Energy Commission⟩ ⟨the Yalta Conference⟩
⟨the Middle Ages⟩ ⟨World War II⟩

8. The names of ships, aircraft, and spacecraft are capitalized.

⟨M.V. *West Star*⟩
⟨Lindbergh's *Spirit of St. Louis*⟩
⟨*Apollo 13*⟩

9. Words designating peoples and languages are capitalized.

⟨Canadians⟩ ⟨Turks⟩
⟨Latin⟩ ⟨Swedish⟩
⟨Iroquois⟩ ⟨Ibo⟩

10. Derivatives of proper names are capitalized when used in their primary sense.

⟨Roman customs⟩
⟨Shakespearean comedies⟩
⟨the Edwardian era⟩
but
⟨macadamize⟩
⟨bowdlerize⟩
⟨jeremiad⟩

11. Words of family relationship preceding the name of a person are capitalized.

⟨Uncle George⟩ ⟨Aunt Jane⟩
⟨Cousin Julia⟩
⟨Grandfather Jones⟩

12. Titles preceding the name of a person and epithets used instead of a name are capitalized.

⟨President Roosevelt⟩
⟨Professor Harris⟩
⟨Pope Paul⟩
⟨Queen Elizabeth⟩
⟨Old Hickory⟩ ⟨the Iron Chancellor⟩

13. The pronoun I is capitalized.

⟨In the play, an ape in a frock coat and other civil appurtenances, recounts his life to members of a literary academy (you and I). —Arthur Sainer⟩

14. Words designating the Deity (and pronouns referring thereto) are often capitalized.

⟨The principal group that disagreed with them . . . did so only in an even greater faith—that when God chose to save the heathen He could do it by Himself.—Elmer Davis⟩
⟨Allah will not subject any believer to eternal punishment . . . because of His readiness to yield to the Prophet's intercession.—G. E. von Grunebaum⟩
⟨An anthropomorphic, vengeful Jehovah became a spiritual, benevolent Supreme Being.—A. R. Katz⟩

15. Personifications are capitalized.

⟨She dwells with Beauty—Beauty that must die;
And Joy, whose hand is ever at his lips
Bidding adieu. —John Keats⟩

16. The days of the week, the months of the year, and holidays and holy days are capitalized.

⟨Tuesday⟩ ⟨June⟩
⟨Thanksgiving⟩
⟨Independence Day⟩
⟨Easter⟩ ⟨Yom Kippur⟩

17. Names of specific courts of law are capitalized.

⟨the Circuit Court of the United States for the 2d Circuit⟩ ⟨the Michigan Court of Appeals⟩

18. Names of treaties are capitalized.

⟨Treaty of Versailles⟩
⟨Kellogg-Briand Pact⟩
⟨Peace of Westphalia⟩

19. Registered trademarks and service marks are capitalized.

⟨Dubonnet⟩ ⟨Orlon⟩
⟨Air Express⟩
⟨Laundromat⟩

20. Geological eras, periods, epochs, strata, and names of prehistoric divisions are capitalized.

⟨Silurian period⟩
⟨Pleistocene epoch⟩
⟨Age of Reptiles⟩
⟨Neolithic age⟩

21. Planets, constellations, asteroids, stars, and groups of stars are capitalized; however, sun, earth, and moon are not capitalized unless they are listed with other capitalized astronomical names.

⟨Venus⟩
⟨Big Dipper⟩
⟨Sirius⟩
⟨Pleiades⟩

22. Genera in binomial scientific names in zoology and botany are capitalized; names of species are not.

⟨a cabbage butterfly (*Pieris rapae*)⟩
⟨a common buttercup (*Ranunculus acris*)⟩
⟨the robin (*Turdus migratorius*)⟩
⟨the haddock (*Melanogrammus aeglefinus*)⟩

23. New Latin names of classes, families, and all groups above genera in zoology and botany are capitalized; however, their derivative adjectives and nouns are not.

⟨Gastropoda⟩ *but* ⟨gastropod⟩
⟨Thallophyta⟩ *but* ⟨thallophyte⟩

● Further information about capitalization may be found at specific vocabulary entries in this dictionary. See, for example, the entries for PST and WASP.

Plurals

The plurals of English nouns are regularly formed by the addition of the suffix *-s* or *-es* to the singular, as

⟨dog → dogs⟩
⟨race → races⟩
⟨guy → guys⟩
⟨monarch → monarchs⟩
⟨grass → grasses⟩
⟨dish → dishes⟩
⟨buzz → buzzes⟩
⟨branch → branches⟩

The plurals of nouns that follow other patterns, as

⟨army → armies⟩
⟨duo → duos⟩
⟨ox → oxen⟩
⟨foot → feet⟩
⟨p. → pp.⟩
⟨sheep → sheep⟩
⟨phenomenon → phenomena⟩
⟨libretto → librettos *or* libretti⟩
⟨curriculum → curricula *also* curriculums⟩
⟨alga → algae⟩
⟨corpus delicti → corpora delicti⟩
⟨sergeant major → sergeants major *or* sergeant majors⟩

are given at the appropriate vocabulary entries in the main body of the dictionary.

● Additional information on the treatment of plurals in this dictionary may be found in the Explanatory Notes, p. 12a.

Footnotes

Footnotes to a text are indicated by Arabic superscript numerals placed immediately after the material to be footnoted, with no intervening space. The numbering may be consecutive throughout a paper, article, or book. If the reference is brief, it may be inserted within parentheses in the text itself, but the first full reference to a work should appear in a note. The footnotes may appear at the end of the complete text, at the end of each chapter, or at the bottom of each page. The samples shown below exemplify only the basic types of footnotes. For more detailed information, the *MLA Style Sheet* may be consulted.

Sample Footnotes

BOOKS

one author	[1] Albert H. Marckwardt, *American English* (New York: Oxford University Press, 1958), p. 94.
multiple authors	[2] De Witt T. Starnes and Gertrude E. Noyes, *The English Dictionary from Cawdrey to Johnson 1604–1775* (Chapel Hill: University of North Carolina Press, 1946), p. 119.
translation and/or edition	[3] Simone de Beauvoir, *The Second Sex*, trans. and ed. H. M. Parshley (New York: Alfred A. Knopf, 1953), p. 600. [4] William Shakespeare, *The Complete Works of Shakespeare*, ed. George Lyman Kittredge (Boston: Ginn and Company, 1936), p. 801.
second or later edition	[5] Albert C. Baugh, *A History of the English Language*, 2nd. ed. (New York: Appleton-Century-Crofts, 1957), p. 300.
a work in a festschrift or collection	[6] Kemp Malone, "The Phonemes of Current English," *Studies for William A. Read*, ed. Nathaniel M. Caffee and Thomas A. Kirby (Baton Rouge: Louisiana State University Press, 1940), pp. 133–165.
corporate author	[7] *Report of the Commission on the Humanities* (New York: American Council of Learned Societies, 1964), p. 130.
book without publisher, date, or pagination	[8] *Photographic View Album of Cambridge* [England], n.d., n.p., n. pag.

ARTICLES

from a journal with continuous pagination throughout the annual volume	[9] Daniel Cook, "A Point of Lexicographical Method," *American Speech*, 34 (1959), 20–25.
from a journal paging each issue separately	[10] Donald K. Ourecky, "Cane and Bush Fruits," *Plants & Gardens*, 27, No. 3 (Autumn 1971), pp. 13–15.
from a monthly magazine	[11] William Irwin Thompson, "Planetary Vistas," *Harper's*, Dec. 1971, pp. 71–78.
from a weekly magazine	[12] Eric F. Goldman, "A Sort of Rehabilitation of Warren G. Harding," *New York Times Magazine*, 26 Mar. 1972, p. 42.
from a newspaper	[13] Haskell Frankel, "Observing the Theater: 'Night Watch' Is First-Class, And Mum's the Word," *National Observer*, 11 Mar. 1972, p. 23, cols. 1–2.
letter to the editor	[14] Arthur M. Cohen, "Letters," *Change*, May 1972, p. 4.
a signed review	[15] Harry Hoijer, rev. of *A Leonard Bloomfield Anthology*, ed. Charles F. Hockett, *Language*, 47 (1971), 911–13.

Forms of Address

Since the relationship between correspondents affects the form of address used in letters, no rigid guidelines can be set down for all occasions. The following generally accepted forms, alphabetically listed in six categories, have been selected as those most likely to be encountered by the average person. When two salutations are shown, it is to be understood that the formal styling precedes the informal. In salutations where the addressee is a woman, it is to be understood that in formal address "Madam" may be substituted for "Sir," and in informal address "Mrs." or "Miss" or "Ms." may be substituted for "Mr."

Addressee	Form of Address	Salutation
	clerical and religious orders	
abbot	The Right Reverend John Smith, O.S.B. Abbot of —	Right Reverend and Dear Father:
archbishop	The Most Reverend Archbishop of — *or* The Most Reverend John Smith Archbishop of —	Your Excellency: Dear Archbishop Smith:
archdeacon	The Venerable the Archdeacon of —	Venerable Sir:
bishop, Catholic	The Most Reverend John Smith Bishop of —	Your Excellency: Dear Bishop Smith:
bishop, Episcopal	The Right Reverend John Smith Bishop of —	Right Reverend Sir: Dear Bishop Smith:
bishop, other denomination(s)	The Reverend John Smith	Reverend Sir: Dear Bishop Smith:
brotherhood, Catholic, member of	Brother James, S.J.	Dear Brother James:
brotherhood, Catholic, superior of	Brother Michael, S.J., Superior	Dear Brother Michael:
cardinal	His Eminence John Cardinal Smith	Your Eminence: Dear Cardinal Smith:
clergyman, Protestant	The Reverend John Smith *or* The Reverend Dr. John Smith (if having a doctor's degree)	Dear Sir: Dear Mr. Smith: *or* Dear Dr. Smith:
dean (of a cathedral)	The Very Reverend John Smith *or* Dean John Smith	Very Reverend Sir: Dear Dean Smith:
monsignor	The Right Reverend Monsignor Smith	Dear Monsignor Smith:

Addressee	Form of Address	Salutation
patriarch (of an Eastern church)	His Beatitude the Patriarch of —	Most Reverend Lord:
pope	His Holiness Pope — *or* His Holiness the Pope	Your Holiness: *or* Most Holy Father:
priest	The Reverend Father Smith *or* The Reverend John Smith	Dear Father Smith: Dear Father:
rabbi	Rabbi John Smith *or* Rabbi John Smith, D.D. (if having a doctor's degree)	Dear Rabbi Smith: *or* Dear Dr. Smith:
sisterhood, member of	Sister Mary Angelica, S.C.	Dear Sister Mary Angelica: Dear Sister:
sisterhood, superior of	The Reverend Mother Superior, S.C.	Reverend Mother: Dear Reverend Mother:

college and university officials

Addressee	Form of Address	Salutation
dean of a college or university	Dean John Smith	Dear Dean Smith:
president of a college or university	President John Smith	Dear President Smith:
professor at a college or university	Professor John Smith	Dear Professor Smith:

diplomats

Addressee	Form of Address	Salutation
ambassador to the U.S.	His Excellency John Smith Ambassador of —	Sir: Dear Mr. Ambassador:
American ambassador	The Honorable John Smith American Ambassador	Sir: Dear Mr. Ambassador:
American chargé d'affaires	John Smith, Esq. American Chargé d'Affaires	Dear Sir:
consul	John Smith, Esq. American Consul	Dear Sir:
minister to the U.S.	The Honorable John Smith Minister of —	Sir: Dear Mr. Minister:
secretary-general, U.N.	His Excellency John Smith Secretary-General of the United Nations	Excellency: Dear Mr. Secretary-General: *or* Dear Mr. Smith:

federal, state, and local government officials

Addressee	Form of Address	Salutation
alderman	The Honorable John Smith	Dear Mr. Smith:
assemblyman	—see REPRESENTATIVE, STATE	
associate justice, Supreme Court	Mr. Justice Smith The Supreme Court of the United States	Dear Mr. Justice:
cabinet officers (as the Secretary of State *and* the Attorney General)	The Honorable John Smith Secretary of State The Honorable John Smith Attorney General of the United States	Dear Sir:

Addressee	Form of Address	Salutation
chief justice, Supreme Court	The Chief Justice of the United States	Dear Mr. Chief Justice:
commissioner	The Honorable John Smith	Dear Mr. Smith:
former U.S. president	The Honorable John Smith	Dear Mr. Smith:
governor	The Honorable John Smith Governor of —	Dear Governor Smith:
judge, federal	The Honorable John Smith United States District Judge	Dear Judge Smith:
judge, state or local	The Honorable John Smith Chief Judge of the Court of Appeals	Dear Judge Smith:
lieutenant governor	The Honorable John Smith Lieutenant Governor of —	Dear Mr. Smith:
mayor	The Honorable John Smith Mayor of —	Dear Mayor Smith:
president, U.S.	The President	Dear Mr. President:
representative, state (same format for assemblyman)	The Honorable John Smith House of Representatives State Capitol	Dear Mr. Smith:
representative, U.S.	The Honorable John Smith The United States House of Representatives	Dear Mr. Smith:
senator, state	The Honorable John Smith The State Senate State Capitol	Dear Senator Smith:
senator, U.S.	The Honorable John Smith United States Senate	Dear Senator Smith:
speaker, U.S. House of Representatives	The Honorable John Smith Speaker of the House of Representatives	Dear Mr. Speaker:
vice-president, U.S.	The Vice-President United States Senate	Dear Mr. Vice-President:

military ranks—a typical but not exhaustive list

Addressee	Form of Address	Salutation
admiral vice admiral rear admiral	*(full rank + full name + comma + abbreviation of branch of service)*	Sir: Dear Admiral Smith:
airman	*(same as above)*	Dear Airman Smith:
cadet	Cadet John Smith United States Military Academy	Dear Mr. Smith:
captain (air force, army, coast guard, marine corps, or navy)	*(full rank + full name + comma + abbreviation of branch of service)*	Dear Captain Smith:
colonel lieutenant colonel (air force, army, or marine corps)	*(same as above)*	Dear Colonel Smith:
commander (coast guard or navy)	*(same as above)*	Dear Commander Smith:
corporal	*(same as above)*	Dear Corporal Smith:

Addressee	Form of Address	Salutation
first lieutenant second lieutenant (air force, army, or marine corps)	*(same as above)*	Dear Lieutenant Smith:
general lieutenant general major general brigadier general (air force, army, or marine corps)	*(same as above)*	Sir: Dear General Smith:
lieutenant commander lieutenant lieutenant (jg) ensign (coast guard or navy)	*(same as above)*	Dear Mr. Smith:
major (air force, army, or marine corps)	*(same as above)*	Dear Major Smith:
master sergeant [a typical example for other enlisted ranks having compound titles not shown here]	*(same as above)*	Dear Sergeant Smith:
midshipman	Midshipman John Smith United States Naval Academy	Dear Midshipman Smith:
petty officer *and* chief petty officer ranks	*(full rank + full name + comma + branch of service)*	Dear Mr. Smith: Dear Mr. Smith: *or* Dear Chief Smith:
private	*(same as above)*	Dear Private Smith:
seaman	*(same as above)*	Dear Seaman Smith:
specialist	*(same as above)*	Dear Specialist Smith:
warrant officer	*(same as above)*	Dear Mr. Smith:
other ranks not here listed	*(same as above)*	Dear + rank + surname:

● Abbreviations of ranks are included in the main vocabulary of this dictionary.

miscellaneous professional ranks and titles

Addressee	Form of Address	Salutation
attorney	Mr. John Smith Attorney-at-Law *or* John Smith, Esq.	Dear Mr. Smith:
dentist	John Smith, D.D.S. (office address) *or* Dr. John Smith (home address)	Dear Dr. Smith:
physician	John Smith, M.D. (office address) *or* Dr. John Smith (home address)	Dear Dr. Smith:
veterinarian	John Smith, D.V.M. (office address) *or* Dr. John Smith (home address)	Dear Dr. Smith:

Style in Business Correspondence

The four main business letter stylings are full block, modified block, modified semi-block, and indented. The choice of styling may depend on personal preference or corporate policy. Examples of these stylings are shown below.

Block

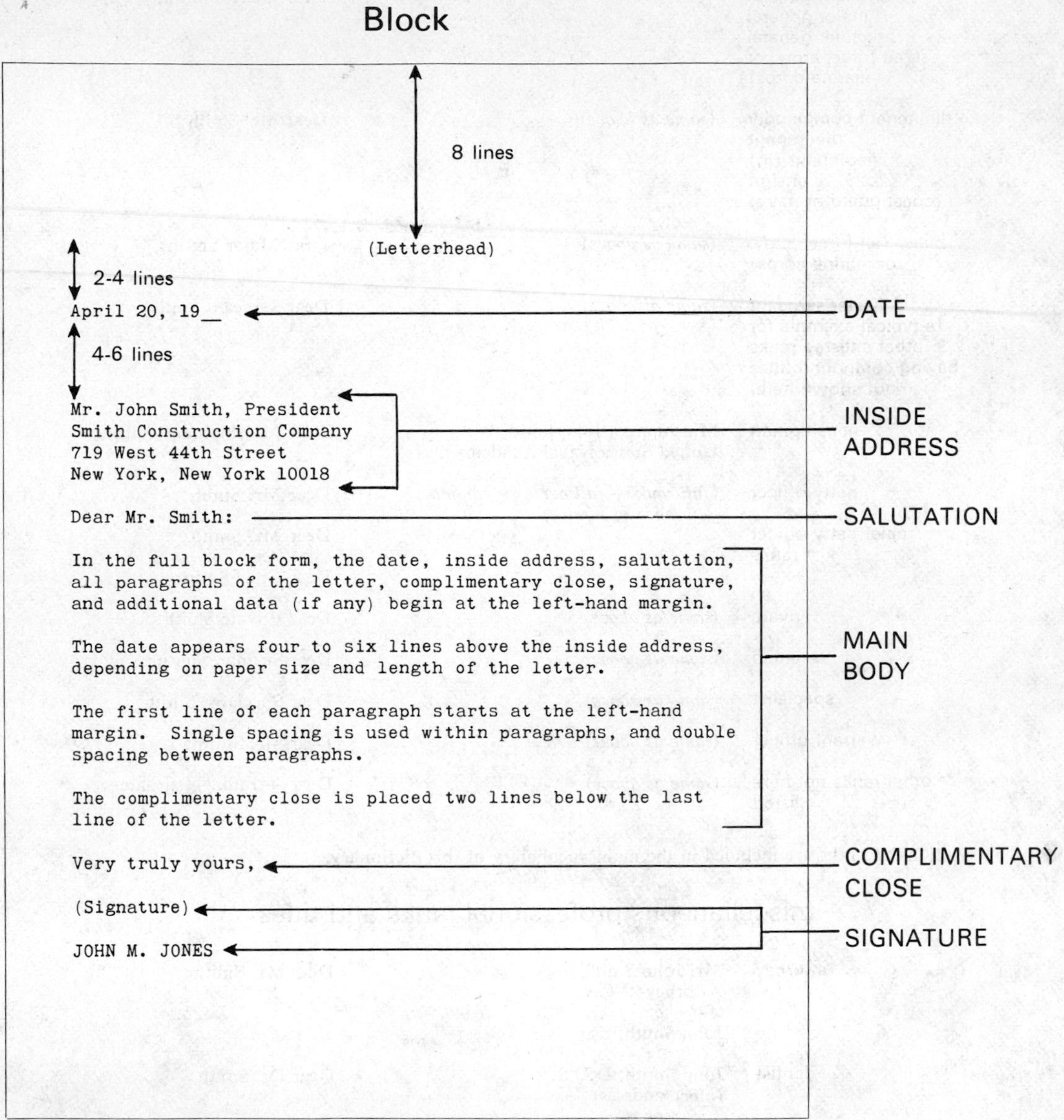